HISTORY

OF THE

CHURCH OF JESUS CHRIST

OF

LATTER-DAY SAINTS

PERIOD I.

History of Joseph Smith, the Prophet

BY HIMSELF

VOLUME I

AN INTRODUCTION AND NOTES

BY

B. H. ROBERTS

PUBLISHED FOR THE CHURCH
Second Edition Revised

THE DESERET BOOK COMPANY
Salt Lake City, Utah

1980

ISBN 0-87747-074-X

PREFACE.

In publishing the HISTORY OF THE CHURCH OF JESUS CHRIST OF LATTER-DAY SAINTS, it is felt that a solemn duty is being performed to the Saints and to the world. The events which make up the history of the Church in this age are the most important that history can chronicle. It is due therefore both to the Saints themselves and to the world that a faithful and complete history of the facts in which the Church of Jesus Christ of Latter-day Saints had its origin, together with the events through which it was subsequently developed, and all the circumstances, experiences and trials through which it passed be made known to mankind. It is important, too, that so far as possible the events which make up the history be related by the persons who witnessed them, since such statements give the reader testimony of the facts at first hand; and there is placed on record at the same time the highest order of historical evidence of the truth of what is stated. It was these considerations which induced the Church authorities, under whose auspices this history is published, to take the narrative of the Prophet Joseph Smith, as found in the manuscript *History of the Church*—now in the archives of the Historian's office—for the body of the work, rather than to authorize the writing of a history in the ordinary way. The editors of the work are not oblivious to the fact that to proceed in the manner followed in these volumes has its disadvantages; that it renders it impossible to correlate the facts, and give unity to the work; that it makes the body of the work more of the nature of annals than of history; with the accompanying result that the conclusion of an event, or even a series of events, is frequently postponed indefinitely, and each reader is left to be his own "philosopher of history" while perusing these pages; that is, to form his own conclusions upon the data here presented to him. To overcome, at least in some small degree, the obvious disadvantages of the style in which it has been determined to publish this history, marginal notes relating to important matters are given, which, while it is not claimed that they overcome the difficulties of the analistic style of the main body of the work, will nevertheless, be of great service to the reader both in this respect and also in here and there enlarging upon the Prophet's narrative where that narrative does not include all the facts known upon the subject.

From the first the Prophet Joseph Smith had a clear apprehension of the importance of keeping a faithful record of the events connected with the great work which God was bringing forth through his instrumentality; and it is to his appreciation of the importance of that fact, and his never tiring energy respecting it, that we are indebted for the minute completeness of our Church annals. While the very rapidity with which events happened, together with the quickly changing circumstances through which the purposes of God were unfolded in the great Dispensation of the Fulness of Times, necessarily occupied the time of the Prophet, and well nigh made it impossible for him to give all the attention to the making of annals that is necessary to such work, still he quite thoroughly supervised the writing of his history, with the result that more complete historical data have been written and preserved respecting the coming forth of the work of God in these last days than any other great movement whatsoever.

One difficulty the Prophet experienced in writing the annals of the Church, which he usually called his history, was the unfaithfulness of some whom he employed in this service, and the frequent change of historians, owing to the ever shifting conditions surrounding the Church in the early years of its existence. It would be marvelous indeed if under all these circumstances there had been no mistakes made in our annals, no conflict of dates, no errors in the relation of events. But whether these conditions are taken into account or not, the manuscript annals of the Church are astonishingly free from errors of dates, relation of facts, or anachronisms of every description. When the Church historians George A. Smith and Wilford Woodruff completed their publication of the *History of Joseph Smith,* down to the 8th of August, 1844, which history was published in instalments in the *Deseret News,* Utah, and in the *Millennial Star,* England, they expressed themselves upon the correctness of what they had published in the following manner:

"The *History of Joseph Smith* is now before the world, and we are satisfied that a history more correct in its details than this was never published. To have it strictly correct, the greatest possible pains have been taken by the historians and clerks engaged in the work. They were eye and ear witnesses of nearly all the transactions recorded in this history, most of which were reported as they transpired, and, where they were not personally present, they have had access to those who were. Moreover, since the death of the Prophet Joseph, the history has been carefully revised under the strict inspection of President Brigham Young, and approved by him, We, therefore, hereby bear our testimony to all the world, unto whom these words shall come, that the *History of Joseph Smith* is true, and is one of the most authentic histories ever written."

Their statement assuredly is true; and yet by a careful revision of the work they did, and the correction of a few errors in dates and other details, the work has been brought to a still higher state of perfection. Where grammatical accuracy was violated in the original record it has been corrected, so far as observed; but no historical or doctrinal statement has been changed. Some changes will be observed in the matter of the biographies of the leading elders of the early days of the Church. When a man of prominence connected himself with the Church, the Prophet Joseph usually gave a biographical sketch of him in his own history, then writing; and sometimes these biographies were long and unduly interrupted the movement of events. To rid the body of the work of this incumbrance it was decided to place all biographical matter in marginal notes; this made it necessary to condense very much those found in the Prophet's narrative, while severe brevity—after accuracy—has been the aim in those prepared by the annotator.

The most careful attention has been given to this work by those engaged in its preparation. The manuscript has been read to the Church Historian, President Anthon H. Lund, with constant reference to the original manuscript history and all copies of it published in the *Times and Seasons* and the *Millennial Star;* and also to various editions of the Doctrine and

Covenants, and the Book of Commandments published at Independence, Missouri, in 1833, where the revelations received by the Prophet Joseph Smith are contained. In the course of this work slight variations in phraseology were discovered in the several editions of the Doctrine and Covenants, that doubtless arose through careless proof reading; and as between the most carefully proof-read editions and the revelations found in the manuscript *History of the Church* there were some slight differences, which were corrected to agree with the original manuscript; but the corrections were never made until first submitted to the First Presidency, and carefully considered and approved by them. We therefore feel that this great care has resulted in presenting to the Church and to the world the revelations which the Prophet Joseph Smith received in their most perfect form; and that a standard is created for all future publication of these revelations. Speaking of the revelations that appear in this book, it is proper to remark that one of the chief values of this volume of the *History of the Church* will arise from the fact that the greater number of those revelations received by the Prophet Joseph Smith is published in it—one hundred and one, out of a hundred and thirty-three found in the Doctrine and Covenants; and as they are published in connection with the circumstances existing when brought forth, the student of the doctrines of the Church will find this volume of almost incalculable benefit to him.

In the Introduction it is believed the reader will find a fitting background from which are projected with majestic boldness the great events and splendid doctrines of the Dispensation of the Fulness of Times.

That dispensation, of which this history is but the chronicle, bears an important relation to all former dispensations since the world began. It is the ocean into which they as streams flow. It is their complement, and unifying force—it makes them all one; and demonstrates that while things to men appear but in parts, God forever stands in the presence of the whole, and dispenses His providences with reference to His perfect comprehension of the end from the beginning. It is to exhibit this relation of dispensations that the Introduction is written, and the importance of the subject must be the apology for its length.

TABLE OF CONTENTS

VOLUME I

CONTENTS

CHAPTER I.

JOSEPH SMITH'S BIRTH AND LINEAGE—THE PROPHET'S FIRST VISION —"THIS IS MY BELOVED SON."

CHAPTER II.

THE VISITATION OF MORONI—EXISTENCE OF THE BOOK OF MORMON MADE KNOWN.

CHAPTER III.

THE NEPHITE RECORD DELIVERED TO JOSEPH—THE ANGEL'S WARNING—THE WORK OF TRANSLATION.

CHAPTER IV.

OLIVER COWDERY BECOMES THE PROPHET'S SCRIBE—THE TRANSLATION OF THE PLATES CONTINUED.

CHAPTER V.

RESTORATION OF THE AARONIC PRIESTHOOD—FIRST BAPTISMS.

CHAPTER VI.

THE TESTIMONY OF THE ESPECIAL WITNESSES TO THE BOOK OF MORMON.

CHAPTER VII.

THE DAY APPOINTED FOR ORGANIZING THE CHURCH—REVELATION ON CHURCH GOVERNMENT.

CHAPTER VIII.

THE BOOK OF MORMON PUBLISHED—THE CHURCH ORGANIZED.

CHAPTER IX.

THE COMMENCEMENT OF THE PUBLIC MINISTRY OF THE CHURCH.

CHAPTER X.

THE MOLESTATION AT COLESVILLE BY MOBS—THE REVELATION EMBODYING THE VISION OF MOSES.

CHAPTER XI.

FURTHER LIGHT RESPECTING THE SACRAMENT—PROPHET'S REMOVAL TO FAYETTE.

CHAPTER XII.

LOST BOOKS OF ANCIENT SCRIPTURE—COMMANDMENT TO THE CHURCH IN NEW YORK TO MOVE TO OHIO.

CHAPTER XIII.

PROSPECTS OF THE CHURCH AT THE OPENING OF THE YEAR 1831—REMOVAL OF THE PROPHET JOSEPH FROM NEW YORK TO OHIO—DOCTRINAL DEVELOPMENT.

CHAPTER XIV.

EFFORT TO OVERWHELM THE CHURCH BY FALSEHOOD—SUNDRY REVELATIONS LEADING TO DOCTRINAL DEVELOPMENT.

CHAPTER XV.

THE IMPORTANT CONFERENCE OF JUNE 3RD-6TH—ARRIVAL OF THE ELDERS IN WESTERN MISSOURI.

CHAPTER XVI.

THE FOUNDING OF ZION.

CHAPTER XVII.

THE APOSTASY OF EZRA BOOTH—PREPARATIONS FOR PUBLISHING THE BOOK OF COMMANDMENTS.

CHAPTER XVIII.

THE AMHERST CONFERENCE—THE VISION OF THE DEGREES OF GLORY IN MAN'S FUTURE LIFE.

CHAPTER XIX.

MOB VIOLENCE AT HIRAM—THE SECOND JOURNEY OF THE PROPHET TO ZION, AND RETURN TO KIRTLAND.

CHAPTER XX.

"THE EVENING AND MORNING STAR."

CHAPTER XXI.

LARGER VIEWS OF THE DOCTRINE OF PRIESTHOOD REVEALED—THE MEETING OF THE PROPHET JOSEPH SMITH, JUN., BRIGHAM YOUNG, AND HEBER C. KIMBALL.

CHAPTER XXII.

THE PROPHECY ON THE WAR OF THE REBELLION—THE OLIVE LEAF—COMMUNICATION TO MR. SEATON—WARNING TO ZION.

CHAPTER XXIII.

THE ENJOYMENT OF SPIRITUAL BLESSINGS IN THE CHURCH—THE WORD OF WISDOM.

CHAPTER XXIV.

KIRTLAND TO BE A STAKE OF ZION—REGULATION OF CHURCH AFFAIRS IN MISSOURI.

CHAPTER XXV.

PREPARATIONS FOR BUILDING THE KIRTLAND TEMPLE—TRIAL AND EXCOMMUNICATION OF "DOCTOR" PHILASTUS HURLBURT.

CHAPTER XXVI.

THE PLAT OF THE CITY OF ZION—ITS TEMPLES—CORRESPONDENCE ON AFFAIRS IN ZION AND EUGENE.

CHAPTER XXVII.

PREPARATION OF THE MOB IN JACKSON COUNTY TO RESORT TO VIOLENCE—IMPORTANT EXCERPTS FROM THE "STAR."

CHAPTER XXVIII.

MOB VIOLENCE IN THE LAND OF ZION.

CHAPTER XXIX.

MINOR EVENTS IN ZION AND KIRTLAND—AN APPEAL TO THE GOVERNOR OF MISSOURI.

CHAPTER XXX

THE PROPHET'S MISSION TO CANADA.

CHAPTER XXXI.

EXPULSION OF THE SAINTS FROM JACKSON COUNTY.

CHAPTER XXXII.

REMEMBRANCE OF CANADA SAINTS—CORRESPONDENCE AND PETITION RELATIVE TO MISSOURI AFFAIRS.

CHAPTER XXXIII.

THE PROPHET'S SYMPATHY FOR THE EXILED SAINTS—REASONS FOR THEIR EXPULSION FROM ZION.

CHAPTER XXXIV.

A PRESS ESTABLISHED AT KIRTLAND—BLESSING UPON THE PROPHET'S FAMILY—RESPONSIBILITY FOR LAWLESS ACTS IN MISSOURI.

CHAPTER XXXV.

IMPORTANT CORRESPONDENCE ON JACKSON COUNTY AFFAIRS, CHIEFLY BETWEEN LEADING OFFICIALS OF THE CHURCH IN ZION AND STATE OFFICIALS OF MISSOURI.

INTRODUCTION

ANTIQUITY OF THE GOSPEL

THE HISTORY OF THE CHURCH OF JESUS CHRIST OF LATTER-DAY SAINTS is also the history of the opening and progress of the Dispensation of the Fulness of Times; and as that dispensation bears an important relation to all dispensations which have preceded it, let us here ascertain in what that relation consists. By doing so we shall have a better appreciation of the full import of those events which make up the history of the Church.

A dispensation, without reference to any specific application or limitation of the term, is the act of dealing out or distributing, such as the dispensation of justice by courts, the dispensation of blessings or afflictions by the hand of Providence. Theologically a dispensation is defined as one of the several systems or bodies of law in which at different periods God has revealed his mind and will to man, such as the Patriarchal Dispensation, the Mosaic Dispensation, or the Christian Dispensation. The word is also sometimes applied to the periods of time during which the said laws obtain. That is, the period from Adam to Noah is usually called the Patriarchal Dispensation. From Noah to the calling of Abraham, the Noachian Dispensation; and from Abraham to the calling of Moses, the Abrahamic Dispensation. But the word dispensation as connected with the Gospel of Jesus Christ means the opening of the heavens to men; the giving out or dispensing to them the word of God; the revealing to men in whole or in part the principles and ordinances of the Gospel; the conferring of divine authority upon certain chosen ones, by which they are empowered to act in the name, that is, in the authority of God, and for Him. That is a dispensation as relating to the Gospel; and the Dispensation of the Fulness of Times is the dispensation which includes all others and gathers to itself all things which bear any relation whatsoever to the work of God. Also it is the last dispensation, the one in which will be gathered together in one all things in Christ, both which are in heaven, and which are on earth; even in Him.* It is the dispensation which will see fulfilled all the decrees of God respecting the salvation of men and the redemption of the earth itself; and bears

*Eph. 1:8-10.

such relation to all other dispensations of the Gospel as the ocean does to all earth's streams. It receives and unites them all in itself.

That there have been many dispensations of the Gospel, many times that divine authority has been conferred upon men, is apparent from the Scripture narrative of such events. And yet, strange as it may seem, in the face of such Scripture narratives, there are those among professing Christians who hold that the Gospel had no earlier origin than the time of Messiah's ministry in the flesh. As a matter of fact, however, the Gospel of Jesus Christ has existed from the very earliest ages of the world. There are, indeed, certain passages of Scripture which lead us to believe that even before the earth was made or ever man was placed upon it, the Gospel had been formulated and was understood by the spirits which inhabited the kingdom of the Father; and who, in course of time, would be blessed with a probation on the earth—an earth-life. If this be not true, of what significance is the Scripture which speaks of Jesus as the Lamb ordained before the foundation of the world, but revealed in this day for the salvation of man?* What of the "Lamb slain from the foundation of the world"?† And further: "They that dwell on the earth shall wonder, whose names were not written in the Book of Life from the foundation of the world."‡ "Where wast thou," asked the Lord of Job, "when I laid the foundations of the earth? * * * When the morning stars sang together, and all the sons of God shouted for joy?"§ There is evidence in these expressions found in Scripture that before the foundations of the earth were laid the sacrifice necessary to the redemption of men was understood, and the "Lamb" for the sacrifice was chosen, Jesus, the Messiah. There is evidence in these expressions from Scripture of the pre-existence of the spirits of men, and the names of some of them at least were written in the "Book of Life" from the foundation of the world, and it is not unlikely that the shouting of all the sons of God for joy at the creation of the earth was in consequence of the prospects which opened before them because of the earth-life and the salvation that would come to them through the Gospel—even in the prospects of that "eternal life, which God that cannot lie promised before the world began."

The Gospel Revealed to Adam.

The Gospel, then, is of great antiquity. Older than the hills,

* I Peter 1: 18-25.

† Rev. xiii: 8.

‡ Rev. xvii: 8.

§ Job xxxviii: 4-6.

older than the earth; for in the heavenly kingdom was it formulated before the foundations of the earth were laid. Nor were men left in ignorance of the plan of their redemption until the coming of the Messiah in the flesh. From the first that plan was known. Our annals are imperfect on that head, doubtless, but enough exists even in the Jewish scriptures to indicate the existence of a knowledge of the fact of the Atonement and of the redemption of man through that means. Abel, the son of Adam, is the first we read of in the Jewish scriptures as offering "the firstlings of his flock" as a sacrifice unto God. How came he to offer sacrifice of the firstlings of his flock? Doubtless behind Abel's sacrifice, as behind similar offerings in subsequent ages, stood the fact of the Christ's Atonement.* In it was figured forth the means of man's redemption—through a sacrifice, and that the sacrifice of the first-born. But where learned Abel to offer sacrifice if not from his father Adam? It is reasonably certain that Adam as well as Abel offered sacrifices, in like manner and for the same intent; and to Adam, though the Jewish scriptures are silent respecting it, God must have revealed both the necessity of offering sacrifice and the great thing of which it was but the symbol. And here, to some advantage, may be quoted a passage from the writings of Moses, as revealed to Joseph Smith, in December, 1830. From what was then made known to the great latter-day Prophet of the writings of Moses, it appears that our book of Genesis does not contain all that was revealed to Moses respecting the revelations of God to Adam and his children of the first generation. According to this more complete account of the revelation to Moses, after Adam was driven from Eden, God gave commandments both to him and his wife, that they should worship the Lord their God, and should offer the firstlings of their flocks for an offering unto the Lord, and Adam was obedient unto the commandment:

> And after many days an angel of the Lord appeared unto Adam, saying: Why doest thou offer sacrfices unto the Lord? And Adam said unto him: I know not, save the Lord commanded me. And the angel spake, saying: This thing is a similitude of the sacrifice of the Only Begotten of the Father, which is full of grace and truth. Wherefore, thou shalt do all that thou doest in the name of the Son, and thou shalt repent and call upon God in the name of the Son for evermore.†

After some time elapsed and men multiplied in the earth and wickedness increased; after Abel, the righteous, was slain and Cain was a vagabond in the earth for the murder; after Lamech had also become a murderer and Satan had great power among the disobedient—then, it is written:

*Paul to Titus 1: 2.

†Pearl of Great Price, Book of Moses, ch. v:6-8, Edition of 1902, quoted throughout.

And God cursed the earth with a sore curse, and was angry with the wicked, with all the sons of men whom he had made; for they would not hearken unto His voice, nor believe on His Only Begotten Son, even Him whom He declared should come in the meridian of time, who was prepared from before the foundation of the world. And thus the Gospel began to be preached, from the beginning, being declared by holy angels sent forth from the presence of God, and by His own voice, and by the gift of the Holy Ghost. And thus all things were confirmed unto Adam, by an holy ordinance, and the Gospel preached, and a decree sent forth, that it should be in the world, until the end thereof.*

Establishment of the Ancient Church.

As the Gospel was thus preached there were those among the children of Adam who obeyed it, and a record of those men was kept, and they constituted the ancient Church of God. Enoch was of the number of righteous ones, and a preacher of righteousness. In these revealed writings of Moses he is represented in the course of his ministry as referring to the manner in which the Gospel was taught to Adam:

And he said unto them: Because that Adam fell, we are, and by his fall came death; and we are made partakers of misery and woe. Behold Satan hath come among the children of men, and tempteth them to worship him; and men have become carnal, sensual, and devilish, and are shut out from the presence of God. But God hath made known unto our fathers that all men must repent. And He called upon our father Adam by His own voice, saying: I am God; I made the world, and men before they were in the flesh. And He also said unto him: If thou wilt turn unto me, and hearken unto my voice, and believe, and repent of all thy transgressions, and be baptized, even in water, in the name of mine Only Begotten Son, who is full of grace and truth, which is Jesus Christ, the only name which shall be given under heaven, whereby salvation shall come unto the children of men, ye shall receive the gift of the Holy Ghost, asking all things in His name, and whatsoever ye shall ask, it shall be given you.†

Adam was obedient to the commandments of the Lord, and taught them to his children, many of whom believed them, obeyed, and became the sons of God.

Enoch, we are told, "walked with God: and he was not; for God took him."‡ Paul, in speaking of him, says: "By faith Enoch was translated that he should not see death; and was not found. because God had translated him."§ But the writings of Moses, as reveled to

* Pearl of Great Price, Book of Moses, ch. v: 56-59.
† Pearl of Great Price, Book of Moses, ch. vi: 48-52.
‡ Gen. v: 24.
§ Heb. xi: 5.

Joseph Smith, and from which I have been quoting, give information that not only was Enoch translated but the Saints inhabiting his city, into which he had gathered his people, and this city was called Zion; "And it came to pass that Zion was not, for God received it up into His own bosom; and from thence went forth the saying, Zion is fled."*

The Gospel versus the Law.

Thus the Gospel was taught to the ancients. Noah was a preacher of it as well as Enoch. So, too, was Melchizedek, priest of the Most High God, King of Salem, who met Abraham in his day and blessed him.† Paul, the Apostle of the Gentiles, bears unmistakable testimony to the fact that the Gospel was preached unto Abraham; and also that it was offered to Israel under Moses before "the law of carnal commandments" was given. "I would not that ye should be ignorant," he says, "how that all our fathers were under the cloud, and all passed through the sea; and were all baptized unto Moses in the cloud and in the sea; and did all eat the same spiritual meat; and did all drink the same spiritual drink: *for they drank of that spiritual Rock that followed them: and that Rock was Christ.*"‡

Referring again to the fact of the presentation of the Gospel to ancient Israel, Paul says that the Gospel was preached unto ancient Israel, as well as unto Israel in his day; but the preaching of the Gospel to ancient Israel was not profitable to them, because they received it not in faith, and as a result displeased God by their unbelief, and the rebellious perished in the wilderness.§

Paul's great controversy with the Christian Jews was in relation to the superiority of the Gospel to the law of Moses. Many of the Christian Jews while accepting Jesus of Nazareth as the promised Messiah, still held to the law with something like superstitious reverence, and could not be persuaded that the Gospel superseded the law, and was, in fact, a fulfilment of all its types and symbols. This controversy culminated in Paul's now celebrated letter to the Galatians, wherein he says:

Know ye therefore that they which are of faith, the same are the children of Abraham. And the Scripture, foreseeing that God would justi-

* Pearl of Great Price, Book of Moses, ch. vii: 69.

† Heb. vii: 1.

‡ 1 Cor. x: 1-4.

§ Heb. iii: 14-19 and iv: 1-2. This cites the close of one chapter and the opening verses of another, but it should be remembered that Paul did not divide his epistle into chapters and verses; and this awkward division is but one of many divisions that exist in the Scriptures.

fy the heathen through faith, *preached before the Gospel unto Abraham,* saying, in thee shall all nations be blessed. * * * * Now to Abraham and his seed were the promises made. He saith not, And to seeds, as of many; but as of one. And to thy seed, which is Christ. And this I say, that the covenant, that was confirmed before of God in Christ, the law, which was four hundred and thirty years after, cannot disannul, that it should make the promise of none effect. * * * * Wherefore then serveth the law? It was added because of transgressions, till the seed should come to whom the promise was made; and it was ordained by angels in the hand of a mediator. * * * Wherefore the law was our schoolmaster to bring us unto Christ, that we might be justified by faith. But after that faith is come, we are no longer under a schoolmaster. For ye are all the children of God by faith in Christ Jesus.*

From Moses to John the Baptist and Messiah

In greater clearness, however, than in these sayings of Paul gathered up from his writings like scattered rays of light from a prism's reflection, the antiquity of the Gospel, as far as it concerns ancient Israel, is stated in a revelation of God to the Prophet Joseph Smith. And not only the antiquity of the Gospel, but in greater clearness also is stated the reasons why, after the Gospel was first preached to ancient Israel, the law of carnal commandments was "added" to the Gospel, or given in its place, to act as a schoolmaster to bring Israel unto Christ. And by the knowledge imparted in that revelation the time between the Mosaic dispensation and the coming of John the Baptist, to prepare the way for the coming of the Christ, is spanned by a statement so rational, that the truth of it cannot be reasonably questioned. Speaking of the Melchizedek Priesthood and its powers in administering the ordinances of the Gospel, and how it came to disappear as an organization in Israel, the passage in question says:

This greater Priesthood administereth the Gospel and holdeth the key of the mysteries of the kingdom, even the key of the knowledge of God. Therefore, in the ordinances thereof, the power of godliness is manifest. And without the ordinances thereof, and the authority of the Priesthood, the power of godliness is not manifest unto men in the flesh; for without this no man can see the face of God, even the Father, and live. Now this Moses plainly taught to the children of Israel in the wilderness, and sought diligently to sanctify his people that they might behold the face of God; but they hardened their hearts and could not endure his presence; therefore, the Lord in his wrath, for his anger was kindled against them, swore that they should not enter into his rest while in the wilderness, which rest is the fulness of his glory. Therefore he took Moses out of their midst, and the Holy Priesthood also; and the lesser Priesthood con-

* Gal. iii.

tinued, which Priesthood holdeth the key of the ministering of angels and the preparatory Gospel; which Gospel is the Gospel of repentance and of baptism, and the remission of sins, and the law of carnal commandments, which the Lord in his wrath, caused to continue with the house of Aaron among the children of Israel until John, whom God raised up, being filled with the Holy Ghost from his mother's womb; for he was baptized while he was yet in his childhood, and was ordained by the angel of God at the time he was eight days old unto this power to overthrow the kingdom of the Jews, and to make straight the way of the Lord before the face of his people, to prepare them for the coming of the Lord, in whose hand is given all power.*

As before remarked, this passage spans the interval of time between Moses and John the Baptist, and gives a fuller explanation than can be found in the writings of Paul or elsewhere, for the reason why and in what manner the law supplanted the Gospel; and what measure of the Priesthood remained with Israel unto the coming of John; in what the mission of John consisted, and in what manner he was qualified to fulfil that mission.

It should be remarked, however, that while the Lord took Moses out of the midst of ancient Israel, and the Holy Melchizedek Priesthood also, as an institution, as an organization, it is evident that subsequently special dispensations of that Priesthood were given to individual prophets, such as Samuel, Nathan, Elijah, Isaiah, Jeremiah, Ezekiel, and Daniel: for these men exercised powers and enjoyed privileges which belong exclusively to the Melchizedek Priesthood.

The Dispensation of the Meridian of Time.

With the period between Moses and John the Baptist spanned, we come to the Dispensation of the Meridian of Time. This dispensation begins with the preaching of John the Baptist in the wilderness. It was made glorious by the personal ministry of Jesus of Nazareth, the Son of God; by His suffering and death, for the redemption of mankind; by His glorious resurrection from the dead; by His subsequent ministry among His followers, and His final ascension into heaven to the throne of His Father; by the faithful ministry of His Apostles, by whom the good tidings of man's salvation were published to the world: by the establishment of the Church as the agency through which the Gospel was to be more widely proclaimed, and those who accepted the Gospel were more thoroughly instructed in its doctrines, guarded from error, and finally perfected in the Christian life. An inspired volume of Scripture, the New Testament, was also

* Doctrine and Covenants, sec. lxxxiv: 19-28.

brought into existence, from the teachings of the inspired Apostles, in which the great fundamental truths of the Gospel were embodied and cast in a form that would be enduring, and to which men could appeal through all the ages to come, as an authoritative statement, not only of what Jesus said and what He did, but also a statement of what doctrines are to be believed; what precepts to be practiced; what ordinances to be observed. By thus embodying the chief doctrines of Christ in a volume of Scripture that should live forever, and be published in all the languages of the world, provision was made for such a dissemination of the knowledge of God, that the world would never again be wholly without that knowledge; and though the Church might become corrupted, as it afterwards did; though men ambitious of distinction and power might usurp authority and establish churches, in which they taught for doctrines the commandments of men, as they certainly did; still in this volume of Scripture men henceforth would have at hand a standard of truth by which to test the utterances of would-be teachers, while at the same time it would keep above the horizon of a world's knowledge the great truths of the Gospel—the existence and character of God; the manifestation of Him through the person and character of Jesus of Nazareth; the relationship existing between God and man; the fall of man; and the redemption provided for him in the atonement of Jesus Christ. All this was achieved in the Dispensation of the Meridian of Time; a mighty work accomplished by the Son of God and His associates; a work sealed not only by the blood of Jesus Christ, but by the blood also of many faithful witnesses, which shall make their testimony of force in the world.

The Identity of the Dispensation of the Meridian of Time and the Dispensation of the Fulness of Times Considered.

At this point we are confronted with a question that must be settled before progress is possible with this Introduction. Owing to the phraseology of certain passages of Scripture, making reference to the coming of Messiah in the flesh, and to the work of God in those days, the Dispensation of the Meridian of Time is mistaken for the Dispensation of the Fulness of Times. In Mark's Gospel, for instance, John the Baptist is represented as saying, "*The time is fulfilled*, and the kingdom of God is at hand: repent ye, and believe the gospel."* The words in Italics are usually understood to make reference to the Dispensation of the Fulness of Times. Again it is written: "*But when the fulness of the time was come*, God sent forth

* Mark i: 15.

His Son, made of a woman, made under the law, to redeem them that were under the law."* The words, "when the fulness of the time was come," are supposed to refer to the Dispensation of the Fulness of Times. Other passages of Scripture referring to the days of Messiah's personal ministry among men in the flesh, speak of them as the "last days." Paul, in the opening sentence of his letter to the Hebrews, does this: "God, who at sundry times and in divers manners spake in time past unto the fathers by the prophets, hath *in these last days* spoken unto us by His Son, whom He hath appointed heir of all things."† So St. John, in addressing the Saints in his day: "Little children, *it is the last time*: and as ye have heard that anti-Christ shall come, even now are there many anti-Christs; whereby we know that *it is the last time*."‡ These, with two other special passages of Scripture to be separately considered, constitute the authority upon which the Meridian Dispensation is confounded with the Dispensation of the Fulness of Times. And yet all these passages are susceptible of quite a different and more natural rendering. Without controversy it will be conceded that the Lord had an appointed time for His Son Jesus to come to earth in the flesh and perform the mission that had been assigned him; to suffer; to die; to arise again from the dead. And when the fulness of this time was come, God indeed sent forth His Son into the world. As for those inspired writers who speak of the "last days," and the "last times"—they speak relatively; that is, with reference to former days and times; and, of course, the days and times in which they lived to them were the last days, and the last times; but they were not the last days of the earth's temporal existence; they were not the last days in any general sense at all, as there have been now some two thousand years of days since then. They were not the "last days" that are understood as immediately preceding the glorious coming of the Son of God.

Joel's Great Prophecy of the Dispensation of the Last Days.

Of the special passages before referred to, and which I said would receive separate consideration, the first is Peter's quotation from the Prophet Joel concerning the outpouring of the Spirit of God upon "all flesh in the last days." This quotation from Joel is regarded as identifying the days in which the Apostle was speaking, as "the last days;" and the dispensation in which he was living as the Dispensation of the Last Days and of the Fulness of Times. The conditions existing when Peter was speaking, and the prophecy of Joel, however,

* Gal. iv: 4.

† Heb i: 1, 2.

‡ I John ii: 18.

admit of no such interpretation. The circumstances were as follows: The Holy Ghost in an extraordinary manner rested upon the Apostles and gave them the power of speaking in other languages than those they had learned. Some in the listening multitude attributed this singular manifestation to drunkenness, whereupon the Apostle Peter arose and refuted the slander, saying: "These are not drunken, as ye suppose, seeing it is but the third hour of the day. But this is *that* which was spoken by the Prophet Joel; and it shall come to pass *in the last days,* saith God, I will pour out of my Spirit upon all flesh: and your sons and your daughters shall prophesy, and your young men shall see visions, and your old men shall dream dreams: and on my servants and on my handmaidens I will pour out in those days of my Spirit; and they shall prophesy: and I will show wonders in heaven above, and signs in the earth beneath; blood, and fire, and vapor of smoke: the sun shall be turned into darkness and the moon into blood, before that great and notable day of the Lord come: and it shall come to pass, that whosoever shall call on the name of the Lord shall be saved."* "For," to finish the passage as it stands in Joel, but which is not in Peter's quotation, "For in Mount Zion and in Jerusalem shall be deliverance, as the Lord hath said, and in the remnant whom the Lord shall call."†

Because Peter, referring to the Spirit that was then resting upon the Twelve Apostles, said, "this is that which was spoken by the Prophet Joel," etc., the very general opinion prevails that Joel's prophecy was then fulfilled; and hence the *last days* were come. This is an entire misapprehension of the purpose of Peter in making the quotation; as also of the quoted passage itself. Beyond all controversy Peter meant only: This Spirit which you now see resting upon these Apostles of Jesus of Nazareth, is that same Spirit which your Prophet Joel says will, in the last days, be poured out upon all flesh. Obiviously he did not mean that this occasion of the Apostles receiving the Holy Ghost was a complete fulfilment of Joel's prediction. To insist upon such an exegesis would be to charge the chief of the Apostles with palpable ignorance of the meaning of Joel's prophecy. On the occasion in question the Holy Ghost was poured out upon the Twelve Apostles, who were given the power to speak in various tongues; Joel's prophecy for its complete fulfilment requires that the Spirit of the Lord, the Holy Ghost, shall be poured out upon *all flesh;* and undoubtedly refers to that time which shall come in the blessed millennium when the enmity shall not only cease between man and man, but even between the beasts of the forests and of the fields; and between man and beast, as described by Isaiah in the following language:

* Acts ii: 15-21.

† Joel ii: 28-32.

The wolf also shall dwell with the Lamb, and the leopard shall lie down with the kid; and the calf and the young lion and the fatling together; and a little child shall lead them. And the cow and the bear shall feed; their young ones shall lie down together: and the lion shall eat straw like the ox. And the suckling child shall play on the hole of the asp, and the weaned child shall put his hand on the cockatrice' den. They shall not hurt nor destroy in all my holy mountain; for the earth shall be full of the knowledge of the Lord, as the waters cover the sea.*

Compare these conditions so vividly described with what Joel himself says of the period when the Spirit of the Lord shall be poured out upon all flesh, and it will at once be clear that the two Prophets are dealing with the same period, and not only dealing with the same period, but that the period itself is certainly far beyond, in time, the days of Peter; in fact is still in the future; for the sun has not yet been turned into blackness; nor the moon into blood; nor have the stars withdrawn their shining. It is obvious that the events upon the day of Pentecost did not fulfil the terms of this prophecy, except in those particulars already pointed out. The mention in this prophecy, however, of those special signs which Jesus refers to as immediately preceding His own second and glorious coming, clearly demonstrate that Joel was speaking of the last days indeed, and not of a circumstance that occurred in connection with a period more properly designated as the Dispensation of the Meridian of Time. Immediately following his prediction of the outpouring of God's Spirit upon all flesh, Joel represents the Lord as saying: "And I will show wonders in the heavens and in the earth, blood, and fire, and pillars of smoke. The sun shall be turned into darkness, and the moon into blood, before the great and the terrible day of the Lord come." And later: "The sun and the moon shall be darkened, and the stars shall withdraw their shining. The Lord also shall roar out of Zion, and utter his voice from Jerusalem; and the heavens and the earth shall shake; but the Lord will be the hope of his people, and the strength of the children of Israel."

Compare this with the Savior's description of conditions in the earth that will precede His own second coming:

Immediately after the tribulation of those days shall the sun be darkened, and the moon shall not give her light, and the stars shall fall from heaven, and the powers of the heavens shall be shaken: and then shall appear the sign of the Son of Man in heaven: and then shall all the tribes of the earth mourn, and they shall see the Son of Man coming in the clouds of heaven with power and great glory. And he shall send his angels with a great sound of a trumpet, and they shall gather together his elect from the four winds, from one end of heaven to the other.†

The same wonders in heaven and earth; the same changes in sun

* Isaiah xi: 6-9.

† Matt. xxiv: 29-31.

and moon, and stars; the same promises of the gathering of God's people as are found in the prophecy of Joel. There can be no question, then, but that the prophecy of Joel refers to the same "last days" that Jesus here alludes to—the days of the coming of the Son of Man——and not to the days of Peter and the other Apostles in the Meridian of time.

The sum of the matter then is, that Peter was not living in the "last days;" that the prophecy of Joel was not in its entirety fulfilled in the outpouring of God's Spirit upon the Apostles on the day of Pentecost; that at no time subsequent to the days of the Apostles has there existed such conditions in the earth as amount to a complete fulfilment of Joel's prophecy; therefore at some time future from the days of the Apostles, we may look forward to a universal outpouring of God's Holy Spirit upon all flesh, resulting in a universal peace and widespread knowledge of God, brought about, unquestionably, by a subsequent dispensation from that in which Peter wrought—the Dispensation of the Fulness of Times, in which God promises to "gather together in one all things in Christ, both which are in heaven and which are on earth; even in Him."*

Daniel's Prophecy of the Rise of the Kingdom of God in the Last Days.

The second special Scripture to which I have promised a separate consideration is the prophecy of Daniel relative to the succession of the great earth empires; and the final establishment of the Kingdom of God, which in "the last days" shall fill the whole earth and remain for ever. By and error on the part of Christian writers Daniel's Prophecy concerning the Kingdom of God to be set up in "the last days" is supposed to have been fulfilled by the founding of "The Spiritual Kingdom of Christ" in the days of Messiah's earthly ministry; and therefore the conclusion is drawn that those days were "the last days," and the dispensation then ushered in, the final dispensation of the Gospel. It is my purpose here to refute that error.

The prophecy in question is familiar, and comes from Daniel's interpretation of the King of Babylon's dream of the great image, whose "brightness was excellent, whose form was terrible." The head of the image was of gold; his breast and arms were of silver; the body and thighs of brass; the legs of iron; and the feet and the toes part of iron and part of clay. The king in his dream also saw a little stone cut out of the mountain without hands, that smote the image upon the feet of mixed clay and iron, and broke it to pieces—until it became like the chaff of the summer threshingfloor, and the wind of heaven

* Eph. i: 10.

carried it away, that no place was found for it: but the little stone cut from the mountain without hands, which smote the image on the feet and ground it to dust, became a great mountain and filled the whole earth. This is the dream; and this is the prophet's interpretation, addressed to the king of Babylon:

> Thou, O king, art a king of kings: for the God of heaven hath given thee a kingdom, power, and strength, and glory. And wheresoever the children of men dwell, the beasts of the field and the fowls of the heaven hath he given into thine hand, and hath made thee ruler over them all. Thou art this head of gold. And after thee shall arise another kingdom inferior to thee, and another third kingdom of brass, which shall bear rule over all the earth. And the fourth kingdom shall be strong as iron: forasmuch as iron breaketh in pieces and subdueth all things: and as iron that breaketh all these, shall it break in pieces and bruise. And whereas thou sawest the feet and toes, part of potters' clay, and part of iron, the kingdom shall be divided: but there shall be in it of the strength of the iron, forasmuch as thou sawest the iron mixed with miry clay. And as the toes of the feet were part of iron, and part of clay, so the kingdom shall be partly strong, and partly broken. And whereas thou sawest iron mixed with miry clay, they shall mingle themselves with the seed of men: but they shall not cleave one to another, even as iron is not mixed with clay. And in the days of these kings shall the God of heaven set up a kingdom, which shall never be destroyed: and the kingdom shall not be left to other people, but it shall break in pieces and consume all these kingdoms, and it shall stand forever. Forasmuch as thou sawest that the stone was cut out of the mountain without hands, and that it brake in pieces the iron, the brass, the clay, the silver, and the gold; the great God hath made known to the king what shall come to pass hereafter: and the dream is certain, and the interpretation thereof sure.*

As understood by the learned, Daniel's interpretation stands thus:

"(1) The *Golden Head*—the Assyrio-Babylonish monarchy (the 6th and 5th century, B. C.);

"(2) The *Silver Breast and Arms*—the Medo-Persian empire (from 538 B. C. to about 330 B. C.);

"(3) The *Brazen Belly and Thighs*—the Greco-Macedonian kingdom, especially after Alexander, those of Egypt and Syria (from about 330 B. C. to 160 B. C.);

"(4) The *Legs of Iron*—the power of Rome, bestriding the east and west, but broken into a number of states, the ten toes, which retained some of its warlike strength (the iron), mingled with elements of weakness (the soft potters' clay), which rendered the whole imperial structure unstable.

* Dan. ii: 37-45.

"(5) The *Stone* cut without hands out of the *Living Rock,* dashing down the image, becoming a great mountain, and filling all the earth—*The Spiritual Kingdom of Christ.*"

The last phrase—"The Spiritual Kingdom of Christ"—meaning of course the "Christian churches" which have existed from the time of Christ, and that now exist, and which, taken together, form Christ's spiritual kingdom.

On the foregoing exegesis, which is the one commonly accepted by orthodox Christians, I make the following several observations:

First: The phrase with reference to the little Stone, "cut out of the Living Rock," is one introduced by Dr. Smith, from whose *Old Testament History** the above analysis of Daniel's interpretation is taken. The language of the Bible is, "cut out of the mountain without hands." Why it is changed by the Doctor one may not conjecture, unless it is to lay the foundation of an argument not warranted by the text of Daniel's interpretation. It is enough here to note that the change in phraseology is wholly gratuitous and unwarranted.

Second: The claim that the "little Stone cut from the mountain without hands," is the *"Spiritual Kingdom of Christ"*—if by that "spiritual kingdom" is meant not a real kingdom, actually existing, visible and tangible—is an assumption of the Doctor's. It is not the language of the Bible, nor is there any evidence in Scripture for believing that the "kingdom," represented by "the stone cut out of the mountain without hands," is any less a *material* kingdom than those which preceded it. The differences between this kingdom of God and the other kingdoms of the vision are not in the kingdom being "spiritual," but in these; (1) that the kingdom which God shall set up will never be destroyed; (2) never left to another people; (3) will break in pieces and consume all other kingdoms; (4) it shall fill the whole earth; (5) and stand forever. We are warranted in the belief, however, that it will be a tangible, *bona fide* government of God on earth, consisting of a king; subordinate officers; laws; subjects; and the whole earth for its territory—for its dominion. The coming forth of such a government, the founding of such a kingdom, is in harmony with all the hopes of all the saints, and the predictions of all the prophets who have touched upon the subject. It is the actual reign of Christ on earth with His Saints, in fulfilment of the hopes held out to them in every dispensation of the Gospel. It is to be the burden of the song of the redeemed out of every kindred, and tongue, and people, and nation, that Christ has made them unto their God kings and priests—"and we shall reign on the earth."† It is to be the chorus in

* Edition of 1878, page 622.

† Rev. v:10.

heaven—the kingdoms of this world are become the kingdoms of our Lord, and of His Christ; and He shall reign for ever and ever."* And the elders in heaven shall say:

> We give thee thanks, O Lord God Almighty, which art, and wast, and art to come; because thou hast taken to thee thy great power, and hast reigned. And the nations were angry, and thy wrath is come, and the time of the dead, that they should be judged, and that thou shouldst give reward unto thy servants the prophets, and to the saints, and them that fear thy name, small and great; and shouldst destroy them which destroy the earth.†

And still again:

> Blessed and holy is he that hath part in the first resurrection: on such the second death hath no power, but they shall be priests of God and of Christ, and shall reign with him a thousand years.‡

It should be observed respecting the last passage and the one preceding it, that "the reign on earth" of the kingdom of God is connected with the resurrection of the righteous saints; so that it will be the "last days" indeed—not in the days of the Roman empire. And this reign of the saints on earth, this kingdom of God which they shall constitute shall be a reign of righteousness, but a veritable kingdom nevertheless.

Third: The orthodox exegesis under consideration omits one important matter of fact, viz., that instead of four great dominant political powers symbolized in the image which Nebuchadnezzar saw, and which Daniel interpreted, there are five: viz., (1) The Head of Gold—Babylonish Kingdom; (2) the Chest and Arms of Silver—the Medo-Persian Monarchy; (3) the Brazen Belly and Thighs—the Greco-Macedonian Empire; (4) the Legs of Iron—Rome; (5) the *Feet and Toes Mixed of Iron and Clay*—the modern kingdoms and states of the world.

This failure to recognize the fifth political power represented by the feet and toes of Daniel's image leads to serious errors with respect to this prophecy. It has led the theologians to assign the setting up of God's kingdom spoken of in the prophecy to the wrong period of the world's history. They say the kingdom represented by the stone cut from the mountain without hands is "the spiritual kingdom of Christ;" and that the said kingdom was set up in the days of Messiah's earthly ministry in the meridian of time. This, however, cannot be correct; for the Church which Jesus established by His personal ministry and which, it is granted, is sometimes spoken of as the Kingdom of

* Rev. xi: 15.

† Ibid xi: 17, 18.

‡ Ibid. xx: 6.

God, was founded in the days of the Roman empire, the fourth world power of Daniel's prophecy; and at a time, too, when imperial Rome was at the very zenith of her glory and power. Whereas the terms of Daniel's prophecy require that the kingdom which God shall establish, and which was represented by the stone cut from the mountain without hands, shall be set up in the days of the fifth political world power—in the days of the kingdom represented by the pieces of iron and clay in the feet and toes of the image. The language of the prophecy on this point is: "And whereas thou sawest the feet and toes, part of potters' clay, and part of iron, the kingdom [i. e. the political power so represented, and that succeeds the fourth power or Roman empire,] shall be divided; but there shall be in it of the strength of the iron, forasmuch as thou sawest the iron mixed with miry clay. And as the toes of the feet were part of iron, and part of clay, * * * they [i. e., the kingdom represented by the pieces of iron and clay,] shall mingle themselves with the seed of men: but they shall not cleave one to another even as iron is not mixed with clay. And in the days of *these kings* [not in the days of the Roman empire]—*in the days of these kings* shall the God of heaven set up a kingdom, which never shall be destroyed."

Fourth: One of the peculiarities of the kingdom of God of Daniel's prophecy is, that when it is established among men it will not only never be destroyed, but *"the kingdom shall not be left to other people."* By which saying we can only conclude that when the kingdom of God shall be set up by the Lord in the last days, it will not be taken from the people to whom it shall come, and be given, or left, to another people. But how stands it with the institution which arose from the preaching of the Gospel in the days of Messiah's earthly ministry, the church, sometimes called the kingdom of God, and the kingdom of heaven? Was it not "left to other people?" Messiah Himself said of the Jews, "Therefore say I unto you, *the kingdom of God shall be taken from you and given to a nation bringing forth the fruits thereof.*" This passage comes, too, as a conclusion to the parable of the householder who let both his house and his vineyard to unworthy husbandmen, who successively beat, stoned, and slew the servants, and even the son and heir whom the master sent to collect his portion of the fruit of the vineyard. "When the Lord of the vineyard cometh, what will he do unto those husbandmen?" asked Jesus of his hearers. "He will miserably destroy these wicked men," they replied, "and will let out his vineyard unto other husbandmen, which shall render him the fruits in their season." They had pronounced judgment upon themselves. The parable presented the case of the Jews to whom Jesus was speaking, exactly, and Jesus quickly made the application of the judgment—

"Therefore say I unto you, The kingdom of God shall be taken from you, and given unto a nation bringing forth the fruits thereof."* There can be no mistaking the meaning of the parable or its application; and some years later we have Paul saying to the contradicting and blaspheming Jews of Antioch in Pisidia: "It was necessary that the word of God should first have been spoken to you; but seeing ye put it from you, and judge yourselves unworthy of everlasting life, lo, we turn to the Gentiles. *For so hath the Lord commanded us*"† And so it came to pass that as Israel in those days rejected the Gospel of the kingdom which was first offered to them, so God also rejected them; and they have stood rejected to this day; smitten and trodden under foot of the Gentile races, a scoff, a hiss, and a byword in every land that they have inhabited; while the kingdom of God first offered to them was left to other people, to the Gentiles, who, for a season, brought forth the fruits thereof. But the fact that the kingdom then preached to the Jews was taken from them and given to another people, is proof positive that it was not the kingdom which was to fulfil the terms of Daniel's great prophecy.

Fifth: Another characteristic of the kingdom of God of Daniel's prophecy is, that it will never be destroyed, but will break in pieces and consume all other kingdoms, and stand for ever. This is not true of that institution brought into existence by the preaching of Messiah and the Apostles, sometimes called the kingdom of God, but more properly the Church of Christ. Saddening as the thought may seem, the Church founded by the labors of Jesus and His Apostles was destroyed from the earth; the Gospel was perverted; its ordinances were changed; its laws were transgressed; its covenant was, on the part of man, broken; and the world was left to flounder in the darkness of a long period of apostasy from God. For the reason, then, that the institution founded by the preaching of the Apostles was destroyed in the earth, as well as for the other reasons considered, the conclusion is forced upon the mind that the Church founded by Jesus and the Apostles was not the fulfilment of Daniel's great prophecy respecting the kingdom which God promised to set up in the last days: and hence we may look for another dispensation beyond the times of the Apostles, which will culminate in subduing the kingdoms of this world and making them the kingdom of our God and His Christ, followed by that reign of righteousness and peace of which all the prophets have spoken.

Having considered the Dispensation of the Meridian of Time and corrected the popular error which confounds that dispensation with the

*Matt. xxi: 43.
†Acts xii: 46, 47.

Dispensation of the Fulness of Times, it is necessary now to consider the decline of the Christian religion.

The Announcement of the Universal Apostasy

It is a most startling announcement with which the Prophet Joseph Smith begins his message to the world. Concerning the question, he asked God—"Which of all the sects is right, and which shall I join?" he says:

*"I was answered that I must join none of them, for they were all wrong, and the personage who addressed me said that all their creeds were abomination in His sight: that those professors were all corrupt; that they draw near to me with their lips, but their hearts are far from me; they teach for doctrines the commandments of men: having a form of godliness, but they deny the power thereof."**

This is a tremendous arraignment of all Christendom. It charges a condition of universal apostasy from God, especially upon Christendom that was dwelling in a fancied security of being the farthest removed from the possibility of such a charge; each division of the so-called Christian Church felicitating itself with the flattering unction that its own particular society possessed the enlightened fullness of the Christian religion. While the boldness of this declaration of the young Prophet is astounding, upon reflection it must be conceded that just such a condition of affairs in the religious world is consistent with the work he, under the direction of divine Providence, was about to inaugurate. Nothing less than a complete apostasy from the Christian religion would warrant the establishment of the Church of Jesus Christ of Latter-day Saints. Of sects there were already enough in existence. Division and subdivision had already created of confusion more than enough, and there was no possible excuse for the introduction of a new Christian sect. But if men through apostasy had corrupted the Christian religion and lost divine authority to administer the ordinances of the Gospel, it was of the utmost importance that a new dispensation of the true Christian religion should be given to the world. It should also be observed at this point, that Joseph Smith, then but a boy, scarcely removed from childhood, was not himself pronouncing judgment upon the status of Christendom. It was not he who declared the sects to be all wrong, their creeds an abomination, and the professors thereof corrupt. He of all persons, both on account of his extreme

**History of the Church*, vol. 1, p. 6.

youthfulness and his lack of general information, was among the least qualified to pronounce upon such a question. Indeed, he himself confesses his unfitness for such an office. His seeking knowledge from God upon this very question—"which of all the sects is right?"' is a confession of his own inability to determine the matter. No human wisdom was sufficient to answer that question. No man in all the world was so pre-eminent as to be justified in proclaiming the divine acceptance of one church in preference to another. Divine wisdom alone was sufficient to pass judgment upon such a question; and there is peculiar force in the circumstance that the announcement which Joseph Smith makes with reference to this subject is not formulated by him nor by any other man, but is given to him of God. God has been the judge of apostate Christendom, Joseph Smith but His messenger, to herald that judgment to the world.

It now becomes my melancholy task to trace through the early Christian centuries the decline of the Christian religion. By this phrase I mean that a really unChristian religion was gradually substituted for the beautiful religion of Jesus Christ; that a universal apostasy from the Christian doctrine and the Christian Church took place. So tracing the decline of Christianity, I shall establish the truth of the first great message with which the modern prophet, Joseph Smith, came to the world; and shall also prove the fact, that a necessity existed for the establishment of such a work as he claims, under God. to have founded, and of which the several volumes of this work are the detailed history.

Character of the Early Christians.

First of all, it should be remarked that the early Christians were not so far removed from the possession of the common weaknesses of humanity as to preclude the possibility of apostatizing from the Christian religion. Owing to our being so far removed from them in time, by which many of their defects are obscured, and the exaggerated celebration of their virtues, extravagant ideas of the sanctity of their lives, and the holiness of their natures have very generally obtained, whereas a little inquiry into the character of the early Saints will prove that they were very human, and men of like passions with ourselves. The mother of Zebedee's children exhibited a rather ambitious spirit, and the two brethren themselves gave much offense to their fellow Apostles by aspiring to sit one on the right hand of Jesus and the other on His left when He should come in His kingdom.* Even Peter, the chief Apostle, exhibited his full share of human weakness

* Matt. xx: 20-24.

when he thrice denied his Lord in the presence of his enemies, through fear, and even confirmed that denial by cursing and swearing.* It was rather a heated controversy, too, that arose in the early Christian Church as to whether those who accepted the Christian faith were still bound to the observances of the law of Moses, and more especially to the rite of circumcision. Although there seems to have been an amicable and authoritative settlement of that question by the decision of what some learned writers have called the first general council of the Church held by the Apostles and Elders at Jerusalem,† yet the old difficulty broke out again and again, not only between the Jewish saints and the Gentile converts, but even among the Apostles themselves, leading to serious accusations one against another, the straining of friendship between fellow-workmen in the ministry, through criminations and recriminations.

After the settlement of this very question of circumcision by the council at Jerusalem, Peter went down to Antioch and at first mingled unreservedly with both Gentile and Jewish converts without distinction, accepting both Jew and Gentile in perfect fellowship, departing entirely from the restraints placed on a Jew by the law of Moses, which rendered it unlawful for one who was a Jew to have such unrestricted fellowship with the Gentiles. But when certain ones came down from James, who resided at Jerusalem, then Peter, fearful of offending "them which were of the circumcision," suddenly withdrew his social fellowship from the Gentile converts. Other Jewish brethren did the same; Barnabas, the friend of Paul, being among the number. Whereupon Paul, as he himself testified, withstood Peter to the face, directly charging him before all the brethren with dissimulation, saying: "If thou, being a Jew, livest after the manner of Gentiles, and not as do the Jews, why compellest thou the Gentiles to live as do the Jews?"‡ Yet this same Paul notwithstanding his loyaly to the Gentile converts on that occasion, his zeal for the decision which had been rendered by the council of the Church at Jerusalem, and notwithstandng his usually strong moral courage subsequently showed, by his conduct, that he, too, was not beyond the weakness of "becoming all things to all men;" for a short time after the incident with Peter at Antioch. when in the province of Galatia, and he desired Timothy to be his companion in the ministry, Paul took him and circumcised him, because it was well known that while his mother was a Jewess, his father was a Greek, and all this for fear of the Jews.§

* Matt. xxvi: 69-75.

† Acts xv

‡ Galatians ii: 1-14.

§ Acts xvi: 1-4.

This question continued to be a cause of contention, even after this sharp disputation at Antioch; for though the decision of the council at Jerusalem was against the contention of the Judaizing party, yet they continued to agitate the question whenever opportunity presented itself, and seemed especially to follow close upon the footsteps of Paul in his missionary journeys; and in Galatia, at least, succeeded in turning the saints of that province from the grace of Christ unto another gospel, perverting the Gospel of Christ.* This question continued to agitate the Church throughout the Apostolic age, and was finally settled through overwhelming numbers of Gentiles being converted, and taking possession of the Church, rather than through any profound respect for the decision of the council at Jerusalem.

The withdrawal of John Mark from the ministry while accompanying Paul and Barnabas on their first mission in Asia Minor, and which withdrawal grew out of a faltering of his zeal or a misunderstanding with his companions, will be readily called to mind.† Subsequently, when Paul proposed to Barnabas that they go again and visit the brethren in every city where they had preached while on their first mission, a sharp contention arose between them about this same John Mark. Barnabas desired to take him again into the ministry, but Paul seriously objected; and so pronounced was the quarrel between them that these two friends and fellow yokemen in the ministry parted company no more to be united. It is just possible also that in addition to this misunderstanding about John Mark, the severe reproof which Paul administered to Barnabas in the affair of dissimulation at Antioch had somewhat strained their friendship.

Turning from these misunderstandings and criminations among the leading officers of the Church, let us inquire how it stood with the members. The epistle of Paul to the church at Corinth discloses the fact that there were serious schisms among them; some boasting that they were of Paul, others that they were of Apollos, others of Cephas, and still others of Christ; which led Paul to ask sharply, "Is Christ divided? was Paul crucified for you?"‡ There were endless strifes as well as divisions among them, which caused Paul to denounce them as carnally minded.§ Among them also was such fornication as was not named among the Gentiles, "that one should have his father's wife!" And this shameful sin had not humbled the church at Corinth, for Paul denounced them for being puffed up in the presence of such a crime, rather than having mourned over it.‖ They were in the habit of

* Gal. i: 6, 7.

† Acts xiii: 13.

‡ I Cor. i: 12-13.

§ I Cor. iii: 3, 4.

‖ I Cor. v: 1-3.

going to law one with another, and that before the world, in violation of the teachings of Jesus Christ.* They desecrated the ordinance of the Lord's Supper by their drunkenness, for which they were sharply reproved by the Apostle.† They ate and drank unworthily, "not discerning the Lord's body; for which cause many were sickly among them, and many slept" (that is, died). There were heresies also among them,‡ some denying the resurrection of the dead, while others possessed not the knowledge of God, which the Apostle declared was their shame.§ It is true, this sharp letter of reproof made the Corinthian saints sorry, and sorry, too, after a godly fashion, in that it brought them to a partial repentance; but even in the second epistle, from which we learn of their partial repentance, the Apostle could still charge that there were many in the church who had not repented of the uncleanness and fornication and lasciviousness which they had committed.‖ From this second letter, also, we learn that there were many in the Church at large who corrupted the word of God;** that there were those, even in the ministry, who were "false prophets, deceitful workers, transforming themselves into the Apostles of Christ."††

Of the churches throughout the province of Galatia, it is scarcely necessary to say more than we have already said concerning the invasion of that province by Judaizing Christian ministers who were turning away the saints from the grace of Christ back to the beggarly elements of the law of carnal commandments; a circumstance which led Paul to exclaim: "I marvel that ye are so soon removed from him that had called you unto the grace of Christ unto another gospel: which is not another; but there be some that trouble you and would pervert the gospel of Christ.‡‡

That there were two distinct parties in the Church at this time, between whom bitter contentions arose, is further evidenced by the letter of Paul to the Philippians. Some preached Christ even of envy and strife, and some of good will. "The one preach Christ of contention, not sincerely," says Paul, "supposing to add affliction to my bonds: but the other of love, knowing that I am set for the defense of the Gospel."§§ "Beware of dogs," said he again to the same people; "beware of evil workers; beware of the concision." ¶¶ "Brethren, be fol-

* I Cor. vi: 1-20, and Matt. xviii: 15, 17.

† I Cor. xi: 2-22 and 29, 30.

‡ I Cor. xi: 19.

§ I Cor. xv:12-34.

‖ II Cor. xi: 21

** II Cor. ii: 17.

†† II Cor. xi: 12-14.

‡‡ Gal. i: 6, 7.

§§ Phil. i: 15, 16.

¶¶ Phil. iii: 2.

lowers together of me," he admonishes them, "and mark them which walk so as ye have us for an example. For many walk, of whom I have told you often, and now tell you even weeping, that they are the enemies of the cross of Christ: whose end is destruction, whose God is their belly, and whose glory is in their shame, who mind earthly things."* To the Colossians Paul found it necessary to say: "Beware lest any man spoil you through philosophy and vain deceit, after the tradition of men, after the rudiments of the world, and not after Christ. * * * Let no man beguile you of your reward in a voluntary humility and worshiping of angels, intruding into those things which he hath not seen, vainly puffed up by his fleshly mind."†

But it is in Paul's pastoral letters that we get a deeper insight into corruptions threatening the early church, and even beginning to lay the foundation for that subsequent apostasy which overwhelmed it. The Apostle sent Timothy to the saints at Ephesus to represent him, that he might charge some to teach no other doctrines than those which he had delivered to them: "Neither give heed to fables and endless genealogies, which minister questions, rather than godly edifying which is in faith," for some had turned aside from the commandment of charity, out of a pure heart, and a good conscience, and faith unfeigned, unto "vain jangling; desiring to be teachers of the law; understanding neither what they say nor whereof they affirm."‡ Others concerning faith had made shipwreck, of whom were Hymenaeus and Alexander, whom Paul had delivered unto Satan that they might learn not to blaspheme.§ Others had "erred concerning the faith", and had "given heed to vain babblings, and opposition of science falsely so called."‖ In his second letter to Timothy, Paul informs him that all the saints in Asia had turned away from him, of whom were Phygellus and Hermogenes."** He admonishes Timothy again to shun "profane and vain babblings," "for," said he, "they will increase unto more ungodliness, and their word will eat as doth a canker; of whom is Hymenaeus and Philetus; who, concerning the truth, have erred, saying that the resurrection is passed already, and overthrown the faith of some."†† Demos, once a fellow-laborer with Paul, had forsaken him, "having loved this present world;"‡‡ and at Paul's first answer, that is, when arraigned before the court at Rome, no man

* Phil. iii: 17, 19.
† Col. ii: 8, 18.
‡ I Tim. i: 4-7.
§ I Tim. i: 19, 20.
‖ I Tim. vi: 20, 21.
** II Tim. i: 15.
†† II Tim. 2: 16, 18.
‡‡ II Tim. iv: 10.

stood with him, but all men forsook him; he prays that God will not lay this to their charge.*

Paul admonished Titus to hold fast to the faith, for there were many unruly and vain talkers and deceivers, especially those of the circumcision; who subverted whole houses, teaching things which they ought not, for filthy lucre's sake; and were giving heed to Jewish fables and commandments of men and turning from the truth.†

Peter also had something to say with reference to the danger of heresies and false teachers which menaced the Church. He declared that there would be false teachers among the saints, who "privily would bring in damnable heresies, even denying the Lord that bought them, and bring upon themselves swift destruction." "And many," said he, "shall follow their pernicious ways: by reason of whom the truth shall be evil spoken of. And through covetousness shall they with feigned words make merchandise of you; whose judgment now for a long time lingereth not, and their damnation slumbereth not. For if God spared not the angels that sinned, but cast them down to hell and delivered them unto chains of darkness to be reserved unto judgment"—he argued that the Lord would not spare these corrupters of the Gospel of Christ, who, like the dog, had turned again to his own vomit, and the sow who was washed to her wallowing in the mire.‡ He charged also that some were wresting the epistles of Paul, as they were some of the "other scriptures," unto their own destruction.§

John, the disciple whom Jesus loved, also bears testimony to the existence of anti-Christs, false prophets, and the depravity of many in the early Church. "It is the last time," said he, "and as ye have heard that anti-Christ shall come, even now there are many anti-Christs, whereby we know that it is the last time;" * * * * "They went out from us * * * * that they might be manifest that they were not all of us."‖ "Try the spirits," said he, in the same epistle, "whether they are of God; because many false prophets are gone out into the world."** Again: "Many deceivers are entered into the world, who confess not that Jesus Christ is come in the flesh. This is a deceiver, an anti-Christ."††

Jude also is a witness against this class of deceivers. He admonished

* II Tim. iv: 16.

† Titus i: 9-14.

‡ II Peter ii.

§ Ibid. iii: 16.

‖ I John ii: 18, 19.

** I John iv: 1.

†† II John vii: 5.

the saints to "contend earnestly for the faith which was once delivered unto the saints;" "for," said he, "there are certain men crept in unawares, * * * ungodly men, turning the grace of our God into lasciviousness and denying the only Lord God, and our Lord Jesus Christ."* The rest of the epistle he devotes to a description of their wickedness, comparing it with the conduct of Satan, and the vileness of the inhabitants of Sodom and Gomorrah.

I have not given this review of the condition of the Church of Christ in the Apostolic age with the view of establishing the idea that the Church at that time was in a complete state of apostasy; nor have I dwelt upon the weaknesses and sins of the early saints for the purpose of holding them up for contempt. My only purpose has been to dispel, first of all, the extravagant ideas that obtain in many minds concerning the absolute sanctity of the early Christians; and secondly, and mainly, to show that there were elements and tendencies existing in the early Church, even in the days of the Apostles, that would, when unrestrained by Apostolic authority and power, lead to its entire overthrow.

We have no good reason to believe that there occurred any change for the better in the affairs of the Church after the demise of the Apostles, no reason to believe that there were fewer hereies or fewer false teachers, or false prophets to lead away the people with their vain philosophies, their foolish babblings, and opposition of science falsely so called. On the contrary, one is forced to believe the prediction of Paul, viz., that evil men and seducers would wax worse and worse, deceiving and being deceived;† for who, after the Apostles were fallen asleep, would stand up and correct the heresies, that were brought into the Church, rebuke the schismatics, the false teachers and false prophets that arose to draw away disciples after them? If false teachers insinuated themselves into the Church, brought in damnable heresies by reason of which the way of truth was evil spoken of, and the pure religion of Jesus Christ corrupted even while inspired Apostles were still in the Church, it is not unreasonable to conclude that all these evils would increase and revel unchecked after the death of the Apostles.

The Rise of False Teachers.

I cannot, of course, in this introduction, enter into even a brief history of false teachers in the early Christian centuries. That of itself would be matter for a volume. I shall therefore content myself with making quotations from reliable authorities that will directly establish the fact of the rapid increase in the number of false teachers, and the

* Jude 3, 4.

† II Tim. iii: 13.

Pernicious effects of their doctrines upon the Christian religion. It should be said before making these quotations, however, that Protestant writers are interested in maintaining that the Christian religion was perpetuated, even through the ages of apostasy, and given back to mankind by the agency of the so-called "Reformation" of the sixteenth century. Hence in their writings, when stating the corruptions of the early Church, they are especially guarded, lest too strong a statement would lead to the belief that the Christian religion had been utterly subverted. Indeed, it is well known that Milner wrote his *Church History*—which should be regarded not so much as the history of the Church as the history of piety—to counteract the influence of Mosheim's *Institutes of Ecclesiastical History*, which work Milner considered too frank in its statements of perversions and abuses of religion. The Protestant writers must need set forth the theory that the Christian religion survived all the abuses and corruptions of it through ages of apostasy, else they would have no logical ground for the sixteenth century "Reformation" to stand upon. They seem not oblivious to the fact, though never mentioning it, that if the Christian religion was displaced by a paganized religion—a false religion—as is fully predicted, as we shall see later, in the New Testament prophecies, and of which the works of Protestant writers go far towards proving—then the only possible way in which the true Christian religion and the Church of Christ could be restored would be by re-opening of the heavens, and the giving forth of a new dispensation of the Gospel, together with a renewal of divine authority to preach it, and administer its ordinances of salvation. Catholics hold that there has been no great apostasy in the Church. Their theory is, that there has been a constant, unbroken, perpetuation of the Christian Church from the days of the Messiah and His Apostles until now; and that the Roman Catholic church is that very Church so perpetuated through the ages. Catholic writers admit that there have been very corrupt periods in the church and many wicked prelates, and some vile popes; yet they hold that the church has persisted, that the Christian religion has been preserved in the earth.

With these remarks on the position of the Protestant and Catholic churches respecting their attitude on the subject of the perpetuation of the Christian religion, I proceed with the quotations promised; and, first, a passage from Neander's *History of the Christian Religion and Church*, on the very great difference between the writings of the Apostles and the writings of the so-called Apostolic Fathers; and the suddenness of that transition, to the disparagement of the productions of the Fathers:

A phenomenon, singular in its kind, is the striking difference between the writings of the apostles and the writings of the Apostolic Fathers, who were so nearly their contemporaries. In other cases, transitions are wont to be gradual; but in this instance we observe a sudden change. There are here no gentle gradations, but all at once an abrupt transition from one style of language to another; a phenomenon which should lead us to acknowledge the fact of a special agency of the Divine Spirit in the souls of the Apostles. After the time of the first extraordinary operations of the Holy Ghost followed the period of the free development of human nature in Christianity; and here, as in all other cases, the beginning must be small and feeble before the effects of Christianity could penetrate more widely, and bring fully under their influence the great powers of the human mind. It was to be shown first, what the divine power could effect by the foolishness of preaching. The writings of the so-called Apostolic Fathers have unhappily, for the most part, come down to us in a condition very little worthy of confidence, partly because under the name of these men, so highly venerated in the Church, writings were early forged for the purpose of giving authority to particular opinions or principles; and partly because their own writings which were extant became interpolated in subservience to a Jewish hierarchical interest which aimed to crush the free spirit of the Gospel.*

There is no authority of scripture for the supposition made here by Dr. Neander that the extraordinary operations of the Holy Ghost were to be confined to the Apostles; the whole tenor of scripture authority is to the contrary. It is the theory of the Gospel itself, that all who receive it, and particularly its ministers, shall have the divine Spirit as a special agency working in their souls, through all time, and there is no warrant for the belief that its operations were to be confined to those who first received it and became its first ministers. Therefore, this sudden transition in the matter of excellence and trustworthiness between the writings of the Apostles and the writings of the Apostolic Fathers indicates not only a deterioration in the character of the teachers in the Church and what is taught, but more especially indicates the progress of the "mystery of iniquity" which was at work subverting the Christian religion and destroying the Church of Christ.

On the question of forged books and writings mentioned in the passage from Neander, Dr. Nathaniel Lardner refers to a dissertation written by Dr. Mosheim, which shows the reasons and causes for the many forged writings produced in the first and second centuries, and then adds: "All own that Christians of all sorts were guilty of this fraud. Indeed we may say it was one great fault of the times; for truth needs no such defenses, and would blush at the sight of them."†

Eusebius, quoting Hegesippus on the subject of false teachers and referring to the condition of the Church about the close of the first century, says:

* Vol. i, pp. 656, 657.

†Lardner's *Works*, vol. viii, p. 330.

The Church continued until then [close of the first century] as a pure and uncorrupt virgin, whilst if there were any at all that attempted to pervert the sound doctrine of the saving Gospel, they were yet skulking in dark retreats: but when the sacred choir of Apostles became extinct, and the generation of those that had been privileged to hear their inspired wisdom had passed away, then also the combinations of impious errors arose by the fraud and delusions of false teachers. These also, as there were none of the Apostles left, henceforth attempted without shame, to preach their false doctrine against the gospel of truth.*

Dr. Mosheim has the following on the same subject:

Not long after the Savior's ascension, various histories of his life and doctrines, full of impositions and fables, were composed by persons of no bad intentions, perhaps, but who were superstitious, simple, and piously fraudulent; and afterwards various other spurious writings were palmed upon the world, falsely inscribed with the names of the holy Apostles.†

This condition of things with reference to the writers in the centuries under consideration, naturally leads one to the reflection, that if there were so much of fraud, and so many forged writings, what must have been the state of the Church at this time with reference to oral teaching? We are justified in believing, I think, that bad as was the state of things with reference to the writings of these early teachers of the Church, the discourses of such as preached may be depended upon as being much worse. In this view of the case, one can readily understand that the "authority of antiquity" so generally urged as a reason for accepting the testimonies of the Fathers, that "handmaid to scripture," as "antiquity" is sometimes called, the whole body of it, written and oral, may indeed "be regarded," as Dr. Jortin remarks, "as Briarean, for she has a hundred hands, and these hands often clash and beat one another."‡

Moreover, it often happens that those who are condemned by some of these Fathers as heretics were not only censured for their heresies, but sometimes for the truths which they held. For example: Papias, a Bishop and Christian Father in the second century, is condemned by Eusebius for saying that he received from Apostolic men—meaning thereby men who were associated with the Apostles—the fact that there would be a corporeal reign of Christ on earth with the saints, after the resurrection, which would continue through a thousand years.§

* Eus. *Ec. Hist.*, bk. iii, ch. 32.

†*Institutes*, bk. i cent. 1, part ii, ch. ii.

‡ Jortin's *Remarks on Ecclesiastical History*, vol. i, p. 248.

§ Eusebius, bk. iii, ch. 39.

Prodicus is censured by Clement of Alexandria for holding that men are by nature the children of Deity.*

Marcion, besides being condemned for his many errors, is also censured by Irenaeus for believing in salvation for the dead, concerning which, it must be acknowledged, Marcion did hold peculiar views; but that is no reason why the general principle should be condemned.† He taught that Jesus Christ went to Hades and preached there, and brought hence all that believed on him. "The ancients," continue Irenaeus, as quoted by Lardner, "being of opinion that eternal life is not to be obtained but through faith in Jesus Christ, and that God is too merciful to let men perish for not hearing the Gospel, supposed that the Lord preached also to the dead, that they might have the same advantage with the living." He further adds, "In the language of Marcion and the fathers, hell does not necessarily mean the place of the damned; in that place is Tartarus, the place of torment, and Paradise, or the bosom of Abraham, a place of rest and refreshment. In that part of Hades Jesus found the just men of the Old Testament. They were not miserable, but were in a place of comfort and pleasure." "For Christ," he continues, "promiseth the Jews after this life, rest in Hades, even in the bosom of Abraham." This far the doctrine of Marcion is in strict agreement with the New Testament, though denounced as blasphemy by his opponent. The unfortunate part of Marcion's doctrine on this head is that he taught that Cain and the wicked of Sodom and the Egyptians, and in fact all the nations in general, though they had lived in all manner of wickedness, were saved by the Lord, but that Abel, Enoch, Noah, and the patriarchs and prophets and other righteous men who walked with God and pleased Him in their earth life, did not obtain salvation because they suspected that in the preaching of Christ in the spirit world there was some scheme of deception to lead them away from their present qualified acceptance with God, and therefore they would not come to Christ nor believe in him, for which reason, as he says, "their souls remained in hell."‡

Marcion is also condemned for believeing in the eternity of matter,§ So, too, Hermogenes is censured by Tertullian for the same cause, and for arguing that God made the world out of matter and could not have made it out of nothing.¶

And so throughout there is censure and counter censure between the orthodox and the heretics, and it is difficult at times to determine which are the orthodox and which heretics, so frequently do they

* Lardner *Works*, vol. viii, p. 418.

† Lardner *Works*, vol. viii, 449:470; also I Peter iii: 18-21; Ibid, iv: 6; I Cor. xv: 29.

‡ Lardner, vol. viii, p. 460.

§ Ibid. p. 581-2.

‖ Lardner, vol. viii, p. 345.

change places. Nor was there any improvement in the ages that succeeded these that have been briefly considered. The editor of Dr. Jortin's learned work on ecclesiastical history, William Trollope, on a passage of Jortin's on the early fathers, says of the fathers of the fourth century:

> After the council of Nice,* a class of writers sprang up, greatly inferior to their predecessors, in whatever light their pretensions are viewed. Sadly deficient in learning, prejudiced in opinion, and inelegant in style, they cannot be admitted for a moment into competition with those who were contemporary with the Apostles and their immediate successors.†

The whole tenor of his remarks is to the effect that while the fathers of the second and third centuries, are not to be relied upon in their interpretations of scripture, were frequently deceived in opinions, and not always to be depended upon in matters of tradition, yet they were greatly to be preferred in all respects to the fathers of succeeding centuries.

The Development of False Doctrines After the Death of the Apostles.

Here, too, I shall rely very largely upon the conclusions of the learned. Dr. Lardner, referring to the development of the heresies, the seeds of which were sown in the days of the Apostles, says:

> Eusebius relates that Ignatius, on his way from Antioch to Rome, exhorted the churches to beware of heresies which were then springing up, and which would increase; and that he afterwards wrote his epistles in order to guard them against these corruptions, and to confirm them in the faith. This opinion that the seeds of these heresies were sown in the time of the Apostles, and sprang up immediately after is an opinion probable in itself and is embraced by several learned moderns; particularly by Vitringa, and by the late Rev. Mr. Brekel of Liverpool.‡

A certain Mr. Deacon attempted to refute the Mr. Brekel referred to by Dr. Lardner, and to maintain the purity of the Church of the first three centuries. On this Mr. Brekel observed that "If this point were thoroughly examined, it would appear that the Christian Church preserved her virgin purity no longer than the Apostolic age, at least if we may give credit to Hegesippus." Relying upon

* Held in 325 A. D.

† Jortin, vol. i, p. 166, note.

‡ Lardner, vol. viii, p. 344.

the support of the ecclesiastical history of Socrates, a writer of the first half of the fifth century, Mr. Brekel also says: "To mention the corruptions and innovations in religion of the four first centuries, is wholly superfluous; when it is so very notorious, that, even before the reign of Constantine, there sprang up a sort of heathenish Christianity which mingled itself with the true Christian religion."*

Of the impending departure from the Christian religion immediately succeeding the days of the apostles, Dr. Neander says:

> Already, in the latter part of the age of St. Paul, we shall see many things different from what they had been originally; and so it cannot appear strange if other changes come to be introduced into the constitution of the (Christian) communities, by the altered circumstances of the times immediately succeeding those of St. Paul or St. John. Then ensued those strongly marked oppositions and schisms, those dangers with which the corruptions engendered by manifold foreign elements threatened primitive Christianity.†

Dr. Philip Smith, the author of the *Students' Ecclesiastical History,* in speaking of the early corruptions of the Christian religion, says:

> The sad truth is that as soon as Christianity was generally diffused, it began to absorb corruption from all the lands in which it was planted, and to reflect the complexion of all their systems of religion and philosophy.‡

Dean Milman, in his preface to his annotated edition of Edward Gibson's great wrok, *The Decline and Fall of the Roman Empire,* and commenting upon that great author's attitude respecting the Christian religion, says:

> If, after all, the view of the early progress of Christianity be melancholy and humiliating, we must beware lest we charge the whole of this on the infidelity of the historian. It is idle, it is disingenuous to deny or to dissemble the early depravations of Christianity, its gradual but rapid reparture from its primitive simplicity and purity, still more from its spirit of universal love. It may be no unsalutary lesson to the Christian world, that this silent, this unavoidable perhaps, *yet fatal change* shall have been drawn by an impartial, or even an hostile hand.§

Dr. Mosheim, in his *Institutes,* deals at length with the abuses which arose in the Church in the second and third centuries, which I abridge to the following, and first as to the second century: Many rites were added without necessity to both public and private reli-

* Lardner, vol. viii, p. 345.

† Neander's *History of the Christian Religion and Church,* vol. i, p. 191.

‡ Student's *Eccles. Hist.,* vol. i, p. 49.

§ Gibbon's *Roman Empire,* Preface by Dean Milman, p. 15.

gious worship, to the great offense of good men; and principally because of the perversity of mankind who are more delighted with the pomp and splendor of external forms and pageantry than with the true devotion of the heart. There is good reason to believe that the Christion bishops purposely multiplied sacred rites for the sake of rendering the Jews and pagans more friendly to them. For both these classes bad always been accustomed to numerous and splendid ceremonies, and believed them an essential part of religion. In pursuance of this policy, and to silence the calumnies of the pagans and the Jews against them—to the effect that the Christians were pronounced atheists, because destitute of temples, altars, victims, priests, and all that pomp in which the vulgar suppose the essence of religion to consist—the Christian leaders introduced many rites, that they might be able to maintain that they really had those things which the pagans had, only they subsisted under different forms. Some of these rites—justified, as was supposed, by a comparison of the Christian oblations with Jewish victims and sacrifices—in time corrupted essentially the doctrine of the Lord's supper, and converted it into a sacrifice. To add further to the dignity of the Christian Religion, the churches of the east feigned mysteries similar to those of the pagan religions; and, as with the pagans, the holy rites of the mysteries were concealed from the vulgar: "And they not only applied the terms used in the pagan mysteries to the Christian institutions, particularly baptism and the Lord's supper, but they gradually introduced also the rites which were designated by those terms." This practice originated in the eastern provinces of the empire, and thence, after the times of Adrian (who first introduced the Grecian mysteries among the Latins), it spread among the Christians of the west. "A large part, therefore, of Christian observances and institutions, even in this century, had the aspect of the pagan mysteries." In like manner many ceremonies and customs of the Egyptians were adopted.*

Speaking of the third century the Doctor says that all the monuments of this century show that there was a great increase of ceremonies in the Church owing to the prevailing passion for the Platonic philosophy. Hence arose the public exorcisms, the multiplication of fasts, the aversion to matrimony, and the painful austerities and penances which were enjoined upon offenders.†

The Revolution of the Fourth Century: Constantine.

It will be observed that I have so far confined my quotations concerning the corruptions which arose in the Church to the first three

* *Institutes,* vol. i, cent. ii, ch. iv.

† Ibid. cent, iii, part ii, ch. iv.

centuries of the Christian Era. I have done so purposely; and chiefly that I might show by such quotations that the forces which were to bring about the destruction of the Christian Church were active during those ages; and also because an event took place in the first part of the fourth century that culminated in the triumph of those forces. This event was the establishment of Christianity as the state religion of Rome. Constantine the Great was the emperor under whose reign this unlooked for revolution took place. He was the son of Constantine Chlorus, emperor of the West in the preceding reign, which reign he had shared with Galerius Maximinus, who ruled the East. Constantine was an "emperor born of an emperor, the pious son of a most pious and virtuous father," is the flattering announcement of his parentage on the paternal side, by his contemporary, Eusebius, the church historian; though he neglects to mention the obscure origin and humble vocation (that of inn keeper) of his mother, Helena, whom her husband repudiated when raised to the dignity of "Caesar" in the reign of Diocletian.

Constantine was proclaimed emperor by the army in Britain on the death of his father at York, 306 A. D.; but civil strife raged through the empire for eighteen years, occasioned by the contending aspirants for the imperial dignity. The future patron of Christianity, however, overcame all his rivals and reigned sole monarch of Rome from 323 A. D., to the time of his death, fourteen years later.

The policy of Constantine's father towards the Christians in his division of the empire, the West, had been one not only of toleration but also of friendship; and this policy the son followed from the commencement of his career as emperor. The fact of both his own and his father's friendliness toward the Church, on the one hand, and the hostility of his rivals against the Church on the other, brought to him the united support of the Christians throughout the empire; and though they were not so numerous as they are frequently represented to be, yet it cannot be denied that the Christians were important factors in determining the course of events in the empire at this time, and truly they were faithful allies to Constantine, and he, on his part, neglected not to meet their anticipations of reward.

A careful study of his life and character will force the conviction upon the mind that Constantine was a most suitable head for the revolution which ended by establishing a pseudo-Christianity as the state religion of the decaying empire. A professed Christian for many years, if we may believe Lactantius and Eusebius he postponed his baptism, after the fashion of his times, until the very last year of his life, in order that, purified at once from all the stains of sin by means of it, he might be sure of entering into bliss. Such the explanation of those who would defend this delay of the emperor's; but one cannot fail to remember that it was quite customary at this time among many professing the Christian religion to put off baptism as long as they dared that they might enjoy a life of sin, and then through the means of baptism, just before death, as by magic, obtain forgiveness.* On the motives that prompted Constantine's acceptance of Christianity, our historians are not agreed. According to Eusebius his conversion was brought about through seeing in the heavens a luminous cross at midday, and above it the inscription: *"By this Conquer."* This miraculous sign was supplemented on the night following by the appearance of Jesus Christ to the emperor in a dream, with the same symbol, the cross, and directed him to make it the ensign of his banners and his protection against the power of the enemy.† According to Theodoret the emperor was converted through the arguments of his Christian mother.‡ According to Zosimus, it was through the arguments of an Egyptian Christian bishop—supposed to be Hosius, Bishop of Corduba—who promised him absolution for his crimes, which included a number of murders, if he would but accept Christianity.§

It is as difficult to settle upon the time of Constantine's conversion as it is the means and nature of it. Neander inclines to the opinion that he was early influenced in favor of Christianity through the example if not the teachings of his parents, who, if not fully converted to the Christian faith, were at least tolerant of it; and may be reasonably counted among that number who at least admitted Christ to be the pantheon of the gods. But an act of his in 308 A. D., after the death of his father, and he himself had been proclaimed emperor of the West, shows that he was at that time still attached to the pagan forms of worship; for hearing that the Franks who had been inclined to rebellion against his government had, on his preparations to make war upon them, laid down their arms, he offered public thanks in a celebrated temple of Apollo and gave a magnificent offering to the god.||

The story of his conversion as related by Eusebius would fix that event in the year 312 A. D.; and surely if the open vision of the luminous cross and the subsequent appearing of Christ in his dream, were realities, Constantine had sufficient grounds for a prompt and unequivocal conversion to the Christian faith. But after that, if we consider the conduct of the emperor, we shall find him, however, astonishing it may seem, still attached to pagan ceremonies of worship. As late as 321, A. D., nine years after the visitation of Christ to him, we find him accused of artfully balancing the hopes and fears of both his pagan and

*Neander *Ch. Hist.*, vol. i, p. 253. *Decline and Fall,* vol. ii, chap. xx.

† Eusebius' *Life of Constantine*, bk. i, 27.

‡ *Hist. Eccles.*, vol. I, bk. i, ch. 17.

§ Zosimus, bk. ii, p. 104.

|| Neander's *Ch. Hist.*, vol. ii, p. 8.

Christian subjects by publishing in the same year two edicts; the first of which enjoined the solemn observance of Sunday; and the second directed the consultation of the Haruspices*—the soothsayers of the old pagan religion. Of this circumstance, Neander, who is disposed to palliate the conduct of Constantine as far as possible, after intimating that this lapse might be accounted for on the grounds of state policy, says, "Yet the other hypothesis, viz., that Constantine had actually fallen back into heathen superstitions may indeed be regarded as the more natural."† Five years after his supposed miraculous conversion "we find marks of the pagan state religion upon the imperial coins."‡ "A medal was struck," says Dr. John W. Draper, doubtless referring to the same thing, "on which was impressed his [Constantine's] title of 'God,' together with the monogram of Christ." "Another," he continues, "represented him as raised by a hand from the sky while seated in the chariot of the Sun. But more particularly the great prophyry pillar, a column one hundred and twenty feet in height, exhibited the true religious condition of the founder of Constantinople. The statue on its summit mingled together the Sun, the Savior, and the Emperor. Its body was a colossal image of Apollo, whose features were replaced by those of Constantine, and around the head, like rays, were fixed the nails of the cross of Christ recently discovered in Jerusalem."§ While on the day Constantinople was formally made the capital of the empire, he honored the statue of Fortune with his gifts. In view of all these acts, ranging as they do over the greater part of the first Christian emperor's life, and through many years after his supposed conversion, I think Gibbon is justified in his remarks upon this part of Constantine's conduct: "It was an arduous task to eradicate the habits and prejudices of his education, to acknowledge the divine power of Christ, and to understand that the truth of *his* revelation was incompatible with the worship of the gods."‖

Turning from the consideration of the equivocal conduct of the emperor to his character, we have a subject about which there is less disagreement among authorities; for even Christian apologists are compelled to admit the wickedness of this first Christian emperor. "Relying, with presumptuous confidence," says Neander, "on the great things which God had done, through him, for the advancement of the Christian Church, he found it easy to excuse or extenuate to his conscience many a wrong deed, into which he had suffered himself to be betrayed

* Gibbon, *Decline and Fall*, vol. iii, ch. xx.

† Neander *Ch. Hist.*, vol. ii, p. 23.

‡ Neander *Ch. Hist.*, vol. ii, p. 21.

§ *Intellectual Development of Europe*, vol. i, p. 280

‖ Gibbon, *Decline and Fall*, ch. xx.

by ambition, the love of rule, the arbitrary exercise of power, or the jealousy of depostism."*

"It is indeed true that Constantine's life was not such as the precepts of Christianity required," Dr. Mosheim remarks, but softens the statement against the emperor by saying that, "It is but too notorious that many persons who look upon the Christian religion as indubitably true and of divine origin, yet do not conform their lives to all its holy precepts."†

Dr. Lardner, after drawing a most favorable outline of Constantine's person and character, and citing the flattery of contemporary panegyrists as a description of the man, says: "Having observed these virtues of Constantine, and other things, which are to his advantage; a just respect to truth obligeth us to take notice of some other things, which seem to cast a reflection upon him. ‡ And then in the most naive manner he adds: "Among these, one of the chief is putting to death so many of his relatives!" He enumerates the victims of the first Christian emperor as follows: "Maximilian Herculius, his wife's father; Bassianus, husband of his sister Anastasia; Crispus, his own son; Fausta, his wife; Licinius, husband of his sister Contantia; and Licinianus, or Licinius, the younger, his nephew, and son of the forementioned Licinius."§ The last named victim was a mere lad when put to death, "not more than a little above eleven years of age, if so much," is Dr. Lardner's own description of him. Fausta was suffocated in a steam bath, though she had been his wife for twenty years and mother of three of his sons. It should be remembered that this is the list of victims admitted by a most learned and pious Christian writer, not a catalogue drawn up by pagan historians, whom we might suspect of malice against one who had deserted the shrines of the ancient gods for the faith of the Christians. But this rather formidable list of murdered victims, admitted by Dr. Lardner, shakes not his faith in the goodness of the first Christian emperor. Some of these "executions" he palliates, if not justifies, on the ground of political necessity; and others on the ground of domestic perfidy; though he almost stumbles in his efforts at excusing the taking off of Crispus, the emperor's own son; Fausta, his wife; and the lad Licinius. "These are the executions," he says, "which above all others cast a reflection upon the reign of Constantine; though there are also hints of the death of some others about the same time, with whom Constantine had till then lived

* Neander *Ch. Hist.*, vol. ii, p. 24.

† Mosheim's *Institutes*, vol. i, p. 214.

‡ Lardner, vol. iv, p. 39.

§ Lardner, vol. iv, p. 39.

in friendship."* After which the Doctor immediately adds—in the very face of all the facts he adduces, and after reciting the condemnation of both heathen and Christian writers of some of these murders—the following: "I do by no means think that Constantine was a man of a cruel disposition; and therefore I am unwilling to touch upon any other actions of a like nature: as his making some German princes taken captive, fight in the theatre; and sending the head of Maxentius to Africa, after it had been made a part of Constantine's triumphal entry at Rome." When one finds a sober Christian writer of the eighteenth century who can thus speak of Constantine; and further remembers that to this day a priest of the Greek church seldom mentions the name of the "imperial saint," without adding the title, *"Equal to the Apostles;"* one is not surprised that while he lived, and at his court a Christian bishop could be found who "congratulated him as constituted by God to rule over all, in the present world, and destined to reign with the son of God in the world to come."† Or that Eusebius, who is spoken of as one of the best bishops of the imperial court, "did not scruple for a moment to ascribe to the purest motives of a true servant of God all those transactions into which the emperor, without evincing the slightest regard to truth or to humanity, had suffered himself to be drawn by an ambition which could not abide a rival, in the struggle with Licinius; when he represents the emperor, in a war which, beyond a doubt, had been undertaken from motives of a purely selfish policy, as marshalling the order of the battle, and giving out the words of command by divine inspiration bestowed in answer to his prayer."‡

Enough of this. Let us look no longer at this first of the Christian emperors through the eyes of churchmen seeking to extol his virtues and hide his crimes, all for the honor of the Church. So odious had he become in Rome for his many murders that a pasquinade which compared his reign to that of the detested Nero was nailed to the palace gates. "The guilty emperor," says one, "in the first burst of anger, was on the point of darkening the tragedy, if such a thing had been possible, by a massacre of the Roman populace who had thus insulted him." His brothers were consulted on this measure of vengeance, however, and the result of their counsel was a resolution to degrade Rome to a subordinate rank, and build a metropolis elsewhere, and hence the new capital of the empire rose on the shores of the Bosphorus.

Reflecting upon the career of Constantine from the days of his young manhood, which had in it something of the quality that makes the successful leader of men, to the time when he fell under the influence of the false priests of a corrupted religion, Draper says:

* Lardner, vol. iv, p. 44.

† Neander, *Ch. Hist.*, vol. ii, p. 25.

‡ Neander, *Ch. Hist.*, vol. ii, p. 25.

> From the rough soldier who accepted the purple at York, how great the change to the effeminate emperor of the Bosphorus, in silken robes stiffened with threads of gold, a diadem of sapphires and pearls, and false hair, stained of various tints; his steps stealthily guarded by mysterious eunuchs flitting through the palace, the streets full of spies, and an ever watchful police! The same man who approaches us as the Roman imperator retires from us as the Asiatic despot. In the last days of his life he put aside the imperial purple, and, assuming the customary white garments, prepared for baptism, that the sins of his long and evil life might all be washed away. Since complete purification can thus be only once obtained, he was desirous to procrastinate that ceremony to the last moment. Profoundly politic, even in his relations with heaven, he thenceforth reclined on a white bed, took no further part in worldly affairs, and, having thus insured a right to the continuance of that prosperity in a future life which he had enjoyed in this, expired.*

And so Gibbon:

> The sublime theory of the gospel had made a much fainter impression on the heart, than on the understanding, of Constantine himself. He pursued the great objects of his ambition through the dark and bloody paths of war and policy; and, after the victory, he abandoned himself, without moderation, to the abuse of his fortune. Instead of asserting his just superiority above the imperfect heroism and profane philosophy of Trajan and the Antonines, the mature age of Constantine forfeited the reputation which he had acquired in his youth. As he gradually advanced in the knowledge of truth, he proportionately declined in the practice of virtue; and the same year of his reign in which he convened the council of Nice, was polluted by the execution, or rather murder of his eldest son (Crispus). * * * * At the time of the death of Crispus, the emperor could no longer hesitate in the choice of religion; he could no longer be ignorant that the church was possessed of an infallible remedy, (baptism) though he chose to defer the application of it till the approach of death had removed the temptation and danger of a relapse. * * * * The example and reputation of Constantine seemed to countenance the delay of baptism. Future tyrants were encouraged to believe that the innocent blood which they might shed in a long reign would instantly be washed away in the waters of regeneration; and the abuse of religion dangerously undermined the foundations of moral virtue.†

Such then, was the first Christian emperor. He uplifted "Christianity" from the condition of a persecuted religion, and made it the state religion of Rome; and also provided means for its wider acceptance. If for this it shall be claimed, as it is, that much in his evil life should be overlooked, it would still be pertinent to ask whether his acts in connection with Christianity did not debase rather than exalt it; and if his provisions for its wider acceptation did not tend rather to the corruption of what remained true in the Christianity then extant, than to the establishment of true religion.

* Draper, *Intellectual Development*, vol. 1, p. 283.

† *Decline and Fall*. ch. xx.

Corrupted Christianity Made a Persecuting Religion

The edict of Milan, by which was intended no more than the establishment of religious liberty in the empire, and which was issued in 313 A. D., by Constantine and his colleague, Licinius, was well enough. Freedom to teach and practice the truth is all the Christian church could ask or expect. Had he stopped here, his action in this particular would have met with universal applause. But he went beyond this. He not only protected the Christians by his laws, but prohibited by express edicts the free exercise of religion to the pagans. His proscriptions were mild at first, going no further than to prohibit soothsaying and divination in private houses or anywhere in secret. Later, however, if we may believe the words of Eusebius, he placed the pagan religion under the ban of the laws. Eusebius says:

> The emperor proceeded to act with great vigor, gave the government of the provinces chiefly to Christians, and when any Gentiles were made governors they were prohibited to sacrifice. Which law comprehended not only presidents of provinces but also higher officers, and even the prætorian præfects. If they were Christians, they were required to act according to their principles. If they were otherwise disposed, still the practice of idolatrous rites were forbidden. * * * * And soon after that were two laws published, at one and the same time, one prohibiting the detestable rites of idolatry hitherto practiced in cities and country places; and that for the future none should erect statues to the gods, nor perform the vain arts of divination, nor offer up any sacrifices. The other law was for enlarging Christian oratories and churches, or for rebuilding them more grand and splendid.*

When contrasting the course of the first Christian emperor with the pagan emperors, Eusebius says, "They commanded the temples to be magnificently adorned; he demolished them to the foundation, especially such as were most respected by superstitious people."† Later he expressly says that throughout the whole Roman empire, the doors of idolatry were shut to the commonalty and to the soldiery; and that "every kind of sacrifice was prohibited." Again he says, that there were several laws, published for these purposes, forbidding sacrifices, divinations, raising statues, and the secret mysteries or rites of initiation. And he says further, that "in Egypt a sort of priesthood, consecrated to the honor of the Nile, was entirely suppressed."‡ I am not unmindful that some respectable authorities question if Constantine really departed from the policy of toleration announced in his edict of Milan; and that even Gibbon is inclined to believe in his toleration of

* *Life of Constantine* (Eusebius) I, ch. ii: 44.

† Ibid, ch. 45.

‡ *Life of Constantine*, (Eusebius) ch. iv: 23, 25.

paganism. The statement here made by Eusebius, the contemporary and biographer of Constantine, however, together with reference to the edicts of suppression quoted by his son Constans in the succeeding reign, and which is quoted by Lardner,* establishes beyond question the policy of intolerance of Constantine toward paganism. Especially when what Eusebius has said is supplemented by the fact that the emperor destroyed a number of heathen temples, and peremptorily ordered the closing of the others. Among the heathen temples destroyed was one at Aegae, in Cilicia, erected to Aesculapius, celebrated for the number of sick that had been healed there, and held in high esteem by men of the better class among the pagans and philosophers. It is said that by its destruction and the public exhibition of certain images of the gods, many tricks of the priests were exposed and, became objects of sport to the populace.† But while this may have been the conduct of some insincere pagans, those who remained heathens, as LeClerc has well said, "were no doubt extremely shocked at the manner in which the statues of their gods were treated; and could not consider the Christians as men of moderation. For, in short, those statues were as dear to them, as anything, the most sacred, could be to the Christians."‡ Eusebius taunted the philosophers about the destruction of the temple, without any interference on the part of the god to whom it had been erected, apparently all unmindful of the fact that just such taunts had been hurled at the Christian martyrs in the days that the "kingdom of God suffered violence, and the violent took it by force." "Had not Eusebius," remarked Lardner, "often heard with his own ears, and read in the history of ancient martyrs, the insults and triumphs of the heathens over the Christians, that they professed themselves the worshipers of the great and only true God, and yet everybody, that pleased, was able to molest and destroy them, as he saw good?"§

The zeal of Christian writers has done all in its power to excuse or palliate the conduct of Constantine in his acts for the suppression of the pagan religion and worship; but after all is said by his apologists that can be said; after every allowance is conceded for the times in which he lived, and the previous conduct of the pagans through two centuries of violence towards the Christians, the fact remains that the first Christian emperor did by his edicts put the ancient religion of the empire under the ban of the law, and by acts of violence destroyed some of its temples and closed the rest by imperial decree, that the pagan gods might not be worshiped; and this, doubtless, with the approval—and it would not

* Lardner, vol. viii, p. 169.

† Neander, *Ch. Hist.*, vol. ii, p. 26, 27.

‡ Lardner, *Works*, vol. iv, p. 49.

§ Lardner, *Works*, vol. iv, p. 50.

be difficult to believe, under all the circumstances, at the suggestion—of Christian bishops who thronged his court. On the foundation of intolerance thus laid by him, others hastened to build. In the succeeding reign, among the first laws enacted was this one against pagan sacrifices:

> Let superstition cease; let the madness of sacrificing be abolished. For whoever shall presume contrary to the constitution of our father, a prince of blessed memory, and contrary to this command of our clemency, to offer sacrifices, let a proper and convenient punishment be inflicted, and execution presently done upon him.*

This edict was supplemented a few years later† by the following edict:

> It is our pleasure that in all places and in all cities, the temples be immediately shut, and carefully guarded that none may have the power of offending. It is likewise our pleasure, that all our subjects should abstain from sacrifices. If any one should be guilty of such an act, let him feel the sword of vengeance; and after his execution, let his property be confiscated to the public use. We denounce the same penalties against the governors of the provinces, if they neglect to punish the criminals.‡

It is not necessary to pursue the subject much further. It will be sufficient to say that during the fourth century, by following the policy of suppression inaugurated by this first Christian emperor, Christianity was changed from a persecuted to a persecuting religion. Without restraint from the ecclesiastical authorities, the Christian emperors issued edicts against the pagan religion, proscribed its followers, destroyed its temples, and confiscated its property to the uses of the rival religion. Even Neander, speaking of this revolution, and constrained as he is to say all that he can for the honor of the Christian Church, is compelled to admit that "the relation of things had become reversed. As in former times the observance of the pagan ceremonies, the religion of the state, had appeared in the light of a civil duty, and the profession of Christianity in that of a crime against the state; so now it was the case, not indeed that the outward profession of Christianity was commanded as a universal civil duty, for against this the spirit of Christianity too earnestly remonstrated; but that the exercise of the pagan religion was made politically dangerous."§ In the pages of this eminent Christian historian one may read that before the close of the century which witnessed the elevation of Christianity to the dignity of the state religion of the empire, wild troops of Christian monks were undertaking campaigns, especially in the country, for the destruction of

* Lardner, *Works*, vol. viii, p. 169.
† In 353 A. D., according to Gothford.
‡ The law is extant in the Theodocian Code
§ Neander, vol. ii, p. 34.

the heathen temples in which sacrifices were alleged to have been performed; of bishops who not only superintended the destruction of heathen temples at the head of bands of soliders and gladiators, but paraded through the streets of the cities the symbols of the heathen faith, provoking civil conflicts which Christian emperors did not hesitate to take advantage of for the more complete suppression of paganism.* Meantime a pagan apologist, Libanius, arises to plead the cause of religious toleration, and in the course of his address to the Christian emperor, Theodosius, he puts to shame the Christianity then in vogue, by showing the emperor how far the Church had departed from the spirit of the Christian religion, by saying: "Force is said not to be permitted, even according to the laws of your own religion: persuasion is said to be praised, but force condemned by them. Why then, do you wreak your fury against the temples, when this surely is not to persuade, but to use force? Thus, then, it is plain you would transgress even the laws of your own religion."† Lardner calls attention to the fact that as under pagan emperors previous to Constantine Christianity had been in a state of persecution, so now, after Constantine, he proceeds to show that paganism under Christian emperors was all along in a state of persecution—"However, I would hope, not so severe and vigorous as that of the Christians in the foregoing period of near three hundred years."‡ And so LeClerc, as quoted by Lardner:

Thus it was that the Christians continued to return to the pagans what they had suffered from them during the first three centuries, instead of gaining them by patience and mildness, which they had so much recommended when they were the weakest. This conduct was proper to make the pagans more obstinate, by teaching them that the Christians affected to speak of humanity and moderation from interest only, and not from a principle of religion as they pretended. At least it is certain, that thereby they lost the right to complain of the manner in which the pagans had treated them in times past, or to boast of the mildness of their religion, which they effectually disparaged by those persecutions. * * * Nor ought we to imagine that the penalties laid by Christians upon the pagans were light. If a sacrifice was offered in a private place, with the knowledge of the proprietor, the place was confiscated; if not, they were to pay a fine of twenty pounds of gold, as much as if it had been done in a temple; and in some cases the penalty of death was appointed. We may look into the oration of Libanius for the temples, where that orator sustains the same character before Theodosius as the Christians had formerly done before pagan emperors. I must acknowledge that this phenomenon, if I may so call it, gives me pain: for I could wish that they who defended the truth had preserved

* Neander, *Ch. Hist.*, vol. ii, pp| 88-110.

† Ibid. p. 67.

‡ Lardner, *Works*, vol. viii, p. 164.

to themselves the honor of being the only persons that were persecuted for religion.*

Persecution of "Heretics."

Once started upon the policy of suppressing by force those of a different religion, Christianity did not stop with the persecution of the pagans; bad and un-Christian as that was, still more serious results occurred from the persecutions inflicted upon so-called heretics in the Church, by those who were considered orthodox. It is true that there were heretics in the Church before the days of Constantine; much progress had been made in the matter of paganizing Christianity, and more or less of intolerance was manifested by Christian sects towards one another; but it was the policy and example of this first Christian emperor that laid the real foundation for that monument of shame and disgrace to the Christian name which rises upon the plains of Christian discord and strife and war waged against heretics in the name and for the glory of Christ. It is this which constitutes the most melancholy page of ecclesiastical history.

In his office of supreme pontiff in the old pagan religion, which he held by virtue of being emperor of Rome, Constantine may naturally have supposed that the supreme headship of the religion he had protected and the Church he had elevated fell to him for the same reason; and with it the right to reconcile differences, compose factions, and determine what should be the orthodox faith. At any rate we find him acting somewhat in this capacity. When contending church parties appealed to him, he at first was indifferent to their disputes, and tried to shame them into harmony by referring to the conduct of the Greek philosophers, who never discussed difficult questions before ignorant multitudes; who could "maintain their arguments without losing their temper; and assert their freedom without violating any friendship."† His efforts at reconciling the differences that arose among Christians over what is known as the Arian controversy were of no avail; and after six years of bitter strife, the emperor summoned the bishops of the Church to Nicea in Bithynia. After long deliberation Arianism was condemned, and orthodox Christianity was established by decree of the council, ratified by the emperor, to which all Christians must conform. Those who resisted the divine judgment of the synod must prepare themselves for immediate exile.‡ How effectual the argument, "belief or banishment," even among the bishops at the council, was, may be determined from the fact that "the opposition to the decision of the

* Lardner, *Works,* vol. viii, p. 276.

† *Decline and Fall,* ch. xxi.

‡ *Decline and Fall,* ch. xxi.

council was almost instantly reduced from seventeen to two."* In his zeal to enforce orthodoxy the emperor forgot his former moderation, and in 326 A. D.—the year following the council of Nicea—he issued a general edict against heretics, in which, after condemning his own past forbearance as occasioning men's being seduced, he says to the various heretical parties:

> Wherefore, since this your pernicious wickedness is no longer to be endured, we by this present law command you, that you no more presume to meet together. And we have given orders that all those places where you are wont to hold assemblies should be taken away. Yea, our concern for this matter is such, that we not only forbid you to assemble in any public place; but we likewise forbid all assemblies of your foolish superstition in private houses, and in all private places whatever. All of you, therefore, who have any sincere love of truth, come to the Catholic church. And that this remedy may have its full effect, we ordain that all your superstitious conventicles, I mean oratories of all heretics, if it be fit to call such houses oratories, be forthwith taken away, and without any opposition delivered to the Catholic church: and that the rest of your places be adjudged to the public.†

"Thus the dens of heretics were laid open by the imperial edict," exultantly exclaims Eusebius, the Christian bishop, "and the wild beasts, the ring leaders of their impiety, were scattered."‡ And thus was the paganized Christian church launched upon that career of persecution of heretics within the church, as well as upon the policy of persecuting those of a different religion; a policy that has filled the world with religious wars, and deeds of cruelty which would better become the reign of a Nero than Christian rulers of Christian nations. It is a terrible arraignment which Gibbon draws against apostate Christendom in the concluding paragraph of his review of the persecutions which had been endured by the followers of Christ in the Christian centuries preceding Constantine. He says:

> We shall conclude this chapter by a melancholy truth, which obtrudes itself on the reluctant mind; that, even admitting, without hesitation or inquiry, all that history has recorded, or devotion has feigned, on the subject of martyrdoms, it must still be acknowledged that the Christians, in the course of their intestine dissensions, have inflicted far greater severities on each other than they have experienced from the zeal of infidels. During the ages of ignorance which followed the subversion if the Roman empire in the west,§ the bishops of the imperial city extended their dominion over the laity as well as clergy of the Latin church. The fabric of superstition

* *Decline and Fall,* ch. xxi.

† Lardner, *Works,* vol. iv, p. 36.

‡ *Life of Constantine,* Eusebius, p. 66.

§ This event occurred about 476 A. D.

which they had erected, and which might long have defied the feeble efforts of reason, was at length assaulted by a crowd of daring fanatics, who, from the twelfth to the sixteenth century, assumed the popular character of reformers. The church of Rome defended by violence the empire which she had acquired by fraud; a system of peace and benevolence was soon disgraced by proscriptions, wars, massacres, and the institution of the holy office; and as the reformers were animated by the love of civil as well as religious freedom, the Catholic princes connected their own interest with that of the clergy, and enforced by fire and sword the terror of spiritual censures. In the Netherlands alone more than one hundred thousand of the subjects of Charles the Fifth are said to have suffered by the hand of the executioner; and this extraordinary number is attested by Grotius, a man of genius and learning, who preserved his moderation amidst the fury of contending sects, and who composed the annals of his own age and century, at the time when the invention of printing had facilitated the means of intelligence and increased the danger of detection. If we are obliged to submit our belief to the authority of Grotius, it must be allowed that the number of protestants who were executed in a single province and a single reign far exceeded that of the primitive martyrs in the space of three centuries, and of the Roman empire!*

Both Guizot and Milman, eminent Christian scholars, annotated the work of Edward Gibbon, the former in French, the latter in an English edition; and at every point where they could modify a statement or soften a passage apparently unjust to Christianity, they did so; but in the presence of the important and terrible passages just quoted, they remained absolutely silent! Nor has any other Christian writer since their day, so far as I know, attempted to contradict the statement of Mr. Gibbon. It is proper to say, however, that in a note Mr. Gibbon himself cites the fact that Fra Paola, an Italian writer, places the number of Belgic martyrs at fifty thousand, but even that computation would still leave the conclusion of Mr. Gibbon's reflections unimpaired.

The circumstance of the Church elevated by Constantine becoming a persecuting Church is a strong evidence of its paganized state; for the true Christian religion is not a persecuting religion; the true Church of Christ is not a persecuting Church. When the Samaritans would not receive the Messiah, some of the Apostles would have them consumed by fire from heaven; but the Master turned and rebuked them, saying, "Ye know not what manner of spirit ye are of. For the Son of man is not come to destroy men's lives, but to save them."† It is true that Messiah said: "Think not that I am come to send peace on earth: I came not to send peace, but a sword. For I am come to set a man at variance against his father, and the daughter against her mother, and the daughter-in-law against her mother-in-law. And a man's foes shall be

* *Decline and Fall*, ch. xvi.

† Luke ix: 54-56.

they of his own household."* This, however, is but a prediction of the effect of the proclamation of the Gospel, not an authorization to force the acceptance of Christianity by the sword; nor does it authorize the Church to invoke the arm of the civil authority to execute by force her doctrinal decrees. The Gospel of Jesus Christ, it is true, did not bring peace, but a sword; the sword, however, was found in the hands of those who rejected the Gospel, not in the hands of those who accepted and preached it. And when the Church departed so far from the spirit of Christ that she grasped the sword in her own hands, or dictated the civil authority to wield it in her behalf, and that became the policy of the Church, the adoption of that policy proclaimed her apostate condition to the world, in a manner to be known and read of all men.

Christianity Before and After Constantine.

I think sufficient has been said to justify the belief that the reign of Constantine marks the period when the paganization of Christianity had become complete. I do not mean by this that there is any particular date which one may set down to show that here true Christianity ceases, and there apostate Christianity begins; which is a point frequently insisted upon by those who contend for the unbroken perpetuity of Christianity from the days of Messiah. They demand to know on what night it was that the whole collection of Christians, of different nationalities and languages, went to bed sound in the Christian faith, to awake the next morning all pagans.† I claim no such sudden revolution brought about the apostasy which I am sure took place. We have seen by what has already been said, that even in the time of the Apostles there was a tendency on the part of the Christians to depart from the religion of Jesus Christ; that after the days of the Apostles there was a steady increase in the number and influence of false teachers; an insidious introduction of heresies; a multiplication of rites and ceremonies well known in the pagan celebration of religious mysteries, but entirely foreign to the Gospel; and an amalgamation of pagan doctrines with Christian principles. It remains to be shown that there was a steady increase of immorality among the professing Christians; a marked loss of spirituality; a rapid growth of pride and worldliness on the part of Christian bishops and other church leaders; and at last, an utter departure from the true and living God and Jesus Christ whom He had sent, and the establishment of a system in its place, as debasing to men as it was dishonorable to God.

Taking then the reign of Constantine as the period beyond which the

* Matt. x: 34-36.

† *End of Religious Controversy*, Milner, Letter 26.

true religion of Christ did not extend, nor the true Church of Christ exist, let us consider Christianity before his reign and after it. Here I shall ask the reader to take into account as part of the consideration of Christianity previous to Constantine what I have already set before him in this introduction concerning the tendency to division and heresies which existed in the Church in the days of the Apostles; and also those quotations I have made from eminent Christian authorities, which give evidence of the early corruption of Christianity, and which too plainly testify that it was in a state of steady decline through the second and third centuries, until it was fit only for such enthronement as a Constantine could give it, when he made it the state religion of a corrupt empire hastening to its decay. If the reader will do this, it will obviate the necessity of my referring to these matters again.

Decline in Moral and Spiritual Living Among Christians.

It will be conceded that the Gospel of Jesus Christ commands a very high order of moral and spiritual living, and that the Apostles enjoined this moral law upon the early saints as essential to the favor of God. Others also after the days of the Apostles, followed in the same admonition, and indeed the sharp contrast that existed between the lives of converts before and after their acceptance of Christianity was a matter of pride not only to St. Paul,* but to Justin Martyr of the second century, who, in reference to the change produced in the lives of Christian converts, said:

> We, who were once slaves of lust, now have delight only in purity of morals; we, who once practiced arts of magic, have consecrated ourselves to the Eternal and Good God; we, who once prized gain above all things, give even what we have to the common use, and share it with such as are in need; we, who once hated and murdered one another, who on account of differences of customs would have no common hearth with strangers, do now, since the appearance of Christ, live together with them; we pray for our enemies; we seek to convince those that hate us without cause, so that they may order their lives according to Christ's glorious doctrine and attain to the joyful hope of receiving like blessings with us from God, the Lord of all.†

It was not long, however, before there was a marked departure from this high moral level among the Christians. In tracing that decline I shall use chiefly the *History of the Church* by Joseph Milner, published in 1794. My reason for doing so is as follows: I have already stated in this writing, that Milner wrote what some regard as his "great history of the Church," to counteract the influence of Dr. Mosheim's splendid *Institutes of Ecclesiastical History,* which is evidently by

* I Cor. vi: 9-11.

† Neander, *Ch. Hist.*, vol. i, p. 250.

some regarded as too much a history of the perversions and abuses of religion. Milner plainly informs his readers that he intends to write the history of those only who have been real, not nominal, Christians, irrespective of the external Church to which they belonged, proceeding upon the theory that these good men constitute the Church of Christ. His history, in other words, is a history of piety, not of the Church. It will be his purpose therefore to exalt the morality of the Christians in all ages; and I quote his work respecting the moral deteriorations of the Christians that I may not be charged with quoting authorities who some think have made too much of Christian shortcomings. Milner says that a gloomy cloud, concerning moral conditions, hung over the close of the first century, and proceeds to argue that the first impressions made by the effusions of the spirit are the strongest; that human depravity overborne for a time arose afresh, particularly in the next generation, and hence the disorders of schisms and heresies in the Church. Neander does not agree with the philosophy of Milner. He says, "Christianity, since it first entered human nature, has operated, wherever it has struck root, with the same divine power for sanctification; and this divine power cannot be weakened by the lapse of ages. In this respect, therefore, the period of the first appearance of Christianity could have no advantage over any of the following ages of the Christian Church."* And he follows this declaration with a statement, that the change which Christianity produced in the lives of those who accepted it appeared so strongly marked by the contrast it presented with what they had previously been when pagans. The correctness of the philosophy I shall leave these two great Christian authorities to settle between themselves. I am concerned more particularly with the facts in the case.

In consequence of the prominence that has been given to the persecutions of the Christians during the first three centuries, the impression very extensively prevails that the early Christian Church was constantly under the hard pressure of continuous and relentless persecutions. This, however, is not the case. There were many periods of peace granted to the Christians. Indeed their periods of persecution were only occasional, and it is a question if these periods of peace were not more detrimental to Christianity than the seasons of persecution. Milner, under the authority of Origen, says that the long peace granted the Church in the third century, during the reign of the several emperors, from about 260 A.D., to the opening of the fourth century, produced a great degree of luke-warmness and religious indecorum. "Let the reader," he says, "only notice the indifference which Origen here describes and the conduct of Christians both in the first and second centuries, and

* Neander, *Ch. Hist.*, vol. i, p. 259.

he will be affected with the greatness of the declension." Then he quotes Origen: "Several come to church only on solemn festivals, and then not so much for instruction as diversion. Some go out again as soon as they have heard the lecture, without conferring or asking the pastors questions. Others stay not till the lecture is ended, and others hear not so much as a single word, but entertain themselves in a corner of the church."*

Coming to the middle of the third century, just previous to that severe persecution inaugurated by the emperor Decius, and speaking of Cyprian, Bishop of Carthage, Milner exclaims: "A star of the first magnitude, when we consider the time in which he lived! Let us recreate ourselves with the contemplation of it. We are fatigued with hunting for Christian goodness, and we have discovered but little and that little with much difficulty. We shall find Cyprian to be a character who partook indeed of the declensions which we have noticed and lamented, but who was still far superior, I apprehend, in real simplicity and piety, to the Christians of the East."† This same Cyprian, in whom Milner delights, speaking of the effects of the long peace upon the Church which preceded the Decian persecution, says:

> Each had been bent on improving his own patrimony, and had forgotten what believers had done under the Apostles, and what they ought always to do. They were brooding over the arts of amassing wealth; the pastors and the deacons each forgot his duty; works of mercy were neglected, and discipline was at the lowest ebb; luxury and effeminacy prevailed; meritricious arts in dress were cultivated; fraud and deception practiced among brethren. Christians would unite themselves in matrimony with unbelievers; could swear, not only without reverence but without veracity. With haughty asperity they despised their ecclesiastical superiors; they railed against one another with outrageous acrimony, and conducted quarrels with determined malice. Even many bishops, who ought to be guides and patterns to the rest, neglected the peculiar duties of their stations, gave themselves up to secular pursuits. They deserted their places of residence and their flocks; they traveled through distant provinces in quest of pleasure and gain; gave no assistance to their needy brethren, but were insatiable in their thirst of money. They possessed estates by fraud and multiplied usury. What have we not deserved to suffer for such conduct? Even the divine word hath foretold us what we might expect: "If his children forsake my law and walk not in my judgments, I will visit their offenses with the rod and their sins with scourges." These things had been denounced and foretold but in vain. Our sins had brought our affairs to that pass, that because we had despised the Lord's directions, we were obliged to undergo a correction of our multiplied evils and a trial of our faith by severe remedies.‡

* Milner's *Ch. Hist.*, vol. i, cent. iii, ch. vi.
† Milner's *Ch. Hist.*, vol. i, cent. iii, ch. vi.
‡ Milner's *Ch. Hist.*, vol. i, cent. iii, ch. viii.

Referring to the long reign of peace in the closing decade of the third century, Milner says:

This new scene [the toleration of Christianity by a pagan government] did not prove favorable to the growth of grace and holiness. In no period since the Apostles was there ever so great a general decay as in this. Not even in particular instances can we discover during this interval much of lively Christianity.*

Here I drop Milner to take up Eusebius, who was an eye witness of the moral declension among the Christians previous to the last great pagan persecution under the emperor Diocletian. Referring to the long period of peace which the Church had enjoyed—a period of forty years—he says:

But when, by reason of excessive liberty, we sunk into negligence and sloth, one envying and reviling another in different ways, and we were almost, as it were, upon the point of taking up arms against each other with words as with darts and spears, prelates inveighing against prelates, and people rising up against people, and hypocrisy and dissimulation had arisen to the greatest height of malignity, then the divine judgment, which usually proceeds with a lenient hand, whilst the multitudes were yet crowding into the Church, with gentle and mild visitations began to afflict the episcopacy; the persecution having begun with those brethren in the army. But as if destitute of all sensibility, we were not prompt in measures to appease and propitiate the Deity; some indeed like atheists, regarding our situation as unheeded and unobserved by a Providence, we added one wickedness and misery to another. But some that appeared to be our pastors deserting the law of piety, were inflamed against each other with mutual strifes, only accumulating quarrels and threats, rivalship, hostility and hatred to each other, only anxious to assert the government as a kind of sovereignty for themselves.†

Here I shall avail myself of some reflections upon this condition which I have elsewhere expressed.‡ Let it be remembered that what is said in the foregoing quotation is from a writer contemporary with the events, and who says, in the very chapter following the one from which I have just quoted, that it was not for him to record the dissensions and follies which the shepherds of the people exercised against each other before the persecution. He also adds: "We shall not make mention of those that were shaken by the persecution, nor of those that suffered shipwreck in their salvation, and of their own accord were sunk in the depths of the watery gulf."§ Then in his *Book of Martyrs*, referring to events that occurred between the edicts ordering the persecution, he says: "But the events that occurred in the intermediate times, besides

* Milner's *Ch. Hist.*, vol. i, cent, iii, ch. xvii.

† Eusebius' *Eccl. Hist.*, bk. viii, ch. i.

‡ *New Witnesses for God*, pp. 75, 76.

§ Eusebius' *Eccl. Hist.*, bk. viii, ch. ii.

those already related, I have thought proper to pass by; I mean more particularly the circumstances of the different heads of the churches, who from being shepherds of the reasonable flocks of Christ, that did not govern in a lawful and becoming manner, were condemned by divine justice, as unworthy of such a charge, to be the keepers of the unreasonable camel. an animal deformed in the structure of his body; and condemned further to be the keepers of the imperial horses. * * * * Moreover, the ambitious aspirings of many to office, and the injudicious and unlawful ordinations that took place, the divisions among the confessors themselves, the great schisms and difficulties industriously fomented by the factions among the new members, against the relics of the Church, devising one innovation after another, and unmercifully thrusting them into the midst of all these calamities, heaping up affliction upon affliction; all this, I say, I have resolved to pass by, judging it foreign to my purpose, wishing, as I said in the beginning, to shun and avoid giving an account of them."* Hence, however bad the condition of the Church is represented to be by ecclesiastical writers, we must know that it was still worse than that; however numerous the schisms; however unholy the ambition of aspiring prelates; however frequent and serious the innovations upon the primitive ordinances of the Gospel; however great the confusion and apostasy in the Church is represented to be; we must know that it is still worse than that, since the Church historians contemporaneous with the events refused to record these things in heir fulness, lest it should prove disastrous to the Church; just as some of our modern scholars professing to write Church history express their determination to close their eyes to the corruption and abuses which form the greater part of the melancholy story of ecclesiastical history, for fear that relating these things would make it appear that real religion scarcely had any existence.†

I shall say no more upon the matter of moral declensions among Christians, except this: If there was such moral declensions among Christians as is represented by the foregoing high authorities on Christian affairs in the centuries preceding Constantine, what moral declension must have prevailed when from a proscribed religion Christianity was exalted to the dignity of the state religion of the empire; and her prelates and clergy were recalled from exile and suffering, poverty and disgrace, and loaded with the wealth and honors that the lord of the Roman world could bestow? Consider, in this connection, the propositions of Constantine at the council of Nicea for the propaganda of Christianity, and pass a candid judgment upon the moral or rather immoral effect they would produce upon the Church. Neander thus states them:

* *Book of Martyrs*, ch. 12.

† See Milner's Introduction to his *Church Hist.*, vol. 1.

"The heathen would be most easily led to salvation, if the condition of the Christians were made to appear to them in all respects enviable.

"They [the bishops] should consider, that the advantage to be derived from preaching could not belong to all.

"Some, he said, might be drawn to the faith by being seasonably supplied with the means of subsistence.

"Others were accustomed to repair to that quarter where they found protection and intercession (alluding to the intercessions of the bishops).

"Others would be won by an an affable reception.

"Others by being honored with presents.

"There were but few who honestly loved the exhibitions of religious doctrine; but few were the friends of truth (therefore but few sincere converts).

*"For this reason they should accommodate themselves to the characters of all, and like skillful physicians, give to each man that which might contribute to his cure, so that in every way the saving doctrine might be glorified in all."**

The effect of adopting such methods for the more rapid propagation of Christianity, as is here proposed by the emperor to the bishops assembled at the council of Nicea, must be apparent to all, and is quite universally lamented by Christian writers of later ages. "A course of proceeding upon such principles," remarks Neander himself, "must entirely have thrown open a wide door for all manner of hypocrisy. Even Eusebius, the panegyrist of Constantine, blinded as he was by the splendor which the latter had cast over the outward Church—even he is obliged to reckon among the grevious evils of this period, of which he was an eye witness, the indescribable hypocrisy of those who gave themselves out as Christians merely for temporal advantage, and who, by their outward show of zeal for the faith, contrived to win the confidence of the emperor, which he suffered them to abuse."† "The piercing eye of ambition and avarice," says Gibbon, "soon discovered that the profession of Christianity might contribute to the interest of the present as well as of a future life. The hopes of wealth and honors, the example of an emperor, his exhortations, his irresistible smiles, diffused conviction among the venal and obsequious crowds which usually fill the apartments of a palace. The cities which signalized a forward zeal by the voluntary destruction of their temples, were distinguished by municipal privileges and rewarded with popular donatives. * * * As the lower ranks of society are governed by imitation, the conversion of those who possessed any eminence of birth, of power, or of riches, was soon followed by dependent multitudes. The salvation of the common people was purchased at an easy rate, if it be true that in one year

* Neander's, *Church Hist.*, vol ii, pp. 29-30.

† Neander's *Church Hist.*, vol. ii, p. 30.

twelve thousand men were baptized at Rome, besides a proportionable number of women and children; and that a white garment, with twenty pieces of gold, had been promised by the emperor to every convert.*

Under all these circumstances it is small wonder if men exclaimed as Augustine did somewhat later in his commentary on St. John—"How many seek Jesus only that He may benefit them in earthly matters! One man has a law suit, so he seeks the intercession of the clergy; another is oppressed by his superior, so he takes refuge in the Church. Others are seeking, one in this way and another in that, to be interceded for in some quarter where they have but little influence themselves. The Church is daily full of such persons. Seldom is Jesus sought for Jesus' sake!"† After nicely balancing the possibility and probability of those who came into the Church for present worldly advantage being converted in time to a true faith in the Christian religion, Neander says: "Beyond all doubt the number was far greater of those who grew hardened in that worldly sense by which from the first they had profaned a holy profession, and who were thus the means of introducing into the Church a great mass of corruption."

"Unhappily," he adds, "there were bishops whose only wish was to make the conversion to Christianity a right easy thing for the pagans. * * * Hence they baptized even those who lived in open sin, and who plainly enough manifested that it was not their purpose to forsake it. They imagined that when these were only baptized and introduced into the fellowship of the Church, it was then time enough to admonish them against sin."‡ Surely it was not difficult among such a mass of unconverted members thus brought into the Church to find elements that would foster the errors, both in ethics and in doctrine, which about this time arose in the Church. It is small wonder that it was well nigh publicly adopted in this age—as we are informed by Mosheim—"That to deceive and lie is a virtue when religion can be promoted by it, and that error in religion ought to be visited with penalties and punishments." The first of these evils resulted in the accumulation of that mass of myth and fable that burdens the annals of the dark ages; the second established the "holy inquisition," alike the shame of the Roman Catholic church and the so-called Christian civilization she has influenced. "It is almost incredible," continues Mosheim, speaking of the first evil referred to, "what a mass of the most insipid fables, and what a host of pious falsehoods have, through all the centuries, grown out of it, to the great detriment of true religion. If some inquisitive person were to examine the conduct and the writings

* *Decline and Fall*, ch. xx.

† Augustine on St. John, tract 25, ch. 10.

‡ Neander's *Ch. Hist.*, vol. ii, p. 120.

of the great and most pious teachers of this century, I fear he would find about all of them infected with this leprosy." "Those idle fictions," he adds, "which a regard for the Platonic philosphy, and for the prevailing opinions of the day had induced most theologians to embrace, even before the time of Constantine, were now in various ways confirmed, extended and embellished. Hence it is that we see, on every side, evident traces of excessive veneration for departed saints; of a purifying fire for the soul when separated from the body; of the celibacy of the clergy; of the worship of images and relics; and of many other opinions, which in process of time almost banished the true religion, or"—and here the Doctor perhaps remembered that he was a Protestant and that his position as such would not admit of conceding the utter subversion of the Christian religion, and hence added—"or at least very much obscured and corrupted it." "Genuine piety" he continues, "was supplanted by a long train of superstitious observances which originated partly from opinions inconsiderately embraced partly from a preposterous disposition to adopt profane rites and combine them with Christian worship, and partly from the natural predilections of mankind in general for a splendid and ostentatious religion."*

The Loss of Spiritual Gifts.

Not only did the moral declensions in the Church, which started soon after the demise of the Apostles, proceed with accelerated pace after Constantine became the patron of the Church, and with such resulting evils as I have pointed out, but there was a like declension in the enjoyment of spiritual gifts in the Church. It is well known that the Apostles promised the Holy Ghost to those who received the Gospel, and the enjoyment of those supernatural gifts which go with it. Indeed Jesus Himself said in His last commission to His disciples:

> Go ye into all the world, and preach the Gospel to every creature. He that believeth and is baptized shall be saved; but he that believeth not shall be damned. And these signs shall follow them that believe: In my name they shall cast out devils; they shall speak with new tongues; they shall take up serpents; and if they drink any deadly thing, it shall not hurt them: they shall lay hands on the sick, and they shall recover.†

Paul, in speaking of the spiritual gifts promised in the Gospel says:

> Now there are diversities of gifts, but the same Spirit. And there are differences of administrations, but the same Lord. And there are diversities

* *Mosheim,* book ii, cent, iv, part ii, chap. iii.
† Mark, xvi: 15-18.

of operations, but it is the same God which worketh all in all. But the manifestation of the Spirit is given to every man to profit withal. For to one is given by the Spirit the word of wisdom; to another the word of knowledge by the same Spirit; to another faith by the same Spirit; to another the gifts of healing by the same Spirit; to another the working of miracles; to another prophecy; to another discerning of spirits; to another diverse kinds of tongues; to another the interpretation of tongues; but all these worketh that one and the self-same Spirit, dividing to every man severally as he will.*

It is well known that the spiritual gifts here enumerated were enjoyed by the saints in the early Christian centuries; and especially in Apostolic times. The New Testament books are replete with reference to the enjoyment of these gifts of the Spirit among the saints. Nor is there any intimation of the discontinuance of them. On the contrary it is reasonable to conclude that so long as the saints shall continue in the enjoyment of the Holy Ghost, that long also will they enjoy the spiritual gifts which proceed from a possession of Him. Moreover, "the fruit of the Spirit is love, joy, peace, longsuffering, gentleness, goodness, faith, meekness, temperance: against such there is no law. And they that are Christ's have crucified the flesh with the affections and lusts."† Such are the effects of the operations of the Holy Ghost upon the nature of man. These fruits of the Spirit indicate the change that the Spirit of God may effect in human nature; by which that which is corrupted through sin may be conformed to that which is pure and holy, according to the working whereby the Spirit is able to subdue all things unto Himself, in them that give place for His indwelling in their souls. This effectual working of the Spirit in the souls of men, by which they were transformed from vileness to holiness, was the boast of the early saints. And, upon reflection, all will concede that the victories of the Spirit in reforming the lives of men and making them in their very nature conform to the likeness of Christ in righteouness, are more to be desired and more to be celebrated than those victories which are physical or intellectual merely in their nature. Indeed these latter fruits of the Spirit derive their chief value from the extent to which they contribute to the production of the former—that is, to the extent that they establish men in the faith, enable them to crucify the flesh with the lusts thereof, and help them to live in harmony with the sweet influence of the Spirit of God. When men live in harmony with that Spirit there will righteousness obtain; there will love abound; there will the Gospel of Christ appear triumphant. Where these fruits do not appear, there the Gospel of Christ is not; there the powers of darkness, for the time being, are triumphant. Yet notwithstanding this promise,

* I Cor., xii: 4-11.

† Gal. v: 22-24.

concerning the enjoyment of the spiritual gifts of the Gospel, the evidence is abundant and conclusive that when all the Apostles were deceased, then there was a marked declension in the manifestation of the spiritual powers of the Gospel. "With the close of the New Testament records," says Dr. Phillip Smith, author of *The Students' Ecclesiastical History*, "and the death of the last surviving Apostle, the history of the Church passes from its sacred to its purely human phase. The miraculous gifts which attested the divine mission of the Apostles ceased; not indeed by any formal record of their withdrawal, but by the clear evidence that they were possessed no longer.*

Dr Jortin bears witness to the same fact. He says:

> The words of Eusebius intimate that he thought those extraordinary powers to be, at least, not very common afterwards—[i. e., the beginning of the second century]. "They went about," says he, "with God's co-operative grace, for even then the divine Spirit performed many miracles by them." * * * This brings the probability of miracles down to the beginning of the second century, in the middle of which Justin Martyr says: "There are prophetic gifts among us even until now:" and amongst these gifts he reckons up miraculous powers, as healing the sick, casting out evil spirits, etc. His words imply an opinion that such gifts were not only exercised in his time, but had been continued down to his time, and he may be justly supposed to speak the sense of his contemporary Christians; and that is all that I cite him for. It seems probable that if we had a full and authentic history of the propagation of the Gospel, from the time of the Apostles to the middle of the second century, composed by eye witnesses and by the preachers of Christianity, we should find miracles wrought for the conversion of the pagans. But from A. D. 70 to 150 is a dark interval, and we have very short accounts of the transactions of those days, unless we should accept of groundless rumors and frivolous tales.†

So, also, Dr. Mosheim, speaking of the second century, and after commenting on the extent to which the extraordinary divine gifts contributed to the extension of the limits of the Church, says: "The gift of foreign tongues appears to have gradually ceased, as soon as many nations became enlightened with the truth; * * * but the other gifts with which God favored the rising Church of Christ, were, as we learn from numerous testimonies of the ancients, still conferred upon particular persons here and there." And when writing of the fourth and succeeding centuries, he, too, bears witness of the declension, and final cessation of these spiritual powers among the Christians; and, indeed, the most of our ecclesiastical writers form the same conclusion.

Thus the Christians lost the enjoyment of the spiritual gifts of the

* *Student's Ecclesiastical History*, vol. i, p. 62.

† Jortin's *Eccl. Hist.*, vol. i, pp. 134-6.

Gospel, such as inspired dreams, prophecies, healings, speaking in new tongues, ministering of angels, and, most to be lamented of all, direct revelation from God, by which the will of God might be made known to His people and His Church preserved from error, from decadence, and from destruction: and by the absence of these spiritual gifts and powers among the Christians of the third and fourth centuries, we may know that a mere man-made religion, having indeed a form of godliness but denying the power thereof, had succeeded to the spiritually gifted religion, of Jesus Christ, wherein the power of God is ever present and outwardly as well as inwardly manifested.

Departure of "Christendom" from the True Doctrine of Deity.

In nothing perhaps was there a wider departure from the real truth of Christianity than in the doctrine concerning God defined by the general council of the Church held within the lifetime of Constantine, and which, in fact, he assembled upon his own authority. This was the celebrated Council of Nicea, in Bithynia, Asia Minor, held in 325 A. D. The main purpose for which the first general Council of the Church was assembled was to settle a dispute between one Arius, a presbyter of Alexandria, and his bishop, Alexander, of the same city, respecting the doctrine of the Godhead. The dispute proved to be far-reaching in its effects, and for three hundred years the rivalry of the contending factions disturbed the peace of Christendom. We shall have clearer conceptions of the subject, however, and be better able to judge of the extent to which there was a departure from the true doctrine respecting the Godhead, by the definitions formulated and enforced upon the Church by the council of Nicea, if we first consider the doctrine of the Godhead as found in the Testament.

The Christian Doctrine of God.

The existence of God both Jesus and the Apostles accepted as a fact. In all the teachings of the former He nowhere seeks to prove God's existence. He assumes that, and proceeds from that basis with His doctrine. He declares the fact that God was His Father, and frequently calls Himself the Son of God.* After His resurrection and departure into heaven, the Apostle taught that He, the Son of God, was with God the Father in the beginning; that He, as well as the Father. was God; that under the direction of the Father He was the Creator of

* John x; Matt. xxvii; Mark xiv: 61, 62.

worlds; that without Him was not anything made that was made.* That in him dwelt all the fulness of the Godhead bodily;† and that He was the express image of the Father's person.‡ Jesus Himself taught that He and the Father were one;§ that whosoever had seen Him had seen the Father also;|| that it was part of His mission to reveal God, the Father, through His own personality; for as was the Son, so too was the Father.** Hence Jesus was God manifested in flesh—a revelation of God to the world.†† That is, a revelation, not only of the *being* of God, but of the *kind* of being God is.

Jesus also taught (and in doing so showed in what the "oneness" of Himself and His Father consisted) that the disciples might be one with Him, and also one with each other, *as* He and the Father were one.‡‡ Not one in person—not all merged into one individual, and all distinctions of personality lost; but one in mind, in knowledge, in love, in will—one by reason of the indwelling in all of the one spirit, even as the mind and will of God the Father was also in Jesus Christ.§§

The Holy Ghost, too, was upheld by the Christian religion to be God.|| || Jesus ascribed to Him a distinct personality; as proceeding from the Father; as sent forth in the name of the Son, as feeling love; experiencing grief; as forbidding; as abiding; as teaching; as bearing witness; as appointing to work; and as interceding for men. All of which clearly establishes for Him a personality.

The distinct personality of these three individual Gods (united however into one Godhead, or Divine Council), was made apparent at the baptism of Jesus; for as He, God the Son, came up out of the water from His baptism at the hands of John, a manifestation of the presence of the Holy Ghost was given in the sign of the dove which rested upon Jesus, while out of the glory of heaven the voice of God the Father was heard saying, "This," referring to Jesus, "is my beloved Son, in whom I am well pleased." The distinctness of the personality of each member of the Godhead is also shown by the commandment to baptize those who believe the Gospel equally in the name of each person of the Holy Trinity. That is, in the name of the Father, and of the Son, and of the

* For all of which see John i: 1-4, 14; Heb. i: 1-3; Matt. xxviii: 18.

† Col. i: 15-19, and ii: 9.

‡ Heb. i: 2, 3.

§ John x: 30; xvii: 11-22.

|| John xiv: 9.

** John xiv: 1-9; John i: 18.

†† I Tim. iii: 16.

‡‡ John xiv: 10, 11, 19, 20; also John xvii.

§§ Eph. iii: 14-19.

|| || Acts v: 1-14. To lie to the Holy Ghost is to lie to God, because the Holy Ghost is God.

Holy Ghost.* And again, also, in the Apostolic benediction, viz., "The grace of the Lord Jesus Christ, and the love of God, and the communion of the Holy Ghost, be with you all."†

These three personages constitute the Christian Godhead, the Holy Trinity. In early Christian theology they were regarded as the Supreme Governing and Creating Power in heaven and in earth. Of which Trinity the Father was worshiped in the name of the Son, while the Holy Ghost bore record of both the Father and the Son. And though the Holy Trinity was made up of three distinct persons, yet did they constitute but one Godhead, or Supreme Governing Power.

This outline of the doctrine of God derived from the New Testament represents Him as anthropomorphic; that is, like a man in form; or, rather, it re-affirms the old doctrine found in the book of Genesis, viz., that man is created in the image of God, and after His likeness. The outline of New Testament doctrine of God also ascribes to Him what are called human attributes and feelings; but as in the foregoing we first say that God is represented as being in human form, and then to get the exact truth say: "Or, rather, man was created in the image and likeness of God," so in this latter case, when we have said that the doctrine of the New Testament ascribes human attributes and feelings to God, to get the exact truth we should say: "Or, rather, man possesses the attributes of God"—the attributes of knowing, willing, judging, loving, etc.—though it should be stated, of course, that man does not possess these attributes in their perfection, as God does. The same may also be said of the physical perfections. While man has been created in the image and likeness of God, yet our bodies in their present state of imperfection—sometimes stunted in growth, diseased, subject to sickness, wasting, decay, and death—cannot be said to be like God's glorious, perfect physical body, yet we have the Divine word that our bodies shall be like His:

"For our conversation is in heaven; from whence also we look for the Savior, the Lord Jesus Christ: who shall change our vile body, that it may be fashioned like unto His glorious body, according to the working whereby he is able even to subdue all things unto himself."‡

So also the attributes of the spirit of man—the attributes of the mind—now imperfect, impure, unholy, and limited in the range of vision and apprehension of things, owing largely to the conditions in which man finds himself placed in this earth-life (and all for a wise purpose in God's economy); yet the time will come that it will be with the spirit as with the body; for God shall change our vile spirit that it may

* Matt. xxviii: 19, 20.

† II Cor. xiii: 14.

‡ Phil. iii: 20, 21.

be fashioned like unto His own glorious spirit, "according to the working whereby He is able even to subdue all things unto Himself." That whereas now we see only as through a glass, darkly, then we shall see as we are seen; that whereas now we know but in part, then we shall know even as we are known.*

The foregoing doctrine of God, taught to the Christians in Apostolic times, awakened their pious reverence without exciting their curiosity. They dealt with no metaphysical abstractions, but were contented to accept the teachings of the Apostles in humble faith, and believed that Jesus Christ was the complete manifestation of Deity, and the express image of God His Father; and hence a revelation to them of God; while the Holy Ghost they accepted as God's witness and messenger to them.

Paganization of the Christian Doctrine of God.

But Christianity, as is well known, came in contact with other doctrines concerning Deity. It was almost immediately brought in touch with the mysticism of the Orient and also with the philosophy of the Greeks, who took so much delight in intellectual subtleties. In the Oriental philosophies, and in the Greek, there was conceived the idea of a trinity in Deity; an idea which possibly may have come down from the doctrines revealed to the patriarchs concerning the Godhead, but which had been corrupted and rendered unintelligible by the vain philosophizings of men. In some of the Oriental systems the trinity or Trimurti consisted of Brahma, the Creator; Vishnu, the Preserver; and Siva, the Destroyer. It will be seen, however, that this trinity is not necessarily one of persons, or individuals, but may be one of attributes, qualities, or even a trinity of functions in *one being;* and in this way it is usually understood.†

Plato's trinity is sometimes stated in the terms, "First Cause; Reason, or Logos; and Soul of the Universe;" but more commonly in these: "Goodness, Intellect, and Will." The nature of the Greek trinity has long been a matter of contention among the learned, and one indeed that is not settled to this day. Is there indicated in his system "a true and proper tri-personality, or merely a personification of three impersonalities," a trinity of attributes or functions? The answers to these questions are varied, and would require too much space for consideration here. Christians having been taught to accept the New Testament doctrine of the Father, Son and Holy Spirit as constituting one Godhead, Christianity no sooner came in contact with the philosophies of the Greeks and Egyptians than there was an effort made to

* I Cor. xiv.

† See Shedd's *History of Christian Doctrine*, vol. i, p. 342, *et seq.* and note.

identify the Christian trinity with that of the Greek and other philosophies. The temptation to do this was very great. Christianity was a proscribed religion and its followers detested. Whenever it could be shown, therefore, that under new symbols the Church really taught the same doctrines that the old philosophers, which were held in esteem, did, it was regarded as a distinct gain to Christianity. The mere fact of Christianity teaching a trinity of any kind was a sufficient basis of comparison, under the temptation offered, and hence in a short time we have the alleged followers of Christ involved in all the metaphysical disputations of the age. The chief difficulty in those speculations was to define the nature of the Logos, or Word of God; a title that is given to our Savior by the Apostle St. John,* be it remembered. Adopting absolute "being" as the postulate of their conception of God, absolute oneness, and therefore absolute singleness, their difficulties arose in trying to reconcile the existence of three persons in the Godhead to the postulate of unity. The disputations were carried on chiefly concerning Christ, the "Word," in His relationship to the Godhead; and the disputants concerned themselves with such questions as these: "Is Jesus the Word?" "If He be the Word, did He emanate from God in time or before time?" "If He emanated from God, is He co-eternal and of the *same*, that is *identical*, substance with Him, or merely of a *similar* substance?" "Is He distinct from the Father, that is, separate from Him, or is He not?" "Is He made or begotten?" "Can He beget in return?" "Has He paternity, or productive virtue without paternity?" Similar questions were asked as to the other Person of the Godhead, the Holy Spirit. These questions were violently agitated at Alexandria by the bishop of that city, Alexander, and one of the presbyters, Arius, 318-321 A. D.; thence spread throughout Christendom, and culminated finally in the Council at Nicea, 325 A. D. Arius held the doctrine that Logos or Word was a dependent or spontaneous production created out of nothing by the will of the Father, hence the Son of God, by whom all things were made, begotten before all worlds; but there had been a time when the Logos *was not;* and also He was of a substance, however similar it might be, different from the Father. This doctrine, in the minds of the opponents of Arius, detracted from the divine nature of Christ, in fact, denied Him true Deity and relegated Him to the position of a creature, against which the piety of a large number of Christians rebelled. After six years of hot disputation and frequent appeals by the contestants to the emperor, the council of Nicea was assembled and the mysteries of the Christian faith submitted to public debate, a portion of the time, at least, in the presence of the emperor, who,

* John i: 1-5, 14.

to some extent, seemed to exercise the functions of president over the assembly. The doctrine of Arius was condemned, and after "long deliberations, among struggles, and scrupulous examinations," the following creed was adopted:

We believe in one God, the Father Almighty, creator of all things visible and invisible; and in one Lord Jesus Christ, the Son of God, only begotten of the Father, that is, of the substance of the Father, God of God, Light of Light, very God of very God, begotten, not made, being of the same substance with the Father, by whom all things were made in heaven and in earth, who for us men and for our salvation came down from heaven, was incarnate, was made man, suffered, rose again the third day, ascended into the heavens, and He will come to judge the living and the dead; and in the Holy Ghost. Those who say there was a time when He was not, and He was not before He was begotten, and He was made of nothing (he was created), or who say that He is of another hypostatis, or of another substance (than the Father), or that the Son of God is created, that he is mutable, or subjec to change, the Catholic church anathematizes.*

Arius himself was condemned as a heretic and banished into one of the remote provinces, Ilyricum, his friends and disciples branded by law, with the odius name of "Porphyrians," because it is supposed that Arius, like Porphyry, had sought to injure Christianity. His writings were condemned to the flames and a capital punishment was pronounced against those in whose possession they should be found. Three years later, however, through the influence of the women at the imperial court, Constantine softened in his demeanor towards Arius and his followers. The exiles were recalled and Arius himself was received at court and his faith approved by a synod of prelates and presbyters at Jerusalem; but on the day that he was to be publicly received in the cathedral church at Constantinople, by the order of the emperor, who, by the way, received the sacrament at the hands of Arius, he expired under circumstances which have led many to believe that other means than the prayers of the orthodox against him were the cause of his death. The leaders of the orthodox party, Athanasius of Alexandria, Eustathius of Antioch, and Paul of Constantinople, were now to feel the wrath of the first Christian emperor. They were deposed on various occasions and by the sentence of numerous councils, and banished into distant provinces. In fact, so far from the adoption of the Nicene creed ending the conflict which had arisen, it was more like the opening of that controversy which agitated Christendom for so long, and resulted in so many shameful conflicts. Councils were arrayed against councils, and though they never could convince one another of error, they never failed, in the spirit of such Christian charity as was then ex-

* *Hist. Christian Councils* (Hefele), p. 294.

tant, to close their decrees with curses. Votes were bartered for and purchased in those councils, and facts justify the latent sarcasm in Gibbon's remark, that "the cause of truth and justice was promoted by the influence of gold." There were persecutions and counter-persecutions, as now one party and then the other prevailed; there were assassinations and bloody battles over this doctrine of Deity, the accounts of which fill, as they also disgrace, our Christian annals. The creed which was adopted at Nicea, however, became the settled doctrine of orthodox Christendom, and remains so to this day.

It is difficult to determine which is really the worst, the creed itself or the explanations of it. At any rate, we do not clearly see the impiety of its doctrines until we listen to the explanations that have been made of it. Athanasius himself has left on record a creed explanatory of the one adopted at Nicea. True, among the learned, many doubt Athanasius being the author of the creed which bears his name; but, however much doubt may be thrown upon that question, no one hesitates to accept it as the orthodox explanation of the doctrine of Deity, and, in fact, it is accepted as one of the important symbols of the Christian faith, and is as follows:

> We worship one God in Trinity, and Trinity in Unity, neither confounding the persons nor dividing the substance. For there is one person of the Father, another of the Son, and another of the Holy Ghost. But the Godhead of the Father, Son and Holy Ghost is all one; the glory equal, the majesty co-eternal. Such as the Father is, such is the Son, and such is the Holy Ghost. The father uncreate, the Son uncreate, and the Holy Ghost uncreate. The Father incomprehensible, the Son incomprehensible, and the Holy Ghost incomprehensible. The Father eternal, the Son eternal, and the Holy Ghost eternal. And yet there are not three eternals, but one eternal. As also there are not three incomprehensibles, nor three uncreate, but one uncreate and one incomprehensible. So likewise the Father is almighty, the Son almighty, and the Holy Ghost almighty; and yet they are not three almighties, but one almighty. So the Father is God, the Son is God, and the Holy Ghost is God; and yet there are not three Gods, but one God.

As already stated, this creed of St. Athanasius is accepted as one of the symbols of the orthodox Christian faith. It is understood that these two creeds teach that God is incorporeal, that is to say, an immaterial being. The Catholic church says: "There is but one God, the creator of heaven and earth, the supreme *incorporeal*, uncreated being who exists of Himself and is infinite in all his attributes."* While the Church of England teaches in her articles of faith "that there is but one living and true God everlasting, *without body*,† parts, or passions, of infinite

* *Catholic Belief* (Bruno), p. 1.

† i. e. without materiality.

power, wisdom and goodness." This view of God as an incorporeal, immaterial, bodiless, partless, passionless being is now and has been from the days of the great apostasy from God and Christ, in the second and third centuries, the doctrine of Deity generally accepted by apostate Christendom. The simple doctrine of the Christian Godhead, set forth in the New Testament is corrupted by the meaningless jargon of these creeds, and their explanations; and the learned who profess a belief in them are wandering in the darkness of the mysticisms of the old pagan philosophies. No wonder that Athanasius himself, whom Gibbon with a quiet sarcasm calls the most sagacious of the Christian theologians, candidly confessed that whenever he forced his understanding to mediate on the divinity of the Logos (and which, of course, involved the whole doctrine of the Godhead), his "toilsome and unavailing efforts recoiled on themselves; and the more he thought, the less he comprehended: and the more he wrote, the less capable was he of expressing his thoughts!" It is a fine passage with which Gibbon closes his reflections upon this subject, and hence I shall give it place here:

> In every step of the inquiry, we are compelled to feel and acknowledge the immeasurable disproportion between the size of the object and the capacity of the human mind. We may try to abstract the notions of time, of space, and of matter, which so closely adhere to all the perceptions of our experimental knowledge; but as soon as we presume to reason of infinite substance, or spiritual generation; as often as we deduce any *positive* conclusions from a *negative* idea, we are involved in darkness, perplexity, and inevitable contradiction.*

Recurrence to the New Testament doctrine of God, and a comparison of it with the doctrine of Deity set forth in the Nicean and Athanasian creeds, will exhibit the wide departure—the absolute apostasy—that has taken place in respect of this most fundamental of all doctrines of religion—the doctrine of God. Truly "Christians" have denied the Lord that bought them,† and turned literally to fables. They have enthroned a conception of a negative idea of "being," which can stand in no possible relationship to man, nor man to it; and to this they ascribe divine attributes and give it title, knee and adoration which belong to God alone. Small wonder that the angel whom John saw flying in the midst of heaven having the everlasting Gospel to commit to the earth in the hour of God's judgment, in the last days, should cry aloud to the inhabitants of the earth, saying, "Fear God, and give glory to Him; * * * and worship him that made

* *Decline and Fall,* xxi.
† II Peter, ii:1.

heaven, and earth, and the sea, and the fountains of waters"*—small wonder, I repeat, that such should be part of this great message, for truly the whole world had departed from the worship of the true and living God.

The Church of Christ Displaced by the Churches of Men.

The departure from the form and spirit of church government was no less marked than the moral and spiritual declension among the Christians of the early centuries of the era, or the departure from the true doctrine of Deity. Beyond filling the vacancy in the council of the Twelve Apostles, occasioned by the fall of Judas, there is no clear and satisfactory evidence that other successors of the Apostles were ever chosen, though the fair implication is that the organization of the Church with Apostles, Prophets, Evangelists, Seventies, Bishops, Teachers, etc., was to be perpetuated as at first established. At least this organization was given for the perfecting of the saints, for the work of the ministry, until the saints should come to a unity of the faith and the knowledge of the Son of God;† so that the plain inference is that so long as there are saints to be perfected, or edified, or united, or brought to the knowledge of God; so long as there is work for a ministry, or the necessity of a Church through the agency of which the truth is to be taught to the world so long it will be necessary to perpetuate the organization given of God for the achievement of those high purposes. To say that man could devise a better organization for the accomplishment of these several objects would be to challenge the wisdom of God. To say that any of these means provided in the Church organization could be dispensed with, would be to contradict the plain teaching of scripture, which, in this very connection forbids the eye to say to the hand, I have no need of thee; or the head to the feet, I have no need of you; that is, one officer of the Church may not say to another officer, I have no need of thee.‡ The doctrine of scripture is that all the officers of the Church together with their several gifts are essential to the Church of Christ; essential to its perfection; essential to the performance of the sacred functions assigned to it. Yet it must be conceded that the organization described in the New Testament did not survive the last of the Apostles; or preserve much beyond that time, the spirit which the Master had impressed upon it.§

The Apostles, while they lived, exercised a general jurisdiction over the Church, to which all submitted without question. In the exercise

* Rev. xiv: 6, 7.

† I Cor. xii; Eph. iv.

‡ I Cor. xii.

§ Matt. xx.

of their general authority they organized branches of the Church, appointed Elders or Bishops to take the oversight of them, and instructed them in Church government, and discipline, and doctrine. After the demise of the Apostles, there seems to have been left no central authority to exercise the functions of general supervision or presidency over the entire Church, such as the Twelve had exercised. That center of unity, together with the power thereof, seems to have vanished from the Church with the Apostles. The bishops and some subordinate officers remained, it is true, but these were local, not general authorities. The Church in each city or district of country after the Apostolic age, seems to have been regarded as a sort of independent republic of itself, without any bond of consociation with any other church beyond that which was the result of possessing a common faith in Christianity, which bond was one of sympathy merely, not of hierarchal association. The rise of the hierarchy with the centralization of its powers in the bishop of Rome, and which ultimately dominated the whole Church, and not only the Church but, directly or indirectly, the western civilized world, came later, and was of gradual development; and when it was finally established, it was not the organization described in the New Testament, the Church with an inspired Priesthood of Apostles, and Prophets, Evangelists, Seventies, and Pastors, etc., but a hierarchy fashioned by man out of such remnants of Church organization as survived Apostolic times. As the number of Christians increased, the bishops of large cities organized new branches of the Church in the suburbs of their cities, and in the towns and villages adjacent, and ordained for them a ministry. It was but natural perhaps that the officers of these new branches of the Church, both the bishops and the subordinate clergy, should look to the one who had brought them into existence as a sort of general presiding authority over them. And hence, in time arose what were called metropolitan bishops, bishops who had under their direction the bishops of neighboring towns and villages—bishops of the "suburbs and the fields," they were sometimes called—and perhaps of the entire province of which the metropolitan city was recognized as the center. As the bishops of the metropolis of a province, in the manner described, became the center of ecclesiastical unity for that province, so, too, in time, the bishops of cities which were the capitals of the three great divisions of the empire—Antioch, Alexandria and Rome—asserted a superior dignity over metropolitan bishops. It was in these cities that the exarchs of the empire resided, and if we may trust the authority of Neander, the bishops of these cities also, at first, took that title, but later made choice of the more ecclesiastical name of Patriarch.* In addition to the importance attached to these cities as

* Neander, *Ch. Hist.*, vol. ii, p. 196.

the capitals of the great divisions of the empire, a superior dignity in the minds of Christians attached to the Churches founded by the Apostles as the surest depositories of the Apostolic teaching and doctrine; and as Apostolic origin could be claimed for the churches in the three cities named, it is not surprising, when their political importance is added, that the bishops of those cities claimed superior dignity for their office, and united under their jurisdiction the metropolitan bishops of the respective three great divisions of the empire. Subsequently the same title was granted to the bishop of Jerusalem, and to the bishop of Constantinople; to the former it was granted in virtue of the peculiar sanctity which attaches to Jerusalem, and the fact that the first Christian Church was planted there; to the latter, because it was made the capital of the empire, "New Rome;" and because also it was peculiarly the city of the first imperial patron of Christianity. Thus five patriarchates were established.

Through circumstances too numerous and intricate to detail here, the bishops of Rome changed the primacy of mere precedence which had been accorded them among associated brethren, to a primacy of power and jurisdiction, which resulted in the bishops of Rome becoming recognized as the supreme head of the Christian Church; and the papacy entered upon that marvelous career which by the impartial can but be regarded as the shame of the Christian name.

Attention has already been called to the corruptions which prevailed in that period of peace in the closing decades of the third century, where bishops are represented as being full of pride and ostentation; as deserting the law of piety and being inflamed against each other with mutual strifes, only accumulating quarrels, threats, rivalships, hostilities, hatred towards each other, and only anxious to assert the Church government as a kind of sovereignty for themselves.* And all this when Christianity was a proscribed religion; and when the Church, and especially its leaders, the bishops, were liable to severest persecution. Reason and a due consideration of human nature both combined to fix upon us the conviction that the bitterness of rivalry, of hatred, of ambition, must have greatly increased when metropolitan and patriarchal bishops, formerly proscribed and hunted like wild beasts, rose to the dignity of civil princes, and took upon them more and ever more of the spirit of worldliness as wealth and honor and popular applause were made the accompaniments of their ecclesiastical offices. History confirms what reason and a knowledge of human nature suggests; for the history of the Church after the elevation of proscribed Christianity to the dignity of the state religion of the Roman empire, is but the melancholy history of unholy ambitions, jealousies, strifes, contentions, murders, and wars between rival bishops and their adherents, on the one

* See pp. lxxiii-lxxv.

hand; and equally unholy struggles for worldly advantages with kings and rulers of this world, on the other. The spirit that actuated the bishops of the Church after their elevation through the policy of Constantine is admirably illustrated by a remark of Gregory of Nazianzus, made in Constantinople, 380 A. D., when deploring the evils of the Church. He says:

> Would to heaven there were no primacy, no eminence of place, and no tyrannical precedence of rank; that we might be known by eminence of virtue alone! But, as the case now stands, the distinction of a seat at the right hand or the left, or in the middle; at a higher or a lower place; of going before or aside of each other, has given rise to many disorders among us, to no salutary purpose whatever, and plunged multitudes in ruin.*

Matters in Church government did not mend with time, but grew worse and worse. Pride increased; rivalship between contending prelates grew more embittered; ambition mounted higher and ever higher in the breasts of the shepherds of the flock of Christ. In his association with his Apostles—to whom he committed the keys of His kingdom—the Master had discouraged ambition and had said that he who would be great among his followers must be their minister; and whosoever would be chief among them, was to be their servant; and the government of His Church was to be distinct in these particulars from the governments of this world.† But all in vain were the instructions of Messiah to the worldly, ambitious prelates of an apostate Christianity which had gradually supplanted the religion of Jesus Christ; and henceforth we may see in that hierarchy which usurped the place of the Church of Christ from the time of Constantine, all the spirit of pride envy, jealousy, contention, strife, selfishness, bitterness, and unholy ambition which characterized the princes and rulers of this world; attended, too, with all the evils that wait upon these passions of rulers when once let loose, viz., secret plottings, usurpations of authority, corrupt elections, cruel imprisonments, banishments, secret and public murders, and wars; all undertaken, of course, in the interest of the gentle religion of Jesus Christ, and the maintenance of that authority which is based on love, and whose control over men is through the means of persuasion and the teaching of true knowledge. Is it not evident that the kigdom of peace, wherein was to dwell righteousness and truth, had become merely one of the kingdoms of this world? And were not the Fratriceli of the thirteenth century, though denounced as heretics, right when they loudly proclaimed their conviction that "the fatal gift of a Christian emperor had been the doom of the true Christian religion?"

* This remark is quoted by Neander, *Ch. Hist.*, vol. ii, p. 198.
† Matt. xx: 26, 27.

The Testimony of Prophecy to the Universal Apostasy.

Clear as the fact is made in this historical review that there was a complete and universal apostasy from the religion established in the Dispensation of the Meridian of Time; and clear as is the proof from the same review that the Church of Christ then established was destroyed, there is yet another line of evidence pointing to the same solemn fact that I can not altogether omit, though often used in our literature, viz., the testimony of prophecy to the apostasy from the Christian religion, and the destruction of the Church of Christ.

The Apostles themselves through the inspiration of the Holy Ghost were fully aware that such an apostasy would take place, as the following several predictions bear witness: Paul passing through Ephesus admonished the Elders of that Church to take heed to the flock "over which the Holy Ghost hath made you overseers; * * * * * for I know this, that after my departing shall grievous wolves enter in among you, not sparing the flock. Also of your own selves shall men arise, speaking perverse things, to draw away disciples after them."*

To Timothy Paul said: "The Spirit speaketh expressly, that in the latter times some shall depart from the faith, giving heed to seducing spirits, and doctrines of devils; speaking lies in hypocrisy; having their conscience seared with a hot iron; forbidding to marry and commanding to abstain from meats."† And again: "I charge thee, * * * preach the word; be instant in season, out of season; reprove, rebuke, exhort with all long suffering and doctrine. For the time will come when they will not endure sound doctrine; but after their own lusts they shall heap to themselves teachers, having itching ears; and they shall turn away their ears from the truth; and shall be turned unto fables."‡

And still again he said to Timothy: "This know also, that in the last days perilous times shall come. For men shall be lovers of their own selves, covetous, boasters, proud, blasphemers, disobedient to parents, unthankful, unholy, without natural affection, truce breakers, false accusers, incontinent, fierce, despisers of those that are good, traitors, heady, highminded, lovers of pleasure more than lovers of God; having a form of Godliness, but denying the power thereof: from such turn away."§

Peter's prophecy concerning the rise of false teachers among the saints, who privately would bring in damnable heresies, even denying the Lord who bought them, and by reason of whom the way of truth would be evil spoken of, we have already quoted.‖

* Acts xx: 28-30.

† I Tim. iv: 1, 2, 3.

‡ II Tim. iv: 1, 2, 3, 4.

§ II Tim. iii: 1-5.

‖ See page xlviii, and II Peter i: 3.

Paul in his second epistle to the Thessalonians gives utterance to a prophecy which covers the whole ground of the absolute and universal apostasy of Christendom. A prophecy which, if the apostasy of so-called Christendom has not been complete and universal, proves beyond all question that the great Apostle of the Gentiles is a false prophet; or if fulfilled, then it proves that the Church of Christ, so far as it existed in the earth was to be destroyed; that another and different religion was to be substituted for the Christian religion; that another church, one founded by men, was to take the place of the Church of Christ, a worldly church dominated by the very spirit of Lucifier, who, under its rule, would oppose and exalt himself above all that is called God; and sit in the temple of God showing himself, so far as this world is concerned, that he is God. Moreover Paul declared in this very prophecy I am about to quote that the forces which would ultimately bring to pass this universal apostasy from the Christian religion—"the mystery of iniquity—" was already at work even in his day. With this introduction, which is also to be considered as my comment upon and interpretation of the passage, I quote Paul's great prediction on the universal Apostasy:

> Now we beseech you, brethren, by the coming of our Lord Jesus Christ, and by our gathering together unto him, that ye be not soon shaken in mind, or be troubled, neither by spirit, nor by word, nor by letter as from us, as that the day of Christ is at hand. Let no man deceive you by any means: for that day shall not come, except there come a falling away first, and that man of sin be revealed, the Son of Perdition; who opposeth and exalteth himself above all that is called God, or that is worshiped; so that he as Gad sitteth in the temple of God, showing himself that he is God. Remember ye not, that, when I was yet with you, I told you these things? And now ye know what withholdeth that he might be revealed in his time. For the mystery of iniquity doth already work: only he who now letteth (hindereth) will let (hinder), until he be taken out of the way. And then shall that Wicked be revealed, whom the Lord shall consume with the spirit of his mouth, and shall destroy with the brightness of his coming: even him whose coming is after the working of Satan with all power and signs and lying wonders, and with all deceivableness of unrighteousness in them that perish; because they receive not the love of the truth, that they might be saved. And for this cause God shall send them strong delusion, that they should believe a lie: that they all might be damned who believe not the truth, but had pleasure in unrighteousness.*

A more ancient prophet than Paul also predicted a like condition of the world in the last days: "Behold," says Isaiah, "the Lord maketh the earth empty, and maketh it waste, and turneth it upside down, and scattereth abroad the inhabitants thereof. And it shall be, as with the people, so with the priest, * * * The land shall be utterly emptied, and utterly spoiled; for the Lord hath spoken this word. The

* II Thes. ii: 1-12.

earth mourneth and fadeth away, the world languisheth and fadeth away, the haughty people of the earth do languish. The earth also is defiled under the inhabitants thereof; because they have transgressed the laws, changed the ordinance, broken the everlasting covenant. Therefore hath the curse devoured the earth, and they that dwell therein are desolate: therefore the inhabitants of the earth are burned, and few men left."*

Clearly all this prophecy of Isaiah's has not yet been fulfilled; for the earth, however much it may have been defiled under the inhabitants thereof, has not yet been burned, and but few men left. That is a judgment that still hangs over the world; and will come upon it as sure as the Lord has spoken the word; and that, too, because men have transgressed the laws; because they have changed the ordinances, because they have broken—not the covenant made with Moses, or with Abraham—but because they have broken the everlasting covenant; of which covenant the blood of Christ is the sign and seal.† In other words, they have broken the Gospel covenant—departed from the Gospel faith—hence the predicted judgment.

If I did not think these two great prophecies foretold completely the universal apostasy of Christendom, I should be tempted to enter into the consideration of the great prophecies to be found in the book of Daniel and the book of Revelation, and show how to both of these prophets, as well as unto Paul and other New Testament writers, the Lord revealed the rise of an earth power that would not only open his mouth in blasphemy against God, to blaspheme His name and them who dwell in heaven;‡ who would speak great words against the Most High, and so magnify himself as to stand up against the Prince of princes§—but who would also make war with the saints and "prevail against them;"‖ who would "wear out the saints of the Most High;"** "destroy the mighty and the holy people;"†† "make war with the saints and overcome them."‡‡ But believeing that the two passages quoted at length entirely cover the subject prophetically, I shall not here enter into further prophetic proofs either as to the corruptions of the Christian religion or the destruction of the Christian Church, deeming that what has already been set forth sufficient on that head.

Conclusion

The sum of the whole matter is:—The purpose of man's creation, and the plan of his redemption, were known to God and the immense

* Isaiah xxiv: 1-6.
† Heb. xiii: 10.
‡ Rev. xiii: 6.
§ Dan. vii: 25; viii: 25.
‖ Dan. vii: 21.
** Dan. vii: 25.
†† Dan. viii: 24.
‡‡ Rev. xiii: 7.

host of the spirits of men before the creation of the earth. Adam came to the new creation, the earth, under the divine commandment to people it with his offspring. From Adam to Messiah numerous dispensations of the Gospel were given to men; but these dispensations were limited in their effectiveness, owing to the proneness of men to reject the truth, and to walk in darkness rather than light because their deeds were evil. Yet God left not Himself without witnesses in the earth; for there were a few in all dispensations who honored Him and His righteous laws. Finally, when the appointed time was come, Jesus of Nazareth, the Son of God, came and made the appointed Atonement for the sins of the world and brought men under the dominion of His mercy. He taught the Gospel; He brought life and immortality to light; He brought into existence His Church, and then ascended on high to His Father. For a time the Gospel in its purity was preached in the world by the chosen Apostles, though even in their day men began to mar it with their vain philosophies, their doctrines of science, falsely so called; and when the Apostles were all fallen asleep, then corruptions ran riot in the Church, doctrines of men were taught for the commandments of God! a church made by men was substituted for the Church of Christ; a church full of pride and worldliness; a church which while it clung to forms of godliness ran riot in excesses and abominations—until spiritual darkness fell like a pall over the nations; and thus they lay for ages. In vain men sought to establish reforms, and through them bring back the religion of Jesus Christ, and the Church of Christ. To do that, however, was beyond the power of these men, however good their intentions. The Gospel taken from the earth, divine authority lost, the Church of Christ destroyed, there was but one way in which all these could be restored, viz.: By re-opening the heavens and dispensing again a knowledge of the Gospel; by once more conferring divine authority upon men, together with a commission to teach all the world, and re-establish the Church of Christ on earth. In a word, it would require the incoming of the Dispensation of the Fulness of Times to restore all things, and gather together in one all things in Christ, both in heaven and in earth. Such Dispensation is promised of God, as we have seen; and now it only remains to add that the History of the Church of Jesus Christ of Latter-day Saints, as set forth in these volumes, is the history of that series of events which has resulted in the restoration of the Gospel in its fullness, and the re-establishment of the Church of Jesus Christ on earth.

HISTORY OF THE CHURCH OF JESUS CHRIST OF LATTER-DAY SAINTS

VOLUME I.

HISTORY
OF THE
CHURCH OF JESUS CHRIST
OF
LATTER-DAY SAINTS

PERIOD I.

HISTORY OF JOSEPH SMITH, THE PROPHET

CHAPTER I.

JOSEPH SMITH'S BIRTH AND LINEAGE—THE PROPHET'S FIRST VISION—"THIS IS MY BELOVED SON."

The Prophet's Introduction.

OWING to the many reports which have been put in circulation by evil-disposed and designing persons, in relation to the rise and progress of the Church of Jesus Christ of Latter-day Saints, all of which have been designed by the authors thereof to militate against its character as a Church and its progress in the world—I have been induced to write this history, to disabuse the public mind, and put all inquirers after truth into possession of the facts, as they have transpired, in relation both to myself and the Church, so far as I have such facts in my possession. In this history I shall present the various events in relation to this Church, in truth and righteousness, as they have transpired, or as they at present exist, being now the eighth* year since the organization of said Church.

Birth and Ancestry.

I was born in the year of our Lord one thousand eight hundred and five, on the twenty-third day of December, in the town of Sharon, Windsor county, state of Vermont. My father, Joseph Smith, was born July 12th, 1771, in Topsfield, Essex county, Massachusetts; his father, Asael Smith, was born March 7th, 1744, in Topsfield, Massachusetts; his father, Samuel Smith, was born January 26th, 1714, in Topsfield, Massachusetts; his father, Samuel Smith, was born January 26th, 1666, in Topsfield, Massachusetts; his father, Robert Smith, came from England. My father, Joseph Smith, Senior, left the state of Vermont, and moved to Palmyra, Ontario (now Wayne) county, in the state of New York, when I was in my tenth year, or thereabouts. In about four years after my father's arrival in Palmyra he moved with his family into Manchester, in the same county of Ontario, his family consisting of eleven souls, namely—my father, Joseph Smith, my mother, Lucy Smith, (whose name, previous to her marriage, was Mack, daughter of Solomon Mack,) † my brothers, Alvin, (who died November 19th, 1824, in the 27th year of his age,) Hyrum, myself, Samuel Harrison, William, Don Carlos, and my sisters Sophronia, Catherine, and Lucy.

Religious Excitement in Western New York.

Some time in the second year after our removal to Manchester, there was in the place where we lived an unusual excitement on the subject of religion. It commenced with the Methodists, but soon became general among all the sects in that region of country. Indeed, the whole district of

* That is, 1838, since the Church was organized April 6th, 1830. The date at which the Prophet began the writing of this History is also indicated on a subsequent page, where reference is made to the final return of the plates to the angel, in whose charge they remained "until this day, the second day of May, 1838."

† The Mack family, at least back to Ebenezer Mack, grandfather of Lucy, was from the state of Connecticut (*Joseph Smith and his Progenitors*, by Lucy Smith, ch. ix.)

country seemed affected by it, and great multitudes united themselves to the different religious parties, which created no small stir and division amongst the people, some crying, "Lo here!" and others, "Lo, there!" Some were contending for the Methodist faith, some for the Presbyterian, and some for the Baptist. For notwithstanding the great love which the converts to these different faiths expressed at the time of their conversion, and the great zeal manifested by the respective clergy, who were active in getting up and promoting this extraordinary scene of religious feeling, in order to have everybody converted, as they were pleased to call it, let them join what sect they pleased—yet when the converts began to file off, some to one party and some to another, it was seen that the seemingly good feelings of both the priests and the converts were more pretended than real; for a scene of great confusion and bad feeling ensued; priest contending against priest, and convert against convert; so that all their good feelings one for another, if they ever had any, were entirely lost in a strife of words and a contest about opinions.

Reflections on Divided Christendom.

I was at this time in my fifteenth year. My father's family was proselyted to the Presbyterian faith, and four of them joined that church, namely—my mother Lucy; my brothers Hyrum and Samuel Harrison; and my sister Sophronia. During this time of great excitement, my mind was called up to serious reflection and great uneasiness; but, though my feelings were deep and often poignant, still I kept myself aloof from all these parties, though I attended their several meetings as often as occasion would permit. In process of time my mind became somewhat partial to the Methodist sect, and I felt some desire to be united with them; but so great were the confusion and strife among the different denominations, that it was impossible for a person young as I was, and so unacquainted with men and things, to come to any certain conclusion who was right and who was wrong. My mind at times was greatly excited, the cry and tumult were so great and incessant. The Presbyterians were most decided against the Baptists and Methodists, and used all the powers of both reason and sophistry to prove their errors, or, at least, to make the people think they were in error. On the other hand, the Baptists and Methodists in their turn were equally zealous in endeavoring to establish their own tenets and disprove all others.

Perplexity of the Prophet.

In the midst of this war of words and tumult of opinions, I often said to myself, what is to be done? Who of all these parties are right; or, are they all wrong together? If any one of them be right, which is it, and how shall I know it? While I was laboring under the extreme difficulties caused by the contests of these parties of religionists, I was one day reading the Epistle of James, first chapter and fifth verse, which reads:

> If any of you lack wisdom, let him ask of God, that giveth to all men liberally, and upbraideth not; and it shall be given him.

The Promise of James Tested.

Never did any passage of Scripture come with more power to the heart of man than this did at this time to mine. It seemed to enter with great force into every feeling of my heart. I reflected on it again and again, knowing that if any person needed wisdom from God, I did; for how to act I did not know and unless I could get more wisdom than I then had, I would never know; for the teachers of religion of the different sects understood the same passage of Scripture so differently as to destroy all confidence in settling the question by an appeal to the Bible. At length I came to the conclusion that I must either remain in darkness and confusion, or else I must do as James directs, that is, ask of God. I at length came to the determination to "ask of God," concluding that if He gave wisdom to them that lacked wisdom, and would give liberally, and not upbraid, I might venture. So, in accordance with this, my determination to Ask God, I retired to the woods to make the attempt. It was on the morning of a beautiful, clear day, early in the spring of eighteen hundred and twenty. It was the first time in my life that I had made such an attempt, for amidst all my anxieties I had never as yet made the attempt to pray vocally.

Effort of Satan to Destroy the Prophet.

After I had retired to the place where I had previously designed to go, having looked around me, and finding myself alone, I kneeled down and began to offer up the desires of my heart to God. I had scarcely done so, when immediately I was seized upon by some power which entirely overcame me, and had such an astonishing influence over me as to bind my tongue so that I could not speak. Thick darkness gathered around me, and it seemed to me for a time as if I were doomed to sudden destruction. But, exerting all my powers to call upon God to deliver me out of the power of this enemy which had seized upon me, and at the very moment when I was ready to sink into despair and abandon myself to destruction—not to an imaginary ruin, but to the power of some actual being from the unseen world, who had such marvelous power as I had never before felt in any being—just at this moment of great alarm, I saw a pillar of light exactly over my head, above the brightness of the sun, which descended gradually until it fell upon me.

The First Vision

It no sooner appeared than I found myself delivered from the enemy which held me bound. When the light rested upon me I saw two personages, whose brightness and glory defy all description, standing above me in the air. One of them spake unto me, calling me by name, and said—pointing to the other—

"THIS IS MY BELOVED SON, HEAR HIM."

My object in going to inquire of the Lord was to know which of all the sects was right, that I might know which to join. No sooner, therefore, did I get possession of myself, so as to be able to speak, than I asked the personages who stood above me in the light, which of all the sects was right—and which I should join. I was answered that I must join none of them, for they were all wrong, and the personage who addressed me said that all their creeds were an abomination in His sight: that those professors were all corrupt; that "they draw near to me with their lips, but their hearts are far from me; they teach for doctrines the commandments of men: having a form of godliness, but they deny the power thereof." He again forbade me to join with any of them: and many other things did he say unto me, which I cannot write at this time. When I came to myself again, I found myself lying on my back, looking up into heaven. When the light had departed, I had no strength; but soon recovering in some degree, I went home. And as I leaned up to the fireplace, mother inquired what the matter was. I replied, "Never mind, all is well—I am well enough off." I then said to my mother, "I have learned for myself that Presbyterianism is not true."

State of Christain World.

It seems as though the adversary was aware, at a very early period of my life, that I was destined to prove a disturber and an annoyer of his kingdom; else why should the powers of darkness combine against me? Why the opposition and persecution that arose against me, almost in my infancy? Some few days after I had this vision, I happened to be in company with one of the Methodist preachers, who was very active in the before-mentioned religious excitement, and, conversing with him on the subject of religion, I took occasion to give him an account of the vision which I had had. I was greatly surprised at his behavior; he treated my communication not only lightly, but with great contempt, saying, it was all of the devil, that there were no such things as visions or revelations in these days; that all such things had ceased with the Apostles, and that

Sectarian Opposition.

there would never be any more of them. I soon found, however, that my telling the story had excited a great deal of prejudice against me among professors of religion, and was the cause of great persecution, which continued to increase; and though I was an obscure boy, only between fourteen and fifteen years of age, and my circumstances in life such as to make a boy of no consequence in the world, yet men of high standing would take notice sufficient to excite the public mind against me, and create a bitter persecution; and this was common among all the sects—all united to persecute me.

Reflections upon Sectarian Opposition.

It caused me serious reflection then, and often has since, how very strange it was that an obscure boy, of a little over fourteen years of age, and one, too, who was doomed to the necessity of obtaining a scanty maintenance by his daily labor, should be thought a character of sufficient importance to attract the attention of the great ones of the most popular sects of the day, and in a manner to create in them a spirit of the most bitter persecution and reviling. But strange or not, so it was, and it was often the cause of great sorrow to myself. However, it was nevertheless a fact that I had beheld a vision. I have thought since, that I felt much like Paul, when he made his defense before King Agrippa, and related the account of the vision he had when he saw a light, and heard a voice; but still there were but few who believed him; some said he was dishonest, others said he was mad; and he was ridiculed and reviled. But all this did not destroy the reality of his vision. He had seen a vision, he knew he had, and all the persecution under heaven could not make it otherwise; and though they should persecute him unto death, yet he knew, and would know to the last breath, that he had both seen a light, and heard a voice speaking unto him, and all the world could not make him think or believe otherwise. So it was with me. I had actually seen a light, and in the midst of that light I saw two personages, and they did in reality speak to me; and though I was hated and persecuted for saying that I had seen a vision, yet it was true; and while they were persecuting me, reviling me, and speaking all manner of evil against me falsely for so saying, I was led to say in my heart, Why persecute me for telling the truth? I have actually seen a vision, and who am I that I can withstand God, or why does the world think to make me deny what I have actually seen? For I had seen a vision; I knew it, and I knew that God knew it, and I could not deny it, neither dared I do it, at least I knew that by so doing I would offend God, and come under condemnation.

All Doubts Settled.

I had now got my mind satisfied so far as the sectarian world was concerned; that it was not my duty to join with any of them, but to continue as I was until further directed. I had found the testimony of James to be true, that a man who lacked wisdom might ask of God, and obtain, and not be upbraided.

CHAPTER II.

THE VISITATION OF MORONI—EXISTENCE OF THE BOOK OF MORMON MADE KNOWN.

I CONTINUED to pursue my common vocation in life until the twenty-first of September, one thousand eight hundred and twenty-three, all the time suffering severe persecution at the hands of all classes of men, both religious and irreligious, because I continued to affirm that I had seen a vision.

Interval of Three Years 1820-23.

During the space of time which intervened between the time I had the vision and the year eighteen hundred and twenty-three—having been forbidden to join any of the religious sects of the day, and being of very tender years, and persecuted by those who ought to have been my friends, and to have treated me kindly, and if they supposed me to be deluded to have endeavored in a proper and affectionate manner to have reclaimed me,—I was left to all kinds of temptations; and mingling with all kinds of society, I frequently fell into many foolish errors, and displayed the weakness of youth, and the foibles of human nature; which, I am sorry to say, led me into divers temptations, offensive in the sight of God. In making this confession, no one need suppose me guilty of any great or malignant sins. A disposition to commit such was never in my nature. But I was guilty of levity, and sometimes associated with jovial company, etc., not consistent with that character which ought to be maintained by one who was called of God as I had been. But this will not seem very

Confession of Errors.

strange to any one who recollects my youth, and is acquainted with my native cheery temperament.*

In consequence of these things, I often felt condemned for my weakness and imperfections; when, on

*With this agrees a letter which the Prophet addressed to Oliver Cowdery upon hearing that it was the intention of the latter to publish a series of articles in the *Saints' Messenger and Advocate*, on "Early Scenes and Incidents in the Church." The letter referred to appeared in vol. 1, no. 3, of the *Messenger and Advocate*, 1834.

LETTER OF JOSEPH SMITH TO OLIVER COWDERY:

Dear Brother:

Having learned from the first number of the *Messenger and Advocate*, that you were not only about to "give a history of the rise and progress of the Church of the Latter-day Saints;" but that said history would necessarily embrace my life and character, I have been induced to give you the time and place of my birth; as I have learned that many of the opposers of those principles which I have held forth to the world, profess a personal acquaintance with me, though when in my presence, represent me to be another person, in age, education, and stature, from what I am.

I was born (according to the record of the same kept by my parents) in the town of Sharon, Windsor county, Vermont, on the 23rd of December, 1805. At the age of ten my father's family removed to Palmyra, New York, where, in the vicinity of which, I lived, or, made it my place of residence, until I was twenty-one; the latter part in the town of Manchester.

During this time, as is common to most, or all youths, I fell into many vices and follies; but as my accusers are, and have been forward to accuse me of being guilty of gross and outrageous violations of the peace and good order of the community, I take the occasion to remark that, though as I have said above, "as is common to most, or all youths, I fell into many vices and follies," I have not, neither can it be sustained, in truth, been guilty of wronging or injuring any man or society of men; and those imperfections to which I allude, and for which I have often had occasion to lament, were a light, and too often, vain mind, exhibiting a foolish and trifling conversation.

This being all, and the worst, that my accusers can substantiate against my moral character, I wish to add that it is not without a deep feeling of regret that I am thus called upon in answer to my own conscience, to fulfil a duty I owe to myself, as well as to the cause of truth, in making this public confession of my former uncircumspect walk, and trifling conversation and more particularly, as I often acted in violation of those holy precepts which I knew came from God. But as the "Articles and Covenants," of this Church are plain upon this particular point, I do not deem it important to proceed further. I only add, that I do not, nor never have, pretended to be any other than a man "subject to passion," and liable, without the assisting grace of the Savior, to deviate from that perfect path in which all men are commanded to walk.

By giving the above a place in your valuable paper, you will confer a lasting favor upon myself as an individual, and, as I humbly hope, subserve the cause of righteousness.

I am, with feelings of esteem, your fellow-laborer in the Gospel of our Lord,

[Signed] JOSEPH SMITH.

the evening of the above-mentioned twenty-first of September, after I had retired to my bed for the night, I betook myself to prayer and supplication to Almighty God for forgiveness of all my sins and follies, and also for a manifestation to me, that I might know of my state and standing before Him; for I had full confidence in obtaining a divine manifestation, as I previously had done. While I was thus in the act of calling upon God, I discovered a light appearing in my room, which continued to increase until the room was lighter than at noonday, when immediately a personage appeared at my bedside, standing in the air, for his feet did not touch the floor. He had on a loose robe of most exquisite whiteness. It was a whiteness beyond anything earthly I had ever seen; nor do I believe that any earthly thing could be made to appear so exceedingly white and brilliant. His hands were naked and his arms also, a little above the wrist, so, also were his feet naked, as were his legs, a little above the ankles. His head and neck were also bare. I could discover that he had no other clothing on but this robe, as it was open, so that I could see into his bosom. Not only was his robe exceedingly white, but his whole person was glorious beyond description, and his countenance truly like lightning. The room was exceedingly light, but not so very bright as immediately around his person.

Appearing of Moroni.

When first I looked upon him, I was afraid; but the fear soon left me. He called me by name, and said unto me that he was a messenger sent from the presence of God to me and that his name was Moroni;* that God had a work for me to do; and that my name should be had for good and evil among all nations, kindreds, and tongues, or that it should

Moroni's Message.

* In the original publication of the history in the *Times and Seasons* at Nauvoo, this name appears as "Nephi," and the *Millennial Star* perpetuated the error in its republication of the History. That it is an error is evident, and it is so noted in the manuscripts to which access has been had in the preparation of this work. See also *Book of Doctrine and Covenants*, section 27, par. 5, and section 128, par. 20.

be both good and evil spoken of among all people. He said there was a book deposited, written upon gold plates, giving an account of the former inhabitants of this continent, and the sources from whence they sprang. He also said that the fullness of the everlasting Gospel was contained in it, as delivered by the Savior to the ancient inhabitants; also that there were two stones in silver bows—and these stones, fastened to a breastplate, constituted what is called the Urim and Thummim—deposited with the plates; and the possession and use of these stones were what constituted "Seers" in ancient or former times; and that God had prepared them for the purpose of translating the book.

Ancient Prophecies Quoted.

After telling me these things, he commenced quoting the prophecies of the Old Testament. He first quoted part of the third chapter of Malachi,* and he quoted also the fourth or last chapter of the same prophecy, though with a little variation from the way it reads in our Bibles. Instead of quoting the first verse as it reads in our books, he quoted it thus:

> For behold the day cometh that shall burn as an oven, and all the proud, yea, and all that do wickedly shall burn as stubble: for they that come shall burn them, saith the Lord of hosts, that it shall leave them neither root nor branch.

And again, he quoted the fifth verse thus:

> Behold I will reveal unto you the Priesthood, by the hand of Elijah the prophet, before the coming of the great and dreadful day of the Lord.

He also quoted the next verse differently:

> And he shall plant in the hearts of the children the promises made to the fathers, and the hearts of the children shall turn to their fathers; if it were not so, the whole earth would be utterly wasted at his coming.

In addition to these, he quoted the eleventh chapter of Isaiah, saying that it was about to be fulfilled. He

*Most likely the first part of the chapter; as that deals with the coming of a messenger to prepare the way for the glorious coming of Messiah.

quoted also the third chapter of Acts, twenty-second and twenty-third verses, precisely as they stand in our New Testament. He said that that Prophet was Christ; but the day had not yet come when "they who would not hear his voice should be cut off from among the people," but soon would come. He also quoted the second chapter of Joel, from the twenty-eighth verse to the last. He also said that this was not yet fulfilled, but was soon to be. And he further stated that the fullness of the Gentiles was soon to come in. He quoted many other passages of Scripture, and offered many explanations which cannot be mentioned here.

Plates not to be Shown.

Again, he told me, that when I got those plates of which he had spoken—for the time that they should be obtained was not yet fulfilled—I should not show them to any person; neither the breast plate with the Urim and Thummim; only to those to whom I should be commanded to show them; if I did I should be destroyed. While he was conversing with me about the plates, the vision was opened to my mind that I could see the place where the plates were deposited, and that so clearly and distinctly that I knew the place again when I visited it.

Second Appearing of Moroni.

After this communication, I saw the light in the room began to gather immediately around the person of him who had been speaking to me, and it continued to do so, until the room was again left dark, except just around me, when instantly I saw, as it were, a conduit open right up into heaven, and he ascended until he entirely disappeared, and the room was left as it had been before this heavenly light had made its appearance. I lay musing on the singularity of the scene and marveling greatly at what had been told to me by this extraordinary messenger; when, in the midst of my meditation, I suddenly discovered that my room was again beginning to get lighted, and in an instant, as it were, the same heavenly messenger was again by my bedside. He commenced, and again related the very same things which he had done at the first visit, without the least variation; which having done, he informed me of great judgments which were coming upon the earth, with great desolations by famine, sword, and pestilence; and that these grievous judgments would come on the earth in this generation. Having related these things, he again ascended as he had done before.

The Third Appearing of Moroni.

By this time, so deep were the impressions made on my mind, that sleep had fled from my eyes, and I lay overwhelmed in astonishment at what I had both seen and heard. But what was my surprise when again I beheld the same messenger at my bedside, and heard him rehearse or repeat over again to me the same things as before; and added a caution to me, telling me that Satan would try to tempt me, (in consequence of the indigent circumstances of my father's family,) to get the plates for the purpose of getting rich. This he forbade me, saying that I must have no other object in view in getting the plates but to glorify God, and must not be influenced by any other motive than that of building His kingdom; otherwise I could not get them. After this third visit, he again ascended into heaven as before, and I was again left to ponder on the strangeness of what I had just experienced; when almost immediately after the heavenly messenger had ascended from me the third time, the cock crowed, and I found that day was approaching, so that our interviews must have occupied the whole of that night.

Fourth Appearing of Moroni.

I shortly after arose from my bed, and, as usual, went to the necessary labors of the day; but in attempting to work as at other times, I found my strength so exhausted as to render me entirely unable. My father, who was laboring along with me, discovered something to be wrong with me, and told be to go home. I started with the intention of going to the house; but, in attempting to cross the fence out of the field where we were, my strength entirely failed me, and I fell helpless on the ground, and for a time was quite unconscious of anything. The first thing that I can recollect was a voice speaking unto me, calling me by name. I looked up, and beheld the same messenger standing over my head, surrounded by light as before. He then again related unto me all that he had related to me the previous night, and commanded me to go to my father and tell him of the vision and commandments which I had received. I obeyed; I returned to my father in the field, and rehearsed the whole matter to him. He replied to me that it was of God, and told me to go and do as commanded by the messenger. I left the field, and went to the place where the messenger had told me the plates were deposited; and owing to the distinctness of the vision which I had had concerning it, I knew the place the instant that I arrived there.

The Hill Cumorah.

Convenient to the village of Manchester, Ontario county, New York, stands a hill of considerable size, and the most elevated of any in the neighborhood.* On the west side of this hill, not far from the top, under a stone of considerable size, lay the plates, deposited in a stone box. This stone was thick and rounding in the middle on the upper side, and thinner towards the edges, so that the middle part

* The following description of Cumorah is from the pen of Oliver Cowdery:

You are acquainted with the mail road from Palmyra, Wayne county, to Canandaigua, Ontario county, New York, and also, as you pass from the former to the latter place, before arriving at the little village of Manchester, say from three to four, or about four miles from Palmyra, you pass a large hill on the east side of the road. Why I say large, is because it is as large perhaps, as any in that country. To a person acquainted with this road a description would be unnecessary, as it is the largest and rises the highest of any on that route. The north end rises quite sudden until it assumes a level with the more southerly extremity, and I think I may say an elevation higher than at the south a short distance, say half or three-fourths of a mile. As you pass toward Canandaigua it lessens gradually until the surface assumes its common level, or is broken by other smaller hills or ridges, water-courses and ravines. I think I am justified in saying that this is the highest hill for some distance round, and I am certain that its appearance, as it rises so suddenly from the plain on the north, must attract the notice of the traveler as he passes by.—*Messenger and Advocate,* 1834.

of it was visible above the ground, but the edge all around was covered with earth.

The Nephite Record.

Having removed the earth, I obtained a lever, which I got fixed under the edge of the stone, and with a little exertion raised it up. I looked in, and there indeed did I behold the plates, the Urim and Thummim, and the breastplate, as stated by the messenger. The box in which they lay was formed by laying stones together in some kind of cement. In the bottom of the box were laid two stones crosswise of the box, and on these stones lay the plates and the other things with them.

Four Annual Visits to Cumorah.

I made an attempt to take them out, but was forbidden by the messenger, and was again informed that the time for bringing them forth had not yet arrived, neither would it, until four years from that time; but he told me that I should come to that place precisely in one year from that time, and that he would there meet with me, and that I should continue to do so until the time should come for obtaining the plates. Accordingly, as I had been commanded, I went at the end of each year, and at each time I found the same messenger there, and received instruction and intelligence from him at each of our interviews, respecting what the Lord was going to do, and how and in what manner His kingdom was to be conducted in the last days.

Story of Being a Money Digger.

As my father's worldly circumstances were very limited, we were under the necessity of laboring with our hands, hiring out by day's work and otherwise, as we could get opportunity. Sometimes we were at home, and sometimes abroad, and by continued labor, were enabled to get a comfortable maintenance. In the year 1824* my father's family met with a great affliction by the death

* A genealogy of the Prophet's family in the Church records gives the date of Alvin's death, November 19, 1825. Lucy Smith's *History of the Prophet* agrees with the text above.—1824, November 19.

of my eldest brother, Alvin. In the month of October, 1825, I hired with an old gentleman by the name of Josiah Stowel, who lived in Chenango county, state of New York. He had heard something of a silver mine having been opened by the Spaniards in Harmony, Susquehanna county, state of Pennsylvania; and had, previous to my hiring to him, been digging, in order, if possible, to discover the mine. After I went to live with him, he took me, with the rest of his hands, to dig for the silver mine, at which I continued to work for nearly a month, without success in our undertaking, and finally I prevailed with the old gentleman to cease digging after it. Hence arose the very prevalent story of my having been a money-digger.

The Prophet's Marriage.

During the time that I was thus employed, I was put to board with a Mr. Isaac Hale, of that place; it was there I first saw my wife (his daughter), Emma Hale.† On the 18th of January, 1827, we were married, while I was yet employed in the service of Mr. Stoal. Owing to my continuing to assert that I had seen a vision, persecution still followed me, and my wife's father's family were very much opposed to our being married. I was, therefore, under the necessity of taking her elsewhere; so we went and were married at the house of Squire Tarbill, in South Bainbridge, Chenango county, New York. Immediately after my marriage, I left Mr. Stoal's and went to my father's, and farmed with him that season.

† Emma Hale was born in the town of Harmony, Susquehanna county, Pennsylvania, July 10, 1804. It will therefore be observed that Emma Hale was in her twenty-third year at the time of her marriage with the Prophet; hence of age; hence, under the law, mistress of her own actions. This is remarked because the Prophet, in works written against him, is charged with having abducted his wife.

CHAPTER III.

THE NEPHITE RECORD DELIVERED TO JOSEPH—THE ANGEL'S WARNING—THE WORK OF TRANSLATION.

The Prophet Receives the Plates.

AT length the time arrived for obtaining the plates, the Urim and Thummim, and the Breastplate. On the twenty-second day of September, one thousand eight hundred and twenty-seven, having gone as usual at the end of another year to the place where they were deposited, the same heavenly messenger delivered them up to me with this charge: that I should be responsible for them; that if I should let them go carelessly, or through any neglect of mine, I should be cut off; but that if I would use all my endeavors to preserve them, until he, the messenger, should call for them, they should be protected.

Efforts of Enemies to Get the Plates.

I soon found out the reason why I had received such strict charges to keep them safe, and why it was that the messenger had said that when I had done what was required at my hand, he would call for them. For no sooner was it known that I had them, than the most strenuous exertions were used to get them from me. Every stratagem that could be invented was resorted to for that purpose. The persecution became more bitter and severe than before, and multitudes were on the alert continually to get them from me if possible. But by the wisdom of God, they remained safe in my hands, until I had accomplished by them what was required at my hand. When, according to arrangements, the messenger called for them, I delivered them up to him; and he has them in his charge until this day, being the second day of May, one thousand eight hundred and thirty-eight.*

The excitement, however, still continued, and rumor with her thousand tongues was all the time employed in circulating falsehoods about my father's family, and about myself. If I were to relate a thousandth part of them, it would fill up volumes. The persecution, however, became so intolerable that I was under the necessity of leaving Manchester, and going with my wife to Susquehanna county, in the state of Pennsylvania.

Misrepresentations.

While preparing to start,—being very poor, and the persecution so heavy upon us that there was no probability that we would ever be otherwise,—in the midst of our afflictions we found a friend in a gentleman by the name of Martin Harris,† who came to us and gave me fifty dollars to assist us on our journey. Mr. Harris was a resident of Palmyra township, Wayne county, in the state of New York, and a farmer of respectability. By this timely aid was I enabled to reach the place of my destination in Pennsylvania; and immediately after my arrival there I commenced copying the characters off the plates. I copied a considerable number of them, and by means of the Urim and Thummim I translated some of them, which I did between the time I arrived at the house of my wife's father, in the month of December, and the February following.

Removal to Pennsylvania.

Some time in this month of February, the aforementioned Mr. Martin Harris came to our place, got the characters which I had drawn off the plates, and started with them to the city of New York. For what took place relative to him and the characters, I refer to his own account of

Words of the Book Given to the Learned.

* See footnote page 2.

† Martin Harris, who subsequently became one of the Three Witnesses to the Book of Mormon, was born in East-town, Saratoga county, New York, on the 18th of May, 1783. When in his ninth year his father moved with his family into Palmyra, Wayne county, so that man and boy Martin Harris had lived in Palmyra some thirty-six years. He had amassed a considerable property in lands, and had established a reputation for business reliability.

the circumstances, as he related them to me after his return, which was as follows:

I went to the city of New York, and presented the characters which had been translated, with the translation thereof, to Professor Charles Anthon, a gentleman celebrated for his literary attainments. Professor Anthon stated that the translation was correct, more so than any he had before seen translated from the Egyptian. I then showed him those which were not yet translated, and he said that they were Egyptian, Chaldaic, Assyric, and Arabic; and he said they were true characters. He gave me a certificate, certifying to the people of Palmyra that they were true characters, and that the translation of such of them as had been translated was also correct. I took the certificate and put it into my pocket, and was just leaving the house, when Mr. Anthon called me back, and asked me how the young man found out that there were gold plates in the place where he found them. I answered that an angel of God had revealed it unto him.

He then said to me, "Let me see that certificate." I accordingly took it out of my pocket and gave it to him, when he took it and tore it to pieces, saying, that there was no such thing now as ministering of angels, and that if I would bring the plates to him, he would translate them. I informed him that part of the plates were sealed, and that I was forbidden to bring them. He replied, "I cannot read a sealed book." I left him and went to Dr. Mitchell, who sanctioned what Professor Anthon had said respecting both the characters and the translation.*

The Loss of 116 Pages of Manuscript.

Mr. Harris, having returned from his tour, left me and went home to Palmyra, arranged his affairs, and returned again to my house about the 12th of April, 1828, and commenced writing for me while I translated from the plates, which we continued until the 14th of June following,

* In a letter to E. D. Howe, of Painesville, Ohio, who published a book against the Church in 1834, Professor Anthon acknowledged the visit of Martin Harris to him and the presentation of the characters in question. He states, however, that Harris, whom he describes as "a plain, apparently simple-hearted farmer," presented him with a note from Dr. Samuel L. Mitchell, of New York, requesting him (Anthon) to decipher, if possible, a paper which the "farmer" would hand to him. The call on Dr. Mitchell, alluded to in Martin Harris' statement above, must, therefore, have referred to a second visit to Dr. Mitchell, after his adventure with Professor Anthon. The latter's communication to Howe bears the date of February 17th, 1834, and is published in *extenso* in Smucker's *History of the Mormons*, pp. 37-39.

by which time he had written one hundred and sixteen pages of manuscript on foolscap paper. Some time after Mr. Harris had begun to write for me, he began to importune me to give him liberty to carry the writings home and show them; and desired of me that I would inquire of the Lord, through the Urim and Thummim, if he might not do so. I did inquire, and the answer was that he must not. However, he was not satisfied with this answer, and desired that I should inquire again. I did so, and the answer was as before. Still he could not be contented, but insisted that I should inquire once more. After much solicitation I again inquired of the Lord, and permission was granted him to have the writings on certain conditions; which were, that he show them only to his brother, Preserved Harris, his own wife, his father and his mother, and a Mrs. Cobb, a sister to his wife. In accordance with this last answer, I required of him that he should bind himself in a covenant to me in a most solemn manner that he would not do otherwise than had been directed. He did so. He bound himself as I required of him, took the writings, and went his way. Notwithstanding, however, the great restrictions which he had been laid under, and the solemnity of the covenant which he had made with me, he did show them to others, and by stratagem they got them away from him, and they never have been recovered unto this day.

Prophet's Journey to Manchester and Return to Pennsylvania.

In the meantime, while Martin Harris was gone with the writings, I went to visit my father's family at Manchester. I continued there for a short season, and then returned to my place in Pennsylvania. Immediately after my return home, I was walking out a little distance, when, behold, the former heavenly messenger appeared and handed to me the Urim and Thummim again—for it had been taken from me in consequence of my having wearied the Lord in asking for the privilege of letting Martin Harris take the writings, which he lost by transgression—and I inquired of the Lord through it, and obtained the following:

*Revelation to Joseph Smith, Jun., given July, 1828, concerning certain manuscripts of the first part of the Book of Mormon, which had been taken from the possession of Martin Harris.**

1. The works, and the designs, and the purposes of God cannot be frustrated, neither can they come to naught.

2. For God doth not walk in crooked paths, neither doth he turn to the right hand nor to the left, neither doth he vary from that which he hath said, therefore his paths are straight, and his course is one eternal round.

3. Remember, remember that it is not the work of God that is frustrated, but the work of men;

4. For although a man may have many revelations, and have power to do many mighty works, yet if he boasts in his own strength, and sets at naught the counsels of God, and follows after the dictates of his own will and carnal desires, he must fall and incur the vengeance of a just God upon him.

5. Behold, you have been entrusted with these things, but how strict were your commandments; and remember also the promises which were made to you, if you did not transgress them.

6. And behold, how oft you have transgressed the commandments and the laws of God, and have gone on in the persuasions of men.

7. For, behold, you should not have feared man more than God. Although men set at naught the counsels of God, and despise his words—

8. Yet you should have been faithful and he would have extended his arm and supported you against all the fiery darts of the adversary; and he would have been with you in every time of trouble.

9. Behold, thou art Joseph, and thou wast chosen to do the work of the Lord, but because of transgression, if thou art not aware thou wilt fall.

10. But remember, God is merciful; therefore, repent of that which thou hast done which is contrary to the commandment which I gave you, and thou art still chosen, and art again called to the work;

11. Except thou do this, thou shalt be delivered up and become as other men and have no more gift.

12. And when thou deliveredst up that which God had given thee sight and power to translate, thou deliveredst up that which was sacred into the hands of a wicked man,

13. Who has set at naught the counsels of God, and has broken the

* Doctrine and Covenants, sec. iii.

most sacred promises which were made before God, and has depended upon his own judgment and boasted in his own wisdom.

14. And this is the reason that thou hast lost thy privileges for a season—

15. For thou hast suffered the counsel of thy director to be trampled upon from the beginning.

16. Nevertheless, my work shall go forth, for inasmuch as the knowledge of a Savior has come into the world, through the testimony of the Jews, even so shall the knowledge of a Savior come unto my people—

17. And to the Nephites, and the Jacobites, and the Josephites, and the Zoramites, through the testimony of their fathers—

18. And this testimony shall come to the knowledge of the Lamanites, and the Lamuelites, and the Ishmaelites, who dwindled in unbelief because of the iniquity of their fathers, whom the Lord has suffered to destroy their brethren the Nephites, because of their iniquities and their abominations.

19. And for this very purpose are these plates preserved which contain these records—that the promises of the Lord might be fulfilled, which he made to his people;

20. And that the Lamanites might come to the knowledge of their fathers, and that they might know the promises of the Lord, and that they may believe the gospel and rely upon the merits of Jesus Christ, and be glorified through faith in his name, and that through their repentance they might be saved. Amen.

After I had obtained the above revelation, both the plates and the Urim and Thummim were taken from me again; but in a few days they were returned to me, when I inquired of the Lord, and the Lord said thus unto me:*

Interpreters and Plates Returned to the Prophet.

Revelation, given to Joseph Smith, Jun., informing him of the alteration of the manuscript of the fore part of the Book of Mormon.†

1. Now, behold, I say unto you, that because you delivered up those writings which you had power given unto you to translate by the

†Doctrine and Covenants, sec. x. This revelation was given at Harmony, Pennsylvania in the summer of 1828, a short time after the revelation known as section 3, in the Doctrine and Covenants.

means of the Urim and Thummim, into the hands of a wicked man, you have lost them.

2. And you also lost your gift at the same time, and your mind became darkened.

3. Nevertheless, it is now restored unto you again; therefore see that you are faithful and continue on unto the finishing of the remainder of the work of translation as you have begun.

4. Do not run faster or labor more than you have strength and means provided to enable you to translate; but be diligent unto the end:

5. Pray always, that you may come off conqueror: yea, that you may conquer Satan, and that you may escape the hands of the servants of Satan that do uphold his work.

6. Behold, they have sought to destroy you; yea, even the man in whom you have trusted has sought to destroy you.

7. And for this cause I said that he is a wicked man, for he has sought to take away the things wherewith you have been entrusted; and he has also sought to destroy your gift.

8. And because you have delivered the writings into his hands, behold, wicked men have taken them from you.

9. Therefore, you have delivered them up, yea, that which was sacred, unto wickedness.

10. And, behold, Satan hath put it into their hearts to alter the words which you have caused to be written, or which you have translated, which have gone out of your hands.

11. And behold, I say unto you, that because they have altered the words, they read contrary from that which you translated and caused to be written;

12. And, on this wise, the devil has sought to lay a cunning plan, that he may destroy this work;

13. For he hath put it into their hearts to do this, that by lying they may say they have caught you in the words which you have pretended to translate.

14. Verily, I say unto you, that I will not suffer that Satan shall accomplish his evil design in this thing.

15. For behold, he has put it into their hearts to get thee to tempt the Lord thy God, in asking to translate it over again.

16. And then, behold, they say and think in their hearts—We will see if God has given him power to translate; if so, he will also give him power again;

17. And if God giveth him power again, or if he translates again, or, in other words, if he bringeth forth the same words, behold, we have the same with us, and we have altered them;

18. Therefore they will not agree, and we will say that he has lied in his words, and that he has no gift, and that he has no power:

19. Therefore we will destroy him, and also the work; and we will do this that we may not be ashamed in the end, and that we may get glory of the world.

20. Verily, verily, I say unto you, that Satan has great hold upon their hearts; he stirreth them up to iniquity against that which is good;

21. And their hearts are corrupt, and full of wickedness and abominations; and they love darkness rather than light, because their deeds are evil: therefore they will not ask of me.

22. Satan stirreth them up, that he may lead their souls to destruction.

23. And thus he has laid a cunning plan, thinking to destroy the work of God; but I will require this at their hands, and it shall turn to their shame and condemnation in the day of judgment.

24. Yea, he stirreth up their hearts to anger against this work.

25. Yea, he saith unto them: Deceive and lie in wait to catch, that ye may destroy; behold, this is no harm. And thus he flattereth them, and telleth them that it is no sin to lie that they may catch a man in a lie, that they may destroy him.

26. And thus he flattereth them, and leadeth them along until he draggeth their souls down to hell; and thus he causeth them to catch themselves in their own snare.

27. And thus he goeth up and down, to and fro in the earth, seeking to destroy the souls of men.

28. Verily, verily, I say unto you, woe be unto him that lieth to deceive because he supposeth that another lieth to deceive, for such are not exempt from the justice of God.

29. Now, behold, they have altered these words, because Satan saith unto them: He hath deceived you—and thus he flattereth them away to do iniquity, to get thee to tempt the Lord thy God.

30. Behold, I say unto you, that you shall not translate again those words which have gone forth out of your hands;

31. For, behold, they shall not accomplish their evil designs in lying against those words. For, behold, if you should bring forth the same words they will say that you have lied and that you have pretended to translate, but that you have contradicted yourself.

32. And, behold, they will publish this, and Satan will harden the hearts of the people to stir them up to anger against you, that they will not believe my words.

33. Thus Satan thinketh to overpower your testimony in this generation, that the work may not come forth in this generation.

34. But behold, here is wisdom, and because I show unto you wisdom, and give you commandments concerning these things, what you shall do, show it not unto the world until you have accomplished the work of translation.

35. Marvel not that I said unto you: Here is wisdom, show it not

unto the world—for I said, show it not unto the world, that you may be preserved.

36. Behold, I do not say that you shall not show it unto the righteous;

37. But as you cannot always judge the righteous, or as you cannot always tell the wicked from the righteous, therefore I say unto you, hold your peace until I shall see fit to make all things known unto the world concerning the matter.

38. And now, verily I say unto you, that an account of those things that you have written, which have gone out of your hands, is engraven upon the plates of Nephi;

39. Yea, and you remember it was said in those writings that a more particular account was given of these things upon the plates of Nephi.

40. And now, because the account which is engraven upon the plates of Nephi is more particular concerning the things which, in my wisdom, I would bring to the knowledge of the people in this account—

41. Therefore, you shall translate the engravings which are on the plates of Nephi, down even till you come to the reign of King Benjamin, or until you come to that which you have translated, which you have retained;

42. And behold, you shall publish it as the record of Nephi; and thus I will confound those who have altered my words.

43. I will not suffer that they shall destroy my work; yea, I will show unto them that my wisdom is greater than the cunning of the devil.

44. Behold, they have only got a part, or an abridgment of the account of Nephi.

45. Behold, there are many things engraven upon the plates of Nephi which do throw greater views upon my gospel; therefore, it is wisdom in me that you should translate this first part of the engravings of Nephi, and send forth in this work.

46. And, behold, all the remainder of this work does contain all those parts of my gospel which my holy prophets, yea, and also my disciples, desired in their prayers should come forth unto this people.

47. And I said unto them, that it should be granted unto them according to their faith in their prayers;

48. Yea, and this was their faith—that my gospel, which I gave unto them that they might preach in their days, might come unto their brethren the Lamanites, and also all that had become Lamanites because of their dissensions.

49. Now, this is not all—their faith in their prayers was that this gospel should be made known also, if it were possible that other nations should possess this land;

50. And thus they did leave a blessing upon this land in their prayers, that whosoever should believe in this gospel in this land might have eternal life;

51. Yea, that it might be free unto all of whatsoever nation, kindred, tongue, or people they may be.

52. And now, behold, according to their faith in their prayers will I bring this part of my gospel to the knowledge of my people. Behold, I do not bring it to destroy that which they have received, but to build it up.

53. And for this cause have I said: If this generation harden not their hearts, I will establish my church among them.

54. Now I do not say this to destroy my church, but I say this to build up my church;

55. Therefore, whosoever belongeth to my church need not fear, for such shall inherit the kingdom of heaven.

56. But it is they who do not fear me, neither keep my commandments but build up churches unto themselves to get gain, yea, and all those that do wickedly and build up the kingdom of the devil—yea, verily, verily, I say unto you, that it is they that I will disturb, and cause to tremble and shake to the center.

57. Behold, I am Jesus Christ, the Son of God. I came unto mine own, and mine own received me not.

58. I am the light which shineth in darkness, and the darkness comprehendeth it not.

59. I am he who said—Other sheep have I which are not of this fold—unto my disciples, and many there were that understood me not.

60. And I will show unto this people that I had other sheep, and that they were a branch of the house of Jacob;

61. And I will bring to light their marvelous works, which they did in my name;

62. Yea, and I will also bring to light my gospel which was ministered unto them, and, behold, they shall not deny that which you have received, but they shall build it up, and shall bring to light the true points of my doctrine, yea, and the only doctrine which is in me.

63. And this I do that I may establish my gospel, that there may not be so much contention; yea, Satan doth stir up the hearts of the people to contention concerning the points of my doctrine; and in these things they do err, for they do wrest the scriptures and do not understand them.

64. Therefore, I will unfold unto them this great mystery;

65. For, behold, I will gather them as a hen gathereth her chickens under her wings, if they will not harden their hearts;

66. Yea, if they will come, they may, and partake of the waters of life freely.

67. Behold, this is my doctrine —whosoever repenteth and cometh unto me, the same is my church.

68. Whosoever declareth more or less than this, the same is not of me, but is against me; therefore he is not of my church.

69. And now, behold, whosoever is of my church, and endureth of my church to the end, him will I establish upon my rock, and the gates of hell shall not prevail against them.

70. And now, remember the words of him who is the life and light of the world, your Redeemer, your Lord and your God. Amen.

Interval in the Work of Translation.

I did not, however, go immediately to translating, but went to laboring with my hands upon a small farm which I had purchased of my wife's father, in order to provide for my family. In the month of February, 1829, my father came to visit us, at which time I received the following revelation for him:

*Revelation to Joseph Smith, Sen., given February, 1829.**

1. Now behold, a marvelous work is about to come forth among the children of men.

2. Therefore, O ye that embark in the service of God, see that ye serve him with all your heart, might, mind and strength, that ye may stand blameless before God at the last day.

3. Therefore, if ye have desires to serve God ye are called to the work;

4. For behold the field is white already to harvest; and lo, he that thrusteth in his sickle with his might, the same layeth up in store that he perisheth not, but bringeth salvation to his soul;

5. And faith, hope, charity and love, with an eye single to the glory of God, qualify him for the work.

6. Remember faith, virtue, knowledge, temperance, patience, brotherly kindness, godliness, charity, humility, diligence.

7. Ask, and ye shall receive, knock, and it shall be opened unto you. Amen.

Three Witnesses Promised.

The following I applied for and obtained, at the request of the aforementioned Martin Harris:

Revelation, given March, 1829.†

1. Behold, I say unto you, that as my servant Martin Harris has de-

* Doctrine and Covenants, sec. iv.

† Doctrine and Covenants, sec. v.

sired a witness at my hand, that you, my servant Joseph Smith, Jun., have got the plates of which you have testified and borne record that you have received of me;

2. And now, behold, this shall you say unto him,—He who spake unto you, said unto you: I, the Lord, am God, and have given these things unto you, my servant Joseph Smith, Jun., and have commanded you that you should stand as a witness of these things;

3. And I have caused you that you should enter into a covenant with me, that you should not show them except to those persons to whom I commanded you; and you have no power over them except I grant it unto you.

4. And you have a gift to translate the plates; and this is the first gift that I bestowed upon you; and I have commanded that you should pretend to no other gift until my purpose is fulfilled in this; for I will grant unto you no other gift until it is finished.

5. Verily, I say unto you, that woe shall come unto the inhabitants of the earth if they will not hearken unto my words;

6. For hereafter you shall be ordained and go forth and deliver my words unto the children of men.

7. Behold, if they will not believe my words, they would not believe you, my servant Joseph, if it were possible that you should show them all these things which I have committed unto you.

8. Oh, this unbelieving and stiffnecked generation—mine anger is kindled against them.

9. Behold, verily I say unto you, I have reserved those things which I have entrusted unto you, my servant Joseph, for a wise purpose in me, and it shall be made known unto future generations;

10. But this generation shall have my word through you;

11. And in addition to your testimony, the testimony of three of my servants, whom I shall call and ordain, unto whom I will show these things, and they shall go forth with my words that are given through you.

12. Yea, they shall know of a surety that these things are true, for from heaven will I declare it unto them.

13. I will give them power that they may behold and view these things as they are;

14. And to none else will I grant this power, to receive this same testimony among this generation, in this the beginning of the rising up and the coming forth of my Church out of the wilderness—clear as the moon, and fair as the sun, and terrible as an army with banners.

15. And the testimony of three witnesses will I send forth of my word.

16. And behold, whosoever believeth on my words, them will I visit with the manifestation of my Spirit; and they shall be born of me, even of water and of the Spirit—

17. And you must wait yet a little while, for ye are not yet ordained—

18. And their testimony shall also go forth unto the condemnation of this generation if they harden their hearts against them;

19. For a desolating scourge shall go forth among the inhabitants of the earth, and shall continue to be poured out from time to time, if they repent not, until the earth is empty, and the inhabitants thereof are consumed away and utterly destroyed by the brightness of my coming.

20. Behold, I tell you these things, even as I also told the people of the destruction of Jerusalem; and my word shall be verified at this time as it hath hitherto been verified.

21. And now I command you, my servant Joseph, to repent and walk more uprightly before me, and to yield to the persuasions of men no more;

22. And that you be firm in keeping the commandments wherewith I have commanded you; and if you do this, behold I grant unto you eternal life, even if you should be slain.

23. And now, again, I speak unto you, my servant Joseph, concerning the man that desires the witness—

24. Behold, I say unto him, he exalts himself and does not humble himself sufficiently before me; but if he will bow down before me, and humble himself in mighty prayer and faith, in the sincerity of his heart, then will I grant unto him a view of the things which he desires to see.

25. And then he shall say unto the people of this generation: Behold, I have seen the things which the Lord hath shown unto Joseph Smith, Jun., and I know of a surety that they are true, for I have seen them, for they have been shown unto me by the power of God and not of man.

26. And I the Lord commanded him, my servant Martin Harris, that he shall say no more unto them concerning these things, except he shall say: I have seen them, and they have been shown unto me by the power of God; and these are the words which he shall say.

27. But if he deny this he will break the covenant which he has before covenanted with me, and behold, he is condemned.

28. And now, except he humble himself and acknowledge unto me the things that he has done which are wrong, and covenant with me that he will keep my commandments, and exercise faith in me, behold, I say unto him, he shall have no such views, for I will grant unto him no views of the things of which I have spoken.

29. And if this be the case, I command you, my servant Joseph, that you shall say unto him, that he shall do no more, nor trouble me any more concerning this matter.

30. And if this be the case, behold, I say unto thee Joseph, when

thou hast translated a few more pages thou shalt stop for a season, even until I command thee again; then thou mayest translate again.

31. And except thou do this, behold, thou shalt have no more gift, and I will take away the things which I have entrusted with thee.

32. And now, because I forsee the lying in wait to destroy thee, yea, I forsee that if my servant Martin Harris humbleth not himself and receive a witness from my hand, that he will fall into transgression;

33. And there are many that lie in wait to destroy thee from off the face of the earth; and for this cause, that thy days may be prolonged, I have given unto thee these commandments.

34. Yea, for this cause I have said: Stop and stand still until I command thee, and I will provide means whereby thou mayest accomplish the thing which I have commanded thee.

35. And if thou art faithful in keeping my commandments, thou shalt be lifted up at the last day. Amen.

CHAPTER IV.

OLIVER COWDERY BECOMES THE PROPHET'S SCRIBE—THE TRANSLATION OF THE PLATES CONTINUED.

Oliver Cowdery.

ON the 5th day of April, 1829, Oliver Cowdery* came to my house, until which time I had never seen him. He stated to me that having been teaching school in the neighborhood where my father resided, and my father being one of those who sent to the school, he went to board for a season at his house, and while there the family related to him the circumstance of my having received the plates, and accordingly he had come to make inquiries of me.† Two days after the arrival of Mr. Cowdery (being the 7th of April) ‡ I commenced to translate the Book of Mor-

* Oliver Cowdery was born in the town of Wells, Rutland county, Vermont, Oct. 3, 1806. He married Elizabeth Ann Whitmer, in Kaw township, Jackson county, Missouri, Dec. 18, 1832. She was born in Fayette, Seneca county, New York, January 22, 1815.

† Previous to joining the Prophet Joseph Smith, Oliver Cowdery had met David Whitmer at Palmyra, and conversed with him concerning the rumors rife in that vicinity about the finding of the Book of Mormon plates. This chance meeting resulted in a friendship between the young men, and finally when Cowdery determined to visit the Prophet in Harmony, he went *via* the Whitmer residence, at Fayette, which was near the town of Waterloo, at the head of Seneca lake, Seneca county, New York; and promised his friend David Whitmer that after visiting the Prophet he would write him his impressions as to the truth or untruth of Joseph Smith's having an ancient record. (See statement of David Whitmer in *Kansas City Journal*, June 5th, 1886; also statement of the same to Orson Pratt and Joseph F. Smith, in 1878. *Millennial Star*, vol. xl, pp. 769-774.

‡ This date, 7th of April, and the one above, 5th of April, 1829, in the History of Joseph Smith, published in the *Millennial Star*, are given as the 15th and 17th of April, respectively. The dates in the Star, however, are typographical errors, as in the original MS of the History the dates are as given in the text. See also Cowdery's letters to W. W. Phelps, published in *Messenger and Advocate*, 1834, where the dates are also given as in the text above—5th and 7th of April.

mon, and he began to write for me, which having continued for some time, I inquired of the Lord through the Urim and Thummim, and obtained the following:

*Revelation given April, 1829, to Oliver Cowdery and Joseph Smith, Jun.**

1. A great and marvelous work is about to come forth unto the children of men.

2. Behold, I am God; give heed unto my word, which is quick and powerful, sharper than a two-edged sword, to the dividing asunder of both joints and marrow; therefore give heed unto my words.

3. Behold, the field is white already to harvest; therefore, who so desireth to reap, let him thrust in his sickle with his might, and reap while the day lasts, that he may treasure up for his soul everlasting salvation in the kingdom of God.

4. Yea, whosoever will thrust in his sickle and reap, the same is called of God.

5. Therefore, if you will ask of me you shall receive; if you will knock it shall be opened unto you.

6. Now, as you have asked, behold, I say unto you, keep my commandments, and seek to bring forth and establish the cause of Zion;

7. Seek not for riches but for wisdom, and behold, the mysteries of God shall be unfolded unto you, and then shall you be made rich. Behold, he that hath eternal life is rich.

8. Verily, verily, I say unto you, even as you desire of me so it shall be unto you; and if you desire, you shall be the means of doing much good in this generation.

9. Say nothing but repentance unto this generation; keep my commandments, and assist to bring forth my work, according to my commandments, and you shall be blessed.

10. Behold thou hast a gift, and blessed art thou because of thy gift. Remember it is sacred and cometh from above—

11. And if thou wilt inquire, thou shalt know mysteries which are great and marvelous: therefore thou shalt exercise thy gift, that thou mayest find out mysteries, that thou mayest bring many to the knowledge of the truth, yea, convince them of the error of their ways.

12. Make not thy gift known unto any save it be those who are of thy faith. Trifle not with sacred things.

13. If thou wilt do good, yea, and hold out faithful to the end, thou shalt be saved in the kingdom of God, which is the greatest of all the gifts of God; for there is no gift greater than the gift of salvation.

* Doctrine and Covenants, section vi.

14. Verily, verily, I say unto thee, blessed art thou for what thou hast done; for thou hast inquired of me, and behold, as often as thou hast inquired, thou hast received instruction of my Spirit. If it had not been so, thou wouldst not have come to the place where thou art at this time.

15. Behold, thou knowest that thou hast inquired of me and I did enlighten thy mind; and now I tell thee these things that thou mayest know that thou hast been enlightened by the spirit of truth;

16. Yea, I tell thee, that thou mayest know that there is none else save God that knowest thy thoughts and the intents of thy heart.

17. I tell thee these things as a witness unto thee—that the words or the work which thou hast been writing are true.

18. Therefore be diligent; stand by my servant Joseph, faithfully, in whatsoever difficult circumstances he may be for the words' sake.

19. Admonish him in his faults and also receive admonition of him. Be patient; be sober; be temperate; have patience, faith, hope and charity.

20. Behold, thou art Oliver, and I have spoken unto thee because of thy desire; therefore treasure up these words in thy heart. Be faithful and diligent in keeping the commandments of God, and I will encircle thee in the arms of my love.

21. Behold, I am Jesus Christ, the Son of God. I am the same that came unto mine own, and mine own received me not. I am the light which shineth in darkness, and the darkness comprehendeth it not.

22. Verily, verily, I say unto you, if you desire a further witness, cast your mind upon the night that you cried unto me in your heart, that you might know concerning the truth of these things.

23. Did I not speak peace to your mind concerning the matter? What greater witness can you have than from God?

24. And now, behold, you have received a witness; for if I have told you things which no man knoweth, have you not received a witness?

25. And, behold, I grant unto you a gift, if you desire of me, to translate, even as my servant Joseph.

26. Verily, verily, I say unto you, that there are records which contain much of my gospel, which have been kept back because of the wickedness of the people;

27. And now I command you, that if you have good desires—a desire to lay up treasures for yourself in heaven—then shall you assist in bringing to light, with your gift, those parts of my scriptures which have been hidden because of iniquity.

28. And now, behold, I give unto you, and also unto my servant Joseph, the keys of this gift, which shall bring to light this ministry; and in the mouth of two or three witnesses shall every word be established.

29. Verily, verily, I say unto you, if they reject my words, and this part of my gospel and ministry, blessed are ye, for they can do no more unto you than unto me;

30. And even if they do unto you even as they have done unto me, blessed are ye, for you shall dwell with me in glory.

31. But if they reject not my words, which shall be established by the testimony which shall be given, blessed are they, and then shall ye have joy in the fruit of your labors.

32. Verily, verily, I say unto you, as I said unto my disciples, where two or three are gathered together in my name, as touching one thing, behold, there will I be in the midst of them—even so am I in the midst of you.

33. Fear not to do good, my sons, for whatsoever ye sow, that shall ye also reap; therefore, if ye sow good ye shall also reap good for your reward.

34. Therefore, fear not, little flock; do good; let earth and hell combine against you, for if ye are built upon my rock, they cannot prevail.

35. Behold, I do not condemn you; go your ways and sin no more; perform with soberness the work which I have commanded you.

36. Look unto me in every thought; doubt not, fear not.

37. Behold the wounds which pierced my side, and also the prints of the nails in my hands and feet; be faithful, keep my commandments, and ye shall inherit the kingdom of heaven. Amen.

After we had received this revelation, Oliver Cowdery stated to me that after he had gone to my father's to board, and after the family had communicated to him concerning my having obtained the plates, that one night after he had retired to bed he called upon the Lord to know if these things were so, and the Lord manifested to him that they were true, but he had kept the circumstance entirely secret, and had mentioned it to no one; so that after this revelation was given, he knew that the work was true, because no being living knew of the thing alluded to in the revelation, but God and himself.

Witness of the Spirit to Cowdery.

During the month of April I continued to translate, and he to write, with little cessation, during which time we received several revelations. A difference of opinion arising between us about the account of John the Apostle, mentioned in the New Testament,* as to whether he died or con-

The Mission of John the Apostle.

*St. John, chap. xxi, verse 22.

tinued to live, we mutully agreed to settle it by the Urim and Thummim and the following is the word which we received:

Revelation, given to Joseph Smith, Jun., and Oliver Cowdery, in Harmony, Pennsylvania, April, 1829, when they desired to know whether John, the beloved disciple, tarried on earth or died. Translated from parchment, written and hid up by himself.†

1. And the Lord said unto me: John, my beloved, what desirest thou? For if you shall ask what you will, it shall be granted unto you.

2. And I said unto him: Lord, give unto me power over death, that I may live and bring souls unto thee.

3. And the Lord said unto me: Verily, verily, I say unto thee, because thou desirest this thou shalt tarry until I come in my glory, and shall prophesy before nations, kindreds, tongues and people.

4. And for this cause the Lord said unto Peter: If I will that he tarry till I come, what is that to thee? For he desired of me that he might bring souls unto me, but thou desiredst that thou mightest speedily come unto me in my kingdom.

5. I say unto thee, Peter, this was a good desire; but my beloved has desired that he might do more, or a greater work yet among men than what he has before done.

6. Yea, he has undertaken a greater work; therefore, I will make him as flaming fire and a ministering angel; he shall minister for those who shall be heirs of salvation who dwell on the earth.

7. And I will make thee to minister for him and for thy brother James; and unto you three I will give this power and the keys of this ministry until I come.

8. Verily I say unto you, ye shall both have according to your desires, for ye both joy in that which ye have desired.

Oliver Desires to Translate.

Whilst continuing the work of translation, during the month of April, Oliver Cowdery became exceedingly anxious to have the power to translate bestowed upon him, and in relation to this desire the following revelations were obtained:

Revelation, given April, 1829.‡

1. Oliver Cowdery, verily, verily, I say unto you, that assuredly as the Lord liveth, who is your God and your Redeemer, even so surely

† Doctrine and Covenants, sec. vii.
‡ Doctrine and Covenants, sec. viii.

shall you receive a knowledge of whatsoever things you shall ask in faith, with an honest heart, believing that you shall receive a knowledge concerning the engravings of old records, which are ancient, which contain those parts of my scripture of which has been spoken by the manifestation of my Spirit.

2. Yea, behold, I will tell you in your mind and in your heart, by the Holy Ghost, which shall come upon you and which shall dwell in your heart.

3. Now, behold, this is the spirit of revelation; behold, this is the spirit by which Moses brought the children of Israel through the Red Sea on dry ground.

4. Therefore this is thy gift; apply unto it, and blessed art thou, for it shall deliver you out of the hands of your enemies, when, if it were not so, they would slay you and bring your soul to destruction.

5. Oh, remember these words, and keep my commandments. Remember, this is your gift.

6. Now this is not all thy gift; for you have another gift, which is the gift of Aaron; behold, it has told you many things;

7. Behold, there is no other power, save the power of God, that can cause this gift of Aaron to be with you.

8. Therefore, doubt not, for it is the gift of God; and you shall hold it in your hands, and do marvelous works; and no power shall be able to take it away out of your hands, for it is the work of God.

9. And, therefore, whatsoever you shall ask me to tell you by that means, that will I grant unto you, and you shall have knowledge concerning it.

10. Remember that without faith you can do nothing; therefore ask in faith. Trifle not with these things; do not ask for that which you ought not.

11. Ask that you may know the mysteries of God, and that you may translate and receive knowledge from all those ancient records which have been hid up, that are sacred; and according to your faith shall it be done unto you.

12. Behold, it is I that have spoken it; and I am the same that spake unto you from the beginning. Amen.

*Revelation, given to Oliver Cowdery, April, 1829.**

1. Behold, I say unto you, my son, that because you did not translate according to that which you desired of me, and did commence again to write for my servant, Joseph Smith, Jun., even so I would

* Doctrine and Covenants, sec. ix.

that ye should continue until you have finished this record, which I have entrusted unto him.

2. And then, behold, other records have I, that I will give unto you power that you may assist to translate.

3. Be patient, my son, for it is wisdom in me, and it is not expedient that you should translate at this present time.

4. Behold, the work which you are called to do is to write for my servant Joseph.

5. And, behold, it is because that you did not continue as you commenced, when you began to translate, that I have taken away this privilege from you.

6. Do not murmur, my son, for it is wisdom in me that I have dealt with you after this manner.

7. Behold, you have not understood; you have supposed that I would give it unto you, when you took no thought save it was to ask me.

8. But, behold, I say unto you, that you must study it out in your mind; then you must ask me if it be right, and if it is right I will cause that your bosom shall burn within you; therefore, you shall feel that it is right.

9. But if it be not right, you shall have no such feelings, but you shall have a stupor of thought that shall cause you to forget the thing which is wrong; therefore, you cannot write that which is sacred save it be given you from me.

10. Now, if you had known this you could have translated; nevertheless, it is not expedient that you should translate now.

11. Behold, it was expedient when you commenced; but you feared, and the time is past, and it is not expedient now;

12. For, do you not behold that I have given unto my servant Joseph sufficient strength, whereby it is made up? and neither of you have I condemned.

13. Do this thing which I have commanded you, and you shall prosper. Be faithful, and yield to no temptation.

14. Stand fast in the work wherewith I have called you, and a hair of your head shall not be lost, and you shall be lifted up at the last day. Amen.

CHAPTER V.

RESTORATION OF THE AARONIC PRIESTHOOD—FIRST BAPTISMIS.

WE still continued the work of translation, when in the ensuing month (May, 1829), we on a certain day went into the woods to pray and inquire of the Lord respecting baptism for the remission of sins, that we found mentioned in the translation of the plates. While we were thus employed, praying and calling upon the Lord, a messenger from heaven descended in a cloud of light, and having laid his hands upon us, he ordained us, saying:

The Aaronic Priesthood Restored.

> Upon you my fellow servants, in the name of Messiah I confer the Priesthood of Aaron, which holds the keys of the ministering of angels, and of the Gospel of repentance, and of baptism by immersion for the remission of sins; and this shall never be taken again from the earth, until the sons of Levi do offer again an offering unto the Lord in righteousness.*

He said this Aaronic Priesthood had not the power of laying on hands for the gift of the Holy Ghost, but that this should be conferred on us hereafter; and he commanded us to go and be baptized, and gave us directions that I should baptize Oliver Cowdery, and afterwards that he should baptize me. Accordingly we went and were baptized. I baptized him first, and afterwards he baptized me, after which I laid my hands upon his head and ordained him to the Aaronic Priesthood, and

Limitations of the Aaronic Priesthood.

* Doctrine and Covenants, sec. xiii.

afterwards he laid his hands on me and ordained me to the same Priesthood—for so we were commanded.

John the Baptist, May 15, 1829.

The messenger who visited us on this occasion, and conferred this Priesthood upon us, said that his name was John, the same that is called John the Baptist in the New Testament, and that he acted under the direction of Peter, James and John who held the keys of the Priesthood of Melchizedek, which Priesthood he said would in due time be conferred on us,* and that I should be called

* RESTORATION OF THE MELCHIZEDEK PRIESTHOOD.—The promise to confer upon Joseph and Oliver the Melchizedek Priesthood was fulfilled; but as there is no definite account of the event in the history of the Prophet Joseph, or, for matter of that, in any of our annals, the evidences of the fact of their ordination to the higher or Melchizedek Priesthood promised them by John the Baptist are presented now, together with a consideration of the place where, and the time when the great event occurred.

The Prophet Joseph, in a communication to the Church, under date of September 6, 1842, makes undoubted allusion to the restoration of the Melchizedek Priesthood in the course of an ecstatic review of the great things God had revealed to him. He said: "And again, what do we hear? Glad tidings from Cumorah. Moroni, an angel from heaven, declaring the fulfilment of the prophets—the book to be revealed. A voice of the Lord in the wilderness of Fayette, Seneca county, declaring the three witnesses to bear record of the book. The voice of Michael on the banks of the Susquehanna, detecting the devil when he appeared as an angel of light. *The voice of Peter, James and John in the wilderness between Harmony, Susquehanna county, and Colesville, Broome county, on the Susquehanna river, declaring themselves as possessing the keys of the kingdom, and of the Dispensation of the Fulness of Times.*" (Doctrine and Covenants, sec. cxxviii: 20.)

In one of the early revelations given to the Prophet Joseph, the Lord makes most direct reference to the restoration of the higher Priesthood through the ministration of Peter, James and John. The subject matter of the revelation is the Sacrament of the Lord's Supper; and in the course of it the Lord promises to "drink of the fruit of the vine" with his servants on earth to whom the revelation is addressed; "and with Moroni, * * * and also Michael, or Adam, the father of all, * * * and also with *Peter, and James, and John, whom I have sent unto you, by whom I have ordained you and confirmed you to be Apostles, and special witnesses of my name,* and bear the keys of your ministry, and of the same things which I revealed unto them; unto whom I have committed the keys of my kingdom, and a dispensation of the gospel for the last times; and for the fulness of times." (Doctrine and Covenants, sec. xxvii). This revelation was given some time early in August, 1830, but only the first four verses were written at that time. The rest of it was written in September of that year. (See chapter xi of this volume). These two allusions—the one by the Prophet and the other by the Lord—to the restoration of the Melchizedek Priesthood not only make clear the fact that the Melchizedek Priesthood was restored in accordance with the promise of John the Baptist when conferring the Aaronic Priesthood, but they make it possible to fix the first Elder of the Church, and he (Oliver Cowdery) the second. It was on the 15th day of May, 1829, that we were ordained under the hand of this messenger and baptized.

upon the place where, and approximately the time when, the event occurred. Undoubtedly the *place* where the ordination was performed was on the banks of the Susquehanna river, in the wilderness between Colesville, in Broome county, New York, and Harmony, in Susquehanna county, Pennsylvania; for it is there the Prophet says the voice of Peter, James and John was heard declaring themselves as "possessing the keys of the kingdom, and of the Dispensation of the Fulness of Times;" for which appearing and declaration there could be no other occasion than the ordination of Oliver and Joseph to the Melchizedek Priesthood in fulfilment of the promises made by John the Baptist. The *time* at which the ordination took place was evidently between the 15th of May, 1829, and August, 1830. The last named date is the one under which the Lord so definitely referred to the circumstance of having sent Peter, James and John to ordain Joseph and others to be Apostles, even special witnesses of His name, and unto whom He had committed the keys of the kingdom. Hence the time of the ordination must have been between those two dates.

From information contained in other revelations, however, this period within which the Melchizedek Priesthood was restored may be considerably reduced. In April, 1830, a revelation was given concerning the organization and government of the Church, and in that revelation the Lord said: "Which commandments [i. e. to organize the Church] were given to Joseph Smith, Jr., who was called of God and ordained an apostle of Jesus Christ to be the first Elder of this Church; and to Oliver Cowdery, who was also called of God, an Apostle of Jesus Christ, to be the second Elder of this Church, and ordained under his hand." (Doctrine and Covenants, sec. xx: 2, 3.) This allusion to the ordination of these men to the apostleship reduces the time of their ordination to the period between the 15th of May, 1829, and April 6, 1830.

But the time within which the ordination took place may be still further reduced. In a revelation bearing the date of June, 1829, making known the calling of the Twelve Apostles in these last days, and addressed to Oliver Cowdery and David Whitmer, the Lord said: "I speak unto you, even as unto Paul mine Apostle, *for you are called even with that same calling with which he was called.*" As this could scarcely be said of men who had not been ordained to the same holy apostleship as that held by Paul, and consequently to the Melchizedek Priesthood, the conclusion is reasonable that the ordination promised by John the Baptist, doubtless occurred some time between May 15, 1829, and the expiration of the month of June of that same year.

That there was a distinct administration of angels in the restoration of the Melchizedek Priesthood is sustained by the testimony of Oliver Cowdery. On the occasion of his returning to the Church at Kanesville, Iowa, in the fall of 1848, after an absence of eleven years from the body of the Saints, in the course of the public address which he then delivered, he said: "I was present with Joseph when an holy angel from God came down from heaven and conferred on us, or restored, the lesser or Aaronic Priesthood, and said to us, at the same time, that it should remain upon the earth while the earth stands. *I was also present with Joseph when the higher or Melchizedek Priesthood was conferred by the holy angel from on high.* This Priesthood, we then conferred on each other by the will and commandment of God." The authority for the foregoing statement is the report of Bishop Reuben Miller, who was present on the occasion of Oliver Cowdery's delivering the address

Outpourings of the Spirit.

Immediately on our coming up out of the water after we had been baptized, we experienced great and glorious blessings from our Heavenly Father. No sooner had I baptized Oliver Cowdery, than the Holy Ghost fell upon him, and he stood up and prophesied many things which should shortly come to pass. And again, so soon as I had been baptized by him, I also had the spirit of prophecy, when standing up, I prophesied concerning the rise of this church, and many other things connected with the Church, and this generation of the children of men. We were filled with the Holy Ghost, and rejoiced in the God of our salvation.*

from which the above is quoted. Bishop Miller's notes of Cowdery's remarks were published in the *Deseret News* of the 13th of April, 1859. It is to be observed that Oliver Cowdery, in this quotation, is represented as saying with reference to the restoration of the Melchizedek Priesthood, that it was by the "holy angel," whereas, according to the statement of the Prophet, that Priesthood was restored by three angels—Peter, James and John. The discrepancy may arise from imperfect recording of Oliver's language. In a signed statement which Oliver Cowdery gave to Samuel W. Richards, under date of January 13, 1849—the statement has been published a number of times in our Church periodicals—being about two months and a half after delivering the address reported by Bishop Miller, he said: "John the Baptist, holding the keys of the Aaronic Priesthood; Peter, James and John, holding the keys of the Melchizedek Priesthood, have also ministered for those who shall be heirs of salvation, and with these administrations ordained men to the same Priesthood. These Priesthoods, with their authority, are now, and must continue to be in the body of the Church of Jesus Christ of Latter-day Saints. * * * Accept assurances, dear brother, of the unfeigned prayer of him who, in connection with Joseph, the Seer, was blessed with the above administrations."

[Signed] OLIVER COWDERY.

* It may be well at this point to call attention to the singular and important fact that the Prophet, neither in his narrative of the above really great and dramatic event, nor in any of those great visions and revelations which precede or follow it, stops to comment or grow eloquent over the importance of an administration or the grandeur of an occasion. He may never have heard the maxim, "A true tale speeds best being plainly told," but had he heard of it and adopted it as his motto, he could not have followed it more closely than unconsciously he has done in his narrative. He seems to have but one object in view, and that is to get on record the plain truth pertaining to the coming forth of the work of God. Oliver Cowdery, however, who shared in this ministration of the angel, John the Baptist, has left upon record a description of the scene and the impressions it left upon his mind, and which, withal is of such singular beauty and power that I think the history of the event should not go to the world without it. After speaking of his own and the Prophet's desire to hear the commandment given, "Arise and be baptized," he says:

"This was not long desired before it was realized. The Lord, who is rich in

Ordination and Baptism Kept Secret.

Our minds being now enlightened, we began to have the Scriptures laid open to our understandings, and the true meaning and intention of their more mysterious passages revealed unto us in a manner which we never could attain to previously, nor ever before had thought of. In the meantime we were forced to keep secret the circumstances of having received the Priesthood and our having been baptized, owing to a spirit of persecution

mercy, and ever willing to answer the consistent prayer of the humble, after we had called upon him in a fervent manner, aside from the abodes of men, condescended to manifest to us His will. On a sudden, as from the midst of eternity, the voice of the Redeemer spake peace to us, while the veil was parted and the angel of God came down clothed with glory and delivered the anxiously looked for message, and the keys of the Gospel of repentance. What joy! what wonder! what amazement! While the world was racked and distracted—while millions were groping as the blind for the wall, and while all men were resting upon uncertainty, as a general mass, our eyes beheld—our ears heard. As in the 'blaze of day;' yes, more—above the glitter of the May sunbeam, which then shed its brilliancy over the face of nature! Then his voice, though mild, pierced to the center, and his words, 'I am thy fellow-servant,' dispelled every fear. We listened, we gazed, we admired! 'Twas the voice of an angel from glory—'twas a message from the Most High, and as we heard we rejoiced, while His love enkindled upon our souls, and we were rapt in the vision of the Almighty! Where was room for doubt? Nowhere; uncertainty had fled, doubt had sunk, no more to rise, while fiction and deception had fled forever. But, dear brother, think further, think for a moment what joy filled our hearts and with what surprise we must have bowed, (for who would not have bowed the knee for such a blessing?) when we received under his hands the Holy Priesthood, as he said, 'Upon you my fellow servants, in the name of Messiah, I confer this Priesthood and this authority, which remain upon earth, that the sons of Levi may yet offer an offering unto the Lord in righteousness!'

"I shall not attempt to paint to you the feelings of this heart, nor the majestic beauty and glory which surrounded us on this occasion; but you will believe me when I say, that earth, nor men, with the eloquence of time, cannot begin to clothe language in as interesting and sublime a manner as this holy personage. No; nor has this earth power to give the joy, to bestow the peace, or comprehend the wisdom which was contained in each sentence as it was delivered by the power of the Holy Spirit! Man may deceive his fellow man; deception may follow deception, and the children of the wicked one may have power to seduce the foolish and untaught, till naught but fiction feeds the many, and the fruit of falsehood carries in its current the giddy to the grave, but one touch with the finger of his love, yes, one ray of glory from the upper world, or one word from the mouth of the Savior, from the bosom of eternity, strikes it all into insignificance, and blots it forever from the mind! The assurance that we were in the presence of an angel; the certainty that we heard the voice of Jesus, and the truth unsullied as it flowed from a pure personage, dictated by the will of God, is to me, past description, and I shall ever look upon this expression of the Savior's goodness with wonder and thanksgiving while I am permitted to tarry, and in those mansions where perfection dwells and sin never comes, I hope to adore in that day which shall never cease."—(*Messenger and Advocate,* 1834.)

which had already manifested itself in the neighborhood. We had been threatened with being mobbed from time to time, and this, too, by professors of religion. And their intentions of mobbing us were only counteracted by the influence of my wife's father's family (under Divine providence), who had become very friendly to me, and who were opposed to mobs, and were willing that I should be allowed to continue the work of translation without interruption; and therefore offered and promised us protection from all unlawful proceedings as far as in them lay.

Conversion of Samuel H. Smith.

After a few days, however, feeling it to be our duty, we commenced to reason out of the Scriptures with our acquaintances and friends, as we happened to meet with them. About this time my brother Samuel H. Smith* came to visit us. We informed him of what the Lord was about to do for the children of men, and began to reason with him out of the Bible. We also showed him that part of the work which we had translated, and labored to persuade him concerning the Gospel of Jesus Christ, which was now about to be revealed in its fulness. He was not, however, very easily persuaded of these things, but after much inquiry and explanation he retired to the woods, in order that by secret and fervent prayer he might obtain of a merciful God, wisdom to enable him to judge for himself. The result was that he obtained revelation for himself sufficient to convince him of the truth of our assertions to him; and on the twenty-fifth day of that same month in which we had been baptized and ordained, Oliver Cowdery baptized him; and he returned to his father's house, greatly glorifying and praising God, being filled with the Holy Spirit.

Not many days afterwards, my brother Hyrum

* Samuel H. Smith was born in Tunbridge, Vt., March 13, 1808. He was the fourth son of Joseph and Lucy Smith.

Smith† came to us to inquire concerning these things, when at his earnest request, I inquired of the Lord through the Urim and Thummim, and received for him the following:

Hyrum Smith's Inquiry.

*Revelation, given to Hyrum Smith, Harmony, Susquenhanna County, Pennsylvania, May, 1829.**

1. A great and marvelous work is about to come forth among the children of men.

2. Behold, I am God; give heed to my word, which is quick and powerful, sharper than a two-edged sword, to the dividing asunder of both joints and marrow; therefore give heed unto my word.

3. Behold, the field is white already to harvest; therefore, whoso desireth to reap let him thrust in his sickle with his might, and reap while the day lasts, that he may treasure up for his soul everlasting salvation in the kingdom of God.

4. Yea, whosoever will thrust in his sickle and reap, the same is called of God.

5. Therefore, if you will ask me, you shall receive; if you will knock it shall be opened unto you.

6. Now, as you have asked, behold, I say unto you, keep my commandments, and seek to bring forth and establish the cause of Zion.

7. Seek not for riches but for wisdom; and, behold, the mysteries of God shall be unfolded unto you, and then shall you be made rich. Behold, he that hath eternal life is rich.

8. Verily, verily, I say unto you, even as you desire of me so it shall be done unto you; and, if you desire, you shall be the means of doing much good in this generation.

9. Say nothing but repentance unto this generation. Keep my commandments, and assist to bring forth my work, according to my commandments, and you shall be blessed.

10. Behold, thou hast a gift, or thou shalt have a gift if thou wilt desire of me in faith, with an honest heart, believing in the power of Jesus Christ, or in my power which speaketh unto thee;

11. For, behold, it is I that speak; behold. I am the light which shineth in darkness, and by my power I give these words unto thee.

12. And now, verily, verily, I say unto thee, put your trust in that Spirit which leadeth to do good—yea, to do justly, to walk humbly, to judge righteously; and this is my Spirit.

13. Verily, verily, I say unto you, I will impart unto you of my Spirit, which shall enlighten your mind, which shall fill your soul with joy;

† Hyrum Smith was born in Tunbridge, Vt., February 9, 1800. He was the second son of Joseph and Lucy Smith, and at this time the oldest son living.

* Doctrine and Covenants, sec. xi.

14. And then shall ye know, or by this shall you know, all things whatsoever you desire of me, which are pertaining unto things of righteousness, in faith believing in me that you shall receive.

15. Behold, I command you that you need not suppose that you are called to preach until you are called.

16 Wait a little longer, until you shall have my word, my rock, my Church, and my gospel, that you may know of a surety my doctrine.

17. And then, behold, according to your desires, yea, even according to your faith shall it be done unto you.

18. Keep my commandments; hold your peace; appeal unto my Spirit;

19. Yea, cleave unto me with all your heart, that you may assist in bringing to light those things of which have been spoken—yea, the translation of my work; be patient until you shall accomplish it.

20. Behold, this is your work, to keep my commandments, yea, with all your might, mind and strength.

21. Seek not to declare my word, but first seek to obtain my word, and then shall your tongue be loosed; then, if you desire, you shall have my Spirit and my word, yea, the power of God unto the convincing of men.

22. But now hold your peace; study my word which hath gone forth among the children of men, and also study my word which shall come forth among the children of men, or that which is now translating, yea, until you have obtained all which I shall grant unto the children of men in this generation, and then shall all things be added thereto.

23. Behold thou art Hyrum, my son; seek the kingdom of God, and all things shall be added according to that which is just.

24. Build upon my rock, which is my gospel;

25. Deny not the spirit of revelation, nor the spirit of prophecy, for woe unto him that denieth these things;

26. Therefore, treasure up in your heart until the time which is in my wisdom that you shall go forth.

27. Behold, I speak unto all who have good desires, and have thrust in their sickle to reap.

28. Behold, I am Jesus Christ, the Son of God. I am the life and the light of the world.

29. I am the same who came unto mine own and mine own received me not;

30. But verily, verily, I say unto you, that as many as receive me, to them will I give power to become the sons of God, even to them that believe on my name. Amen.

About the same time an old gentleman came to visit us of whose name I wish to make honorable mention—Mr. Joseph Knight, Sen.,* of Colesville, Broome county, New York, who, having heard of the manner in which we were occupying our time, very kindly and considerately brought us a quantity of provisions, in order that we might not be interrupted in the work of translation by the want of such necessaries of life; and I would just mention here, as in duty bound, that he several times brought us supplies, a distance of at least thirty miles, which enabled us to continue the work when otherwise we must have relinquished it for a season.

Assistance from Joseph Knight, Sen.

* There is no record in the Church annals of the time and place of the birth of Joseph Knight, Sen. He was well advanced in life, however, when the work of God in these last days began to come forth. From the journal of his son, Newel Knight, it is learned that Joseph Knight, Sen., married Polly Peck; that he moved into the state of New York and settled on the Susquehanna river, near the great bend, in Chenango county, in 1809. Two years later he removed to Colesville, Broome county, New York, where he remained nineteen years. "My father," says Newel Knight in his journal, "owned a farm, a grist mill and carding machine. He was not rich, yet he possessed enough of this world's goods to secure to himself and family, not only the necessaries, but also the comforts of life. His family, consisting of my mother, three sons and four daughters, he reared in a genteel and respectable manner, and gave his children a good, common school education. My father was a sober, honest man, generally respected and beloved by his neighbors and acquaintances. He did not belong to any religious sect, but was a believer in the Universalian doctrine." The business in which Joseph Knight, Sen., engaged, made it necessary at times for him to hire men, and the Prophet Joseph was occasionally employed by him. To the Knight family, who were greatly attached to him, the young Prophet related many of the things God had revealed respecting the Book of Mormon, then as yet, to come forth. So far at least was the elder Knight taken into the Prophet's confidence that he purposely so arranged his affairs as to be at the Smith family residence, near Manchester, at the time the plates of the Book of Mormon were given into Joseph's possession. Mr. Knight had driven to the Smith residence with a horse and carriage, and in this conveyance, according to the statement of both Lucy Smith, mother of the Prophet, (See Lucy Smith's *History of the Prophet*, ch. xxiii), and Joseph Knight, Sen., Joseph, in company with his wife Emma, drove away very early—before daylight—on the morning of September the 22nd. It is presumed, of course, the Prophet drove to Cumorah, and there received from Moroni the plates of the Book of Mormon, the Urim and Thummim and Breastplate, which were, for some time—excepting the Urim and Thummim—concealed in the woods. Mr. Knight remained at the Smith residence several days, and was there the day Joseph brought home the plates; and in company with Joseph Smith, Sen., and Mr. Stoal—who was also present at the Smith residence in company with Mr. Knight—went in search of those men who had assailed the Prophet while on his way home with the plates, but they did not find them. From Joseph's narrative in the text it will be seen that the senior Joseph Knight's interest in the work continued.

Being very anxious to know his duty as to this work, I inquired of the Lord for him, and obtained the following:

*Revelation, given to Joseph Knight, Sen., at Harmony, Susquehanna County, Pennsylvania, May, 1829.**

1. A great and marvelous work is about to come forth among the children of men.

2. Behold, I am God; give heed to my word, which is quick and powerful, sharper than a two-edged sword, to the dividing asunder of both joints and marrow; therefore, give heed unto my word.

3. Behold, the field is white already to harvest; therefore, whoso desireth to reap let him thrust in his sickle with his might, and reap while the day lasts, that he may treasure up for his soul everlasting salvation in the kingdom of God.

4. Yea, whosoever will thrust in his sickle and reap, the same is called of God.

5. Therefore, if you will ask of me you shall receive; if you will knock it shall be opened unto you.

6. Now, as you have asked, behold, I say unto you, keep my commandments, and seek to bring forth and establish the cause of Zion.

7. Behold, I speak unto you, and also to all those who have desires to bring forth and establish this work;

8. And no one can assist in this work except he shall be humble and full of love, having faith, hope, and charity, being temperate in all things, whatsoever shall be entrusted to his care.

9. Behold, I am the light and the life of the world, that speak these words, therefore give heed with your might, and then you are called. Amen.

The Prophet's Removal to Fayette.

Shortly after commencing to translate, I became acquainted with Mr. Peter Whitmer,† of Fayette, Seneca county, New York, and also with some of his family. In the beginning of the month of June, his son, David Whitmer,‡ came

* Doctrine and Covenants, sec, xii.

† Peter Whitmer, Sen., was born April 14, 1773. Of the place of his birth there is no record in the Church annals, but it was doubtless in the state of Pennsylvania. He married Mary Musselman, who was born 27th of August, 1778; and to them were born eight children. The elder Whitmer was a strict Presbyterian, and trained his children in that faith. In the early years of the 19th century he moved from the state of Pennsylvania to New York, and settled in Fayette township, about three miles south of Waterloo, where the Prophet made his acquaintance.

‡ David Whitmer was born near Harrisburg, Pennsylvania, January 7th, 1805, and was the fourth son of Peter Whitmer, Sen., and Mary Musselman Whitmer.

to the place where we were residing, and brought with him a two-horse wagon, for the purpose of having us accompany him to his father's place, and there remain until we should finish the work. It was arranged that we should have our board free of charge, and the assistance of one of his brothers to write for me, and also his own assistance when convenient. Having much need of such timely aid in an undertaking so arduous, and being informed that the people in the neighborhood of the Whitmers were anxiously awaiting the opportunity to inquire into these things, we accepted the invitation, and accompanied Mr. Whitmer to his father's house, and there resided until the translation was finished and the copyright secured. Upon our arrival, we found Mr. Whitmer's family very anxious concerning the work, and very friendly toward ourselves. They continued so, boarded and lodged us according to arrangements; and John Whitmer,* in particular, assisted us very much in writing during the remainder of the work.

David, John and Peter Whitmer, Jun., as Assistants.

In the meantime, David, John and Peter Whitmer, Jun.,† became our zealous friends and assistants in the work; and being anxious to know their respective duties, and having desired with much earnestness that I should inquire of the Lord concerning them, I did so, through the means of the Urim and Thummim, and obtained for them in succession the following revelations:

Revelation, given to David Whitmer, at Fayette, Seneca County, New York, June, 1829.‡

1. A great and marvelous work is about to come forth unto the children of men.

2. Behold, I am God; give heed to my word, which is quick

* John Whitmer was born August 27th, 1802. He was the third son of Peter Whitmer, Sen., and Mary Musselman Whitmer.

† Peter Whitmer, Jun., was born September 27th, 1809, and was the fifth son, but sixth child of Mary Musselman and Peter Whitmer, Sen.

‡ Doctrine and Covenants, sec. xiv.

and powerful, sharper than a two-edged sword, to the dividing asunder of both joints and marrow; therefore give heed unto my word.

3. Behold, the field is white already to harvest; therefore whoso desireth to reap, let him thrust in his sickle with his might, and reap while the day lasts, that he may treasure up for his soul everlasting salvation in the kingdom of God.

4. Yea, whosoever will thrust in his sickle and reap, the same is called of God.

5. Therefore, if you will ask of me you shall receive; if you will knock it shall be opened unto you.

6. Seek to bring forth and establish my Zion. Keep my commandments in all things.

7. And, if you keep my commandments and endure to the end you shall have eternal life, which gift is the greatest of all the gifts of God.

8. And it shall come to pass, that if you shall ask the Father in my name, in faith believing, you shall receive the Holy Ghost, which giveth utterance, that you may stand as a witness of the things of which you shall both hear and see, and also that you may declare repentance unto this generation.

9. Behold, I am Jesus Christ, the Son of the living God, who created the heavens and the earth, a light which cannot be hid in darkness;

10. Wherefore, I must bring forth the fulness of my gospel from the Gentiles unto the house of Israel.

11. And behold, thou art David, and thou art called to assist; which thing if ye do, and are faithful, ye shall be blessed both spiritually and temporally, and great shall be your reward. Amen.

*Revelation given to John Whitmer, June, 1829.**

1. Hearken, my servant John, and listen to the words of Jesus Christ, your Lord and your Redeemer,

2. For behold, I speak unto you with sharpness and with power, for mine arm is over all the earth,

3. And I will tell you that which no man knoweth save me and thee alone—

4. For many times you have desired of me to know that which would be of the most worth unto you.

5. Behold, blessed are you for this thing, and for speaking my words which I have given you according to my commandments.

6. And now, behold, I say unto you, that the thing which will be of the most worth unto you will be to declare repentance unto this

* Doctrine and Covenants, sec xv.

people, that you may bring souls unto me, that you may rest them in the kingdom of my Father. Amen.

*Revelation to Peter Whitmer, Jun., June, 1829.**

1. Harken, my servant Peter, and listen to the words of Jesus Christ, your Lord and your Redeemer,

2. For behold, I speak unto you with sharpness and with power, for mine arm is over all the earth,

3. And I will tell you that which no man knoweth save me and thee alone—

4. For many times you have desired of me to know that which would be of the most worth unto you.

5. Behold, blessed are you for this thing, and for speaking my words which I have given unto you according to my commandments.

6. And now, behold, I say unto you, that the thing which will be of the most worth unto you will be to declare repentance unto this people, that you may bring souls unto me, that you may rest with them in the kingdom of my Father. Amen.

Early Baptisms.

We found the people of Seneca county in general friendly, and disposed to enquire into the truth of these strange matters which now began to be noised abroad. Many opened their houses to us, in order that we might have an opportunity of meeting with our friends for the purpose of instruction and explanation. We met with many from time to time who were willing to hear us, and who desired to find out the truth as it is in Christ Jesus, and apparently willing to obey the Gospel, when once fairly convinced and satisfied in their own minds; and in this same month of June, my brother Hyrum Smith, David Whitmer, and Peter Whitmer, Jun., were baptized in Seneca lake, the two former by myself, the latter by Oliver Cowdery. From this time forth many became believers, and some were baptized whilst we continued to instruct and persuade as many as applied for information.

* Doctrine and Covenants, sec. xvi.

CHAPTER VI.

THE TESTIMONY OF THE ESPECIAL WITNESSES TO THE BOOK OF MORMON.

Provision Made for Special Witnesses.

In the course of the work of translation, we ascertained that three special witnesses* were to be provided by the Lord, to whom He would grant that they should see the plates from which this work (the Book of Mormon) should be translated; and that these witnesses should bear record of the same, as will be found recorded, Book of Mormon, page 581 [Book of Ether, chapter 5, verses 2, 3 and 4, p. 487, edition 1920], also page 86 [II Nephi, chapter 11, verse 3, p. 73, edition 1920].† Almost immediately after we had made this discovery,

* See also revelation given March, 1829, page 29.

† In the original manuscript copy of the History, the reference here made are to the first edition of the Book of Mormon, but to avoid confusion, the pages, chapters and verses of the later and prevailing editions are given. In the first edition [now very rare] the reference from the Book of Ether is on page 548, toward the middle of chapter 2; and that from Nephi is on page 86, toward the beginning of chapter 8. The quotations are as follows:

"And behold, ye may be privileged that ye may show the plates unto those who shall assist to bring forth this work; and unto three shall they be shown by the power of God; wherefore they shall know of a surety that these things are true. And in the mouth of three witnesses shall these things be established; and the testimony of three, and this work, in the which shall be shown forth the power of God and also his word, of which the Father, and the Son, and the Holy Ghost bear record:—and all this shall stand as a testimony against the world at the last day."—*Book of Ether*, v: 2-4.

'And my brother, Jacob, also has seen him as I have seen him; wherefore, I will send their words forth unto my children to prove unto them that my words are true. Wherefore, by the words of three, God hath said, I will establish my word. Nevertheless, God sendeth more witnesses, and he proveth all his words."—*II Nephi* xi: 3.

it occurred to Oliver Cowdery, David Whitmer and the aforementioned Martin Harris (who had come to inquire after our progress in the work) that they would have me inquire of the Lord to know if they might not obtain of him the privilege to be these three special witnesses; and finally they became so very solicitous, and urged me so much to inquire that at length I complied; and through the Urim and Thummim, I obtained of the Lord for them the following:

*Revelation to Oliver Cowdery, David Whitmer, and Martin Harris, at Fayette, Seneca County, New York, June, 1829, given previous to their viewing the plates containing the Book of Mormon.**

1. Behold, I say unto you, that you must rely upon my word, which if you do with full purpose of heart, you shall have a view of the plates, and also the breastplate, the sword of Laban, the Urim and Thummim, which were given to the brother of Jared upon the mount, when he talked with the Lord face to face, and the miraculous directors which were given to Lehi while in the wilderness, on the borders of the Red Sea.

2. And it is by your faith that you shall obtain a view of them, even by that faith which was had by the prophets of old.

3. And after that you have obtained faith, and have seen them with your eyes, you shall testify of them, by the power of God;

4. And this you shall do that my servant Joseph Smith, Jun., may not be destroyed, that I may bring about my righteous purposes unto the children of men in this work.

5. And ye shall testify that you have seen them, even as my servant Joseph Smith, Jun., has seen them; for it is by my power that he has seen them, and it is because he had faith.

6. And he has translated the book, even that part which I have commanded him, and as your Lord and your God liveth it is true.

7. Wherefore you have received the same power, and the same faith, and the same gift like unto him;

8. And if you do these last commandments of mine, which I have given you, the gates of hell shall not prevail against you; for my grace is sufficient for you, and you shall be lifted up at the last day.

9. And, I, Jesus Christ, your Lord and your God, have spoken it unto you, that I might bring about my righteous purposes unto the children of men. Amen.

* Doctrine and Covenants, sec. xvii.

Seeking the Fulfilment of the Promise.

Not many days after the above commandment was given, we four, viz., Martin Harris, David Whitmer, Oliver Cowdery and myself, agreed to retire into the woods, and try to obtain, by fervent and humble prayer, the fulfilment of the promises given in the above revelation—that they should have a view of the plates. We accordingly made choice of a piece of woods convenient to Mr. Whitmer's house, to which we retired, and having knelt down, we began to pray in much faith to Almighty God to bestow upon us a realization of these promises.

The Order of Prayer.

According to previous arrangement, I commenced by vocal prayer to our Heavenly Father, and was followed by each of the others in succession. We did not at the first trial, however, obtain any answer or manifestation of divine favor in our behalf. We again observed the same order of prayer, each calling on and praying fervently to God in rotation, but with the same result as before.

The Visitation of the Angel—Viewing the Plates.

Upon this, our second failure, Martin Harris proposed that he should withdraw himself from us, believing, as he expressed himself, that his presence was the cause of our not obtaining what we wished for. He accordingly withdrew from us, and we knelt down again, and had not been many minutes engaged in prayer, when presently we beheld a light above us in the air, of exceeding brightness; and behold, an angel stood before us. In his hands he held the plates which we had been praying for these to have a view of. He turned over the leaves one by one, so that we could see them, and discern the engravings theron distinctly. He then addressed himself to David Whitmer, and said, "David, blessed is the Lord, and he that keeps His commandments;" when, immediately afterwards, we heard a voice from out of the bright light above us, saying,

"These plates have been revealed by the power of God, and they have been translated by the power of God. The translation of them which you have seen is correct, and I command you to bear record of what you now see and hear."

Martin Harris also Views the Plates.

I now left David and Oliver, and went in pursuit of Martin Harris, whom I found at a considerable distance, fervently engaged in prayer. He soon told me, however, that he had not yet prevailed with the Lord, and earnestly requested me to join him in prayer, that he also might realize the same blessings which we had just received. We accordingly joined in prayer, and ultimately obtained our desires, for before we had yet finished, the same vision was opened to our view, at least it was again opened to me, and I once more beheld and heard the same things; whilst at the same moment, Martin Harris cried out, apparently in an ecstasy of joy, "'Tis enough; 'tis enough; mine eyes have beheld; mine eyes have beheld;" and jumping up, he shouted, "Hosanna," blessing God, and otherwise rejoiced exceedingly.*

* There are some other details connected with the obtaining of the testimony of the Three Witnesses which ought not to be omitted at this point. The day on which the Three Witnesses received their manifestation the usual morning family service was held at the Whitmer residence, namely, scripture-reading, singing, and prayer. Besides the Whitmer family, the Prophet and his wife and Oliver Cowdery, there were present the Prophet's father and mother and Martin Harris. As soon as Joseph rose from his knees, he approached Martin Harris and said, "with a solemnity that thrills through my veins to this day," says the Prophet's mother, who relates this circumstance: "Martin Harris, you have got to humble yourself before your God this day, that you may obtain a forgiveness of your sins. If you do, it is the will of God that you should look upon the plates in company with Oliver Cowdery and David Whitmer." (*History of the Prophet Joseph*, by Lucy Smith, ch. xxxi.) When the former transgression of Martin Harris in the matter of betraying the trust of the Prophet, by which part of the translation of the Book of Mormon had been lost (see p. 21)—when this and the pride and self-will of the man's character are taken into account, there was certainly a necessity for the admonition which the Prophet gave Martin Harris that morning. The circumstance also affords an explanation of Martin's difficulty in obtaining a testimony which, after his withdrawal from them, appears to have been given so readily to Oliver Cowdery and David Whitmer.

Another circumstance is related by Lucy Smith which is here *apropos*, namely, the joy of the Prophet in having other witnesses than himself to the truth of the work the Lord was then bringing forth to the world. Speaking of the witnesses returning to the Whitmer home after seeing the plates, she says: "When they returned to the house, it was between three and four o'clock p. m. Mrs. Whitmer, Mr. Smith, and myself were sitting in the bedroom at the time. On coming in,

Statement of the Witnesses.

Having thus, through the mercy of God, obtained these glorious manifestations, it now remained for these three individuals to fulfil the commandment which they had received, viz., to bear record of these things; in order to accomplish which, they drew up and subscribed* the following document:†

The Testimony of Three Witnesses.

BE IT KNOWN unto all nations, kindreds, tongues, and people, unto whom this work shall come: That we, through the grace of God the

Joseph threw himself down beside me, and exclaimed, 'Father, mother, you do not know how happy I am; the Lord has now caused the plates to be shown to three more besides myself. They have seen an angel, who has testified to them, and they will have to bear witness to the truth of what I have said, for now they know for themselves that I do not go about to deceive the people, and I feel as if I was relieved of a burden which was almost too heavy for me to bear, and it rejoices my soul that I am not any longer to be entirely alone in the world.' Upon this, Martin Harris came in. He seemed almost overcome with joy, and testified boldly to what he had both seen and heard. And so did David and Oliver, adding that no tongue could express the joy of their hearts and the greatness of the things which they had both seen and heard."—*History of the Prophet Joseph*, ch. xxxi.

* In an extended interview between Elders Orson Pratt, Joseph F. Smith (both of the council of the Twelve Apostles) and David Whitmer, at the home of Mr. Whitmer, in Richmond, Missouri, in September, 1878, the question was asked the then aged witness if he and the other witnesses did or did not sign the testimonies themselves. Whitmer replied that each signed his own name.—Pratt and Smith Report, *Millennial Star*, vol. xi, nos. 49, 50. Report is dated Sept. 17, 1878.

† In the first edition of the Book of Mormon the testimony of Three Witnesses, and also the Testimony of Eight Witnesses appear at the end—or on the last two pages of the volume, instead of being, as in the later editions, on the page following the title-page. The first edition also had the following:

PREFACE.

TO THE READER—

As many false reports have been circulated respecting the following work, and also many unlawful measures taken by evil designing persons to destroy me, and also the work, I would inform you that I translated, by the gift and power of God, and caused to be written, one hundred and sixteen pages, the which I took from the book of Lehi, which was an account abridged from the plates of Lehi, by the hand of Mormon; which said account, some person or persons have stolen and kept from me, notwithstanding my utmost exertions to recover it again—and being ocmmanded of the Lord that I should not translate the same over again, for Satan had put it into their hearts to tempt the Lord their God, by altering the words, that they did read contrary from that which I translated and caused to be written; and if I should bring forth the same words again, or, in other words, if I should translate the same over again, they would publish that which they had stolen, and Satan would stir up the hearts of this generation, that they might not receive this work: but behold, the

Father, and our Lord Jesus Christ, have seen the plates which contain this record, which is a record of the people of Nephi, and also of the Lamanites, their brethren, and also of the people of Jared, who came from the tower of which hath been spoken. And we also know that they have been translated by the gift and power of God, for his voice hath declared it unto us; wherefore we know of a surety that the work is true. And we also testify that we have seen the engravings which are upon the plates; and they have been shown unto us by the power of God, and not of man. And we declare with words of soberness, that an angel of God came down from heaven, and he brought and laid before our eyes, that we beheld and saw the plates, and the engravings thereon; and we know that it is by the grace of God the the Father, and our Lord Jesus Christ, that we beheld and bear record that these things are true. And it is marvelous in our eyes. Nevertheless, the voice of the Lord commanded us that we should bear record of it; wherefore, to be obedient unto the commandments of God, we bear testimony of these things. And we know that if we are faithful in Christ, we shall rid our garments of the blood of all men, and be found spotless before the judgment seat of Christ, and shall dwell with him eternally in the heavens. And the honor be to the Father, and to the Son, and to the Holy Ghost, which is one God. Amen.

OLIVER COWDERY
DAVID WHITMER
MARTIN HARRIS

Soon after these things had transpired, the following additional testimony was obtained:*

The Testimony of Eight Witnesses.

BE IT KNOWN unto all nations, kindreds, tongues, and people, unto whom this work shall come: that Joseph Smith, Jun., the translator

Lord said unto me, I will not suffer that Satan shall accomplish his evil design in this thing; therefore thou shalt translate from the plates of Nephi, until ye come to that which ye have translated, which ye have retained; and behold ye shall publish it as the record of Nephi; and thus I will confound those who have altered my words. I will not suffer that they shall destroy my work; yea, I will show unto them that my wisdom is greater than the cunning of the devil. Wherefore to be obedient unto the commandments of God, I have through His grace and mercy, accomplished that which He hath commanded me, respecting this thing. I would also inform you that the plates of which hath been spoken, were found in the township of Manchester, Ontario county, New York.

THE AUTHOR

*According to Lucy Smith (see *History of the Prophet Joseph,* ch. xxxi) the eight witnesses obtained a view of the plates near the Smith residence at Manchester.

of this work,* has shown unto us the plates of which hath been spoken, which have the appearance of gold; and as many of the leaves as the said Smith has translated we did handle with our hands; and we also saw the engravings thereon, all of which has the appearance of ancient work, and of curious workmanship. And this we bear record with words of soberness, that the said Smith has shown unto us, for we have seen and hefted, and know of a surety that the said Smith has got the plates of which we have spoken. And we give our names unto the world to witness unto the world that which we have seen. And we lie not, God bearing witness of it.

CHRISTIAN WHITMER
JACOB WHITMER
PETER WHITMER, JUN.
JOHN WHITMER
HIRAM PAGE
JOSEPH SMITH, SEN.
HYRUM SMITH
SAMUEL H. SMITH

It was on the occasion of the Prophet Joseph's coming over to Manchester from Fayette, accompanied by several of the Whitmers and Hiram Page, to make arrangements about getting the Book of Mormon printed. After arriving at the Smith residence, Joseph Smtih, Sen., Hyrum Smith, and Samuel H. Smith, joined Joseph's company from Fayette, and together they repaired to a place in the woods where members of the Smith family were wont to hold secret prayer, and there the plates were shown to these eight witnsss by the Prophet himself. The difference between the testimony given the Three Witnesses and that given to the Eight, is that the former was attended by a splendid display of the glory and power of God and the ministration of an angel, while the latter was attended by no such display, but was a plain, matter-of-fact exhibition of the plates by the Prophet to his friends; and they not only saw the plates, but handled them and examined the engravings upon them.

*In the first edition, the words "Author and Proprietor" appear instead of the word "translator." The reason for this is obvious. Under the laws then existing the copyright was secured to "authors and proprietors;" and hence on the title page of the first edition, "Joseph Smith, Junior, author and proprietor," takes the place of the line "Translated by Joseph Smith, Jun.," in the later editions. The Prophet merely adopted the phraseology of the law. Preceding the preface to the first edition appears the following certificate of copyright, which is interesting not only as explaining the foregoing point, but also as preserving an important date in Church history:

Northern District of New York, to wit:

BE IT REMEMBERED, That on the eleventh day of June, in the fifty-third year of the independence of the United States of America, A. D. 1829, JOSEPH SMITH, JUN., of the said district, hath deposited in this office the title of a Book, the right whereof he claims as author, in the words following to wit: [Here follows the title page with the words, "By Joseph Smith, Junior, Author and Proprietor, Palmyra: Printed by E. B. Grandin for the Author. 1830."]

In conformity to the act of the Congress of the United States, entitled "An act

Early Progress in the Work.

Meantime we continued to translate, at intervals, when not under the necessity of attending to the numerous inquirers who now began to visit us—some for the sake of finding the truth others for the purpose of putting hard questions, and trying to confound us. Among the latter class were several learned priests, who generally came for the purpose of disputation. However, the Lord continued to pour out upon us His Holy Spirit, and as often as we had need, He gave us in that moment what to say; so that although unlearned and inexperienced in religious controversies, yet we were able to confound those learned priests of the day; whilst at the same time we were enabled to convince the honest in heart that we had obtained, through the mercy of God, the true and everlasting Gospel of Jesus Christ; and occasionally we administered the ordinance of baptism for the remission of sins to such as believed.

for the encouragement of learning, by securing the copies of Maps, Charts and Books, to the authors and proprietors of such copies, during the times therein mentioned;" and also the act, entitled, "An act supplementary to an act, entitled, 'An act for the encouragement of learning, by securing the copies, of Maps, Charts, and Books, to to the authors and proprietors of such copies, during the times therein mentioned,' and extending the benefits thereof to the arts of designing, engraving, and etching historical and other prints." R. R. LANSING,

Clerk of the Northern District of New York.

CHAPTER VII.

THE DAY APPOINTED FOR ORGANIZING THE CHURCH—REVELATION ON CHURCH GOVERNMENT.

Directions for the Organization of the Church.

We now became anxious to have that promise realized to us, which the angel that conferred upon us the Aaronic Priesthood had given us, viz., that provided we continued faithful, we should also have the Melchizedek Priesthood, which holds the authority of the laying on of hands for the gift of the Holy Ghost. We had for some time made this matter a subject of humble prayer, and at length we got together in the chamber of Mr. Whitmer's house, in order more particularly to seek of the Lord what we now so earnestly desired; and here, to our unspeakable satisfaction, did we realize the truth of the Savior's promise—"Ask, and it shall be given you; seek, and ye shall find; knock, and it shall be opened unto you"—for we had not long been engaged in solemn and fervent prayer, when the word of the Lord came unto us in the chamber,*commanding us that I should ordain Oliver

*This occasion is unquestionably the one that the Prophet Joseph alludes to in his letter to the Saints in Nauvoo, under date of September 6th, 1842, (Doctrine and Covenants, sec. 128: 21) where he says: "Again what do we hear * * * *the voice of God in the chamber of old Father Peter Whitmer, in Fayette, Seneca county,* and at sundry times, and in divers places through all the travels and tribulations of this Church of Jesus Christ of Latter-day Saints."

It must not be thought because of the reference in the text above to the desire of Joseph and Oliver to have the Melchizedek Priesthood conferred upon them, and the commandment given that they should ordain each other Elders of the Church—it must not be thought because of this, I repeat, that there is any conflict between what is here stated in the text and what has been said with reference to the restoration of the keys of the Melchizedek Priesthood by Peter, James and John. This "voice of God

Cowdery to be an Elder in the Church of Jesus Christ; and that he also should ordain me to the same office; and then to ordain others, as it should be made known unto us from time to time. We were, however, commanded to defer this our ordination until such times as it should be practicable to have our brethren, who had been and who should be baptized, assembled together, when we must have their sanction to our thus proceeding to ordain each other, and have them decide by vote whether they were willing to accept us as spiritual teachers or not; when also we were commanded to bless bread and break it with them, and to take wine, bless it, and drink it with them; afterward proceed to ordain each other according to commandment; then call out such men as the Spirit should dictate, and ordain them; and then attend to the laying on of hands for the gift of the Holy Ghost, upon all those whom we had previously baptized, doing all things in the name of the Lord. The following commandment will further il-

in the chamber of old Father Peter Whitmer, in Fayette," commanding Joseph and Oliver to ordain each other "Elders of the Church," but also commanding them to defer said ordinations until their brethren who had been and should be baptized could be assembled together to give their sanction to such procedure—was all previous to their ordination to the Apostleship under the hands of Peter, James and John; and is to be regarded as instruction to them as to how they should proceed in the matter of ordaining each other, and calling and ordaining others to the same ministry, after they themselves should have received the keys of this Melchizedek Priesthood. The ordination of each other to be Elders of the Church was deferred until the meeting at which the Church was organized, the 6th of April, 1830. (See p. 75.) But this voice of God in Peter Whitmer's chamber, which told them how to proceed in the matter of ordaining each other, was given in or before June, 1829. The evidence of this is in the fact that the revelation in Whitmer's chamber, about ordaining each other "Elders of the Church," precedes the one immediately following the paragraph of narrative above: and that revelation, making known the calling of the Twelve Apostles, was given in June, 1829, ten months before the instructions relative to ordaining each other to be Elders in the Church was carried out. Meantime, as we have seen (see note pp. 40, 41, 42,) before the 6th of April, 1830, and probably before that very month of June, 1829, had expired Peter, James and John had come and conferred upon Joseph and Oliver the keys of the Melchizedek Priesthood, the holy apostleship, by which authority they were authorized to organize the Church, ordain each other Elders, and also call and ordain others to the same office.

lustrate the nature of our calling to this Priesthood, as well as that of others who were yet to be sought after:

*Revelation to Joseph Smith, Jun., Oliver Cowdery and David Whitmer, making known the calling of Twelve Apostles in these last days; and also instructions relative to building up the Church of Christ according to the fulness of the Gospel. Given in Fayette, New York, June, 1829.**

1. Now, behold, because of the thing which you, my servant Oliver Cowdery, have desired to know of me, I give unto you these words:

2. Behold, I have manifested unto you, by my Spirit in many instances, that the things which you have written are true; wherefore you know that they are true.

3. And if you know that they are true, behold, I give unto you a commandment, that you rely upon the things which are written;

4. For in them are all things written concerning the foundation of my church, my gospel, and my rock.

5. Wherefore, if you shall build up my church, upon the foundation of my gospel and my rock, the gates of hell shall not prevail against you.

6. Behold, the world is ripening in iniquity; and it must needs be that the children of men are stirred up unto repentance, both the Gentiles and also the house of Israel.

7. Wherefore, as thou hast been baptized by the hands of my servant Joseph Smith, Jun., according to that which I have commanded him, he hath fulfilled the thing which I commanded him.

8. And now, marvel not that I have called him unto mine own purpose, which purpose is known in me; wherefore, if he shall be diligent in keeping my commandments he shall be blessed unto eternal life; and his name is Joseph.

9. And now, Oliver Cowdery, I speak unto you, and also unto David Whitmer, by the way of commandment; for, behold, I command all men everywhere to repent, and I speak unto you, even as unto Paul mine apostle, for you are called even with that same calling with which he was called.

10. Remember the worth of souls is great in the sight of God;

11. For, behold, the Lord your Redeemer suffered death in the flesh; wherefore he suffered the pain of all men, that all men might repent and come unto him.

12. And he hath risen again from the dead, that he might bring all men unto him, on conditions of repentance.

13. And how great is his joy in the soul that repenteth!

14. Wherefore, you are called to cry repentance unto this people.

*Doctrine and Covenants, sec. xviii.

15. And if it so be that you should labor all your days in crying repentance unto this people, and bring, save it be one soul unto me, how great shall be your joy with him in the kingdom of my Father!

16. And now, if your joy will be great with one soul that you have brought unto me into the kingdom of my Father, how great will be your joy if you should bring many souls unto me!

17. Behold, you have my gospel before you, and my rock, and my salvation.

18. Ask the Father in my name, in faith believing that you shall receive, and you shall have the Holy Ghost, which manifesteth all things which are expedient unto the children of men.

19. And if you have not faith, hope, and charity, you can do nothing.

20. Contend against no church, save it be the church of the devil.

21. Take upon you the name of Christ, and speak the truth in soberness.

22. And as many as repent and are baptized in my name, which is Jesus Christ, and endure to the end, the same shall be saved.

23. Behold, Jesus Christ is the name which is given of the Father, and there is none other name given whereby man can be saved;

24. Wherefore, all men must take upon them the name which is given of the Father, for in that name shall they be called at the last day;

25. Wherefore, if they know not the name by which they are called, they cannot have place in the kingdom of my Father.

26. And now, behold, there are others who are called to declare my gospel, both unto Gentile and unto Jew:

27. Yea, even twelve; and the Twelve shall be my disciples, and they shall take upon them my name; and the Twelve are they who shall desire to take upon them my name with full purpose of heart.

28. And if they desire to take upon them my name with full purpose of heart, they are called to go into all the world to preach my gospel unto every creature.

29. And they are they who are ordained of me to baptize in my name, according to that which is written;

30. And you have that which is written before you; wherefore, you must perform it according to the words which are written.

31. And now I speak unto you, the Twelve—Behold, my grace is sufficient for you: you must walk uprightly before me and sin not.

32. And, behold, you are they who are ordained of me to ordain priests and teachers; to declare my gospel, according to the power of the Holy Ghost which is in you, and according to the callings and gifts of God unto men;

33. And I, Jesus Christ, your Lord and your God, have spoken it.

34. These words are not of men, nor of man, but of me; wherefore, you shall testify they are of me and not of man;

35. For it is my voice which speaketh them unto you; for they are given by my Spirit unto you, and by my power you can read them

one to another; and save it were by my power you could not have them;

36. Wherefore, you can testify that you have heard my voice, and know my words.

37. And now, behold, I give unto you, Oliver Cowdery, and also unto David Whitmer, that you shall search out the Twelve, who shall have the desires of which I have spoken;

38. And by their desires and their works you shall know them.

39. And when you have found them, you shall show these things unto them.

40. And you shall fall down and worship the Father in my name,

41. And you must preach unto the world, saying: You must repent and be baptized, in the name of Jesus Christ;

42. For all men must repent and be baptized, and not only men, but women, and children who have arrived at the years of accountability.

43. And now, after that you have received this, you must keep my commandments in all things;

44. And by your hands I will work a marvelous work among the children of men, unto the convincing of many of their sins, that they may come unto repentance, and that they may come unto the kingdom of my Father.

45. Wherefore, the blessings which I give unto you are above all things.

46. And after that you have received this, if you keep not my commandments you cannot be saved in the kingdom of my Father.

47. Behold, I, Jesus Christ, your Lord and your God, and your Redeemer, by the power of my Spirit have spoken it. Amen.

Instructions on Church Organization.

In this manner did the Lord continue to give us instructions from time to time, concerning the duties which now devolved upon us; and among many other things of the kind, we obtained of Him the following, by the spirit of prophecy and revelation; which not only gave us much information, but also pointed out to us the precise day upon which, according to His will and commandment, we should proceed to organize His Church once more here upon the earth:

*A Revelation on Church Government.**

1. The rise of the Church of Christ in these last days, being one thousand eight hundred and thirty years since the coming of our Lord

*Doctrine and Covenants, section xx.

and Savior Jesus Christ in the flesh, it being regularly organized and established agreeable to the laws of our country, by the will and commandments of God, in the fourth month, and on the sixth day of the month which is called April—

2. Which commandments were given to Joseph Smith, Jun., who was called of God, and ordained an apostle of Jesus Christ, to be the first elder of this Church;

3. And to Oliver Cowdery, who was also called of God, an apostle of Jesus Christ, to be the second elder of this church, and ordained under his hand;

4. And this according to the grace of our Lord and Savior Jesus Christ, to whom be all glory, both now and for ever. Amen.

5. After it was truly manifested unto this first elder that he had received a remission of his sins, he was entangled again in the vanities of the world;

6. But after repenting, and humbling himself sincerely, through faith, God ministered unto him by an holy angel, whose countenance was as lightning, and whose garments were pure and white above all other whiteness;

7. And gave unto him commandments which inspired him;

8. And gave him power from on high, by the means which were before prepared, to translate the Book of Mormon;

9. Which contains a record of a fallen people, and the fulness of the gospel of Jesus Christ to the Gentiles and to the Jews also;

10. Which was given by inspiration, and is confirmed to others by the ministering of angels, and is declared unto the world by them—

11. Proving to the world that the Holy Scriptures are true, and that God does inspire men and call them to his holy work in this age and generation, as well as in generations of old;

12. Thereby showing that he is the same God yesterday, today, and for ever. Amen.

13. Therefore, having so great witnesses, by them shall the world be judged, even as many as shall hereafter come to a knowledge of this work.

14. And those who receive it in faith, and work righteousness, shall receive a crown of eternal life;

15. But those who harden their hearts in unbelief, and reject it, it shall turn to their own condemnation—

16. For the Lord God hath spoken it; and we, the elders of the church, have heard and bear witness to the words of the glorious Majesty on high, to whom be glory for ever and ever. Amen.

17. By these things we know that there is a God in heaven, who is infinite and eternal, from everlasting to everlasting the same un-

changeable God, the framer of heaven and earth, and all things which are in them;

18. And that he created man, male, and female, after his own image and in his own likeness, created he them;

19. And gave unto them commandments that they should love and serve him, the only living and true God, and that he should be the only being whom they should worship.

20. But by the transgression of these holy laws man became sensual and devilish, and became fallen man.

21. Wherefore, the Almighty God gave his Only Begotton Son, as it is written in those scriptures which have been given of him.

22. He suffered temptations but gave no heed unto them.

23. He was crucified, died, and rose again the third day;

24. And ascended into heaven, to sit down on the right hand of the Father, to reign with almighty power according to the will of the Father;

25. That as many sa would believe and be baptized in his holy name, and endure in faith to the end, should be saved—

26. Not only those who believe after he came in the meridian of time, in the flesh, but all those from the beginning, even as many as were before he came, who believed in the words of the holy prophets, who spake as they were inspired by the gift of the Holy Ghost, who truly testified of him in all things, should have eternal life,

27. As well as those who should come after, who should believe in the gifts and callings of God by the Holy Ghost, which beareth record of the Father and of the Son;

28. Which Father, Son, and Holy Ghost are one God, infinite and eternal, without end. Amen.

29. And we know that all men must repent and believe on the name of Jesus Christ, and worship the Father in his name, and endure in faith on his name to the end, or they cannot be saved in the kingdom of God.

30. And we know that justification through the grace of our Lord and Savior Jesus Christ is just and true;

31. And we know also, that sanctification through the grace of our Lord and Savior Jesus Christ is just and true, to all those who love and serve God with all their mights, minds, and strength.

32. But there is a possibility that man may fall from grace and depart from the living God;

33. Therefore let the church take heed and pray always, lest they fall into temptation;

34. Yea, and even let those who are sanctified take heed also.

35. And we know that these things are true and according to the

revelations of John, neither adding to, nor diminishing from the prophecy of his book, the holy scriptures, or the revelations of God which shall come hereafter by the gift and power of the Holy Ghost, the voice of God, or the ministering of angels.

36. And the Lord God has spoken it; and honor, power and glory be rendered to his holy name, both now and ever. Amen.

37. *And again, by way of commandment to the Church concerning the manner of baptism*—All those who humble themselves before God, and desire to be baptized, and come forth with broken hearts and contrite spirits, and witness before the church that they have truly repented of all their sins, and are willing to take upon them the name of Jesus Christ, having a determination to serve him to the end, and truly manifest by their works that they have received of the Spirit of Christ unto the remission of their sins, shall be received by baptism into his church.

38. *The duty of the elders, priests, teachers, deacons, and members of the church of Christ*—An apostle is an elder, and it is his calling to baptize;

39. And to ordain other elders, priests, teachers, and deacons;

40. And to administer bread and wine—the emblems of the flesh and blood of Christ—

41. And to confirm those who are baptized into the church, by the laying on of hands for the baptism of fire and the Holy Ghost, according to the scriptures;

42. And to teach, expound, exhort, baptize, and watch over the church;

43. And to confirm the church by the laying on of the hands, and the giving of the Holy Ghost;

44. And to take the lead of all meetings.

45. The elders are to conduct the meetings as they are led by the Holy Ghost, according to the commandments and revelations of God.

46. The priest's duty is to preach, teach, expound, and exhort, and baptize, and administer the sacrament,

47. And visit the house of each member, and exhort them to pray vocally and in secret and attend to all family duties.

48. And he may also ordain other priests, teachers, and deacons.

49. And he is to take the lead of meetings when there is no elder present;

50. But when there is an elder present, he is only to preach, teach, expound, exhort, and baptize,

51. And visit the house of each member, exhorting them to pray vocally and in secret and attend to all family duties.

52. In all these duties the priest is to assist the elder if occasion requires.

53. The teacher's duty is to watch over the church always, and be with and strengthen them;

54. And see that there is no iniquity in the church, neither hardness with each other, neither lying, back biting, nor evil speaking;

55. And see that the church meet together often, and also see that all the members do their duty.

56. And he is to take the lead of meetings in the absence of the elder or priest—

57. And is to be assisted always, in all his duties in the church, by the deacons, if occasion requires.

58. But neither teachers nor deacons have authority to baptize, administer the sacrament, or lay on hands;

59. They are, however, to warn, expound, exhort, and teach, and invite all to come unto Christ.

60. Every elder, priest, teacher, or deacon is to be ordained according to the gifts and callings of God unto him; and he is to be ordained by the power of the Holy Ghost, which is in the one who ordains him.

61. The several elders composing this church of Christ are to meet in conference once in three months, or from time to time as said conferences shall direct or appoint;

62. And said conferences are to do whatever church business is necessary to be done at the time.

63. The elders are to receive their licenses from other elders, by vote of the church to which they belong, or from the conferences.

64. Each priest, teacher, or deacon, who is ordained by a priest, may take a certificate from him at the time, which certificate, when presented to an elder, shall entitle him to a license, which shall authorize him to perform the duties of his calling; or he may receive it from a conference.

65. No person is to be ordained to any office in this church, where there is a regularly organized branch of the same, without the vote of that church;

66. But the presiding elders, traveling bishops, high councilors, high priests, and elders, may have the privilege of ordaining, where there is no branch of the church that a vote may be called.

67. Every president of the high priesthood (or presiding elder), bishop, high councilor and high priest, is to be ordained by the direction of a high council or general conference.*

68. *The duty of the members after they are received by baptism.*— The elders or priests are to have a sufficient time to expound all

*Verses 65, 66 and 67 were added by the Prophet some time after the rest of the revelation was given.

things concerning the church of Christ to their understanding, previous to their partaking of the sacrament and being confirmed by the laying on of the hands of the elders, so that all things may be done in order.

69. And the members shall manifest before the church, and also before the elders, by a godly walk and conversation, that they are worthy of it, that there may be works and faith agreeable to the Holy Scriptures—walking in holiness before the Lord.

70. Every memger of the church of Christ having children is to bring them unto the elders before the church, who are to lay their hands upon them in the name of Jesus Christ, and bless them in his name.

71. No one can be received into the church of Christ, unless he has arrived unto the years of accountability before God, and is capable of repentance.

72. Baptism is to be administered in the following manner unto all those who repent—

73. The person who is called of God and has authority from Jesus Christ to baptize, shall go down into the water with the person who has presented himself or herself for baptism, and shall say, calling him or her by name: Having been commissioned of Jesus Christ, I baptize you in the name of the Father, and of the Son, and of the Holy Ghost. Amen.

74. Then shall he immerse him or her in the water, and come forth again out of the water.

75. It is expedient that the church meet together often to partake of bread and wine in the remembrance of the Lord Jesus;

76. And the elder or priest shall administer it; and after this manner shall he administer it—he shall kneel with the church and call upon the Father in solemn prayer, saying:

77. O God, the Eternal Father, we ask thee in the name of thy Son, Jesus Christ, to bless and sanctify this bread to the souls of all those who partake of it, that they may eat in remembrance of the body of thy Son, and witness unto thee, O God, the Eternal Father, that they are willing to take upon them the name of thy Son, and always remember him and keep his commandments which he has given them; that they may always have his Spirit to be with them. Amen.

78. The manner of administering the wine—he shall take the cup also, and say:

79. O God, the Eternal Father, we ask thee in the name of thy Son, Jesus Christ, to bless and sanctify this wine to the souls of all those who drink of it, that they may do it in remembrance of the blood of thy Son, which was shed for them; that they may witness

unto thee, O god, the Eternal Father, that they do always remember him, that they may have his Spirit to be with them. Amen.

80. Any member of the church of Christ transgressing, or being overtaken in a fault, shall be dealt with as the scriptures direct.

81. It shall be the duty of the several churches, composing the church of Christ, to send one or more of their teachers to attend the several conferences held by the elders of the church,

82. With a list of the names of the several members uniting themselves with the church, since the last conference; or send by the hand of some priest; so that a regular list of all the names of the whole church may be kept in a book by one of the elders whomsoever the other elders shall appoint from time to time;

83. And also, if any have been expelled from the church, so that their names may be blotted out of the general church record of names.

84. All members removing from the church where they reside, if going to a church where they are not known, may take a letter, certifying that they are regular members and in good standing, which certificate may be signed by any elder or priest if the member receiving the letter is personally acquainted with the elder or priest, or it may be signed by the teachers or deacons of the church.

CHAPTER VIII

THE BOOK OF MORMON PUBLISHED—THE CHURCH ORGANIZED.

Price for Publishing Book of Mormon.

MEANTIME, our translation drawing to a close, we went to Palmyra, Wayne county, New York, secured the copyright, and agreed with Mr. Egbert B. Grandin to print five thousand copies for the sum of three thousand dollars.

The Title Page.

I wish to mention here that the title-page of the Book of Mormon is a literal translation, taken from the very last leaf, on the left hand side of the collection or book of plates, which contained the record which has been translated, the language of the whole running the same as all Hebrew writing in general;* and that said title page is not by any means a modern composition, either of mine or of any other man who has lived or does live in this generation. Therefore, in order to correct an error, which generally exists concerning it, I give below that part of the title-page of the English version of the Book of Mormon, which is a genuine and literal translation of the title-page of the original Book of Mormon as recorded on the plates:

THE BOOK OF MORMON.

An account written by the hand of Mormon, upon Plates, taken from the Plates of Nephi.

Wherefore, it is an abridgment of the record of the people of Nephi. and also of the Lamanites—Written to the Lamanites, who are a rem-

*That is, from right to left.

nant of the house of Israel; and also to Jew and Gentile—Written by way of commandment, and also by the spirit of prophecy and of revelation—Written and sealed up, and hid up unto the Lord, that they might not be destroyed—To come forth by the gift and power of God unto the interpretation thereof—Sealed by the hand of Moroni, and hid up unto the Lord, to come forth in due time by way of the Gentile—The interpretation thereof by the gift of God.

An abridgment taken from the Book of Ether also, which is a record of the people of Jared, who were scattered at the time the Lord confounded the language of the people, when they were building a tower to get to heaven—Which is to show unto the remnant of the house of Israel what great things the Lord hath done for their fathers; and that they may know the covenants of the Lord, that they are not cast off forever—And also to the convincing of the Jew and Gentile that *Jesus* is the *Christ*, the *Eternal God*, manifesting himself unto all nations—And now, if there are faults they are the mistakes of men; wherefore, condemn not the things of God, that ye may be found spotless at the judgment-seat of Christ.

The remainder of the title-page is, of course, modern.

*A Commandment of God and not of man, to Martin Harris, given (Manchester, New York, March, 1830,) by Him who is Eternal.**

1. I am Alpha and Omega, Christ the Lord; yea, even I am he, the beginning and the end, the Redeemer of the world.

2. I, having accomplished and finished the will of him whose I am, even the Father, concerning me—having done this that I might subdue all things unto myself—

3. Retaining all power, even to the destroying of Satan and his works at the end of the world, and the last great day of judgment, which I shall pass upon the inhabitants thereof, judging every man according to his works and the deeds which he hath done.

4. And surely every man must repent or suffer, for I, God, am endless.

5. Wherefore, I revoke not the judgments which I shall pass, but woes shall go forth, weeping, wailing and gnashing of teeth, yea, to those who are found on my left hand.

*Doctrine and Covenants, section xix. No words of the Prophet introduce this revelation in his History. Nothing is known of the circumstances which called it forth. And yet there are few revelations that have been given in the present dispensation of the Gospel more important than this one. The doctrine of the atonement of the Lord Jesus, as directly applying to the individual, and God's exposition of "Eternal Punishment," as here set forth, give it a place of first importance in the doctrinal development of the Church.

6. Nevertheless, it is not written that there shall be no end to this torment, but it is written *endless torment.*

7. Again, it is written *eternal damnation;* wherefore it is more express than other scriptures, that it might work upon the hearts of the children of men, altogether for my name's glory.

8. Wherefore, I will explain unto you this mystery, for it is meet unto you to know even as mine apostles.

9. I speak unto you that are chosen in this thing, even as one, that you may enter into my rest.

10. For, behold, the mystery of godliness, how great is it! For, behold, I am endless, and the punishment which is given from my hand is endless punishment, for Endless is my name, wherefore—

11. Eternal punishment is God's punishment.

12. Endless punishment is God's punishment.

13. Wherefore, I command you to repent, and keep the commandments which you have received by the hand of my servant Joseph Smith, Jun., in my name;

14. And it is by my almighty power that you have received them;

15. Therefore I command you to repent—repent, lest I smite you by the rod of my mouth, and by my wrath, and by my anger, and your sufferings be sore—how sore you know not, how exquisite you know not, yea, how hard to bear you know not.

16. For behold, I, God, have suffered these things for all, that they might not suffer if they would repent;

17. But if they would not repent, they must suffer even as I;

18. Which suffering caused myself, even God, the greatest of all, to tremble because of pain, and to bleed at every pore, and to suffer both body and spirit—and would that I might not drink the bitter cup, and shrink—

19. Nevertheless, glory be to the Father, and I partook and finished my preparations unto the children of men.

20. Wherefore, I command you again to repent, lest I humble you with my almighty power; and that you confess your sins, lest you suffer these punishments of which I have spoken, of which in the smallest, yea, even in the least degree you have tasted at the time I withdrew my Spirit.

21. And I command you, that you preach naught but repentance and show not these things unto the world until it is wisdom in me.

22. For they cannot bear meat now, but milk they must receive; wherefore, they must not know these things, lest they perish.

23. Learn of me, and listen to my words; walk in the meekness of my Spirit, and you shall have peace in me.

24. I am Jesus Christ; I came by the will of the Father, and I do his will.

25. And again, I command thee that thou shalt not covet thy neighbor's wife; nor seek thy neighbor's life.

26. And again, I command thee that thou shalt not covet thine own property, but impart it freely to the printing of the Book of Mormon, which contains the truth and the word of God—

27. Which is my word to the Gentile, that soon it may go to the Jew, of whom the Lamanites are a remnant, that they may believe the gospel, and look not for a Messiah to come who has already come.

28. And again, I command thee that thou shalt pray vocally as well as in thy heart; yea, before the world as well as in secret, in public as well as in private.

29. And thou shalt declare glad tidings, yea, publish it upon the mountains, and upon every high place, and among every people that thou shalt be permitted to see.

30. And thou shalt do it with all humility, trusting in me, reviling not against revilers.

31. And of tenets thou shalt not talk, but thou shalt declare repentance and faith on the Savior, and remission of sins by baptism and by fire, yea, even the Holy Ghost.

32. Behold, this is a great and the last commandment which I shall give unto you concerning this matter; for this shall suffice for thy daily walk, even unto the end of thy life.

33. And misery thou shalt receive if thou wilt slight these counsels, yea, even the destruction of thyself and property.

34. Impart a portion of thy property, yea, even part of thy lands, and all save the support of thy family.

35. Pay the debt thou hast contracted with the printer. Release thyself from bondage.

36. Leave thy house and home, except when thou shalt desire to see thy family;

37. And speak freely to all; yea, preach, exhort, declare the truth, even with a loud voice, with a sound of rejoicing, crying—Hosanna, hosanna, blessed be the name of the Lord God!

38. Pray always, and I will pour out my Spirit upon you, and great shall be your blessing—yea, even more than if you should obtain treasures of earth and corruptibleness to the extent thereof.

39. Behold, canst thou read this without rejoicing and lifting up thy heart for gladness?

40. Or canst thou run about longer as a blind guide?

41. Or canst thou be humble and meek, and conduct thyself wisely before me? yea, come unto me thy Savior. Amen.

Whilst the Book of Mormon was in the hands of the

printer,* we still continued to bear testimony and give information, as far as we had opportunity; and also made known to our brethren that we had received a commandment to organize the Church; and accordingly we met together for that

Procedure in the Organization of the Church.

*Nothing is said by the Prophet in his History of the difficulties that arose "whilst the Book of Mormon was in the hands of the printer;" nor of the care that was taken to prevent the manuscript falling into the hands of enemies of the work. It is proper, however, that these matters should be stated at this point. It appears that when the arrangements were completed with Mr. Grandin for printing the Book of Mormon, the Prophet went down to Harmony, in Pennsylvania. Before taking his departure, however, it was arranged:

First: that Oliver Cowdery transscribe the whole manuscript; hence it came about that there were two manuscript copies of the Book of Mormon, the original, which was taken in charge by the Prophet after the publication of the book, and the copy made by Oliver Cowdery for the printer's use, and which finally was given by him into the custody of David Whitmer, with whose family it remains to this day (1901).

Second: that the copy made by Cowdery from the original manuscript only should be taken to the printers, so that if that should be destroyed the original would remain in the hands of the Prophet and his associates, from which it could be replaced; and even this copy was supplied the printer in small quantities at a time, usually enough only for a single day's work of the printer.

Third: that in going to and from the office whoever carried the manuscript—usually it was Oliver Cowdery—should always have a guard to attend him.

Fourth: that a guard should be kept constantly upon the watch, both night and day, about the house, to protect the manuscript from malicious persons, who might seek to destroy it. (The authorities for the above are: Lucy Smith's *History of the Prophet Joseph*, ch. xxxi; the statements of Stephen S. Harding, who a number of times visited Grandin's establishment while the Book of Mormon was being printed; his statement is published in *The Prophet of Palmyra*, by Thomas Gregg, pp. 34-56—this is that same Stephen S. Harding who was governor of Utah Territory from July, 1862, to July, 1863; also the statement of J. H. Gilbert, the principal compositor on the Book of Mormon. The extreme care in allowing the printer to have but a small amount of copy at a time is a subject of ridicule in nearly all anti-"Mormon" books that treat of this period. In addition to all this is the evidence of the manuscript in the hands of the Whitmer family, nearly every page of which is in the handwriting of Oliver Cowdery, and by being divided into "takes" clearly bears evidence of having passed through the printer's hands. The evidence also in the existence of portions of the original manuscript, now in the possession of President Joseph F. Smith, which was taken from its depository in one of the corner stones of the Nauvoo House, where it was placed by the hands of Joseph the Prophet, with other relics, on the occasion of laying the corner stone of that building on the 2nd of October, 1841. Unfortunately a great part of the manuscript was destroyed by dampness, but enough is preserved to establish the fact that it is the original).

Notwithstanding all the precautions taken by the little group of brethren engaged in publishing the book, the Nephite record, mutilated by interlineations of human invention, omissions, and added vulgarisms intended to destroy the work, came nearly being given to the world before the Book of Mormon itself was published. This was

purpose, at the house of Mr. Peter Whitmer, Sen., (being six in number,)* on Tuesday, the sixth day of

the work of one Esquire Cole, ex-justice of the peace, who undertook to publish the Book of Mormon, in instalments, in a weekly periodical called *Dogberry Paper on Winter Hill.* He obtained the use of Grandin's press nights and on Sundays, and surely must have obtained the advance sheets of the printed forms of the Book of Mormon, which he was using, with the knowledge of Mr. Grandin; at least it is difficult to conceive how he could obtain and use them without his knowledge. Hyrum Smith, feeling uneasy concerning the security of that part of the Book of Mormon in the hands of the printer, induced Oliver Cowdery one Sunday to go with him to the printer's to see if all was well, and there they found Squire Cole at work on his *Dogberry Paper,* and publishing mutilated extracts from the Book of Mormon. He refused to desist from his unlawful course; but Joseph was sent for and came up during the week from Harmony, and by firmly asserting his rights under the copyright law, and by threatening to prosecute those who infringed them, Cole was induced to abandon his intention of publishing the Book of Mormon in his paper.

This difficulty past, another arose. The people of Palmyra and vicinity held a mass meeting and passed a resolution pledging themselves not to purchase the Book of Mormon when published, and to use their influence to prevent others from purchasing it. This had the effect of causing Mr. Grandin to suspend printing until he could obtain renewed assurance of receiving the amount agreed upon for printing the edition of five thousand. Again the Prophet was sent for, and again he made the journey from Harmony to Palmyra, quieted the fears of Mr. Grandin by renewed assurances on the part of himself and Martin Harris that the amount agreed upon would be paid. The work proceeded, and at last issued from the press, notwithstanding all the difficulties it had encountered (See Lucy Smith's *History of the Prophet Joseph,* ch. xxxiii).

*The following statement is interesting as furnishing the names of these six:

Names of the six members of the Church as they were organized April 6, 1830—

Oliver Cowdery,
Joseph Smith, Jun.,
Hyrum Smith,
Peter Whitmer, Jun.,
Samuel H. Smith,
David Whitmer.

Some of these had been baptized previously; but were all baptized on the day of organization.

These names were given to Joseph Knight by Oliver Cowdery.

(Signed) JOSEPH KNIGHT.

G. S. L. City
Aug. 11th, 1862.

Witnesses

G. A. SMITH,
ROBT. L. CAMPBELL,
THOS. BULLOCK,
JOHN V. LONG.

(*Copy*)

There has been some question as to the number that had been baptized previous to the organization of the Church on the 6th day of April, 1830. David Whitmer in his "Address to All Believers in Christ," a pamphlet of seventy-five pages, published in 1887, says that there were six Elders and about seventy members before April 6th, 1830. Others have estimated the number at thirty, thirty-five, and forty.

April, A. D., one thousand eight hundred and thirty. Having opened the meeting by solemn prayer to our Heavenly Father, we proceeded, according to previous commandment, to call on our brethren to know whether they accepted us as their teachers in the things of the Kingdom of God, and whether they were satisfied that we should proceed and be organized as a Church according to said commandment which we had received. To these several propositions they consented by a unanimous vote. I then laid my hands upon Oliver Cowdery, and ordained him an Elder of the

These estimates, however, are beyond all question too large. In the minutes of the second conference of the Church, held at Fayette, New York, on the 26th of September, 1830, this statement is made: "Number of the several members uniting to this Church, since the last conference, thity-five: making in whole now belonging to this Church, sixty-two." "The last conference," referred to was one held on the 9th of June, 1830. If there were but sixty-two members in September, 1830, and thirty-five of them were added since the conference of the Church held on the 9th of June of that year, then there were but twenty-seven in the Church on the said 9th of June. In the last week of May, 1830, Newel Knight was baptized—*one*; on the 18th of April, 1830, Oliver Cowdery baptized *seven*, (the names are given on p. 81); on the 11th of April, Oliver baptized *six* persons (their names are also given on p. 81); on the 6th of April, 1830, the same day that the Church was organized, there were *four* persons baptized, two of whom were the father and mother of the Prophet (see p. 79). This makes a total of eighteen baptized between the 9th of June conference and the 6th of April meeting; and as there were but *twenty-seven* in the Church on the 9th of June, the number that had been baptized up to the 6th of April, 1830, must have been but *nine*. *The Far West Record*, containing the minutes of the conferences of the 9th of June, and the 26th of September, was kept by the clerks of the High Council in Missouri, and the minutes of the two conferences above referred to, and which give the information here set forth, occupy pages *one* and *two* of that record. The accuracy of the minutes of the conference of the 26th of September, 1830, which fix the membership of the Church at that time at *sixty-two*, is confirmed by the following remark of the Prophet, to be found in his history in December of that same year, which remark immediately preceedes extracts from the prophecy of Enoch in this volume (ch. xii): "To the joy of the little flock, which in all, from Colesville to Canandaigua, New York, numbered about *seventy members*, did the Lord reveal the following," etc. When it is remembered that the Prophet is here speaking of conditions existing in December, 1830, and the figures given are exclusive of the additions which had been made in Kirtland, Ohio, it strongly sustains the correctness of the minutes of the conference of September 26th, which record the membership of the Church at that time to be but *sixty-two*. The correctness of this number is also still further confirmed by a brief historical sketch of "The Rise and Progress of the Church of Christ," published in the *Evening and Morning Star* under date of April, 1833, where it is said: "In October, 1830, the number of disciples had increased to between seventy and eighty." (p. 169.)

"Church of Jesus Christ of Latter-day Saints;" after which, he ordained me also to the office of an Elder of said Church. We then took bread, blessed it, and brake it with them; also wine, blessed it, and drank it with them. We then laid our hands on each individual member of the Church present, that they might receive the gift of the Holy Ghost, and be confirmed members of the Church of Christ. The Holy Ghost was poured out upon us to a very great degree—some prophesied, whilst we all praised the Lord, and rejoiced exceedingly. Whilst yet together, I received the following commandment:

Joseph Smith, Jun., Appointed a Prophet, Seer and Revelator to the Church.

*Revelation to Joseph Smith, Jun., given at Fayette, Seneca County, New York, April 6th, 1830.**

1. Behold, there shall be a record kept among you; and in it thou shall be called a seer, a translator, a prophet, an apostle of Jesus Christ, an elder of the church through the will of God the Father, and the grace of your Lord Jesus Christ,

2. Being inspired of the Holy Ghost to lay the foundation thereof, and to build it up unto the most holy faith,

3. Which church was organized and established in the year of your Lord eighteen hundred and thirty, in the fourth month, and on the sixth day of the month, which is called April.

4. Wherefore, meaning the church, thou shalt give heed unto all his words and commandments which he shall give unto you as he receiveth them, walking in all holiness before me;

5. For his word ye shall receive, as if from mine own mouth, in all patience and faith.

6. For by doing these things the gates of hell shall not prevail against you; yea, and the Lord God will disperse the powers of darkness from before you, and cause the heavens to shake for your good, and his name's glory.

7. For thus saith the Lord God, him have I inspired to move the cause of Zion in mighty power for good, and his diligence I know, and his prayers I have heard.

8. Yea, his weeping for Zion I have seen, and I will cause that he shall mourn for her no longer; for his days of rejoicing are come unto the remission of his sins, and the manifestations of my blessings upon his works.

9. For, behold, I will bless all those who labor in my vineyard with a mighty blessing, and they shall believe on his words, which are given

*Doctrine and Covenants, sec. xxi.

him through me by the Comforter, which manifesteth that Jesus was crucified by sinful men for the sins of the world, yea, for the remission of sins unto the contrite heart.

10. Wherefore it behooveth me that he should be ordained by you, Oliver Cowdery, mine apostle;

11. This being an ordinance unto you, that you are an elder under his hand, he being the first unto you, that you might be an elder unto this church of Christ, bearing my name—

12. And the first preacher of this church unto the church, and before the world, yea, before the Gentiles; yea, and thus saith the Lord God, lo, lo! to the Jews also. Amen.

The Church of Jesus Christ Begins its Career.

We now proceeded to call out and ordain some others of the brethren to different offices of the Priesthood, according as the Spirit manifested unto us: and after a happy time spent in witnessing and feeling for ourselves the powers and blessings of the Holy Ghost, through the grace of God bestowed upon us, we dismissed with the pleasing knowledge that we were now individually members of, and acknowledged of God, "The Church of Jesus Christ," organized in accordance with commandments and revelations given by Him to ourselves in these last days, as well as according to the order of the Church as recorded in the New Testament. Several persons who had attended the above meeting, became convinced of the truth and came forward shortly after, and were rceived into the Church; among the rest, my own father and mother were baptized, to my great joy and consolation; and about the same time, Martin Harris and Orrin Porter Rockwell.

*Revelation to the Church of Christ which was established in these last days, in the year of our Lord, one thousand eight hundred and thirty. Given at Manchester, New York, April, 1830, in consequence of some desiring to unite with the Church without rebaptism, who had previously been baptized.**

1. Behold, I say unto you that all old covenants have I caused to be done away in this thing; and this is a new and an everlasting covenant, even that which was from the beginning.

*Doctrine and Covenants, sec. xxii.

2. Wherefore, although a man should be baptized an hundred times it availeth him nothing, for you cannot enter in at the strait gate by the law of Moses, neither by your dead works.

3. For it is because of your dead works, that I have caused this last covenant and this church to be built up unto me, even as in days of old.

4. Wherefore, enter ye in at the gate, as I have commanded, and seek not to counsel your God. Amen.

Word of the Lord to Several Persons.

The following persons being anxious to know of the Lord what might be their respective duties in relation to this work, I enquired of the Lord, and received for them the following:

*Revelation to Oliver Cowdery, Hyrum Smith, Samuel H. Smith, Joseph Smith, Sen., and Joseph Knight, Sen. Given at Manchester, New York, April, 1830.**

1. Behold, I speak unto you, Oliver, a few words. Behold, thou art blessed, and art under no condemnation. But beware of pride, lest thou shouldst enter into temptation.

2. Make known thy calling unto the church, and also before the world, and thy heart shall be opened to preach the truth from henceforth and forever. Amen.

3. Behold, I speak unto you, Hyrum, a few words; for thou also art under no condemnation, and thy heart is opened, and thy tongue loosed; and thy calling is to exhortation, and to strengthen the church continually. Wherefore thy duty is unto the church forever, and this because of thy family. Amen.

4. Behold, I speak a few words unto you, Samuel; for thou also art under no condemnation, and thy calling is to exhortation, and to strengthen the church; and thou art not as yet called to preach before the world. Amen.

5. Behold, I speak a few words unto you, Joseph; for thou also art under no condemnation, and thy calling also is to exhortation, and to strengthen the church; and this is thy duty from henceforth and forever. Amen.

6. Behold, I manifest unto you, Joseph Knight, by these words, that you must take up your cross, in the which you must pray vocally before the world as well as in secret, and in your family, and among your friends, and in all places.

7. And, behold, it is your duty to unite with the true church, and give your language to exhortation continually, that you may receive the reward of the laborer. Amen.

Doctrine and Covenants, sec. xxiii.

CHAPTER IX.

THE COMMENCEMENT OF THE PUBLIC MINISTRY OF THE CHURCH.

The First Public Discourse.

ON Sunday, April 11th, 1830, Oliver Cowdery preached the first public discourse that was delivered by any of our number. Our meeting was held, by previous appointment, at the house of Mr. Peter Whitmer, Sen., Fayette. Large numbers of people attended, and the same day the following were baptized, viz., Hiram Page, Katharine Page, Christian Whitmer, Anne Whitmer, Jacob Whitmer, Elizabeth Whitmer; and on the 18th day, Peter Whitmer, Sen., Mary Whitmer, William Jolly, Elizabeth Jolly, Vincent Jolly, Richard B. Peterson, and Elizabeth Anne Whitmer—all by Oliver Cowdery, in Seneca lake.

The Prophet's Ministry at Colesville.

During this month of April, I went on a visit to the residence of Mr. Joseph Knight, of Colesville, Broome county, New York, with whom and his family I had been for some time acquainted, and whose name I had previously mentioned as having been so kind and thoughtful towards us while translating the Book of Mormon. Mr. Knight and his family were Universalists, but were willing to reason with me upon my religious views, and were, as usual, friendly and hospitable. We held several meetings in the neighborhood; we had many friends, and some enemies. Our meetings were well attended, and many began to pray fervently to Almighty God, that He would give them wisdom to understand the truth.

Labors of the Prophet with Newel Knight.

Amongst those who attended our meetings regularly, was Newel Knight, son of Joseph Knight. He and I had many serious conversations on the important subject of man's eternal salvation. We had got into the habit of praying much at our meetings, and Newel had said that he would try and take up his cross, and pray vocally during meeting; but when we again met together, he rather excused himself. I tried to prevail upon him, making use of the figure, supposing that he should get into a mud-hole, would he not try to help himself out? And I further said that we were willing now to help him out of the mud-hole. He replied, that provided he had got into a mud-hole through carelessness, he would rather wait and get out himself, than to have others help him; and so he would wait until he could get into the woods by himself, and there he would pray. Accordingly, he deferred praying until next morning, when he retired into the woods; where, according to his own account afterwards, he made several attempts to pray, but could scarcely do so, feeling that he had not done his duty, in refusing to pray in the presence of others. He began to feel uneasy, and continued to feel worse both in mind and body, until, upon reaching his own house, his appearance was such as to alarm his wife very much. He requested her to go and bring me to him. I went and found him suffering very much in his mind, and his body acted upon in a very strange manner; his visage and limbs distorted and twisted in every shape and appearance possible to imagine; and finally he was caught up off the floor of the apartment, and tossed about most fearfully.

The First Miracle in the Church.

His situation was soon made known to his neighbors and relatives, and in a short time as many as eight or nine grown persons had got together to witness the scene. After he had thus suffered for a time, I succeded in getting hold of him by the hand, when almost immediately he spoke to me, and with great earnestness requested me to cast the devil out of him, saying that he knew he was in him, and that he also knew that I could cast him out.

I replied, "If you know that I can, it shall be done;" and then almost unconsciously I rebuked the devil, and commanded him in the name of Jesus Christ to depart from him; when immediately Newel spoke out and said that he saw the devil leave him and vanish from his sight. This was the first miracle which was done in the Church, or by any member of it; and it was done not by man, nor by the power of man, but it was done by God, and by the power of godliness; therefore, let the honor and the praise, the dominion and the glory, be ascribd to the Father, Son, and Holy Spirit, for ever and ever. Amen.

Remarkable Experience of Newel Knight.

This scene was now entirely changed, for as soon as the devil had departed from our friend, his countenance became natural, his distortions of body ceased, and almost immediately the Spirit of the Lord descended upon him, and the visions of eternity were opened to his view. So soon as consciousness returned, his bodily weakness was such that we were obliged to lay him upon his bed, and wait upon him for some time. He afterwards related his experience as follows:

> I now began to feel a most pleasing sensation resting on me, and immediately the visions of heaven were opened to my view. I felt myself attracted upward, and remained for some time enwrapt in contemplation, insomuch that I knew not what was going on in the room. By and by, I felt some weight pressing upon my shoulder and the side of my head, which served to recall me to a sense of my situation, and I found that the Spirit of the Lord had actually caught me up off the floor, and that my shoulder and head were pressing against the beams.

All this was witnessed by many, to their great astonishment and satisfaction, when they saw the devil thus cast out, and the power of God, and His Holy Spirit thus made manifest. As may be expected, such a scene as this contributed much to make believers of those who witnessed it, and finally the greater part of them became members of the Church.

Effect of Publishing the Book of Mormon.

Soon after this occurrence I returned to Fayette, Seneca county. The Book of Mormon (the stick of Joseph in the hands of Ephraim,) had now been published for some time, and as the ancient prophet had predicted of it, "it was accounted as a strange thing." No small stir was created by its appearance. Great opposition and much persecution followed the believers of its authenticity. But it had now come to pass that truth had sprung out of the earth, and righteousness had looked down from heaven, so we feared not our opponents, knowing that we had both truth and righteousness on our side, that we had both the Father and the Son, because we had the doctrines of Christ, and abided in them; and therefore we continued to preach and to give information to all who were willing to hear.

During the last week in May, the above-mentioned Newel Knight came to visit us at Fayette, and was baptized by David Whitmer.

The First Conference of the Church.

On the ninth day of June,* 1830, we held our first conference as an organized Church. Our numbers were about thirty, besides whom many assembled with us, who were either believers or anxious to learn. Having opened by singing and prayer, we partook together of the emblems of the body and blood of our Lord Jesus Christ. We then proceeded to confirm several who had lately been baptized, after which we called out and ordained several to the various offices of the Priesthood. Much

*The date of this conference, in the *History of the Prophet*, published in the *Times and Seasons* and the *Millennial Star*, as also in the History in manuscript in the custody of the Church Historian—from which the history published in those periodicals was taken—is given as the "first day of June;" but the minutes of the conference, written, as the minutes themselves state, by Oliver Cowdery, and recorded in the *Far West Record*, are dated "June 9th," 1830. It is for this reason that the date is changed in the text. These minutes also state that this conference of June 9th, was adjourned to convene again at the same place on the "26th of September, 1830"

exhortation and instruction was given, and the Holy Ghost was poured out upon us in a miraculous manner —many of our number prophesied, whilst others had the heavens opened to their view, and were so overcome that we had to lay them on beds or other convenient places; among the rest was Brother Newel Knight, who had to be placed on a bed, being unable to help himself. By his own account of the transaction, he could not understand why we should lay him on the bed, as he felt no sense of weakness. He felt his heart filled with love, with glory, and pleasure unspeakable, and could discern all that was going on in the room; when all of a sudden a vision of the future burst upon him. He saw there represented the great work which through my instrumentality was yet to be accomplished. He saw heaven opened, and beheld the Lord Jesus Christ, seated at the right hand of the majesty on high, and had it made plain to his understanding that the time would come when he would be admitted into His presence to enjoy His society for ever and ever. When their bodily strength was restored to these brethren, they shouted hosannas to God and the Lamb, and rehearsed the glorious things which they had seen and felt, whilst they were yet in the spirit.

Effect of Spiritual Manifestations.

Such scenes as these were calculated to inspire our hearts with joy unspeakable, and fill us with awe and reverence for that Almighty Being, by whose grace we had been called to be instrumental in bringing about, for the children of men, the enjoyment of such glorious blessings as were now at this time poured out upon us. To find ourselves engaged in the very same order of things as observed by the holy Apostles of old; to realize the importance and solemnity of such proceedings; and to witness and feel with our own natural senses, the like glorious manifestations of the powers of the Priesthood, the gifts and blessings of the Holy Ghost, and the goodness and condescension of a merciful God unto such as obey the everlasting Gospel of our Lord Jesus Christ, combined to create within us sensations of rapturous gratitude, and inspire us with fresh zeal and energy in the cause of truth.

Baptisms.

Shortly after this conference, David Whitmer baptized the following persons, in Seneca lake: viz., John Poorman, John Jolly, Julia Anne Jolly, Harriet Jolly, Jerusha Smith, Katherine Smith, William Smith, Don C. Smith, Peter Rockwell, Caroline Rockwell, and Electa Rockwell.

Labor of the Prophet at Colesville.

Immediately after conference I returned to my own house, and from thence, accompanied by my wife, Oliver Cowdery, John Whitmer and David Whitmer, went again on a visit to Mr. Knight, of Colesville, Broome county. We found a number in the neighborhood still believing, and now anxious to be baptized. We appointed a meeting for the Sabbath, and on the afternoon of Saturday we erected a dam across a stream of water, which was convenient, for the purpose of there attending to the ordinance of baptism; but during the night a mob collected and tore down our dam, which hindered us from attending to the baptism on the Sabbath. We after ward found out that this mob had been instigated to this act of molestation by certain sectarian priests of the neighborhood, who began to consider their craft in danger, and took this plan to stop the progress of the truth; and the sequel will show how determinedly they prosecuted their opposition, as well as to how little purpose in the end. The Sabbath arrived, and we held our meeting. Oliver Cowdery preached, and others of us bore testimony to the truth of the Book of Mormon, the doctrine of repentance, baptism for the remission of sins, and laying on of hands for the gift of the Holy Ghost, etc. Amongst our audience were those who had torn down our dam, and who seemed desirous to give us trouble, but did not until after the meeting was dismissed, when they immediately commenced talking to those whom they considered our friends, and tried to turn them against us and our doctrines.

Adventures of Emily Coburn.

Amongst the many present at this meeting, was one Emily Coburn, sister to the wife of Newel Knight. The Rev. Mr. Shearer, a divine of the Presbyterian faith, who had considered himself her pastor, came to understand that she was likely to believe our doctrine, and had, a short time previous to this meeting, come to labor with her. But having spent some time with her without being able to persuade her against us, he endeavored to have her leave her sister's house and go with him to her father's, who lived at a distance. For this purpose, he had recourse to stratagem; he told her that one of her brothers was waiting at a certain place desirous to have her go with him. He succeeded thus in getting her a little distance from the house, when, seeing that her brother was not in waiting for her, she refused to go any further with him; upon which he took hold of her by the arm to force her along. But her sister was soon with them, and as the two women were too many for him to cope with, he was forced to sneak off without accomplishing his errand, after all his labor and ingenuity. Nothing daunted, however, he went to her father, representing to him some thing or other, which induced the old gentleman to give him a power of attorney, which, as soon as our meeting was over, on the above-named Sunday evening, he immediately served upon her, and carried her off to her father's residence by open violence against her will. All his labor was in vain, however, for the said Emily Coburn in a short time afterwards, was baptized and confirmed a member of the Church of Jesus Christ of Latter-day Saints.

Baptisms.

Early on Monday morning we were on the alert, and before our enemies were aware of our proceedings, we had repaired the dam, and the following thirteen persons baptized, by Oliver Cowdery; viz., Emma Smith, Hezekiah Peck and wife, Joseph Knight, Sen., and wife, William Stringham and wife, Joseph Knight, Jun., Aaron Culver and wife, Levi Hale, Polly Knight, and Julia Stringham.

Mobbings.

Before the baptizing was entirely finished, the mob began again to collect, and shortly after we had retired, they amounted to about fifty men. They surrounded the house of Mr. Knight—whither we had retired—raging with anger, and apparently determined to commit violence upon us. Some asked us questions, others threatened us, so that we thought it wisdom to leave and go to the house of Newel Knight. There also they followed us, and it was only by the exercise of great prudence on our part, and reliance in our heavenly Father, that they were kept from laying violent hands upon us; and so long as they chose to stay, we were obliged to answer them various unprofitable questions, and bear with insults and threatenings without number.

The Prophet Arrested.

We had appointed a meeting for this evening, for the purpose of attending to the confirmation of those who had been the same morning baptized. The time appointed had arrived and our friends had nearly all collected together, when to my surprise, I was visited by a constable, and arrested by him on a warrant, on the charge of being a disorderly person, of setting the country in an uproar by preaching the Book of Mormon, etc. The constable informed me, soon after I had been arrested, that the plan of those who had got out the warrant was to get me into the hands of the mob, who were now lying in ambush for me; but that he was determined to save me from them, as he had found me to be a different sort of person from what I had been represented to him. I soon found that he had told me the truth in this matter, for not far from Mr. Knight's house, the wagon in which we had set out was surrounded by a mob, who seemed only to await some signal from the constable; but to their great disappointment, he gave the horse the whip, and drove me out of their reach.

The Prophet Escapes the Mob.

Whilst driving in great haste one of the wagon wheels came off, which left us once more very nearly surrounded by them, as they had come on in close pursuit. However, we managed to replace the wheel and again left them behind us. He drove on to the town of South Bainbridge, Chenango county, where he lodged me for the time being in an upper room of a tavern; and in order that all might be right with himself and with me also, he slept during the night with his feet against the door, and a loaded musket by his side, whilst I occupied a bed which was in the room; he having declared that if we were interrupted unlawfully, he would fight for me, and defend me as far as it was in his power.

Excitement Over the Prophet's Case.

On the day following, a court was convened for the purpose of investigating those charges which had been preferred against me. A great excitement prevailed on account of the scandalous falsehoods which had been circulated, the nature of which will appear in the sequel. In the meantime, my friend, Joseph Knight, had repaired to two of his neighbors, viz., James Davidson and John Reid, Esqrs., respectable farmers, men renowned for their integrity, and well versed in the laws of their country; and retained them on my behalf during my trial.

The Trial.

At length the trial commenced amidst a multitude of spectators, who in general evinced a belief that I was guilty of all that had been reported concerning me, and of course were very zealous that I should be punished according to my crimes. Among many witnesses called up against me, was Mr. Josiah Stoal—of whom I have made mention as having worked for him some time—and examined to the following effect:

"Did not the prisoner, Joseph Smith, have a horse of you?"

"Yes."

"Did not he go to you and tell you that an angel had appeared unto him and authorized him to get the horse from you?"

"No, he told me no such story."

"Well, how had he the horse of you?"

"He bought him of me as any other man would."

"Have you had your pay?"

"That is not your business."

The question being again put, the witness replied:

"I hold his note for the price of the horse, which I consider as good as the pay; for I am well acquainted with Joseph Smith, Jun., and know him to be an honest man; and if he wishes, I am ready to let him have another horse on the same terms."

Mr. Jonathan Thompson was next called up and examined:

"Has not the prisoner, Joseph Smith Jun., had a yoke of oxen of you?"

"Yes."

"Did he not obtain them of you by telling you that he had a revelation to the effect that he was to have them?"

"No, he did not mention a word of the kind concerning the oxen; he purchased them the same as any other man would."

Daughters of Mr. Stoal as Witnesses.

After a few more such attempts, the court was detained for a time, in order that two young women, daughters of Mr. Stoal, with whom I had at times kept company, might be sent for, in order, if possible, to elicit something from them which might be made a pretext against me. The young ladies arrived, and were severally examined touching my character and conduct in general, but particularly as to my behavior towards them, both in public and private; when they both bore such testimony in my favor as left my enemies without a pretext on their account. Several other attempts were made to prove something against me, and even circumstances which were alleged to have taken place in Broome county, were brought forward, but these my lawyers would not admit of as testimony against me; in consequence of which my persecutors managed to detain the court until they had succeeded in obtaining a warrant from Broome county, which warrant they served upon me at the very moment that I was acquitted by this court.

The Acquittal.

The constable who served this second warrant upon me had no sooner arrested me than he began to abuse and insult me; and so unfeeling was he with me, that although I had been kept all the day in court without anything to eat since the morning, yet he hurried me off to Broome county, a distance of about fifteen miles, before he allowed me any kind of food whatever. He took me to a tavern, and gathered in a number of men, who used every means to abuse, ridicule and insult me. They spit upon me, pointed their fingers at me, saying, "Prophesy, prophesy!" and thus did they imitate those who crucified the Savior of mankind, not knowing what they did.

The Prophet's Second Arrest.

We were at this time not far distant from my own house. I wished to be allowed the privilege of spending the night with my wife at home, offering any wished for security for my appearance; but this was denied be. I applied for something to eat. The constable ordered me some crusts of bread and water, which was the only food I that night received. At length we retired to bed. The constable made me lie next the wall. He then laid himself down by me and put his arm around me, and upon my moving in the least, would clench me fast, fearing that I intended to escape from him; and in this very disagreeable manner did we pass the night.

Unnecessary Severity.

Next day I was brought before the magistrate's court

at Colesville, Broome county, and put upon my trial. My former faithful friends and lawyers were again at my side; my former persecutors were arrayed against me. Many witnesses were again called forward and examined, some of whom swore to the most palpable falsehoods, and like the false witnesses which had appeared against me the day previous, they contradicted themselves so plainly that the court would not admit their testimony. Others were called, who showed by their zeal that they were willing enough to prove something against me, but all they could do was to tell something which somebody else had told them.

The Second Trial.

In this frivolous and vexatious manner did they proceed for a considerable time, when, finally, Newel Knight was called up and examined by Lawyer Seymour, who had been especially sent for on this occasion. One Lawyer Burch, also, was on the side of the prosecution; but Mr. Seymour seemed to be a more zealous Presbyterian, and appeared very anxious and determined that the people should not be deluded by any one professing the power of godliness, and not "denying the power thereof."

Newel Knight vs. Lawyer Seymour.

Mr. Knight was sworn, and Mr. Seymour interrogated him as follows:

"Did the prisoner, Joseph Smith, Jun., cast the devil out of you?"

"No, sir."

"Why, have not you had the devil cast out of you?"

"Yes, sir."

"And had not Joe Smith some hand in its being done?"

"Yes, sir."

"And did not he cast him out of you?"

"No, sir; it was done by the power of God, and Joseph Smith was the instrument in the hands of God, on the occasion. He commanded him to come out of me in the name of Jesus Christ."

"And are you sure that it was the devil?"

"Yes, sir."

"Did you see him after he was cast out of you?"

"Yes, sir! I saw him."

"Pray, what did he look like?"

[Here one of my lawyers informed the witness that he need not answer the question.] The witness replied:

"I believe I need not answer your last question, but I will do it, provided I be allowed to ask you one question first, and you answer me, viz., Do you, Mr. Seymour, understand the things of the spirit?"

"No," answered Mr. Seymour, "I do not pretend to such big things."

"Well, then," replied Knight, "it would be of no use to tell you what the devil looked like, for it was a spiritual sight, and spiritually discerned; and of course you would not understand it were I to tell you of it."

The lawyer dropped his head, whilst the loud laugh of the audience proclaimed his discomfiture.

Plea for the State.

Mr. Seymour now addressed the court, and in a long and violent harangue endeavored to blacken my character and bring me in guilty of the charges which had been brought against me. Among other things, he brought up the story of my having been a money-digger; and in this manner proceeded, hoping evidently to influence the court and the people against me.

Plea for the Defendant.

Mr. Davidson and Mr. Reid followed on my behalf. They held forth in true colors the nature of the prosecution, the malignancy of intention, and the apparent disposition to persecute their client, rather than to afford him justice. They took up the different arguments which had been brought by the lawyers for the prosecution, and having shown their utter futility and misapplication, then proceeded to scrutinize the evidence which had been adduced, and each, in his turn, thanked God that he had been engaged in so good a cause as that of defending a man whose character stood so well the test of such a strict investigation. In fact, these men, although not regular lawyers, were upon this occasion able to put to silence their opponents, and convince the court that I was innocent. They spoke like men inspired of God, whilst those who were arrayed against me trembled under the sound of their voices, and quailed before them like criminals before a bar of justice.*

*In a speech made at a public gathering in Nauvoo, on the 17th of May, 1844, the above-mentioned Mr. Reid, who defended the Prophet in these early prosecutions before the courts of New York, very strongly corrobrates the statements of the Prophet's History with reference to those court trials and the Prophet's vindication in them. Mr. Reid never became a member of the Church, but was always the Prophet's staunch and true friend. His remarks on the occasion referred to were as follows:

The first acquaintance I had with Gen. Smith was about the year 1823. He came into my neighborhood, being then about eighteen years of age, and resided there two years; during which time I became intimately acquainted with him. I do know that his character was irreproachable; that he was well known for truth and uprightness; that he moved in the first circles of the community, and he was often spoken of as a young man of intelligence and good morals, and possessing a mind susceptible of the highest intellectual attainments.

I early discovered that his mind was constantly in search of truth, expressing an anxious desire to know the will of God concerning His children here below, often speaking of those things which professed Christians believe in. I have often observed to my best informed friends (those that were free from superstition and bigotry) that I thought Joseph was predestinated by his God from all eternity to be an instrument in the hands of the great Dispenser of all good, to do a great work; what it was I knew not. After living in that neighborhood about three years, enjoying the good feelings of his acquaintances, as a worthy youth, he told his particular friends that he had had a revelation from God to go to the west about eighty miles, to his father's, in which neighborhood he would find hid in the earth an old history written on golden plates, which would give great light and knowledge concerning the will of God towards His people in this generation; unfolding the destiny of all nations, kindreds and tongues; he said that he distinctly heard the voice of Him that spake. Joseph Knight, one of the fathers of your Church, a worthy man and my intimate friend, went with him. When I reflect upon our former friendship, Mr. Chairman, and upon the scenes that he (i. e. Joseph Knight) has passed through in consequence of mal-administration, mobocracy and cruelty, I feel to lift up my voice to high heaven and pray God to bless the aged veteran, and that his silver locks may go down to the grave in peace, like a shock of corn fully ripe. In a few days his friends returned with the glad news that Joseph had found the plates and had gone down to his father-in-law's for the purpose of translating them. I believe he remained there until he finished the translation. After the book was published, he came to live in the neighbordood of Father Knight's, about four miles from me, and began to preach the Gospel, and many were pricked in their hearts, believed and were baptized in the name of the Lord Jesus. He soon formed a church at Colesville, his meetings were numerously attended; the eyes of all people were upon him with astonishment. O, Mr. Chairman, the world was turned up side down at once, and the devil, always ready to assist and help along in all difficulties that arise among men, personified in some of the religionists, begun to prick up his ears and jump and kick and run about like Jim Crow, calling for rotten eggs to help in the wake; you would have thought, sir, that Gog and Magog were let loose on the young man. He

The majority of the assembled multitude had now begun to find that nothing could be sustained against me. Even the constable who arrested me, and treated me so badly, now came and apologized to me, and asked my forgiveness for his be-

Change in Sentiment.

called upon the world's people, (as they are called) but got no help; he then flew about in the sectarian churches like lightning, and they immediately came to his aid, and uniting their efforts, roared against him like the thunders of Mount Sinai. When those fiery bigots were let loose, they united in pouring the red hot vials of their wrath upon his head. The cry of "False prophet! false prophet!" was sounded from village to village, and every foul epithet that malice and wicked ingenuity could invent was heaped upon him. Yes, sir, the same spirit that influenced the Presbyterians of Massachusetts, about one hundred and fifty years ago, in their persecution of the Quakers, when they first began to preach their doctrines in that state, was fully manifested by those religious bigots who were afraid if they let them alone their doctrines would come to nought. * * * But, Mr. Chairman, I am wandering too far from the subject. I will return to the persecutions which followed General Smith, when his cheeks bloosomed with the beauty of youth, and his eyes sparked with innocence. Those bigots soon made up a false accusation against him and had him arraigned before Joseph Chamberlain, a justice of the peace, a man that was always ready to deal justice to all, and a man of great discernment of mind. The case came on about 10 o'clock a. m. I was called upon to defend the prisoner. The prosecutors employed the best counsel they could get, and ransacked the town of Bainbridge and county of Chenango for witnesses that would swear hard enough to convict the prisoner; but they entirely failed. *Yes, sir, let me say to you that not one blemish nor spot was found against his character, he came from that trial, notwithstanding the mighty efforts that were made to convict him of crime by his vigilant persecutors, with his character unstained by even the appearance of guilt.* The trial closed about 12 o'clock at night. After a few moments' deliberation, the court pronounced the words "not guilty," and the prisoner was discharged. But alas! the devil, not satisfied with his defeat, stirred up a man not unlike himself, who was more fit to dwell among the fields of hell than to belong to the human family, to go to Colesville and get another writ, and take him to Broome county for another trial. They were sure they could send that boy to hell, or Texas, they did not care which; and in half an hour after he was discharged by the court, he was arrested again, and on the way to Colesville for another trial. I was again called upon by his friends to defend him against his malignant persecutors, and clear him from the false charges they had preferred against him. I made every reasonable excuse I could, as I was nearly worn down through fatigue and want of sleep; as I had been engaged in law suits for two days, and nearly the whole of two nights. But I saw the persecution was great against him; and here let me say, Mr. Chairman, singular as it may seem, while Mr Knight was pleading with me to go, a peculiar impression or thought struck my mind, that I must go and defend him, for he was the Lord's anointed. I did not know what it meant, but thought I must go and clear the Lord's anointed. I said I would go, and started with as much faith as the Apostles had when they could remove mountains, accompanied by Father Knight, who was like the old patriarchs that followed the ark of God to the city of David. * * * * * The next morning about 10 o'clock the court was organized. The prisoner was to be tried by three justices of the peace, that his departure out of the county

havior towards me; and so far was he changed, that he informed me that the mob were determined, if the court acquitted me, that they would have me, and rail-ride me, and tar and feather me; and further, that he was willing to favor me and lead me out in safety by a private way.

The Prophet Acquitted.

The court found the charges against me not sustained; I was accordingly acquitted, to the great satisfaction of my friends and vexation of my enemies, who were still determined upon molesting me. But through the instrumentality of my new friend the constable, I was enabled to escape them and make my way in safety to my wife's sister's house, where I found my wife awaiting with much anxiety the issue of those ungodly proceedings, and in company with her I arrived next day in safety at my own house.

might be made sure. Neither talents nor money were wanting to insure them success. They employed the ablest lawyer in that county, and introduced twenty or thirty witnesses before dark, but proved nothing. They then sent out runners and ransacked the hills and vales, grog shops and ditches, and gathered together a company that looked as if they had come from hell and had been whipped by the soot boy thereof; which they brought forward to testify one after the other, but with no better success than before, although they wrung and twisted into every shape, in trying to tell something that would criminate the prisoner. Nothing was proven against him whatever. Having got through with the examination of their witnesses about 2 o'clock in the morning, the case was argued about two hours. There was not one particle of testimony against the prisoner. No, sir, he came out like the three children from the fiery furnace, without the smell of fire upon his garments. The court deliberated upon the case for half an hour with closed doors, and then we were called in. The court arraigned the prisoner and said: "Mr. Smith, we have had your case under consideration, examined the testimony and find nothing to condemn you, and therefore you are discharged." They then proceeded to reprimand him severely; not because anything derogatory to his character in any shape had been proven against him by the host of witnesses that had testified during the trial, but merely to please those fiends in human shape who were engaged in the unhallowed persecution of an innocent man, sheerly on account of his religious opinions.

After they had got through, I arose and said: "This court puts me in mind of a certain trial held before Felix of old, when the enemies of Paul arraigned him before the venerable judge for some alleged crime, and nothing was found in him worthy of death or of bonds. Yet, to please the Jews, who were his accusers, he was left bound contrary to law; and this court has served Mr. Smith in the same way, by their unlawful and uncalled for reprimand after his discharge, to please his accusers." We got him away that night from the midst of three hundred people without his receiving any injury; but I am well aware that we were assisted by some higher power than man; for to look back on the scene, I cannot tell how we succeeded in getting him away. I take no glory to myself; it was the Lord's work and marvelous in our eyes.—*Times and Seasons, vol. v. pp.* 549-552.

CHAPTER X.

FURTHER MOLESTATION AT COLESVILLE BY MOBS—THE REVELATION EMBODYING THE VISION OF MOSES.

AETER a few days I returned to Colesville, in company with Oliver Cowdery, for the purpose of confirming those whom we had been forced to leave for a time. We had scarcely arrived at Mr. Knight's, when the mob was seen collecting together to oppose us, and we considered it wisdom to leave for home, which we did, without even waiting for any refreshments. Our enemies pursued us, and it was oftentimes as much as we could do to elude them. However, we managed to get home, after having traveled all night, except a short time, during which we were forced to rest ourselves under a large tree by the wayside, sleeping and watching alternately.

Second Flight from Colesville.

Thus were we persecuted on account of our religious faith—in a country the Constitution of which guarantees to every man the indefeasible right to worship God according to the dictates of his own conscience—and by men, too, who were professors of religion, and who were not backward to maintain the right of religious liberty for themselves, though they could thus wantonly deny it to us. For instance, Cyrus McMaster, a Presbyterian of high standing in his church, was one of the chief instigators of these persecutions; and he at one time told me personally that he considered me guilty without judge or jury. The celebrated Dr. Boyington, also a Presbyterian, was another instigator of these deeds of outrage; whilst a young man named Benton, of the same religious faith, swore out the first warrant against me.

Reflections on Persecution.

I could mention many others also, but for brevity's sake, will make these suffice for the present.

The Srength which God Gave.

I will say, however, that amid all the trials and tribulations we had to wade through, the Lord, who well knew our infantile and delicate situation, vouchsafed for us a supply of strength, and granted us "line upon line of knowledge —here a little and there a little," of which the following was a precious morsel:

*Revelation to Joseph Smith, Jun., given June, 1830.**

1. *The words of God, which he spake unto Moses at a time when Moses was caught up into an exceedingly high mountain,*

2. *And he saw God face to face, and he talked with him, and the glory of God was upon Moses; therefore Moses could endure his presence.*

3. And God spake unto Moses, saying: Behold, I am the Lord God Almighty, and Endless is my name; for I am without beginning of days or end of years; and is not this endless?

4. And, behold, thou art my son; wherefore look, and I will show thee the workmanship of mine hands; but not all, for my works are without end, and also my words, for they never cease.

5. Wherefore, no man can behold all my works, except he behold all my glory; and no man can behold all my glory, and afterwards remain in the flesh on the earth.

6. And I have a work for thee, Moses, my son; and thou art in the similitude of mine Only Begotten; and mine Only Begotten is and shall be the Savior, for he is full of grace and truth; but there is no God beside me, and all things are present with me, for I know them all.

7. And now, behold, this one thing I show unto thee, Moses, my son; for thou art in the world, and now I show it unto thee.

8. And it came to pass that Moses looked, and beheld the world upon which he was created; and Moses beheld the world and the ends thereof, and all the children of men which are, and which were created; of the same he greatly marveled and wondered.

9. And the presence of God withdrew from Moses, that his glory was not upon Moses; and Moses was left unto himself. And as he was left unto himself, he fell unto the earth.

10. And it came to pass that it was for the space of many hours before Moses did again receive his natural strength like unto man: and he said unto himself: Now, for this cause I know that man is nothing, which thing I never had supposed.

* Pearl of Great Price.

11. But now mine own eyes have beheld God; but not my natural, but my spiritual eyes, for my natural eyes could not have beheld; for I should have withered and died in his presence; but his glory was upon me; and I beheld his face, for I was transfigured before him.

12. And it came to pass that when Moses had said these words, behold, Satan came tempting him, saying: Moses, son of man, worship me.

13. And it came to pass that Moses looked upon Satan and said: Who art thou? For behold, I am a son of God, in the similitude of his Only Begotten; and where is thy glory, that I should worship thee?

14. For behold, I could not look upon God, except his glory should come upon me, and I were strengthened before him. But I can look upon thee in the natural man. Is it not so, surely?

15. Blessed be the name of my God, for his Spirit hath not altogether withdrawn from me, or else where is thy glory, for it is darkness unto me? And I can judge between thee and God; for God said unto me: Worship God, for him only shalt thou serve.

16. Get thee hence, Satan; deceive me not; for God said unto me: Thou art after the similitude of mine Only Begotten.

17. And he also gave me commandments when he called unto me out of the burning bush, saying: Call upon God in the name of mine Only Begotten, and worship me.

18. And again Moses said: I will not cease to call upon God, I have other things to inquire of him: for his glory has been upon me, wherefore I can judge between him and thee. Depart hence, Satan.

19. And now, when Moses had said these words, Satan cried with a loud voice, and rent upon the earth, and commanded, saying: I am the Only Begotten, worship me.

20. And it came to pass that Moses began to fear exceedingly; and as he began to fear, he saw the bitterness of hell. Nevertheless, calling upon God, he received strength, and he commanded, saying: Depart from me, Satan, for this one God only will I worship, which is the God of glory.

21. And now Satan began to tremble, and the earth shook; and Moses received strength, and called upon God, saying: In the name of the Only Begotten, depart hence, Satan.

22. And it came to pass that Satan cried with a loud voice, with weeping and wailing and gnashing of teeth; and he departed hence, even from the presence of Moses, that he beheld him not.

23. And now of this thing Moses bore record; but because of wickedness it is not had among the children of men.

24. And it came to pass that when Satan had departed from the presence of Moses, that Moses lifted up his eyes unto heaven, being

filled with the Holy Ghost, which beareth record of the Father and the Son;

25. And calling upon the name of God, he beheld his glory again, for it was upon him; and he heard a voice, saying: Blessed art thou, Moses, for I, the Almighty, have chosen thee, and thou shalt be made stronger than many waters; for they shall obey thy command as if thou wert God.

26. And lo, I am with thee, even unto the end of thy days; for thou shalt deliver my people from bondage, even Israel my chosen.

27. And it came to pass, as the voice was still speaking, Moses cast his eyes and beheld the earth, yea, even all of it; and there was not a particle of it which he did not behold, discerning it by the Spirit of God.

28. And he beheld also the inhabitants thereof, and there was not a soul which he beheld not; and he discerned them by the Spirit of God; and their numbers were great, even numberless as the sand upon the sea shore.

29. And he beheld many lands; and each land was called earth, and there were inhabitants on the face thereof.

30. And it came to pass that Moses called upon God, saying: Tell me, I pray thee, why these things are so, and by what thou madest them?

31. And behold, the glory of the Lord was upon Moses, so that Moses stood in the presence of God, and talked with him face to face. And the Lord God said unto Moses: For mine own purpose have I made these things. Here is wisdom and it remaineth in me.

32. And by the word of my power, have I created them, which is mine Only Begotten Son, who is full of grace and truth.

33. And worlds without number have I created; and I also created them for mine own purpose; and by the Son I created them, which is mine Only Begotten.

34. And the first man of all men have I called Adam, which is many.

35. But only an account of this earth, and the inhabitants thereof, give I unto you. For behold, there are many worlds that have passed away by the word of my power. And there are many that now stand, and innumerable are they unto man; but all things are numbered unto me, for they are mine and I know them.

36. And it came to pass that Moses spake unto the Lord, saying: Be merciful unto thy servant, O God, and tell me concerning this earth, and the inhabitants thereof, and also the heavens, and then thy servant will be content.

37. And the Lord God spake unto Moses, saying: The heavens, they are many, and they cannot be numbered unto man, but they are numbered unto me, for they are mine.

38. And as one earth shall pass away, and the heavens thereof, even

so shall another come; and there is no end to my works, neither to my words.

39. For behold, this is my work and my glory—to bring to pass the immortality and eternal life of man.

40. And now, Moses, my son, I will speak unto thee concerning this earth upon which thou standest; and thou shalt write the things which I shall speak.

41. And in a day when the children of men shall esteem my words as naught and take many of them from the book which thou shalt write, behold, I will raise up another like unto thee; and they shall be had again among the children of men—among as many as shall believe.

42. These words were spoken unto Moses in the mount, the name of which shall not be known among the children of men. And now they are spoken unto you. Show them not unto any except them that believe. Even so. Amen.

Meantime, and notwithstanding all the rage of our enemies, we had much consolation, and many things occurred to strengthen our faith and cheer our hearts.

Encouragement From Inspired Dreams.

After our departure from Colesville, after the trial, the Church there were very anxious, as might be expected, concerning our again visiting them, during which time Sister Knight, wife of Newel Knight, had a dream, which enabled her to say that we would visit them that day, which really came to pass, for a few hours afterwards we arrived; and thus was our faith much strengthened concerning dreams and visions in the last days, foretold by the ancient Prophet Joel; and although we this time were forced to seek safety from our enemies by flight, yet did we feel confident that eventually we should come off victorious, if we only continued faithful to Him who had called us forth from darkness into the marvelous light of the everlasting Gospel of our Lord Jesus Christ.

Shortly after our return home, we received the following commandments

*Revelation to Joseph Smith, Jun., and Oliver Cowdery, given at Harmony, Pennsylvania, July, 1830.**

1. Behold thou wast called and chosen to write the Book of Mor-

*Doctrine and Covenants, sec. xxiv.

mon, and to my ministry; and I have lifted thee up out of thine afflictions, and have counseled thee, that thou hast been delivered from all thine enemies, and thou hast been delivered from the powers of Satan and from darkness!

2. Nevertheless, thou art not excusable in thy transgressions; nevertheless, go thy way and sin no more.

3. Magnify thine office; and after thou hast sowed thy fields and secured them, go speedily unto the church which is in Colesville, Fayette, and Manchester, and they shall support thee; and I will bless them both spiritually and temporally;

4. But if they receive thee not, I will send upon them a cursing instead of a blessing.

5. And thou shalt continue in calling upon God in my name, and writing the things which shall be given thee by the Comforter, and expounding all scriptures unto the church,

6. And it shall be given thee in the very moment what thou shalt speak and write, and they shall hear it, or I will send unto them a cursing instead of a blessing.

7. For thou shalt devote all thy service in Zion; and in this thou shalt have strength.

8. Be patient in afflictions, for thou shalt have many; but endure them, for, lo, I am with thee, even unto the end of thy days.

9. And in temporal labors thou shalt not have strength, for this is not thy calling. Attend to thy calling and thou shalt have wherewith to magnify thine office, and to expound all Scriptures, and continue in laying on of the hands and confirming the churches.

10. And thy brother Oliver shall continue in bearing my name before the world, and also to the church. And he shall not suppose that he can say enough in my cause; and lo, I am with him to the end.

11. In me he shall have glory, and not of himself, whether in weakness or in strength, whether in bonds or free;

12. And at all times, and in all places, he shall open his mouth and declare my gospel as with the voice of a trump, both day and night. And I will give unto him strength such as is not known among men.

13. Require not miracles, except I shall command you, except casting out devils, healing the sick, and against poisonous serpents, and against deadly poisons;

14. And these things ye shall not do, except it be required of you by them who desire it, that the scriptures might be fulfilled; for ye shall do according to that which is written.

15. And in whatsoever place ye shall enter, and they receive you not in my name, ye shall leave a cursing instead of a blessing, by casting off the dust of your feet against them as a testimony, and cleansing your feet by the wayside.

16. And it shall come to pass that whosoever shall lay their hands upon you by violence, ye shall command to be smitten in my name; and, behold, I will smite them according to your words, in mine own due time.

17. And whosoever shall go to law with thee shall be cursed by the law.

18. And thou shalt take no purse nor scrip, neither staves, neither two coats, for the church shall give unto thee in the very hour what thou needest for food and for raiment, and for shoes and for money, and for scrip.

19. For thou art called to prune my vineyard with a mighty pruning, yea, even for the last time; yea, and also all those whom thou hast ordained, and they shall do even according to this pattern. Amen.

*Revelation given at Harmony, Pennsylvania, July, 1830.**

1. Hearken unto the voice of the Lord your God, while I speak unto you, Emma Smith, my daughter; for verily I say unto you, all those who receive my gospel are sons and daughters in my kingdom.

2. A revelation I give unto you concerning my will; and if thou art faithful and walk in the paths of virtue before me, I will preserve thy life, and thou shalt receive an inheritance in Zion.

3. Behold, thy sins are forgiven thee, and thou art an elect lady, whom I have called.

4. Murmur not because of the things which thou hast not seen, for they are withheld from thee and from the world, which is wisdom in me in a time to come.

5. And the office of thy calling shall be for a comfort unto my servant, Joseph Smith, Jun., thy husband, in his afflictions, with consoling words, in the spirit of meekness.

6. And thou shalt go with him at the time of his going, and be unto him for a scribe, while there is no one to be a scribe for him, that I may send my servant, Oliver Cowdery, whithersoever I will.

7. And thou shalt be ordained under his hand to expound scriptures, and to exhort the church, according as it shall be given thee by my Spirit.

8. For he shall lay his hands upon thee, and thou shalt receive the Holy Ghost, and thy time shall be given to writing, and to learning much.

9. And thou needest not fear, for thy husband shall support thee in the church; for unto them is his calling, that all things might be revealed unto them, whatsoever I will, according to their faith.

10. And verily I say unto thee that thou shalt lay aside the things of this world, and seek for the things of a better.

*Doctrine and Covenants, sec. xxv.

11. And it shall be given thee, also, to make a selection of sacred hymns, as it shall be given thee, which is pleasing unto me, to be had in my church.

12. For my soul delighteth in the song of the heart; yea, the song of the righteous is a prayer unto me, and it shall be answered with a blessing upon their heads.

13. Wherefore, lift up thy heart and rejoice, and cleave unto the covenants which thou hast made.

14. Continue in the spirit of meekness, and beware of pride. Let thy soul delight in thy husband, and the glory which shall come upon him.

15. Keep my commandments continually, and a crown of righteousness thou shalt receive. And except thou do this, where I am you cannot come.

16. And verily, verily, I say unto you, that this is my voice unto all. Amen.

*Revelation to Joseph Smith, Jun., Oliver Cowdery, and John Whitmer, given at Harmony, Pennsylvania, July, 1830.**

1. Behold, I say unto you that you shall let your time be devoted to the studying of the scriptures, and to preaching, and to confirming the church at Colesville, and to performing your labors on the land, such as is required, until after you shall go to the west to hold the next conference; and then it shall be made known what you shall do.

2. And all things shall be done by common consent in the church, by much prayer and faith, for all things you shall receive by faith. Amen.

Compilation of Revelations.

Shortly after we had received the above revelations, Oliver Cowdery returned to Mr. Peter Whitmer's, Sen., and I began to arrange and copy the revelations, which we had received from time to time; in which I was assisted by John Whitmer, who now resided with me.

Cowdery's Error.

Whilst thus employed in the work appointed me by my Heavenly Father, I received a letter from Oliver Cowdery, the contents of which gave me both sorrow and uneasiness. Not having that letter now in my possession, I cannot of course give it here in full, but merely an extract of the most prominent parts, which I can yet, and expect long to, remember.

*Doctrine and Covenants, sec. xxvi.

He wrote to inform me that he had discovered an error in one of the commandments—Book of Doctrine and Covenants: "And truly manifest by their works that they have received of the Spirit of Christ unto a remission of their sins."*

The above quotation, he said, was erroneous, and added: "I command you in the name of God to erase those words, that no priestcraft be amongst us!"

I immediately wrote to him in reply, in which I asked him by what authority he took upon him to command me to alter or erase, to add to or diminish from, a revelation or commandment from Almighty God.

The Prophet's Correction of the Error.

A few days afterwards I visited him and Mr. Whitmer's family, when I found the family in general of his opinion concerning the words above quoted, and it was not without both labor and perseverance that I could prevail with any of them to reason calmly on the subject. However, Christian Whitmer at length became convinced that the sentence was reasonable, and according to Scripture; and finally, with his assistance, I succeeded in bringing, not only the Whitmer family, but also Oliver Cowdery to acknowledge that they had been in error, and that the sentence in dispute was in accordance with the rest of the commandment. And thus was this error rooted out, which having its rise in presumption and rash judgment, was the more particularly calculated (when once fairly understood) to teach each and all of us the necessity of humility and meekness before the Lord, that He might teach us of His ways, that we might walk in His paths, and live by every word that proceedeth forth from His mouth.

*Part of paragraph 37, sec. xx, Doctrine and Covenants.

CHAPTER XI.

FURTHER LIGHT RESPECTING THE SACRAMENT—THE PROPHET'S REMOVAL TO FAYETTE.

Instructions on the Sacrament.

EARLY in the month of August Newel Knight and his wife paid us a visit at my place in Harmony, Pennsylvania; and as neither his wife nor mine had been as yet confirmed, it was proposed that we should confirm them, and partake together of the Sacrament, before he and his wife should leave us. In order to prepare for this I set out to procure some wine for the occasion, but had gone only a short distance when I was met by a heavenly messenger, and received the following revelation, the first four paragraphs of which were written at this time, and the remainder in the September following:

*Revelation given at Harmony, Pennsylvania, August, 1830.**

1. Listen to the voice of Jesus Christ, your Lord, your God, and your Redeemer, whose word is quick and powerful.

2. For, behold, I say unto you, that it mattereth not what ye shall eat, or what ye shall drink, when ye partake of the sacrament, if it so be that ye do it with an eye single to my glory—remembering unto the Father my body which was laid down for you, and my blood which was shed for the remission of your sins.

3. Wherefore, a commandment I give unto you, that you shall not purchase wine, neither strong drink of your enemies;

4. Wherefore, you shall partake of none except it is made new among you; yea, in this my Father's kingdom which shall be built up on the earth.

* Doctrine and Covenants, section xxvii.

5. Behold, this is wisdom in me: wherefore, marvel not, for the hour cometh that I will drink of the fruit of the vine with you on the earth, and with Moroni, whom I have sent unto you to reveal the Book of Mormon, containing the fulness of my everlasting gospel, to whom I have committed the keys of the record of the stick of Ephraim;

6. And also with Elias, to whom I have committed the keys of bringing to pass the restoration of all things spoken by the mouth of all the holy prophets since the world began, concerning the last days;

7. And also John the son of Zacharias, which Zacharias he (Elias) visited and gave promise that he should have a son, and his name should be John, and he should be filled with the spirit of Elias;

8. Which John I have sent unto you, my servant, Joseph Smith, Jun., and Oliver Cowdery, to ordain you unto the first Priesthood which you have received, that you might be called and ordained even as Aaron;

9. And also Elijah, unto whom I have committed the keys of the power of turning the hearts of the fathers to the children, and the hearts of the children to the fathers, that the whole earth may not be smitten with a curse;

10. Anr also with Joseph and Jacob, and Isaac, and Abraham, your fathers, by whom the promises remain;

11. And also with Michael, or Adam, the father of all, the prince of all, the ancient of days;

12. And also with Peter, and James, and John, whom I have sent unto you, by whom I have ordained you and confirmed you to be apostles, and especial witnesses of my name, and bear the keys of your ministry and of the same things which I revealed unto them;

13. Unto whom I have committed the keys of my kingdom, and a dispensation of the gospel for the last times; and for the fulness of times, in the which I will gather together in one all things, both which are in heaven, and which are on earth;

14. And also with all those whom my Father hath given me out of the world.

15. Wherefore, lift up your heart and rejoice, and gird up your loins, and take upon you my whole armor, that ye may be able to withstand the evil day, having done all, that ye may be able to stand.

16. Stand, therefore, having your loins girt about with truth, having on the breastplate of righteousness, and your feet shod with the preparation of the gospel of peace, which I have sent mine angels to commit unto you;

17. Taking the shield of faith wherewith ye shall be able to quench all the fiery darts of the wicked;

18. And take the helmet of salvation, and the sword of my Spirit, which I will pour out upon you, and my word which I reveal unto

you, and be agreed as touching all things whatsoever ye ask of me, and be faithful until I come, and ye shall be caught up, that where I am ye shall be also. Amen.

A Confirmation Meeting.

In obedience to the above commandment, we prepared some wine of our own making, and held our meeting, consisting only of five, viz., Newel Knight and his wife, myself and my wife, and John Whitmer. We partook together of the Sacrament, after which we confirmed these two sisters into the Church, and spent the evening in a glorious manner. The Spirit of the Lord was poured out upon us, we praised the Lord God, and rejoiced exceedingly.

The Prophet's Father-in-law Embittered.

About this time a spirit of persecution began again to manifest itself against us in the neighborhood where I now resided, which was commenced by a man of the Methodist persuasion, who professed to be a minister of God. This man had learned that my father-in-law and his family had promised us protection, and were friendly, and inquiring into the work; and knowing that if he could get him turned against me, my friends in that place would be but few, he visited my father-in-law, and told him falsehoods concerning me of the most shameful nature, which turned the old gentleman and his family so much against us, that they would no longer promise us protection nor believe our doctrines.*

The Eyes of Enemies Blinded Through Faith.

Towards the latter end of August, in company with John and David Whitmer, and my brother Hyrum Smith, I visited the Church at Colesville, New York. Well knowing the determined hostility of our enemies in that quarter, and also knowing that it was our duty to visit the Church, we had called upon our Heavenly Father, in mighty

* Mr. Hale, the Prophet's father-in-law, retained the bitterness then engendered in his mind; and some years later—namely, in 1834—made an affidavit concerning the character of Joseph the Prophet, which has been very generally quoted in anti-"Mormon" works.

prayer, that He would grant us an opportunity of meeting with them, that he would blind the eyes of our enemies, so that they would not know us, and that we might on this occasion return unmolested. Our prayers were not in vain, for when within a little distance of Mr. Knight's place, we encountered a large company at work upon the public road, amongst whom were several of our most bitter enemies. They looked earnest-at us, but not knowing us, we passed on without interruption. That evening we assembled the Church, and confirmed them, partook of the Sacrament, and held a happy meeting, having much reason to rejoice in the God of our salvation, and sing hosannas to His holy name. Next morning we set out on our return home, and although our enemies had offered a reward of five dollars to any one who would give them information of our arrival, yet did we get out of the neighborhood, without the least annoyance, and arrived home in safety. Some few days afterwards, however, Newel Knight came to my place, and from him we learned that, very shortly after our departure, the mob came to know of our having been there, when they immediately collected together, and threatened the brethren, and very much annoyed them during all that day.

The Prophet Finds an Asylum in Fayette.

Meantime, Brother Knight had come with his wagon, prepared to move my family to Fayette, New York. Mr. Whitmer, having heard of the persecutions against us at Harmony, Pennsylvania, had invited us to go and live with him; and during the last week in August we arrived at Fayette, amidst the congratulations of our brethren and friends.

Spurious Revelations Through Hiram Page.

To our great grief, however, we soon found that Satan had been lying in wait to deceive, and seeking whom he might devour. Brother Hiram Page had in his possesson a certain stone, by which he had obtained certain "revelations" concerning the upbuilding of Zion, the order of the

Church, etc., all of which were entirely at variance with the order of God's house, as laid down in the New Testament, as well as in our late revelations. As a conference meeting had been appointed for the 26th* day of September, I thought it wisdom not to do much more than to converse with the brethren on the subject, until the conference should meet. Finding, however, that many, especially the Whitmer family and Oliver Cowdery, were believing much in the things set forth by this stone, we thought best to inquire of the Lord concerning so important a matter; and before conference convened, we received the following:

Revelation to Oliver Cowdery, given at Fayette, New York, September, 1830.†

1. Behold, I say unto thee, Oliver, that it shall be given unto thee. that thou shalt be heard by the church in all things whatsoever thou shalt teach them by the Comforter, concerning the revelations and commandments which I have given.

2. But, behold, verily, verily, I say unto thee, no one shall be appointed to receive commandments and revelations in this Church excepting my servant Joseph Smith, Jun., for he receiveth them even as Moses.

3. And thou shalt be obedient unto the things which I shall give

*In the manuscript of the Prophet Joseph's History this conference is said to have been appointed for the "first day of September;" but in the *Far West Record*, a manuscript record kept by the clerks of the High Council in Missouri—and to which reference has before been made—are the minutes of the 9th of June conference (1830), which state that that conference adjourned to meet again on the 26th of September. The record also contains the minutes of the above conference bearing the date of September 26th. In addition to these reasons for changing the date in the text is the fact that immediately, or at least very soon after the close of the conference, a revelation was sought and obtained concerning the mission to the Lamanites, to which, even previous to the conference, Oliver Cowdery had been appointed (Doctrine and Covenants, xxviii: 8-10). The said revelation bears the date of "October, 1830." (Doctrine and Covenants, sec. xxxii), which would scarcely be the case if the conference had been held on the first, rather than near the close of September, as there is every reason to believe from the record that this revelation was received immediately after the conference closed. Moreover, the 26th of September, 1830, came on Sunday; whereas the first of September came on Wednesday, and as the conference lasted but three days, the brethren would scarcely arrange such a gathering without appointing it for such days as would include a Sunday.

† Doctrine and Covenants, sec. xxviii.

unto him, even as Aaron, to declare faithfully the commandments and the revelations, with power and authority unto the Church.

4. And if thou art led at any time by the comforter to speak or teach or at all times by the way of commandment unto the Church, thou mayest do it.

5. But thou shalt not write by way of commandment, but by wisdom;

6. And thou shalt not command him who is at thy head, and at the head of the church;

7. For I have given him the keys of the mysteries, and the revelations which are sealed, until I shall appoint unto them another in his stead.

8. And now, behold, I say unto you that you shall go unto the Lamanites and preach my gospel unto them; and inasmuch as they receive thy teachings, thou shalt cause my church to be established among them; and thou shalt have revelations, but write them not by way of commandment.

9. And now, behold, I say unto you that it is not revealed, and no man knoweth where the city of Zion shall be built, but it shall be given hereafter. Beholr, I say unto you that it shall be on the borders by the Lamanites.

10. Thou shalt not leave this place until after the conference; and my servant Joseph shall be appointed to preside over the conference by the voice of it, and what he saith to thee thou shalt tell.

11. And again, thou shalt take thy brother, Hiram Page, between him and thee alone, and tell him that those things which he hath written from that stone are not of me, and that Satan deceiveth him;

12. For, behold, these things have not been appointed unto him, neither shall anything be appointed unto any of this church contrary to the church covenants.

13. For all things must be done in order, and by common consent in the church, by the prayer of faith.

14. And thou shalt assist to settle all these things, according to the covenants of the church, before thou shalt take thy journey among the Lamanites.

15. And it shall be given thee from the time thou shalt go, until the time thou shalt return, what thou shalt do.

16. And thou must open thy mouth at all times, declaring my gospel with the sound of rejoicing. Amen.

*Revelation, given in the presence of Six Elders, in Fayette, New York, September, 1830.**

1. Listen to the voice of Jesus Christ, your Redeemer, the Great I AM, whose arm of mercy hath atoned for your sins;

* Doctrine and Covenants, sec. xxix.

2. Who will gather his people even as a hen gathereth her chickens under her wings, even as many as will hearken to my voice and humble themselves before me, and call upon me in mighty prayer.

3. Behold, verily, verily, I say unto you, that at this time your sins are forgiven you, therefore ye receive these things; but remember to sin no more, lest perils shall come upon you.

4. Verily, I say unto you that ye are chosen out of the world to declare my gospel with the sound of rejoicing, as with the voice of a trump.

5. Lift up your hearts and be glad, for I am in your midst, and am your advocate with the Father; and it is his good will to give you the kingdom.

6. And, as it is written—Whatsoever ye shall ask in faith, being united in prayer according to my command, ye shall receive.

7. And ye are called to bring to pass the gathering of mine elect; for mine elect hear my voice and harden not their hearts;

8. Wherefore the decree hath gone forth from the Father that they shall be gathered in unto one place upon the face of this land, to prepare their hearts and be prepared in all things against the day when tribulation and desolation are sent forth upon the wicked.

9. For the hour is nigh and the day soon at hand when the earth is ripe; and all the proud and they that do wickedly shall be as stubble; and I will burn them up, saith the Lord of Hosts, that wickedness shall not be upon the earth;

10. For the hour is nigh, and that which was spoken by mine apostles must be fulfilled; for as they spoke, so shall it come to pass;

11. For I will reveal myself from heaven with power and great glory, with all the hosts thereof, and dwell in righteousness with men on earth a thousand years, and the wicked shall not stand.

12. And again, verily, verily, I say unto you, and it hath gone forth in a firm decree, by the will of the Father, that mine apostles, the Twelve which were with me in my ministry at Jerusalem, shall stand at my right hand at the day of my coming in a pillar of fire, being clothed with robes of righteousness, with crowns upon their heads, in glory even as I am, to judge the whole house of Israel, even as many as have loved me and kept my commandments, and none else.

13. For a trump shall sound both long and loud, even as upon Mount Sinai, and all the earth shall quake, and they shall come forth—yea, even the dead which died in me, to receive a crown of righteousness, and to be clothed upon, even as I am, to be with me, that we may be one.

14. But, behold, I say unto you that before this great day shall come the sun shall be darkened, and the moon shall be turned into blood, and the stars shall fall from heaven, and there shall be greater signs in heaven above, and in the earth beneath;

15. And there shall be weeping and wailing among the hosts of men;

16. And there shall be a great hailstorm sent forth to destroy the crops of the earth.

17. And it shall come to pass because of the wickedness of the world, that I will take vengeance upon the wicked, for they will not repent; for the cup of mine indignation is full; for behold, my blood shall not cleanse them if they hear me not.

18. Wherefore, I the Lord God will send forth flies upon the face of the earth, which shall take hold of the inhabitants thereof, and shall eat their flesh, and shall cause maggots to come in upon them;

19. And their tongues shall be staid that they shall not utter against me; and their flesh shall fall from off their bones, and their eyes from their sockets;

20. And it shall come to pass that the beasts of the forest and the fowls of the air shall devour them up.

21. And the great and abominable church, which is the whore of all the earth, shall be cast down by devouring fire, according as it is spoken by the mouth of Ezekiel the prophet, who spoke of these things, which have not come to pass but surely must, as I live, for abominations shall not reign.

22. And again, verily, verily, I say unto you that when the thousand years are ended, and men again begin to deny their God, then will I spare the earth but for a little season;

23. And the end shall come, and the heaven and the earth shall be consumed and pass away, and there shall be a new heaven and a new earth,

24. For all old things shall pass away, and all things shall become new, even the heaven and the earth, and all the fulness thereof, both men and beasts, the fowls of the air, and the fishes of the sea;

25. And not one hair, neither mote, shall be lost, for it is the workmanship of mine hand.

26. But, behold, verily I say unto you, before the earth shall pass away, Michael, mine archangel, shall sound his trump, and then shall all the dead awake, for their graves shall be opened, and they shall come forth—yea, even all.

27. And the righteous shall be gathered on my right hand unto eternal life; and the wicked on my left hand will I be ashamed to own before the Father;

28. Wherefore I will say unto them—Depart from me, ye cursed, into everlasting fire, prepared for the devil and his angels.

29. And now, behold, I say unto you, never at any time have I declared from mine own mouth that they should return, for where I am they cannot come, for they have no power.

30. But remember that all my judgments are not given unto men: and as the words have gone forth out of my mouth, even so shall they be fulfilled, that the first shall be last, and that the last shall be first in all things whatsoever I have created by the word of my power, which is the power of my spirit.

31. For by the power of my spirit created I them; yea, all things both spiritual and temporal—

32. Firstly spiritual, secondly temporal, which is the beginning of my work; and again, first temporal, and secondly spiritual, which is the last of my work—

33. Speaking unto you that you may naturally understand; but unto myself my works have no end, neither beginning; but it is given unto you that ye may understand, because ye have asked it of me and are agreed.

34. Wherefore, verily I say unto you that all things unto me are spiritual, and not at any time have I given unto you a law which was temporal; neither any man, nor the children of men; neither Adam, your father, whom I created.

35. Behold, I gave unto him that he should be an agent unto himself; and I gave unto him commandment, but no temporal commandment gave I unto him, for my commandments are spiritual; they are not natural nor temporal, neither carnal nor sensual.

36. And it came to pass that Adam, being tempted of the devil —for, behold, the devil was before Adam, for he rebelled against me, saying, Give me thine honor, which is my power; and also a third part of the hosts of heaven turned he away from me because of their agency;

37. And they were thrust down, and thus came the devil and his angels;

38. And, behold, there is a place prepared for them from the beginning, which place is hell.

39. And it must needs be that the devil should tempt the children of men, or they could not be agents unto themselves; for if they never should have bitter they could not know the sweet—

40. Wherefore, it came to pass that the devil tempted Adam, and he partook of the forbidden fruit and transgressed the commandment, wherein he became subject to the will of the devil, because he yielded unto temptation.

41. Wherefore, I, the Lord God, caused that he should be cast out from the Garden of Eden, from my presence, because of his transgression, wherein he became spiritually dead, which is the first death, even that same death which is the last death, which is spiritual, which shall be pronounced upon the wicked when I shall say: Depart, ye cursed.

42. But, behold, I say unto you that I, the Lord God, gave unto

Adam and unto his seed that they should not die as to the temporal death, until I, the Lord God, should send forth angels to declare unto them repentance and redemption, through faith on the name of mine Only Begotten Son.

43. And thus did I, the Lord God, appoint unto man the days of his probation—that by his natural death he might be raised in immortality unto eternal life, even as many as would believe;

44. And they that believe not unto eternal damnation; for they cannot be redeemed from their spiritual fall, because they repent not;

45. For they love darkness rather than light, and their deeds are evil, and they receive their wages of whom they list to obey.

46. But, behold, I say unto you, that little children are redeemed from the foundation of the world through mine Only Begotten:

47. Wherefore, they cannot sin, for power is not given unto Satan to tempt little children, until they begin to become accountable before me;

48. For it is given unto them even as I will, according to mine own pleasure, that great things may be required at the hand of their fathers.

49. And, again, I say unto you, that whoso having knowledge, have I not commanded to repent?

50. And he that hath no understanding, it remaineth in me to do according as it is written. And now I declare no more unto you at this time. Amen.

The Conference of September 26th.

At length our conference assembled. The subject of the stone previously mentioned was discussed, and after considerable investigation, Brother Page, as well as the whole Church who were present, renounced the said stone, and all things connected therewith, much to our mutual satisfaction and happiness. We now partook of the Sacrament, confirmed and ordained many, and attended to a great variety of Church business on the first and the two following days of the conference, during which time we had much of the power of God manifested amongst us; the Holy Ghost came upon us, and filled us with joy unspeakable; and peace, and faith, and hope, and charity abounded in our midst.

Before we separated we received the following:

*Revelation to David Whitmer, Peter Whitmer, Jun., and John Whitmer, given September, 1830.**

1. Behold, I say unto you, David, that you have feared man and have not relied on me for strength as you ought.

2. But your mind has been on the things of the earth more than on the things of me, your Maker, and the ministry whereunto you have been called; and you have not given heed unto my Spirit, and to those who were set over you, but have been persuaded by those whom I have not commanded.

3. Wherefore, you are left to inquire for yourself at my hand, and ponder upon the things which you have received.

4. And your home shall be at your father's house until I give unto you further commandments. And you shall attend to the ministry in the church, and before the world, and in the regions round about. Amen.

5. Behold, I say unto you, Peter, that you shall take your journey with your brother Oliver; for the time has come that it is expedient in me that you shall open your mouth to declare my gospel; therefore, fear not, but give heed unto the words and advice of your brother, which he shall give you.

6. And be you afflicted in all his afflictions, ever lifting up your heart unto me in prayer and faith, for his and your deliverance; for I have given unto him power to build up my church among the Lamanites;

7. And none have I appointed to be his counselor over him in the church concerning church matters, except it is his brother, Joseph Smith, Jun.

8. Wherefore, give heed unto these things and be diligent in keeping my commandments, and you shall be blessed unto eternal life. Amen.

9. Behold, I say unto you, my servant John, that thou shalt commence from this time forth to proclaim my gospel, as with the voice of a trump.

10. And your labor shall be at your brother Philip Burroughs', and in that region round about, yea, wherever you can be heard, until I command you to go from hence.

11. And your whole labor shall be in Zion, with all your soul, from henceforth; yea, you shall ever open your mouth in my cause, not fearing what man can do, for I am with you. Amen.

Revelation to Thomas B. Marsh, Given September, 1830.†

1. Thomas, my son, blessed are you because of your faith in my work.

2. Behold, you have had many afflictions because of your family;

* Doctrine and Covenants, sec. xxx.

† Doctrine and Covenants, sec. xxxi.

nevertheless, I will bless you and your family, yea, your little ones; and the day cometh that they will believe and know the truth and be one with you in my church.

3. Lift up your heart and rejoice, for the hour of your mission is come; and your tongue shall be loosed, and you shall declare glad tidings of great joy unto this generation.

4. You shall declare the things which have been revealed to my servant, Joseph Smith, Jun. You shall begin to preach from this time forth, yea, to reap in the field which is white already to be burned.

5. Therefore, thrust in your sickle with all your soul, and your sins are forgiven you, and you shall be laden with sheaves upon your back, for the laborer is worthy of his hire. Wherefore, your family shall live.

6. Behold, verily I say unto you, go from them only for a little time, and declare my word. and I will prepare a place for them.

7. Yea, I will open the hearts of the people, and they will receive you. And I will establish a church by your hand;

8. And you shall strengthen them and prepare them against the time when they shall be gathered.

9. Be patient in afflictions, revile not against those that revile. Govern your house in meekness, and be steadfast.

10. Behold, I say unto you that you shall be a physician unto the church, but not unto the world, for they will not receive you.

11. Go your way withersoever I will, and it shall be given you by the Comforter what you shall do and whither you shall go.

12. Pray always, lest you enter into temptation and lose your reward.

13. Be faithful unto the end, and lo, I am with you. These words are not of man nor of men, but of me, even Jesus Christ, your Redeemer, by the will of the Father. Amen.*

*Thomas Baldwin Marsh, to whom the foregoing revelation was given through the Prophet Joseph, was born in Massachusetts, November 1, 1799, and after his marriage to Elizabeth Godkin in 1820, he went into the grocery business in New York, afterwards engaging in a type foundry in Boston. Here he joined the Methodist church, but on comparing its principles with the Scripture, and failing to make them correspond, he withdrew from all sects, but expected and indeed predicted the rise of a new church which should have the truth in its purity. He was moved by the Spirit to make a journey west, during which he heard of the Book of Mormon. He met Martin Harris at the office where it was being printed, and secured proof sheets of the first sixteen pages. He later met Oliver Cowdery, and remained with him two days, receiving from him full information as to the coming forth of the Book of Mormon. Returning to his home near Boston, he kept up a correspondence with the Prophet and Oliver for about a year; and upon learning of the organization of the Church, he moved to Palmyra in September, 1830, and was baptized by David Whitmer, and a few days later was ordained an Elder by Oliver Cowdery.

During this conference, which continued three days, the utmost harmony prevailed, and all things were settled satisfactorily to all present, and a desire was manifested by all the Saints to go forward and labor with all their powers to spread the great and glorious principles of truth, which had been revealed by our Heavenly Father. A number were baptized during the conference, and the word of the Lord spread and prevailed.

Satisfactory Results of the Conference.

At this time a great desire was manifested by several of the Elders respecting the remnants of the house of Joseph, the Lamanites, residing in the west—knowing* that the purposes of God were great respecting that people, and hoping that the time had come when the promises of the Almighty in regard to them were about to be accomplished, and that they would receive the Gospel, and enjoy its blessings. The desire being so great, it was agreed that we should inquire of the Lord respecting the propriety of sending some of the Elders† among them, which we accordingly did, and received the following:

Mission to the Lamanites.

Revelation to Parley P. Pratt and Ziba Peterson, given October, 1830‡

1. And now concerning my servant Parley P. Pratt,§ behold, I say

*Of course this knowledge arose from what the brethren had learned from the Book of Mormon of the promises of God to the Lamanites.

†The consideration of the "propriety" of sending Elders among the Lamanites here referred to was doubtless restricted to the propriety of increasing the number of Elders to go among them; for before the conference convened the propriety of sending Elders to the Lamanites had been settled by the word of the Lord. In a revelation received before the conference of September 26th, Oliver Cowdery was appointed to go on a mission to the Lamanites, though instructed not to leave Fayette until after the conference. (See p. 111; also Doctrine and Covenants, sec. xxviii: 8-10.) And before the conference adjourned another revelation was received in which Peter Whitmer, Jun., was appointed to accompany Oliver Cowdery on his mission. (See p. 116; and Doctrine and Covenants, sec. xxx: 5-6. Hence these inquiries after the conference concerning the "propriety" of sending Elders among the Lamanites, I repeat, must have had reference merely to the propriety of increasing the number that should go. It will be observed also that the revelation which follows in the text merely appoints Parley P. Pratt and Ziba Peterson to accompany Elders Cowdery and Whitmer.

‡Doctrine and Covenants, sec. xxxii.

§Parley Parker Pratt was born on the 12th day of April, 1807, in Burlington,

unto him that as I live I will that he shall declare my gospel and learn of me, and be meek and lowly at heart.

2. And that which I have appointed unto him is that he shall go with my servants Oliver Cowdery and Peter Whitmer, Jun., into the wilderness among the Lamanites.

3. And Ziba Peterson also shall go with them; and I myself will go with them and be in their midst; and I am their advocate with the Father, and nothing shall prevail against them.

Otsego county, state of New York. He was the third son of Jared and Charity Pratt. Jared was the son of Obediah and Jemima Pratt; Obediah was the son of Christopher and Sarah Pratt; Christopher was the son of William and Hannah Pratt; William was the son of Joseph Pratt; Joseph was the son of Lieutenant William and Elizabeth Pratt, who were found among the first settlers of Hartford, Connecticut, in the year 1639.

This William Pratt was a member of the legislature for some twenty-five or thirty sessions; and the general court gave him one hundred acres of land in Saybrook, Connecticut, for services performed as lieutenant in the Pequot war; he was one of the judges of the first court in New London county. Parley P. Pratt is a lineal descendant, of the seventh generation, from that distinguished pilgrim and humble pioneer to the new world.

Parley P. Pratt was reared to hard work on a farm, and though his opportunities for acquiring an education were extremely limited, he was brought up in the strictest school of morals. Even in early youth he gave evidence of a profoundly religious nature, and while yet in his teens became identified with the Baptist church. In 1826 he left New York state and settled some thirty miles west of the town of Cleveland, in the state of Ohio, and laid the foundation of a wilderness home. The next year, 1827, he returned to Canaan, Columbia county, New York,—the county where much of his boyhood was spent, the home, too, of his parents—and there married Thankful Halsey, on the 9th of September, 1827. The same month the newly married couple returned to the wilderness home west of Cleveland. About eighteen months later Sidney Rigdon, who was connected with Alexander Campbell, Walter Scott and others in that aggressive reform movement among the Christian sects, which resulted in the founding of the sect of the "Disciples" or "Campbellites," came into Mr. Pratt's neighborhood preaching the doctrines of faith, repentance and baptism. As his doctrine more nearly conformed to the scriptures than any other Mr. Pratt had heard, he accepted Sydney Rigdon's teachings, joined the "Disciples," and became a minister in that church He determined to take up the ministry as his life's labor, sold his possessions and started first of all to call upon his relatives in New York. En route, however, he was moved upon by the spirit to stop off at Newark, in New York, while his wife continued her journey to her father's home. At Newark, Mr. Pratt first heard of and saw the Book of Mormon, and, without delay, hastened to Palmyra to investigate the story of its coming forth. At the home of the Smiths, near Manchester, he met with Hyrum, brother of the Prophet, and from him learned the particulars of the work. In company with Hyrum Smith he went to Fayette, where he met with Oliver Cowdery; and about the first of September he was baptized by him in Seneca Lake, and straightway was ordained an Elder of the Church. After these events he continued his journey to the home of his kindred in Columbia county, New York, where he baptized his brother Orson, then a youth of nineten yars. He returned to Fayette in time to attend the conference, where he met the Prophet Joseph, and received the appointment to the Lamanite mission as related in the text.

4. And they shall give heed to that which is written, and pretend to no other revelation, and they shall pray always that I may unfold the same to their understanding.

5. And they shall give heed unto these words and trifle not, and I will bless them. Amen.

Departure of the Lamanite Mission.

Immediately on receiving this revelation, preparations were made for the journey of the brethren therein designated, to the borders of the Lamanites, and a copy of the revelation was given them. They bade adieu to their brethren and friends, and commenced their journey, preaching by the way, and leaving a sealing testimony behind them, lifting up their voice like a trump in the different villages through which they passed.* They continued their journey until they came to Kirtland, Ohio, where they tarried some time, there being quite a number in that place and vicinity who believed their testimony, and came forward and obeyed the Gospel. Among the number was Mr. Sidney Rigdon,† and a large portion of the church over which he presided.

Arrival at Kirtland.

*After traveling for some days the Lamanite mission called at some Indian encampments near the city of Buffalo, where they spent part of a day instructing them in the knowledge of their forefathers. These Indians were of the Catteraugus tribe, and kindly received the brethren, who left with certain of their number who could read English, two copies of the Book of Mormon, and then continued their journey westward. (*Autobiography of Parley P. Pratt*, pp. 49, 61.)

†Sidney Rigdon was born in Saint Clair township, Allegheny county, state of Pennsylvania, on the 19th of February, A. D. 1793, and was the youngest son of William and Nancy Rigdon. William Rigdon, his father, a native of Hartford county, state of Maryland, was born A. D. 1743, and died Moy 26th, A. D. 1810. William Rigdon was the son of Thomas Baker and Ann Lucy Rigdon. Thomas Baker Rigdon was a native of the state of Maryland, and was the son of Thomas Baker Rigdon, who came from Great Britain. Ann Lucy Rigdon, grandmother of Sidney Rigdon, was a native of Ireland, and emigrated to the city of Boston, Massachusetts, and was there married to Thomas Baker Rigdon. Nancy Rigdon's mother was a native of Freehold, Monmouth county, New Jersey; she was born March 16th, 1759, and died October 3rd, 1839, and was the eldest daughter of Byrant Gallacher, who was a native of Ireland. Elizabeth Gallaher, mother to the aforesaid Nancy Rigdon, was the second wife of the said Byrant Gallaher, and her maiden name was Reed. She was a native of Monmouth county, New Jersey. Her parents were natives of Scotland.

The early days of Sidney Rigdon's life were uneventful. His youth and the early years of his manhood were spent at his father's farm in St. Clair township, Allegheny county, Pennsylvania. When Sidney was seventeen years old his father died,

Previous to this, Elder Parley P. Pratt had been a preacher in the same church with Mr. Rigdon, and resided in the town of Amherst, Loraine county, in Ohio, and had been sent into the state of New York on a mission, where he be-

Previous Relations of Pratt and Rigdon.

but he continued on the same farm with his mother until he was twenty-six. In his twenty-fifth year he joined the "Regular Baptist" society or church. The pastor in charge was the Rev. David Phillips, a clergyman from Wales. In March, 1819, Mr. Rigdon left the farm and made his home with the Rev. Andrew Clark, of Pittsburg, also a Baptist minister. While residing with Mr. Clark he took out a license and began from that time his career as a minister. In May, 1819, he removed from from Pennsylvania to Trumbull county, Ohio. In July of the same year he made his home with Adamson Bentley, a minister of the same faith. While residing at Bentley's he met Phebe Brook, to whom he was married on the 12th day of June, 1820. She was a native of the state of New Jersey, Bridgetown, Cumberland county, but had previously removed to Trumbull county, Ohio.

Sidney Rigdon continued to preach throughout Trumbull county until November, 1821. Passing through Pittsburgh about that time, for the purpose of visiting his relatives at the old homestead in St. Clair township, Allegheny county, Pennsylvania, he was invited to preach to the Baptist society of Pittsburg, which he did the following and several succeeding Sundays. As the congregation had no regular pastor they invited him to take charge and become their regular minister; a "call" which he accepted and removed from Warren in Trumbull county, Ohio, to Pittsburg, in February, 1822. Meantime misgivings arose in his mind with reference to some of the doctrines of the church with which he was connceted, especially with reference to the fate of unbaptized infants. Finally, after serving his congregation about two years and six months, he gave up his charge in August, 1824, and retired from the ministry. After taking this step he joined his wife's brother, Richard Brook, in the tanning business. Together they started a small tannery in which Mr. Rigdon worked as a journeyman for some two years. Meantime he had formed the acquaintance of Mr.. Alexander Campbell, generally regarded as the founder of the sect of the "Disciples," or "Campbellites," and Mr. Walter Scott, a Scotchman by birth, but at this time a resident of Pittsburg and a dissenter from a Scandinavian church with which he had formerly been associated. These three gentlemen often met and discussed the subject of religion, the necessity for a universal reformation among the churches, the abandonment of their creeds, etc. The consultations they held led ultimately to the establishment of the church or sect of the "Disciples."

Mr. Rigdon left Pittsburg in 1826, and went to Bainbridge, Geaugo county, Ohio, where the people urged him tc speak to them. He did so, following in his teachings that line of doctrine which in his consultation with Messrs. Campbell and Scott they had considered were essential to Christian spiritual life, viz., faith in God, repentance of sins, baptism by immersion in water for the remission of sins, and holiness of life—a godly walk and conversation. Mr. Rigdon continued to labor in Bainbridge for about one year, when the people of Mentor, in the same county, but some thirty miles distant from Bainbridge, invited him to reside among them and preach. This he consented to do, and notwithstanding he at first met with some opposition, he prevailed against it and extended his labors into surrounding townships and counties until he had in a number of places a large following. Such were his circumstances and such his labor when the message of "Mormonism" found him —when Parley P. Pratt presented him with the Book of Mormon and its attendant message.

came acquainted with the circumstances of the coming forth of the Book of Mormon, and was introduced to Joseph Smith, Jun., and other members of the Church. The belief that there were many in the church with which he had formerly been united, who were honest seekers after truth, induced Elder Pratt, while on his journey to the west, to call upon his friends, and make known the great things which the Lord had brought to pass.

Presentation of the Book of Mormon to Sidney Rigdon.

The first house at which they called in the vicinity of Kirtland, was Mr. Rigdon's, and after the usual salutations, they presented him with the Book of Mormon, stating that it was a revelation from God. This being the first time he had ever heard of, or seen, the Book of Mormon,* he felt

*The circumstance of Oliver Cowdery, Parley P. Pratt and their associates presenting Sidney Rigdon with the Book of Mormon is thus related in the *Life of Sidney Rigdon*, by his son, John W. Rigdon (Ms. p. 18): "In the fall of 1830, Parley P. Pratt, Ziba Peterson, Oliver Cowdery, and Peter Whitmer called at the home of Sidney Rigdon, in the town of Mentor, Ohio, and Parley P. Pratt presented to him a bound volume of the Book of Mormon in the presence of his wife and his oldest child, Athalia Rigdon, now Athalia Robinson, who was then a girl ten years old, and now (1900) living in the town of Friendship, Allegheny county, state of New York; and who remembers the transaction as well as any incident of her life. Parley P. Pratt, at the time he handed the book to Sidney Rigdon, said it was a "Revelation from God."

Again referring to this circumstance near the close of the sketch of his father's life, John W. Rigdon relates how, in the fall of 1863, he visited the territory of Utah, where he spent the winter among the "Mormon" people. He was not favorably impressed with their religious life, and came to the conclusion that the Book of Mormon itself was a fraud. He determined in his own heart that if ever he returned home and found his father, Sidney Rigdon, alive, he would try and find out what he knew of the origin of the Book of Mormon. "Although," he adds, "he had never told but one story about it, and that was that Parley P. Pratt and Oliver Cowdery presented him with a bound volume of that book in the year 1830, while he (Sidney Rigdon) was preaching Campbellism at Mentor, Ohio." What John W. Rigdon claims to have seen in Utah, however, together with the fact that Sidney Rigdon had been charged with writing the Book of Mormon, made him suspicious; "and," he remarks, "I concluded I would make an investigation for my own satisfaction and find out if I could if he had all these years been deceiving his family and the world, by telling that which was not true, and I was in earnest about it. If Sidney Rigdon, my father, had thrown his life away by telling a falsehood and bringing sorrow and disgrace upon his family, I wanted to know it and was determined to find out the facts, no matter what the consequences might be. I reached home in the fall of 1865, found my father in good health and [he] was very much pleased to see me. As he had not heard anything from me for some time, he was afraid that I had been killed by the Indians. Shortly after I had arrived home,

very much surprised at the assertion, and replied that he had the Bible which he believed was a revelation from God, and with which he pretended to have some acquaintance; but with respect of the book they had

I went to my father's room; he was there and alone, now was the time for me to commence my inquiries in regard to the origin of the Book of Mormon, and as to the truth of the 'Mormon' religion. I told him what I had seen at Salt Lake City, and I said to him that what I had seen at Salt Lake had not impressed me very favorably toward the 'Mormon' Church, and as to the origin of the Book of Mormon I had some doubts. You have been charged with writing that book and giving it to Joseph Smith to introduce to the world. You have always told me one story; that you never saw the book until it was presented to you by Parley P. Pratt and Oliver Cowdery; and all you ever knew of the origin of that book was what they told you and what Joseph Smith and the witnesses who claimed to have seen the plates had told you. Is this true? If so, all right; if it is not, you owe it to me and your family to tell it. You are an old man and you will soon pass away, and I wish to know if Joseph Smith, in your intimacy with him for fourteen years, has not said something to you that led you to believe he obtained that book in some other way than what he had told you. Give me all you know about it, that I may know the truth. My father, after I had finished saying what I have repeated above, looked at me a moment, raised his hand above his head and slowly said, with tears glistening in his eyes: 'My son, I can swear before high heaven that what I have told you about the origin of that book is true. Your mother and sister, Mrs. Athalia Robinson, were present when that book was handed to me in Mentor, Ohio, and all I ever knew about the origin of that book was what Parley P. Pratt, Oliver Cowdery, Joseph Smith and the witnesses who claimed they saw the plates have told me, and in all my intimacy with Joseph Smith he never told me but the one story, and that was that he found it engraved upon gold plates in a hill near Palmyra, New York, and that an angel had appeared to him and directed him where to find it; and I have never, to you or to anyone else, told but the one story, and that I now repeat to you.' I believed him, and now believe he told me the truth. He also said to me after that that 'Mormonism' was true; that Joseph Smith was a Prophet, and this world would find it out some day. After my father's death, my mother, who survived him several years, was in the enjoyment of good health up to the time of her last sickness, she being eighty-six years old. A short time before her death I had a conversation with her about the origin of the Book of Mormon, and wanted to know what she remembered about its being presented to my father. She said to me in that conversation that what my father had told me about the book being presented to him was true, for she was present at the time and knew that was the first time he ever saw it, and that the stories told about my father writing the Book of Mormon were not true. This she said to me in her old age and when the shadows of the grave were gathering around her and I believe her." (*Life of Sidney Rigdon*, by his son, John W. Rigdon, Ms, pp. 188-195).

Our author also mentions in his sketch of his father's life, an affidavit given to him by his sister, Athalia Robinson, to the same effect as the statement of Sidney Rigdon and his wife, relative to the coming of Pratt and Cowdery to their home in Mentor, and presenting to her father a bound copy of the Book of Mormon. Athalia was ten years old at the time, and distinctly remembered throughout her life the circumstance. (Ibid, Ms. pp. 195-6).

presented him, he must say that he had considerable doubt. Upon this, they expressed a desire to investigate the subject, and argue the matter. But he replied, "No, young gentleman, you must not argue with me on the subject; but I will read your book, and see what claims it has upon my faith, and will endeavor to ascertain whether it be a revelation from God or not."

Public Ministry at Mentor.

After some further conversation they expressed a desire to lay the subject before the people, and requested the privilege of preaching in Mr. Rigdon's chapel, to which he readily consented. The appointment was accordingly published, and a large and respectable congregation assembled. Oliver Cowdery and Parley P. Pratt severally addressed the meeting. At the conclusion, Mr. Rigdon arose, and stated to the congregation that the information they had that evening received was of an extraordinary character, and certainly demanded their most serious consideration; and as the Apostle advised his brethren to "prove all things, and hold fast that which is good," so he would exhort his brethren to do likewise, and give the matter a careful investigation, and not turn against it without being fully convinced of its being an imposition, lest they should, possibly, resist the truth.

The Work Opened at Kirtland.

A few miles from Mr. Rigdon's home in Mentor, at the town of Kirtland, lived a number of the members of his church. They lived together and had all things common—from which circumstance has risen the idea that this was the case with the Church of Jesus Christ. To that place the Elders immediately repaired, and proclaimed the Gospel unto them, with considerable success; for their testimony was received by many of the people, and seventeen came forward in obedience to the Gospel.

While thus engaged, they visited Mr. Rigdon occasionally, and found him very earnestly reading the Book of Mormon,—praying to the Lord for direction, and meditating on the things he heard and read; and after a fortnight from the time the book was put into his hands, he was fully convinced of the truth of the work, by a revelation from Jesus Christ, which was made known to him in a remarkable manner, so that he could exclaim, "Flesh and blood hath not revealed it unto me, but my Father which is in heaven." Accordingly he and his wife were both baptized into the Church of Jesus Christ; and, together with those who had been previously admitted to baptism, made a little branch of the Church, in this section of Ohio, of about twenty members.

The Conversion of Sidney Rigdon.

This much accomplished, the brethren bound for the borders of the Lamanites, bade an affectionate farewell to the Saints in Kirtland and vicinity; and, after adding one of their new converts to their number—Dr. Frederick G. Williams*—they went on their way rejoicing.

*Frederick Granger Williams was born in Suffield, Hartford county, Connecticut, October 28th, 1787. He was therefore a man of forty-three years of age when the Gospel was brought to him at Kirtland by Oliver Cowdery and associates. He was a man of considerable influence in the community where he resided. He owned a farm near Kirtland, but at the time the Gospel found him he was practicing medicine, and was widely known as Dr. Williams. He abandoned the practice of his profession, however, for the work of the ministry, and accompanied the Lamanite mission to Missouri.

CHAPTER XII.

LOST BOOKS OF ANCIENT SCRIPTURE—COMMANDMENT TO THE CHURCH IN NEW YORK TO MOVE TO OHIO.

THE LORD, who is ever ready to instruct such as diligently seek in faith, gave the following revelation at Fayette, New York:

Readiness of the Lord to Impart Knowledge.

*Revelation to Ezra Thayre and Northrop Sweet, given October, 1830.**

1. Behold, I say unto you, my servants Ezra and Northrop, open ye your ears and hearken to the voice of the Lord your God, whose word is quick and powerful, sharper than a two-edged sword, to the dividing asunder of the joints and marrow, soul and spirit; and is a discerner of the thoughts and intents of the heart.

2. For verily, verily, I say unto you that ye are called to lift up your voices as with the sound of a trump, to declare my gospel unto a crooked and perverse generation.

3. For behold, the field is white already to harvest; and it is the eleventh hour, and the last time that I shall call laborers into my vineyard.

4. And my vineyard has become corrupted every whit; and there is none which doeth good save it be a few; and they err in many instances because of priestcrafts, all having corrupt minds.

5. And verily, verily, I say unto you, that this Church have I established and called forth out of the wilderness.

6. And even so will I gather mine elect from the four quarters of the earth, even as many as will believe in me, and hearken unto my voice.

7. Yea, verily, verily, I say unto you, that the field is white already to harvest; wherefore, thrust in your sickles, and reap with all your might, mind, and strength.

8. Open your mouths and they shall be filled, and you shall become even as Nephi of old, who journeyed from Jerusalem in the wilderness.

*Doctrine and Covenants, sec. xxxiii.

9. Yea, open your mouths and spare not, and you shall be laden with sheaves upon your backs, for lo, I am with you.

10. Yea, open your mouths and they shall be filled, saying: Repent, repent, and prepare ye the way of the Lord, and make his paths straight; for the kingdom of heaven is at hand;

11. Yea, repent and be baptized, every one of you, for a remission of your sins; yea, be baptized even by water, and then cometh the baptism of fire and of the Holy Ghost.

12. Behold, verily, verily, I say unto you, this is my gospel, and remember that they shall have faith in me, or they can in no wise be saved;

13. And upon this rock I will build my church; yea, upon this rock ye are built, and if ye continue, the gates of hell shall not prevail against you.

14. And ye shall remember the church articles and covenants to keep them.

15. And whoso having faith you shall confirm in my church, by the laying on of the hands, and I will bestow the gift of the Holy Ghost upon them.

16. And the Book of Mormon and the Holy Scriptures are given of me for your instruction; and the power of my Spirit quickeneth all things.

17. Wherefore, be faithful, praying always, having your lamps trimmed and burning, and oil with you, that you may be ready at the coming of the Bridegroom—

18. For behold, verily, verily, I say unto you, that I come quickly. Even so. Amen.

Orson Pratt Seeks to Know the Will of the Lord.

In the fore part of November, Orson Pratt,* a young man nineteen years of age, who had been baptized at the first preaching of his brother, Parley P. Pratt, September 19th (his birthday), about six weeks previous, in Canaan, New York,

*Orson Pratt was born September 19, 1811, in Hartford, Washington county, New York. His ancestors are enumerated in the biographical note of his brother, Parley P. Pratt, pp. 118, 119. The humble circumstances of his parents compelled him to seek employment where he could obtain it in various places, mainly at farming, during which time, however, he managed to get some schooling, paying especial attention to arithmetic, and gaining an acquaintance also with bookkeeping, grammar, geography and surveying. The early lessons of morality and religion taught at his father's home made deep impressions on his youthful mind, and led him in the autumn of 1829, particularly to seek the Lord. For this purpose he retired frequently to the lonely fields or the woods for prayer. This continued till September, 1830, when his brother Parley P. Pratt, an Elder of the Church of Jesus Christ of Latter-day Saints, came into the neighborhood where he resided, and as related in the text was converted at the first preaching of his brother Parley P. Pratt.

came to inquire of the Lord what his duty was, and received the following answer:

*A Revelation to Orson Pratt, given November, 1830.**

1. My son Orson, hearken and hear and behold what I, the Lord God, shall say unto you, even Jesus Christ your Redeemer;

2. The light and the life of the world, a light which shineth in darkness and the darkness comprehendeth it not;

3. Who so loved the world that he gave his own life, that as many as would believe might become the sons of God. Wherefore you are my son;

4. And blessed are you because you have believed;

5. And more blessed are you because you are called of me to preach my gospel—

6. To lift up your voice as with the sound of a trump, both long and loud, and cry repentance unto a crooked and perverse generation, preparing the way of the Lord for his second coming.

7. For behold, verily, verily, I say unto you, the time is soon at hand that I shall come in a cloud with power and great glory,

8. And it shall be a great day at the time of my coming, for all nations shall tremble.

9. But before that great day shall come, the sun shall be darkened, and the moon be turned into blood; and the stars shall refuse their shining, and some shall fall, and great destruction await the wicked.

10. Wherefore, lift up your voice and spare not, for the Lord God hath spoken; therefore prophesy, and it shall be given by the power of the Holy Ghost.

11. And if you are faithful, behold, I am with you until I come—

12. And verily, verily, I say unto you, I come quickly. I am your Lord and your Redeemer. Even so. Amen.

Sidney Rigdon and Edward Partridge Visit the Prophet.

In December Sidney Rigdon came to inquire of the Lord, and with him came Edward Partridge;† the latter was a pattern of piety, and one of the Lord's great men. Shortly after the arrival of these two brethren, thus spake the Lord:

*Doctrine and Covenants, section xxxiv.

†Edward Partridge was born in Pittsfield, Berkshire county, Massachusetts, on the 27th of August, 1793, of William and Jemima Partridge. His father's ancestor emigrated from Berwick, Scotland, during the seventeenth century, and settled at Hadley, Massachusetts, on Connecticut river. Nothing worthy of note transpired

*Revelation to Joseph Smith, Jun., and Sidney Rigdon, given at Fayette, New York, December, 1830.**

1. Listen to the voice of the Lord your God, even Alpha and Omega, the beginning and the end, whose course is one eternal round, the same today as yesterday, and forever.

2. I am Jesus Christ, the Son of God, who was crucified for the sins of the world, even as many as will believe on my name, that they may become the sons of God, even one in me as I am one in the Father, as the Father is one in me, that we may be one.

3. Behold, verily, verily, I say unto my servant Sidney, I have looked upon thee and thy works. I have heard thy prayers, and prepared thee for a greater work.

4. Thou art blessed, for thou shalt do great things. Behold thou wast sent forth, even as John, to prepare the way before me, and before Elijah which should come and thou knewest it not.

5. Thou didst baptize by water unto repentance, but they received not the Holy Ghost;

6. But now I give unto thee a commandment, that thou shalt baptize by water, and they shall receive the Holy Ghost by the laying on of the hands, even as the apostles of old.

7. And it shall come to pass that there shall be a great work in the land, even among the Gentiles, for their folly and their abominations shall be made manifest in the eyes of all people.

8. For I am God, and mine arm is not shortened; and I will show miracles, signs, and wonders, unto all those who believe on my name.

in his youth, with this exception, that he remembered, (though the precise time he could not recollect) that the Spirit of the Lord strove with him a number of times, insomuch that his heart was made tender, and he went and wept; and sometimes he went silently and poured the effusions of his soul to God in prayer.

At the age of sixteen he went to learn the hatter's trade, and continued as an apprentice for about four years. At the age of twenty he had become disgusted with the religious world. He saw no beauty, comeliness, or loveliness in the character of God as represented by the teaching of the various religious sects. He however heard a Universal Restorationer preach upon the love of God: this sermon gave him exalted opinions of God, and he concluded that Universal Restoration was right according to the Bible. He continued in this belief till 1828, when he and his wife were baptized into the "Campbellite" church by Sidney Rigdon, in Mentor, though they resided in Painesville, Ohio. He continued a member of this church, though doubting at times its being the true one, until Elders Parley P. Pratt, Oliver Cowdery, Peter Whitmer, Jun., and Ziba Peterson came with the Book of Mormon, when he began to investigate the subject of religion anew. As stated in the text he accompanied Sidney Rigdon to Fayette, New York, where, on the 11th of December, he was baptized by the Prophet Joseph Smith in the Seneca river.

*Doctrine and Covenants, sec. xxxv.

9. And whoso shall ask it in my name in faith, they shall cast out devils; they shall heal the sick; they shall cause the blind to receive their sight, and the deaf to hear, and the dumb to speak, and the lame to walk.

10. And the time speedily cometh that great things are to be shown forth unto the children of men;

11. But without faith shall not anything be shown forth except desolations upon Babylon, the same which has made all nations drink of the wine of the wrath of her fornication.

12. And there are none that doeth good except those who are ready to receive the fulness of my gospel which I have sent forth unto this generation.

13. Wherefore, I call upon the weak things of the world, those who are unlearned and despised, to thresh the nations by the power of my Spirit;

14. And their arm shall be my arm, and I will be their shield and their buckler; and I will gird up their loins, and they shall fight manfully for me; and their enemies shall be under their feet; and I will let fall the sword in their behalf, and by the fire of mine indignation will I preserve them.

15. And the poor and the meek shall have the gospel preached unto them, and they shall be looking forth for the time of my coming, for it is nigh at hand—

16. And they shall learn the parable of the fig-tree, for even now already summer is nigh,

17. And I have sent forth the fulness of my gospel by the hand of my servant Joseph; and in weakness have I blessed him;

18. And I have given unto him the keys of the mystery of those things which have been sealed, even things which were from the foundation of the world, and the things which shall come from this time until the time of my coming, if he abide in me, and if not, another will I plant in his stead.

19. Wherefore, watch over him that his faith fail not, and it shall be given by the Comforter, the Holy Ghost, that knoweth all things.

20. And a commandment I give unto thee—that thou shalt write for him; and the scriptures shall be given, even as they are in mine own bosom, to the salvation of mine own elect;

21. For they will hear my voice, and shall see me, and shall not be asleep, and shall abide the day of my coming; for they shall be purified, even as I am pure.

22. And now I say unto you, tarry with him, and he shall journey with you; forsake him not, and surely these things shall be fulfilled.

23. And inasmuch as ye do not write, behold, it shall be given unto

him to prophesy; and thou shalt preach my gospel, and call on the holy prophets to prove his words, as they shall be given him.

24. Keep all the commandments and covenants by which ye are bound; and I will cause the heavens to shake for your good, and Satan shall tremble and Zion shall rejoice upon the hills and flourish;

25. And Israel shall be saved in mine own due time; and by the keys which I have given shall they be led, and no more be confounded at all.

26. Lift up your hearts and be glad, your redemption draweth nigh.

27. Fear not, little flock, the kingdom is yours until I come. Behold, I come quickly. Even so. Amen.

And the voice of the Lord to Edward Partridge was:

*A Revelation to Edward Partridge, given December, 1830.**

1. Thus saith the Lord God, the Mighty One of Israel: Behold, I say unto you, my servant Edward, that you are blessed, and your sins are forgiven you, and you are called to preach my gospel as with the voice of a trump;

2. And I will lay my hand upon you by the hand of my servant Sidney Rigdon, and you shall receive my Spirit, the Holy Ghost, even the Comforter, which shall teach you the peaceable things of the kingdom;

3. And you shall declare it with a loud voice, saying: Hosanna, blessed be the name of the most high God.

4. And now this calling and commandment give I unto you concerning all men—

5. That as many as shall come before my servants Sidney Rigdon and Joseph Smith, Jun., embracing this calling and commandment, shall be ordained and sent forth to preach the everlasting gospel among the nations—

6. Crying repentance, saying: Save yourselves from this untoward generation, and come forth out of the fire, hating even the garments spotted with the flesh.

7. And this commandment shall be given unto the elders of my church, that every man which will embrace it with singleness of heart may be ordained and sent forth, even as I have spoken.

8. I am Jesus Christ, the Son of God; wherefore, gird up your loins and I will suddenly come to my temple. Even so. Amen.

It may be well to observe here, that the Lord greatly encouraged and strengthened the faith of His little flock, which had embraced the fulness of the everlast-

*Doctrine and Covenants, sec. xxxvi.

ing Gospel, as revealed to them in the Book of Mormon, by giving some more extended information upon the Scriptures, a translation of which had already commenced. Much conjecture and conversation frequently occurred among the Saints, concerning the books mentioned, and referred to, in various places in the Old and New Testaments, which were now nowhere to be found.* The common remark was, "They are *lost books*;" but it seems the Apostolic Church had some of these writings, as Jude mentions or quotes the Prophecy of Enoch, the seventh from Adam. To the joy of the little flock, which in

Of the Lost Books of Scripture.

*The most prominent of the "lost books" of the Old Testament are mentioned in the following passages: I Chronicles, xxix: 29; II Chronicles ix: 29; II Chronicles, xii: 15; I Samuel, x: 25; I Kings, iv: 32, 33. The following is the list of "lost books" mentioned in the New Testament:

Scripture of Abraham's Time: "And the scripture, foreseeing that God would justify the heathen through faith, preached before the Gospel unto Abraham." (Galatians, iii: 8.) The Christian world says, "Moses was God's first pen," but it appears from the above quotation that some one wrote scriptures even before Abraham's day, and he read them, learned the Gospel from them and also learned that God would justify the heathen through faith.

Prophecy of Enoch: Speaking of characters who are like "raging waves of the sea, foaming out their own shame," Jude says: "And Enoch also, the seventh from Adam, prophesied of these, saying, Behold, the Lord cometh with ten thousands of His saints, to execute judgment upon all," etc. (Jude, 14, 15.) From this it appears that Enoch had a revelation concerning the glorious coming of the Son of God to judgment. May not the prophecy of Enoch have been among the scriptures with which Abraham was acquainted?

Another Epistle of Jude: "When I gave all diligence to write unto you of the common salvation, it was needful for me to write unto you, and exhort you that ye should earnestly contend for the faith which was once delivered unto the Saints." (Jude 3.) We have but one epistle of Jude. Would not the epistle on the "common salvation" be as important as the one the only one we now have from Jude's pen?

Another Epistle to the Ephesians: In Ephesians, iii and 3rd, Paul alludes to another epistle which he had written to that people, but of which the world has no knowledge except from this reference which is made by its author. This epistle contained a revelation from God.

An Epistle to the Laodiceans: "When the epistle [Colossians] is read among you, cause that it be read also in the church of the Laodiceans; and that ye likewise read the epistle from Laodicea." (Colossians, iv: 16.) The epistles to the Laodiceans is among the lost scripture.

Another Epistle to the Corinthians: In the "first letter to the Corinthians" is this statement: "I wrote you in an epistle not to company with fornicators" (I Corinthians, v: 9). From this it would appear that our so-called first epistle to the Corinthians is really not the first, since Paul in it speaks of a former letter he had written to the Corinthians, and which was doubtless as good scripture as the two which have been preserved.

all, from Colesville to Canandaigua, New York, numbered about seventy members, did the Lord reveal the following doings of olden times, from the prophecy of Enoch:*

*Extracts from the Prophecy of Enoch.**

1. And it came to pass that Enoch continued his speech, saying: Behold, our father Adam taught these things, and many have believed and become the sons of God, and many have believed not, and have perished in their sins, and are looking forth with fear, in torment, for the fiery indignation of the wrath of God to be poured out upon them.

2. And from that time forth Enoch began to prophesy, saying unto the people, That: As I was journeying, and stood upon the place Mahujah, and cried unto the Lord, there came a voice out of heaven, saying—Turn ye, and get ye upon the Mount Simeon.

3. And it came to pass that I turned and went up on the mount; and as I stood upon the mount, I beheld the heavens open, and I was clothed upon with glory;

4. And I saw the Lord; and he stood before my face, and he talked with me, even as a man talketh one with another, face to face; and he said unto me: Look, and I will show unto thee the world for the space of many generations.

5. And it came to pass that I beheld in the valley of Shum, and lo, a great people which dwelt in tents, which were the people of Shum.

6. And again the Lord said unto me: Look; and I looked towards the north, and I beheld the people of Canaan, which dwelt in tents.

7. And the Lord said unto me; prophesy; and I prophesied, saying: Behold the people of Canaan, which are numerous, shall go forth in battle array against the people of Shum, and shall slay them that they shall utterly be destroyed; and the people of Canaan shall divide themselves in the land, and the land shall be barren and unfruitful, and none other people shall dwell there but the people of Canaan;

8. For behold, the Lord shall curse the land with much heat, and the barrenness thereof shall go forth forever; and there was a blackness came upon all the children of Canaan, that they were despised among all people.

9. And it came to pass that the Lord said unto me: Look; and I

*This prophecy of Enoch is contained in the "Writings of Moses," which about this time were revealed to the Prophet, and are now published in the "Pearl of Great Price." It will be understood, then, by the reader, that the "Prophecy of Enoch" itself is found in the "Writings of Moses," and that in the text above we have but a few extracts of the most prominent parts of "Enoch's Prophecy." For the complete prophecy the reader is referred to the "Pearl of Great Price." (Chapter vii.)

looked, and I beheld the land of Sharon, and the land of Enoch, and the land of Omner, and the land of Heni, and the land of Shem, and the land of Haner, and the land of Hanannihah, and all the inhabitants thereof;

10. And the Lord said unto me: Go to this people, and say unto them—Repent, lest I come out and smite them with a curse, and they die.

11. And he gave unto me a commandment that I should baptize in the name of the Father, and of the Son, which is full of grace and truth, and of the Holy Ghost, which beareth record of the Father and the Son.

12. And it came to pass that Enoch continued to call upon all the people, save it were the people of Canaan, to repent;

13. And so great was the faith of Enoch, that he led the people of God, and their enemies came to battle against them; and he spake the word of the Lord, and the earth trembled, and the mountains fled, even according to his command; and the rivers of water were turned out of their course; and the roar of the lions was heard out of the wilderness; and all nations feared greatly, so powerful was the word of Enoch, and so great was the power of the language which God had given him.

14. There also came up a land out of the depth of the sea, and so great was the fear of the enemies of the people of God, that they fled and stood afar off, and went upon the land which came up out of the depths of the sea.

15. And the giants of the land, also, stood afar off; and there went forth a curse upon all people that fought against God;

16. And from that time forth there were wars and bloodshed among them; but the Lord came and dwelt with his people, and they dwelt in righteousness.

17. The fear of the Lord was upon all nations, so great was the glory of the Lord, which was upon his people. And the Lord blessed the land, and they were blessed upon the mountains, and upon the high places, and did flourish.

18. And the Lord called his people Zion, because they were of one heart and one mind, and dwelt in righteousness; and there was no poor among them.

19. And Enoch continued his preaching in righteousness unto the people of God. And it came to pass in his days, that he built a city that was called the city of Holiness, even Zion.

20. And it came to pass that Enoch talked with the Lord; and he said unto the Lord: Surely Zion shall dwell in safety forever. But the Lord said unto Enoch: Zion have I blessed, but the residue of the people have I cursed.

21. And it came to pass that the Lord showed unto Enoch all the inhabitants of the earth; and he beheld, and lo, Zion, in process of

time, was taken up into heaven. And the Lord said unto Enoch: Behold mine abode forever.

22. And Enoch also beheld the residue of the people which were the sons of Adam; and they were a mixture of all the seed of Adam, save it were the seed of Cain, for the seed of Cain were black, and had not place among them.

23. And after that Zion was taken up into heaven, Enoch beheld, and lo, all the nations of the earth were before him; and there came generation upon generation;

24. And Enoch was high and lifted up, even in the bosom of the Father, and of the Son of Man; and behold, the power of Satan was upon all the face of the earth.

25. And he saw angels descending out of heaven; and he heard a loud voice saying: Wo, wo be unto the inhabitants of the earth.

26. And he beheld Satan; and he had a great chain in his hand, and it veiled the whole face of the earth with darkness; and he looked up and laughed and his angels rejoiced.

27. And Enoch beheld angels descending out of heaven, bearing testimony of the Father and the Son; and the Holy Ghost fell on many, and they were caught up by the powers of heaven into Zion.

28. And it came to pass that the God of heaven looked upon the residue of the people, and he wept; and Enoch bore record of it, saying: How is it that the heavens weep, and shed forth their tears as the rain upon the mountains?

29. And Enoch said unto the Lord: How is it that thou canst weep, seeing thou art holy, and from all eternity to all eternity?

30. And were it possible that man could number the particles of the earth, yea millions of earths like this, it would not be a beginning to the number of thy creations; and thy curtains are stretched out still; and yet thou art there, and thy bosom is there; and also thou art just; thou art merciful and kind forever;

31. And thou hast taken Zion to thine own bosom, from all thy creations, from all eternity to all eternity; and nought but peace, justice, and truth is the habitation of thy throne; and mercy shall go before thy face and have no end; how is it thou canst weep?

32. The Lord said unto Enoch: Behold these thy brethren; they are the workmanship of mine own hands, and I gave unto them their knowledged, in the day I created them; and in the Garden of Eden, gave I unto man his agency;

33. And unto thy brethren have I said, and also given commandment, that they should love one another, and that they should choose me, their Father; but behold, they are without affection, and they hate their own blood.

34. And the fire of mine indignation is kindled against them; and in my hot displeasure will I send in the floods upon them, for my fierce anger is kindled against them.

35. Behold, I am God; Man of Holiness is my name; Man of Counsel is my name; and Endless and Eternal is my name, also.

36. Wherefore, I can stretch forth mine hands and hold all the creations which I have made; and mine eye can pierce them also, and among all the workmanship of mine hands there has not been so great wickedness as among thy brethren.

37. But behold, their sins shall be upon the heads of their fathers; Satan shall be their father, and misery shall be their doom; and the whole heavens shall weep over them, even all the workmanship of mine hands; wherefore should not the heavens weep, seeing these shall suffer?

38. But behold, these which thine eyes are upon shall perish in the floods; and behold, I will shut them up; a prison have I prepared for them.

39. And That which I have chosen hath plead before my face. Wherefore, he suffereth for their sins; inasmuch as they will repent in the day that my Chosen shall return unto me, and until that day they shall be in torment;

40. Wherefore, for this shall the heavens weep, yea, and all the workmanship of mine hands.

41. And it came to pass that the Lord spake unto Enoch, and told Enoch all the doings of the children of men; wherefore Enoch knew, and looked upon their wickedness, and their misery, and wept and stretched forth his arms, and his heart swelled wide as eternity; and his bowels yearned; and all eternity shook.

42. And Enoch also saw Noah, and his family; that the posterity of all the sons of Noah should be saved with a temporal salvation;

43. Wherefore Enoch saw that Noah built an ark; and that the Lord smiled upon it, and held it in his own hand; but upon the residue of the wicked the floods came and swallowed them up.

44. And as Enoch saw this, he had bitterness of soul, and wept over his brethren, and said unto the heavens: I will refuse to be comforted; but the Lord said unto Enoch: Lift up your heart, and be glad; and look.

45. And it came to pass that Enoch looked; and from Noah, he beheld all the families of the earth; and he cried unto the Lord, saying: When shall the day of the Lord come? When shall the blood of the Righteous be shed, that all they that mourn may be sanctified, and have eternal life?

46. And the Lord said: It shall be in the meridian of time, in the days of wickedness and vengeance.

47. And behold, Enoch saw the day of the coming of the Son of Man even in the flesh; and his soul rejoiced, saying: The Righteous is lifted up, and the Lamb is slain from the foundation of the world; and through faith I am in the bosom of the Father, and behold, Zion is with me.

48. And it came to pass that Enoch looked upon the earth; and he heard a voice from the bowels thereof, saying: Wo, wo is me, the mother of men; I am pained, I am weary, because of the wickedness of my children. When shall I rest, and be cleansed from the filthiness which has gone forth out of me? When will my Creator sanctify me that I may rest, and righteousness for a season abide upon my face?

49. And when Enoch heard the earth mourn, he wept, and cried unto the Lord, saying: O Lord, wilt thou not have compassion upon the earth? Wilt thou not bless the children of Noah?

50. And it came to pass that Enoch continued his cry unto the Lord, saying: I ask thee, O Lord, in the name of thine Only Begotten even Jesus Christ, that thou wilt have mercy upon Noah and his seed, that the earth might never more be covered by the floods.

51. And the Lord could not withhold; and he covenanted with Enoch, and sware unto him with an oath, that he would stay the floods; that he would call upon the children of Noah;

52. And he sent forth an unalterable decree, that a remnant of his seed should always be found among all nations, while the earth should stand;

53. And the Lord said: Blessed is he through whose seed Messiah shall come; for he saith—I am Messiah, the King of Zion, the Rock of Heaven, which is broad as eternity; whoso cometh in at the gate and climbeth up by me shall never fall; wherefore, blessed are they of whom I have spoken, for they shall come forth with songs of everlasting joy.

54. And it came to pass that Enoch cried unto the Lord, saying: When the Son of Man cometh in the flesh, shall the earth rest? I pray thee, show me these things.

55. And the Lord said unto Enoch: Look, and he looked and beheld the Son of Man lifted up on the cross, after the manner of men;

56. And he heard a loud voice; and the heavens were veiled; and all the creations of God mourned; and the earth groaned; and the rocks were rent; and the Saints arose, and were crowned at the right hand of the Son of Man, with crowns of glory;

57. And as many of the spirits as were in prison came forth, and stood on the right hand of God; and the remainder were reserved in chains of darkness until the judgment of the great day.

58. And again Enoch wept and cried unto the Lord, saying: When shall the earth rest?

59. And Enoch beheld the Son of Man ascend up unto the Father; and he called unto the Lord, saying: Wilt thou not come again upon the earth? For as much as thou art God, and I know thee, and thou hast sworn unto me, and commanded me that I should ask in the name of thine Only Begotten; thou hast made me, and given unto me a right to thy throne, and not of myself, but through Thine own grace; wherefore, I ask thee if thou wilt not come again on the earth.

60. And the Lord said unto Enoch: As I live, even so will I come in the last days, in the days of wickedness and vengeance, to fulfil the oath which I have made unto you concerning the children of Noah;

61. And the day shall come that the earth shall rest, but before that day the heavens shall be darkened, and a veil of darkness shall cover the earth; and the heavens shall shake, and also the earth; and great tribulations shall be among the children of men, but my people will I preserve;

62. And righteousness will I send down out of heaven; and truth will I send forth out of the earth, to bear testimony of mine Only Begotten; his resurrection from the dead; yea, and also the resurrection of all men; and righteousness and truth will I cause to sweep the earth as with a flood, to gather out mine elect from the four quarters of the earth, unto a place which I shall prepare, an Holy City, that my people may gird up their loins, and be looking forth for the time of my coming; for there shall be my tabernacle, and it shall be called Zion, a New Jerusalem.

63. And the Lord said unto Enoch: Then shalt thou and all thy city meet them there, and we will receive them into our bosom, and they shall see us; and we will fall upon their necks, and they shall fall upon our necks, and we will kiss each other;

64. And there shall be mine abode, and it shall be Zion, which shall come forth out of all the creations which I have made; and for the space of a thousand years the earth shall rest.

65. And it came to pass that Enoch saw the day of the coming of the Son of Man, in the last days, to dwell on the earth in righteousness for the space of a thousand years;

66. But before that day he saw great tribulations among the wicked; and he also saw the sea, that it was troubled, and men's hearts failing them, looking forth with fear for the judgments of the Almighty God, which should come upon the wicked.

67. And the Lord showed Enoch all things, even unto the end of the world; and he saw the day of the righteous, the hour of their redemption; and receivevd a fulness of joy;

68. And all the days of Zion, in the days of Enoch, were three hundred and sixty-five years.

69. And Enoch and all his people walked with God, and he dwelt in the midst of Zion; and it came to pass that Zion was not, for God received it up into his own bosom; and from thence went forth the saying, Zion is fled.

Commanded to go to Ohio.

Soon after the words of Enoch were given, the Lord gave the following commandment:

*A Revelation to Joseph Smith, Jun., and Sidney Rigdon, given December, 1830.**

1. Behold, I say unto you that it is not expedient in me that ye should translate any more until ye shall go to the Ohio, and this because of the enemy and for your sakes.

2. And again, I say unto you that ye shall not go until ye have preached my gospel in those parts, and have strenthened up the church whithersoever it is found, and more especially in Colesville; for, behold, they pray unto me in much faith.

3. And again, a commandment I give unto the church, that it is expedient in me that they should assemble together at the Ohio, against the time that my servant Oliver Cowdery shall return unto them.

4. Behold, here is wisdom, and let every man choose for himself until I come. Even so. Amen.

*Doctrine and Covenants, section xxxvii.

CHAPTER XIII.

PROSPECTS OF THE CHURCH AT THE OPENING OF THE YEAR 1831—REMOVAL OF THE PROPHET JOSEPH FROM NEW YORK TO OHIO—DOCTRINAL DEVELOPMENT.

Prospects of the Church—1831.

THE year 1831 opened with a prospect great and glorious for the welfare of the kingdom; for on the 2nd of January, 1831, a conference was held in the town of Fayette, New York, at which the ordinary business of the Church was transacted; and in addition, the following revelation was received:

*Revelation, given January 2nd, 1831.**

1. Thus saith the Lord your God, even Jesus Christ, the Great I AM, Alpha and Omega, the beginning and the end, the same which looked upon the wide expanse of eternity, and all the seraphic hosts of heaven, before the world was made:

2. The same which knoweth all things, for all things are present before mine eyes;

3. I am the same which spake, and the world was made, and all things came by me.

4. I am the same which have taken the Zion of Enoch into mine own bosom; and verily, I say, even as many as have believed in my name, for I am Christ, and in mine own name, by the virtue of the blood which I have spilt, have I pleaded before the Father for them.

5. But behold, the residue of the wicked have I kept in chains of darkness until the judgment of the great day, which shall come at the end of the earth;

6. And even so will I cause the wicked to be kept, that will not hear my voice but harden their hearts, and wo, wo, wo, is their doom.

*Doctrine and Covenants, sec. xxxviii.

7. But behold, verily, verily, I say unto you that mine eyes are upon you. I am in your midst, and ye cannot see me;

8. But the day soon cometh that ye shall see me, and know that I am; for the veil of darkness shall soon be rent, and he that is not purified shall not abide the day.

9. Wherefore, gird up your loins and be prepared. Behold, the kingdom is yours, and the enemy shall not overcome.

10. Verily I say unto you, ye are clean, but not all; and there is none else with whom I am well pleased;

11. For all flesh is corrupted before me; and the powers of darkness prevail upon the earth, among the children of men, in the presence of all the hosts of heaven—

12. Which causeth silence to reign, and all eternity is pained, and the angels are waiting the great command to reap down the earth, to gather the tares that they may be burned; and, behold, the enemy is combined.

13. And now I show unto you a mystery, a thing which is had in secret chambers, to bring to pass even your destruction in process of time, and ye knew it not;

14. But now I tell it unto you, and ye are blessed, not because of your iniquity, neither your hearts of unbelief; for verily some of you are guilty before me, but I will be merciful unto your weakness.

15. Therefore, be ye strong from henceforth; fear not, for the kingdom is yours.

16. And for your salvation I give unto you a commandment, for I have heard your prayers, and the poor have complained before me, and the rich have I made, and all flesh is mine, and I am no respecter of persons.

17. And I have made the earth rich, and behold it is my footstool, wherefore, again I will stand upon it.

18. And I hold forth and deign to give unto you greater riches, even a land of promise, a land flowing with milk and honey, upon which there shall be no curse when the Lord cometh;

19. And I will give it unto you for the land of your inheritance, if you seek it with all your hearts.

20. And this shall be my covenant with you, ye shall have it for the land of your inheritance, and for the inheritance of your children forever, while the earth shall stand, and ye shall possess it again in eternity, no more to pass away.

21. But, verily I say unto you that in time ye shall have no king nor ruler, for I will be your king and watch over you.

22. Wherefore, hear my voice and follow me, and you shall be a

free people, and ye shall have no laws but my laws when I come, for I am your law-giver, and what can stay my hand?

23. But, verily I say unto you, teach one another according to the office wherewith I have appointed you;

24. And let every man esteem his brother as himself, and practise virtue and holiness before me.

25. And again I say unto you, let every man esteem his brother as himself.

26. For what man among you having twelve sons, and is no respecter of them, and they serve him obediently, and he saith unto the one: Be thou clothed in robes and sit thou here; and to the other: Be thou clothed in rags and sit thou there, and looketh upon his sons and saith I am just?

27. Behold, this I have given unto you as a parable, and it is even as I am. I say unto you, be one; and if ye are not one ye are not mine.

28. And again, I say unto you that the enemy in the secret chambers seeketh your lives.

29. Ye hear of wars in far countries, and you say that there will soon be great wars in far countries, but ye know not the hearts of men in your own land.

30. I tell you these things because of your prayers; wherefore, treasure up wisdom in your bosoms, let the wickedness of men reveal these things unto you by their wickedness, in a manner which shall speak in your ears with a voice louder than that which shall shake the earth; but if ye are prepared, ye shall not fear.

31. And that ye might escape the power of the enemy, and be gatherd unto me a righteous people, without spot and blameless—

32. Wherefore, for this cause I gave unto you the commandment that ye should go to the Ohio; and there I will give unto you my law; and there you shall be endowed with power from on high;

33. And from thence, whosoever I will, shall go forth among all nations, and it shall be told them what they shall do; for I have a great work laid up in store, for Israel shall be saved, and I will lead them whithersoever I will, and no power shall stay my hand.

34. And now, I give unto the church in these parts a commandment, that certain men among them shall be appointed, and they shall be appointed by the voice of the church.

35. And they shall look to the poor and the needy, and administer to their relief that they shall not suffer; and send them forth to the place which I have commanded them;

36. And this shall be their work, to govern the affairs of the property of this church.

37. And they have farms that cannot be sold, let them be left or rented as seemeth them good.

38. See that all things are preserved; and when men are endowed with power from on high and sent forth, all these things shall be gathered unto the bosom of the church.

39. And if ye seek the riches which it is the will of the Father to give unto you, ye shall be the richest of all people, for ye shall have the riches of eternity; and it must needs be that the riches of the earth are mine to give; but beware of pride, lest ye become as the Nephites of old.

40. And again, I say unto you, I give unto you a commandment, that every man, both elder, priest, teacher, and also member, go to with his might, with the labor of his hands, to prepare and accomplish the things which I have commanded.

41. And let your preaching be the warning voice, every man to his neighbor, in mildness and in meekness.

42. And go ye out from among the wicked. Save yourselves. Be ye clean that bear the vessels of the Lord. Even so. Amen.

James Covill.

Not long after this conference of the 2nd of January closed, there was a man came to me by the name of James Covill, who had been a Baptist minister for about forty years, and covenanted with the Lord that he would obey any command that the Lord would give to him through me, as His servant, and I received the following:

*Revelation to James Covill, given at Fayette, New York, January 5th, 1831.**

1. Hearken and listen to the voice of him who is from all eternity to all eternity, the Great I AM, even Jesus Christ—

2. The light and life of the world; a light which shineth in darkness and the darkness comprehendeth it not:

3. The same which came in the meridian of time unto mine own, and mine own received me not;

4. But to as many as received me, gave I power to become my sons; and even so will I give unto as many as will receive me, power to become my sons.

5. And verily, verily, I say unto you, he that receiveth my gospel receiveth me; and he that receiveth not my gospel receiveth not me.

* Doctrine and Covenants, sec. xxxix.

6. And this is my gospel—repentance and baptism by water, and then cometh the baptism of fire and the Holy Ghost, even the Comforter, which showeth all things, and teacheth the peaceable things of the kingdom.

7. And now, behold, I say unto you, my servant James, I have looked upon thy works and I know thee.

8. And verily I say unto thee, thine heart is now right before me at this time; and, behold, I have bestowed great blessings upon thy head;

9. Nevertheless, thou hast seen great sorrow, for thou hast rejected me many times because of pride and the cares of the world.

10. But, behold, the days of thy deliverance are come, if thou wilt hearken to my voice, which saith unto thee: Arise and be baptized, and wash away your sins, calling on my name, and you shall receive my Spirit, and a blessing so great as you never have known.

11. And if thou do this, I have prepared thee for a greater work. Thou shalt preach the fulness of my gospel, which I have sent forth in these last days, the covenant which I have sent forth to recover my people, which are of the house of Israel.

12. And it shall come to pass that power shall rest upon thee; thou shalt have great faith, and I will be with thee and go before thy face.

13. Thou art called to labor in my vineyard, and to build up my church, and to bring forth Zion, that it may rejoice upon the hills and flourish.

14. Behold, verily, verily, I say unto thee, thou art not called to go into the eastern countries, but thou art called to go to the Ohio.

15. And inasmuch as my people shall assemble themselves at the Ohio, I have kept in store a blessing such as is not known among the children of men, and it shall be poured forth upon their heads. And from thence men shall go forth into all nations.

16. Behold, verily, verily, I say unto you, that the people in Ohio call upon me in much faith, thinking I will stay my hand in judgment upon the nations, but I cannot deny my word.

17. Wherefore lay to with your might and call faithful laborers into my vineyard, that it may be pruned for the last time.

18. And inasmuch as they do repent and receive the fulness of my gospel, and become sanctified, I will stay mine hand in judgment.

19. Wherefore, go forth, crying with a loud voice, saying: The kingdom of heaven is at hand; crying: Hosanna! blessed be the name of the Most High God.

20. Go forth baptizing with water, preparing the way before my face for the time of my coming;

21. For the time is at hand; the day or the hour no man knoweth; but it surely shall come.

22. And he that receiveth these things receiveth me; and they shall be gathered unto me in time and in eternity.

23. And again, it shall come to pass, that on as many as ye shall baptize with water, ye shall lay your hands, and they shall receive the gift of the Holy Ghost, and shall be looking forth for the signs of my coming, and shall know me.

24. Behold, I come quickly. Even so. Amen.

Why Covill Rejected the Commandment.

As James Covill rejected the word of the Lord, and returned to his former principles and people, the Lord gave unto me and Sidney Rigdon the following revelation, explaining why he obeyed not the word:

*Revelation given at Fayette, New York, January, 1831.**

1. Behold, verily I say unto you, that the heart of my servant James Covill was right before me, for he covenanted with me that he would obey my word,

2. And he received the word with gladness, but straightway Satan tempted him; and the fear of persecution and the cares of the world caused him to reject the word.

3. Wherefore he broke my covenant, and it remaineth with me to do with him as seemeth me good. Amen.

The Prophet Removes to Ohio.

The latter part of January, in company with Brothers Sidney Rigdon and Edward Partridge, I started with my wife for Kirtland, Ohio, where we arrived about the first of February, and were kindly received and welcomed into the house of Brother Newel K. Whitney.† My wife and I lived in

*Doctrine and Covenants, sec. xl.

† Newel Kimball Whitney was descended from the Whitneys of Watertown, Mass., who emigrated from England in 1635. His mother was a native of the "Bay State," and his father of the state of Vermont. There, also, Newel was born, in Marlborough, Windham county, February 5, 1795. A natural business man, he made his own way in the world, and after figuring as a sutler during the war of 1812, and taking part in the battle of Plattsburgh, near Lake Champlain, he established himself as an Indian trader at Green Bay, Lake Michigan. He next settled in Ohio, where he made the acquaintance of Algernon Sidney Gilbert, a merchant of Paines-

the family of Brother Whitney several weeks, and received every kindness and attention which could be expected, and especially from Sister Whitney.

The Branch of the Church at Kirtland.

The branch of the Church in this part of the Lord's vineyard, which had increased to nearly one hundred members, were striving to do the will of God, so far as they knew it, though some strange notions and false spirits had crept in among them. With a little caution and some wisdom, I soon assisted the brethren and sisters to overcome them. The plan of "common stock," which had existed in what was called "the family,"* whose members generally had embraced the everlasting Gospel,

ville, whose partner he became in the successful firm of Gilbert and Whitney at Kirtland. In October, 1822, he married Elixabeth Ann Smith, a young lady from Connecticut, who is known in Church history as "Mother Whitney." When Oliver Cowdery and his fellow missionaries came to Kirtland, en route to Missouri, the Whitneys were Campbellites, members of Sidney Rigdon's flock, but upon hearing the fulness of the Gospel as preached by those Elders, they embraced it. In the Whitney family folk lore the incident of the Prophet's arrival at Kirtland is thus related: "About the first of February, 1831, a sleigh containing four persons drove through the streets of Kirtland and drew up in front of the store of Gilbert and Whitney. One of the men, a young and stalwart personage alighted, and springing up the steps walked into the store and to where the junior partner was standing. 'Newel K. Whitney! Thou art the man!' he exclaimed, extending his hand cordially, as if to an old and familiar acquaintance. 'You have the advantage of me,' replied the merchant, as he mechanically took the proffered hand, 'I could not call you by name as you have me.' 'I am Joseph the Prophet,' said the stranger smiling. 'You've prayed me here, now what do you want of me?' " The Prophet, it is said, while in the East had seen the Whitneys, in vision, praying for his coming to Kirtland. "Mother Whitney" also tells how on a certain night prior to the advent of Elder Cowdery and his companions, while she and her husband were praying to the Lord to know how they might obtain the gift of the Holy Ghost, which of all things they desired, they saw a vision as of a cloud of glory resting upon their house, and heard a voice from heaven saying, "Prepare to receive the word of the Lord, for it is coming." Shortly afterwards Oliver Cowdery and his associates came with the Book of Mormon, and with the message of the restored Gospel. Moreover, in further fulfilment of this vision, under the rooftree of the Whitneys the Prophet received a number of the revelations contained in this volume.

*This organization, called "the family," came into existence before the Gospel was preached in Kirtland, through an effort of the people of this neighborhood to live as the early Christians are said to have lived, viz., "And the multitude of them that believed were of one heart and of one soul: neither said any of them that ought of the things which he possessed was his own; but they had all things common."—(Acts iv:32.)

was readily abandoned for the more perfect law of the Lord; and the false spirits were easily discerned and rejected by the light of revelation.

The Lord gave unto the Church the following:

*Revelation, given at Kirtland, Ohio, February 4th, 1831.**

1. Hearken and hear, O ye my people, saith the Lord and your God, ye whom I delight to bless with the greatest of all blessings, ye that hear me; and ye that hear me not will I curse, that have professed my name, with the heaviest of all cursings.

2. Hearken, O ye elders of my church whom I have called, behold I give unto you a commandment, that ye shall assemble yourselves together to agree upon my word;

3. And by the prayer of your faith ye shall receive my law, that ye may know how to govern my church and have all things right before me.

4. And I will be your ruler when I come; and behold, I come quickly, and ye shall see that my law is kept.

5. He that receiveth my law and doeth it, the same is my disciple; and he that saith he receiveth it and doeth it not, the same is not my disciple, and shall be cast out from among you;

6. For it is not meet that the things which belong to the children of the kingdom, shall be given to them that are not worthy, or to dogs, or the pearls to be cast before swine.

7. And again, it is meet that my servant Joseph Smith, Jun., should have a house built, in which to live and translate.

8. And again, it is meet that my servant Sidney Rigdon should live as seemeth him good, inasmuch as he keepeth my commandments.

9. And again, I have called my servant, Edward Partridge, and I give a commandment, that he should be appointed by the voice of the church, and ordained a bishop unto the church, to leave his merchandise and to spend all his time in the labors of the church;

10. To see to all things as it shall be appointed unto him in my laws in the day that I shall give them.

11. And this because his heart is pure before me, for he is like unto Nathaniel of old, in whom there is no guile.

12. These words are given unto you, and they are pure before me; wherefore, beware how you hold them, for they are to be answered upon your souls in the day of judgment. Even so. Amen.

* Doctrine and Covenants, sec. xli.

Revelation Giving the Law of the Church.

On the 9th of February, 1831, at Kirtland, in the presence of twelve Elders, and according to the promise heretofore made,* the Lord gave the following revelation, embracing the law of the Church:

Revelation, given February, 1831.†

1. Hearken, O ye elders of my church, who have assembled yourselves together in my name, even Jesus Christ the Son of the living God, the Savior of the world; inasmuch as ye believe on my name and keep my commandments.

2. Again I say unto you, hearken and hear and obey the law which I shall give unto you.

3. For verily I say, as ye have assembled yourselves together according to the commandment wherewith I commanded you, and are agreed as touching this one thing, and have asked the Father in my name, even so ye shall receive.

4. Behold, verily I say unto you, I give unto you this first commandment, that ye shall go forth in my name, every one of you, excepting my servants Joseph Smith, Jun., and Sidney Rigdon.

5. And I give unto them a commandment that they shall go forth for a little season, and it shall be given by the power of the Spirit when they shall return.

6. And ye shall go forth in the power of my Spirit, preaching my gospel, two by two, in my name, lifting up your voices as with the sound of a trump, declaring my word like unto angels of God·

7. And ye shall go forth baptizing with water, saying: Repent ye, repent ye, for the kingdom of heaven is at hand.

8: And from this place ye shall go forth into the regions westward; and inasmuch as ye shall find them that will receive you ye shall build up my church in every region—

9. Until the time shall come when it shall be revealed unto you from on high, when the city of the New Jerusalem shall be prepared, that ye may be gathered in one, that ye may be my people and I will be your God.

10. And again, I say unto you, that my servant Edward Partridge shall stand in the office whereunto I have appointed him. And it shall come to pass, that if he transgress, another shall be appointed in his stead. Even so. Amen.

* This refers to the promise which the Lord gave in the revelation of Januarv 1831, see p. 142, verse 32.

† Doctrine and Covenants, sec. xlii.

11. Again, I say unto you, that it shall not be given to any one to go forth to preach my gospel, or to build up my church, except he be ordained by some one who has authority, and it is known to the church that he has authority and has been regularly ordained by the heads of the church.

12. And again, the elders, priests and teachers of this church shall teach the principles of my gospel, which are in the Bible and the Book of Mormon, in the which is the fulness of the gospel;

13. And they shall observe the covenants and church articles to do them, and these shall be their teachings, as they shall be directed by the Spirit.

14. And the Spirit shall be given unto you by the prayer of faith; and if ye receive not the Spirit, ye shall not teach,

15. And all this ye shall observe to do as I have commanded concerning your teaching, until the fulness of my scriptures is given.

16. And as ye shall lift up your voices by the Comforter, ye shall speak and prophesy as seemeth me good;

17. For, behold, the Comforter knoweth all things, and beareth record of the Father and of the Son.

18. And now, behold, I speak unto the church. Thou shalt not kill; and he that kills shall not have forgiveness in this world, nor in the world to come.

19. And again, I say, thou shalt not kill; but he that killeth shall die.

20. Thou shalt not steal; and he that stealeth and will not repent shall be cast out.

21. Thou shalt not lie; he that lieth and will not repent, shall be cast out.

22. Thou shalt love thy wife with all thy heart, and shalt cleave unto her and none else.

23. And he that looketh upon a woman to lust after her shall deny the faith, and shall not have the Spirit; and if he repents not he shall be cast out.

24. Thou shalt not commit adultery; and he that committeth adultery, and repenteth not, shall be cast out.

25. But he that has committed adultery and repents with all his heart, and forsaketh it, and doeth it no more, thou shalt forgive;

26. But if he doeth it again, he shall not be forgiven, but shall be cast out.

27. Thou shalt not speak evil of thy neighbor, nor do him any harm.

28. Thou knowest my laws concerning these things are given in my scriptures; he that sinneth and repenteth not shall be cast out.

29. If thou lovest me, thou shalt serve me and keep all my commandments.

30. And behold, thou wilt remember the poor, and consecrate of thy properties for their support that which thou hast to impart unto them, with a covenant and a deed which cannot be broken.

31. And inasmuch as ye impart of your substance unto the poor, ye will do it unto me; and they shall be laid before the bishop of my church and his counselors, two of the elders, or high priests,* such as he shall appoint or has appointed and set apart for the purpose.

32. And it shall come to pass, that after they are laid before the bishop of my church, and after that he has received these testimonies concerning the consecration of the properties of my church, that they cannot be taken from the church, agreeable to my commandments, every man shall be made accountable unto me, a steward over his own property, or that which he has received by consecration, as much as is sufficient for himself and family.

33. And again, if there shall be properties in the hands of the Church, or any individuals of it, more than is necessary for their support after this first consecration, which is a residue to be consecrated unto the bishop, it shall be kept to administer to those who have not, from time to time, that every man who has need may be amply supplied and receive according to his wants.

34. Therefore, the residue shall be kept in my storehouse, to administer to the poor and the needy, as shall be appointed by the high council of the church, and the bishop and his council;

35. And for the purpose of purchasing lands for the public benefit of the church, and building houses of worship, and building up of the New Jerusalem which is hereafter to be revealed—

36. That my covenant people may be gathered in one in that day when I shall come to my temple. And this I do for the salvation of my people.

37. And it shall come to pass, that he that sinneth and repenteth not shall be cast out of the church, and shall not receive again that which he has consecrated unto the poor and the needy of my Church, or in other words, unto me—

38. For inasmuch as ye do it unto the least of these, ye do it unto me.

39. For it shall come to pass, that which I spake by the mouths of my prophets, shall be fulfilled; for I will consecrate of the riches of those who embrace my gospel among the Gentiles unto the poor of my people who are of the house of Israel.

* "The words, 'or High Priests,' were added by the Prophet some years after: and also the words, 'High Council,' in the 34th verse."—*Orson Pratt.*

40. And again, thou shalt not be proud in thy heart; let all thy garments be plain, and their beauty the beauty of the work of thine own hands;

41. And let all things be done in cleanliness before me.

42. Thou shalt not be idle; for he that is idle shall not eat the bread nor wear the garments of the laborer.

43. And whosoever among you are sick, and have not faith to be healed, but believe, shall be nourished with all tenderness, with herbs and mild food, and that not by the hand of an enemy.

44. And the elders of the church, two or more, shall be called, and shall pray for and lay their hands upon them in my name; and if they die they shall die unto me, and if they live they shall live unto me.

45. Thou shalt live together in love, insomuch that thou shalt weep for the loss of them that die, and more especially for those that have not hope of a glorious resurrection.

46. And it shall come to pass that those that die in me, shall not taste of death, for it shall be sweet unto them;

47. And they that die not in me, wo unto them, for their death is bitter.

48. And again, it shall come to pass that he that hath faith in me to be healed, and is not appointed unto death, shall be healed.

49. He who hath faith to see shall see.

50. He who hath faith to hear shall hear.

51. The lame who hath faith to leap shall leap.

52. And they who have not faith to do these things, but believe in me, have power to become my sons; and inasmuch as they break not my laws thou shalt bear their infirmities.

53. Thou shalt stand in the place of thy stewardship.

54. Thou shalt not take thy brother's garment; thou shalt pay for that which thou shalt receive of thy brother.

55. And if thou obtainest more than that which would be for thy support; thou shalt give it into my store-house, that all things may be done according to that which I have said.

56. Thou shalt ask, and my Scriptures shall be given as I have appointed, and they shall be preserved in safety;

57. And it is expedient that thou shouldst hold thy peace concerning them, and not teach them until ye have received them in full.

58. And I give unto you a commandment that then ye shall teach them unto all men; for they shall be taught unto all nations, kindreds, tongues and people.

59. Thou shalt take the things which thou hast received, which have been given unto thee in my Scriptures for a law, to be my law to govern my church;

60. And he that doeth according to these things shall be saved, and he that doeth them not shall be damned, if he so continue.

61. If thou shalt ask, thou shalt receive revelation upon revelation, knowledge upon knowledge, that thou mayest know the mysteries and peaceable things—that which bringeth joy, that which bringeth life eternal.

62. Thou shalt ask, and it shall be revealed unto you in mine own due time where the New Jerusalem shall be built.

63. And behold, it shall come to pass that my servants shall be sent forth to the east and to the west, to the north and to the south.

64. And even now, let him that goeth to the east teach them that shall be converted to flee to the west, and this in consequence of that which is coming on the earth, and of secret combinations.

65. Behold, thou shalt observe all these things, and great shall be thy reward; for unto you it is given to know the mysteries of the kingdom, but unto the world it is not given to know them.

66. Ye shall observe the laws which ye have received and be faithful.

67. And ye shall hereafter receive church covenants, such as shall be sufficient to establish you, both here and in the New Jerusalem.

68. Therefore, he that lacketh wisdom, let him ask of me, and I will give him liberally and upbraid him not.

69. Lift up your hearts and rejoice, for unto you the kingdom, or in other words, the keys of the church have been given. Even so. Amen.

70. The priests and teachers shall have their stewardships, even as the members.

71. And the elders, or high priests,* who are appointed to assist the bishop as counselors in all things, are to have their families supported out of the property which is consecrated to the bishop, for the good of the poor, and for other purposes, as before mentioned;

72. Or they are to receive a just remuneration for all their services, either a stewardship or otherwise, as may be thought best or decided by the counselors and bishop.

73. And the bishop, also, shall receive his support, or a just remuneration for all his services in the church.

74. †Behold, verily I say unto you, that whatever persons among you, having put away their companions for the cause of fornication, or in other words, if they shall testify before you in all lowliness of heart that this is the case, ye shall not cast them out from among you;

* The words, "or High Priests," were added by the Prophet some years after.—*Orson Pratt.*

† Verses 74 to 93 inclusive, were given some days after the first 73 verses.—*Orson Pratt.*

75. But if ye shall find that any persons have left their companions for the sake of adultery, and they themselves are the offenders, and their companions are living, they shall be cast out from among you.

76. And again, I say unto you, that ye shall be watchful and careful, with all inquiry, that ye receive none such among you if they are married;

77. And if they are not married, they shall repent of all their sins or ye shall not receive them.

78. And again, every person who belongeth to this church of Christ, shall observe to keep all the commandments and covenants of the church.

79. And it shall come to pass, that if any persons among you shall kill they shall be delivered up and dealt with according to the laws of the land; for remember that he hath no forgiveness; and it shall be proved according to the laws of the land.

80. And if any man or woman shall commit adultery, he or she shall be tried before two elders of the church, or more, and every word shall be established against him or her by two witnesses of the church, and not of the enemy; but if there are more than two witnesses it is better.

81. But he or she shall be condemned by the mouth of two witnesses; and the elders shall lay the case before the church, and the church shall lift up their hands against him or her, that they may be dealt with according to the law of God.

82. And if it can be, it is necessary that the bishop be present also.

83. And thus ye shall do in all cases which shall come before you.

84. And if a man or woman shall rob, he or she shall be delivered up unto the law of the land.

85. And if he or she shall steal, he or she shall be delivered up unto the law of the land.

86. And if he or she shall lie, he or she shall be delivered up unto the law of the land.

87. And if he or she do any manner of iniquity, he or she shall be delivered up unto the law, even that of God.

88. And if thy brother or sister offend thee, thou shalt take him or her between him or her and thee alone; and if he or she confess thou shalt be reconciled.

89. And if he or she confess not, thou shalt deliver him or her up unto the church, not to the members, but to the elders. And it shall be done in a meeting, and that not before the world.

90. And if thy brother or sister offend many, he or she shall be chastened before many.

91. And if any one offend openly, he or she shall be rebuked

openly, that he or she may be ashamed. And if he or she confess not, he or she shall be delivered up unto the law of God.

92. If any shall offend in secret, he or she shall be rebuked in secret, that he or she may have opportunity to confess in secret to him or her whom he or she has offended, and to God, that the church may not speak reproachfully of him or her.

93. And thus shall ye conduct in all things.

Pretentions of a Woman to Revelations, etc.

Soon after the foregoing revelation was received, a woman* came making great pretensions of revealing commandments, laws and other curious matters; and as almost every person has advocates for both theory and practice, in the various notions and projects of the age, it became necessary to inquire of the Lord, when I received the following:

Revelation given at Kirtland, February, 1831.†

1. O hearken, ye elders of my church, and give ear to the words which I shall speak unto you.

2. For behold, verily, verily, I say unto you, that ye have received a commandment for a law unto my church, through him whom I have appointed unto you to receive commandments and revelations from my hand.

3. And this ye shall know assuredly—that there is none other appointed unto you to receive commandments and revelations until he be taken, if he abide in me.

4. But verily, verily, I say unto you, that none else shall be appointed unto this gift except it be through him; for if it be taken from him he shall not have power except to appoint another in his stead.

5. And this shall be a law unto you, that ye receive not the teachings of any that shall come before you as revelations or commandments;

6. And this I give unto you that you may not be deceived, that you may know they are not of me.

7. For verily I say unto you, that he that is ordained of me shall

* This woman's name, according to the history of the church kept by John Whitmer, was Hubble. "She professed to be a prophetess of the Lord, and professed to have many revelations, and knew the Book of Mormon was true, and that she should become a teacher in the church of Christ. She appeared to be very sanctimonious and deceived some who were not able to detect her in her hypocrisy; others, however, had the spirit of discernment and her follies and abominations were manifest." John Whitmer's *History of the Church*, ch. iii.

† Doctrine and Covenants, sec. xliii.

come in at the gate and be ordained as I have told you before, to teach those revelations which you have received and shall receive through him whom I have appointed.

8. And now, behold, I give unto you a commandment, that when ye are assembled together ye shall instruct and edify each other, that ye may know how to act and direct my church, how to act upon the points of my law and commandments, which I have given.

9. And thus ye shall become instructed in the law of my church, and be sanctified by that which ye have received, and ye shall bind yourselves to act in all holiness before me—

10. That inasmuch as ye do this, glory shall be added to the kingdom which ye have received. Inasmuch as ye do it not, it shall be taken, even that which ye have received.

11. Purge ye out the iniquity which is among you; sanctify yourselves before me;

12. And if ye desire the glories of the kingdom, appoint ye my servant Joseph Smith, Jun., and uphold him before me by the prayer of faith.

13. And again, I say unto you, that if ye desire the mysteries of the kingdom, provide for him food and raiment, and whatsoever thing he needeth to accomplish the work wherewith I have commanded him;

14. And if ye do it not, he shall remain unto them that have received him, that I may reserve unto myself a pure people before me.

15. Again I say, hearken ye elders of my church, whom I have appointed: Ye are not sent forth to be taught, but to teach the children of men the things which I have put into your hands by the power of my Spirit;

16. And ye are to be taught from on high. Sanctify yourselves and ye shall be endowed with power, that ye may give even as I have spoken.

17. Hearken ye, for, behold, the great day of the Lord is nigh at hand.

18. For the day cometh that the Lord shall utter his voice out of heaven; the heavens shall shake and the earth shall tremble, and the trump of God shall sound both long and loud, and shall say to the sleeping nations: Ye saints, arise and live; ye sinners, stay and sleep until I shall call again.

19. Wherefore gird up your loins lest ye be found among the wicked.

20. Lift up your voices and spare not. Call upon the nations to repent, both old and young, both bond and free, saying: Prepare yourselves for the great day of the Lord;

21. For if I, who am a man, do lift up my voice and call upon you to repent, and ye hate me, what will ye say when the day cometh

when the thunders shall utter their voices from the ends of the earth, speaking to the ears of all that live, saying—Repent, and prepare for the great day of the Lord?

22. Yea, and again, when the lightnings shall streak forth from the east unto the west, and shall utter forth their voices unto all that live, and make the ears of all tingle that hear, saying these words—Repent ye, for the great day of the Lord is come?

23. And again, the Lord shall utter his voice out of heaven, saying: Hearken, O ye nations of the earth, and hear the words of that God who made you.

24. O, ye nations of the earth, how often would I have gathered you together as a hen gathereth her chickens under her wings, but ye would not!

25. How oft have I called upon you by the mouth of my servants, and by the ministering of angels, and by mine own voice, and by the voice of thunderings, and by the voice of lightnings, and by the voice of tempests, and by the voice of earthquakes, and great hailstorms, and by the voice of famines and pestilences of every kind, and by the great sound of a trump, and by the voice of judgment, and by the voice of mercy all the day long, and by the voice of glory and honor and the riches of eternal life, and would have saved you with an everlasting salvation, but ye would not!

26. Behold the day has come, when the cup of the wrath of mine indignation is full.

27. Behold, verily I say unto you, that these are the words of the Lord your God.

28. Wherefore, labor ye, labor ye in my vineyard for the last time —for the last time call upon the inhabitants of the earth.

29. For in mine own due time will I come upon the earth in judgment, and my people shall be redeemed and shall reign with me on earth,

30. For the great Millennium, of which I have spoken by the mouth of my servants, shall come.

31. For Satan shall be bound, and when he is loosed again he shall only reign for a little season, and then cometh the end of the earth.

32. And he that liveth in righteousness shall be changed in the twinkling of an eye, and the earth shall pass away so as by fire.

33. And the wicked shall go away into unquenchable fire, and their end no man knoweth on earth, nor ever shall know, until they come before me in judgment.

34. Hearken ye to these words. Behold, I am Jesus Christ, the Savior of the world. Treasure these things up in your hearts, and let the solemnities of eternity rest upon your minds.

35. Be sober. Keep all my commandments. Even so. Amen.

The latter part of February I received the following revelation, which caused the Church to appoint a conference to be held early in the month of June ensuing:

A Special Conference, 3rd-6th of June.

*Revelation to Joseph Smith, Jun., and Sidney Rigdon, given at Kirtland, February, 1831.**

1. Behold, thus saith the Lord unto you my servants, it is expedient in me that the elders of my church should be called together, from the east and from the west, and from the north and from the south, by letter or some other way.

2. And it shall come to pass, that inasmuch as they are faithful, and exercise faith in me, I will pour out my Spirit upon them in the day that they assemble themselves together.

3. And it shall come to pass that they shall go forth into the regions round about, and preach repentance unto the people.

4. And many shall be converted, insomuch that ye shall obtain power to organize yourselves according to the laws of man;

5. That your enemies may not have power over you; that you may be preserved in all things; that you may be enabled to keep my laws; that every bond may be broken wherewith the enemy seeketh to destroy my people.

6. Behold, I say unto you, that ye must visit the poor and the needy and administer to their relief, that they may be kept until all things may be done according to my law which ye have received. Amen.

* Doctrine and Covenants, sec. xliv.

CHAPTER XIV.

EFFORT TO OVERWHELM THE CHURCH BY FALSEHOOD —SUNDRY REVELATIONS LEADING TO DOCTRINAL DEVELOPMENT.

Efforts Through the Press to Retard the Work.

AT this age of the Church [i. e., early in the spring of 1831] many false reports, lies, and foolish stories, were published in the newspapers, and circulated in every direction, to prevent people from investigating the work, or embracing the faith. A great earthquake in China, which destroyed from one to two thousand inhabitants, was burlesqued in some papers, as " 'Mormonism' in China."* But to the joy of the Saints who had to struggle against every thing that prejudice and wickedness could invent, I received the following:

*This earthquake in China is a matter of some interest in connection with the history of the church, since it was the means of bringing Simonds Ryder, a somewhat noted preacher of the Campbellite faith, into the Church. According to *Hayden's History of the Disciples on the Western Reserve* (a Campbellite book), Mr. Ryder was much perplexed over "Mormonism," and for a time was undecided whether to join the Church or not. "In the month of June," (1831), writes Mr. Hayden, "he read in a newspaper an account of the destruction of Pekin in China, and he remembered that six weeks before, a young 'Mormon' girl had predicted the destruction of that city." J. H. Kennedy, in his *Early Days of Mormonism* (Scribner's & Sons, 1888), refers to the same thing, and adds: "This appeal to the superstitious part of his nature was the final weight in the balance and he threw the whole power of his influence upon the side of 'Mormonism.' His surrender caused an excitement almost equal to that which followed the fall of Rigdon," (pp. 103-4). It was doubtless this prophecy and the conversion connected with it that led the papers mentioned in the text to refer to it as " 'Mormonism' in China." The discrepancy in dates, Hayden and Kennedy referring to the published accounts of the events as appearing in June, and the Prophet making reference to it previous to the 7th of March, need cause no confusion. It will be seen that the Prophet alludes to it in connection with a number of other things as taking place "at this age of the Church"—a very indefinite reference as to the time in which a thing may have occurred.

*Revelation at Kirtland, given March 7th, 1831.**

1. Hearken, O ye people of my church, to whom the kingdom has been given; hearken ye and give ear to him who laid the foundation of the earth, who made the heavens and all the hosts thereof, and by whom all things were made which live, and move, and have a being.

2. And again I say, hearken unto my voice, lest death shall overtake you; in an hour when ye think not the summer shall be past, and the harvest ended, and your souls not saved.

3. Listen to him who is the advocate with the Father, who is pleading your cause before him—

4. Saying: Father, behold the sufferings and death of him who did no sin, in whom thou wast well pleased; behold the blood of thy Son which was shed, the blood of him whom thou gavest that thyself might be glorified;

5. Wherefore, Father, spare these my brethren that believe on my name, that they may come unto me and have everlasting life.

6. Hearken, O ye people of my church, and ye elders listen together, and hear my voice while it is called today, and harden not your hearts,

7. For verily I say unto you that I am Alpha and Omega, the beginning and the end, the light and the life of the world—a light that shineth in darkness and the darkness comprehendeth it not.

8. I came unto mine own, and mine own received me not; but unto as many as received me gave I power to do many miracles, and to become the sons of God; and even unto them that believed on my name gave I power to obtain eternal life.

9. And even so I have sent mine everlasting covenant into the world, to be a light to the world, and to be a standard for my people, and for the Gentiles to seek to it, and to be a messenger before my face to prepare the way before me.

10. Wherefore, come ye unto it, and with him that cometh I will reason as with men in days of old, and I will show unto you my strong reasoning,

11. Wherefore, hearken ye together and let me show unto you even my wisdom—the wisdom of him whom ye say is the God of Enoch, and his brethren,

12. Who were separated from the earth, and were received unto myself—a city reserved until a day of righteousness shall come—a day which was sought for by holy men, and they found it not because of wickedness and abominations;

13. And confessed they were strangers and pilgrims on the earth;

* Doctrine and Covenants, sec. xlv.

14. But obtained a promise that they should find it and see it in their flesh.

15. Wherefore, hearken and I will reason with you, and I will speak unto you and prophesy, as unto men in days of old.

16. And I will show it plainly, as I showed it unto my disciples as I stood before them in the flesh, and spake unto them, saying: As ye have asked of me concerning the signs of my coming in the day when I shall come in my glory in the clouds of heaven, to fulfil the promises that I have made unto your fathers,

17. For as ye have looked upon the long absence of your spirits from your bodies to be a bondage, I will show unto you how the day of redemption shall come, and also the restoration of the scattered Israel.

18. And now ye behold this temple which is in Jerusalem, which ye call the house of God, and your enemies say that this house shall never fall.

19. But, verily I say unto you, that desolation shall come upon this generation as a thief in the night, and this people shall be destroyed and scattered among all nations.

20. And this temple which ye now see shall be thrown down that there shall not be left one stone upon another.

21. And it shall come to pass, that this generation of Jews shall not pass away until every desolation which I have told you concerning them shall come to pass.

22. Ye say that ye know that the end of the world cometh; ye say also that ye know that the heavens and the earth shall pass away;

23. And in this ye say truly, for so it is; but these things which I have told you shall not pass away until all shall be fulfilled,

24. And this I have told you concerning Jerusalem; and when that day shall come, shall a remnant be scattered among all nations;

25. But they shall be gathered again; but they shall remain until the times of the Gentiles be fulfilled.

26. And in that day shall be heard of wars and rumors of wars, and the whole earth shall be in commotion, and men's hearts shall fail them, and they shall say that Christ delayeth his coming until the end of the earth.

27. And the love of men shall wax cold, and iniquity shall abound.

28. And when the times of the Gentiles is come in, a light shall break forth among them that sit in darkness, and it shall be the fulness of my gospel;

29. But they receive it not; for they perceive not the light, and they turn their hearts from me because of the precepts of men.

30. And in that generation shall the times of the Gentiles be fulfilled.

31. And there shall be men standing in that generation, that shall not pass until they shall see an overflowing scourge; for a desolating sickness shall cover the land.

32. But my disciples shall stand in holy places, and shall not be moved; but among the wicked, men shall lift up their voices and curse God and die.

33. And there shall be earthquakes also in divers places and many desolations; yet men will harden their hearts against me, and they will take up the sword, one against another, and they will kill one another.

34. And now, when I the Lord had spoken these words unto my disciples, they were troubled.

35. And I said unto them: Be not troubled, for, when all these things shall come to pass, ye may know that the promises which have been made unto you shall be fulfilled.

36. And when the light shall begin to break forth, it shall be with them like unto a parable which I will show you—

37. Ye look and behold the fig trees, and ye see them with your eyes, and ye say when they begin to shoot forth, and their leaves are yet tender, that summer is now nigh at hand;

38. Even so it shall be in that day when they shall see all these things, then shall they know that the hour is nigh.

39. And it shall come to pass that he that feareth me shall be looking forth for the great day of the Lord to come, even for the signs of the coming of the Son of Man.

40. And they shall see signs and wonders, for they shall be shown forth in the heavens above, and in the earth beneath.

41. And they shall behold blood, and fire, and vapors of smoke.

42. And before the day of the Lord shall come, the sun shall be darkened, and the moon be turned into blood, and the stars fall from heaven.

43. And the remnant shall be gathered unto this place;

44. And then they shall look for me, and, behold, I will come; and they shall see me in the clouds of heaven, clothed with power and great glory, with all the holy angels; and he that watches not for me shall be cut off.

45. But before the arm of the Lord shall fall, an angel shall sound his trump, and the saints that have slept shall come forth to meet me in the cloud.

46. Wherefore, if ye have slept in peace, blessed are you; for as you now behold me and know that I am, even so shall ye come unto me and your souls shall live, and your redemption shall be perfected; and the saints shall come forth from the four quarters of the earth.

47. Then shall the arm of the Lord fall upon the nations.

48. And then shall the Lord set his foot upon this mount, and it shall cleave in twain, and the earth shall tremble, and reel to and fro, and the heavens also shall shake.

49. And the Lord shall utter his voice, and all the ends of the earth shall hear it; and the nations of the earth shall mourn, and they that have laughed shall see their folly,

50. And calamity shall cover the mocker, and the scorner shall be consumed; and they that have watched for iniquity shall be hewn down and cast into the fire.

51. And then shall the Jews look upon me and say: What are these wounds in thine hands and in thy feet?

52. Then shall they know that I am the Lord; for I will say unto them: These wounds are the wounds with which I was wounded in the house of my friends. I am he who was lifted up. I am Jesus that was crucified. I am the Son of God.

53. And then shall they weep because of their iniquities; then shall they lament because they persecuted their king.

54. And then shall the heathen nations be redeemed, and they that knew no law shall have part in the first resurrection; and it shall be tolerable for them.

55. And Satan shall be bound, that he shall have no place in the hearts of the children of men.

56. And at that day, when I shall come in my glory, shall the parable be fulfilled which I spake concerning the ten virgins.

57. For they that are wise and have received the truth, and have taken the Holy Spirit for their guide, and have not been deceived—verily I say unto you, they shall not be hewn down and cast into the fire, but shall abide the day.

58. And the earth shall be given unto them for an inheritance; and they shall multiply and wax strong, and their children shall grow up without sin unto salvation,

59. For the Lord shall be in their midst, and his glory shall be upon them, and he will be their king and their lawgiver.

60. And now, behold, I say unto you, it shall not be given unto you to know any further concerning this chapter, until the New Testament be translated, and in it all these things shall be made known;

61. Wherefore I give unto you that ye may now translate it, that ye may be prepared for the things to come.

62. For verily I say unto you, that great things await you;

63. Ye hear of wars in foreign lands; but, behold, I say unto you, they are nigh, even at your doors, and not many years hence ye shall hear of wars in your own lands.

64. Wherefore I, the Lord, have said, Gather ye out from the eastern lands, assemble ye yourselves together ye elders of my church; go ye forth into the western countries, call upon the inhabitants to repent, and inasmuch as they do repent, build up churches unto me.

65. And with one heart and with one mind, gather up your riches that ye may purchase an inheritance which shall hereafter be appointed unto you,

66. And it shall be called the New Jerusalem, a land of peace, a city of refuge, a place of safety for the saints of the Most High God;

67. And the glory of the Lord shall be there, and the terror of the Lord also shall be there, insomuch that the wicked will not come unto it, and it shall be called Zion.

68. And it shall come to pass among the wicked, that every man that will not take his sword against his neighbor must needs flee unto Zion for safety.

69. And there shall be gathered unto it out of every nation under heaven; and it shall be the only people that shall not be at war one with another.

70. And it shall be said among the wicked: Let us not go up to battle against Zion, for the inhabitants of Zion are terrible; wherefore we cannot stand.

71. And it shall come to pass that the righteous shall be gathered out from among all nations, and shall come to Zion, singing with songs of everlasting joy.

72. And now I say unto you, keep these things from going abroad unto the world until it is expedient in me, that ye may accomplish this work in the eyes of the people, and in the eyes of your enemies, that they may not know your works until ye have accomplished the thing which I have commanded you;

73. That when they shall know it, that they may consider these things.

74. For when the Lord shall appear he shall be terrible unto them, that fear may seize upon them, and they shall stand afar off and tremble.

75. And all nations shall be afraid because of the terror of the Lord, and the power of his might. Even so. Amen.

The next day after the above was received, I also received the following revelation, relative to the gifts of the Holy Ghost:

The Gifts of the Holy Ghost.

*Revelation, given at Kirtland, March 8th, 1831.**

1. Hearken, O ye people of my church; for verily I say unto you,

* Doctrine and Covenants, sec. xlvi. With reference to the matters mentioned in verses 1-7, in this revelation, John Whitmer writes: "In the beginning of the Church,

that these things were spoken unto you for your profit and learning.

2. But notwithstanding those things which are written, it always has been given to the elders of my church from the beginning, and ever shall be, to conduct all meetings as they are directed and guided by the Holy Spirit.

3. Nevertheless ye are commanded never to cast any one out from your public meetings, which are held before the world.

4. Ye are also commanded not to cast any one who belongeth to the church out of your sacrament meetings; nevertheless, if any have trespassed, let him not partake until he make reconciliation.

5. And again I say unto you, ye shall not cast any out of your sacrament meetings who are earnestly seeking the kingdom—I speak this concerning those who are not of the church.

6. And again I say unto you, concerning your confirmation meetings, that if there be any that are not of the church, that are earnestly seeking after the kingdom, ye shall not cast them out.

7. But ye are commanded in all things to ask of God, who giveth liberally; and that which the Spirit testifies unto you even so I would that ye should do in all holiness of heart, walking uprightly before me, considering the end of your salvation, doing all things with prayer and thanksgiving, that ye may not be seduced by evil spirits, or doctrines of devils, or the commandments of men; for some are of men, and others of devils.

8. Wherefore, beware lest ye are deceived; and that ye may not be deceived seek ye earnestly the best gifts, always remembering for what they are given;

9. For verily I say unto you, they are given for the benefit of those who love me and keep all my commandments, and him that seeketh so to do; that all may be benefited that seek or that ask of me, that ask and not for a sign that they may consume it upon their lust.

10. And again, verily I say unto you, I would that ye should always remember, and always retain in your minds what those gifts are, that are given unto the church,

11. For all have not every gift given unto them; for there are many gifts, and to every man is given a gift by the Spirit of God.

while yet in her infancy, the disciples used to exclude unbelievers, which caused some to marvel and converse of this matter because of the things written in the Book of Mormon [III Nephi xviii: 22-34.] Therefore the Lord deigned to speak on this subject, that His people might come to understanding, and said that He had always given to His Elders to conduct all meetings as they were led by the Spirit."
—John Whitmer's *History of the Church*, ch. iv.

12. To some is given one, and to some is given another, that all may be profited thereby.

13. To some it is given by the Holy Ghost to know that Jesus Christ is the Son of God, and that he was crucified for the sins of the world.

14. To others it is given to believe on their words, that they also might have eternal life if they continue faithful.

15. And again, to some it is given by the Holy Ghost to know the differences of administration, as it will be pleasing unto the same Lord, according as the Lord will, suiting his mercies according to the conditions of the children of men.

16. And again, it is given by the Holy Ghost to some to know the diversities of operations, whether they be of God, that the manifestations of the Spirit may be given to every man to profit withal.

17. And again, verily I say unto you, to some is given, by the Spirit of God, the word of wisdom.

18. To another is given the word of knowledge, that all may be taught to be wise and to have knowledge.

19. And again, to some it is given to have faith to be healed,

20. And to others it is given to have faith to heal.

21. And again, to some is given the working of miracles;

22. And to others it is given to prophesy;

23. And to others the discerning of spirits.

24. And again, it is given to some to speak with tongues;

25. And to another is given the interpretation of tongues.

26. And all these gifts come from God, for the benefit of the children of God.

27. And unto the bishop of the church, and unto such as God shall appoint and ordain to watch over the church, and to be elders unto the church, are to have it given unto them to discern all those gifts lest there shall be any among you professing and yet be not of God.

28. And it shall come to pass that he that asketh in Spirit shall receive in Spirit;

29. That unto some it may be given to have all those gifts, that there may be a head, in order that every member may be profited thereby.

30. He that asketh in the Spirit, asketh according to the will of God; wherefore it is done even as he asketh.

31. And again, I say unto you, all things must be done in the name of Christ, whatsoever you do in the Spirit;

32. And ye must give thanks unto God in the Spirit for whatsoever blessings ye are blessed with.

33. And ye must practice virtue and holiness before me continually. Even so. Amen.

John Whitmer Appointed Historian.

The same day that I received the foregoing revelation, I also received the following, setting apart John Whitmer as a historian,* inasmuch as he is faithful:

Revelation to Joseph Smith, Jun., and John Whitmer, given at Kirtland, March 8th, 1831.†

1. Behold, it is expedient in me that my servant John should write and keep a regular history, and assist you, my servant Joseph, in transcribing all things which shall be given you, until he is called to further duties.

2. Again, verily I say unto you that he can also lift up his voice in meetings, whenever it shall be expedient.

3. And again, I say unto you that it shall be appointed unto him to keep the church record and history continually, for Oliver Cowdery I have appointed to another office.

4. Wherefore, it shall be given him, inasmuch as he is faithful, by the Comforter, to write these things. Even so. Amen.

On the Purchase of Lands in Ohio.

Upon inquiry how the brethren should act in regard to purchasing lands to settle upon,‡ and where they should finally make a permanent location, I received the following:

Revelation, given at Kirtland, March, 1831.§

1. It is necessary that ye should remain for the present time in your places of abode, as it shall be suitable to your circumstances.

2. And inasmuch as ye have lands, ye shall impart to the eastern brethren;

3. And inasmuch as ye have not lands, let them buy for the pres-

* Previous to this Oliver Cowdery, had acted as historian and recorder. John Whitmer, according to his own representations, said he would rather not keep the Church history, but observed—"The will of the Lord be done, and if He desires it, I wish that He would manifest it through Joseph the Seer."—John Whitmer's *History of the Church*, ch. vi.—Accordingly the revelation was given.

† Doctrine and Covenants, sec. xlvii.

‡ This question was agitating the minds of the brethren in consequence of the expected arrival in the near future, of the Saints from New York, who had been commanded to gather to Ohio, and for whose reception it was necessary to make preparations.

§ Doctrine and Covenants, section xlviii.

ent time in those regions round about, as seemeth them good, for it must needs be necessary that they have places to live for the present time.

4. It must needs be necessary, that ye save all the money that ye can, and that ye obtain all that ye can in righteousness, that in time ye may be enabled to purchase land for an inheritance, even the city.

5. The place is not yet to be revealed; but after your brethren come from the east there are to be certain men appointed, and to them it shall be given to know the place, or to them it shall be revealed.

6. And they shall be appointed to purchase the lands, and to make a commencement to lay the foundation of the city; and then shall ye begin to be gathered with your families, every man according to his family, according to his circumstances, and as is appointed to him by the presidency and the bishop of the church, according to the laws and commandments which ye have received, and which ye shall hereafter receive. Even so. Amen.

The Shaking Quakers.

At about this time came Leman Copley, one of the sect called Shaking Quakers,* and embraced the fulness of the everlasting Gospel, apparently honest-hearted, but still retaining the idea that the Shakers were right in some particulars of their faith. In order to have more perfect understanding on the subject, I inquired of the Lord, and received the following:

Revelation to Sidney Rigdon, Parley P. Pratt, and Leman Copley, given March, 1831.†

1. Hearken unto my word, my servants Sidney, and Parley, and

*"This sect of Christians arose in England, and Ann Lee has the credit of being its founder. They derive their name from their manner of worship, which is performed by singing and dancing, and clapping their hands in regular time, to a novel but rather pleasant kind of music. This sect was persecuted in England, and came to America in 1774. They first settled in Watervliet, near Albany, New York. They have, or think they have, revelations from heaven, or gifts from the Holy Spirit, which direct them in the choice of their leaders, and in other important concerns. Their dress and manners are similar to those of the society of Friends (Quakers); hence they are often called Shaking Quakers."—Hayward's *Book of All Religions*, pp. 84-85. "They assert, with the Quakers, that all external ordinances, especially baptism and the Lord's supper, ceased in the apostolic age; and that God had sent no one to preach since that time till they were raised up, to call in the elect in a new dispensation. They deny the doctrine of the Trinity and a vicarious atonement, as also the resurrection of the body."—Burder's *History of All Religions*, p. 502.

† Doctrine and Covenants, sec. xlix.

Leman; for behold, verily I say unto you, that I give unto you a commandment that you shall go and preach my gospel which ye have received, even as ye have received it, unto the Shakers.

2. Behold, I say unto you, that they desire to know the truth in part, but not all, for they are not right before me and must needs repent.

3. Wherefore, I send you, my servants Sidney and Parley to preach the gospel unto them;

4. And my servant Leman shall be ordained unto this work, that he may reason with them, not according to that which he has received of them, but according to that which shall be taught him by you my servants; and by so doing I will bless him, otherwise he shall not prosper.

5. Thus saith the Lord; for I am God, and have sent mine Only Begotten Son into the world for the redemption of the world, and have decreed that he that receiveth him shall be saved, and he that receiveth him not shall be damned—

6. And they have done unto the Son of Man even as they listed; and he has taken his power on the right hand of his glory, and now reigneth in the heavens, and will reign till he descends on the earth to put all enemies under his feet, which time is nigh at hand—

7. I, the Lord God, have spoken it; but the hour and the day no man knoweth, neither the angels in heaven, nor shall they know until he comes.

8. Wherefore, I will that all men shall repent, for all are under sin, except those which I have reserved unto myself, holy men that ye know not of.

9. Wherefore, I say unto you, that I have sent unto you mine everlasting covenant, even that which was from the beginning.

10. And that which I have promised I have so fulfilled, and the nations of the earth shall bow to it; and, if not of themselves, they shall come down, for that which is now exalted of itself shall be laid low of power.

11. Wherefore, I give unto you a commandment that ye go among this people, and say unto them, like unto mine apostle of old, whose name was Peter:

12. Believe on the name of the Lord Jesus, who was on the earth, and is to come, the beginning and the end;

13. Repent and be baptized in the name of Jesus Christ, according to the holy commandment, for the remission of sins;

14. And whoso doeth this shall receive the gift of the Holy Ghost, by the laying on of the hands of the elders of the church.

15. And again, verily I say unto you, that whoso forbiddeth to marry is not ordained of God, for marriage is ordained of God unto man.

16. Wherefore, it is lawful that he should have one wife, and they twain shall be one flesh, and all this that the earth might answer the end of its creation;

17. And that is might be filled with the measure of man, according to his creation before the world was made.

18. And whoso forbiddeth to abstain from meats, that man should not eat the same, is not ordained of God;

19. For, behold, the beasts of the field and the fowls of the air, and that which cometh of the earth, is ordained for the use of man for food and for raiment, and that he might have in abundance.

20. But it is not given that one man should possess that which is above another, wherefore the world lieth in sin.

21. And wo be unto man that sheddeth blood or that wasteth flesh and hath no need.

22. And again, verily I say unto you, that the Son of Man cometh not in the form of a woman, neither of a man traveling on the earth.

23. Wherefore, be not deceived, but continue in steadfastness, looking forth for the heavens to be shaken, and the earth to tremble and to reel to and fro as a drunken man, and for the valleys to be exalted, and for the mountains to be made low, and for the rough places to become smooth—and all this when the angel shall sound his trumpet.

24. But before the great day of the Lord shall come, Jacob shall flourish in the wilderness, and the Lamanites shall blossom as the rose.

25. Zion shall flourish upon the hills and rejoice upon the mountains, and shall be assembled together unto the place which I have appointed.

26. Behold, I say unto you, go forth as I have commanded you; repent of all your sins; ask and ye shall receive; knock and it shall be opened unto you.

27. Behold, I will go before you and be your rearward; and I will be in your midst, and you shall not be confounded.

28. Behold, I am Jesus Christ, and I come quickly. Even so. Amen.*

* Elders Rigdon and Pratt fulfilled the mission appointed to them by this revelation. In company with Leman Copley, who at his own earnest request had been ordained to the Priesthood, (John Whitmer's *History of the Church*, p. 20.) they visited the settlement of the Shakers, near Cleveland, Ohio, and preached the Gospel to them; "but," writes Elder Pratt, "they utterly refused to hear or obey the Gospel." —*Autobiography of Parley P. Pratt*, p. 65 (first ed.). John Whitmer also remarks upon this incident: "The above-named brethren went and proclaimed [the Gospel] according to the revelation given them, but the Shakers hearkened not to their words and received not the Gospel at that time, for they are bound in tradition and priestcraft; and thus they are led away with foolish and vain imaginations." —John Whitmer's *History of the Church*. Ms. p. 20.

During the month of April, I continued to translate the Scriptures as time would allow. In May, a number of Elders being present, and not understanding the different spirits* abroad in the earth, I inquired and received from the Lord the following:

Inquiry on Spiritual Manifestations.

Revelation, given May, 1831.†

1. Hearken, O ye elders of my church, and give ear to the voice of the living God; and attend to the words of wisdom which shall be given unto you, according as ye have asked and are agreed as touching the church, and the spirits which have gone abroad in the earth.

2. Behold, verily I say unto you, that there are many spirits which are false spirits, which have gone forth in the earth, deceiving the world.

3. And also Satan hath sought to deceive you, that he might overthrow you.

4. Behold, I, the Lord, have looked upon you, and have seen abominations in the church that profess my name.

5. But blessed are they who are faithful and endure, whether in life or in death, for they shall inherit eternal life.

6. But wo unto them that are deceivers and hypocrites, for, thus saith the Lord, I will bring them to judgment.

7. Behold, verily I say unto you, there are hypocrites among you, who have deceived some, which has given the adversary power; but behold such shall be reclaimed;

* This is a very brief allusion to very important and strange phenomena. Elder Parley P. Pratt, in his *Autobiography*, has a much more extended account of the spirit manifestations which called forth the revelation upon the subject. "As I went forth among the different branches," he says, alluding to the branches in the vicinity of Kirtland, "some very strange spiritual operations were manifested, which were disgusting rather than edifying. Some persons would seem to swoon away and make unseemly gestures, and be drawn or disfigured in their countenances. Others would fall into ecstasies and be drawn into contortions, cramp, fits, etc. Others would seem to have visions, and revelations, which were not edifying and which were not congenial to the doctrine and spirit of the Gospel. In short, a false and lying spirit seemed to be creeping into the Church. All these things were new and strange to me, and had originated in the Church during our absence, and previous to the arrival of President Joseph Smith from New York. Feeling our weakness and inexperience, and lest we should err in judgment concerning these spiritual phenomena, myself, John Murdock, and several other Elders, went to Joseph Smith and asked him to inquire of the Lord concerning these spirits or manifestations. After we had joined in prayer in his translating room, he dictated in our presence the following revelation." This is the revelation given in the text above on spiritual manifestations.

† Doctrine and Covenants, sec. L.

8. But the hypocrites shall be detected and shall be cut off, either in life or in death, even as I will; and wo unto them who are cut off from my Church, for the same are overcome of the world.

9. Wherefore, let every man beware lest he do that which is not in truth and righteousness before me.

10. And now come, saith the Lord, by the Spirit, unto the elders of his church, and let us reason together, that ye may understand;

11. Let us reason even as a man reasoneth one with another face to face.

12. Now, when a man reasoneth he is understood of man, because he reasoneth as a man; even so will I the Lord, reason with you, that you may understand.

13. Wherefore, I the Lord ask you this question—Unto what were ye ordained?

14. To preach my gospel by the Spirit, even the Comforter which was sent forth to teach the truth.

15. And then received ye spirits which ye could not understand, and received them to be of God; and in this are ye justified?

16. Behold ye shall answer this question yourselves; nevertheless, I will be merciful unto you; he that is weak among you hereafter shall be made strong.

17. Verily I say unto you, he that is ordained of me and sent forth to preach the word of truth by the Comforter, in the Spirit of truth, doth he preach it by the Spirit of truth or some other way?

18. And if it be by some other way it is not of God.

19. And again, he that receiveth the word of truth, doth he receive it by the Spirit of truth or some other way?

20. If it be some other way it is not of God.

21. Therefore, why is it that ye cannot understand and know that he that receiveth the word by the Spirit of truth, receiveth it as it is preached by the Spirit of truth?

22. Wherefore, he that preacheth and he that receiveth, understand one another, and both are edified and rejoice together.

23. And that which doth not edify is not of God, and is darkness.

24. That which is of God is light; and he that receiveth light, and continueth in God, receiveth more light; and that light groweth brighter and brighter until the perfect day.

25. And again, verily I say unto you, and I say it that you may know the truth, that you may chase darkness from among you;

26. He that is ordained of God and sent forth, the same is appointed to be the greatest, notwithstanding he is the least and the servant of all.

27. Wherefore, he is possessor of all things; for all things are subject unto him, both in heaven and on the earth, the life and the light,

the Spirit and the power, sent forth by the will of the Father, through Jesus Christ, his Son.

28. But no man is possessor of all things except he be purified and cleansed from all sin.

29. And if ye are purified and cleansed from all sin, ye shall ask whatsoever you will in the name of Jesus and it shall be done.

30. But know this, it shall be given you what you shall ask; and as ye are appointed to the head, the spirits shall be subject unto you.

31. Wherefore, it shall come to pass, that if you behold a spirit manifested that you cannot understand, and you receive not that spirit, ye shall ask of the Father in the name of Jesus; and if he give not unto you that spirit, then you may know that it is not of God.

32. And it shall be given unto you, power over that spirit; and you shall proclaim against that spirit with a loud voice that it is not of God—

33. Not with railing accusation, that ye be not overcome, neither with boasting nor rejoicing, lest you be seized therewith.

34. He that receiveth of God, let him account it of God; and let him rejoice that he is accounted of God worthy to receive.

35. And by giving heed and doing these things which ye have received, and which ye shall hereafter receive—and the kingdom is given you of the Father, and power to overcome all things which are not ordained of him—

36. And behold, verily I say unto you, blessed are you who are now hearing these words of mine from the mouth of my servant, for your sins are forgiven you.

37. Let my servant Joseph Wakefield, in whom I am well pleased, and my servant Parley P. Pratt go forth among the churches and strengthen them by the word of exhortation;

38. And also my servant John Corrill, or as many of my servants as are ordained unto this office, and let them labor in the vineyard; and let no man hinder them doing that which I have appointed unto them—

39. Wherefore in this thing my servant Edward Partridge is not justified; nevertheless let him repent and he shall be forgiven.

40. Behold, ye are little children and ye cannot bear all things now; ye must grow in grace and in the knowledge of the truth.

41. Fear not, little children, for you are mine, and I have overcome the world, and you are of them that my Father hath given me;

42. And none of them that my Father hath given me shall be lost.

43. And the Father and I are one. I am in the Father and the Father in me: and inasmuch as ye have received me, ye are in me and I in you.

44. Wherefore, I am in your midst, and I am the good shepherd, and the stone of Israel. He that buildeth upon this rock shall never fall.

45. And the day cometh that you shall hear my voice and see me, and know that I am.

46. Watch, therefore, that ye may be ready. Even so. Amen.*

Not long after the foregoing was received, the Saints from the State of New York began to come on, and it seemed necessary to settle them; therefore at the solicitation of Bishop Partridge, I inquired, and received the following:

Arrival in Ohio of the New York Saints.

Revelation, given May, 1831.†

1. Hearken unto me, saith the Lord your God, and I will speak unto my servant Edward Partridge, and give unto him directions; for it must needs be that he receive directions how to organize this people.

2. For it must needs be that they be organized according to my laws; it otherwise, they will be cut off.

3. Wherefore, let my servant Edward Partridge, and those whom he has chosen, in whom I am well pleased, appoint unto this people their portions, every man equal according to his family, according to his circumstances and his wants and needs.

4. And let my servant Edward Partridge, when he shall appoint a man his portion, give unto him a writing that shall secure unto him his portion, that he shall hold it, even this right and this inheritance in the church, until he transgresses and is not accounted worthy by

* Elder Parley P. Pratt, in his *Autobiography*, referring to this revelation. for he was present when it was given—indeed it was obtained chiefly at his own and Elder John Murdock's solicitation—takes occasion to relate how this and other revelations were given through the Prophet. "Each sentence," says he, "was uttered slowly and very distinctly, and with a pause between each, sufficiently long for it to be recorded by an ordinary writer in long hand. This was the manner in which all his written revelations were dictated and written. There was never any hesitation, reviewing, or reading back, in order to keep the run of the subject; neither did any of these communications undergo revisions, interlinings or corrections. As he dictated them so they stood, so far as I have witnessed; and I was present to witness the dictation of several communications of several pages each."—*Aut.* Parley P. Pratt, pp. 65-66. This statement of Elder Pratt's is true in a general way, and valuable as a description of the manner in which revelations were dictated by the Prophet; and needs modifying only to the extent of saying that some of the early revelations first published in the "Book of Commandments," in 1833, were revised by the Prophet himself in the way of correcting errors made by the scribes and publishers; and some additional clauses were inserted to throw increased light upon the subjects treated in the revelations, and paragraphs added, to make the principles or instructions apply to officers not in the Church at the time some of the earlier revelations were given. The addition of verses, 65, 66 and 67 in sec. xx of the Doctrine and Covenants, is an example.

† Doctrine and Covenants, sec. li.

the voice of the church according to the laws and covenants of the church, to belong to the church.

5. And if he shall transgress and is not accounted worthy to belong to the church, he shall not have power to claim that portion which he has consecrated unto the bishop for the poor and needy of my church; therefore, he shall not retain the gift, but shall only have claim on that portion that is deeded unto him.

6. And thus all things shall be made sure, according to the laws of the land.

7. And let that which belongs to this people be appointed unto this people.

8. And the money which is left unto this people—let there be an agent appointed unto this people, to take the money to provide food and raiment, according to the wants of this people.

9. And let every man deal honestly, and be alike among this people, and receive alike, that ye may be one, even as I have commanded you.

10. And let that which belongeth to this people not be taken and given unto that of another church.

11. Wherefore, if another church would receive money of this church, let them pay unto this church again according as they shall agree;

12. And this shall be done through the bishop or the agent, which shall be appointed by the voice of the church.

13. And again, let the bishop appoint a storehouse unto this church; and let all things both in money and in meat, which are more than is needful for the wants of this people, be kept in the hands of the bishop.

14. And let him also reserve unto himself for his own wants, and for the wants of his family, as he shall be employed in doing this business.

15. And thus I grant unto this people a privilege of organizing themselves according to my laws.

16. And I consecrate unto them this land for a little season, until I, the Lord, shall provide for them otherwise, and command them to go hence;

17. And the hour and the day is not given unto them, wherefore let them act upon this land as for years, and this shall turn unto them for their good.

18. Behold, this shall be an example unto my servant Edward Partridge, in other places, in all churches.

19. And whoso is found a faithful, a just, and a wise steward shall enter into the joy of his Lord, and shall inherit eternal life.

20. Verily, I say unto you, I am Jesus Christ, who cometh quickly, in an hour you think not. Even so. Amen.

CHAPTER XV.

THE IMPORTANT CONFERENCE OF JUNE 3RD-6TH—ARRIVAL OF THE ELDERS IN WESTERN MISSOURI.

Important Conference of June 3rd-6th, at Kirtland.

ON the 3rd* of June, the Elders from the various parts of the country where they were laboring, came in; and the conference before appointed, convened in Kirtland; and the Lord displayed His power to the most perfect satisfaction of the Saints. The man of sin was revealed,† and the au-

* This date in the Prophet's narrative is given the 6th of June, but the minutes of the conference in the *Far West Record* are dated "June 3rd." In John Whitmer's *History of the Church* it is written: "June 3rd, 1831, a general conference was called, and a blessing promised if the Elders were faithful and humble before Him [i. e., the Lord]. Therefore the Elders assembled from the east and from the west, from the north and the south, and also many members." (p. 21.) Whitmer, however, speaks of the conference as continuing several days (p. 22); and then under date of "the 6th of June" states that the revelation was given which Joseph, the Prophet, in the text of his *History* above, speaks of as having been given the day following the close of the conference. The 3rd of June, 1831, fell upon Friday, so that the great probability is that this important conference commenced on Friday and continued through Saturday and Sunday; and then, before the Elders dispersed on Monday, the 6th, the revelation alluded to by the Prophet, was given. Previous conferences of a general character usually occupied three days, see p. 118, and hence it is likely that this one did.

† The manner in which the man of sin was revealed and the authority of the Melchizedek Priesthood manifested, is related by John Whitmer, in his *History of the Church* (ch. vii). After giving the names of those who were ordained High Priests the day on which the two powers were manifested, he says: "Joseph Smith, Jun., prophesied the day previous that the man of sin would be revealed. While the Lord poured out His Spirit upon His servants, the devil took a notion to make known his power. He bound Harvey Whitlock and John Murdock so that they could not speak, and others were affected but the Lord showed to Joseph, the seer, the design of the thing; he commanded the devil in the name of Christ, and he departed, to our joy and comfort."

Parley P. Pratt also alludes to this subject in his *Autobiography*: "In this conference much instruction was given by President Smith, who spoke in great power, as he was moved upon by the Holy Ghost; and the spirit of power and of testimony rested down upon the Elders in a marvelous manner. Here also were some strange manifestations of false spirits, which were immediately rebuked." (p. 72.)

thority of the Melchizedek Priesthood was manifested and conferred for the first time upon several of the Elders.* It was clearly evident that the Lord gave us power in proportion to the work to be done, and strength according to the race set before us, and grace and help as our needs required.† Great harmony prevailed; several were ordained; faith was strengthened;

* A misapprehension has arisen in the minds of some respecting the statement—"The authority of the Melchizedek Priesthood was manifested and conferred for the first time upon several of the Elders." It has been supposed that this passage meant that the higher or Melchizedek Priesthood was now for the first time conferred upon men in this dispensation. This of course is an error, since even before the Church was organized, the Apostleship, the highest authority in the Melchizedek Priesthood, was conferred upon Joseph Smith and Oliver Cowdery, and very probably upon David Whitmer also. (See pp. 40-42, note.) The Prophet does not mean that the Melchizedek Priesthood was given for the first time in the Church. It was at this conference, however, that the special office of High Priest was for the first time conferred upon men in this dispensation, except in so far as Apostles are also High Priests (Doctrine and Covenants, sec. lxxxiv: 63); and of course as there were men who had been ordained to the apostleship before this conference of June, 1831, in that manner there had been High Priests in the Church, but not otherwise.

† In addition to the spiritual manifestations already mentioned as having occurred at this conference of June 3rd-6th, it should be said that. according to John Whitmer's *History of the Church* (ch. v): "The Spirit of the Lord fell upon Joseph in an unusual manner, and he prophesied that John the Revelator was then among the Ten Tribes of Israel who had been led away by Shalmaneser, king of Assyria, to prepare them for their return from their long dispersion, to again possess the land of their fathers. He prophesied many more things that I have not written. After he had prophesied he laid his hands upon Lyman Wight and ordained him to the High Priesthood [i. e., ordained him a High Priest], after the holy order of God. And the Spirit fell upon Lyman, and he prophesied concerning the coming of Christ. He said that there were some in the congregation that should live until the Savior should descend from heaven with a shout, with all the holy angels with Him. He said the coming of the Savior should be like the sun rising in the east, and will cover the whole earth. So with the coming of the Son of Man; yea, He will appear in His brightness and consume all [the wicked] before Him; and the hills will be laid low, and the valleys be exalted, and the crooked be made straight, and the rough smooth. And some of my brethren shall suffer martyrdom for the sake of the religion of Jesus Christ, and seal their testimony of Jesus Christ, and seal their testimony of Jesus with their blood. He saw the heavens opened and the Son of Man sitting on the right hand of the Father, making intercession for his brethren, the Saints. He said that God would work a work in these last days that tongue cannot express and the mind is not capable to conceive. The glory of the Lord shone around.'"

"The congregation at this conference numbered two thousand souls."—Cannon's *Life of Joseph Smith the Prophet*, p. 113.

This was the fourth general conference of the Church, the others were held on the 9th of June, 1830; the 26th of September, 1830; and the 2nd of January, 1831, respectively; and all at Fayette, Seneca County, New York.

and humility, so necessary for the blessing of God to follow prayer, characterized the Saints.

The next day, as a kind continuation of this great work of the last days, I received the following:

*Revelation, given June, 1831.**

1. Behold, thus saith the Lord unto the elders whom he hath called and chosen in these last days, by the voice of his Spirit—

2. Saying: I, the Lord, will make known unto you what I will that ye shall do from this time until the next conference, which shall be held in Missouri, upon the land which I will consecrate unto my people, which are a remant of Jacob, and those who are heirs according to the covenant.

3. Wherefore, verily I say unto you, let my servants Joseph Smith, Jun., and Sidney Rigdon take their journey as soon as preparations can be made to leave their homes, and journey to the land of Missouri.

4. And inasmuch as they are faithful unto me, it shall be made known unto them what they shall do;

5. And it shall also, inasmuch as they are faithful, be made known unto them the land of your inheritance.

6. And inasmuch as they are not faithful, they shall be cut off, even as I will, as seemeth me good.

7. And again, verily I say unto you, let my servant Lyman Wight and my servant John Corrill take their journey speedily;

8. And also my servant John Murdock, and my servant Hyrum Smith, take their journey unto the same place by the way of Detroit.

9. And let them journey from thence preaching the word by the way, saying none other things than that which the prophets and apostles have written, and that which is taught them by the Comforter through the prayer of faith.

10. Let them go two by two, and thus let them preach by the way in every congregation, baptizing by water, and the laying on of the hands by the water's side.

11. For thus saith the Lord, I will cut my work short in righteousness, for the days come that I will send forth judgment unto victory.

12. And let my servant Lyman Wight beware, for Satan desireth to sift him as chaff.

13. And behold, he that is faithful shall be made ruler over many things.

14. And again, I will give unto you a pattern in all things, that ye

* Doctrine and Covenants, sec. lii.

may not be deceived; for Satan is abroad in the land, and he goeth forth deceiving the nations—

15. Wherefore he that prayeth, whose spirit is contrite, the same is accepted of me if he obey mine ordinances.

16. He that speaketh, whose spirit is contrite, whose language is meek and edifieth, the same is of God if he obey mine ordinances.

17. And again, he that trembleth under my power shall be made strong, and shall bring forth fruits of praise and wisdom, according to the revelations and truths which I have given you.

18. And again, he that is overcome and bringeth not forth fruits, even according to this pattern, is not of me.

19. Wherefore, by this pattern ye shall know the spirits in all cases under the whole heavens.

20. And the days have come; according to men's faith it shall be done unto them.

21. Behold, this commandment is given unto all the elders whom I have chosen.

22. And again, verily I say unto you, let my servant Thomas B. Marsh and my servant Ezra Thayre, take their journey also, preaching the word by the way unto this same land.

23. And again, let my servant Isaac Morley, and my servant Ezra Booth take their journey, also preaching the word by the way unto this same land.

24. And again, let my servants Edward Partridge and Martin Harris take their journey with my servants Sidney Rigdon and Joseph Smith, Jun.

25. Let my servants David Whitmer and Harvey Whitlock also take their journey, and preach by the way unto this same land.

26. And let my servants Parley P. Pratt and Orson Pratt take their journey, and preach by the way, even unto this same land.

27. And let my servants Solomon Hancock and Simeon Carter also take their journey unto this same land, and preach by the way.

28. Let my servants Edson Fuller and Jacob Scott also take their journey.

29. Let my servants Levi W. Hancock and Zebedee Coltrin also take their journey.

30. Let my servants Reynolds Cahoon and Samuel H. Smith also take their journey.

31. Let my servants Wheeler Baldwin and William Carter also take their journey.

32. And let my servants Newel Knight and Selah J. Griffin, both be ordained, and also take their journey.

33. Yea, verily I say, let all these take their journey unto one

place, in their several courses, and one man shall not build upon another's foundation, neither journey in another's track.

34. He that is faithful, the same shall be kept and blessed with much fruit.

35. And again, I say unto you, let my servants Joseph Wakefield and Solomon Humphrey take their journey into the eastern lands;

36. Let them labor with their families, declaring none other things than the prophets and apostles, that which they have seen and heard and most assuredly believe, that the prophecies may be fulfilled.

37. In consequence of transgression, let that which was bestowed upon Heman Bassett be taken from him, and placed upon the head of Simonds Ryder.

38. And again, verily I say unto you, let Jared Carter be ordained a priest, and also George James be ordained a priest.

39. Let the residue of the elders watch over the churches, and declare the word in the regions round about them: and let them labor with their own hands that there be no idolatry nor wickedness practiced.

40. And remember in all things the poor and the needy, the sick and the afflicted, for he that doeth not these things, the same is not my disciple.

41. And again, let my servant Joseph Smith, Jun., and Sidney Rigdon, and Edward Partridge take with them a recommend from the church. And let there be one obtained for my servant Oliver Cowdery also.

42. And thus, even as I have said, if ye are faithful ye shall assemble yourselves together to rejoice upon the land of Missouri, which is the land of your inheritance, which is now the land of your enemies.

43. But, behold, I, the Lord, will hasten the city in its time, and will crown the faithful with joy and with rejoicing.

44. Behold, I am Jesus Christ, the Son of God, and I will lift them up at the last day. Even so. Amen.

Shortly after the foregoing was received, at the request of Algernon Sidney Gilbert I inquired, and obtained the following:

*Revelation, given June, 1831.**

1. Behold, I say unto you, my servant Sidney Gilbert, that I have heard your prayers, and you have called upon me that it should be made known unto you, of the Lord your God, concerning your calling

* Doctrine and Covenants, sec. liii.

and election in the church, which I, the Lord, have raised up in these last days.

2. Behold, I, the Lord, who was crucified for the sins of the world, give unto you a commandment that you shall forsake the world.

3. Take upon you mine ordination, even that of an elder, to preach faith and repentance and remission of sins, according to my word, and the reception of the Holy Spirit by the laying on of hands;

4. And also to be an agent unto this church in the place which shall be appointed by the bishop, according to commandments which shall be given hereafter.

5. And again, verily I say unto you, you shall take your journey with my servants Joseph Smith, Jun., and Sidney Rigdon.

6. Behold these are the first ordinances which you shall receive; and the residue shall be made known in a time to come, according to your labor in my vineyard.

7. And again, I would that ye should learn that he only is saved who endureth unto the end. Even so. Amen.

Difficulty in the Thompson Branch.

The branch of the Church in Thompson, on account of breaking the covenant,* and not knowing what to do, they sent in Newel Knight and other Elders, to ask me to inquire of the Lord for them; which I did, and received the following:

* It is difficult to determine with exactness in what the transgressions of the Saints at Thompson consisted; but it is evident that selfishness and rebellion were at the bottom of their trouble, and that Leman Copley and Ezra Thayre were immediately concerned in it. The Saints comprising the Colesville branch, when they arrived at the gathering place, in Ohio, were advised to remain together and were settled at Thompson, a place in the vicinity of Kirtland. On their arrival Bishop Edward Partridge urged the Prophet Joseph to inquire of the Lord concerning the manner of settling them, and providing for them. Whereupon the Prophet inquired of the Lord and received the revelation found on page 173. It will bee senn from that revelation that the Saints of the Colesville branch were to be organized under the law of consecration and stewardship. That is, in brief, the Saints were to make a consecration of whatsoever things they possessed unto the Bishop, and then each man receive from the Bishop a stewardship. Every man was to be equal in his stewardship, according to his family, his circumstances, and his needs. For details in the matter the reader is referred to the revelation itself. It is evident that some of the brethren already living at Thompson, had agreed to enter into the law of consecration and stewardship with the Saints from Colesville; and that afterwards they broke this covenant. Among these were Leman Copley and Ezra Thayre. "A man by the name of Copley," says Newel Knight in his journal, "had a considerable tract of land there [in Thompson] which he offered to let the Saints occupy. Consequently a contract was agreed upon, and we commenced work in good faith. But in a short time Copley broke the engagement, and I went to Kirtland to see Brother Joseph," etc. *Scraps of Biography*,

*Revelation to Newel Knight, given at Kirtland, June, 1831.**

1. Behold, thus saith the Lord, even Alpha and Omega, the beginning and the end, even he who was crucified for the sins of the world—

2. Behold, verily, verily, I say unto you, my servant Newel Knight, you shall stand fast in the office wherewith I have appointed you.

3. And if your brethren desire to escape their enemies, let them repent of all their sins, and become truly humble before me and contrite.

4. And as the covenant which they made unto me has been broken, even so it has become void and of none effect.

5. And wo to him by whom this offense cometh, for it had been better for him that he had been drowned in the depth of the sea.

6. But blessed are they who have kept the covenant and observed the commandment, for they shall obtain mercy.

7. Wherefore, go to now and flee the land, lest your enemies come upon you; and take your journey, and appoint whom you will to be your leader, and to pay monies for you.†

8. And thus you shall take your journey into the regions westward, unto the land of Missouri, unto the borders of the Lamanites.

9. And after you have done journeying, behold, I say unto you, seek ye a living like unto men, until I prepare a place for you,

10. And again be patient in tribulation until I come; and, behold, I came quickly, and my reward is with me, and they who have sought me early shall find rest to their souls. Even so. Amen.

The Elders now began to go to the western country, two and two, according to the word of the Lord.

From Parley P. Pratt, who during the spring had returned from his mission of last fall, we had verbal

in which is published Newel Knight's journal, ch. vi.) Of this matter, John Whitmer, then the Church Historian, writes: "At this time [the early part of June] the Church at Thompson, Ohio, was involved in difficulty because of the rebellion of Leman Copley, who would not do as he had previously agreed, which thing confused the whole Church, and finally the Lord spake through Joseph the Prophet, saying:" He then quotes the revelation to Newel Knight given in the text above.—(John Whitmer's *History of the Church*, chap. viii.) For Ezra Thayre's part in the proceedings at Thompson, see the revelation given to Thomas B. Marsh, pp. 186, 187.

* Doctrine and Covenants, sec. liv.

† "The Church at Thompson," says John Whitmer, "made all possible haste to leave for Missouri, and left, and none of their enemies harmed them."—John Whitmer's *History of the Church*, chap. viii. Newel Knight was appointed the leader of this company, which was made up of the Colesville branch, and under his leadership they made the entire journey from Thompson to Missouri.

information; and from letters from the still remaining Elders we had written intelligence; and as the mission to Western Missouri and the gathering of the Saints to that place was the most important subject which then engrossed the attention of the Church, I will here insert the copy of a letter, received about this time from that section, dated at Kaw Township, Missouri, May 7, 1831:

Report of Oliver Cowdery on Conditions in Western Missouri.

Our Dearly Beloved Brethren:—I have nothing particular to write as concerning the Lamanites; because of a short journey which I have just returned from, and in consequence of which I have not written to you since the 16th of last month. Brother Ziba Peterson and myself went into the county east, which is Lafayette, about forty miles; and, in the name of Jesus, we called on the people to repent, many of whom are, I believe, earnestly searching for truth, and if sincerely, I pray they may find that precious treasure, for it seems to be wholly fallen in the streets, and equity cannot enter.

The letter we received from you informed us that the opposition was great against you. Now, our beloved brethren, we verily believe that we also can rejoice that we are counted worthy to suffer shame for His name; for almost the whole country, consisting of Universalists Atheists, Deists, Presbyterians, Methodists, Baptists, and other professed Christians, priests and people; with all the devils from the infernal pit are united, and foaming out their own shame [against us]. God forbid that I should bring a railing accusation against them, for vengeance belongeth to Him who is able to repay; and herein, brethren, we confide.

I am lately informed of another tribe of Lamanites, who have abundance of flocks of the best kinds of sheep and cattle; and they manufacture blankets of a superior quality. The tribe, is very numerous; they live three hundred miles west of Santa Fe, and are called Navashoes.* Why I mention this tribe is because I feel under obligations to communicate to my brethren any information concerning the Lamanites that I meet with in my labors and travels; believing, as I do, that much is expected from me in the cause of our Lord; and doubting not that I am daily remembered before the throne of the Most High by all my brethren, as well by those who have not seen my face in the flesh as by those who have.

We begin to expect our brother Parley P. Pratt soon; we have heard from him only when he was at St. Louis. We are all well, bless

* It was doubtless the Navajo Indians, whose reservation is now located in northeastern Arizona, of whom Oliver heard.

the Lord; and preach the Gospel we will, if earth and hell oppose our way—for we dwell in the midst of scorpions—and in Jesus we trust. Grace be with you all. Amen. OLIVER COWDERY.

P. S.—I beseech Brother Whitney to remember and write, and direct to me, Independence, Jackson County, Missouri.*

* THE MISSION TO THE LAMANITES.—As the "mission to the Lamanites" is a very prominent event in early Church history, it is proper that the labors of the brethren engaged in it should be spoken of more fully than appears anywhere in the Prophet's narrative, and at this point, following the letter of Oliver Cowdery, seems as appropriate a place as will be found to speak of it. It has already been said that the brethren of the mission called upon the Catteraugus tribe, near Buffalo, New York, (p. 120 note). After leaving Kirtland, on their journey westward, they visited the Wyandot tribe of Indians near Sandusky, Ohio, with whom they spent several days. "We were well received," writes Elder Parley P. Pratt, "and had an opportunity of laying before them the record of their forefathers, which we did. They rejoiced in the tidings, bid us Godspeed and desired us to write to them in relation to our success among the tribes further west, who had already removed to the Indian territory, where these expected soon to go."—*Aut.* P. P. Pratt, p. 54.

On arriving at Independence two of the company secured employment, while the other three crossed the frontier and began their labors among the Indians. They visited the Shawnees, spending one night with them, and the next day crossed the Kansas river and began their labors among the Delawares. They sought an interview with the chief of the Delawares, known among the whites as Chief Anderson. He was the grand sachem of ten nations or tribes, and consequently possessed of large influence. He had always opposed the introduction of missionaries among his people, and therefore did not at first extend a very hearty welcome to the brethren. However, through an interpreter, the brethren made known their errand and explained to him the Book of Mormon and the information it contained for his people. They asked to be heard before a full council of his nation, a proposition which the chief took under consideration until the next day. Next morning the conversation with the Delaware Chief was renewed, but he was not inclined at first to call the council. But as he began to understand better the nature of the Book of Mormon, he changed his mind and asked the brethren to suspend their conversation until the council could be assembled. A runner was dispatched to the tribes, and in about an hour forty leading men were assembled and seated in grave silence to hear the message concerning the book of their forefathers. At the request of the chief, Oliver Cowdery in substance delivered the following address:

OLIVER COWDERY'S SPEECH TO THE DELAWARES.

"Aged Chief, and Venerable Council of the Delaware nation: we are glad of this opportunity to address you as our red brethren and friends. We have traveled a long distance from towards the rising sun to bring you glad news; we have traveled the wilderness, crossed the deep and wide rivers, and waded in the deep snows, and in the face of the storms of winter, to communicate to you great knowledge which has lately come to our ears and hearts and which will do the red man good as well as the pale face.

"Once the red men were many; they occupied the country from sea to sea—from the rising to the setting sun; the whole land was theirs; the Great Spirit gave it to them, and no pale faces dwelt among them. But now they are few in numbers; their possessions are small, and the pale faces are many.

"Thousands of moons ago, when the red men's forefathers dwelt in peace and possessed this whole land, the Great Spirit talked with them, and revealed His law and

About the middle of June, while we were preparing for our journey to Missouri, William W. Phelps and

His will, and much knowledge to their wise men and prophets. This they wrote in a Book, together with their history and the things which should befall their children in the latter days.

"This Book was written on plates of gold and handed down from father to son for many ages and generations.

"It was then that the pople prospered and were strong and mighty; they cultivated the earth, built buildings and cities and abounded in all good things, as the pale faces now do.

"But they became wicked; they killed one another and shed much blood; they killed their prophets and wise men, and sought to destroy the Book. The Great Spirit became angry and would speak to them no more; they had no more good and wise dreams; no more visions; no more angels sent among them by the Great Spirit; and the Lord commanded Mormon and Moroni, their last wise men and prophets to hide the Book in the earth, that it might be preserved in safety and be found and made known in the latter-day to the pale faces who should possess the land, that they might again make it known to the red men, in order to restore them to the knowledge of the will of the Great Spirit and to His favor. And if the red men would then receive this Book and learn the things written in it and do according thereunto, they should be restored to all their rights and privileges; should cease to fight and kill one another; should become one people; cultivate the earth in peace, in common with the pale faces, who were willing to believe and obey the same Book and be good men and live in peace.

"Then should the red men become great and have plenty to eat and good clothes to wear, and should be in favor with the Great Spirit and be His children, while He would be their Great Father and talk with them, and raise up prophets and wise and good men among them again, who should teach them many things.

"This Book, which contained these things, was hid in the earth by Moroni, in a hill called by him Cumorah, which hill is now in the State of New York, near the village of Palmyra, in Ontario county.

"In that neighborhood there lived a young man named Joseph Smith, who prayed to the Great Spirit much, in order that he might know the truth, and the Great Spirit sent an angel to him and told him where this Book was hid by Moroni, and commanded him to go and get it. He accordingly went to the place and dug in the earth and found the Book written on golden plates.

"But it was written in the language of the forefathers of the red men; therefore this young man, being a pale face, could not understand it; but the angel told him and showed him and gave him knowledge of the language and how to interpret the Book. So he interpreted it into the language of the pale faces, and wrote it on paper and caused it to be printed, and published thousands of copies of it among them, and then sent us to the red men to bring some copies of it to them, and to tell them this news. So we have now come from him, and here is a copy of the Book, which we now present to our red friend, the Chief of the Delawares, which we hope he will cause to be read and known among his tribe; it will do them good."

We then presented him with a Book of Mormon.

There was a pause in the council and some conversation in their own language, after which the chief made the following reply:

THE CHIEF'S REPLY.

"We feel truly thankful to our white friends who have come so far and been at

his family arrived among us—"to do the will of the Lord," he said: so I inquired of the Lord concerning him and received the following:

*Revelation given June, 1831.**

1. Behold, thus saith the Lord unto you, my servant William, yea, even the Lord of the whole earth, thou art called and chosen; and after thou hast been baptized by water, which if you do with an eye single to my glory, you shall have a remission of your sins and a reception of the Holy Spirit by the laying on of hands;

2. And then thou shalt be ordained by the hand of my servant Joseph Smith, Jun., to be an elder unto this church, to preach repentance and remission of sins by way of baptism in the name of Jesus Christ the Son of the living God.

3. And on whomsoever you shall lay your hands, if they are contrite before me, you shall have power to give the Holy Spirit.

4. And again, you shall be ordained to assist my servant Oliver Cowdery to do the work of printing, and of selecting and writing books for schools in this Church, that little children also may receive instruction before me as is pleasing unto me.

such pains to tell us good news, and especially this new news concerning the Book of our forefathers; it makes us glad in here"—placing his hand on his heart. "It is now winter; we are new settlers in this place; the snow is deep; our cattle and horses are dying; our wigwams are poor; we have much to do in the spring—to build houses and fence and make farms; but we will build a council house and meet together, and you shall read to us and teach us more concerning the Book of our fathers and the will of the Great Spirit."

Elder Parley P. Pratt in his report of the matter adds: "We continued for several days to instruct the old Chief and many of his tribe. The interest became more and more intense on their part, from day to day, until at length nearly the whole tribe began to feel a spirit of inquiry and excitement on the subject. We found several among them who could read, and to them we gave copies of the Book, explaining to them that it was the Book of their forefathers. Some began to rejoice exceedingly and took great pains to tell the news to others in their own language. The excitement now reached the frontier settlements in Missouri, and stirred up the jealousy and envy of the Indian agents and sectarian missionaries to that degree that we were soon ordered out of the Indian country as disturbers of the peace, and even threatened with the military in case of non-compliance. We accordingly departed from the Indian country and came over the line, and commenced laboring in Jackson county, Missouri, among the whites We were well received and listened to by many, and some were baptized and added to the Church.

"Thus ended our first Indian mission, in which we had preached the Gospel in its fulness and distributed the record of their forefathers among three tribes, viz.: the Catteraugus Indians,near Buffalo, N. Y.; the Wyandots, of Ohio; and the Delawares, west of Missouri."—*Aut.* P. P. Pratt, pp. 56-61.

* Doctrine and Covenants, sec. lv.

5. And again, verily I say unto you, for this cause ye shall take your journey with my servants Joseph Smith, Jun., and Sidney Rigdon, that you may be planted in the land of your inheritance to do this work.

6. And again, let my servant Joseph Coe also take his journey with them. The residue shall be made known hereafter, even as I will. Amen.*

Marsh and Thayre Separated as Missionary Companions.

Soon after I received the foregoing, Elder Thomas B. Marsh came to inquire what he should do; as Elder Ezra Thayre, his yoke-fellow in the ministry, could not get ready to start on his mission as soon as he (Marsh) would; and I inquired of the Lord, and received the following:

Revelation, given at Kirtland, June, 1831.†

1. Hearken, O ye people who profess my name, saith the Lord your God; for behold, mine anger is kindled against the rebellious, and they shall know mine arm and mine indignation, in the day of visitation and of wrath upon the nations.

2. And he that will not take up his cross and follow me, and keep my commandments, the same shall not be saved.

3. Behold, I, the Lord, command; and he that will not obey shall be cut off in mine own due time, after I have commanded and the commandment is broken.

4. Wherefore I, the Lord, command and revoke, as it seemeth me good; and all this to be answered upon the heads of the rebellious, saith the Lord.

5. Wherefore, I revoke the commandment which was given unto my servants Thomas B. Marsh and Ezra Thayre, and give a new commandment unto my servant Thomas, that he shall take up his journey speedily to the land of Missouri, and my servant Selah J. Griffin shall also go with him.

6. For behold, I revoke the commandment which was given unto my servants Selah J. Griffin and Newel Knight, in consequence of the stiffneckedness of my people which are in Thompson and their rebellions.

* William Wine Phelps, spoken of in the foregoing revelation, was born at Hanover, Morris county, New Jersey, February 17th, 1792. He was therefore in his fortieth year when he came to the Church at Kirtland, to cast in his lot with the Saints. It appears that before making his appearance at Kirtland, he had resided chiefly in the state of New York; and had been somewhat active in politics. He had been the editor of a partisan newspaper; and had aspired to be the candidate for the office of lieutenant-governor of New York. On the 28th of April, 1815, he married Sally Waterman, at Smyrna, Chenango county, New York.

† Doctrine and Covenants, sec lvi.

7. Wherefore, let my servant Newel Knight remain with them, and as many as will go may go, that are contrite before me, and be led by him to the land which I have appointed.

8. And again, verily I say unto you, that my servant Ezra Thayre must repent of his pride, and of his selfishness, and obey the former commandment which I have given him concerning the place upon which he lives.

9. And if he will do this, as there shall be no divisions made upon the land, he shall be appointed still to go to the land of Missouri;

10. Otherwise he shall receive the money which he has paid, and shall leave the place, and shall be cut off out of my church, saith the Lord God of hosts;

11. And though the heaven and the earth pass away, these words shall not pass away, but shall be fulfilled.

12. And if my servant Joseph Smith, Jun., must needs pay the money, behold, I, the Lord, will pay it unto him again in the land of Missouri, that those of whom he shall receive may be rewarded again according to that which they do;

13. For according to that which they do they shall receive, even in lands for their inheritance.

14. Behold, thus saith the Lord unto my people—you have many things to do and to repent of; for behold, your sins have come up unto me, and are not pardoned, because you seek to counsel in your own ways.

15. And your hearts are not satisfied. And ye obey not the truth, but have pleasure in unrighteousness.

16. Wo unto you rich men, that will not give your substance to the poor, for your riches will canker your souls; and this shall be your lamentation in the day of visitation, and of judgment, and of indignation: The harvest is past, the summer is ended, and my soul is not saved!

17. Wo unto you poor men, whose hearts are not broken, whose spirits are not contrite, and whose bellies are not satisfied, and whose hands are not stayed from laying hold upon other men's goods, whose eyes are full of greediness, and who will not labor with your own hands!

18. But blessed are the poor who are pure in heart, whose hearts are broken, and whose spirits are contrite, for they shall see the kingdom of God coming in power and great glory unto their deliverance; for the fatness of the earth shall be theirs.

19. For behold, the Lord shall come, and his recompense shall be with him, and he shall reward every man, and the poor shall rejoice;

20. And their generations shall inherit the earth from generation

to generation, for ever and ever. And now I make an end of speaking unto you. Even so. Amen.*

The Departure of the Prophet and Company for Missouri.

On the 19th of June, in company with Sidney Rigdon, Martin Harris, Edward Partridge, William W. Phelps, Joseph Coe, Algernon S. Gilbert and his wife, I started from Kirtland, Ohio, for the land of Missouri, agreeable to the commandment before received, wherein it was promised that if we were faithful, the land of our inheritance, even the place for the city of the New Jerusalem, should be revealed. We went by wagon, canal boats, and stages to Cincinnati, where I had an interview with the Rev. Walter Scott, one of the founders of the Campbellites, or Newlight church.† Before the close of our interview, he manifested one of the bitterest spirits against the doctrine of the New Testament (that "these signs shall follow them that believe," as recorded in Mark the 16th chapter,) that I ever witnessed among men. We left Cincinnati in a steamer, and landed at Louisville, Kentucky, where we were detained three days in waiting for a steamer to convey us to St. Louis. At St. Louis, myself, Brothers Harris, Phelps, Partridge and Coe, went by land on foot to Independence, Jackson county, Missouri, where we arrived about the middle of July, and the rest of the company came by water a few days later.

Treatment by the Way.

Notwithstanding the corruptions and abominations of the times, and the evil spirit manifested towards us on account of our belief in the Book of Mormon, at many places and among various persons, yet the Lord continued His watchful

* The phrase in the ninth verse of the foregoing revelation, "*As there shall be no divisions made upon the land,*" undoubtedly has reference to the land upon which Ezra Thayre was living at Thompson, and which he had covenanted, under some arrangement for compensation, to grant to the Church, and which contract he attempted, at least, to repudiate.

† Reference is made to both Mr. Alexander Campbell and Mr. Scott, and the founding of the "Campbellite" or "Disciples" sect in the biographical sketch of Sidney Rigdon; as also Rigdon's connection with that movement.—See pp. 120, 121.

care and loving kindness to us day by day; and we made it a rule wherever there was an opportunity, to read a chapter in the Bible, and pray; and these seasons of worship gave us great consolation.

The meeting of our brethren, who had long awaited our arrival, was a glorious one, and moistened with many tears. It seemed good and pleasant for brethren to meet together in unity. But our reflections were many, coming as we had from a highly cultivated state of society in the east, and standing now upon the confines or western limits of the United States, and looking into the vast wilderness of those that sat in darkness; how natural it was to observe the degradation, leanness of intellect, ferocity, and jealousy of a people that were nearly a century behind the times, and to feel for those who roamed about without the benefit of civilization, refinement, or religion; yea, and exclaim in the language of the Prophets: "When will the wilderness blossom as the rose? When will Zion be built up in her glory, and where will Thy temple stand, unto which all nations shall come in the last days?" Our anxiety was soon relieved by receiving the following:

Arrival in Missouri.

Reflections on State of Society in Missouri.

Questions and the Answer by Revelation.

*Revelation, given in Zion, July, 1831.**

1. Hearken, O ye elders of my church, saith the Lord your God, who have assembled yourselves together, according to my commandments, in this land, which is the land of Missouri, which is the land which I have appointed and consecrated for the gathering of the Saints.
2. Wherefore, this is the land of promise, and the place for the city of Zion.
3. And thus saith the Lord your God, if you will receive wisdom here is wisdom. Behold, the place which is now called Independence is the center place; and the spot for the temple is lying westward, upon a lot which is not far from the court-house.
4. Wherefore, it is wisdom that the land should be purchased by the Saints, and also every tract lying westward, even unto the line running directly between Jew and Gentile.

* Doctrine and Covenants, sec. lvii.

5. And also every tract bordering by the prairies, inasmuch as my disciples are enabled to buy lands. Behold, this is wisdom, that they may obtain it for an everlasting inheritance.

6. And let my servant Sidney Gilbert stand in the office to which I have appointed him, to receive monies, to be an agent unto the church, to buy land in all the regions round about, inasmuch as can be done in righteousness, and as wisdom shall direct.

7. And let my servant Edward Partridge stand in the office to which I have appointed him, and divide unto the Saints their inheritance, even as I have commanded; and also those whom he has appointed to assist him.

8. And again, verily I say unto you, let my servant Sidney Gilbert plant himself in this place, and establish a store, that he may sell goods without fraud, that he may obtain money to buy lands for the good of the Saints, and that he may obtain whatsoever things the disciples may need to plant them in their inheritance.

9. And also let my servant Sidney Gilbert obtain a license—behold here is wisdom, and whoso readeth let him understand—that he may send goods also unto the people, even by whom he will as clerks employed in his service.

10. And thus provide for my saints, that my gospel may be preached unto those who sit in darkness, and in the region and shadow of death.

11. And again, verily I say unto you, let my servant William W. Phelps be planted in this place, and be established as a printer unto the church.

12. And lo, if the world receive his writings—behold here is wisdom—let him obtain whatsoever he can obtain in righteousness, for the good of the Saints.

13. And let my servant Oliver Cowdery assist him, even as I have commanded, in whatsoever place I shall appoint unto him, to copy, and to correct, and select, that all things may be right before me, as it shall be proved by the Spirit through him.

14. And thus let those of whom I have spoken be planted in the land of Zion, as speedily as can be, with their families, to do those things even as I have spoken.

15. And now concerning the gathering—Let the bishop and the agent make preparations for those families which have been commanded to come to this land, as soon as possible, and plant them in their inheritance.

And unto the residue of both elders and members further directions shall be given hereafter. Even so. Amen.

The First Sabbath in Zion.

The first Sabbath after our arrival in Jackson county, Brother W. W. Phelps preached to a western audience over the boundary of the United States, wherein were present specimens of all the families of the earth; Shem, Ham and Japheth; several of the Lamanites or Indians—representative of Shem; quite a respectable number of negroes—descendants of Ham; and the balance was made up of citizens of the surrounding country, and fully represented themselves as pioneers of the West. At this meeting two were baptized, who had previously believed in the fulness of the Gospel.

During this week the Colesville branch, referred to in the latter part of the last revelation,* and Sidney Rigdon, Sidney Gilbert and wife and Elders Morley and Booth, arrived. I received the following:

Arrival of the Colesville Branch.

Revelation, given in Zion, August, 1831.†

1. Hearken, O ye elders of my church, and give ear to my word, and learn of me what I will concerning you, and also concerning this land unto which I have sent you.

2. For verily I say unto you, blessed is he that keepeth my commandments, whether in life or in death; and he that is faithful in tribulation, the reward of the same is greater in the kingdom of heaven.

3. Ye cannot behold with your natural eyes, for the present time, the design of your God concerning those things which shall come hereafter, and the glory which shall follow after much tribulation.

4. For after much tribulation come the blessings. Wherefore the day cometh that ye shall be crowned with much glory; the hour is not yet, but is nigh at hand.

5. Remember this, which I tell you before, that you may lay it to heart, and receive that which is to follow.

6. Behold, verily I say unto you, for this cause I have sent you—that you might be obedient, and that your hearts might be prepared to bear testimony of the things which are to come;

7. And also that you might be honored in laying the foundation, and in bearing record of the land upon which the Zion of God shall stand;

8. And also that a feast of fat things might be prepared for the poor; yea, a feast of fat things, of wine on the lees well refined, that the earth may know that the mouths of the prophets shall not fail;

* Verse fifteen.

† Doctrine and Covenants, sec. lviii.

9. Yea, a supper of the house of the Lord, well prepared, unto which all nations shall be invited.

10. First, the rich and the learned, the wise and the noble;

11. And after that cometh the day of my power; then shall the poor, the lame, and the blind, and the deaf, come in unto the marriage of the Lamb, and partake of the supper of the Lord, prepared for the great day to come.

12. Behold, I, the Lord, have spoken it.

13. And that the testimony might go forth from Zion, yea, from the mouth of the city of the heritage of God—

14. Yea, for this cause I have sent you hither, and have selected my servant Edward Partridge, and have appointed unto him his mission in this land.

15. But if he repent not of his sins, which are unbelief and blindness of heart, let him take heed lest he fall.

16. Behold his mission is given unto him, and it shall not be given again.

17. And whoso standeth in this mission is appointed to be a judge in Israel, like as it was in ancient days, to divide the lands of the heritage of God unto his children;

18. And to judge his people by the testimony of the just, and by the assistance of his counselors, according to the laws of the kingdom which are given by the prophets of God.

19. For verily I say unto you, my law shall be kept on this land.

20. Let no man think he is ruler; but let God rule him that judgeth, according to the counsel of his own will; or, in other words, him that counseleth or sitteth upon the judgment seat.

21. Let no man break the laws of the land, for he that keepeth the laws of God hath no need to break the laws of the land.

22. Wherefore, be subject to the powers that be, until he reigns whose right it is to reign, and subdues all enemies under his feet.

23. Behold, the laws which ye have received from my hand are the laws of the church, and in this light ye shall hold them forth. Behold, here is wisdom.

24. And now as I spake concerning my servant Edward Partridge, this land is the land of his residence, and those whom he has appointed for his counselors; and also the land of the residence of him whom I have appointed to keep my store-house;

25. Wherefore, let them bring their families to this land, as they shall counsel between themselves and me.

26. For behold, it is not meet that I should command in all things; for he that is compelled in all things, the same is a slothful and not a wise servant; wherefore he receiveth no reward.

27. Verily I say, men should be anxiously engaged in a good cause,

and do many things of their own free will, and bring to pass much righteousness;

28. For the power is in them, wherein they are agents unto themselves. And inasmuch as men do good they shall in nowise lose their reward.

29. But he that doeth not anything until he is commanded, and receiveth a commandment with doubtful heart, and keepeth it with slothfulness, the same is damned.

30. Who am I that made man, saith the Lord, that will hold him guiltless that obeys not my commandments?

31. Who am I, saith the Lord, that have promised and have not fulfilled?

32. I command and men obey not; I revoke and they receive not the blessing.

33. Then they say in their hearts: This is not the work of the Lord, for his promises are not fulfilled. But wo unto such, for their reward lurketh beneath, and not from above.

34. And now I give unto you further directions concerning this land.

35. It is wisdom in me that my servant Martin Harris should be an example unto the church, in laying his monies before the bishop of the church.

36. And also, this is a law unto every man that cometh unto this land to receive an inheritance; and he shall do with his monies according as the law directs.

37. And it is wisdom also that there should be lands purchased in Independence, for the place of the store-house, and also for the house of the printing.

38. And other directions concerning my servant Martin Harris shall be given him of the Spirit, that he may receive his inheritance as seemeth him good;

39. And let him repent of his sins, for he seeketh the praise of the world.

40. And also let my servant William W. Phelps stand in the office which I have appointed him, and receive his inheritance in the land;

41. And also he hath need to repent, for I, the Lord, am not well pleased with him, for he seeketh to excel, and he is not sufficiently meek before me.

42. Behold, he who has repented of his sins, the same is forgiven, and I, the Lord, remember them no more.

43. By this ye may know if a man repenteth of his sins—behold, he will confess them and forsake them.

44. And now, verily, I say concerning the residue of the elders of my church, the time has not yet come, for many years, for them to

receive their inheritance in this land, except they desire it through the prayer of faith, only as it shall be appointed unto them of the Lord.

45. For, behold, they shall push the people together from the ends of the earth.

46. Wherefore, assemble yourselves together; and they who are not appointed to stay in this land, let them preach the gospel in the regions round about; and after that let them return to their homes.

47. Let them preach by the way, and bear testimony of the truth in all places, and call upon the rich, the high and the low, and the poor to repent.

48. And let them build up churches, inasmuch as the inhabitants of the earth will repent.

49. And let there be an agent appointed by the voice of the church, unto the church in Ohio, to receive monies to purchase lands in Zion.

50. And I give unto my servant Sidney Rigdon a commandment, that he shall write a description of the land of Zion, and a statement of the will of God, as it shall be made known by the Spirit unto him;

51. And an epistle and subscription, to be presented unto all the churches to obtain monies, to be put into the hands of the bishop. of himself or the agent, as seemeth him good or as he shall direct, to purchase lands for an inheritance for the children of God.

52. For, behold, verily I say unto you, the Lord willeth that the disciples, and the children of men should open their hearts, even to purchase this whole region of country, as soon as the time will permit.

53. Behold, here is wisdom. Let them do this lest they receive none inheritance, save it be by the shedding of blood.

54. And again, inasmuch as there is land obtained, let there be workmen sent forth of all kinds unto this land, to labor for the saints of God.

55. Let all these things be done in order; and let the privileges of the lands be made known from time to time, by the bishop or the agent of the church.

56. And let the work of the gathering be not in haste, nor by flight; but let it be done as it shall be counseled by the elders of the church at the conferences, according to the knowledge which they receive from time to time.

57. And let my servant Sidney Rigdon consecrate and dedicate this land, and the spot for the temple unto the Lord.

58. And let a conference meeting be called; and after that let my servants Sidney Rigdon and Joseph Smith, Jun., return, and also Oliver Cowdery with them, to accomplish the residue of the work which I have appointed unto them in their own land, and the residue as shall be ruled by the conferences.

59. And let no man return from this land except he bear record by the way of that which he knows and most assuredly believes.

60. Let that which has been bestowed upon Ziba Peterson be taken from him; and let him stand as a member in the church, and labor with his own hands, with the brethren, until he is sufficiently chastened for all his sins; for he confesseth them not, and he thinketh to hide them.

61. Let the residue of the elders of this church, who are coming to this land, some of whom are exceedingly blessed even above measure, also hold a conference upon this land.

62. And let my servant Edward Partridge direct the conference which shall be held by them.

63. And let them also return, preaching the gospel by the way, bearing record of the things which are revealed unto them.

64. For, verily, the sound must go forth from this place into all the world, and unto the uttermost parts of the earth—the gospel must be preached unto every creature, with signs following them that believe.

65. And behold the Son of man cometh. Amen.

CHAPTER XVI.

THE FOUNDING OF ZION.

The First Act in the Founding of Zion.

On the second day of August, I assisted the Colesville branch of the Church* to lay the first log, for a house, as a foundation of Zion in Kaw township, twelve miles west of Independence. The log was carried and placed by twelve men, in honor of the twelve tribes of Israel. At the same time, through prayer, the land of Zion was consecrated and dedicated by Elder Sidney Rigdon for the gathering of the Saints.†It was a season of joy to those present, and afforded a glimpse of the future, which time will yet unfold to the satisfaction of the faithful.

* The Colesville branch of the Church numbered about sixty souls.—Statement made by Oliver Cowdery in *John Whitmer's History of the Church*, ch. ix.

† Speaking of this second of August meeting, in addition to what the Prophet relates in his narrative, John Whitmer, in his *History of the Church*, (ch. ix), gives the following interesting details from a statement of Oliver Cowdery's: "On the second day of August, 1831, Rigdon stood up and asked, saying,

" 'Do you receive this land for the land of your inheritance with thankful hearts from the Lord?'

"Answer from all: 'We do.'

" 'Do you pledge yourselves to keep the law of God in this land which you never have kept in your own lands?'

" 'We do.'

" 'Do you pledge yourselves to see that others of your brethren who shall come hither do keep the laws of God?'

" 'We do.'

"After prayer, he arose and said: 'I now pronounce this land consecrated and dedicated unto the Lord for a possession and inheritance for the Saints, and for all the faithful servants of the Lord to the remotest ages of time. In the name of Jesus Christ, having authority from Him. Amen.' "

As we had received a commandment for Elder Rigdon to write a description of the land of Zion, we sought for all the information necessary to accomplish so desirable an object. The country is unlike the timbered states of the East. As far as the eye can reach the beautiful rolling prairies lie spread out like a sea of meadows; and are decorated with a growth of flowers so gorgeous and grand as to exceed description; and nothing is more fruitful, or a richer stockholder in the blooming prairie than the honey bee. Only on the water courses is timber to be found. There in strips from one to three miles in width, and following faithfully the meanderings of the streams, it grows in luxuriant forests. The forests are a mixture of oak, hickory, black walnut, elm, ash, cherry, honey locust, mulberry, coffee bean, hackberry, boxelder, and bass wood; with the addition of cottonwood, butterwood, pecan, and soft and hard maple upon the bottoms. The shrubbery is beautiful, and consists in part of plums, grapes, crab apple, and persimmons.

Description of the Land of Zion.

The soil is rich and fertile; from three to ten feet deep, and generally composed of a rich black mould, intermingled with clay and sand. It yields in abundance, wheat, corn, sweet potatoes, cotton and many other common agricultural products. Horses, cattle and hogs, though of an inferior breed, are tolerably plentiful and seem nearly to raise themselves by grazing in the vast prairie range in summer, and feeding upon the bottoms in winter. The wild game is less plentiful of course where man has commenced the cultivation of the soil, than in the wild prairies. Buffalo, elk, deer, bear, wolves, beaver and many smaller animals here roam at pleasure. Turkeys, geese, swans, ducks, yea a variety of the feathered tribe, are among the rich abundance that grace the delightful regions of this goodly land—the heritage of the children of God.

Agricultural Products.

Animals, Domestic and Wild.

The Climate.

The season is mild and delightful nearly three quarters of the year, and as the land of Zion, situated at about equal distances from the Atlantic and Pacific oceans, as well as from the Alleghany and Rocky mountains, in the thirty-ninth degree of north latitude, and between the sixteenth and seventeenth degrees of west longitude,* it bids fair—when the curse is taken from the land—to become one of the most blessed places on the globe. The winters are milder than the Atlantic states of the same parallel of latitude, and the weather is more agreeable; so that were the virtues of the inhabitants only equal to the blessings of the Lord which He permits to crown the industry of those inhabitants, there would be a measure of the good things of life for the benefit of the Saints, full, pressed down, and running over, even an hundredfold. The disadvantages here, as in all new countries, are self-evident—lack of mills and schools; together with the natural privations and inconveniences which the hand of industry, the refinement of society, and the polish of science, overcome.

The Future Glory of Zion.

But all these impediments vanish when it is recollected what the Prophets have said concerning Zion in the last days; how the glory of Lebanon is to come upon her; the fir tree, the pine tree, and the box tree together, to beautify the place of His sanctuary, that He may make the place of His feet glorious. Where for brass, He will bring gold; and for iron, He will bring silver; and for wood, brass; and for stones, iron; and where the feast of fat things will be given to the just; yea, when the splendor of the Lord is brought to our consideration for the good of His people, the calculations of men and the vain glory of the world vanish, and we exclaim, "Out of Zion the perfection of beauty, God hath shined."

*This is the Washington longitude. It is between ninety-five and ninety-six degrees west longitude from Greenwich.

On the third day of August, I proceeded to dedicate the spot for the Temple, a little west of Independence, and there were also present Sidney Rigdon, Edward Partridge, W. W. Phelps, Oliver Cowdery, Martin Harris and Joseph Coe.

Dedication of the Temple Site.

The 87th Psalm was read:—

His foundation is in the holy mountains.

The Lord loveth the gates of Zion more than all the dwellings of Jacob.

Glorious things are spoken of thee, O city of God. Selah.

I will make mention of Rahab and Babylon to them that know me: behold Philistia, and Tyre, with Ethiopia; this man was born there.

And of Zion it shall be said, This and that man was born in her: and the Highest Himself shall establish her.

The Lord shall count, when he writeth up the people, that this man was born there. Selah.

As well the singers as the players on instruments shall be there: all my springs are in thee.

The scene was solemn and impressive.

On the 4th I attended the first conference in the land of Zion. It was held at the house of Brother Joshua Lewis, in Kaw township, in the presence of the Colesville branch of the Church. The Spirit of the Lord was there.

First Conference in Zion.

On the 7th, I attended the funeral of Sister Polly Knight, the wife of Joseph Knight, Sen. This was the first death in the Church in this land, and I can say, a worthy member sleeps in Jesus till the resurrection.*

Death of Polly Knight.

I also received the following:

* Polly Knight's health had been failing for some time, according to a statement made by her son, Newel. She was very ill during her journey from Kirtland to Missouri. "Yet," says her son, "she would not consent to stop traveling; her only, or her greatest desire was to set her feet upon the land of Zion, and to have her body interred in that land. I went on shore and bought lumber to make a coffin in case she should die before we arrived at our place of destination—so fast did she fail. But the Lord gave her the desire of her heart, and she lived to stand upon that land." —*Scraps of Biography*, p. 70.

*Revelation, given in Zion, August 7th, 1831.**

1. Behold, blessed, saith the Lord, are they who have come up unto this land with an eye single to my glory, according to my commandments.

2. For those that live shall inherit the earth, and those that die shall rest from all their labors, and their works shall follow them; and they shall receive a crown in the mansions of my Father, which I have prepared for them.

3. Yea, blessed are they whose feet stand upon the land of Zion, who have obeyed my gospel; for they shall receive for their reward the good things of the earth, and it shall bring forth in its strength.

4. And they shall also be crowned with blessings from above, yea, and with commandments not a few, and with revelations in their time—they that are faithful and diligent before me.

5. Wherefore, I give unto them a commandment, saying thus: Thou shalt love the Lord thy God with all thy heart, with all thy might, mind, and strength; and in the name of Jesus Christ thou shalt serve him.

6. Thou shalt love thy neighbor as thyself. Thou shalt not steal; neither commit adultery, nor kill, nor do anything like unto it.

7. Thou shalt thank the Lord thy God in all things.

8. Thou shalt offer a sacrifice unto the Lord thy God in righteousness, even that of a broken heart and a contrite spirit.

9. And that thou mayest more fully keep thyself unspotted from the world, thou shalt go to the house of prayer and offer up thy sacraments upon my holy day;

10. For verily this is a day appointed unto you to rest from your labors, and to pay thy devotions unto the Most High;

11. Nevertheless thy vows shall be offered up in righteousness on all days and at all times;

12. But remember that on this, the Lord's day, thou shalt offer thine oblations and thy sacraments unto the Most High, confessing thy sins unto thy brethren, and before the Lord.

13. And on this day thou shalt do none other thing, only let thy food be prepared with singleness of heart that thy fasting may be perfect, or, in other words, that thy joy may be full.

14. Verily, this is fasting and prayer, or in other words rejoicing and prayer.

15. And inasmuch as ye do these things with thanksgiving, with cheerful hearts and countenances, not with much laughter, for this is sin, but with a glad heart and a cheerful countenance—

* Doctrine and Covenants, sec. lix.

16. Verily I say, that inasmuch as ye do this, the fulness of the earth is yours, the beasts of the field and the fowls of the air, and that which climbeth upon the trees and walketh upon the earth;

17. Yea, and the herb, and the good things which come of the earth, whether for food or for raiment, or for houses, or for barns, or for orchards, or for gardens, or for vineyards;

18. Yea, all things which come of the earth, in the season thereof, are made for the benefit and the use of man, both to please the eye and to gladden the heart;

19. Yea, for food and for raiment, for taste and for smell, to strengthen the body and to enliven the soul.

20. And it pleaseth God that he hath given all these trings unto man; for unto this end were they made to be used, with judgment, not to excess, neither by extortion.

21. And in nothing doth man offend God, or against none is his wrath kindled, save those who confess not his hand in all things, and obey not his commandments.

22. Behold, this is according to the law and the prophets; wherefore, trouble me no more concerning this matter.

23. But learn that he who doeth the works of righteousness shall receive his reward, even peace in this world and eternal life in the world to come.

24. I, the Lord, have spoken it, and the Spirit beareth record. Amen.

On the 8th, as there had been some inquiry among the Elders what they were to do, I received the following:

Directions for the Elders.

*Revelation, given August, 1831.**

1. Behold, thus saith the Lord unto the elders of his church, who are to return speedily to the land from whence they came: Behold, it pleaseth me, that you have come up hither;

2. But with some I am not well pleased, for they will not open their mouths, but they hide the talent which I have given unto them, because of the fear of man. Wo unto such, for mine anger is kindled against them.

3. And it shall come to pass, if they are not more faithful unto me, it shall be taken away, even that which they have.

4. For I, the Lord, rule in the heavens above, and among the armies of the earth; and in the day when I shall make up my jewels, all men shall know what it is that bespeaketh the power of God.

5. But, verily, I will speak unto you concerning your journey unto

Doctrine and Covenants, sec. lx.

the land from whence you came. Let there be a craft made, or bought, as seemeth you good, it mattereth not unto me, and take your journey speedily for the place which is called St. Louis.

6. And from thence let my servants, Sidney Rigdon, Joseph Smith, Jun., and Oliver Cowdery, take their journey for Cincinnati;

7. And in this place let them lift up their voice and declare my word with loud voices, without wrath or doubting, lifting up holy hands upon them. For I am able to make you holy, and your sins are forgiven you.

8. And let the residue take their journey from St. Louis, two by two, and preach the word, not in haste, among the congregations of the wicked, until they return to the churches from whence they came.

9. And all this for the good of the churches; for this intent have I sent them.

10. And let my servant Edward Partridge impart of the money which I have given him, a portion unto mine elders who are commanded to return;

11. And he that is able, let him return it by the way of the agent; and he that is not, of him it is not required.

12. And now I speak of the residue who are to come unto this land.

13. Behold, they have been sent to preach my gospel among the congregations of the wicked; wherefore, I give unto them a commandment, thus: Thou shalt not idle away thy time, neither shalt thou bury thy talent that it may not be known.

14. And after thou hast come up unto the land of Zion, and hast proclaimed my word, thou shalt speedily return, proclaiming my word among the congregations of the wicked, not in haste, neither in wrath nor with strife.

15. And shake off the dust of thy feet against those who receive thee not, not in their presence, lest thou provoke them; but in secret and wash thy feet, as a testimony against them in the day of judgment.

16. Behold, this is sufficient for you, and the will of him who hath sent you.

17. And by the mouth of my servant Joseph Smith, Jun., it shall be made known concerning Sidney Rigdon and Oliver Cowdery. The residue hereafter. Even so. Amen.

Prophet and Others Depart for Kirtland.

On the 9th, in company with ten Elders, I left Independence landing for Kirtland. We started down the river in canoes, and went the first day as far as Fort Osage, where we had an excellent wild turkey for supper. Nothing very important occurred till the third day, when many of the dangers so common upon the western waters, manifested themselves; and after we had encamped upon the bank of the river, at McIlwaine's Bend, Brother Phelps, in open vision by daylight, saw the destroyer in his most horrible power, ride upon the face of the waters; others heard the noise, but saw not the vision.

The next morning after prayer, I received the following:

*Revelation, given August, 1831.**

1. Behold, and hearken unto the voice of him who has all power, who is from everlasting to everlasting, even Alpha and Omega, the beginning and the end.

2. Behold, verily thus saith the Lord unto you, O ye elders of my church, who are assembled upon this spot, whose sins are now forgiven you, for I, the Lord, forgive sins, and am merciful unto those who confess their sins with humble hearts;

3. But verily I say unto you, that it is not needful for this whole company of mine elders to be moving swiftly upon the waters, whilst the inhabitants on either side are perishing in unbelief.

4. Nevertheless, I suffered it that ye might bear record; behold, there are many dangers upon the waters, and more especially hereafter;

5. For I, the Lord, have decreed in mine anger many destructions upon the waters; yea, and especially upon these waters.

6. Nevertheless, all flesh is in mine hand, and he that is faithful among you shall not perish by the waters.

7. Wherefore, it is expedient that my servant Sidney Gilbert and my servant William W. Phelps, be in haste upon their errand and mission.

8. Nevertheless, I would not suffer that ye should part until you were chastened for all your sins, that you might be one, that you might not perish in wickedness;

9. But now, verily I say, it behooveth me that ye should part. Where fore let my servants Sidney Gilbert and William W. Phelps take their former company, and let them take their journey in haste that they may fill their mission, and through faith they shall overcome;

10. And inasmuch as they are faithful they shall be preserved, and I, the Lord, will be with them.

11. And let the residue take that which is needful for clothing.

* Doctrine and Covenants, sec. lxi.

12. Let my servant Sidney Gilbert take that which is not needful with him, as you shall agree.

13. And now, behold, for your good I gave unto you a commandment concerning these things; and I, the Lord, will reason with you as with men in days of old.

14. Behold, I, the Lord, in the beginning blessed the waters, but in the last days, by the mouth of my servant John, I cursed the waters;

15. Wherefore, the days will come that no flesh shall be safe upon the waters.

16. And it shall be said in days to come that none is able to go up to the land of Zion upon the waters, but he that is upright in heart.

17. And, as I, the Lord, in the beginning cursed the land, even so in the last days have I blessed it, in its time, for the use of my Saints, that they may partake the fatness thereof.

18. And now I give unto you a commandment that what I say unto one I say unto all, that you shall forewarn your brethren concerning these waters, that they come not in journeying upon them, lest their faith fail and they are caught in snares;

19. I, the Lord, have decreed, and the destroyer rideth upon the face thereof, and I revoke not the decree;

20. I, the Lord, was angry with you yesterday, but today mine anger is turned away.

21. Wherefore, let those concerning whom I have spoken, that should take their journey in haste—again I say unto you, let them take their journey in haste.

22. And it mattereth not unto me, after a little, if it so be that they fill their mission, whether they go by water or by land; let this be as it is made known unto them according to their judgments hereafter.

23. And now, concerning my servants Sidney Rigdon, and Joseph Smith, Jun., and Oliver Cowdery, let them come not again upon the waters, save it be upon the canal, while journeying unto their homes; or in other words they shall not come upon the waters to journey, save upon the canal.

24. Behold, I, the Lord, have appointed a way for the journeying of my Saints; and behold this is the way—that after they leave the canal, they shall journey by land, inasmuch as they are commanded to journey and go up unto the land of Zion;

25. And they shall do like unto the children of Israel, pitching their tents by the way.

26. And, behold, this commandment you shall give unto all your brethren.

27. Nevertheless, unto whom it is given power to command the waters, unto him it is given by the Spirit to know all his ways;

28. Wherefore, let him do as the Spirit of the living God commandeth him, whether upon the land or upon the waters, as it remaineth with me to do hereafter.

29. And unto you it is given the course for the saints, or the way for the saints of the camp of the Lord, to journey.

30. And again, verily I say unto you, my servants, Sidney Rigdon, Joseph Smith, Jun., and Oliver Cowdery, shall not open their mouths in the congregations of the wicked, until they arrive at Cincinnati;

31. And in that place they shall lift up their voices unto God against that people; yea unto him whose anger is kindled against their wickedness, a people who are well-nigh ripened for destruction.

32. And from thence let them journey for the congregations of their brethren, for their labors even now are wanted more abundantly among them than among the congregations of the wicked.

33. And now, concerning the residue, let them journey and declare the word among the congregations of the wicked, inasmuch as it is given;

34. And inasmuch as they do this they shall rid their garments, and they shall be spotless before me.

35. And let them journey together, or two by two, as seemeth them good, only let my servant Reynolds Cahoon, and my servant Samuel H. Smith, with whom I am well pleased, be not separated until they return to their homes, and this for a wise purpose in me.

36. And now, verily I say unto you, and what I say unto one I say unto all, be of good cheer, little children, for I am in your midst, and I have not forsaken you;

37. And inasmuch as you have humbled yourselves before me, the blessings of the kingdom are yours.

38. Gird up your loins and be watchful and be sober, looking forth for the coming of the Son of Man, for he cometh in an hour you think not.

39. Pray always that you enter not into temptation, that you may abide the day of his coming, whether in life or in death. Even so. Amen.

A Chance Meeting of Elders.

On the 13th [August] I met several of the Elders on their way to the land of Zion, and after the joyful salutations with which brethren meet each other, who are actually "contending for the faith once delivered to the Saints," I received the following:

*Revelation, given August, 1831.**

1. Behold, and hearken, O ye elders of my church, saith the Lord your God, even Jesus Christ, your advocate, who knoweth the weakness of man and how to succor them who are tempted.

2. And verily mine eyes are upon those who have not as yet gone up unto the land of Zion; wherefore your mission is not yet full.

3. Nevertheless, ye are blessed, for the testimony which ye have borne is recorded in heaven for the angels to look upon; and they rejoice over you, and your sins are forgiven you.

4. And now continue your journey. Assemble yourselves upon the land of Zion; and hold a meeting and rejoice together, and offer a sacrament unto the Most High.

5. And then you may return to bear record, yea, even all together, or two by two, as seemeth you good, it mattereth not unto me; only be faithful, and declare glad tidings unto the inhabitants of the earth, or among the congregations of the wicked.

6. Behold, I, the Lord, have brought you together that the promise might be fulfilled, that the faithful among you should be preserved and rejoice together in the land of Missouri. I, the Lord, promised the faithful and cannot lie.

7. I, the Lord, am willing, if any among you desire to ride upon horses, or upon mules, or in chariots, he shall receive this blessing, if he receive it from the hand of the Lord, with a thankful heart in all things.

8. These things remain with you to do according to judgment and the directions of the Spirit.

9. Behold, the kingdom is yours. And behold, and lo, I am with the faithful always. Even so. Amen.

Arrival of the Prophet and Party at Kirtland.

After this meeting with the Elders, Sidney Rigdon, Oliver Cowdery, and myself, continued our journey by land to St. Louis, where we overtook Brothers Phelps and Gilbert. From this place we took stage, and they went by water to Kirtland, where we arrived safe and well on the 27th [August]. Many things transpired upon this journey to strengthen our faith, and which displayed the goodness of God in such a marvelous manner, that we could not help beholding the exertions of Satan to blind the eyes of the people, so as to hide the true light that lights every man that comes into the world.

* Doctrine and Covenants, sec. lxii.

In these infant days of the Church, there was a great anxiety to obtain the word of the Lord upon every subject that in any way concerned our salvation; and as the land of Zion was now the most important temporal object in view, I enquired of the Lord for further information upon the gathering of the Saints, and the purchase of the land, and other matters, and received the following:

Anxiety of the Saints to Receive the Word of the Lord.

*Revelation, given in Kirtland, August, 1831.**

1. Hearken, O ye people, and open your hearts and give ear from afar; and listen, you that call yourselves the people of the Lord, and hear the word of the Lord and his will concerning you.

2. Yea, verily, I say, hear the word of him whose anger is kindled against the wicked and rebellious;

3. Who willeth to take even them whom he will take, and preserveth in life them whom he will preserve;

4. Who buildeth up at his own will and pleasure; and destroyeth when he pleases, and is able to cast the soul down to hell.

5. Behold, I, the Lord, utter my voice, and it shall be obeyed.

6. Wherefore, verily I say, let the wicked take heed, and let the rebellious fear and tremble; and let the unbelieving hold their lips, for the day of wrath shall come upon them as a whirlwind, and all flesh shall know that I am God.

7. And he that seeketh signs shall see signs, but not unto salvation.

8. Verily, I say unto you, there are those among you who seek signs, and there have been such even from the beginning;

9. But, behold, faith cometh not by signs, but signs follow those that believe.

10. Yea, signs come by faith, not by the will of men, nor as they please, but by the will of God.

11. Yea, signs come by faith, unto mighty works, for without faith no man pleaseth God; and with whom God is angry he is not well pleased; wherefore, unto such he showeth no sign, only in wrath unto their condemnation.

12. Wherefore, I, the Lord, am not pleased with those among you who have sought after signs and wonders for faith, and not for the good of men unto my glory.

13. Nevertheless, I gave commandments, and many have turned away from my commandments and have not kept them.

* Doctrine and Covenants, sec. lxiii.

14. There were among you adulterers and adulteresses; some of whom have turned away from you, and others remain with you that hereafter shall be revealed.

15. Let such beware and repent speedily, lest judgment shall come upon them as a snare, and their folly shall be made manifest, and their works shall follow them in the eyes of the people.

16. And verily I say unto you, as I have said before, he that looketh upon a woman to lust after her, or if any shall commit adultery in their hearts, they shall not have the Spirit, but shall deny the faith and shall fear.

17. Wherefore I, the Lord, have said that the fearful, and the unbelieving, and all liars, and whosoever loveth and maketh a lie, and the whoremonger, and the sorcerer, shall have their part in that lake which burneth with fire and brimstone, which is the second death.

18. Verily I say, that they shall not have part in the first resurrection.

19. And now behold, I, the Lord, say unto you that ye are not justified because these things are among you.

20. Nevertheless, he that endureth in faith and doeth my will, the same shall overcome, and shall receive an inheritance upon the earth when the day of transfiguration shall come;

21. When the earth shall be transfigured, even according to the pattern which was shown unto mine apostles upon the mount; of which account the fulness ye have not yet received.

22. And now, verily I say unto you, that as I said that I would make known my will unto you, behold I will make it known unto you, not by the way of commandment, for there are many who observe not to keep my commandments.

23. But unto him that keepeth my commandments I will give the mysteries of my kingdom, and the same shall be in him a well of living water, springing up unto everlasting life.

24. And now, behold, this is the will of the Lord your God concerning his saints, that they should assemble themselves together unto the land of Zion, not in haste, lest there should be confusion, which bringeth pestilence.

25. Behold, the land of Zion, I, the Lord, hold it in mine own hands;

26. Nevertheless, I, the Lord, render unto Cæsar the things which are Cæsar's.

27. Wherefore, I the Lord will that you should purchase the lands, that you may have advantage of the world, that you may have claim on the world, that they may not be stirred up unto anger.

28. For Satan putteth it into their hearts to anger against you, and to the shedding of blood.

29. Wherefore, the land of Zion shall not be obtained but by purchase or by blood, otherwise there is none inheritance for you.

30. And if by purchase, behold you are blessed;

31. And if by blood, as you are forbidden to shed blood, lo, your enemies are upon you, and ye shall be scourged from city to city, and from synagogue to synagogue, and but few shall stand to receive an inheritance.

32. I, the Lord, am angry with the wicked; I am holding my Spirit from the inhabitants of the earth.

33. I have sworn in my wrath, and decreed wars upon the face of the earth, and the wicked shall slay the wicked, and fear shall come upon every man;

34. And the Saints also shall hardly escape; nevertheless, I, the Lord, am with them, and will come down in heaven from the presence of my Father and consume the wicked with unquenchable fire.

35. And behold, this is not yet, but by and by.

36. Wherefore, seeing that I, the Lord, have decreed all these things upon the face of the earth, I will that my Saints should be assembled upon the land of Zion;

37. And that every man should take righteousness in his hands and faithfulness upon his loins, and lift a warning voice unto the inhabitants of the earth; and declare both by word and by flight, that desolation shall come upon the wicked.

38. Wherefore, let my disciples in Kirtland arrange their temporal concerns, who dwell upon this farm.

39. Let my servant Titus Billings, who has the care thereof, dispose of the land, that he may be prepared in the coming spring to take his journey up unto the land of Zion, with those that dwell upon the face thereof, excepting those whom I shall reserve unto myself, that shall not go until I shall command them.

40. And let all the monies which can be spared, it mattereth not unto me whether it be little or much, be sent up unto the land of Zion, unto them whom I have appointed to receive.

41. Behold, I, the Lord, will give unto my servant Joseph Smith, Jun., power that he shall be enabled to discern by the Spirit those who shall go up unto the land of Zion, and those of my disciples who shall tarry.

42. Let my servant Newel K. Whitney retain his store, or in other words, the store, yet for a little season.

43. Nevertheless, let him impart all the money which he can impart, to be sent up unto the land of Zion.

44. Behold, these things are in his own hands, let him do according to wisdom.

45. Verily I say, let him be ordained as an agent unto the disciples that shall tarry, and let him be ordained unto this power;

46. And now speedily visit the churches, expounding these things unto them, with my servant Oliver Cowdery. Behold, this is my will, obtaining moneys even as I have directed.

47. He that is faithful and endureth shall overcome the world.

48. He that sendeth up treasures unto the land of Zion shall receive an inheritance in this world, and his works shall follow him, and also a reward in the world to come.

49. Yea, and blessed are the dead that die in the Lord, from henceforth, when the Lord shall come, and old things shall pass away, and all things become new, they shall rise from the dead and shall not die after, and shall receive an inheritance before the Lord, in the holy city.

50. And he that liveth when the Lord shall come, and hath kept the faith, blessed is he; nevertheless, it is appointed to him to die at the age of man.

51. Wherefore, children shall grow up until they become old; old men shall die; but they shall not sleep in the dust, but they shall be changed in the twinkling of an eye.

52. Wherefore, for this cause preached the apostles unto the world the resurrection of the dead.

53. These things are the things that ye must look for; and, speaking after the manner of the Lord, they are now nigh at hand, and in a time to come, even in the day of the coming of the Son of Man.

54. And until that hour there will be foolish virgins among the wise; and at that hour cometh an entire separation of the righteous and the wicked; and in that day will I send mine angels to pluck out the wicked and cast them into unquenchable fire.

55. And now behold, verily I say unto you, I, the Lord, am not pleased with my servant Sidney Rigdon; he exalted himself in his heart, and received not counsel, but grieved the Spirit;

56. Wherefore his writing is not acceptable unto the Lord, and he shall make another; and if the Lord receive it not, behold he standeth no longer in the office to which I have appointed him.

57. And again, verily I say unto you, those who desire in their hearts, in meekness, to warn sinners to repentance, let them be ordained unto this power.

58. For this is a day of warning, and not a day of many words. For I, the Lord, am not to be mocked in the last days.

59. Behold, I am from above, and my power lieth beneath. I am over all and in all, and through all, and search all things, and the day cometh that all things shall be subject unto me.

60. Behold, I am Alpha and Omega, even Jesus Christ.

61. Wherefore, let all men beware how they take my name in their lips—

62. For behold, verily I say, that many there be who are under this condemnation, who use the name of the Lord, and use it in vain, having not authority.

63. Wherefore, let the church repent of their sins, and I, the Lord, will own them; otherwise they shall be cut off.

64. Remember that that which cometh from above is sacred, and must be spoken with care, and by constraint of the Spirit; and in this there is no condemnation, and ye receive the Spirit through prayer; wherefore, without this there remaineth condemnation.

65. Let my servants, Joseph Smith, Jun., and Sidney Rigdon, seek them a home, as they are taught through prayer by the Spirit.

66. These things remain to overcome through patience that such may receive a more exceeding and eternal weight of glory, otherwise, a greater condemnation. Amen.

Preparations to Move to Hiram.

The early part of September was spent in making preparations to remove to the town of Hiram, and renew our work on the translation of the Bible. The brethren who were commanded to go up to Zion were earnestly engaged in getting ready to start in the coming October. On the 11th of September I received the following:

*Revelation, given in Kirtland.**

1. Behold, thus saith the Lord your God unto you, O ye elders of my church, hearken ye and hear, and receive my will concerning you.

2. For verily I say unto you, I will that ye should overcome the world; wherefore I will have compassion upon you.

3. There are those among you who have sinned; but verily I say, for this once, for mine own glory, and for the salvation of souls, I have forgiven you your sins.

4. I will be merciful unto you, for I have given unto you the kingdom.

5. And the keys of the mysteries of the kingdom shall not be taken from my servant Joseph Smith, Jun., through the means I have appointed, while he liveth, inasmuch as he obeyeth mine ordinances.

6. There are those who have sought occasion against him without cause;

* Doctrine and Covenants, sec. lxiv.

7. Nevertheless, he has sinned; but verily I say unto you, I, the Lord, forgive sins unto those who confess their sins before me and ask forgiveness, who have not sinned unto death.

8. My disciples, in days of old, sought occasion against one another and forgave not one another in their hearts; and for this evil they were afflicted and sorely chastened.

9. Wherefore, I say unto you, that ye ought to forgive one another; for he that forgiveth not his brother his trespasses standeth condemned before the Lord; for there remaineth in him the greater sin.

10. I, the Lord, will forgive whom I will forgive, but of you it is required to forgive all men.

11. And ye ought to say in your hearts—let God judge between me and thee, and reward thee according to thy deeds.

12. And him that repenteth not of his sins, and confesseth them not, ye shall bring before the church, and do with him as the scripture saith unto you, either by commandment or by revelation.

13. And this ye shall do that God may be glorified—not because ye forgive not, having not compassion, but that ye may be justified in the eyes of the law, that ye may not offend him who is your lawgiver—

14. Verily I say, for this cause ye shall do these things.

15. Behold, I, the Lord, was angry with him who was my servant Ezra Booth, and also my servant Isaac Morley, for they kept not the law, neither the commandment;

16. They sought evil in their hearts, and I, the Lord, withheld my Spirit. They condemned for evil that thing in which there was no evil; nevertheless I have forgiven my servant Isaac Morley.

17. And also my servant Edward Partridge, behold, he hath sinned, and Satan seeketh to destroy his soul; but when these things are made known unto them and they repent of the evil, they shall be forgiven.

18. And now, verily I say that it is expedient in me that my servant Sidney Gilbert, after a few weeks, shall return upon his business, and to his agency in the land of Zion;

19. And that which he hath seen and heard may be made known unto my disciples, that they perish not. And for this cause have I spoken these things.

20. And again, I say unto you, that my servant Isaac Morley may not be tempted above that which he is able to bear, and counsel wrongfully to your hurt, I gave commandment that his farm should be sold.

21. I will not that my servant Frederick G. Williams should sell his farm, for I, the Lord, will to retain a strong hold in the land of Kirtland, for the space of five years, in the which I will not overthrow the wicked, that thereby I may save some.

22. And after that day, I, the Lord, will not hold any guilty that

shall go with an open heart up to the land of Zion; for I, the Lord, require the hearts of the children of men.

23. Behold, now it is called today until the coming of the Son of Man, and verily it is a day of sacrifice, and a day for the tithing of my people; for he that is tithed shall not be burned at his coming.

24. For after today cometh the burning—this is speaking after the manner of the Lord—for verily I say, tomorrow all the proud and they that do wickedly shall be as stubble; and I will burn them up, for I am the Lord of Hosts; and I will not spare any that remain in Babylon.

25. Wherefore, if ye believe me, ye will labor while it is called today.

26. And it is not meet that my servants, Newel K. Whitney and Sidney Gilbert, should sell their store and their possessions here; for this is not wisdom until the residue of the church, which remaineth in this place, shall go up unto the land of Zion.

27. Behold, it is said in my laws, or forbidden, to get in debt to thine enemies;

28. But behold, it is not said at any time that the Lord should not take when he please, and pay as seemeth him good.

29. Wherefore, as ye are agents, ye are on the Lord's errand; and whatever ye do according to the will of the Lord is the Lord's business.

30. And he hath set you to provide for his saints in these last days, that they may obtain an inheritance in the land of Zion.

31. And behold, I, the Lord, declare unto you, and my words are sure and shall not fail, that they shall obtain it.

32. But all things must come to pass in their time.

33. Wherefore, be not weary in well-doing, for ye are laying the foundation of a great work. And out of small things proceedeth that which is great.

34. Behold, the Lord requireth the heart and a willing mind; and the willing and obedient shall eat the good of the land of Zion in these last days.

35. And the rebellious shall be cut off out of the land of Zion, and shall be sent away, and shall not inherit the land.

36. For, verily I say that the rebellious are not of the blood of Ephraim, wherefore they shall be plucked out.

37. Behold, I, the Lord, have made my church in these last days like unto a judge sitting on a hill or in a high place, to judge the nations.

38. For it shall come to pass that the inhabitants of Zion shall judge all things pertaining to Zion.

39. And liars and hypocrites shall be proved by them, and they who are not apostles and prophets shall be known.

40. And even the bishop, who is a judge, and his counselors, if they are not faithful in their stewardships shall be condemned, and others shall be planted in their stead.

41. For, behold, I say unto you that Zion shall flourish, and the glory of the Lord shall be upon her;

42. And she shall be an ensign unto the people, and there shall come unto her out of every nation under heaven.

43. And the day shall come when the nations of the earth shall tremble because of her, and shall fear because of her terrible ones. The Lord hath spoken it. Amen.

CHAPTER XVII.

THE APOSTASY OF EZRA BOOTH—PREPARATIONS FOR PUBLISHING THE BOOK OF COMMANDMENTS.

On the 12th of September, I removed with my family to the township of Hiram, and commenced living with John Johnson. Hiram was in Portage county, and about thirty miles southeasterly from Kirtland. From this time until the forepart of October, I did little more than prepare to re-commence the translation of the Bible.*

The Prophet Moves to Hiram.

About this time Ezra Booth came out as an apostate. He came into the Church upon seeing a person healed of an infirmity of many years standing.† He had been a Methodist priest for some time previous to his embracing the fulness of the

Ezra Booth's Apostasy.

* It would be more proper to say "revision of the Bible" than "translation" of it; as the Prophet did not at any time pretend to a knowledge of the ancient languages that would enable him to translate from the Hebrew or the Greek as "translation" is commonly understood. But what he did was to revise the English text of the Bible under the inspiration of God; and that led him not only to give different renderings of various passages, but also to supply missing parts.

†The miracle here referred to is thus related in *Hayden's History of the Disciples* (a Campbellite work), pp. 250-1. "Ezra Booth, of Mantua, a Methodist preacher of much more than ordinary culture, and with strong natural abilities, in company with his wife, Mr. and Mrs. Johnson, and some other citizens of this place [Hiram], visited Smith at his home in Kirtland, in 1831. Mrs. Johnson had been afflicted for some time with a lame arm, and was not at the time of the visit able to lift her hand to her head. The party visited Smith partly out of curiosity, and partly to see for themselves what there might be in the new doctrine. During the interview the conversation turned on the subject of supernatural gifts, such as were conferred in the days of the apostles. Some one said, 'Here is Mrs. Johnson with a lame arm; has God given any power to men now on the earth to cure her?'

Gospel, as developed in the Book of Mormon; and upon his admission into the Church he was ordained an Elder. As will be seen by the foregoing revelations,* he went up to Missouri as a companion of Elder Morley; but when he actually learned that faith, humility, patience, and tribulation go before blessing, and that God brings low before He exalts; that instead of the "Savior's granting him power to smite men and make them believe," (as he said he wanted God to do in his own case)—when he found he must become all things to all men, that he might peradventure save some; and that, too, by all diligence, by perils by sea and land, as was the case in the days of Jesus—then he was disappointed. In the 6th chapter of St. John's Gospel, 26th verse, it is written: "Verily, verily I say unto you, Ye seek me, not because ye saw the miracles, but because ye did eat of the loaves, and were filled." So it was with Booth; and when he was disappointed by his own evil heart, be turned away, and, as said before. became an apostate, and wrote a series of letters,†

A few moments later, when the conversation had turned in another direction, Smith rose, and walking across the room, taking Mrs. Johnson by the hand, said in the most solemn and impressive manner: 'Woman, in the name of the Lord Jesus Christ I command thee to be whole,' and immediately left the room. The company were awe-stricken at the infinite presumption of the man, and the calm assurance with which he spoke. The sudden mental and moral shock—I know not how better to explain the well-attested fact—electrified the rheumatic arm—Mrs. Johnson at once lifted it up with ease, and on her return home the next day she was able to do her washing without difficulty or pain."

* See page 212, verses 15, 16.

†It is generally supposed that Ezra Booth was the first to turn away from the faith; but this is an error. Others denied the faith before him, but he was the first apostate, I think, to publish anything against the Church. That he was not the first apostate, however, is evident from the fact that John Whitmer in his history makes mention of others turning from the faith even before the journey of the Elders to Missouri was undertaken; whereas Booth did not announce his apostasy until his return from that journey in the month of September. Writing of a time previous to the assembling of the conference of June 3rd-6th, 1831, John Whitmer remarks: "About these days the disciples arrived from the state of New York to this place, Kirtland, Ohio. They had some difficulty between themselves because of some that did not continue faithful—who denied the truth and turned to fables." (Ch. viii.) Again in chapter viii he says: "After some of the Elders had left [i. e., for Missouri], and the time for Joseph Smith, Jun., and others to leave [had come]—some of those who had been commanded to take their journey speedily, had denied the faith and

which, by their coloring, falsity, and vain calculations to overthrow the work of the Lord, exposed his weakness, wickedness and folly, and left him a monument of his own shame, for the world to wonder at.*

The Purchase of a Press.

A conference was held in which Brother W. W. Phelps was instructed to stop at Cincinnati on his way to Missouri and purchase a press and type, for the purpose of establishing and publishing a monthly paper at Independence, Jackson county, Missouri, to be called the *Evening and Morning Star*.

The first Sunday in October, Orson Hyde,† a clerk in Brother Sidney Gilbert and Newel K. Whitney's store, in Kirtland, was baptized, and became a member of the Church. He was soon after designated as one of the chosen men of the Lord, to bear His word to the nations.

turned from the truth." And still speaking of a time previous to the apostasy of Booth, and before detailing the events which happened on the land of Zion among the Elders who went there, he says: "There was much trouble and unbelief among those who called themselves disciples of Christ; some apostatized and became enemies to the cause of God, and persecuted the Saints." (Chapter ix.) All this was before Booth's apostasy. In the minutes of a conference held on the 6th of September, 1831, and signed by Oliver Cowdery, it is recorded: "Upon testimony satisfactory to this conference, it was voted that Ezra Booth be silenced from preaching as an Elder in this Church."

*The series of letters referred to in the text above were nine in number, and first appeared in the *Ohio Star*, published at Ravenna, the county seat of Portage county. Afterwards they were published in E. D. Howe's Book, *Mormonism Unveiled*, pp. 175-221.

† Orson Hyde was born January 8th, 1805, at Oxford, New Haven county, Connecticut. He was the son of Nathan and Sally Hyde. His father served in the United States army in the war of 1812. When Orson was seven years old his mother died, and the large family of Nathan Hyde, consisting of nine sons and three daughters, were scattered. Orson was taken in charge by a man of the name of Nathan Wheeler. Seven years later, or when young Hyde was fourteen years of age, Mr. Wheeler moved from the state of Connecticut to Ohio, settling in the vicinity of Kirtland. Orson accompanied him and continued to live with him in Ohio for about four years, after which he engaged in various occupations on his own account, at last becoming a clerk in the firm of Gilbert & Whitney, merchants. In the year 1827 a religious revival of unusual fervor occurred in Kirtland and vicinity, and under its influence Orson Hyde became a convert to the Methodist faith; and shortly afterwards was made a class leader. "At about the same time," writes Edward Tullidge, in a biographical sketch of him, "he heard that a 'golden Bible' had been dug out of a rock in the state of New York. It was treated, however, as a hoax; but, on

A Prayer Revealed.

In the fore part of October, I received the following prayer through revelation:

*Revelation**

1. Hearken, and lo, a voice as of one sent down from on high, who is mighty and powerful, whose going forth is unto the ends of the earth, yea, whose voice is unto men—Prepare ye the way of the Lord, make his paths straight.

2. The keys of the kingdom of God are committed unto man on the earth, and from thence shall the gospel roll forth unto the ends of the earth, as the stone which is cut out of the mountain without hands shall roll forth, until it has filled the whole earth.

3. Yea, a voice crying—Prepare ye the way of the Lord, prepare ye the supper of the Lamb, make ready for the Bridegroom.

4. Pray unto the Lord, call upon his holy name, make known his wonderful works among the people.

5. Call upon the Lord, that his kingdom may go forth upon the earth, that the inhabitants thereof may receive it, and be prepared for the days to come, in the which the Son of Man shall come down in heaven, clothed in the brightness of his glory, to meet the kingdom of God which is set up on the earth.

6. Wherefore, may the kingdom of God go forth, that the kingdom of heaven may come, that thou, O God, mayest be glorified in heaven so on earth, that thine enemies may be subdued; for thine is the honor, power and glory, forever and ever. Amen.

reading the report, Hyde remarked: 'Who knows but that this 'golden Bible' may break up our religion and change its whole features and bearing." (*Utah and her Founders*, Biographical Sketches, p. 70). Some time subsequent to his becoming a Methodist he heard Sidney Rigdon preach the Campbellite faith, and being convinced that the doctrine Rigdon advocated was more scriptural than that which he had embraced, he accepted it and was baptized into the Campbellite church. He also became a theological student under his new teacher's instruction, with a view of becoming a minister of the new church; and, in fact, began to preach and had already assisted in founding several Campbellite congregations in Lorain and Huron counties. In 1830, he was made pastor over these congregations. In the fall of that year the Lamanite mission of the Church of Jesus Christ arrived in the northeast part of Ohio, and soon the whole country was agitated by the presentation of the Book of Mormon and its attendant message, the restored Gospel of Jesus Christ. At first Orson Hyde, at the request of members of the Campbellite faith, opposed the Book of Mormon in public addresses; but feeling reproved by the Spirit for this course, he suspended his opposition in order to make further inquiry, with the result that after much prayer and some hesitancy he accepted the great latter-day message, and was baptized, as related in the text.

* Doctrine and Covenants, sec. lxv.

Soon after the above revelation was received, I renewed my work on the translation of the Scriptures, in company with Elder Rigdon, who had removed to Hiram, to act in his office of scribe to me.

Revision of the Bible Renewed.

On the 11th of October, a conference was held at Brother Johnson's where I was living, at which the Elders were instructed in the ancient manner of conducting meetings, of which knowledge most of them were ignorant. A committee of six was appointed to instruct the several branches of the Church. Elders David Whitmer and Reynolds Cahoon were appointed as two of the said committee; with the further duty on their mission of setting forth the condition of Brothers Joseph Smith, Jun., and Sidney Rigdon, that they might obtain means to continue the translation. This conference was adjourned till the 25th of October, to meet at the house of Irenus Burnett, in Orange, Cuyahoga county.

Instructions and Appointments of the Conference of October 11th.

On the 21st, I attended a special conference, to settle a difficulty which had occurred in Kirtland, on account of William Cahoon and Peter Devolue, having abused one of Brother Whitney's children. Elder Rigdon and myself were appointed to go to Kirtland and settle the difficulty, which we did.

Special Conference of October 21st.

At the conference on the 25th, at Orange, twelve High Priests, seventeen Elders, four Priests, three Teachers, and four Deacons, together with a large congregation attended. Much business was done, and the four remaining members of the committee, authorized by the conference at Hiram on the 11th, were appointed, and consisted of Simeon Carter, Orson Hyde, Hyrum Smith, and Emer Harris.*

Conference at Orange, Ohio, October 25th.

*This was a very important conference, and continued through two days, the 25th and 26th of October—Tuesday and Wednesday. The minutes of it are contained in the *Far West Record*, pp. 10-15. Very many of the brethren holding the Priesthood addressed the conference, and each one expressed his willingness to consecrate all he possessed to God and His cause. The minutes of the Prophet's remarks

At the request of William E. M'Lellin,* I inquired of the Lord, and received the following:

Revelation, given October, 1831.†

1. Behold, thus saith the Lord unto my servant William E.

upon this subject, as relating to his own willingness to consecrate all to the Lord, are of particular interest. It stands as follows in the record: "Brother Joseph Smith, Jun., said that he had nothing to consecrate to the Lord of the things of the earth, yet he felt to consecrate himself and family. Was thankful that God had given him a place among His Saints; felt willing to labor for their good" (p. 13). It appears at this time that the Prophet and other leading Elders of the Church were much embarrassed in the work of translating the Scriptures and preaching the Gospel, in consequence of the difficulty they encountered to do this work of the ministry and at the same time provide for their families. It appears also that the Saints were somewhat backward in providing means for the support of the ministry of the Church. Referring to the subject the Prophet, according to the minutes above referred to, said: "The Lord held the Church bound to provide for the families of the absent Elders while proclaiming the Gospel. Further said that God had often sealed up the heavens because of covetousness in the Church" (p. 13).

The remarks of Simeon Carter, one of the High Priests in attendance at the conference, are of interest and importance, owing to the light they throw upon the views of the faithful brethren respecting the journey to the land of Zion and the work that had been accomplished there. The minute of his remarks stands as follows: "Brother Simeon Carter said that he was thankful that he had been spared and preserved to go to the land of Zion according to the commandment of the Lord, for he received it as from His mouth; and also thanked the Lord that his feet had trodden upon the consecrated ground which was the inheritance of the Saints. Testified that the Book of Mormon was true. Mourned because of the falling away [in Kirtland] since he took his journey to the land of Zion" (p. 12).

Another item of interest will be found in the following circumstance: Several of the brethren took occasion to testify to the truth of the Book of Mormon; and now the minutes—"Brother Hyrum Smith said that he thought best that the information of the coming forth of the Book of Mormon be related by Joseph himself to the Elders present, that all might know for themselves."

"Brother Joseph Smith, Jun., said that it was not intended to tell the world all the particulars of the coming forth of the Book of Mormon; and also said that it was not expedient for him to relate these things" (p. 13). This will account for the Prophet confining himself to the merest generalities in all his statements concerning the coming forth of the Book of Mormon.

*The exact date of the birth of William E. M'Lellin cannot be ascertained. He was born in the state of Tennessee, about the year 1806. He first heard the Gospel preached by Elders Samuel H. Smith and Reynolds Cahoon, while those brethren were en route from Kirtland to Independence, Missouri, in the early summer of 1831. He closed up his affairs as soon as possible and followed these missionaries to Jackson county. On the way to that place he was baptized and ordained an Elder. During the same summer he made his way to Kirtland, where we find him in attendance at the special conference of October 25th, seeking to learn the will of the Lord, through the Prophet, respecting himself.

† Doctrine and Covenants, sec. lxvi.

M'Lellin—Blessed are you, inasmuch as you have turned away from your iniquities, and have received my truths, saith the Lord your Redeemer, the Savior of the world, even of as many as believe on my name.

2. Verily I say unto you, blessed are you for receiving mine everlasting covenant, even the fulness of my gospel, sent forth unto the children of men, that they might have life and be made partakers of the glories which are to be revealed in the last days, as it was written by the prophets and apostles in days of old.

3. Verily I say unto you, my servant William, that you are clean, but not all; repent, therefore, of those things which are not pleasing in my sight, saith the Lord, for the Lord will show them unto you.

4. And now, verily, I, the Lord, will show unto you what I will concerning you, or what is my will concerning you.

5. Behold, verily I say unto you, that it is my will that you should proclaim my gospel from land to land, and from city to city, yea, in those regions round about where it has not been proclaimed.

6. Tarry not many days in this place; go not up unto the land of Zion as yet; but inasmuch as you can send, send; otherwise, think not of thy property.

7. Go unto the eastern lands, bear testimony in every place, unto every people and in their synagogues, reasoning with the people.

8. Let my servant Samuel H. Smith go with you, and forsake him not, and give him thine instructions; and he that is faithful shall be made strong in every place; and I, the Lord, will go with you.

9. Lay your hands upon the sick, and they shall recover. Return not till I, the Lord, shall send you. Be patient in affliction. Ask, and ye shall receive; knock, and it shall be opened unto you.

10. Seek not to be cumbered. Forsake all unrighteousness. Commit not adultery—a temptation with which thou hast been troubled.

11. Keep these sayings, for they are true and faithful; and thou shalt magnify thine office, and push many people to Zion with songs of everlasting joy upon their heads.

12. Continue in these things even unto the end, and you shall have a crown of eternal life at the right hand of my Father, who is full of grace and truth.

13. Verily, thus saith the Lord your God, your Redeemer, even Jesus Christ. Amen.

Special Conference November 1st.

I returned from the conference at Orange, to Hiram; and as Oliver Cowdery and John Whitmer were to start for Independence, Missouri, a special conference was appointed for the first of November,* at which I received the following:

Revelation.†

1. Hearken, O ye people of my church, saith the voice of him who dwells on high, and whose eyes are upon all men; yea, verily I say: Hearken ye people from afar; and ye that are upon the islands of the sea, listen together.

2. For verily the voice of the Lord is unto all men, and there is none to escape; and there is no eye that shall not see, neither ear that shall not hear, neither heart that shall not be penetrated.

3. And the rebellious shall be pierced with much sorrow; for their iniquities shall be spoken upon the housetops, and their secret acts shall be revealed.

4. And the voice of warning shall be unto all people, by the mouths of my disciples, whom I have chosen in these last days.

5. And they shall go forth and none shall stay them, for I the Lord have commanded them.

6. Behold, this is mine authority, and the authority of my servants, and my preface unto the book of my commandments, which I have given them to publish unto you, O inhabitants of the earth.

7. Wherefore, fear and tremble, O ye people, for what I the Lord have decreed in them shall be fulfilled.

*This special conference at Hiram on November 1st, should receive larger notice. The number of copies in the edition of the Book of Commandments to be printed was considered, and the decision reached that ten thousand should be published. The conference lasted two days. In the afternoon of the first day of the conference, according to the minutes of the meeting, the preface to the Book of Commandments was "received by inspiration." The same afternoon, the following occurred: "Brother Joseph Smith, Jun., said that inasmuch as the Lord had bestowed a great blessing upon us in giving commandments and revelations, he asked the conference what testimony they were willing to attach to these commandments which would shortly be sent to the world. A number of the brethren arose and said that they were willing to testify to the world that they knew that they were of the Lord." (*Far West Record*, p. 16.)

In the second day's proceedings of the conference it is recorded: "The revelation of last evening read by the moderator [this was Oliver Cowdery]. The brethren then arose in turn and bore witness to the truth of the Book of Commandments; after which Brother Joseph Smith, Jun., arose and expressed his feelings and gratitude concerning the commandments and preface received yesterday." (*Far West Record*, p. 16.)

† Doctrine and Covenants, sec. i. This revelation which, in the current edition, and in fact in all editions of the Doctrine and Covenants, stands as section i, is the Lord's Preface to the revelations which He has given to this Dispensation of the Fulness of Times.

8. And verily I say unto you, that they who go forth, bearing these tidings unto the inhabitants of the earth, to them is power given to seal both on earth and in heaven, the unbelieving and rebellious;

9. Yea, verily, to seal them up unto the day when the wrath of God shall be poured out upon the wicked without measure—

10. Unto the day when the Lord shall come to recompense unto every man according to his work, and measure to every man according to the measure which he has measured to his fellow man.

11. Wherefore the voice of the Lord is unto the ends of the earth, that all that will hear may hear:

12. Prepare ye, prepare ye for that which is to come, for the Lord is nigh;

13. And the anger of the Lord is kindled, and his sword is bathed in heaven, and it shall fall upon the inhabitants of the earth.

14. And the arm of the Lord shall be revealed; and the day cometh that they who will not hear the voice of the Lord, neither the voice of his servants, neither give heed to the words of the prophets and apostles, shall be cut off from among the people;

15. For they have strayed from mine ordinances, and have broken mine everlasting covenant;

16. They seek not the Lord to establish his righteousness, but every man walketh in his own way, and after the image of his own God, whose image is in the likeness of the world, and whose substance is that of an idol, which waxeth old and shall perish in Babylon, even Babylon the great, which shall fall.

17. Wherefore, I the Lord, knowing the calamity which should come upon the inhabitants of the earth, called upon my servant Joseph Smith, Jun., and spake unto him from heaven, and gave him commandments;

18. And also gave commandments to others, that they should proclaim these things unto the world; and all this that it might be fulfilled, which was written by the prophets—

19. The weak things of the world shall come forth and break down the mighty and strong ones, that man should not counsel his fellow man, neither trust in the arm of flesh—

20. But that every man might speak in the name of God the Lord, even the Savior of the world;

21. That faith also might increase in the earth;

22. That mine everlasting covenant might be established;

23. That the fulness of my gospel might be proclaimed by the weak and the simple unto the ends of the world, and before kings and rulers.

24. Behold, I am God and have spoken it; these commandments are of me, and were given unto my servants in their weakness, after

the manner of their language, that they might come to understanding.

25. And inasmuch as they erred it might be made known;

26. And inasmuch as they sought wisdom they might be instructed:

27. And inasmuch as they sinned they might be chastened, that they might repent;

28. And inasmuch as they were humble they might be made strong, and blessed from on high, and receive knowledge from time to time.

29. And after having received the record of the Nephites, yea, even my servant Joseph Smith, Jun., might have power to translate through the mercy of God, by the power of God, the Book of Mormon.

30. And also those to whom these commandments were given, might have power to lay the foundation of this church, and to bring it forth out of obscurity and out of darkness, the only true and living church upon the face of the whole earth, with which I, the Lord, am well pleased, speaking unto the church collectively and not individually—

31. For I the Lord cannot look upon sin with the least degree of allowance;

32. Nevertheless, he that repents and does the commandments of the Lord shall be forgiven;

33. And he that repents not, from him shall be taken even the light which he has received; for my Spirit shall not always strive with man, saith the Lord of Hosts.

34. And again, verily I say unto you, O inhabitants of the earth: I the Lord am willing to make these things known unto all flesh;

35. For I am no respecter of persons, and will that all men shall know that the day speedily cometh; the hour is not yet, but is nigh at hand, when peace shall be taken from the earth, and the devil shall have power over his own dominion.

36. And also the Lord shall have power over his saints, and shall reign in their midst, and shall come down in judgment upon Idumea, or the world.

37. Search these commandments, for they are true and faithful, and the prophecies and promises which are in them shall all be fulfilled.

38. What I the Lord have spoken, I have spoken, and I excuse not myself; and though the heavens and the earth pass away, my word shall not pass away, but shall all be fulfilled, whether by mine own voice or by the voice of my servants, it is the same.

39. For behold, and lo, the Lord is God, and the Spirit beareth record, and the record is true, and the truth abideth forever and ever. Amen.

Language of Revelations Criticised.

After this revelation was received, some conversation was had concerning revelations and language. I received the following:

*Revelation, given November, 1831.**

1. Behold and hearken, O ye elders of my church, who have assembled yourselves together, whose prayers I have heard, and whose hearts I know, and whose desires have come up before me.

2. Behold and lo, mine eyes are upon you, and the heavens and the earth are in mine hands, and the riches of eternity are mine to give.

3. Ye endeavored to believe that ye should receive the blessing which was offered unto you; but behold, verily I say unto you there were fears in your hearts, and verily this is the reason that ye did not receive.

4. And now I, the Lord, give unto you a testimony of the truth of these commandments which are lying before you.

5. Your eyes have been upon my servant Joseph Smith, Jun., and his language you have known, and his imperfections you have known; and you have sought in your hearts knowledge that you might express beyond his language; this you also know.

6. Now, seek ye out of the Book of Commandments, even the least that is among them, and appoint him that is the most wise among you;

7. Or, if there be any among you that shall make one like unto it, then ye are justified in saying that ye do not know that they are true;

8. But if ye cannot make one like unto it, ye are under condemnation if ye do not bear record that they are true.

9. For ye know that there is no unrighteousness in them, and that which is righteous cometh down from above, from the Father of lights.

10. And again, verily I say unto you that it is your privilege, and a promise I give unto you that have been ordained unto this ministry, that inasmuch as you strip yourselves from jealousies and fears, and humble yourselves before me, for ye are not sufficiently humble, the veil shall be rent and you shall see me and know that I am—not with the carnal neither natural mind, but with the spiritual.

11. For no man has seen God at any time in the flesh, except quickened by the Spirit of God.

12. Neither can any natural man abide the presence of God, neither after the carnal mind.

13. Ye are not able to abide the presence of God now, neither the ministering of angels; wherefore, continue in patience until ye are perfected.

14. Let not your minds turn back; and when ye are worthy, in mine own due time, ye shall see and know that which was conferred upon you by the hands of my servant Joseph Smith, Jun. Amen.

*Doctrine and Covenants, sec. lxvii.

After the foregoing was received, William E. M'Lellin, as the wisest man, in his own estimation, having more learning than sense, endeavored to write a commandment like unto one of the least of the Lord's, but failed; it was an awful responsibility to write in the name of the Lord. The Elders and all present that witnessed this vain attempt of a man to imitate the language of Jesus Christ, renewed their faith in the fulness of the Gospel, and in the truth of the commandments and revelations which the Lord had given to the Church through my instrumentality; and the Elders signified a willingness to bear testimony of their truth to all the world. Accordingly I received the following:

The Folly of William E. M'Lellin.

The testimony of the witnesses to the book of the Lord's commandments, which He gave to His Church through Joseph Smith, Jun., who was appointed by the voice of the Church for this purpose; we therefore feel willing to bear testimony to all the world of mankind, to every creature upon the face af all the earth and upon the islands of the sea, that the Lord has borne record to our souls, through the Holy Ghost, shed forth upon us, that these commandments were given by inspiration of God, and are profitable for all men, and are verily true. We give this testimony unto the world, the Lord being our helper; and it is through the grace of God, the Father, and His Son, Jesus Christ, that we are permitted to have this privilege of bearing this testimony unto the world, that the children of men may be profited thereby.*

* This "Testimony" to the truth of the "Book of Commandments" was doubtless drawn up with the intention of having it signed by the Elders present at the conference; but whether that was done or not does not appear in the Ms. of the Prophet's history. The testimony itself, however, is in the manuscript History. This is remarked because it has not been published heretofore in the History of the Prophet. The matter appears to stand thus: Each of the Elders present at the conference testified to the truth of the revelations then about to be published; and, as already seen (p. 222 note), expressed a willingness to testify to the truth of the revelations to all the world. Accordingly this testimony was prepared with the intention of having it signed and published in the "Book of Commandments." It may have been signed, too, and carried to Missouri, but owing to the fact that the printing press was destroyed by a mob before the "Book of Commandments" was all printed, the "Testimony" does not appear in the part of it that was printed. The names of the Elders present at this special conference, according to the minutes of it in the *Far West Record* (p. 15), are as follows: Joseph Smith, Jun., Oliver Cowdery, David Whitmer, John Whitmer, Peter Whitmer, Jun., Sidney Rigdon, William E. M'Lellin, Orson Hyde, Luke Johnson, Lyman E. Johnson.

As the following Elders—Orson Hyde, Luke Johnson, Lyman E. Johnson, and William E. M'Lellin—were desirous to know the mind of the Lord concerning themselves, I inquired, and received the following:

*Revelation, given November, 1831.**

1. My servant, Orson Hyde, was called by his ordination to proclaim the everlasting gospel, by the Spirit of the living God, from people to people, and from land to land, in the congregations of the wicked, in their synagogues, reasoning with and expounding all scriptures unto them.

2. And, behold, and lo, this is an ensample unto all those who were ordained unto this priesthood, whose mission is appointed unto them to go forth—

3. And this is the ensample unto them, that they shall speak as they are moved upon by the Holy Ghost.

4. And whatsoever they shall speak when moved upon by the Holy Ghost shall be scripture, shall be the will of the Lord, shall be the mind of the Lord, shall be the word of the Lord, shall be the voice of the Lord, and the power of God unto salvation.

5. Behold, this is the promise of the Lord unto you, O ye my servants.

6. Wherefore, be of good cheer, and do not fear, for I the Lord am with you, and will stand by you; and ye shall bear record of me, even Jesus Christ, that I am the Son of the living God, that I was, that I am, and that I am to come.

7. This is the word of the Lord unto you, my servant Orson Hyde, and also unto my servant Luke Johnson, and unto my servant Lyman Johnson, and unto my servant William E. M'Lellin, and unto all the faithful elders of my church—

8. Go ye into all the world, preach the gospel to every creature, acting in the authority which I have given you, baptizing in the name of the Father, and of the Son, and of the Holy Ghost.

9. And he that believeth and is baptized shall be saved, and he that believeth not shall be damned.

10. And he that believeth shall be blest with signs following, even as it is written.

11. And unto you it shall be given to know the signs of the times, and the signs of the coming of the Son of Man;

12. And of as many as the Father shall bear record, to you shall be given power to seal them up unto eternal life. Amen.

* Doctrine and Covenants, sec. lxviii.

13. And now, concerning the items in addition to the covenants and commandments, they are these—

14. There remain hereafter, in the due time of the Lord, other bishops to be set apart unto the church, to minister even according to the first;

15. Wherefore they shall be high priests who are worthy, and they shall be appointed by the First Presidency of the Melchizedek Priesthood, except they be literal descendants of Aaron.

16. And if they be literal descendants of Aaron they have a legal right to the bishopric, if they are the firstborn among the sons of Aaron;

17. For the firstborn holds the right of the presidency over this priesthood, and the keys or authority of the same.

18. No man has a legal right to this office, to hold the keys of this priesthood, except he be a literal descendant and the firstborn of Aaron.

19. But, as a high priest of the Melchizedek Priesthood has authority to officiate in all the lesser offices he may officiate in the office of bishop when no literal descendant of Aaron can be found, provided he is called and set apart and ordained unto this power, under the hands of the First Presidency of the Melchizedek Priesthood.

20. And a literal descendant of Aaron, also, must be designated by this Presidency, and found worthy, and anointed, and ordained under the hands of this Presidency, otherwise they are not legally authorized to officiate in their priesthood.

21. But, by virtue of the decree concerning their right of the priesthood descending from father to son, they may claim their anointing if at any time they can prove their lineage, or do ascertain it by revelation from the Lord under the hands of the above named Presidency.

22. And again, no bishop or high priest who shall be set apart for this ministry shall be tried or condemned for any crime, save it be before the First Presidency of the church;

23. And inasmuch as he is found guilty before this Presidency, by testimony that cannot be impeached, he shall be condemned;

24. And if he repent he shall be forgiven, according to the covenants and commandments of the church.

25. And again, inasmuch as parents have children in Zion, or in any of her stakes which are organized, that teach them not to understand the doctrine of repentance, faith in Christ the Son of the living God, and of baptism and the gift of the Holy Ghost by the laying on of the hands, when eight years old, the sin be upon the heads of the parents.

26. For this shall be a law unto the inhabitants of Zion, or in any of her stakes which are organized.

27. And their children shall be baptized for the remission of their

sins when eight years old, and receive the laying on of the hands.

28. And they shall also teach their children to pray, and to walk uprightly before the Lord.

29. And the inhabitants of Zion shall also observe the Sabbath day to keep it holy.

30. And the inhabitants of Zion also shall remember their labors, inasmuch as they are appointed to labor, in all faithfulness; for the idler shall be had in remembrance before the Lord.

31. Now, I, the Lord, am not well pleased with the inhabitants of Zion, for there are idlers among them; and their children are also growing up in wickedness; they also seek not earnestly the riches of eternity but their eyes are full of greediness.

32. These things ought not to be, and must be done away from among them; wherefore, let my servant Oliver Cowdery carry these sayings unto the land of Zion.

33. And a commandment I give unto them—that he that observeth not his prayers before the Lord in the season thereof, let him be had in remembrance before the judge of my people.

34. These sayings are true and faithful; wherefore, transgress them not, neither take therefrom.

35. Behold, I am Alpha and Omega, and I come quickly. Amen.

Preparation of the Revelations for Publication, Nov. 1st-15th.

It had been decided by the conference that Elder Oliver Cowdery should carry the commandments and revelations to Independence, Missouri, for printing, and that I should arrange and get them in readiness by the time that he left, which was to be by—or, if possible, before—the 15th of the month [November]. At this time there were many things which the Elders desired to know relative to preaching the Gospel to the inhabitants of the earth, and concerning the gathering; and in order to walk by the true light, and be instructed from on high, on the 3rd of November, 1831, I inquired of the Lord and received the following important revelation, which has since been added to the book of Doctrine and Covenants, and called the Appendix:

*Revelation, given November 3, 1831.**

1. Hearken, O ye people of my church, saith the Lord your God, and hear the word of the Lord concerning you—

* Doctrine and Covenants, sec. cxxxiii.

2. The Lord who shall suddenly come to his temple; the Lord who shall come down upon the world with a curse to judgment; yea, upon all the nations that forget God, and upon all the ungodly among you.

3. For he shall make bare his holy arm in the eyes of all the nations, and all the ends of the earth shall see the salvation of their God.

4. Wherefore, prepare ye, prepare ye, O my people; sanctify yourselves; gather ye together, O ye people of my church, upon the land of Zion, all you that have not been commanded to tarry.

5. Go ye out from Babylon. Be ye clean that bear the vessels of the Lord.

6. Call your solemn assemblies, and speak often one to another. And let every man call upon the name of the Lord.

7. Yea, verily I say unto you again, the time has come when the voice of the Lord is unto you: Go ye out of Babylon; gather ye out from among the nations, from the four winds, from one end of heaven to the other.

8. Send forth the elders of my church unto the nations which are afar off; unto the islands of the sea; send forth unto foreign lands; call upon all nations, first upon the Gentiles, and then upon the Jews.

9. And behold, and lo, this shall be their cry, and the voice of the Lord unto all people: Go ye forth unto the land of Zion, that the borders of my people may be enlarged, and that her stakes may be strengthened, and that Zion may go forth unto the regions round about.

10. Yea, let the cry go forth among all people: Awake and arise and go forth to meet the Bridegroom; behold and lo, the Bridegroom cometh; go ye out to meet him. Prepare yourselves for the great day of the Lord.

11. Watch, therefore, for ye know neither the day nor the hour.

12. Let them, therefore, who are among the Gentiles, flee unto Zion.

13. And let them who be of Judah flee unto Jerusalem, unto the mountains of the Lord's house.

14. Go ye out from among the nations, even from Babylon, from the midst of wickedness, which is spiritual Babylon.

15. But verily, thus saith the Lord, let not your flight be in haste, but let all things be prepared before you; and he that goeth, let him not look back lest sudden destruction shall come upon him.

16. Hearken and hear, O ye inhabitants of the earth. Listen, ye elders of my church together, and hear the voice of the Lord; for he calleth upon all men, and he commandeth all men everywhere to repent.

17. For behold, the Lord God hath sent forth the angel crying through the midst of heaven, saying: Prepare ye the way of the Lord, and make his paths straight, for the hour of his coming is nigh—

18. When the Lamb shall stand upon Mount Zion, and with him a hundred and forty-four thousand, having his Father's name written on their foreheads.

19. Wherefore, prepare ye for the coming of the Bridegroom; go ye, go ye out to meet him.

20. For behold, he shall stand upon the mount of Olivet, and upon the mighty ocean, even the great deep, and upon the islands of the sea, and upon the land of Zion.

21. And he shall utter his voice out of Zion, and he shall speak from Jerusalem, and his voice shall be heard among all people;

22. And it shall be a voice as the voice of many waters, and as the voice of a great thunder, which shall break down the mountains, and the valleys shall not be found.

23. He shall command the great deep, and it shall be driven back into the north countries, and the islands shall become one land;

24. And the land of Jerusalem and the land of Zion shall be turned back into their own place, and the earth shall be like as it was in the days before it was divided.

25. And the Lord, even the Savior, shall stand in the midst of his people, and shall reign over all flesh.

26. And they who are in the north countries shall come in remembrance before the Lord; and their prophets shall hear his voice, and shall no longer stay themselves; and they shall smite the rocks, and the ice shall flow down at their presence.

27. And an highway shall be cast up in the midst of the great deep.

28. Their enemies shall become a prey unto them.

29. And in the barren deserts there shall come forth pools of living water; and the parched ground shall no longer be a thirsty land.

30. And they shall bring forth their rich treasures unto the children of Ephraim, my servants.

31. And the boundaries of the everlasting hills shall tremble at their presence.

32. And there shall they fall down and be crowned with glory, even in Zion, by the hands of the servants of the Lord, even the children of Ephraim.

33. And they shall be filled with songs of everlasting joy.

34. Behold, this is the blessing of the everlasting God upon the tribes of Israel, and the richer blessing upon the head of Ephraim and his fellows.

35. And they also of the tribe of Judah, after their pain shall be

sanctified in holiness before the Lord, to dwell in his presence day and night, forever and ever.

36. And now, verily saith the Lord, that these things might be known among you, O inhabitants of the earth, I have sent forth mine angel flying through the midst of heaven, having the everlasting gospel, who hath appeared unto some and hath committed it unto man, who shall appear unto many that dwell on the earth.

37. And this gospel shall be preached unto every nation, and kindred, and tongue, and people.

38. And the servants of God shall go forth, saying with a loud voice: Fear God and give glory to him, for the hour of his judgment is come;

39. And worship him that made heaven, and earth, and the sea, and the fountains of waters—

40. Calling upon the name of the Lord day and night, saying: O that thou wouldst rend the heavens, that thou wouldst come down, that the mountains might flow down at thy presence.

41. And it shall be answered upon their heads; for the presence of the Lord shall be as the melting fire that burneth, and as the fire which causeth the waters to boil.

42. O Lord, thou shalt come down to make thy name known to thine adversaries, and all nations shall tremble at thy presence—

43. When thou doest terrible things, things they look not for;

44. Yea, when thou comest down, and the mountains flow down at thy presence, thou shalt meet him who rejoiceth and worketh righteousness, who remembereth thee in thy ways.

45. For since the beginning of the world have not men heard nor perceived by the ear, neither hath any eye seen, O God, besides thee, how great things thou hast prepared for him that waiteth for thee.

46. And it shall be said: Who is this that cometh down from God in heaven with dyed garments; yea, from the regions which are not known, clothed in his glorious apparel, traveling in the greatness of his strength?

47. And he shall say: I am he who spake in righteousness, mighty to save.

48. And the Lord shall be red in his apparel, and his garments like him that treadeth in the wine-vat.

49. And so great shall be the glory of his presence that the sun shall hide his face in shame, and the moon shall withhold its light, and the stars shall be hurled from their places.

50. And his voice shall be heard: I have trodden the winepress alone, and have brought judgment upon all people; and none were with me;

51. And I have trampled them in my fury, and I did tread upon them in mine anger, and their blood have I sprinkled upon my gar-

ments, and stained all my raiment; for this was the day of vengeance which was in my heart.

52. And now the year of my redeemed is come; and they shall mention the loving kindness of their Lord, and all that he has bestowed upon them according to his goodness, and according to his loving kindness, forever and ever.

53. In all their afflictions he was afflicted. And the angel of his presence saved them; and in his love, and in his pity, he redeemed them, and bore them, and carried them all the days of old;

54. Yea, and Enoch also, and they who were with him; the prophets who were before him; and Noah also, and they who were before him; and Moses also, and they who were before him;

55. And from Moses to Elijah, and from Elijah to John, who were with Christ in his resurrection, and the holy apostles, with Abraham, Isaac, and Jacob, shall be in the presence of the Lamb.

56. And the graves of the saints shall be opened; and they shall come forth and stand on the right hand of the Lamb, when he shall stand upon Mount Zion, and upon the holy city, the New Jerusalem; and they shall sing the song of the Lamb, day and night forever and ever.

57. And for this cause, that men might be made partakers of the glories which were to be revealed, the Lord sent forth the fulness of his gospel, his everlasting covenant, reasoning in plainness and simplicity—

58. To prepare the weak for those things which are coming on the earth, and for the Lord's errand in the day when the weak shall confound the wise, and the little one become a strong nation, and two shall put their tens of thousands to flight.

59. And by the weak things of the earth the Lord shall thrash the nations by the power of his Spirit.

60. And for this cause these commandments were given; they were commanded to be kept from the world in the day that they were given, but now are to go forth unto all flesh—

61. And this according to the mind and will of the Lord, who ruleth over all flesh.

62. And unto him that repenteth and sanctifieth himself before the Lord shall be given eternal life.

63. And upon them that hearken not to the voice of the Lord shall be fulfilled that which was written by the prophet Moses, that they should be cut off from among the people.

64. And also that which was written by the prophet Malachi: For, behold, the day cometh that shall burn as an oven, and all the proud, yea, and all that do wickedly, shall be stubble; and the day that cometh

shall burn them up, saith the Lord of hosts, that it shall leave them neither root nor branch.

65. Wherefore, this shall be the answer of the Lord unto them:

66. In that day when I came unto mine own, no man among you received me, and you were driven out.

67. When I called again there was none of you to answer; yet my arm was not shortened at all that I could not redeem, neither my power to deliver.

68. Behold, at my rebuke I dry up the sea. I make the rivers a wilderness; their fish stink, and die for thirst.

69. I clothe the heavens with blackness, and make sackcloth their covering.

70. And this shall ye have of my hand—ye shall lie down in sorrow.

71. Behold, and lo, there are none to deliver you; for ye obeyed not my voice when I called to you out of the heavens; ye believed not my servants, and when they were sent unto you ye received them not.

72. Wherefore, they sealed up the testimony and bound up the law, and ye were delivered over unto darkness.

73. These shall go away into outer darkness, where there is weeping, and wailing, and gnashing of teeth.

74. Behold the Lord your God hath spoken it. Amen.

Dedication of the Book of Commandments.

The Book of Commandments and Revelations was to be dedicated by prayer to the service of Almighty God by me; and after I had done this, I inquired of the Lord concerning these things, and received the following:

*Revelation, given November, 1831.**

* Doctrine and Covenants, sec. lxix. It must not be understood from the first paragraph of this revelation that Oliver Cowdery was untrustworthy, and therefore it was necessary that a companion be provided for him. The fact was that much of the journey between Kirtland and Independence, or Zion, was through a sparsely settled country, the western portion of it through a frontier country where there is always a gathering, more or less, of lawless people; and it was at considerable risk that a person traveled through such a country, especially when alone and carrying money with him. It was wisdom then, for the sake of Oliver Cowdery, and to insure the safety of the money and the sacred things he was to carry with him, that one should go with him that would be a true and faithful companion, hence the appointment of John Whitmer.

1. Hearken unto me, saith the Lord your God, for my servant Oliver Cowdery's sake. It is not wisdom in me that he should be entrusted with the commandments and the moneys which he shall carry unto the land of Zion, except one go with him who will be true and faithful.

2. Wherefore, I, the Lord, will that my servant, John Whitmer, should go with my servant Oliver Cowdery;

3. And also that he shall continue in writing and making a history of all the important things which he shall observe and know concerning my church;

4. And also that he receive counsel and assistance from my servant Oliver Cowdery and others.

5. And also my servants who are abroad in the earth should send forth the accounts of their stewardships to the land of Zion;

6. For the land of Zion shall be a seat and a place to receive and do all these things.

7. Nevertheless, let my servant John Whitmer travel many times from place to place, and from church to church, that he may the more easily obtain knowledge—

8. Preaching and expounding, writing, copying, selecting, and obtaining all things which shall be for the good of the church, and for the rising generations that shall grow up on the land of Zion, to possess it from generation to generation, forever and ever. Amen.

Esteem in which the Conference Held the Book of Commandments and Book of Mormon.

My time was occupied closely in reviewing the commandments and sitting in conference, for nearly two weeks; for from the first to the twelfth of November we held four special conferences. In the last which was held at Brother Johnson's, in Hiram, after deliberate consideration, in consequence of the book of revelations, now to be printed, being the foundation of the Church in these last days, and a benefit to the world, showing that the keys of the mysteries of the kingdom of our Savior are again entrusted to man; and the riches of eternity within the compass of those who are willing to live by every word that proceedeth out of the mouth of God—therefore the conference voted that they prize the revelations to be worth to the Church the riches of the whole earth, speaking temporally. The great benefits to the world which result from the Book of Mormon and the revelations which the Lord has seen fit in His infinite wisdom to grant unto us for our salvation, and for the salvation of all that will believe, were duly appreciated;* and in answer to an inquiry, I received the following:

Revelation, given November, 1831.†

1. Behold, and hearken, O ye inhabitants of Zion, and all ye people of my church who are afar off, and hear the word of the Lord which I give unto my servant Joseph Smith, Jun., and also unto my servant Martin Harris, and also unto my servant Oliver Cowdery, and also unto my servant John Whitmer, and also unto my servant Sidney Rigdon, and also unto my servant William W. Phelps, by the way of commandment unto them.

2. For I give unto them a commandment; wherefore hearken and hear, for thus saith the Lord unto them—

3. I, the Lord, have appointed them, and ordained them to be stewards over the revelations and commandments which I have given unto them, and which I shall hereafter give unto them;

4. And an account of this stewardship will I require of them in the day of judgment.

5. Wherefore, I have appointed unto them, and this is their business in the church of God, to manage them and the concerns thereof, yea, the benefits thereof.

* In the minutes of the special conference of November 12th, spoken of in the foregoing by the Prophet, occurs the following account of what took place in addition to what the Prophet has written: "Brother Joseph Smith, Jun., said one item he wished acted upon was that our brothers Oliver Cowdery and John Whitmer and the sacred writings which they have entrusted to them to carry to Zion—be dedicated to the Lord by the prayer of faith. Secondly, Brother Oliver has labored with me from the beginning in writing, &c. Brother Martin has labored with me from the beginning and Brothers John Whitmer and Sidney Rigdon also for a considerable time, and as these sacred writings are now going to the Church for its benefit, that we may have claim on the Church for recompense—if this conference think these things worth prizing to be had on record to show hereafter—I feel that it will be according to the mind of the Spirit, for by it these things were put into my heart which I know to be the Spirit of truth.

"Voted; that Joseph Smith, Jun., be appointed to dedicate and consecrate these brethren and the sacred writings and all they have entrusted to their care, to the Lord. Done accordingly. * * * * Voted; that in consequence of the diligence of our brethren, Joseph Smith, Jun., Oliver Cowdery, John Whitmer, and Sidney Rigdon in bringing to light by the grace of God these sacred things,—[they] be appointed to manage them according to the laws of the Church and the commandments of the Lord. And also that in consequence of the families of Joseph Smith, Hyrum Smith, Peter Whitmer, Christian Whitmer, Jacob Whitmer, Hiram Page and David Whitmer administering to their wants in temporal things; and also [on account of] the labors of Samual H. Smith, Peter Whitmer,Jun., William Smith and Don Carlos Smith—voted by the conference that the above named brethren be remembered to the Bishop in Zion as being worthy of inheritances among the people of the Lord according to the laws of said Church."—*Far West Record*, pp. 18, 19.

† Doctrine and Covenants, sec. lxx.

6. Wherefore, a commandment I give unto them, that they shall not give these things unto the church, neither unto the world;

7. Nevertheless, inasmuch as they receive more than is needful for their necessities and their wants, it shall be given into my storehouse;

8. And the benefits shall be consecrated unto the inhabitants of Zion, and unto their generations, inasmuch as they become heirs according to the laws of the kingdom.

9. Behold, this is what the lord requires of every man in his stewardship, even as I, the Lord, have appointed or shall hereafter appoint unto any man.

10. And behold, none are exempt from this law who belong to the church of the living God;

11. Yea, neither the bishop, neither the agent who keepeth the Lord's storehouse, neither he who is appointed in a stewardship over temporal things.

12. He who is appointed to administer spiritual things, the same is worthy of his hire, even as those who are appointed to a stewardship to administer in temporal things;

13. Yea, even more abundantly, which abundance is multiplied unto them through the manifestations of the Spirit.

14. Nevertheless, in your temporal things you shall be equal, and this not grudgingly, otherwise the abundance of the manifestations of the Spirit shall be withheld.

15. Now, this commandment I give unto my servants for their benefit while they remain, for a manifestation of my blessings upon their heads, and for a reward of their diligence and for their security;

16. For food and for raiment; for an inheritance; for houses and for lands, in whatsoever circumstances I, the Lord, shall place them, and whithersoever I, the Lord, shall send them.

17. For they have been faithful over many things, and have done well inasmuch as they have not sinned.

18. Behold, I, the Lord, am merciful and will bless them, and they shall enter into the joy of these things. Even so. Amen.

CHAPTER XVIII.

THE AMHERST CONFERENCE—THE VISION OF THE DEGREES OF GLORY IN MAN'S FUTURE LIFE.

The Labors of the Prophet and Sidney Rigdon.

After Oliver Cowdery and John Whitmer had departed for Jackson county, Missouri, I resumed the translation of the Scriptures, and continued to labor in this branch of my calling with Elder Sidney Rigdon as my scribe, until I received the following:

*Revelation, given December 1st, 1831.**

1. Behold, thus saith the Lord unto you my servants Joseph Smith, Jun., and Sidney Rigdon, that the time has verily come that it is necessary and expedient in me that you should open your mouths in proclaiming my gospel, the things of the kingdom, expounding the mysteries thereof out of the scriptures, according to that portion of Spirit and power which shall be given unto you, even as I will.

2. Verily I say unto you, proclaim unto the world in the regions round about, and in the church also, for the space of a season, even until it shall be made known unto you.

3. Verily this is a mission for a season, which I give unto you.

4. Wherefore, labor ye in my vineyard. Call upon the inhabitants of the earth, and bear record, and prepare the way for the commandments and revelations which are to come.

5. Now, behold this is wisdom; whoso readeth, let him understand and receive also;

6. For unto him that receiveth it shall be given more abundantly, even power.

7. Wherefore, confound your enemies; call upon them to meet you both in public and in private; and inasmuch as ye are faithful their shame shall be made manifest.

* Doctrine and Covenants, sec. lxxi.

8. Wherefore, let them bring forth their strong reasons against the Lord.

9. Verily, thus saith the Lord unto you—there is no weapon that is formed against you shall prosper;

10. And if any man lift his voice against you he shall be confounded in mine own due time.

11. Wherefore, keep my commandments; they are true and faithful. Even so. Amen.

The Prophet's Earnest Labors in Kirtland.

Knowing now the mind of the Lord, that the time had come that the Gospel should be proclaimed in power and demonstration to the world, from the Scriptures, reasoning with men as in days of old, I took a journey to Kirtland, in company with Elder Sidney Rigdon on the 3rd day of December, to fulfil the above revelation. On the 4th, several of the Elders and members assembled together to learn their duty, and for edification, and after some time had been spent in conversing about our temporal and spiritual welfare, I received the following:

*Revelation Given December 4th, 1831**

1. Hearken, and listen to the voice of the Lord, O ye who have assembled yourselves together, who are the high priests of my church, to whom the kingdom and power have been given.

2. For verily thus saith the Lord, it is expedient in me for a bishop to be appointed unto you, or of you, unto the church in this part of the Lord's vineyard.

3. And verily in this thing ye have done wisely, for it is required of the Lord, at the hand of every steward, to render an account of his stewardship, both in time and in eternity.

4. For he who is faithful and wise in time is accounted worthy to inherit the mansions prepared for him of my Father.

5. Verily I say unto you, the elders of the church in this part of my vineyard shall render an account of their stewardship unto the bishop, who shall be appointed of me in this part of my vineyard.

6. These things shall be had on record, to be handed over unto the bishop in Zion.

7. And the duty of the bishop shall be made known by the commandments which have been given, and the voice of the conference.

* Doctrine and Covenants, sec. lxxii.

8. And now, verily I say unto you, my servant Newel K. Whitney is the man who shall be appointed and ordained unto this power. This is the will of the Lord your God, your Redeemer. Even so. Amen.

9. The word of the Lord, in addition to the law which has been given, making known the duty of the bishop who has been ordained unto the church in this part of the vineyard, which is verily this—

10. To keep the Lord's storehouse; to receive the funds of the church in this part of the vineyard;

11. To take an account of the elders as before has been commanded; and to administer to their wants, who shall pay for that which they receive, inasmuch as they have wherewith to pay;

12. That this also may be consecrated to the good of the church, to the poor and needy.

13. And he who hath not wherewith to pay, an account shall be taken and handed over to the bishop of Zion, who shall pay the debt out of that which the Lord shall put into his hands.

14. And the labors of the faithful who labor in spiritual things, in administering the gospel and the things of the kingdom unto the church, and unto the world, shall answer the debt unto the bishop in Zion;

15. Thus it cometh out of the church, for according to the law every man that cometh up to Zion must lay all things before the bishop in Zion.

16. And now, verily I say unto you, that as every elder in this part of the vineyard must give an account of his stewardship unto the bishop in this part of the vineyard—

17. A certificate from the judge or bishop in this part of the vineyard, unto the bishop in the vineyard, unto the bishop in Zion, rendereth every man acceptable, and answereth all things, for an inheritance, and to be received as a wise steward and as a faithful laborer;

18. Otherwise he shall not be accepted of the bishop of Zion.

19. And now, verily I say unto you, let every elder who shall give an account unto the bishop of the church in this part of the vineyard be recommended by the church or churches, in which he labors, that he may render himself and his accounts approved in all things.

20. And again, let my servants who are appointed as stewards over the literary concerns of my church have claim for assistance upon the bishop or bishops in all things—

21. That the revelations may be published, and go forth unto the ends of the earth; that they also may obtain funds which shall benefit the church in all things;

22. That they also may render themselves approved in all things, and be accounted as wise stewards.

23. And now, behold, this shall be an ensample for all the extensive

branches of my church, in whatsoever land they shall be established. And now I make an end of my sayings. Amen.

24. A few words in addition to the laws of the kingdom, respecting the members of the church—they that are appointed by the Holy Spirit to go up unto Zion, and they who are privileged to go up unto Zion—

25. Let them carry up unto the bishop a certificate from three elders of the church, or a certificate from the bishop;

26. Otherwise he who shall go up unto the land of Zion shall not be accounted as a wise steward. This is also an ensample. Amen.

Effectiveness of the Prophet's and Sidney Rigdon's Labors.

From this time until the 8th or 10th of January, 1832, myself and Elder Rigdon continued to preach in Shalersville, Ravenna, and other places, setting forth the truth, vindicating the cause of our Redeemer; showing that the day of vengeance was coming upon this generation like a thief in the night; that prejudice, blindness and darkness filled the minds of many, and caused them to persecute the true Church, and reject the true light; by which means we did much towards allaying the excited feelings which were growing out of the scandalous letters then being published in the *Ohio Star*, at Ravenna, by the before-mentioned apostate, Ezra Booth.* On the 10th of January, I received the following revelation making known the will of the Lord concerning the Elders of the Church until the convening of the next conference.†

Revelation of January 10th, 1832‡

1. For verily, thus saith the Lord, it is expedient in me that they should continue preaching the gospel, and in exhortation to the churches in the regions round about, until conference;

2. And then, behold, it shall be made known unto them, by the voice of the conference, their several missions.

3. Now, verily I say unto you my servants, Joseph Smith, Jun., and Sidney Rigdon, saith the Lord, it is expedient to translate again;

4. And, inasmuch as it is practicable, to preach in the regions round

*These are the letters referred to at p. 217, note.

†This conference had been appointed to meet on the 25th of January, at Amherst, Lorain county, Ohio.

‡ Doctrine and Covenants, sec. lxxiii.

about until conference; and after that it is expedient to continue the work of translation until it be finished.

5. And let this be a pattern unto the elders until further knowledge, even as it is written.

6. Now I give no more unto you at this time. Gird up your loins and be sober. Even so. Amen.

Translation Renewed.

Upon the reception of the foregoing word of the Lord, I recommenced the translation of the Scriptures, and labored diligently until just before the conference, which was to convene on the 25th of January. During this period, I also received the following, as an explanation of the First Epistle to the Corinthians, 7th chapter, 14th verse:

*Revelation.**

1. For the unbelieving husband is sanctified by the wife, and the unbelieving wife is sanctified by the husband; else were your children unclean, but now are they holy.

2. Now, in the days of the apostles the law of circumcision was had among all the Jews who believed not the gospel of Jesus Christ.

3. And it came to pass that there arose a great contention among the people concerning the law of circumcision, for the unbelieving husband was desirous that his children should be circumcised and become subject to the law of Moses, which law was fulfilled.

4. And it came to pass that the children, being brought up in subjection to the law of Moses, gave heed to the traditions of their fathers and believed not the gospel of Christ, wherein they became unholy.

5. Wherefore, for this cause the apostle wrote unto the church, giving unto them a commandment, not of the Lord, but of himself, that a believer should not be united to an unbeliever; except the law of Moses should be done away among them.

6. That their children might remain without circumcision; and that the tradition might be done away, which saith that little children are unholy; for it was had among the Jews;

7. But little children are holy, being sanctified through the atonement of Jesus Christ; and this is what the scriptures mean.

The Amherst Conference.

A few days before the conference was to commence in Amherst, Lorain county, I started with the Elders that lived in my own vicinity, and arrived in good time. At this conference much har-

* Doctrine and Covenants, sec. lxxiv.

mony prevailed, and considerable business was done to advance the kingdom, and promulgate the Gospel to the inhabitants of the surrounding country.* The Elders seemed anxious for me to inquire of the Lord that they might know His will, or learn what would be most pleasing to Him for them to do, in order to bring men to a sense of their condition; for, as it was written, all men have gone out of the way, so that none doeth good, no, not one. I inquired and received the following:

Revelation, given January, 1832.†

1. Verily, verily, I say unto you, I who speak even by the voice of my spirit, even Alpha and Omega, your Lord and your God—

2. Hearken, O ye who have given your names to go forth to proclaim my gospel, and to prune my vineyard.

3. Behold, I say unto you that it is my will that you should go forth and not tarry, neither be idle but labor with your might—

4. Lifting up your voices as with the sound of a trump, proclaiming the truth according to the revelations and commandments which I have given you.

5. And thus, if ye are faithful ye shall be laden with many sheaves, and crowned with honor, and glory, and immortality, and eternal life.

6. Therefore, verily I say unto my servant William E. M'Lellin, I revoke the commission which I gave unto him to go unto the eastern countries;

7. And I give unto him a new commission and a new commandment, in the which I, the Lord, chasten him for the murmurings of his heart;

8. And he sinned; nevertheless, I forgive him and say unto him again, Go ye into the south countries.

9. And let my servant Luke Johnson go with him, and proclaim the things which I have commanded them—

10. Calling on the name of the Lord for the Comforter, which shall teach them all things that are expedient for them—

11. Praying always that they faint not; and inasmuch as they do this, I will be with them even unto the end.

12. Behold, this is the will of the Lord your God concerning you. Even so. Amen.

13. And again, verily thus saith the Lord, let my servant Orson

*The chief item of interest connected with this Amherst conference held on the 25th of January, 1832, is the fact that it was here that the Prophet Joseph was sustained and ordained as President of the High Priesthood.

†Doctrine and Covenants, sec. lxxv.

Hyde and my servant Samuel H. Smith take their journey into the eastern countries, and proclaim the things which I have commanded them; and inasmuch as they are faithful, lo, I will be with them even unto the end.

14. And again, verily I say unto my servant Lyman Johnson, and unto my servant Orson Pratt, they shall also take their journey into the eastern countries; and behold, and lo, I am with them also, even unto the end.

15. And again, I say unto my servant Asa Dodds, and unto my servant Calves Wilson, that they also shall take their journey unto the western countries, and proclaim my gospel, even as I have commanded them.

16. And he who is faithful shall overcome all things, and shall be lifted up at the last day.

17. And again, I say unto my servant Major N. Ashley, and my servant Burr Riggs, let them take their journey also into the south country.

18. Yea, let all those take their journey, as I have commanded them, going from house to house, and from village to village, and from city to city.

19. And in whatsoever house ye enter, and they receive you, leave your blessing upon that house.

20. And in whatsoever house ye enter, and they receive you not, ye shall depart speedily from that house, and shake off the dust of your feet as a testimony against them.

21. And you shall be filled with joy and gladness; and know this, that in the day of judgment you shall be judges of that house, and condemn them;

22. And it shall be more tolerable for the heathen in the day of judgment, than for that house; therefore, gird up your loins and be faithful, and ye shall overcome all things and be lifted up at the last day. Even so. Amen.

23. And again, thus saith the Lord unto you, O ye elders of my church, who have given your names that you might know his will concerning you—

24. Behold, I say unto you, that it is the duty of the church to assist in supporting the families of those, and also to support the families of those who are called and must needs be sent unto the world to proclaim the gospel unto the world.

25. Wherefore, I, the Lord, give unto you this commandment, that ye obtain places for your families inasmuch as your brethren are willing to open their hearts.

26. And let all such as can obtain places for their families, and sup-

port of the church for them, not fail to go into the world, whether to the east, or to the west, or to the north, or to the south.

27. Let them ask and they shall receive, knock and it shall be opened unto them, and be made known from on high, even by the Comforter, whither they shall go.

28. And again, verily I say unto you, that every man who is obliged to provide for his own family, let him provide, and he shall in nowise lose his crown; and let him labor in the church.

29. Let every man be diligent in all things. And the idler shall not have place in the church, except he repent and mend his ways.

30. Wherefore, let my servant Simeon Carter and my servant Emer Harris be united in the ministry;

31. And also my servant Ezra Thayre and my servant Thomas B. Marsh;

32. Also my servant Hyrum Smith and my servant Reynolds Cahoon;

33. And also my servant Daniel Stanton and my servant Seymour Brunson;

34. And also my servant Sylvester Smith and my servant Gideon Carter;

35. And also my servant Ruggles Eames and my servant Stephen Burnett;

36. And also my servant Micah B. Welton and also my servant Eden Smith. Even so. Amen.

Revelation on the Degrees of Future Glory.

Upon my return from Amherst conference, I resumed the translation of the Scriptures. From sundry revelations which had been received, it was apparent that many important points touching the salvation of man, had been taken from the Bible, or lost before it was compiled. It appeared self-evident from what truths were left, that if God rewarded every one according to the deeds done in the body the term "Heaven," as intended for the Saints' eternal home must include more kingdoms than one. Accordingly, on the 16th of February, 1832, while translating St. John's Gospel, myself and Elder Rigdon saw the following vision:

*Vision of the Glories.**

1. Hear, O ye heavens, and give ear, O earth, and rejoice ye in-

* Doctrine and Covenants, sec. lxxvi.

habitants thereof, for the Lord is God, and beside him there is no Savior.

2. Great is his wisdom, marvelous are his ways, and the extent of his doings none can find out.

3. His purposes fail not, neither are there any who can stay his hand.

4. From eternity to eternity he is the same, and his years never fail.

5. For thus saith the Lord—I, the Lord, am merciful and gracious unto those who fear me, and delight to honor those who serve me in righteousness and in truth unto the end.

6. Great shall be their reward and eternal shall be their glory.

7. And to them will I reveal all mysteries, yea, all the hidden mysteries of my kingdom from days of old, and for ages to come, will I make known unto them the good pleasure of my will concerning all things pertaining to my kingdom.

8. Yea, even the wonders of eternity shall they know, and things to come will I show them, even the things of many generations.

9. And their wisdom shall be great, and their understanding reach to heaven; and before them the wisdom of the wise shall perish, and the understanding of the prudent shall come to naught.

10. For by my Spirit will I enlighten them, and by my power will I make known unto them the secrets of my will—yea, even those things which eye has not seen, nor ear heard, nor yet entered into the heart of man.

11. We, Joseph Smith, Jun., and Sidney Rigdon, being in the Spirit on the sixteenth day of February, in the year of our Lord one thousand eight hundred and thirty-two—

12. By the power of the Spirit our eyes were opened and our understandings were enlightened, so as to see and understand the things of God—

13. Even those things which were from the beginning before the world was, which were ordained of the Father, through his Only Begotten Son, who was in the bosom of the Father, even from the beginning;

14. Of whom we bear record; and the record which we bear is the fulness of the gospel of Jesus Christ who is the Son, whom we saw and with whom we conversed in the heavenly vision.

15. For while we were doing the work of translation, which the Lord had appointed unto us, we came to the twenty-ninth verse of the fifth chapter of John, which was given unto us as follows:

16. Speaking of the resurrection of the dead, concerning those who shall hear the voice of the Son of Man, and shall come forth—

17. They who have done good in the resurrection of the just, and they who have done evil in the resurrection of the unjust—

18. Now this caused us to marvel, for it was given unto us of the Spirit.

19. And while we meditated upon these things, the Lord touched the eyes of our understandings and they were opened, and the glory of the Lord shone round about.

20. And we beheld the glory of the Son, on the right hand of the Father, and received of his fulness;

21. And saw the holy angels, and them who are sanctified before his throne, worshiping God, and the Lamb, who worship him forever and ever.

22. And now, after the many testimonies which have been given of him, this is the testimony, last of all, which we give of him: That he lives!

23. For we saw him, even on the right hand of God; and we heard the voice bearing record that he is the Only Begotten of the Father—

24. That by him, and through him, and of him, the worlds are and were created, and the inhabitants thereof are begotten sons and daughters unto God.

25. And this we saw also, and bear record, that an angel of God who was in authority in the presence of God, who rebelled against the Only Begotten Son whom the Father loved and who was in the bosom of the Father, was thrust down from the presence of God and the Son,

26. And was called Perdition, for the heavens wept over him—he was Lucifer, a son of the morning.

27. And we beheld, and lo, he is fallen! is fallen, even a son of the morning!

28. And while we were yet in the Spirit, the Lord commanded us that we should write the vision; for we beheld Satan, that old serpent, even the devil, who rebelled against God, and sought to take the kingdom of our God and his Christ—

29. Wherefore, he maketh war with the saints of God, and encompasseth them round about.

30. And we saw a vision of the sufferings of those with whom he made war and overcame, for thus came the voice of the Lord unto us:

31. Thus saith the Lord concerning all those who know my power, and have been made partakers thereof, and suffered themselves through the power of the devil to be overcome, and to deny the truth and defy my power—

32. They are they who are the sons of perdition, of whom I say that it had been better for them never to have been born;

33. For they are vessels of wrath, doomed to suffer the wrath of God, with the devil and his angels in eternity;

34. Concerning whom I have said there is no forgiveness in this world nor in the world to come—

35. Having denied the Holy Spirit after having received it, and having denied the Only Begotten Son of the Father, having crucified him unto themselves and put him to an open shame.

36. These are they who shall go away into the lake of fire and brimstone, with the devil and his angels—

37. And the only ones on whom the second death shall have any power;

38. Yea, verily, the only ones who shall not be redeemed in the due time of the Lord, after the sufferings of his wrath.

39. For all the rest shall be brought forth by the resurrection of the dead, through the triumph and the glory of the Lamb, who was slain, who was in the bosom of the Father before the worlds were made.

40. And this is the gospel, the glad tidings, which the voice out of the heavens bore record unto us—

41. That he came into the world, even Jesus, to be crucified for the world, and to bear the sins of the world, and to sanctify the world, and to cleanse it from all unrighteousness;

42. That through him all might be saved whom the Father had put into his power and made by him;

43. Who glorifies the Father, and saves all the works of his hands, except those sons of perdition who deny the Son after the Father has revealed him.

44. Wherefore, he saves all except them—they shall go away into everlasting punishment, which is endless punishment, which is eternal punishment, to reign with the devil and his angels in eternity, where their worm dieth not, and the fire is not quenched, which is their torment—

45. And the end thereof, neither the place thereof, nor their torment, no man knows;

46. Neither was it revealed, neither is, neither will be revealed unto man, except to them who are made partakers thereof;

47. Nevertheless, I, the Lord, show it by vision unto many, but straightway shut it up again;

48. Wherefore, the end, the width, the height, the depth, and the misery thereof, they understand not, neither any man except those who are ordained unto this condemnation.

49. And we heard the voice, saying: Write the vision, for lo, this is the end of the vision of the sufferings of the ungodly.

50. And again we bear record—for we saw and heard, and this is the testsimony of the gospel of Christ concerning them who shall come forth in the resurrection of the just—

51. They are they who received the testimony of Jesus, and believed on his name and were baptized after the manner of his burial,

being buried in the water in his name, and this according to the commandment which he has given—

52. That by keeping the commandments they might be washed and cleansed from all their sins, and receive the Holy Spirit by the laying on of the hands of him who is ordained and sealed unto this power;

53. And who overcome by faith, and are sealed by the Holy Spirit of promise, which the Father sheds forth upon all those who are just and true.

54. They are they who are the church of the Firstborn.

55. They are they into whose hands the Father has given all things—

56. They are they who are priests and kings, who have received of his fulness, and of his glory;

57. And are priests of the Most High, after the order of Melchizedek, which was after the order of Enoch, which was after the order of the Only Begotten Son.

58. Wherefore, as it is written, they are gods, even the sons of God—

59. Wherefore, all things are theirs, whether life or death, or things present, or things to come, all are theirs and they are Christ's. and Christ is God's.

60. And they shall overcome all things.

61. Wherefore, let no man glory in man, but rather let him glory in God, who shall subdue all enemies under his feet.

62. These shall dwell in the presence of God and his Christ forever and ever.

63. These are they whom he shall bring with him, when he shall come in the clouds of heaven to reign on earth over his people.

64. These are they who shall have part in the first resurrection.

65. These are they who shall come forth in the resurrection of the just.

66. These are they who are come unto Mount Zion, and unto the city of the living God, the heavenly place, the holiest of all.

67. These are they who have come to an innumerable company of angels, to the general assembly and church of Enoch, and of the Firstborn.

68. These are they whose names are written in heaven, where God and Christ are the judge of all.

69. These are they who are just men made perfect through Jesus the mediator of the new covenant, who wrought out this perfect atonement through the shedding of his own blood.

70. These are they whose bodies are celestial, whose glory is that of the sun, even the glory of God, the highest of all, whose glory the sun of the firmament is written of as being typical.

71. And again, we saw the terrestrial world, and behold and lo, these are they who are of the terrestrial, whose glory differs from that

of the church of the Firstborn who have received the fulness of the Father, even as that of the moon differs from the sun in the firmament.

72. Behold, these are they who died without law;

73. And also they who are the spirits of men kept in prison, whom the Son visited, and preached the gospel unto them, that they might be judged according to men in the flesh;

74. Who received not the testimony of Jesus in the flesh, but afterwards received it.

75. These are they who are honorable men of the earth, who were blinded by the craftiness of men.

76. These are they who receive of his glory, but not of his fulness.

77. These are they who receive of the presence of the Son, but not of the fulness of the Father.

78. Wherefore, they are bodies terrestrial, and not bodies celestial, and differ in glory as the moon differs from the sun.

79. These are they who are not valiant in the testimony of Jesus; wherefore, they obtain not the crown over the kingdom of our God.

80. And now this is the end of the vision which we saw of the terrestrial, that the Lord commanded us to write while we were yet in the Spirit.

81. And again, we saw the glory of the telestial, which glory is that of the lesser, even as the glory of the stars differs from that of the glory of the moon in the firmament.

82. These are they who received not the gospel of Christ, neither the testimony of Jesus.

83. These are they who deny not the Holy Spirit.

84. These are they who are thrust down to hell.

85. These are they who shall not be redeemed from the devil until the last resurrection, until the Lord, even Christ the Lamb, shall have finished his work.

86. These are they who receive not of his fulness in the eternal world, but of the Holy Spirit through the ministration of the terrestrial;

87. And the terrestrial through the ministration of the celestial.

88. And also the telestial receive it of the administering of angels who are appointed to minister for them, or who are appointed to be ministering spirits for them; for they shall be heirs of salvation.

89. And thus we saw, in the heavenly vision, the glory of the telestial, which surpasses all understanding;

90. And no man knows it except him to whom God has revealed it.

91. And thus we saw the glory of the terrestrial which excels in all things the glory of the telestial, even in glory, and in power, and in might, and in dominion.

92. And thus we saw the glory of the celestial, which excels in all

things—where God, even the Father, reigns upon his throne forever and ever;

93. Before whose throne all things bow in humble reverence, and give him glory forever and ever.

94. They who dwell in his presence are the church of the Firstborn; and they see as they are seen, and know as they are known, having received of his fulness and of his grace;

95. And he makes them equal in power, and in might, and in dominion.

96. And the glory of the celestial is one, even as the glory of the sun is one.

97. And the glory of the terrestrial is one, even as the glory of the moon is one.

98. And the glory of the telestial is one, even as the glory of the stars is one; for as one star differs from another star in glory, even so differs one from another in glory in the telestial world;

99. For these are they who are of Paul, and of Apollos, and of Cephas.

100. These are they who say they are some of one and some of another—some of Christ and some of John, and some of Moses, and some of Elias, and some of Esaias, and some of Isaiah, and some of Enoch;

101. But received not the gospel, neither the testimony of Jesus, neither the prophets, neither the everlasting covenant.

102. Last of all, these all are they who will not be gathered with the saints, to be caught up unto the church of the Firstborn, and received into the cloud.

103. These are they who are liars, and sorcerers, and adulterers, and whoremongers, and whosoever loves and makes a lie.

104. These are they who suffer the wrath of God on earth.

105. These are they who suffer the vengeance of eternal fire.

106. These are they who are cast down to hell and suffer the wrath of Almighty God, until the fulness of times, when Christ shall have subdued all enemies under his feet, and shall have perfected his work;

107. When he shall deliver up the kingdom, and present it unto the Father, spotless, saying: I have overcome and have trodden the wine-press alone, even the wine-press of the fierceness of the wrath of Almighty God.

108. Then shall he be crowned with the crown of his glory, to sit on the throne of his power to reign forever and ever.

109. But behold, and lo, we saw the glory and the inhabitants of the telestial world, that they were as innumerable as the stars in the firmament of heaven, or as the sand upon the seashore;

110. And heard the voice of the Lord, saying: These all shall bow

the knee, and every tongue shall confess to him who sits upon the throne forever and ever;

111. For they shall be judged according to their works, and every man shall receive according to his own works, his own dominion, in the mansions which are prepared;

112. And they shall be servants of the Most High; but where God and Christ dwell they cannot come, worlds without end.

113. This is the end of the vision which we saw, which we were commanded to write while we were yet in the Spirit.

114. But great and marvelous are the works of the Lord, and the mysteries of his kingdom which he showed unto us, which surpass all understanding in glory, and in might, and in dominion;

115. Which he commanded us we should not write while we were yet in the Spirit, and are not lawful for man to utter;

116. Neither is man capable to make them known, for they are only to be seen and understood by the power of the Holy Spirit, which God bestows on those who love him, and purify themselves before him;

117. To whom he grants this privilege of seeing and knowing for themselves;

118. That through the power and manifestation of the Spirit, while in the flesh, they may be able to bear his presence in the world of glory.

119. And to God and the Lamb be glory, and honor, and dominion forever and ever. Amen.

The Prophet's Views on the Foregoing Revelation.

Nothing could be more pleasing to the Saints upon the order of the kingdom of the Lord, than the light which burst upon the world through the foregoing vision. Every law, every commandment, every promise, every truth, and every point touching the destiny of man, from Genesis to Revelation, where the purity of the scriptures remains unsullied by the folly of men, go to show the perfection of the theory [of different degrees of glory in the future life] and witnesses the fact that that document is a transcript from the records of the eternal world. The sublimity of the ideas; the purity of the language; the scope for action; the continued duration for completion, in order that the heirs of salvation may confess the Lord and bow the knee; the rewards for faithfulness, and the punishments for sins, are so much beyond the narrow-mindedness of men, that every honest man is constrained to exclaim: *"It came from God."*

About the first of March, in connection with the translation of the Scriptures, I received the following explanation of the Revelation of St. John:

A Key to St. John's Book of Revelation.

*Revelation, given at Hiram, Portage County, Ohio.**

1. Q. What is the sea of glass spoken of by John, 4th chapter, and 6th verse of the Revelation?

A. It is the earth, in its sanctified, immortal, and eternal state.

2. Q. What are we to understand by the four beasts, spoken of in the same verse?

A. They are figurative expressions, used by the Revelator, John, in describing heaven, the paradise of God, the happiness of man, and of beasts, and of creeping things, and of the fowls of the air; that which is spiritual being in the likeness of that which is temporal; and that which is temporal in the likeness of that which is spiritual; the spirit of man in the likeness of his person, as also the spirit of the beast, and every other creature which God has created.

3. Q. Are the four beasts limited to individual beasts, or do they represent classes or orders?

A. They are limited to four individual beasts, which were shown to John, to represent the glory of the classes of beings in their destined order or sphere of creation, in the enjoyment of their eternal felicity.

4. Q. What are we to understand by the eyes and wings, which the beasts had?

A. Their eyes are a representation of light and knowledge, that is, they are full of knowledge; and their wings are a representation of power, to move, to act, etc.

5. Q. What are we to understand by the four and twenty elders, spoken of by John?

A. We are to understand that these elders whom John saw, were elders who had been faithful in the work of the ministry and were dead; who belonged to the seven churches, and were then in the paradise of God.

6. Q. What are we to understand by the book which John saw, which was sealed on the back with seven seals?

A. We are to understand that it contains the revealed will, mysteries, and works of God; the hidden things of his economy concerning

* Doctrine and Covenants, sec. **lxxvii.**

this earth during the seven thousand years of its continuance, or its temporal existence.

7. Q. What are we to understand by the seven seals with which it was sealed?

A. We are to understand that the first seal contains the things of the first thousand years, and the second also of the second thousand years, and so on until the seventh.

8. Q. What are we to understand by the four angels, spoken of in the 7th chapter and 1st verse of Revelation?

A. We are to understand that they are four angels sent forth from God, to whom is given power over the four parts of the earth, to save life and to destroy; these are they who have the everlasting gospel to commit to every nation, kindred, tongue, and people; having power to shut up the heavens, to seal up unto life, or to cast down to the regions of darkness.

9. Q. What are we to understand by the angel ascending from the east, Revelation 7th chapter and 2nd verse?

A. We are to understand that the angel ascending from the east is he to whom is given the seal of the living God over the twelve tribes of Israel; wherefore, he crieth unto the four angels having the everlasting gospel, saying: Hurt not the earth, neither the sea, nor the trees, till we have sealed the servants of our God in their foreheads. And, if you will receive it, this is Elias which was to come to gather together the tribes of Israel and restore all things.

10. Q. What time are the things spoken of in this chapter to be accomplished?

A. They are to be accomplished in the sixth thousand years, or the opening of the sixth seal.

11. Q. What are we to understand by sealing the one hundred and forty-four thousand, out of all the tribes of Israel—twelve thousand out of every tribe?

A. We are to understand that those who are sealed are high priests, ordained unto the holy order of God, to administer the everlasting gospel; for they are they who are ordained out of every nation, kindred, tongue, and people, by the angels to whom is given power over the nations of the earth, to bring as many as will come to the church of the Firstborn.

12. Q. What are we to understand by the sounding of the trumpets, mentioned in the 8th chapter of Revelation?

A. We are to understand that as God made the world in six days, and on the seventh day he finished his work, and sanctified it, and also formed man out of the dust of the earth, even so, in the beginning of the seventh thousand years will the Lord God sanctify the earth, and complete the salvation of man, and judge all things, and shall redeem all things, except that which he hath not put into his power, when he shall have sealed all things, unto the end of all things; and the sounding of the trumpets of the seven angels are the preparing and finishing of his work, in the beginning of the seventh thousand years—the preparing of the way before the time of his coming.

13. Q. When are the things to be accomplished, which are written in the 9th chapter of Revelation?

A. They are to be accomplished after the opening of the seventh seal, before the coming of Christ.

14. Q. What are we to understand by the little book which was eaten by John, as mentioned in the 10th chapter of Revelation?

A. We are to understand that it was a mission, and an ordinance, for him to gather the tribes of Israel; behold, this is Elias, who, as it is written, must come and restore all things.

15. Q. What is to be understood by the two witnesses, in the eleventh chapter of Revelation?

A. They are two prophets that are to be raised up to the Jewish nation in the last days, at the time of the restoration, and to prophesy to the Jews after they are gathered and have built the city of Jerusalem in the land of their fathers.

Besides the work of translating, previous to the 20th of March, I received the four following revelations:—

Sundry Revelations.

Revelation, given March, 1832. The Order given of the Lord to Enoch, [Joseph Smith, Jun.,] for the purpose of establishing the poor.†*

1. The Lord spake unto Enoch [Joseph Smith, Jun.], saying: Hearken unto me, saith the Lord your God, who are ordained unto the high priesthood of my church, who have assembled yourselves together;

2. And listen to the counsel of him who has ordained you from on high, who shall speak in your ears the words of wisdom, that salvation may be unto you in that thing which you have presented before me, saith the Lord God.

3. For verily I say unto you, the time has come, and is now at hand; and behold, and lo, it must needs be that there be an organization

* It was not always desirable that the individuals whom the Lord addressed in revelations should at the time be known by the world, and hence in this and in some subsequent revelations the brethren were addressed by other than their own names. The temporary necessity having passed for keeping the names of the individuals addressed unknown, their real names were subsequently given in brackets.

† Doctrine and Covenants, sec. lxxviii.

of my people, in regulating and establishing the affairs of the storehouse for the poor of my people, both in this place and in the land of Zion—

4. Or in other words, the city of Enoch [Joseph], for a permanent and everlasting establishment and order unto my church, to advance the cause, which ye have espoused, to the salvation of man, and to the glory of your Father who is in heaven;

5. That you may be equal in the bonds of heavenly things, yea, and earthly things also, for the obtaining of heavenly things.

6. For if ye are not equal in earthly things ye cannot be equal in obtaining heavenly things;

7. For if you will that I give unto you a place in the celestial world, you must prepare yourselves by doing the things which I have commanded you and required of you.

8. And now, verily thus saith the Lord, it is expedient that all things be done unto my glory, by you who are joined together in this order;

9. Or, in other words, let my servant Ahashdah [Newel K. Whitney]and my servant Gazelam, or Enoch [Joseph Smith, Jun.,] and my servant Pelagoram [Sidney Rigdon], sit in council with the saints which are in Zion;

10. Otherwise Satan seeketh to turn their hearts away from the truth, that they become blinded and understand not the things which are prepared for them.

11. Wherefore, a commandment I give unto you, to prepare and organize yourselves by a bond or everlasting covenant that cannot be broken.

12. And he who breaketh it shall lose his office and standing in the church, and shall be delivered over to the buffetings of Satan until the day of redemption.

13. Behold, this is the preparation wherewith I prepare you, and the foundation, and the ensample which I give unto you, whereby you may accomplish the commandments which are given you;

14. That through my providence, notwithstanding the tribulation which shall descend upon you, that the church may stand independent above all other creatures beneath the celestial world;

15. That you may come up unto the crown prepared for you, and be made rulers over many kingdoms, saith the Lord God, the Holy One of Zion, who hath established the foundations of Adam-ondi-Ahman;

16. Who hath appointed Michael your prince, and established his feet, and set him upon high, and given unto him the keys of salvation under the counsel and direction of the Holy One, who is without beginning of days or end of life.

17. Verily, verily, I say unto you, ye are little children, and ye have not as yet understood how great blessings the Father hath in his own hands and prepared for you;

18. And ye cannot bear all things now; nevertheless, be of good cheer, for I will lead you along. The kingdom is yours and the blessings thereof are yours, and the riches of eternity are yours.

19. And he who receiveth all things with thankfulness shall be made glorious; and the things of this earth shall be added unto him even an hundred fold, yea, more.

20. Wherefore, do the things which I have commanded you, saith your Redeemer, even the Son Ahman, who prepareth all things before he taketh you;

21. For ye are the church of the Firstborn, and he will take you up in a cloud, and appoint every man his portion.

22. And he that is a faithful and wise steward shall inherit all things. Amen.

*Revelation, given March, 1832.**

1. Verily I say unto you, that it is my will that my servant Jared Carter should go again into the eastern countries, from place to place, and from city to city, in the power of the ordination wherewith he has been ordained, proclaiming glad tidings of great joy, even the everlasting gospel.

2. And I will send upon him the Comforter, which shall teach him the truth and the way whither he shall go;

3. And inasmuch as he is faithful, I will crown him again with sheaves.

4. Wherefore, let your heart be glad, my servant Jared Carter, and fear not, saith your Lord, even Jesus Christ. Amen.

Revelation, given March, 1832.†

1. Verily, thus saith the Lord unto you my servant Stephen Burnett: Go ye, go ye into the world and preach the gospel to every creature that cometh under the sound of your voice.

2. And inasmuch as you desire a companion, I will give unto you my servant Eden Smith.

3. Wherefore, go ye and preach my gospel, whether to the north or to the south, to the east or to the west, it mattereth not, for ye cannot go amiss.

4. Therefore, declare the things which ye have heard, and verily believe, and know to be true.

5. Behold, this is the will of him who hath called you, your Redeemer, even Jesus Christ. Amen.

Revelation, given March, 1832.‡

1. Verily, verily, I say unto you my servant Frederick G. Williams:

* Doctrine and Covenants, sec. lxxix.
† Doctrine and Covenants, sec. lxxx.
‡ Doctrine and Covenants, sec. lxxxi.

Listen to the voice of him who speaketh, to the word of the Lord your God, and hearken to the calling wherewith you are called, even to be a high priest in my church, and a counselor unto my servant Joseph Smith, Jun.;

2. Unto whom I have given the keys of the kingdom, which belong always unto the Presidency of the High Priesthood:*

3. Therefore, verily I acknowledge him and will bless him, and also thee, inasmuch as thou art faithful in counsel, in the office which I have appointed unto you, in prayer always, vocally and in thy heart, in public and in private, also in thy ministry in proclaiming the gospel in the land of the living, and among thy brethren.

4. And in doing these things thou wilt do the greatest good unto thy fellow beings, and wilt promote the glory of him who is your Lord.

5. Wherefore, be faithful; stand in the office which I have appointed unto you; succor the weak, lift up the hands which hang down, and strengthen the feeble knees.

6. And if thou art faithful unto the end thou shalt have a crown of immortality, and eternal life in the mansions which I have prepared in the house of my Father.

7. Behold, and lo, these are the words of Alpha and Omega, even Jesus Christ. Amen.

*It has been said that there was no First Presidency in the Church of Jesus Christ in former days and that this body is peculiar to the Dispensation of the Fulness of Times. Here the Lord declares that the keys of the kingdom "belong always unto the Presidency of the High Priesthood." In other words they belong to the Presidency of the Church. In a discourse delivered July 2, 1839, the Prophet Joseph Smith said that Adam held the keys of the First Presidency, then Noah also held this office. He said: "The Priesthood is everlasting. The Savior, Moses and Elias, gave the keys to Peter, James and John, on the mount, when they were transfigured before him." This being true, then Peter, James and John were chosen by the Lord as a First Presidency and served in that capacity in the Church of Jesus Christ in their dispensation. It was by virtue of this calling that they were sent to confer upon Joseph Smith and Oliver Cowdery the keys of the kingdom. (D. & C. 27:13.)

CHAPTER XIX

MOB VIOLANCE AT HIRAM—THE SECOND JOURNEY OF THE PROPHET TO ZION, AND RETURN TO KIRTLAND.

I RECEIVED a letter from the brethren who went up to the land of Zion, stating that they had arrived at Independence, Missouri, in good health and spirits, with a printing press and a store of goods. Agreeable to the instructions of the fall conference, they also sent me the prospectus of a monthly paper, *The Evening and Morning Star.**

Prospectus of *The Evening and Morning Star.*

* The prospectus of *The Evening and Morning Star*, referred to above, is a lengthy document, from which the following is condensed: it is announced that the *Star* will be devoted to unfolding the meaning of the revelations of God from the earliest times to the present, but more especially those revelations which God has given in the present dispensation; that God made choice of Israel in ancient times through whom to make known His will unto mankind; but owing to transgression Israel was taken captive and scattered among all nations; God, however, promised that in the last days He would gather Israel then scattered, and bring them again into their own lands where they should be wonderfully prospered.

The time for the accomplishment of these things is rapidly approaching. It will be attended with the sore judgments of God upon the wicked. And as in all past ages, before allowing judgments to fall upon the wicked, God has sent them a word of warning and an opportunity to repent, so too in the crisis pending the Lord will not bring the threatened calamity upon mankind without sending forth due warning. "Therefore, in the fear of Him (the Lord), and to spread the truth among all nations, kindreds, tongues and people, this paper is sent forth, that a wicked world may know that Jesus Christ, the Redeemer, who shall come to Zion will soon appear." *The Evening and Morning Star*—in addition to being a herald of Israel's return to the favor of God, and a messenger of the everlasting Gospel—will also contain whatever of truth or information that will benefit the Saints of God temporally as well as spiritually, "without interfering with politics, broils, or the gainsaying of the world." It is also announced that from the *Star* press it may be expected, as soon as wisdom directs, that there will be issued "many sacred records which have slept for ages." The Star was to be a royal quarto sheet, issued monthly, at one dollar a year, until it should be deemed proper to publish it oftener. The prospectus was issued in February, and signed by W W. Phelps.

The Prophet's Life in Hiram.

According to previous intentions, we now began to make preparations to visit the brethren who had removed to the land of Missouri. Before going to Hiram to live with Father Johnson,* my wife had taken two children (twins), of John Murdock's, to rear.† She received them when only nine days old; they were now nearly eleven months. I would remark that nothing important had occurred since I came to reside in Father Johnson's house in Hiram, except that I had held meetings on the Sabbaths and evenings, and baptized a number.

A Prophecy on Olmsted Johnson.

Father Johnson's son, Olmsted Johnson, about this time came home on a visit, during which I told him if he did not obey the Gospel, the spirit he was of would lead him to destruction, and when he went away, he would never return or see his father again. He went to the Southern States and Mexico; on his return he took sick and died in Virginia.

Apostates.

In addition to the apostate Ezra Booth, Simonds Ryder,‡ Eli Johnson, Edward Johnson and John Johnson, Jun., had apostatized.

* The Johnson family was one of the typical American families of old colonial times—the men were large, strong, brave, sensible, honest, well-to-do. "My grandfather, Israel Johnson," writes Luke Johnson in his autobiographical sketch, "lived in Chesterfield, New Hampshire, and was much respected by his neighbors for his honesty, integrity and industry. My father, John Johnson, was born in Chesterfield, New Hampshire, April 11th, 1779. He followed the occupation of farming on a large scale, and was noted for paying his debts and living independently. He moved from Pomfret, Vermont, to Hiram, Portage county, Ohio. He was connected with the Methodist church for about five years previous to receiving the Gospel." Luke Johnson then relates the circumstance of the Prophet, through the power of God, healing his mother of chronic rheumatism in the arm, which converted Ezra Booth as already related on page 215, and then resumes: "My father was satisfied in regard to the truth of 'Mormonism,' and was baptized by Joseph Smith, Jun., in the winter of 1830-1, and furnished him and his family a home, while he translated a portion of the Bible."

† Their names were Joseph S. and Julia. They were born in Orange, Cuyahoga county, Ohio, April 30, 1831. Emma Smith, the Prophet's wife, had given birth to twins, a boy and girl—on the same date. They lived but three hours and Emma Smith took the motherless Murdock twins in the fond hope that they would fill the void in her life occasioned by the loss of her own.

‡Mention has already been made of Simonds Ryder's conversion to the Gospel

Mob Violence at Hiram.

On the 24th of March, the twins before mentioned, which had been sick of the measles for some time, caused us to be broken of our rest in taking care of them, especially my wife. In the evening I told her she had better retire to rest with one of the children, and I would watch with the sicker child. In the night she told me I had better lie down on the trundle bed, and I did so, and was soon after awakened by her screaming murder, when I found myself going out of the door, in the hands of about a dozen men; some of whose hands were in my hair, and some had hold of my shirt, drawers and limbs. The foot of the trundle bed was towards the door, leaving only room enough for the door to swing open. My wife heard a gentle tapping on the windows which she then took no particular notice of (but which was unquestionably designed for ascertaining whether or not we were all asleep), and soon after the mob burst open the door and surrounded the bed in an instant, and, as I said, the first I knew I was going out of the door in the hands of an infuriated mob. I made a desperate struggle, as I was forced out, to extricate myself, but only cleared one leg, with which I made a pass at one man, and he fell on the door steps. I was immediately overpowered again; and they swore by G— —, they would kill me if I did not be still, which quieted me. As they passed

through the fulfilment of a prophecy relating to an earthquake in Pekin, China (see p. 158). The initial point of his apostasy is equally interesting. It appears that some time after his baptism he was ordained an Elder of the Church (*Far West Record*, p. 4); and somewhat later informed by a communication signed by the Prophet Joseph and Sidney Rigdon, that it was the will of the Lord, made known by the Spirit, that he should preach the Gospel. Both in the letter he received and in the official commission to preach, however, his name was spelled R-i-d-e-r, instead of R-y-d-e-r, and is soberly stated in the *History of the Disciples on the Western Reserve* (Hayden), that he thought if the "Spirit" through which he had been called to preach could err in the matter of spelling his name, it might have erred in calling him to the ministry as well; or, in other words, he was led to doubt if he were called at all by the Spirit of God, because of the error in spelling his name! The same circumstance is referred to in *Kennedy's Early Days of Mormonism* (p. 104). Kennedy also remarks that while in the uncertain mood excited by this incident Ezra Booth returned from Missouri, and a comparison of experiences led to a complete overthrow of all belief in the new creed in the minds of both.

around the house with me, the fellow that I kicked came to me and thrust his hand, all covered with blood, into my face and with an exulting hoarse laugh, muttered: *"Ge, gee, G— d—ye, I'l fix ye."**

Brutality of the Mob.

They then seized me by the throat and held on till I lost my breath. After I came to, as they passed along with me, about thirty rods from the house, I saw Elder Rigdon stretched out on the ground, whither they had dragged him by his heels. I supposed he was dead. I began to plead with them, saying, "You will have mercy and spare my life, I hope." To which they replied, "G—d—ye, call on yer God for help, we'll show ye no mercy;" and the people began to show themselves in every direction; one coming from the orchard had a plank; and I expected they would kill me, and carry me off on the plank. They then turned to the right, and went on about thirty rods further; about sixty rods from the house, and thirty from where I saw Elder Rigdon, into the meadow, where they stopped, and one said, "Simonds, Simonds," (meaning, I supposed, Simonds Ryder,) "pull up his drawers, pull up his drawers, he will take cold." Another replied: *"Ain't ye going to kill 'im? ain't ye going to kill 'im?"* when a group of mobbers collected a little way off, and said: "Simonds, Simonds, come here;" and "Simonds" charged those who had hold of me to keep me from touching the ground (as they had done all the time), lest I should get a spring upon them. They held a council, and as I could occasionally overhear a word, I supposed it was to know whether or not it was best to kill me. They returned after a while, when I learned that they had

* The man whom the Prophet struck was named Waste. He was regarded, says Luke Johnson, as the strongest man in the Western Reserve, and had boasted that he could take the Prophet out of the house alone. "At the time they [the mob] were taking him [the Prophet] out of the house, Waste had hold of one foot. Joseph drew up his leg and gave him a kick, which sent him sprawling into the street. He afterwards said that the Prophet was the most powerful man he ever had hold of in his life." (*History of Luke Johnson*, by himself: *Millennial Star*, vol. xxvi, p. 835.)

concluded not to kill me, but to beat and scratch me well, tear off my shirt and drawers, and leave me naked. One cried, "Simonds, Simonds, *where's the tar bucket?*" "I don't know," answered one, "*where 'tis, Eli's left it.*" They ran back and fetched the bucket of tar, when one exclaimed, with an oath, "*Let us tar up his mouth;*" and they tried to force the tar-paddle into my mouth; I twisted my head around, so that they could not; and they cried out, "*G—d—ye, hold up yer head and let us giv ye some tar.*" They then tried to force a vial into my mouth, and broke it in my teeth. All my clothes were torn off me except my shirt collar; and one man fell on me and scratched my body with his nails like a mad cat, and then muttered out: "*G—d—ye, that's the way the Holy Ghost falls on folks!*"

The Prophet's Pitiable Condition.

They then left me, and I attempted to rise, but fell again; I pulled the tar away from my lips, so that I could breathe more freely, and after a while I began to recover, and raised myself up, whereupon I saw two lights. I made my way towards one of them, and found it was Father Johnson's. When I came to the door I was naked, and the tar made me look as if I were covered with blood, and when my wife saw me she thought I was all crushed to pieces, and fainted. During the affray abroad, the sisters of the neighborhood had collected at my room. I called for a blanket, they threw me one and shut the door; I wrapped it around me and went in.

A Case of Mistaken Identity.

In the meantime, Brother John Poorman heard an outcry across the corn field, and running that way met Father Johnson, who had been fastened in his house at the commencement of the assault, by having his door barred by the mob, but on calling to his wife to bring his gun, saying he would blow a hole through the door, the mob fled, and Father Johnson, seizing a club, ran after the party that had Elder Rigdon, and knocked down one man, and raised his club to level another, exclaiming, "*What are you doing* *here?*" when they left Elder Rigdon and turned upon Father Johnson, who, turning to run toward his own house, met Brother Poorman coming out of the corn field; each supposing the other to be a mobber, an encounter ensued, and Poorman gave Johnson a severe blow on the left shoulder with a stick or stone, which brought him to the ground.* Poorman ran immediately towards Father Johnson's, and arriving while I was waiting for the blanket, exclaimed, "I'm afraid I've killed him." Killed who? asked one; when Poorman hastily related the circumstances of the rencounter near the corn field, and went into the shed and hid himself. Father Johnson soon recovered so as to come to the house, when the whole mystery was quickly solved concerning the difficulty between him and Poorman, who, on learning the facts, joyfully came from his hiding place.

The Prophet's Undaunted Spirit.

My friends spent the night in scraping and removing the tar, and washing and cleansing my body; so that by morning I was ready to be clothed again. This being the Sabbath morning, the people assembled for meeting at the usual hour of worship, and among them came also the mobbers; viz.: Simonds Ryder, a Campbellite preacher and leader of the mob; one McClentic, who had his hands in my hair; one Streeter, son of a Campbellite minister; and Felatiah Allen, Esq., who gave the mob a barrel of whiskey to raise their spirits. Besides these named, there were many others in the mob. With my flesh all scarified and defaced, I preached to the congregation as usual, and in the afternoon of the same day baptized three individuals.†

* This blow broke his collar bone, according to the statement of his son, Luke Johnson. David Whitmer laid his hands upon him, and he was immediately healed. (*Millennial Star*, vol. xxvi, p. 835)

†According to the statement of Luke Johnson (autobiographical sketch, *Millennial Star*, vol. xxvi, p. 834-5), there were about forty or fifty in the mob that attacked the Prophet on this occasion. He also states that a Dr. Dennison, a man of considerable influence in the community, was a member of this mob, and threatened to do the Prophet great bodily injury, but when he saw the Prophet in the hands of his enemies his heart failed him. Carnot Mason was the one who first seized the Prophet and dragged him from his bed. Speaking of the fate that overtook some of the members of the mob, Johnson remarks that Mason, soon after the mobbing, "had an at-

The next morning I went to see Elder Rigdon, and found him crazy, and his head highly inflamed, for they had dragged him by his heels, and those, too, so high from the ground that he could not raise his head from the rough, frozen surface, which lacerated it exceedingly; and when he saw me he called to his wife to bring him his razor. She asked him what he wanted of it; and he replied, to kill me. Sister Rigdon left the room, and he asked me to bring his razor; I asked him what he wanted of it, and he replied he wanted to kill his wife; and he continued delirious some days. The feathers which were used with the tar on this occasion, the mob took out of Elder Rigdon's house. After they had seized him, and dragged him out, one of the banditti returned to get some pillows; when the women shut him in and kept him a prisoner some time.

Elder Rigdon's Condition.

During the mobbing one of the twins contracted a severe cold, continued to grow worse until Friday, and then died.* The mobbers were composed of various religious parties, but mostly Campbellites, Methodists and Baptists, who continued to molest and menace Father Johnson's house for a long time. Elder Rigdon removed to Kirtland with his family —then sick with the measles— the following Wednesday; and, on account of the mob, he went to Chardon† on Saturday, March 31st.

Composition of the Mob.

April first, I started for Missouri, in company with Newel K. Whitney, Peter Whitmer, and Jesse Gause, to fulfil the revelation. Not wishing to go by Kirtland, as another mob existed in that neighborhood (and indeed, the spirit of

The Prophet Starts on his Second Visit to Zion.

tack of spinal affection." Fullars, another of the mob, died of cholera, in Cleveland, Ohio; and Dr. Dennison was sent to the penitentiary for ten years (but for what offense he does not say) and died before the term expired.

* This was Joseph S. Murdock, whose death occurred March 29, 1832, his age being one day less than eleven months.

†Chardon was the county seat of Geauga county, and about five miles from Kirtland.

mobocracy was very prevalent through that whole region of country at the time), brother George Pitkin took us in his wagon by the most expeditious route to Warren, where we arrived the same day, and were there joined by Elder Rigdon, who left Chardon in the morning; and proceeding onward, we arrived at Wellsville the next day, and the day following at Steubenville, where we left the wagon; and on Wednesday, the 4th of April, we took passage on board a steam packet for Wheeling, Virginia; where we purchased a lot of paper for the press in Zion, then in care of W. W. Phelps.

Incidents by the Way.

After we left Hiram, fearing for the safety of my family, on account of the mob, I wrote to my wife (in connection with Bishop Whitney) suggesting that she go to Kirtland and tarry with Brother Whitney's family until our return. From Wheeling we took passage on board the steamer Trenton. While at the dock, during the night, the boat was twice on fire burning the whole width of the boat through into the cabin, but with so little damage that the boat went on in the morning; and when we arrived at Cincinnati, some of the mob which had followed us, left us, and we arrived at Louisville the same night. Captain Brittle offered us protection on board of his boat, and gave us supper and breakfast gratuitously. At Louisville we were joined by Elder Titus Billings,* who was journeying with a company of Saints from Kirtland to Zion, and we took passage on the steamer *Charleston* for St. Louis, where we parted from Brother Billings and company, and by stage arrived at Independence, Missouri, on the twenty-fourth of April, having traveled a distance of about three hundred miles from St. Louis. We found the brethren in Zion, generally enjoying health and faith; and they were extremely glad to welcome us among them.

*Titus Billings was born on March 25th, 1793, at Greenfield, Franklin county, Massachusetts. He is said to be the second person baptized in Kirtland, Ohio, the baptism taking place in November, 1830.

On the 26th, I called a general council of the Church, and was acknowledged as the President of the High Priesthood, according to a previous ordination at a conference of High Priests, Elders and members, held at Amherst, Ohio, on the 25th of January, 1832. The right hand of fellowship was given to me by the Bishop, Edward Partridge, in behalf of the Church. The scene was solemn, impressive and delightful. During the intermission, a difficulty or hardness which had existed between Bishop Partridge and Elder Rigdon, was amicably settled, and when we came together in the afternoon, all hearts seemed to rejoice and I received the following:*

The Prophet Acknowledged President of the High Priesthood.

Revelation, given April, 1832, showing the order given to Enoch, and the Church in his day.†

1. Verily, verily, I say unto you, my servants, that inasmuch as you have forgiven one another your trespasses, even so I, the Lord, forgive you.

2. Nevertheless, there are those among you who have sinned exceedingly; yea, even all of you have sinned; but verily I say unto you, beware from henceforth, and refrain from sin, lest sore judgments fall upon your heads.

3. For of him unto whom much is given much is required; and he who sins against the greater light shall receive the greater condemnation.

4. Ye call upon my name for revelations, and I give them unto you; and inasmuch as ye keep not my sayings, which I give unto you, ye become transgressors; and justice and judgment are the penalty which is affixed unto my law.

5. Therefore, what I say unto one I say unto all: Watch, for the adversary spreadeth his dominions, and darkness reigneth;

6. And the anger of God kindleth against the inhabitants of the earth; and none doeth good, for all have gone out of the way.

7. And now, verily I say unto you, I, the Lord, will not lay any sin to your charge; go your ways and sin no more; but unto that soul who sinneth shall the former sins return, saith the Lord your God.

*"All differences," says the minutes of this meeting, recorded in the *Far West Record*—"all differences settled, and the hearts of all were united together in love." —(p. 25.)

†Doctrine and Covenants, sec. lxxxii.

8. And again, I say unto you, I give unto you a new commandment, that you may understand my will concerning you;

9. Or, in other words, I give unto you directions how you may act before me, that it may turn to you for your salvation.

10. I, the Lord, am bound when ye do what I say; but when ye do not what I say, ye have no promise.

11. Therefore, verily I say unto you, that it is expedient for my servants Alam and Ahashdah [Newel K. Whitney], Mahalaleel and Pelagoram [Sidney Rigdon], and my servant Gazelam [Joseph Smith], and Horah and Olihah [Oliver Cowdery], and Shalemanasseh and Mahemson [Martin Harris], to be bound together by a bond and covenant that cannot be broken by transgression, except judgment shall immediately follow, in your several stewardships—

12. To manage the affairs of the poor, and all things pertaining to the bishopric both in the land of Zion and in the land of Shinehah [Kirtland];

13. For I have consecrated the land of Shinehah [Kirtland] in mine own due time for the benefit of the saints of the Most High, and for a stake to Zion.

14. For Zion must increase in beauty, and in holiness; her borders must be enlarged; her stakes must be strengthened; yea, verily I say unto you, Zion must arise and put on her beautiful garments.

15. Therefore, I give unto you this commandment, that ye bind yourselves by this covenant, and it shall be done according to the laws of the Lord.

16. Behold, here is wisdom also in me for your good.

17. And you are to be equal, or in other words, you are to have equal claims on the properties, for the benefit of managing the concerns of your stewardships, every man according to his wants and his needs, inasmuch as his wants are just—

18. And all this for the benefit of the church of the living God, that every man may improve upon his talent, that every man may gain other talents, yea, even an hundred fold, to be cast into the Lord's storehouse, to become the common property of the whole church—

19. Every man seeking the interest of his neighbor, and doing all things with an eye single to the glory of God.

20. This order I have appointed to be an everlasting order unto you, and unto your successors, inasmuch as you sin not.

21. And the soul that sins against this covenant, and hardeneth his heart against it, shall be dealt with according to the laws of my church, and shall be delivered over to the buffetings of Satan until the day of redemption.

22. And now, verily I say unto you, and this is wisdom, make

unto yourselves friends with the mammon of unrighteousness, and they will not destroy you.

23. Leave judgment alone with me, for it is mine and I will repay. Peace be with you; my blessings continue with you.

24. For even yet the kingdom is yours, and shall be forever, if you fall not from your steadfastness. Even so. Amen.

On the 27th, we transacted considerable business for the salvation of the Saints, who were settling among a ferocious set of mobbers, like lambs among wolves. It was my endeavor to so organize the Church, that the brethren might eventually be independent of every incumbrance beneath the celestial kingdom, by bonds and covenants of mutual friendship, and mutual love.

The Purposes the Prophet Seeks to Effect Through Church Organization.

On the 28th and 29th, I visited the brethren above Big Blue river, in Kaw township, a few miles west of Independence, and received a welcome only known by brethren and sisters united as one in the same faith, and by the same baptism, and supported by the same Lord. The Colesville branch, in particular, rejoiced as the ancient Saints did with Paul.* It is good to rejoice with the people of God. On the 30th, I returned to Independence, and again sat in council with the brethren, and received the following:

A Visit to the Colesville Saints.

Revelation, given April, 1832.†

1. Verily, thus saith the Lord, in addition to the laws of the church concerning women and children, those who belong to the church, who have lost their husbands or fathers:

2. Women have claim on their husbands for their maintenance, until their husbands are taken; and if they are not found transgressors they shall have fellowship in the church.

3. And if they are not faithful they shall not have fellowship in

*It should be remembered that these Colesville Saints were among the first to receive the Gospel under the teachings of the Prophet, and hence his heart was naturally tender toward them, and this visit was doubtless especially delightful both to the Saints and the Prophet.

†Doctrine and Covenants, sec. lxxxiii.

the church; yet they may remain upon their inheritances according to the laws of the land.

4. All children haye claim upon their parents for their maintenance until they are of age.

5. And after that, they have claim upon the church, or in other words upon the Lord's storehouse, if their parents have not wherewith to give them inheritances.

6. And the storehouse shall be kept by the consecrations of the church; and widows and orphans shall be provided for, as also the poor. Amen.

Literary Affairs of the Church Considered.

Our council was continued on the 1st of May, when it was ordered that three thousand copies of the Book of Commandments be printed in the first edition;* that William W. Phelps, Oliver Cowdery, and John Whitmer, be appointed to review and prepare such revelations for the press as shall be deemed proper for publication, and print them as soon as possible at Independence, Missouri; the announcement to be made that they are "Published by W. W. Phelps & Co." It was also ordered that W. W. Phelps correct and print the hymns which had been selected by Emma Smith in fulfilment of the revelation.

Transaction of Temporal Business.

Arrangements were also made for supplying the Saints with stores in Missouri and Ohio, which action, with a few exceptions, was hailed with joy by the brethren.† Before we left Independence, Elder Rigdon preached two most powerful discourses, which, so far as outward appear-

*This action of course, annulled the resolution at the Kirtland conference to publish an edition of ten thousand. (See p. 222.)

†The arrangements here referred to for the establishment of stores in Missouri and Ohio, as disclosed by the minutes of these council meetings of the 26th, 27th, 30th of April, and the 1st of May, were that the brethren in mercantile pursuits in Kirtland and Zion should be united in one firm; and the establishments in Kirtland and Zion respectively were regarded merely as branches of the one firm. Still it was resolved that each of these branches should have a separate company name. The name of the branch in Zion was to be "Gilbert, Whitney & Company," and the one in Kirtland "Newel K. Whitney & Company." W. W. Phelps and A. S. Gilbert were appointed to draft the bond for the united firm. A. S. Gilbert and Newel K. Whitney were appointed to be the agents of the new firm. It was also resolved that whenever any special business should arise it would be the duty of the united firm by its branches at Jackson county, Missouri, and Geauga county, Ohio, to regulate the same by special agency. It was also resolved that the united firm negotiate a loan of fifteen thousand dollars at six per centum. The firm of Newel K. Whitney & Co. was appointed to transact the business.

ance was concerned, gave great satisfaction to the people.

Return Journey to Kirtland—Incidents by the Way.

On the 6th of May I gave the parting hand to the brethren in Independence, and, in company with Brothers Rigdon and Whitney, commenced a return to Kirtland, by stage to St. Louis, from thence to Vincennes, Indiana; and from thence to New Albany, near the falls of the Ohio river. Before we arrived at the latter place, the horses became frightened, and while going at full speed Bishop Whitney attempted to jump out of the coach, but having his coat fast, caught his foot in the wheel, and had his leg and foot broken in several places; at the same time I jumped out unhurt. We put up at Mr. Porter's public house, in Greenville, for four weeks, while Elder Rigdon went directly forward to Kirtland. During all this time, Brother Whitney lost not a meal of victuals or a night's sleep, and Dr. Porter, our landlord's brother, who attended him, said it was a pity we had not got some "Mormon" there, as they could set broken bones or do anything else. I tarried with Brother Whitney and administered to him till he was able to be moved. While at this place I frequently walked out in the woods, where I saw several fresh graves; and one day when I rose from the dinner table, I walked directly to the door and commenced vomiting most profusely. I raised large quantities of blood and poisonous matter, and so great were the muscular contortions of my system, that my jaw in a few moments was dislocated. This I succeeded in replacing with my own hands, and made my way to Brother Whitney (who was on the bed), as speedily as possible; he laid his hands on me and administered to me in the name of the Lord, and I was healed in an instant, although the effect of the poison was so powerful, as to cause much of the hair to become loosened from my head. Thanks be to my Heavenly Father for His interference in my behalf at this critical moment, in the name of Jesus Christ. Amen.

The Foreknowledge of a Seer.

Brother Whitney had not had his foot moved from the bed for nearly four weeks, when I went into his room, after a walk in the grove, and told him if he would agree to start for home in the morning, we would take a wagon to the river, about four miles, and there would be a ferry-boat in waiting which would take us quickly across, where we would find a hack which would take us directly to the landing, where we should find a boat, in waiting, and we would be going up the river before ten o'clock, and have a prosperous journey home. He took courage and told me he would go. We started next morning, and found everything as I had told him,* for we were passing rapidly up the river before ten o'clock, and, landing at Wellsville, took stage coach to Chardon, from thence in a wagon to Kirtland, where we arrived some time in June.

*This is an instance of the Prophet Joseph's power as a seer. Another example is given by David Whitmer in his account of going to Harmony, Pennsylvania, after the Prophet and Oliver Cowdery, in order to take them to his father's home in Fayette, New York, in the summer of 1829, when the Book of Mormon was in course of translation. "When I arrived at Harmony," says David, "Joseph and Oliver were coming toward me, and met me some distance from the house. Oliver told me that Joseph had informed him when I started from home, where I had stopped the first night, how I read the sign at the tavern, where I stopped the next night, etc., and that I would be there that day before dinner, and this was why they had come out to meet me; all of which was exactly as Joseph had told Oliver, at which I was greatly astonished." (David Whitmer's Statement to Orson Pratt and Joseph F. Smith, *Millennial Star*, vol. xl, nos. 49, 50.)

CHAPTER XX.

"THE EVENING AND MORNING STAR."

As soon as I could arrange my affairs, I recommenced the translation of the Scriptures, and thus I spent most of the summer. In July, we received the first number of *The Evening and Morning Star,* which was a joyous treat to the Saints. Delightful, indeed, was it to contemplate that the little band of brethren had become so large, and grown so strong, in so short a time as to be able to issue a paper of their own, which contained not only some of the revelations, but other information also,—which would gratify and enlighten the humble inquirer after truth.

Occupation of the Prophet, Summer of 1832.

So embittered was the public mind against the truth, that the press universally had been arrayed against us; and although many newspapers published the prospectus of our paper, yet it appeared to have been done more to calumniate the editor, than give publicity to the forthcoming periodical. Editors thought to do us harm, while the Saints rejoiced that they could do nothing against the truth but for it.

Opposition of the Press.

The following are extracts from *The Evening and Morning Star,* Independence, Missouri, June, 1832—first number:

TO MAN.

With the help of God, the first number of *The Evening and Morning Star* comes to the world for the objects specified in its prospectus, which was published last winter. That we should now recapitulate some of its leading objects, and briefly add a few remarks, will naturally be expected; and we cheerfully do so, that this generation may know—

That the *Star* comes in these last days as the friend of man, to persuade him to turn to God and live, before the great and terrible day of the Lord sweeps the earth of its wickedness;

That it comes not only as the messenger of truth, to bring the revelations and commandments of God which have been, but to publish those that God gives now, as in the days of old, for He is the same God yesterday, today, and for ever; * * * *

That it comes as the harbinger of peace and good will to them that serve the Lord with a determination to have part in the first resurrection, and finally become Kings and Priests to God the Father in the celestial kingdom, where God and Christ are, and where they will be for eternity; * * * * * *

That it comes according to the will of God from those who are not ashamed to take upon them the name of Christ, and walk lowly in the valley of humiliation, and let the solemnities of eternity rest upon them: knowing that the great day of the Lord will soon usher in the Sabbath of creation, for the rest of the Saints, that the Savior may reign His thousand years of peace upon the earth while Satan is bound;

That is comes in meekness and mercy to all mankind, that they may do works meet for repentance and be saved in the first resurrection, and afterwards dwell with the spirits of just men made perfect in the celestial kingdom;

That it comes to bring good tidings of great joy to all people, but more especially to the house of Israel scattered abroad, that the day of their redemption is near, for the Lord hath set His hand again the second time to restore them to the lands of their inheritance;

That it comes to show that the ensign is now set up unto which all nations shall come, and worship the Lord, the God of Jacob, acceptably;

That it comes when war, and the plague, or pestilence as it is called, are sweeping their thousands and tens of thousands to the grave, to show that the day of tribulation spoken of by our Savior is nigh at hand, even at the doors;

That it comes to repeat the great caution of Paul: Beware lest any man spoil you (the disciples of Christ), through philosophy and vain deceit, after the traditions of men and the rudiments of the world;

That it comes to prepare the way of the Lord, that when He comes He may have a holy people ready to receive Him;

That it comes to show that no man can be too good to be saved, but that many may be too bad:

That it comes to declare that goodness consists in doing good, not merely in preaching it;

That it comes to show that all men's religion is vain without charity;

That it comes to open the way for Zion to rise and put on her beautiful garments and become the glory of the earth, that her land may be joined, or married (according to the known translation of Isaiah) to Jerusalem again, and they be one as they were in the days of Peleg.

* * * * * *

Man, being created but little below the angels, only wants to know for himself, and not by another, that, by obeying the commands of his Creator, he can rise again after death, in the flesh, and reign with Christ a thousand years on the earth without sin; be changed in the twinkling of an eye, and become a King and Priest to God in eternity—to forsake his sins, and say: Lord, I am thine! The first words of which we have any account that Jesus Christ spake concerning the things of eternal life, were, Suffer it to be so now: for thus it becometh us to fulfil all righteousness. Then he was baptized: and truly, if it became the Savior of the world, holy as He was, to be baptized in the meridian of time, to fulfil all righteousness, how much more necessary it is for man to be baptized in order to be saved. * * *

As this paper is devoted to the great concerns of eternal things and the gathering of the Saints, it will leave politics, the gainsaying of the world, and many other matters, for their proper channels, endeavoring by all means to set an example before the world, which, when followed, will lead our fellow-men to the gates of glory, where the wicked cease from troubling, and where the weary will find rest. That there may be errors both in us and in the paper, we readily admit, but we mean to grow better, till from little children, we all come into the unity of the faith and of the knowledge of the Son of God, unto a perfect man, unto the measure of the stature of the fulness of Christ, which we pray may be the happy lot of thousands, before He comes with the hundred and forty and four thousand that are without guile.*

TO THE CHURCH OF CHRIST ABROAD IN THE EARTH.

It is the duty of the Church of Christ, in Zion, to stand as an ensign to all nations, that the Lord has set His hand the second time to restore the house of Israel to the lands of their inheritance; and it behooves the members of this Church to manifest before the world by a godly walk, by a noble example, as well as by sterling precept; by

*The salutatory address was signed by W. W. Phelps.

prudence in living, by plainness in dress, by industry, by economy, by faith and works, and, above all, by solemnity, humility and patience, that this is a day of warning and not a day of many words.

This being the order in Zion, how much more necessary is it, that the churches of Christ, which have not yet come up to this land should show the world, by well ordered conduct in all things, that they are the children of the living God! It is all-important, and the salvation of many souls depends upon their faultless example. They will, therefore, knowing that the Lord will suddenly come to His temple, do their part in preparing the way, by observing the Sabbath day, and keeping it holy; by teaching their children the Gospel, and teaching them to pray; by avoiding extremes in all matters; by shunning every appearance of evil; by studying to be approved, and doing unto others as they would have others do unto them; by bearing trouble and persecution patiently, without a murmur, knowing that Michael, the Arch-angel, when contending with the devil—he disputed about the body of Moses—durst not bring against him a railing accusation, but said, The Lord rebuke thee. They will not only set an example worthy of imitation, but they will let their light so shine that others, seeing their good works, may go and do likewise. Example is the great thing that defies the world with all its vain glory; by letting their moderation be known unto all men, both in dress and in living; in words and in deeds; in watching and in praying; in love and in labor, and in works as well as in faith, they [the Saints] preach the world a lecture, they set the inquirer an example, and teach all Christendom a lesson, that studied preaching and pulpit eloquence have failed to accomplish.

COMMON SCHOOLS.

The disciples should lose no time in preparing schools for their children, that they may be taught as is pleasing unto the Lord, and brought up in the way of holiness. Those appointed to select and prepare books for the use of schools, will attend to that subject as soon as more weighty matters are finished.* But the parents and guardians in the Church of Christ need not wait—it is all-important that children to become good should be taught [good]. Moses, while delivering the words of the Lord to the congregation of Israel, that is, to the parents, says, "And these words which I command thee this day, shall be in thy heart: and thou shalt teach them diligently unto thy children, and

*This is in plain allusion to the revelation on page 185 where W. W. Phelps and Oliver Cowdery are appointed a committee to prepare books for schools in the Church, that little children might receive instruction, which is pleasing before the Lord. That revelation and the above article from the *Star* of June, 1832, plainly foreshadow the great interest the Church would take in education.

shalt talk of them when thou sittest in thy house, and when thou walkest by the way, and when thou liest down, and when thou risest up. And thou shalt bind them for a sign upon thy hand, and they shall be as frontlets between thine eyes." If it were necessary then to teach their children diligently, how much more necessary is it now, when the Church of Christ is to be an ensign, yea, even an ensample to the world, for good? A word to the wise ought to be sufficient, for children soon become men and women. Yes, they are they that must follow us, and perform the duties which not only appertain to this world, but to the second coming of the Savior, even preparing for the Sabbath of creation, and for eternity.

THE "STAR" OFFICE.

The *Star* office is situated within twelve miles of the west line of the state of Missouri; which at present is the western limits of the United States, and about 120 miles west of any press in the state, in about 39 degrees of north latitude, and about 17½ degrees of west longitude, 2½ miles south of Missouri river; 280 miles by land, or 500 by water, west of St. Louis; nearly 1,200 miles west of Washington; 1,300 miles from New York, and more than 1,500 miles from Boston.

In August we were again delighted to receive the *Star*. The following is extracted from the second [July] number:

Second No. of the *Star*.

THE ELDERS IN THE LAND OF ZION, TO THE CHURCH OF CHRIST SCATTERED ABROAD.

Brethren, we think it proper to give you some general information respecting the present state of the Church in Zion, and also the work of the gathering. Notwithstanding that nearly all Christendom doubt the propriety of receiving revelations for the government of the Church of Christ in this age, and generally adopt the Scriptures of the Old and New Testaments as the only rule of faith and practice, yet we believe, from the Scriptures of truth, that to every church in past ages which the Lord recognized to be His, He gave revelations, wisely calculated to govern them in the peculiar situation and circumstances under which they were placed, and to enable them by authority to do the peculiar work which they were to perform. The Bible contains revelations given at different times to different people, under different circumstances, as will be seen by editorial articles in this paper. The old world was destroyed for rejecting the revelations of God given to them through Noah. The Israelites were destroyed in the wilderness for despising the revelations given to them through Moses; and Christ said that the world, in the days of the Apostles, would be condemned for not receiving the word of God through them: Thus we see that the judgments of God in the past ages have come upon the people, not so much for neglecting the revelations given to their forefathers, as for rejecting those given immediately to themselves. Of the blessings of heaven it may be said, that they always rested upon the heads of those to whom they were promised. Therefore, seeing that it not only was, but, as long as God remains the same, always will be, the privilege of the true Church to receive revelations containing blessings and cursings, peculiarly adapted to itself as a Church, we conclude that it is a mistaken notion that the Scriptures of the Old and New Testaments are the only rule of faith and practice; nevertheless, inasmuch as the precepts and examples contained in them are truly applicable to us under our particular circumstances, we are bound to be governed by them; and we also can receive much benefit from such prophecies as point out the events that shall take place in our day and age. Of these there are many, both in the Old and the New Testaments. They speak plainly of great things that shall be accomplished in the last days;—such as preaching the everlasting Gospel to all nations; the gathering of the elect from the four winds of heaven; the building up of Zion and Jerusalem, or the ingathering of the remnants of Jacob, and the planting them in the lands of their fathers' inheritance; the necessary preparation to meet the Savior at His second coming, with all the Saints, to dwell with them in the millennial reign. And now, who with the Bible in his hand, can suppose that these great and marvelous works can be accomplished by the Church without more revelations from the Lord? We cannot, for we worship the God of Israel, in whom is neither variableness nor shadow of turning;— consequently as in days of old, so in these last days, He has given us revelations by which we may know how to organize the Church of Christ, and by His authority to perform the work which He has enjoined upon us. And now brethren, if we wish for blessings upon this Church, we must walk humbly before the Lord, and observe to keep all His commandments. Notwithstanding the work of the gathering will be accomplished, we believe in a speedy manner, yet the Lord has commanded that it shall not be done in haste, nor by flight, but that all things shall be prepared before you; and for this purpose He has made it the duty of the Bishop or agent in the land of Zion to make known, from time to time, the privileges of the land to the conferences, which may determine and make known how many can be accommodated. And the Saints will remember that the Bishop in the land of Zion will not receive any, as wise stewards, without they bring a recommend from the Bishop in Ohio, or from three Elders. The Elders therefore, will be careful not to recommend and send up churches to this place, without first receiving information from the Bishop in Ohio, or in the land of Zion, that they can be accommodated when they arrive, so as to be settled without confusion, which would produce pestilence. Therefore, if a church is desirous to come to the land of Zion, we would recommend that first, by letter or otherwise, they make known their desires and their situation to the Bishop in Ohio, or in the land of Zion, and receive information from them before they start. Brethren will perceive as well as we, that where churches of fifty or a hundred souls each, are coming to the land of Zion, from different parts of the nation, and, as soon will be the case, from different nations, without a knowledge of each other, they would, when they arrive, be in a state of confusion, and labor under many disadvantages which might be avoided by strictly observing the rules and regulations of the Church. Moreover by being in haste, and forcing the sale of property, unreasonable sacrifices have been made, and although this is a day of sacrifice and tithing, yet to make lavish and unreasonable sacrifices is not well pleasing in the sight of the Lord.

It is about one year since the work of the gathering commenced, in which time between three and four hundred have arrived here, and are mostly located upon their inheritances, and are generally in good health and spirits and are doing well. The expense of journeying and settling here, together with the establishment of a printing office and store, have probably exceeded the expectations of our brethren abroad, and although Zion, according to the Prophets, is to become like Eden, or the garden of the Lord, yet, at present it is as it were but a wilderness and desert, and the disadvantages of settling in a new country, you know, are many and great. Therefore, prudence would dictate the churches abroad, at present, not to come up to Zion, until preparations can be made for them, and they receive information as above. The prospect for crops in this region of country is, at present, tolerably good, but calls for provisions will undoubtedly be considerable, for besides the emigration of the whites, the government of the United States is settling the Indians (or remnants of Joseph), immediately to the west, and they must be fed.

Brethren, we drop the above remarks for your benefit, until you can have the revelations to peruse for yourselves, which will be published as soon as they consistently can be. Although the Lord has said, that it is His business to provide for His Saints in these last days, yet remember He is not bound so to do, unless we observe His sayings and keep them.

TO THE ELDERS OF THE CHURCH OF CHRIST, WHO PREACH GOOD TIDINGS TO THE WORLD.

Brethren, as stars of the ensign which is now set up for the benefit of all nations, you are to enlighten the world, you are to prepare the way for the people to come up to Zion; you are to instruct men how to receive the fulness of the Gospel, and the everlasting covenants, even them that were from the beginning; you are to carry the ark of safety before the wondering multitudes, without fear, entreating and beseeching all men to be saved; you are to set an example of meekness and humility before Saints and sinners, as did the Savior; and when reviled you are not to revile again; you are to reason with men, as in days of old, to bear patiently and answer as the spirit of truth shall direct, allowing all credit for every item of good. You are to walk in the valley of humility, and pray for the salvation of all; yes, you are to pray for your enemies; and warn in compassion without threatening the wicked with judgments which are to be poured out upon the world hereafter. You have no right to take the judgments, which fell upon the ungodly before the flood, and pour them upon the head of this generation; you have no authority to use the judgments which God sent upon Pharaoh in Egypt, to terrify the inhabitants of America, neither have you any direction by commandment, to collect the calamities of six thousand years and paint them upon the curtain of these last days to scare mankind to repentance; no, you are to preach the Gospel, which is the power of God unto salvation, even glad tidings of great joy unto all people.

Again, you are not to take the blessings of an individual, or of a church, from the days of Enoch to the days of the Apostles, and place them upon an individual or a church in these last days; but you are to teach all men that they shall be judged according to their works. For, if God is the same yesterday, today, and for ever, His reward is always with Him; and His revelations and blessings and judgments, before the flood, were fitted for that people and that time; in the days of Abraham, for that man and that time; in the days of Moses, for that man and that time; in the days of David, for that man and that time; in the days of Paul, for that man and that time; and now, for this generation and this time. You therefore, must reason from the Bible and the Book of Mormon, with great care and not pervert the meaning of God's sacred word. If our Heavenly Father saw fit to destroy Sodom and Gomorrah for their wickedness, Nineveh for its abomination, and Jerusalem for a transgression of His commandments, what have their destruction to do with the salvation of the world now? The Lord says, Vengeance is mine, and I will repay. Teach all men to trust in God and not in man, and do works meet for repentance. Again, teach all men that God is a God of the living and not of the dead. Finally, whatever you do, do it with an eye single to the glory of God. You are the light of the world in matters of pure religion, and many souls may be required at your hands. Let the idea not leave you, that not only the eyes of the world, but the eyes of the angels and of God are upon you.

FOREIGN NEWS.

It is a day of strange appearances. Everything indicates something more than meets the eye. Every nation is opening events which astonish mankind. Even the heart of man begins to melt at the prospect before him. The unquenchable thirst for news; the continuity of emigration; the wars and rumors of wars, with many other signs of the distress of nations, from the old world—as the land is called across the ocean—whisper so loud to the understanding, that he who runs may read the label on the eastern sky—The end is nigh. France is filled with a spirit of rebellion, and when the cholera was sweeping its thousands mobs were collecting to slay their tens of thousands. While the hospitals were crowded with the sick, and the groans of the dying filled the air, the fashionable French were holding cholera balls and dancing at the judgments of the Almighty. In England, where an anxious multitude have been waiting for reformation in government for years, disappointment is destruction. The house of lords has rejected the Reform Bill, and the proud-hearted Englishman says: Reform or Revolution! No stop there; for the sound comes across the Atlantic: Reform or ruin! All the kingdoms of the east seem to be preparing to act the part allotted to them, when the Lord rebukes the nations. As on a morning of some great festival, the church bell, the cannon, the small arms, the music, and the cheers of the multitude, arouse all to what is going on, and thunder to man: Behold the day! So also earthquakes, wars and rumors of wars, the distress of nations, the constant tide of emigration to the west, the wide spreading ravages of the cholera, and the joy of the Saints of God as they come out of Babylon, alarm the world, and whisper to every mortal: Watch ye, for the time is at hand for the second coming of Jesus Christ, the Redeemer of Israel, with peace on earth and good will to man. Watch the signs of His coming, that ye be not deceived.

ITEMS FOR THE PUBLIC.

In connection with the *Star,* we publish a weekly paper, entitled the *Upper Missouri Advertiser*. It will contain sketches of the news of the day, politics, advertisements, and whatever tends to promote the interest of the great west.

The August number of the *Star,* [no. 3] contained the following:

THE CHOLERA.

This desolating sickness is spreading steadily over the United States. The account of its ravages in many places, we cannot give. The whole number of cases in New York, to July 31st, is 3,731. Deaths, 1,520.

No man can stop the work of the Lord, for God rules the pestilence, and the pestilence rules men. Forts, sentinels, and oceans may hinder men, or money may bribe, but when the pestilence rides on the wings of the wind, the sentinel has no power; the fort is no obstacle, the ocean is no barrier; and money has no value; the destroying angel goes waving the banner of death over all; and who shall escape his pointed arrow? Not he that could brave death at the cannon's mouth, but shrinks at the sound of the cholera; not he that worshiped his God in some stately chapel, every Sabbath till the cholera comes, and then flees for his life; no; none but he that trusts in God, shall be able to stand when a thousand shall fall at his side, and ten thousand at his right hand by the noisome pestilence.

TO THE HONORABLE MEN OF THE WORLD.

To the honorable searchers for truth: we, in a spirit of candor and meekness are bound by every tie that makes man the friend of man, by every endowment of heaven, that renders intelligent beings seekers of happiness to show you the way to salvation. In fact, we are not only bound to do thus for those that seek the riches of eternity, but, to walk in the tracks of our Savior, we must love our enemies; bless them that curse us; do good to them that hate us, and pray for them that despitefully use us, and persecute us, or else you and the world may know that we are not the children of God. Therefore to be obedient to the precepts of our divine Master, we say unto you—Search the Scriptures—search the revelations which we publish, and ask your Heavenly Father, in the name of His Son Jesus Christ, to manifest the truth unto you, and if you do it with an eye single to His glory, nothing doubting, He will answer you by the power of His Holy Spirit. You will then know for yourselves and not for another. You will not then be dependent on man for the knowledge of God; nor will there be any room for speculation. No; for when men receive their instruction from Him that made them, they know how he will save them. Then again we say: Search the Scriptures, search the Prophets, and learn what portion of them belongs to you and the people of the nineteenth century. You, no doubt, will agree with us, and say, that you have no right to claim the promises of the inhabitants before the flood; that you cannot found your hopes of salvation upon the obedience of the children of Israel when journeying in the wilderness; nor can you expect that the blessings which the Apostles pronounced upon the churches of Christ, eighteen hundred years ago, were intended for you. Again, if others' blessings are not your blessings, others' curses are not your curses; you stand then in these last days, as all have stood before you, agents unto yourselves, to be judged according to your works.

Every man lives for himself. Adam was made to open the ways of the world, and for dressing the garden. Noah was born to save seed of everything, when the earth was washed of its wickedness by the flood; and the Son of God came into the world to redeem it from the fall. But except a man be born again, he cannot see the kingdom of God. This eternal truth settles the question of all men's religion. A man may be saved, after the judgment, in the terrestrial kingdom, or in the telestial kingdom, but he can never see the celestial kingdom of God without being born of the water and the Spirit. He may receive a glory like unto the moon [i. e. of which the light of the moon is typical], or a star [i. e. of which the light of the stars is typical], but he can never come unto Mount Zion, and unto the city of the living God, the heavenly Jerusalem, and to an innumerable company of angels; to the general assembly and Church of the First-born, which are written in heaven, and to God the judge of all, and to the spirits of just men made perfect, and to Jesus the Mediator of the new covenant, unless he becomes as a little child, and is taught by the Spirit of God. Wherefore, we again say, search the revelations of God: study the prophecies, and rejoice that God grants unto the world Seers and Prophets. They are they who saw the mysteries of godliness; they saw the flood before it came; they saw angels ascending and descending upon a ladder that reached from earth to heaven: they saw the stone cut out of the mountain, which filled the whole earth; they saw the Son of God come from the regions of bliss and dwell with men on earth; they saw the deliverer come out of Zion, and turn away ungodliness from Jacob; they saw the glory of the Lord when He showed the transfiguration of the earth on the mount; they saw every mountain laid low and every valley exalted when the Lord was taking vengeance upon the wicked; they saw truth spring out of the earth, and righteousness look down from heaven in the last days, before the Lord came the second time to gather His elect; they saw the end of wickedness on earth, and the Sabbath of creation crowned with peace; they saw the end of the glorious thousand years, when Satan was loosed for a little season; they saw the day of judgment when all men received according to their works, and they saw the heaven and earth flee away to make room for the city of God, when the righteous receive an inheritance in eternity. And, fellow sojourners upon earth, it is your privilege to purify yourselves and come up to the same glory, and see for yourselves, and know for yourselves. Ask, and it shall be given you; seek, and ye shall find; knock, and it shall be opened unto you.

CHAPTER XXI.

LARGER VIEWS ON THE DOCTRINE OF PRIESTHOOD REVEALED—THE MEETING OF THE PROPHET JOSEPH SMITH, JUN., BRIGHAM YOUNG, AND HEBER C. KIMBALL.

Baptism of Elder George A. Smith.

ON September the 10th, George A. Smith was baptized by Joseph H. Wakefield, at Potsdam, St. Lawrence county, New York; and confirmed by Elder Solomon Humphry.*

*George Albert Smith was born at Potsdam, St. Lawrence county, New York, on the 26th of June, 1817. He was the son of John Smith, the sixth son of Asael and Mary Smith. John Smith was therefore a brother of the Prophet's father, and George Albert and the Prophet were cousins. In the fall of 1828, Asael Smith, grandfather of the subject of this note, received a letter from Joseph Smith, Sen., informing him of some of the visions the youthful Prophet had received. Soon after this a letter from the young Prophet himself was received by John Smith, and read in the hearing of George Albert. The letter declared that the judgments of God would overtake the wicked of this generation unless they repented. The letter made a deep impression upon George Albert; while his father remarked that "Joseph wrote like a prophet." In August, 1830, Joseph Smith, Sen., visited his brother John, bringing with him the Book of Mormon, a copy of which he left at the former's residence. During the temporary absence of his uncle, who was visiting other branches of the family, George Albert championed the Book of Mormon, and answered objections urged against it by the neighbors who came in to examine it. Meantime he formulated some objections of his own, which his Uncle Joseph on his return answered to his complete satisfaction; and he never afterwards ceased to advocate the divine authenticity of the Book of Mormon. Notwithstanding this conviction, however, he was not baptized until some two years had elapsed as will be seen by reference to the date of his baptism in the text of the Prophet's narrative.

At this point I think it proper that a letter written by Asael Smith, grandfather of the Prophet Joseph Smith, Jun., should be introduced. A copy of the letter was obtained by George A. Smith, the subject of the foregoing biographical note, while on a visit to Topsfield, in 1872. The original was in the hands of a son of Mr. Jacob Town, then the town clerk of Topsfield, and who, while unwilling to part with the original, because written to and received by his father, permitted President George A. Smith to copy it.

On the outside of the letter, besides the superscription, "Mr. Jacob Town, Topsfield, Commonwealth of Massachusetts," is this: "Rec'd Feb. 14, 1796, from Asael

Return of Elders from Missouri.

The Elders during the month of September began to return from their missions to the Eastern States, and present the histories of their several stewardships in the Lord's vineyard; and while together in these seasons of joy, I inquired

Smith." From which it appears, when compared with the date under which it was written, the letter was one month on the journey from Tunbridge, Vt., to Topsfield. a distance of 150 miles, and was probably carried by private conveyance.

The letter is produced here for two reasons: first for its own intrinsic interest as a literary relic of one of the Prophet's ancestors, and of the American Revolutionary period; second, as showing the character of the stock from which the Prophet Joseph descended. This letter exhibits in Asael Smith a noble independence of character, united with a childlike humility before God, together with unbounded faith and trust in the wisdom of Providence and of His over-ruling hand in the affairs of nations. Loyalty to his country and faith in the stability of the government under the over-ruling providences of God are equally conspicuous. The letter will go far towards refuting the slanders which untruthful writers have been pleased to circulate concerning the character of that race from which the Prophet descended.

ASAEL SMITH'S LETTER TO MR. JACOB TOWN.

"TUNBRIDGE, Jan. 14th, 1796.

"Respected Sir:—Having a favorable opportunity, altho' on very short notice, I with joy and gratitude, embrace it, returning herewith my most hearty thanks for your respect shown in your favor of the 30th of November, by Mr. Willis, which I view as a singular specimen of friendship, which has very little been practiced by any of my friends in Topsfield, altho' often requested.

"My family are all, through the goodness of the Divine Benediction, in a tolerable good state of health, and desire to be remembered to you and to all inquiring friends.

"I have set me up a new house since Mr. Willis was here and expect to remove into it next spring, and begin again on an entire new farm, and my son Joseph will live on the old farm (if this that has been but four years occupied can be called old), and carry it on at the halves, which half I hope will nearly furnish my family with food, whilst I with my four youngest sons shall endeavor to bring to another farm, etc.

"As to news, I have nothing, as I know of, worth noticing, except that grain has taken a sudden rise amongst us, about one-third.

"As to the Jocobin party, they are not very numerous here, or if they are thev are pretty still; there are some in this state, viz., in Bennington, who like other children crying for a rattle, have blared out against their rulers, in hopes to wrest from them, if possible, what they esteem the plaything of power and trust. But they have been pretty well whipped and have become tolerably quiet again, and I am in hopes if they live to arrive to the years of discretion, when the empire of reason shall take place, that they will then become good members of society, notwithstanding their noisy, nucious behavior in their childhood, for which they were neither capable of hearing or giving any reason.

of the Lord, and received on the 22nd and 23rd of September, the following revelation on Priesthood:

*Revelation.**

1. A revelation of Jesus Christ unto his servant Joseph Smith, Jun., and six elders, as they united their hearts and lifted their voices on high.

"For my part, I am so willing to trust the government of the world in the hands of the Supreme Ruler of universal nature, that I do not at present wish to try to wrest it out of His hands, and I have so much confidence in His abilities to teach our senators wisdom, that I do not think it worth while for me to interpose, from the little stock of knowledge that He has favored me with, in the affair, either one way or the other. He has conducted us through a glorious Revolution and has brought us into the promised land of peace and liberty, and I believe that He is about to bring all the world into the same beatitude in His own time and way; which, altho' His ways may appear never so inconsistent to our blind reason, yet may be perfectly consistent with His designs. And I believe that the stone is now cut out of the mountain without hands, spoken of by Daniel, and has smitten the image upon his feet, by which the iron, the clay, the brass, the silver and the gold, (viz.) all the monarchial and ecclesiastical tyranny will be broken to pieces and become as the chaff of the summer threshing floor, the wind shall carry them all away, that there shall be no place found for them.

"Give my best regards to your parents and tell them that I have taken up with the eleventh commandment, that the negro taught to the minister, which was thus—

"The minister asked the negro how many commandments there were, his answer was 'Eleben, sir.' 'Aye,' replied the other, 'what is the eleventh? That is one I never heard of.' 'The eleventh commandment, sir, is mind your own business.'

"So I choose to do, and give myself but little concern about what passes in the political world.

"Give my best regards to Dr. Meriam, Mr. Willis, Joseph Dorman and Mr. Cree, and tell Mr. Cree I thank him for his respects and hope he will accept of mine. Write to me as often and as large as you can and oblige your sincere friend and well-wisher.

(Signed) ASAEL SMITH.

"Mr. Jacob Town, Jun."

The following appears on the back of the first page of the letter, being evidently of the nature of a postscript—

"Give my hearty thanks to Mr. Charles Rogers for his respects shown in writing me a few lines, and tell him that I should a wrote to him now, had I had time, but now waive it for the present, as I have considerable part of what I intended to a writ to you.

"If I should live and do well, I expect to come to Topsfield myself next winter, which, if I do, I shall come and pay you a visit. Farewell.

"Tell Mr. Joseph Cree that if he will come here and set up his trade, I will warrant him as much work as he can do, and good pay."

On the margin of the second page of the letter appears the following—

"I expect my son Joseph will be married in a few days."

*Doctrine and Covenants, sec. lxxxiv.

2. Yea, the word of the Lord concerning his church, established in the last days for the restoration of his people, as he has spoken by the mouth of his prophets, and for the gathering of his saints to stand upon Mount Zion, which shall be the city of New Jerusalem.

3. Which city shall be built, beginning at the temple lot, which is appointed by the finger of the Lord, in the western boundaries of the State of Missouri, and dedicated by the hand of Joseph Smith, Jun., and others with whom the Lord was well pleased.

4. Verily this is the word of the Lord, that the city New Jerusalem shall be built by the gathering of the saints, beginning at this place, even the place of the temple, which temple shall be reared in this generation.

5. For verily this generation shall not all pass away until an house shall be built unto the Lord, and a cloud shall rest upon it, which cloud shall be even the glory of the Lord, which shall fill the house.

6. And the sons of Moses, according to the Holy Priesthood which he received under the hand of his father-in-law, Jethro;

7. And Jethro received it under the hand of Caleb;

8. And Caleb received it under the hand of Elihu;

9. And Elihu under the hand of Jeremy;

10. And Jeremy under the hand of Gad;

11. And Gad under the hand of Esaias;

12. And Esaias received it under the hand of God.

13. Esaias also lived in the days of Abraham, and was blessed of him—

14. Which Abraham received the priesthood from Melchizedek, who received it through the lineage of his fathers, even till Noah;

15. And from Noah till Enoch, through the lineage of their fathers;

16. And from Enoch to Abel, who was slain by the conspiracy of his brother, who received the priesthood by the commandments of God, by the hand of his father Adam, who was the first man—

17. Which priesthood continueth in the church of God in all generations, and is without beginning of days or end of years.

18. And the Lord confirmed a priesthood also upon Aaron and his seed, throughout all their generations, which priesthood also continueth and abideth forever with the priesthood which is after the holiest order of God.

19. And this greater priesthood administereth the gospel and holdeth the key of the mysteries of the kingdom, even the key of the knowledge of God.

20. Therefore, in the ordinances thereof, the power of godliness is manifest.

21. And without the ordinances thereof, and the authority of the

priesthood, the power of godliness is not manifest unto men in the flesh;

22. For without this no man can see the face of God, even the Father, and live.

23. Now this Moses plainly taught to the children of Israel in the wilderness, and sought diligently to sanctify his people that they might behold the face of God;

24. But they hardened their hearts and could not endure his presence; therefore, the Lord in his wrath, for his anger was kindled against them, swore that they should not enter into his rest while in the wilderness, which rest is the fulness of his glory.

25. Therefore, he took Moses out of their midst, and the Holy Priesthood also;

26. And the lesser priesthood continued, which priesthood holdeth the key of the ministering of angels and the preparatory gospel;

27. Which gospel is the gospel of repentance and of baptism, and the remission of sins, and the law of carnal commandments, which the Lord in his wrath caused to continue with the house of Aaron among the children of Israel until John, whom God raised up, being filled with the Holy Ghost from his mother's womb.

28. For he was baptized while he was yet in his childhood, and was ordained by the angel of God at the time he was eight days old unto this power, to overthrow the kingdom of the Jews, and to make straight the way of the Lord before the face of his people, to prepare them for the coming of the Lord, in whose hand is given all power.

29. And again, the offices of elder and bishop are necessary appendages belonging unto the high priesthood.

30. And again, the offices of teacher and deacon are necessary appendages belonging to the lesser priesthood, which priesthood was confirmed upon Aaron and his sons.

31. Therefore, as I said concerning the sons of Moses—for the sons of Moses and also the sons of Aaron shall offer an acceptable offering and sacrifice in the house of the Lord, which house shall be built unto the Lord in this generation, upon the consecrated spot as I have appointed—

32. And the sons of Moses and of Aaron shall be filled with the glory of the Lord, upon Mount Zion in the Lord's house, whose sons are ye; and also many whom I have called and sent forth to build up my church.

33. For whoso is faithful unto the obtaining these two priesthoods of which I have spoken, and the magnifying their calling, are sanctified by the Spirit unto the renewing of their bodies.

34. They become the sons of Moses and of Aaron and the seed of Abraham, and the church and kingdom, and the elect of God.

35. And also all they who receive this priesthood receive me, saith the Lord;

36. For he that receiveth my servants receiveth me;

37. And he that receiveth me receiveth my Father;

38. And he that receiveth my Father receiveth my Father's kingdom; therefore all that my Father hath shall be given unto him.

39. And this is according to the oath and covenant which belongeth to the priesthood.

40. Therefore, all those who receive the priesthood, receive this oath and covenant of my Father, which he cannot break, neither can it be moved.

41. But whoso breaketh this covenant after he hath received it, and altogether turneth therefrom, shall not have forgiveness of sins in this world nor in the world to come.

42. And wo unto all those who come not unto this priesthood which ye have received, which I now confirm upon you who are present this day, by mine own voice out of the heavens; and even I have given the heavenly hosts and mine angels charge concerning you.

43. And I now give unto you a commandment to beware concerning yourselves, to give diligent heed to the words of eternal life.

44. For you shall live by every word that proceedeth forth from the mouth of God.

45. For the word of the Lord is truth, and whatsoever is truth is light, and whatsoever is light is Spirit, even the Spirit of Jesus Christ.

46. And the Spirit giveth light to every man that cometh into the world; and the Spirit enlighteneth every man through the world, that hearkeneth to the voice of the Spirit.

47. And every one that hearkeneth to the voice of the Spirit cometh unto God, even the Father.

48. And the Father teacheth him of the covenant which he has renewed and confirmed upon you, which is confirmed upon you for your sakes, and not for your sakes only, but for the sake of the whole world.

49. And the whole world lieth in sin, and groaneth under darkness and under the bondage of sin.

50. And by this you may know they are under the bondage of sin, because they come not unto me.

51. For whoso cometh not unto me is under the bondage of sin.

52. And whoso receiveth not my voice is not acquainted with my voice, and is not of me.

53. And by this you may know the righteous from the wicked, and that the whole world groaneth under sin and darkness even now.

54. And your minds in times past have been darkened because of unbelief, and because you have treated lightly the things you have received—

55. Which vanity and unbelief have brought the whole church under condemnation.

56. And this condemnation resteth upon the children of Zion, even all.

57. And they shall remain under this condemnation until they repent and remember the new covenant, even the Book of Mormon and the former commandments which I have given them, not only to say, but to do according to that which I have written—

58. That they may bring forth fruit meet for their Father's kingdom; otherwise there remaineth a scourge and judgment to be poured out upon the children of Zion.

59. For shall the children of the kingdom pollute my holy land? Verily, I say unto you, Nay.

60. Verily, verily, I say unto you who now hear my words, which are my voice, blessed are ye inasmuch as you receive these things;

61. For I will forgive you of your sins with this commandment—that you remain steadfast in your minds in solemnity and the spirit of prayer, in bearing testimony to all the world of those things which are communicated unto you.

62. Therefore, go ye into all the world; and unto whatsoever place ye cannot go ye shall send, that the testimony may go from you into all the world unto every creature.

63. And as I said unto mine apostles, even so I say unto you, for you are mine apostles, even God's high priests; ye are they whom my Father hath given me; ye are my friends;

64. Therefore, as I said unto mine apostles I say unto you again, that every soul who believeth on your words, and is baptized by water for the remission of sins, shall receive the Holy Ghost.

65. And these signs shall follow them that believe—

66. In my name they shall do many wonderful works;

67. In my name they shall cast out devils;

68. In my name they shall heal the sick;

69. In my name they shall open the eyes of the blind, and unstop the ears of the deaf;

70. And the tongue of the dumb shall speak;

71. And if any man shall administer posion unto them it shall not hurt them;

72. And the poison of a serpent shall not have power to harm them.

73. But a commandment I give unto them, that they shall not boast themselves of these things, neither speak them before the world; for these things are given unto you for your profit and for salvation.

74. Verily, verily I say unto you, they who believe not on your words, and are not baptized in water in my name, for the remission

of their sins, that they may receive the Holy Ghost, shall be damned, and shall not come into my Father's kingdom where my Father and I am.

75. And this revelation unto you, and commandment, is in force from this very hour upon all the world, and the gospel is unto all who have not received it.

76. But, verily I say unto all those to whom the kingdom has been given—from you it must be preached unto them, that they shall repent of their former evil works; for they are to be upbraided for their evil hearts of unbelief, and your brethren in Zion for their rebellion against you at the time I sent you.

77. And again I say unto you, my friends, for from henceforth I shall call you friends, it is expedient that I give unto you this commandment, that ye become even as my friends in days when I was with them, traveling to preach the gospel in my power;

78. For I suffered them not to have purse or scrip, neither two coats

79. Behold, I send you out to prove the world, and the laborer is worthy of his hire.

80. And any man that shall go and preach this gospel of the kingdom, and fail not to continue faithful in all things, shall not be weary in mind, neither darkened, neither in body, limb, nor joint; and a hair of his head shall not fall to the ground unnoticed. And they shall not go hungry, neither athirst.

81. Therefore, take ye no thought for the morrow, for what ye shall eat or what ye shall drink, or wherewithal ye shall be clothed.

82. For, consider the lilies of the field, how they grow, they toil not, neither do they spin; and the kingdoms of the world, in all their glory, are not arrayed like one of these.

83. For your Father, who is in heaven, knoweth that you have need of all these things.

84. Therefore, let the morrow take thought for the things of itself.

85. Neither take ye thought beforehand what ye shall say; but treasure up in your minds continually the words of life, and it shall be given you in the very hour that portion that shall be meted unto every man.

86. Therefore, let no man among you, for this commandment is unto all the faithful who are called of God in the church unto the ministry, from this hour take purse or scrip, that goeth forth to proclaim this gospel of the kingdom.

87. Behold, I send you out to reprove the world of all their unrighteous deeds, and to teach them of a judgment which is to come.

88. And whoso receiveth you, there I will be also, for I will go before your face. I will be on your right hand and on your left,

and my Spirit shall be in your hearts, and mine angels round about you, to bear you up.

89. Whoso receiveth you receiveth me; and the same will feed you, and clothe you, and give you money.

90. And he who feeds you, or clothes you, or gives you money, shall in nowise lose his reward.

91. And he that doeth not these things is not my disciple; by this you may know my disciples.

92. He that receiveth you not, go away from him alone by yourselves, and cleanse your feet even with water, pure water, whether in heat or in cold, and bear testimony of it unto your Father which is in heaven, and return not again unto that man.

93. And in whatsoever village or city ye enter, do likewise.

94. Nevertheless, search diligently and spare not; and wo unto that house, or that village or city that rejecteth you, or your words, or your testimony concerning me.

95. Wo, I say again, unto that house, or that village or city that rejecteth you, or your words, or your testimony of me;

96. For I, the Almighty, have laid my hands upon the nations, to scourge them for their wickedness.

97. And plagues shall go forth, and they shall not be taken from the earth until I have completed my work, which shall be cut short in righteousness—

98. Until all shall know me, who remain, even from the least unto the greatest, and shall be filled with the knowledge of the Lord, and shall see eye to eye, and shall lift up their voice, and with the voice together sing this new song, saying:

99. The Lord hath brought again Zion;
The Lord hath redeemed his people, Israel,
According to the election of grace, which was brought to pass by the faith
And covenant of their fathers.

100. The Lord hath redeemed his people;
And Satan is bound and time is no longer.
The Lord hath gathered all things in one.
The Lord hath brought down Zion from above.
The Lord hath brought up Zion from beneath.

101. The earth hath travailed and brought forth her strength;
And truth is established in her bowels;
And the heavens have smiled upon her;
And she is clothed with the glory of her God;
For he stands in the midst of his people.

102. Glory, and honor, and power, and might,

Be ascribed to our God; for he is full of mercy,
Justice, grace and truth, and peace,
Forever and ever, Amen.

103. And again, verily, verily, I say unto you, it is expedient that every man who goes forth to proclaim mine everlasting gospel, that inasmuch as they have families, and receive money by gift, that they should send it unto them or make use of it for their benefit, as the Lord shall direct them, for thus it seemeth me good.

104. And let all those who have not families, who receive money, send it up unto the bishop in Zion, or unto the bishop in Ohio, that it may be consecrated for the bringing forth of the revelations and the printing thereof, and for establishing Zion.

105. And if any man shall give unto any of you a coat, or a suit, take the old and cast it unto the poor, and go on your way rejoicing.

106. And if any man among you be strong in the Spirit, let him take with him him that is weak, that he may be edified in all meekness, that he may become strong also.

107. Therefore, take with you those who are ordained unto the lesser priesthood, and send them before you to make appointments, and to prepare the way, and to fill appointments that you yourselves are not able to fill.

108. Behold, this is the way that mine apostles, in ancient days, built up my church unto me.

109. Therefore, let every man stand in his own office, and labor in his own calling; and let not the head say unto the feet it hath no need of the feet; for without the feet how shall the body be able to stand?

110. Also the body hath need of every member, that all may be edified together, that the system may be kept perfect.

111. And behold, the high priests should travel, and also the elders, and also the lesser priests; but the deacons and teachers should be appointed to watch over the church, to be standing ministers unto the church.

112. And the bishop, Newel K. Whitney, also should travel round about and among all the churches, searching after the poor to administer to their wants by humbling the rich and the proud.

113. He should also employ an agent to take charge and to do his secular business as he shall direct.

114. Nevertheless, let the bishop go unto the city of New York, also to the city of Albany, and also to the city of Boston, and warn the people of those cities with the sound of the gospel, with a loud voice, of the desolation and utter abolishment which await them if they do reject these things.

115. For if they do reject these things the hour of their judgment is nigh, and their house shall be left unto them desolate.

116. Let him trust in me and he shall not be confounded; and a hair of his head shall not fall to the ground unnoticed.

117. And verily I say unto you, the rest of my servants, go ye forth as your circumstances shall permit, in your several callings, unto the great and notable cities and villages, reproving the world in righteousness of all their unrighteous and ungodly deeds, setting forth clearly and understandingly the desolation of abomination in the last days.

118. For, with you saith the Lord Almighty, I will rend their kingdoms; I will not only shake the earth, but the starry heavens shall tremble.

119. For I, the Lord, have put forth my hand to exert the powers of heaven; ye cannot see it now, yet a little while and ye shall see it, and know that I am, and that I will come and reign with my people.

120. I am Alpha and Omega, the beginning and the end. Amen.

The Prophet's Visit to Eastern Cities.

I continued the translation of the Bible and ministering to the Church, through the fall, excepting a hurried journey to Albany, New York and Boston, in company with Bishop Whitney, from which I returned on the 6th of November, immediately after the birth of my son Joseph Smith, the third.*

About the 8th of November I received a visit from Elders Joseph Young,† Brigham Young, and Heber

*Three children had previously been born to Joseph and Emma: a son, on June 15, 1828, who died the same hour; and a son and daughter, on April 30, 1831, who lived three hours. These latter children were born the same day as the Murdock twins, whose adoption into Joseph's family at the age of nine days, is mentioned on page 260.

†Joseph Young, mentioned above, was named for his grandfather Joseph Young, a physician and surgeon in the British-American army during the French and Indian war. John Young, the father of Joseph Young, subject of this note, was a native of Hopkinton, Middlesex county, Massachusetts. He married Nabby Howe, who bore to him eleven children, of whom Joseph was the seventh child and second son. Joseph was born on the 7th of April, 1797, in Hopkinton, Middlesex county, Massachusetts. In early life he became attached to religion, and was very moral and devout. In his youth he assisted his father in agricultural pursuits. He was a Methodist preacher for a number of years, and labored in the United States and Canada. On April 6th, 1832, he was baptized into the Church of Jesus Christ of Latter-day Saints, by Elder Daniel Bowen, in Columbia, Pennsylvania; and was ordained an Elder a few days

C. Kimball* of Mendon, Monroe county, New York. They spent four or five days at Kirtland, during which we had many interesting moments. At one of our interviews, Brother Brigham Young† and John P. Greene spoke in

The Arrival of the Youngs at Kirtland.

afterwards under the hands of Ezra Landon. After preaching in the state of New York for several months, he took a mission to Canada, in the summer of 1832, in company with his brother Phinehas, Eleazer Miller and others. They organized two small branches, and returned to Mendon in about four months. He then went to Kirtland with Heber C. Kimball and his brother Brigham, as related in the text.

*Heber Chase Kimball was born June 14, 1801, in Sheldon, Franklin county, Vermont. His parents were American born, though of Scotch extraction, the ancient name of the family being, it is believed, Campbell. His opportunities for acquiring an education even of the common school order were extremely limited. At the age of nineteen he was apprenticed to his elder brother, Charles, to learn the potter's trade. He served some two years as an apprentice and then worked for his brother as a journeyman potter. While yet in the employ of his brother they together moved to Mendon, Monroe county, where the latter established a pottery. While living here Heber married Vilate Murray, of Victor, a town near Mendon, but in the adjoining county of Ontario. Soon after his marriage he joined the Baptist church. Three weeks later, and some time in the winter of 1831, a number of the Elders of the Church of Jesus Christ of Latter-day Saints began preaching in the town of Victor, and Heber C. Kimball and a number of the Youngs attended their meetings. Then followed the visit to the branch of the Church in Columbia, Pennsylvania, mentioned in the biographical note of Brigham Young. After his return from Columbia he was baptized by Alpheus Gifford, on the 15th of April, 1832. During the summer of 1832 Heber C. Kimball was ordained an Elder and with the Youngs labored part of his time in the ministry, and succeeded in raising up several small branches of the Church. In September he made the journey to Kirtland, spoken of by the Prophet in his narrative.

†Brigham Young was born in Whitingham, Windham county, Vermont, June 1, 1801. He was the ninth child and fourth son of John and Nabby Howe Young. He was early taught by his parents to live a strictly moral life, it was not until he was in his twenty-second year that he gave serious thought to religion. He soon afterwards joined the Methodist church. On the 8th of October he married Miriam Works, daughter of Asa and Jerusha Works, and for a number of years followed the trade of carpenter and joiner, painter and glazier. In the spring of 1829 he made his home at Mendon, a small town some fifteen miles south and east of Rochester, in Monroe county, where his father also resided. A year later he saw for the first time the Book of Mormon, a copy that was left at the house of his brother, Phinehas H. Young, by Samuel H. Smith, brother of the Prophet. In the fall of 1831 Elders Alpheus Gifford, Elial Strong and others appeared in the vicinity of Mendon, preaching the restored Gospel, as revealed through Joseph Smith the Prophet, and Brigham believed their testimony. In company with his brother, Phinehas, and Heber C. Kimball he visited a branch of the Church in Columbia, Bradford county, Pennsylvania. The three brethren remained with the branch of the Church about a week, during which time their faith was much strengthened in the mission of the modern Prophet. On returning to Mendon, Brigham Young in company with John P. Greene started

tongues, which was the first time I had heard this gift among the brethren; others also spoke, and I received the gift myself.*

In answer to letters received from the brethren in Missouri, I wrote as follows:

KIRTLAND, Nov. 27th, 1832.

BROTHER WILLIAM W. PHELPS:—I say brother, because I feel so

for Canada to find Joseph Young, an elder brother of Brigham's, then a preacher in the Methodist church. On meeting his brother Brigham related what he had learned of the new dispensation and Joseph rejoiced at hearing the glad tidings. Together they returned to Mendon, where they arrived in March, 1832; and on the 14th of April following, Brigham was baptized by Eleazer Miller, and confirmed a member of the Church at the water's edge. Almost immediately afterwards Miller ordained him an Elder in the Church. During the summer of 1832 he preached in Mendon and vicinity and assisted in raising up several branches of the Church. On the 8th of September his wife died of consumption, leaving him with two small children, both girls. After the death of his wife he made his home with Heber C. Kimball, the latter's wife taking in charge his motherless babes. In the same month of September, in company with Heber C. Kimball and his brother Joseph, he went to Kirtland on his visit to the Prophet, as related in the text.

*The above incident is thus related by President Brigham Young in his own history:—In September, 1832, Brother Heber C. Kimball took his horse and wagon, Brother Joseph Young and myself accompanying him, and started for Kirtland to see the Prophet Joseph. We visited many friends on the way, and some branches of the Church. We exhorted them and prayed with them, and I spoke in tongues. Some pronounced it genuine and from the Lord, and others pronounced it of the devil. We proceeded to Kirtland and stopped at John P. Greene's, who had just arrived there with his family. We rested a few minutes, took some refreshments and started to see the Prophet. We went to his father's house and learned that he was in the woods chopping. We immediately repaired to the woods, where we found the Prophet, and two or three of his brothers, chopping and hauling wood. Here my joy was full at the privilege of shaking the hand of the Prophet of God, and receiving the sure testimony, by the spirit of prophecy, that he was all that any man could believe him to be as a true prophet. He was happy to see us and bid us welcome. We soon returned to his house, he accompanying us.

In the evening, a few of the brethren came in, and we conversed upon the things of the kingdom. He called upon me to pray; in my prayer I spoke in tongues. As soon as we arose from our knees, the brethren flocked around him, and asked his opinion concerning the gift of tongues that was upon me. He told them it was the pure Adamic language. Some said to him they expected he would condemn the gift Brother Brigham had, but he said, "No, it is of God."—*Millennial Star*, vol. xxv, p. 439.

The gift of tongues here spoken of was first exercised in one of the Pennsylvania branches; next at Mendon, where the Youngs and Kimballs resided; then in the branches between Mendon and Kirtland; then in Kirtland under the circumstances above related, and shortly afterwards it was a gift quite generally exercised by the Saints in Ohio. "And it came to pass," writes John Whitmer in his history of the Church (chap. x), "that in the fall of 1832, the disciples in Ohio received the gift of tongues, and in June, 1833, we received the gift of tongues in Zion."

from the heart, and although it is not long since I wrote a letter unto you, yet I feel as though you would excuse me for writing this, as I have many things which I wish to communicate. Some things which I will mention in this letter, which are lying with great weight on my mind. I am well, and my family also; God grant that you may enjoy the same, and yours, and all the brethren and sisters who remember to inquire after the commandments of the Lord, and the welfare of Zion and such a being as myself; and while I dictate this letter, I fancy to myself that you are saying or thinking something similar to these words:—"My God, great and mighty art Thou, therefore show unto Thy servant what shall become of those who are essaying to come up unto Zion, in order to keep the commandments of God, and yet receive not their inheritance by consecrations, by order of deed from the Bishop, the man that God has appointed in a legal way, agreeably to the law given to organize and regulate the Church, and all the affairs of the same."

Brother William, in the love of God, having the most implicit confidence in you as a man of God, having obtained this confidence by a vision of heaven, therefore I will proceed to unfold to you some of the feelings of my heart, and to answer the question.

Firstly, it is the duty of the Lord's clerk,* whom He has appointed, to keep a history, and a General Church Record of all things that transpire in Zion, and of all those who consecrate properties and receive inheritances legally from the Bishop; and also their manner of life, their faith, and works and also of the apostates who apostatize after receiving their inheritances. It is contrary to the will and commandment of God, that those who receive not their inheritance by consecration, agreeably to His law, which he has given, that He may tithe His people, to prepare them against the day of vengeance and burning, should have their names enrolled with the people of God; neither is their genealogy to be kept, or to be had where it may be found on any of the records or history of the Church; their names shall not be found neither the names of the fathers, nor the names of the children written in the book of the law of God, saith the Lord of hosts. Yea, thus saith the still small voice, which whispereth through and pierceth all things, and oftentimes it maketh my bones to quake while it maketh manifest, saying: and it shall come to pass, that I, the Lord God, will send one mighty and strong, holding the sceptre of power in his hand, clothed with light for a covering, whose mouth shall utter words, eternal words;

*The part of the above letter, beginning with the words, "It is the duty of the Lord's clerk, etc., and ending with the words, "As will be found recorded in the second chapter and sixty-first and sixty-second verses of Ezra," was accepted afterwards as the word of the Lord, that is, as a revelation upon the matters treated therein, and appears in the Doctrine and Covenants as section lxxxv.

while his bowels shall be a fountain of truth, to set in order the house of God, and to arrange by lot the inheritances of the Saints, whose names are found, and the names of their fathers, and of their children enrolled in the book of the law of God: while that man, who was called of God, and appointed, that putteth forth his hand to steady the ark of God, shall fall by the shaft of death, like as a tree that is smitten by the vivid shaft of lightning; and all they who are not found written in the book of remembrance, shall find none inheritance in that day but they shall be cut asunder, and their portion shall be appointed them among unbelievers, where are wailing and gnashing of teeth. These things I say not of myself; therefore, as the Lord speaketh, He will also fulfil. And they who are of the High Priesthood, whose names are not found written in the book of the law, or that are found to have apostatized, or to have been cut off from the Church; as well as the lesser Priesthood, or the members, in that day, shall not find an inheritance among the Saints of the Most High; therefore it shall be done unto them as unto the children of the priest, as will be found recorded in the second chapter, and sixty-first and sixty-second verses of Ezra.*

Now, Brother William, if what I have said is true, how careful men ought to be what they do in the last days, lest they are cut short of their expectations, and they that think they stand should fall, because they keep not the Lord's commandments; whilst you, who do the will of the Lord and keep His commandments, have need to rejoice with unspeakable joy, for such shall be exalted very high, and shall be lifted up in triumph above all the kingdoms of this world; but I must drop this subject at the beginning [of it].

Oh, Lord, when will the time come when Brother William, Thy servant, and myself, shall behold the day that we may stand together and gaze upon eternal wisdom engraven upon the heavens, while the majesty of our God holdeth up the dark curtain until we may read the round of eternity, to the fulness and satisfaction of our immortal souls? Oh, Lord, deliver us in due time from the little, narrow prison, almost as it were, total darkness of paper, pen and ink;—and a crooked, broken, scattered and imperfect language.

I have obtained ten subscribers for the *Star*. Love for all the brethren.

Yours in bonds. Amen.
JOSEPH SMITH, JUN.

*"And the children of the priests: the children of Habaiah, the children of Koz, the children of Barzillai; which took a wife of the daughters of Barzillai the Gileadite, and was called after their name: these sought their register among those that were reckoned by genealogy, but they were not found, therefore were they, as polluted, put from the priesthood."—Ezra ii: 61, 62.

On the 6th of December, 1832, I received the following revelation explaining the parable of the wheat and tares:

*Revelation.**

1. Verily, thus saith the Lord unto you my servants, concerning the parable of the wheat and of the tares:

2. Behold, verily I say, the field was the world, and the apostles were the sowers of the seed;

3. And after they have fallen asleep, the great persecutor of the church, the apostate, the whore, even Babylon, that maketh all nations to drink of her cup, in whose hearts the enemy, even Satan, sitteth to reign—behold he soweth the tares; wherefore, the tares choke the wheat and drive the church into the wilderness.

4. But behold, in the last days, even now while the Lord is beginning to bring forth the word, and the blade is springing up and is yet tender—

5. Behold, verily I say unto you, the angels are crying unto the Lord day and night, who are ready and waiting to be sent forth to reap down the fields;

6. But the Lord saith unto them, pluck not up the tares while the blade is yet tender (for verily your faith is weak), lest you destroy the wheat also.

7. Therefore, let the wheat and the tares grow together until the harvest is fully ripe; then ye shall first gather out the wheat from among the tares, and after the gathering of the wheat, behold and lo, the tares are bound in bundles, and the field remaineth to be burned.

8. Therefore, thus saith the Lord unto you, with whom the priesthood hath continued through the lineage of your fathers—

9. For ye are lawful heirs, according to the flesh, and have been hid from the world with Christ in God—

10. Therefore your life and the priesthood have remained, and must needs remain through you and your lineage until the restoration of all things spoken by the mouths of all the holy prophets since the world began.

11. Therefore, blessed are ye if ye continue in my goodness, a light unto the Gentiles, and through this priesthood, a savior unto my people Israel. The Lord hath said it. Amen.

*Doctrine and Covenants, sec. lxxxvi.

CHAPTER XXII.

THE PROPHECY ON THE WAR OF THE REBELLION—THE OLIVE LEAF—COMMUNICATION TO MR. SEATON—WARNING TO ZION.

State of the World at the Close of 1832.

APPEARANCES of troubles among the nations became more visible this season than they had previously been since the Church began her journey out of the wilderness. The ravages of the cholera were frightful in almost all the large cities on the globe. The plague broke out in India, while the United States, amid all her pomp and greatness, was threatened with immediate dissolution. The people of South Carolina, in convention assembled (in November), passed ordinances, declaring their state a free and independent nation; and appointed Thursday, the 31st day of January, 1833, as a day of humiliation and prayer, to implore Almighty God to vouchsafe His blessings, and restore liberty and happiness within their borders. President Jackson issued his proclamation against this rebellion, called out a force sufficient to quell it, and implored the blessings of God to assist the nation to extricate itself from the horrors of the approaching and solemn crisis.

On Christmas day [1832], I received the following revelation and prophecy on war.

*Revelation and Prophecy.**

1. Verily, thus saith the Lord concerning the wars that will shortly come to pass, beginning at the rebellion of South Carolina, which will eventually terminate in the death and misery of many souls;

2. And the time will come that war will be poured out upon all nations, beginning at this place.

3. For behold, the Southern States shall be divided against the Northern States, and the Southern States will call on other nations, even the nation of Great Britain, as it is called, and they shall also

*Doctrine and Covenants, sec. lxxxvii.

call upon other nations, in order to defend themselves against other nations; and then war shall be poured out upon all nations.

4. And it shall come to pass, after many days, slaves shall rise up against their masters, who shall be marshaled and discipled for war.

5. And it shall come to pass also that the remnants who are left of the land will marshal themselves, and shall become exceedingly angry, and shall vex the Gentiles with a sore vexation.

6. And thus, with the sword and by bloodshed the inhabitants of the earth shall mourn; and with famine, and plague, and earthquake, and the thunder of heaven, and the fierce and vivid lightning also, shall the inhabitants of the earth be made to feel the wrath, and indignation, and chastening hand of an Almighty God, until the consumption decreed hath made a full end of all nations;

7. That the cry of the saints, and of the blood of the saints, shall cease to come up into the ears of the Lord of Sabaoth, from the earth, to be avenged of their enemies.

8. Wherefore, stand ye in holy places, and be not moved, until the day of the Lord come; for behold, it cometh quickly, saith the Lord. Amen.

Two days after the preceding prophecy, on the 27th of December, I received the following:

*Revelation.**

1. Verily, thus saith the Lord unto you who have assembled yourselves together to receive his will concerning you:

2. Behold, this is pleasing unto your Lord, and the angels rejoice over you; the alms of your prayers have come up into the ears of the Lord of Sabaoth, and are recorded in the book of the names of the sanctified, even them of the celestial world.

3. Wherefore, I now send upon you another Comforter, even upon you my friends, that it may abide in your hearts, even the Holy Spirit of promise; which other Comforter is the same that I promised unto my disciples, as is recorded in the testimony of John.

4. This Comforter is the promise which I give unto you of eternal life, even the glory of the celestial kingdom;

5. Which glory is that of the church of the Firstborn, even of God, the holiest of all, through Jesus Christ his Son—

6. He that ascended up on high, as also he descended below all

*Doctrine and Covenants, sec. lxxxviii. This is the revelation referred to as "The Olive Leaf," plucked from the Tree of Paradise, in the Prophet's letter of January 11, 1833. See page 316.

things, in that he comprehended all things, that he might be in all and through all things, the light of truth;

7. Which truth shineth. This is the light of Christ. As also he is in the sun, and the light of the sun, and the power thereof by which it was made.

8. As also he is in the moon, and is the light of the moon, and the power thereof by which it was made;

9. As also the light of the stars, and the power thereof by which they were made;

10. And the earth also, and the power thereof, even the earth upon which you stand.

11. And the light which shineth, which giveth you light, is through him who enlighteneth your eyes, which is the same light that quickeneth your understandings;

12. Which light proceedeth forth from the presence of God to fill the immensity of space—

13. The light which is in all things, which giveth life to all things, which is the law by which all things are governed, even the power of God who sitteth upon his throne, who is in the bosom of eternity, who is in the midst of all things.

14. Now, verily I say unto you, that through the redemption which is made for you is brought to pass the resurrection from the dead.

15. And the spirit and the body are the soul of man.

16. And the resurrection from the dead is the redemption of the soul.

17. And the redemption of the soul is through him that quickeneth all things, in whose bosom it is decreed that the poor and the meek of the earth shall inherit it.

18. Therefore, it must needs be sanctified from all unrighteousness, that it may be prepared for the celestial glory;

19. For after it hath filled the measure of its creation, it shall be crowned with glory, even with the presence of God the Father;

20. That bodies who are of the celestial kingdom may possess it forever and ever; for, for this intent was it made and created, and for this intent are they sanctified.

21. And they who are not sanctified through the law which I have given unto you, even the law of Christ, must inherit another kingdom, even that of a terrestrial kingdom, or that of a telestial kingdom.

22. For he who is not able to abide the law of a celestial kingdom cannot abide a celestial glory.

23. And he who cannot abide the law of a terrestrial kingdom cannot abide a terrestrial glory.

24. And he who cannot abide the law of a telestial kingdom cannot abide a telestial glory; therefore he is not meet for a kingdom of

glory. Therefore he must abide a kingdom which is not a kingdom of glory.

25. And again, verily I say unto you, the earth abideth the law of a celestial kingdom, for it filleth the measure of its creation, and transgresseth not the law—

26. Wherefore, it shall be sanctified; yea, notwithstanding it shall die, it shall be quickened again, and shall abide the power by which it is quickened, and the righteous shall inherit it.

27. For notwithstanding they die, they also shall rise again, a spiritual body.

28. They who are of a celestial spirit shall receive the same body which was a natural body; even ye shall receive your bodies, and your glory shall be that glory by which your bodies are quickened.

29. Ye who are quickened by a portion of the celestial glory shall then receive of the same, even a fulness.

30. And they who are quickened by a portion of the terrestrial glory shall then receive of the same, even a fulness.

31. And also they who are quickened by a portion of the telestial glory shall then receive of the same, even a fulness.

32. And they who remain shall also be quickened; nevertheless, they shall return again to their own place, to enjoy that which they are willing to receive, because they were not willing to enjoy that which they might have received.

33. For what doth it profit a man if a gift is bestowed upon him, and he receive not the gift? Behold, he rejoices not in that which is given unto him, neither rejoices in him who is the giver of the gift.

34. And again, verily I say unto you, that which is governed by law is also preserved law and perfected and sanctified by the same.

35. That which breaketh a law, and abideth not by law, but seeketh to become a law unto itself, and willeth to abide in sin, and altogether abideth in sin, cannot be sanctified by law, neither by mercy, justice, nor judgment. Therefore, they must remain filthy still.

36. All kingdoms have a law given;

37. And there are many kingdoms; for there is no space in the which there is no kingdom; and there is no kingdom in which there is no space, either a greater or a lesser kingdom.

38. And unto every kingdom is given a law; and unto every law there are certain bounds also and conditions.

39. All beings who abide not in those conditions are not justified.

40. For intelligence cleaveth unto intelligence: wisdom receiveth wisdom; truth embraceth truth; virtue loveth virtue; light cleaveth unto light; mercy hath compassion on mercy and claimeth her own; justice continueth its course and claimeth its own; judgment goeth be-

fore the face of him who sitteth upon the throne and governeth and executeth all things.

41. He comprehendeth all things, and all things are before him, and all things are round about him; and he is above all things, and in all things, and is through all things, and is round about all things; and all things are by him, and of him, even God, forever and ever.

42. And again, verily I say unto you, he hath given a law unto all things, by which they move in their times and their seasons;

43. And their courses are fixed, even the courses of the heavens and the earth, which comprehend the earth and all the planets.

44. And they give light to each other in their times and in their seasons, in their minutes, in their hours, in their days, in their weeks, in their months, in their years—all these are one year with God, but not with man.

45. The earth rolls upon her wings, and the sun giveth his light by day, and the moon giveth her light by night, and the stars also give their light, as they roll upon their wings in their glory, in the midst of the power of God.

46. Unto what shall I liken these kingdoms, that ye may understand?

47. Behold, all these are kingdoms, and any man who hath seen any or the least of these hath seen God moving in his majesty and power.

48. I say unto you, he hath seen him; nevertheless, he who came unto his own was not comprehended.

49. The light shineth in darkness, and the darkness comprehendeth it not; nevertheless, the day shall come when you shall comprehend even God, being quickened in him and by him.

50. Then shall ye know that ye have seen me, that I am, and that I am the true light that is in you, and that you are in me; otherwise ye could not abound.

51. Behold, I will liken these kingdoms unto a man having a field, and he sent forth his servants into the field to dig in the field.

52. And he said unto the first: Go ye and labor in the field, and in the first hour I will come unto you, and ye shall behold the joy of my countenance.

53. And he said unto the second: Go ye also into the field, and in the second hour I will visit you with the joy of my countenance.

54. And also unto the third, saying: I will visit you;

55. And unto the fourth, and so on unto the twelfth.

56. And the lord of the field went unto the first in the first hour, and tarried with him all that hour, and he was made glad with the light of the countenance of his lord.

57. And then he withdrew from the first that he might visit the second also, and the third, and the fourth, and so on unto the twelfth.

58. And thus they all received the light of the countenance of their lord, every man in his hour, and in his time, and in his season—

59. Beginning at the first, and so on unto the last, and from the last unto the first, and from the first unto the last;

60. Every man in his own order, until his hour was finished, even according as his lord had commanded him, that his lord might be glorified in him, and he in his lord, that they all might be glorified.

61. Therefore, unto this parable I will liken all these kingdoms, and the inhabitants thereof—every kingdom in its hour, and in its time, and in its season, even according to the decree which God hath made.

62. And again, verily I say unto you, my friends, I leave these sayings with you to ponder in your hearts, with this commandment which I give unto you, that ye shall call upon me while I am near—

63. Draw near unto me and I will draw near unto you; seek me diligently and ye shall find me; ask, and ye shall receive; knock, and it shall be opened unto you.

64. Whatsoever ye ask the Father in my name it shall be given unto you, that is expedient for you;

65. And if ye ask anything that is not expedient for you, it shall turn unto your condemnation.

66. Behold, that which you hear is as the voice of one crying in the wilderness—in the wilderness, because you cannot see him—my voice, because my voice is Spirit; my Spirit is truth; truth abideth and hath no end; and if it be in you it shall abound.

67. And if your eye be single to my glory, your whole bodies shall be filled with light, and there shall be no darkness in you; and that body which is filled with light comprehendeth all things.

68. Therefore, sanctify yourselves that your minds become single to God, and the days will come that you shall see him; for he will unveil his face unto you, and it shall be in his own time, and in his own way, and according to his own will.

69. Remember the great and last promise which I have made unto you; cast away your idle thoughts and your excess of laughter far from you.

70. Tarry ye, tarry ye in this place, and call a solemn assembly, even of those who are the first laborers in this last kingdom.

71. And let those whom they have warned in their traveling call on the Lord, and ponder the warning in their hearts which they have received, for a little season.

72. Behold, and lo, I will take care of your flocks, and will raise up elders and send unto them.

73. Behold, I will hasten my work in its time.

74. And I give unto you, who are the first laborers in this last kingdom, a commandment that you assemble yourselves together, and or-

ganize yourselves, and prepare yourselves, and sanctify yourselves; yea, purify your hearts, and cleanse your hands and your feet before me, that I may make you clean;

75. That I may testify unto your Father, and your God, and my God, that you are clean from the blood of this wicked generation; that I may fulfil this promise, this great and last promise, which I have made unto you, when I will.

76. Also, I give unto you a commandment that ye shall continue in prayer and fasting from this time forth.

77. And I give unto you a commandment that you shall teach one another the doctrine of the kingdom.

78. Teach ye diligently and my grace shall attend you, that you may be instructed more perfectly in theory, in principle, in doctrine, in the law of the gospel, in all things that pertain unto the kingdom of God, that are expedient for you to understand;

79. Of things both in heaven and in the earth, and under the earth; things which have been, things which are, things which must shortly come to pass; things which are at home, things which are abroad; the wars and the perplexities of the nations, and the judgments which are on the land; and a knowledge also of countries and of kingdoms—

80. That ye may be prepared in all things when I shall send you again to magnify the calling whereunto I have called you, and the mission with which I have commissioned you.

81. Behold, I sent you out to testify and warn the people, and it becometh every man who hath been warned to warn his neighbor.

82. Therefore, they are left without excuse, and their sins are upon their own heads.

83. He that seeketh me early shall find me, and shall not be forsaken.

84. Therefore, tarry ye, and labor diligently, that you may be perfected in your ministry to go forth among the Gentiles for the last time, as many as the mouth of the Lord shall name, to bind up the law and seal up the testimony, and to prepare the saints for the hour of judgment which is to come;

85. That their souls may escape the wrath of God, the desolation of abomination which awaits the wicked, both in this world and in the world to come. Verily, I say unto you, let those who are not the first elders continue in the vineyard until the mouth of the Lord shall call them, for their time is not yet come; their garments are not clean from the blood of this generation.

86. Abide ye in the liberty wherewith ye are made free; entangle not yourselves in sin, but let your hands be clean, until the Lord comes.

87. For not many days hence and the earth shall tremble and reel

to and fro as a drunken man; and the sun shall hide his face, and shall refuse to give light; and the moon shall be bathed in blood; and the stars shall become exceedingly angry, and shall cast themselves down as a fig that falleth from off a fig-tree.

88. And after your testimony cometh wrath and indignation upon the people.

89. For after your testimony cometh the testimony of earthquakes, that shall cause groanings in the midst of her, and men shall fall upon the ground and shall not be able to stand.

90. And also cometh the testimony of the voice of thunderings, and the voice of lightnings, and the voice of tempests, and the voice of the waves of the sea heaving themselves beyond their bounds.

91. And all things shall be in commotion; and surely, men's hearts shall fail them; for fear shall come upon all people.

92. And angels shall fly through the midst of heaven, crying with a loud voice, sounding the trump of God, saying: Prepare ye, prepare ye, O inhabitants of the earth; for the judgment of our God is come. Behold, and lo, the Bridegroom cometh; go ye out to meet him.

93. And immediately there shall appear a great sign in heaven, and all people shall see it together.

94. And another angel shall sound his trump, saying: That great church, the mother of abominations, that made all nations drink of the wine of the wrath of her fornication, that persecuteth the saints of God, that shed their blood—he who sitteth upon many waters, and upon the islands of the sea—behold, she is the tares of the earth; she is bound in bundles, her bands are made strong, no man can loose them; therefore, she is ready to be burned. And he shall sound his trump both long and loud, and all nations shall hear it.

95. And there shall be silence in heaven for the space of half an hour; and immediately after shall the curtain of heaven be unfolded, as a scroll is unfolded after it is rolled up, and the face of the Lord shall be unveiled;

96. And the saints that are upon the earth, who are alive, shall be quickened and be caught up to meet him.

97. And they who have slept in their graves shall come forth, for their graves shall be opened; and they also shall be caught up to meet him in the midst of the pillar of heaven—

98. They are Christ's, the first fruits, they who shall descend with him first, and they who are on the earth and in their graves, who are first caught up to meet him; and all this by the voice of the sounding of the trump of the angel of God.

99. And after this another angel shall sound, which is the second trump; and then cometh the redemption of those who are Christ's at

his coming; who have received their part in that prison which is prepared for them, that they might receive the gospel, and be judged according to men in the flesh.

100. And again, another trump shall sound, which is the third trump; and then come the spirits of men who are to be judged, and are found under condemnation;

101. And these are the rest of the dead; and they live not again until the thousand years are ended, neither again, until the end of the earth.

102. And another trump shall sound, which is the fourth trump, saying: There are found among those who are to remain until that great and last day, even the end, who shall remain filthy still.

103. And another trump shall sound, which is the fifth trump, which is the fifth angel who committeth the everlasting gospel—flying through the midst of heaven, unto all nations, kindreds, tongues, and people;

104. And this shall be the sound of his trump, saying to all people, both in heaven and in earth, and that are under the earth—for every ear shall hear it, and every knee shall bow, and every tongue shall confess, while they hear the sound of the trump, saying: Fear God, and give glory to him who sitteth upon the throne, forever and ever; for the hour of his judgment is come.

105. And again, another angel shall sound his trump, which is the sixth angel, saying: She is fallen who made all nations drink of the wine of the wrath of her fornication; she is fallen, is fallen!

106. And again, another angel shall sound his trump, which is the seventh angel, saying: It is finished; it is finished! The Lamb of God hath overcome and trodden the wine-press alone, even the wine-press of the fierceness of the wrath of Almighty God.

107. And then shall the angels be crowned with the glory of his might, and the saints shall be filled with his glory, and receive their inheritance and be made equal with him.

108. And then shall the first angel again sound his trump in the ears of all living, and reveal the secret acts of men, and the mighty works of God in the first thousand years.

109. And then shall the second angel sound his trump, and reveal the secret acts of men, and the thoughts and intents of their hearts, and the mighty works of God in the second thousand years—

110. And so on, until the seventh angel shall sound his trump; and he shall stand forth upon the land and upon the sea, and swear in the name of him who sitteth upon the throne, that there shall be time no longer; and Satan shall be bound, that old serpent, who is called the devil, and shall not be loosed for the space of a thousand years.

111. And then he shall be loosed for a little season, that he may gather together his armies.

112. And Michael, the seventh angel, even the archangel, shall gather together his armies, even the hosts of heaven.

113. And the devil shall gather together his armies; even the hosts of hell, and shall come up to battle against Michael and his armies.

114. And then cometh the battle of the great God; and the devil and his armies shall be cast away into their own place, that they shall not have power over the saints any more at all.

115. For Michael shall fight their battles, and shall overcome him who seeketh the throne of him who sitteth upon the throne, even the Lamb.

116. This is the glory of God, and the sanctified; and they shall not any more see death.

117. Therefore, verily I say unto you, my friends, call your solemn assembly, as I have commanded you.

118. And as all have not faith, seek ye diligently and teach one another words of wisdom; yea, seek ye out of the best books words of wisdom; seek learning, even by study and also by faith.

119. Organize yourselves; prepare every needful thing; and establish a house, even a house of prayer, a house of fasting, a house of faith, a house of learning, a house of glory, a house of order, a house of God;

120. That your incomings may be in the name of the Lord; that your outgoings may be in the name of the Lord; that all your salutations may be in the name of the Lord, with uplifted hands unto the Most High.

121. Therefore, cease from all your light speeches, from all laughter, from all your lustful desires, from all your pride and light-mindedness, and from all your wicked doings.

122. Appoint among yourselves a teacher, and let not all be spokesmen at once; but let one speak at a time and let all listen unto his sayings, that when all have spoken that all may be edified of all, and that every man may have an equal privilege.

123. See that ye love one another; cease to be covetous; learn to impart one to another as the gospel requires.

124. Cease to be idle; cease to be unclean; cease to find fault one with another; cease to sleep longer than is needful; retire to thy bed early, that ye may not be weary; rise early, that your bodies and your minds may be invigorated.

125. And above all things, clothe yourselves with the bond of charity, as with a mantle, which is the bond of perfectness and peace.

126. Pray always, that ye may not faint, until I come. Behold, and lo, I will come quickly, and receive you unto myself. Amen.

127. And again, the order of the house prepared for the presidency of the school of the prophets, established for their instruction in all things that are expedient for them, even for all the officers of the church, or in other words, those who are called to the ministry in the church, beginning at the high priests, even down to the deacons—

128. And this shall be the order of the house of the presidency of the school: He that is appointed to be president, or teacher, shall be found standing in his place, in the house which shall be prepared for him.

129. Therefore, he shall be first in the house of God, in a place that the congregation in the house may hear his words carefully and distinctly, not with loud speech.

130. And when he cometh into the house of God, for he should be first in the house—behold, this is beautiful, that he may be an example—

131. Let him offer himself in prayer upon his knees before God, in token or remembrance of the everlasting covenant.

132. And when any shall come in after him, let the teacher arise, and, with uplifted hands to heaven, yea, even directly, salute his brother or brethren with these words:

133. Art thou a brother or brethren? I salute you in the name of the Lord Jesus Christ, in token or remembrance of the everlasting covenant, in which covenant I receive you to fellowship, in a determination that is fixed, immovable, and unchangeable, to be your friend and brother through the grace of God in the bonds of love, to walk in all the commandments of God blameless, in thanksgiving, forever and ever. Amen.

134. And he that is found unworthy of this salutation shall not have place among you; for ye shall not suffer that mine house shall be polluted by him.

135. And he that cometh in and is faithful before me, and is a brother, or if they be brethren, they shall salute the president or teacher with uplifted hands to heaven, with this same prayer and covenant, or by saying Amen, in token of the same.

136. Behold, verily, I say unto you, this is an ensample unto you for a salutation to one another in the house of God, in the school of the prophets.

137. And ye are called to do this by prayer and thanksgiving, as the Spirit shall give utterance in all your doings in the house of the Lord, in the school of the prophets, that it may become a sanctuary, a tabernacle of the Holy Spirit to your edification.

138. And ye shall not receive any among you into this school save he is clean from the blood of this generation;

139. And he shall be received by the ordinance of the washing of feet, for unto this end was the ordinance of the washing of feet instituted.

140. And again, the ordinance of washing feet is to be administered by the president, or presiding elder of the church.

141. It is to be commenced with prayer; and after partaking of bread and wine, he is to gird himself according to the pattern given in the thirteenth chapter of John's testimony concerning me. Amen.

I wrote to N. E. Seaton, Esq.,* editor of the——. as follows:†

KIRTLAND, January 4th, 1833.

Mr. Editor:—Sir, Considering the liberal principles upon which your interesting and valuable paper is published, myself being a subscriber, and feeling a deep interest in the cause of Zion, and in the happiness of my brethren of mankind, I cheerfully take up my pen to contribute my mite at this very interesting and important period.

For some length of time I have been carefully reviewing the state of things, as it now appears, throughout our Christian land; and have looked at it with feelings of the most painful anxiety. While upon one hand I behold the manifest withdrawal of God's Holy Spirit, and the veil of stupidity which seems to be drawn over the hearts of the people; upon the other hand, I behold the judgments of God that have swept, and are still sweeping, hundreds and thousands of our race (and I fear unprepared) down to the shades of death. With this solemn and alarming fact before me, I am led to exclaim, "O that my head were

*This name is also spelled Sexton in the Ms. History. Mr. Seaton lived at Rochester, New York, and published a paper there, but the name of the paper cannot be ascertained.

†The Prophet states subsequently that he wrote this communication by commandment of the Lord. The general condition of the world as noted by the Prophet at the commencement of this chapter, was doubtless the occasion of the Lord sending forth such a note of warning to the inhabitants of the earth as is here presented. It should be said, however, in addition to what is here set down, i. e. at the beginning of the chapter—that the "plague," or Asiatic cholera, which first broke out in India, spread also throughout the United States in that same year. One historian, speaking of its ravages in the United States, says: "It was on the 21st of June, 1832, that the eastern plague, known as the Asiatic cholera, made its first appearance in the United States, in the city of New York. Its rapid spread produced universal panic, though it was less fatal in the South Atlantic States than in the north and in the valley of the Mississippi. Thousands of persons of all ages and conditions died of it within a few months. The most robust constitutions in many instances became victims of its malignancy within thirty-six hours from its first attack."—*History U. S.*, Stephens, p. 450.

waters, and mine eyes a fountain of tears, that I might weep day and night."

I think that it is high time for a Christian world to awake out of sleep, and cry mightily to that God, day and night, whose anger we have justly incurred. Are not these things a sufficient stimulant to arouse the faculties and call forth the energies of every man, woman or child that possesses feelings of sympathy for their fellows, or that is in any degree endeared to the budding cause of our glorious Lord? I leave an intelligent community to answer this important question, with a confession, that this is what has caused me to overlook my own inability, and expose my weakness to a learned world; but, trusting in that God who has said that these things are hid from the wise and prudent and revealed unto babes, I step forth into the field to tell you what the Lord is doing, and what you must do, to enjoy the smiles of your Savior in these last days.

The time has at last arrived when the God of Abraham, of Isaac, and of Jacob, has set His hand again the second time to recover the remnants of his people, which have been left from Assyria, and from Egypt, and from Pathros, and from Cush, and from Elam, and from Shinar, and from Hamath, and from the islands of the sea, and with them to bring in the fulness of the Gentiles, and establish that covenant with them, which was promised when their sins should be taken away. See Isaiah xi, Romans xi: 25, 26 and 27, and also Jeremiah xxxi: 31, 32 and 33. This covenant has never been established with the house of Israel, nor with the house of Judah, for it requires two parties to make a covenant, and those two parties must be agreed, or no covenant can be made.

Christ, in the days of His flesh, proposed to make a covenant with them, but they rejected Him and His proposals, and in consequence thereof, they were broken off, and no covenant was made with them at that time. But their unbelief has not rendered the promise of God of none effect: no, for there was another day limited in David, which was the day of His power; and then His people, Israel, should be a willing people;—and He would write His law in their hearts, and print it in their thoughts; their sins and their iniquities He would remember no more.

Thus after this chosen family had rejected Christ and His proposals, the heralds of salvation said to them, "Lo, we turn unto the Gentiles;" and the Gentiles received the covenant, and were grafted in from whence the chosen family were broken off: but the Gentiles have not continued in the goodness of God, but have departed from the faith that was once delivered to the Saints, and have broken the covenant in which their fathers were established (See Isaiah xxiv: 5); and have become high-minded, and have not feared; therefore, but few of them will be gathered with the chosen family. Have not the pride, high-mindedness, and unbelief of the Gentiles, provoked the Holy One of Israel to withdraw His Holy Spirit from them, and send forth His judgments to scourge them for their wickedness? This is certainly the case.

Christ said to His disciples (Mark xvi: 17 and 18), that these signs should follow them that believe:—"In my name shall they cast out devils; they shall speak with new tongues; they shall take up serpents; and if they drink any deadly thing it shall not hurt them; they shall lay hands on the sick, and they shall recover;" and also, in connection with this, read 1st Corinthians, 12th chapter. By the foregoing testimonies we may look at the Christian world and see the apostasy there has been from the apostolic platform; and who can look at this and not exclaim in the language of Isaiah, "The earth also is defiled under the inhabitants thereof; because they have transgressed the laws, changed the ordinances, and broken the everlasting covenant?"

The plain fact is this, the power of God begins to fall upon the nations, and the light of the latter-day glory begins to break forth through the dark atmosphere of sectarian wickedness, and their iniquity rolls up into view, and the nations of the Gentiles are like the waves of the sea, casting up mire and dirt, or all in commotion, and they are hastily preparing to act the part allotted them, when the Lord rebukes the nations, when He shall rule them with a rod of iron, and break them in pieces like a potter's vessel. The Lord declared to His servants, some eighteen months since, that He was then withdrawing His Spirit from the earth; and we can see that such is the fact, for not only the churches are dwindling away, but there are no conversions, or but very few: and this is not all, the governments of the earth are thrown into confusion and division; and *Destruction*, to the eye of the spiritual beholder, seems to be written by the finger of an invisible hand, in large capitals, upon almost every thing we behold.

And now what remains to be done, under circumstances like these? I will proceed to tell you what the Lord requires of all people, high and low, rich and poor, male and female, ministers and people, professors of religion and non-professors, in order that they may enjoy the Holy Spirit of God to a fulness and escape the judgments of God, which are almost ready to burst upon the nations of the earth. Repent of all your sins, and be baptized in water for the remission of them, in the name of the Father, and of the Son, and of the Holy Ghost, and receive the ordinance of the laying on of the hands of him who is ordained and sealed unto this power, that ye may receive the Holy Spirit of God; and this is according to the Holy Scriptures, and the Book of Mormon; and the only way that man can enter into the celestial kingdom. These are the requirements of the new covenant, or first principles of the Gospel of Christ; then "Add to your faith, virtue; and to virtue, knowledge; and to knowledge, temperance; and to temperance, patience; and to patience, godliness; and to godliness, brotherly kindness; and to brotherly kindness, charity [or love]; for if these things be in you, and abound, they make you that ye shall neither be barren nor unfruitful, in the knowledge of our Lord Jesus Christ."

The Book of Mormon is a record of the forefathers of our western tribes of Indians; having been found through the ministration of an holy angel, and translated into our own language by the gift and power of God, after having been hid up in the earth for the last fourteen hundred years, containing the word of God which was delivered unto them. By it we learn that our western tribes of Indians are descendants from that Joseph which was sold into Egypt, and that the land of America is a promised land unto them, and unto it all the tribes of Israel will come, with as many of the Gentiles as shall comply with the requisitions of the new covenant. But the tribe of Judah will return to old Jerusalem. The city of Zion spoken of by David, in the one hundred and second Psalm, will be built upon the land of America, "And the ransomed of the Lord shall return, and come to Zion with songs and everlasting joy upon their heads" (Isaiah xxxv: 10); and then they will be delivered from the overflowing scourge that shall pass through the land. But Judah shall obtain deliverance at Jerusalem. See Joel ii:32; Isaiah xxvi: 20 and 21; Jeremiah xxxi: 12; Psalm 1: 5; Ezekiel xxxiv: 11, 12 and 13. These are testimonies that the Good Shepherd will put forth His own sheep, and lead them out from all nations where they have been scattered in a cloudy and dark day, to Zion, and to Jerusalem; besides many more testimonies which might be brought.

And now I am prepared to say by the authority of Jesus Christ, that not many years shall pass away before the United States shall present such a scene of *bloodshed* as has not a parallel in the history of our nation; pestilence, hail, famine, and earthquake will sweep the wicked of this generation from off the face of the land, to open and prepare the way for the return of the lost tribes of Israel from the north country. The people of the Lord, those who have complied with the requirements of the new covenant, have already commenced gathering together to Zion, which is in the state of Missouri; therefore I declare unto you the warning which the Lord has commanded to declare unto this generation, remembering that the eyes of my Maker are upon me, and that to him I am accountable for every word I say, wishing nothing worse to my fellow-men than their eternal salvation; therefore, "Fear God, and give glory to Him, for the hour of His judgment is come." Repent ye, repent ye, and embrace the everlasting covenant, and flee to Zion, before the overflowing scourge overtake you, for there are those now living upon the earth whose eyes shall not be closed in death until they see all these things, which I have spoken, fulfilled. *Remember* these things; call upon the Lord while He is near, and seek Him while He may be found, is the exhortation of your unworthy servant.

[Signed] JOSEPH SMITH, JUN.

IMPORTANT CORRESPONDENCE WITH THE BRETHREN IN ZION

KIRTLAND, January 14, 1833.

Brother William W. Phelps:

I send you the "olive leaf" which we have plucked from the Tree of Paradise,* the Lord's message of peace to us; for though our brethren in Zion indulge in feelings towards us, which are not according to the requirements of the new covenant, yet, we have the satisfaction of knowing that the Lord approves of us, and has accepted us, and established His name in Kirtland for the salvation of the nations; for the Lord will have a place whence His word will go forth, in these last days, in purity; for if Zion will not purify herself, so as to be approved of in all things, in His sight, He will seek another people; for His work will go on until Israel is gathered, and they who will not hear His voice, must expect to feel His wrath. Let me say unto you, seek to purify yourselves, and also all the inhabitants of Zion, lest the Lord's anger be kindled to fierceness. Repent, repent, is the voice of God to Zion; and strange as it may appear, yet it is true, mankind will persist in self-justification until all their iniquity is exposed, and their character past being redeemed, and that which is treasured up in their hearts be exposed to the gaze of mankind. I say to you (and what I say to you I say to all,) hear the warning voice of God, lest Zion fall, and the Lord sware in His wrath the inhabitants of Zion shall not enter into His rest.

The brethren in Kirtland pray for you unceasingly, for, knowing the terrors of the Lord, they greatly fear for you. You will see that the Lord commanded us, in Kirtland, to build a house of God, and establish a school for the Prophets,† this is the word of the Lord to us, and we must, yea, the Lord helping us, we will obey: as on conditions of our obedience He has promised us great things; yea, even a visit from the heavens to honor us with His own presence. We greatly fear before the Lord lest we should fail of this great honor, which our

*This is the revelation beginning on p. 302, and section lxxxviii of the Doctrine and Covenants.

†See pp. 310, 311, verses 119-136.

Master proposes to confer on us; we are seeking for humility and great faith lest we be ashamed in His presence. Our hearts are greatly grieved at the spirit which is breathed both in your letter and that of Brother Gilbert's, the very spirit which is wasting the strength of Zion like a pestilence; and if it is not detected and driven from you, it will ripen Zion for the threatened judgments of God. Remember God sees the secret springs of human action, and knows the hearts of all living.

Brother, suffer us to speak plainly, for God has respect to the feelings of His Saints, and He will not suffer them to be tantalized with impunity. Tell Brother Gilbert that low insinuations God hates; but He rejoices in an honest heart, and knows better who is guilty than he does. We send him this warning voice, and let him fear greatly for himself, lest a worse thing overtake him; all we can say by way of conclusion is, if the fountain of our tears be not dried up, we will still weep for Zion. This from your brother who trembles for Zion, and for the wrath of heaven, which awaits her if she repent not.

[Signed] JOSEPH SMITH, JUN.

P. S.—I am not in the habit of crying peace, when there is no peace; and, knowing the threatened judgments of God, I say, Wo unto them who are at ease in Zion; fearfulness will speedily lay hold of the hypocrite. I did not suspect you had lost the commandments, but thought from your letters you had neglected to read them, otherwise you would not have written as you did.

It is in vain to try to hide a bad spirit from the eyes of them who are spiritual, for it will show itself in speaking and in writing, as well as in all our other conduct. It is also needless to make great pretensions when the heart is not right; the Lord will expose it to the view of His faithful Saints. We wish you to render the *Star* as interesting as possible, by setting forth the rise, progress, and faith of the Church, as well as the doctrine; for if you do not render it more interesting than at present, it will fall, and the Church suffer a great loss thereby.

[Signed] J. S. JUN.

KIRTLAND MILLS,* GEAUGA CO., OHIO,
January 14, 1833.

From a Conference of Twelve High Priests, to the Bishop, his Council and the Inhabitants of Zion.

Orson Hyde, and Hyrum Smith being appointed by the said confer-

*"Kirtland Mills" and "Kirtland" are identical. The name "Kirtland Mills" arose from the existence of some mills on the banks of the branch of the Chagrin river on which Kirtland is situated.

ence to write this epistle in obedience to the commandment, given the 22nd and 23rd of September last, which says: "But verily I say unto all those to whom the kingdom has been given—from you it must be preached unto them, that they shall repent of their former evil works: for they are to be upbraided for their evil hearts of unbelief, and your brethren in Zion for their rebellion against you at the time I sent you."*

Brother Joseph, and certain others, have written to you on this all-important subject, but you have never been apprised of these things by the united voice of the conference of those High Priests that were present at the time this commandment was given.

We therefore, Orson and Hyrum, the committee appointed by said conference to write this epistle, having received the prayers of said conference, that we might be enabled to write the mind and will of God upon this subject, now take up our pen to address you in the name of the conference, relying upon the arm of the Great Head of the Church.

In the commandment above alluded to, the children of Zion were all, yea, even every one, under condemnation, and were to remain in that state until they repented and remembered the new covenant, even the Book of Mormon, and the former commandments, which the Lord had given them, not only to say, but to do them, and bring forth fruit meet for the Father's kingdom; otherwise there remaineth a scourge and a judgment to be poured out upon the children of Zion: for "shall the children of the kingdom pollute my holy land? I say unto you, Nay."†

The answers received from those letters, which have been sent to you upon this subject, have failed to bring to us that satisfactory confession and acknowledgment, which the spirit of our Master requires. We, therefore, feeling a deep interest for Zion, and knowing the judgments of God that will come upon her except she repent, resort to these last, and most effectual means in our power, to bring her to a sense of her standing before the Most High.

At the time Joseph, Sidney, and Newel left Zion, all matters of hardness and misunderstanding were settled and buried (as they supposed), and you gave them the hand of fellowship; but, afterwards, you brought up all these things again, in a censorious spirit, accusing Brother Joseph in rather an indirect way of seeking after monarchial power and authority. This came to us in Brother Corrill's letter of June 2nd. We are sensible that this is not the thing Brother Joseph is seeking after, but to magnify the high office and calling whereunto he has been called and appointed by the command of God, and the united

*See p. 292, verse 76.

†See p. 291, verses 55-59.

voice of this Church. It might not be amiss for you to call to mind the circumstances of the Nephites, and the children of Israel rising up against their Prophets, and accusing them of seeking after kingly power, and see what befel them, and take warning before it is too late.

Brother Gilbert's letter of December 10th, has been received and read attentively, and the low, dark, and blind insinuations, which were in it, were not received by us as from the fountain of light, though his claims and pretensions to holiness were great. We are not unwilling to be chastened or rebuked for our faults, but we want to receive it in language that we can understand, as Nathan said to David, "Thou art the man." We are aware that Brother Gilbert is doing much, and has a multitude of business on hand; but let him purge out all the old leaven, and do his business in the spirit of the Lord, and then the Lord will bless him, otherwise the frown of the Lord will remain upon him. There is manifestly an uneasiness in Brother Gilbert, and a fearfulness that God will not provide for His Saints in these last days, and these fears lead him on to covetousness. This ought not so to be; but let him do just as the Lord has commanded him, and then the Lord will open His coffers, and his wants will be liberally supplied. But if this uneasy, covetous disposition be cherished by him, the Lord will bring him to poverty, shame, and disgrace.

Brother Phelps' letter of December 15th is also received and carefully read, and it betrays a lightness of spirit that ill becomes a man placed in the important and responsible station that he is placed in. If you have fat beef, and potatoes, eat them in singleness of heart, and boast not yourselves in these things. Think not, brethren, that we make a man an offender for a word; this is not the case; but we want to see a spirit in Zion, by which the Lord will build it up; that is the plain, solemn, and pure spirit of Christ. Brother Phelps requested in his last letter that Brother Joseph should come to Zion; but we say that Brother Joseph will not settle in Zion until she repent, and purify herself, and abide by the new covenant, and remember the commandments that have been given her, to do them as well as say them.

You may think it strange that we manifest no cheerfulness of heart upon the reception of your letters; you may think that our minds are prejudiced so much that we can see no good that comes from you, but rest assured, brethren, that this is not the case.

We have the best of feelings, and feelings of the greatest anxiety for the welfare of Zion: we feel more like weeping over Zion than we do like rejoicing over her, for we know that the judgments of God hang over her, and will fall upon her except she repent, and purify herself before the Lord, and put away from her every foul spirit. We now say to Zion, this once, in the name of the Lord, Repent! repent!

awake, awake, put on thy beautiful garments, before you are made to feel the chastening rod of Him whose anger is kindled against you. Let not Satan tempt you to think we want to make you bow to us, to domineer over you, for God knows this is not the case; our eyes are watered with tears, and our hearts are poured out to God in prayer for you, that He will spare you, and turn away His anger from you.

There are many things in the last letters from Brothers Gilbert and Phelps that are good, and we esteem them much. The idea of having "certain ones appointed to regulate Zion, and Traveling Elders have nothing to do with this part of the matter," is something we highly approbate, and you will doubtless know before this reaches you, why William E. M'Lellin opposed you in this move. We fear there was something in Brother Gilbert, when he returned to this place from New York last fall, in relation to his brother William, that was not right; for Brother Gilbert was asked two or three times about his brother William, but gave evasive answers, and at the same time, he knew that William was in Cleveland: but the Lord has taken him. We merely mention this, that all may take warning to work in the light, for God will bring every secret thing to light.

We now close our epistle by saying unto you, the Lord has commanded us to purify ourselves, to wash our hands and our feet, that He may testify to His Father and our Father, to His God and our God, that we are clean from the blood of this generation; and before we could wash our hands and our feet, we were constrained to write this letter. Therefore, with the feelings of inexpressible anxiety for your welfare, we say again, Repent, repent, or Zion must suffer, for the scourge and judgment must come upon her.

Let the Bishop read this to the Elders, that they may warn the members of the scourge that is coming, except they repent. Tell them to read the Book of Mormon, and obey it; read the commandments that are printed, and obey them; yea, humble yourselves under the mighty hand of God, that peradventure He may turn away His anger from you. Tell them that they have not come up to Zion to sit down in idleness, neglecting the things of God, but they are to be diligent and faithful in obeying the new covenant.

There is one clause in Brother Joseph's letter which you may not understand; that is this, "If the people of Zion did not repent, the Lord would seek another place, and another people." Zion is the place where the temple will be built, and the people gathered, but all people upon that holy land being under condemnation, the Lord will cut off, if they repent not, and bring another race upon it, that will serve Him. The Lord will seek another place to bring forth and prepare his word to go forth to the nations, and as we said before, so we say again.

Brother Joseph will not settle in Zion, except she repent, and serve God, and obey the new covenant. With this explanation, the conference sanctions Brother Joseph's letter.

Brethren, the conference meets again this evening to hear this letter read, and if it meet their minds, we have all agreed to kneel down before the Lord, and cry unto Him with all our hearts, that this epistle, and Brother Joseph's and the revelations also, may have their desired effect, and accomplish the thing whereunto they are sent, and that they may stimulate you to cleanse Zion, that she mourn not. Therefore when you get this, know ye that a conference of twelve High Priests have cried unto the Lord for you, and are still crying, saying, Spare thy people, O Lord, and give not thy heritage to reproach. We now feel that our garments are clean from you, and all men, when we have washed our feet and hands, according to the commandment.

We have written plainly at this time, but we believe not harshly. Plainness is what the Lord requires, and we should not feel ourselves clear, unless we had done so; and if the things we have told you be not attended to, you will not long have occasion to say, or to think rather, that we may be wrong in what we have stated. Your unworthy brethren are determined to pray unto the Lord for Zion, as long as we can shed the sympathetic tear, or feel any spirit to supplicate the throne of grace in her behalf.

The School of the Prophets will commence, if the Lord will, in two or three days. It is a general time of health with us. The cause of God seems to be rapidly advancing in the eastern country; the gifts are beginning to break forth so as to astonish the world, and even believers marvel at the power and goodness of God. Thanks be rendered to His holy name for what He is doing. We are your unworthy brethren in the Lord, and may the Lord help us all to do His will, that we may at last be saved in His kingdom.

ORSON HYDE,
HYRUM SMITH.

N. B.—We stated that Brother Gilbert, when he was in Kirtland, knew that William was in Cleveland last fall. We wrote this upon the strength of hearsay; but William being left at St. Louis, strengthened our suppositions that such was the fact. We stated further respecting this matter, or this item, than the testimony will warrant us. With this exception the conference sanctions this letter.

O. H.
H. S.

CHAPTER XXIII.

THE ENJOYMENT OF SPIRITUAL BLESSINGS IN THE CHURCH—THE WORD OF WISDOM.

The Enjoyment of Spiritual Gifts.

THIS winter [1832-33] was spent in translating the Scriptures; in the School of the Prophets; and sitting in conferences. I had many glorious seasons of refreshing. The gifts which follow them that believe and obey the Gospel, as tokens that the Lord is ever the same in His dealings with the humble lovers and followers of truth, began to be poured out among us, as in ancient days;—for as we, viz.: Joseph Smith, Jun., Sidney Rigdon, Frederick G. Williams, Newel K. Whitney, Hyrum Smith, Zebedee Coltrin,* Joseph Smith, Sen., Samuel H. Smith, John Murdock, Lyman E. Johnson,† Orson Hyde, Ezra Thayer, High Priests; and Levi Hancock,‡ and William Smith,§ Elders, were assem-

*Zebedee Coltrin was born at Ovid, Seneca county, New York, September 7, 1804. He was the son of John and Sarah Coltrin; and was baptized into the Church soon after its organization.

†Lyman E. Johnson was born in Pomfret, Windsor county, Vermont, October 24, 1811. He was baptized into the Church in February, 1831, by Sidney Rigdon, and was ordained an Elder under the hands of the Prophet Joseph Smith.

‡Levi Ward Hancock was born April 7, 1803, in Old Springfield, Hampden county, Massachusetts. He was the youngest son of Thomas Hancock and Amy Ward Hancock. When Levi was about two years old his family removed from Massachusetts to Ohio, settling in Chagrin, Cayahoga county, not far from Kirtland. Here Levi grew to manhood, occupied chiefly in farming with his father. In 1827, however he purchased a farm in Ashtabula county, which is in the extreme northeast part of Ohio. He was directly in the pathway of Elders Cowdery, Pratt, Whitmer and Peterson, when journeying westward on their mission to the Lamanites; and shortly after they passed through his neighborhood he followed them to Kirtland, where he was baptized on the 16th of November, 1830, by Elder Parley P. Pratt, and was soon afterwards ordained an Elder under the hands of Oliver Cowdery.

§William Smith was the fifth son of Joseph Smith, Sen., and Lucy Smith. He was born in Royalton, Windsor county, Vermont, March 13, 1811; and was baptized soon after the Church was organized.

bled in conference, on the 22nd day of January, I spoke to the conference in another tongue, and was followed in the same gift by Brother Zebedee Coltrin, and he by Brother William Smith, after which the Lord poured out His Spirit in a miraculous manner, until all the Elders spake in tongues, and several members, both male and female, exercised the same gift. Great and glorious were the divine manifestations of the Holy Spirit. Praises were sung to God and the Lamb; speaking and praying, all in tongues, occupied the conference until a late hour at night, so rejoiced were we at the return of these long absent blessings.

Ordinance of the Washing of Feet.

On the 23rd of January, we again assembled in conference; when, after much speaking, singing, praying, and praising God, all in tongues, we proceeded to the washing of feet (according to the practice recorded in the 13th chapter of John's Gospel), as commanded of the Lord. Each Elder washed his own feet first, after which I girded myself with a towel and washed the feet of all of them, wiping them with the towel with which I was girded. Among the number, my father presented himself, but before I washed his feet, I asked of him a father's blessing, which he granted by laying his hands upon my head, in the name of Jesus Christ, and declaring that I should continue in the Priest's office until Christ comes. At the close of the scene, Brother Frederick G. Williams, being moved upon by the Holy Ghost, washed my feet in token of his fixed determination to be with me in suffering, or in journeying, in life or in death, and to be continually on my right hand; in which I accepted him in the name of the Lord.

The Elders Pronounced Clean.

I then said to the Elders, As I have done so do ye; wash ye, therefore, one another's feet; and by the power of the Holy Ghost I pronounced them all clean from the blood of this generation; but if any of them should sin wilfully after they were thus cleansed, and sealed up unto eternal life, they should be given over unto the buffetings of

Satan until the day of redemption. Having continued all day in fasting, and prayer, and ordinances, we closed by partaking of the Lord's supper. I blessed the bread and wine in the name of the Lord, when we all ate and drank, and were filled; then we sang a hymn, and the meeting adjourned.

Revision of the New Testament Completed.

I completed the translation and review of the New Testament, on the 2nd of February, 1833 and sealed it up, no more to be opened till it arrived in Zion.*

AN EPISTLE

Of the First Presidency, to the Church of Christ in Thompson, Geauga County, Ohio.

KIRTLAND, February 6th, 1833.

Dear Brethren:

We salute you, by this our epistle, in the bonds of love, rejoicing in your steadfastness in the faith which is in Christ Jesus our Lord: and we desire your prosperity in the ways of truth and righteousness, praying for you continually, that your faith fail not, and that you may overcome all the evils with which you are surrounded, and become pure and holy before God, even our Father, to whom be glory for ever and ever. Amen.

It has seemed good unto the Holy Spirit and unto us, to send this our epistle to you by the hand of our beloved Brother Salmon Gee, your messenger, who has been ordained by us, in obedience to the commandments of God, to the office of Elder to preside over the

*It was the intention of the Prophet to have this revised version of the Scriptures, which he had made with such laborious care, published in Zion, at the printing establishment of the Church in that place, (New Testament and Book of Mormon to be published together; see p. 341), but before the work could even be commenced, the persecution arose which made the undertaking impracticable. And such was the unsettled state of the Church throughout the remaining years of the Prophet's life that he found no opportunity to publish the revised Scriptures, and to this day there is no authoritative publication of his translation of the Old and New Testaments given to the world, except in such excerpts as appear in the Pearl of Great Price. On this subject the late President George Q. Cannon, in his *Life of Joseph Smith*, remarks in a foot note (p. 142)—"We have heard President Brigham Young state that the Prophet, before his death, had spoken to him about going through the translation of the Scriptures again and perfecting it upon points of doctrine which the Lord had restrained him from giving in plainness and fulness at the time of which we write [2nd Feb., 1833]."

Church in Thompson, taking the oversight thereof, to lead you and to teach the things which are according to godliness; in whom we have great confidence, as we presume also you have, we therefore say to you, yea, not us only, but the Lord also, receive him as such, knowing that the Lord has appointed him to this office for your good, holding him up by your prayers, praying for him continually that he may be endowed with wisdom and understanding in the knowledge of the Lord, that through him you may be kept from evil spirits, and all strifes and dissensions, and grow in grace and in the knowledge of our Lord and Savior Jesus Christ.

Brethren beloved, continue in brotherly love, walk in meekness, watching unto prayer, that you be not overcome. Follow after peace, as said our beloved brother Paul, that you may be the children of our Heavenly Father, and not give occasion for stumbling, to Saint or sinner. Finally, brethren, pray for us, that we may be enabled to do the work whereunto we are called, that you may enjoy the mysteries of God, even a fulness; and may the grace of our Lord Jesus Christ be with you all. Amen.

JOSEPH SMITH, JUN.,
SIDNEY RIGDON,
FREDERICK G. WILLIAMS.

John Murdock's Message to the Thompson Branch.

The following letter was written by John Murdock, a High Priest, (who had previously been with the Church in Thompson), to Salmon Gee, Elder of the Church in Thompson:

KIRTLAND, February 11, 1833.

Beloved brethren and sisters in the Lord and Savior Jesus Christ, I beseech you in the bowels of mercy to remember the exhortation which I gave you while I was yet present with you, to beware of delusive spirits. I rejoice that our Heavenly Father hath blessed you greatly, as He also has me, in enabling me to speak the praises of God and the mysteries of the kingdom in other tongues according to promise: and this without throwing me down or wallowing me on the ground, or any thing unbecoming or immoral; also, without any external operation of the system, but it is the internal operation and power of the Spirit of God, so that I know that those odd actions and strange noises are not caused by the Spirit of the Lord as is represented by Brother King. Therefore in the name of the Lord Jesus Christ, by the Spirit of the living God, according to the authority of the Holy Priesthood committed to me, I command Brother Thomas King, (as though I were present), to cease from your diabolical acts of enthusiasm, and also from acting as an Elder in this Church of Christ, until you come and give full testimony to the High Priests in Kirtland, that you are worthy of that holy calling; because those are the things of God, and are to be used in the fear of God: and I now not only command you, but exhort you in behalf of your soul's salvation, to submit, and let Brother Gee be upheld by the prayer of faith of every brother and sister, and if there be this union of spirit, and prayer of faith, every false spirit shall be bound, and cast out from among you.

My beloved children in the bonds of the Gospel, and the bowels of mercy, which is the everlasting love of God, I do beseech you to live faithful and in obedience to the commandments of God; and in the name of the Lord Jesus, I say, the blessings of God shall attend you.

JOHN MURDOCK.

Concerning the Prophet's Communication to Seaton.

February 12.—Having received Seaton's paper, from Rochester, New York, containing a part of my communication, written on the 4th of January, I wrote as follows:

To N. E. Seaton, Rochester.

DEAR SIR:—I was somewhat disappointed on receiving my paper with only a part of my letter inserted in it. The letter which I wrote you for publication, I wrote by the commandment of God, and I am quite anxious to have it all laid before the public, for it is of importance to them: but I have no claim upon you, neither do I wish to urge you, beyond that which is reasonable, to do it. I have only to appeal to your extended generosity to all religious societies that claim that Christ has come in the flesh; and also to tell you what will be the consequence of a neglect to publish it.

Some parts of the letter were very severe upon the wickedness of sectarianism, I acknowledge; and the truth, remember, is hard and severe against all iniquity and wickedness, but this is no reason why it should not be published, but the very reason why it should be. I lay the ax at the root of the tree, and I long to see many of the sturdy oaks, which have long cumbered the ground, fall prostrate. I now say unto you, that if you wish to clear your garments from the blood of your readers, I exhort you to publish that letter entire; but if not, the sin be upon your head. Accept, sir, the good wishes and tender regard of your unworthy servant,

JOSEPH SMITH, JUN.

February 13.—A council of High Priests assembled to investigate the proceedings of Brother Burr Riggs, who was accused of failing to magnify his calling as High Priest, and had been guilty of neglect of duty, of abusing the Elders, and of treating their admonitions with contempt. After the council had considered the case, Brother Riggs agreed to make satisfaction, but did not show much humility.

Case of Burr Riggs.

February 15.—In a council I ordained Harpin Riggs, and Isaac McWethy, Elders.

February 17.—In conference I ordained John Johnson to the office of Elder.

February 26.—A special council of High Priests assembled in Zion, to take into consideration my letter to Brother Phelps, of the 11th of January, and the revelation called the Olive Leaf, referred to in my letter, and the epistle of Orson Hyde and Hyrum Smith of the 14th of January, in behalf of the conference of High Priests: and Oliver Cowdery, William W. Phelps, and John Corrill were appointed a committee to write an epistle from the conference to the brethren in Kirtland; which was written and sanctioned by the conference.

Consideration of Missouri Correspondence of the 11th and 12th of January.

The same day a conference of High Priests was again called in Kirtland, concerning Brother Burr Riggs, who was accused of neglecting to make satisfaction to the Church as he had agreed, and disgracing the High Priesthood by neglect of duty, and saying he did not care how soon he was cut off from the Church. He was cut off by a unanimous vote of the council.

Excommunication of Burr Riggs.

February 27.—I received the following revelation:

THE WORD OF WISDOM.*

1. A Word of Wisdom, for the benefit of the council of high priests, assembled in Kirtland, and the church, and also the saints in Zion—

*Doctrine and Covenants, sec. lxxxix.

2. To be sent greeting; not by commandment or constraint, but by revelation and the word of wisdom, showing forth the order and will of God in the temporal salvation of all saints in the last days—

3. Given for a principle with promise, adapted to the capacity of the weak and the weakest of all saints, who are or can be called saints.

4. Behold, verily, thus saith the Lord unto you: In consequence of evils and designs which do and will exist in the hearts of conspiring men in the last days, I have warned you, and forewarn you, by giving unto you this word of wisdom by revelation—

5. That inasmuch as any man drinketh wine or strong drink among you, behold it is not good, neither meet in the sight of your Father, only in assembling yourselves together to offer up your sacraments before him.

6. And, behold, this should be wine, yea, pure wine of the grape of the vine, of your own make.

7. And, again, strong drinks are not for the belly, but for the washing of your bodies.

8. And again, tobacco is not for the body, neither for the belly, and is not good for man, but is an herb for bruises and all sick cattle, to be used with judgment and skill.

9. And again, hot drinks are not for the body or belly.

10. And again, verily I say unto you, all wholesome herbs God hath ordained for the constitution, nature, and use of man—

11. Every herb in the season thereof, and every fruit in the season thereof; all these to be used with prudence and thanksgiving.

12. Yea, flesh also of beasts and of the fowls of the air, I, the Lord, have ordained for the use of man with thanksgiving; nevertheless they are to be used sparingly;

13. And it is pleasing unto me that they should not be used, only in times of winter, or of cold, or famine.

14. All grain is ordained for the use of man and of beasts, to be the staff of life, not only for man but for the beasts of the field, and the fowls of heaven, and all wild animals that run or creep on the earth;

15. And these hath God made for the use of man only in times of famine and excess of hunger.

16. All grain is good for the food of man; as also the fruit of the vine; that which yieldeth fruit, whether in the ground or above the ground—

17. Nevertheless, wheat for man, and corn for the ox, and oats for the horse, and rye for the fowls and for swine, and for all beasts

of the field, and barley for all useful animals, and for mild drinks, as also other grain.

18. And all saints who remember to keep and do these sayings, walking in obedience to the commandments, shall receive health in their naval and marrow to their bones;

19. And shall find wisdom and great treasures of knowledge, even hidden treasures;

20. And shall run and not be weary, and shall walk and not faint.

21. And I, the Lord, give unto them a promise, that the destroying angel shall pass by them, as the children of Israel, and not slay them. Amen.

A Word of Comfort to the Prophet

March 8.—I received the following revelation:

*Revelation.**

1. Thus saith the Lord, verily, verily I say unto you my son, thy sins are forgiven thee, according to thy petition, for thy prayers and the prayers of thy brethren have come up into my ears.

2. Therefore, thou art blessed from henceforth that bear the keys of the kingdom given unto you; which kingdom is coming forth for the last time.

3. Verily I say unto you, the keys of this kingdom shall never be taken from you, while thou art in the world, neither in the world to come;

4. Nevertheless, through you shall the oracles be given to another, yea, even unto the church.

5. And all they who receive the oracles of God, let them beware how they hold them lest they are accounted as a light thing, and are brought under condemnation thereby, and stumble and fall when the storms descend, and the winds blow, and the rains descend, and beat upon their house.

6. And again, verily I say unto thy brethren, Sidney Rigdon and Frederick G. Williams, their sins are forgiven them also, and they are accounted as equal with thee in holding the keys of this last kingdom;

7. As also through your administration the keys of the school of the prophets, which I have commanded to be organized;

8. That thereby they may be perfected in their ministry for the salvation of Zion, and of the nations of Israel, and of the Gentiles, as many as will believe;

*Doctrine and Covenants, sec. xc.

9. That through your administration they may receive the word, and through their administration the word may go forth unto the ends of the earth, unto the Gentiles first, and then, behold, and lo, they shall turn unto the Jews.

10. And then cometh the day when the arm of the Lord shall be revealed in power in convincing the nations, the heathen nations, the house of Joseph, of the gospel of their salvation.

11. For it shall come to pass in that day, that every man shall hear the fulness of the gospel in his own tongue, and in his own language, through those who are ordained unto this power, by the administration of the Comforter, shed forth upon them for the revelation of Jesus Christ.

12. And now, verily I say unto you, I give unto you a commandment that you continue in the ministry and presidency.

13. And when you have finished the translation of the prophets, you shall from thenceforth preside over the affairs of the church and the school;

14. And from time to time, as shall be manifested by the Comforter, receive revelations to unfold the mysteries of the kingdom;

15. And set in order the churches, and study and learn, and become acquainted with all good books, and with languages, tongues, and people.

16. And this shall be your business and mission in all your lives, to preside in council, and set in order all the affairs of this church and kingdom.

17. Be not ashamed, neither confounded; but be admonished in all your high-mindedness and pride, for it bringeth a snare upon your souls.

18. Set in order your houses; keep slothfulness and uncleanness far from you.

19. Now, verily I say unto you, let there be a place provided, as soon as it is possible, for the family of thy counselor and scribe, even Frederick G. Williams.

20. And let mine aged servant, Joseph Smith, Sen., continue with his family upon the place where he now lives; and let it not be sold until the mouth of the Lord shall name.

21. And let my counselor, even Sidney Rigdon, remain where he now resides until the mouth of the Lord shall name.

22. And let the bishop search diligently to obtain an agent, and let him be a man who has got riches in store—a man of God, and of strong faith—

23. That thereby he may be enabled to discharge every debt; that the storehouse of the Lord may not be brought into disrepute before the eyes of the people.

24. Search diligently, pray always, and be believing, and all things shall work together for your good, if ye walk uprightly and remember the covenant wherewith ye have covenanted one with another.

25. Let your families be small, especially mine aged servant Joseph Smith's, Sen., as pertaining to those who do not belong to your families;

26. That those things that are provided for you, to bring to pass my work, be not taken from you and given to those that are not worthy—

27. And thereby you be hindered in accomplishing those things which I have commanded you.

28. And again, verily I say unto you, it is my will that my handmaid Vienna Jaques should receive money to bear her expenses, and go up unto the land of Zion;

29. And the residue of the money may be consecrated unto me, and she be rewarded in mine own due time.

30. Verily I say unto you, that it is meet in mine eyes that she should go up unto the land of Zion, and receive an inheritance from the hand of the bishop;

31. That she may settle down in peace inasmuch as she is faithful, and not be idle in her days from thenceforth.

32. And behold, verily I say unto you, that ye shall write this commandment, and say unto your brethren in Zion, in love greeting, that I have called you also to preside over Zion in mine own due time.

33. Therefore, let them cease wearying me concerning this matter.

34. Behold, I say unto you that your brethren in Zion begin to repent, and the angels rejoice over them.

35. Nevertheless, I am not well pleased with many things; and I am not well pleased with my servant William E. M'Lellin, neither with my servant Sidney Gilbert; and the bishop also, and others have many things to repent of.

36. But verily I say unto you, that I, the Lord, will contend with Zion, and plead with her strong ones, and chasten her until she overcomes and is clean before me.

37. For she shall not be removed out of her place. I, the Lord, have spoken it. Amen.

The Apocrypha.

March 9.—Having come to that portion of the ancient writings called the Apocrypha, I received the following:

*Revelation.**

1. Verily, thus saith the Lord unto you concerning the Apocrypha

*Doctrine and Covenants, sec. xci.

—There are many things contained therein that are true, and it is mostly translated correctly;

2. There are many things contained therein that are not true, which are interpolations by the hands of men.

3. Verily, I say unto you, that it is not needful that the Apocrypha should be translated.

4. Therefore, whoso readeth it, let him understand, for the Spirit manifesteth truth;

5. And whoso is enlightened by the Spirit shall obtain benefit therefrom;

6. And whoso receiveth not by the Spirit, cannot be benefited. Therefore it is not needful that it should be translated. Amen.

A Mission to the East Appointed.

March 12.—A council of High Priests assembled in the school room and decided that Horace Cowin and Zerubbabel Snow, Amasa M. Lyman* and William F. Cahoon, Jenkins Salisbury and Truman Wait, journey east on a mission, two by

*Amasa Mason Lyman was born in the township of Lyman, Grafton county, New Hampshire, on the 30th of March, 1813. He was the third son of Boswell Lyman and Martha Mason. His father dying when Amasa was about eight years of age, and some time later his mother marrying again, he was reared in the home of his grandfather, on the maternal side, Perez Mason, until he was eleven years of age. Perez Mason then retired from his farm to live with his eldest son, Perley Mason; with whom also, according to the wishes of his mother, Amasa lived during the next seven years. When young Lyman was in his eighteenth year he became thoughtful on the subject of religion and earnestly sought the favor of the Lord by righteous deportment, though without connecting himself with any of the religious sects. About one year later Elders Orson Pratt and Lyman E. Johnson passed through the section of New Hampshire where young Lyman lived, on a preaching tour. He believed the message proclaimed by these new evangels and was baptized on the 27th of April, 1832, by Elder Lyman E. Johnson, and confirmed on the following day by Elder Orson Pratt. In consequence of the ill feelings which arose in his uncle's family, owing to his joining the Church, Amasa departed from the home of his kindred, and set out on foot for the gathering place of the Saints in Ohio. After a journey of some seven hundred miles, in which he endured many hardships—for much of the journey was made on foot and with but scant means of subsistence—he arrived at Hiram in Portage county, and engaged to work for Father Johnson at ten dollars a month. It was at this time that the Prophet was making his home at Father Johnson's, though on the arrival of young Lyman at Hiram he was absent in Missouri. About the first of July, however, Joseph returned from his western journey, and Amasa had the joy of meeting the Prophet of the new dispensation. Of that meeting and the impressions it produced, he says: "Of the impressions produced I will here say, although there was nothing strange or different from other men in his personal appearance, yet when he grasped my hand in that cordial way (known to those who have met him in the honest simplicity of truth), I felt as one of old in the presence of the Lord; my strength

two, paired as their names are written. Brothers Cowin and Salisbury were ordained at the same time.

March 15.—A council was called to consider the case of Brother Lake, from Wooster, Wayne county, Ohio, who came professing to have received revelations. On investigation, it was unanimously agreed, that said Brother Lake was under the influence of an evil spirit, and that his license as Priest be taken from him.

Case of Brother Lake.

The same day I received the following:

*Revelation to Enoch (Joseph Smith, Jun.,) given to the Saints in Kirtland.**

1. Verily, thus saith the Lord, I give unto the united order, organized agreeable to the commandment previously given, a revelation and commandment concerning my servant Shederlaomach [Frederick G. Williams], that ye shall receive him into the order. What I say unto one I say unto all.

2. And again, I say unto you my servant Shederlaomach [Frederick G. Williams], you shall be a lively member in this order; and inasmuch as you are faithful in keeping all former commandments you shall be blessed forever. Amen.

seemed to be gone, so that it required an effort on my part to stand on my feet; but in all this there was no fear, but the serenity and peace of heaven pervaded my soul, and the still small voice of the Spirit whispered its living testimony in the depths of my soul, where it has ever remained, that he was the man of God."—Autobiographical Sketch of Amasa M. Lyman, *Millennial Star*, vol. xxvii, p. 473.

*Doctrine and Covenants, sec. xcii.

CHAPTER XXIV.

KIRTLAND TO BE A STAKE OF ZION—REGULATION OF CHURCH AFFAIRS IN MISSOURI.

March 18.—Great joy and satisfaction continually beamed in the countenances of the School of the Prophets, and the Saints, on account of the things revealed, and our progress in the knowledge of God. The High Priests assembled in the school room of the Prophets, and were organized according to revelation; prayer by Sidney Rigdon.

The School of the Prophets.

"Doctor" Hurlburt was ordained an Elder; after which Elder Rigdon expressed a desire that himself and Brother Frederick G. Williams should be ordained to the offices to which they had been called, viz., those of Presidents of the High Priesthood, and to be equal in holding the keys of the kingdom with Brother Joseph Smith, Jun., according to the revelation given on the 8th of March, 1833. Accordingly I laid my hands on Brothers Sidney and Frederick, and ordained them to take part with me in holding the keys of this last kingdom, and to assist in the Presidency of the High Priesthood, as my Counselors; after which I exhorted the brethren to faithfulness and diligence in keeping the commandments of God, and gave much instruction for the benefit of the Saints, with a promise that the pure in heart should see a heavenly vision; and after remaining a short time in secret prayer, the promise was verified; for many present had the eyes of their understanding opened by the Spirit of God, so as to behold many things. I then

Rigdon and Williams Ordained Presidents.

blessed the bread and wine, and distributed a portion to each. Many of the brethren saw a heavenly vision of the Savior, and concourses of angels, and many other things, of which each one has a record of what he saw.

Kirtland a Stake of Zion.

March 23.—A council was called for the purpose of appointing a committee to purchase land in Kirtland, upon which the Saints might build a Stake of Zion. Brother Joseph Coe and Moses Dailey were appointed to ascertain the terms of sale of certain farms; and Brother Ezra Thayre to ascertain the price of Peter French's farm. The brethren agreed to continue in prayer and fasting for the ultimate success of their mission. After an absence of about three hours Brothers Coe and Dailey returned and reported that Elijah Smith's farm could be obtained for four thousand dollars; and Mr. Morley's for twenty-one hundred; and Brother Thayre reported that Peter French would sell his farm for five thousand dollars. The council decided to purchase the farms, and appointed Ezra Thayre and Joseph Coe to superintend the purchase; and they were ordained under the hands of Sidney Rigdon, and set apart as general agents of the Church for that purpose.

Matters Relating to Church Government in Zion Settled.

On the 26th of March a council of High Priests, twenty-one in number, convened for the general welfare of the Church, in what was then called Zion, in Jackson county, Missouri. On account of a revelation, my letter, and an epistle from the Church in Kirtland, a solemn assembly had been called, and a sincere and humble repentance manifested, insomuch that on the 26th of February, one month previous, a general epistle had been written in conference, which was satisfactory to the Presidency and Church at Kirtland. At the sitting of the council of the 26th of March, according to the plan taught at the solemn assembly, which was, that the seven High Priests who were sent from Kirtland to build up Zion, viz.—Oliver Cowdery, W. W.

Phelps, John Whitmer, Algeron Sidney Gilbert, Bishop Partridge and his two counselors—should stand at the head of affairs relating to the Church, in that section of the Lord's vineyard; and these seven men, with the common consent of the branches comprising the Church were to appoint presiding Elders, to take the watch-care of the several branches, as they were appointed: Now, therefore, as many of the High Priests and Elders —whose calling was to travel and preach to the world —went up to Zion, and commenced regulating and setting the branches in order, and claiming for themselves as much power by the authority of their Priesthood, and gift of the Holy Ghost, as those set apart and appointed to preside over the branches, it became necessary to call the council now spoken of, to set in order the Elders of Israel. After a long discussion, it was decided from the revelations, that the order taught in the solemn assembly was correct; and that the Elders, when they arrived at Zion, were bound by the authorities set in the Church, to be submissive to the powers that be; their labors and calling being more particularly to push the people together from the ends of the earth to the places the Lord had appointed. This decision in council gave general satisfaction, and the Elders soon saw the beauty of every man standing in his place.

Purchase of the French Farm.

April 2.—F. G. Williams was appointed by a council of High Priests, an agent to superintend and employ men to labor in the brick-yard on the French farm, also to rent the farm. The French farm was purchased on account of the facilities found there for making brick, which was essential to the building up of the city. The council also instructed Brother Ezra Thayre to purchase the tannery of Arnold Mason, in Kirtland.

Conference in Zion.

On the 6th of April, in the land of Zion, about eighty officials, together with some unofficial members of the Church, met for instruction and the service of God, at the Ferry on Big Blue river near the western limits of Jackson county, which is the boundary line of the state of Missouri and also of the United States. It was an early spring, and the leaves and blossoms enlivened and gratified the soul of man like a glimpse of Paradise. The day was spent in a very agreeable manner, in giving and receiving knowledge which appertained to this last kingdom—it being just 1800 years since the Savior laid down His life that men might have everlasting life, and only three years since the Church had come out of the wilderness, preparatory for the last dispensation. The Saints had great reason to rejoice: they thought upon the time when this world came into existence, and the morning stars sang together, and all the sons of God shouted for joy; they thought of the time when Israel ate the "Passover," as wailing came up for the loss of the first-born of Egypt; they felt like the shepherds who watched their flocks by night, when the angelic choir sweetly sang the electrifying strain, *"Peace on earth, good will to man;"* and the solemnities of eternity rested upon them. This was the first attempt made by the Church to celebrate the anniversary of her birthday, and those who professed not our faith talked about it as a strange thing.

The State of the World.

While the Church was thus rejoicing, the news from abroad was, that 30,000 out of a population of 100,000 had died of starvation, in consequence of the famine produced by three year's drouth, followed by a flood, in the Cape Verde Islands; that sixteen shocks of earthquake had been felt the previous February, at St. Kitts and Nevis, in the West Indian Islands; that the Polish Jews were about to visit Jerusalem; that war was raging between Turkey and Egypt; that a great fire had occurred in Liverpool; that volcanic eruptions, wars and rumors of wars, were prevailing in different sections of the earth, and fire-balls and fearful signs were seen in the heavens, with many other alarming appearances, which caused the hearts of the wicked to tremble, none of which was more awful than the continued spread of the Asiatic cholera in Europe, which had already swept from the earth, in the short space of fifteen years, about sixty millions of inhabitants.*

Brother Jared Carter presented me a letter, which he had received from his brother, and requested me to answer it, which I did as follows:

KIRTLAND, April 13, 1833.

Dear Brother Carter:—Your letter to Brother Jared is just put into my hand, and I have carefully perused its contents, and embrace this opportunity to answer it. We proceed to answer your questions: first concerning your labor in the region where you live; we acquiesce in your feelings on this subject until the mouth of the Lord shall name. Respecting the vision you speak of we do not consider ourselves bound to receive any revelation from any one man or woman without his being legally constituted and ordained to that authority, and giving sufficient proof of it.

I will inform you that it is contrary to the economy of God for any member of the Church, or any one, to receive instructions for those in authority, higher than themselves; therefore you will see the impropriety of giving heed to them; but if any person have a vision or a visitation from a heavenly messenger, it must be for his own benefit and instruction; for the fundamental principles, government, and doctrine of the Church are vested in the keys of the kingdom. Respecting an apostate, or one who has been cut off from the Church, and who wishes to come in again, the law of our Church expressly says that such shall repent, and be baptized, and be admitted as at the first.

The duty of a High Priest is to administer in spiritual and holy things, and to hold communion with God; but not to exercise monarchial government, or to appoint meetings for the Elders without their consent. And again, it is the High Priests' duty to be better qualified to teach principles and doctrines, than the Elders; for the office of Elder is an appendage to the High Priesthood, and it concentrates and centers in one. And again, the process of laboring with members: We are to deal with them precisely as the Scriptures direct. If thy brother trespass against thee, take him between him and thee alone; and, if he make thee satisfaction, thou hast saved thy brother; and if not, proceed to take another with thee, etc., and when there is no

*The above on the state of the world is condensed from the *Evening and Morning Star* for April, 1833.

Bishop, they are to be tried by the voice of the Church; and if an Elder, or a High Priest be present, he is to take the lead in managing the business; but if not, such as have the highest authority should preside.

With respect to preparing to go to Zion:—First it would be pleasing to the Lord that the church or churches going to Zion should be organized, and a suitable person appointed who is well acquainted with the condition of the church, and he be sent to Kirtland to inform the Bishop, and procure a license from him agreeable to the revelation: by so doing you will prevent confusion and disorder, and escape many difficulties that attend an unorganized band in journeying in the last days.

And again, those in debt, should in all cases pay their debts; and the rich are in no wise to cast out the poor, or leave them behind, for it is said that the poor shall inherit the earth.

You quoted a passage in Jeremiah, with regard to journeying to Zion; the word of the Lord stands sure, so let it be done.

There are two paragraphs in your letter which I do not commend, as they were written blindly. Speaking of the Elders being sent like lightning from the bow of Judah; the second, no secrets in the councils of Zion. You mention these as if fear rested upon your mind, otherwise we cannot understand it. And again we never inquire at the hand of God for special revelation only in case of there being no previous revelation to suit the case; and that in a council of High Priests.

For further information on the subject about which you have written, I will refer you to the Elders who have recently left here for the east, by commandment, some of whom you will probably see soon. You may depend on any information you may receive from them that are faithful. You may expect to see Brothers Orson Pratt and Lyman E. Johnson for whom we have great fellowship.

It is a great thing to inquire at the hands of God, or to come into His presence; and we feel fearful to approach Him on subjects that are of little or no consequence, to satisfy the queries of individuals, especially about things the knowledge of which men ought to obtain in all sincerity, before God, for themselves, in humility by the prayer of faith; and more especially a Teacher or a High Priest in the Church. I speak these things not by way of reproach, but by way of instruction; and I speak as if acquainted with you, whereas we are strangers to each other in the flesh.

I love your soul, and the souls of the children of men, and pray and do all I can for the salvation of all.

I now close by sending you a salutation of peace in the name of the Lord Jesus Christ. Amen.

The blessing of our Lord Jesus Christ be and abide with you all. Amen. JOSEPH SMITH, JUN.

P. S.—If it be convenient to send a delegate to Kirtland, to procure license for the brethren to go to Zion, it can be done by two or more Elders. We have received two letters from Brother Sherwood, stating the order and condition of the Church, and respecting the vision of his wife, but on account of a multitude of business they have not been answered by us; you will please read this letter to Brother Sherwood. J. S.

In April the School of the Prophets closed to commence again in the fall.

A LETTER TO THE BRETHREN IN ZION.

KIRTLAND, April 21, 1833.

Dear Brethren in Zion:

Agreeable to a notice we gave you, in Brother Whitney's last letter to you with respect to answering your letters, we now commence, after giving thanks to our Heavenly Father for every expression of His goodness in preserving our unprofitable lives to the present time, and for the health and other blessings which we now enjoy through His mercies.

With joy we received your general epistle, written the 26th of February, which contained the confession of our brethren concerned, all of which was to our entire satisfaction.

It was read by the brethren in Kirtland with feelings of the deepest interest, knowing as we did, that the anger of the Lord was kindled against you, and nothing but repentance, of the greatest humility, would turn it away; and I will assure you that expressions of joy beamed on every countenance when they saw that our epistle and the revelation had been received by our brethren in Zion, and had had the desired effect.

For your satisfaction, I here insert a revelation given to Shederlaomach [Frederick G. Williams], the 15th of March, 1833, constituting him a member of the United Firm.*

With respect to Brother Gilbert's letter of the 10th of December, I would say to him: firstly, he wrote it in all sincerity of heart, and we were pleased with the style, and composition; but upon mature reflection, and inquiry at the hands of the Lord, we find some things that are unreconcilable, especially to some; I mean with respect to hints given that are not clearly explained.

As every letter that comes from Zion must go the rounds of the

*Here follows the revelations on page 333.

brethren for inspection, it is necessary that there should be no disguise in them, but that every subject written upon by the brethren should be plain to the understanding of all, that no jealousy may be raised, and when we rebuke, do it in all meekness. The letter written the 24th of February was not written in that contrition of heart in which it should have been, for it appears to have been written in too much of a spirit of justification; but the letter to Brother Whitney of the 20th of March, was written to our entire satisfaction.

Now I would say to Brother Gilbert, that I do not write this by way of chastisement, but to show him the absolute necessity of having all his communications written in a manner to be clearly understood. We are well aware of the great care upon his mind, in consequence of much business, but he must put his trust in God, and he may rest assured that he has our prayers day and night, that he may have strength to overcome every difficulty. We have learned of the Lord that it is his duty to assist all the poor brethren that are pure in heart, and that he has done wrong in withholding credit from them, as they must have assistance; and the Lord established him in Zion for that express purpose.

It is not the will of the Lord to print any of the New Translation in the *Star;* but when it is published, it will all go to the world together, in a volume by itself; and the New Testament and the Book of Mormon will be printed together.

With respect to Brother Oliver's private letter to me on the subject of giving deeds, and receiving contributions from brethren, I have nothing further to say on the subject than to recommend that you make yourselves acquainted with the commandments of the Lord, and the laws of the state, and govern yourselves accordingly. Brother Elliot was here yesterday and showed me a letter from Brother Phelps, and we were well pleased with the spirit in which it was written. The probability is that he [Elliot] will not go to Zion at present, as he has bought [lands] in Chagrin.

We rejoice to hear that the Seminary lands are reduced in price, and are coming into market; and be assured that we shall use our influence to send brethren to Zion who are able to help you in the purchase of lands.

We have just received a letter from Brother Sidney, he has built up a church of eight members, in Medina county, Ohio, and has prospects of more. With respect to the deaths in Zion, we feel to mourn with those that mourn, but remember that the God of all the earth will do right. And now, my beloved brethren, I commend you to God and His grace, praying Him to keep and preserve you blameless, of the coming of our Lord Jesus Christ. Amen.

JOSEPH SMITH, JUN.

P. S.—Say to Brother Corrill that his confession gave me great satisfaction, and all things are now settled on my part.

J. S.

First Assembling of the Mob in Zion.

In the month of April, the first regular mob rushed together, in Independence, to consult upon a plan, for the removal, or immediate destruction, of the Church in Jackson county. The number of the mob was about three hundred. A few of the first Elders met in secret, and prayed to Him who said to the wind, "Be still," to frustrate them in their wicked designs. The mob, therefore, after spending the day in a fruitless endeavor to unite upon a general scheme for "moving the Mormons out of their diggings" (as they asserted), became a little the worse for liquor and broke up in a regular Missouri "row," showing a determined resolution that every man would "carry his own head."

Conference of High Priests in Kirtland.

April 30.—A conference of High Priests assembled at the school room, in Kirtland, and appointed Brother Albert Brown a committee to circulate a subscription, to procure money to pay for the use of the house where meetings had been held the past season. John P. Greene was instructed to go and take charge of the branch of the Church in Parkham county, carrying with him an epistle to the brethren; and as soon as convenient he was to remove his family to that place. It was also decided that Sister Vienna Jaques should not proceed immediately on her journey to Zion, but wait until William Hobert was ready, and go in company with him.

Another Conference of High Priests.

May 4.—A conference of High Priests assembled in Kirtland, to take into consideration the necessity of building a school house, for the accommodation of the Elders, who should come together to receive instruction preparatory for their missions, and ministry, according to a revelation on that subject, given March 8, 1833,* and by unanimous voice of the conference; Hyrum Smith, Jared

*See p. 329.

Carter, and Reynolds Cahoon were appointed a committee to obtain subscriptions, for the purpose of erecting such a building.

A council had previously been held in Norton Township, Medina county, Ohio, at which Sidney Rigdon presided. The council took into consideration the standing of Baldwin Welton, Aaron Smith, and——Hays, Elders; and James Braden, Priest; and decided that their ordinations were illegal, and that the churches should not receive them in their several offices. The doings of the council were reviewed, and sanctioned by the First Presidency, viz: Joseph Smith, Jun., Sidney Rigdon, Frederick G. Williams, and entered on record in Kirtland.

Council Proceedings Approved.

May 6.—I received the following:

*Revelation.**

1. Verily, thus saith the Lord: It shall come to pass that every soul who forsaketh his sins and cometh unto me, and calleth on my name, and obeyeth my voice, and keepeth my commandments, shall see my face and know that I am:

2. And that I am the true light that lighteth every man that cometh into the world;

3. And that I am in the Father, and the Father in me, and the Father and I are one—

4. The Father because he gave me of his fulness, and the Son because I was in the world and made flesh my tabernacle, and dwelt among the sons of men.

5. I was in the world and received of my Father, and the works of him were plainly manifest.

6. And John saw and bore record of the fulness of my glory, and the fulness of John's record is hereafter to be revealed.

7. And he bore record, saying: I saw his glory, that he was in the beginning, before the world was;

8. Therefore, in the beginning the Word was, for he was the Word, even the messenger of salvation—

9. The light and the Redeemer of the world; the Spirit of truth, who came into the world, because the world was made by him, and in him was the life of men and the light of men.

*Doctrine and Covenants, sec. xciii.

10. The worlds were made by him; men were made by him; all things were made by him, and through him, and of him.

11. And I, John, bear record that I beheld his glory, as the glory of the Only Begotten of the Father, full of grace and truth, even the Spirit of truth, which came and dwelt in the flesh, and dwelt among us.

12. And I, John, saw that he received not of the fulness at the first, but received grace for grace;

13. And he received not of the fulness at first, but continued from grace to grace, until he received a fulness;

14. And thus he was called the Son of God, because he received not of the fulness at the first.

15. And I, John, bear record, and lo, the heavens were opened, and the Holy Ghost descended upon him in the form of a dove, and sat upon him, and there came a voice out of heaven saying: This is my beloved Son.

16. And I, John, bear record that he received a fulness of the glory of the Father;

17. And he received all power, both in heaven and on earth, and the glory of the Father was with him, for he dwelt in him.

18. And it shall come to pass, that if you are faithful you shall receive the fulness of the record of John.

19. I give unto you these sayings that you may understand and know how to worship, and know what you worship, that you may come unto the Father in my name, and in due time receive of his fulness.

20. For if you keep my commandments you shall receive of his fulness, and be glorified in me as I am in the Father; therefore, I say unto you, you shall receive grace for grace.

21. And now, verily I say unto you, I was in the beginning with the Father, and am the Firstborn;

22. And all those who are begotten through me are partakers of the glory of the same, and are the church of the Firstborn.

23. Ye were also in the beginning with the Father; that which is Spirit, even the Spirit of truth;

24. And truth is knowledge of things as they are, and as they were, and as they are to come;

25. And whatsoever is more or less than this is the spirit of that wicked one who was a liar from the beginning.

26. The Spirit of truth is of God. I am the Spirit of truth, and John bore record of me, saying: He received a fulness of truth, yea, even of all truth;

27. And no man receiveth a fulness unless he keepeth his commandments.

28. He that keepeth his commandments receiveth truth and light, until he is glorified in truth and knoweth all things.

29. Man was also in the beginning with God. Intelligence, or the light of truth, was not created or made, neither indeed can be.

30. All truth is independent in that sphere in which God has placed it, to act for itself, as all intelligence also; otherwise there is no existence.

31. Behold, here is the agency of man, and here is the condemnation of man; because that which was from the beginning is plainly manifest unto them, and they receive not the light.

32. And every man whose spirit receiveth not the light is under condemnation.

33. For man is spirit. The elements are eternal, and spirit and element, inseparably connected, receive a fulness of joy;

34. And when separated, man cannot receive a fulness of joy.

35. The elements are the tabernacle of God; yea, man is the tabernacle of God, even temples; and whatsoever temple is defiled, God shall destroy that temple.

36. The glory of God is intelligence, or, in other words, light and truth.

37. Light and truth forsake that evil one.

38. Every spirit of man was innocent in the beginning; and God having redeemed man from the fall, men became again, in their infant state, innocent before God.

39. And that wicked one cometh and taketh away light and truth, through disobedience, from the children of men, and because of the tradition of their fathers.

40. But I have commanded you to bring up your children in light and truth.

41. But verily I say unto you, my servant Frederick G. Williams, you have continued under this condemnation;

42. You have not taught your children light and truth, according to the commandments; and that wicked one hath power, as yet, over you, and this is the cause of your affliction.

43. And now a commandment I give unto you—if you will be delivered you shall set in order your own house, for there are many things that are not right in your house.

44. Verily, I say unto my servant Sidney Rigdon, that in some things he hath not kept the commandments concerning his children; therefore, first set in order thy house.

45. Verily, I say unto my servant Joseph Smith, Jun., or in other words, I will call you friends, for you are my friends, and ye shall have an inheritance with me—

46. I called you servants for the world's sake, and ye are their servants for my sake—

47. And now, verily I say unto Joseph Smith, Jun.—You have not kept the commandments, and must needs stand rebuked before the Lord;

48. Your family must needs repent and forsake some things, and give more earnest heed unto your sayings, or be removed out of their place.

49. What I say unto one I say unto all; pray always lest that wicked one have power in you, and remove you out of your place.

50. My servvant Newel K. Whitney also, a bishop of my church, hath need to be chastened, and set in order his family, and see that they are more diligent and concerned at home, and pray always, or they shall be removed out of their place.

51. Now, I say unto you, my friends, let my servant Sidney Rigdon go on his journey, and make haste, and also proclaim the acceptable year of the Lord, and the gospel of salvation, as I shall give him utterance; and by your prayer of faith with one consent I will uphold him.

52. And let my servants Joseph Smith, Jun., and Frederick G. Williams make haste also, and it shall be given them even according to the prayer of faith; and inasmuch as you keep my sayings you shall not be confounded in this world, nor in the world to come.

53. And, verily I say unto you, that it is my will that you should hasten to translate my scriptures, and to obtain a knowledge of history, and of countries, and of kingdoms, of laws of God and man, and all this for the salvation of Zion. Amen.

The same date (May 6th) I received the following:

*Revelation.**

1. And again, verily I say unto you, my friends, a commandment I give unto you, that ye shall commence a work of laying out and preparing a beginning and foundation of the city of the stake of Zion, here in the land of Kirtland, beginning at my house.

2. And behold, it must be done according to the pattern which I have given unto you.

3. And let the first lot on the south be consecrated unto me for the building of a house for the presidency, for the work of the presidency, in obtaining revelations; and for the work of the ministry of the presidency, in all things pertaining to the church and kingdom.

4. Verily I say unto you, that it shall be built fifty-five by sixty-five feet in the width thereof and in the length thereof, in the inner court.

5. And there shall be a lower court and a higher court, according to the pattern which shall be given unto you hereafter.

*Doctrine and Covenants, sec. xciv.

6. And it shall be dedicated unto the Lord from the foundation thereof, according to the order of the priesthood, according to the pattern which shall be given unto you hereafter.

7. And it shall be wholly dedicated unto the Lord for the work of the presidency.

8. And ye shall not suffer any unclean thing to come in unto it; and my glory shall be there, and my presence shall be there.

9. But if there shall come into it any unclean thing, my glory shall not be there; and my presence shall not come into it.

10. And again, verily I say unto you, the second lot on the south shall be dedicated unto me for the building of a house unto me, for the work of the printing of the translation of my scriptures, and all things whatsoever I shall command you.

11. And it shall be fifty-five by sixty-five feet in the width thereof and the length thereof, in the inner court; and there shall be a lower and a higher court.

12. And this house shall be wholly dedicated unto the Lord from the foundation thereof, for the work of the printing, in all things whatsoever I shall command you, to be holy, undefiled, according to the pattern in all things as it shall be given unto you.

13. And on the third lot shall my servant Hyrum Smith receive his inheritance.

14. And on the first and second lots on the north shall my servants Reynolds Cahoon and Jared Carter receive their inheritances—

15. That they may do the work which I have appointed unto them, to be a committee to build mine houses, according to the commandment, which I, the Lord God, have given unto you.

16. These two houses are not to be built until I give unto you a commandment concerning them.

17. And now I give unto you no more at this time. Amen.

Signs of the Times.

The signs of the times continued to attract the attention of the world. The cholera had broken out at Havana, and it was reported that five hundred were perishing daily, and Oporto, in the province of Entre-Minho-e-Douro, Portugal, was experiencing the same calamity. The influenza was raging at St. Petersburg, Russia; more than one hundred thousand were suffering from its effects, and it was reported to be more violent at Moscow. So dreadful were the effects of the cholera. which spread consternation among the inhabitants of the earth, that it was reported that the eyes of some of the afflicted burst from their sockets.

Removal of Indians.

A treaty was entered into about this time with several tribes of Indians, some to be located on the east of Winnebago lake, and others to be removed west of the Mississippi.*

Arrival of the Prophet's Relatives in Kirtland.

May 25.—My uncle, John Smith and family arrived in Kirtland, from Potsdam, New York, my uncle being an Elder in the Church; and his wife and eldest son, George Albert Smith, a lad of fifteen, were members. They were the first of my father's relatives who obeyed the Gospel.†

*The above items of plagues and removal of Indians are from the *Evening and Morning Star,* for May, 1833.

†For an account of their conversation to the Gospel see page 285.

CHAPTER XXV.

PREPARATION FOR BUILDING THE KIRTLAND TEMPLE—TRIAL AND EXCUMMUNICATION OF "DOCTOR" PHILASTUS HURLBURT.

June 1.—Great preparations were making to commence a house of the Lord; and notwithstanding the Church was poor, yet our unity, harmony and charity abounded to strengthen us to do the commandments of God. The building of the house of the Lord in Kirtland was a matter that continued to increase in its interest in the hearts of the brethren, and the building committee issued the following circular to the different branches of the Church:

The House of the Lord at Kirtland.

CIRCULAR.

KIRTLAND, June 1, 1833.

To the Church of Christ in————

We feel under obligations to write to you as well as to all the brethren of the different branches; and we do this, that you, with us, may exert yourselves to bring about the fulfilment of the command of the Lord concerning the establishing, or preparing a house, wherein the Elders who have been commanded of the Lord so to do, may gather themselves together, and prepare all things, and call a solemn assembly, and treasure up words of wisdom, that they may go forth to the Gentiles for the last time; and now, in order to accomplish this, we are directed, yea, we are under the necessity, to call upon the whole Church as a body, that they make every possible exertion to aid temporally, as well as spiritually, in this great work that the Lord is beginning, and is about to accomplish. And unless we fulfil this command, viz: establish an house, and prepare all things necessary whereby the elders may gather into a school, called the School of the Prophets, and receive that instruction which the Lord designs they should receive, we may all despair of obtaining the great blessing that God has promised to the faithful of the Church of Christ; therefore it is as important, as our salvation, that we obey this above-mentioned command, as well as all the commandments of the Lord.

Therefore, brethren, we write this epistle to you, to stir up your minds to make that exertion which the Lord requires of you, to lend a temporal aid in these things above written; and in order that you may know how to conduct the business, we will relate what we have done and are doing here.

We have met in conference, and agreed to form a subscription, and circulate it through the churches. The conference also appointed Hyrum Smith, Reynolds Cahoon, and Jared Carter, a committee to superintend this business, viz: that of circulating subscriptions to establish a fund to build a house, and to aid the Elders to attend this school. The subscriptions are now in circulation among us, and our Heavenly Father is opening the hearts of our brethren beyond the expectation of many; and not one brother among us, as yet, refuses to exert himself to do something in a temporal way to bring about the establishing of this house and school; and we say, may our Heavenly Father open your hearts also, that you, with us, may gather together something to aid as a temporal benefit.

Probably you had better call the officers of the Church immediately together, and appoint someone to circulate a subscription that each individual, after signing, may have a sufficient time to make preparations to pay what he subscribes; for it will be necessary, wherever the brethren are at a distance from Kirtland, that they exert themselves to send on their gift or assistance as soon as they can to Kirtland; though-they can, if they believe best, wait on those that sign until the first of September, and then collect and send it to Kirtland.

These considerations we have written to you, knowing it to be our duty thus to do, and may the Lord help you to exert yourselves with us, in raising the means to bring about the glorious work of the Lord; and may we all be kept by the grace of God unto eternal life. Amen.

HYRUM SMITH,
REYNOLDS CAHOON,
JARED CARTER,
Committee.

The same day [June 1st] I received the following:

*Revelation.**

1. Verily, thus saith the Lord unto you whom I love, and whom

*Doctrine and Covenants, sec. xcv.

I love I also chasten that their sins may be forgiven, for with the chastisement I prepare a way for their deliverance in all things out of temptation, and I have loved you—

2. Wherefore, ye must needs be chastened and stand rebuked before my face;

3. For ye have sinned against me a very grievous sin, in that ye have not considered the great commandment in all things, that I have given unto you concerning the building of mine house;

4. For the preparation wherewith I design to prepare mine apostles to prune my vineyard for the last time, that I may bring to pass my strange act, that I may pour out my Spirit upon all flesh—

5. But behold, verily I say unto you, that there are many who have been ordained among you, whom I have called but few of them are chosen.

6. They who are not chosen have sinned a very grievous sin, in that they are walking in darkness at noon-day.

7. And for this cause I gave unto you a commandment that you should call your solemn assembly, that your fastings and your mourning might come up into the ears of the Lord of Sabaoth, which is by interpretation, the creator of the first day, the beginning and the end.

8. Yea, verily I say unto you, I gave unto you a commandment that you should build a house, in the which house I design to endow those whom I have chosen with power from on high;

9. For this is the promise of the Father unto you; therefore I command you to tarry, even as mine apostles at Jerusalem.

10. Nevertheless, my servants sinned a very grievous sin; and contentions arose in the school of the prophets; which was very grievous unto me, saith your Lord; therefore I sent them forth to be chastened.

11. Verily I say unto you, it is my will that you should build a house. If you keep my commandments you shall have power to build it.

12. If you keep not my commandments, the love of the Father shall not continue with you, therefore you shall walk in darkness.

13. Now here is wisdom, and the mind of the Lord—let the house be built, not after the manner of the world, for I give not unto you that ye shall live after the manner of the world;

14. Therefore, let it be built after the manner which I shall show unto three of you, whom ye shall appoint and ordain unto this power.

15. And the size thereof shall be fifty and five feet in width, and let it be sixty-five feet in length, in the inner court thereof.

16. And let the lower part of the inner court be dedicated unto me for your sacrament offering, and for your preaching, and your fasting, and your praying, and the offering up of your most holy desires unto me, saith your Lord.

17. And let the higher part of the inner court be dedicated unto me for the school of mine apostles, saith Son Ahman; or, in other words, Alphus; or, in other words, Omegus; even Jesus Christ your Lord. Amen.

June 3.—A conference of High Priests convened in the translating room in Kirtland. The first case presented was that of "Doctor" Philastus Hurlburt, who was accused of un-Christian conduct with women, while on a mission to the east. On investigation it was decided that his commission be taken from him, and that he be no longer a member of the Church of Christ.

Trial of "Doctor" Hurlburt.

The next matter before the conference was to ascertain what should be the dimensions or size of the house, that is to be built for a house of worship and for the School of the Prophets. I had received a revelation on the size of the house in which the word of the Lord was that it should be fifty-five feet wide, and sixty-five feet long, in the inner court. The conference appointed Joseph Smith, Jun., Sidney Rigdon and Frederick G. Williams to obtain a draft or construction of the inner court of the house.

The House of the Lord to be Built at Kirtland.

June 4.—A similar conference assembled at the same place, and took into consideration how the French farm should be disposed of. The conference could not agree who should take charge of it, but all agreed to inquire of the Lord; accordingly we received the following:

The French Farm.

Revelation to Enoch [*Joseph Smith, Jun.*] *Showing the Order of the City or Stake of Zion, in Shinehah* [*Kirtland,*] *given for a Sample to the Saints in Kirtland.**

1. Behold, I say unto you, here is wisdom, whereby ye may know how to act concerning this matter, for it is expedient in me that this stake that I have set for the strength of Zion should be made strong.

2. Therefore, let my servant Ahashdah [Newel K. Whitney] take

*Doctrine and Covenants, sec. xcvi.

charge of the place which is named among you, upon which I design to build mine holy house.

3. And again, let it be divided into lots, according to wisdom, for the benefit of those who seek inheritances, as it shall be determined in council among you.

4. Therefore, take heed that ye see to this matter, and that portion that is necessary to benefit mine order, for the purpose of bringing forth my word to the children of men.

5. For behold, verily I say unto you, this is the most expedient in me, that my word should go forth unto the children of men, for the purpose of subduing the hearts of the children of men for your good. Even so. Amen.

6. And again, verily I say unto you, it is wisdom and expedient in me, that my servant Zombre [John Johnson] whose offering I have accepted, and whose prayers I have heard, unto whom I give a promise of eternal life inasmuch as he keepeth my commandments from henceforth—

7. For he is a descendant of Seth [Joseph] and a partaker of the blessings of the promise made unto his fathers—

8. Verily I say unto you, it is expedient in me that he should become a member of the order, that he may assist in bringing forth my word unto the children of men.

9. Therefore ye shall ordain him unto this blessing, and he shall seek diligently to take away incumbrances that are upon the house named among you, that he may dwell therein. Even so. Amen.

John Johnson Ordained a High Priest.

Zombre [John Johnson] was ordained by the conference to the High Priesthood, and admitted according to the revelation.

Ground Broken for Kirtland Temple.

June 5.—George A. Smith hauled the first load of stone for the Temple, and Hyrum Smith and Reynolds Cahoon commenced digging the trench for the walls of the Lord's house, and finished the same with their own hands.

Action of Conference with Reference to the Temple.

June 6.—A conference of High Priests assembled, and chose Orson Hyde a clerk to the Presidency of the High Priesthood. This conference was more especially called to counsel the committee, who had been appointed to take the oversight of the building of the house of the Lord. The conference voted that the committee, (Reynolds Cahoon, Jared Carter, and Hyrum Smith), proceeded immediately to commence building the house; or to obtaining materials, stone, brick, lumber, etc., for the same.

June 21.—"Doctor" Hurlburt being dissatisfied with the decision of the council on his case presented the following appeal:

Hurlburt's Appeal.

> I, Doctor Philastus Hurlburt, having been tried before the Bishop's council of High Priests on a charge of unChristian-like conduct with the female sex, and myself being absent at the time, and considering that strict justice was not done me, I do, by these presents, most solemnly enter my appeal unto the President's council of high priests for a re-hearing, according to the privilege guaranteed to me in the laws of the Church, which council is now assembled in the school room, in Kirtland, this 21st day of June, 1833.

It was voted by the council present, when this was received, that Brother Hurlburt be granted a re-hearing; and after prayer (which was customary at the opening of all councils of the Church), the council proceeded to ordain two High Priests, to make out the number, (twelve) that the council, or Church court, might be organized. By the choice of the council Brothers John and William Smith were ordained under the hands of Elder Rigdon.

Brother Hurlburt's case was then laid before the court, and the testimony against him given by Orson Hyde and Hyrum Smith, and duly investigated. The decision of the court was, that Brother Hurlburt should be forgiven, because of the liberal confession which he made. This court also decided that the Bishop's council decided correctly on the case, and that Brother Hurlburt's crime was sufficient to cut him off from the Church; but on his confession he was restored.

The President's court also took Brother Daniel Copley's Priest's license and membership from him, because he refused to fulfil his mission according to the council of the High Priesthood of the holy order of God.

Copley's Case.

June 23.—"Doctor" Philastus Hurlburt was again called in question, by a general council; and Brother Gee, of Thompson, testified that Brother Hurlburt said that he deceived Joseph Smith's God, or the spirit by which he is actuated. There was also corroborating testimony brought against him by Brother Hodges. The council cut him off from the Church.*

Excommunication of "Doctor" Hulburt.

A council of the Elders of the Church was held at Westfield, New York, the same day. Elder Gladden Bishop was president, and Brother Chester L. Heath clerk. Brother Paul entered a complaint against Brother James Higby, an Elder, for circulating false and slanderous reports, and not observing the order of the Gospel, and presented evidence unimpeachable, to substantiate the same to the satisfaction of the council; upon which evidence—and from Brother Higby's own mouth, and the spirit he manifested—

Case of James Higby.

*Owing to the subsequent prominence of this man, "Doctor" Philastus Hurlburt, as a bitter anti-"Mormon," more should be said of him than is given in the Prophet's narrative. He was not a physician, as the title "Doctor" would seem to indicate; but being the seventh son in his father's family, according to the old folklore superstition that the seventh son would possess supernatural qualities that would make him a physician, he was called "Doc," or "Doctor," "This said 'Doctor,' " wrote Sidney Rigdon in 1839, to the *Boston Journal*, "was never a physician at any time, nor anything else but a base ruffian. He was the seventh son and his parents called him 'Doctor;' it was his name, and not the title of his profession. He once belonged to the Methodist church, and was excluded for immoralities. He afterwards imposed himself on the Church of Latter-day Saints, and was excluded for using obscene language to a young lady, a member of the said Church, who resented his insult with indignation which became both her character and profession." Joseph E. Johnson, in a communication to the *Deseret Evening News*, under date of December 28, 1880, says of "Doctor" Hurlburt: "In the year A. D. 1833, then living in Kirtland, Ohio, I became acquainted with a man subsequently known as Dr. Hurlburt, who came to investigate the truth of 'Mormonism.' Claiming to be satisfied, he was baptized and became a member in full fellowship. He was a man of fine physique, very pompous, good looking, and very ambitious, with some energy, though of poor education. Soon after his arrival he came to my mother's house to board, where he remained for nearly a year, while he made an effort to get into a good practice of medicine, sought position in the Church and was ever striving to make marital connection with any of the first families. Finally * * * he was charged with illicit intercourse with the sex, was tried and cut off from the Church. He denied, expostulated, threatened, but to no use, the facts were too apparent, and he at once avowed himself the enemy of the Church."

he was declared guilty by the council, and he was cut off from the Church. The council then demanded his license and the Church record, which he utterly refused to give up; therefore, resolved that the proceedings of the council be sent to Kirtland, that it may be known among the different branches of the Church.*

*The account of the council of Elders at Westfield was copied into the Kirtland Church record on the 29th of June, 1833.

CHAPTER XXVI.

THE PLAT OF THE CITY OF ZION—ITS TEMPLES—CORRESPONDENCE ON AFFAIRS IN ZION AND EUGENE.

An explanation of the plat of the city of Zion, sent to the brethren in Zion, the 25th of June, 1833:

The General Plan of the City of Zion.

THE plat contains one mile square; all the squares in the plat contain ten acres each, being forty rods square. You will observe that the lots are laid off alternately in the squares; in one square running from the south and north to the line through the center of the square; and in the next, the lots run from the east and west to the center line. Each lot is four perches in front and twenty back, making one half of an acre in each lot, so that no one street will be built on entirely through the street; but on one square the houses will stand on one street, and on the next one, another, except the middle range of squares, which runs north and south, in which range are the painted squares. The lots are laid off in these squares, north and south, all of them; because these squares are forty perches by sixty, being twenty perches longer than the others, their greatest length being east and west, and by running all these squares, north and south, it makes all the lots in the city of one size.

The Blocks Set Aside for Temples.

The painted squares in the middle are for public buildings. The one without any figures is for store-houses for the Bishop, and to be devoted to his use. Figure first is for temples for the use of the presidency; the circles inside of the squares, are the places for the temples. You will see it contains twelve figures, two are for the temples of the lesser Priesthood. It is also to contain twelve temples.

The whole plot is supposed to contain from fifteen to twenty thousand people: you will therefore see that it will require twenty-four buildings to supply them with houses of worship, schools, etc.; and none of these temples are to be smaller than the one of which we send you a draft. This temple is to be built in the square marked figure 1; and to be built where the circle is which has a cross on it on the north end.

Location of Lands for the Agriculturist.

South of the plot where the line is drawn, is to be laid off for barns, stables, etc., for the use of the city; so that no barns or stables will be in the city among the houses; the ground to be occupied for these must be laid off according to wisdom. On the north and south are to be laid off the farms for the agriculturist, and sufficient quantity of land to supply the whole plot; and if it cannot be laid off without going too great a distance from the city, there must also be some laid off on the east and west.

Zion a Group of Cities.

When this square is thus laid off and supplied, lay off another in the same way, and so fill up the world in these last days; and let every man live in the city, for this is the city of Zion. All the streets are of one width, being eight perches wide. Also the space round the outer edge of the painted squares, is to be eight perches between the temple and the street on every side. No one lot, in this city, is to contain more than one house, and that to be built twenty-five feet back from the street, leaving a small yard in front, to be planted in a grove, according to the taste of the builder; the rest of the lot for gardens; all the houses are to be built of brick and stone. The scale of the plot is forty perches to the inch.

Names of the Temples.

The names of the temples to be built on the painted squares as represented on the plot of the city of Zion, which is now about to be forwarded thither:—numbers 10, 11, and 12, are to be called, House of the Lord, for the Presidency of the High and most Holy Priesthood, after the order of Melchizedek, which was after the order of the Son of God, upon Mount Zion, City of the New Jerusalem. Numbers 7, 8, and 9, the Sacred Apostolic Repository, for the use of the Bishop. Numbers 4, 5, and 6, the Holy Evangelical House, for the High Priesthood of the Holy Order of God. Numbers 1, 2, and 3, the House of the Lord, for the Elders of Zion, an Ensign to the Nations. Numbers 22, 23, and 24, House of the Lord for the Presidency of the High Priesthood, after the Order of Aaron, a Standard for the People. Numbers 19, 20, and 21, House of the Lord, the Law of the Kingdom of Heaven, and Messenger to the People; for the Highest Priesthood after the Order of Aaron. Numbers 16, 17, and 18, House of the Lord for the Teachers in Zion, Messenger to the Church. Numbers 13, 14, and 15, House of the Lord for the Deacons in Zion, Helps in Government. Underneath must be written on each house—

HOLINESS TO THE LORD.

A description of the House of the Lord, which is to be built first in Zion:

The House of the Lord for the Presidency.

The house of the Lord for the Presidency, is eighty-seven feet long and sixty-one feet wide, and ten feet taken off of the east end for the stairway, leaves the inner court, seventy-eight feet by sixty-one, which is calculated and divided for seats in the following manner, viz: the two aisles four feet wide each; the middle block of pews are eleven feet ten inches long, and three feet wide each; and the two lines drawn through the middle are four inches apart; in which space a curtain is to drop at right angles, and divide the house into four parts if necessary. The pews of the side blocks are fourteen and a half feet long, and three feet wide. The five pews in each corner of the house, are twelve feet six inches long. The open spaces between the corner and side pews are for fireplaces; those in the west are nine feet wide, and the east ones are eight feet and eight inches wide, and the chimneys carried up in the wall where they are marked with a pencil.

The Pulpits of the Temple.

The pulpit in the west end of the house is to be occupied by the High Priesthood, as follows:—Number 1, is for the President and his council; number 2, for the Bishop and his council; number 3, for the High Priests; and number 4 for the Elders: each of these is eight feet long, containing three coves or stands for the respective speakers; and those seats opposite them are for visiting officers, who are to occupy seats according to their respective grades. The two spaces in the middle are stairs two feet wide. The middle pulpit is to be elevated; the first seats one foot, the second two feet, the third three feet, and the fourth four feet. And those upon each side are also to be elevated: the first one eight inches, the second sixteen, the third tweny-four, the fourth thirty-two. The corner seats are to be occupied by singers, and elevated —the first seat six inches, the second twelve, the third eighteen, the fourth twenty-four, and the fifth thirty-two inches. The pulpit in the east end of the house is to be occupied by the Lesser Priesthood. Number 1, is for the Presidency of the Lesser Priesthood; nubber 2, for the Priests; number 3, for the Teachers; and number 4, for the Deacons; and the seats by their sides, are also to be occupied by visiting officers; each one opposite his respective grade. The pulpits are to be finished with panel work, in the best workmanlike manner; and the building to be constructed of stone and brick of the best quality. Observe particularly that as there are pulpits at each end of the house, the backs of the congregation must be to one of them, and they will want occasionally to change. In order for this the house must have pews instead of slips, and in the pews let the seats be loose, that they may slip from one side of the pew to the other, so as to face either pulpit, as occasion may require.

The Windows.

The side view represents five windows in each story. The windows are to have each forty-eight lights, of seven by nine glass, six one way and eight the other; the sides and lintels of the windows to be of hewn stone, and on the top of the lintel is to be a Gothic top, as you see, but the windows must have a lintel; and so with the outside doors, all with Gothic tops.

General Dimensions.

Make your house fourteen feet high between the floors. There will not be a gallery but a chamber; each story to be fourteen feet high, arched overhead with an elliptic arch. Let the foundation of the house be of stone; let it be raised sufficiently high to allow of banking up so high as to admit of a descent every way from the house, so far as to divide the distance between this house, and the one next to it. On the top of the foundation, above the embankment, let there be two rows of hewn stone, and then commence the brick-work on the hewn stone. The entire height of the house is to be twenty-eight feet, each story being fourteen feet; make the wall a sufficient thickness for a house of this size. The end view represents five windows of the same size as those at the side, the middle window excepted, which is to be the same, with the addition of side lights. This middle window is designed to light the rooms both above and below, as the upper floor is to be laid off in the same way as the lower one, and arched overhead;

with the same arrangement of curtains, or veils, as before mentioned.

The doors are to be five feet wide, and nine feet high, and to be in the east end of the house. The west end is to have no doors, but in other respects is to be like the east, except the windows are to be opposite the alleys which run east and west. The roof of the house is to have one-fourth pitch, the door to have Gothic top, the same as the windows. The shingles of the roof to be painted before they are put on. There is to be a fanlight, as you see. The windows and doors are all to have venetian blinds. A belfry is to be in the east end, and a bell of very large size.

Arrangement of Curtains.

You will be careful to have hooks and rings to suspend your veils on, so that they can be let down or raised at any time, at pleasure. Also, as you see, the pulpits are to have four seats, rising one above another; for instance, the Elder's seat is the lowest, next comes the High Priest's, next the Bishop's; so each of these must have a veil that is suspended from the upper floor, so as to be let down; which will at any time when necessary be let down, and shut off each stand or seat by itself.

Important Letter to Brethren in Zion.

The same day [June 25th], we wrote to Brother W. W. Phelps, and others in Zion, from Kirtland, as follows:

Brethren:—We have received your last, containing a number of questions which you desire us to answer; this we do the more readily as we desire with all our hearts the prosperity of Zion, and the peace of her inhabitants; for we have as great an interest in the welfare of Zion, as you can have.

First, as respects getting the Book of Commandments bound, we think it is not necessary. They will be sold well without binding, and there is no bookbinder to be had that we know of, nor are there materials to be had for binding, without keeping the books too long from circulation.

With regard to the copies of the Book of Mormon, which are in the hands of Brother Burkett, we say to you, get them from Brother

Burkett, and give him a receipt for them in the name of the Literary Firm. Let Brother Gilbert pay Brother Chapin his money.

We have not found the Book of Jasher, nor any other of the lost books mentioned in the Bible as yet; nor will we obtain them at present. Respecting the Apocrypha, the Lord said to us that there were many things in it which were true, and there were many things in it which were not true, and to those who desire it, should be given by the Spirit to know the true from the false.

We have received some revelations within a short time back, which you will obtain in due season. As soon as we can get time, we will review the manuscripts of the Book of Mormon, after which they will be forwarded to you.

We commend the plan highly of your choosing a teacher to instruct the High Priests, that they may be able to silence gainsayers. Concerning Bishops, we recommend the following: Let Brother Isaac Morley be ordained second Bishop in Zion, and let Brother John Corrill be ordained third.

Let Brother Edward Partridge choose as counselors in their place, Brother Parley P. Pratt and Brother Titus Billings, ordaining Brother Billings to the High Priesthood.

Let Brother Morley choose for his counselors, Brother Christian Whitmer, whom ordain to the High Priesthood, and Brother Newel Knight. Let Brother Corrill choose Brother Daniel Stanton and Brother Hezekiah Peck, for his counselors; let Brother Hezekiah also, be ordained to the High Priesthood.

Zombre [John Johnson] has been received as a member of the firm, by commandment, and has just come to Kirtland to live; as soon as we get a power of attorney signed agreeably to law, for Alam [Edward Partridge] we will forward it to him, and will immediately expect one from that part of the firm to Ahashdah [Newel K. Whitney], signed in the same manner. We would again say to Alam [Edward Partridge], be sure to get a form according to law for securing a gift. We have found by examining the law, that a gift cannot be retained without this.

The truth triumphs gloriously in the east; multitudes are embracing it. I, Sidney, who write this letter in behalf of the Presidency, had the privilege of seeing my aged mother baptized into the faith of the Gospel, a few weeks since, at the advanced age of seventy-five. She now resides with me.

We send by this mail, a draft of the city of Zion, with explanations, and a draft of the house to be built immediately in Zion, for the Presidency, as well as for all purposes of religion and instruction.

Kirtland, the stake of Zion, is strengthening continually. When the enemies look at her they wag their heads and march along. We anticipate the day when the enemies will have fled away and be far from us.

You will remember that the power of agency must be signed by the wives as well as the husbands, and the wives must be examined in the matter separate and apart from the husbands, the same as signing a deed, and a specification to that effect inserted at the bottom, by the justice before whom such acknowledgment is made, otherwise the power of attorney will be of none effect.

Should you not understand the explanations sent with the drafts, you will inform us, so that you may have a proper understanding, for it is meet that all things should be done according to the pattern.

We have found the following errors in the Commandments, as printed: fortieth chapter, tenth verse, third line, instead of "corruptable," put corrupted. Fourteenth verse of the same chapter, fifth line, instead of "respecter to persons," put respecter of persons. Twenty-first verse, second line of the same chapter, instead of "respecter to," put respecter of. Forty-fourth chapter, twelfth verse, last line, instead of "hands," put heads.

ITEMS OF INSTRUCTION CONCERNING THE CONSECRATION OF PROPERTY.

Brother Edward Partridge:

SIR:—I proceed to answer your questions, concerning the consecration of property:—First, it is not right to condescend to very great particulars in taking inventories. The fact is this, a man is bound by the law of the Church, to consecrate to the Bishop, before he can be considered a legal heir to the kingdom of Zion; and this, too, without constraint; and unless he does this, he cannot be acknowledged before the Lord on the Church Book therefore, to condenscend to particulars, I will tell you that every man must be his own judge how much he should receive and how much he should suffer to remain in the hands of the Bishop. I speak of those who consecrate more than they need for the support of themselves and their families.

The matter of consecration must be done by the mutual consent of both parties; for to give the Bishop power to say how much every man shall have, and he be obliged to comply with the Bishop's judgment, is giving to the Bishop more power than a king has; and upon the other hand, to let every man say how much he needs, and the Bishop be obliged to comply with his judgment, is to throw Zion into confusion, and make a slave of the Bishop. The fact is, there must be a balance or equilibrium of power, between the Bishop and the people, and thus harmony and good will may be preserved among you.

Therefore, those persons consecrating property to the Bishop in

Zion, and then receiving an inheritance back, must reasonably show to the Bishop that they need as much as they claim. But in case the two parties cannot come to a mutual agreement, the Bishop is to have nothing to do about receiving such consecrations; and the case must be laid before a council of twelve High Priests, the Bishop not being one of the council, but he is to lay the case before them.*

Say to Brother Gilbert that we have no means in our power to assist him in a pecuniary way, as we know not the hour when we shall be sued for debts which we have contracted ourselves in New York. Say to him that he must exert himself to the utmost to obtain means himself, to replenish his store, for it must be replenished, and it is his duty to attend to it.

We were not a little surprised to hear that some of our letters of a public nature, which we sent for the good of Zion, have been kept back from the Bishops. This is conduct which we highly disapprobate.

ANSWERS TO QUERIES TO BROTHER PHELPS' LETTER OF JUNE 4TH.

First, in relation to the poor: When the Bishops are appointed according to our recommendation, it will devolve upon them to see to the poor, according to the laws of the Church.

In regard to the printing of the New Translation: It cannot be done until we can attend to it ourselves, and this we will do as soon as the Lord permits.

As to Shederlaomach, [F. G. Williams], all members of the United Firm are considered one. The order of the Literary Firm is a matter

*The first of the following deed-forms was used in consecrating property to the Church; the second, in securing the stewardships to those entering into the law of consecration and stewardship, sometimes called the Order of Enoch, because it was the law under which the Partriarch Enoch and his people lived. These deed forms were found in the private papers of Bishop Edward Partridge:

I.

BE IT KNOWN, THAT I, Titus Billings of Jackson county, and the state of Missouri, having become a member of the Church of Christ, organized according to law, and established by the revelations of the Lord, on the 6th day of April, 1830, do, of my own free will and accord, having first paid my just debts, grant and hereby give unto Edward Partridge of Jackson county, and state of Missouri, Bishop of said Church, the following described property, viz.:—sundry articles of furniture valued fifty-five dollars twenty-seven cents; also two beds, bedding and extra clothing valued seventy-three dollars twenty-five cents; also farming utensils valued forty-one dollars; also one horse, two wagons, two cows and two calves, valued one hundred forty-seven dollars.

For the purpose of purchasing lands in Jackson county, Mo., and building up the New Jerusalem, even Zion, and for relieving the wants of the poor and needy. For which I, the said Titus Billings, do covenant and bind myself and my heirs forever,

of stewardship, which is of the greatest importance; and the mercantile establishment God commanded to be devoted to the support thereof, and God will bring every transgression unto judgment.

Say to the brothers Hulet and to all others, that the Lord never authorized them to say that the devil, his angels or the sons of perdition, should ever be restored; for their state of destiny was not revealed to man, is not revealed, nor ever shall be revealed, save to those who are made partakers thereof: consequently those who teach this doctrine, have not received it of the Spirit of the Lord. Truly Brother Oliver declared it to be the doctrine of devils. We therefore command that this doctrine be taught no more in Zion. We sanction the decision of the Bishop and his council, in relation to this doctrine being a bar to communion.

The number of disciples in Kirtland is about one hundred and fifty. We have commenced building the house of the Lord, in this place, and it goes on rapidly. Good news from the east and south of the success of the laborers is often saluting our ears. It is a general time of health

to release all my right and interest to the above described property, unto him, the said Edward Partridge, Bishop of said Church.

And I, the said Edward Partridge, Bishop of said Church, having received the above described property, of the said Titus Billings, do bind myself, that I will cause the same to be expended for the above mentioned purposes of the said Titus Billings to the satisfaction of said Church; and in case I should be removed from the office of Bishop of said Church, by death or otherwise, I hereby bind myself and my heirs forever, to make over to my successor in office, for the benefit of said Church, all the above described property, which may then be in my possession.

IN TESTIMONY WHEREOF, we have hereunto set our hands and seals this.......... day of.........., in the year of our Lord, one thousand, eight hundred and thirty.......

In the presence of { ______________________,
____

Signed, { TITUS BILLINGS,
EDWARD PARTRIDGE.

II.

BE IT KNOWN, THAT I, Edward Partridge, of Jackson county, state of Missouri, Bishop of the Church of Christ, organized according to law, and established by the revelations of the Lord, on the 6th day of April, 1830, have leased and by these presents do lease unto Titus Billings, of Jackson county, and state of Missouri, a member of said Church, the following described piece or parcel of land, being a part of section No. three, township No. forty-nine, range No. thirty-two, situated in Jackson county, and state of Missouri, and is bounded as follows, viz:— Beginning eighty rods E. from the S. W. corner of said section; thence N. one hundred and sixty rods; thence E. twenty-seven rods, twenty-five links; thence S. one hundred and sixty rods; thence W. seventy-seven rods, twenty-five links, to the place of beginnning, containing twenty-seven and one-half acres, be the same more or less, subject to roads and highways. And also have loaned the following described

among us; families all well, and day and night we pray for the salvation of Zion.

We deliver Brother Ziba Peterson over to the buffetings of Satan, in the name of the Lord, that he may learn not to transgress the commandments of God. We conclude our letter by the usual salutation, in token of the new and everlasting covenant. We hasten to close, because the mail is just going.

JOSEPH SMITH, JUN.,
SIDNEY RIGDON,
F. G. WILLIAMS.

P. S.—We feel gratified with the way in which Brother William W.

property, viz:—Sundry articles of furniture, valued fifty-five dollars twenty-five cents; also two beds, bedding and clothing, valued seventy-three dollars twenty-seven cents; also sundry farming utensils, valued forty-one dollars; also one horse, two cows, two calves, and two wagons, valued one hundred forty-seven dollars, to have and to hold the above described property, by him, the said Titus Billings, to be used and occupied as to him shall seem meet and proper.

And as a consideration for the use of the above described property, I, the said Titus Billings, do bind myself to pay the taxes, and also to pay yearly unto the said Edward Partridge, Bishop of said Church, or his successor in office, for the benefit of said Church, all that I shall make or accumulate more than is needful for the support and comfort of myself and family. And it is agreed by the parties that this lease and loan shall be binding during the life of the said Titus Billings, unless he transgresses and is not deemed worthy by the authority of the Church, according to its laws, to belong to the Church. And in that case I, the said Titus Billings, do acknowledge that I forfeit all claim to the above described leased and loaned property, and hereby bind myself to give back the lease, and also pay an equivalent, for the loaned [articles] for the benefit of said Church, unto the said Edward Partridge, Bishop of said Church, or his successor in office. And further, in case of said Titus Billings' or family's inability in consequence of infirmity or old age to provide for themselves while members of this Church, I, the said Edward Partridge, Bishop of said Church, do bind myself to administer to their necessities out of any fund in my hands appropriated for that purpose, not otherwise disposed of, to the satisfaction of the Church. And further, in case of the death of the said Titus Billings, his wife or widow, being at the time a member of said Church, has claim upon the above described leased and loaned property, upon precisely the same conditions that her said husband had them, as above described; and the children of the said Titus Billings, in case of the death of both their parents, also have claim upon the above described property, for their support, until they shall become of age, and no longer; subject to the same conditions yearly that their parents were; provided, however, should the parents not be members of said Church, and in possession of the above described property at the time of their deaths, the claim of the children as above described, is null and void.

IN TESTIMONY WHEREOF we have hereunto set our hands and seals this........day of............, in the year of our Lord, one thousand eight hundred and thirty...........

In presence of { ....
{ ....

Signed, { EDWARD PARTRIDGE,
{ TITUS BILLINGS.

Phelps is conducting the *Star* at present, we hope he will seek to render it more and more interesting. In relation to the size of Bishoprics: When Zion is once properly regulated there will be a Bishop to each square of the size of the one we send you with this; but at present it must be done according to wisdom. It is needful, brethren, that you should be all of one heart, and of one mind, in doing the will of the Lord.

There should exist the greatest freedom and familiarity among the rulers in Zion.

We were exceedingly sorry to hear the complaint that was made in Brother Edward Partridge's letter, that the letters attending the Olive Leaf had been kept from him, as it is meet that he should know all things in relation to Zion, as the Lord has appointed him to be a judge in Zion. We hope, dear brethren, that the like occurrence will not take place again. When we direct letters to Zion to any of the High Priests, which pertain to the regulation of her affairs, we always design that they should be laid before the Bishop, so as to enable him to perform his duty. We say so much, hoping it will be received in kindness, and our brethren will be careful of one anothers' feelings, and walk in love, honoring one another more than themselves, as is required by the Lord. Yours as ever, J. S.,

S. R.,

F. G. W.

A SECOND COMMUNICATION TO THE BRETHREN IN ZION.

KIRTLAND, July 2nd, 1833.

To the Brethren in Zion:

We received your letters of June 7th: one from Brothers William W. Phelps and Oliver Cowdery; one from Brother David Whitmer; and one from Brother Sidney Gilbert, for which we are thankful to our Heavenly Father, as also to hear of your welfare, and the prosperity of Zion. Having received your letters in the mail of today, we hasten to answer, in order that our reply may go with tomorrow's mail.

We are exceedingly fatigued, owing to a great press of business. We this day finished the translating of the Scriptures, for which we returned gratitude to our Heavenly Father, and sat immediately down to answer your letters. We rejoiced greatly to hear of the safe arrival of Sister Vienna Jaques and Brother William Hobert, and thank our Heavenly Father that their lives have been spared them till their arrival. The health of the brethren and sisters in Kirtland is good at present; no case of sickness known to us. Brother Joseph C. Kingsbury's wife is declining fast, and cannot continue much longer, but will soon be in the paradise of God.

We are engaged in writing a letter to Eugene* respecting the two Smiths, as we have received two letters from them; one from John Smith, the other from the Elder of the Church.† As to the gift of tongues, all we can say is, that in this place, we have received it as the ancients did: we wish you, however, to be careful lest in this you be deceived. Guard against evils which may arise from any accounts given by women, or otherwise; be careful in all things lest any root of bitterness spring up among you, and thereby many be defiled. Satan will no doubt trouble you about the gift of tongues, unless you are careful; you cannot watch him too closely, nor pray too much. May the Lord give you wisdom in all things. In a letter mailed last week, you will doubtless, before you receive this, have obtained information about the New Translation. Consign the box of the Book of Commandments to N. K. Whitney & Co., Kirtland, Geauga, county, Ohio, care of Kelly and Walworth, Cleveland, Cuyahoga county, Ohio.

I, Sidney, write this in great haste, in answer to yours to Brother Joseph, as I am going off immediately, in company with Brother Frederick to proclaim the Gospel; we think of starting tomorrow. Having finished the translation of the Bible, a few hours since, and needing some recreation, we know of one way we can spend our time more to divine acceptance than in endeavoring to build up His Zion in these last days, as we are not willing to idle any time away which can be spent to useful purposes. Doors are opening continually for proclaiming the Gospel. The spirit of bitterness among the people is fast subsiding, and a spirit of inquiry is taking its place. I preached last Sunday at Chardon, our county seat; I had the court house; there was a general turn-out, good attention, and a pressing invitation for more meetings, which will be granted, if the Lord will, when we return from this tour.

Brother Joseph is going to take a tour with Brother George James, of Brownhelm, as soon as Brother George comes to this place. We hope, our brethren, that the greatest freedom and frankness will exist between you and the Bishop, not withholding from one another any information from us, but communicating with the greatest freedom, lest you should produce evils of a serious character, and the Lord become offended: for know assuredly, if we, by our wickedness, bring

*This was a settlement in Ohio where a branch of the Church had been organized.

†This was Eden Smith, son of the John Smith previously named, and president of the branch of the Church at Eugene. He is mentioned in a revelation given in March, 1832.—(See p. 257) where he is appointed to travel as a missionary companion to Stephen Burnett.

evil on our own heads, the Lord will let us bear it till we get weary and hate iniquity. Brother Frederick wants you to say to Brother Burke, that the man from whom he expected to get the mill stones, has run off, so he will not be able to get them; but Brother Burke can get them of the same man's make, in St. Louis.

We conclude by giving our heartiest approbation to every measure caluculated for the spread of the truth, in these last days; and our strongest desires, and sincerest prayers for the prosperity of Zion. Say to all the brethren and sisters in Zion, that they have our hearts, our best wishes, and the strongest desires of our spirits for their welfare, temporal, spiritual, and eternal. As ever, we salute you in the name of the Lord Jesus. Amen.

SIDNEY RIGDON,
JOSEPH SMITH, JUN.,
F. G. WILLIAMS.

CORRESPONDENCE OVER TROUBLES IN THE EUGENE BRANCH OF THE CHURCH.

KIRTLAND, July 2nd, 1833.

Brother John Smith:

We have just received your letter, of the 8th of June, which seems to have been written in a spirit of justification on your part. You will recollect that previous to your leaving this place, you were tried before the Bishop's court, which found you guilty of misdemeanor, and decided that you should no longer retain your authority in the Church; all of which we, as Presidents of the High Priesthood, sanction. You name something in your letter, that took place at Brother Olney's in Shalersville, on the 27th and 28th of August, which we perfectly recollect, and had you made such confession as you were required to, at Chippeway, all things would have worked together for your good, and as I told you; but you did not manifest that degree of humility to the brethren that was required, but remained obstinate; for that reason God withdrew His Spirit from you, and left you in darkness. In your letter you say many hard things against the brethren, especially against Father Joseph Smith, Brother Reynolds Cahoon, and Bishop Whitney, all of which we highly disapprove. It seems also that your son Eden is confederate with you, and needs to be reproved, together with yourself, in all humility before the Lord, or you must expect to be dealt with according to the laws of the Church. We say you are no more than a private member in the Church.

JOSEPH SMITH, JUN., }
F. G. WILLIAMS, } Presidents.

KIRTLAND, July 2nd, 1833.

To the Church at Eugene:

DEAR BRETHREN:—It is truly painful to be under the necessity of writing on a subject which engages our attention at this time, viz: the case of John Smith, and Eden Smith, his son. We have just received a letter from you concerning their standing in the Church. We do not hold them in fellowship. We would inform you that John Smith has been dealt with, and his authority taken from him; and you are required not to receive his teachings, but to treat him as a transgressor, until he repents and humbles himself before the Lord, to the entire satisfaction of the Church: and also, you have authority to call a conference, and sit in judgment on Eden's case, and deal with him as the law directs.

We feel to rebuke the Elders of that branch of the Church of Christ, for not magnifying their office, and letting the transgressor go unpunished. We, therefore, enjoin upon you, to be watchful on your part, and search out iniquity, and put it down wherever it may be found. You will see by this, brethren, that you have authority to sit in council on the Smiths; and if found guilty, to deal with them accordingly. We have this day directed a letter to John Smith, thereby making known to him our disapprobation of the course he has pursued. We commend you to God and His grace, ever praying He will keep and preserve you blameless till He come.

JOSEPH SMITH, JUN.,
SIDNEY RIGDON,
F. G. WILLIAMS.

Postscript by Bishop Whitney, same date:

DEAR BRETHREN:—Yours of the 3rd of June, came safe to hand the last mail, and John Smith's, which was directed to Brother Joseph. Now, my brethren, on this sheet you have Brother Joseph's sanction to my proceedings, and the letter I last wrote you, and you will govern yourselves accordingly, for you have full power and authority to call the two brothers Smith to an account for their conduct; and, unless they repent and make satisfaction, not only to your branch of the Church, but also to this branch, they must be cut off from the body; for under existing circumstances, we have no fellowship with them. Brother John Smith's authority, as an officer in the Church, was taken from him before he left, and he ought to have given up his license; but he went away without doing so, and it seems he has made use of it to impose upon you. As to the two sisters you spoke of in your last, if there is no testimony on either side, all you can do is to forbid them to partake of the Sacrament unworthily; and pray much, and God will bring all things to light. N. K. WHITNEY, Bishop.

CHAPTER XXVII.

PREPARATIONS OF THE MOB IN JACKSON COUNTY TO RESORT TO VIOLENCE—IMPORTANT EXCERPTS FROM THE *STAR*.

The Rise of Mob Force in Jackson County.

JULY, which once dawned upon the virtue and independence of the United States, now dawned upon the savage barbarity and mobocracy of Missouri. Most of the clergy acting as missionaries to the Indians, or to the frontier inhabitants, were among the most prominent characters, that rose up and rushed on to destroy the rights of the Church, as well as the lives of her members. One Reverend Pixley*, who had been sent by the Mission-

*The Reverends Finis Ewing and Isaac McCoy were equally bitter and nearly as active. The former was the head and front of the Cumberland Presbyterian church, and is credited with publishing this statement: "The 'Mormons' are the common enemies of mankind and ought to be destroyed."

Of this Reverend Pixley and the part taken by the clergy against the Saints generally in these Jackson county troubles, Elder Newel Knight, in his journal, published in *Scraps of Biography*, page 76, says: "The sectarian priests and missionaries around us were among the first to come out both secretly and openly against us. Among the more active of these was a Mr. Pixley, who did not content himself in slandering us to the people of Jackson county, but also wrote to eastern papers telling horrible lies about us, with the evident intention of rousing a spirit of hatred against us. His talk was of the bitterest kind, his speeches perfectly inflammatory; and he appeared to have an influence among the people to carry them with him in his hellish designs. Nor did he confine his actions to the white settlers, but tried to stir up the Indians against us, and use every means in his power to accomplish his purposes. His efforts were seconded by such men as Reverends McCoy, Fitzhugh, Bogard, Kavanaugh, Lovelady, Likens, Hunter, and others; and by their perseverance at last, the public mind became so excited that on the 20th of July a meeting was called and largely attended by not only the rabble of the county, but also the men holding official positions."

ary Society to civilize and Christianize the heathen of the west, was a black rod in the hands of Satan; as well as a poisoned shaft in the hands of our other foes He wrote horrible falsehoods about the Saints which he sent to the religious papers in the East, from time to time, in order to sour the public mind against them; and used his influence among both Indians and whites to overthrow the Church in Jackson county. On the first of July, he wrote a slanderous tract entitled, "Beware of False Prophets," which he carried from house to house, to incense the inhabitants against the Church, to mob them, and drive them away. The July number of *The Evening and Morning Star,* pursued a mild and pacific course; the first article therein, entitled, "Beware of False Prophets," was calculated to disabuse the honest public mind from Pixley's falsehoods;* and the caution against "Free People of Color," settling in Missouri, was sufficient to silence the fears of every sober mind, yet, it was all in vain; the hour of trial must come: notwithstanding the constitution of Missouri—as published in the same paper —says:

*As stated in the Prophet's narrative, the article in the *Star,* "Beware of False Prophets," written as an answer to Reverend Pixley's tract, was of a mild and pacific character. It proceeds to place in contrast, merely, the course and character of true Prophets and false ones—fixing many of the marks of false prophets, however, on the sectarian ministers of the times who, while clinging to forms of godliness, were denying the power thereof. It makes no direct allusion to the tract of Rev. Pixley, nor does it say a personal word of the course he was pursuing: but indirectly it evidently refers to him and his nefarious work in the following passages: "When, therefore, any man, no matter who, or how high his standing may be, utters or publishes anything which afterwards proves to be untrue, he is a false prophet. And if he does it uncalled for, for the purpose of injuring his fellow-beings, or for the sake of gain, or to deceive any man by putting a false coloring upon a matter of religion, to lead astray or prejudice the minds of any to hinder them from receiving the truth, wo unto him, he is a false prophet! * * * * Here then we can say, where we find a person uttering or publishing what he does not know to be a truth, merely to make a noise, whereby the least saint on earth might be offended—beware of false prophets. * * * * Did you ever hear, or have you ever read of a true prophet that spake evil of any man, or that would lie to further the cause of God or anything else? If you have, brethren, then has the hypocrite an excuse for leaving his own fault unexposed, and publishing his neighbor's to the world. Then has the false prophet an opportunity to plead his right to send his lying words abroad, that he may obtain the praise and glory of this world, and deceive the simple."

Article 4th. That all men have a natural and indefeasible right to worship Almighty God according to the dictates of their own consciences; and that no man can be compelled to erect, support, or attend any place of worship, or to maintain any minister of the Gospel, or teacher of religion; that no human authority can control or interfere with the rights of conscience; that no person can ever be hurt, molested, or restrained in his religious professions, or sentiments, if he do not disturb others in their religious worship.

5th. That no person, on account of his religious opinions, can be rendered ineligible to any office of trust or profit under this state; that no preference can ever be given by law, to any sect or mode of worship.*

The Mob Ignores the Constitutional Guarantee of Religious Freedom.

Yet, because the Saints in spiritual things believed and taught differently from their neighbors—although both the faith and the teachings of the Saints were according to the laws of heaven—the mob drew up and published the following manifesto:

THE MANIFESTO OF THE MOB.†

We, the undersigned, citizens of Jackson county, believing that an important crisis is at hand, as regards our civil society, in consequence of a pretended religious sect of people that have settled, and are still settling in our county, styling themselves "Mormons;" and intending, as we do, to rid our society, "peaceably if we can, forcibly if we must," and believing as we do, that the arm of the civil law does not afford us a guarantee, or at least a sufficient one, against the evils which are now inflicted upon us, and seem to be increasing, by the said religious sect, deem it expedient, and of the highest importance, to form ourselves into a company for the better and easier accomplishment of our purpose—a purpose which we deem it almost superfluous to say, is justified as well by the law of nature, as by the law of self-preservation.

*The comment of the editor of the *Star* on this clause of Missouri's constitution is—"It shows a liberality of opinion of the great men of the west, and will vie with that of any other state. It is good; it is just, and it is the citizen's right."

†This document is sometimes referred to as *"The secret constitution,"* and was doubtless regarded as a "constitution" by the mob, by which they were bound together to accomplish the objects set forth in the document itself. The Saints became aware of its existence and the fact of its being circulated among the old settlers about the middle of July; how long before that it had been circulated is not known, but it was doubtless drawn up early in that month.

It is more than two years since the first of these fanatics, or knaves, (for one or the other they undoubtedly are) made their first appearance amongst us, and pretended as they did, and now do, to hold personal communication and converse face to face with the Most High God; to receive communications and revelations direct from heaven; to heal the sick by laying on hands; and, in short, to perform all the wonder-working miracles wrought by the inspired Apostles and Prophets of old.

We believed them deluded fanatics, or weak and designing knaves, and that they and their pretensions would soon pass away; but in this we were deceived. The arts of a few designing leaders amongst them have thus far succeeded in holding them together as a society; and since the arrival of the first of them, they have been daily increasing in numbers; and if they had been respectable citizens in society and thus deluded, they would have been entitled to our pity rather than to our contempt and hatred; but from their appearance, from their manners, and from their conduct since their coming among us, we have every reason to fear that, with but very few exceptions, they were of the very dregs of that society from which they came, lazy, idle, and vicious. This we conceive is not idle assertion, but a fact susceptible of proof, for with these few exceptions above named, they brought into our country little or no property with them and left less behind them, and we infer that those only yoke themselves to the "Mormon" car who had nothing earthly or heavenly to lose by the change; and we fear that if some of the leaders amongst them, had paid the forfeit due to crime, instead of being chosen ambassadors of the Most High, they would have been inmates of solitary cells. But their conduct here stamps their characters in their true colors. More than a year since, it was ascertained that they had been tampering with our slaves, and endeavoring to sow dissensions and raise seditions amongst them. Of this their "Mormon" leaders were informed, and they said they would deal with any of their members who should again in like case offend. But how spacious are appearances. In a late number of the *Star*, published in Independence by the leaders of the sect, there is an article inviting free negroes and mulattoes from other states to become "Mormons," and remove and settle among us. This exhibits them in still more odious colors. It manifests a desire on the part of their society, to inflict on our society an injury that they know would be to us entirely insupportable, and one of the surest means of driving us from the country; for it would require none of the supernatural gifts that they pretend to, to see that the introduction of such a caste amongst us would corrupt our blacks, and instigate them to bloodshed.

They openly blaspheme the Most High God, and cast contempt on

His holy religion, by pretending to receive revelations direct from heaven, by pretending to speak unknown tongues, by direct inspiration, and by divers pretenses derogatory to God and religion, and to the utter subversion of human reason.

They declare openly that their God hath given them this county of land, and that sooner or later they must and will have possession of our lands for an inheritance; and, in fine, they have conducted themselves on many other occasions, in such a manner, that we believe it a duty we owe to ourselves, our wives, and children, to the cause of public morals, to remove them from among us, as we are not prepared to give up our pleasant places and goodly possessions to them or to receive into the bosom of our families, as fit companions for our wives and daughters, the degraded and corrupted free negroes and mulattoes that are now invited to settle among us.

Under such a state of things, even our beautiful county would cease to be a desirable residence, and our situation intolerable. We, therefore, agree (that after timely warning, and receiving an adequate compensation for what little property they cannot take with them, they refuse to leave us in peace, as they found us—we agree to use such means as may be sufficient to remove them, and to that end we each pledge to each other our bodily powers, our lives, fortunes and sacred honors.

We will meet at the court house, at the town of Independence, on Saturday next, the 20th inst., [July], to consult on subsequent movements.

Among the hundreds of names attached to the above document were:

Lewis Franklin, *jailor;* Samuel C. Owens, *county clerk;* Russel Hicks, *deputy county clerk;* R. W. Cummins, *Indian agent;* James H. Flournoy, *postmaster;* S. D. Lucas, *colonel and judge of the court;* Henry Chiles, *attorney-at-law;* N. K. Olmstead, *M. D.;* John Smith, *justice of the peace;* Samuel Weston, *justice of the peace;* William Brown, *constable;* Abner F. Staples, *captain;* Thomas Pitcher, *deputy constable;* Moses G. Wilson, and Thomas Wilson, *merchants.**

*Relative to the charges against the Saints in the foregoing documents, Elder Parley P. Pratt has the following pertinent comment in his *History of the Persecution of the Saints*, pages 26-29:

"I will briefly notice a few items of the foregoing bond of conspiracy, for I consider most of it as too barefaced to need any comment. In the first place I would inquire whether our belief as set forth in this declaration, as to gifts, miracles, revelations and tongues, is not the same that all the Apostles and disciples taught, believed and practiced, and the doctrine of the New Testament?

Secondly—I would inquire when the New Testament religion ceased, and a law revealed or instituted, which made blasphemy of the belief and practice of it? or what holy religion the Jackson mob were speaking of, which was thrown into contempt by the revival of the New Testament religion?

Thirdly—They complain of our society being very poor as to property; but have

FREE PEOPLE OF COLOR.*

To prevent any misunderstanding among the churches abroad, respecting free people of color, who may think of coming to the western boundaries of Missouri, as members of the Church, we quote the following clauses from the laws of Missouri:

"Section 4.—Be it further enacted, that hereafter no free negro or mulatto, other than a citizen of someone of the United States, shall come into or settle in this state under any pretext whatever; and upon complaint made to any justice of the peace, that such person is in his county, contrary to the provisions of this section, if it shall appear that such person is a free negro or mulatto, and that he hath come into this state after the passage of this act, and such person shall not produce a certificate, attested by the seal of some court of record in someone of the United States, evidencing that he is a citizen of such state, the justice shall command him forthwith to depart from this state; and in case such negro or mulatto shall not depart from the state within thirty days after being commanded so to do as aforesaid, any justice of the peace, upon complaint thereof to him made may

they never read in the New Testament that God had chosen the poor in this world, rich in faith, and heirs of the kingdom of God? And when did poverty become a crime known to the law?

Fourthly—Concerning free negroes and mulattoes. Do not the laws of Missouri provide abundantly for the removal from the state of all free negroes and mulattoes (except certain privileged ones)? And also for the punishment of those who introduce or harbor them? The statement concerning our invitation to them to become "Mormons," and remove to this state, and settle among us, is a wicked fabrication, as no such thing was ever published in the *Star*, or anywhere else, by our people, or anything in the shadow of it; and we challenge the people of Jackson [county], or any other people, to produce such a publication from us. *In fact one dozen free negroes or mulattoes never belonged to our society in any part of the world, from its first organization to this day* (1839).

Fifthly—As to crime or vice, we solemnly appeal to all the records of the courts of Jackson county, and challenge the county to produce the name of any individual of our society on the list of indictments, from the time of our first settlement in the county, to the time of our expulsion, a period of more than two years.

Sixthly—As it respects the ridiculous report of our threatening that we would have their lands for a possession, it is too simple to require a notice, as the laws of the country guarantee to every man his rights, and abundantly protect him in their full enjoyment. And we hereby declare, that we settled no lands, only such as our money purchased, and that no such thing ever entered our hearts, as possessing any inheritance in any other way.

Seventhly—We ask what public morals were in danger of being corrupted where officers of the peace could openly violate their several oaths in the most awful manner, and join with hundreds of others in murder, treason, robbery, house burning, stealing, etc.

*This article, "Free People of Color," referred to in the Prophet's *History*, but not quoted *in extenso* anywhere by him, is here given entire, and is followed with

cause such person to be brought before him and may commit him to the common gaol of the county in which he may be found, until the next term of the circuit court to be held in such county. And the said court shall cause such person to be brought before them and examine into the cause of commitment; and if it shall appear that such person came into the state contrary to the provisions of this act, and continued therein after being commanded to depart as aforesaid, such court may sentence such person to receive ten lashes on his or her bare back, and order him to depart the state; and if he or she shall not depart, the same proceedings shall be had and punishment inflicted, as often as may be necessary, until such person shall depart the state.

"Sec. 5.—Be it further enacted, that if any person shall, after the taking effect of this act, bring into this state any free negro or mulatto, not having in his possession a certificate of citizenship as required by this act, (he or she) shall forfeit any pay, for every person so brought, the sum of five hundred dollars, to be recovered by action of debt in the name of the state, to the use of the university, in any court having competent jurisdiction; in which action the defendant may be held to bail, of right and without affidavit; and it shall be the duty of the attorney-general or circuit attorney of the district in which any person so offending may be found, immediately upon information given of such offenses to commence and prosecute an action as aforesaid."

Slaves are real estate in this and other states, and wisdom would dictate great care among the branches of the Church of Christ on this subject. So long as we have no special rule in the Church, as to people of color, let prudence guide, and while they, as well as we, are in the hands of a merciful God, we say: Shun every appearance of evil.

"THE EVENING AND MORNING STAR" EXTRA.*

July 16, 1833.

Having learned with extreme regret, that an article entitled, "Free

The Evening and Morning Star extra, published on the 16th of July, 1833. The importance of these documents justifies their introduction in this manner. It will be observed that the mob in their manifesto charge that the Saints in the first article in question, "Invite free negroes and mulattoes from other states to become 'Mormons,' and remove and settle among us." On this false accusation the mob pretended to found the following apprehensions: "This exhibits them in still more odious colors. It manifests a desire on the part of their society, to inflict on our society an injury that they know would be to us entirely unsupportable, and one of the surest means of driving us from the country; for it would require none of the supernatural gifts that they pretend to, to see that the introduction of such a caste among us would corrupt our blacks, and instigate them to bloodshed."

The publication of the article, "Free People of Color," completely refutes the false accusation of the mob against the Saints.

*This "Extra," as soon as the brethren learned what construction was being

People of Color," in the last number of the *Star*, has been misunderstood, we feel in duty bound to state, in this *Extra*, that our intention was not only to stop free people of color from emigrating to this state, but to prevent them from being admitted as members of the Church.

On the second column of the one hundred and eleventh page of the same paper, may be found this paragraph:—"Our brethren will find an extract of the law of this state, relative to free people of color, on another page of this paper. Great care should be taken on this point. The Saints must shun every appearance of evil. As to slaves, we have nothing to say; in connection with the wonderful events of this age much is doing towards abolishing slavery, and colonizing the blacks in Africa.

We often lament the situation of our sister states in the south, and we fear, lest, as has been the case, the blacks should rise and spill innocent blood, for they are ignorant, and a little may lead them to disturb the peace of society. To be short, we are opposed to having free people of color admitted into the state; and we say, that none will be admitted into the Church; for we are determined to obey the laws and constitutions of our country, that we may have that protection which the sons of liberty inherit from the legacy of Washington, through the favorable auspices of a Jefferson and Jackson.

The Elders Stationed in Zion, to the Churches Abroad, in Love Greeting: (From *The Evening and Morning Star*, July number.)

DEAR BRETHREN:—One year having passed since we addressed the

put upon the article "Free People of Color," was printed in the form of a handbill and circulated as promptly as possible. In it, however, the editor of the *Star* goes too far when he says that no free people of color "will be admitted into the Church." Such was never the doctrine or policy of the Church. Indeed in the article "Free People of Color," the editor himself had said: "So long as we have no special rule in the Church as to free people of color, let prudence guide." And again, in the "Address of the Elders Stationed in Zion to the Churches Abroad," published in the July number of the *Star*, and also found on page 379 of this volume, occurs the following: "Our brethren will find an extract of the law of this state relative to free people of color on another page of this paper. Great care should be taken on this point. The Saints must shun every appearance of evil. As to slaves we have nothing to say. In connection with the wonderful events of this age, much is doing towards abolishing slavery, and colonizing the blacks in Africa." This, with the passage from the article "Free People of Color," is quoted to show that the Church had formulated no doctrine or policy with reference to slaves or free people of color; and in forming his judgment of this matter the reader must remember that the statement about not admitting such people into the Church is merely the view at that time of the editor of the *Star*, and by no means represents the policy of the Church. As a matter of fact there were very few, if any, people of color in the Church at that time. The "fears" of the Missourians on that head were sheer fabrications of evil-disposed minds.

churches abroad, on the situation of Zion and the state of the gathering it seems to be our duty to again address the Saints on the same subjects. Although you frequently learn through the medium of the *Star* our situation and progress, yet we indulge a hope, that a circular from us, particularly setting these things forth at this time, will be received by you in fellowship. We have abundant reason to thank the Lord for His goodness and mercy manifested unto us, since we were planted in this land. With the exception of the winter season, the gathering has continued slowly. At present we have not the exact number of the disciples; but suppose that there are near seven hundred,—include with these their children and those who belong to families, and the number will probably amount to more than twelve hundred souls. Many have been planted upon their inheritances, where, blessed with a fruitful soil, and a healthy climate,they are beginning to enjoy some of the comforts of life.

This in connection with peace and satisfaction of pure and undefiled religion; which is to visit the widow and fatherless in their afflictions and to keep ourselves unspotted from the world, brings down the blessings of peace and love from our Father, and confirms our faith in the promise, that we shall see Him in the flesh, when He comes to be glorified in His Saints, and to be admired in all them that believe in that day.

Here let us remark, that our duty urges us to notice a few letters which have been sent from this place, by persons seeking the loaves and fishes, or by such as have lost their standing among men of character in the world. In the letters alluded to, are some facts; but most of the statements are false. It is said that women go out to work; this is a fact, and not only women, but men, too; for in the Church of Christ, all that are able have to work to fulfil the commandments of the Lord; and the situation in which many have come up here, has brought them under the necessity of seeking employment from those who do not belong to the Church. Yet, we can say as far as our knowledge extends, that they have been honorably compensated. And we are willing to decree concerning mankind, Thou shalt eat thy bread by the sweat of thy brow, should be fulfilled. Members of the Church have, or will have, "deeds" [to their lands] in their own name.

One Bates, from New London, Ohio—who subscribed fifty dollars for the purpose of purchasing lands, and the necessaries for the Saints—after his arrival here, sued (Bishop) Edward Partridge, and obtained a judgment for the same. Bates shortly after denied the faith, and ran away on Sunday, leaving debts unpaid. We do not mention this to cast reflection, but to give a sample of his work manifested since he came to this land. No man that has consecrated property to the

Lord, for the benefit of the poor and the needy, by a deed of gift according to the laws of the land, has thought of suing for it, any more than the men of the world, who give, or donate to build meeting houses, and colleges; or send missionaries to India or the Cape of Good Hope. Every Saint that has come to this land to escape the desolations which await the wicked, and prepare for the coming of the Lord, is well satisfied with the country, and the order of the kingdom of our God; and we are happy to say that the inhabitants of Zion are growing in grace, and in the knowledge of those things which lead to peace and eternal glory. And our hearts are filled with thanksgiving for the privilege of bearing this testimony concerning our brethren on this land. One object in writing this epistle is, to give some instructions to those who come up to the land of Zion. Through a mistaken idea many of the brethren abroad, that had property, have given some away, and sacrificed some, they hardly know how. This is not right nor according to the commandments. We would advise in the first place, that every disciple, if in his power, pay his just debts so as to owe no man, and then if he has any property left, let him be careful of it; and he can help the poor, by consecrating some for their inheritances; for as yet, there has not been enough consecrated to plant the poor in inheritances, according to the regulation of the Church and the desire of the faithful.

This might have been done, had such as had property been prudent. It seems as though a notion was prevalent in Babylon, that the Church of Christ was a common stock concern. This ought not so to be, for it is not the case. When a disciple comes to Zion for an inheritance, it is his duty, if he has anything to consecrate to the Lord for the benefit of the poor and needy, or to purchase lands, to consecrate it according to the law of the Lord, and also according to the law of the land, and the Lord has said, that in keeping his laws we have no need to break the laws of the land; and we have abundant reason to be thankful, that we are permitted to establish ourselves under the protection of a government that knows no exceptions to sect or society, but gives all its citizens the privilege of worshiping God according to their own desire. Again, while in the world, it is not the duty of a disciple to exhaust all his means in bringing the poor to Zion; and this because if all should do so, there would be nothing to put in the storehouse in Zion for the purpose which the Lord has commanded.

Do not think, brethren, by this, that we would advise or direct that the poor be neglected in the least; this is not the desire of our hearts; for we are mindful of the word of our Father, which informs us that in His bosom it is decreed that the poor and the meek of the earth shall possess it.

The welfare of the poor has always a place in our hearts; yet we are confident that our experience, even had we nothing else to prompt us to advise on this point, and that wholly for the good of the cause in which we labor, would be sufficient in the minds of our brethren abroad, to excuse a plainness on this important part of our subject. To see numbers of disciples come to this land, destitute of means to procure an inheritance, and much less the necessaries of life, awakens a sympathy in our bosoms of no ordinary feeling; and we should do injustice to the Saints were we to remain silent, when, perhaps, a few words, by way of advice, may be the means of instructing them, that hereafter great difficulties may be avoided. For the disciples to suppose that they can come to this land without ought to eat, or to drink, or to wear, or anything to purchase these necessaries with, is a vain thought. For them to suppose that the Lord will open the windows of heaven, and rain down angel's food for them by the way, when their whole journey lies through a fertile country, stored with the blessings of life from His own hand for them to subsist upon, is also vain. For them to suppose that their clothes and shoes will not wear out upon the journey, when the whole of it lies through a country where there are thousands of sheep from which wool in abundance can be procured to make them garments, and cattle upon a thousand hills, to afford leather for shoes, is just as vain.

The circumstances of the Saints in gathering to the land of Zion in these last days are very different from those of the children of Israel, after they despised the promised rest of the Lord, after they were brought out of the land of Egypt. Previous to that, the Lord promised them, if they would obey His voice and keep His commandments, that He would send the hornet before them, and drive out those nations which then inhabited the promised land, so that they might have peaceable possession of the same, without the shedding of blood. But in consequence of their unbelief and rebellion, they were compelled to obtain it by the sword, with the sacrifice of many lives.

But to suppose we can come up here and take possession of this land by the shedding of blood, would be setting at naught the law of the glorious Gospel and also the word of our great Redeemer: and to suppose we can take possession of this country without making regular purchases of the same, according to the laws of our nation, would be reproaching this great republic, in which the most of us were born, and under whose auspices we all have protection.

We feel as though enough was said on this point, knowing that a word to the wise is sufficient; and that all our brethren are aware of the fact, that all the tithes cannot be gathered into the storehouse of the Lord, that the windows of heaven may be opened, and a blessing be poured out that there is not room enough to contain it, if all the means of the Saints are exhausted, before they reach the place where they can have the privilege of so doing. Do not conclude from these remarks, brethren, that we doubt in the least, that the Lord will provide for His Saints in these last days; or think that we would extend our hands to steady the ark; for this is not the case. We know that the Saints have the unchangeable word of God that they shall be provided for; yet we know, if any are imprudent, or lavish, or negligent, or indolent, in taking that proper care, and making that proper use of what the Lord has made them stewards over, they are not counted wise; for a strict account of every one's stewardship is required, not only in time, but will be in eternity. Neither do we apprehend that we shall be considered putting out our hands to steady the ark of God by giving advice to our brethren upon important points relative to their coming to Zion, when the experience of almost two years' gathering, has taught us to revere that sacred word from heaven, "Let not your flight be in haste, but let all things be prepared before you."

Then, brethren, we would advise, that where there are many poor in a church, that the Elders counsel together, and make preparations to send a part at one time, and a part at another. And let the poor rejoice in that they are exalted, but the rich in that they are made low, for there is no respect of persons in the sight of the Lord.

The disciples of Christ, blessed with immediate revelations from Him, should be wise and not take the way of the world, nor build air-castles, but consider that when they have been gathered to Zion, means will be needed to purchase their inheritances, and means will be needed to purchase food and raiment for at least one year; or at any rate, food; and where disciples, or churches, are blessed with means to do as much as this, they would be better off in Zion than in the world, troubled as it is, and will shortly be, with plagues, famines, pestilences, and utter destruction upon the ungodly.

On the subject of false reports, which are put in circulation by evil-minded men, to ridicule the idea of the gathering of Israel in these last days, we would say to our brethren abroad, believe them not; *The Evening and Morning Star* was established expressly to publish the truth, and the word of the Lord, that the Saints might not be deceived, by such as make broad the borders of their garments, and love the uppermost rooms at feasts; yea, by such as bind heavy burdens which are grievous to be borne, and lay them upon men's shoulders, but will not move them with one of their fingers. Yea, we give this caution that the disciples may not give heed to the gainsaying of those who seek the honor of this world and the glory of the same, rather than seek the honor of God and His glory; nor those who have turned away from the Church of Christ, and denied the faith delivered to His Saints in these last days.

Brethren, the Lord has begun to gather His children, even Israel, that they may prepare to enter into and enjoy His rest when He comes in His glory, and He will do it. No matter what your ideas or notions may be upon the subject; no matter what foolish reports the wicked may circulate to gratify an evil disposition, the Lord will continue to gather the righteous, and destroy the wicked, till the sound goes forth—*it is finished*.

It ought to be known abroad that much improvement is needed in the cattle, sheep, and hogs in this part of the country. As cows here are worth from ten to fifteen dollars, our brethren would do well, and we would advise them, to purchase before they arrive in this region. In fact, if they journey according to the commandments of the Lord, pitching their tents by the way, like Israel in days of old, it would be no more than right to drive cows enough to supply every family or company with milk on the way. They would then have them when they arrived here, and if they selected of the best breeds, they would lay a foundation for improvement. A thing of which all our brethren who are acquainted with raising stock will at once see the propriety.

The sheep of this state are large, but as their wool is coarse, the breed would soon be improved if our brethren would drive with them some merinos or saxons. As soon as wool and flax are had among the brethren, sufficient for the purpose, they will manufacture cloth for their own use in the Church. The swine in this country are not good, being the old fashioned shack breed, and much inferior to the large, white grass breed of the eastern states. If any could introduce this breed, what little pork might be wanted in the winter, would be much better, and easier raised.

It is a matter of much surprise to us, that our brethren should come up to the land of Zion, as many do, without bringing garden seeds, and even seeds of all kinds. The Jaredites and Nephites took with them of all kinds; and the Jaredites, all kinds of animals. And although the Lord has said that it was His business to provide for His Saints, yet He has not said that He would do it, unless they kept His commandments.

And notwithstanding the fulness of the earth is for the Saints, they can never expect it unless they use the means put into their hands to obtain the same in the manner provided by our Lord. When you flee to Zion, we enjoin the word, prepare all things, that you may be ready to labor for a living, for the Lord has promised to take the curse off the land of Zion in His own due time, and the willing and the obedient, not the idle, will eat the good of the same; for they are to be had in remembrance before the Lord.

One very important requisition for the Saints that come up to the land of Zion is, that before they start, they procure a certificate from three Elders of the Church, or from the Bishop in Ohio, according to the commandments; and when they arrive, to present it to the Bishop in Zion; otherwise they are not considered wise stewards, and cannot be received into fellowship with the Church, till they prove themselves by their own goodness.

Some of our brethren may think, at the first instant, perhaps, that this is useless and formal, but a few reflections will be sufficient for them to see the propriety of it, and more especially, when they learn that it is a commandment given us of the Lord.

On another page of this paper, our brethren will find an extract of the law of this state relative to free people of color. Great care should be taken on this point. The Saints must shun every appearance of evil. As to slaves, we have nothing to say. In connection with the wonderful events of this age, much is doing towards abolishing slavery, and colonizing the blacks in Africa.

The foregoing remarks have been addressed to our brethren abroad, considered as one general body, and have been designed as general information to all. We cannot close this epistle, compatible with our duty, without particularly addressing ourselves to our brethren, the Elders, to whom is entrusted the preaching of the everlasting Gospel,—the glad tidings of salvation to Israel, and to all the Gentiles, if they will listen to the invitation.

Brethren, we are aware of your many afflictions, or at least in part, some of us having been eye witnesses to the things of God, and having been called to bear testimony of the same from the first, since this Gospel has been proclaimed in these last days. The desire of our hearts for your prosperity we can truly say is inexpressible; for when you are prospered, we are, and when you are blessed, we are blessed also. The affliction which you are necessarily called to undergo in these days of tribulation and vengeance upon the wicked, call forth from our hearts unceasing prayers to our common parents in your behalf, that you may be enabled to deliver His message in the demonstration of His Spirit, and call together His elect from the ends of the earth, to the place of the name of the Lord of hosts, even to Mount Zion.

By those few expressions, you will see brethren, how important we view your calling. We do not consider that it is our duty to direct you in your missions; but we will give you in few words what we have reason to expect relative to the gathering of the Saints, according to the revelations of the Lord.

By the authority of your calling and ordination, you, no doubt, will admit that it will be expected that you know your duty, and at all times and in all places, teach the disciples theirs; but we are sorry to say, that in some instances, some of our brethren have failed to do so.

We will remind our brethren of a clause in the covenants, which informs us that all who are ordained in this Church, are to be ordained according to the gifts and callings of God unto them, by the power of the Holy Ghost which is in the one who ordains them. We would also remind them of one valuable caution recorded in Paul's first letter to Timothy, which says, "Lay hands suddenly on no man, neither be partaker of other men's sins."

Those cautions, however, are particularly addressed to our young brethren in the ministry. We know that many of our brethren are wise in these important parts of their labors, and have rid their garments of the blood of this generation, and are approved before the Lord.

We will proceed further, brethren, to notice some particular items immediately connected with your duties, and what, as we said before, we have reason to expect from you, according to the revelations. In one given December 4th, 1831, we learn that it is the duty of the Elders of the Church in the East to render an account of their stewardship unto the Bishop appointed unto the Church in that part of the Lord's vineyard.

The Lord says, "And now, verily I say unto you, that as every Elder in this part of the vineyard, (the East) must give an account of his stewardship unto the Bishop in this part of the vineyard, a certificate from the judge or Bishop in this part of the vineyard, unto the Bishop in Zion, rendereth every man acceptable, and answereth all things for an inheritance, and to be received as a wise steward, and as a faithful laborer; otherwise he shall not be accepted of the Bishop in Zion.

"And now, verily I say unto you, let every Elder who shall give an account unto the Bishop of the Church, in this part of the vineyard, (the East) be recommended by the church or churches, in which he labors, that he may render himself and his accounts approved in all things."

We hope brethren, that you will be particular to teach the disciples abroad prudence and economy in all things. Teach them in plainness, that without regular recommends, they cannot be received in fellowship with the Church in Zion, until after they have proven themselves worthy by their godly walk. And those who are recommended by you, we expect will be such as are personally known to you to be disciples indeed, and worthy the confidence of all Saints.

Viewing the quotation relative to your obtaining a certificate from the Bishop in the East concerning your worthiness, you cannot blame us brethren if we are strict on this point. It may be understood, therefore, by our brethren, the Elders, who come from the East and do not bring a regular certificate showing that their labors have been accepted there, that they cannot be accepted in Zion. We do not set ourselves up as judges in this; we have only a desire to see the order of our Redeemer's kingdom observed in all things; for His commandments are precious with us; we have them in our hands, and they are sacred to our hearts.

Our brethren who labor in the churches a distance to the west of the residence of the Bishop in the East, who do not render their accounts to him, should be particular to bring recommends from the churches in which they do labor, and present them with the accounts of their labors to the Bishop immediately after their arrival here. And those Elders who labor continually in preaching the Gospel to the world, should also be particular to render their account of the same, that they may show themselves approved in all things, and be known to be worthy of the high office in which they stand in the Church of Christ.

Having said considerable concerning those particular points which are necessary to be observed by our brethren who journey to this land, and also a few words to the Elders, we deem it a privilege before we conclude, to say something more to the Church at large. In the previous remarks, however, we presume our brethren may make many improvements; and perhaps discover some errors; if so, we can say that the best of motives has prompted us to write to our brethren; and if some small errors are to be found, we are certain that the general ideas are correct, and will be a means of doing good, if those who are immediately interested in the same, give heed to them.

Dear brethren in the New Covenant, accept this as a token for a salutation in the name of the Lord Jesus Christ, from your brethren in Zion. While we are permitted to witness the great things which are continually taking place in fulfilment of the prophecies concerning the last days, as the children of God are gathered home to prepare themselves for the supper of the Lamb, our language, that is. the English tongue, fails to express our joy.

EXTRACTS FROM THE ELDERS' LETTERS TO THE EDITOR OF THE "EVENING AND MORNING STAR," JULY NUMBER.

PALMYRA, MISSOURI, May 16th, 1833.

The Lord is opening the eyes of the blind, and blessing our labors. We have baptized eighteen members in this settlement.

G. M. HINKLE,
ELISHA H. GROVES.

SIX MILES FROM QUINCY, MO., June 3, 1833.

Every few days there are some honest souls born into the kingdom of God. Persecution rages to a considerable extent. It seems as if every denomination, sect, party, and club, were prepared to fight against the work of the Lord. A man has just told me that in Palmyra, in forty-eight hours, the cholera had taken forty-seven to their graves. The disease is in the country as well as the town, and carries off all ages, colors and conditions, sparing none.

GEORGE M. HINKLE.

CHENANGO POINT, N. Y., May 16, 1833.

Dear Brothers:—It is about six weeks since I left Kirtland to take a mission to the East; since which time I have visited twelve churches, and passed three others in coming to this place; all of which are nearly in the course from Kirtland to Chenango, N. Y.; so grows, and so spreads the mighty work of the Lord. Some of said churches are composed of nearly one hundred members; and in nearly all of them, the work is still going on. O, may the Lord cause His glorious voice to be heard, until error and superstition shall give way to the everlasting Gospel of Jesus. I feel much weakness as a man, but in the strength of Christ, I am resolved to blow the trumpet of the Gospel until the people of God are delivered from the merchants and traffickers of souls unto the glorious liberty of the Gospel. I have baptized four since I left Kirtland. As for myself I intend, if possible, to attend the school at the *latter* Jerusalem, to which I am confident, it is my privilege to go, as often as the old Apostles went to the *former* Jerusalem.

I have traveled about five hundred miles in about six weeks, and held fifteen meetings, and I trust that I shall continue to receive the grace of God to support me even to the end. SYLVESTER SMITH.

STATE OF THE WORLD.

(From the July *Star*.)

The flood of waters, occasioned by the great rains in the eastern and middle states, did immense damage: war between Turkey and Russia continued to rage: and the epidemic disease of London continued its frightful ravages; so terrible were its effects as to close all the principal places of amusement and suspend the court of reform for the metropolis.

Council of Elders in Kirtland.

July 13.—Elder Brigham Young having returned from his mission to Canada, accompanied by some twenty or thirty of the brethren, a council of Elders assembled in Kirtland. There were present at the council Gideon H. Carter,

Jacob Wood, Dennis Lake, Brigham Young, James Lake, Newel K. Whitney, John Smith, Luke S. Johnson, and myself. Elder James Lake desired to know the will of the Lord, whether he should proceed on to Zion, or remain in Kirtland. It was decided that he should remain in Kirtland.

CHAPTER XXVIII.

MOB VIOLENCE IN THE LAND OF ZION.

Demands of the Mob.

ON the 20th of July, the mob collected,* and demanded the discontinuance of the Church printing establishment in Jackson county, the closing of the store, and the cessation of all mechanical labors. The brethren refused compliance, and the consequence was that the house of W. W. Phelps, which contained the printing establishment, was thrown down, the materials taken possession of by the mob, many papers destroyed, and the family and furniture thrown out of doors.†

The Mob's Treatment of Edward Partridge.

The mob then proceeded to violence towards Edward Partridge, the Bishop of the Church, as he relates in his autobiography:

I was taken from my house by the mob, George Simpson being their leader, who escorted me about half a mile, to the court house, on the public square in Independence; and then and there, a few rods from said court house, surrounded by hundreds of the mob, I was stripped of my hat, coat and vest and daubed with tar from head to foot, and then had a quantity of feathers put upon me; and all this because I

*The mob consisted of from three to five hundred.—*Times and Seasons*, vol. 1, p. 18.

†The incident is thus described in the *Times and Seasons*, vol. 1, p. 18: "In a short time hundreds of the mob gathered around the printing office, which was a two story brick building, which they soon threw down. The press was thrown from the upper story, and also the apparatus, book work, paper, type, etc. A family residing in the lower story was also thrust out in great haste. After dtstroying the printing establishment, they proceeded to Gilbert & Whitney's store for the same purpose, but Gilbert agreeing to box the goods, soon, they concluded to let it alone."

would not agree to leave the county, and my home where I had lived two years.

Before tarring and feathering me I was permitted to speak. I told them that the Saints had suffered persecution in all ages of the world; that I had done nothing which ought to offend anyone; that if they abused me, they would abuse an innocent person; that I was willing to suffer for the sake of Christ; but, to leave the country, I was not then willing to consent to it. By this time the multitude made so much noise that I could not be heard: some were cursing and swearing, saying, "call upon your Jesus," etc.; others were equally noisy in trying to still the rest, that they might be enabled to hear what I was saying.

Until after I had spoken, I knew not what they intended to do with me, whether to kill me, to whip me, or what else I knew not. I bore my abuse with so much resignation and meekness, that it appeared to astound the multitude, who permitted me to retire in silence, many looking very solemn, their sympathies having been touched as I thought; and as to myself, I was so filled with the Spirit and love of God, that I had no hatred towards my persecutors or anyone else.

Charles Allen.

Charles Allen was next stripped and tarred and feathered, because he would not agree to leave the county, or deny the Book of Mormon. Others were brought up to be served likewise or whipped.*

But from some cause the mob ceased operations, and adjourned until Tuesday, the 23rd. Elder Sidney Gilbert, the keeper of the store, agreed to close it; and that may have been one reason why the work of destruction was suddenly stopped for two days.

Reflections of the Prophet.

In the course of this day's wicked, outrageous, and unlawful proceedings, many solemn realities of human degradation, as well as thrilling incidents were presented to the Saints. An armed and well organized mob, in a government professing to be governed by law, with the Lieutenant Governor (Lil-

*They succeeded in taking Charles Allen, whom they tarred and feathered upon the public square, surrounded by hundreds of the mob. A number more were taken, but they succeded in making their escape, through the over anxiety of their keepers, who wished to have the "sport" of seeing those who were being tarred.—*Times and Seasons*, vol. I, p. 18.

burn W. Boggs), the second officer in the state, calmly looking on, and secretly aiding every movement, saying to the Saints, "You now know what our Jackson boys can do, and you must leave the county;" and all the justices, judges, constables, sheriffs, and military officers, headed by such western missionaries and clergymen as the Reverends McCoy, Kavanaugh, Hunter, Fitzhugh, Pixley, Likens, and Lovelady, consisting of Methodists, Baptists, Presbyterians, and all the different sects of religionists that inhabited that country, with that great moral reformer, and register of the land office at Lexington, forty miles east, known as the head and father of the Cumberland Presbyterians, even the Reverend Finis Ewing, publicly publishing that "Mormons were the common enemies of mankind, and ought to be destroyed"—all these solemn realities were enough to melt the heart of a savage; while there was not a *solitary offense* on record, or proof, that a Saint had broken the law of the land.*

When Bishop Partridge, who was without guile, and Elder Charles Allen, walked off, coated like some

*The Prophet's statement on this head is abundantly sustained even by those historians who become apologists for the actions of the mob, and also by the declaration put forth by the mob themselves. It will be remembered that in the "Mob Manifesto," or "Secret Constitution," (p. 374, this volume) those who signed it justified their determination "to rid their society of the Mormons" by resorting to mob violence because, said they, "we believe that the arm of the civil law does not afford us a guarantee, or at least a sufficient one, against the evils which are now inflicted upon us." In the address adopted at their meeting of the 20th of July, which was published in the *Western Monitor* (see p. 396) the mob further excuse their lawless intentions by saying: "*The evil is one that no one could have foreseen, and therefore is unprovided for by the laws;* and the delays incident to legislation would put the mischief beyond remedy." In all of which one plainly sees unconscious admission that the Saints were not guilty of infraction of the laws of the land. As to the historian apologists referred to in the opening sentence of this note, I quote the following statements from the *History of Jackson County, Missouri,* published by the Union Historical Company, Kansas City, Missouri, 1881: "Assuming this that they [the Saints] were the holy people of the Lord, that the Lord was the real owner of all things, and that all His possessions were free to them, they were not calculated to be very respectful of the rights and interests of their non-'Mormon' neighbors. *But though no overt acts of transgression upon such rights were being committed,* the rapidly gathering members of the 'Mormons' * * * made the new sect an object of profound solicitude to the people." (See also comment of Parley P. Pratt on charges of the mob, 5th paragraph in note at p. 377 this volume).

unnamed, unknown bipeds, one of the sisters cried aloud: *"While you, who have done this wicked deed, must suffer the vengeance of God, they, having endured persecution, can rejoice, for henceforth for them, is laid up a crown eternal in the heavens."*

Surely this was a time for awful reflection; man, unrestrained, like the brute beast, may torment the body; but God will punish the soul!

Aftermath of Mob Violence.

After the mob had retired, and while evening was spreading her dark mantle over the scene, as if to hide it from the gaze of day, men, women, and children, who had been driven or frightened from their homes, by yells and threats, began to return from their hiding places in thickets, corn-fields, woods, and groves, and view with heavy hearts the scene of desolation and wo: and while they mourned over fallen man, they rejoiced with joy unspeakable that they were accounted worthy to suffer in the glorious cause of their Divine Master. There lay the printing office a heap of ruins; Elder Phelps's furniture strewed over the garden as common plunder; the revelations, book works, papers, and press in the hands of the mob, as the booty of highway robbers; there was Bishop Partridge, in the midst of his family, with a few friends, endeavoring to scrape off the tar which, from its eating his flesh, seemed to have been prepared with lime, pearl-ash, acid, or some flesh-eating substance, to destroy him; and there was Charles Allen in the same awful condition. The heart sickens at the recital, how much more at the picture! More than once, those people, in this boasted land of liberty, were brought into jeopardy, and threatened with expulsion or death, because they desired to worship God according to the revelations of heaven, the constitution of their country, and the dictates of their own consciences. Oh, liberty, how art thou fallen! Alas, clergymen, where is your charity!

Early in the morning of the 23rd of July, the mob again assembled, armed with weapons of war, and bearing a red flag; whereupon the Elders, led by the Spirit of God, and in order to save time, and stop the effusion of blood, entered into a treaty with the mob, to leave the county within a certain time.* The treaty was as follows:

The Second Gathering of the Mob.

Memorandum of argeement between the undersigned of the Mormon Society in Jackson County, Missouri, and a committee appointed by a public meeting of the citizens of said county, made on the 23rd day of July, 1833.

It is understood that the undersigned members of the society, do give their solemn pledges, each for himself, as follows, to-wit:—

That Oliver Cowdery, W. W. Phelps, William M'Lellin, Edward Partridge, Lyman Wight, Simeon Carter, Peter and John Whitmer, and Harvey H. Whitlock shall remove with their families out of this county on or before the first day of January next, and that they, as well as the two hereinafter named, use all their influence to induce all the brethern now here to remove as soon as possible: one half, say, by the first of January next, and all by the first day of April next; to advise and try all means in their power to stop any more of their sect from moving to this county; and as to those now on the road, they will use their influence to prevent their settling permanently in the county, but that they shall only make arrangements for temporary shelter, till a new location is agreed on for the society. John Corrill and Algernon Sidney Gilbert, are allowed to remain as general agents to wind up the business of the society, so long as necessity shall require; and said Gilbert may sell out his merchandise now on hand, but is to make no new importation.

The *Star* is not again to be published nor a press set up by any of the society in this county.

If the said Edward Partridge and W. W. Phelps move their families by the first day of January, as aforesaid, that they themselves will be allowed to go and come, in order to transact and wind up their business.

The committee pledge themselves to use all their influence to prevent

*It was at this point, too, that several of the brethren stepped forward and offered themselves as a ransom for the Church, expressing themselves as being willing to be scourged or to die if that would appease the anger of the mob against the Saints. The mob would not accept the sacrifice of the brethren, however, but renewed their threats of violence against the whole Church. The brethren who offered themselves as a ransom for the Saints were *John Corrill, John Whitmer, William W. Phelps, Algernon S. Gilbert, Edward Partridge, and Isaac Morley.*

any violence being used, so long as a compliance with the foregoing terms is observed by the parties concerned, to which agreement is subscribed the names of the above named committee, as also those of the Mormon brethren named in the report as having been present.*

Which report of the committee was unanimously adopted by the meeting, and thereupon the meeting adjourned *sine die*.

RICHARD SIMPSON, Chairman.

S. D. LUCAS,
J. H. FLOURNOY, } Secretaries.

The execution of this treaty presented an opportunity for the brethren in Zion to confer with the Presidency of the Church in Ohio concerning their situation, which they improved two or three days later by sending Elder Oliver Cowdery as a special messenger to Kirtland.

A Messenger Sent to Kirtland.

On the second day of August, the *Western Monitor*, printed at Fayette,† Missouri, edited by Weston F. Birch, published the proceedings of the mob, as follows:

The *Western Monitor* on Jackson County Troubles.

MORMONISM.

At a meeting of the citizens of Jackson county, Missouri, called for the purpose of adopting measures to rid themselves of the sect of fanatics, called Mormons, held at Independence on the 20th day of July, 1833,—which meeting was composed of gentlemen from every part of the county, there being present between four and five hundred persons: the meeting was organized by calling Colonel Richard Simpson to the chair and appointing James H. Flournoy and Colonel Samuel D. Lucas, secretaries,—it was resolved, that a committee of seven be appointed to report an address to the public, in relation to the object of this meeting; and the chair named the following gentlemen to wit: Russel Hicks, Esq., Robert Johnson, Henry Chiles, Esq., Colonel James Hambright, Thomas Hudspeth, Joel F. Chiles and James M. Hunter. The meeting then adjourned, and convened again, when

*This agreement was signed on the part of the brethren by Edward Partridge, Isaac Morley, John Corrill, W. W. Phelps, Algernon S. Gilbert, and John Whitmer; and on the part of the mob by the Mob Committee whose names are given in the article from the *Western Monitor*, page 399.

†Fayette was the county seat of Howard county, about one hundred and fifty miles directly east of Independence.

Robert Johnson, the chairman of the said committee, submitted for the consideration of the meeting, the following address:

"This meeting, professing to act, not from the excitement of the moment, but under a deep and abiding conviction, that the occasion is one that calls for cool deliberation, as well as energetic action, deem it proper to lay before the public an expose of our peculiar situation, in regard to this singular sect of pretended Christians; and a solemn declaration of our unalterable determination to amend it.

"The evil is one that no one could have foreseen, and is therefore unprovided for by the laws; and the delays incident to legislation would put the mischief beyond remedy.

"But little more than two years ago, some two or three of these people made their appearance on the Upper Missouri, and they now number some twelve hundred souls in this county; and each successive autumn and spring pours forth its swarms among us, with a gradual falling of the character of those who compose them; until it seems that those communities from which they come, were flooding us with the very dregs of their composition. Elevated, as they mostly are, but little above the condition of our blacks, either in regard to property or education; they have become a subject of much anxiety on that part, serious and well grounded complaints having been already made of their corrupting influence on our slaves.

"We are daily told, and not by the ignorant alone, but by all classes of them, that we, (the Gentiles,) of this county are to be cut off, and our lands appropriated by them for inheritances. Whether this is to be accomplished by the hand of the destroying angel, the judgments of God, or the arm of power, they are not fully agreed among themselves.

"Some recent remarks in the *Evening and Morning Star*, their organ in this place, by their tendency to moderate such hopes, and repress such desires, show plainly that many of this deluded and infatuated people have been taught to believe that our lands were to be won from us by the sword. From this same *Star* we learn that for want of more honest or commendable employment, many of their society are now preaching through the states of New York, Ohio, and Illinois; and that their numbers are increased beyond every rational calculation; all of whom are required as soon as convenient to come up to Zion, which name they have thought proper to confer on our little village. Most of those who have already come, are characterized by the profoundest ignorance, the grossest superstition, and the most abject poverty.

"Indeed, it is a subject of regret by the *Star* itself, that they have come not only unable to buy an inheritance, which means some fifteen acres of wild land for each family, but destitute of the means of procuring bread and meat. When we reflect on the extensive field in which the sect is operating, and that there exists in every country a leaven of superstition that embraces with avidity, notions the most extravagant and unheard of, and that whatever can be gleaned by them from the purlieus of vice, and the abodes of ignorance, is to be cast like a waif into our social circle it requires no gift of prophecy to tell that the day is not far distant when the civil government of the county will be in their hands; when the sheriff, the justices, and the county judges will be Mormons, or persons wishing to court their favor from motives of interest or ambition.

"What would be the fate of our lives and property, in the hands of jurors and witnesses, who do not blush to declare, and would not upon occasion hesitate to swear, that they have wrought miracles, and have been the subjects of miraculous and supernatural cures, have converse with God and His angels, and possess and exercise the gifts of divination and of unknown tongues, and fired with the prospect of obtaining inheritances without money and without price—may be better imagined than described.

"One of the means resorted to by them, in order to drive us to emigrate, is an indirect invitation to the free brethren of color in Illinois, to come up like the rest, to the land of Zion. True, they say this was not intended to invite, but to prevent their emigration; but this weak attempt to quiet our apprehension, is but a poor compliment to our understanding. The article alluded to, contained an extract from our laws, and all necessary directions and *cautions* to be observed by colored brethren, to enable them upon their arrival here, to claim and exercise the rights of citizenship. Contemporaneous with the appearance of this article, was the expectation among the brethren here, that a considerable number of this degraded caste were only awaiting this information before they should set out on their journey. With the corrupting influence of these on our slaves, and the stench, both physical and moral, that their introduction would set afloat in our social atmosphere, and the vexation that would attend the civil rule of these fanatics, it would require neither a visit from the destroying angel, nor the judgments of an offended God, to render our situation here insupportable. True, it may be said, and truly no doubt, that the fate has marked the rise and fall of Johanna Southcote and Ann Lee, will also attend the progress of Joe Smith; but this is no opiate to our fears, for when the fabric falls, the rubbish will remain.

"Of their pretended revelations from heaven—their personal intercourse with God and His angels—the maladies they pretend to heal by the laying on of hands—and the contemptible gibberish with which they habitually profane the Sabbath, and which they dignify with the appellation of unknown tongues, we have nothing to say; vengeance belongs to God alone. But as to the other matters set forth in this paper we feel called on by every consideration of self-preservation, good society, public morals, and the fair prospects, that if not blasted in the germ, await this young and beautiful county, at once to declare, and we do hereby most solemnly declare;—

" '1—That no Mormon shall in future move and settle in this county.

" '2—That those now here, who shall give a definite pledge of their intention, within a reasonable time to remove out of the county, shall be allowed to remain unmolested until they have sufficient time to sell their property, and close their business, without any material sacrifice.

" '3—That the editor of the *Star* be required forthwith to close his office, and discontinue the business of printing in this county; and as to all other stores and shops belonging to the sect, their owners must in every case strictly comply with the terms of the second article of this declaration; and upon failure prompt and efficient measures will be taken to close the same.

" '4—That the Mormon leaders here, are required to use their influence in preventing any further emigration of their distant brethren to this county, and to counsel and advise their brethren here to comply with the above requisitions.

" '5—That those who fail to comply with these requisitions, be referred to those of their brethren who have the gifts of divination, and of unknown tongues, to inform them of the lot that awaits them.'

"Which address being read and considered, was unanimously adopted. And thereupon it was resolved that a committee of twelve be appointed forthwith to wait on the Mormon leaders, and see that the foregoing requisitions are strictly complied with by them; and upon their refusal, that said committee do, as the organ of this county, inform them that it is our unwavering purpose and fixed determination, after the fullest consideration of all the consequences and responsibilites under which we act, to use such means as shall insure their full and complete adoption; and that said committee, so far as may be within their power, report to this present meeting. And the following gentlemen were named as said committee:—

"Robert Johnson, James Campbell, Colonel Moses Wilson, Joel F. Chiles, Hon. Richard Fristoe, Abner F. Staples, Garr Johnson, Lewis Franklin, Russell Hicks, Esq., Colonel S. D. Lucas, Thomas Wilson and James M. Hunter, to whom was added Colonel R. Simpson, chairman.

And after an adjournment of two hours, the meeting again convened, and the committee of twelve reported that they had called on Mr. Phelps, the editor of the *Star;* Edward Partridge, the Bishop of the sect;

and Mr. Gilbert, the keeper of the Lord's store house; and some others; and that they declined giving any direct answer to the requisitions made of them, and wished an unreasonable time for consultation, not only with their brethren here, but in Ohio.

"Whereupon it was unanimously resolved by the meeting, that the *Star* printing office should be razed to the ground, the type and press secured. Which resolution was, with the utmost order, and the least noise and disturbance possible, forthwith carried into execution, as also some other steps of a similar tendency; but no blood was spilled, nor any blows inflicted. The meeting then adjourned till the 23rd instant, to meet again to know further concerning the determination of the Mormons.

"Resolved, that a copy of these proceedings be posted up at the post-office in this place, for the information of all concerned; and that the secretaries of this meeting send copies of the same to the principal editors in the eastern and middle states for publication; that the Mormon brethren may know at a distance that the gates of Zion are closed against them—that their interests will be best promoted by remaining among those who know and appreciate their merits."

RICHARD SIMPSON, Chairman.

S. D. LUCAS,
J. H. FLOURNOY, } Secretaries.

The citizens' meeting again convened on the 23rd day of July, 1833, which was composed of gentlemen from all parts of the county, and much more unanimously attended than the meeting of the 20th instant.

The meeting was organized by the chairman taking his seat, when the following gentlemen were appointed a committee, to wit:—

Henry Chiles, Esq., Dr. N. K. Olmstead, H. L. Brazile, Esq., Zachariah Waller, Samuel Weston, Esq., William L. Irwin, Leonidas Oldham, S. C. Owens, Esq., George Simpson, Captain Benjamin Majors, James C. Sadler, Colonel William Bowers, Henry Younger, Russell Hicks, Esq., Aaron Overton, John Harris, and Harmon Gregg, to wait upon the Mormon leaders, who had intimated a wish to have a conference with said committee.

After an adjournment of two hours, the meeing again convened, when the committee reported to the meeting that they had waited on most of the Mormon leaders, consisting of the Bishop, Mr. Partridge; Mr. Phelps, Editor of the *Star;* Mr. Gilbert, the keeper of the Lord's store house, and Messrs, Corrill, Whitmer, and Morley, Elders of the Church; and that the said committee had entered into an amicable agreement with them, which they had reduced to writing, which they submitted: and that the committee have assured Mr. Phelps, that when ever he was ready to move, that the amount of all his loses should be paid to him by the citizens. The written agreement is as follows:*

The Prophet's Comment on the *Monitor* Article.

The foregoing is copied entire to give one sample of hypocritical bombast, and current falsehoods, with which the country was flooded in the early days of this Church. The declaration of the mob, by which they pledged to each other their lives, their bodily powers, fortunes, and sacred honors to remove the Church from Jackson county, is a very good climax for all the arguments used, falsehoods set forth, and even a full interpretation of the sublime admission that "vengeance belongs to God alone." The events that followed from this time till November, explain the *modus operandi* much more clearly than the publication in the *Monitor*, or other papers that generally were so willing to give the western missionaries, the doctors, lawyers, judges, justices, sheriffs, constables, military officers and other distinguished personages a fair chance against the Mormons.

Corner Stones of Kirtland Temple Laid.

On the same day (July 23rd), while the brethren in Missouri were preparing to leave the county, through the violence of the mob, the corner stones of the Lord's House were laid in Kirtland, after the order of the Holy Priesthood.

August 2.—I received the following:

Revelation.†

1. Verily I say unto you my friends, I speak unto you with my voice, even the voice of my Spirit, that I may show unto you my will concerning your brethren in the land of Zion, many of whom are truly humble and are seeking diligently to learn wisdom and to find truth.

*The document is already printed in full on pages 394, 395.

†Doctrine and Covenants, sec. xcvii. Respecting the School of the Prophets referred to in the above revelation, Elder Parley P. Pratt, whose course is so highly commended in the revelation, writes in his *Autobiography*, page 100: "In the latter part of the summer (1833) and in the autumn, I devoted almost my entire time in ministering among the churches, holding meetings, visiting the sick, comforting the afflicted, and giving counsel. A school of Elders was also organized, over which I

2. Verily, verily I say unto you, blessed are such, for they shall obtain; for I, the Lord, show mercy unto all the meek, and upon all whomsoever I will, that I may be justified when I shall bring them unto judgment.

3. Behold, I say unto you, concerning the school in Zion, I, the Lord, am well pleased that there should be a school in Zion, and also with my servant Parley P. Pratt, for he abideth in me.

4. And inasmuch as he continueth to abide in me he shall continue to preside over the school in the land of Zion until I shall give unto him other commandments.

5. And I will bless him with a multiplicity of blessings, in expounding all scriptures and mysteries to the edification of the school, and of the church in Zion.

6. And to the residue of the school, I, the Lord, am willing to show mercy; nevertheless, there are those that must needs be chastened, and their works shall be made known.

7. The ax is laid at the root of the trees; and every tree that bringeth not forth good fruit shall be hewn down and cast into the fire. I, the Lord, have spoken it.

8. Verily I say unto you, all among them who know their hearts are honest, and are broken, and their spirits contrite, and are willing to observe their covenants by sacrifice—yea, every sacrifice which I, the Lord, shall command—they are accepted of me.

9. For I, the Lord, will cause them to bring forth as a very fruitful tree which is planted in a goodly land, by a pure stream, that yieldeth much precious fruit.

10. Verily I say unto you, that it is my will that a house should be built unto me in the land of Zion, like unto the pattern which I have given you.

11. Yea, let it be built speedily, by the tithing of my people.

12. Behold, this is the tithing and the sacrifice which I, the Lord, require at their hands, that there may be a house built unto me for the salvation of Zion—

13. For a place of thanksgiving for all saints, and for a place of

was called to preside. This class, to the number of about sixty, met for instructions once a week. The place of meeting was in the open air, under some tall trees, in a retired place in the wilderness, where we prayed, preached and prophesied, and exercised ourselves in the gifts of the Holy Spirit. Here great blessings were poured out, and many great and marvelous things were manifested and taught. The Lord gave me great wisdom, and enabled me to teach and edify the Elders, and comfort and encourage them in their preparations for the great work which lay before us. I was also much edified and strengthened. To attend this school I had to travel on foot, and sometimes with bare feet at that, about six miles. This I did once a week, besides visiting and preaching in five or six branches a week.

instruction for all those who are called to the work of the ministry in all their several callings and offices;

14. That they may be perfected in the understanding of their ministry, in theory, in principle, and in doctrine, in all things pertaining to the kingdom of God on the earth, the keys of which kingdom have been conferred upon you.

15. And inasmuch as my people build a house unto me in the name of the Lord, and do not suffer any unclean thing to come into it, that it be not defiled my glory shall rest upon it;

16. Yea, and my presence shall be there, for I will come into it, and all the pure in heart that shall come into it shall see God.

17. But if it be defiled I will not come into it, and my glory shall not be there; for I will not come into unholy temples.

18. And, now, behold, if Zion do these things she shall prosper, and spread herself and become very glorious, very great, and very terrible.

19. And the nations of the earth shall honor her, and shall say: Surely Zion is the city of our God, and surely Zion cannot fall, neither be moved out of her place, for God is there, and the hand of the Lord is there;

20. And he hath sworn by the power of his might to be her salvation and her high tower.

21. Therefore, verily, thus saith the Lord, let Zion rejoice, for this is Zion—THE PURE IN HEART; therefore, let Zion rejoice, while all the wicked shall mourn.

22. For behold, and lo, vengeance cometh speedily upon the ungodly as the whirlwind; and who shall escape it?

23. The Lord's scourge shall pass over by night and by day, and the report thereof shall vex all people; yea, it shall not be stayed until the Lord come;

24. For the indignation of the Lord is kindled against their abominations and all their wicked works.

25. Nevertheless, Zion shall escape if she observe to do all things whatsoever I have commanded her.

26. But if she observe not to do whatsoever I have commanded her, I will visit her according to all her works, with sore affliction, with pestilence, with plague, with sword, with vengeance, with devouring fire.

27. Nevertheless, let it be read this once to her ears, that I, the Lord, have accepted of her offering; and if she sin no more none of these things shall come upon her;

28. And I will bless her with blessings, and multiply a multiplicity of blessings upon her, and upon her generations forever and ever, saith the Lord your God. Amen.*

*"This revelation," writes Elder Pratt (*Autobiography*, p. 102)," was not com-

August 6th.—I received the following:

*Revelation.**

1. Verily I say unto you my friends, fear not, let your hearts be comforted; yea rejoice evermore, and in everything give thanks;

2. Waiting patiently on the Lord, for your prayers have entered into the ears of the Lord of Sabaoth, and are recorded with this seal and testament—the Lord hath sworn and decreed that they shall be granted.

3. Therefore, he giveth this promise unto you, with an immutable covenant that they shall be fulfilled; and all things wherewith you have been afflicted shall work together for your good, and to my name's glory, saith the Lord.

4. And now, verily I say unto you concerning the laws of the land, it is my will that my people should observe to do all things whatsoever I command them.

5. And that law of the land which is constitutional, supporting that principle of freedom in maintaining rights and privileges, belongs to all mankind, and is justifiable before me.

6. Therefore, I, the Lord, justify you, and your brethren of my church, in befriending that law which is the constitutional law of the land;

7. And as pertaining to law of man, whatsoever is more or less than this cometh of evil.

8. I, the Lord God, make you free, therefore ye are free indeed; and the law also maketh you free.

9. Nevertheless, when the wicked rule the people mourn.

10. Wherefore, honest men and wise men should be sought for diligently, and good men and wise men ye should observe to uphold; otherwise whatsoever is less than these cometh of evil.

11. And I give unto you a commandment, that ye shall forsake all evil and cleave unto all good, that ye shall live by every word which proceedeth forth out of the mouth of God.

12. For he will give unto the faithful line upon line, precept upon precept; and I will try you and prove you herewith.

13. And whoso layeth down his life in my cause, for my name's sake, shall find it again, even life eternal.

14. Therefore, be not afraid of your enemies, for I have decreed

plied with by the leaders and Church in Missouri as a whole (notwithstanding many were humble and faithful); therefore, the threatened judgment was poured out to the uttermost, as the history of the five following years will show."

*Doctrine and Covenants, sec. xcviii.

in my heart, saith the Lord, that I will prove you in all things, whether you will abide in my covenant, even unto death, that you may be found worthy.

15. For if ye will not abide in my covenant ye are not worthy of me.

16. Therefore, renounce war and proclaim peace, and seek diligently to turn the hearts of the children to their fathers, and the hearts of the fathers to the children;

17. And again, the hearts of the Jews unto the prophets, and the prophets unto the Jews; lest I come and smite the whole earth with a curse, and all flesh be consumed before me.

18. Let not your hearts be troubled; for in my Father's house are many mansions, and I have prepared a place for you; and where my Father and I am, there ye shall be also.

19. Behold, I, the Lord, am not well pleased with many who are in the church at Kirtland;

20. For they do not forsake their sins, and their wicked ways, the pride of their hearts, and their covetousness, and all their detestable things, and observe the words of wisdom and eternal life which I have given unto them.

21. Verily I say unto you, that I, the Lord, will chasten them and will do whatsoever I list, if they do not repent and observe all things whatsoever I have said unto them.

22. And again I say unto you, if ye observe to do whatsoever I command you, I, the Lord, will turn away all wrath and indignation from you, and the gates of hell shall not prevail against you.

23. Now, I speak unto you concerning your families—if men will smite you, or your families, once, and ye bear it patiently and revile not against them, neither seek revenge, ye shall be rewarded;

24. But if ye bear it not patiently, it shall be accounted unto you as being meted out as a just measure unto you.

25. And again, if your enemy shall smite you the second time, and you revile not against your enemy, and bear it patiently, your reward shall be an hundredfold.

26. And again, if he shall smite you the third time, and ye bear it patiently, your reward shall be doubled unto you four-fold;

27. And these three testimonies shall stand against your enemy if he repent not, and shall not be blotted out.

28. And now, verily I say unto you, if that enemy shall escape my vengeance, that he be not brought into judgment before me, then ye shall see to it that ye warn him in my name, that he come no more upon you, neither upon your family, even your children's children unto the third and fourth generation.

29. And then, if he shall come upon you or your children, or your children's children unto the third and fourth generation, I have delivered thine enemy into thine hands;

30. And then if thou wilt spare him, thou shalt be rewarded for thy righteousness; and also thy children and thy children's children unto the third and fourth generation.

31. Nevertheless, thine enemy is in thine hands; and if thou rewardest him according to his works thou art justified; if he has sought thy life, and thy life is endangered by him, thine enemy is in thine hands and thou art justified.

32. Behold, this is the law I gave unto my servant Nephi, and thy fathers, Joseph, and Jacob, and Isaac, and Abraham, and all mine ancient prophets and apostles.

33. And again, this is the law that I gave unto mine ancients, that they should not go out unto battle against any nation, kindred, tongue, or people, save I, the Lord, commanded them.

34. And if any nation, tongue, or people should proclaim war against them, they should first lift a standard of peace unto that people, nation, or tongue;

35. And if that people did not accept the offering of peace, neither the second nor the third time, they should bring these testimonies before the Lord;

36. Then I, the Lord, would give unto them a commandment, and justify them in going out to battle against that nation, tongue, or people.

37. And I, the Lord, would fight their battles, and their children's battles, and their children's children, until they had avenged themselves on all their enemies, to the third and fourth generation.

38. Behold, this is an ensample unto all people, saith the Lord your God, for justification before me.

39. And again, verily I say unto you, if after thine enemy has come upon thee the first time, he repent and come unto thee praying thy forgiveness, thou shalt forgive him, and shalt hold it no more as a testimony against thine enemy—

40. And so on unto the second and third time; and as oft as thine enemy repenteth of the trespass wherewith he has trespassed against thee, thou shalt forgive him, until seventy times seven.

41. And if he trespass against thee and repent not the first time, nevertheless thou shalt forgive him.

42. And if he trespass against thee the second time, and repent not, nevertheless thou shalt forgive him.

43. And if he trespass against thee the third time, and repent not, thou shalt also forgive him.

44. But if he trespass against thee the fourth time thou shalt not forgive him, but shalt bring these testimonies before the Lord; and they shall not be blotted out until he repent and reward thee four-fold in all things wherewith he has trespassed against thee.

45. And if he do this, thou shalt forgive him with all thine heart; and if he do not this, I, the Lord, will avenge thee of thine enemy an hundred-fold;

46. And upon his children, and upon his children's children of all them that hate me, unto the third and fourth generation.

47. But if the children shall repent, or the children's children, and turn to the Lord their God, with all their hearts and with all their might, mind, and strength, and restore four-fold for all their trespasses wherewith they have trespassed, or wherewith their fathers have trespassed, or their father's fathers, then thine indignation shall be turned away;

48. And vengeance shall no more come upon them, saith the Lord thy God, and their trespasses shall never be brought any more as a testimony before the Lord against them. Amen.

CHAPTER XXIX.

MINOR EVENTS IN ZION AND KIRTLAND—AN APPEAL TO THE GOVERNOR OF MISSOURI.

August 21.—At a council of High Priests in Zion, Elder Christian Whitmer was ordained to the High Priesthood. And on the 28th, the council resolved, that no High Priest, Elder, or Priest, shall ordain any Priest, Elder, or High Priest in the land of Zion, without the consent of a conference of High Priests.*

Soon after the arrival of Oliver Cowdery at Kirtland,† arrangements were made to dispatch Elders Orson Hyde and John Gould‡ to Jackson county, Missouri, with advice to the Saints in their unfortunate situation, through the late outrage of the mob.

September 4.—I wrote as follows to Sister Vienna Jaques, at Independence, Missouri:

Prophet's Letter to Vienna Jaques.

Dear Sister:—Having a few leisure moments, I sit down to communicate to you a few words, which I know I am under obligation to improve for your satisfaction, if it should be a satisfaction for you to receive a few words from your unworthy brother in Christ. I re-

*There were twenty High Priests present at the council meeting. The minutes of the meeting are found in the *Far West Record* pages 35, 36.

†The exact date of Elder Cowdery's arrival in Kirtland as a special messenger from the brethren in Zion cannot be ascertained.

‡This was the same John Gould who was subsequently ordained a member of the First Council of Seventy.

ceived your letter some time since, containing a history of your journey and your safe arrival, for which I bless the Lord; I have often felt a whispering since I received your letter, like this: "Joseph, thou art indebted to thy God for the offering of thy Sister Vienna, which proved a savor of life as pertaining to thy pecuniary concerns. Therefore she should not be forgotten of thee, for the Lord hath done this, and thou shouldst remember her in all thy prayers and also by letter, for she oftentimes calleth on the Lord, saying, O Lord, inspire thy servant Joseph to communicate by letter some word to thine unworthy handmaiden, and say all my sins are forgiven, and art thou not content with the chastisement wherewith thou hast chastised thy handmaiden?" Yea, sister, this seems to be the whispering of a spirit, and judge ye what spirit it is. I was aware when you left Kirtland that the Lord would chasten you, but I prayed fervently in the name of Jesus that you might live to receive your inheritance, agreeable to the commandment which was given concerning you. I am not at all astonished at what has happened to you, neither to what has happened to Zion, and I could tell all the whys and wherefores of all these calamities. But alas, it is in vain to warn and give precepts, for all men are naturally disposed to walk in their own paths as they are pointed out by their own fingers and are not willing to consider and walk in the path which is pointed out by another, saying, This is the way, walk ye in it, although he should be an unerring director, and the Lord his God sent him. Nevertheless, I do not feel disposed to cast any reflections, but I feel to cry mightily unto the Lord that all things, which have happened may work together for good; yea, I feel to say, O Lord, let Zion be comforted, let her waste places be built up and established an hundred fold; let Thy Saints come unto Zion out of every nation; let her be exalted to the third heavens, and let Thy judgment be sent forth unto victory; and after this great tribulation, let Thy blessing fall upon Thy people, and let Thy handmaid live till her soul shall be satisfied in beholding the glory of Zion; for notwithstanding her present affliction, she shall yet arise and put on her beautiful garments, and be the joy and glory of the whole earth. Therefore let your heart be comforted; live in strict obedience to the commandments of God, and walk humbly before Him, and He will exalt thee in His own due time. I will assure you that the Lord has respect unto the offering you made. Brother David W. Patten has just returned from his tour to the east, and gives us great satisfaction as to his ministry. He has raised up a church of about eighty-three members in that part of the country where his friends live—in the state of New York. Many were healed through his instrumentality, several cripples were restored. As many as twelve that were afflicted came at a time from a distance to be healed; he and others administered in the name of Jesus, and they were made whole. Thus you see that the laborers in the Lord's vineyard are laboring with their might, while the day lasts, knowing "the night soon cometh when no man can work."

[Signed] JOSEPH SMITH.

September 11.—The followng members, residing in Kirtland, viz.: F. G. Williams, Sidney Rigdon, N. K. Whitney, with myself, and Oliver Cowdery, delegate to represent the residue of the members in Independence, Missouri, met in council, to consider the expediency of establishing a printing press in Kirtland, when it was

Resolved, unanimously, that a press be established, and conducted under the firm name of F. G. Williams & Co.

Resolved, that the above firm publish a paper, as soon as arrangements can be made, entitled the *Latter-day Saints' Messenger and Advocate.*

Resolved, also, that *The Evening and Morning Star,* formerly published in Jackson county, Missouri, by the firm of F. G. Williams & Co., to be conducted by Oliver Cowdery, one of the members of the firm, until it is transferred to its former location.

The same day Bishop Partridge was acknowledged by the council in Zion, to be the head of the Church in Zion at that time; and by virtue of his office, was acknowledged the moderator or president of the councils or conferences.

Ten High Priests were appointed to watch over the ten branches of the Church in Zion.*

A hymn, concerning the travels, toils, troubles, and tribulations of the Nephites, was sung in tongues by Elder W. W. Phelps, interpreted by Elder Lyman Wight.

September 26.—The council again assembled in

*The minutes of the council are contained in the *Far West Record,* page 36. The names of the presidents of the branches and the number of the branch each presided over respectively are given as follows: Newel Knight, Branch No. 1; Daniel Stanton, Branch No. 2; David Whitmer, Branch No. 3; John Corrill, Branch No. 4; Thomas B. Marsh, Branch No. 5; Peter Dustin, Branch No. 6; Lyman Wight, Branch No. 7; Parley P. Pratt, Branch No. 8; Simeon Carter, Branch No. 9; Calvin Beebe, Branch No. 10.

Zion, and ordained Jesse Hitchcock, Elias Higbee,* and Isaac Higbee,† High Priests.

Brother John Tanner‡ sent his two sons to Kirtland to learn the will of the Lord, whether he should remove to Zion or Kirtland. It was decided by the unanimous voice of the council, on the 28th of September, that it was the will of the Lord for all who were able and willing, to build up and strengthen the stake in Kirtland. Brother Tanner was counseled accordingly.

About this time, Elders Hyde and Gould arrived in Zion, and the Church having made the necessary preparations, Elders W. W. Phelps and Orson Hyde were dispatched to the Governor of Missouri, residing at Jefferson City, the capital of the state, with the following:

PETITION.

September 28, 1833.

To His Excellency Daniel Dunklin, Governor of the State of Missouri:

We, the undersigned, citizens of the Republic of the United States of America, inhabitants of the state of Missouri, and residents of Jackson county, members of the Church of Christ, vulgarly called "Mor-

*The Higbee family subsequently became very prominent in the Church. Elias Higbee was the son of Isaac and Sophia Higbee. He was born 23rd of October, 1795, in Galloway, Gloucester county, New Jersey. At the age of twenty-two he married Sarah Ward and removed to Cincinnati. He received the Gospel in the spring of 1832, and during the summer following went to Jackson county, Missouri, but returned to Cincinnati the following winter, where he was ordained an Elder by his Brother Isaac, on the 20th of February, 1833. He returned to Missouri with his family, arriving in Zion in the month of March, 1833, and on the 26th of September following he was ordained a High Priest.—(*Millennial Star*, vol. xxi, page 203; also *Far West Record*, page 37.)

†Isaac Higbee was also the son of Isaac and Sophia Higbee. He was born in Galloway, Gloucester county, New Jersey, on the 23rd of December, 1797. When between five and six years old he removed with his parents to Ohio. February 11th, 1819, he married Heziah String. About the first of May, 1832, his parents received the Gospel, and a few months afterwards himself and wife did the same. In the spring of 1833, he removed with his family to Zion, and in September following, as stated by the Prophet, was ordained a High Priest.

‡John Tanner was the son of Joshua and Thankful Tefft Tanner. He was born at Hopkinton, Rhode Island, August 15, 1778. According to the tradition of the family, Francis Tanner, the grandfather of John Tanner, the subject of this sketch, came from England with his two brothers—Nathan and William—and settled in the state of Rhode Island, about the year 1718.

mons," believing in God, and worshiping Him according to His revealed wili contained in the Holy Bible, and the fulness of the Gospel contained in the Book of Mormon, and the revelations and commandments of God through Jesus Christ, respectfully show:—

That we, your petitioners, having purchased lands of the United States, and of the State of Missouri, and of the inhabitants of said state, for the purpose of improving the same, and peaceably enjoying our rights, privileges, immunities, and religion, according to the constitution and laws of the state and national governments, have suffered unjustly and unlawfully in property, in person, and in reputation, as follows:—

First, in the spring of 1832, some persons, in the deadly hours of the night, commenced stoning or brick-batting some of our houses, and breaking in our windows, disturbing ourselves, our wives, and our children; and also, some few days after, they called a county meeting to consult measures to remove us, but after some confusion among themselves, they dispersed with doing no more than threatening on that day. In the fall of the same year, they, or some one, burned a large quantity of hay in the stack, and soon after commenced shooting into some of our houses, and at many times insulting with abusive language.

Secondly, about the middle of July last, yea, in fact, previous, they commenced brick-batting our houses again, and breaking in our windows. At this time, July 18th, the following document was in circulation:* * * * * * * * *

On Saturday, the 20th of July last, according to the foregoing document, there assembled, suddenly, in the town of Independence, at the court house, between four and five hundred persons, who sent Robert Johnson, James Campbell, Moses Wilson, Joel F. Chiles, Richard Bristoe, Abner F. Staples, Garr Johnson, Lewis Franklin, Russell Hicks, S. D. Lucas, Thomas Wilson, James M. Hunter, and Richard Simpson to some of your petitioners; namely, Edward Partridge, A. S. Gilbert, John Corrill, Isaac Morley, John Whitmer, and W. W. Phelps, and demanded that we should immediately stop the publication of the *Evening and Morning Star,* and close printing in Jackson county; and that we, as Elders of said Church, should agree to remove out of the county forthwith. We asked for three months for consideration. They would not grant it. We asked for ten days. They would not grant it, but said fifteen minutes was the longest, and refused to hear any reasons. Of course the conversation broke up.

The four or five hundred persons, as a *mob,* then proceeded to demolish or raze to the ground, the printing office and dwelling house of W. W. Phelps & Co. Mrs. Phelps, with a sick infant and the

*Document will be found on pages 374-376. It was the mob's "secret constitution."

rest of her children, together with the furniture in the house, were thrown out of doors— the press was broken, the type pied—the book-work, furniture, apparatus, property, etc., of the office, were principally destroyed, and the office thrown down, whereby seven hands were thrown out of employment, and three families left destitute of the means of subsistence.

The loss of the whole office, including the stoppage of *The Evening and Morning Star*, a monthly paper, and the *Upper Missouri Advertiser*, a weekly paper, was about six thousand dollars, without the damages which must result in consequence of their suspension.

The mob then proceeded to demolish the store-house and destroy the goods of Gilbert, Whitney & Co.; but Mr. Gilbert assuring them the goods should be packed by the 23rd inst., [July] they then stopped the destruction of property, and proceeded to do personal violence. They took Edward Partridge, the Bishop of the Church, from his dwelling house by force, and a Mr. Allen, and stripping them of their coats, vests, and hats, or causing them to do it themselves, tarred and feathered them in the presence of the mob, before the court house. They caught other members of the Church to serve them in like manner, but they made their escape. With horrid yells and the most blasphemous epithets they sought for other leading Elders, but found them not. It being late, they adjourned until the 23rd inst.

On the 23rd inst., early in the day, the mob again assembled to the number of about five hundred, many of them armed with rifles, dirks, pistols, clubs and whips; one or two companies riding into town bearing the red flag, raising again the *horrid yell*. They proceeded to take some of the leading Elders by force, declaring it to be their intention to whip them with from fifty to five hundred lashes apiece, to demolish their dwelling houses, and let their negroes loose to go through our plantations, and lay open our fields for the destruction of our crops.

Whereupon John Corrill, John Whitmer, W. W. Phelps, A. S. Gilbert, Edward Partridge, and Isaac Morley, made no resitance, but offered themselves a ransom for the Church, willing to be scourged or die, if that would appease their anger towards the Church, but were assured by the mob, that every man, woman, and child would be whipped or scourged, until they were driven out of the county, as the mob declared that either they or the "Mormons" must leave the county, or they, or the "Mormons" must die.

The mob then chose a new committee, consisting of Samuel C. Owens, Leonidas Oldham, G. W. Simpson, M. L. Irwin, John Harris, Henry Chiles, Harvey H. Younger, Hugh L. Brazile, N. K. Olmstead, James C. Sadler, William Bowers, Benjamin Majors, Zachariah Waller, Harman Gregg, Aaron Overton, and Samuel Weston, who with Edward Partridge, Isaac Morley, John Corrill, W. W. Phelps, A. S. Gilbert, and John Whitmer, entered into the following stipulation:—

"Memorandum of agreement between the undersigned of the Mormon society in Jackson county, Missouri, and a committee appointed by a public meeting of the citizens of said county, made the 23rd day of July, 1833.

" It is understood that the undersigned members of the society, do give their solemn pledge each for himself, as follows, to wit:—

"That Oliver Cowdery, W. W. Phelps, William E. M'Lellin, Edward Partridge, Lyman Wight, Simeon Carter, Peter and John Whitmer, and Harvey Whitlock, shall remove with their families out of this county on or before the first day of January next; and that they, as well as the two hereinafter named, use all their influence to induce all the brethren now here, to remove as soon as possible—one half, say, by the first of January next, and all by the first day of April next; to advise and try all means in their power, to stop any more of their sect from moving to this county, and as to those now on the road, they will use their influence to prevent their settling permanently in the county, but that they shall only make arrangements for temporary shelter, till a new location is agreed on for the society. John Corrill and Algernon S. Gilbert, are allowed to remain as general agents to wind up the business of the society, so long as necessity shall require; and said Gilbert may sell out his merchandise now on hand, but is to make no new importations.

"The *Star* is not again to be published, nor a press set up by any of the society in this county.

"If the said Edward Partridge and W. W. Phelps move their families by the first day of January as aforesaid, they themselves will be allowed to go and come in order to transact and wind up their business.

"The committee pledge themselves to use all their influence to prevent any violence being used so long as a compliance with the foregoing terms is observed by the parties concerned.

"To which agreement are subscribed the names of the above-named committee, as also those of the Mormon brethren named in the report as having been present."

The damages which your petitioners have sustained in consequence of this outrage and stipulation are, at present, incalculable. A great number of industrious inhabitants who were dependent on their labors for support, have been thrown out of employment, and are kept so by the threatenings of those who compose the mob. [See their resolutions as published in the *Western Monitor*, numbers 1, 2, 3, 4 and 5, August 2, 1833.] In estimating the damages which have resulted from the beginning to this time from those illegal and inhuman proceedings against your poor and persecuted petitioners, were they to name many thousands of dollars, it would be short of a remuneration. Most of the mechanic's shops have been closed; two pair of blacksmith's bellows have been cut in pieces; our merchant, as you will see by the foregoing stipulation, has been forbidden to import or bring into the country any more goods, by which his business has been ruined.

Soon after the above stipulation was made, some of your petitioners proceeded to make a new location in Van Buren county on the south, but the settlers in that county drew up an agreement among themselves to drive us from that county, after we had commenced laboring there; they threatened to shoot our cattle, and destroy our labor, and in fact, "the foxes have holes, and the birds of the air have nests, but we have not where to lay our heads." We were obliged to return.

Since the stipulation was entered into, some of our houses have been broken open, and the inmates threatened to be shot if they stirred; and also some of our houses have been stoned or brick-batted.

Also, that since some publications have appeared in the *Western Monitor* and other papers, censuring the conduct of the mob, the *leaders have begun to threaten life,* declaring that if any of the Mormons attempted to seek redress by law or otherwise, for character, person, or property, they shall *die!*

Now therefore, for ourselves, as members of the Church, we declare, with the exception of poverty, which has not yet become a crime by the laws of the land, that the crimes charged against us, so far as we are acquainted, contained in the documents above written, and those in the proceedings of the mob, as published in the *Western Monitor* of August 2nd, *are not true.* In relation to inviting free people of color to emigrate to this section of country, and other matters relative to our society, see the 109th, 110th, and 111th pages of *The Evening and Morning Star,* and the *Extra* accompanying the same, dated July 16th, which are annexed to this petition. Our situation is a critical one; we are located upon the western limits of the state, and of the United States; where desperadoes can commit outrages, and even murder, and escape in a few minutes beyond the reach of process; where the most abandoned of all classes from almost every state may too often pass to the Mexican states, or to the more remote regions of the Rocky Mountains to escape the grasp of justice; where numerous tribes of Indians, located by the General Government amid the corrupting influence of mid-day mobs, might massacre our defenseless women and children, with impunity.

Influenced by the precepts of our beloved Savior when we have been smitten on the one cheek, we have turned the other also; when we have been sued at the law, and our coat been taken, we have given them our cloak also; when they have compelled us to go with them a mile, we have gone with them twain; we have borne the above outrages without murmuring; but we cannot patiently bear them any longer; according to the laws of God and man, we have borne enough. Believing with all honorable men, that whenever that fatal hour shall arrive that the poorest citizen's person, property, or rights and privileges, shall be trampled upon by a lawless mob with impunity, that moment a dagger is plunged into the heart of the constitution, and the union must tremble! Assuring ourselves that no republican will suffer the liberty of the press, the freedom of speech, and the liberty of conscience, to be silenced by a mob, without raising a helping hand to save his country from disgrace, we solicit assistance to obtain our rights, holding ourselves amenable to the laws of our county whenever we transgress them.

Knowing as we do, that the threats of this mob, in most cases, have been put into execution, and knowing also that every officer, civil and military, with a very few exceptions, has pledged his life and honor to force us from the county, dead or alive; and believing that civil process cannot be served without the aid of the executive; and not wishing to have the blood of our defenseless women and children to stain the land which has once been stained by the blood of our fathers to purchase our liberty, we appeal to the Governor for aid, asking him to raise by express proclamation, or otherwise, a sufficient number of troops, who, with us, may be empowered to defend our rights, that we may sue for damages for the loss of property, for abuse, for defamation, as to ourselves, and if advisable try for treason against the government; that the law of the land may not be defiled, or nullified, but peace be restored to our country. And we will ever pray.

This petition was signed by Edward Partridge and nearly all the members of the Church in Jackson county.

CHAPTER XXX.

THE PROPHET'S MISSION TO CANADA.

The Prophet Starts for Canada.

October 5.—I started on a journey to the east, and to Canada, in company with Elders Rigdon and Freeman Nickerson,* and arrived the same day at Lamb's tavern, in Ashtabula;† and the day following, the Sabbath, we arrived in Springfield, whilst the brethren were in meeting, and Elder Rigdon spoke to the congregation. A large and attentive congregation assembled at Brother Rudd's in the evening, to whom we bore our testimony.‡ We

*Freeman Nickerson was born in South Dennis, Barnstable county, Massachusetts, February 5, 1778. His father's name was Eleazer Nickerson, his mother's Thankful Chase Nickerson. Her father was a seaman. In 1800 Freeman emigrated to Vermont, and settled in Windsor county; and here he married Huldah Chapman, daughter of Eliphalet and Abigail Chase Chapman, on January 10, 1801. He served in the war of 1812 and was commissioned a lieutenant. He received the Gospel at Dayton, Catteraugus county, New York, in April, 1833, being baptized by Elder Zerubbabel Snow, and was soon after ordained a Deacon. Brother Nickerson performed a mission among the Saints in Kirtland and vicinity in the early fall of 1833, and on the 5th of October started for Canada in company with the Prophet and Sidney Rigdon, taking them on this journey with his own team and conveyance.—"Obituary Record," (Ms.), page 45.

†Ashtabula is in Ashtabula county, Ohio, some forty miles northeast of Kirtland.

‡While on this journey to Canada the Prophet kept a daily journal, from which the narrative he gives in the text was evidently taken. This journal is in the Prophet's own handwriting, and is one of the interesting relics among the records of the Church. At various points in the Prophet's narrative of this mission, I shall quote whatever may be of interest in addition to the narrative given in the text. Of this meeting at Rudd's the Prophet says: "Had a great congregation—paid good attention. O God, seal our testimony to their hearts!"—(Page 6.)

§Springfield is in the western part of Erie county, Pennsylvania.

continued at Springfield§ until the 8th of October, when we removed to Brother Roundy's at Elk Creek; and continuing our journey on the evening of the 9th, we arrived at a tavern, and on the 10th, at Brother Job Lewis,' in Westfield* where we met the brethren according to previous appointment, and spoke to them as the Spirit gave utterance, greatly to their gratification.

This day, October 10th, Elder Frederick G. Williams wrote as follows from Kirtland to the Saints in Missouri:

Letter to Saints in Zion.

Dear Brethren:—It is a long time since we have received any intelligence from you, save a letter received by Brother Elliott from Elder John Whitmer, which informed us that he had written four letters since Elder Oliver Cowdery left, but we have not received any of them, nor any others from Zion, except one from Bishop Partridge, of August 13th, and have had no information, to be depended upon, concerning the riot, and the situation of the brethren in Zion; and considering that the enemy have commenced intercepting our letters, I direct this to Mrs. Billings, thinking, by so doing, that you may get it. The brethren here are all engaged in the work of the Lord, and are using every exertion in their power for the welfare of Zion and for the promotion of the great cause of our Redeemer. Immediately after the arrival of Oliver Cowdery, we sat in council to know what should be done. The decision of the council was, that measures should be immediately taken to seek redress by the laws of our country, for your grievances; accordingly two messengers were dispatched for that purpose. (Let this suffice, for this may fall into the hands of the enemy). We have not received any revelation for a long time (which has been written), and none concerning the present situation of Zion; but it has been manifested to Joseph, and communicated to me by him, that the brethren in Zion should not sell any of their inheritances, nor move out of the county, save those who signed the agreement to go, and if it becomes necessary for those to move for their personal safety, let them be directed by wisdom, and seek for homes where the Lord shall open the way.

If Elder Phelps is obliged to move from that place, let him take his family and Elder Cowdery's wife, and come to Kirtland, but not to bring anything with him, except his bedding and clothing; and let Elder Gilbert furnish him with the means to bear his expenses; but it would not be expedient for Elder Phelps to come, provided the prospect is favorable for a reconciliation to the extent that the Saints are

§Springfield is in the western part of Erie county, Pennsylvania.

*Westfield was in Chautauqua county, New York, near the shore of Lake Erie.

not obliged to leave the county. We can do no more for you than we are doing; but we have this great consolation, that God will deliver Zion, and establish you upon the land of your everlasting inheritance. Remember that this is only for the trial of your faith, and he that overcomes and endures to the end, will be rewarded a hundred fold in this world, and in the world to come will receive eternal life; so, brethren, you have great reason to rejoice, for your redemption draweth nigh.

Presidents Smith and Rigdon are absent on a mission, and we do not expect their return until some time in November. They have gone down the lake to Niagara, from thence they expect to go into Upper Canada, as far as Long Point, and preach in all the most noted places on their way.

We held a council meeting this morning, on the subject of building, etc. It was decided by the council that we should discontinue the building of the Temple during the winter, for want of materials; and to prepare and get all things in readiness to recommence it early in the spring. It was also agreed that we should set the hands immediately to erect a house for the printing office, which is to be thirty by thirty-eight feet on the ground; the first story to be occupied for the School of the Prophets this winter, and the upper story for the printing press.

Oliver Cowdery started for New York on the first of October for the printing establishment, with eight hundred dollars. There will be as many hands employed upon the house as can work, and every exertion made to get the printing into operation, republish the *Star*, commencing from the last number printed, to be conducted by Oliver Cowdery (until an opportunity offers to transfer it again to Zion, to be conducted by W. W. Phelps & Co., as usual), and also publish a paper under the firm-name of F. G. Williams & Co., entitled the *Latter-day Saints' Messenger and Advocate*, which will be forwarded to subscribers for the *Star* by the first of December. Oliver has written to you for the names and residences of the subscribers for the *Star*, and if you have not sent them, we wish you to send them immediately, that there may be no delay in the papers going to subscribers as soon as they can be printed.

Bishop Whitney, also, started for New York at the same time, to replenish his store in Kirtland, with money enough to pay all the debts of both establishments, and expects to bring a larger supply of goods than at any former time. Thus you see the goodness and mercy of God in providing for His Saints. Not one week before Bishop Whitney started, the way seemed hedged up, and ten or twelve hundred dollars was the most that he had, and knew not where to obtain the amount he wanted; but by a remarkable interposition of Divine Providence, he was furnished with all he wanted, for which let us raise our hearts in gratitude to God, and praise His holy name, that He is a present help in every time of need.

We have seen a letter, written to Sister Whitney, in Nelson, that has a great deal to say about the gift of tongues, and the interpretation which was given by way of prophecy, namely, "that Zion would be delivered by judgments;" and that certain ones named, would go to such and such places among the Lamanites, and "great things would be done by them;" and also, that two Lamanites were at a meeting, and the following prophecy was delivered to them:—"That they were our friends, and that the Lord had sent them there; and the time would soon come, when they would embrace the Gospel;" and, also, "that if we will not fight for ourselves, the Indians will fight for us." Though all this may be true, yet, it is not needful that it should be spoken, for it is of no service to the Saints, and has a tendency to stir up the people to anger.

No prophecy spoken in tongues should be made public, for this reason:—Many who pretend to have the gift of interpretation are liable to be mistaken, and do not give the true interpretation of what is spoken; therefore, great care should be taken as respects this thing, but, if any speak in tongues a word of exhortation, or doctrine, or the principles of the Gospel, etc., let it be interpreted for the edification of the Church.

When you receive this letter, I wish you to write immediately, and direct your letters to David Elliott, Chagrin, Cuyahoga county, Ohio, and put this mark "X" on the back of it, if you do not wish it broken open, and he will forward it to us; and you will please to name in your letter, where and to whom we shall direct our reply, and thus we may evade interception. Yours in the bonds of love,

F. G. WILLIAMS.

Distraction About Zion.

At this time the evil and designing circulated a report, that Zion was to be extended as far east as Ohio, which in some degree tended to distract the minds of the Saints, and produced a momentary indecision about removing thither, according to the commandments; but the report was soon corrected, and the brethren continued to remove to Zion and Kirtland.

Narrative of Canada Journey Renewed.

On the 11th of October, we left Westfield, and continuing our journey, staid that night with a man named Nash, an infidel, with whom we reasoned, but to no purpose.* On the 12th,

*The Prophet in his Journal also says under this date (11th of October): "I feel very well in my mind. The Lord is with us, but have much anxiety about my family."—(Journal, page 7).

arrived at Father Nickerson's, at Perrysburg, New York,* where I received the following revelation:

Revelation. †

1. Verily, thus saith the Lord unto you, my friends Sidney and Joseph, your families are well; they are in mine hands, and I will do with them as seemeth me good; for in me there is all power.

2. Therefore, follow me, and listen to the counsel which I shall give unto you.

3. Behold, and lo, I have much people in this place, in the regions round about; and an effectual door shall be opened in the regions round about in this eastern land.

4. Therefore, I, the Lord, have suffered you to come unto this place; for thus it was expedient in me for the salvation of souls.

5. Therefore, verily I say unto you, lift up your voices unto this people; speak the thoughts that I shall put into your hearts, and you shall not be confounded before men;

6. For it shall be given you in the very hour, yea, in the very moment, what ye shall say.

7. But a commandment I give unto you, that ye shall declare whatsoever thing ye declare in my name, in solemnity of heart, in the spirit of meekness, in all things.

8. And I give unto you this promise, that inasmch as ye do this the Holy Ghost shall be shed forth in bearing record unto all things whatsoever ye shall say.

9. And it is expedient in me that you, my servant Sidney, should be a spokesman unto this people; yea, verily, I will ordain you unto this calling, even to be a spokesman unto my servant Joseph.

10. And I will give unto him power to be mighty in testimony.

11. And I will give unto thee power to be mighty in expounding all scriptures, that thou mayest be a spokesman unto him, and he shall be a revelator unto thee, that thou mayest know the certainty of all things pertaining to the things of my kingdom on the earth.

12. Therefore, continue your journey and let your hearts rejoice; for behold, and lo, I am with you even unto the end.

13. And now I give unto you a word concerning Zion. Zion shall be redeemed, although she is chastened for a little season.

14. Thy brethren, my servants Orson Hyde and John Gould, are in my hands; and inasmuch as they keep my commandments they shall be saved.

*This was Brother Freeman Nickerson who was conveying them to Canada, and this Perrysburg, Cattaraugus county, New York, was his place of residence.

†Doctrine and Covenants, sec. c.

15. Therefore, let your hearts be comforted; for all things shall work together for good to them that walk uprightly, and to the sanctification of the church.

16. For I will raise up unto myself a pure people, that will serve me in righteousness;

17. And all that call upon the name of the Lord, and keep his commandments, shall be saved. Even so. Amen.

On the day following (October 13th), Elder Rigdon preached to a large congregation, at Freeman Nickerson's, and I bore record while the Lord gave His Spirit in a remarkable manner.

At "Father" Nickerson's.

Monday, 14.—Continued our journey towards Canada, and arrived at Lodi, where we had an appointment, and preached in the evening to a small assembly, and made an appointment for Tuesday, the 15th, at 10 o'clock a. m., to be in the Presbyterian meeting house. When the hour arrived, the keeper of the house refused to open the doors, and the meeting was thus prevented. We came immediately away, leaving the people in great confusion, and continued our journey till Friday, the 18th, when we arrived at the house of Freeman A. Nickerson, in Upper Canada, having passed through a fine and well-cultivated country, after entering the province, and having had many peculiar feelings in relation to both the country and people. We were kindly received by Freeman A. Nickerson, who lived at Mount Pleasant, which was near Brantford, the county seat of Brant county.

Through Upper Canada.

Sunday, 20.—At 10 o'clock we met an attentive congregation at Brantford; and the same evening a large assembly at Mount Pleasant, at Mr. Nickerson's. The people gave good heed to the things spoken.

Meeting at Brantford.

Tuesday, 22.—We went to the village of Colburn; and although it snowed severely, we held a meeting by candle-light on Wednesday evening, and were publicly opposed by a Wesleyan Methodist. He was very tumultuous, but exhibited a great lack of

At Colburn.

reason, knowledge, and wisdom, and gave us no opportunity to reply.

At Waterford.

Thursday, 24.—At the house of Mr. Beman, in Colburn, whence we left for Waterford,* where we spoke to a small congregation; thence to Mount Pleasant, and preached to a large congregation the same evening, when Freeman A. Nickerson and his wife declared their belief in the work, and offered themselves for baptism. Great excitement prevailed in every place we visited.†

Meetings and Baptisms at Mt. Pleasant.

Saturday, 26.—Preached at Mount Pleasant; the people were very tender and inquiring.

Sunday, 27.—Preached to a large congregation at Mount Pleasant, after which I baptized twelve, and others were deeply impressed, and desired another meeting, which I appointed for the day following.

Monday, 28.—In the evening, we broke bread, and laid on hands for the gift of the Holy Ghost, and for confirmation, having baptized two more. The Spirit was given in great power to some, and peace to others.‡

Tuesday, 29.—After preaching at 10 o'clock a. m., I baptized two, and confirmed them at the water's side. Last evening we ordained F. A. Nickerson an Elder; and one of the sisters received the gift of tongues, which made the Saints rejoice exceedingly.§ Tuesday, the 29th of October, also we took our departure from Mount Pleasant, on our return to Kirtland, and arrived at Buffalo, New York, on the 31st.

Return to Kirtland.

Friday, November 1.—I left Buffalo, New York, at 8 o'clock a. m., and arrived at my house in Kirtland on Monday, the 4th, 10 a. m.

*Waterford is immediately south of Brantford, in the adjoining county of Norfolk.

†"The result is in the hands of God," adds the Prophet. (Journal, page 14.) I also add the Prophet's entry for the 25th, which is omitted in his narrative. Friday, 25th. "This afternoon, at a Mr. Patrick's, expect to hold a meeting this evening. People very superstitious. O God, establish thy word among this people. Held a meeting this evening; had an attentive congregation; the Spirit gave utterance." (Page 14.)

‡"May God carry on His work in this place," adds the Prophet, "till all shall know Him. Amen." (Page 16.)

§"May God," adds the Prophet, "increase the gifts among them for His Son's

and found my family well, according to the promise of the Lord in the revelation of October 12th, for which I felt to thank my Heavenly Father.

Action of Governor Dunklin on Petition.

On the 8th of October Elders Phelps and Hyde had presented the petition of the Saints in Jackson county to the Governor of Missouri, who at that time gave them for an answer that the Attorney-General of the State was absent, but promised that on his return he would inform them of his conclusions by mail, addressed at Independence, whither the brethren immediately returned. About the 28th of October, in pursuance of Governor Dunklin's promise, the brethren in Zion received the following communication from him in reply to their petition of September 28:

CITY OF JEFFERSON, EXECUTIVE DEPARTMENT,

October 19, 1833.

To Edward Partridge, W. W. Phelps, Isaac Morley, John Corrill, A. S. Gilbert, John Whitmer and others:

Your memorial, soliciting my interposition against violence threatened you, and redress for injuries received by a portion of the citizens of Jackson county, has been received, and its contents duly considered. I should think myself unworthy the confidence with which I have been honored by my fellow-citizens, did I not promptly employ all the means which the constitution and laws have placed at my disposal, to avert the calamities with which you are threatened.

Ours is a government of laws; to them we owe all obedience; and their faithful administration is the best guarantee for the enjoyment of our rights.

sake." (Journal, page 17.) On the 29th the Prophet's party started for home. "May the Lord prosper our journey. Amen," he writes in his Journal, page 17.

These excerpts from the Prophet's Daily Journal omitted from the narrative made up from it, have been reproduced in these notes in order that the deeply religious and prayerful nature of the Prophet might be observed. They are indeed gems of expression, and exhibit the Prophet's profound reliance upon God and his blessings." "O God, seal our testimony to their hearts:" "I feel very well in my mind." "The Lord is with us;" "The Lord gave His Spirit in a remarkable manner to some Saints, for which I am thankful to the God of Abraham," he exclaims. "Lord bless my family, and preserve them," is a frequent prayer. "This day we expect to start for Canada. Lord be with us on our journey. Amen." And thus in all things he remembers the Lord, seeks the guidance of His Spirit, trusts in Him, relies upon Him for success, and pleads for the presence of His protecting power.

No citizen, nor number of citizens, have a right to take the redress of their grievances, whether real or *imaginary*, into their own hands. Such conduct strikes at the very existence of society, and subverts the foundation on which it is based. Not being willing to persuade myself that any portion of the citizens of the state of Missouri are so lost to a sense of these truths as to require the exercise of *force*, in order to ensure a respect for them, after advising with the Attorney-General, and exercising my best judgment, I would advise you to make a trial of the efficacy of the laws. The judge of your circuit is a conservator of the peace; if an affidavit is made before him by any of you, that your lives are threatened, and you believe them in danger, it would be his duty to have the offenders apprehended and bind them to keep the peace. Justices of the peace in their respective counties, have the same authority, and it is made their duty to exercise it. Take, then, this course:—obtain a warrant, let it be placed in the hands of the proper officer, and the experiment will be tested, whether the laws can be peaceably executed or not. In the event they cannot be, and that fact is officially notified to me, my duty will require me to take such steps as will enforce a faithful execution of them.

With regard to the injuries you have sustained by destruction of property, etc., the law is open to redress; I cannot permit myself to doubt that the courts will be open to you, nor [believe] that you will find difficulty in procuring legal advocates to sue for damages therein.

Respectfully, your obedient servant,

DANIEL DUNKLIN.

W. W. Phelps, Esq., Independence, Jackson County, Mo.

Preparation for Asserting Rights.

Immediately on receipt of the Governor's letter, the members of the Church generally, (though they had lain idle since the outrage in July), began to labor as usual, and build and set in order their houses, gardens, etc. The brethren in Zion were also busily engaged in devising means of redress for their grievances; and having consulted with four lawyers from Clay county, then attending court in Independence, they received from them the following letter on the day written; which I will copy entire, that the principles by which the lawyers of this generation are actuated may be recorded, as well as the difficulties the Saints had to encounter in following the Governor's instructions:

INDEPENDENCE, Oct. 30, 1833.

GENTLEMEN:—The first thing necessary to be done, under circumstances like ours, is to ascertain and fix upon the amount of fee to be paid, and to secure the payment thereof by the necessary papers: and then the responsibility of advising falls upon us. We are now laboring under all the disadvantages of an engagement without any of its advantages; it therefore becomes us to know whether we can agree as to the fee or not; and that we should be paid, too, according to the situation in which we place ourselves. We have been doing a practice here among these people, to a considerable extent, and by this engagement we must expect to lose the greatest part of it, which will be to all of us a considerable loss; besides that, the amount involved must be very considerable, and the amount involved must be generally the criterion of the fee. Taking all these matters into consideration we propose to you to bring all the suits you may want brought, and attend to them jointly throughout, for the sum of two hundred and fifty dollars each, making for all four, of us, the sum of one thousand dollars.

This may seem to be a large sum for a fee for lawyers in this country, but the circumstances here involved make it necessary. This matter must be attended to in the first place, and then such advice, for the present, as may seem to be dictated by wisdom, and be necessary, we will give you; and in the proper time we will bring the suits. If this proposal suits, you will please execute notes, and send them to us; and if not agreed to, apprise us by letter immediately, for we can be engaged on the opposite side in all probability. We prefer to bring your suits, as we have been threatened by the mob, we wish to show them we disregard their empty bravadoes.

(Signed)

WOOD,
REESE,
DONIPHAN,
ATCHISON.

Counsel Employed.

As a *dernier ressort,* the brethren accepted the foregoing propostition, and Brothers Phelps and Partridge gave their note of one thousand dollars, endorsed by Gilbert & Whitney. No sooner had this news spread among the mob, than they began to congregate and prepare for battle.

CHAPTER XXXI.

EXPULSION OF THE SAINTS FROM JACKSON COUNTY.

Attack on the Saints Settled on Big Blue.

THURSDAY night, the 31st of October, gave the Saints in Zion abundant proof that no pledge on the part of their enemies, written or verbal, was longer to be regarded; for on that night, between forty and fifty persons in number, many of whom were armed with guns, proceeded against a branch of the Church, west of the Big Blue, and unroofed and partly demolished ten dwelling houses; and amid the shrieks and screams of the women and children, whipped and beat in a savage and brutal manner, several of the men: while their horrid threats frightened women and children into the wilderness. Such of the men as could escape fled for their lives; for very few of them had arms, neither were they organized; and they were threatened with death if they made any resistance; such therefore as could not escape by flight, received a pelting with stones and a beating with guns and whips. On Friday, the first of November, women and children sallied forth from their gloomy retreats, to contemplate with heartrending anguish the ravages of a ruthless mob, in the lacerated and bruised bodies of their husbands, and in the destruction of their houses, and their furniture. Houseless and unprotected by the arm of the civil law in Jackson county, the dreary month of November staring them in the face and loudly proclaiming an inclement season at hand; the continual threats of the mob that they would drive every "Mormon" from the county; and the inability of many to move, because of their poverty, caused an anguish of heart indescribable.

The Saints at the Prairie Settlement Attacked.

On Friday night, the 1st of November, a party of the mob proceeded to attack a branch of the Church settled on the prairie, about twelve or fourteen miles from the town of Independence. Two of their number were sent in advance, as spies, viz., Robert Johnson, and ——— Harris, armed with two guns and three pistols. They were discovered by some of the Saints, and without the least injury being done to them, said mobber Robert Johnson struck Parley P. Pratt over the head with the breech of his gun, after which they were taken and detained till morning; which action, it was believed, prevented a general attack of the mob that night. In the morning the two prisoners, notwithstanding their attack upon Parley P. Pratt the evening previous, were liberated without receiving the least injury.*

Mobbing at Independence.

The same night, (Friday), another party in Independence commenced stoning houses, breaking down doors and windows and destroying furniture. This night the brick part attached to the dwelling house of A. S. Gilbert, was partly pulled down, and the windows of his dwelling broken in with brickbats and rocks, while a gentleman, a stranger, lay sick with fever in his house. The same night three doors of the store of Messrs. Gilbert &

*It was evening. I was out in the act of posting guards a short distance from the dwellings, when two men assailed us, armed with guns and pistols; and supposing it against our principles to make any defense, they attacked the guards. I was without arms, but stepped forward to interfere between them, when one of them drew his gun backwards, and, with both hands, struck the barrel of it across the top of my head. I staggered back, but did not fall; the blood came streaming down my face, and I was for an instant stunned by the blow; but, recovering myself, I called help from the house and disarmed them, and put them under guard till morning. Their arms were then restored, and they let go in peace. The taking of these two men proved a preventive against an attack that night. They were the advance of a party of men who were about to come upon the settlement, but were disconcerted by this means. (*Autobiography of P. P. Pratt*, p. 103.)

Whitney were split open, and after midnight the goods, such as calicos, handkerchiefs, shawls, cambrics, lay scattered in the streets. An express came from Independence after midnight to a party of the brethren who had organized about half a mile from the town for the safety of their lives, and brought the information that the mob were tearing down houses, and scattering goods of the store in the streets. Upon receiving this information the company of brethren referred to marched into Independence, but the main body of the mob fled at their approach. One Richard McCarty, however, was caught in the act of throwing rocks and brickbats into the doors, while the goods lay scattered around him in the streets. He was immediately taken before Samuel Weston, Esq., justice of the peace, and complaint was then made to said Weston, and a warrant requested, that McCarty might be secured; but Weston refused to do anything in the case at that time, and McCarty was liberated.*

Other **Incidents** at Independence.

The same night some of the houses of the Saints in Independence had long poles thrust through the shutters and sash into the rooms of defenseless women and children, from whence their husbands and fathers had been driven by the dastardly attacks of the mob, which were made by ten, fifteen, or twenty men upon a house at a time. Saturday, the 2nd of November, all the families of the Saints in Independence moved with their goods about half a mile out of town and organized to the number of thirty, for the preservation of life and personal effects. The same night a party from Independence met a party from west of the Blue, and made an attack upon a

*"McCarty was arrested and taken before Squire Weston," says Lyman Wight, in an affidavit upon the subject, "and although seven persons testified against him, he was acquitted without delay. The next day the witnesses were taken before the same man (Squire Weston) for false imprisonment, and by the testimony of this one burglar were found guilty and committed to jail." In relation to this matter, John Corrill tersely remarked, "Although we could not obtain a warrant against him for breaking open the store, yet he had gotten one for us for catching him at it."

branch of the Church located at the Blue, about six miles from the village of Independence. Here they tore the roof from one dwelling and broke open another house; they found the owner, David Bennett, sick in bed, and beat him most inhumanly, swearing they would blow out his brains. They discharged a pistol at him, and the ball cut a deep gash across the top of his head. In this skirmish a young man of the mob, was shot in the thigh; but by which party the shot was fired is not known.

An Appeal to the Circuit Court.

The next day, Sunday, November 3rd, four of the brethren, viz., Joshua Lewis, Hiram Page, and two others,* were dispatched for Lexington to see the circuit judge, and obtain a peace warrant. Two other brethren called on Esquire Silvers, in Independence, and asked him for a peace warrant, but he refused to issue one on account, as he afterwards declared, of his fears of the mob. This day many of the citizens, professing friendship, advised the Saints to leave the county as speedily as possible; for the Saturday night affray had enraged the whole county, and the people were determined to come out on Monday and massacre indiscriminately; and, in short, it was commonly declared among the mob, that *"Monday would be a bloody day."*

Events of Monday, November 4th.

Monday came, and a large party of the mob gathered at the Blue, took the Ferry boat belonging to the Church, threatened lives, etc. But they soon abandoned the ferry, and went to Wilson's store, about one mile west of the Blue. Word had been previously sent to a branch of the Church, several miles west of the Blue, that the mob were destroying property on the east side of the river, and the sufferers there wanted help to preserve lives and

*The other two members were Parley P. Pratt and "Mr. Marsh," supposed to be Thomas B. Marsh. They called upon Judge Ryland at Lexington and made oath concerning the outrages committed against them and the Saints in Jackson county, but the judge refused to issue any process against the mob, and advised that the Saints fight and kill the mob whenever the latter came upon them.—Pratt's *Persecutions*, page 37.

property. Nineteen men volunteered, and started to their assistance; but discovering that fifty or sixty of the mob had gathered at said Wilson's they turned back. At this time two small boys passed on their way to Wilson's who gave information to the mob, that the "Mormons" were on the road west of them. Between forty and fifty of the mob armed with guns, immediately started on horseback and on foot in pursuit; after riding about two or two and a half miles, they discovered them, when the said company of nineteen brethren immediately dispersed, and fled in different directions. The mob hunted them, turning their horses meantime into a corn field belonging to the Saints. Corn fields and houses were searched, the mob at the same time threatening women and children that they would pull down their houses and kill them if they did not tell where the men had fled. Thus they were employed in hunting the men and threatening the women, when a company of thirty of the brethren from the prairie, armed with seventeen guns, made their appearance.*

The Battle.

The former company of nineteen had dispersed, and fled, and but one or two of them returned in time to take part in the subsequent battle. On the approach of the latter company of thirty men, some of the mob cried, "Fire, *G—d—ye,* fire." Two or three guns were then fired by the mob, which fire was returned by the other party without loss of time. This company is the same that is represented by the mob as having gone forth in the evening of the above incident bearing the olive branch of peace. The mob retreated immediately after the first fire, leaving some of their horses in Whitmer's corn field, and two of their number, Hugh L. Brazeale and Thomas Linvill dead on the ground. Thus fell Hugh L. Brazeale, who had been heard to say, "With ten fellows, I will wade to my knees in blood, but that I will drive the 'Mormons' from Jackson county." The next morning

*This company of brethren was led by David Whitmer. (See John Whitmer's *History of the Church*, chapter 10.)

the corpse of Brazeale was discovered on the battle ground with a gun by his side. Several were wounded on both sides, but none mortally among the brethren except Andrew Barber, who expired the next day.* This attack of the mob was made about sunset, Monday, November the 4th; and the same night, runners were dispatched in every direction under pretense of calling out the militia; spreading every rumor calculated to alarm and excite the uninformed as they went; such as that the "Mormons" had taken Independence, and that the Indians had surrounded it, the "Mormons" and Indians being colleagued together.

Gilbert *et al* on Trial.

The same evening, November 4th—not being satisfied with breaking open the store of Gilbert & Whitney, and demolishing a part of the dwelling house of said Gilbert the Friday night previous—the mob permitted the said McCarty, who was detected on Friday night as one of the breakers of the store doors, to take out a warrant, and arrest the said Gilbert and others of the Church, for a pretended assault, and false imprisonment of said McCarty. Late in the evening, while the court was proceeding with their trial in the court house, a gentleman unconnected

*Andrew Barber, who fell on this occasion was the first direct martyr to the cause. Among those wounded was Philo Dibble of Ohio. He was wounded in the abdomen at the first fire of the mob. Newel Knight in his Journal, (*Scraps of Biography*, page 81,) says that he was examined by a surgeon of great experience who had served in the Mohawk War, and he said he never knew a man to live who was wounded in such a manner. Knight also gives the following account of his visit to the wounded man, and the manner in which he was healed by the power of God: "The next day (November 5th), I went to see Brother Dibble, and found the house where he lay surrounded by the mob. I managed to get in, and went to the bed; two men came and seated themeslves at the door; as I looked upon Brother Dibble lying there in extreme agony, I drew the bed curtains with one hand and laid the other on his head, praying secretly to our Heavenly Father in his behalf. I then left, as I did not want to put myself into the power of the mob; and the next day business took me some ten miles from the place, where I met Brother Dibble making his escape from the county. He told me that as soon as I placed my hand upon his head, the pain and soreness seemed gradually to move as before a power driving it, until in a few minutes it left his body. He then discharged about a gallon of putrid matter, and the balls and pieces of clothing which had passed into his body."

with the court, as was believed, perceiving the prisoners to be without counsel and in imminent danger, advised Brother Gilbert and his brethren, to go to jail as the only alternative to save life; for the north door of the court house was already barred, and an infuriated mob thronged the house, with a determination to beat and kill; but through the interposition of this gentleman (Samuel C. Owens, clerk of the county court, so it was afterwards learned), said Gilbert and four of his brethren were committed to the county jail of Jackson county, the dungeon of which must have been a palace compared with a court room where dignity and mercy were strangers, and naught but the wrath of man as manifested in horrid threats shocked the ears of the prisoners.

Assault on the Prisoners.

The same night, the prisoners, Gilbert, Morley, and Corrill, were liberated from the jail, that they might have an interview with their brethren, and try to negotiate some measures for peace; and on their return to jail about 2 o'clock, Tuesday morning, in the custody of the deputy sheriff, an armed force of six or seven men stood near the jail and hailed them. They were answered by the sheriff, who gave his name and the names of the prisoners, crying, *"Don't fire, don't fire, the prisoners are in my charge."* They, however, fired one or two guns, when Morley and Corrill retreated; but Gilbert stood, firmly held by the sheriff, while several guns were presented at him. Two, more desperate than the rest, attempted to shoot, but one of their guns flashed, and the other missed fire. Gilbert was then knocked down by Thomas Wilson, who was a grocer living at Independence. About this time a few of the inhabitants of the town arrived, and Gilbert again entered the jail, from which he, with three of his brethren, were liberated about sunrise, without further prosecution of the trial. William E. M'Lellin was one of the prisoners.

On the morning of the 5th of November, Independence began to be crowded with individuals from different parts of the county armed with guns and other weapons; and report said the militia had been called out under the sanction or at the instigation of Lieutenant Governor Boggs; and that one Colonel Pitcher had the command. Among this militia (so-called) were included the most conspicuous characters of the mob; and it may truly be said that the appearance of the ranks of this body was well calculated to excite suspicion of their horrible designs.

Incidents of the 5th of November.

Very early on the same morning, several branches of the Church received intelligence that a number of their brethren were in prison, and the determination of the mob was to kill them; and that the branch of the Church near the town of Independence was in imminent danger, as the main body of the mob was gathered at that place. In this critical situation, about one hundred of the Saints, from different branches, volunteered for the protection of their brethren near Independence,* and proceeded on the road towards Independence, and halted about one mile west of the town, where they awaited further information concerning the movements of the mob. They soon learned that the prisoners were not massacred, and that the mob had not fallen upon the branch of the Church near Independence, as had been reported. They were also informed, that the militia had been called out for their protection; but in this they placed little confidence, for the body congregated had every appearance of a mob; and subsequent events fully verified their suspicions.

One Hundred Volunteers.

On application to Colonel Pitcher, it was found that there was no alternative, but for the Church to leave the county forthwith, and deliver into his hands certain men to be tried for murder, said to have been committed by them in the

The Demands of the Mob-Militia.

*This company of volunteers was led by Lyman Wight, a bold and courageous man. (Wight's Affidavit before Municipal Court of Nauvoo.—*Millennial Star*, vol. xxi, page 506).

battle, as he called it, of the previous evening. The arms of the Saints were also demanded by Colonel Pitcher. Among the committee appointed to receive the arms of the brethren were several of the most unrelenting of the old July mob committee, who had directed in the demolishing of the printing office, and the personal injuries inflicted on brethren that day, viz., Henry Chiles, Abner Staples, and Lewis Franklin, who had not ceased to pursue the Saints, from the first to the last, with feelings the most hostile.

These unexpected requisitions of the Colonel, made him appear like one standing at the head of both civil and military law, stretching his authority beyond the constitutional limits that regulate both civil and military power in our Republic. Rather than to have submitted to these unreasonable requirements, the Saints would have cheerfully shed their blood in defense of their rights, the liberties of their country and of their wives and children; but the fear of violating law, in resisting this pretended militia, and the flattering assurance of protection and honorable usage promised by Lieutenant Governor Boggs, in whom, up to this time, they had reposed confidence, induced the Saints to submit, believing that he did not tolerate so gross a violation of all law, as had been practiced in Jackson county.* But as so glaringly exposed in the sequel, it was the design and craft of this man to rob an innocent people of their arms by stratagem, and leave more than one thousand defenseless men, women and child-

*Another circumstance which embarrassed the Saints not a little in their movements against the mob was the fact that they were divided as to what action it would be proper for them to take in the premises. Parley P. Pratt in his *Persecutions of the Saints*, page 31, says that the Saints, "having passed through the most aggravating insults and injuries without making the least resistance, a general inquiry prevailed at that time throughout the Church as to the propriety of self-defense. Some claimed the right of defending themselves and their families from destruction, while others doubted the propriety of self-defense." Under these conditions it can be readily understood that the defense of the Saints was not so effective against their enemies as it might have been had they been perfectly agreed as to the extent to which they would be justified in defending themselves and their families against the violence of the mob.

ren to be driven from their homes among strangers in a strange land to seek shelter from the stormy blast of winter. All earth and hell cannot deny that a baser knave, a greater traitor, and a more wholesale butcher, or murderer of mankind ever went untried, unpunished, and unhung—since hanging is the popular method of execution among the Gentiles in all countries professing Christianity, instead of blood for blood, according to the law of heaven.* The conduct of Colonels Lucas and Pitcher, had long proven them to be open and avowed enemies of the Saints. Both of these men had their names attached to the mob circular, as early as the July previous, the object of which was to drive the Saints from Jackson county. But with assurances from the Lieutenant Governor and others that the object was to disarm the combatants on both sides, and that peace would be the result, the brethren surrendered their arms to the number of fifty or upwards.†

The men present, who were accused of being in the battle the evening before, also gave themselves up for trial; but after detaining them one day and a night on a pretended trial for murder, in which time they were

*"Whoso sheddeth man's blood, by man shall his blood be shed." Gen. ix: 6. Newel Knight, in his Journal, *Scraps of Biography*, page 85, speaks of Governor Boggs as follows: "Although Governor Boggs did not come out and show himself openly in his true colors, we have sufficient evidence that he sustained all the moves of the mob and even directed them. He it was who put in motion the movements of July [20th and 23rd], and continued his exertions until he had accomplished all his hellish designs."

†Lyman Wight in an affidavit before the Municipal Court of Nauvoo, in 1843, said of this incident of disarming the Saints: "I here agreed that the Church would give up their arms provided the said Colonel Pitcher would take the arms from the mob. To this the Colonel cheerfully agreed, and pledged his honor with that of Lieutenant Governor Boggs, Owens and others. This treaty entered into, we returned home resting assured on their honor, that we should not be further molested; but this solemn contract was violated in every sense of the word. The arms of the mob were never taken away, and the majority of the militia, to my certain knowledge, were engaged the next day with the mob, Colonel Pitcher and Boggs not excepted, going from house to house in gangs of from sixty to seventy in number, threatening the lives of women and children if they did not leave forthwith."—(*Millennial Star*, xxi: 506.) Wight's statement is also supported by John Corrill. *Brief History of the Church of Christ*, page 20, 1839.)

threatened and brick-batted, Colonel Pitcher, after receiving a watch of one of the prisoners to satisfy "costs of court," took them into a corn field, and said to them, "*Clear!*" [Meaning, of course, clear out, leave.]

Savagery of the Mob.

After the Saints had surrendered their arms, which had been used only in self-defense, the tribes of Indians in time of war let loose upon women and children, could not have appeared more hideous and terrific, than did the companies of ruffians who went in various directions, well armed, on foot and on horseback, bursting into houses without fear, knowing the arms were secured; frightening distracted women with what they would do to their husbands if they could catch them; warning women and children to flee immediately, or they would tear their houses down over their heads, and massacre them before night. At the head of these companies appeared the *Reverend Isaac McCoy,* with a gun upon his shoulder, ordering the Saints to leave the county forthwith, and surrender what arms they had. Other pretended preachers of the Gospel took a conspicuous part in the persecution, calling the "Mormons" the "common enemy of mankind," and exulting in their afflictions.

Events of 5th and 6th of November.

On Tuesday and Wednesday nights, the 5th and 6th of November, women and children fled in every direction before the merciless mob. One party of about one hundred and fifty women and children fled to the prairie, where they wandered for several days with only about six men to protect them. Other parties fled to the Missouri river, and took lodging for the night where they could find it. One Mr. Barnet opened his house for a night's shelter to a wandering company of distressed women and children, who were fleeing to the river. During this dispersion of the women and children, parties of the mob were hunting the men, firing upon some, tying up and whipping others, and pursuing others with horses for several miles.

Thursday, November 7th, the shores of the Missouri river began to be lined on both sides of the ferry, with men, women and children; goods, wagons, boxes, chests, and provisions; while the ferrymen were busily employed in crossing them over. When night again closed upon the Saints, the wilderness had much the appearance of a camp meeting. Hundreds of people were seen in every direction; some in tents, and some in the open air, around their fires, while the rain descended in torrents. Husbands were inquiring for their wives, and women for their husbands; parents for children, and children for parents. Some had the good fortune to escape with their families, household goods, and some provisions; while others knew not the fate of their friends, and had lost all their effects. The scene was indescribable, and would have melted the hearts of any people upon earth, except the blind oppressor, and the prejudiced and ignorant bigot. Next day the company increased, and they were chiefly engaged in felling small cottonwood trees, and erecting them into temporary cabins, so that when night came on, they had the appearance of a village of wigwams, and the night being clear, the occupants began to enjoy some degree of comfort.

Scenes on the Banks of the Missouri.

Lieutenant Governor Boggs has been represented as merely a curious and disinterested observer of these events;* yet he was evidently the head and front of the mob; for as may easily be seen by what follows, no important move was made without his sanction. He certainly was the secret mover in the affairs of the 20th and 23rd of July; and, as will appear in the sequel, by his authority the mob was converted into militia, to effect by stratagem what he knew, as well as his hellish host, could not be done by legal force. As Lieutenant Governor, he had only to wink, and the mob went from maltreatment to

Lieutenant Governor Boggs.

*See *History of the Mormons,* Samuel M. Smucker, pp. 89, 90.

murder. The horrible calculations of this second Nero were often developed in a way that could not be mistaken. Early on the morning of the 5th, say at 1 o'clock a. m., he came to Phelps, Gilbert, and Partridge, and told them to flee for their lives. Now, unless he had given the order to murder no one would have attempted it, after the Church had agreed to go away. His conscience, however, seemed to vacillate at its moorings, and led him to give the secret alarm to these men.*

In Exile.

The Saints who fled from Jackson county, took refuge in the neighboring counties, chiefly in Clay county, the inhabitants of which received them with some degree of kindness. Those who fled to the county of Van Buren were again driven, and compelled to flee, and these who fled to Lafayette county, were soon expelled, or the most of them, and had to move wherever they could find protection.†

*Elders W. W. Phelps, A. S. Gilbert, and William E. M'Lellin (the last named had also been imprisoned with the others), after their escape through the warning of Boggs, went into Clay county and made an affidavit embodying substantially the foregoing narrative concerning events which had occurred in Jackson county from the 31st of October, and forwarded the same to Governor Dunklin by express.

†Of the extent of the injuries inflicted upon the Saints in this Jackson county persecution I would add that according to a statement made in a petition to Congress for redress of their Jackson county grievances, it is represented that "The houses of the Mormons in the county of Jackson, amounting to about two hundred, were burned down or otherwise destroyed by the mob, as well as much of their crops, furniture, and stock. The damage done to the property of the Mormons by the mob in the county of Jackson, as above related, as near as they can ascertain, would amount to the sum of $175,000.00. The number of Mormons thus driven from the county of Jackson amounted to about twelve hundred souls."—(*Millennial Star*, vol. 17, page 435.)

According to a statement made in an affidavit before the Municipal Court of Nauvoo, Parley P. Pratt also states that the number driven from the county was twelve hundred, and that two hundred and three houses were destroyed. Lyman Wight, in an affidavit before the same body also says of the mob, that "they burned two hundred and three houses and one grist mill, these being the only residences of the Saints in Jackson county."

Of the spirit of cruelty with which the mob prosecuted their determination to expel the Saints from Jackson county, the following instances are given in addition to what is said in the Prophet's narrative. Lyman Wight, in the before mentioned affidavit, says: "I saw one hundred and ninety women and children driven thirty miles across the prairie in the month of November, with three decrepit men only in their company; the ground was thinly crusted with sleet, and I could easily follow on their trail by the blood that flowed from their lacerated feet on the stubble of

November 13.—About 4 o'clock a. m. I was awakened by Brother Davis knocking at my door, and calling on me to arise and behold the signs in the heavens. I arose, and to my great joy, beheld the stars fall from heaven like a shower of hailstones; a literal fulfilment of the word of God, as recorded in the holy Scriptures, and a sure sign that the coming of Christ is close at hand. In the midst of this shower of fire, I was led to exclaim, "How marvelous are Thy works, O Lord! I thank Thee for Thy mercy unto Thy servant; save me in Thy kingdom for Christ's sake. Amen."

The "Stars" Fall.

The appearance of these signs varied in different sections of the country: in Zion, all heaven seemed enwrapped in splendid fireworks, as if every star in the broad expanse had been suddenly hurled from its course, and sent lawless through the wilds of ether. Some at times appeared like bright shooting meteors, with long trains of light following in their course, and in numbers resembled large drops of rain in sunshine. These seemed to vanish when they fell behind the trees, or came near the ground. Some of the long trains of light following the meteoric stars, were visible for some seconds; these streaks would curl and twist up like serpents writhing. The appearance was beautiful, grand, and sublime beyond description; and it

the burnt prairie. This company not knowing the situation of the country or the extent of Jackson county, built quite a number of cabins that proved to be in the border of Jackson county. The mob, infuriated at this, rushed on them in the month of January, 1834, burned these scanty cabins and scattered the inhabitants to the four winds, from which cause many were taken suddenly ill and of this illness died."—(*Millennial Star*, vol. xxi, page 506.)

Another instance is thus related by Newel Knight in his Journal, *Scraps of Biography*, pages 84 and 85: "I must not omit to mention one act of cruelty, which, if possible, seems to surpass all others. In one of the settlements [in Jackson county] were four families of very old men, infirm and very poor. They seemed to think that they would not be molested and so remained behind, but no sooner did the mob learn of it, than they went to their houses, broke their windows and doors, and hurled great stones into their rooms, endangering their lives: thus were these poor old men, and their families, driven before the ruthless mob in midwinter. These men had served in the Revolutionary War—and Brother Jones had been one of General Washington's body guard—but this availed them nothing, for they were of the hated people. Thus were all the Saints compelled to flee into Clay county, where the sympathies of the people were extended toward them."

seemed as if the artillery and fireworks of eternity were set in motion to enchant and entertain the Saints, and terrify and awe the sinners of the earth. Beautiful and terrific as was the scenery, it will not fully compare with the time when the sun shall become black like sack-cloth of hair, the moon like blood, and the stars fall to the earth—Rev. vi: 13.*

*Speaking of this event as it appeared to the exiled Saints bivouacked on the Missoui bottoms, Elder Parley P. Pratt in his *Autobiography,* (page 110) says: "About 2 o'clock the next morning [November 13th], we were called up by the cry of signs in the heavens. We arose, and to our great astonishment all the firmament seemed involved in splendid fireworks, as if every star in the broad expanse had been hurled from its course, and sent lawless through the wilds of ether. Thousands of bright meteors were shooting through space in every direction, with long trains of light following in their course. This lasted for several hours, and was only closed by the dawn of the rising sun. Every heart was filled with joy at this majestic display of signs and wonders, showing the near approach of the coming of the Son of God." Stephens in his *History of the United States* (page 455), thus speaks of the same event: "During the fall of 1833 occurred a natural phenomenon of a most wonderful character. This was on the night of the 13th of November. It was what is known as the 'meteoric shower,' or the 'falling of the stars.' It was witnessed with amazement and astonishment throughout the entire limits of the United States."

CHAPTER XXXII.

REMEMBRANCE OF CANADA SAINTS—CORRESPONDENCE AND PETITION RELATIVE TO MISSOURI AFFAIRS.

November 19.—I wrote as follows, from Kirtland, to Moses C. Nickerson, Mount Pleasant, Upper Canada:

Letter to Moses C. Nickerson.

Brother Moses:—We arrived at this place on the fourth ultimo, after a fatiguing journey, during which we were blessed with usual health. We parted with Father and Mother Nickerson at Buffalo, in good health, and they expressed a degree of satisfaction for the prosperity and blessings of their journey.

Since our arrival here, Brother Sidney has been afflicted with sore eyes, which is probably the reason why you have not previously heard from us, as he was calculating to write you immediately. But though I expect he will undoubtedly write you soon, as his eyes are evidently better, yet lest you should be impatient to learn something concerning us, I have thought that perhaps a few lines from me, though there may be a lack of fluency according to the *literati* of the age, might be received with a degree of satisfaction on your part, at least, when you call to mind the near relation with which we are united by the everlasting ties of the Gospel of our Lord Jesus Christ.

We found our families and the Church in this place well, generally. Nothing of consequence happened while we were absent, except the death of one of our brethren—David Johnson—a young man of great worth as a private citizen among us, the loss of whom we justly mourn.

We were favored with frequent intelligence from different sections of our country, respecting the progress of the Gospel, and our prayers are daily to our Father, that it may greatly spread, even till all nations shall hear the glorious news and come to a knowledge of the truth.

We have received letters from our brethren in Missouri of late, but we cannot tell, from their contents, the probable extent to which those persons who are desirous to expel them from that country will carry their unlawful and unrighteous purposes. Our brethren have applied to the executive of the state, who has promised them all the assistance that the civil law can give; and in all probability a suit has been commenced ere this.

We are informed, however, that those persons are very violent, and threaten immediate extermination upon all those who profess our doctrine. How far they will be suffered to execute their threats, we know not, but we trust in the Lord, and leave the event with Him to govern in his own wise providence.

I shall expect a communication from you on receipt of this, and hope you will give me information concerning the brethren, their health, faith, etc., also inform me concerning our friends with whom we formed acquaintance.

You are aware, no doubt, dear brother, that anxieties inexpressible crowd themselves continually upon my mind for the Saints, when I consider the many temptations to which we are subject, from the cunning and flattery of the great adversary of our souls: and I can truly say, with much fervency have I called upon the Lord for our brethren in Canada. And when I call to mind with what readiness they received the word of truth by the ministry of Brother Sidney and myself, I am truly under great obligations to humble myself before Him.

When I contemplate the rapidity with which the great and glorious day of the coming of the Son of Man advances, when He shall come to receive His Saints unto Himself, where they shall dwell in His presence, and be crowned with glory and immortality; when I consider that soon the heavens are to be shaken, and the earth tremble and reel to and fro; and that the heavens are to be unfolded as a scroll when it is rolled up; and that every mountain and island are to flee away, I cry out in my heart, What manner of persons ought we to be in all holy conversation and godliness!

You remember the testimony which I bore in the name of the Lord Jesus, concerning the great work which He has brought forth in the last days. You know my manner of communication, how that in weakness and simplicity, I declared to you what the Lord had brought forth by the ministering of His holy angels to me for this generation. I pray that the Lord may enable you to treasure these things in your mind, for I know that His Spirit will bear testimony to all who seek diligently after knowledge from Him. I hope you will search the Scriptures to see whether these things are not also consistent with those things which the ancient Prophets and Apostles have written.

I remember Brother Freeman and wife, Ransom also, and Sister Lydia, and little Charles, with all the brethren and sisters. I entreat for an interest in all your prayers before the throne of mercy, in the name of Jesus. I hope the Lord will grant that I may see you all again, and above all that we may overcome, and sit down together in the kingdom of our Father.

Your brother, etc.,

JOSEPH SMITH.

Nothing of note occurred from the falling of the stars on the 13th, to this date, November 19th, when my heart is somewhat sorrowful, but I feel to trust in the Lord, the God of Jacob. I have learned in my travels that man is treacherous and selfish, but few excepted.

The Prophet's Reflections.

Brother Sidney is a man whom I love, but he is not capable of that pure and steadfast love for those who are his benefactors that should characterize a President of the Church of Christ. This, with some other little things, such as selfishness and independence of mind, which too often manifested destroy the confidence of those who would lay down their lives for him—these are his faults. But notwithstanding these things, he is a very great and good man; a man of great power of words, and can gain the friendship of his hearers very quickly. He is a man whom God will uphold, if he will continue faithful to his calling. O God, grant that he may, for the Lord's sake. Amen.

Sidney Rigdon.

And again, blessed be Brother Sidney: notwithstanding he shall be high and lifted up, yet he shall bow down under the yoke like unto an ass that croucheth beneath his burthen, that learneth his master's will by the stroke of the rod; thus saith the Lord: yet, the Lord will have mercy on him, and he shall bring forth much fruit, even as the vine of the choice grape, when her clusters are ripe, before the time of the gleaning of the vintage; and the Lord shall make his heart merry as with sweet wine, because of Him who putteth forth His hand, and lifteth him up out of deep mire, and pointeth him out the way, and guideth his feet when he stumbles, and humbleth him in his pride. Blessed are his generations: nevertheless one shall hunt

A Prophecy.

after them as a man hunteth after an ass that has strayed in the wilderness, and straightway findeth him and bringeth him into the fold. Thus shall the Lord watch over his generation, that they may be saved. Even so. Amen.

The Prophet's Maxims.

The man who willeth to do well, we should extol his virtues, and speak not of his faults behind his back. A man who wilfully turneth away from his friend without a cause, is not easily forgiven. The kindness of a man should never be forgotten. That person who never forsaketh his trust, should ever have the highest place of regard in our hearts, and our love should never fail, but increase more and more, and this is my disposition and these my sentiments.

Frederick G. Williams.

Brother Frederick G. Williams is one of those men in whom I place the greatest confidence and trust, for I have found him ever full of love and brotherly kindness. He is not a man of many words, but is ever winning, because of his constant mind. He shall ever have place in my heart, and is ever entitled to my confidence. He is perfectly honest and upright, and seeks with all his heart to magnify his Presidency in the Church of Christ, but fails in many instances, in consequence of a want of confidence in himself. God grant that he may overcome all evil. Blessed be Brother Frederick, for he shall never want a friend, and his generation after him shall flourish. The Lord hath appointed him an inheritance upon the land of Zion: yea, and his head shall blossom, and he shall be as an olive branch that is bowed down with fruit. Even so. Amen.

Attorney-General's Letter to the Exiles' Counsel.

The following is a copy of a letter from the Attorney-General of Missouri to the counsel employed by the Church to prosecute the mob in Jackson county:

CITY OF JEFFERSON,
November 21, 1833.

Messrs. Doniphan and Atchison:

GENTLEMEN: From conversation I have had with the Governor, I believe I am warranted in saying to you, and through you to the Mormons, that if they desire to be replaced in possession of their property, that is, their houses in Jackson county, an adequate force will be sent forthwith to effect that object. Perhaps a direct application had better be made to him for that purpose, if they wish thus to be re-possessed. The militia have been ordered to hold themselves in readiness.

If the Mormons will organize themselves into regular companies, or a regular company of militia, either volunteers or otherwise, they will, I have no doubt, be supplied with public arms. This must be upon application therefor. A volunteer company must be accepted by the Colonel, and that is a matter in *his* discretion. Perhaps the best way would be to organize and elect officers as is done in ordinary cases—*not* volunteers; you could give them the necessary directions on these points. If the Colonel should refuse to order an election of company officers, after they have reported themselves to him for that purpose, he would, I presume, be court-martialed, on representation to the Governor of the facts. As only a certain quantity of public arms can be distributed in each county, those who first apply will be most likely to receive them. The less, therefore, that is said upon the subject the better.

I am, with great respect, your obedient servant,

(Signed) R. W. WELLS.

Judge Ryland's Letter to Amos Reese.

Again, Judge Ryland wrote Amos Reese, Esq., Circuit Attorney, also of counsel for the exiled Saints, as follows:

NEW LEXINGTON,
November 24, 1833.

Dear Sir:—I have been requested by the Governor, to inform him about the outrageous acts of unparalleled violence that have lately happened in Jackson county, and have also been requested to examine into these outrages, and take steps to punish the guilty and screen the innocent.

I cannot proceed unless some person shall be willing to make the proper information before me. I now request you to inform me whether the "Mormons" are willing to take legal steps against the citizens of Jackson county; whether they wish to return there or not; and let me know all the matters connected with this unhappy affair. It will be necessary for you to see the persons injured, and be informed of their desires and intentions. The military force will repair to Jackson county, to aid the execution of any order I make on this subject. Be particular in your information to me. I am willing to go any time to Jackson county, for the purpose of holding a court of inquiry, and binding over to keep the peace such persons as I shall think ought to be restrained.

It is a disgrace to the state for such acts to happen within its limits, and the disgrace will attach to our official characters, if we neglect to take proper means to insure the punishment due such offenders.

I wish to know whether Joshua Lewis and Hyrum Page handed the writ to the sheriff of Jackson county, that I made and issued on their affidavit, against some of the ringleaders of the mob in Jackson county, dated the sixth of this month.

I will know why he refused to execute the writ, if it ever came to his hands. Inquire into this subject and let me know. I should be glad to see you, and agree upon what course to take. After you have sufficiently informed yourself, come down and see me. As you live near the scene of these outrages, you are better able to receive all information necessary, and prepare for future action, than I am.

Write me as soon as you are properly informed, and state when you can come down and see me on this business. Keep copies of all the letters you write on this subject.

Your friend,
(Signed) JOHN F. RYLAND.

November 22.—My brother Don Carlos came to live with me and learn the art of printing.

Hyde and Gould Return to Kirtland.

Elders Orson Hyde and John Gould returned from Missouri to Kirtland on the 25th, and brought the melancholy intelligence of the mob in Jackson county persecuting the brethren.

Elder A. S. Gilbert wrote the Governor of Missouri as follows:

(*Confidential.*)

LIBERTY, CLAY COUNTY,
November 29, 1833.

Dear Sir:—Yesterday I saw Mr. Doniphan, an attorney of this place, who informed me that he saw the Attorney-General, Mr. Wells, in Saline county, last Saturday week, and that Mr. Wells had acquainted him with your intention of ordering a court of inquiry to be held in Jackson county, in relation to the late riotous proceedings in that county. Mr. Doniphan is of opinion, from the conversation he had with Mr. Wells, that said order will be suspended till a communication is received from our people, or their counsel. This is therefore to acquaint your Excellency, that most of the heads of our Church had an interview yesterday on the subject of an *immediate* court of inquiry, to be held in Jackson county; and by their request to me, I hasten to lay before your Excellency serious difficulties attending our people on an *immediate* court of inquiry being called.

Our Church is at this time scattered in every direction: some in the new county of Van Buren; a part in this county; and a part in Lafayette, and Ray. Some of our principal witnesses would be women and children, and while the rage of the mob continues, it would be impossible to gather them in safety at Independence. That your Excellency may know of the unabating fury with which the last remnant of our people remaining in that county are pursued at this time, I here state that a few families, perhaps fifteen or twenty, who settled themselves more than two years ago on the prairie about fifteen miles from the county seat of Jackson county, had hoped from the obscurity of their location that they might escape the vengeance of the enemy through the winter; consequently they remained on their plantations, receiving occasionally, a few individual threats, till last Sunday, when a mob made their appearance among them; some with pistols cocked, and presented to their breasts, commanded them to leave the county in three days, or they would tear their houses down over their heads, etc., etc.

Two expresses arrived here from said neighborhood last Monday morning, for advice, and counsel advised their speedy removal for the preservation of life and their personal effects. I suppose these families will be out of the county of Jackson this week. In this distressed situation, in behalf of my brethren, I pray your Excellency to await a further communication, which will soon follow this, setting forth among other things the importance of our people being restored to their possessions, that they may have an equal chance with their enemies in producing important testimony before the court, which the enemy are now determined to deprive them of. I trust that your Excellency will perceive the agitation and consternation that must necessarily prevail among most of our people at this day, from the unparalleled usage they have received, and many of them wandering at this time destitute of shelter.

An *immediate* court of inquiry called while our people are thus situated, would give our enemies a decided advantage in point of testimony, while they are in possession of their *own* homes, and *ours* also; with no enemy in the county to molest or make them afraid.

Very respectfully, your obedient servant,

A. S. GILBERT.

To his Excellency Daniel Dunklin, Jefferson City, Mo.

I have seen and read the above letter, and on reflection, I concur entirely in the opinion therein expressed. I also think that at the next regular term of the court, an examination of the criminal matter cannot be gone into, without a guard for the court and witnesses.

(Signed) AMOS REESE.

Remnants Scattered.

Those who were threatened by the mob on Sunday, the 24th, fled into Clay county, and encamped on the banks of the Missouri river. A number of the families went into Van Buren county: their whole number of men, women, and children, being upwards of one hundred and fifty.

New Church Press.

About the 1st of December, Elder Cowdery and Bishop Whitney arrived at Kirtland with a new press and type, and on the 4th commenced distributing the type.

December 5.—I wrote to Bishop Partridge, Liberty, Clay county, Missouri, as follows:

KIRTLAND, December 5, 1833.

Dear Brethren:—We have just received a letter from Brother Phelps, dated 6th and 7th November, at Liberty, which gives us the painful intelligence of the rage of the enemy, and your present unsettled situation. But I must inform you that there is a great dubiety resting upon our minds, with regard to the true state of affairs of Zion; for there seems to be some difference in the statements of Elder Phelps' letter, and that of Elder Hyde's communication to the editors of the *Missouri Republican.** Elder Hyde states that "on Monday, the 4th, the mob collected in Independence, to the number of two or three hundred, well armed; that a part of their number went above Blue, to drive away our people, and destroy our property; but they were met by a party of our people, who, being prepared, poured a deadly fire upon them: two of their number fell dead on the ground, and a number were mortally wounded, among the former was Brazeale.

"Tuesday morning there were a number of the mob missing, and could not be accounted for; and while we were at Liberty landing, on Wednesday, a messenger rode up, saying that he had just come from

*The slight discrepancies which the Prophet notes between the report of Elder Hyde and the communications of W. W. Phelps lie chiefly from the inaccuracy of the reports current at that time. It will be seen that they are not very important, but doubtless on account of the anxiety of the Prophet and brethren at Kirtland, seemed so at the time, and at any rate were somewhat confusing.

the seat of war, and that the night before, another battle was fought, in which Mr. Hicks fell, having three balls and some buck-shot through his body, and about twenty more shared a similar fate; and also, that one or two of our men were killed, and as many wounded; and he (Hyde) heard the cannonading distinctly; and also, stated that the man who broke open the store, took Gilbert, Phelps, and one more, for false imprisonment, and put them in prison, and as near as he could learn, never to let them escape alive."

This statement of Elder Hyde is somewhat different from that of Elder Phelps, who states that "on Friday night the brethren had mustered about forty or fifty men, armed, and marched into the village, took one prisoner, and fired one gun (through mistake); and on Saturday the mob fell upon our brethren above Blue, and one of Manship's sons was mortally wounded. On Monday a regular action was fought near Christian Whitmer's, under the command of Elder David Whitmer. We had four wounded; they had five wounded and two killed, viz.: Linvill and Brazeale. From Friday till Tuesday, our brethren were under arms, when one hundred and fifty of them came forth, like Moroni, to battle. On Tuesday morning the mob had collected to the number of three hundred, and before any blood was shed, we agreed to go away immediately, and the enemy took our guns."

Elder Phelps also states that "since the above was written (viz.: on the 6th), another horrid scene has transpired: after our people surrendered their arms, a party of the mob went above Blue, and began to whip, and even murder; and the brethren have been driven into the woods, and are fleeing to the ferry; and also the mob have hired the ferrymen to carry them across the river (but they made the brethren pay the ferryage); and it was reported that the mob had killed two more of the brethren."

It appears, brethren, that the above statements were made mostly from reports, and there is no certainty of their being correct; therefore, it is difficult for us to advise, and we can only say, that the destinies of all people are in the hands of a just God, and He will do no injustice to any one; and this one thing is sure, that they who will live godly in Christ Jesus, shall suffer persecution; and before their robes are made white in the blood of the Lamb, it is to be expected, according to John the Revelator, they will pass through great tribulation.

I wish, when you receive this letter, that you would collect every particular, concerning the mob, from the beginning, and send us a correct statement of facts, as they occurred from time to time, that we may be enabled to give the public correct information on the subject, and inform us also of the situation of the brethren, with respect to their means of sustenance.

I would inform you, that it is not the will of the Lord for you to sell your lands in Zion, if means can possibly be procured for your sustenance without. Every exertion should be made to maintain the cause you have espoused, and to contribute to the necessities of one another, as much as possible, in this your great calamity, and remember not to murmur at the dealings of God with His creatures. You are not as yet brought into as trying circumstances as were the ancient Prophets and Apostles. Call to mind a Daniel, the three Hebrew children, Jeremiah, Paul, Stephen, and many others, too numerous to mention, who were stoned, sawn asunder, tempted, slain with the sword, and wandered about in sheep skins and goat skins, being destitute, afflicted, tormented, of whom the world was not worthy. They wandered in deserts and in mountains, and hid in dens and caves of the earth; yet they all obtained a good report through faith; and amidst all their afflictions they rejoiced that they were counted worthy to receive persecutions for Christ's sake.

We know not what we shall be called to pass through before Zion is delivered and established; therefore, we have great need to live near to God, and always to be in strict obedience to all His commandments, that we may have a conscience void of offense toward God and man. It is your privilege to use every lawful means in your power to seek redress for your grievances from your enemies, and prosecute them to the extent of the law; but it will be impossible for us to render you any temporal assistance, as our means are already exhausted, and we are deeply in debt, and know of no means whereby we shall be able to extricate ourselves.

The inhabitants of this county threaten our destruction, and we know not how soon they may be permitted to follow the example of the Missourians; but our trust is in God, and we are determined, His grace assisting us, to maintain the cause and hold out faithful unto the end, that we may be crowned with crowns of celestial glory, and enter into the rest that is prepared for the children of God.

We are now distributing the type, and intend to commence setting today, and issue a paper the last of this week, or beginning of next. We wrote to Elder Phelps some time since, and also sent by Elder Hyde, for the list of names of subscribers to the *Star*, which we have not yet received, and, until we receive it, the most of the subscribers will be deprived of the paper; and when you receive this, if you have not sent the list, I wish you to attend to it immediately, as much inconvenience will follow a delay.

We expect shortly to publish a political paper, weekly, in favor of the present administration; the influential men of that party have offered a liberal patronage to us, and we hope to succeed, for thereby we can show the public the purity of our intention in supporting the government under which we live.

We learn by Elder Phelps, that the brethren have surrendered their arms to the Missourians and are fleeing across the river. If that is the case, it is not meet that they should recommence hostilities with them; but if not, you should maintain the ground as long as there is a man left, as the spot of ground upon which you are located, is the place appointed of the Lord for your inheritance, and it is right in the sight of God that you contend for it to the last.

You will recollect that the Lord has said, that Zion should not be removed out of her place; therefore the land should not be sold, but be held by the Saints, until the Lord in His wisdom shall open a way for your return; and until that time, if you can purchase a tract of land in Clay county for present emergencies, it is right you should do so, if you can do it, and not sell your land in Jackson county. It is not safe for us to send you a written revelation on the subject, but what is stated above is according to wisdom. I haste to a close to give room for Brother Oliver, and remain yours in the bonds of the everlasting covenant,

JOSEPH SMITH, JUN.

Dedication of the New Press.

December 6.—Being prepared to commence our labors in the printing business, I ask God in the name of Jesus, to establish it for ever, and cause that His word may speedily go forth to the nations of the earth, to the accomplishing of His great work in bringing about the restoration of the house of Israel.

This day, also, the Elders in Missouri sent the following petition:

To his Excellency, Daniel Dunklin, Governor of the State of Missouri:

We, the undersigned, leading members of the Church of Christ, vulgarly called "Mormons," would respectfully represent to your Excellency—in addition to the petition presented to you by Messrs. Phelps and Hyde, and the affidavit of Messrs Phelps, Gilbert, and M'Lellin, after having read also the letters of the Attorney-General and District Judge of this circuit to Mr. Rees:—that whereas, our society, men, women, and children, after having been in some cases wounded, scourged, and threatened with death, have been driven by force of arms from their lands, houses and much of their property in Jackson county—most of which lands, houses, and property, have been possessed by the mob of Jackson county, or others, and are now unlawfully detained from the use and possession of our people; that whereas our people have been driven and scattered into the counties of Clay, Ray, Van Buren, Lafayette, and others, where, in many cases, they are destitute of the common necessaries of life even in this winter season; that whereas, the guns which were taken from our people, as set forth in the affidavit, are kept from them; therefore, in behalf of our society, which is so scattered and suffering, we, your petitioners, ask aid and assistance of your Excellency, that we may be restored to our lands, houses, and property, and protected in them by the militia of the state, if legal, or by a detachment of the United States Rangers, which might be located at Independence, instead of at Cantonment Leavenworth, till peace can be restored. This could be done, probably, by conferring with the President, or perhaps with Colonel Dodge. Also, we ask that our men may be organized into companies of Jackson Guards, and be furnished with arms by the state, to assist in maintaining their rights against the unhallowed power of the mob of Jackson county.

And then, when arrangements are made to protect us in our persons and property (which cannot be done without an armed force, nor would it be prudent to risk our lives there without guards, till we receive strength from our friends to protect ourselves), we wish a court of inquiry instituted, to investigate the whole matter of the mob against the "Mormons:" and we will ever pray.

W. W. PHELPS,
JOHN WHITMER,
JOHN CORRILL,
ISAAC MORLEY,
EDWARD PARTRIDGE,
A. S. GILBERT.

The following letter accompanied the foregoing petition:

LIBERTY, December 6, 1833.

Dear Sir:—Your Excellency will perceive by the petition, bearing date with this letter, that we intend to return to Jackson county as soon as arrangements can be made to protect us after we are reinstated in our possessions.

We do not wish to go till we know that our lives are not in danger from a lawless mob. Your Excellency will understand that at this inclement season it will require time to restore us, and troops to protect us after we are there, for the threats of the mob have not ceased.

Your obedient servant,
W. W. PHELPS.

To Daniel Dunklin, Governor of Missouri.

CHAPTER XXXIII.

THE PROPHET'S SYMPATHY FOR THE EXILED SAINTS—REASONS FOR THEIR EXPULSION FROM ZION.

*A Letter from the Prophet Joseph Smith to the Exiled Saints in Missouri.**

KIRTLAND MILLS, OHIO,
December 10, 1833.

Edward Partridge, W. W. Phelps, John Whitmer, A. S. Gilbert, John Corrill, Isaac Morley, and all the Saints whom it may concern.

BELOVED BRETHREN:—This morning's mail brought letters from Bishop Partridge, and Elders Corrill and Phelps, all mailed at Liberty, November 19th, which gave us the melancholy intelligence of your flight from the land of your inheritance, having been driven before the face of your enemies in that place.

From previous letters we learned that a number of our brethren had been slain, but we could not learn from the letters referred to above, that there had been more than one killed, and that one Brother Barber, and that Brother Dibble was wounded in the bowels. We were thankful to learn that no more had been slain, and our daily prayers are that the Lord will not suffer His Saints, who have gone up to His land to keep His commandments, to stain His holy mountain with their blood.

I cannot learn from any communication by the Spirit to me, that Zion has forfeited her claim to a celestial crown, notwithstanding the Lord has caused her to be thus afflicted, except it may be some individuals, who have walked in disobedience, and forsaken the new covenant; all such will be made manifest by their works in due time. I have always expected that Zion would suffer some affliction, from what I could learn from the commandments which have been given. But I would remind you of a certain clause in one which says, that after *much* tribulation cometh the blessing.† By this, and also others, and also one received of late, I know that Zion, in the due time of the Lord,

*This letter was, as will be seen by the text of it, written after the first definite and detailed account of what had taken place in Missouri reached the Prophet's hand. We know of nothing written by him that better manifests the nobility of his soul, or the gentle sympathy of his nature, than this communication.

†Page 191, verses 3 and 4.

will be redeemed; but how many will be the days of her purification, tribulation, and affliction, the Lord has kept hid from my eyes; and when I inquire concerning this subject, the voice of the Lord is: Be still, and know that I am God! all those who suffer for my name shall reign with me, and he that layeth down his life for my sake shall find it again.

Now, there are two things of which I am ignorant; and the Lord will not show them unto me, perhaps for a wise purpose in Himself—I mean in some respects—and they are these: Why God has suffered so great a calamity to come upon Zion, and what the great moving cause of this great affliction is; and again, by what means He will return her back to her inheritance, with songs of everlasting joy upon her head. These two things, brethren, are in part kept back that they are not plainly shown unto me; but there are some things that are plainly manifest which have incurred the displeasure of the Almighty. When I contemplate upon all things that have been manifested, I am aware that I ought not to murmur, and do not murmur, only in this, that those who are innocent are compelled to suffer for the iniquities of the guilty; and I cannot account for this, only on this wise, that the saying of the Savior has not been strictly observed: "If thy right eye offend thee, pluck it out, and cast it from thee; or if thy right arm offend thee, cut it off, and cast it from thee." Now the fact is, if any of the members of our body is disordered, the rest of our body will be affected with it, and then all are brought into bondage together; and yet, notwithstanding all this, it is with difficulty that I can restrain my feelings when I know that you, my brethren, with whom I have had so many happy hours—sitting, as it were, in heavenly places in Christ Jesus; and also, having the witness which I feel, and ever have felt, of the purity of your motives—are cast out, and are as strangers and pilgrims on the earth, exposed to hunger, cold, nakedness, peril, sword—I say when I contemplate this, it is with difficulty I can keep from complaining and murmuring against this dispensation; but I am sensible that this is not right, and may God grant that notwithstanding your great afflictions and sufferings, there may not anything separate us from love of Christ.

Brethren, when we learn your sufferings, it awakens every sympathy of our hearts; it weighs us down; we cannot refrain from tears, yet, we are not able to realize, only in part, your sufferings: and I often hear the brethren saying, they wish they were with you, that they might bear a part of your sufferings; and I myself should have been with you, had not God prevented it in the order of His providence, that the yoke of affliction might be less grievous upon you, God having forewarned me, concerning these things, for your sake; and also, Elder

Cowdery could not lighten your afflictions by tarrying longer with you, for his presence would have so much the more enraged your enemies; therefore God hath dealt mercifully with us. O brethren, let us be thankful that it is as well with us as it is, and we are yet alive and preadventure, God hath laid up in store great good for us in this generation, and may grant that we may yet glorify His name.

I feel thankful that there have no more denied the faith; I pray God in the name of Jesus that you all may be kept in the faith unto the end; let your sufferings be what they may, it is better in the eyes of God that you should die, than that you should give up the land of Zion, the inheritances which you have purchased with your moneys; for every man that giveth not up his inheritance, though he should die, yet, when the Lord shall come, he shall stand upon it, and with Job in his flesh he shall see God. Therefore, this is my counsel, that yo retain your lands, even unto the uttermost, and employ every lawfu means to seek redress of your enemies; and pray to God, day and night, to return you in peace and in safety to the lands of your inheritance: and when the judge fail you, appeal unto the executive; and when the executive fail you, appeal unto the president; and when the president fail you, and all laws fail you, and the humanity of the people fail you, and all things else fail you but God alone, and you continue to weary Him with your importunings, as the poor woman did the unjust judge, He will not fail to execute judgment upon your enemies, and to avenge His own elect that cry unto Him day and night.

Behold He will not fail you! He will come with ten thousand of His Saints, and all His adversaries shall be destroyed with the breath of His lips! All those who keep their inheritances, notwithstanding they should be beaten and driven, shall be likened unto the wise virgins who took oil in their lamps. But all those who are unbelieving and fearful, will be likened unto the foolish virgins, who took no oil in their lamps: and when they shall return and say unto the Saints, Give us of your lands—behold, there will be no room found for them. As respects giving deeds, I would advise you to give deeds as far as the brethren have legal and just claims for them, and then let every man answer to God for the disposal of them.

I would suggest some ideas to Elder Phelps, not knowing that they will be of any real benefit, but suggest them for consideration. I would be glad if he were here, were it possible for him to come, but dare not advise, not knowing what shall befall us, as we are under very heavy and serious threatenings from a great many people in this place.

But, perhaps, the people in Liberty may feel willing, God having power to soften the hearts of all men, to have a press established there; and if not, in some other place; any place where it can be the most convenient, and it is possible to get to it; God will be willing to have it in any place where it can be established in safety. We must be wise as serpents and harmless as doves. Again, I desire that Elder Phelps should collect all the information, and give us a true history of the beginning and rise of Zion, and her calamities.

Now hear the prayer of your unworthy brother in the new and everlasting covenant:—O My God! Thou who hast called and chosen a few, through Thy weak instrument, by commandment, and sent them to Msisouri, a place which Thou didst call Zion, and commanded Thy servants to consecrate it unto Thyself for a place of refuge and safety for the gathering of Thy Saints, to be built up a holy city unto Thyself; and as Thou hast said that no other place should be appointed like unto this, therefore, I ask Thee in the name of Jesus Christ, to return Thy people unto their houses and their inheritances, to enjoy the fruit of their labors; that all the waste places may be built up; that all the enemies of Thy people, who will not repent and turn unto Thee may be destroyed from off the face of the land; and let a house be built and established unto Thy name; and let all the losses that Thy people have sustained, be rewarded unto them, even more than four-fold, that the borders of Zion may be enlarged forever; and let her be established no more to be thrown down; and let all thy Saints, when they are scattered, as sheep, and are persecuted, flee unto Zion, and be established in the midst of her; and let her be organized according to Thy law; and let this prayer ever be recorded before Thy face. Give Thy Holy Spirit unto my brethren, unto whom I write; send Thine angels to guard them, and deliver them from all evil; and when they turn their faces toward Zion, and bow down before Thee and pray, may their sins never come up before Thy face, neither have place in the book of Thy remembrance; and may they depart from all their iniquities. Provide food for them as Thou doest for the ravens; provide clothing to cover their nakedness, and houses that they may dwell therein; give unto them friends in abundance, and let their names be recorded in the Lamb's book of life, eternally before Thy face. Amen.

Finally, brethren, the grace of our Lord Jesus Christ be with you all until His coming in His kingdom. Amen.

JOSEPH SMITH, JUN

December 12.—An express arrived at Liberty, from Van Buren county, with information that those families, which had fled from Jackson county, and located there, were about to be driven from that county, after building their houses and

Expulsion of Saints from Van Buren County.

carting their winter's store of provisions, grain, etc., forty or fifty miles. Several families are already fleeing from thence. The contaminating influence of the Jackson county mob, is predominant in this new county of Van Buren, the whole population of which is estimated at about thirty or forty families. The destruction of crops, household furniture, and clothing, is very great, and much of their stock is lost. The main body of the Church is now in Clay county, where the people are as kind and accommodating as could reasonably be expected. The continued threats of deaths to individuals of the Church, if they make their appearance in Jackson county, prevent the most of them, even at this day, from returning to that county, to secure personal property, which they were obliged to leave in their flight.

The following is an extract of a letter to me, from Elder Phelps, dated—

Sad Condition of the Saints.

CLAY COUNTY, Missouri.
December 15, 1833.

The condition of the scattered Saints is lamentable, and affords a gloomy prospect. No regular order can be enforced, nor any usual discipline kept up; among the world, yea, the most wicked part of it, some commit one sin, and some another (I speak of the rebellious, for there are Saints that are as immovable as the everlasting hills), and what can de done? We are in Clay, Ray, Lafayette, Jackson, Van Buren and other counties, and cannot hear from one another oftener than we do from you. I know it was right that we should be driven out of the land of Zion, that the rebellious might be sent away. But, brethren, if the Lord will, I should like to know what the honest in heart shall do? Our clothes are worn out; we want the necessaries of life, and shall we lease, buy, or otherwise obtain land where we are, to till, that we may raise enough to eat? Such is the common language of the honest, for they want to do the will of God. I am sensible that we shall not be able to live again in Zion, till God or the President rules out the mob.

The Governor is willing to restore us, but as the constitution gives him no power to guard us when back, we are not willing to go. The mob swear if we come we shall die! If, from what has been done in Zion, we, or the most of us, have got to be persecuted from city to city, and from synagogue to synagogue, we want to know it; for there are those among us that would rather earn eternal life on such conditions than lose it; but we hope for better things and shall wait patiently for the word of the Lord.

Our people fare very well, and when they are discreet, little or no persecution is felt. The militia in the upper counties is in readiness at a moment's warning, having been ordered out by the Governor, to guard a court martial and court of inquiry; but we cannot attend a court of inquiry, on account of expense, till we are restored and protected.

(Signed) W. W. PHELPS.

December 16.—I received the following:

*Revelation.**

1. Verily I say unto you, concerning your brethren who have been afflicted, and persecuted, and cast out from the land of their inheritance—

2. I, the Lord, have suffered the affliction to come upon them, wherewith they have been afflicted, in consequence of their transgressions;

3. Yet I will own them, and they shall be mine in that day when I shall come to make up my jewels.

4. Therefore, they must needs be chastened and tried, even as Abraham, who was commanded to offer up his only son.

5. For all those who will not endure chastening, but deny me, cannot be sanctified.

6. Behold, I say unto you, there were jarrings, and contentions, and envyings, and strifes, and lustful and covetous desires among them; therefore by these things they polluted their inheritances.

7. They were slow to hearken unto the voice of the Lord their God; therefore, the Lord their God is slow to hearken unto their prayers, to answer them in the day of their trouble.

8. In the day of their peace they esteemed lightly my counsel; but, in the day of their trouble, of necessity they feel after me.

9. Verily I say unto you, notwithstanding their sins, my bowels are filled with compassion towards them. I will not utterly cast them off; and in the day of wrath I will remember mercy.

10. I have sworn, and the decree hath gone forth by a former commandment which I have given unto you, that I would let fall the sword of mine indignation in behalf of my people; and even as I have said, it shall come to pass.

*Doctrine and Covenants, sec. ci. The revelation explains why the Saints were driven from Zion.

11. Mine indignation is soon to be poured out without measure upon all nations; and this will I do when the cup of their iniquity is full.

12. And in that day all who are found upon the watch-tower, or in other words, all mine Israel, shall be saved.

13. And they that have been scattered shall be gathered.

14. And all they who have mourned shall be comforted.

15. And all they who have given their lives for my name shall be crowned.

16. Therefore, let your hearts be comforted concerning Zion; for all flesh is in mine hands; be still and know that I am God.

17. Zion shall not be moved out of her place, notwithstanding her children are scattered.

18. They that remain, and are pure in heart, shall return, and come to their inheritances, they and their children, with songs of everlasting joy, to build up the waste places of Zion—

19. And all these things that the prophets might be fulfilled.

20. And, behold, there is none other place appointed than that which I have appointed; neither shall there be any other place appointed than that which I have appointed, for the work of the gathering of my saints—

21. Until the day cometh when there is found no more room for them; and then I have other places which I will appoint unto them, and they shall be called stakes, for the curtains or the strength of Zion.

22. Behold, it is my will, that all they who call on my name, and worship me according to mine everlasting gospel, should gather together, and stand in holy places;

23. And prepare for the revelation which is to come, when the veil of the covering of my temple, in my tabernacle, which hideth the earth, shall be taken off, and all flesh shall see me together.

24. And every corruptible thing, both of man, or of the beasts of the field, or of the fowls of the heavens, or of the fish of the sea, that dwells upon all the face of the earth, shall be consumed;

25. And also that of element shall melt with fervent heat; and all things shall become new, that my knowledge and glory may dwell upon all the earth.

26. And in that day the enmity of man, and the enmity of beasts, yea, the enmity of all flesh, shall cease from before my face.

27. And in that day whatsoever any man shall ask, it shall be given unto him.

28. And in that day Satan shall not have power to tempt any man.

29. And there shall be no sorrow because there is no death.

30. In that day an infant shall not die until he is old; and his life shall be as the age of a tree;

31. And when he dies he shall not sleep, that is to say in the earth, but shall be changed in the twinkling of an eye, and shall be caught up, and his rest shall be glorious.

32. Yea, verily I say unto you, in that day when the Lord shall come, he shall reveal all things—

33. Things which have passed, and hidden things which no man knew, things of the earth, by which it was made, and the purpose and the end thereof—

34. Things most precious, things that are above, and things that are beneath, things that are in the earth, and upon the earth, and in heaven.

35. And all they who suffer persecution for my name, and endure in faith, though they are called to lay down their lives for my sake yet shall they partake of all this glory.

36. Wherefore, fear not even unto death; for in this world your joy is not full, but in me your joy is full.

37. Therefore, care not for the body, neither the life of the body; but care for the soul, and for the life of the soul.

38. And seek the face of the Lord always, that in patience ye may possess your souls, and ye shall have eternal life.

39. When men are called unto mine everlasting gospel, and covenant with an everlasting covenant, they are accounted as the salt of the earth and the savor of men;

40. They are called to be the savor of men; therefore, if that salt of the earth lose its savor, behold, it is thenceforth good for nothing only to be cast out and trodden under the feet of men.

41. Behold, here is wisdom concerning the children of Zion, even many, but not all; they were found transgressors, therefore they must needs be chastened—

42. He that exalteth himself shall be abased, and he that abaseth himself shall be exalted.

43. And now, I will show unto you a parable, that you may know my will concerning the redemption of Zion.

44. A certain nobleman had a spot of land, very choice; and he said unto his servants: Go ye unto my vineyard, even upon this very choice piece of land, and plant twelve olive-trees;

45. And set watchmen round about them, and build a tower, that one may overlook the land round about, to be a watchman upon the tower, that mine olive-trees may not be broken down when the enemy shall come to spoil and take unto themselves the fruit of my vineyard.

46. Now, the servants of the nobleman went and did as their lord commanded them, and planted the olive-trees, and built a hedge round about, and set watchmen, and began to build a tower.

47. And while they were yet laying the foundation thereof, they began to say among themselves: And what need hath my lord of this tower?

48. And consulted for a long time, saying among themselves: What need hath my lord of this tower, seeing this is a time of peace?

49. Might not this money be given to the exchanges? For there is no need of these things.

50. And while they were at variance one with another they became very slothful, and they hearkened not unto the commandments of their lord.

51. And the enemy came by night, and broke down the hedge; and the servants of the nobleman arose and were affrighted, and fled; and the enemy destroyed their works, and broke down the olive-trees.

52. Now, behold, the nobleman, the lord of the vineyard, called upon his servants, and said unto them, Why! what is the cause of this great evil?

53. Ought ye not to have done even as I commanded you, and—after ye had planted the vineyard, and built the hedge round about, and set watchmen upon the walls thereof—built the tower also, and set a watchman upon the tower, and watched for my vineyard, and not have fallen asleep, lest the enemy should come upon you?

54. And behold, the watchman upon the tower would have seen the enemy while he was yet afar off; and then ye could have made ready and kept the enemy from breaking down the hedge thereof, and saved my vineyard from the hands of the destroyer.

55. And the lord of the vineyard said unto one of his servants: Go and gather together the residue of my servants, and take all the strength of mine house, which are my warriors, my young men, and they that are of middle age also among all my servants, who are the strength of mine house, save those only whom I have appointed to tarry;

56. And go ye straightway unto the land of my vineyard, and redeem my vineyard; for it is mine; I have bought it with money.

57. Therefore, get ye straightway unto my land; break down the walls of mine enemies; throw down their tower, and scatter their watchmen.

58. And inasmuch as they gather together against you, avenge me of mine enemies, that by and by I may come with the residue of mine house and possess the land.

59. And the servant said unto his lord: When shall these things be?

60. And he said unto his servant: When I will; go ye straightway, and do all things whatsoever I have commanded you;

61. And this shall be my seal and blessing upon you—a faithful and wise steward in the midst of mine house, a ruler in my kingdom.

62. And his servant went straightway, and did all things whatsoever his lord commanded him; and after many days all things were fulfilled.

63. Again, verily I say unto you, I will show unto you wisdom in me concerning all the churches, inasmuch as they are willing to be guided in a right and proper way for their salvation—

64. That the work of the gathering together of my saints may continue, that I may build them up unto my name upon holy places; for the time of harvest is come, and my word must needs be fulfilled.

65. Therefore, I must gather together my people, according to the parable of the wheat and the tares, that the wheat may be secured in the garners to possess eternal life, and be crowned with celestial glory, when I shall come in the kingdom of my Father to reward every man according as his work shall be;

66. While the tares shall be bound in bundles, and their bands made strong, that they may be burned with unquenchable fire.

67. Therefore, a commandment I give unto all the churches, that they shall continue to gather together unto the places which I have appointed.

68. Nevertheless, as I have said unto you in a former commandment, let not your gathering be in haste, nor by flight; but let all things be prepared before you.

69. And in order that all things be prepared before you, observe the commandment which I have given concerning these things—

70. Which saith, or teacheth, to purchase all the lands with money, which can be purchased for money, in the region round about the land which I have appointed to be the land of Zion, for the beginning of the gathering of my saints;

71. All the land which can be purchased in Jackson county, and the counties round about, and leave the residue in mine hand.

72. Now, verily I say unto you, let all the churches gather together all their moneys; let these things be done in their time, but not in haste; and observe to have all things prepared before you.

73. And let honorable men be appointed, even wise men, and send them to purchase these lands.

74. And the churches in the eastern countries; when they are built up, if they will harken unto this counsel they may buy lands and gather together upon them; and in this way they may establish Zion.

75. There is even now already in store sufficient, yea, even an abundance, to redeem Zion, and establish her waste places, no more to

be thrown down, were the churches, who call themselves after my name, willing to hearken to my voice.

76. And again I say unto you, those who have been scattered by their enemies, it is my will that they should continue to importune for redress, and redemption, by the hands of those who are placed as rulers and are in authority over you—

77. According to the laws and constitution of the people, which I have suffered to be established, and should be maintained for the rights and protection of all flesh, according to just and holy principles;

78. That every man may act in doctrine and principle pertaining to futurity, according to the moral agency which I have given unto him, that every man may be accountable for his own sins in the day of judgment.

79. Therefore, it is not right that any man should be in bondage one to another.

80. And for this purpose have I established the Constitution of this land, by the hands of wise men whom I raised up unto this very purpose, and redeemed the land by the shedding of blood.

81. Now, unto what shall I liken the children of Zion? I will liken them unto the parable of the woman and the unjust judge, for men ought always to pray and not to faint, which saith—

82. There was in a city a judge which feared not God, neither regarded man.

83. And there was a widow in that city, and she came unto him, saying: Avenge me of mine adversary.

84. And he would not for a while, but afterward he said within himself: Though I fear not God, nor regard man, yet because this widow troubleth me I will avenge her, lest by her continual coming she weary me.

85. Thus will I liken the children of Zion.

86. Let them importune at the feet of the judge;

87. And if he heed them not, let them importune at the feet of the governor;

88. And if the governor heed them not, let them importune at the feet of the president;

89. And if the president heed them not, then will the Lord arise and come forth out of his hiding place, and in his fury vex the nation;

90. And in his hot displeasure, and in his fierce anger, in his time, will cut off those wicked, unfaithful, and unjust stewards, and appoint them their portion among hypocrites, and unbelievers;

91. Even in outer darkness, where there is weeping, and wailing, and gnashing of teeth.

92. Pray ye, therefore, that their ears may be opened unto your cries, that I may be merciful unto them, that these things may not

come upon them.

93. What I have said unto you must needs be, that all men may be left without excuse;

94. That wise men and rulers may hear and know that which they have never considered;

95. That I may proceed to bring to pass my act, my strange act, and perform my work, my strange work, that men may discern between the righteous and the wicked, saith your God.

96. And again, I say unto you, it is contrary to my commandment and my will that my servant Sidney Gilbert should sell my storehouse, which I have appointed unto my people, into the hands of mine enemies.

97. Let not that which I have appointed be polluted by mine enemies, by the consent of those who call themselves after my name;

98. For this is a very sore and grievous sin against me, and against my people, in consequence of those things which I have decreed and which are soon to befall the nations.

99. Therefore, it is my will that my people should claim, and hold claim upon that which I have appointed unto them, though they should not be permitted to dwell thereon.

100. Nevertheless, I do not say they shall not dwell thereon; for inasmuch as they bring forth fruit and works meet for my kingdom they shall dwell thereon.

101. They shall build, and another shall not inherit it; they shall plant vineyards, and they shall eat the fruit thereof. Even so. Amen.

CHAPTER XXXIV.

A PRESS ESTABLISHED AT KIRTLAND—BLESSINGS UPON THE PROPHET'S FAMILY—RESPONSIBILITY FOR LAWLESS ACTS IN MISSOURI.

Dedication of the Printing Press.

December 18.—The Elders assembled in the printing office, and bowed down before the Lord, and I dedicated the printing press, and all that pertained thereunto, to God, which dedication was confirmed by Elder Rigdon, and my brother, Hyrum Smith. We then proceeded to take the first proof sheet of the reprinted *Star,** edited by Elder Oliver Cowdery.

Strength and Weakness of Oliver Cowdery.

Blessed of the Lord is Brother Oliver, nevertheless there are two evils in him that he must needs forsake, or he cannot altogether escape the buffetings of the adversary. If he forsake these evils he shall be forgiven, and shall be made like unto the bow which the Lord hath set in the heavens; he shall be a sign and an ensign unto the nations. Behold, he is blessed of the Lord for his constancy and steadfastness in the work of the Lord; wherefore, he shall be blessed in his generation, and they shall never be cut off, and he shall be helped out of many troubles; and if he keep the commandments, and hearken unto the counsel of the Lord, his rest shall be glorious.

And again, blessed of the Lord is my father, and also

*All the numbers of *The Evening and Morning Star* from the first issued, in June, 1832, up to and including the number for July, 1833 (fourteen numbers in all,) were reprinted at Kirtland: though in the reprint the page was changed from quarto to octavo form. The last number issued in Zion was in July, 1833; the first reprinted number was issued in Kirtland in December of the same year.

my mother, and my brothers and my sisters; for they shall yet find redemption in the house of the Lord, and their offspring shall be a blessing, a joy, and a comfort unto them.

The Prophet's Blessing upon his Father's House.

Blessed is my mother, for her soul is ever filled with benevolence and philanthropy; and notwithstanding her age, yet she shall receive strength, and shall be comforted in the midst of her house, and she shall have eternal life.

His Mother.

And blessed is my father, for the hand of the Lord shall be over him, for he shall see the affliction of his children pass away; and when his head is fully ripe, he shall behold himself as an olive tree, whose branches are bowed down with much fruit; he shall also possess a mansion on high.

His Father.

Blessed of the Lord is my brother Hyrum, for the integrity of his heart; he shall be girt about with truth, and faithfulness shall be the strength of his loins: from generation to generation he shall be a shaft in the hands of his God to execute judgment upon his enemies; and he shall be hid by the hand of the Lord, that none of his secret parts shall be discovered unto his hurt; his name shall be accounted a blessing among men; and when he is in trouble, and great tribulation hath come upon him, he shall remember the God of Jacob; and He will shield him from the power of Satan; and he shall receive counsel in the house of the Most High, that he may be strengthened in hope, that the goings of his feet may be established for ever.

His Brother Hyrum.

Blessed of the Lord is my brother Samuel, because the Lord shall say unto him, Samuel, Samuel; therefore he shall be made a teacher in the house of the Lord, and the Lord shall mature his mind in judgment, and thereby he shall obtain the esteem and fellowship of his brethren, and his soul shall be established and he shall benefit the house of the Lord, because he shall obtain answer to prayer in his faithfulness.

His Brother Samuel.

Brother William is as the fierce lion, which divideth not the spoil because of his strength; and in the pride of his heart he will neglect the more weighty matters until his soul is bowed down in sorrow; and then he shall return and call on the name of his God, and shall find forgiveness, and shall wax valiant, therefore, he shall be saved unto the uttermost; and as the roaring lion of the forest in the midst of his prey, so shall the hand of his generation be lifted up against those who are set on high, that fight against the God of Israel; fearless and undaunted shall they be in battle, in avenging the wrongs of the innocent, and relieving the oppressed; therefore, the blessings of the God of Jacob shall be in the midst of his house, notwithstanding his rebellious heart.

Prophecy on the Head of his Brother William.

And now, O God, let the residue of my father's house ever come up in remembrance before Thee, that Thou mayest save them from the hand of the oppressor, and establish their feet upon the Rock of Ages, that they may have place in Thy house, and be saved in Thy kingdom; and let all things be even as I have said, for Christ's sake. Amen.

A Prayer.

December 19.—William Pratt and David Patten took their journey to the land of Zion, for the purpose of bearing dispatches to the brethren in that place, from Kirtland, O may God grant that they may be a blessing to Zion, as kind angels from heaven. Amen.

Messengers to Zion.

The following circular was published in the December number of the *Star*:

THE ELDERS IN KIRTLAND TO THEIR BRETHREN ABROAD.

Dear Brethren in Christ, and Companions in Tribulation:—It seemeth good unto us to drop a few lines to you, giving you some instruction relative to conducting the affairs of the kingdom of God, which has been committed unto us in these latter times, by the will and testament of our Mediator, whose intercessions in our behalf are lodged in the bosom of the Eternal Father, and ere long will burst with blessings upon the heads of all the faithful.

We have all been children, and are too much so at the present time; but we hope in the Lord that we may grow in grace and be prepared for all things which the bosom of futurity may disclose unto us. Time is rapidly rolling on, and the prophecies must be fulfilled. The days of tribulation are fast approaching, and the time to test the fidelity of the Saints has come. Rumor with her ten thousand tongues is diffusing her uncertain sounds in almost every ear; but in these times of sore trial, let the Saints be patient and see the salvation of God. Those who cannot endure persecution, and stand in the day of affliction, cannot stand in the day when the Son of God shall burst the veil, and appear in all the glory of His Father, with all the holy angels.

On the subject of ordination, a few words are necessary. In many instances there has been too much haste in this thing, and the admonition of Paul has been too slightingly passed over, which says, "Lay hands suddenly upon no man." Some have been ordained to the ministry, and have never acted in that capacity, or magnified their calling at all. Such may expect to lose their appointment, except they awake and magnify their office. Let the Elders abroad be exceedingly careful upon this subject, and when they ordain a man to the holy ministry, let him be a faithful man, who is able to teach others also; that the cause of Christ suffer not. It is not the multitude of preachers that is to bring about the glorious millennium! but it is those who are "called, and chosen, and faithful."

Let the Elders be exceedingly careful about unnecessarily disturbing and harrowing up the feelings of the people. Remember that your business is to preach the Gospel in all humility and meekness, and warn sinners to repent and come to Christ. Avoid contentions and vain disputes with men of corrupt minds, who do not desire to know the truth. Remember that "it is a day of warning, and not a day of many words." If they receive not your testimony in one place, flee to another, remembering to cast no reflections, nor throw out any bitter sayings. If you do your duty, it will be just as well with you, as though all men embraced the Gospel.

Be careful about sending boys to preach the Gospel to the world; if they go, let them be accompanied by some one who is able to guide them in the proper channel, lest they become puffed up, and fall under condemnation, and into the snare of the devil. Finally, in these critical times, be careful; call on the Lord day and night; beware of pride; beware of false brethren, who will creep in among you to spy out your liberties. Awake to righteousness, and sin not; let your light shine, and show yourselves workmen that need not be ashamed, rightly dividing the word of truth. Apply yourselves diligently to study, that your minds may be stored with all necessary information.

We remain your brethren in Christ, anxiously praying for the day of redemption to come, when iniquity shall be swept from the earth, and everlasting righteousness brought in. Farewell.

A Life Guard of Washington Driven from Jackson County.

Monday night, the 24th of December, four aged families, living near the town of Independence, whose penury and infirmities, incidents to old age, forbade a speedy removal, were driven from their homes by a party of the mob, who tore down their chimneys, broke in their doors and windows, and hurled large stones into their houses, by which the life of old Mr. Miller, in particular, was greatly endangered. Mr. Miller is aged sixty-five years, and the youngest man in the four families. Some of these men have toiled and bled in the defense of their country; and old Mr. Jones, one of the sufferers, served as life guard to General George Washington, in the Revolution. Well may the soldier of "Seventy-six" contemplate with horror the scenes which surround him at this day in Jackson county, where liberty, law, and equal rights, are trodden under foot. It is now apparent that no man embracing the faith of the Latter-day Saints, whatever be his age or former standing in society, may hope to escape the wrath of the Jackson county mob whenever it is in their power to inflict abuse.

Court of Inquiry.

A court of inquiry was held at Liberty, Clay county, Missouri, the latter part of this month, to inquire into the conduct of Colonel Pitcher, for driving the Saints, or "Mormons," from Jackson county, which resulted in his arrest for further trial by a court-martial.

December 26.—James Blanchard and Alonzo Rider were cut off from the Church by a council of Elders, in Kirtland, for repeated transgressions, and promising to reform, and never fulfiling. Nelson Acre was also cut off, on account of his absenting himself from the meetings, and saying that he wanted no more of the Church, and that he desired to be cut off. None of these being present, the council notified them of their expulsion by letters. This evening a Bishop's court was called to investigate the case of Elder Ezekiel Rider, who had said many hard things against Bishop Whitney: that Brother Whitney was not fit for a Bishop; that he treated the brethren who came into the store with disrespect; that he was overbearing, and fain would walk on the necks of the brethren. Brother Story was also in a similar transgression. I rebuked them sharply, and told them that the Church must feel the wrath of God except they repent of their sins and cast away their murmurings and complainings one of another. Elder Rigdon also lectured them on the same principles. Brothers Rider and Story confessed their wrongs, and all forgave one another.

Excommunications at Kirtland.

December 27.—A bishop's court was called to investigate complaints made against Brothers Elliot, Haggart, and Babbitt, and their wives, and Jenkins Salisbury, all of whom were present; but the accusers not being present, the court adjourned *sine die.*

Elliot, Haggart, and Babbitt Cases.

The mob in Jackson county sold the materials, or rather gave Messrs. Davis and Kelly leave to take *The Evening and Morning Star* establishment to Liberty, Clay county, where they commenced the publication of *The Missouri Enquirer,* a weekly paper. They (that is, Davis and Kelly) also paid our lawyers, employed as counsel against the mob, three hundred dollars, on the one thousand dollar note, on agreement; a small amount towards an establishment which, with book work and furniture, had cost some three or four thousand dollars.

Disposition of the *Star* Press.

From the very features of the celebrated mob circular, previously inserted,* it will be seen that they meditated a most daring infraction of the constitution of our

*Pages 374-6.

country that they might gratify a spirit of persecution against an innocent people. To whom shall blame be attached in this tragedy? In July last they boldly made known their determination to drive the "Mormons" from Jackson county, "peaceably if they could, forcibly if they must," openly declaring, that "the arm of the civil law did not afford them a sufficient guarantee against the increasing evils of this religious sect;" and in their circular they further say, "We deem it expedient, and of the highest importance, to form ourselves into a company for the better and easier accomplishment of our purposes;" and conclude with these hightoned words: "We therefore agree, that after timely warning, and upon receiving an adequate compensation for what little property they cannot take with them, they refuse to leave us in peace, as they found us—we agree to use such means as may be sufficient to remove them; and to this end, we each pledge to each other our lives, our bodily powers, fortunes, and sacred honors."

Where Responsibility Rests.

In answer to their bold and daring resolves to guard against anticipated evils, I give the following extract from the Governor's letter in relation to this affair, dated October 19th, 1833:

> No citizen nor number of citizens, have a right to take the redress of their grievances, whether real or imaginary, into their own hands; such conduct strikes at the very existence of society, and subverts the foundation on which it is based.

I ask again, to whom shall blame be attached for this tragedy? When the mob previously and publicly declared their intentions; and the principles involved were understood by the Executive, as appears by the foregoing; and also by the judiciary, according to Judge Ryland's letter;* while the constitution of the land guarantees equal rights and privileges to all—all this considered, to whom should blame be attached, but to Jackson county mobbers, and to Missouri?

*Page 445.

CHAPTER XXXV.

IMPORTANT CORRESPONDENCE ON JACKSON COUNTY AFFAIRS CHIEFLY BETWEEN LEADING OFFICIALS OF THE CHURCH IN ZION AND STATE OFFICIALS OF MISSOURI.*

ALGERNON SIDNEY GILBERT'S LETTER TO GOVERNOR DUNKLIN.

LIBERTY, CLAY COUNTY, MO.,
January 9, 1834.

Dear Sir:—Since my communication of the 29th of November, and a petition dated 6th of December last, to which my name was attached, I am induced to trespass again upon your patience, with further particulars in relation to the unfortunate faction in Jackson county, on which subject I should be silent, were it not that I entertain a hope of suggesting some ideas that may ultimately prove useful in ameliorating the present suffering conditions of my brethren, and in some degree restoring peace to both parties.

Being particularly acquainted with the situation of both parties at this day, my desire is to write impartially; notwithstanding I feel very sensibly the deep wound that has been inflicted upon the Church of which I am a member, by the citizens of Jackson county, The petition to your Excellency, dated the 6th of December last, was drawn up hastily by Mr. Phelps, and signed by several of us, just before the closing of the mail; and there is one item in particular in said petition that needs some explanation: the request that "our men may be organized into companies of Jackson Guards, and furnished with arms by the state," was made at the instance of disinterested advisers; and also a communication from the Attorney General to Messrs. Doniphan and Atchison, dated the 21st of November last, gives his views as to the propriety of organizing into regular companies, etc. The necessity of being compelled to resort to arms, to regain our possessions in Jackson county, is by no means agreeable to the feelings of the Church and would never be thought of but from pure necessity.

In relation to a court of inquiry, serious difficulties continue to exist, well calculated to preclude the most important testimony of our

*In order to group the correspondence concerning the troubles in Jackson county as close to the recital of those events in the text of the Prophet's narrative as may be, several of the communications in this chapter are taken from the place assigned them by previous editors and given in this concluding chapter of Volume I.

Church; and there appears to be no evil which man is capable of inflicting upon his fellow-man, but what our people are threatened with, at this day by the citizens of Jackson county. This intimidates a great many, particularly women and children, and no military guard would diminish their fears so far as to induce them to attend the court in that county. This, with other serious difficulties, will give a decided advantage to the offenders, in a court of inquiry, while they triumph in power, numbers, etc.

The citizens of Jackson county are well aware that they have this advantage, and the leaders of the faction, if they must submit to such a court, would gladly hasten it. The Church are anxious for a thorough investigation into the whole affair, if their testimony can be taken without so great peril as they have reason to fear. It is my opinion, from present appearances, that not one-fourth of the witnesses of our people can be prevailed upon to go into Jackson county to testify. The influence of the party that compose that faction is considerable, and this influence operates in some degree upon the drafted militia, so far as to lessen confidence in the loyalty of that body; and I am satisfied that the influence of the Jackson county faction will not be entirely put down while they have advocates among certain religious sects.

Knowing that your Excellency must be aware of the unequal contest in which we are engaged, and that the little handful that compose our Church are not the only suffers that feel the oppressive hand of priestly power; with these difficulties existing, and many others not enumerated, it would be my wish to adopt such measures as are best calculated to allay the rage of Jackson county, and restore the injured to their rightful possessions; and to this end, I would suggest the propriety of purchasing the possessions of the most violent leaders of the faction; and if they assent to this proposition, if the holdings of about twenty of the most influential in that county (which would embrace the very leaders of the faction) could be obtained, I think the majority would cease in their persecutions, at least, when a due exercise of executive counsel and authority was manifested. I suggest this measure because it is of a pacific nature, well knowing that no legal steps are calculated to subdue their obduracy, only when pushed with energy by the highest authorities of the state.

In this proposal, I believe that I should have the concurrence of my brethren. I therefore give this early intimation of an intention, on the part of some of the leading men in the Church, to purchase out some of the principal leaders of the faction, if funds sufficient can be raised; hoping thereby to regain peaceful possession of their homes; and in making a trial of this measure at a future day, we would deem it important, and of great utility, if we could avail ourselves of counsel and directions from your Excellency, believing there will be a day, in negotations for peace, in which an executive interposition would produce a salutary effect upon both parties.

In this communication, with honesty of heart, I have endeavored briefly to touch upon a few interesting points, in plain truth, believing that I have given no wrong bias on either side, and with earneset prayers to our great Benefactor, that the chief ruler of this state may come to a full knowledge of the gross outrages in Jackson county, I subscribe myself,

Your obedient servant,
ALGERNON S. GILBERT.

To his Excellency, Daniel Dunklin, Jefferson City, Missouri.

LETTER OF THE FIRST PRESIDENCY TO THE SCATTERED SAINTS.

Greeting:

We your companions in tribulation, embrace the present opportunity of sending you this token of our love and good will, assuring you that our bowels are filled with compassion, and that our prayers are daily ascending to God in the name of Jesus Christ, in your behalf.

We have just received intelligence from you, through the medium of Brother Elliott, of Chagrin, making inquiries concerning the course which you are to pursue. In addition to the knowledge contained in the above on this subject, we say, if it is not the duty of the Governor to call out and keep a standing force in Jackson county to protect you on your lands (which it appears must be done, as we understand the mob are determined to massacre you, if the Governor take you back upon your lands, and leave you unprotected), it will become your duty to petition the Governor to petition the President to send a force there to protect you, when you are reinstated.

The Governor proposes to take you back to your lands whenever you are ready to go (if we understand correctly); but cannot keep up an army to guard you; and while the hostile feelings of the people of Jackson county remain unabated, probably you dare not go back to be left unguarded. Therefore, in your petition to the Governor, set all these things forth in their proper light, and pray him to notify the President, of your situation; and also petition the President yourselves, according to the direction of the Lord. We have petitioned Governor Dunklin in your behalf, and enclosed in it a printed revelation, the same as this which we now send you. The petition was signed by something like sixty brethren, and mailed for Jefferson city, one week ago: and he will probably receive it two weeks before you receive this.

We also intend to send a petition and this revelation to the President forthwith, in your behalf, and then we will act the part of the poor widow to perfection, if possible, and let our rulers read their destiny if they do not lend a helping hand. We exhort you to prosecute and try every lawful means to bring the mob to justice as fast as circumstances will permit. With regard to your tarrying in Clay county, we cannot advise, you must be governed by circumstances; perhaps you will have to hire out, and take farms to cultivate, to obtain bread until the Lord delivers you.

We sent you a fifty dollar United States note some time ago; if you have received it, please acknowledge the receipt of it to us, that we may be satisfied you received it. We shall do all that is in our power to assist you in every way we can. We know your situation is a trying one, but be patient, and murmur not against the Lord, and you shall see that all these things shall turn to your greatest good.

Inquire of Elder Marsh, and find out the entire secret of mixing and compounding lead and antimony, so as to make type metal, and write us concerning it. Joseph has sent you another fifty dollar note, making in all one hundred dollars; write us concerning it. There is a prospect of the eastern churches doing something handsome towards the deliverance of Zion, in the course of a year, if Zion is not delivered otherwise.

Though the Lord said this affliction came upon you because of your sins, polluting your inheritances, etc., yet there is an exception of some, namely, the heads of Zion; for the Lord said, Your brethren in Zion begin to repent, and the angels rejoice over them. You will also see an exception at the top of the second column of this revelation; therefore this affliction came upon the Church to chasten those in transgression, and prepare the hearts of those who had repented, for an endowment from the Lord.

We shall not be able to send you any more money at present, unless the Lord puts it into our hands unexpectedly. There is not quite so much danger of a mob upon us as there has been. The hand of the Lord has thus far been stretched out to protect us. Doctor Philastus Hurlburt, an apostate Elder from this Church, has been to the state of New York, and gathered up all the ridiculous stories that could be invented, and some affidavits respecting the character of Joseph and the Smith family; and exhibited them to numerous congregations in Chagrin, Kirtland, Mentor, and Painsville; and he has fired the minds of the people with much indignation against Joseph and the Church.

Hurlburt also made many harsh threats, that he would take the life of Joseph, if he could not destroy "Mormonism" without. Brother Joseph took him with a peace warrant, and after three days' trial, and investigating the merits of our religion, in the town of Painsville, by able attorneys on both sides, he was bound over to the county court. Thus his influence was pretty much destroyed, and since the trial, the spirit of hostility seems to be broken down in a good degree; but how long it will continue so, we cannot say.

You purchased your inheritances with money, therefore, behold you are blessed: you have not purchased your lands by the shedding of blood, consequently you do not come under the censure of this commandment which says, "If by blood, lo your enemies are upon you, and ye shall be driven from city to city;" give yourselves no uneasiness on this account.

Farewell, in the bonds of the new covenant, and partakers in tribulation.

(Signed) ORSON HYDE,
Clerk of the Presidency of the Church.

GOVERNOR DUNKLIN TO THE BRETHREN IN MISSOURI.

CITY OF JEFFERSON,
February 4, 1834.

Gentlemen:—Your communication of the 6th December, was regularly received, and duly considered; and had I not expected to have received the evidence brought out on the inquiry ordered into the military conduct of Colonel Pitcher, in a short time after I received your petition, I should have replied to it long since.

Last evening I was informed that the further inquiry of the court was postponed until the 20th inst. Then, before I could hear anything from this court, the court of civil jurisdiction will hold its session in Jackson county; consequently, I cannot receive anything from one, preparatory to arrangements for the other.

I am very sensible indeed of the injuries your people complain of, and should consider myself very remiss in the discharge of my duties were I not to do everything in my power consistent with the legal exercise of them, to afford your society the redress to which they seem entitled. One of your requests needs no evidence to support the right to have it granted; it is that your people be put in possession of their homes, from which they have been expelled. But what may be the duty of the Executive after that, will depend upon contingencies.

If, upon inquiry, it is found that your people were wrongfully dispossessed of their arms by Colonel Pitcher, then an order will be issued to have them returned; and should your men organize according to law—which they have a right to do, indeed it is their duty to do so, unless exempted by religious scruples—and apply for public arms, the Executive could not distinguish between their right to have them, and the right of every other description of people similarly situated.

As to the request for keeping up a military force to protect your people, and prevent the commission of crimes and injuries, were I to comply, it would transcend the powers with which the Executive of this state is clothed. The Federal Constitution has given to Congress the power to provide for calling forth the militia to execute the laws of the Union, suppress insurrection, or repel invasion; and for these purposes, the President of the United States is authorized to make the call upon the executive of the respective states; and the laws of this state empower the "commander-in-chief, in case of actual or threatened invasion, insurrection or war, or public danger, or other emergency, to call forth into actual service, such portion of the militia as he may deem expedient." These, together with the general provision of our state constitution that "the Governor shall take care that the laws are faithfully executed," are all upon this branch of executive powers. None of these, as I consider, embraces this part of your request. The words, "or other emergency," in our militia law, seem quite broad; but the emergency to come within the object of that provision, should be of a public nature.*

Your case is certainly a very emergent one, and the consequences as important to *your society*, as if the war had been waged against the whole state, yet the *public* has no other interest in it, than that the laws be faithfully executed; thus far I presume the whole community feel a deep interest; for that which is the case of the *"Mormons"* today, may be the case of the *Catholics* tomorrow, and after them, any other sect that may become obnoxious to a majority of the people of any section of the state. So far as a faithful execution of the laws is concerned, the Executive is disposed to do everything consistent with the means furnished him by the legislature, and I think I may safely say the same of the judiciary.

As now advised, I am of the opinion that a military guard will be necessary to protect the state witnesses and officers of the court, and to assist in the execution of its orders, while sitting in Jackson county. By this mail I write to Mr. Reese, enclosing him an order on the captain of the "Liberty Blues," requiring the captain to comply with the requisition of the circuit attorney, in protecting the court and officers,

*In my judgment, it does seem that under the powers conferred upon the executive by the provision of the fundamental law of the state—the constitution—and the militia law he quotes, the governor could have granted the request of the Saints to be protected in their homes, until peace was restored. Surely the clause, "or other emergency," in the section of the law just referred to, was broad enough to justify him in protecting, by the State militia, twelve hundred citizens of the United States in their homes until mob-violence had subsided—until respect for the civil law had been restored, and these citizens allowed to dwell in safety upon the lands they had purchased from the general government. Under these provisions he could have "curbed those cruel devils of their will," without "doing even a little wrong, in order to do a great right"—without "wresting the law to his authority."

and executing their precepts and orders during the progress of these trials. Under the protection of this guard, your people can, if they think proper, return to their homes in Jackson county, and be protected in them during the progress of the trial in question, by which time, facts will be developed upon which I can act more definitely.* The Attorney-General will be required to assist the Circuit Attorney, if the latter deem it necessary.

On the subject of civil injuries, I must refer you to the courts; such questions rest with them exclusively. The laws are sufficient to afford a remedy for every injury of this kind; and, whenever you make out a case entitling you to damages, there can be no doubt entertained of their ample award. Justice is sometimes slow in its progress, but is not less sure on that account.

Very respectfully, your obedient servant,

(Signed) DANIEL DUNKLIN.

To Messrs. W. W. Phelps, Isaac Morley, John Whitmer, Edward Partridge, John Corrill and A. S. Gilbert.

LETTER OF ALGERNON S. GILBERT TO A. LEONARD, ESQ., ATTORNEY.

LIBERTY, CLAY COUNTY, MISSOURI,
February 13, 1834.

A. Leonard, Esq.:

DEAR SIR:—I have received a line from William Pratt, who called on you a few weeks since, to inquire if your services could be secured in the prosecution of claims for damages by our Church against the citizens of Jackson county; and by his letter it appears that you are willing to engage in our case. So far as I have conversed with the principal leaders of our Church, they are desirous to secure your services, which also meets the approbation of our counsel in this county, viz., Messrs. Reese, Doniphan, Atchison and Wood.

I write this a few moments before closing the mail, and have not time to state particulars as to the extent of the suits, but believe that four or five suits have been brought by Phelps & Co., for the destruction of the printing office, etc., etc., and by Partridge and others for personal abuse. I understand that at the next Monday term of the circuit court, petition will be made for a change of venue in Jackson county, and I suppose no case can be tried before next June or October

*It required no great wisdom, however, to forsee that for the Saints to return to their homes, and then be left there without protection—left to the mercy of human wretches, in whose veins ran none of the milk of human kindness—would not be far removed from suicide, as the mob greatly outnumbered the Saints. To return under these circumstances would only be laying the foundation for a greater tragedy than the one already enacted; and the brethren wisely concluded not to attempt to regain possession of their homes, until some measure was adopted to protect them when there—until "God or the President ruled out the mob."

term. If it is expedient, some one of our people will call on you in a few days, and during the interim, wish you to drop me a line if convenient.

We have this day received a communication of the 4th instant, from the Governor, in which he states, that he is of opinion that a military guard will be necessary, to protect the state witnesses and officers of the court, and to assist in the execution of its orders, while sitting in Jackson county.

By this mail I write to Mr. Reese, enclosing him an order on the captain of the "Liberty Blues," requiring the captain to comply with the requisition of the circuit attorney, in protecting the court and officers, and executing their precepts and orders during the progress of these trials.

The foregoing relates to a court of inquiry into criminal matters, to be held in Jackson county, next Monday week.

Very respectfully, your obedient servant,

ALGERNON S. GILBERT.

THE BRETHREN IN CLAY COUNTY, MISSOURI, TO JUDGE RYLAND.

LIBERTY, February 19, 1834.

To the Hon. John F. Ryland, Judge of the Fifth Circuit Court, Missouri:

SIR:—Learning that a court of inquiry is to be held in Jackson county, at the next regular term of the circuit court for that county, or that some kind of legal proceeding is to be commenced for the purpose of obtaining the facts, as far as can be, or bringing to punishment the guilty in that county,—We, therefore, pray your honor to avail yourself of every means in your power to execute the law and make it honorable; and believing that the testimony of some of the members of our Church will be important, and deeming it unsafe to risk our persons in that county without a guard, we request that the order from the Executive, already transmitted, may be put in force.

Respectfully, etc.,

EDWARD PARTRIDGE,
A. S. GILBERT,
W. W. PHELPS,
JOHN CORRILL,
JOHN WHITMER.

Another request similar to the above was sent, same date, to Amos Reese, Circuit Attorney.

LETTER OF W. W. PHLEPS *et al.* TO JUDGE WOODWARD.

LIBERTY, February 19, 1834.

George Woodward, Judge Advocate, in the case of the State of Missouri, versus Colonel Thomas Pitcher:

SIR:—The undersigned request of you, if it be consistent with custom and law, an official copy of the proceedings recorded by you, in the above stated case, for the purpose of preservation, as an important link in the history of our unfortunate society.

Respectfully,
W. W. PHELPS,
EDWARD PARTRIDGE,
ALGERNON S. GILBERT.

AFFIDAVIT OF ABIGAIL LEONARD.

I, Abigail Leonard, depose and say, that on the night of the 20th of February, 1833, in the county of Jackson and State of Missouri, a company of men, about fifty or sixty in number, armed with whips and guns, came to the house of my husband: among them were John Young, Mr. Yocum, Mr. Cantrell, Mr. Patterson and Mr. Noland. Five of the number entered the house; among them was John Young. They ordered my husband to leave the house, threatening to shoot him if he did not. He not complying with their desire, one of the five took a chair and struck him upon the head, knocking him down, and then dragging him out of the house; I, in the meantime, begging of them to spare his life, when one of the number called to the others, telling them to take me into the house, for I would *"overpower every devil of them."* Three of the company then approached me, and, presenting their guns, declared with an oath, if I did not go in, they would blow me through. While this was happening Mr. Patterson jumped upon my husband with his heels; my husband then got up, they stripped all his clothes from him excepting his pantaloons, then five or six attacked him with whips and gun sticks, and whipped him till he could not stand, and he fell to the ground. I then went to them, and took their whips from them; I then called to Mrs. Bruce, who lived in the same house with us, to come out and help me carry my husband into the house. When carried in he was very much lacerated and bruised, and unable to lie upon a bed, and also unable to work for a number of months. Also, at the same time and place. Mr. Josiah Sumner was taken from the house, and came in very bloody and bruised from whipping.

(Signed) ABIGAIL LEONARD.

The following letter from W. W. Phelps reacned the hand of the Prophet at Kirtland at a time when he had received some eastern papers deploring the success attending upon the preaching of "Mormonism" in the East. The Prophet introduces the letter of Elder Phelps in his history in the following language: "Thus, while the press was mourning the prosperity of the work, and the Saints were rejoicing in the East, troubles changed and multiplied in the West, as may be seen by the following letter:"

LETTER OF WM. W. PHELPS TO THE BRETHREN IN KIRTLAND, DETAILING THE FARCICAL EFFORT OF THE OFFICERS OF MISSOURI TO ENFORCE THE LAW.

CLAY COUNTY, MISSOURI, Feb. 27, 1834.

Dear Brethren—The times are so big with events, and the anxiety of everybody so great to watch them, that I feel somewhat impressed to write oftener than I have done, in order to give you more of the "strange acts" of this region. I have just returned from Independence, the seat of war in the West. About a dozen of our brethren, among whom were Bishop Partridge, Elder Corrill and myself, were subpœnaed in behalf of the state; and on the 23rd of February, about 12 o'clock, we were on the bank opposite Everett's Ferry, where we found Captain Atchison's company of "Liberty Blues"—nearly fifty rank and file—ready to guard us into Jackson county. The soldiers were well armed with United States muskets, bayonets fixed, etc., and to me the scene was "passing strange," and long to be remembered; the martial law in force to guard the civil! About twenty-five men crossed over to effect a landing in safety, and when they came near the warehouse they fired six or eight guns, though the enemy had not gathered to witness the landing.

After we were all across, and waiting for the baggage wagon, it was thought most advisable to encamp in the woods, and the witnesses, with half the company, marched nearly a mile towards Independence, to build night fires, as we were without tents, and the weather cold enough to snow a little. While on the way, the quartermaster and others, that had gone on ahead to prepare quarters in town, sent an express back, which was not of the most pacific appearance. Captain Atchison continued the express to Colonel Allen for the two hundred drafted militia, and also to Liberty for more ammunition; and the night passed off in warlike style, with the sentinels marching silently at a proper distance from the watch fires.

Early in the morning we marched, strongly guarded by the troops, to the seat of war, and quartered in the blockhouse, formerly the tavern stand of S. Flournoy; after breakfast we were visited by the District Attorney, Mr. Reese, and the Attorney-General, Mr. Wells. From them we learned that all hopes of criminal prosecutions were at an end. Mr. Wells had been sent by the governor to investigate, as far as possible, the Jackson outrage; but the bold front of the mob; bound even unto death (as I have heard), was not to be penetrated by civil law, or awed by executive influence. Shortly after, Captain

Atchison informed me that he had just received an order from the judge that his company's service was no longer wanted in Jackson county; and we were marched out of town to the tune of Yankee Doodle, in quick time, and soon returned to our camp without the loss of any lives. This order was issued by the court, apparently, on account of the speedy gathering of the old mob, or citizens of Jackson county, and their assuming such a boisterous and mobocratic appearance. Much credit is due to Captain Atchison for his gallantry and hospitality, and I think I can say of the officers and company that their conduct as soldiers and men is highly reputable; so much the more so, knowing as I do, the fatal results of the trial had the militia come or not come. I can add that the Captain's safe return refreshed my mind with Xenophon's safe retreat of the Ten Thousand! Thus ends all hope of "redress," even with a guard ordered by the Governor for the protection of the court and witnesses.*

Before a crop is harvested it becomes ripe of itself. The dreadful deeds now done in Jackson county, with inpunity, must bring matters to a focus shortly. Within two or three weeks past some of the most savage acts ever witnessed have been committed by these bitter branches. Old Father Lindsey, whose locks have been whitened by the blasts of nearly seventy winters, had his house thrown down, after he was driven from it; his goods, corn, etc. piled together and fire put to it, but fortunately after the mob retired, his son extinguished it.

The mob has quit whipping and now beats with clubs. Lyman Leonard, one of the number that returned from Van Buren county had two chairs broken to splinters upon him, and was then dragged out of doors and beat with clubs till he was supposed to be dead, but

*Thus ended the only effort that was ever made by the officers of Missouri to bring to justice these violators of the law. One class of citizens had conspired against the liberties of another class, and being the stronger had, without the authority of the law, or shadow of justification, driven twelve hundred of them from their possessions, and there was not virtue enongh in the executive of the state and his associates to punish the offenders. The determination of the mob to resist the law was stronger than the determination of the state officers to execute it and make it honorable. And yet the constitution of the state made it the imperative duty of the executive to "take care that the laws are faithfully executed;" and the laws of the state empowered the commander-in-chief of the militia (the governor) "in case of * * * insurrection, or war, or public danger, or other emergency, to call forth into actual service such portion of the militia as he might deem expedient." With this power placed in his hands by the laws of the state, Governor Dunklin permitted mobs to overawe the court of inquiry he himself had ordered, and allowed them to continue unchecked in their unhallowed deeds of devastation and violence. And while the mobocrats triumphed over law and order, the governor's letters to the leading Elders of the Church contained many pretty, patriotic sentiments, but he lacked the moral courage to execute the law of the state.

he is yet alive. Josiah Sumner and Barnet Cole were severely beaten at the same time. The mob have commenced burning houses, stacks, etc.; and we shall not think it out of their power, by any means, to proceed to murder any of our people that shall try to live in that county, or perhaps, only go there.

Such scenes as are happening around us are calculated to arouse feelings and passions in all, and to strengthen the faith and fortify the hearts of the Saints for great things. Our Savior laid down His life for our sakes, and shall we, who profess to live by every word that proceeds out of the mouth of God—shall we, the servants of the Lord of the vineyard, who are called and chosen to prune it for the last time—shall we, yea, verily we, who are enlightened by the wisdom of heaven—shall we fear to do at least this much for Jesus who has done so much for us? No; we will obey the voice of the Spirit that God may overcome the world.

I am a servant, etc.,
W. W. PHELPS.

SECOND PETITION TO THE PRESIDENT OF THE UNITED STATES.

LIBERTY, CLAY COUNTY, MISSOURI, April 10, 1834.

To the President of the United States of America:

We, the undersigned, your petitioners, citizens of the United States of America, and residents of the county of Clay, in the state of Missouri, being members of the Church of Christ, reproachfully called "Mormon," beg leave to refer the President to our former petition, dated in October last; and also to lay before him the accompanying hand-bill, dated December 12th, 1833, with assurances that the said hand-bill exhibits but a faint sketch of the sufferings of your petitioners and their brethren, up to the period of its publication.

The said hand-bill shows, that at the time of dispersion a number of our families fled into the new and unsettled county of Van Buren; but being unable to procure provisions in that county through the winter, many of them were compelled to return to their homes in Jackson county or perish of hunger. But they had no sooner set foot upon that soil—which a few months before they had purchased of the United States—than they were again met by the cititzens of Jackson county, and a renewal of savage barbarities was inflicted upon these families by beating with clubs and sticks, presenting knives and fire arms, and threatenings of death if they did not flee from the county. These inhuman assaults upon a number of these families were repeated at two or three different times through the past winter, till they were compelled at last to abandon their possessions in Jackson county, and flee with their wounded bodies into this county, here to mingle their tears and unite their supplications, with hundreds of their brethren, to our Heavenly Father and the chief ruler of our nation.

Between one and two thousand of the people called "Mormons" had been driven by force of arms from the county of Jackson in this state since the first of November last, being compelled to leave their highly cultivated fields—the greater part of their lands having been bought of the United States—and all this on account of our belief in direct revelation from God to the children of men according to the Holy Scriptures. We know that such illegal violence has not been inflicted upon any sect or community of people by the citizens of the United States since the Declaration of Independence.

That this is a religious persecution is notorious throughout our country; for while the officers of the county, both civil and military, were accomplices in these unparalleled outrages, engaged in the destruction of the printing office, dwelling houses, etc., yet the records of the judicial tribunals of that county are not stained by any record of crime committed by our people. Our numbers being greatly inferior to the enemy were unable to stand in self defense; and our lives, at this day, are continually threatened by that infuriated people, so that our personal safety forbids one of our number going into that county on business.

We beg leave to state that no impartial investigation into this criminal matter can be made, because the offenders must be tried in the county where the offense was committed, and the inhabitants of the county, both magistrates and people, with the exception of a few, being combined, justice cannot be expected. At this day your petitioners do not know of a solitary family belonging to our Church in Jackson county but what has been violently expelled from that county by the inhabitants thereof.

Your petitioners have not gone into detail with an account of their individual sufferings from death, and bruised bodies, and the universal distress which prevails at this day, in a greater or less degree throughout our community. Not only have those sacred rights guaranteed to every religious sect been publicly invaded, in open hostility to the spirit and genius of our free government; but such of their houses as have not been burnt, and their lands and most of the products of the labor of their hands for the last year, have been wrested from them by a band of outlaws congregated in Jackson county, on the western frontiers of the United States, and this within about thirty miles of the United States military post at Fort Leavenworth, on the Missouri river.

Your petitioners say that they do not enter into a minute detail of their sufferings in this petition lest they should weary the patience of their venerable chief, whose arduous duties they know are great, and daily accumulating. We only hope to show him that this is an unprecedented emergency in the history of our country, that the magistracy thereof is set at defiance, and justice checked in open violation of its laws; and that we, your petitioners, who are almost wholly native born citizens of these United States, of whom we purchased our lands in Jackson county, Missouri, with intent to cultivate the same as peaceable cititzens, are now forced from them, and are now dwelling in the counties of Clay, Ray and Lafayette, in the state of Missouri, without permanent homes, and suffering all the privations which must necessarily result from such inhuman treatment. Under these sufferings your petitioners petitioned the governor of this state in December last, in answer to which they received the following letter:*

* * * * * * * * * *

By the foregoing letter from the Governor, the President will perceive a disposition manifested by him to enforce the laws as far as means have been furnished him by the legislature of this state. But the powers vested in the executive of this state appear to be inadequate for relieving the distresses of your petitioners in their present emergency. He is willing to send a guard to conduct our families back to their possessions, but is not authorized to direct a military force to be stationed any length of time for the protection of your petitioners. This step would be laying the foundation for a more fatal tragedy than the first, as our numbers at present are too small to contend single handed with the mob of said county; and as the Federal Constitution has given to Congress the power to provide for calling forth the militia to execute the laws of the Union, suppress insurrections, or repel invasions: and for these purposes the President of the United States is authorized to make the call upon the executive of the respective states; therefore, we your petitioners, in behalf of our society, which is so scattered and suffering, most humbly pray that we may be restored to our lands, houses, and property in Jackson county, and protected in them by an armed force, till peace can be restored. And as in duty bound, will ever pray.

Here followed one hundred and fourteen signatures, among whom were: Edward Partridge, John Corrill, John Whitmer, Isaac Morley, A. S. Gilbert, W. W. Phelps, etc., etc.

LETTER OF ALGERNON S. GILBERT *et al.* TO THE PRESIDENT ACCOMPANYING FOREGOING PETITION.

LIBERTY, CLAY COUNTY, MISSOURI, April 10, 1834.

To the President of the United States:

We, the undersigned, some of the leading members of the Church

*The letter here referred to will be found on pages 476-8.

of Christ, whose names are subscribed to the accompanying petition, beg leave to refer the President to the petition and hand-bill herewith. We are not insensible to the multiplicity of business and numerous petitions, by which the cares and perplexities of our chief ruler are daily increased; and it is with diffidence that we venture to lay before the executive, at this emergent period, these two documents, wherein is briefly portrayed the most unparalled persecution and flagrant outrage of law that has disgraced the country since the adoption of the Declaration of Independence, but knowing the independent fortitude, and vigorous energy for preserving the rights of the citizens of this republic, which has hitherto marked the course of our chief magistrate, we are encouraged to hope, that this communication will not pass unnoticed, but that the President will consider our location on the extreme western frontier of the United States, exposed to many ignorant and lawless ruffians, who are already congregated, and determined to nullify all law that will secure to your petitioners the peaceable possession of their lands in Jackson county. We again repeat, that our society are wandering in adjoining counties at this day, bereft of their houses and lands, and threatened with death by the aforesaid outlaws of Jackson county.

And lest the President should have been deceived in regard to our true situation, by the misrepresentations of certain individuals, who, from religious, political, and speculative motives, are disposed to cover the gross outrages of the mob, we beg leave to refer him to the Governor of this state, at the same time informing him that the number of men composing the mob of Jackson county, may be estimated at from three to five hundred, most of them equipped with fire-arms.

After noting the statements here made, if it should be the disposition of the President to grant aid, we most humbly entreat that *early* relief may be extended to suffering families, who are now expelled from their possessions by force of arms. Our lands in Jackson county, are about thirty miles distant from Fort Leavenworth, on the Missouri river.

With due respect, we are, sir, your obedient servants,

A. S. GILBERT,
W. W. PHELPS,
EDWARD PARTRIDGE.

P. S.—In February last a number of our people were marched under a guard furnished by the governor of the state, into Jackson county, for the purpose of prosecuting the mob criminally; but the Attorney-General of the state, and the District Attorney, knowing the force and power of the mob, advised us to relinquish all hope of criminal prosecution to effect anything against that band of outlaws, and we returned under guard, without the least prospect of ever obtaining our rights and possessions in Jackson county, by any other means than a few companies of the United States regular troops, to guard and assist us till we are safely settled.

A. S. G.
W. W. P.
E. P.

The foregoing letter and petition were forwarded by mail the same day, April 10th; also the following:

LETTER OF THE BRETHREN TO GOVERNOR DUNKLIN ASKING HIM TO WRITE THE PRESIDENT IN CONNECTION WITH THEIR PETITION.

LIBERTY, CLAY COUNTY, MISSOURI,
April 10, 1834.

To His Excellency, Daniel Dunklin, Governor of Missouri:

DEAR SIR:—Notwithstanding you may have become somewhat tired of receiving communications from us, yet we beg of your Excellency to pardon us for this, as we have this day forwarded a petition to the President of the United States, setting forth our distressed condition, together with your Excellency's views of it, as well as the limited powers with which you are clothed, to afford that protection which we need, to enjoy our rights and lands in Jackson county. A few lines from the Governor of the state, in connection with our humble entreaties for our possessions and privileges, we think would be of considerable consequence towards bringing about the desired result, and would be gratefully acknowledged by us, and our society, and we may add, by all honorable men.

We therefore, as humble petitioners, ask as a favor of your Excellency to write to the President of the United States, that he may assist us, or our society, in obtaining our rights in Jackson county, and help protect us when there, till we are safe. As in duty bound, we will ever pray.

(Signed)

W. W. PHELPS,
JOHN WHITMER,
A. S. GILBERT,
EDWARD PARTRIDGE,
JOHN CORRILL.

LETTER OF W. W. PHELPS TO U. S. SENATOR BENTON OF MISSOURI ON THE SUBJECT OF THE PETITION TO THE PRESIDENT.

LIBERTY, CLAY COUNTY, MISSOURI,
April 10, 1834.

DEAR SIR:—As our society has just sent a petition and hand-bill to the President of the United States, setting forth their distressed condition since expelled from their homes by the Jackson county mob; and as you may remember that I was about to establish last summer, previous to the destruction of my office by the mob, a weekly newspaper, in favor of the present administration. I have thought best to address this communication to your honor, and refer you to said petition and hand-bill, and assure you, at the same time, that my determination is to publish a weekly paper, in Jackson county, in favor of the present administration as soon as our society is restored to its legal rights and possessions.

As a people we are bound to support our republican government and its institutions; and more than all, my press, which was wrested from me, is now printing a mean opposition paper, by "Kelly and Davis." Any communication from you will be well received by

Your obedient servant,

W. W. PHELPS.

Hon. Thomas H. Benton.

LETTER FROM GOVERNOR DUNKLIN TO THE BRETHREN, ANSWERING THE ONE INVITING HIM TO WRITE THE PRESIDENT ON THE SUBJECT OF THE SAINTS' PETITION.

CITY OF JEFFERSON,
April 20, 1834.

To Messrs. W. W. Phelps, Edward Partridge, John Corrill, John Whitmer, and A. S. Gilbert:

GENTLEMEN:—Yours of the 10th inst., was received yesterday, in which you request me as executive of this state to join you in an appeal to the President of the United States for protection in the enjoyment of your rights in Jackson county. It will readily occur to you, no doubt, the possibility of your having asked of the President protection in a way that he, no more than the executive of this state, can render. If you ask for that which I may be of opinion he has power to grant, I should have no objection to join in urging it upon him; but I could no more ask the President—however willing I am to see your society restored and protected in their rights—to do that which I may believe he has no power to do, than I could do such an act myself. If you will send me a copy of your petition to the President, I will judge of his right to grant it; and if of opinion he possesses the power, I will write in favor of its exercise.

I am now in correspondence with the federal government, on the subject of deposits of munitions of war on our northern and western borders, and have no doubt but I shall succeed in procuring one, which will be located, if left to me, (and the Secretary of War seems willing to be governed by the opinion of the executive of this state), somewhere near the state line, either in Jackson or Clay county. The establishment will be an "arsenal," and will probably be placed under the command of a lieutenant of the army. This will afford you the best means of military protection, the nature of your case will admit. Although I can see no direct impropriety in making the subject of this paragraph public, yet I should prefer it not to be so considered for the present, as the erection of an arsenal is only in expectancy.

Permit me to suggest to you, that as you now have greatly the advantage of your adversaries, in public estimation, there is a great propriety in retaining that advantage, which you can easily do by keeping your adversaries in the wrong. The laws, both civil and military, seem deficient in affording your society proper protection; nevertheless, public sentiment is a powerful corrector of error, and you should make it your policy to continue to deserve it.

With much respect, and great regard,
I am your obedient servant,
DANIEL DUNKLIN.

THE BRETHREN IN MISSOURI TO GOVERNOR DUNKLIN, INFORMING HIM THAT THEY EXPECT THE ARRIVAL OF REINFORCEMENTS FROM THEIR BRETHREN IN THE EAST.

LIBERTY, CLAY COUNTY, MO.,
April 24, 1834.

DEAR SIR:—In our last communication of the 10th instant, we omitted to make inquiry concerning the evidence brought up before the court of inquiry, in the case of Colonel Pitcher. The court met pursuant to adjournment, on the 20th of February last, and for some reason unknown to us, we have not been able to obtain information concerning the opinion or decision of that court; we hoped that the testimony would have been transmitted to your Excellency before this, that an order might be issued for the return of our arms, of which we have been wrongfully dispossessed, as we believe will clearly appear to the commander-in-chief, when the evidence is laid before him.

As suggested in your communication of the 4th of February, we have concluded to organize according to law, and apply for public arms; but we feared that such a step, which must be attended with public ceremonies, might produce some excitement; and we have thus far delayed any movement of that nature, hoping to regain our arms from Jackson county, that we might independently equip ourselves, and be prepared to assist in the maintenance of our constitutional rights and liberties, as guaranteed to us by our country; and also to defend our persons and property from a lawless mob, when it shall please the executive at some future day, to put us in possession of our homes, from which we have been most wickedly expelled. We are happy to make an expression of our thanks for the willingness manifested by the executive to enforce the laws, so far as he can consistently "with the means furnished him by the legislature;" and we are firmly persuaded that a future day will verify to him that whatever aid we may receive from the executive has not been lavished upon a band of traitors, but upon a people whose respect and veneration for the laws of our country, and its pure republican principles are as great as that of any other society in these United States.

As our Jackson foes and their correspondents are busy in circulating slanderous and wicked reports concerning our people, their views, etc., we have deemed it expedient to inform your Excellency that we have received communications from our friends in the East, informing us that a number of our brethren, perhaps two or three hundred, would remove to Jackson county in the course of the ensuing summer; and we are satisfied that when the Jackson mob get the intelligence that a large number of our people are about to remove into that county, they will raise a great hue-and-cry, and circulate many bugbears through the medium of their favorite press; but we think your Excellency is well aware that our object is purely to defend ourselves and possessions against another outrageous attack from the mob, inasmuch as the executive of this state cannot keep up a military force "to protect our people in that county, without transending his powers." We want, therefore, the privilege of defending ourselves and the constitution of our country, while God is willing we should have a being on His footstool.

We do not know at what time our friends will arrive, but expect more certain intelligence in a few weeks. Whenever they do arrive, it would be the wish of our people in this county, to return to our homes, in company with our friends, under guard; and when once in legal possession of our homes in Jackson county, we shall endeavor to take care of them, without further wearying the patience of our worthy chief magistrate. We will write hereafter, or send an express. During the intermediate time, we would be glad to hear of the prospects of recovering our arms.

With due respect, we are, sir, your obedient servants,

(Signed)

A. S. Gilbert,
Edward Partridge,
W. W. Phelps,
John Corrill,
John Whitmer.

P. S. Many of the brethren who are expected here soon, had made arrangements to emigrate to this state before the outrages of the mob last fall. We hope the painful emergency of our case will plead an excuse for our frequent communications.

LETTER OF GOVERNOR DUNKLIN REPLYING TO THE COMMUNICATION OF APRIL 24TH FROM THE BRETHREN IN CLAY COUNTY.

CITY OF JEFFERSON, May 2, 1834.

To Messrs. W. W. Phelps and others:

GENTLEMEN:—Yours of the 24th ultimo is before me, in reply to which I can inform you, that becoming impatient at the delay of the court of inquiry in making their report in the case of Lieutenant-Colonel Pitcher,—on the 11th ultimo I wrote to General Thompson for the reasons of such delay: last night I received his reply, and with it the report of the court of inquiry, from the tenor of which, I find no difficulty in deciding that the arms your people were required to surrender on the 5th of last November, should be returned; and have issued an order to Colonel Lucas to deliver them to you or your order, which order is here enclosed.

Respectfully, your obedient servant,

(Signed) DANIEL DUNKLIN.

Following is the order referred to above:

CITY OF JEFFERSON, May 2, 1834.

To Samuel D. Lucas, Col. 33rd Regiment:

SIR:—The court ordered to inquire into the conduct of Lieutenant-Colonel Pitcher, in the movement he made on the 5th of November last, report it as their unanimous opinion that there was no insurrection on that day, and that Colonel Pitcher was not authorized to call out his troops on the 5th of November, 1833. It was then unnecessary to require the Mormons to give up their arms. Therefore, you will deliver to W. W. Phelps, Edward Partridge, John Corrill, John Whitmer, and A. S. Gilbert, or their order, the fifty-two guns and one pistol reported by Lieutenant-Colonel Pitcher to you on the 3rd of December last, as having been received by him from the Mormons on the 5th of the preceding October, [November].

Respectfully,
DANIEL DUNKLIN,
Commander-in-Chief.

LETTER TO GOVERNOR DUNKLIN ANSWERING HIS OF APRIL THE 20TH WHEREIN HE CAUTIONED THE SAINTS TO KEEP THEIR ENEMIES IN THE WRONG.

LIBERTY, CLAY COUNTY, May 7, 1834.

DEAR SIR:—Your favor of the 20th ultimo, came to hand the 1st instant, which gives us a gleam of hope that the time will come when we may experience a partial mitigation of our sufferings. The salutary advice at the conclusion of your letter is received with great deference.

Since our last of the 24th ultimo, the mob of Jackson county have burned our dwellings; as near as we can ascertain, between one hundred and one hundred and fifty were consumed by fire in about one week; our arms were also taken from the depository (the jail) about ten days since, and distributed among the mob. Great efforts are now making by said mob to stir up the citizens of this county (Clay) and Lafayette, to similiar outrages against us; but we think they will fail of accomplishing their wicked designs in this county. We here annex a copy of the petition to the President, signed by about one hundred and twenty.

With great respect, etc.,
(Signed)
A. S. GILBERT,
W. W. PHELPS.

Daniel Dunklin, Governor of Missouri.

LETTER TO COLONEL S. D. LUCAS ASKING ABOUT ARMS SURRENDERED AT INDEPENDENCE.

LIBERTY, CLAY COUNTY, MISSOURI,
May 15, 1834.

Colonel S. D. Lucas:

SIR:—We have this day received a communication from the Governor of this state, covering the order herewith, and we hasten to forward the said order to you by the bearer, Mr. Richardson, who is instructed to receive your reply. We would further remark that under existing circumstances, we hope to receive our arms on this side the river, and we would name a place near one of the ferries for your convenience: as the arms are few in number, we request that they may be delivered with as little delay as possible.

Respectfully yours,
(Signed)
A. S. GILBERT,
W. W. PHELPS,
JOHN CORRILL,
EDWARD PARTRIDGE,
JOHN WHITMER.

P. S.—We will thank you for a written communication, in answer to this letter, and the accompanying order.*

*The arms were never returned to their owners. Before Lucas received the Governor's order, forwarded to him by the brethren, he had left Jackson county, settled in Lexington, Missouri, and resigned his commission. Subsequently Gov-

All hope for relief from the general government was destroyed on receipt of the following communication from the city of Washington:

REPLY OF THE GENERAL GOVERNMENT TO THE PETITION OF THE SAINTS.

WAR DEPARTMENT, May 2, 1834.

GENTLEMEN:—The President has referred to this department the memorial and letter addressed to him by yourselves and other citizens of Missouri, requesting his interposition in order to protect your persons and property.

In answer, I am instructed to inform you, that the offenses of which you complain, are violations of the laws of the state of Missouri, and not of the laws of the United States. The powers of the President under the constitution and laws, to direct the employment of a military force, in cases where the ordinary civil authority is found insufficient, extend only to proceedings under the laws of the United States.

Where an insurrection in any state exists, against the government thereof, the President is required on the application of such state, or of the executive (when the legislature cannot be convened), to call forth such number of the militia, as he may judge sufficient to suppress such insurrection.

But this state of things does not exist in Missouri, or if it does, the fact is not shown in the mode pointed out by law. The President cannot call out a military force to aid in the execution of the state laws, until the proper requisition is made upon him by the constituted authorities.

Very respectfully, your most obedient servant,

(Signed) LEWIS CASS.

To Messrs. A. S. Gilbert, W. W. Phelps, Edward Partridge, and others, Liberty, Clay County, Missouri.

ernor Dunklin issued a second requisition for the arms, this time directing it to Colonel Pitcher; but between the issuing of the two orders, the first to Lucas and the second to Pitcher, the arms were distributed among the mob, and they insolently boasted that the arms should not be returned, notwithstanding the order of the chief executive of the state.

END OF VOLUME I.

INDEX TO VOLUME I

D

E

F

J

K

L

Y

Z

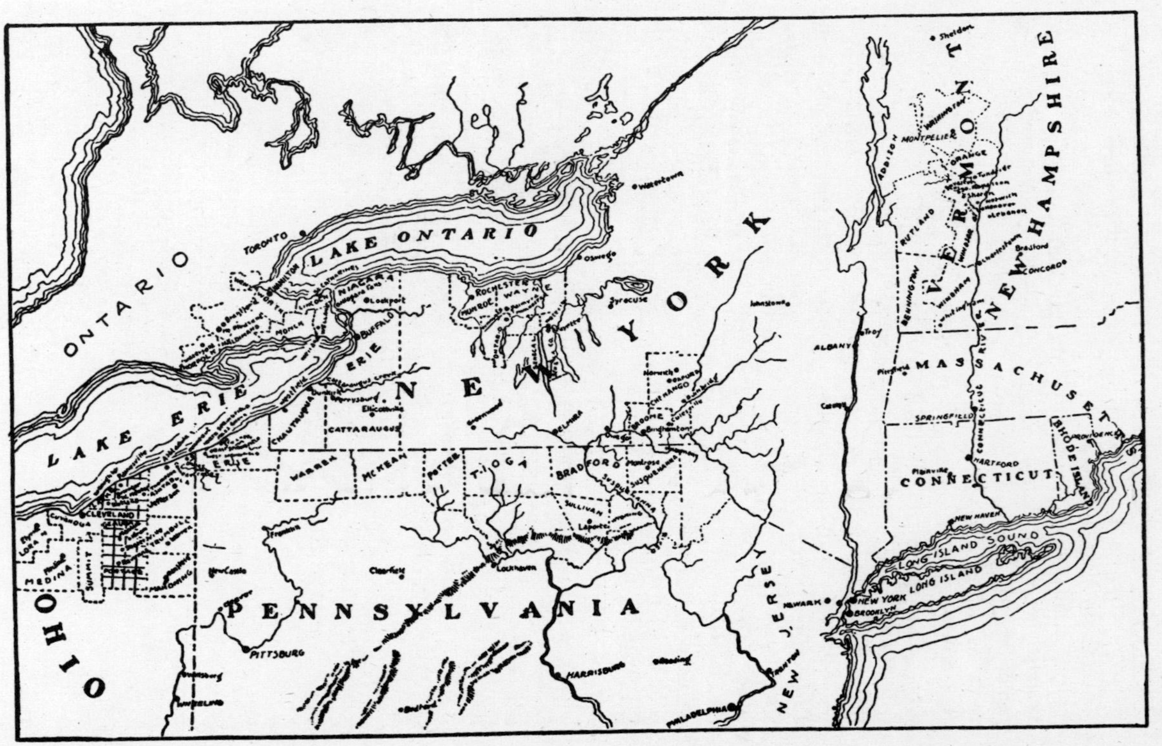

ONTARIO
LAKE ONTARIO
TORONTO
LAKE ERIE
NIAGARA
Lockport
BUFFALO
ERIE
CATTARAUGUS
CHAUTAUQUA
ROCHESTER
MONROE
WAYNE
Oswego
Syracuse
Watertown
Johnstown
NEW YORK
CHENANGO
BROOME
Binghamton
ALBANY
Troy
WARREN
McKEAN
POTTER
TIOGA
BRADFORD
SUSQUEHANNA
SULLIVAN
Laporte
Clearfield
Lockhaven
PENNSYLVANIA
PITTSBURG
HARRISBURG
PHILADELPHIA
NEW JERSEY
NEWARK
NEW YORK
BROOKLYN
LONG ISLAND
LONG ISLAND SOUND
NEW HAVEN
HARTFORD
CONNECTICUT
RHODE ISLAND
SPRINGFIELD
MASSACHUSETTS
Pittsfield
BENNINGTON
RUTLAND
ADDISON
MONTPELIER
ORANGE
WINDHAM
WINDSOR
VERMONT
Sheldon
NEW HAMPSHIRE
CONCORD
OHIO
CLEVELAND
MEDINA
SUMMIT

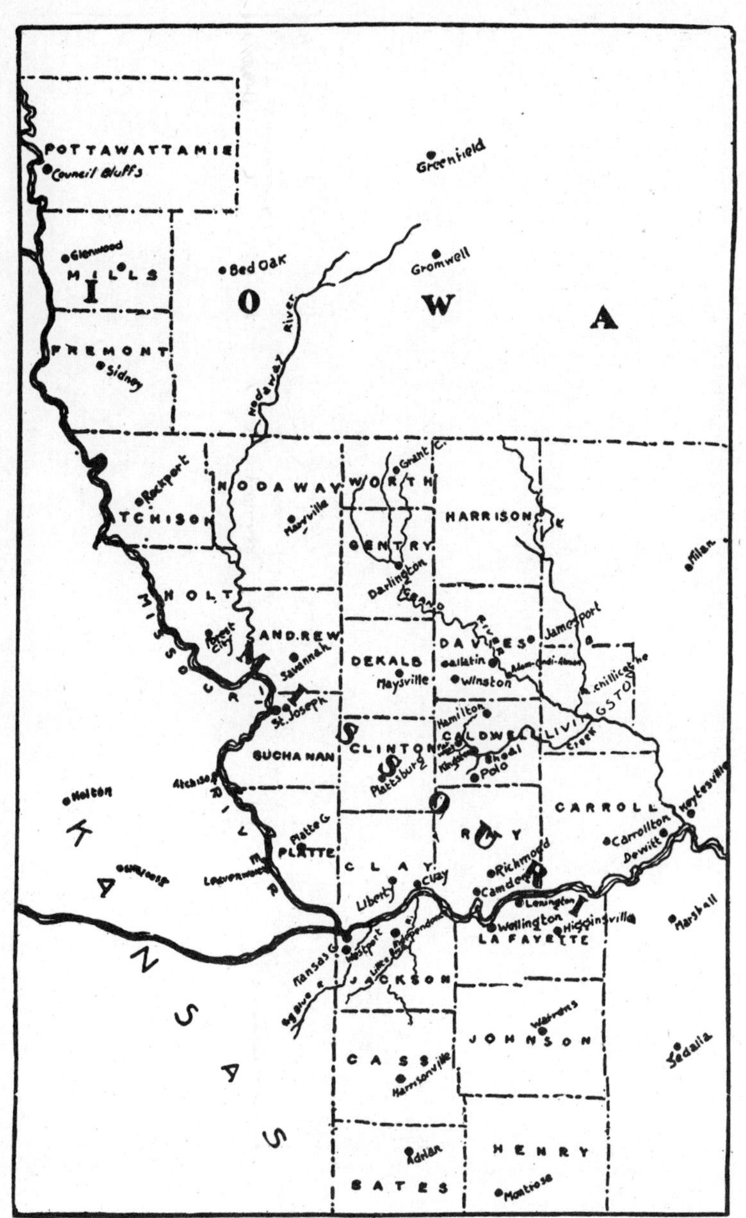

I O W A
POTTAWATTAMIE
Council Bluffs
Greenfield
Glenwood
MILLS
Cromwell
FREMONT
Sidney
Nodaway River
NODAWAY
WORTH
Grant C.
Rockport
ATCHISON
Maryville
HARRISON
GENTRY
Darlington
Grand River
Milan
HOLT
Forest City
ANDREW
Savannah
DEKALB
Maysville
DAVIESS
Gallatin
Winston
Jamesport
Adam-ondi-Ahman
Chillicothe
LIVINGSTON
St. Joseph
Hamilton
CALDWELL
Shoal Creek
Kingston
Polo
BUCHANAN
CLINTON
Plattsburg
Atchison
Holton
CARROLL
Carrollton
Dewitt
Keytesville
Platte C.
PLATTE
RAY
Richmond
Camden
Leavenworth
CLAY
Liberty
Lexington
Wellington
Higginsville
Marshall
LA FAYETTE
Kansas C.
Westport
Independence
Little Blue
Big Blue
JACKSON
Warrensburg
JOHNSON
Sedalia
CASS
Harrisonville
K A N S A S
MISSOURI RIVER
M I S S O U R I
Adrian
HENRY
BATES
Montrose

HISTORY

OF THE

CHURCH OF JESUS CHRIST

OF

LATTER-DAY SAINTS

PERIOD I.

History of Joseph Smith, the Prophet

BY HIMSELF

VOLUME II

AN INTRODUCTION AND NOTES

BY

B. H. ROBERTS

PUBLISHED FOR THE CHURCH
Second Edition Revised

THE DESERET BOOK COMPANY
Salt Lake City, Utah
1976

ISBN-O-87747-075-8

TABLE OF CONTENTS.

VOLUME II.

CHAPTER I

THE YEAR EIGHTEEN HUNDRED AND THIRTY-FOUR—AFFAIRS IN ZION AND KIRTLAND.

CHAPTER II.

ORGANIZATION OF THE HIGH COUNCIL—FIRST CASES BEFORE THE COUNCIL.

CHAPTER III.

THE CAUSE AND OBJECT OF THE JACKSON COUNTY PERSECUTION—THE PROPHET'S MISSION THROUGH WESTERN NEW YORK.

CHAPTER IV.

TRIAL AND CONVICTION OF HURLBURT—EFFORTS IN BEHALF OF THE REDEMPTION OF ZION—DISSOLUTION OF THE UNITED ORDER OF ZION AND KIRTLAND.

CHAPTER V.

ZION'S CAMP—IT'S JOURNEY FROM KIRTLAND TO MISSOURI.

CHAPTER VI.

ZION'S CAMP IN MISSOURI—LETTERS OF GOVERNOR DUNKLIN AND OTHERS.

CHAPTER VII.

ZION'S CAMP IN MISSOURI—EFFORTS AT ARBITRATION—THE WORD OF THE LORD.

CHAPTER VIII.

ZION'S CAMP DISBANDED—AN APPEAL.

CHAPTER IX.

RETURN OF THE PROPHET TO KIRTLAND—SUNDRY EVENTS IN MISSOURI.

CHAPTER X.

CHARGES AGAINST THE PROPHET ON HIS RETURN FROM ZION'S CAMP EXPEDITION—TRIAL OF ELDER SYLVESTER SMITH.

CHAPTER XI.

A MOMENT'S PEACE—COUNCIL MEETINGS IN OHIO AND MISSOURI.

CHAPTER XII.

CHANGE IN CHURCH PERIODICALS—THE COVENANT OF TITHING—CLOSE OF THE YEAR 1834.

CHAPTER XIII—1.*

THE LECTURES ON FAITH—TWELVE APOSTLES CHOSEN AND ORDAINED.

CHAPTER XIII—2.*

THE ORGANIZATION OF THE SEVENTIES—BLESSING OF THE FAITHFUL ELDERS AND SAINTS.

* By typographical error there are two chapters numbered xiii.

CHAPTER XIV.

THE GREAT REVELATION ON PRIESTHOOD.

CHAPTER XV.

THE FIRST MISSION OF THE TWELVE.

CHAPTER XVI.

PROGRESS OF AFFAIRS AT KIRTLAND—DISCOVERY OF THE BOOK OF ABRAHAM.

CHAPTER XVII.

SUNDRY COUNCIL MEETINGS IN VERMONT, OHIO AND NEW YORK.

CHAPTER XVIII.

THE BOOK OF DOCTRINE AND COVENANTS PRESENTED TO THE GENERAL ASSEMBLY OF THE PRIESTHOOD AND THE CHURCH.

CHAPTER XIX.

THE PROPHET'S RETURN FROM MICHIGAN TO KIRTLAND—HIS ADDRESS TO THE ELDERS OF THE CHURCH.

CHAPTER XX.

SUNDRY AFFAIRS AT KIRTLAND—THE PLEDGE TO REDEEM ZION.

CHAPTER XXI.

INCIDENTS FROM THE PROPHET'S EXPERIENCE IN KIRTLAND AND VICINITY.

CHAPTER XXII.

THE MINISTRY OF THE PROPHET IN KIRTLAND.

CHAPTER XXIII.

THE MINISTRY OF THE PROPHET IN KIRTLAND.

CHAPTER XXIV.

MISCELLANEOUS LABORS OF THE PROPHET IN KIRTLAND.

CHAPTER XXV.

THE TROUBLES OF ORSON HYDE AND WILLIAM SMITH—THE BOOK OF ABRAHAM—CLOSE OF THE YEAR.

CHAPTER XXVI.

OPENING OF THE YEAR 1836—THE AMERICAN INDIANS—SPECIAL COUNCIL MEETING IN KIRTLAND.

CHAPTER XXVII.

RECONCILIATION OF THE FIRST PRESIDENCY AND TWELVE APOSTLES—PENTECOSTAL TIMES IN KIRTLAND.

CHAPTER XXVIII.

THE PROPHET'S MINISTRY AND STUDIES IN KIRTLAND.

CHAPTER XXIX.

DEDICATION OF THE KIRTLAND TEMPLE—SPIRITUAL MANIFESTATIONS.

CHAPTER XXX.

THE ORDINANCE OF WASHING OF FEET—VISIONS IN THE KIRTLAND TEMPLE—THE PROPHET ON ABOLITION.

CHAPTER XXXI.

PREDICTION OF THE PROPHET'S GRANDPARENTS—AGITATION FOR THE REMOVAL OF THE SAINTS FROM CLAY COUNTY, MISSOURI.

CHAPTER XXXII.

THE PROPHET'S MISSION—LABORS IN MASSACHUSETTS—THE ORGANIZATION OF THE KIRTLAND SAFETY SOCIETY.

CHAPTER XXXIII.

MEETINGS OF THE QUORUMS OF PRIESTHOOD IN THE KIRTLAND TEMPLE—THE PROPHET'S INSTRUCTIONS ON PRIESTHOOD.

CHAPTER XXXIV.

AFFAIRS IN ZION—APOSTASY AT KIRTLAND—APPOINTMENT OF THE BRITISH MISSION—ITS DEPARTURE FOR ENGLAND.

CHAPTER XXXV.

FINANCIAL CONDITIONS IN VARIOUS NATIONS—PROGRESS OF THE BRITISH MISSION—CONFERENCES AT FAR WEST AND KIRTLAND.

CHAPTER XXXVI.

THE GATHERING SAINTS—INCREASE IN THE NUMBER OF STAKES CONTEMPLATED—COUNCILS IN ZION AND KIRTLAND—CLOSE OF THE VOLUME.

INTRODUCTION TO VOLUME II.

Summary Review of Volume One.

THE events which make up the first volume of the History of the Church moved forward from the back ground of successive dispensations of the Gospel which preceded the Dispensation of the Fullnes of Times. That volume covered the period from the birth of the Prophet Joseph Smith, 1805, to the close of the year 1833, and included as its chief events: the birth of the Prophet: his first vision of the Father aud the Son; the coming forth of the Book of Mormon; the organization of the Church, April 6th, 1830; the mission to the Lamanites; the gathering of the people from the state of New York, first to Kirtland, Ohio, and subsequently the gathering of many of them to Jackson county, Missouri; the location of the site of the future city of Zion and its temple; the introduction of the doctrine of consecration and stewardship; the experience of the Elders of Israel in their movements back and forth between Kirtland and Zion; the spread of the work throughout the states of the American Union and Canada; the Prophet's own mission to the latter place; the founding of the first Church periodical, *The Evening and Morning Star;* the selection of a number of the revelations of God for publication under the title, "The Book of Commandments;" the establishment of the Mercantile and Literary firms of Zion and Kirtland; the laying of the corner stones of the Kirtland Temple; the planting of a number of settlements in Jackson county, Missouri; the awakening jealousy of the old settlers against the more progressive Saints; the fanning of these flames of jealousy by sectarian priests; the rise of that religio-political persecution which culminated in the terrible suffering of the Saints—the destruction of their printing establishment, the burning of their homes, their final expulsion from Jackson county; also the negotiations between the Saints and the civil authorities of the state of Missouri for reinstatement of the exiles upon their lands. The first volume closed with the narration of these circumstances of discouragement which befell the Saints in their efforts to establish Zion in Missouri.

Summary of Volume Two.

In this second volume is recorded the arrival of a delegation from the exiled Saints in Missouri, seeking advice and the word of the Lord from the Prophet; the organization of Zion's Camp for the deliverance of Zion; its march from Kirtland to Missouri; its rich educational experiences; its disbandment and the return of many of the brethren to Ohio; the establishment of a school for the Elders at Kirtland, the first educational movement in the Church; the discovery of the Book of Abraham; the organization of the first, or Kirtland High Council; the organization of the quorums of the foreign ministry; the Twelve and the Seventy; the publication of the Doctrine and Covenants; the completion and dedication of the Kirtland Temple; the purification and spiritual endowment of the Elders of the Church; the appearance of Messiah in the Temple declaring His acceptance of it; the appearance of Moses, Elias and Elijah, on the same occasion, delivering the keys of their respective dispensations to the Prophet of the Dispensation of the Fullness of Times; the commencement of the ministry of the Twelve among the branches of the Church in the eastern States of the American Union; the misunderstandings that arose between them and the Presidency of the Church; the revelations of God which came in consequence of their misunderstandings, more clearly defining the rights, powers, and relations of the respective quorums of the Priesthood; the peaceful exodus of the Saints from Clay county, Missouri, and the founding of Far West; the opening of the first foreign mission by sending two of the Twelve and several Elders to England; the attempt to mass the several industrial pursuits and temporal interests of the Saints under one general concern, the "Kirtland Safety Society Company;" the failure of that concern in the general financial maelstrom that swept over the country in 1837, hastened also— sad to relate—by the unwise management and dishonesty of some of the incorporators and directors; the manifestation of excessive pride and worldliness on the part of some of the Saints at Kirtland; the disaffection of many hitherto leading Elders of the Church against the Prophet Joseph; the extensive apostasy of many Elders and Saints in Kirtland; with the account of which calamitous events this volume closes.

The Expedition of Zion's Camp.

The time covered by this volume may properly be called the Kirtland period of the Church History, since that city is the chief center of activity. The four years which comprise the period are marked, on the one hand, by rapid doctrinal development, institutional growth, outward enlargement and internal spiritual progress; and, on the other hand, are marked by internal dissensions, abundant manifestations of human weakness and wickedness, resulting in bitterness and apostasy. The period is one in which the Church is manifestly militant, and not always, from surface appearances, triumphant. Yet removed from that period by well nigh three-quarters of a century, one may see now that it was a glorious period, notwithstanding sombre shadows are now and then cast athwart the pathway of the Church's progress. Who can rightly estimate the value of the experiences of that movement for the redemption of Zion, called Zion's Camp? Nothing so completely reveals the worth or worthlessness of human character as expeditions of this description. Men are thrown into such relations with each other that all that is in them, good or bad, comes to the surface. As opportunities in time of war reveal noble or debased natures, so in expeditions such as Zion's Camp the base or exalted phases of human nature are forced to the surface, and are known and read of men. God, it appears, was about to choose His foreign ministry, His Especial Witnesses to the world, the Twelve and the Seventy. After the expedition of Zion's Camp He could choose them from among men who had offered their all in sacrifice—even to life itself—for the work's sake. Are not such manifestly fitter witnesses than those who are untried? Will it be argued that to the All-knowing the untried are as well known as the tried, and that God needed no such demonstration of fidelity as was afforded by the expedition of Zion's Camp in order to guide Him in the choice of His Witnesses to the nations of the earth? If so, my answer would be an acquiescence—God needs no such expedition in order to reveal to Him the worthiness of those who shall be His special Witnesses. But what of the world—what of men? Do not they need some such evidence back of those who shall testify of a new dispensation of the Gospel? Will not men have more regard for the testimony of Witnesses who have offered their all in sacrifice for any given work, than for the testimony of witnesses who have made no such sacrifice? Undoubtedly. Not for God's guidance, then, but for the qualification of the Witnesses in the eyes of men was the expedition of Zion's Camp in part conceived and executed. Also that those men who, under God—the Prophet Joseph Smith and the Three Witness to the Book of Mormon—were to make choice of especial Witnesses might know whom to select because of actually demonstrated fitness and worthiness.

Moreover there were men in that expedition who later will be called upon to conduct larger expeditions much of the same character—an exodus of thousands from Missouri; an exodus of tens of thousands from the confines of the United States, a thousand miles into the wilderness of the Rocky Mountains. May not the Lord have designed in part this expedition of Zion's Camp for their instruction, for their training? The leaders of these later movements are all there—Brigham Young, Heber C. Kimball, Orson Pratt, Parley P. Pratt, Charles C Rich, George A. Smith, Wilford Woodruff and many more. It is significant, too, that Brigham Young at least sensed the true importance of the Zion's Camp expedition. That expedition for the redemption of Zion was regarded by many weak-faithed Saints as a sad failure, a humiliation of a presumptuous prophet. One of these attempted to ridicule it in the presence of Brigham Young, as a case of marching men up a hill to march them down again. "Well," said the scoffer, "what did you gain on this useless journey to Missouri with Joseph Smith?" "All we went for," promptly replied Brigham Young. "I would not exchange the *experience* gained in that expedition for all the wealth of Geauga county." A remark which proves that Brigham Young had a keen insight into the purpose of the Zion's Camp movement.

First Educational Movement of the Church.

The value of the educational movement in the Church by the establishment of a school for the Elders in Kirtland, cannot be fully appreciated even yet. It stands as a direct contradiction to the oft-repeated charges that Mormonism seeks to thrive through the ignorance of its devotees. "Seek ye diligently, and teach one another words of wisdom," was an admonition the Church in the Kirtland period of its history sought earnestly to carry into effect. "Yea, seek ye out of the best books words of wisdom: seek learning even by study, and also by faith." To the sphere of their learning there were no limitations set. "Teach ye diligently," said the Lord, "and my grace shall attend you, that you may be instructed more perfectly in theory, in principle, in doctrine, in the law of the Gospel, in all things that pertain unto the kingdom of God, that are expedient for you to understand; of things both in heaven and in the earth, and under the earth; things which have been, things which are, things which must shortly come to pass; things which are at home, things which are abroad; the wars and the perplexities of the nations, and the judgments which are on the land, and a knowledge also of countries and of kingdoms." I know of nothing that lies outside this boundless field of research into which the Elders of the Church especially were invited—nay, commanded, to enter. It comprehends the whole possible sphere of human investigation; and furnishes all necessary contradiction to the theory that the Church at any time contemplated an ignorant ministry. By intelligence, not stupidity; by knowledge, not ignorance, has the Church from the very beginning hoped to succeed in her mission.

The Organization of the Foreign Ministry.

It is during the Kirtland period of her history also that the Church raised her eyes and for the first time gazed out upon the world-wide sphere of her future activities. Until now she had confined her missions and labors to the United States and Canada. But lo! a foreign minis try had been organized, a quorum of Twelve Apostles and two quorums of Seventy had been called into existence and ordained. Was that without significance? Do ordinations count for nothing, or is there virtue in divine appointment? Undoubtedly there is power in ordinances, in divine appointments: "Joshua the son of Nun was full of the spirit of wisdom; for Moses had laid his hands upon him and the children of Israel hearkened unto him and did as the Lord commanded Moses." While Timothy, the young Christian evangelist, was admonished by Paul to stir up the gift of God which was in him by the putting on of the Apostle's hands. Since, then, there is virtue in ordinations of divine appointing, it is but to be expected that the Church of Christ in this last dispensation would be influenced by the appointment and ordination of her foreign ministry. It was but a proper sequence of the appointment of this ministry that Apostles and their associates should be sent to England. The Church of Jesus Christ of Latter-day Saints was never intended to be merely an American sect of religion. It is a new and the last dispensation of the Christian religion—the Dispensation of the Fullness of Times, the dispensation into which will be gathered all former dispensations of the Gospel of Christ; all keys of authority, all powers, all gifts, all graces essential to the welfare and salvation of man—all that is essential to the completion of the mission of the Christian religion. The mission of the Church in such a dispensation is general not local, world-embracing. Had it been less than one of the world's great movements, Mormonism had been inadequate to the world's needs—less than sufficient for a world's redemption. There was marked, therefore, a mighty bound forward in the progress of the work when the foreign ministry of the Church was organized, and a mission appointed to England. The work would have perished had it not taken this step forward. The Church had reached that stage of its development when there must be a forward movement. Things do not stand inert in this world. Inertia is death. In progress only is there life. The thing that does not grow dies. The very rocks increase or decay. For the time being the elements on which the Church lived were exhausted in the land where it came forth. The material which had been gathered into it was passing through tne crucible. There was need of an enlargement of action, a necessity for new elements being brought into the body religious. That enlargement of action was found in opening the British mission. The new elements essential to the preservation of the work were found in the English people; for among them were given the evidences of the existence of the spiritual light and life which had characterized the work at its coming forth: and as that mission had been directly appointed by the Prophet Joseph Smith, it supplied the proofs that God was still with him, honored the authority which had been given him, and still directed his movements in the administration of the affairs of the Church; for it was the prompting of the Spirit of God in the Prophet, that led to the appointment of this first foreign mission. These considerations made the opening of the British mission an epoch in the history of the Church.

The Restoration of the Keys for the Gathering of Israel.

The work of God was also greatly enlarged during this Kirtland period, by the appearance of Moses and Elias and Elijah, and bestowing upon the Prophet the keys of their respective dispensations. Let us contemplate the event. "Moses appeared before us," says the Prophet, "and committed unto us the keys of the gathering of Israel, from the four parts of the earth, and the leading of the ten tribes from the land of the north." Who, at the time comprehended the full import of this incident? Who comprehends it now? From the beginning of the great Latter-day work men had their attention directed to the gathering of Israel and the establishment of Zion and Jerusalem as a part of the purposes of God to be accomplished in the work. The angel Moroni on the occasion of his first visit to the Prophet Joseph, quoted a number of Old Testament scriptures referring to the Lord's promises concerning the redemption of Judah and Jerusalem;* also concerning the gathering of Israel from all the lands whither they had been driven.† Numerous are the prophecies relating to the return of Israel from the land of the north, and other parts of the earth, into which they were driven in the day of their rebellion and apostasy;‡ but it occurred to no one that before these prophecies could be fulfilled Israel's great prophet, Moses, who held the keys of the dispensation pertaining to the gathering of Israel, must come and give to men the authority to proceed with that work. The moment he appears, however, and gives such authority, the propriety of it, the fitnes of it is apparent. The appearance of Moses was also in proper sequence of events in the development of the great Latter-day work. Although, as already stated, the gathering of Israel in the last days had been made a prominent feature in the communication of Moroni to the Prophet Joseph, and the subject also of some other early revelations to the Church § not until the foreign ministry had been organized—the Twelve and the Seventy—the quorums of Priesthood on which rests the re-

* See Mal. iii: 1-7.

† Isaiah xi: 11-16; also History of the Church, vol. I, pp. 12, 13.

‡ Following are a few of the most prominent of these prophecies: Deut. xxx: 1-6; Isaiah ii: 1-4; Jeremiah iii, 12-18. Also xvi: 4-18; xxiii: 1-8, and xxxi: 7-14.

§ See Doc. & Cov. sec. xlv: 15-71, this revelation was given in 1831; also Doc. & Cov. sec. cxxxiii. This is the revelation called the appendix and was given November 3, 1831.

sponsibility to travel in all the world and preach the Gospel and gather Israel—not until this ministry was organized did Moses appear and commit the keys of the gathering of Israel from the four parts of the earth. What order is here? The organization of the foreign ministry to go into all the nations of earth, and then the coming of Moses to commit the keys of the gathering of Israel from the four parts of the earth, and the leading of the ten tribes from the land of the north. In this incident as in a thousand others in the great work of God in the last days, the evidence of a divine wisdom having regard for the eternal fitness of things, for the proper sequence in the order of events in the development of the Lord's purposes, is apparent. Note, too, the spiritual effect opon the Saints of the restoration of these keys of the gathering of Israel. Before the mission for England under Elders Kimball and Hyde departed, the prophet enjoined them to adhere strictly to the first principles of the Gospel, and say nothing for the present in relation to the gathering; this, doubtless on account of the unsettled condition of the Church at the time. Similar instructions, and for the same reason, were given to the Twelve Apostles in 1839 when they went on their mission to England. But the Saints could not be kept in ignorance of these matters. No sooner were the people baptized than they were seized with a desire to gather with the main body of the Church. "I find it is difficult to keep anything from the Saints," writes Elder Taylor in his journal of this period, "for the Spirit of God reveals it to them. * * * * Some time ago Sister Mitchell dreamed that she, her husband and a number of others were on board a vessel, and that there were other vessels, loaded with Saints, going somewhere. She felt very happy and was rejoicing in the Lord." Another sister, Elder Taylor informs us, had a similar dream, and was informed that all the Saints were going. Neither of these sisters nor any of the Saints at that time, knew anything about the principle of gathering, yet all were anxious to leave their homes, their kindred and the associations of a lifetime, to join the main body of the Church in a distant land, the members of which were total strangers to them.* The same spirit has rested upon the people in every nation where the Gospel has been received. There has been little need of preaching the gathering, the people as a rule have had to be restrained rather than encouraged in the matter of gathering to Zion and her stakes.

The Spirit of Gathering on the Jews.

During the last ten years the world has witnessed a remarkable change of spirit come over the Jewish race. We hear of Jewish aspirations for national existence; for the perpetuation of the Jewish customs

* Life of John Taylor, p. 96.

and Jewish ideals. After saying so long, "May we celebrate the next Passover in Jerusalem," the thought at last seems to have occurred to some Jewish minds that if that expressed wish is ever realized, some practical steps must be taken looking to the actual achievement of that possibility—which has given rise among the Jews to what is called the "Zionite Movement." The keynotes of that movement are heard in the following utterances of some of the leaders in explanation of it: "We want to resume the broken thread of our national existence; we want to show to the world the moral strength, the intellectual power of the Jewish people. We want a place where the race can be centralized."* "It is for these Jews [of Russia, Roumania and Galicia] that the name of their country [Palestine] spells 'Hope.' I should not be a man if I did not realize that for these persecuted Jews, Jerusalem spells reason, justice, manhood and integrity"† "Jewish nationalism on a modern basis in Palestine, the old home of the people."‡ "Palestine needs a people, Israel needs a country. Give the country without a people, to the people without a country."§ In a word, it is the purpose of "Zionism" to redeem Palestine and give it back to Jewish control—create, in fact, a Jewish state in the land promised to their fathers.

Of course, for hundreds of years there has been talk of the Jews returning to Jerusalem, and from time to time societies have been formed to keep alive that hope, and keep the Jew's face turned toward the chief city and land of his forefathers; but little was achieved by those societies, however, except to foster the hope of Israel's return in the heart of a widely dispersed, persecuted and discouraged race, who have waited long for the realization of the promises made to their fathers. I say but "little" was accomplished by the various Jewish societies existing before the Zionite movement began beyond fostering the hope of Israel based on the predictions of their prophets; but that "little" was much. It was nourishing in secret and through ages of darkness that spark of fire which when touched with the breath of God should burst forth into a flame that not all the world could stay. They made possible this larger movement, now attracting the attention of the world, and known as the "Zionite Movement;" which, in reality, is but the federation of all Jewish societies which have had for their purpose the realization of the hopes of scattered Israel.

"Zionism" is considered to have grown out of the persecution of the Jews during the last eighteen years in such European countries as Russia, France, Germany, and Roumania. It held its first general confer-

* Leon Zeltekoff

† Rabbi Emil G. Hirsch.

‡ Max Nordau.

§ Israel Zangwill.

ence in August, 1897, in Basle, Switzerland; and since then has continued to hold annual conferences that have steadily increased both in interest and the number of delegates representing various Jewish societies, until now it takes on the appearance of one of the world's great movements. It is not so much a religious movement as a racial one: for prominent Jews of all shades of both political and religious opinions have participated in it under the statesmanlike leadership of Doctor Herzel of Austria. Not to persecution alone, however, is due this strange awakening desire on the part of the Jews to return to the city and the land of their fathers; but to the fact of the restoration of the keys of the gathering of Israel by Moses to the Prophet of the Dispensation of the Fullness of Times. Under the divine authority restored by Moses, Joseph Smith sent an Apostle of the Lord Jesus Christ to the land of Palestine to bless it and dedicate it once more to the Lord for the return of His people. This Apostle was Orson Hyde, and he performed his mission in 1840-2. In 1872 an Apostolic delegation consisting of the late Presidents George A. Smith and Lorenzo Snow were sent to Palestine. The purpose of their mission, in part, is thus stated in President Young's letter of appointment to George A. Smith: "When you get to the land of Palestine, we wish you to dedicate and consecrate that land to the Lord, that it may be blessed with fruitfulness, preparatory to the return of the Jews, in fulfillment of prophecy and the accomplishment of the purposes of our heavenly Father."*

Acting, then, under the divine authority restored to earth by the Prophet Moses, this Apostolic delegation—as well as the Apostle first sent—from the summit of Mount Olivet blessed the land, and again dedicated it for the return of the Jews. It is not strange, therefore, to those who look upon such a movement as Zionism in connection with faith in God's great latter-day work, to see this spirit now moving upon the minds of the Jewish people prompting their return to the land of their fathers. It is but the breath of God upon their souls turning their hearts to the promises made to the fathers. It is but the fulfillment in part of one of the many prophecies of the Book of Mormon relating to the gathering of Israel, viz: "It shall come to pass that the Lord God shall commence His work among all nations, kindreds, tongues, and people, to bring about the restoration of His people upon the earth." The spirit attendant upon the restoration of the keys of authority to gather Israel from the four quarters of the earth, and the exercise of that divine authority, though unrecognized as yet by the world, is the real cause of this movement Palestine-ward by the Jews.

Elijah's Mission.

The work accomplished by Elijah in giving to the Prophet Joseph the particular dispensation of the Priesthood which should plant in the

* Biography of Lorenzo Snow, p. 496.

hearts of the children the promises made to the fathers—lest the whole earth should be utterly wasted at His coming*—is attended by evidences of virtue and power of God no less palpable than those which bear witness to the virtue and power of God in the work accomplished by Moses in giving to the Prophet the keys of authority for the gathering of Israel. The work done by Elijah was to open the door of salvation for the dead. From that event comes the knowledge of the principles by which the saving power of the Gospel may be applied to men who have died without receiving its benefits in this life, From of old men had read in the scriptures that Messiah would bring out the prisoners from the prison, and them that sit in darkness out of the prison house;† that in addition to being given as a restorer of the tribes of Jacob and a light to the gentiles, the Messiah should have power to say to the prisoners, "Go forth; to them that sit in darkness, show yourselves;"‡ "to proclaim liberty to the captives, and the opening of the prison to them that are bound."§ From the beginning of Christianity men had read in the New Testament how Jesus had once suffered for sins, the just for the unjust; and how that being put to death in the flesh He was quickened by the Spirit by which He went and preached to the spirits in prison which were disobedient when the long suffering of God waited in the days of Noah.‖ Also they read how for this cause was the Gospel preached to them that are dead that they might be judged as men are in the flesh, but live according to God in the spirit;** also the reasoning of Paul to the effect that if there was no resurrection of the dead, why, then, were the Saints baptized for the dead;†† also how the fathers without those of later generations cannot be made perfect.‡‡ All of which passages, however, have been regarded as among the mysteries of the word of God, incomprehensible, dark. But touched by the Prophet Elijah's hand, imparting to them their true import, how bright they glow with spiritual light and life! and what a sense of largeness and power is given to the Gospel of Jesus Christ when from this mission of Elijah's there comes the power to apply the principles and ordinances of salvation to all the children of men (save the sons of perdition; and these, thank God! are but few) in all ages of the world, and whether living or dead! How the horizon of things respecting the Gospel of Christ is pushed back from the walled-in limits of that pseudo-Christianity current among men, by this spirit and power of Elijah that has come into the

* Church History Vol. I p. 12, also Mal. iv: 5, 6.

† Isaiah xlii: 7.

‡ Ibid. xlix: 6-9.

§ Ibid. lxi: I.

‖ I Peter iii: 18-20.

** Ibid. iv: 6.

†† I. Cor. xv: 29

‡‡ Heb. xi.

world! The fact that such a spirit has come into the world is sustained by palpable evidences. The truth of my statement will be recognized when I say that within the last fifty years there has arisen throughout the world an increased spirit of interest among men concerning their ancestors that scarcely stops this side of the marvelous. In all lands men are earnestly seeking for their genealogies, and many volumes are issued from the press annually in which the pedigrees of men of all sorts and conditions are given. Some may be said to be possessed almost of a mania, on this subject so ardent are they in seeking for a knowledge of their fore-fathers, and this all quite apart from any direct work that is being done along the same lines by the Latter-day Saints; though the work of the Saints in the temples for their dead is greatly helped by this outside circumstance to which I call attention. Why and whence this spirit in the hearts of the children which turns the attention of men to the fathers of former generations, if it is not a consequence of the fulfillment of Elijah's predicted mission that before the great and dreadful day of the Lord should come he [Elijah] would be sent to turn the heart of the children to the fathers, and the heart of the fathers to the children?*

Of the work done by the Latter-day Saints in consequence of the restoration of these special keys of the Priesthood by the hand of Elijah I need scarcely speak. That the spirit which came into the world by reason of Elijah's special dispensation of authority to Joseph Smith is working upon the hearts of the Latter-day Saints is evidenced by the building of the beautiful temple at Nauvoo, and by the erection of the world-famed temple in Salt Lake City; also by the erection of magnificent temples in Logan, Manti and St. George—all in Utah. These temples have all been erected in response to the diffusion of that spirit that attended upon Elijah's mission; and are evidences in stone that the Saints have partaken of that spirit which turns the hearts of the children to the fathers. Another palpable evidence to the same great truth is seen in the throngs which daily visit these temples to perform the ordinances of salvation for the dead; not only baptism for the dead, but also the confirmations, ordinations and sealings by which the fathers shall be prepared for the kingdom of God, and all the families of men be set in order, united together by bonds, covenants and established relations that shall be in harmony with that heavenly kingdom which the redeemed of God shall inherit. The full importance of this work—its height and depth—is not yet appreciated by the children of men; but so great it is that the period of our Church History which witnesses its beginning—even if it were the only achievement—must ever be regarded as an important period.

* Mal. 4; 5, 6.

Calamitous Events.

As for the calamitous events of the Church during the Kirtland period, what shall we say of them? Are they to be accounted wholly deplorable, or as part of that experience of the Church which makes for advancement? Unquestionably every experience is of value to an individual or an organization. Some experiences may be sad, and accounted at the time as disastrous; but are they really so? The rough wind which shakes it helps the young and slow-growing oak; for by reason of this very shaking the tree takes firmer hold of the earth; wider spread the roots; deeper down into the soil are they thrust, until the sapling, once so easily shaken, becomes a monarch in the forest, mocks the howling tempest, until its height and frame become worthy of the land and atmosphere in which it grows a giant tree. So may grow a government—civil or ecclesiastical—so may grow the Church, helped by the adverse circumstances which shake it to the very foundations on which it rests. Profitable if not sweet are the uses of adversity. As the winter's wind when it bites and blows upon man's body is no flatterer, but feelingly persuades him what he is, so the adverse circumstances which overtake an organization, such as the Church of Christ, may be very profitable to it. Such rebellions and apostasies as occurred in this Kirtland period of the Church's history but test and exhibit the strength of the fabric. Such circumstances force a review of the work as far as accomplished. The whole is re-examined to see if in it there is any flaw or defect; if any worthless material is being worked into its structure. Hence periods usually considered calamitous are accompanied by corrections of what may be wrong; and the body religious is purified by the expulsion of those whose rebellion and apostasy but prove them unworthy of the Lord's work. Let me be rightly understood here. I am not contending that adverse circumstances, rebellions and apostasies are in themselves good. Whatever may be the over-ruled results to the body religious, rebellion and apostasy spell condemnation and the destruction of spiritual life for the individuals overtaken by such calamities. But so long as human nature is what it now is—weak and sinful—just so long as out of that intractable material the Church of Christ has the mission to prepare men for the Father's kingdom, just so long will there be occasional calamities periods in the history of the Church such as was the year 1837 at Kirtland. But what after all are such periods but times of purification, of cleansing? During the previous years of success in the ministry, there had been gathered into the Church all classes of men. As in former dispensations of the Gospel, so in this last dispensation; the kingdom of heaven is like unto a net cast into the sea, that gathers of every kind of fish; and when it is full, they draw it to shore, and sit down, and gather the good into vessels, and cast the bad away. The first step in the process of correcting human nature is to discover its defects. It may not always follow that when the defects are made known they will be corrected. But it is true that no correction will be made until the necessity of correction is manifest, until the defects are pointed out. Hence God has said: "If men will come unto me, I will show unto them their weaknesses." But, unhappily, it sometimes is the case that men resist God, they love their sins, they become hardened in their iniquity, they resist the Spirit, and prove themselves unworthy of the Father's kingdom. What then? Shall they pollute that kingdom, or shall they be cast out as material unfitted for the Master's use, and of their own volition choose to remain so? There can be but one reasonable answer to the question. They refuse to go peaceably, however. They are boisterous, they accuse the innocent, they justify their own course, they seek to wreck the Church, to bring to pass chaos; and in the midst of this disorder they are cast out; and although this may not always end their power to work mischief, or create annoyance for the body-religious—for the power to work evil is still with them—yet the Church is rid of them, and in no way can be regarded as responsible for their wickedness. It is our custom to enumerate such scenes as among the calamitous events of the Church; and they are so, in some aspects of the case. As already remarked it is a calamitous time for those who are cast out, for they are overcome of the evil one; and as the heavens wept when the Son of the Morning and his following were cast out of heaven, so it is to be expected that the Saints will be sad, and sorrow over those who are overcome of the adversary. But for the Church herself it is well that this intractable material is gotten rid of; that the body religious is purged of those who can only be a source of weakness and of shame to her. She is helped by the event; purified by it; strengthened; made more acceptable with God and pleasing to reasonable men. It is only in a modified sense, then, that this latter part of the Kirtland period of the Church's history can be regarded as a calamitous time. There is more adversity yet to follow in the experience of the Saints; much distress and many sore trials: and so shall there continue to be such times of trial as long as the Church remains the Church militant. Not until she becomes the Church triumphant, and is glorified by the presence of her Great Head, the Lord Jesus Christ, can the Saints hope for an absolute discontinuance of the occasional recurrence of what are generally considered trying or calamitous events.

HISTORY

OF THE

Church of Jesus Christ of Latter-day Saints

VOL. II.

HISTORY

OF THE

CHURCH OF JESUS CHRIST

—OF—

LATTER-DAY SAINTS.

PERIOD I.

HISTORY OF JOSEPH SMITH, THE PROPHET.

CHAPTER I.

THE YEAR EIGHTEEN HUNDRED AND THIRTY-FOUR—AFFAIRS IN ZION AND KIRTLAND.

January 1, 1834.—The scattered Saints in Missouri commenced the year eighteen hundred and thirty-four, with a conference, which they held in Clay county, on the first day of January, at which Bishop Partridge presided. After transacting much business relative to comforting and strengthening the scattered members of the Church, it was

Condition of the Saints in Missouri.

Resolved, That Lyman Wight and Parley P. Pratt be sent as special messengers, to represent the situation of the scattered brethren in Missouri, to the Presidency and Church in Kirtland, and ask their advice.

On the evening of the 2nd of January, a Bishop's court assembled in Kirtland to investigate the case of Wesley Hurlburt, against whom charges had been preferred by Harriet Howe and others to the effect "that Hurlburt had denied the faith, spoken reproachfully of the Church, did not believe Joseph was a true Prophet," etc. Hurlburt was in the place, but did not appear before the court, consequently was cut off.

Excommunication of Wesley Hurlburt.

The threats of the mob about Kirtland through the fall and winter had been such as to cause the brethren to be constantly on the lookout, and those who labored on the temple were engaged at night watching to protect the walls they had laid during the day, from threatened violence. On the morning of the 8th of January, about 1 o'clock, the inhabitants of Kirtland were alarmed by the firing of about thirteen rounds of cannon, by the mob, on the hill about half a mile northwest of the village.*

Mob Threats at Kirtland.

On the evening of the 11th of January, Joseph Smith, Jun., Frederick G. Williams, Newel K. Whitney, John Johnson, Oliver Cowdery, and Orson Hyde united in prayer, and asked the Lord to grant the following petitions:

A Prayer.

1.—That the Lord would grant that our lives might be precious in His sight; that He would watch over our persons, and give His angels charge concerning us and our families, that no evil nor unseen hand might be permitted to harm us.

2.—That the Lord would also hold the lives of all the United Order as sacred, and not suffer that any of them should be taken.

* Of these days in Kirtland Elder Heber C. Kimball in his Journal says: "The Church was in a state of poverty and distress, in consequence of which it appeared almost impossible that the commandments could be fulfilled [relative to the Kirtland Temple]; at the same time our enemies were raging and threatening destruction upon us, and we had to guard ourselves night after night, and for weeks were not permitted to take off our clothes, and were obliged to lay with our fire locks in our arms."—*Times and Seasons*, vol. vi, p. 771.

3.—That the Lord would grant that Brother Joseph might prevail over his enemy, even Dr. Hurlburt, who has threatened his life, whom Joseph has caused to be taken with a precept; that the Lord would fill the heart of the court with a spirit to do justice, and cause that the law of the land may be magnified in bringing Hurlburt to justice.

4.—That the Lord in the order of His providence, would provide the Bishop of this Church [at Kirtland] with means sufficient to discharge every debt, in due season, that the Order owes, that the Church may not be brought into disrepute, and the Saints be afflicted by the hands of their enemies.

5.—That the Lord would protect our printing press from the hands of evil men, and give us means to send forth His record, even His Gospel, that the ears of all may hear it; and also that we may print His Scriptures; and also that He would give those who were appointed to conduct the press, wisdom sufficient that the cause may not be hindered, but that men's eyes may thereby be opened to see the truth.

6.—That the Lord would deliver Zion, and gather in His scattered people to possess it in peace; and also, while in their dispersion, that He would provide for them that they perish not from hunger or cold; and finally, that God, in the name of Jesus, would gather His elect speedily, and unveil His face, that His Saints might behold His glory, and dwell with Him. Amen.

Efforts of Sectarian Priests Against Restoration of Exiles.

As soon as the Governor of Missouri intimated, or the news began to circulate, that the "Mormons" (as the people called the members of the Church), would be restored to their possessions in Jackson county (if they desired to be), the priests of all denominations, as the men behind the scene, with the mob, began to set their springs in motion, and by their secret councils, and false publications and insinuations, soured the public mind, and prevented the administration of the laws, so that anything like a return to their houses and lands, or recovery of damages for losses sustained, seemed as distant as the day of judgment. The powers of wickedness and darkness walked hand in hand together, and the Saints mourned.

January 16.—I visited Brother Jenkins Salisbury, and spent the night. O Lord! keep us and my family safe, until I return unto them; O my God, have mercy on my brethren in Zion, for Christ's sake. Amen.

January 22.—The Presidency of the High Priesthood wrote from Kirtland to the brethren in Christ Jesus, scattered from Zion—scattered abroad from the land of their inheritance:

THE ELDERS OF THE CHURCH IN KIRTLAND, TO THEIR BRETHREN ABROAD.*

Dear Brethren in Christ, and Companions in Tribulation:

When we call to remembrance the ties with which we are bound to those who embrace the everlasting covenant, and the fellowship and love with which the hearts of the children of our Lord's kingdom should be united, we cherish a belief that you will bear with us, when we take this course to communicate to you some of the many thoughts which occupy our minds, and press with continued weight upon our hearts, as we reflect upon the vast importance and responsi-

* The use of "abroad" here does not have reference to foreign lands, but means those who were scattered from their homes in Missouri.

This communication of the Elders of the Church at Kirtland, to their brethren scattered abroad, does not appear in the History of the Prophet, but is found in the *Evening and Morning Star*, Vol. II, Nos. 17, 18, 19. The document is evidently dictated by the Prophet and is of such doctrinal importance that it is thought proper to give it place in the body of the Church History. It treats of the origin of law, human and divine, and man's relations thereto; the antiquity of the Gospel; the virtue of the atonement of Christ; the importance of men in this age being in communication with God through the means of revelation; the bitterness and fate of apostates. The document is a complete refutation of the charges of bad motives behind the conduct of the Saints. No man, I believe, can read this document and then believe that those who issued it were evil disposed men bent on deceiving mankind.

The late President Daniel H. Wells was wont to say that some time previous to his joining the Church he was satisfied that Joseph Smith was an inspired man because of his intuitive knowledge of the fundamental principles of law—a view that will be confirmed by a perusal of the parts of this communication which deal with the origin, force, and relations of law.

bility of your callings, in the sight of the Master of the vineyard. And though our communications to you may be frequent, yet we believe they will be received on your part with brotherly feelings; and that from us your unworthy brethren, you will suffer a word of exhortation to have place in your hearts, as you see the great extent of the power and dominion of the prince of darkness, and realize how vast the numbers are who are crowding the road to death without ever giving heed to the cheering sound of the Gospel of our Lord Jesus Christ.

Consider for a moment, brethren, the fulfillment of the words of the prophet; for we behold that darkness covers the earth, and gross darkness the minds of the inhabitants thereof—that crimes of every description are increasing among men—vices of great enormity are practiced—the rising generation growing up in the fullness of pride and arrogance—the aged losing every sense of conviction, and seemingly banishing every thought of a day of retribution—intemperance, immorality, extravagance, pride, blindness of heart, idolatry, the loss of natural affection; the love of this world, and indifference toward the things of eternity increasing among those who profess a belief in the religion of heaven, and infidelity spreading itself in consequence of the same—men giving themselves up to commit acts of the foulest kind, and deeds of the blackest dye, blaspheming, defrauding, blasting the reputation of neighbors, stealing, robbing, murdering; advocating error and opposing the truth, forsaking the covenant of heaven, and denying the faith of Jesus—and in the midst of all this, the day of the Lord fast approaching when none except those who have won the wedding garment will be permitted to eat and drink in the presence of the Bridegroom, the Prince of Peace!

Impressed with the truth of these facts what can be the feelings of those who have been partakers of the heavenly gift and have tasted the good word of God, and the powers of the world to come? Who but those who can see the awful precipice upon which the world of mankind stands in this generation, can labor in the vineyard of the Lord without feeling a sense of the world's deplorable situation? Who but those who have duly considered the condescension of the Father of our spirits, in providing a sacrifice for His creatures, a plan of redemption, a power of atonement, a scheme of salvation, having as its great objects, the bringing of men back into the presence of the King of heaven, crowning them in the celestial glory, and making them heirs with the Son to that inheritance which is incorruptible, undefiled, and which fadeth not away—who but such can realize the importance of a perfect walk before all men, and a diligence in calling upon all men to partake of these blessings? How indescribably glorious are these things to mankind! Of a truth they may be considered tidings of great joy to all people; and tidings, too, that ought to fill the earth and cheer the hearts of every one when sounded in his ears. The reflection that everyone is to receive according to his own diligence and perseverance while in the vineyard, ought to inspire everyone who is called to be a minister of these glad tidings, to so improve his talent that he may gain other talents, that when the Master sits down to take an account of the conduct of His servants, it may be said, Well done, good and faithful servant: thou hast been faithful over a few things; I will now make thee ruler over many things: enter thou into the joy of thy Lord.

Some may pretend to say that the world in this age is fast increasing in righteousness; that the dark ages of superstition and blindness have passed, when the faith of Christ was known and held only by a few, when ecclesiastic power had an almost universal control over Christendom, and the consciences of men were bound by the strong chains of priestly power: but now, the gloomy cloud is burst, and the Gospel is shining with all the resplendent glory of an apostolic day; and that the kingdom of the Messiah is greatly spreading, that the Gospel of our Lord is carried to divers nations of the earth, the Scriptures translating into different tongues; the ministers of truth crossing the vast deep to proclaim to men in darkness a risen Savior, and to erect the standard of Emanuel where light has never shone; and that the idol is destroyed, the temple of images forsaken; and those who but a short time previous followed the traditions of their fathers and sacrificed their own flesh to appease the wrath of some imaginary god, are now raising their voices in the worship of the Most High, and are lifting their thoughts up to Him with the full expectation that one day they will meet with a joyful reception in His everlasting kingdom!

But a moment's candid reflection upon the principles of these systems, the manner in which they are conducted, the individuals employed, the apparent object held out as an inducement to cause them to act, we think, is sufficient for every candid man to draw a conclusion in his own mind whether this is the order of heaven or not. We deem it a just principle, and it is one the force of which we believe ought to be duly considered by every individual, that all men are created equal, and that all have the privilege of thinking for themselves upon all matters relative to conscience. Consequently, then, we are not disposed, had we the power, to deprive any one of exercising that free independence of mind which heaven has so graciously bestowed upon the human family as one of its choicest gifts; but we take the liberty (and this we have a right to do) of looking at this order of things a few moments, and contrasting it with the order of God as we find it in the sacred Scriptures. In this review, however, we shall present the points as we consider they were really designed by the great Giver to be understood, and the happy result arising from a performance of the requirements of heaven as revealed to every one who obeys them; and the consequence attending a false construction, a misrepresentation, or a forced meaning that was never designed in the mind of the Lord when He condescended to speak from the heavens to men for their salvation.

Previous to entering upon a subject of so great moment to the human family there is a prominent item which suggests itself to our minds, which, here, in few words, we wish to discuss: All regularly organized and well established governments have certain laws by which, more or less, the innocent are protected and the guilty punished. The fact admitted, that certain laws are good, equitable and just, ought to be binding upon the individual who admits this, and lead him to observe in the strictest manner an obedience to those laws. These laws when violated, or broken by the individual, must, in justice, convict his mind with a double force, if possible, of the extent and magnitude of his crime; because he could have no plea of ignorance to produce; and his act of transgression was openly committed against light and knowledge. But the individual who may be ignorant and imperceptibly transgresses or violates laws, though the voice of the country requires that he should suffer, yet he will never feel that remorse of conscience that the other will, and that keen, cutting reflection will never rise in his breast that otherwise would, had he done the deed, or committed the offense in full conviction that he was breaking the law of his country, and having previously acknowledged the same to be just. It is not our intention by these remarks, to attempt to place the law of man on a parallel with the law of heaven; because we do not consider that it is formed in the same wisdom and propriety; neither do we consider that it is sufficient in itself to bestow anything on man in comparison with the law of heaven, even should it promise it. The laws of men may guarantee to a people protection in the honorable pursuits of this life, and the temporal happiness arising from a protection against unjust insults and injuries: and when this is said, all is said, that can be in truth, of the power, extent, and influence of the laws of men, exclusive of the law of God. The law of heaven is presented to man, and as such guarantees to all who obey it a reward far beyond any earthly consideration; though it does not promise that the believer in every age should be exempt from the afflictions and troubles arising from different sources in consequence of the acts of wicked men on earth. Still in the midst of all this there is a promise predicated upon the fact that it is the law of heaven, which transcends the law of man, as far as eternal life the temporal; and as the blessings which God is able to give, are greater than those which can be given by man. Then, certainly, if the law of man is binding upon man when acknowledged, how much more must the law of heaven be! And as much as the law of heaven is more perfect than the law of man, so much greater must be the reward if obeyed. The law of man promises safety in temporal life; but the law of God promises that life which is eternal, even an inheritance at God's own right hand, secure from all the powers of the wicked one.

We consider that God has created man with a mind capable of instruction, and a faculty which may be enlarged in proportion to the heed and diligence given to the light communicated from heaven to the intellect; and that the nearer man approaches perfection, the clearer are his views, and the greater his enjoyments, till he has overcome the evils of his life and lost every desire for sin; and like the ancients, arrives at that point of faith where he is wrapped in the power and glory of his Maker, and is caught up to dwell with Him. But we consider that this is a station to which no man ever arrived in a moment: he must have been instructed in the government and laws of that kingdom by proper degrees, until his mind is capable in some measure of comprehending the propriety, justice, equality, and consistency of the same. For further instruction we refer you to Deut. xxxii, where the Lord says, that Jacob is the lot of his inheritance. He found him in a desert land, and in the waste, howling wilderness; He led him about, He instructed him, He kept him as the apple of His eye, etc.; which will show the force of the last item advanced, that it is necessary for men to receive an understanding concerning the laws of the heavenly kingdom, before they are permitted to enter it: we mean the celestial glory. So dissimilar are the governments of men, and so divers are their laws, from the government and laws of heaven, that a man, for instance, hearing that there was a country on this globe called the United States of North America, could take his journey to this place without first learning the laws of government; but the conditions of God's kingdom are such, that all who are made partakers of that glory, are under the necessity of learning something respecting it previous to their entering into it. But the foreigner can come to this country without knowing a syllable of its laws, or even subscribing to obey them after he arrives. Why? Because the government of the United States does not require it: it only requires an obedience to its laws after the individual has arrived within its jurisdiction.

As we previously remarked, we do not attempt to place the law of man on a parallel with the law of heaven; but we will bring forward another item, to further urge the propriety of yielding obedience to the law of heaven, after the fact is admitted, that the laws of man are binding upon man. Were a king to extend his dominion over the habitable earth, and send forth his laws which were of the most perfect kind, and command his subjects one and all to yield obedience to the same, and add as a reward to those who obeyed them, that at a certain period they should be called to attend the marriage of his son, who in due time was to receive the kingdom, and they should be made equal with him in the same; and fix as a penalty for disobedience that every individual guilty of it should be cast out at the marriage feast, and have no part nor portion with his government, what rational mind could for a moment accuse the king with injustice for punishing such rebellious subjects? In the first place his laws were just, easy to be complied with, and perfect: nothing of a tyrannical nature was required of them; but the very construction of the laws was equity and beauty; and when obeyed would produce the happiest condition possible to all who adhered to them, beside the last great benefit of sitting down with a royal robe in the presence of the king at the great, grand marriage supper of his son, and be made equal with him in all the afiairs of the kingdom.

When these royal laws were issued, and promulgated throughout the vast dominion, every subject, when interrogated whether he believed them to be from his sovereign or not, answered, Yes; I know they are, I am acquainted with the signature, for it is as usual. *Thus saith the King!* This admitted, the subject is bound by every consideration of honor to his country, his king, and his own personal character, to observe in the strictest sense every requisition in the royal edict. Should any escape the search of the ambassadors of the king and never hear these last laws, giving his subjects such exalted privileges, an excuse might be urged in their behalf, and they escape the censure of the king. But for those who had heard, who had admitted, and who had promised obedience to these just laws no excuse could be urged; and when brought into the presence of the king, certainly, justice would require that they should suffer a penalty. Could that king be just in admitting these rebellious individuals into the full enjoyment and privileges with his son, and those who had been obedient to his commandments? Certainly not. Because they disregarded the voice of their lawful king; they had no regard for his virtuous laws, for his dignity, nor for the honor of his name; neither for the honor of their country, nor their private virtue. They regarded not his authority enough to obey him, neither did they regard the immediate advantages and blessings arising from these laws if kept, so destitute were they of virtue and goodness; and above all, they regarded so little the joy and satisfaction of a legal seat in the presence of the king's only son, and to be made equal with him in all the blessings, honors, comforts, and felicities of his kingdom, that they turned away from a participation in them, and considered that they were beneath their present notice though they had no doubt as to the real authenticity of the royal edict.

We ask, again, would the king be just in admitting these rebels to all the privileges of his kingdom, with those who had served him with the strictest integrity? We again answer, No. Such individuals would be dangerous characters in any government: good and wholesome laws they despise; just and perfect principles they trample under their feet as something beneath their notice; and the commands of their sovereign which they had once acknowledged to be equitable they entirely disregard. How could a government be conducted with harmony if its administrators were possessed with such different dispositions and different principles? Could it prosper? Could it flourish? Would harmony prevail? Would order be established, and could justice be executed in righteousness in all branches of its departments? No! In it were two classes of men as dissimilar as light and darkness, virtue and vice, justice and injustice, truth and falsehood, holiness and sin. One class were perfectly harmless and virtuous: they knew what virtue was for they had lived in the fullest enjoyment of it, and their fidelity to truth had been fairly tested by a series of years of faithful obedience to all its heavenly precepts. They knew what good order was, for they had been orderly and obedient to the laws imposed on them by their wise sovereign, and had experienced the benefits arising from a life spent in his government till he has now seen proper to make them equal with his son. Such individuals would indeed adorn any court where perfection was one of its main springs of action, and shine far more faire than the richest gem in the diadem of the prince.

The other class were a set of individuals who disregarded every principle of justice and equity; and this is demonstrated from the fact, that when just laws were issued by the king, which were perfectly equitable, they were so lost to a sense of righteousness that they disregarded those laws, notwithstanding an obedience to them would have produced at the time, as regards their own personal comfort and advantage, the happiest result possible. They were entirely destitute of harmony and virtue, so much so that virtuous laws they despised. They had proven themselves unworthy a place in the joys of the prince, because they had for a series of years lived in open violation of his government. Certainly, then, those two classes of men could not hold the reins of the same government at the same time in peace; for internal jars, broils, and discords would rack it to the center, were such a form of government to exist under such a system. The virtuous could not enjoy peace in the constant and unceasing schemes and evil plans of the wicked; neither could the wicked have enjoyment in the constant perseverance of the righteous to do justly. That there must be an agreement in this government, or it could not stand, must be admitted by all. Should the king convey the reins into the hands of the rebellious the government must soon fall; for every government, from the creation to the present, when it ceased to be virtuous, and failed to execute justice, sooner or later has been overthrown. And without virtuous principles to actuate a government all care for justice is soon lost, and the only motive which prompts it to act is ambition and selfishness. Should the king admit these rebels into his house to make them equal with the others, he would condescend beneath his dignity, because he once issued virtuous laws which were received by a part of his subjects, and the reward affixed was a seat at the marriage feast, and an adoption into his own family as lawful heirs. So that should he now offer any thing different he would destroy forever that government which he once so diligently labored to establish and preserve and which he once had wisdom to organize. Such indivinuals as the last named, would be a bane to a virtuous government, and would prove its overthrow if suffered to hold a part in conducting it.

We take the sacred writings into our hands, and admit that they were given by direct inspiration for the good of man. We believe that God condescended to speak from the heavens and declare His will concerning the human family, to give them just and holy laws, to regulate their conduct, and guide them in a direct way, that in due time He might take them to Himself, and make them joint heirs with His Son. But when this fact is admitted, that the immediate will of heaven is contained in the Scriptures, are we not bound as rational creatures to live in accordance to all its precepts? Will the mere admission, that this is the will of heaven ever benefit us if we do not comply with all its teachings? Do we not offer violence to the Supreme Intelligence of heaven, when we admit the truth of its teachings, and do not obey them? Do we not descend below our own knowledge, and the better wisdom which heaven has endowed us with, by such a course of conduct? For these reasons, if we have direct revelations given us from heaven, surely those revelations were never given to be trifled with, without the trifler's incurring displeasure and vengence upon his own head, if there is any justice in heaven; and that there is must be admitted by every individual who admits the truth and force of God's teachings, His blessings and cursings, as contained in the sacred volume.

Here, then, we have this part of our subject immediately before us for consideration: God has in reserve a time, or period appointed in His own bosom, when He will bring all His subjects, who have obeyed His voice and kept His commandments, into His celestial rest. This rest is of such perfection and glory, that man has need of a preparation before he can, according to the laws of that kingdom, enter it and enjoy its blessings. This being the fact, God has given certain laws to the human family, which, if observed, are sufficient to prepare them to inherit this rest. This, then, we conclude, was the purpose of God in giving His laws to us: if not, why, or for what were they given? If the whole family of man were as well off without them as they might be with them, for what purpose or intent were they ever given? Was it that God wanted to merely show that He could talk? It would be nonsense to suppose that He would condescend to talk in vain: for it would be in vain, and to no purpose whatever [if the law of God were of no benefit to man]: because, all the commandments contained in the law of the Lord, have the sure promise annexed of a reward to all who obey, predicated upon the fact that they are really the promises of a Being who cannot lie, One who is abundantly able to fulfill every tittle of His word: and if man were as well prepared, or could be as well prepared, to meet God without their ever having been given in the first instance, why were they ever given? for certainly, in that case they can now do him no good.

As we previously remarked, all well established and properly organized governments have certain fixed and prominent laws for the regulation and management of the same. If man has grown to wisdom and is capable of discerning the propriety of laws to govern nations, what less can be expected from the Ruler and Upholder of the universe? Can we suppose that He has a kingdom without laws? Or do we believe that it is composed of an innumerable company of beings who are entirely beyond all law? Consequently have need of nothing to govern or regulate them? Would not such ideas be a reproach to our Great Parent, and at variance with His glorious intelligence? Would it not be asserting that man had found out a secret beyond Deity? That he had learned that it was good to have laws, while God after existing from eternity and having power to create man, had not found out that it was proper to have laws for His government? We admit that God is the great source and fountain from whence proceeds all good; that He is perfect intelligence, and that His wisdom is alone sufficient to govern and regulate the mighty creations and worlds which shine and blaze with such magnificence and splendor over our heads, as though touched with His finger and moved by His Almighty word. And if so, it is done and regulated by law; for without law all must certainly fall into chaos. If, then, we admit that God is the source of all wisdom and understanding, we must admit that by His direct inspiration He has taught man that law is necessary in order to govern and regulate His own immediate interest and welfare: for this reason, that law is beneficial to promote peace and happiness among men. And as before remarked, God is the source from whence proceeds all good; and if man is benefitted by law, then certainly, law is good; and if law is good, then law, or the principle of it emanated from God; for God is the source of all good; consequently, then, he was the first Author of law, or the principle of it, to mankind.

We would remind you, brethren, of the fatigues, trials, privations, and persecutions, which the ancient saints endured for the sole purpose of persuading men of the excellency and propriety of the faith of Christ, were it in our opinion necessary, or if it would serve in any respect to stimulate you to labor in the vineyard of the Lord with any more diligence. But we have reason to believe (if you make the holy Scriptures a sufficient part of your studies), that their perseverance is known to you all; as also that they were willing to sacrifice the present honors and pleasures of this world, that they might obtain an assurance of a crown of life from the hand of our Lord; and their excellent example in labor, which manifests their zeal to us in the cause which they embraced, you are daily striving to pattern. And not only these examples of the Saints, but the commandments of our Lord, we hope are constantly revolving in your hearts, teaching you, not only His will in proclaiming His Gospel, but His meekness and perfect walk before all, even in those times of severe persecutions and abuse which were heaped upon Him by a wicked and adulterous generation. Remember, brethren, that He has called you unto holiness; and need we say, to be like Him in purity? How wise, how holy; how chaste, and how perfect, then, you ought to conduct yourselves in His sight; and remember, too, that His eyes are continually upon you. Viewing these facts in a proper light, you cannot be insensible, that without a strict observance of all His divine requirements, you may, at least, be found wanting; and if so, you will admit, that your lot will be cast among the unprofitable servants. We beseech you, therefore, brethren, to improve upon all things committed to your charge, that you lose not your reward.

No doubt, the course which we pursued in our last communication to you, is yet familiar to your minds; that we there endeavored to show, as far as possible, the propriety, in part, of adhering to the law of heaven; and also, the consistency in looking to heaven for a law or rule to serve us as a guide in this present state of existence, that we may be prepared to meet that which inevitably awaits us, as well as all mankind. There is an importance, perhaps, attached to this subject, which the world has not so fully examined as it requires. Think for a moment, of the greatness of the Being who created the Universe; and ask, could He be so unconsistent with his own character, as to leave man without a law or rule by which to regulate his conduct, after placing him here, where, according to the formation of his nature he must in a short period sink into the dust? Is there nothing further; is there no existence beyond this vail of death which is so suddenly to be cast over all of us? If there is, why not that Being who had power to place us here, inform us something of the hereafter? If we had power to place ourselves in this present existence, why not have power to know what shall follow when that dark vail is cast over our bodies? If in this life we receive our all; if when we crumble back to dust we are no more, from what source did we emanate, and what was the purpose of our existence? If this life were all, we should be led to query, whether or not there was really any substance in existence, and we might with propriety say, "Let us eat, drink, and be merry, for to morrow we die!" But if this life is all, then why this constant toiling, why this continual warfare, and why this unceasing trouble? But this life is not all, the voice of *reason*, the language of *inspiration*, and the Spirit of the living God, our Creator, teaches us, as we hold the record of truth in our hands, that this is not the case, that this is not so; for, the heavens declare the glory of a God, and the firmament showeth His handiwork; and a moment's reflection is sufficient to teach every man of common intelligence, that all these are not the mere productions of *chance*, nor could they be supported by any power less than an Almigthy hand; and He that can mark the power of Omnipotence, inscribed upon the heavens, can also see God's own handwriting in the sacred volume: and he who reads it oftenest will like it best, and he who is acquainted with it, will know the hand wherever he can see it; and when once discovered, it will not only receive an acknowledgment, but an obedience to all its heavenly precepts. For a moment reflect: what could have been the purpose of our Father in giving to us a law? Was it that it might be obeyed, or disobeyed? And think further, too, not only of the propriety, but of the importance of attending to His laws in every particular. If, then, there is an importance in this respect, is there not a responsibility of great weight resting upon those who are called to declare these truths to men? Were we capable of laying any thing before you as a just comparison, we would cheerfully do it; but in this our ability fails, and we are inclined to think that man is unable, without assistance beyond what has been given to those before, of expressing in words the greatness of this important subject. We can only say, that if an anticipation of the joys of the celestial glory, as witnessed to the hearts of the humble is not sufficient, we will leave to yourselves the result of your own diligence; for God ere long, will call

all His servants before Him, and there from His own hand they will receive a just recompense and a righteous reward for all their labors.

* * * * * * * * * * * * *

It is reasonable to suppose, that man departed from the first teachings, or instructions which he received from heaven in the first age, and refused by his disobedience to be governed by them. Consequently, he formed such laws as best suited his own mind, or as he supposed, were best adapted to his situation. But that God had influenced man more or less since that time in the formation of law for His benefit we have no hesitancy in believing; for, as before remarked, being the source of all good, every just and equitable law was in a greater or less degree influenced by Him. And though man in his own supposed wisdom would not admit the influence of a power superior to his own, yet for wise and great purposes, for the good and happiness of His creatures, God has instructed man to form wise and wholesome laws, since he had departed from Him and refused to be governed by those laws which God had given by His own voice from on high in the beginning. But notwithstanding the transgression, by which man had cut himself off from an immediate intercourse with his Maker without a Mediator, it appears that the great and glorious plan of His redemption was previously provided; the sacrifice prepared; the atonement wrought out in the mind and purpose of God, even in the person of the Son, through whom man was now to look for acceptance, and through whose merits he was now taught that he alone could find redemption, since the word had been pronounced, Unto dust thou shalt return.

But that man was not able himself to erect a system, or plan with power sufficient to free him from a destruction which awaited him, is evident from the fact that God, as before remarked, prepared a sacrifice in the gift of His own Son who should be sent in due time, to prepare a way, or open a door through which man might enter into the Lord's presence, whence he had been cast out for disobedience. From time to time these glad tidings were sounded in the ears of men in different ages of the world down to the time of Messiah's coming. By faith in this atonement or plan of redemption, Abel offered to God a sacrifice that was accepted, which was the firstlings of the flock. Cain offered of the fruit of the ground,and was not accepted,because he could not do it in faith,he could have no faith,or could not exercise faith contrary to the plan of heaven. It must be shedding the blood of the Only Begotten to atone for man;for this was the plan of redemption, and without the shedding of blood was no remission; and as the sacrifice was instituted for a type,by which man was to discern the great Sacrifice which God had prepared; to offer a sacrifice contrary to that, no faith could be exercised, because redemption was not purchased in that way, nor the power of atonement instituted after that order; consequently Cain could have no faith; and whatsoever is not of faith, is sin. But Abel offered an acceptable sacrifice, by which he obtained witness that he was righteous, God Himself testyfying of his gifts. Certainly, the shedding of the blood of a beast could be beneficial to no man, except it was done in imitation, or as a type, or explanation of what was to be offered through the gift of God Himself; and this performance done with an eye looking forward in faith on the power of that great Sacrifice for a remission of sins. But however various may have been, and may be at the present time, the opinions of men respecting the conduct of Abel, and the knowledge which he had on the subject of atonement, it is evident in our minds, that he was instructed more fully in the plan than what the Bible speaks of, for how could he offer a sacrifice in faith, looking to God for a remission of his sins in the power of the great atonement, without having been previously instructed in that plan? And further, if he was accepted of God, what were the ordinances performed further than the offering of the firstlings of the flock?

It is said by Paul in his letter to the Hebrew brethren, that Abel obtained witness that he was righteous, God testifying of his gifts. To whom did God testify of the gifts of Abel, was it to Paul? We have very little on this important subject in the forepart of the Bible. But it is said that Abel himself obtained witness that he was righteous. Then certainly God spoke to him: indeed, it is said that God talked with him: and if He did, would He not, seeing that Abel was righteous,deliver to him the whole plan of the Gospel. And is not the Gospel the news of the redemption? How could Abel offer a sacrifice and look forward with faith on the Son of God for a remission of his sins, and not understand the Gospel? The mere shedding of the blood of beasts or offering anything else in sacrifice, could not procure a remission of sins, except it were performed in faith of something to come; if it could, Cain's offering must have been as good as Abel's. And if Abel was taught of the coming of the Son of God, was he not taught also of His ordinances? We all admit that the Gospel has ordinances, and if so, had it not always ordinances, and were not its ordinances alwas the same? Perhaps our friends will say that the Gospel and its ordinances were not known till the days of John, the son of Zacharias, in the days of Herod, the king of Judea. But we will here look at this point: For our own part we cannot believe that the ancients in all ages were so ignorant of the system of heaven as many suppose, since all that were ever saved, were saved through the power of this great plan of redemption, as much before the coming of Christ as since; if not, God has had different plans in operation (if we may so express it), to bring men back to dwell with Himself; and this we cannot believe, since there has been no change in the constitution of man since he fell; and the ordinance or institution of offering blood in sacrifice, was only designed to be performed till Christ was offered up and shed His blood —as said before—that man might look forward in faith to that time. It will be noticed that, according to Paul, (see Gal. iii: 8) the Gospel was preached to Abraham. We would like to be informed in what name the Gospel was then preached, whether it was in the name of Christ or some other name. If in any other name, was it the Gospel? And if it was the Gospel, and that preached in the name of Christ, had it any ordinances? If not, was it the Gospel? And if it had ordinances what were they? Our friends may say, perhaps, that there were never any ordinances except those of offering sacrifices before the coming of Christ, and that it could not be possible for the Gospel to have been administered while the law of sacrifices of blood was in force. But we will recollect that Abraham offered sacrifice, and notwithstanding this, had the Gospel preached to him. That the offering of sacrifice was only to point the mind forward to Christ, we infer from these remarkable words of Jesus to the Jews: "Your Father Abraham rejoiced to see my day: and he saw it, and was glad" (John viii: 56.) So, then, because the ancients offered sacrifice it did not hinder their hearing the Gospel; but served, as we said before, to open their eyes, and enable them to look forward to the time of the coming of the Savior, and rejoice in His redemption. We find also, that when the Israelites came out of Egypt they had the Gospel preached to them, according to Paul in his letter to the Hebrews, which says: "For unto us was the Gospel preached, as well as unto them: but the word preached did not profit them, not being mixed with faith in them that heard it" (see Heb. iv:2). It is said again, in Gal. iii:19, that the law (of Moses, or the Levitical law) was "added" because of transgression. What, we ask, was this law added to, if it was not added to the Gospel? It must be plain that it was added to the Gospel, since we learn that they had the Gospel preached to them. From these few facts, we conclude that whenever the Lord revealed Himself to men in ancient days, and commanded them to offer sacrifice to Him, that it was done that they might look forward in faith to the time of His coming, and rely upon the power of that atonement for a remission of their sins. And this they have done, thousands who have gone before us, whose garments are spotless, and who are, like Job, waiting with an assurance like his, that they will see Him in the *latter day* upon the earth, even in their flesh.

We may conclude, that though there were different dispensations, yet all things which God communicated to His people were calculated to draw their minds to the great object, and to teach them to rely upon God alone as the author of their salvation, as contained in His law.

From what we can draw from the Scriptures relative to the teachings of heaven, we are induced to think that much instruction has been given to man since the beginning which we do not possess now. This may not agree with the opinions of some of our friends who are bold to say that we have everything written in the Bible which God ever spoke to man since the world began, and that if he had ever said anything more we should certainly have received it. But we ask, does it remain for a people who never had faith enough to call down one scrap of revelation from heaven, and for all they have now are indebted to the faith of another people who lived hundreds and thousands of years before them, does it remain for them to say how much God has spoken and how much he has not spoken? We have what we have, and the Bible contains what it does contain: but to say that God never said anything more to man than is there recorded, would be saying at once that we have at last received a revelation; for it must require one to advance thus far, because it is nowhere said in that volume by the mouth of God, that He would not, after giving, what is there contained, speak again; and if any man has found out for a fact that the Bible contains all that God ever revealed to man he has ascertained it by an immediate revelation, other than has been previously written by the prophets and apostles. But through the kind providence of our Father a portion of His word which He delivered to His ancient saints, has fallen into our hands, is presented to us with a promise of a reward if obeyed, and with a penalty if disobeyed. That all are deeply interested in these laws or teachings, must be admitted by all who acknowledge their divine authenticity.

It may be proper for us to notice in this place a few of the many blessings held out in this law of heaven as a reward to those who obey its teachings. God has appointed a day in which He will judge the world, and this He has given an assurance of in that He raised up His Son Jesus Christ from the dead—the point on which the hope of all who believe the inspired record is founded for their future happiness and enjoyment; because, "If Christ be not risen," said Paul to the Corinthians, "your faith is vain; ye are yet in your sins. Then they also which are fallen asleep in Christ have perished" (see I Cor. xv). If the resurrection from the dead be not an important point, or item in our faith, we must confess that we know nothing about it; for if there be no resurrection from the dead, then Christ has not risen; and if Christ has not risen He was not the Son of God; and if He was not the Son of God, there is not nor cannot be a Son of God, if the present book called the Scriptures is true; because the time has gone by when, according to that book, He was to make His appearance. On this subject, however, we are reminded of the words of Peter to the Jewish Sanhedrim, when speaking of Christ, he says that God raised Him from the dead, and we (the apostles) are His witnesses of these things, and so is the Holy Ghost, whom God had given to them that obey Him (see Acts v). So that after the testimony of the Scriptures on this point, the assurance is given by the Holy Ghost, bearing witness to those who obey Him, that Christ Himself has assuredly risen from the dead; and if He has risen from the dead, He will, by His power, bring all men to stand before Him: for if He has risen from the dead the bands of the temporal death are broken that the grave has no victory, If then, the grave has no victory, those who keep the sayings of Jesus and obey His teachings have not only a promise of a resurrection from the dead, but an assurance of being admitted into His glorious kingdom; for, He Himself says, "Where I am there also shall my servant be" (see John xii).

In the 22nd chapter of Luke's account of the Messiah, we find the kingdom of heaven likened unto a king who made a marriage for his son. That this son was the Messiah will not be disputed, since it was the kingdom of heaven that was represented in the parable; and that the Saints, or those who are found faithful to the Lord, are the individuals who will be found worthy to inherit a seat at the marriage-supper, is evident from the sayings of John in the Revelation where he represents the sound which he heard in heaven to be like a great multitude, or like the voice of mighty thunderings, saying, the Lord God Omnipotent reigneth. Let us be glad and rejoice, and give honor to Him; for the marriage of the Lamb is come, and His wife hath made herself ready. And to her was granted that she should be arrayed in fine linen, clean and white: For the fine linen is the righteousness of Saints (Rev. xix).

That those who keep the commandments of the Lord and walk in His statutes to the end, are the only individuals permitted to sit at this glorious feast, is evident from the following items in Paul's last letter to Timothy, which was written just previous to his death,—he says: "I have fought a good fight, I have finished my course, I have kept the faith: henceforth there is laid up for me a crown of righteousness which the Lord, the righteous Judge shall give me at that day: and not to me only, but unto all them also that love His appearing." No one who believes the account, will doubt for a moment this assertion of Paul which was made, as he knew, just before he was to take his leave of this world. Though he once, according to his own word, persecuted the Church of God and wasted it, yet after embracing the faith, his labors were unceasing to spread the glorious news: and like a faithful soldier, when called to give his life in the cause which he had espoused, he laid it down, as he says, with an assurance of an eternal crown. Follow the labors of this Apostle from the time of his conversion to the time of his death, and you will have a fair sample of industry and patience in promulgating the Gospel of Christ. Derided, whipped, and stoned, the moment he escaped the hands of his persecutors he as zealously as ever proclaimed the doctrine of the Savior. And all may know that he did not embrace the faith for honor in this life, nor for the gain of earthly goods. What, then, could have induced him to undergo all this toil? It was, as he said, that he might obtain the crown of righteousness from the hand of God. No one, we presume, will doubt the faithfulness of Paul to the end. None will say that he did not keep the faith, that he did not fight the good fight, that he did not preach and persuade to the last. And what was he to receive? A crown of righteousness. And what shall others receive who do not labor faithfully, and continue to the end? We leave such to search out their own promises if any they have; and if they have any they are welcome to them, on our part, for the Lord says that every man is to receive according to his works. Reflect for a moment, brethren, and enquire, whether you would consider yourselves worthy a seat at the marriage feast with Paul and others like him,if you had been unfaithful? Had you not fought the good fight, and kept the faith, could you expect to receive? Have you a promise of receiving a crown of righteousness from the hand of the Lord, with the Church of the First Born? Here then, we understand, that Paul rested his hope in Christ,because he had kept the faith, and loved his appearing and from His hand he had a promise of receiving a crown of righteousness. If the Saints are not to reign, for what purpose are they crowned? In an exhortation of the Lord to a certain church in Asia, which was built up in the days of the Apostles, unto whom He communicated His word on that occasion by His servant John,He says,"Behold, I come quickly: hold that fast which thou hast, that no man take thy crown." And again, "To him that overcometh will I grant to sit with me in my throne,even as I also overcame, and am set down with my Father in His throne" (see Rev. iii). And again, it is written, "Behold, now are we the sons of God, and it doth not yet appear what we shall be: but we know that, when He shall appear,we shall be like Him; for we shall see Him as He is. And every man that hath this hope in him, purifieth himself, even as He is pure" (I John iii: 2, 3). How is it that these old Apostles should say so much on the subject of the coming of Christ? He certainly had once come; but Paul says, To all who love His appearing, shall be given the crown: and John says, When He shall appear, we shall be like Him; for we shall see Him as He is. Can we mistake such language as this? Do we not offer violence to our own good judgment when we deny the second coming of the Messiah? When has He partaken of the fruit of the vine new with His ancient Apostles in His Father's kingdom, as He promised He would just before He was crucified? In Paul's epistle to the

Philippians, (iii: 20, 21), he says: "For our conversation is in heaven; from whence also we look for the Savior, the Lord Jesus Christ; who shall change our vile body, that it may be fashioned like unto His glorious body, according to the working whereby He is able even to subdue all things unto Himself." We find another promise to individuals living in the church at Sardis who had not defiled their garments: "And they shall walk with me in white: for they are worthy. He that overcometh, the same shall be clothed in white raiment; and I will not blot out his name out of the book of life, but I will confess his name before my Father, and before His angels." John represents the sound which he heard from heaven, as giving thanks and glory to God, saying that the Lamb was worthy to take the book and to open its seals; because He was slain, and had made them kings and priests unto God: and they should reign on the earth (see Rev. v). In the 20th chapter we find a length of time specified, during which Satan is to be confined in his own place, and the Saints reign in peace, all these promises and blessings we find contained in the law of the Lord, which the righteous are to enjoy; and we might enumerate many more places where the same or similar promises are made to the faithful, but we do not deem it of importance to rehearse them here, as this epistle is now lengthy; and our brethren, no doubt, are familiar with them all.

Most assuredly it is, however, that the ancients, though persecuted and afflicted by men, obtained from God promises of such weight and glory, that our hearts are often filled with gratitude that we are even permitted to look upon them while we contemplate that there is no respect of persons in His sight, and that in every nation, he that feareth God and worketh righteousness, is acceptable with Him. But from the few items previously quoted we can draw the conclusion that there is to be a day when all will be judged of their works, and rewarded according to the same; that those who have kept the faith will be crowned with a crown of righteousness; be clothed in white raiment; be admitted to the marriage feast; be free from every affliction, and reign with Christ on the earth, where, according to the ancient promise, they will partake of the fruit of the vine new in the glorious kingdom with Him; at least we find that such promises were made to the ancient Saints. And though we cannot claim these promises which were made to the ancients for they are not our property, merely because they were made to the ancient Saints, yet if we are the children of the Most High, and are called with the same calling with which they were called, and embrace the same covenant that they embraced, and are faithful to the testimony of our Lord as they were, we can approach the Father in the name of Christ as they approached Him, and for ourselves obtain the same promises. These promises, when obtained, if ever by us, will not be because Peter, John, and the other Apostles, with the churches at Sardis, Pergamos, Philadelphia, and elsewhere, walked in the fear of God and had power and faith to prevail and obtain them; but it will be because we,ourselves, have faith and approach God in the name of His Son Jesus Christ, even as they did; and when these promises are obtained, they will be promises directly to us, or they will do us no good. They will be communicated for our benefit, being our own property (through the gift of God), earned by our own diligence in keeping His commandments, and walking uprightly before Him. If not, to what end serves the Gospel of our Lord Jesus Christ, and why was it ever communicated to us?

Previous to commencing this letter we designed giving you some instruction upon the regulation of the Church; but that will be given hereafter.

In our own country, surrounded with blessings innumerable, to which thousands of our fellow men are strangers, enjoying unspeakable benefits and inexpressible comforts, when once our situation is compared with the ancient Saints, as followers of the Lamb of God who has taken away our sins by His own blood, we are bound to rejoice and give thanks to Him always. Since the organization of the Church of Christ, or the Church of the Latter-day Saints, on the 6th of April, 1830, we have had the satisfaction of witnessing the spread of the truth into various parts of our land, notwithstanding its enemies have exerted their unceasing diligence to stop its course and prevent its progress; though evil and designing men have combined to destroy the innocent, because their own craft was in danger; and these have been assisted in raising mobs and circulating falsehoods by a miserable set of apostates who have for wicked and unbecoming conduct been expelled from the body of which they were once members, yet the glorious Gospel in its fullness is spreading and daily gaining converts; and our prayer to God is, that it may continue, and numbers be added of such as shall be eternally saved.

The Messiah's kingdom on earth is of that kind of government, that there has always been numerous apostates, for the reason that it admits of no sins unrepented of without excluding the individual from its fellowship. Our Lord said, "Strive to enter in at the straight gate; for many, I say unto you, will seek to enter in, and shall not be able." And again, many are called, but few are chosen. Paul said to the elders of the Church at Ephesus, after he had labored three years with them, that he knew that some of their own number would turn away from the faith, and seek to lead away disciples after them. None, we presume, in this generation will pretend that he has the experience of Paul in building up the Church of Christ; and yet, after his departure from the

Church at Ephesus,many, even of the elders,turned away from the truth; and what is almost always the case, sought to lead away disciples after them. Strange as it may appear at first thought,yet it is no less strange than true, that notwithstanding all the professed determination to live godly, apostates after turning from the faith of Christ, unless they have speedily repented, have sooner or later fallen into the snares of the wicked one, and have been left destitute of the Spirit of God, to manifest their wickedness in the eyes of multitudes. From apostates the faithful have received the severest persecutions. Judas was rebuked and immediately betrayed his Lord into the hands of His enemies,because Satan entered into him. There is a superior intelligence bestowed upon such as obeyed the Gospel with full purpose of heart, which, if sinned against, the apostate is left naked and destitute of the Spirit of God, and he is, in truth, nigh unto cursing, and his end is to be burned. When once that light which was in them is taken from them they become as much darkened as they were previously enlightened, and then, no marvel, if all their power should be enlisted against the truth, and they, Judas like, seek the destruction of those who were their greatest benefactors. What nearer friend on earth, or in heaven, had Judas than the Savior? And his first object was to destroy Him. Who, among all the Saints in these last days, can consider himself as good as our Lord? Who is as perfect? Who is as pure? Who is as holy as He was? Are they to be found? He never transgressed or broke a commandment or law of heaven—no deceit was in His mouth, neither was guile found in His heart. And yet one that ate with Him,who had often drunk of the same cup, was the first to lift up his heel against Him. Where is one like Christ? He cannot be found on earth. Then why should His followers complain, if from those whom they once called brethren, and considered as standing in the nearest relation in the everlasting covenant they should receive persecution? From what source emanated the principle which has ever been manifested by apostates from the true Church to persecute with double diligence, and seek with double perseverance, to destroy those whom they once professed to love, with whom they once communed, and with whom they once covenanted to strive with every power in righteousness to obtain the rest of God? Perhaps our brethren will say the same that caused Satan to seek to overthrow the kingdom of God, because he himself was evil, and God's kingdom is holy. * * * * * * * * * *

The great plan of salvation is a theme which ought to occupy our strict attention, and be regarded as one of heaven's best gifts to mankind. No consideration whatever ought to deter us from showing ourselves approved in the sight of God, according to His divine requirement. Men not unfrequently forget that they are dependent upon heaven for every blessing which they are permitted to enjoy, and that for every opportunity granted them they are to give an account. You know, brethren, that when the Master in the Savior's parable of the stewards called his servants before him he gave them several talents to improve on while he should tarry abroad for a little season, and when he returned he called for an accounting. So it is now. Our Master is absent only for a little season, and at the end of it He will call each to render an account; and where the five talents were bestowed, ten will be required; and he that has made no improvement will be cast out as an unprofitable servant, while the faithful will enjoy everlasting honors. Therefore we earnestly implore the grace of our Father to rest upon you, through Jesus Christ His Son, that you may not faint in the hour of temptation, nor be overcome in the time of persecution.

Prayer of the First Presidency.

On the evening of the 28th of January, Brothers Oliver Cowdery, Frederick G. Williams, and myself, being agreed, bowed before the Lord, and united in prayer, that God would continue to deliver me and my brethren from "Doctor" Hurlburt,* that he may not prevail against us in the law-suit that is pending; and also that God would soften the hearts of Eden Smith, —— Jones, —— Lowd, —— Lyman, and also Mr. Bardsley, that they might obey the Gospel; or if they would not repent, that the Lord would send faithful Saints to purchase their farms, that this Stake may be strengthened. and its borders enlarged. O Lord, grant it for Christ's sake. Amen.

January 31.—It is my prayer to the Lord that three thousand subscribers may be added to the STAR in the time of three years.

Preparations for Returning Exiles to Zion.

February 1.—Every expedient preparation was making by the Church in Kirtland, and Clay county, to have those who have been driven from their possessions in Jackson county, returned.

February 9.—A conference of High Priests, Elders and officers of the Church of Christ in New Portage, Medina county, Ohio, was called at the house of Brother

* The case of Joseph Smith *vs.* "Doctor" Hurlburt did not come to trial until the 4th of April, 1834, when the "Doctor" was bound over to keep the peace.

Kirlins, which I attended. It had been suggested that Elder Rigdon might remove from Kirtland to New Portage; but after listening to the proceedings of a previous conference in Portage, from Brothers Palmer and Bosworth, it was decided that Elder Rigdon should not remove; and that the brethren in New Portage should assist all in their power to build the Lord's House in Kirtland; and that the brethren erect only a temporary or cheap place for meeting in Portage, as that was not to be established as a Stake of Zion at present; and that course would enable them to do more for the House in Kirtland.

Conference of High Priests and Elders at New Portage.

At a council of the High Priests and Elders, (Orson Hyde, clerk,) at my house in Kirtland, on the evening of the 12th of February, I remarked that I should endeavor to set before the council the dignity of the office which had been conferred on me by the ministering of the angel of God, by His own voice, and by the voice of this Church; that I had never set before any council in all the order in which it ought to be conducted, which, perhaps, has deprived the councils of some or many blessings.

And I continued and said, no man is capable of judging a matter, in council, unless his own heart is pure; and that we are frequently so filled with prejudice, or have a beam in our own eye, that we are not capable of passing right decisions.

But to return to the subject of order; in ancient days councils were conducted with such strict propriety, that no one was allowed to whisper, be weary, leave the room, or get uneasy in the least, until the voice of the Lord, by revelation, or the voice of the council by the Spirit, was obtained, which has not been observed in this Church to the present time. It was understood in ancient days, that if one man could stay in council, another could; and if the president could spend his time, the members could also; but in our councils, generally, one will be uneasy, another asleep; one praying,

Order in Ancient Councils.

another not; one's mind on the business of the council, and another thinking on something else.

Responsibility of Those who sit in Judgment.

Our acts are recorded, and at a future day they will be laid before us, and if we should fail to judge right and injure our fellow-beings, they may there, perhaps, condemn us; there they are of great consequence, and to me the consequence appears to be of force, beyond anything which I am able to express. Ask yourselves, brethren, how much you have exercised yourselves in prayer since you heard of this council; and if you are now prepared to sit in council upon the soul of your brother.

The Prophet's Predicted Triumph.

I then gave a relation of my situation at the time I obtained the record [Book of Mormon], the persecutions I met with, and prophesied that I would stand and shine like the sun in the firmament, when my enemies and the gainsayers of my testimony shall be put down and cut off, and their names blotted out from among men.

Trial of Martin Harris.

The council proceeded to investigate certain charges presented by Elder Rigdon against Martin Harris; one was, that he told A. C. Russell, Esq., that Joseph drank too much liquor when he was translating the Book of Mormon; and that he wrestled with many men and threw them; and that he (Harris) exalted himself above Joseph, in that he said, "Brother Joseph knew not the contents of the Book of Mormon, until it was translated, but that he himself knew all about it before it was translated."

Brother Harris did not tell Esq. Russell that Brother Joseph drank too much liquor while translating the Book of Mormon, but this thing occurred previous to the translating of the Book; he confessed that his mind was darkened, and that he had said many things inadvertently, calculated to wound the feelings of his brethren, and promised to do better. The council forgave him, with much good advice.

Brother Leonard Rich was called in question for transgressing the Word of Wisdom, and for selling the revelations at an extortionate price, while he was journeying east with Father Lyons, Brother Rich confessed, and the council forgave him upon his promising to do better and reform his life.

Trial of Leonard Rich.

CHAPTER II.

ORGANIZATION OF THE HIGH COUNCIL—FIRST CASES BEFORE THE COUNCIL.

*Minutes of the Organization of the High Council of the Church of Christ of Latter-day Saints, Kirtland, February 17, 1834.**

1. This day a general council of twenty-four High Priests assembled at the house of Joseph Smith, Jun., by revelation, and proceeded to organize the High Council of the Church of Christ, which was to consist of twelve High Priests, and one or three Presidents, as the case might require.

2. The High Council was appointed by revelation for the purpose of settling important difficulties which might arise in the Church, which could not be settled by the Church or the Bishop's council to the satisfaction of the parties.

3. Joseph Smith, Jun., Sidney Rigdon, and Frederick G. Williams, were acknowledged Presidents by the voice of the Council; and Joseph Smith, Sen., John Smith, Joseph Coe, John Johnson, Martin Harris, John S. Carter, Jared Carter, Oliver Cowdery, Samuel H.Smith, Orson Hyde, Sylvester Smith, and Luke Johson, High Priests, were chosen to be a standing Council for the Church, by the unanimous voice of the Council.

4. The above-named Councilors were then asked whether they accepted their appointments, and whether they would act in that office according to the law of heaven: to which they all answered that they accepted their appointments, and would fill their offices according to the grace of God bestowed upon them.

5. The number composing the Council, who voted in the name and for the Church, in appointing the above named Councilors were forty-three, as follows:—Nine High Priests, seventeen Elders, four Priests, and thirteen members.

5. Voted: that the High Council cannot have power to act without seven of the above-named Councilors, or their regularly appointed successors, are present.

7. These seven shall have power to appoint other High Priests, whom they may consider worthy and capable to act in the place of absent Councilors.

* Doctrine and Covenants, sec. cii.

8. Noted: that whenever any vacancy shall occur by the death, removal from office for transgression, or removal from the bounds of this Church government, of any one of the above-named Councilors, it shall be filled by the nomination of the President or Presidents, and sanctioned by the voice of a general council of High Priests, convened for that purpose, to act in the name of the Church.

9. The President of the Church, who is also the President of the Council, is appointed by revelation, and acknowledged in his administration, by the voice of the Church.

10. And it is according to the dignity of his office that he should preside over the Council of the Church; and it is his privilege to be assisted by two other Presidents, appointed after the same manner he himself was appointed;

11. And in case of the absence of one or both of those who are appointed to assist him, he has power to preside over the Council without an assistant: and in case he himself is absent, the other Presidents have power to preside in his stead, both, or either of them.

12. Whenever a High Council of the Church of Christ is regularly organized, according to the foregoing pattern, it shall be the duty of the twelve Councilors to cast lots by numbers, and thereby ascertain, who of the twelve shall speak first, commencing with number one, and so in succession to number twelve.

13. Whenever this Council convenes to act upon any case, the twelve Councilors shall consider whether it is a difficult one or not; if it is not, two only of the Councilors shall speak upon it, according to the form above written.

14. But if it is thought to be difficult, four shall be appointed; and if more difficult, six; but in no case shall more than six be appointed to speak.

15. The accused, in all cases, has a right to one half of the Council, to prevent insult or injustice;

16. And the Councilors appointed to speak before the Council, are to present the case after the evidence is examined, in its true light before the Council, and every man is to speak according to equity and justice.

17. Those Councilors who draw even numbers, that is 2, 4, 6, 8, 10, and 12, are the individuals who are to stand up in behalf of the accused, and prevent insult and injustice.

18. In all cases the accuser and accused shall have a privilege of speaking for themselves before the Council after the evidences are heard, and the Councilors who are appointed to speak on the case, have finished their remarks.

19. After the evidences are heard, the Councilor, accuser and accused have spoken, the President shall give a decision according to the

understanding which he shall have of the case, and call upon the twelve Councilors to sanction the same by their vote.

20. But should the remaining Councilors, who have not spoken, or any one of them, after hearing the evidences and pleadings impartially, discover an error in the decision of the President, they can manifest it, and the case shall have a re-hearing;

21. And if, after a careful re-hearing, any additional light is shown upon the case, the decision shall be altered accordingly;

22. But in case no additional light is given, the first decision shall stand, the majority of the Council having power to determine the same.

23. In case of difficulty, respecting doctrine or principle, (if there is not a sufficiency written to make the case clear to the minds of the Council,) the President may inquire and obtain the mind of the Lord by revelation.

24. The High Priests, when abroad, have power to call and organize a Council after the manner of the foregoing to settle difficulties when the parties, or either of them, shall request it;

25. And the said Council of High Priests shall have power to appoint one of their own number, to preside over such Council for the time being.

26. It shall be the duty of said Council to transmit immediately, a copy of their proceedings, with a full statement of the testimony accompanying their decision, to the High Council of the seat of the First Presidency of the Church,

27. Should the parties, or either of them be dissatisfied with the decision of said Council, they may appeal to the High Council of the seat of the First Presidency of the Church, and have a re-hearing, which case shall there be conducted, according to the former pattern written, as though no such decision had been made.

28. The Council of High Priests abroad, is only to be called on the most difficult cases of Church matters; and no common or ordinary case is to be sufficient to call such Council.

29. The traveling or located High Priests abroad, have power to say whether it is necessary to call such a Council or not.

30. There is a distinction between the High Council of traveling High Priests abroad, and the traveling High Council composed of the Twelve Apostles, in their decisions.

31. From the decision of the former there can be an appeal, but from the decision of the latter there cannot.

32. The latter can only be called in question by the general authorities of the Church in case of transgression.

33. Resolved, that the President or Presidents of the seat of the First Presidency of the Church, shall have power to determine whether any

such case, as may be appealed, is justly entitled to a re-hearing, after examining the appeal and the evidences and statements accompanying it.

34. The twelve Councilors then proceeded to cast lots or ballot, to ascertain who should speak first, and the following was the result, namely:—

1 Oliver Cowdery,
2 Joseph Coe,
3 Samuel H. Smith,
4 Luke Johnson,
5 John S. Carter,
6 Sylvester Smith,
7 John Johnson,
8 Orson Hyde,
9 Jared Carter,
10 Joseph Smith, Sen.,
11 John Smith,
12 Martin Harris.

After prayer the conference adjourned.

Oliver Cowdery,
Orson Hyde, } Clerks.

Supplementary Proceedings in the Organization of the High Council.

On the 18th of January I reviewed and corrected the minutes of the organization of the High Council, and on the 19th of February, the Council assembled according to adjournment, from the 17th, (Oliver Cowdery and Orson Hyde, clerks,) when the revised minutes were presented and read to the Council. I urged the necessity of prayer, that the Spirit might be given, that the things of the Spirit might be judged thereby, because the carnal mind cannot discern the things of God. The minutes were read three times, and unanimously adopted and received for a form and constitution of the High Council of the Church of Christ hereafter; with this provision, thas if the President should hereafter discover anything lacking in the same, he should be privileged to supply it.

The number present who received the above-named document, was twenty-six High Priests, eighteen Elders, three Priests, one Teacher, and fourteen private members, making in all sixty-two.

After giving such instruction as the Spirit dictated, I laid my hands upon the heads of the two assistant Presidents severally and blessed them, that they might have wisdom to magnify their office and power to prevail over the adversary.

I also laid my hands upon the twelve Councilors, and commanded a blessing to rest upon them, that they might have wisdom and power to counsel in righteousness, upon all subjects that might be laid before them. I also prayed that they might be delivered from those evils to which they were most exposed, and that their lives might be prolonged on the earth.

My father, Joseph, then laid his hands upon my head, and said,

Joseph, I lay my hands upon thy head, and pronounce the blessings of thy progenitors upon thee, that thou mayest hold the keys of the mysteries of the kingdom of heaven until the coming of the Lord. Amen.

He also laid his hands upon the head of his son Samuel, and said,

Samuel, I lay my hands upon thy head, and pronounce the blessings of thy progenitors upon thee, that thou mayest remain a Priest of the Most High God, and like Samuel of old, hear His voice, saying, Samuel, Samuel. Amen.

Father John Johnson, also, laid his hands upon the head of his son Luke, and said,

My Father in heaven, I ask Thee to bless this my son, according to the blessings of his forefathers; that he may be strengthened in his ministry, according to his holy calling. Amen.

I then gave the assistant Presidents a solemn charge to do their duty in righteousness, and in the fear of God; I also charged the twelve Councilors in a similar manner, all in the name of Jesus Christ.

We all raised our hands to heaven in token of the everlasting covenant, and the Lord blessed us with His Spirit. I then declared the council organized according to the ancient order, and also according to the mind of the Lord.

The following complaint was then presented before the Council, by Ezra Thayer, a High Priest:

First Case before the High Council.

KIRTLAND, February 19, 1834.

To the President of the High Council of the Church of Christ.

The following charges I prefer against Elder Curtis Hodges, Sen., of this Church: First, for an error in spirit; second, for an error in the manner of his address, which consisted in loud speaking, and a want of clearness in articulation, which was calculated to do injury to the cause of God; and also, for contending that that was a good and proper spirit that actuated him thus to speak—all of which I consider unbecoming in an Elder in this Church, and request a hearing before the High Concil.

(Signed) EZRA THAYER.

Elder Hodges pleaded "not guilty" of the above charges.

Father Lions was called on to substantiate the above charges, and his testimony was pointed against Brother Hodges. Brother Story testified that Elder Hodges talked so loud at a prayer meeting that the neighbors came out to see if some one was hurt. At another meeting, he said that Elder Thayer rebuked him for his error, but he did not receive the rebuke; that he raised his voice so high, that he could not articulate so as to be understood; and that his teaching brought a damper upon the meeting, and was not edifying. Brother Erastus Babbitt was then called upon, who testified that Elder Hodges was guilty of hollowing so loud that in a measure he lost his voice, and uttered but little else distinctly than "Glory to heaven's King." His testimony against Brother Hodges was pointed. Brother Truman Wait testified much to the same effect.

Councilor Oliver Cowdery stood up on the part of the accuser, and opened the case clearly.

Councilor Joseph Coe stood up on the part of the accused, but could say but a few words.

The accuser and the accused then spoke for themselves, after which the President arose and laid open the case still more plainly, and gave his decision, which was, that the charges in the declaration had been sustained by good witnesses; also, that Elder Hodges ought to have confessed when rebuked by Elder Thayer; also, if he had the Spirit of the Lord at the meetings, where he hollowed, he must have abused it, and grieved it away. All the Council agreed with the decision.

Elder Hodges then rose and said he now saw his error, but never saw it before; and appeared to feel thankful that he saw it. He said he had learned more during this trial than he had since he came into the Church; confessed freely his error, and said he would attend to the overcoming of that evil, the Lord being his helper.

The Council forgave him, and adjourned to the evening of the 20th.

February 20.—The High Council met this evening to determine concerning the Elders going out to preach.

Minutes of the High Council.

The president opened the Council by prayer.

At a church meeting, held in Pennsylvania, Erie county, and Springfield township, by Orson Pratt and Lyman E. Johnson, High Priests, some of the members of that church refused to partake of the Sacrament, because the Elder administering it did not observe the Word of Wisdom to obey it. Elder Johnson argued that they were justified in so doing, because the Elder was in transgression. Elder Pratt argued that the church was bound to receive the Supper under the administration of an Elder, so long as he retained his office or license. Voted that six Councilors should speak upon the subject.

The Council then proceeded to try the question, whether disobedience to the Word of Wisdom was a transgression sufficient to deprive an official member from holding office in the Church, after having it sufficiently taught him.

Councilors Samuel H. Smith, Luke S. Johnson, John S. Carter, Sylvester Smith, John Johnson and Orson Hyde, were called to speak upon the case then before the Council. After the Councilors had spoken, the President proceeded to give the decision:

No official member in this Church is worthy to hold an office, after having the Word of Wisdom properly taught him, and he, the official member, neglecting to comply with or obey it; which decision the Council confirmed by vote.

The President then asked if there were any Elders present who would go to Canada, and preach the Gospel to that people; for they have written a number of letters for help. And the whole Council felt as though the Spirit required the Elders to go there. It was, therefore, decided by the Council, that Lyman E. Johnson and Milton Holmes should travel together into Canada; that Zebedee Coltrin and Henry Herriman travel together into Canada; and that Jared Carter and Phineas Young travel together, if they can so arrange their affairs at home as to be liberated.

It was also decided that Elder Oliver Granger should travel eastward as soon as his circumstances would permit, and that he could travel alone on account of his age; it was also decided that Elder Martin Harris should travel alone whenever he travels; that Elders John S. Carter and Jesse Smith travel east together as soon as they can; and that Elder Brigham Young should travel alone, it being his own choice; also that James Durfee and Edward Marvin should travel together eastward; that Sidney Rigdon and John P. Greene go to Strongville, that Orson Pratt and Harrison Sagers travel together for the time being; and that there should be a general conference held at Saco, in the state of Maine, on the 13th day of June, 1834.

It was furthermore voted that Elder Orson Hyde, accompanied by Elder Orson Pratt, go east to obtain donations for Zion, and means to redeem the farm on which the house of the Lord stands.

The Church and Council then prayed with uplifted hands, that they might be prospered in their mission.

ORSON HYDE,
OLIVER COWDERY, } Clerks.

CHAPTER III.

THE CAUSE AND OBJECT OF THE JACKSON COUNTY PERSECUTION—THE PROPHET'S MISSION THROUGH WESTERN NEW YORK.

February 24.—I received the following:

*Revelation.**

1. Verily I say unto you, my friends, behold I will give unto you a revelation and commandment, that ye may know how to act in the discharge of your duties concerning the salvation and redemption of your brethren who have been scattered on the land of Zion;

2. Being driven and smitten by the hand of mine enemies, on whom I will pour out my wrath without measure in mine own time;

3. For I have suffered them thus far, that they might fill up the measure of their iniquities, that their cup might be full;

4. And that those who call themselves after my name might be chastened for a little season with a sore and grievous chastisement, because they did not hearken altogether unto the precepts and commandments which I gave unto them.

5. But verily I say unto you, that I have decreed a decree which my people shall realize, inasmuch as they hearken from this very hour, unto the counsel which I, the Lord their God, shall give unto them.

6. Behold they shall, for I have decreed it, begin to prevail against mine enemies from this very hour,

7. And by hearkening to observe all the words which I, the Lord their God, shall speak unto them, they shall never cease to prevail until the kingdoms of the world are subdued under my feet, and the earth is given unto the saints, to possess it for ever and ever.

8. But inasmuch as they keep not my commandments, and hearken not to observe all my words, the kingdoms of the world shall prevail against them,

9. For they were set to be a light unto the world, and to be saviors of men;

* Doctrine and Covenants, sec. ciii.

10. And inasmuch as they are not the saviors of men, they are as salt that has lost its savor, and is thenceforth good for nothing but to be cast out and trodden under foot of men.

11. But verily I say unto you, I have decreed that your brethren which have been scattered shall return to the lands of their inheritances, and shall build up the waste places of Zion.

12. For after much tribulation, as I have said unto you in a former commandment, cometh the blessing.

13. Behold, this is the blessing which I have promised after your tribulations, and the tribulations of your brethren: your redemption, and the redemption of your brethren, even their restoration to the land of Zion, to be established no more to be thrown down;

14. Nevertheless, if they pollute their inheritances they shall be thrown down, for I will not spare them if they pollute their inheritances.

15. Behold, I say unto you, the redemption of Zion must needs come by power;

16. Therefore, I will raise up unto my people a man, who shall lead them like as Moses led the children of Israel,

17. For ye are the children of Israel, and of the seed of Abraham, and ye must needs be led out of bondage by power, and with a stretched out arm:

18. And as your fathers were led at the first, even so shall the redemption of Zion be.

19. Therefore let not your hearts faint, for I say unto you as I said unto your fathers, mine angel shall go up before you, but not my presence;

20. But I say unto you, mine angels shall go up before you, and also my presence, and in time ye shall possess the goodly land.

21. Verily, verily I say unto you, that my servant Baurak Ale (Joseph Smith, Jun.,) is the man to whom I likened the servant to whom the Lord of the vineyard spake in the parable which I have given unto you.

22. Therefore let my servant Baurak Ale (Joseph Smith, Jun.,) say unto the strength of my house, my young men and the middle aged, gather yourselves together unto the land of Zion, upon the lands which I have bought with money that has been consecrated unto me:

23. And let all the churches send up wise men with their moneys, and purchase lands even as I have commanded them;

24. And inasmuch as mine enemies come against you to drive you from my goodly land, which I have consecrated to be the land of Zion: even from your own lands after these testimonies, which ye have brought before me against them, ye shall curse them;

25. And whomsoever ye curse, I will curse, and ye shall avenge me of mine enemies;

26. And my presence shall be with you even in avenging me of mine enemies, unto the third and fourth generation of them that hate me.

27. Let no man be afraid to lay down his life for my sake, for whoso layeth down his life for my sake shall find it again;

28. And whoso is not willing to lay down his life for my sake, is not my disciple.

29. It is my will that my servant Sidney Rigdon shall lift up his voice in the congregations in the eastern countries, in preparing the churches to keep the commandments which I have given unto them concerning the restoration and redemption of Zion.

30. It is my will that my servant Parley P. Pratt and my servant Lyman Wight should not return to the land of their brethren, until they have obtained companies to go up unto the land of Zion, by tens, or by twenties, or by fifties, or by an hundred, until they have obtained to the number of five hundred of the strength of my house.

31. Behold this is my will; ask and ye shall receive, but men do not always do my will;

32. Therefore, if you cannot obtain five hundred, seek diligently, that peradventure you may obtain three hundred;

33. And if you cannot obtain three hundred, seek diligently, that peradventure ye may obtain one hundred.

34. But verily I say unto you, a commandment I give unto you, that ye shall not go up unto the land of Zion, until you have obtained a hundred of the strength of my house, to go up with you unto the land of Zion.

35. Therefore as I said unto you, ask and ye shall receive; pray earnestly that peradventure my servant Baurak Ale (Joseph Smith, Jun.,) may go with you, and preside in the midst of my people, and organize my kingdom upon the consecrated land, and establish the children of Zion upon the laws and commandments which have been, and which shall be, given unto you.

36. All victory and glory is brought to pass unto you through your diligence, faithfulness and prayers of faith.

37. Let my servant Parley P. Pratt journey with my servant Joseph Smith, Jun.

38. Let my servant Lyman Wight journey with my servant Sidney Rigdon.

39. Let my servant Hyrum Smith journey with my servant Frederick G. Williams.

40. Let my servant Orson Hyde journey with my servant Orson Pratt,

whithersoever my servant Joseph Smith, Jun., shall counsel them, in obtaining the fulfillment of these commandments which I have given unto you, and leave the residue in my hands. Even so. Amen.

The High Council of the Church also met this day at my house for the purpose of giving an audience or hearing to Lyman Wight and Parley P. Pratt, delegates from the Church in Missouri, to represent to us the state of the Church in that place.

Arrival of Delegation from the Church in Missouri.

Minutes of Council Meeting.

President Joseph opened the Council by prayer. Two of the standing Councilors were absent, namely, Joseph Coe and John Smith. Hyrum Smith was chosen to act in the place of John Smith, and John P. Greene to act in the place of Joseph Coe. Thus the High Council was organized, and six Councilors were appointed to speak. Brothers Parley P. Pratt and Lyman Wight, messengers from Zion, arose, and laid their business before the Council, and delivered their message, the substance of which was: when, how and by what means Zion was to be redeemed from her enemies. They said that our brethren who had been driven away from their lands and scattered abroad, had found so much favor in the eyes of the people [of Clay county, Mo.,] that they could obtain food and raiment of them for their labor, insomuch that they were comfortable. But the idea of their being driven away from the land of Zion pained their very souls, and they desired of God, by earnest prayer, to return with songs of everlasting joy, as said Isaiah, the prophet.

They also said that none of their lands were sold into the hands of our enemies, except a piece of thirty acres owned by Brother William E. McLellin, which he sold into the hands of the enemy, and seven acres more which he would have sold to the enemy if a brother had not come forward and purchased it and paid him his money.

Brother Joseph then arose, and said that he was going to Zion, to assist in redeeming it. He called for the voice of the Council to sanction his going, which was given without a dissenting voice. He then called for volunteers to go with him, when some thirty or forty volunteered to go, who were present at the Council. It was a question whether the company should go by water or by land, and after a short investigation it was decided unanimously that they go by land. Joseph Smith, Jun., was nominated to be the commander-in-chief of the armies of Israel, and the leader of those who volunteered to go and assist in the redemption of Zion: the nomination was seconded and carried by the vote of all present. Council then adjourned by prayer and thanksgiving.

ORSON HYDE,
OLIVER COWDERY, } Clerks.

The Prophet seeks Volunteers to Redeem Zion.

February 26.—I started from home to obtain volunteers for Zion, in compliance with the foregoing revelation and action of the High Council; and on the 27th, stayed at Brother Roundy's.

To show the feelings of a certain portion of the public, at this period, I copy the following from the February number of the *Evening and Morning Star*, page 271:

We copy the following article from the *North Star*, headed "The Mormons," printed in Danville, Vermont, by E. Eaton:

"We have received the first number of the 'Mormon' *Morning and Evening Star* [the *Evening and Morning Star*], resusciated in Kirtland, Ohio. *It is the same assuming, mysterious publication as its original.*"

Cheering Words.

While the press and many of the public were breathing the spirit of bitterness against the work of God, I received letters from many of our friends, which gave us occasion for rejoicing: amongst them, I extract from Brother Moses Chapman Nickerson's letter of December 20, 1833:*

Your labors in Canada have been the beginning of a good work; there are thirty-four members attached to the Church at Mount Pleasant, all of whom appear to live up to their profession, five of whom have spoken in tongues, and three have sung in tongues; and we live at the top of the mountain.

Also from Saco, Maine:

January 20, 1834.

BRETHREN IN THE LORD,—I have baptized about fourty in this section, and there are more convinced of the truth, but are still lingering on the threshhold of the Church, and I think the Lord will gather some of them into His kingdom. Brother Evan M. Greene labored with me

* This Mount Pleasant branch of the Church, it will be remembered, was organized by the Prophet and Sidney Rigdon, in the October previous. See vol. I, chap. XXX.

from the 16th of January, 1833, till the October following; while we were together, we baptized about one hundred and thirty. Brethren, pray for me, that I may have words of wisdom, and a door of utterance to declare the whole counsel of God, and rightly divide the word of truth, giving to every man his portion in due season; for my determination is, with the stick of Joseph [the Book of Mormon] in one hand, and the stick of Judah [the Bible] in the other, to labor diligently in this world, that my skirts may be clear from the blood of all men, and I stand acquitted before the bar of God.

I am yours in Christ

(Signed) JOHN F. BOYNTON.

Incidents in the Prophet's Journey through Western New York.

We continued our journey, and, on the 28th of February stayed at a stranger's, who entertained us very kindly; and on the first of March arrived at Brother Lewis', in Westfield.

On the 2nd, which was the Sabbath, Brother Parley P. Pratt preached, and I spoke in the evening; we had a good meeting. There is a small church in this place, which seems strong in the faith. O may God keep them in the faith, and save them, and lead them to Zion.

March 3.—We intended to start on our journey east, but concluded to tarry another day. O may God bless us with the gift of utterance to accomplish the journey and errand on which we are sent, and return safe to the land of Kirtland, and find my family all well. O Lord, bless my little children with health and long life, to do good in their generation, for Christ's sake. Amen.

Since leaving Kirtland, we passed through Thompson, Springfield, Elk Creek, Erie, Livonia, Silver Creek, Perrysburgh, Collins, China, Warsaw, Geneseo, Centreville, Catlin and Spafford, before we arrived at Westfield.

On the 4th instant, we continued our journey from Westfield, accompanied by Elder Gould; and after a ride of thirty-three miles arrived at Villanova, and tarried all night with a Brother McBride.

The next morning, March 5th, we went to Brother Nickerson's, and found him and his household full of faith and of the Holy Spirit.

We called the church together, and related unto them what had happened to our brethren in Zion, and opened to them the prophecies and revelations concerning the order of the gathering to Zion, and the means of her redemption; and I prophesied to them, and the Spirit of the Lord came mightily upon me, and with all readiness the young and middle-aged volunteered for Zion. The same evening we held two meetings, three or four miles distant from each other.

March 6.—We held another meeting at Brother Nickerson's. The few unbelievers that attended were outrageous, and the meeting ended in complete confusion.

March 7.—We proceeded on our journey, accompanied by Brother Nickerson, leaving Brothers Gould and Matthews to prepare and gather up the companies in the churches in that region, and meet us in Ohio, ready to start for Zion on the first of May. We arrived after dark at Ellicotville, the county seat of Cataraugus, and tried for lodgings at every tavern in the place. It being court time we found no room; but were obliged to ride on in the dark, through mud and rain; and, after traveling about one mile, we found shelter, for which we paid more than tavern fare.

On the 8th, we arrived at Palmersville, at the house of Elder McGown, where we were invited to go to Esquire Walker's to spend the evening. We found them very friendly and somewhat believing, and tarried all night.

Sunday, March 9.—We preached in a school house, and had great attention. We found a few disciples who were firm in the faith; and, after meeting found many believing and could hardly get away from them, and appointed a meeting in Freedom for Monday the 10th, and stayed at Mr. Warren A. Cowdery's, where we were blessed with a full enjoyment of temporal and spiritual blessings, even all we needed, or were worthy to receive.

Monday 10.—Met our appointment, and preached to a great congregation; and at evening again preached to an overflowing house. After meeting, I proposed if any wished to obey, and would make it manifest, we would stay to administer to another meeting. A young man of the Methodist order arose and testified his faith in the fullness of the Gospel and desired to be baptized. We appointed another meeting for the next day.

Tuesday 11.—Fulfilled our appointment and baptized Heman T. Hyde,* after which we rode nine miles, and put up at Steward's tavern.

Wednesday 12.—We arrived at Father Bosley's, after a ride of thirty-six miles.

Thursday 13.—I preached.

Friday 14.—At Father Beaman's.†

March 15.—While at Father Beaman's, Elders Rigdon and Wight arrived, much to the joy of their souls and the Saints in Livonia.

* Of this incident Elder Parley P. Pratt, who was the Prophet's traveling companion on this mission, says: "We baptized a young man named Heman Hyde; his parents were Presbyterians, and his mother, on account of the strength of her traditions, thought that we were wrong, and told me afterwards that she would much rather have followed him to an earthly grave than to have seen him baptized. Soon afterwards, however, herself, her husband, and the rest of the family, with some thirty or forty others, were all baptized and organized into a branch of the Church—called the Freedom branch—from which nucleus the light spread and souls were gathered into the fold in all the regions round. Thus mightily grew the word of God, or the seed sown by that extraordinary personage, the Prophet and Seer of the nineteenth century." (Autobiography of Parley P. Pratt, p. 117.)

Speaking of the pleasure of his companionship with the Prophet, Elder Pratt also says: "As we journeyed day after day, and generally lodged together, we had much sweet communion concerning the things of God and the mysteries of His kingdom, and I received many admonitions and instructions which I shall never forget." (Ibid., p. 117.)

† Speaking of "Father Beaman" and his interesting family, Elder Parley P. Pratt has the following interesting passage, which discloses the fact that "Father Beaman" was acquainted with the work during the time that the Book of Mormon was translating: "Among those whose hospitality we shared in that vicinity [Geneseo] was old Father Beaman and his amiable and interesting family. He was a good singer, and so were his three daughters; we were much edified and comforted in their society, and were deeply interested in hearing the old gentleman and Brother Joseph converse on their early acquaintance and history. He [Beaman] had been intimate with Joseph long before the first organization of the Church; had assisted him to preserve the plates of the Book of Mormon from the enemy, and had at one time had them concealed under his own hearth." (Ibid,, pp. 117, 118.)

Sunday 16.—Elder Rigdon preached to a large congregation in Geneseo, Elder Pratt preached in the afternoon of Monday, the 17th.

The Conference at Avon, Livingston County.

There was also the same day, March 17, a conference of Elders at Avon, Livingston county, New York, at the house of Alvah Beaman, which I attended. There were present also Sidney Rigdon, Parley P. Pratt, Lyman Wight, John Murdock, Orson Pratt and Orson Hyde, High Priests; and six Elders. I stated that the object of the Conference was to obtain young and middle-aged men to go and assist in the redemption of Zion, according to the commandment; and for the Church to gather up their riches, and send them to purchase lands according to the commandment of the Lord; also to devise means, or obtain money for the relief of the brethren in Kirtland, say two thousand dollars, which sum would deliver the Church in Kirtland from debt; and also determine the course which the several companies shall pursue, or the manner they shall journey when they shall leave this place.

It was voted by the Council, that Fathers Bosley and Nickerson, Elder McWithey, and Brother Roger Orton, should exert themselves to obtain two thousand dollars, for the present relief of Kirtland. They all agreed to do what they could to obtain it, firmly believing that it could be accomplished by the first of April. It was also decided that Elder Orson Hyde should tarry and preach in the regions round about, till the money should be obtained, and then carry it with him to Kirtland. It was also voted that I should return to Kirtland, accompanied by Elders Sidney Rigdon and Lyman Wight. Elders John Murdock and Orson Pratt were appointed to journey to Kirtland, preaching by the way; and Elders Parley P. Pratt and Henry Brown to visit the churches in Black River country, and obtain all the means they could to help Zion.

Tuesday, March 18.—Tarried at Father Bosley's through the day. On the 19th commenced my journey for

Kirtland, and stayed that night at Brother McWithey's tavern.

March 20.—Continued our journey. Dined at Brother Joseph Holbrook's, and at night tried three times to procure lodgings in the names of disciples, but could not succeed. After night had commenced we found a man, in China, named Reuben Wilson, who would keep us for money; thus we learn there are more places for money than for the disciples of Jesus, the Lamb of God.

March 21.-We came to the house of a man named Starks, six miles east of Springville; and on the 22nd arrived at Brother Vinson Knight's in Perrysburgh, Cataraugus county. On the 23rd we arrived at Father Nickerson's, in Perrysburgh, where we held meeting. On the 24th, I was not able to start, but felt determined to go the next morning.

March 25.—Journeyed from Father Nickerson's to Father Lewis', in Westfield, accompanied by Father Nickerson. On the 26th, continued our journey to Elk Creek, and stayed with Elder Hunt. The 27th, I came to Springfield, where I found Elder Sidney Rigdon, who had come on by a different route; and we arrived that night within sixteen miles of Painesville. Arrived home at Kirtland on the 28th of March, finding my family all well. The Lord be praised for this blessing!

March 27.—Remained at home and had great joy with my family. Sunday, the 30th, was at home, except going to hear Elder Rigdon preach.

CHAPTER IV.

TRIAL AND CONVICTION OF HURLBURT—EFFORTS IN BEHALF OF THE REDEMPTION OF ZION—DISSOLUTION OF THE UNITED ORDER OF ZION AND KIRTLAND.

Monday, *March 31*.—This day, Ira J. Willis, a young man who had been in the Church for some time, and who was driven from Jackson county into Clay county, returned thither to look for a stray cow, and while at the house of Esquire Manship, a justice of the peace (where he had called with Brother John Follet, to prove his title to the cow), was caught by that unhung land pirate and inhuman monster, Moses Wilson, and whipped in a most cruel and savage manner, while surrounded by some half dozen of the old mobbers. This was an unpardonable act; all that know Mr. Willis can bear testimony that he is a young man, honest, peaceable and unoffending, working righteousness, and molesting no one. May God reward Moses Wilson according to his works.

The Whipping of Ira J. Willis.

I went to Chardon today to attend the court in the case of "Doctor" Philastus Hurlburt.

April 1.—This day at Brother Rider's in Chardon. The court has not brought forward Hurlburt's trial yet, and we were engaged in issuing subpœnas for witnesses. My soul delighteth in the law of the Lord, for He forgiveth my sins, and will confound mine enemies. The Lord shall destroy him who has lifted his heel against me, even that wicked man Dr. Philastus Hurlburt; He will deliver him to the fowls of heaven, and his bones shall be cast to the blasts of the wind, for he lifted his arm against the Almighty, therefore the Lord shall destroy him.

The Trial of "Doctor" Hurlburt for Threatening the Prophet's Life.

Wednesday, April the 2nd, and Thursday, the 3rd, attended the court. Hurlburt was on trial for threatening my life. Friday morning I returned home, and in the evening attended Council, of which the following are the minutes:

Minutes of Council.

KIRTLAND, April 4, 1834.

This evening a Council of High Priests assembled at the house of President Joseph Smith, Jun., to reconsider the case of Brother George F. James. President Joseph Smith, Jun., presiding.

Brother George said that he had often promised to take up his cross and magnify his calling, but had failed, and ought to have written to the President ere this time and given him the information that his pecuniary affairs called his attention at home, which prevented his fulfilling the promise he made to President Joseph Smith, in going out to proclaim the Gospel; and he sincerely asked pardon of the Lord, and of his brethren, and particularly of Brother Joseph. He also said he was willing to ask the forgiveness of this Church. He said relative to certain charges, which were, that he "had not attended meetings, and had treated lightly some of the weak," etc.; that he had attended meetings generally; and as far as speaking or treating lightly any brother because of his weakness, that was foreign from his mind, and was that which he had never done, nor could he ever find such principles in his bosom.

President Joseph Smith said he had no hardness; he only wished Brother George to consider this as a chastisement, and that the Council were bound to take notice of his conduct heretofore; but now, if Brother George was willing to walk according to the new covenant, he should have his hand of fellowship. The Council then expressed their satisfaction at Brother George's confession.

(Signed) OLIVER COWDERY, Clerk.

April 5—I went to Chardon as a witness for Father Johnson, and returned in the evening. Mr. Russell, the state's attorney for Portage county, called on me. He approached me in a gentlemanly manner, and treated me with great respect.

Special Prayer.

April 7.—Bishop Whitney, Elder Frederick G. Williams, Oliver Cowdery, Heber C. Kimball, and myself, met in the council room, and bowed down before the Lord, and prayed that He would furnish the means to deliver the Firm from debt, that they might be set at liberty; also, that I might prevail against that wicked man, Hurlburt, and that he might be put to shame.

The Presidency wrote Elder Orson Hyde, who yet remained in the state of New York, as follows:

KIRTLAND, April 7, 1834.

DEAR BROTHER ORSON:—We received yours of the 31st ultimo in due course of mail, and were much grieved on learning that you were not likely to succeed according to our expectations. Myself, Brothers Newel, Frederick and Oliver, retired to the translating room, where prayer was wont to be made, and unbosomed our feelings before God; and cannot but exercise faith yet that you, in the miraculous providences of God, will succeed in obtaining help. The fact is, unless we can obtain help, I myself cannot go to Zion, and if I do not go, it will be impossible to get my brethren in Kirtland, any of them, to go; and if we do not go, it is in vain for our eastern brethren to think of going up to better themselves by obtaining so goodly a land, (which now can be obtained for one dollar and one quarter per acre,) and stand against that wicked mob; for unless they do the will of God, God will not help them; and if God does not help them, all is vain.

Now the fact is, this is the head of the Church and the life of the body; and those able men, as members of the body, God has appointed to be hands to administer to the necessities of the body. Now if a man's hand refuses to administer to the necessities of his body, it must perish of hunger; and if the body perish, all the members perish with it; and if the head fail, the whole body is sickened, the heart faints, and the body dies, the spirit takes its exit, and the carcase remains to be devoured by worms.

Now, Brother Orson, if this Church, which is essaying to be the Church of Christ will not help us, when they can do it without sacrifice, with those blessings which God has bestowed upon them, I prophesy —I speak the truth, I lie not—God shall take away their talent, and give it to those who have no talent, and shall prevent them from ever obtaining a place of refuge, or an inheritance upon the land of Zion; therefore they may tarry, for they might as well be overtaken where they are, as to incur the displeasure of God, and fall under His wrath by the way side, as to fall into the hands of a merciless mob, where there is no God to deliver, as salt that has lost its savor, and is thenceforth good for nothing, but to be trodden under foot of men.

We therefore adjure you to beseech them, in the name of the Lord, by the Son of God, to lend us a helping hand; and if all this will not soften their hearts to administer to our necessity for Zion's sake, turn your back upon them, and return speedily to Kirtland; and the blood of

Zion be upon their heads, even as upon the heads of her enemies; and let their recompense be as the recompense of her enemies; for thus shall it come to pass, saith the Lord of Hosts, who has the cattle upon a thousand hills, who has put forth His Almighty hand to bring to pass His strange act; and what man shall put forth his hand to steady the ark of God, or be found turning a deaf ear to the voice of His servant? God shall speak in due time, and all will be declared. Amen.

Your brethren in the New Covenant,

JOSEPH SMITH, JUN.,
FREDERICK G. WILLIAMS,
OLIVER COWDERY.

April 9.—After an impartial trial, the court decided that Dr. Philastus Hurlburt be bound over, under two hundred dollar bonds, to keep the peace for six months, and pay the cost, which amounted to nearly three hundred dollars, all of which was in answer to our prayers, for which I thank my Heavenly Father.*

Judgment Against Hurlburt.

On the 10th, had a council of the United Order, in which it was agreed that the Order should be dissolved, and each one have his stewardship set off to him.

Dissolution of the United Order in Kirtland.

The same day the brethren in Clay county, Missouri, executed the following letters and petitions, according to the revelation.†

* The closing paragraph of the order of the court in the Hurlburt case is as follows: "Wherefore it is ordered and adjudged by the court that the said Doctor P. Hurlburt enter into a new recognizance, with good and sufficient security, in the sum of two hundred dollars, hereafter to keep the peace and be of good behavior to the citizens of the state of Ohio generally, and to the said Joseph Smith, Junior, in particular, for the period of six months; and it is further ordered, that the said Doctor P. Hurlburt pay the costs of this prosecution, taxed at the sum of one hundred and twelve dollars and fifty-nine cents. And thereupon came the said Doctor P. Hurlburt, with Charles A. Holmes and Elijah Smith as his sureties, in open court, entered into a recognizance in the penal sum of two hundred dollars each, conditioned that the said Doctor P. Hurlburt shall, for the period of six months from and after this day, keep the peace and be of good behavior to all the citizens of the state of Ohio generally, and to the said Joseph Smith, Jun., in particular.

(Signed) "M. BIRCHARD, P. J."

† See vol. I., pp. 483-488. The papers alluded to include a second petition to the President of the United States; a letter from A. S. Gilbert *et al.* accompanying same; one from W. W. Phelps *et al.* to Governor Dunklin, informing him of the petition to the President; and one from W. W. Phelps to Senator Thomas H. Benton, informing him of the petition to the President, etc.

Friday, April 11.—I attended meeting, and Father Tyler was restored to the fellowship of the Church.

On the 12th, I went to a place near Lake Erie, and spent the day in fishing, and visiting the brethren.

Sunday, 13.—Was sick, and unable to attend meeting.

Monday, 14.—I purchased some hay and oats, and got them home.

Tuesday, 15.—Hauled a load of hay; and on Wednesday plowed and sowed oats for Brother Frederick G. Williams.

Deliverance of Zion Considered.

Thursday, April 17.—I attended a meeting agreeable to appointment, at which time the important subjects of the deliverance of Zion and the building of the Lord's House in Kirtland were discussed by Elder Rigdon. After the lecture, I requested the brethren and sisters to contribute all the money they could for the deliverance of Zion; and received twenty-nine dollars and sixty-eight cents.

An Assault Thwarted by the Spirit.

April 18.—In company with Elders Sidney Rigdon, Oliver Cowdery and Zebedee Coltrin, I left Kirtland for New Portage, to attend a conference; dined at W. W. Williams', in Newburg, and continuing our journey, after dark, we were hailed by a man who desired to ride. We were checked by the Spirit, and refused. He professed to be sick, but in a few minutes was joined by two others, who followed us hard, cursing and swearing; but we were successful in escaping their hands, through the providence of the Lord, and stayed that night at a tavern, where we were treated with civility.

An Occasion of Prayer and Blessing.

April 19.—Continuing our journey, dined at Brother Joseph Bosworth's, in Copley, Medina county. Brother Bosworth was strong in the faith, and if faithful may do much good. We arrived the same day at Brother Jonathan Taylor's, in Norton, where we were received with kindness. We soon retired to the wilderness, where we united in prayer and supplication for the blessings of the Lord to be given unto His Church. We called upon the Father in the name of Jesus, to go with the brethren who were going to the land of Zion; and that I might have strength, and wisdom, and understanding sufficient to lead the people of the Lord, and to gather and establish the Saints upon the land of their inheritances, and organize them according to the will of Heaven, that they may be no more cast down forever. We then united in the laying on of hands.

Elders Rigdon, Cowdery and Coltrin laid their hands on my head, and conferred upon me all the blessings necessary to qualify me to stand before the Lord, in my calling, and return again in peace and triumph, to enjoy the society of my brethren.

Those present then laid their hands upon the head of Elder Rigdon, and confirmed upon him the blessings of wisdom and knowledge to preside over the Church in my absence, also to have the Spirit to assist Elder Cowdery in conducting the *Star*, in arranging the Book of Covenants; and pronounced the blessings of old age and peace upon him, till Zion is built up, and Kirtland established, till all his enemies are under his feet, and he receive a crown of eternal life in the kindom of God with us.

Previous to blessing Elder Rigdon, we laid hands on Elder Oliver Cowdery, and confirmed upon him the blessings of wisdom and understanding sufficient for his station that he be qualified to assist Elder Rigdon in arranging the Church Book of Covenants, which is soon to be published, and have intelligence in all things to do the work of printing.

After blessing Elder Rigdon, we laid our hands upon Brother Zebedee Coltrin, and confirmed the blessings of wisdom to preach the Gospel, even till it spreads to the islands of the seas, and to be spared to see three score years and ten, and see Zion built up, and Kirtland established forever, and even at last to receive a crown of life. Our hearts rejoiced, and we were comforted with the Holy Spirit.

Sunday, April 20.—Elder Rigdon entertained a large congregation of Saints with an interesting discourse upon the Fullness of Times.

April 21.—I attended conference, and had a glorious time. Some few volunteered to go to Zion, and others donated sixty-six dollars and thirty-seven cents for the benefit of the scattered brethren in Zion. The following is an extract from the minutes of the conference:

Minutes of Conference.

NORTON, MEDINA COUNTY, OHIO, April 21, 1834.

This day a conference of Elders assembled at the dwelling house of Brother Carpenter. President Joseph Smith, Jun., read the second chapter of Joel's prophecy, prayed, and addressed the conference as follows:

"It is very difficult for us to communicate to the churches all that God has revealed to us, in consequence of tradition; for we are differently situated from any other people that ever existed upon this earth; consequently those former revelations cannot be suited to our conditions; they were given to other people, who were before us; but in the last days, God was to call a remnant, in which was to be deliverance, as well as in Jerusalem and Zion. Now if God should give no more revelations, where will we find Zion and this remnant? The time is near when desolation is to cover the earth, and then God will have a place of deliverance in His remnant, and in Zion."

The President then gave a relation of obtaining and translating the Book of Mormon, the revelation of the Priesthood of Aaron, the organization of the Church in 1830, the revelation of the High Priesthood, and the gift of the Holy Ghost poured out upon the Church; and said:

"Take away the Book of Mormon and the revelations, and where is our religion? We have none; for without Zion, and a place of deliverance, we must fall; because the time is near when the sun will be darkened, and the moon turn to blood, and the stars fall from heaven, and the earth reel to and fro. Then, if this is the case, and if we are not sanctified and gathered to the places God has appointed, with all our former professions and our great love for the Bible, we must fall; we cannot stand; we cannot be saved; for God will gather out His Saints from the Gentiles, and then comes desolation and destruction, and none can escape except the pure in heart who are gathered."

Elder Rigdon addressed the conference, and said:

"On two points hang all the revelations that have ever been given, and these are the two advents of the Messiah. The first is past, and the second is now just before us; and consequently those who desire a part in this era which the angels desired to look into, have to be assembled with the Saints; for if they are not gathered, they must wail because of His coming. There is no part of His creation which will not feel a shock at this grand display of His power, for the ancient Saints will reign with Christ a thousand years. The gathered Saints will dwell under that reign, and those who are not gathered may expect to endure His wrath that length of time; for the rest of the dead are not to live till tne thousand years are ended.

"It is vain for men of this generation to think of laying up and providing inheritances for their children, except they lay it up in the place where deliverance is appointed by the voice of God; for these are the days of vengeance, as were the days of Jeremiah; because, before his eyes were closed in death, the Jews were led captive, and the land possessed by another people. And so in this day; while the father is laying up gold for his son, the destroyer may lay him lifeless at his feet, and where then is all his treasure? Therefore if we, the islands of the sea, and all the ends of the earth, desire an inheritance for ourselves and our children, and themselves and their children, it must be obtained where God has appointed the places of deliverance."

Elder Rigdon adverted to the former covenants to Abraham, Isaac, and Jacob, and others of the ancients, which were to be realized in the last days; and spoke at some length upon the deliverance of Zion, the endowment of the Elders with power from on high according to former promises, and the spreading of the word of the Lord to the four winds. He first referred to the situation of the brethren in Missouri, and urged the importance of those who could, giving heed to the revelations by going up to their assistance; and those who could not go, to help those who are going with means for their expenses.

Elder Cowdery gave a brief relation of the mobbing in Missouri, and called for a contribution.

Elders Ambrose Palmer and Salmon Warner followed on the same subject.

Brother Joseph Bosworth spoke on the deliverance of Zion, and said he had no property, but if necessary for her deliverance he would sell his clothes at auction, if he might have left him as good a garment as the Savior had in the manger.

Others also spoke on the deliverance of Zion.

President Joseph Smith, Jun., prophesied.

"If Zion is not delivered, the time is near when all of this Church, wherever they may be found, will be pesecuted and destroyed in like manner."

Elder Rigdon gave an account of the endowment of the ancient apostles, and laid before the conference the dimensions of the House to be built in Kirtland, and rehearsed the promise to the Elders in the last days, which they were to realize after the House of the Lord was built.

Brother Bosworth then related a few items of a vision, as a testimony of those things contained in the revelation read by Elder Rigdon, and his remarks thereon.

President Smith explained the revelation concerning the building of the Lord's House.

Elder Rigdon then spoke on the spreading of the word of the Lord; followed by several of the brethren.

The conference voted that Thomas Tripp be excluded from the Church in consequence of his imprudent conduct, with the privilege of an appeal to the Bishop's Council in Kirtland.

President Smith then laid hands on certain children, and blessed them in the name of the Lord.

Elder Rigdon administered the Sacrament.

There were present seven High Priests, and thirteen Elders.

Adjourned to the Monday preceding the second Sunday in September.

Closed by singing "Now my remnant of days," etc.

(Signed) OLIVER COWDERY,
Clerk of the Conference.

April 22.—I returned to Kirtland.

Return of the Prophet and Party to Kirtland.

April 23.—Assembled in Council with Elders Sidney Rigdon, Frederick G. Williams, Newel K. Whitney, John Johnson, and Oliver Cowdery; and united in asking the Lord to give Elder Zebedee Coltrin influence over Brother Jacob Myres, to obtain the money which he has gone to borrow for us, or cause him to come to this place and bring it himself. I also received the following:

*Revelation given April 23, 1834, to Enoch [Joseph Smith, Jun.,] concerning the Order of the Church for the benefit of the poor.**

1. Verily I say unto you, my friends, I give unto you counsel, and a commandment, concerning all the properties which belong to the order which I commanded to be organized and established, to be an

* Doctrine and Covenants, sec. civ.

united order, and an everlating order for the benefit of my Church, and for the salvation of men until I come,

2. With promise immutable and unchangeable, that inasmuch as those whom I commanded were faithful, they should be blessed with a multiplicity of blessings;

3. But inasmuch as they were not faithful, they were nigh unto cursing.

4. Therefore, inasmuch as some of my servants have not kept the commandment but have broken the covenant through covetousness, and with feigned words, I have cursed them with a very sore and grievous curse;

5. For I, the Lord, have decreed in my heart, that inasmuch as any man belonging to the order shall be found a transgressor, or, in other words, shall break the covenant with which ye are bound, he shall be cursed in his life, and shall be trodden down by whom I will,

6. For I, the Lord, am not to be mocked in these things;

7. And all this, that the innocent among you may not be condemned with the unjust, and that the guilty among you may not escape, because I, the Lord, have promised unto you a crown of glory at my right hand.

8. Therefore, inasmuch as you are found transgressors, ye cannot escape my wrath in your lives;

9. Inasmuch as ye are cut off for transgression, ye cannot escape the buffetings of Satan until the day of redemption.

10. And now I give unto you power from this very hour, that if any man among you, of the order, is found a transgressor, and repenteth not of the evil, that ye shall deliver him over unto the buffetings of Satan, and he shall not have power to bring evil upon you.

11. It is wisdom in me; therefore, a commandment I give unto you, that ye shall organize yourselves and appoint every man his stewardship,

12. That every man may give an account unto me of the stewardship which is appointed unto him;

13. For it is expedient that I, the Lord, should make every man accountable as a steward over earthly blessings, which I have made and prepared for my creatures.

14. I, the Lord, stretched out the heavens, and built the earth, my very handy-work, and all things therein are mine;

15. And it is my purpose to provide for my Saints, for all things are mine;

16. But it must needs be done in mine own way; and behold this is the way that I, the Lord, have decreed to provide for my Saints, that the poor shall be exalted, in that the rich are made low;

17. For the earth is full, and there is enough and to spare; yea, I prepared all things, and have given unto the children of men to be agents unto themselves.

18. Therefore, if any man shall take of the abundance which I have made, and impart not his portion, according to the law of my gospel, unto the poor and the needy, he shall, with the wicked, lift up his eyes in hell, being in torment.

19. And now, verily I say unto you, concerning the properties of the order.

20. Let my servant Pelagoram (Sidney Rigdon) have appointed unto him the place where he now resides, and the lot of Tahhanes (the tannery) for his stewardship, for his support while he is laboring in my vineyard, even as I will, when I shall command him;

21. And let all things be done according to the counsel of the order, and united consent or voice of the order, which dwell in the land of Shinehah (Kirtland).

22. And this stewardship and blessing I, the Lord, confer upon my servant Pelagoram (Sidney Rigdon), for a blessing upon him, and his seed after him;

23. And I will multiply blessings upon him, inasmuch as he will be humble before me.

24. And again, let my servant Mahemson (Martin Harris) have appointed unto him, for his stewardship, the lot of land which my servant Zombre (John Johnson) obtained in exchange for his former inheritance, for him and his seed after him.

25. And inasmuch as he is faithful, I will multiply blessings upon him and his seed after him.

26. And let my servant Mahemson (Martin Harris) devote his moneys for the proclaiming of my words, according as my servant Gazelam (Joseph Smith, Jun.,) shall direct.

27. And again, let my servant Shederlaomach (Frederick G. Williams) have the place upon which he now dwells.

28. And let my servant Olihah (Oliver Cowdery) have the lot which is set off joining the house, which is to be for the Laneshine-house (printting office), which is lot number one, and also the lot upon which his father resides.

29. And let my servants Shederlaomach (Frederick G. Williams) and Olihah (Oliver Cowdery) have the Laneshine-house (printing office), and all things that pertain unto it;

30. And this shall be their stewardship which shall be appointed unto them:

31. And inasmuch as they are faithful, behold I will bless, and multiply blessings upon them.

32. And this is the beginning of the stewardship which I have appointed them, for them and their seed after them;

33. And inasmuch as they are faithful, I will multiply blessings upon them, and their seed after them, even a multiplicity of blessings.

34. And again, let my servant Zombre (John Johnson) have the house in which he lives, and the inheritance—all, save the ground which has been reserved for the building of my houses, which pertains to that inheritance, and those lots which have been named for my servant Olihah (Oliver Cowdery).

35. And, inasmuch as he is faithful, I will multiply blessings upon him.

36. And it is my will that he should sell the lots that are laid off for the building up of the city of my Saints, inasmuch as it shall be made known to him by the voice of the Spirit, and according to the counsel of the order, and by the voice of the order.

37. And this is the beginning of the stewardship which I have appointed unto him, for a blessing unto him, and his seed after him;

38. And inasmuch as he is faithful, I will multiply a multiplicity of blessings upon him.

39. And let my servant Ahashdah (Newel K. Whitney) have appointed unto him the houses and lot where he now resides, and the lot and building on which the Ozondah (mercantile establishment) stands, and also the lot which is now on the corner south of the Ozondah (mercantile establishment), and also the lot upon which the Shule (ashery) is situated.

40. And all this I have appointed unto my servant Ahashdah (Newel K. Whitney) for his stewardship, for a blessing upon him and his seed after him, for the benefit of the Ozondah (mercantile establishment) of my order which I have established for my Stake in the land of Shinehah (Kirtland).

41. Yea, verily, this is the stewardship which I have appointed unto my servant Ahashdah (N. K. Whitney), even this whole Ozondah (mercantile establishment), him and his agent, and his seed after him;

42. And inasmuch as he is faithful in keeping my commandments which I have given unto him, I will multiply blessings upon him, and his seed after him, even a multiplicity of blessings.

43 And again, let my servant Gazelam (Joseph Smith, Jun.,) have appointed unto him the lot which is laid off for the building of my house, which is forty rods long, and twelve wide, and also the inheritance upon which his father now resides.

44. And this is the beginning of the stewardship which I have appointed unto him, for a blessing upon him, and upon his father.

45. For, behold, I have reserved an inheritance for his father, for his

support; therefore he shall be reckoned in the house of my servant Gazelam (Joseph Smith, Jun.)

46. And I will multiply blessings upon the house of my servant Gazelam (Joseph Smith, Jun.,) inasmuch as he is faithful, even a multiplicity of blessings.

47. And now, a commandment I give unto you concerning Zion, that you shall no longer be bound as an United Order to your brethren of Zion, only on this wise:

48. After you are organized, you shall be called the United Order of the Stake of Zion, the city of Shinehah (Kirtland). And your brethren, after they are organized, shall be called the United Order of the City of Zion.

49. And they shall be organized in their own names, and in their own name; and they shall do their business in their own name, and in their own names;

50. And you shall do business in your own name, and in your own names.

51. And this I have commanded to be done for your salvation, and also for their salvation, in consequence of their being driven out and that which is to come.

52. The covenants being broken through transgression, by covetousness and feigned words;

53. Therefore you are dissolved as a United Order with your brethren, that you are not bound only up to this hour unto them, only on this wise, as I said, by loan as shall be agreed by this order in council, as your circumstances will admit and the voice of the council direct.

54. And again a commandment I give unto you concerning your stewardships which I have appointed unto you.

55. Behold, all these properties are mine, or else your faith is vain, and ye are found hypocrites, and the covenants which ye have made unto me are broken;

56. And if the properties are mine, then ye are stewards, otherwise ye are no stewards.

57. But, verily I say unto you, I have appointed unto you to be stewards over mine house, even stewards indeed;

58. And for this purpose I have commanded you to organize yourselves, even to shinelah (print) my words, the fullness of my scriptures, the revelations which I have given unto you, and which I shall hereafter, from time to time, give unto you,

59. For the purpose of building up my Church and Kingdom on the earth, and to prepare my people for the time when I shall dwell with them, which is nigh at hand.

60. And ye shall prepare for yourselves a place for a treasury, and consecrate it unto my name;

61. And ye shall appoint one among you to keep the treasury, and he shall be ordained unto this blessing;

62. And there shall be a seal upon the treasury, and all the sacred things shall be delivered into the treasury, and no man among you shall call it his own, or any part of it, for it shall belong to you all with one accord;

63. And I give it unto you from this very hour; and now see to it, that ye go to and make use of the stewardship which I have appointed unto you, exclusive of the sacred things, for the purpose of shinelane (printing) these sacred things as I have said;

64. And the avails of the sacred things shall be had in the treasury, and a seal shall be upon it, and it shall not be used or taken out of the treasury by any one, neither shall the seal be loosed which shall be placed upon it, only by the voice of the order, or by commandment.

65. And thus shall ye preserve the avails of the sacred things in the treasury for sacred and holy purposes:

66. And this shall be called the sacred treasury of the Lord; and a seal shall be kept upon it that it may be holy and consecrated unto the Lord.

67. And again, there shall be another treasury prepared, and a treasurer appointed to keep the treasury, and a seal shall be placed upon it;

68. And all moneys that you receive in your stewardships, by improving upon the properties which I have appointed unto you, in houses, or in lands, or in cattle, or in all things save it be the holy and sacred writings, which I have reserved unto myself, for holy and sacred purposes, shall be cast into the treasury as fast as you receive moneys, by hundreds, or by fifties, or by twenties, or by tens, or by fives;

69. Or in other words, if any man among you obtain five talents (dollars), let him cast them into the treasury; or if he obtain ten, or twenty, or fifty, or an hundred, let him do likewise;

70. And let not any among you say that it is his own, for it shall not be called his, nor any part of it;

71. And there shall not any part of it be used, or taken out of the treasury, only by the voice and common consent of the order.

72. And this shall be the voice and common consent of the order; that any man among you say to the treasurer, I have need of this to help me in my stewardship;

73. If it be five talents (dollars), or if it be ten talents (dollars,) or twenty, or fifty, or a hundred, the treasurer shall give unto him the sum which he requires, to help him in his stewardship.

74. Until he be found a transgressor, and it is manifest before the council of the order plainly, that he is an unfaithful and an unwise steward;

75. But so long as he is in full fellowship, and is faithful, and wise in his stewardship, this shall be his token unto the treasurer, that the treasurer shall not withhold.

76. But in case of transgression, the treasurer shall be subject unto the council and voice of the order.

77. And in case the treasurer is found an unfaithful and an unwise steward, he shall be subject to the council and voice of the order, and shall be removed out of his place, and another shall be appointed in his stead.

78. And again, verily I say unto you, concerning your debts, behold it is my will that you shall pay all your debts;

79. And it is my will that you shall humble yourselves before me, and obtain this blessing by your diligence and humility, and the prayer of faith;

80. And inasmuch as you are diligent and humble, and exercise the prayer of faith, behold, I will soften the hearts of those to whom you are in debt, until I shall send means unto you for your deliverance.

81. Therefore write speedily to Cainhannoch (New York), and write according to that which shall be dictated by my Spirit, and I will soften the hearts of those to whom you are in debt, that it shall be taken away out of their minds to bring affliction upon you.

82. And inasmuch as ye are humble and faithful, and call upon my name, behold I will give you the victory.

83. I give unto you a promise, that you shall be delivered this once out of your bondage;

84. Inasmuch as you obtain a chance to loan money by hundreds, or thousands, even until you shall loan enough to deliver yourselves from bondage, it is your privilege:

85. And pledge the properties which I have put into your hands, this once, by giving your names by common consent or otherwise, as it shall seem good unto you

86. I give unto you this privilege, this once, and behold, if you proceed to do the things which I have laid before you, according to my commandments, all these things are mine, and ye are my stewards, and the master will not suffer his house to be broken up. Even so. Amen.

CHAPTER V.

ZION'S CAMP—ITS JOURNEY FROM KIRTLAND TO MISSOURI.

ABOUT the last of April I received, by letters from friends in the East, and of brethren in Kirtland, the sum of two hundred and fifty-one dollars and sixty cents, towards the deliverance of Zion.

Aid for the Redemption of Zion.

May 1.—More than twenty of the brethren left Kirtland for Missouri, according to previous appointment, accompanied by four baggage wagons. They traveled to New Portage, and there tarried with the church until the remainder of the Kirtland company, who were not in readiness to start with them, arrived.

Gathering of Zion's Camp at New Portage.

The following letter from Elder Phelps to us, clearly shows the necessity there was of the Saints in Missouri receiving assistance:

LIBERTY, May 1, 1834.

DEAR BRETHREN—There are great moves in the west. Last week an alarm was spread in Jackson county, the seat of iniquity and bloodshed, that the "Mormons" were crossing the Missouri, to take possession of their lands, and nearly all the county turned out, "prepared for war;" on Saturday and on Sunday took the field, near old McGee's, above Blue; but no "Mormons" came; neither did Arthur* go over to

* The circumstance here alluded to is that a Mr. Arthur, a respectable and wealthy planter of Clay county, sent one of his black servants into Jackson county with a large wagon load of whisky, flour and bacon. After the servant had crossed the river, a stranger came out of the woods and began to burst open the barrels and destroy the flour, threatening the life of the negro if he should ever come into that county again. Mr. Arthur, it is needless to say, was not a member of the Church of Latter-day Saints, nor a member of any other religious society. Whether he was taken for a "Mormon" or not does not appear. (See *Evening and Morning Star*, vol. ii, p. 319.)

see about his "spilt whisky," so that the scene closed by burning our houses, or many of them. Our people had about one hundred and seventy buildings in Jackson, and a bonfire of nearly all of them at once made a light large enough to glare on their dark deed and cup of iniquity running over at midnight.

The crisis has come; all who will not take up arms with the mob and prepare to fight the "Mormons," have to leave Jackson county. I understand some have left the county, because they refused to fight an innocent people. It is said the mob will hold a "general muster" this week, for the purpose of learning who is who. We have reason to believe that they begin to slip over the Missouri, and commit small depredations upon our brethren settled near the river.

It is said to be enough to shock the stoutest heart to witness the drinking, swearing and ravings of most of the mob; nothing but the power of God can stop them in their latter-day crusade against the Church of Christ.

Our brethren are very industrious in putting in spring crops; and they are generally in good health, and the faithful are in strong hope of a glorious hereafter.

I remain yours, etc.,
W. W. PHELPS.

May 3.—Kirtland.

*Minutes of a Conference of the Elders of the Church of Christ, which Church was organized in the township of Fayette, Seneca county, New York, on the 6th of April, A.D. 1830.**

President Joseph Smith, Jun., was chosen moderator, and Frederick G. Williams and Oliver Cowdery were appointed clerks.

After prayer, the conference proceeded to discuss the subject of

* The minutes of this conference are to be found in the *Evening and Morning Star*, vol. ii, p. 352. It will be observed from the heading that the Elders assembled in the conference are called *the Elders of the Church of Christ.* This is pointed out in order that it may be seen that while the conference adopted the title "The Church of the Latter-day Saints," and the Church was for some years called by that name, it was not the intention to regard the Church as any other than the Church of Christ. In an editorial upon this subject in the May number of the *Star* [minutes of the conference, however, designating the above name of the Church were not published until the July number of the *Star* was issued] the following occurs as a comment upon the action of this conference: "It is now more than four years since this Church was organized in these last days, and though the conferences have always shown by their minutes that they took no other name than the name of Christ, the Church has, particularly abroad, been called 'Mormonite.' As the members of this Church profess a belief in the truth of the Book of Mormon, the

names and appellations, when a motion was made by Sidney Rigdon, and seconded by Newel K. Whitney, that this Church be known hereafter by the name of "The Church of the Latter-day Saints." Remarks were made by the members, after which the motion passed by unanimous vote.

"Resolved, that this conference recommend to the conferences and churches abroad, that in making out and transmitting minutes of their proceedings, such minutes and proceedings be made out under the above title.

"Resolved, that these minutes be signed by the moderator and clerks, and published in the *Evening and Morning Star*.

JOSEPH SMITH, JUN., Moderator.
FREDERICK G. WILLIAMS, } Clerks.
OLIVER COWDERY, }

Departure of the Prophet from Kirtland for Missouri.

May 5.—Having gathered and prepared clothing and other necessaries to carry to our brethren and sisters, who had been robbed and plundered of nearly all their effects; and having provided for ourselves horses, and wagons, and firearms, and all sorts of munitions of war of the most portable kind for self-defense—as our enemies are thick on every hand—I started with the remainder of the company from Kirtland for Missouri. This day we went as far as the town of Streetsborough, twenty-seven miles from Kirtland. We stayed in Mr. Ford's barn, where Uncle John Smith and Brigham Young had been preaching three months before. This day Brothers Brigham and Joseph Young went to Israel Barlow's, about three-quarters of a mile, and tarried over night. Brother Barlow returned with them in the morning and joined the camp. Brother Brigham Young

world, either out of contempt and ridicule, or to distinguish us from others, have been very lavish in bestowing the title of 'Mormonite.' Others may call themselves by their own, or by other names, and have the privilege of wearing them without our changing them or attempting so to do; but *we* do not accept the above title [Mormonite], nor shall we wear it as *our* name, though it may be lavished upon us double to what it has heretofore been. And when the bitterness of feeling now cherished in the bosoms of those who profess to be the followers of Christ, against the Church of the Latter-day Saints, shall cease to exist, and when fabrications and desipient reports concerning this society are no longer considered a virtue, it will take its rank, at least with others, and these stigmas will forever sleep with their inventors." (*Evening and Morning Star*, vol. ii, p. 317.)

had taken the families of Solomon Angel and Lorenzo Booth into his house, that they might accompany us to Missouri.

On the 6th we arrived at New Portage, about fifty miles distance from Kirtland, and joined our brethren who had gone before.

My company from Kirtland consisted of about one hundred men, mostly young men, and nearly all Elders, Priests, Teachers or Deacons. As our wagons were nearly filled with baggage, we had mostly to travel on foot.

On the 7th we made preparations for traveling, gathered all the moneys of every individual of the company, and appointed Frederick G. Williams paymaster to disburse the funds thus collected; and Zerubbabel Snow was chosen commissary general. The whole company now consisted of more than one hundred and thirty men, accompanied by twenty baggage wagons. We left but few men in Kirtland, viz.: Elders Sidney Rigdon, Oliver Cowdery, a few working on the Temple, and the aged.

Organization of Zion's Camp.

Through the remainder of this day I continued to organize the company, appoint such other officers as were required, and gave such instructions as were necessary for the discipline, order, comfort and safety of all concerned. I also divided the whole band into companies of twelve, leaving each company to elect its own captain, who assigned each man in his respective company his post and duty, generally in the following order: Two cooks, two firemen; two tent men, two watermen, one runner, two wagoners and horsemen, and one commissary. We purchased flour and meal, baked our own bread, and cooked our own food, generally, which was good, though sometimes scanty; and sometimes we had johnny-cake, or corndodger, instead of flour bread. Every night before retiring to rest, at the sound of the trumpet, we bowed before the Lord in the several tents, and presented our thank-offerings with prayer and supplication; and at the sound of the morning trumpet, about four o'clock, every man was again on his knees before the Lord, imploring His blessing for the day.

The March of Zion's Camp.

On the 8th we recommenced our march towards Zion, and pitched our tents for the night in a beautiful grove at Chippeway, twelve miles from New Portage.

On the morning of the 9th we completed our organization by companies and proceeded onward, and encamped near Wooster; and on Saturday the 10th, passing through Mansfield, encamped for the Sabbath in Richfield township. About one hour after we had encamped, Elders Lyman E. Johnson, Willard Snow and a number of others joined the camp from the north part of Vermont.

Sunday 11.—Elder Sylvester Smith preached, and the company received the Sacrament of bread and wine. Here we were increased in number by eight brethren, in company of Elder Elias Benner, from Richland and Stark counties, most of whom were Germans.

Incidents in Zion's Camp.

Monday, May 12.—We left Richfield, traveled about thirty-five miles, passed the Bucyrus, and encamped on the Sandusky plains, at a short distance from the place where the Indians roasted General Crawford, and near the Indian settlements.

On the 13th we passed through a long range of beech woods, where the roads were very bad. In many instances we had to fasten ropes to the wagons to haul them out of the sloughs and mud holes. Brother Parley P. Pratt broke his harness; the brethren fastened their ropes to his wagon, and drew it about three miles to the place of encampment on the Scioto river, while he rode singing and whistling.

Wednesday, May 14.—We passed on to Belle Fontaine, where we discovered refractory feelings in Sylvester Smith, who expressed great dissatisfaction because we were short of bread, although we had used all diligence to procure a supply, and Captain Brigham Young had previously sent two men ahead to provide supplies for his company.

Thursday, *May 15*.—We forded Mad river, and passing through a beautiful country, encamped a little west of Springfield. This night Moses Martin fell asleep on sentry duty, and I went and took his sword, and left him asleep.

Friday, *May 16*.—About nine o'clock, while I was riding in a wagon with Brother Hyrum, Ezra Thayer and George A. Smith, we came into a piece of thick woods of recent growth, where I told them that I felt much depressed in spirit and lonesome, and that there had been a great deal of bloodshed in that place, remarking that whenever a man of God is in a place where many have been killed, he will feel lonesome and unpleasant, and his spirits will sink.

In about forty rods from where I made this observation we came through the woods, and saw a large farm, and there near the road on our left, was a mound sixty feet high, containing human bones. This mound was covered with apple trees, and surrounded with oat fields, the ground being level for some distance around.

At dinner time some of the brethren expressed considerable fear on account of milk sickness, with which the people were troubled along our route. Many were afraid to use milk or butter, and appealed to me to know if it was not dangerous. I told them to use all they could get, unless they were told it was "sick." Some expressed fears that it might be sold to us by our enemies for the purpose of doing us injury. I told them not to fear; that if they would follow my counsel, and use all they could get from friend or enemy, it should do them good, and none be sick in consequence of it; and although we passed through neighborhoods where many of the people and cattle were infected with the sickness, yet my words were fulfilled.

While passing through Dayton, Ohio, great curiosity was manifested, various reports of our numbers and designs having gone before us. Some of the inhabitants inquired of the company where they were from, when Captain Young replied: "From every place but this, and we will soon be from this." "Where are you going?" 'To the West." *

Delegation from Dayton.

Some ten or a dozen gentlemen came over from Dayton to ascertain our numbers, which they reported to be at least six hundred. These gentlemen also inquired of almost every man in the camp where he was from and where he was going, and what was his business. They returned to Dayton and reported that every man in the company was a gentleman and gave a respectful answer to every question asked, but they could not ascertain where we were going, or what was our business.

This evening a courtmartial was held in the camp for the trial of Moses Martin for falling asleep while on picket duty. Brother Martin pleaded his own case, say-

* The late President Wilford Woodruff, who was a member of Zion's Camp, speaking at the celebration of the thirty-third anniversary (July 24, 1880,) of the entrance of the Pioneers into Salt Lake valley, speaking of Zion's Camp, said:

"We were followed by spies hundreds of miles to find out the object of our mission. We had some boys in the camp. George A. Smith was among the youngest. When they could get him alone they would question him, thinking that he looked green enough for them to get what they wanted out of him. The following questions were frequently put and answered:

" 'My boy, where are you from?'

" 'From the East.'

" 'Where are you going?'

" 'To the West.'

" 'What for?'

" 'To see where we can get land cheapest and best.'

" 'Who leads the camp?'

" 'Sometimes one, sometimes another.'

" 'What name?'

" 'Captain Wallace, Major Bruce, Orson Hyde, James Allred,' etc.

"This was about the information the spies obtained from any of the camp that were questioned." ("The Utah Pioneers," p. 18.)

ing that he was overcome with fatigue, and so overpowered that he could not keep awake, etc. I decided that he should be acquitted with a warning never to go to sleep again on watch, which was sanctioned by the court, and I took occasion from this circumstance to give the brethren much useful instruction.

The Camp Enters Indiana.

We forded the Miami river with our baggage wagons, most of the men wading through the water. On the 17th of May we crossed the state line of Ohio, and encamped for the Sabbath just within the limits of Indiana, having traveled about forty miles that day. Our feet were very sore and blistered, our stockings wet with blood, the weather being very warm. At night a spy attempted to get into our camp, but was prevented by our guard. We had our sentinels posted every night, on account of spies who were continually striving to harass us, steal our horses, etc.

Difficulties Within the Camp.

This evening there was a difficulty between some of the brethren and Sylvester Smith, on occasion of which I was called to decide in the matter. Finding a rebellious spirit in Sylvester Smith, and to some extent in others, I told them they would meet with misfortunes, difficulties and hindrances, and said, "and you will know it before you leave this place," exhorting them to humble themselves before the Lord and become united, that they might not be scourged. A very singular occurrence took place that night and the next day, concerning our teams. On Sunday morning, when we arose, we found almost every horse in the camp so badly foundered that we could scarcely lead them a few rods to the water. The brethren then deeply realized the effects of discord. When I learned the fact, I exclaimed to the brethren, that for a witness that God overruled and had His eye upon them, all those who would humble themselves before the Lord should know that the hand of God was in this misfortune, and their horses should be restored to health immediately; and by twelve o'clock the same day the horses were as nimble as ever, with the exception of one of Sylvester Smith's, which soon afterwards died.

Sunday, May 18.—We had preaching as usual, and the administration of the Sacrament.

About this time the Saints in Clay county, Missouri, established an armory, where they commenced manufacturing swords, dirks, pistols, stocking rifles, and repairing arms in general for their own defense against mob violence; many arms were purchased; for the leading men in Clay county rendered every facility in their power, in order, as they said, "to help the 'Mormons' settle their own difficulties, and pay the Jackson mob in their own way."

Monday, May, 19.—We traveled thirty-one miles and encamped in Franklin township, Henry county, in the beech woods.

Tuesday, May 20.—We encamped near Greenfield, having traveled about twenty-five miles, some part of the way being so bad I walked over the tops of my boots in mud, helping to pull through the wagons with ropes.

Spies from the West in the Camp.

While we were eating dinner three gentlemen came riding up on very fine looking horses and commenced their inquiries of various ones concerning our traveling in so large a body, asking where we were from, and where we were going. The reply was as usual—some from the state of Maine; another would say, "I am from York state;" some from Massachusetts; some from Ohio; and some replied, "we are from the East, and as soon as we have done eating dinner we shall be going to the West again." They then addressed themselves to Dr. Frederick G. Williams to see if they could find out who the leader of the camp was. The doctor replied, "We have no one in particular." They asked if we had not a general to take the lead of the company. The reply was, "No one in particular." "But," said they, "is there not some one among you whom you call your captain, or leader, or who is superior to the rest?" He answered, "Sometimes one and sometimes another takes charge of the company, so as not to throw the burden upon any one in particular." These spies, who had come from the west, passed us several times that same day and the next.

Indianapolis Incident.

Although threatened by our enemies that we should not pass through Indianapolis, we passed through that city on the 21st unmolested. All the inhabitants were quiet. At night we encamped a few miles west of Indianapolis. There had previously been so many reports that we should never be permitted to pass through this place, and that the governor would have us dispersed, that some of the brethren were afraid that we might have difficulty there. But I had told them, in the name of the Lord, we should not be disturbed and that we would pass through Indianapolis without the people knowing it. When near the place many got into the wagons, and, separating some little distance, passed through the city, while others walked down different streets, leaving the inhabitants wondering "when that big company would come along."

Since the 18th we had followed the national road where it was passable, but frequently we had to take by-roads which were miry and led through thick woods.

Thursday, *May 22.*—We encamped on a small stream of water in a grove near Belleville.

Friday, *May 23.*—We encamped about four miles from Greencastle, after a hard drive.

Saturday, *May*, *24.*—We crossed the Wabash river at Clinton in ferry boats, in quick time, and pushed on to the state line, where we arrived late in the evening, and encamped in an oak opening in Edgar county, Illionois.

A Jackson County Spy in Camp.

Sunday, *May 25.*—We had no meeting, but attended to washing, baking, and preparing to resume our journey. A man in disguise, having on an old sealskin cap, came into our camp. He swore we were going up to Jackson county, and that we would never get over the Mississippi river alive. It was evident he was a spy, and I recollected having seen him in Jackson county, Missouri.

Precept *vs.* Example—a Lesson.

Monday, May 26.—A very hot day. We traveled through Paris and across a sixteen mile prairie; at noon we stopped to bait at a slough, about six miles from the timber, having no water to drink but such as was filled with living animals commonly called wigglers, and as we did not like to swallow them we strained the water before using it. This was the first prairie of any extent that we had come to on our journey, and was a great curiosity to many of the brethren. It was so very level that the deer miles off appeared but a short distance away; some of the brethren started out in pursuit before they were apprised of their mistake as to the distance. We continued our march, pulling our wagons through a small creek with ropes, and came to the house of Mr. Wayne, the only settler in the vicinity, where we found a well of water, which was one of the greatest comforts we could have received, as we were almost famished, and it was a long time before we could, or dared to satisfy our thirst. We crossed the Embarras river and encamped on a small branch of the same about one mile west. In pitching my tent we found three massasaugas or prairie rattlesnakes, which the brethren were about to kill, but I said, "Let them alone—don't hurt them! How will the serpent ever lose his venom, while the servants of God possess the same disposition, and continue to make war upon it? Men must become harmless, before the brute creation; and when men lose their vicious dispositions and cease to destroy the animal race, the lion and the lamb can dwell together, and the sucking child can play with the serpent in safety." The brethren took the serpents carefully on sticks and carried them across the creek. I exhorted the brethren not to kill a serpent, bird, or an animal of any kind during our journey unless it became necessary in order to preserve ourselves from hunger.

I had frequently spoken on this subject, when on a certain occasion I came up to the brethren who were watching a squirrel on a tree, and to prove them and to know if they would heed my counsel, I took one of their guns, shot the squirrel and passed on, leaving the squirrel on the ground. Brother Orson Hyde, who was just behind, picked up the squirrel, and said, "We will cook this, that nothing may be lost." I perceived that the brethren understood what I did it for, and in their practice gave more heed to my precept than to my example, which was right.

This evening Brother Parley P. Pratt and Amasa Lyman returned from the Eugene branch, Indiana (where I had sent them), with a company of about a dozen men.

A Call to Arms.

The reports of mobs which were continually saluting our ears caused the brethren to be constantly alive to the subject, and about eleven o'clock this evening our picket guards reported that they saw the fires of the mob on the southeast of us. I instantly arose and discovered the mistake; but wishing the brethren to enjoy the scene as well as myself, immediately discharged my gun, which was a signal to call all men to arms. When the companies were all paraded and ready for battle, I pointed them to the reflection of the rising moon resting on points of timber in the east, which gave the appearance of the reflection of the light of a number of camp fires. The scenery was most delightful, and was well worth the trouble of any man rising from his couch to witness, who had never seen the like on the broad prairie before. This circumstance proved that nearly every man in the camp was ready for battle, except Dean Gould, who was not baptized, and Captain Jazeniah B. Smith, who was suddenly taken with the colic, and did not leave his tent. The whole incident was very amusing.

Tuesday, May 27.—Notwithstanding our enemies were continually breathing threats of violence, we did not fear, neither did we hesitate to prosecute our journey, for God was with us, and His angels went before us, and the faith of our little band was unwavering. We know that angels were our companions, for we saw them.*

Angels Attend the Camp.

We arrived at the Okaw branch of the Kaskaskia, where we found log canoes, which we lashed together, and ferried our baggage across the stream. We then swam our horses and wagons, and when arrived at the opposite shore, the brethren fastened ropes to the wagon tongues and helped the teams out of the water and up the steep, miry banks. Some of the brethren felled a tall tree across the river, on which they passed over, and carried some of their baggage on their backs. While we were passing over, George A. Smith discovered a spring that with a little digging furnished us with an abundant supply of excellent water, which afterwards received the name of "the Mormon Spring." This afternoon, Elder Solomon Humphreys, an aged brother of the camp,

* On this point Elder Parley P. Pratt, in his Autobiography, relates a most interesting incident. Elder Pratt was chiefly engaged as a recruiting officer along the line of the camp's march, and would fall in with the camp from time to time, with additional men, arms, stores, money, etc., as opportunity afforded. And now his story:

"On one occasion, I had traveled all night to overtake the camp with some men and means, and having breakfasted with them and changed horses, I again started ahead on express to visit other branches and do business, to again overtake them. At noon I had turned my horse loose from the carriage to feed on the grass in the midst of a broad level plain. No habitation was near; stillness and repose reigned around me; I sank down overpowered in a deep sleep, and might have lain in a state of oblivion till the shades of night had gathered around me, so completely was I exhausted for want of sleep and rest; but I had only slept a few moments till the horse had grazed sufficiently, when a voice, more loud and shrill than I had ever before heard, fell on my ear and thrilled through every part of my system; it said: 'Parley, it is time to be up and on your journey.' In the twinkling of an eye I was perfectly aroused; I sprang to my feet so suddenly that I could not recollect where I was or what was before me to perform. I related the circumstance afterwards to Brother Joseph Smith, and he bore testimony that it was the angel of the Lord who went before the camp who found me overpowered with sleep, and thus awoke me." (Autobiography of Parley P. Pratt, pp. 122, 123.)

having become exceedingly weary, lay down on the prairie to rest himself and fell asleep. When he awoke he saw, coiled up within one foot of his head, a rattlesnake lying between him and his hat, which he had in his hand when he fell asleep. The brethren gathered around him, saying, "It is a rattlesnake, let us kill it;" but Brother Humphreys said, "No, I'll protect him; you shan't hurt him, for he and I had a good nap together."

Wednesday, May 28.—We passed on as usual, except suffering much from want of water and provisions; and arrived at Decatur township. We encamped on a small stream of water, and here one of Brother Tanner's horses died.

Camp Diversions.

Thurday, May 29.—Having to buy a horse we were detained until near noon. There was some murmuring among the brethren, many wishing to go on and not tarry with the rest of the company for the day, and some were already started. I sent for them to return and collected the whole company together, and instructed them not to scatter. I told them if they went ahead of the camp in a scattered condition they would become weary, lie down on the ground when their blood was heated, and they would be liable to take diseases, such as fever and ague, which are prevalent in this climate. They would also be in danger of being killed by an enemy, and none of us be the wiser for it.

I then proposed for a diversion that we divide the camp into three parts and have a sham battle, which was agreed to. Brother Roger Orton led one division, Frederick G. Williams another division, while I remained in the camp with the third division. They retired to the woods with their divisions, and soon attacked the camp, which we defended by various maneuvers for some time. Many of our captains showed considerable tact and more acquaintance with military matters than I had expected. Everything passed off with good feelings, although Captain Heber C. Kimball, in receiving a charge, grasped Captain Lewis Zobriski's sword, and in endeavoring to take it from him, had the skin cut from the palm of his hand. After the sham battle was over, I called the camp together and cautioned the men to be careful in the future and control their spirits in such circumstances so as never to injure each other.

We traveled across the prairie and encamped in a strip of timber. When we stopped to dine, I wrote a letter to the brethren in Missouri, dated "Camp of Israel," requesting some of them to meet us as soon as possible and give me information of the state of things in Upper Missouri, and sent the letter to Springfield post office by Dr. Frederick G. Williams.

At this place I discovered that a part of my company had been served with sour bread, while I had received good, sweet bread from the same cook. I reproved Brother Zebedee Coltrin for this partiality, for I wanted my brethren to fare as well as I did.

Proposition to Divide Jackson County between Saints and the Mob.

The same day (May 29th) the brethren in Clay county wrote the following letter to his Excellency Daniel Dunklin:

LIBERTY, MISSOURI, May 29, 1834.

SIR—Your communication to us of May 2nd, containing or enclosing an order on Colonel S. D. Lucas for the arms which were forcibly taken from us last November, was received on the 15th instant, and the order forwarded to Colonel Lucas at Independence, on the 17th, giving him the privilege of returning our arms at one of the several ferries in this county. His reply to the order was, that he would write what he would do by the next mail, May 22nd. But as he has removed to Lexington without writing, we are at a loss to knew whether he means to delay returning them for a season, or entirely to refuse to restore them.

At any rate, the excitement, or rather spite, of the mob, runs so high against our people, that we think best to request your Excellency to have said arms returned through the agency of Colonel Allen or Captain Atchison. Report says the arms will not be returned, and much exertion is making by the mob to prevent our return to our possessions in Jackson county. We also understand that the mob is employing certain influential gentlemen to write to your Excellency, to persuade us to compromise our matters in difference with the Jackson mob, and probably *divide Jackson county*. We ask for our rights and no more.

Respectfully, your Excellency's servants,

(Signed) W. W. PHELPS,
ALGERNON S. GILBERT,
JOHN CORRILL,
EDWARD PARTRIDGE.

Passage of Camp through Springfield, Illinois.

Friday, May 30.—Frederick G. Williams and Almon W. Babbitt* went ahead of the camp into Springfield in disguise, to learn the feeling of the people and procure some powder. We passed through Springfield; our appearance excited considerable curiosity, and a great many questions were asked. The spies who had followed us so long pursued us very closely, changing their dress and horses several times a day.

Brother Eleazer Miller with others joined the company with three horses about noon, a little east of Rochester. This reinforcement was very seasonable, as many of our horses were afflicted as they very frequently are in changing country, climate and food. Many of the horses after eating the dry corn and prairie grass would be seized with colic and bloat very badly. Brother Ezra Thayre administered medicine mixed in a quart stone bottle, prepared as follows: A threepenny paper of tobacco, half an ounce of copperas and two table-spoonsfull of cayenne pepper, and the bottle filled with water when he could not procure whisky. One-half of a bottle constituted a dose, and would almost invariably cure a sick horse in a few minutes, and is worthy of remembrance. Brother Thayre called his medicine "18 by 24."

We encamped about three miles from Springfield on Spring Creek. Frederick G. Williams and Almon W.

* Almon W. Babbitt was born October 1, 1813, in Berkshire county, Mass. He was the son of Ira and Nancy Babbitt.

Babbitt returned to the camp with two kegs of powder, and reported that the people were somewhat excited, more however from a curiosity to know where we were going than from a desire to hinder us. A brother came to see us with the news that my brother Hyrum had passed on west the day before with a company, about fifty miles north of us, saying, "he has a fine company, and they all look mighty *pert*." I asked him to accompany us to Missouri, but he replied, "I cannot." He went and stayed at a tavern over night with the spies, who said they followed us three hundred miles on purpose to take some advantage of us.

Arrival at Jacksonville, Illinois.

Saturday, May 31.—In the morning this brother came to me and said: "I would be mighty glad to go with you, but my business is such I cannot. Will a hundred dollars do you any good?" I replied, "Yes, it will, for we are short of money." He immediately remounted his horse and rode to Springfield, and within an hour after the camp had started he returned and said to me: "I am mighty sorry I cannot go with you. Here is a hundred dollars, and if I had had a few days' notice I could have got more."

At noon we halted for dinner. A man, apparently drunk, came to the camp and said he had a large farm and forty cows a little way ahead, and if we would go there, he would give us all we wanted to eat and drink, feed our horses, etc. But I soon discovered that he was more sober than drunk, and that he was probably a spy.

Near night we arrived at a small stream of water about one mile from Jacksonville, where we found a pawpaw bush in the road, which had been dropped by Dr. Frederick G. Williams as a signal for us to camp. I had sent Dr. Williams forward in the morning on horseback to select a camp ground and watch the movements of our enemies. We pitched our tents in the place he had selected.

Agreeable to my instructions, about sunset Brother Roger Orton proclaimed aloud that there would be preaching under the trees within the camp at half-past ten o'clock on the morrow. There was only one stranger in the camp to hear the appointment. Dr. Williams had gone on to Jacksonville with his pill bags to spend the night.

A Puzzling Religious Service.

Sunday, June 1.—We had preaching, and many of the inhabitants of the town came to hear. Elder John Carter, who had formerly been a Baptist preacher, spoke in the morning, and was followed by four other Elders in the course of the day, all of whom had formerly been preachers for different denominations. When the inhabitants heard these Elders they appeared much interested, and were very desirous to know who we were, and we told them one had been a Baptist preacher, and one a Campbellite; one a Reformed Methodist, and another a Restorationer. During the day many questions were asked, but none could learn our names, professions, business, or destination; and, although they suspected we were "Mormons," they were very civil.*

* In addition to confirming the above narrative of the services on June 1, Elder Heber C. Kimball, in his journal, adds some very interesting details, as follows:

"On Sunday, June 1, we preached all day, and many of the inhabitants of the town came out to hear. Brother John Carter preached in the morning. By this time the inhabitants began to flock down in companies to hear preaching, as they understood we were professors of religion and had had a meeting in the morning. Brother Joseph then proposed that some of the brethren should set forth different portions of the Gospel in their discourses, as held by the religious world. He called upon Brother Joseph Young to preach upon the principle of free salvation. He then called upon Brigham Young to speak, who set forth baptism as essential to salvation. He was followed by Brother Orson Hyde, who proved by the scriptures that baptism was for the remission of sins. He next called upon Brother Lyman E. Johnson, who spoke at some length upon the necessity of men being upright in their walk, and keeping the Sabbath day holy. He then called upon Brother Orson Pratt, who delivered an excellent discourse on the principle of the final restoration of all things. The services of the day were concluded by a powerful exhortation from Eleazer Miller. * * * After the day's services were over at this place, many strangers were in our camp making remarks upon the preaching which they had heard. They said Brother Joseph Young, by his preaching, they should jndge was a Methodist. They thought Brother Brigham Young was a close communion Baptist. Brother Orson Hyde they supposed was a Campbellite or Reformed Baptist. Brother Lyman E. Johnson they supposed was a Presbyterian, and Brother Orson Pratt a Restorationer. They inquired if we all bolonged to one

Our enemies had threatened that we should not cross the Illinois river, but on Monday the 2nd we were ferried over without any difficulty. The ferryman counted, and declared there were five hundred of us, yet our true number was only about one hundred and fifty. Our company had been increased since our departure from Kirtland by volunteers from different branches of the Church through which we had passed. We encamped on the bank of the river until Tuesday the 3rd.

The Finding of Zelph.

During our travels we visited several of the mounds which had been thrown up by the ancient inhabitants of this country—Nephites, Lamanites, etc., and this morning I went up on a high mound, near the river, accompanied by the brethren. From this mound we could overlook the tops of the trees and view the prairie on each side of the river as far as our vision could extend, and the scenery was truly delightful.

On the top of the mound were stones which presented the appearance of three altars having been erected one above the other, according to the ancient order; and the remains of bones were strewn over the surface of the ground. The brethren procured a shovel and a hoe, and removing the earth to the depth of about one foot, discovered the skeleton of a man, almost entire, and between his ribs the stone point of a Lamanitish arrow, which evidently produced his death. Elder Burr Riggs retained the arrow. The contemplation of the scenery around us produced peculiar sensations in our bosoms; and subsequently the visions of the past being opened to my understanding by the Spirit of the Almighty, I discovered that the person whose skeleton was before us was a white Lamanite, a large, thick-set man, and a man of God. His name was Zelph. He was a warrior and chieftain under the great prophet Onandagus, who was known from the Hill Cumorah, or eastern sea

denomination. The answer was, We *were* some of us Baptists, some Methodists, some Presbyterians, some Campbellites, and some Restorationers." (*Times and Seasons*, vol. vi, pp. 772-3.)

to the Rocky mountains. The curse was taken from Zelph, or, at least, in part—one of his thigh bones was broken by a stone flung from a sling, while in battle, years before his death. He was killed in battle by the arrow found among his ribs, during the last great struggle of the Lamanites and Nephites.*

A Prophecy.

While we were refreshing ourselves and teams about the middle of the day [June 3rd], I got up on a wagon wheel, called the people together, and said that I would deliver a prophecy. After giving the brethren much good advice, exhorting them to faithfulness and humility, I said the Lord had revealed to me that a scourge would come upon the camp in consequence of the fractious and unruly spirits that appeared among them, and they should die like sheep with the rot; still, if they would repent and humble themselves before the Lord, the scourge, in a great measure, might be turned away; but, as the Lord lives, the members of this camp will suffer for giving way to their unruly temper.†

Proposition of Colonel Ross.

When we arrived at Atlas, I had a conversation with Colonel Ross, a wealthy gentleman of the neighborhood, who gave us a flattering account of the country, and wished to employ one hundred men, for which he proposed to make ready payment. He wanted brickmakers, builders, etc.

Here our commissary purchased twenty-five gallons of honey at twenty-five cents per gallon, and a dozen Mis-

* According to Elder Kimball's journal, the facts concerning the person whose bones had been found in the mound were not revealed to the Prophet Joseph until the camp had departed from the mound. He says:

"While on our way we felt anxious to know who the person was who had been killed by the arrow. It was made known to Joseph that he had been an officer who fell in battle in the last destruction among the Lamanites, and his name was Zelph. This caused us to rejoice much, to think that God was so mindful of us as to show these things to His servant. Brother Joseph had inquired of the Lord, and it was made known in a vision." (*Times and Seasons*, vol. vi, p. 788.)

† Elder Heber C. Kimball corroborates this prediction of the 3rd of June, closing his reference to it in his journal in these words: "Which [predicted calamity] afterwards actually did take place, to the sorrow of the brethren." (*Times and Seasons*, vol. vi, p. 788.)

souri cured hams, which proved to have been a little injured on the outside. There not being enough to supply one for every company, my company agreed to do without. Our supper consisted of mush and honey, as we had been unable to procure flour on account of the scarcity of mills. After the fatigues of the day it hardly satisfied hunger; but when we had finished, some six of the hams were brought to our tent door and thrown down in anger, the remark being, "We don't eat stinking meat." I called on Brother Zebedee Coltrin, our cook, and told him to be quick and fry some ham, as I had not had my hunger fairly allayed for forty-eight hours. He immediately commenced cooking the ham, and for once my company feasted to their full satisfaction.

Report of Luke S. Johnson.

We had just retired to rest when the picket guard announced Luke S. Johnson. He came into our camp and made his report. He had visited a number of influential men, among the rest a Baptist minister, who expressed great anxiety that our company should be stopped, and went to a magistrate to inquire if there was not some law or pretext for stopping us. He, the priest, said to the magistrate, "That company march and have guns like an army. They pitch their tents by the side of the road; they set out guards, and let nobody pass into their camp in the night; and they are Mormons, and I believe they are going to kill the people up in Jackson county, Missouri, and retake their lands." The magistrate replied, "If you were traveling, and did not wish to put up at public houses, or there were none in the country, would you not camp by the road side in a tent? And if you were afraid that your horses and property would be stolen in a strange country, would you not watch and keep guards?" "Why, yes," said the priest; "but they are Mormons!" "Well, I can't hear but they mind their own business, and if you and this stranger [meaning Luke S. Johnson] will mind your own business, everything will be right." This Bap tist priest treated Brother Luke S. Johnson with great politeness. He gave him his dinner, his wife washed his stockings; he gave him letters of introduction to men in Jackson county, and delivered to his charge some letters which he had received from Jackson county, which Brother Luke brought into the camp. He also stated that he had seen a man that morning who informed him that four hundred men were in readiness on the Missouri side, with ten hours' notice, to use up all the camp, and he was on his way to give them the notice.

A False Alarm.

A little before midnight we heard several guns fired to the west of us, which appeared to be answered by one directly east. There was no settlement west of us nearer than the state of Missouri. This appearing so much like a signal, in addition to the many threats of our being attacked on crossing the Mississippi, I considered sufficient cause of alarm to put out a double picket guard and put the camp in a state of defense, so that every man might be ready at a moment's notice. It however proved to be a false alarm.*

Continuing our journey on the 4th, we encamped on the banks of the Mississippi river. At this place we were somewhat afflicted, and our enemies strongly threatened that we should not cross over into Missouri. The river being a mile and a half wide, and having but one ferry boat, it took two days for us to pass over.† While some were ferrying, others were engaged in hunting, fishing,

* Of this incident about the firing of the guns on the 3rd, Elder Kimball, in his journal, says: "There was a great excitement in the country through which we had passed, and also ahead of us; the mob threatened to stop us. Guns were fired in almost all directions through the night. Brother Joseph did not sleep much, if any, but was through the camp pretty much during the night."

† This account, given under date of the 4th of June, really covers both the 4th and 5th, and the journey was made from Atlas to the Missouri side of the Mississippi during the two days, the 4th and 5th. While encamped on Snye island, the brethren manifested a disposition to scatter through the woods for hunting, "but I advised them to the contrary," said the prophet. He then continues: "Some of the brethren went on to the sand bar and got a quantity of turtles' eggs, as they supposed. I told them they were snakes' eggs, and they must not eat them; but some of them thought they knew more about it than I did, and still

etc. As we arrived, we encamped on the bank, within the limits of Missouri.

While at this place, Sylvester Smith rebelled against the order of the company, and gave vent to his feelings against myself in particular. This was the first outbreak of importance which had occurred to mar our peace since we commenced our journey.*

persisted they were turtles' eggs. I said they were snakes' eggs—eat snakes' eggs, will you? The man that eats them will be sorry for it; you will be sick. Notwithstanding all I said, several brethren ate them, and were sick all the day after it."

* Of Sylvester Smith's rebellion against the order of the camp, Elder Kimball, in his journal, relates the following interesting circumstances:

"When we had all got over [the Mississippi], we camped about one mile back from the little town of Louisiana, in a beautiful oak grove, which is immediately on the bank of the river. At this place there were some feelings of hostility manifested again by Sylvester Smith, in consequence of a dog growling at him while he was marching his company up to the camp, he being the last that came over the river. The next morning Brother Joseph told the camp that he would descend to the spirit that was manifested by some of the brethren, to let them see the folly of their wickedness. He rose up and commenced speaking by saying, 'If any man insults me, or abuses me, I will stand in my own defense at the expense of my life; and if a dog growls at me, I will let him know that I am his master.' At this moment Sylvester Smith, who had just returned from where he had turned out his horses to feed, came up, and hearing Brother Joseph make those remarks, said, 'If that dog bites me, I'll kill him.' Brother Joseph turned to Sylvester and said, 'If you kill that dog, I'll whip you,' and then went on to show the brethren how wicked and unchristianlike such conduct appeared before the eyes of truth and justice."

CHAPTER VI.

ZION'S CAMP IN MISSOURI—LETTERS OF GOVERNOR DUNKLIN AND OTHERS.

THE Elders in Clay county wrote Governor Dunklin as follows:

LIBERTY, June 5, 1834.

DEAR SIR—We think the time is just at hand when our society will be glad to avail themselves of the protection of a military guard, that they may return to Jackson county. We do not now know the precise day, but Mr. Reese gives his opinion, that there would be no impropriety in petitioning your Excellency for an order on the commanding officer, to be sent by return mail, that we might have it in our hands to present when our people get ready to start. If this should meet your approbation, and the order sent by return mail, we think it would be of great convenience to our society.

We would also be obliged to your Excellency for information concerning the necessary expenses of ferriage, etc. Are our people bound to pay the ferriage on their return? As they have already sustained heavy losses, and many of them have lost their all, a mitigation of expenses on their return at this time, where they could legally be reduced, would afford great relief; not only ferriage across the Missouri river, but other items of expense that could lawfully be reduced.

We remain, your Excellency's most obedient servants,

A. S. GILBERT,
W. W. PHELPS,
EDWARD PARTRIDGE.

Copy of a letter from Daniel Dunklin, Governor of the State of Missouri, to Colonel J. Thornton, dated—

CITY OF JEFFERSON, June 6, 1834.

DEAR SIR—I was pleased at the receipt of your letter, concurred in by Messrs. Reese, Atchison and Doniphan, on the subject of the Mormon difficulties. I should be gratified indeed if the parties could compromise upon the terms you suggest, or, indeed, upon any other terms satisfactory to themselves. But I should travel out of the line of strict duty, as chief executive officer of the government, were I to take upon myself the task of effecting a compromise between the parties. Had I not supposed it possible, yes, probable, that I should, as executive of the state, have to act, I should, before now, have interfered individually in the way you suggest, or in some other way, in order if possible to effect a compromise. Uncommitted as I am to either party, I shall feel no embarrassment in doing my duty—though it may be done with the most extreme regret. My duty in the relation which I now stand to the parties, is plain and straightforward. By an official interposition I might embarrass my course, and urge a measure for the purpose of effecting a compromise, and [if] it should fail, and in the end, should I feel it my duty to act contrary to the advice I had given, it might be said, that I either advised wrong, or that I was partial to one side or the other, in giving advice that I would not as an officer follow.

A more clear and indisputable right does not exist, than that of the Mormon people, who were expelled from their homes in Jackson county, to return and live on their lands; and if they cannot be persuaded, as a matter of policy, to give up that right, or to qualify it, my course, as the chief executive of the state, is a plain one. The constitution of the United States declares "that the citizens of each state shall be entitled to all privileges and immunities of citizens in the several states." Then we cannot interdict any people, who have a political franchise in the United States, from immigrating to this state, nor from choosing what part of the state they will settle in, provided they do not trespass on the property or rights of others. Our state constitution declares that the people's "right to bear arms, in defense of themselves and of the state, cannot be questioned." Then it is their constitutional right to arm themselves. Indeed, our military law makes it the duty of every man, not exempted by law, between the ages of eighteen and forty-five, to arm himself with a musket, rifle, or some firelock, with a certain quantity of ammunition, etc.; and again, our constitution says, "that all men have a natural and indefeasible right to worship Almighty God according to the dictates of their own consciences."

I am fully persuaded that the eccentricity of the religious opinions and practices of the Mormons is at the bottom of the outrages committed against them. They have the right constitutionally guaranteed to them, and it is indefeasible, to worship Joe Smith as a man, an angel, or even as the only true and living God, and to call their habitation Zion, the Holy Land, or even heaven itself. Indeed, there is nothing so absurd or ridiculous that they have not a right to adopt as their religion, so that in its exercise they do not interfere with the rights of others.

It is not long since an impostor assumed the character of Jesus Christ and attempted to minister as such; but I never heard of any combination to deprive him of his rights.

I consider it the duty of every good citizen of Jackson county and the adjoining counties to exert himself to effect a compromise of these difficulties; and were I assured that I would not have to act in my official capacity in the affair, I would visit the parties in person and exert myself to the utmost to settle it. My first advice would be to the Mormons, to sell out their lands in Jackson county, and to settle somewhere else, where they could live in peace, if they could get a fair price for them, and reasonable damages for injuries received. If this failed, I would try the citizens, and advise them to meet and rescind their illegal resolves of last summer, and agree to conform to the laws in every particular, in respect to the Mormons. If both these failed, I would then advice the plan you have suggested, for each party to take separate territory, and confine their members within their respective limits with the exception of the public right of ingress and egress upon the highway. If all these failed, then the simple question of legal right would have to settle it. It is this last that I am afraid I shall have to conform my action to in the end, and hence the necessity of keeping myself in the best situation to do my duty impartially.

Rumor says that both parties are preparing themselves with cannon. That would be illegal: it is not necessary to self-defense, as guaranteed by the constitution, and as there are no artillery companies organized in this state, nor field pieces provided by the public, any preparation of that kind will be considered as without right, and, in the present state of things, would be understood to be with criminal intent, I am told that the people of Jackson county expect assistance from the adjoining counties, to oppose the Mormons in taking or keeping possession of their lands. I should regret it extremely if any should be so imprudent as to do so; it would give a different aspect to the affair.

The citizens of Jackson county have a right to arm themselves and parade for military duty in their own county independent of the commander-in-chief; but if citizens march there in arms from other counties without order from the commander-in-chief or some one authorized by him, it would produce a very different state of things. Indeed, the Mormons have no right to march to Jackson county in arms, unless by order or permission of the commander-in-chief; men must not "levy war" in taking possession of their rights, any more than others should in opposing them in taking possession.

As you have manifested a deep interest in a peaceable compromise of this important affair, I presume you will not be unwilling to be placed in a situation in which, perhaps, you can be more serviceable to these parties. I have therefore taken the liberty of appointing you an aid to the commander-in-chief, and I hope it will be agreeable to you to accept. In this situation you can give your propositions all the influence they would have were they to emanate from the executive, without committing yourself or the commander-in-chief, in the event of failure. I should be glad if you, or some of the other gentlemen who joined you in your communication, would keep in close correspondence with these parties, and by each mail write to me.

The character of the state has been injured in consequence of this unfortunate affair; and I sincerely hope it may not be disgraced by it in the end;

With high respect, your obedient servant,

(Signed) DANIEL DUNKLIN.

Arrival of the Camp at Salt River.

June 6.—We resumed our journey,* and on the evening of the 7th† encamped in a piece of woods, near a spring of water, at Salt River. Here was a branch of the Church.

Arrival of Hyrum Smith and Lyman Wight.

Sunday, June 8.—We had preaching, and in the course of the day were joined by Brothers Hyrum Smith and Lyman Wight, with a company of volunteers which they had gathered in Michigan.‡ The whole company now consisted of two hundred and five men, and twenty-five baggage

* A note in the "Addenda" of the manuscript History to the "We resumed our journey"—etc., adds: "The men who had previously followed us passed us several times during the day, and were in search of us this evening. The guard heard them say, 'They have turned aside, damn 'em, we can't find 'em.' Elders Seth Johnson and Almon W. Babbitt, who had been sent to the Bowling Green branch to gather recruits, returned to the camp on the morning of the 7th with a small company, two wagons and several horses."

† A note in the "Addenda" to the manuscript History adds this statement, under the events of the 7th: "One of the camp walked on ahead to procure some milk. A number of men armed with guns met him and said: 'Here's one damn Mormon alone—let's kill him.' But at the same instant they discovered a number of others just coming over the hill, when they immediately rode off in great haste. In the evening encamped in a grove near a spring, in Monroe county. A branch of the Church, known as the Salt River branch, but frequently called the Allred Settlement, was located here. We remained at this place several days, washing our clothes, and preparing to pursue our journey."

‡ The following is given in the "Addenda" of the manuscript History as a fuller account of the events under the date of the 8th: "Sunday, 8th, we were joined by my brother Hyrum Smith and Lyman Wight, with another company, who started from

wagons with two or three horses each. We remained at Salt River until the 12th, refreshing and reorganizing the camp, which reorganizing was done by electing Lyman Wight general of the camp.* I chose twenty men for my life guards, of whom my Brother Hyrum was chosen captain, and George A. Smith was my armor bearer. The remainder of the company was organized according to the pattern at New Portage. While at Salt River, General Wight marched the camp on the prairie, inspected our firelocks, ordered a discharge of the same at targets by platoons, drilled us half a day, and returned to camp.

Messengers Sent to Governor Dunklin.

About this time I dispatched Elders Orson Hyde and Parley P. Pratt to Jefferson City with a message to Governor Dunklin, to ascertain if he was ready to fulfill the proposition which he had previously made to the brethren to reinstate them on

Pontiac, Michigan Territory, May 5th, the same day we started from Kirtland having passed through Ann Arbor, Jacksonsburgh, Spring Arbor, Constantine, Elkhart, crossed the Illinois river one mile below Ottawa, Pleasant Grove, Pekin, Quincy and Palmyra. Elijah Fordham was their historian; Lyman Wight, steward; Hyrum Smith and Samuel Bent, moderators. We had agreed to meet at this point, and the first company that arrived was to wait for the other. Soon after the arrival of Brother Hyrum and his company, I dispatched Brother Luke Johnson and Almon W. Babbitt with messages to the brethren in Clay county, fearing that the letter which I sent from Springfield had miscarried. James Allred, Sen., and ten others of this branch joined our camp, which now numbered two hundred and five men, all armed and equipped as the law directs. It was delightful to see the company, for they were all young men, except one company whom we called the Silver Greys, and who ate at my table. We were all in good spirits, and were taught the sword practice by Brother William Cherry (who was a native of Ireland), an expert drill master, who had been in the British dragoon service for upwards of twenty years, and deserves much credit for his unwearied exertions in imparting all he knew to the brethren. This was our first attempt at learning the sword exercise. Brothers Hiram Stratton and Nelson Tubbs procured a shop of Myres Mobley and repaired every firelock that was out of order, and David Elliott shod our horses. Here Brother James Foster was taken sick. I proposed to him to remain behind. He said, 'Brother Joseph, let me go with you if I die on the road.' I told him in the name of the Lord, that if that was his faith, to go on his bed in the wagon, and he should get better every day until he recovered, which was literally fulfilled."

* Joseph Smith, however, was the commander-in-chief. The following occurs in the "Addenda" to the manuscript History: "We organized the camp. I was acknowledged commander-in-chief and Lyman Wight general."

their lands in Jackson county, and leave them there to defend themselves.*

On June 9th Governor Dunklin wrote to W. W. Phelps and others: mailed at—

CITY OF JEFFERSON, June 9, 1834.

Herewith you have a second order for the delivery of your arms now in the possession of the militia of Jackson county. Colonel Lucas has resigned his command, he informs me. If Lieut.-Colonel Pitcher should be arrested before you receive this, you will please hold up the order until I am informed who may be appointed to the command of the regiment.

Respectfully,
(Signed) DANIEL DUNKLIN.

The foregoing letter enclosed the following order:

CITY OF JEFFERSON, June 4, 1834.

Thomas Pitcher, Lieut.-Colonel commandant of the Thirty-third Regiment.

SIR—On the 2nd day of last May I issued an order to Colonel Lucas to deliver the fifty-two guns and one pistol, which you received from the Mormons on the 4th day of November last, and reported to him on the 3rd day of the succeeding December—to W. W. Phelps, Edward Partridge, John Corrill, John Whitmer, and A. S. Gilbert, or their order. On the 24th ultimo, Colonel Lucas wrote and informed me that he had resigned his commission and left the county of Jackson. You, as commandant of said regiment, are therefore commanded to collect the said arms, if they are not already in your possession, and deliver them to the aforesaid gentlemen or their order.

Respectfully,
DANIEL DUNKLIN, Commander-in-Chief.

The day following Judge Ryland wrote the following:

RICHMOND, June 10, 1834.

Mr. A. S. Gilbert:

SIR—Deeply impressed with a desire to do all in my power to settle or allay the disturbances between the Mormons and the citizens of Jackson county, I have concluded that it might have some tendency to effectuate this object by having the Mormons called together at Liberty next Monday, and there explain to them my notions and views of their present situation, and of the circumstances attendant. I therefore request you, sir, to use all your influence with your brethren, to

* This paragraph is a note in the "Addenda" of manuscript History.

get them to meet me next Monday in Liberty. I much fear and dread the consequences that are yet to ensue, unless I should succeed in my wishes to restore peace. It is the duty of all good men to use all proper and laudable means to establish peace. I expect a deputation of some of the most respectable citizens of Jackson county will meet me on Monday next at Liberty. I call upon you, in the name of humanity, therefore, to leave no efforts untried to collect your brethren at Liberty as requested. Should my efforts to make peace fail of success, there can be no wrong, sir, in the attempt, and I shall enjoy the consolation of having done my duty as a man, as well as a Christian.

I hope, sir, you will duly appreciate the motive which prompts me to address this letter to you, and will aid me with all your influence with your brethren in the prosecution of an object so much to be desired by all good men and citizens.

Yours very respectfully,

JOHN F. RYLAND.

Departure of Camp from Salt River.

June 12.—We left Salt River and traveled about fourteen miles. The inhabitants of Salt River manifested a great respect for us, and many of them accompanied us some distance on our journey. I instructed the camp in the morning that if a gun was fired it would be considered an alarm; but in the course of the day, while I was a little ahead, I shot a squirrel for Brother Foster, when several of the brethren came running up to see what was the matter. I told them Brother Foster was sick; "I want you to pray for him." *

Reproof of Williams and Orton.

Friday 13.—Elder Kimball's horses, through the negligence of the guards, got loose and went back ten miles with others. He pursued them and returned with them to camp. Frederick G. Williams and Roger Orton received a very severe chastisement for neglect of orders in not taking care of the teams when in charge of the guard. The reproof given to Roger Orton was more particularly for suffering Elder Kimball to go back after the horses, and he was one of my life guards, and it belonged to Orton to see that the team

* This paragraph is from notes in the "Addenda" of the manuscript History.

was attended to. But as the team was Kimball's, and he had taken the care of it all through, Orton still threw the care on him. The Silver Grey company, numbering fourteen, were attached to my mess, making it twenty-eight in number.*

Saturday 14.—Brother Joseph Hancock and another of the brethren were chased a considerable portion of the day by four suspicious fellows on horseback, armed with guns, whom they eluded by traveling in the brush and thickets where horsemen could not ride. It was late when they returned to the camp.*

Enemies Eluded.

At night we encamped in an unsafe and unpleasant situation in a ravine, the only place we could get water for some miles. The country was a wild and uncultivated region.

In answer to Judge Ryland, the Elders wrote as follows:

NEAR LIBERTY, June 14, 1834.

Hon. J. F. Ryland:

DEAR SIR—Your communication of the 9th instant from Richmond was duly received, and at a public meeting of our society this day its contents were made known. Our brethren unanimously tender their thanks for the laudable disposition manifested on your part to effect peace between our society and the inhabitants of Jackson county; and as many as conveniently can will be present on Monday next. Entertaining some fears that your honor, in your zeal for peace, might unwarily recommend a sale of our lands in Jackson county, we have thought it expedient to give you reasonable notice, that no such proposition could possibly be acceded to by our society.

We have not heard that it was the intention of your honor to urge any such measure, but our enemies in Jackson county have long been trying to effect this object. In a letter from the governor to us, he says: "I have been requested to advise the Mormons to sell out and move away; but believing that it would have no good effect, I have withheld my advice." We give this quotation from the governor's letter to disprove the statement made in the *Upper Missouri Enquirer* of last Wednesday, and conclude by adding that "home is home," and that we

* Paragraph is from notes in the "Addenda" of the manuscript History.

want possession of our homes—from which we have been wickedly expelled—and those rights which belong to us as native free-born citizens of the United States.

Very respectfully, your friends and servants,

JOHN CORRILL, Chairman.
A. S. GILBERT, Secretary.

The foregoing was enclosed in the following letter to their lawyers:

GENTLEMEN—Will you be so good as to read the enclosed, then seal and hand it to the judge? We have given him an early hint, fearing that he might be induced by the solicitations of our enemies to propose a sale of our lands, which you well know would be like selling our children into slavery; and the urging of such a measure would avail nothing unless to produce an excitement against us in this county. As requested last Thursday, we hope you will be present on Monday.*

Your friends and servants,

JOHN CORRILL,
A. S. GILBERT.

To Messrs. Doniphan and Atchison.

* The same day, June 14, Elder John Corrill wrote to the editor of the *Evening and Morning Star*, giving an account of affairs in Jackson county; and as his communication gives a description of things in Jackson county not found elsewhere, I quote so much of the letter as was published in the *Star*, vol. ii. pp. 333, 334:

"The leaders of the mob are yet striving to keep up the same spirit of opposition, by instilling falsehoods into the minds of the people. They tell them that the 'Mormons' are coming upon them, *mob like*, to kill their women and children. They raised an alarm a few days ago which set the whole county of Jackson in an uproar—men riding in different directions and proclaiming, 'the Mormons are coming—they are now crossing the river—they are coming to kill, destroy,' etc. Some women and children left their houses, and fled to the woods and elsewhere, while the men, two hundred or three hundred, gathered together to oppose the 'Mormons,' as they supposed, in their return. They repaired to the different ferries on the river, to guard them, and I have been credibly informed that they have since continued to guard the river at the different crossing places from one end of Jackson county to the other. And for fear that we would return and enjoy our dwellings again, they set fire to and burned them down, and then raised the report that the 'Mormons' went over and burnt their houses, and I am informed that they have burnt them all, except a very few which are occupied by other families; and I have been told that they have destroyed our fences and other property that remained. What was the cause of this great alarm among them, I know not; for we are at home attending to our own business, and had not thought of returning at that time. Neither have we any thoughts of ever returning in the night time, or in the mob like manner which they represent to the people; for as we design to be governed in all cases by the laws of the land, we shall therefore return under the protection of the governor, as he has promised us. We therefore have no need to return and take them on surprise, as they falsely represent to the people; for we mean only to act on the principles of self-defense in all cases. But they state falsehoods to the people, for the purpose, I suppose, of keeping their strength good to oppose our return, which, I understand, they are determined to do, even to the shedding of blood; and it is said by the mob, that the whole county is combined together. They are arming themselves, and they have distributed our guns among them. But it is easy to be seen, that fear and consternation prevail among them; some of their leaders have already cleared out. Colonel S.D.Lucas has taken his goods and gone down the river; both the Chiles [Henry and Joel F.] have lately gone to the south on a long visit. Lawyer Hicks says, if no compromise is made he shall seek a location somewhere else; and I have been told that L.Franklin is going away soon; some other families, I have heard, are leaving through fear. As nearly as I can learn, the rumber that is determined to stand and oppose our return, even unto bloodshed, is about one hundred and fifty, or two hundred, in that county, though it is said that many from other counties will come to their assistance.

"They are trying to excite the people of this county [Clay] to drive us from here, and for this purpose, it is said, they are circulating a paper, and have got some signers; but the authorities of this county do not countenance them in this thing, and I think they cannot succeed; but it is said they are lurking about and seeking a chance to do private injury, but the brethren are on the lookout, and are preparing themselves with arms for self-defense, and I think if we firmly continue and persevere, according to the laws of the land, that we shall be enabled shortly to overcome the mob and obtain our rights.

"Yours, etc.,

"JOHN CORRILL."

CHAPTER VII.

ZION'S CAMP IN MISSOURI—EFFORTS AT ARBITRATION—THE WORD OF THE LORD.

*Sunday, June 15.**—Traveled twelve miles. While on the way Orson Hyde and Parley P. Pratt returned to us from Jefferson City, and reported that Governor Dunklin refused to fulfill his promise to reinstate the brethren on their lands in Jackson county on the ground of impracticability.†

Governor Dunklin refuses to Reinstate the Saints on their lands.

* This paragraph is a note in the "Addenda" of the Ms. Church History, page 13, Book A.

† This refusal of Governor Dunklin to reinstate the Saints on their lands in Jackson county must have been a severe blow to the hopes of Zion's Camp and the Saints scattered in Clay county. From the time of their expulsion from Jackson county the governor repeatedly said that the exiles had a right to be reinstated upon their lands, and had promised that he would call out the militia of the State to reinstate them whenever they were ready and willing to return. In his communication to Messrs. W. W. Phelps, Morley, *et al.*, under date of Feb. 4, 1834 (see Ch. Hist. Vol. I, p. 476) he said in answer to their petition to be reinstated: "One of your requests needs no evidence to support the right to have it granted; it is that your people be put in possession of their homes, from which they had been expelled. But what may be the duty of the Executive after that, will depend upon contingencies." Even a few days before his interview with Messrs. Hyde and Pratt, in his letter to Colonel J. Thornton, under date of June 6th, he had said: "A more clear and indisputable right does not exist, than that of the Mormon people, who were expelled from their homes in Jackson county, to return and live on their lands; and if they cannot be persuaded as a matter of policy to give up that right, or to qualify it, my course, as the chief, executive officer of the state, is a plain one. The constitution of the United States declares, that the citizens of each state shall be entitled to all privileges and immunities of citizens in the several states. Then we cannot interdict any people, who have a political franchise in the United States, from immigrating to this state, nor from choosing what part of the state they will settle in, provided they do not trespass on the property or rights of others." (See p. 85.)

In the face of this and other utterances the position now assumed by Governor Dunklin was a manifestation of weakness truly lamentable.

We crossed the Chariton river at its mouth and encamped on the west bank. Bishop Partridge came into the camp from Clay county. We received much information from him concerning the hostile feelings and prejudices that existed against us in Missouri in all quarters, but it gave us great satisfaction to receive intelligence from him of the union and good feeling that prevailed among the brethren. We were in perils and threatened all the while, we were much troubled to get provisions, and had to live principally on corn meal, and were glad to get that. Here Dean Gould was baptized by Lyman Wight.

Arrival of Bishop Partridge in Camp.

*Monday, June 16.**—Traveled to Grand river, ferried over it, and encamped on its bank. The ferryman intended charging seventeen dollars; the brethren said they would not pay it, but would sooner make a raft and ferry themselves over. He then agreed to take them over for twelve dollars which offer we accepted. This morning was excessively hot, no air stirring, and traveling in the thick woods, a thunder shower coming on, the brethren caught all the water they could on the brims of their hats, and not catching enough to satisfy their thirst, they drank out of the horse tracks.

The Camp Crosses Grand River.

Martin Harris having boasted to the brethren that he could handle snakes with perfect safety, while fooling with a black snake with his bare feet, he received a bite on his left foot. The fact was communicated to me, and I took occasion to reprove him, and exhort the brethren never to trifle with the promises of God. I told them it was presumption for any one to provoke a serpent to bite him, but if a man of God was accidentally bitten by a poisonous serpent, he might have faith, or his brethren might have faith for him, so that the Lord would hear his prayer and he might be healed; but when a man designedly provokes a serpent to bite him,

Martin Harris Trifles with a Promise of God.

* This and the paragraph following concerning Martin Harris, are notes in "Addenda" of the Ms. History. p. 14, Book A.

the principle is the same as when a man drinks deadly poison knowing it to be such. In that case no man has any claim on the promises of God to be healed.*

Important Meeting at Liberty Court House.

On this day, June 16th, the citizens of Clay county, to the number of eight hundred or a thousand, among whom were the brethren, assembled at the court house in Liberty, in accordance with the request of Judge Ryland, expressed in his letter of the 10th instant, a deputation from Jackson county also attended the meeting and presented the following:—

Propositions of the people of Jackson county to the Mormons.

The undersigned committee, being fully authorized by the people of Jackson county, hereby propose to the Mormons, that they will buy all the land that the said Mormons own in the county of Jackson, and also all the improvements which the said Mormons had on any of the public lands in said county of Jackson, as they existed before the first disturbance between the people of Jackson and the Mormons, and for such as they have made since. They further propose that the value of said land and improvements shall be ascertained by three disinterested arbitrators, to be chosen and agreed to by both parties. They further propose, that should the parties disagree in the choice of arbitrators, then ———————is to choose them. They further propose, that twelve of the Mormons shall be permitted to go along with the arbitrators to show them their land and improvements while valuing the same, and such others of the Mormons as the arbitrators shall wish to do so, to give them information; and the people of Jackson hereby guarantee their entire safety while doing so. They further propose, that when the arbitrators report the value of the land and improvements, as aforesaid, the people of Jackson will pay the valuation, with one hundred per cent, added thereon, to the Mormons, within thirty days thereafter. They further propose, that the Mormons are not to make any effort, ever

* How beautifully in harmony is this counsel with the words of the Savior to Lucifer when the latter took him up and stood him on a pinnacle of the temple, and said: "If thou be the Son of God, cast thyself down: for it is written, He shall give his angels charge concerning thee: and in their hands they shall bear thee up, lest at any time thou dash thy foot against a stone. Jesus said unto him, It is written again, Thou shalt not tempt the Lord thy God" (Matt. iv: 6, 7.] Moreover, in this last dispensation when the promise of the spiritual gifts was renewed to the Saints, including the promise that "the poison of a serpent should not have power to harm them"—yet, saith the Lord, "a commandment I give unto them, that they shall not boast themselves of these things, neither speak them before the world, for these things are given unto you for your profit and for salvation" (Doc. & Cov., Sec. lxxxiv: 73).

after, to settle, either collectively or individually, within the limits of Jackson county. The Mormons are to enter into bonds to insure the conveyance of their land in Jackson county, according to the above terms, when the payment shall be made; and the committee will enter into a like bond, with such security as may be deemed sufficient for the payment of the money, according to the above proposition. While the arbitrators are investigating and deciding upon the matters referred to them, the Mormons are not to attempt to enter Jackson county, or to settle there, except such as are by the foregoing propositions permitted to go there.

They further propose that the people of Jackson will sell all their lands and improvements on public lands, in Jackson county, to the Mormons, the valuation to be obtained in the same manner, the same per cent in addition to be paid, and the time the money is to be paid is the same as the above set forth in our propositions to buy; the Mormons to give good security for the payment of the money, and the undersigned will give security that the land will be conveyed to the Mormons. They further propose, that all parties are to remain as they are till the payment is made, at which time the people of Jackson will give possession.

(Signed) SAMUEL C. OWENS,
RICHARD FRISTOE,
THOS. HAYTON, SEN.,
THOS. CAMPBELL,
JOHN DAVIS,
THOS. JEFFREYS,
SMALLWOOD NOLAND,
ROBERT RICKMAN,
ABRAHAM MCCLELLAN,
S. V. NOLAND.

Stirring Incidents at the Liberty Meeting.

On presentation of the foregoing, Samuel C. Owens made a flaming war-speech, and General Doniphan replied on the side of peace.

The Rev. Mr. Riley, a Baptist priest, made a hot speech against the "Mormons," and said, "The Mormons have lived long enough in Clay county; and they must either clear out, or be cleared out."

Mr. Turnham, the moderator of the meeting, answered in a masterly manner; saying, "Let us be republicans; let us honor our country, and not disgrace it like Jackson county. For God's sake don't disfranchise or drive away the Mormons. They are better citizens than many of the old inhabitants."

General Doniphan exclaimed, "That's a fact, and as the Mormons have armed themselves, if they don't fight they are cowards. I love to hear that they have brethren coming to their assistance. Greater love can no man show, than he who lays down his life for his brethren."

At this critical instant, the cocking of pistols, and the unsheathing of other implements of death, denoted desperation. One moved "adjournment," another cried "go on," and in the midst of this awful crisis a person bawled in at the door, "a man stabbed!" The mass instantly rushed out to the spot, in hopes, as some said, that "a Mormon had got killed," but as good luck would have it, only one Missourian had dirked another, (one Calbert, a blacksmith, had stabbed one Males, who had previously whipped one Mormon nearly to death. and boasted of having whipped many more). The wound was dangerous, but the incident appeared providential as it seemed as though the occurrence was necessary to break up the meeting without further bloodshed, and give the Saints a chance to consult what would be the most advisable thing to do in such a critical instant. They immediately penned the following answer to the propositions from Jackson county, presented by Mr. Owens *et al.*

Answer of the Mormons to the Proposition of the People of Jackson County.

GENTLEMEN—Your propositions for an adjustment of the difficulties between the citizens of Jackson county and the Mormons, is before us; and as explained to you in the court house this day, we are not authorized to say to you that our brethren will submit to your proposals; but we agree to spread general notice, and call a meeting of our people, the present week, and lay before you an answer as soon as Saturday or Monday next. We can say for ourselves, and in behalf of our brethren, that peace is what we desire and what we are disposed to cultivate with all men; and to effect peace, we feel disposed to use all our influence, as far as it will be required at our hands as free-born citizens of these United States; and as fears have been expressed, that we design hostilities against the inhabitants of Jackson county, we hereby pledge ourselves to them, and to the hospitable citizens of Clay county, that we will not, and neither have we designed, as a people, to commence hostilities against the aforesaid citizens of Jackson county, or any other people.

Our answer shall be handed to Judge Turnham, the chairman of the meeting, even earlier than the time before stated, if possible.

(Signed) W. W. PHELPS,
WM. E. M'LELLIN,
A. S. GILBERT,
JOHN CORRILL,
ISAAC MORLEY.

N.B.—As we are informed that large numbers of our people are on their way removing to Jackson county, we agree to use our influence immediately to prevent said company from entering into Jackson county, until you shall receive an answer to the propositions aforenamed.

Reflections on the Jackson County Proposition.

It may be thought, at first view, that the mob committee made a fair proposition to the Saints, in offering to buy their lands at a price fixed by disinterested arbitrators and one hundred per centum added thereto, payment to be made in thirty days, and offering theirs on the same terms; but when it is understood that the mob held possession of a much larger quantity of land than the Saints, and that they only offered thirty days for the payment, having previously robbed the Saints of nearly everything, it will be readily seen that they were only making a sham to cover their previous unlawful conduct.

A Mobber's Threat and God's Vengeance.

The tempest of an immediate conflict seemed to be checked, and the Jackson mob to the number of about fifteen, with Samuel C. Owens and James Campbell at their head, started for Independence, Jackson county, to raise an army sufficient to meet me, before I could get into Clay county. Campbell swore, as he adjusted his pistols in his holsters, "The eagles and turkey buzzards shall eat my flesh if I do not fix Joe Smith and his army so that their skins will not hold shucks, before two days are passed." They went to the ferry and undertook to cross the Missouri river after dusk, and the angel of God saw fit to sink the boat about the middle of the river, and seven out of twelve that attempted to cross, were drowned. Thus, suddenly and justly, went they to their own place. Campbell was among the missing. He floated down the river some four or five miles, and lodged upon a pile of drift wood, where the eagles, buzzards, ravens, crows, and wild animals ate his flesh from his bones, to fulfill his own words, and left him a horrible example of God's vengeance. He was discovered about three weeks after by one Mr.Purtle. Owens saved his life only, after floating four miles down the stream, where he lodged upon an island, "swam off naked about day light, borrowed a mantle to hide his shame, and slipped home rather shy of the vengeance of God."

Incidents of Insubordination in the Camp.

Tuesday, *June 17.*—At noon we crossed the Wakenda; it being high, we had to be ferried over. We were informed here that a party of men were gathered together on the Missouri river with the intention of attacking us that night. The prairie ahead of us was twenty-three miles long without any timber or palatable, healthy water. Some of the brethren wished to stop near the timber, and were about making arrangements to pitch their tents. We had but little provisions. I proposed to get some wood and water to carry with us, and go on into the prairie eight or ten miles. My brother Hyrum said he knew, in the name of the Lord, that it was best to go on to the prairie; and as he was my elder brother, I thought best to heed his counsel, though some were murmuring in the camp. We accordingly started. When Lyman Wight crossed the river he disapproved of our moving on to the prairie, upon which Sylvester Smith placed himself in the road, turned back all that he could by saying, "Are you following your general, or some other man?" and twenty stayed behind with Lyman Wight. We drove about eight miles on the prairie and encamped out of sight of timber.

The sun apparently went down, and rose again next morning in the grass. Our company had filled a couple of empty powder kegs with water; it tasted so bad we could not drink it, and all the water that we had was out of a slough filled with red living animals, and was putrid. About eleven o'clock Lyman Wight arrived with the company that had remained with him. I called them together and reproved them for tarrying behind, and not obeying my counsel, and told Lyman Wight never to do so again. He promised that he would stand by me forever, and never forsake me again, let the consequence be what it would; but Sylvester Smith manifested very refractory feelings.*

The Prophet's Illness.

Wednesday, June 18.—As Hyrum Stratton and his companion were taking up their blankets this morning, they discovered two prairie rattle-snakes quietly sleeping under them, which they carefully carried out of the camp. This day my health was so poor I left the affairs of the camp to the management of General Wight. Having no provisions, we traveled seventeen miles before breakfast, and I rode in Elder Kimball's wagon. We crossed a slough half a mile wide through which most of the brethren were obliged to wade waist deep in mud and water. General Lyman Wight, who had traveled from Kirtland without a stocking on his foot, carried Brother Joseph Young through on his back. Our breakfast consisted entirely of corn meal mush, or hasty pudding. We had not meal enough in our company to make the mush of the consistence of good starch.

The Prophet's Anxiety for the Safety of the Camp.

After our ten o'clock breakfast we passed on to within one mile of Richmond. We encamped in a very small prairie surrounded by a thicket of hazel brush. When I arrived where the camp had pitched their tents, and viewed our unsafe

* This paragraph is a note in the "Addenda" of the Ms. History, Book A, p. 14.

location, considering the danger of an attack from our enemies, I almost forgot my sickness, went some distance in the brush, bowed down and prayed my Heavenly Father to suffer no evil to come upon us, but keep us safe through the night. I obtained an assurance that we should be safe until morning, notwithstanding about fifty of the Jackson county mob crossed the Lexington Ferry that evening for the purpose of joining the Ray county mob and of making an attack upon us. All was quiet in the camp through the night. While the brethren were making their bed in Captain Brigham Young's tent, one of them discovered a very musical rattlesnake which they were about to kill. Captain Young told them not to hurt him but carry him out of the tent, whereupon Brother Carpenter took him in his hands, carried him beyond all danger, and left him to enjoy his liberty, telling him not to return.*

Threats of the Mob.

Thursday, June 19.—At daybreak, feeling that we were in a very unsafe situation, I counseled the camp to move forward without delay, and continued a lively march for about nine miles, when we stopped for breakfast. While passing through Richmond, Brother Luke Johnson observed a black woman in a gentleman's garden near the road. She beckoned to him and said, "Come here, Massa." She was evidently much agitated in her feelings. He went up to the fence, and she said to him, "There is a company of men lying in wait here, who are calculating to kill you this morning as you pass through." We halted for breakfast on an eminence near a farm house. The owner furnished us with a large quantity of milk, which gave a great relish to our bacon and corn dodger, which our commissary had procured that morning. When we asked the price of his milk he replied: "He is a mean man that will sell milk; I could have let you have more, if I had known you had been coming."

* This paragraph and the one preceding it, under same date, are notes in the "Addenda" of the Ms. History, Book A, p. 14.

He further said: "You have many enemies about here, and you may meet with some trouble; and it is a damned shame that every man can't come up and enjoy his religion, and everything else without being molested." It was near noon when we finished our breakfast, and we passed on in fine spirits, determined to go through and meet the brethren in Clay county. We traveled but a short distance when one wagon broke down, and the wheels ran off from others; and there seemed to be many things to hinder our progress, although we strove with all diligence to speed our way forward. This night we camped on an elevated piece of land between Little Fishing and Big Fishing rivers, which streams were formed by seven small streams or branches.*

As we halted and were making preparations for the night, five men armed with guns rode into our camp, and told us we should "see hell before morning;" and their accompanying oaths partook of all the malice of demons. They told us that sixty men were coming from Richmond, Ray county, and seventy more from Clay county, to join the Jackson county mob, who had sworn our utter destruction.

During this day, the Jackson county mob, to the number of about two hundred, made arrangements to cross the Missouri river, above the mouth of Fishing river, at Williams' ferry, into Clay county, and be ready to meet the Richmond mob near Fishing river ford, for our utter destruction; but after the first scow load of about forty had been set over the river, the scow in returning was met by a squall, and had great difficulty in reaching the Jackson side by dark.

A Timely Storm.

When these five men were in our camp, swearing vengeance, the wind, thunder, and rising cloud indicated an approaching storm, and in a short time after they left the rain and hail began to

* This paragraph is a note in the "Addenda" of the Ms. History, Book A, p. 15.

fall.* The storm was tremendous; wind and rain, hail and thunder met them in great wrath, and soon softened their direful courage, and frustrated all their designs to "kill Joe Smith and his army." Instead of continuing a cannonading which they commenced when the sun was about one hour high, they crawled under wagons, into hollow trees, and filled one old shanty, till the storm was over, when their ammunition was soaked, and the forty in Clay county were extremely anxious in the morning to return to Jackson, having experienced the pitiless pelting of the storm all night; and as soon as arrangements could be made, this "forlorn hope" took the "back track" for Independence, to join the main body of the mob, fully satisfied, as were those survivors of the company who were drowned, that when Jehovah fights they would rather be absent. The gratification is too terrible.

Very little hail fell in our camp, but from half a mile to a mile around, the stones or lumps of ice cut down the crops of corn and vegetation generally, even cutting limbs from trees, while the trees, themselves were twisted into withes by the wind. The lightning flashed incessantly.

* Wilford Woodruff says that when the five men entered the camp there was not a cloud to be seen in the whole heavens, but as the men left the camp there was a small cloud like a black spot appeared in the north west, and it began to unroll itself like a scroll, and in a few minutes the whole heavens were covered with a pall as black as ink. This indicated a sudden storm which soon broke upon us with wind, rain, thunder and lightning and hail. Our beds were soon afloat and our tents blown down over our heads. We all fled into a Baptist meetinghouse. As the Prophet Joseph came in shaking the water from his hat and clothing he said, "Boys, there is some meaning to this. God is in this storm." We sang praises to God, and lay all night on benches under cover while our enemies were in the pelting storm. It was reported that the mob cavalry who fled into the schoolhouse had to hold their horses by the bridles between the logs, but when the heavy hail storm struck them they broke away, skinning the fingers of those who were holding them. The horses fled before the storm and were not found for several days. It was reported that the captain of the company in the schoolhouse said it was a strange thing that they could do nothing against the Mormons but what there must be some hail storm or some other thing to hinder their doing anything, but they did not feel disposed to acknowledge that God was fighting our battles. (Wilford Woodruff's note in Ms. History of the Church, Book A p. 332.)

which caused it to be so light in our camp through the night, that we could discern the most minute objects; and the roaring of the thunder was tremendous. The earth trembled and quaked, the rain fell in torrents, and, united, it seemed as if the mandate of vengeance had gone forth from the God of battles, to protect His servants from the destruction of their enemies, for the hail fell on them and not on us, and we suffered no harm, except the blowing down of some of our tents, and getting wet; while our enemies had holes made in their hats, and otherwise received damage, even the breaking of their rifle stocks, and the fleeing of their horses through fear and pain.

Many of my little band sheltered in an old meetinghouse through this night, and in the morning the water in Big Fishing river was about forty feet deep, where, the previous evening, it was no more than to our ankles, and our enemies swore that the water rose thirty feet in thirty minutes in the Little Fishing river. They reported that one of their men was killed by lightning, and that another had his hand torn off by his horse drawing his hand between the logs of a corn crib while he was holding him on the inside. They declared that if that was the way God fought for the Mormons, they might as well go about their business.

Care of Arms During the Storms.

Friday 20.—This morning I counseled the brethren to discharge all their firearms, when it was found we had nearly six hundred shots, very few of which missed fire, which shows how very careful the brethren had been in taking care of their arms during the storm.

The Visit of Col. Sconce to the Camp.

We drove five miles on to the prairie where we could procure food for ourselves and horses, and defend ourselves from the rage of our enemies. While camped here on Saturday the 21st, Colonel Sconce, with two other leading men from Ray county, came to see us, desiring to know what our intentions were; "for," said he, "I see that there is an Almighty power that protects this people, for I started from Richmond, Ray county, with a company of armed men, having a fixed dertermination to destroy you, but was kept back by the storm, and was not able to reach you." When he entered our camp he was seized with such a trembling that he was obliged to sit down to compose himself; and when he had made known the object of their visit, I arose, and, addressing them, gave a relation of the sufferings of the Saints in Jackson county, and also our persecutions generally, and what we had suffered by our enemies for our religion; and that we had come one thousand miles to assist our brethren, to bring them clothing, etc., and to reinstate them upon their own lands; and that we had no intention to molest or injure any people, but only to administer to the wants of our afflicted friends; and that the evil reports circulated about us were false, and got up by our enemies to procure our destruction. When I had closed a lenghty speech, the spirit of which melted them into compassion, they arose and offered me their hands, and said they would use their influence to allay the excitement which everywhere prevailed against us; and they wept when they heard of our afflictions and persecutions, and learned that our intentions were good. Accordingly they went forth among the people, and made unwearied exertions to allay the excitement.*

Cholera Breaks out in the Camp.

Brother Ezra Thayre and Joseph Hancock are sick with the cholera. Thomas Heyes was taken today. Previous to crossing the Mississippi river I had called the camp together† and told them that in consequence of the disobedience of some who had been unwilling to listen to my words, but had rebelled, God

* It is said of the prophet Joseph that if he could but once get the attention even of his bitterest enemies his native eloquence, inspired by the truth and the pathos of his people's sufferings, usually overwhelmed them; and in no instance was his triumph more marked than in the one just related.

† The prediction will be found at p. 80.

had decreed that sickness should come upon the camp, and if they did not repent and humble themselves before God they should die like sheep with the rot; that I was sorry, but could not help it.* The scourge must come; repentance and humility may mitigate the chastisement, but cannot altogether avert it. But there were some who would not give heed to my words.

The brethren in Clay county wrote the committee of the Jackson mob the same day as follows:—

CLAY COUNTY, June 21, 1834.

GENTLEMEN—Your propositions of Monday last have been generally made known to our people, and we are instructed to inform you that they cannot be acceded to.

Honorable propositions to you are now making on our part, and we think we shall be enabled to deliver the same to you the early part of next week. We are happy to have it in our power to give you assurances that our brethren here, together with those who have arrived from the east, are unanimously disposed to make every sacrifice for an honorable adjustment of our differences, that could be required of free citizens of the United States.

Negotiations at the camp are now going on between some gentlemen of this county, and our brethren, which are calculated to allay the great excitement in your county. We are informed that the citizens of Jackson entertain fears that our people intend to invade their territory in a hostile manner. We assure you that their fears are groundless, such is not and never was our intention.

(Signed) W. W. PHELPS,
A. S. GILBERT,
W. E. M'LELLIN,
JOHN CORRILL,
ISAAC MORLEY.

To S. C. Owens, and others of the Jackson committee.

June 22.—Brother Lyman Smith received a wound from the accidental discharge of a horse-pistol, from which he recovered in about three days.

* When he [the Prophet Joseph] spoke these things it pierced me like a dart, having a testimony that so it would be. (Extracts from H. C. Kimball's journal, *Times and Seasons*, Vol. vi, p. 804.)

Visit of Clay County Sheriff to the Camp.

Cornelius Gillium, the sheriff of Clay county, came to our camp to hold consultation with us. I marched my company into a grove near by, and formed in a circle, with Gillium in the centre. Gillium commenced by saying that he had heard that Joseph Smith was in the camp, and if so he would like to see him. I arose and replied, "I am the man." This was the first time that I had been discovered or made known to my enemies since I left Kirtland. Gillium then gave us instruction concerning the manners, customs, and dispositions of the people, and what course we ought to pursue to secure their favor and protection, making certain inquiries, to which we replied, which were afterwards published, and will appear under date of publication.

I received the following:—

*Revelation given on Fishing River, Missouri, June 22, 1834.**

1. Verily I say unto you who have assembled yourselves together that you may learn my will concerning the redemption of mine afflicted people:

2. Behold, I say unto you, were it not for the transgressions of my people, speaking concerning the Church and not individuals, they might have been redeemed even now;

3. But behold, they have not learned to be obedient to the things which I required at their hands, but are full of all manner of evil, and do not impart of their substance as becometh saints, to the poor and afflicted among them,

4. And are not united according to the union required by the law of the celestial kingdom;

5. And Zion cannot be built up unless it is by the principles of the law of the celestial kingdom, otherwise I cannot receive her unto myself;

6. And my people must needs be chastened until they learn obedience, if it must needs be, by the things which they suffer.

7. I speak not concerning those who are appointed to lead my people, who are the first Elders of my Church, for they are not all under this condemnation;

* Doctrine and Covenants, sec. cv.

8. But I speak concerning my churches abroad—there are many who will say, Where is their God? Behold, He will deliver them in time of trouble, otherwise we will not go up unto Zion, and will keep our moneys.

9. Therefore, in consequence of the transgressions of my people, it is expedient in me that mine Elders should wait for a little season for the redemption of Zion,

10. That they themselves may be prepared, and that my people may be taught more perfectly, and have experience, and know more perfectly concerning their duty, and the things which I require at their hands.

11. And this cannot be brought to pass until mine Elders are endowed with power from on high;

12. For behold, I have pepared a great endowment and blessing to be poured out upon them, inasmuch as they are faithful and continue in humility before me;

13. Therefore it is expedient in me that mine Elders should wait for a little season, for the redemption of Zion;

14. For behold, I do not require at their hands to fight the battles of Zion; for, as I said in a former commandment, even so will I fulfill—I will fight your battles.

15. Behold the destroyer I have sent forth to destroy and lay waste mine enemies: and not many years hence they shall not be left to pollute mine heritage, and to blaspheme my name upon the lands which I have consecrated for the gathering together of my saints.

16. Behold, I have commanded my servant Baurak Ale (Joseph Smith, Jun.,) to say unto the strength of my house, my warriors, my young men, and middle-aged, to gather together for the redemption of my people, and throw down the towers of mine enemies and scatter their watchmen;

17. But the strength of mine house have not hearkened unto my words;

18. But inasmuch as there are those who have hearkened unto my words, I have prepared a blessing and an endowment for them, if they continue faithful.

19. I have heard their prayers, and will accept their offering; and it is expedient in me, that they should be brought thus far for a trial of their faith.

20. And now, verily I say unto you, a commandment I give unto you, that as many as have come hither, that can stay in the region round about, let them stay;

21. And those that cannot stay, who have families in the east, let them tarry for a little season, inasmuch as my servant Joseph shall appoint unto them;

22. For I will counsel him concerning this matter, and all things whatsoever he shall appoint unto them shall be fulfilled.

23. And let all my people who dwell in the regions round about be very faithful, and prayerful, and humble before me, and reveal not the things which I have revealed unto them, until it is wisdom in me that they should be revealed.

24. Talk not of judgments, neither boast of faith, nor of mighty works, but carefully gather together, as much in one region as can be consistently with the feelings of the people;

25. And behold, I will give unto you favor and grace in their eyes, that you may rest in peace and safety, while you are saying unto the people, Execute judgment and justice for us according to law, and redress us of our wrongs.

26. Now, behold, I say unto you, my friends, in this way you may find favor in the eyes of the people, until the army of Israel becomes very great;

27. And I will soften the hearts of the people, as I did the heart of Pharaoh, from time to time, until my servant Baurak Ale (Joseph Smith, Jun.,) and Baneemy (mine Elders), whom I have appointed, shall have time to gather up the strength of my house,

28. And to have sent wise men, to fulfill that which I have commanded concerning the purchasing of all the lands in Jackson county that can be purchased, and in the adjoining counties round about;

29. For it is my will that these lands should be purchased, and after they are purchased that my Saints should possess them according to the laws of consecration which I have given;

30. And after these lands are purchased, I will hold the armies of Israel guiltless in taking possession of their own lands, which they have previously purchased with their moneys, and of throwing down the towers of mine enemies that may be upon them, and scattering their watchmen, and avenging me of mine enemies unto the third and fourth generation of them that hate me.

31. But firstly, let my army become very great, and let it be sanctified before me, that it may become fair as the sun, and clear as the moon, and that her banners may be terrible unto all nations;

32. That the kingdoms of this world may be constrained to acknowledge, that the kingdom of Zion is in very deed the kingdom of our God and His Christ; therefore let us become subject unto her laws.

33. Verily I say unto you, it is expedient in me that the first Elders of my Church should receive their endowment from on high in my house, which I have commanded to be built unto my name in the land of Kirtland;

34. And let those commandments which I have given concerning Zion and her law be executed and fulfilled, after her redemption;

35. There has been a day of calling, but the time has come for a day of choosing, and let those be chosen that are worthy;

36. And it shall be manifest unto my servant, by the voice of the Spirit, those that are chosen, and they shall be sanctified;

37. And inasmuch as they follow the counsel which they receive, they shall have power after many days to accomplish all things pertaining to Zion.

38. And again I say unto you, sue for peace not only to the people that have smitten you, but also to all people;

39. And lift up an ensign of peace, and make a proclamation of peace unto the ends of the earth;

40. And make proposals for peace unto those who have smitten you, according to the voice of the Spirit which is in you, and all things shall work together for your good;

41. Therefore be faithful, and behold, and lo, I am with you even unto the end. Even so. Amen.

CHAPTER VIII.

ZION'S CAMP DISBANDED—AN APPEAL.

June 23.—We resumed our march for Liberty, Clay county, taking a circuitous course around the heads of Fishing river, to avoid the deep water. When within five or six miles of Liberty, we were met by General Atchison and other gentlemen, who desired us not to go to Liberty because the feelings of the people were so much enraged against us. At their solicitation we turned our course, wheeling to the left, and crossing the prairie and woodland, came to Brother Algernon Sidney Gilbert's residence, and encamped on the bank of Rush creek, in Brother Burket's* field.

A council of High Priests assembled in fulfillment of the revelation given the day previous, and the following individuals were called and chosen, as they were made manifest unto me by the voice of the Spirit and revelation, to receive their endowments:

Edward Partridge was called and chosen, to go to Kirtland and receive his endowment with power from on high, and also, to stand in his office as Bishop to purchase lands in the state of Missouri.

William W. Phelps was called and chosen, and it was appointed unto him to receive his endowment with power from on high, and help to carry on the printing establishment in Kirtland, until Zion is redeemed.

Isaac Morley and John Corrill were called and chosen, and it was appointed unto them to receive their endowment with power from on high in Kirtland, and assist in

* Also given "Burghart's" in some of the Church records.

gathering up the strength of the Lord's house, and preach the Gospel.

John Whitmer and David Whitmer were called and chosen, and appointed to receive their endowment in Kirtland, and continue in their offices.

Algernon Sidney Gilbert was called and chosen, and appointed to receive his endowment in Kirtland, and to assist in gathering up the strength of the Lord's house, and to proclaim the everlasting Gospel until Zion is redeemed. But he said he "could not do it."

Peter Whitmer, Jun., Simeon Carter, Newel Knight, Parley P. Pratt, Christian Whitmer and Solomon Hancock were called and chosen; and it was appointed unto them to receive their endowment in Kirtland, with power from on high; to assist in gathering up the strength of the Lord's house; and to preach the everlasting Gospel.

Thomas B. Marsh was called and chosen; and it was appointed unto him to receive his endowment in Kirtland, his office to be made known hereafter.

Lyman Wight was called and chosen; and it was appointed unto him to receive his endowment in Kirtland, with power from on high; and return to Zion and have his office appointed unto him hereafter.

The same day the Elders made the following reply, before referred to, to "Samuel C. Owens and others, committee" of the Jackson county mob:

We, the undersigned committee, having full power and authority to settle and adjust all matters and differences existing between our people or society and the inhabitants of Jackson county, upon honorable and constitutional principles; therefore, if the said inhabitants of Jackson county will not let us return to our lands in peace, we are willing to propose first: that twelve disinterested men, six to be chosen by our people, and six by the inhabitants of Jackson county; and these twelve men shall say what the lands of those men are worth in that county, who cannot consent to live with us, and they shall receive their money for the same in one year from the time the treaty is made, and none of our people shall enter the county to reside till the money is paid. The said twelve men shall have power also to say what the damages shall be for the injuries we have sustained in the destruction of property and in being driven from our possessions, which amount of damages shall be deducted from the amount for their lands. Our object is peace, and an early answer will be expected.

(Signed) W. W. PHELPS,
EDWARD PARTRIDGE,
ISAAC MORLEY,
JOHN CORRILL,
JOHN WHITMER,
A. S. GILBERT.

June 24.—This night the cholera burst forth among us, and about midnight it was manifested in its most virulent form. Our ears were saluted with cries and moanings, and lamentations on every hand; even those on guard fell to the earth with their guns in their hands, so sudden and powerful was the attack of this terrible disease. At the commencement, I attempted to lay on hands for their recovery, but I quickly learned by painful experience, that when the great Jehovah decrees destruction upon any people, and makes known His determination, man must not attempt to stay His hand. The moment I attempted to rebuke the disease I was attacked, and had I not desisted in my attempt to save the life of a brother, I would have sacrificed my own. The disease seized upon me like the talons of a hawk, and I said to the brethren: "If my work were done, you would have to put me in the ground without a coffin."

Cholera in the Camp.

Early on the morning of the 25th, the camp was separated into small bands, and dispersed among the brethren living in the vicinity; and I wrote and sent by express, to "Messrs. Thornton, Doniphan, and Atchison," as follows:

Zion's Camp Disbanded.

RUSH CREEK, CLAY COUNTY, June 25, 1834.

GENTLEMEN—Our company of men advanced yesterday from their encampment beyond Fishing river to Rush Creek, where their tents are again pitched. But feeling disposed to adopt every pacific measure, without jeopardizing our lives, to quiet the prejudices and fears of some part of the citizens of this county, we have concluded that our company shall be immediately dispersed, and continue so till every effort for an adjustment of differences between us and the people of Jackson has been made on our part, that would in any wise be required of us by disinterested men of republican principles.

I am respectfully, your obedient servant,

JOSEPH SMITH, JUN.

N.B.—You are now corresponding with the governor, (as I am informed); will you do us the favor to acquaint him of our efforts for a compromise. This information we want conveyed to the governor, inasmuch as his ears are stuffed with reports from Jackson, of our hostile intentions. J. S.

Fear of the Cholera.

I left Rush Creek the same day in company with David Whitmer and two other brethren, for the western part of Clay county. While traveling, we called at the house of a Mr. Moss for a drink of water. The woman of the house shouted from the door, that they had "no water for Mormons," that they were "afraid of the cholera," etc., at the same time throwing out her arms as if defending herself from the cholera in the form of a personage. We turned and departed, according to the commandment, and before a week had passed, the cholera entered that house, and that woman and three others of the family were dead.

First Victims of the Cholera.

When the cholera made its appearance, Elder John S. Carter was the first man who stepped forward to rebuke it, and upon this, was instantly seized, and became the first victim in the camp. He died about six o'clock in the afternoon; and Seth Hitchcock died in about thirty minutes afterwards. Erastus Rudd died about the same moment, although a half a mile distant. He was buried by Jesse Smith, George A. Smith and two or three others, and while burying him, Jesse Smith was attacked with the cholera. As it was impossible to obtain coffins, the brethren rolled the corpses in blankets, carried them on a horse-sled about half a mile, buried them on the bank of a small stream, which empties into Rush creek, all of which was accomplished by dark. When they had returned from the burial, the brethren unitedly covenanted and prayed, hoping the disease would be stayed; but in vain, for while thus covenanting, Eber Wilcox died; and while some were digging the grave, others stood sentry with their fire arms, watching their enemies.*

* Of these sorrowful scenes Elder Heber C. Kimball in his journal, gives the following description, which ought not to be lost to the reader of Church History:

"When the Cholera first broke out in the camp, Brother John S. Carter was the first who went forth to rebuke it, but [he] himself, was immedaitely seized by it, and as before stated, was the first who was slain. In about thirty minutes after his death, Seth Hitchcock followed him; and it appeared as though we must sink under the destroyer with them. We were not able to obtain boards to make coffins, [for those who died], but were under the necessity of rolling them up in their blankets, and burying them in that manner. So we placed them on a sled, which was drawn by a horse about half a mile, where we buried them in a little bluff by the side of a small stream that emptied into Rush creek. This we accomplished by dark, and returned. Our hopes were that no more would die, but while we were uniting in a covenant to pray once more with uplifted hands to God, we looked at our beloved brother, Elder Wilcox, and he was gasping his last. At this scene my feelings were beyond expression. Those only who witnessed it, can realize anything of the nature of our sufferings, and I felt to weep, and pray to the Lord that He would spare my life that I might behold my dear family again. I felt to covenant with my brethren, and I felt in my heart never to commit another sin while I lived. We felt to sit and weep over our brethren, and so great was our sorrow that we could have washed them with our tears, to realize that they had traveled one thousand miles through so much fatigue to lay down their lives for our brethren—and who hath greater love than he who is willing to lay down his life for his brethren? This increased our love to them. About 12 o'clock at night we placed Brother Wilcox on a small sled, which we drew to the place of interment, with one hand hold of the rope, and in the other we bore our firelocks for our defense. While one or two were digging the grave, the rest stood with their arms to defend them. This was our situation, the enemies around us, and the destroyer in our midst. Soon after we returned another brother was taken away from our little band; thus it continued until five out of ten [attacked] were taken away. It was truly affecting to see the love manifested among the brethren for one another, during the affliction; Brother Joseph, seeing the sufferings of his brethren, stepped forward to rebuke the destroyer, but was immediately seized with the disease himself; and I assisted him a short distance from the place, when it was with difficulty he could walk. All that kept our enemies from us was the fear of the destroyer which the Lord so sent among us. After burying these five brethren, or about this time, I was seized by the hand of the destroyer, as I had gone in the woods to pray. I was instantly struck blind, and saw no way whereby I could free myself from the disease, only to exert myself by jumping and thrashing myself about, until my sight returned to me, and my blood began to circulate in my veins. I started and ran some distance, and by this means, through the help of God, I was enabled to extricate myself from the grasp of death. This circumstance took place in a piece of woods just behind Brother Sidney Gilbert's house. * * * * * * Two other brethren died at Brother Gilbert's house about this same time. One of these was a cousin to Brother Joseph Smith, the Prophet."

June 26.—The Elders wrote Governor Dunklin as follows:

SIR—A company of our people, exceeding two hundred men, arrived in this county the 19th instant, and encamped about twelve miles from Liberty, where they were met by several gentlemen from this [Clay] and Ray county,who went by request of the people, to ascertain the motives and designs of our people in approaching this county; and as the deputation was composed of gentlemen who appeared to possess humane feelings and republican principles, our people were rejoiced at the opportunity of an interchange of feelings, and an open and frank avowal of all their views and intentions in emigrating to this country with their arms. A full explanation having been given in a public address by our brother, Joseph Smith, Jun., which produced great satisfaction, the same in substance was afterwards reduced to writing, and handed to the aforesaid gentlemen, that it might be made public. The shedding of blood is, and ever has been, foreign and revolting to our feelings; for this reason, we have patiently endured the grossest indignities that freemen of this republic have ever been called to suffer; and we still continue to bear with heart-rending feelings, a deprivation of our rights. We commenced negotiations with the inhabitants of Jackson county for a compromise, wherein proposals on our part have been made which have been acknowledged by every disinterested man to be highly honorable and liberal. An answer to our proposition has not yet been received from the people of Jackson county.

If we fail in this attempt, we intend to make another effort and go all lenghts that could be required by human or divine law. As our proposals and correspondence with the inhabitants of Jackson county will doubtless hereafter be published, we think it unnecessary to detail the same in this communication. Our right to our soil in Jackson county we shall for ever claim, but to obtain peaceful possession we are willing to make great sacrifices. To allay excitement in this county, the aforesaid company of emigrants have dispersed to await the final end of all negotiations that can be made with the said county of Jackson.

Within the last week, one of our men being near the ferry, was seized by some Jackson citizens, while in this county, threatened with death if be made resistance, and carried over the river, a prisoner, to Independence, where he was put under guard one day, and after hearing many threats, was liberated. The houses of several of our brethren in this county have been forcibly entered by some of the inhabitants of Jackson, and a number of guns and small arms taken therefrom. We have been informed and have no doubt of the fact that where the men were absent from their houses, loaded guns were presented to the females, and their lives threatened if they made resistance.

Your second order of the restoration of our arms, was received last mail; we have not yet done anything with it. Hoping that the influence of the inhabitants of Jackson county will materially lessen in the surrounding counties, and the people become more tranquil, we think it wisdom to defer petitioning for a guard, while there exists a hope of a compromise.

We believe that the President would render us assistance in obtaining possession of our lands, if aided by the executive of this state in a petition, and thereby put an end to serious evils that are growing out of the Jackson county outrage.

In a letter from your Excellency, of April 20th, we had a word on the subject of petitioning. We should be pleased to hear further, and would here observe that no communication from the executive, giving his opinion or advice, will be made public, if requested not to do so.

We are respectfully, and with great regard,

Your obedient servants,

A. S. GILBERT,
W. W. PHELPS,
JOHN CORRILL.

Death of Algernon Sidney Gilbert.

The drafting and signing of the above, was the last public act of the keeper of the Lord's storehouse Algernon Sidney Gilbert, for he was attacked with the cholera the same day, and died about the 29th. He had been called to preach the Gospel, but had been known to say that he "would rather die than go forth to preach the Gospel to the Gentiles." *

* Heber C. Kimball remarks: "The Lord took him at his word." Extracts from Kimball's journal, *Times and Seasons*, Vol. vi, p. 839.

The remarks in the body of the history, and this expression from Elder Kimball's journal are liable to create a misunderstanding concerning Brother Algernon Sidney Gilbert, than whom the Lord has had few more devoted servants in this dispensation. The place and date of his birth cannot now be ascertained. His father's family resided in Huntington, Connecticut. Besides himself, there was a younger brother who joined the Church, but he died of cholera in St. Louis, Missouri, the same year as his elder brother. Elder Gilbert for some years was a successful merchant in Painesville, Ohio; and subsequently, with Newel K. Whitney, he founded the successful mercantile firm of Gilbert and Whitney in Kirtland, Ohio. at which place the Gospel found him in the year 1830. Later, he was called to go to Missouri, and was appointed keeper of the Lord's storehouse, and upon him also devolved the responsibility of purchasing lands for the Saints. He was devoted to the interest of the Saints and the Church. In the persecutions which came upon the people in Jackson county

The following is from the chairman of the committee of the Jackson county mob, to our lawyer:

INDEPENDENCE, MISSOURI, JUNE 26, 1834.

Mr. Amos Reese:

DEAR SIR—Since my return from Liberty, I have been busily engaged in conversing with the most influential men of our county, endeavoring to find out, if possible, what kind of a compromise will suit with the Mormons on their part. The people here, *en masse*, I find out, will do nothing like acceding to their last proposition. We will have a meeting if possible, on Monday next, at which time the proposals of the Mormons will be answered. In the meantime, I would be glad that they, the Mormons, would cast an eye back of Clinton, and see if that is not a country calculated for them.

Yours respectfully,
S. C. OWENS.

List of the Victims of Cholera.

The cholera continued its ravages for about four days, when a remedy for the purging, vomiting, and cramping, was discovered; viz., dipping the persons afflicted in cold water, or pouring it upon them, and giving them whisky thickened with flour to the consistency of starch. Whisky was the only kind of spirits that could be procured at this place. About

he sacrificed all his goods, and was among the six who offered their own lives for the lives of their friends in the Jackson county trouble. As to his refusing to accept the appointment to go and preach the Gospel to the Gentiles, that refusal did not arise from any lack of faith in the truth of God's great work, but from a native diffidence and a lack of confidence in his own ability to preach. He was a man of rare good sense, conservative and of sound judgment. All of which appears in the many communications drawn up in Missouri by him during the troublous times through which the Church passed in those days. Much of the correspondence between the Missouri brethren and Governor Dunklin was the work of Elder Gilbert, and it bears witness to the truth of what is here said of him. Nor did he entirely refuse to bear witness of the truth of the Gospel to others. In a communication to the *Messenger and Advocate* from Huntington, Connecticut, under date of September 24, 1834, his aged father, Eli Gilbert, describing the visit of his son to that place some two years previous, says: "He continued with us about two weeks, and in that time was pressed by his friends and acquaintances to meet them and others, and inform them concerning the people, and the Book of Mormon. This he cheerfully did, as often as his low state of health would permit; and although threatened and abused by some of our pious persecutors, yet [he was] not much hurt nor interrupted. When a meeting was held, a goodly number were brought to serious inquiry concerning these things, and several would gladly have received baptism, as they afterwards told me. And, thank God, some retain that desire and determination yet."

sixty-eight of the Saints suffered from this disease, of which number fourteen died, viz.: John S. Carter, Eber Wilcox, Seth Hitchcock, Erastus Rudd, Algernon Sidney Gilbert, Alfred Fisk, Edward Ives, Noah Johnson, Jesse B. Lawson, Robert McCord, Elial Strong, Jesse J. Smith, Warren Ingalls and Betsy Parrish.

Among the most active of those who were engaged in taking care of the sick at the camp, burying the dead, etc., were John D. Parker, John Tanner, Nathan Tanner, Joseph B. Noble, Brigham Young, Joseph Young, Heber C. Kimball, Luke S. Johnson and Eleazar Miller.

I sent Hiram Page with instructions to bring Jesse J. Smith and George A. Smith to me at all hazards to the west part of the county, having had intimations that they were sick. He found that Jesse had been severely racked with the cholera all day, George A. Smith had taken care of him for upwards of thirty hours. Dr. Frederick G. Williams decided that the cholera had left him, and he would recover if not moved. On the morning of the 28th, George A. Smith was attacked and was immediately mounted on a hard-riding horse, rode fifteen miles, and came to me.

The last days of June I spent with my old Jackson county friends, in the western part of Clay county.

On the 1st of July Jesse J. Smith died. I crossed the Missouri river, in company with a few friends, into Jackson county, to set my feet once more on the "goodly land;" and on the 2nd I went down near Liberty, and visited the brethren. A considerable number of the Camp met me at Lyman Wight's. I told them if they would humble themselves before the Lord and covenant to keep His commandments and obey my counsel, the plague should be stayed from that hour, and there should not be another case of the cholera among them. The brethren covenanted to that effect with uplifted hands, and the plague was stayed.

The Prophet in the Goodly Land.

This day the *Enquirer* published the correspodence between the sheriff, Cornelius Gillium, and Zion's Camp, of the 22nd of June, as follows:

Gillium's Communication.

Being a citizen of Clay county, and knowing that there is considerable excitement amongst the people thereof, and also knowing that different reports are arriving almost hourly; and being requested by the Hon. J. F. Ryland to meet the Mormons under arms, and obtain from the leaders thereof the correctness of the various reports in circulation, the true intent and meaning of their present movements, and their views generally regarding the difficulties existing between them and Jackson county,—I did, in company with other gentlemen, call upon the said leaders of the Mormons, at their camp in Clay county; and now give to the people of Clay county their written statement, containing the substance of what passed between us.

(Signed) CORNELIUS GILLIUM.

"*Propositions of the Mormons.*

"Being called upon by the above-named gentlemen, at our camp in Clay county, to ascertain from the leaders of our men our intentions, views, and designs, in approaching this county in the manner we have, we therefore the more cheerfully comply with their request, because we are called upon by gentlemen of good feelings, and who are disposed for peace and an amicable adjustment of the difficulties existing between us and the people of Jackson county. The reports of our intentions are various, and have gone abroad in a light calculated to arouse the feelings of almost every man. For instance, one report is, that we intend to demolish the printing office in Liberty; another report is, that we intend crossing the Missouri river on Sunday next, and falling upon women and children, and slaying them; another is, that our men were employed to perform this expedition, being taken from manufacturing establishments in the east, that had closed business; also that we carried a flag, bearing 'Peace' on one side, and 'War or Blood' on the other; and various other reports too numerous to mention, all of which a plain declaration of our intentions, from under our own hands will show are not correct.

"In the first place, it is not our intention to commit hostilities against any man, or set of men; it is not our intention to injure any man's person or property, except in defending ourselves. Our flag has been exhibited to the above gentlemen, who will be able to describe it. Our men were not taken from any manufacturing establishment. It is our intention to go back upon our lands in Jackson county, by order of the executive of the state, if possible. We have brought our arms with us for the purpose of self defense, as it is well known to almost every man of the State, that we have every reason to put ourselves in an attitude of defense, considering the abuse we have suffered in Jackson county. We are anxious for a settlement of the difficulties existing between us, upon honorable and constitutional principles.

"We are willing for twelve disinterested men, six to be chosen by each party, and these men shall say what the possessions of those men are worth who cannot live with us in the county; and they shall have their money in one year; and none of the Mormons shall enter that county to reside until the money is paid. The damages that we have sustained in consequence of being driven away, shall also be left to the above twelve men; or they may all live in the county, if they choose, and we will never molest them if they let us alone, and permit us to enjoy our rights. We want to live in peace with all men; and equal rights is all we ask. We wish to become permanent citizens of this State; and wish to bear our proportion in support of the government, and to be protected by its laws. If the above propositions are complied with, we are willing to give security on our part; and we shall want the same of the people of Jackson county for the performance of this agreement. We do not wish to settle down in a body, except where we can purchase the land with money; for to take possession by conquest or the shedding of blood is entirely foreign to our feelings. The shedding of blood we shall not be guilty of, until all just and honorable means among men prove insufficient to restore peace."

(Signed) JOSEPH SMITH, JUN.,
FREDERICK G. WILLIAMS.
LYMAN WIGHT,
ROGER ORTON,
ORSON HYDE,
JOHN S. CARTER.

June 21st.

To John Lincoln, John Sconce, George R. Morehead, Jas. H. Long, James Collins.

Organization of the High Council in Missouri.

On the third of July, the High Priests of Zion assembled in the yard of Col. Arthurs, where Lyman Wight lived, in Clay county, and I proceeded to organize a High Council, agreeable to the revelation and pattern given at Kirtland, for the purpose of settling important business that might come before them, which could not be settled by the Bishop and his council. David Whitmer was elected president, and William W. Phelps and John Whitmer assistant presidents. The following High Priests, viz.: Christian Whitmer, Newel Knight, Lyman Wight, Calvin Beebe, Wm. E. M'Lellin, Solomon Hancock, Thomas B. Marsh, Simeon Carter, Parley P. Pratt, Orson Pratt, John Murdock, and Levi Jackman, were appointed councilors; and the Council adjourned to Monday. Frederick G. Williams was clerk of the meeting.

Members of the Camp Discharged.

I authorized General Lyman Wight to give a discharge to every man of the Camp who had proved himself faithful, certifying that fact and giving him leave to return home.*

* This formal order to discharge every man of Zion's Camp and release him to return home may be considered as the termination of Zion's Camp expedition for the redemption of Zion. Had Governor Dunklin possessed the courage to enforce the law of the State; had he called out the militia of Missouri to reinstate the exiles in their homes as at one time he expressed a willingness to do, the history of Zion's Camp might have had a different ending; for the exiles reinstated in their lands, and reinforced by the two hundred brethren who constituted Zion's Camp, might have been able to have maintained their inheritances on that land; but Governor Dunklin when the crisis came, lacked the necessary courage to fulfill his promise, and without the moral assistance which the reinstatement of the Saints upon their lands by the military forces of the State would give, the exiles and Zion's Camp were powerless. Perhaps also another view is admissible. Had the members of Zion's Camp been more faithful, less contentious, more united; had the Saints in the eastern branches had more faith—faith to send up to Zion more men and more money with which to strengthen the hands of the Saints on the land of Zion—the history of Zion's Camp might have been different: for with a larger force they would doubtless have been able to hold their lands against the mob, independent of the action of the State authorities. But thus it is: what men and great movements might attain to is often defeated, sometimes by the actions of enemies, sometimes by the lack of devotion and faith and energy on the part of those into whose hands great enterprises are committed. While God's general purposes will never ultimately be defeated by man, still upon each side of the general purposes of God a margin somewhat wide seems to have been left in which those both for and against those purposes may write what history they please—one that will meet with the approval of God, or one that will meet only with condemnation—herein is the agency of man. But in the exercise of that agency God's purposes will not be thwarted, for man's agency will not extend so far as that; if it did, it would interfere with God's agency and decrees. The order above, I again remark, closed the history of this first march of Zion's Camp; and the redemption of Zion has been left to other hands, and to other times. But that its redemption will come no one doubts who believes in the firm decrees of God.

Instructions to the High Council.

From this time I continued to give instruction to the members of the High Council, Elders, those who had traveled in the Camp with me, and such others as desired information, until the 7th, when the Council assembled according to adjournment at the house of Elder Lyman Wight; present, fifteen High Priests, eight Elders, four Priests, eight Teachers, three Deacons, and several members. After singing and prayer, I gave the Council such instructions in relation to their high calling, as would enable them to proceed to minister in their office agreeable to the pattern heretofore given; read the revelation on the subject; and told them that if I should now be taken away, I had accomplished the great work the Lord had laid before me, and that which I had desired of the Lord; and that I had done my duty in organizing the High Council, through which council the will of the Lord might be known on all important occasions, in the building up of Zion, and establishing truth in the earth.

It was voted that those who were appointed on the 3rd, should be confirmed in their appointments.

The Missouri Presidency and High Council.

I then ordained David Whitmer, president, and W. W. Phelps and John Whitmer, assistants; and the twelve councilors. The twelve councilors then proceeded to cast lots, to know who should speak first, and the order of speaking, which resulted as follows, viz.:

Simeon Carter,	1	Parley P. Pratt,	2
Wm. E. M'Lellin,	3	Calvin Beebe,	4
Levi Jackman,	5	Solomon Hancock,	6
Christian Whitmer,	7	Newel Knight,	8
Orson Pratt,	9	Lyman Wight,	10
Thomas B. Marsh,	11	John Murdock.	12

Blessings.

Father Peter Whitmer came forward and blessed his three sons, David, John and Christian Whitmer, in the name of the Lord. Also Father Knight blessed his son Newel.

Bishop Partridge stated to the Council that a greater responsibility rested upon him than before their organization, as it was not his privilege to counsel with any of them, except the president, and his own counselors; and desired their prayers that he might be enabled to act in righteousness.

I next presented the case of William W. Phelps to the Council, to have their decision whether or not he should take his family to Kirtland, and if so, when he should start; as it had been deemed necessary for him to assist in the printing establishment. It was moved and carried that four of the councilors speak on the subject, two on each side, viz., Simeon Carter and Wm. E. M'Lellin, for William W. Phelps; and Parley P. Pratt and Calvin Beebe, for the church. After hearing the pleas, the president decided that it was the duty of William W. Phelps to go to Kirtland to assist in printing, and that his family remain in the region where they are, and that he have an honorable discharge from his station in Zion for a season, (as soon as he can accomplish his business). Signed by the president and clerk.

Sundry Items Determined by the High Council.

It was then proposed by W. W. Phelps, that David Whitmer, the president of the church in Zion, should go to Kirtland, and assist in promoting the cause of Christ, as being one of the three witnesses. This case was argued by Levi Jackman and Christian Whitmer in behalf of David Whitmer; and by Solomon Hancock and Newel Knight for the church; after which it was decided, as before, that Brother David Whitmer go to the East and assist in the great work of the gathering, and be his own judge as to leaving his family or taking them with him.

It was also decided that John Whitmer and Wm. E. M'Lellin go east, as soon as convenient.

The High Priests, Elders, Priests, Teachers, Deacons and members present, then covenanted with hands uplifted to heaven, that they would uphold Brother David

Whitmer, as president in Zion, in my absence; and John Whitmer and William W. Phelps, as assistant presidents or counselors; and myself as First President of the Church; and to uphold one another by faith and prayer.

Previous to entering into this covenant, and in pursuance of the revelation to the Saints to sue for and proclaim peace to the ends of the earth, the following appeal was written, and sanctioned by the High Council and First Presidency of the Church, at the foregoing sitting.

President Whitmer closed the Council by prayer.

FREDERICK G. WILLIAMS, Clerk.

*An Appeal.**

Whereas the Church of Christ, recently styled the Church of the Latter-day Saints, contumeliously called "Mormons," or "Mormonites," has suffered many privations, afflictions, persecutions and losses on account of the religious belief and faith of its members, which belief and faith are founded in the revealed Word of God, as recorded in the Holy Bible, or the Book of Mormon, the Revelations and Commandments of our Savior Jesus Christ; and whereas the said Church, through revelation, commenced removing to the western boundaries of the State of Missouri, where lands were purchased of the government, and where it was calculated to purchase of those who were unwilling to reside with the Church, as a society, all lands that could be bought, for the purpose of building up a holy city unto God, a New Jerusalem, a place which we were desirous to call Zion, a place of refuge from the scourges and plagues that are so often mentioned in the Bible by the

* The editor of the *Evening and Morning Star* (Oliver Cowdery) thus concluded an editorial which preceded this "Appeal," published in the number of the *Star* above quoted:

"With the most of individuals and societies who have been traduced, and their characters and designs misrepresented, their last appeal has been made to the world or nation at large; here they rested their claim, and here the matter, with them, was brought to a final close. If the community approved their course, they triumphed; if not, it sank forever; but this is not the last resort of a people whose interest is in heaven, and whose hope is built upon the everlasting word of Omnipotence. When earthly courts and tribunals fail, and when the voice of the people is not given in their favor, and a place on earth is denied them, and their helpless, innocent posterity, their last great refuge is Jehovah; and if, like the ancients, they are driven from the face of society, that even a lodging place is forbidden them, they can wander in obscurity, not 'accepting deliverance,' till their change comes, and they 'obtain a better resurrection.'" *Evening and Morning Star*, vol. ii, p. 361.

prophets and apostles, which should be poured out upon the earth in the last days; and whereas the inhabitants of Jackson county, Missouri, have leagued and combined themselves against said Church, and have driven the Saints from their lands, and have taken their arms from them, and burned down many of their houses without any provocation; and whereas, we have petitioned the governor of this state and the President of the United States for the redress of wrongs—the law being put to defiance in Jackson county—and for the redemption of rights, that we might be legally repossessed of our lands and property; and whereas the said inhabitants of Jackson county have not only bound themselves to keep us out of that county, but have armed themselves *cap a pie*, and even with cannon for war; and whereas, our people residing in Upper Missouri, have recently armed themselves for military duty and self-defense, seeing their arms taken from them by the inhabitants of Jackson county, were purposely kept from them; and whereas, a number of the members of the Church in the East have emigrated to this region of country, to settle and join with their brethren, with arms to answer the military law, which has created some excitement among the inhabitants of the upper counties of this state; whereupon, to show that our object was only the peaceable possession of our rights and property, and to purchase more lands in the regions round about, we met a committee from Jackson county for compromise, and our emigrating brethren met some gentlemen from Clay and other counties, to satisfy them that their motives were good, and their object peace, which they did; and whereas, the propositions of the Jackson county committee could not be accepted on our part, because they proposed to "buy or sell," and to sell our land would amount to a denial of our faith, as that land is the place where the Zion of God shall stand, according to our faith and belief in the revelations of God, and upon which Israel will be gathered, according to the prophets; and, secondly, the propositions were unfair, notwithstanding they offered double price for our lands, in thirty days, or to sell theirs at the same rate, for this plain reason, that the whole large county of Jackson would be as thirty to one, or nearly so, in comparison with the matter in question, and in supposition, for one thousand dollars, two thousand dollars to our people was asking for three hundred thousand dollars, the exorbitant sum of six hundred thousand dollars, taking the land, rich and poor, within thirty days, with the reproachable, vicious, un-American, and unconstitutional proviso, that the committee on our part bind themselves "that no Mormons should ever settle in Jackson county;" and whereas, our committee proposed to the said Jackson committee (if they would not grant us our rights otherwise), that our people would buy the land of those who were unwilling to live among our people, in that county, and pay them in one year, they allowing the damage we have sustained in the loss of a printing office, apparatus and book-work, houses, property, etc., to come out of the purchase-money, but no answer returned; and whereas, to show our honest intentions, and awaken the friends of virtue, humanity, and equal rights, it becomes our duty to lay our case before the world, to be weighed in the balances of public opinion.

Now, therefore, as citizens of the United States and leading Elders in the Church of the Latter-day Saints, residing in the State of Missouri, in behalf of the Church, we, the undersigned, do make this solemn appeal to the people and constitutional authorities of this nation, and to the ends of the earth, for peace; that we may have the privilege of enjoying our religious rights and immunities, and worship God according to the dictates of our own consciences, as guaranteed to every citizen by the constitution of the national and state governments; that although the laws have been broken, and are defied in Jackson county, we may be enabled to regain and enjoy our rights and property, agreeable to law, in this boasted land of liberty.

Since the disgraceful combination of the inhabitants of Jackson county has set the law at defiance, and put all hope of criminal prosecution against them, in that vicinage, beyond the reach of judge or jury, and left us but a distant expectation of civil remuneration for the great amount of damages we have sustained, necessity compels us to complain to the world; and if our case and calamity are not sufficient to excite the commiseration of the humane, and open the hearts of the generous, and fire the spirits of the patriotic, then has sympathy lost herself in the wilderness, and justice fled from power; then has the dignity of the ermine shrunk at the gigantic front of a mob, and the sacred mantle of freedom been caught up to heaven, where the weary are at rest and the wicked cannot come.

To be obedient to the commandments of our Lord and Savior, some of the leaders of the Church commenced purchasing lands in the western boundaries of the State of Missouri, according to the revelation of God, for the city of Zion; in doing which, no law was evaded no rights infringed, and no principle of religion neglected; but the laudable foundation of a glorious work was begun, for the salvation of mankind in the last days, agreeable to our faith, and according to the promises in the sacred Scriptures of God. We verily believed—knowing that the national and state constitutions, and the statute laws of the land, and the commandments of the Lord allowed all men to worship as they please—that we should be protected, not only by the laws of a free republic, but by every republican throughout the realms of freedom.

The holy prophets have declared, that "it shall come to pass in the last days that the mountain of the Lord's house shall be established in the top of the mountains, and shall be exalted above the hills; and all nations shall flow unto it. And many people shall go and say, Come ye, and let us go up to the mountain of the Lord, to the house of the God of Jacob; and He will teach us of His ways, and we will walk in His paths: for out of Zion shall go forth the law, and the word of the Lord from Jerusalem." And again, it was said by Joel, seemingly to strengthen the faith of the Latter-day Saints in the above, "that whosoever shall call on the name of the Lord shall be delivered: for in Mount Zion and in Jerusalem shall be deliverance, as the Lord hath said, and in the remnant whom the Lord shall call." The Book of Mormon, which we hold equally sacred with the Bible, says, "that a New Jerusalem should be built up upon this land, unto the remnant of the seed of Joseph, for the which things there has been a type."

In fact, all the prophets, from Moses to John the Revelator, have spoken concerning these things. And in all good faith, by direct revelation from the Lord, as in days of old, we commenced the glorious work, that a holy city, a new Jerusalem, even Zion, might be built up, and a temple reared in this generation, whereunto, as saith the Lord, all nations shall be invited. First, the rich and the learned, the wise and the noble, were to be invited; and after that cometh the day of His power. But the inhabitants of Jackson county arrayed themselves against us because of our faith and belief, and destroyed our printing establishment to prevent the spread of the work, and drove men, women and children from their lands, houses, and homes, to perish in the approaching winter. Every blast carried the wailing of women and the shrieks of children across the widespread prairie, sufficiently horrible to draw tears from the savage or melt a heart of stone.

Now, that the world may know that our faith in the work and word of the Lord is firm and unshaken; and to show all nations, kindreds, tongues and people, that our object is good, for the good of all, we come before the great family of mankind for peace, and ask their hospitality and assistance for our comfort, and the preservation of our persons and property, and solicit their charity for the great cause of God. We are well aware that many slanderous reports and ridiculous stories are in circulation against our religion and society; but as wise men will hear both sides and then judge, we sincerely hope and trust that the still, small voice of truth will be heard, and our great revelations read and candidly compared with the prophecies of the Bible, that the great cause of our Redeemer may be supported by a liberal share of public opinion, as well as by the unseen power of God.

It will be seen by reference to the Book of Commandments, page 135, that the Lord has said to the Church—and we mean to live by His words: "Let no man break the laws of the land, for he that keepeth the laws of God hath no need to break the laws of the land."* Therefore, as the people of God, we come before the world, and claim protection by law of the common officers of justice in every neighborhood where our people may be. We claim the same at the hands of the governors of the several states, and of the President of the United States, and of the friends of humanity and justice in every clime and country on the globe.

By the desperate acts of the inhabitants of Jackson county, many hundreds of American citizens are deprived of their lands and rights. It is reported, we mean to regain our possessions, and even Jackson county, "by the shedding of blood;" but if any man will take the pains to read the 153rd page of the Book of Commandments he will find it there said:

"Wherefore the land of Zion shall not be obtained but by purchase or by blood; otherwise there is none inheritance for you. And if by purchase, behold you are blessed; and if by blood, *as you are forbidden to shed blood*, lo, your enemies are upon you, and you shall be scourged from city to city, and from synagogue to synagogue, and but few shall stand to receive an inheritance."†

So we declare that we have ever meant and now mean to purchase the land of our inheritance of the government, like all honest men, and of those who would rather sell their farms than live in our society; and, as thousand have done before us, we solicit the aid of the children of men, and of government, to help us to obtain our rights in Jackson county, and the land whereon the Zion of God, according to our faith, shall stand in the last days, for the salvation and gathering of Israel.

Let no man be alarmed because our society has commenced gathering to build a city and a house for the Lord, as a refuge from present evils and coming calamities. Our forefathers came to this goodly land of America to shun persecution and enjoy their religious opinions and rights, as they thought proper; and the Lord, after much tribulation, blessed them; and has said that we should continue to importune for redress and redemption by the hands of those who are placed as rulers and are in authority over us, according to the laws and constitution of the people, which he has suffered to be established, and should be maintained for the rights and protection of all flesh, according to just and holy principles; that every man may act in doctrine and in principle pertaining to futurity according to the moral agency which He has given unto him; that every man may be accountable for his own sins in that day of judgment; and for this purpose He has established the

* Doctrine and Covenants, sec. lviii: 21.

† Doctrine and Covenants, sec. lxiii: 29-31.

constitution of this land by the hands of wise men, whom He raised up unto this very purpose, and redeemed the land by the shedding of blood.*

Now we seek peace, and ask our rights, even redress and redemption, at the hands of the rulers of this nation; not only our lands and property in Jackson county, but for free trade with all men, and unmolested emigration to any part of the Union, and for our inherent right to worship God as we please. We ask the restoration of these rights, because they have been taken from us or abridged by the violence and usurpation of the inhabitants of Jackson county. As a people we hold ourselves amenable to the laws of the land; and while the government remains as it is, the right to emigrate from state to state, from territory to territory, from county to county, and from vicinity to vicinity, is open to all men of whatever trade or creed, without hindrance or molestation; and as long as we are justifiable and honest in the eyes of the law, we claim it—whether we remove by single families or in bodies of hundreds—with that of carrying the necessary arms and accoutrements for military duty; and we believe that all honest men, who love their country and their country's glory, and have a wish to see the law magnified and made honorable, will not only help to perpetuate the great legacy of freedom that came unimpaired from the hands of our venerable fathers to us, but they will also protect us from insult and injury, and aid the work of God, that they may reap a reward in the regions of bliss, when all men receive according to their works.

In relation to our distress from the want of our lands in Jackson county, and for the want of property destroyed by fire and waste, rather than do any act contrary to law, we solemnly appeal to the people with whom we tarry, for protection from insult and harm, and for the comforts of life, by labor or otherwise, while we seek peace and satisfaction of our enemies through every possible and honorable means which humanity can dictate, or philanthropy urge, or religion require. We are citizens of this republic, and we ask our rights as republicans, not merely in our restoration to our lands and property in Jackson county, Missouri, but in being considered honest in our faith; honest in our deal, and honest before God, till, by due course of law, we may be proved otherwise; reserving the right of every man's being held amenable to the proper authority for his own crimes and sins.

"Crowns won by blood, by blood must be maintained;" and to avoid blood and strife, and more fully satisfy the world that our object is peace and good will to all mankind, we hereby APPEAL for peace to the ends of the earth and ask the protection of all people. We shall use

* Doctrine and Covenants, sec. ci: 76-80.

every fair means in our power to obtain our rights and immunities without force; setting an example for all true believers that we will not yield our faith and principles for any earthly consideration, whereby a precedent might be established that a majority may crush any religious sect with impunity. If we give up our rights in Jackson county, farewell to society! farewell to religion! farewell to our rights! farewell to property! farewell to life! The fate of our Church now might become the fate of the Methodists next week, the Catholics next month, and the overthrow of all societies next year, leaving nation after nation a wide waste, where reason and friendship once were.

Another, and the great object which we mean to help to accomplish, is the salvation of the souls of men. To bring to pass this glorious work, like many other religious denominations in all ages, we shall license Elders to preach the everlasting Gospel to all nations, according to the great commandment of our Lord and Savior Jesus Christ, as recorded in Matthew: "Go ye therefore, and teach all nations, baptizing them in the name of the Father, and of the Son, and of the Holy Ghost: teaching them to observe all things whatsoever I have commanded you: and, lo, I am with you alway, even unto the end of the world."

Thus we shall send laborers into the Lord's vineyard, to gather the wheat, and prepare the earth against the day when desolations shall be poured out without measure; and as it now is and ever has been considered one of the most honorable and glorious employments of men to carry good tidings to the nations, so we shall expect the clemency of all men, while we go forth, for the last time, to gather Israel for the glory of God, that He may suddenly come to His temple; that all nations may come and worship in His presence, when there shall be none to molest or make afraid, but the earth shall be filled with His knowledge and glory.

We live in an age of fearful imagination; with all the sincerity that common men are endowed with, the Saints have labored without pay, to instruct the United States that the gathering had commenced in the western boundaries of Missouri, to build a holy city, where, as may be seen in the eighteenth chapter of Isaiah, the present should "be brought unto the Lord of Hosts of a people scattered and peeled, and from a people terrible from their beginning hitherto; a nation meted out and trodden under foot, whose land the rivers have spoiled, to the place of the name of the Lord of Hosts, the Mount Zion:" and how few have come forth rejoicing that the hour of redemption was nigh! And some that came have turned away, which may cause thousands to exclaim, amid the general confusion and fright of the times, "Remember Lot's wife."

It would be a work of supererogation to labor to show the truth of the gathering of the children of Israel in these last days; for the prophet told us long ago, that it should "no more be said, The Lord liveth, that brought the children of Israel out of the land of Egypt, but, The Lord liveth, that brought up the children of Israel from the land of the north, and from all the lands whither He had driven them," and so it must be for the honor and glory of God.

The faith and religion of the Latter-day Saints are founded upon the old Scriptures, the Book of Mormon, and direct revelation from God; and while every event that happens around us is evidence of the truth of them, and an indicator that the great and terrible day of the Lord is near, we entreat the philanthropist, the moralist, and the honorable men of all creeds and sects, to read our publications, to examine the Bible, the Book of Mormon, and the Commandments, and listen to the fullness of the Gospel, and judge whether we are entitled to the credit of the world for honest motives and pure principles.

A cloud of bad omen seems to hang over this generation; men start up at the impulse of the moment, and defy and outstrip all law, while the destroyer is also abroad in the earth, wasting flesh without measure, and none can stay his course. In the midst of such portentous times, we feel an anxious desire to prepare, and help others to prepare, for coming events; and we candidly believe that no honest man will put forth his hand to stop the work of the Lord or persecute the Saints. In the name of Jesus Christ, we intreat the people of this nation to pause before they reject the works of the Lord or His servants; these, like all flesh, may be imperfect, but God is pure; hear ye Him.

While we ask peace and protection for the Saints, wherever they may be, we also solicit the charity and benevolence of all the worthy of the earth, to purchase the righteous a holy home, a place of rest, and a land of peace; believing that no man who knows he has a soul will keep back his mite, but cast it in for the benefit of Zion; thus, when time is no longer, he, with all the ransomed of the Lord, may stand in the fullness of joy, and view the grand pillar of heaven, which was built by the faith and charity of the Saints, beginning at Adam, with his motto in the base, "Repent and live," surrounded with a beautiful circle sign, supported by a cross about midway up its lofty column, staring the world in letters of blood, "The Kingdom of Heaven is at hand;" and finished with a plain top towering up in the midst of the celestial world-around which is written by the finger of Jehovah, "Eternal Life is the greatest gift of God."

Although we may fail to show all men the truth of the fullness of the Gospel, yet we hope to be able to convince some that we are neither deluded nor fanatics; but, like other men, have a claim on the world for land and for a living, as good and as great as our venerable fathers had for independence and liberty; that though the world has been made to believe, by false reports and vague stories, that the Saints—called "Mormons"—were meaner than the savages, still God has been our help in time of trouble, and has provided for us in due season, and, to use the language of Pope, He has let the work "spread undivided" and "operate unspent."

For the honor of our beloved country, and the continuation of its free government, we appeal for peace, for an example of forbearance, and the diffusion of the everlasting Gospel; we appeal to the humanity of all nations, and for the glory of God, before whom we must all answer for the deeds done in life, and for the hope of holiness hereafter, we mean to remain faithful to the end, continuing to pray to the Lord to spare us and the people from whatever is evil and not calculated to humble us, and prepare us for His presence and glory; at the same time beseeching Him, in the name of Jesus, to extend His blessings to whom He will, and His mercy to all; till by righteousness, the kingdoms of this world become fair as the sun and clear as the moon.

(Signed) W. W. PHELPS,
DAVID WHITMER,
JOHN WHITMER,
EDWARD PARTRIDGE,
JOHN CORRILL,
ISAAC MORLEY,
PARLEY P. PRATT,
LYMAN WIGHT,
NEWEL KNIGHT,
THOMAS B. MARSH,
SIMEON CERTER,
CALVIN BEEBE.

Missouri, United States, July, 1834.

CHAPTER IX.

RETURN OF THE PROPHET TO KIRTLAND—SUNDRY EVENTS IN MISSOURI.

The Prophet Returns to Kirtland.

On the 8th of July I went to the eastern part of Clay county, and held a meeting in the evening at the house of Thomas B. Marsh. Those present were chiefly High Priests and Elders. On the 9th I started for Kirtland, in company with my brother Hyrum, Frederick G. Williams, William E. M'Lellin and others, in a wagon.

July 10.—Elder Corrill wrote as follows:

Samuel C. Owens, Esq.:

SIR—The last time I saw you in Liberty you said that an answer to our proposals, you thought, would be forwarded soon; but it has not been done. We are anxiously waiting to have a compromise effected, if possible. Respecting our wheat in Jackson county, can it be secured so that we can receive the avails of it, or not, seeing that we are at present prohibited the privilege [of harvesting it]?

JOHN CORRILL.

P. S.—Please hand the following to Colonel Pitcher.

J. C.

LIBERTY, July 10, 1834.

Colonel Thomas Pitcher:

SIR—The following is a true copy of an order from the governor for our arms. Have the goodness to return an answer as soon as possible, that we may know whether we can have the arms upon said order or not; also, when. Send word when we can receive them, and we will appoint an agent to receive and receipt the same. Be assured we do not wish to obtain them from any hostile intentions, but merely because the right of property is ours. If I remember right, there is one gun and a sword more than the order calls for.

JOHN CORRILL.

[Here followed a copy of the Governor's order of May 2, to Colonel Lucas.]*

Assembling of the High Council in Missouri.

On the 12th the High Council of Zion assembled in Clay county, and appointed Edward Partridge, Orson Pratt, Isaac Morley and Zebedee Coltrin to visit the scattered and afflicted brethren in that region, and teach them the ways of truth and holiness, and set them in order according as the Lord shall direct; but it was decided that it was not wisdom for the Elders generally to hold public meetings in that region.

It was also decided that Amasa Lyman assist Lyman Wight in his mission of gathering the strength of the Lord's house, to which labor I had appointed him.

July 31.—The High Council of Zion assembled, and heard the report of Edward Partridge, Orson Pratt, Zebedee Coltrin, and Isaac Morley, concerning the mission appointed them at the previous council.

The Counsel of David Whitmer.

President David Whitmer gave the council some good instructions, to the effect that it was their duty to transact all business in order, and when any case is brought forward for investigation, every member should be attentive and patient to what is passing in all cases, and avoid confusion and contention, which are offensive in the sight of the Lord. He also addressed the Elders, and said it was not pleasing in the sight of the Lord for any man to go forth and preach the Gospel of peace, unless he is qualified to set forth its principles in plainness to those whom he endeavors to instruct; and also he should be informed as to the rules and regulations of the Church of the Latter-day Saints; for just

* Vol. i, p. 491.

as a man is, and as he teaches and acts, so will his followers be, let them be ever so full of notions and whims. He also addressed the congregation, and told them it was not wisdom for the brethren to vote at the approaching election; and the council acquiesced in the instructions of the president.

Proposition of W. W. Phelps.

William W. Phelps proposed to the council to appoint a certain number of Elders to hold public meetings in that section of country [Clay county], as often as should be deemed necessary, to teach the disciples how to escape the indignation of their enemies, and keep in favor with those who were friendly disposed. Simeon Carter, John Corrill, Parley P. Pratt and Orson Pratt were appointed by the unanimous voice of the council and congregation to fill the mission.

Charges Against Samuel Brown.

Elder Nathan West preferred charges against Samuel Brown, High Priest, for teaching contrary to counsel, namely, encouraging the brethren in practicing gifts (speaking in tongues,) in ordaining Sylvester Hulet a High Priest (without counsel) in a clandestine manner; asserting that he had obtained a witness of the Lord, which was a command to perform the same on receiving the gift of tongues, which gift he had never before received, but afterwards said that he had been in possession of that gift for the space of a year; and in undervaluing the authority and righteousness of the High Council by charging Elder West not to say anything that would tend to prejudice their minds, lest they might not judge righteously.

The charges were sustained by the testimony of Leonard Rich, Charles English, Brother Bruce, Edward Partridge, Hiram Page, Roxa Slade, Caleb Baldwin, and Sylvester Hulet. President David Whitmer gave the following decision, which was sanctioned by the council:

"According to testimony and the voice of the Holy Spirit, which is in us, we say unto you, that God, in His infinite mercy, doth yet grant you a space for repentance; therefore, if you confess all the charges which have been alleged against you to be just, and in a spirit that we can receive it, then you [Samuel Brown] can stand as a private member in this Church, otherwise we have no fellowship for you; and also, that the ordination of Sylvester Hulet, by Samuel Brown, is illegal and not acknowledged by us to be of God, and therefore it is void.

Brother Brown confessed the charges, and gave up his license, but retained his membership.*

Letter of Appointment to the Elders.

Council adjourned on the evening of the first of August; but previous to adjourning, the Council gave the following letter to the Elders appointed to visit the churches in Clay county:

To the Latter-day Saints who have been driven from the land of their inheritance, and also those who are gathering in the regions round about, in the western boundaries of Missouri. The High Council established according to the pattern given by our blessed Savior Jesus Christ, send greeting:

DEAR BRETHREN—We have appointed our beloved brother and companion in tribulation, John Corrill, to meet you in the name of the Lord Jesus. He, in connection with others also duly appointed, will visit you alternately for the purpose of instructing you in the necessary qualifications of the Latter-day Saints; that they may be perfected, that the officers and members of the body of Christ may become very prayerful and very faithful, strictly keeping all the commandments, and walking in holiness before the Lord continually; that all that mean to have the destroyer pass over them, as the children of Israel, and not slay them, may live according to the "word of wisdom;" that the Saints, by industry, diligence, faithfulness, and the prayer of faith, may become purified, and enter upon their inheritance, to build up Zion, according to the word of the Lord.

We are sure if the Saints are very humble, very watchful, and very prayerful, that few will be deceived by those who have not authority to teach, or who have not the spirit to teach according to the power of the

* The closing words in the decision signed by David Whitmer and W. W. Phelps as moderators and John Whitmer, clerk, are: "Therefore Brother Brown stands as a private member in this Church—all this by the voice of the councilors." (Far West Record of High Council (Ms.), p. 57.)

Holy Ghost, and the scriptures. Lest any man's blood be required at your hands, we beseech you, as you value the salvation of souls, who are within, to set an example worthy to be followed by those who are without the kingdom of our God and His Christ, that peace by grace, and blessings by righteousness, may attend you, until you are sanctified and redeemed.

Dated, Clay county, August 1, 1834.

Arrival of the Prophet in Kirtland.

About this t me I arrived in Kirtland, after a tedious journey from the midst of enemies; mobs, cholera, and excessively hot weather, having parted from those whom I started with on the 9th ultimo, at different points of the journey.

August 4.—[Kirtland.] A council of Elders ordained Thomas Colburn, Elder; and resolved to send Elder Zerubbabel Snow to Canada, to labor in the ministry.

Charges Against the Hulet Branch.

August 6.—The High Council of Zion assembled in Clay county, and resolved that Leonard Rich act in the place of Parley P. Pratt, who was absent, and Amasa Lyman in place of William E. M'Lellin, absent.

The following charge was then preferred:

This may certify, that whereas, the brethren and sisters comprising that part of the Church known by the name of the Hulet Branch, have imbibed certain principles concerning the gifts that are not thought to be correct by the remainder of the Church; which principles seem to have a tendency to cause disunion in the Church.

I, therefore, as a well wisher in the cause of Christ, and for the peace, and love, and upholding of the great cause of God, do hereby pray that the High Council will take into consideration the above report, that we all may come to understanding and grow until we all come unto the perfect stature of men and women in Christ Jesus.

(Signed) NATHAN WEST.

Testimony Against the Hulet Branch

Charles English testified that tne Hulet Branch believed that they received the word of the Lord by the gift of tongues, and would not proceed to their temporal business without receiving the word of the Lord. Sylvester Hulet would speak, and

Sally Crandall interpret. Said they would not receive the teachings of ordained members, even Brother Joseph Smith, Jun., himself, unless it agreed with their gifts. Said they received the word of the Lord while they were in Jackson county, that they were to be persecuted by their brethren in Clay county, and now it had come. Also said that the heads of the Church would have to come down and receive the gifts as they did. Said that they, the Hulet Branch, had come up to their privileges more than the rest of the Church. They thought they were right; but if they could be convinced that they were wrong, they would retract. Sister Crandall professed to know and see men's hearts.

Philo Dibble concurred in the foregoing testimony, and also testified that Sister Crandall saw the hearts of King Follett and Hiram Page, and they were not right.

Hiram Page testified that Lyman Leonard said, if it was necessary to lay aside the gifts for a season, they would receive a knowledge of it through the gifts.

Nathan West concurred in the foregoing testimony, also testified that Sally Crandall saw his heart, that it was full of eyes; also eyes in others' hearts, some few, some many eyes.

Daniel Stanton testified that Sally Crandall said she saw his heart and saw two books in it, and that there was a Nephite standing behind him to push him into his duty; also that Sylvester Hulet spoke in tongues in meeting, and Sally Crandall interpreted thus: Verily, verily, thus saith the Lord unto you, little band, ye must beware, for there are many who are seeking to pry into your privileges.

Absalom Crichfield testified that when he was in Jackson county last spring, the Hulet Branch said, in tongues, that they would be safe, during the night, from any interruption by the mob; but, before morning, Lyman Leonard and Josiah Sumner were whipped; they also said that they saw my heart, and three young women in it.

Brother Batson and Alpheus Gifford concurred in much

of the foregoing testimony, and also other similar circumstances in addition.

After an adjournment of three-quarters of an hour, the president instructed the speakers not to seek to excel, but speak according to truth and equity; and that they ought to chase darkness from their minds, and be exercised on the subject upon which they were to speak, in order that they might touch upon points of doctrine, bring hidden things to light, and make dark things, clear, etc.

After councilors had spoken, the president said: "As for the gift of tongues in the manner it was used in the Hulet Branch, the devil deceived them, and they obtained not the word of the Lord, as they supposed, but were deceived; and as for the gift of "seeing," as held by the Hulet Branch, it is of the devil, saith the Lord God."

Decision of the Council in the Hulet Branch Case.

The council were unanimous in sanctioning the decision, and appointed Amasa Lyman and Simeon Carter to go and labor with Brother Hulet and Sister Crandall, and others of like faith, and set the truth in order before them.

I have been thus particular in giving the history of this council, as the gift of tongues is so often made use of by Satan to deceive the Saints.

The council adjourned to the 7th, when about twenty Elders were sent forth to preach the Gospel to the world, but not in Jackson or Clay counties, or their vicinity.

Elders Sent Forth to Preach.

President David Whitmer testified to the council that William Batson was not capable of filling his office of Elder, because he had not discretion and understanding sufficient to act wisely in that capacity, whereupon the council voted unanimously, that his office and license be taken from him; to which he consented, and gave up his license.

The Case of William Batson.

Elias and Isaac Higbee, and Jesse Hitchcock, were ordained to the High Priesthood, and council adjourned to the 21st of August.

CHAPTER X.

CHARGES AGAINST THE PROPHET ON HIS RETURN FROM ZION'S CAMP EXPEDITION—TRIAL OF ELDER SYLVESTER SMITH.

Minutes of a Council held at Kirtland, August 11, 1834.

This day a number of High Priests and Elders of the Church of the Latter-day Saints, assembled in the new school house, for the purpose of investigating a matter of difficulty growing out of certain reports, or statements, made by Elder Sylvester Smith, one of the High Councilors of this Church, accusing President Joseph Smith, Jun., with criminal conduct during his journey to and from Missouri this spring and summer.

After calling the meeting to order, President Joseph Smith spoke at considerable length upon the circumstances of their journey to and from Missouri, and very minutely laid open the causes out of which the jealousies of Brother Sylvester Smith and others had grown. He made a satisfactory statement concerning his rebukes and chastisements upon Sylvester Smith and others, and also concerning the distribution of monies and other properties, calling on brethren present who accompanied him, to attest the same, all of which was satisfactory to the brethren present, as appeared by their own remarks afterwards.

After President Joseph Smith had closed his lengthy remarks, Brother Sylvester Smith made some observations relative to the subject of their difficulties, and began to make a partial confession for his previous conduct, asking forgiveness for accusing Brother Joseph publicly, on the Saturday previous, of prophesying lies in the name of the Lord; and for abusing (as he had said) his (Sylvester's) character before the brethren, while journeying to the west.

Elder Rigdon made some remarks, by way of reproof, upon the conduct of Sylvester Smith.

Elder John P. Greene spoke: others also, followed by the clerk [Oliver Cowdery]: after which, on motion of Elder Rigdon, the assembly arranged itself into a council, Bishop Newel K. Whitney presiding, and proceeded to discuss how this difficulty should be disposed of.

Elder John Smith thought that for Brother Sylvester to make a public confession in the *Star*, would be the way to heal the wound.

Elder Cahoon followed with nearly the same remarks.

Elder Isaac Hill thought it ought to be quashed and go no further: followed with the same from Elder I. Bishop.

Samuel H. Smith said that it was his opinion that Brother Sylvester ought to make a more public confession and send by letter, to those who are in the same transgression with himself, and inform them of this decision; and then, if necessary, make it public in the *Star*.

Elder Orson Hyde thought the confession ought to be as liberal as the accusation, or that it ought to be written and published.

Elder John P. Greene said, that if Brother Sylvester would view this thing in its proper light, he would be willing to make a public confession, and send it forth; and he advised him to do this for the salvation of the churches abroad.

Elder Isaac Story said, that it was his opinion, that the plaster ought to be as large as the wound; that a proper statement ought to be published abroad.

The clerk [Oliver Cowdery] then proposed that the council send a certificate or resolution, informing the churches abroad, that the conduct of President Joseph Smith has been investigated, and that he has acted in a proper manner, and in every respect has conducted himself to the satisfaction of the Church in Kirtland; and also let Brother Sylvester make a proper confession, following the same minutes.

Elders Amasa Lyman, Peter Shirts, Truman Wait, Roswell Evans, Alpheus Cutler, and Thomas Burdick, made remarks to the same effect.

Elder Sidney Rigdon made a few remarks upon the attitude in which Sylvester stood before the world, in endeavoring to preach the Gospel.

Elder Orson Hyde moved for a decision relative to the first question, viz., What is to be done to arrest the evil.

The moderator [Bishop Newel K. Whitney] then proceeded, after a few remarks, to give a decision according to a motion previously made, viz., that an article be published in the *Evening and Morning Star*, by the direction of the Council, that the Church in Kirtland has investigated the conduct of President Joseph Smith, Jun., while journeying to the west, and returning; and that we find that he has acted in every respect in an honorable and proper manner with all monies and other properties entrusted to his charge; after which a vote was taken and carried to the above effect.

A motion was then made by Orson Hyde, and seconded by Sidney Rigdon, that a committee of three be appointed to write the article for the *Star*, agreeable to the decision.

Oliver Cowdery, Thomas Burdick and Orson Hyde, were nominated and appointed a committee by unanimous vote.

Brother Sylvester then said that he was willing to publish a confession in the *Star*.

OLIVER COWDERY, Clerk.

The Prophet Reports His Vindication to the Elders in Missouri.

I wrote to Lyman Wight, Edward Partridge, John Corrill, Isaac Morley, and others of the High Council of Zion, from Kirtland, August 16, 1834, as follows:

DEAR BRETHREN—After so long a time, I dictate a few lines to you, to let you know that I am in Kirtland, and that I found all well when I arrived, as pertaining to health; but our common adversary had taken the advantage of our Brother Sylvester Smith, and others, who gave a false coloring to almost every transaction, from the time we left Kirtland, until we returned, and thereby stirred up a great difficulty in the Church against me. Accordingly I was met in the face and eyes, as soon as I had got home, with a catalogue of charges as black as the author of lies himself; and the cry was Tyrant—Pope—King—Usurper—Abuser of men—Angel—False Prophet—Prophesying lies in the name of the Lord—Taking consecrated monies—and every other lie to fill up and complete the catalogue. Such experiences may be necessary to perfect the Church, and render our traducers mete for the devourer, and the shaft of the destroying angel. In consequence of having to combat all these, I have not been able to regulate my mind, so as to give you counsel, and the information that you needed; but that God who rules on high, and thunders judgments upon Israel when they transgress, has given me power from the time I was born into the kingdom to stand; and I have succeeded in putting all gainsayers and enemies to flight, unto the present time; and notwithstanding the adversary laid a plan, which was more subtle than all others, as you will see by the next *Star*, I now swim in good, clean water, with my head out.

I shall now proceed to give you such counsel as the Spirit of the Lord may dictate. You will recollect that your business must be done by your High Council. You will recollect that the first Elders are to receive their endowment in Kirtland, before the redemption of Zion. You will recollect that Council will have power to say who of the first Elders among the children of Zion are accounted worthy; and you will also recollect that you have my testimony in behalf of certain ones, previous to my departure. You will recollect that the sooner these ambassadors of the Most High are dispatched to bear testimony, to lift up a warning voice, and proclaim the everlasting Gospel, and to use every convincing proof and faculty with this generation, while on their journey to Kirtland—the better it will be for them and for Zion. Inasmuch as the indignation of the people sleepeth for a while our time should be employed to the best advantage; although it is not the will of God, that these ambassadors should hold their peace after they have started upon their journey. They should arouse the sympathy of the people.

I would recommend to Brother Phelps, (if he be yet there,) to write a petition, such as will be approved by the High Council; and let every signer be obtained that can be, in the State of Missouri by them while they are on their journey to this place [Kirtland] that peradventure we may learn whether we have friends or not in these United States.

This petition is to be sent to the governor of Missouri, to solicit him to call on the President of the United States for a guard to protect our brethren in Jackson county, upon their own lands, from the insults and abuse of the mob.

And I would recommend to Brother Wight to enter complaint to the governor as often as he receives any insults or injury; and in case that they proceed to endeavor to take life, or tear down houses, and if the citizens of Clay county do not befriend us, to gather up the little army, and be set over immediately into Jackson county, and trust in God, and do the best he can in maintaining the ground. But, in case the excitement continues to be allayed, and peace prevails, use every effort to prevail on the churches to gather to those regions and locate themselves, to be in readiness to move into Jackson county in two years from the eleventh of September next, which is the appointed time for the redemption of Zion. If—verily I say unto you—if the Church with one united effort perform their duties; if they do this, the work shall be complete—if they do not this in all humility, making preparation from this time forth, like Joseph in Egypt, laying up store against the time of famine, every man having his tent, his horses, his chariots, his armory, his cattle, his family, and his whole substance in readiness against the time when it shall be said: To your tents, O Israel! Let not this be noised abroad; let every heart beat in silence, and every mouth be shut.

Now, my beloved brethren, you will learn by this we have a great work to do, and but little time to do it in; and if we do not exert ourselves to the utmost in gathering up the strength of the Lord's house that this thing may be accomplished, behold there remaineth a scourge for the Church, even that they shall be driven from city to city, and but few shall remain to receive an inheritance; if those things are not kept, there remaineth a scourge also; therefore, be wise this once, O ye children of Zion! and give heed to my counsel, saith the Lord.

I would inform Bishop Partridge that the bill I received from him was good, and when I can get our money changed for another, I will mail it to him.

The brethren, up to now, have generally arrived from Clay county in health, notwithstanding the warm season. I would also inform Bishop Partridge that I am not satisfied with Brother Hulet concerning the colt, and so long as unrighteous acts are suffered in the Church, it cannot be sanctified, neither can Zion be redeemed; and also that I was obliged to leave the consecrated horn in Illinois, also Brother William E. M'Lellin, who was sick. We expect when he recovers that he will come to Kirtland. He was very humble, and I entertain no doubt as to his standing while he continues so. We have a desire to hear concerning the cholera, and whether Sister Bunnel is yet alive. Inform us as to all deaths, and give the names and standing of all those who are called away.

The cholera is raging in Detroit, Cleveland, Fairport, Buffalo, and other places. We found it in Chariton as we came through and almost every other place. It is an awful and solemn day, but this is only the foreshadowing of what is to come.

The churches seem to be in a cold, languid and disconsolate state; and as the revolution of the earth is once in twenty-four hours, so we may look for frequent revolutions among this wicked and perverse generation, and also in the Church of Christ. When the head is sick, the whole body is faint; and when the Church lifts up the head, the angel will bring us good tidings. Even so. Amen.

JOSEPH SMITH, JUN.

The Plague of Cholera in Cleveland.

August 21.—Doctor Frederick G. Williams returned from Cleveland and told us concerning the plague, and after much consultation, we agreed that Dr. Williams should go to Cleveland and commence administering to the sick, for the purpose of obtaining blessings for them, and for the glory of the Lord. Accordingly, we (Joseph, Frederick, and Oliver,) united in prayer before the Lord for this thing. Now, O Lord, grant us these blessings in the name of Jesus Christ. Amen.

The same day the High Council of Zion assembled at

the house of Lyman Wight, and Elders Simeon Carter and Amasa Lyman made a report concerning their mission to the Hulet branch. They found the church willing to receive the decision of the last council respecting the false spirits with which they had been troubled.

Affairs in Missouri—Hulet Branch Troubles.

John Corrill entered a complaint against Lyman Wight for teaching that "all disease in this Church is of the devil, and that medicine administered to the sick is of the devil; for the sick in the Church ought to live by faith."

Charge Against Lyman Wight.

Elder Wight acknowledged that he had taught the doctrine, and rather believed it to be correct.

The President decided that it was not lawful to teach the Church that all disease is of the devil, but if there is anyone who has this faith, let him have it to himself; and if there are any who believe that roots and herbs administered to the sick, and all wholesome vegetables which God has ordained for the use of man—and if any say that such things applied to the sick, in order that they may receive health, and this medicine is applied by any member of the Church—if there are any among you that teach that these things are of Satan, such teaching is not of God.

On the 23rd of August, a council convened for the purpose of hearing the resolutions designed for the *Star*, which were to be drawn up by Elders Oliver Cowdery, Thomas Burdick, and Orson Hyde, on the subject of the difficulty existing between President Joseph Smith, Jun., and Sylvester Smith.

Resolutions of Vindication.

Elder Reynolds Cahoon presided in consequence of the ill health of Bishop Whitney.

The following preamble and resolutions were read and adopted, to wit:—

Whereas a report having come to this place [Kirtland] censuring the conduct of President Joseph Smith, Jun., relative to his proceedings during his late journey to and from Missouri; and whereas said report was calculated to create an unfavorable influence as regards the moral character and honesty of our brother, it becomes necessary for us to investigate the matter, and report the same to our brethren abroad; Therefore,—

Resolved: That after hearing from the mouths of some that a suspicion rested upon their minds relative to the conduct of our President as regards his honesty and godly walk, we have investigated his whole proceedings by calling upon those who accompanied him to and from Missouri, and we are happy to have it in our power to say to our brethren abroad, one and all, that we are satisfied with his conduct, having learned from the clearest evidence, that he has acted in every respect worthy his high and responsible station in this Church, and has prudently and cautiously preserved the good of this society at large, and is still worthy of our esteem and fellowship, and that those reports could have originated in the minds of none except such as either from a natural misunderstanding, or a natural jealousy, are easily led to conceive of evils where none exists.

Resolved: That we say to our brethren that while we are surrounded by thousands eager to grasp at a shadow, if they have a hope of turning it into a falsehood for the injury of the Gospel, we exhort them to be steadfast and immovable in the truth, resting assured that while they continue to walk in the Holy Covenant they have confessed to embrace, that nothing can in the end operate against their good; and that while wickedness abounds, as in days of old, the characters of those seeking the greatest good for their fellow men will be shamefully traduced and every act of their lives misrepresented, and a false shade thrown over their worthy deeds, all this is calculated to create an evil prejudice in the minds of the community, to prevent, if possible, the increase of light, the better to effect evil purposes and keep man in error. We say, dear brethren, may peace and the blessings of our Lord Jesus Christ be multiplied unto you through the knowledge of truth, forever.

Resolved: That the minutes be signed by the moderator and clerk, and published to the churches in the *Evening and Morning Star*.

REYNOLDS CAHOON, Moderator.
OLIVER COWDERY, Clerk.

We, the undersigned, members of the above named Conference, for the satisfaction of our brethren abroad, feel it to be our duty to say to those with whom we have a personal acquaintance, that we were present during the foregoing investigation, and cheerfully concur in the spirit of the above minutes, and join in saying that we are perfectly satisfied that whatever impressions may have gone abroad, or whatever may remain with any in this vicinity, relative to the conduct of our President, Joseph Smith, Jun, we are certain (from evidence) that he conducted himself in all respects as set forth in the resolutions of this Conference. We are induced to make these statements that the innocent may not suffer wrongfully, and that the minds of our brethren and friends may be satisfied, that every appearance of evil is, in this place, searched out, and that nothing urbecoming a society of people professing godliness is suffered to exist among them.

IRA AMES, Benson, Vermont.
ASA LYMAN, Parishville, New York.
JOHN RUDD, Springfield, Erie county, Pennsylvania.
ISAAC STOREY, Warsaw, New York.
WILLIAM BURGESS, Bolton, New York.
JONAS PUTNAM, Bolton, New York.
J. B. BOSWORTH, from the church in Norton.
ROSWELL EVANS, Waterford, Vermont.
JOHN SMITH, Potsdam, New York.
ORSON JOHNSON, Bath, New Hampshire.
OLIVER HIGLEY, Jamestown.
ALMAN SHERMAN, Pomfret, New York.
JACOB BUMP, Silver Creek, New York.
ISAAC HILL, East Liverpool, Ohio.
LORENZO YOUNG, the same.

The undersigned members of this Conference, having accompanied President Joseph Smith, Jun., to and from Missouri, certify that the above is a correct statement concerning his character and conduct.

LYMAN E. JOHNSON.
HEBER C. KIMBALL.*

Sylvester Smith Refuses to Accept the Decision of the Council.

Brother Sylvester Smith objected to abiding by the decision of the former council, and proceeded to justify himself in his former conduct; and after much discussion, the following resolution was offered by the clerk, and passed by unanimous vote:—

Resolved: That in consequence of the stand our brother, Sylvester Smith, has taken against the former decision of this council, that we judge him guilty of a misdemeanor, unbecoming a man in his high sta.

* The foregoing resolutions to this point were all published in the *Evening and Morning Star*, Vol. II, No. 23, August, 1834.

tion, and except a humble confession be made to this council, he stands rebuked, and disqualified to act further in his office in the Church, until he make proper satisfaction, or till a trial before the Bishop, assisted by twelve High Priests can be had.

OLIVER COWDERY,
Clerk of Council.

Formal Trial of Sylvester Smith.

August 28, 1834.—This day the High Council assembled according to the direction of Bishop Whitney, to try Brother Sylvester Smith, charged with a misdemeanor. The following is a copy of the complaint:—

To Newel K. Whitney, Bishop of the Church of Latter-day Saints in Kirtland,

Sir, I prefer the following charges against Sylvester Smith, a High Priest of said Church:—

1st. He has refused to submit to the decision of a council of the High Priests and Elders of this Church, held in this place on the 11th of this month, given in a case of difficulty between said Sylvester Smith and Joseph Smith, Jun.

2nd. He continues to charge said Joseph Smith, contrary to the decision of the before mentioned council, with improper conduct in his proceedings as President of the Church of the Latter-day Saints, during his journey the past season to the State of Missouri.

As these things are exceedingly grievous to many of the Saints in Kirtland, and very prejudicial to the cause of truth in general, I therefore require that you summon the High Council of this Church to investigate this case, that a final decision may be had upon the same. I say the High Council because it is a case affecting the Presidency of said Church.*

SIDNEY RIGDON.

Kirtland, Ohio, August 23, 1834.

* This has reference to the special High Council of the Church authorized to try the President of the High Priesthood, who is also the President of the Church, should he be found in transgression. The Council consists of the Presiding Bishop of the Church, assisted by twelve High Priests, agreeable to the revelation which says: "And inasmuch as a President of the High Priesthood shall transgress, he shall be had in remembrance before the common Council of the Church, who shall be assisted by twelve counselors of the High Priesthood; and their decision upon his head shall be an end of controversy concerning him. Thus, none shall be exempt from the justice and the laws of God, that all things may be done in order and in solemnity before Him, according to truth and righteousness."—Doctrine and Covenants, Sec. cvii: 82-84.

As remarked by Elder Rigdon, inasmuch as this case was one involving charges against the Presidency of the Church, it was proper that it should be heard by this special council of the Church.

Bishop Whitney notifies Sylvester Smith of the Cnarge.

KIRTLAND, OHIO, August 27, 1834.

BROTHER SYLVESTER SMITH—Whereas complaint has been made to me by Counselor Sidney Rigdon, setting forth that you have been violating the laws of the Church of the Latter-day Saints, you are therefore, notified to appear before the High Council of High Priests, to be held in the Council House, in Kirtland, on the 28th day of August, at ten o'clock, a. m., to answer to said charges, agreeably to the laws of the Church.

N. K. WHITNEY, Bishop.

The presidents proceeded to nominate a High Priest to fill the vacancy in the council, occasioned by the death of Elder John C. Carter, viz.: Orson Johnson—which nomination was carried unanimously, and he was ordained High Councilor under the hands of Counselor Sidney Rigdon.

Councilor Luke S. Johnson said he wished to be excused from sitting in this council, because he had been previously tempted on some matters, and that he had sinned, and wished to make a more public confession than he could make here.

After some remarks from the councilors, it was decided that Elder Johnson continue his seat in the council.

Elder John P. Greene was appointed to act in the place of Sylvester Smith; also Elder Amos Durfee in the place of John Johnson, Sen., who was absent; also Lyman Johnson in the place of Martin Harris.

The council was organized and complaint read. It was agreed that six councilors speak on the case. The Bishop then charged the council in the name of the Lord, to act according to truth and righteousness.

Elder Reynolds Cahoon testified that the testimony given before a council, on the 11th instant, was, that President Joseph Smith, Jun., had conducted himself in a proper manner, while journeying to and from Missouri; and that the council considered that Sylvester Smith had accused President Joseph Smith wrongfully, and was entirely in the fault. He further considered that everything bearing on or relating to this affair had been brought before the council, and from this they gave their decision.

Elder John P. Greene concurred in the foregoing statements, and he supposed that Brother Sylvester, on the 11th instant, saw the affair in the same light in consequence of his [Sylvester's] saying at the time, that he was not previously aware of the spirit that possessed him at the time he made his charges againt President Joseph Smith.

Elder Alpheus Cutler said that he considered that the evidence given before the council on the 27th was sufficient to prove that President

Joseph Smith had conducted himself in an honorable manner during his late journey to and from Missouri, and that he considered that the evidence there given was such that it could not be invalidated.

Elder Jacob Bump said that previous to the council on the 11th his mind had been agitated, and it was in consequence, in part, of reports which had been put in ciculation respecting President Smith's conduct during his late journey to and from Missouri; but when he heard the case investigated before that council his mind was satisfied that he had been misinformed, and was fully satisfied that President Joseph Smith had not acted in any respect contrary to righteousness before the Lord.

Elder Asa Lyman said, that previous to the council his mind had been agitated also, but was satisfied at the council; and he verily believed from the evidence there given that President Joseph Smith had not acted contrary to justice.

Elder Jacob Bump said that his mind was excited still further after conversing with Brother Sylvester, previous to the 11th, which served in a degree to excite his mind further.

Elder Edmund Bosley said that he understood the case on the 11th in the same light as stated by Brothers Cahoon and Whitney.

Elders John Rudd, Ezekiel Rider and Samuel H. Smith viewed the case in the same light.

Elder Orson Hyde said that he considered that Brother Sylvester was to publish a confession in the *Evening and Morning Star*, and that he himself had been in the fault, and that President Smith had not committed fault, as he [Sylvester had] previously stated.

Elders Alpheus Cutler, J. P. Greene, Ezekiel Rider, Jacob Bump, Samuel H. Smith, John Rudd and Frederick G. Williams concurred.

Elder Oliver Cowdery said, that after listening to all the reports and evidences, from the beginning up to the decision on the 11th instant, he considered that Brother Sylvester was to acknowledge that all the charges previously preferred in public against President Joseph Smith were ungrounded, and that he [Sylvester] was the one, and the only one in fault, touching all circumstances occurring between himself and President Joseph Smith, and that the other charges indirectly preferred as grievances of others, were also without foundation.

Elder John Smith concurred in the above.

Elder C. Durfee said that he considered that President Smith was acquitted, as not being guilty of any misdemeanor before the council on the 11th.

Elder Orson Hyde said that he had accompanied President Smith to Missouri from Mansfield in Ohio, except leaving him for a short time to visit the governor of Missouri. He was present when Brother Sylvester reproved President Smith concerning a certain difficulty arising about a dog; that he considered President Smith's reproofs were just at the time, as he well recollects stating the same in substance to President Smith. He said he did not consider this reproof had any tendency to lessen the esteem of the brethren for President Smith; but if it had, in consequence of a confession in general terms from President Smith about that time, he thought that sufficient to heal any hard feeling then existing against him, or that might exist; and that during his journey to the west, he could not say that he had seen anything in President Smith's conduct contrary to the true principles of his profession as a man of God.

Elder Luke S. Johnson said that he fell in company with President Joseph Smith at Mansfield, Ohio, and accompanied him most of the way to Missouri; and that during the whole course of the journey he did not see anything in his conduct to lessen his esteem for him as a man of God. But he said he heard President Joseph Smith reprove Brother Sylvester concerning a certain matter respecting some bread; he did not hear the whole, and thought at the time the reproofs were rather severe, but had learned since they were not any more severe than just.

President Joseph Smith was then called upon to make a statement concerning the transactions as they happened at the time these reproofs were given. He said that Brother John S. Carter came to him to know whether Brother Sylvester had conducted himself right in the affairs between him [Sylvester] and Brother Parley P. Pratt, when Brother Pratt called upon Brother Sylvester for some bread for supper. He learned from Brother Pratt's mouth that Brother Sylvester had more bread than he needed at the time, yet directed him to some one else, who, he [Brother Sylvester] said, had sufficient. President Smith then went with Brothers Pratt and John S. Carter to Brother Sylvester's tent, where Brother Sylvester justified himself in not imparting a portion of his bread to Brother Pratt. He then rebuked Brother Sylvester for contending that he had done right in this case, because, if this was so, brethren might frequently retire to rest without food, and as long as he [Brother Sylvester] had bread he was bound to impart to those who had none; and that, under these circumstances, Brother Sylvester had conducted himself contrary to the principles of Christ; and that his [Sylvester's] mind was darkened in consequence of this covetous spirit.

The moderator then adjourned the council until nine o'clock, a. m., tomorrow, at this place.

Elder Hyrum Smith closed by prayer.

August 29th, nine o'clock, a. m., council being organized in due form, the testimony was continued as follows:

Elder Luke S. Johnson said, in relation to a circumstance that occurred on the twenty-five mile prairie in Missouri, that by a direction from the leader of the camp he had been back to inspect the crossing at a certain creek; that when he came up with the camp he found it moving, and as he was behind, he went on till he came up with Brother Wight's and Sylvester's company, and found them out of the road building a fire to cook supper. As the teams passed on Brother Sylvester called to the leaders of companies (those who were yet behind), and asked them whom they were following; whether General Wight or some other man. Some hesitated a little and went on. After taking supper he [Luke] went on with their company.

When he came up with the camp from the creek he found that the ensign or flag commonly carried ahead for the camp to follow, was then moving forward. He further said that he understood that Joseph was appointed to lead the camp; that he always, or generally, gave orders when the camp should move forward, and when it should stop; that when on his way to the creek the second time he met President Smith, who told him that he Joseph should order the camp to move into the prairie. When the camp came to order on the prairie in the evening, Brothers Wight and Sylvester were called upon to state why they had sought to divide the camp. They both acknowledged that they had been out of the way by so doing, and were reproved for their conduct. Relative to an assertion heretofore made, that President Smith did at the time throw a trumpet or horn at Brother Sylvester, he did not consider at the time that the President had any intention of throwing it at Brother Sylvester, because he might have hit him with it, being so near to him as he was; it only fell to the ground near to them (himself and Brother Sylvester), but supposed that he had had it in his hand, and only threw it down as usual. He further said that the reproofs given by President Smith at the time were no more severe than he had often heard him give previously; that he did not consider him angry, as he has been represented.

Elder Hyrum Smith said, that when the camp first came to the creek he and his brother Joseph were forward; that while the teams were crossing Brother Joseph asked whether it was advisable to move into the prairie to camp. After consultation it was first advised to camp in the bushes in the edge of the prairie. While making preparations to encamp they were informed that a mob intended to make an attack upon them that night. They further consulted upon their situation, and himself and Brother Thayer were requested by Brother Joseph to go on to the edge of the prairie, where they might encamp. They looked out a place, but it was near the bushes, and Brother Joseph gave an order to go forward on to the prairie. Some complained of the order because they could not find fuel with which to cook their supper. They were told that it would be advisable to carry wood for that purpose. Some further remarks were offered on the subject of a visit from a mob, and preparations were made with the guns, etc. Some fears were entertained for the teams and families yet crossing the creek, and it was thought advisable to send back a company, among whom was Luke S. Johnson, to guard and assist them over. He then took the flag or standard—as he had previously carried it—and gave the word to move forward, and the teams immediately began to follow. After the company had come upon the prairie, himself and Elder Roger Orton received an order to call on Lyman Wight to place a strong guard around the camp that night; but he [Wight] refused doing anything further, because he supposed that he [Hyrum] had ordered the camp on to the prairie without an order from the commander of the company. He was then informed by Brother Joseph that it was by his [Joseph's] order that the camp moved on to the prairie. He was present when Brother Joseph reproved Lyman Wight and Sylvester Smith, and saw the transactions concerning the trumpet or horn; and as to Brother Joseph's intention or design to throw it at Sylvester, he had no such thought at the time, nor could he have had such thought since; that at the time when Joseph had finished his remarks to Lyman Wight and Sylvester Smith he threw the horn on the ground, and Brother Wight told him the next day that he had had a jealousy existing in his mind against him [Hyrum] for some days, but now his mind was satisfied, and he now had no hardness or jealousy. He further said, that when he received the order for moving the camp on the prairie, Brothers Lyman and Sylvester were near by.

Adjourned to one o'clock p. m.

Council met according to adjournment. The clerk called the names of the councilors and parties, when business was resumed.

Elder Brigham Young said, that he was in company with President Joseph Smith, Jun., from about twenty-seven miles of this place [Kirtland till they arrived in Clay county, Missouri; that at the time the difficulty occurred on the Twenty-five Mile Prairie, when the camp was divided, he concurred in what Brother Hyrum had said, and that he could not relate it any more circumstantially than he had done. He further said that he had not seen anything in President Smith's conduct to justify the charge previously made by Brother Sylvester "that his heart was corrupt." So far from this, he had not seen the least shadow of anything of the kind. He had not seen anything in his [Joseph's] conduct, during his journey to the west, unbecoming his profession as a man of God.

Question by Sylvester Smith.—Did you not think that my character was injured in the minds of the weaker part of the camp in consequence of those reproofs and chastisements which were given me by Brother Joseph?

Answer.—I did not.

Elder Young further said in regard to a certain difficulty over a dog, that on a certain evening after crossing the Mississippi river, Brother Sylvester came up with the remaining part of the camp, when the dog came out and barked at him; he knew not whether the dog bit him or not. The next morning, after hearing considerable complaint and murmuring concerning the dog, President Smith spoke to several brethren present and said, "I will descend to that spirit that is in the camp, to show you the spirit you are of, for I want to drive it from the camp. *The man that kills that dog, (or my dog),I will whip him.*" He thought that about this time Brother Sylvester came up, and said, "*If that dog bites me I will kill him.*" Joseph replied, "If you do, I will whip you." Sylvester said, "If you do, I shall defend myself the best way that I can!" Brother Joseph then said that he "would do it in the name of the Lord."

President Smith then asked the brethren if they were not ashamed of such a spirit. Said he, "*I am.*"

He then proceeded to reprove them for condescending to that spirit; that they ought to be above it; that it was the spirit of a dog; and men ought never to place themselves on a level with the beasts; but be possessed of a more noble disposition. He [Joseph] then said, he had condescended to that spirit, in order to show the spirit which was among them.

Elder Young further said, that this explanation gave general satisfaction, and the most of the brethren saw that he had only made these remarks for the purpose of instructing them, and warning them against such a spirit or disposition.

Elders Lyman E. Johnson and Heber C. Kimball concurred.

Elder David Elliot said he was not present when those reproofs were given in the morning; that the circumstances were related to him afterwards, which unfavorably affected his mind, and gave him some disagreable feelings; that at noon he heard President Joseph give a further explanation, which perfectly satisfied him.

He further said, that during the forenoon he learned there were many of the brethren dissatisfied with President Smith's remarks in the morning concerning the dog, but that after the explanation at noon so generally given, he thought that every one in the camp might have understood President Smith's purpose.

Elder Lorenzo Booth concurred in the statement of Elder Young; though he was not present in the morning when the reproofs were given concerning the dog; that he was with President Smith from twenty-seven miles from this place [Kirtland] to Missouri, and a part of the way home; that he did not see anything in President Smith's character derogatory to a man professing religion; that he was present during a certain transaction which occurred during their journey home, respecting certain articles of bedding: that he had heard since his return that President Smith and Ezra Thayer had fought; that he was present during the whole transaction, and there was no fighting.

He further said, in relation to a certain report which had come to his knowledge since his return from Missouri, that President Smith had taken a bed quilt which was not his property; that while at New Portage, Ohio, on their way to Missouri, one of the brethren gave him [Joseph] two bed quilts, which he [Booth] had charge of, as he was the individual who drove the team for President Smith, and had charge of the baggage; that before leaving Clay county, Missouri, he [Booth] took them to be washed, and after starting for home he put them on board of the wagon, the baggage of which he had the charge during their journey home; that he brought the same back with him, has seen them since, and knows that the one which was said to be the property of another individual, is the one which was given President Smith at Norton.

Counselor Frederick G. Williams said, while at Norton certain articles were handed him to mark, among which were two bed quilts, which he marked with common ink; has seen certain bed quilts since his return, and has no doubt but this one in question is the one he marked.

Elder Brigham Young further said relative to a difficulty about some bread, that Elder John S. Carter, on their journey to Missouri, on the line between Ohio and Indiana, said to President Smith, "Is this thing right?" "What thing?" "Concerning Parley P. Pratt's asking Brother Sylvester for some bread for supper."

He then learned that Brother Pratt had asked Brother Sylvester for some bread; that Sylvester had bread at the time, but directed Brother Pratt to some one else, who he [Sylvester] said had sufficient; that Elder Pratt called upon that individual, and could not obtain any; that he was present when President Smith told Brother Sylvester that he had not acted right in the matter, that he ought to impart when he had it instead of directing one where he was not certain he could obtain, that by so doing some might be deprived of food at times.

He further said, that Brother Sylvester contended he had been right, and justified his own conduct in the matter; that Joseph reasoned with Sylvester to convince him that he [Sylvester] was in fault; but he continued to justify his course till President Smith reproved him sharply.

He frequently heard the brethren speak of this circumstance, and all whom he had heard say anything on the subject, manifested a satisfaction with President Smith, and thought his observations correct, and the principles which he advanced, just.

Elder Lyman Sherman said that he concurred in Elder Young's statement concerning the bread; that he thought it was generally known that Elder Pratt, in consequence of Brother Sylvester's not furnishing him with bread, was deprived of bread that night; that at the time he [Joseph] told him [Sylvester] that Brother Parley did not obtain any bread in consequence of Brother Sylvester not supplying him with it.

Elder Jacob Bump said, that since the brethren's return from the west he had gone with Sylvester to Elder Rigdon to advise concerning the adjusting of certain complaints which were in circulation respecting President Joseph Smith's conduct on the journey to and from Missouri; that Brother Sylvester told Brother Rigdon that Elder Pratt did obtain bread of the individual to whom he sent him.

Elder Orson Hyde said, that he concurred in the statements of Elder Brigham Young concerning the circumstances which occurred at the time the difficulty arose about the bread.

Elders Lyman Johnson and Heber C. Kimball concurred in the same statement.

Elder Orson Hyde then exhibited an account current, taken from the receipts of monies and other property expended during their late journey to and from Missouri.

This account was taken from documents during the journey by Counselor Frederick G. Williams, who said that the account exhibited was correctly taken from his accounts, as he had the charge of the monies, and attended to paying them out, etc.

The case was then submitted to the council, and the councilors severally spoke in their turns, followed by the complainant and accused, as follows:—First, the councilors: Jared Carter commenced fifteen minutes before six o'clock, p.m., and spoke twenty-five minutes. Joseph Smith,Sen., commenced ten minutes past six o'clock and spoke five minutes. John Smith commenced fifteen minutes past six o'clock and spoke ten minutes. Lyman E. Johnson commenced twenty-five minutes past six o'clock and spoke one minute. Oliver Cowdery commenced twenty-eight minutes past six and spoke two hours and twelve minutes. Joseph Coe commenced twenty minutes before nine o'clock and spoke five minutes.

The accuser, Sidney Rigdon, commenced fifteen minutes before nine o'clock and spoke five minutes. Oliver Cowdery spoke seven minutes more.

The accused, Sylvester Smith, commenced eighteen minutes before ten o'clock and spoke one hour and eighteen minutes.

The Moderator then gave the following decision:

"That if Brother Sylvester Smith will acknowledge the following items of complaint before this council, and publish the same in print; that he can remain yet a member of this Church, otherwise he is expelled from the same, viz.: First, he is to acknowledge that he has wickedly and maliciously accused our President, Joseph Smith, Jun., with prophesping lies in the name of the Lord, once on the line between Ohio and Indiana, and at another time after crossing the Mississippi river, and at another time, after leaving the Church in Missouri, at Florida; that he is to acknowledge, that in making these charges against President Joseph Smith, Jun., he has himself wilfully and maliciously lied; that he has maliciously told falsehoods in saying that President Joseph Smith, Jun., has abused him with insulting and abusive language, and also in injuring his character and standing before the brethren while journeying to Missouri; that he further cast out insinuations concerning President Joseph Smith's character, which was also an evil and malicious design to injure President Smith's standing in the Church; that he further acknowledge that he has abused the former councils which have sat upon this case, and wickedly and maliciously insulted their just and righteous decisions; that he has further tantalized this present council, in seeking to excuse himself contrary to the advice of the counselors, after acknowledging that it was organized by the direction of revelation; and further, that he has wilfully and maliciously lied, by saying that Brother Joseph Smith, Jun., had prohibited the liberty of speech on their journey to Missouri; that he also acknowledge that he has wickedly and maliciously lied by charging President Joseph Smith, Jun., of being possessed of a heart as corrupt as hell."

The councilors were then called upon to give their assent to the foregoing decision, and they concurred unanimously.

"I hereby certify that the foregoing charges or complaint are just and true, and hereby acknowledge the same, as set forth in the decisions of this council, by signing my own proper name to their minutes, with my own hand.

(Signed) "SYLVESTER SMITH."

The above was signed for fear of punishment.*

* This remark assigning a "fear of punishment" as the reason why Sylvester Smith signed the above acquiescence in the decision of the council, may have been true at the time it was signed; but in justice to Sylvester Smith the fact ought to be known that after time to reflect upon his conduct and his accusation against the Prophet his mind underwent a very radical change: for in a communication to the *Messenger and Advocate*, under date of October 28, 1834, he

The council then proceeded to other business, President Joseph Smith presiding.

Council agreed that the Church in Kirtland be instructed in their particular duties, etc., on Sunday next, by President Joseph Smith, Jun. It was further decided that Elder Brigham Young be appointed to take the lead in singing in our meetings.

The council then closed, at fifteen minutes before three o'clock, a. m., on the 30th of August, 1834. Brother Reynolds Cahoon prayed.

OLIVER COWDERY,
ORSON HYDE,
Clerks.

volunteered a most complete vindication of the Prophet's course while on the Zion's Camp expedition, and made a most humble confession of his own shortcomings. Following is the communication referred to:

Dear Brother:

"Having heard that certain reports are circulating abroad, prejudicial to the character of Brother Joseph Smith, Jun., and that said reports purport to have come from me, I have thought proper to give the public a plain statement of the facts concerning this matter. It is true, that some difficulties arose between Brother Joseph Smith, Jun., and myself, in our travels the past summer to Missouri; and that on our return to this place I laid my grievances before a general council, where they were investigated in full, in an examination which lasted several days, and the result showed to the satisfaction of all present, I believe, but especially to myself, that in all things Brother Joseph Smith, Jun., had conducted worthily, and adorned his profession as a man of God, while journeying to and from Missouri. And it is no more than just that I should confess my faults by saying unto all people, so far as your valuable and instructive paper has circulation, that the things that I accused Brother Smith of were without foundation; as most clearly proven, by the evidence which was called, to my satisfaction. And in fact, I have not at any time withdrawn my confidence and fellowship from Brother Joseph Smith, Jun., but thought that he had inadvertently erred, being but flesh and blood, like the rest of Adam's family. But I am now perfectly satisfied that the errors of which I accused him before the council, did not exist, and were never committed by him; and my contrition has been and still continues to be deep, because I admitted thoughts into my heart which were not right concerning him; and because that I have been the means of giving rise to reports which have gone abroad, censuring the conduct of Brother Joseph Smith, Jun., which reports are without foundation. And I hope that this disclosure of the truth, written by my own hand, and sent abroad into the world, through the medium of the *Messenger and Advocate*, will put a final end to all evil reports and censurings which have sprung out of anything that I have said or done.

"I wish still further to state for the relief of my own feelings, which you must be sensible are deeply wounded in consequence of what has happened, that I know for myself, because I have received testimony from the heavens that the work of the Lord, brought forth by means of the Book of Mormon, in our day through the instrumentality of Brother Joseph Smith Jun., is eternal truth, and must stand, though the heavens and the earth pass away.

"Please give publication to the above, and oblige a lover of righteousness and truth. Yours in the testimony of Jesus,

"SYLVESTER SMITH."

"To O. Cowdery, Kirtland, October 28, 1834."

CHAPTER XI.

A MOMENT'S PEACE—COUNCIL MEETINGS IN OHIO AND MISSOURI.

THE excitement of the people began to subside and the Saints, both in Missouri and Ohio, began to enjoy a little peace. The elders began to go forth, two and two, preaching the word to all that would hear, and many were added to the Church daily.*

Temporary Peace.

September 1.—I continued to preside over the Church, and in forwarding the building of the house of the Lord in Kirtland. I acted as foreman in the Temple stone quarry, and when other duties would permit, labored with my own hands.

The Prophet as Foreman.

September 2. — Conference wrote Brother William Cherry, by Orson Hyde, clerk, to correct a report to the effect that "he had been cut off from the Church;" and advising the brethren not to find fault with one another, after having returned from such an arduous journey as that to Missouri had been, and especially since their offerings had been accepted of the Lord; also encouraging Brother Cherry and others to move west.

Message to Wm. Cherry.

On the 4th, Elder Edmund Bosley said that, if he could obtain the management of his property, in one year, he would consecrate it for the printing of the word of the Lord.

Covenant of Edmund Bosley.

* End of manuscript "Record A."

Minutes of a Conference of Elders, at New Portage, Ohio, held September 8, 1834.

After prayer, President Joseph Smith, Jun., and Oliver Cowdery united in anointing with oil and laying hands upon a sick sister. She said she was healed, but requested us to pray that her faith fail not, saying if she did not doubt she would not be afflicted any more.

President Joseph Smith then made remarks upon the subject of false spirits.

Elder Ambrose Palmer presented a case that had previously occasioned some difficulty in the Church, which was that Brother Carpenter had been tried for a fault before the Church, and the Church gave him a certain time to reflect whether he would acknowledge his error or not. Brother Gordon, at the time, spoke in tongues, and declared that Brother Carpenter should not be shown any lenity. Elder Palmer wished instruction on this point, whether they had proceeded right or not, as Brother Carpenter was dissatisfied.

President Joseph Smith then gave an explanation of the gift of tongues, that it was particularly instituted for the preaching of the Gospel to other nations and languages, but it was not given for the government of the Church.

He further said, if Brother Gordon introduced the gift of tongues as a testimony against Brother Carpenter, it was contrary to the rules and regulations of the Church, because in all our decisions we must judge from actual testimony.

Elder Gordon said the testimony was received and the decision given before the gift of tongues was manifested.

President Smith advised that we speak in our own language in all such matters, and then the adversary cannot lead our minds astray.

Elder Palmer stated that when he was presiding in a conference, several of the brethren spoke out of order, and Elder J. B. Bosworth refused to submit to order according to his request; and he wished instructions on this point, whether he or some one else should preside over this branch of the Church; and also whether such conduct could be approved in conferences.

Brother Gordon made some remarks on the same subject.

President Smith said, relative to the first question, that Brother Gordon's tongue in the end did operate as testimony, as, by his remarks in tongues, the former decision was set aside and his [given in tongues] taken; that it was his [President Smith's] decision that Brother Gordon's manifestation was incorrect, and from a suspicious mind. He approved the first decision, but discarded the second.

Brother Joseph Keeler acknowledged that in the former decision he had acted hastily himself in urging Brother Carpenter to make acknowledgment without having time to reflect; and asked forgiveness wherein he had erred.

Brother Gordon said he discovered that he was in error, and was satisfied with the counsel, and was willing to ask forgiveness of the brethren and of the Lord.

Decision was then given on the second question, that Elder Bosworth was out of his place in opposing Elder Palmer when the latter presided in the conference.

The two decisions were confirmed by unanimous vote of the conference.

A motion was then made and passed by unanimous vote that a letter be written to Brother J.B. Bosworth, informing him of the last decision —that he acted out of place in opposing Elder Palmer in a former conference when requested to take his seat that the business might proceed according to order—and that such letter be signed by the clerk of this conference.

The case of Elder Milton Stow was then presented. when it was proven that he had delivered prophecies at two different times that were not true; at one time in saying that Zion was already redeemed, and at another in saying that Brother Carpenter was cut off forever and also in saying that Sister Carpenter was dead.

It was decided by vote, that Brother Milton Stow be and by the decision of this conference is, suspended from the privileges of this Church of Latter-day Saints, and from acting in the authority of an Elder in said Church of the Latter-day Saints, till he appear before the Bishop's council in Kirtland and make proper satisfaction.

Conference closed by prayer.

OLIVER COWDERY, Clerk of Conference.

The following letter was written according to the instruction of the conference, as recorded in the foregoing minutes:—

NEW PORTAGE, OHIO, September 8, 1834.

To Joseph B. Bosworth, a High Priest in the Church of Latter-day Saints.

DEAR BROTHER:—By a decision of this conference I am directed to inform you that a difficulty has been presented to this body which arose in a former conference between yourself and Elder Ambrose Palmer, to the effect that in a former conference where Elder Palmer presided, according to the office of his appointment as president of this [New Portage] branch of the Church of the Latter-day Saints, you, when requested by him to be seated, refused to submit to his decision, and spoke disrespectfully to our brother while acting in his calling, which has occasioned offense to the conference. It is the decision, therefore, of this conference, that you come before the Church, (as you are not present to do it at this conference) and make the proper confession required in the law of the Lord. Why I say disrespectfully is because when you were requested to be seated and to desist from speaking, you said you had as much right to speak as Elder Palmer.

OLIVER COWDERY, Clerk of Conference.

Extracts from the minutes of the High Council of Zion, assembled in Clay County, September 10, 1834.

The following brethren were chosen to fill the places of absent members:—Zebedee Coltrin for Parley P. Pratt; Hazen Aldrich for Solomon Hancock; Elias Higbee for Newell Knight; Isaac Higbee for William E. M'Lellin; Peter Dustin for Orson Pratt.

Elisha H. Groves was ordained a High Priest.

A letter was read from President Joseph Smith to W. W. Phelps, dated 16th of August; also a petition written by W. W. Phelps to the governor of the state of Missouri was read and accepted.

Calvin Beebe and Levi Jackman were nominated as first Elders to go forth to Kirtland, preaching by the way, and if approved by President Joseph Smith, should be accounted worthy, and numbered as such.*

It was decided by the President, and sanctioned by the Council, that the first Elders go forth as soon as they can get ready, and preach by the way to Kirtland.

Voted, that those Elders that came up in the camp apply for a release from Lyman Wight,† and receive a recommandation to Bishop Partridge, to go forth to preach the Gospel.

THOMAS B. MARSH, Secretary pro tem.

* That is, they should be numbered among the Elders to receive their endowments in Kirtland, if approved by the Prophet, Seer, and Revelator, Joseph Smith, as provided by the revelation of June 22nd. (See p. 108.)

† Who, it will be remembered, was appointed "General of the Camp" (p.88); and n the absence of the "Commander-in-Chief," was first in command; hence the direction to apply to him for release.

Minutes of the High Council at Kirtland, September 24, 1834.

Joseph Smith, Jun., presiding, assisted by Sidney Rigdon and Frederick G. Williams, counselors.

Jared Carter and Martin Harris were absent.

After prayer, the president made some remarks; when the case of Sylvester Smith was called up to inquire whether or not, under existing circumstances, he can fill the office of High Councilor.

It was decided that four Councilors speak on the case, viz.: Samuel H. Smith and Orson Johnson, Luke Johnson and Orson Hyde.

The Councilors severally spoke in their course, followed by Brother Sylvester; after which the assistent-presidents spoke; when the president gave a decision, that Brother Sylvester stand no longer a High Councilor, but that he retain the office of High Priest, and continue to lift up his voice in the name of Jesus in preaching the Gospel—to which the council assented, and Brother Sylvester gave his assent with thankfulness.

The President nominated Hyrum Smith to fill the office vacated by Sylvester Smith. The nomination was seconded by the clerk. The Councilors and all present voted for the nomination.

The President led in prayer, and then he ordained Hyrum Smith to the office of High Councilor, pronouncing blessings upon him in the name of the Lord; after which Joseph Smith, Sen., blessed his son Hyrum in the name of the Lord, confirming the same blessings.

Elders John P. Greene and Brigham Young were then appointed to fill the vacancies occasioned by the absence of Councilors Jared Carter and Martin Harris.

The council then proceeded to appoint a commitee to arrange the items of the doctrine of Jesus Christ, for the government of the Church of Latter-day Saints, which Church was organized and commenced its rise on the 6th of April, 1830. These items are to be taken from the Bible, Book of Mormon, and the revelations which have been given to the Church up to this date, or that shall be given until such arrangements are made.

Councilor Samuel H. Smith nominated President Joseph Smith, Jun., Oliver Cowdery, Sidney Rigdon, and Frederick G. Williams to compose said committee, which was seconded by Councilor Hyrum Smith. The Councilors then gave their vote in the affirmative, which was also agreed to by the whole conference.

The council then decided that said committee, after arranging and publishing said Book of Covenants, have the avails of the same.

The council then decided that a notice be published to the churches and conferences abroad that High Priests be ordained hereafter, in the High Council at Kirtland, and receive licence signed by the clerk of the council.

The council decided that Bishop Whitney be privileged, considering his present embarrassed circumstances, to make such arrangements with his store as he shall deem most advisable.

Closed by prayer.

OLIVER COWDERY,
ORSON HYDE,
Clerks.

CHAPTER XII.

CHANGE IN CHURCH PERIODICALS—THE COVENANT OF TITHING—CLOSE OF THE YEAR 1834.

October 1-15.—Great exertions were made to expedite the work of the Lord's house, and notwithstanding it was commenced almost with nothing, as to means, yet the way opened as we proceeded, and the Saints rejoiced. The former part of October was spent in arranging matters respecting the Lord's house and the printing office, for it had previously been published that the *Evening and Morning Star* would be discontinued, and a new paper issued in its place, entitled *The Latter-day Saints Messenger and Advocate.**

"Messenger and Advocate" Founded.

* The following is the explanation given in the *Evening and Morning Star* for this change in the name of the Church periodical: "As the *Evening and Morning Star* was designed to be published at Missouri, it was considered that another name would be more appropriate for a paper in this place [Kirtland], consequently, as the name of this Church has lately been entitled the Church of the Latter-day Saints, and since it is destined, at least for a season, to bear the reproach and stigma of this world, it is no more than just that a paper disseminating the doctrines believed by the same, and advocating its character and rights should be entitled *The Latter-day Saints Messenger and Advocate.*"

There was also a change announced in the form of the Church periodical. The *Evening and Morning Star* as first published was a quarto, but the *Messenger and Advocate* was to be published in octavo form for greater convenience in binding and preserving. It was also announced that the two volumes of the *Star* would be reprinted in octavo form; which, by the way, was done.

This first number of the *Messenger and Advocate* contained a summary of the most prominent points of doctrine believed in by the Church at that time, signed by Oliver Cowdery; and as the doctrine development in the Church is a prominent feature of this work, that summary is here appended:

"We believe in God, and His Son Jesus Christ. We believe that God, from the beginning, revealed Himself to man, and that whenever He has had a people on earth, He always has revealed Himself to them by the Holy Ghost, the ministering

Having accomplished all that could be done at present, on the 16th of the month, in company with my brother Hyrum Smith, and Elders David Whitmer, Frederick G. Williams, Oliver Cowdery, and Roger Orton, left Kirtland for the purpose of visiting some Saints in the state of Michigan, where, after a tolerably pleasant journey, we arrived at Pontiac on the 20th.

The Prophet's Labors in Michigan.

While on our way up the lake on board the steamer *Monroe*, Elder Cowdery had a short discussion with a man calling his name Ellmer. He said that he was "personally acquainted with Joe Smith, had heard him preach his lies,

of angels or His own voice. We do not believe that He ever had a church on earth without revealing Himself to that church; consequently there were apostles, prophets, evangelists, pastors, and teachers in the same.

"We believe that God is the same in all ages, and that it requires the same holiness, purity, and religion to save a man now as it did anciently; and that, as He is no respecter of persons, always has, and always will reveal Himself to men when they call upon Him.

"We believe that God has revealed Himself to men in this age, and commenced to raise up a church preparatory to His second advent, when He will come in the clouds of heaven with power and great glory.

"We believe that the popular religious theories of the day are incorrect; that they are without parallel in the revelations of God, as sanctioned by Him; and that however faithfully they may be adhered to, or however jealously or warmly they may be defended, they will never stand the strict scrutiny of the word of life.

"We believe that all men are born free and equal; that no man, combination of men, or government of men has power or authority to compel or force others to embrace any system of religion, or religious creed, or to use force or violence to prevent others from enjoying their own opinions, or practicing the same, so long as they do not molest or disturb others in a manner to deprive them of their privileges as free citizens, or of worshiping God as they choose, and that any attempt to do so is an assumption unwarrantable in the revelations of heaven, and strikes at the root of civil liberty, and is a subversion of all equitable principles between man and man.

"We believe that God has set His hand the second time to recover the remnant of His people, Israel; and that the time is near when He will bring them from the four winds with songs of everlasting joy, and reinstate them upon their own lands which He gave their fathers by covenant.

"And further, we believe in embracing good wherever it may be found; of proving all things, and holding fast to that which is righteous. This, in short, is our belief, and we stand ready to defend it upon its own foundation whenever it is assailed by men of character and respectability. And while we act upon these broad principles, we trust in God that we shall never be confounded.

"OLIVER COWDERY."

"Kirtland, Ohio, October, 1834."

and now, since he was dead, he was glad! He had heard Joe Smith preach in Bainbridge Chenango county, New York, five years since; he knew it to be him, that he [Joseph Smith] was a dark complexioned man,'' etc. Ellmer appeared to exult most in that ''Joe'' was dead, and made his observations in my presence. I concluded that he learned it from the popular priests of the day, who, through fear that their craft will be injured, if their systems are compared with the truth, seek to ridicule those who teach the truth, and thus I am suffering under the tongue of slander for Christ's sake, unceasingly. God have mercy on such, if they will quit their lying. I need not state my complexion to those that have seen me, and those who have read my history thus far, will recollect that five years ago I was not a preacher, as Ellmer represented; neither did I ever preach in Bainbridge.*

After preaching, and teaching the Saints in Michigan as long as our time would allow, we returned to Kirtland, greatly refreshed from our journey, and much pleased with our friends in that section of the Lord's vineyard.

Preparation of the School for the Elders.

It now being the last of the month, and the Elders beginning to come in, it was necessary to make preparations for the school for the Elders, wherein they might be more perfectly instructed in the great things of God, during the coming winter. A building for a printing office was nearly finished, and the lower story of this building was set apart for that pur-

* In a communication to the first number of the *Messenger and Advocate*, October, 1834, Elder Oliver Cowdery gives substantially the same account of this incident. After a somewhat lengthy statement of how he refuted Ellmer's assertion that the Savior had not been seen since His ascension, he continues:

''How far this conversation was, or will be, productive of good, I am unable to say; but by that means numbers heard, and no doubt felt an increased anxiety to learn something further relative to this 'strange work.' One individual purchased a Book of Mormon, notwithstanding Mr. Ellmer's bitter cry of 'Joe Smith' and 'false prophets,' and will thus have the privilege of hearing the truth, though he may be separated far from those who have authority to administer the ordinances of the everlasting Gospel. May heaven inspire his heart to seek diligently until he obtains a certain knowledge of the kingdom of our God in these last days.''

pose, (the school) when it was completed. So the Lord opened the way according to our faith and works, and blessed be His name.

Strenuous Life of the Prophet.

No month ever found me more busily engaged than November; but as my life consisted of activity and unyielding exertions, I made this my rule: *When the Lord commands, do it.* Among other matters, the following letter was sent to George James, Brownhelm, Ohio, by order of the High Council:

KIRTLAND, November 10, 1834.

DEAR BROTHER:—There having been serious complaints presented to us against you, we sincerely request you to come to Kirtland immediately, as it will be necessary that a proper notice be taken of the same. We do not write the above with a view to accuse you ourselves, but you know the great responsibility resting upon us and the propriety of noticing charges, especially when they are preferred against men in important and interesting stations in the Church of the Saints. We have truly written the above with feelings of deep interest for your own welfare and standing in the Church; and we do hope you will not fail to come down immediately, as the representations made to us will require immediate notice. It is necessary for us to inform you that until you appear and make the satisfaction requisite, you are suspended from acting in the authority of the office to which you have been previously ordained.

With feelings of respect we subscribe ourselves, your brethren in the New Covenant,

JOSEPH SMITH, JUN.
SIDNEY RIGDON.

OLIVER COWDERY,
Clerk of the High Council.

I continued my labors daily, preparing for the school, and received the following:

*Revelation given November 25, 1834.**

1. It is my will that my servant Warren A. Cowdery should be appointed and ordained a presiding High Priest over my Church in the land of Freedom and the regions round about;

* Doctrine and Covenants, sec. civ

2. And should preach my everlasting Gospel, and lift up his voice and warn the people, not only in his own place, but in the adjoining counties.

3. And devote his whole time to this high and holy calling which I now give unto him, seeking diligently the kingdom of heaven and its righteousness, and all things necessary shall be added thereunto, for the laborer is worthy of his hire.

4. And again, verily I say unto you, the coming of the Lord draweth nigh, and it overtaketh the world as a thief in the night:

5. Therefore, gird up your loins that you may be the children of light, and that day shall not overtake you as a thief.

6. And again, verily I say unto you, there was joy in heaven when my servant Warren bowed to my sceptre, and separated himself from the crafts of men.

7. Therefore, blessed is my servant Warren, for I will have mercy on him, and notwithstanding the vanity of his heart, I will lift him up, inasmuch as he will humble himself before me;

8. And I will give him grace and assurance wherewith he may stand, and if he continue to be a faithful witness and a light unto the Church, I have prepared a crown for him in the mansions of my Father. Even so. Amen.

The same day, Hon. J. T. V. Thompson, Missouri state senator, wrote Elder Phelps, at Liberty, as follows:

JEFFERSON CITY, Nov. 25, 1834.

DEAR SIR:—I will say to you that your case with the Jackson people has been mentioned to the highest officer in the state, the governor. He speaks of it in his message, and so much of his message will be referred to a commitee. I am not able to say what will be their report, but I will write you again.

I have the honor, etc.,

J. T. V. THOMPSON.

The following is that portion of the governor's message referred to in the foregoing letter:

In July, 1833, a large portion of the citizens of Jackson county organized themselves and entered into resolutions to expel from that county a religious sect called Mormons, who had become obnoxious to them. In November following, they effected their object; not, however, without the loss of several lives.

In the judicial inquiry into these outrages, the civil authorities who had cognizance of them, deemed it proper to have a military guard for the purpose of giving protection during the progress of the trials. This was ordered, and the Attorney-General was requested to give his attention during the investigation, both of which were performed, but all to no purpose. As yet none has been punished for these outrages, and it is believed that, under our present laws, conviction for any violence committed against a Mormon cannot be had in Jackson county. These unfortunate people are now forbidden to take possession of their homes, and the principal part of them, I am informed, are at this time living in an adjoining county, in a great measure upon the charity of its citizens. It is for you to determine what amendements the laws may require so as to guard against such acts of violence for the future.

Minutes of a Council held at Kirtland, November 28th.

A council convened this evening to transact business according to the regulations of the Church; Joseph Smith, Jun., Sidndy Rigdon and Frederick G. Williams presiding. Eight councilors present.

John Johnson and Hyrum Smith were appointed to speak.

A letter from the church in Lewis, Essex county, New York, was presented by Brothers John H. Tippits, and Joseph H. Tippits, and read by the clerk. Said letter contained an account of money and other property sent by the church in Lewis, in the care of said brethren, to carry to Missouri to purchase land. These Elders wished the advice of the council, whether they had better pursue their journey or not.

The two Councilors spoke on the case, followed by President Williams, Councilor Orson Hyde and the clerk; after which President Rigdon gave a decision that our brethren be advised to tarry in this place during the winter; in which the council concurred.

The two brethren then arose respectively and said they were perfectly satisfied with the decision of the council.

The amount donated by the church in Lewis is, according to their letter, in cash, $473.29. The amount in *Star* property is $375.11. Total, $848.40.

The council then decided that President Joseph Smith, Jun., take such amount of said money as those brethren can part with for the present, by giving sufficient security, to be paid with interest by the 15th of April, 1835.

It was ascertained by the council that Sister Caroline Tippits held $149.75 of the money mentioned in said letter, she was accordingly called into the council, and expressed a willingness to loan the same.

One note of $280 was drawn in favor of John H. Tippits, and another of $150, in favor of Caroline Tippits, each due April 15, 1835. Signed by Joseph Smith, Jun., Oliver Cowdery, and Frederick G. Williams. OLIVER COWDERY, Clerk.

The following letter was presented by John H. Tippits, and formed the subject for consideration by the preceding council, written to President Joseph Smith, Jun., and the High Council in Kirtland, by Alvah L. Tippits, to be sent greeting:

President Smith will recollect the time I left Kirtland last winter in order to come to dispose of the property I had in possession, which I have been striving to do from that time till about the first of September last, but I have felt very uneasy while the commandment has gone forth for the eastern churches to flee unto the West.

The 1st, or about the 1st of September, with two of my brethren, I took the revelation concerning the redemption of Zion and read it, and then we agreed to ask God to enable us to obey the same. As we live in the eastern states, our minds were impressed with these important lines:

"Therefore, a commandment I give unto all the churches, that they shall continue to gather together unto the places which I have appointed; nevertheless as I have said unto you in a former commandment, let not your gathering be in haste, nor by flight; but let all things be prepared before you: and in order that all things be prepared before you, observe the commandment which I have given concerning these things, which saith, or teacheth, to purchase all the lands with money, which can be purchased or money, in the region round about the land which I have appointed to be the land of Zion, for the beginning of the gathering of my Saints; all the land which can be purchased in Jackson county and the counties round about, and leave the residue in mine hand. Now, verily I say unto you, let all the churches gather together all their monies; let these things be done in their time, but not in haste, and observe to have all things prepared before you. And let honorable men be appointed, even wise men, and send them to purchase these lands; and the churches in the eastern countries, when they are built up, if they will hearken unto this counsel, they may buy lands and gather together upon them; and in this way they may establish Zion."*

After further consideration and much prayer, we carried the case before the church in this place, which met the approbation of the same

* Doctrine and Covenants; sec. ci: 67-74.

Accordingly we strove to become of one heart and one mind, and appointed a day for fasting and prayer, and asked the Lord to enable us to collect all our monies; and appointed a day for the church to come together for counsel.

Accordingly we came together, and after conversation, chose a moderator and clerk to keep the records of the church; counseled concerning property owned by the church, and commenced to make sale and collect pay according to the voice of the church, in order to collect all monies owned by the church, and send by the hands of wise men, who were appointed by the voice of the church; one Elder and one Priest, according to the will of God.

ALVAH L. TIPPITS.

Lewis, County of Essex,
New York, October 20, 1834.

The members of a branch of the Church of the Latter-day Saints, agreeable to the requirement of heaven, have striven to unite their hearts and views, in order to be found spotless before the blazing throne of the Great Jehovah when He comes to make up His jewels, and for this end to send property by the hands of wise men, appointed by the voice of the church, agreeable to the revelation concerning the redemption of Zion, for the purpose of purchasing land in Jackson county, or counties round about, for the inheritance of the Church. Agreeable to this, we give our names with the affixed sums annexed:

	Cash	*Property*
Joseph H. T ipp ts	$98.67	$120.37
Alvah Tippits	34.63	80.00
John H. Tippits	171.05	51.93
Henry Adams	11.13	8.75
Zebulon Adams	1.75	
Caroline Tippits	151.06	107.00
David Bragg	5.00	1.06
Gustavus A. Perry		6.00

Total, $848.40; $100.00 for boots and shoes, to be left in Kirtland.

The wise men appointed are John H. Tippits and Joseph H. Tippits.

On the evening of the 29th of November, I united in prayer with Brother Oliver for the continuance of blessings. After giving thanks for the relief which the Lord had lately sent us by opening the hearts of the brethren from the east, to loan us $430; after commencing and rejoicing before the Lord on this occasion, we agreed to enter into the following covenant with the Lord, viz.:

The Covenant of Tithing.

That if the Lord will prosper us in our business and open the way before us that we may obtain means to pay our debts; that we be not troubled nor brought into disrepute before the world, nor His people; after that, of all that He shall give unto us, we will give a tenth to be bestowed upon the poor in His Church, or as He shall command; and that we will be faithful over that which He has entrusted to our care, that we may obtain much; and that our children after us shall remember to observe this sacred and holy covenant; and that our children, and our children's children, may know of the same, we have subscribed our names with our own hands.

(Signed) JOSEPH SMITH, JUN.
OLIVER COWDERY.

A Prayer.

And now, O Father, as Thou didst prosper our father Jacob, and bless him with protection and prosperity wherever he went, from the time he made a like covenant before and with Thee; as Thou didst even the same night, open the heavens unto him and manifest great mercy and power, and give him promises, wilt Thou do so with us his sons; and as his blessings prevailed above his progenitors unto the utmost bounds of the everlasting hills, even so may our blessings prevail like his; and may Thy servants be preserved from the power and influence of wicked and unrighteous men; may every weapon formed against us fall upon the head of him who shall form it; may we be blessed with a name and a place among Thy Saints here, and Thy sanctified when they shall rest. Amen.

November 30.—While reflecting on the goodness and mercy of God this evening, a prophecy was put into our hearts, that in a short time the Lord would arrange His providences in a merciful manner and send us assistance to deliver us from debt and bondage.

A Prophecy.

December 1.—Our school for the Elders was now well

attended, and with the lectures on theology,* which were regularly delivered, absorbed for the time being everything else of a temporal nature. The classes, being mostly Elders gave the most studious attention to the all-important object of qualifying themselves as messengers of Jesus Christ, to be ready to do His will in carrying glad tidings to all that would open their eyes, ears and hearts.

School at Kirtland for the Elders.

According to the direction of the Holy Spirit, on the evening of the 5th of December, while assembled with Sidney Rigdon, Frederick G. Williams, and Oliver Cowdery, conversing upon the welfare of the Church, I laid my hands on Brother Oliver Cowdery, and ordained him an assistant-president, saying these words: "In the name of Jesus Christ, who was crucified for the sins of the world, I lay my hands upon thee and ordain thee an assistant-president to the High and Holy Priesthood, in the Church of the Latter-day Saints."†

Oliver Cowdery Ordained an Assistant President.

* These "Lectures on Theology" here referred to were afterwards prepared by the Prophet, (see page 180) and published in the Doctrine and Covenants under the title "Lectures on Faith." They are seven in number, and occupy the first seventy-five pages in the current editions of the Doctrine and Covenants. They are not to be regarded as of equal authority in matters of doctrine with the revelations of God in the Doctrine and Covenants, but as stated by Elder John Smith, who, when the book of Doctrine and Covenants was submitted to the several quorums of the Priesthood for acceptance, (August 17, 1835,) speaking in behalf of the Kirtland High Council, "bore record that the revelations in said book were true, and that the lectures judicially were written and compiled, and were profitable for doctrine." The distinction which Elder John Smith here makes should be observed as a marking the difference between the Lectures on Faith and the revelations of God in the Doctrine and Covenants.

† This meeting of the 5th of December was a most interesting occasion. The minutes of it are found in the hand writing of Oliver Cowdery in the back of Record A, Ms. It would appear, according to these minutes, that the express purpose of the meeting of the brethren named in the Prophet's history was to recognize Oliver Cowdery in his station as the second Elder in the Church, a position for which he was designated in the revelations of God, and to which he was ordained under the hand of the Prophet, (Doctrine and Covenants, sec.20: 3,4). It is explained in the minutes that the reason why he had not been able to officiate in his calling as said second Elder in the Church was because of his necessary absence in Zion (Missouri) to assist W. W. Phelps in conducting the printing business of the Church, etc.; hence Sidney Rigdon and Frederick G. Williams had been ordained as assistant-presidents in the Church during this necessary absence of Elder Cowdery. Another

On the 11th, Elder Phelps wrote from Liberty, Clay county, to J. T. V. Thompson, Jefferson City, in reply to his letter of the 25th November, expressive of thankfulness to his Excellency, Governor Dunklin, for introducing the sufferings of the Saints in his message; also asking counsel "whether it would avail anything for the society to petition the legislature for an act to reinstate them in their rights," etc.; and requesting him to confer with his friends and his Excellency on the subject, and give an early answer.

Thanks to Governor Dunklin.

About the middle of the month, the message of Governor Dunklin, of Missouri, to the legislature, arrived at Kirtland. It was read with great interest, and revived the hopes of the Church for the scattered brethren of Jackson county.

Revived Hopes.

Elder Phelps wrote again to Esquire Thompson, on the 18th as follows:

DEAR SIR—By this mail I have forwarded to Captain Atchison, of the lower house, a petition and documents, on the subject of our rights in Jackson county. He will hand them to you for the senate, when they are through with them in the house. I shall be greatly obliged, if you will lay them before your honorable body; and any information

item of interest recorded in these minutes is the word of the Lord by way of reproof through the Spirit concerning the failure of the brethren and the Church in general to properly recognize each other by their official titles in the Church. This item appears in the minutes as follows: "After assembling we received a rebuke for our former uncultivated and disrespectful manner of communication and salutation with and unto each other by the voice of the Spirit, saying unto us: 'Verily, condemnation resteth upon you, who are appointed to lead my Church, and to be saviors of men; and also upon the Church; and there must needs be a repentance and a reformation among you, in all things, in your examples before the Church and before the world, in all your manners, habits and customs, and salutations one toward another; rendering unto every man the respect due the office, calling, and priesthood whereunto I, the Lord, have appointed and ordained you. Amen.' " "It is only necessary to say," continue the minutes, "relative to the foregoing reproof and instruction, that though it was given in sharpness, it occasioned gladness and joy, and we were willing to repent and reform in every particular, according to the instruction given. It is also proper to remark that after the reproof was given, we all confessed, voluntarily, that such had been the manifestation of the Spirit a long time since, in consequence of which, the rebuke came with great sharpness."

you may require, or even personal attendance, write, and you shall have it if it is in my power. As a people, all we ask is our rights.

With esteem, etc.,

W. W. PHELPS.

On the 20th Messrs. Thompson and Atchison wrote Elder Phelps from the "'Senate Chamber,'' acknowledging the receipt of his letter, stating that the committee on the Governor's message had not reported, and recommending the Saints to get up a petition to the legislature, with as many signatures as possible, promising their assistance and influence to obtain redress of grievances. A petition was accordingly forwarded; but the year closed without bringing anything to pass for the relief of the Saints in Missouri.*

Thompson and Atchison Promise Assistance.

* The following letter from Governor Dunklin, in response to the petitions referred to in the text above, is found as an addenda in the manuscript history for 1835, Note A:

"To the petitions which we sent up to Missouri, Governor Dunklin replied as follows:

"CITY OF JEFFERSON, January 22, 1836.

"*To Messrs. W. W. Phelps and others,*

"GENTLEMEN:—Your numerous petitions, post-marked 'Kirtland,' came safe to hand. It is unnecessary for me to repeat to you my feelings on the subject of your grievances; what they were you have been already apprised; and they have undergone no change. Your case was presented by me to the last General Assembly of this state. They did not legislate upon the subject. I am, however, persuaded that it was for want of a constitutional power to pass any law that could afford you a proper remedy prevented their acting upon the subject. Your feelings are very natural when such causes exist to produce them, but you misconceive your case, and consequently do not advert to the proper remedy; you cannot make a case of invasion or insurrection out of the outrages committed on your persons or property in Jackson county, and unless one of those could be made out, it would be idle to address the President of the United States. If such a case had been made out, as executive of this state, I should have immediately ordered out a military force to repell or suppress it. The mob in New York to which you cite me, is not in point. The military force was then resorted to for the purpose of quelling the mob. You wish this kind of force used to restore justice. However palpable and grievous the outrages have been upon you, your only remedy for injuries done, must be in and through the courts of justice. On a former occasion I informed you I was then in correspondence with the General Government for a depot of arms on the Missouri river, near out western boundary line. For reasons unknown to me, the Secretary of War has taken no steps during the last year towards the fulfillment of that object. I have renewed the subject through our delegation in Congress this winter. When this object shall be attained, it may furnish you a place of resort for protection, in case of emergency, should you think proper to risk yourselves on your lands in Jackson county again.

Respectfully,

DANIEL DUNKLIN.

CHAPTER XIII.

THE LECTURES ON FAITH—TWELVE APOSTLES CHOSEN AND ORDAINED.

January, 1835.—During the month of January, I was engaged in the school of the Elders, and in preparing the lectures on theology for publication in the book of Doctrine and Covenants, which the committee appointed last September were now compiling.

The Lectures on Theology.

Certain brethren from Bolton, New York, came for counsel, relative to their proceeding to the West; and the High Council assembled on the 18th. After a long investigation I decided that Elder Tanner assist with his might to build up the cause by tarrying in Kirtland; which decision received the unanimous vote of the council.

Brethren Moving West Halted at Kirtland.

The school of the Elders will continue, and arrangements were also made, according to the revelation of June, 1829,* for choosing "the Twelve Apostles" to be especial messengers to bear the Gospel among the nations.

On the Sabbath previous to the 14th of February, (February 8th) Brothers Joseph and Brigham Young came to my house after meeting, and sung for me; the Spirit of the Lord was poured out upon us, and I told them I wanted to see those brethren together, who went up to Zion in the camp, the previous summer, for I had a

* Doctrine and Covenants, sec. xviii.

blessing for them; and a meeting was appointed of which the following are the minutes:*

Minutes of the Meetings at which the Twelve Apostles were Chosen, Ordained and Instructed.

Kirtland, February 14, 1835.—This day, a meeting was called of those who journeyed last season to Zion for the purpose of laying the foundation of its redemption, together with as many other of the brethren and sisters as were disposed to attend.

President Joseph Smith, Jun., presiding, read the 15th chapter of John, and said: Let us endeavor to solemnize our minds that we may receive a blessing, by calling on the Lord. After an appropriate and

* Elder Joseph Young gives the following interesting account of the above meeting mentioned by the Prophet: "On the 8th day of February, in the year of our Lord 1835, the Prophet Joseph Smith called Elders Brigham and Joseph Young to the chamber of his residence, in Kirtland, Ohio, it being on the Sabbath day. After they were seated and he had made some preliminaries, he proceeded to relate a vision to these brethren, of the state and condition of those men who died in Zion's Camp, in Missouri. He said, 'Brethren, I have seen those men who died of the cholera in our camp; and the Lord knows, if I get a mansion as bright as theirs, I ask no more.' At this relation he wept, and for some time could not speak. When he had relieved himself of his feelings, in describing the vision, he resumed the conversation, and addressed himself to Brother Brigham Young. He said to him, 'I wish you to notify all the brethren living in the branches, within a reasonable distance from this place, to meet at a general conference on Saturday next. I shall then and there appoint twelve Special Witnesses, to open the door of the Gospel to foreign nations, and you,' said he (speaking to Brother Brigham), 'will be one of them.' He then proceeded to enlarge upon the duties of their calling. The interest that was taken on the occasion of this announcement, produced in the minds of the two Elders present a great sensation and many reflections; having previously notified Brother Brigham Young that he would be one of the Witnesses, but said nothing to Joseph, until he had exhausted much of his feelings in regard to the Twelve, which took up some little time. He then turned to Elder Joseph Young with quite an earnestness, as though the vision of his mind was extended still further, and addressing him, said, 'Brother Joseph, the Lord has made you President of the Seventies.' They had heard of Moses and seventy Elders of Israel, and of Jesus appointing 'other Seventies,' but had never heard of Twelve Apostles and of Seventies being called in this Church before. It was a strange saying, 'The Lord has made you President of the Seventies,' as though it had already taken place, and it caused these brethren to marvel. The Prophet did not say that any others would be called to be the bearers of this message abroad, but the inference might be clearly drawn, that this was his meaning, from the language he used at the time. Agreeable to his request to Elder Brigham Young, the branches were all notified, and a meeting of the brethren in general conference was held in Kirtland, in the new school house under the printing office, on the following Saturday, February 14th, when the Twelve were appointed and ordained, and the conference adjourned for two weeks."—"History of the organization of the Seventies," by Joseph Young, Sen. (1878) pp. 1, 2.

affecting prayer, the brethren who went to Zion [in Zion's camp] were requested to take their seats together in a part of the house by themselves.

President Smith then stated that the meeting had been called, because God had commanded it; and it was made known to him by vision* and by the Holy Spirit. He then gave a relation of some of the circumstances attending us while journeying to Zion—our trials, sufferings; and said God had not designed all this for nothing, but He had it in remembrance yet;† and it was the will of God that those who went to Zion, with a determination to lay down their lives, if necessary, should be ordained to the ministry, and go forth to prune the vineyard for the last time, or the coming of the Lord, which was nigh—even fifty-six years should wind up the scene.

The President also said many things; such as the weak things, even the smallest and weakest among us, shall be powerful and mighty, and great things shall be accomplished by you from this hour; and you shall begin to feel the whisperings of the Spirit of God; and the work of God shall begin to break forth from this time; and you shall be endowed with power from on high.

President then called up all those who went to Zion, if they were agreed with him in the statement which he had made, to arise; and they all arose and stood upon their feet.

He then called upon the remainder of the congregation, to know if they also sanctioned the move, and they all raised their right hand.

* This vision, in which the Prophet evidently saw the order of the Church organization, is several times alluded to by him. By reference to the note on page 181 it will be observed that President Smith there refers to the vision in such a manner as to lead one to believe that he saw that Brigham Young would be one of the Twelve, and Joseph Young President of the Seventies. He also refers to this vision in the revelation which appears in chapter xiv; (Doctrine and Covenants, sec. cvii, 93). Describing the order of the Seventies, he says: "And it is according to the *vision*, showing the order of the Seventy, that there shall be seven Presidents to preside over them, chosen out of the number of the Seventy." It was doubtless in this vision also that the Prophet saw the manner in which the Twelve should be chosen.

† Elder Joseph Young in his "History of the Organization of the Seventies," (page 14) says that the following sentiment was delivered by the Prophet Joseph Smith in an address to the Elders assembled in Kirtland soon after the Seventies were organized: "Brethren, some of you are angry with me, because you did not fight in Missouri; but let me tell you, God did not want you to fight. He could not organize His kingdom with twelve men to open the Gospel door to the nations of the earth, and with seventy men under their direction to follow in their tracks, unless He took them from a body of men who had offered their lives, and who had made as great a sacrifice as did Abraham. Now the Lord has got His Twelve and His Seventy, and there will be other quorums of Seventies called, who will make the sacrifice, and those who have not made their sacrifices and their offerings now, will make them hereafter."

The names of those who went to Zion in the camp are as follows:*

Hazen Aldrich,
Joseph S. Allen,
Isaac Allred,
James Allred,
Martin Allred,
Milo Andrus,
Solomon Angel,
Allen A. Avery,
Almon W. Babbitt,
Alexander Badlam,
Samuel Baker,
Nathan Bennett Baldwin,
Elam Barber,
Israel Barlow,
Lorenzo D. Barnes,
Edson Barney,
Royal Barney,
Henry Benner,
Samuel Bent,
Hiram Backman,
Lorenzo Booth,
George W. Brooks,
Albert Brown,
Harry Brown,
Samuel Brown,
John Brownell,
Peter Buchanan,
Alden Burdick,
Harrison Burgess,
David Byur,
William F. Cahoon,
John Carpenter,
John S. Carter,
Daniel Cathcart,
Solon Foster,
Jacob Gates,
Benjamin Gifford,
Alonzo Champlin,
Jacob Chapman,
William Cherry,
John M. Chidester,
Alden Childs,
Nathaniel Childs,
Stephen Childs,
Albert Clements,
Thomas Colborn,
Alanson Colby,
Zera S. Cole,
Zebedee Coltrin,
Libeus T. Coon,
Horace Cowan,
Lyman Curtis,
Mecham Curtis,
Solomon W. Denton,
Peter Doff,
David D. Dort,
John Duncan,
James Dunn,
Philemon Duzette,
Philip Ettleman,
Bradford W. Elliot,
David Elliot,
David Evans,
Asa Field,
Edmund Fisher,
Alfred Fisk,
Hezekiah Fisk,
Elijah Fordham,
George Fordham,
Frederick Forney,
John Fossett,
James Foster,
William S. Ivie,
William Jessop,

* A full list of those who went up to Zion, including women and children, is here published in place of the partial list heretofore published in the History of Joseph Smith in the *Millennial Star*, volume xv, page 205.

Levi Gifford,
Sherman Gilbert,
Tru Glidden,
Dean C. Gould,
Jedediah M. Grant,
Addison Green,
Michael Griffith,
Everett Griswold,
Elisha Groves,
Joseph Hancock,
Levi W. Hancock,
Joseph Harmon,
Henry Herriman,
Martin Harris,
Joseph Hartshorn,
Thomas Hayes,
Nelson Higgins,
Seth Hitchcock,
Amos Hogers,
Chandler Holbrook,
Joseph Holbrook,
Milton Holmes,
Osmon Houghton,
Marshal Hubbard,
Solomon Humphrey,
Joseph Huntsman,
John Hustin,
Elias Hutchins,
Heman T. Hyde,
Orson Hyde,
Warren S. Ingalls,
Edward Ivie,
James R. Ivie,
John A. Ivie;
David W. Patten,
William D. Pratt,
Leonard Rich,
Darwin Richardson,
Burr Riggs,
Harpin Riggs,
Nathaniel Riggs,
Milcher Riley,
Alanson Ripley,
Luke S. Johnson,
Lyman E. Johnson,
Noah Johnson,
Seth Johnson,
Isaac Jones,
Levi Jones,
Charles Kelley,
Heber C. Kimball,
Samuel Kingsley,
Dennis Lake,
Jesse B. Lawson,
L. S. Lewis,
Josiah Littlefield,
Lyman O. Littlefield,
Waldo Littlefield,
Amasa M. Lyman,
Moses Martin,
Edward W. Marvin,
Reuben McBride,
Robert McCord,
Eleazer Miller,
John Miller,
Justin Morse,
John Murdock,
Freeman Nickerson,
Levi S. Nickerson,
Uriah C. Nickerson,
Joseph Nicholas,
Joseph B. Noble,
Ur. North,
Roger Orton,
John D. Parker,
Warren Parrish,
Orson Pratt,
Parley P. Pratt,
Charles C. Rich,
Samuel Thompson,
Wm. P. Tippetts,
Tinney Thomas,
Nelson Tribbs,
Joel Vaughn,
Salmon Warner,
William Weden,

Lewis Robbins,
Erastus Rudd,
William Henry Sagers,
Wilkins Jenkins Salisbury,
Henry Sherman,
Lyman Sherman,
Henry Shibley,
Cyrus Smalling,
Avery Smith,
George A. Smith,
Hyrum Smith,
Jackson Smith,
Zechariah B. Smith,
Joseph Smith,
Lyman Smith,
Sylvester Smith,
William Smith,
Willard Snow,
Harvey Stanley,
Hyrum Stratton,
Zerubbabel Snow,
Daniel Stephens,
Elias Strong,
John Joshua Tanner,
Ezra Thayer,
Nathan Tanner,
James L. Thompson,
Elias Wells,
Alexander Whitesides,
Andrew W. Whitlock,
Lyman Wight,
Eber Wilcox,
Sylvester B. Wilkinson,
Frederick G. Williams.
Alonzo Winchester,
Benjamin Winchester,
Lupton Winchester,
Alvin Winegar,
Samuel Winegar,
Hiram Winter,
Henry Wissmiller,
Wilford Woodruff,
Brigham Young,
Joseph Young.

WOMEN IN ZION'S CAMP.

Charlotte Alvord,
Sophronia Curtis,
Mary Snow Gates,
Nancy Lambson Holbrook,
Betsy Parrish,
Ada Clements,
Mary Chidester,
Diana Drake,
Eunice Holbrook,
Mrs. Houghton,
——— Ripley.

CHILDREN IN ZION'S CAMP.

Diana Holbrook, daughter of Chandler Holbrook,
Sarah Lucretia Holbrook, daughter of Joseph Holbrook,
Charlotte Holbrook, daughter of Joseph Holbrook,
———————, daughter of Alvin Winegar,
Sarah Pulsipher, daughter of Zera Pulsipher,
John P. Chidester, son of John M. Chidester,
Eunice Chidester, daughter of John M. Chidester.

President Joseph Smith, Jun., after making many remarks on the subject of choosing the Twelve, wanted an expression from the brethren, if they would be satisfied to have the Spirit of the Lord dictate in the choice of the Elders to be Apostles; whereupon all the Elders present expressed their anxious desire to have it so.

A hymn was then sung, "Hark, listen to the trumpeters."* President Hyrum Smith prayed, and meeting was dismissed for one hour.

Assembled pursuant to adjournment, and commenced with prayer.

President Joseph Smith, Jun., said that the first business of the meeting was, for the Three Witnesses† of the Book of Mormon, to pray, each

* The hymn was peculiarly suited to the occasion. Some of the stanzas follow:

"Hark! listen to the trumpeters!
They sound for volunteers;
On Zion's bright and flowery mount
Behold the officers.

"Their horses white, their armor bright,
With courage bold they stand,
Enlisting soldiers for their king,
To march to Zion's land.

* * *

"We want no cowards in our bands,
Who will our colors fly:
We call for valiant-hearted men,
Who're not afraid to die.

"To see our armies on parade,
How martial they appear!
All armed and dressed in uniform,
They look like men of war.

"They follow their great General.
The great Eternal Lamb—
His garments stained in his own blood—
King Jesus is His name."

† It was made known to the Prophet and Oliver Cowdery as early as June, 1829, that there would be Twelve Apostles chosen in this dipensation. In that revelation (Doctrine and Covenants, sec. xviii: 37) the Lord, addressing Oliver Cowdery and David Whitmer, said: "And now, behold, I give unto you Oliver Cowdery, and also unto David Whitmer, that you shall search out the Twelve, who shall have the desires of which I have spoken." That is, desires to take upon them the name of Jesus Christ with full purpose of heart. It will be observed that in this revelation only two of the Three Witnesses are named, yet Martin Harris was associated with his fellow Witnesses in choosing and ordaining the Twelve Apostles. I think it was designed from the first that the Three Witnesses should choose the Twelve Special Witnesses of the name and mission of the Lord Jesus Christ—the Twelve Apostles; but at the time the revelation of June, 1829, was given, making known that Twelve Apostles would be called, and designating Oliver Cowdery and David Whitmer as the ones to choose them, Martin Harris was out of favor with the Lord, and I suggest that it was for that reason doubtless that his name was omitted at that time. The evidence that Martin Harris was wavering about that time in his adherence to the Prophet and the work of God is found in Doctrine and Covenants, sec. xix, given in the month of June, 1829; in which revelation Martin Harris is sharply reproved for such wavering; for his

one, and then proceed to choose twelve men from the Church, as Apostles, to go to all nations, kindreds, tongues, and people.

The Three Witnesses, viz., Oliver Cowdery, David Whitmer, and Martin Harris, united in prayer.

These Three Witnesses were then blessed by the laying on of the hands of the Presidency.

The Witnesses then, according to a former commandment, proceeded to make choice of the Twelve. Their names are as follows:

1. Lyman E. Johnson,
2. Brigham Young,
3. Heber C. Kimball,
4. Orson Hyde,
5. David W. Patten,
6. Luke S. Johnson,
7. William E. M'Lellin,
8. John F. Boynton,
9. Orson Pratt,
10. William Smith,
11. Thomas P. Marsh,
12. Parley P. Pratt,

Lyman E. Johnson, Brigham Young and Heber C. Kimball came forward; and the Three Witnesses laid their hands upon each one's head and prayed, separately.*

covetousness; for hesitating to dispose of his land to meet the obligations entered into with the printer. He is commanded to repent of all these things, which, happily he did; but evidently not before the revelation concerning the choosing of the Twelve (Doctrine and Covenants, sec. xviii) was given, for which reason doubtless his name is not there associated with those of his fellow Witnesses when they were designated to choose the Twelve Apostles. As already stated, however, in the vision in which the Prophet Joseph saw more perfectly the organization of the Church, and the manner in which the Twelve were to be chosen, he undoubtedly learned that it was in harmony with the order of things that the Three Witnesses should choose the Twelve Special Witnesses, and hence appointed Martin Harris to assist Oliver Cowdery and David Whitmer in choosing the Apostles.

A word, by the way, in relation to the appropriateness of the Three Witnesses choosing the Twelve. In the revelation defining the special calling of the Twelve Apostles it is written: "The Twelve traveling counselors are called to be the Twelve Apostles, or special witnesses of the name of Christ in all the world; thus differing from other officers in the Church in the duties of their calling. (Doctrine and Covenants, sec. cvii: 23). From this it appears that the *special* calling of the Twelve is to be Witnesses for the Lord Jesus Christ in all the world; hence it was preeminently proper that these Twelve Witnesses should be chosen by the Three very special Witnesses—witnesses of the Book of Mormon in particular, and of God's marvelous work in general.

* Much interest has been manifested in the Church concerning who was mouth in ordaining respectively the brethren of the first Twelve. Most likely the Three Witnesses who ordained the Apostles were mouth in the order in which they have always stood as Witnesses, viz., Oliver Cowdery first, David Whitmer second, and Martin Harris third. If they officiated in this order then Oliver Cowdery ordained Lyman E. Johnson; David Whitmer, Brigham Young; and Martin Harris, Heber C. Kimball. It has been suggested by some that the Prophet Joseph may have joined the Three Witnesses in ordaining the Twelve, and in that event would be mouth first, and therefore ordained Lyman E. Johnson, leaving Oliver Cowdery to ordain Brigham

The blessing of Lyman E. Johnson was, in the name of Jesus Christ, that he should bear the tidings of salvation to nations, tongues, and people, until the utmost corners of the earth shall hear the tidings; and that he shall be a witness of the things of God to nations and tongues, and that holy angels shall administer to him occasionally; and that no power of the enemy shall prevent him from going forth and doing the work of the Lord; and that he shall live until the gathering is accomplished, according to the holy prophets; and he shall be like unto Enoch; and his faith shall be like unto his; and he shall be called great among all the living; and Satan shall tremble before him; and he shall see the Savior come and stand upon the earth with power and great glory.

The blessing of Brigham Young was that he should be strong in body, that he might go forth and gather the elect, preparatory to the great day of the coming of the Lord; and that he might be strong and mighty, declaring the tidings to nations that know not God; that he may add ten talents; that he may come to Zion with many sheaves. He shall go forth from land to land and from sea to sea; and shall behold heavenly messengers going forth; and his life shall be prolonged; and the Holy

Young, David Whitmer, Heber C. Kimball. This, however, is not likely since but three of those who had been chosen were called up at the above meeting to be ordained, one for each Witness. Besides, the express language of the minutes of the proceedings is, "The Three Witnesses laid their hands upon each one's head and prayed separately; that is each ordained his man. The statement of Heber C. Kimball in the published extracts of his journal, also confirms this view of the matter. After giving the names of the Twelve men chosen he says: "After having expressed our feeling on this occasion, we were severally called into the stand, and there received our ordinations, *under the hands of Oliver Cowdery, David Whitmer, and Martin Harris. These brethren ordained us to the Apostleship*, and predicted many things which should come to pass, that we should have power to heal the sick, cast out devils, raise the dead, give sight to the blind, have power to remove mountains, and all things should be subject to us through the name of Jesus Christ, and angels should minister unto us, and many more things, too numerous to mention." He also adds the following interesting item with reference to the ordinations of that day: "After we [referring to the first three called up to receive ordination] had been thus ordained by these brethren, the First Presidency laid their hands on us and confirmed these blessings and ordinations, and likewise predicted many things which should come to pass." (*Times and Seasons*, vol. vi, p. 868). While these statements make it very clear that the Prophet Joseph did not join with the Three Witnesses in ordaining the Apostles—except in the way of confirming the ordination they received from the Witnesses, as described by Elder Kimball—the minutes of the meeting held February 21st, at which Parley P. Pratt was ordained, state that he was "ordained one of the Twelve by President Joseph Smith, Jun., David Whitmer, and Oliver Cowdery." Martin Harris must have been absent, and the Prophet evidently joined Oliver Cowdery and David Whitmer on that occasion because of the absence of Harris; but whether or not the Prophet was mouth on that occasion does not appear in the minutes or in Elder Pratt's autobiography.

Priesthood is conferred on him, that he may do wonders in the name of Jesus; that he may cast out devils, heal the sick, raise the dead, open the eyes of the blind, go forth from land to land and from sea to sea; and that heathen nations shall even call him God himself, if he do not rebuke them.

Heber C. Kimball's blessing was, in substance, that he shall be made like unto those who have been blessed before him; and be favored with the same blessing. That he might receive visions; the ministration of angels, and hear their voice; and even come into the presence of God; that many millions may be converted by his instrumentality; that angels may waft him from place to place, and that he may stand unto the coming of our Lord, and receive a crown in the Kingdom of our God; that he be made acquainted with the day when Christ shall come; that he shall be made perfect in faith; and that the deaf shall hear, the lame shall walk, the blind shall see, and greater things than these shall he do; that he shall have boldness of speech before the nations, and great power.

A hymn was then sung, "Glorious things of thee are spoken," etc.; and the congreagation was dismissed by President Joseph Smith, Jun.

Sunday, February 15.—The congregation again assembled.

President Cowdery made some observations upon the nature of the meeting, calling upon the Lord for his assistance; after which a number of certificates from brethren that had recently returned from Zion were read and accepted.

President Cowdery then called forward Orson Hyde, David W. Patten and Luke Johnson, and proceeded to their ordinations and blessings.

Orson Hyde's Blessing:—Oliver Cowdery called upon the Lord to smile upon him; that his faith be made perfect, and that the blessings pronounced may be realized; that he be made mighty, and be endued with powers from on high, and go forth to the nations of the earth to proclaim the Gospel, that he may escape all the pollutions of the world; that the angels shall uphold him; and that he shall go forth according to the commandment, both to Jew and Gentile, and to all nations, kingdoms and tongues; that all who hear his voice shall acknowledge him to be a servant of God; that he shall be equal with his brethren in holding the keys of the kingdom; that he may stand on the earth and bring souls till Christ comes. We know that he loves Thee, O, Lord, and may this Thy servant be able to walk through pestilence and not be harmed; and the powers of darkness have no ascendency over him; may he have power to smite the earth with pestilence; to divide waters, and lead through the Saints; may he go from land to land and from sea to sea, and may he be like one of the three Nephites.

David W. Patten's blessing:—O God, give this Thy servant, a knowledge of Thy will; may he be like one of old, who bore testimony of Jesus; may he be a new man from this day forth. He shall be equal with his brethren, the Twelve, and have the qualifications of the prophets before him. May his body be strong and never be weary; may he walk and not faint. May he have power over all diseases, and faith according to his desires; may the heavens be opened upon him speedily; that he may bear testimony from knowledge; that he may go to nations and isles afar off. May he have a knowledge of the things of the Kingdom, from the beginning, and be able to tear down priestcraft like a lion. May he have power to smite his enemies before him, with utter destruction. May he continue till the Lord comes. O Father, we seal these blessings upon him. Even so. Amen.

Luke S. Johnson's Blessing:—Our Father in heaven, look down in mercy upon us, and upon this Thy servant, whom we ordain to the ministry of the Twelve. He shall be prepared and preserved, and be like those we have blessed before him. The nations shall tremble before him. He shall hear the voice of God; he shall comfort the hearts of the Saints always. The angels shall bear him up till he shall finish his ministry. He shall be delivered, and come forth with Israel. He shall bear testimony to the kings of the earth, and hold communion with the Father, with the Son, and with the general assembly and Church of the first-born. If cast into prison, he shall be able to comfort the hearts of his comrades. His tongue shall be loosed, and he shall have power to lead many to Zion, and sit down with them; the Ancient of Days shall pronounce this blessing, that he has been faithful; he shall have strength, wisdom, and power; he shall go among the covenant people and speak all their tongues where he shall go. All these blessings we confirm upon him in the name of Jesus. Amen.

William E. M'Lellin's Blessing:—In the name of the Lord, wisdom and intelligence shall be poured out upon him, to enable him to perform the great work that is incumbent upon him; that he may be spared until the Saints are gathered; that he may stand before kings and rulers to bear testimony, and be upheld by holy angels; and the nations of the earth shall acknowledge that God has sent him; he shall have power to overcome his enemies; and his life shall be spared in the midst of pestilence and destruction, and in the midst of his enemies. He shall be a prince and savior to God's people. The tempter shall not overcome him, nor his enemies prevail against him; the heavens shall be opened unto him, as unto men in days of old. He shall be mighty in the hands of God, and shall convince thousands that God has sent him; and his days may be prolonged until the coming of the Son of Man. He shall be wafted as on eagles' wings, from country to country, and from people to people; and be able to do wonders in the midst of this generation. Even so. Amen.

John F. Boynton's Blessing:—Thou hast prevailed and thou shalt prevail, and thou shalt declare the Gospel unto many nations. Thou shalt be made mighty before God; and although thou shalt be cast out from the face of men, yet thou shalt have power to prevail. Thou shalt lead the elect triumphantly to the places of refuge; thou shalt be like the brethren who have been blessed before thee. Thou shalt stand in that day of calamity when the wicked shall be consumed, and present unto the Father, spotless, the fruits of thy labor. Thou shalt overcome all the evils that are in the world; thou shalt have wisdom to put to silence all the wisdom of the wise; and thou shalt see the face of thy Redeemer in the flesh. These blessings are pronounced and sealed upon thee. Even so. Amen.

William Smith's Blessing:—We pray that he may be purified in heart; that he may have communion with God; that he may be equal with his brethren in holding the keys of this ministry; that he may be kept and be instrumental in leading Israel forth, that he may be delivered from the hands of those who seek to destroy him; that he may be enabled to bear testimony to the nations that Jesus lives; that he may stand in the midst of pestilence and destruction. He shall be mighty in the hands of God, in bringing about the restoration of Israel. The nations shall rejoice at the greatness of the gifts which God has bestowed upon him: that his tongue shall be loosed; he shall have power to do great things in the name of Jesus. He shall be preserved and remain on the earth, until Christ shall come to take vengeance on the wicked. Adjourned.

Kirtland, February 21st, 1835: Pursuant to adjournment, a meeting of the Church was held, and after prayer by President David Whitmer, and a short address by President Oliver Cowdery to the congregation, Elder Parley P. Pratt was called to the stand, and ordained one of the Twelve, by President Joseph Smith, Jun., David Whitmer, and Oliver Cowdery. O Lord, smile from heaven upon this thy servant; forgive his sins, sanctify his heart, and prepare him to receive the blessing. Increase his love for Thee and for Thy cause; increase his intelligence; communicate to him all that wisdom, that prudence, and that understanding, which he needs as a minister of righteousness and to magnify the Apostleship whereunto he is called. May a double portion of that Spirit which was communicated to the disciples of our Lord and Savior to lead them unto all truth, rest down upon him, and go with him where he goes, that nothing shall prevail against him, that he may be delivered from prisons, from the power of his enemies, and from the adversary of all righteousness. May he be able to mount up on wings as an eagle, to run and not be weary, to walk and not faint; may he have great wisdom and intelligence, and be able to lead thine elect through this thorny maze. Let sickness and death have no power over him; let him be equal with his brethren in bringing many sons and daughters to glory, and many nations to a knowledge of the truth. Great blessings shall rest upon thee; thy faith shall increase; thou shalt have great power to prevail. The vail of the heavens shall be rolled up; thou shalt be permitted to gaze within it, and receive instructions from on high. No arm that is formed and lifted against thee shall prosper; no power shall prevail; for thou shalt have power with God, and shalt proclaim His Gospel. Thou wilt be afflicted, but thou shalt be delivered, and conquer all thy foes. Thine office shall never be taken from thee; thou shalt be called great; angels shall carry thee from place to place. Thy sins are forgiven, and thy name written in the Lamb's Book of Life. Even so. Amen.

Apostolic Charge given by Oliver Cowdery to Parley P. Pratt:

I am aware, dear Brother, that the mind naturally claims something new; but the same thing rehearsed frequently profits us. You will have the same difficulties to encounter in fulfilling this ministry, that the ancient Apostle had. You have enlisted in a cause that requires your whole attention; you ought, therefore, to count the cost; and to become a polished shaft, you must be sensible, requires the labor of years; and your station requires a perfect polish. It is required of you not merely to travel a few miles in the country, but in distant countries: you must endure much labor, much toil, and many privations, to become perfectly polished. Your calling is not like that of the husbandman, to cultivate a stinted portion of the planet on which we dwell, and when heaven has given the former and the latter rain, and mellow autumn ripened his fruit, gathers it in, and congratulates himself for a season in the intermission of his toils, while he anticipates his winter evenings of relaxation and fire-side enjoyments. But, dear Brother, it is far otherwise with you. Your labor must be incessant, and your toil great; you must go forth and labor till the great work is done. It will require a series of years to accomplish it; but you will have this pleasing consolation, that your heavenly Father requires it; the field is His; the work is His; and He will not only cheer you, animate you, and buoy you up in your pilgrimage, in your arduous toils; but when your work is done, and your labor over, He will take you unto Himself. But before this consummation of your felicity, bring your mind to bear upon what will be imperiously required of you to accomplish, viz., the great work that lies before you. Count well the cost. You have read of the persecutions and trials of ancient days. Has not bitter experience taught you that they are the same now? You will be dragged before the authorities for the religion you profess; and it were better not to set out, than to start and look back, or shrink when dangers thicken around you, or appalling death stares you in the face. I have spoken these things, dear brother, because I have seen them in visions. There are strong dungeons and gloomy prisons for you. These should not appal you. You must be called a good or a bad man. The ancients passed through the same experience. They had this testimony—that they had seen the Savior after He rose from the dead. You must bear the same testimony; or your mission, your labor, your toil, will be in vain. You must bear the same testimony, that there is but one God, one Mediator; he that hath seen Him, will know Him, and testify of Him. Beware of pride; beware of evil; shun the very appearance of it; for the time is coming when, if you do not give heed to these things, you will have a fall. Among your many afflictions, you will have many blessings also; but you must pass through many afflictions, in order to receive the glory that is in reserve for you. You will meet thousands, who, when they first see you, will know nothing about salvation by Jesus Christ; you shall see a nation born in a day. A great work lies before you, and the time is near when you must bid farewell to your native land, cross the mighty deep, and sound the tocsin of alarm to other nations, kindreds, tongues, and people. Remember that all your hopes of deliverance from danger and from death, will rest upon your faithfulness to God; in His cause, you must necessarily serve Him with a perfect heart and a willing mind. Avoid strife and vain glory; think not yourself better than your brethren, but pray for them, as well as for yourself; and if you are faithful, great will be your blessings; but if you are not, your stewardship will be taken from you, and another appointed in your stead.

Elder Pratt gave his hand to President Oliver Cowdery, and said he had received ordination, and should fulfill the ministry according to the grace given him; to which the President replied, Go forth, and angels shall bear thee up; and thou shalt come forth at the last day, bringing many with thee.

Thomas B. Marsh and Orson Pratt were absent on a mission.

Elder Marsh returned to Kirtland on the 25th of April, and Elder Orson Pratt on the 26th, and received their ordinations and blessings, which are recorded in this place, in connection with the ordinations and blessings of their brethren.*

Thomas B. Marsh's Blessing by President Oliver Cowdery.—Dear Brother—You are to be a minister of righteousness, and to this ministry and apostleship you are now to be ordained; and may all temporal and spiritual blessings attend you. Your sins are forgiven you, and you are to go forth and preach the everlasting Gospel. You shall travel from kingdom to kingdom and from nation to nation. Angels shall bear thee up, and thou shalt be instrumental in bringing thousands of the redeemed of the Lord to Zion. Sealed by President David Whitmer. Even so. Amen.

Orson Pratt's Blessing.—Dear Brother—You are chosen and set apart, to be ordained to this apostleship and this ministry; you shall go forth and preach the Gospel, and do a mighty work. You shall be sustained; the Holy Spirit shall enlighten thy mind; thou shalt travel from nation to nation; the Lord God shall preserve thee, and return thee safe, with songs of everlasting joy upon thy head. Confirmed by President David Whitmer.

General Charge to the Twelve.

The following general charge was given to the Twelve by President Oliver Cowdery:—Dear Brethren—Previous to delivering the charge, I shall read a part of a revelation. It is known to you, that previous to the organization of this Church in 1830, the Lord gave revelations, or the Church could not have been organized. The people of this Church were weak in faith compared with the ancients. Those who embarked in this cause were desirous to know how the work was to be conducted.

* According to Heber C. Kimball's Journal, Orson Pratt's ordination took place on the 5th of April, 1835, under the following circumstances: "Sunday morning, April 5, 1835.—The Twelve had not all as yet been together, for the last three mentioned [Orson Pratt, Thomas B. Marsh and Parley P. Pratt] were not present at the time of choosing, and as the time drew near that we should travel to the east, we appointed this day to bear our testimony unto our brethren and friends. We were all assembled together, with the exception of Brother Orson Pratt, who had not yet been with us. At this time, while we were praying, and wishing for his arrival, while opening the meeting, he entered the house. We rejoiced at his presence, and thanked the Lord for it. He was then ordained and we proceeded to speak according to our ages, the eldest speaking first. This day Brother Thomas B. Marsh, Brigham Young, David W. Patten, and myself spake." (*Times and Seasons*, vol. vi, p. 869.) The incident is given as Elder Kimball relates it because of its interest, but he is in error as to the date of the occurrence, since Elder Pratt himself, as well as the Prophet, gives the date of the former's ordination 26th of April, 1835. Elder Pratt also makes this entry in his journal: "April 24—Took the stage, and arrived in Kirtland on the 26th, about ten o'clock in the forenoon; walked into the meeting and learned that they had been prophesying that I would arrive there, so as to attend that meeting, although not one of them knew where I was. I was much rejoiced at meeting with the Saints."

They read many things in the Book of Mormon concerning their duty, and the way the great work ought to be done; but the minds of men are so constructed that they will not believe, without a testimony of seeing or hearing. The Lord gave us a revelation that, in process of time, there should be twelve men chosen to preach His Gospel to Jew and Gentile. Our minds have been on a constant stretch, to find who these twelve were; when the time should come we could not tell; but we sought the Lord by fasting and prayer to have our lives prolonged to see this day, to see you, and to take a retrospect of the difficulties through which we have passed; but having seen the day, it becomes my duty to deliver to you a charge; and first, a few remarks respecting your ministry. You have many revelations put into your hands—revelations to make you acquainted with the nature of your mission; you will have difficulties by reason of your visiting all the nations of the world. You will need wisdom in a tenfold proportion to what you have ever had; you will have to combat all the prejudices of all nations.

He then read the revelation,* and said: Have you desired this ministry with all your hearts? If you have desired it you are called of God, not of man, to go into the world.

He then read again, from the revelation, what the Lord said unto the Twelve. Brethren, you have had your duty presented in this revelation. You have been ordained to this holy Priesthood, you have received it from those who have the power and authority from an angel; you are to preach the Gospel to every nation. Should you in the least degree come short of your duty, great will be your condemnation; for the greater the calling the greater the transgression. I therefore warn you to cultivate great humility; for I know the pride of the human heart. Beware, lest the flatterers of the world lift you up; beware, lest your affections be captivated by worldly objects. Let your ministry be first. Remember, the souls of men are committed to your charge; and if you mind your calling, you shall always prosper.

You have been indebted to other men, in the first instance, for evidence; on that you have acted; but it is necessary that you receive a testimony from heaven for yourselves; so that you can bear testimony to the truth of the Book of Mormon, and that you have seen the face of God. That is more than the testimony of an angel. When the proper time arrives, you shall be able to bear this testimony to the world. When you bear testimony that you have seen God, this testimony God will never suffer to fall, but will bear you out; although many will not give heed, yet others will. You will therefore see the necessity of getting this testimony from heaven.

Never cease striving until you have seen God face to face. Strengthen your faith; cast off your doubts, your sins, and all your unbelief; and

* Doctrine and Covenants, sec. xviii.

nothing can prevent you from coming to God. Your ordination is not full and complete till God has laid His hand upon you. We require as much to qualify us as did those who have gone before us; God is the same. If the Savior in former days laid His hands upon His disciples, why not in latter days?

With regard to superiority, I must make a few remarks. The ancient apostles sought to be great; but lest the seeds of discord be sown in this matter; understand particularly the voice of the Spirit on this occasion. God does not love you better or more than others. You are to contend for the faith once delivered to the saints. Jacob, you know, wrestled till he had obtained. It was by fervent prayer and diligent search that you have obtained the testimony you are now able to bear. You are as one; you are equal in bearing the keys of the Kingdom to all nations. You are called to preach the Gospel of the Son of God to the nations of the earth; it is the will of your heavenly Father, that you proclaim His Gospel to the ends of the earth and the islands of the sea.

Be zealous to save souls. The soul of one man is as precious as the soul of another. You are to bear this message to those who consider themselves wise; and such may persecute you—they may seek your life. The adversary has always sought the life of the servants of God; you are therefore to be prepared at all times to make a sacrifice of your lives, should God require them in the advancement and building up of His cause. Murmur not at God. Be always prayerful; be always watchful. You will bear with me while I relieve the feelings of my heart. We shall not see another day like this; the time has fully come—the voice of the Spirit has come—to set these men apart.

You will see the time when you will desire to see such a day as this, and you will not see it. Every heart wishes you peace and proserity, but the scene with you will inevitably change. Let no man take your bishopric, and beware that you lose not your crowns. It will require your whole souls, it will require courage like Enoch's.

The time is near when you will be in the midst of congregations who will gnash their teeth upon you. The Gospel must roll forth, and it will until it fills the whole earth. Did I say congregations would gnash their teeth at you? Yea, I say, nations will oppose you—you will be considered the worst of men. Be not discouraged at this. When God pours out His Spirit, the enemy will rage; but God. remember, is on your right hand, and on your left. A man, though he be considered the worst, has joy, who is conscious that he pleases God.

The lives of those who proclaim the true Gospel will be in danger; this has been the case ever since the days of righteous Abel. The same opposition has been manifest whenever man came forward to publish the Gospel. The time is coming when you will be considered the worst of men by many, and by some the best. The time is coming when you will be perfectly familiar with the things of God. This testimony will make those who do not believe your testimony, seek your lives; but there are whole nations who will receive your testimony. They will call you good men. Be not lifted up when ye are called good men. Remember you are young men, and ye shall be spared. I include the other three. Bear them in mind in your prayers—carry their cases to the throne of grace; although they are not present, yet you and they are equal. This appointment is calculated to create for you an affection for each other, stronger than death. You will travel to other nations; bear each other in mind. If one or more be cast into prisons, let the others pray for them, and deliver them by their prayers. Your lives shall be in great jeopardy; but the promise of God is, that you shall be delivered.

Remember, you are not to go to other nations till you receive your endowments. Tarry at Kirtland until you are endowed with power from on high. You need a fountain of wisdom, knowledge and intelligence such as you never had. Relative to the endowment, I make a remark or two, that there may be no mistake. The world cannot receive the things of God. He can endow you without worldly pomp or great parade. He can give you that wisdom, that intelligence, and that power, which characterized the ancient saints, and now characterizes the inhabitants of the upper world.

The greatness of your commission consists in this: you are to hold the keys of this ministry; you are to go to the nations afar off—nations that sit in darkness. The day is coming when the work of God must be done. Israel shall be gathered: the seed of Jacob shall be gathered from their long dispersion. There will be a feast to Israel, the elect of God. It is a sorrowful tale, but the Gospel must be preached, and God's ministers rejected: but where can Israel be found and receive your testimony, and not rejoice? Nowhere! The prophecies are full of great things that are to take place in the last days. After the elect are gathered out, destructions shall come on the inhabitants of the earth; all nations shall feel the wrath of God, after they have been warned by the Saints of the Most High. If you will not warn them, others will, and you will lose your crowns.

You must prepare your minds to bid a long farewell to Kirtland, even till the great day come. You will see what you never expected to see; you will need the mind of Enoch or Elijah, and the faith of the brother of Jared; you must be prepared to walk by faith, however appalling the prospect to human view; you, and each of you, should feel the force of the imperious mandate, Son, go labor in my vineyard, and cheerfully receive what comes; but in the end you will stand while others will fall. You have read in the revelation concerning ordination: Beware how you ordain, for all nations are not like this nation; they will willingly receive the ordinances at your hands to put you out of the way. There will be times when nothing but the angels of God can deliver you out of their hands.

We appeal to your intelligence, we appeal to your understanding, that we have so far discharged our duty to you. We consider it one of the greatest condescensions of our heavenly Father, in pointing you out to us; you will be stewards over this ministry; you have a work to do that no other men can do; you must proclaim the Gospel in its simplicity and purity; and we commend you to God and the word of His grace. You have our best wishes, you have our most fervent prayers, that you may be able to bear this testimony, that you have seen the face of God. Therefore call upon Him in faith in mighty prayer till you prevail, for it is your duty and your privilege to bear such testimony for yourselves. We now exhort you to be faithful to fulfill your calling; there must be no lack here; you must fulfill in all things; and permit us to repeat, all nations have a claim on you; you are bound together as the Three Witnesses were; notwithstanding you can part and meet, and meet and part again, till your heads are silvered over with age.

He then took them separately by the hand, and said, "Do you with full purpose of heart take part in this ministry, to proclaim the Gospel with all diligence, with these your brethren, according to the tenor and intent of the charge you have received?" Each of them answered in the affirmative.*

Important Items of Instructions to the Twelve.

KIRTLAND, February 27.

This evening, nine of the Twelve, viz., Lyman Johnson, Brigham Young, Heber C. Kimball, Orson Hyde, David W. Patten, Luke Johnson, William E. M'Lellin, John F. Boynton, and William Smith, assembled at the house of President Joseph Smith, Jun., who was present, with Frederick G. Williams, Sidney Rigdon, Bishop Whitney, and three Elders. Parley P. Pratt had gone to New Partage, and Orson Pratt and Thomas B. Marsh had not yet arrived to receive their ordination.

After prayer by President Joseph Smith, Jun., he said, if we heard patiently, he could lay before the council an item which would be of importance. He had for himself, learned a fact by experience, which, on recollection, always gave him deep sorrow. It is a fact, if I now had in my possession, every decision which had been had upon impor-

* Elder Parley P. Pratt, in his autobiography (page 127) refers to this question put to each of the Twelve Apostles by Elder Cowdery as the "Oath and Covenant of the Apostleship."

tant items of doctrine and duties since the commencement of this work, I would not part with them for any sum of money; but we have neglected to take minutes of such things, thinking, perhaps, that they would never benefit us afterwards; which, if we had them now, would decide almost every point of doctrine which might be agitated. But this has been neglected, and now we cannot bear record to the Church and to the world, of the great and glorious manifestations which have been made to us with that degree of power and authority we otherwise could, if we now had these things to publish abroad.

Since the Twelve are now chosen, I wish to tell them a course which they may pursue, and be benefited thereafter, in a point of light of which they are not now aware. If they will, every time they assemble, appoint a person to preside over them during the meeting, and one or more to keep a record of their proceedings, and on the decision of every question or item, be it what it may, let such decision be written, and such decision will forever remain upon record, and appear an item of covenant or doctrine. An item thus decided may appear, at the time, of little or no worth, but should it be published, and one of you lay hands on it after, you will find it of infinite worth, not only to your brethren, but it will be a feast to your own souls.

Here is another important item. If you assemble from time to time, and proceed to discuss important questions, and pass decisions upon the same, and fail to note them down, by and by you will be driven to straits from which you will not be able to extricate yourselves, because you may be in a situation not to bring your faith to bear with sufficient perfection or power to obtain the desired information; or, perhaps, for neglecting to write these things when God had revealed them, not esteeming them of sufficient worth, the Spirit may withdraw and God may be angry; and there is, or was, a vast knowledge, of infinite importance, which is now lost. What was the cause of this? It came in consequence of slothfulness, or a neglect to appoint a man to occupy a few moments in writing all these decisions.

Here let me prophesy. The time will come, when, if you neglect to do this thing, you will fall by the hands of unrighteous men. Were you to be brought before the authorities, and be accused of any crime or misdemeanor, and be as innocent as the angels of God, unless you can prove yourselves to have been somewhere else, your enemies will prevail against you; but if you can bring twelve men to testify that you were in a certain place, at that time, you will escape their hand. Now, if you will be careful to keep minutes of these things, as I have said, it will be one of the most important records ever seen; for all such decisions will ever after remain as items of doctrine and covenants.

The council then expressed their approbation concerning the foregoing remarks of President Smith, and appointed Orson Hyde and William E. M'Lellin clerks of the meeting.

President Smith proposed the following question: What importance is there attached to the calling of these Twelve Apostles, different from the other callings or officers of the Church?

After the question was discussed by Councilors Patten, Young, Smith, and M'Lellin, President Joseph Smith, Jun., gave the following decision:

They are the Twelve Apostles, who are called to the office of the Traveling High Council, who are to preside over the churches of the Saints, among the Gentiles, where there is a presidency established; and they are to travel and preach among the Gentiles, until the Lord shall command them to go to the Jews. They are to hold the keys of this ministry, to unlock the door of the Kingdom of heaven unto all nations, and to preach the Gospel to every creature. This is the power, authority, and virtue of their apostleship.

OLIVER COWDERY, Clerk.

Report of the Kirtland School.

KIRTLAND, OHIO, February 27, 1835.

Having been requested by the trustees of the "Kirtland School" to give a sketch of the number of students who have attended the institution, and of their progress in the different sciences, I cheerfully comply with the request, having been an instructor therein from its commencement in December last.

The school has been conducted under the immediate care and inspection of Joseph Smith, Jun., Frederick G. Williams, Sidney Rigdon, and Oliver Cowdery, trustees. When the school first commenced, we received into it both large and small, but in about three weeks the classes became so large and the house so crowded, that it was thought advisable to dismiss all the small students, and continue those only who wished to study penmanship, arithmetic, English grammar, and geography. Before we dismissed the small pupils, there were in all about one hundred and thirty who attended; since that time there have been upon an average about one hundred; the most of whom have received lectures upon English grammar; and for the last four weeks about seventy have been studying geography one-half the day, and grammar and writing the other part. Burdick's Arithmetic, Kirkham's Grammar, and Olney's Geography have been used, and Noah Webster's Dictionary as standard. Since the year 1827, I have taught school in five different states, and visited many schools in which I was not engaged as teacher; in none, I can say, with certainty, I have seen students make more rapid progress than in this.

WILLIAM E. M'LELLIN.

CHAPTER XIII.

THE ORGANIZATION OF THE SEVENTIES—BLESSING OF THE FAITHFUL ELDERS AND SAINTS.

On the 28th of February, the Church in council assembled, commenced selecting certain individuals to be Seventies,* from the number of those who went up to Zion with me in the camp; and the following are the names of those who were ordained

The Calling of Seventies.

* The organization of quorums of Seventy in the Church was regarded as a very strange thing in modern times, but that such an organization had existed in the Church of God, both in the days of Moses and also in the days of Messiah, is evident from the scriptures. The Lord said to Moses: "Come up unto the Lord, thou, and Aaron, Nadab, and Abihu, and seventy of the elders of Israel; and worship ye afar off. * * * Then went up Moses, and Aaron, Nadab, and Abihu, and seventy of the elders of Israel. * * * And upon the nobles of the children of Israel He laid not His hand: also they saw God, and did eat and drink" (Exodus xxiv: 1, 9, 11). And again, "And the Lord said unto Moses, Gather unto me seventy men of the elders of Israel, whom thou knowest to be the elders of the people, and officers over them; and bring them unto the tabernacle of the congregation, that they may stand there with thee. And I will come down and talk with thee there: and I will take of the spirit which is upon thee, and will put it upon them; and they shall bear the burden of the people with thee, that thou bear it not thyself alone. * * * And Moses went out, and told the people the words of the Lord, and gathered the seventy men of the elders of the people, and set them round about the tabernacle. And the Lord came down in a cloud, and spake unto him, and took of the Spirit that was upon him, and gave it unto the seventy elders: and it came to pass, that, when the Spirit rested upon them, they prophesied, and did not cease" (Numbers xi: 16, 17, 24, 25).

It is not clear from the Old Testament just what the functions of the Seventy were in the Hebrew Priesthood, but they certainly were endowed with prophetic powers, and it is quite probable that the Sanhedrim (consisting of seventy-one members, inclusive of the president,) of later Jewish times had some relation to this earlier council of Seventy.

The organization of the Seventy by the Savior is alluded to in the tenth chapter

and blessed at that time, to begin the organization of the first quorum of Seventies, according to the visions* and revelations which I have received. The Seventies are to constitute traveling quorums, to go into all the earth, whithersoever the Twelve Apostles shall call them.†

of Luke as follows: "After these things the Lord appointed other seventy also, [from this it appears that quorums of seventy had been appointed previous to this] and sent them two and two before His face into every city and place, whither He Himself would come. Therefore said He unto them, The harvest truly is great, but the laborers are few: pray ye therefore the Lord of the harvest, that He would sent forth laborers into His harvest. Go your way: behold, I send you forth as lambs among wolves. Carry neither purse nor scrip, nor shoes: and salute no man by the way. And into whatsoever house ye enter, first say, Peace be to this house. And if the Son of peace be there, your peace shall rest upon it: if not, it shall turn to you again. And in the same house remain, eating and drinking such things as they give: for the laborer is worthy of his hire. Go not from house to house." That is, while these men were sent forth without purse and scrip, it was evidently not the intention of the Lord that they should beg from door to door. Continuing His instructions, the Master said: "And into whatsoever city ye enter, and they receive you, eat such things as are set before you: and heal the sick that are therein, and say unto them, The kingdom of God is come nigh unto you. But into whatsoever city ye enter, and they receive you not, go your ways out into the streets of the same, and say, Even the very dust of your city, which cleaveth on us, we do wipe off against you. notwithstanding be ye sure of this, that the kingdom of God is come nigh unto you But I say unto you, that it shall be more tolerable in that day for Sodom, than for that city. * * He that heareth you heareth me; and he that despiseth you despiseth me and he that despiseth me despiseth Him that sent me." The Seventy, it appears went forth under these instructions and were successful, for Luke continues: "And the seventy returned again with joy, saying, Lord, even the devils are subject unto us through Thy name." After this very plain allusion to this order of the Priesthood called the Seventy, these instructions, and the definitions given of their duties and callings, there can be no doubt as to their constituting an important factor in the Christian Church organization. The absence of such quorums of Priesthood in modern church establishments is but one among many other evidences that the Church of Christ had ceased from among men.

* See page 182 (note).

† The quorums of Seventy, in other words—in connection with the Twelve Apostles, under whose direction they labor—constitute the foreign ministry of the Church; and when the kind of labor they are expected to perform is taken into account, it will be found that their organization is admirably adopted for their work—the means are adequate to the end proposed. In all other quorums of the high Priesthood, excepting the Twelve, the presidency consists of a president and two counselors, but the presidency of the quorum of Seventy consists of seven presidents, equal in authority. For the sake of order, however, precedence is recognized in seniority of ordination; that is, the senior president by ordination—not of age—presides in the council, and over the quorum; and in the event of his absence, then the next senior president by ordination has the right of initiative and presides, and so on down the line of presidents. The order established in the Church for the work of the foreign ministry is for Elders to travel two and two. This doubtless for the reason that the Lord would establish His word by the mouths of two wit-

*Names of the Presidents and Members of the First Quorum of Seventies, Ordained Under the Hand of the Prophet Joseph Smith, with his two Counselors, Sidney Rigdon and Oliver Cowdery.**

PRESIDENTS.

Hazen Aldrich,
Joseph Young,
Levi W. Hancock,
Leonard Rich,
Zebedee Coltrin,
Lyman Sherman
Sylvester Smith.

MEMBERS.

Elias Hutchings,
Cyrus Smalling,
Levi Gifford,
Stephen Winchester,
Roger Orton,
Peter Buchannan,
John D. Parker,
David Elliot,
Samuel Brown,
Salmon Warner,
Jacob Chapman,
Charles Kelly,
Edmund Fisher,
Warren Parrish,
Joseph Hancock,
Alden Burdick,
Hiram Winters,
Harpin Riggs,
Edson Barney,
Joseph B. Noble,
Henry Benner,
David Evans,
Nathan B. Baldwin,
Burr Riggs,
Lewis Robbins,
Alexander Whitesides,
George W. Brooks,
Michael Griffith,
Royal Barney,
Libbeus T. Coons,
Willard Snow,
Jesse D. Harmon,
Heman T. Hyde,
Lorenzo D. Barnes.

nesses at least, to say nothing of the pleasure that would be derived from the companionship subsisting between two Elders while traveling among strangers, and even among enemies. A quorum of Seventy, if sent out into the world as a body, is capable of realizing all the advantages conceivable from organization. It can be broken up into just seven groups of ten members; with each group would be a president; these groups can be sub-divided into five pairs, who could scatter out into various neighborhoods, occasionally meet in conference with the group of ten to which the respective pairs belonged, and at greater intervals, the several groups could be called together for quorum conference. Thus a quorum of Seventy can be a veritable flying column, making proclamation of the Gospel, the like of which is to be found nowhere outside the Church of Christ.

* Instead of giving the forty names that here follow the statement of the Prophet in his history, I give the entire list of names that constituted the first quorum of Seventy, as written by the late President Joseph Young, in his "History of the Organization of the Seventies." All the brethren given in this list were not ordained on this 28th day of February, 1835, but all who were ordained on that date, of course, are included in this list. Of this organization of the quorum of Seventy, the statement of Elder Joseph Young, who became the senior president of the first council, has already been given at page 181.

Hiram Blackman,	Hiram Stratton,
William D. Pratt,	Moses Martin,
Zera S. Cole,	Lyman Smith,
Jesse Huntsman,	Harvey Stanley,
Solomon Angel,	Almon W. Babbitt,
Henry Herriman,	William F. Cahoon,
Israel Barlow,	Darwin Richardson,
Wilkins Jenkins Salisbury	Milo Andrus,
Nelson Higgins,	True Glidden,
Harry Brown,	Henry Shibley,
Jezeniah B. Smith,	Harrison Burgess,
Lorenzo Booth,	Jedediah M. Grant,
Alexander Badlam,	Daniel Stephens,
Zerubbabel Snow,	Amasa M. Lyman,

George A. Smith.

The council adjourned to the day following, March 1st, when, after attending the funeral of Seth Johnson, several who had recently been baptized, were confirmed, and the sacrament was administered to the Church. Previous to the administration, I spoke of the propriety of this institution in the Church, and urged the importance of doing it with acceptance before the Lord, and asked, How long do you suppose a man may partake of this ordinance unworthily, and the Lord not withdraw His Spirit from him? How long will he thus trifle with sacred things, and the Lord not give him over to the buffetings of Satan until the day of redemption! The Church should know if they are unworthy from time to time to partake, lest the servants of God be forbidden to administer it. Therefore our hearts ought to be humble, and we to repent of our sins, and put away evil from among us.

The Prophet's Remarks on the Sacrament.

After sacrament the council continued the ordination and blessing of those previously called; also John Murdock and S. W. Denton were ordained and blessed; Benjamin Winchester, Hyrum Smith, and Frederick G. Williams were blessed; and Joseph Young and Sylvester Smith were ordained presidents of Seventies.

More Ordinations.

The Blessing of those who assisted in Building the House of the Lord at Kirtland.

March 7.—This day a meeting of the Church of Latter-day Saints was called for the purpose of blessing, in the name of the Lord, those who have heretofore assisted in building, by their labor and other means, the House of the Lord in this place.

The morning was occupied by President Joseph Smith, Jun., in teaching the Church the propriety and necessity of purifying itself. In the afternoon, the names of those who had assisted to build the house were taken, and further instructions received from President Smith. He said that those who had distinguished themselves thus far by consecrating to the upbuilding of the House of the Lord, as well as laboring thereon, were to be remembered; that those who build it should own it, and have the control of it.

After further remarks, those who performed the labor on the building voted unanimously that they would continue to labor thereon, till the house should be completed.

President Sidney Rigdon was appointed to lay on hands and bestow blessings in the name of the Lord.

The Presidents were blessed; and Reynolds Cahoon, Hyrum Smith, and Jared Carter, the building committee, though the last two were not present, yet their rights in the house were preserved.

The following are the names of those who were blessed in consequence of their labor on the house of the Lord in Kirtland, and those who consecrated to its upbuilding:

Sidney Rigdon,
Joseph Smith, Jun.,
F. G. Williams,
Joseph Smith, Sen.,
Oliver Cowdery,
Newel K. Whitney,
Reynolds Cahoon,
Hyrum Smith
Jared Carter,
Jacob Bump,
Artemus Millet,
Alpheus Cutler,
Asa Lyman,
Josiah Butterfield,
Noah Packard,
James Putnam,
Isaac Hill,
Maleum C. Davis,
Jaman Aldrich,
John Young, Sen.,
Ezra Strong,
Joel McWithy,
Matthew Foy,
James Randall,
John P. Greene,
Aaron E. Lyon,
Thomas Burdick,
Truman Wait,
Edmund Bosley,
William Bosley,
William Perry,
Don Carlos Smith,
Shadrach Roundy,
Joel Johnson,

Edmund Durfee, Sen.,
Edmund Durfee, Jun.,
Gideon Ormsby,
Albert Miner,
Ira Ames,
Salmon Gee,
Peter Shirts,
Isaac Hubbard,
Horace Burgess,
Dexter Stillman,
Amos F. Herrick,
Mayhew Hillman,
William Carter,
William Burgess,
Giles Cook,
Almon Sherman,
Warren Smith,
Moses Bailey,
Sebe Ives,
Andrew H. Aldrich,
Ebenezar Jennings,
Oliver Granger,
Orson Johnson,
James Lake,
William Redfield,
Cyrus Lake,
Harvey Smith,
Isaac Cleveland,
William Barker,
Samuel S. Brannan,
John Wheeler,
Henry Baker,
William Fisk,
Henry Wilcox,
George Gee,
Lorenzo D. Young,
David Clough,
James Durfee,
Joseph Coe,
Thomas Gates,
Loren Babbitt,
Blake Baldwin,
Oliver Higley,
Evan M. Greene,
Levi Osgood,
Alpheus Harmon,
Joseph C. Kingsbury,
Ira Bond,
Z. H. Brewster,
Samuel Thomson,
John Ormsby,
Luman Carter,
John Smith,
Samuel H. Smith,
Thomas Fisher,
Starry Fisk,
Amos R. Orton,
Gad Yale,
John Johnson,
John Tanner,
Henry G. Sherwood,
Sidney Tanner,
Joseph Tippits,
Robert Quigley,
Erastus Babbitt,
Samuel Canfield,
Phineas H. Young,
Samuel Rolfe,
Calvin W. Stoddard,
Josiah Fuller,
Erastus Rudd,
Isaac G. Bishop,
Roswell Murray,
Benjamin Wells,
Nehemiah Harman,
Oliver Wetherby,
Thomas Hancock,
Josuah Grant,
William Draper,
Ransom Van Leuven,
Tunis Rappellee,
John Reed,
Samuel Wilcox,
Benjamin Johnson,
Joseph B. Bosworth.

The blessings and ordinations of particular individuals of the foregoing were as follows:—Reynolds Cahoon, Jacob Bump, and Artemus Millet, were blessed with the blessings of heaven and a right in the house of the Lord in Kirtland, agreeable to the labor they had performed thereon, and the means they had contributed.

Alpheus Cutler, Asa Lyman, Josiah Butterfield, Noah Packard, Jonas Putnam, and Isaac Hill received the same blessing. The blessing referred to was according to each man's labor or donation, and in addition, Elder Packard was promised wisdom and ability to proclaim the Gospel. Edmund Durfee, Sen., Edmund Durfee, Jun., and Gideon Ormsby received the same blessing, and Edmund Durfee, Jun., was ordained an Elder. Albert Miner, Ira Ames, Salmon Gee, Peter Shirts, Isaac Hubbard, and Horace Burgess were blessed, and Peter Shirts and Horace Burgess were ordained Elders. Dexter Stillman, Amos F. Herrick, and Matthew Hillman were blessed. William Burgess, Jaman Aldrich, and John Young, Sen., were blessed. Giles Cook, Jun., and M. C. Davis were blessed and ordained Elders. Wm. Carter, who was blind, was promised a restoration of sight, if faithful. Ezra Strong, Joel McWithy, Matthew Foy, James Randall, and Aaron C. Lyon were blessed. John P. Greene was ordained a missionary to the Lamanites, after others have unlocked the door, with a promise of gathering many to Zion, and of returning with great joy at the end of his mission, to enjoy the blessings of his family. Thomas Burdick, Truman Wait and Edmund Bosley were blessed, and Elder Bosley was told that God had a work for him, viz.: to go and preach the Gospel to the sectarian priests of this age, to call after them and hunt them up, wherever he could hear of them, and preach the Gospel to them whether they will hear or forbear. William Bosley and William Berry were blessed and ordained Elders. Don Carlos Smith was blessed with a promise of wisdom to proclaim the Gospel, and also to write in wisdom. Shadrach Roundy, Joel Johnson, and Oliver Higbee were blessed.

Adjourned till tomorrow.

March 8th.—Met pursuant to adjournment. Evan M. Greene, Levi Osgood, Alpheus Harmon, Joseph C. Kingsbury, Ira Bond, Z. H. Brewster, Samuel Tompkins, John Ormsby, Luman Carter, John Smith, Samuel H. Smith, Thomas Fisher, Starry Fisk, Amos R. Orton and Almon Sherman were blessed. Amos R. Orton was ordained an Elder and a missionary to the Lamanites. Andrew H. Aldrich, Thomas Bailey, Seba Ives, Ebenezer Jennings, Oliver Granger, Orson Johnson, Warren Smith, James Lake, and William Redfield were blessed, and William Redfield was ordained an Elder. Cyrus Lake,

Harvey Smith, Isaac Cleveland, William Baker, Samuel S. Brannan, John Wheeler, Henry Baker, William Fisk, Henry Wilcox, George W. Gee, David Clough, and Lorenzo D. Young were blessed, and Elder Young was set apart as a missionary to the Lamanites. Jas. Durfee, Jos. Coe, Thos. Gates, Loren Babbitt, Blake Baldwin, and Jos. B. Baldwin were blessed. John Johnson, John Tanner and Gad Yale were blessed; and Gad Yale, being one who went to the relief of the brethren in Missouri, was blessed accordingly. Henry G. Sherwood, Sidney Tanner, Joseph H. Tippits, Robert Quigley, and Erastus Babbitt were blessed, and Samuel Canfield was blessed and ordained an Elder. Phineas H. Young, Samuel Rolfe, and Calvin H. Stoddard were blessed, and Elder Young was ordained a missionary to the Lamanites. Erastus Rudd, Josiah Fuller, Isaac H. Bishop, Roswell Murray, Benjamin Wells, Nehemiah Harman, Thomas Hancock, Oliver Wetherby, Joshua Grant, Jun., William Draper, Jun., Ransom Van Leuven, Tunis Rappellee, John Rudd, and Samuel Wilcox were blessed. Moses Martin, who went to Missouri, was set apart to be one of the Seventies, and blessed and warned as follows: "If thou art not purified, thou wilt not be able to execute thy commission. Thou wilt fall into the snares and into the hands of enemies who will take thy life; thou must begin to make a complete reformation in thyself."

Oliver Cowdery,
Clerk.

The following belong to the Seventies, but the date of their ordinations is not definitely known: Milo Andrus, Joseph Winchester, Zerubbabel Snow, Heman T. Hyde, Henry Brown, Nelson Higgins, (Hezekiah Fisk was blessed, but was not one of the Seventies,) Henry Beaman, Jesse Huntsman, Royal Barney, Zebedee Coltrin, Henry Herriman, and Lorenzo D. Barnes. James L. Thompson was blessed, but not ordained.

CHAPTER XIV.

THE GREAT REVELATION ON PRIESTHOOD.

Minutes of Meetings of the Twelve.

KIRTLAND, March 12, 1835.—This evening the Twelve assembled, and the Council was opened by President Joseph Smith, Jun., and he proposed we take our first mission through the Eastern States, to the Atlantic Ocean, and hold conferences in the vicinity of the several branches of the Church for the purpose of regulating all things necessary for their welfare.

It was proposed that the Twelve leave Kirtland on the 4th day of May, which was unanimously agreed to.

It was then proposed that during their present mission, Elder Brigham Young should open the door of the Gospel to the remnants of Joseph, who dwell among the Gentiles, which was carried.

It was voted that the Twelve should hold their first conference in Kirtland, May 2nd; in Westfield, New York, May 9th; in Freedom, N.Y., May 22nd; in Lyonstown, N.Y., June 5th; at Pillow Point, June 10th; in West Loboro', Upper Canada, June 29th; in Johnsbury, Vermont, July 17th; in Bradford, Massachusetts, August 7th; in Dover, New Hampshire, September 4th; in Saco, Maine, September 18th; Farmington, Maine, October 2nd.

ORSON HYDE,
WM. E. M'LELLIN, Clerks.

KIRTLAND, March 28th.

This afternoon the Twelve met in council, and had a time of general confession. On reviewing our past course we are satisfied, and feel to confess also, that we have not realized the importance of our calling to that degree that we ought; we have been light-minded and vain, and in many things have done wrong. For all these things we have asked the forgiveness of our heavenly Father; and wherein we have grieved or wounded the feelings of the Presidency, we ask their forgiveness. The time when we are about to separate is near; and when we shall meet again, God only knows; we therefore feel to ask of him whom we have acknowledged to be our Prophet and Seer, that he inquire of God for us, and obtain a revelation, (if consistent) that we may look upon it when we are separated, that our hearts may be comforted. Our worthiness has not inspired us to make this request, but our unworthiness. We have unitedly asked God our heavenly Father to grant unto us through His Seer, a revelation of His mind and will concerning our duty the coming season, even a great revelation, that will enlarge our hearts, comfort us in adversity, and brighten our hopes amidst the powers of darkness.

ORSON HYDE,
WM. E. M'LELLIN, Clerks.

To President Joseph Smith, Jun., Kirtland, Ohio.

In compliance with the above request,* I inquired of the Lord, and received for answer the following:

Revelation on Priesthood.†

1. There are in the Church two Priesthoods, namely, the Melchisedek and the Aaronic, including the Levitical Priesthood.

* At this point it may be well to note a singular thing with reference to nearly all the revelations that have been received in this dispensation; they came in response to enquiry, in response to prayer. "Ask and ye shall receive;" "Seek and ye shall find," seems to have been the principle on which the Lord has acted with reference to giving revelations. For instance, the Lord revealed Himself and His Son Jesus Christ to the Prophet Joseph in answer to the latter's earnest prayer to know the truth respecting the various religions; Moroni came three years later in response to the young Prophet's earnest prayer to know his standing before the Lord; nearly all the early revelations to individuals in the Church, to Joseph Smith, Sen., Hyrum Smith, Oliver Cowdery, Joseph Knight, David, Peter, John and Christian Whitmer were given in answer to the enquiry of these men to know their duty in respect of the work of the Lord then coming forth; the revelation on Church Organization and Government (Doc. and Cov. sec. 20), was given in response to Joseph and Oliver's prayers and enquiries concerning those things; so with reference to the revelations given to the Witnesses to the Book of Mormon; and in fact throughout the whole course of the work's development. This great revelation on Priesthood and the relations of the quorums to each other in the Church is also given in response to a most humble petition to the Prophet on the part of the Twelve; and, the Prophet says: *"I inquired of the Lord, and received for answer the following revelation,"* then follows the revelation.

† According to the explanatory note in the Doctrine and Covenants, sec. cvii, the fore part of this revelation, the first fifty-eight verses, was given March 28th, the same day the Twelve ask the Prophet to enquire of the Lord for them, the other items were revealed at sundry times.

2. Why the first is called the Melchisedek Priesthood, is because Melchisedek was such a great High Priest;

3. Before his day it was called *the Holy Priesthood after the Order of the Son of God.*

4. But out of respect or reverence to the name of the Supreme Being, to avoid the too frequent repetition of His name, they, the Church in ancient days, called that Priesthood after Melchisedek, or the Melchisedek Priesthood.

5. All other authorities or offices in the Church are appendages to this Priesthood;

6. But there are two divisions, or grand heads; one is the Melchisedek Priesthood, and the other is the Aaronic or Levitical Priesthood.

7. The office of an Elder comes under the Priesthood of Melchisedek.

8. The Melchisedek Priesthood holds the right of presidency, and has power and authority over all the offices in the Church, in all ages of the world, to administer in spiritual things.

9. The Presidency of the High Priesthood, after the Order of Melchisedek, have a right to officiate in all the offices in the Church.

10. High Priests after the Order of the Melchisedek Priesthood, have a right to officiate in their own standing, under the direction of the Presidency, in administering spiritual things, and also in the office of an Elder, Priest (of the Levitical order), Teacher, Deacon and member.

11. An Elder has a right to officiate in his stead, when the High Priest is not present.

12. The High Priest and Elder are to administer in spiritual things, agreeable to the covenants and commandments of the Church; and they have a right to officiate in all these offices of the Church, when there are no higher authorities present.

13. The second Priesthood is called the Priesthood of Aaron, because it was conferred upon Aaron and his seed, throughout all their generations.

14. Why it is called the lesser Priesthood, is because it is an appendage to the greater, or the Melchisedek Priesthood, and has power in administering outward ordinances.

15. The Bishopric is the Presidency of this Priesthood, and holds the keys or authority of the same.

16. No man has a legal right to this office, to hold the keys of this Priesthood, except he be a literal descendant of Aaron.

17. But as a High Priest of the Melchisedek Priesthood has authority to officiate in all the lesser offices, he may officiate in the office of Bishop, when no literal descendant of Aaron can be found, provided he is called,

and set apart, and ordained unto this power, by the hands of the Presidency of the Melchisedek Priesthood.

18. The power and authority of the higher, or Melchisedek Priesthood, is to hold the keys of all the spiritual blessings of the Church.

19. To have the privilege of receiving the mysteries of the kingdom of heaven, to have the heavens opened unto them, to commune with the general assembly and Church of the first-born, and to enjoy the communion and presence of God the Father, and Jesus, the Mediator of the New Covenant.

20. The power and authority of the lesser, or Aaronic Priesthood, is to hold the keys of the ministering of angels, and to administer in outward ordinances, the letter of the Gospel, the baptism of repentance for the remission of sins, agreeable to the covenants and commandments.

21. Of necessity there are Presidents, or presiding officers, growing out of, or appointed of, or from among those who are ordained to the several offices in these two Priesthoods.

22. Of the Melchisedek Priesthood three presiding High Priests, chosen by the body, appointed and ordained to that office, and upheld by the confidence, faith, and prayer of the Church, form a quorum of the Presidency of the Church.

23. The Twelve traveling councilors are called to be the Twelve Apostles, or especial witnesses of the name of Christ, in all the world, thus differing from other officers in the Church, in the duties of their calling;

24. And they form a quorum equal in authority and power to the three Presidents previously mentioned.

25. The Seventy are also called to preach the Gospel, and to be especial witnesses unto the Gentiles and in all the world; thus differing from other officers in the Church in the duties of their calling;

26. And they form a quorum equal in authority to that of the Twelve especial witnesses or Apostles, just named.

27. And every decision made by either of these quorums, must be by the unanimous voice of the same; that is, every member in each quorum must be agreed to its decisions, in order to make their decisions of the same power or validity one with the other.

28. (A majority may form a quorum when circumstances render it impossible to be otherwise.)

29. Unless this is the case, their decisions are not entitled to the same blessings which the decisions of a quorum of three Presidents were anciently, who were ordained after the order of Melchisedek, and were righteous and holy men.

30. The decisions of these quorums or either of them, are to be made in all righteousness, in holiness and lowliness of heart, meekness

and long-suffering, and in faith, and virtue, and knowledge, temperance, patience, godliness, brotherly kindness, and charity;

31. Because the promise is, if these things abound in them they shall not be unfruitful in the knowledge of the Lord.

32. And in case that any decision of these quorums is made in unrighteousness, it may be brought before a general assembly of the several quorums, which constitute the spiritual authorities of the Church, otherwise there can be no appeal from their decision.

33. The Twelve are a traveling, presiding High Council, to officiate in the name of the Lord, under the direction of the Presidency of the Church, agreeable to the institution of heaven, to build up the Church, and regulate all the affairs of the same, in all nations, first unto the Gentiles, and secondly unto the Jews.

34. The Seventy are to act in the name of the Lord, under the direction of the Twelve, or the Traveling High Council, in building up the Church, and regulating all the affairs of the same in all nations; first unto the Gentiles, and then to the Jews;

35. The Twelve being sent out, holding the keys to open the door by the proclamation of the Gospel of Jesus Christ, and first unto the Gentiles and then unto the Jews.

36. The standing High Councils at the Stakes of Zion form a quorum equal in authority, in the affairs of the Church, in all their decisions, to the quorum of the Presidency, or to the traveling High Council.

37. The High Council in Zion form a quorum equal in authority, in the affairs of the Church, in all their decisions, to the councils of the Twelve at the Stakes of Zion.

38. It is the duty of the traveling High Council, to call upon the Seventy, when they need assistance, to fill the several calls for preaching and administering the Gospel, instead of any others.

39. It is the duty of the Twelve, in all large branches of the Church, to ordain evangelical ministers, as they shall be designated unto them by revelation.

40. The order of this Priesthood was confirmed to be handed down from father to son, and rightly belongs to the literal descendants of the chosen seed, to whom the promises were made.

41. This order was instituted in the days of Adam, and came down by lineage in the following manner:

42. From Adam to Seth, who was ordained by Adam at the age of sixty-nine years, and was blessed by him three years previous to his (Adam's) death, and received the promise of God, by his father, that his posterity should be the chosen of the Lord, and that they should be preserved unto the end of the earth.

43. Because he (Seth) was a perfect man, and his likeness was the express likeness of his father insomuch that he seemed to be like unto his father in all things, and could be distinguished from him only by his age.

44. Enos was ordained at the age of an hundred and thirty-four years and four months, by the hand of Adam.

45. God called upon Cainan in the wilderness, in the fortieth year of his age, and he met Adam in journeying to the place Shedolamak; he was eighty-seven years old when he received his ordination.

46. Mahalaleel was four hundred and ninety-six years and seven days old, when he was ordained by the hand of Adam, who also blessed him.

47. Jared was two hundred years old when he was ordained under the hand of Adam, who also blessed him.

48. Enoch was twenty-five year old when he was ordained under the hand of Adam, and he was sixty-five when Adam blessed him.

49. And he saw the Lord, and he walked with Him, and was before His face continually; and he walked with God three hundred and sixty-five years, making him four hundred and thirty year old when he was translated.

50. Methuselah was one hundred years old when he was ordained under the hand of Adam.

51. Lamech was thirty-two years old when he was ordained under the hand of Seth.

52. Noah was ten years old when he was ordained under the hand of Methuselah.

53. Three years previous to the death of Adam, he called Seth, Enos, Cainan, Mahalaleel, Jared, Enoch, and Methuselah, who were all High Priests, with the residue of his posterity, who were righteous, into the valley of Adam-ondi Ahman, and there bestowed upon them his last blessing.

54. And the Lord appeared unto them, and they rose up and blessed Adam, and called him Michael the Prince, the Archangel.

55. And the Lord administered comfort unto Adam, and said unto him, I have set thee to be at the head; a multitude of nations shall come of thee; and thou art a prince over them for ever.

56. And Adam stood up in the midst of the congregation, and notwithstanding he was bowed down with age, being full of the Holy Ghost, predicted whatsoever should befall his posterity unto the latest generation.

57. These things were all written in the Book of Enoch, and are to be testified of in due time.

58. It is the duty of the Twelve, also, to ordain and set in

order all the other officers of the Church agreeable to the revelation which says:

59. To the Church of Christ in the land of Zion, in addition to the Church laws, respecting Church business.

60. Verily, I say unto you, saith the Lord of Hosts, there must needs be presiding Elders, to preside over those who are of the office of an Elder;

61. And also Priests to preside over those who are of the office of a Priest;

62. And also Teachers to preside over those who are of the office of a Teacher, in like manner; and also the Deacons;

63. Wherefore from Deacon to Teacher, and from Teacher to Priest, and from Priest to Elder, severally as they are appointed, according to the covenants and commandments of the Church;

64. Then comes the High Priesthood, which is the greatest of all.

65. Wherefore, it must needs be that one be appointed, of the High Priesthood, to preside over the Priesthood; and he shall be called President of the High Priesthood of the Church,

66. Or in other words, the presiding High Priest over the High Priesthood of the Church.

67. From the same comes the administering of ordinances, and blessings upon the Church, by the laying on of the hands.

68. Wherefore, the office of a Bishop is not equal unto it; for the office of a Bishop is in administering all temporal things;

69. Nevertheless, a Bishop must be chosen from the High Priesthood unless he is a literal descendant of Aaron;

70. For unless he is a literal descendant of Aaron he cannot hold the keys of that Priesthood;

71. Nevertheless,a High Priest, that is,after the order of Melchisedek, may be set apart unto the ministering of temporal things, having a knowledge of them by the Spirit of truth,

72. And also to be a judge in Israel, to do the business of the Church, to sit in judgment upon transgressors, upon testimony, as it shall be laid before him, according to the laws, by the assistance of his counselors, whom he has chosen, or will choose among the Elders of the Church;

73. This is the duty of a Bishop who is not a literal descendant of Aaron, but has been ordained to the High Priesthood after the order of Melchisedek.

74. Thus shall he be a judge, even a common judge among the inhabitants of Zion, or in a Stake of Zion, or in any branch of the Church where he shall be set apart unto this ministry, until the borders

of Zion are enlarged, and it becomes necessary to have other Bishops or judges in Zion, or elsewhere;

75. And inasmuch as there are other Bishops appointed, they shall act in the same office.

76. But a literal descendant of Aaron has a legal right to the Presidency of this Priesthood, to the keys of this ministry, to act in the office of Bishop independently, without counselors, except in a case where the President of the High Priesthood, after the order of Melchisedek, is tried; to sit as a judge in Israel:

77. And the decision of either of these councils, agreeable to the commandment, which says:

78. Again, verily I say unto you, the most important business of the Church, and the most difficult cases of the Church, inasmuch as there is not satisfaction upon the decision of the Bishop, or judges, it shall be handed over and carried up unto the Council of the Church, before the Presidency of the High Priesthood;

79. And the Presidency of the Council of the High Priesthood, shall have power to call other High Priests, even twelve, to assist as counselors; and thus the Presidency of the High Priesthood, and its counselors, shall have power to decide upon testimony, according to the laws of the Church;

80. And after this decision, it shall be had in remembrance no more before the Lord; for this is the highest Council of the Church of God; and a final decision upon controversies in spiritual matters.

81. There is not any person belonging to the Church who is exempt from this Council of the Church.

82. And inasmuch as a President of the High Priesthood shall transgress, he shall be had in remembrance before the common council of the Church, who shall be assisted by twelve counselors of the High Priesthood,

83. And their decision upon his head shall be an end of controversy concerning him.

84. Thus none shall be exempted from the justice and the laws of God; that all things may be done in order and in solemnity before him, according to truth and righteousness.

85. And again, verily I say unto you, the duty of a president over the office of a Deacon, is to preside over twelve Deacons, to sit in council with them, and to teach them their duty, edifying one another, as it is given according to the covenants.

86. And also the duty of the president over the office of the Teachers, is to preside over twenty-four of the Teachers, and to sit in council with them, teaching them the duties of their office as given in the covenants.

87. Also the duty of the president over the Priesthood of Aaron, is to preside over forty-eight Priests, and sit in council with them, to teach them the duties of their office, as it is given in the covenants;

88. This president is to be a Bishop; for this is one of the duties of this Priesthood.

89. Again, the duty of the president over the office of Elders, is to preside over ninety-six Elders, and to sit in council with them, and to teach them according to the covenants.

90. This presidency is a distinct one from that of the Seventy, and is designed for those who do not travel into all the world.

91. And again, the duty of the President of the office of the High Priesthood, is to preside over the whole Church, and to be like unto Moses.

92. Behold, here is wisdom; yea, to be a Seer, a Revelator, a Translator, and a Prophet, having all the gifts of God which He bestows upon the head of the Church.

93. And it is according to the vision showing the order of the Seventy, that they should have seven presidents to preside over them, chosen out of the number of the Seventy;

94. And the seventh president of these presidents is to preside over the six;

95. And these seven presidents are to choose other seventy beside the first seventy, to whom they belong; and are to preside over them;

96. And also other seventy, till seven times seventy, if the labor in the vineyard of necessity requires it;

97. And these seventy are to be traveling ministers unto the Gentiles first, and also unto the Jews;

98 Whereas other officers of the Church, who belong not unto the Twelve, neither to the Seventy, are not under the responsibility to travel among all nations, but are to travel as their circumstances shall allow; notwithstanding, they may hold as high and responsible offices in the Church.

99. Wherefore, now, let every man learn his duty, and to act in the office in which he is appointed, in all diligence.

100. He that is slothful shall not be counted worthy to stand, and he that learns not his duty and shows himself not approved, shall not be counted worthy to stand. Even so. Amen.

CHAPTER XV.

THE FIRST MISSION OF THE TWELVE.

Close of the Elders' School.

THE school in Kirtland closed the last week in March, to give the Elders an opportunity to go forth and proclaim the Gospel, preparatory to the endowment.

Public Discussion at Huntsburgh.

Sunday, March 29.—I preached about three hours, at Huntsburgh—where William E. M'Lellin had been holding a public discussion, on a challenge from J. M. Tracy, a Campbellite preacher, the two days previous, on the divinity of the Book of Mormon—at the close of which two were baptized; and, on Monday, four more came forward for baptism.

Minutes of Conference held at Freedom, N. Y.

April 3rd and 4th, a conference of the Saints was held at Freedom, New York, Sidney Rigdon presiding.

Fifteen branches of the Church were represented, five of which had not been previously represented at any conference, numbering about fifty members.

Elder Chester L. Heath, of Avon, was expelled from the Church, for breach of covenant, and not observing the Word of Wisdom.

WARREN A. COWDERY, Clerk.

Minutes of a Conference of the Twelve and the Seventies.

On the 26th of April the Twelve Apostles, and the Seventies who had been chosen, assembled in the temple (although unfinished), with a numerous concourse of people, to receive their charge and instructions from President Joseph Smith, Jun., relating to their mission and duties. The congregation being assembled, Elder Orson Pratt arrived from the south part of the state, making our number complete, Elder Thomas B. Marsh having arrived the day previous.

Meeting of the Twelve.

April 28.—The Twelve met this afternoon at the schoolroom, for the purpose of prayer and consultation. Elder David W. Patten opened the meeting by prayer.

Moved and carried, that when any member of the council wishes to speak, he shall arise and stand upon his feet.

Elder M'Lellin read the commandment given concerning the choosing of the Twelve; when it was voted that we each forgive one another every wrong that has existed among us, and that from henceforth each one of the Twelve love his brother as himself, in temporal as well as in spiritual things, always inquiring into each other's welfare.

Decided that the Twelve be ready and start on their mission from Elder Johnson's tavern on Monday, at two o'clock a. m., May 4th.

Elder Brigham Young then closed by prayer.

ORSON HYDE,
W. E. M'LELLIN,
Clerks.

Minutes of a General Council of the Priesthood.

May 2.—A grand council was held in Kirtland, composed of the following officers of the Church, viz: Presidents Joseph Smith, Jun., David Whitmer, Oliver Cowdery, Sidney Rigdon, Frederick G. Williams, Joseph Smith, Sen., and Hyrum Smith, with the council of the Twelve Apostles, Bishop Partridge and counselors, Bishop Whitney and counselors, and some of the Seventies, with their presidents, viz. Sylvester Smith, Leonard Rich, Lyman Sherman, Hazen Aldrich, Joseph Young, and Levi Hancock; and many Elders from different parts of the country. President Joseph Smith, Jun., presiding.

After the conference was opened, and the Twelve had taken their seats, President Joseph Smith, Jun., said that it would be the duty of the Twelve, when in council, to take their seats together according to age, the oldest to be seated at the head, and preside in the first council, the next oldest in the second, and so on until the youngest had presided; and then begin at the oldest again.*

* It should be observed here, that this arrangement has reference only to the first organization of the quorum of the Twelve. After this first arrangement, the brethren of that quorum held and now hold their place in it and preside according to seniority of ordination, not of age. Though it must be admitted, that this order was not always strictly observed; for instance, the late President Woodruff, for a number of years, ranked in the quorum of the Twelve before Elder John Taylorr; although the

The Twelve then took their seats according to age as follows: Thomas B. Marsh, David W. Patten, Brigham Young, Heber C. Kimball, Orson Hyde, William E. M'Lellin, Parley P. Pratt, Luke S. Johnson William Smith, Orson Pratt, John F. Boynton, and Lyman E. Johnson.

Items of Instruction to the Twelve and the Seventy.

President Joseph Smith then stated that the Twelve will have no right to go into Zion, or any of its stakes, and there undertake to regulate the affairs thereof, where there is a standing high council; but it is their duty to go abroad and regulate all matters relative to the different branches of the Church. When the Twelve are together, or a quorum of them, in any church, they will have authority to act independently, and make decisions, and those decisions will be valid. But where there is not a quorum, they will have to do business by the voice of the Church. No standing High Council has authority to go into the churches abroad, and regulate the matters thereof, for this belongs to the Twelve. No standing High Council will ever be established only in Zion, or one of her stakes.* When the Twelve pass a decision, it is in the name of the Church, therefore it is valid.

No official member of the Church has authority to go into any branch thereof, and ordain any minister for that Church, unless it is by the

latter was ordained first, and actually assisted in the ordination of President Woodruff at Far West in the spring of 1839. I think this case illustrates the inconsistency of the idea that seniority of age should govern in fixing the standing of the members in the quorum of the Twelve. Surely it would be nothing short of an absurdity in order, for one just ordained to out-rank one that had taken part in his ordination. The slight irregularity here noticed was corrected by President Brigham Young some two years before his death, and President Taylor was accorded his place, which gave him priority of standing in the quorum to Elder Woodruff. President Taylor himself gives the following explanation of the matter: "Through some inadvertency, or perhaps mixed up with the idea of seniority of age taking the precedence, Wilford Woodruff's name was placed on the records at the time, and for many years after, before that of John Taylor. This matter was investigated, some time afterwards, by President Young and his council, sanctioned also by the Twelve, whether [or not] John Taylor held the precedency and stood in gradation prior to Brother Wilford Woodruff; and it was voted on and decided that his name be placed before Wilford Woodruff's, although Wilford Woodruff was the older man. The reason assigned for this change was, that although both were called at the same time, John Taylor was ordained into the Twelve prior to Wilford Woodruff; and another prominent reason would be, that as John Taylor assisted in the ordination of Elder Wilford Woodruff, he therefore must precede him in the council." (Succession in the Priesthood, a Discourse by President John Taylor—October, 1881—p. 16).

* But a *temporary* High Concil of High Priests abroad may be organized when necessity requires it, the High Priests abroad (i. e., outside organized stakes of Zion) having the power to determine when the organization of such High Council is necessary. (See the revelation at page 30 this volume, verses 24-32).

voice of that branch. No Elder has authority to go into any branch of the Church, and appoint meetings, or attempt to regulate the affairs of the church, without the advice and consent of the presiding Elder of that branch.

If the first Seventy are all employed, and there is a call for more laborers, it will be the duty of the seven presidents of the first Seventy to call and ordain other Seventy and send them forth to labor in the vineyard, until, if needs be, they set apart seven times seventy, and even until there are one hundred and forty-four thousand thus set apart for the ministry.*

The Seventy are not to attend the conferences of the Twelve, unless they are called upon or requested so to do by the Twelve. The Twelve and the Seventy have particularly to depend upon their ministry for their support, and that of their families; and they have a right, by virtue of their offices, to call upon the churches to assist them.

Elder Henry Herriman was ordained one of the Seventy.

The circumstances of the presidents of the Seventy were severally considered, relative to their traveling in the vineyard: and it was unanimously agreed that they should hold themselves in readiness to go, at the call of the Twelve, when the Lord opens the way. Twenty-seven of the Seventy were also considered, and it was decided they should hold themselves in readiness to travel in the ministry, at the call of the president of the Seventy, as the Lord opens the way.

After an adjournment of one hour, the council re-assembled.

Ezra Thayre was suspended as an Elder and member, until investigation could be had before the bishop's court, complaint having been preferred against him by Oliver Granger.

Lorenzo D. Barnes was ordained one of the Seventy; also Henry Benner, Michael Griffiths, Royal Barney, and Lebbeus T. Coon, who, together with twenty others, were called upon to hold themselves in readiness to travel when circumstances might permit.

The Elders in Kirtland and its vicinity were then called upon, or their circumstances considered, and their names enrolled. President Joseph Smith, Jun., arose with the lists in his hand, and made

* In his notes on Church History, John Whitmer, who was the Church Historian at that time, says concerning the organization of the Seventy: "About the same time [i. e., that the quorum of the Twelve was organized] there were seventy High Priests chosen, who were called to be under the direction of the Twelve, and assist them according to their needs; and if seventy were not enough, call seventy more, until seventy times seventy." (Ms. p. 51.) John Whitmer, however, is mistaken in saying that they were High Priests that were chosen. They were chiefly chosen from among the Elders, and the few High Priests that were called into the quorum were afterwards requested to take their place with the High Priests again, and others were chosen to fill the vacancies thus created. (See "History of the Organization of the Seventies," Joseph Young, pp. 4, 5.)

some very appropriate remarks, relative to the deliverance of Zion; and, so much of the authority of the Church being present, moved that we never give up the struggle for Zion, even until death, or until Zion is redeemed.

The vote was unanimous, and given with deep feeling.

Voted, that all the Elders of the Church are bound to travel in the world to preach the Gospel, with all their might, mind, and strength, when their circumstances will admit of it; and that the door is now opened.

Voted, that Elders Brigham Young, John P, Greene, and Amos Orton be appointed to go and preach the Gospel to the remnants of Joseph, the door to be opened by Elder Brigham Young, and this will open the door to the whole house of Joseph.

Voted, that when another Seventy is required, the presidency of the first Seventy shall choose, ordain, and set them apart from among the most experienced of the Elders of the Church.

Voted, that whenever the labor of other Seventy is required, they are to be set apart and ordained to that office; those who are residing at Kirtland and the regions round about, who can come to Kirtland, to be set apart and ordained by the direction of the Presidency of the Church in Kirtland.

WM. E. M'LELLIN, Clerk.

The First Mission of the Twelve.

The Twelve left Kirtland this morning [May 4th],* and embarked on board the steamer *Sandusky*, at Fairport, and landed at Dunkirk, New York, 5 o'clock p. m., and after preaching in those regions a few days, met in conference at Westfield, May 9th, according to previous appointment; the church being present, and Thomas B. Marsh, the oldest of the quorum, presiding.

The following items were suggested for the consideration of the council:

Resolved, 1st: That the limits of this conference extend south and west to the line of Pennsylvania, north as far as Lake Erie, and east as far as Lodi, embracing the branches of Westfield, Silver Creek, Perrysburgh, and Lavona, to be called the "Westfield Conference."

* Presumably on the 4th of May, since that was the date fixed for starting on this mission by the Twelve at their meeting on the 28th of April preceding (see p. 219). John Whitmer, in his notes on Church History, however, fixes the date on the 5th of May. He says: "On the morning of the 5th of May, the Twelve took leave of their families and brethren, to fill their first mission under their commission, being commissioned to carry the Gospel to Gentile and also unto Jew, having the keys of the Gospel to unlock, and then call upon others to promulgate the same." (Whitmer's Ms., p. 50.)

2nd. Inquire into the standing of all the Elders within the bounds of this conference.

3rd. Inquire into the manner of their teaching, doctrines, etc.

4th. Inquire into the teaching, conduct, and faithfulness of all traveling Elders who have recently labored within the bounds of this conference.

5th. Hear a representation of the several branches of the Church.

On investigation, the standing and teaching of the Elders present met the approbation of the council, except the teaching of Elder Joseph Rose, which was, "that the Jewish church was the sun, and the Gentile church was the moon, etc.; when the Jewish church was scattered, then sun was darkened: and when the Gentile church is cut off, the moon will be turned to blood;" also some things relative to the apocalyptic beast with seven heads and ten horns.

He was shown his error, and willingly made a humble confession.

The faithfulness of all the traveling Elders was found to be good.

The members of the Westfield branch were represented as in good standing, but with a difficulty in the minds of some, relative to the baptism of Brother Lloyd L. Lewis, inasmuch as he was baptized by a traveling Elder without the church being called together to know if they would receive him to fellowship.

The council decided that if there was a fault, it was in the administrator, and not in the candidate. The branch numbered seventy-five.

The Lavona branch numbered twenty in good standing, but lacking in the enjoyment of the Spirit in consequence of a neglect to keep the Word of Wisdom.

After further instructions on general principles, the conference adjourned until 8 o'clock a. m., Monday, May 11.

Sunday, May 10.—Elders Marsh and Patten preached to an attentive congregation of about five hundred; after Sacrament, five persons desired baptism, which was attended to by Elder M'Lellin.

Monday, 11.—Conference met pursuant to adjournment.

Resolved unanimously—That this conference go to, immediately, and appoint their "wise men," and gather up their riches, and send them to Zion to purchase land, according to previous commandment, that all things be prepared before them in order to their gathering.

Much was said to the conference upon these important things; and the Saints covenanted before the Lord, that they would be strict to attend to our teaching.

After preaching by Elder Young at 3 o'clock p. m., and the farewell exhortation of the Twelve, seven individuals were baptized by Elder Orson Hyde, and they were confirmed in the evening.

After laying hands on many sick, who obtained relief, adjourned to the 22nd instant, to meet in Freedom, New York.

ORSON HYDE, Clerk.

The Conference at Freedom.

May 22.—The Twelve met in conference with the church in Freedom, New York, when, after an agreeable salutation and rejoicing in each other's prosperity, Elder David W. Patten being chairman, conference was opened by singing, and prayer by the President.

[Here let it be remarked, that it was the universal custom of the Twelve and the Presidency of the Church, to open and close all conferences and councils by prayer, and generally singing, so that this need not be named in this history hereafter.]

Resolved—That the limits of this conference extend from Lodi in the west, so far east as to include Avon, south to Pennsylvania, and north to Lake Ontario, called the "Freedom Conference," including the branches of Freedom, Rushford, Portage, Grove, Burns, Genesee, Avon, Java, Holland, Aurora, Greenwood, and Niagara.

The report concerning the labors and teachings of the Elders in the conference, and those who had recently traveled through the branches, was good.

The branch in Freedom numbered sixty-five; Rushford, twenty-eight; Burns, thirty; Holland, fifteen—represented by P. P. Pratt as having suffered much from false teachings by hypocrites and knaves; Aurora, four; Niagara, four; the numbers of the remaining branches not ascertained, but generally reported in good standing.

The council gave instruction concerning the "Word of Wisdom," the gift of tongues, prophesying, etc., and adjourned until tomorrow morning.

May 23.—Conference met to take into consideration the redemption of Zion.

After addresses by five of the council, the church expressed their determination to put into practice the teachings we had given, when the conference adjourned.

May 25.—The Twelve met in council to pray for one another until they should meet again; and,

Resolved—That we recommand and counsel Elders John Murdock and Lloyd Lewis to go to the churches at Chenango Point, New York, and Springville, Pennsylvania (among whom we understand there is some difficulty), and set in order the things that are wanting in those branches.

Resolved—That Elder Brigham Young go immediately from this place to an adjacent tribe of the remnants of Joseph, and open the door of salvation to that long dejected and afflicted people. The council, according to his request, laid their hands upon him, that he might have their faith and prayers, to fill, with humility and power, that very important mission.

They also laid hands on Elders John P. Greene and Amos Orton, for the same purpose, as they expected to accompany him.

ORSON HYDE, Clerk.

On the 5th of June, nine of the Twelve met in council at Rose, or Lyonstown, New York. There being so few of the brethren in that region, it was resolved that it was not necessary to establish a conference, after which council adjourned. After they had preached several sermons in the vicinity, Elders Brigham Young, Orson Hyde and William Smith returned to Kirtland, as witnesses in a certain case wherein President Joseph Smith, Jun., was concerned before the county court, in which he righteously triumphed over his enemies.*

ORSON HYDE, Clerk.

On the 19th of June, nine of the traveling High Council met with the church in conference at Pillow Point, New York, and resolved that the limits of the conference embrace all the northern part of the State, to be called the "Black River Conference." The Elders of the conference had been diligent in their callings. Their manner of teaching in some respects needed correction, which they gladly received.

The church at Pillow Point numbered twenty-one, but did not generally observe the Word of Wisdom. The church at Sackets Harbor numbered nineteen; Burville, seven; Champion, six; Ellesburg, thirty-three; Henderson, four; Alexandria, four· Lyme, four; and two in Orleans, three in Potsdam, and six in Stockholm.

After hearing the report of the churches, five of the council successively addressed the conference, upon the principles of church government, the nature and exercise of spiritual gifts, the Word of Wisdom, and the propriety of choosing wise men and sending them with moneys to purchase lands in Zion, so that they might not gather in confusion; and the conference unanimously acquiesced in the teachings of the council. Adjourned until the 20th, then met, and John Elmer was charged with holding very incorrect principles; such, for instance, that the Spirit of God sometimes took him and threw him down, and that he could die the death of the righteous, and of the wicked; and in order to show his power with God, he also stated that he had passed through a kind of death so as to become immortal, and would exist forever without any other death or

* What the case in question was cannot now be ascertained.

change, only growing brighter and brighter eternally. He persisted in these things, and would not receive teaching from the council, therefore was cut off. On Monday, five were baptized, and our public meeting closed.

ORSON HYDE, Clerk.

CHAPTER XVI.

PROGRESS OF AFFAIRS AT KIRTLAND—DISCOVERY OF THE BOOK OF ABRAHAM.

About the middle of May, W. W. Phelps and John Whitmer, Presidents of the Church in Missouri, arrived at Kirtland, and John Whitmer was appointed to take the place of President Oliver Cowdery, in conducting the *Messenger and Advocate.*

Change of Editors on the "Messenger and Advocate."

Frederick G. Williams was appointed to edit the *Northern Times*, a weekly newspaper, which we had commenced in February last, in favor of Democracy; and W. W. Phelps (with his son Waterman) made his home with my family, and assisted the committee in compiling the Book of Doctrine and Covenants.

The "Northern Times."

Minutes of Conference held at New Portage, June 6th.

The Elders and brethren assembled in conference, June 6th, at New Portage, Oliver Cowdery, presiding.

Elder David Matthews, who was suspended at a previous conference, for unchristian conduct, was present.

After hearing the testimony, the council unanimously agreed that there had been due contrition of spirit manifested by him, in his walk and conversation since his suspension; and Elder Matthews was restored.

Elder Barkdall preferred a claim against Elder Keeler, for services said to be rendered some eight or nine years since, and to have been awarded by a former council.

It appeared there had been a decision in favor of Elder Barkdall, but no testimony was produced by either of the parties to substantiate a claim, or prove a payment. It was, therefore, Resolved:—That both the accuser and the accused nave manifested a bad spirit, and deserve the severe rebuke of this council.

Elder Milo Hays was tried for not obeying the Word of Wisdom, and for covenant breaking.

Both charges were sustained by testimony, and Elder Hays was excluded from the Church.

Several other cases of discipline were attended to, and conference adjourned at 12 o'clock at night.

Sunday morning, President Oliver Cowdery preached, after which four were baptized.

The council again organized in the evening, and ordained Jacob Myers an Elder.

The case of Elders Barkdall and Keeler was again called up; four councilors spoke on the subject, when it was decided that they have one week and no more to settle their differences with each other, and make confession to the Church, or lose their standing.

W. A. COWDERY, Clerk.

Instructions of the Prophet to the Elders and Saints in Missouri.

The Presidency, Bishop, and High Council of Zion, having removed to Kirtland, or gone forth in the vineyard, I caused it to be published in the June number of the *Messenger and Advocate*, that according to the order of the kingdom begun in the last days, to prepare men for the rest of the Lord, the Elders in Zion or in her immediate region, have no authority or right to meddle with her spiritual affairs, to regulate her concerns, or hold councils for the expulsion of members, in her unorganized condition. The High Council has been expressly organized to administer in all her spiritual affairs; and the Bishop and his council are set over her temporal matters; so that the Elders' acts are null and void. *Now*, the Lord wants the wheat and tares to grow together; for Zion must be redeemed with judgment, and her converts with righteousness. Every Elder that can, after providing for his family (if he has any) and paying his debts, must go forth and clear his skirts from the blood of this generation. While they are in that region, [Missouri] instead of trying members for transgression, or offenses, let every one labor to prepare himself for the vineyard, sparing a little time to comfort the mourners, to bind up the broken-hearted, to reclaim the backslider, to bring back the wanderer, to re-invite into the kingdom such as have been cut off, by encouraging them to lay to while the day lasts, and work righteousness, and, with one heart and one mind, prepare to help to redeem Zion, that goodly land of promise, where the willing and obedient shall be blessed.*

* The whole article is so valuable that, notwithstanding to publish it entire leads to a repetition of part of the above, it is placed here in a foot note.

"TO THE SAINTS SCATTERED ABROAD.

"Dear Brethren:—It is a duty which every Saint ought to render to his brethren freely—to always love them, and ever succor them. To be justified before God we must love one another: we must overcome evil; we must visit the fatherless and the widow in their affliction, and we must keep ourselves unspotted from the world: for such virtues flow from the great fountain of pure religion. Strengthening our faith by adding every good quality that adorns the children of the blessed Jesus, we can pray in the season of prayer; we can love our neighbor as ourselves, and be faithful in tribulation, knowing that the reward of such is greater in the kingdom of heaven. What a consolation! What a joy! Let me live the life of the righteous, and let my reward be like this!

According to the order of the kingdom begun in the last days, to prepare men for the rest of the Lord, the Elders in Zion, or in her immediate region, have no authority or right to meddle with her spiritual affairs, to regulate her concerns, or hold councils for the expulsion of members in her unorganized condition. The High Council has been expressly organized to administer in all her spiritual affairs; and the Bishop and his council, are set over her temporal matters: so that the Elders' acts are null and void. Now the Lord wants the tares and wheat to grow together: for Zion must be redeemed with judgment, and her converts with righteousness. Every Elder that can, after providing for his family (if he has any) and paying his debts, must go forth and clear his skirts from the blood of this generation. While they are in that region instead of trying members for transgressions, or offenses, let every one labor to prepare himself for the vineyard, sparing a little time to comfort the mourners; to bind up the broken-hearted; to reclaim the backslider; to bring back the wanderer; to re invite into the kingdom such as have been cut off, by encouraging them to lay to while the day lasts, and work righteousness, and, with one heart and one mind, prepare to help redeem Zion, that goodly land of promise, where the willing and the obedient shall be blessed. Souls are as precious in the sight of God as they ever were; and the Elders were never called to drive any down to hell, but to persuade and invite all men everywhere to repent, that they may become the heirs of salvation. It is the acceptable year of the Lord: liberate the captives that they may sing hosanna. The Priests, too, should not be idle: their duties are plain, and unless they do them diligently, they cannot expect to be approved. Righteousness must be the aim of the Saints in all things, and when the covenants are published, they will learn that great things must be expected from them. Do good and work righteousness with an eye single to the glory of God, and you shall reap your reward when the Lord recompenses every one ac-

About this time, I received an introduction to Mr. Hewitt, a preacher who had come out from Europe, with his wife, to examine this work; he stated that he was delegated by his church for this purpose, and presented a letter of commendation, a copy of which follows:

The mission of Mr. Hewitt.

To the Saints of the Most High:

Dear Brethren in the Lord.—At a council of the pastors of our church, held March 28th, 1835, upon the propriety of Reverend John

cording to his work. The Teachers and Deacons are the standing ministers of the Church, and in the absence of other officers, great things and holy walk are required of them. They must strengthen the members' faith; persuade such as are out of the way to repent, and turn to God and live; meekly persuade and urge every one to forgive one another all their trespasses, offenses and sins, that they may work out their own salvation with fear and trembling. Brethren, bear and forbear one with another, for so the Lord does with us. Pray for your enemies in the Church and curse not your foes without: for vengeance is mine, saith the Lord, and I will repay. To every ordained member, and to all, we say, be merciful and you shall find mercy. Seek to help save souls, not to destroy them: for verily you know, that "there is more joy in heaven, over one sinner that repents, than there is over ninety and nine just persons that need no repentance." Strive not about the mysteries of the kingdom; cast not your pearls before swine, give not the bread of the children to dogs, lest you and the children should suffer, and you thereby offend your righteous Judge. Your brethren who leave their families, with whom they have enjoyed an earthly measure of peace and joy, to carry glad tidings around the world, expect great things of you, while you are privileged to enjoy the blessings of the Saints' society. They pray our heavenly Father that you may be very prayerful, very humble, and very charitable; working diligently, spiritually and temporally for the redemption of Zion, that the pure in heart may return with songs of everlasting joy to build up her waste places, and meet the Lord when He comes in His glory. Brethren, in the name of Jesus Christ, we entreat you to live worthy of the blessings that shall follow after much tribulation, to satiate the souls of them that hold out faithful to the end."—*Messenger and Advocate*, vol. 1, No. 8, pp. 137-8.

The substance of the foregoing article from the *Messenger and Advocate* is also contained, according to John Whitmer's history (manuscript page 52) in a letter to Hezekiah Peck, signed by Joseph Smith, Jun., Oliver Cowdery, Sidney Rigdon, Frederick G. Williams, W. W. Phelps and John Whitmer; the opening paragraph of which is as follows:

"The Presidency of Kirtland and Zion say that the Lord has manifested by revelation of His Spirit, that the High Priests, Teachers, Priests, and Deacons, or in other words, all the officers in the land of Clay County, Missouri, belonging to the Church, are more or less in transgression, because they have not enjoyed the Spirit of God sufficiently to be able to comprehend their duties respecting themselves and the welfare of Zion; thereby having been left to act in a manner that is detrimental to the interest, and also a hindrance to the redemption of Zion. Now if they will be wise, they will humble themselves in a peculiar manner that God may open the eyes of their understanding. It will be clearly manifested what the

Hewitt visiting you, it was resolved and approved that as he had an anxious desire to go to America to see things that are spoken of in one of your papers brought here by a merchant from New York, he should have, as he desired, the sanction of the council, and if it pleased the Lord, His approval. The Lord hath seen our joy and gladness to hear that He was raising up a people for Himself in that part of the New World, as well as here. O, may our faith increase that He may have Evangelists, Apostles, and Prophets, filled with the power of the Spirit, and performing His will in destroying the works of darkness.

The Reverend Mr. Hewitt was professor of mathematics in Rotherham Independent Seminary, and four years pastor of Barnsley Independent church. He commenced preaching the doctrines we taught, about two years since, and was excommunicated. Many of his flock followed him, so that he was eventually installed in the same church, and the Lord's work prospered. As he is a living epistle, you will have, if all be well, a full explanation. Many will follow, should he approve of the country, etc., who will help the cause, because the Lord hath favored them with this world's goods. We had an utterance during our meeting, which caused us to sing for joy. The Lord was pleased with our brother's holy determination to see you; and we understand that persecution had been great among you, or would be, but we were commanded not to fear, for He would be with us. Praise the Lord.

The time is at hand when distance shall be no barrier between us; but when on the wings of love, Jehovah's messages shall be communicated by His Saints. The Lord bless our brother, and may he prove a blessing to you. Be not afraid of our enemies; they shall,

design and purposes of the Almighty are with regard to them, and the children of Zion, that they should let the High Council, which is appointed of God and ordained for that purpose, make and regulate all the affairs of Zion, and that it is the will of God that her children should stand still and see the salvation of redemption." Then follows the substance of the *Messenger and Advocate* article. This letter has the following *post script* written personally by the Prophet, to Brother Peck, and is a gem which manifests the profound sympathy of the Prophet for the faithful in Israel:

"P. S.—Brother Hezekiah Peck: We remember your family with all the first families of the Church who first embraced the truth. We remember your losses and sorrows; our first ties are not broken; we participate with you in the evil as well as the good, in the sorrows as well as the joys; our union, we trust, is stronger than death, and shall never be severed. Remember us unto all who believe in the fullness of the Gospel of our Lord and Savior Jesus Christ. We hereby authorize you, Hezekiah Peck, our beloved brother, to read this epistle and communicate it unto all the brotherhood in all that region of country.

"Dictated by me, your unworthy brother, and fellow laborer in the testimony of the Book of Mormon. Signed by my own hand in the token of the everlasting covenant. *Joseph Smith, Jun.*"

unless they repent, be cast down by the Lord of Hosts. The workers of iniquity have been used by the prince of darkness to play the counterfeit; but discernment has been given to us, that they were immediately put to shame, by being detected, so that the flock never suffered as yet by them.

Grace, mercy, and peace be unto you from God our Father, and from the Spirit, Jesus Christ our Lord. Amen.

I am, dear sir,

Your brother in the Gospel,

THOMAS SHAW.

Barnsley, April 21, 1835.*

The interview with Mr. Hewitt was brief, and he left with the understanding that he would call again and renew his investigations. As he did not return according to agreement, and hearing he was at Fairport, the council of the Presidency sent him the following letter:—

To the Reverend Mr. Hewitt:

Sir—In consequence of your not returning as we understood you would at your introduction to us, it was resolved and approved in council, on the evening of the 14th instant, that the bearer of this communication, Oliver Cowdery, one of the presiding Elders of our Church, should proceed to Fairport, and ascertain if possible, the cause of your delay; and this is done as one reason, that we feel an anxious desire for the salvation of the souls of men, and to satisfy your inquiries concerning the religion we profess. If at Fairport it is the sincere desire of the council, that Mr. Hewitt return, that we may satisfy him concerning our religion, and he satisfy us concerning his; for we feel as great a desire for the welfare of his people, as he can for ours.

With respect, etc.,

W. W. PHELPS, Clerk.

* This communication in the Prophet's history as published in the *Millennial Star* appears under the date of April 21st, 1835; but it was thought to be a better grouping of events to bring it down to this date—first half of June—where the whole incident may be disposed of in a single reference to it. Following is a remark of the Prophet's respecting the letter as published in the *Star*, but which under our present arrangement of the matter is not necessary in the text of the History: "One object, and only one, has induced us to lay the foregoing letter from England, before our readers; and that is, the good of the cause of God. It might have remained in our possession, perhaps for years, in silence, had it not been for circumstances, which we will briefly mention hereafter." These "circumstances" are those relating to the indifferent actions of Mr. Hewitt, as set forth in the text.

Elder Cowdery immediately repaired to Fairport, and on the day following reported to the Council that Mr. Hewitt was not in the place: that he left their letter with Mrs. Hewitt, who informed him that her "husband had frequently spoken of his wish to become further acquainted with the people whom he had come out from Europe to see." But the next we heard of the Reverend John Hewitt was that he had opened a school in Painsville, Ohio.

The indifference of Mr. Hewitt

Mr. Hewitt was an elder of the Irvingite* church, in Barn-

* This is not the name accepted by the church which Mr. Hewitt represented. The religious body usually called "Irvingites" object to any designation "which implies sectarianism" and therefore, they themselves use no other name than the "Catholic Apostolic Church," of which the congregation at Barnsley, England, was but a branch. Such was the prominence, however, for learning, social and ecclesiastical standing of Reverend Edward Irving that when he gave the influence of his name and standing to what was probably a really spiritual awakening among some of the people in western and southern Scotland, the movement received his name, hence "Irvingites." Mr. Irving was born in Annan, Dumfrieshire, August 15, 1792, and in his early ministry was associated with such men as Doctors Chalmers and Canning. He created no little stir in higher circles of religious society in London for a time; but his announcement of the near approach of the coming of the Son of Man, attended by the judgments of God, together with his strictures against the looseness of fashionable life, soon displeased the worldly who for a time flocked to hear him; and the people of fashion soon separated from his congregation. He taught the doctrine that the spiritual gifts of the Gospel were to continue forever in the church, together with the New Testament organization of the church. The Irvingite views of this New Testament organization are set forth in the following: "There are, as in the apostolic times, four ministeries: 1st, that of 'apostle;' 2nd, that of 'prophet;' 3rd, that of 'evangelist;' and 4th, that of 'pastor.' The apostles are invested with spiritual prerogatives; they alone can administer the Holy Ghost by laying on of hands; to them the mysteries of God are revealed and unfolded to the church; and they decide on matters of order and discipline. Nothing that transpires in any church in the way of 'prophetic utterance' can be authoritatively explained save by them; and the various 'angels of the churches' are bound to bring all such utterances under their cognizance, in order that they may be rightly interpreted. The function of the 'prophet' has been already indicated. The work of an 'evangelist' mainly consists in endeavoring to 'bring' in, those who are without. The 'angel' of the Catholic Apostolic Church, corresponds with the bishop of other Christian denominations. The ministers of each full congregation comprise an angel, with a four-fold ministry (consisting of elders, prophets, evangelists, and pastors;) and a ministry of deacons to take charge of temporal matters. This ministry is supported by tithes, the people giving a tenth of their income for the support of the priesthood. Church affairs were managed by a council of ministers of all classes, whose selection and arrangement are conceived to have been foreshadowed in the structure of the Mosaic tabernacle." The sympathy of the members of the Catholic Apostolic Church at Barnsley who believed in the spirit-

sley, England, and was sent as a delegate from that church, as expressed in the letter from Mr. Shaw, of April 21st, to visit the Saints in America, and ascertain their faith and principles; and if Mr. Hewitt found them as they expected, the Saints in America might expect help from them (the church in Barnsley) as they were rich in temporal things, and had received the gift of tongues in the church.

June 18.—Nine hundred and fifty dollars were subscribed for the temple, by the Saints in Kirtland. Great anxiety was manifested to roll on the work.

Subscriptions for the Temple.

The twenty-first, being Sunday, I preached in Kirtland on the Evangelical Order.*

Thursday, June 25.—There was a meeting in Kirtland to subscribe for the building of the Temple; and $6,232.50 was added to the list. Joseph Smith subscribed $500; Oliver Cowdery, $750; W. W. Phelps, $500; John Whitmer, $500; and Frederick G. Williams, $500; of the above, all of which they paid within one hour, and the people were astonished.

ual gifts of the Gospel, and what they understood to be the New Testament organization of the church, readily explains the interest they would naturally feel in the Latter-day Saints in America, when they would come to hear of the things which God had established among them; and it is regretted that they did not send a more faithful representative than Mr. Hewitt to enquire into the work of the Lord as developed in divine manifestations to the Prophet Joseph. "This Mr. Hewitt," says John Whitmer in his manuscript history of the Church, page 52, "did not obey the Gospel; neither would he investigate the matter. Thus ended the mission of Mr. Hewitt."

* Of the evangelical or patriarchal order of Priesthood in the Church it is said in the revelations of God: "The order of this Priesthood was confirmed to be handed down from father to son, and rightly belongs to the literal descendants of the chosen seed, to whom the promises were made. This order was instituted in the days of Adam, and came down by lineage in the following manner." Then follow the names of those who successively held the evangelical Priesthood in ancient times (Doctrine and Covenants, sec. cvii). According to the word of the Lord, at the time this order of Priesthood was conferred upon Hyrum Smith, brother of the Prophet, it is said "The Patriarch holds the keys of the patriarchal blessings upon the heads of all my people, that whoever he blesses shall be blessed, and whoever he curses shall be cursed; that whatsoever he shall bind on earth shall be bound in heaven; and whatsoever he shall loose on earth shall be loosed in heaven." (Doctrine and Covenants, cxxiv, 92, 93.) It was undoubtedly upon this order of priesthood that the Prophet spoke in the meeting of the twenty-first of June.

June 29.—Six of the traveling High Council, viz.:—David W. Patten, Heber C. Kimball, Luke S. Johnson, Orson Pratt, John F. Boynton, and Lyman E. Johnson, assembled in conference with the church in Loborough, Upper Canada. The church in Loborough, composed of twenty-five members, were uninformed in many principles of the new covenant, not having had the same privilege of instruction as the churches in the United States.

Conference in Canada.

Brothers Henry and Jacob Wood, who had been suspended, had a rehearing, but were cut off. Elder Frederick M. Van Leuven, was appoinded presiding Elder, and a number were added to the Church during their stay.

On the 3rd of July, Michael H. Chandler came to Kirtland to exhibit some Egyptian mummies. There were four human figures, together with some two or more rolls of papyrus covered with hieroglyphic figures and devices. As Mr. Chandler had been told I could translate them, he brought me some of the characters, and I gave him the interpretation, and like a gentleman, he gave me the following certificate:

Michael H. Chandler and the Egyptian Mummies.

KIRTLAND, July 6, 1835.

This is to make known to all who may be desirous, concerning the knowledge of Mr. Joseph Smith, Jun., in deciphering the ancient Egyptian hieroglyphic characters in my possession, which I have, in many eminent cities, showed to the most learned; and, from the information that I could ever learn, or meet with, I find that of Mr. Joseph Smith, Jun., to correspond in the most minute matters.

MICHAEL H. CHANDLER,
Traveling with, and proprietor of, Egyptian mummies.*

Sunday 5.—I preached in the afternoon.

Michael H. Barton tried to get into the Church, but he was not willing to confess and forsake all his sins—and he was rejected.

The case of Michael H. Barton.

* Mr. Chandler is responsible for the English of the above certificate, and I do not feel at liberty to edit it.

The Writings of Abraham and Joseph.

Soon after this, some of the Saints at Kirtland purchased the mummies and papyrus, a description of which will appear hereafter, and with W. W. Phelps and Oliver Cowdery as scribes, I commenced the translation of some of the characters or hieroglyphics, and much to our joy found that one of the rolls contained the writings of Abraham, another the writings of Joseph of Egypt, etc.,—a more full account of which will appear in its place, as I proceed to examine or unfold them. Truly we can say, the Lord is beginning to reveal the abundance of peace and truth.

Edmund Bosley Tried for Breaking Covenant.

On the 9th I rode to Cleveland, in company with Elder Cowdery and others. On the 14th a charge was preferred against Elder Edmund Bosley, to a council of the Presidency, for unchristian-like conduct, in breaking a certain sacred covenant, made September 4, 1834.

I instructed the council on points of duty, such as observing covenants, etc., and testified to the truth of the above covenant.

President Oliver Cowdery testified that he himself framed the covenant alluded to, and that at the time when Bosley said that he had a witness that it was the will of the Lord that he should consecrate the surplus of his property over and above what would be needful for his and his family's support.

Bishop Whitney stated that Elder Bosley agreed to let the Presidency and others have money on loan, for the printing of the Revelations, if he could control his property in one year, or, as soon as he obtained it.

Decided that Elder Bosley broke the covenant which he made September 4, 1834—therefore he is not a member of this Church, unless he make satisfaction to those whom he injured.

Also Isaac H. Bishop was complained of as having spoken evil of the High Council, by saying that "the High Council had the wrong tree to bark up," which was testified to by J. M. Corrill, President Rigdon and others.

It was decided that Isaac H. Bishop shall make public confession to the satisfaction of the injured, and walk as a Saint in all things.

The hand of the Lord shall be upon them, until they repent in sackcloth and ashes, and shall effect their temporal and spiritual interests unless they repent.

CHAPTER XVII.

SUNDRY COUNCIL MEETINGS IN VERMONT, OHIO, AND NEW YORK.

Minutes of the Vermont Conference.

July 17th.—The Twelve met in conference, agreeably to previous appointment, at St. Johnsbury, Vermont.

Resolved:—That this State be within the limits of this conference, and include the branches in Littleton, Dalton, and Landaff, in New Hampshire, to be called the Vermont Conference.

The St. Johnsbury branch numbered forty-one members; Danville, twenty-three; Charlton, twenty-one; Jay, eleven; Dalton, fifteen; Landaff, four; Littleton, ten; Andover, Vermont, fifteen; Beneeon, seven; and Lewis, New York, seventeen.

Six of the council addressed the conference on principles of faith and action.

Adjourned to the 18th, when the remaining six members of the council enforced the necessity of sending up wise men, and purchasing lands, according to the commandments—which the Saints readily agreed to do.

Sunday, 19th.—Our public meeting was attended by more than a thousand people, and during our conference nine were baptized.

ORSON HYDE,
WM. E. M'LELLIN,
Clerks.

The remainder of this month, I was continually engaged in translating an alphabet to the Book of Abraham, and arranging a grammar of the Egyptian language as practiced by the ancients.

The Prophet at work on the Book of Abraham.

August 2nd, being the Sabbath, I preached a part of the day.

Minutes of the High Council at Kirtland.

Kirtland, August 4th, 1835, a High Council of the Church of Christ of Latter day Saints assembled in conference, consisting of Presidents Joseph Smith, Jun., Oliver Cowdery, Sidney Rigdon, Hyrum Smith, David Whitmer, John Whitmer, and W. W. Phelps, and others, to take into consideration certain items contained in letters from abroad—one from Warren A. Cowdery. Presiding Elder of the Freedom Conference, and one from Elder William E. M'Lellin. The first reads as follows:

"FREEDOM, July 29th, 1835.

"DEAR BROTHER:—Elder Jared Carter called on this church last Thursday, on his way east, soliciting donations and subscriptions for finishing the house in your place. Although the subject of such a mission, in connection with his name, had been mentioned in the *Messenger and Advocate*, still, as no other method had been taken to impress the subject on our minds, it had measurably passed out, or ceased to make any impression—therefore, we were in some degree taken on surprise. To the recollection of any of the church, neither the Twelve, the Bishop, nor any others clothed with authority have ever mentioned this subject to us, except incidentally. It surely was never made a subject of public instruction—as Brother Carter had just reasons to expect it had been, he felt an embarrassment peculiar to such a situation. He undertook to preach to us yesterday, but from the aforesaid embarrassment, or the deadness, or the covetousness of the church, he could get none of the Spirit of the Lord to assist him. I am free to say that I attributed more to the latter cause than the former; yet notwithstanding, we made out in donations and subscriptions which I trust will realize $341.37½. May the Lord bless and prosper him, and all His faithfull servants; and may they find favor in the sight of God and man, is the prayer of your unworthy brother,

"WARREN A. COWDERY.

"*To Oliver Cowdery.*"

From this short letter we discover that the Elders failed in the outset to fill their great and important mission, as they know the Lord has commanded us to build a house, in which to receive an endowment, previous to the redemption of Zion; and that Zion could not be redeemed until this takes place. Knowing that the committee were to journey for the express purpose of soliciting donations, they have failed to hold them up and set forth this first important thing; and in consequence God has not blessed them as He otherwise would. We remind you of these things in the name of the Lord, and refer you to the Book of

Covenants, 2nd section, 2nd part, and 12th paragraph, and ask, did we not instruct you to remember first the house, secondly the cause of Zion, and then the publishing of the word to the nations?

The other item referred to is an extract from Elder William E. M'Lellin's letter to his wife, as follows:—

"You say that it will not be in your power to go to school this summer. I am glad that it is not, since Elder Hyde has returned and given me a description of the manner in which it is conducted; though we do not wish to cast any reflections."

This the Council considered to be a libel on the face of it. Elder M'Lellin says, "We do not wish to cast any reflections," when the highest insult and reflections are cast by it upon the Church, the Presidency, and those who are held in much higher estimation in the sight of God and this Church than themselves.

The vote of the Council was: We hereby inform Elders M'Lellin and Hyde that we withdraw our fellowship from them until they return and make satisfaction face to face.

We further inform the Twelve, that as far as we can learn from the churches through which we have traveled, you have set yourselves up as an independent council, subject to no authority of the Church, a kind of outlaws! This impression is wrong, and will, if persisted in, bring down the wrath and indignation of heaven upon your heads. The other ten are directed to proceed on and finish the conferences, and the two may act upon their own judgment whether to proceed or return.

President Joseph Smith, Jun., read to the Council a letter from Elder William Smith, which was approved, and filled our hearts with joy.

A letter was presented from Elder Thomas B. Marsh. The Council referred him to the commandment, which requires none to leave or bring his family without revelation or decision of the High Council.

We discover an error in Elder Marsh's letter—he says, "to the able preaching of William E. M'Lellin and Parley P. Pratt." We conclude that if it had been the preaching of the Lord, as it should have been, He would have had the honor, and not these men. To close, we add that unless this epistle is heeded in all its parts, in its full force, those who rebel against it shall be dealt with by the Lord accordingly, for we ask this, being agreed as touching this thing. We wish you to understand that your duty requires you to seek first the kingdom of heaven and its righteousness; that is, attend to the first things first, and then all things will be added, and that complaint about your families will be less frequent. Don't preach yourselves crucified for your wives' sake, but remember that Christ was crucified, and you are sent out to be special witnesses of this thing. Men do not wish to hear these little things, for there is no salvation in them, but there is in the other.

Let the hands of the ten be strengthened, and let them go forth in the name of the Lord, in the power of their mission, giving diligent heed to the direction of the Holy Spirit. We say, be strong in the Lord, and in the power of His might; for great things await you, and great blessings are in store for you. Let the power of the two be upon the Seventy until the two make full satisfaction; for the Seventy shall be blessed, and are blessed. The man who presumes to speak evil of the dignities which God has set in His Church, to his family, or to anybody else, shall be cursed in his generation. Remember the 109th Psalm. His bishopric shall be taken from him unless he speedily repents. Be it known that God is God, and when He speaks, let all the congregation say, Amen. We have evil insinuations enough in Kirtland to grapple with that are suggested by the father of lies, without having them from those who are sent out to put down insinuations. May God bless you to be more wise in the future. Amen.*

OLIVER COWDERY, Clerk.

Minutes of the Massachusetts Conference.

Bradford, Massachusetts, August 7th. Nine of the traveling High Council met and decided that the limits of the conference embrace the State of Massachusetts, to be called the Massachusetts Conference.

Elder Chase had his license and membership taken from him because of gambling for money, and then breaking bread to the Saints before he confessed his sins.

Elder Holmes' license was taken from him in consequence of a disagreement between him and his wife, which was of long standing. It was therefore considered that if a man cannot preserve peace in his own family, he is not qualified to rule the Church of God.

A letter of complaint was written to Kirtland by Elder Gibson Smith, of Norfolk, Connecticut, against Elder Gladden Bishop, upon which he was suspended, and referred to the conference at Bradford for trial. No one appeared to substantiate the complaint against Elder Bishop, who was, therefore, acquitted on that point; but upon further inquiry, it was proved that he had erred in spirit and in doctrine, and was considerably inclined to [excessive] enthusiasm, and much lifted up. The council therefore took his license from him, until he became more instructed, and also get his spirit and feelings more amalgamated with his brethren.

Elder James Patten of North Providence, Rhode Island, was excommunicated for improper conduct, and refusing to give up his license. This action was ordered to be published in the *Messenger and Advocate*.

* It appears that the minutes of this High Council at Kirtland were intended to be sent to the Twelve as a communication.

The people in this region were generally hard and unbelieving, and but little preaching called for, except by the Church.

The appointment for our conference at Dover, New Hampshire, was recalled on account of the small number of disciples in that place, and no business of importance to be transacted. Also the conferences at Saco and Farmington were altered so as to close at Farmington one month earlier than the former appointment, and notices accordingly were forwarded by mail.

ORSON HYDE, Clerk.

Blessing the "Sons of Zion."

August 8th, a council was held in Kirtland, for the purpose of laying hands on Father Duncan and others of the sons of Zion.

Minutes of the High Council.

The High Council of Kirtland assembled, August 10th, to hear complaint of President Joseph Smith, Jun., against Elder Reynolds Cahoon, in that the latter had failed to do his duty in correcting his children, and instructing them in the way of truth and righteousness; which was proved and decision given accordingly. Elder Cahoon confessed the correctness of the decision and promised to make public acknowledgment before the Church.

OLIVER COWDERY, Clerk.

CHAPTER XVIII.

THE BOOK OF DOCTRINE AND COVENANTS PRESENTED TO THE GENERAL ASSEMBLY OF THE PRIESTHOOD AND THE CHURCH.

A general assembly of the Church of Latter-day Saints was held at Kirtland on the 17th of August, 1835, to take into consideration the labors of a committee appointed by a general assembly of the Church on the 24th of September, 1834, for the purpose of arranging the items of the doctrine of Jesus Christ for the government of the Church. The names of the committee were: Joseph Smith, Jun., Sidney Rigdon, Oliver Cowdery and Frederick G. Williams, who, having finished said book according to the instructions given them, deem it necessary to call a general assembly of the Church to see whether the book be approved or not by the authorities of the Church: that it may, if approved, become a law and a rule of faith and practice to the Church. Wherefore, Oliver Cowdery and Sidney Rigdon, members of the First Presidency, (Presidents Joseph Smith, Jun., and Frederick G. Williams being absent on a visit to the Saints in Michigan,) appointed Thomas Burdick, Warren Parrish, and Sylvester Smith clerks, and proceeded to organize the whole assembly as follows:

They organized* the High Council of the church at Kirtland, and Presidents W. W. Phelps and John Whitmer organized the High Council of the church in Missouri.

Bishop Newel K. Whitney organized his counselors of the church in

* The use of the term "organized" here means merely that the various councils and quorums were arranged by their respective presidencies in the order proper for that assembly, not that they were then organized in the sense of bringing them into existence.

Kirtland, and acting Bishop John Corrill organized the counselors of the church in Missouri.

Presidents Leonard Rich, Levi W. Hancock, Sylvester Smith and Lyman Sherman organized the council of the Seventy. Elder John Gould, acting president, organized the Elders. Ira Ames, acting president, organized the Priests. Erastus Babbitt, acting president, organized the Teachers. William Burgess, acting president, organized the Deacons. And they also, as the assembly was large, appointed Thomas Gates, John Young, William Cowdery, Andrew H. Aldrich, Job L. Lewis and Oliver Higley assistant presidents of the day, to assist in preserving order in the whole assembly.

Elder Levi W. Hancock being appointed chorister, a hymn was sung, and the services for the day opened by the prayer of President Oliver Cowdery, and the solemnities of eternity rested upon the audience.

Another hymn was then sung. After transacting some business for the Church, such as ordaining Morris Phelps to the High Priesthood; Warren Parrish, to the First Seventy; Sherman Gilbert, an Elder; and blessing James Foster, Dean Gould, Benjamin Gifford, Elisha H.Groves and Joseph Hartshorn, the assembly adjourned for one hour.

Afternoon: A hymn was sung, when President Rigdon arose and rebuked some of the authorities for not being in their seats at the time appointed.

President Cowdery arose and introduced the "Book of Doctrine and Covenants of the Church of the Latter-day Saints," in behalf of the committee. He was followed by President Rigdon, who explained the manner by which they intended to obtain the voice of the assembly for or against said book.

According to said arrangement, W. W. Phelps bore record that the book presented to the assembly was true. President John Whitmer, also, rose and testified that it was true.

Elder John Smith, taking the lead of the High Council in Kirtland, bore record that the revelations in said book were true, and that the lectures were judiciously arranged and compiled, and were profitable for doctrine. Whereupon, the High Council of Kirtland accepted and acknowledged them as the doctrine and covenants of their faith by a unanimous vote.

Elder Levi Jackman, taking the lead for the High Council of the church in Missouri, bore testimony that the revelations in said book were true, and the said High Council of Missouri accepted and acknowledged them as the doctrine and covenants of their faith, by a unanimous vote.

President W. W. Phelps then read the written testimony of the Twelve, as follows:

TESTIMONY OF THE TWELVE APOSTLES TO THE TRUTH OF THE BOOK OF DOCTRINE AND COVENANTS.

"*The testimony of the Witnesses to the Book of the Lord's Commandments, which commandments He gave to His Church through Joseph Smith, Jun., who was appointed by the voice of the Church, for this purpose.*

"We therefore feel willing to bear testimony to all the world of mankind, to every creature upon the face of all the earth, that the Lord has borne record to our souls, through the Holy Ghost shed forth upon us, that these Commandments were given by inspiration of God, and are profitable for all men, and are verily true. We give this testimony unto the world, the Lord being our helper; and it is through the grace of God the Father, and His Son Jesus Christ, that we are permitted to have this privilege of bearing this testimony unto the world, in the which we rejoice exceedingly, praying the Lord always that the children of men may be profited thereby.

(Signed) "THOMAS B. MARSH,
"DAVID W. PATTEN,
"BRIGHAM YOUNG,
"HEBER C. KIMBALL,
"ORSON HYDE,
"WM. E. M'LELLIN,
"PARLEY P. PRATT,
"LUKE S. JOHNSON,
"WILLIAM SMITH,
"ORSON PRATT,
"JOHN F. BOYNTON,
"LYMAN E. JOHNSON."*

Elder Leonard Rich bore record of the truth of the book, and the council of the Seventy accepted and acknowledged it as the doctrine and covenants of their faith, by a unanimous vote.

Bishop Newel K. Whitney bore record of the truth of the book, and

* In this testimony of the Twelve to the Book of Doctrine and Covenants, as published in the History of Joseph Smith in the *Millennial Star*, the names of the Apostles were not appended, but it is thought proper that they should be inserted here in the order in which they stood in the quorum. The document was undoubtedly prepared before the departure of the Twelve for the east, as it was well known that the work of the committee on selection and compilation would present the Doctrine and Covenants to a general assembly before the Twelve would return.

with his counselors accepted and acknowledged it as the doctrine and covenants of their faith, by a unanimous vote.

Acting Bishop John Corrill bore record of the truth of the book, and with his counselors accepted and acknowledged it as the doctrine and covenants of their faith, by a unanimous vote.

Acting President John Gould gave his testimony in favor of the book, and with the Elders accepted and acknowledge it as the doctrine and covenants of their faith, by a unanimous vote.

Ira Ames, acting president of the Priests, gave his testimony in favor of the book, and with the Priests accepted and acknowledged it as the doctrine and covenants of their faith, by a unanimous vote.

Erastus Babbitt, acting president of the Teachers, gave his testimony in favor of the book, and they accepted and acknowledged it as the doctrine and covenants of their faith, by a unanimous vote.

William Burgess, acting president of the Deacons, bore record of the truth of the book, and they accepted and acknowledged it as the doctrine and covenants of their faith, by a unanimous vote.

The venerable assistant president, Thomas Gates, then bore record of the truth of the book, and with his five silver-haired assistants, and the whole congregation, accepted and acknowledged it as the doctrine and covenants of their faith, by a unanimous vote.

The several authorities and the general assembly, by a unanimous vote, accepted the labors of the committee.

President W. W. Phelps then read the following article on marriage,* which was accepted and adopted and ordered to be printed in said book, by a unanimous vote, namely:

Article on Marriage.

"According to the custom of all civilized nations, marriage is regulated by laws and ceremonies; therefore we believe that all marriages in this Church of Christ of Latter-day Saints should be solemnized in a public meeting or feast prepared for that purpose, and that the solemnization should be performed by a Presiding High Priest, High Priest, Bishop, Elder or Priest, not even prohibiting those persons who are desirous to get married, of being married by other authority. We believe that it

* It should be observed that this "Article on Marriage" presented by W. W. Phelps, and also the one on "Government and Laws in General," presented by Oliver Cowdery, were not presented as revelations and were not published as such at the time, but were expressions, of course, of the belief of the Saints at that period on those subjects. It should also be noted that these two articles were presented and acted upon in the absence of the Prophet who was at the time visiting Saints and preaching in Michigan.

is not right to prohibit members of this Church from marrying out of the Church, if it be their determination so to do; but such persons will be considered weak in the faith of our Lord Jesus Christ.

"Marriage should be celebrated with prayer and thanksgiving, and at the solemnization, the persons to be married, standing together, the man on the right and the woman on the left, shall be addressed by the person officiating as he shall be directed by the Holy Spirit, and if there be no legal objections, he shall say, calling each by name: 'You both mutually agree to be each other's companion, husband and wife, observing the legal rights belonging to this condition: that is, keeping yourselves wholly for each other, and from all others, during your lives?' And when they have both answered 'yes,' he shall pronounce them 'husband and wife,' in the name of the Lord Jesus Christ, and by virtue of the laws of the country and authority vested in him. 'May God add His blessings and keep you to fulfill your covenants from henceforth and forever. Amen.'

"The clerk of every church should keep a record of all marriages solemnized in his branch. All legal contracts of marriage made before a person is baptized into this Church should be held sacred and fulfilled. Inasmuch as this Church of Christ has been reproached with the crime of fornication and polygamy, we declare that we believe that one man should have one wife, and one woman but one husband, except in case of death, when either is at liberty to marry again. It is not right to persuade a woman to be baptized contrary to the will of her husband; neither is it lawful to influence her to leave her husband. All children are bound by law to obey their parents, and to influence them to embrace any religious faith, or be baptized, or leave their parents without their consent, is unlawful and unjust. We believe that husbands, parents, and masters, who exercise control over their wives, children and servants, and prevent them from embracing the truth, will have to answer for that sin."

President Oliver Cowdery then read the following article on "Governments and Laws in General," which was accepted and adopted and ordered to be printed in said book, by a unanimous vote:

Of Governments and Laws in General.

"That our belief with regard to earthly governments and laws in general may not be misinterpreted nor misunderstood, we have thought proper to present, at the close of this volume, our opinion concerning the same.

"We believe that governments were instituted of God for the benefit of man, and that he holds men accountable for their acts in relation to them, both in making laws and administering them for the good and safety of society.

"We believe that no government can exist in peace, except such laws are framed and held inviolate as will secure to each individual the free exercise of conscience, and the right and control of property, and the protection of life.

"We believe that all governments necessarily require civil officers and magistrates to enforce the laws of the same, and that such as will administer the law in equity and justice should be sought for, and upheld by the voice of the people (if a republic,) or the will of the sovereign.

"We believe that religion is instituted of God, and that men are amenable to Him, and to Him only, for the exercise of it, unless their religious opinions prompt them to infringe upon the rights and liberties of others; but we do not believe that human law has a right to interfere in prescribing rules of worship to bind the consciences of men, or dictate forms for public or private devotion; that the civil magistrate should restrain crime, but never control conscience; should punish guilt, but never suppress the freedom of the soul.

"We believe that all men are bound to sustain and uphold the respective governments in which they reside, while protected in their inherent and inalienable rights by the laws of such governments; and that sedition and rebellion are unbecoming every citizen thus protected, and should be punished accordingly; and that all governments have a right to enact such laws as in their own judgments are best calculated to secure the public interest; at the same time, however, holding sacred the freedom of conscience.

"We believe that every man should be honored in his station: ruler or magistrate as such—being placed for the protection of the innocent and the punishment of the guilty; and that to the laws all men owe respect and deference, as without them peace and harmony would be supplanted by anarchy and terror; human laws being instituted for the express purpose of regulating our interests as individuals and nations between man and man; and divine laws given of heaven prescribing rules on spiritual concerns, for faith and worship, both to be answered by man to his Maker.

"We believe that rulers, states, and governments have a right, and are bound to enact laws for the protection of all citizens in the free exercise of their religious belief; but we do not believe that they have a right, in justice, to deprive citizens of this privilege, or proscribe them in their opinions, so long as a regard and reverence are shown to the laws, and such religious opinions do not justify sedition or conspiracy.

"We believe that the commission of crime should be punished according to the nature of the offense, that murder, treason, robbery, theft, and the breach of the general peace, in all respects, should be punished according to their criminality, and their tendency to evil among men, by the laws of that government in which the offense is committed; and for the public peace and tranquility all men should step forward and use their ability in bringing offenders against good laws to punishment.

"We do not believe it just to mingle religious influence with civil government, whereby one religious society is fostered and another proscribed in its spiritual privileges, and the individual rights of its members, as citizens, denied.

"We believe that all religious societies have a right to deal with their members for disorderly conduct, according to the rules and regulations of such societies; provided that such dealings be for fellowship and good standing; but we do not believe that any religious society has authority to try men on the right of property or life, to take from them this world's goods, or to put them in jeopardy of either life or limb; or to inflict any physical punishment upon them; they can only excommunicate them from their society, and withdraw from them their fellowship.

"We believe that men should appeal to the civil law for redress of all wrongs and grievances where personal abuse is inflicted, or the right of property or character infringed, where such laws exist as will protect the same; but we believe that all men are justified in defending themselves, their friends and property, and the government from the unlawful assaults and encroachments of all persons in times of exigency when immediate appeal cannot be made to the laws, and relief afforded.

"We believe it just to preach the Gospel to the nations of the earth, and warn the righteous to save themselves from the corruption of the world; but we do not believe it right to interfere with bond servants; neither preach the Gospel to, nor baptize them contrary to the will and wish of their masters; nor to meddle with or influence them in the least to cause them to be dissatisfied with their situations in this life, thereby jeopardizing the lives of men; such interference we believe to be unlawful, and unjust, and dangerous to the peace of every government allowing human beings to be held in servitude."

A hymn was then sung. President Sidney Rigdon returned thanks;

after which the assembly was blessed by the Presidency with uplifted hands, and dismissed.

OLIVER COWDERY,
SIDNEY RIGDON,
Presidents.

THOMAS BURDICK,
WARREN PARRISH,
SYLVESTER SMITH,
Clerks.*

* Following is the title page and preface of the first edition of the Doctrine and Covenants.

DOCTRINE AND COVENANTS

OF

THE CHURCH OF THE LATTER-DAY SAINTS:

CAREFULLY SELECTED

FROM THE REVELATIONS OF GOD,

AND COMPILED BY

Joseph Smith, Junior,
Oliver Cowdery,
Sidney Rigdon,
Frederick G. Williams,
(Presiding Elders of the Church,)

PROPRIETORS.

KIRTLAND, OHIO,
PRINTED BY F. G. WILLIAMS & CO.,
For the Proprietors.
1835.

PREFACE.

To the Members of the Church of the Latter-day Saints,

DEAR BRETHREN:—We deem it to be unnecessary to entertain you with a lengthy preface to the following volume, but merely to say that it contains in short the leading items of the religion which we have professed to believe.

The first part of the book will be found to contain a series of lectures as delivered before a theological class in this place, and in consequence of their embracing the important doctrine of salvation, we have arranged them in the following work.

The second part contains items or principles for the regulation of the Church as taken from the revelations which have been given since its organization, as well as from former ones.

There may be an aversion in the minds of some against receiving anything purporting to be articles of religious faith, in consequence of there being so many now extant; but if men believe a system, and profess that it was given by inspiration, certainly the more intelligibly they can present it, the better. It does not make a principle untrue to print it, neither does it make it true not to print it.

The Church, viewing this subject to be of importance, appointed, through their servants and delegates the High Council, your servants to select and compile this work. Several reasons might be adduced in favor of this move of the Council, but we only add a few words. They knew that the Church was evil spoken of in many places, its faith and belief misrepresented, and the way of truth thus subverted. By some it was represented as disbelieving the Bible; by others as being an enemy to all good order and uprightness; and by others as being injurious to the peace of all governments, civil and political.

We have, therefore, endeavored to present, though in few words, our belief, and when we say this, humbly trust, the faith and principles of this society as a body.

We do not present this little volume with any other expectation than that we are to be called to answer to every principle advanced, in that day when the secrets of all hearts will be revealed, and the reward cf every man's labor be given him.

With sentiments of esteem and sincere respect, we subscribe ourselves your brethren in the bonds of the Gospel of our Lord Jesus Christ,

JOSEPH SMITH, JUN.,
OLIVER COWDERY,
SIDNEY RIGDON,
FREDERICK G. WILLIAMS.

KIRTLAND, OHIO, February 17, 1835.

CHAPTER XIX.

THE PROPHET'S RETURN FROM MICHIGAN TO KIRTLAND—HIS ADDRESS TO THE ELDERS OF THE CHURCH.

Minutes of the High Council at Kirtland—Trial of Almon W. Babbitt.

On the 19th, a charge was preferred before a council of the Presidency, against Elder Almon W. Babbitt, for not keeping the Word of Wisdom; for stating the Book of Mormon was not essential to our salvation, and that we have no articles of faith except the Bible.

Elder J. B. Smith testified that Elder Babbitt had assumed the prerogative of dictating to him in his preaching; and that he was not keeping the Word of Wisdom.

Elder Babbitt said that he had taken the liberty to break the Word of Wisdom, from the example of President Joseph Smith, Jun., and others, but acknowledged that it was wrong; that he had taught the Book of Mormon and Commandments as he had thought to be wisdom, and for the good of the cause; that he had not intended to dictate to Elder J. B. Smith, but only to advise with him.

The council reproved Elder Babbitt, and instructed him to observe the Word of Wisdom, and commandments of the Lord in all things; also that it is not advisable for any Elder to take his wife with him on a mission to preach.

WARREN PARRISH, Clerk.

Conference at Saco, Maine.

Seven of the Twelve met in conference at Saco, Maine, August 21st.

The church in that place numbered fifty-seven; the Dover branch in New Hampshire, eight.

The council gave instructions on the redemption of Zion, the building of the Temple in Kirtland, and the printing of the word of God to the nations, etc., etc.; and some were added to the Church during their stay.

The church in Saco contributed seventy or eighty dollar, to assist the

Twelve to return home, which the Twelve recorded as a memento in their behalf, according to covenant.

Return of the Prophet to Kirtland.

Sunday, August 23.—I arrived at Kirtland from my visit to Michigan.

On the 24th the High Council at Kirtland ordained Jonathan Stevens an Elder, and instructed him and his sons, Uzziel and Lyman, and his son-in-law, John E. Page,* Elders, to locate their families and then go forth and preach the Gospel; also that Joseph H. Tippits and J. W. Tippits go to Missouri this fall to purchase land for the church in Essex, New York, according to previous appointment by the voice of said church.

John E. Page.

August 28.—This day I preached on the duty of wives.

The traveling High Council assembled in conference at Farmington, Maine, and resolved—that this be called the "Maine Conference." The church at Farmington numbered thirty-two; in Sitter B., twenyt-two; in Akwry, twenty-five; in Errol, New Hampshire, twenty; all in good standing.

The Conference at Farmington, Maine.

September 1.—I wrote the following communication to John Whitmer, Esq., editor, which was published in the *Messenger and Advocate*, page 179, *et seq.*:

The Prophet's Letter to the Elders.

TO THE ELDERS OF THE CHURCH OF LATTER-DAY SAINTS:†

After so long a time, and after so many things have been said, I feel it my duty to drop a few hints, that perhaps the Elders traveling through the world, to warn the inhabitants of the earth to flee the wrath to come, and save themselves from this untoward generation—

* John E. Page was born February 25, 1799, in Trenton Township, Oneida County, New York. He was baptized by the brother of Martin Harris—Emar Harris—in August, 1833, in Ohio, and ordained an Elder in September, 1833. He was now, on his removal to Kirtland, in his thirty-sixth year.

† This is a most important document, since in it the Prophet reviews the actions and motives of himself and associates in settling the Church in Missouri. It is a most just and conservative statement of the case, a statement in which the errors and overzeal of some of the Elders and Saints are admitted and deplored. It also admirably portrays the Prophet as the conservative force in the Church, and gives an insight into the greatness and inspiration of his mind.

may be aided in a measure, in doctrine, and in the way of their duty. I have been laboring in this cause for eight years, during which time I have traveled much, and have had much experience. I removed from Seneca County, New York, to Geauga County, Ohio, in February, 1831.

I received, by a heavenly vision, a commandment in June following, to take my journey to the western boundaries of the State of Missouri, and there designate the very spot which was to be the central place for the commencement of the gathering together of those who embrace the fullness of the everlasting Gospel. Accordingly I undertook the journey, with certain ones of my brethren, and after a long and tedious journey, suffering many privations and hardships, arrived in Jackson County, Missouri, and after viewing the country, seeking diligently at the hand of God, He manifested Himself unto us, and designated, to me and others, the very spot upon which He designed to commence the work of the gathering, and the upbuilding of an "holy city," which should be called Zion — Zion, because it is a place of righteousness, and all who build thereon are to worship the true and living God, and all believe in one doctrine, even the doctrine of our Lord and Savior Jesus Christ. "Thy watchmen shall lift up the voice; with the voice together shall they sing: for they shall see eye to eye, when the Lord shall bring again Zion" (Isaiah lii: 8).

Here we pause for a moment to make a few remarks upon the idea of gathering to this place. It is well known that there were lands belonging to the government, to be sold to individuals, and it was understood by all, at least we believed so, that we lived in a free country, a land of liberty and of laws, guaranteeing to every man, or any company of men, the right of purchasing lands, and settling and living upon them; therefore we thought no harm in advising the Latter-day Saints, or "Mormons," as they are reproachfully called, to gather to this place, inasmuch as it was their duty (and it was well understood so to be) to purchase with money, lands, and live upon them, not infringing upon the rights of any individual, or community of people; always keeping in view the saying, "Do unto others as you would wish others to do unto you;" following also the good injunction, "Deal justly, love mercy, and walk humbly with thy God."

These were our motives in teaching the people, or Latter-day Saints, to gather together, beginning at this place; and inasmuch as there are those who have had different views from this, we feel that it is a cause of deep regret. Be it known unto all men, that our principles concerning this thing have not been such as have been represented by those who, we have every reason to believe, are designing and wicked men, that have said that this was our doctrine: "To infringe upon the rights of a people who inhabit our civil and free country, such as to drive the inhabitants of Jackson County from their lands, and take possession thereof unlawfully." Far, yea, far be such a principle from our hearts. It never entered into our minds; and we only say, that God shall reward such in that day when He shall come to make up His jewels.

But to return to my subject. After having ascertained the very spot, and having the happiness of seeing quite a number of the families of my brethren comfortably situated upon the land, I took leave of them and journeyed back to Ohio, and used every influence and argument that lay in my power to get those who believed in the everlasting covenant, whose circumstances would admit, and whose families were willing to remove to the place which I had designated to be the land of Zion; and thus the sound of the gathering, and of the doctrine, went abroad into the world; and many, having a zeal not according to knowledge, and not understanding the pure principles of the doctrine of the Church, have, no doubt, in the heat of enthusiasm, taught and said many things which were derogatory to the genuine character and principles of the Church; and for these things we are heartily sorry, and would apologize, if apology would do any good.

But we pause here, and offer a remark upon the saying which we learn has gone abroad, and has been handled in a manner detrimental to the cause of truth, by saying, "that in preaching the doctrine of gathering, we break up families, and give license for men to leave their families, women their husbands, children their parents and slaves their masters, thereby deranging the order and breaking up the harmony and peace of society." We shall here show our faith, and thereby, as we humbly trust, put an end to these false and wicked misrepresentations, which have caused, we have every reason to believe, thousands to think they were doing God's service, when they were persecuting the children of God; whereas, if they could have enjoyed the true light, and had a just understanding of our principles, they would have embraced them with all their hearts, and been rejoicing in the love of the truth. And now to show our doctrine on this subject, we shall commence with the first principles of the Gospel, which are faith, repentance, and baptism for the remission of sins, and the gift of the Holy Ghost by the laying on of the hands. This we believe to be our duty—to teach to all mankind the doctrine of repentance, which we shall endeavor to show from the following quotations:

"Then opened He their understandings, that they might understand the scriptures, and said unto them, Thus it is written, and thus it behoved Christ to suffer, and to rise from the dead the third day: and that repentance and remission of sins should be preached in His name among all nations, beginning at Jerusalem" (Luke xxiv: 45, 46, 47).

By this we learn that it behoved Christ to suffer, and to be crucified, and rise again on the third day, for the express purpose that repentance and remission of sins should be preached to all nations.

"Then Peter said unto them, Repent, and be baptized every one of you in the name of Jesus Christ for the remission of sins, and ye shall receive the gift of the Holy Ghost. For the promise is unto you, and to your children, and to all that are afar off, even as many as the Lord our God shal call" (Acts ii: 38, 39).

By this we learn that the promise of the Holy Ghost is made unto as many as those to whom the doctrine of repentance was to be preached, which was unto all nations. And we discover also, that the promise was to extend by lineage; for Peter says, not only unto you, but "to your children, and to all that are afar off." From this we infer, that the promise was to continue unto their children's children, and even unto as many as the Lord their God should call. We discover here that we are blending two principles together in these quotations. The first is the principle of repentance, and the second is the principle of the remission of sins; and we learn from Peter that remission of sins is to be obtained by baptism in the name of the Lord Jesus Christ; and the gift of the Holy Ghost follows inevitably, for, says Peter, "you shall receive the Holy Ghost."

Therefore we believe in preaching the doctrine of repentance in all the world, both to old and young, rich and poor, bond and free, as we shall endeavor to show hereafter how, and in what manner, and how far, it is binding on the consciences of mankind, making proper distinctions between old and young, men, women, children and servants. But we discover, in order to be benefitted by the doctrine of repentance, we must believe in obtaining the remission of sins. And in order to obtain the remission of sins, we must believe in the doctrine of baptism in the name of the Lord Jesus Christ. And if we believe in baptism for the remission of sins, we may expect a fulfillment of the promise of the Holy Ghost, for the promise extends to all whom the Lord our God shall call; and hath He not surely said, as you will find in the last chapter of Revelation—"And the Spirit and the bride say, Come. And let him that heareth say, Come. And let him that is athirst come. And whosoever will, let him take the water of life freely" (Rev. xxii: 17).

Again, the Savior says, "Come unto me, all ye that labor, and are heavy laden, and I will give you rest. Take my yoke upon you, and learn of me; for I am meek and lowly in heart: and ye shall find rest unto your souls. For my yoke is easy, and my burden is light" (Matt. xi: 28, 29, 30).

Again, Isaiah says, "Look unto me, and be ye saved, all the ends of the earth: for I am God, and there is none else. I have sworne by myself, the word is gone out of my mouth in righteousness and shall not return, That unto me every knee shall bow, every tongue shall swear. Surely shall one say, in the Lord have I righteousness and strength: even to Him shall men come; and all that are incensed against Him shall be ashamed" (Isaiah xlv: 22-24).

And to show further connections in proof of the doctrine above named, we quote the following scriptures:

"Him hath God exalted with His right hand, to be a Prince and a Savior, for to give repentance to Israel, and forgiveness of sins. And we are His witnesses of these things; and so is also the Holy Ghost, whom God hath given to them that obey Him" (Acts v: 31, 32).

"But when they believed Philip, preaching the things concerning the Kingdom of God, and the name of Jesus Christ, they were baptized, both men and women. Then Simon, himself, believed also: and when he was baptized, he continued with Philip, and wondered, beholding the miracles and signs which were done. Now when the apostles which were at Jerusalem heard that Samaria had received the word of God, they sent unto them Peter and John: who, when they were come down, prayed for them, that they might receive the Holy Ghost: (for as yet he was fallen upon none of them, only they were baptized in the name of the Lord Jesus.) Then laid they their hands on them, and they received the Holy Ghost."

"And as they went on their way, they came unto a certain water, and the eunuch said, See, here is water, what doth hinder me to be baptized? And Philip said, If thou believest with all thine heart, thou mayest. And he answered and said, I believe that Jesus Christ is the Son of God. And he commanded the chariot to stand still, and they went down both into the water, both Philip and the eunuch, and he baptized him. And when they were come up out of the water, the Spirit of the Lord caught away Philip, and the eunuch saw him no more, and he went on his way rejoicing. But Philip was found at Azotus; and passing through, he preached in all the cities, till he came to Cesarea" (Acts viii: 12-17; 36-40).

"While Peter yet spake these words, the Holy Ghost fell on all them which heard the word. And they of the circumcision, which believed, were astonished, as many as came with Peter, because that on the Gentiles also was poured out the gift of the Holy Ghost, for they heard them speak with tongues and magnify God. Then answered Peter, Can any man forbid water, that these should not be baptized, which have received the Holy Ghost as well as we? And he commanded them to be baptized in the name of the Lord. Then prayed they him to tarry certain days" (Acts x: 44-48).

"And on the Sabbath, we went out of the city, by a river side where prayer was wont to be made; and we sat down and spake unto the women which resorted thither. And a certain woman, named Lydia, a seller of purple, of the city of Thyatira, which worshiped God, heard us; whose heart the Lord opened, that she attended unto the things spoken of by Paul. And when she was baptized, and her household, she besought us, saying, If ye have judged me to be faithfu to the Lord. come into my house, and abide there; and she constrained us" (Acts xvi: 13-15).

"And at midnight Paul and Silas prayed, and sang praises to God; and the prisoners heard them. And suddenly there was a great earthquake, so that the foundations of the prison were shaken; and immediately all the doors were opened, and every one's bands were loosed. And the keeper of the prison awaking out of his sleep, and seeing the prison doors open, he drew out his sword and would have killed himself, supposing the prisoners had been fled. But Paul cried with a loud voice, saying, Do thyself no harm, for we are all here. Then he called for a light, and sprang in, and came trembling and fell down before Paul and Silas, and brought them out, and said, Sirs, what must I do to be saved? And they said, Believe on the Lord Jesus Christ, and thou shalt be saved, and thy house. And they spoke unto him the word of the Lord, and to all that were in the house. And he took them the same hour of the night, and washed their stripes, and was baptized, he and all his straightway. And when he had brought them into his house, he set met before them, and rejoiced, believing in God, with all his house" (Acts xvi: 25-34).

"And it came to pass that while Apollos was at Corinth, Paul, having passed through the upper coasts, came to Ephesus, and finding certain disciples, he said unto them, Have ye received the Holy Ghost since ye believed? And they said unto him, we have not so much as heard whether there be any Holy Ghost. And he said unto them, Unto what then were ye baptized? And they said, Unto John's baptism. Then said Paul, John verily baptized with the baptism of repentance, saying unto the people, that they should believe on Him which should come after him, that is on Christ Jesus. When they heard this, they were baptized in the name of the Lord Jesus. And when Paul had laid his hands upon them, the Holy Ghost came on them, and they spake with tongues and prophesied" (Acts xix: 1-6).

"And one Ananias, a devout man according to the law, having a good report of all the Jews which dwelt there, came unto me, and stood and said unto me, Brother Saul, receive thy sight. And the same hour I looked upon him, and he said, The God of our fathers hath chosen thee that thou shouldst know His will, and see that Just One, and shouldst hear the word of His mouth. For thou shalt be his witness unto all men, of what thou hast seen and heard. And now, why tarriest thou? Arise and be baptized, and wash away thy sins, calling on the name of the Lord" (Acts xxii: 12-16).

"For when for the time ye ought to be teachers, ye have need that one teach you again which be the first principles of the oracles of God, and are become such as have need of milk and not of strong meat. For every one that useth milk is unskillful in the word of righteousness, for he is a babe. But strong meat belongeth to them that are of full age, even those who by reason of use, have their senses exercised to discern both good and evil" (Heb. v: 12-14).

"Therefore, leaving the principles of the doctrine of Christ, let us go on unto perfection; not laying again the foundation of repentance from dead works, and of faith toward God, and of the doctrine of baptisms, and of laying on of hands, of resurrection of the dead, and of eternal judgment. And this will we do, if God permit. For it is impossible for those who were once enlightened, and have tasted of the heavenly gift, and were made partakers of the Holy Ghost, and have tasted the good word of God, and the powers of the world to come, if they shall fall away, to renew them again unto repentance, seeing they crucify to themselves the Son of God afresh, and put Him to an open shame" (Heb. vi: 1-6).

These quotations are so plain, in proving the doctrine of repentance and baptism for the remission of sins, I deem it unnecessary to enlarge this letter with comments upon them; but I shall continue the subject in my next.

In the bonds of the new and everlasting covenant,

JOSEPH SMITH, JUN.

II.

TO THE ELDERS OF THE CHURCH OF THE LATTER-DAY SAINTS.*

At the close of my letter in the September number of the *Messenger and Advocate* I promised to continue the subject there commenced. I do so with a hope that it may be a benefit and a means of assistance in the labors of the Elders, while they are combating the prejudices of a crooked and preverse generation, by having in their possession the facts of my religious principles, which are misrepresented by almost all those whose crafts are in danger by the same; and also, to aid those who are anxiously inquiring, and have been excited to do so from rumor,

* It has been decided to let the several divisions of this communication to the Elders of the Church appear together in this one chapter. There were three separate communication of the Prophet, as they appear in the *Messenger and Advocate* for September, November and December, 1835, respectively; but as they constitute one continuous address, it is believed that it will in every way be better to have them appear together in one chapter.

to ascertain correctly what my principles are. I have been drawn into this course of proceeding by persecution, that is brought upon us from false rumors and misrepresentations concerning my sentiments.

But to proceed. In the letter alluded to, the principles of repentance and baptism for the remission of sins were not only set forth, but many passages of scripture were quoted, clearly elucidating the subject; let me add, I do positively rely upon the truth of those principles inculcated in the New Testament, and then pass on from the above named items, to the item or subject of the gathering, and show my views upon this point. It is a principle I esteem to be of the greatest importance to those who are looking for salvation in this generation, or in these, that may be called, "the latter times." All that the prophets that have written, from the days of righteous Abel, down to the last man that has left any testimony on record for our consideration, in speaking of the salvation of Israel in the last days, goes directly to show that it consists in the work of the gathering.

First, I shall begin by quoting from the prophecy of Enoch, speaking of the last days: "Righteousness will I sent down out of heaven, and truth will I send forth out of the earth, to bear testimony of mine Only Begotten, His resurrection from the dead (this resurrection I understand to be the corporeal body); yea, and also the resurrection of all men; righteousness and truth will I cause to sweep the earth as with a flood, to gather out mine own elect from the four quarters of the earth, unto a place which I shall prepare, a holy city, that my people may gird up their loins, and be looking forth for the time of my coming, for there shall be my tabernacle, and it shall be called Zion, a new Jerusalem" (Pearl of Great Price, ch. vii: 62, 1902 edition).

Now I understand by this quotation, that God clearly manifested to Enoch the redemption which He prepared, by offering the Messiah as a Lamb slain from before the foundation of the world; and by virtue of the same, the glorious resurrection of the Savior, and the resurrection of all the human family, even a resurrection of their corporeal bodies, is brought to pass; and also righteousness and truth are to sweep the earth as with a flood. And now, I ask, how righteousness and truth are going to sweep the earth as with a flood? I will answer. Men and angels are to be co-workers in bringing to pass this great work, and Zion is to be prepared, even a new Jerusalem, for the elect that are to be gathered from the four quarters of the earth, and to be established an holy city, for the tabernacle of the Lord shall be with them.

Now Enoch was in good company in his views upon this subject: "And I heard a great voice out of heaven, saying, Behold, the tabernacle of God is with men, and He will dwell with them, and they shall be His people and God Himself shall be with them, and be their God" (Revelation xxi: 3).

I discover by this quotation, that John upon the isle of Patmos, saw the same thing concerning the last days, which Enoch saw. But before the tabernacle can be with men, the elect must be gathered from the four quarters of the earth. And to show further upon this subject of the gathering, Moses, after having pronounced the blessing and cursing upon the children of Israel, for their obedience or disobedience, says thus:

"And it shall come to pass, when all these things are come upon thee, the blessing and the curse which I have set before thee, and thou shalt call them to mind, among all the nations whither the Lord thy God hath driven thee, and shalt return unto the Lord thy God, and shalt obey His voice, according to all that I command thee, this day, thou and thy children, with all thine heart, and with all thy soul, then the Lord thy God will turn thy captivity, and have compassion upon thee, and will return and gather thee from all the nations whither the Lord thy God hath scattered thee. If any of thine be driven out unto the outmost parts of heaven, from thence will the Lord thy God gather thee, and from thence will He fetch thee" (Deut. xxx: 1-4).

It has been said by many of the learned and wise men, or historians, that the Indians or aborigines of this continent, are of the scattered tribes of Israel. It has been conjectured by many others, that the aborigines of this continent are not of the tribes of Israel, but the ten tribes have been led away into some unknown regions of the north. Let this be as it may, the prophecy I have just quoted "will fetch them," in the last days, and place them in the land which their fathers possessed. And you will find in the 7th verse of the 30th chapter, quoted, "And the Lord thy God will put all these curses upon thine enemies, and on them that hate thee, which persecuted thee."

Many may say that this scripture is fulfilled, but let them mark carefully what the prophet says: "If any are driven out unto the utmost parts of heaven," (which must mean the breadth of the earth). Now this promise is good to any, if there should be such, that are driven out, even in the last days, therefore, the children of the fathers have claim unto this day. And if these curses are to be laid over on the heads of their enemies, wo be unto the Gentiles. (See Book of Mormon III Nephi, ch. xvi, current edition.) "Wo unto the unbelieving of the Gentiles, saith the Father." And again (see Book of Mormon, III Nephi xx: 22, current edition, which says), "Behold this people will I establish in this land, unto the fulfilling of the covenant which I made with your father Jacob, and it shall be a New Jerusalem." Now we learn from the Book of Mormon the very identical continent and spot of land upon which the New Jerusalem is to stand, and it must be caught up according to the vision of John upon the isle of Patmos.

Now many will feel disposed to say, that this New Jerusalem spoken of, is the Jerusalem that was built by the Jews on the eastern continent. But you will see, from Revelation xxi: 2, there was a New Jerusalem coming down from God out of heaven, adorned as a bride for her husband; that after this, the Revelator was caught away in the Spirit, to a great and high mountain, and saw the great and holy city descending out of heaven from God. Now there are two cities spoken of here. As everything cannot be had in so narrow a compass as a letter, I shall say with brevity, that there is a New Jerusalem to be established on this continent, and also Jerusalem shall be rebuilt on the eastern continent (See Book of Mormon, Ether xiii: 1-12). "Behold, Ether saw the days of Christ, and he spake also concerning the house of Israel, and the Jerusalem from whence Lehi should come; after it should be destroyed, it should be build up again, a holy city unto the Lord, wherefore it could not be a New Jerusalem, for it had been in a time of old." This may suffice, upon the subject of gathering, until my next.

I now proceed, at the close of my letter, to make a few remarks on the duty of Elders with regard to their teaching parents and children, husbands and wives, masters and slaves, or servants, as I said I would in my former letter.

And first, it becomes an Elder when he is traveling through the world, warning the inhabitants of the earth to gather together, that they may be built up an holy city unto the Lord, instead of commencing with children, or those who look up to parents or guardians to influence their minds, thereby drawing them from their duties, which they rightfully owe these legal guardians, they should commence their labors with parents, or guardians; and their teachings should be such as are calculated to turn the hearts of the fathers to the children, and the hearts of children to the fathers; and no influence should be used with children, contrary to the consent of their parents or guardians; but all such as can be persuaded in a lawful and righteous manner, and with common consent, we should feel it our duty to influence them to gather with the people of God. But otherwise let the responsibility rest upon the heads of parents or guardians, and all condemnation or consequences be upon their heads, according to the dispensation which he hath committed unto us; for God hath so ordained, that His work shall be cut short in righteousness, in the last days; therefore, first teach the parents, and then, with their consent, persuade the children to embrace the Gospel also. And if children embrace the Gospel, and their parents or guardians are unbelievers, teach them to stay at home and be obedient to their parents or guardians, if they require it; but if they consent to let them gather with the people of God, let them do so, and there shall be no wrong; and let all things be done carefully and righteously and God will extend to all such His guardian care.

And secondly, it is the duty of Elders, when they enter into any house, to let their labors and warning voice be unto the master of that house; and if he receive the Gospel, then he may extend his influence to his wife also, with consent, that peradventure she may receive the Gospel; but if a man receive not the Gospel, but gives his consent that his wife may receive it, and she believes, then let her receive it. But if a man forbid his wife, or his children, before they are of age, to receive the Gospel, then it should be the duty of the Elder to go his way, and use no influence against him, and let the responsibility be upon his head; shake off the dust of thy feet as a testimony against him, and thy skirts shall then be clear of their souls. Their sins are not to be answered upon such as God hath sent to warn them to flee the wrath to come, and save themselves from this untoward generation. The servants of God will not have gone over the nations of the Gentiles, with a warning voice, until the destroying angel will commence to waste the inhabitants of the earth, and as the prophet hath said. "It shall be a vexation to hear the report." I speak thus because I feel for my fellow men; I do it in the name of the Lord, being moved upon by the Holy Spirit. Oh, that I could snatch them from the vortex of misery, into which I behold them plunging themselves, by their sins; that I might be enabled by the warning voice, to be an instrument of bringing them to unfeigned repentance, that they might have faith to stand in the evil day!

Thirdly, it should be the duty of an Elder, when he enters into a house, to salute the master of that house, and if he gain his consent, then he may preach to all that are in that house; but if he gain not his consent, let him not go unto his slaves, or servants, but let the responsibility be upon the head of the master of that house, and the consequences thereof, and the guilt of that house is no longer upon his skirts, he is free; therefore, let him shake off the dust of his feet, and go his way. But if the master of that house give consent, the Elder may preach to his family, his wife, his children and his servants, his man-servants, or his maid-servants, or his slaves; then it should be the duty of the Elder to stand up boldly for the cause of Christ, and warn that people with one accord to repent and be baptized for the remission of sins, and for the Holy Ghost, always commanding them in the name of the Lord, in the spirit of meekness, to be kindly affectionate one toward another, that the fathers should be kind to their children, husbands to their wives, masters to their slaves or servants, children obedient to their parents, wives to their husbands, and slaves or servants to their masters.

"Wives submit yourselves unto your own husbands, as unto the Lord, for the husband is the head of the wife, even as Christ is the head of the Church; and He is the Savior of the body. Therefore, as the Church is subject unto Christ, so let the wives be to their own husbands, in everything. Husbands, love your wives, even as Christ also loved the Church and gave Himself for it, that He might sanctify and cleanse it with the washing of water by the Word, that He might present it to Himself a glorious Church, not having spot or wrinkle, or any such thing, but that it should be holy and without blemish, so ought men to love their own wives as their own bodies. He that loveth his wife, loveth himself, for no man ever yet hated his own flesh, but nourisheth and cherisheth it, even as the Lord the Church, for we are members of His body, of His flesh, and of His bones. For this cause shall a man leave his father and mother, and shall be joined unto his wife, and they two shall be one flesh" (Ephesians v: 22-31).

Wives, submit yourselves unto your own husbands, as it is fit in the Lord. Husbands, love your wives, and be not bitter against them. Children, obey your parents in all things, for this is well pleasing unto the Lord. Fathers, provoke not your children to anger, lest they be discouraged. Servants, obey in all things your masters, according to the flesh, not with eye-service, as men-pleasers, but in singleness of heart, fearing God (Colossians iii: 18-22).

But I must close this letter, and resume the subject in another number.

In the bonds of the New and Everlasting Covenant,

JOSEPH SMITH, JUN.

III.

TO THE ELDERS OF THE CHURCH OF LATTER-DAY SAINTS.

I have shown unto you, in my last, that there are two Jerusalems spoken of in holy writ, in a manner I think satisfactory to your minds; at any rate I have given my views upon the subject. I shall now proceed to make some remarks from the sayings of the Savior, recorded in the 13th chapter of His Gospel according to St. Matthew, which, in my mind, afford us as clear an understanding upon the important subject of the gathering, as anything recorded in the Bible. At the time the Savior spoke these beautiful sayings and parables contained in the chapter above quoted, we find Him seated in a ship on account of the multitude that pressed upon Him to hear His words; and He commenced teaching them, saying:

"Behold, a sower went forth to sow, and when he sowed, some seeds fell by the way side, and the fowls came and devoured them up: some fell upon stony places, where they had not much earth; and forthwith they sprang up because they had no deepness of earth: and when the sun was up they were scorched: and because they had no root they withered away. And some fell among thorns; and the thorns sprung up and choked them: but other fell in good ground, and brought forth fruit, some an hundred fold, some sixty fold, some thirty fold. Who hath ears to hear, let him hear.

"And the disciples came and said unto Him, Why speakest thou unto them in parables? [I would here remark, that the 'them' made use of in this interrogation, is a personal pronoun, and refers to the multitude.] He answered and said unto them, [that is unto the disciples,] because it is given unto *you* to know the mysteries of the Kingdom of Heaven, but to *them*, [that is, unbelievers,] it is not given; for whosoever hath, to him shall be given, and he shall have more abundance; but whosoever hath not, from him shall be taken away even that he hath."

We understand from this saying, that those who had been previously looking for a Messiah to come, according to the testimony of the Prophets, and were then, at that time looking for a Messiah, but had not sufficient light, on account of their unbelief, to discern Him to be their Savior; and He being the true Messiah, consequently they must be disappointed, and lose even all the knowledge, or have taken away from them all the light, understanding, and faith which they had upon this subject; therefore he that will not receive the greater light, must have taken away from him all the light which he hath; and if the light which is in you become darkness, behold, how great is that darkness! "Therefore," says the Savior, "speak I unto them in parables, because they, seeing, see not, and hearing, they hear not, neither do they understand: and in them is fulfilled the prophecy of Esaias which saith, "By hearing ye shall hear, and shall not understand; and seeing ye shall see, and not perceive."

Now we discover that the very reason assigned by this prophet, why they would not receive the Messiah, was, because they did not or would not understand; and seeing, they did not perceive; "for this people's heart is waxed gross, and their ears are dull of hearing, their eyes have closed, lest at any time they should see with their eyes, and hear with their ears, and understand with their heart, and should be converted, and I should heal them." But what saith He to His disciples? "Blessed are your eyes for they see, and your ears for they hear, for verily I say unto you, that many prophets and righteous men have desired to see those things which ye see, and have not seen them; and to hear those things which ye hear, and have not heard them."

We again make remark here—for we find that the very principle upon which the disciples were accounted blessed, was because they were permitted to see with their eyes and hear with their ears—that the condemnation which rested upon the multitude that received not His saying, was because they were not willing to see with their eyes, and hear with their ears; not because they could not, and were not privileged to see and hear, but because their hearts were full of iniquity and abominations; "as your fathers did, so do ye." The prophet, foreseeing that they would thus harden their hearts, plainly declared it; and herein is the condemnation of the world; that light hath come into the world, and men choose darkness rather than light, because their deeds are evil. This is so plainly taught by the Savior, that a wayfaring man need not mistake it.

And again—hear ye the parable of the sower. Men are in the habit, when the truth is exhibited by the servants of God, of saying, All is mystery; they have spoken in parables, and, therefore, are not to be understood. It is true they have eyes to see, and see not, but none are so blind as those who will not see; and, although the Savior spoke this to such characters, yet unto His disciples he expounded it plainly; and we have reason to be truly humble before the God of our fathers, that He hath left these things on record for us, so plain, that notwithstanding the exertions and combined influence of the priests of Baal, they have not power to blind our eyes, and darken our understanding, if we will but open our eyes, and read with candor, for a moment.

But listen to the explanation of the parable of the Sower: "When any one heareth the word of the Kingdom, and understandeth it not, then cometh the wicked one, and catcheth away that which was sown in his heart." Now mark the expression—that which was sown in his heart. This is he which receiveth seed by the way side. Men who have no principle of righteousness in themselves, and whose hearts are full of iniquity, and have no desire for the principles of truth, do not understand the word of truth when they hear it. The devil taketh away the word of truth out of their hearts, because there is no desire for righteousness in them. "But he that receiveth seed in stony places, the same is he that heareth the word, and anon, with joy receiveth it; yet hath he not root in himself, but dureth for a while: for when tribulation or persecution ariseth because of the word, by and by, he is offended. He also that receiveth seed among the thorns, is he that heareth the word; and the care of this world, and the deceitfulness of riches choke the word, and he becometh unfruitful. But he that received seed into the good ground is he that heareth the word, and understandeth it, which also beareth fruit, and bringeth forth, some an hundred fold, some sixty, some thirty." Thus the Savior Himself explains unto His disciples the parable which He put forth, and left no mystery or darkness upon the minds of those who firmly believe on His words.

We draw the conclusion, then, that the very reason why the multitude, or the world, as they were designated by the Savior, did not receive an explanation upon His parables, was because of unbelief. To you, He says, (speaking to His disciples,) it is given to know the mysteries of the Kingdom of God. And why? Because of the faith and confidence they had in Him. This parable was spoken to demonstrate the effects that are produced by the preaching of the word; and we believe that it has an allusion directly, to the commencement, or the setting up of the Kingdom in that age; therefore we shall continue to trace His sayings concerning this Kingdom from that time forth, even unto the end of the world.

"Another parable put He forth unto them, saying, [which parable has an allusion to the setting up of the Kingdom, in that age of the world also.] The Kingdom of Heaven is likened unto a man which sowed good seed in his field, but while men slept, his enemy came and sowed tares among the wheat, and went his way. But when the blade was sprung up, and brought forth fruit, then appeared the tares also; so the servants of the householder came and said unto him, Sir, didst not thou sow good seed in thy field? From whence, then, hath it tares? He said unto them, An enemy hath done this. The servants said unto him, Wilt thou then that we go and gather them up? But he said, Nay; lest while ye gather up the tares, ye root up also the wheat with them. Let both grow together until the harvest: and in the time of harvest I will say to the reapers, Gather ye together first the tares, and bind them in bundles to burn them, but gather the wheat into my barn."

Now we learn by this parable, not only the setting up of the Kingdom in the days of the Savior, which is represented by the good seed, which produced fruit, but also the corruptions of the Church, which are represented by the tares, which were sown by the enemy, which His disciples would fain have plucked up, or cleansed the Church of, if their views had been favored by the Savior. But He, knowing all things, says, Not so. As much as to say, your views are not correct, the Church is in its infancy, and if you take this rash step, you will destroy the wheat, or the Church, with the tares; therefore it is better to let them grow together until the harvest, or the end of the world, which means the destruction of the wicked, which is not yet fulfilled, as we shall show hereafter, in the Savior's explanation of the parable, which is so plain that there is no room left for dubiety upon the mind, notwithstanding the cry of the priests—"parables, parables! figures,

figures! mystery, mystery! all is mystery!" But we find no room for doubt here, as the parables were all plainly elucidated.

And again, another parable put He forth unto them, having an allusion to the Kingdom that should be set up, just previous to or at the time of the harvest, which reads as follows—"The Kingdom of Heaven is like a grain of mustard seed, which a man took and sowed in his field: which indeed is the least of all seeds: but, when it is grown, it is the greatest among herbs, and becometh a tree, so that the birds of the air come and lodge in the branches thereof." Now we can discover plainly that this figure is given to represent the Church as it shall come forth in the last days. Behold, the Kingdom of Heaven is likened unto it. Now, what is like unto it?

Let us take the Book of Mormon, which a man took and hid in his field, securing it by his faith, to spring up in the last days, or in due time; let us behold it coming forth out of the ground, which is indeed accounted the least of all seeds, but behold it branching forth, yea, even towering, with lofty branches, and God-like majesty, until it, like the mustard seed, becomes the greatest of all herbs. And it is truth, and it has sprouted and come forth out of the earth, and righteousness begins to look down from heaven, and God is sending down His powers, gifts and angels, to lodge in the branches thereof.

The Kingdom of heaven is like unto a mustard seed. Behold, then is not this the Kingdom of heaven that is raising its head in the last days in the majesty of its God, even the Church of the Latter-day Saints, like an impenetrable, immovable rock in the midst of the mighty deep, exposed to the storms and tempests of Satan, but has, thus far, remained steadfast, and is still braving the mountain waves of opposition, which are driven by the tempestuous winds of sinking crafts, which have [dashed] and are still dashing with tremendous foam across its triumphant brow; urged onward with redoubled fury by the enemy of righteousness, with his pitchfork of lies, as you will see fairly represented in a cut contained in Mr. Howe's *Mormonism Unveiled?* And we hope that this adversary of truth will continue to stir up the sink of iniquity, that the people may the more readily discern between the righteous and the wicked.

We also would notice one of the modern sons of Sceva, who would fain have made people believe that he could cast out devils, by a certain pamphlet, the *Millennial Harbinger*, that went the rounds through our country; who felt so fully authorized to brand "Jo" Smith with the appellation of Elymas the sorcerer, and to say with Paul, "O full of all subtlety, and all mischief, thou child of the devil, thou enemy of all righteousness, wilt thou not cease to pervert the right ways of the Lord?" We would reply to this gentleman, Paul we know, and Christ we know, but who are ye? And with the best of feeling would say to him, in the language of Paul to those who said they were John's disciples, but had not so much as heard there was a Holy Ghost—to repent and be baptized for the remission of sins, by those who have legal authority, and under their hands you shall receive the Holy Ghost, according to the Scriptures:*

"Then laid they *their* hands upon them, and they received the Holy Ghost (Acts viii: 17.) "And when Paul had laid his hands upon them the Holy Ghost came on them and they spake with tongues and prophesied" (Acts xix: 6). "Of the doctrine of baptism, and of laying on of hands, and of resurrection of the dead and of eternal judgment" (Hebrews vi: 2). "How, then, shall they call on him in whom they have not believed? And how shall they believe in him of whom they have not heard? And how shall they hear without a preacher? And how shall they preach, except they be sent? As it is written, How beautiful are the feet of them that preach the Gospel of peace, and bring glad tidings of good things" (Romans x: 14, 15). But if this man will not take our admonition, but will persist in his wicked course, we hope that he will continue trying to cast out devils, that we may have the clearer proof that the kingdom of Satan is divided against itself, and consequently cannot stand; for a kingdom divided against itself, speedily hath an end.

If we were disposed to take this gentleman upon his own ground, and justly heap upon him that which he so readily and unjustly heaps upon others, we might go farther—we might say that he has wickedly and maliciously lied about, villified and traduced the characters of innocent men. We might invite the gentleman to a public investigation of these matters, yea, and we do challenge him to an investigation upon any or all principles wherein he feels opposed to us, in public or in private. We might farther say that we could introduce him to *Mormonism Unveiled*, also to the right honorable Dr. Philastus Hurlburt, who is the

* In this and several of the following paragraphs the Prophet alludes to Alexander Campbell, founder of the sect of the "Disciples;" and also to an article which appeared in the *Millennial Harbinger*, Vol. 2 (1831), pages 86-96. The reference to Elymas, to which the Prophet so strongly replies, stands thus in Campbell's aritcle—which was afterwards circulated as a pamphlet: "I have never felt so fully authorized to address mortal man in the style in which Paul addressed Elymas the sorcerer as I feel towards this atheist Smith." (*Millennial Harbinger*, Vol. 2, p. 96). That is, "O full of all subtlety and all mischief, thou child of the devil, thou enemy of all righteousness, wilt thou not cease to pervert the right ways of the Lord" (Acts xiii: 10).

The paragraph dealing with the laying on of hands, and the passages of scripture quoted in support of that doctrine, will also be the better understood when it is known that while Mr. Campbell and his associates taught faith in God, repentance and baptism for the remission of sins, they rejected wholly the doctrine of the laying on of hands for the gift of the Holy Ghost, and the enjoyment of the spiritual blessings which accompany the possession of that Spirit.

legitimate author of the same. who is not so much a doctor of physics as of falsehood, or doctor by name.

We could also give him an introduction to the Reverend Mr. Howe, the illegitimate author of *Mormonism Unveiled,* in order to give currency to the publication, as Mr. Hurlburt about this time was bound over to court for threatening life. He is also an associate of the celebrated Mr. Clapp, who has of late immortalized his name, by swearing that he would not believe a Mormon under oath; and by his polite attention to Hurlburt's wife, which cost him (as we are informed) a round sum. Also his son Matthew testified, that the Book of Mormon had been proved false an hundred times, by Howe's book; and also that he would not believe a Mormon under oath. And also we could mention the Rev. Mr. Bentley, who, we believe, has been actively engaged in injuring the character of his brother-in-law, viz., Elder Sidney Rigdon.

Now the above statements are according to our best information, and we believe them to be true, and this is as fair a sample of the doctrine of Campbellism as we ask, taking the statements of these gentlemen, and judging them by their fruits; and we might add many more to the black catalogue; even the ringleaders not of the Nazarenes, (for how can any good thing come out of Nazareth) but of the far-famed Mentor mob, all sons and legitimate heirs of the same spirit of Alexander Campbell, and *Mormonism Unveiled*, according to the representation of the cut spoken of above.

The above clouds of darkness have long been beating like mountain waves upon the immovable rock of the Church of the Latter-day Saints; and notwithstanding all this, the mustard seed is still towering its lofty branches, higher and higher, and extending itself wider and wider; and the chariot wheels of the Kingdom are still rolling on, impelled by the mighty arm of Jehovah; and in spite of all opposition, will still roll on, until His words are all fulfilled.

Our readers will excuse us for deviating from the subject, when they take into consideration the abuses that have been heaped upon us heretofore, which we have tamely submitted to, until forbearance is no longer required at our hands. Having frequently turned both the right and left cheek, we believe it our duty now to stand up in our own defense. With these remarks we shall proceed with the subject of the gathering.

"And another parable spake He unto them. The Kingdom of heaven is like unto leaven which a woman took and hid in three measures of meal till the whole was leavened." It may be understood that the Church of the Latter-day Saints has taken its rise from a little leaven that was put into three witnesses. Behold, how much this is like the parable! It is fast leavening the lump, and will soon leaven the whole. But let us pass on.

"All these things spake Jesus unto the multitude in parables; and without a parable spake He not unto them: that it might be fulfilled which was spoken by the prophet, saying, I will open my mouth in parables; I will utter things which have been kept secret from the foundation of the world. Then Jesus sent the multitude away, and went into the house: and His disciples came unto Him, saying, Declare unto us the parable of the tares of the field. He answered and said unto them, He that soweth the good seed is the Son of Man; the field is the world; the good seed are the children of the Kingdom; but the tares are the children of the wicked one." Now let our readers mark the expression—"the field is the world, the tares are the children of the wicked one, the enemy that sowed them is the devil, the harvest is the end of the world, [let them carefully mark this expression—*the end of the world*,] and the reapers are the angels."

Now men cannot have any possible grounds to say that this is figurative, or that it does not mean what it says; for he is now explaining what He has previously spoken in parables; and according to this language, the end of the world is the destruction of the wicked, the harvest and the end of the world have an allusion directly to the human family in the last days, instead of the earth, as many have imagined; and that which shall precede the coming of the Son of Man, and the restitution of all things spoken of by the mouth of all the holy prophets since the world began; and the angels are to have something to do in this great work, for they are the reapers. As, therefore, the tares are gathered and burned in the fire, so shall it be in the end of the world; that is, as the servants of God go forth warning the nations, both priests and people, and as they harden their hearts and reject the light of truth, these first being delivered over to the buffetings of Satan, and the law and the testimony being closed up, as it was in the case of the Jews, they are left in darkness, and delivered over unto the day of burning; thus being bound up by their creeds, and their bands being made strong by their priests, are prepared for the fulfillment of the saying of the Savior—"The Son of Man shall send forth His angels, and gather out of His Kingdom all things that offend, and them which do iniquity, and shall cast them into a furnace of fire, there shall be wailing and gnashing of teeth." We understand that the work of gathering together of the wheat into barns, or garners, is to take place while the tares are being bound over, and preparing for the day of burning; that after the day of burnings, the righteous shall shine forth like the sun, in the Kingdom of their Father. Who hath ears to hear, let him hear.

But to illustrate more clearly this gathering: We have another parable—"Again, the Kingdom of heaven is like a treasure hid in a field, the which, when a man hath found, he hideth, and for joy thereof, goeth and selleth all that he hath, and buyeth that field!" The Saints work after this pattern. See the Church of the Latter-day Saints, selling all that they have, and gathering themselves together unto a place that they may purchase for an inheritance, that they may be together and bear each other's afflictions in the day of calamity.

"Again, the Kingdom of heaven is like unto a merchantman seeking goodly pearls, who, when he had found one pearl of great price, went and sold all that he had, and bought it." The Saints again work after this example. See men traveling to find places for Zion and her stakes or remnants, who, when they find the place for Zion, or the pearl of great price, straightway sell that they have, and buy it.

"Again, the Kingdom of heaven is like unto a net that was cast into the sea, and gathered of every kind, which when it was full they drew to shore, and sat down, and gathered the good into vessels, but cast the bad away." For the work of this pattern, behold the seed of Joseph, spreading forth the Gospel net upon the face of the earth, gathering of every kind, that the good may be saved in vessels prepared for that purpose, and the angels will take care of the bad. So shall it be at the end of the world—the angels shall come forth and sever the wicked from among the just, and cast them into the furnace of fire, and there shall be wailing and gnashing of teeth.

"Jesus saith unto them, Have you understood all these things? They say unto Him, Yea, Lord." And we say, yea, Lord; and well might they say, yea, Lord; for these things are so plain and so glorious that every Saint in the last days must respond with a hearty Amen to them.

"Then said He unto them, therefore every scribe which is instructed in the kingdom of heaven, is like unto a man that is an householder, which bringeth forth out of his treasure things that are new and old."

For the works of this example, see the Book of Mormon coming forth out of the treasure of the heart. Also the covenants given to the Latter-day Saints, also the translation of the Bible—thus bringing forth out of the heart things new and old, thus answering to three measures of meal undergoing the purifying touch by a revelation of Jesus Christ, and the ministering of angels, who have already commenced this work in the last days, which will answer to the leaven which leavened the whole lump. Amen.

So I close, but shall continue the subject in another number.*

In the bonds of the New and Everlasting Covenant,

JOSEPH SMITH, JUN.

* Notwithstanding this promise of the Prophet, the subject was not again renewed by him. About this time he was so overwhelmed with work and a multitude of other subjects that he did not find time to complete the work he had outlined in these papers.

CHAPTER XX.

SUNDRY AFFAIRS AT KIRTLAND—THE PLEDGE TO REDEEM ZION.

I WENT to New Portage on the 2nd of September, in company with Oliver Cowdery and Sidney Rigdon, to attend a conference; and returned on the 8th. I was engaged in various spiritual and temporal matters for several days.

Conference at New Portage.

September 14.—In a meeting of a High Council and the Presidency at Kirtland, it was decided that, as the laborer is worthy of his hire, whenever President Jossph Smith, Sen., is called upon to pronounce Patriarchal blessings upon the Church, he be paid for his services at the rate of ten dollars per week and his expenses. It was further decided that President Frederick G. Williams be appointed and hereafter serve as scribe, to attend blessing meetings, and that he receive for his services, at the same ratio, having his expenses borne also. It was further decided that President Oliver Cowdery be appointed, and that he act hereafter as Recorder for the Church. It was further decided that Sister Emma Smith proceed to make a selection of Sacred Hymns, according to the revelation;* and that President W. W. Phelps be appointed to revise and arrange them for printing.

Provision Made for Remunerating the Patriarch.

Oliver Cowdery Appointed Church Recorder.

September 16.—The Presidency of the Church assembled and appointed David Whitmer and Samuel H. Smith a committee and general agents to act in the name of, and for, the "Literary Firm."

Agents for the "Literary Firm" of the Church Appointed.

* See Vol. I, p. 104. Doctrine and Covenants, sec. xxv

MINUTES OF A HIGH COUNCIL HELD IN KIRTLAND, SEPTEMBER 16th, 1835.

The Trial of Elder Henry Green—Sidney Rigdon, Oliver Cowdery and Frederick G. Williams presiding.

A complaint was preferred by President Joseph Smith, Jun., against Brother Henry Green, for accusing President Joseph Smith, Jun., "of rebuking Brother Aldridge wrongfully, and under the influence of an evil spirit."

Brother Green being absent, President Rigdon arose and said, that it was the decision of the Presidency, that the Council proceed to examine the charge preferred, because Brother Green had been regularly summoned by himself.

The Council appointed one to speak on each side; after which the following testimony was heard:

Elder Sylvester Smith testified that Brother Green, on Monday morning last, said that Brother Aldridge was justified in what he said, and that Presidents Joseph and Hyrum Smith were wrong in abusing the old man; and after Elder Smith explained the matter to him, said, that if any man should do so by him, he should call him a scoundrel; and that he should say that any man who would talk as Joseph did, must have the devil in him.

Elder Lorin Babbitt said he was present when the above conversation took place, and heard a considerable part of it, and fully concurred in the statement of Elder Smith; and he heard Brother Green say, previous to the above talk, that although they accused Brother Aldridge of having an evil spirit, yet, if the truth were known, the devil was in them, (namely, Presidents Joseph and Hyrum); for if any man should ask my opinion, and then abuse me in that way, I should call him a scoundrel or a knave.

President Cowdery stated to the Council, that Brother Aldridge was not called upon to give his opinion concerning the book, but said what he did without being called upon to speak; for the book was only handed to him and others to look at, that they might see the quality and goodness.

President Joseph Smith arose and stated that he knew that Brother Aldridge was under the influence of an evil spirit, and had been for a long time.

Councilor Orson Johnson also said that he knew that this was so, by what he had seen and learned, and that he had heard from credible authority, that the old gentleman had been in the habit, for a long time, of neglecting prayer and family worship.

Councilor Samuel H. Smith said, that President Joseph Smith was in the line of his duty when he reproved Brother Aldridge for his evil; and, consequently, Brother Green must have been wrong in opposing him, and saying he [Joseph] acted like a scoundrel, and that the devil was in him.

Councilor Levi Jackman said that Brother Green could not be justified in opposing the servant of the Lord, while in the actual discharge of his duty, and that it was evident that Satan hath sought to make divisions in the Church, and had taken advantage of the occasion of presenting the book, to do this.

The book referred to, was purchased for recording "The Patriarchal Blessings."

President Frederick G. Williams said, that the wickedness of Brother Green in condemning President Smith is evident from the testimony; and that Brother Aldridge also did act foolishly, and by the influence of a wrong spirit, in questioning the integrity of the head of the Church, in the purchase of the book, and that President Smith was and is justifiable in doing as he has done in the matter, and should not be censured, as he has been by Brother Green.

President Oliver Cowdery then arose, and showed, by a few plain remarks who Satan had sought, from the beginning, to destroy the Book of Mormon; and in order to do this, had been actually levelling his shafts against the servants of God, who were called to bring it forth and bear testimony of it to the world; and now had sought occasion against the servants of God, in tempting brethren to say they had equivocated in the price of the record book, which was presented last Sabbath; and that Brother Aldridge, and perhaps others, fell under this evil influence, and Brother Green justifies them in this thing, and condemns President Smith, and is not, and ought not to be justified in so doing.

President Cowdery went on to show that the book was purchased as cheap as it could be, and was actually worth what was given for it, namely, twelve dollars.

Elder Cahoon requested leave to interrupt President Cowdery a moment, to inform the Council that, a moment before, Brother Green passed the house, and when the speaker told him the Council was considering his case, and requested him to come in, he said he should go about his own business, so went on his way regardless of the Council.

President Cowdery resumed, showing that the design of Brother Aldridge, or at least of the spirit that was in him, was to destry the character of the heads of the Church, by charging that we intended to speculate out of the brethren, and extort from them more than the cost of the book; and now, instead of regarding our feelings, he disregards us altogether, and shows that he has no faith in the High Council.

Soon afterwards Brother Green came in, and said that he had been detained longer than he intended, having been to Chagrin on business, and had to deliver the horse and harness to the owner before he could attend the Council.

President Rigdon then arose and decided that Brother Green should not have been hindered from being here, by any other business; and if so, he should have notified the Council, and requested an adjournment.

President Cowdery then observed, that he thought the case sufficiently brought before the Council, and would say no more. And President Rigdon proceeded to give his decision—that Brother Green should have gone, if he were grieved with President Smith, and told him of his difficulty, and should not have said anything about it to his neighbor. And again, that Mr. Aldridge, as has been shown, has been guilty of neglecting his prayers before God, and therefore has not had the Spirit of God to preserve him from the temptations of Satan, and has fallen into evil, and actually did do wrong in raising objections to the price of the book presented last Sabbath, and was under the influence of an evil spirit.

Brother Green fellowships the evil spirit in Brother Aldridge, and says he is justified in what he has done, and therefore it is evident that an evil spirit is reigning in the breast of Brother Green. And it is also as evident, that President Joseph Smith, Jun., was justified in rebuking that evil spirit, and it was not only justifiable in President Smith to rebuke that evil spirit, but it was also his duty as President and First High Priest in the Church of Christ, appointed of God to lead the same in all righteousness.

The decision, then, of the Presidency of the High Council is, in short, that Brother Green be and is now, excluded from this Church, and shall be a member no more, until he comes in by the ordinance of baptism, as appointed by the Gospel, to be done in the Church.

This was agreed to by all the Councilors except Joseph Coe, who queried whether Mr. Green should not have the privilege of confessing his faults, and still be retained in the Church. He therefore thought that it was the privilege of Brother Green to have a re-organization of the Council, and a rehearing. This was about to be granted and the council to be adjourned till tomorrow, but Councilor Coe requested some explanation from the President, and was instructed as follows:—

"When a serious offense is committed, and indignity offered to the High Council, then it is the privilege of the Presidency of the High Council to stamp it with indignation under foot, and cut off the offender as in the case just decided."

Councilor Coe then withdrew his objection to the decision of the

Presidency, which was acknowledged by the whole house, and council adjourned.

SYLVESTER SMITH, Clerk.

Minutes of a High Council held in Kirtland, September 19, 1835. The trial of Elder Jared Carter. President Joseph Smith, Jun., Oliver Cowdery, David Whitmer, Frederick G. Williams, Sidney Rigdon, and W. W. Phelps, present.

COUNCILORS.

John Smith,	Joseph Smith, Sen.,
Orson Johnson,	Joseph Coe,
Newel Knight,	Hyrum Smith,
John Whitmer,	Levi Jackman,
Samuel H. Smith,	Noah Packard,
John Johnson,	Roger Orton,

The object of the Council was stated by President Joseph Smith, Jun., as follows: "Some weeks since Elder Jared Carter preached on the Sabbath in the Church, and some of the brethren found fault with his teachings; and this Council is called upon to decide this matter, and to see who was in fault."

Six were appointed to speak.

Elder Jared Carter proceeded to speak largely, and explain his designs in teaching as he did, saying he believed God directed him by His Spirit, and afterwards being rebuked by Presidents Cowdery, Rigdon and Phelps, he called upon the Lord, and received again a witness of the Spirit that he was right, and the Presidents were wrong. Elder Carter taught in his concluding remarks, that God had shown him by laying His hand upon him in judgment, and delivering him therefrom, that he was thus rebuked by heaven for his iniquity, and that he was made an example to the whole Church, and God would curse them if they did not hold up the committee,* for he was made an example in this thing.

President Rigdon arose and said that he attended the meeting in which Elder Carter spoke, and was certain, and is certain, that he did not have the spirit of wisdom to direct; and after he had sat down, and Elder Samuel H. Smith had occupied some half an hour, filled with the Spirit, he arose again and said, that if any man spoke against the committee, God would curse him, and set the committee away above the common brethren, and said that God would take care of the committee, and the brethren had nothing to do with them, for their

* This was the temple building committee.

station was appointed them of God, and not of man; therefore God will curse any man or woman in the Church who shall speak evil of the committee. He told Elder Carter at the time, in private, that he did wrong; and in company with other of the Presidents, advised him after he should fill a certain mission to the east, that he should make a confession to the Church, in order to satisfy many of the brethren who were aggrieved with him.

President Phelps then arose, and said President Rigdon had truly related the matter, as far as he had gone; but one thing more—Elder Carter commanded the brethren to pray for the committee, and demanded it in the name of the Lord, with an authoritative voice and gesticulation, which are not according to the meekness of the spirit of Jesus.

President Oliver Cowdery arose and said: I do not intend to occupy much time in speaking for those who have spoken have expressed pretty much my mind and feelings on the subject; that in the advice which he and the other two Presidents had given Elder Carter, in the talk they had with him, they did have the spirit of meekness, and only desired to do him good, and had no personal feelings against him, and did not express any, but to the contrary.

President John Whitmer concurred in the statements of the above brethren, and said that he did not believe that God had made an example of Elder Carter, for he was not before the Church as such; and God had not so revealed it to the Saints; and again, it is vain that Elder Carter should command the Saints to pray for the committee, for in so doing, if they did not fellowship him, they must pray for his removal, and so all his designs would be frustrated.

Several others were called upon, and all testified that these things which have been expressed above were true and as they understood them; and one thing further, Elder Carter did say that even the faults of the committee might be charged back upon the brethren if they neglected to pray for them.

After hearing the testimony, the six Councilors spoke, and the sum of their conviction upon the matter was as follows:

Councilor John Smith said he thought that Elder Carter did not express the feelings of his heart, so as to be understood, and perhaps his heart was not so hard as his words.

Father Joseph Smith said that Elder Carter was exalted, and did not receive the admonitions of the Presidents, and in consequence lost the true spirit, and so has erred since the time of his discourse, and needs admonishing.

Councilor Orson Johnson agreed with the above.

Councilor Joseph Coe said that Elder Carter had a small degree of the Spirit in his discourse, and a greater degree in his remarks afterwards, but was awkward in expressing his views, not having much of the Spirit, and that the feelings of his heart were not as expressed by his words,

An inquiry was made of the Court whether this Councilor [Joseph Coe] was correct in appealing to the feelings of men's hearts, and not to the words and actions, as they appeared.

The Court decided that the Council must be confined to facts, words, and actions; and not go into feelings and designs which were not expressed.

The other Councilors concurred in the above.

Councilor Hyrum Smith said that Elder Carter had been blessed of God, and by the prayer of faith the sick had been healed under his administration; yet he does not always have the gift of God and wisdom to direct; so in the case before the Council. Pride had engendered in Elder Carter's heart a desire to excel, and the spirit of meekness was withdrawn, and he was left to err, as has been shown by the testimony, because he is not yet perfect. But he erred in understanding, and his words were wrong; yet the spirit of his heart, or the integrity of the same, might be good in the main.

Elder Carter then arose and said that he was willing to acknowledge his faults, and that he lacked wisdom. He went on to explain how he had erred, and why—being seized with the cholera while at the east, he called upon God for deliverance, and finally received the Spirit of God which healed him, and he then thought it was the same spirit which he had when preaching in Kirtland.

When he was through, President Oliver Cowdery arose, and said that Presidents Rigdon and Phelps had requested him to speak, and they would say nothing as it was getting late, and the case was already plain before the Court. He showed that a man might be highly excited and yet neither have the Spirit of God nor the spirit of Satan; but it came by his own spirit and judgment; therefore some things may be of God, others of men, and others from the adversary; and Elder Carter had in his sermon some of the Spirit of God, but in his last remarks he had it not, but his own spirit of justification and pride, commanding in the name of Jesus, and not by the spirit of Jesus or of meekness, and was very wrong in this thing, also in exalting the committee above the brethren, as if they might not be touched by the brethren; and again, when Elder Carter was healed, it came in answer to his earnest prayer before God; but his impressions about being made an example to the Church were not an answer to prayer, and might be wrong.

President Frederick G. Williams gave his decision, that Brother Carter did err with his lips in speaking, and also erred in understanding the Presidents who labored with him for it, and misinterpreted their admonitions, which led him into what followed, and finally has brought him before this Council.

President David Whitmer said, that according to the testimony it is plain that Elder Carter has lacked in humility, and also in confidence in his brethren, and erred as expressed by President Williams.

President Joseph Smith, Jun., arose, and said, that the decision of his mind was, that Brother Jared Carter erred in judgment in not understanding what the brethren desired of him when they labored with him; and he erred in spirit when he taught in the Church the things testified of here; and that the hand of the destroyer was laid upon him because he had a rebellious spirit from the beginning; and the word of the Lord has been spoken by my mouth, that it should come upon him, and this Council should see it, and now that he has been seized by the destroyer comes in fulfillment of His [the Lord's] word; and God requires him to bear testimony of it before the Church, and warn them to be careful, and not to do as he had done. But instead of doing this, he said he would prove the Book of Mormon, and one thing or another, not being sufficiently humble to deliver just the message that was required, and so he stumbled and could not get the Spirit, and the brethren were not edified, and he did not do the thing that God required, but erred in choosing words to communicate his thoughts; such as commanding the prayers of the Church instead of soliciting them, and also of making himself an example for the Church, when it was only the things that he suffered which were to be as a check upon transgression.

His rebelling against the advice and counsel of the Presidents was the cause of his falling into the hands of the destroyer again, as he had done before when he rebelled against the counsel that had been given him by the authorities of the Church; and that in all this, Elder Carter has not designed to do wickedly, but he erred in judgment, and deserves reproof, and the decision is—that he shall acknowledge his errors on the morrow, before the congregation, and say, Brethren, I am fully convinced that I have erred in spirit, in my remarks before you, when I spoke here a few Sabbaths since; and now I ask your forgiveness. And if he do this in full faith, and is truly humble before God, God will bless him abundantly as He hath been wont to do.

Elder Carter arose, and justified the decision of the Court, and promised to comply.

SYLVESTER SMITH, Clerk.

I labored in obtaining blessings, which were written by Oliver Cowdery. We were thronged with company, so that our labor in this thing was hindered; but we obtained many precious things, and our souls were blessed. O Lord, may Thy Holy Spirit be with Thy servants forever. Amen.

The Prophet Seeks for Blessings.

September 23.—I was at home writing blessings for my most beloved brethren, but was hindered by a multitude of visitors. The Lord has blessed our souls this day, and may God grant to continue His mercies unto my house this night, for Christ's sake. This day my soul has desired the salvation of Brother Ezra Thayer. Also Brother Noah Packard came to my house and loaned the committee one thousand dollars to assist building the house of the Lord. Oh! may God bless him a hundred fold, even of the things of the earth, for this righteous act. My heart is full of desire today, to be blessed of the God of Abraham with prosperity, until I shall be able to pay all my debts, for it is the delight of my soul to be honest. O Lord, that thou knowest right well. Help me, and I will give to the poor.

Delight of the Prophet in Being Honest.

Brothers William, John and Joseph Tippits started for Missouri, the place designated for Zion, or the Saints' gathering place. They came to bid us farewell. The brethren came in to pray with them, and Brother David Whitmer acted as spokesman. He prayed in the spirit, and a glorious time succeeded his prayer; joy filled our hearts and we blessed them and bid them God speed, and promised them a safe journey, and took them by the hand and bid them farewell for a season. May God grant them long life and good days. These blessings I ask upon them for Christ's sake. Amen.

Rejoicing with Brethren Bound for Zion.

The High Council met at my house on the 24th to take into consideration the redemption of Zion. And it was the voice of the Spirit of the Lord that we petition the

Governor, that is, those who have been driven out, shall petition to be set back on their own lands next spring, and that we go next season, to live or die on our own lands, which we have purchased in Jackson County, Missouri. We truly had a good time, and covenanted to struggle for this thing, until death shall dissolve the union; and if one falls, that the remainder be not discouraged, but pursue this object until it be accomplished; which may God grant unto us in the name of Jesus Christ our Lord. Also, this day drew up a subscription for enrolling the names of those who are willing to go up to Missouri next spring and settle; and I ask God in the name of Jesus that we may obtain eight hundred or one thousand emigrants.

The Covenant to Work for the Redemption of Zion.

I spent the 25th of September at home.

CHAPTER XXI.

INCIDENTS FROM THE PROPHET'S EXPERIENCE IN KIRTLAND AND VICINITY.

September 26.—This morning the Twelve returned from their mission to the East, and on the same day the Council of the Presidency of the Church, consisting of Joseph Smith, Jun., Sidney Rigdon, David Whitmer, W. W. Phelps, John Whitmer, Hyrum Smith and Oliver Cowdery, met to consider the case of the Twelve who had previously been reproved in consequence of certain letters and reports coming to the ears of the Council. First, the items contained in Warren A. Cowdery's letter, in connection with certain other reports, derogatory to the character and teaching of the Twelve, were considered; and from the testimony of several witnesses (the Twelve) it was proved before the Council that said complaints originated in the minds of persons who were darkened in consequence of covetousness, or some other cause, rather than the spirit of truth. Second, one item contained in Elder Wm. E. M'Lellin's letter to his wife, expressing dissatisfaction with President Rigdon's school. Elder Orson Hyde was also designated with him [M'Lellin] or blamed in the matter, in which they were found to be in the fault, which they frankly confessed, and were forgiven and all things were satisfactorily settled.

Return of the Twelve.

Sunday 27.—I attended meeting. Elders Thomas B. Marsh, David W. Patten, Brigham Young and Heber C. Kimball preached and broke bread. The Lord poured out His Spirit and my soul was edified.

Minutes of the High Council at Kirtland. Trial of Gladden Bishop,

The High Council met for the trial of Gladden Bishop, on a charge preferred by the Twelve, "for advancing heretical doctrines, which were derogatory to the character of the Church."

Elder William Smith testified that when Elder Bishop was conversing with a brother concerning the two witnesses mentioned by the Prophets [Rev. xi] he said that he [Bishop] might be one of them, and that he [the brother] might be one himself; that he [Bishop] intended to prophesy the night that an advertisement was put up by an enemy, saying that the Mormon Prophet and others were to be sold by auction in public, that he would not be surprised if the man who put up the advertisement should die at the time of sale.

Elder Brigham Young corroborated the foregoing, and said that Bishop was very erroneous in his tenets of faith.

Elder John Boynton concurred.

Elder Thomas B. Marsh said that Bishop frequently told of women falling in love with him, and observed frequently when passing people that they felt his spirit; also that he was so indolent his presence was oppressive.

Elder L. Johnson testified that on a former trial before the Twelve for error in doctrine, such as, that he might be one of the two witnesses, and that he ought not to travel and preach on account of the women so often falling in love with him, he was not humble when reproved, but justified himself, and preferred a charge against the Council for harsh treatment.

Elder William Smith said, that Bishop, after taking a stand against the Council, finally said it was all right, they had dealt with him in righteousness.

Elders Marsh and Young corroborated the above, that he yielded after being overcome, also that he was capable of magnifying his office if he would.

Elder Heber C. Kimball concurred in the above, also that Bishop said, after he saw his case was hopeless, that the Council had turned him wrong side out.

Elder John P. Greene concurred in full, and, in addition to the above, said that Bishop was so indolent that he would not help himself to a drink of water.

After the pleas of the Councilors and the case was submitted for decision, Brother Bishop arose and made a humble confession for his transgression, and asked forgiveness of the High Council and all the Church, saying that he intended to learn wisdom from the revelations that God had given, and submitted himself to the decision of the Court, being perfectly satisfied with the whole course of the trial.

After much instruction, the President decided that the counsel of the Twelve in this case was given in righteousness, also that Brother Bishop's confession be published in the *Messenger and Advocate*, and he be received in full fellowship, and receive his ordination and license as before; which the Council concurred in, and Brother Bishop was ordained by the Court an Elder.

WARREN PARRISH, Clerk.

The Authority to which the Twelve are Amenable.

An attempt was made in the foregoing Council to criminate the Twelve before the High Council for cutting off Gladden Bishop at their Bradford conference, but their attempt totally failed. I decided that the High Council had nothing to do with the Twelve, or the decisions of the Twelve. But if the Twelve erred they were accountable only to the General Council of the authorities of the whole Church, according to the revelations.

Trial of Lorenzo L. Lewis.

In the afternoon a charge of adultery was preferred against Lorenzo L. Lewis, on general report circulating among the brethren, to which he pleaded not guilty, and the charge was changed to "an illicit intercourse with a female." Lewis confessed that he had disgraced the girl, himself, and the Church, but [was] not guilty of the charge. After hearing the testimony of witnesses, Elders Marsh, M'Lellin, Patten and William Smith, and the pleadings, Elder Lewis confessed that he had done wickedly and had made all the reparation he could, in his confession in the early part of this trial and required his name to be taken off the Church records, or dispose of him according to the mind of the Spirit, and submitted to the decision of the Council. The Council decided that Brother Lorenzo L. Lewis be cut off from the Church, being satisfied that the charge preferred is substantiated by evidence, and the Spirit of the Lord; but if he repent, and humble himself to the satisfaction of the Church, he should be received into it again and receive his license. The Council adjourned till morning.

The High Council met on the 29th, and heard a charge against Elder Allen Avery, on an appeal case from an Elders' Court in Zion, which took away his license for rebelling against their decision. Brother Avery frankly and readily complied with the requisition of the Council, and the President decided that he be restored to fellowship, and receive his license.

Trial of Elder Allen Avery.

In these cases I acted on the part of the defense for the accused, to plead for mercy. The Lord blessed my soul, and the Council was greatly blessed also, and much good will result from our labors.

The Prophet on the Part of the Accused.

I was at home on the 30th, and was visited by many who came to inquire after the work of the Lord.

October 1.—This afternoon I labored on the Egyptian alphabet, in company with Brothers Oliver Cowdery and W. W. Phelps, and during the research, the principles of astronomy as understood by Father Abraham and the ancients unfolded to our understanding, the particulars of which will appear hereafter.

The Prophet Learns the Principles of Astronomy as Understood by Abraham.

On the 2nd of October I wrote the following letter for publication in the *Messenger and Advocate*, (continued from the 1st of September.)*

October 3.—I attended the High Council to investigate charges preferred by Reynolds Cahoon against Elder John Gould "for making expressions calculated to injure the cause we have espoused, and manifesting a strong dissatisfaction with the teachings of the Presidency." Also against Dean Gould for speaking unadvisedly against Elder Rigdon and other Elders.

Charges Against the Goulds.

In the case of John Gould, the accuser and defendant agreed the matter should be talked over, by which all difference of feeling was allayed. Gould confessed and was forgiven.

* For this communication see Article II, Chapter XIX. (Note.)

Dean Gould acknowledged that he spoke unadvisedly against President Rigdon, and was forgiven.

In the afternoon I waited on most of the Twelve, at my house, and exhibited to them the ancient records, and gave explanations. This day passed off with the blessing of the Lord.

Sunday, 4.—I started early in the morning, with Brother John Corrill, to hold a meeting in Perry. When about a mile from home we discovered two deer playing in the field, which diverted our minds by giving an impetus to our thoughts upon the subject of the creation of God. We conversed on many topics. The day passed off very agreeably, and the Lord blessed our souls. When we arrived at Perry, we were disappointed of a meeting, through mis-arrangement, but conversed freely with Brother Corrill's relatives, which allayed much prejudice. May the Lord have mercy on their souls.

The Prophet's Journey with John Corrill.

Monday, 5.—I returned home, being much fatigued from riding in the rain. Spent the remainder of the day in reading and meditation, and in the evening attended a Council of the Twelve Apostles; had a glorious time, and gave them much instruction concerning their duties for time to come; told them that it was the will of God they should take their families to Missouri next season; also this fall to attend the solemn assembly of the first Elders, for the organization of the School of the Prophets; and attend to the ordinance of the washing of feet; and to prepare their hearts in all humility for an endowment with power from on high; to which they all agreed with one accord, and seemed to be greatly rejoiced. May God spare the lives of the Twelve to a good old age, for Christ the Redeemer's sake. Amen.

The Prophet's Meeting With the Twelve.

Tuesday, 6.—At home. Elder Stevens came to my house and loaned Frederick G. Williams and Co. six hundred dollars, which greatly relieved us of our present difficulties. May God bless and preserve his soul forever.

A Timely Loan.

In the afternoon called to visit my father, who was very sick with a fever: somewhat better towards evening. Spent the rest of the day in reading and meditation.

Illness of Joseph Smith, Sen.

Wednesday, 7.—Went to visit my father, found him very low, administered some mild herbs, agreeably to the commandment. May God grant to restore him immediately to health for Christ the Redeemer's sake. Amen.

Bishop Whitney and Brother Hyrum Smith started by stage for Buffalo, New York, to purchase goods to replenish the committee's store. May God grant, in the name of Jesus, that their lives may be spared, and they have a safe journey, and no accident or sickness of the least kind befall them, that they may return in health and in safety to the bosom of their families.

The Prophet's Blessing on Bishop Whitney.

Blessed of the Lord is Brother Whitney, even the Bishop of the Church of Latter-day Saints, for the Bishopric shall never be taken away from him while he liveth. And the time cometh that he shall overcome all the narrow-mindedness of his heart, and all his covetous desires that so easily beset him; and he shall deal with a liberal hand to the poor and the needy, the sick and afflicted, the widow and the fatherless. And marvelously and miraculously shall the Lord his God provide for him, even that he shall be blessed with a fullness of the good things of this earth, and his seed after him from generation to generation. And it shall come to pass, that according to the measure that he meteth out with a liberal hand to the poor, so shall it be measured to him again by the hand of his God, even an hundred fold. Angels shall guard his house, and shall guard the lives of his posterity, and they shall become very great and very numerous on the earth. Whomsoever he blesseth, they shall be blessed; and whomsoever he curseth, they shall be cursed; and when his enemies seek him unto his hurt and destruction, let him rise up and curse, and the hand of God shall be upon his enemies in judgment, they shall be utterly confounded and brought to desolation. Therefore he shall be preserved unto the utmost, and his life shall be precious in the sight of the Lord, he shall rise up and shake himself, as a lion riseth out of his lair and roareth until he shaketh the hills; and as a lion goeth forth among the lesser beasts, so shall the going forth of him be whom the Lord hath anointed to exalt the poor, and to humble the rich, therefore his name shall be on high, and his rest among the sanctified. This afternoon I re-commenced translating the ancient records.

Translation of the Writings of Abraham Begun.

Thursday, *8.*—At home. I attended on my father with great anxiety.

Friday, *9.*—At home. Waited on my father.

Saturday, *10.*—At home, and visited the house of my father, found him failing very fast.

Sunday, *11.*—Waited on my father again, who was very sick. In secret prayer in the morning, the Lord said, "My servant, thy father shall live." I waited on him all this day with my heart raised to God in the name of Jesus Christ, that He would restore him to health, that I might be blessed with his company and advice, esteeming it one of the greatest earthly blessings to be blessed with the society of parents, whose mature years and experience render them capable of administering the most wholesome advice. At evening Brother David Whitmer came in. We called on the Lord in mighty prayer in the name of Jesus Christ, and laid our hands on him, and rebuked the disease. And God heard and answered our prayers—to the great joy and satisfaction of our souls. Our aged father arose and dressed himself, shouted, and praised the Lord. Called Brother William Smith, who had retired to rest, that he might praise the Lord with us, by joining in songs of praise to the Most High.

The Prophet's Care of His Father.

Monday, 12.—Rode to Willoughby, in company with my wife, to purchase some goods at William Lyon's store. On our return we found a Mr. Bradley lying across the road. He had been thrown from his wagon, and was much injured by the fall.

Tuesday, 13—Visited my father, who was very much recovered from his sickness, indeed, which caused us to marvel at the might, power, and condescension of our Heavenly Father, in answering our prayers in his behalf.

Wednesday, 14.—At home.

Thursday, 15.—Labored in father's orchard, gathering apples.

Friday, 16.—Was called into the printing office, to settle some difficulties in that department. In the evening I baptized Ebenezer Robinson.* The Lord poured out His Spirit upon us and we had a good time.

Baptism of Ebenezer Robinson.

Saturday, 17.—Called my family together and arranged my domestic concerns, and dismissed my boarders.

Sunday, 18.—Attended meeting in the chapel, confirmed several that had been baptized, and blessed several children with the blessings of the New and Everlasting Covenant. Elder Parley P. Pratt preached in the forenoon, and Elder John F. Boynton in the afternoon. We had an interesting time.

The Book of Abraham.

Monday, 19.—At home. Exhibited the records of antiquity to a number who called to see them.

* Ebenezer Robinson, afterwards somewhat prominent in the Church in Missouri and Illinois as editor. printer and publisher, was born in the town of Floyd, Oneida County, New York, May 25, 1816; and was the son of Nathan and Mary Robinson. He was already a printer of considerable experience when he came to Kirtland in May, 1835, and began work in the Church printing establishment, then running under the firm name of F. G. Williams & Co., though not a member of the Church. For six months he boarded in the families of Oliver Cowdery, F. G. Williams and the Prophet Joseph. "We found them all very pious, good Christian people," he remarks, "(who) asked a blessing at the table and all attended to family worship morning and evening." (The "Return," Vol. I, p. 58). Mr. Robinson did not become immediately converted to the Gospel, but conviction gradually dawned upon his mind, and he finally declared his faith and was baptized by the Prophet as stated in the text.

Tuesday, 20.—At home. Preached in the evening in the school house.

Wednesday, 21.—At home.

Thursday, 22.—At home, attending to my domestic concerns.

Prayer for Special Blessings.

Friday 23.—At home. At four o'clock, afternoon, Oliver Cowdery, David Whitmer, Hyrum Smith, John Whitmer, Sidney Rigdon, Samuel H. Smith, Frederick G. Williams and W. W. Phelps assembled, and we united in prayer, with one voice, before the Lord, for the following blessings: That the Lord would give us means sufficient to deliver us from all our afflictions and difficulties wherein we are placed by reason of our debts; that He would open the way and deliver Zion in the appointed time, and that without the shedding of blood; that He would hold our lives precious, and grant that we may live to the common age of man, and never fall into the hands nor power of the mob in Missouri, nor in any other place; that He would also preserve our posterity, that none of them fall, even unto the end of time; that He would give us blessings of the earth sufficient to carry us to Zion, and that we may purchase inheritances in that land, even enough to carry on and accomplish the work unto which He has appointed us; and also that He would assist all others who desire, according to His commandments, to go up and purchase inheritances, and all this easily and without perplexity and trouble; and finally, that in the end He would save us in His celestial kingdom. Amen.

Saturday, 24.—Mr. Goodrich and wife called to see the ancient [Egyptian] records, and also Dr. Frederick G. Williams to see the mummies. Brothers Hawkes and Carpenter, from Michigan, visited us and tarried over night.

Sunday, 25.—Attended meeting with Brothers Hawkes and Carpenter. President Rigdon preached in the fore noon, Elder Lyman E. Johnson in the afternoon, after which Elder Seymour Brunson joined Brother William Perry and Sister Eliza Brown in matrimony, and I blessed them with long life and prosperity in the name of Jesus Christ.

Meetings in Kirtland.

In the evening I attended prayer meeting, opened it, and exhorted the brethren and sisters about one hour. The Lord poured out His Spirit, and some glorious things were spoken in the gift of tongues and interpreted concerning the redemption of Zion.

Monday, 26.—Went to Chardon to attend the County Court in company with my brothers Hyrum, Samuel H., and Don Carlos Smith. Brother Samuel was called in question before this Court for not doing military duty, and was fined because we had not our conference minutes with us for testimony to prove that Frederick G. Williams was clerk of the conference. This testimony we should have carried with us had it not been for the neglect of our counsel or lawyer, who did not put us in possession of this information [i. e. that we would need such testimony]. This we felt was a want of fidelity to his client, and we consider it a base insult, practiced upon us on account of our faith, that the ungodly might have unlawful power over us, and trample us under their unhallowed feet. And in consequence of this neglect, a fine was imposed upon Brother Samuel of twenty dollars, including costs, for which he was obliged to sell his cow to defray the expenses of the same. And I say, in the name of Jesus Christ, that the money which they have thus unjustly taken shall be a testimony against them, and canker, and eat their flesh as fire.

Trial of Samuel Smith for Neglect of Military Duty

Tuesday, 27.—In the morning I was called to visit at Brother Samuel Smith's. His wife was confined and in a dangerous condition. Brother Carlos went to Chardon after Dr. Williams. I went out into the field and bowed before the Lord and called upon Him in mighty prayer in her behalf. And the word of the

A Prayer and Promise.

Lord came unto me, saying, "My servant Frederick shall come, and shall have wisdom given him to deal prudently, and my handmaid shall be delivered of a living child, and be spared." The doctor came in about one hour afterwards, and in the course of two hours she was delivered, and thus what God had manifested to me was fulfilled every whit. This evening I preached in the school house to a crowded congregation.

Wednesday, 28.—At home, attending to my family affairs.

Thursday, 29.—Brother Warren Parrish commenced writing for me, at fifteen dollars per month. I paid him sixteen dollars in advance out of the committee's store. Father and Mother Smith visited us. While we sat writing Bishop Partridge passed our window, just returned from the East.

Warren Parrish Becomes the Prophet's Scribe.

I was called to appear before the High Council, which was then sitting, to give my testimony in an action brought by Brother William Smith against Brother David Elliot, for whipping his daughter unreasonably. My testimony was in Brother Elliot's favor, from conversation with the parents and the girl at their house in Chagrin, I was satisfied that the girl was in the fault, and that the neighbors were trying to create a difficulty.

Trial of David Elliot.

Returned to our writing room, went to Dr. Williams' after my large journal; made some observations to my scribe concerning the plan of the city, which is to be built up hereafter on this ground consecrated for a Stake of Zion.

While at the doctor's, Bishop Edward Partridge came in in company with President Phelps. I was much rejoiced to see him. We examined the mummies, returned home, and my scribe commenced writing in my journal a history of my life; concluded President Cowdery's second letter to W. W. Phelps, which President Williams had begun.

Bishop Whitney and his wife, with his father and mother, called to visit us. His parents having lately arrived here from the East, called to make inquiry concerning the coming forth of the Book of Mormon. Bishop Partridge and some others came in. I then sat down and related to them the history of the coming forth of the book, the administration of the angel to me, and taught them the rudiments of the Gospel of Christ. They appeared well satisfied, and I expect to baptize them in a few days, though they have made no request of the kind.*

The Visit of Bishop Whitney's Parents to the Prophet

Went to the Council. The Presidency arose and adjourned. On my return Elder Boynton observed that long debates were bad. I replied that it was generally the case that too much altercation was indulged in on both sides, and their debates protracted to an unprofitable length.

Of Debates in Council.

We were called to supper. While seated at table we indulged in a free interchange of thought, and Bishop Whitney observed to Bishop Partridge that the thought had just occurred to his mind that perhaps in about one year from this time they might be seated together around a table on the land of Zion. My wife observed she hoped it might be the case, that not only they, but the rest of the company present, might be seated around her table on that land of promise. The same sentiment was reciprocated from the company around the table, and my heart responded, Amen. God grant it, I ask in the name of Jesus Christ.

Hopes for Zion's Redemption.

After supper I went to the High Council in company with my wife and some others that belonged to my household. I was solicited to take a seat with the Presidency and preside on a trial of Sister Elliot. I did so. My mother was called upon for testimony, and began to relate circumstances that had been brought before the Church and settled. I objected

Disorder in a Council Meeting.

* The expectation was realized on the last day of October, see p. 297.

to such testimony. The complainant, Brother William Smith, arose and accused me of invalidating or doubting my mother's testimony, which I had not done, nor did I desire to do so. I told him he was out of order, and asked him to sit down. He refused. I repeated my request. He became enraged. I finally ordered him to sit down. He said he would not, unless I knocked him down. I was agitated in my feelings on account of his stubbornness, and was about to leave the house, but my father requested me not to do so. I complied, and the house was brought to order after much debate on the subject, and we proceeded to business.

The decision of the Council in the case of Brother Elliot was, "that the complaint was not without foundation, yet the charge has not been fully sustained, but he has acted injudiciously and brought a disgrace upon himself, his daughter, and upon this Church, because he ought to have trained his child in a way that she would not have required the rod at the age of fifteen years." Brother Elliot made his confession and was forgiven. Sister Elliot confessed her wrong and promised to do better, consequently the Council forgave her. And they were both restored to fellowship.

A Methodist's Inquiry into Conditions at Kirtland.

Friday, *30*.—At home. Mr. Francis Porter, from Jefferson County, New York, a member of the Methodist church, called to make some inquiry about lands in this place (Kirtland), whether there were any valuable farms for sale, and whether a member of our Church could move into this vicinity and purchase lands and enjoy his own possessions and property without making them common stock. He had been requested to make this inquiry by some brethren who live in the town of Leroy, New York. I replied that I had a valuable farm joining the Temple lot I would sell, and that there were other lands for sale in this place and that we had no common stock business among us; that every man enjoys his own property, or can, if he is disposed, consecrate liberally or illiberally to the support of the poor and needy, or the building up of Zion. He also inquired how many members there were in this Church. I told him there were about five or six hundred who communed at our chapel, and perhaps a thousand in this vicinity.

William Smith's Self-justification.

In the evening I was presented with a letter from Brother William Smith, the purport of which is, that he is censured by the brethren on account of what took place at the Council last night, and wishes to have the matter settled to the understanding of all, that he may not be censured unjustly, considering that his cause was a just one and that he had been materially injured. I replied that I thought we parted with the best of feelings, that I was not to blame on account of the dissatisfaction of others. I invited him to call and talk with me, and that I would talk with him in the spirit of meekness and give him all the satisfaction I could. This reply was by letter.

Hyrum Smith as Peace-maker.

Saturday, *31*.—In the morning Brother Hyrum Smith came in and said he had been much troubled all night and had not slept any, that something was wrong. While talking, Brother William Smith came in, according to my request last night. Brother Hyrum said that he must go to the store. I invited him to stay. He said he would go and do his business and return. He did so. While he was gone Brother William introduced the subject of our difficulty at the Council. I told him I did not want to converse upon the subject until Hyrum returned. He soon came in. I then proposed to relate the occurrences of the Council before named, and wherein I had been out of the way I would confess it, and ask his forgiveness, and then he should relate his story, and make confession wherein he had done wrong, and then leave it to Brother Hyrum Smith and Brother Parrish to decide the matter between us, and I would agree to the decision and be satisfied therewith.

William observed that he had not done wrong, and that I was always determined to carry my points whether right or wrong, and therefore he would not stand an equal chance with me. This was an insult, but I did not reply to him in a harsh manner, knowing his excitable disposition, but tried to reason with him and show him the propriety of a compliance with my request. I finally succeeded with the assistance of Brother Hyrum, in obtaining his assent to the proposition that I had made. I then related my story, and wherein I had been wrong I confessed it, and asked his forgiveness. After I got through he made his statements, justifying himself throughout in transgressing the order of the Council, and treating the authority of the Presidency with contempt. After he had got through Brother Hyrum began to make some remarks in the spirit of meekness. He (William) became enraged. I joined Brother Hyrum in trying to calm his stormy feelings, but to no purpose, he insisted that we intended to add abuse to injury, his passion increased, he arose abruptly, declared that he wanted no more to do with us. He rushed out at the door. We tried to prevail on him to stop, but all to no purpose. He went away in a passion, and soon after sent his license to me. He went home and spread the leaven of iniquity among my brothers, and especially prejudiced the mind of Brother Samuel. I soon learned that he was in the street exclaiming against me, and no doubt our enemies rejoiced at it. And where the matter will end I know not, but I pray God to forgive him and them, and give them humility and repentance.

The Rebellion of William Smith.

The feelings of my heart I cannot express on this occasion, I can only pray my Heavenly Father to open their eyes, that they may discover where they stand, that they may extricate themselves from the snare they have fallen into.

After dinner I rode out in company with my wife and

children, Brother Don Carlos and some others. We visited Brother Roundy* and family, who live near Willoughby.

Visit to Shadrach Roundy.

We had an interesting visit. As soon as I returned I was called upon to baptize Samuel Whitney and his wife and daughter. After baptism we returned to their house and offered our thanks in prayer. I obtained a testimony that my brother William would return to the Church, and repair the wrong he had done,

* This is Shadrach Roundy who afterwards became prominent in Church affairs. He was born in Rockingham, Windham County, Vermont, January 1, 1789. At twenty-five he married Betsy Quimby. He first heard of the Gospel on moving from Vermont to Onondaga County, New York, and in the winter of 1830-1 sought out the Prophet, then residing at Fayette, Seneca County, New York. After his first interview he was baptized; and subsequently his wife and all his children of sufficient age received the Gospel. He removed with the New York Saints to Ohio, settling near Willoughby, where the Prophet frequently visited him.

CHAPTER XXII.

THE MINISTRY OF THE PROPHET IN KIRTLAND.

Reproof of Reynolds Cahoon.

Sunday, November 1.—Verily thus said the Lord unto me, His servant, Joseph Smith, Jun.—

Revelation.

Mine anger is kindled against my servant Reynolds Cahoon, because of his iniquities, his covetous and dishonest principles, in himself and family, and he doth not purge them away and set his house in order. Therefore, if he repent not, chastisement awaiteth him, even as it seemeth good in my sight, therefore go and declare unto him these words.

I went immediately and delivered this message according as the Lord commanded me. I called him in, and read what the Lord had said concerning him. He acknowledged that it was verily so, and expressed much humility. I then went to meeting. Elder John Corrill preached a fine discourse.

In the afternoon President Phelps continued the services of the day by reading the fifth chapter of Matthew, also the laws regulating the High Council, and made some remarks upon them, after which, Sacrament was administered. I then confirmed a number who had been baptized, and blessed a number of children, in the name of Jesus Christ, with the blessings of the New and Everlasting Covenant. Notice was then given that the Elders' school would commence on the morrow.

Monday, November 2.—I was engaged in regulating the affairs of the school, after which I had my team prepared, and Sidney Rigdon, Oliver Cowdery, Frederick G. Williams, my scribe, and a number of others, went to Willoughby to hear Dr. Piexotto deliver a lecture on the theory and practice of physics. Called at Mr. Cushman's, dined, attended the lecture. Was treated with great respect throughout, and returned home.

School for the Elders Opened.

Lyman Wight arrived from Zion, also George A. and Lyman Smith returned from a mission to the east, after an absence of five months. The question was agitated whether Frederick G. Williams or Oliver Cowdery should go to New York, to make arrangements respecting a book-bindery. They referred the matter to me for a decision. And thus came the word of the Lord to me, saying—

Revelation.

It is not my will that my servant Frederick should go to New York, inasmuch as he wishes to go and visit his relations, that he may warn them to flee the wrath to come, let him go and see them for that purpose, and let that be his only business, and behold, in this thing, he shall be blessed with power to overcome their prejudices, verily thus saith the Lord. Amen.

Tuesday, November 3.—Thus came the word of the Lord unto me concerning the Twelve, saying—

Revelation to the Twelve.

Behold they are under condemnation, because they have not been sufficiently humble in my sight, and in consequence of their covetous desires, in that they have not dealt equally with each other in the division of the monies which came into their hands, nevertheless, some of them dealt equally, therefore they shall be rewarded; but verily I say unto you, they must all humble themselves before me, before they will be accounted worthy to receive an endowment, to go forth in my name unto all nations.

As for my servant William, let the Eleven humble themselves in prayer and in faith, and wait on me in patience, and my servant William shall return, and I will yet make him a polished shaft in my quiver, in bringing down the wickedness and abominations of men; and there shall be none mightier than he, in his day and generation, nevertheless if he repent not speedily, he shall be brought low, and shall be chastened sorely for all his iniquities he has committed against me; nevertheless the sin which he has sinned against me is not even now more grievous than the sin with which my servant David W. Patten, and my servant Orson Hyde, and my servant William E. M'Lellin have sinned against me, and the residue are not sufficiently humble before me.

Behold the parable which I spake concerning a man having twelve sons: for what man among you, having twelve sons, and is no respecter of them, and they serve him obediently, and he saith unto one, Be thou clothed in robes, and sit thou here; and to the other, Be thou clothed in rags, and sit thou there, and looketh upon his sons, and saith, I am just? Ye will answer, and say, no man; and ye answer truly; therefore, verily thus saith the Lord your God, I appoint these Twelve that they should be equal in their ministry, and in their portion, and in their evangelical rights; wherefore they have sinned a very grievous sin, inasmuch as they have made themselves unequal, and have not hearkened unto my voice; therefore, let them repent speedily, and prepare their hearts for the solemn assembly, and for the great day which is to come, verily thus saith the Lord. Amen.

Object of the Elders' School.

I then went to assist in organizing the Elders' school. I called it to order and made some remarks upon the object of this school, and the great necessity of our rightly improving our time and reining up our minds to the sense of the great object that lies before us, viz—the glorious endowment that God has in store for the faithful.

I then dedicated the school in the name of the Lord Jesus Christ.

After the school was dismissed, I attended a patriarchal meeting at brother Samuel Smith's; his wife's parents were blessed, also his child, named Susannah.

In the evening I preached in the school house, to a crowded congregation.

Wednesday, November 4.—At home in the morning. Attended school during school hours, made rapid progress in our studies. In the evening lectured on grammar at home. King Follet arrived from Zion this day.

Thursday, November 5.—Attended school. Isaac Morley came in from the east.

This morning I was called to visit Thomas Burdick, who was sick. I took my scribe with me, and we prayed for and laid our hands on him in the name of the Lord Jesus Christ, and rebuked his affliction.

William E. M'Lellin and Orson Hyde came in and desired to hear the Revelation concerning the Twelve. My scribe read it to them. They expressed some little dissatisfaction, but after examining their own hearts, they acknowledged it to be the word of the Lord, and said they were satisfied. After school, Brigham Young came in, and desired also to hear it read; after hearing it, he appeared perfectly satisfied.

Inquiries About the Revelation to the Twelve.

In the evening I lectured on grammar.

Friday, November 6.—At home. Attended school during school hours, returned and spent the evening at home.

Reflections on the Nature of Prophets.

I was this morning introduced to a man from the east. After hearing my name, he remarked that I was nothing but a man, indicating by this expression, that he had supposed that a person to whom the Lord should see fit to reveal His will, must be something more than a man. He seemed to have forgotten the saying that fell from the lips of St. James, that Elias was a man subject to like passions as we are, yet he had such power with God, that He, in answer to his prayers, shut the heavens that they gave no rain for the space of three years and six months; and again, in answer to his prayer, the heavens gave forth rain, and the earth gave forth fruit. Indeed, such is the darkness and ignorance of this generation, that they look upon it as incredible that a man should have any intercourse with his Maker.

Isaac Morley and Edward Partridge Commended.

Saturday, November 7.—Spent the day at home attending to my domestic concerns. The word of the Lord came unto me saying—

Revelation.

Behold I am well pleased with my servant Isaac Morley, and my servant Edward Partridge, because of the integrity of their hearts in laboring in my vineyard, for the salvation of the souls of men. Verily I say unto you, their sins are forgiven them; therefore say unto them.

in my name, that it is my will that they should tarry for a little season, and attend the school, and also the solemn assembly, for a wise purpose in me. Even so. Amen.

Sunday, November 8.—Went to meeting in the morning at the usual hour. Zerubbabel Snow preached a very interesting discourse; in the afternoon Joseph Young preached. After preaching, Isaac Hill came forward to make some remarks by way of confession. He had previously been excommunicated from the Church for lying, and for an attempt to seduce a female. His confession was not satisfactory to my mind, and John Smith arose and made some remarks respecting the doings of the High Council, in the case of said Hill; that is, that he should make a public confession of his crime, and have it published in the *Messenger and Advocate.* He proposed that Mr. Hill should now make his confession before the congregation, and then immediately observed that he had forgiven Mr. Hill, which was in contradiction to the sentiment he first advanced. This I attributed to an error in judgment, not in design.

The Case of Isaac Hill.

President Rigdon then arose, and very abruptly militated against the sentiment of Uncle John, which had a direct tendency to destroy his influence, and bring him into disrepute in the eyes of the Church, which was not right. He also misrepresented Mr. Hill's case, and spread darkness rather than light upon the subject.

A vote of the Church was then called on Brother Hill's case, and he was restored without any further confession, viz., that he should be received into the Church by baptism, which was administered accordingly.

After I returned home, I labored with Uncle John, and convinced him that he was wrong; and he made his confession, to my satisfaction. I then went and labored with President Rigdon, and succeeded in convincing him also of his error, which he confessed to my satisfaction.

Labors of the Prophet with the Erring.

The word of the Lord came unto me, saying, that President Phelps and President John Whitmer were under condemnation before the Lord for their errors. For which they made satisfaction the same day.

I also took up a labor with John Corrill, for not partaking of the Sacrament; he made his confession. Also my wife, for leaving the meeting before Sacrament; she made no reply, but manifested contrition by weeping.

Monday, November 9.—After breakfast, Mary Whitcher came in and wished to see me. I granted her request.

Case of Mary Whitcher.

She gave a relation of her grievances, which are unfathomable at present, and if true, sore indeed; and I pray my Heavenly Father, to bring the truth of the case to light, that the reward due to evil doers may be given them, and that the afflicted and oppressed may be delivered.

While sitting in my house, between ten and eleven this morning, a man came in and introduced himself to me by the name of "Joshua, the Jewish Minister."

Joshua, the Jewish Minister.

His appearance was something singular, having a beard about three inches in length, quite grey; also his hair was long and considerably silvered with age; I thought him about fifty or fifty-five years old; tall, straight, slender built, of thin visage, blue eyes, and fair complexion; wore a sea-green frock coat and pantaloons, black fur hat with narrow brim; and, while speaking, frequently shut his eyes, with a scowl on his countenance. I made some inquiry after his name, but received no definite answer. We soon commenced talking on the subject of religion, and, after I had made some remarks concerning the Bible, I commenced giving him a relation of the circumstances connected with the coming forth of the Book of Mormon, as recorded in the former part of this history.

While I was relating a brief history of the establishment of the Church of Christ in the last days, Joshua seemed to be highly entertained. When I had closed my narration,

I observed that the hour of worship and dinner had arrived, and invited him to tarry, to which he consented. After dinner, the conversation was resumed, and Joshua proceeded to make some remarks on the prophecies, as follows—he observed that he was aware that I could bear stronger meat than many others, therefore he should open his mind the more freely:

The Doctrines of "Joshua the Jewish Minister."

Daniel has told us that he is to stand in his proper lot, in the latter days; according to his vision he had a right to shut it up, and also to open it again after many days, or in latter times. Daniel's image, whose head was gold, and body, arms, legs and feet, were composed of the different materials described in his vision, represents different governments. The golden head was to represent Nebuchadnezzar, King of Babylon; the other parts, other kings and forms of governments which I shall not now mention in detail, but confine my remarks more particularly to the feet of the image. The policy of the wicked spirit is to separate what God has joined together, and unite what He has separated, which the devil has succeeded in doing to admiration in the present state of society, which is like unto iron and clay.

There is confusion in all things, both political and religious; and notwithstanding all the efforts that are made to bring about a union, society remains disunited, and all attempts to unite it are as fruitless as to attempt to unite iron and clay. The feet of the image are the government of these United States. Other nations and kingdoms are looking up to her for an example of union, freedom, and equal rights, and therefore worship her as Daniel saw in the vision; although they are beginning to lose confidence in her, seeing the broils and discord that rise on her political and religious horizon. This image is characteristic of all governments.

We should leave Babylon. Twenty-four hours of improvement now, are worth as much as a year a hundred years ago. The spirits of the fathers that were cut down, or those that were under the altar, are now rising; this is the first resurrection. The Elder that falls first will rise last. We should not form any opinion only for the present, and leave the result of futurity with God. I have risen up out of obscurity, but was looked up to in temporal things when but a youth. It is not necessary that God should give us all things in His first commission to us, but in His second. John saw the angel deliver the Gospel in the last days. The small lights that God has given are sufficient to lead us out of Babylon; when we get out, we shall have the greater light.

I told Joshua I did not understand his remarks on the

resurrection, and wished him to explain. He replied that he did not feel impressed by the Spirit to unfold it further at present, but perhaps he might at some future time.

I then withdrew to transact some business with a gentleman who had called to see me, when Joshua informed my scribe that he was born in Cambridge, Washington County, New York. He says that all the railroads, canals, and other improvements are projected by the spirits of the resurrection. The silence spoken of by John the Revelator, which is to be in heaven for the space of half an hour, is between 1830 and 1851, during which time the judgments of God will be poured out, after that time there will be peace.

Additional Views of Joshua.

Curiosity to see a man that was reputed to be a Jew, caused many to call during the day, and more particularly in the evening.

Suspicions were entertained that the said Joshua was the noted Matthias of New York, spoken so much of in the public prints, on account of the trials he endured in that place, before a court of justice, for murder, man-slaughter, contempt of court, whipping his daughter, etc.; for the last two crimes he was imprisoned, and came out about four months since. After some equivocating, he confessed that he really was Matthias.

Matthias *not* Joshua.

After supper I proposed that he should deliver a lecture to us. He did so, sitting in his chair.

He commenced by saying, God said, let there be light, and there was light, which he dwelt upon throughout his discourse. He made some very excellent remarks, but his mind was evidently filled with darkness.

After the congregation dispersed, he conversed freely upon the circumstances that occurred in New York. His name is Robert Matthias. He says that Joshua is his priestly name. During all this time I did not contradict his sentiments, wishing to draw out all that I could concerning his faith.

Mr. Beaman, of New York, came to ask advice of me

whether or not he had better purchase lands in this vicinity, as he could not arrange his business to go to Missouri next spring. I advised him to come here and settle until he could move to Zion.

Matthias Dismissed by the Prophet.

Tuesday, November 10.—I resumed conversation with Matthias, and desired him to enlighten my mind more on his views respecting the resurrection.

He said that he posessed the spirit of his fathers, that he was a literal descendant of Matthias, the Apostle, who was chosen in the place of Judas that fell; that his spirit was resurrected in him; and that this was the way or scheme of eternal life—this transmigration of soul or spirit from father to son.

I told him that his doctrine was of the devil, that he was in reality in possession of a wicked and depraved spirit, although he professed to be the Spirit of truth itself; and he said also that he possessed the soul of Christ.

He tarried until Wednesday, 11th, when, after breakfast, I told him, that my God told me, that his god was the devil, and I could not keep him any longer, and he must depart. And so I, for once, cast out the devil in bodily shape, and I believe a murderer.

Attended school during school hours. Spent the evening around my fireside, teaching my family grammar. It commenced snowing this afternoon; wind very heavy.

The Prophet's Meeting with the Twelve.

Thursday, November 12.—Attended school again during school hours; rain and snow still falling, about one inch in depth and wind very heavy; the weather extremely unpleasant. The laborers who were finishing the outside of the chapel, were obliged to break off from their business at the commencement of this storm, on the 11th instant.

This evening, at 6 o'clock, met with the Council of the Twelve, by their request. Nine of them were present. Council opened by singing and prayer. And I made some remarks as follows—

The Prophet's Remarks to the Twelve.

I am happy in the enjoyment of this opportunity of meeting with this Council on this occasion. I am satisfied that the Spirit of the Lord is here, and I am satisfied with all the brethren present; and I need not say that you have my utmost confidence, and that I intend to uphold you to the uttermost, for I am well aware that you have to sustain my character against the vile calumnies and reproaches of this ungodly generation, and that you delight in so doing.

Darkness prevail sat this time as it did at the time Jesus Christ was about to be crucified. The powers of darkness strove to obscure the glorious Sun of rightousness, that began to dawn upon the world, and was soon to burst in great blessings upon the heads of the faithful; and let me tell you, brethren, that great blessings await us at this time, and will soon be poured out upon us, if we are faithful in all things, for we are even entitled to greater spiritual blessings than they were, because they had Christ in person with them, to instruct them in the great plan of salvation. His personal presence we have not, therefore we have need of greater faith, on account of our peculiar circumstances; and I am determined to do all that I can to uphold you, although I may do many things inadvertently that are not right in the sight of God.

You want to know many things that are before you, that you may know how to prepare yourselves for the great things that God is about to bring to pass. But there is one great deficiency or obstruction in the way, that deprives us of the greater blessings; and in order to make the foundation of this Church complete and permanent, we must remove this obstruction, which is, to attend to certain duties that we have not as yet attended to. I supposed I had established this Church on a permanent foundation when I went to Missouri, and indeed I did so, for if I had been taken away, it would have been enough, but I yet live, and therefore God requires more at my hands. The item to which I wish the more particularly to call your attention to-night, is the ordinance of washing of feet. This we have not done as yet, but it is necessary now, as much as it was in the days of the Savior; and we must have a place prepared, that we may attend to this ordinance aside from the world.

We have not desired as much from the hand of the Lord through faith and obedience, as we ought to have done, yet we have enjoyed great blessings, and we are not so sensible of this as we should be. When or where has God suffered one of the witnesses or first Elders of this Church to fall? Never, and no where. Amidst all the calamities and judgments that have befallen the inhabitants of the earth, His almighty arm has sustained us, men and devils have raged and spent their malice in vain. We must have all things prepared, and call our solemn assembly as the Lord has commanded us, that we may be able to accomplish His great work, and it must be done in God's own way. The house of the Lord must be prepared, and the solemn assembly called and organized in it, according to the order of the house of God; and in it we must attend to the ordinance of washing of feet. It was never intended for any but official members. It is calculated to unite our hearts, that we may be one in feeling and sentiment, and that our faith may be strong, so that Satan cannot overthrow us, nor have any power over us here.

The endowment you are so anxious about, you cannot comprehend now, nor could Gabriel explain it to the understanding of your dark minds; but strive to be prepared in your hearts, be faithful in all things, that when we meet in the solemn assembly, that is, when such as God shall name out of all the official members shall meet, we must be clean every whit. Let us be faithful and silent, brethren, and if God gives you a manifestation, keep it to yourselves; be watchful and prayerful, and you shall have a prelude of those joys that God will pour out on that day. Do not watch for iniquity in each other, if you do you will not get an endowment, for God will not bestow it on such. But if we are faithful, and live by every word that proceeds forth from the mouth of God, I will venture to prophesy that we shall get a blessing that will be worth remembering, if we should live as long as John the Revelator; our blessings will be such as we have not realized before, nor received in this generation. The order of the house of God has been, and ever will be, the same, even after Christ comes; and after the termination of the thousand years it will be the same; and we shall finally enter into the celestial Kingdom of God, and enjoy it forever.

You need an endowment, brethren, in order that you may be prepared and able to overcome all things; and those that reject your testimony will be damned. The sick will be healed, the lame made to walk, the deaf to hear, and the blind to see, through your instrumentality. But let me tell you, that you will not have power, after the endowment to heal those that have not faith, nor to benefit them, for you might as well expect to benefit a devil in hell as such as are possessed of his spirit, and are willing to keep it; for they are habitations for devils, and only fit for his society. But when you are endowed and prepared to preach the Gospel to all nations, kindred, and tongues, in their own languages, you must faithfully warn all, and bind up the testimony, and seal up the law, and the destroying angel will follow close at your heels, and exercise his tremendous mission upon the children of disobedience; and destroy the workers of iniquity, while the Saints will be gathered out from among them, and stand in holy places ready to meet the Bridegroom when he comes.

I feel disposed to speak a few words more to you, my brethren, concerning the endowment: All who are prepared, and are sufficiently pure to abide the presence of the Savior, will see Him in the solemn assembly.

The brethren expressed their gratification for the instruction I had given them. We then closed by prayer, when I returned home and retired to rest.

CHAPTER XXIII.

THE MINISTRY OF THE PROPHET IN KIRTLAND.

Friday, November 13.—Attended school during school hours: after school, returned home. Mr. Messenger, a Universalist minister, of Bainbridge, Chenango county, New York, came in to make some inquiries about Hezekiah Peck's family. We entered into conversation upon religious subjects, and went to President Rigdon's and spent the evening in conversation. We preached the Gospel to him, and bore testimony of what we had seen and heard.

The visit of Mr. Messenger.

He attempted to raise some objections, but the force of truth bore him down, and he was silent, although unbelieving.

I returned home and retired to rest.

Saturday, 14.—Thus came the word of the Lord unto me, saying:

Revelation to Warren Parrish.

Verily thus saith the Lord unto my servant Joseph, concerning my servant Warren Parrish. Behold his sins are forgiven him, because of his desires to do the works of righteousness. Therefore, inasmuch as he will continue to hearken unto my voice, he shall be blessed with wisdom, and with a sound mind, even above his fellows. Behold, it shall come to pass in his day, that he shall see great things show forth themselves unto my people; he shall see much of my ancient records, and shall know of hidden things, and shall be endowed with a knowledge of hidden languages; and if he desire and shall seek it at my hands, he shall be privileged with writing much of my word, as a scribe unto me for the benefit of my people; therefore this shall be his calling until I shall order it otherwise in my wisdom, and it shall be said of him in time to come, Behold Warren, the Lord's scribe for the Lord's Seer, whom He hath appointed in Israel. Therefore, if he will keep my commandments, he shall be lifted up at the last day. Even so. Amen.

Inquiries by Erastus Holmes.

This afternoon, Erastus Holmes, of Newbury, Ohio, called on me to inquire about the establishment of the Church, and to be instructed in doctrine more perfectly.

I gave him a brief relation of my experience while in my juvenile years, say from six years old up to the time I received my first vision, which was when I was about fourteen years old; also the revelations that I received afterwards concerning the Book of Mormon, and a short account of the rise and progress of the Church up to this date.

He listened very attentively, and seemed highly gratified, and intends to unite with the Church.

On Sabbath morning, 15th, he went with me to meeting, which was held in the schoolhouse, as the plastering of the chapel was not yet finished.

President Rigdon preached on the subject of men being called to preach the Gospel, their qualifications, etc. We had a fine discourse, it was very interesting indeed. Mr. Holmes was well satisfied, and returned and dined with me. Said Holmes has been a member of the Methodist church, and was excommunicated for receiving the Elders of the Latter-day Saints into his house.

Went to meeting in the afternoon. Before partaking of the Sacrament, Isaac Hill's case was agitated again, and settled after much controversy. He was retained in the Church, by making a humble acknowledgement before the Church, and consenting to have his confession published in the *Messenger and Advocate;* after which the ordinance of the Lord's Supper was administered, and the meeting closed late. Returned home and spent the evening.

Monday 16.—At home. Dictated the following letter for publication in the *Messenger and Advocate.**

* This refers to the Prophet's second communication to the *Messenger and Advocate* and will be found at page 259 *et seq.*

The same day, I received a letter from Harvey Whitlock, of which the following is a copy—

The Case of Harvey Whitlock.

Harvey Whitlock's Letter.

DEAR SIR.—Having a few leisure moments, I have at last concluded to do what my own judgment has long dictated would be right, but the allurements of many vices have long retarded the hand that would wield the pen to make intelligent the communication that I wish to send to you; and even now, that ambition, which is a prevailing and predominant principle among the great mass of natural men, forbids that plainness of sentiment with which I wish to write; for know assuredly, sir, to you I wish to unbosom my feelings, and unveil the secrets of my heart, as before the omniscient Judge of all the earth. Be not surprised, when I declare unto you, as the Spirit will bear record, that my faith is firm and unshaken in the things of the everlasting Gospel, as it is proclaimed by the servants of the Latter-day Saints.

Dear Brother Joseph, (if I may be allowed the expression,) when I consider the happy times, and peaceful moments, and pleasant seasons I have enjoyed with you and this people, contrasted with my now degraded state; together with the high and important station I have held before God, and the abyss into which I have fallen—it is a subject that swells my heart too big for utterance, and I am overwhelmed with feelings that language cannot express. As I desire to know the will of God concerning me, and believing it is my duty to make known unto you my real situation, I shall dispassionately proceed to give a true and untarnished relation.

I need not tell you that in former times I have preached the word, and endeavored to be instant in season, and out of season—to reprove, rebuke, exhort, and faithfully to discharge that trust reposed in me. But oh! with what grief, and lamentable sorrow, and anguish, do I have to relate that I have fallen from that princely station whereunto our God has called me. Reasons why are unnecessary, may the fact suffice, and believe me when I tell you, that I have sunk myself (since my last separation from this body) in crimes of the deepest dye. And that I may the better enable you to understand what my real sins are, I will mention (although pride forbids it) some that I am not guilty of. My hands have not been stained with innocent blood, neither have I lain couched around the cottages of my fellow men, to seize and carry off the booty; nor have I slandered my neighbor, nor borne false testimony, nor taken unlawful hire, nor oppressed the widow or fatherless, neither have I persecuted the Saints. But my hands are swift to do iniquity, and my feet are fast running in the paths of vice and folly, and my heart is quick to devise wicked imaginations; nevertheless, I am impressed with the sure thought that I am fast hastening into a world of disembodied beings, without God, and with but one hope in the world, which is to know that to err is human, but to forgive is divine.

Much I might say in relation to myself, and the original difficulties with the Church, but I will forbear; and inasmuch as I have been charged with things that I am not guilty of, I am now more than doubly guilty, and am now willing to forgive and forget, only let me know that I am within the reach of mercy. If I am not, I have no reflections to cast, but say that I have sealed my own doom, and pronounced my own sentence. If the day is passed by with me, may I here beg leave to entreat of those who are still toiling up the rugged ascent, to make their way to the realms of endless felicity and delight, to stop not for anchors here below, follow not my example, but steer their course onward in spite of all the combined powers of earth and hell, for know that one misstep here is only retrievable by a thousand groans and tears before God.

Dear Brother Joseph, let me entreat you, on the reception of this letter, as you regard the salvation of my soul, to inquire at the hand of the Lord, in my behalf; for I this day, in the presence of God, do covenant to abide the word that may be given, for I am willing to receive any chastisement that the Lord sees I deserve. Now hear my prayer, and suffer me to break forth in the agony of my soul. O ye angels! that surround the throne of God, princes of heaven that excel in strength, ye who are clothed with transcendent brightness, plead, O plead for one of the most wretched of the sons of men. O ye heavens! whose azure arches rise immensely high, and stretch immeasurably wide—grand amphitheatre of nature, throne of the Eternal God, bow to hear the prayer of a poor, wretched, bewildered, way-wanderer to eternity. O! Thou great omnipotent and omnipresent Jehovah! Thou who sittest upon the throne, before whom all things are present; Thou maker, moulder, and fashioner of all things visible and invisible, breathe, O breathe into the ears of Thy servant the Prophet, words suitably adapted to my case and situation. Speak once more, make known Thy will concerning me; which favors I ask in the name of the Son of God. Amen.

Yours respectfully,

HARVEY WHITLOCK.

To Joseph Smith.

N.B.—I hope you will not let any business prevent you from answering this letter in haste.

I answered as follows:

KIRTLAND, November 16, 1835.

BROTHER HARVEY WHITLOCK—I have received your letter of the 28th of September, 1835, and I have read it twice, and it gave me sensations that are better imagined than described, let it suffice that I say that the very flood gates of my heart were broken up—I could not refrain from weeping. I thank God that it has entered into your heart to try to return to the Lord, and to this people, if it so be that He will have mercy upon you. I have inquired of the Lord concerning your case; these words came to me:

Revelation to Harvey Whitlock.

"Verily, thus saith the Lord unto you—Let him who was my servant Harvey, return unto me, and unto the bosom of my Church, and forsake all the sins wherewith he has offended against me, and pursue from henceforth a virtuous and upright life, and remain under the direction of those whom I have appointed to be pillars and heads of my Church. And behold, saith the Lord your God, his sins shall be blotted out from under heaven, and shall be forgotten from among men, and shall not come up in mine ears, nor be recorded as a memorial against him, but I will lift him up, as out of deep mire, and he shall be exalted upon the high places, and shall be counted worthy to stand among princes, and shall yet be made a polished shaft in my quiver for bringing down the strongholds of wickedness among those who set themselves up on high, that they may take counsel against me, and against my anointed ones in the last days. Therefore, let him prepare himself speedily and come unto you, even to Kirtland. And inasmuch as he shall hearken unto all your counsel from henceforth, he shall be restored unto his former state, and shall be saved unto the uttermost, even as the Lord your God liveth. Amen."

Thus you see, my dear brother, the willingness of our heavenly Father to forgive sins, and restore to favor all those who are willing to humble themselves before Him, and confess their sins, and forsake them, and return to Him with full purpose of heart, acting no hypocrisy, to serve Him to the end.

Marvel not that the Lord has condescended to speak from the heavens, and give you instructions whereby you may learn your duty. He has heard your prayers and witnessed your humility, and holds forth the hand of paternal affection for your return; the angels rejoice over you, while the Saints are willing to receive you again into fellowship.

I hope, on the receipt of this, you will lose no time in coming to Kirtland, for if you get here in season, you will have the privilege of attending the school of the Prophets, which has already commenced, and also receive instructions in doctrine and principle, from those whom God has appointed, whereby you may be qualified to go forth, and declare the true doctrines of the Kingdom, according to the mind and will of God; and when you come to Kirtland, it will be explained to you why God has condescended to give you a revelation according to your request.

Please give my respects to your family, and be assured I am yours in the bonds of the new and everlasting covenant,

JOSEPH SMITH, JUN.

In the courseof the day, Father Beaman, Elder Strong, and others, called to counsel with me. In the evening a council was called at my house to counsel with Alva Beaman on the subject of his moving to Missouri. I had previously told him that the Lord had said that he had better go to Missouri next spring; however, he wished a council called. The council met, and President David Whitmer arose and said, the Spirit manifested to him that it was Brother Beaman's duty to go. Others bore the same testimony.

Council Concerning Brethren Going to Missouri.

The same night, I received the word of the Lord on Mr. Holmes' case. He had desired that I would inquire at the hand of the Lord, whether it was his duty to be baptized here, or wait until he returned home. The word of the Lord came unto me, saying, Mr. Holmes had better not be baptized here; that he had better not return by water; also that there were three men seeking his destruction; he must beware of his enemies.

The Word of the Lord as to Mr. Holmes' Baptism.

Tuesday 17.—Exhibited the alphabet of the ancient records, to Mr. Holmes, and some others. Went with him to Fredrick G. Williams', to see the mummies. We then took the parting hand, and he started for home, being strong in the faith of the Gospel of Jesus Christ, and determined to obey its requirements. I returned home and spent the day in dictating and comparing letters. A fine, pleasant day, although cool.

This evening, at early candle light, I preached at the schoolhouse.

Wednesday, 18.—At home in the forenoon, until about

eleven o'clock. I then went to Preserved Harris', to preach his father's funeral sermon, by the request of his family. I preached on the subject of the resurrection. The congregation were very attentive. My wife, my mother, and my scribe, accompanied me to the funeral. Pleasant outing, but cool and cloudy on our return.

Minutes of a Council Meeting at New Portage.

This day a Council of High Priests and Elders of the Church of Latter-day Saints, was held at New Portage, to hear the complaint of Sister Clarissa Matthews, against Elder Reuben Keeler, for prosecuting in a court of law, and taking her property on execution, (notwithstanding he had received his pay, or the most part of it) and refusing to allow her for what she had paid to him; also forfeiting his word, as he had frequently stated to her that he would not take her property in such a manner; and also for oppressing her family in an unchristian-like manner.

Elder Keeler pleaded not guilty, but the Council decided that he was guilty of the first and last charges; and gave judgment accordingly; with which Elder Keeler refused to comply, and said he would appeal to the High Council at Kirtland.

AMBROSE PALMER, Presiding Elder.
JOSEPH B. BOSWORTH, Clerk.

Debate on the Question of Miracles.

In the evening, Bishop Whitney, his wife, father, mother, and sister-in-law, came and invited me and my wife to go with them and visit Father Smith and family. My wife was unwell, and could not go, but my scribe and I went.

When we arrived, some of the young Elders were about engaging in a debate on the subject of miracles. The question—"Was it, or was it not, the design of Christ to establish His Gospel by miracles?" After an interesting debate of three hours or more, during which time much talent was displayed, it was decided, by the President of the debate, in the negative, which was a righteous decision.

I discovered in this debate, much warmth displayed, too much zeal for mastery, too much of that enthusiasm that characterizes a lawyer at the bar, who is determined to defend his cause, right or wrong. I therefore availed myself of this favorable opportunity to drop a few words upon this subject, by way of advice, that they might improve their minds and cultivate their powers of intellect in a proper manner, that they might not incur the displeasure of heaven; that they should handle sacred things very sacredly, and with due deference to the opinions of others, and with an eye single to the glory of God.

Thursday, 19.—Went, in company with Dr. Williams and my scribe, to see how the workmen prospered in finishing the House of the Lord. The masons in the inside had commenced putting on the finishing coat of plaster. On my return, I met Lloyd and Lorenzo Lewis, and conversed with them upon the subject of their being disaffected. I found that they were not so, as touching the faith of the Church, but were displeased with some of the members. I returned home and spent the day in translating the Egyptian records. A warm and pleasant day.

Translating the Egyptian Records.

Friday, 20.—At home in the morning. Weather warm and rainy. We spent the day in translating, and made rapid progress.

In the evening, President Cowdery returned from New York, bringing with him a quantity of Hebrew books, for the benefit of the school. He presented me with a Hebrew Bible, Lexicon, and Grammar, also a Greek Lexicon, and Webster's English Dictionary. President Cowdery had a prosperous journey, according to the prayers of the Saints in Kirtland.

Return of Oliver Cowdery from New York.

Saturday, 21.—Spent the day at home, in examining my books, and studying the Hebrew alphabet.

Arrangement for Studying Hebrew.

At evening, met with our Hebrew class, to make some arrangements about a teacher. It was decided, by the voice of the school, to send to New York, for a Jew to teach us the language, if we could get released from the engagements we had made with Dr. Piexotto to teach us, having ascertained that he was not qualified to give us the knowledge we wished to acquire of the Hebrew.

Sunday, 22.—Went to meeting at the usual hour. Simeon Carter preached from the 7th of Matthew. President Rigdon's brother-in-law and other relatives were at meeting.

In the afternoon the meeting was held in the school-house.

In the evening, a Council of High Priests and Elders was held in the presence of the members of the Church, when Mr. Andrew Jackson Squires, who had been an ordained Elder in the Church, and for a time had preached the Gospel successfully, but after a while sent his license to President Smith, in a letter, came before the Council, and confessed that he had been in temptation, and fallen into error, so much as to join the Methodists; yet said he had no faith in their doctrine. He desired to return to the fellowship of the Church, asked forgiveness of the brethren, and restoration of his license.

Case of Andrew Jackson Squires.

I spoke of the impropriety of turning away from the truth, and going after a people so destitute of the spirit of righteousness as the Methodists.

President Rigdon showed the folly of fellowshiping any doctrine or spirit aside from that of Christ.

Mr. Squires arose and said he felt firm in the determination of doing the will of God in all things, or as far as in him lies the power; was sorry for his faults, and, by the grace of God, would forsake them in future.

Council and Church voted to restore him to fellowship, and the office of Elder also, and that the clerk give him a license.

Monday, 23.—Several brethren called to converse with me, and see the records. Received a letter from Jared

Carter. Spent the day in conversation, and in studying the Hebrew. A stormy day.

Tuesday, 24.—At home. Spent the forenoon instructing those that called to inquire concerning the things of God in the last days.

In the afternoon we translated some of the Egyptian records.

I had an invitation to attend a wedding at Brother Hyrum Smith's in the evening; also to solemnize the matrimonial ceremony between Newel Knight and Lydia Goldthwaite. My wife accompanied me. On our arrival a considerable company had collected. The bridegroom and bride came in, and took their seats, which gave me to understand that they were ready. After prayers, I requested them to rise, and join hands. I then remarked that marriage was an institution of heaven, instituted in the garden of Eden; that it was necessary it should be solemnized by the authority of the everlasting Priesthood. The ceremony was original with me, and in substance as follows—You covenant to be each other's companions through life, and discharge the duties of husband and wife in every respect; to which they assented. I then pronounced them husband and wife in the name of God, and also pronounced upon them the blessings that the Lord conferred upon Adam and Eve in the garden of Eden, that is, to multiply and replenish the earth, with the addition of long life and prosperity. Dismissed them and returned home. Freezing cold, some snow on the ground.

The Marriage of Newel Knight.

Wednesday, 25.—Spent the day in translating. Harvey Redfield and Jesse Hithcock arrived from Missouri. The latter says that he has no doubt but a dose of poison was administered to him, in a bowl of milk, but God delivered him.

Translating the Egyptian Records.

Thursday, 26.—Spent the day in translating Egyptian characters from the papyrus, though severely afflicted with a cold. Robert Rathbone and George Morey arrived from Zion.

Friday, 27.—Much afflicted with my cold, yet I am determined to overcome in the name of the Lord Jesus Christ. Spent the day at home, reading Hebrew. Brother Parrish, my scribe, being afflicted with a cold, asked me to lay my hands on him in the name of the Lord. I did so, and in return I asked him to lay his hands on me. We were both relieved.

Saturday, 28.—Spent the morning in comparing our Journal. Elder Josiah Clark, from the state of Kentucky, called on me. Considerably recovered from my cold. Cold and stormy, snow falling, and winter seems fast to be closing in, all nature shrinks before the chilling blasts of rigid winter. Elder Clark, above mentioned, whose residence is about three miles from Cincinnati, was bitten by a mad dog some three or four years since; has doctored much, and received some benefit, but is much afflicted notwithstanding He came here that he might be benefitted by the prayers of the Church. Accordingly we prayed for him and laid hands on him in the name of the Lord Jesus Christ, and anointed him with oil, and rebuked his afflictions, praying our heavenly Father to hear and answer our prayers, according to our faith. Cold and snowy.

The case of Josiah Clark.

Sunday, 29.—Went to meeting at the usual hour. Elder Morley preached; and in the afternoon, Bishop Partridge. These discourses were well adapted to the times in which we live, and the circumstances under which we are placed. Their words were words of wisdom, like apples of gold in pictures of silver, spoken in the simple accents of a child, yet sublime as the voice of an angel. The Saints appeared to be much pleased with the beautiful discourses of these two fathers in Israel. After these services closed, three of the Zion brethren came forward and received their blessings, and Solon Foster was ordained an Elder. The Lord's Supper

Preaching of Morley and Partridge.

was administered. Spent the evening at home. Snow fell about one foot deep. Very cold.

Monday, *30*.—The snow continues to fall—an uncommon storm for this country, and this season of the year. Spent the day in reviewing and copying the letter I dictated on the 16th, concerning the gathering, for the *Messenger and Advocate*. Henry Capron, an old acquaintance from Manchester, New York, called on me. I showed him the Egyptian records.

CHAPTER XXIV.

MISCELLANEOUS LABORS OF THE PROPHET IN KIRTLAND.

December 1.—At home. Spent the day in writing for the *Messenger and Advocate.* Fine sleighing, and the snow yet falling.

Insolent Treatment of the Prophet.

Wednesday, 2.—A fine morning. I started to ride to Painesville with my family and scribe. When we were passing through Mentor Street, we overtook a team, with two men in the sleigh; I politely asked them to let me pass. They granted my request, and as we passed them they bawled out, "Do you get any revelations lately?" with an addition of blackguard language that I did not understand. This is a fair sample of the character of Mentor Street inhabitants, who are ready to abuse and scandalize men who never laid a straw in their way; and, in fact, those whose faces they never saw, and [whom they] cannot bring an accusation against, either of a temporal or spiritual nature, except their firm belief in the fullness of the Gospel. I was led to marvel at the longsuffering and condescension of our heavenly Father in permitting these ungodly wretches to possess this goodly land, which is indeed as beautifully situated, and its soil is as fertile, as any in this region of country, and its inhabitants are wealthy even blessed above measure in temporal things; and fain would God bless them with spiritual blessings, even eternal life, were it not for their evil hearts of unbelief. And we are led to mingle our prayers with those of the Saints that have suffered the like treatment before us, whose souls are under the altar, crying to the Lord for vengeance upon those that dwell upon the earth. And we rejoice that the time is at hand, when the wicked who will not repent will be swept from the earth as with a besom of destruction, and the earth become an inheritance of the poor and the meek.

When we arrived at Painesville, we called at Sister Harriet Howe's, and left my wife and family to visit her, while we rode into town to do some business. Called and visited H. Kingsbury. Dined with Sister Howe and returned home. Had a fine ride—sleighing good, weather pleasant.

Thursday, 3.—At home. Wrote a letter to David Dort, Rochester, Michigan; another to Almira Schoby, Liberty, Clay County, Missouri.

At evening, visited with my wife at Thomas Carrico's.

Marriage of Warren Parrish.

A respectable company awaited our arrival. After singing and prayer I delivered an address on matrimony, and joined in marriage Warren Parrish and Martha H. Raymond. Closed by singing and prayer. After refreshments, returned home, having spent the evening very agreeably.

Friday, 4.—In company with Vinson Knight, drew

Financial Transactions.

three hundred and fifty dollars out of Painesville Bank, on three months' credit, for which we gave the names of Frederick G. Williams & Co., Newel K. Whitney, John Johnson and Vinson Knight. Settled with Brother Hyrum Smith and Vinson Knight, and paid Knight two hundred and forty-five dollars; also have it in my power to pay J. Lewis, for which blessing I feel heartily thankful to my heavenly Father, and ask Him, in the name of Jesus Christ, to enable us to extricate ourselves from all embarrassments whatever, that we may not be brought into disrepute, that our enemies may not have any power over us. Spent the day at home, a part of the day studying Hebrew. Warm, with some rain, snow fast melting.

This evening a Mr. John Hollister, of Portage County, Ohio, called to see me on the subject of religion, and I spent the evening conversing with him. He tarried over night with me, and acknowledged in the morning that, although he had thought he knew something about religion, he was now sensible that he knew but little; which was the greatest trait of wisdom I could discover in him.

Conversation on Religion.

Saturday, 5.—Weather cold and freezing, with a moderate fall of snow. In the forenoon studying Hebrew with Dr. Frederick G. Williams and President Cowdery. I am laboring under some indisposition of health. Slept awhile, and arose feeling tolerably well, through the mercy of God. I received a letter from Reuben McBride, Vilanovia, New York; also another from Parley P. Pratt's mother-in-law, Herkimer County, New York, of no consequence as to what it contained, but it cost me twenty-five cents for postage. I mention this, as it is a common occurrence, and I am subjected to a great deal of expense by those whom I know nothing about, only that they are destitute of good manners; for if people wish to be benefitted with information from me, common respect and good breeding would dictate them to pay the postage on their letters.

A Matter of Postage.

I addressed the following letter to the editor of the *Messenger and Advocate:*

DEAR BROTHER—I wish to inform my friends and all others abroad, that whenever they wish to address me through the postoffice, they will be kind enough to pay the postage on the same. My friends will excuse me in this matter, as I am willing to pay postage on letters to hear from them; but I am unwilling to pay for insults and menaces; consequently must refuse all unpaid.

Yours in the Gospel,

JOSEPH SMITH, JUN.

Sunday, 6.—Went to meeting at the usual hour. Gideon Carter preached a splendid discourse. In the afternoon we had an exhortation and communion service. Some two or three weeks since, Brother Draper insisted on leaving the meeting before communion, and could not be prevailed on to tarry a few moments, although we invited him to do so, as we did not wish to have the house thrown into confusion. He observed that he "would not," if we excluded him from the Church. Today he attempted to make a confession, but it was not satisfactory to me, and I was constrained by the Spirit to deliver him over to the buffetings of Satan, until he should humble himself and repent of his sins, and make satisfactory confession before the Church.

An Unruly Member.

Monday, 7.—Received a letter from Milton Holmes, and was much rejoiced to hear from him, and of his success in proclaiming the Gospel. Wrote him a letter requesting him to return to Kirtland. Spent the day in reading Hebrew. Mr. John Hollister called to take the parting hand with me, and remarked that he had been in darkness all his days, but had now found the truth and intended to obey it.

This evening a number of brethren called to see the records, which I exhibited and explained. Fine sleighing.

Tuesday, 8.—At home. Read Hebrew in company with Dr. Williams, President Cowdery, Brother Hyrum Smith and Orson Pratt. In the evening, preached at the school house as usual, had great liberty in speaking, congregation attentive. After the services closed, the brethren proposed to haul wood for me.

Kindness of the Saints to the Prophet.

Wednesday, 9.—At home. Wind south, strong, and chilly. Elder Packard came in this morning, and made me a present of twelve dollars, which he held in a note against me. May God bless him for his liberality. Also, James Aldrich sent me my note by the hand of Jesse Hitchcock, on which there was twelve dollars due. And may God bless him for his kindness to me. Also the brethren whose names are written below opened their hearts in great liberality, and paid me, at the committee's store, the sums set opposite their respective names, to wit:

John Corrill . .	$5 00	Salmon Gee . . .	$0 75
Levi Jackman . .	3 25	Harvey Stanley . .	1 00
Elijah Fordham .	5 25	Zemira Draper . .	1 00
James Emmet . .	5 00	Emer Harris . . .	1 00
Newel Knight . .	2 00	Truman Jackson . .	1 00
Truman O. Angell	3 00	Samuel Rolf . . .	1 25
William Felshaw .	3 00	Elias Higbee . . .	1 00
Albert Brown . .	3 00	George Morey . . .	1 00
William F. Cahoon	1 00	John Rudd	0 50
Harlow Crosier .	0 50	Alex. Badlam . . .	1 00
			$40 50
With the addition of the two notes above . . .			24 00
		Total . .	$64 50

My heart swells with gratitude inexpressible when I realize the great condescension of my heavenly Father, in opening the hearts of these my beloved brethren to administer so liberally to my wants. And I ask God, in the name of Jesus Christ, to multiply blessings without number upon their heads, and bless me with much wisdom and understanding, and dispose of me to the best advantage for my brethren, and the advancement of His cause and kingdom. And whether my days are many or few, whether in life or in death, I say in my heart, O Lord, let me enjoy the society of such brethren.

Gratitude of the Prophet.

Elder Tanner brought me half of a fatted hog for the benefit of my family. A few days since, Elder Shadrach Roundy brought me a quarter of beef. And may all the blessings named above be poured upon their heads, for their kindness towards me.

Thursday, 10.—This morning a number of brethren called to see the records, [Egyptian] which I exhibited to their satisfaction. This day my brethren met according to previous arrangement to chop and haul wood for me. Beautiful morning, indeed, and fine sleighing.

Healing of Angeline Works.

This afternoon I was called, in company with President David Whitmer, to visit Angeline Works. We found her very sick, and so much deranged that she did not recognize her friends and intimate acquaintances. We prayed for her and laid hands on her in the name of Jesus Christ, and commanded her in His name to receive her senses, which were immediately restored. We also prayed that she might be restored to health; and she said she was better.

Fire in the Kirtland Board Kiln.

The board kiln had taken fire, and on our return we found the brethren engaged in extinguishing the flames. After laboring about one hour against this destructive element, we succeeded in conquering it, and probably saved about one-fourth part of the lumber. I do not know the amount of loss the committee have sustained, but it must have been considerable, as there was much lumber in the kiln. There were about two hundred brethren engaged on this occasion; they displayed much activity and interest, and deserve much credit. The brethren have also been very industrious, and supplied me with my winter's wood, for which I am sincerely grateful to each and every one of them, and shall remember, with warm emotions, this expression of their goodness to me. And in the name of Jesus Christ I invoke the rich benediction of heaven to rest upon them and their families; and I ask my heavenly Father to preserve their health, and that of their wives and children, that they may have strength of body to perform their labors in their several occupations in life, and the use and activity of their limbs, also powers of intellect and understanding hearts, that they may treasure up wisdom, understanding and intelligence above measure, and be preserved from plagues, pestilence, and famine, and from the power of the adversary, and the hands of evil-designing men, and have power over all their enemies, and the way be prepared for them that they may journey to the land of Zion, and be established on their inheritances, to enjoy undisturbed peace and happiness forever, and ultimately be crowned with everlasting life in the celestial Kingdom of God, which blessing I ask in the name of Jesus of Nazareth. Amen.

The Prophet's Blessing on Leonard Rich.

I would remember Elder Leonard Rich, who was the first one that proposed to the brethren to assist me in obtaining wood for the use of my family, for which I pray my heavenly Father to bless him with all the blessings named above. And I shall ever remember him with much gratitude, for this testimony of benevolence and respect, and thank the great I AM for putting into his heart to do me this kindness. And I say in my heart, I will trust in Thy goodness and mercy forever, O Lord, for Thy wisdom and benevolence, are unbounded, and beyond the comprehension of men, and all of Thy ways cannot be found out.

The petitions of the people from all parts of the United States to the Governor of Missouri to restore the Saints to their possessions, were arranged and mailed at Kirtland, this day, for Missouri. The petitions were numerous, and the package large, the postage thereon being five dollars. It was directed to the governor.

Friday, 11.—A fire broke out in a shoemaker's shop, owned by Orson Johnson, but the flames were soon extinguished by the active exertions of the brethren. A pleasant morning. Spent the day in reading and instructing those who called for advice.

The Prophet Reproves a Young Lady.

Saturday, 12.—Spent the forenoon in reading. About twelve o'clock a number of young persons called to see the Egyptian records. My scribe exhibited them. One of the young ladies who had been examining them, was asked if they had the appearance of antiquity. She observed, with an air of contempt, that they had not. On hearing this, I was surprised at the ignorance she displayed, and I observed to her, that she was an anomaly in creation, for all the wise and learned that had examined them, without hesitation pronounced them ancient. I further remarked, that it was downright wickedness, ignorance, bigotry and superstition had caused her to make the remark; and that I would put it on record. And I have done so, because it is a fair sample of the prevailing spirit of the times, showing that the victims of priestcraft and superstition would not believe though one should rise from the dead.

Debate at William Smith's.

In the evening attended a debate at Brother William Smith's, on the following question—Was it necessary for God to reveal Himself to mankind in order for their happiness? I was on the affirmative, and the last to speak on that side of the question; but, while listening with interest to the ingenuity displayed on both sides, I was called away to visit Sister Angeline Works, who was supposed to be dangerously sick. Elder John Corrill and myself went and prayed for her and laid hands on her in the name of Jesus Christ; and leaving her apparently better, returned home.

Sunday, 13.—At the usual hour, ten a. m., attended meeting at the school house on the flats. Elder Jesse Hickcock preached a very feeling discourse.

Experiences of Elders Whitmer and Williams.

In the afternoon, Elder Peter Whitmer related his experience; after which, President Frederick G. Williams related his also. They both spoke of many things connected with the rise and progress of this Church, which were interesting. After this, the Sacrament of the Lord's Supper was administered under the superintendence of President David Whitmer, after which, I made some remarks respecting prayer meetings, and our meeting was closed by invoking the blessing of heaven. I returned home and ordered my horse, and myself and scribe rode to Mr. E. Jenning's, where I joined Ebenezer Robinson and Angeline Works in matrimony, according to previous engagements. Miss Works had so far recovered from her illness as to be able to sit in her easy chair while I pronounced the marriage ceremony.

Marriages in Kirtland.

We then rode to Mr. McWhithy's a distance of about three miles from town, where I had been solicited to attend another marriage. We found a large and respectable number of friends present. I had been requested to make some preliminary remarks on the subject of matrimony, touching the design of the Almighty in its institution, also the duties of husbands and wives towards each other. And after opening our interview with singing and prayer, I delivered a lecture of about forty minutes, in which all seemed interested, except one or two individuals, who manifested a spirit of groveling contempt, which I was constrained to reprove and rebuke sharply. After I had closed my remarks, I sealed the matrimonial engagement between Mr. E. Webb and Miss E. A. McWhithy, in the name of God, and pronouncing the blessings of heaven upon their heads, closed by returning thanks. A sumptuous feast was then spread, and the company invited to seat themselves at the table by pairs, male and female, commencing with the eldest. The festival was conducted with propriety and decorum, and cheerfulness prevailed. After spending the evening agreeable until nine o'clock, we pronounced a blessing upon the company and returned home. This day the board kiln took fire again.

Monday, 14.—A number of brethren from New York called to visit me and see the Egyptian records. Also Elder Harris returned from Palmyra, New York, and Brother Francis Eaton of the same place, and Sister Harriet Howe called to visit us.

After dinner, attended the funeral of Sylvester Smith's youngest child. And in the evening met, according to previous notice, to make arrangements to guard against fire, and organize a company for this purpose; also counseled on other affairs of a temporal nature.

Precautions Against Incendiaries.

Samuel Barnum came to my house, much afflicted with a swollen arm. As he had not sufficient faith to be healed, my wife applied a poultice of herbs, and he tarried over night. I spent the day at home reading Hebrew, and visiting with friends who called to see me.

CHAPTER XXV.

THE TROUBLES OF ORSON HYDE AND WILLIAM SMITH—THE BOOK OF ABRAHAM—CLOSE OF THE YEAR.

Tuesday, December 15.—At home, and, as usual, was blessed with much company. Samuel Barnum is very sick, his arm much inflamed.

This afternoon, Elder Orson Hyde handed me a letter, the purport of which was, that he was dissatisfied with the committee* in their dealings with him, in temporal affairs, that is, that they did not deal as liberal with him as they did with Elder William Smith; also requested me to reconcile the revelation given to the Twelve since their return from the east.† That unless these things and others named in the letter, could be reconciled to his mind, his honor would not stand united with them. This I believe is the amount of the contents of the letter, although much was written.

Complaints of Orson Hyde.

My feelings on this occasion were much lacerated, knowing that I had dealt in righteousness with him in all things, and endeavored to promote his happiness and well being as much as lay in my power. And I feel that

* This committee was the one having in charge the building of the Kirtland Temple. They were also managers of a store in Kirtland, through which much of the business connected with the construction of the temple was accomplished. The committee consisted of Hyrum Smith, Reynolds Cahoon and Jared Carter.

† That is, Elder Hyde desired that the Prophet would reconcile the conduct of the above named committee with some of the revelations which in Elder Hyde's opinion taught that the Twelve were to be equal in both temporal and spiritual things. See Elder Hyde's letter, page 335.

these reflections are ungrateful, and founded in jealousy, and that the adversary is striving with all his subtle devices and influence to destroy him, by causing a division among the Twelve whom God has chosen to open the Gospel kingdom to all nations. But I pray Thee, my heavenly Father, in the name of Jesus of Nazareth, that he may be delivered from the power of the destroyer, that his faith fail not in this hour of temptation, and prepare him, and all the Elders, to receive an endowment in Thy house, even according to Thine own order from time to time, as Thou seest them worthy to be called into Thy solemn assembly.

Wednesday, 16.—Weather extremely cold. I went to the Council room to lay before the Presidency, the letter that I received yesterday from Elder Orson Hyde; but when I arrived, I found that I had lost said letter, but I laid the substance of it, as far as I could recollect it, before the Council; but they had not time to attend to it on account of other business; accordingly adjourned until Monday evening, the 20th inst. Returned home.

Elders William E. M'Lellin, Brigham Young, and Jared Carter, called and paid me a visit with which I was much gratified. I exhibited and explained the Egyptian records to them, and explained many things concerning the dealing of God with the ancients, and the formation of the planetary system.

Visit of Elders M'Lellin, Young, and Carter With the Prophet.

This evening, according to adjournment, I went to Brother William Smith's to take part in the debate that was commenced Saturday evening last. After the debate was concluded, and a decision given in favor of the affirmative of the question, some altercation took place upon the propriety of continuing the school [debate] fearing that it would not result in good. Brother William Smith opposed these measures, and insisted on having another question proposed, and at length became much enraged,

The Prophet Assaulted by Wm. Smith.

particularly at me, and used violence upon my person, and also upon Elder Jared Carter, and some others, for which I am grieved beyond measure, and can only pray God to forgive him, inasmuch as he repents of his wickedness, and humbles himself before the Lord.

Thursday, 17.—At home, quite unwell. Elder Orson Hyde called to see me, and presented me with a copy of the letter he handed me on Tuesday last, which I had lost. The following is the copy—

Orson Hyde's Letter of Complaint.

DECEMBER 15th, 1835.

President Smith: Sir—You may esteem it a novel circumstance to receive a written communication from me at this time. My reasons for writing are the following—I have some things which I wish to communicate to you, and feeling a greater liberty to do it by writing alone by myself, I take this method, and it is generally the case you are thronged with business, and not convenient to spend much time in conversing upon subjects of the following nature. Therefore let these excuses palliate the novelty of the circumstance, and patiently hear my recital.

After the committee received their stock of fall and winter goods, I went to Elder Cahoon and told him I was destitute of a cloak, and wanted him to trust me, until spring, for materials to make one. He told me that he would trust me until January, but must then have his pay, as the payment for the goods became due at that time. I told him I knew not from whence the money would come, and I could not promise it so soon. But, in a few weeks after, I unexpectedly obtained the money to buy a cloak, and applied immediately to Elder Cahoon for one, and told him that I had the cash to pay for it; but he said the materials for cloaks were all sold, and that he could not accommodate me; and I will here venture a guess, that he has not realized the cash for one cloak pattern.

A few weeks after this, I called on Elder Cahoon again, and told him that I wanted cloth for some shirts, to the amount of four or five dollars. I told him that I would pay him in the spring, and sooner if I could. He let me have it. Not long after, my school was established, and some of the hands who labored on the house, attended, and wished to pay me at the committee's store for their tuition. I called at the store to see if any negotiation could be made, and they take me off where I owed them; but no such negotiation could be made. These, with some other circumstances of a like character, called forth the following reflection:

In the first place, I gave the committee $275.00 in cash, besides some more, and during the last season, have traveled through the Middle and Eastern states to support and uphold the store; and in so doing, have reduced myself to nothing, in a pecuniary point. Under these circumstances, this establishment refused to render me that accommodation which a worldling's establishment gladly would have done; and one, too, which never received a donation from me, or in whose favor I never raised my voice, or exerted my influence. But after all this, thought I, it may be right, and I will be still—until, not long since, I ascertained that Elder William Smith could go to the store and get whatever he pleased, and no one to say, why do ye so? until his account has amounted to seven hundred dollars, or thereabouts, and that he was a silent partner in the concern, but not acknowledged as such, fearing that his creditors would make a haul upon the store.

While we [the Twelve] were abroad this last season, we strained every nerve to obtain a little something for our families, and regularly divided the monies equally for aught I know, not knowing that William had such a fountain at home, from whence he drew his support. I then called to mind the Revelation in which myself, M'Lellin, and Patten were chastened, and also the quotation in that revelation of the parable of the twelve sons, as if the original meaning referred directly to the Twelve Apostles of the Church of Latter-day Saints. I would now ask if each one of the Twelve has not an equal right to the same accommodations from that store, provided they are alike faithful? If not, with such a combination, mine honor be not thou united. If each one has the same right, take the baskets from off our noses, and put one to William's nose; or if this cannot be done, reconcile the parable of the twelve sons, with the superior privileges that William has. Pardon me if I speak in parables or parody.

A certain shepherd had twelve sons, and he sent them out one day to go and gather his flock which was scattered upon the mountains and in the valleys afar off. They were all obedient to their father's mandate, and at evening they returned with the flock, and one son received wool enough to make him warm and comfortable, and also received of the flesh and milk of the flock, the other eleven received not so much as one kid to make merry with their friends.

These facts, with some others, have disqualified my mind for studying the Hebrew language, at present; and believing as I do, that I must sink or swim, or in other words, take care of myself, I have thought that I should take the most efficient means in my power to get out of debt; and to this end I proposed taking the school; but if I am not thought competent to take the charge of it, or worthy to be placed in that station, I must devise some other means to help myself, although having been ordained to that office under your own hand, with a promise that it should not be taken from me.

The conclusion of the whole matter is: I am willing to continue and do all I can, provided we can share equal benefits, one with the other, and upon no other principle whatever. If one has his support from the "public crib," let them all have it; but if one is pinched, I am willing to be, provided we are all alike. If the principle of impartiality and equity can be observed by all, I think that I will not peep again. If I am damned, it will be for doing what I think is right. There have been two applications made to me to go into business since I talked of taking the school, but it is in the world, and I had rather remain in Kirtland, if I can consistently. All I ask is right.

I am, sir, with respect,

Your obedient servant,

ORSON HYDE.

To President J. Smith, Jun.,
Kirtland, &c.

Reconciliation of Orson Hyde with the Prophet.

Elder Orson Hyde read the foregoing copy himself, and I explained the objections he had set forth in it, and satisfied his mind upon every point, perfectly. And he observed, after I got through, that he was more than satisfied, and would attend the Hebrew school, and took the parting hand with me with every expression of friendship that a gentleman and a Christian could manifest; which I felt to reciprocate with cheerfulness, and entertain the best of feeling for him, and most cheerfully forgive him the ingratitude which was manifested in his letter, knowing that it was for want of correct information, that his mind was disturbed, as far as his reflections related to me; but on the part of the committee he was not treated right in all things; however, all things are settled amicably, and no hardness exists between us and them.

I told Elder Cahoon, of the Temple committee, that we must sustain the Twelve, and not let them go down; if we do not, they must go down, for the burden is on them and is coming on them heavier and heavier. If the Twele go down, we must go down, but we must sustain them.

Charge to Elder Cahoon to Sustain the Twelve.

My father and mother called this evening to see me upon the subject of the difficulty that occurred at their house, on Wednesday evening, between me and my brother William. They were sorely afflicted in mind on account of that occurrence. I conversed with them and convinced them that I was not to blame in taking the course I did, but had acted in righteousness in all things on that occasion. I invited them to come and live with me. They consented to do so as soon as it was practicable.

Sorrow of Father and Mother Smith over William Smith's Difficulty.

Friday, *18.*—Brother Hyrum Smith called to see me, and read a letter that he received from William, in which he asked forgiveness for the abuse he offered to him (Hyrum) at the debate. He tarried most of the forenoon, and conversed freely with me upon the subject of the difficulty existing between me and Brother William. He said that he was perfectly satisfied with the course I had taken in rebuking William in his wickedness, but he is wounded to the very soul, because of the conduct of William; and although he experiences the tender feelings of a brother towards him, yet he can but look upon his conduct as an abomination in the sight of God. And I could pray in my heart that all my brethren were like unto my beloved brother Hyrum, who possesses the mildness of a lamb, and the integrity of a Job, and in short, the meekness and humility of Christ; and I love him with that love that is stronger than death, for I never had occasion to rebuke him, nor he me, which he declared when he left me to-day.

The Sympathy Between the Prophet and his Brother Hyrum.

This day received the following letter from Brother William Smith:

William Smith's Letter to the Prophet.

BROTHER JOSEPH—Though I do not know but I have forfeited all right and title to the word brother, in consequence of what I have done, (for I consider, myself, that I am unworthy to be called one,) after coming to myself, and considering what I have done, I feel as though it was a duty to make a humble confession to you, for what I have done, or what took place the other evening; but leave this part of the subject at present. I was called to an account, by the Twelve, yesterday, for my conduct; or they desired to know my mind or determination, and what I was going to do. I told them that on reflection upon the many difficulties that I had had with the Church, and the much disgrace I had brought upon myself in consequence of these things, and also that my health would not permit me to go to school to make any preparations for the endowment, and that my health was such that I was not able to travel, that it would be better for them to appoint one, in the office, that would be better able to fill it, and by doing this they would throw me into the hands of the Church, and leave me where I was before I was chosen, then I would not be in a situation to bring so much disgrace upon the cause, when I fall into temptation; and perhaps, by this I might obtain salvation. You know my passions and the danger of falling from so high a station; and thus by withdrawing from the office of the Apostleship, while there is salvation for me, and remaining a member of the Church—I feel afraid, if I don't do this, it will be worse for me some other day.

And again, my health is poor, and I am not able to travel and it is necessary the office should not be idle. And again, I say, you know my passions, and I am afraid it will be the worse for me by and by. Do so, if the Lord will have mercy on me, and let me remain as a member in the Church, and then I can travel and preach when I am able. Do not think I am your enemy for what I have done. Perhaps you may say or ask why I have not remembered the good that you have done to me. When I reflect upon the injury I have done you, I must confess that I do not know what I have been about. I feel sorry for what I have done, and humbly ask your forgiveness. I have not confidence as yet to come and see you, for I feel ashamed of what I have done; and as I feel now, I feel as though all the confessions that I could make, verbally or by writing, would not be sufficient to atone for the transgression. Be this as it may, I am willing to make all the restitution you shall require. If I can stay in the Church as a member, I will try to make all the satisfaction possible.

Yours with respect,

WILLIAM SMITH.

P.S.—Do not cast me off for what I have done, but strive to save me in the Church as a member. I do repent of what I have done to you and ask your forgiveness. I consider the transgression, the other evening, of no small magnitude; but it is done, and I cannot help it now. I know, Brother Joseph, you are always willing to forgive; but I sometimes think, when I reflect upon the many injuries I have done you, I feel as though confession was hardly sufficient. But have mercy on me this once, and I will try to do so no more.

The Twelve called a Council yesterday, and sent over after me, and I went over. This Council, remember, was called together by themselves and not by me. W. S.

To the foregoing I gave the following answer the same day.

Letter of the Prophet to his Brother William.

BROTHER WILLIAM—Having received your letter, I now proceed to answer it, and shall first proceed to give a brief narration of my feelings and motives since the night I first came to the knowledge of your having a debating school, which was at the time I happened in with Bishop Whitney, his father and mother, &c.; and from that time I took an interest in it, and was delighted with it, and formed a determination to attend the school, for the purpose of obtaining information, and with the idea of imparting the same, through the assistance of the Spirit of the Lord, if by any means I should have faith to do so. And with this intent, I went to the school on last Wednesday night, not with the idea of breaking up the school, neither did it enter into my heart that there was any wrangling or jealousies in your heart against me. Notwithstanding, previous to my leaving home, there were feelings of solemnity rolling across my breast, which were unaccountable to me; and also these feelings continued by spells to depress my spirits, and seemed to manifest that all was not right, even after the school commenced, and during the debate, yet I strove to believe that all would work together for good. I was pleased with the power of the arguments that were used, and did not feel to cast any reflections upon any one that had spoken; but I felt it was the duty of old men that sat as Presidents, to be as grave, at least, as young men, and that it was our duty to smile (not) at solid arguments and sound reasonings; and be impressed with solemnity, which should be manifested in our countenances, when folly which militates against truth and righteousness, rears its head.

Therefore, in the spirit of my calling, and in view of the authority of the Priesthood that has been conferred upon me, it would be my duty to reprove whatever I esteemed to be wrong, fondly hoping in my heart, that all parties would consider it right, and therefore humble themselves, that Satan might not take the advantage of us, and hinder the progress of our school.

Now, Brother William, I want you should bear with me, notwithstanding my plainness. I would say to you that my feelings were grieved at the interruption you made upon Elder M'Lellin. I thought you should consider your relationship with him in your Apostleship, and not manifest any division of sentiment between you and him, for a surrounding multitude to take advantage of you; therefore, by way of entreaty, on account of the anxiety I had for your influence and welfare, I said unto you: Do not have any feelings; or something to that amount. Why I am thus particular, is, that if you have misconstrued my feelings towards you, you may be corrected. But to proceed. After the school was closed, Brother Hyrum requested the privilege of speaking; you objected; however, you said if he would not abuse the school, he might speak, and that you would not allow any man to abuse the school in your house. Now, you had no reason to suspect that Hyrum would abuse the school; therefore, my feelings were mortified at these unnecessary observations. I undertook to reason with you, but you manifested an inconsiderate and stubborn spirit. I then despaired of benefitting you, on account of the spirit you manifested, which drew from me the expression that you were as ugly as the devil. Father then commanded silence, and I formed a determination to obey his mandate, and was about to leave the house, with the impression that you was under the influence of a wicked spirit: you replied that you would say what you pleased in your own house. Father said: Say what you please, but let the rest hold their tongues. Then a reflection rushed through my mind, of the anxiety and care I have had for you and your family, in doing what I did in finishing your house, and providing flour for your family, &c.; and also, father had possession* in the house as well as yourself; and when at any time have I transgressed the commandments of my father, or sold my birthright, that I should not have the privilege of speaking in my father's house, or in other words, in my father's family, or in your house, (for so we will call it, and so it shall be,) that I should not have the privilege of reproving a younger brother? Therefore I said, I will speak, for I built the house, and it is as much mine as yours; or something to that effect. I should have said, that I helped to finish the house. I said it merely to show that it could not be the right spirit that would rise up for trifling matters, and undertake to put me to silence. I saw that your indignation was kindled against me, and you made towards me. I was not then to be moved, and I thought to pull off my loose coat, lest it should tangle me, and you be left to hurt me, but not with the intention of hurting you. But you were too quick for me, and having once fallen into the hands of a mob, and been wounded in my side, and now into the hands

* That is, Father Smith had assisted in building the house, and was also at that time making his home with William.

of a brother, my side gave way. And after having been rescued from your grasp, I left your house with feelings indescribable—the scenery had changed, and all those expectations that I had cherished, when going to your house, and brotherly kindness, charity, forbearance, and natural affection, that in duty bind us not to make each other offenders for a word. But alas! abuse, anger, malice, hatred, and rage, with a lame side, with marks of violence heaped upon me by a brother, were the reflections of my disappointment; and with these I returned home, not able to sit down or rise up without help, but, through the blessing of God, I am now better.

I received your letter and perused it with care. I have not entertained a feeling of malice against you. I am older than you and have endured more suffering, having been marred by mobs. The labors of my calling, a series of persecutions and injuries continually heaped upon me—all serve to debilitate my body; and it may be that I cannot boast of being stronger than you. If I could or could not, would this be an honor or dishonor to me? If I could boast, like David, of slaying a Goliah, who defied the armies of the living God; or, like Paul, of contending with Peter, face to face, with sound arguments, it might be an honor; but to mangle the flesh, or seek revenge upon one who never did you any wrong, cannot be a source of sweet reflection to you nor to me, neither to an honorable father and mother, brothers and sisters. And when we reflect with what care, and with what unremitting diligence our parents have striven to watch over us, and how many hours of sorrow and anxiety they have spent, over our cradles and bed-sides, in times of sickness, how careful we ought to be of their feelings in their old age! It cannot be a source of sweet reflection to us, to say or do anything that will bring their gray hairs down with sorrow to the grave.

In your letter you ask my forgiveness, which I readily grant. But it seems to me, that you still retain an idea that I have given you reasons to be angry or disaffected with me. Grant me the privilege of saying then, that however hasty and harsh I may have spoken at any time to you, it has been done for the express purpose of endeavoring to warn, exhort, admonish, and recue you from falling into difficulties and sorrows, which I foresaw you plunging into, by giving way to that wicked spirit, which you call your passions, which you should curb and break down, and put under your feet; which if you do not, you never can be saved, in my view, in the Kingdom of God. God requires the will of His creatures to be swallowed up in His will.

You desire to remain in the Church, but forsake your Apostleship. This is the stratagem of the evil one; when he has gained one advantage, he lays a plan for another. But by maintaining your Apostleship, in rising up and making one tremendous effort, you may overcome your passions and please God. And by forsaking your Apostleship, is not to be willing to make that sacrifice that God requires at your hands, and is to incur His displeasure; and without pleasing God, we do not think it will be any better for you. When a man falls one step, he must regain that step again, or fall another; he has still more to gain, or eventually all is lost.

I desire, Brother William, that you will humble yourself. I freely forgive you, and you know my unshaken and unchangeable disposition; I know in whom I trust; I stand upon the rock; the floods cannot, no, they shall not, overthrow me. You know the doctrine I teach is true, you know that God has blessed me. I brought salvation to my father's house, as an instrument in the hands of God when they were in a miserable situation. You know that it is my duty to admonish you, when you do wrong. This liberty I shall always take, and you shall have the same privilege. I take the liberty to admonish you, because of my birthright; and I grant you the privilege, because it is my duty to be humble, and receive rebuke and instruction from a brother, or a friend.

As it regards what course you shall pursue hereafter, I do not pretend to say; I leave you in the hands of God and His Church. Make your own decision; I will do you good, although you mar me, or slay me. By so doing, my garments shall be clear of your sins. And if at any time you should consider me to be an imposter, for heaven's sake leave me in the hands of God, and not think to take vengeance on me yourself. Tyranny, usurpation, and to take men's rights, ever has been and ever shall be banished from my heart. David sought not to kill Saul, although he was guilty of crimes that never entered my heart.

And now may God have mercy upon my father's house; may God take away enmity from between me and thee; and may all blessings be restored, and the past be forgotten forever. May humble repentance bring us both to Thee, O God, and to Thy power and protection, and a crown, to enjoy the society of father, mother, Alvin, Hyrum, Sophronia, Samuel, Catherine, Carlos, Lucy, the Saints, and all the sanctified in peace, forever, is the prayer of your brother,

JOSEPH SMITH, JUN.

To William Smith.

Saturday, 19.—At home. Sent the above letter to Brother William Smith. I have had many solemn feelings this day concerning my brother William, and have prayed in my heart fervently, that the Lord will not cast him off, but that he

Desire of the Prophet for William's Salvation.

may return to the God of Jacob, and magnify his Apostleship and calling. May this be his happy lot, for the Lord of glory's sake. Amen.

Sunday, 20.—At home all day. Took solid comfort with my family. Had many serious reflections. Brothers Palmer and Taylor called to see me. I showed them the sacred records to their joy and satisfaction. O! may God have mercy upon these men, and keep them in the way of everlasting life, in the name of Jesus. Amen.

Sundry Prayers of the Prophet for the Welfare of Various Brethren.

Monday, 21.—Spent this day at home, endeavoring to treasure up knowledge for the benefit of my calling. The day passed off very pleasantly. I thank the Lord for His blessings to my soul, His great mercy over my family in sparing our lives. O continue Thy care over me and mine, for Christ's sake.

Tuesday, 22.—At home. Continued my studies. O may God give me learning, even language; and endue me with qualifications to magnify His name while I live.

I also delivered an address to the Church, this evening. The Lord blessed my soul. My scribe is unwell. O may God heal him. And for his kindness to me, O my soul, be thou grateful to him, and bless him. And he shall be blessed of God for ever, for I believe him to be a faithful friend to me, therefore my soul delighteth in him. Amen.

Wednesday, 23.—In the forenoon, at home, studying the Greek language. And also waited upon the brethren who came in, and exhibited to them the papyrus. Afternoon, visited Brother Leonard Rich, with the relatives of Brother Oliver Cowdery. Had not a very agreeable visit, for I found them filled with prejudice against the work of the Lord, and their minds blinded with superstition and ignorance.

Thursday, 24.—The forenoon, at home. In the afternoon, I assisted the commissioner appointed by the [county] court, in surveying a road across my farm.

Friday, *25.*—Enjoyed myself at home with my family, all day, it being Christmas, the only time I have had this privilege so satisfactorily for a long period. Brother Jonathan Crosby called this evening.

The Prophet's Christmas at Home.

Saturday, *26.*—Commenced again studying the Hebrew language, in company with Brothers Parrish and Williams. In the meantime, Brother Lyman Sherman came in, and requested to have the word of the Lord through me; "for," said he, "I have been wrought upon to make known to you my feelings and desires, and was promised that I should have a revelation which should make known my duty."

The Prophet's Renewal of the Study of Hebrew.

Revelation given to Lyman Sherman, December 26, 1835.

Verily thus saith the Lord unto you, my servant Lyman, your sins are forgiven you, because you have obeyed my voice in coming up hither this morning to receive counsel of him whom I have appointed. Therefore, let your soul be at rest concerning your spiritual standing, and resist no more my voice; and arise up and be more careful henceforth, in observing your vows which you have made, and do make, and you shall be blessed with exceeding great blessings. Wait patiently until the solemn assembly shall be called of my servants, then you shall be remembered with the first of mine Elders, and receive right by ordination with the rest of mine Elders, whom I have chosen. Behold, this is the promise of the Father unto you if you continue faithful; and it shall be fulfilled upon you in that day that you shall have right to preach my Gospel wheresoever I shall send you, from henceforth from that time. Therefore, strengthen your brethren in all your conversation, in all your prayers, in all your exhortations, and in all your doings; and behold, and lo! I am with you to bless you, and deliver you forever. Amen.

Sunday, *27.*—At the usual hour, attending meeting at the school house. President Cowdery delivered a very able and interesting discourse.

Sunday Services.

In the afternoon, Brother Hyrum Smith and Bishop Partridge delivered each a short and interesting lecture, after which Sacrament was administered.

While chopping wood at my door, on the 25th instant,

two gentlemen called, and requested an interview with the heads of the Church, which I agreed to grant them this morning, but they did not come, and I consider they were trifling characters.

Trifling Visitors.

Monday, *28*.—Having previously preferred a charge against Almon W. Babbitt, for traducing my character, he was this morning called before the High Council, and I attended with my witnesses, and substantiated the charge against him; and he in part acknowledged his fault, but not satisfactorily to the Council; and after parleying with him a long time, and granting him every indulgence that righteousness required, the Council adjourned without obtaining a full confession from him.

Arraignment of Almon W. Babbitt.

This day the Council of the Seventy met to render an account of their travels and ministry, since they were ordained to that Apostleship. The meeting was interesting indeed, and my heart was made glad while listening to the relation of those that had been laboring in the vineyard of the Lord, with such marvelous success. And I pray God to bless them with an increase of faith and power, and keep them all, with the endurance of faith in the name of Jesus Christ to the end.

First Report of the Seventies.

Tuesday, *29*.—The following charges were preferred:

To the Honorable Presidency of the Church of Christ of Latter-day Saints, against Elder William Smith.

1st. Unchristianlike conduct in speaking disrespectfully of President Joseph Smith, Jun., and the revelations and commandments given through him.

2nd. For attempting to inflict personal violence on President Joseph Smith, Jun.

ORSON JOHNSON.

I remained at home until about ten o'clock. I then attended a blessing meeting at Oliver Olney's, in company with my wife, and father and mother, who had come to live with me. Also

Patriarchal Blessing Meeting.

my scribe went with us. A large company assembled, when Father Smith made some appropriate remarks. A hymn was sung and father opened the meeting by prayer. About fifteen persons then received patriarchal blessings under his hands. The services were concluded as they commenced. A table was crowned with the bounties of nature; and after invoking the benediction of heaven upon the rich repast, we fared sumptuously; and suffice it to say that we had a glorious meeting throughout, and I was much pleased with the harmony that existed among the brethren and sisters. We returned home, and at early candle-light I preached at the school house to a crowded congregation, who listened with attention about three hours. I had liberty in speaking. Some Presbyterians were present, as I afterwards learned; and I expect that some of my sayings sat like a garment that was well fitted, as I exposed their abominations in the language of the scriptures; and I pray God that it may be like a nail in a sure place, driven by the master of assemblies.

Hebrew Studies.

Wednesday, *30*.—Spent the day reading Hebrew at the council room, in company with my scribe, who is recovering his health, which gives me much satisfaction, for I delight in his company.

Questions of the Twelve Concerning Trial of William Smith.

Thursday, *31*.—At home. After attending to the duties of my family, retired to the council room to pursue my studies. The Council of the Twelve convened in the upper room, in the printing office, directly over the room where we were assembled in our studies. They sent for me, and the Presidency, or a part of them, to receive counsel from us on the subject of the council which is to be held on Saturday next.

In the afternoon I attended at the chapel to give directions concerning the upper rooms, and more especially the west room, which I intend occupying for a translating room, which will be prepared this week.

An Account of the Book of Abraham.

The public mind has been excited of late, by reports which have been circulated concerning certain Egyptian mummies and ancient records, which were purchased by certain gentlemen of Kirtland, last July. It has been said that the purchasers of these antiquities pretend they have the bodies of Abraham, Abimelech, (the king of the Philistines,) Joseph, who was sold into Egypt, &c., &c., for the purpose of attracting the attention of the multitude, and gulling the unwary; which is utterly false. Who these ancient inhabitants of Egypt were, I do not at present say. Abraham was buried on his own possession "in the cave of Machpelah, in the field of Ephron, the son of Zohah, the Hittite, which is before Mamre," which he purchased of the sons of Heth. Abimelech lived in the same country, and for aught we know, died there; and the children of Israel carried Joseph's bones from Egypt, when they went out under Moses; consequently, these could not have been found in Egypt, in the nineteenth century. The record of Abraham and Joseph, found with the mnmmies, is beautifully written on papyrus, with black, and a small part red, ink or paint, in perfect preservation. The characters are such as you find upon the coffins of mummies—hieroglyphics, etc.; with many characters of letters like the present (though probably not quite so square) form of the Hebrew without points. The records were obtained from one of the catacombs in Egypt, near the place where once stood the renowned city of Thebes, by the celebrated French traveler, Antonio Sebolo, in the year 1831. He procured license from Mehemet Ali, then Viceroy of Egypt, under the protection of Chevalier Drovetti, the French Consul, in the year 1828, and employed four hundred and thirty-three men, four months and two days (if I understand correctly)—Egyptian or Turkish soldies, at from four to six cents per diem, each man. He entered the catacomb June 7, 1831, and obtained eleven mummies. There were several hundred mummies in the same catacomb; about one hundred embalmed after the first order, and placed in niches, and two or three hundred after the second and third orders, and laid upon the floor or bottom of the grand cavity. The two last orders of embalmed were so decayed, that they could not be removed, and only eleven of the first, found in the niches. On his way from Alexandria to Paris, he put in at Trieste, and, after ten days' illness, expired. This was in the year 1832. Previous to his decease, he made a will of the whole, to Mr. Michael H. Chandler, (then in Philadelphia, Pa.,) his nephew, whom he supposed to be in Ireland. Accordingly, the whole were sent to Dublin, and Mr. Chandler's friends ordered them to New York, where they were received at the Custom House, in the winter or spring of 1833. In April, of the same year, Mr. Chandler paid the duties and took possession of his mummies. Up to this time, they had not been taken out of the coffins, nor the coffins opened. On opening the coffins, he discovered that in connection with two of the bodies, was something rolled up with the same kind of linen, saturated with the same bitumen, which, when examined, proved to be two rolls of papyrus, previously mentioned. Two or three other small pieces of papyrus, with astronomical calculations, epitaphs, &c., were found with others of the mummies. When Mr. Chandler discovered that there was something with the mummies, he supposed or hoped it might be some diamonds or valuable metal, and was no little chagrined when he saw his disappointment. "He was immediately told, while yet in the custom house, that there was no man in that city who could translate his roll: but was referred, by the same gentleman, (a stranger,) to Mr. Joseph Smith, Jun., who, continued he, possesses some kind of power or gifts, by which he had previously translated similar characters." I was then unknown to Mr. Chandler, neither did he know that such a book or work as the record of the Nephites, had been brought before the public. From New York, he took his collection on to Philadelphia, where he obtained the certificate of the learned,* and from thence came on to Kirtland, as before related, in July. Thus I have given a brief history of the manner in which the writings of the fathers, Abraham

* The account here given of how the Prophet came into possession of the writings of Abraham, and of Joseph, the son of Jacob, was adapted from an article in the *Messenger and Advocate*, (Volume II, Number 3, pages 233, 236, bearing date of December, 1835) signed by Oliver Cowdery. The article is addressed to William Frye, Esq., of Gilead, Calhoun County, Ill. The certificate of the "learned" referred to, is in the body of the article. It seems that Michael H. Chandler, the owner of the Egyptian mummies and the papyrus, exhibited his treasures in Philadelphia, and, while there, obtained the following opinion of several prominent doctors:

"Having examined with considerable attention and deep interest, a number of mummies from the Catacombs, near Thebes, in Egypt, and now exhibiting in the Arcade, we beg leave to recommend them to the observation of the curious inquirer on subjects of a period so long elapsed; probably not less than three thousand years ago. The features of some of these mummies are in perfect expression. The papyrus covered with black or red ink, or paint, in excellent preservation, are very interesting. The undersigned, unsolicited by any person connected by interest with this exhibition, have voluntarily set their names hereunto, for the simple purpose of calling the attention of the public to an interesting collection, not sufficiently know in this city."

JOHN REDMAN COXE, M. D.,
RICHARD HARLAN, M. D.,
J. PANCOAST, M. D.,
WILLIAM P. C. BARTON, M. D.,
E. F. RIVINUS, M. D.,
SAMUEL G. MORGAN, M. D.

"I concur in the above sentiments, concerning the collection of mummies in the Philadelphia Arcade, and consider them highly deserving the attention of the curious.

"W. E. HORNER, M. D."

Another paragraph in the article explains how it came about that Mr. Chandler gave the Prophet a certificate, concerning his belief in the Prophet's ability to decipher the Egyptian hieroglyphics of the papyrus—which certificate will be found at page 235, of this volume, under the date of the purchase of the mummies and papyrus by certain persons in Kirtland. From the paragraph referred to, it appears that on the morning that Mr. Chandler first presented his papyrus to the Prophet Joseph Smith, he was shown by the latter, a number of characters which had been copied from the Nephite plates, and found that there were some points of resemblance between some of the Nephite characters and some of the characters on the Egyptian papyrus. Mr. Chandler then asked the Prophet's opinion concerning the antiquity of the Egyptian papyrus, and also requested him to give a translation of the characters. The Prophet gave Mr. Chandler a translation of some few of the Egyptian characters, which agreed with the interpretation given by learned men in other cities, where the mummies and papyrus had been exhibited, whereupon Mr. Chandler gave the Prophet a certificate, stating that fact.

and Joseph, have been preserved, and how I came in possession of the same—a correct translation of which I shall give in its proper place.

Tone of the American Press Toward the Prophet.

To show the spirit of the public journals, such as the *Philadelphia Saturday Courier*, *New York Daily Advertiser*, *Sunday Morning News*, and the press generally, the past year, towards me and the cause of God, which I have fearlessly espoused, I quote the following, as a specimen of the whole, from M. M. Noah's *New York Evening Star:*

HEATHEN TEMPLE ON LAKE ERIE.

That bold-faced imposter, Joe Smith, of Gold Bible and Mormon memory, has caused his poor fanatic followers to erect on the shores of Lake Erie, near Painesville, Ohio, a stone building, 58 by 78 feet, with dormer windows, denominating the same "The Temple of the Lord." We should think this work of iniquity extorted out of the pockets of his dupes, as it reflects its shadows over the blue Lake, would make the waters crimson with shame at the prostitution of its beautiful banks to such unhallowed purposes.

Thus much from M. M. Noah, a Jew, who had used all the influence in his power, to dupe his fellow Jews, and make them believe that the New Jerusalem for them, was to be built on Grand Island, whose banks are surrounded by the waters of the same Lake Erie. The Lord reward him according to his deeds.

CHAPTER XXVI.

OPENING OF THE YEAR 1836—THE AMERICAN INDIANS—SPECIAL COUNCIL MEETINGS IN KIRTLAND.

Friday Morning, January 1, 1836.—This being the beginning of a new year, my heart is filled with gratitude to God that He has preserved my life, and the lives of my family, while another year has passed away. We have been sustained and upheld in the midst of a wicked and preverse generation, although exposed to all the afflictions, temptations, and misery that are incident to human life; for this I feel to humble myself in dust and ashes, as it were, before the Lord. But notwithstanding the gratitude that fills my heart on retrospecting the past year, and the multiplied blessings that have crowned our heads, my heart is pained within me, because of the difficulty that exists in my father's family. The devil has made a violent attack on my brother William and Calvin Stoddard, and the powers of darkness seem to lower over their minds, and not only over theirs, but they also cast a gloomy shade over the minds of my brethren and sisters, which prevents them from seeing things as they really are; and the powers of earth and hell seem combined to overthrow us and the Church, by causing a division in the family; and indeed the adversary is bringing into requisition all his subtlety to prevent the Saints from being endowed, by causing a division among the Twelve, also among the Seventy, and bickering and jealousies among the Elders and the official members of the Church; and so the leaven of iniquity

Reflections of the Prophet.

ferments and spreads among the members of the Church. But I am determined that nothing on my part shall be lacking to adjust and amicably dispose of and settle all family difficulties on this day, that the ensuing year and years, be they few or many, may be spent in righteousness before God. And I know that the cloud will burst, and Satan's kingdom be laid in ruins, with all his black designs; and that the Saints will come forth like gold seven times tried in the fire, being made perfect through sufferings and temptations, and that the blessings of heaven and earth will be multiplied upon their heads; which may God grant for Christ's sake. Amen.

Reconciliation of the Prophet and his Brother William.

Brothers William and Hyrum, and Uncle John Smith, came to my house, and we went into a room by ourselves, in company with father and Elder Martin Harris. Father Smith then opened our interview by prayer, after which he expressed himself on the occasion in a very feeling and pathetic manner, even with all the sympathy of a father, whose feelings were deeply wounded on account of the difficulty that was existing in the family; and while he addressed us, the Spirit of God rested down upon us in mighty power, and our hearts were melted. Brother William made a humble confession and asked my forgiveness for the abuse he had offered me. And wherein I had been out of the way, I asked his forgiveness. And the spirit of confession and forgiveness was mutual among us all, and we covenanted with each other, in the sight of God, and the holy angels, and the brethren, to strive thenceforward to build each other up in righteousness in all things, and not listen to evil reports concerning each other; but, like brothers indeed, go to each other, with our grievances, in the spirit of meekness, and be reconciled, and thereby promote our happiness, and the happiness of the family, and, in short, the happiness and well-being of all. My wife and mother and my scribe were then called in, and we repeated the covenant to them that we had entered into; and while gratitude swelled our bosoms, tears flowed from our eyes. I was then requested to close our interview, which I did, with prayer; and it was truly a jubilee and time of rejoicing; after which we all unitedly administered, by laying on of hands, to my cousin George A. Smith, who was immediately healed of a severe rheumatic affection all over the body, which caused excruciating pain.

Saturday, January 2.—According to previous arrangement, I went to the Council at nine o'clock. This Council was called to sit in judgment on a complaint preferred against Brother William Smith, by Orson Johnson, on the 29th of December.

Settlement of William Smith's case Before the Council.

The Council organized and proceeded to business, but before entering on trial, Brother William arose and humbly confessed the charges preferred against him, and asked the forgiveness of the Council and the whole congregation.

A vote was then called to know whether his confession was satisfactory, and whether the brethren would extend again to him the hand of fellowship. With cheerfulness the whole congregation raised their hands to receive him.

Elder Almon W. Babbitt also confessed the charges which I preferred against him in a previous Council; and was received into fellowship.

Council voted that Vinson Knight and Thomas Grover should be ordained Elders. And some other business was transacted in union and fellowship, and the best of feeling seemed to prevail among the brethren, and our hearts were made glad on the occasion, and there was joy in heaven, and my soul doth magnify the Lord, for His goodness and mercy endure forever.

Elijah Fordham, Hyrum Dayton, Samuel James and John Herrot were also appointed by Council to be ordained Elders under my hands.

Sunday, 3.—Went to meeting at the usual hour. President Rigdon delivered a fine lecture upon the subject of Revelation.

In the afternoon I confirmed ten or twelve persons who had been baptized, among whom was Malcham C. Davis, who was baptized during the intermission today. Brother William Smith made his confession to the Church to their satisfaction, and was cordially received into fellowship again. The Lord's Supper was administered, and Brother William gave out an appointment to preach in the evening at early candle-light, and preached a fine discourse; and this day has been a day of rejoicing to me. The cloud that has been hanging over us has burst with blessings on our heads, and Satan has been foiled in his attempts to destroy me and the Church, by causing jealousies to arise in the hearts of some of the brethren; and I thank my heavenly Father for the union and harmony which now prevail in the Church.

Monday, 4.—Met and organized our Hebrew school according to the arrangements that were made on Saturday last. We had engaged Doctor Piexotto to teach us in the Hebrew language, when we had our room prepared. We informed him that we were ready and our room was prepared. And he agreed to wait on us this day, and deliver his introductory lecture. Yesterday he sent us word that he could not come until Wednesday next. A vote was then called to know whether we would submit to such treatment or not; and carried in the negative; and Elder Sylvester Smith was appointed clerk to write him on the subject, and inform him that his services were not wanted; and Elders William E. M'Lellin and Orson Hyde despatched to Hudson Seminary to hire a teacher. They were appointed by the voice of the school to act in their behalf. However, we concluded to go on with our school and do the best we could until we obtained a teacher; and by the voice of the school I con-

Preparation for the Hebrew School.

sented to render them all the assistance I was able to for the time being.

We are occupying the translating room for the use of the school, until another room can be prepared. It is the west room in the upper part of the Temple, and was consecrated this morning by prayer, offered up by Father Smith. This is the first day we have occupied it. This is a rainy time, and the roads are extremely muddy.

Met this evening at the Temple, to make arrangements for a singing school. After some discussion, a judicious arrangement was made, a committee of six was chosen to take charge of the singing department.

Tuesday, 5.—Attended the Hebrew school, divided it into classes. Had some debate with Elder Orson Pratt concerning the pronunciation of a Hebrew letter. He manifested a stubborn spirit, at which I was much grieved.

A Difference Between the Prophet and Orson Pratt.

Wednesday, 6.—Attended school and spent most of the forenoon in settling the unpleasant feelings that existed in the breast of Elder Orson Pratt. After much controversy, he confessed his fault for entering into any controversy concerning so small a matter as the sound of a Hebrew letter, and asked the forgiveness of the whole school, and was cheerfully forgiven by all.

A New Teacher in Hebrew Employed.

Elder M'Lellin returned from Hudson, and reported to the school that he had hired a teacher to teach us the term of seven weeks, for three hundred and twenty dollars; that is, forty scholars for that amount; to commence in about fifteen days. He is highly celebrated as a Hebrew scholar, and proposes to give us sufficient knowledge during the above term to start us in reading and translating the language.

Vacancies in the High Council Filled.

A High Council assembled at Kirtland for the purpose of filling the vacancies of the High Council of Zion. Presidents David Whitmer, John Whitmer and W. W. Phelps, and fifteen High

Priests and Elders present. President Phelps announced the death of Christian Whitmer on the 27th of November, 1835. Four councilors, namely Parley P. Pratt, Orson Pratt, William E. M'Lellin and Thomas B. Marsh, had been chosen Apostles, or especial witnesses; and Elisha H. Groves was appointed to take the place of Parley P. Pratt in the High Council of Zion, John Hitchcock in the place of William E. M'Lellin, George M. Hinkle of Orson Pratt, Elias Higbee of Thomas B.Marsh, and Peter Whitmer, Jun., of Christian Whitmer, deceased; who were ordained at the time to their office as councilors.

The Gathering of Israel and the American Indians.

Much has been said and done of late by the general government in relation to the Indians (Lamanites) within the territorial limits of the United States. One of the most important points in the faith of the Church of the Latter-day Saints, through the fullness of the everlasting Gospel, is the gathering of Israel (of whom the Lamanites constitute a part)—that happy time when Jacob shall go up to the house of the Lord, to worship Him in spirit and in truth, to live in holiness; when the Lord will restore His judges as at the first, and His counselors as at the beginning; when every man may sit under his own vine and fig tree, and there will be none to molest or make afraid; when He will turn to them a pure language, and the earth will be filled with sacred knowledge, as the waters cover the great deep; when it shall no longer be said, the Lord lives that brought up the children of Israel out of the land of Egypt, but the Lord lives that brought up the children of Israel from the land of the north, and from all the lands whither He has driven them. That day is one, all important to all men.

In view of its importance, together with all that the prophets have said about it before us, we feel like dropping a few ideas in connection with the official statements from the government concerning the Indians. In speaking of the gathering, we mean to be understood as speaking of it according to scripture, the gathering of the elect of the Lord out of every nation on earth, and bringing them to the place of the Lord of Hosts, when the city of righteousness shall be built, and where the people shall be of one heart and one mind, when the Savior comes; yea, where the people shall walk with God like Enoch, and be free from sin. The word of the Lord is precious; and when we read that the vail spread over all nations will be destroyed, and the pure in heart see God, and reign with Him a thousand years on earth, we want all honest men to have a chance to gather and build up a city of righteousness, where even upon the bells of the horses shall be written *Holiness to the Lord.*

Policy of the Government of the United States Respecting the Indians.

The Book of Mormon has made known who Israel is, upon this continent. And while we behold the government of the United States gathering the Indians, and locating them upon lands to be their own, how sweet it is to think that they may one day be gathered by the Gospel! Our venerable President of these United States (Andrew Jackson) speaks of the Indians as follows:

President Andrew Jackson's Views on the Policy of the General Government with Reference to the Indians.

The plan of removing the aboriginal people who yet remain within the settled portions of the United States, to the country west of the Mississippi River, approaches its consummation. It was adopted on the most mature consideration of the condition of this race, and ought to be persisted in till the object is accomplished, and prosecuted with as much vigor as a just regard to their circumstances will permit, and as far as their consent can be obtained. All preceding experiments for the improvement of the Indians have failed. It seems now to be an established fact, that they cannot live in contact with a civilized community and prosper. Ages of fruitless endeavors have at length brought us to a knowledge of this principle of intercommunication with them. The past we cannot recall, but the future we can provide for,

Independently of the treaty stipulations into which we have entered with the various tribes for the usufructuary rights ceded to us, no one can doubt the moral duty of the government of the United States to protect, and, if possible, to preserve and perpetuate the scattered remnants of this race which are left within our borders. In the discharge of this duty, an extensive region in the west has been assigned for their permanent residence. It has been divided into districts, and allotted among them. Many have already removed, and others are preparing to go; and, with the exception of two small bands, living in Ohio and Indiana, not exceeding fifteen hundred persons, and of the Cherokees, all the tribes on the east side of the Mississippi, and extendig from Lake Michigan to Florida, have entered into engagements which will lead to their transplantation.

The plan for their removal and re-establishment is founded upon the knowledge we have gained of their character and habits, and has been dictated by a spirit of enlarged liberality. A territory exceeding in extent to that relinquished has been granted to each tribe. Of its climate, fertility, and capability to support an Indian population, the representations are highly favorable. To these districts the Indians are removed at the expense of the United States, and with certain supplies of clothing, arms, ammunition, and other indispensable articles; they are also furnished gratuitously with provisions for the period of a year after their arrival at their new homes. In that time, from the nature of the country, and of the products raised by them, they can subsist themselves by agricultural labor, if they choose to resort to that mode of life. If they do not, they are on the skirts of the great prairies, where countless herds of buffalo roam, and a short time suffices to adapt their own habits to the changes which a change of the animals destined for their food may require.

Ample arrangements have also been made for the support of schools; in some instances, council houses and churches are to be erected, dwellings to be constructed for the chiefs, and mills for cotton use. Funds have been set apart for the maintenance of the poor, the most necessary mechanical arts have been introduced, and blacksmiths, gunsmiths, wheelwrights, millwrights, etc., are supported among them. Steel and iron, and sometime salt are purchased for them; and plows and other farming utensils.

Domestic animals, looms, spinning wheels, cards, etc., are presented to them; and besides these beneficial arrangements, annuities are in all cases paid, amounting in some instances to more than thirty dollars for each individual of the tribe, and in all cases sufficiently great, if justly divided and prudently expended, to enable them, in addition to their own exertions, to live comfortably. And as a stimulus for exertion, it is now provided by law, that in all cases of the appointment of interpreters, or other persons employed for the benefit of the Indians, a preference shall be given to persons of Indian descent, if such can be found, who are properly qualified for the discharge of the duties.

Such are the arrangements for the physical comfort and for the moral improvement of the Indians. The necessary measures for their political advancement and for their separation from our citizens have not been neglected. The pledge of the United States has been given by Congress, that the country designated for the residence of this people shall be "forever secured and guaranteed to them." A country west of Missouri and Arkansas has been assigned to them, into which the white settlements are not to be pushed. No political communities can be formed in that extensive region, except those that are established by the Indians themselves, or by the United States for them and with their concurrence. A barrier has thus been raised for their protection against the encroachments of the citizens, and guarding the Indians as far as possible, from those evils which have brought them to their present condition.

Summary authority has been given by law, to destroy all ardent spirits found in their country without waiting the doubtful result and slow process of a legal seizure.

I consider the absolute and unconditional interdiction of this article, among these people, as the first great step in their amelioration. Half-way measures will answer no purpose. These cannot successfully contend against the cupidity of the seller and the overpowering appetite of the buyer; and the destructive effects of the traffic are marked in every page of the history of our Indian intercourse.

Some general legislation seems necessary for the regulation of the relations which will exist in this new state of things between the government and people of the United States and those transplanted Indian tribes, and for the establishment among the latter, with their own consent, some of the principles of intercommunication which their juxtaposition will call for; that moral may be substituted for physical force; the authority of a few simple laws, for the tomahawk; and that an end may be put to those bloody wars, whose prosecution seems to have made a part of their social system.

After the further detail of the arrangements are completed, with a very general supervision over them, they ought to be left to the progress of events. These, I indulge the hope, will secure their prosperity and improvement; and a large portion of the moral debt we owe them will be paid.

In addition to the above, we extract the following from the report on Indian affairs, made to Congress at the present session. We add and arrange according to circumstances:

The United Nation—Chippewas, Ottowas and Pottawatamies —about 1,000 in number, removed since September, 1834—possess 5,000,000 of acres of land on the east side of the Missouri and lying north-west of the north-west corner of Missouri [All these tribes may be rated at about 7,000]	1,000
The Choctaws, about 19,000, in humber, have 15,000,000 of acres, lying between the Red River and the Canadian	19,000
A small band of Quapaws, 200 or 300, perhaps near 95,000 acres, between the western boundary of the State of Missouri and the eastern boundary of the Osages	300
The Creeks, about 3,000 or 4,000, have 13,140,000 acres on Arkansas and Canadian rivers	4,000
The Seminoles, and other Florida Indians, to the number of say 25,000, included as the owners of the above 13,140,000 acres	25,000
The Cherokees, amounting to say 16,000, have 13,000,000 of acres, near the 36th degree of north latitude	16,000
The Kickapoos, something less than 1,000, have 160,000 acres north of Fort Leavenworth	1,000
The Delawares, nearly 1,000, have 200,000 acres west and south of the Kickapoos	1,000
The Shawnees, 1,200 or 1,400, have 1,600,000 acres south side of Kansas River	1,400
The Ottawas, about 200, have 30,000 acres south of the Shawnees	200
The Weas, Pinkeshaws, Peoria, and Kashaskias, say 500 in all, have 260,000 acres south of the Shawnees	500
The Senecas and Shawnees, say 500, have 100,000 acres on the western boundaries of the State of Missouri	500

Of the native tribes west of the Mississippi, the report is as follows:

Sioux	27,000
Iowas	1,200
Sacs of the Missouri	500
Omahas	1,400
Ottoes and Missourias	1,600
Pawnees	10,000
Camanches	7,000
Mandans	15,000

Minatares	15,000
Assinaboins	8,000
Crees	3,000
Gros Ventres	3,000
Crows	4,500
Quapaws	450
Caddoes*	2,000
Poncas	800
Arickarees	3,000
Cheyennes	2,000
Blackfeet	30,000
Foxes	1,600
Anepahas, Kioways, etc	14,000
Osages	5,120
Kansas	1,471
Sacs	4,800

Hopes of the Prophet in Behalf of the Indians.

The joy that we shall feel, in common with every honest American, and the joy that will eventually fill their bosoms on account of nationalizing the Indians, will be reward enough when it is shown that gathering them to themselves, and *for themselves*, to be associated with themselves, is a wise measure, and it reflects the highest honor upon our government. May they all be gathered in peace, and form a happy union among themselves, to which thousands may shout, *Esto perpetua*.

A Feast at Bishop Whitney's.

Thursday, 7.—Attended a sumptuous feast at Bishop Newel K. Whitney's. This feast was after the order of the Son of God—the lame, the halt, and the blind were invited, according to the instructions of the Savior. Our meeting was opened by singing, and prayer by Father Smith; after which Bishop Whitney's father and mother, and a number of others, were blessed with a patriarchal blessing. We then received a bountiful refreshment, furnished by the liberality of the Bishop. The company was large, and before we partook we had some of the songs of Zion sung; and our hearts were made glad by a foretaste of those joys that will be

* The agent reported these Indians as upwards of 2,000.

poured upon the heads of the Saints when they are gathered together on Mount Zion, to enjoy one another's society for evermore, even all the blessings of heaven, when there will be none to molest or make us afraid. Returned home, and spent the evening.

Progress of Work on Kirtland Temple.

Friday, *8*.—Spent the day in the Hebrew school, and made rapid progress in our studies. The plastering and hard-finishing on the outside of the Lord's house was commenced on the 2nd of November, 1835, and finished this day. The job was let to Artemas Millet and Lorenzo Young, at one thousand dollars. Jacob Bump took the job of plastering the inside of the house throughout, at fifteen hundred dollars, and commenced the same on the 9th of November last. He is still continuing the work, notwithstanding the inclemency of the weather.

Saturday, *9*.—Attended school in the forenoon. About eleven o'clock received the following note:

Bishop Whitney's Unique Invitation to the Prophet.

Thus saith the voice of the Spirit to me—If thy brother Joseph Smith, Jun., will attend the feast at thy house, this day (at twelve o'clock), the poor and the lame will rejoice in his presence, and also think themselves honored.

Yours in friendship and love,

NEWEL K. WHITNEY.

January 9, 1836.

I dismissed the school to accept this polite invitation, with my wife, father and mother. A large congregation assembled, a number were blessed under the hands of Father Smith, and we had a good time. Spent the evening at home.

Sunday, *10*.—Attended meeting at the usual hour. Elder Wilbur Denton and Wilkins J. Salisbury preached in the forenoon, and Brothers Samuel and Don Carlos Smith in the afternoon. They all did well, considering their youth. Administered the Sacrament during intermission. Elder Martin Harris baptized three. Spent the evening at home.

Monday, 11.—There being no school, I spent the day at home. Many brethren called to see me, among whom was Alva Beaman, from Genesee County, New York, who had come to attend the solemn assembly. I delight in the society of my brethren and friends, and pray that the blessings of heaven and earth may be multiplied upon their heads.

Visit of Alva Beaman to the Prophet.

Tuesday, 12.—I called on the Presidency of the Church, and made arrangements to meet tomorrow at ten o'clock, a. m. to take into consideration the subject of the solemn assembly. This afternoon, a young man called to see the Egyptian manuscripts, which I exhibited. Also Brother Joseph Rose introduced to me, Russel Weaver, a Christian or Unitarian preacher, so-called, from Cambray, New York. We had some little controversy on prejudice, but soon came to an understanding. He spoke of the Gospel, and said he believed it, adding that it was good tidings of great joy. I replied that it was one thing to proclaim good tidings, and another to tell what these tidings were. He waived the conversation and withdrew.

Preparations for the Solemn Assembly.

Wednesday, 13.—At ten o'clock I met in council with the Presidency of Kirtland and Zion, namely, Joseph Smith, Sen., Sidney Rigdon, Hyrum Smith, David Whitmer, John Whitmer, and W. W. Phelps; also the Twelve Apostles, the High Council of Zion, and the High Council of Kirtland, the Bishops of Zion and Kirtland, the Presidency of the Seventies, and many more of the Elders. Some of the Councilors, both of Zion and Kirtland, were absent.

The council came to order, sung Adam-ondi-Ahman,*

* Adam-ondi-Ahman was known to the Saints at this time as the place where the Lord appeared unto Adam our Father, three years previous to his death, and ministered unto the righteous among his posterity assembled at that place; on which occasion Adam was called "Michael," "the Prince," "the Archangel," and the Lord administered unto Adam and said unto him, "I have set thee at the head: a multitude of nations shall come of thee, and thou art a prince over them." It was

and opened by prayer offered up by Joseph Smith, Sen.; when I made some remarks, in my introductory lecture before the autorities of the Church, in general terms, laying before them the business of the day, which was to supply some deficiencies in the Bishop's Council in this place, also in the High Council.

Vinson Knight Ordained into Kirtland Bishopric.

After some consideration upon the most proper manner of proceeding, Elder Vinson Knight was nominated as a counselor in the Bishopric at Kirtland. The nomination was made by the Bishop and seconded by the Presidency. The vote was then called from the Presidency, and carried; next from the High Council of Zion, and carried; from the Twelve, and carried; from the Council of the Seventy, and carried; from the Bishop of Zion and his Council, and carried. And Elder Knight was received by the universal voice and consent of all the authorities of the Church.

Elder Knight was then ordained under the hands of Bishop Newel K. Whitney, to the office of High Priest

this knowledge that inspired the hymn sung on that occasion, composed by W. W Phelps, and here follows:

This earth was once a garden place,
With all her glories common;
And men did live a holy race,
And worship Jesus face to face,
In Adam-ondi-Ahman.

We read that Enoch walked with God,
Above the power of Mammon;
While Zion spread herself abroad,
And saints and angels sang aloud,
In Adam-ondi-Ahman.

Her land was good and greatly blessed,
Beyond old Israel's Canaan;
Her fame was known from east to west;
Her peace was great and pure the rest
Of Adam-ondi-Ahman.

Hosanna to such days to come—
The Savior's second coming,
When all the earth in glorious bloom
Affords the Saints a holy home,
Like Adam-ondi-Ahman.

(L. D. S. Hymn Book, p. 277.

and Bishop's counselor, to fill the place of Elder Hyrum Smith, who had been ordained to the Presidency of the High Council of Kirtland.

Council adjourned for one hour, by singing, "Come let us rejoice," etc.

Council assembled again at one o'clock p. m.

John P. Greene was nominated and seconded by the Presidency, a member of the High Council of Kirtland, and carried by the unanimous voice of all the authority of the Church, to supply the place of President Oliver Cowdery, who had been elected to the Presidency of the High Council of Kirtland.

Vacancies in the Kirtland High Council Filled.

Elder Thomas Grover was elected in like manner, a Councilor in the High Council, to fill the vacancy occasioned by Luke S. Johnson's having been ordained one of the Twelve Apostles.

Elder Noah Packard was elected a member of the High Council of Kirtland, to fill the place of Sylvester Smith, who had been ordained to the Presidency of the Seventy.

Elder John E. Page was nominated, but being absent, his name was dropped.

Elder Joseph Kingsbury was unanimously chosen a High Councilor in Kirtland, to fill the vacancy occasioned by Orson Hyde's being ordained one of the Twelve Apostles.

Elder Samuel James was unanimously chosen a member of the High Council of Kirtland, in place of Joseph Smith, Sen.

The newly elected Councilors were then called forward in order as they were elected, and ordained under the hands of Presidents Rigdon, Joseph Smith, Jun., and Hyrum Smith, to be High Priests, and Councilors in this Stake of Zion. Many great and glorious blessings were pronounced upon the heads of these Councilors, by President Rigdon, who was spokesman on the occasion.

The Council next proceeded to fill the vacancies in the

High Council of Zion, occasioned by the absence of Councilors John Murdock and Solomon Hancock. And Elders Alva Beaman and Isaac McWithy were appointed to serve as Councilors in the High Council of Zion, for the time being.

Vacancies Filled in the High Council of Zion.

Elders Nathaniel Milliken and Thomas Carrico were appointed by unanimous vote to officiate as doorkeepers in the House of the Lord.

Presidents Joseph Smith, Jun., Sidney Rigdon, W. W. Phelps, David Whitmer and Hyrum Smith were appointed to draft rules and regulations to govern the House of the Lord.

By unanimous voice of the assembly, moved, seconded, and carried, that no whispering shall be allowed in our councils or assemblies, nor any one allowed (except he be called upon or asks permission) to speak aloud upon any consideration whatever; and no man shall be interrupted while speaking, unless he is speaking out of place; and every man shall be allowed to speak in his turn.

Elder Milliken objected to officiate in the House of the Lord as doorkeeper, on account of his health; and was released by the voice of the assembly.

The minutes of the Council were then read, and Council adjourned until Friday, the 15th instant, at nine a. m., to the west school room, in the upper part of the temple.

President Sidney Rigdon requested some of the Presidency to lay their hands upon him, and rebuke a severe affliction in the face, which troubles him most at night. Elders Hyrum Smith and David Whitmer, by request, laid hands upon him and prayed for him, and rebuked his disease in the name of the Lord Jesus Christ. The whole assembly responded, Amen.

Sidney Rigdon's Ailment.

Elder David W. Patten requested our prayers in behalf of his wife, that she might be healed. I offered up a prayer for her recovery, and the assembly responded, Amen.

President Rigdon arose and made some very appropriate remarks touching the endowment, and dismissed the assembly by prayer.

This has been one of the best days that I ever spent; there has been an entire union of feeling expressed in all our proceedings this day; and the spirit of the God of Israel has rested upon us in mighty power, and it has been good for us to be here in this heavenly place in Christ Jesus; and although much fatigued with the labors of the day, yet my spiritual reward has been very great indeed. Spent the evening at home.

The Prophet's Joy.

Thursday, 14.—Nine o'clock. Met the Hebrew class at the school room in the Temple, and made some arrangements about our anticipated teacher, Mr. Joshua Seixas, of Hudson, Ohio.

The Coming of Professor Seixas.

I then returned to the council room in the printing office, to meet my colleagues who were appointed with myself to draft rules and regulations to be observed in the "House of the Lord," in Kirtland, built by the Church of the Latter-day Saints, in the year of our Lord 1834, which rules are as follows:

Rules and Regulations to be Observed in the House of the Lord in Kirtland.

I. It is according to the rules and regulations of all regularly and legally organized bodies to have a president to keep order.

II. The bodies thus organized are under obligation to be in subjection to that authority.

III. When a congregation assembles in this house, it shall submit to the following rules, that due respect may be paid to the order of worship, viz.:

1st. No man shall be interrupted who is appointed to speak by the Presidency of the Church, by any disorderly person or persons in the congregation, by whispering, by laughing, by talking, by menacing gestures, by getting up and running out in a disorderly manner, or by offering indignity to the manner of worship, or the religion, or to any officer of said Church while officiating in his office, in anywise whatsoever, by any display of ill manners or ill breeding, from old or young, rich or poor, male or female, bond or free, black or white, believer or unbeliever. And if any of the above insults are offered, such measures will be taken as are lawful, to punish the aggressor or aggressors, and eject them from the house.

2nd. An insult offered to the presiding Elder of said Church shall be considered an insult to the whole body. Also, an insult offered to any of the officers of said Church, while officiating, shall be considered an insult to the whole body.

3rd. All persons are prohibited from going up the stairs in times of worship.

4th. All persons are prohibited from exploring the house, except waited upon by a person appointed for that purpose.

5th. All persons are prohibited from going into the several pulpits, except the officers who are appointed to officiate in the same.

6th. All persons are prohibited from cutting, marking or marring the inside or outside of the house with a knife, pencil, or any other instrument whatever, under pain of such penalty as the law shall inflict.

7th. All children are prohibited from assembling in the house, above or below, or any part of it, to play, or for recreation, at any time: and all parants, guardians, or masters, shall be amenable for all damage that shall accrue in consequence of their children's misconduct.

8th. All persons, whether believers or unbelievers, shall be treated with due respect by the authorities of the Church.

9th. No imposition shall be practiced upon any members of the Church, by depriving them of their rights in the house.

Council adjourned *sine die.*

Return of Oliver Cowdery from Columbus, Ohio.

Returned home and spent the afternoon. Towards evening President Cowdery returned from Columbus, the capital of the State. I could spend but little time with him, being under obligation to attend at Mrs. Wilcox's, to join Mr. John Webb and Mrs. Catherine Wilcox in matrimony: also Mr. Thomas Carrico and Miss Elizabeth Baker, at the same place; all of which I performed in the customary manner in the midst of a large assembly. We then partook of some refreshments, and our hearts were made glad with the fruit of the vine. This is according to the pattern set by our Savior Himself, and we feel disposed to patronize all the institutions of heaven.

Friday, *15*.—At nine a. m., met in council agreeable to adjournment, at the Council room in the Temple, and seated the authorities of the Church agreeable to their respective offices. I then made some observations respecting the order of the day, and the great responsibility we were under to transact all our business in righteousness before God, inasmuch as our decisions will have a bearing upon all mankind, and upon all generations to come.

The Council Meeting in the Kirtland Temple.

Minutes of a Priesthood Meeting Held in Kirtland Temple, January 15, 1836.

Council opened in usual form, and proceeded to business by reading the rules and regulations to govern the house of the Lord, three times.

The vote of the Presidency was then called upon these rules, followed by the High Council of Kirtland, the High Council of Zion, the Twelve, the Seventy, the Bishops of Zion and Kirtland, with their Counselors, each in turn; and after a few queries, answers, and debates, the above rules passed the several quorums in their order, by the unanimous voice of the whole, and are therefore received and established as a law to govern the House of the Lord in Kirtland.

In the investigation of the subject, it was found that many who had deliberated upon it, were darkened in their minds, which drew forth some remarks from President Smith respecting the privileges of the authorities of the Church, that each should speak in his turn and in his place, and in his time and season, that there may be perfect order in all things; and that every man, before he makes an objection to any item that is brought before a council for consideration, should be sure that he can throw light upon the subject rather than spread darkness, and that his objection be founded in righteousness, which may be done by men applying themsolves closely to study the mind and will of the Lord, whose Spirit always makes manifest and demonstrates the truth to the understanding of all who are in possession of the Spirit.

After one hour's adjournment of the Council, Elder Don Carlos Smith was nominated to be ordained to the High Priesthood, also to officiate as President, to preside over that body in Kirtland. The vote of the quorums was called for in their order, and their nomination passed through the whole house by unanimous voice.

Elder Alva Beaman was chosen in the same manner to preside over the Elders in Kirtland.

William Cowdery was nominated to officiate as President over the Priests of the Aaronic Priesthood in Kirtland.

The vote of the assembly was called, beginning at the Bishop's Council, and passing through the several authorities, until it came to the presidency of the High Council in Kirtland, and received their sanction, having been carried unanimously in all the departments below.

Oliver Olney was unanimously elected to preside over the Teachers in Kirtland.

Ira Bond was unanimously chosen to preside over the deacons in Kirtland.

Elders Don Carlos Smith and Alva Beaman were ordained to the offices to which they had been elected, under the hands of Presidents Joseph Smith, Jun., Sidney Rigdon, and Hyrum Smith, with many blessings.

Bishop Whitney, of Kirtland, then proceeded to ordain William Cowdery, Oliver Olney and Ira Bond, and pronounced many blessings upon them according to their offices and standing.

Moved, seconded, and carried, that all the several quorums take their turn in performing the office of doorkeeper in the House of the Lord; also, that Nathaniel Milliken, Thomas Carrico, Amos R. Orton, and Samuel Rolfe be appointed assistant doorkeepers.

Moved and carried, that the presidency of the High Council hold the keys of the House of the Lord, except the keys of one vestry, which is to be held by the Bishopric of the Aaronic Priesthood.

Moved, and carried unanimously, that John Corrill be appointed to take charge of the House of the Lord in Kirtland immediately, and that the laws regulating the House of the Lord go into effect from this time, and that Elder Corrill see that they are enforced, with the privilege of calling as many as he chooses to assist him.

Council adjourned *sine die.*

ORSON HYDE, Clerk

CHAPTER XXVII.

RECONCILIATION OF THE FIRST PRESIDENCY AND TWELVE APOSTLES—PENTECOSTAL TIMES IN KIRTLAND.

Saturday, 16.—By request I met with the Council of the Twelve in company with my Counselors, Frederick G. Williams and Sidney Rigdon.

Special Council Meeting with the Twelve.

Council opened with singing, and prayer by Thomas B. Marsh, President of the Twelve. He arose and requested the privilege, in behalf of his colleagues, of each speaking in his turn without being interrupted; which was granted them.

Elder Marsh proceeded to unbosom his feelings touching the mission of the Twelve, and more particularly respecting a certain letter which they received from the Presidency of the High Council in Kirtland, while attending a conference in the state of Maine; also spoke of being placed, in the council on Friday last, below the Councils of Kirtland and Zion, having been previously placed next the Presidency in our assemblies; also observed that they were hurt on account of some remarks made by President Hyrum Smith, on the trial of Gladden Bishop, (who had been previously tried before the Council of the Twelve, while on their mission in the east,) who had by their request, thrown his case before the High Council in Kirtland, for investigation; and the Twelve considered that their proceedings with him, were in some degree discountenanced.

Elder Marsh then gave way to his brethren, and they arose and spoke in turn until they had all spoken, acquiescing in the observations of Elder Marsh, and made some additions to his remarks, which, in substance, were as follows: That the letter in question, which they received from the Presidency, in which two of their members were suspended, and the rest severely chastened, and that, too, upon testimony which was unwarranted; and particular stress was laid upon a certain letter which the Presidency had received from Dr. Warren E. Cowdery, of Freedom, New York, in which he preferred charges against them, which were false, and upon which the Presidency had acted in chastening them; and therefore the Twelve had concluded that the Presidency had lost confidence in them; and that whereas, the Church in this place had caressed them at the time of their appointment to the Apostleship, they now treated them coolly, and also appeared to have lost confidence in them.

They spoke of their having been in the work from the beginning almost, and had borne the burden in the heat of the day, and passed through many trials, and that the Presidency ought not to suspect their fidelity, nor lose confidence in them, neither ought they to have chastened them upon such testimony as was lying before them; also urged the necessity of an explanation upon the letter which they received from the Presidency, and the propriety of their having information respecting their duties, authority, etc., that they might come to an understanding in all things, that they might act in perfect unison and harmony before the Lord, and be prepared for the endowment; also that they had preferred a charge against Doctor Cowdery, for his unchristian conduct, which the Presidency had disregarded; also that President Oliver Cowdery, on a certain occasion, had made use of language to one of the Twelve that was unchristian and unbecoming any man; and that they would not submit to such treatment. The remarks of the Twelve were made in a very forcible and explicit manner, yet cool and deliberate.

President Smith observed that the Presidency had heard them patiently, and, in turn, should expect to be heard patiently also. And first, he remarked that it was necessary that the Twelve should state whether they were determined to persevere in the work of the Lord, whether the Presidency were able to satisfy them or not.

Vote called, and carried in the affirmative, unanimously.

President Smith then said to the Twelve that he had not lost confidence in them; they had no reason to suspect his confidence; and that he would be willing to be weighed in the scale of truth, today, in this matter, and risk it in the day of judgment. Respecting the chastening contained in the letter in question, which he acknowledged might have been expressed in too harsh language, which was not intentional, he asked their forgiveness, inasmuch as he had hurt their feelings; but nevertheless, the letter that Elder M'Lellin wrote back to Kirtland, while the Twelve were in the east, was harsh also, and he was willing to set the one against the other.

President Smith next proceeded to explain the duty of the Twelve, and their authority, which is next to the present Presidency, and that the arrangement of the assembly in this place, on the 15th instant, in placing the High Councils of Kirtland next the Presidency, was because the business to be transacted, was business relating to that body in particular, which was to fill the several quorums in Kirtland, not because they were first in office, and that the arrangements were the most judicious that could be made on the occasion; also the Twelve are not subject to any other than the first Presidency, viz., "myself," said the Prophet, "Sidney Rigdon, and Frederick G. Williams, who are now my Counselors; and where I am not, there is no First Presidency over the Twelve."

The Prophet also stated to the Twelve that he did not countenance the harsh language of President Cowdery to them, neither would he countenance it in himself nor in any other man, "although," said he, "I have sometimes spoken too harshly from the impulse of the moment, and inasmuch as I have wounded your feelings, brethren, I ask your forgiveness, for I love you and will hold you up with all my heart in all righteousness, before the Lord, and before all men; for be assured, brethren, I am willing to stem the torrent of all opposition, in storms and in tempests, in thunders and in lightnings, by sea and by land, in the wilderness or among false brethren, or mobs, or wherever God in His providence may call us. And I am determined that neither heights nor depths, principalities nor powers, things present or things to come, or any other creature, shall separate me from you. And I will now covenant with you before God, that I will not listen to or credit any derogatory report against any of you, nor condemn you upon any testimony beneath the heavens, short of that testimony which is infallible, until I can see you face to face, and know of a surety; and I do place unremitted confidence in your word, for I believe you to be men of truth. And I ask the same of you, when I tell you anything, that you place equal confidence in my word, for I will not tell you I know anything that I do not know. But I have already consumed more time than I intended when I commenced, and I will now give way to my colleagues."

President Rigdon arose next and acquiesced in what President Smith had said, and acknowledged to the Twelve that he had not done as he ought, in not citing Dr. Warren A. Cowdery to trial on the charges that were put into his hands by the Twelve; that he neglected his duty in this thing, for which he asked their forgiveness, and would now attend to it, if they desired him to do so;* and President Rigdon also observed

* Evidently this matter concerning Warren A. Cowdery was afterwards taken up and settled amicably, as the Doctor published the following note of explanation and acknowledgment in the February, 1836, number of the *Messenger and Advocate:*

"NOTICE.

"I hereby give to all whom it may concern, that Messrs. T. B. Marsh and others, denominated the 'Twelve,' while on their mission to the East, last season, received a letter from the Presidency of the Church in which they were censured for neglecting to teach the Church in Freedom, Cattaraugus County, N. Y., the neces-

to the Twelve, if he had spoken or reproved too harshly at any time, and had injured their feelings by so doing, he asked their forgiveness.

President Williams arose and acquiesced in the above sentiments, expressed by the Prophet and President Rigdon, in full, and said many good things.

The President of the Twelve then called a vote of that body, to know whether they were perfectly satisfied with the explanations given them, and whether they would enter into the covenant the Presidency had proposed to them, which was most readily manifested in the affirmative, by raising their hands to heaven in testimony of their willingness and desire to enter into this covenant, and their entire satisfaction with the explanation upon all tho difficulties that were on their minds. The brethren then took each other by the hand in confirmation of the covenant, and there was a perfect union of feeling on this occasion, and the hearts of all overflowed with blessings, which the brethren pronounced upon one another's heads as the Spirit gave them utterance.

In conclusion, the Prophet said: "My scribe is included in that covenant, and these blessings with us, for I love him for the truth and integrity that dwell in him. And may God enable us to perform our vows and covenants with each other, in all fidelity and righteousness before Him, that our influence may be felt among the nations of the earth, in mighty power, even to rend the kingdoms of darkness asunder, and triumph over priestcraft and spiritual wickedness in high places, and break in pieces all kingdoms that are opposed to the kingdom of Christ, and spread the light and truth of the everlasting Gospel from the rivers to the ends of the earth."

Elder Beaman came in for counsel, to know whether it was best for him to return before the solemn assembly or not. After consideration, the Council advised him to tarry.

Council dismissed by singing and prayer.

WARREN PARRISH, Clerk.

Sunday, 17.—Attended meeting at the school house at the usual hour; a large congregation assembled. I pro-

sity of contributing of their earthly substance for the building of the House of the Lord in this place. The rebuke from the Presidency, (as the undersigned has been informed) was predicated upon a letter addressed by him, to the presidents or some one of them, stating that they, the Twelve, taught no such thing. The undersigned although actuated by the purest motives at the time he wrote believing he had stated nothing but the truth, has since become satisfied from the best of evidence, that that particular item in their instructions was not omitted as he had represented, he, therefore, most deeply regrets it, being sensible as he now is, that he was the cause (although innocent) of wounding the best of feelings, and depressing spirits buoyant with hope, while in the field of useful labor at a distance from home."—W. A. COWDERY.

ceeded to arrange the several quorums present, first the Presidency, then the Twelve, and the Seventy who were present, also the Councilors of Kirtland and Zion.

Testimonies of Presidency and Twelve.

President Rigdon then arose and observed that instead of preaching the time would be occupied by the Presidency and Twelve, in speaking each in his turn until they had all spoken. The Lord poured out His Spirit upon us, and the brethren began to confess their faults one to the other, and the congregation was soon overwhelmed in tears, and some of our hearts were too big for utterance. The gift of tongues came on us also, like the rushing of a mighty wind, and my soul was filled with the glory of God.

In the afternoon I joined three couple in matrimony, in the public congregation, viz: William F. Cahoon and Maranda Gibbs, Harvey Stanley and Larona Cahoon, Tunis Rapley and Louisa Cutler. We then administered the Sacrament, and dismissed the congregation, which was so large that it was very unpleasant for all. We were then invited to a feast at Elder Cahoon's which was prepared for the occasion, and had a good time while partaking of the rich repast; and I verily realized that it was good for brethren to dwell together in unity, like the dew upon the mountains of Israel, where the Lord commanded blessings, even life forevermore. Spent the evening at home.

Marriage and Sacrament.

Monday, 18.—Attended the Hebrew school. This day the Elders' school was removed into the Temple, in the room adjoining the Hebrew school.

Tuesday, 19.—Spent the day at school. The Lord blessed us in our studies. This day we commenced reading in our Hebrew Bibles with much success. It seems as if the Lord opens our minds in a marvelous manner, to understand His word in the original language; and my prayer is that God will speedily endow us with a knowledge of all languages and

Progress in Study of Hebrew.

tongues, that His servants may go forth for the last time the better prepared to bind up the law, and seal up the testimony.

FORM OF MARRIAGE CERTIFICATE.

I hereby certify, that, agreeable to the rules and regulations of the Church of Jesus Christ of Latter-day Saints, on matrimony, Mr. William F. Cahoon and Miss Nancy M. Gibbs, both of this place, were joined in marriage, on Sabbath, the 17th, instant.

JOSEPH SMITH, JUN., { Presiding Elder of said Church.

Kirtland, Ohio, January 19th, 1836.

Wednesday, 20.—Attended school at the usual hour, and spent the day in reading and lecturing, and made some advancement in our studies.

In the evening I attended a matrimonial occasion with my family, at Mr. John Johnson's, having been invited to join Elder John F. Boynton and Miss Susan Lowell in marriage; a large and respectable company assembled, and were seated by Elders Orson Hyde and Warren Parrish, in the following order—The Presidency and their companions in the first seats, the Twelve Apostles in the second, the Seventy in the third, and the remainder of the congregation seated with their companions. Elder Boynton and lady, with their attendants, came in and were seated in front of the Presidency.

Marriage of J. F. Boynton.

A hymn was sung, after which I addressed the throne of grace. I then arose and read aloud a license, (according to the law of the land) granting any minister of the Gospel the privilege of solemnizing the rights of matrimony, and after calling for objection, if any there were, against the anticipated alliance between Elder Boynton and Miss Lowell; after waiting a sufficient time and hearing no objection, I observed that all forever after this must hold their peace. I then invited them to join hands. I pronounced the ceremony, according to the rules and regulations of the Church of the Latter-day Saints, in the name of God, and in the name of Jesus Christ. I pronounced upon them the blessings of Abraham, Isaac, and Jacob, and such other blessings as the Lord put into my heart; and being much under the influence of a cold, I then gave way, and President Rigdon arose and delivered a very forcible address, suited to the occasion, and closed the services of the evening by prayer.

The Marriage Feast.

Elders Orson Hyde, Luke S. Johnson, and Warren Parrish, then presented the Presidency with three servers of glasses filled with wine, to bless. And it fell to my lot to attend to this duty, which I cheerfully discharged. It was then passed round in order, then the cake in the same order; and suffice it to say, our hearts were made glad while partaking of the bounty of earth which was presented, until we had taken our fill; and joy filled every bosom, and the countenances of old and young seemed to bloom alike with cheerfulness and smiles of youth; and an entire unison of feeling seemed to pervade the congregation, and indeed I doubt whether the pages of history can boast of a more splendid and innocent wedding and feast than this, for it was conducted after the order of heaven, which has a time for all things; and this being a time of rejoicing, we heartily embraced it and conducted ourselves accordingly. Took leave of the company and returned home.

J. W. Olived and the Prophet.

Thursday, 21.—This morning, a minister from Connecticut, by the name of John W. Olived, called at my house and inquired of my father: "Does the Prophet live here?" My father replied he did not understand him. Mr. Olived asked the same question again and again, and received the same answer. He finally asked: "Does Mr. Smith live here?" Father replied: "O yes, sir, I understand you now." Father then stepped into my room and informed me that a gentleman had called to see me. I went into the room where he was, and the first question he asked me, after passing a compliment was: "How many members have you in your Church?" I replied that we had between fifteen hundred and two thousand in this branch. He then asked: "Wherein do you differ from other Christian denominations?" I replied, that we believe the Bible, and they do not. However, he affirmed that he believed the Bible. I told him then to be batized. He replied that he did not realize it to be his duty. But when I laid before him the principles of the Gospel, viz: faith and repentance; baptism, for the remission of sins; and the laying on of hands, for the reception of the Holy Ghost, he manifested much surprise. I observed that the hour for school had arrived, and I must attend. The man appeared astonished at our doctrine, but by no means hostile.

About three o'clock, p. m., I dismissed the school, and the Presidency retired to the attic story of the printing office, where we attended the ordinance of washing our bodies in pure water. We also perfumed our bodies and our heads, in the name of the Lord.

Washing and Anointings in Kirtland Temple.

At early candle-light I met with the Presidency at the west school room, in the Temple, to attend to the ordinance of anointing our heads with holy oil; also the Councils of Kirtland and Zion met in the two adjoining rooms, and waited in prayer while we attended to the ordinance. I took the oil in my left hand, Father Smith being seated before me, and the remainder of the Presidency encircled him round about. We then stretched our right hands towards heaven, and blessed the oil, and consecrated it in the name of Jesus Christ.

We then laid our hands upon our aged Father Smith, and invoked the blessings of heaven. I then anointed his head with the consecrated oil, and sealed many blessings upon him. The Presidency then in turn laid their hands upon his head, beginning at the oldest, until they had all laid their hands upon him, and pronounced such blessings upon his head,

The Prophet Blessed to Lead Israel in the Last Days.

as the Lord put into their hearts, all blessing him to be our Patriarch, to anoint our heads, and attend to all duties that pertain to that office. The Presidency then took the seat in their turn, according to their age, beginning at the oldest, and received their anointing and blessing under the hands of Father Smith. And in my turn, my father anointed my head, and sealed upon me the blessings of Moses, to lead Israel in the latter days, even as Moses led him in days of old; also the blessings of Abraham, Isaac and Jacob. All of the Presidency laid their hands upon me, and pronounced upon my head many prophecies and blessings, many of which I shall not notice at this time. But as Paul said, so say I, let us come to visions and revelations.

The Prophet's Vision of the Celestial Kingdom.

The heavens were opened upon us, and I beheld the celestial kingdom of God, and the glory thereof, whether in the body or out I cannot tell. I saw the transcendent beauty of the gate through which the heirs of that kingdom will enter, which was like unto circling flames of fire; also the blazing throne of God, whereon was seated the Father and the Son. I saw the beautiful streets of that kingdom, which had the appearance of being paved with gold. I saw Fathers Adam and Abraham, and my father and mother, my brother, Alvin, that has long since slept, and marvelled how it was that he had obtained an inheritance in that kingdom, seeing that he had departed this life before the Lord had set His hand to gather Israel the second time, and had not been baptized for the remission of sins.

Alvin Smith.

Thus came the voice of the Lord unto me, saying—

Revelation.

All who have died without a knowledge of this Gospel, who would have received it if they had been permitted to tarry, shall be heirs of the celestial kingdom of God; also all that shall die henceforth without a knowledge of it, who would have received it with all their hearts, shall be heirs of that kingdom, for I, the Lord, will judge all men according to their works, according to the desire of their hearts.

And I also beheld that all children who die before they arrive at the years of accountability, are saved in the celestial kingdom of heaven. I saw the Twelve Apostles of the Lamb, who are now upon the earth, who hold the keys of this last ministry, in foreign lands, standing together in a circle, much fatigued, with their clothes tattered and feet swollen, with their eyes cast downward, and Jesus standing in their midst, and they did not behold Him. The Savior looked upon them and wept.

The Salvation of Children.

I also beheld Elder M'Lellin in the south, standing upon a hill, surrounded by a vast multitude, preaching to them, and a lame man standing before him supported by his crutches; he threw them down at his word and leaped as a hart, by the mighty power of God. Also, I saw Elder Brigham Young standing in a strange land, in the far south and west, in a desert place, upon a rock in the midst of about a dozen men of color, who appeared hostile. He was preaching to them in their own tongue, and the angel of God standing above his head, with a drawn sword in his hand, protecting him, but he did not see it. And I finally saw the Twelve in the celestial kingdom of God. I also beheld the redemption of Zion, and many things which the tongue of man cannot describe in full.

The Prophet's Vision of the Twelve.

Many of my brethren who received the ordinance with me saw glorious visions also. Angels ministered unto them as well as to myself, and the power of the Highest rested upon us, the house was filled with the glory of God, and we shouted Hosanna to God and the Lamb. My scribe also received his anointing with us, and saw, in a vision, the armies of heaven protecting the Saints in their return to Zion, and many things which I saw.

Ministrations of Angels.

The Bishop of Kirtland with his Counselors, and the Bishop of Zion with his Counselors, were present with us, and received their anointings under the hands of Father

Smith, and this was confirmed by the Présidency, and the glories of heaven were unfolded to them also.

High Councils of Zion and Kirtland Anointed.

We then invited the High Councilors of Kirtland and Zion into our room, and President Hyrum Smith anointed the head of the President of the Councilors in Kirtland, and President David Whitmer the head of the President of the Councilors of Zion. The President of each quorum then anointed the heads of his colleagues, each in his turn, beginning at the oldest.

Further Visions and Revelations.

The visions of heaven were opened to them also. Some of them saw the face of the Savior, and others were ministered unto by holy angels, and the spirit of prophecy and revelation was poured out in mighty power; and loud hosannas, and glory to God in the highest, saluted the heavens, for we all communed with the heavenly host. And I saw in my vision all of the Presidency in the celestial kingdom of God, and many others that were present. Our meeting was opened by singing, and prayer was offered up by the head of each quorum; and closed by singing, and invoking the benediction of heaven, with uplifted hands. Retired between one and two o'clock in the morning.

Friday 22.—Attended at the school room at the usual hour, but instead of pursuing our studies, we spent the time in rehearsing to each other the glorious scenes that occurred on the preceding evening, while attending to the ordinance of holy anointing.

Anointing of the Twelve and Seventy.

In the evening we met at the same place, with the Council of the Twelve, and the Presidency of the Seventy, who were to receive this ordinance [of anointing and blessing]. The High Councils of Kirtland and Zion were present also.

After calling to order and organizing, the Presidency proceeded to consecrate the oil.

We then laid our hands upon Elder Thomas B. Marsh, who is President of the Twelve, and ordained him to the authority of anointing his brethren. I then poured the consecrated oil upon his head, in the name of Jesus Christ, and sealed such blessings upon him as the Lord put into my heart. The rest of the Presidency then laid their hands upon him and blessed him, each in his turn, beginning at the oldest. He then anointed and blessed his brethren from the oldest to the youngest. I also laid my hands upon them, and pronounced many great and glorious things upon their heads. The heavens were opened, and angels ministered unto us.

The Twelve then proceeded to anoint and bless the Presidency of the Seventy, and seal upon their heads power and authority to anoint their brethren.

The heavens were opened unto Elder Sylvester Smith, and he, leaping up, exclaimed: "The horsemen of Israel and the chariots thereof."

Brother Don C. Smith was also anointed and blessed to preside over the High Priests' quorum.

Blessing of the Lord's Anointed.

President Rigdon arose to conclude the services of the evening by invoking the blessing of heaven upon the Lord's anointed, which he did in an eloquent manner; the congregation shouted a long hosanna: the gift of tongues fell upon us in mighty power, angels mingled their voices with ours, while their presence was in our midst, and unceasing praises swelled our bosoms for the space of half-an-hour.

I then observed to the brethren, that it was time to retire. We accordingly closed our interview and returned home at about two o'clock in the morning, and the Spirit and visions of God attended me through the night.

To the petitions which we sent up to Missouri, Governor Dunklin replied as follows: *

CITY OF JEFFERSON, Jan. 22nd, 1836.

To Messrs. W. W. Phelps and Others,

GENTLEMEN:—Your numerous petitions, post-marked "Kirtland,"

* The communication from Governor Dunklin, of Missouri, which follows, is found as "Note H," in the addenda of the manuscript History, Book "B." And is placed here in the Prophet's narrative, under the date on which it was written, *viz.* January 22, 1836.

came safe to hand. It is unnecessary for me to repeat to you my feelings on the subject of your grievances. What they were you have been already apprised, and, they have undergone no change. Your case was presented by me to the last General Assembly of the state. They did not legislate upon the subject. I am, however, persuaded, that it was for want of a constitutional power to pass any law that could afford you a proper remedy, prevented their acting upon the subject. Your feelings are very natural, when such causes exist to produce them; but you misconceive your case, and, consequently, do not advert to the proper remedy. You cannot make a case of *invasion* or *insurrection* of the outrages committed upon your persons or property in Jackson County. And, unless one of those could be made out, it would be idle to address the President of the United States. If such a case had been made out, as Executive of this state, I should have immediately ordered out a military force to repel or suppress it. The mob in New York, to which you cite me, is not in point. The military force was there resorted to, for the purpose of *quieting* the mob. You wish this kind of a force used to *restore* justice. However palpable and grievous the outrages have been upon you, your only remedy for injuries done must be in and through the courts of justice. On a former occasion I informed you I was then in correspondence with the General Government, for a depot of arms, on the Missouri river, near our western boundary line. For reasons unknown to me, the Secretary of War has taken no steps during the last year towards the fulfillment of the subject. I have renewed the subject through our delegation in Congress, this winter. When this object shall be attained, it may furnish you a place of resort, for protection, in case of emergency, should you think proper to risk yourselves on your lands, in Jackson County, again.

Respectfully,

[Signed] DANL. DUNKLIN.

Doubts of Alva Beaman.

Saturday, 23.—Attended at the school room, as usual, and we came together filled with the Spirit, as on the past evening, and did not feel like studying, but commenced conversing upon heavenly things, and we spent the day agreeably and profitably. Elder Alva Beaman had been tempted to doubt the things which we received the evenings before, and he made an humble confession, and asked forgiveness of the school, which was joyfully accorded him, and he said he would try to resist Satan in the future.

Sunday, 24.—Met the several quorums in the room under the printing office, and, after organizing and opening by prayer, called upon the High Council of Kirtland to proceed and confess their sins, as they might be directed by the Spirit, and they occupied the first part of the day, and confessed and exhorted as the Spirit led.

Continuation of Spiritual Meetings.

In the afternoon, attended meeting again, and saw the bread and wine administered to the quorums and brethren who were present.

In the evening met the Presidency in the chamber over the printing room, and counseled on the subject of endowment, and the preparation for the solemn assembly, which is to be called when the house of the Lord is finished.

Monday, 25.—Received a line from my scribe, informing me of his ill health, as follows—

Illness of Warren Parrish.

BROTHER JOSEPH—My great desire is to be in your company and in the assembly of the Saints, where God opens the heavens, and exhibits the treasures of eternity. It is the only thing that has stimulated me, for a number of days past, to leave my house; for be assured, dear brother, my bodily affliction is severe. I have a violent cough, more especially at night, which deprives me of my appetite, and my strength fails, and writing has a particular tendency to injure my lungs, while I am under the influence of such a cough. I therefore, with reluctance, send your journal to you, until my health improves.

Yours in haste,

WARREN PARRISH.

P. S.—Brother Joseph, pray for me, and ask the prayers of the class on my account also. W. P.

Appointed Elder Sylvester Smith, acting scribe, for the time being, or, till Elder Parrish shall recover his health. Spent the day at home, receiving visitors.

Tuesday, *26*.—Mr. Seixas arrived from Hudson, to teach the Hebrew language, and I attended upon the organizing of the class, for the purpose of receiving lectures upon Hebrew grammar. His hours of instruction are from ten to eleven, a. m.; and from two to

Arrival of Prof. Seixas.

three, p. m. His instruction pleased me much. I think he will be a help to the class in learning Hebrew.

Wednesday, *27*.—Attended school as usual, and also attended to other matters which came before me.

Thursday, *28*.—Attended school at the usual hour.

Continuation of Ministrations and Visions.

In the evening met the quorum of High Priests, in the west room of the upper loft of the Lord's house, and, in company with my counselors, consecrated and anointed the counselors of the presidents of the High Priests' quorum, and, having instructed them and set the quorum in order, I left them to perform the holy anointing, and went to the quorum of Elders at the other end of the room. I assisted in anointing the counselors of the president of the Elders, and gave the instruction necessary for the occasion, and left the president and his counselors to anoint the Elders, while I should go to the adjoining room, and attend to organizing and instructing the quorum of the Seventy.

I found the Twelve Apostles assembled with this quorum, and I proceeded, with the quorum of the Presidency, tc instruct them, and also the seven presidents of the Seventy Elders, to call upon God with up-lifted hands, to seal the blessings which had been promised to them by the holy anointing. As I organized this quorum, with the presidency in this room, President Sylvester Smith saw a pillar of fire rest down and abide upon the heads of the quorum, as we stood in the midst of the Twelve.

When the Twelve and the seven presidents were through with their sealing prayer, I called upon President Sidney Rigdon to seal them with uplifted hands; and when he had done this, and cried hosanna, that all the congregation should join him, and shout hosanna to God and the Lamb, and glory to God in the highest. It was done so, and Elder Roger Orton saw a mighty angel riding upon a horse of fire, with a flaming sword in his hand, followed by five others, encircle the house, and protect the Saints, even the Lord's anointed, from the power of Satan and a host of evil spirits, which were striving to disturb the Saints.

President William Smith, one of the Twelve, saw the heavens opened, and the Lord's host protecting the Lord's anointed.

President Zebedee Coltrin, one of the seven presidents of the Seventy, saw the Savior extended before him, as upon the cross, and a little after, crowned with glory upon his head above the bsightness of the sun.

After these things were over, and a glorious vision, which I saw, had passed, I instructed the seven presidents to proceed and anoint the Seventy, and returned to the room of the High Priests and Elders, and attended to the sealing of what they had done, with up-lifted hands.

The Lord assisted my brother, Don Carlos, the president of the High Priests, to go forward with the anointing of the High Priests, so that he had performed it to the acceptance of the Lord, notwithstanding he was very young and inexperienced in such duties; and I felt to praise God with a loud hosanna, for His goodness to me and my father's family, and to all the children of men. Praise the Lord, all ye, His Saints, praise His holy name.

After these quorums were dismissed, I retired to my home, filled with the Spirit, and my soul cried hosanna to God and the Lamb, through the silent watches of the night; and while my eyes were closed in sleep, the visions of the Lord were sweet unto me, and His glory was round about me. Praise the Lord.

Friday, 29.—Attended school and read Hebrew. I received a line from the presidency of the Elders' quorum, they wishing to know whom they should receive into their quorum, I answered verbally.

Afternoon, I called in all my father's family and made a feast, and related my feelings towards them. My father pronounced patriarchal blessings on the heads of Henry Gannet, Charles H. Smith, Marietta Carter, Angeline Carter, Johanna Carter, and

The Prophet Feasts his Father's Family.

Nancy Carter. This was a good time to me, and all the family rejoiced together. We continued the meeting till about eight o'clock in the evening, and related the goodness of God to us, in opening our eyes to see the visions of heaven, and in sending His holy angels to minister unto us the word of life. We sang the praise of God in animated strains, and the power of union and love was felt and enjoyed.

Saturday, 30.—Attended school, as usual, and waited upon several visitors, and showed them the record of Abraham. Mr. Seixas, our Hebrew teacher, examined it with deep interest, and pronounced it to be original beyond all doubt. He is a man of excellent understanding, and has a knowledge of many languages which were spoken by the ancients, and he is an honorable man, so far as I can judge yet.

Resolutions.

At a conference of the Presidency of the Church, it was resolved that no one be ordained to an office in the Church in Kirtland, without the voice of the several quorums, when assembled for Church business.

Resolved—That Alva Beaman, president of the Elders, be directed to give to the Presidents of the Church a list of the names of the several Elders, comprising his quorum, and all other Elders in Kirtland, not belonging to any quorum now established.

Resolved—That Harvey Whitlock be restored to the Church, in full fellowship, on his being rebaptized, and after, be ordained to the High Priesthood.

OLIVER COWDERY, Clerk.

In the evening, went to the upper rooms of the Lord's house, and set the different quorums in order. Instructed the presidents of the Seventy concerning the order of their anointing, and requested them to proceed and anoint the Seventy. Having set all the quorums in order, I returned to my house, being weary with continual anxiety and labor, in putting all the authorities in order, and in striving to purify them for the solemn assembly, according to the commandment of the Lord.

Anointing the Seventy.

Sunday, 31.—Attended divine service in the school house, arranged the several quorums of the authorities of the Church, appointed doorkeepers to keep order about the door, because of the crowd, and to prevent the house from being excessively crowded. The High Council of Zion occupied the first part of the day, in speaking as they were led, and relating experiences, trials, etc.

Afternoon. House came to order, as usual, and President Sidney Rigdon delivered a short discourse, and we attended to the breaking of bread.

In the evening, my father attended to the blessing of three brethren, at President Oliver Cowdery's. Spent the evening at home.

CHAPTER XXVIII.

THE PROPHET'S MINISTRY AND STUDIES IN KIRTLAND.

Monday, February 1, 1836.—Attended school as usual, and in company with the other members of the committee organized another class of thirty, to receive Mr. Seixas' lectures on the Hebrew.

Further Arrangements for the Study of Hebrew.

In the evening, attended to the organizing of the quorums of High Priests, Elders, Seventy, and Bishops, in the upper rooms of the house of the Lord, and after blessing each quorum in the name of the Lord, I returned home. I had another interview with Mr. Seixas, our Hebrew teacher, and related to him some of the dealings of God with me, and gave him some of the evidence of the truth of the work of the latter days. He listened cordially and did not oppose.

Tuesday 2.—Attended school as usual, and to various other duties.

Went to the school house in the evening, and heard an animated discourse delivered by President Rigdon. He touched on the outlines of our faith, showed the scattering and gathering of Israel, from the Scriptures, and the stick of Joseph in the hands of Ephraim, as also from the scriptures of Moses. It was an interesting meeting, the Spirit bore record that the Lord was well pleased.

The Gathering of Israel.

Wednesday, 3.—Morning, attended our Hebrew lecture.

Afternoon, studied with Oliver Cowdery and Sylvester Smith. Received many visitors, and showed them the

Records of Abraham. My father blessed three with a patriarchal blessing. President Alva Beaman handed in seventy of his quorum designed for another Seventy if God will.

Names for the Second Quorum of Seventy.

Thursday, 4.—Attended school, and assisted in forming a class of twenty-two members to read at three o'clock, p. m. The other twenty-three read at eleven o'clock. The first class recites at a quarter before ten, a. m., and the second a quarter before two, p. m. We have a great want of books, but are determined to do the best we can. May the Lord help us to obtain this language, that we may read the Scriptures in the language in which they were given.

Hebrew Class Arrangements

Friday, 5.—Attended school, and assisted the committee to make arrangements to supply the third and fourth classes with books; concluded to divide a Bible into several parts, for the benefit of said classes; continued my studies in the Hebrew; received several visitors, and attended various duties.

Saturday, 6.—Called the anointed together to receive the seal of all their blessings. The High Priests and Elders in the council room as usual, the Seventy with the Twelve in the second room, and the Bishops in the third. I labored with each of these quorums for some time to bring them to the order which God had shown to me, which is as follows: The first part to be spent in solemn prayer before God, without any talking or confusion; and the conclusion with a sealing prayer by President Rigdon, when all the quorums were to shout with one accord a solemn hosanna to God and the Lamb, with an Amen, Amen and Amen; and then all take seats and lift up their hearts in silent prayer to God, and if any obtain a prophecy or vision, to rise and speak that all may be edified and rejoice together.

Arrangements of Quorums to Receive Spiritual Blessings.

I had considerable trouble to get all the quorums united in this order. I went from room to room repeatedly, and charged each separately, assuring them that it was according to the mind of God, yet, notwithstanding all my labor, while I was in the east room with the Bishops' quorum, I felt, by the Spirit, that something was wrong in the quorum of Elders in the west room, and I immediately requested Presidents Oliver Cowdery and Hyrum Smith to go in and see what was the matter. The quorum of Elders had not observed the order which I had given them, and were reminded of it by President Don Carlos Smith, and mildly requested to preserve order, and continue in prayer. Some of them replied that they had a teacher of their own, and did not wish to be troubled by others. This caused the Spirit of the Lord to withdraw; this interrupted the meeting, and this quorum lost their blessing in a great measure.

The other quorums were more careful, and the quorum of the Seventy enjoyed a great flow of the Holy Spirit. Many arose and spoke, testifying that they were filled with the Holy Ghost, which was like fire in their bones, so that they could not hold their peace, but were constrained to cry hosanna to God and the Lamb, and glory in the highest.

Visions in the Kirtland Temple.

President William Smith, one of the Twelve, saw a vision of the Twelve, and Seven in council together, in old England, and prophesied that a great work would be done by them in the old countries, and God was already beginning to work in the hearts of the people.

President Zebedee Coltrin, one of the Seven, saw a vision of the Lord's host. And others were filled with the Spirit, and spake with tongues and prophesied. This was a time of rejoicing long to be remembered. Praise the Lord.

Sunday, 7.—Attended meeting at the usual hour. The quorums were seated according to their official standing in the Church. The Bishop of Zion and his counselors occupied the forenoon in confession and exhortation. The

Bishop of Kirtland and his counselors occupied the stand in the afternoon. The discourses of these two quorums were very interesting. A number of letters of commendation were presented and read, a vote was called, and all were received into the Church in Kirtland. Bread was broken and blessed, and while it was passing, President Rigdon commenced speaking from Acts ii, and continued about fifteen minutes. His reasoning was good. The wine was then blessed and passed, after which meeting dismissed.

In the evening, met with the Presidency in the loft of the printing office, in company with the presidency of the Seventy, to choose other Seventy also. Blessed one of the Zion brethren. Dismissed and retired.

Monday, *8*.—Attended school at the usual hour.

Warren Parrish Resumes his Duty as Scribe.

In the afternoon, lectured in the upper room of the printing office with some of the brethren. At evening, visited Mr. Seixas, in company with Presidents Rigdon and Cowdery. He conversed freely; is an interesting man. Elder Parrish, my scribe, received my journal again. His health is so much improved, that he thinks he will be able, with the blessing of God, to perform his duty.

Tuesday, *9*.—Spent the day in studying the Hebrew language. Fine weather and sleighing. Evening at home.

Wednesday, *10*.—At ten o'clock, met at the school room to read Hebrew.

Afternoon, read in the upper room of the printing office.

Hyrum Smith Meets with an Accident.

At four o'clock, called at the school room in the Temple to make some arrangements concerning the classes. On my return, I was informed that Brother Hyrum Smith had cut himself. I immediately repaired to his house, and found him badly wounded in his left arm, he had fallen on his ax, which caused a wound about four or five inches in length. Doctor Williams sewed it up and dressed it, and I feel to thank God that it is no worse, and I ask my Heavenly Father in the name of Jesus Christ to heal my brother

Hyrum, and bless my father's family, one and all, with peace and plenty, and eternal life.

Thursday, 11.—Attended school, and read Hebrew with the morning class.

Spent the afternoon in reading, and in exhibiting the Egyptian records to those who called to see me, and heaven's blessings have attended me.

Friday, 12.—Spent the day in reading Hebrew, and attending to the duties of my family, and the duties of the Church.

Remarks of the Prophet on Those Unworthy of the Ministry.

I met in company with the several quorums in the school room in the temple, at evening, to take into consideration the subject of ordination. I made some remarks upon the subject of our meeting, which were as follows: Many are desiring to be ordained to the ministry, who are not called, consequently the Lord is displeased. Secondly, many already have been ordained, who ought not to hold official stations in the Church, because they dishonor themselves and the Church, and bring persecution swiftly upon us, in consequence of their zeal without knowledge. I requested the quorums to take some measures to regulate the same. I proposed some resolutions, and remarked to the brethren that the subject was now before them, and open for discussion.

The subject was discussed by Presidents Sidney Rigdon and Oliver Cowdery, and Elder Martin Harris, and others, and resolutions were drafted by my scribe (who served as clerk on the occasion), read, and rejected. It was then proposed that I should indite resolutions, which I did as follows:

The Prophet's Draft of Resolutions.

First. Resolved—That no one be ordained to any office in the Church in this stake of Zion, at Kirtland, without the unanimous voice of the several bodies that constitute this quorum, who are appointed to do Church business in the name of said Church, viz., the Presidency of the Church; the Twelve Apostles of the Lamb; the twelve High

Councilors of Kirtland; the twelve High Councilors of Zion; the Bishop of Kirtland and his counselors; the Bishop of Zion and his counselors; and the seven presidents of Seventies; until otherwise ordered by said quorums.

Second. And further Resolved—That no one be ordained in the branches of said Church abroad, unless they are recommended by the voice of the respective branches of the Church to which they belong, to a general conference appointed by the heads of the Church, and from that conference receive their ordination. The foregoing resolutions were concurred in by the presidents of the Seventies.

Saturday, 13.—Spent the day in reading Hebrew.

At noon I prepared a horse and sleigh for Professor Seixas to go to Hudson and see his family.

Action of the Twelve on the Resolutions Governing Ordinations.

At one o'clock p. m. the council of the Twelve Apostles met in the house of the Lord, and after prayer and consultation upon the nature and expediency of the preceding resolutions offered in council on the 12th instant, it was unanimously agreed to offer the following amendment to the second resolution, (perfectly acquiescing in the first) viz.: That none be ordained to any office in the branches to which they belong; but to be recommended to a general conference appointed by those, or under the direction of those, who are designated in the book of Doctrine and Covenants, as having authority to ordain and set in order all the officers of the Church abroad, and from that conference receive their ordination.

THOMAS B. MARSH,
Chairman,
ORSON HYDE,
WM. E. M'LELLIN,
Clerks.

Sunday, 14.—Attended to the ordinance of baptism before meeting.

At the usual hour attended meeting. The presidents of the Seventy expressed their feelings on the occasion, and their faith in the Book of Mormon and the revelations, also their entire confidence in all the quorums that are organized in the Church of Latter-day Saints. A good time—the Spirit of God

The Faith and Confidence of Seventy.

rested upon the congregation. Administered the Sacrament, and confirmed a number that had been baptized, and then dismissed the meeting.

Monday 15.—Attended school at the usual hours.

Spent the afternoon in reading Hebrew and in receiving and waiting on visitors. On this day we commenced translating the Hebrew language, under the instruction of Professor Seixas, and he stated that we were the most forward of any class he ever instructed for the same length of time.

Progress in the Study of Hebrew.

Tuesday, 16.—Attended school at the usual hour. Resumed our translating, and made rapid progress. Many called to see the House of the Lord, and the Egyptian manuscript, and to visit me. Extremely cold weather, and fine sleighing.

Wednesday, 17.—Attended the school and read and translated with my class as usual. My soul delights in reading the word of the Lord in the original, and I am determined to pursue the study of the languages, until I shall become master of them, if I am permitted to live long enough. At any rate, so long as I do live, I am determined to make this my object; and with the blessing of God, I shall succeed to my satisfaction.

Elder Coe called to make some arrangements about the Egyptian mummies and records. He proposes to hire a room at John Johnson's Inn, and exhibit them there from day to day, at certain hours, that some benefit may be derived from them. I complied with his request, and only observed that they must be managed with prudence and care, especially the manuscripts.

Action of the Kirtland High Council on the Resolutions on Ordinations.

The High Council of Kirtland met in the House of the Lord at six o'clock, p. m., to discuss the subject of ordination, as laid before the Council on the 12th instant; and also the proposed amendment of the Twelve Apostles of the 13th. After discussing the resolutions drawn

by President Smith, it was voted unanimously that they should remain entire, and the proposed amendment of the Twelve Apostles be rejected.

JOSEPH C. KINGSBURY, Clerk.

Thursday, 18.—Spent the day as usual in attending to my family concerns, receiving and waiting upon those who called for instructions, and attending to my studies.

Action of the High Council of Zion on the Resolution on Ordinations.

The High Council of Zion met in the upper room of the printing office at seven o'clock p.m. to discuss the subject of ordination, as laid before them in the council of the 12th instant, and also the amendment of the Twelve Apostles. After discussing the resolutions drawn up by the President, it was voted unanimously that they should remain, and that we perfectly acquiesce in said resolutions without any alteration or amendment.

ELIAS HIGBEE, Clerk.

Friday, 19.—Attended with the morning class and translated. Professor Seixas handed me the names of a few whom he had selected from the first class, and requested us to meet together this afternoon and lecture, which we did, in the upper room of the printing office. The names are as follows: Presidents Sidney Rigdon, Oliver Cowdery, William W. Phelps, Bishop Edward Partridge, Elders William E. M Lellin, Orson Hyde, Orson Pratt, Sylvester Smith, myself, and scribe. These, and Prof. Seixas, to meet one hour earlier on the following morning.

The Prophet's Regard for Prof. Seixas.

I conversed with Mr. Seixas on the subject of religion, at my house this afternoon. He listened with attention, and appeared interested with my remarks. And I believe the Lord is striving with him, by His Holy Spirit, and that he will eventually embrace the new and everlasting covenant, for he is a chosen vessel unto the Lord to do His people good; but I forbear lest I get to prophesying upon his head.

This evening President Rigdon and myself called at Mr. Seixas' lodgings and conversed with him upon the subject of the school. Had a pleasant interview.

Saturday, *20*.—At home attending to my domestic concerns.

At nine o'clock attended the school, and translated with the morning class.

Spent the afternoon with my class in the printing office and the evening at home.

Sunday, *21*.—Spent the day at home in reading, meditation and prayer. I reviewed my lesson in Hebrew.

The Varied Activities of the Prophet.

Some three or four persons were baptized, and the powers of darkness seem to be giving way on all sides. Many who have been enemies to the work of the Lord, are beginning to enquire into the faith of the Latter-day Saints, and are friendly.

Monday, *22*.—Translated Hebrew with the first class in the morning. Returned home and made out my returns, to the county clerk on eleven marriages which I had solemnized within three months—eight by license from the clerk of the court of common pleas in Geauga County, Ohio, and three by publishment. Sent them to Chardon by Elijah Fuller. I baptized John O. Waterman.

Spent the afternoon translating with my scribe, Elder Warren Parrish, at his house.

At four o'clock met Professor Seixas and the school committee at the printing office, to make some arrangements for the advancement of the several classes.

Action of the First Presidency on the Resolutions on Ordinations.

The Presidency of the Church met and took in consideration the resolutions presented to the Twelve Apostles, (dated Feb. 12th), the presidents of Seventies, the High Councils of the Church for Zion and Kirtland. After due deliberation it was unanimously agreed that the original resolutions be adopted without amendments.

OLIVER COWDERY, Clerk of Council.

The lower room of the Temple is now prepared for painting. Elder Brigham Young was obliged to leave the Hebrew class and superintend the painting of the lower room until finished.*

This afternoon the sisters met to make the veil of the Temple. Father Smith presided over them, and gave them much good instruction. Closed by singing and prayer, which is customary at the commencement and close of all councils and meetings of the Church of Latter-day Saints, although not always mentioned in this record.

Tuesday, *23.*—Read and translated Hebrew.

This afternoon the sisters met again at the Temple to work on the veil.†

Towards the close of the day I met with the Presidency and many of the brethren in the house of the Lord, and made some remarks from the pulpit upon the rise and progress of the Church of Christ of Latter-day Saints, and pronounced a blessing upon the sisters, for their liberality in giving their services so cheerfully, to make the veil for the Lord's House; also upon the congregation; and dismissed.

Wednesday, *24.*—Attended to my studies as usual.

In the evening, met the quorums at the school room in the Temple to take into consideration the propriety or im-

* Elder Brigham Young, it should be remembered, in the town of Aurelius, Cayuga County, New York, had for twelve years followed the occupation of carpenter, joiner, painter and glazier. (See Life of Brigham Young, Tullidge, p. 77). Hence this appointment to supervise the work mentioned.

† "The Temple was so constructed that with white canvas curtains that could be dropped and raised at pleasure, the lower story was, whenever occasion reqnired, divided into four sections or compartments. * * * * The two sets of pulpits, one on the east and the other to the west end of the building were intersected by the curtains extending from east to west, so as to leave half their lengths in each apartment, and they were occupied by the presiding officers who directed the services. Thus four separate meetings could be in session at the same time without in the least interfearing with each other, giving opportunity for four to exercise instead of one."—(Eliza R. Snow, Autobiography and Family Record of Lorenzo Snow, p. 12). It was upon these canvas curtains or "veils" tha the sisters were at work as stated in the text.

propriety of ordaining a large number of individuals who wish to be ordained to official stations in the Church. Each individual's name was presented and the voice of the assembly called; and William Wightman, Charles Wightman, David Cluff, Truman Jackson, Reuben Barton, Daniel Miles, and Moses Daily, were received, and nineteen were rejected. Their ordinations deferred until another time. Presidents Orson Hyde, Oliver Cowdery, and Sylvester Smith, were nominated to draft rules and regulations concerning licenses, and by vote of the assembly passed unanimously.

The Selection of Men for the Ministry.

Thomas Burdick was chosen by nomination to officiate as clerk, to record licenses, and is to receive pay for his services. Also voted that the Twelve and Seventy see that the calls for preaching in the region round about Kirtland be attended to, and filled by judicious Elders of this Church.

Thursday, *25*.—Attended to my studies as usual, and made some advancement.

In the afternoon I was called upon by Elder Rigdon to go and see his wife, who was very sick. I did so in company with my scribe. We prayed for her and anointed her in the name of the Lord, and she began to recover from that very hour. Returned home and spent the evening there.

Friday, *26*.—Read Hebrew with the first class in the morning.

Spent the afternoon in the printing office. Settled some misunderstanding between Brother William Smith and Professor Seixas.

Saturday 27.—Cold, and fine sleighing. I prepared my horse and sleigh for Mr. Seixas to ride to Hudson and visit his family, to return on Monday next. Attended with my class at the printing office, both in the forenoon and afternoon, lectured and also translated Hebrew.

Sunday, *28*.—This morning two gentlemen, late from

Scotland, called to see me, to make inquiries about the work of the Lord in these last days. They treated me with respect, and the interview was pleasing to me, and I presume interesting to them. They attended our meeting with me, and expressed satisfaction at what they heard. They spoke of Irving,* the religious reformer, and his prophecies. After meeting I returned home and spent the after part of the day and evening in reading and translating the Hebrew.

Respectful Inquiries About the Work.

Monday, 29.—Spent the day in studying as usual. A man called to see the House of the Lord, in company with another gentleman. On entering the door they were politely invited, by the gentleman who had charge of the house, to take off their hats. One of them replied with the request unhesitatingly, while the other observed that he would not take off his hat nor bow to "Jo Smith," but that he had made "Jo" bow to him at a certain time. He was immediately informed by Elder Morey, the keeper of the house, that his first business was to leave, for when a man insulted Joseph Smith he, Brother Morey, was himself insulted. The man manifested much anger, but left the house. For this independence and resolution of Elder Morey, I respect him, and for the love he manifested towards me; and may Israel's God bless him, and give him an ascendency over all his enemies.

The Manliness of Elder Morey.

This afternoon Professor Seixas returned from Hudson and brought a few more Hebrew Bibles and one grammar of his second edition. Weather warm and sleighing failing fast.

Tuesday, March 1, 1836.—Attended school in the forenoon.

In the afternoon, at the printing office, and read and translated with my class until four o'clock. Returned home and attended to my domestic concerns. We have

* This is Mr. Edward Irving, the Scotch clergyman who founded the sect of the Irvingites. See pp. 233-4 this volume.

as yet fine sleighing, which is uncommon in this country at this season of the year.

Wednesday, 2.—Pursued my studies as usual.

At seven o'clock in the evening the first class met, agreeable to the request of Mr. Seixas, at Elder Orson Hyde's, to spend one hour in translating. Returned at eight o'clock.

Misunderstanding Over Sale of Bibles.

Thursday, 3.—Attended to my studies in the Hebrew school. Some misunderstanding took place between Professor Seixas and some of his scholars respecting the sale of Bibles. His feelings were much hurt, apparently. He made some remarks concerning it to each class. At noon he called on the school committee, his feelings much depressed. We gave him all the satisfaction we could in righteousness, and his feelings were measurably allayed.

This evening the several quorums met agreeable to adjournment, and were organized according to their official standing in the Church. I then arose and made some remarks on the object of our meeting, as follows:

First—To receive or reject certain resolutions that were drafted by a committee chosen for that purpose, at a preceding meeting, respecting licenses for Elders and other official members.

Second—To sanction, by the united voice of the quorums, certain resolutions respecting ordaining members that have passed through each quorum separately, without any alteration or amendment, excepting in the quorum of the Twelve.

Final Action on Resolutions on Ordinations and Licenses.

After singing and prayer, President Oliver Cowdery, chairman of the committee appointed on the 24th ultimo, to draft resolutions respecting licenses, arose and made report in behalf of the committee, which was read three times by the chairman. The third time he read the resolutions he gave time and opportunity, after reading each article, for objections to be made, if any there were. No objections were raised, or alterations made, but an addition was made to the sixth article extending the powers of the chairman and clerk *pro tem.* to sign licenses, etc.

I then observed that these resolutions must needs pass through each quorum separately, beginning at the presidency of each quorum, and consequently it must first be thrown into the hands of the president of the Deacons and his council, as equal rights and privileges is my motto; and one man is as good as another, if he behaves as well; and that all men should be esteemed alike, without regard to distinctions of an official nature. The resolutions were passed by the president of the Deacons and his council by unanimous voice.

It was then presented before the presidents of the several quorums and their counselors in the following order, and in the same manner as before, viz: the Teachers, Priests, Bishop of Kirtland, Bishop of Zion, Elders, High Priests, Seventy, High Council of Zion, High Council of Kirtland, the Twelve, and, lastly, passed into the hands of the Presidency of the Church, and all the quorums, and received their unanimous sanction. The resolutions are as follows:

Resolutions on Ordinations and Licenses.

Whereas, the records of the several conferences held by the Elders of the Church, and the ordination of many of the official members of the same, in many cases, have been imperfectly kept since its organization. to avoid ever after any inconvenience, difficulty or injury, in consequence of such neglect, your committee recommend:

First—That all licenses hereafter granted by these autorities assembled as a quorum, or by general conference held for the purpose of transacting the business of the Church, be recorded at full length by a clerk appointed for that purpose, in a book to be kept in this branch of the Church, until it shall be thought advisable by the heads of the Church to order other books and appoint other clerks, to record licenses as above; and that said recording clerk be required to indorse a certificate under his own hand and signature, on the back of said licenses, specifying the time when, and place where, such license was recorded, and also a reference to the letter and page of the book containing the same.

Second—That this quorum appoint two persons to sign licenses given as aforesaid, one as chairman, and the other as clerk of conference; and that it shall be the duty of said persons appointed to sign licenses as clerk of conference immediately hereafter, to deliver the same into the hands of the recording clerk.

Third—That all general conferences abroad give each individual whom they ordain, a certificate, signed by the chairman and clerk of said conference, stating the time and place of such conference, and the office to which the individual has been ordained; and that when such certificate has been forwarded to the person hereafter authorized to sign licenses as clerk of conference, such person shall, together with chairman of conference, immediately sign a license; and said clerk of conference shall, after the same has been recorded, forward to the proper person.

Fourth—That all official members in good standing and fellowship in the various branches of this Church, be requested to forward their present licenses, accompanied by a certificate of their virtuous and faithful walk before the Lord, signed by the chairman and clerk of a general conference, or by the clerk of a branch of the Church in which such official member resides, by the advice and direction of such Church, to the clerk of conference, whose duty it shall be to fill a new license, as directed in the third article; and that all licenses, signed, recorded, and endorsed, as specified in the first article, shall be considered good, and valid to all intents and purposes, in the business and spiritual affairs of this Church, as a religious society, or before any court of record of this or any other country, wherein preachers of the Gospel are entitled to special privileges, answering in all respects as an original record, without the necessity of referring to any other document.

Fifth—That the recording clerk be required to publish quarterly, in paper published by some member or members of this Church, a list of the names of the several persons for whom he has recorded licenses within the last quarter of a year.

Sixth—That this quorum appoint two persons to sign licenses as chairman and clerk of conference *pro tem.* for the standing chairman and clerk, who shall be appointed as named in the second article, and also to act in their absence, in signing other licenses, as specified in the foregoing article.

President Joseph Smith, Jun., was nominated as chairman, Frederick G. Williams, as clerk, and Sidney Rigdon as chairman *pro tem.* and Oliver Cowdery as clerk *pro tem.* Vote from the several quorums called, in their order, and passed unanimously.

President Joseph Smith, Jun., made some remarks upon the resolution offered to the Council on the 12th of February. Followed by President Thomas B. Marsh, who called a vote of his quorum to ascertain whether they would repeal their amendment of the 13th of February. And nine of the Twelve voted in the affirmative, and three, viz., John F. Boynton, Lyman E. Johnson, and Orson Pratt, in the negative. And the original resolution of the 12th of February was passed.

Dismissed by prayer, half-past nine o'clock.

OLIVER COWDERY, Clerk.

Friday, 4.—Attended school as usual. The sleighing is failing fast, the icy chains of winter seem to be giving way under the influence of the returning sun, and spring will soon open to us with all its charms.

Saturday, 5.—Attended school. In the afternoon the board kiln took fire, and the lumber was principally consumed. To the best of my recollection this is the fifth or sixth time it has burned this winter.

The Board Kiln Again Fired.

Sunday, 6.—Spent the day at home in the enjoyment of the society of my family, around the social fireside.

Monday, 7.—Spent the day in attending to my studies, At the evening, met with my class at Professor Seixas' room and translated the 17th chapter of Genesis.

After the class was dismissed I was requested to tarry, with the rest of the committee, to make some arrangements about paying Mr. Seixas for his instruction, and to engage him for another quarter. We did not arrive at anything definite upon the point. However, Mr. Seixas has agreed to teach us three weeks longer, and perhaps a quarter, after having a vacation of two weeks, at the expiration of the present course.

Tuesday, 8.—Attended school and translated most of the 22nd chapter of Genesis. After my class was dismissed, retired to the printing office and translated ten verses of the 3rd of Exodus, which, with the first and second Psalms, are our next lesson.

Wednesday, 9.—Attended school as usual.

Thursday, 10.—Attended school in the morning Afternoon, read Hebrew in the office.

At evening went down to the Professor's room, to be instructed by him in the language. On account of the storm the class did not meet.

Friday, *11*.—Met with the morning class at nine o'clock.

Further Arrangements of Hebrew Classes.

At ten, went into the office and made a division of our class for private studies, for our better accommodation and advancement in the language we are studying.

Presidents Rigdon, Phelps, and Cowdery, met at the printing office; Elders Orson Pratt, Sylvester Smith, and Bishop Partridge, at Luke S. Johnson's; Elders M'Lellin, Orson Hyde, and Warren Parrish, on the Flats.

This evening our class met at Mr. Seixas' room and spent an hour in our studies. Class dismissed and retired, except the school committee, who tarried and made some arrangements with Mr. Seixas about continuing longer with us and bringing his family to this place. This has been a very stormy day, and the snow is still falling fast, and the prospect is fair for another run of sleighing, which is uncommon for this country at this season of the year.

Saturday, *12*.—Engaged a team to go to Hudson after Mr. Seixas' family and goods, also a horse and carriage for himself and wife. Cold weather and fine sleighing. I was informed today that a man by the name of Clark, who was under the influence of ardent spirits froze to death last night, near this place. How long, O Lord, will this monster intemperance find its victims on the earth! I fear until the earth is swept with the wrath and indignation of God, and Christ's kingdom becomes universal. O, come, Lord Jesus, and cut short Thy work in righteousness.

The Prophet's Reflection on Intemperance

Elder Solomon Hancock received a letter from Missouri bearing the painful intelligence of the death of his wife. May the Lord bless him and comfort him in this hour of affliction.

Sunday, *13*.—Met with the Presidency and some of

the Twelve, and counseled with them upon the subject of removing to Zion this spring. We conversed freely upon the importance of her redemption, and the necessity of the Presidency removing to that place, that their influence might be more effectually used in gathering the Saints to that country; and we finally resolved to emigrate on or before the 15th of May next, if kind Providence smiles upon us and opens the way before us.

Removal of the Presidency and Twelve to Zion Contemplated.

Monday, 14.—Attended school as usual. Professor Seixas returned from Hudson with his family.

Tuesday, 15.—At school in the forenoon.

In the afternoon met in the printing office. Received and waited upon those who called to see me, and attended to my domestic concerns.

In the evening met in the printing office and listened to a lecture on grammar.

Wednesday, 16.—Pursued my studies in the Hebrew language.

In the evening met the choir of singers in the Temple. They performed admirably considering the opportunities they have had.

The Temple Choir.

Thursday, 17.—At school in the morning; in the afternoon in the office.

In the evening met with the quorum in the west school room of the Lord's House to receive or reject certain individuals whose names were submitted for ordination, Erastus B. Whitman, Osmon M. Duel, Chapman Duncan, Joshua Bosley, and Heman Hyde, were received, and four were rejected by the united voice of the assembly.

Friday, 18.—Attended school with the morning class.

At ten o'clock went to the school house to attend the funeral of Susan Johnson, daughter of Ezekiel Johnson. She was a member of the Church of Latter-day Saints, and remained strong in the faith until her spirit took its departure from time into eternity. May God bless and comfort her afflicted parents, family,

Death of Susan Johnson.

connections and friends. President Rigdon delivered a fine discourse on the occasion, and much solemnity prevailed.

Saturday, 19.—Read Hebrew with the morning class. Spent the day in attending to my domestic concerns and the affairs of the Church.

Withdrawal of Objections to the Resolutions on Ordinations.

Elders Orson Pratt, John F. Boynton, and Lyman E. Johnson, met the Presidency of the Church and verbally withdrew all objections to the second resolution presented to the quorums by the Presidency, on the 12th of February, for the regulation of ordinations.

OLIVER COWDERY,
Clerk of Conference.

Sunday, 20.—Attended the house of worship. The quorum of High Priests delivered short addresses to the congregation, in a very feeling and impressive manner. One individual was baptized during intermission.

In the afternoon administered the Lord's Supper, as we are wont to do on every Sabbath, and the Lord blessed our souls with the outpouring of His Spirit, and we were made to rejoice in His goodness.

Elders Obtain from the Courts Licenses to Perform Marriages.

Monday, 21.—At school in the morning. After school went to the printing office and prepared a number of Elders' licenses, to send by Elder Palmer to the court of Medina County, in order to obtain licenses to marry, as the court in this county will not grant us this privilege. Ten persons were baptized in this place.

Tuesday, 22.—Read Hebrew with the morning class. Five young men were received into the Church by baptism in this place today. This is a stormy day, the snow is nearly a foot deep, an uncommon storm for this season of the year.

Wednesday, 23.—Attended school. A pleasant day and fine sleighing. Two were received into the Church by baptism.

Thursday, 24.—Attended school as usual.

In the evening met with my class at the printing office and listened to a lecture by Professor Seixas, upon the Hebrew language. After we were dismissed, we called at the school room to hear the choir of singers perform, which they did admirably. Five more were received into the Church by baptism this day.

Friday, 25.—Attended school with the morning class, also at five o'clock p. m., and heard a lecture upon the Hebrew grammar. We have pleasant weather and good sleighing.

Saturday, 26.—At home in the morning attending to my domestic concerns. After breakfast met with the Presidency to make arrangements for the solemn assembly; this business occupied the remainder of the day.

CHAPTER XXIX.

DEDICATION OF THE KIRTLAND TEMPLE—SPIRITUAL MANIFESTATIONS.

Sunday, March 27.—The congregation began to assemble at the Temple, at about seven o'clock, an hour earlier than the doors were to be opened. Many brethren had come in from the regions round about, to witness the dedication of the Lord's House and share in His blessings; and such was the anxiety on this occasion that some hundreds (probably five or six) assembled before the doors were opened. The presidents entered with the doorkeepers, and stationed the latter at the inner and outer doors; also placed our stewards to receive donations from those who should feel disposed to contribute something to defray the expense of building the House of the Lord. We also dedicated the pulpits, and consecrated them to the Lord.

Gathering of the Saints to the Dedication.

The doors were then opened. Presidents Rigdon, Cowdery and myself seated the congregation as they came in, and, according to the best calculation we could make, we received between nine and ten hundred, which were as many as could be comfortably seated. We then informed the doorkeepers that we could receive no more, and a multitude were deprived of the benefits of the meeting on account of the house not being sufficiently capacious to receive them; and I felt to regret that any of my brethren and sisters should be deprived of the meeting, and I recom-

The Number at the First Meeting.

mended them to repair to the schoolhouse and hold a meeting, which they did, and filled that house also, and yet many were left out.

Arrangement of the Assembly.

The assembly was then organized in the following manner, viz.: west end of the house, Presidents Frederick G. Williams, Joseph Smith, Sen., and William W. Phelps occupying the first pulpit for the Melchisedek Priesthood; Presidents Joseph Smith, Jun., Hyrum Smith, and Sidney Rigdon, the second pulpit; Presidents David Whitmer, Oliver Cowdery, and John Whitmer, the third pulpit; the fourth was occupied by the President of the High Priests' quorum and his counselors, and two choristers. The Twelve Apostles on the right, in the three highest seats. The President of the Elders, his counselors and clerk, in the seat immediately below the Twelve. The High Council of Kirtland, consisting of twelve, on the left in the three first seats. The fourth seat, and next below the High Council, was occupied by Elders Warren A. Cowdery and Warren Parrish, who served as scribes. The pulpits in the east end of the house, for the Aaronic Priesthood, were occupied as follows: The Bishop of Kirtland and his counselors, in the first pulpit; the Bishop of Zion and his counselors, in the second pulpit; the president of the Priests and his counselors, in the third pulpit: the president of the Teachers and his counselors, and one chorister, in the fourth pulpit; the High Council of Zion, consisting of twelve counselors, on the right; the president of the Deacons and his counselors, in the seat below them; the seven presidents of Seventies, on the left. The choir of singers were seated in the four corners of the room, in seats prepared for that purpose.

Received by contribution—nine hundred and sixty-three dollars.

At nine o'clock a. m. President Sidney Rigdon commenced the services of the day by reading the 96th and 24th Psalms.

An excellent choir of singers, led by M. C. Davis, sung the following hymn:

TUNE—*Sterling.*

Ere long the veil will rend in twain,
The King descend with all His train;
The earth shall shake with awful fright,
And all creation feel His might.

The angel's trumpet long shall sound,
And wake the nations under ground;
Throughout the vast domain of space
'Twill echo forth from place to place.

Lift up your heads, ye Saints, in peace,
The Savior comes for your release;
The day of the redeemed has come;
The Saints shall all be welcomed home.

Behold the church! it soars on high,
To meet the Saints amid the sky,
To hail the King in clouds of fire,
And strike and tune th' immortal lyre.

Hosanna! now the trump shall sound,
Proclaim the joys of heaven around,
When all the Saints together join
In songs of love, and all divine.

With Enoch here we all shall meet,
And worship at Messiah's feet,
Unite our hands and hearts in love,
And reigh on thrones with Christ above.

The city that was seen of old,
Whose walls were jasper, streets were gold,
We'll now inherit, throned in might—
The Father and the Son's delight.

Celestial crowns we shall receive,
And glories great our God shall give;
While loud hosannas we'll proclaim,
And sound aloud our Savior's name.

Our hearts and tongues shall join in one,
To praise the Father and the Son;
While all the heavens shall shout again,
And all creation say, Amen.*

President Rigdon addressed the throne of grace in a devout and appropriate manner, and the following hymn was sung:

TUNE—*Weymouth.*

O happy souls, who pray
Where God appoints to hear!
O happy Saints, who pay
Their constant service there
We'll praise Him still,
And happy we
Who love the way
To Zion's hill.

No burning heats by day,
Nor blasts of evening air,
Shall take our health away,
If God be with us there.
He is our sun,
And He our shade
To guard the head
By night or noon.

God is the only Lord,
Our shield and our defense;
With gifts His hands are stored;
We draw our blessings thence.
He will bestow
On Jacob's race
Peculiar grace,
And glory too.†

Elder Rigdon's Discourse.

President Rigdon then read the 18th, 19th and 20th verses of the 18th chapter of Matthew, and preached more particularly from the 20th verse: "Verily I say unto you, whatsoever ye shall bind on earth, shall be bound in heaven; and

* Parley P. Pratt, author.
† W. W. Phelps, author.

whatsoever ye shall loose on earth, shall be loosed in heaven. Again I say unto you, that if two of you shall agree on earth as touching any thing that they shall ask, it shall be done for them of my Father which is in heaven. For where two or three are gathered together in my name, there am I in the midst of them." He spoke two hours and a half in his usual logical manner. His prayer and address were very forcible and sublime, and well adapted to the occasion. At one time, in the course of his remarks, he was rather pathetic, and drew tears from many eyes. He was then taking a retrospective view of the toils, privations, and anxieties of those who had labored upon the walls of the house to erect them; and added, there were those who had wet them with their tears, in the silent shades of night, while they were praying to the God of heaven to protect them, and stay the unhallowed hands of ruthless spoilers, who had uttered a prophecy, when the foundation was laid, that the walls would never be reared.

In reference to his main subject, he assumed as a postulate that in the days of the Savior there were synagogues where the Jews worshiped God, and in addition to them, the splendid temple at Jerusalem, yet, when on a certain occasion,one proposed to follow Christ, whithersoever He went, He, though heir of all things, cried out like one in the bitterness of His soul in abject poverty—"The foxes have holes, and the birds of the air have nests; but the Son of Man hath not where to lay His head." This, said the speaker, was evidence to his mind, that the Most High did not put His name there, and that He did not accept the worship of those who paid their vows and adorations there. This was evident from the fact that they would not receive Him, but thrust Him from them, saying: "Away with Him, crucify Him! crucify Him!" It was therefore abundantly evident that His Spirit did not dwell in them. They were the degenerate sons of noble sires, but they had long since slain the Prophets and Seers, through whom the Lord revealed Himself to the children of men. They were not led by revelation. *This*, said the speaker, was the grand difficulty among them—*their unbelief in present revelation.*

He further remarked, that their unbelief in present revelation, was the means of dividing that generation into the various sects and parties that existed. They were zealous worshipers according to outward forms, but such worship was not required of them, nor was it acceptable to God. The Redeemer Himself, who knew the hearts of all men, called them a generation of vipers. It was proof positive to the speaker's mind, there being Pharisees, Sadducees, Herodians, and Essenes, all differing from one another, that they were led by the precepts and commandments of men. Each had something peculiar to himself, but all agreed in one thing, viz., to oppose the Savior; so that we discover He could, with the utmost propriety, exclaim, notwithstanding their synagogue and temple-worship: "The foxes have holes, and the birds of the air have nests, but the Son of Man hath not where to lay His head."

Remarks on Revelation.

He took occasion here to remark that such diversity of sentiment ever had, and ever would obtain, when people were not led by present revelation. This brought him to the inevitable conclusion, that the various sects of the present day, from their manifesting the same spirit, rested under the same condemnation, with those who were contemporary with the Savior. He admitted there were many houses, many sufficiently large, built for the worship of God, but not one except this, on the face of the whole earth, that was built by divine revelation; and were it not for this the dear Redeemer might, in this day of science, this day of intelligence, this day of religion, say to those who would follow Him: "The foxes have holes, the birds of the air have nests, but the Son of Man hath not where to lay His head."

The Consequence of Rejecting Present Revelation.

After closing his discourse he called upon the several quorums, commencing with the Presidency, to manifest, by rising, their willingness to acknowledge me as a Prophet and Seer, and uphold me as such, by their prayers of faith. All the quorums, in turn, cheerfully complied with this request. He then called upon all the congregation of Saints, also, to give their assent by rising on their feet, which they did unanimously.

Joseph Smith, Jun., Sustained as the Prophet and Seer of the Church.

The following hymn was then sung:

TUNE—*Hosanna.*

Now let us rejoice in the day of salvation,
No longer as strangers on earth need we roam;
Good tidings are sounding to us and each nation,
And shortly the hour of redemption will come;
When all that was promised the Saints will be given,
And none will molest them from morn until even,
And earth will appear as the Garden of Eden,
And Jesus will say to all Israel, Come home.

We'll love one another, and never dissemble,
But cease to do evil, and ever be one;
And while the ungodly are fearing and tremble,
We'll watch for the day when the Savior will come:
When all that was promised the Saints will be given,
And none will molest them from morn until even,
And earth will appear as the Garden of Eden,
And Jesus will say to all Israel, Come home.

In faith we'll rely on the arm of Jehovah
To guide through these last days of trouble and gloom;
And, after the scourges and harvest are over,
We'll rise with the just when the Savior doth come.
Then all that was promised the Saints will be given,
And they will be crowned as the angels of heaven,
And earth will appear as the garden of Eden,
And Christ and His people will ever be one.*

After an intermission of twenty minutes, during which

* W. W. Phelps, author.

time the congregation kept their seats, the services of the day were resumed by singing "Adam-ondi-Ahman:"

This earth was once a garden place,
  With all her glories common;
And men did live a holy race,
And worship Jesus face to face,
  In Adam-ondi-Ahman.

We read that Enoch walked with God,
  Above the power of Mammon;
While Zion spread herself abroad,
And Saints and angels sang aloud,
  In Adam-ondi-Ahman.

Her land was good and greatly blest,
  Beyond old Israel's Canaan;
Her fame was known from east to west;
Her peace was great and pure the rest
  Of Adam-ondi-Ahman.

Hosanna to such days to come—
  The Savior's second coming,
When all the earth in glorious bloom
Affords the Saints a holy home,
  Like Adam-ondi-Ahman.*

Presidency of Church and Twelve Apostles Sustained as Prophets, Seers and Revelators.

I then made a short address, and called upon the several quorums, and all the congregation of Saints, to acknowledge the Presidency as Prophets and Seers, and uphold them by their prayers. They all covenanted to do so, by rising.

I then called upon the quorums and congregation of Saints to acknowledge the Twelve Apostles, who were present, as Prophets, Seers, Revelators, and special witnesses to all the nations of the earth, holding the keys of the kingdom, to unlock it, or cause it to be done, among them, and uphold them by their prayers, which they assented to by rising.

* W. W. Phelps, author.

I next called upon the quorums and congregation of Saints to acknowledge the presidents of Seventies, who act as their representatives, as Apostles and special witnesses to the nations, to assist the Twelve in opening the Gospel kingdom among all people, and to uphold them by their prayers, which they did by rising.

The Seventies Sustained as Apostles and Special Witnesses.

I then called upon the quorums and congregation of Saints to acknowledge the High Council of Kirtland, in all the authority of the Melchisedek Priesthood, and uphold them by their prayers, which they assented to by rising.

High Councils and Bishoprics Sustained

I then called upon the quorums and congregation of Saints to acknowledge, and uphold by their prayers, the Bishops of Kirtland and Zion, and their counselors, in all the authority of the Aaronic Priesthood, which they did by rising.

I next called upon the quorums and congregation of Saints to acknowledge the High Council of Zion, and uphold them by their prayers, in all the authority of the High Priesthood, which they did by rising.

I then called upon the quorums and all the Saints to acknowledge the president of the Elders, and his counselors, and uphold them by their prayers, which they did by rising.

Presidency of Elders Quorum Sustained.

The quorums and congregation of Saints were then called upon to acknowledge, and uphold by their prayers, the presidents and counselors, of the Priests, Teachers and Deacons, which they did by rising.

The Presidencies of the Quorum of the Lesser Priesthood Sustained.

The vote was unanimous in every instance, and I prophesied to all, that inasmuch as they would uphold these men in their several stations, (alluding to the different quorums in the Church), the Lord would bless them; yea, in the name of Christ, the blessings of heaven should be theirs; and when the Lord's anointed go forth to proclaim the word, bearing

The Prophet's Promise and Prediction.

testimony to this generation, if they receive it they shall be blessed; but if not, the judgments of God will follow close upon them, until that city or that house which rejects them, shall be left desolate.

The following hymn was then sung:

TUNE—*Dalston.*

How pleased and blessed was I
To hear the people cry:
"Come, let us seek our God today!"
Yes, with a cheerful zeal,
We'll haste to Zion's hill,
And there our vows and honors pay.

Zion, thrice happy place,
Adorned with wondrous grace,
And walls of strength embrace thee round,
In thee our tribes appear,
To praise and pray and hear
The sacred Gospel's joyful sound.

There, David's greater Son
Has fixed his royal throne;
He sits for grace and judgment there;
He bids the Saints be glad,
He makes the sinner sad,
And humble souls rejoice with fear.

May peace attend thy gate,
And joy within thee wait,
To bless the soul of every guest!
The man that seeks thy peace,
And wishes thine increase,
A thousand blessings on him rest.

My tongue repeats her vows,
"Peace to this sacred house!
For here my friends and kindred dwell;"
And since my glorious God
Makes thee His blest abode,
My soul shall ever love thee well.*

Watts, author.

The dedicatory prayer was then offered:

*The following Prayer was given by Revelation to Joseph, the Seer, and was Repeated in the Kirtland Temple at the time of its Dedication, March 27, 1836.**

PRAYER.

1. Thanks be to Thy name, O Lord God of Israel, who keepest covenant and shewest mercy unto Thy servants who walk uprightly before Thee, with all their hearts;

2. Thou who hast commanded Thy servants to build a house to Thy name in this place (Kirtland).

3. And now Thou beholdest, O Lord, that Thy servants have done according to Thy commandment,

4. And now we ask Thee, Holy Father, in the name of Jesus Christ, the Son of Thy bosom, in whose name alone, salvation can be administered to the children of men, we ask Thee, O Lord, to accept of this house, the workmanship of the hands of us, Thy servants, which Thou didst command us to build;

5. For Thou knowest that we have done this work through great tribulations; and out of our poverty we have given of our substance, to build a house to Thy name, that the Son of Man might have a place to manifest Himself to His people.

6. And as Thou hast said in a revelation, given to us, calling us Thy friends, saying, "Call your solemn assembly, as I have commanded you;

7. And as all have not faith, seek ye diligently, and teach one another words of wisdom; yea, seek ye out of the best books, words of wisdom, seek learning even by study, and also by faith.

8. Organize yourselves; prepare every needful thing, and establish a house, even a house of prayer, a house of fasting, a house of faith, a house of learning, a house of glory, a house of order, a house of God,

9. That your incomings may be in the name of the Lord, that your outgoings may be in the name of the Lord, that all your salutations may be in the name of the Lord, with uplifted hands unto the Most High."

10. And now, Holy Father, we ask Thee to assist us, Thy people, with Thy grace, in calling our solemn assembly, that it may be done to Thy honor, and to Thy divine acceptance,

11. And in a manner that we may be found worthy, in Thy sight, to secure a fulfillment of the promises which Thou hast made unto us, Thy people, in the revelations given unto us;

* Doctrine and Covenants, sec. cix.

12. That Thy glory may rest down upon Thy people, and upon this Thy house, which we now dedicate to Thee, that it may be sanctified and consecrated to be holy, and that Thy holy presence may be continually in this house,

13. And that all people who shall enter upon the threshold of the Lord's House, may feel Thy power, and feel constrained to acknowledge that Thou hast sanctified it, and that it is Thy house, a place of Thy holiness.

14. And do Thou grant, Holy Father, that all those who shall worship in this house, may be taught words of wisdom out of the best books, and that they may seek learning even by study, and also by faith, as Thou hast said;

15. And that they may grow up in Thee, and receive a fullness of the Holy Ghost, and be organized according to Thy laws, and be prepared to obtain every needful thing;

16. And that this house may be a house of prayer, a house of fasting, a house of faith, a house of glory and of God, even Thy house;

17. That all the incomings of Thy people, into this house, may be in the name of the Lord;

18. That all their outgoings from this house may be in the name of the Lord;

19. And that all their salutations may be in the name of the Lord, with holy hands, uplifted to the Most High;

20. And that no unclean thing shall be permitted to come into Thy house to pollute it;

21. And when Thy people transgress, any of them, they may speedily repent, and return unto Thee, and find favor in Thy sight, and be restored to the blessings which Thou hast ordained to be poured out upon those who shall reverence Thee in Thy house.

22. And we ask Thee, Holy Father, that Thy servants may go forth from this house, armed with Thy power, and that Thy name may be upon them, and Thy glory be round about them, and Thine angels have charge over them;

23. And from this place they may bear exceedingly great and glorious tidings, in truth, unto the ends of the earth, that they may know that this is Thy work, and that Thou hast put forth Thy hand, to fulfill that which Thou hast spoken by the mouths of the Prophets concerning the last days.

24. We ask Thee, Holy Father, to establish the people that shall worship, and honorably hold a name and standing in this Thy house to all generations, and for eternity,

25. That no weapon formed against them shall prosper; that he who diggeth a pit for them shall fall into the same himself.

26. That no combination of wickedness shall have power to rise up and prevail over Thy people upon whom Thy name shall be put in this house;

27. And if any people shall rise against this people, that Thine anger be kindled against them,

28. And if they shall smite this people, Thou wilt smite them, Thou wilt fight for Thy people as Thou didst in the day of battle, that they may be delivered from the hands of all their enemies.

29. We ask Thee, Holy Father, to confound, and astonish, and to bring to shame and confusion, all those who have spread lying reports, abroad, over the world, against Thy servant, or servants, if they will not repent, when the everlasting Gospel shall be proclaimed in their ears,

30. And that all their works may be brought to naught, and be swept away by the hail, and by the judgments which Thou wilt send upon them in Thine anger, that there may be an end to lyings and slanders against Thy people;

31. For Thou knowest, O Lord, that Thy servants have been innocent before Thee in bearing record of Thy name, for which they have suffered these things;

32. Therefore we plead before Thee for a full and complete deliverance from under this yoke;

33. Break it off, O Lord; break it off from the necks of Thy servants, by Thy power, that we may rise up in the midst of this generation and do Thy work.

34. Jehovah, have mercy upon this people, and as all men sin, forgive the transgressions of Thy people, and let them be blotted out forever.

35. Let the anointing of Thy ministers be sealed upon them with power from on high;

36. Let it be fulfilled upon them, as upon those on the day of Pentecost, let the gift of tongues be poured out upon Thy people, even cloven tongues as of fire, and the interpretation thereof,

37. And let Thy house be filled, as with a rushing mighty wind, with Thy glory.

38. Put upon Thy servants the testimony of the covenant, that when they go out and proclaim Thy word, they may seal up the law, and prepare the hearts of Thy Saints for all those judgments Thou art about to send, in Thy wrath, upon the inhabitants of the earth, because of their transgressions, that Thy people may not faint in the day of trouble.

39. And whatsoever city Thy servants shall enter, and the people of that city receive their testimony, let Thy peace and Thy salvation be

upon that city, that they may gather out of that city the righteous, that they may come forth to Zion, or to her stakes, the places of Thine appointment, with songs of everlasting joy,

40. And until this be accomplished, let not Thy judgments fall upon that city.

41. And whatsoever city Thy servants shall enter, and the people of that city receive not the testimony of Thy servants, and Thy servants warn them to save themselves from this untoward generation, let it be upon that city according to that which Thou hast spoken by the mouths of Thy Prophets;

42. But deliver Thou, O Jehovah we beseech Thee, Thy servants from their hands, and cleanse them from their blood.

43. O Lord, we delight not in the destruction of our fellow men; their souls are precious before Thee;

44. But Thy word must be fulfilled; help Thy servants to say, with Thy grace assisting them, Thy will be done, O Lord, and not ours.

45. We know that Thou hast spoken by the mouth of Thy Prophets terrible things concerning the wicked, in the last days—that Thou wilt pour out Thy judgments, without measure;

46. Therefore, O Lord, deliver Thy people from the calamity of the wicked; enable Thy servants to seal up the law, and bind up the testimony, that they may be prepared against the day of burning.

47. We ask Thee, Holy Father, to remember those who have been driven by the inhabitants of Jackson county, Missouri, from the lands of their inheritance, and break off, O Lord, this yoke of affliction that has been put upon them,

48. Thou knowest, O Lord, that they have been greatly oppressed and afflicted by wicked men, and our hearts flow out with sorrow, because of their grievous burdens.

49. O Lord, how long wilt Thou suffer this people to bear this affliction, and the cries of their innocent ones to ascend up in Thine ears, and their blood come up in testimony before Thee, and not make a display of Thy testimony in their behalf?

50. Have mercy, O Lord, upon the wicked mob, who have driven Thy people, that they may cease to spoil, that they may repent of their sins, if repentance is to be found;

51. But if they will not, make bare Thine arm, O Lord, and redeem that land which Thou didst appoint a Zion unto Thy people!

52. And if it cannot be otherwise, that the cause of Thy people may not fail before Thee, may Thine anger be kindled, and Thine indignation fall upon them, that they may be wasted away, both root and branch, from under heaven;

53. But inasmuch as they will repent, Thou art gracious and merci-

ful, and wilt turn away Thy wrath, when Thou lookest upon the face of Thine anointed.

54. Have mercy, O Lord, upon all the nations of the earth, have mercy upon the rulers of our land, may those principles which were so honorably and nobly defended, viz., the Constitution of our land, by our fathers, be established forever;

55. Remember the kings, princes, the nobles, and the great ones of the earth, and all people, and the churches, all the poor, the needy, and afflicted ones of the earth,

56. That their hearts may be softened, when Thy servants shall go out from Thy house, O Jehovah, to bear testimony of Thy name, that their prejudices may give way before the truth, and Thy people may obtain favor in the sight of all,

57. That all the ends of the earth may know that we Thy servants have heard Thy voice, and that Thou hast sent us,

58. That from among all these, Thy servants, the sons of Jacob, may gather out the righteous to build a holy city to Thy name, as Thou hast commanded them.

59. We ask Thee to appoint unto Zion other stakes, besides this one which Thou hast appointed, that the gathering of Thy people may roll on in great power and majesty, that Thy work may be cut short in righteousness.

60. Now these words, O Lord, we have spoken before Thee, concerning the revelations and commandments which Thou hast given unto us, who are identified with the Gentiles;

61. But Thou knowest that Thou hast a great love for the children of Jacob, who have been scattered upon the mountains, for a long time, in a cloudy and dark day;

62. We therefore ask Thee to have mercy upon the children of Jacob, that Jerusalem, from this hour, may begin to be redeemed,

63. And the yoke of bondage may begin to be broken off from the house of David.

64. And the children of Judah may begin to return to the lands which Thou didst give to Abraham, their father;

65. And cause that the remnants of Jacob, who have been cursed and smitten, because of their transgression, be converted from their wild and savage condition to the fullness of the everlasting Gosgel,

66. That they may lay down their weapons of bloodshed, and cease their rebellions;

67. And may all the scattered remnants of Israel, who have been driven to the ends of the earth, come to a knowledge of the truth, believe in the Messiah, and be redeemed from oppression, and rejoice before Thee.

68. O Lord, remember Thy servant, Joseph Smith, Jun., and all his afflictions and persecutions—how he has covenanted with Jehovah, and vowed to Thee, O mighty God of Jacob—and the commandments which Thou hast given unto him, and that he hath sincerely striven to do Thy will.

69. Have mercy, O Lord, upon his wife and children, that they may be exalted in Thy presence, and preserved by Thy fostering hand;

70. Have mercy upon all their immediate connections, that their prejudices may be broken up, and swept away as with a flood, that they may be converted and redeemed with Israel, and know that Thou art God.

71. Remember, O Lord, the presidents, even all the presidents of Thy Church, that Thy right hand may exalt them, with all their families, and their immediate connections, that their names may be perpetuated, and had in everlasting remembrance, from generation to generation.

72. Remember all Thy Church, O Lord, with all their families, and all their immediate connections, with all their sick and afflicted ones, with all the poor and meek of the earth, that the kingdom which Thou hast set up without hands, may become a great mountain, and fill the whole earth;

73. That Thy Church may come forth out of the wilderness of darkness, and shine forth fair as the moon, clear as the sun, and terrible as an army with banners;

74. And be adorned as a bride for that day when Thou shalt unveil the heavens, and cause the mountains to flow down at Thy presence, and the valleys to be exalted, the rough places made smooth; that Thy glory may fill the earth,

75. That when the trump shall sound for the dead we shall be caught up in the clouds to meet Thee, that we may ever be with the Lord,

76. That our garments may be pure, that we may be clothed upon with robes of righteousness, with palms in our hands, and crowns of glory upon our heads, and reap eternal joy for all our sufferings.

77. O Lord God Almighty, hear us in these our petitions, and answer us from heaven, Thy holy habitation, where Thou sittest enthroned, with glory, honor, power, majesty, might, dominion, truth, justice, judgment, mercy, and an infinity of fullness, from everlasting to everlasting.

78. O hear, O hear, O hear us O Lord! and answer these petitions, and except the dedication of this house unto Thee, the work of our hands, which we have built unto Thy name.

79. And also this Church, to put upon it Thy name; and help us by the power of Thy Spirit, that we may mingle our voices with those

bright, shining seraphs around Thy throne, with acclamations of praise, singing hosanna to God and the Lamb;

80. And let these Thine anointed ones be clothed with salvation, and Thy Saints shout aloud for joy. Amen and amen.

The choir then sang:

TUNE—*Hosanna.*

The Spirit of God like a fire is burning!
The latter-day glory begins to come forth;
The visions and blessings of old are returning,
The angels are coming to visit the earth.

CHORUS.

We'll sing and we'll shout with the armies of heaven—
Hosanna, hosanna to God and the Lamb!
Let glory to them in the highest be given,
Henceforth and forever: amen and amen.

The Lord is extending the Saints' understanding,
Restoring their judges and all as at first;
The knowledge and power of God are expanding;
The veil o'ver the earth is beginning to burst.
We'll sing and we'll shou, etc.

We'll call in our solemn assemblies in spirit,
To spread forth the kingdom of heaven abroad,
That we through our faith may begin to inherit
The visions and blessings and glories ot God.
We'll sing and we'll shout, etc.

We'll wash and be washed, and with oil be anointed,
Withal not omitting the washing of feet;
For he that receiveth his penny appointed
Must surely be clean at the harvest of wheat.
We'll sing and we'll shout, etc.

Old Israel, that fled from the world for his freedom,
Must come with the cloud and the pillar amain;
And Moses and Aaron and Joshua lead him,
And feed him on manna from heaven again.
We'll sing and we'll shout, etc.

How blessed the day when the lamb and the lion
Shall lie down together without any ire,
And Ephraim be crowned with his blessing in Zion,
As Jesus descends with His chariots of fire!

We'll sing and we'll shout with the armies of heaven—
Hosanna, hosanna to God and the Lamb!
Let glory to them in the highest be given,
Henceforth and forever: amen and amen! *

I then asked the several quorums separately, and then the congregation, if they accepted the dedication prayer, and acknowledged the house dedicated. The vote was unanimous in the affirmative, in every instance.

Dedication of the Temple Accepted by the Priesthood and the Saints.

The Lord's Supper was then administered; President Don Carlos Smith blessed the bread and the wine, which was distributed by several Elders to the Church; after which I bore record of my mission, and of the ministration of angels.

The Lord's Supper and Testimonies.

President Don Carlos Smith also bore testimony of the truth of the work of the Lord in which we were engaged.

President Oliver Cowdery testified of the truth of the Book of Mormon, and of the work of the Lord in these last days.

President Frederick G. Williams arose and testified that while President Rigdon was making his first prayer, an angel entered the window and took his seat between Father Smith and himself, and remained there during the prayer.

President David Whitmer also saw angels in the house.

President Hyrum Smith made some appropriate remarks congratulating those who had endured so many toils and privations to build the house.

President Rigdon then made a few appropriate closing remarks, and a short prayer, at the close of which we sealed the proceedings of the day by shouting hosanna,

* W. W. Phelps.

hosanna, hosanna to God and the Lamb, three times, sealing it each time with amen, amen, and amen.

President Brigham Young gave a short address in tongues, and David W. Patten interpreted, and gave a short exhortation in tongues himself, after which I blessed the congregation in the name of the Lord, and the assembly dispersed a little past four o'clock, having manifested the most quiet demeanor during the whole exercise.

I met the quorums in the evening and instructed them respecting the ordinance of washing of feet, which they were to attend to on Wednesday following; and gave them instructions in relation to the spirit of prophecy, and called upon the congregation to speak, and not to fear to prophesy good concerning the Saints, for if you prophesy the falling of these hills and the rising of the valleys, the downfall of the enemies of Zion and the rising of the kingdom of God, it shall come to pass. Do not quench the Spirit, for the first one that opens his mouth shall receive the Spirit of prophecy.

Spiritual Manifestations in the Kirtland Temple.

Brother George A. Smith arose and began to prophesy, when a noise was heard like the sound of a rushing mighty wind, which filled the Temple, and all the congregation simultaneously arose, being moved upon by an invisible power; many began to speak in tongues and prophesy; others saw glorious visions; and I beheld the Temple was filled with angels, which fact I declared to the congregation. The people of the neighborhood came running together (hearing an unusual sound within, and seeing a bright light like a pillar of fire resting upon the Temple), and were astonished at what was taking place. This continued until the meeting closed at eleven p. m.

The number of official members present on this occasion was four hundred and sixteen, being a greater number than ever assembled on any former occasion.

CHAPTER XXX.

THE ORDINANCE OF WASHING OF FEET—VISIONS IN THE KIRTLAND TEMPLE—THE PROPHET ON ABOLITION.

Monday, March 28.—Attended school. Very warm, like spring.

Tuesday, 29.—Attended school, which was the last day of our course of lectures in Hebrew, by Professor Seixas.

Seeking the Word and Will of the Lord.

At eleven o'clock, a.m., Presidents Joseph Smith, Jun., Frederick G. Williams, Sidney Rigdon, Hyrum Smith, and Oliver Cowdery, met in the most holy place in the Lord's House, and sought for a revelation from Him concerning the authorities of the Church going to Zion, and other important matters. After uniting in prayer, the voice of the Spirit was that we should come into this place three times, and also call the other presidents, the two Bishops and their counselors, each to stand in his place, and fast through the day and also the night, and that during this, if we would humble ourselves, we should receive further communications from Him. After this word was received we immediately sent for the other brethren, who came.

The Presidency proceeded to ordain George Boosinger to the High Priesthood, and anoint him. This was in consequence of his having administered unto us in temporal things in our distress, and also because he left the place just previous to the dedication of the Lord's House, to bring us the temporal means, previously named. Soon after this, the word of the Lord came, through President Joseph Smith, Jun., that those who had entered the holy place, must not leave the house until morning, but send for such things as were necessary, and, also, during our stay, we must cleanse our feet and partake of the Sacrament that we might be made holy before Him, and thereby be qualified to officiate in our calling, upon the morrow, in washing the feet of the Elders.

The Washing of Feet.

Accordingly we proceeded to cleanse our faces and our feet, and then proceeded to wash one another's feet. President Sidney Rigdon first washed President Joseph Smith, Junior's feet, and then, in turn, was washed by him; after which President Rigdon washed President Joseph Smith, Sen., and Hyrum Smith. President Joseph Smith, Jun., washed President Frederick G. Williams, and then President Hyrum Smith washed President David Whitmer's and President Oliver Cowdery's feet. Then President David Whitmer washed President William W. Phelps' feet, and in tu:n President Phelps washed President John Whitmer's feet. The Bishops and their Counselors were then washed, after which we partook of the bread and wine. The Holy Spirit rested down upon us, and we continued in the Lord's House all night, prephesying and giving glory to God.

Continuance of the Ordinance of Feet Washing.

Wednesday, *30*.—At eight o'clock, according to appointment, the Presidency, the Twelve, the Seventies, the High Council, the Bishops and their entire quorums, the Elders and all the official members in this stake of Zion, amounting to about three hundred, met in the Temple of the Lord to attend to the ordinance of washing of feet. I ascended the pulpit, and remarked to the congregation that we had passed through many trials and afflictions since the organization of the Church, and that this is a year of jubilee to us, and a time of rejoicing, and that it was expedient for us to prepare bread and wine sufficient to make our hearts glad, as we should not, probably, leave this house until morning; to this end we should call on the brethren to make a contribution. The stewards passed round and took up a liberal contribution, and messengers were despatched for bread and wine.

Tubs, water, and towels were prepared, and I called the house to order, and the Presidency proceeded to wash the feet of the Twelve, pronouncing many prophecies and blessings upon them in the name of the Lord Jesus; and then the Twelve proceeded to wash the feet of the Presidents of the several quorums. The brethren began to prophesy upon each other's heads, and upon the enemies of Christ, who inhabited Jackson county, Missouri; and continued prophesying, and blessing, and sealing them with hosanna and amen, until nearly seven o'clock in the evening.

The bread and the wine were then brought in, and I observed that we had fasted all the day, and lest we faint, as the Savior did so shall we do on this occasion; we shall bless the bread, and give it to the Twelve, and they to the multitude. While waiting, I made the following remarks: that the time that we were required to tarry in Kirtland to be endowed, would be fulfilled in a few days, and then the Elders would go forth, and each must stand for himself, as it was not necessary for them to be sent out, two by two, as in former times, but to go in all meekness, in sobriety, and preach Jesus Christ and Him crucified; not to contend with others on account of their faith, or systems of religion, but pursue a steady course. This I delivered by way of commandment; and all who observe it not, will pull down persecution upon their heads, while those who do, shall always be filled with the Holy Ghost; this I pronounced as a prophecy, and sealed with hosanna and amen. Also that the Seventies are not called to serve tables, or preside over churches, to settle difficulties, but are to preach the Gospel and build them up, and set others, who do not belong to these quorums, to preside over them,

The Prophet's Instruction to the Elders Who Engage in the Ministry.

who are High Priests. The Twelve also are not to serve tables, but to bear the keys of the Kingdom to all nations, and unlock the door of the Gospel to them, and call upon the Seventies to follow after them, and assist them. The Twelve are at liberty to go wheresoever they will, and if any one will say, I wish to go to such a place, let all the rest say amen.

The Seventies are at liberty to go to Zion if they please, or go wheresoever they will, and preach the Gospel; and let the redemption of Zion be our object, and strive to effect it by sending up all the strength of the Lord's House, wherever we find them; and I want to enter into the following covenant, that if any more of our brethren are slain or driven from their lands in Missouri, by the mob, we will give ourselves no rest, until we are avenged of our enemies to the uttermost. This covenant was sealed unanimously, with a hosanna and an amen.

I then observed to the quorums, that I had now completed the organization of the Church, and we had passed through all the necessary ceremonies, that I had given them all the instruction they needed, and that they now were at liberty, after obtaining their licenses, to go forth and build up the Kingdom of God, and that it was expedient for me and the Presidency to retire, having spent the night previously in waiting upon the Lord in His Temple, and having to attend another dedication on the morrow, or conclude the one commenced on the last Sabbath, for the benefit of those of my brethren and sisters who could not get into the house on the former occasion, but that it was expedient for the brethren to tarry all night and worship before the Lord in His house.

The Day—March 30th—A Pentecost.

I left the meeting in the charge of the Twelve, and retired about nine o'clock in the evening. The brethren continued exhorting, prophesying, and speaking in tongues until five o'clock in the morning. The Savior made His appearance to some, while angels ministered to others, and it was a Pentecost and an endowment indeed, long to be remembered, for the sound shall go forth from this place into all the world, and the occurrences of this day shall be handed down upon the pages of sacred history, to all generations; as the day of Pentecost, so shall this day be numbered and celebrated as a year of jubilee, and time of rejoicing to the Saints of the Most High God.

Thursday, *31.*—This day being set apart to perform again the ceremonies of the dedication, for the benefit of those who could not get into the house on the preceding Sabbath, I repaired to the Temple at eight, a. m., in company with the Presidency, and arranged our door keepers and stewards as on the former occasion. We then opened the doors, and a large congregation entered the house, and were comfortably seated. The authorities of the Church were seated in their respective places, and the services of the day were commenced, prosecuted and terminated in the same manner as at the former dedication, and the Spirit of God rested upon the congregation, and great solemnity prevailed.

The Second Day of Dedicatory Service.

Friday, *April 1.*—At home most of the day. Many brethren called to see me, some on temporal and some on spiritual business; among the number was Leman Copley, who testified against me in a suit I brought against Dr. Philastus Hurlburt for threatening my life. He confessed that he bore a false testimony against me in that suit, but verily thought, at the time, that he was right, but on calling to mind all the circumstances connected with the things that happened at that time, he was convinced that he was wrong, and humbly confessed it, and asked my forgiveness, which was readily granted. He also wished to be received into the Church again, by baptism, and was received according to his desire. He gave me his confession in writing.

Confession of Leman Copley to Bearing False Witness

Saturday, *2.*—Transacted business of a temporal nature in the upper room in the printing office, in company with

Frederick G. Williams, Sidney Rigdon, Oliver Cowdery, William W. Phelps and John Whitmer, which was to have a bearing upon the redemption of Zion. After mature deliberation the council decided that Oliver Cowdery and myself should act as a board or committee to raise, in righteousness, all the money we could for a season, to send by, or to, certain wise men appointed to purchase lands in Zion in obedience to a revelation or commandment of the Lord, for the mutual benefit of the council.

The Prophet and Oliver Cowdery Appointed to Raise Money for the Redemption of Zion.

Also, it was agreed by the council that Sidney Rigdon and Frederick G. Williams exert themselves in devising ways and means with the stock on hand, the available outstanding claims of the company, and such other means as they shall deem most proper, to discharge the company's debts. It was also agreed that W. W. Phelps, John Whitmer, and David Whitmer have five hundred books of Doctrine and Covenants, when bound, and five hundred Hymn Books, together with the subscription list for the *Messenger and Advocate* and *Northern Times*,* now due in Clay County, Missouri; and that Messrs. Phelps and John Whitmer be released from the responsibility of claims on them, or either of them, as joint partners in the firm.

As soon as the above plans were settled, I started with President Cowdery on our mission, and our success was such in one half day as to give us pleasing anticipations that we were doing the will of God, and assurance that His work prospered in our hands.

Sunday, 3.—Attended meeting in the Lord's House, and assisted the other Presidents of the Church in seating the congregation, and then became an attentive listener to the preaching from the stand. Thomas B. Marsh and David W. Patten spoke in the forenoon to an attentive

* This was the weekly newspaper which had been started in February, 1835, in support of Democracy; and which was edited by Frederick G. Williams.

audience of about one thousand persons. In the afternoon, I assisted the other Presidents in distributing the Lord's Supper to the Church, receiving it from the Twelve, whose privilege it was to officiate at the sacred desk this day. After having performed this service to my brethren, I retired to the pulpit, the veils being dropped, and bowed myself, with Oliver Cowdery, in solemn and silent prayer. After rising from prayer, the following vision was opened to both of us—

*Vision Manifested to Joseph the Seer and Oliver Cowdery.**

1. The veil was taken from our minds, and the eyes of our understanding were opened.

2. We saw the Lord standing upon the breastwork of the pulpit, before us, and under His feet was a paved work of pure gold in color like amber.

3. His eyes were as a flame of fire, the hair of His head was white like the pure snow, His countenance shone above the brightness of the sun, and His voice was as the sound of the rushing of great waters, even the voice of Jehovah, saying—

4. I am the first and the last, I am He who liveth, I am He who was slain, I am your advocate with the Father.

5. Behold, your sins are forgiven you, you are clean before me, therefore lift up your heads and rejoice.

6. Let the hearts of your brethren rejoice, and let the hearts of all my people rejoice, who have, with their might, built this house to my name.

7. For behold, I have accepted this house, and my name shall be here, and I will manifest myself to my people in mercy in this House.

8. Yea, I will appear unto my servants, and speak unto them with mine own voice, if my people will keep my commandments, and do not pollute this holy house.

9. Yea the hearts of thousands and tens of thousands shall greatly rejoice in consequence of the blessings which shall be poured out, and the endowment with which my servants have been endowed in this house;

10. And the fame of this house shall spread to foreign lands, and this is the beginning of the blessing which shall be poured out upon the heads of my people. Even so. Amen.

11. After this vision closed, the heavens were again opened unto us, and Moses appeared before us, and committed unto us the keys of the

* Doctrine and Covenants, sec. cx.

gathering of Israel from the four parts of the earth, and the leading of the Ten Tribes from the land of the north.

12. After this, Elias appeared, and committed the dispensation of the Gospel of Abraham, saying, that in us, and our seed, all generations after us should be blessed.

13. After this vision had closed, another great and glorious vision burst upon us, for Elijah the Prophet, who was taken to heaven without tasting death, stood before us, and said—

14. Behold, the time has fully come, which was spoken of by the mouth of Malachi, testifying that he [Elijah] should be sent before the great and dreadful day of the Lord come.

15. To turn the hearts of the fathers to the children, and the children to the fathers, lest the whole earth be smitten with a curse.

16. Therefore the keys of this dispensation are committed into your hands, and by this ye may know that the great and dreadful day of the Lord is near, even at the doors.

Monday, 4.—The Elders began to spread abroad in all parts of the land, preaching the word.

Leading Elders Return to Zion—Missouri.

Saturday, 9.—Myself and the principal heads of the Church, accompanied the wise men of Zion, namely, Bishop Partridge and his counselors, Isaac Morley and John Corrill, and President W. W. Phelps, on their way home, as far as Chardon; and after staying with them all night, blessed them in the morning, and returned to Kirtland.

Soon after I wrote an article for the *Messenger and Advocate*, which was published in the April number as follows:—

The Prophet's Views on Abolition.

Brother Oliver Cowdery,

DEAR SIR:—This place [Kirtland] having recently been visited by a gentleman who advocated the principles or doctrines of those who are called Abolitionists, and his presence having created an interest in that subject, if you deem the following reflections of any service, or think they will have a tendency to correct the opinions of the Southern public, relative to the views and sentiments I entertain, as an individual, and which I am able to say from personal knowledge are the sentiments of others, you are at liberty to give them publicity in the columns of the *Advocate*. In one respect I am prompted to this course in consequence of many Elders having gone into the Southern States, besides there being now many in that country who have already embraced the fulness of the Gospel, as revealed through the Book of Mormon. I have learned by experience that the enemy of truth does not slumber, nor cease his exertions to bias the minds of communities against the servants of the Lord, by stirring up the indignation of men upon all matters of importance or interest; therefore I fear that the sound might go out, that "an Abolitionist" had held forth several times to this community, and that the public feeling was not aroused to create mobs or disturbances, leaving the impression that all he said was concurred in, and received as Gospel, and the word of salvation. I am happy to say that no violence, or breach of the public peace, was attempted; so far from this, all, except a very few, attended to their own vocations, and left the gentleman to hold forth his own arguments to nearly naked walls. I am aware that many, who profess to preach the Gospel, complain against their brethren of the same faith, who reside in the South, and are ready to withdraw the hand of fellowship, because they will not renounce the principle of slavery, and raise their voice against every thing of the kind. This must be a tender point, and one which should call forth the candid reflections of all men, and more especially before they advance in an opposition calculated to lay waste the fair states of the South, and let loose upon the world a community of people, who might, peradventure, overrun our country, and violate the most sacred principles of human society, chastity and virtue.

No one will pretend to say that the people of the free states are as capable of knowing the evils of slavery, as those who hold slaves. If slavery be an evil, who could we expect would first learn it: Would the people of the free states, or the people of the slave states? All must readily admit, that the latter would first learn this fact. If the fact were learned first by those immediately concerned, who would be more capable than they of prescribing a remedy? And besides, are not those who hold slaves, persons of ability, discernment and candor? Do they not expect to give an account at the bar of God for their conduct in this life? It may no doubt with propriety be said that many who hold slaves live without the fear of God before their eyes; but the same may be said of many in the free states. Then who is to be the judge in this matter? So long, then, as the people of the free states, are not interested in the freedom of the slaves, in any other way than upon the mere abstract principles of equal rights, and of the Gospel; and are ready to admit that there are men of piety, who reside in the South, who are immediately concerned, and until *they* complain and call for assistance, why not cease this clamor, and no further urge the slave to acts of murder, and the master to vigorous discipline, rendering both miserable, and unprepared to pursue that course which might otherwise lead them both to better their conditions? I do not believe that the people of the North have any more right to say that the South *shall not* hold slaves, than the South have to say the North shall.

And further, what benefit will it ever be to the slaves for persons to run over the free states, and excite indignation against their masters in the minds of thousands and tens of thousands, who understand nothing relative to their circumstances, or conditions? I mean particularly those who have never traveled in the South, and who in all their lives have scarcely ever seen a negro.

How any community can ever be excited with the chatter of such persons, boys and others, who are too indolent to obtain their living by honest industry, and are incapable of pursuing any occupation of a professional nature, is unaccountable to me; and when I see persons in the free states, signing documents against slavery, it is no less, in my mind, than an army of influence, and a declaration of hostilities, against the people of the South. What course can sooner divide our union?

After having expressed myself so freely upon this subject, I do not doubt, but those who have been forward in raising their voices against the South, will cry out against me as being uncharitable, unfeeling, unkind, and wholly unacquainted with the Gospel of Christ. It is my privilege then to name certain passages from the Bible, and examine the teachings of the ancients upon the matter as the fact is uncontrovertible that the first mention we have of slavery is found in the Holy Bible, pronounced by a man who was perfect in his generation, and walked with God. And so far from that prediction being averse to the mind of God, it remains as a lasting monument of the decree of Jehovah, to the shame and confusion of all who have cried out against the South, in consequence of their holding the sons of Ham in servitude. "And he said, Cursed be Canaan; a servant of servants shall he be unto his brethren." "Blessed be the Lord God of Shem; and Canaan shall be his servant" (Gen. ix: 25, 26).

Trace the history of the world from this notable event down to this day, and you will find the fulfillment of this singular prophecy. What could have been the design of the Almighty in this singular occurrence is not for me to say; but I can say, the curse is not yet taken off from the sons of Canaan, neither will be until it is affected by as great a power as caused it to come; and the people who interfere the least with the purposes of God in this matter, will come under the least condemnation before Him; and those who are determined to pursue a course, which shows an opposition, and a feverish restlessness against the decrees of the Lord, will learn, when perhaps it is too late for their own good, that God can do His own work, without the aid of those who are not dictated by His counsel.

I must not pass ever a notice of the history of Abraham, of whom so much is spoken in the Scripture. If we can credit the account, God conversed with him from time to time, and directed him in the way he should walk, saying, I am the Almighty; walk before me, and be thou perfect." Paul says the Gospel was preached to this man. And it is further said, that he had sheep and oxen, men-servants and maid-servants, etc. From this I conclude, that if the principle had been an evil one, in the midst of the communications made to this holy man, he would have been instructed to that effect, and if he was instructed against holding men servants and maid-servants, he never ceased to do it; consequently must have incurred the displeasure of the Lord, and thereby lost His blessings; which was not the fact.

Some may urge that the names man servant and maid-servant, only mean hired persons, who were at liberty to leave their masters or employers at any time. But we can easily settle this point, by turning to the history of Abraham's descendants, when governed by a law from the mouth of Jehovah Himself. I know that when an Israelite had been brought into servitude, in consequence of debt, or otherwise, at the seventh year he went from the task of his former master, or employer; but to no other people or nation was this granted in the law of Israel. And if after a man had served six years, he did not wish to be free, then the master was to bring him unto the judges—bore his ear with an awl, and that man was "to serve him forever." The conclusion I draw from this, is, that this people were led and governed by revelation, and if such a law was wrong, God only is to be blamed, and abolitionists are not responsible.

Now, before proceeding any farther, I wish to ask one or two questions: Were the Apostles men of God, and did they preach the Gospel? I have no doubt that those who believe the Bible, will admit that they were; and that they also knew the mind and will of God concerning what they wrote to the churches, which they were instrumental in building up. This being admitted, the matter can be put to rest without much argument, if we look at a few items in the New Testament. Paul says: "Servants be obedient to them that are your masters according to the flesh, with fear and trembling, in singleness of your heart, as unto Christ; not with eyeservice as men-pleasers; but as the servants of Christ, doing the will of God from the heart; with good will doing service, as to the Lord, and not to men: knowing that whatsoever good thing any man doeth, the same shall be received of the Lord, whether he be bond or free. And, ye masters, do the same things unto them, forbearing threatening: knowing that your Master also is in heaven: neither is there respect of persons with him" (Eph. vi: 5, 6, 7, 8, 9). Here is a lesson which might be profitable for all to learn; and the principle upon which the Church was anciently governed, is so plainly set forth, that an eye of truth might see and understand. Here certainly, are represented the master, and servant; and so far from instructions to the servant to leave his master, he is commanded to be in obedience, as unto the Lord; the master in turn, is required to treat him with kindness before God; understanding, at the same time, that he is to give an account. The hand of fellowship is not withdrawn from him in consequence of his having servants.

The same writer, in his first epistle to Timothy, the sixth chapter, and the first five verses, says,—"Let as many servants as are under the yoke count their own masters worthy of all honor, that the name of God and His doctrine be not blasphemed. And they that have believing masters, let them not despise them, because they are brethren; but rather do them service, because they are faithful and beloved, partakers of the benefit. These things teach and exhort. If any man teach otherwise, and consent not to wholesome words, even the words of our Lord Jesus Christ, and to the doctrine which is according to godliness; he is proud, knowing nothing, but doting about questions and strifes of words, whereof cometh envy, strife, railings, evil surmisings, perverse disputing of men of corrupt minds, and destitute of the truth, supposing that gain is godliness: from such withdraw thyself." This is so perfectly plain, that I see no need of comment. The Scripture stands for itself; and I believe that these men were better qualified to teach the will of God, than all the abolitionists in the world.

Before closing this communication, I beg leave to drop a word to the traveling Elders. You know, brethren, that great responsibility rests upon you; and that you are accountable to God, for all you teach the world. In my opinion, you will do well to search the Book of Covenants, in which you will see the belief of the Church, concerning masters and servants. All men are to be taught to repent; but we have no right to interfere with slaves, contrary to the mind and will of their masters. In fact it would be much better, and more prudent, not to preach at all to slaves, until after their masters are converted, and then teach the masters to use them with kindness; remembering that they are accountable to God, and the servants are bound to serve their masters with singleness of heart, without murmuring.

I do most sincerely hope that no one who is authorized from this Church to preach the Gospel, will so far depart from the Scriptures, as to be found stirring up strife and sedition against our brethren of the South. Having spoken frankly and freely, I leave all in the hands of God, who will direct all things for His glory, and the accomplishment of His work. Praying that God may spare you to do much good in this life, I subscribe myself your brother in the Lord,

JOSEPH SMITH, JUN.

CHAPTER XXXI.

PREDICTION OF THE PROPHET'S GRANDPARENTS—AGITATION FOR THE REMOVAL OF THE SAINTS FROM CLAY COUNTY, MISSOURI.

THE remainder of this month [April] and May also, was devoted to the spiritual interests of the brethren; and particularly in devising ways and means to build up Kirtland.

Labors of Elder Heber C. Kimball.

May 10.--Brother Heber C. Kimball came to me for counsel, to know whether he should go into the vineyard to proclaim the Gospel, or go to school. I told him he might do either that he should choose, for the Lord would bless him. He chose to go into the vineyard; and immediately went down through the State of New York, into Vermont, his native State. He stopped a short time, and then returned to the city of Ogdensburg, on the St. Lawrence river, where he built up a church of twenty members. When about leaving that place, my father, and uncle John Smith, came to him, and blessed the church with patriarchal blessings. When they came to Brother Kimball, they were very much depressed in spirits, for when they came through the town of Potsdam, their brother, Jesse Smith, having a spite against them in consequence of their religion, swore out an execution against my father, and levied upon his horse and wagon; and to settle the affair, and get out of his clutches, my uncle, Silas Smith, (who had returned to that place on private business) stepped forward and paid fifty dollars, in order that they might pursue their journey home.

May, 16.—President Oliver Cowdery having preferred, to the High Council, a charge of unchristianlike conduct against Wilkins J. Salisbury, the Council assembled in the Lord's House, when it was proved that he had so conducted himself as to bring unnecessary persecution on me; that he had neglected his family, leaving them without wood, without provisions, or telling them where he was going, or when he would return; that he used strong drink and had been intimate with other women.

Dealing with Sundry Transgressors.

Elder Salisbury confessed his propensity for tale-bearing, and drinking strong liquor, but denied the other charges. The Council decided that he could no longer be an Elder or member in the Church until there was a thorough reformation.

Charges of unchristianlike conduct were also preferred against Sisters Hannah Brown, and L. Elliot. They confessed they had been guilty of telling falsehoods.

The Council reproved them, but permitted them to retain their standing in the Church.

The Council then withdrew fellowship from Elder Charles Kelly.*

My cousin, Elias Smith, arrived from St. Lawrence county, New York, with the information that his father and family, and Uncle Silas and family, were on their way to Kirtland, and that my grandmother [Mary Duty Smith, wife of Asael Smith] was at Fairport.

May 17.—I went in company with my brother Hyrum, in a carriage to Fairport, and brought home my grandmother, Mary Smith, aged ninety-theree years. She had not been baptized, on account of the opposition of Jesse Smith, her eldest son, who has always been an euemy to the work. She had

Arrival of the Prophet's Relatives in Kirtland.

* Charles Kelly was a member of Zion's Camp, also a member of the first quorum of Seventy. His offenses are named at page 444.

come five hundred miles to see her children, and knew all of us she had ever seen. She was much pleased at being introduced to her great grand-children, and expressed much pleasure and gratification on seeing me.

My grandfather, Asael Smith, long ago predicted that there would be a prophet raised up in his family, and my grandmother was fully satisfied that it was fulfilled in me. My grandfather Asael died in East Stockholm, St. Lawrence county, New York, after having received the Book of Mormon, and read it nearly through; and he declared that I was the very Prophet that he had long known would come in his family.

On the 18th, my uncle Silas Smith and family arrived from the east. My father, three of his brothers, and their mother, met the first time for many years. It was a happy day, for we had long prayed to see our grandmother and uncles in the Church.

Death of the Prophet's Grandmother.

On May 27, after a few days' visit with her children, which she enjoyed extremely well, my grandmother fell asleep without sickness, pain or regret. She breathed her last about sunset, and was buried in the burial ground near the Temple, after a funeral address had been delivered by Sidney Rigdon.* She had buried one daughter, Sarah; two Sons, Stephen and Samuel; and her husband, who died October 30, 1830, and left five sons and three daughters still living. At the death of my grandfather, who had kept a record, there were one hundred and ten children, grand children and great grand children. My uncle Stephen, and aunt Sarah, were buried side by side in the burial grounds in Royalton, Windsor county, Vermont. Stephen died July 25th, 1802, aged seventeen years, three months, and eleven days.

May 23.—The case of Elder Charles Kelly was again

* "She died firm in the faith of the Gospel, although she had never yielded obedience to any of its ordinances."—*Hist. of the Prophet Joseph, by Lucy Smith, ch. xii.*

brought before the High Council, then in session, and it was proved that he left his family in a destitute condition, about the time of the solemn assembly, which, together with other unchristianlike conduct, led the Council to decide that he be expelled from the Church.

Case of Chas. Kelley.

Also Asael Perry was cut off from the Church for unchristianlike conduct.

Job L. Lewis was excommunicated, for treating the Church with contempt.

May 17.—Died, in Kirtland, Miss Mary Smith, in the thirty-fifth year of her age. The deceased was a member of the Church of Latter-day Saints, and died in the triumphs of faith.

June 2.—President Phelps wrote a letter from Liberty, Missouri, to President Oliver Cowdery, from which I make the following extracts:

Letter from W. W. Phelps to the Brethren in Kirtland.

Since I returned home to Missouri, I have been out on two expeditions, examining the regions of the "Far West." Soon after our return, Bishop Partridge and myself passed from Liberty to the northwest corner of Clay county, and examined the mills and streams, and country around Mr. Smith's, generally denominated "Yankee Smith." It is customary, you know, for the sake of *provincialism*, among nations, kindreds and people, to nick-name [people] by their religion, or province or ancestry; so that one can be distinguished by being an Israelite, a Canaanite, a Christian, a "Mormon," a Methodist, or a Corn Cracker, or a Mighty Hunter, &c., according to fancy or favor.

From Mr. Smith's, we proceeded north-easterly through some timber and some prairie to Plattsburg, the county seat for Clinton county, "a smart little town," containing from fifteen to twenty hewed log cabins, and a two-story court house, thirty-two feet square. This town is located on the west side of Horse and Smith's fork of the Little Platte, contiguous to the timber on these streams, twenty-five miles north of Liberty. The timber, mill, and water privileges may answer a very small population, but for a large population they would be nothing. There are now three stores, and soon will be four. Clinton county is mostly prairie, with here and there a few fringes or spots of timber on the creeks that run into the Little Platte and Grand River.

From this town we made the best course we could to the waters of Grand River. We had a "sort of road" towards Busby Fork, then we had to contend with naked prairie, patches of scrubby timber, deep banked creeks and branches, together with a rainy morning, and no compass; but with the blessing of the Lord, we came to "some house" in the afternoon, and passed into Ray county. On Shoal creek, where there is water, there are some tolerable mill sites; but the prairies—those "old clearings," peering one over another, as far as the eye can glance, flatten all common calculation as to timber for boards, rails, or future wants, for a thick population, according to the natural reasoning of men.

What the design of our heavenly Father was, or is, as to these vast prairies of the Far West, I know no further than we have revelation. The Book of Mormon terms them, the land of desolation; and when I get into a prairie so large that I am out of sight of timber, just as a seaman is "out of sight of land on the ocean," I have to exclaim—What are man and his works, compared with the Almighty and His creations? Who hath viewed His everlasting fields? Who hath counted His buffaloes? Who hath seen all His deer on a thousand prairies? The pinks variegate these wide-spread lawns, without the hand of man to aid them, and the bees of a thousand groves banquet on the flowers, unobserved, and sip the honey-dews of heaven. Nearly every skirt of timber to the state line on the north, I am informed, has some one in it. The back settlers are generally very honorable, and more hospitable than any people I ever saw, you are in most instances, welcome to the best they have.

W. W. PHELPS.

Case of Preserved Harris and Isaac McWithy.

The High Council assembled in the Lord's house in Kirtland on the 16th of June, Presidents Sidney Rigdon, and Frederick G Williams presiding, to investigate the charges of "A want of benevolence to the poor, and charity to the Church," which I had previously preferred against Brother Preserved Harris and Elder Isaac McWithy. After a full and lengthy investigation, the Council decided that the charges were fully sustained against Preserved Harris, and that the hand of fellowship be withdrawn from him, until he shall see that the course he is pursuing is contrary to the Gospel of Jesus.

In the pleas of the Councilors, in the case of Elder Mc

Withy, they decided that the charges had been fully sustained; after which, I spoke in my turn as accuser, and stated that I called on the accused, in company with President Oliver Cowdery, for money to send up to Zion, but could get none; afterwards saw him, and asked him if he would sell his farm. He at first seemed willing, and wished to build up Zion. He pleaded excuse in consequence of his liberality to the poor. We offered him three thousand dollars for his farm, would give him four or five hundred dollars to take him to Zion, and settle him there, and an obligation for the remainder, with good security and interest. He went and told Father Lyon that we demanded all his property, and so we lost four or five hundred dollars; because the accused told him [Lyon] such a story, [that] he calculated to keep it [the aforesaid four or five hundred dollars] himself.

The accused, Elder McWithy, arose and said it was the first time he had been called upon to clear himself before a High Council. He complained of being called contrary to the rules of the Gospel, before the Council. The president decided that as the case was now before the Council, this pl a could not now be urged, but should have been made in the beginning. Elder McWithy pleaded that he had relieved the wants of the poor, and did so many good things that he was astonished that he should hear such things as he had heard today, because he did not give all he had got to one man. If he had done wrong he asked forgiveness of God and the Church.

During the quarter ending the 3rd of June, 1836, two hundred and forty-four Elders', eleven Priests', three Teachers', and five Deacons' licenses were recorded in the license Records, in Kirtland, Ohio.

Departure of the Patriarch and John Smith on a Mission.

June 22.—My father and Uncle John Smith started on a mission to visit the branches of the Church in the Eastern States, to set them in order, and confer on the brethren their patriarchal blessings. I took my mother and Aunt Clarissa (my Uncle John's wife,) in a carriage, and accompanied them to Painsville, where we procured a bottle of wine, broke bread, ate and drank, and parted after the ancient order, with the blessings of God.

June 28.—Elder Warren Parrish wrote from Hickman county, Tennessee, stating that:—

Many citizens of the county of Benton, and some of Carroll had met in convention, headed by a Methodist priest, who was called to the chair, and the county clerk appointed secretary. They drew up resolutions to drive all the "Mormon preachers from their coast," signed by the sheriff and many who were sworn to be civil, peace-officers, also colonels, majors, &c. We enjoyed our meeting unmolested at Brother Utley's, on Saturday, the 19th instant. Hundreds had entered into the conspiracy. In the afternoon, a little before sunset, a company of some forty or fifty men made their appearance; some on foot, others mounted, two on a horse, with guns, sticks, clubs, &c. They were led by a sheriff, colonel, first and second major, other officers, and a Methodist priest, with a gun on his shoulder.

The sheriff informed us that he had states' warrant for David W. Patten, Warren Parrish, and Wilford Woodruff; issued on complaint of the Methodist priest, Matthew Williams, chairman as above; who swore that we had put forth the following false and pretended prophecy; viz.: that Christ would come the second time before this generation passes away; also that four individuals should receive the Holy Ghost within four and twenty hours. The company consisted, as we were informed, of Baptists, Methodists, Presbyterians, liars, drunkards, hog and horse thieves. So determined were they, to force us off at that late hour, that it was with much difficulty we could prevail on them to show us any lenity; however, they protracted the time of our appearance at court until Tuesday by giving our bond, with surety of two brethren, in the sum of one thousand dollars.

They intended to have led us into the woods, under the dark curtain of night with the pretension of taking us before the magistrate that they might the better execute their diabolical designs upon us.

On Tuesday, in company with about twenty brethren and warm friends, who were ready and willing to lay down their lives for us, we went before our rulers, and found about one hundred persons assembled, armed with guns, pistols, dirks, clubs, sticks, &c. At a late hour we prevailed on the sheriff to have the court called, which consisted of three magistrates, one of whom was rejected from the judgment-seat, because some of his family were members of our Church.

The sheriff, with leave of court, divested us of our arms, consisting of walking sticks and a pocket knife. A man by the name of Perkins, (who report says, had run his county for hog stealing, and also had been guilty of concealing a stolen horse, for which he had lost part of his nose,) was appointed by the court to act as states' attorney; or in other words mob solicitor-general, to abuse the innocent and screen the guilty.

After the conspirators had witnessed against us, the court refused to hear any testimony on our part, being controlled by the bandits. Perkins made a plea against us, but we were not permitted to reply. The verdict of the court was, that they concluded that the charges preferred against us had been sustained, and that we were bound over to court for trial. Our accusers did not attempt to prove that those who were promised the Holy Ghost did not receive it; and the candid can judge whether he who prophesies that Christ will come the second time in this generation, is a false prophet. Also our complainant testified that these crimes, were committed in 1834, and it is a well known fact that Elder Woodruff, whose name is on the warrant, (though not arrested,) was not in this state until 1835. So much for an oath from a Methodist priest.

While the court was preparing our bonds, another warrant was served on Elder Patten; the mob without, and the mob within, whose intoxicating zeal had arisen to its zenith, were threatening our lives, and seemed only to wait the dark shades of night, which were fast gathering round, to cover them, while they should wreak their hands in our blood; the influence of our friends, as instruments in the hands of our God, kept this gathering storm from bursting upon our heads. About this time the sheriff proposed to us that if we would leave the county in ten days, and pay the cost, they would set us at liberty; at the same time informing us it was the only way to escape the hands of the mob, who were hardly restrained from acts of violence. One of the brethren present offered to pay the cost, and all advised us to accept the offer; which, in itself, proved that we were innocent of any crime, although in its nature most insulting.

(Signed) WARREN PARRISH.

Minutes of a Public Meeting at Liberty, Missouri.

On the 29th of June, a respectable number of the citizens being previously notified of the meeting, met at the court-house, in the town of Liberty, Missouri. On motion, John Bird was called to the chair, and John F. Doherty appointed secretary. The object of the meeting, was, by request of the chair, explained in a few appropriate remarks, by Colonel Wood; when on motion of Colonel William T. Wood, a committee of nine was appointed to draft resolutions expressive of the sense of this meeting; whereupon the following gentlemen were chosen—namely: John Thornton, Esq., Peter Rogers, Esq., Andrew Robertson, Esq., James T. V. Thompson, Colonel W. T. Wood, Doctor Woodson, J. Moss, James H. Hughes, Esq., David R. Atchison, Esq., and A. W. Doniphan, Esq., who retired and in a short time returned and made, through their chairman, Colonel John Thornton, the following unanimous report, which was read:

REPORT.

It is apparent to every reflecting mind that a crisis has arisen in this country, that requires the deep, cool, dispassionate consideration, and immediate action of every lover of peace, harmony and good order. We cannot conceal from ourselves the fact that at this moment the clouds of civil war are rolling up their fearful masses, and hanging over our devoted country. Solemn, dark and terrible. This painful state of things has been produced mainly by the rapid and increasing emigration of that people commonly called Mormons, during the last few months. It is known to all, that in November, 1833, these people were expelled from their homes in Jackson county, without money, without property, without the means of subsistence for themselves, their wives and their children, and like Noah's dove, without a resting place for their feet.

They came to our county thus friendless and penniless, (seeking as they said) but a temporary asylum from the storm of persecution by which they were then buffeted. Their destitute and miserable condition, at that inclement season of the year, excited the deep sympathies of the philanthropic and hospitable citizens of this county; and notwithstanding the thousand reports that were borne on the wings of the wind, charging them with almost every crime known to the laws of our country, yet our feelings of kindness and sympathy for human suffering prevailed over every obstacle, and they were received with friendship and treated with toleration, and often with remarks of peculiar kindness. They always declared that they looked not upon this county as their home, but as a temporary asylum; and that, whenever, a respectable portion of the citizens of this county should request it, they would promptly leave us in peace as they found us.

That period has now arrived. Duty to ourselves, to our families, and to the best interests of our country, requires at our hands, to demand the fulfillment of that pledge. They are charged by those who are opposed to them with an unfriendly determination to violate that pledge. Their rapid emigration, their large purchases, and offers to purchase lands, the remarks of the ignorant and imprudent portion of them, that this country is destined by heaven to be theirs are received and looked upon, by a large portion of this community, as strong and convincing proofs that they intend to make this county their permanent home, the centre and general rendezvous of their people.

These are some of the reasons why these people have become objects of the deepest hatred and detestation to many of our citizens. They are eastern men, whose manners, habits, customs, and even dialect, are essentially different from our own. They are *non*-slaveholders, and opposed to slavery, which in this peculiar period, when abolitionism has reared its deformed and haggard visage in our land, is well calculated to excite deep and abiding prejudices in any community where slavery is tolerated and protected.

In addition to all this, they are charged, as they have hitherto been, with keeping up a constant communication with our Indian tribes on our frontiers, with declaring, even from the pulpit, that the Indians are a part of God's chosen people, and are destined by heaven to inherit this land, in common with themselves. We do not vouch for the correctness of these statements; but whether they are true or false, their effect has been the same in exciting our community. In times of greater tranquility, such ridiculous remarks might well be regarded as the offspring of frenzied fanaticism; but at this time, our defenseless situation on the frontier, the bloody disasters of our fellow citizens in Florida, and other parts of the South, all tend to make a portion of our citizens regard such sentiments with horror, if not alarm. These and many other causes, have combined to raise a prejudice against them; and a feeling of hostility, that the first spark may, and we deeply fear will, ignite into all the horrors and desolations of a civil war, the worst evil that can befall any country.

We therefore feel it our duty to come forward, as mediators, and use every means in our power to prevent the occurrence of so great an evil. As the most efficacious means to arrest the evil, we urge on the Mormons to use every means to put an immediate stop to the emigration of their people to this county. We earnestly urge them to seek some other abiding place, where the manners, the habits, and customs of the people will be more consonant with their own.

For this purpose we would advise them to explore the territory of Wisconsin. This country is peculiarly suited to their conditions and their wants. It is almost entirely unsettled; they can there procure large bodies of land together, where there are no settlements, and none to interfere with them. It is a territory in which slavery is prohibited, and it is settled entirely with emigrants from the North and East.

The religious tenets of this people are so different from the present churches of the age, that they always have, and always will, excite deep prejudices against them in any populous country where they may locate. We, therefore, in a spirit of frank and friendly kindness, do advise them to seek a home where they may obtain large and separate bodies of land, and have a community of their own. We further say to them, if they regard their own safety and welfare, if they regard the welfare of their families, their wives and children, they will ponder with deep and solemn reflection on this friendly admonition.

If they have one spark of gratitude, they will not willingly plunge a people into civil war, who held out to them the friendly hand of assistance in that hour of dark distress, when there was few to say God save them. We can only say to them if they still persist in the blind course they have heretofore followed in flooding the country with their people, that we fear and firmly believe that an immediate civil war is the inevitable consequence. We know that there is not one among us who thirsts for the blood of that people.

We do not contend that we have the least right, under the Constitution and laws of the country, to expel them by force. But we would indeed be blind, if we did not foresee that the first blow that is struck, at this moment of deep excitement, must and will speedily involve every individual in a war, bearing ruin, woe, and desolation in its course. It matters but little how, where, or by whom, the war may begin, when the work of destruction commences, we must all be borne onward by the storm, or crushed beneath its fury. In a civil war, when our homes are the theatre on which it is fought, there can be no neutrals; let our opinions be what they may, we must fight in self-defense.

We want nothing, we ask nothing, we would have nothing from this people, we only ask them, for their own safety, and for ours, to take the least of the two evils. Most of them are destitute of land, have but little property, are late emigrants to this country, without relations, friends, or endearing ties to bind them to this land. At the risk of such imminent peril to them and to us, we request them to leave us, when their crops are gathered, their business settled, and they have made every suitable preparation to remove. Those who have forty acres of land, we are willing should remain until they can dispose of it without loss, if it should require years. But we urge, most strongly urge, that emigration cease, and cease immediately, as nothing else can or will allay for a moment, the deep excitement that is now unhappily agitating this community.

If the Mormons will comply with these friendly requisitions, we will use every exertion among our own citizens, to arrest this evil before it is forever too late; but if they are disregarded, we can promise neither them nor ourselves, a long continuation of the blessings of peace and harmony.

1st. Therefore be it Resolved by this meeting, that we view with feelings of the deepest regret the present unhappy situation of our country.

2nd. That it is the fixed and settled conviction of this meeting, that unless the people commonly called Mormons will agree to stop immediately the emigration of their people to this county, and take measures to remove themselves from it, a civil war is inevitable.

3rd. That a committee of ten be appointed to make known to the leaders of that people, the views of this meeting, and to urge upon them the propriety of acceding to these propositions.

4th. The said committee consisting of Andrew Robertson, Michael Arthur, Littlebury Sublet, John Baxter, James M. Hughes, W. J. Moss, John Bird, Peter Rogers, W. T. Wood and J. T. V. Thompson, who shall meet on the morrow at the house of Mr. Cowan, and confer with the Mormons, and report at this meeting, as soon thereafter as convenient, the reply of the Mormons to these requisitions.

5th. That if the Mormons agree to these propositions, we will use every means in our power to allay the excitement among our own citizens, and to get them to await the result of these things. That it is the opinion of this meeting that the recent emigrants among the Mormons should take measures to leave this county immediately, as they have no crops on hand, and nothing to lose by continuing their journey to some more friendly land. On motion of Wm. T. Wood, the preamble and resolutions were unanimously adopted. Be it resolved that this meeting adjourn until Saturday next.

JOHN BIRD, Chairman,
JOHN F. DOHERTY, Secretary.

Minutes of a Public Meeting of the Saints in Clay County, Missouri, Held to Consider the Proposition of the Citizens of Clay County that the Latter-day Saints Move into another Part of the State.

July 1, 1836. At a very large meeting of the Elders of the Church of Latter-day Saints, assembled in Clay county, Missouri, W. W. Phelps was called to the chair, and John Corrill appointed secretary. The preamble and resolutions from a meeting of citizens of the 29th ultimo, was read, and a committee of twelve, viz., Edward Partridge, Isaac Morley, Lyman Wight, Thomas B. Marsh, Elias Higby, Calvin Bebee, Isaac Hitchcock, Isaac Higby, Samuel Bent, Titus Billings, James Emmet, and R. Evans, were appointed, who retired, and after a short time reported the following preamble and resolutions:

Resolved, that we (the "Mormons," so called), are grateful for the kindness which has been shown to us by the citizens of Clay county since we have resided with them; and being desirous for peace, and wishing the good rather than the ill-will of mankind, we will use all honorable means to allay the excitement, and so far as we can, remove any foundation for jealousies against us as a people. We are aware that many rumors prejudicial to us as a society are afloat, and time only can prove their falsity to the world at large.

We deny having claim to this, or any other county, or country, further than we shall purchase the land with money, or more than the Constitution and laws allow us as free American citizens. We have taken no part for or against slavery; but are opposed to the abolitionists, and consider that men have a right to hold slaves or not, according to law.

We believe it just to preach the Gospel to the nations of the earth, and warn the righteous to save themselves from the corruptions of the world; but we do not believe it right to interfere with bond-servants, nor preach the Gospel to them, nor meddle with nor influence them in the least to cause them to be dissatisfied with their situation in this life; thereby jeopardizing the lives of men. Such interference we believe to be unlawful and unjust, and dangerous to the peace of every government allowing human beings to be held in servitude.

We deny holding any communications with the Indians; and mean to hold ourselves as ready to defend our country against their barbarous ravages, as any other people. We believe that all men are bound to sustain and uphold the respective governments in which they reside, while protected in their inherent and inalienable rights by the laws of such governments; and that sedition and rebellion are unbecoming every citizen thus protected, and should be punished accordingly. It is needless to enter into any further detail of our faith, or mention our sufferings; therefore—

First. Resolved: For the sake of friendship, and to be in a covenant of peace with the citizens of Clay county, and they to be in a covenant of peace with us, notwithstanding the necessary loss of property, and expense we incur in moving, we comply with the requisitions of their resolutions in leaving Clay county, as explained by the preamble accompanying the same; and that we will use our exertions to have the Church do the same; and that we will also exert ourselves to stop the tide of emigration of our people to this county.

Second. Resolved: That we accept the friendly offer verbally tendered to us by the committee yesterday, to assist us in selecting a location, and removing to it.

Third. Resolved, unanimously: That this meeting accept and adopt the above preamble and resolutions, which are here presented by the committee.

Fourth. Resolved: That Thomas B. Marsh, Lyman Wight, and Samuel Bent, be a committee to carry the minutes of these proceedings to the meeting of the citizens of Clay county, to be held tomorrow at Liberty. The foregoing resolutions were unanimously adopted by the meeting.

W. W. PHELPS, Chairman,
JOHN CORRILL, Secretary.

Mtnutes of the Second Meeting of the Citizens of Clay County.

The citizens of Clay county met pursuant to adjournment. The chairman and secretary resumed their stations, when the committee appointed by the pulic meeting of the citizens at the court house, in Liberty, on the 29th ultimo, reported through their chairman, W. J. Moss, the foregoing preamble and resolutions of the Elders of the Church of Latter-day Saints, on the 1st instant, whereupon it was

Resolved, That this meeting do accept and receive the reply of the Mormons to the resolution passed on Wednesday, the 29th of June, as perfectly satisfactory.

Be it further *Resolved* by this meeting, that we will use our utmost endeavors to carry into effect the object contained in the preamble and resolutions passed on Wednesday, the 29th, as agreed to by the Mormons.

Be it further *Resolved*, That we urge it on our fellow citizens to keep the peace towards the Mormons, as good faith, justice, morality and religion require.

Be it further *Resolved*, That a committee of ten persons, two in each township, be appointed to raise money by subscription to aid those of the Mormons who may from necessity require it, to leave this county.

Resolved, That Samuel Tillery Jeremiah Minger and Abraham Shafer be appointed a committee to receive the pecuniary aid by subscription for the purpose of aiding the poor persons that may belong to the Mormons in removing from this county to their place of abode, and that the Elders of the Church be requested to report the above-named persons to the aforesaid committee, who will judge of the proofs and facts entitling the Mormons to pecuniary aid, and appropriate the funds accordingly.

Resolved, That the said committee be authorized to employ some suitable person to accompany those that may wish to examine a new country. It is also understood that if the money which may be received by the committee is not appropriated for the purpose above named, it shall be refunded back in proportion to the amount subscribed.

Resolved, That the chair appoint five persons in each township to carry the object of the above resolutions into effect.

The following gentlemen were then appointed in the different townships: For Liberty township, John Thornton, Joel Turnham, Peter

Rogers, John Bird, David R. Atchison; for Fishing River township, Elisha Cameron, E. Price, G. Withers, M. Welton, James Kazey; for Platte township, T. C. Gordon, S. Harris, W. Owen, L. Rollins, I. Marsh; for Washington township, B. Riley, S. Crawford, T. Findley, G. McIlvaine, P. Y. G. Bartee; for Gallatin township, D. Dale, N. Nash, William Todd, B. Ricketts, R. Forboin.

Be it further *Resolved,* That this meeting recommend the Mormons to the good treatment of the citizens of the adjoining counties. We also recommend the inhabitants of the neighboring counties to assist the Mormons in selecting some abiding place for their people where they will be, in a measure, the only occupants; and where none will be anxious to molest them.

Resolved, That the proceedings of this meeting be handed over to the publishers of the *Far West* with a request that it be printed, which was severally read and unanimously adopted, and meeting adjourned.

JOHN BIRD, Chairman,
JOHN F. DOHERTY, Secretary.

LIBERTY, July 2nd, 1836.

Letter from the Brethren at Kirtland to the Brethren in Missouri.

KIRTLAND, July 25th, 1836.

To W. W. Phelps and Others:

DEAR BRETHREN:—Yours of the first inst., accompanying the proceedings of a public meeting held by the people of Clay county, was duly received. We are sorry that this disturbance has broken out, but we do not consider it our fault. You are better acquainted with circumstances than we are, and, of course, have been directed by wisdom in your moves relative to leaving the county.

We forward you our letter to Mr. Thornton and others that you may know all that we have said. We advise that you be not the first aggressors. Give no occasion, and if the people will let you, dispose of your property, settle your affairs, and go in peace. You have thus far had an asylum, and now seek another, as God may direct.

Relative to your going to Wisconsin, we cannot say, we should think if you could stop short, in peace, you had better do so. You know our feelings relative to not giving the first offense, and also of protecting your wives and little ones in case a mob should seek their lives. We shall publish the proceedings of the public meeting, with your answer, as well as our letter. We mean that the world shall know all things as they transpire. If we are persecuted and driven men shall know it.

Be wise; let prudence dictate all your counsels; preserve peace with all men, if possible; stand by the Constitution of your country; observe its principles; and above all, show yourselves men of God, worthy citizens, and we doubt not, the community, ere long, will do you justice, and rise in indignation against those who are the instigators of your sufferings and afflictions.

In the bonds of brotherly love we subscribe ourselves, as ever,

JOSEPH SMITH, JUN.,
SIDNEY RIGDON,
OLIVER COWDERY,
F. G. WILLIAMS,
HYRUM SMITH.

The letter to Mr. Thornton referred to above was as follows:

KIRTLAND, GEAUGA COUNTY, OHIO,
July 25, 1836.

To John Thornton, Esq., Peter Rogers, Esq., Andrew Robertson, Esq., James T. V. Thompson, Esq., Colonel William T. Wood, Doctor Woodson, I. Moss, James H. Hughes, Esq., David R. Atchison, Esq., and A. W. Doniphan, Esq.:

GENTLEMEN:—We have just perused, with feelings of deep interest, an article in the *Far West*, printed at Liberty, Clay county, Missouri, containing the proceeding of a public meeting of the citizens of said county on the subject of an excitement now prevailing among you, occasioned either from false reports against the Church of Latter-day Saints, or from the fact that said Church is considered dangerous to the welfare of your country; and will, if suffered among you under existing circumstances, cause the ties of peace and friendship, so desirable among all men, to be burst asunder, and bring war and desolation upon your own pleasant homes.

While rumor is afloat with her accustomed cunning, and while public opinion is fast rising, like a flood tide against the members of the Church, we cannot but admire the candor with which your preambles and resolutions were clothed, as presented to the citizens of Clay county on the 29th of June last; though, as you expressed in your report to said meeting, "We do not contend that we have the least right, under the Constitution and laws of the country, to expel them by force." yet communities may be at times unexpectedly thrown into a situation when wisdom, prudence, and that first item in nature's law, self defense, would dictate that the responsible and influential part [of a community] should step forward and guide the public mind in a course to save difficulty, preserve rights and spare the innocent blood from staining that soil so dearly purchased with the lives and fortunes of our fathers. As you have come forward as "mediators" to prevent the effusion of blood and save disasters consequent upon civil war, we take this opportunity to present to you, though strangers, and through you, if you wish, to the people of Clay county, our heart-felt gratitude for every kindness rendered our friends in affliction, when driven from their peaceful homes; and to yourselves, also, for the prudent course in the present excited state of your community; but in doing this, justice to ourselves, as communicants of that Church to which our friends belong, and duty towards them as acquaintances and former fellow citizens, require us to say something to exonerate them from the foul charges brought against them, to deprive them of their constitutional privileges and drive them from the face of society.

They have been charged, in consequence of the whims and vain notions of some few uninformed [persons], with claiming that upper country, [north-western Missouri], and that ere long they were to possess it at all hazards and in defiance of all consequences. This is unjust and far from having a foundation in truth; a thing not expected or looked for—not desired by this society as a people, and where the idea could have originated is unknown to us. We do not, neither did we ever, insinuate a thing of this kind, or hear it from the leading men of the society now in your country. There is nothing in all our religious faith to warrant it, but on the contrary, the most strict injunctions to live in obedience to the laws and follow peace with all men; and we doubt not but a recurrence to the Jackson county difficulties with our friends will fully satisfy you, that at least heretofore such has been the course followed by them, that instead of fighting for their own rights they have sacrificed them for a season to wait the redress guaranteed in the law and so anxiously looked for at a time distant from this.

We have been, and are still, clearly under the conviction that had our friends been disposed they might have maintained their possessions in Jackson county. They might have resorted to the same barbarous means with their neighbors, throwing down dwellings, threatening lives, driving innocent women and children from their homes, and thereby have annoyed their enemies equally at least; but to their credit—and it must ever remain upon the page of time to their honor—this they did not do. They had possessions, they had homes, they had sacred rights, and more still, they had helpless, harmless innocence, with an approving conscience that they had violated no law of their country or their God to urge them forword; but to show to all that they were willing to forego these for the peace of their country they tamely submitted, and have since been wanderers among strangers (though hospitable) without homes. We think these sufficient reasons to show to your patriotic minds that our friends, instead of having a wish to expel a community by force of arms, would suffer their rights to be taken from them before shedding blood.

Another charge brought against our friends is that of being dangerous in societies "where slavery is tolerated and practiced." Without occupying time here we refer you to the April (1836) number of the *Latter-day Saints' Messenger and Advocate*, printed at this place, a copy of which we forward to each of you. From the length of time which has elapsed since its publication, you can easily see it was put forth for no other reason than to correct the public mind generally, without a reference or expectation of any excitement of the nature of the one now in your county. Why we refer you particularly to this publication is because many of our friends who are now in the West were in this place when this paper made its appearance, and from personal observation gave it their decided approbation, and declared those sentiments to be their own in the fullest particular.

Another charge of great magnitude is brought against our friends in the West, that of "keeping up a constant communication with the Indian tribes on the frontier; with declaring even from the pulpit that the Indians are a part of God's chosen people, and are destined by heaven to inherit this land, in common with themselves." We know of nothing under the present aspect of our Indian relations calculated to arouse the fears of the people of the Upper Missouri more than a combination or influence of this nature; and we cannot look upon it as being other than one of the most subtle purposes of those whose feelings are embittered against our friends to turn the eye of suspicion upon them from every man who is acquainted with the barbarous cruelty of rude savages. Since a rumor was afloat that the western Indians were showing signs of war we have received frequent private letters from our friends who have not only expressed fears for their own safety, in case the Indians should break out, but a decided determination to be among the first to repel any invasion and defend the frontier from all hostilities. We mention the last fact because it was wholly uncalled for on our part and came previous to any excitement on the part of the people of Clay county against our friends and must definitely show that this charge is also untrue.

Another charge against our friends and one that is urged as a reason why they must immediately leave Clay county, is, that they are making, or are likely to make the same "their permanent home, the center and general rendezvous of their people." We have never understood such to be the purpose, wish, or design of this society; but on the contrary, have ever supposed that those who resided in Clay county only designed it as a temporary residence until the law and authority of our country should put them in the quiet possession of their homes in Jackson county; and such as had not possessions there could purchase to the entire satisfaction and interest of the people of Jackson county.

Having partially mentioned the leading objections urged against our friends, we would here add, that it has not been done with a view, on our part, to dissuade you from acting in strict conformity with your preamble and resolutions offered to the people of Clay county on the 29th ult., but from a sense of duty to a people embarrassed, persecuted and afflicted; for you are aware, gentlemen, that in times of excitement virtues are transformed into vices; acts, which in other cases and other circumstances would be considered upright and honorable, are interpreted contrary to their real intent and made objectionable and criminal; and from whom could we look for forbearance and compassion, with confidence and assurance, more than from those whose bosoms are warmed with those pure principles of patriotism with which you have been guided in the present instance, to secure the peace of your county and save a persecuted people from further violence and destruction?

It is said that our friends are poor; that they have but little or nothing to bind their feelings or wishes to Clay county, and that in consequence they have a less claim upon that county. We do not deny the fact that our friends are poor; but their persecutions have helped to render them so. While other men were peacefully following their vocations and extending their interests they have been deprived of the right of citizenship, prevented from enjoying their own, charged with violating the sacred principles of our Constitution and laws, made to feel the keenest aspersions of the tongue of slander, waded through all but death, and are now suffering under calumnies calculated to excite the indignation and hatred of every people among whom they dwell, thereby exposing them to destruction and inevitable ruin.

If a people, a community, or a society can accumulate wealth, increase in worldly fortune, improve in science and arts, rise to eminence in the eyes of the public, surmount these difficulties, so much as to bid defiance to poverty and wretchedness, it must be a new creation, a race of beings superhuman. But in all their poverty and wants we have yet to learn for the first time that our friends are not industrious and temperate; and wherein they have not always been the last to retaliate or resent an injury. and the first to overlook and forgive. We do not urge that there are no exceptions to be found; all communities, all societies and associations are cumbered with disorderly and less virtuous members—members who violate in a greater or less degree, the principles of the same; but this can be no just criterion by which to judge a whole society; and further still where a people are laboring under constant fear of being dispossessed; very little inducement is held out to excite them to be industrious.

We think, gentlemen, that we have pursued the subject far enough, and we here express to you, as we have in a letter accompanying this to our friends, our decided disapprobation to the idea of shedding blood, if any other course can be followed to avoid it; in which case, and which alone, we have urged upon our friends to desist, only in extreme cases of self defense; and in this case not to give the offense or provoke their fellow men to acts of violence, which we have no doubt they will observe as they ever have done; for you may rest assured, gentlemen, that we would be the last to advise our friends to shed the blood of men or commit one act to endanger the public peace. We have no doubt but our friends will leave your county, sooner or later; they have not only signified the same to us, but we have advised them so to do as fast as they can without incurring too much loss. It may be said that they have but little to lose if they lose the whole. But if they have but little that little is their all, and the necessities of the helpless urge them to make a prudent disposal of the same. We are highly pleased with a proposition in your preamble, suffering them to remain peaceably until a disposition can be made of their land, etc., which, if suffered, our fears are at once hushed, and we have every reason to believe that during the remaining part of the residence of our friends in your county the same feelings of friendship and kindness will continue to exist that have heretofore, and that when they leave you, you will have no reflection of sorrow that they have been sojourners among you.

To what distance or place they will remove we are unable to say; in that they must be dictated by judgment and prudence. They may explore the territory of Wisconsin, they may remove there, or they may stop on the other side, of this we are unable to say; but be they where they will we have this gratifying reflection, that they have never been the first, in an unjust manner, to violate the laws, injure their fellow men, or disturb the tranquility and peace under which any part of our country has heretofore reposed; and we cannot but believe that ere long, the public mind must undergo a change, when it will appear to the satisfaction of all that this people have been illy treated and abused without cause, and when as justice would demand, those who have been the instigators of their sufferings will be regarded as their true characters demand.

Our religious principles are before the world ready for the investigation of all men, yet we are aware that all the persecution against our friends has arisen in consequence of calumnies and misconstructions without foundation in truth and righteousness. This we have endured in common with all other religious societies at their first commencement. Should Providence order that we rise not as others before us to respectability and esteem, but be trodden down by the ruthless force of extermination, posterity will do us justice when our persecutors are equally low in the dust with ourselves, to hand down to succeeding generations the virtuous acts and forbearance of a people who sacrificed their reputation for their religion; and their earthly fortunes and happiness to preserve peace and save this land from being further drenched in blood.

We have no doubt but your very seasonable mediation in the time of so great an excitement will accomplish your most sanguine desires in preventing further disorder; and we hope, gentlemen, that while you reflect upon the fact that the citizens of Clay county are urgent for our friends to leave you, that you will also bear in mind that by their complying with your request to leave they are surrendering some of the dearest rights guaranteed in the Constitution of our country; and that human nature can be driven to a certain extent when it will yield no further. Therefore, while our friends suffer so much and forego so many sacred rights, we sincerely hope, and we have every reason to expect it, that a suitable forbearance may be shown by the people of Clay county; which, if done, the cloud which has been obscuring your horizon will disperse and you be left to enjoy peace, harmony and prosperity.

With sentiments of esteem and profound respect, we are, gentlemen, your obedient servants,

JOSEPH SMITH, JUN.,
SIDNEY RIGDON,
OLIVER COWDERY,
FREDERICK G. WILLIAMS,
HYRUM SMITH.

The following letter was received at Liberty, Clay county, Missouri, on the 28th of July:

Letter from Daniel Dunklin to the Saints in Missouri.

CITY OF JEFFERSON, July 18th, 1836.

Messrs. W. W. Phelps and Others:

GENTLEMEN:—The treatment your people have received, and are now receiving, is of an extraordinary character, such as is seldom experienced in any country by any people. As an individual I sympathize with you, and as the executive of the state, deeply deplore such a state of things. Your appeal to the executive is a natural one; but a proper understanding of our institutions will show you that yours is a case not for the special cognizance of the executive. It is a case, or, I may say, they are cases of individual wrongs. These, as I have before told you, are subjects for judicial interference; and there are cases sometimes of individual outrage which may be so popular as to render the action of courts of justice nugatory, in endeavoring to afford a remedy. I would refer you to the charge of Judge Lawless, made to the grand jury of St. Louis. Public sentiment may become paramount law; and when one man or society of men become so obnoxious to that sentiment as to determine the people to be rid of him or them, it is useless to run counter to it.

The time was when the people (except those in Jackson county) were divided, and the major part in your favor; that does not now seem to be the case. Why is this so? Does your conduct merit such censures as exist against you? It is not necessary for me to give my opinion. Your neighbors accuse your people of holding illicit communication with the Indians, and of being opposed to slavery. You deny. Whether the charge or the denial is true I cannot tell. The fact exists and your neighbors seem to believe it true; and whether true or false, the consequences will be the same (if your opponents are not merely gasconading), unless you can, by your conduct and arguments, convince them of your innocence. If you cannot do this, all I can say to you is that in this Republic the *vox populi* is the *vox Dei*.

Yours repectfully,

DANIEL DUNKLIN.

CHAPTER XXXII.

THE PROPHET'S MISSION—LABORS IN MASSACHUSETTS—THE ORGANIZATION OF THE KIRTLAND SAFETY SOCIETY.

On Monday afternoon, July 25th, in company with Sidney Rigdon, Brother Hyrum Smith, and Oliver Cowdery, I left Kirtland, and at seven o'clock the same evening, we took passage on board the steamer *Charles Townsend*, S. Fox, master, at Fairport, and the next evening, about ten o'clock we arrived at Buffalo, New York, and took lodgings at the "Farmer's Hotel." Here we met with Elders Orson Hyde and Moses C. Nickerson, the former on his way to Canada, and the latter from that province.

Departure of the Prophet from Kirtland

To avoid the crowding, fisting, fighting, racing and rioting of the packets, we took passages on a line boat for Utica, where we arrived about eight o'clock a. m. of the 29th, just in time to take the railroad car for Schenectady, the first passenger car on the new road.* We were more than six hours traveling eighty miles. The locomotive had hardly stopped before the cry was, "Albany baggage: the cars start in five minutes." Amid a scene

* This was the Albany & Schenectady Railway, the first railroad contracted for in New York; it began to operate in September, 1831. It was at that time called the Mohawk & Hudson railroad and ran from Albany to Schenectady. Its charter was issued in 1826 and is generally regarded as the earliest charter given in the United States for the construction of a railroad.

of confusion, bustle, and crowding, we succeeded, after a good share of scuffling and pulling, in getting our trunks on board the luggage car for Albany where we arrived the same evening.

A Steamboat Race.

On the 30th, at seven o'clock a. m., we went on board the steamer *John Mason*, which took us to the *Erie*, lying over the bar. While the passengers were stepping off the *John Mason*, the steamer *Rochester* passed us: "Now for a race," was the cry from different parts, and a race trial of speed it was; however, as fate or steam power of engine would have it, the *Erie*, after touching at Catskill and West Point, where the *Rochester* did not, went into New York a few minutes "ahead." By such undue pressure of steam the lives of thousands have been sacrificed, and I thanked God that myself and friends were safely landed.

The Great Fire in New York City.

While in New York I visited the burnt district—the part of the city where it was estimated fifteen millions of property was consumed by fire on the 16th of December, 1835,* according to the prediction of the ancient Prophets, that there should be "fire and vapor of smoke" in the last days.

Arrival of the Prophet's Party in Salem, Mass.

From New York we continued our journey to Providence, on board a steamer; from thence to Boston, by steam cars, and arrived in Salem, Massachusetts, early in August, where we hired a house, and occupied the same during the month, teaching the people from house to house, and preaching publicly, as opportunity presented; visiting occasionally, sections of the surrounding country, which are rich in the history of the Pilgrim Fathers of New England, in Indian warfare, religious superstition, bigotry, persecution, and learned ignorance.

The early settlers of Boston (the Emporium of New

* The fire here alluded to broke out on the night of the 16th of December, 1835, and in fourteen hours there was consumed over seventeen million dollars' worth of property. The burnt district covered several acres of ground in the most prominent business part of the city.

England), who had fled from their mother country to avoid persecution and death, soon became so lost to principles of justice and religious liberty as to whip and hang the Baptist and the Quaker, who like themselves, had fled from tyranny to a land of freedom; and the fathers of Salem from 1692 to 1693, whipped, imprisoned, tortured, and hung many of their citizens for supposed witchcraft; and quite recently,—while boasting of her light and knowledge, of her laws and religion, as surpassed by none on earth,—has New England been guilty of burning a Catholic convent in the vicinity of Charleston, and of scattering the inmates to the four winds; yes, in sight of the very spot where the fire of American Independence was first kindled, where a monument is now erecting in memory of the battle of Bunker Hill, and the fate of the immortal Warren, who bled, who died, on those sacred heights, to purchase religious liberty for his country—in sight of this very spot, have the religionists of the nineteenth century, demolished a noble brick edifice, hurling its inhabitants forth upon a cold, unfeeling world for protection and subsistence.

Reflections of the Prophet on Religious Intolerance.

Well did the Savior say concerning such, "by their fruits you shall know them." And if the wicked mob who destroyed the Charleston convent, and the cool, calculating religious lookers on, who inspired their hearts with deeds of infamy, do not arise, and redress the wrong, and restore the injured four-fold, they in turn, will receive of the measure they have meted out till the just indignation of a righteous God is satisfied. When will man cease to war with man, and wrest from him his sacred rights of worshiping his God according as his conscience dictates? Holy Father, hasten the day.

I received the following:

*Revelation given in Salem, Massachusetts, August 6th, 1836.**

1. I, the Lord your God, am not displeased with your coming this journey, notwithstanding your follies;

* See Doctrine and Covenants sec. cxi.

2. I have much treasure in this city for you, for the benefit of Zion; and many people in this city whom I will gather out in due time for the benefit of Zion, through your instrumentality.

3. Therefore it is expedient that you should form acquaintance with men in this city, as you shall be led, and as it shall be given you;

4. And it shall come to pass in due time, that I will give this city into your hands; that you shall have power over it, insomuch that they shall not discover your secret parts; and its wealth pertaining to gold and silver shall be yours.

5. Concern not yourselves about your debts, for I will give you power to pay them.

6. Concern not yourselves about Zion, for I will deal mercifully with her.

7. Tarry in this place, and in the regions round about;

8. And the place where it is my will that you should tarry, for the main, shall be signalized unto you by the peace and power of my Spirit, that shall flow unto you.

9. This place you may obtain by hire, etc. And inquire diligently concerning the more ancient inhabitants and founders of this city;

10. For there are more treasures than one for you in this city;

11. Therefore be ye as wise as serpents and yet without sin, and I will order all things for your good, as fast as ye are able to receive them. Amen.

While here [at Salem] Brothers Brigham Young and Lyman E. Johnson arrived. Brother Young had been through New York, Vermont, and Massachusetts, in company with his brother Joseph Young. They visited their relations in this country, and baptized a good number into the Church; they remained in Boston two or three weeks, and baptized seventeen persons. We had a good visit with the brethren, for which I feel very thankful.

Thus I continued in Salem and vicinity until I returned to Kirtland, some time in the month of September. During this month the Church in Clay county, Missouri, commenced removing to their newly selected location on Shoal Creek, in the territory attached to Ray County.

Success of the Ministry.

During the quarter ending September 3rd, fifty-two Elders', six Priests', three Teachers', and two Deacons' licenses were recorded in the license records, in Kirtland, Ohio, by Thomas Burdick. The intelligence from the Elders abroad was interesting. Elder Parley P. Pratt still continued his labors in Upper Canada, Toronto, and vicinity, with good success. Elder Lyman E. Johnson had been laboring in New Brunswick, and other places on the sea-board; and on the 12th, 13th, and 14th of August a conference was held by Elders Brigham Young and Lyman E. Johnson, at Newry, Maine, where seventeen branches were represented, numbering in all three hundred and seventeen members.

Labors of the Patriarch Joseph Smith, Sen.

October 2nd, 1836.—My father and Uncle John Smith returned to Kirtland from their mission to the Eastern States, having traveled about two thousand four hundred miles, and visited nearly all the branches of the Church in New York, Vermont, New Hampshire, and Pennsylvania. During this mission they baptized many, conferred blessings upon many hundreds, and preached the Gospel to many thousands. They also visited their friends and relatives in the land of their nativity. My cousin, George A. Smith, returned the same day from his mission to Richland County, Ohio. Brother Heber C. Kimball returned to Kirtland, having been absent nearly five months, during which time he baptized thirty persons into the Church of the Latter-day Saints, this being in fulfillment of a blessing that I had conferred upon his head before he started on his mission.

Movements of the Saints in Missouri.

Through the month of October the Saints continued to gather at Shoal Creek, Missouri, and my attention was particularly directed to the building up of Kirtland, and the spiritual interests of the Church.

Organization of Kirtland Safety Society

On the 2nd of November the brethren at Kirtland drew up certain articles of agreement, preparatory to the organization of a banking institution, to be called the "Kirtland Safety Society."* President Oliver Cowdery was delegated to Philadelphia

* "Kirtland Safety Society Bank" was the full title of the proposed institution, and Oliver Cowdery had the plates on which bank notes were to be printed so engraved.

to procure plates for the institution; and Elder Orson Hyde to repair to Columbus with a petition to the legislature of Ohio, for an act of incorporation, which was presented at an early period of their session, but because we were "Mormons" the legislature raised some frivolous excuse on which they refused to grant us those banking privileges they so freely granted to others. Thus Elder Hyde was compelled to return without accomplishing the object of his mission, while Elder Cowdery succeeded at a great expense in procuring the plates, and bringing them to Kirtland.

Licenses.

Forty-four Elders' licenses were recorded in the license records at Kirtland during the quarter ending December 1st; also five Priests' and one Teachers' license, by Thomas Burdick.

Organization of Caldwell County.

The Saints having gathered in considerable numbers on Shoal Creek, Missouri, petitioned for an act of incorporation for a new county, which was granted about the middle of December, under the name of Caldwell County, from which time a fresh impetus was given to the gathering, and the county grew like Jonah's gourd.

Minutes of a Conference held in the House of the Lord at Kirtland on the 22nd of December, 1836.

The authorities of the Church being present, viz.: The First Presidency, the High Council of Kirtland, the quorum of the Twelve, the presidents of the Seventies, the president of the Elders and his counselors, and many other official members, such as Priests, Teachers, Deacons etc., the house was called to order, and the following motions were made and carried by the unanimous voice of the assembly:

First—That it has been the case that a very improper and unchristianlike course of conduct has been pursued by the Elders of this Church, and the churches abroad, in sending their poor from among them to this place, without the necessary means of subsistence. Whereas the Church in this place being poor from the beginning, having had to pay an extraordinate price for their lands, provisions, etc ; and having a serious burthen imposed upon them by comers and goers, from most parts of the world, and in assisting traveling Elder and theirs the families, while they themselves have been laboring in the vineyard of the Lord, to preach the Gospel; and also having suffered great loss in endeavoring to benefit Zion, it (the thing complained of) has become a serious matter which ought to be considered by us.

Therefore, after deliberate discussion upon the subject, it was moved seconded, and unanimously carried, that we have borne our part of this burden, and that it becomes the duty, henceforth, of all the churches abroad to provide for those who are objects of charity, that are not able to provide for themselves; and not send them from their midst, to burden the Church in this place, unless they come and prepare a place for them, and provide means for their support.

Second—That there be a stop put to churches or families gathering or moving to this place, without their first coming or sending their wise men to prepare a place for them, as our houses are all full, and our lands mostly occupied, except those houses that do not belong to the Church, which cannot be obtained without great sacrifice, especially when brethren with their families are crowding in upon us, and are compelled to purchase at any rate, and consequently are thrown into the hands of speculators, and extortioners, with which course the Lord is not well pleased. Also that the churches abroad be required to do according to the revelation contained in the book of Doctrine and Covenants, commencing at section 101: 72-74, which is as follows:

"Now verily I say unto you, let all the churches gather together all their monies; let these things be done in their time, be not in haste; and observe to have all things prepared before you, and let honorable men be appointed, even wise men, and send them to purchase these lands; and all branches of the Church in the eastern countries when they are built up, if they will harken unto this counsel, they may buy lands and gather together upon them, and in this way they may establish Zion."

JOSEPH SMITH, Chairman,
WARREN PARRISH, Clerk.

Baptism of Doctor Richards.

On the 31st of December, at the setting of the sun, Dr. Willard Richards was baptized at Kirtland, under the hands of President Brigham Young, in the presence of Heber C. Kimball and others, who had spent the afternoon in cutting the ice to prepare for the baptism.*

* Dr. Willard Richards was born at Hopkinton, Middlesex County, Massachusetts, June 24, 1804, and from the religious teachings of his parents (Joseph and Rhoda Richards), he was the subject of religious impressions from his earliest moments, although careless and indifferent in his external deportment. At the

Minutes of a Meeting of the Members of the "Kirtland Safety Society," held on the 2nd day of January, 1837.

At a special meeting of the "Kirtland Safety Society," two-thirds of the members being present, Sidney Rigdon was called to the chair, and Warren Parrish chosen secretary.

The house was called to order, and the object of the meeting explained by the chairman; which was—1st, to annul the old constitution, which was adopted by the society, on the second day of November, 1836; which was, on motion by the unanimous voice of the meeting, annulled. 2nd, to adopt articles of agreement, by which the "Kirtland Safety Society" is to be governed.

After much discussion and investigation, the following preamble and articles of agreement were adopted by the unanimous voice of the meeting:

We, the undersigned subscribers, for the promotion of our temporal interests, and for the better management of our different occupations,

age of ten years he removed with his father's family to Richmond, in the same state, where he witnessed several sectarian "revivals," and offered himself to the Congregational church in that place, at the age of seventeen, having previously passed the painful ordeal of conviction and conversion, according to that order, even to the belief that he had committed the unpardonable sin; but the total disregard of that church to his request for admission, led him to a more thorough investigation of the principles of religion, when he became convinced that the sects were all wrong, and that God had no church on earth, but that He would soon have a church whose creed would be the truth, the whole truth, and nothing but the truth, and from that time kept himself aloof from sectarian influence, boldly declaring his belief to all who wished to learn his views; until the summer of 1835, while in the practice of medicine near Boston, the Book of Mormon, which President Brigham Young had left with his cousin Lucius Parker, at Southborough, accidentally or providentially fell in his way, which was the first he had seen or heard of the Latter-day Saints, except the scurrilous reports of the public prints, which amounted to nothing more than that "a boy named Jo Smith, somewhere out west, had found a gold Bible." He opened the book without regard to place, and totally ignorant of its design or contents, and before reading half a page, declared "God or the Devil has had a hand in that book, for man never wrote it." He read it twice through in about ten days, and so firm was his conviction of the truth, that he immediately commenced settling his accounts, selling his medicine, and freeing himself from every incumbrance, that he might go to Kirtland, seven hundred miles west, the nearest point he could hear of a Saint, and give the work a thorough investigation; firmly believing that if the doctrine was true, God had some greater work for him to do than to peddle pills. But no sooner did he commence a settlement than he was smitten with palsy, from which he suffered exceedingly, and was prevented executing his design until October, 1836, when he arrived at Kirtland, in company with his brother (Doctor Levi Richards, who attended him as physician), where he was most cordially and hospitably received and entertained by his cousin, President Brigham Young, with whom he tarried, and gave the work an unceasing and untiring investigation until the day of his baptism.

which consist in agriculture, mechanical arts, and merchandising, do hereby form ourselves into a firm or company for the before-mentioned objects, by the name of the "Kirtland Safety Society Anti-Banking Company," for the proper management of said firm, we individually and jointly enter into and adopt the following articles of agreement:

Article 1st. The capital stock of said society or firm shall not be less than four millions of dollars; to be divided into shares of fifty dollars each; and may be increased to any amount, at the discretion of the managers.

Art. 2nd. The management of said company shall be under the superintendence of thirty-two managers, to be chosen annually, by, and from among, the members of the same; each member being entitled to one vote for each share, which he, she, or they, may hold in said company; and said votes may be given by proxy or in *propria persona.*

Art. 3rd. It shall be the duty of said managers, when chosen, to elect from their number, a treasurer and secretary. It shall be the further duty of said managers to meet in the upper room of the office of said company, on the first Mondays of November and May, of each year, at 9 o'clock a. m., to inspect the books of said company, and transact such other business as may be deemed necessary.

Art. 4th. It shall be the duty of said managers to choose from among their number, seven men, who shall meet in the upper room of said office on Tuesday of each week, at 4 o'clock p. m., to inquire into and assist in all matters pertaining to said company.

Art. 5th. Each manager shall receive from the company one dollar per day for his services when called together at the annual and semi-annual meetings. The treasurer and secretary and the seven the committee of the managers, shall receive a compensation for their services as shall be agreed by the managers at their semi-annual meetings.

Art. 6th. The first election of managers, as set forth in the second article, shall take place at the meeting of the members to adopt this agreement, who shall hold their offices until the first Monday of November, 1837, unless removed by death or misdemeanor, and until others are duly elected. Every annual election of managers shall take place on the first Monday of November in each year. It shall be the duty of the treasurer and secretary of said company to receive the votes of the members by ballot, and declare the election.

Art. 7th. The books of the company shall be always open for the inspection of the members.

Art. 8th. It shall be the duty of the managers of the company to declare a divided once in six months; which dividend shall be apportioned among the members, according to the installments by them paid in.

Art. 9th. All persons subscribing stock in said firm shall pay their first installment at the time of subscribing, and other installments from time to time, as shall be required by the managers.

Art. 10th. The managers shall give thirty days notice in some public paper, printed in this county, previous to an installment being paid in. All subscribers residing out of the state, shall be required to pay in half the amount of their subscriptions at the time of subscribing; and the remainder, or such part thereof as shall be required at any time by the managers, after thirty days notice.

Art. 11th. The treasurer shall be empowered to call special meetings of the managers whenever he shall deem it necessary, separate and aside from the annual and semi-annual meetings.

Art. 12th. Two-thirds of the managers shall form a quorum to act at the semi-annual meetings, and any number of the seven, the committee of the managers, with the treasurer and secretary, or either of them, may form a quorum to transact business at the weekly meetings, and in case none of the seven is present at the weekly meetings, the treasurer and secretary must transact the business.

Art. 13th. The managers shall have power to enact such by-laws as they may deem necessary from time to time, provided they do not infringe upon these articles of agreement.

Art. 14th. All notes given by said society shall be signed by the treasurer and secretary thereof, and we, the individual members of said firm, hereby hold ourselves bound for the redemption of all such notes.

Art. 15th. The notes given for the benefit of said society shall be given to the treasurer in the following form: "Ninety days after date, we jointly, and severally, promise to pay A. B. or order,——dollars and——cents, value received." A record of which shall be made in the books at the time, of the amount, and by whom given, and when due, and deposited with the files and papers of said society.

Art. 16th. Any article in this agreement may be altered at any time, annulled, added unto, or expunged by the vote of two-thirds of the members of said society, except the 14th article, that shall remain unaltered during the existence of said company. For the true and faithful fulfillment of the above covenant and agreement, we individually bind ourselves to each other, under the penal sum of one hundred thousand dollars. In witness whereof we have hereunto set our hands and seals, the day and date first above written.

The Prophet's Remarks on the Kirtland Safety Society

In connection with the above articles of agreement of the "Kirtland Safety Society," I published the following remarks to all who were preparing themselves, and appointing their wise men, for the purpose of building up Zion and her stakes in the January number of the *Messenger and Advocate:*

It is wisdom and according to the mind of the Holy Spirit, that you should call at Kirtland, and receive counsel and instruction upon those principles that are necessary to further the great work of the Lord, and to establish the children of the kingdom, according to the oracles of God; as they are had among us: and further, we invite the brethren from abroad, to call on us, and take stock in our Safety Society; and we would remind them also of the sayings of Isaiah, contained in the 60th chapter and more particularly the 9th and 17th verses, which are as follows: "Surely the isles shall wait for me, and the ships of Tarshish first, to bring thy sons from far, their silver and their gold [not their bank notes] with them, unto the name of the Lord thy God, and to the Holy One of Israel, because He hath glorified thee. * * * For brass I will bring gold, and for iron I will bring silver, and for wood, brass, and for stone, iron: I will also make thy officers peace, and thine exactors righteousness." Also 62nd chapter, 1st verse: "For Zion's sake will I not hold my peace, and for Jerusalem's sake I will not rest, until the righteousness thereof go forth as brightness, and the salvation thereof as a lamp that burneth."

JOSEPH SMITH, JUN.

CHAPTER XXXIII.

MEETINGS OF THE QUORUMS OF PRIESTHOOD IN THE KIRTLAND TEMPLE—THE PROPHET'S INSTRUCTIONS ON PRIESTHOOD.

The Arrangements for Classes and Meetings in Kirtland Temple.

During the winter, the House of the Lord at Kirtland was filled to overflowing with attentive hearers, mostly communicants; and in the evenings the singers met under the direction of Elders Luman Carter and Jonathan Crosby, Jun., who gave instruction in the principles of vocal music. On Monday evenings the quorum of High Priests meet in the west room of the attic story, where they transact the business of their particular quorum. On Tuesday evenings the Seventies occupy the same room. On Wednesday evenings the rooms are occupied by the quorum of Elders. And on Thursday evening a prayer meeting is held in the lower part of the house, free to all, though generally conducted by Patriarch Joseph Smith, Sen. The Twelve, the High Council and other quorums, generally meet each week to transact business, and during the week the "Kirtland High School is taught in the attic story, by H. M. Hawes, Esq., professor of the Greek and Latin languages. The school numbers from one hundred and thirty-five to one hundred and forty students, divided into three departments—the classic, where the languages only are taught; the English department, where mathematics, common arithmetic, geography, English grammar, writing, and reading are taught; and the juve nile department, the last two having each an assistant instructor. The school commenced in November, and on the first Wednesday in January the several classes passed a public examination in presence of the trustees of the school, parents and guardians, and their progress in study was found of the highest order.

Owing to the multiplicity of letters with which I was crowded from almost every quarter, I was compelled to decline all not postpaid, and gave notice of the same in the *Messenger and Advocate*.

Gathering of the Saints in Missouri.

The brethren in Missouri were very busy in gathering into Caldwell county, entering United States land, building houses, and preparing to put in crops in the spring.

Firm of Cowdery & Co. Dissolved.

On the first of February, 1837, the firm of Oliver Cowdery & Co. was dissolved by mutual consent, and the entire establishment was transferred to Joseph Smith, Jun., and Sidney Rigdon; and Warren A. Cowdery acted as their agent in the printing office and bookbindery, and editor of the *Messenger and Advocate*.

Licenses.

During the quarter ending March the 3rd, thirty-two Elders', seven Priests', three Teachers', and two Deacons' licenses were recorded in the license records in Kirtland, by Thomas Burdick.

Notice of a Solemn Assembly.

A brief notice only was given, that a solemn assembly would be called, of the official members of the Church, on the 6th of April, for the purpose of washing, anointing, washing of feet, receiving instructions, and the further organization of the ministry. Meetings were held by the different quorums on Monday, 3rd, Tuesday, 4th, and Wednesday, 5th, to anoint such of their respective members as had not been washed and anointed, that all might be prepared for the meeting on the 6th.

At an early hour on Thursday, the 6th of April, the official members asssembled in the House of the Lord, when the time for the first two or three hours was spent by the different quorums in washing of feet, singing, praying, and preparing to receive instructions from the Presidency. The Presidents, together with the Seventies and their presidents, repaired to the west room in the attic story, where, for want of time the preceding evening, it became necessary to seal the anointing of those who had recently been anointed and not sealed.

Washing of Feet.

Another subject of vital importance to the Church, was the establishing of the grades of the different quorums. It was ascertained that all but one or two of the presidents of the Seventies were High Priests, and when they had ordained and set apart any from the quorums of Elders, into the quorum of Seventies, they had conferred upon them the High Priesthood, also.* This was declared to be wrong, and not according to the order of heaven. New Presidents of the Seventies were accordingly ordained to fill the places of such of them as were High Priests,† and the *ex-officio* presidents, and such of the Seventies as had been legally ordained to be High Priests, were directed to unite with the High Priests' quorum. All the quorums then assembled in the lower room of the Lord's House, where they were addressed by the presidents from the stand. The following, in substance, is what was said:

Regulation of the Seventies.

* That is they ordained them High Priests. Since they were Elders, however, they already possessed the High Priesthood, and hence it was only necessary to ordain them to the office of Seventy in that Priesthood; but the brethen who had immediate charge of ordaining Seventies (the first presidents of Seventies) seemed to have thought it necessary to ordain them High Priests in order for them to hold the High Priesthood, hence the correction made by the Prophet.

† In the selection and ordination of the council composed of the first seven presidents of Seventy, it had been overlooked, evidently, that the revelation on Priesthood, given March 28, 1835, specifically stated: "And it is according to the vision, showing the order of the Seventy, that they should have seven presidents to preside over them, *chosen out of the number of the Seventy*."—(Doc. and Cov., sec. 107, verse 93). Five of those chosen to make up the first council were High Priests; therefore to make the action of the Church conform to the word of God, these High Priests were invited by the Prophet to take their place in the High Priests' quorum, that the first council might be made up of men "chosen out of the number of the Seventy" as provided by the law of God.

President Joseph Smith, Jun., addressed the assembly and said, the Melchizedek High Priesthood was no other than the Priesthood of the Son of God; that there are certain ordinances which belong to the Priesthood, from which flow certain results; and the Presidents or Presidency are over the Church; and revelations of the mind and will of God to the Church, are to come through the Presidency. This is the order of heaven, and the power and privilege of this Priesthood. It is also the privilege of any officer in this Church to obtain revelations, so far as relates to his particular calling and duty in the Church. All are bound by the principles of virtue and happiness, but one great privilege of the Priesthood is to obtain revelations of the mind and will of God. It is also the privilege of the Melchizedek Priesthood, tc reprove, rebuke, and admonish, as well as to receive revelation. If the Church knew all the commandments, one half they would condemn through prejudice and ignorance.

The Prophet on the Subject of Priesthood.

A High Priest, is a member of the same Melchizedek Priesthood with the Presidency, but not of the same power or authority in the Church. The Seventies are also members of the same Priesthood, [i. e. the High Priesthood], are a sort of traveling council or Priesthood, and may preside over a church or churches, until a High Priest can be had. The Seventies are to be taken from the quorum of Elders, and are not to be High Priests. They are subject to the direction and dictation of the Twelve, who have the keys of the ministry. All are to preach the Gospel, by the power and influence of the Holy Ghost; and no man can preach the Gospel without the Holy Ghost.

The High Priests.

The Bishop is a High Priest, and necessarily so, because he is to preside over that particular branch of Church affairs, that is denominated the Lesser Priesthood, and because we have no direct lineal descendant of Aaron, to whom it would of right

Bishops.

belong. This is the same, or a branch of the same, Priesthood, which may be illustrated by the figure of the human body, which has different members, which have different offices to perform; all are necessary in their place, and the body is not complete without all the members.

From a retrospect of the requirements of the servants of God to preach the Gospel, we find few qualified even to be Priests, and if a Priest understands his duty, his calling, and ministry, and preaches by the Holy Ghost, his enjoyment is as great as if he were one of the Presidency; and his services are necessary in the body, as are also those of Teachers and Deacons. Therefore, in viewing the Church as a whole, we may strictly denominate it one Priesthood. President Smith also said:

The Dignity of the Lesser Officers.

"I frequently rebuke and admonish my brethren, and that because I love them, not because I wish to incur their displeasure, or mar their happiness. Such a course of conduct is not calculated to gain the good will of all, but rather the ill will of many; therefore, the situation in which I stand is an important one; so, you see, brethren, the higher the authority, the greater the difficulty of the station; but these rebukes and admonitions become necessary, from the perverseness of the brethren, for their temporal as well as spiritual welfare. They actually constitute a part of the duties of my station and calling. Others have other duties to perform, that are important, and far more enviable, and may be just as good, like the feet and hands, in their relation to the human body—neither can claim priority, or say to the other, I have no need of you. After all that has been said, the greatest and most important duty is to preach the Gospel.

Necessity for Occasional Reproofs.

"There are many causes of embarrassment, of a pecuniary nature now pressing upon the heads of the Church. They began poor; were needy, destitute, and were truly afflicted by their enemies; yet the Lord commanded them to go forth and preach the Gospel, to sacrifice their time, their talents, their good name, and jeopardize their lives; and in addition to this, they were to build a house for the Lord, and prepare for the gathering of the Saints. Thus it is easy to see this must [have] involved them [in financial difficulties]. They had no temporal means in the beginning commensurate with such an undertaking; but this work must be done; this place [Kirtland] had to be built up. Large contracts have been entered into for lands on all sides, where our enemies have signed away their rights. We are indebted to them, but our brethren from abroad have only to come with their money, take these contracts, relieve their brethren from the pecuniary embarrassments under which they now labor, and procure for themselves a peaceable place of rest among us. This place must and will be built up, and every brother that will take hold and help secure and discharge those contracts that have been made, shall be rich."

Pecuniary Embarrassments of the Presidency.

At 4 p. m. President Hyrum Smith addressed the assembly, principally in relation to the temporal affairs of the Church, and censured those who counseled such brethren as moved to this place, when they were not authorized to give advice. He also alluded, in terms of disapprobation, to the practice of some individuals, in getting money from brethren that come in, when it ought to be appropriated to the discharge of heavy debts that are now hanging over the heads of the Church, or for the payments of the land contracts which had been made for the benefit of the Saints in this place.

Remarks of Hyrum Smith

Twenty-five minutes before five, President Oliver Cowdery spoke, opposing the idea of Elders attempting to preach or teach that which they did not know, etc.

Oliver Cowdery.

President Sidney Rigdon rose a little before 5 p.m., and

after referring to the gathering, and the preaching of the Gospel, as the first things, alluded to the debt which had been contracted for building the Lord's House, and other purposes, and stated three principal items that constituted nearly the aggregate of debt that now remained unliquidated.

Sidney Rigdon's Remarks on Church Debts.

First a charge of six thousand dollars which was appropriated and expended in consequence of the brethren being driven by a lawless mob from their possessions in Jackson county. The second was the building of the Lord's House, the unliquidated debt of which was rising of thirteen thousand dollars. The third item of debt was for the purchase of land, that there might be a place of rest, a place of safety, a place that the Saints might lawfully call their own. All this is to lay a foundation for the gathering of Israel, and when the Elders go abroad they can speak understandingly, and urge the necess ty and propriety of the gathering, from the fact that we have a place for them, and it is the will of God they should come. Prey not one upon another, brethren, and for the time being say not, Pay me what thou owest; but contribute all in your power to discharge the great debts that now hang over the Church.

The Sacrament—Use of Water.

At half-past five, bread and water* were distributed liberally among the quorums, and it was truly a refreshing season to spirit and body. Many brethren and sisters assembled in the evening for prayer and exhortation, and some tarried nearly all night.

* In the revelation given in August 1830 (Sec. 27) the Lord said "it mattereth not what ye shall eat or what ye shall drink when ye partake of the Sacrament, if it so be that ye do it with an eye single to my glory," etc. This is the first occasion on record where water was used instead of wine, but it is possible that water may have been used in the Sacrament before this time.

CHAPTER XXXIV.

AFFAIRS IN ZION—APOSTASY AT KIRTLAND—APPOINTMENT OF THE BRITISH MISSION—ITS DEPARTURE FOR ENGLAND.

Minutes of the High Council at Far West.

FAR WEST, MO., April 7th.

At a meeting of the Presidency of the Church in Missouri, the High Council, Bishop and counselors, it was resolved that the city plat of Far West retain its present form; and that the alleys be opened by a majority of the owners of each square, or block, when they shall desire it; that the price and sale of the town lots be left to W. W. Phelps, John Whitmer, Edward Partridge, Isaac Morley, and John Corrill; that Jacob Whitmer, Elisha H. Groves, and George M. Hinkle be a building committee of the House of the Lord in this city (Far West); that Jacob Whitmer be received as High Councilor until the arrival of President David Whitmer; also that President David Whitmer, John Whitmer, and W. W. Phelps, superintend the building of the Lord's House, in this city, and receive revelations, visions, etc. concerning said house.

JOHN CORRILL, Clerk.

Charge Against Lyman Wight.

David W. Patten preferred a charge against Lyman Wight, for teaching erroneous doctrines, which was investigated by the High Council at Far West, April 24, 1837.

Seymour Brunson, George P. Dykes, and others, testified that Lyman Wight said that we (the Church) were under a telestial law, because God does not whip under a celestial law, therefore He took us (the Church) out of doors to whip us, as a parent took his children out of doors to chastise them; and that the book of Doctrine and Covenants was a telestial law; and the Book of Commandments (a part of the revelations printed in Jackson county) was a celestial law.

The Presidency decided, with the approbation of the Council, that Lyman Wight had taught erroneous doctrine, and that he be required to make an acknowledgment to the Council; also that he go and acknowledge to the churches where he had preached such abominable doctrine.

NATHAN WEST, Clerk.

Complaint against J. M. Patten.

Joshua Fairchild, David Pettigrew, Benjamin Johnson, and Sheffield Daniels entered a complaint against John Patten, for not fulfilling his contracts, or covenants, in consequence of which they were materially injured; which was proved by Lyman Wight and Abigail Daniels, before the High Council at Far West, May 22nd, 1837.

After a long investigation by the Councilors and parties, the Presidency, W. W. Phelps and John Whitmer, [it was decided] that both accuser and accused should be disfellowshiped, if they did not settle their difficulties. Jesse Hitchcock was then cut off from the High Council.

James Emmet, who had previously been disfellowshiped, made satisfaction, and was restored to fellowship; and John Corrill was appointed agent to the Church, and keeper of the Lord's Store House.

HARVEY GREEN, Clerk.

Case of John Patten.

On the 28th of May a charge was preferred by John Corrill and others against John Patten, for not complying with his agreement, which charge being sustained by testimony, the High Council decided that John Patten be disfellowshiped until he make satisfaction.

James Emmet Disfellowshiped.

About this time the Presidency of the Church at Far West called a general meeting of the Church, at which were present the High Council, two of the Twelve Apostles, ten of the Seventies, the Bishop, and one counselor, when it was resolved that we withdraw fellowship from James Emmet, for unwise conduct, until he returns and makes satisfaction.

Action in Relation to the Word of Wisdom.

Resolved unanimously, that we will not fellowship any ordained member who will not, or does not, observe the Word of Wisdom according to its literal reading.

Literary Firm Sustained.

Resolved unanimously, that we sanction the Literary Firm, and give them our voice and prayers, to manage all the affairs of the same, as far as it concerns this place, according to the revelation in book of Doctrine and Covenants, first edition, published at Kirtland, Ohio, page 152, section 26th, given November, 1831, (current edition, section 70).*

* A short time previous to the above recorded actions, viz., in the early part of April preceding, an important meeting of the High Council of Zion was convened and before it Presidents W. W. Phelps and John Whitmer (David Whitmer, the President of Zion being absent) were arraigned for some irregularity in their conduct; and as the action of that Council will have an important bearing upon facts which will later appear in the body of this history, I here give *in extenso* the minutes of that Council meeting, which continued from the third to the seventh of April.

Minutes of the High Council at Far West.

At a meeting of the High Council in Far West, April 3, 1837, seven of the standing councilors were present. John Murdock was appointed moderator, and Elias Higbee clerk.

Resolved, That the Council request the Presidents W. W. Phelps and John Whitmer to give explanation of the following items:

First—By what authority was this place [Far West] pointed out as a city and [a place for a] house of the Lord, and by whom?

Second—By what authority was a committee appointed and ordained to superintend the building of the House of the Lord?

Third—By what authority was Jacob Whitmer ordained to the High Priesthood?

Fourth—Have two presidents authority to lay out a city, and build a House of God; independent of the counsel of the High Council?

Fifth—By what authority was one of the High Councilors disfellowshiped in the name of the High Council without their knowledge?

Sixth—Has any individual or individuals a right to prefer a charge to the Presidency in Kirtland against any High Councilor, [of this Council] without the knowledge of the Council or [the] individual?

Seventh—Should not the High Council and Bishop of Zion, who are appointed to do business for Zion, receive their inheritance in the care of that city in preference to one who is not particularly called to labor for Zion, or an unbeliever?

Eight—Shall any intelligence relative to the building up of Zion be withheld from the Council of Zion?

Ninth—Are the two presidents entitled to the profits arising from the sale of land, on which the city is to be built in this place, independent of the authorities who have been appointed to labor with them for Zion and have suffered like tribulations with them?

The Council then agreed to invite Presidents W. W. Phelps and John Whitmer, also the Bishop, Edward Partridge, and his counselors; also the two Apostles, viz., Thomas B. Marsh and David W. Patten, to meet with them on the 5th, inst, that the above named presidents might explain [answer] the foregoing questions and that the subject might be investigated. The Concil then adjourned to the 5th at ten o'clock.

Far West, April 5th, 1837.

The Council convened agreeable to adjournment with the aforementioned Presidents, the Bishops and counselors; also the two Apostles. The Council opened by prayer; but previous to proceeding to business the said presidents proposed that the Bishop and his counselors, with the above named Apostles leave the Council; which was objected to by the Council, the Bishop and Apostles. The presidents still insisted on having a private council in the absence of the Bishop and his

Minutes of a High Council held in the Lord's House, in Kirtland, Monday, May 29, 1837, ten o'clock a. m.

Isaac Rogers, Artemas Millet, Abel Lamb, and Harlow Redfield, appeared as complainants against Presidents Frederick G. Williams and David Whitmer, and Elders Parley P. Pratt, Lyman Johnson, and Warren Parrish.

Sidney Rigdon presiding.

COUNCILORS.

John Smith,	John Johnson,
Jared Carter,	John P. Greene,
Noah Packard,	Oliver Granger,
Joseph Kingsbury,	Samuel H. Smith,
Joseph Coe,	Martin Harris,
Gideon Carter,	Willard Woodstock.

President Rigdon then read the following complaint:

"*To the Presidency of the Church of Latter-day Saints:*

"We, the undersigned, feeling ourselves aggrieved with the conduct

counselors and the Apostles. All opposed the two presidents. The Bishops and the two Apostles gave them to understand that they had a right to remain, and that they therefore should remain. President Phelps then said he would dissolve the Council, upon which Thomas B. Marsh declared that if the Council should be dissolved he would prepare acharge against the two presidents, before the Bishop and twelve High Priests. The presidents then said they were willing to let all present remain in the house. The Council then proceeded to the investigation of the above named questions. They were not generally satisfactorily answered, which led the Council and others to strongly rebuke the late improper proceedings of the presidents. David W. Patten spoke against them with apparent indignation; stating that their proceedings had been iniquitous and fraudulent in the extreme, in unrighteously appropriating Church funds to their own enrichment, which had been plainly proven. April 6th was occupied in like discussions. April 7th, Council convened agreeable to appointment. The Bishop and counselors present, also the two Apostles. The above named presidents agreed to give up the town plat of Far West with four eighties on the commons to be disposed of by the High Council, the Bishop and his counselors and the said Apostles. After which, on motion, the Council adjourned. The Council met in Far West to take into consideration the affairs relative to the town plat; at which the council resolved, (it being agreed by all parties) to make over or that W. W. Phelps and John Whitmer make over, or transfer the town plat with four eighties, which are on the commons, into the hands of the Bishop of Zion; and that the avails arising from the sale of said lands should be appropriated to the benefit and upbuilding of "Poor, Bleeding Zion." In the above resolution, W.W. Phelps and John Whitmer acquiesced. Also resolved that whereas W. W. Phelps and John Whitmer had subscribed $1,000 each to the House of the Lord to be built in this place—which they were before intending to pay out of the avails of the town plat—be considered exempt from paying that subscription."—*Far West Record* [Ms.] pp. 72, 73.

of Presidents David Whitmer and Frederick G. Williams, and also with Elders Lyman E. Johnson, Parley P. Pratt, and Warren Parrish, believing that their course for some time past has been injurious to the Church of God, in which they are high officers, we therefore desire that the High Council should be assembled, and we should have an investigation of their behavior, believing it to be unworthy of their high calling—all of which we respectfully submit.

"ABEL LAMB,
"NATHAN HASKINS,
"HARLOW REDFIELD,
"ARTEMAS MILLET,
"ISAAC ROGERS.

"KIRTLAND, MAY, 1837."

Elder Warren Parrish then stated that the declaration just read was not in accordance with the copy which they [the accused] received of the charges preferred against them.

The resolution was then offered and carried, that three speak on a side.

The Council was then opened by prayer, by President Rigdon.

After a short address to the Councilors, by President Rigdon, President Frederick G. Williams arose, and wished to know by what authority he was called before the present Council; that according to the Book of Covenants, he ought to be tried before the Bishop's court.

After some discussion between Presidents Rigdon and Williams, President Rigdon gave his decision that President Williams should be tried before the present Council.

President David Whitmer also objected to being tried before the present Council.

President Williams then expressed a willingness to be tried for his conduct, and if this was the proper tribunal, he would be tried before it, but still thought it was not.

President David Whitmer objected to being tried before the present Council, stating that he thought the instructions in the Book of Covenants showed that this was not the proper authority to try him.

Councilor Greene gave it as his opinion that the present Council was not the proper authority to try Presidents Williams and Whitmer.

President Rigdon then submitted the case to the Councilors.

Councilor John Smith then put the question to the Council for decision, in substance as follows: Have the present Council authority, from the Book of Covenants, to try Presidents Williams and Whitmer? A majority of the Council decided that they could not conscientiously proceed to try Presidents Williams and Whitmer, and they were accordingly discharged.

After one hour's adjournment, the Council sat again at one o'clock p. m. Sidney Rigdon and Oliver Cowdery presiding.

Councilor John Smith stated that he had selected three High Priests to sit in the Council to fill vacancies, and asked the Council if they accepted the selection he had made. Council decided in the affirmative.

On motion of Warren Parrish, the Councilors were directed to sit as they were originally chosen, or according to the form in the book of Doctrine and Covenants as far as possible.

Resolved, that three speak on each side.

Councilor Martin Harris moved that President Frederick G. Williams take a seat with the presidents.

After much discussion as to the propriety of his sitting, motion carried, and President Williams took his seat.

Elder Parley P. Pratt then arose and objected to being tried by President Rigdon or Joseph Smith, Jun., in consequence of their having previously expressed their opinion against him, stating also that he could bring evidence to prove what he then said.

President Rigdon then stated that he had previously expressed his mind repecting the conduct of Elder Pratt, and that he had felt and said that Elder Pratt had done wrong, and he still thought so, and left it with the Council to decide whether, under such circumstances, he should proceed to try the case.

After much discussion between the councilors and parties, President Rigdon said that, under the present circumstances, he could not conscientiously proceed to try the case, and after a few remarks left the stand.

President Oliver Cowdery then said that although he might not be called upon to preside, yet if he should be, he should also be unfit to judge in the case, as he had previously expressed his opinion respecting the conduct of Elder Parley P. Pratt and others, and left the stand.

President Williams then arose and said, that as he had been implicated with the accused, he should be unwillig to preside in the case, and left the stand.

The Council and assembly then dispersed in confusion.

F. W. Cowdery, Clerk.

Transfer of the *Messenger and Advocate*.

Some time this month, the *Messenger and Advocate* office and contents were transferred to William Marks,* of Portage, Allegheny County, New York, and Joseph Smith and Sidney Rigdon continued the office, by power of attorney from said Marks.

* William Marks was born November 15, 1792, in Rutland, Rutland County, Vermont. This is the first mention of his name in the Prophet's narrative, and nothing can be learned of his career previous to this time.

At this time the spirit of speculation in lands and property of all kinds, which was so prevalent throughout the whole nation,* was taking deep root in the Church. As the fruits of this spirit, evil surmisings, fault-finding, disunion, dissension, and apostasy followed in quick succession, and it seemed as though all the powers of earth and hell were combining their influence in an especial manner to overthrow the Church at once, and make a final end.† Other banking

Conditions in Kirtland.

* As additional evidence that this financial maelstrom in which the "Kirtland Safety Society" met disaster was national and not merely local, I quote here the description of the wide-spread financial panic of 1837, as given in the History of the United States by Alexander H. Stephens: "Soon after Mr. Van Buren became President occurred a great commercial crisis. This was in April, 1837, and was occasioned by a reckless spirit of speculation, which had, for two or three preceding years, been fostered and encouraged by excessive banking, and the consequent expansion of paper currency beyond all the legitimate wants of the country. During the months of March and April of this year the failures in New York City alone amounted to over $100,000,000. The state of affairs became so distressing that petitions were sent to the President from several quarters, and a deputation of merchants and bankers of New York waited upon him in person, and solicited him to defer the immediate collection of duties, for which bonds had been given, and to rescind the treasury orders which had been issued under Jackson's administration, requiring dues to the government to be paid in specie. They also asked that an extra session of Congress should be called to adopt measures of relief. He granted their request so far only as to suspend suits on bonds, which had been given for the collection of duties. In a few days after his response to this deputation was made known in New York, all the banks in that city stopped specie payments, and their example was soon followed by nearly all the banks in all the states. In this emergency, Mr. Van Buren was compelled to convene an extra session of Congress, to provide for meeting demands on the treasury with legal currency. He accordingly summoned the Twenty-fifth Congress to meet at the capitol on the 4th day of September, 1837. The session lasted five or six weeks. In his message to Congress, Mr. Van Buren assigned as the causes of the unhappy condition of the country, the excessive issues of bank paper; the great fire in New York, in December, 1835; the large investments that had been made in unproductive lands, and other speculative enterprises. To meet the exigencies of the treasury, as well as to provide for the public relief, as far as to them seemed proper, Congress passed an act authorizing the issue of treasury notes to the amount of '10,-000,000' "—(History of the United States, by Alexander H. Stephens, p. 460).

† Of the condition of affairs in Kirtland at this time Eliza R. Snow, in her Biography of her brother, the late President Lorenzo Snow, says: "A spirit of speculation had crept into the hearts of some of the Twelve, and nearly, if not every quorum was more or less infected. Most of the Saints were poor, and now prosperity was dawning upon them—the Temple was completed, and in it they had been recipients of marvelous blessings, and many who had been humble and faithful to the performance of every duty—ready to go and come at every call of the Priesthood, were getting haughty in their spirits, and lifted up in the pride of

institutions refused the "Kirtland Safety Society's" notes. The enemy abroad, and apostates in our midst, united in their schemes, flour and provisions were turned towards other markets, and many became disaffected toward me as though I were the sole cause of those very evils I was most strenuously striving against, and which were actually brought upon us by the brethren not giving heed to my counsel.

No quorum in the Church was entirely exempt from the influence of those false spirits who are striving against me for the mastery; even some of the Twelve were so far lost to their high and responsible calling, as to begin to take sides, secretly, with the enemy.*

their hearts. As the Saints drank in the love and spirit of the world, the Spirit of the Lord withdrew from their hearts, and they were filled with pride and hatred toward those who maintained their integrity. They linked themselves together in an opposing party—pretended that they constituted the Church, and claimed that the Temple belonged to them, and even attempted to hold it."

* Among those who were embittered against the Prophet at this time was Elder Parley P. Pratt, and of this incident in his experience he says: About this time, (summer of 1837) after I had returned from Canada, there were jarrings and discords in the Church at Kirtland, and many fell away and became enemies and apostates. There were also envyings, lyings, strifes and divisions, which caused much trouble and sorrow. By such spirits I was also accused, misrepresented and abused. And at one time, I also was overcome by the same spirit in a great measure, and it seemed as if the very powers of darkness which war against the Saints were let loose upon me. But the Lord knew my faith, my zeal, my integrity of purpose, and He gave me the victory. I went to Brother Joseph Smith in tears, and, with a broken heart and contrite spirit, confessed wherein I had erred in spirit, murmured, or done or said amiss. He frankly forgave me, prayed for me and blessed me. Thus, by experienc, I learned more fully to discern and to contrast the two spirits, and to resist the one and cleave to the other. And, being tempted in all points, even as others, I learned how to bear with, and excuse, and succor those who are tempted."—(Autobiography of Parley P. Pratt, pp. 183-4).

In the midst of these troubles there were reputations made as well as some lost. Among those who were developed rather than destroyed by the troubles and temptations of these times was the late President John Taylor. Referring to a visit which Elder Taylor made to Kirtland in the spring of 1837 his Biography states: "At that time there was a bitter spirit of apostasy rife in Kirtland. A number in the quorum of the Twelve were disaffected toward the Prophet, and the Church seemed on the point of disintegration. Among others, Parley P. Pratt was floundering in darkness, and coming to Elder Taylor told him of some things wherein he considered the Prophet Joseph in error. To his remarks Elder Taylor replied: 'I am surprised to hear you speak so, Brother Parley. Before you left Canada you bore a strong testimony to Joseph Smith being a Prophet of God, and to the truth of the work he has inaugurated; and you said you knew these things by revelation, and the gift of the Holy Ghost. You gave to me a strict charge to the effect that though

The British Mission Projected.

In this state of things, and but a few weeks before the Twelve were expecting to meet in full quorum, (some of them having been absent for some time), God revealed to me that something new must be done for the salvation of His Church. And on or about the first of June, 1837, Heber C. Kimball, one of the Twelve, was set apart by the spirit of prophecy and revelation, prayer and laying on of hands, of the First Presidency, to preside over a mission to England, to be the first foreign mission of the Church of Christ in the last days.* While we were about ordaining him, Orson

you or an angel from heaven was to declare anything else I was not to believe it. Now Brother Parley, it is not man that I am following, but the Lord. The principles you taught me led me to Him, and I now have the same testimony that you then rejoiced in. If the work was true six months ago, it is true today; if Joseph was then a Prophet, he is now a Prophet.' To the honor of Elder Pratt, be it said, he sought no further to lead Elder Taylor astray; nor did he use much argument in the first place. 'He and many others,' says Elder Taylor, 'were passing under a dark cloud; he soon made all right with the Prophet Joseph, and was restored to full fellowship.' It was about this time that Elder Taylor first came prominently before the Church. The apostates met frequently in the Temple, and on one of these occasions, on a Sunday—the Prophet Joseph was absent—Warren Parrish made a violent attack upon the character of the Prophet, in which he was warmly sustained by many of those present. Towards the close of the meeting, Elder Taylor asked the privilege of speaking. It was granted him. He referred, in opening his remarks, to the ancient Israelites, and to their murmurings against God and Moses, and then asked: 'From whence do we get our intelligence, and knowledge of the laws, ordinances and doctrines of the kingdom of God? Who understood even the first principles of the doctrines of Christ? Who in the Christian world taught them? If we, with our learning and intelligence, could not find out the first principles, which was the case with myself and millions of others, how can we find out the mysteries of the kingdom? It was Joseph Smith, under the Almighty, who developed the first principles, and to him we must look for further instructions. If the spirit which he manifests does not bring blessings, I am very much afraid that the one manifested by those who have spoken, will not be very likely to secure them. The children of Israel, formerly, after seeing the power of God manifested in their midst, fell into rebellion and idolatry, and there is certainly very great danger of our doing the same thing.' While the apostates were neither convinced nor silenced by the remarks of Elder Taylor, the faithful Saints were strengthened, and saw in that fearless defender of the Prophet, a champion of innocence and truth. While on his part, in commenting on this circumstance, Elder Taylor remarks: 'I was pained on the one hand to witness the hard feelings and severe expressions of apostates; while on the other, I rejoiced to see the firmess, faith, integrity and joy of the faithful.' "—(Life of John Taylor, pp. 39, 40, 41.)

* Of this call of Heber C. Kimball to the Presidency of the British mission his biographer (Bishop O. F. Whitney, his grandson) gives the following account:

Hyde, another of the Twelve, came in, and upon listening to what was passing, his heart melted within him, (for he had begun to drink of the cup filled with the overflowings of speculation), he acknowledged all his faults, asked forgiveness, and offered to accompany President Kimball on his mission to England. His offer was accepted, and he was set apart for that purpose.*

Licenses.

Thirty-five Elders', three Priests', two Teachers', and two Deacons' licenses were recorded in the license records in Kirtland, during the quarter ending June 3rd, by Thomas Burdick.

On the 10th of June, 1837, a conference of the Church

"On Sunday, the 4th day of June, 1837," says Heber C. Kimball, "the Prophet Joseph came to me, while I was seated in front of the stand, above the sacrament table, on the Melchisedek side of the Temple, in Kirtland, and whispering to me, said, 'Brother Heber, the Spirit of the Lord has whispered to me: Let my servant Heber go to England and proclaim my Gospel, and open the door of salvation to that nation.'" The thought was overpowering. He had been surprised at his call to the Apostleship; now he was overwhelmed. Like Jeremiah he staggered under the weight of his own weakness, exclaiming in self-humiliation: "O, Lord, I am a man of stammering tongue, and altogether unfit for such a work; how can I go to preach in that land, which is so famed throughout Christendom for learning, knowledge and piety; the nursery of religion; and to a people whose intelligence is proverbial! Feeling my weekness to go upon such an errand. I asked the Prophet if Brother Brigham might go with me. He replied that he wanted Brother Brigham to stay with him, for he had something else for him to do. The idea of such a mission was almost more than I could bear up under. I was almost ready to sink under the burden which was placed upon me. However, all these considerations did not deter me from the path of duty; the moment I understood the will of my heavenly Father, I felt a determination to go at all hazards, believing that He would support me by His almighty power, and endow me with every qualification that I needed; and although my family was dear to me, and I should have to leave them almost destitute, I felt that the cause of truth, the Gospel of Christ, outweighed every other consideration."—(Life of Heber C. Kimball, by O. F. Whitney, pp. 116, 117).

* The British mission was really an outgrowth of the work in Canada. "Several of the Saints in Canada," says Parley P. Pratt, in speaking of his labors there in the early spring of 1837, "were English, who had friends in England. Letters had already been sent to them with information of the rise of the Church, and of its principles. Several of the Canadian Elders felt a desire to go on a mission to their friends in that country. At length, Joseph Fielding, Isaac Russell, John Goodson and John Snider, of the Canadian Elders, were selected for a mission to England. Elders Heber C. Kimball and Orson Hyde, of the Quorum of the Twelve, were selected to go at the head of the mission, and Elder Willard Richards was appointed to accompany them."—(Autobiography of Parley P. Pratt, p. 183.)

was held at Portland, district of Johnstown, upper Canada, at which Elder John E. Page presided. There were present thirteen Elders, five Priests, eight Teachers, and six Deacons; and there were seven Elders, nine Priests, eleven Teachers and five Deacons ordained. West Bastard, Bedford, Bathurst, North Bathurst, East Bastard, Williamsburg, Leeds, and South Crosby branches were represented at the conference, comprising three hundred members in good standing, and five baptized at conference, total three hundred and five, being the fruits of the labors of Elder John E. Page in the last thirteen months.

Church Conference in Upper Canada.

Minutes of a High Council Meeting in Missouri.

At a meeting of the High Council, at the Committee Store, Far West, June 11, 1837, John Whitmer and W. W. Phelps presiding, Resolved by the Council and all present that the building committee be upheld in the mercantile business, by our prayers; that Lyman Wight, Simeon Carter and Elias Higbee be upheld in conducting a leather store; that John Corrill, Isaac Morley, and Calvin Bebee engage in the mercantile business if they choose; that the right of no man shall be infringed upon, to do as he choose according to the law of God and man; and that the above named men shall be upheld in purchasing goods as other men.

It was reported that certain individuals, not of the Church, were desirious, or were about to establish themselves as grocers, retailers of spirituous liquors, and so forth, in Far West, whereupon it was resolved that we will not uphold any man or men to take a partner out of the Church to trade or traffic in this line of business, or sell for any man or men out of the Church, in his name, or on commission.

David W. Patten requested that the Church pay his debts, and take him for security, that he might go forth and preach the Gospel.

Resolved that Elder Patten's request be granted, and that David W. Patten and Thomas B. Marsh, receive each a lot in the town of Far West, free of charge, and that the Bishop, if he approve, give a title.

JOHN CORRILL, Clerk.

The same evening, [11th of June] while I was engaged

in giving some special instructions to Elders Kimball and Hyde, and Priest Joseph Fielding,* concerning their mission to England, President Brigham Young came into my house, where we were sitting, accompanied by Dr. Willard Richards, who had just returned from a special business mission to New York, Boston, and other eastern cities, on which he started with President Young on the 14th of March—Dr. Richards having been previously ordained an Elder, viz., on the 6th of March, and President Young having returned from the mission a few days previous. My instructions to the brethren were, when they arrived in England, to adhere closely to the first principles of the Gospel, and remain silent concerning the gathering, the vision, and the Book of Doctrine and Covenants, until such time as the work was fully established, and it should be clearly made manifest by the Spirit to do otherwise.

The Prophet's Instructions to the British Missionaries.

Monday, *June 12.*—I was taken sick, and kept my room, unable to attend to business.

Elder Willard Richards, having reported his mission, requested the privilege of fulfilling a covenant which he made with President Kimball in January, which was, that he should, agreeable to his desire, accompany the Twelve on their first foreign mission. President Hyrum Smith and Sidney Rigdon granted his petition, laid their hands upon his head, and set him apart for the English mission.

Willard Richards Added to the British Mission.

Tuesday, *13.*—My afflictions continued to increase, and were very severe, insomuch that I was unable to raise my head from my pillow when the brethren called to bid me farewell; and at nine o'clock a. m. Elders Heber C. Kimball, Orson Hyde, Will-

Illness of the Prophet.

* Joseph Fielding was born in Honeydon, Bradfordshire, England, and was the son of John and Rachel Fielding. He emigrated from England and located in Upper Canada, near Toronto, in 1832. Together with his two sisters, Mary and Rachel, he received the Gospel under the ministry of Elder Parley P. Pratt in May, 1832, and soon after was ordained a Priest and joined the mission to England as recorded in the text of the history above.

ard Richards, and Joseph Fielding, a Priest, a native of Honeydon, England, left Kirtland in company with President Brigham Young and several of the Kirtland brethren and sisters, who continued with them as far as Fairport, on Lake Erie, where the missionaries took a steamer for Buffalo, directing their course for New York City.

Wednesday, 14.—I continued to grow worse and worse until my sufferings were excruciating, and although in the midst of it all I felt to rejoice in the salvation of Israel's God, yet I found it expedient to call to my assistance those means which a kind Providence had provided for the restoration of the sick, in connection with the ordinances; and Dr. Levi Richards, at my request, administered to me herbs and mild food, and nursed me with all tenderness and attention; and my heavenly Father blessed his administrations to the easing and comforting of my system, for I began to amend in a short time, and in a few days I was able to resume my usual labors.

Employment of Supplementary Means for Healing the Sick.

This is one of the many instances in which I have suddenly been brought from a state of health, to the borders of the grave, and as suddenly restored, for which my heart swells with gratitude to my heavenly Father, and I feel renewedly to dedicate myself and all my powers to His service.

While I was thus afflicted, the enemy of all righteousness was suggesting, apostates reporting, and the doubtful believing that my afflictions were sent upon me, because I was in transgression, and had taught the Church things contrary to godliness; but of this the Lord judge between me and them, while I pray my Father to forgive them the wrong they do.

Dastardly Suggestions of Apostates.

The brethren appointed to the mission to England, landed at Buffalo, and went down the canal. While walking on its bank, President Kimball found an iron ring, about one and one-fourth inch diameter, which he presented to Elder Richards, saying, "I will make you a present of this, keep it in remembrance of me, for our friendship shall be as endless as this ring."

Progress of the British Mission.

The brethren having been disappointed in not receiving funds from Canada, while at Buffalo, Elder Richards left the company at Albany, and in company with President Kimball visited his friends in Richmond, Massachusetts, where they obtained means sufficient to continue their journey; and arrived in New York on the eve of the 22nd of June, where they found Elder Hyde and Brother Fielding, also three brethren from Canada, viz., John Goodson,* one of the Seventies, Elder Isaac Russell,† and John Snyder,‡ a Priest, who had gone forward to join the mission; and on the 23rd they engaged passage to Liverpool in the second cabin of the merchant ship *Garrick.*

Arrival of British Mission in New York.

The brethren found but one member of the Church in the City of New York, viz., Elder Elijah Fordham, who was very attentive, and rendered them assistance ac-

* Concerning the place and time of the birth of John Goodson nothing can be learned. He was, however, among those whom Elder Parley P. Pratt converted in Upper Canada during his memorable mission in that land.

† Isaac Russell was born April 13, 1807, in Windy Hall, Cumberland County, England. His father's name was William Russell, and Isaac was the youngest of thirteen children. The family emigrated to America about 1817, settling in Upper Canada. In June, 1829, he married Mary Walton and made his home in Toronto, where he received the Gospel under the ministry of Elder Parley P. Pratt. He was ordained an Elder and engaged in missionary work in Upper Canada until he joined the British mission under the leadership of Elder Heber C. Kimball, as stated in the text.

‡ John Snyder was born in New Brunswick, Nova Scotia, November 11, 1800. He removed with his father's family to Upper Canada, near Toronto. His father died while John was yet a youth, but under the influence of his mother, a woman of strong character and upright life, young Snyder grew to manhood with strong religious sentiments. In 1835, he joined, with the late President John Taylor, an association of students of the Scriptures who were seeking for a profounder knowledge of the truth. It was to this association that Elder Parley P. Pratt was directed in 1836 and to whom he so frequently preached the Gospel that quite a number of them united with the Church, John Snyder among them. Soon after John Snyder was ordained to the Priesthood and joined the British mission as stated in the text.

cording to his means, but they, being short of funds to pay their passage, etc., removed from their lodgings at Mrs. Fordham's (Elder Fordham's sister-in-law), on the 24th, and, hiring a room in an unfurnished store house of Elder Fordham's father, took lodgings on the floor, and ate their bread and drank their water, until they went on shipboard.

Kindness of Elijah Fordham.

Sunday, 25.—The brethren remained in their lodgings fasting, praying and counciling for the success of the mission, and had a joyful time. In the afternoon two sectarian priests came in to talk and find fault, but they were soon confounded, and left. On the 28th the brethren deposited one of Orson Hyde's "Timely Warnings," in the New York postoffice, for each of the sectarian priests in the city, amounting to some hundreds. They went on board the *Garrick* on the 29th, and left the dock; on the 30th, lay at anchor in East River; and at 7:30 a. m., on the first of July, were towed out of harbor by a steamer, hoisted sail, and were out of sight of land at 4:30 p. m.

Warning to New York Ministers—Departure for England.

CHAPTER XXXV.

FINANCIAL CONDITION IN VARIOUS NATIONS—PROGRESS OF THE BRITISH MISSION—CONFERENCES AT FAR WEST AND KIRTLAND.

The following is an extract from a letter to the brethren in Kirtland, written at—

FAR WEST, MISSOURI, July 7, 1837.

Monday, the 3rd of July, was a great and glorious day in Far West, more than fifteen hundred Saints assembled at this place, and at half-past eight in the morning, after prayer, singing, and an address, they proceeded to break the ground for the Lord's House. The day was beautiful; the Spirit of the Lord was with us. An excavation for this great edifice, one hundred and ten feet long by eighty feet broad was nearly finished. Tuesday, the 4th, we had a large meeting, and several of the Missourians were baptized; our meetings, held in the open prairie, were larger than they were in Kirtland, when I was there. We have more or less to bless, confirm, and baptize, every Sabbath. This same day, our school section was sold at auction, and although entirely a prairie, it brought, on a year's credit, from $3.50 to $10.20 per acre, making our first school fund five thousand and seventy dollars. Land cannot be had around town now much less than ten dollars per acre.

Our numbers increase daily, and notwithstanding the season has been cold and backward no one has lacked a meal or went hungry. Provisions have risen in price, but not as high as accounts say they were abroad. Public notice has been given by the mob in Daviess county, north of us, for the Mormons to leave that county by the first of August and go into Caldwell: our enemies will not slumber till Satan knows how vain is his plotting. Our town gains some, we have about one hundred buildings, eight of which are stores. If the brethren abroad are wise and will come on with means and help enter the land and populate the county and build the Lord's House, we shall soon have one of the most precious spots on the globe; God grant that it may be so. Of late we receive little news from you, and we think much of that is exaggerated.

As ever,

W. W. PHELPS.

N. B.—Please say in your *Messenger and Advocate* "A postoffice has been established at Far West, Caldwell county, Missouri."

The same day (July 7th), the *Garrick* passed the banks of Newfoundland.

The Prophet Resigns his Office in the "Safety Society."

Some time previous to this I resigned my office in the "Kirtland Safety Society," disposed of my interest therein, and withdrew from the institution; being fully aware, after so long an experiment, that no institution of the kind, established upon just and righteous principles for a blessing not only to the Church but the whole nation, would be suffered to continue its operations in such an age of darkness, speculation and wickedness. Almost all banks throughout the country, one after the other, have suspended specie payment, and gold and silver have risen in value in direct ratio with the depreciation of paper currency. The great pressure of the money market is felt in England as well as America, and bread stuffs are everywhere high. The season has been cool, wet and backward.

Status of Various Nations.

Mexico, unwilling to acknowledge the independence of Texas, considers her inhabitants as rebellious subjects. Spain is divided against herself, wasting her blood and treasure in her own destruction. Portugal is rapidly exhausting her resources in princely luxuries. Poland has lost her rank among the nations to gratify the ambition of Nicholas, the Russian autocrat. The government of Buenos Ayres has declared war against Peru, and nearly all the republics of South America are mingled in the strife, while the Indians continue their depredations on the inhabitants of Florida. Trouble and distress are the grand topics of conversation amongst politicians, merchants, mechanics and demagogues; and crimes, misdemeanors, and casualties, occupy a large space in the public journals.

Sunday, July 16.—Elder Hyde preached on the quarter-deck of the *Garrick* concerning the prophecies; the cabin passengers listened with attention, and were particularly affected during prayer, also a little child belonging to some of the steerage passengers, that was sick until it was considered hopeless, was healed by the power of God, President Kimball laying his hands upon it secretly.

On the 18th the *Garrick* entered St. George's Channel, in sight of Cape Clear.

On Thursday morning, July 20th, the *Garrick* anchored in the River Mersey, opposite Liverpool, and while the cable chains were yet rattling the merchant ship *South America*, which left New York at the same time with the *Garrick*, under a bet, it is said, of $10,000, as to which would be in Liverpool first, came alongside, having kept in sight daily during the voyage but never getting ahead of the *Garrick;* and in all the different stages from Kirtland to Liverpool, no vessel was permitted to go past the mission.

The Landing.

While the passengers were going on board a steamer Elders Kimball, Hyde, Richards, and Goodson jumped into a small boat and were rowed toward shore. When within leaping distance Elder Kimball sprang from the boat as if impelled by some superior power and alighted on the steps of the dock, followed instantly by Elders Hyde and Richards, all three of whom had not one farthing on earth at their command, while Elder Goodson, having a heavy purse of silver in his hand, waited until the vessel touched shore.

"Truth will Prevail."

On the bretnren went to Preston, about thirty miles from Liverpool, and as they alighted from the coach a large flag was unfurled nearly over their heads, with this inscription, in letters of gold, "Truth will Prevail," it being election day for members of Parliament. King William the Fourth had recently died and Queen Victoria was about to organize her cabinet. Taking lodgings in Wilford street, some of the Elders had an interview that evening with the Rev. James Fielding, brother of Joseph Fielding, who had a chapel in that place, where all the seven brethren went to hear him preach on Sunday, 23rd. After his sermon in the morning Mr. Fielding gave notice to his congregation that there were present some ministers from America, and they would occupy his pulpit in the afternoon. This unexpected offer was unsolicited but joyfully received, and in the afternoon President Kimball gave a brief relation of the history of the Church from the commencement, followed by Elder Hyde, who bore testimony to the same; thus was the key turned and the door of salvation opened to the inhabitants of England. At the close of the meeting Mr. Fielding offered his pulpit for the evening, when Elder Goodson preached and Brother Fielding bore testimony.

Kindness of Rev. James Fielding.

The same day that the Gospel was first preached in England I received the following

*Revelation given at Kirtland, Ohio, July, 23rd, 1837. The word of the Lord unto Thomas B. Marsh, concerning the Twelve Apostles of the Lamb.**

1. Verily thus saith the Lord unto you, my servant Thomas, I have heard thy prayers, and thine alms have come up as a memorial before me, in behalf of those thy brethren who were chosen to bear testimony of my name, and to send it abroad among all nations, kindreds, tongues, and people, and ordained through the instrumentality of my servants.

2. Verily I say unto you, there have been some few things in thine heart and with thee with which I, the Lord, was not well pleased;

3. Nevertheless, inasmuch as thou hast abased thyself thou shalt be exalted, therefore all thy sins are forgiven thee.

4. Let thy heart be of good cheer before my face, and thou shalt bear record of my name, not only unto the Gentiles but also unto the Jews; and thou shalt send forth my word unto the ends of the earth.

5. Contend thou therefore morning by morning, and day after day let thy warning voice go forth, and when the night cometh, let not the inhabitants of the earth slumber because of thy speech.

6. Let thy habitation be known in Zion, and remove not thy house.

* Doctrine and Covenants, sec. cxii.

for I, the Lord, have a great work for thee to do, in publishing my name among the children of men;

7. Therefore gird up thy loins for the work. Let thy feet be shod, also, for thou art chosen, and thy path lieth among the mountains, and among many nations;

8. And by thy word many high ones shall be brought low, and by thy word many low ones shall be exalted.

9. Thy voice shall be a rebuke unto the transgressor, and at thy rebuke let the tongue of the slanderer cease its perverseness.

10. Be thou humble, and the Lord thy God shall lead thee by the hand, and give thee answer to thy prayers.

11. I know thy heart, and have heard thy prayers concerning thy brethren. Be not partial toward them in love above many others; but let thy love be for them as for thyself, and let thy love abound unto all men, and unto all who love my name.

12. And pray for thy brethren of the Twelve. Admonish them sharply for my name's sake, and let them be admonished for all their sins, and be ye faithful before me unto my name.

13. And after their temptations and much tribulation, behold, I, the Lord, will feel after them, and if they harden not their hearts, and stiffen not their necks against me, they shall be converted and I will heal them.

14. Now, I say unto you, and what I say unto you I say unto all the Twelve, Arise and gird up your loins, take up your cross, follow me, and feed my sheep.

15. Exalt not yourselves; rebel not against my servant Joseph, for verily I say unto you, I am with him, and my hand shall be over him; and the keys which I have given unto him, and also to youward, shall not be taken from him till I come.

16. Verily I say unto you my servant Thomas, thou art the man whom I have chosen to hold the keys of my kingdom (as pertaining to the Twelve) abroad among all nations,

17. That thou mayest be my servant to unlock the door of the kingdom in all places where my servant Joseph, and my servant Sidney, and my servant Hyrum cannot come;

18. For on them have I laid the burden of all the churches for a little season;

19. Wherefore whithersoever they shall send you, go ye, and I will be with you; and in whatsoever place ye shall proclaim my name, an effectual door shall be opened unto you that they may receive my word;

20. Whosoever receiveth my word receiveth me, and whosoever receiveth me receiveth those (the First Presidency) whom I have sent, whom I have made counselors for my name's sake unto you.

21. And again, I say unto you, that whomsoever ye shall send in my name, by the voice of your brethren the Twelve, duly recommended and authorized by you, shall have power to open the door of my kingdom unto any nation, whithersoever ye shall send them,

22. Inasmuch as they shall humble themselves before me, and abide in my word, and harken to the voice of my Spirit.

23. Verily, verily I say unto you, darkness covereth the earth, and gross darkness the minds of the people, and all flesh has become corrupt before my face.

24. Behold, vengeance cometh speedily upon the inhabitants of the earth, a day of wrath, a day of burning, a day of desolation, of weeping, of mourning, and of lamentation, and as a whirlwind it shall come upon all the face of the earth, saith the Lord.

25. And upon my house shall it begin, and from my house shall it go forth, saith the Lord.

26. First among those among you, saith the Lord, who have professed to know my name, and have not known me, and have blasphemed against me in the midst of my house, saith the Lord.

27. Therfore see to it that you trouble not yourselves concerning the affairs of my Church in this place, saith the Lord;

28. But purify your hearts before me, and then go ye into all the world, and preach my Gospel unto every creature who has not received it,

29. And he that believeth and is baptized shall be saved, and he that believeth not and is not baptized, shall be damned.

30. For unto you (the Twelve) and those (the First Presidency) who are appointed with you, to be your counselors and your leaders, is the power of this Priesthood given, for the last days and for the last time, in the which is the dispensation of the fullness of times.

31. Which power you hold in connection with all those who have received a dispensation at any time from the beginning of the creation;

32. For verily I say unto you, the keys of the dispensation which ye have received have come down from the fathers, and last of all being sent down from heaven unto you.

33. Verily I say unto you, behold, how great is your calling. Cleanse your hearts and your garments, lest the blood of this generation be required at your hands.

34. Be faithful until I come, for I come quickly, and my reward is with me to recompense every man according as his work shall be. I am Alpha and Omega. Amen.

Albert P. Rockwood,* of Holliston, Massachusetts,

* Albert P. Rockwood was born June 5, 1805, in Holliston, Middlesex county, Massachusetts.

having heard of the Saints, through Elders Young and Richards, came to Kirtland to investigate, and was baptized on the 25th of July, by President Brigham Young.

Baptism of Albert P. Rockwood.

Wednesday, 26.—Elder Hyde preached in the evening in Mr. Fielding's chapel, and Elder Richards bore testimony. Much feeling was manifested by the congregation, and many were convinced of the truth; but Mr. Fielding, fearing for the loss of his society, more than the displeasure of heaven, closed his doors against the brethren from that time, and opposed the work with all his power. Invitations were given to the Elders to preach in private houses in different parts of Preston, which opportunities were improved daily, after the close of the factories.

Progress of the British Mission.

Thursday, 27.—I started from Kirtland in company with Elders Rigdon and Marsh for the purpose of visiting the Saints in Canada. Brother Rockwood on his return home, Elder Brigham Young on a mission to the eastern cities, started with us. When we arrived at Painsville we were detained all day by malicious and vexatious law suits. About sun-set I got into my carriage to return home to Kirtland; at this moment the sheriff sprang into the carriage, seized my lines, and served another writ on me, which was sworn out by a man who had a few weeks previously brought a new fashioned cooking stove to Kirtland, and prevailed on me to put it up in my kitchen, saying it would give credit to his stove, wishing to have it tested by our people; and now he thought would be a good time to get pay for it. I gave my watch to the officer for security and we all returned home.

Vexatious Law Suits at Painesville.

The following day I remained at home until evening, when we set out again in Brother S. B. Stoddard's wagon to Ashtabula, a distance of thirty miles and arrived there a little after daybreak and stayed till afternoon and enjoyed ourselves very much in walking

Second Start for Canada.

on the beach and bathing in the beautiful, clear water of the lake. At four p. m. we took a deck passage on board the steamer for Buffalo. At night we all lay down to rest on the upper deck of the boat, and for pillows some took their boots, others their valises, and had a comfortable night's repose. We arrived at Buffalo the next morning in safety. Here we separated from Brothers Brigham Young and Albert P. Rockwood, they going to the Eastern States; and myself, Brothers Sidney Rigdon and Thomas B. Marsh started for Toronto, Upper Canada.

The British Mission—Attacked by Evil Spirits.

About daybreak Sunday, July 30th, Elder Isaac Russell, who had been appointed to preach on the Obelisk in Preston market-place that day, and who slept in the second story of their lodgings in Wilford street, went up to the third loft where Elders Hyde and Kimball were sleeping, and called upon them to pray for him, that he might be delivered from the evil spirits that were tormenting him to such a degree that he felt he could not live long unless he obtained relief. They immediately arose and laid hands on him and prayed that the Lord would have mercy on His servant and rebuke the devil. While thus engaged Elder Kimball was struck with great force by some invisible power and fell senseless on the floor; and the first thing Elder Kimball recollected was being supported by Elders Hyde and Russell beseeching the throne of grace in his behalf. They then laid him on the bed but his agony was so great he could not endure it, and arose, fell on his knees and prayed; then he arose and sat upon the bed while the brethren distinctly saw the evil spirits, who foamed and gnashed upon them with their teeth, by legions for the space of some minutes; Elder Richards was present the latter part of the time. About ten o'clock in the morning the brethren repaired to the river Ribble, according to previous appointment, and, in the midst of a large collection of people, baptized nine individuals, one of whom was George D. Watt, the first man baptized in England in this dispensation.

Spread of the Work in England.

On Monday, the 31st of July, the Elders held a council and appointed Elders Goodson and Richards a mission to Bedford, and Elders Russell and Snyder to Alton, Cumberland county, continuing in prayer until morning, August 1st, when they took their departure for their several stations.

Affairs at Far West.

The same day (August 1st) a general meeting of the Presidency, High Council, Bishop, and counselors and the Saints assembled at Far West. The High Council elected Thomas Grover a High Councilor in place of Jesse Hitchcock; and George Morey in place of Peter Whitmer, Jun., deceased; and Titus Billings was elected Bishop's counselor in place of John Corrill. Voted unanimously by the whole assembly that in the absence of the Presidency, Councilors, Bishop and counselors at Kirtland, the Elders in Missouri had no authority [to act as a Council for the Church], consequently their acts in that capacity during that space of time are considered null and void; and that every president of High Priests and Elders be ordained by some higher authority; and the president of any quorum having counselors may ordain them himself.

Opening of the Work in Bedford.

Elders Goodson and Richards arrived in Bedford on the 2nd and were joyfully received by the Rev. Timothy R. Mathews, to whom they had letters of introduction from his brother-in-law, Joseph Fielding, and were invited to preach in his chapel in the evening to his congregation.

First Confirmation in England.

Friday, 4.—Elder Kimball baptized Jennetta Richards* at Preston, daughter of the Rev. John Richards, of Walkerfold, Chaidgley, fifteen miles from Preston, and confirmed her at the water side. This was the first confirmation in England. Sister Richards returned home the day following, Saturday, 5th, and

* Jennetta Richards was born August 21, 1817, in Lancashire, England, and was the daughter of John and Ellen Richards.

persuaded her father to write to Elder Kimball to come and preach in his chapel.

The same day, August 5th, the Presidency, High Council, and all the authorities of the Church in Missouri, assembled in council at Far West, and unanimously resolved to go on moderately and build a house unto the name of the Lord in Far West, as they had means, and appointed Edward Partridge treasurer, to receive all the donations and subscriptions for the erection of the House of the Lord; Isaac Morley to be his secretary. Also voted that the committee, viz., Jacob Whitmer, Elisha H. Groves, and George M. Hinkle stand [as the building committee of the Lord's House at Far West]* until President David Whitmer goes to and returns from Kirtland; also, that the building committee of the House of the Lord have no store connected with building the house, but that every firm or individual that embarks in that business have, own, and claim such property as their own private individual property and stewardship.

Affairs in Far West—Building the Lord's House.

The Elders at Bedford continued to lecture in the basement of Mr. Matthews' chapel from evening to evening, with the most flattering prospects until this evening, when Elder Goodson, contrary to the most positive instructions of President Kimball, and without advising with any one, read publicly the vision from the Doctrine and Covenants, which turned the current of feeling generally, and nearly closed the door in all that region. Mr. Matthews wished the meetings to be removed from his house, but continued to attend the meetings occasionally and investigated the subject to considerable extent.

Goodson's Violation of Instructions.

In the August number of the *Messenger and Advocate* was published a prospectus for a new paper, to be published at Kirtland, Ohio, called the *Elders' Journal* of the Church of Latter-day Saints, to commence in October, edited by Joseph Smith, Jun.

The *Elders' Journal*.

* See page 481.

Elders Kimball and Hyde and Brother Fielding having continued their labors in Preston, Elder Hyde preached to a great multitude in the market place Sunday, the 6th of August, opposed by one Reverend gentleman who was quickly confounded by the spirit of truth; and in the evening they met at the house of Sister Ann Dawson and confirmed between forty and fifty who had been baptized, most of whom had been members of Mr. James Fielding's church, so mightily grew the word, this being only the third Sabbath of the brethren in Preston. Mr. Fielding persecuted and called the Elders "thieves, sheep stealers," etc., acknowledging them good judges, having "stolen all the best of his flock." Sister Dawson (a widown) kindly received the Elders into her house and lodged them, which was a great blessing to the brethren, as they were quite destitute, most of the people extremely poor, and lodgings scarce; while they went from house to house as invited, to procure their daily meals.

Confirmations at Preston.

Elder Kimball, having received a letter from Mr. John Richards, inviting him to preach in his chapel, repaired to Walkerfold, where he was most hospitably received, and the day following preached three times in Mr. Richards' pulpit.

The Work in Walkerfold.

Elders Goodson and Richards baptized five at Bedford, among whom, and the first, was Mrs. Ann Braddock, a widow, who was obliged to support her family by her industry, yet she received the Elders and lodged them.

Baptisms at Bedford.

Timothy R. Matthews, having investigated the work, acknowledged the truth, and having previously borne testimony of the same to his church in public, and urged them to go forward, agreed with Elders Goodson and Richards to meet them on the bank of the river Ouse one hour before sunset and be baptized. The hour and the Elders arrived, but Mr. Matthews was not there, he had gone out into the country to preach.

The Failure of Mr. Matthews.

Elder Kimball preached on Monday and Wednesday evenings in Mr. Richards' chapel at Walkerfold, and on Thursday baptized six individuals. Mr. Matthews baptized himself in the river, and then went to baptizing his people, denouncing the Elders as false teachers and the doctrines of the Latter-day Saints as having come from hell, while he went to preaching the same doctrine, baptizing all, even infants, and laid on hands for confirmation.

Tuesday, 15.—The quorum of High Priests organized at Far West, Missouri, this day. Charles C. Rich* was ordained President of the High Priests' quorum in Missouri; and Henry Green president of the Elders in Caldwell county, August 20th.

Charles C. Rich Made President of High Priests in Missouri.

The same day Elders Wilford W. Woodruff and Jonathan H. Hale landed at Vinalhaven, on North Fox Island,† and commenced preaching.

Opening in the Fox Islands.

In the August number of the *Messenger and Advocate* I published the following

CAUTION.

To the brethren and friends of the Church of the Latter-day Saints: I am disposed to say a word relative to the bills of the "Kirtland Safety Society Bank." I hereby warn them to beware of speculators, renegades, and gamblers, who are duping the unwary and unsuspecting, by palming upon them those bills, which are of no worth here. I discountenance and disapprove of any and all such practices. I know

* Charles C. Rich was born August 21, 1809, in Campbell county, Kentucky; and was the son of Joseph Rich and Nancy O. Neal. He was baptized by Ira M. Hinckley in Tazewell county, Illinois, on the first of April, 1832, and later was ordained an Elder by Zebedee Coltrin. He removed with his father to Far West, Missouri, in 1836. February 11, 1837, he married Sarah D. Pea.

† Fox Islands are off the south coast of Maine, directly east of Rockland. The principal town is Vinalhaven. The population of the islands at the time of Elder Woodruff's first visit is given at eighteen hundred, and the following is his description of the people and islands: "The inhabitants are generally wealthy, intelligent, industrious, generous and hospitable to strangers. North Island is nine miles long and two wide, population eight hundred; South Island is ten miles long and five wide, population one thousand." Elder Woodruff met with great success in his labors in this island and soon had a flourishing branch organized.

them to be detrimental to the best interests of society, as well as to the principles of religion.

[Signed] JOSEPH SMITH, JUN.

The Alston Branch.

In this month Elder Isaac Russell succeeded in establishing a small branch in Alston, England.

The Prophet's Work in Canada.

At this time I was engaged in visiting the churches in Canada, preaching, baptizing, blessing the Saints and strengthening the branches.

I returned to Kirtland about the last of August and wrote the following letter, which I sent by the hand of Thomas B. Marsh:

KIRTLAND, GEAUGA, COUNTY, OHIO,
September 4, 1837.

Joseph Smith, Jun., President of the Church of Christ of the Latter-day Saints in all the world, to John Corrill and the whole Church in Zion, sendeth greeting.

Blessed be the God and Father of our Lord Jesus Christ who has blessed you with many blessings in Christ, and who has delivered you many times from the hands of your enemies, and planted you many times in a heavenly or holy place. My respects and love to you all, and my blessings upon all the faithful and true hearted in the New and Everlasting Covenant. Forasmuch as I have desired for a long time to see your faces and converse with you and instruct you in those things which have been revealed to me pertaining to the kingdom of God in the last days, I now write unto you offering as an apology my being bound with cords of affliction by the workers of iniquity, and also by the labors of the Church, endeavoring in all things to do the will of God for the salvation of the Church, both in temporal as well as spiritual things.

Brethren, we have waded through affliction and sorrow thus far for the will of God, that language is inadequate to describe. Pray ye therefore with more earnestness for our redemption. You have undoubtedly been informed by letter and otherwise of our difficulties in Kirtland, which are now about being settled; and that you may have a knowledge of the same, I inclose you the following minutes of the committee of the whole Church in Kirtland, the authorities, etc., referring you to my brother Hyrum and Brother Thomas B. Marsh for further particulars; also that you may know how to proceed to set in order and regulate the affairs of the Church in Zion whenever they become disorganized.

Minutes of a Conference Assembled in Committee of the whole Church at Kirtland on Sunday, the 3rd of September, 1837.

At nine o'clock in the morning George W. Robinson was called upon to take minutes of the conference. Sidney Rigdon then presented Joseph Smith, Jun., to the Church to know if they still looked upon and would still receive and uphold him as the President of the whole Church, and the vote was unanimous in the affirmative.

President Smith then presented Sidney Rigdon and Frederick G. Williams as his counselors, and to constitute with himself the three first Presidents of the Church. Voted unanimously in the affirmative, except for Frederick G. Williams, which was not carried unanimously.

President Smith then introduced Oliver Cowdery, Joseph Smith, Sen., Hyrum Smith, and John Smith for assistant counselors. These last four, together with the first three, are to be considered the heads of the Church. Carried unanimously.

Voted, that Newel K. Whitney hold his office as Bishop and continue to act as such in Kirtland, and that Reynolds Cahoon and Vinson Knight continue to act as counselors to the Bishop.

The Twelve Apostles were then presented one by one, when Thomas B. Marsh, David W. Patten, Brigham Young, Heber C. Kimball, Orson Hyde, Parley P. Pratt, Orson Pratt, William Smith, and William E. M'Lellin were received unanimously in their Apostleship, Luke S. Johnson, Lyman E. Johnson, and John F. Boynton were rejected and disfellowshiped, though privileged with confessing and making satisfaction.

Elder Boynton (who was the only one of the three present at the time) arose and endeavored to confess, justifying himself in his former conduct by reason of the failure of the bank.

His conduct was strongly protested against by Elder Brigham Young in a plain and energetic manner, stating various reasons why he could not receive him into fellowship until a hearty repentance and confession were manifested.

Elder Young was followed by Elder Marsh, who acquiesced in testimony and resolutions.

President Rigdon then addressed the assembly, showing the cause of the difficulty with Elders Boynton and Johnson in leaving their calling to attend to other occupations.

Elder Boynton again rose and still attributed his difficulties to the failure of the bank, stating that he understood the bank was instituted by the will of God, and he had been told that it should never fail, let men do what they would.

President Smith then arose and stated that if this had been declared no one had authority from him for so doing, for he had always said that unless the institution was conducted on righteous principles it would not stand.

A vote was then taken to know if the congregation was satisfied with Elder Boynton's confession; carried in the negative.

Conference adjourned for one hour.

Conference reassembled at two o'clock in the afternoon; opened by reading, singing, and prayer.

The President then arose and said he would call upon the Church to know if they were satisfied with their High Council, and should proceed to name them individually.

John Johnson, Joseph Coe, Joseph C. Kingsbury, and Martin Harris were objected to, also John P. Greene, but his case went over until he should be present.

Noah Packard, Jared Carter, Samuel H. Smith, were sustained.

Oliver Granger, Henry G. Sherwood, William Marks, Mayhew Hillman, Harlow Redfield, Asahel Smith, Phinehas Richards, and David Dort, were chosen to fill the places of those objected to, (and Thomas Grover having moved west) John Smith, chosen one of the presidents of the Church, all having belonged to the High Council.

The President then called upon the congregation to know if the recently appointed presidents of the Seventies should stand in their calling.

Voted that John Gaylord, James Forster, Salmon Gee, Daniel S. Miles, Joseph Young, Josiah Butterfield, and Levi W. Hancock, should reatain their offices as presidents of Seventies; John Gould was objected to.

The President then arose and made some remarks concerning the former presidents of the Seventies, the calling and authority of their Priesthood, etc.

Voted that the old presidents of the Seventies [who were High Priests] be referred to the quorum of High Priests; and also, that if any members of the quorum of the Seventies should be dissatisfied and would not submit to the present order and receive these last presidents, the latter should have power to demand their licenses, and the former should no longer be considered members of the Church.

Conference closed by prayer by the President.

JOSEPH SMITH, JUN., President,
GEORGE W. ROBINSON, Clerk.

Announcement concerning Oliver Cowdery.

DEAR BRETHREN—Oliver Cowdery has been in transgression, but as he is now chosen as one of the presidents or counselors, I trust that he will yet humble himself and magnify his calling, but if he should not, the Church will soon be under the necessity of raising their hands against him; therefore pray for him.

David Whitmer, Leonard Rich, and others have been in transgression, but we hope that they may be humble and ere long make satisfaction to the Church, otherwise they cannot retain their standing; therefore we say unto you, beware of all disaffected characters, for they come not to build up, but to destroy and scatter abroad. Though we or an angel from heaven preach any other Gospel, or introduce an order of things other than those things which ye have received, and are authorized to receive from the First Presidency, let him be accursed.

May God Almighty bless you all and keep you unto the coming and kingdom of our Lord and Savior Jesus Christ.

Yours in the bond of the New Covenant,

JOSEPH SMITH, JUN.

I received the following:

Revelation given at Kirtland, Ohio, September 4, 1837, making known the transgression of John Whitmer and William W. Phelps.

Verily thus saith the Lord unto you my servant Joseph—my servants John Whitmer and William W. Phelps have done those things which are not pleasing in my sight, therefore if they repent not they shall be removed out of their places. Amen.

September 9.—The High Council of Kirtland met in the Lord's House and organized by electing Jared Carter, president, and Phinehas Richards, clerk. The members elected on the 3rd were ordained and drew for their numbers, and the whole were arranged as follows: John P. Greene, No. 1; Asahel Smith, No. 2; Samuel H. Smith, 3; Mayhew Hillman, 4; William Marks, 5; Noah Packard, 6; Oliver Granger, 7; David Dort, 8; Jared Carter, 9; Phinehas Richards, 10; Henry G. Sherwood, 11; and Harlow Redfield, 12.

The High Council of Kirtland withdrew the hand of fellowship from Uriah and Lydia Ann Hawkins for unlawful matrimony, deceiving, and unchristianlike conduct.

Minutes of a Meeting in the Kirtland Temple.

Sunday, September 10th, 2 o'clock, afternoon, in an assembly of the Church in the Lord's House, Kirtland, President Rigdon read the rules and regulations of the House of the Lord, as passed by the different quorums on the 18th of January, 1836, when the Church voted to receive the same, and be governed by them.

The minutes of the High Council of the 9th instant were read, after which those of the Twelve who were disfellowshiped the previous Sabbath had opportunity to speak; and Luke S. Johnson, Lyman E. Johnson, and John F. Boynton made their confessions and were received into fellowship by vote of the Church, also to retain their apostleship.

President Smith read a letter from Elder Thomas B. Marsh to the Church, stating that before he started from Missouri he had received satisfaction from these Elders. Elder Young alse stated the same.

High Councilor John P. Greene made some confessions to the Church, stating wherein he had been wrong for a short time past; and the Church voted that he be received into fellowship and retain his office.

President Rigdon made some observations on the business transacted last Sabbath, reproving some for the conjectures they had respecting President Smith and himself conniving together to remove certain individuals from office, etc., or at least to use their influence to do so. This he informed them was a mistake, for not one word had passed between them on the subject, neither had he a premiditated thought upon the subject.

President Smith then corrected some mistakes of certain individuals which had been circulated by them concerning what he had said on the last Sabbath.

The Lord's Supper was administered by Elders Luke S. and Lyman E. Johnson, and John F. Boynton.

GEORGE W. ROBINSON, Clerk.

When a lying spirit is abroad it is difficult for truth to be understood.

CHAPTER XXXVI.

THE GATHERING SAINTS — INCREASE IN THE NUMBER OF STAKES CONTEMPLATED—COUNCILS IN ZION AND KIRTLAND—CLOSE OF THE VOLUME.

At a conference of the authorities of the Church and the Saints in the House of the Lord at Kirtland, September 17th, Bishop Newel K. Whitney said the time had arrived when it became necessary for him to travel, and necessarily he must have an agent to act in his absence agreeable to the provisions made in the revelations. He nominated William Marks, who was elected agent to the Bishop by unanimous vote.

Bishop's Agent Appointed.

George W. Robinson was unanimously elected general Church recorder in place of Oliver Cowdery, who had removed to Missouri.

The Church Recorder.

After taking into consideration the situation of Zion and the Church in general, the conference decided that it was of great importance to the cause of truth in general, and the prosperity of the work, that the Bishop and his counselors send abroad their memorial to all the Saints throughout the land, as well as to all well-wishers to the cause of Zion, and that their appeal go forth in the name and by the authority of the Church to all the Saints scattered abroad.

The Bishop's Memorial.

The same evening the Elders assembled in conference in the House of the Lord when I addressed them on the subject of the gathering of the Saints in the last days, and the duties of the different quorums in relation thereto.

The Prophet on the Gathering.

It appeared manifest to the conference that the places appointed for the gathering of the Saints were at this time crowded to overflowing, and that it was necessary that there be more stakes of Zion appointed in order that the poor might have a place to gather to, "wherefore it was moved, seconded and voted unanimously that President Joseph Smith, Jun., and Sidney Rigdon be requested by this conference to go and appoint other stakes, or places of gathering, and that they receive a certificate of their appointment, signed by the clerk of the Church."

Other Stakes of Zion to be Appointed.

Elder William Marks, who had previously been appointed agent to the Bishop, being called upon arose and said that he would comply with the request of the Church, and the Lord being his helper he would discharge the duties of his office to the best of his ability. After which the Elders present who were in a situation to travel were called upon to number themselves, and there were numbered one hundred and nine, and they were divided into eight companies in the following order—number one to thirteen, called the first company, were appointed to travel east; No. 14 to 26, were to travel southeast; No, 27 to 39, south; No. 40 to 52, southwest; No. 53 to 65, west; No. 66 to 78, northwest; No. 79 to 91, north; No. 92 to 104, northeast. Five being left after this division, No. 105 was appointed to travel with the company going southeast; No. 106, with the company northwest; 107, south; 108, east; 109, with the north company. It was further appointed that those who might desire to travel a different course from the one which was appointed to the division to which they belonged, might have the privilege of changing with those of another division. And lastly it was appointed that the different divisions hold their own meetings, to make such arrangements as they should think proper in relation to their journeying.

Arrangements for Preaching the Gospel.

Agreeable to the vote of the conference on the 17th,

Bishop Whitney and counselors issued the memorial as follows:

KIRTLAND, OHIO, September 18th, 1837.

To the Saints Scattered Abroad, the Bishop of Kirtland and his Counselors send Greeting:

Whereas the Church in Kirtland has taken into consideration the affairs of the Latter-day Saints in general, having opportunities of making themselves acquainted with the situation of the Saints throughout the continent, and the very flattering prospects of the prosperity of the cause of God in our land, and also of the peculiar condition of the city of Kirtland, which is a kind of first fruits of the cities which the Lord has begun to build unto Himself in these last days, it has been deemed of great importance to the prosperity of the cause of truth in general, that the Bishop and his counselors send abroad this their memorial to all the Saints throughout the land, as well as to all well wishers to the cause of Zion in this our most happy country.

It is a fact well known that the Saints in the city of Kirtland have been called to endure great affliction for the truth's sake, and to bear a heavy burden in order that the foundation of the kingdom of God might be laid on a sure and certain basis, so that the prophetic vision of Daniel might most certainly be fulfilled, that this kingdom might break in pieces all other kingdoms and stand for ever. The exertions of the enemy to prevent this have been very great; and through their great exertions they have given to the Saints great trouble, and caused them much expense. In addition to this, they have had to publish the word of the Lord, which has been attended with great expense. These things, together with building the House of the Lord, have embarrassed them very much; for when subscriptions failed they went on and accomplished the work of building the house themselves, plighting all that they had, property, credit, and reputation, and by these means accomplished this great work which is the wonder and admiration of the world. This they have done in faith, believing that, as the multitude of Saints increased, their liberality would abound towards those who, regarding nothing but the salvation of the world, have thus exposed themselver to financial ruin in order that the work of the gathering might not fail. And besides all this there have been a large number of poor who have had to receive assistance from the donations of the Church, which have tended to increase its embarrassments; and now so numerous are the Saints grown that it is impracticable for them all to gather to the places which are now appointed for this purpose.

The Church at Kirtland has, therefore, required at the hand of our beloved brethren, Joseph Smith, Jun., and Sidney Rigdon, men who have not thought their lives dear unto them in order that the cause of God might be established, presidents whom God has appointed to preside over the whole Church, and the persons to whom this work belongs, that they should go forth and lay off other stakes of Zion, or places of gathering, so that the poor may have a place of refuge, or places of refuge, in the day of tribulation which is coming swiftly on the earth. All these things will be attended with expense. Feeling ourselves under great responsibility by virtue of our office and calling in the Church of God, we present this our memorial to all the Saints, making a most solemn appeal to the feelings, benevolence and philanthropy of all the Saints into whose hands this our memorial comes, in faith and confidence that this appeal will not be made in vain.

It is the fixed purpose of our God, and has been so from the beginning, as appears by the testimony of the ancient Prophets, that the great work of the last days was to be accomplished by the tithing of His Saints. The Saints were required to bring their tithes into the store house, and after that, not before, they were to look for a blessing that there should not be room enough to receive it. (See Malachi 3rd chapter, 10th verse). Our appeal, then, to the Saints is founded on the best of testimony, that which no Saint will feel to gainsay, but rejoice to obey. The Saints of God will rejoice in all that the Lord does, and in doing all that the Lord requires. The sacrifice of righteousness which the Lord requires will be offered with a willing heart and ready mind, and with great joy, because they are accounted worthy to offer up sacrifice for His name.

In making this appeal to the benevolence of the Saints of God we do not only take into consideration the situation of the poor, the embarrassments of the stake of Kirtland, but also their own interests, for every Saint has an equal interest in building up the Zion of our God, for it is after the Lord has built up Zion that He will appear in His glory (Psalm cii: 16). We all look for the appearing of the great God and our Savior Jesus Christ, but we shall look in vain until Zion is built, for Zion is to be the dwelling place of our God when He comes (Joel iii: 21). Anyone who will read this chapter with attention will see that it treats of the last days, and of the Zion of the last days. How, then, is the Lord to dwell in Zion if Zion be not built up? This question we leave the Saints to answer. The salvation of the Saints one and all depends on the building up of Zion, for without this there is no salvation, for deliverance in the last days is found in Zion and in Jerusalem, and in the remnant whom the Lord our God shall call, or in other words, in the stakes which He shall appoint (Joel ii: 32)

It is in Zion where the Lord is to create upon every dwelling place and upon her assemblies a cloud of smoke by day and the shining of a flaming fire by night. It is upon the glory of Zion that there will be a defense. It is in Zion that there shall be a tabernacle for a shadow in the day time from the heat, and for a place of refuge and for a covert from storm and from rain (Isaiah iv: 5, 6). It is upon the walls of Zion where the watchmen shall see eye to eye (Isaiah lii: 8).

Whatever is glorious, whatever is desirable, whatever pertains to salvation, either temporal or spiritual, our hopes, our expectations, our glory, and our reward, all depend on our building up Zion according to the testimony of the Prophets, for unless Zion is built our hopes perish, our expectations fail, our prospects are blasted, our salvation withers, and God will come and smite the whole earth with a curse. Hear, then, O ye Saints of the last days! And let this our appeal have a favorable reception among you. Let every Saint consider well the nature of his calling in the last days, and the great responsibility which rests upon him or her, as one to whom God has revealed His will; and make haste not only to the relief of Kirtland, but also to the building up of Zion. Let every man and every woman give heed the very instant that they embrace the Gospel, and exert themselves with energy to send on means to build up Zion, for our God bids us to hasten the building of the city, saying the time has come when the city must be pushed forward with unceasing exertions, for behold, the day of calamity draweth nigh, and unless the Saints hasten the building of the city they will not escape.

Be admonished, then, O ye Saints! And let not covetousness, which is idolatry, nor worldly ambition hinder you; but gather up your gold and your silver and all the means you have and send on to the Saints who are engaged in this great work of building the Zion of God, that there may be a place of refuge for you and for your children in the day of God's vengeance, when He shall come down on Idumea, or the world, in His fury and stamp them down in His wrath, and none shall escape but the inhabitants of Zion. What we say unto one we say unto all, haste, haste, and delay not! for the hour of desolation does not linger, and with all the power that the Saints have, and with all the diligence they can use they will scarcely escape.

The time is not far distant when some of those who now deride and mock the Saints for devoting their all to build up the Zion of God, will bless their name for having provided a city of refuge for them and their children, regardless of the ravings of ungodly priests, and the mockings of a stupid and ignorant people. In the confidence which we have in the good sense and righteous principles of the multitude of the

Saints, we send this our memorial in the name of our Master, Jesus, believing that this appeal will be received with great kindness, and will be attended to with untiring perseverance until the object for which it has been sent shall be accomplished. And may the God of all grace pour out His richest blessings on your heads, and crown you with abundance, that the Zion of our God may flourish and cease not until the righteousness thereof shall go forth as the light and the salvation thereof as a lamp which burneth, is the prayer of your brethren in Christ Jesus.

NEWEL K. WHITNEY,
REYNOLDS CAHOON,
VINSON KNIGHT.

The Voice of Warning.

About this time Elder Parley P. Pratt, who was laboring in New York, published his Voice of Warning, consisting of 216 pages.*

The Prophet's Departure for Missouri.

I started from Kirtland on the 27th of September, in company with Brother Sidney Rigdon, to fulfill the mission appointed us on the 18th of September by a conference of Elders, in establishing places of gathering for the Saints; Brothers William Smith and Vinson Knight accompanying us.

October 1.—Elder Lyman Sherman was elected High Councilor at Kirtland in place of Jared Carter, removed to Far West.

October 2.—Samuel H. Smith was elected president of the High Council, and council voted that if a councilor

* The above named publication, "A Voice of Warning and Instruction to all People," is the first argumentative and doctrinal work published by any of the Elders; and it is no disparagement of other works to say that this pioneer book of its class is not only the first in the matter of time when issued, but first also in excellence. It has been a most successful missionary; and thousands have been brought to a conviction of the truth through reading its pages. The first edition—three thousand copies—sold in about two years. A second edition—two thousand five hundred copies—was issued; and such was the increase in the demand for it that by 1846, the author could congratulate himself upon having seen it pass through five editions. During more than half a century since then "The Voice of Warning" has passed through many editions in English, and has been translated into seven foreign languages, and in a number of these several editions have been issued. The author, of honored memory, is to be congratulated upon the attainment of his fondest hopes respecting this work, as so prophetically expressed in the preface of the first European edition: "And should the author be called to sacrifice his life for the *Truth*, he will have the consolation that it will be said of him, as it was of Abel—'*He being dead, yet speaketh.*'"

absented himself from their meetings without a reasonable excuse, he should be reported to the Church as a delinquent. The High Council at Kirtland voted that the clerk grant licenses to the members of the council (who wished to travel), signed by the president and clerk.

President of High Council Elected.

We arrived at Terre Haute, Indiana, on the 12th, about midway from Kirtland to Far West.

My brother Hyrum's wife, Jerusha Barden Smith, died on the 13th of October while I was at Terre Haute, and her husband at Far West. She left five small children and numerous relatives to mourn her loss; her demise was severely felt by all. She said to one of her tender offspring when on her dying bed, "Tell your father when he comes that the Lord has taken your mother home and left you for him to take care of." She died in full assurance of a part in the first resurrection.

Death of Hyrum Smith's Wife.

October 15.—The High Priests' quorum at Kirtland decided to take Doctor Sampson Avard's license until he returns and make satisfaction; and the High Council concurred.

Minutes of High Council.

October 18.—The High Council and presidents of the different quorums met in the Lord's House, Samuel H. Smith presiding, and after a lengthy discussion concerning existing evils, agreed that it was time to commence the work of reform, and voted unanimously to meet again in the Lord's House on Monday evening next, and invite the different quorums to meet at the same time, and commence pruning the vine of God in Kirtland, and thus continue the work evening after evening until it shall be wisdom to stay their hands.

PHINEHAS RICHARDS, Clerk of the High Council.

Sunday 22.—The Church in Kirtland disfellowshiped twenty-two brethren and sisters until they make satisfaction for uniting with the world in a dance the Thursday previous.

Twenty-two Disfellowshiped.

Minutes of High Council.

October 23.—The High Council of Kirtland appointed Luke S. Johnson, Reynolds Cahoon, and John Gould a committee to visit John Johnson, Jun., and see if he would desist from selling spirituous liquors to those who were in the habit of getting intoxicated, and report to the authorities of the Church those members who might drink spirits at his house. Also voted that the Church see that all difficulties and differences be settled as speedily as possible; and that unruly children be reported to their parents, and if they neglect to take suitable notice of it, then the parents shall be reported to the authorities of the Church and dealt with accordingly.

Voted that we discountenance the use of ardent spirits in any way to sell or to be brought into this place for sale or use.

PHINEHAS RICHARDS, Clerk.

Confessions.

Sunday, October 29.—Nine more of the brethren and sisters were reported to the Church as having been engaged in the recreations of the 19th instant and eleven of the thirty-one that had been reported made confession.

Norris Brewster.

On the 30th of October, Brothers Norris, Brewster, and others, presented to the High Council a plan for the better organization of the Church in temporal affairs, stating that Moroni had appeared to Collins Brewster. The council decided that it was a trick of the devil.

More Confessions.

Most of those who were complained of for participating in the recreation on the 19th and had not confessed, acknowledged their fault to the High Council on the first of November, and the remainder were required so to do or be cut off from the Church.

Action Against Loungers.

November 2.—The High Council voted that loungers about the streets should be labored with, and appointed a committee of three for that purpose.

The Egyptian Records.

The Church in Kirtland voted to sanction the appointment of Brother Phinehas Richards and Reuben Hedlock, by the Presidency, to transact business for the Church in procuring means to translate and print the records taken from the Catacombs of Egypt, then in the Temple.

I arrived at Far West some time in the latter part of October or first of November. A meeting of some of the Church was called on the sixth to counsel on certain affairs of the Church, which I attended with Brothers Rigdon and Hyrum Smith. There were present also Elders Thomas B. Marsh, William E. M'Lellin, Lyman E. Johnson, William Smith, and Vinson Knight, from Ohio, the High Council of the Church of Far West, and some other Elders. Prayer by W. W. Phelps. Several topics were discussed, when it was unanimously voted that it be recommended to the propıietors of the corporation of Far West tc petition the trustees of said corporation to alter the streets or lessen them so as to make each block contain four acres of ground, and each block to be divided into four lots. Also voted unanimously that it is the opinion of this council that there is sufficient room in this country for the churches to continue gathering from abroad; also that the building of the House of the Lord be postponed until the Lord shall reveal it to be His will to have it commenced.

Arrival of the Prophet at Far West.

Adjourned until early candle light, and met accordingly, when remarks were made by many of the authorities present upon the previous disposition of the town plat, the purchase of land, etc.; and all difficulties were satisfactorily settled except a matter between Oliver Cowdery, Thomas B. Mash, and myself, which was referred to us with the agreement that our settlement of the affair would be sufficient for the council.

The Settlement of Difficulties.

W. W. Phelps presided at this meeting, and Oliver Cowdery acted as clerk.

Minutes of a High Council at Kirtland.

The High Council and Bishop of Kirtland met in the Lord's House on Tuesday evening, November 7th to discuss the question, "Who presides when the presidents are absent?" but upon discussion were not able to come to any conclusion.

Thomas Burdick was appointed High Councilor in the place and absence of Phinehas Richards; and Harlow Redfield clerk for the time being.

President Joseph Smith, Sen., proposed that Brother Phinehas Richards be ordained under the hands of President John Smith and Bishop Whitney, and he was accordingly blessed for his mission.

PHINEHAS RICHARDS, Clerk.

Minutes of a Conference at Far West, Missouri, November 7th, 1837.

At a general assembly of the Church of Latter-day Saints, assembled at Far West to take into consideration and transact the business of said Church, Elder Thomas B. Marsh was chosen as moderator and Oliver Cowdery clerk.

After singing the moderator addressed the throne of grace in prayer, after which President Sidney Rigdon explained the object of the meeting, giving a relation of the recent reorganization of the Church in Kirtland. The minutes of said meeting at Kirtland were read by the moderator who also nominated Joseph Smith, Jun., the first President of the whole Church, to preside over the same.

All were requested (male and female) to vote; and he was unanimously chosen.

President Smith then made a few remarks accepting the appointment, requesting the prayers of the Church in his behalf. He also nominated President Sidney Rigdon to be one of his counselors, and he was unanimously chosen.

He then nominated Frederick G. Williams to be his second counselor, but he was objected to by Elder Lyman Wight in a few remarks referring to a certain letter written to this place by the said Frederick G. Williams.

Also Elder Marsh objected to President Williams.

Elder James Emmet also objected to President Williams.

Bishop Edward Partridge said he seconded President Williams' nomination and should vote for him; and as to said letter, he had heard it and saw nothing so criminal in it.

President David Whitmer also made a few remarks in President Williams' favor.

Elder Marsh made further remarks.

Elder Thomas Grover also objected to President Williams.

President Sidney Rigdon then nominated President Hyrum Smith to take President Williams' place.

The moderator called for a vote in favor of President Williams, but he was rejected.

He then called for a vote in favor of President Hyrum Smith, which was carried unanimously.

Some few remarks were made by Presidents David Whitmer and Sidney Rigdon.

David Whitmer was nominated as the President of this branch of the Church, but was objected to by Elder Marsh.

Bishop Edward Partridge said he should vote for President Whitmer.

Elder William E. M'Lellin made a few marks.

Elder George M. Hinkle and Elder King Follet made a few remarks in favor of President Whitmer.

Elders Caleb Baldwin and Seymour Brunson spoke against President Whitmer.

Elder Elisha H. Groves spoke in favor of President Whitmer.

Further remarks from Elder M'Lellin, by request of President Whitmer, gave general satisfaction.

Remarks were also made by President Joseph Smith, Jun., who called for an expression, which was carried by almost a unanimous vote in favor of President Whitmer.

President Joseph Smith, Jun., then nominated John Whitmer for an assistant president, who was objected to, and Elder Marsh spoke in opposition to him, and read a list of charges from a written document against him and President Phelps.

President John Whitmer then spoke a few words by way of confession, and was followed by Elder Isaac Morley.

The vote sustaining him was called, and carried unanimously.

The meeting adjourned for one hour.

Meeting convened according to adjournment, a hymn was sung and prayer offered by the moderator.

W. W. Phelps was nominated for an assistant president for this branch of the Church by President Joseph Smith, Jun.

Brother Phelps rose and made certain remarks on the subject of the charges referred to above by way of confession, whereupon the vote was put by President Rigdon and passed unanimously.

Elders John Murdock, Solomon Hancock, Elias Higbee, Calvin Bebee, John M. Hinkle, Thomas Grover, and Simeon Carter were unanimously chosen High Councilors.

Lyman Wight was nominated a member of the High Council but was objected to by John Anderson; they went aside to converse.

Newel Knight was unanimously chosen. George M. Hinkle was nominated, and objected to by Elder James Emmet, because he was too noisy; by King Follet because of his military office; and by James Durfee because he was a merchant.

Elder Hinkle made a few remarks.

The vote was called and was unanimous in Elder Hinkle's favor.

Levi Jackman and Elisha H. Groves were unanimously chosen.

John Anderson then took the stand and made his objections to Lyman Wight; after which Elder Wight also spoke.

The vote was called and Elder Wight was unanimously chosen.

The Twelve Apostles were then called, namely, Thomas B. Marsh, David W. Patten, Brigham Young, Heber C. Kimball, Orson Hyde, William E. M'Lellin, Parley P. Pratt, William Smith, Luke Johnson, Orson Pratt, John F. Boynton, and Lyman E. Johnson, and were unanimously sustained.

Bishop Edward Partridge was nominated to still act as Bishop, and was unanimously chosen; he then nominated Isaac Morley and Titus Billings for his counselers, who were also unanimously chosen.

Elder Isaac Morley was unanimously appointed Patriarch of this branch of the Church.

Elder John Corrill was chosen to be keeper of the Lord's Store House.

Elder Isaac Morley was then ordained to the office of Patriarch under the hands of Presidents Joseph Smith, Jun., Sidney Rigdon and Hyrum Smith.

The congregation, after a few remarks from Sidney Rigdon, unanimously voted not to support stores and shops selling spirituous liquors, tea, coffee, or tobacco.

A vote was called on the subject of the presidents of the Seventies; and those who have recently been appointed to that office, were unanimously received.

The congregation then united with President Sidney Rigdon, who, in the closing prayer, called upon their Lord to dedicate this land for the gathering of the Saints, and their inheritances.

THOMAS B. MARSH, Moderator,
OLIVER COWDERY, Clerk.

FAR WEST, MISSOURI, November 10, 1837.

At a general meeting of the ordained members of the Church in this place Elder Thomas B. Marsh opened the meeting by prayer, and President Sidney Rigdon read the memorial of the Bishop of Kirtland and his counselors, of September 18th, 1837, to the churches abroad. He then laid before the meeting the subject of laying off cities, of consecrating lands for public purposes, and for remunerating those who lay them off. It was unanimously voted that all city plats hereafter laid off, after remunerating those for their labor who may be engaged in appointing and laying off the same shall be consecrated for the public benefit of the Church, for building houses for public worship, or such other purposes as the Church shall say.

President Rigdon then read the prospectus of the *Elders' Journal*, which was unanimously received.

It was then unanimously voted that the persons present use their exertions to support said paper.

It was then voted that the town of Far West be enlarged so that it contain four sections, that is, two miles square.

Voted that Bishop Partridge and his counselors be appointed a committee to appraise the land adjacent to the present town plat and see that it is enlarged according to the above vote, provided the present holders of those lands will take such a price for the same as the above appraisers think them to be worth; and that the same be then disposed of as voted above.

A call was then made for those whose circumstances were such as to permit them to go out to preach to present themselves. There were twenty-three who arose.

Sylvester H. Earl, Henry Jackman, Harrison Sagers, and John W. Clark were ordained Elders, and William J. Levans was ordained a Priest.

President Rigdon then closed the meeting by prayer.

THOMAS B. MARSH, Moderator,
OLIVER COWDERY, Clerk.

About this time I left Far West on my return to Kirtland.

Minutes of a High Council at Kirtland.

Kirtland, November 20th. The High Council met in the Lord's House, John Smith presiding.

Reuben Hedlock preferred the following charge against Zenos H. Brewster, Jane Brewster, Collins Brewster, D. H. Dustin and wife, Moses R. Norris and wife, Eliza Norris, Samuel Barnet, Jemima Butler, Osman M. Duel, ——Butler, and Roxanna Repsher, for giving heed to revelations said to be translated from the Book of Moroni by Collins Brewster, and for entering into a written covenant different from the articles and covenants of the Church of Latter-day Saints, and following a vain and delusive spirit.

Two were appointed to speak on each side.

The writings and revelations kept and received by the accused were presented, and read by the clerk of the Council.

The accused pleaded not guilty.

Brother Felshaw was called forward by the plaintiff, who stated that he had visited the accused and labored with them according to the law of the Church; that the accused justified themselves, seeing the Church had not lived according to the former revelations, and they considered the High Council and others were in transgression; and that most of the accused appeared to be determined to pursue their own way, whether right or wrong.

Brother Allen said the accused appeared to manifest a hard spirit against the Presidents of the Church and the High Council.

Brother Dunn concurred.

Brother Sawyer stated that he heard Brother Norris say that those in authority were against him and if he could not establish an order of things here to his mind he would go out among the Gentiles and do it.

Brother Knight confirmed the foregoing testimony.

The accused called Brother Freeman, who stated that he had attended a number of the meetings of the accused and saw nothing out of the way.

Brother E. Strong confirmed Brother Freeman's statement, but did not know when he attended the meetings at which they received revelations for themselves.

Brother J. Foster agreed with the last two witnesses.

Brother Preston was called by the accuser, who testified that the accused refused to admit him into their meetings and that others were rejected.

Several witnesses testified that they attended their meetings and saw nothing wrong.

Others testified they had heard them speak against the heads of the Church and that Brother Joseph had many things to repent of, and one of them said he thought some put too much stress on the Priesthood, and that he was informed that Brother Norris laid his hands on Collins Brewster and ordained him a prophet, and that one of the accused said he was determined to pursue his own course whether it suited the High Council or not.

After the pleas of his councilors the accused spoke in justification of their course generally, when the Council decided that the charge had been fully sustained and withdrew fellowship from those who persisted in their course of conduct as before mentioned.

HARLOW REDFIELD, Clerk.

Reuben Hedlock Chosen President of Elders.

At a conference of Elders, consisting of all the authorities of the Church in Kirtland, November 27th, Elder Reuben Hedlock was chosen President of the Elders' quorum, in place of Elder Beaman, deceased.

November 30.—Daniel S. Miles presented a complaint

against Roger Orton "for abusing Elder Brigham Young, and for a general course of unchristianlike conduct." The accused having been notified to appear and answer for his conduct, and having refused, the High Council decided that he be cut off, for showing contempt to the authorities of the Church.

Excommunication of Rodger Orton.

Far West, December 6th.—The High Council and Bishop and counselors appointed Elias Higbee, Simeon Carter, and Elisha H. Groves, a committee to consider the propriety of proposing to the Church to pay the High Council for their time while engaged in council. Bishop Partridge, John Corrill, and Isaac Morley were appointed a committee to report upon the subject of raising a revenue to defray the expenses of the Church.

A Question of Compensation

David Whitmer was appointed to sign Elders' licenses, as chairman of the Council, and W. W. Phelps, as clerk; and Frederick G. Williams, to sign licenses as chairman *pro tempore*, in the absence of President Whitmer; and John Whitmer, as clerk *pro tempore;* and Oliver Cowdery, recording clerk, standing clerk of the Council, and recorder of patriarchal blessings at Far West.

Various Appointments

The committee on pay for the Council reported:

It is our united opinion that the Presidency, High Council, Bishop and conselors, clerk of the council, Patriarch and agents of the Church, (also any others who may be employed in Church business), receive per day, each, one dollar and fifty cents.

[Signed] SIMEON CARTER,
ELIAS HIGBEE,
ELISHA H. GROVES.

Bishop Partridge reported to the Council that he had paid six hundred dollars to the lawyers to carry on suits against the Jackson mob, and three hundred dollars costs in carrying on said suits for which he had involved himself, and was paying ten per cent interest on the same; and petitioned the Council for leave to liquidate the debt out of the properties consecrated

Bishop Partridge's Report

for the benefit of the Church, and charge the Church for the same. The Council granted the petition.

Voted that the recorder of licenses and patriarchal blessings receive, for each one hundred words, ten cents.

Council adjourned to December 7th.

Council assembled on the 7th, according to adjournment, and heard the report of their Committee on raising a revenue to pay the officers of the Church for their services, and after much discussion and adjournment from time to time, dismissed the subject as being anti-scriptural.

I returned to Kirtland on or about the 10th of December. During my absence in Missouri Warren Parrish, John F. Boynton, Luke S. Johnson, Joseph Coe, and some others united together for the overthrow of the Church. Soon after my return this dissenting band openly and publicly renounced the Church of Christ of Latter-day Saints and claimed themselves to be the old standard, calling themselves the Church of Christ, excluding the word "Saints," and set me at naught, and the whole Church, denouncing us as heretics, not considering that the Saints shall possess the kingdom according to the Prophet Daniel.

Apostasy in Kirtland.

The *Elders' Journal* No. 2 for November was the last paper printed at Kirtland. Our printing establishment was attached to satisfy an unjust judgment of the county court, and soon after the whole printing apparatus and office were burned to the ground.

Last Paper Printed in Kirtland.

The work began to spread in England with great rapidity. On the 12th of September Elder Goodson left Bedford for Preston, and about the 1st of October sailed for America, in company with Brother Snyder, taking with him two hundred Books of Mormon, which the Elders in vain tried to persuade him to leave. Branches were established in Eccleston, Wrightington, Heskin, Euxton Bath, Daubers Lane, Chorley, Whittle, Leyland Moss, Ribchester, Thornley, Clithero, Wadding-

The Work in England.

ton, Downham, and other places round about Preston, where the brethren hired the "Cock Pit," a large and convenient building for preaching, but, being disturbed by some Methodist priests, were obliged to have the house licensed by the civil courts, according to the statutes of the realm, which, with the aid of two constables who voluntarily proffered their services, restored peace and order. And on Christmas day, December 25th, Elders Kimball and Hyde, and Joseph Fielding (who had previously been ordained an Elder) assembled in the "Cock Pit" with about three hundred Saints, several of whom were ordained to the lesser Priesthood, fourteen were confirmed, and about one hundred children were blessed by the Elders. This was the first public conference of the Church in England, and at this conference the Word of Wisdom was first publicly taught in that country.

Progress of the British Mission.

While the work was thus rapidly progressing in Lancashire it continued gradually to progress at Bedford, also a branch was established at Bassynburn, and another at Peter's Green, by Elder Richards.

Flight of Brigham Young from Kirtland

On the morning of the 22nd of December, 1837, Brother Brigham Young left Kirtland in consequence of the fury of the mob spirit that prevailed in the apostates who had threatened to destroy him because he would proclaim publicly and privately that he knew by the power of the Holy Ghost that I was a Prophet of the Most High God, that I had not transgressed and fallen as the apostates declared.

Close of the Year 1837.

Apostasy, persecution, confusion, and mobocracy strove hard to bear rule at Kirtland, and thus closed the year 1837.

END OF VOL. II.

INDEX TO VOLUME II.

D

M

R

T

HISTORY

OF THE

CHURCH OF JESUS CHRIST

OF

LATTER-DAY SAINTS.

PERIOD I.

History of Joseph Smith, the Prophet.

BY HIMSELF.

VOLUME III.
REVISED

AN INTRODUCTION AND NOTES
BY
B. H. ROBERTS.

PUBLISHED BY THE CHURCH.

DESERET BOOK COMPANY
Salt Lake City, Utah
1980

Lithographed by
DESERET PRESS
in the United States of America

TABLE OF CONTENTS.

VOLUME III.

INTRODUCTION.

CHAPTER I.

THE PROPHET JOSEPH'S DEPARTURE FROM KIRTLAND AND ARRIVAL IN MISSOURI.

CHAPTER II.

EXCOMMUNICATION OF OLIVER COWDERY AND DAVID WHITMER—THE WORK IN ENGLAND.

CHAPTER III.

READJUSTMENT AND SETTLEMENT OF AFFAIRS AT FAR WEST.

CHAPTER IV.

SELECTION OF LANDS IN CALDWELL AND DAVIESS COUNTIES FOR SETTLEMENT—ADAM-ONDI-AHMAN.

CHAPTER V.

INDEPENDENCE DAY AT FAR WEST—SUNDRY EVENTS AND REVELATIONS—EPISTLE OF DAVID W. PATTEN.

CHAPTER VI.

THE BEGINNING OF TROUBLE IN CALDWELL AND DAVIESS COUNTIES.

CHAPTER VII.

INCREASING DIFFICULTIES BETWEEN THE SAINTS AND THE MOBS OF DAVIESS AND CALDWELL COUNTIES.

CHAPTER VIII.

MOB MOVEMENTS IN CALDWELL, DAVIESS AND CARROLL COUNTIES—ARRIVAL OF KIRTLAND CAMP AT FAR WEST.

CHAPTER IX.

THE ORGANIZATION AND JOURNEY OF KIRTLAND CAMP.

CHAPTER X.

THE JOURNEY OF KIRTLAND CAMP (CONTINUED).

CHAPTER XI.

EXPULSION OF THE SAINTS FROM DE WITT, CARROLL COUNTY, MISSOURI.

CHAPTER XII.

MOVEMENTS OF THE MOB UPON DE WITT—BATTLE OF CROOKED RIVER —EXTERMINATING ORDER OF GOVERNOR BOGGS.

CHAPTER XIII.

MOB MOVEMENTS ABOUT FAR WEST—TREACHERY OF COLONEL HINKLE—SORROWFUL SCENES.

CHAPTER XIV.

RIVALRY AMONG THE MILITIA GENERALS FOR POSSESSION OF THE PRISONERS—"TRIAL" AT RICHMOND.

CHAPTER XV.

THE CASE OF THE SAINTS PRESENTED TO THE MISSOURI LEGISLATURE—THE PROPHET'S COMMUNICATION TO THE SAINTS FROM LIBERTY PRISON.

CHAPTER XVI.

CASE OF THE "MORMONS" BEFORE THE MISSOURI LEGISLATURE—CLOSE OF THE YEAR 1838.

CHAPTER XVII.

PREPARATIONS FOR LEAVING MISSOURI—ACTION OF THE STATE LEGISLATURE.

CHAPTER XVIII.

THE EXILED SAINTS GATHER AT QUINCY—PROPOSITION TO SETTLE AT COMMERCE.

CHAPTER XIX.

LETTERS TO THE PROPHET—AFFAIRS IN ENGLAND—PETITIONS.

CHAPTER XX.

SUNDRY MOVEMENTS IN THE INTEREST OF THE EXILED SAINTS—THE PROPHET'S LETTERS FROM LIBERTY PRISON.

CHAPTER XXI.

STIRRING SCENES ABOUT FAR WEST—THE EPISTLE OF THE PROPHET AND HIS FELLOW PRISONERS.

CHAPTER XXII.

THE PROPHET'S ACCOUNT OF HIS EXPERIENCES IN MISSOURI—FULFILLMENT OF A PROPHETIC REVELATION—COMPLETE EXODUS OF THE SAINTS FROM MISSOURI.

CHAPTER XXIII.

SETTLEMENT IN COMMERCE, ILLINOIS.

CHAPTER XXIV.

ADVENTURES OF THE PRISONERS REMAINING IN MISSOURI—THE PROPHET'S NARRATIVE OF PERSONAL EXPERIENCES IN MISSOURI.

CHAPTER XXV.

COMMERCE—THE PROPHET'S HISTORY—DOCTRINAL DEVELOPMENT.

CHAPTER XXVI.

THE PROPHET'S MINISTRY IN THE VICINITY OF COMMERCE—ADDRESS TO THE TWELVE.

CHAPTER XXVII.

BAPTISM OF ISAAC GALLAND—EPISTLE OF THE TWELVE TO THE CHURCH.

CHAPTER XXVIII.

THE ESCAPE OF PARLEY P. PRATT AND HIS FELLOW PRISONERS FROM MISSOURI—THE CLOSE OF AN EPOCH.

APPENDIX TO VOLUME III.

AFFIDAVITS OF HYRUM SMITH *et al.* ON AFFAIRS IN MISSOURI, 1831-39; OFFICIALLY SUBSCRIBED TO BEFORE THE MUNICIPAL COURT OF NAUVOO THE FIRST DAY OF JULY, 1843.

INTRODUCTION TO VOLUME III.

Enlightenment a Factor in Determining Responsibility for Conduct.

VOLUME THREE concludes,for the present, the history of the Church in Missouri. I think it proper, therefore, that here should be considered the causes of the Missouri persecutions, which resulted in the expulsion of the entire Church from that state.

There have been, of course, more extensive persecutions than those inflicted on the Saints in Missouri; but I doubt if there has ever been a persecution more cruel or terror-laden in its character. Viewed from the standpoint of its net results there were some fifty people, men, women, and children, killed outright; about as many more were wounded or cruelly beaten, and many more perished indirectly because of the exposure to which they were subjected through the winters of 1833-4 and 1838-9.

In round numbers it is estimated that between twelve and fifteen thousand people, citizens of the United States, after being dispossessed of their lands, were forcibly driven from the state. It is known that they paid to the United States government for land alone, three hundred and eighteen thousand dollars, which, at the minimum price of one dollar and a quarter per acre, would give them land holdings of over two hundred and fifty thousand acres, which represented for that day very large interests.*

To this list of results must be added the more horrible one of several cases of ravishment at Far West; and also, after barely escaping from the sentence of death pronounced by a court martial, the cruel imprisonment through weary months of a number of Church leaders.

In passing judgment upon such matters as these account must be taken of the age and country in which they occurred; likewise the pretensions to right views of life, and devotion to freedom on the part of the perpetrators of the injustice. Undoubtedly a heavier debt is incurred to history, to humanity and to God, when the parties who resort to such acts of mob violence and injustice live in an enlightened age, and where the free institutions of their country guarantee both the freedom and security of its citizens.

* See "American Commonwealths," Missouri, (Houghton, Mifflin & Company, 1888), p. 181.

If in the jungle a man meets a tiger and is torn to pieces, no one thinks of holding the tiger to any moral accountability. Perhaps the hunt will be formed to destroy the beast, but that is merely to be rid of a dangerous animal, and prevent the repetition of the deed. If another meets a cruel death among savages in heathen lands, while some moral responsibility would hold against them, according to their degree of enlightenment, yet the fact that it was an act of savages would be held to reduce the degree of moral turpitude. And likewise even in civilized states, in localities to which the vicious may gravitate, when acts of violence are committed there, some allowance may be, and generally is, made for the ignorance and general brutality of the particular neighborhood.

By this process of reasoning I think it will appear quite clear that moral responsibility,both on the part of individuals and communities or nations, increases in proportion to their enlightenment. If, therefore, this principle be kept in view, the persecution of the Latter-day Saints by the people of Missouri was a very heinous offense.

True it may be said that the worst acts of cruelty were perpetrated by low, brutish men among the mob or in the militia—for these bodies were convertible from one to the other on shortest possible notice, and wholly as the exigencies of the enemies of the Saints demanded—but these were led and abetted by quite a different order of men: by lawyers, members of the state legislature, by county and district judges, by physicians, by professed ministers of the gospel, by merchants, by leading politicians, by captains, majors, colonels, and generals—of several grades—of the militia, by many other high officials of the state including the Governor and Lieutenant Governor, and finally by the action of the state legislature which appropriated two hundred thousand dollars to defray the expenses incurred by the mob-militia in carrying out the Governor's order, exterminating the Saints from the state. These facts are made apparent in the pages of this and the two preceding volumes of the HISTORY OF THE CHURCH. The facts cannot be questioned. They are written out most circumstantially in the Prophet's story. Times, places, and names are given of the incidents related, and the more important of these may be corroborated by histories of these events other than our own.

The persecutions then of the Latter-day Saints in Missouri, and their final expulsion from that state, were crimes against the enlightenment of the age and of the state where the acts occurred; a crime against the constitutions and institutions both of the state of Missouri and of the United States; as also a crime against the Christian religion. All this we have in mind when speaking of the severity and cruelty of these compared with other persecutions. The state of Missouri was guilty of a greater crime when it persecuted the Latter-day Saints than states were which in the barbarous times of the dark ages persecuted their people; though when estimated in net results there may have been more murders and robberies, greater destruction of property, and more wide-spread suffering in the latter than in the former.

It is in the light of the principle here laid down that I propose to review the causes of the persecutions of the Latter-day Saints in Missouri.

The People of Missouri and the Saints.

The people of the state of Missouri, and especially those living in western and upper Missouri, in the early decades of the nineteenth century, were chiefly from the states of the South—from Kentucky, Tennessee, Virginia, and the Carolinas. This is not stated as a matter of reproach, for among the American people there have been no better or nobler citizens of the Republic than the people of the states enumerated. I merely make the statement in order to present a fact, and because other facts grow out of it. To say that Missouri was settled by emigrants from the states of the South carries with it the explanation why Missouri was one of the slave states, and her people attached to the social and industrial methods of life attendant upon that circumstance. That is to say, they looked with contempt upon manual labor; regarding it as menial and proper only for slaves to perform. With that idea is closely related another; namely, that white people who from circumstances were compelled to perform manual labor, or who followed it from principle, in the eyes of the people of the South were of an inferior class; contemptuously characterized by some as "white trash," and by others, inclined to be more polite, as "poor whites."

Freedom from manual labor gave to those of active dispositions in such communities an opportunity to follow the more desirable vocations of professional life; the law, medicine, the Christian ministry, merchandizing and general business; or leisure for political or military activities; or the pursuit of pleasure, fishing, hunting, horse racing, and social life generally. These conditions naturally resulted in pride, often in arrogance, and a desperate sort of courage, which held honor high and weakness and cowardice in contempt; also something of intolerance for those disposed to set themselves against such an order of things.

The reader will recognize, of course, that I have so far in mind only the better element of the population, the least of the evils and some of the advantages resulting from such industrial and social conditions. There were, however, quite different and more serious results than any yet noted arising from this system of society. While those disposed to activity and inclined to honorable pursuits might enjoy certain advantages from the system, on the other hand, it fostered man's natural inclination to idleness and love of ease that comes of idleness; and fostered jealousy and bitterness against those more industrious and successful. In such a class the system led to ignorance, irreligion, and criminal tendencies; constituting them a dangerous element in the community. It was doubtless this class the Prophet Joseph had in mind when he said soon after his first arrival in western Missouri: "Our reflections were great, coming as we had from a highly cultivated state of society in the East, and standing now upon the confines or western limits of the United States, and looking into the vast wilderness of those that sat in darkness. How natural it was to observe the degradation, leanness of intellect, ferocity and jealousy of a people that were nearly a century behind the times, and to feel for those who roamed about without the benefit of civilization, refinement, or religion!"

Many of the positions in the higher walks of life, in western Missouri, were sought by the unworthy, the corruptible and the vicious—men who sought all the advantages of the southern ideals of life without possessing the refining virtues which for generations in the older states of the south made some of the evils of the social system that obtained there at least tolerable. Such were the Brazeales, the Wilsons, the Hunters, the Kavanaughs, the Likens, the Loveladys, the McCartys, the McCoys, the Pixleys, the Simsons, the Silvers, the Westons, the Gilliams, the Birches, the Blacks, the Bogarts, the Clarks, the Liveseys, and the Penistons.

Another circumstance which influenced somewhat the character of western Missouri's population in the early decades of the nineteenth century, was the fact that these sections of the state constituted part of the frontiers of the United States, and here had gravitated a more or less lawless class which sought the security of proximity to the boundary lines of the United States, from whose confines they could make their escape in the event of being hard pressed for violations of law in the older states whence they had come, or in their new habitat. Such were the Lovels, the Hawkins, the Heatherleys and many others.

The Latter-day Saints who settled in Missouri from 1831 to 1839 had come for the most part from the New England States and New York. There were, therefore, marked differences in character between them and the old settlers of Missouri; differences of ideas as to industrial and social life; of moral and religious life. The Saints were descendants chiefly of the Puritans, and both by inheritance and training had fallen heirs to the Puritan's strict views of industry, religion and morality. The Puritans taught that all labor was honorable, and industry a duty. Religion occupied a large share of their attention—entered in fact into all the affairs of life—though its duties meant largely a regular attendance upon church service; a strict observance of the proprieties while there; a rigid observance throughout of the Sabbath day. Neither work nor amusements were tolerated on that day. In the olden time among some of their forefathers it had been unlawful to sit in Boston Common on the Sabbath or to walk in the streets of Boston, except to church. Once a man was publicly whipped for shooting a fowl on Sunday. A woman was threatened with banishment for smiling in church. A person absent from church for more than one Sunday was in danger of being fined, whipped, or set in the stocks. Swearing was prohibited in nearly all the New England colonies, and a split stick was sometimes placed on the swearer's tongue.*

Both food and dress were plain, and the latter, in some instances, was regulated by law. Amusements were few. Dancing and card-playing were forbidden, and there was little music. The state sought to take entire charge of the individual, and supposed that tendency toward immorality could be stemmed by legislation. In early Connecticut no one under twenty was allowed to use tobacco, and none to use it more than once a day. The laws were severe and the penalties cruel. The stocks and whipping-post and pillory were in frequent requisition to correct moral delinquents. An offender might be made to stand on a stool in church with the name of his misdemeanor displayed on his breast. Among the common punishments were cropping or boring the ears and branding with a hot iron.†

Of course in later years there was a general relaxation from these severities, and many of these customs and laws, by the time our generation of Saints came on the scene, were obsolete. Still, the moral and spiritual atmosphere in which the Saints and their fathers had been reared was austere in its moral character, and stood in marked contrast to the moral atmosphere of the South, where, in respect of such things as church attendance, religious observances, personal liberty in eating, drinking and amusements, there was wider freedom.

In the sparsely settled country of western Missouri, the descendants of the old cavaliers and their following, who settled the South, and the descendants of the Puritans, who settled the North, were to meet: and very naturally one may see in these antagonistic elements—aside from the cause of antagonism which will be found in the newly revealed religion of the Latter-day Saints—natural causes of irritation between them founded in the differences of character, and their respective conceptions of industrial, moral, and religious duties. That the old settlers

* "History of the United States," (Morris) p. 132.

† Ibid, pp. 135-7.

in Missouri, even those friendly disposed towards the Saints, recognized the incompatibility of the two classes is evident from the public utterances of a mass meeting held at Liberty, in Clay county, when the Saints were urged to seek a new locality where they could live by themselves. "They are eastern men," said the address, "whose manners, habits, customs, and even dialect, are essentially different from our own. We earnestly urge them to seek some other abiding place, where the manners, the habits, and customs of the people will be more consonant with their own."*

This difference of character between the Saints and the old settlers I account one of the causes of the Missouri persecutions.

The Question of Slavery.

The question of slavery in Missouri was a delicate one. It will perhaps be remembered that it was the application of the territory of Missouri for admission into the Union, 1818-19, that brought the question of slavery into one of its acute stages before the country; and inaugurated a long series of debates in the National Congress on the subject. It was upon the admission of Missouri into the Union in 1821 that the great Compromise which bears the state's name settled,not the question of slavery itself, but, for the time, the agitation of it.

That Compromise consisted finally in this: that while Missouri herself was admitted with a clause in her constitution permitting slavery, and also prohibiting free people of color from immigrating into the state, slavery was forever to be prohibited in all territory of the United States north of the line thirty-six degrees and thirty minutes north latitude (the southern boundary line of the state of Missouri); and Missouri was required "by a solemn, public act" of her legislature, to declare that the clause in her constitution relating to the immigration of free negroes into the state, should never be construed to authorize the passage of any law by which any citizen of either of the states in this Union shall be excluded from the enjoyment of any of the privileges and immunities to which he is entitled under the Constitution of the United States.

These historical facts are referred to here that the reader may be reminded that slavery was a delicate question in Missouri; that her people were super-sensitive about it since she was the first territory upon which the National Congress sought to impose the prohibition of slavery as a condition precedent to her admission into the Union, which, up to that time, had been a matter left to the people of the territory seeking admission to determine for themselves. Of course this attempt at re-

* History of the Church, Vol. II, p. 450.

striction of slavery was made by northern members of the national Congress.* All the sentiment for the restriction of slavery was in the North. In 1831 the sentiment for the positive abolition of slavery had made such progress in Massachusetts, that William Lloyd Garrison established in Boston "*The Liberator*," a paper which advocated "the immediate and unconditional emancipation of every slave in the United States." As a result of this agitation anti-slavery societies were formed and active measures taken to advocate these opinions by means of lectures and pamphlets. These extreme measures against slavery did not meet with the approval of all or even the majority of the people of New England, much less with the approval of the people of other northern states. Still this agitation arose and was chiefly supported in New England. It will not be difficult to understand, therefore, that any considerable number of people from that section of the Union immigrating into a slave state would arouse suspicion; especially when that immigration was into a slave state upon which, when as a territory she had made application for admission into the Union, prohibition of slavery was sought to be enforced by the northern members of the National Congress. Nor will it be sufficient to dispel this suspicion to aver that these particular immigrants from New England, and other northern states are not abolitionists; that they take no part with, and do not share the fanatical sentiments of, the abolitionists; that their objects and purposes are of an entirely different and larger character.

The answer to all this was given in a public document drawn up to voice the sentiment of a great mass meeting of the people of Clay county—a people, be it remembered, who at the time (1836) were not unfriendly towards the Saints, but a people who a few years before had received the Saints into their homes, and given them shelter when they were exiles from Jackson county, and who, at the time of the utterance I am about to quote was published, were in a covenant of peace with the Saints, and the Saints in a covenant of peace with them—I say the answer to all disclaimers on the part of the Saints respecting their not being abolitionists was found in this public utterance: "They are eastern men, whose manners, habits, customs and even dialect are essentially different from our own. They are non-slaveholders, and opposed to slavery, which in this peculiar period, when abolitionism has reared its deformed and haggard visage in our land, is well calculated to excite deep and abiding prejudices in any community where slavery is tolerated and protected."

I call attention to these facts that the student of the history of the Church may appreciate the weight of influence they would have in cre-

* Mr. Tallmadge, a representative from the state of New York, offered the restricting provision.

ating popular sentiment against the Saints; a matter which hitherto, if I may be permitted to say so, has not been fully appreciated. One can readily see what a potent factor this sentiment against New England and other northern states people would be in the hands of political demagogues and sectarian priests seeking to exterminate what they would respectively consider an undesirable element in politics and a religious rival. That both political demagogues and sectarian priests made the most of the opportunity which hostile sentiment in Missouri against abolition and abolitionists afforded, abundantly appears in the pages of the first volume of the Church History. That sentiment was appealed to from the first; indeed in the very first manifesto of the mob —known as "The Secret Constitution,"*—issued against the Saints in Missouri, it was a prominent feature. This was at Independence, in July, 1833. In that "Manifesto" the following passage occurs: "More than a year since, it was ascertained that they [the Saints] had been tampering with our slaves, and endeavoring to sow dissensions and raise seditions amongst them. Of this their Mormon leaders were informed, and they said they would deal with any of their members who should again in like case offend. But how specious are appearances. In a late number of the *Star*, published in Independence by the leaders of the sect, there is an article inviting free negroes and mulattoes from other states to become Mormons, and remove and settle among us. This exhibits them in still more odious colors. It manifests a desire on the part of their society, to inflict on our society an injury that they know would be to us entirely insupportable, and one of the surest means of driving us from the country; for it would require none of the supernatural gifts that they pretend to, to see that the introduction of such a caste amongst us would corrupt our blacks, and instigate them to bloodshed."

The article on "Free People of Color" referred to appeared in the *Evening and Morning Star* for July. The charge of sowing dissensions and inspiring seditions among the slaves, and inviting free negroes to settle in Missouri, had no foundation in truth. Concerning such people the Missouri laws provided that: If any negro or mulatto came into the state of Missouri, without a certificate from a court of record in some one of the United States, evidencing that he was a citizen of such state, on complaint before any justice of the peace, such negro or mulatto could be commanded by the justice to leave the state; and if the colored person so ordered did not leave the state within thirty days, on complaint of any citizen, such person could be again brought before the justice who might commit him to the common jail of the county, until

* HISTORY OF THE CHURCH, vol. 1, p. 374, et seq.

the convening of the circuit court, when it became the duty of the judge of the circuit court to inquire into the cause of commitment; and if it was found that the negro or mulatto had remained in the state contrary to the provisions of this statute, the court was authorized to sentence such person to receive ten lashes on his or her bare back, and then order him or her to depart from the state; if the person so treated should still refuse to go, then the same proceedings were to be repeated and punishment inflicted as often as was necessary until such person departed.

And further: If any person brought into the state of Missouri a free negro or mulatto, without the aforesaid certificate of citizenship, for every such negro or mulatto the person offending was liable to a forfeit of five hundred dollars; to be recovered by action of debt in the name of the state.

The editor of the *Star* commenting upon this law said: "Slaves are real estate in this and other states, and wisdom would dictate great care among the branches of the Church of Christ on this subject. So long as we have no special rule in the Church as to people of color, let prudence guide; and while they, as well as we, are in the hands of a merciful God, we say: shun every appearance of evil."

Publishing this law and the above comment was construed by the old settlers to be an invitation to free people of color to settle in Jackson county! Whereupon an extra was published to the July number of the *Star* on the sixteenth of the month, which said: "The intention in publishing the article, "Free People of Color," was not only to stop free people of color from immigrating to Missouri, but to prevent them from being admitted as members of the Church. * * * * * To be short, we are opposed to having free people of color admitted into the State."*

But in the face of all this the Missourians still claimed that the article was merely published to give directions and cautions to be observed by "colored brethren," to enable them upon their arrival in Missouri, to "claim and exercise the rights of citizenship." "Contemporaneous with the appearance of this article"—the above article in the *Star*

* In making the statement that it was the intention of the *Star* article not only to stop "free people of color" immigrating to Missouri, but also to "prevent them from being admitted as members of the Church," the editor of the *Star*, of course went too far; if not in his second article, explaining the scope and meaning of the first, then in the first article; for he had no authority to seek to prevent "free people of color" from being admitted members of the Church. But as a matter of fact there were very few if any "free people of color" in the Church at that time. The "fears" of the Missourians on that head were sheer fabrications of evil disposed minds.

—continued the charge published in the *Western Monitor*—"was the expectation among the brethren, that a considerable number of this degraded caste were only waiting this information before they should set out on their journey."* And this base falsehood was used to inflame the minds of the old settlers against the Saints.

I do not refer to this question of slavery in connection with the persecution of the Saints in Missouri in order to set it down as one of the causes of that persecution; because, as a matter of fact, the views of the Saints, and especially of the leading Elders of the Church on that question were such that they could never be truthfully charged with being a menace to that institution. The Prophet Joseph himself, at the time of the Jackson county troubles and subsequently, held very conservative views on the subject of slavery, surprisingly conservative views when his own temperament and environment are taken into account, of which fact any one may convince himself by reading his paper on the subject of abolition in Volume II of the Church History, pages 436-40.

Finally, it was given by the inspiration of God to the Prophet first to utter the most statesman-like word upon this vexed question of slavery, and had the nation and people of the United States but given heed to his recommendations it would have settled the question in harmony with the convictions of the people of the North, and without injustice to the South. Here follows his statesman-like word, published throughout the United States in 1844—eleven years before Ralph Waldo Emerson made substantially the same recommendation, and for which the philosopher received no end of praise:—

"Petition, also, ye goodly inhabitants of the slave states, your legislators to abolish slavery by the year 1850, or now, and save the abolitionist from reproach and ruin, and infamy and shame. Pray Congress to pay every man a reasonable price for his slaves out of the surplus revenue arising from the sale of the public lands, and from the deduction of pay from the members of Congress. Break off the shackles from the poor black man, and hire him to labor like other human beings; for an hour of virtuous liberty is worth a whole eternity of bondage."†

But now to return to the course of the Missourians in misrepresenting the views of the Saints on the subject of slavery. Notwithstanding the explicit denials through the "*Evening and Morning Star*," that the article on "Free People of Color" was intended to invite such a class into the state; and the further declaration that the Saints were opposed to such persons coming into the state; as also the fact that it is

* *Western Monitor* for the 2nd of August, 1833.

† Joseph Smith's "Views of the Powers and Policy of the Government of the United States," *Mill. Star*, Vol. XXII. p. 743.

doubtful if there were any free negroes who were members of the Church—notwithstanding all this, their enemies continued to misrepresent them, and their views on the subject of slavery. They saw in the fact that many of them were from New England, where abolition sentiment was rife, their opportunity to charge them with abolition sentiments and intention to interfere with slavery, with every prospect of having it quite generally believed—hence the charge was made and became a pretext if not a cause of acts of aggression upon the Saints, and as such is a factor that must be taken account of in these pages.

Political Fears.

I know of no circumstances which developed what the political faith of the Saints really was during their sojourn in the state of Missouri; and doubt if any data exists from which it could be determined whether a majority of them were Whigs or Republican-Democrats, as the party now designated as the Democratic party was then called. In fact, politics, local or national, concerned the Saints but very little during their stay in Missouri. Their minds were occupied by quite other, and I may say, larger and higher things; and their activities were concerned with other issues than those political. They were concerned about the redemption of Zion, her establishment, the proclamation of the Gospel, the salvation of men, the preparation of the earth for the incoming of that Kingdom whose King is the Lord. Their mission encompassed the whole world, it was not confined to the state of Missouri and her petty political affairs; nor even to the political affairs of the United States, important as they were. "Mormonism" was a world-movement, not merely a national one. It concerned itself with the deeper and broader subject of religion, rather than with the principles and methods of the administration of government, state or national. Still, in common with other people of the county, state and nation of which they were citizens, they possessed civil and political rights and privileges, accompanied as such rights and privileges always are in a republic with certain duties both to the state and themselves, among which the exercise of the elective franchise. As this made them a power in the community, their actual and prospective influence in the affairs of the counties where they resided, and in the state, was a matter of frequent discussion among the old settlers in Missouri. I do not know that it was ever charged that they were Whigs, and that by acting with that party in Missouri they could wrest the control of the state from the Republican-Democratic party then in power; though that they were Whigs might have been inferred from the fact of their being chiefly from New England and other northern states; yet this was not charged.

There was repeatedly expressed, however, a fear of their political power. In the document issued by the mob meeting at Independence on the 20th of July, 1833, it is said: "When we reflect on the extensive field in which the sect is operating, and that there exists in every country a leaven of superstition that embraces with avidity, notions the most extravagant and unheard of, and that whatever can be gleaned by them from the purlieus of vice and the abodes of ignorance, is to be cast like a waif into our social circle, it requires no gift of prophecy to tell that the day is not far distant when the civil government of the county will be in their hands; when the sheriff, the justices, and the county judges will be Mormons, or persons wishing to court their favor from motives of interest or ambition."

It was an effort to prevent members of the Church from voting at an election at Gallatin, Daviess county, in August, 1838, which led to the commencement of those acts of hostility against the Saints which ended ultimately in their expulsion from that state. There was no political offense even charged against the Saints; only that if permitted to exercise the franchise they would in time obtain control of the counties where they resided, so rapidly were they increasing in numbers; and the old settlers would lose the offices; and as these old settlers were dear lovers of office, it was political jealousy born of fear which prompted in part the acts of aggression against the Saints. When such jealousy is awakened, pretexts for the justification of its existence are not difficult to find, and in this instance the old settlers in Missouri relied upon the false charges of ignorance, superstition, and general unworthiness of the Saints to be considered good citizens of the state. The charge was not that they were all of one political faith; or that they voted solidly; or that they were under the political dictation of their religious leaders; or that religious influence was dragged into political affairs. None of these charges were made: it was simply a fear that the old settlers would lose the offices, and the new settlers, the Saints, being in the majority, would hold them. How much justification there was for this "fear" may not be determined, since it was based upon no accomplished fact, but regarded as the natural outcome of the operation of the political system obtaining in the United States; namely, the right of the majority to choose the public officers; and if the Saints happened to be in the majority it was regarded as likely that they would elect their friends to office, among whom, at least, would have been some members of their own faith. How the matter would have terminated in the event of the Saints having been permitted to remain in Missouri—what would have been the political alignment of the members of the Church I mean, no one can say. The only political utterance made by any Church leader was that given out by the Prophet Joseph soon after his arrival in Missouri, and called at the time "*The Political Motto of the Church.*" I quote it:

"*The Constitution of our country formed by the Fathers of Liberty; peace and good order in society; love to God, and good will to man. All good and wholesome laws; virtue and truth above all things, and Aristarchy* [a government by good men] *live for ever; but woe to tyrants, mobs, aristocracy, anarchy and toryism, and all those who invent or seek out unrighteous or evasive law suits, under the pretext and color of law or office, either religious or political. Exalt the standard of Democracy! Down with that of priestcraft, and let all the people say Amen! That the blood of the fathers may not cry from the ground against us. Sacred is the memory of that blood which bought for us our liberty.*"

This surely is sufficiently non-partisan, cosmopolitan and patriotic. Is it not of the essence of Americanism? And under such sentiments would not every member of the Church be able to perform his political duty in either of the great American parties then existing or afterwards to arise?

It is not necessary to pursue this subject further. It is enough to say that the political fears of the old settlers of Missouri, though based upon conjecture as to what could or might happen, were real fears, and became one of the causes of the Missouri persecutions.

The Saints and the Indians.

The interest of the Saints in the American Indians grows out of the knowledge they have of their forefathers, revealed through the Book of Mormon. From the historical parts of that book they learned the origin of these Indians; that they are of the house of Israel: from the prophetic parts of the book they learn of their future, that it is to be glorious; that fallen as their fortunes now are, they will not always remain so; extinction is not their fate, but before many generations shall pass away they will become a white and a delightsome people, favored of God, and prominent in bringing to pass His purposes in the land of Zion—the two Americas. It was a mission to the Lamanites or Indians which first brought several of the Elders of the Church of Christ to western Missouri. When the people of Missouri learned in what esteem the Saints held the forefathers of the Indians, and also the Indians themselves, both on account of their forefathers and the promises of God to them, it was but reasonable that they should conclude there was—as indeed there is—a strong sympathy on the part of the Saints towards the Indians; and there was great reason to believe that this sympathy might become mutual.

It was in this substratum of truth that the false accusations against the Saints were founded to the effect that they were seeking to enter into an alliance with the Indian tribes of the west for the purpose of driving the old settlers from their possessions in western Missouri, in order that the Saints with the Indians might possess the land to the exclusion of the "Gentiles."

To appreciate the seriousness of this charge, it should be remembered that the Indian tribes formerly residing east o the Mississippi, about this time—during President Jackson's two presidential terms, 1829-1837—were being transplanted into the country immediately west of Missouri, so that there were great numbers of these people—amounting to many thousands—being massed just beyond the boundaries of the state. Many of the tribes were in no amiable mood either. In some instances the terms of the treaties by which they accepted lands in the Indian territory west of Missouri, for lands that constituted their old homes in the East and South, were forced upon them after—to them—disastrous wars; so that it might well be suspected that they would be ready to follow any leader who would hold out promise of regaining their lost possessions, or who would give them the hope of revenge upon their despoilers.

Let these facts be considered and given their due weight, and the reader will not find it difficult to perceive what a potent factor against the Saints this charge of holding communication with the Indians for the purpose of dispossessing the people of western Missouri of their homes would be; and, as in the case of the slavery question, their enemies were not slow to see the advantage, and made the most of it. It was not until the agitation for the removal of the Saints from Clay county began, however, 1836, that this charge of holding communication with the Indians for the purposes already set forth, was publicly made. Then in the document adopted at the mass meeting setting forth the several reasons of the old settlers for asking the Saints to remove from Clay county, this passage occurs:

"In addition to all this, they are charged, as they have hitherto been, with keeping up a constant communication with our Indian tribes on the frontiers; with declaring, even from the pulpit, that the Indians are a part of God's chosen people, and are destined by heaven to inherit this land, in common with themselves. We do not vouch for the correctness of these statements; but whether they are true or false, their effect has been the same in exciting the community. In times of greater tranquility, such ridiculous remarks might well be regarded as the offspring of frenzied fanaticism; but at this time, our defenseless situation on the frontier, the bloody disasters of our fellow citizens in Florida and other parts of the South, all tend to make a portion of our citizens regard such sentiments with horror, if not alarm. These and many other causes have combined to raise a prejudice against them, and a feeling of hostility, that the first spark may, and we deeply fear will, ignite into all the horrors and desolations of a civil war, the worst evil that can befall any country."

Governor Dunklin, shortly after this, in answer to appeals made to him by the Saints for protection, by the execution of the law, on this charge of holding communication with the Indians, said: "Your neighbors accuse your people with holding illicit communication with the Indians, and of being opposed to slavery. You deny. Whether the charge or the denial is true, I cannot tell. The fact exists, and your neighbors seem to believe it true; and whether true or false, the consequences will be the same (if your opponents are not merely gasconading), unless you can, by your conduct and arguments, convince them of your innocence. If you cannot do this, all I can say to you is that in this Republic the *vox populi* is the *vox Dei.*"

Of course this false accusation was emphatically denied by the Saints. In a public meeting held by the members of the Church to draw up a reply to the request of the people of Clay county, that the Saints remove from that county, they said: "We deny holding any communication with the Indians, and mean to hold ourselves as ready to defend our country against their barbarous ravages as any other people. We believe that all men are bound to sustain and uphold the respective governments in which they reside, while protected in their inherent and inalienable rights by the laws of such governments; and that sedition and rebellion are unbecoming every citizen thus protected, and should be punished accordingly."

In a communication signed by the Prophet Joseph and several other presiding officers of the Church, and addressed to the leading men of Clay county, referring to the Indian charge, this was said: "Another charge of great magnitude is brought against our friends in the west, that of keeping up a constant communication with the Indian tribes on the frontier; with declaring, even from the pulpit, that the Indians are a part of God's chosen people, and are destined by heaven to inherit this land, in common with themselves. We know of nothing under the present aspect of our Indian relations calculated to arouse the fears of the people of the Upper Missouri more than a combination of influences of this nature; and we cannot look upon it as being other than one of the most subtle purposes of those whose feelings are embittered against our friends, to turn the eye of suspicion upon them from every man who is acquainted with the barbarous cruelty of rude savages. Since a rumor was afloat that the western Indians were showing signs of war, we have received frequent private letters from our friends, who have not only expressed fears for their own safety, in case the Indians should break out, but a decided determination to be among the first to repel any invasion and defend the frontier from all hostilities. We mention the last fact because it was wholly uncalled for on our part, and came previous to any excitement on the part of the people of Clay county against our friends, and must definitely show that this charge is untrue."

But all these denials went for nothing. As remarked by Governor Dunklin, whether the denial or the charge was true, people at a distance, at least, might not tell; quite generally, however, the charge was believed, and helped to swell the volume of prejudice—already too great—against the Saints. Indeed, so potent a factor was this charge of holding illicit communication with the Indians, in arousing prejudice against the Saints, that it was used against them with great effect after their settlement in Utah. It was one of the charges made against them at the time the general government of the United States was induced by their enemies to send out an army to suppress a rebellion in Utah that had no existence except in the hate-frenzied minds of the detractors of the Saints.

"It is charged," said Stephen A. Douglas in a speech at Springfield, Illinois, on the 12th of June, 1857*—"It is charged * * * * that the Mormon government, with Brigham Young at its head, is now forming alliances with Indian tribes in Utah and adjoining territories, stimulating the Indians to acts of hostility, and organizing bands of his own followers, under the name of Danites or destroying angels, to prosecute a system of robbery and murders upon American citizens who support the authority of the United States, and denounce the infamous and disgusting practices and institutions of the Mormon government."

The army came only to find the foregoing with other charges that had induced the general government to send it to Utah, untrue. But this is digression.

Mormon communication with the American Indians for the purpose of despoiling the Gentiles and taking possession of their lands can never be set down as one of the causes of the Missouri persecution; for such communication never took place—the charge of it was untrue. It was, however, one of a number of pretexts, and became a factor in creating public prejudice, which alone made possible the expulsion of the Saints from Missouri.

The Unwisdom of the Saints.

I come now to one of the most delicate subdivisions of this Introduc-

* The speech appears in the *Missouri Republican* of June 18th, 1857.

tion; namely, the unwisdom of the Saints. To appreciate this as a factor in the Missouri persecutions one needs to take into account not only human nature, but also human nature under the stress of religious impulse and influence. First, however, as to the facts involved.

To the Saints of those times had been given a dispensation of the Gospel—a new revelation of it. They had been blessed with the spirit of faith to receive it. To them it was made known that God had again spoken from heaven; He had again conferred divine authority upon men to act in His name—many of the brethren, the majority of the male membership of the Church in fact, held that divine authority, the priesthood of God; the terms of man's salvation were restated; the spiritual powers and gifts of the Gospel were guaranteed anew and plenteously enjoyed by the Saints. To them was made known the truth of a new volume of scripture, the Book of Mormon. The knowledge imparted by that book was in itself, and especially to them, wonderful. From it they learned that the ancient inhabitants of the American continents, the ruins of whose civilization challenged the curiosity of men and excited their wonder, were of the house of Israel; the American Indians were their fallen descendants and, of course, also of the house of Israel and heirs to the general promises made to that people, to say nothing of special promises made to them as direct descendants of the house of the patriarch Joseph, son of Jacob. Messiah in his resurrected and glorified state had visited America and its inhabitants shortly after His resurrection at Jerusalem, and established the Christian institution,—a Christian ministry, and a Christian Church, followed by a veritable golden age of peace, prosperity, and righteousness; and although the descendants of that ancient God-favored people were now fallen from the high estate of their fathers, yet were the promises and prophecies great concerning them. God would again visit them by His grace, they should be redeemed from their ignorance and barbarism, and they should yet be important factors in establishing a "New Jerusalem," the Zion of God on this land of America, given to the descendants of the ancient patriarch Joseph, whose descendants principally the Indians are. The Saints had been even so far favored as to have the place for the chief city of refuge and safety pointed out to them by revelation; as also the site of its temple—Independence, Missouri; and they were required by the commandments of God to bear witness to the world of these things. In view of all this—the fact that they were made at once the depository and witnesses of these great revelations, is it not likely that they would regard themselves as a people peculiarly favored of God? And is it matter of astonishment if some among them, not possessed of the soundest judgment, should run into an excess of zeal and give expression to unwise, as also to unwarranted conclusions?

Moreover, the Lord had spoken of the future glory of Zion—of the city, the location of which the Elders were to testify; also of the glory of the temple, with its future cloud by day and pillar of fire by night; of the future union of this New-World Zion with the ancient Zion of Enoch, where the Lord will make His abode, "and for the space of a thousand years shall the earth rest;"* also of his covenant with them concerning Zion, both as pertaining to time and eternity, wherein He said: "I have made the earth rich; and behold it is my footstool, wherefore, again I will stand upon it; and I hold forth, and deign to give unto you greater riches, even a land of promise, a land flowing with milk and honey, upon which there shall be no curse when the Lord cometh: and I will give it unto you for the land of your inheritance, if you seek it with all your hearts. And this shall be my covenant with you,you shall have it for the land of your inheritance, and for the inheritance of your children forever,while the earth shall stand,and you shall possess it again in eternity, no more to pass away."†

The Lord said again concerning Zion: "Wherefore I, the Lord, have said, gather ye out from the eastern lands, assemble yourselves together ye elders of my Church; go ye forth into the western countries, call upon the inhabitants to repent, and inasmuch as they do repent, build up churches unto me; and with one heart and with one mind, gather up your riches that ye may purchase an inheritance which shall hereafter be appointed unto you, and it shall be called the New Jerusalem, a land of peace, a city of refuge,a place of safety for the Saints of the Most High God; and the glory of the Lord shall be there, insomuch that the wicked will not come unto it, and it shall be called Zion. And it shall come to pass, among the wicked, that every man that will not take his sword against his neighbor, must needs flee unto Zion for safety. And there shall be gathered unto it out of every nation under heaven; and it shall be the only people that shall not be at war one with another. And it shall be said among the wicked, Let us not go up to battle against Zion, for the inhabitants of Zion are terrible; wherefore we cannot stand."‡

These promises to the Saints respecting Zion; these descriptions given to them of her future sanctified and glorified state; their connection with a work so exalted and far-reaching, was apt to fire their minds with a zeal not always tempered with wisdom. It was in vain that limitations of time and conditions were placed upon these general descriptions of the future greatness and glory of the city of God; nor could they understand that their own relationship to these great things

---

* Pearl of Great Price, pp. 44, 45, 1902 edition.

† Doc. & Cov. Sec. 38.

‡ Doc. and Cov. Sec. 45.

was merely to lay the foundation of them, to locate the site of the future city and temple, and then bear witness of it to the world. Yet that their work in connection with the founding of Zion was chiefly this, is clearly to be seen in the revelations of God to them.

The immediate and triumphant establishment of Zion, though expected by many of the Saints, was nowhere contemplated in the revelations of God to the Church. That hope of immediate establishment and glorification of Zion was the result of faulty deductions from the revelations of God; but the Lord was not blind respecting the events about to take place on the land of Zion, nor did He hold out any false hope to His people had they but read His revelations aright. A few days before the first conference held by the Elders on the land of Zion, the Lord said to them through His Prophet:

"Hearken, O ye elders of my Church, and give ear to my word, and learn of me what I will concerning you, and also concerning this land unto which I have sent you: For verily I say unto you, blessed is he that keepeth my commandments, whether in life or in death; and he that is faithful in tribulation, the reward of the same is greater in the kingdom of heaven. Ye cannot behold with your natural eyes, for the present time, the design of your God concerning those things which shall come hereafter, and the glory which shall follow *after much tribulation. For after much tribulation comes the blessings.* Wherefore the day cometh that ye shall be crowned with much glory; the hour is not yet, but is nigh at hand. Remember this, which I tell you before, that you may lay it to heart, and receive that which shall follow. Behold, verily I say unto you, for this cause I have sent you that you might be obedient, and that your hearts might be prepared to bear testimony of the things which are to come; and also that you might be honored of laying the foundation, and of bearing record of the land upon which the Zion of God shall stand; * * * * and that the testimony might go forth from Zion, yea, from the mouth of the city of the heritage of God. * * * * And now, verily, I say, concerning the residue of the elders of my Church, *the time has not yet come, for many years*, for them to receive their inheritance in this land, except they desire it through the prayer of faith, only as it shall be appointed unto them of the Lord. For, behold, they shall push the people together from the ends of the earth."*

These statements, when rightly considered, dispel all notion of the immediate establishment of Zion. The Lord distinctly warns His servants against any such supposition. He predicts "tribulation" before the glory shall come. It is only after "much tribulation" that the blessings are

* Doc. & Cov. Sec. 58.

promised. He reminds them that He has "told them before" of this, and asks them "to lay it to heart," and gives them to understand that it will be "*many years*" before some of the Elders of His Church will receive their inheritance in the goodly land.

The Lord still further foreshadowed the trouble which afterwards overtook His people by urging them to make arrangements for the purchase of the whole region that had been designated as the center place of Zion. "For, behold, verily I say unto you, the Lord willeth that the disciples, and the children of men should open their hearts, even to purchase this whole region of country, as soon as time will permit. Behold, here is wisdom. Let them do this lest they receive none inheritance, save it be by the shedding of blood."*

In this same month of August the Lord again said: "Behold, the land of Zion, I, the Lord, hold it in mine own hands; nevertheless, I, the Lord, render unto Cæsar the things which are Cæsar's: wherefore, I, the Lord, will that you should purchase the lands that you may have advantage of the world, that you may have claim on the world, that they may not be stirred up unto anger; for Satan putteth it into their hearts to anger against you, and to the shedding of blood; wherefore the land of Zion shall not be obtained but by purchase or by blood, otherwise there is none inheritance for you. And if by purchase behold you are blessed; and if by blood, *as you are forbidden to shed blood, lo, your enemies are upon you, and ye shall be scourged from city to city, and from synagogue to synagogue, and but few shall stand to receive an inheritance.*"†

About a month after this word, the Lord said: "Behold the Lord requireth the heart and a willing mind; and the willing and obedient shall eat the good of the land of Zion in these last days; and the rebellious shall be cut off out of the land of Zion, and shall be sent away, and shall not inherit the land; for, verily, I say that the rebellious are not of the blood of Ephraim, wherefore they shall be plucked out."‡

All this makes it very clear that while great things were promised concerning the establishment of Zion and the glory that is to be hers, yet all was predicated upon the faithfulness of the Saints in keeping the commandments of the Lord—in purchasing the lands that constituted the center place of Zion, and living upon them in all righteousness.

This they failed to do. In a revelation given in November, 1831, a few months after the land had been dedicated unto the Lord for the gathering of His people, He thus complained of those who had assembled in western Missouri:

---

* Doc. and Cov., Sec. 58, verses 52-3.

† Doc. and Cov., Sec. 63, verses 25-31.

‡ Doc. and Cov., Sec. 64, verses 34-36.

"And the inhabitants of Zion shall also observe the Sabbath day to keep it holy. And the inhabitans of Zion also shall remember their labors, inasmuch as they are appointed to labor, in all faithfulness; for the idler shall be had in remembrance before the Lord. Now, I, the Lord, am not well pleased with the inhabitants of Zion, for there are idlers among them; and their children are also growing up in wickedness; they also seek not earnestly the riches of eternity, but their eyes are full of greediness. These things ought not to be, and must be done away from among them: wherefore let my servant, Oliver Cowdery carry these sayings unto the land of Zion. And a commandment I give unto them, that he that observeth not his prayers before the Lord in the season thereof, let him be had in remembrance before the judge of my people. These sayings are true and faithful; wherefore transgress them not, neither take therefrom."*

In addition to these evils there were jealousies and bickerings among some of the brethren in Zion, and also between some of the Elders in Zion, and leading Elders in Kirtland. In the spring of 1832 the Prophet visited the Saints in Jackson county, and there were reconciliations among the brethren, and forgiveness of sins obtained from the Lord;† but shortly after the Prophet's departure for Kirtland these ill feelings broke out again with renewed bitterness; carelessness as to keeping the commandments of God characterized the conduct of the Saints in Zion, and there arose some confusion also in the government of the Church there, owing to conflicting claims of authority between traveling Elders and the standing ministry in the branches of the Church. This led to the following reproof from the Lord in a revelation given on the 22nd and 23rd of September, 1832:

"And your minds in times past have been darkened because of unbelief, and because you have treated lightly the things you have received, which vanity and unbelief hath brought the whole Church under condemnation. And this condemnation resteth upon the children of Zion, even all: and they shall remain under this condemnation until they repent and remember the new covenant, even the Book of Mormon, and the former commandments which I have given them,‡ not only to say, but to do according to that which I have written, that they may bring forth fruit meet for their Father's kingdom, *otherwise there remaineth a scourge and a judgment to be poured out upon the children of Zion:* for shall the children of the kingdom pollute my holy land? Verily, I say unto you, Nay."§

* Doc. and Cov., sec. 68, verses 29-34.

† See "History of the Church," Vol. I, ch. 19.

‡ Including of course, and I may say especially including, the commandment to purchase the lands of Jackson county.

§ Doc. and Cov., sec. 84, verses 54-59.

When this revelation, given early in January, 1833, was sent to the Elders in Zion, it was accompanied also by a letter from the Prophet, sharply reproving the brethren and Saints in Zion, in which the following passage occurs:

"Let me say unto you, seek to purify yourselves, and also the inhabitants of Zion, lest the Lord's anger be kindled to fierceness. *Repent, repent, it is the voice of God to Zion;* and strange as it may appear, yet it is true, mankind will persist in self-justification until all their iniquity is exposed, and their character past being redeemed, and that which is treasured up in their hearts be exposed to the gaze of mankind. I say to you (and what I say to you, I say to all), hear the warning voice of God, *lest Zion fall, and the Lord swear in His wrath, 'The inhabitants of Zion shall not enter into my rest.'* "*

Hyrum Smith and Orson Hyde were appointed by a Council of the High Priests in Kirtland at this time, to write a letter of reproof and warning to the brethren in Zion. In this communication the conduct of the Saints in Zion was reviewed in great plainness. The whole spirit of the communication may be judged by the following paragraph:

"We feel more like weeping over Zion than rejoicing over her, *for we know that the judgments of God hang over her, and will fall upon her except she repent,* and purify herself before the Lord, and put away from her every foul spirit. We now say to Zion, this once, in the name of the Lord, Repent! repent! awake! awake! put on thy beautiful garments, before you are made to feel the chastening rod of Him whose anger is kindled against you. Let not Satan tempt you to think we want to make you bow to us, to domineer over you, for God knows this is not the case; our eyes are watered with tears, and our hearts are poured out to God in prayer for you, that He will spare you, and turn away His anger from you. * * * Therefore, with the feelings of inexpressible anxiety for your welfare, we say again, Repent, repent, *or Zion must suffer, for the scourge and judgment must come upon her.*"†

All this reproof and warning, however, only produced a partial repentance, and in July following acts of violence began to be perpetrated upon the Saints by the old settlers of Missouri, and in the month of November, under circumstances of great cruelty, all the Saints were driven from Jackson county, and later more than two hundred of their homes, together with their public improvements, were destroyed.

When the Lord revealed to the Prophet Joseph why this affliction had befallen the people, He said: "Verily I say unto you concerning your

* History of the Church, Vol. I p 316.

† *Ibid*, pp 317-21.

brethren who have been afflicted, and persecuted, and cast out from the land of their inheritance, I, the Lord, have suffered the affliction to come upon them wherewith they have been afflicted, in consequence of their transgressions; yet I will own them, and they shall be mine in that day when I shall come to make up my jewels. Therefore, they must needs be chastened and tried, even as Abraham, who was commanded to offer up his only son; for all those who will not endure chastening, but deny me, cannot be sanctified. Behold, I say unto you, there were jarrings, and contentions, and envyings, and strifes and lustful and covetous desires among them; therefore, by these things they polluted their inheritances. They were slow to hearken unto the voice of the Lord their God, therefore the Lord their God is slow to hearken unto their prayers, to answer them in the day of their trouble. In the day of their peace they esteemed lightly my counsel; but in the day of their trouble, of necessity they feel after me. Verily I say unto you, notwithstanding their sins my bowels are filled with compassion towards them; I will not utterly cast them off; and in the day of wrath I will remember mercy.*

From this it is very clear that the reason why the Saints were prevailed against by their enemies and driven from the center place of Zion, was because of their failure to live up to the high requirements made of them by the Lord. In subsequent efforts to redeem Zion, by attempting to return the exiles to Jackson county, the Saints in all parts of the land again failed to respond with sufficient promptness and fulness to the requirements of the Lord, for He commanded them again to consecrate money to purchase lands in Jackson county and in the counties round about, saying to the Church: "There is even now already in store a sufficient, yea even abundance, to redeem Zion, and establish her waste places, no more to be thrown down, were the churches who call themselves after my name willing to hearken to my voice."†

The Lord also commanded them to gather up their forces and to go in sufficient strength to possess the land, and maintain their inheritance against their enemies. This, however, they failed to do. Instead of raising five hundred men, as they were commanded to do,‡ they started from Kirtland in "Zion's Camp" with a company of only about one hundred and thirty men ,and twenty baggage wagons. This number was increased by additions *en route* to one hnndred and eighty-two men,but even this number fell far short of the strength required to accomplish the purpose for which the camp was organized. In the matter of rais-

---

* Doc. and Cov., sec. 101, vereses 1-9.

† Ibid, verse 75.

‡ Ibid, sec. 103.

ing money for the purchase of lands the failure was more conspicuous than in raising men to take possession of them, and hence this effort to redeem Zion failed.

Here let me pause in pointing out the unwisdom of the Saints, to make an explanation, lest there should be a misunderstanding of what is thus far set down respecting their transgressions, by reason of which they were prevailed against by their enemies. These transgressions, be it understood, were no violations of the laws of the land, nor did they consist in any acts of aggression or of trespass upon their Missouri neighbors. The old settlers of Missouri themselves are our witnesses here; for in all their procedure in this Jackson county persecution there is no accusation made against the Saints of violations of the law. On the contrary, in their public utterances against the Saints and in justification of their own course, the old settlers declare—after expressing their determination to rid their society of the Saints, peacefully if they could, but forcibly if they must—"*that the arm of the civil law does not afford us a guarantee, or at least a sufficient one, against the evils which are now inflicted upon us, and seem to be inreasing by the said religious sect.*"* A more emphatic acknowledgement that the alleged offenses of the Saints were not cognizable by the laws, that the Saints had not violated the laws of the land, could not be made.

In their second manifesto the mob said: "*The evil is one that no one could have foreseen, and is therefore unprovided for by the laws; and the delays incident to legislation would put the mischief beyond remedy.*"† Another admission that amounts to a declaration, that the Saints, whatever the nature of the complaints made against them were, had not violated any of the laws of the state, that their offending was not cognizable by the laws of the land.

The transgressions and sinfulness referred to in the revelations and letters of reproof and warning quoted, and for which transgressions the Saints were left in the hands of their enemies, were sins against each other and the Lord—unbelief in the word of God, hardness of heart towards each other, rejection of the servants of God, fault-finding, bickerings, jealousies, covetousness, pride, idleness, boastfulness, levity of thought and conduct, disregard of the scriptures, especially of the Book of Mormon, neglecting to instruct their children in sacred things and to bring them up in the fear and admonition of the Lord; all of which were displeasing to the Lord, contrary to His commandments, and a violation of the conditions upon which He had promised to redeem Zion and preserve His people from their enemies. "Ye call

---

* First Manifesto of the Mob, History of the Church, Vol. I, p. 374.

† History of the Church, Vol. I, p. 396.

upon my name for revelations;" said the Lord to the Elders in Zion, "and I give them unto you; and inasmuch as ye keep not my sayings, which I give unto you, ye become transgressors, and justice and judgment are the penalty which is affixed to my law. * * * I, the Lord, am bound when ye do what I say; but when ye do not what I say, ye have no promise."*

This, then, was the nature of their offenses; they sinned against the Lord in the particulars named; they sinned against each other in the manner described; they did not trespass against their non-Mormon neighbors, nor break the laws of the land; but they failed to live in accordance with the high moral and spiritual law of the Gospel; they failed to meet the conditions on which God was pledged to their maintenance upon the land of Zion, and hence were left in the hands of their enemies.

At the commencement of this subdivision of the Introduction I called attention to the great things which God had revealed to the Saints, the greatness of the dispensation committed unto them, accompanied by the promise to establish Zion and give unto the Saints the land thereof as an everlasting inheritance. It would be marvelous indeed, and past all human experience, if these great things did not turn the heads of some of the weak-minded, and make them vain-glorious and boastful. I doubt not for a moment that many vain and foolish things were said by such characters in the presence of, and perhaps directly to, the old settlers of Jackson county, about the Saints taking possession of the land, and the wicked being driven away. There was doubtless enough of this kind of talk to give color to what the Missourians charged on this head, viz., "They [the Saints] declare openly that their God hath given them this county of land, and that sooner or later they must and will take possession of our lands for an inheritance."

The Missourians made much of, and attached a sinister meaning to the following expression in one of the revelations to the Saints: "*The land of Zion shall not be obtained but by purchase or by blood, otherwise there is none inheritance for you.*"† This the Missourians pretended to regard as a threat to take possession of their land by armed conquest. Had they read the context of the passage they would have known how entirely groundless were their fears, if indeed they had any fears, for I am convinced that all their expressed apprehensions on this head were mere pretense. The passage and its context are: "Wherefore the land of Zion shall not be obtained but by purchase or by blood, otherwise there is none inheritance for you. *And if by purchase, behold you*

* Doc. and Cov., sec. 83.

† Doc. and Cov., sec. 63.

are blessed; and if by blood, as you are forbidden to shed blood, lo, your enemies are upon you, and ye shall be scourged from city to city, and from synagogue to synagogue and but few shall stand to receive an inheritance."*

Clearly this is a warning to the Saints, not a threat to the Missourians. If the Saints obtained the land by purchase they were blessed. If by blood—since the Saints were forbidden to shed blood, lo their enemies would be upon them and they would be driven from city to city —not the Missourians, but the Saints. In consequence of the agitation of this matter by the foolish, the following passage occurred in *The Evening and Morning Star* for July, 1833, addressed to the churches scattered abroad: "To suppose that we can come up here and take possession of this land by the shedding of blood, would be setting at nought the law of the glorious Gospel, and also the word of our great Redeemer. And to suppose that we can take possession of this country without making regular purchases of the same according to the laws of our nation, would be reproaching this great Republic, in which the most of us were born, and under whose auspices we all have protection."†

Of this the Missourians said that whether they were to be dispossessed of their lands "by the hand of the destroying angel, the judgments of God, or the arm of power, they [the Saints] are not fully agreed among themselves. Some recent remarks in the *Evening and Morning Star*, their organ in this place, by their tendency to moderate such hopes, and repress such desires, show plainly that many of this deluded and infatuated people have been taught to believe that our lands were to be won from us by the sword!"‡

Thus the very efforts of the Church to correct the misconceptions and silence the utterances of the over-zealous and foolish members, were made to contribute as proof that the Saints contemplated the very armed conquest of the land which they disclaimed. History, however, will do the Saints justice, and it will say, and now says, that neither their general principles, nor the special commandments under which they moved into the land of Zion, nor any act of theirs warranted the least suspicion that they at any time contemplated taking possession of the land by force, or in any other manner whatsoever except by purchase and possession under the laws of the state of Missouri and the United States. And while history will do them this justice it will at the same time say that the "fears" of the Missourians on this head were simulated; that to the foolish boasts of a few ignorant persons they attached an undue importance because it happened to give a coloring to their pretended fears in the eyes of those at a distance who had no oppor-

* Doc. and Cov., sec. 63: 29-31.

† Evening and Morning Star, p. 220.

‡ "History of the Church," Vol. I, p. 396.

tunity to learn the truth, and tended to prejudice the public mind against the Saints, and thus served the purpose of their enemies.

In like manner there may have been some talk among the same class of people—the ignorant and over-zealous Church members—respecting the Indians, and their future union with the Saints in redeeming the land of Zion; a circumstance which led the good people of Clay county and Governor Dunklin,to refer to the charge of the Saints holding illicit communication with the Indians, designing to employ them in taking possession of the land of Zion. Of this charge also history will and does vindicate the Saints. It will, and does say, that they disclaimed holding any such communication; that neither their general principles nor any special commandment from God, and particularly that no action of theirs warranted any suspicion on the subject, much less justified the charge of such a diabolical purpose.

After the Saints withdrew from Clay county and at the suggestion of her citizens—including some of the most influential men in western Missouri, some of whom afterwards attained national reputations—located in the sparsely settled counties of Caldwell and Daviess, the situation became somewhat changed. For two years the work of purchasing lands, locating settlements, opening farms, establishing merchantile houses, and preparing for manufacturing and commercial enterprises went steadily on. In Caldwell and adjoining counties, by the autumn of 1838, the Saints had opened two thousand farms, and paid to the general government three hundred and eighteen thousand dollars for land, which at the minimum price for government land would give them over two hundred and fifty thousand acres.* One hundred and fifty houses had been erected in Far West; there were four dry goods stores, three family groceries, half a dozen blacksmith's shops, and two hotels.† The excavation for a temple 120 by 80 feet had been made, and a large commodious schoolhouse had been erected on the public square.‡ The town of Adam-Ondi-Ahman was also making rapid progress.

* These estimates are by the late President George A. Smith, Church Historian, and hence are entirely reliable. They are quoted by Lucien Carr in his History of Missouri, "American Commonwealths," p. 181, and are also to be found in an Historical Address by George A. Smith, Journal of Discourses, Vol. XIII, pp. 103, *et seq.*

† "History of Caldwell county" (National Historical Company, 1886) p. 121.

‡ "In the fall of 1836, a large and comfortable schoolhouse was built and here courts were held after the location of the county seat until its removal to Kingston. The Mormons very early gave attention to educational matters. There were many teachers among them and schoolhouses were among their first buildings. The schoolhouse in Far West was used as a Church, as a town hall and as a court house, as well as for a schoolhouse. It first stood in the southwest quarter of town, but upon the establishment of the county seat it was removed to the center of the square." ("History of Caldwell County," p. 121.—National Historical Company, 1886).

By this time the Prophet Joseph and other leading men of the Church had left Kirtland and located with the Saints in Missouri, and everything looked propitious for the permanent establishment of the Saints in the borders of Zion. The Saints had now been driven bodily from Jackson county; and their homes, store houses and printing establishment had been destroyed. The courts of Missouri had proven powerless to restore to them their homes, their lands and other property. The executive of the state confessed himself powerless to return them to their possessions in Jackson county, and maintain them there against the wishes of the people of that county. Indeed, Governor Dunklin had weakly given up the vindication of the outraged laws of the state, as we have seen, saying that whether the charges of their enemies or the denials by the Saints were true he could not tell; their neighbors seemed to believe them true, and whether true or false the consequences would be the same, unless the Saints by their conduct and argument could convince the Missourians of their innocence. "If you cannot do this," said the governor, "all I can say to you is that in this Republic the *vox populi is the vox Dei!*" The Saints at some considerable sacrifice had withdrawn from Clay county at the request of her citizens, in the interests of peace, and had settled in the new counties of Caldwell and Daviess, where settlers were few and the country less desirable than in Jackson and Clay counties. In doing these things they had repeatedly sacrificed their rights as citizens, both of Missouri and of the United States. Smitten on the one cheek—speaking figuratively—they had turned the other; sued at the law for their coat, they had given their cloak also; compelled to go one mile with their enemy, they had gone with him twain. After doing all this for the sake of peace and the friendship of the Missourians, when the Saints saw forming again those elements which threatened their peace; when old enemies appeared upon the new scene of the Saints' activities, and openly threatened their peace and boasted that they would again prosper by despoiling them of their new possessions; when they saw the red right hand of a relentless persecution arming again to plague them, it is small wonder if righteous anger flushed their cheek, made bright their eyes with indignation and led them instinctively to form the resolution that they would submit no more to such acts of despoliation, injustice and outrage.

It was this sense of outraged justice and humanity which led to the deliverance of a very noted "Oration" by Sidney Rigdon at Far West, on the Fourth of July, 1838, in the course of which there was expressed a strong determination to no more submit quietly to mob violence, and acts of pillage. At this distance of time from that occasion, and balancing against the heated utterances of the speaker the subsequent uses made of them to incite the public mind to that series of acts which culminated in the expulsion of the Saints from the state, we say those utterances were untimely, extreme, and unwise. So indeed they were. The speaker seems to have thrown discretion to the winds, and in the fervor of his rhetoric made threats of retaliation on behalf of the Saints, if assailed, that went beyond all bounds of reason and humanity, and proved a very damaging as also a very potent factor against the Saints in the subsequent movements of their enemies against them.

But while this oratorical outburst against injustice was unwise, it was a very natural thing. The marvel is not that it came at the time it did, but that it did not come earlier, more vehemently, and that some of the things it threatened were not effectively carried out. What the Prophet thought, and how he felt respecting the repeated acts of injustice heaped upon himself and the Saints in Missouri; how he felt and what he proposed for the future is made clear in his journal entry for September 1st, 1838; and, fortunately, is more temperately expressed than in the oration of July the fourth. He said:

"There is great excitement at present among the Missourians, who are seeking if possible an occasion against us. They are continually chafing us, and provoking us to anger if possible, one sign of threatening after another, but we do not fear them, for the Lord God, the Eternal Father is our God, and Jesus the Mediator is our Savior, and in the great I Am is our strength and confidence.

"We have been driven time after time, and that without cause; and smitten again and again, and that without provocation; until we have proved the world with kindness, and the world has proved us, that we have no designs against any man or set of men, that we injure no man, that we are peaceable with all men, minding our own business, and our business only. We have suffered our rights and our liberties to be taken from us; we have not avenged ourselves of those wrongs; we have appealed to magistrates, to sheriffs, to judges, to government and to the President of the United States, all in vain; yet we have yielded peaceably to all these things. We have not complained at the great God, we murmured not, but peaceably left all, and retired into the back country, in the broad and wild prairies, in the barren and desolate plains, and there commenced anew; we made the desolate places to bud and blossom as the rose; and now the fiend-like race is disposed to give us no rest. Their father the devil, is hourly calling upon them to be up and doing, and they, like willing and obedient children, need not the second admonition; but in the name of Jesus Christ, the Son of the living God, we will endure it no longer, if the great God will arm us with courage, with strength and with power, to resist them in their persecutions. We will not act on the offensive, but always on the defensive; our rights and our liberties shall not be taken from us, and we peaceably submit to it as we have done heretofore, but we will avenge ourselves of our enemies, inasmuch as they will not let us alone."

No one can marvel at the conclusion here arrived at if he will but pay attention to and give due weight to the enumerated wrongs which precede it. It would be asking the Saints to be more than human if we say they ought not to have indulged, much less to have expressed, such feelings of resentment.

Meantime, however, we may not close our eyes to the fact that there was unwisdom manifested on the part of a few of the Saints, which gave advantage to their enemies, by affording pretexts for some of their accusations. That unwisdom, as we have seen, consisted of boasting as to what the Lord would do in the immediate future in giving them possession of western Missouri as an inheritance; perhaps some unwise allusions to the supposed part the Lamanites would take in the establishment and redemption of Zion; and the vehement threats of retaliation in the event of their being further assailed. These unwise utterances, however, were made, for the most part, by the overzealous and ignorant. Men who had no grasp of the real genius of the great work whose foundations were then being laid; men who, in common with men of like nature in all ages and in all great movements, have been trouble-breeders; who, in their contemplation of ultimate results to be achieved, overleaped the intervening space through which the movement must pass, the difficulties it must encounter and overcome, the experiences its adherents must gain, the great and varied labors they must perform. They seem not to undestand that great movements require time for the achievement of their ends; that time with God is one thing, with man quite another thing; that the thing which is "nigh at hand" with the Lord may be to men afar off; and overlooking these important facts leads such men into many errors of thought and action. It was wholly reprehensible, unwarranted, and cowardly, however, on the part of the Missourians to take advantage of the unwise utterances of such characters and charge their sentiments and folly to the whole body religious, that never entertained such sentiments nor contemplated the actions such sentiments suggest. And this is to be said even of those who were unwise enough to give the advantage here noted to the enemies of the Saints, they at no time or place were ever guilty of attempting in any manner to carry into effect by any action of their own the unwise and unwarranted opinions they entertained and expressed. Their boastings and vain speculations were in relation to what the Lord was going to do, not what they themselves purposed doing. These utterances were merely the effervescence of overwrought minds, of overzealous, foolish, but well meaning and harmless people. Unhappily, however, what they said gave the enemy an advantage that he was not slow to avail himself of, and the unwisdom of some of the Saints is a factor that must be reckoned with in dealing with the causes of the persecutions of the Saints in Missouri.

The Real Cause of the Missouri Persecutions.

Having considered those facts and circumstances which may be regarded as the minor causes and pretexts of the Missouri persecutions, let us now come to the heart of the matter, to the real cause of the persecution of the Saints.

It was against the Saints as a religious sect that the Missourians first complained. It was "in consequence of a pretended religious sect of people" that had settled, and was still settling in their country, "styling themselves Mormons," that led the Missourians of Jackson county to pretend to believe that an important crisis regarding their civil society was at hand. "It is more thant wo years," they said, "since the first of these fanatics, or knaves (for one or other they undoubtedly are), made their first appearance amongst us, and pretended as they did, and do now, to hold personal communication and converse face to face with the Most High; to receive communications and revelations direct from heaven; to heal the sick hy laying on hands; and, in short, to perform all the wonder-working miracles wrought by the inspired apostles and prophets of old. We believed them deluded fanatics, or weak and designing knaves, and that they and their pretensions would soon pass away; but in this we were deceived. * * * They openly blaspheme the Most High God, and cast contempt on His holy religion, by pretending to receive revelations direct from heaven, by pretending to speak unknown tongues by direct inspiration, and by divers pretenses derogatory to God and religion, and to the utter subversion of human reason."*

The foregoing is quoted from the first "Manifesto," or "Secret Constitution" of the mob. Somewhat later, in a second manifesto issued to the public in justification of their contemplated acts of violence against the Saints, they say: "What would be the fate of our lives and property, in the hands of jurors and witnesses, who do not blush to declare, and would not upon occasion hesitate to swear, that they have wrought miracles, and have been the subjects of miraculous and supernatural cures, have conversed with God and His angels, and possess and exercise the gifts of divination and of unknown tongues, and fired with the prospect of obtaining inheritances without money and without price—may be better imagined than described. * * * Of their pretended revelations from heaven—their personal intercourse

* "History of the Church," Vol., 1, pp. 375-6.

with God and His angels—the maladies they pretend to heal by the laying on of hands—and the contemptible gibberish with which they habitually profane the Sabbath, and which they dignify with the appellation of unknown tongues, we have nothing to say: vengeance belongs to God alone."*

Yet it was because the Saints entertained these religious beliefs that the mob of Jackson county issuing this "manifesto," proceeded to take "vengeance" into their own hands, and wreak it upon the Saints. All their other accusations against them,—namely, idleness, ignorance, inviting "free negroes" into the state, inciting the slaves to insubordination to their masters, claiming Jackson county as their inheritance to be obtained by force if not bloodshed, and poverty—all these charges, except, perhaps the last (for some of the Saints were very poor, though I have yet to learn that that is a crime), were absolutely untrue. The Saints, however, did claim the existence of spiritual power in their religion; that the channel of communication between God and men by means of revelation, the visitation of angels, and the inspiration of the Holy Ghost, had been opened anew; that gifts of the Gospel—tongues, interpretations, visions, inspired dreams, healings—that all the spiritual powers and graces of the Gospel, in fact, were manifested in the religion they had accepted. By this religion, also, they were admonished to righteousness of life; to the strict observance of the Sabbath; to respect for the name of Deity; to temperance; to industry; to true speaking and true acting; to patience—in a word, to godliness; all of which but to live was to place themselves in marked contrast to those about them, and their righteous lives were a great rebuke to the general dissolute conduct of the Missourians. It was this effort at a godly walk and conversation, and the religion which commanded it, that was offensive in the eyes of the Missourians, and which led them to form their strong determination to be rid of a people and a religion which made their own lives a reproach.

That this was regarded as the chief, if not the sole cause of their persecution, appears in the subsequent discussion of the Jackson county difficulties, both *pro et con.* All other questions, all the minor causes and pretexts were lost sight of in that discussion. Governor Dunklin, in a communication to Colonel J. Thornton, in answer to a letter written by that gentleman proposing a compromise between the Saints and their enemies in Jackson county, recognizes what he calls "the eccentricity of the religious opinions of the Mormons" as being the cause of their persecution. "I am fully persuaded," he remarks, "that the eccentricity of the religious opinions and practices of the Mormons is at the bottom of the outrages committed against them."

---

* "History of the Church," Vol. I, p. 397.

In this important communication he no where considers anything else as the cause of their persecution, but argues at length in favor of their right to the entertainment of their religious views, eccentric howsoever they might be, so long as they did not interfere with the rights of others. "They have the right constitutionally guaranteed to them," he remarks, "and it is indefeasible, to worship Joe Smith as a man, an angel, or even as the only true and living God, and to call their habitation Zion, the Holy Land, or even heaven itself. Indeed, there is nothing so absurd or ridiculous that they have not a right to adopt as their religion, so that in its exercise they do not interfere with the rights of others."*

The people of Clay county when they called upon the Saints to peaceably remove from their borders and seek a locality where they could form a community that should be largely, if not exclusively, made up of their own Church membership, indicated very clearly that it was the religion of the Saints that was the chief cause of complaint against them. In a document they published setting forth the reasons why they suggested such removal, they said: "The religious tenets of this people are so different from the present churches of the age, that they always have, and always will, excite deep prejudices against them in any populous country where they may locate. We, therefore, in a spirit of frank and friendly kindness, do advise them to seek a home where they may obtain large and separate bodies of land, and have a community of their own."*

Again, after the surrender at Far West, when the Church leaders had been betrayed into bondage; after the Saints had delivered up their arms; after they had signed over their properties to defray the expenses of the "war;" and when the whole body of the Church was making hasty preparations to depart from the state, a number of the brethren were assembled on the temple square at Far West, and in the course of a long speech, which he read† to them, General John B. Clark said:

"I am sorry, gentlemen, to see so great a number of apparently intelligent men found in the situation you are; and oh! that I could invoke that Great Spirit, the Unknown God, to rest upon you, and make you sufficiently intelligent to break that chain of superstition, and liberate you from those fetters of fanaticism with which you are bound—that you no longer worship a man! I would advise you to scatter abroad, and never again organize yourselves with Bishops, Presidents,

* "History of the Church," Vol. II, p. 85.

* "History of the Church," Vol. II, p. 450.

† "History of Caldwell and Livingston Counties," compiled by the St. Louis National and Historical Company, 1886, p. 140.

etc., lest you excite the jealousies of the people, and subject yourselves to the same calamities that have now come upon you."

This to a people whose leaders had been betrayed into the hands of their enemies; who themselves had been disarmed, though acting only in defense of their homes and families; who had been compelled at the muzzle of the musket to sign away their property to defray the expenses of the militia mobs that had brought their calamities upon them; who were then under an order of expulsion from the state and making hurried preparations for their enforced departure—this to men who had sacrificed or had been robbed of the most sacred rights of American citizenship! And he who thus addressed the brethren impudently told them in the very speech from which I quote, that he approved of all that had been done to them! But the foregoing quotation is not made in order to point out the mockery of the speech; or the mixture of hypocrisy and blasphemy in it; or the utter contemptibility of him who delivered it. I quote the passage merely to point out the fact that it was hatred of their alleged "superstition" and "fanaticism," in other words the religion of the Saints that was the cause of their persecution. The crimes against which the Saints are warned for the future—under penalty of having their present troubles revisited upon them—is gathering together in large bodies, and organizing themselves with Bishops, Presidents, etc. In other words it was the religion of the people and the organization which was both the depository of its doctrines, and the instrumentality by which they were promulgated—the Church—which was the object of the Missourians' animosity, the thing they were determined to destroy.

Later, when the Prophet Joseph and other leading brethren were under examination before Judge Austin A. King at Richmond, Ray county, special inquiry was made as to the belief of the witnesses in the declaration of the Prophet Daniel: "And in the days of these kings shall the God of heaven set up a kingdom, which shall never be destroyed: and the kingdom shall not be left to other people, but it shall break in pieces and consume all these kingdoms, and it shall stand for ever."*

The judge on being answered that the Saints believed the prophecy, turned to the clerk and told him to write the answer down as it was "*a strong point for treason*!"† I call it another evidence that it was the religious beliefs of the Saints that constituted their offense. True the Prophet and several other brethren were technically held for trial on

* Daniel 2: 44.

† Autobiography of Parley P. Pratt, p. 230, also History of the Church, Vol. III p. 212.

the charge of "treason, murder, arson, burglarly, robbery, larceny and perjury," but no one in Missouri ever seriously believed the charges since they were wholly untrue or grew out of those acts of self defense, and defense of their families against the aggressions of mob violence—a course which all men have a right to take in the protection of their own lives and the preservation of their homes from the hand of the despoiler.

The meeting of discordant elements of society—New England people and people from the Southern States, descendants of Puritans and descendants of Cavaliers—may have been a cause of dislike, and, on the part of the Missourians, a cause of irritation against the Saints; the suspected existence of anti-slavery sentiments among the Saints may have been to the Missourians a cause of distrust; the interest of the Saints in the Indians and the beliefs of the former in the future rehabilitation of the latter as a people favored of God, may have been, under all the circumstances, a cause of uneasiness to the Missourians; and the desire to plunder the Saints and to profit by dispossessing them of their lands and homes might have been, and doubtless was, an incentive to many of the mob who participated in the events which culminated in the expulsion of the Saints from the state; but, at bottom, I repeat, it was the destruction of the religion of the Saints, and of the organization that taught its doctrines, and controlled its membership in ecclesiastical affairs, that were the objectives of all that agitation, violence and injustice, which make up the persecution of the Latter-day Saints in Missouri. But how shall the truth of this be established beyond reasonable doubt? Listen:—

The author of the "*Decline and Fall of the Roman Empire*" gives the following pen-picture of conditions with reference to religious toleration which obtained in the empire under the reign of the Antonines, Adrian and Marcus Aurelius, second century, A. D. "The firm edifice of Roman power was raised and preserved by the wisdom of ages. The obedient provinces of Trajan and the Antonines were united by laws, and adorned by arts. They might occasionally suffer from the partial abuse of delegated authority; but the general principle of government was wise, simple, and beneficent. They enjoyed the religion of their ancestors, whilst in civil honors and advantages they were exalted, by just degrees, to an equality with their conquerors. The policy of the emperors and the senate, as far as it concerned religion, was happily seconded by the reflections of the enlightened, and the habits of the superstitious, part of their subjects. The various modes of worship, which prevailed in the Roman world, were all considered by the people as equally true; by the philosopher, as equally false; and by the magistrate, as equally useful. And thus toleration produced not only mutual indulgence, but even religious concord. The superstition of the people was not embittered by any mixture of theological rancor; nor was it confined by the chains of any speculative system. The devout polytheist, though fondly attached to his national rites, admitted with implicit faith the different religions of the earth. Fear, gratitude, and curiosity, a dream or an omen, a singular disorder, or a distant journey, perpetually disposed him to multiply the articles of his belief, and to enlarge the list of his protectors. The thin texture of the Pagan mythology was interwoven with various but not discordant materials. As soon as it was allowed that sages and heroes, who had lived or who had died for the benefit of their country, were exalted to a state of power and immortality, it was universally confessed that they deserved, if not the adoration, at least the reverence, of all mankind. The deities of a thousand groves and a thousand streams possessed in peace their local and respective influence: nor could the Roman who deprecated the wrath of the Tiber, deride the Egyptian who presented his offering to the beneficent genius of the Nile. The visible powers of nature, the planets, and the elements, were the same throughout the universe. The invisible governors of the moral world were inevitably cast in a similar mould of fiction and allegory. Every virtue, and even vice, acquired its divine representative; every art and profession its patron, whose attributes, in the most distant ages and countries, were uniformly derived from the character of their peculiar votaries. A republic of gods of such opposite tempers and interests required, in every system, the moderating hand of a supreme magistrate, who, by the progress of knowledge and flattery, was gradually invested with the sublime perfections of an eternal parent, and an omnipotent monarch. Such was the mild spirit of antiquity, that the nations were less attentive to the difference, than to the resemblance, of their religious worship. The Greek, the Roman, and the Barbarian, as they met before their respective altars, easily persuaded themselves, that under various names, and with various ceremonies, they adored the same deities. * * * * Rome, the capital of a great monarchy, was incessantly filled with subjects and strangers from every part of the world, who all introduced and enjoyed the favorite superstitions of their native country. Every city in the empire was justified in maintaining the purity of its ancient ceremonies; and the Roman senate, using the common privilege, sometimes interposed to check this inundation of foreign rites. The Egyptian superstition, of all the most contemptible and abject, was frequently prohibited; the temples of Serapis and Isis demolished, and their worshipers banished from Rome and Italy. But the zeal of fanaticism prevailed over the cold and feeble efforts of policy. The exiles returned, the proselytes multiplied, the temples were restored with increasing splendor, and Isis and Serapis at length assumed their place among the Roman deities. * * * * Rome gradually became the common temple of her subjects; and the freedom of the city was bestowed on all the gods of mankind."*

Some Christian editors of Gibbon's great work, in their annotations, hold that the author of the "Decline and Fall" gives in the foregoing a too favorable view of pagan-religious toleration; but after giving due weight to the instances of intolerance they cite in evidence of their contention, and viewing them in connection with the extent of the empire and the period of time covered by Gibbon's description, I do not regard them as of sufficient importance to warrant any change in the representation made by our author of conditions as to religious toleration in the Roman empire at the time of which he writes. Especially, since Gibbon himself in a foot note admits that "some obscure traces of an intolerant spirit appears in the conduct of the Egyptians," the case chiefly relied upon by his critics to disprove his description of universal religious toleration in the empire; and in the same note he refers to the Christians and the Jews as forming an important exception; so important an exception indeed that he promises, and subsequently gives, a distinct chapter to the discussion of the subject.†

It is to Christianity as the chief exception to the Roman policy of universal religious toleration that I wish now to direct attention. Let it be borne in mind that the spirit of universal religious toleration within the Roman empire claimed for the second century of our era, largely obtained also in the first century. It was in this reign of universal religious toleration that the Christian religion was brought forth and developed. Christ was born in the eighteenth year of the reign of Tiberius Cæsar, in the Roman province of Palestine, in which, also, His personal labors as religious teacher and reformer were chiefly confined. In the villages of Galilee, and subsequently in Samaria and Judea and in the ancient city of Jerusalem, He went about doing good; speaking words of encouragement to the oppressed and the poor; healing the sick; opening the eyes of the blind; cleansing the lepers; teaching, as no one ever taught before, the fatherhood of God, the brotherhood of men, and proclaiming Himself the Son of God and the Redeemer of the world. He gathered about Him a few devout followers, and from their number He established a priesthood and organized a Church to perpetuate the gentle doctrines He Himself taught. Strangely enough, notwithstanding the beauty and purity of His moral precepts, and the gentleness of His own deportment, proclamation of His doctrines everywhere incited hostility. The people of the village in which He was reared rejected Him.

* "Decline and Fall of the Roman Empire," Vol. I, Chapter II.

† "This is Chapter XVI of the "Decline and Fall."

His own people, the Jews, were so hostile that they at last clamored for His execution; and so deep was their hatred that they were willing that responsibility for the shedding of His blood should be upon their heads and upon the heads of their children after them, if only the Roman authorities would sanction His execution! He was finally crucified amid the rejoicings of His enemies.

After His resurrection He appeared among His disciples and commissioned them to evangelize the world. As they went about this work they encountered the same spirit of opposition that had met their Master. Whippings, imprisonment, and martyrdom confronted them on every hand, and when they extended their labors beyond the borders of Palestine, notwithstanding the general religious tolerance that obtained in the Roman empire, the Christians were everywhere spoken against, and their ministers everywhere opposed and persecuted.

Passing by the persecutions inflicted upon the Christians by the Jews —the whipping of Peter and John, under the order of the Jewish Sanhedrim, the martyrdom of Stephen, the execution of Saint James, the repeated mobbing and whippings of Paul—I call attention to the first great pagan persecution under the cruel edict of the Emperor Nero, in the second half of the first Christian century. The emperor having set on fire the city of Rome in order that he might view a great conflagration, and wishing to divert suspicion from himself, he first accused and then tried to compel the Christians to confess the crime. At this point I summon Tacitus, the renowned Roman annalist, to tell the remainder of the story:

"With this view he inflicted the most exquisite tortures on those men who, under the vulgar appellation of Christians, were already branded with deserved infamy. They derived their name and origin from Christ, who, in the reign of Tiberius, had suffered death by the sentence of the procurator Pontius Pilate. For awhile this dire superstition was checked, but it again burst forth, and not only spread itself over Judea, the first seat of this mischievous sect, but was even introduced into Rome, the common asylum, which receives and protects whatever is impure, whatever is atrocious. The confessions of those that were seized discovered a great multitude of their accomplices, and they were all convicted not so much for the crime of setting fire to the city, as for their hatred of human kind. They died in torments, and their torments were embittered by insults and derision. Some were nailed on crosses; others sewn up in the skins of wild beasts and exposed to the fury of dogs; others, again, smeared over with combustible materials, were used as torches to illuminate the darkness of the night. The gardens of Nero were destined for the melancholy spectacle, which was accompanied with a horse race, and honored with the presence of the emperor, who mingled with the populace in the dress and attitude of a charioteer. The guilt of the Christians deserved indeed the most exemplary punishments, but the public abhorrence was changed into commiseration from the opinion that those unhappy wretches were sacrificed, not so much to the public welfare as to the cruelty of a jealous tyrant."*

This first great persecution of the Christians under the authority of the Roman emperor, is sufficiently characteristic to describe the other persecutions which were intermittingly perpetrated upon the Christians through the two succeeding centuries. What seems to be the most incongruous circumstance connected with these persecutions is, that they occurred not only under such wretches as Nero and Domitian, but under such virtuous emperors as Trajan, Adrian, Marcus Aurelius and Diocletian. Intermittingly, then, through three troubled centuries, and under circumstances of the utmost cruelty, persecution raged against the Christians. As the highest authority on Roman history remarks: "If the empire had been afflicted by any recent calamity, by a plague, a famine, or an unsuccessful war; if the Tiber had, or the Nile had not risen above its banks; if the earth had shaken, or if the temperate order of the seasons had been interrupted, the superstitious pagans were convinced that the crimes and impurities of the Christians, who were spared by the excessive lenity of the government, had at length provoked the divine justice."† And however virtuous the emperors were, or however mild and equitable in character the governors of the provinces, it is certain that they did not hesitate to appease the rage of the people by sacrificing the obnoxious Christian victims. All this at a time, too, when religious tolerance and in large measure even religious freedom were enjoyed by those of all other religions within the empire, and in fact we may say that the persecution of the Christians was the only circumstance which broke in upon the religious concord of the world. From the apologies of the early church fathers, addressed to some of the emperors of the second and third centuries, we find them making the most pathetic complaints to the effect, "that the Christians who obeyed the dictates, and solicited the liberty of conscience, were alone, among all the subjects of the Roman empire, excluded from the common benefits of their auspicious government."

Why was this? Surely it did not arise from any vicious principle inherent in the Christian religion itself. "If we seriously consider the purity of the Christian religion," remarks Gibbon, in the opening paragraph of his great treatise on the "*Conduct of the Roman Government Toward the Christians*," "the sanctity of its moral precepts, and the

* Tacitus Annal., lib. XV, ch. 44.

† "Decline and Fall," Vol. I, ch. 15.

innocence as well as the austere lives of the greater number of those who, during the first ages, embraced the faith of the gospel, we should naturally suppose that so benevolent a doctrine would have been received with due reverence even by the unbelieving world; that the learned and polite, however they might deride the miracles, would have esteemed the virtues of the new sect; and that the magistrates, instead of persecuting, would have protected an order of men who yielded the most passive obedience to the laws, though they declined the active cares of war and government. If, on the other hand, we recollect the universal tolerance of polytheism, as it was invariably maintained by the faith of the people, the incredulity of philosophers, and the policy of the Roman senate and emperors, we are at a loss to discover what new offense the Christians had committed, what new provocation could exasperate the mild indifference of antiquity, and what new motives could urge the Roman princes, who beheld without concern a thousand forms of religion subsisting in peace under their gentle sway, to inflict a severe punishment upon any part of their subjects who had chosen for themselves a singular but an inoffensive mode of faith and worship."*

What, then, I again ask, was the cause of the singular departure from the enlightened policy of the empire in granting religious toleration and even large religious freedom to its subjects? I am sure that modern Christians will scarcely be satisfied with the various causes assigned for this strange conduct on the part of the Roman emperors who persecuted the Christians. These causes, or at least the principal ones, are conceded by both infidel and Christian authorities to be:

First, the Christians were a sect and not a nation, and were open to the charge that they had deserted the faith of their forefathers, a thing inexplicable to the Roman mind. It could be claimed on the part of the Christians, of course, that this was not true; that so far were they from deserting the faith of their fathers, that their present Christian faith was but the complement of their fathers' faith, the fulfillment alike of its prophecies and symbols—in a word, the gospel was the fulfillment of the law. This, however, was a refinement of explanation to which the haughty Romans could not be expected to give attention.

Second, the Christians condemned and abhorred the public religion of the state, so closely connected with the affairs of the government, and hence they were judged to be enemies of the state, a circumstance which made them objects of detestation to those intrusted with the administration of the laws.

* "History of the Decline and Fall of the Roman Empire," ch. 16.

Third, the Christians in their worship employed no images, nor temples, nor incense, nor sacrifices; neither did they represent their God by any corporeal figure or symbol, therefore they were adjudged to be atheists, and accordingly detested.

Fourth, the gloom and austere aspect of the Christians, and their thorough abhorrence of the common business and pleasures of life, their denunciation of war, together with their frequent predictions of impending divine judgments, caused them to be regarded as the enemies of mankind.

Fifth, the secrecy in which they conducted their religious services (a policy first born of necessity, because of the fear of their adversaries, and afterwards continued under the false notion that it would render their sacred institutions more respectable) drew upon them the suspicion that they only "concealed what they would have blushed to disclose;" and this left them open to the misrepresentation and calumny of their enemies, by which the fury of the multitude was aroused against them.

Sixth, the severe simplicity of the Christian mode of worship, employing as it did neither sacrifices nor an elaborate priesthood—excited the animosity of the pagan priests and their servitors, in exact proportion as the Christians became a menace to their occupation; for it was painfully apparent to them that if Christianity was successful there would be no need of the pagan priesthood—its occupation would be gone.

All these alleged causes for the persecution of the Christians within the Roman empire may be allowed, though some of them may be more properly regarded as pretexts for, than causes of the persecution. But back of all the assigned causes—which are at best but secondary in their nature—one may see moving a force, the primary cause of the persecution, of which the apprehensions of magistrates, the hatred of the pagan priesthood, and the clamor of the multitude were but the outward manifestations. That primary cause of the persecution of the Christians is to be found in the bitter hatred of that dark spirit who in heaven, before he fell from his high estate, was known under the splendid appellation of "The Light Bearer," "Lucifer," "Son of the Morning," as high in favor as in station, before his sin of rebellion against the Father-God.*

Beyond the mere fact that he impiously did rebel in heaven against God, and that he was impelled thereto by a vaulting ambition which overleaped itself, the Hebrew scriptures give us little information concerning Lucifer. No cause for the rebellion is assigned, though evidence

* Isaiah 14: 12-15. Doc. and Cov., sec. 76: 25-9.

of the fact and reality of the rebellion is abundant.* In some ancient scripture revealed to Joseph Smith, however, the cause of that Lucifer-led rebellion is stated. It was immediately connected with man's earth-life, and the means and conditions of his salvation.

In order that the reader may appreciate the force of the truth to be presented, it is necessary to remind him that the spirit of man had an existence before he dwelt in his body of flesh and bones—a self-conscious existence, in which he possessed all the faculties and attributes that the spirit or mind of man now possesses; that the time had come when the present earth-life became necessary to his continued progress; that all that would take place in that earth-life was known to God—the fall of man, the wickedness of the human race, the redemption through the atonement of a sinless sacrifice—all was known, and for all these events ample provisions were to be made; one chosen to open the series of dispensations that should make up the history of man's earth-life; one chosen to redeem man from his fallen state. It was at this point that Lucifer came before the grand council in heaven saying: Behold—here am I, send me, I will be Thy son, and I will redeem all mankind, that one soul shall not be lost, and surely *I will do it;* wherefore give me Thine honor. "But, behold," said the Lord, "My Beloved Son, which was My Beloved and Chosen from the beginning, said unto Me—Father, Thy will be done, and the glory be Thine forever. Wherefore, because that Satan rebelled against Me, and sought to destroy the agency of man, which I, the Lord God, had given him; and also that I should give unto him Mine own power; by the power of Mine Only Begotten, I caused that he should be cast down; and he became Satan, yea, even the devil, the father of all lies, to deceive and to blind men, and to lead them captive at his will, even as many as would not hearken unto My voice."†

This discloses the reason of Lucifer's rebellion—opposition to the plan of man's redemption—a counter plan that involved the destruction of the agency of man. Then what?

"I beheld Satan," says Jesus, "as lightning fall from heaven."‡

"And the angels which kept not their first estate, but left their own habitation, He hath reserved in everlasting chains, under darkness, unto the judgment of the great day."§

"And there was war in heaven: Michael and his angels fought

* See Luke 10: 17, 18. John 8: 44. Rev. 12. In the light of these references consider also Isaiah 14: 12-5, and Doc. and Cov. section 76: 25-9.

† Pearl of Great Price, chapter 4: 1-4.

‡ Luke 10: 18.

§ Jude 1: 6

against the dragon: and the dragon fought and his angels, and prevailed not; neither was their place found any more in heaven. And the great dragon was cast out, that old serpent, called the devil, and Satan, which deceiveth the whole world; he was cast out into the earth, and his angels were cast out with him. And I heard a loud voice saying in heaven, Now is come salvation, and strength, and the kingdom of our God, and the power of His Christ: for the accuser of our brethren is cast down, which accused them before our God day and night. And they overcame him by the blood of the Lamb, and by the word of their testimony; and they loved not their lives unto the death. Therefore rejoice, ye heavens, and ye that dwell in them. Woe to the inhabiters of the earth, and of the sea! for the devil is come down unto you, having great wrath, because he knoweth that he hath but a short time."*

Lucifer, then, becomes a factor to be reckoned with in the persecution of the Saints. In heaven he opposed the gospel of Jesus Christ; cast out into the earth will he not oppose it there? Herein lies the real cause of the persecution of the Christians within the Roman empire. So long as the inhabitants of the earth were content with the pagan superstitions, wherein there was no power of God unto salvation; so long as they were content with conflicting pagan philosophies, wherein was no power of God unto salvation, it was a matter of indifference to Lucifer whether they worshiped Jupiter Olympus, or Isis; Apollo, or Minerva; or bowed at the philosopher's shrine of the Unknown God—all were equally barren of saving power and left the kingdom of Lucifer undiminished in its strength and numbers; left all nations in his thraldom. But when the Christ and His apostles came preaching repentance and the coming of the kingdom of heaven; making known the origin of man and his relationship to Deity; making known the purpose of God to redeem him from his fallen state; establishing His Church as the depository of divine truth, and the instrumentality for conveying to man divine instruction—then Lucifer saw cause for alarm, for it was evident that the days of his dominion were numbered; his kingdom must decline if Christianity prevailed; his sway over the kingdoms of the earth must be broken if Christ was preached: and hence in all the bitterness of hatred, with all the strength of his cunning, with all the power of his resourcefulness, and using every instrumentality he could command—corrupted human nature over which he had influence; the apprehension of magistrates; the jealousy of pagan priesthoods—all were employed to destroy that institution wrought out in the wisdom of God to bring to pass the salvation of man; and hence the fire, the

* Rev. 12: 7-12.

sword and the rack; the lions, the dungeons,—in a word, the pagan persecutions of the Saints of God; Lucifer and his hatred of the truth the primary cause of all, all other causes and pretexts but secondary, mere instrumentalities used by him to impede the progress of and destroy, if possible, the truth, the gospel, wherein lies the power of man's salvation.

* * * * * * * *

It is said that history repeats itself; and this in matters of religion as in other things. In the introduction to the first volume of the Church History, the paganization of Christianity was discussed at some length, and when the Lord would again prepare the way for the incoming of the last dispensation of the Gospel—the dispensation of the fullness of times—as part of that preparation, He established a great republic in the New World, the chief corner stone of whose temple of liberty was religious freedom. The Congress of the United States, by express provision of the Constitution, is prohibited from making any law respecting an establishment of religion, or prohibiting the free exercise thereof.* Similar guarantees of religious freedom are provided for in the constitutions of all the states. The clause in Missouri's constitution on the subject was as follows:

"All men have a natural and indefeasible right to worship Almighty God according to the dictates of their own consciences; that no man can be compelled to erect, support or attend any place of worship, or to maintain any minister of the gospel or teacher of religion; that no human authority can control or interfere with the rights of conscience; that no person can ever be hurt, molested or restrained in his religious professions or sentiments, if he do not disturb others in their religious worship: that no person, on account of his religious opinions, can be rendered ineligible to any office of trust or profit under this state; that no preference can ever be given by law to any sect or mode of worship; and that no religious corporation can ever be established in this state."

Under these guarantees of religious liberty, in both state and national constitutions, infidels, Jews, and all sects of the Christian religion lived in unbroken peace. In the colonial history of the country there had been some intolerance and acts of violence practiced by the sects of Christians on one another, but in the main, and especially since the establishment of the republic of the United States, under its present Constitution, there had been absolute religious freedom. But now a strange thing occurred. A youth, yet in his early teens, startled the neighborhood in which he resided with the announcement that he had received a revelation from God; a new dispensation of the Gospel of Christ had been committed to him; he is authorized to found again the very

* First Amendment, Constitution of the United States.

Church of Christ; men are to teach once more by divine authority; and the world is to be made ready for the incoming of the glorious kingdom, whose king shall be the resurrected, glorified Christ; and peace and truth and righteousness are to abound. Strangely enough, notwithstanding all the guarantees of religious freedom in the state and national constitutions, this proclamation is resented by the people, and those who advocate it are persecuted in various ways, until at the last, as set forth in the three volumes of the Church History now published, it culminated in the death and misery of many souls, and the final expulsion of from twelve to fifteen thousand Saints from the state of Missouri, under all the circumstances of cruelty detailed in this history.

Why is this violence done to the principle of religious freedom, a principle that is both the pride and boast of the American people? Why are constitutions and institutions violated in efforts made by the authorities of the sovereign state of Missouri to destroy this religion and this Church of Christ? What is the cause of these Missouri persecutions? In view of the principles already set forth in these pages, the primary cause of these persecutions in Missouri will not be difficult to find. In them, as in the Roman persecutions of the Christians, the cunning and power of Lucifer will be apparent. So long as only apostate forms of Christianty obtained; so long as men adhered to mere forms of godliness and denied the power thereof, so long Lucifer cared not with what devotion they clung to these lifeless forms of religion. He laughed; his kingdom was undiminished; the nations were held in his thraldom. But when the Prophet of the dispensation of the fulness of times announced his revelation; when God again stood revealed once more before a witness; when the divine plan of life and salvation was again communicated to men through an inspired prophet; when the Church of Christ in all its completeness and power was restored to the earth, then it behoved Lucifer to look to his dominions, to strengthen his forces, and to prepare for the final conflict for possession of this world; for now God had taken it in hand to complete His work of redeeming the earth, of saving men, and overthrowing Lucifer and his power so far as this earth is concerned; and hence when Joseph Smith announced his new revelation, the incoming of the dispensation of the fulness of times, Lucifer with all the cunning and power at his command, and setting in motion every force—the fears and jealousies of men, misrepresentation and calumny, hatred of righteousness and truth, in a word, every force that he could summons, every pretext that he could suggest to men of evil disposed minds was employed to destroy the inauguration of that work which was to subdue his power, conquer his dominions, and render men free from his influence. Lucifer's bitterness, then, his hatred, his cunning, his devisements were the cause of the Missouri persecutions. All else was secondary, pretext, his instrumentalities, nothing more.

Retribution.

But what of Missouri? Missouri, who had violated her constitution which guaranteed religious freedom to all who came within her borders! Missouri, whose officers from the Governor down entered into a wicked conspiracy, contrary to all law and righteousness, and drove the Saints from the state! Missouri, who had violated not only her own constitution by becoming a party to a religious persecution, but had also violated the spirit of our times, and outraged the civilization of the nineteenth century—what of Missouri? Did she pay any penalty for her wrong-doing? Are states such entities as may be held to an accounting for breaches of public faith and public morals—constitutional immoralities? Is there within the state a public conscience to which an appeal can be made; and in the event of the public conscience being outraged is there retribution?

I answer these questions in the affirmative; and hold that Missouri paid dearly for the violations of her guarantees of religious freedom, and her lawlessness and her cruelties practiced towards the Latter-day Saints.

I have already referred to the relationship which the state of Missouri sustained to the great question of slavery. By the political compromise which bore her name, Missouri became a "cape of slavery thrust into free territory." Except for the state of Missouri alone, her southern boundary line was to mark the furthermost point northward beyond which slavery must not be extended into the territory of the United States. In 1854, however, the Missouri compromise was practically overthrown by the introduction into Congress of the "Kansas-Nebraska Act," by Stephen A. Douglas, United States senator from Illinois. This act provided for the organization of two new territories from the Louisiana purchase, west of Missouri and Iowa. The act proposed that the new territories should be open to slavery, if their inhabitants desired it. This left the question of slavery in the status it occupied previous to the Missouri Compromise, and left the people in the prospective states to determine for themselves whether slavery should or should not prevail in their state. This opened again the slavery question, and there was begun that agitation which finally resulted in the great American Civil War.

As soon as it became apparent that the people of new territories were to determine for themselves the question of slavery, very naturally each party began a struggle for possession of the new territory according as its sentiments or interests dictated. The struggle began by the abolition party of the north organizing "Emigrant Aid Societies," and sending emigrants of their own faith into Kansas. The slave holders of Missouri also sent settlers representing their faith and interests into the new territory in the hope of bringing it into the Union as a slave state. This brought on a border warfare in which the settlements of western Missouri and eastern Kansas alternately suffered from the raids and counter raids of the respective parties through some six years before the outbreak of the Civil War. As to which were the more lawless or cruel, the fanatical abolitionists or the pro-slavery party, the "jayhawkers," as the organized bands of ruffians of the former party were called, or the "bushwhackers," as the similarly organized bands of the pro-slavery men were called, is not a question necessary for me to discuss here. Both held the laws in contempt, and vied with each other in committing atrocities. The western counties of Missouri, where the Latter-day Saints had suffered so cruelly at the hands of people of those counties some eighteen or twenty years before, were in this border warfare laid desolate, and all the hardships the Missourians had inflicted upon the Saints were now visited upon their heads, only more abundantly.

Speaking of the situation in Missouri in 1861, the out-going Governor, Robert M. Stewart, in his address to the legislature, and referring to Missouri and her right to be heard on the slavery question, said:

"Missouri has a right to speak on this subject, because she has suffered. Bounded on three sides by free territory, her border counties have been the frequent scenes of kidnapping and violence, and this state has probably lost as much, in the last two years, in the abduction of slaves, as all the rest of the Southern States. *At this moment several of the western counties are desolated, and almost depopulated, from fear of a bandit horde, who have been committing depredations—arson, theft, and foul murder—upon the adjacent border*"*

Brigadier-General Daniel M. Frost, who had been employed in repressing lawlessness in the western counties of Missouri, in reporting conditions prevailing there in November, 1860, said:

"The deserted and charred remains of once happy homes, combined with the general terror that prevailed amongst the citizens who still clung to their possessions, gave but too certain proof of the persecution to which they had all been subjected, and which they would again have to endure, with renewed violence, so soon as armed protection should be withdrawn."* "In view of this condition of affairs," continues the historian of Missouri I am quoting, "and in order to carry out fully Governor Stewart's order to repel invasions and restore peace to the border, General Frost determined to leave a considerable force in

* "The Fight for Missouri," (Snead) p. 14.

the threatened district. Accordingly, a battalion of volunteers, consisting of three companies of rangers and one of artillery, was enlisted, and Lieutenant-Colonel John S. Bowen, who afterwards rose to high rank in the Confederate service, was chosen to the command."*

"With the organization of this force, and perhaps owing also, in some degree, to the inclemency of the season, 'jayhawking,' as such, came to an end, though the thing itself, during the first two or three years of the Civil War, and, in fact, as long as there was anything left on the Missouri side of the border worth taking, flourished more vigorously than ever. The old jayhawking leaders, however, now came with United States commissions in their pockets and at the head of regularly enlisted troops, in which guise they carried on a system of robbery and murder that left a good portion of the frontier south of the Missouri river as perfect a waste as Germany was at the end of the Thirty Years' War."†

While this description confines the scenes of violence and rapine to the border counties south of the Missouri river,—it included Jackson county, however, which was one of the heaviest sufferers both in this border warfare and subsequently during the Civil War—still, the counties north of that stream also suffered from lawlessness and violence.

At the outbreak of the Civil War Missouri was peculiarly situated. She was surrounded on three sides by free states. The great majority of her own people were for the Union, but her government, with Clairborne Jackson as the state executive, was in sympathy with the South. As the extreme Southern States one after another seceded from the Union, Missouri was confronted with the question: What position she ought to assume in the impending conflict. The question was referred to a state convention in which appeared no secessionists. Indeed, the people of Missouri in this election by a majority of eighty thousand decided against secession. The convention, in setting forth the attitude of the state on the subject, said that Missouri's position was, "Evidently that of a state whose interests are bound up in the maintenance of the Union, and whose kind feelings and strong sympathies are with the people of the Southern States, with whom we are connected by ties of friendship and blood. We want the peace and harmony of the country restored, and we want them with us. To go with them as they are now * * * * is to ruin ourselves without doing them any good."‡

While this doubtless voiced the sentiment of a great majority of Mis-

* "American Commonwealths, Missouri," p. 258.

† "American Commonwealths, Missouri," p. 259.

‡ "American Commonwealths, Missouri," (Carr) p. 288.

souri's people, the government of the state and many thousands of its inhabitants sympathized with the South. The general assembly of the state authorized the raising and equipment of large military forces held subject, of course, to the orders of the governor, under the pretense of being prepared to repel invasion from any quarter whatsoever, and enable the state to maintain a neutral attitude. The governor refused to raise Missouri's quota of four regiments under President Lincoln's first call for seventy-five thousand men to suppress the rebellion, on the ground that these regiments were intended to form "part of the President's army, to make war upon the people of the seceded states." This he declared to be illegal, unconstitutional, and therefore could not be complied with. This precipitated a conflict between the state and national forces that resulted in a civil war within the state since some of her citizens sided with the general government and some with the state.

On the 20th of April, 1861, the state militia under the governor's orders captured the Federal arsenal at Liberty, Clay county, and in the nineteen months following that event "over three hundred battles and skirmishes were fought within the limits of the state," and it is assumed that in the last two years of the war, there were half as many more; "and it may be said of them," continues our historian, "that they were relatively more destructive of life, as by this time the contest had degenerated into a disgraceful internecine struggle."*

In the fall of 1864, General Sterling Price penetrated the state at the head of twelve thousand men; captured Lexington, in Ray county, and Independence, in Jackson county, and thence made his escape into Arkansas. "In the course of this raid he marched 1,434 miles, fought forty-three battles and skirmishes, and according to his own calculation destroyed upwards of 'ten million dollars' worth of property,' a fair share of which belonged to his own friends."†

In August, 1863, the celebrated Military Order No. 11 was issued from Kansas City, by General Thomas Ewing, by which "all persons living in Cass, Jackson, and Bates counties, Missouri, and in that part of Vernon included in this district, except those living within one mile of the limits of Independence, Hickman's Mills, Pleasant Hill, and Harrisonville, and except those in that part of Kaw township, Jackson county, north of Brush creek and west of the Big Blue, embracing Kansas City and Westport, are hereby ordered to remove from their present places of residence within fifteen days from the date hereof.

* "American Commonwealths, Missouri." p. 342.

† History of Missouri, Carr, p. 360. General Price was the Colonel Sterling Price, who held the Prophet Joseph in custody at Richmond in 1838, who shackled the brethren and whose scurrilous guards were so severely rebuked by the Prophet.—History of the Church, Vol. III, p. 208, Note.

Those who, within that time, establish their loyalty to the satisfaction of the commanding officer of the military station nearest their present place of residence, will receive from him certificates stating the fact of their loyalty, and the names of the witnesses by whom it can be shown. All who receive such certificates will be permitted to remove to any military station in this district, or to any part of the state of Kansas, except the counties on the eastern borders of the state. All others shall remove out of this district. Officers commanding companies and detachments serving in the counties named will see that this paragraph is promptly obeyed."*

The admonition in the last clause to commanding officers was rigidly followed; and within the district named scenes of violence and cruelty were appalling. This order with its cruel execution has been more severely criticized than any other act during the entire Civil War. The justification for it has been urged on the ground that Jackson county afforded a field of operations for Confederates; that here the bushwhacking marauders recruited their forces, and found the means of support; that the policy was necessary on the ground of putting an end to that kind of warfare. On the other hand, it is contended that "tried by any known standard," the people in that section of Missouri were as loyal to the Union as were their neighbors in Kansas. "They had voted against secession; they had not only, thus far, kept their quota in the Union army full, and that without draft or bounty, but they continued to do so; and if they did not protect themselves against the outrages alike of Confederate bushwhackers and Union jayhawkers, it was because early in the war they had been disarmed by Federal authority and were consequently without the means of defense."†

By the execution of the order, however, the people in the districts named "were driven from their homes, their dwellings burned, their farms laid waste, and the great bulk of their movable property handed over, without let or hindrance, to the Kansas 'jayhawkers.' It was a brutal order, ruthlessly enforced, but so far from expelling or exterminating the guerrillas, it simply handed the whole district over to them." "Indeed," continues Lucien Carr, "we are assured by one who was on the ground, that from this time until the end of the war, no one wearing the Federal uniform dared risk his life within the devatasted region. The only people whom the enforcement of the order did injure were some thousands of those whom it was Ewing's duty to protect."‡

* "History of Caldwell and Livingston Counties," p. 51.

† "American Commonwealths, Missouri," p. 351.

‡ Ibid, p. 351.

Whether justified or not by the attitude of the Jackson county people in the Civil War, the execution of Order No. 11 certainly was but a re-enactment, though upon a larger scale, of those scenes which the inhabitants of that section of the country thirty years before had perpetrated upon the Latter-day Saints in expelling them from Jackson county. The awful scenes then enacted inspired the now celebrated painting by G. C. Bingham, bearing the title "Civil War," and dedicated by the artist "to all who cherish the principles of civil liberty."

Connected with the scenes of civil strife in Missouri, is a prophecy uttered by Joseph Smith many years before they began, and recently published in a very able paper by Elder Junius F. Wells, in the November number of the *Improvement Era* for 1902. Elder Wells, it appears, had the pleasure of an interview with the Hon. Leonidas M. Lawson, of New York city, formerly a resident of Clay county, Missouri, and a brother-in-law of General Alexander W. Doniphan, whose name so frequently occurs in our pages, dealing with events in the history of the Church while in Missouri.

In the course of the interview, which took place at the University Club, New York city, Mr. Lawson referred to an incident connected with a visit to General Doniphan in 1863. General Doniphan, it will be remembered by those acquainted with his history, took no part in the Civil War beyond that of a sorrowful spectator. On the occasion of Mr. Lawson's visit to him, just referred to, they rode through Jackson county together, and in a letter to Elder Wells, under date of February 7, 1902, Mr. Lawson relates the following incident, which is part of a biographical sketch of General Doniphan, prepared by Mr. Lawson:

"In the year 1863, I visited General A. W. Doniphan at his home in Liberty, Clay county, Missouri. This was soon after the devastation of Jackson county, Missouri, under what is known as 'Order No. 11.' This devastation was complete. Farms were everywhere destroyed, and the farmhouses were burned. During this visit General Doniphan related the following historical facts and personal incidents:

"About the year 1831-2, the Mormons settled in Jackson county, Mo., under the leadership of Joseph Smith. The people of Jackson county became dissatisfied with their presence, and forced them to leave; and they crossed the Missouri river and settled in the counties of De Kalb, Caldwell and Ray. They founded the town of Far West, and began to prepare the foundation of a temple. It was here that the troubles arose which culminated in the expulsion of the Mormons from the state of Missouri according to the command of Governor Lilburn W. Boggs. This was known in Missouri annals as the Mormon War. There were many among those who obeyed the order of the governor, in the state militia, who believed that the movement against the Mormons was unjust and cruel, and that the excitement was kept up by those who coveted the homes, the barns and the fields of the Mormon people. The latter, during their residence in the state of Missouri, paid, in entry fees for the land they claimed, to the United States government land office, more than $300,000, which, for that period represented a tremendous interest. During their sojourn in Missouri the Mormons did not practice or teach polygamy, so that question did not enter into it.

"Following the early excitement, Joseph Smith was indicted for treason against the state of Missouri, and General Doniphan was one of the counsel employed to defend him, he having shown a friendly interest in Smith, whom he considered very badly treated. Joseph Smith was placed in prison in Liberty, Missouri, to await his trial. This place was the residence of General Doniphan. His partner in the practice of law was James H. Baldwin.

"On one occasion General Doniphan caused the sheriff of the county to bring Joseph Smith from the prison to his law office, for the purpose of consultation about his defense. During Smith's presence in the office, a citizen of Jackson county, Missouri, came in for the purpose of paying a fee which was due by him to the firm of Doniphan and Baldwin, and offered in payment a tract of land in Jackson county.

"Doniphan told him that his partner, Mr. Baldwin, was absent at the moment, but as soon as he had an opportunity he would consult him and decide about the matter. When the Jackson county man retired, Joseph Smith, who had overheard the conversation, addressed General Doniphan about as follows:

" '*Doniphan, I advise you not to take that Jackson county land in payment of the debt. God's wrath hangs over Jackson county. God's people have been ruthlessly driven from it, and you will live to see the day when it will be visited by fire and sword. The Lord of Hosts will sweep it with the besom of destruction. The fields and farms and houses will be destroyed, and only the chimneys will be left to mark the desolation.*' "

"General Doniphan said to me that the devastation of Jackson county forcibly reminded him of this remarkable prediction of the Mormon prophet." (signed) L. M. LAWSON.

"There is a prediction of the Prophet Joseph," remarks Elder Wells, in commenting upon Mr. Lawson's story, "not before put into print, and history has recorded its complete fulfillment."

That a just retribution overtook the entire state, as well as the inhabitants of Jackson county, and other western counties, I think must be conceded by all who are familiar with the events of her history in the Civil War. That which she did to an inoffensive people was done to her inhabitants, especially to those living within the districts formerly occupied by the Latter-day Saints; only the measure meted out to the Missourians was heaped up, pressed down, and made to run over.

The Missourians had complained that the Latter-day Saints were eastern men, whose manners, habits, customs, and even dialect were different from their own;* but the Missourians lived to see great throngs of those same eastern men flock into an adjoining territory and infest their border, so that the settlers of western Missouri became accustomed to, and learned to endure the strange manners, customs and dialect so different from their own.

The Missourians complained of the rapidity with which the Saints were gathering into the state to establish their Zion; but the Missourians lived to see hordes of the detested easterners gather into their region of country by continuous streams of emigrant trains, sent there by "Emigrant Aid Companies" of New England.

The Missourians falsely charged that the coming of "Zion's Camp" into western Missouri to aid their brethren to repossess their homes in Jackson county, was an armed invasion of the state; but the Missourians lived to see formidable hosts of eastern and northern men gather upon their frontiers and frequently invade the state. "The character of much of this emigration may be gathered," says one historian, "from the fact that the Kansas Emigration Societies, Leagues and Committees * * * *sent out men only*;" and that in some of their bands Sharp's rifles were more numerous than agricultural implements."† Of course the "Blue Lodges" of Missouri were organized largely on the same principle as the "Emigrant Aid Companies" of New England, and adopted practically the same methods, expecting to add Kansas to the list of slave states. But "certainly," remarks Lucien Carr, "if a company of so-called northern emigrants, in which there were two hundred and twenty-five men and only five women, whose wagons contained no visible furniture, agricultural implements or mechanical tools, but abounded in all the requisite articles for camping and campaigning purposes, were considered as *bona fide* settlers and permitted to vote, there could not have been a sufficient reason for ruling out any band of Missourians who ever crossed the border and declared their intention of remaining, even though they left the next day."‡

Among the men sent to the borders of Missouri by the "Emigrant Aid Companies" of New England were some of the most desperate adventurers; and the Missourians who had pretended to be alarmed at the coming of "Zion's Camp," and feigned to regard it as an armed invasion

* Minutes of Citizen Meeting, Liberty, Clay county, Church History Vol. III, p. 450.

† History of Missouri, Carr, p. 343, Note.

‡ History of Missouri, Carr, 245.

of the state, saw their state repeatedly invaded—especially Jackson county—by the bands of Union "jayhawkers" organized from among these desperate eastern and northern men, who ruthlessly laid waste their homes and farms.

The Missourians had falsely charged the Saints with abolition madness, with tampering with their slaves, with inviting free negroes into the state to corrupt their blacks, whose very presence would render their institution of slave labor insecure; but they lived to see their system of slave labor abolished by the setting free of some one hundred and fifteen thousand slaves, valued at $40,000,000, eight thousand of whom were "martialed and disciplined for war" in the Federal armies, and many of them marched to war against their former masters.

Governor Dunklin and his advisors in the government of Missouri claimed that there was no warrant of authority under the laws and constitution of the state for calling out a permanent military force to protect the Saints in the peaceful possession of their homes until the civil authority proved itself competent to keep the peace and protect the citizens in the enjoyment of their guaranteed rights; but the people in the western part of Missouri saw the time come when they themselves prayed for the same protection; and Governor Stewart, unlike Governor Dunklin, approved the appointment of a battalion of volunteers consisting of three companies of rangers and one of artillery, all of which were placed under command of Lieutenant-Colonel John L. Bowen, to do the very thing the Saints had prayed might be done in their case.* But even this provision for their protection did not avail; for their old jayhawking enemies soon reappeared under new conditions —which will be stated in the next paragraph—under which they renewed their incursions of rapine and murder.

The state authorities of Missouri converted the mobs which had plundered the Saints, burned their homes and laid waste their lands, into the state militia, which gave the former mob a legal status, under which guise they plundered the Saints, compelled them to sign away their property and agree to leave the state. To resist this mob-militia was to be guilty of treason; but the people of western Missouri lived to see a like policy pursued towards them. They suffered much in Jackson and other western counties in the border war, previous to the opening of the Civil War, from the inroads of abolition "jayhawkers" in the interest of anti-slavery. For a time this was in part suppressed by the state militia under General Frost and by the permanent force stationed on the border under Lieutenant-Colonel Bowen. But later, and when the Civil War broke out, these old "jayhawking" leaders "now came with United States commissions in their pockets, and at the head of regularly enlisted troops, in which guise they carried on a sys-

* History of Missouri, Carr, p. 158.

tem of robbery and murder that left a good portion of the frontier south of the Missouri river as perfect a waste as Germany was at the end of the Thirty Years' War."*

Such wretches as Generals Lane and Jennison, though Union officers, and denounced alike by Governor Robinson of Kansas—of course a strong Union man—and General Halleck,† commander-in-chief of the western armies of the Union, were permitted to disgrace alike the Union cause and our human nature by their unspeakable atrocities. But they were retained in office, nevertheless. It was the outrages committed by these men and their commands, and the Kansas "Red Legs" that led to the equally savage reprisals on the people of Kansas. In revenge for what western Missouri had suffered, outlawed Missourians sacked Lawrence, Kansas, a Union city, massacred one hundred and eighty-three of its inhabitants, and left it in flames. In justification of their act of savagery, they declared: "Jennison has laid waste our homes, and the 'Red Legs' have perpetrated unheard of crimes. Houses have been plundered and burned, defenseless men shot down, and women outraged. We are here for revenge—and we have got it."‡ How nearly this language of the Missourians—and there can be no question that it describes what had been done in Missouri by Lane, Jennison, and their commands, and the Kansas "Red Legs"§—follows the complaint justly made by the Latter-day Saints years before against the Missourians! But thank God, there is recorded against the Saints no such horrible deeds of reprisal.

The Missourians falsely charged that the Saints held illicit communication with the Indian tribes then assembled near the frontiers of the state, and pretended to an alarm that their state might be invaded by the savages, prompted thereto by "Mormon" fanaticism; but these same Missourians lived to see cause for real fear of such an invasion when the Governor of an adjoining state—Arkansas—authorize Brigadier General Albert Pike to raise two mounted regiments of Choctaw and Chickasaw Indians to actually invade the state. These regiments of savages were engaged in the battle of Pea Ridge, on the southwest

* History of Missouri, Carr, p. 259.

† General Halleck when he learned that the "jayhawking" leader, Lane, had been promoted to the command of a brigade, declared that such an appointment was "offering a premium for rascality and robbing generally;" and that it would "take twenty thousand men to counteract its effect in the state." History of Missouri, Carr, p. 348.

‡ Spring's Kansas, p. 287.

§ These were bands of Kansas robbers, whose custom it was at intervals to dash into Missouri, seize horses and cattle—not omitting other and worse crimes on occasion—then to repair with their booty to Lawrence, where it was defiantly sold at auction." History of Missouri, Carr, p. 348.

borders of Missouri. General Pike, who led them in that battle, dressed himself in gaudy, savage costume, and wore a large plume on his head —*a la Niel Gilliam* at Far West—to please the Indians. It is also charged that before the battle of Pea Ridge, he maddened his Indians with liquor "that they might allow the savage nature of their race to have unchecked development. In their fury they respected none of the usages of civilized warfare, but scalped the helpless wounded, and committed atrocities too horrible to mention."* The "fear" expressed by the Missourians respecting the alleged illicit communication of the Saints with the Indians was mere feigning, but with this example before them, and knowing that there were many thousands of Indians on their frontiers that might be similarly induced to take up arms, their former feigned fears became real ones.

The Missourians instead of demanding the execution of the law in support of the liberties of the Saints, expressed the fear that the presence of the Saints would give rise to "Civil War," in which none could be neutrals, since their homes must be the theatre on which it would be fought,† so they drove the Saints away; but the Missourians lived to see the outbreak of a civil war in their state that was one of the most appalling men ever witnessed; and Missouri, when all things are considered, and especially western Missouri, suffered more than any other state of the Union. In other states the war lasted at most but four years; but counting her western border warfare in the struggle for Kansas, the war was waged in western Missouri from 1855 to 1865, ten years; and for many years after the close of the Civil War, a guerrilla warfare was intermittently carried on by bands of outlaws harbored in western Missouri—especially in Jackson, Ray, Caldwell and Clay counties—that terrorized the community and shocked the world by the daring and atrocity of their crimes—including bank robberies in open day, express train wrecking and robberies, and murders. Not until 1881 was this effectually stopped by the betrayal and murder of the outlaw chief of these bands.

Missouri sent into the Union Armies one hundred and nine thousand of her sons, including eight thousand negroes. About thirty thousand enlisted in the confederate army. According to official reports the percentage of troops to population in the western states and territories was 13.6 per cent, and in the New England states 12 per cent; whilst in Missouri, if there be added to her quota sent to the northern army the thirty thousand sent to the confederate army, her percentage was fourteen per cent, *or sixty per cent of those who were subject to military duty.* Of the deaths among these enlisted men, only approximate esti-

* History of the United States, Lossing, p. 592—*note*.

† History of the Church, Vol. II, p. 450-1.

mates may be made, since of the mortality among the Confederates no official records were kept. But of those who entered the Union service, thirteen thousand eight hundred and eighty-five deaths are officially reported. The rate of mortality in the Confederate forces, owing to the greater hardships they endured, and the lack of medical attendants to care for the wounded, was much higher, and is generally estimated at twelve thousand, (most of whom were from western Missouri), which added to the deaths of those in the Union army would aggregate the loss among the troops from Missouri to twenty-five thousand eight hundred and eighty-five. "This estimate," says Lucien Carr, "does not cover those who were killed in the skirmishes that took place between the home guards and the guerrillas; nor does it include those who were not in either army, but who were shot down by "bushwhackers" and "bushwhacking" Federal soldiers. Of these latter there is no record, though there were but few sections of the state in which such scenes were not more or less frequent. Assuming the deaths from these two sources to have been 1,200, and summing up the results, it will be found that the number of Missourians who were killed in the war and died from disease during their term of service amounted to not less than 27,000 men."*

The loss in treasure was in full proportion to the loss in blood. The state expended $7,000,000 in fitting out and maintaining her Union troops in the field.† She lost $40,000,000 in slave property; and four years after the close of the war—two of which, 1867-8, were remarkably prosperous—the taxable wealth of the state was $46,000,000 less than it was in 1860. "In many portions of the state," says the historian to whom I am indebted for so many of the facts relating to Missouri in these pages, "especially in the southern and western borders, whole counties had been devastated. The houses were burned, the fences destroyed, and the farms laid waste. Much of the live stock of the state had disappeared; and everywhere, even in those sections that were comparatively quiet and peaceful, the quantity of land in cultivation was much less than it had been at the outbreak of the war. Added to these sources of decline, and in some measure a cause of them, was the considerable emigration from the state which now took place, and particularly from those regions that lay in the pathway of the armies, or from those neighborhoods that were given over to the "bushwhackers." The amount of loss from these different sources cannot be accurately gauged, but some idea may be formed of it, and of the unsettled condition of affairs, from the fact that only 41 out of the 113 counties in the state

* History of Missouri, Carr, p. 358.

† It is but proper, however, to say that the state was afterwards reimbursed for this amount by the general government.

receipted for the tax books for 1861; and in these counties, only $250,000 out of the $600,000 charged against them were collected."*

This only in a general way indicates the losses in property sustained by the state during the period under consideration, but it assists one to understand somewhat the enormity of those losses.

It is in no spirit of gloating exultation that these facts in Missouri's history are referred to here. It gives no gratification to the writer to recount the woes of Missouri, and his hope is that it will give none to the reader. These facts of history are set down only because they are valuable for the lesson they teach. It may be that visible retribution does not always follow in the wake of state or national wrong-doing; but it is well that it should sometimes do so, lest men should come to think that Eternal Justice sleeps, or may be thwarted, or, what would be worst of all, that she does not exist. I say it is well, therefore, that sometimes visible retribution should follow state and national as well as individual transgressions, that the truth of the great principle that "as men sow, so shall they reap," may be vindicated. Missouri in her treatment of the Latter-day Saints during the years 1833-9, sowed the wind; in the disastrous events which overtook her during the years 1855-65, she reaped the whirlwind. Let us hope that in those events Justice was fully vindicated so far as the state of Missouri is concerned; and that the lessons of her sad experience may not be lost to the world. May the awful and visible retribution visited upon Missouri teach all states and nations that when they feel power they must not forget Justice; may it teach all peoples that states and nations in their corporate capacity are such entities as may be held accountable before God and the world for their actions; that righteousness exalteth a nation, while injustice is a reproach to any people. May the retribution that was so palpably visited upon the state of Missouri satisfy and encourage the Latter-day Saints; not that I would see them rejoice in the suffering of the wicked; but rejoice rather in the evidence that Justice slumbereth not; that their wrongs are not hidden from the All-seeing eye of God; that they are within the circle of His love; that they cannot be unjustly assailed with impunity, however humble and weak they may be. From all these considerations may they be established in peace, hope, confidence and charity; knowing that God is their friend; that His arm is strong to protect; or, if in the course of God's economy in the management of the affairs of the world it must needs be that for a time they suffer at the hands of oppressors, that He will avenge them of their enemies; and amply reward them for their sufferings in His cause.

* History of Missouri, Carr, p. 359.

HISTORY

OF THE

CHURCH OF JESUS CHRIST OF LATTER-DAY SAINTS.

VOL. III.

HISTORY

OF THE

CHURCH OF JESUS CHRIST

OF

LATTER-DAY SAINTS.

PERIOD I.

HISTORY OF JOSEPH SMITH, THE PROPHET.

CHAPTER I.

THE PROPHET JOSEPH'S DEPARTURE FROM KIRTLAND AND ARRIVAL IN MISSOURI.

January, 1838.—A new year dawned upon the Church in Kirtland in all the bitterness of the spirit of apostate mobocracy; which continued to rage and grow hotter and hotter, until Elder Rigdon and myself were obliged to flee from its deadly influence, as did the Apostles and Prophets of old, and as Jesus said, "when they persecute you in one city, flee to another." On the evening of the 12th of January, about ten o'clock, we left Kirtland, on horseback, to escape mob violence, which was about to burst upon us under the color of legal process to cover the hellish designs of our enemies, and to save themselves from the just judgment of the law.

Flight of the Prophet and Sidney Rigdon from Kirtland.

We continued our travels during the night, and at eight o'clock on the morning of the 13th, arrived among the brothren in Norton Township, Medina county, Ohio, a distance of sixty miles from Kirtland. Here we tarried about thirty-six hours, when our families arrived; and on the 16th we pursued our journey with our families, in covered wagons towards the city of Far West, in Missouri. We passed through Dayton and Eaton, in Ohio, and Dublin, Indiana; in the latter place we tarried nine days, and refreshed ourselves.

About January 16, 1838, being destitute of money to pursue my journey, I said to Brother Brigham Young: "You are one of the Twelve who have charge of the kingdom in all the world; I believe I shall throw myself upon you, and look to you for counsel in this case." Brother Young thought I was not earnest, but I told him I was. Brother Brigham then said, "If you will take my counsel it will be that you rest yourself, and be assured you shall have money in plenty to pursue your journey."

Brigham Young to the Prophet's Rescue.

There was a brother living in the place who had tried for some time to sell his farm but could not; he asked counsel of Brother Young concerning his property; Brother Young told him that if he would do right, and obey counsel, he should have an opportunity to sell. In about three days Brother Tomlinson came to Brother Brigham and said he had an offer for his place; Brother Brigham told him that this was the manifestation of the hand of the Lord to deliver Brother Joseph Smith from his present necessities. Brother Brigham's promise was soon verified, and I got three hundred dollars from Brother Tomlinson, which enabled me to pursue my journey.*

The weather was extremely cold, we were obliged to secrete ourselves in our wagons, sometimes, to elude the

* This incident occurred at Dublin, Indiana, where, and after, the Prophet had sought for a job at cutting and sawing wood to relieve his necessities.—"Life of Brigham Young, (Tullidge), p. 85.

grasp of our pursuers, who continued their pursuit of us more than two hundred miles from Kirtland, armed with pistols and guns, seeking our lives. They frequently crossed our track, twice they were in the houses where we stopped, once we tarried all night in the same house with them, with only a partition between us and them; and heard their oaths and imprecations, and threats concerning us, if they could catch us; and late in the evening they came in to our room and examined us, but decided we were not the men. At other times we passed them in the streets, and gazed upon them, and they on us, but they knew us not. One Lyons was one of our pursuers.

The Bitterness of the Prophet's Enemies.

I parted with Brother Rigdon at Dublin, and traveling different routes we met at Terre Haute, where, after resting, we separated again, and I pursued my journey, crossing the Mississippi river at Quincy, Illinois.

The Prophet's Arrival in Missouri.

TRIAL OF THE FAR WEST PRESIDENCY OF THE CHURCH.

Minutes of the Proceedings of the Committee of the whole Church in Zion, in General Assembly, at the following places, to-wit: At Far West, February 5, 1838; Carter's Settlement on the 6th; Durphy's Settlement, on the 7th; Curtis' Dwelling-house on the 8th; and Haun's Mills on the 9th. Thomas B. Marsh, Moderator, John Cleminson, Clerk.

After prayer, the Moderator stated the object of the meeting, giving a relation of the recent organization of the Church here and in Kirtland. He also read a certain revelation given in Kirtland, September 3, 1837, which made known, that John Whitmer and W. W. Phelps, were in transgression, and if they repented not, they should be removed out of their places;* also read a certain clause contained in the appeal published in the old *Star*, on the 183rd page as follows:

"And to sell our lands would amount to a denial of our faith, as that is the place where the Zion of God shall stand, according to our faith and belief in the revelations of God."

Elder John Murdock then took the stand and showed to the congregation, why the High Council proceeded thus was that the Church

* See Vol. II, p. 511.

might have a voice in the matter; and that he considered it perfectly legal according to the instructions of President Joseph Smith, Jun.

Elder George M. Hinkle then set forth the way in which the Presidency of Far West had been labored with, that a committee of three, of whom he was one, had labored with them. He then read a written document, containing a number of accusations against the three presidents. He spoke many things against them, setting forth in a plain and energetic manner the iniquity of Elders Phelps and Whitmer, in using the monies which were loaned to the Church. Also David Whitmer's wrong-doing in persisting in the use of tea, coffee, and tobacco.

Bishop Partridge then arose and endeavored to rectify some mistakes of minor importance, made by Elder Hinkle; also the Bishop spoke against the proceedings of the meeting, as being hasty and illegal, for he thought they ought to be had before the Common Council, and said that he could not lift his hand against the Presidency at present. He then read a letter from President Joseph Smith, Jun.

A letter from William Smith was then read by Thomas B. Marsh, who made some comments on the same, and also on the letter read by Bishop Partridge.

Elder George Morey, who was one of the committee sent to labor with the Missouri Presidency, spoke, setting forth in a very energetic manner, the proceedings of that Presidency, as being iniquitous.

Elder Thomas Grover, also, being one of the committee, spoke against the conduct of the Presidency, and of Oliver Cowdery, on their visit to labor with them.

Elder David W. Patten spoke with much zeal against the Presidency, and in favor of Joseph Smith, Jun., and that the wolves alluded to, in his letter, were the dissenters in Kirtland.

Elder Lyman Wight stated that he considered all other accusations of minor importance compared to Brothers Phelps and Whitmer selling their lands in Jackson county; that they had set an example which all the Saints were liable to follow. He said that it was a hellish principle on which they had acted, and that they had flatly denied the faith in so doing.

Elder Elias Higbee sanctioned what had been done by the Council, speaking against the Presidency.

Elder Murdock stated that sufficient had been said to substantiate the accusations against them.

Elder Solomon Hancock pleaded in favor of the Presidency, stating that he could not raise his hand against them.

Elder John Corrill then spoke against the proceedings of the High Council and labored hard to show that the meeting was illegal, and that the Presidency ought to be arraigned before a proper tribunal, which he considered to be a Bishop and twelve High Priests. He labored in favor of the Presidency, and said that he should not raise his hands against them at present, although he did not uphold the Presidents in their iniquity.

Simeon Carter spoke against the meeting as being hasty.

Elder Groves followed Brother Carter in like observations.

Elder Patten again took the stand in vindication of the cause of the meeting.

Elder Morley spoke against the Presidency, at the same time pleading mercy.

Titus Billings said he could not vote until they had a hearing in the Common Council.*

Elder Marsh said that the meeting was according to the direction of Brother Joseph, he therefore considered it legal.

Elder Moses Martin spoke in favor of the legality of the meeting, and against the conduct of the Presidency, with great energy, alleging that the present corruptions of the Church here, were owing to the wickedness and mismanagement of her leaders.

The Moderator then called the vote in favor of the Missouri Presidency; the negative was then called, and the vote against David Whitmer, John Whitmer, and William W. Phelps was unanimous, excepting eight or ten, and this minority only wished them to continue in office a little longer, or until Joseph Smith, Jun., arrived.

THOMAS B. MARSH, Moderator,
JOHN CLEMINSON, Clerk.

Minutes of Proceedings in Other Settlements than Far West.

In Simeon Carter's settlement the Saints assembled on the 6th instant, when they unanimously rejected the three above-named Presidents. On

* The question raised here several times by the brethren, and hereafter alluded to by the defendants in the case, concerning the illegality of the Council attempting then to try David Whitmer, John Whitmer, and William W. Phelps, constituting the local Presidency of the Church in Missouri, grew out of a misapprehension of a council provided for in the revelations of God for the trial of a President of the High Priesthood, who is also of the Presidency of the whole Church. The said revelation provides that if a President of the High Priesthood, shall transgress, he shall be brought before the Presiding Bishop, or bishopric, of the Church, who are to be assisted by twelve counselors chosen from the High Priesthood. Here the President's conduct may be investigated, and the decision of that council upon his head is to be the end of controversy concerning him. (See Doc. and Cov., sec. 107: 76, 81, 82, 83). But the Presidency of the Church in Missouri was a local presidency, hence they could not plead the illegality of a local council of the Church to try them.

the 7th, the Saints assembled at Edmond Durphy's, agreeable to appointment, where the above-named Presidents were unanimously rejected; also on the 8th at Nahum Curtis' dwelling-house, they were unanimously rejected by the assembly; also at Haun's Mills, on the 9th, the Saints unanimously rejected them.

At a meeting of the High Council the Bishop and his counsel, February 10, 1838, it was moved, seconded, and carried, that Oliver Cowdery, William W. Phelps, and John Whitmer, stand no longer as chairman and clerks to sign and record licenses.

Voted that Thomas B. Marsh and David W. Patten be authorized to attend to such business for the time being.

Also voted that Thomas B. Marsh and David W. Patten be presidents, pro tempore, of the Church of Latter-day Saints in Missouri, until Presidents Joseph Smith, Jun., and Sidney Rigdon, arrive in the land of Zion.

J. MURDOCK, Moderator,
T. B. MARSH, Clerk.

High Council Meeting at Far West.

The High Council of Zion met in Far West, on Saturday, March 10, 1838, agreeable to adjournment; when after discussion it was resolved,

First—That the High Council recommend by writing to the various branches of this Church, that all those who wish to receive ordination, procure recommends from the branches to which they belong, and have such recommends pass through the hands of the different quorums for inspection, previous to the applicants' ordination.

Second—Resolved that the High Council recommend to all those who hold licenses, between the ages of eighteen and forty-five, and do not officiate in their respective offices, be subject to military duty.*

A charge was then preferred against William W. Phelps and John Whitmer, for persisting in unchristian-like conduct.

Six councilors were appointed to speak, viz., Simeon Carter, Isaac Higbee, and Levi Jackman, on the part of the accuser; and Jared Carter, Thomas Grover, and Samuel Bent, on the part of the accused; when the following letter, belonging to Thomas B. Marsh, was read by

* The law of Missouri excused from military duty all licensed ministers of the Gospel, and as nearly all the adult members of the Church who were worthy had received ordination to the Priesthood, it left the community in Far West, then a frontier country and liable to be raided by warlike tribes of Indians, without militia companies and state arms for its protection; hence the recommendation of the Council that the brethren within the ages specified, and not actively employed in the ministry, place themselves in a position to accept militia service.

Brother Marcellus F. Cowdery, bearer of the same, previous to giving it to its rightful owner:

"FAR WEST, March 10, 1838.

"Sir—It is contrary to the principles of the revelations of Jesus Christ and His gospel, and the laws of the land, to try a person for an offense by an illegal tribunal, or by men prejudiced against him, or by authority that has given an opinion or decision beforehand, or in his absence.

"Very respectfully we have the honor to be,

"DAVID WHITMER,
"WILLIAM W. PHELPS,
"JOHN WHITMER,
"Presidents of the Church of Christ in Missouri.

"To Thomas B. Marsh, one of the [Twelve] Traveling Councilors."

Attested: OLIVER COWDERY,
Clerk of the High Council of the Church of Christ in Missouri.

I certify the foregoing to be a true copy from the original.

OLIVER COWDERY,
Clerk of the High Council.

All the effect the above letter had upon the Council, was to convince them still more of the wickedness of those men, by endeavoring to palm themselves off upon the Church, as her Presidents, after the Church had by a united voice, removed them from their presidential office, for their ungodly conduct; and the letter was considered no more nor less than a direct insult or contempt cast upon the authorities of God, and the Church of Jesus Christ; therefore the Council proceeded to business.

A number of charges were sustained against these men, the principal of which was claiming $2,000 Church funds, which they had subscribed for building a house to the Lord in this place, when they held in their possession the city plat, and were sitting in the presidential chair; which subscription they were intending to pay from the avails of the town lots; but when the town plat was transferred into the hands of the Bishop for the benefit of the Church, it was agreed that the Church should take this subscription off the hands of W. W. Phelps and John Whitmer; but in the transaction of the business, they bound the Bishop in a heavy mortgage, to pay them the above $2,000, in two years from the date thereof, a part of which they had already received, and claimed the remainder.

The six councilors made a few appropriate remarks, but none felt to plead for mercy, as it had not been asked on the part of the accused, and all with one consent declared that justice ought to have her demands.

After some remarks by Presidents Marsh and Patten, setting forth the iniquity of those men in claiming the $2,000 spoken of, which did not belong to them, any more than to any other person in the Church, it was decided that William W. Phelps and John Witmer be no longer members of the Church of Christ of Latter-day Saints, and be given over to the buffetings of Satan, until they learn to blaspheme no more against the authorities of God, nor fleece the flock of Christ.

The Council was then asked if they concurred with the decision, if so, to manifest it by rising; they all arose.

The vote was then put to the congregation, and was carried unanimously.

The negative was called, but no one voted.

Brother Marcellus F. Cowdery arose and said he wished to have it understood that he did not vote either way, because he did not consider it a legal tribunal. He also offered insult to the High Council, and to the Church, by reading a letter belonging to Thomas B. Marsh, before giving it to him, and in speaking against the authorities of the Church.

A motion was then made by President Patten, that fellowship be withdrawn from Marcellus F. Cowdery, until he make satisfaction, which was seconded and carried unanimously.

THOMAS B. MARSH,
DAVID W. PATTEN,
Presidents.
EBENEZER ROBINSON,
Clerk of High Council.

The Prophet's Reception in Zion.

When I had arrived within one hundred and twenty miles of Far West, the brethren met me with teams and money to help me forward; and when eight miles from the city, we were met by an escort, viz., Thomas B. Marsh and others, who received us with open arms; and on the 13th of March, with my family and some others I put up at Brother Barnard's for the night. Here we were met by another escort of the brethren from the town, who came to make us welcome to their little Zion.

On the 14th of March, as we were about entering Far West, many of the brethren came out to meet us, who also with open arms welcomed us to their bosoms. We were immediately received under the hospitable roof of Brother George W. Harris, who treated us with all possible kindness, and we refreshed ourselves with much satisfaction, after our long and tedious journey, the brethren bringing in such things as we had need of for our comfort and convenience.

After being here two or three days, my brother Samuel arrived with his family.

Shortly after his arrival, while walking with him and certain other brethren, the following sentiments occurred to my mind:

The Political Motto of the Church of Latter-day Saints.

The Constitution of our country formed by the Fathers of liberty. Peace and good order in society. Love to God, and good will to man. All good and wholesome laws, virtue and truth above all things, and aristarchy, live for ever! But woe to tyrants, mobs, aristocracy, anarchy, and toryism, and all those who invent or seek out unrighteous and vexatious law suits, under the pretext and color of law, or office, either religious or political. Exalt the standard of Democracy! Down with that of priestcraft, and let all the people say Amen! that the blood of our fathers may not cry from the ground against us. Sacred is the memory of that blood which bought for us our liberty.

JOSEPH SMITH, JUN.,
THOMAS B. MARSH,
DAVID W. PATTEN,
BRIGHAM YOUNG,
SAMUES H. SMITH,
GEORGE M. HINKLE,
JOHN CORRILL,
GEORGE W. ROBINSON.

*The Prophet's Answers to Questions on Scripture.**

Who is the Stem of Jesse spoken of in the 1st, 2nd, 3rd, 4th, and 5th verses of the 11th chapter of Isaiah?

Verily thus saith the Lord, it is Christ.

What is the rod spoken of in the first verse of the 11th chapter of Isaiah that should come of the Stem of Jesse?

* Doctrine and Covenants, sec. cxiii.

Behold, thus saith the Lord, it is a servant in the hands of Christ, who is partly a descendant of Jesse as well as of Ephraim, or of the House of Joseph, on whom there is laid much power.

What is the root of Jesse spoken of in the 10th verse of the 11th chapter?

Behold, thus saith the Lord, it is a descendant of Jesse, as well as of Joseph, unto whom righty belongs the Priesthood, and the keys of the Kingdom, for an ensign, and for the gathering of my people in the last days.

Questions by Elias Higbee:

"What is meant by the command in Isaiah, 52nd chapter, 1st verse, which saith, put on thy strength O Zion? And what people had Isaiah reference to?"

He had reference to those whom God should call in the last days, who should hold the power of Priesthood to bring again Zion, and the redemption of Israel; and to put on her strength is to put on the authority of the Priesthood, which she (Zion) has a right to by lineage; also to return to that power which she had lost.

"What are we to understand by Zion loosing herself from the bands of her neck; 2nd verse?"

We are to understand that the scattered remnants are exhorted to return to the Lord from whence they have fallen, which if they do, the promise of the Lord is that He will speak to them, or give them revelation. See the 6th, 7th and 8th verses. The bands of her neck are the curses of God upon her, or the remnants of Israel in their scattered condition among the Gentiles.

The Prophet's Letter to the Presidency of the Church of Jesus Christ of Latter-day Saints in Kirtland.

FAR WEST, March 29, 1838.

Dear and Well Beloved Brethren—Through the grace and mercy of our God, after a long and tedious journey of two months and one day, my family and I arrived safe in the city of Far West, having been met at Huntsvills, one hundred and twenty miles from this place, by my brethren with teams and money, to forward us on our journey. When within eight miles of the city of Far West, we were met by an escort of brethren from the city, viz.: Thomas B. Marsh, John Corrill, Elias Higbee, and several others of the faithful of the West, who received us with open arms and warm hearts, and welcomed us to the bosom of their society. On our arrival in the city we were greeted on every hand by the Saints, who bid us welcome to the land of their inheritance.

Dear brethren, you may be assured that so friendly a meeting and reception paid us well for our long seven years of servitude, persecution, and affliction in the midst of our enemies, in the land of Kirtland; yea, verily our hearts were full; and we feel grateful to Almighty God for His kindness unto us. The particulars of our journey, brethren, cannot well be written, but we trust that the same God who has protected us will protect you also, and will, sooner or later, grant us the privilege of seeing each other face to face, and of rehearsing all our sufferings.

We have heard of the destruction of the printing office, which we presume to believe must have been occasioned by the Parrish party, or more properly the aristocrats or anarchists.

The Saints here have provided a room for us, and daily necessaries, which are brought in from all parts of the country to make us comfortable; so that I have nothing to do but to attend to my spiritual concerns, or the spiritual affairs of the Church.

The difficulties of the Church had been adjusted before my arrival here, by a judicious High Council, with Thomas B. Marsh and David W. Patten, who acted as presidents *pro tempore* of the Church of Zion, being appointed by the voice of the Council and Church, William W. Phelps and John Whitmer having been cut off from the Chuch, David Whitmer remaining as yet. The Saints at this time are in union; and peace and love prevail throughout; in a word, heaven smiles upon the Saints in Caldwell. Various and many have been the falsehoods written from Kirtland to this place, but [they] have availed nothing. We have no uneasiness about the power of our enemies in this place to do us harm.

Brother Samuel H. Smith and family arrived here soon after we did, in good health. Brothers Brigham Young, Daniel S. Miles, and Levi Richards arrived here when we did. They were with us on the last part of our journey, which ended much to our satisfaction. They also are well. They have provided places for their families, and are now about to break the ground for seed.

Having been under the hands of [men who urged against me] wicked and vexatious law suits for seven years past, my business [in Kirtland] was so deranged that I was not able to leave it in so good a situation as I had anticipated; but if there are any wrongs, they shall all be noticed, so far as the Lord gives me ability and power to do so.

Say to all the brethren, that I have not forgotten them, but remember them in my prayers. Say to Mother Beaman that I remember her, also Brother Daniel Carter, Brother Strong and family, Brother Granger and family; finally I cannot enumerate them all for want of room, I will just name Brother Knight, the Bishop, etc.; my best respects to them all, and I commend them and the Church of God in Kirtland to our Heavenly Father, and the word of His grace, which is able to make you wise unto salvation.

I would just say to Brother Marks, that I saw in a vision while on the road, that whereas he was closely pursued by an innumerable concourse of enemies, and as they pressed upon him hard, as if they were about to devour him, and had seemingly obtained some degree of advantage over him, but about this time a chariot of fire came, and near the place, even the angel of the Lord put forth his hand unto Brother Marks and said unto him, "Thou art my son, come here," and immediately he was caught up in the chariot, and rode away triumphantly out of their midst. And again the Lord said, I will raise thee up for a blessing unto many people." Now the particulars of this whole matter cannot be written at this time, but the vision was evidently given to me that I might know that the hand of the Lord would be on his behalf.

I transmit to you the Motto of the Church of Latter-day Saints.

We left President Rigdon thirty miles this side of Paris, Illinois, in consequence of the sickness of Brother George W. Robinson's wife.

On yesterday Brother Robinson arrived here, who informed us that his father-in-law (Sidney Rigdon) was at Huntsville, detained on account of the ill health of his wife. They will probably be here soon.

Choice seeds of all kinds of fruit, also choice breeds of cattle, would be in much demand; and best blood of horses, garden seeds of every description, and hay seeds of all sorts, are much needed in this place.

Very respectfully I subscribe myself your servant in Christ, our Lord and Savior.

JOSEPH SMITH, JUN.,
President of the Church of Christ of Latter-day Saints.

CHAPTER II.

EXCOMMUNICATION OF OLIVER COWDERY AND DAVID WHITMER —THE WORK IN ENGLAND.

PRESIDENT RIGDON arrived at Far West with his family, Wednesday, April 4th, having had a tedious journey, and his family having suffered many afflictions.

Arrival of Sidney Rigdon at Far West.

Minutes of a General Conference of the Church at Far West.

FAR WEST, April 6, 1838.

Agreeable to a resolution passed by the High Council of Zion, March 3, 1838, the Saints in Missouri assembled in this place to celebrate the anniversary of the Church of Jesus Christ of Latter-day Saints, and to transact Church business, Joseph Smith, Jun., and Sidney Rigdon, presiding.

The meeting was opened by singing, and prayer by David W. Patten, after which President Joseph Smith, Jun., read the order of the day as follows: Doors will be opened at 9 o'clock a. m., and the meeting will commence by singing and prayer. A sexton will then be appointed as a door keeper, and other services in the House of the Lord. Two historians will then be appointed to write and keep the Church history; also a general recorder to keep the records of the whole Church, and to be the clerk of the First Presidency. And a clerk will be appointed for the High Council, and to keep the Church records of this Stake. Three presidents will be appointed to preside over this Church of Zion, after which an address will be delivered by the Presidency. Then an intermission of one hour, when the meeting will again convene, and open by singing and prayer. The Sacrament will then be administered, and the blessing of infants attended to.

The meeting proceeded to business. George Morey was appointed sexton, and Dimick Huntington assistant; John Corrill and Elias Higbee, historians; George W. Robinson, general Church recorder and clerk to the First Presidency; Ebenezer Robinson, Church clerk and recorder for Far West and clerk of the High Council; Thomas B. Marsh, President *pro tempore* of the Church in Zion, and Brigham Young and David W. Patten, his assistant Presidents.

After one hour's adjournment, meeting again opened by David W. Patten. The bread and wine were administered, and ninety-five infants were blessed.

JOSEPH SMITH, JUN., President.
EBENEZER ROBINSON, Clerk.

Minutes of the First Quarterly Conference at Far West.

Agreeable to a resolution of the High Council, March 3, 1838, the general authorities of the Church met, to hold the Quarterly Conference of the Church of Latter-day Saints, at Far West, on the 7th of April, 1838.

President Joseph Smith, Jun., Sidney Rigdon, Thomas B. Marsh, David W. Patten, and Brigham Young, took the stand, after which the several quorums, the High Council, the High Priests, the Seventies, the Elders, the Bishops, the Priests, Teachers and Deacons, were organized by their Presidents.

President Joseph Smith, Jun., made some remarks and also gave some instructions respecting the order of the day. After singing, prayer by Brigham Young, and singing again, President Smith then addressed the congregation at considerable length, followed by President Rigdon.

Adjourned twenty minutes.

Opened by David W. Patten, who also made some remarks respecting the Twelve Apostles. He spoke of Thomas B. Marsh, Brigham Young, Heber C. Kimball, Orson Hyde, Parley P. Pratt, and Orson Pratt, as being men of God, whom he could recommend with cheerfulness and confidence. He spoke somewhat doubtful of William Smith, for something he had heard respecting his faith in the work. He also spoke of William E. McLellin, Luke S. Johnson, Lyman E. Johnson, and John F. Boynton, as being men whom he could not recommend to the conference.

President John Murdock represented the High Council. The report was favorable. The seats of Elisha H. Groves, Calvin Bebee, and Lyman Wight were vacant in consequence of their having moved so far away they could not attend the Council.

Thomas B. Marsh nominated Jared Carter, to fill the seat of Elisha H. Groves; John P. Greene that of Calvin Bebee, and George W. Harris that of Lyman Wight; which nominations were severally and unanimously sanctioned.

George W. Harris was ordained a High Priest.

On motion, conference adjourned to the 8th, 9 o'clock a. m.

Sunday, April 8th, 9 o'clock a. m., conference convened and opened as usual, prayer by Brigham Young.

President Joseph Smith, Jun., made a few remarks respecting the Kirtland Bank. He was followed by Brigham Young, who gave a short history of his travels to Massachusetts and New York.

President Charles C. Rich represented his quorum of High Priests, and read their names. The principal part were in good standing.

President Daniel S. Miles and Levi W. Hancock represented the Seventies.

The quorum of Elders were represented by their President, Harvey Green, numbering one hundred and twenty-four in good standing.

President Joseph Smith, Jun., made a few remarks on the Word of Wisdom, giving the reason of its coming forth, saying it should be observed.

Adjourned for one hour.

Conference convened agreeable to adjournment, and opened as usual, after which Bishop Partridge represented his Council and the Lesser Priesthood, and made a report of receipts and expenditures of Church funds which had passed through his hands.

It was then moved, seconded and carried, that the First Presidency be appointed to sign the licenses of the official members of the Church.

Conference adjourned until the first Friday in July next.

JOSEPH SMITH, JUN., President.
EBENEZER ROBINSON, Clerk.

Demand on John Whitmer for the Church Records.

The following letter was sent to John Whitmer, in consequence of his withholding the records of the Church in the city of Far West, when called for by the clerk.

Mr. John Whitmer, Sir: We were desirous of honoring you by giving publicity to your notes on the history of the Church of Latter-day Saints, after making such corrections as we thought would be necessary, knowing your incompetency as a historian, and that writings coming from your pen, could not be put to press without our correcting them, or else the Church must suffer reproach. Indeed, sir, we never supposed you capable of writing a history, but were willing to let it come out under your name, notwithstanding it would really not be yours but ours. We are still willing to honor you, if you can be made to know your own interest, and give up your notes, so that they can be corrected and made fit for the press; but if not, we have all the materials for another, which we shall commence this week to write.

Your humble servants,

JOSEPH SMITH, JUN.,

SIDNEY RIGDON,

Presidents of the whole Church of Latter-day Saints.

Attest: EBENEZER ROBINSON, Clerk.

Charges Against Oliver Cowdery.

Wednesday, April 11, Elder Seymour Brunson preferred the following charges against Oliver Cowdery, to the High Council at Far West:*

To the Bishop and Council of the Church of Jesus Christ of Latter-day Saints, I prefer the following charges against President Oliver Cowdery:

"First—For persecuting the brethren by urging on vexatious law suits against them, and thus distressing the innocent.

"Second—For seeking to destroy the character of President Joseph Smith, Jun., by falsely insinuating that he was guilty of adultery.

"Third—For treating the Church with contempt by not attending meetings.

"Fourth—For virtually denying the faith by declaring that he would not be governed by any ecclesiastical authority or revelations whatever, in his temporal affairs.

"Fifth—For selling his lands in Jackson county, contrary to the revelations.

"Sixth—For writing and sending an insulting letter to President Thomas B. Marsh, while the latter was on the High Council, attending to the duties of his office as President of the Council, and by insulting the High Council with the contents of said letter.

"Seventh—For leaving his calling to which God had appointed him by revelation, for the sake of filthy lucre, and turning to the practice of law.

Eighth—For disgracing the Church by being connected in the bogus business, as common report says.

"Ninth—For dishonestly retaining notes after they had been paid; and finally, for leaving and forsaking the cause of God, and returning to the beggarly elements of the world, and neglecting his high and holy calling, according to his profession."

The Bishop and High Council assembled at the Bishop's

* The charges were drawn up and dated the 7th of April, and handed to Bishop Partridge.

office, April 12, 1838. After the organization of the Council, the above charges of the 11th instant were read, also a letter from Oliver Cowdery, as will be found recorded in the Church record of the city of Far West, Book A. The 1st, 2nd, 3rd, 7th, 8th, and 9th charges were sustained. The 4th and 5th charges were rejected, and the 6th was withdrawn. Consequently he (Oliver Cowdery) was considered no longer a member of the Church of Jesus Christ of Latter-day Saints.* Also voted by the High Council that

Trial of Oliver Cowdery.

* The following letter from Oliver Cowdery respecting his difficulties at this time in the Church, is copied from the Far West Record of the High Council, and is an interesting document for several reasons: First, it shows the spirit of Oliver Cowdery at that time, also his misapprehensions of the policy of the authorities in the government of the Church, for it is to be noted that the two principal points covered in this letter, numbers four and five of Elder Brunson's charges, were rejected by the Council as not being proper to be considered, and the sixth charge also is withdrawn, so that Oliver Cowdery was not disfellowshiped from the Church on the points raised in his letter at all, but on the first, second, third, seventh, eighth and ninth charges in Elder Brunson's formal accusation, and since these charges were sustained upon testimony of witnesses, as the minutes of the High Council proceedings in the Far West Record clearly show, it is to be believed that the Church had sufficient cause for rejecting him.

Elder Cowdery's Letter.

Far West, Missouri, April 12, 1838.

Dear Sir:—I received your note of the 9th inst., on the day of its date, containing a copy of nine charges preferred before yourself and Council against me, by Elder Seymour Brunson.

I could have wished that those charges might have been deferred until after my interview with President Smith; but as they are not, I must waive the anticipated pleasure with which I had flattered myself of an understanding on those points which are grounds of different opinions on some Church regulations, and others which personally interest myself.

The fifth charge reads as follows: "For selling his lands in Jackson County contrary to the revelations." So much of this charge, "for selling his lands in Jackson County," I acknowledge to be true, and believe that a large majority of this Church have already spent their judgment on that act, and pronounced it sufficient to warrant a disfellowship; and also that you have concurred in its correctness, consequently, have no good reason for supposing you would give any decision contrary.

Now, sir, the lands in our country are allodial in the strictest construction of that term, and have not the least shadow of feudal tenures attached to them, consequently, they may be disposed of by deeds of conveyance without the consent or even approbation of a superior.

The fourth charge is in the following words, "For virtually denying the faith

Oliver Cowdery be no longer a committee to select locations for the gathering of the Saints.

Charges against David Whitmer.

April 13.—The following charges were preferred against David Whitmer, before the High Council at Far West, in council assembled.

"First—For not observing the Word of Wisdom.

"Second—For unchristian-like conduct in neglecting to attend meet-

by declaring that he would not be governed by any ecclesiastical authority nor revelation whatever in his temporal affairs."

With regard to this, I think I am warranted in saying, the judgment is also passed as on the matter of the fifth charge, consequently, I have no disposition to contend with the Council; this charge covers simply the doctrine of the fifth, and if I were to be controlled by other than my own judgment, in a compulsory manner, in my temporal interests, of course, could not buy or sell without the consent of some real or supposed authority. Whether that clause contains the precise words, I am not certain—I think however they were these, "I will not be influenced, governed, or controlled, in my temporal interests by any ecclesiastical authority or pretended revelation whatever, contrary to my own judgment." Such being still my opinion shall only remark that the three great principles of English liberty, as laid down in the books, are "the right of personal security, the right of personal liberty, and the right of private property." My venerable ancestor was among the little band, who landed on the rocks of Plymouth in 1620—with him he brought those maxims, and a body of those laws which were the result and experience of many centuries, on the basis of which now stands our great and happy government; and they are so interwoven in my nature, have so long been inculcated into my mind by a liberal and intelligent ancestry that I am wholly unwilling to exchange them for anything less liberal, less benevolent, or less free.

The very principle of which I conceive to be couched in an attempt to set up a kind of petty government, controlled and dictated by ecclesiastical influence, in the midst of this national and state government. You will, no doubt, say this is not correct; but the bare notice of these charges, over which you assume a right to decide, is, in my opinion, a direct attempt to make the secular power subservient to Church direction—to the correctness of which I cannot in conscience subscribe—I believe that principle never did fail to produce anarchy and confusion.

This attempt to control me in my temporal interests, I conceive to be a disposition to take from me a portion of my Constitutional privileges and inherent right—I only, respectfully, ask leave, therefore, to withdraw from a society assuming they have such right.

So far as relates to the other seven charges, I shall lay them carefully away, and take such a course with regard to them, as I may feel bound by my honor, to answer to my rising posterity.

I beg you, sir, to take no view of the foregoing remarks, other than my belief in the outward government of this Church. I do not charge you, or any other person who differs with me on these points, of not being sincere, but such difference does exist, which I sincerely regret.

With considerations of the highest respect, I am, your obedient servant,

[Signed.] OLIVER COWDERY.

Rev. Edward Partridge, Bishop of the Church of Latter-day Saints.

ings, in uniting with and possessing the same spirit as the dissenters.

"Third—In writing letters to the dissenters in Kirtland unfavorable to the cause, and to the character of Joseph Smith, Jun.

"Fourth—In neglecting the duties of his calling, and separating himself from the Church, while he had a name among us.

"Fifth—For signing himself President of the Church of Christ in an insulting letter to the High Council after he had been cut off from the Presidency."

After reading the above charges, together with a letter sent to the President of said Council,* the Council held that the charges were sustained, and consequently considered David Whitmer no longer a member of the Church of Latter-day Saints.

* The letter referred to is to be found in the Far West Record. It is as follows

"FAR WEST, Mo., April 13, 1838.

"JOHN MURDOCK:

"Sir:—I received a line from you bearing date the 9th inst., requesting me as a High Priest to appear before the High Council and answer to five several charges on this day at 12 o'clock.

"You, sir, with a majority of this Church have decided that certain councils were legal by which it is said I have been deprived of my office as one of the Presidents of this Church. I have thought, and still think, they were not agreeable to the revelations of God, which I believe; and by now attending this Council, and answering to charges, as a High Priest, would be acknowledging the correctness and legality of those former assumed councils, which I shall not do.

"Believing as I verily do, that you and the leaders of the councils have a determination to pursue your unlawful course at all hazards, and bring others to your standard in violation of the revelations, to spare you any further trouble I hereby withdraw from your fellowship and communion—choosing to seek a place among the meek and humble, where the revelations of heaven will be observed and the rights of men regarded.

"DAVID WHITMER."

In the minutes of the council in which this letter was read appear also the following paragraphs:

"After the reading of the above letter it was not considered necessary to investigate the case, as he [David Whitmer] had offered contempt to the Council by writing the above letter, but it was decided to let the councilors speak what they had to say upon the case, and pass decision.

"The councilors then made a few remarks in which they spoke warmly of the contempt offered to the Council in the above letter, therefore, thought he [David Whitmer] was not worthy a membership in the Church.

"Whereupon President Marsh made a few remarks, and decided that David Whitmer be no longer considered a member of the Church of Jesus Christ of Latter-day Saints."

The Council sustained the decision of President Marsh and David Whitmer was excommunicated. The letters of both Oliver Cowdery and David Whitmer to the High Council, setting forth their position respecting matters involved, are here

The same day three charges were preferred against Lyman E. Johnson, which were read, together with a letter from him, in answer to the one recorded in Far West Record.* The charges were sustained, and he was cut off from the Church.

Charges against Lyman E. Johnson.

The work continued to prosper in England, and Elders Richards and Russell having previously been called to Preston, to prepare for their return to America, a general conference was held in the Temperance Hall, (Cock Pit) Preston, on Sunday, April 1st, for the purpose of setting in order the churches, etc. Brother Joseph Fielding was chosen President over the whole Church in England, and Willard Richards and William Clayton† were chosen his Counselors, and were ordained to the High Priesthood and to the Presidency. This was the first notice given Elder Richards that he would be required to continue in England. At this conference eight Elders were ordained, among whom was Thomas Webster, and several Priests, Teachers and Deacons; about forty were confirmed, who had previously been baptized; about sixty children were blessed, and twenty baptized that day. Conference continued without intermission from 9 a.m. to 5 p.m. About fifty official members met in council in the evening.

The Work in England—Conference in Preston.

presented that I might call attention to this fact: neither of them deny or even slight the great facts in which Mormonism had its origin—the coming forth of the Book of Mormon, and the ministration of the angels of heaven to both Joseph Smith and themselves. Had there been any fraud or collusion entered into between Joseph Smith and Oliver Cowdery and David Whitmer, I take it that it would have been a very natural thing for men smarting under what they regarded as injustice, to have manifested that fact in one way or another in these communications. Their silence at this critical time of their experience, and in the experience of the Church, constitutes very strong presumptive evidence of the reality of those facts which brought Mormonism into existence.

* A copy of which may be found in Far West Record, Book A, p. 128.

† William Clayton was born in Penworthan, Lancashire, England, July 17, 1814. He was baptized soon after the arrival of the Mormon Elders in England in 1837. Soon after his ordination to the Holy Priesthood and Presidency of the British mission he abandoned all other business and gave himself to the ministry, in which he was remarkably successful.

From the 1st to the 8th of April Presidents Kimball and Hyde visited the churches a short distance from Preston, and on the 8th attended meeting in the "Cock Pit." After preaching by Elder Richards, they bore their farewell testimony to the truth of the work. After they had closed, and while Elder Russell was speaking, the enemy severed the gas pipes which lighted the house, and threw the assembly into darkness in an instant. The damage was soon repaired, and the design of breaking up the meeting frustrated.

Farewell Meetings with the Saints.

On Tuesday, the 10th of April, at 12 o'clock, Elders Kimball and Hyde left Preston by coach for Liverpool.

While the Elders were in Liverpool they wrote as follows:

A Prophecy.

LIVERPOOL, GOOD FRIDAY, April 13, 1838.

DEAR BROTHERS AND SISTERS IN PRESTON:—It seemeth good unto us, and also to the Holy Spirit, to write you a few words which cause pain in our hearts, and will also pain you when they are fulfilled before you, yet you shall have joy in the end. Brother Thomas Webster will not abide in the Spirit of the Lord, but will reject the truth, and become the enemy of the people of God, and expose the mysteries that have been committed to him, that a righteous judgment may be executed upon him, unless he speedily repent. When this sorrowful prediction shall be fulfilled, this letter shall be read to the Church, and it shall prove a solemn warning to all to beware.

Farewell in the Lord,

HEBER C. KIMBALL,
ORSON HYDE.

The foregoing letter was written and sealed in the presence of Presidents Joseph Fielding and Willard Richards, who had gone to Liverpool to witness the brethren sail, and, by the writers, committed to their special charge, that no one should know the contents until the fulfillment thereof.

Previous to this period, very few of the foolish and wicked stories which filled the weekly journals and pamphlets in America concerning the "Mormons," as the Saints were termed, had found their way into the English prints; but immediately after Elders Kimball and Hyde left Preston, on or about the 15th of April, one Livesey (a Methodist priest, who had previously spent some years in America, and said he heard nothing about the Saints in America) came out with a pamphlet, made up of forged letters, apostate lies, and "walk on the water" stories, he found in old American papers, which he had picked up while in America. But he stopped the circulation of his own pamphlet by stating to a public congregation, that he had accidentally found the contents of his pamphlet in old papers in his trunk, which was quite providential, to stop such abominable work as the Saints were engaged in; and in the same lecture said he "wished the people to purchase his pamphlet, as he had been at a great expense to procure the materials for writing it!" His hearers retired.

American Slanders Reach England.

On the 20th of April Elders Kimball and Hyde sailed from Liverpool on the ship *Garrick*.

CHAPTER III.

READJUSTMENT AND SETTLEMENT OF AFFAIRS AT FAR WEST.

April 17.—I received the following:

*Revelation Given at Far West.**

1. Verily thus saith the Lord, it is wisdom in my servant David W. Patten, that he settle up all his business as soon as he possibly can, and make a disposition of his merchandise, that he may perform a mission unto me next spring, in company with others, even twelve, including himself, to testify of my name, and bear glad tidings unto all the world;
2. For verily thus saith the Lord, that inasmuch as there are those among you who deny my name, others shall be planted in their stead, and receive their bishopric. Amen.

I also received the following:

Revelation Given to Brigham Young at Far West.

Verily thus saith the Lord, let my servant Brigham Young go unto the place which he has bought, on Mill Creek, and there provide for his family until an effectual door is opened for the support of his family, until I shall command him to go hence, and not to leave his family until they are amply provided for. Amen.

April 26.—I received the following:

Revelation Given at Far West making known the will of God concerning the building up of that place, and of the Lord's House.†

1. Verily thus saith the Lord unto you, my servant Joseph Smith, Jun., and also my servant Sidney Rigdon, and also my servant Hyrum Smith, and your counselors who are and shall be appointed hereafter;
2. And also unto you my servant Edward Partridge, and his counselors;

* Doctrine and Covenants, sec. cxiv.

† Doctrine and Covenants, sec. cxv. It will be observed that in verses three and

3. And also unto my faithful servants, who are of the High Council of my Church in Zion (for thus it shall be called), and unto all the Elders and people of my Church of Jesus Christ of Latter-day Saints, scattered abroad in all the world;

4. For thus shall my Church be called in the last days, even the Church of Jesus Christ of Latter-day Saints.

5. Verily I say unto you all, Arise and shine forth, that thy light may be a standard for the nations,

6. And that the gathering together upon the land of Zion, and upon her stakes, may be for a defense, and for a refuge from the storm, and from wrath when it shall be poured out without mixture upon the whole earth.

7. Let the city, Far West, be a holy and consecrated land unto me, and it shall be called most holy, for the ground upon which thou standest is holy;

8. Therefore I command you to build an house unto me, for the gathering together of my Saints, that they may worship me;

9. And let there be a beginning of this work, and a foundation, and a preparatory work, this following summer;

10. And let the beginning be made on the 4th day of July next, and from that time forth let my people labor diligently to build an house unto my name,

11. And in one year from this day let them re-commence laying the foundation of my house:

12. Thus let them from that time forth labor diligently until it shall

four of this revelation the Lord gives to the Church its official name, "The Church of Jesus Christ of Latter-day Saints." Previous to this the Church had been called "The Church of Christ," "The Church of Jesus Christ," "The Church of God,"and by a conference of Elders held at Kirtland in May, 1834, (see Church History, vol. 2, pp. 62-3), it was given the name"The Church of the Latter-day Saints." All these names, however, were by this revelation brushed aside, and since then the official name given in this revelation has been recognized as the true title of the Church,though often spoken of as"The Mormon Church," the "Church of Christ," etc. The appropriateness of this title is self evident, and in it there is a beautiful recognition of the relationship both of the Lord Jesus Christ and of the Saints to the organization. It is "The Church of Jesus Christ." It is the Lord's; He owns it, He organized it. It is the Sacred Depository of His truth. It is His instrumentality for promulgating all those spiritual truths with which He would have mankind acquainted. It is also His instrumentality for the perfecting of the Saints, as well as for the work of the ministry. It is His in all these respects; but it is an institution which also belongs to the Saints. It is their refuge from the confusion and religious doubt of the world. It is their instructor in principle, doctrine, and righteousness. It is their guide in matters of faith and morals. They have a conjoint ownership in it with Jesus Christ, which ownership is beautifully recognized in the latter part of the title. "The Church of Jesus Christ of Latter day Saints," is equivalent to "The Church of Jesus Christ," and "The Church of the Latter-day Saints."

be finished, from the corner stone thereof unto the top thereof, until there shall not any thing remain that is not finished.

13. Verily I say unto you, let not my servant Joseph, neither my servant Sidney, neither my servant Hyrum, get in debt any more for the building of an house unto my name;

14. But let an house be built unto my name according to the pattern which I will show unto them.

15. And if my people shall build it not according to the pattern which I shall show unto their Presidency, I will not accept it at their hands.

16. But if my people do build it according to the pattern which I shall show unto their Presidency, even my servant Joseph and his counselors, then I will accept it at the hands of my people.

17. And again, verily I say unto you, it is my will that the city of Far West should be built up speedily by the gathering of my Saints,

18. And also that other places should be appointed for stakes in the region round about, as they shall be manifested unto my servant Joseph, from time to time;

19. For behold, I will be with him, and I will sanctify him before the people, for unto him have I given the keys of this kingdom and ministry. Even so. Amen.

The Teachers' quorum voted today [April 26th] not to hold any member of the quorum in fellowship, who would not settle his own difficulties in the Church, and show himself approved in all things; and that they would not hold any member of the quorum in fellowship who would take unlawful interest.

April 27.—This day I chiefly spent in writing a history of the Church from the earliest period of its existence, up to this date.

Minutes of the High Council.

Saturday, April 28, 1838. This morning Presidents Joseph Smith, Jun., and Sidney Rigdon attended the High Council, by invitation.

The business before the Council was an appeal case, from the branch of the Church near Guymon's Mill. A Brother Jackson was accuser, and Aaron Lyon accused. Thomas B. Marsh and David W. Patten presiding.

It appeared, in calling the Council to order, that some of the seats were vacant, which the Council proceeded to fill, but as there were not a sufficient number present who were eligible for the station, Presidents

Smith and Rigdon were strongly solicited to act as Councilors, or to preside and let the presiding officers act as Councilors.

They accepted the former proposal, and President Smith was chosen to act on the part of the defense, and to speak upon the case, together with George W. Harris.

President Rigdon was chosen to speak on the part of the prosecution, together with George M. Hinkle.

After some discussion as to whether witnesses should be admitted to testify against Aaron Lyon, or whether he should have the privilege of confessing his own sins, it was decided that witnesses should be admitted, and also the written testimony of the wife of a brother of the name of Jackson.

[This trial is written up at great length in the minutes of the Far West Record, and also in G. W. Robinson's summary of the proceedings heretofore printed. Condensed, the account of the fault of Brother Aaron Lyon was this: He claimed to have had a revelation that a Sister Jackson, who was a married woman, and whose husband was still living, was to become his wife. Lyon claimed that it had been revealed to him that the woman's husband was dead. He exerted undue influence in persuading her of these things, and she consented to be his wife; but before they were married the woman's husband appeared on the scene, with the result, of course, that the prospective marriage did not take place. The witnesses were permitted to testify, although Brother Lyon confessed the facts and admitted his error. The conclusion of the matter follows as stated by G. W. Robinson, clerk of the Council].

Council decided that, inasmuch as this man had confessed his sins, and asked forgiveness, and promised to make well the paths of his feet, and do, as much as lies in his power, what God should require at his hands, he should give up his license as High Priest, and stand as a member in the Church; and this in consequence of his being considered incapable of magnifying that office.

G. W. Robinson.

Sundry Employments of the Prophet.

Sunday, *29*.—I spent the day chiefly in meeting with the Saints, ministering the words of life.

Monday, *30*.—The First Presidency were engaged in writing the Church history and in recitation of grammar lessons, which recitations at this period were usually attended each morning before writing.

May 1st, *2nd*, *3rd*, *and 4th*.—The First Presidency were engaged in writing Church history and administering to the sick. Received a letter from John E. Page on the 4th.

Saturday, 5.—The Presidency wrote for the *Elders' Journal;* also received intelligence from Canada by Brother Bailey, that two hundred wagons, with families, would probably be here in three weeks; also listened to an address on political matters delivered by General Wilson, Federal candidate for Congress.

Sunday, May 6.—I preached to the Saints, setting forth the evils that existed, and that would exist, by reason of hasty judgment, or decisions upon any subject given by any people, or in judging before they had heard both sides of a question. I also cautioned the Saints against men who came amongst them whining and growling about their money, because they had kept the Saints, and borne some of the burden with others, and thus thinking that others, who are still poorer, and have borne greater burdens than they themselves, ought to make up their losses. I cautioned the Saints to beware of such, for they were throwing out insinuations here and there, to level a dart at the best interests of the Church, and if possible destroy the character of its Presidency. I also gave some instructions in the mysteries of the kingdom of God; such as the history of the planets, Abraham's writings upon the planetary systems, etc.

The Prophet's Discourse on Evils of Hasty Judgment.

In the afternoon I spoke again on different subjects: the principle of wisdom, and the Word of Wisdom.

The Teachers' quorum at Far West numbered twenty-four members.

Monday, 7.—I spent the day in company with Judge Morain, one of our neighboring county judges, and Democratic candidate for the state senate.

I also visited with Elders Reynolds Cahoon and Parley P. Pratt, who had this day arrived in Far West, the former from Kirtland, the latter from New York City, where he had been preaching for some time; and our hearts were made glad with the pleasing intelligence of the gatering of the Saints from all parts of the earth to this place, to avoid

Arrival of Elder Parley P. Pratt at Far West.

the destructions which are coming upon this generation, as spoken by all the holy prophets since the world began.

Death of Jas. G. Marsh.

James G. Marsh, son of Thomas B. Marsh, aged fourteen years, eleven months, and seven days, died this day, in the full triumph of the everlasting Gospel.

The Prophet's Answers to Sundry Questions

Tuesday, 8.—I spent the day with Elder Rigdon in visiting Elder Cahoon at the place he had selected for his residence, and in attending to some of our private, personal affairs; also in the afternoon I answered the questions which were frequently asked me, while on my last journey but one from Kirtland to Missouri, as printed in the *Elders' Journal*, vol. I, Number II, pages 28 and 29, as follows:

First—"Do you believe the Bible?"

If we do, we are the only people under heaven that does, for there are none of the religious sects of the day that do.

Second—"Wherein do you differ from other sects?"

In that we believe the Bible, and all other sects profess to believe their interpretations of the Bible, and their creeds.

Third—"Will everybody be damned, but Mormons?"

Yes, and a great portion of them, unless they repent, and work righteousness.

Fourth—"How and where did you obtain the Book of Mormon?'"

Moroni, who deposited the plates in a hill in Manchester, Ontario county, New York, being dead and raised again therefrom, appeared unto me, and told me where they were, and gave me directions how to obtain them. I obtained them, and the Urim and Thummim with them, by the means of which I translated the plates; and thus came the Book of Mormon.

Fifth—"Do you believe Joseph Smith, Jun., to be a Prophet?"

Yes, and every other man who has the testimony of Jesus. For the testimony of Jesus is the spirit of prophecy.—Revelation, xix: 10th verse.

Sixth—"Do the Mormons believe in having all things in common?"

No.

Seventh—"Do the Mormons believe in having more wives than one?"

"No, not at the same time. But they believe that if their companion dies, they have a right to marry again. But we do disapprove of the custom, which has gained in the world, and has been practiced among us, to our great mortification, in marrying in five or six weeks, or even in two or three months, after the death of their companion. We believe that due respect ought to be had to the memory of the dead, and the feelings of both friends and children.

Eighth—"Can they [the Mormons] raise the dead?"

No, nor can any other people that now lives, or ever did live. But God can raise the dead, through man as an instrument.

Ninth—"What signs does Joseph Smith give of his divine mission?"

The signs which God is pleased to let him give, according as His wisdom thinks best, in order that He may judge the world agreeably to His own plan.

Tenth—"Was not Joseph Smith a money digger?"

Yes, but it was never a very profitable job for him, as he only got fourteen dollars a month for it.

Eleventh —"Did not Joseph Smith steal his wife?"

Ask her, she was of age, she can answer for herself.

Twelfth—"Do the people have to give up their money when they join his Church?"

No other requirement than to bear their proportion of the expenses of the Church, and support the poor.

Thirteenth—"Are the Mormons abolitionists?"

No, unless delivering the people from priestcraft, and the priests from the power of Satan, should be considered abolition. But we do not believe in setting the negroes free.

Fourteenth—"Do they not stir up the Indians to war, and to commit depredations?"

No, and they who reported the story knew it was false when they put it in circulation. These and similar reports are palmed upon the people by the priests, and this is the only reason why we ever thought of answering them.

Fifteenth—"Do the Mormons baptize in the name of 'Joe' Smith?"

No, but if they did, it would be as valid as the baptism administered by the sectarian priests.

Sixteenth—"If the Mormon doctrine is true, what has become of all those who died since the days of the Apostles?"

All those who have not had an opportunity of hearing the Gospel, and being administered unto by an inspired man in the flesh, must have it hereafter, before they can be finally judged.

Seventeenth—"Does not 'Joe' Smith profess to be Jesus Christ?"

No, but he professes to be His brother, as all other Saints have done and now do: Matt., xii: 49, 50, "And He stretched forth His hand toward His disciples and said, Behold my mother and my brothren; for whosoever shall do the will of my Father, which is in heaven, the same is my brother, and sister, and mother."

Eighteenth—"Is there anything in the Bible which licenses you to believe in revelation now-a-days?"

Is there anything that does not authorize us to believe so? If there is, we have, as yet, not been able to find it.

Nineteenth—"Is not the canon of the Scriptures full?"

If it is, there is a great defect in the book, or else it would have said so.

Twentieth—"What are the fundamental principles of your religion?"

The fundamental principles of our religion are the testimony of the Apostles and Prophets, concerning Jesus Christ, that He died, was buried, and rose again the third day, and ascended into heaven; and all other things which pertain to our religion are only appendages to it. But in connection with these, we believe in the gift of the Holy Ghost, the power of faith, the enjoyment of the spiritual gifts according to the will of God, the restoration of the house of Israel, and the final triumph of truth.

I published the foregoing answers to save myself the trouble of repeating the same a thousand times over and over again.

Wednesday, 9.—I attended the funeral of James G. Marsh, and complied with the request that I should preach on the occasion.

Elder Rigdon's Political Address.

Thursday, 10.—I listened to an address on the political policy of our nation, delivered by President Rigdon, at the school house, in the southwest quarter of the city, to a large concourse of people from all sections of the county, and from other counties also. Although President Rigdon was suffering under a severe cold and great hoarseness, yet being assisted by the Spirit of God, he was enabled clearly to elucidate the policy of the Federal and Democratic parties from their rise in our country to the present time, to the understanding of all present, giving an impartial review to both sides of the question. This address was delivered in consequence of a partial electioneering Federal speech of General Wilson at the same place a short time previously, and the politics of the Church of

Latter-day Saints, generally being Democratic,* it seemed desirable to hear an elucidation of the principles of both parties, with which I was highly edified.

Friday, 11.—I attended the trial of William E. McLellin and Dr. McCord, for transgression, before the Bishop's court.

Trial of Wm. E. McLellin and Dr. McCord.

McCord said he was sorry to trouble the Council on his account, for he had intended to withdraw from the Church before he left the place; that he had no confidence in the work of God, or His Prophet, and should go his way. He gave up his license and departed.

William E. McLellin stated about the same as McCord, and that he had no confidence in the heads of the Church, believing they had transgressed, and had got out of the way, consequently he quit praying and keeping the commandments of God, and indulged himself in his lustful desires, but when he heard that the First Presidency had made a general settlement, and acknowledged their sins, he began to pray again. When I interrogated him, he said he had seen nothing out of the way himself, but he judged from hearsay.†

Saturday, 12.—President Rigdon and myself attended the High Council for the purpose of presenting for their cosideration some business relating to our pecuniary concerns.

Remuneration of the Prophet and Sidney Rigdon for Temporal Labors in the Church.

We stated to the Council our situation, as to maintaining our families, and the relation we now stand in to the Church, spending as we have for eight years, our time, talents, and property, in the service of the Church: and being reduced as it were to beggary, and being still detained in the business and

* Of course what is meant by this statement is that the individuals composing the Church were quite generally Democrats, not that the Church as an organization was democratic or had any politics.

† It will be observed that the text is silent in relation to what action was taken respecting William E. McLellin, and the Far West Record is silent upon the subject also. In fact the minutes of the trial before the Bishop are not written in that record at all. It is known, however, from other sources that William E. McLellin was finally excommunicated from the Church at Far West. Thence for-

service of the Church, it appears necessary that something should be done for the support of our families by the Church, or else we must do it by our own labors; and if the Church say to us, "Help yourselves," we will thank them and immediately do so; but if the Church say, "Serve us," some provision must be made for our sustenance.

The Council investigated the matter, and instructed the Bishop to make over to President Joseph Smith, Jun., and Sidney Rigdon, each an eighty-acre lot of land from the property of the Church, situated adjacent to the city corporation; also appointed three of their number, viz., George W. Harris, Elias Higbee and Simeon Carter, a committee to confer with said Presidency, and satisfy them for their services the present year; not for preaching, or for receiving the word of God by revelation, neither for instructing the Saints in righteousness, but for services rendered in the printing establishment, in translating the ancient records, etc., etc. Said committee agreed that Presidents Smith and Rigdon should receive $1,100 each as a just remuneration for their services this year.

Sunday, 13.—Elder Reynolds Cahoon preached in the forenoon. In the afternoon President Rigdon preached a

ward he took an active part in the persecution of the Saints in Missouri, and at one time expressed the desire to do violence to the person of Joseph Smith, while the latter was confined in Liberty prison. Subsequently he attempted what he called a reorganization of the Church, and called upon David Whitmer to take the presidency thereof, claiming that he was ordained by Joseph Smith on the 8th of July, 1834, as his (the Prophet Joseph's) successor. The Prophet himself, according to the minutes of the High Council held in Far West, on the 15th of March, 1838, referred to his ordaining of David Whitmer in July, 1834, and this is the account of what he said:

"President Joseph Smith, Jun., gave a history of the ordination of David Whitmer which took place in July, 1834, to be a leader or a Prophet to this Church, which (ordination) was on conditions that he (Joseph Smith, Jun.,) did not live to God himself. President Joseph Smith, Jun., approved of the proceedings of the High Council after hearing the minutes of the former councils."—Far West Record, page 108.

The minutes of the councils here referred to, and which the Prophet approved, gave the account of deposing David Whitmer from the local Presidency of the Church in Missouri.

funeral sermon on the death of Swain Williams, son of Frederick G. Williams.

Monday, 14.—I spent in plowing my garden, while Elder Rigdon was preparing and correcting some matter for the press. Elder Harlow Redfield arrived from Kirtland, Ohio.

CHAPTER IV.

SELECTION OF LANDS IN CALDWELL AND DAVIESS COUNTIES FOR SETTLEMENT—ADAM-ONDI-AHMAN.

Friday, May 18.—I left Far West, in company with Sidney Rigdon, Thomas B. Marsh, David W. Patten, Bishop Partridge, Elias Higbee, Simeon Carter, Alanson Ripley, and many others, for the purpose of visiting the north country, and laying off a stake of Zion; making locations, and laying claim to lands to facilitate the gathering of the Saints, and for the benefit of the poor, in upholding the Church of God. We traveled to the mouth of Honey Creek, which is a tributary of Grand river, where we camped for the night. We passed through a beautiful country the greater part of which is prairie, and thickly covered with grass and weeds, among which is plenty of game, such as deer, turkey, and prairie hen. We discovered a large, black wolf, and my dog gave him chase, but he outran us. We have nothing to fear in camping out, except the rattlesnake, which is native to this country, though not very numerous. We turned our horses loose, and let them feed on the prairie.

The Prophet Leaves Far West to Locate Settlements.

Saturday, 19.—This morning we struck our tents and formed a line of march, crossing Grand River at the mouth of Honey Creek and Nelson's Ferry. Grand River is a large, beautiful, deep and rapid stream, during the high waters of Spring, and will undoubtedly admit of navigation by steamboat and other water craft. At the mouth of Honey Creek is a good landing. We pursued our course up the river,

The Prophet and Party Reach Tower Hill.

mostly through timber, for about eighteen miles, when we arrived at Colonel Lyman Wight's home. He lives at the foot of Tower Hill (a name I gave the place in consequence of the remains of an old Nephite altar or tower that stood there), where we camped for the Sabbath.

Adam-ondi-Ahman.

In the afternoon I went up the river about half a mile to Wight's Ferry, accompanied by President Rigdon, and my clerk, George W. Robinson, for the purpose of selecting and laying claim to a city plat near said ferry in Daviess County, township 60, ranges 27 and 28, and sections 25, 36, 31, and 30, which the brethren called "Spring Hill," but by the mouth of the Lord it was named Adam-ondi-Ahman,* because, said He, it is the place where Adam shall come to visit his people, or the Ancient of Days shall sit, as spoken of by Daniel the Prophet.†

* See Doctrine and Covenants, sec. 116. This is not the first time that the name or phrase "Adam-ondi-Ahman" is used in the revelations of the Lord. Some six years before this, viz., in the year 1832, it is used incidentally in one of the revelations where the Lord in addressing a number of the brethren who had been ordained to the High Priesthood, said that notwithstanding the tribulations through which they should pass, He had so ordered events that they might come unto the crown prepared for them, "and be made rulers over many kingdoms, saith the Lord God, the Holy One of Zion, who hath established the foundations of *Adam-ondi-Ahman.*" (Doctrine and Covenants, sec. lxxviii: 15). Some years afterwards, viz., in 1835, W. W. Phelps composed his beautiful hymn bearing the name of Adam-ondi-Ahman, which was first published in the *Messenger and Advocate* (No. 9, vol. I); see also History of the Church, Vol. II, p 365.

This hymn was a great favorite among the early Saints, although they, perhaps, did not understand at that time the significance of the name, nor even now do they understand its full significance. All that is known of its meaning is what the Lord revealed to the Prophet, viz., that it is significant of the fact that it designates the place where the Lord will come and meet with His people as described by Daniel the Prophet.

† Daniel's description of the events here referred to is found in the 7th chapter of his prophecies. The description is very imposing, hence I quote it: "I beheld till the thrones were cast down, and the Ancient of Days did sit, whose garment was white as snow, and the hair of his head like the pure wool: his throne was like the fiery flame, and his wheels as burning fire. A fiery stream issued and came forth from before him: thousand thousands ministered unto him, and ten thousand times ten thousand stood before him: the judgment was set, and the books were opened. * * * * * * I saw in the night visions, and, behold, one like the Son of man came with the clouds of heaven, and came to the Ancient of Days, and they brought him near before Him. And there was given Him dominion, and glory, and a kingdom, that all people, nations, and languages,

Sunday, *20*.—This day was spent by our company principally at Adam-ondi-Ahman; but near the close of the day, we struck our tents, and traveled about six miles north and encamped for the night with Judge Morin and company, who were also traveling north.

Monday, *21*.—This morning, after making some locations in this place, which is in township 61, ranges 27 and 28, we returned to Robinson's Grove, about two miles, to secure some land near Grand River, which we passed the day previous; and finding a mistake in the former survey, I sent the surveyor south five or six miles to obtain a correct line, while some of us tarried to obtain water for the camp.

Council called to determine Location of Settlements.

In the evening, I called a council of the brethren, to know whether it was wisdom to go immediately into the north country, or tarry here and hereabouts, to secure land on Grand River, etc. The brethren spoke their minds freely on the subject, when I stated to the council that I felt impressed to tarry and secure all the land near by, that is not secured between this and Far West, especially on Grand River. President Rigdon concurred, and the council voted unanimously to secure the land on Grand River, and between this and Far West.

Elders Kimball and Hyde this day (21st May) arrived at Kirtland from England.

American Antiquities Discovered.

Tuesday, *22*.—President Rigdon went east with a company, and selected some of the best locations in the county,* and returned with a good report of that vicinity, and with information of

should serve Him: His dominion is an everlasting dominion, which shall not pass away, and His kingdom that which shall not be destroyed."

The Prophet Daniel also saw in this connection that earthly powers would make war upon the Saints and prevail against them—until the Ancient of Days should come. "And [then] the kingdom and dominion, and the greatness of the kingdom under the whole heaven, shall be given to the people of the Saints of the Most High, whose kingdom is an everlasting kingdom, and all dominions shall serve and obey Him."

* This most likely was Livingstone county, which borders both Daviess and Caldwell counties on the east.

valuable locations which might be secured. Following awhile the course of the company, I returned to camp in Robinson's Grove, and thence went west to obtain some game to supply our necessities. We discovered some antiquities about one mile west of the camp, consisting of stone mounds, apparently erected in square piles, though somewhat decayed and obliterated by the weather of many years. These mounds were probaby erected by the aborigines of the land, to secrete treasures. We returned without game.

Wednesday, *23.*—We all traveled east, locating lands, to secure a claim, on Grove Creek, and near the city of Adam-ondi-Ahman. Towards evening I accompanied Elder Rigdon to Colonel Wight's, and the remainder of the company returned to their tents.

Varied Movements of the Prophet's Company.

Thursday, *24.*—This morning the company returned to Grove Creek to finish the survey, accompanied by President Rigdon and Colonel Wight, and I returned to Far West.

Friday, *25.*—The company went up Grand River and made some locations. In the afternoon they struck their tents and removed to Colonel Wight's.

Saturday, *26.*—The company surveyed lands on the other side of the river opposite Adam-ondi-Ahman.

Sunday, *27.*—The company locating lands spent the day at Colonel Wight's.

Monday, *28.*—The company started for home (Far West), and I left Far West the same day in company with Brother Hyrum Smith and fifteen or twenty others, to seek locations in the north, and about noon we met President Rigdon and his company going into the city, where they arrived the same evening.

President Hyrum Smith returned to Far West on the 30th, and I returned on the 1st of June, on account of my family, for I had a son born unto me.*

Birth of Alexander Hale Smith.

*The birth of the son took place on the 2nd of June. It was Alexander Hale Smith.

Monday, June 4.—I left Far West with President Rigdon, my brother Hyrum and others for Adam-ondi-Ahman, and stayed at Brother Moses Dailey's over night; and on the morning of the 5th, went to Colonel Lyman Wight's in the rain. We continued surveying, building houses, day after day, for many days, until the surveyor had completed the city plat.

The Prophet's Return to Adam-ondi-Ahman.

Monday, June 11.—President Joseph Fielding was married to Hannah Greenwood, Preston, England.

June 16.—My uncle, John Smith, and family, with six other families, arrived in Far West, all in good health and spirits. I counseled them to settle at Adam-ondi-Ahman.

Minutes of the Meeting which Organized the Stake of Zion called Adam-ondi-Ahman.

Adam-ondi-Ahman, Missouri, Daviess county, June 28, 1838. A conference of Elders and members of the Church of Jesus Christ of Latter-day Saints was held in this place this day, for the purpose of organizing this Stake of Zion, called Adam-ondi-Ahman.

The meeting convened at 10 o'clock a. m., in the grove near the house of Elder Lyman Wight.

President Joseph Smith, Jun., was called to the chair. He explained the object of the meeting, which was to organize a Presidency and High Council to preside over this Stake of Zion, and attend to the affairs of the Church in Daviess county.

It was then moved, seconded and carried by the unanimous voice of the assembly, that John Smith* should act as President of the Stake of Adam-ondi-Ahman.

Reynolds Cahoon was unanimously chosen first counselor, and Lyman Wight second counselor.

After prayer the presidents ordained Elder Wight as second counselor.

Vinson Knight was chosen acting Bishop *pro tempore* by the unanimous voice of the assembly.

President John Smith then proceeded to organize the High Council. The councilors were chosen according to the following order, by a unanimous vote: John Lemon, first; Daniel Stanton, second; Mayhew Hillman, third; Daniel Carter, fourth; Isaac Perry, fifth; Harrison Sagers, sixth; Alanson Brown, seventh; Thomas Gordon, eighth; Lorenzo D.

* The Prophet's uncle, who had but recently arrived at "Diahman.'

Barnes, ninth; George A. Smith, tenth; Harvey Olmstead, eleventh; Ezra Thayer, twelfth.

After the ordination of the councilors who had not previously been ordained to the High Priesthood, President Joseph Smith, Jun., made remarks by way of charge to the presidents and counselors, instructing them in the duties of their callings, and the responsibility of their stations, exhorting them to be cautious and deliberate in all their councils, and be careful and act in righteousness in all things.

President John Smith, Reynolds Cahoon, and Lyman Wight then made some remarks.

Lorenzo D. Barnes was unanimously chosen clerk of this Council and Stake. After singing the well known hymn, Adam-ondi-Ahman, the meeting closed by prayer by President Cahoon, and a benediction by President Joseph Smith, Jun.

LORENZO D. BARNES,
ISAAC PERRY,
Clerks.

Description of Adam-ondi-Ahman.

Adam-ondi-Ahman is loated immediately on the north side of Grand River, in Daviess county, Missouri, about twenty-five miles north of Far West. It is situated on an elevated spot of ground, which renders the place as healthful as any part of the United States, and overlooking the river and the country round about, it is certainly a beautiful location.*

* Perhaps the following more detailed description of Adam-ondi-Ahman, as also the allusion to at least one stirring event which occurred there in the past, may not be without interest: Adam-ondi-Ahman, or "Diahman," as it is familiarly known to the Saints, is located on the north bank of Grand River. It is situated, in fact, in a sharp bend of that stream. The river comes sweeping down from the northwest and here makes a sudden turn and runs in a meandering course to the northeast for some two or three miles, when it as suddenly makes another bend and flows again to the southeast. Grand River is a stream that has worn a deep channel for itself, and left its banks precipitous; but at "Diahman" that is only true of the south bank. The stream as it rushes from the northwest, strikes the high prairie land which at this point contains beds of limestone, and not being able to cut its way through, it veered off to the northeast, and left that height of land standing like palisades which rise very abruptly from the stream to a height of from fifty to seventy-five feet. The summit of these bluffs is the common level of the high rolling prairie, extending off in the direction of Far West. The bluffs on the north bank recede some distance from the stream, so that the river bottom at this point widens out to a small valley. The bluffs on the north bank of the river are by no means as steep as those on the south, and are covered with a light growth of timber. A ridge runs out from the main line of the bluffs into the river bottom some two or three hundred yards, approach-

June 28.—This day Victoria was crowned queen of England.

ing the stream at the point where the bend of the river is made. The termination of the bluff is quite abrupt, and overlooks a considerable portion of the river bottom. On the brow of the bluff stood the old stone altar, and near the foot of it was built the house of Lyman Wight. When the altar was first discovered, according to those who visited it frequently, it was about sixteen feet long, by nine or ten feet wide, having its greatest extent north and south. The height of the altar at each end was some two and a half feet, gradually rising higher to the center, which was between four and five feet high—the whole surface being crowning. Such was the altar at "Diahman" when the Prophet's party visited it. Now, however, it is thrown down, and nothing but a mound of crumbling stones mixed with soil, and a few reddish boulders mark the spot which is doubtless rich in historic events. It was at this altar, according to the testimony of Joseph Smith, that the patriarchs associated with Adam and his company, assembled to worship their God. Here their evening and morning prayer ascended to heaven with the smoke of the burning sacrifice, prophetic and symbolic of the greater sacrifice then yet to be, and here angels instructed them in heavenly truths.

North of the ridge on which the ruins of the altar were found, and running parallel with it, is another ridge, separated from the first by a depression varying in width from fifty to a hundred yards. This small valley with the larger one through which flows Grand River, is the valley of Adam-ondi-Ahman. Three years previous to the death of Adam, declares one of the Prophet Joseph's revelations, the Patriarchs Seth, Enos, Cainan, Mahalaleel, Jared, Enoch, and Methuselah, together with all their righteous posterity, were assembled in this valley we have described, and their common father, Adam, gave them his last blessing. And even as he blessed them, the heavens were opened, and the Lord appeared, and in the presence of God, the children or Adam arose and blessed him, and called him Michael, the Prince, the Archangel. The Lord also blessed Adam, saying: "I have set thee to be the head—a multitude of nations shall come of thee, and thou art a prince over them for ever." So great was the influence of this double blessing upon Adam, that, though bowed down with age, under the outpouring of the Spirit of God, he predicted what should befall his posterity to their latest generation. (Doctrine and Covenants, sec. cvii). Such is one of the great events which occurred on this old historic land of Adam-ondi-Ahman.

CHAPTER V.

INDEPENDENCE DAY AT FAR WEST—SUNDRY EVENTS AND REVELATIONS—EPISTLE OF DAVID W. PATTEN.

July 4.—The day was spent in celebrating the Declaration of Independence of the United States of America, and also by the Saints making a "Declaration of Independence" from all mobs and persecutions which have been inflicted upon them, time after time, until they could bear it no longer; having been driven by ruthless mobs and enemies of truth from their homes, and having had their property confiscated, their lives exposed, and their all jeopardized by such barbarous conduct. The corner stones of the Houses of the Lord, agreeable to the commandments of the Lord unto us, given April 26, 1838, were laid.

Celebration of Independence Day at Far West.

Joseph Smith, Jun., was president of the day; Hyrum Smith, vice-president; Sidney Rigdon, orator; Reynolds Cahoon, chief marshal; George M. Hinckle and J. Hunt, assistant marshals; and George W. Robinson, clerk.

The Officers.

The order of the day was splendid. The procession commenced forming at 10 o'clock a. m., in the following order: First, the infantry (militia); second, the Patriarchs of the Church; the president, vice-president, and orator; the Twelve Apostles, presidents of the stakes, and High Council; Bishop and counselors; architects, ladies and gentlemen. The cavalry brought up the rear of the large procession, which marched to music, and formed a circle, with the ladies in front, round the excavation. The southeast corner stone of the Lord's House in Far West, Missouri, was then laid by the

The Procession.

presidents of the stake, assisted by twelve men. The southwest corner, by the presidents of the Elders, assisted by twelve men. The northwest corner by the Bishop, assisted by twelve men. The northeast corner by the president of the Teachers, assisted by twelve men. This house is to be one hundred and ten feet long, and eighty feet broad.

The Oration.

The oration was delivered by President Rigdon,* at the close of which was a shout of Hosanna, and a song, composed for the occasion by Levi W. Hancock, was sung by Solomon Hancock. The most perfect order prevailed throughout the day.†

* The oration soon afterwards appeared in *The Far West*, a periodical published at Liberty, Clay County, Missouri. It was also published in pamphlet form from the office of the "*Elders' Journal.*" (See statement of Ebenezer Robinson in *The Return*, vol. 1, p. 170). This oration by Sidney Rigdon has always been severely criticised as containing passages that were ill-advised and vehemently bitter. Especially those passages which threatened a war of extermination upon mobs should they again arise to plague the Saints. But when such criticism is made, the rank injustice, the destruction of property and the outrages committed upon the persons of many of the members of the Church, by the Jackson county mob, should also be remembered. Also the failure on the part of the officers of the State to protect the Saints in the enjoyment of their civil and religious liberties or even to return them to their homes in Jackson county—from which failure to magnify the law the Saints were still suffering. When, therefore, they saw mobocracy again threatening them, it is small wonder if they gave way for a moment to anger, and denounced in strong terms those who were likely to disturb their peace and repeat the outrages under which they had so long suffered.

† Following this account of the 4th of July celebration at Far West the Prophet in his history, as heretofore published, takes up the account of the organization of "Kirtland Camp," an organization effected by the First Seven Presidents of the Seventies, assisted by Elder Hyrum Smith. The object of the organization was to move the Saints, who desired to go, in a body, from Kirtland to Missouri. The Prophet in his history gives an account, as already stated, of the organization of this camp and its departure from Kirtland. Then from day to day as more or less important events took place in the camp, he records such events in his own personal history, with the result that his narrative is frequently interrupted by brief paragraphs from the camp's Journal. But as we have the full daily journal of the camp's progress from Kirtland to Far West, written in a most careful and commendable style by the camp's Historian, Elias Smith, it has been decided to publish the history of the camp from the time it met for organization in Kirtland (March, 1838), until its arrival at Far West, (on the 2nd day of October, 1838), without other interruptions; and then omit from the narrative of the Prophet those occasional paragraphs taken from the said journal of the camp. This arrangement will relieve the Prophet's narrative of so many interruptions, and on the other hand it will give an unbroken narrative from an original document of one of the most remarkable organizations and journeys in the early history of the

July 6.—This day I received a letter from Heber C. Kimball and Orson Hyde, dated at Kirtland, Ohio, expressing their good feelings, firmness in the faith and prosperity.

A Word from Elders Kimball and Hyde

Also another letter from my brother Don Carlos Smith, as follows:

NINE MILES FROM TERRE HAUTE, INDIANA.

Brother Joseph:—I sit down to inform you of our situation at the present time. I started from Norton, Ohio, the 7th of May, in company with father, William, Wilkins Jenkins Salisbury, William McClary and Lewis Robbins, and families, also Sister Singly. We started with fifteen horses, seven wagons, and two cows. We have left two horses by the way sick, and a third horse (our main dependence) was taken lame last evening, and is not able to travel, and we have stopped to doctor him. We were disappointed on every hand before we started in getting money. We got no assistance whatever, only as we have taken in Sister Singly, and she has assisted us as far as her means extended. We had, when we started, $75 in money. We sold the two cows for $13.50 per cow. We have sold of your goods to the amount of $45.74, and now we have only $25 to carry twenty-eight souls and thirteen horses five hundred miles.

We have lived very close and camped out at night, notwithstanding the rain and cold, and my baby only two weeks old when we started. Agnes* is very feeble; father and mother are not well and very much fatigued; mother has a severe cold, and in fact it is nothing but the prayer of faith and the power of God, that will sustain them and bring them through. Our courage is good, and I think we shall be brought through. I leave it with you and Hyrum to devise some way to assist us to some more expense money. We have unaccountably bad roads, had our horses down in the mud, and broke one wagon tongue and thills, and broke down the carriage twice, and yet we are all alive and encamped on a dry place for almost the first time. Poverty is a heavy load, but we are all obliged to welter under it.

It is now dark and I close. May the Lord bless you all, and bring us together, is my prayer. Amen. All the arrangements that brother Hyrum left for getting money failed; they did not gain us one cent.

DON C. SMITH.

Church. This promised history will be inserted at the point of the Prophet's narrative where the camp arrives at Far West.

* This refers to Don Carlos Smith's wife, who before her marriage to him in Kirtland, on July 30, 1835, was Agnes Coolbirth.

The three revelations* which I received January 12, 1838, the day I left Kirtland, were read in the public congregation at Far West; and the same day I inquired of the Lord, "O Lord! Show unto thy servant how much thou requirest of the properties of thy people for a tithing," and received the following answer, which was also read in public:

Missing Revelations.

Revelation, Given at Far West, July 8, 1838.†

1. Verily, thus saith the Lord, I require all their surplus property to be put into the hands of the Bishop of my Church of Zion,

2. For the building of mine house, and for the laying of the foundation of Zion and for the Priesthood, and for the debts of the Presidency of my Church;

3. And this shall be the beginning of the tithing of my people;

4. And after that, those who have thus been tithed, shall pay one-tenth of all their interest annually; and this shall be a standing law unto them forever, for my holy Priesthood, saith the Lord.

5. Verily I say unto you, it shall come to pass, that all those who gather unto the Land of Zion shall be tithed of their surplus properties, and shall observe this law, or they shall not be found worthy to abide among you.

6. And I say unto you, if my people observe not this law, to keep it holy, and by this law sanctify the land of Zion unto me, that my statutes and my judgments may be kept thereon, that it may be most holy, behold, verily I say unto you, it shall not be a land of Zion unto you;

7. And this shall be an ensample unto all the stakes of Zion. Even so. Amen.

Also I received the following:

Revelation, given July 8, 1838, making known the disposition of the properties tithed as named in the preceding revelation.‡

Verily, thus saith the Lord, the time is now come that it shall be disposed of by a council composed of the First Presidency of my Church, and of the Bishop and his council, and by my High Council, and by mine own voice unto them, saith the Lord. Even so. Amen.

* The three revelations here referred to do not appear in the Doctrine and Covenants nor in any other publication. Diligent search also has been made for them through the several packages of Church documents in the Historian's Office, but they have not been found.

† Doctrine and Covenants, sec. cxix.

‡ Doctrine and Covenants, sec. cxx.

Also I received the following:

*Revelation given to William Marks, Newel K. Whitney, Oliver Granger and others, at Far West, July 8, 1838.**

1. Verily thus saith the Lord unto my servant William Marks, and also unto my servant N. K. Whitney, let them settle up their business speedily and journey from the land of Kirtland, before I, the Lord, send again the snows upon the earth;

2. Let them awake, and arise, and come forth, and not tarry, for I, the Lord, command it;

3. Therefore if they tarry it shall not be well with them.

4. Let them repent of all their sins, and of all their covetous desires, before me, saith the Lord, for what is property unto me, saith the Lord?

5. Let the properties of Kirtland be turned out for debts, saith the Lord. Let them go, saith the Lord, and whatsoever remaineth, let it remain in your hands, saith the Lord;

6. For have I not the fowls of heaven, and also the fish of the sea, and the beasts of the mountains? Have I not made the earth? Do I not hold the destinies of all the armies of the nations of the earth?

7. Therefore will I not make solitary places to bud and to blossom, and to bring forth in abundance, saith the Lord?

8. Is there not room enough upon the mountains of Adam-ondi-Ahman, and on the plains of Olaha Shinehah, or the land where Adam dwelt, that you should covet that which is but the drop, and neglect the more weighty matters?

9. Therefore come up hither unto the land of my people, even Zion.

10. Let my servant William Marks be faithful over a few things, and he shall be ruler over many. Let him preside in the midst of my people in the city of Far West, and let him be blessed with the blessings of my people.

11. Let my servant N. K. Whitney be ashamed of the Nicholatine band and of all their secret abominations, and of all his littleness of soul before me, saith the Lord, and come up to the land of Adam-ondi-Ahman, and be a Bishop unto my people, saith the Lord, not in name but in deed, saith the Lord.

12. And again, I say unto you, I remember my servant Oliver Granger, behold, verily I say unto him, that his name shall be had in sacred remembrance from generation to generation, for ever and ever, saith the Lord.

13. Therefore let him contend earnestly for the redemption of the

* Doctrine and Covenants, sec. cxvii.

First Presidency of my Church, saith the Lord, and when he falls he shall rise again, for his sacrifice shall be more sacred unto me, than his increase, saith the Lord;

14. Therefore let him come up hither speedily, unto the land of Zion, and in the due time he shall be made a merchant unto my name, saith the Lord, for the benefit of my people;

15. Therefore let no man despise my servant Oliver Granger, but let the blessings of my people be on him for ever and ever.

16. And again, verily I say unto you, let all my servants in the land of Kirtland remember the Lord their God, and mine house also, to keep and preserve it holy, and to overthrow the money changers in mine own due time, saith the Lord. Even so. Amen.

Also I received the following:

*Revelation given at Far West, July 8, 1838, in answer to the question, Show unto us thy will O Lord concerning the Twelve.**

1. Verily, thus saith the Lord, let a conference be held immediately, let the Twelve be organized, and let men be appointed to supply the place of those who are fallen.

2. Let my servant Thomas remain for a season in the land of Zion, to publish my word.

3. Let the residue continue to preach from that hour, and if they will do this in all lowliness of heart, in meekness and humility, and long-suffering, I, the Lord, give unto them a promise that I will provide for their families, and an effectual door shall be opened for them, from henceforth;

4. And next spring let them depart to go over the great waters, and there promulgate my gospel, the fullness thereof, and bear record of my name.

5. Let them take leave of my Saints in the city Far West, on the

* Doctrine and Covenants,sec. cxviii. This date,the 8th of July, 1838, is remakable for the many revelations given. In addition to the foregoing which are printed in the Doctrine and Covenants, in the sections indicated in the foot notes, the following was also received, which is not published in the Doctrine and Covenants nor elsewhere. It is found on file in Package XVI at the Historian's Office: Revelation given July 8, 1838, making known the duty of William W. Phelps and Frederick G. Williams.

"Verily, thus saith the Lord,in consequence of their transgressions their former standing has been taken away from them, and now, if they will be saved, let them be ordained as Elders in my Church to preach my Gospel and travel abroad from land to land and from place to place, to gather mine elect unto me, saith the Lord, and let this be their labors from henceforth. Amen.

26th day of April next, on the building spot of my house, saith the Lord.

6. Let my servant John Taylor, and also my servant John E. Page, also my servant Wilford Woodruff, and also my servant Willard Richards, be appointed to fill the places of those who have fallen, and be officially notified of their appointment.

Minutes of a Meeting of the Twelve.

Far West, July 9, 1838, a conference of the Twelve Apostles assembled at Far West, agreeable to the revelation, given July 8, 1838. Present, Thomas B. Marsh, David W. Patten, Brigham Young, Parley P. Pratt and William Smith: T. B. Marsh, presiding.

Resolved 1st. That the persons who are to fill the places of those who are fallen, be immediately notified to come to Far West; as also, those of the Twelve who are not present.

Resolved 2nd. That Thomas B. Marsh notify Wilford Woodruff, that Parley P. Pratt notify Orson Pratt, and that President Rigdon notify Willard Richards, who is now in England.

Voted that President Marsh publish the same in next number of *The Elders' Journal.*

President Rigdon gave some counsel concerning the provisions necessary to be made for the families of the Twelve, while laboring in the cause of their Redeemer, advising them to instruct their converts to move without delay to the places of gathering, and there to strictly attend to the law of God.

T. B. MARSH, President.
G. W. ROBINSON, Clerk.

Tuesday, 10.—About this time I visited Adam-ondi-Ahman in company with President Rigdon, Brother Hyrum, and George W. Robinson.

Thursday, 26.—The First Presidency, High Council, and Bishop's court assembled at Far West to dispose of the public properties of the Church in the hands of the Bishop, many of the brethren having consecrated their surplus property according to the revelations.

The Disposition of Public Church Properties.

It was agreed that the First Presidency should keep all their properties that they could dispose of to advantage, for their support, and the remainder be put into the hands of the Bishop or Bishops, according to the commandments.

Moved, seconded, and carried unanimously:

"First—That the First Presidency shall have their expenses defrayed in going to, and returning from Adam ondi-Ahman; equally by the Bishop of each place.

"Second—That all the traveling expenses of the First Presidency shall be defrayed.

"Third—That the Bishop be authorized to pay orders coming from the east, inasmuch as they will consecrate liberally, but this is to be done under the inspection of the First Presidency.

"Fourth—That the First Presidency shall have the prerogative to direct the Bishop as to whose orders shall or may be paid by him in this place, or in his jurisdiction.

"Fifth—That the Bishop of Zion receive all consecrations from those living east, west, and south, who are not in the jurisdiction of a Bishop of any other stake.

"Sixth—That we use our influence to put a stop to the selling of liquors in the city Far West, or in our midst, that our streets may not be filled with drunkenness; and that we use our influence to bring down the price of provisions.

"Seventh—That Brother William W. Phelps be requested to draw up a petition to locate the county seat at Far West."

Arrival of Saints from Canada.

Saturday, 28.—I left Far West for Adam-ondi-Ahman, in company with President Rigdon, to transact some important business, and to settle some Canadian brethren in that place, as they are emigrating rapidly to this land from all parts of the country.

Elder Babbitt, with his company from Canada has arrived, and Brother Theodore Turley is with him.

Sunday, 29.—Elders Kimball and Hyde having just returned from England, preached in Far West.

Monday, 30.—The circuit court sat in Far West, Judge King presiding.

I returned this evening from Adam-ondi-Ahman to Far West, with President Rigdon.

Tuesday, 31.—Attended the circuit court awhile, and received a visit from Judge King.

Some time in July we succeeded in publishing the third

number of the *Elders' Journal;* Joseph Smith, Jun., editor; Thomas B. Marsh, printer and publisher. In this number of the *Journal* was published the following Epistle of David W. Patten, one of the Twelve Apstles of the last days:

Publication of the *Elders' Journal.*

The Epistle of Elder David W. Patten.

To the Saints Scattered Abroad:

DEAR BRETHREN:—Whereas many have taken in hand to set forth the kingdom of God on earth, and have testified of the grace of God, as given unto them to publish unto you, I also feel it my duty to write unto you, touching the grace of God given unto me, to you-ward, concerning the dispensation we have received, which is the greatest of all dispensations, and has been spoken of by the mouth of all the holy Prophets since the world began.

In this my communication to you, I design to notice some of these prophecies. Now, the Apostle Paul says on this wise: "For I would not, brethren, that ye should be ignorant of this mystery, lest ye should be wise in your own conceits; that blindness in part is happened to Israel, until the fullness of the Gentiles be come in. And so all Israel shall be saved: as it is written, There shall come out of Sion the Deliverer, and shall turn away ungodliness from Jacob." What is it that he says? "For I would not have you ignorant." Ignorant of what? Why of this mystery, that blindness in part had happened unto Israel. And to what end? Why, that salvation might come unto the Gentiles. "Now if the fall of them be the riches of the world, and the diminishing of them the riches of the Gentiles; how much more their fullness!" "For I speak to you Gentiles, inasmuch as I am the Apostle of the Gentiles, I magnify mine office." (See Rom., xi: 12, 13). Now we are to understand the Apostle, as speaking of the return of Israel, when he said, "How much more their fullness," in their return. "For I would not have you ignorant concerning this matter," that blindnesss will depart from them in the day that the fullness of the Gentiles is come in. And the reason is very obvious, because it is said, that "Out of Sion shall come the deliverer;" and for what cause? Why? That the word of God might be fulfilled, that this deliverer might, through the grace and mercy of God, "turn away ungodliness from Jacob." This work evidently commences at the time God begins to take the darkness from the minds of Israel, for this will be the work of God by the deliverer, for He shall turn away ungodliness from the whole family of Jacob, "for this is my covenant unto them, when I shall take away their sins."

Now, then, we can see that this deliverer is a kind of harbinger or forerunner, that is, one that is sent to prepare the way for another, and this deliverer is such a one, for he comes to turn away ungodliness from Jacob, consequently he must receive a dispensation and an authority suitable to his calling, or he could not turn away ungodliness from Jacob, nor fulfill the Scriptures. But the words of the prophets must be fulfilled, and in order to do this, to this messenger must be given the dispensation of the fullness of times, according to the prophets. For Paul says again, in speaking of the dispensation of the fullness of times, "Having made known unto us the mystery of His will, according to His good pleasure, which He hath purposed in Himself: that in the dispensation of the fullness of times, He might gather together in one all things in Christ, both which are in heaven, and which are on earth; even in Him." (Ephesians, i: 9). And Isaiah says, "And it shall come to pass in that day, that the Lord shall set His hand again the second time to recover the remnant of His people." (chapter xi: 11). Now is the time that the deliverer shall come out of Zion and turn away ungodliness from the house of Israel. Now the Lord has said that He would set His hand the second time, and we ask, for what, but to recover the house of Jacob? For what have they fallen? Most assuredly they have broken the covenant that God had made with their fathers, and through their fathers with them. For Paul says, "Thou wilt say then, The branches were broken off, that I might be grafted in. Well; because of unbelief they were broken off, and thou standest by faith. Be not highminded, but fear."—Rom., xi: 18, 20.

Now it is evident that the Jews did forsake the Lord, and by that means they broke the covenant, and now we see the need of the Lord setting His hand the second time to gather His people according to Eph., i: 10, "That in the dispensation of the fullness of times, he might gather together in one all things in Christ, both which are in heaven, and which are on earth." Now, I ask, what is a dispensation? I answer, it is power and authority to dispense the word of God, and to administer in all the ordinances thereof. This is what we are to understand by it, for no man ever had the Holy Ghost to deliver the Gospel, or to prophesy of things to come, but had liberty to fulfill his mission; consequently the argument is clear; for it proves itself; nevertheless I will call on the Scriptures to prove the assertion: "If ye have heard of the dispensation of the grace of God, which is given me to you-ward: how that by revelation he made known unto me the mystery;(as I wrote afore in few words)." (Ephesians, iii: 2.) And also, Colossians, i: 25. "Whereof I am made a minister, according to the dispensation of God which is given to me for you, to fulfill the word of God." It is evident, then, that the dispensation given to the Apostle, came to him by revelation from God. Then by this we may understand, in some degree, the power by which he spake, and also the dispensation of the fullness of times.

Now this, at first thought, would appear very small to some who are not acquainted with the order of God from the beginning; but when we take under consideration the plan of God for the salvation of the world, we can readily see that plan carried out most faithfully in all its bearings. Soon after the fall of Adam, the plan of salvation was made known to him of God Himself; who in like manner, in the meridian of time, revealed the same in sending His first begotten Son Jesus Christ, who also revealed the same to the Apostles; and God raised him from the dead to perfect the plan, and the Apostles were made special witnesses of that plan, and testified that in the dispensation of the fullness of times, God would gather together in one all things in Christ, whether they be things in heaven, or things on the earth.

Now the thing to be known is, what the fullness of times means, or the extent or authority thereof. It means this, that the dispensation of the fullness of times is made up of all the dispensations that ever have been given since the world began, until this time. Unto Adam first was given a dispensation. It is well known that God spake to him with His own voice in the garden, and gave him the promise of the Messiah. And unto Noah also was a dispensation given; for Jesus said, "As it was in the days of Noah, so shall it be also in the days of the Son of man;" and as the righteous were saved then, and the wicked destroyed, so it will be now. And from Noah to Abraham, and from Abraham to Moses, and from Moses to Elias, and from Elias to John the Baptist, and from then to Jesus Christ, and from Jesus Christ to Peter, James, and John, the Apostles—all received in their time a dispensation by revelation from God, to accomplish the great scheme of restitution, spoken of by all the holy prophets since the world began; the end of which is the dispensation of the fullness of times, in the which all things shall be fulfilled that have been spoken of since the earth was made.

Now the question is, unto whom is this dispensation to be given? Or by whom to be revealed? The answer is, to the deliverer that is to come out of Zion, and be given to him by the angel of God. "And I saw another angel, fly in the midst of heaven, having the everlasting Gospel to preach unto them that dwell on the earth, and to every nation. and kindred, and tongue, and people, saying with a loud voice, Fear God, and give glory to Him: for the hour of His judgment is come: and worship Him that made heaven, and earth, and the sea, and the fountains of waters." (Revelation, xiv: 6, 7). Now observe, this angel delivers the everlasting Gospel to man on the earth, and that, too, when the hour of the judgments of God had come on the generation in which the Lord should set His hand the second time to gather His people, as stated above. Now we have learned that this deliverer must be clothed with the power of all the other dispensations, or his dispensation could not be called the dispensation of the fullness of times, for this it means, that all things shall be revealed both in heaven and on earth; for the Lord said there is nothing secret that shall not be revealed, or hid that shall not come abroad, and be proclaimed upon the house top, and this may with propriety be called the fullness of times.

The authority connected with the ordinances, renders the time very desirable to the man of God, and renders him happy amidst all his trials and afflictions. To such a one through the grace of God we are indebted for this dispensation, as given by the angel of the Lord. But to what tribe of Israel was it to be delivered? We answer, to Ephraim, because to him were the greater blessings given. For the Lord said to his father Joseph, A seer shall the Lord thy God raise up of the fruit of thy loins, and he shall be a choice seer unto the fruit of thy loins. Yea, he truly said, Thus saith the Lord, a choice seer will I raise up out of the fruit of thy loins, and he shall be esteemed highly, and unto him will I give commandment that he shall do a work for the fruit of thy loins, his brethren, which shall be of great worth unto them, even to the bringing of them to the knowledge of the covenants which I have made with their fathers. And I will give unto him a commandment that he shall do none other work save the work which I shall command him, and I will make him great in mine eyes, for he shall do my work, and he shall be great like unto Moses; and out of weakness he shall be made strong, in that day when my work shall commence among all people, unto the restoring of the house of Israel, saith the Lord.

And thus prophesied Joseph, saying—Behold, that seer will the Lord bless, and they that seek to destroy him shall be confounded. Behold, I am sure of the fulfillment of this promise, and his name shall be called after the name of his father, and he shall be like unto me, for the thing which the Lord shall bring forth by his hand, by the power of the Father, shall bring forth my people unto salvation.

And thus prophesied Joseph, "I am sure of this thing, even as I am sure of the promise of Moses." (II Nephi, iii: 6-16). And again, Jesus says, as recorded in the Book of Mormon, page 526: "Behold my servant shall deal very prudently; he shall be exalted and extolled, and be very high. As many as were astonished at thee. * * * So shall he sprinkle many nations; the kings shall shut their mouths at him, for that which had been told them shall they see; and that which they had not heard shall they consider." Upon this servant is bestowed the keys of the dispensation of the fullness of times, that from him the Priesthood of God, through our Lord Jesus Christ, might be given to many, and the order of this dispensation established on the earth. And to the Church He has said by commandment, "Wherefore, meaning the Church, thou shalt give heed unto all his words and commandments, which he shall give unto you as he receiveth them, walking in all holiness before me; for his word ye shall receive as if from my own mouth, in all patience and faith; for by doing these things, the gates of hell shall not prevail against you."—Doctrine and Covenants, sec. xxi.

Now, my readers, you can see in some degree the grace given to this man of God, to us-ward: that we, by the great mercy of God, should receive from under his hands, the Gospel of Jesus Christ, having the promise of partaking of the fruit of the vine on the earth with him, and with the holy Prophets and Patriarchs, our fathers. For those holy men are angels now; and these are they who make the fullness of times complete with us; and they who sin against this authority given to him (the aforementioned man of God), sin not againt him only, but against Moroni, who holds the keys of the stick of Ephraim [Book of Mormon], and also Elias, who holds the keys of bringing to pass the restitution of all things, and also John, the son of Zacharias, which Zacharias Elias visited, and gave promise that he should have a son, and his name should be John, and he should be filled with the spirit of Elias, which John I have sent unto you, my servants Joseph Smith, Jun, and Oliver Cowdery, to ordain you to this first Priesthood, even as Aaron; and also Elijah who holds the keys of committing the power to turn the hearts of the fathers to the children, and the hearts of the children to the fathers, that the whole earth may not be smitten with a curse; and also Joseph and Jacob and Isaac and Abraham, your fathers, by whom the promises remain; and also Michael, or Adam, the Father of all, the Prince of all, the Ancient of Days; and also Peter and James and John, whom I have sent unto you, by whom I have ordained you, and confirmed you to be Apostles and especial witnesses of my name, and bear the keys of your ministry, and of the same things I revealed unto them, unto whom I have committed the keys of my kingdom, and a dispensation of the Gospel for the last times, and for the fullness of times, in the which I will gather together in one all things, both which are in heaven, and which are on earth. (Doctrine and Covenants, sec. xxvii.)

Therefore, brethren, beware concerning yourselves, that you sin not against the authority of this dispensation, nor think lightly of those whom God has counted worthy for so great a calling, and for whose sake He hath made them servants unto you, that you might be made the heirs of God to inherit so great a blessing, and be prepared for the great assembly, and sit there with the Ancient of Days, even Adam our father, who shall come to prepare you for the coming of Jesus Christ our Lord; for the time is at hand, therefore gather up your effects, and gather together upon the land which the Lord has appointed for your safety.

DAVID W. PATTEN.

CHAPTER VI.

THE BEGINNING OF TROUBLE IN CALDWELL AND DAVIESS COUNTIES.

Wednesday, August 1.—I tarried at home with my family, also the 2nd and 3rd, to refresh myself after my many late fatigues and arduous duties which I had been called upon to perform.

The Prophet Rests.

Sunday, 5.—I attended meeting. Elder Erastus Snow* preached, after which I addressed the congregation, and particularly the Elders, on the principle of wisdom, etc. President Rigdon preached in the afternoon, and several were confirmed, among whom was Frederick G. Williams, who had recently been re-baptized.

Monday, 6.—This morning my council met me at my house, to consider the conduct of certain Canada brethren, who had settled on the forks of Grand river, contrary to counsel. On investigation, it was resolved that they must return to Adam-ondi-Ahman, according to counsel, or they would not be considered one with us.

Reproof of Canadian Brethren.

This day the citizens of Caldwell county assembled at Far West, and organized by calling Elias Higbee to the chair, and appointing George W. Robinson secretary.

* Erastus Snow was the son of Levi and Lucina Snow. His ancestors were among the early settlers of the Massachusetts colony. He was born on the 9th of November, 1818, and converted to the Gospel in the Spring of 1832, through the ministry of Elders Orson Pratt and Luke S. Johnson. Though converted to the Gospel by these Elders he was baptized by his elder brother, William, on the 3rd of February, 1833, and soon afterwards was ordained a teacher and commenced his work in the ministry. Previous to his arrival at Far West he had been active in the ministry for several years, preaching extensively in Ohio, New York and Pennsylvania. He was a member of the second quorum of Seventies, and had already given evidence of his sterling integrity and untiring efforts as a minister of the Lord Jesus Christ which so characterized all the subsequent years of his long life.

W. W. Phelps having resigned the office of postmaster, it was voted unanimously that Sidney Rigdon be recommended to the Postmaster General, as the person of our choice to fill the place of W. W. Phelps, as postmaster in this city.

A Citizens' Meeting at Far West.

In the afternoon, the citizens of Far West assembled in the school house and organized the meeting by calling Judge Elias Higbee to the chair, and appointing George W. Robinson, secretary. I stated to the meeting, that the time had come when it was necessary that we should have a weekly newspaper, to unite the people, and give the news of the day. It was unanimously agreed that such a paper be established, and that President Sidney Rigdon should be the editor. It was also voted that a petition be circulated to locate the county seat at Far West. I addressed the meeting on the propriety of the measure, and also on the duty of the brethren to come into cities to build and live, and carry on their farms out of the cities, according to the order of God. President Rigdon and Brother Hyrum Smith spoke upon the same subject.

Judge Morin's Friendly Warning.

Some two weeks previous to this, Judge Morin, who lived at Mill Port, informed John D. Lee* and Levi Stewart, that it was determined by the mob to prevent the "Mormons" from voting at the election on the sixth day of August, and thereby elect Colonel William P. Peniston, who led the mob in Clay county. He also advised them to go prepared for an attack, to stand their ground, and have their rights.

The brethren, hoping better things, gave little heed to Judge Morin's friendly counsel, and repaired to the polls at Gallatin, the shire town of Daviess county, without weapons.

About eleven o'clock a. m., William P. Peniston mounted a barrel, and harangued the electors for the pur-

* John D. Lee was born on the 6th of September, 1812, in the town of Kaskaskia, Randolph County, Illinois; and was the son of Ralph Lee, of Virginia, and the daughter of John Doyle, of Nashville, Tennessee.

pose of exciting them against the "Mormons," saying, "The Mormon leaders are a set of horse thieves, liars, counterfeiters, and you know they profess to heal the sick, and cast out devils, and you all know that is a lie." He further said that the members of the Church were dupes, and not too good to take a false oath on any common occasion; that they would steal, and he did not consider property safe where they were; that he was opposed to their settling in Daviess county; and if they suffered the "Mormons" to vote, the people would soon lose their suffrage; "and," said he, addressing the Saints, "I headed a mob to drive you out of Clay county, and would not prevent your being mobbed now."

Peniston's Harangue.

Richard (called Dick) Welding, the mob bully, just drunk enough for the occasion, began a discussion with Brother Samuel Brown, by saying, "The Mormons were not allowed to vote in Clay county no more than the negroes," and attempted to strike Brown, who gradually retreated, parrying the blow with his umbrella, while Welding continued to press upon him, calling him a liar, etc., and meanwhile trying to repeat the blow on Brown. Perry Durphy sought to suppress the difficulty by holding Welding's arm, when five or six of the mobbers seized Durphy and commenced beating him with clubs, boards, and crying, "*Kill him, kill him*, when a general scuffle commenced with fists and clubs, the mobbers being about ten to one of the brethren. Abraham Nelson was knocked down, and had his clothes torn off, and while trying to get up was attacked again, when his brother, Hyrum Nelson, ran in amongst them, and knocked the mobbers down with the butt of his whip. Riley Stewart struck Welding on the head, which brought him to the ground. The mob cried out, "Dick Weldin's dead; who killed Dick?" And they fell upon Riley, knocked him down, kicked him, crying, "Kill him, kill him; shoot him," and they would have killed him, had not

"Dick" Welding's Row.

John L. Butler sprung in amongst them and knocked them down. During about five minutes it was one succession of knock downs, when the mob dispersed to get fire arms.

Very few of the brethren voted. Riley, escaping across the river, had his wounds dressed, and returned home.

John L. Butler's speech.

John L. Butler called the brethren together and made a speech, saying, "We are American citizens; our fathers fought for their liberty, and we will maintain the same principles." The authorities of the county finally came to the brethren, and requested them to withdraw, stating that it was a premeditated thing to prevent the "Mormons" from voting.

Gathering of the Mob

The brethren held a council about one-fourth of a mile out of town, where they saw mob recruits coming in, in small parties, from five and ten, to twenty-five in number cursing and swearing, and armed with clubs, pistols, dirks, and some guns. The brethren not having arms, thought it wisdom to return to their farms, collect their families, and hide them in a thicket of hazel bush, which they did, and stood guard around them through the night, while the women and children lay on the ground in the rain.

Reports of Gallatin Trouble Reach Far West.

Tuesday, 7.—A report came to Far West this morning, by way of those not belonging to the Church, to the effect that at the election at Gallatin, yesterday, two or three of our brethren were killed by the Missourians, and left upon the ground, and not suffered to be interred; that the brethren were prevented from voting, and a majority of the inhabitants of Daviess county were determined to drive the Saints from that county.

The Departure of the Prophet for Gallatin.

On hearing this report, I started for Gallatin, to assist the brethren, accompanied by President Rigdon, Brother Hyrum Smith, and fifteen or twenty others, who were armed for their own protection; and the command of the company was given to George W. Robinson.

On our way we were joined by the brethren from different parts of the county, some of whom were attacked by the mob, but we all reached Colonel Wight's that night in safety, where we found some of the brethren who had been mobbed at Gallatin, with others, waiting for our counsel. Here we received the cheering intelligence that none of the brethren were killed, although several were badly wounded.

The Prophet Commends the Brethren for Standing for Their Rights.

From the best information, about one hundred and fifty Missourians warred against from six to twelve of our brethren, who fought like lions. Several Missourians had their skulls cracked. Blessed be the memory of those few brethren who contended so strenuously for their constitutional rights and religious freedom, against such an overwhelming force of desperadoes!

Interview with Adam Black.

Wednesday, 8.—After spending the night in counsel at Colonel Wight's, I rode out with some of the brethren to view the situation of affairs in that region, and among others, called on Adam Black, justice of the peace, and judge elect for Daviess county, who had some time previous sold his farm to Brother Vinson Knight, and received part pay according to agreement, and afterwards united himself with a band of mobbers to drive the Saints from, and prevent their settling in, Daviess county. On interrogation, he confessed what he had done, and in consequence of this violation of his oath as magistrate, we asked him to give us some satisfaction so that we might know whether he was our friend or enemy, whether or not he would administer the law in justice; and politely requested him to sign an agreement of peace, but being jealous, he would not sign it, but said he would write one himself to our satisfaction, and sign it, which he did, as follows—

Adam Black's Agreement.

I, Adam Black, a Justice of the Peace of Daviess county, do hereby

Sertify to the people, *coled Mormin*, that he is bound to *suport* the Constitution of this State, and of the United State, and he is not attached to any mob, nor will not attach himself to any such people, and so long as they will not molest me, I will not molest them. This the 8th day of August, 1838.

ADAM BLACK, J. P.*

Hoping he would abide his own decision, and support the law, we left him in peace, and returned to Colonel Wight's at Adam-ondi-Ahman.

Interview with Citizens of Mill Port.

In the evening some of the citizens from Mill Port called on us, and we agreed to meet some of the principal men of the county in council, at Adam-ondi-Ahman the next day at twelve o'clock, noon.

Thursday, 9.—The Committee assembled at Adam-ondi-Ahman at twelve, according to previous appointment, viz., on the part of Mill Port citizens, Joseph Morin, senator elect: John Williams, representative elect; James B. Turner, clerk of the circuit court, and others: on the part of the Saints, Lyman Wight, Vinson Knight, John Smith, Reynolds Cahoon, and others. At this meeting both parties entered into a covenant of peace, to preserve each other's rights, and stand in each other's defense; that if men did wrong, neither party would uphold them or endeavor to screen them from justice, but deliver up all offenders to be dealt with according to law and justice. The assembly dispersed on these friendly terms, myself and friends returning to Far West, where we arrived about midnight and found all quiet.

Friday, 10.—Being somewhat fatigued I spent the day with my family, transacting but little business.

Treaties of Peace of Little Avail.

The spirit of mobocracy continued to stalk abroad, notwithstanding all our treaties of peace, as will be seen by the following affidavit—

* The original orthography and composition of this note are preserved in the above copy.

Peniston's Affidavit.

STATE OF MISSOURI, }
RAY COUNTY. } ss.

Personally appeared before me, the undersigned, judge of the Fifth Judicial Circuit, William P. Peniston, and makes oath that he has good reason to believe, and that he verily does believe, that there is now collected and embodied in the County of Daviess, a large body of armed men, whose movements and conduct are of a highly insurrectionary and unlawful character; that they consist of about five hundred men, and that they, or a part of them, to the number of one hundred and twenty, have committed violence against Adam Black, by surrounding his house, and taking him in a violent manner, and subjecting him to great indignities, by forcing him, under threats of immediate death, to sign a paper writing of a very disgraceful character, and by threatening to do the same to all the old settlers and citizens of Daviess county; and that they have, as a collected and armed body, threatened to put to instant death this affiant on sight; and that he verily believes they will accomplish that act without they are prevented; and also that they have threatened the same to Wm. Bowman and others; and this affiant states that he verily believes all the above facts to be true, and that the body of men now assembled do intend to commit great violence to many of the citizens of Daviess county, and that they have already done so to Adam Black; and this affiant verily believes, from information of others, that Joseph Smith, Jun., and Lyman Wight are the leaders of this body of armed men, and the names of others thus combined are not certainly known to this affiant; and he further states the fact to be that it is his opinion, and he verily believes, that it is the object of this body of armed men, to take vengeance for some injuries, or imaginary injuries, done to some of their friends, and to intimidate and drive from the county all the old citizens, and possess themselves of their lands, or to force such as do not leave, to come into their measures and submit to their dictation.

WILLIAM P. PENISTON.

Sworn to and subscribed before me the undersigned judge, as aforesaid, this 10th day of August, 1838.

AUSTIN A. KING.

Reflections of the Prophet

The above was also sworn to by William Bowman, Wilson McKinney, and John Netherton. So it is that when men's hearts become hardened and corrupt, they will more readily swear to lies than speak the truth.

At this time some of the brethren had removed with

their families from the vicinity of Gallatin, to Diahman and Far West, for safety.

Saturday, 11.—This morning I left Far West, with my council and Elder Almon W. Babbitt, to visit the brethren on the Forks of Grand river, who had come from Canada with Elder Babbitt, and settled at that place contrary to counsel.

Inquiry at Far West concerning Gallatin Affair.

In the afternoon, after my departure, a committee from Ray county arrived at Far West, to inquire into the proceedings of our society in going armed into Daviess county, complaint having been entered in Ray county by Adam Black, William P. Peniston, and others. The committee from Ray county requested an interview with a committee of Caldwell, and a general meeting was called at the city hall, at six in the evening, when it was stated that they were assembled to take into consideration the doings of the citizens of Ray county, wherein they have accused the "Mormons" of this place of breaking the peace, in defending their rights and those of their brethren in the county of Daviess. The meeting was organized by appointing Bishop Edward Partridge, chairman; and Geo. W. Robinson, clerk. The meeting adopted the following—

Resolutions.

"Resolved 1st. That a committee of seven be appointed to confer with the committee from Ray county.

"Resolved 2nd. That this committee, with their secretary, be authorized to answer such questions as may be offered by the committee from Ray county, and as are named in the document presented to this meeting, purporting to be the preamble and resolutions of the citizens of Ray county.

"Resolved 3rd. That whereas the document referred to has no date or signature, our committee judge of the fact, and act accordingly.

"Resolved 4th. That our committee report their proceedings to this meeting as soon as possible.

"EDWARD PARTRIDGE, Chairman,
"GEO. W. ROBINSON, Clerk."

Sunday, 12.—I continued with the brethren at the Forks

of Grand river, offering such counsel as their situation required.

Monday, 13.—I returned with my council to Far West. We were chased ten or twelve miles, by some evil designing men, but we eluded their pursuit. When within about eight miles of home, we met some brethren who had come to inform us that a writ had been issued by Judge King, for my arrest, and that of Lyman Wight, for attempting to defend our rights against the mob.*

Chased by a Mob.

Tuesday and Wednesday, 14 and 15.—I spent principally at home, engaged in domestic affairs.

Thursday, 16.—I spent principally at home.

The sheriff of Daviess county, accompanied by Judge Morin, called and notified me, that he had a writ to take me to Daviess county, for trial, for visiting that county on the seventh instant.

The Prophet's Interview with the Sheriff of Daviess County.

It had been currently reported that I would not be apprehended by legal process, and that I would not submit to the laws of the land; but I told the sheriff that I intended always to submit to the laws of our country, but I wished to be tried in my own county, as the citizens of Daviess county were highly exasperated at me, and that the laws of the country gave me this privilege. Upon hearing this, the sheriff declined serving the writ, and said he would go to Richmond, and see Judge King on the subject. I told him I would remain at home until his return.

The sheriff returned from Richmond, and found me at home (where I had remained during his absence), and informed me very gravely, that I was out of his jurisdiction, and that he could not act in Caldwell county, and retired.

August 20.—Nothing peculiar transpired at Far West, from the sixteenth to this day, when the inhabitants of the different parts of the county met to organize

* The warrant was issued on the misrepresentations of what the Prophet and Lyman Wight did on their visit to Adam Black on the 8th of August.

themselves into Agricultural Companies. I was present and took part in their deliberations. One company was formed, called the "Western Agricultural Company," which voted to enclose one field for grain containing twelve sections, seven thousand six hundred and eighty acres of land. Another company was also organized, called the "Eastern Agricultural Company," the extent of the field not decided.

Organization of Agriculture Companies.

Tuesday, *21*.—Another company was formed, called the "Southern Agricultural Company," the field to be as large as the first mentioned.

Wednesday, *22*.—I spent part of the day in counseling with several brethren upon different subjects.

The brethren continued to gather to Zion daily.

Some time this month the Saints were warned by the mob to leave De Witt, Carroll county.

Thursday, *23*.—This day I spent transacting a variety of business about the city.

Friday, *24*.—I was at home. Also on the 25th, 26th, 27th, 28th, 29th, and 30th.

Affidavit of Adam Black.

STATE OF MISSOURI, }
COUNTY OF DAVIESS. } ss.

Before me, William Dryden, one of the justices of the peace of said county, personally came Adam Black, who being duly sworn according to law, deposeth and saith: that on or about the 8th day of August, 1838, in the county of Daviess, there came an armed force of men, said to be one hundred and fifty-four, to the best of his information, and surrounded his house and family, and threatened him with instant death if he did not sign a certain instrument of writing, binding himself, as a justice of the peace for said county of Daviess, not to molest the people called Mormons; and threatened the lives of himself and other individuals, and did say they intended to make every citizen sign such obligation, and further said they intended to have satisfaction for abuse they had received on the Monday previous, and that they could not submit to the laws: and further saith, that from the best information and his own personal knowledge, that Andrew [Alanson] Ripley, George A. Smith, Ephraim Owens, Harvey Humstead, Hiram Nelson, A. Brown, John L.

Butler, Cornelius [P.] Lott, John Wood, H. Redfield, Riley Stewart, James Whitaker, Andrew Thor, Amos Tubbs, Dr. Gourze, and Abram Nelson was guilty of aiding and abetting in committing and perpetrating the above offense.

ADAM BLACK.

Sworn to and subscribed this the 28th of August, 1838.

W. DRYDEN,
Justice of the Peace of the County aforesaid.

Comment on Adam Black.

This document, with that of the 8th of August, of said Black, shows him in his true light—a detestable, unprincipled mobocrat and *perjured man*.

Thursday, 30.—This day Governor Boggs issued the following order to General Atchison—

Proclamation of Governor Boggs.

HEADQUARTERS OF MILITIA, ADJUTANT GENERAL'S OFFICE,
August 30th, 1838.

General David R. Atchison, 3rd Division, Missouri Militia.

SIR—Indications of Indian disturbances on our immediate frontier, and the recent civil disturbances in the counties of Caldwell, Daviess, and Carroll, render it necessary, as a precautionary measure, that an effective force of the militia be held in readiness to meet either contingency. The Commander-in-Chief therefore orders that you cause to be raised immediately, within the limits of your division, to be held in readiness, and subject to further orders, four hundred mounted men, armed and equipped as infantry or riflemen, and formed into companies according to law, under officers already in commission. The Commander-in-Chief suggests the propriety of your causing the above to be carried into effect, in a manner calculated to produce as little excitement as possible, and report your proceedings to him through the Adjutant General.

By order of the Commander-in-Chief,
B. M. LISLE, Adjutant-General.

A similar letter was also addressed to Major Generals John B. Clark, Samuel D. Lucas, David Willock, Lewis Bolton, Henry W. Crawther, and Thomas D. Grant.

I spent considerable time to day in conversation with Brother John Corrill, in consequence of some expressions made by him, in presence of several brethren who had not been long in the place. Brother Corrill's conduct for some time had been very unbecoming, especially in a man in whom so much confidence had been placed. He said he would not yield his judgment to anything proposed by the Church, or any individuals of the Church, or even the Great I Am, given through the appointed organ, as revelation, but would always act upon his own judgment, let him believe in whatever religion he might. He stated he would always say what he pleased, for he was a Republican, and as such would do, say, act, and believe what he pleased.

Conduct of John Corrill Reproved.

Mark such republicanism as this! A man to oppose his own judgment to the judgment of God, and at the same time to profess to believe in that same God, who has said: "The foolishness of God is wiser than man; and the weakness of God is stronger, than man."

President Rigdon also made some observations to Brother Corrill, which he afterwards acknowledged were correct, and that he understood things different after the interview from what he did before.

CHAPTER VII.

INCREASING DIFFICULTIES BETWEEN THE SAINTS AND THE MOBS OF DAVIESS AND CALDWELL COUNTIES.

Saturday, September 1, 1838.—The First Presidency, with Judge Higbee, as surveyor, started this morning for the half-way house, as it is called, kept by Brother Littlefield, some fourteen or fifteen miles from Far West, directly north—for the purpose of appointing a city of Zion, for the gathering of the Saints in that place, for safety, and from the storm which will soon come upon this generation, and that the brethren may be together, and that they may receive instructions to prepare them for that great day which will come upon this generation as a thief in the night.

The Prophet Leaves Far West to Found a City of Zion.

There is great excitement at present among the Missourians, who are seeking if possible an occasion against us. They are continually chafing us, and provoking us to anger if possible, one sign of threatening after another, but we do not fear them, for the Lord God, the Eternal Father is our God, and Jesus the Mediator is our Savior, and in the great I Am is our strength and confidence.

Excitement Among the Missourians.

We have been driven time after time, and that without cause; and smitten again and again, and that without provocation; until we have proved the world with kindness, and the world has proved us, that we have no designs against any man or set of men, that we injure no man, that we are peaceable with all men, minding our own business, and our business only. We have suffered our rights and our liberties to be taken from us; we have not avenged ourselves of those wrongs; we have appealed to magistrates, to sheriffs, to judges, to

The Prophet's Review of the Wrongs of the Saints.

government and to the President of the United States, all in vain; yet we have yielded peaceably to all these things. We have not complained at the Great God, we murmured not, but peaceably left all; and retired into the back country, in the broad and wild prairies, in the barren and desolate plains, and there commenced anew; we made the desolate places to bud and blossom as the rose; and now the fiend-like race is disposed to give us no rest. Their father the devil, is hourly calling upon them to be up and doing, and they, like willing and obedient children, need not the second admonition; but in the name of Jesus Christ the Son of the living God, we will endure it no longer, if the great God will arm us with courage, with strength and with power, to resist them in their persecutions. We will not act on the offensive, but always on the defensive; our rights and our liberties shall not be taken from us, and we peaceably submit to it, as we have done heretofore, but we will avenge ourselves of our enemies, inasmuch as they will not let us alone.

Site for a City Selected.

But to return again to our subject. We found the place for the city, and the brethren were instructed to gather immediately into it, and soon they should be organized according to the laws of God. A more particular history of this city may be expected hereafter, perhaps at its organization and dedication. We found a new route home, saving, I should think, three or four miles. We arrived at Far West about the close of day.

The High Priests met at Brother Pea's at Far West, and received Levi Richards into their quorum.

Rumors of Mobs Gathering.

Sunday, 2.—The First Presidency attended meeting as usual in the morning. I tarried at home in the evening to examine the Church records, and spent a part of the time in company with a gentleman from Livingston county, who had become considerably excited, on account of a large collection of people, as he said, to take Joseph Smith, Jun., and Lyman Wight, for going to one Adam Black's in Daviess county; and as the said

President Smith and Colonel Wight had resisted the officer who had endeavored to take them, accordingly these men are assembling to take them—as they say. They are collecting from every part of the country, to Daviess county. Report says that they are collecting from eleven counties, to help take two men who had never resisted the law or officer, nor had they thought of doing so, and this their enemies knew at the same time, or many of them at least knew it. This looks a little too much like mobocracy, it foretells some evil intentions. The whole of upper Missouri is in an uproar and confusion.

An Appeal to Gen. Atchison.

This evening I sent for General Atchison, of Liberty, Clay county, who is the major general of this division—to come and counsel with us, and to see if we could not put a stop to this collection of people, and to put a stop to hostilities in Daviess county. I also sent a letter to Judge King containing a petition for him to assist in putting down and scattering the mob collecting in Daviess county.

Monday, 3.—Nothing of importance occurred today. Reports come in concerning the collection of a mob in Daviess county, which has been collecting ever since the election in Daviess county, on the sixth of August last. I was at home most of the day.

This evening General Atchison arrived in Far West.

Consultation with General Atchison.

Tuesday, 4.—This day I spent in council with General Atchison. He says he will do all in his power to disperse the mob. We employed him and Alexander Doniphan (his partner) as our counsel in law. They are considered the first lawyers in upper Missouri.

The Prophet and Sidney Rigdon Study Law.

President Rigdon and myself commenced this day the study of law, under the instruction of Generals Atchison and Doniphan. They think, by diligent application, we can be admitted to the bar in twelve months.

The result of our consultation with our lawyers was

that myself and Colonel Wight volunteer to be tried by Judge King in Daviess county. Colonel Wight was present, having been previously notified to attend the consultation. Accordingly, Thursday next, was appointed for the trial, and word to that effect was sent to Judge King (who had previously agreed to try the case). All are to meet at Brother Littlefield's, near the county line in the southern part of Daviess county. I was at home in the evening after six o'clock.

The Prophet and Lyman Wight to submit to Trial.

Wednesday, *5*.—I gave the following affidavit, that the truth might appear before the public in the matter in controversy:

The Prophet's Affidavit on the Adam Black Incident.

STATE OF MISSOURI, }
CALDWELL COUNTY. } ss.

Before me, Elias Higbee, one of the justices of the county court, within and for the county of Caldwell aforesaid, personally came Joseph Smith, Jun., who, being duly sworn according to law, deposeth and saith: That on the seventh day of August, one thousand eight hundred and thirty-eight, being informed that an affray had taken place in Daviess county, at the election, in the town of Gallatin, in which two persons were [reported] killed, and one person badly wounded, and fled to the woods to save his life; all of which were said to be persons belonging to the society of the Church of Latter-day Saints; and further, said informant stated that those persons who committed the outrage would not suffer the bodies of those who had been killed to be taken off the ground and buried.

These reports, with others, one of which was that the Saints had not the privilege of voting at the polls as other citizens; another was that those opposed to the Saints were determined to drive them from Daviess county, and also that they were arming and strengthening their forces and preparing for battle; and that the Saints were preparing and making ready to stand in self defense—these reports having excited the feelings of the citizens of Far West and vicinity, I was invited by Dr. Avard and some others to go out to Daviess county, to the scene of these outrages; they having previously determined to go out and learn the facts concerning said reports.

Accordingly some of the citizens, myself among the number, went out, two, three, and four, in companies, as they got ready. The reports and excitement continued until several of those small companies through the day were induced to follow the first, who were all eager to learn the facts concerning this matter. We arrived in the evening at the house of Lyman Wight, about three miles from Gallatin, the scene of the reported outrages. Here we learned the truth concerning the said affray, which had been considerably exaggerated, yet there had been a serious outrage committed. We there learned that the mob was collected at Millport, to a considerable number; that Adam Black was at their head; and that they were to attack the Saints the next day, at the place we then were in, called Adam-ondi-Ahman. This report we were still inclined to believe might be true, as this Adam Black, who was said to be their leader, had been, but a few months before, engaged in endeavoring to drive those of the society who had settled in that vicinity, from the county. This had become notorious, from the fact that said Black had personally ordered several of said society to leave the county.

The next morning we dispatched a committee to said Black's, to ascertain the truth of these reports, and to know what his intentions were; and as we understood he was a peace officer, we wished to know what we might expect from him. They reported that Mr. Black, instead of giving them any assurance of peace, insulted them and gave them no satisfaction. Being desirous of knowing the feelings of Mr. Black for myself, and being in want of good water, and understanding that there was none nearer than Mr. Black's spring, myself with several others mounted our horses and rode up to Mr. Black's fence.

Dr. Avard, with one or two others who had ridden ahead, went into Mr. Black's house; myself and some others went to the spring for water. I was shortly after sent for by Mr. Black, and invited into the house, being introduced to Mr. Black by Dr. Avard. Mr. Black wished me to be seated. We then commenced a conversation on the subject of the late difficulties, and present excitement. I found Mr. Black quite hostile in his feelings toward the Saints; but he assured us he did not belong to the mob, neither would he take any part with them; but said he was bound by his oath to support the Constitution of the United States, and the laws of the State of Missouri. Deponent then asked him if he would make said statement in writing, so as to refute the statement of those who had affirmed that he (Black) was one of the leaders of the mob. Mr. Black answered in the affirmative. Accordingly he did so, which writing is in possession of the deponent. The deponent further saith, that no violence was offered to any individual in his presence, or within his knowledge; and that no insulting language was given by either party, except on the part of Mrs. Black, who, while Mr. Black was engaged in making out the above-named writing, (which he made with his own hand), gave to this deponent, and others of his society, highly insulting language and false accusations, which were calculated in their nature to greatly irritate, if possible, the feelings of the bystanders belonging to said society, in language like this—being asked by the deponent if she knew anything in the "Mormon" people derogatory to the character of gentlemen, she answered in the negative, but said she did not know but the object of their visit was to steal something from them. After Mr. Black had executed the writing, deponent asked Mr. Black if he had any unfriendly feelings towards the deponent, and if he [the deponent] had not treated him genteelly. He answered in the affirmative. Deponent then took leave of said Black and repaired to the house of Lyman Wight. The next day he returned to Far West, and further this deponent saith not.

JOSEPH SMITH, JUN.

Sworn to and subscribed this fifth day of September, A. D. 1838.

ELIAS HIGBEE, J. C. C. C.

Judge King at Far West.

Judge King arrived at Far West, on his way to Daviess to meet the proposed trial. General Atchison had gone before Judge King arrived, and the judge tarried all night. I was at home after six o'clock in the evening.

Start for the Place of Trial.

Thursday, 6.—At half-past seven this morning, I started on horseback, accompanied by several brethren, among whom were my brother Hyrum and Judge Elias Higbee, to attend my trial at Brother Littlefield's. I thought it not wisdom to make my appearance before the public at the county seat of Daviess county, in consequence of the many threats made against me, and the high state of excitement. The trial could not proceed, on account of the absence of the plaintiff, and lack of testimony, and the court adjourned until tomorrow at ten o'clock in the morning, at a Mr. Raglin's, some six or eight miles further south, and within half a mile of the line of Caldwell. Raglin is a regular mob character. We all returned to Far West, where we arrived before dark.

The Trial at Raglin's.

Friday, 7.—About sunrise I started with my friends, and arrived at Mr. Raglin's at the appointed hour. We did not know but there would be a disturbance among the mob characters today; we accordingly had a company of men placed at the county line, so as to be ready at a minute's warning, if there should be any difficulty at the trial.

The trial commenced; William P. Peniston, who was the prosecutor, had no witnesses but Adam Black, but he contrived to swear to a great many things that never had an existence, and I presume never entered into the heart of any other man, and in fine, I think he swore by the job, and that he was employed so to do by Peniston.

The witnesses on the part of the defense were Dimick B. Huntington, Gideon Carter, Adam Lightner, and George W. Robinson.

The Prophet and Lyman Wight Bound Over.

The judge bound Colonel Wight and myself over to court in a five hundred dollar bond. There was no proof against us to criminate us, but it is supposed he did it to pacify, as much as possible, the feelings of the mobbers. The judge stated afterwards, in the presence of George W. Robinson, that there was nothing proven against us worthy of bonds, but we submitted without murmuring a word, gave the bonds, with sufficient securities, and all returned home the same evening.

A Committee of Inquiry from Chariton County.

I found two persons in Daviess county at the trial, who were sent from Chariton county as a committe, to inquire into all this matter, as the mobbers had sent to that place for assistance, they said, to take Smith and Wight; but their real object was to drive the brethren from the county of Daviess, as had been done in Jackson county. They said the people in Chariton county did not see proper to send help without knowing for what purpose they were doing it, and this they said was their errand. They accompanied us to Far West, to hold a council with us, in order to learn the facts of this great excitement, which is, as it were, turning the world upside down. We arrived home in the evening.

The Presidency met in council with the committee from

Chariton county, together with General Atchison, where a relation was given of our affairs in general, the present state of excitement, and the cause of all this confusion. The gentlemen from Chariton expressed their fullest satisfaction upon the subject, and considered they had been outrageously imposed upon in this matter. They left this afternoon apparently perfectly satisfied with the interview.

Rumors of an Attack upon "Diahman."

News came this evening that the mob were to attack Adam-ondi-Ahman, and a few of the brethren from Far West started to assist the brethren to defend themselves.

Sunday, *9*.—This morning a company in addition to that which went last evening went to Adam-ondi-Ahman to assist the brethren there in their defense against the mob.

Capture of Arms Intended for the Mob

Captain William Allred took a company of ten mounted men and went to intercept a team with guns and ammunition, sent from Richmond to the mob in Daviess county. They found the wagon broken down, and the boxes of guns drawn into the high grass near by the wagon; there was no one present that could be discovered. In a short time two men on horseback came from towards the camp of the mob, and immediately behind them was a man with a wagon; they all came up and were taken by virtue of a writ on the supposition that they were abetting the mob, by carrying guns and ammunition to them. The men were taken together with the guns to Far West; the guns were distributed among the brethren, for their defense, and the prisoners were held in custody. This was a glorious day indeed, the plans of the mob were frustrated in losing their guns, and all their efforts appeared to be blasted. Captain Allred acted under the civil authorities in Caldwell, who issued the writ for securing the arms and arresting the carriers. The prisoners were brought to Far West for trial.

The mob continue to take prisoners at their pleasure; some they keep, and some they let go. They try all in their power to make us commit the first act of violence. They frequenty send in word that they are torturing the prisoners to death, in the most cruel manner, but we understand all their ways, and their cunning and wisdom are not past finding out.

The Mob Take Prisoners.

Monday, 10.—This day the prisoners taken by Captain Allred on Sunday, viz., John B. Comer, William L. McHoney, and Allen Miller, were brought before Albert Petty, justice of the peace, for examination. The prisoners asked for bail, to allow time to get counsel. The law allowed no bail, but the court adjourned till Wednesday to give time to the prisoners to get counsel.

Allred's Prisoners.

After the arrest the facts were communicated to Judge King by letter, under date of Richmond, September 10th, asking his advice how to dispose of the guns and prisoners.

Judge King advised by letter to turn the prisoners loose, and let them receive kind treatment; that the guns were government property, in the care of Captain Pollard of his vicinity, but whether they went by his authority or permission he could not say, he was at a loss to give any advice about them; but said that they should not, through any agency of his, be taken from us to be converted and used for illegal purposes. The letter was signed by A. A. King (directed to Messrs. Smith and Rigdon).

Advice from Judge King.

Under the same date Judge King advised General Atchison "to send two hundred or more men, and dispel the forces in Daviess county and all the assembled armed forces in Caldwell, and cause those 'Mormons' who refuse to give up, to surrender, and be recognized, for it will not do to compromise the law with them." What compromise need there be, Judge King, for no "Mormons" had refused to surrender to the requisitions of the law? It is mob violence, alone, that the "Mormons" are contending against.

Judge King's Apparent Double Dealing.

Petition from Ray County.

A petition was this day made out by the citizens of Ray county, directed to General Atchison, asking him to call out the militia to suppress the insurrection in Caldwell and Daviess counties, and save the effusion of blood, which must speedily take place unless prevented. Signed by Jesse Coates and twenty-eight others.

The Trial of Allred's Prisoners.

Wednesday, 12.—This day the prisoners, [Allred's] John B. Comer and his comrades, were put upon trial. It was proven to the court that the guns were taken by one of the prisoners and that he with the others were taking them to Daviess county to arm the mob. It was also proved that the mob was collecting for the purpose of driving the Saints from their homes. The prisoners were held to bail for their appearance at the circuit court, Comer as principal, the others were merely in his service.

The Citizens of Daviess County to the Governor.

This day also a communication was sent to Governor Boggs, dated Daviess county, containing all the falsehoods and lies that the evil genius of mobocrats, villains, and murderers could invent, charging the "Mormons" with every crime they themselves had been guilty of, and calling the "Mormons" impostors, rebels, Canadian refugees, emissaries of the prince of darkness, and signed, "The Citizens of Daviess and Livingston Counties."

Atchison Orders Out the Militia.

Under this date, General Atchison informed the Governor, by letter from headquarters at Richmond, that on the solicitation of the citizens and the advice of the judge of the circuit, he had ordered out four companies of fifty men each from the militia of Clay county, and a like number from Ray; also four hundred men to hold themselves in readiness if required, all mounted riflemen, except one company of infantry. The troops were to proceed immediately to the scene of excitement and insurrection.

CHAPTER VIII.

MOB MOVEMENTS IN CALDWELL, DAVIESS AND CARROLL COUNTIES—ARRIVAL OF KIRTLAND CAMP AT FAR WEST.

Trouble at De Witt Begins.

About this time [September 12th] sixty or more mobbers entered De Witt* and warned the brethren to leave that place.

Friday, 14.—I was at home after three o'clock in the evening.

Dryden's Report to the Governor.

William Dryden, Justice of the Peace in Daviess county, stated to the Governor, in a long communication, that he had issued a writ against Alanson Ripley, George A. Smith, and others, for assaulting and threatening Adam Black, on the eighth of August last; and that the officer, with a guard of ten men, in attempting to serve the writ, was forcibly driven from the town where the offenders were supposed to be, and that the "Mormons" were so well armed and so numerous in Caldwell and Daviess, that the judicial power of those counties was wholly unable to execute a writ against a "Mormon," and that the "Mormons" held the "institutions of the country in utter contempt," with many more such falsehoods of the blackest kind. Upon this representation Governor Boggs issued an order to General David R. Atchison, of the third Division of Missouri militia, through the Adjutant General, B. M. Lisle, to raise a sufficient force of troops under his command, and aid the civil officers in Daviess county, to execute all writs and other processes, in their charge, and especially assist the officer

* De Witt is located in the southeast corner of Carroll county, about fifty miles southeast of Far West, and near the point where Grand river empties into the Missouri. During the summer of 1838 a number of the Saints settled there, some of whom, when the above warning was given, were still encamped in their wagons and tents.

charged with the execution of a writ issued by William Dryden, Justice of the Peace, on the twenty-ninth of August last, for the arrest of Alanson Ripley, George A. Smith and others, and bring the offenders to justice.

The following letter gives a tolerably fair view of the movements of the militia for a few days past:

Doniphan's Report to Atchison.

HEADQUARTERS, FIRST BRIGADE, 3RD DIVISION MISSOURI MILITIA, CAMP AT GRAND RIVER, September 15, 1838.

Major General David R. Atchison, Commanding 3rd Division Missouri Militia:

SIR:—In pursuance of your orders, dated 11th instant, I issued orders to Colonel William A. Dunn, commanding the 28th regiment, to raise four companies of mounted riflemen, consisting of fifty men each; also to Colonel John Boulware, commanding 70th regiment, to raise two companies of mounted riflemen, consisting each of like number to start forthwith for service in the counties of Caldwell and Daviess.

On the same day, Colonel Dunn obtained the four companies of volunteers required from the 28th regiment, and on the morning of the 12th I took the command in person, and marched to the line of Caldwell, at which point, I ordered the colonels to march the regiments to the timber of Crooked river. I then started for Far West, the county seat of Caldwell, accompanied by my aid alone.

On arriving at that place, I found Comer, Miller, and McHoney, the prisoners mentioned in your order. I demanded of the guard, who had them in confinement, to deliver them over to me, which was promptly done. I also found that the guns that had been captured by the Sheriff and citizens of Caldwell, had been distributed and placed in the hands of the soldiery, and scattered over the country; I ordered them to be immediately collected and delivered up to me. I then sent an express to Colonel Dunn to march the regiment by daylight, for that place, where he arrived about seven a. m., making forty miles since ten o'clock, a. m., on the previous day.

When my command arrived, the guns were delivered up, amounting to forty-two stand, three stand could not be produced, as they had probably gone to Daviess county. I sent these guns under a guard to your command in Ray county, together with the prisoner Comer, the other two being citizens of Daviess I retained, and brought with me to this county, and released them on parol of honor, as I conceived their detention illegal.

At eight o'clock a. m., we took up the line of march, and proceeded through Millport in Daviess county, thirty-seven miles from our former encampment, and arrived at the camp of the citizens of Daviess and other adjoining counties, which amounted to between two and three hundred, as their commander, Dr. Austin, of Carroll county, informed me. Your order requiring them to disperse, which had been forwarded in advance of my command, by your aid, James M. Hughes, was read to them, and they were required to disperse. They professed that their object for arming and collecting was solely for defense, but they were marching and counter marching guards out; and myself and others who approached the camp were taken to task and required to wait the approach of the sergeant of the guard. I had an interview with Dr. Austin, and his professions were all pacific. But they still continue in arms, marching and counter marching.

I then proceeded with your aid, J. M. Hughes, and my aid, Benjamin Holliday, to the Mormon encampment commanded by Colonel Lyman Wight. We held a conference with him, and he professed entire willingness to disband and surrender up to me every one of the Mormons accused of crime, and required in return that the hostile forces, collected by the other citizens of the county, should also disband. At the camp commanded by Dr. Austin, I demanded the prisoner, demanded in your order, who had been released on the evening after my arrival in their vicinity.

I took up my line of march, and encamped in the direct road between the two hostile encampments, where I have remained since, within about two and a half miles of Wight's encampment, and sometimes the other camp is nearer, and sometimes further from me. I intend to occupy this position until your arrival, as I deem it best to preserve peace, and prevent an engagement between the parties, and if kept so for a few days, they will doubtless disband without coercion. I have the honor to be, yours with respect,

A. W. Doniphan,
Brig-General 1st Brigade, 3rd Division Missouri Militia.

The Prophet's Comment.

By this it is clearly seen that the officers and troops acting under the Governor's orders had very little regard for the laws of the land, otherwise Comer, Miller, and McHoney would not have been discharged by them.

I was at and about home this day, attending to my business as usual.

Sunday, 16.—Held meeting in the afternoon, had

preaching and breaking of bread. I was at home all day with my family.

Monday, 17.—I was counseling with the brethren at home and about the city.

Atchison's Report to the Governor.

HEADQUARTERS 3RD DIVISION, MISSOURI MILITIA,
GRAND RIVER, Sep. 17, 1838,

To His Excellency the Commander-in-Chief:

SIR:—I arrived at the county seat of this county, Daviess, on the evening of the 15th instant, with the troops raised from the militia of Ray county, when I was joined by the troops from Clay county under the command of General Doniphan. In the same neighborhood I found from two to three hundred men in arms, principally from the counties of Livingston, Carroll and Saline. These men were embodied under the pretext of defending the citizens of Daviess county, against the Mormons, and were operating under the orders of a Dr. Austin from Carroll county. The citizens of Daviess, or a large portion of them, residing on each side of Grand river, had left their farms, and removed their families either to the adjoining counties, or collected them together at a place called the Camp Ground. The whole county on the east side of Grand river appears to be deserted, with the exception of a few who are not so timid as their neighbors. The Mormons of Daviess county have also left their farms, and have encamped for safety at a place immediately on the east bank of Grand river, called Adam-ondi-Ahman. The numbers are supposed to be about two hundred and fifty men, citizens of Daviess county, and from fifty to one hundred men, citizens of Caldwell county; both parties have been scouting through the country, and occasionally taking prisoners, and threatening and insulting each other, but as yet no blood has been shed. I have ordered all armed men from adjoining counties to repair to their homes; and Livingston county men, and others, to the amount of one hundred men, have returned, and there remain now about one hundred and fifty, who will, I am in hopes, return in a few days. I have been informed by the Mormons, that all of those who have been charged with a violation of the laws will be in today for trial; when that is done, the troops under my command will be no longer required in this county, if the citizens of other counties will return to their respective homes. I have proposed to leave two companies of fifty men each, in this county, and discharge the remainder of the troops; said two companies will remain for the preservation of order, until peace and confidence are restored. I also enclose to your Excellency the report of General Doniphan, and refer you for particulars to Major Rogers.

I have the honor to be your obedient servant,

D. R. ATCHISON,

Major General 3rd Division Missouri Militia.

Tuesday, 18.—I have been at home all day, considerably unwell, but am somewhat better this evening.

Marching Orders to the Militia.

This day the Governor ordered Captain Childs to have the Boonville Guards mounted, with ten days' provisions, and in readiness to march on his arrival at the end of the week. The Governor also ordered General S. D. Lucas, of the fourth division to march immediately with four hundred mounted men to the scene of difficulty, and co-operate with General Atchison. Similar orders were issued to Major Generals Lewis Bolton, John B. Clark, and Thomas D. Grant.

Wednesday, 19.—I was at and about home.

Thursday, 20.—I was at home until about ten o'clock, when I rode out on horseback. I returned a little before sunset, and was at home through the evening.

Movements of the Militia.

The following extracts from General Atchison's letter of this date, to the Governor, from Liberty, will give a pretty correct view of the movements of the militia:

Excerpts of Atchison's Letter to the Governor.

SIR:—The troops ordered out for the purpose of putting down the insurrection supposed to exist in the counties of Daviess and Caldwell, were discharged on the 20th instant, with the exception of two companies of the Ray militia, now stationed in the county of Daviess, under the command of Brigadier General Parks. It was deemed necessary in the state of excitement in that county that those companies should remain there for a short period longer, say some twenty days, until confidence and tranquility should be restored. All the offenders against the law in that county, against whom process was taken out, were arrested and brought before a court of inquiry, and recognized to appear at the Circuit Court. Mr. Thomas C. Birch attended to the prosecution on the part of the State. The citizens of other counties who came in armed, to the assistance of the citizens of Daviess county, have dispersed and returned to their respective homes, and the Mormons have also returned to their respective homes, so that I consider the insurrection, for the present at least, to be at an end. From the best information I can get, there are about two hundred and fifty Mormon families in Daviess county, nearly one half of the population, and the whole of the Mormon forces in Daviess, Caldwell, and the adjoining counties, is estimated at from thirteen to fifteen hundred men, capable of bearing arms. The Mormons of Daviess county, as I stated in a former report, were encamped in a town called Adam-ondi-Ahman, and are headed by Lyman Wight, a bold, brave, skillful, and I may add, a desperate man; they appeared to be acting on the defensive, and I must further add, gave up the offenders with a good deal of promptness. The arms taken by the Mormons, and prisoners were also given up upon demand, with seeming cheerfulness.

The mob this day again threatened De Witt.

Friday, 21.—I was about home.

Saturday, 22.—I went out early in the morning, returned to breakfast at half past seven, and took an airing on horseback at nine in the morning.

Petition of the Saints of De Witt to Governor Boggs.

DE WITT, CARROLL COUNTY, STATE OF MISSOURI,
September 22, 1838.

To His Excellency Lilburn W. Boggs, Governor of the State of Missouri:

Your Petitioners, citizens of the county of Carroll, do hereby petition your Excellency, praying for relief: That whereas, your petitioners have on the 20th instant, been sorely aggrieved, by being beset by a lawless mob, certain inhabitants of this and other counties, to the injury of the good citizens of this and the adjacent places; that on the aforesaid day, there came from one hundred to one hundred and fifty armed men, and threatened with force and violence, to drive certain peaceable citizens from their homes, in defiance of all law, and threatened then to drive said citizens out of the county. but, on deliberation, concluded to give them, said citizens, till the first of October next, to leave said county; and threatened, if not gone by that time, to exterminate them, without regard to age or sex, and destroy their chattels, by throwing them into the river. We therefore pray you to take such steps as shall put a stop to all lawless proceeding; and we, your Petitioners, will ever pray, &c.

Benj. Kendrick. John Tillford,
Dudley Thomas, H. G. Sherwood,

William P. Lundow,
Jno. Kendrick,
Thos. Dehart,
Francis Brown,
Albert Loree
Samuel Lake,
Asa Manchester,
Wm. Winston,
John Clark,
Thos. Hollingshead,
Asa W. Barnes,
Elijah T. Rogers,
John Dougherty,
Moses Harris,
Perry Thayer,
B. B. Bartley,
Jonathan Harris,
Wm. J. Hatfield,
Oliver Olney,
John Thorp,
H. T. Chipman,
David Dixon,
Benj. Hensley,
John Murdock,
G. M. Hinkle,
James Valance,
Jabez Lake,
H. M. Wallace,
D. Thomas, (non-(Mormon,
Nathan Harrison,
Elizabeth Smith,
Henry Root,
A. L. Caldwell,
Rufus Allen,
Ezekiel Barnes,
D. H. Barnes,
Wm. S. Smith,
James Hampton,
Robert Hampton,
Jonathan Hampton,
George Peacock,
Daniel Clark,
John Proctor,
James McGuin,
Smith Humphrey,
Franklin N. Thayer.

Sunday, 23.—I attended meeting both forenoon and afternoon, and was at home in the evening.

Monday, 24.—I was at home until half-past eight a. m., when I rode out on horseback, and returned about five in the evening.

The governor, having heard that peace had been restored in Daviess and Caldwell counties, ordered Generals Clark, Crowther, Lewis, and Bolton to discharge their troops. The order was dated at Jonesborough.

General Parks' Report to Governor Boggs.

Tuesday, 25.—General Parks wrote the governor from Mill Port, that he had been in the upper part of Daviess county to assist the constable in bringing offenders to justice, and that the major-general, with the troops from Ray and Clay counties on the 18th instant, (except two companies from

Ray under his command) were disbanded. In this letter General Parks said:

Whatever may have been the disposition of the people called Mormons, before our arrival here, since we have made our appearance they have shown no disposition to resist the laws, or of hostile intentions. There has been so much prejudice and exaggeration concerned in this matter, that I found things entirely different from what I was prepared to expect. When we arrived here, we found a large body of men from the counties adjoining, armed and in the field, for the purpose, as I learned, of assisting the people of this county against the Mormons, without being called out by the proper authorities.

P. S.—Since writing the above, I received information that if the committee do not agree,*the determination of the Daviess county men is to drive the Mormons with powder and lead.

The same day, General Parks wrote General Atchison as follows:

I am happy to be able to state to you, that the deep excitement existing between the parties, has in a great degree ceased; and so far I have had no occasion to resort to force, in assisting the constables. On tomorrow, a committee from Daviess county meets a committee of the Mormons at Adam-ondi-Ahman, to propose to them to buy or sell, and I expect to be there.

Wednesday, *26*.—Fifteen or twenty of the Mormons were cited to trial at Gallatin where Lyman Wight has pledged himself to me that they will attend.

I was at home until ten or eleven o'clock in the morning, when I rode out, and returned home and spent the evening.

Agreement to Buy Out the Mob.

The mob committee met a committee of the brethren, and the brethren entered into an agreement to purchase all the lands and possessions of those who desired to sell and leave Daviess county. The High Council of Adam-ondi-Ahman was immediately called and Elders Don C. Smith, George A. Smith, Lorenzo D. Barnes and Harrison Sagers were appointed to go immediately to the churches in the south and east and raise men and means to fulfill the contract. The commit-

*This has reference to the committee appointed by the respective parties to negotiate terms for buying or selling on the part either of the mob oı the Saints.

tee arrived at Far West late in the evening, and called upon me and gave me the foregoing information. I approved of the action of the brethren.

Thursday, 27.—I was home and about the city.

Extract of a Letter from General Atchison to Governor Boggs, Dated—

LIBERTY, September 27th, 1838.

The force under General Parks is deemed sufficient to execute the laws and keep the peace in Daviess county. Things are not so bad in that county as represented by rumor, and, in fact, from affidavits I have no doubt your Excellency has been deceived by the exaggerated statements of designing or half crazy men. I have found there is no cause of alarm on account of the Mormons; they are not to be feared; they are very much alarmed.

Friday, 28.—I was about home until near sundown, when I rode out.

Elder John E. Page arrived at De Witt with his Canada company sometime this week.

Saturday, 29.—I rode out on horseback, returning about three in the afternoon and spent the evening at home.

Sunday, 30.—I left home about ten o'clock in the morning.

Monday, October 1.—I returned home about five o'clock where I tarried the remainder of the evening. The mob having left Daviess county (after they were organized into a militia by Atchison, Doniphan and Parks and disbanded) went to Carroll county and gathered at De Witt, threatening vengeance to the Saints without regard to age, sex or condition; but Daviess county was for a season freed from those peace disturbers.

Mob Activities Shifted to De Witt.

Tuesday, 2.—The mob pressed harder upon De Witt and fired upon the Saints.

The Kirtland Camp arrived in Far West from Kirtland. I went in company with Sidney Rigdon, Hyrum Smith, Isaac Morley and George W. Robinson, and met them some miles out, and escorted them into the city, where they encamped on the

Arrival of Kirtland Camp at Far West.

public square directly south, and close by the excavation for the Lord's House. Here friends greeted friends in the name of the Lord. Isaac Morley, Patriarch at Far West, furnished a beef for the camp. President Rigdon provided a supper for the sick, and the brethren provided for them like men of God, for they were hungry, having eaten but little for several days, and having traveled eleven miles this day; eight hundred and sixty miles from Kirtland, the way the camp traveled.

CHAPTER IX.

THE ORGANIZATION AND JOURNEY OF KIRTLAND CAMP.*

The Meeting of the Seventies.

At a meeting of the Seventies in the House of the Lord in Kirtland, on the sixth day of March, 1838, the moving of the Saints from Kirtland to the land of Missouri, in accordance with the commandments and revelations of God, was spoken of and also the practicability of the quorum of the Seventies locating in as compact a body as possible in some stake of Zion in the west, where they could meet together when they were not laboring in the vineyard of the Lord; and also could receive counsel from the Twelve and the First Presidency in matters pertaining to their mission to the nations with greater facilities than they would if scattered here and there over all the face of the land.

The subject was discussed at some length, and a resolution was passed requesting the Councilors to consult together and make a report on the subject at the next meeting of the quorum. The meeting was then adjourned to Saturday, the 10th instant, at one o'clock p. m.

The Report of the Presidents.

At that time the quorum met again and the Presidents reported that they had consulted together on the subject referred to them at the last meeting, and that they were of the opinion that the subject should be laid before the First Presidency of the Church for their counsel and advice; and also if it would be thought expedient to appoint the place for their location in Far West or some other place where it should seem good unto them.

The measures proposed by the Councilors were unanimously approved of by the members of the quorum pres-

* This chapter and the one following contain the uninterrupted history of Kirtland camp promised at p. 42, and is taken from the camp's daily journal, kept by the late Judge Elias Smith.

ent. The Presidents further stated that they had taken into consideration the extreme poverty of the Seventies in Kirtland and vicinity, and that it seemed to them almost an impossible thing for the quorum [as such] to move from this place under existing circumstances; that the measures entered into by the High Council and High Priests for removing the Saints had failed and they had given up making any further attempts after their scheme of going by water had fallen through, and that they had further advised every individual of the Church wishing to go up unto Zion to look out for himself individually and make the best of it he could.

To Move in a Body not Thought Practicable.

Much was said on the subject; and while the subject of going up in a body—which seemed to be the prevailing desire of the members present—was under discussion, the Spirit of the Lord came down in mighty power, and some of the Elders began to prophesy that if the quorum would go up in a body together, and go according to the commandments and revelations of God, pitching their tents by the way, that they should not want for anything on the journey that would be necessary for them to have; and further that there should be nothing wanting towards removing the whole quorum of Seventies that would go in a body, but that there should be a sufficiency of all things for carrying such an expedition into effect.

The Subject Discussed.

President James Foster arose in turn to make some remarks on the the subject, and in the course of his address he declared that he saw a vision in which was shown unto him a company (he should think of about five hundred) starting from Kirtland and going up to Zion. That he saw them moving in order, encamping in order by the way, and that he knew thereby that it was the will of God that the quorum should go up in that manner.

Foster's Vision.

The Spirit bore record of the truth of his assertions for

it rested down on the assembly in power, insomuch that all present were satisfied that it was the will of God that the quorum should go up in a company together to the land of Zion, and that they should proceed immediately to make preparations for the journey. The Councilors were requested to devise the best course to be pursued to carry the plan into effect, and the meeting adjourned to Tuesday, 13th, at one p. m.

"God Wills It."

In the forenoon of that day the Council of the Seventies met and invited President Hyrum Smith, and sent for President William Marks, but he was not at home, and consequently did not attend. Benjamin S. Wilber, in absence of the clerk, was invited to act as clerk *pro tem.* After the meeting was opened by President Hyrum Smith by prayer, they proceeded to draw up under the supervision of President Smith the outlines of the following Constitution for the organization and government of the camp, which was adopted at the meeting in the afternoon.*

Meeting of the 13th of March.

At the time appointed in the afternoon the quorum met according to adjournment. Several of the High Council and High Priests attended the meeting. The Spirit of God was manifested as before. The subject was discussed and the Constitution presented, which was approved by the quorum and by the visiting Elders who testified that the movement was of God and recommended it to the brethren of the Church; and said that they should lay the subject immediately before their own quorums. On motion it was resolved that two of the quorum should be appointed to act as members of the Council, *pro tem*, in the place of Daniel S. Miles and Levi Hancock—who were then in the west—till the camp should arrive at Far West. This to be in accordance with the first article of the Constitution, which recognized the whole seven [First Seven Presidents of the Seventy] as councilors of the camp.

Presidents *pro tem.* Appointed.

* See page 90.

On motion it was resolved that the President of Seventies should have the right of nominating the two assistant councilors and all other officers of the camp required by the Constitution, or on the journey, up to the land of Zion. In accordance with the above resolution Elias Smith, clerk of the Council, and Benjamin S. Wilber, were nominated and received the unanimous vote of the quorum as Councilors of the camp. The Constitution was read and explained to the meeting item by item, that there might be no misunderstanding concerning any part of it or of the motives and designs of the Seventies in the movement then in agitation; and those who subscribed to the Constitution were exhorted to make all preparations in their power to carry into effect the object of the camp, and the meeting was adjourned to Saturday, 17th, at one p. m.

Power of Nominating Officers Vested in First Council.

The Constitution.

The council of the Seventies met this day in the attic story of the Lord's House and took into consideration the propriety and necessity of the body of the Seventies going up to the land of Zion in a company together the present season, and adopted the following rules and laws, for the organization and government of the camp:

First—That the Presidents of the Seventies, seven in number, shall be the Councilors [i. e. leaders] of the camp; and that there shall be one man appointed as treasurer, who shall by the advice of the Councilors manage the financial concerns during the journey, and keep a just and accurate account of all monies received and expended for the use of the camp.

Second—That there shall be one man appointed to preside over each tent, to take charge of it; and that from the time of their appointment the tent-men shall make all necessary arrangements for the providing of teams and tents for the journey; and they shall receive counsel and advice from the Councilors; and furthermore, shall see that cleanliness and decency are observed in all cases, the commandments kept, and the Word of Wisdom heeded, that is, no tobacco, tea, coffee, snuff or ardent spirits of any kind are to be taken internally.

Third—That every man shall be the head of his own family, and shall see that they are brought into subjection according to the order of the camp.

Fourth—That all those who shall subscribe to the resolutions, rules and regulations, shall make every exertion, and use all lawful means to provide for themselves and their families, and for the use and benefit of the camp to which they belong; and also to hand over to the Seven Councilors all monies appropriated for that purpose on or before the day the camp shall start.

Fifth—That the money shall be retained in the hands of the Councilors, being divided proportionately among them for safety and to be paid over to the Treasurer as circumstances may require.

Sixth—That any faithful brethren wishing to journey with us can do so by subscribing to, and observing these rules and regulations.

Seventh—That every individual shall at the end of the journey—when a settlement is to be made, or as soon thereafter as their circumstances will admit—pay their proportional part of the expenses of the journey. By expenses it is understood all that is necessarily paid out for the use of a team, wagon or cow, if they safely arrive at the place where the camp shall finally break up.

Eighth—That these rules and laws shall be strictly observed, and every person who shall behave disorderly and not conform to them shall be disfellowshiped by the camp and left by the wayside.

Ninth—That this shall be the law of the camp in journeying from this place up to the land of Zion, and that it may be added unto or amended as circumstances may require by the voice of those who shall subscribe unto it.

[The names of the persons and number in their respective families, who subscribed to the foregoing constitution].

NAME	NO. IN FAMILY	NAME	NO. IN FAMILY
James Foster	6	Eleazer King, Jun.	3
Josiah Butterfield	4	Thomas G. Fisher	4
Zerah Pulsipher	7	Alfred Brown	2
Joseph Young	5	Stephen Headlock	2
Henry Harriman	2	John R. Folger	4
Elias Smith	3	Nathan K. Knight	9
W. S. Wilbur	2	Joel Judd	3
Joshua S. Holman	8	Thomas Nickerson	4
J. D. Parker	3	Brother Nickerson's family	5
Duncan McArthur	9	David D. Demming	2
Stephen Starks	6	Nancy Richerson	3
Anson Call	3	Joseph McCaseland	4
Amos B. Fuller	3	Hiram H. Byington	4
Jeremiah Willey	4	David Gray	8

Hiram Dayton........................12
Truman O. Angell................. 4
Dominicus Carter................. 6
Jonathan H. Holmer.............. 3
J. B. Noble.......................... 7
Levi B. Wilder...................... 6
James S. Holmon.................. 7
Amos Nickerson.................... 6
Lewis Eager.......................... 3
Stephen Shumway 3
Enoch S. Sanborn................. 5
Jonathan Crosby................... 2
Jonathan Hampton................ 4
Otis Shumway....................... 7
Frederick M. Vanleuven......... 6
Benjamin Butterfield 7
Eleazer King. 7
John Tanner..........................10
Alanson Pettingill................ 5
William Perry 4
Warren Smith........................ 7
Samuel Barnet...................... 5
William Carpenter................ 5
John Greabble...................... 8
Arnold Healey..................... 3
Joel Harvey.......................... 5
Justin Blood.......................... 5
Reuben Daniels..................... 7
Jonas Putnam............... 6
Daniel Pulsipher.................. 4
Charles Thompson................ 2
Nathan B. Baldwin................ 2
Michael Griffith.................... 6
Henry Stevens...................... 3
Levi Osgood.......................... 5
Cyrus B. Fisher.................... 6
Elijah Merriam...................... 2
Samuel Hale.......................... 3
Martin Hanchet..................... 5
Orin Cheney.......................... 9
George Stringham................. 6
Mary Parker 4
Julia Johnson........................ 8
Alexander Wright................ 1
Adonijah Cooley.................... 5
Elijah Cheney........................ 2
Jesse Baker........................... 2
Elias Pulsipher...... 8
Jason Brunett........................ 7
E. B. Gayland........................ 6
Samuel Fowler...................... 8
David K. Dustin. 2
Charles Bird.......................... 7
Thomas Butterfield............... 3
William Field.................. .. 5
William Shuman.................... 7
Cornelius Vanleuven.............. 3
Benjamin K. Hull....... 6
Oliver Olney............... 9
William Bosley...................... 2
Joseph Pine........................... 6
Noah Packard........................ 9
John M. King........................ 4
Jonathan Dunham................. 4
Joel H. Johnson.................... 6
Austin W. Cowles.................. 9
Jonathan H. Hale.................. 5
George W. Brooks................. 4
Abraham Wood...................... 4
Shearman A. Gilbert............. 3
William B. Pratt.................... 4
Samuel Parker....................... 4
Daniel Bowen........................ 7
Richard Brasier..................... 4
John Pulsipher. 2
Alba Whittle.......................... 6
Joel Drury............................. 5
Jonathan Fisher..................... 5
Benjamin Baker 6
Amasa Cheney....................... 6
Josiah Miller..........................10
Amos Baldwin........................12
John Sweat........ 10
Daniel Allen, Jun.................. 4
Stephen Richardson.............. 8
Martin H. Peck......... 6

Zemira Draper	6	John Lameraux	6
Isaac Rogers	4	Jesse P. Harmon	6
Abram Boynton	7	John Vanleuven, Jun	9
Michael McDonald	5	Aaron Cheney	6
James Brown	7	Nathan Cheney	4
Alexander Campbell		Edwin P. Merriam	3
Joseph C. Clark	6	Henry Munroe	3
Jared Porter	3	Ira P. Thornton	7
William Earl	11	Oliver Rowe	6
Daniel Bliss	2	Stephen Rowe	6
Isaac W. Pierce	5	John Thorp	7
Jabez Lake	5	Daniel L. Nuptire	3
Samuel Mulliner	5	William Gribble	3
Aaron M. York	4	Charles N. Baldwin	2
James Strop	6	William Draper, Sen	2
Reuben Hedlock	8	Laban Morris	2
Andrew Lamereaux	7	Lucius N. Scovil	4
William Wilson	3	Aaron Johnson	4
John Carter	2	Joseph Coon	4
Samuel Parker	4	Nathan Staker	6
Isaac Dewitt	8	Asa Wright	10
Hiram Griffiths	3	Zephaniah W. Brewster	9
John Hamond	6	Munro Crosier	2
Arnold Stevens	6	Asaph Blanchard	1
Gardner Snow	3	Ethan A. Moore	8
George Snow	2	William Carey	
Thomas Draper		James Lethead	
Abram Bond	3	John Rulison	8

The Movement Commended.

March 17.—Met again agreeable to adjournment in the attic story of the Lord's House, at 1 p. m. A general attendance of those belonging to the camp and many others belonging to the different quorums of the Church came in. The room was full to overflowing. Elder Josiah Butterfield, presided. After opening by prayer the object of the meeting was stated by the chairman, viz., the removing of the Saints to Zion. Elder James Foster next laid before the meeting the movements of the Seventies in relation to that desired object and was followed by Elders Joseph Young, Henry Harriman, Zera Pulsipher, and by others of the different quorums, who highly approved of the proceedings of the quorum of Seventies in relation to the order of removing and of the organization of the camp. The Constitution was read by the clerk, which was spoken of in terms of commendation by all who spoke. Much of the Spirit of God was manifested on this occasion and the hearts of all made glad in anticipation of their deliverance from Kirtland.

Hyrum Smith on Previous Movements.

President Hyrum Smith came in and addressed the meeting at some length on the movements of the Saints in Kirtland in relation to their emigration to the land of Zion since the commandment had gone forth for the honest in heart to rise up and go up unto that land. He stated that what he had said and done in reference to chartering a steamboat, for the purpose of removing the Church as a body,he had done according to his own judgment without reference to the testimony of the Spirit of God; that he had recommended that course and had advised the High Council and High Priests to adopt that measure, acting solely by his own wisdom, for it had seemed to him that the whole body of the Church in Kirtland could be removd with less expense in the way he had proposed than in any other. He said further that the Saints had to act oftentimes upon their own responsibility without any reference to the testimony of the Spirit of God in relation to temporal affairs, that he has so acted in this matter and has never had any testimony from God that the plan of going by water was approved of by Him, and that the failure of the scheme was evidence in his mind that God did not approve of it.

Hyrum Smith Commends the Seventies.

He then declared that he knew by the Spirit of God that the movements that were making by the quorum of the Seventies for their removal and the plan of their journeying was according to the will of the Lord. He advised all who were calculating to go up to Zion at present, whose circumstances would admit, to join with the Seventies in their plan and go up with them; and if he were so situated that he could join the camp himself and go with them, he would do so, and strictly comply with the rules which had been adopted for the regulation of the camp on the journey. It would be his delight to go as an individual without having any concern whatever in the management of affairs, either directly or indirectly, during the journey.

Advantage of a Large Company.

In answer to an inquiry that was made about the difficulties that might attend the movements of so large a body, he observed that no fears need be entertained by any on that score, for there would no difficulty attend the camp, if there should be 5,000 persons in it. The more the better; and the advantages of their going altogether would be greater than they could possibly be if they should go in small companies, as provisions and other necessities could be purchased in large quantities much cheaper than they could by small squads who would be under the necessity of buying at great disadvantage.

Caution as to the Word of Wisdom.

After advising the camp not to be too particular in regard to the Word of Wisdom and advised them to have the assistance of the High Council in carrying the plan into execution, and giving other advice about organizing the camp, President Hyrum Smith retired.

The Constitution being read again, about forty who did not belong to the quorum of Seventies came forward and subscribed their names to it, making in all about eighty. The meeting was then adjourned to Tuesday, March 20th, at 1 p. m.

Practical Steps.

March 20.—In the afternoon the Seven Councilors met to consult on the best measures to be pursued for procuring teams and tents and other things necessary for the journey. After considering the subject carefully it was thought that two good teams and one tent, if no more could be obtained, would suffice for eighteen persons; and that it would be advisable to appoint the overseers of tents at the meeting to be held in the afternoon, whose duty according to the Constitution would be to form their companies of eighteen, or as near that number as circumstances will admit of, and proceed immediately to procure teams and a tent for the same, and to make all necessary arrangements for the journey.

Views of Oliver Granger *et al.*

Elders Oliver Granger, Mayhew Hillman and Harvey Redfield and some others attended who were requested to express their views of the expedition, as a rumor had gone forth that they considered it an impracticable undertaking and one that would never be accomplished. Elder Granger said that he considered it would be the greatest thing ever accomplished since the organization of the Church or even since the exodus of Israel from Egypt if the Saints in Kirtland, considering their poverty, should succeed in going from that place in a body, and that it would require great wisdom and prudence and the most determined perseverance to effect such a measure, though he considered it possible to do it and believed God would bless them in so doing.

Elder Redfield spoke at some length and said that in consequence of the rumors which were afloat he had thought the Seventies were taking unwarrantable ground, and had expressed his views freely on the subject, and rather justified himself on that score, though he condemned the principle of believing reports which were put in circulation without first considering their foundation and the source from which they came. He said he was convinced that the things he had heard were untrue concerning some movements which he had heard the Seventies were making, and the declarations and denunciations they gave some of the other quorums, which had come to his ears, were likewise without foundation. He said he was heart and hand with the Council of the Seventies in their endeavors to remove the Saints in Kirtland to the land of Zion, and the Spirit testified to him that the movements were in righteousness and according to the will of God.

Elder Hillman spoke in confirmation of what his brethren had said, approved of the movement and said that the High Priests and High Council had at a meeting held a day or two previous passed a resolution to uphold and support the Seventies in their undertaking.

A selection of names for overseers of tents was made and the meeting adjourned.

Admonitions.

At one p. m. the members of the camp and others who attended met in the upper court of the Lord's House. Elder Henry Harriman presided, and opened by prayer. He also addressed the meeting, followed by Elder Foster, both setting forth the greatness of the undertaking in hand, of the necessity of every individual bestirring himself and making every exertion to prepare for the journey. The names of those who had signed the Constitution were read over, that if there were any objection against their going in the camp in consequence of any difficulty that might exist or of disobedience to the commandments of the Lord it might be made manifest by those who might know of the existence of any such thing.

The names of those selected for overseers of tents were read over one by one and were voted in by the voice of the camp, and Jonathan H. Hale was appointed treasurer, and the meeting was then adjourned.

Sundry Meetings and the Object of Them.

After the 20th of March the Council met often to counsel on the things which from time to time pressed themselves upon their attention relative to the preparation necessary for the journey, things both spiritual and temporal; and to ask counsel and give their advice that they might decide in righteousness all things pertaining to their calling and the affairs of the camp, and to implore their heavenly Father to provide means to soften the hearts of the enemies of the Saints, in Kirtland, and in the region round about:

that His people might be delivered from their power, as they have fallen into the hands of their enemies like Israel of old, in consequence of disobedience and their slowness of heart to obey the commandments of the Lord which He had given unto them; and that He would have mercy upon them and deliver them from bondage in this land, that they might go up to the land of Zion according to the commandments and revelations of the Lord by His servant Joseph Smith, Jun., and according to the pattern given unto them.

In these meetings for counsel and prayer God truly verified His promises; for when His servants asked they received, and His Spirit was poured out upon them abundantly, from time to time manifesting the will of the Lord concerning the movements necessary to be made in order to carry the arduous undertaking into effect, in removing the quorum of Seventies, and those that joined with them, from Kirtland to the land of Zion.

Difficulties Encountered.

The extreme poverty of the majority of those belonging to the camp and the depression of their spirits in consequence thereof and the downfall of Kirtland; the opposition of those who had dissented from the Church and of those who from the beginning had opposed the commandments of God which He had established in the last days among the children of men, and last of all, though not least, the opposition of many who called themselves Saints, were obstacles which presented themselves in formidable aspect against the exertions of the Council to bring about the order of things to be entered into in order to accomplish the work, and to unite the feelings of the brethren and to restore their confidence in each other, which had in a great measure been lost during the past year, or since the failure of their imaginary means of speculation, of grandeur and wealth.

Thursday, July 5.—The camp commenced organizing on a piece of land in the rear of the house formerly occupied by Mayhew Hillman, about one hundred rods south of the

House of the Lord, in Kirtland. The morning was beautiful. At an early hour the heavens were overspread with a cloud which continued to hide the scorching rays of the sun till towards evening, when it moved away. The horizon at every point that was unobstructed by intervening objects was clear, and everything seemed to indicate that the God of heaven has His all-searching eye upon the camp of the Saints, and had prepared the day for the express purpose of organizing the camp, that the Saints might start on their journey in the order which had been shown in the beginning. About twenty tents were pitched in the course of the day and several other companies came on late who had not time to pitch their tents. Many spectators from the towns round about came to behold the scene, and, with few exceptions, they behaved with the greatest decorum. The day was solemn to all concerned and the greatest solemnity was visible on the countenances of the Saints who expected to tarry for a season in Kirtland, and also on the countenances of many of the unbelievers in the everlasting Gospel of Jesus Christ and of the great work of the gathering of the Saints of the Most High in these last days of wickedness before God's judgments shall have been poured out without measure upon the wicked, to sweep them off from the face of the earth.

Assembling of the Camp.

Between four and five hundred of the camp tented on the ground during the night. The spectators retired at a late hour and left the camp in quietude. The night was clear and the encampment and all around was solemn as eternity; which scene, together with the remembrance of those other scenes through which the Saints in Kirtland had passed during the last two years all presented themselves to the thinking mind; and, together with the greatness of the undertaking, the length of the journey, and many other things combined, could not fail to awaken sensations that could be better felt than described.

Solemn Reflections.

Friday, July 6.—At an early hour in the morning the

people began to assemble to witness the exodus of the camp, and several hundred persons had gathered together before all things could be arranged in order to move off from the ground without confusion, all of which consumed most of the forenoon. At twelve o'clock, noon, the camp began to move, and at half-past twelve the whole company had left the ground in order, and took up their line of march towards Chester, south from Kirtland, where they encamped at six o'clock p. m., a distance of seven miles from Kirtland.

The Start.

After the tents were pitched and all things arranged an enumeration of the camp was taken, when it was ascertained that there were in the camp 529 souls present—a few necessarily absent—of which 256 were males, and 273 females. There were 105 families, all on the ground excepting five, which had not time to get ready in season to start with the camp, two of which came up in the evening; of the others Elder Martin H. Peck joined at Petersburgh; the other two, Elders S. Shumway and Brother Charles Wood, joined the camp at the same place a few hours after. President William Marks and some other brethren from Kirtland accompanied the camp to Chester, and on parting with the Councilors blessed them, in the name of the Lord, and left his blessing with them, and with the camp, covenanting to uphold them by the prayer of faith and required the same of the Councilors and of the brethren of the camp.

Number in the Camp.

The feelings of the brethren on leaving Kirtland and parting with those who were left behind were somewhat peculiar, notwithstanding the scenes they had passed through in Kirtland; but the consciousness of doing the will of their heavenly Father, and obeying His commandments in journeying to Zion, over balanced every other consideration that could possibly be presented to their minds, and buoyed up their spirits, and helped them to overcome the weaknesses and infirmities

Sorrow at Parting.

of human nature which men are subject to here on the earth.

Saturday, July 7.—Started from Chester about half-past six in the morning, and camped in Aurora, Portage county—thirteen miles from Chester—at four p. m., on the farm of Mr. Lacey. The road between Chester and Aurora, through Russell and Bainbridge, in Geauga county, was bad and somewhat hilly. The weather being extremely warm and the camp not being sufficiently accustomed to moving and acting in concert, all contributed to make some confusion in the camp during the latter part of the day. One wagon, Andrew Lamereaux's, broke down twice and some other small accidents happened, but nothing very serious. During the day several children were sick, some dangerously so, and some adults were attacked by the destroyer.

First Experiences.

Sunday, July 8.—Public worship at eleven o'clock, Elder Joseph Young preached. Many came in the course of the day to visit the camp. They generally treated us with great civility, though there were some exceptions. In the afternoon about half-past five the heads of families were called together and were instructed by Elders Foster, Pulsipher, Butterfield and Dunham to keep their families in more strict subjection to the laws of God, and to adhere strictly to the Constitution of the camp. They were told that the destroyer was in the camp and some would fall victims to his power if they did not comply with the requisitions of the Lord.

A Renewal of Covenants.

A vote was called and the camp covenanted anew strictly to observe the laws of the camp and the commandments of the Lord. Soon after night-fall a company of marauders were heard about the camp, but we were not molested during the night.

Monday, July 9.—At seven in the morning the camp began to move, passed through the village of Aurora, through the corner of Streetsborough to Hudson, a handsome village, in which is situ-

Incidents of a Day.

ated the "Western Reserve College." Stopped at one o'clock near the south line of that town. David Elliot broke his wagon down near Streetsborough, and Samuel Hale's wagon tongue was broken a little south of the village of Hudson. The fourth division of the camp came up about two o'clock, at which time the first moved on and passed through Stowe Corners, so called, across the Pittsburgh and Akron canal (which is yet in an unfinished state at the falls on the Cuyahoga river, which empties into Lake Erie at Cleveland), and encamped for the night on Mr. Camp's farm, at Talmadge, at half-past six in the evening. The first, second and third divisions came on to the grounds together, the fourth, composed chiefly of ox teams, did not come up till ten o'clock. The roads were generally good, the country level, with few exceptions, the weather extremely warm, but nearly all withstood the fatigue of the day with fortitude and patience, feeling thankful for the blessings which the Lord bestowed upon the camp of His Saints.

The country through which we passed this day was better adapted to pasturage than tillage, the grass generally looked well, some fine fields of wheat were seen which had began to whiten for the harvest.

Joel H. Johnson's oxen failed and were left behind, and some others were very much fatigued and did not arrive at the encampment until late at night. Traveled twenty miles, which was three or four more than we should have done if accommodations for the teams could have been obtained short of that distance.

Additional Camp Regulations.

Tuesday, Juld 10.—Before starting the Council drew up the following resolutions for the further organization of the camp, which were unanimously adopted:

Resolved—First. That the engineer of the camp shall receive advice from the Councilors concerning the duties of his office, and that he shall call on his assistants to perform those duties which he cannot attend to himself, and that he shall be relieved from the arduous task of [personally] superintending the movements of the camp during the journey.

Second —That the horn shall be blown for rising at four o'clock, and at twenty minutes past four for prayer every morning, at which time each overseer shall see that the inmates of his tent are in order, that worship may commence throughout the camp at the same time, immediately after the blowing of the horn.

Third—That the head of each division shall keep a roll of all able-bodied men, and that he shall call out as many men each night as the engineer shall require of his division to stand on guard. One-half of which guard shall stand the fore part of the night, and the other the latter part, being regularly relieved by the engineer or one of his assistants at one o'clock in the morning.

Fourth—That every company in the camp is entitled to an equal proportion of the milk whether the cows are owned by the individuals of the several tents or not, and that it shall be so distributed, as near as may be, among the several companies in the camp.

Fifth—That Thomas Butterfield shall be appointed herdsman of the camp, whose duty it shall be to superintend the driving of the cows and other stock, and to see that they are well taken care of on the journey, and that he shall call on as many as shall be necessary to assist him in performing those duties.

Sixth—That in no case at present shall the camp move more than fifteen miles in one day, unless circumstances shall absolutely require it.

Joel H. Johnson sold one of his oxen for ten dollars, the other came up with the camp.

The First Deserter.

The camp began to move at nine o'clock and passed through the village of Talmadge, one mile, then turned southwest to Middleburg, a fine village situated on a branch of the Cuyahoga, three miles from Talmadge, and encamped for the night in the town of Coventry, about one mile from the village of Akron, which is situated on the Ohio and Erie canal. At twelve o'clock, for the purpose of lightening our loads, we left some of our goods on the canal boats to be conveyed by water. The wind rose high and the roads were dusty which made it hard traveling on account of the dust. In the afternoon we had a small shower of rain, the first that had fallen since the camp started Benjamin Butterfield left the camp in the morning and started off by himself. Traveled this day six miles. Brother John Hammond broke his wagon, the only accident.

Wednesday, July 11.—After the goods that were to be sent by water were conveyed to Akron, the camp moved on, all but the first division which waited to attend to the burial of Brother and Sister Wilbur's little son, aged six months and twelve days, who died at 11 o'clock a. m. and was interred in an orchard on the farm of Israel Allen in Coventry, at 2 p. m. He had been sick two or three days, and some other children in the camp had also been sick, but all recovered excepting Brother Wilbur's son. Passed this day through New Portage on the Ohio canal, which we crossed two or three miles below that place, and encamped on the farm of Mr. Bockmans, in Chippeway township, county of Wayne. A heavy shower of rain fell in the afternoon and the whole company got thoroughly wet for the first time since we started; but very few complained, however, and all retired to rest wet and weary after the usual duties of the evening were ended.

The First Death.

The country through which we passed this day was somewhat uneven and swampy. Near New Portage it is low and to all appearance must be quite unhealthful. The crops of wheat, corn and grass look well, the wheat being generally about ripe and ready to harvest. John Hammond broke his wagon again today and was left behind to repair it, and did not get up to the encampment at night. Traveled this day eleven miles.

Thursday, July 12.—Left the encampment at half-past eight; passed through the village of Doylestown, situated on a hill in the township of Chippeway. Crossed Chippeway creek; some of the headwaters of the Muskingum river came through the township of Milton, where we stopped at one p. m. to feed. Then passed through the township of Green into Wayne, and encamped on the farm of Mr. ————,

Nature of the Country Traversed.

two miles from Wooster, at seven in the evening. The road was rough in some places, in some places stony, and, in consequence of the shower of rain which fell the day before, in some places muddy.

The country through which we passed today is somewhat hilly, the soil productive and the crops of wheat, corn and oats look fine and beautiful. Timber, principally of oak, with some chestnut and some other kinds of forest trees, is scattered here and there.

Difficulties by the way.

John Hammond overtook us in the morning on horseback, his wagon had broken again, the third time, so it could not be easily mended. The Council advised him to go back and get the brethren residing near New Portage to assist him in exchanging it for another, or let him have one to go up to Zion with, and have it returned to them, as he had now fallen so far behind that we could not well assist him without hindering many others.

Nathan B. Baldwin broke one of his wagon tires, and Henry Harriman one of his axle-trees, and stopped near Chippeway creek to have them mended. Brother Baldwin came up in the evening and Henry Harriman the next morning.

It rained a little in the course of the day, the air was cool and the horses and oxen performed the journey with greater ease than any other day since the camp started. Traveled in the course of the day about seventeen miles.

Descriptions of Country.

Friday, July 13.—The fourth division left the encampment about eight o'clock, the third and second followed, and the first left at nine. Passed through Wooster, the county seat of Wayne county, a large and beautiful village surrounded by a fertile country and is a place of considerable business. There are eight or ten public houses and several synagogues for worship, and many other commodious and elegant buildings in the village which is in Wayne township.

At Wooster we took the road to Mansfield, west from

Wooster thirty-three miles. Passed through the village of Jefferson, a small place in the township of Plain, thence to Reedsborough in Mohican township, and encamped a little after five p. m. on the farm of William Crothers, in Mohican, thirteen miles from Wooster, making this day sixteen miles.

The country west of Wooster is rather hilly, some beautiful flats on the creeks, though not in so good a state of cultivation as in many other places. Crossed Apple creek east of Wooster, and Killbuck west of the town, a branch of the White Woman and Mohican creek, which fall into the same stream in Coshocton county. The roads were somewhat better than between New Portage and Wooster, though more hilly. On the flats of Mohican the road was bad, being muddy and stony. The country west of Wooster is not so productive as it is north of that place through which we passed on the twelfth inst., yet some beautiful fields of grain were seen. Two wagons failed this day, Joseph C. Clark's and Edwin P. Merriam's. The first was mended at Wooster, the other broke down just at the entrance of the field in which we pitched our tents. Bought four barrels of flour, the first provisions we purchased after the camp started. The people between Kirtland and Wooster were generally apprised of our coming before we arrived, and were not so much surprised to see us as they were west of that place. After we left the main road to Columbus, as we followed along, they seemed astonished and filled with wonder and amazement at seeing so large a body moving together, and some did not fail to express their feelings with warmth to the brethren as they passed along, declaring against the "fallacy", as they called it, of "Jo Smith's" prophecies, and expressing their pity for the deluded believers in modern revelation. We saw this day the first harvesting of grain of any kind, though many of the farmers in Wayne county had done most of their haying.

Sorrow for the "Deluded" Saints.

Saturday, July 14.—Struck our tents at seven a. m. and

the fourth division left the encampment followed by the third and second, the first left at eight. We passed through Jeromeville, a small village situated on a branch of the Mohican, thence through the village of Haysville in Vermillion township, county of Richland, and pitched our tents on the farm of Mr. Solomon Braden, in the town of Petersborough. The country we passed through this day is beautifully diversified with hills and valleys. The timbered lands were covered principally with oak, the roads good, the weather warm and dry. Brother William Perry turned over his wagon and his wife and children were hurt, though not dangerously. A young woman, a daughter of John Vanleuven, Jun., came very near being killed by having a wagon run over her, these were the only accidents that occurred during the day. This was the first day since we left Kirtland that we traveled without breaking down one or more wagons. Pitched our tents at two p. m. on a hill near the east line of Petersburg township and washed and prepared for the Sabbath. In the afternoon a complaint was prepared by N. B. Baldwin against Abram Bond for murmuring and other unchristian-like conduct. The Council, after hearing the complaint and the defense, referred the case to the company in their own tent to settle among themselves. This was the second complaint made to the Council of any consequence on the way from Kirtland. Traveled this day ten miles.

Preparations for the Sabbath.

Sunday, July 15.—The Council met in the morning and made some arrangements about the order of the day. Elder Josiah Butterfield and Joseph Young were appointed to preside during the day.

Public Worship.

At eleven o'clock public worship commenced. Many of the citizens of the town attended, most of whom behaved well, and treated us with respect. Elder Jonathan Dunham delivered a discourse on the first principles of the Gospel, from Mark, 16th chapter, followed by several others of the Elders.

Martin H. Peck came up and joined the camp about noon, and Stephen Shumway and Charles Wood came up in the afternoon.

Some left by the Way Re-join the Camp.

John Hammond, who was left behind at New Portage in consequence of breaking his wagon, also joined us again. Benjamin Butterfield, who left the camp at Talmadge, Portage county, found his way into camp again in the course of the day.

Monday, July 16.—Started in our usual order in the morning, traveling west toward Mansfield, through which we passed in the afternoon about four o'clock. Passed through the village of Petersburg two miles from our encampment, then through Mifflic township, three or four miles east of Mansfield. In Madison township we were met by the sheriff and a deputy, and a Mr. Stringer, who had taken out a warrant for several of the brethren for Kirtland Safety Society money, and took Josiah Butterfield, Jonathan Dunham and Jonathan H. Hale for Joseph Young, and committed them to jail. As we came to Mansfield we were *honored* by the discharge of artillery, but as the Lord would have it we were not enjoined nor molested more than by insulting language from some of the numerous crowd of persons that thronged the streets. From Mansfield we came through Newcastle, in the township of Springfield, and encamped on the farm of Frederick Cassel over night. Mansfield is a fine village, the county seat of Richland, situated on a hill surrounded by a fertile country. Traveled this day sixteen miles.

Prominent Elders Arrested.

Benjamin Butterfield left the camp again before night in ill humor and went off by himself.

Tuesday, July 17.—Started at eight in the morning; passed through the village of Ontario in Springfield, thence through the town of Sandusky into Jackson, in Crawford county, and encamped six miles east of Bucyrus, the county seat of Crawford county. Traveled sixteen miles.

On the Head-waters of the Sciota and Sandusky.

The country we passed through between Mansfield and Bucyrus is the highest in the State of Ohio, being on the headwaters of the Sciota which falls into the Ohio, and of the Sandusky that falls into Erie, the country though high is generally level.

Just at dark the brethren who had been committed to prison came up. They were discharged by the court at 12 o'clock, noon, after which they traveled twenty-two miles.

The court for Richland county was in session and would have been adjourned the evening the brethren, Josiah, Butterfield Jonathan Dunham and Jonathan H. Hale, were arrested, had it not been for that occurrence. Their case was called on the same evening and adjourned till eight o'clock next morning. Dominicus Carter went back from our camp and staid with them till they were liberated. We were all glad and thanked the Lord for their deliverance out of the hands of our enemies.

Instructions to Overseers.

Wednesday, July 18.—The Council met in the morning and called together the overseers of tents and gave them some instructions concerning their duty in presiding over their tents, and Dominicus Carter was appointed commissary of the camp, and Aaron M. York chosen overseer of tent No. 3, third division, in his place; and the tent removed to No. 5, first division. About eight the camp started, passed through Benjamin and took the road to upper Sandusky, and stopped at one p. m. on the edge of a prairie to rest. For the first time we had the privilege of encamping without pay. The road in the afternoon in some places was rather bad in the groves between the openings of the grand prairie, the edge of which bordered on the right of our road from our encampment east of Bucyrus till we encamped at night in the town of Grand Prairie, county of Marion, on the line between that county and Crawford, ten miles south-west from Bucyrus. Passed through the township of Antrim, in Crawford county, in the afternoon. Traveled this day sixteen miles. As we passed through Bucyrus the people seemed much agitated and made many remarks concerning us. One man said he had received a liberal education and had prepared himself for the ministry, but it now availed him nothing. The movements of the "Mormons" were actions and not words, and looked more like love and like the spirit of union than anything that had come under his observation.

Thursday, July 19.—The second, third and fourth divisions started about eight o'clock, the first stayed on the ground, some of them until afternoon, to repair wagons. Traveled through a prairie country to Little Sandusky, a little north of west from the place of our encampment on the night of the eighteenth. Then turned west and pitched our tents on the west side of the prairie, about a mile and a half from the village of Sandusky. Traveled this day seven and one-half miles. No particular occurrence through the day worthy of notice. Encamped for the first time in a straight line, and being on a prarie the tents and wagons presented a beautiful picture to a distant beholder, and could not fail to bring to the mind of anyone familiar with the history of the journeyings of Israel from Egypt, the prophecy of Balaam, concerning Israel's prosperity, and his pathetic exclamation, when he beheld them abiding in their tents from the top of Peor: "How goodly are thy tents, O Jacob, and thy tabernacles, O Israel! As the valleys, as they spread forth, as gardens by the river side, as the trees of lignaloes which the Lord hath planted, and as cedar trees beside the waters."

Friday, July 20.—The Council met in the morning to attend to another complaint preferred by E. B. Gaylord,* superintendent of the fourth division, against Abram Bond, for murmuring and complaining, and for personal abuse. Elder Zera Pulsipher, who presided, gave him a severe reprimand for his conduct in general on the journey and for abusing others without

Reproofs Administered.

*By typographical error this name, in the list of those who signed the camp's constitution (p 92), is given as E. B. Gayland.

any provocation, and he was informed that he would be left by the wayside if he did not reform, and behave more like a man of God than he had of late, or for a few days past. Some other business relative to our circumstances and situation in journeying was talked over and the Council unanimously decided that the camp should be called together before we started and some instructions given to them concerning their duties, and also to reprimand some for indulging themselves in covetousness and murmuring against the Council, and also others of the camp who held important stations as captains of divisions or overseers of tents.

The camp was accordingly called together and such instructions given them as the Spirit of the Lord dictated, by Elders Pulsipher, Young, Butterfield, Foster and Harriman, which had the desired effect in restoring good order and the spirit of union in the camp.

The Council Relieved of Guard Duty.

On motion of Samuel Parker it was unanimously resolved that the Councilors should be excused from standing on guard during the journey, that they might have more time to counsel together and to attend to those duties which necessarily devolved upon them as Councilors of the camp. James A. Clark, Jared Porter and Daniel Bliss were appointed to assist the herdsman in taking care of the herds, as it was found too arduous for one. The camp started about nine and traveled westwardly two miles to Bowsherville, which is one hundred and forty-three miles from Detroit; thence four miles in the same direction, and then turned south and came through the village of Burlington, situated on Taymockty creek, a branch of the Sandusky, and pitched our tents in the highway near a schoolhouse, about one-half mile from Burlington, in the township of Grand, Marion county, between three and four o'clock p. m.

A heavy shower of rain fell soon after we encamped and it continued to rain most of the night. Most of the company got thoroughly wet. Distance this day nine and one-half miles.

Saturday, July 21.—Started about eight a. m.; traveled southwesterly through the township of Goshen, Hardin county to the Sciota river, in the township of Dudley, where we stopped to refresh ourselves and teams, at Judge Wheeler's. From thence we came to Mr. Bosman's, in township of Jackson, where we encamped in the highway, seven miles from Sciota, making in all sixteen miles. It was quite cool and comfortable traveling, but the road was extremely bad, being in some places almost impassable, but the Lord attended us and His blessings were multiplied upon us so that no accident of any account happened to us during the day. Newel K. Knight broke an axle-tree out of his wagon which was mended in a short time.

Sunday, July 22.—On account of forage we were under the necessity of traveling about five miles through Rush creek, and pitched our tents on a rise of ground, by the wayside, on the farm of Mr. Partial, inn-keeper in the town of Rush Creek, Logan county, and held public meeting at five p. m. Attended to offering our sacraments to the Most High, breaking bread for the first time on our journey. The first two Sabbaths after we started on our journey we were so circumstanced and thronged with visitors that we omitted attending to the ordinance of the Lord's Supper. At our meeting in the afternoon the Lord blessed us by the outpouring of His Spirit, our hearts were comforted and most of the camp felt thankful for the blessings conferred upon us by our heavenly Father, thus far on the journey to the land of Zion.

As we passed along the road in the morning, molesting no one, some of the company were saluted in modern style by having eggs thrown at them by some ruffians from their dwellings near the road, but on seeing some of our company stop, they desisted from their course fearing the consequences from appearances, and even showed three or four bayonets, intimating that they would defend themselves in case of assault. No one, however, intended doing any harm to them, and only wished them to understand that we noticed their intrusion upon our privileges as citizens to travel the high road unmolested. Sometime in the night a luminous body about the size of a cannon ball came down from over the encampment near the ground then whirled round some forty or fifty times and moved off in a horizontal direction, soon passing out of sight.

Monday, July 23.—The camp began to move at a quarter past seven a. m., and came through the village of Rushsylvania, where we were threatened before our arrival with prosecution for "Kirtland Bank Money," signed by F. G. Williams, president, and Warren Parrish, cashier. Some of the company passed on from our encampment in the morning to find out what was intended against us, but no person made any attempt to stop any one, and we passed on in safety. From Rushsylvania we came through the village of Bellefontaine, the county seat of Logan county; twelve miles thence to McKee's creek, a branch of the Miami, in the township of Union, and camped at the side of the creek at seven o'clock. Traveled this day sixteen miles.

Threats of Arrest Made.

On the road near Bellefontaine one of the sons of Martin H. Peck, had a wagon wheel run over his leg, but as the Lord would have it, and to the astonishment of all—considering the weight of the load on the wagon—he received no particular injury, although the wheel ran over the boy's leg on a hard road without any obstruction whatever. The wheel made a deep cut in the limb, but after hands were laid on him in the name of the Lord, the boy was able to walk considerable in the course of the afternoon. This was one, but not the first, of the wonderful manifestations of God's power unto us on the journey.

A Case of Healing.

After we left Bucyrus hill we came to Bellefontaine,

the road was in many places very bad, especially in the backwoods. In Marion and Hardin counties provisions were scarce and could not be obtained, consequently we were obliged to do with what we had; and here was another manifestation of the power of Jehovah, for seven and a half bushels of corn sufficed for the whole camp, consisting of six hundred and twenty souls, for the space of three days, and none lacked for food, though some complained and murmured because they did not have that to eat which their souls lusted after.

Scarcity of Food.

Tuesday, July 24.—We lay in our encampment at McKee's creek through the day to wash our clothes and refresh our teams, as they were very much fatigued by traveling for several days on a rough and muddy road. We took two jobs, one of chopping cord wood, and one of shoemaking, and earned about twenty dollars, besides mending and repairing several wagons and putting things in order in the camp.

A Day of Rest.

Wednesday, July 25.—Started on our journey and came through West Liberty, situated on Mad river, thence into the township of Salem, Champaign county, and encamped about two miles north of Terbana, on the farm of Joseph Vance, Governor of the state of Ohio. The encampment was formed near his residence, at six o'clock, having traveled twelve miles this day. The country in the valley of Mad river is level and beautiful and very fertile. We saw extensive fields of wheat on each side of the way, mostly reaped, and crops of all kinds were far better than any we had seen elsewhere on our journey.

Camp at the Farm of the Governor of Ohio.

In the evening the camp was called together by the Council, and some of them severely reprimanded in general terms for their unchristian-like conduct, and much instruction given concerning our duties to God, and to one another, in order to move on our journey in righteousness, that we might obtain the favor of the Lord, and have His blessings attend us from day to day.

After the assembly was dismissed, the Council returned and listened to a complaint presented by B. S. Wilbur against Stephen Starks, for some unchristian-like conduct during the day. The trouble was amicably settled to the satisfaction of all concerned. The Council adjourned, after transacting some other business, at eleven o'clock p. m. From Kirtland to our encampment in Salem, is two hundred and fifteen miles.

Thursday, July 26.—Camp began to move at eight o'clock; the first division, however, did not leave the grounds until after eleven. Several of the brethren went out to labor both yesterday and today, in order to procure means to further us on our journey, and they did not come up with us at night. We traveled south through the village of Urbana, the county seat of Champaign county; thence into the township of Moneyfield, Clark county, and camped on the farm of Mr. A. Breneman, four and one half miles off the National road at Springfield. Traveled twelve miles, plus two hundred and fifteen miles from Kirtland, equals two hundred and twenty-seven miles.

Camp Labors.

The camp was called together in the evening and a timely lecture was given by Elder Pulsipher, on our situation, and all were exhorted to be united in heart and hand in order to join together. The Spirit of the Lord was manifested and we returned to our tents feeling thankful for the blessings of the Lord upon us.

Admonitions.

Friday, July 27.—Continued our journey to Springfield on the National road, one hundred and seventy-one miles from Wheeling, in Virginia. Crossed Buck creek, a branch of Mad river, just before entering the village on the north. Springfield is a large and beautiful village, the county seat of Clark county, containing about three thousand inhabitants. There are many elegant buildings of brick, and it seems to be a place of considerable trade.

Through Springfield.

A little west of Springfield we left the National road and took the road to Dayton, distance from Springfield twenty-five miles, and passed through the township of Mad river, and a small village called Washington in the same township, and pitched our tents just at dark in a grove near Lenox, in Mad river township. The day was excessively warm and the road dusty, but we all arrived safely at our encampment in the evening, except some of those who stopped to labor. Many of the people all along the road seemed quite astonished to see so many in the company. Some judging there were three hundred teams, and made some curious remarks concerning us and "Jo Smith;" and one man threatened to shoot Elder Dunham if he did not immediately leave his premises when he called to procure forage for our teams at noon. After we encamped a stage went by and the passengers behaved as they passed us more like the savages of the west than anything we have seen since the commencement of our journey. Distance traveled today, fifteen miles. J. D. Parker, who had left Kirtland some time after we did, overtook us at our encampment this evening and staid with us till Monday morning.

Astonishment Created by the Camp.

Saturday, July 28.—We removed from Mad river township and came to Fairfield, three miles, thence to Bath township and encamped about noon half a mile from the road on the banks of Mad river in Green county, five and one half miles from Dayton. Distance this day nine miles. Distance from Kirtland, two hundred and fifty-one miles.

Sunday, July 29.—We held a public meeting in a grove on a farm of Mr. Houghman, about one fourth of a mile from our encampment, at eleven o'clock, Elder Zera Pulsipher preached.

In the afternoon we had a sacrament meeting on the camp grounds. Elder Duncan McArthur, after the administration of the Lord's Supper, bore testimony of the truth of the revelations of the Lord in these last days to the numerous spectators who were present, and in a brief way made known unto them some of those things that the Lord was doing in the earth; and others that would shortly come to pass among the inhabitants thereof. The Spirit of God attended his testimony and we had a joyful meeting.

The Sacrament Administered.

The Council met in the morning to regulate some things relative to the duties of the day, and adjourned till five p. m. At that time they met again and took into consideration the case of Abram Bond, and unanimously resolved that for his murmuring and not giving heed to the regulations of the camp, he should be disfellowshiped by the camp and left to the care of himself, which decision was made known unto him and approbated by those who were present at the time. He accordingly left the camp the next day. Warren Smith, who left Kirtland about the first of June, came into the camp with his family and joined us. William Gribble—whose wife accompanied us from Kirtland—also joined the camp this day. We found many of the Saints from Kirtland and other places, and Elder John E. Page, with a part of his company that started from Oak Point, in St. Lawrence county, New York, whither they had fled in the course of the past winter, from the commotions and rumors of war in Canada.* They were scattered along the

Abram Bond Di-fellowshiped.

John E. Page's Company.

* The war rumors here mentioned have reference to what is known in Canadian history as the "Canadian Rebellion." It was the culmination of agitation begun as early as 1831, on the part of the people of Canada, under popular leaders, such as Papineau, Brown, Nielson, McKenzie and others, for enlarged measures of home rule for the Dominion. The popular leaders marshaled their forces against the government during the winter of 1837-8, and a number of skirmishes took place. Canadian independence was much talked of, and the people in the United States along the Canadian border were much excited, and volunteers began to flock in considerable numbers to aid the cause of the "patriots," as the insurgents were called. "But," to quote a Canadian historian, "the American President, Mr. Van-Buren, issued two successive proclamations warning the people of the penalties to which they would expose themselves by engaging in hostilities with a friendly power, and also appointed General Scott to take command of the disturbed fron-

road from Springfield to Dayton, some of them laboring for means to prosecute their journey and some had stopped to recruit their teams as well as their purses, that they might continue their journey after the warm season had passed. Many of them came to visit us and were received with feelings of gratitude for the goodness of our heavenly Father for the preservation of our lives and for the privilege of meeting each other in this land of strangers.

The weather has been extremely hot and dry in the land, and in the southwestern part of the state of Ohio, for many weeks: and rain was much needed, and supplication was made to the God of Israel for rain on the land in this region of country, at the meeting in the forenoon, and at the close of the service in the afterpart of the day. Elder Dunham and Elder Charles Thompson each held a meeting in the afternoon, about two miles from camp.

Prayer for Rain.

Monday, July 30.—We remained in our encampment during the day and were visited by several gentlemen, and were solicited to tarry in this place for a season and take a job on the Springfield and Dayton turnpike. Some of the brethren went out to make what discoveries they could relative to labor, and partly engaged some small jobs on condition that we tarried here for a few days. In the afternoon and evening it rained on each side of us, that is, to the north and to the south, and at no great distance from us quite hard, to all appearances; and we also had a small shower in the afternoon, though not enough to water the earth sufficiently, yet it cooled the air and greatly revived both the animal and vegetable kingdoms, for which we thank that

Rain.

tier and enforce a strict neutrality." After the arrival of General Scott on the frontiers, effective measures were taken to prevent further supplies and recruits from reaching the "patriots," and the militia ordered out by the Canadian government, after some severe fighting, dispersed the insurgents, many of whom fled to the United States. The British parliament subsequently granted some of the legislative reforms demanded by the people.

Being that rules the armies of heaven and the inhabitants of the earth, and sendeth rain both upon the just and upon the unjust.

Elder John E. Page, who preached about one mile from us in the evening, tarried with us over night and left us in the morning to go to his family at Fairfield, five miles and one half distant, where they had resided for a few weeks since the Canada camp (John E. Page's company) had stopped.

Tuesday, *July 31*.—A part of our company went off to work on a job of raising a levee for Mr. Hushman, and some one way and some another to labor during the day. In the morning all the men in the camp were called out and were made acquainted with our pecuniary circumstances, and an inquiry made who, if any, wished to leave the camp and look out for themselves. One man, Brother Asa Wright, said that his wife had always been opposed to going in the camp, and that he had told some of the brethren in the camp that in consequence of that and some other things it was his choice to leave. Elder Stephen Headlock also complained of the murmuring of some of the camp, and said that he had rather leave the camp—though he desired with all his heart to go in it up to the land of Zion—than to hear so much complaining as he had for a few days past, and had freely expressed his mind before to that effect to some of the brethren.

Some Leave the Camp.

He was reprimanded by Elder Pulsipher for his own neglect of duty and told to set his own tent in order, and then if he knew of any infringement on the rules of the camp by others, to try, as the law of God required, to reclaim the offenders and restore them to order that the blessings of God might be poured out upon the camp during the long and tedious journey which still lay before it. A vote was taken to see how many were desirous of stopping and laboring, if the Council thought advisable to do so. Some further inquiries were

A Reproof.

made concerning the conditions that had been or might be offered to the camp to make a piece of turn pike road or do any other work that might be obtained by the Council, and under their superintendency, when all, with a few exceptions,—and they were persons unable to labor—voted to abide by the advice of the Council, and would stay or go, as they should advise or direct.

Elder Page Exhorts the Camp.

Elder John E. Page made a short speech, exhorting all to fulfill their covenants, let what would come, life or death, inasmuch as they were in righteousness before God; and said that all our deeds would be had in remembrance; that we would be rewarded for them, whether good or evil, both in time and in eternity; and further observed that the journeying of the Saints to Zion in obedience to the commandments of the Lord afforded an opportunity for them to become what they desired; either to be as great and as noble as they could or to sink into obscurity in the eyes of God and His Saints and be the least in this last kingdom which God has set His hand to build up upon the earth. After making many appropriate remarks he implored the blessings of heaven upon us, which was responded to by a hearty amen, and then all dispersed to attend to the duties of the day.

Work on the Turnpike.

In the course of the day we took a job of making half a mile of turnpike, and removed our encampment into a beautiful grove near the edge of a prairie about one-fourth of a mile, and about the same distance from Mad river. Here we began to make preparations to commence work, but made little progress, for most of the laboring men were absent, and we did not get our tents pitched till nearly night.

Wednesday, August 1.—Began at an early hour to make arrangements to commence our job. Sent off part of the men to finish the levee and some to build a fence around our camp, and about twelve o'clock made a beginning on the road. A few sick in the camp this day, but most of us were in good health and satisfied with our situation.

Thursday, August 2.—Very warm and dry as it had been for many days, with the exception of the showers on Monday evening.

Progressed with our labors on the road rather slowly, for we were not in condition to work to good advantage, as we had not tools enough, and had been on our journey so long that it was rather fatiguing to labor hard in the commencement. Some sickness in the camp, but no more than would be expected, owing to our change of climate, and the extreme heat and drouth in the land.

Friday, August 3.—Made great progress in the turnpike, and the desponding spirits of some began to revive, for laboring had looked to some to be rather a hard way to procure means to prosecute our journey, though but few complained. Some new cases of sickness, but many of those who were unwell the day before were recovering fast. The men and boys in camp were called together in the evening and instructed by the Council as the Spirit of the Lord manifested unto them concerning cleanliness and decency and the importance of being industrious in laboring with their hands to procure means to go on our way. The covenant to put our strength, our properties and monies together for the purpose of going together in the camp to Zion, and of delivering the poor from their poverty and oppression in the land of Kirtland was adverted to by Elders Pulsipher and Foster, and all exhorted and entreated to give heed to it if they wished to enjoy the blessings of the Lord.

Renewed Diligence.

The Council at a meeting held in the afternoon had taken into consideration the propriety of appointing three men to sit as councilors or judges [known as an Assistant Council, see p. 128] to settle matters and difficulties between brethren, that the Council might be relieved in some measure from the arduous duties of settling controversies and have more

An Assistant Council Appointed.

time to devote to other things that devolved upon them as Presidents of the camp. Duncan McArthur, Gordon Snow and George Stringham were nominated, and the subject was laid before the meeting in the evening to receive the unanimous approbation of all present. The many blessings conferred on us by our Heavenly Father since He first made known His will unto the Council of Seventies, that it was His will that the Seventies should go to Zion in a camp together, were recapitulated and our hearts were made glad and we rejoiced in the Rock of our salvation whose mercies had been extended unto us, notwithstanding our murmurings against Him and slowness of heart to believe His words, and the many promises which He had made unto us. At the close of the meeting our united prayers ascended to God in the name of His Son, Jesus Christ, for the recovery of Elder Jacob Chapman's family who resided near the city of Dayton, and had sent unto us for some of the Elders to go and lay hands on them in the name of the Lord, as they were sorely afflicted with disease, and for the recovery of the sick in our own camp, and that the destroyer might cease to make inroads among us.

Saturday, August 4.—Our circumstances about the same as on the day previous. A heavy shower towards evening cooled the air and greatly revived the vegetation which was suffering for want of rain in the country round about. In the evening the camp was called together again and the names of those who had absented themselves from labor were read over and those who had no excuse for their absence were severely reprimanded, and the overseers of tents instructed by the Council to withhold the usual rations allotted from such individuals as could but would not labor, that the idler should not eat the bread of the laborer, according to the commandments of the Lord.—Doctrine and Covenants, sec. xlii.

CHAPTER X.

THE JOURNEY OF KIRTLAND CAMP. (CONTINUED).

Sunday, August 5.—One month had passed away since the camp was organized and we were all present in the camp with few exceptions. Elder Joseph Young preached from Acts xvi, and 30th verse, on the principles of salvation through the Gospel of Jesus Christ. A respectable congregation of strangers assembled with us and gave the best attention to what was declared unto them. The sacrament of the Lord's supper was administered in the afternoon by Elders Foster and Wilbur and the services of the day were closed by singing and imploring the blessings of God upon us and upon the Saints of the Most High in every land, and for the triumph of Christ's kingdom on the earth. The Council met after the public services of the day were ended, to transact some business of the camp which seemed to be necessary; and after that was disposed of Elder Zera Pulsipher suggested the propriety of ordaining George Stringham to the office of an Elder, and said that the Spirit had borne witness to him for some time that it was the will of the Lord that he should be ordained to that office. The subject was taken into consideration and the Council decided that he should be ordained if it was congenial to his own feelings. On being interrogated he said that he was willing to be ordained and would do anything the Lord required of him for the building up of His kingdom on the earth. Elder James Foster with some others then proceeded to ordain him according to the rules of the Church of Latter-day Saints, an Elder in said Church. The Council then adjourned.

Preaching of Elder Young.

Monday, August 6.—Some complaining in the camp and some sick, principally children and aged persons. We progressed finely in our labors on the road, and a greater interest seemed to be manifested for the welfare of the whole body than had been since the camp stopped. John Hammond lost one of his horses in the night, the first one that had died during our journey.

An Increase of Interest in the Camp.

Tuesday, August 7.—No occurrence worthy of note during the day. The destroyer continued to afflict us with sickness as a body, and many of the men were unable to labor. In the evening the laborers were called together and some instructions were given to them concerning our labors and the necessity of diligence impressed upon those who manifested an indifference to the general interest of the whole camp.

Exhortations.

Wednesday, August 8.—This morning found another of our horses dead, one that had been bought for the benefit of the camp, and before noon we had to kill another that had his leg broken. It belonged to John Matthews who had left the camp a few days before without the consent of the Council. Sickness still prevailed among us though the laboring men were in better health than usual and the spirit of love and union was manifested by most of the camp and all that were able labored cheerfully without a murmur during the day. In the evening a child of Hiram H. Byington died, which was the second time death had entered our camp on the road from Kirtland to this place.

Death of Horses.

Thursday, August 9.—Brother Byington's child was buried at twelve o'clock. Some sickness in the camp this day, but not quite so much as there has been for a few days past. A little shower about noon cooled the air though enough did not fall to water the earth which was suffering from want of rain and had been for some time, insomuch that the shower that fell on the 4th instant did not suffice to water it enough to restore

A Burial.

vegetation to its natural state, and the crops of corn and other grains were suffering almost beyond description in the region of country round about.

Friday, August 10.—The weather continued extremely hot and dry. Elder James Foster took his tent in company with J. S. Holman, S. Shumway of the 3rd division and Joel Harvey of the 4th, with the inmates of their tents and went to work on a job of building a levee for Mr. Hushman about two miles from the camp, where E. B. Gaylord of the 4th division had moved his tent a few days before, and was digging a ditch for the same individual. In the evening a daughter of Thomas Carico, aged one year and five months, died, and was buried the next day.

More Employment.

Saturday, August 11.—One or two showers of rain cooled the air and revived the languid and drooping spirits of those in the camp, and symptoms of better health were visible on the countenances of the afflicted. In the fore part of the night Sarah Emily, daughter of Dominicus Carter, aged about two years and three months, died, being the fourth one the destroyer took from our midst.

Showers.

Sunday, August 12.—Elder Pulsipher preached in the forenoon to a large congregation of strangers most of whom gave the best attention. At two p. m. the funeral of Elder Carter's child was attended, and at four Elder John E. Page, who had been invited, preached a sermon on the gathering of Israel and the location of Mount Zion,* after which the Council met

Charles Thompson Corrected.

*In speaking of the services this 12th day of August, and the discourse of Elder John E. Page, Brother Samuel D. Tyler, who, as well as Judge Elias Smith, kept a most excellent journal of the camp's proceedings day by day, says: "Elder John E. Page of the Canada camp preached at three o'clock to us, and many spectators. Text. Jer. 31: 6. In his discourse he proved that America was the land given to Joseph's posterity, and that the Indians are the descendants of Joseph, and that they would be gathered to Zion and the Jews to Jerusalem and that the watchmen shall lift up their voices on Mount Zion, etc. In short, he preached the truth with power. At the close he said he had been preaching in Fairfield and had the confidence and good feeling of the people, and he advised that none of less talent

to regulate and set in order some things that seemed to be necessary in the camp, in order to preserve harmony and union among us. Elder Charles Thompson was called in question for something he had taught concerning the order of moving of the camp. After being shown the impropriety of his conduct, and the fallacy of some of his views and the effect the promulgating of them had and would have in the camp, he made ample retraction before the Council, and before the camp which was called together for that purpose in the evening.

Several brethren from Elder Page's camp and others that resided in this region of country spent the Sabbath with us. Among the number were Elder Nelson and Brother Ide, who resided near the city of Dayton. Several of the brethren who had resided in Kirtland, being now on the way to the land of Zion, had stopped to labor near us and they were also present, and met with us at communion which was administered by Elders John E. Page and Jonathan H. Hale at the close of the meeting in the afternoon.

Spirit of Union Manifested.

Monday, *August 13.*—Richard D. Blanchard joined the camp by the consent of the Council. Somewhat cooler towards evening than it had been for some time. About twenty sick in the camp, mostly women and children, but none are dangerously ill. The laborers were called together again in the evening and some instructions given them concerning our labors and prospects in relation to means to prosecute our journey, and a spirit of union was manifested which cheered our hearts and made us thankful to the God of Israel for that and the many other blessings we daily received from His liberal hand.

Tuesday, *August 14.*—The day passed away as usual.

than himself, should venture to preach to them, lest they should injure the cause. He said he did not say this to boast, but I think he had better not [have] said it, for I think it was not according to scripture and the Spirit of God; for God has chosen the weak and foolish things of the world to confound the wisdom of the wise and prudent. Now, if the Lord will send poor, weak Elders to any people to preach to them, I doubt not that He will risk them, yea, and risk His cause with them also.

For some time past most of the laborers were able to perform the work assigned them, and but few comparatively were sick in the camp, and these generally were growing better.

Wednesday, August 15.—It rained most of the afternoon which hindered us from our labors a considerable part of the time.

Jonas Putnam Commended.

Brother Jonas Putnam and family by the advice of the Council left the camp and moved about twelve miles on to a farm belonging to Brother Ide to take charge of it while he [Brother Ide] went to prepare a place for himself and the small branch of the Church in this vicinity in some of the Stakes of Zion in the west. We were not willing that Brother Putnam should leave the camp upon any other principle than that of mutual consent of all concerned, for he was esteemed by all as a just man, and devout, and one that was worthy of the fellowship of the Saints. Elder Elijah Cheney who had left Kirtland before the camp with his family came into our encampment in the forenoon having been blessed of the Lord on his journey and was received with a hearty welcome by the brethren of the camp.

Thursday, August 16.—Elder B. S. Wilbur took about twenty men with Elder George Stringham and his tent and company and went to the city of Dayton to do a job of work which had been engaged by the advice of the Council.

Expulsion from the Camp.

In the evening G. W. Brooks and wife were called before the Council and inquiry made into some things which had been in circulation for some days respecting them, and in the course of the investigation it was acknowledged that Brother Brooks' wife had used tea most of the time on the road, and had used profane language, and she declared she would still pursue the same course, and it was not in the power of her husband or the Council to stop it. She further said that she was not a member of the Church and did not expect to come under the rules of the camp.

The decision of the Council was that they must leave the camp, and Brother Brooks was severely reprimanded for not keeping his tent in order according to the Constitution of the camp, and not keeping his family in subjection, as a man of God, especially as an Elder of Israel.

Further Investigation of Camp Members.

Friday, August 17.—Elders J. Foster and Henry Harriman, having finished the job of embankment [levee], came back into the encampment themselves but did not bring back their tents. In the afternoon the Council met and several of the members of the camp were tried for breach of the Constitution, and Nathan K. Knight presented an appeal from a decision of the Assistant Council on a charge preferred against himself and wife by Amos Jackson, overseer of his tent, for some misdemeanor in respect to the order of the camp and unchristian-like conduct on the journey, which decision was that they had violated the Constitution of the camp and disregarded their covenant to observe and keep it, and consequently must be left by the wayside. After an inquiry into the affair the decision made [by the Assistant Council] was confirmed by the Council of the camp.

Josiah Miller was advised, in consequence of the conduct of his son-in-law, Aaron Dolph, who was not a member of the Church, and would not conform to the order of the camp, to take his family and go by himself.

Expulsions from Camp.

Nathan Staker was requested to leave the camp in consequence of the determination of his wife, to all appearances, not to observe the rules and regulations of the camp. There had been contentions in the tent between herself and Andrew Lamereaux, overseer of the tent, and also contentions with his family several times on the road, and after the camp stopped in this place. The Council had become weary of trying to settlethese contentions between them. Andrew Lamereaux having gone to Dayton to labor, taking his family with him, was not present at the Council, neither was there any new complaint made, but the impossibility of Brother Staker to keep his family in order was apparent to all, and it was thought to be the best thing for him to take his family and leave the camp. Some other things were brought before the Council and inquiry made into the conduct of several individuals, and the Council had come to the determination to put iniquity from the camp wherever it could be found, that God's anger might be turned away and His blessings rest down upon us.

Saturday, August 18.—Josiah Miller, agreeable to the counsel given him, took his family and left the camp with the best of feelings existing between him and the Council of the camp; he left it only in consequence of the disposition of his son-in-law, Aaron Dolph, to set at naught the Constitution by which the camp were bound by agreement to put their strength, properties and monies together in order to move the camp to the land of Zion.

Another child died this day, aged about three years, a daughter of Martha Higby, who was in company with Z. H.* Brewster. Sister Higby's husband had left her some time before the camp started. The brethren finished their job at Mr. Harshman's on Friday, and at Dayton on Saturday. The health of the camp was much better than usual since we stopped here.

Sunday, August 19.—As usual a large congregation met with us and gave good attention to the services of the day. Elder Joel H. Johnson, by the request of Elders Young and Harriman, who presided, preached on the first principles of the Gospel from Galatians i, in the forenoon. In the afternoon the sacrament was administered agreeable to the commandments of the Lord.

Religious Service.

Monday, August 20.—Nathan K. Knight and George W. Brooks, who had been excluded from the camp as before stated, left the camp. Daniel Bliss went with George W. Brooks by the consent of the Council—at his own request—

* By an error this initial in the list of names is given as W.

as he was not well provided for as to a place for his family to ride on the road.

Tuesday, August 21.—Two boys born in the camp in the morning. One, the son of Gardner Snow, the other of Frederick M. Vanleuven. The Council held a consultation in the afternoon and concluded to make preparations to start on our journey as soon as possible, if the Lord did not open the way clearly before us to tarry longer in this place. J. A. Clark was excluded from the camp.

Births in Camp.

Wednesday, August 22.—Finished our job of grading in the morning and the remainder of the day most of us rested ourselves, and made some preparation to start again on our way. Extremely hot, and the earth parched with drought to a greater degree than has been known for many years in this region of country.

TurnpikeContract finished.

Andrew J. Squires called on us on his way to Kirtland on Tuesday afternoon, and left again after having some consultation with the Council of the Seventies about his standing in the Church, and went on his way to Kirtland.

Thursday, August 23.—The Council met to regulate some things and concluded to start on Monday, the 27th instant, and to labor all the time we could till that time. Several resolutions were passed among which was the following: That those of the camp who were absent should come back to the encampment and that the vacancies in overseers of tents be filled and then all called together and instructed more particularly concerning the duties of their office before the camp shall start again; that the camp shall be reorganized, inasmuch as some have left since its organization.

Arrangements for Renewal of the Journey.

John Hammond was expelled by the assistant Council from the camp for not standing at the head of his family, his wife making much disturbance in the tent, of which Brother Hammond was the overseer.

Friday, August 24.—Most of the brethren who

were absent came into the camp during the day to make preparations to go on our journey.

Gathering of the Absent.

Elder Joseph Young went to Dayton to attend the funeral of William Tenny, late of Kirtland, who died yesterday.

Saturday, August 25.—In the afternoon the overseers of the tents were called together by the Council, and inquiry made into the affairs of each tent to see if there were any difficulties existing among them or any other persons in the camp. The inquiry resulted in discovering much that was not as it should be. Several tents were in disorder, and the Council proceeded to make inquiry and to set in order the inmates of those tents that were in a state of confusion. Most of the difficulties were amicably settled, one exception. John Rulison was turned out of the camp by the assistant Council. The same Council were directed to go to Brother Nickerson's tent and set it in order; breaking the Word of Wisdom and disbelief in some of the revelations constituted the difficulties in this tent.

Sunday, August 26.—As usual a public meeting was held in the forenoon and a sacrament meeting in the afternoon. The Spirit of the Lord was poured out on the assembly and some were convinced of the truth of what was declared unto them.

Monday, August 27.—Having finished our turnpike contract, we made every possible exertion to continue our journey on the morrow, by shoeing horses and fixing wagons. We had a blacksmith shop in operation in the camp for several days, doing the necessary work. In the evening a heavy shower of rain fell which was greatly needed, and it seemed for some time past that it would be almost impossible for us to travel in consequence of the drought, and the dust that flew on the highway; but as the Lord had been merciful to us before, so He was in this instance, for which we felt thankful in very deed.

Preparations for the Journey.

Tuesday, August 28.—Made every exertion in our power to start, but found it impossible about noon, as we had to make provisions for several families who had been deprived of a team by those who were turned out of the camp taking their teams with them.

Charles Wood was expelled from the camp by two of the Council, James Foster and Henry Harriman, on the 27th. Brother Wood was tenting about two miles from our encampment with two or three other families, who for some misdemeanor had been expelled from the camp. Brothers Foster and Harriman, by the consent of all concerned, acted in this matter without a majority of the Council being present, but this was not the practice of the Council, as a majority was considered necessary to have a trial or council concerning any matter relating to the affairs of the camp; but in this instance no exceptions were made by any. In the evening the brethren in the camp were called together and our labors and tribulations were talked over. The Spirit of God rested down upon the camp with power, and after singing the hymn, "The Spirit of God like a fire is burning," we concluded by a song, "Hosanna to God and the Lamb," and retired with joyful hearts to our tents.

Wednesday, August 29.—Early in the morning we began to leave the ground, having the previous day reorganized as far as possible.

The Camp Resumes its Journey.

Z. H. Brewster and his father-in-law, J. Higby who was with him, were left behind for want of a team to carry them with their families.

We passed through the city of Dayton, situated near the junction of Mad river with the Great Miami, and took the road to Eaton and traveled through the township of Jefferson and put up in the township of Jackson, near the village of Johnsville, twelve miles from Dayton, and pitched our tents in the highway, having traveled eighteen miles. Having been at work one month we all were thankful for the privilege of again marching on our way.

Our labors in Bath and its vicinity amounted to about ——.*

Thursday, August 30.—Traveled through Twin township on the north line, and through Washington township, in Preble county; passed through the village of Alexander, in Twin township, and then through the village of Eaton, twelve miles from Johnsville, and pitched our tents on the line of Indiana and Ohio, eleven miles from Eaton, having traveled twenty-four miles, and are now two hundred and ninety-three miles from Kirtland.

On the Indiana Line.

The land from Dayton to the Ohio line is generally bad, and covered with maple, beach, elm, ash, whitewood and other northern timber; and the soil after leaving the bottoms of the Miami is not so fertile as the lands on that [Miami] and Mad river. The road was generally good, and the weather extremely fine. Our teams stood the journey much better than when we first started from Kirtland.

On Thursday a daughter of Otis Shumway died, at Eaton, on the road, and was buried in the woods near where we camped at night, in the township of Jackson, Preble county, Ohio.

Friday, August 31.—Started early, crossed the line of Indiana a few rods from our encampment into the township of Wayne, Wayne county, Indiana. We came to the village of Richmond, on the east branch of Whitewater, four miles. Richmond is a flourishing place on the national road, which we came to soon after we passed the line, or between there and Richmond. From Richmond we came to Centerville, the county seat of Wayne county, six miles; and thence we came to the village of Germantown, eight miles, and encamped for the night near that village, about sunset. Crossed during the day several tributary streams of the

Camp Enters the State of Indiana.

* The amount is not stated in the camp journal.

Whitewater, the principal of which was Nolands Fork, west of Centerville. Traveled fourteen miles.

Course of Journey.

September 1.—The camp started at eight a. m. We came through a small village called Cambridge, one mile from Germantown; then through Dublin three miles; through Louisville, nine miles; then to Flatrock, in Franklin township, Henry county; thence to Roysville, on the east side of Blue river, and Knight's Town, on the east side ten miles, and encamped by the side of the way one mile west of Knight's Town, just at dark. The air was cool in the evening and after the fires were built, which was necessary for our comfort and convenience, our encampment looked beautiful, and we attracted the attention of all who passed by, and of the citizens of the neighborhood who declared that our company exceeded any they had before seen in all their lives. Distance from Kirtland three hundred and thirty-five miles

A Sunday Journey.

Sunday, September 2.—Frost seen in the morning. It being quite cool, we thought it our duty to go on our way, so we started at eight o'clock, and came through the small villages of Liberty and Portland, and stopped at noon in Center township, Hancock county, at Mr. Caldwell's, about nine miles from our encampment. Here the son of E. P. Merriam died; the body was carried on to our place of encampment at night. In the afternoon we came through Greenfield, the county seat of Hancock county. Crossed Sugar creek, nine miles, and encamped at night on Buck creek on the west line of Hancock county, and east line of Marion county, having traveled twenty-one miles through a low, level country of clay soil and hard road. The crops of corn were small, and all grain scarce. The weather is cool and the roads good, but from appearances they had been almost impassable. Three hundred and fifty-six miles from Kirtland.

Monday, September 3.—Cold and frosty in the morning.

We arose at four, as usual, and at half-past five Sister Bathsheba Willey, who was sick when we started from Kirtland, died and was buried together with Brother Merriam's child in the northeast corner of T. Ruther's orchard, Jones township, Hancock county, about one-fourth of a mile east from Buck creek. The stage broke Lucius N. Scovil's wagon down.* We came this day to Indianapolis, on the east side of White river, the metropolis of the state of Indiana, and pitched our tents at night six and one-sixth miles west of the city, in Wayne township, on the farm of Brother Miller. Distance from Kirtland, three hundred and seventy-three miles.

Death of Bathsheba Willey.

Tuesday, September 4.—In the morning B. S. Wilbur, who had been left behind in Dayton, Ohio, to transact some business, came up in the stage about four o'clock. The camp was called together in the morning, and warned by the Council of the displeasure of our heavenly Father with some for their wickedness, and that His judgments would fall upon them with greater weight than they had if there was not a speedy repentance. The Council also entreated all to be humble and pray much, for the destroyer was in our midst and many were afflicted. Ira Thornton, overseer of tent No. eight, third division, by leave of the Council, stayed behind to go up to the land of Zion with his father-in-law, who resided near our encampment, and was going to start in a few days. Brother Thornton during the journey had been a faithful brother, and stopped now merely on his wife's account, and not that he was or had been disaffected with the movements in the camp or with the management of the Council.

Warning and Exhortation.

Josiah Butterfield stopped to get a wagon wheel made, and the camp started at a late hour. We came through

* This incident is related by Samuel D. Tyler, under date of Sunday, September 2nd, as follows: "This afternoon a miserable drunken stage driver maliciously ran aside out of his course and struck the fore wheel of one of our wagons and stove it in and dropped it; then drove off exulting in his mischief. The stage he drove was marked "*J. P. Voorhees.*"

Cumberland village, two miles; thence through Plainfield, in Guilford township, Hendricks county, five miles; and stopped at noon in Liberty township, two miles east of Bellville, five miles from Plainfield, through which we passed in the afternoon; thence through the village of Bellville eight miles, and encamped late in the evening about three miles west of Bellville, having traveled twenty-three miles. David Elliot left the camp this morning. Distance from Kirtland, three hundred and ninety-six miles.

Wednesday, September 5.—Thomas Nickerson's child died in the night, and was buried where we stopped at noon on the farm of Noal Fouts, west of the village of Putnamville. Passed this day through Mt. Meridian. Putnamville, and Manhattan. Crossed Walnut and McCray creek and encamped by the side of the way just west of Clay county, having traveled twenty miles. Distance from Kirtland, four hundred and sixteen miles.

Thursday, September 6.—Traveled thirteen miles through a fine country, good road, and pitched our tents between two and three miles east of Terre Haute, the county seat of Vigo county, situated on the west side of the Wabash, on a swell of land in a beautiful prairie surrounded by a fruitful and fertile country. Distance from Kirtland, four hundred and thirty-three miles.

Arrival at Terre Haute.

Friday, September 7.—Sometime in the night a daughter of Otis Shumway died; and in the morning a child of J. A. Clark died. Both were buried in the graveyard in Terre Haute through which we passed, and crossed the Wabash about twelve o'clock at both ferries, and left the national road and turning to the right, took the North Arm Prairie road to Paris. Traveled nine miles, and encamped in LaFayette township, three-fourths of a mile east of the Illinois line. The distance from Kirtland, the way we came, to Terre Haute is four hundred and thirty-six miles. E. Cherry did not come up, and was left behind; his family was sick.

Saturday, September 8.—Crossed the Illinois line in the

morning into Edgar county; crossed the North Arm Prairie, so-called; crossed Sugar creek and came through Paris, the county seat of Edgar county, and traveled fourteen miles on a prairie, and put up for the night at a late hour, pitching our tents on the prairie near the house of Mr. Keller, who appeared friendly and obliging. Traveled today twenty-five miles. Distance from Kirtland, four hundred and seventy miles.

In Illinois.

Sunday, September 9.—Started early, and came to Ambro creek, in a grove, two miles, and encamped during the day. The fourth division came up just as we started in the morning; for they were unable to travel as fast as the other divisions owing to the heat of the day on Saturday. Distance from Kirtland, four hundred and seventy-two miles.

The Council met after we encamped, and after much consultation concluded to call the heads of families together and lay before them our situation with respect to means and the prospects before us and the apparent impossibility of our obtaining labor for ourselves and for the support of our families in the city of Far West during the coming winter; and to advise them, especially those that did not belong to the Seventies, to commence looking for places for themselves where they could procure a subsistence during the Winter and procure means sufficient to remove them to Missouri in the Spring. Accordingly in the afternoon the camp were called together and those things laid before them for their consideration, which seemed to meet with the approval of a large majority of the heads of families in the camp. Distance from Kirtland, four hundred and seventy-two miles.

Serious Difficulties Considered.

Monday, September 10.—Considerable anxiety seemed to be manifested by some concerning the advice of the Council, and some complained, like ancient Israel, and said that they did not thank the Council for bringing them so far, and had rather been left

Dissatisfaction in Camp.

in Kirtland, and some said one thing and some another. Among the number were Aaron Cheney, Nathan Cheney, William Draper and Thomas Draper and Henry Munroe, who were sent for, to come and settle with the clerks and look out for quarters immediately. Themira Draper, Alfred Draper and Cornelius Vanleuven left the camp with them. Reuben Daniels, whose wife was sick and had a son born in the night, together with Ethan A. Moore and Joel Harvey, also left the camp to stop for a few days and then pursue their journey by themselves. After the camp started Joseph Coon stopped because his wife was sick. We traveled five or six miles west of the little Ambarras, where we encamped. We passed through a small place called Independence, which is in an oak opening, in which we had encamped. It was about six miles through it, and then we crossed through a prairie fifteen miles, and encamped on the west side of the East Ocha or Kaskaskias, some of the teams not coming up to the encampment till twelve o'clock. Traveled twenty-two miles. Distance from Kirtland, four hundred and ninety-four miles.

Tuesday, September 11.—Crossed another prairie, fourteen miles, and encamped at four p. m. on the west side of the West Ocha, in Macon county, having traveled sixteen miles. Distance from Kirtland, five hundred and ten miles.

Increased Sickness.

Many in the camp at this time were sick and afflicted. Some with fever and ague, and some with one thing and some with another. The most dangerous were Elder Josiah Willey and John Wright, son of Asa Wright, aged about fourteen years.

Wednesday, September 12.—Started at eight o'clock and crossed another prairie twelve miles, then through a piece of timber land on the headwaters of San Juan river, then over a three-mile prairie, and stopped to refresh our teams in the edge of the wood a little after noon, sixteen miles from our encampment of the night before. In the afternoon crossed over a prairie four miles, then through a piece of timbered land, then another prairie two miles, and encamped by the side of a small creek, having traveled this day twenty-two miles. Distance from Kirtland, five hundred and thirty-nine miles.

Thursday, September 13.—In the morning it was ascertained that George Stringham and Benjamin Baker, with Joseph C. Clark had stopped behind, or could not come up because of the failure of their teams. Asa Wright did not come up at night, but came up in the morning by himself before we started, to settle his accounts. His son being sick was the reason of his staying behind. Alba Whittle and Joel H. Johnson also settled their accounts, as they expected to stop at Springfield or sooner if they could find a place.

Started at a late hour and traveled fourteen miles through a prairie country down the Sangamon river, which ran on the right of the road in a westerly course to the Illinois. We encamped about three p. m. on a piece of land laid out for a village called Boliva or Bolivar. Here Ira Thornton's child died. Distance from Kirtland, five hundred and fifty-three miles.

Friday, September 14.—Before the first division left the ground Elder Stringham and Benjamin Baker came up, but we left them there. We came this day to Springfield, eighteen miles, crossing several small creeks and passing through a small place called Rochester. From Springfield we came four miles, and encamped for the night. We could not procure anything for our teams to eat and were obliged to fasten them to our wagons and give them a little corn or turn them onto dry prairie almost destitute of vegetation. Springfield is destined to be the seat of government of Illinois and the state house is now in course of building. It is situated on a beautiful prairie and looks like a flourishing place though it is yet in its infancy. Elder J. H. Johnson and his mother and their families, together with

Camp Passes Through Springfield.

Alba Whittle, Jonathan and Cyrus B. Fisher, Edwin P. Merriam and Samuel Hale—who was sick—and wife, also stopped at Springfield or near there, and Richard Brasher went to Huron, three miles west from Springfield to stop with his friends for a short season. Traveled twenty-two miles. Distance from Kirtland, five hundred and seventy-five miles.

Saturday, September 15.—William Gribble left the camp in the morning to stop at Springfield during the winter, and Ira Thornton left and went on with Allen Wait.

We started before breakfast and traveled fourteen miles. Passed through a small village called Berlin and camped on Spring creek in Island Grove. Here T. P. Pierce's child died, and was buried on Sunday, near Elder Keeler's house. Elder Keeler was late from New Portage, Ohio. Here we tarried till Monday morning. Distance from Kirtland, five hundred and eighty-nine miles.

Sunday, September 16.—We held a meeting in the afternoon and attended to communion. We had but few spectators in the camp during the day. A spirit of union rarely manifested was felt at the meeting, and our souls rejoiced in the Holy One of Israel.

More Departures from the Camp.

Monday, September 17.—This morning Elias Pulsipher, Daniel Pulsipher, Steven Starks, Hiram H. Byington and Monro Crosier settled their accounts and stopped behind. Traveled this day through Jacksonville, a fine village, the county seat of Morgan county, which we entered about fourteen miles east of Jacksonville. From thence we came to Geneva, a small, dusty place, and encamped near David Orton's, on a prairie, having traveled twenty-five miles. Most of the camp was late in arriving on the ground, and some did not come up till morning Distance from Kirtland, six hundred and fourteen miles.

Tuesday, September 18.—Warren Smith, Jonas Putnam, Stephen Shumway and D. C. Demming and Joseph

Young stopped at Geneva, Morgan county, and in the course of the day, Asaph Blanchard, Stephen Headlock and B. K. Hall also stopped near Exeter, and James C. Snow, whom we found near Geneva, joined us. We came through Exeter to Philip's ferry on the Illinois river, four miles below Naples, which is on the same river, on the straight road from Jacksonville to Quincy on the Mississippi, which we left and traveled six miles east of the ferry. We arrived at the ferry about four p. m., and some of the teams went over and encamped on the west side of the river in Pike county. In the night David Elliot, whom we had left in Putnam county, Indiana, came up on horseback, having arrived with his family within fifteen miles of us in the evening and left us again to hasten on his team that he might overtake us at Louisville, Missouri. Distance from Kirtland, six hundred and twenty-nine miles.

First Tidings from Far West.

Wednesday, September 19.—We all got over the Illinois at half-past one p. m. and came to Griggsville, then to Pittsfield, the county seat of Pike county, twelve miles, and encamped on a small hill one mile west of the village. While we were crossing the river two brethren arrived from Far West and brought us the first direct information from that place or from any of the brethren in the West since we started on our journey. The country between the Illinois river and Pittsfield is more rolling than it is on the east of that river, especially east of Springfield. Distance traveled from Kirtland, six hundred and forty-two miles.

Thursday, September 20.—Started on our journey and came to Atlas, a small village, the former county seat of Pike county, twelve miles through a rolling prairie country, then to the Snye, a branch of the Mississippi, about six miles from the river where we crossed in the afternoon, all but three wagons, into the town of Louisiana, in the state of Missouri; and encamped about three-fourths of a mile west of the town. Traveled twenty miles. Distance from Kirtland, six hundred and sixty-two miles.

A Missouri Storm.

Friday, September 21.—Traveled about seventeen miles throug a hot country and encamped in a wood near a prairie in a heavy rain which fell all the afternoon, and was the first that had fallen on us since we left Bath, Ohio, and was the most tedious time we had passed through. In the evening it thundered and rained powerfully, most of us went to bed without our supper, and tied our horses to our wagons. We thought it a perilous time, but few complained, nearly all bore it patiently. Duncan McArthur broke down his wagon in the forenoon and did not come up at night.

Bad Roads.

Saturday, September 22.—Traveled this day eighteen miles, eight miles of which was the worst road we had on the journey. The other ten miles prairie. Thomas Carico broke down his wagon and stopped and mended it, and did not overtake the camp at night. Eleaser King and sons, who left Kirtland before the camp, came up and encamped with us at night. The air was cool and chilly and towards night uncomfortably cold. We encamped about one-half mile east of Lick creek, in Monroe county. Distance from Kirtland, six hundred and ninety-seven miles.

Sunday, September 23.—A heavy frost in the morning, but after the sun arose it was pleasant and warm. We thought it our duty to travel and accordingly started on our way. The road very rough and bad part of the way, especially in the timbered land. Duncan McArthur and Thomas Carico, who had been left behind in consequence of breaking down their wagons, overtook us in the morning before we all started, some having to stay behind to find their horses, which went back across the prairie about nine miles in the night. E. B. Gaylord broke down his wagon and got badly hurt, and did not overtake us till Monday night. We traveled to Paris, the county seat of Monroe county, twenty miles, and encamped one mile west of the town late in the evening near a prairie. Crossed south fork of Salt river, five miles east of Paris, and several other tributary streams of the same river, most of which were dry by reason of the extreme drought which had prevailed in this land during the summer. Traveled today twenty-one miles. Distance from Kirtland, seven hundred and eighteen miles.

Monday, September 24.—Reorganized the camp which had become rather disorganized by reason of so many stopping by the way. The third division was put into the first and second, as that division had become quite small. The Council called the camp together and laid before them the scanty means in their hands, and wanted the brethren to furnish such things as they had to dispose of to purchase corn, etc., for our cattle and horses, that we might continue our journey. Traveled twenty miles before sunset, most of the way prairie, and encamped on the Elk fork of Salt river. We found the inhabitants in commotion and volunteering, under the order of Governor Boggs, as we were repeatedly told, to go up and fight the "Mormons" in Far West and that region of country. We were very correctly informed that one hundred and ten men had left Huntsville in the morning on that expedition; and that the govenor had called on five thousand from the upper counties ,and if we went any farther we should meet with difficulty and even death as they would as leave kill us as not.

Reorganization of the Camp.

We had been saluted with such reports every day after we came through Jacksonville, Illinois; but we paid little attention to it, trusting in that God for protection which had called upon us to gather ourselves together to the land of Zion, and who had thus far delivered us out of the hands of all our enemies, on every hand, not only in Kirtland, but on all our journey. Traveled this day twenty miles. Distance from Kirtland, seven hundred and thirty-eight miles.

Tuesday, September 25.—Thomas Nickerson lost his

horses and could not find them before the camp started, and did not overtake us at night.

We came through Huntsville, the county seat of Randolph county, eleven miles, where we were told before we arrived there, that we should be stopped, but nothing of the kind occurred when we came through the town, and we even heard no threats whatever, but all appeared friendly. A mile and a half west of Huntsville we crossed the east branch of Chariton, and one and a half miles west of the river we found Ira Ames and some other brethren near the place where the city of Manti is to be built, and encamped for the night on Dark creek, six miles from Huntsville. Traveled this day seventeen miles. Distance from Kirtland, seven hundred and fifty-five miles.

Wednesday, September 26.—In the morning Elder James Foster at a late hour proposed to disband and break up the camp in consequence of some rumors he had heard from the west which he said he believed. Elder Pulsipher being away only five of the Councilors could be present. The other four objected to this proposal, but so far yielded as to consent to have the camp stop till an embassy could be sent to Far West to see the state of things in that region and ascertain whether it would be wisdom or not for us to go into that or any of the western states this winter.

Proposition to Disband the Camp.

The camp was called together and the subject was partially laid before them by Elder Foster, which produced a sadness of countenance seldom seen in the course of our journey. While we were talking over the subject Elder Pulsipher came up, just as a gentleman by the name of Samuel Bend, of Pike county, Missouri, came along, and without knowing our intentions or destination, told us of the state of affairs in Far West, and Adam-ondi-Ahman, and everything we desired to know concerning some particular things. On being told that our intentions were to stop for a while, he advised us to go right along. He told us about the Daviess county mob and that the volunteers called for by the governor, which had rendezvoused at Keatsville, would be discharged at twelve o'clock, noon.

On reconsidering the subject a motion was made to go on which was carried unanimously. Accordingly we moved on and came to Chariton river in Chariton county, sixteen miles, and encamped about four p. m. on the west side of the river. In the afternoon before we started from the place where we stopped to feed on the seven mile prairie, near Brother Kellog's, the militia volunteers began to go by on their return home, and we continued to meet them most of the afternoon. Most of them passed us civilly, but some of them were rather saucy, few replies, however, were made to them. We met some brethren from Far West during the day which confirmed what we had been told in the morning by Mr. Bend. Brother Nickerson overtook us having found his horses, and eight or ten wagons of brethren from Huron county, Ohio, and other places, also Ira O. Thompson, who had formerly been with us as a member of the camp, stayed with us at night. Traveled sixteen miles this day. Distance from Kirtland, seven hundred and seventy-one miles.

Proposition Rejected.

Thursday, September 27.—Started in the morning in some confusion, owing to some misunderstanding, and came to Keatsville on a branch of the Chariton, two miles, and about half a mile west of the town, which is the county seat of Chariton county. We left the state road and took the road to Chillicothe and went up on the east side of Grand river, crossed a prairie about eighteen miles, beautifully diversified with valleys and rolling swells which give it a truly picturesque appearance. It has been surveyed and allotted for military purposes, and for that reason is still unoccupied. We encamped at night at the confluence of the forks of Yellow creek, having traveled twenty-two miles.

On Grand River.

Elder James Foster left us at Keatsville to go by the

way of De Witt, to see his son-in-law, Jonathan Thompson. In the evening the Council met to settle some difficulties and set in order some things that seemed to require attention to enable us to move in order and in peace the remainder of the journey. Traveled twenty-two miles today. Distance from Kirtland, seven hundred and ninety-three miles.

Friday, September 28.—Crossed Turkey creek, seven miles; Locus, four; and pitched our tents on the east side of Parson's creek, in Linn county, six miles from Locus creek, making seventeen miles. Distance from Kirtland, eight hundred and ten miles.

Saturday, September 29.—Came to Mr. Gregory's on Madison creek, six miles; thence to Chillicothe, a town lately laid out for the county seat of Livingston county, eight miles; and encamped about a mile west toward Grand river.

Thomas Carico's and J. H. Holmes' wagons were turned over in the course of the day, but no particular injury was done to any person. The road was new, and in some places rough, especially in the timbered land on the creeks. Traveled fifteen miles today. Distance from Kirtland, eight hundred and twenty-five miles.

Sunday, September 30.—Came to Grand river, two and one-half miles, crossed over and came to a small collection of houses, called Utica; two and one-half miles, here we found Brother Sliter from Kirtland, and some other brethren. From Utica we came through a rough and rolling country for ten miles to Brother Walker's, on Shoal creek, crossed the creek and camped on the west side near the prairie. Richard Blanchard, who joined the camp at Bath, left the camp and went to join his friends who lived near Chillicothe. Traveled fifteen miles today. Distance from Kirtland, eight hundred and forty miles.

Monday, October 1.—Came from Elder Walker's across the prairie, about nineteen miles, and encamped on

Brushy creek. Joshua S. Holman, by permission of one or two of the Council, went on Sunday evening to visit Elder Jacob Myers, formerly from Richland county, Ohio, and early in the morning started on his way without waiting for the camp, disregarding the advice of the Council, and in the evening, at a meeting of the camp, his proceedings were condemned by a unanimous vote. Traveled twenty miles and encamped on Brushy fork of Shoal creek, on the prairie. The entire distance from Kirtland, eight hundred and sixty miles.

Tuesday, October 2.—Crossed Long, Log, and Goose creeks, and arrived in Far West about five p. m. Here we were received with joyful salutations by the brethren in that city. Five miles from the city we were met by the First Presidency of the Church of Latter-day Saints, Joseph Smith, Jun., Sidney Rigdon and Hyrum Smith, together with Isaac Morley, Patriarch of Far West, and George W. Robinson, and by several other brethren between there and the city, who received us with open arms, and escorted us into the city. We encamped on the public square round the foundation of the Temple. Traveled this day ten miles. Whole distance from Kirtland, eight hundred and seventy miles.

[Here the camp journal's narrative ends. The two following entries which complete the history of this remarkable journey are taken from the Prophet's account of the proceedings relative to the camp on its arrival.]

Wednesday, October 3.—The camp continued their journey to Ambrosial creek, where they pitched their tents. I went with them a mile or two, to a beautiful spring, on the prairie, accompanied by Elder Rigdon, brother Hyrum and Brigham Young, with whom I returned to the city, where I spent the remainder of the day.

Thursday, October 4.—This is a day long to be remembered by that part of the Church of Jesus Christ of Latter-day Saints, called the Camp, or Kirtland Camp No. 1, for they arrived at their destination and began to pitch their tents about sunset, when one of the brethren living in the place proclaimed with a loud voice:

"*Brethren, your long and tedious journey is now ended; you are now on the public square of Adam-ondi-Ahman. This is the place where Adam blessed his posterity, when they rose up and called him Michael, the Prince, the Archangel, and he being full of the Holy Ghost predicted what should befall his posterity to the latest generation.*"—*Doctrine and Covenants.*

CHAPTER XI.

EXPULSION OF THE SAINTS FROM DE WITT, CARROLL COUNTY, MISSOURI.

Wednesday, October 3.—Sister Alice Hodgin died at Preston on the 2nd of September, 1838. And it was such a wonderful thing for a Latter-day Saint to die in England, that Elder Willard Richards was arraigned before the Mayor's Court at Preston, on the 3rd of October, charged with "killing and slaying" the said Alice with a "black stick," etc., but was discharged without being permitted to make his defense, as soon as it was discovered that the iniquity of his accusers was about to be made manifest.

Vexatious Persecution of Willard Richards.

The mob continued to fire upon the brethren at De Witt.

The following is an extract from General Parks' express to General Atchison:

Mob Movements at De Witt.

DEAR SIR:—I received this morning an affidavit from Carroll county. The following is a copy: "Henry Root, on his oath, states that on the night of the first of October, there was collected in the vicinity of De Witt, an armed force, consisting of from thirty to fifty persons, and on the morning of the second of October they came into the town of De Witt and fired on the civil inhabitants of that place. Thirteen of said individuals were seen by me in that place, and I believe there is actually an insurrection in that place.

"HENRY ROOT.

"Subscribed and sworn to this 3rd day of October, 1838.

"WILLIAM B. MORTON, J. P."

In consequence of which information, and belief of an attack being made on said place, I have ordered out the two companies raised by your order, to be held in readiness under the commands of Captains Bogart and Houston, to march for De Witt, in Carroll county, by eight o'clock tomorrow morning, armed and equipped as the law directs, with six days' provisions and fifty rounds of powder and ball. I will proceed with these troops in person, leaving Colonel Thomas in command of Grand river. As soon as I reach De Witt, I will advise you of the state of affairs more fully. I will use all due precaution in the affair, and deeply regret the necessity of this recourse.

H. G. PARKS,
Brigadier-General 2nd Brigade, 3rd Division.

Thursday, October 4.—I spent most of this day with my family.

The mob again fired upon the Saints at De Witt, who were compelled to return the fire in self-defense.

Scattering Firebrands.

To show how firebrands, arrows and death were scattered through the State, and that too by men high in authority, and who were sworn to preserve the public peace, I quote the following from a communication of General Lucas to the governor dated Boonville, Missouri, October 4, 1838:

Letter of General Lucas to Governor Boggs.

DEAR SIR:—As we passed down the Missouri river, on Monday last, we saw a large force of Mormons at De Witt, in Carroll county, under arms. Their commander, Colonel Hinkle, formerly of Caldwell county, informed me that there were two hundred, and that they were hourly expecting an attack from the citizens of Carroll county, who he said were then encamped only six miles from there, waiting for a reinforcement from Saline county. Hinkle said they had determined to fight. News had just been received at this place, through Dr. Scott of Fayette, that a fight took place on yesterday, and that several persons were killed. Dr. Scott informed me that he got his information from a gentleman of respectability, who had heard the firing of their guns as he passed down. If a fight has actually taken place, of which I have no doubt, it will create excitement in the whole of upper Missouri, and those base and degraded beings will be exterminated from the face of the earth. If one of the citizens of Carroll should be killed, before five days I believe that there will be from four to five thousand volunteers in the field against the Mormons, and nothing but their blood will satisfy them. It is an unpleasant state of affairs. The remedy I do not pretend to suggest to your Excellency. My troops of the Fourth Division were only dismissed subject to further orders, and can be called into the field at an hour's warning.

SAMUEL D. LUCAS.

"*Base and degraded beings!*" Whoever heard before of high-minded and honorable men condescending to sacrifice their honor, by stooping to wage war, without cause or provocation, against "base and degraded beings." But General Lucas is ready with his whole Division, at "an hour's warning," to enter the field of battle on such degraded terms, if his own statement is true. But General Lucas knew better. He knew the Saints were an innocent, unoffending people, and would not fight, only in self-defense, and why write such a letter to the governor to influence his mind? Why not keep to truth and justice? Poor Lucas! The annals of eternity will unfold to you who are the "base beings," and what it will take to "satisfy" for the shedding of "Mormon blood."

The Prophet's Comment.

Friday, October 5.—Report of the committee of Chariton county:

The undersigned committee were appointed at a public meeting by the citizens of Chariton county, on the 3rd day of October for the purpose of repairing to De Witt, in Carroll county, to inquire into the nature of the difficulties between the citizens of Carroll and the Mormons. We arrived at the place of difficulties on the 4th of October, and found a large portion of the citizens of Carroll and the adjoining counties assembled near De Witt, well armed. We inquired into the nature of the difficulties. They said that there was a large portion of the people called Mormons embodied in De Witt, from different parts of the world. They were unwilling for them to remain there, which is the cause of their waging war against them. To use the gentlemen's language, "they were waging a war of extermination, or to remove them from the said county." We also went into De Witt, to see the situation of the Mormons. We found them in the act of defense, begging for peace, and wishing for the civil authorities to repair there as early as possible, to settle the difficulties between the parties. Hostilities have commenced and will continue until they are stopped by the civil authorities. This we believe to be a correct statement of both parties. This the 5th day of October, 1838.

John W. Price,
Wm. H. Logan.

Subscribed to and sworn before me, the undersigned, one of the

Justices of the Peace within and for Chariton county, and State of Missouri, the 5th day of October, 1838.

JOHN MORSE, J. P.

This day also [October 5] General Atchison wrote the governor from Boonville, that in Carroll county the citizens were in arms for the purpose of driving the "Mormons" from that county.

The third Quarterly Conference of the Church in Caldwell county was held at Far West, President Brigham Young presiding. As there was not a sufficient number of members present to form a quorum for business, after singing and prayer, conference adjourned till 2 p. m., when they met and opened as usual, Presidents Marsh and Young presiding. There was not a sufficient number of the members of the High Council or any other quorum to do business as a quarterly Conference. They voted to ordain a few Elders, appointed a few missions, and adjourned till tomorrow at ten o'clock a. m.

Conference at Far West.

About this time I took a journey in company with some others, to the lower part of the county of Caldwell, for the purpose of selecting a location for a town. While on my journey, I was met by one of the brethren from De Witt, in Carroll county, who stated that our people who had settled in that place were and had been some time, surrounded by a mob, who had threatened their lives, and had shot at them several times; and that he was on his way to Far West, to inform the brethren there of the facts.

News of Mob Violence from De Witt.

I was surprised on receiving this intelligence, although there had, previous to this time, been some manifestations of mobs, but I had hoped that the good sense of the majority of the people, and their respect for the Constitution, would have put down any spirit of persecution which might have been manifested in that neighborhood.

The Prophet's Hopes of Peace Disappointed.

Immediately on receiving this intelligence I made preparations to go to that place, and endeavor, if possible, to allay the feelings of the citizens, and save the lives of my brethren who were thus exposed to their wrath.

The Prophet Arrives at De Witt.

Saturday, October 6.—I arrived at De Witt, and found that the accounts of the situation of that place were correct; for it was with much difficulty, and by traveling unfrequented roads, that I was able to get there, all the principal roads being strongly guarded by the mob, who refused all ingress as well as egress. I found my brethren, who were only a handful in comparison to the mob by which they were surrounded, in this situation, and their provisions nearly exhausted, and no prospect of obtaining any more. We thought it necessary to send immediately to the governor, to inform him of the circumstances, hoping to receive from the executive the protection which we needed; and which was guaranteed to us in common with other citizens. Several gentlemen of standing and respectability, who lived in the immediate vicinity who were not in any way connected with the Church of Latter-day Saints, who had witnessed the proceedings of our enemies, came forward and made affidavits to the treatment we had received, and concerning our perilous situation; and offered their services to go and present the case to the governor themselves.

Continuance of Far West Conference.

The Quarterly Conference convened at Far West this day [October 6th] at ten o'clock according to adjournment, Presidents Marsh and Young presiding. Elder Benjamin L. Clapp* said he had just returned from Kentucky, where he had been laboring, and that many doors were open there. A call was made for volunteers to go into the vineyard and preach, when Elders James Carroll, James Galliher, Lu-

* Benjamin L. Clapp, who afterwards became one of the First Council of Seventy, was born in the state of Alabama, August 19, 1814. He had joined the Church in an early day, and had already performed successful missions in the South, especially in the state of Kentucky.

man A. Shurtliff, James Dana, Ahaz Cook, Isaac Decker, Cornelius P. Lott and Alpheus Gifford offered themselves. President Marsh instructed them not to go forth boasting of their faith, or of the judgments of the Lord, but to go in the spirit of meekness, and preach repentance.*

Elder John Taylor† from Canada, by request, gave a statement of his feelings respecting his having been appointed as one of the Twelve, saying that he was willing to do anything that God would require of him; whereupon it was voted that Brother John

John Taylor Sustained to be an Apostle.

* This missionary movement at a time when it may be said that the whole country was "up in arms" against the Church, and its fortunes were apparently desperate, is truly an astonishing thing. And yet such missionary movements have become quite characteristic of the Church of Jesus Christ of Latter-day Saints. Its fortunes have never been at so low an ebb but what it could always undertake some great missionary enterprise. For example, when apostasy was rife in Kirtland, and the powers of darkness seemed massed for its overthrow, the Prophet, "to save the Church," organized and sent forth a mission to Great Britain; and now from upper Missouri, when the whole organization seemed to be in danger of disintegration, a mission is nevertheless organized to go into the Southern States to preach the Gospel. In later volumes of this work we shall also see that in 1850, when the whole body of the Mormon people had been expatriated from their country and fled into the desert wilderness of the Rocky mountain region, and when it was generally supposed that the world had practically seen the last of Mormonism, and when the Saints still had before them the task of subduing a wilderness, and many thousands of their people yet to gather from the East, where they were in a scattered condition, and the very existence of the people to human eyes seemed precarious, lo! a world-wide mission was organized and members of the quorum of Apostles were sent from the Church in the wilderness, into Scandinavia, France, Germany, Italy and Switzerland. This missionary spirit so characteristic of the Church, and to which it so staunchly adheres in all its fortunes, proclaims the genius of the work. The primary purpose of the Church's existence is to proclaim the truth of which it is the sacred depository, and after that to perfect the lives of those who receive its message. In proportion to its devotion to these two grand objects of its existence, has been and always will be the measure of its success.

† John Taylor was born November 1st, 1808, in Milnthorp, a small town near the head of Morecombe bay, and not far from Windemere, the "Queen of English Lakes," in the county of Westmoreland, England. His father's name was James Taylor, whose forefathers for many generations had lived on an estate known as Craig Gate, in Ackenthwaite. John Taylor's mother's name was Agnes; her maiden name was also Taylor. Her grandfather, Christopher Taylor, lived to be ninety-seven years of age. His son John, father of Agnes, held an office in the excise under the government from his first setting out in life to the age of about sixty. The maiden name of Agnes Taylor's mother was Whittington, a descendant of the family made famous by Richard Whittington, the younger son of Sir William Whittington.

Taylor fill one of the vacancies in the quorum of the Twelve. Stephen Chase was ordained president of the Elders' quorum in Far West. Isaac Laney, Horace Alexander and Albert Sloan were ordained Elders under the hands of the presidents. Samuel Bent and Isaac Higbee were appointed to fill the places of John Murdock and George M. Hinkle in the High Council, the two last named brethren having removed to De Witt. Conference adjourned to the first Friday and Saturday in January next, at ten a. m.

EBENEZER ROBINSON, Clerk.

England.

There were seven cut off from the Church in Preston, England, this day.

De Witt.

General Parks wrote General Atchison from Brigade Headquarters, five miles from De Witt, Carroll county:

Communication of Clark to Atchison on Affairs at De Witt.

SIR:—Immediately after my express to you by Mr. Warder was sent, I proceeded to this place, which I reached yesterday with two companies of mounted men from Ray county. I ordered Colonel Jones to call out three companies from this county, to hold themselves in readiness to join me at Carrolton on the fifth instant, which order has not been carried into effect. None of Carroll county regiment is with me.

At the age of seventeen Elder Taylor was made a Methodist exhorter or local preacher, and was very active and earnest in his ministerial labors. In 1832 he removed with his family to Toronto, upper Canada, and here engaged in preaching under the auspices of the Methodist church. Within a year after his arrival in Canada he married Leonora Cannon, daughter of Captain George Cannon (grandfather of the late George Q. Cannon). Leonora Cannon had come to Canada as the companion of the wife of Mr. Mason, the private secretary of Lord Aylmer, Governor-General of Canada. She was a devout Methodist, and through attendance upon church became acquainted with Mr. Taylor. While living in Toronto Elder Taylor associated himself with a number of gentlemen of education and refinement who were not quite satisfied with the doctrines of their respective churches, as those doctrines did not agree with the teachings of the Bible. Through this organization, they were seeking for greater religious light, and it was under these circumstances that Elder Parley P. Pratt arrived in Toronto with a letter of introduction to Elder Taylor, and several times addressed this association of gentlemen who were seeking the truth. The end of the matter was that John Taylor accepted the Gospel under the ministration of Elder Pratt; and was soon afterwards ordained an Elder in the Church, and commenced his missionary labors. Of his journey to Kirtland and defense of the Prophet against the fulminations of apostates we have already spoken. [See vol. II, p. 488—Note]. Elder Taylor had come to Missouri in response to the notification he had received that he was chosen an Apostle of the Lord Jesus Christ by revelation. (See revelation of 8th of July, 1838, pp. 46, 47).

On arriving in the vicinity of De Witt, I found a body of armed men under the command of Dr. Austin, encamped near De Witt, besieging that place, to the number of two or three hundred, with a piece of artillery ready to attack the town of De Witt. On the other side, Hinkle has in that place three or four hundred Mormons to defend it, and says he will die before he will be driven from thence.

On the 4th instant they had a skirmish—fifteen or thirty guns fired on both sides, one man from Saline county wounded in the hip.

The Mormons are at this time too strong, and no attack is expected before Wednesday or Thursday next, at which time Dr. Austin hopes his forces will amount to five hundred men, when he will make a second attempt on the town of De Witt, with small arms and cannon. In this posture of affairs, I can do nothing but negotiate between the parties until further aid is sent me.

I received your friendly letter of the 5th instant, by Mr. Warder, authorizing me to call on General Doniphan, which call I have made on him for five companies from Platte, Clay and Clinton counties, with two companies I ordered from Livingston, of which I doubt whether these last will come; if they do, I think I will have a force sufficient to manage these belligerents. Should these troops arrive here in time, I hope to be able to prevent bloodshed. Nothing seems so much in demand here (to hear the Carroll county men talk) as Mormon scalps; as yet they are scarce. I believe Hinkle, with the present force and position, will beat Austin with five hundred of his troops. The Mormons say they will die before they will be driven out, etc. As yet they have acted on the defensive, as far as I can learn. It is my settled opinion, the Mormons will have no rest until they leave; whether they will or not, time only can tell.

H. G. Parks.

The Mob's Appeal to Howard County for Help.

Under the same date, [October 6th] from the mob camp near De Witt, eleven blood-thirsty fellows, viz., Congrave Jackson, Larkin H. Woods, Thomas Jackson, Rolla M. Daviess, James Jackson, Jun., Johnson Jackson, John L. Tomlin, Sidney S. Woods, Geo. Crigler. William L. Banks, and Whitfield Dicken, wrote a most inflammatory, lying and murderous communication to the citizens of Howard county, calling upon them as friends and fellow citizens, to come to their immediate rescue, as the "Mormons" were then firing upon them and they would have to act on the defensive until they could procure more assistance.

A. C. Woods, a citizen of Howard county, made a certificate to the same lies, which he gathered in the mob camp; he did not go into De Witt, or take any trouble to learn the truth of what he certified. While the people will lie and the authorities will uphold them, what justice can honest men expect?

Tuesday, October 9.—General Clark wrote the governor from Boonville, that the names subscribed to the paper named above, are worthy, prudent and patriotic citizens of Howard county, yet these men would leave their families and everything dear, and go to a neighboring county to seek the blood of innocent men, women and children! If this constitutes "worth, prudence and patriotism," let me be worthless, imprudent and unpatriotic.

General Clark's Endorsement of the Mob.

The messenger, Mr. Caldwell, who had been dispatched to the governor for assistance, returned, but instead of receiving any aid or even sympathy from his Excellency, we were told that "the quarrel was between the Mormons and the mob," and that "we might fight it out."

The Governor's Answer to the Saints.

About this time a mob, commanded by Hyrum Standly, took Smith Humphrey's goods out of his house, and said Standly set fire to Humphrey's house and burned it before his eyes, and ordered him to leave the place forthwith, which he did by fleeing from De Witt to Caldwell county. The mob had sent to Jackson county and got a cannon, powder and balls, and bodies of armed men had gathered in, to aid them, from Ray, Saline, Howard, Livingston, Clinton, Clay, Platte counties and other parts of the state, and a man by the name of Jackson, from Howard county, was appointed their leader.

House Burning and Robbing.

The Saints were forbidden to go out of the town under pain of death, and were shot at when they attempted to go out to get food, of which they were destitute. As fast as their cattle or horses got where the mob could get hold of them, they were taken as spoil, as also other kinds of property. By these outrages the brethren were obliged, most of them, to live in wagons or tents.

Application had been made to the judge of the Circuit Court for protection, and he ordered out two companies of militia, one commanded by Captain Samuel Bogart, a Methodist minister, and one of the worst of the mobocrats. The whole force was placed under the command of General Parks, another mobber, if his letter speaks his feelings, and his actions do not belie him, for he never made the first attempt to disperse the mob, and when asked the reason of his conduct, he always replied that Bogart and his company were mutinous and mobocratic, that he dare not attempt a dispersion of the mob. Two other principal men of the mob were Major Ashly, member of the Legislature, and Sashiel Woods, a Presbyterian clergyman.

Mob Leaders Made Commanders of Militia.

General Parks informed us that a greater part of his men under Captain Bogart had mutinied, and that he would be obliged to draw them off from the place, for fear they would join the mob; consequently he could offer us no assistance.

We had now no hopes whatever of successfully resisting the mob, who kept constantly increasing; our provisions were entirely exhausted, and we were worn out by continually standing on guard, and watching the movements of our enemies, who, during the time I was there, fired at us a great many times. Some of the brethren perished from starvation; and for once in my life, I had the pain of beholding some of my fellow creatures fall victims to the spirit of persecution, which did then, and has since, prevailed to such an extent in Upper Missouri. They were men, too, who were virtuous and against whom no legal process could for one moment be sustained, but who, in consequence of their love of God, attachment to His cause, and their determination to

Hardships of the Saints.

keep the faith, were thus brought to an untimely grave.

In the meantime Henry Root and David Thomas, who had been the soul cause of the settlement of our people in De Witt, solicited the Saints to leave the place. Thomas said he had assurances from the mob, that if they would leave the place they would not be hurt, and that they would be paid for all losses which they had sustained, and that they had come as mediators to accomplish this object, and that persons should be appointed to set a value on the property which they had to leave, and that they should be paid for it. The Saints finally, through necessity, had to comply, and leave the place. Accordingly the committee was appointed—Judge Erickson was one of the committee, and Major Florey, of Rutsville, another, the names of others are not remembered. They appraised the real estate, that was all.

Proposals for the Departure of the Saints.

When the people came to start, many of their horses, oxen and cows were gone, and could not be found. It was known at the time, and the mob boasted of it, that they had killed the oxen and lived on them. Many houses belonging to my brethren were burned, their cattle driven away, and a great quantity of their property was destroyed by the mob. The people of De Witt utterly failed to fulfill their pledge to pay the Saints for the losses they sustained. The governor having turned a deaf ear to our entreaties, the militia having mutinied, the greater part of them being ready to join the mob, the brethren, seeing no prospect of relief, came to the conclusion to leave that place, and seek a shelter elsewhere. Gathering up as many wagons as could be got ready, which was about seventy, with a remnant of the property they had been able to save from their ruthless foes, they left De Witt and started for Caldwell county on the afternoon of Thursday, October 11, 1838. They traveled that day about twelve miles, and encamped in a grove of timber near the road.

A Sad Journey.

That evening a woman, of the name of Jensen, who

had some short time before given birth to a child, died in consequence of the exposure occasioned by the operations of the mob, and having to move before her strength would properly admit of it. She was buried in the grove, without a coffin.

During our journey we were continually harassed and threatened by the mob, who shot at us several times, whilst several of our brethren died from the fatigue and privation which they had to endure, and we had to inter them by the wayside, without a coffin, and under circumstances the most distressing. We arrived in Caldwell on the twelfth of October.

CHAPTER XII.

MOVEMENTS OF THE MOB UPON DE WITT—BATTLE OF CROOKED RIVER—EXTERMINATING ORDER OF GOVERNOR BOGGS.

Plan of the Mob to Dispossess the Saints.

No sooner had the brethren left De Witt than Sashiel Woods called the mob together, and made a speech to them to the effect that they must hasten to assist their friends in Daviess county. The land sales, he said, were coming on, and if they could get the "Mormons" driven out, they could get all the lands entitled to pre-emptions, and that they must hasten to Daviess county in order to accomplish their object; that if they would join and drive out the Saints, the old settlers could get all the lands back again, as well as all the pay they had received for them. He assured the mob that they had nothing to fear from the state authorities in so doing, for they had now full proof that those authorities would not assist the "Mormons," and that they [the mob] might as well take their property from them as not. His proposition was agreed to, and accordingly the whole banditti started for Daviess county, taking with them their cannon.

In the meantime, Cornelius Gilliam was busily engaged in raising a mob in Platte and Clinton counties, to aid Woods in his effort to drive peaceable citizens from their homes and take their property.

Plans of Doniphan to Protect the Saints

On my arrival in Caldwell, I was informed by General Doniphan, of Clay county, that a company of mobbers, eight hundred strong, were marching toward a settlement of our people in Daviess county. He ordered out one of the officers to raise a force and march immediately to what he called Wight's

Town [Adam-ondi-Ahman], and defend our people from the attacks of the mob, until he should raise the militia in his [Clay] and the adjoining counties to put them down. A small company of militia, who were on their way to Daviess county, and who had passed through Far West, he ordered back again, stating that they were not to be depended upon, as many of them were disposed to join the mob, and to use his own expression, were "damned rotten hearted."

Sunday, October 14.—I preached to the brethren at Far West from the saying of the Savior: "Greater love hath no man than this, that he lay down his life for his brethren." At the close I called upon all that would stand by me to meet me on the public square the next day.

State of Affairs in England.

There were seven cut off from the Church in Preston, England, this day. It was a general time of pruning in England. The powers of darkness raged, and it seemed as though Satan was fully determined to make an end of the work in that kingdom. Elders Joseph Fielding and Willard Richards had as much as they could do for some time, to see to the branches already planted, without planting new ones.

Organization for Defense.

Monday, October 15.—The brethren assembled on the public square of Far West and formed a company of about one hundred, who took up a line of march for Adam-ondi-Ahman. Here let it be distinctly understood that this company were militia of the county of Caldwell, acting under Lieutenant-Colonel George M. Hinkle, agreeable to the order of General Doniphan, and the brethren were very careful in all their movements to act in strict accordance with the constitutional laws of the land.

Mob Depredations at "Diahman."

The special object of this march was to protect Adam-ondi-Ahman, and repel the attacks of the mob in Daviess county. Having some property in that county, and having a house building there, I went up at the same time. While I was there a number of houses belonging to our people were burned by the mob, who committed many other depredations, such as driving off horses, sheep, cattle, hogs, etc. A number of those whose houses were burned down, as well as those who lived in scattered and lonely situations, fled into the town for safety, and for shelter from the inclemency of the weather, as a considerable snowstorm took place on the 17th and 18th. Women and children, some in the most delicate condition, were thus obliged to leave their homes and travel several miles in order to effect their escape. My feelings were such as I cannot describe when I saw them flock into the village, almost entirely destitute of clothes, and only escaping with their lives.

During this state of affairs, General Parks arrived in Daviess county, and was at the house of Colonel Lyman Wight on the 18th, when the intelligence was brought that the mob were burning houses; and also when women and children were fleeing for safety, among whom was Agnes M. Smith, wife of my brother, Don Carlos Smith, who was absent on a mission in Tennessee. Her house had been plundered and burned by the mob, and she had traveled nearly three miles, carrying her two helpless babes, and had to wade Grand river.

Affairs at Millport.

Colonel Wight, who held a commission in the 59th regiment under his (General Parks') command, asked what was to be done. Parks told him that he must immediately call out his men and go and put the mob down. Accordingly a force was immediately raised for the purpose of quelling the mob, and in a short time was on its march, with a determination to disperse the mob, or die in the attempt; as the people could bear such treatment as was being inflicted upon them no longer.

Parks' Order to Wight to Disperse the Mob.

The mob, having learned the orders of General Parks, and likewise being aware of the determination of the oppressed, broke up their encampment and fled. The mob seeing that they could not succeed by force, now resorted to strategem; and after re-

Strategem of the Mob.

moving their property out of their houses, which were nothing but log cabins, they fired them, and then reported to the authorities of the state that the "Mormons" were burning and destroying all before them.*

Friday, October 19.—Elder William Clayton quitted his temporal business in England, and gave himself wholly to the ministry, and soon commenced preaching and baptizing in Manchester.

Beginning of Wm. Clayton's Ministry

As I was driven away from Kirtland without the privilege of settling my business, I had, previous to this, employed Colonel Oliver Granger as my agent, to close all my affairs in the east; and as I have been accused of "running away, cheating my creditors, etc., I will insert one of the many cards and letters I have received from gentlemen who have had the best opportunity of knowing my busi-

Vindication of the Prophet's Business Course in Kirtland.

* It was a cunning piece of diabolism which prompted the mob of Daviess county to set fire to their own log cabins, destroy some of their own property and then charge the crime to the Saints. But it was not without a precedent in Missouri. Two years before that, something very similar occurred in Mercer county, just northeast of Daviess. In June of the year 1836, the Iowa Indians, then living near St. Joseph, made a friendly hunting excursion through the northern part of the state, and their line of travel led them through what was known as the "Heatherly settlement," in Mercer county. The Heatherlys, who were ruffians of the lowest type, took advantage of the excitement produced by the incursion of the Indians, and circulated a report that they were robbing and killing the whites. During the excitement these Heatherlys murdered a man by the name of Dunbar, and another man against whom they had a grudge, and then fled to the settlements along the Missouri river, representing that they were fleeing from the Indians for their lives. This produced great excitement in the settlements in the surrounding counties; the people not knowing at what hour the Indians might be upon them. The militia was called out for their protection; but it was soon ascertained that the alarm was a false one. The Heatherlys were arrested, tried for murder, and some of them sent to the penitentiary. This circumstance occurring only two years before the action of the mob about Millport, and in a county adjacent to Daviess county, doubtless suggested the course pursued by the mob in burning their own houses and fleeing to all parts of the state with the report that the "Mormons" had done it, and were murdering and plundering the old settlers. These false rumors spread by the mob, were strengthened in the public ear by such men as Adam Black, Judge King of Richmond, and other prominent men who were continually writing inflammatory communications to the governor.—For the Heatherly incident, see "History of Livingston County, Missouri," written and compiled by the National Historical Company (1886), chapter 3, pp. 710, 713.

ness transactions, and whose testimony comes unsolicited:

A Card.

PAINSVILLE, October 19, 1838.

We, the undersigned, being personal acquaintances of Oliver Granger, firmly believe that the course which he has pursued in settling the claims, accounts, etc., against the former citizens of Kirtland township, has done much credit to himself, and all others that committed to him the care of adjusting their business with this community, which also furnishes evidence that there was no intention on their part of defrauding their creditors.

[Signed] THOMAS GRIFFITH,
JOHN S. SEYMOUR.

Crimes of the Mob Charged to the Saints.

About this time William Morgan, sheriff of Daviess county, Samuel Bogart, Colonel William P. Penniston, Doctor Samuel Venable, Jonathan J. Dryden, James Stone and Thomas J. Martin, made communications or affidavits of the most inflammatory kind, charging upon the "Mormons" those depredations which had been committed by the mob, endeavoring thereby to raise the anger of those in authority, rallying a sufficient force around their standard, and produce a total overthrow, massacre, or banishment of the "Mormons" from the state. These and their associates were the ones who fired their own houses and then fled the country crying "fire and murder."

Departure of Orson Hyde from Far West.

It was reported in Far West today [October 19th] that Orson Hyde had left that place, the night previous, leaving a letter for one of the brethren, which would develop the secret.

Return of the Prophet to Far West.

Monday, 22.—On the retreat of the mob from Daviess county, I returned to Caldwell, with a company of the brethren, and arrived at Far West about seven in the evening, where I had hoped to enjoy some respite from our enemies, at least for a short time; but upon my arrival there, I was informed that a mob had commenced hostilities on the borders of Caldwell county, adjoining Ray county, and that they had taken some of our brethren prisoners, burned some houses, and had committed depredations on the peaceable inhabitants.

The Saints Flock into Far West.

Tuesday, *23*.—News came to Far West, this morning, that the brethren had found the cannon, which the mob brought from Independence, buried in the earth, and had secured it by order of General Parks. The word of the Lord was given several months since, for the Saints to gather into the cities, but they have been slow to obey until the judgments were upon them, and now they are gathering by flight and haste, leaving all their effects, and are glad to get off at that. The city of Far West is literally crowded, and the brethren are gathering from all quarters.

Inflammatory Letters to the Governor.

Fourteen citizens of Ray county, one of whom was a Mr. Hudgins, a postmaster, wrote the governor an inflammatory epistle. Thomas C. Burch, of Richmond, wrote a similar communication. Also the citizens of Ray county, in public meeting, appealed to the governor of the state, to give the people of Upper Missouri protection from the fearful body of "thieves and robbers;" while the fact is the Saints were minding their own business, only as they were driven from it by those who were crying thieves and robbers.

The Mail Robbed.

The mail came in this evening, but not a single letter to anybody, from which it is evident there is no deposit sacred to those marauders who are infesting the country and trying to destroy the Saints.

The Course of King and Black.

Wednesday, *24*.—Austin A. King and Adam Black renewed their inflammatory communications to the governor, as did other citizens of Richmond, viz., C. R. Morehead, William Thornton, and Jacob Gudgel, who scrupled at no falsehood or exaggeration, to raise the governor's anger against us.

Thomas B. Marsh, formerly president of the Twelve,

having apostatized, repaired to Richmond and made affidavit before Henry Jacobs, justice of the peace, to all the vilest slanders, aspersions, lies and calumnies towards myself and the Church, that his wicked heart could invent. He had been lifted up in pride by his exaltation to office and the revelations of heaven concerning him, until he was ready to be overthrown by the first adverse wind that should cross his track, and now he has fallen, lied and sworn falsely, and is ready to take the lives of his best friends. Let all men take warning by him, and learn that he who exalteth himself, God will abase. Orson Hyde was also at Richmond and testified to most of Marsh's statements.*

The Apostasy of Thomas B. Marsh.

* The chief points in the affidavit of Thomas B. Marsh, referred to in the text, are as follows: "They have among them a company, considered true Mormons, called the Danites, who have taken an oath to support the heads of the Church in all things that they say or do, *whether right or wrong.* Many, however, of this band are much dissatisfied with this oath, as being against moral and religious principles. On Saturday last, I am informed by the Mormons, that they had a meeting at Far West, at which they appointed a company of twelve, by the name of the 'Destruction Company,' for the purpose of burning and destroying, and that if the people of Buncombe came to do mischief upon the people of Caldwell, and committed depredations upon the Mormons, they were to burn Buncombe; and if the people of Clay and Ray made any movement against them, this destroying company were to burn Liberty and Richmond. * * * * The Prophet inculcates the notion, and it is believed by every true Mormon, that Smith's prophecies are superior to the laws of the land. I have heard the Prophet say that he would yet tread down his enemies, and walk over their dead bodies; and if he was not let alone, he would be a second Mohammed to this generation, and that he would make it one gore of blood from the Rocky mountains to the Atlantic ocean; that like Mohammed, whose motto in treating for peace was, 'the Alcoran or the Sword.' So should it be eventually with us, 'Joseph Smith or the Sword.' These last statements were made during the last summer. The number of armed men at Adam-ondi-Ahman was between three and four hundred.

"THOMAS B. MARSH.

"Sworn to and subscribed before me, the day herein written.

"HENRY JACOBS,

"J. P. Ray county, Missouri.

"Richmond, Missouri, October 24, 1838."

"AFFIDAVIT OF ORSON HYDE.

"The most of the statements in the foregoing disclosure I know to be true; the remainder I believe to be true.

"ORSON HYDE.

"Richmond, October 24, 1838.

"Sworn to and subscribed before me, on the day above written.

"HENRY JACOBS, J. P."

Of this testimony and the action of Marsh and Hyde the late President Taylor in

The following letter, being a fair specimen of the "truth and honesty" of many others which I shall notice, I give it in full:

Communication of Woods and Dickson to Governor Boggs.

CARROLTON, MISSOURI, October 24, 1838.

SIR:—We were informed, last night, by an express from Ray county, that Captain Bogart and all his company, amounting to between fifty and sixty men were massacred by the Mormons at Buncombe, twelve miles north of Richmond, except three. This statement you may rely on as being true, and last night they expected Richmond to be laid in ashes this morning. We could distinctly hear cannon, and we know the Mormons had one in their possession. Richmond is about twenty-five

his discourse on Succession in the Presidency, makes these pertinent remarks: "Testimonies from these sources are not always reliable, and it is to be hoped, for the sake of the two brethren, that some things were added by our enemies that they did not assert, but enough was said to make this default and apostasy very terrible. I will here state that I was in Far West at the time these affidavits were made, and was mixed up with all prominent Church affairs. I was there when Thomas B. Marsh and Orson Hyde left there; and there are others present who were there at the same time. And I know that these things, referred to in the affidavits, are not true. I have heard a good deal about Danites, but I never heard of them among the Latter-day Saints. If there was such an organization, I never was made acquainted with it * * * * * * Thomas B. Marsh was unquestionably instigated by the devil when he made this statement, which has been read in your hearing [the foregoing affidavit]. The consequence was, he was cut off from the Church. * * * * * * It would be here proper to state, however, that Orson Hyde had been sick with a violent fever for some time, and had not yet fully recovered therefrom, which, with the circumstances with which we were surrounded, and the influence of Thomas B. Marsh, may be offered as a slight palliation for his default. * * * * * * It may be proper here again to say a few words with regard to Brother Orson Hyde, whose endorsement of the terrible charges made by Thomas B. Marsh in his affidavit, has already been read. Suffice it to say, in addition to what has previously been stated, he was cut off from the Church, and of course lost his apostleship; and when he subsequently returned, and made all the satisfaction that was within his power, he was forgiven by the authorities and the people and was again re-instated in the quorum."

Schuyler Colfax, vice-president of the United States, in his discussion with the late President John Taylor on the "Mormon Question," quoted this Marsh-Hyde affidavit, and Elder Taylor in reply said: "I am sorry to say that Thomas B. Marsh did make that affidavit, and that Orson Hyde stated that he knew part of it and believed the other; and it would be disingenuous in me to deny it; but it is not true that these things existed, for I was there and knew to the contrary; and so did the people of Missouri, and so did the governor of Missouri. How do you account for their acts? Only on the score of the weakness of our common humanity. We were living in troublous times, and all men's nerves are not proof against such shocks as we then had to endure."

miles west of this place, on a straight line. We know not the hour or minute we will be laid in ashes—our country is ruined—for God's sake give us assistance as quick as possible.

Yours, etc.,
SASHIEL WOODS,
JOSEPH DICKSON.

These mobbers must have had very accute ears to hear cannon, (a six pounder) thirty-seven miles! So much for the lies of a priest of this world. Now for the truth of the case. This day about noon, Captain Bogart, with some thirty or forty men called on Brother Thoret Parsons, at the head of the east branch of Log creek, where he was living, and warned him to be gone before next day at ten in the morning, declaring also that he would give Far West thunder and lightning before next day at noon, if he had good luck in meetin Neil Gillum, (Cornelius Gilliam) who would camp about six miles west of Far West that night, and that he should camp on Crooked creek. He then departed towards Crooked creek.

The Prophet's Statement of the Buncombe Affair.

Brother Parsons dispatched a messenger with this news to Far West, and followed after Bogart to watch his movements. Brothers Joseph Holbrook and David Juda, who went out this morning to watch the movements of the enemy, saw eight armed mobbers call at the house of Brother Pinkham, where they took three prisoners, Nathan Pinkham, Brothers William Seely and Addison Green, and four horses, arms, etc. When departing they threatened Father Pinkham that if he did not leave the state immediately they "would have his damned old scalp." Having learned of Bogart's movements the brethren returned to Far West near midnight, and reported their proceedings and those of the mob.

Raid on the Pinkham Residence.

On hearing the report, Judge Elias Higbee, the first judge of the county, ordered Lieutenant Colonel Hinkle, the highest officer in command in Far West, to send out a company to disperse the mob and retake their prisoners, whom, it was reported, they intended to murder that night. The trumpet sounded, and the brethren were assembled on the public square about midnight, when the facts were stated, and about seventy-five volunteered to obey the judge's order, under command of Captain David W. Patten, who immediately commenced their march on horseback, hoping without the loss of blood to surprise and scatter the camp, retake the prisoners and prevent the attack threatening Far West.

Crooked River Battle.

Thursday, *25*.—Fifteen of the company were detached from the main body while sixty continued their march till they arrived near the ford of Crooked river, (or creek) where they dismounted, tied their horses, and leaving four or five men to guard them, proceeded towards the ford, not knowing the location of the encampment. It was just at the dawning of light in the east, when they were marching quietly along the road, and near the top of the hill which descends to the river that the report of a gun was heard, and young Patrick O'Banion reeled out of the ranks and fell mortally wounded. Thus the work of death commenced, when Captain Patten ordered a charge and rushed down the hill on a fast trot, and when within about fifty yards of the camp formed a line. The mob formed a line under the bank of the river, below their tents. It was yet so dark that little could be seen by looking at the west, while the mob looking towards the dawning light, could see Patten and his men, when they fired a broadside, and three or four of the brethren fell. Captain Patten ordered the fire returned, which was instantly obeyed, to great disadvantage in the darkness which yet continued. The fire was repeated by the mob, and returned by Captain Patten's company, who gave the watchword "God and Liberty." Captain Patten then ordered a charge, which was instantly obeyed. The parties immediately came in contact, with their swords, and the mob were soon put to flight, crossing the river at the ford and such places as they could get a chance. In the pursuit, one of the mob fled from behind a tree, wheeled, and shot Captain Patten, who instantly fell, mortally wounded, having received a large ball in his bowels.

The ground was soon cleared, and the brethren gathered up a wagon or two, and making beds therein of tents, etc, took their wounded and retreated towards Far West. Three brethren were wounded in the bowels, one in the neck, one in the shoulder, one through the hips, one through both thighs, one in the arms, all by musket shot. One had his arm broken by a sword. Brother Gideon Carter was shot in the head, and left dead on the ground so defaced that the brethren did not know him. Bogart reported that he had lost one man. The three prisoners were released and returned with the brethren to Far West. Captain Patten was carried some of the way in a litter, but it caused so much distress that he begged to be left by the way side. He was carried into Brother Winchester's, three miles from the city of Far West, where he died that night. Patrick O'Banion died soon after, and Brother Carter's body was also brought from Crooked river, when it was discovered who he was.

List of Casualties. Death of Patten and O'Banion.

I went with my brother Hyrum and Lyman Wight to meet the brethren on their return, near Log creek, where I saw Captain Patten in a most distressing condition. His wound was incurable.

Brother David Patten was a very worthy man, beloved by all good men who knew him. He was one of the Twelve Apostles, and died as he had lived, a man of God, and strong in the faith of a glorious resurrection, in a world where mobs will have no power or place. One of his last expressions to his wife was—"Whatever you do else, O! do not deny the faith."

The Prophet's Reflections on the Death of David W. Patten.

How different his fate to that of the apostate, Thomas

B. Marsh, who this day vented all the lying spleen and malice of his heart towards the work of God, in a letter to Brother and Sister Abbot, to which was annexed an addenda by Orson Hyde.

The following letter will show the state of public feeling in the country at this time:

E. M. Ryland's Letter to Messrs. Rees and Williams.

LEXINGTON, six o'clock p. m.
October 25, 1838.

To Messrs. Amos Rees and Wiley C. Williams:

GENTLEMEN:—This letter is sent on after you on express by Mr. Bryant, of Ray county, since you left this morning. Mr. C. R. Morehead came here on express for men to assist in repelling a threatened attack upon Richmond tonight. He brought news that the Mormon armed force had attacked Captain Bogart this morning at daylight, and had cut off his whole company of fifty men. Since Mr. Morehead left Richmond, one of the company (Bogart's) has come in and reported that there were ten of his comrades killed and the remainder were taken prisoners, after many of them had been severely wounded; he stated further that Richmond would be sacked and burned by the Mormon banditti tonight. Nothing can exceed the consternation which this news gave rise to. The women and children are flying from Richmond in every direction. A number of them have repaired to Lexington, amongst whom is Mrs. Rees. We will have sent from this county since one o'clock this evening about one hundred well-armed and daring men, perhaps the most effective our county can boast of. They will certainly give them (the Mormons) a warm reception at Richmond tonight. You will see the necessity of hurrying on to the City of Jefferson, and also of imparting correct information to the public as you go along. My impression is, that you had better send one of your number to Howard, Cooper and Boone counties, in order that volunteers may be getting ready and flocking to the scene of trouble as fast as possible. They must make haste and put a stop to the devastation which is menaced by these infuriated fanatics, and they must go prepared and with the full determination to exterminate or expel them from the state *en masse*. Nothing but this can give tranquility to the public mind, and re-establish the supremacy of the laws. There must be no further delaying with this question any where. The Mormons must leave the state, or we will, one and all, and to this complexion it must come at last. We have great reliance upon your ability, discretion and fitness for the task you have undertaken, and we have only time to say, God speed you.

Yours truly,
E. M. RYLAND, Judge.

The brethren had *not thought* of going to Richmond—it was a lie out of whole cloth.

Governor Boggs' Order to General John B. Clark.

FRIDAY, HEADQUARTERS OF THE MILITIA,
CITY OF JEFFERSON October 26, 1838.

General John B. Clark, 1st Division Missouri Militia:

SIR:—Application has been made to the commander-in-chief, by the citizens of Daviess county, in this state, for protection, and to be restored to their homes and property, with intelligence that the Mormons, with an armed force, have expelled the inhabitants of that county from their homes, have pillaged and burnt their dwellings, driven off their stock, and were destroying their crops; that they (the Mormons) have burnt to ashes the towns of Gallatin and Millport in said county; the former being the county seat of said county, and including the clerk's office and all the public records of the county, and that there is not now a civil officer within said county. The commander-in-chief therefore orders that there be raised, from the 1st, 4th, 5th, 6th and 12th Divisions of the militia of this state, four hundred men each, to be mounted and armed as Infantry or Riflemen, each man to furnish himself with at least fifty rounds of ammunition, and at least fifteen days provisions. The troops from the 1st, 5th, 6th and 12th, will rendezvous at Fayette, in Howard county, on Saturday, the 3rd day of next month (November) at which point they will receive further instructions as to their line of march. You will therefore cause to be raised the quota of men required of your division (four hundred men) without delay, either by volunteer or drafts, and rendezvous at Fayette, in Howard county, on Saturday, the third day of next month (November) and there join the troops from the 5th, 6th and 12th divisions. The troops from the 4th division will join you at Richmond in Ray county. You will cause the troops raised in your division, to be formed into companies according to law, and placed under officers already in commission. If volunteer companies are raised, they shall elect their own officers. The preference should always be given to volunteer companies already organized and commissioned. You will also detail the necessary field and staff officers. For the convenience of transporting the camp equipage, provisions and hospital stores for the troops under your command, you are authorized to employ two or three baggage wagons.

By order of the Commander-in-Chief,

B. M. LISLE, Adj.-General.

Letters of Horace Kingsbury and John W. Hawden on the Business Integrity of the Prophet and his Agents in Kirtland.

To all persons that are or may be interested. I, Horace Kingsbury, of Painsville township, Geauga county, and state of Ohio, feeling the importance of recommending to remembrance every worthy citizen who has by his conduct commended himself to personal acquaintance by his course of strict integrity, and desire for truth and common justice, feel it my duty to state that Oliver Granger's management in the arrangement of the unfinished business of people that have moved to the Far West, in redeeming their pledges and thereby sustaining their integrity, has been truly praiseworthy, and has entitled him to my highest esteem, and ever grateful recollection.

HORACE KINGSBURY.

Painesville, October 26, 1838.

To whom it may concern. This may certify that during the year of eighteen hundred and thirty-seven, I had dealings with Messrs. Joseph Smith, Junior, and Sidney Rigdon, together with other members of the [Mormon] society, to the amount of about three thousand dollars, and during the spring of eighteen hundred and thirty-eight, I have received my pay in full of Colonel Oliver Granger to my satisfaction. And I would here remark that it is due Messrs. Smith and Rigdon, and the [Mormon] society generally, to say that they have ever dealt honorably and fair with me: and I have received as good treatment from them as I have received from any other society in this vicinity; and so far as I have been correctly informed and made acquainted with their business transactions generally, they have, so far as I can judge, been honorable and honest, and have made every exertion to arrange and settle their affairs. And I would further state, that the closing up of my business with said society has been with their agent, Colonel Granger, appointed by them for that purpose; and I consider it highly due Colonel Granger from me, here to state that he has acted truly and honestly in all his business with me, and has accomplished more than I could reasonably have expected. And I have also been made acquainted with his business in that section; and wherever he has been called upon to act, he has done so and with good management he has accomplished and effected the close of a large amount of business for said society,and as I believe, to the entire satisfaction of all concerned.

JOHN W. HAWDEN.

Painesville, Geauga county, Ohio, October 27, 1838.

Saturday, 27.—Brother Patten was buried this day at Far West, and before the funeral, I called at Brother Patten's house, and while meditating on the scene before me in presence of his friends, I could not help pointing to his lifeless body and testifying, "There lies a man that has done just as he said he would—he has laid down his life for his friends."

Funeral of David W. Patten.

Governor Boggs' Exterminating Order.

HEADQUARTERS MILITIA, CITY OF JEFFERSON,
October 27, 1838.

SIR:—Since the order of the morning to you, directing you to cause four hundred mounted men to be raised within your division, I have received by Amos Rees, Esq., and Wiley C. Williams, Esq., one of my aids, information of the most appalling character, which changes the whole face of things, and places the Mormons in the attitude of open and avowed defiance of the laws, and of having made open war upon the people of this state. Your orders are, therefore, to hasten your operations and endeavor to reach Richmond, in Ray county, with all possible speed. The Mormons must be treated as enemies and *must be exterminated* or driven from the state, if necessary for the public good. Their outrages are beyond all description. If you can increase your force, you are authorized to do so, to any extent you may think necessary. I have just issued orders to Major-General Wallock, of Marion county, to raise five hundred men, and to march them to the northern part of Daviess and there to unite with General Doniphan, of Clay, who has been ordered with five hundred men to proceed to the same point for the purpose of intercepting the retreat of the Mormons to the north. They have been directed to communicate with you by express; and you can also communicate with them if you find it necessary. Instead, therefore, of proceeding as at first directed, to reinstate the citizens of Daviess in their homes, you will proceed immediately to Richmond, and there operate against the Mormons. Brigadier-General Parks, of Ray, has been ordered to have four hundred men of his brigade in readiness to join you at Richmond. The whole force will be placed under your command.

L. W. BOGGS,
Governor and Commander-inChief.

To General Clark.

Great excitemet now prevailed, and mobs were heard

of in every direction, who seemed determined on our destruction. They burned the houses in the country, and took off all the cattle they could find. They destroyed corn fields, took many prisoners, and threatened death to all the Mormons.

Excitement in Upper Missouri.

The Appeal of Atchison and Lucas to Governor Boggs, Asking his Presence at the seat of War.

HEADQUARTERS OF THE 3RD AND 4TH DIVISION, MISSOURI MILITIA, RICHMOND, October 28, 1838.

To the Commander-in-Chief, Missouri Militia:

SIR:—From late outrages committed by the *Mormons, civil war* is inevitable. They have set the laws of the country at defiance, and are in open rebellion. We have about two thousand men under arms to keep them in check. The presence of the commander-in-chief is deemed absolutely necessary, and we most respectfully urge that your excellency be at the seat of *war* as soon as possible.

Your most obedient servants,

DAVID R. ATCHISON, M. G. 3rd Div.*

SAMUEL D. LUCAS, M. G. 4th Div.

* It is to be regretted that General David R. Atchison joined with General Lucas in signing the above communication. Up to this time Major General Atchison had apparently exercised his influence counseling moderation in dealing with the "Mormons." He was a resident of Clay county when the Saints were driven into that county from Jackson. He, with General Doniphan and Amos Rees, had acted as counsel for the exiles, and had seen the doors of the temple of justice closed in their faces by mob violence, and all redress denied them. He was acquainted with the circumstances which led to their removal from Clay county, to the unsettled prairies of what afterwards became Caldwell county. He knew how deep and unreasonable the prejudices were against the Saints. Can it be possible that he did not know how utterly unjustifiable the present movement against them was? Whether he was blinded by the false reports about Millport and Gallatin and Crooked river, or whether his courage faltered, and he became afraid longer to defend a people against whom every man's hand was raised, I cannot now determine, but one or the other must have been the case. General Atchison, however, was afterwards "dismounted," to use a word of General Doniphan's in relating the incident, and sent back to Liberty in Clay county by special order of Governor Boggs, on the ground that he was inclined to be too merciful to the "Mormons," so that he was not active in the operations about Far West. But how he could consent to join with Lucas in sending such an untruthful and infamous report to the governor about the situation in Upper Missouri, is difficult to determine. The Saints had not set the laws at defiance, nor were they in open rebellion. But when all the officers of the law refused to hear their complaints, and both civil and military authority delivered them into the hands of merciless mobs to be plundered and outraged at their brutal pleasure, and all petitions for protection at the hands of the governor had been answered with: "It is a quarrel be-

tween the Mormons and the mob, and they must fight it out," what was left for them to do but to arm themselves and stand in defense of their homes and families? The movement on Gallatin by Captain Patten and that on Millport by Colonel Wight was ordered by General Parks, who called upon Colonel Wight to take command of his company of men, when the militia under Parks' command mutinied, and dispersed all mobs wherever he found them. Gallatin was not burned, nor were the records of the county court, if they were destroyed at all, destroyed by the Saints. What houses were burned in Millport had been set on fire by the mob. The expedition to Crooked river was ordered by Judge Higbee, the first judge in Caldwell county and the highest civil authority in Far West, and was undertaken for the purpose of dispersing a mob which had entered the house of a peaceable citizen—one Pinkham—and carried off three people prisoners, four horses and other property, and who had threatened to "give Far West hell before noon the next day." So that in their operations the acts of the Saints had been strictly within the law, and only in self defense.

CHAPTER XIII.

MOB MOVEMENTS ON FAR WEST—TREACHERY OF COLONEL HINKLE—SORROWFUL SCENES.

The Prophet's Comment on Governor Boggs.

LILBURN W. BOGGS had become so hardened by mobbing the Saints in Jackson county, and his conscience so "seared as with a hot iron," that he was considered a fit subject for the gubernatorial chair; and it was probably his hatred to truth and the "Mormons," and his blood-thirsty, murderous disposition, that raised him to the station he occupied. His *exterminating order* of the twenty-seventh aroused every spirit in the state, of the like stamp of his own; and the Missouri mobocrats were flocking to the standard of General Clark from almost every quarter.

General Clark

Clark, although not the ranking officer, was selected by Governor Boggs as the most fit instrument to carry out his murderous designs; for bad as they were in Missouri, very few commanding officers were yet sufficiently hardened to go all lengths with Boggs in this contemplated inhuman butchery, and expulsion from one of the should-be free and independent states of the Republic of North America, where the Constitution declares, that "*every man shall have the privilege of worshiping God according to the dictates of his own conscience;*" and this was all the offense the Saints had been guilty of.

Doctor Sampson Avard.

And here I would state, that while the evil spirits were raging up and down in the state to raise mobs against the "Mormons," Satan himself was no less busy in striving to stir up mischief in the camp of the Saints: and among the most conspicuous of his willing devotees was one Doctor Sampson Avard, who had been in the Church but a short time, and who, although he had generally behaved with a tolerable degree of external decorum, was secretly aspiring to be the greatest of the great, and become the leader of the people. This was his pride and his folly, but as he had no hopes of accomplishing it by gaining the hearts of the people openly he watched his opportunity with the brethren—at a time when mobs oppressed, robbed, whipped, burned, plundered and slew, till forbearance seemed no longer a virtue, and nothing but the grace of God without measure could support men under such trials—to form a secret combination by which he might rise a mighty conqueror, at the *expense and the overthrow of the Church.* This he tried to accomplish by his smooth, flattering, and winning speeches, which he frequently made to his associates, while his room was well guarded by some of his followers, ready to give him the signal on the approach of anyone who would not approve of his measures.

Avard's Danites.

In these proceedings he stated that he had the sanction of the heads of the Church for what he was about to do; and by his smiles and flattery, persuaded them to believe it, and proceeded to administer to the few under his control, an oath, binding them to everlasting secrecy to everything which should be communicated to them by himself. Thus Avard initiated members into his band, firmly binding them, by all that was sacred, in the protecting of each other in all things that were lawful; and was careful to picture out a great glory that was then hovering over the Church, and would soon burst upon the Saints as a cloud by day, and a pillar of fire by night, and would soon unveil the slumbering mysteries of heaven, which would gladden the hearts and arouse the stupid spirits of the Saints of the latter-day, and fill their hearts with that love which is unspeakable and full of glory, and arm them with power, that the gates of hell could not prevail against them; and would often affirm to his company that the principal men of the Church had put him forward as a spokesman, and a leader of this band, which *he* named *Danites*.

Thus he duped many, which gave him the opportunity of figuring as a person of importance. He held his meetings daily, and carried on his crafty work in great haste, to prevent mature reflection upon the matter by his followers, until he had them bound under the penalties of death to keep the secrets and certain signs of the organization by which they were to know each other by day or night.

Avard's Manner of Proceeding.

After those performances, he held meetings to organize his men into companies of tens and fifties, appointing a captain over each company. After completing this organization, he went on to teach the members of it their duty under the orders of their captains; he then called his captains together and taught them in a secluded place, as follows:

Avard's Instructions to His Captains.

My brethren, as you have been chosen to be our leading men, our captains to rule over this last kingdom of Jesus Christ—and you have been organized after the ancient order—I have called upon you here today to teach you, and instruct you in the things that pertain to your duty, and to show you what your privileges are, and what they soon will be. Know ye not, brethren, that it soon will be your privilege to take your respective companies and go out on a scout on the borders of the settlements, and take to yourselves spoils of the goods of the ungodly Gentiles? for it is written, the riches of the Gentiles shall be consecrated to my people, the house of Israel; and thus you will waste away the Gentiles by robbing and plundering them of their property; and in this way we will build up the kingdom of God, and roll forth the little stone that Daniel saw cut out of the mountain without hands, and roll forth until it filled the whole earth. For this is the very way that God destines to build up His kingdom in the last days. If any of us should be recognized, who can harm us? for we will stand by each other and defend one another in all things. If our enemies swear against us, we can swear also. [The captains were confounded at this, but Avard continued]. Why do you startle at this, brethren? As the Lord liveth, I would swear to a lie to clear any of you; and if this would not do, I would put them or him under the sand as Moses did the Egyptian; and in this way we will consecrate much unto the Lord, and

build up His kingdom; and who can stand against us? And if any of us transgress, we will deal with him amongst ourselves. And if any one of this Danite society reveals any of these things, I will put him where the dogs *cannot bite him.*

At this lecture all of the officers revolted, and said it would not do, they would not go into any such measures, and it would not do to name any such thing; "such proceedings would be in open violation of the laws of our country, would be robbing our fellow citizens of their rights, and are not according to the language and doctrine of Christ, or of the Church of Latter-day Saints."

Revolt of Avard's Officers.

Avard replied, and said there was no laws that were executed in justice, and he cared not for them, this being a different dispensation, a dispensation of the fullness of times; in this dispensation he learned from the Scriptures that the kingdom of God was to put down all other kingdoms, and the Lord Himself was to reign, and His laws alone were the laws that would exist.

Avard's teachings were still manfully rejected by all. Avard then said that they had better drop the subject, although he had received his authority from Sidney Rigdon the evening before. The meeting then broke up; the eyes of those present were opened, Avard's craft was no longer in the dark, and but very little confidence was placed in him, even by the warmest of the members of his Danite scheme.

Avard's Teachings Rejected.

When a knowledge of Avard's rascality came to the Presidency of the Church, he was cut off from the Church, and every means proper used to destroy his influence, at which he was highly incensed, and went about whispering his evil insinuations, but finding every effort unavailing, he again turned conspirator, and sought to make friends with the mob.

Avard Excommunicated.

And here let it be distinctly understood, that these companies of tens and fifties got up by Avard, were altogether separate and distinct from those companies of tens and fifties organized by the brethren for self defense, in case of an attack from the mob. This latter organization was called into existence more particularly that in this time of alarm no family or person might be neglected; therefore, one company would be engaged in drawing wood, another in cutting it, another in gathering corn, another in grinding, another in butchering, another in distributing meat, etc., etc., so that all should be employed in turn, and no one lack the necessaries of life. Therefore, let no one hereafter, by mistake or design, confound this organization of the Church for good and righteous purposes, with the organization of the "Danites," of the apostate Avard, which died almost before it had existed.

Distinction in Organization Pointed Out.

The mob began to encamp at Richmond on the twenty-sixth, and by this time amounted to about two thousand men, all ready to fulfill the exterminating order, and join the standard of the governor. They took up a line of march for Far West, traveling but part way, where they encamped for the night.

Gathering of the Mob at Richmond.

Tuesday, October 30.—The advance guard of the mob were patrolling the country and taking many prisoners, among whom were Brother Stephen Winchester, and Brother Carey, whose skull they laid open by a blow from a rifle barrel. In this mangled condition, the mob laid him in their wagon and went on their way, denying him every comfort, and thus he remained that afternoon and night.

General Clark was in camp at Chariton under a forced march to Richmond, with about a thousand men, and the governor's exterminating order.

Gen. Clark's Movements.

For the history of this day at Haun's Mills, on Shoal creek, I quote the following affidavit of Elder Joseph Young, First President of the Seventies:

Joseph Young's Narrative of the Massacre at Haun's Mills.

On the sixth day of July last, I started with my family from Kirtland, Ohio, for the state of Missouri, the county of Caldwell, in the upper part of the state, being the place of my destination.

On the thirteenth day of October I crossed the Mississippi at Louisiana, at which place I heard vague reports of the disturbances in the upper country, but nothing that could be relied upon. I continued my course westward till I crossed Grand river, at a place called Compton's Ferry, at which place I heard, for the first time, that if I proceeded any farther on my journey, I would be in danger of being stopped by a body of armed men. I was not willing, however, while treading my native soil, and breathing republican air, to abandon my object, which was to locate myself and family in a fine, healthy country, where we could enjoy the society of our friends and connections. Consequently, I prosecuted my journey till I came to Whitney's Mills, situated on Shoal creek, in the eastern part of Caldwell county.

After crossing the creek and going about three miles, we met a party of the mob, about forty in number, armed with rifles, and mounted on horses, who informed us that we could go no farther west, threatening us with instant death if we proceeded any farther. I asked them the reason of this prohibition; to which they replied, that we were "Mormons;" that everyone who adhered to our religious faith, would have to leave the state in ten days, or *renounce* their religion. Accordingly they drove us back to the mills above mentioned.

Here we tarried three days; and, on Friday, the twenty-sixth, we recrossed the creek, and following up its banks, we succeeded in eluding the mob for the time being, and gained the residence of a friend in Myer's settlement.

On Sunday, twenty-eighth October, we arrived about twelve o'clock, at Haun's Mills, where we found a number of our friends collected together, who were holding a council, and deliberating on the best course for them to pursue, to defend themselves against the mob, who were collecting in the neighborhood under the command of Colonel Jennings, of Livingston county, and threatening them with house burning and killing. The decision of the council was, that our friends there should place themselves in an attitude of self defense. Accordingly about twenty-eight of our men armed themselves, and were in constant readiness for an attack of any small body of men that might come down upon them.

The same evening, for some reason best known to themselves, the mob sent one of their number to enter into a treaty with our friends, which was accepted, on the condition of mutual forbearance on both sides, and that each party, as far as their influence extended, should exert themselves to prevent any further hostilities upon either party.

At this time, however, there was another mob collecting on Grand river, at William Mann's, who were threatening us, consequently we remained under arms.

Monday passed away without molestation from any quarter.

On Tuesday, the 30th, that bloody tragedy was acted, the scene of which I shall never forget. More than three-fourths of the day had passed in tranquility, as smiling as the preceding one. I think there was no individual of our company that was apprised of the sudden and awful fate that hung over our heads like an overwhelming torrent, which was to change the prospects, the feelings and the circumstances of about thirty families. The banks of Shoal creek on either side teemed with children sporting and playing, while their mothers were engaged in domestic employments, and their fathers employed in guarding the mills and other property, while others were engaged in gathering in their crops for their winter consumption. The weather was very pleasant, the sun shone clear, all was tranquil, and no one expressed any apprehension of the awful crisis that was near us—even at our doors.

It was about four o'clock, while sitting in my cabin with my babe in my arms, and my wife standing by my side, the door being open, I cast my eyes on the opposite bank of Shoal creek and saw a large company of armed men, on horses, directing their course towards the mills with all possible speed. As they advanced through the scattering trees that stood on the edge of the prairie they seemed to form themselves into a three square position, forming a vanguard in front.

At this moment, David Evans, seeing the superiority of their numbers, (there being two hundred and forty of them, according to their own account), swung his hat, and cried for peace. This not being heeded, they continued to advance, and their leader, Mr. Nehemiah Comstock, fired a gun, which was followed by a solemn pause of ten or twelve seconds, when, all at once, they discharged about one hundred rifles, aiming at a blacksmith shop into which our friends had fled for safety; and charged up to the shop, the cracks of which between the logs were sufficiently large to enable them to aim directly at the bodies of those who had there fled for refuge from the fire of their murderers. There were several families tented in the rear of the shop, whose lives were exposed, and amidst a shower of bullets fled to the woods in different directions.

After standing and gazing on this bloody scene for a few minutes, and finding myself in the uttermost danger, the bullets having reached the house where I was living, I committed my family to the protection of heaven, and leaving the house on the opposite side, I took a path which led up the hill, following in the trail of three of my brethren that had fled from the shop. While ascending the hill we were discovered by the mob, who immediately fired at us, and continued so to do till we reached the summit. In descending the hill, I secreted myself in a thicket of bushes, where I lay till eight o'clock in the evening, at which time I heard a female voice calling my name in an under tone, telling me that the mob had gone and there was no danger. I immediately left the thicket, and went to the house of Benjamin Lewis, where I found my family (who had fled there) in safety, and two of my friends mortally wounded, one of whom died before morning. Here we passed the painful night in deep and awful reflections on the scenes of the preceding evening.

After daylight appeared, some four or five men, who with myself, had escaped with our lives from the horrid massacre, and who repaired as soon as possible to the mills, to learn the condition of our friends, whose fate we had but too truly anticipated. When we arrived at the house of Mr. Haun, we found Mr. Merrick's body lying in the rear of the house, Mr. McBride's in front, literally mangled from head to foot. We were informed by Miss Rebecca Judd, who was an eye witness, that he was shot with his own gun, after he had given it up, and then cut to pieces with a corn cutter by a Mr. Rogers of Daviess county, who keeps a ferry on Grand river, and who has since repeatedly boasted of this act of savage barbarity. Mr. York's body we found in the house, and after viewing these corpses, we immediately went to the blacksmith's shop, where we found nine of our friends, eight of whom were already dead; the other, Mr. Cox, of Indiana, struggling in the agonies of death and soon expired. We immediately prepared and carried them to the place of interment. The last office of kindness due to the remains of departed friends, was not attended with the customary ceremonies or decency, for we were in jeopardy, every moment expecting to be fired upon by the mob, who, we supposed, were lying in ambush, waiting for the first opportunity to despatch the remaining few who were providentially preserved from the slaughter of the preceding day. However, we accomplished without molestation this painful task. The place of burying was a vault in the ground, formerly intended for a well, into which we threw the bodies of our friends promiscuously. Among those slain I will mention Sardius Smith, son of Warren Smith, about nine years old, who, through fear, had crawled under the bellows in the shop, where he remained till the massacre was over, when he was discovered by a Mr. Glaze, of Carroll county, who presented his rifle near the boy's head, and literally blowed off the upper part of it. Mr. Stanley, of Carroll, told me afterwards that Glaze boasted of this fiend-like murder and heroic deed all over the country.

The number killed and mortally wounded in this wanton slaughter was eighteen or nineteen, whose names as far as I recollect were as follows: Thomas McBride, Levi N. Merrick, Elias Benner, Josiah Fuller, Benjamin Lewis, Alexander Campbell, Warren Smith, Sardius Smith, George S. Richards, Mr. William Napier, Augustine Harmer, Simon Cox, Mr. [Hiram] Abbott, John York, Charles Merrick, (a boy eight or nine nears old), [John Lee, John Byers], and three or four others, whose names I do not recollect, as they were strangers, to me. Among the wounded who recovered were Isaac Laney, Nathan K. Knight, Mr. [William] Yokum, two brothers by the name of [Jacob and George] Myers, Tarlton Lewis, Mr. [Jacob] Haun, and several others, [Jacob Foutz, Jacob Potts, Charles Jimison, John Walker, Alma Smith, aged about nine years]. Miss Mary Stedwell, while fleeing, was shot through the hand, and, fainting, fell over a log, into which they shot upwards of twenty balls.

To finish their work of destruction, this band of murderers, composed of men from Daviess, Livingston, Ray, Carroll, and Chariton counties, led by some of the principal men of that section of the upper country, (among whom I am informed were Mr. Ashby, of Chariton, member of the state legislature; Colonel Jennings, of Livingston county, Thomas O. Bryon, clerk of Livingston county; Mr. Whitney, Dr. Randall, and many others), proceeded to rob the houses, wagons, and tents, of bedding and clothing; drove off horses and wagons, leaving widows and orphans destitute of the necessaries of life; and even stripped the clothing from the bodies of the slain. According to their own account, they *fired seven* rounds in this awful butchery, making upwards of sixteen hundred shots at a little company of men, about thirty in number. I hereby certify the above to be a true statement of facts, according to the best of my knowledge.

JOSEPH YOUNG.

STATE OF ILLINOIS, }
COUNTY OF ADAMS. } ss.

I hereby certify that Joseph Young this day came before me, and made oath in due form of law, that the statements contained in the foregoing sheet are true, according to the best of his knowledge and belief. In testimony whereof I have hereunto set my hand and affixed the seal of the Circuit Court at Quincy, this fourth day of June, in the year of our Lord one thousand eight hundred and thirty-nine.

C. M. WOODS,
Clerk Circuit Court, Adams Co., Ill.

A younger brother of the boy here killed, aged eight, was shot through the hip. The little fellow himself states that seeing his father and brother both killed, he thought they would shoot him again if he stirred, and so feigned himself dead, and lay perfectly still, till he heard his mother call him after dark.

Additional Events of the Massacre.

Nathan K. Knight saw a Missourian cut down Father McBride with a corn-cutter, and also saw them stripping the dying, and heard the boys crying for mercy. Brother Knight made his escape across the mill-dam, after receiving wounds through his lungs and finger. After the massacre was over, he was led to a house by a woman, and whilst lying there wounded he heard Mr. Jesse Maupin say that he blew one of the boys' brains out. Some time later whilst walking the streets of Far West Brother Knight was met by three Missourians who threatened to butcher him, and one of them by the name of Rogers drew a butcher knife, and said that he had not got his corn-cutter with him, that he cut down McBride with, "but by —— I have got something that will do as well:" but by a great chance Brother Knight made his escape from the ruffian.

General Atchison withdrew from the army at Richmond as soon as the governor's extermination order was received. Up to this time we were ignorant at Far West of the movements of the mob at Richmond, and the governor's order of extermination.

Atchison Withdraws from "Militia."

On the 30th of October a large company of armed soldiers were seen approaching Far West. They came up near to the town, and then drew back about a mile, and encamped for the night. We were informed that they were militia, ordered out by the governor for the purpose of stopping our proceedings, it having been represented to his excellency, by wicked and designing men from Daviess that we were the aggressors, and had committed outrages in Daviess county. They had not yet got the governor's order of

Arrival of more Mob-Militia.

extermination, which I believe did not arrive till the next day.

Wednesday, October 31.—The militia of Far West guarded the city the past night, and arranged a temporary fortification of wagons, timber, etc., on the south. The sisters, many of them, were engaged in gathering up their most valuable effects, fearing a terrible battle in the morning, and that the houses might be fired and they obliged to flee. The enemy was five to one against us.

Prepartions for a Battle.

About eight o'clock a flag of truce was sent from the enemy, which was met by several of our people, and it was hoped that matters would be satisfactorily arranged after the officers had heard a true statement of all the circumstances. Colonel Hinkle went to meet the flag, and secretly made the following engagement: First, to give up their [the Church's] leaders to be tried and punished; second, to make an appropriation of the property of all who had taken up arms, for the payment of their debts, and indemnify for the damage done by them; third, that the remainder of the Saints should leave the state, and be protected while doing so by the militia; but they were to be permitted to remain under protection until further orders were received from the commander-in-chief; fourth, to give up their arms of every description, which would be receipted for.

Col. Hinkle's Treachery.

The enemy was reinforced by about one thousand five hundred men today, and news of the destruction of property by the mob reached us from every quarter.

Reinforcement of the Mob.

Towards evening I was waited upon by Colonel Hinkle, who stated that the officers of the militia desired to have an interview with me and some others, hoping that the difficulties might be settled without having occasion to carry into effect the exterminating orders which they had received from the governor. I immediately complied with the request, and in

Betrayal of the Prophet *et al.*

company with Elders Sidney Rigdon and Parley P. Pratt, Colonel Wight and George W. Robinson, went into the camp of the militia. But judge of my surprise, when, instead of being treated with that respect which is due from one citizen to another, we were taken as prisoners of war, and treated with the utmost contempt.* The officers would not converse with us, and the soldiers, almost to a man, insulted us as much as they felt disposed, breathing out threats against me and my companions. I

* Elder Parley P. Pratt in his Autobiography referring to this betrayal of the brethren on the part of Hinkle and their reception and treatment by the mob, says: "Colonel George M. Hinkle, who was at that time the highest officer of the militia assembled for the defense of Far West, waited on Messrs. Joseph Smith, Sidney Rigdon, Hyrum Smith, Lyman Wight, George W. Robinson and myself, with a request from General Lucas that we would repair to his camp, with the assurance that as soon as peaceable arrangements could be entered into we should be released. We had no confidence in the word of a murderer and robber, but there was no alternative but to put ourselves into the hands of such monsters, or to have the city attacked, and men, women and children massacred. We, therefore, commended ourselves to the Lord, and voluntarily surrendered as sheep into the hands of wolves. As we approached the camp of the enemy General Lucas rode out to meet us with a guard of several hundred men. The haughty general rode up, and, without speaking to us, instantly ordered his guards to surround us. They did so very abruptly, and we were marched into camp surrounded by thousands of savage looking beings, many of whom were dressed and painted like Indian warriors. These all set up a constant yell, like so many bloodhounds let loose upon their prey, as if they had achieved one of the most miraculous victories that ever graced the annals of the world. If the vision of the infernal regions could suddenly open to the mind, with thousands of malicious fiends, all clamoring, exulting, deriding, blaspheming, mocking, railing, raging and foaming like a troubled sea, then could some idea be formed of the hell which we had entered.

In camp we were placed under a strong guard, and were without shelter during the night, lying on the ground in the open air, in the midst of a great rain. The guards during the whole night kept up a constant tirade of mockery, and the most obscene blackguardism and abuse. They blasphemed God; mocked Jesus Christ; swore the most dreadful oaths; taunted Brother Joseph and others; demanded miracles; wanted signs, such as 'Come, Mr. Smith, show us an angel.' 'Give us one of your revelations.' 'Show us a miracle.' 'Come, there is one of your brethren here in camp whom we took prisoner yesterday in his own house, and knocked his brains out with his own rifle, which we found hanging over his fireplace; he lays speechless and dying; speak the word and heal him, and then we will all believe ' 'Or, if you are Apostles or men of God, deliver yourselves, and then we will be Mormons" Next would be a volley of oaths and blasphemies; then a tumultuous tirade of lewd boastings of having defiled virgins and wives by force, etc., much of which I dare not write; and, indeed, language would fail me to attempt more than a faint description. Thus passed this dreadful night, and before morning several other captives were added to our number, among whom was Brother Amasa Lyman."—Autobiography of Parley P. Pratt, pp. 203-205.

cannot begin to tell the scene which I there witnessed. The loud cries and yells of more than one thousand voices, which rent the air and could be heard for miles, and the horrid and blasphemous threats and curses which were poured upon us in torrents, were enough to appall the stoutest heart. In the evening we had to lie down on the cold ground, surrounded by a strong guard, who were only kept back by the power of God from depriving us of life. We petitioned the officers to know why we were thus treated, but they utterly refused to give us any answer, or to converse with us. After we arrived in the camp, Brother Stephen Winchester and eleven other brethren who were prisoners, volunteered, with permission of the officers, to carry Brother Carey into the city to his family, he having lain exposed to the weather for a show to the inhuman wretches, without having his wound dressed or being nourished in any manner. He died soon after he reached home.

The Prophet and Companions Condemned to be Shot.

Thursday, November 1.—Brothers Hyrum Smith and Amasa Lyman were brought prisoners into camp. The officers of the militia held a court martial, and sentenced us to be shot, on Friday morning, on the public square of Far West as a warning to the "Mormons."* However, notwithstanding their sentence and determination, they were

* This incident of sentencing the Prophet and his companion prisoners to be shot on the public square at Far West is also referred to in the History of Caldwell county, compiled by the St. Louis National Historical Company, and the formal orders of General Lucas to Brigadier-General Doniphan and also Doniphan's reply are given. I quote the following: "Yielding to the pressure upon him, it is alleged that General Lucas, at about midnight, issued the following order to General Doniphan, in whose keeping the hostages were:

" '*Brigadier-General Doniphan:*

" 'SIR:—You will take Joseph Smith and the other prisoners into the public square of Far West, and shoot them at 9 o'clock to-morow morning.

" 'SAMUEL D. LUCAS,
" 'Major-General Commanding.'

But General Doniphan, in great and righteous indignation, promptly returned the following reply to his superior:

" 'It is cold-blooded murder. I will not obey your order. My brigade shall march

not permitted to carry their murderous sentence into execution. Having an opportunity of speaking to General Wilson, I inquired of him why I was thus treated. I told him I was not aware of having done anything worthy of such treatment; that I had always been a supporter of the Constitution and of democracy. His answer was, "I know it, and that is the reason why I want to kill you, or have you killed."

Robbings of the Militia.

The militia went into the town, and without any restraint whatever, plundered the houses, and abused the innocent and unoffending inhabitants and left many destitute. They went to my house, drove my family out of doors, carried away most of my property. General Doniphan declared he would have nothing to do with such cold-blooded murder, and that he would withdraw his brigade in the morning.

Governor Boggs wrote General Clark from Jefferson City, that he considered full and ample powers were

for Liberty tomorrow morning, at 8 o'clock; and if you execute these men, I will hold you responsible before an earthly tribunal, so help me God.

" 'A. W. Doniphan,

" 'Brigadier-General.'

The prisoners somehow heard of the order, and kneeled in prayer, and prayed fervently that it might not be executed. And it was not. Flagrantly insubordinate as was General Doniphan's refusal, he was never called to account for it. The 'Mormons' have always remembered General Doniphan's humanity on this occasion, as well as on others, and when, in 1873, he went to Salt Lake City, he was received with much feeling, and shown every regard and attention by Brigham Young and the other authorities of the Church and city, and by even the masses of the people."—(History of Caldwell County, p. 137).

Parley P. Pratt, referring to this incident, says: "We were informed that the general officers held a secret council during most of the night, which was dignified by the name of court martial; in which, without a hearing, or, without even being brought before it, we were all sentenced to be shot. The day and hour was also appointed for the execution of this sentence, viz., next morning at 8 o'clock, in the public square at Far West. Of this we were informed by Brigadier-General Doniphan, who was one of the council, but who was so violently opposed to this cold-blooded murder that he assured the council that he would revolt and withdraw his whole brigade, and march them back to Clay county as soon as it was light, if they persisted in so dreadful an undertaking. Said he, 'It is cold-blooded murder, and I wash my hands of it.' His firm remonstrance, and that of a few others, so alarmed the haughty murderer and his accomplices that they dare not put the decree in execution."

vested in him [Clark] to carry into effect the former orders; says Boggs:

Excerpt from Governor Boggs' Communication to General Lucas.

The case is now a very plain one—the "Mormons" must be subdued; and peace restored to the community; you will therefore proceed without delay to execute the former orders. Full confidence is reposed in your ability to do so; your force will be amply sufficient to accomplish the object. Should you need the aid of artillery, I would suggest that an application be made to the commanding officer of Fort Leavenworth, for such as you may need. You are authorized to request the loan of it in the name of the state of Missouri. The ringleaders of this rebellion should be made an example of; and if it should become necessary for the public peace, the "Mormons" should be exterminated, or expelled from the state.

Citizens of Far West Disarmed.

This morning General Lucas ordered the Caldwell militia to give up their arms. Hinkle, having made a treaty with the mob on his own responsibility, to carry out his treachery, marched the troops out of the city, and the brethren gave up their arms, their own property, which no government on earth had a right to require.

High Handed Procedure of the Mob.

The mob (called Governor's troops) then marched into town, and under pretense of searching for arms, tore up floors, upset haystacks, plundered the most valuable effects they could lay their hands on, wantonly wasted and destroyed a great amount of property, compelled the brethren at the point of the bayonet to sign deeds of trust to pay the expenses of the mob, even while the place was desecrated by the chastity of women being violated. About eighty men were taken prisoners, the remainder were ordered to leave the state, and were forbidden, under threat of being shot by the mob to assemble more than three in a place.

Avard's Treachery.

Friday, November 2.—About this time Sampson Avard was found by the mob secreted in the hazel brush some miles from Far West, and brought into camp, where he and they were "hail fellows well met;'' for Avard told them that Daniteism was an order of the Church, and by his lying tried to make the Church a scape-goat for his sins.

Myself and fellow prisoners were taken to the town, into the public square, and before our departure we, after much entreaty, were suffered to see our families, being attended all the while by a strong guard. I found my wife and children in tears, who feared we had been shot by those who had sworn to take our lives, and that they would see me no more. When I entered my house, they clung to my garments, their eyes streaming with tears, while mingled emotions of joy and sorrow were manifested in their countenances. I requested to have a private interview with them a few minutes, but this privilege was denied me by the guard. I was then obliged to take my departure. Who can realize the feelings which I experienced at that time, to be thus torn from my companion, and leave her surrounded with monsters in the shape of men, and my children, too, not knowing how their wants would be supplied; while I was to be taken far from them in order that my enemies might destroy me when they thought proper to do so. My partner wept, my children clung to me, until they were thrust from me by the swords of the guards. I felt overwhelmed while I witnessed the scene, and could only recommend them to the care of that God whose kindness had followed me to the present time, and who alone could protect them, and deliver me from the hands of my enemies, and restore me to my family.*

* Of these scenes connected with the separation of the prisoners from their families, Parley P. Pratt writes as follows: "We were now marched to Far West, under the conduct of the whole army; and while they halted in the public square, we were permitted to go with a guard for a change of linen, and to take final leave of our families, in order to depart as prisoners to Jackson county, a distance of sixty miles.

"This was the most trying scene of all. I went to my house, being guarded by two or three soldiers, the cold rain was pouring down without, and on entering my little cottage, there lay my wife sick of a fever, with which she had been for some time confined. At her breast was our son Nathan, an infant of three months, and

After this painful scene I was taken back to the camp, and with the rest of my brethren, namely, Sidney Rigdon, Hyrum Smith, Parley P. Pratt, Lyman Wight, Amasa Lyman, and George W. Robinson, started off for

by her side a little girl of five years. On the foot of the same bed lay a woman in travail, who had been driven from her house in the night, and had taken momentary shelter in my hut of ten feet square—my larger house having been torn down. I stepped to the bed; my wife burst into tears; I spoke a few words of comfort, telling her to try to live for my sake and the children's; and expressing a hope that we should meet again though years might separate us. She promised to try to live. I then embraced and kissed the little babies and departed. Till now I had refrained from weeping; but, to be forced from so helpless a family, who were destitute of provisions and fuel, and deprived almost of shelter in a bleak prairie, with none to assist them, exposed to a lawless banditti who were utter strangers to humanity, and this at the approach of winter, was more than nature could well endure. I went to General Moses Wilson in tears, and stated the circumstances of my sick, heart-broken and destitute family in tears which would have moved any heart that had a latent spark of humanity yet remaining. But I was only answered with an exultant laugh, and a taunt of reproach by this hardened murderer. As I returned from my house towards the troops in the square, I halted with the guard at the door of Hyrum Smith, and heard the sobs and groans of his wife, at his parting words. She was then near confinement; and needed more than ever the comfort and consolation of a husband's presence. As we returned to the wagon we saw Sidney Rigdon taking leave of his wife and daughters, who stood at a little distance, in tears of anguish indescribable. In the wagon sat Joseph Smith, while his aged father and venerable mother came up overwhelmed with tears, and took each of the prisoners by the hand with a silence of grief too great for utterance. In the meantime hundreds of the brethren crowded around us, anxious to take a parting look, or a silent shake of the hand; for feelings were too intense to allow of speech. In the midst of these scenes orders were given and we moved slowly away, under the conduct of General Wilson and his whole brigade."—Autobiography of Parley P. Pratt, pp. 207, 208.

The Prophet's mother describes these scenes of sorrow and parting in the following vivid manner:

"At the time when Joseph went into the enemy's camp, Mr. Smith and myself stood in the door of the house in which we were then living, and could distinctly hear their horrid yellings. Not knowing the cause, we supposed they were murdering him. Soon after the screaming commenced, five or six guns were discharged. At this, Mr. Smith, folding his arms tight across his heart, cried out, 'Oh, my God! my God! they have killed my son! they have murdered him! and I must die, for I cannot live without him!'

"I had no word of consolation to give him, for my heart was broken within me—my agony was unutterable. I assisted him to the bed and he fell back upon it helpless as a child, for he had not strength to stand upon his feet. The shrieking continued; no tongue can describe the sound which was conveyed to our ears; no heart can imagine the sensation of our breasts, as we listened to those awful screams. Had the army been composed of so many bloodhounds, wolves, and panthers, they could not have made a sound more terrible. * * * *

"When they [the division of the mob in charge of the prisoners] were about starting from Far West, a messenger came and told us that if we ever saw our sons alive, we must go immediately to them, for they were in a wagon that would

Independence, Jackson county, and encamped at night on Crooked river, under a strong guard commanded by Generals Lucas and Wilson.

The following letter gives the particulars relating to the movements of the governor's troops in conjunction with the mob:

Report of General S. D. Lucas to Governor Boggs.

HEADQUARTERS, CAMP NEAR FAR WEST,
November 2, 1838.

To His Excellency, L. W. Boggs, Commander-in-Chief, Missouri Militia:

SIR:—On Monday, October 29th, the troops ordered out by Major-General Atchison and myself (as per our report to you of said date), took up their line of march from camp near Richmond, for Far West. We encamped on the night of the 29th at Linville's creek (a short distance from the road), about sixteen miles from Far West, at which point we received an express from Brigadier-General Doniphan, informing us that he was then encamped on Log creek with a force of five hundred men, and that he would join us at the crossing of said creek, on the road from Richmond to Far West, by ten o'clock the next morning.

start in a few minutes for Independence, and in all probability they would never return alive. Receiving this intimation, Lucy and myself set out directly for the place. On coming within about a hundred yards of the wagon, we were compelled to stop, for we could press no further through the crowd. I therefore appealed to those around me, exclaiming, 'I am the mother of the Prophet—is there not a gentleman here who will assist me to that wagon, that I may take a last look at my children, and speak to them once more before I die?' Upon this, one individual volunteered to make a pathway through the army, and we passed on, threatened with death at every step, till at length we arrived at the wagon. The man who led us through the crowd spoke to Hyrum, who was sitting in front, and, telling him that his mother had come to see him, requested that he should reach his hand to me. He did so, but I was not allowed to see him; the cover was of strong cloth, and nailed down so close that he could hardly get his hand through. We had merely shaken hands with him, when we were ordered away by the mob, who forbade any conversation between us, and, threatening to shoot us, they ordered the teamster to drive over us. Our friend then conducted us to the back part of the wagon, where Joseph sat, and said, 'Mr. Smith, your mother and sister are here, and wish to shake hands with you.' Joseph crowded his hand through between the cover and wagon, and we caught hold of it; but he spoke not to either of us, until I said, 'Joseph, do speak to your poor mother once more—I cannot bear to go till I hear your voice.' 'God bless you, mother!' he sobbed out. Then a cry was raised, and the wagon dashed off, tearing him from us just as Lucy pressed his hand to her lips, to bestow upon it a sister's last kiss—for he was then sentenced to be shot."—History of the Prophet Joseph by his Mother, Lucy Smith, pp. 249, 250.

On the 30th of October, the troops got together at the last named point, when we mustered about eighteen hundred men. Whilst at this place we received your orders of the 26th ultimo, and I received an order of the 27th ultimo, and a letter from you of the same date. At this point Major-General Atchison left me for Liberty, when I was left in sole command. I then took up my line of march for Goose creek, one mile south of Far West, which point we reached about one hour by sun in the evening. Just as the troops were encamping, I received intelligence from General Doniphan, from his position on the right, that he had discovered a party of mounted Mormons approaching Far West from the east, and requested permission to intercept them, if possible. Leave was granted, and his brigade started off at nearly full speed to accomplish the order, but the Mormons succeeded in reaching the fort. General Doniphan approached within two hundred yards of their fortress, when they displayed a force of about eight hundred [150] men. At this juncture, I ordered General Graham's brigade (holding General Parks' and part of General Wilson's mounted in reserve) to march full speed to the relief of the First Brigade, Third Division, but from the inequality of the force of the first detachment, (being only two hundred and fifty strong at that time, and the "Mormons eight hundred [150] it was considered prudent to withdraw the troops, and march against them in the morning, which was accordingly done, and they all returned, as dark set in, to camp. At this place I established my headquarters, and continued there during the expedition against the Mormons. The detachment under General Wilson returned about nine o'clock p. m.

The next morning, 31st of October, I received a message from Colonel Hinkle, the commander of the Mormon forces [Caldwell militia], requesting an interview with me on an eminence near Far West, which he would designate by hoisting a white flag. I sent him word I would meet him at two o'clock p. m., being so much engaged in receiving and encamping fresh troops, who were hourly coming in, that I could not attend before. Accordingly at that time, I started with my staff officers and Brigadier-Generals Wilson, Doniphan and Graham, General Parks being left in command. We met him and some other Mormons at the point before mentioned. He stated that his object in asking me to meet him there, was to know if there could not be some compromise or settlement of the difficulty without a resort to arms.

After giving him to understand the nature of your orders, I made him the following propositions, which I furnished him a copy of, also a copy of your order, viz.:

"First—To give up their [the Church's] leaders to be tried and punished.

"Second—To make an appropriation of their property, all who have taken up arms, to the payment of their debts, and indemnify for damages done by them.

"Third—That the balance should leave the state, and be protected out by the militia, but to be permitted to remain under protection until further orders were received from the commander-in-chief.

"Fourth—To give up the arms of every description, to be receipted for."

Colonel Hinkle agreed to the proposition readily, but wished to postpone the matter until morning. I then told him that I would require Joseph Smith, Jun., Sidney Rigdon, Lyman Wight, Parley P. Pratt, and George W. Robinson, as hostage for his faithful compliance with the terms, and would pledge myself and each one of the officers present, that in case he, after reflecting and consulting upon the proposition during the night, declined acceding to them, that the hostages should be returned to him in the morning, at the same point they were received, but it was understood in case they did comply, they were to be held for trial as part of the leaders called for by the first stipulation; I then gave him until one hour by sun in the evening to produce and deliver them. We then returned to camp, and I directed the troops to make preparations to march to Far West by an hour and a half by the sun, with a determination in case the hostages were not produced to make an attack upon the town forthwith.

I directed General Parks' brigade to be mounted, and to form on the right of the division, to act as flankers if necessary, and if required to pass entirely around the town, and form on the north side, with instructions to make the attack at the report of the cannon, which was to be the signal for the general attack. General Graham's brigade was mounted, and formed on the extreme left to act as flankers, and if required to form the line on the west side, with similar instructions as to the commencement of the attack.

General Doniphan's brigade was ordered to parade on foot, and to form on the left of General Parks, with instructions to form the line of battle on the south side, with the same instructions as to commencement of attack.

The artillery company, with one piece of ordnance, was placed at the head of General Doniphan's and General Wilson's brigade, with instructions to occupy an eminence within three hundred yards of the town.

The army being disposed of in this manner, at the appointed time I took up the line of march in direction of Far West. When the troops got within about six hundred yards, I discovered the flag and the hostages advancing. I immediately halted the army, and rode out and met them, received the hostages, and placed a guard over them for their safety and protection, and ordered the forces back to our encampment. I cannot forbear, at this point, expressing my gratification and approbation of the good conduct and gallant bravery* evinced by all the officers and men under my command. They marched up with as much determination and deliberation as old veterans—not knowing but that the charge would be sounded every moment for surrounding the town.† There was no noise or confusion, nothing but an eager anxiety upon the countenance of every man to get at the work.

When the hostages were received, the troops, with some slight exceptions, marched back‡ in profound silence.

November 1st. I ordered the whole forces, amounting to two thousand five hundred men, to parade at nine o'clock a. m., and to take up the line of march for Far West at half-past nine o'clock, to receive the prisoners and their arms.

The troops marched out and formed in the prairie about two hundred yards southeast of the town. General Wilson's brigade formed the west line, General Doniphan's the east line, General Graham and General Parks the south line, with the artillery company and the cannon in the center of the two latter, leaving one side of the square open.

The "Mormon" army, reduced to about six hundred men by desertion and otherwise, under their commander, ColonelHinkle marched out of their town through the space into our square, formed a hollow square, and grounded their arms. Colonel Hinkle then rode forward and delivered up to me his sword and pistols.

I then directed a company from the respective brigades to form a front, rear, right and left flank guards, and to march the prisoners back to Far West, and protect and take charge of them until the next morning. I then detailed a company from General Doniphan's command to take charge of the arms. Then, in order to gratify the army and to let the "Mormons" see our forces, marched around the town, and through the principal streets and back to headquarters.

* On this passage the Prophet makes the following comments:

"Gallant bravery," that some thousands of men should be so anxious to wash their hands in the blood of five hundred poor Saints? I claim not the honor of commanding such a brave army.

† Again the Prophet comments:

"The wicked flee when no man pursueth " This saying was truly verified in the first retreat of this army—they fled precipitately through fear and a great proportion of the men were anxious to get back to the creek, where they could dispense with some of their clothing and wash themselves in the water.

‡ "Profound silence." It might have been silence to the general for aught I know; for the shoutings, bellowings and yells of this army of mobocrats was sufficient to deafen anyone, not guarded by some higher spirit, and could only be equalled in the savage war whoop, and the yells of the damned.

Considering the war at an end in this place I issued orders for General Doniphan's brigade, with the exception of one company, and General Graham's brigade, to take up their line of march for their respective headquarters and dismiss their men, and directed General Wilson to take charge of the prisoners (demanded for trial) and arms, and to march them to my headquarters at Independence, to await further orders, and to dismiss all except a guard for the prisoners and arms.

November 2nd. I relieved the guard placed over the prisoners at Far West by four companies of General Parks' brigade, and placed them under the command of Colonel Thompson, Second brigade, Third division, with instructions to report to General Clark. The balance of General Parks' brigade, with Captain Gillium's company of General Doniphan's brigade, under the command of General Parks, I ordered to Adam-ondi-Ahman, a Mormon town in Daviess county, with instructions to disarm the Mormon forces at that place and to leave a guard of fifty men for the protection of prisoners, and to report to General Clark.

In order to carry the treaty and stipulations into effect I have required your aid-de-camp, Colonel Williams, together with Colonel Burch, and Major A. Rees, of Ray, to attend to drawing up the papers legally, and directed Colonel Thompson to wait on them with a portion of his command, and to cause all their orders and requirements, consistent with the stipulations, to be carried into effect.

This day, about twelve o'clock, there was a battalion of one hundred men from Platte arrived at Far West, which I ordered back, having understood that Major-General Clark would be on in a day or two with sufficient force to operate in Daviess and Livingston, and for any service that may be required.

SAMUEL D. LUCAS,
Major-General Commanding.

CHAPTER XIV.

RIVALRY AMONG THE MILITIA GENERALS FOR POSSESSION OF THE PRISONERS—"TRIAL" AT RICHMOND.

Saturday, 3.—We continued our march and arrived at the Missouri river, which separated us from Jackson county, where we were hurried across the ferry when but few troops had passed.* The truth was, General Clark had sent an express from Richmond to General Lucas, to have the prisoners sent to him, and thus prevent our going to Jackson county, both armies being competitors for the honor of possessing "the royal prisoners." Clark wanted the privilege of putting us to death himself, and Lucas and his troops were desirous of exhibiting us in the streets of Independence.†

Rival Efforts for Possession of the Prisoners.

Sunday, 4.—We were visited by some ladies and gentlemen. One of the women came up, and very candidly inquired of the troops which of the prisoners was the Lord

* It was during this march between Crooked river and the Missouri that the Prophet predicted that none of the prisoners would lose their lives during their captivity. The incident is thus related by Parley P. Pratt: "As we arose and commenced our march on the morning of the 3rd of November, Joseph Smith spoke to me and the other prisoners, in a low, but cheerful and confidential tone; said he: '*Be of good cheer, brethren; the word of the Lord came to me last night that our lives should be given us, and that whatever we may suffer during this captivity, not one of our lives shall be taken.*' Of this prophecy I testify in the name of the Lord, and, though spoken in secret, its public fulfillment and the miraculous escape of each one of us is too notorious to need my testimony."—Autobiography of Parley P. Pratt, p. 210.

† On this matter of competition for possession of the prisoners Parley P. Pratt, one of the prisoners, repeats a statement made by General Wilson as follows: "It was repeatedly insinuated, by the other officers and troops that we should hang you prisoners on the first tree we came to on the way to Independence. But I'll be d——d if anybody shall hurt you. We just intend to exhibit you in Independence, let the people look at you, and see what a d——d set of fine fellows you are. And, more particularly, to keep you from that old bigot of a General Clark and his troops, from down country who are so stuffed with lies and prejudice that they would shoot you down in a moment."—Autobiography of Parley P. Pratt, p. 209.

whom the "Mormons" worshiped? One of the guard pointed to me with a significant smile, and said, "This is he." The woman then turning to me inquired whether I professed to be the Lord and Savior? I replied, that I professed to be nothing but a man, and a minister of salvation, sent by Jesus Christ to preach the Gospel.

Prophet's Interview with a Lady,

This answer so surprised the woman that she began to inquire into our doctrine, and I preached a discourse, both to her and her companions, and to the wondering soldiers, who listened with almost breathless attention while I set forth the doctrine of faith in Jesus Christ, and repentance, and baptism for remission of sins, with the promise of the Holy Ghost, as recorded in the second chapter of the Acts of the Apostles.

The woman was satisfied, and praised God in the hearing of the soldiers, and went away, praying that God would protect and deliver us. Thus was fulfilled a prophecy which had been spoken publicly by me, a few months previous—that a sermon should be preached in Jackson county by one of our Elders, before the close of 1838.

The troops having crossed the river about ten o'clock, we proceeded on and arrived at Independence, past noon, in the midst of a great rain, and a multitude of spectators who had assembled to see us, and hear the bugles sound a blast of triumphant joy, which echoed through the camp. We were ushered into a vacant house prepared for our reception, with a floor for our beds and blocks of wood for our pillows.

Arrival of the Prisoners in Independence

General Clark arrived at Far West with one thousand six hundred men, and five hundred more were within eight miles of the city.

Thus, Far West has been visited by six thousand men in one week, when the militia of the city (before any were taken prisoners) amounted only to about five hundred. After depriving these of their arms the mob continued to hunt the brethren like wild beasts, and shot several, ravished the women, and killed one near the city. No Saint was permitted to go in or out of the city; and meantime the Saints lived on parched corn.

Overwhelming Numbers of Mob Militia.

General Clark ordered General Lucas, who had previously gone to Adam-ondi-Aham with his troops, "to take the whole of the men of the 'Mormons' prisoners, and place such a guard around them and the town as will protect the prisoners and secure them until they can be dealt with properly," and secure all their property, till the best means could be adopted for paying the damages the citizens had sustained.

Monday, 5.—We were kept under a small guard, and were treated with some degree of hospitality and politeness, while many flocked to see us. We spent most of our time in preaching and conversation, explanatory of our doctrines and practice, which removed mountains of prejudice, and enlisted the populace in our favor, notwithstanding their old hatred and wickedness towards our society.

Severity in the Treatment of Prisoners Modified.

The brethren at Far West were ordered by General Clark to form a line, when the names of fifty-six present were called and made prisoners to await their trial for something they knew not what. They were kept under a close guard.

Fifty-six Additional Prisoners.

Tuesday, 6.—General Clark paraded the brethren at Far West, and then addressed them as follows.

General Clark's Harrangue to the Brethren.

Gentlemen, you whose names are not attached to this list of names, will now have the privilege of going to your fields and providing corn, wood, etc., for your families. Those who are now taken will go from this to prison, be tried, and receive the due demerit of their crimes. But you (except such as charges may hereafter be preferred against) are now at liberty, as soon as the troops are removed that now guard the place, which I shall cause to be done immediately. It now devolves upon you to fulfill the treaty that you have entered into, the leading items of which I shall now lay before you:

The first requires that your leading men be given up to be tried according to law; this you have already complied with.

The second is, that you deliver up your arms; this has been attended to.

The third stipulation is, that you sign over your properties to defray the expenses of the war; this you have also done.

Another article yet remains for you to comply with, and that is, that you leave the state forthwith; and whatever may be your feelings concerning this, or whatever your innocence, it is nothing to me; General Lucas, who is equal in authority with me, has made this treaty with you—I approve of it—I should have done the same had I been here—I am therefore determined to see it fulfilled. The character of this state has suffered almost beyond redemption, from the character, conduct and influence that you have exerted, and we deem it an act of justice to restore her character to its former standing among the states, by every proper means.

The orders of the governor to me were, that you should be exterminated, and not allowed to remain in the state, and had your leaders not been given up, and the terms of the treaty complied with, before this, you and your families would have been destroyed and your houses in ashes.

There is a discretionary power vested in my hands which I shall exercise in your favor for a season; for *this* lenity you are indebted to *my* clemency. I do not say that you shall go now, but you must not think of staying here another season, or of putting in crops, for the moment you do this the citizens will be upon you. If I am called here again, in case of a non-compliance of a treaty made, do not think that I shall act any more as I have done—you need not expect any mercy, but extermination, for I am determined the governor's order shall be executed. As for your leaders, do not once think—do not imagine for a moment—do not let it enter your mind that they will be delivered, or that you will see their faces again, for their *fate is fixed—their die is cast—their doom is sealed.*

I am sorry, gentlemen, to see so great a number of apparently intelligent men found in the situation that you are; and oh! that I could invoke that *Great Spirit, the unknown God,* to rest upon you, and make you sufficiently intelligent to break that chain of superstition, and liberate you from those fetters of fanaticism with which you are bound —that you no longer worship a man.

I would advise you to scatter abroad, and never again organize yourselves with Bishops, Presidents, etc., lest you excite the jealousies of the people, and subject yourselves to the same calamities that have now come upon you.

You have always been the aggressors—you have brought upon yourselves these difficulties by being disaffected and not being subject to rule—and my advice is, that you become as other citizens, lest by a recurrence of these events you bring upon yourselves irretrievable ruin.*

The governor wrote General Clark as follows:

It will also be necessary that you hold a military court of inquiry in Daviess county, and arrest the Mormons who have been guilty of the late outrages, committed towards the inhabitants of said county. My instructions to you are to settle this whole matter completely, if possible, before you disband your forces; if the Mormons are disposed voluntarily to leave the state, of course it would be advisable in you to promote that object, in any way deemed proper. The *ringleaders of this rebellion, though, ought by no means to be permitted to escape the punishment they merit.*

The prisoners at Far West were started off for Richmond, under a strong guard.

Wednesday, 7.—The following order was issued at Far West by General Clark:

Brigadier-General Robert Wilson will take up the line of march with his brigade on this morning for Adam-ondi-Ahman, in Daviess county, and take possession of the prisoners at that place, and proceed to ascertain those who committed crimes, and when done, to put them under close guard, and when he moves, take them to Keytesville, after having them recognized by the proper authority.

Thursday, 8.—There was a severe snowstorm yesterday and today. General Wilson arrived at Adam-ondi-Ahman; he placed guards around the town so that no persons

* This speech of General Clark's is to be found in the "History of Caldwell and Livingston counties, Missouri, written and compiled by the St. Louis National Historical Company," 1886, and is introduced as follows: "A few days after his arrival General Clark removed a portion of the restraint he had imposed upon the Mormons' allowing them to go out for wood, provisions, etc. He assembled the multitude on the temple square and delivered to them a written speech, a copy of which is here given. It goes far to prove that General Clark was ordered to 'exterminate' the Mormons, not excepting the women and children, and burn their houses and otherwise destroy their property."—History of Caldwell and Livington Counties, p. 140.

might pass out or in without permission. All the men in town were then taken and put under guard, and a court of inquiry was instituted, with Adam Black on the bench; the said Adam Black belonged to the mob, and was one of the leaders of it from the time mobbing first commenced in Daviess county. The attorney belonged to General Clark's army.

Progress of Affairs at Diahman.

Shortly after our arrival in Jackson county, Colonel Sterling Price, from the army of General Clark, came with orders from General Clark, who was commander-in-chief of the expedition, to have us forwarded forthwith to Richmond. Accordingly, on Thursday morning, we started with three guards only, and they had been obtained with great difficulty, after laboring all the previous day to get them. Between Independence and Roy's Ferry, on the Missouri river, they all got drunk, and we got possession of their arms and horses.

The Prophet and his Fellow Prisoners Sent to Richmond.

It was late in the afternoon, near the setting of the sun. We traveled about half a mile after we crossed the river, and put up for the night.

Friday, 9.—This morning there came a number of men, some of them armed. Their threatenings and savage appearance were such as to make us afraid to proceed without more guards. A messenger was therefore dispatched to Richmond to obtain them. We started before their arrival, but had not gone far before we met Colonel Price with a guard of about seventy-four men, and were conducted by them to Richmond, and put into an old vacant house, and a guard set.

Prisoners not Sufficiently Protected by Guards.

Some time through the course of that day General Clark came in, and we were introduced to him. We inquired of him the reason why we had been thus carried from our homes, and what were the charges against us. He said that he was not then able to determine, but would be in a short time; and with very little more conversation withdrew.

Meeting of the Prophet and Gen. Clark.

Some short time after he had withdrawn Colonel Price came in with two chains in his hands, and a number of padlocks. The two chains he fastened together. He had with him ten men, armed, who stood at the time of these operations with a thumb upon the cock of their guns. They first nailed down the windows, then came and ordered a man by the name of John Fulkerson, whom he had with him, to chain us together with chains and padlocks, being seven in number. After that he searched us, examining our pockets to see if we had any arms. He found nothing but pocket knives, but these he took away with him.

The Prisoners Chained.

Saturday, November 10.—The following is a true specimen of Missouri liberty.

Form of Permit.

I permit David Holman to remove from Daviess to Caldwell county, there to remain during the winter, or to pass out of the state.

R. WILSON, Brigadier-General.
By F. G. COCKNU, Aid.

November 10, 1838.

General Clark had spent his time since our arrival at Richmond in searching the laws to find authority for trying us by court martial. Had he not been a lawyer of eminence, I should have supposed it no very difficult task to decide that quiet, peaceful unoffending, and private citizens too, except as ministers of the Gospel, were not amenable to a *military tribunal*, in a country governed by *civil laws.* But be this as it may, General Clark wrote the governor that he had—

General Clark Desires to Try the Prophet by Court Martial.

General Clark's Report to Governor Boggs.

Detained General White and his field offices here a day or two for the purpose of holding a court martial, if necessary. I this day made out charges against the prisoners, and called on Judge King to try them as a committing court; and I am now busily engaged in procuring witnesses and submitting facts. There being no civil officers in Caldwell,

I have to use the military to get witnesses from there, which I do without reserve. The most of the prisoners here I consider guilty of *treason;* and I believe will be convicted; and the only difficulty in law is, can they be tried in any county but Caldwell? If not, they cannot be there indicted, until a change of population. In the event the latter view is taken by the civil courts, I suggest the propriety of trying Jo Smith and those leaders taken by General Lucas, by a court martial, for mutiny. This I am in favor of only as *dernier resort.* I would have taken this course with Smith at any rate; but it being doubtful whether a court martial has jurisdiction or not in the present case—that is, whether these people are to be treated as in time of war, and the mutineers as having mutinied in time of war—and I would here ask you to forward to me the attorney-general's opinion on this point. It will not do to allow these leaders to return to their treasonable work again, on account of their not being indicted in Caldwell. They have committed *treason, murder, arson, burglary, robbery, larceny, and perjury.*

The three days' investigation having closed at Adam-ondi-Ahman, every man was honorably acquitted, Adam Black being judge.

Hardships Inflicted on the "Diahman" Saints.

General Wilson then ordered every family to be out of Diahman in ten days, with permission to go to Caldwell, and there tarry until spring, and then leave the state under pain of extermination. The weather is very cold, more so than usual for this season of the year.

In keeping the order of General Wilson the Saints had to leave their crops and houses, and to live in tents and wagons, in this inclement season of the year. As for their flocks and herds, the mob had relieved them from the trouble of taking care of them, or from the pain of seeing them starve to death—by stealing them.

An arrangement was made in which it was stipulated that a committee of twelve, which had been previously appointed, should have the privilege of going from Far West to Daviess county, for the term of four weeks, for the purpose of conveying their crops from Daviess to Caldwell. The committee were to wear white badges on their hats for protection.

About thirty of the brethren have been killed, many wounded, about a hundred are missing, and about sixty at Richmond awaiting their trial—for what they know not.

Casualties of the Mobbing.

Sunday, *11*.—While in Richmond we were under the charge of Colonel Price from Chariton county, who allowed all manner of abuses to be heaped upon us. During this time my afflictions were great, and our situation was truly painful.*

* It was during this time that the very remarkable circumstance of the Prophet rebuking the prison guards occurred. The matter is related by Elder Parley P. Pratt in his Autobiography. It appears that during the imprisonment at Richmond Elder Rigdon was taken very ill from the hardships and exposure he had to endure. He was chained next to his son-in-law, George W. Robinson, and compelled to sleep on the hard floor notwithstanding his delirium, the result of fever. Mrs. Robinson, the daughter of Elder Rigdon, had accompanied her hushand and father into the prison for the purpose of caring for the latter during his illness. She is represented as being a very delicate woman with an infant at the breast. She continued by the side of her father until he recovered from his illness notwithstanding the loathsomeness of the prison and the vileness of the guards. And now the story of the rebuke as related by Elder Pratt: "In one of those tedious nights we had lain as if in sleep till the hour of midnight had passed, and our ears and hearts had been pained, while we had listened for hours to the obscene jests, the horrid oaths, the dreadful blasphemies and filthy language of our guards, Colonel Price at their head, as they recounted to each other their deeds of rapine, murder, robbery, etc., which they had committed among the "Mormons" while at Far West and vicinity. They even boasted of defiling by force wives, daughters and virgins, and of shooting or dashing out the brains of men, women and children. I had listened till I became so disgusted, shocked, horrified, and so filled with the spirit of indignant justice that I could scarcely refrain from rising upon my feet and rebuking the guards; but had said nothing to Joseph, or anyone else, although I lay next to him and knew he was awake. On a sudden he arose to his feet, and spoke in a voice of thunder, or as the roaring lion, uttering, as nearly as I can recollect, the following words:

" '*Silence*, ye fiends of the infernal pit! In the name of Jesus Christ I rebuke you, and command you to be still; I will not live another minute and hear such language. Cease such talk, or you or I die *this instant!*'

He ceased to speak. He stood erect in terrible majesty. Chained, and without a weapon; calm, unruffled and dignified as an angel, he looked upon the quailing guards, whose weapons were lowered or dropped to the ground; whose knees smote together, and who, shrinking into a corner, or crouching at his feet, begged his pardon, and remained quiet till a change of guards.

"I have seen the ministers of justice, clothed in magisterial robes, and criminals arraigned before them, while life was suspended on a breath, in the courts of England; I have witnessed a Congress in solemn session to give laws to nations; I have tried to conceive of kings, of royal courts, of thrones and crowns; and of emperors assembled to decide the fate of kingdoms; but dignity and majesty have I seen but once, as it stood in chains, at midnight in a dungeon, in an obscure village in Missouri."—Autobiography of Parley P. Pratt, pp. 228-230.

General Clark informed us that he would turn us over to the civil authorities for trial. Joseph Smith, Jun., Hyrum Smith, Sidney Rigdon, Parley P. Pratt, Lyman Wight, Amasa Lyman, George W. Robinson, Caleb Baldwin, Alanson Ripley, Washington Voorhees, Sidney Turner, John Buchanan, Jacob Gates, Chandler Holbrook, George W. Harris, Jesse D. Hunter, Andrew Whitlock, Martin C. Allred, William Allred, George D. Grant, Darwin Chase, Elijah Newman, Alvin G. Tippets, Zedekiah Owens, Isaac Morley, Thomas Beck, Moses Clawson, John J. Tanner, Daniel Shearer, Daniel S. Thomas, Alexander McRae, Elisha Edwards, John S. Higbee, Ebenezer Page, Benjamin Covey, Ebenezer Robinson, Luman Gibbs, James M. Henderson, David Pettegrew, Edward Partridge, Francis Higbee, David Frampton, George Kimball, Joseph W. Younger, Henry Zobriskie, Allen J. Stout, Sheffield Daniels, Silas Maynard, Anthony Head, Benjamin Jones, Daniel Garn, John T. Earl, and Norman Shearer, were brought before Austin A. King, at Richmond, for trial, charged with the several crimes of high treason against the state, murder, burglary, arson, robbery, and larceny.

List of the Prisoners.

Monday, 12.—The first act of the court was to send out a body of armed men, without a civil process, to obtain witnesses.

Tuesday, 13.—We were placed at the bar, Austin A. King presiding, and Thomas C. Burch, the state's attorney. Witnesses were called and sworn at the point of the bayonet.

Dr. Sampson Avard was the first brought before the court. He had previously told Mr. Oliver Olney that if he [Olney] wished to save himself, he must swear hard against the heads of the Church, as they were the ones the court wanted to criminate; and if he could swear hard against them, they would not (that is, neither court nor mob) disturb him. "I intend to do

The Villainy of Avard.

it," said he, "in order to escape, for if I do not, they will take my life."

This introduction is sufficient to show the character of his testimony, and he swore just according to the statement he had made, doubtless thinking it a wise course to ingratiate himself into the good graces of the mob.

List of Witnesses against the Saints

The following witnesses were examined in behalf of the state, many of whom, if we may judge from their testimony, swore upon the same principle as Avard, they were: Wyatt Cravens, Nehemiah Odle, Captain Samuel Bogart, Morris Phelps, John Corrill, Robert Snodgrass, George Walton, George M. Hinkle, James C. Owens, Nathaniel Carr, Abner Scovil, John Cleminson, Reed Peck, James C. Owens (re-examined), William Splawn, Thomas M. Odle, John Raglin, Allen Rathbun, Jeremiah Myers, Andrew J. Job, Freeburn H. Gardner, Burr Riggs, Elisha Camron, Charles Bleckley, James Cobb, Jesse Kelly, Addison Price, Samuel Kimball, William W. Phelps, John Whitmer, James B. Turner, George W. Worthington, Joseph H. McGee, John Lockhart, Porter Yale, Benjamin Slade, Ezra Williams, Addison Green, John Taylor, Timothy Lewis, and Patrich Lynch.

Sunday, 18.—While our suit was going forward General Wilson gave the following permit, in Daviess county:

Permit.

I permit the following persons, as a committee on the part of the Mormons, to pass and re-pass in and through the county of Daviess during the winter, to-wit.: William Huntington, John Reed, Benjamin S. Wilbur, Mayhew Hillman, Z. Wilson, E. B. Gaylord, Henry Herriman, Daniel Stanton, Oliver Snow, William Earl, Jonathan H. Hale, Henry Humphrey—upon all lawful business.

R. WILSON, Brig.-Gen. Commanding.
By F. G. COCKNU, Aid.

November 18, 1838.

We were called upon for our witnesses, and we gave the names of some forty or fifty. Captain Bogart was despatched with a company of militia to procure them. He arrested all he could find, thrust them into prison, and we were not allowed to see them.

Treatment of Witnesses for the Defense.

During the week we were again called upon most tauntingly for witnesses; we gave the names of some others, and they were thrust into prison, so many as were to be found.

In the meantime Malinda Porter, Delia F. Pine, Nancy Rigdon, Jonathan W. Barlow, Thoret Parsons, Ezra Chipman, and Arza Judd, Jun., volunteered, and were sworn, on the defense, but were prevented as much as possible by threats from telling the truth. We saw a man at the window by the name of Allen, and beckoned him to come in, and had him sworn, but when he did not testify to please the court, several rushed upon him with their bayonets, and he fled the place; three men took after him with loaded guns, and he barely escaped with his life. It was of no use to get any more witnesses, even if we could have done so.

Thus this mock investigation continued from day to day, till Saturday, when several of the brethren were discharged by Judge King, as follows—

Some Prisoners Discharged.

Defendants against whom nothing is proven, viz., Amasa Lyman, John Buchanan, Andrew Whitlock, Alvah L. Tippets, Jedediah Owens, Isaac Morley, John J. Tanner, Daniel S. Thomas, Elisha Edwards, Benjamin Covey, David Frampton, Henry Zobriskie, Allen J. Stout, Sheffield Daniels, Silas Maynard, Anthony Head, John T. Earl, Ebenezer Brown, James Newberry, Sylvester Hulett, Chandler Holbrook, Martin C. Allred, William Allred. The above defendants have been discharged by me, there being no evidence against them.

AUSTIN A. KING, Judge, etc.

November 24, 1838.

Our Church organization was converted, by the testimony of the apostates, into a temporal kingdom, which was to fill the whole earth, and subdue all other kingdoms.

Misconception of the Church Organization.

The judge, who by the by was a Methodist, asked much concerning our views of the prophecy of Daniel: "In the days of these kings shall the God of heaven set up a kingdom which shall break in pieces all other kingdoms, and stand forever," * * * * "and the kingdom and the greatness of the kingdom, under the whole heaven, shall be given to the Saints of the Most High." As if it were treason to believe the Bible.*

Ashby's Report of Haun's Mills Massacre.

Wednesday, *28.*—Daniel Ashby, a member of the state senate, wrote General Clark that he was in the battle [massacre] at Haun's Mills, that thirty-one "Mormons" were killed, and seven of his party wounded.

Prisoners Discharged and Retained.

The remaining prisoners were all released or admitted to bail, except Lyman Wight, Caleb Baldwin, Hyrum Smith, Alexander McRae, Sidney Rigdon, and myself, who were sent to Liberty, Clay county, to jail, to stand our trial for treason and murder. Our treason consisted of having whipped the mob out of Daviess county, and taking their cannon from them; the murder, of killing the man in the Bogart battle; also Parley P. Pratt, Morris Phelps, Luman Gibbs, Darwin Chase, and Norman Shearer, who were put into Richmond jail to stand their trial for the same "crimes."

Legal Advice to Cease Defense.

During the investigation we were confined in chains and received much abuse. The matter of driving away witnesses or casting them into prison, or chasing them out of the county, was carried to such length that our lawyers, General Doniphan and Amos Rees, told us not to bring our witnesses

* Respecting this inquiry concerning the passage in Daniel's prophecy, Elder Parley P. Pratt writes: "This court of inquisition inquired diligently into our belief of the seventh chapter of Daniel concerning the kingdom of God, which should subdue all other kingdoms and stand forever. And when told that we believed in that prophecy, the court turned to the clerk and said: 'Write that down; it is a strong point for treason.' Our lawyer observed as follows: 'Judge, you had better make the Bible treason.' The court made no reply."—Autobiography of Parley P. Pratt, p. 230.

there at all; for if we did, there would not be one of them left for final trial; for no sooner would Bogart and his men know who they were, than they would put them out of the country.

As to making any impression on King, Doniphan said, if a cohort of angels were to come down, and declare we were innocent, it would all be the same; for he (King) had determined from the beginning to cast us into prison. We never got the privilege of introducing our witnesses at all; if we had, we could have disproved all the evidence of our enemies.

M. Arthur, Esq., to the Representatives from Clay County.

LIBERTY, November 29, 1838.

RESPECTED FRIENDS:—Humanity to an injured people prompts me at present to address you thus: You were aware of the treatment (to some extent before you left home) received by that unfortunate race of beings called the Mormons, from Daviess, in the form of human beings inhabiting Daviess, Livingston, and part of Ray counties; not being satisfied with the relinquishment of all their rights as citizens and human beings, in the treaty forced upon them by General Lucas, by giving up their arms, and throwing themselves upon the mercy of the state, and their fellow citizens generally, hoping thereby protection of their lives and property, they are now receiving treatment from those demons, that makes humanity shudder, and the cold chills run over any man, not entirely destitute of the feelings of humanity. These demons are now constantly strolling up and down Caldwell county, in small companies armed, insulting the women in any way and every way, and plundering the poor devils of all the means of subsistence (scanty as it was) left them, and driving off their horses, cattle, hogs, etc., and rifling their houses and farms of everything therein, taking beds, bedding, wardrobes, and such things as they see they want, leaving the poor Mormons in a starving and naked condition.

These are facts I have from authority that cannot be questioned, and can be maintained and substantiated at any time. There is now a petition afloat in our town, signed by the citizens of all parties and grades, which will be sent you in a few days, praying the legislature to make some speedy enactment applicable to their case. They are entirely willing to leave our state, so soon as this inclement season is over; and a number have already left, and are leaving daily, scattering themselves to the four winds of the earth.

Now, sirs, I do not want by any means to dictate to you the course to be pursued, but one fact I will merely suggest. I this day was conversing with Mr. George M. Pryer, who is just from Far West, relating the outrages there committed daily. I suggested to him the propriety of the legislature's placing a guard to patrol on the lines of Caldwell county, say, of about twenty-five men, and give them, say, about one dollar or one and a half per day, each man, and find their provisions, etc., until, say, the first day of June next; these men rendering that protection necessary to the Mormons, and allowing them to follow and bring to justice any individuals who have heretofore or will hereafter be guilty of plundering or any violation of the laws. I would suggest that George M. Pryer be appointed captain of said guard, and that he be allowed to raise his own men, if he is willing thus to act. He is a man of correct habits, and will do justice to all sides, and render due satisfaction.

Should this course not be approved of, I would recommend the restoration of their [the Mormons'] arms for their own protection. One or the other of these suggestions is certainly due the Mormons from the state. She has now their leaders prisoners, to the number of fifty or sixty, and I apprehend no danger from the remainder in any way until they will leave the state.

M. ARTHUR.

Mr. Arthur is not a "Mormon," but a friend of man.

Attested Copy of the Mittimus under which Joseph Smith, Jun., and Others, were sent from Judge King to the Jailer of Liberty Prison, in Clay County, Missouri.

STATE OF MISSOURI, }
RAY COUNTY. }

To the Keeper of the Jail of Clay County:

GREETING:—Whereas, Joseph Smith, Jun., Hyrum Smith, Lyman Wight, Alexander McRae, and Caleb Baldwin, as also Sidney Rigdon, have been brought before me, Austin A. King, judge of the fifth judicial circuit in the state of Missouri, and charged with the offense of treason against the state of Missouri, and the said defendants, on their examination before me, being held to answer further to said charge, the said Joseph Smith, Jun., Hyrum Smith, Lyman Wight, Alexander McRae, and Caleb Buldwin, to answer in the county of Daviess, and the said Sidney Rigdon to answer further in the county of Caldwell, for said charge of treason, and there being no jail in said counties; these are therefore to command that you receive the said Joseph Smith, Jun., Hyrum Smith, Lyman Wight, Alexander

McRae, Caleb Baldwin, and Sidney Rigdon into your custody in the jail of the said county of Clay, there to remain until they be delivered therefrom by due course of law.

Given under my hand and seal the 29th day of November, 1838.

AUSTIN A. KING.

State of Missouri, County of Clay.

I, Samuel Hadley, sheriff of Clay county, do hereby certify that the above is a true copy of the mittimus to me, directed in the cases therein named.

SAMUEL HADLEY, Jailer.
By SAMUEL TILLERY, Deputy Jailer.

Clay County, Missouri.

Friday, 30.—About this time those of us who had been sentenced thereto, were conveyed to Liberty jail, put in close confinement, and all communication with our friends cut off.

In Liberty Prison.

During our trial William E. McLellin, accompanied by Burr Riggs and others, at times were busy in plundering and robbing the houses of Sidney Rigdon, George Morey, the widow Phebe Ann Patten, and others, under pretense or color of law, on an order from General Clark, as testified to by the members of the different families robbed.*

Course of Wm. E. McLellin and Burr Riggs.

Saturday, December 1, 1838.—A committee on the part

* Further concerning the apostasy and conduct of William E. McLellin, soon after the Prophet and his associates were taken prisoners at Far West, Parley P. Pratt says: "While thus confined, William E. McLellin, once my fellow laborer in the Gospel, but now a Judas, with hostile weapon in hand to destroy the Saints, came to me and observed: 'Well, Parley, you have now got where you are certain never to escape; how do you feel as to the course you have taken in religion?' I answered, that I had taken the course which I should take if I had my life to live over again. He seemed thoughtful for a moment, and then replied: 'Well, I think, if I were you, I should die as I had lived; at any rate, I see no possibility of escape for you and your friends.'"—Autobiography of Parley P. Pratt, p. 206.

While the brethren were imprisoned at Richmond it is said that "McLellin, who was a large and active man, went to the sheriff and asked for the privilege of flogging the Prophet. Permission was granted on condition that Joseph would fight. The sheriff made known to Joseph McLellin's earnest request, to which Joseph consented, if his irons were taken off. McLellin then refused to fight unless he could have a club, to which Joseph was perfectly willing; but the sheriff would not allow them to fight on such unequal terms. McLellin was a man of superficial education, though he had a good flow of language. He adopted the profession of medicine."—Mill. Star, vol, xxxvi: pp. 808, 809.

of the "Mormons" and a like committee on the part of the citizens of Daviess county, met at Adam-ondi-Ahman, on the first of December, 1838, the following propositions by the "Mormon" committee were made and agreed to by the Daviess county committee:

First—That the Mormon committee be allowed to employ, say twenty teamsters for the purpose of hauling off their property.

Second—That the Mormon committee collect whatever stock they may have in Daviess county at some point, and some two or three of the Daviess county committee be notified to attend for the purpose of examining said stock, and convey or attend the Mormon committee out of the limits of the county; and it is further understood, that the Mormon committee is not to drive or take from this county any stock of any description, at any other time, nor under any other circumstances, than these mentioned.

As witness our hands,

William P. Peniston,
Dr. K. Kerr,
Adam Black,
Committee.

The above propositions were made and agreed to by the undersigned committee on the part of the Mormons.

William Huntington,
B. S. Wilbur,
J. H. Hale,
Henry Herriman,
Z. Wilson.

CHAPTER XV.

THE CASE OF THE SAINTS PRESENTED TO THE MISSOURI LEGISLATURE—THE PROPHET'S COMMUNICATION TO THE SAINTS FROM LIBERTY PRISON.

Wednesday, December 5.—The Missouri Legislature having assembled, Governor Boggs laid before the House of Representatives all the information in his possession relative to the difficulties between the mob and the "Mormons."

Report of Governor Boggs to the Legislature.

Monday, December 10.—

Memorial of a Committee to the State Legislature of Missouri in Behalf of the Citizens of Caldwell County.

To the Honorable Legislature of the State of Missouri in Senate and House of Representatives convened:

We, the undersigned petitioners and inhabitants of Caldwell county, Missouri, in consequence of the late calamity that has come upon us taken in connection with former afflictions, feel it a duty we owe to ourselves and our country to lay our case before your honorable body for consideration. It is a well known fact, that a society of our people commenced settling in Jackson county, Missouri, in the summer of 1831, where they, according to their ability, purchased lands, and settled upon them, with the intention and expectation of becoming permanent citizens in common with others.

Soon after the settlement began, persecution commenced; and as the society increased, persecution also increased, until the society at last was compelled to leave the county; and although an account of these persecutions has been published to the world, yet we feel that it will not be improper to notice a few of the most prominent items in this memorial.

On the 20th of July, 1833, a mob convened at Independence—a committee of which called upon a few of the men of our Church there, and stated to them that the store, printing office, and indeed all other mechanic shops must be closed forthwith, and the society leave the county immediately.

These propositions were so unexpected, that a certain time was asked for to consider on the subject, before an answer should be returned, which was refused, and our men being individually interrogated, each one answered that he could not consent to comply with their propositions. One of the mob replied that he was sorry, for the work of destruction would commence immediately.

In a short time the printing-office, which was a two story brick building, was assailed by the mob and soon thrown down, and with it much valuable property destroyed. Next they went to the store for the same purpose; but Mr. Gilbert, one of the owners, agreeing to close it, they abandoned their design. Their next move was the dragging of Bishop Partridge from his house and family to the public square, where, surrounded by hundreds, they partially stripped him of his clothes, and tarred and feathered him from head to foot. A man by the name of Allen was also tarred at the same time. This was Saturday, and the mob agreed to meet the following Tuesday, to accomplish their purpose of driving or massacring the society.

Tuesday came, and the mob came also, bearing with them a red flag in token of blood. Some two or three of the principal men of the society offered their lives, if that would appease the wrath of the mob, so that the rest of the society might dwell in peace upon their lands. The answer was, that unless the society would leave *en masse*, every man should die for himself. Being in a defenseless situation, to save a general massacre, it was agreed that one half of the society should leave the county by the first of the next January, and the remainder by the first of the following April. A treaty was entered into and ratified, and all things went on smoothly for awhile. But sometime in October, the wrath of the mob began again to be kindled, insomuch that they shot at some of our people, whipped others, and threw down their houses, and committed many other depredations; indeed the society of Saints were harassed for some time both day and night; their houses were brick-batted and broken open and women and children insulted. The store-house of A. S. Gilbert and Company was broken open, ransacked, and some of the goods strewed in the streets.

These abuses, with many others of a very aggravated nature, so stirred up the indignant feelings of our people, that when a party of them, say about thirty, met a company of the mob of about double their number, a skirmish took place, in which some two or three of the mob, and one of our people, were killed. This raised, as it were, the whole county in arms, and nothing would satisfy the mob but an im mediate surrender of the arms of our people, who forthwith were to leave the county. Fifty-one guns were given up, which have never been returned, or paid for, to this day. The next day, parties of the mob, from fifty to seventy, headed by priests, went from house to house, threatening women and children with death if they were not gone before they returned. This so alarmed our people that they fled in different directions; some took shelter in the woods, while others wandered in the prairies till their feet bled; and the weather being very cold, their sufferings in other respects were great.

The society made their escape to Clay county as fast as they possibly could, where the people received them kindly, and administered to their wants. After the society had left Jackson county, their buildings, amounting to about two hundred, were either burned or otherwise destroyed, and much of their crops, as well as furniture and stock; which if properly estimated would make a large sum, for the loss of which they have not as yet received any remuneration.

The society remained in Clay county nearly three years; when, at the suggestion of the people there, they removed to that section of the state known as Caldwell county. Here the people bought out most of the former inhabitants, and also entered much of the wild land. Many soon owned a number of eighties [eighty acres] while there was scarcely a man who did not secure to himself at least a forty [forty acres]. Here we were permitted to enjoy peace for a season; but as our society increased in numbers, and settlements were made in Daviess and Carroll counties, the mob spirit spread itself again. For months previous to our giving up our arms to General Lucas' army, we heard little else than rumors of mobs collecting in different places and threatening our people. It is well known that the people of our Church, who had located themselves at De Witt, had to give up to a mob, and leave the place, notwithstanding the militia were called out for their protection.

From De Witt the mob went towards Daviess county, and while on their way there they took two of our men prisoners, and made them ride upon the cannon, and told them that they would drive the "Mormons" from Daviess to Caldwell, and from Caldwell to hell; and that they would give them no quarter, only at the cannon's mouth. The threats of the mob induced some of our people to go to Daviess to help to protect their brethren who had settled at Adam-ondi-Ahman, on Grand river. The mob soon fled from Daviess county; and after they were dispersed and the cannon taken, during which time no blood was shed, the people of Caldwell returned to their homes, in hopes of enjoying peace and quiet; but in this they were disappointed; for a large mob was soon found to be collecting on the Grindstone fork of Grand river from ten to fifteen miles off, under the command of Cornelius Gillium, a scouting party of which came within four miles of Far West, in open daylight, and drove off stock belonging to our people.

About this time, word came to Far West that a party of the mob had come into Caldwell county to the south of Far West; that they were taking horses and cattle, burning houses and ordering the inhabitants to leave their homes immediately; and that they had then actually in their possession three men prisoners. This report reached Far West in the evening, and was confirmed about midnight. A company of about sixty men went forth under the command of David W. Patten to disperse the mob, as they supposed. A battle was the result, in which Captain Patten and three of his men were killed, and others wounded. Bogart, it appears, had but one killed and others wounded. Notwithstanding the unlawful acts committed by Captain Bogart's men previous to the battle, it is now asserted and claimed that he was regularly ordered out as a militia captain, to preserve the peace along the line of Ray and Caldwell counties. The battle was fought four or five days previous to the arrival of General Lucas and his army. About the time of the battle with Captain Bogart, a number of our people who were living near Haun's mill, on Shoal creek, about twenty miles below Far West, together with a number of emigrants who had been stopped there in consequence of the excitement, made an agreement with the mob in that vicinity that neither party should molest the other, but dwell in peace. Shortly after this agreement was made, a mob party of from two to three hundred, many of whom are supposed to be from Chariton county, some from Daviess, and also those who had agreed to dwell in peace, came upon our people there, whose number in men was about forty, at a time they little expected any such thing, and without any ceremony, notwithstanding they begged for quarter, shot them down as they would tigers or panthers. Some few made their escape by fleeing. Eighteen were killed and a number more were severely wounded.

This tragedy was conducted in the most brutal and savage manner. An old man [Father Thomas McBride] after the massacre was partially over, threw himself into their hands and begged for quarter, when he was instantly shot down; that not killing him. they took an old corn cutter and literally mangled him to pieces.* A lad of ten years of age, after being shot down, also begged to be spared, when one of the mob placed the muzzle of his gun to the boy's head and blew out his brains.

* This barbarous deed is vividly described by President John Taylor in his controversy with Mr. Schuyler Colfax, Vice-President of the United States, 1870: "My mind wanders back upwards of thirty years ago, when, in the state of Missouri, Mr. McBride, an old, grey-haired, venerable veteran of the Revolution, with

The slaughter of these not satisfying the mob, they then proceeded to rob and plunder. The scene that presented itself after the massacre, to the widows and orphans of the killed, is beyond description. It was truly a time of weeping, mourning and lamentation.

As yet we have not heard of any one being arrested for these murders, notwithstanding there are men boasting about the country that they did kill on that occasion more than one "Mormon;" whereas all our people who were in the battle with Captain Patten against Bogart, that can be found, have been arrested, and are now confined in jail to await their trial for murder.

When General Lucas arrived near Far West, and presented the Governor's order, we were greatly surprised; yet we felt willing to submit to the authorities of the state. We gave up our arms without reluctance. We were then made prisoners, and confined to the limits of the town for about a week, during which time the men from the country were not permitted to go to their families, many of whom were in a suffering condition for want of food and firewood, the weather being very cold and stormy.

Much property was destroyed by the troops in town during their stay there, such as burning house logs, rails, corn-cribs, boards; the using of corn and hay, the plundering of houses, the killing of cattle, sheep and hogs, and also the taking of horses not their own; and all this without regard to owners, or asking leave of any one. In the meantime men were abused, women insulted and abused by the troops; and all this while we were kept prisoners.

Whilst the town was guarded, we were called together by the order of General Lucas, and a guard placed close around us, and in that situation we were compelled to sign a deed of trust for the purpose of making our individual property, all holden, as they said, to pay all the debts of every individual belonging to the Church, and also to pay for all damages the old inhabitants of Daviess may have sustained in consequence of the late difficulties in that county.

General Clark had now arrived, and the first important move made by him was the collecting of our men together on the square and selecting about fifty of them, whom he immediately marched into a house, and placed in close confinement. This was done without the aid of the

feeble frame and tottering steps, cried to a Missouri patriot: 'Spare my life, I am a Revolutionary soldier, I fought for liberty. Would you murder me? What is my offense, I believe in God and revelation?' This frenzied disciple of misplaced faith said: 'Take that, you —— —— Mormon,' and with the butt of his gun he dashed his brains out, and he lay quivering there,—his white locks clotted with his own brains and gore, on that soil that he had heretofore shed his blood to redeem—a sacrifice at the shrine of liberty! Shades of Franklin, Jefferson and Washington, were you there? Did you gaze on this deed of blood? Did you see your companion in arms thus massacred?"

sheriff, or any legal process. The next day forty-six of those taken, were driven off to Richmond, like a parcel of menial slaves, not knowing why they were taken, or what they were taken for. After being confined in Richmond more than two weeks, about one half were liberated; the rest, after another week's confinement, were required to appear at court, and have since been let to bail. Since General Clark withdrew his troops from Far West, parties of armed men have gone through the country, driving off horses, sheep and cattle, and also plundering houses; the barbarity of General Lucas' troops ought not to be passed over in silence. They shot our cattle and hogs merely for the sake of destroying them, leaving them for the ravens to eat. They took prisoner an aged man by the name of John Tanner, and without any reason for it, he was struck over the head with a gun, which laid his skull bare. Another man by the name of Carey was also taken prisoner by them, and without any provocation had his brains dashed out by a gun. He was laid in a wagon and there permitted to remain for the space of twenty-four hours; during which time no one was permitted to administer to him comfort or consolation; and after he was removed from that situation, he lived but a few hours.

The destruction of property at and about Far West is very great. Many are stripped bare, as it were, and others partially so; indeed take us as a body at this time, we are a poor and afflicted people; and if we are compelled to leave the state in the Spring, many, yes a large portion of our society, will have to be removed at the expense of the state; as those who might have helped them are now debarred that privilege in consequence of the deed of trust we were compelled to sign; which deed so operated upon our real estate, that it will sell for but little or nothing at this time.

We have now made a brief statement of some of the most prominent features of the troubles that have befallen our people since our first settlement in this state; and we believe that these persecutions have come in consequence of our religious faith, and not for any immorality on our part. That instances have been, of late, where individuals have trespassed upon the rights of others, and thereby broken the laws of the land, we will not pretend to deny; but yet we do believe that no crime can be substantiated against any of the people who have a standing in our Church of an earlier date than the difficulties in Daviess county. And when it is considered that the rights of this people have been trampled upon from time to time with impunity, and abuses almost innumerable heaped upon them it ought in some degree to palliate for any infraction of the law which may have been made on the part of our people.

The late order of Governor Boggs to drive us from the state, or exterminate us, is a thing so novel, unlawful, tyrannical, and oppressive, that we have been induced to draw up this memorial, and present this statement of our case to your honorable body, praying that a law may be passed, rescinding the order of the governor to drive us from the state, and also giving us the sanction of the legislature to possess our lands in peace. We ask an expression of the legislature, disapproving the conduct of those who compelled us to sign a deed of trust, and also disapproving of any man or set of men taking our property in consequence of that deed of trust, and appropriating it to the payment of debts not contracted by us or for the payment of damages sustained in consequence of trespasses committed by others.

We have no common stock; our property is individual property, and we feel willing to pay our debts as other individuals do; but we are not willing to be bound for other people's debts. The arms which were taken from us here, which we understand to be about six hundred and thirty, besides swords and pistols, we care not so much about, as we do the pay for them; only we are bound to do military duty, which we are willing to do, and which we think was sufficiently manifested by the raising of a volunteer company last fall at Far West when called upon by General Parks to raise troops for the frontier.

The arms given up by us, we consider were worth between twelve and fifteen thousand dollars; but we understand they have been greatly damaged since taken, and at this time probably would not bring near their former value. And as they were, both here and in Jackson county, taken by the militia, and consequently by the authority of the state, we therefore ask your honorable body to cause an appropriation to be made by law, whereby we may be paid for them, or otherwise have them returned to us, and the damages made good.

The losses sustained by our people in leaving Jackson county are such that it is impossible to obtain any compensation for them by law, because those who have sustained them are unable to prove those trespasses upon individuals. That the facts do exist that the buildings, crops, stock, furniture, rails, timber, etc., of the society have been destroyed in Jackson county, is not doubted by those who are acquainted in this upper country [the part of the state north of the Missouri river was so called]; and since these trespasses cannot be proven upon individuals, we ask your honorable body to consider this case; and if in your liberality and wisdom you can conceive it to be proper to make an appropriation by law to these sufferers, many of whom are still pressed down with poverty in consequence of their losses, they would be able to pay their debts, and also in some degree be relieved from poverty and woe; whilst the widow's heart would be made to rejoice, and the orphan's tear measurably dried up, and the prayers of a grateful people ascend on high, with thanksgiving and praise to the Author of our existence for such beneficent act.

In laying our case before your honorable body, we say that we are willing, and ever have been, to conform to the Constitution and laws of the United States, and of this state. We ask, in common with others, the protection of the laws. We ask for the privilege guaranteed to all free citizens of the United States, and of this state, to be extended to us that we may be permitted to settle and live where we please, and worship God according to the dictates of our conscience without molestation. And while we ask for ourselves this privilege, we are willing all others should enjoy the same.

We now lay our case at the feet of you legislators, and ask your honorable body to consider it, and do for us, after mature deliberation, that which your wisdom, patriotism and philanthropy may dictate. And we, as in duty bound, will ever pray.

EDWARD PARTRIDGE,
HEBER C. KIMBALL,
JOHN TAYLOR,
THEODORE TURLEY,
BRIGHAM YOUNG,
ISAAC MORLEY,
GEORGE W. HARRIS,
JOHN MURDOCK,
JOHN M. BURK.

A committee appointed by the citizens of Caldwell county, to draft the memorial and sign it in their behalf.

Far West, Caldwell county, Missouri, December 10, 1838.

Minutes of a High Council Held at Far West, Thursday, December 13, 1838.

Agreeable to appointment, the standing High Council met, when it was found that several were absent, who, (some of them) have had to flee for their lives; therefore it being necessary that those vacancies be filled, the meeting was called for that purpose, and also to express each other's feelings respecting the word of the Lord; President Brigham Young presiding.

The council was opened by prayer by Elder Kimball. After prayer, President Young made a few remarks, saying he thought it all important to have the Council reorganized, and prepared to do business. He advised the councilors to be wise and judicious in all their movements, and not hasty in their transactions. As for his faith, it was the same as ever; and he fellowshiped all such as loved the Gospel of our Lord and Savior Jesus Christ, in act as well as word.

Elder Kimball arose and said he felt as formerly, for he had endeavored to keep a straightforward course; but wherein he had been out of the way in any manner, he meant to mend in that thing; and he was determined, as far as possible, to do as he would be done by; and his faith was as good as ever; he was in fellowship with all who wanted to do right.

Simeon Carter said, as to his faith in the work it was the same as ever; he did not think that Joseph was a fallen Prophet, but he believed in every revelation that had come through him; still he thought that perhaps Joseph had not acted in all things according to the best wisdom; yet how far he had been unwise he could not say. He did not think that Joseph would be removed and another planted in his stead; but he believed that he would still perform his work. He was still determined to persevere and act in righteousness in all things, so that he might at last gain a crown of glory, and reign in the kingdom of God.

Jared Carter, responded to President Brigham Young's feelings, and wished all to walk with the brethren.

Thomas Grover said he was firm in the faith, and he believed the time would come when Joseph would stand before kings, and speak marvelous words.

David Dort expressed his feelings in a similar manner.

Levi Jackman says his faith is the same as ever, and he has confidence in Brother Joseph, as ever.

Solomon Hancock says he is a firm believer in the Book of Mormon and Doctrine and Covenants, and that Brother Joseph is not a fallen prophet, but will yet be exalted and become very high.

John Badger says his confidence in the work is the same as ever, and his faith, if possible, is stronger than ever. He believes that it was necessary that these scourges should come.

George W. Harris says that, as it respects the scourges which have come upon us, the hand of God was in it.

Samuel Bent says that his faith is as it ever was, and that he feels to praise God in prisons and in dungeons, and in all circumstances.

After some consultation it was thought expedient to nominate High Priests to fill the vacancies.

The Council was organized as follows: Simeon Carter, No. 1; Jared Carter, 2; Thomas Grover 3; David Dort, 4; Levi Jackman, 5; Solomon Hancock, 6; John Badger, 7; John Murdock, 8; John E. Page, 9; George W. Harris, 10; John Taylor, 11; Samuel Bent, 12.

Voted that John Murdock fill the vacancy of John P. Greene, No. 4, and David Dort the place of Elias Higbee, No. 11, and John Badger the place of George Morey, No. 7, and Lyman Sherman the place of Newel Knight, until he returns.

Council adjourned until Friday evening, six o'clock. Closed by prayer by President Brigham Young.

E. ROBINSON, Clerk.

Isaac Russell, who had become connected with a small camp of the Saints, of about thirty families, going west, turned from his course at Louisiana, and led them north ten miles on the Spanish claims, where they built huts or lived in tents through the winter in great suffering. Russell turned prophet (apostate). He said Joseph had fallen and he was appointed to lead the people.

Chandler Rogers, who was moving west, was met by a mob at Huntsville, and compelled to turn back, and fell in with Russell's camp. Russell said he was "the chosen of the Lord;" and when they left the place, they would have to go on foot, and take nothing with them, and they must sell their teams. Some would not sell and he cursed them.

Sunday, December 16.—I wrote the following letter:

The Prophet's Letter to the Church.

LIBERTY JAIL, MISSOURI,
December 16, 1838.

To the Church of Jesus Christ of Latter-day Saints in Caldwell county, and all the Saints who are scattered abroad, who are persecuted, and made desolate, and who are afflicted in divers manners for Christ's sake and the Gospel's, by the hands of a cruel mob and the tyrannical disposition of the authorities of this state; and whose perils are greatly augmented by the wickedness and corruption of false brethren, greeting:

May grace, mercy, and the peace of God be and abide with you; and notwithstanding all your sufferings, we assure you that you have our prayers and fervent desires for your welfare, day and night. We believe that that God who seeth us in this solitary place, will hear our prayers, and reward you openly.

Know assuredly, dear brethren, that it is for the testimony of Jesus that we are in bonds and in prison. But we say unto you, that we consider that our condition is better (notwithstanding our sufferings) than that of those who have persecuted us, and smitten us, and borne false witness against us; and we most assuredly believe that those who do bear false witness against us, do seem to have a great triumph over us for the present. But we want you to remember Haman and Mordecai: you know that Haman could not be satisfied so long as he saw Mordecai at the king's gate, and he sought the life of Mordecai and the destruction of the people of the Jews. But the Lord so ordered it, that Haman was hanged upon his own gallows.

So shall it come to pass with poor Haman in the last days, and those who have sought by unbelief and wickedness and by the principle of mobocracy to destroy us and the people of God, by killing and scattering them abroad, and wilfully and maliciously delivering us into the hands of murderers, desiring us to be put to death, thereby having us dragged about in chains and cast into prison. And for what cause? It is because we were honest men, and were determined to defend the lives of the Saints at the expense of our own. I say unto you, that those who have thus vilely treated us, like Haman, shall be hanged upon their own gallows; or, in other words, shall fall into their own gin, and snare, and ditch, and trap, which they have prepared for us, and shall go backwards and stumble and fall, and their name shall be blotted out, and God shall reward them according to all their abominations.

Dear brethren, do not think that our hearts faint, as though some strange thing had happened unto us, for we have seen and been assured of all these things beforehand, and have an assurance of a better hope than that of our persecutors. Therefore God hath made broad our shoulders for the burden. We glory in our tribulation, because we know that God is with us, that He is our friend, and that He will save our souls. We do not care for them that can kill the body; they cannot harm our souls. We ask no favors at the hands of mobs, nor of the world, nor of the devil, nor of his emissaries the dissenters, and those who love, and make, and swear falsehoods, to take away our lives. We have never dissembled, nor will we for the sake of our lives.

Forasmuch, then, as we know that we have been endeavoring with all our mind, might, and strength, to do the will of God, and all things whatsoever He has commanded us; and as to our light speeches, which may have escaped our lips from time to time, they have nothing to do with the fixed purposes of our hearts; therefore it sufficeth us to say, that our souls were vexed from day to day. We refer you to Isaiah, who considers those who make a man an offender for a word, and lay a snare for him that reproveth in the gate. We believe that the old Prophet verily told the truth: and we have no retraction to make. We have reproved in the gate, and men have laid snares for us. We have spoken words, and men have made us offenders. And notwithstanding all this, our minds are not yet darkened, but feel strong in the

Lord. But behold the words of the Savior: "If the light which is in you become darkness, behold how great is that darkness." Look at the dissenters. Again, "If you were of the world the world would love its own." Look at Mr. Hinkle—a wolf in sheep's clothing. Look at his brother John Corrill. Look at the beloved brother Reed Peck, who aided him in leading us, as the Savior was led, into the camp of His enemies, as a lamb prepared for the slaughter, as a sheep dumb before his shearers; so we opened not our mouths.

But these men, like Balaam, being greedy for reward, sold us into the hands of those who loved them, for the world loves his own. I would remember William E. McLellin, who comes up to us as one of Job's comforters. God suffered such kind of beings to afflict Job—but it never entered into their hearts that Job would get out of it all. This poor man who professes to be much of a prophet, has no other dumb ass to ride but David Whitmer,* to forbid his madness when he goes up to curse Israel; and this ass not being of the same kind as Balaam's, therefore, the angel notwithstanding appeared unto him, yet he could not penetrate his understanding sufficiently, but that he brays out cursings instead of blessings. Poor ass! Whoever lives to see it, will see him and his rider perish like those who perished in the gainsaying of Korah, or after the same condemnation. Now as for these and the rest of their company, we will not presume to say that the world loves them; but we presume to say they love the world, and we classify them in the error of Balaam, and in the gain-sayings of Korah, and with the company of Korah, Dathan, and Abiram.

Perhaps our brethren will say, because we thus write, that we are offended at these characters. If we are, it is not for a word, neither because they reproved in the gate—but because they have been the means of shedding innocent blood. Are they not murderers then at heart? Are not their consciences seared as with a hot iron? We confess that we are offended; but the Savior said, "It must needs be that offenses come, but woe unto them by whom they come." And again, "Blessed are ye when men shall revile you, and persecute you, and shall say all manner of evil against you falsely for my sake; rejoice and be exceeding glad, for great is your reward in heaven, for so persecuted they the Prophets which were before you."

Now, dear brethren, if any men ever had reason to claim this promise, we are the men; for we know that the world not only hate us,

* In order to appreciate the allusions here made to David Whitmer it will be necessary to remember that William E. M'Lellin claimed that President Joseph Smith was a fallen prophet and himself sought to bring into existence a re-organized church with David Whitmer as the president thereof. See foot note in this volume at pages 31, 32.

but they speak all manner of evil of us falsely, for no other reason than that we have been endeavoring to teach the fullness of the Gospel of Jesus Christ.

After we were bartered away by Hinkle, and were taken into the militia camp, we had all the evidence we could have asked for that the world hated us. If there were priests among them of all the different sects, they hated us, and that most cordially too. If there were generals, they hated us; if there were colonels, they hated us; and the soldiers, and officers of every kind, hated us; and the most profane, blasphemous, and drunkards; and whoremongers, hated us—they all hated us, most cordially. And now what did they hate us for? Purely because of the testimony of Jesus Christ. Was it because we were liars? We know that it has been so reported by some, but it has been reported falsely. Was it because we have committed treason against the government in Daviess county, or burglary, or larceny, or arson, or any other unlawful act in Daviess county? We know that we have been so reported by priests, and certain lawyers, and certain judges, who are the instigators, aiders, and abettors of a certain gang of murderers and robbers, who have been carrying on a scheme of mobocracy to uphold their priestcraft, against the Saints of the last days; and for a number of years have tried, by a well contemplated and premeditated scheme, to put down by physical power a system of religion that all the world, by their mutual attainments, and by any fair means whatever, were not able to resist.

Hence mobbers were encouraged by priests and Levites, by the Pharisees, by the Sadducees, and Essenes, and Herodians, and the most worthless, abandoned, and debauched, lawless, and inhuman, and the most beastly set of men that the earth can boast of—and indeed a parallel cannot be found anywhere else—to gather together to steal, to plunder, to starve, and to exterminate, and burn the houses of the "Mormons."

These are characters that, by their treasonable and overt acts, have desolated and laid waste Daviess county. These are the characters that would fain make all the world believe that we are guilty of the above named acts. But they represent us falsely; we stood in our own defense, and we believe that no man of us acted only in a just, a lawful, and a righteous retaliation against such marauders.

We say unto you, that we have not committed treason, nor any other unlawful act in Daviess county. Was it for murder in Ray county, against mob-militia; who was as a wolf in the first instance, hide and hair, teeth, legs and tail, who afterwards put on a militia sheep skin with the wool on; who could sally forth, in the day time, into the flock, and snarl, and show his teeth, and scatter and devour the flock, and satiate himself upon his prey, and then sneak back into the bramble in order that he might conceal himself in his well tried skin with the wool on?

We are well aware that there is a certain set of priests and satellites, and mobbers that would fain make all the world believe that we were guilty of the doings of this howling wolf that made such havoc among the sheep, who, when he retreated, howled and bleated at such a desperate rate, that if one could have been there, he would have thought that all the wolves, whether wrapped up in sheep skins or in goat skins, or in some other skins, and in fine all the beasts of the forest, were awfully alarmed, and catching the scent of innocent blood, they sallied forth with one tremendous howl and crying of all sorts; and such a howling, and such a tremendous havoc never was known before; such inhumanity, and relentless cruelty and barbarity as were practiced against the Saints in Missouri can scarcely be found in the annals of history.

Now those characters if allowed to would make the world believe that we had committed murder, by making an attack upon this howling wolf, while the fact is we were at home and in our bed, and asleep, and knew nothing of that transaction any more than we know what is going on in China while we are within these walls. Therefore we say again unto you, we are innocent of these things, and they have represented us falsely.

Was it for committing adultery that we were assailed? We are aware that that false slander has gone abroad, for it has been reiterated in our ears. These are falsehoods also. Renegade "Mormon" dissenters are running through the world and spreading various foul and libelous reports against us, thinking thereby to gain the friendship of the world, because they know that we are not of the world, and that the world hates us; therefore they [the world] make a tool of these fellows [the dissenters]; and by them try to do all the injury they can, and after that they hate them worse than they do us, because they find them to be base traitors and sycophants.

Such characters God hates; we cannot love them. The world hates them, and we sometimes think that the devil ought to be ashamed of them.

We have heard that it is reported by some, that some of us should have said, that we not only dedicated our property, but our families also to the Lord; and Satan, taking advantage of this, has perverted it into licentiousness, such as a community of wives, which is an abomination in the sight of God.

When we consecrate our property to the Lord it is to administer to the wants of the poor and needy, for this is the law of God; it is not for the benefit of the rich, those who have no need; and when a man consecrates or dedicates his wife and children, he does not give them to his brother, or to his neighbor, for there is no such law: for the law of God is, Thou shalt not commit adultery. Thou shalt not covet thy neighbor's wife. He that looketh upon a woman to lust after her, has committed adultery already in his heart. Now for a man to consecrate his property, wife and children, to the Lord, is nothing more nor less than to feed the hungry, clothe the naked, visit the widow and fatherless, the sick and afflicted, and do all he can to administer to their relief in their afflictions, and for him and his house to serve the Lord. In order to do this, he and all his house must be virtuous, and must shun the very appearance of evil.

Now if any person has represented anything otherwise than what we now write, he or she is a liar, and has represented us falsely—and this is another manner of evil which is spoken against us falsely.

We have learned also since we have been prisoners, that many false and pernicious things, which were calculated to lead the Saints far astray and to do great injury, have been taught by Dr. Avard as coming from the Presidency, and we have reason to fear that many other designing and corrupt characters like unto himself, have been teaching many things which the Presidency never knew were being taught in the Church by anybody until after they were made prisoners. Had they known of such things they would have spurned them and their authors as they would the gates of hell. Thus we find that there have been frauds and secret abominations and evil works of darkness going on, leading the minds of the weak and unwary into confusion and distraction, and all the time palming it off upon the Presidency, while the Presidency were ignorant as well as innocent of those things which those persons were practicing in the Church in their name. Meantime the Presidency were attending to their own secular and family concerns, weighed down with sorrow, in debt, in poverty, in hunger, essaying to be fed, yet finding [*i. e.* supporting] themselves. They occasionally received deeds of charity, it is true; but these were inadequate to their subsistence; and because they received those deeds, they were envied and hated by those who professed to be their friends.

But notwithstanding we thus speak, we honor the Church, when we speak of the Church as a Church, for their liberality, kindness, patience, and long suffering, and their continual kindness towards us.

And now, brethren, we say unto you—what more can we enumerate? Is not all manner of evil of every description spoken of us falsely, yea, we say unto you falsely. We have been misrepresented and misunderstood, and belied, and the purity and integrity and uprightness of our hearts have not been known—and it is through ignorance—yea, the very depths of ignorance is the cause of it; and not only ignorance, but on the part of some, gross wickedness and hypocrisy also; for some, by a long face and sanctimonious prayers, and very pious sermons, had power to lead the minds of the ignorant and unwary, and thereby obtain such influence that when we approached their iniquities the devil gained great advantage—would bring great trouble and sorrow upon our heads; and, in fine, we have waded through an ocean of tribulation and mean abuse, practiced upon us by the ill bred and the ignorant, such as Hinkle, Corrill, Phelps, Avard, Reed Peck, Cleminson, and various others, who are so very ignorant that they cannot appear respectable in any decent and civilized society, and whose eyes are full of adultery, and cannot cease from sin. Such characters as McLellin, John Whitmer, David Whitmer, Oliver Cowdery, and Martin Harris, are too mean to mention; and we had liked to have forgotten them. Marsh and "another," whose hearts are full of corruption, whose cloak of hypocrisy was not sufficient to shield them or to hold them up in the hour of trouble, who after having escaped the pollutions of the world through the knowledge of their Lord and Savior Jesus Christ, became again entangled and overcome—their latter end is worse than the first. But it has happened unto them according to the word of the Scripture: "The dog has returned to his vomit, and the sow that was washed to her wallowing in the mire."

Again, if men sin wilfully after they have received the knowledge of the truth, there remaineth no more sacrifice for sin, but a certain fearful looking for of judgment and fiery indignation to come, which shall devour these adversaries. For he who despised Moses' law died without mercy under two or three witnesses. Of how much more severe punishment suppose ye, shall he be thought worthy, who hath sold his brother, and denied the new and everlasting covenant by which he was sanctified, calling it an unholy thing, and doing despite to the Spirit of grace.

And again we say unto you, that inasmuch as there is virtue in us, and the Holy Priesthood has been conferred upon us—and the keys of the kingdom have not been taken from us, for verily thus saith the Lord, "Be of good cheer, for the keys that I gave unto you are yet with you"—therefore we say unto you, dear brethren, in the name of the Lord Jesus Christ, we deliver these characters unto the buffetings of Satan until the day of redemption, that they may be dealt with according to their works; and from henceforth their works shall be made manifest.

And now dear and well beloved brethren—and when we say brethren, we mean those who have continued faithful in Christ, men, women and children—we feel to exhort you in the name of the Lord Jesus, to be strong in the faith in the new and everlasting covenant, and nothing frightened at your enemies. For what has happened unto us is an evident token to them of damnation; but unto us, of salvation, and that of God. Therefore hold on even unto death; for "he that seeks to save his life shall lose it; and he that loses his life for my sake, and the Gospel's, shall find it," saith Jesus Christ.

Brethren, from henceforth, let truth and righteousness prevail and abound in you; and in all things be temperate; abstain from drunkenness, and from swearing, and from all profane language, and from everything which is unrighteous or unholy; also from enmity, and hatred, and covetousness, and from every unholy desire. Be honest one with another, for it seems that some have come short of these things, and some have been uncharitable, and have manifested greediness because of their debts towards those who have been persecuted and dragged about with chains without cause, and imprisoned. Such characters God hates—and they shall have their turn of sorrow in the rolling of the great wheel, for it rolleth and none can hinder. Zion shall yet live, though she seem to be dead.

Remember that whatsoever measure you mete out to others, it shall be measured to you again. We say unto you, brethren, be not afraid of your adversaries; contend earnestly against mobs, and the unlawful works of dissenters and of darkness.

And the very God of peace shall be with you, and make a way for your escape from the adversary of your souls. We commend you to God and the word of His grace, which is able to make us wise unto salvation. Amen.

JOSEPH SMITH, JUN.

CHAPTER XVI.

CASE OF THE "MORMONS" BEFORE THE MISSOURI LEGISLATURE—CLOSE OF THE YEAR 1838.

THIS day [16th December] Elder David H. Redfield arrived in Jefferson City, and on Monday, 17th, presented the petition of the brethren to General David R. Atchison and others, who were very anxious to hear from Caldwell, as there were many reports in circulation, such as "the Mormons kept up the Danite system," "were going to build the Lord's house," and "more blood would be spilled before they left the state," which created a hardness in the minds of the people.

Varied Reports as to the Intentions of the Saints.

In the afternoon Brother Redfield had an interview with Governor Boggs, who inquired about our people and property with as much apparent interest as though his whole soul was engaged for our welfare; and said that he had heard that "the citizens were committing depredations on the 'Mormons,' and driving off their stock."

Interview Beween David H. Redfield and Governor Boggs.

Brother Redfield informed him that armed forces came in the place and abused men, women and children, stole horses, drove off cattle, and plundered houses of everything that pleased their fancy.

Governor Boggs said that he would write Judge King and Colonel Price, to go to Far West, and put down every hostile appearance. He also stated that "the stipulations entered into by the 'Mormons' to leave the state, and to sign the deed of trust, were unconstitutional, and not valid."

Brother Redfield replied, "We want the legislature to pass a law to that effect, showing that the stipulations and deeds of trust are not valid and are unconstitutional; and unless you do pass such a law, we shall not consider ourselves safe in the state. You say there has been a stain upon the character of the state, and now is the time to pass some law to that effect; and unless you do, farewell to the virtue of the state; farewell to her honor and good name; farewell to her Christian virtue, until she shall be peopled by a different race of men; farewell to every name that binds man to man; farewell to a fine soil and a glorious home; they are gone, they are rent from us by a lawless banditti."

Tuesday, December 18.—Mr. Turner, from the joint committee on the "Mormon" investigation, submitted a report, preamble and resolutions, as follows:

*The Turner Committee Report to the Missouri Legislature,**

In Senate, Tuesday, December 18, 1838.

Mr. Turner, from the joint committee on the Mormon investigation, submitted the following report, preamble and resolutions:

The joint committee to whom was referred so much of the governor's message as relates to the recent difficulties between the people called Mormons, and a part of the people of this state, with instructions to inquire into the causes of said disturbances, and the conduct of the military operations in suppressing them, have taken the same under consideration, and would respectfully submit the following report and resolutions:

They have thought it unwise and injudicious under all the existing circumstances of this case, to predicate a report upon the papers, documents, etc., purporting to be copies of the evidence taken before an examining court, held in Richmond, in Ray county, for the purpose of inquiring into the charges alleged against the people called Mormons, growing out of the late difficulties between that people and other citizens of this state.

They consider the evidence adduced in the examination there held, in a great degree, *exparte*, and not of the character which should be desired for the basis of a fair and candid investigation. Moreover, the papers, documents, etc., have not been certified in such manner as to satisfy the committee of their authenticity.

* In the previous publication of this history only part of this report is given, but here the whole document is inserted.

It has been represented to them that the examining court has sent on for further trial, many of that class of citizens called Mormons, charged with various crimes and offenses; under the charge of treason, six; for murder and as accessories thereto, before and after the fact, eight; and for other felonies, twenty-seven. Special terms of the circuit court are expected to be held in the several counties, in which the above mentioned crimes are represented to have been committed. Grand juries will then have these charges against said people before them, and must act upon the same documentary evidence which the committee would necessarily be compelled to examine, by which circumstance two co-ordinate branches of this government may be brought into collision—a contingency that should be studiously avoided and cautiously guarded against.

Another insuperable objection that has presented itself to the mind of the committee, and which would induce them to suspend an investigation, under present and existing circumstances, would be the consequences likely to result from a publication of their report. Those persons who have been sent on for further trial, have guaranteed to them the sacred and constitutional right of "a speedy trial by an impartial jury of the vicinage," and if the guilt of the accused should be confirmed by the report of the committee, it would so prejudice public sentiment against them, as to deprive them of that right, which should not be taken away by any consideration involved in this inquiry.

If the committee were to find it necessary in the prosecution of their object, to have access to the papers, documents, etc., connected with this difficulty, the probable interference of the several courts being in session, might seriously interrupt their views. It might reasonably be expected that all the evidence of every description, would be in the possession of the courts, to be used on the final trial, and by that means the investigation would be protracted to a much greater length than would be necessary under different circumstances. They would therefore recommend, in order to avoid all the difficulties that have been presented, that a committee, after the adjournment of the general assembly, go into the vicinity of the scene of difficulties, and make their investigation, and report at such time, and in such manner, as the legislature may direct. If this course should be adopted, the committee believe that the session would be much shortened, and heavy expenses saved to the state, which otherwise would necessarily be incurred in sending for witnesses, and bringing them from so great a distance. By a resolution of both houses, the special message of the governor in relation to the subject of inquiry, with the accompanying documents, was referred to the committee, with instructions to select such documents as in their opinion ought to be published with the message, and report to their respective houses. The committee after a full consideration of the subject, with due regard to its importance, are of opinion that it is inexpedient at this time, to publish any of the documents, under the authority of the general assembly, and submit to the two houses the leading reasons for that opinion.

The documents may be divided into several classes:

First—The affidavits and correspondence preceding each series of authorized military operations.

Second—The orders issued upon such evidence.

Third—The military operations and correspondence consequent thereon; and

Fourth—The evidence taken before a court of inquiry, held for the investigation of criminal charges against individuals.

It was found by the joint committee, at an early period after their organization, that, in order to a full and satisfactory investigation of the subjects referred to them, a mass of additional testimony, oral and written, would be required. This becomes apparent to the committee, from the contents of the documents referred to them. These documents, although they are serviceable in giving direction to the courts of inquiry, are none of them, except the official orders and correspondence, such as ought to be received as conclusive evidence of the facts stated; nor are their contents such as would, without the aid of further evidence, enable the committee to form a satisfactory opinion in relation to the material points of the inquiry.

The copy of the examination taken before the criminal court of inquiry, is manifestly not such evidence as ought to be received by the committec:

First—Because it is not authenticated; and

Second—It is confined chiefly to the object of that inquiry; namely: the investigation of criminal charges against individuals under arrest; for these reasons, but above all, for the reason that it would be a direct interference with the administration of justice, this document ought not to be published, with the sanction of the legislature.

The committee conclude, that it would not be proper to publish the official orders and correspondence between the officers in command, and the executive, without the evidence on which they were founded; and that evidence is not sufficiently full and satisfactory to authorize its publication. To publish the whole together might tend to give a direction to the public mind, prejudicial to an impartial administration of justice in pending cases, while it will not afford the means of forming any satisfactory conclusion as to the cause of the late disturbances, or the conduct of the military operations in suppressing them.

The committee therefore recommend to each house to adopt the following resolutions:

Resolved, That it is inexpedient at this time, to prosecute further the inquiry into the causes of the late disturbances and the conduct of the military operations in suppressing them.

Resolved, That it is inexpedient to publish at this time, any of the documents accompanying the governor's message in relation to the late disturbances.

Resolved, That it is expedient to appoint a joint committee, composed of ——— senators, and ——— representatives, to investigate the cause of said disturbances, and the conduct of the military operations in suppressing them, to meet at such time, and to be invested with such powers as may be prescribed by law.*

Wednesday, December 19.—Mr. John Corrill presented the petition† to the house. While it was reading the members were silent as the house of death; after which the debate commenced, and excitement increased till the house was in an uproar; their faces turned red; their eyes flashed fire, and their countenances spoke volumes.

The Debate on the Petition.

Mr. Childs, of Jackson county, said, there was not one word of truth in it, so far as he had heard, and that it ought never to have been presented to that body. Not long ago we appropriated two thousand dollars to their relief, and now they have petitioned for the pay for their lands, which we took away from them. We got rid of a great evil when we drove them from Jackson county, and we have had peace there ever since; and the state will always be in difficulty so long as they suffer them to live in the state; and the

* The above report is taken from a book containing the documents, the correspondence, orders, etc., in relation to the disturbances with the "Mormons;" and the evidence given before the Hon. Austin A. King, judge of the Fifth Judicial Circuit of the state of Missouri, at the courthouse in Richmond, in a criminal court of inquiry, begun November 12, 1838, on the trial of Joseph Smith, Jun., and others, for high treason and other crimes against the state, pp. 1-4. The book is published by order of the general assembly.

† This was the petition of the 10th of December, signed by Edward Partridge, Heber C. Kimball, John Taylor *et al.* in behalf of the citizens of Caldwell county, which petition appears in chapter xv. of this volume. Subsequently, viz., in 1841, when the Missouri legislature published, by order of the general assembly, what is alleged to be the documents in relation to the disturbances with the "Mormons," etc., neither this document nor any account of the debate which followed its introduction, as here referred to appears.

quicker they get that petition from before this body the better.

Mr. Ashley, from Livingston, said the petition was false from beginning to end, and that himself and the "Mormons" could not live together, for he would always be found fighting against them, and one or the other must leave the state. He gave a history of the Haun's Mill massacre, and said he saw Jack Rogers cut up McBride with a corn-cutter.

Mr. Corrill corrected Mr. Childs, and stated facts in the petition which he was acquainted with, and that Mr. Childs ought to know that there could not be the first crime established against the "Mormons" while in Jackson county.

One member hoped the matter would not be looked over in silence, for his constituents required of him to know the cause of the late disturbances.

Mr. Young, of Lafayette, spoke very bitterly against the petition and the "Mormons."

An aged member from St. Charles moved a reference of the bill to a select committee; and, continued he, "as the gentleman that just spoke, and other gentlemen, want the petition ruled out of the house for fear their evil doings will be brought to light; this goes to prove to me and others, that the petition is true."

Mr. Redman, of Howard county, made a long speech in favor of a speedy investigation of the whole matter; said he, "The governor's order has gone forth, and the Mormons are leaving; hundreds are waiting to cross the Mississippi river, and by and by they are gone, and our state is blasted; her character is gone; we gave them no chance for a fair investigation. The state demands of us that we give them a speedy investigation."

Nature of the Testimony.

Mr. Gyer, from St. Louis, agreed with the gentleman from Howard county, that the committee should have power to call witnesses from any part of the state, and defend them; and unless the governor's order was rescinded, he for one would leave the state. Other gentlemen made similar remarks.

The testimony presented the committee of investigation, before referred to, was the governor's orders, General Clark's reports, the report of the *ex parte* trial at Richmond, and a lot of papers signed by nobody, given to nobody, and directed to nobody, containing anything our enemies were disposed to write.

Minutes of the High Council at Far West.

The High council of Zion met in Far West, Wednesday, December 19, 1838.

The Council was organized as follows: Ebenezer Robinson, No. 1; Jared Carter, No. 2; Thomas Grover, 3; Reynolds Cahoon, 4; Theodore Turley, 5; Solomon Hancock, 6; John Badger, 7; John Murdock, 8; Harlow Redfield, 9; George W. Harris, 10; David Dort, 11; Samuel Bent 12. The Council was opened by prayer by President Brigham Young, who presided.

Harlow Redfield gave a statement of his feelings. He said his faith was as good as it ever was, notwithstanding he did not feel to fellowship all the proceedings of his brethren in Daviess county; he thought they did not act as wisely as they might have done.

Voted by the Council that John E. Page and John Taylor* be or-

* Of John Taylor a biographical note has already been given. See page 154. The following facts concerning John E. Page are given by himself:

The subscriber was born of Ebenezer and Rachael Page, their first child, February 25th, A. D. 1799. My father was of pure English extraction; my mother of English, Irish, and Welsh extraction. My place of birth was Trenton Township, Oneida county, State of New York. I embraced the faith of the Church of Jesus Christ of Latter-day Saints, and was baptized August the 18th, 1833, by the hands of Elder Emer Harris (own brother to Martin Harris, one of the Three Witnesses to the divinity of the Book of Mormon). I was ordained an Elder under the hands of Elders Nelson Higgins, Ebenezer Page, Jun., and others. My baptism took place in Brownhelm, Lorain county, Ohio; my ordination in Florence, Huron county, of the same state, on the 12th of September, 1833.

I moved to Kirtland, Geauga county Ohio, in the fall of 1835.

On the 31st day of May, 1836, I started on a mission to Canada West, Leeds county. I was gone from my family seven months and twenty days.

On the 16th day of February, 1837, I again left Kirtland with my family, a wife and two small children, taking with me all the earthly goods I possessed, which consisted of one bed and our wearing apparel of the plainest kind, to continue my mission in the same region of country as before.

In July following the commandment came forth for me to occupy a place in the quorum of the Twelve.

dained to the Apostleship, to fill vacancies in the quorum of the Twelve. They came forward and received their ordination under the hands of Brigham Young and Heber C. Kimball.

Voted that we send a petition to the general government, and send it by mail.

Voted that Edward Partridge and John Taylor be a committee to draft the above-mentioned petition; also it is their privilege to choose another person to assist them.

Council adjourned until next Wednesday at one o'clock, at same place.

E. ROBINSON, Clerk.

Tuesday, December 25.—My brother, Don Carlos, and my cousin George A. Smith returned, [from missions through Kentucky and Tennessee], having traveled fifteen hundred miles—nine hundred on foot, and the remainder by steamboat and otherwise. They visited several branches, and would have accomplished the object of their mission, had it not been for the troubles at Far West.

Return of Don Carlos Smith and George A. Smith.

When nearly home they were known and pursued by the mob, which compelled them to travel one hundred miles in two days and nights. The ground at the time was slippery, and a severe northwest wind was blowing in their faces; they had but little to eat, and narrowly escaped freezing both nights.

On the 14th day of May, 1838, I started with a company of Saints, made up of men, women and their children, for the state of Missouri, where we landed with a company occupying thirty wagons, in the first week of October, at a place called De Witt, some six miles above the outlet of Grand river, on the north side of the Missouri river, where we were attacked by an armed mob, and by them barbarously treated for nearly two weeks. We then went to Far West, Caldwell county, where we united with the general body of the Church, and with them participated in all the grievous persecutions practiced on the Church by means of a furious mob, by which means I buried one wife and two children as martyrs to our holy religion, since they died through extreme suffering for the want of the common comforts of life—which I was not allowed to provide even with my money.

On the 19th of December, 1838, at Far West, Elder John Taylor and myself were ordained as Apostles under the hands of Elders Brigham Young and Heber C. Kimball, in the quorum of the Twelve, to fill some vacancies in the quorum, which had occurred by apostasies. In two year's time I had baptized upwards of six hundred persons, and traveled more than five thousand miles, principally on foot and under the most extreme poverty, relative to earthly means, being sustained alone by the power of God and not of man, or the wisdom of the world.—JOHN E. PAGE.

Wednesday, December 26.—David H. Redfield having returned to Far West, made his report, and the High Council voted that they were satisfied with his proceedings.*

Redfield's Report.

Thursday, December 27.—Anson Call went to Ray county, near Elk Horn, to sell some property, and was taken by ten of the mob and one old negro. Some of the mob were two of Judge Dickey's sons, a Mr. Adams, and a constable. They ordered him to disarm himself. He told them he had no arms about his person. They ordered him to turn his pockets wrong side out. They then said they would peel off his naked back before morning, with a hickory gad. They beat him with their naked hands times without number; they struck him in the face with a bowie knife, and severely hurt him a number of times.

Experience of Anson Call.

After abusing him about four hours, saying he was a —— "Mormon," and they would serve him as they had others, tie him with a hickory withe and gad him, and keep him till morning, they then started off and came to a hazel grove; while consulting together what course to pursue with him, he leaped into the bush, when they pursued him, but he made his escape and returned to Far West.

After much controversy and angry disputation, as the papers of Missouri, published at the time, abundantly testify, our petition and memorial was laid on the table until the 4th of July following; thus utterly refusing to grant the request of the memorialists to investigate the subject.†

Action of Missouri Legislature.

After we were cast into prison, we heard nothing but

*David H. Redfield, it will be remembered, was the messenger from the citizens of Caldwell county to the Missouri state legislature, bearing with him the petition of the 10th of December, and it is, of course, from his report of the manner in which the petition was received and the report of the debate thereon that the Prophet makes up his account of that affair.

†The bill providing for an investigation of the "Mormon" difficulties was finally laid upon the table until the 4th of July in the house by a vote of 48 in favor of such action and 37 against such procedure. Seven members were absent. The matter was not again taken up until the legislature of 1840, of which more later.

threatenings, that, if any judge or jury, or court of any kind, should clear any of us, we should never get out of the state alive.

State Appropriation of $2,000.

The state appropriated two thousand dollars to be distributed among the people of Daviess and Caldwell counties, the "Mormons" of Caldwell not excepted. The people of Daviess thought they could live on "Mormon" property, and did not want their thousand, consequently it was pretended to be given to those of Caldwell. Judge Cameron, Mr. McHenry, and others attended to the distribution. Judge Cameron would drive in the brethren's hogs (many of which were identified) and shoot them down in the streets; and without further bleeding, and half dressing, they were cut up and distributed by McHenry to the poor, at a charge of four and five cents per pound; which, together with a few pieces of refuse goods, such as calicoes at double and treble prices soon consumed the two thousand dollars; doing the brethren very little good, or in reality none, as the property destroyed by them, [i. e. the distributing commission] was equal to what they gave the Saints.*

Course of the Minority in the Legislature.

The proceedings of the legislature were warmly opposed by a minority of the house—among whom were David R. Atchison, of Clay county, and all the members from St. Louis, and Messrs. Rollins and Gordon, from Boone county, and by various other members from other counties; but the mob majority carried the day, for the guilty wretches feared an investigation—knowing that it would endanger their lives and liberties. Some time during this

* Of this matter of distributing the legislature's appropriation the late President John Taylor in his discussion with Schuyler Colfax, Vice-President of the United States, 1870, says: "The legislature of Missouri, to cover their infamy, appropriated the munificent (?) sum of $2,000 to help the suffering 'Mormons.' Their agent took a few miserable traps, the sweepings of an old store; for the balance of the patrimony he sent into Daviess county and killed our hogs, which we were then prevented from doing, and brought them to feed the poor 'Mormons' as part of the legislative appropriation. This I saw."

session the legislature appropriated two hundred thousand dollars to pay the troops for driving the Saints out of the state.

Many of the state journals tried to hide the iniquity of the state by throwing a covering of lies over her atrocious deeds. But can they hide the govenor's cruel order for banishment or extermination? Can they conceal the facts of the disgraceful treaty of the generals with their own officers and men at the city of Far West? Can they conceal the fact that twelve or fifteen thousand men, women and children, have been banished from the state without trial or condemnation? And this at an expense of two hundred thousand dollars—and this sum appropriated by the state legislature, in order to pay the troops for this act of lawless outrage? Can they conceal the fact that we have been imprisoned for many months, while our families, friends and witnesses have been driven away? Can they conceal the blood of the murdered husbands and fathers, or stifle the cries of the widows and the fatherless? Nay! The rocks and mountains may cover them in unknown depths, the awful abyss of the fathomless deep may swallow them up, and still their horrid deeds will stand forth in the broad light of day, for the wondering gaze of angels and of men! They cannot be hid.

Course of the State Press.

Some time in December Heber C. Kimball and Alanson Ripley were appointed, by the brethren in Far West, to visit us at Liberty jail as often as circumstances would permit, or occasion required, which duty they faithfully performed. We were sometimes visited by our friends, whose kindness and attention I shall ever remember with feelings of lively gratitude; but frequently we were not suffered to have that privilege. Our food was of the coarsest kind, and served up in a manner which was disgusting.

Thus, in a land of liberty, in the town of Liberty, Clay county, Missouri, my fellow prisoners and I in chains, and dungeons, saw the close of 1838.

CHAPTER XVII.

PREPARATIONS FOR LEAVING MISSOURI—ACTION OF THE STATE LEGISLATURE.

Tuesday, January 1, 1839.—The day dawned upon us as prisoners of hope, but not as sons of liberty. O Columbia, Columbia! How thou art fallen! "The land of the free, the home of the brave!" "The asylum of the oppressed"—oppressing thy noblest sons, in a loathsome dungeon, without any provocation, only that they have claimed to worship the God of their fathers according to His own word, and the dictates of their own consciences. Elder Parley P. Pratt and his companions in tribulation were still held in bondage in their doleful prison in Richmond.

Reflections on the Opening Year.

Monday, January 7.—Anson Call returned to his farm on the three forks of Grand river, to see if he could secure any of the property he had left in his flight to Adam-ondi-Ahman, and was there met by the mob, and beaten with a hoop pole about his limbs, body and head; the man that used the pole about his person was George W. O'Neal. With much difficulty Brother Call returned to Far West, with his person much bruised, and from that time gave up all hopes of securing any of his property.

Anson Call Beaten.

Tuesday, January 8.—About this time England and Ireland were visited by a tremendous storm of wind from the northwest, which unroofed and blew down many houses in the cities and in the country, doing much damage to the shipping; many hundreds of persons were turned out of doors, many lives lost on the land and sea, and an immense amount of property was destroyed.

Storm in England.

Such a wind had not been witnessed by any one living; and some began to think that the judgments were about to follow the Elders' preaching.

Thursday, January 10.—

Missouri State Senate Resolutions on Mormon Difficulties.

Resolved by the Senate, the House of Representatives concurring therein, that the three resolutions of the 18th of December be referred to a joint committee of the two Houses, heretofore raised, on the subject of the Mormon difficulties, with the instructions to report a bill in conformity thereto, as soon as they can conveniently prepare the same; which was agreed to.*

Wednesday, January 16.—Mr. Turner, from the joint select committee, introduced to the Senate, "*A Bill to provide for the investigation of the late disturbances in this state.*" This bill consists of twenty-three sections, of which the following is the first:

1st. A joint committee shall be appointed to investigate the causes of the late disturbances between the people called Mormons and other inhabitants of this state, and the conduct of the military operations in repressing them; which committee shall consist of two senators, to be elected by the Senate and three representatives, to be elected by the House of Representatives.

Other Provisions of the Bill.

The bill further provided that the committee should meet at Richmond, Ray county, on the first Monday in May, and thereafter at such times and places as they should appoint; that they should choose a chairman, clerk, sergeant-at-arms and assistants; issue subpœnas and other processes; admin-

* The above resolutin was offered by Mr. William M. Campbell in the Senate, and the three resolutions of the 18th of December were in Mr. Turner's report to the Senate of that date, and are as follows:

Resolved, That it is inexpedient at this time,to prosecute further the inquiry into the causes of the late disturbances and the conduct of the military operations in suppressing them.

Resolved, That it is inexpedient to publish at this time. any of the documents accompanying the governor's message in relation to the late disturbances.

Resolved, That it is expedient to appoint a joint committee composed of —— Senators, and —— Representatives to investigate the cause of said disturbances, and the conduct of the military operations in suppressing them, to meet at such time, and to be invested with such powers as may be prescribed by law." See the whole report of Mr. Turner's, at pp. 235-8.

ister oaths; keep a record; furnish rooms; pay witnesses one dollar and fifty cents per day out of the treasury; receive their pay as members of the legislature; clerk four dollars per day, and one dollar and fifty cents for each arrest. In short, all parties concerned were to be paid the highest price—and this committee were to be clothed with all the powers of the highest courts of record. This bill did not concern the "Mormons," as the exterminating order of Governor Boggs, and the action of General Clark thereon, would compel all the Saints to be out of the state before the court would sit, so that they would have no testimony but from mobbers and worse, apostates; and this was evidently their object in postponing the time so long.

About this time President Brigham Young proposed to Bishop Partridge to help the poor out of the state. The Bishop replied, "The poor may take care of themselves, and I will take care of myself." President Brigham Young replied, "If you will not help them out, I will."

Proposition to Help the Poor.

Thursday, January 24.—I wrote as follows from Liberty jail:

The Prophet's Petition to the Missouri Legislature.

To the Honorable Legislature of Missouri:

Your memorialists, having a few days since solicited your attention to the same subject,* would now respectfully submit to your honorable body a few additional facts in support of their prayer.

They are now imprisoned under a charge of treason against the state of Missouri, and their lives, and fortunes, and characters, are suspended upon the result of the trial on the criminal charges preferred against them. Therefore your honorable body will excuse them for manifesting the deep concern they feel in relation to their trial for a crime so enormous as that of treason.

It is not our object to complain—to asperse any one. All we ask is a fair and impartial trial. We ask the sympathies of no one. We ask sheer justice; 'tis all we expect, and all we merit, but we merit that. We know the people of no county in this state to which we would ask our final trial to be sent, who are prejudiced in our favor. But we be-

* The previous document here referred to, does not appear in this history as heretofore published, nor is it to be found in any of the manuscrips in the historian's office.

lieve that the state of excitement existing in most of the upper counties is such that a jury would be improperly influenced by it. But that excitement, and the prejudice against us in the counties comprising the fifth Judicial Circuit, are not the only obstacles we are compelled to meet. We know that much of that prejudice against us is not so much to be attributed to a want of honest motives amongst the citizens as it is to misrepresentation.

It is a difficult task to change opinions once formed. The other obstacle which we candidly consider one of the most weighty, is the feeling which we believe is entertained by Hon. Austin A. King against us, and his consequent inability to do us impartial justice. It is from no disposition to speak disrespectfully of that high officer, that we lay before your honorable body the facts we do; but simply that the legislature may be apprised of our real condition. We look upon Judge King as like all other mere men, liable to be influenced by his feelings, his prejudices, and his previously formed opinions. From his reputation we consider him as being partially, if not entirely, committed against us. He has written much upon the subject of our late difficulties, in which he has placed us in the wrong. These letters have been published to the world. He has also presided at an excited public meeting as chairman, and no doubt sanctioned all the proceedings. We do not complain of the citizens who held that meeting, they were entitled to that privilege. But for the judge before whom the very men were to be tried for a capital offense to participate in an expression of condemnation of these same individuals, is to us, at least,apparently wrong;and we cannot think that we should, after such a course on the part of the judge, have the same chance of a fair and impartial trial as all admit we ought to have.

We believe that the foundation of the feeling against us, which we have reason to think Judge King entertains, may be traced to the unfortunate troubles which occurred in Jackson county some few years ago; in a battle between the "Mormons" and a portion of the citizens of that county, Mr. Brazeale, the brother-in-law of Judge King, was killed. It is natural that the judge should have some feelings against us, whether we were right or wrong in that controversy.

We mention these facts, not to disparage Judge King; we believe that from the relation he bears to us, he would himself prefer that our trials should be had in a different circuit, and before a different court. Many other reasons and facts we might mention, but we forebear.

Postscript to the Petition.

This letter was directed to James M. Hughes, Esq., member of the House of Representatives, Jefferson City, with the following request:

Will you be so kind as to present this to the House. The community here would, I believe, have no objection for the trial of these men being transferred to St. Louis.

P. H. B.*

Saturday, 26.—

Minutes of a Public Meeting at Far West.

A meeting of a respectable number of the citizens of Caldwell county, members of the Church of Jesus Christ of Latter-day Saints, was held in Far West, according to previous notice, to devise and take into consideration such measures as might be thought necessary in order to comply with the orders of the Executive to remove from the state of Missouri immediately, as made known by General Clark to the citizens of said county, in the month of November last.

The meeting was called to order by Don C. Smith; and on motion, John Smith was unanimously called to the chair, and Elias Smith appointed secretary.

The object of the meeting was then stated by the chairman, who briefly adverted to the causes which had brought about the present state of affairs, and called for an expression of sentiment on the best course to be pursued in the present emergency.

Several gentlemen addressed the meeting on the subject of our removal from the state and the seeming impossibility of complying with the orders of the governor of Missouri, in consequence of the extreme poverty of many, which had come upon them by being driven from place to place, deprived of their constitutional rights and privileges, as citizens of this, and the United States, and were of the opinion that an appeal to the citizens of Upper Missouri ought to be made, setting forth our condition, and claiming their assistance towards furnishing means for the removal of the poor of this county out of the state, as being our right and our due in the present case.

On motion, resolved: That a committee of seven be appointed to make a draft of a preamble and resolutions in accordance with the foregoing sentiments to be presented to a future meeting for their consideration.

The following were then appointed, viz.,—John Taylor, Alanson Ripley, Brigham Young, Theodore Turley, Heber C. Kimball, John Smith and Don C. Smith.

Resolved: That the committee be further instructed to ascertain the

* Whom these initials represent cannot be ascertained, or whether they represent one person or three They evidently represent secret friends or a friend of the Prophet at Liberty, Clay county, willing to urge this matter upon the attention of Mr. Hughes and also upon the House.

number of families who are actually destitute of means for their removal, and report at the next meeting.

Resolved: That it is the opinion of this meeting that an exertion should be made to ascertain how much can be obtained from individuals of the society [the Church], and that it is the duty of those who have, to assist those who have not, that thereby we may, as far as possible, within and of ourselves, comply with the demands of the Executive.

Adjourned to meet again on Tuesday, the 29th instant, at twelve o'clock, m.

JOHN SMITH, Chairman.
ELIAS SMITH, Secretary.

Tuesday, 29.—

Minutes of the Second Meeting at Far West.

The brethren met again according to adjournment. John Smith was again called to the chair, and Elias Smith appointed secretary.

The committee appointed to draw up a preamble and resolutions to be presented to the meeting for consideration, presented by their chairman, John Taylor, a memorial of the transactions of the people of Missouri towards us since our first settlement in this state, in which was contained some of our sentiments and feelings on the subject of our persecutions by the authority of the state, and our deprivation of the rights of citizenship guaranteed to us by the Constitution. The document under preparation by the committee was yet in an unfinished state, owing to causes which were stated by the committee; and they further apologized for not drawing it up in the form of resolutions, agreeable to the vote of the former meeting.

The report was accepted as far as completed, and by a vote of the meeting, the same committee were directed to finish it, and prepare it for and send it to the press for publication, and they were instructed to dwell minutely on the subject relating to our arms, and the fiend-like conduct of the officers of the militia in sequestering all the best of them after their surrender on condition of being returned to us again, or suffering them to be exchanged for others, not worth half their value, in violation of their bond, and of the honor of the commander of the forces sent against us by the state.

On motion of President Brigham Young, it was resolved that we this day enter into a covenant to stand by and assist each other to the utmost of our abilities in removing from this state, and that we will never desert the poor who are worthy, till they shall be out of the reach of the exterminating order of General Clark, acting for and in the name of the state.

After an expression of sentiments by several who addressed the meeting on the propriety of taking efficient measures to remove the poor from the state, it was resolved, that a committee of seven be appointed to superintend the business of our removal, and to provide for those who have not the means of moving, till the work shall be completed.

The following were then appointed, viz., William Huntington, Charles Bird, Alanson Ripley, Theodore Turley, Daniel Shearer, Shadrach Roundy, and Jonathan H. Hale.

Resolved: That the secretary draft an instrument expressive of the sense of the covenant entered into this day, by those present, and that those who were willing to subscribe to the covenant should do it, that their names might be known, which would enable the committee more expeditiously to carry their business into effect.

The instrument was accordingly drawn, and by vote of the meeting the secretary attached the names of those who were willing to subscribe to it.

Adjourned to meet again on Friday, the 1st of February next, at twelve o'clock, m.

JOHN SMITH, Chairman.
ELIAS SMITH, Secretary.

The following is the covenant referred to in the preceding minutes, with the names which were then and afterwards attached to it, as far as they have been preserved:

We, whose names are hereunder written, do for ourselves individually hereby covenant to stand by and assist one another, to the utmost of our abilities, in removing from this state in compliance with the authority of the state; and we do hereby acknowledge ourselves firmly bound to the extent of all our available property, to be disposed of by a committee who shall be appointed for the purpose of providing means for the removing from this state of the poor and destitute who shall be considered worthy, till there shall not be one left who desires to remove from the state: with this proviso, that no individual shall be deprived of the right of the disposal of his own property for the above purpose, or of having the control of it, or so much of it as shall be necessary for the removing of his own family, and to be entitled to the over-plus, after the work is effected; and furthermore, said committee shall give receipts for all property, and an account of the expenditure of the same.

Far West, Missouri, January 29, 1839.

List of Names Subscribed to the Foregoing.

John Smith,
Wm. Huntington,
James McMillan,
Chandler Holbrook,

Charles Bird,
Alanson Ripley,
Theodore Turley,
Daniel Shearer,
Shadrach Roundy,
Jonathan H. Hale,
Elias Smith,
Brigham Young,
James Burnham,
Leicester Gaylord,
Samuel Williams,
John Miller,
Aaron M. York,
George A. Smith,
Daniel Howe,
James Bradin,
Jonathan Beckelshimer
David Jones,
Wm. M. Fossett,
Charles N. Baldwin,
Jesse N. Reed,
Benjamin Johnson,
Jonathan Hampton,
Anson Call,
Peter Dopp,
Samuel Rolph,
Abel Lamb,
Daniel McArthur,
William Gregory,
Zenas Curtis,
John Reed,
William R. Orton,
Samuel D. Tyler,
John H. Goff,
Thomas Butterfield,
Dwight Hardin,
Norvil M. Head,
Stephen V. Foot,
Jacob G. Bigler,
Eli Bagley,
William Milam,
Lorenzo Clark,
William Allred,
Alexander Wright,
William Taylor,
John Taylor,
Reuben P. Hartwell,
John Lowry,
Welcome Chapman,
Solomon Hancock,
Arza Adams,
Henry Jacobs,
James Carroll,
David Lyons,
John Taylor,
Don Carlos Smith,
William J. Stewart,
Isaac B. Chapman,
Roswell Stephens,
Reuben Headlock,
David Holman,
Joel Goddard,
Phineas R. Bird,
Duncan McArthur,
Allen Talley,
James Hampton,
Sherman A. Gilbert,
James S. Holman,
Andrew Lytle,
Aaron Johnson,
Heber C. Kimball,
George W. Harris,
George W. Davidson,
Harvey Strong,
Elizabeth Mackley,
Sarah Mackley,
Andrew More,
Harvey Downey,
John Maba,
Lucy Wheeler,
John Turpin,
William Earl,
Zenos H. Gurley,
Joseph W. Coolidge.
Anthony Head,
S. A. P. Kelsey,

Wm. Van Ausdall,
Nathan K. Knight,
John Thorp,
Andrew Rose,
John S. Martin,
Albert Sloan,
John D. Lee,
Eliphas Marsh,
Joseph Wright,
John Badger,
Levi Richards.
Erastus Bingham,
Elisha Everett,
John Lytle,
Levi Jackman,
Thomas Guyman,
Nahum Curtis,
Lyman Curtis,
Philip Ballard,
William Gould,
Reuben Middleton,
William Harper,
Seba Joes,
Charles Butler,
Richard Walton,
Isaac Kerron,
Joseph Rose,
David Foot,
L. S. Nickerson,
Moses Daley,
David Sessions,
Perrigrine Sessions,
Alford P. Childs,
James Daley,
Noah T. Guyman,
David Winters,
John Pack,
Sylvanus Hicks,
Horatio N. Kent,
Joseph W. Pierce,
Thomas Gates,
Squire Bozarth,
Nathan Lewis,
Moses Evord,
Ophelia Harris,
Zuba McDonald,
Mary Goff,
Harvey J. Moore,
Francis Chase,
Stephen Markham,
John Outhouse,
Wm. F. Leavens,
Daniel Tyler,
Noah Rogers,
Stephen N. St. John,
Francis Lee,
Eli Lee,
Benjamin Covey,
Michel Borkdull,
Miles Randall,
Horace Evans,
David Dort,
Levi Hancock,
Edwin Whiting,
William Barton,
Elisha Smith,
James Gallaher,
Robert Jackson,
Lemuel Merrick,
James Dunn,
Orin Hartshorn,
Nathan Hawke,
Pierce Hawley,
Thomas J. Fisher,
James Leithead,
Alfred Lee,
Stephen Jones,
Eleazer Harris,
Elijah B. Gaylord,
Thomas Grover,
Alexander Badlam,
Phebe Kellog,
Albert Miner,
William Woodland,
Martin C. Allred,
Jedediah Owen,

Philander Avery,	Orin P. Rockwell,
Benjamin F. Bird,	Nathan B. Baldwin,
Charles Squire,	Truman Brace,
Jacob Curtis,	Sarah Wixom,
Rachel Medfo,	Lewis Zobriski,
Lyman Stevens,	Henry Zobriski,
Roswell Evans,	Morris Harris,
Leonard Clark,	Absolom Tidwell,
Nehemiah Harmon,	Alvin Winegar,
Daniel Cathcart,	Samuel T. Winegar,
Gershom Stokes,	John E. Page,
Rachel Page,	Levi Gifford,
Barnet Cole,	Edmund Durfee,
William Thompson,	Josiah Butterfield,
Nathan Cheney,	John Killion,
James Sherry,	John Patten,
David Frampton,	John Wilkins,
Elizabeth Pettigrew,	Abram Allen,
Charles Thompson,	William Felshaw.

Activity of the Committee on Removal.

The committee who had been appointed for removing the poor from the state of Missouri, viz.: William Huntington, Charles Bird, Alanson Ripley, Theodore Turley, Daniel Shearer, Shadrach Roundy, and Jonathan H. Hale, met in the evening of that day [January 29, 1839], at the house of Theodore Turley, and organized by appointing William Huntington chairman, Daniel Shearer treasurer, and Alanson Ripley clerk, and made some arrangements for carrying into operation the business of removing the poor. President Brigham Young got eighty subscribers to the covenant the first day, and three hundred the second day.

Investigation Ordered.

Thursday, *31.*—Mr. Turner's bill of the 16th instant passed the senate. I sent the poor brethren a hundred dollar bill from jail, to assist them in their distressed situation.

Friday, *February 1:*

Minutes of a Meeting of the Cammittee on Removal.

The committee met according to adjournment, at the house of Theodore Turley; John Smith was present and acted as chairman, and Elias Smith as secretary. The meeting was called to order by the chairman.

On motion, Resolved: That the covenant entered into at the last meeting be read by the Secretary, which was done accordingly.

The chairman then called for the expression of sentiments on the subject of the covenant.

Resolved, That the committee be increased to eleven.

The following were then appointed: Elias Smith, Erastus Bingham, Stephen Markham, and James Newberry.

Several of the committee addressed the meeting on the arduous task before them, and exhorted all to exert themselves to relieve and assist them in the discharge of the duties of their office, to the utmost of their abilities.

Elders Taylor and Young, in the most forcible manner addressed the assembly on the propriety of union in order to carry our resolutions into effect, and exhorted the brethren to use wisdom in the sale of their property.

JOHN SMITH, Chairman,
ELIAS SMITH, Secretary.

The committee met again in the evening at Theodore Turley's. Alanson Ripley declined acting as clerk, and Elias Smith was appointed in his stead.

Resolved, That exertions be made to remove the families of the Presidency and the other prisoners first.

Several of the committee made report of what had been done by them towards carrying the business of the committee into operation. Elder John Taylor had also been appointed to visit the branches of the Church on Log and Upper Goose creeks, and made a report of his proceedings.

Resolved, That Charles Bird be appointed to go down towards the Mississippi river and establish deposits of corn for the brethren on the road, and make contracts for ferriage, etc.

Monday, February 4.—Mr. Turner's bill of 16th January came up for the first reading, "when Mr Wright moved that the bill be laid on the table until the 4th day of July next; and upon this question Mr. Primm desired the yeas and nays, which were ordered, and the decision was in the affirmative" by eleven majority, which by many was considered an approval of all the wrongs the Saints had sustained in the state.*

6th and 7th.† The committee on the removal of the Saints from Missouri were in session. Stephen Markham started for Illinois, with my wife and children, and Jonathan Holmes and wife.

* At any rate Mr. Turner's bill providing for an elaborate investigation was never taken from the table. In the legislature, however, which convened in 1840-41, the subject of the "Mormon" difficulties was again taken up on recommendation of Governor Boggs, who concludes what he had to say in his message in this language. "To explain the attitude which we have been made to assume I would recommend the publication of all the events relating to the occurrence, and distributing the same to the chief authorities of each state." In pursuance of this recommendation the joint committee appointed from the senate and house made a collection of documents on the subject covering 162 pages. In the collection, however, there are none of the statements, petitions, or representations made to the public or the legislature by the Saints. The documents consist in part of the action of the respective houses in the appointment of committees and reports of those committees recommending investigations, etc.; of the reports and military orders of the militia generals; while the remainder of the pamphlet is made up of the *ex parte* testimony taken before Judge King at Richmond, concerning which testimony the Turner senate committee in reporting to the senate, under date of December 18, 1838, said: It "is manifestly not such evidence as ought to be received by the committee:

"First, *because it is not authenticated;* and,

"Second, it is confined chiefly to the object of the inquiry, namely, the investigation of criminal charges against individuals under arrest."

The action of the legislature in the matter was a "white-washing affair," to use a phrase common in such cases. It was an attempt to vindicate the state of Missouri in her treatment of the Latter-day Saints. The effort, however, was in vain. The truths in relation to those transactions, in spite of all the efforts of the legislature, were known, and the state's attempt to deny them by a publication of documents giving a hearing to but one side of the case, only emphasized the crime.

† February 7th. An event occurred on this date which ought not to be omitted from this history, as it throws great light upon the prison life of the Prophet and his associates, upon the character of the Prophet himself, and the great faith his associates had in his prophetic powers. This event, and some others of equal interest were related by Alexander McRae, one of the fellow prisoners of the Prophet, in two communications to the *Deseret News*, under the dates of October 9th, and November 1st, respectively, of the year 1854. At that time "The History of Joseph Smith" was being published in current numbers of the *News*, and Brother McRae, then Bishop of the Eleventh Ward of Salt Lake City, being surprised at the omission in the narrative of the Prophet of many items of interest concerning their prison life, wrote the two following letters to the *News:*

Letter of Alexander McRae to the Deseret News.

SALT LAKE CITY, UTAH, Oct. 9, 1854.

Mr. Editor:—In reading the History of Joseph Smith as published in the *News* last winter, and especially that part of it which relates to his imprisonment in

Liberty jail, Missouri, I see there are many interesting facts which are omitted; and as I had the honor of being a fellow prisoner with him, I thought I would write some of those incidents for the satisfaction of any of your readers who may feel interested in them.

During our imprisonment, we had many visitors, both friends and enemies. Among the latter, many were angry with Brother Joseph, and accused him of killing a son, a brother, or some relative of theirs, at what was called the Crooked River Battle. This looked rather strange to me, that so many should claim a son, or a brother killed there, *when they reported only one man killed.*

Among our friends who visited us, were Presidents Brigham Young and Heber C. Kimball [now—i. e. at the time this letter was written, 1854], of the First Presidency—the latter several times; George A. Smith, of the quorum of the Twelve; Don C. Smith, brother of Joseph, came several times, and brought some of our families to see us. Benjamin Covey, Bishop of the Twelfth Ward of this city, brought each of us a new pair of boots, and made us a present of them. James Sloan, his wife and daughter, came several times. Alanson Ripley also visited us, and many others, whom to name would be too tedious. Orin P. Rockwell brought us refreshments many times; and Jane Bleven and her daughter brought cakes, pies, etc., and handed them in at the window. These things helped us much, as our food was very coarse, and so filthy that we could not eat it until we were driven to it by hunger.

After we had been there some time, and had tried every means we could to obtain our liberty by the law, without effect (except Sidney Rigdon who was bailed out), and also having heard, from a reliable source, that it had been stated in the public street, by the most influential men in that part of the country, that "the Mormon prisoners would have to be condemned or the character of the state would have to go down," we came to the conclusion that we would try other means to effect it.

Accordingly, on the 7th day of February, 1839, after counseling together on the subject, we concluded to try to go that evening when the jailor came with our supper; but Brother Hyrum, before deciding fully, and to make it more sure, asked Brother Joseph to inquire of the Lord as to the propriety of the move. He did so, and received answer to this effect—that if we were all agreed, we could go clear that evening; and if we would ask, we should have a testimony for ourselves. I immediately asked, and had not no more than asked, until I received as clear a testimony as ever I did of anything in my life, that it was true. Brother Hyrum Smith and Caleb Baldwin bore testimony to the same: but Lyman Wight said we might go if we chose, but he would not. After talking with him for some time, he said, "if we would wait until the next day, he would go with us." Without thinking we had no promise of success on any other day than the one above stated, we agreed to wait.

When nignt came, the jailor came alone with our supper, threw the door wide open, put our supper on the table, and went to the back part of the room, where a pile of books lay, took up a book, and went to reading, leaving us between him and the door, thereby giving us every chance to go if we had been ready. As the next day was agreed upon, we made no attempt to go that evening.

When the next evening came, the case was very different; the jailer brought a double guard with him, and with them six of our brethren, to-wit.: Erastus Snow, William D. Huntington, Cyrus Daniels, David Holeman, Alanson Ripley and Watson Barlow. I was afterwards informed that they were sent by the Church. The jailer seemed to be badly scared; he had the door locked and everything made secure. It looked like a bad chance to get away, but we were determined to try it; so when the jailer started out, we started too Brother Hyrum took hold of the door, and the rest followed; but before we were able to render him the assistance he needed, the jailer and guard succeeded in closing the door, shutting the brethren in with us, except Cyrus Daniels, who was on the outside.

As soon as the attempt was made inside, he took two of the guards, one under each arm, and ran down the stairs that led to the door, it being in the second story. When he reached the ground they got away from him; and seeing we had failed to get out, he started to run, but put his foot in a hole and fell, a bullet from one of the guards passed very close to his head, and he thinks the fall saved his life.

The scene that followed this defies description. I should judge, from the number, that all the town, and many from the country, gathered around the jail, and every mode of torture and death that their imagination could fancy, was proposed for us, such as blowing up the jail, taking us out and whipping us to death, shooting us, burning us to death, tearing us to pieces with horses, etc. But they were so divided among themselves that they could not carry out any of their plans, and we escaped unhurt.

During this time, some of our brethren spoke of our being in great danger; and I confess I felt that we were. But Brother Joseph told them "not to fear, that not a hair of their heads should be hurt, and that they should not lose any of their things, even to a bridle, saddle, or blanket; that everything should be restored to them; they had offered their lives for us and the Gospel; that it was necessary the Church should offer a sacrifice, and the Lord accepted the offering."

The brethren had next to undergo a trial, but the excitement was so great that they [the officers] dare not take them out until it abated a little. While they were waiting for their trial, some of the brethren employed lawyers to defend them. Brother [Erastus] Snow asked Brother Joseph whether he had better employ a lawyer or not. Brother Joseph told him to plead his own case. "But," said Brother Snow, "I do not understand the law." Brother Joseph asked him if he did not understand justice; he thought he did. "Well," said Brother Joseph, "go and plead for justice as hard as you can, and quote Blackstone and other authors now and then, and they will take it all for law."

He did as he was told, and the result was as Joseph had said it would be; for when he got through his plea, the lawyers flocked around him, and asked him where he had studied law, and said they had never heard a better plea. When the trial was over Brother Snow was discharged, and all the rest were held to bail, and were allowed to bail each other, by Brother Snow going bail with them; and they said they got everything that was taken from them, and nothing was lost, although no two articles were in one place. More anon.

Yours respectfully,

ALEXANDER MCRAE.

Second Letter of Alexander McRae to the Deseret News.

SALT LAKE CITY, UTAH, Nov. 1, 1854.

Mr. Editor:—Sometime during our stay in Liberty jail an attempt was made to destroy us by poison. I supposed it was administered in either tea or coffee, but as I did not use either, I escaped unhurt, while all who did were sorely afflicted, some being blind two or three days, and it was only by much faith and prayer that the effect was overcome.

We never suffered ourselves to go into any important measure without asking Brother Joseph to inquire of the Lord in relation to it. Such was our confidence in him as a Prophet, that when he said "Thus saith the Lord," we were confident it would be as he said; and the more we tried it, the more confidence we had, for we never found his word fail in a single instance.

A short time before we were to go to Daviess county for trial, word came to us that either General Atchison or Doniphan, would raise a military force, and go with us to protect us from the wrath of that people. The matter was discussed by the brethren (except Brother Joseph), and they naturally enough concluded it would be best; and although I had nothing to say, I concurred with them in my feelings. Brother Hyrum asked Brother Joseph what he thought of it. Brother Joseph hung his head a few moments, and seemed in a deep study, and then raised up and said, "Brother Hyrum, it will not do; we must trust in the Lord; if we take a guard with us we shall be destroyed."

This was very unexpected to us, but Brother Hyrum remarked, "If you say it in the name of the Lord, we will rely on it." Said Brother Joseph, "In the name of the Lord, if we take a guard with us, we will be destroyed; but if we put our trust in the Lord, we shall be safe, and no harm shall befall us, and we shall be better treated than we have ever been since we have been prisoners."

This settled the question, and all seemed satisfied, and it was decided that we should have no extra guard, and they had only such a guard as they chose for our safe keeping. When we arrived at the place where the court was held, I began to think he was mistaken for once, for the people rushed upon us *en masse*, crying, "Kill them: —— —— them, kill them." I could see no chance for escape, unless we could fight our way through, and we had nothing to do it with. At this, Brother Joseph, at whom all seemed to rush, rose up and said, "We are in your hands; if we are guilty, we refuse not to be punished by the law." Hearing these words, two of the most bitter mobocrats in the country—one by the name of William Peniston and the other Kinney, or McKinney, I do not remember which—got up on benches and began to speak to the people, saying, "Yes, gentlemen, these men are in our hands; let us not use violence, but let the law have its course; the law will condemn them, and they will be punished by it. We do not want the disgrace of taking the law into our own hands."

In a very few minutes they were quieted, and they seemed now as friendly as they had a few minutes before been enraged. Liquor was procured, and we all had to drink in token of friendship. This took place in the court-room (a small log cabin about twelve feet square), during the adjournment of the court; and from that time until we got away, they could not put a guard over us who would not become so friendly that they dare not trust them, and the guard was very frequently changed. We were seated at the first table with the judge, lawyers, etc., and had the best the country afforded, with feather beds to sleep on—a privilege we had not before enjoyed in all our imprisonment.

On one occasion, while we were there, the above-named William Peniston, partly in joke and partly in earnest, threw out a rather hard insinuation against some of the brethren This touched Joseph's feelings, and he retorted a good deal in the same way, only with such power that the earth seemed to tremble under his feet, and said, "Your heart is as black as your whiskers," which were as black as any crow. He seemed to quake under it and left the room.

The guards, who had become friendly, were alarmed for our safety, and exclaimed, "O, Mr. Smith, do not talk so; you will bring trouble upon yourself and companions." Brother Joseph replied, "Do not be alarmed; I know what I am about." He always took up for the brethren, when their characters were assailed, sooner than for himself, no matter how unpopular it was to speak in their favor.

Yours as ever,

ALEXANDER MCRAE.

CHAPTER XVIII.

THE EXILED SAINTS GATHER AT QUINCY, ILLINOIS—PROPOSITION TO SETTLE AT COMMERCE.

SOME time this month there was a conference of the Church at Quincy, a report of which is as follows:

Minutes of a Conference of the Church Held at Quincy.

At a meeting of the Church of Jesus Christ of Latter-day Saints, held in the town of Quincy, February —, 1839, to take into consideration the expediency of locating the Church in some place, Brother William Marks was chosen president and Robert B. Thompson, clerk.

Elder John P. Greene, by request, then stated the object of the meeting, and stated that a liberal offer had been made by a gentleman, of about twenty thousand acres, lying between the Mississippi and Des Moines rivers, at two dollars per acre, to be paid in twenty annual installments, without interest; that a committee had examined the land and reported very favorably respecting it, and thought it every way suited for a location for the Church.

Brother Rogers then made some statements, and gave information respecting the land, being one of the committee appointed to examine it.

President William Marks observed that he was altogether in favor of making the purchase, providing that it was the will of the Lord that we should again gather together; but from the circumstances of being driven from the other places, he almost was led to the conclusion that it was not wisdom that we should do so, but hoped that the brethren would speak their minds; the Lord would undoubtedly manifest His will by His Spirit.

Brother Israel Barlow thought that it might be in consequence of not building according to the pattern, that we had thus been scattered.

Brother Mace spoke in favor of an immediate gathering.

Bishop Partridge then spoke on the subject, and thought it was not expedient under the present circumstances to collect together, but thought it was better to scatter into different parts and provide for the poor, which would be acceptable to God.

Judge Higbee said that he had been very favorable to the proposition of purchasing the land and gathering upon it, but since the Bishop had expressed his opinion, he was willing to give up the idea.

Several of the brethren then spoke on the subject, after which it was moved and seconded, and unanimously agreed upon, that it would not be deemed advisable to locate on the lands for the present.

A committee was appointed to draft a petition to the General government, stating our grievances, and one likewise to be presented to the citizens [of the United States] for the same object.

Tuesday, February 12.—The committee [on removal] sent a delegation to Sister Murie to ascertain her necessities. Daniel Shearer and Erastus Bingham went. Applications for assistance were made from Sister Morgan L. Gardner, Jeremiah Mackley's family, Brother Forbush, Echoed Cheney, T. D. Tyler, D. McArthur and others.

Applications for Assistance.

Wednesday, February 13.—Voted that Theodore Turley be appointed to superintend the management of the teams provided for removing the poor, and see that they are furnished for the journey.

Thursday, February 14.—The persecution was so bitter against Elder Brigham Young (on whom devolved the presidency of the Twelve by age,* Thomas B. Marsh having apostatized) and his life was so diligently sought for, that he was compelled to flee; and he left Far West on this day for Illinois.

Persecution of Brigham Young.

My brother Don Carlos Smith had carried a petition to the mob, to get assistance to help our father's family out of Missouri. I know not how much he obtained, but my father and mother started this day for Quincy, with an ox team.

Petition to Help the Smith Family From Mo.

The committee on removal discussed the propriety of paying the debts of the Saints in Clay county. Alanson

* It will be remembered that when the first quorum of the Twelve was organized the Prophet arranged the members in the order of their standing according to their age. Thereafter and now they hold their places in the quorum according to seniority of ordination. A full explanation of this matter is given in the HISTORY OF THE CHURCH, volume II, pp. 219-20. See foot notes.

Ripley was requested to call on lawyer Barnet, who was in town, and make arrangements concerning the matter. A letter of attorney was drawn up for the brethren to sign, who felt willing to dispose of their real estate to discharge their debts, appointing Alanson Ripley their attorney for that purpose. This was not exactly according to the minds of the committee, for they only directed Brother Ripley to confer with the person above named, for the purpose of obtaining information without reference to his being appointed an attorney for that purpose, independent of any other person or persons.

Arrangements for paying the Debts of the Saints.

Friday, February 15.—My family arrived at the Mississippi, opposite Quincy, after a journey of almost insupportable hardships, and Elder Markham returned immediately to Far West.

Monday, 18.—

The Governor's Order to Return the Arms Belonging to the Saints.

EXECUTIVE DEPARTMENT, CITY OF JEFFERSON,
February 18, 1839.

To Colonel Wiley C. Williams, Aid to the Commander-in-Chief:

SIR:—You will take the measures as soon as practicable, to cause the arms surrendered by the Mormons, to be delivered to the proper owners upon their producing satisfactory evidence of their claims. If in any case you think an improper use would be made of them, you can retain such, using a sound discretion in the matter. You will call upon Captain Pollard or any other person who may have arms in possession, and take charge of them; and this will be your authority for so doing.

I am respectfully,
Your obedient servant,
LILBURN W. BOGGS.

Little benefit would have resulted from this order, even if it had been promptly executed, as many of the brethren who owned the arms had left the state and it would be very difficult to decide what would be satisfactory evidence of claims.

Tuesday, February 19.—The committee on removal appointed Charles Bird to visit the several parts of Caldwell county, and William Huntington the town of Far West, to ascertain the number of families that would have to be assisted in removing, and solicit means from those who are able to give for the assistance of the needy, and make report as soon as possible.

Labors in the Interests of the Poor.

Thursday, February 21—Elder Markham arrived at Far West, and in the evening the committee on removal were in council. Elders Bingham, Turley, and Shearer, were appointed to sell the house of Joseph Smith, Sen., to a gentleman from Clay county.

Charles Bird was sent to Liberty relative to a power of attorney.

Committee Resolutions.

Resolved: To send Stephen Markham to Illinois, to visit the brethren there and obtain a power of attorney from such as had left their lands without selling them. A report of the committee appointed to visit the different parts of the country to ascertain the number of families who were destitute of teams for their removal, was made. William Huntington reported thirty-two families, and Charles Bird seven, as far as they had prosecuted their labors.

Resolved: To send Erastus Bingham to visit the north-west part of Caldwell county for the same purpose, and then adjourned till Monday next.

Saturday, February 25.—At a meeting of the Democratic Association, held this evening at Quincy, Adams county, Illinois, Mr. Lindsay introduced a resolution setting forth that the people called "Latter-day Saints" were many of them in a situation requiring the aid of the citizens of Quincy, and recommending that measures be adopted for their relief, which resolution was adopted, and a committee consisting of eight persons appointed by the chair; of which committee J. W. Whitney was chairman. The association then adjourned to meet on Wednesday evening next after instructing the committee to procure the Congregational church as a place of meeting, and to invite as many of

Action of the Democratic Committee of Quincy.

our people to attend as should choose to do so; for it was in their behalf that the meeting was to be held. Also all other citizens of the town who felt to do so were invited to attend. The committee not being able to obtain the meeting house, procured the Court House for that purpose.

Determination of the Prisoners to Escape.

After we were cast into prison, we heard nothing but threatenings, that if any judge or jury, or court of any kind, should clear any of us, we should never get out of the state alive.

This soon determined our course, and that was to escape out of their hands as soon as we could, and by any means we could. After we had been some length of time in prison, we demanded a habeas corpus of Judge Turnham, one of the county judges, which with some considerable reluctance, was granted. Great threatenings were made at this time, by the mob, that if any of us were liberated, we should never get out of the county alive.

Sidney Rigdon's Departure from Prison.

After the investigation, Sidney Rigdon was released from prison by the decision of the judge; the remainder were committed to jail; he, however, returned with us until a favorable opportunity offered for his departure. Through the friendship of the sheriff, Mr. Samuel Hadley, and the jailor, Mr. Samuel Tillery, he was let out of the jail secretly in the night, after having declared in prison, that the sufferings of Jesus Christ were a fool to his; and being solemnly warned by them to be out of the state with as little delay as possible, he made his escape. Being pursued by a body of armed men, it was through the direction of a kind Providence that he escaped out of their hands, and safely arrived in Quincy, Illinois.

Importunities for the Release of the Prisoners.

About this time, Elders Heber C. Kimball and Alanson Ripley were at Liberty, where they had been almost weekly importuning at the feet of the judges; and while performing this duty on a certain occasion, Judge Hughes stared them full in the face, and observed to one of his associates, that "by the look of these men's eyes, they are whipped, but not conquered; and let us beware how we treat these men; for their looks bespeak innocence;" and at that time he entreated his associates to admit of bail for all the prisoners; but the hardness of their hearts would not admit of so charitable a deed. But the brethren continued to importune at the feet of the judges, and also to visit the prisoners. No one of the ruling part of the community disputed the innocence of the prisoners, but said, in consequence of the fury of the mob, that even-handed justice could not be administered; Elders Kimball and Ripley were therefore compelled to abandon the idea of importuning at the feet of the judges, and leave the prisoners in the hands of God.

Meeting of Elder Israel Barlow and Isaac Galland.

When Elder Israel Barlow left Missouri in the fall of 1838, either by missing his way, or some other cause, he struck the Des Moines river some distance above its mouth. He was in a destitute situation; and making his wants known, found friends who assisted him, and gave him introductions to several gentlemen, among whom was Dr. Isaac Galland, to whom he communicated the situation of the Saints; the relation of which enlisted Mr. Galland's sympathies, or interest, or both united, and hence a providential introduction of the Church to Commerce [the place of residence of Mr. Galland] and its vicinity; for Brother Barlow went direct to Quincy, the place of his destination, and made known his interview with Dr. Galland to the Church.

Communication of Isaac Galland.

COMMERCE, ILLINOIS, February 26, 1839.

Mr. D. W. Rogers:

DEAR SIR:—Yours of the 11th instant was received yesterday. I perceive that it had been written before your brethren visited my house. I had also written to Mr. Barlow before I received yours, and which is herewith also sent. I wish here to remark that about ten or fifteen houses or cabins can be had in this neighborhood, and several farms may be rented here, on the half breed lands. I think that more than fifty families can be accommodated with places to dwell in, but not a great quantity of cultivated land, as the improvements on that tract are generally new; there are, however, several farms which can also be rented.

Since writing to Mr. Barlow, I have conversed with a friend of mine, who has also conversed with Governor Lucas, of Iowa territory, in relation to your Church and people. Governor Lucas says that the people called Mormons were good citizens in the state of Ohio, and that he respects them now as good and virtuous citizens, and feels disposed to treat them as such.

I wish also to say, through you, to your people, that Isaac Van Allen, Esq., the attorney-general of Iowa territory, is a personal and tried friend of mine; and I feel fully authorized, from a conversation which I have had with him on the subject, to say that I can assure you of his utmost endeavors to protect you from insult or violence.

I will here repeat what I have written to Mr. Barlow, that I do believe that under a territorial form of government which is directly connected with the general government of the United States, your Church will be better secured against the capriciousness of public opinion, than under a state government, where murder, rapine and robbery are admirable (!) traits in the character of a demagogue; and where the greatest villains often reach the highest offices. I have written to Governor Lucas on the subject; and when I receive his answer, I will communicate it to your Church.

I desire very much to know how your captive brethren in Missouri are faring. I should like to know if Joseph Smith, Jun., is at liberty or not, and what his prospects are. I shall be at Carthage, our county seat, during the fore part of next week, and soon after that, (perhaps the next week following) I expect to go to Burlington, Iowa territory, when I expect to see the governor and converse with him on the subject. I will probably be at home from the 6th until the 12th of March. I shall be pleased to see you or any of your people at my house at any time when you can make it convenient. It is now necessary that something definite should be done in relation to renting farms, as the season for commencing such operations is fast approaching us. A Mr. Whitney, a merchant in Quincy, is owner and proprietor of several farms in this vicinity, and it might be well to see him on the subject.

I wish to serve your cause in any matter which Providence may afford me the opportunity of doing, and I therefore request that you feel no hesitancy or reluctance in communicating to me your wishes, at all times and on any subject. I should be much gratified if it could be convenient for Mr. Rigdon, or some one or more of the leading members of your Church to spend some time with me in traveling through the tract, and in hearing and learning the state of the public mind, and feelings of the community, in relation to the location of the Church.

I feel that I am assuming a very great responsibility in this undertaking, and I wish to be governed by the dictates of wisdom and discretion, while at the same time I am aware that we are often disposed to view things as we would wish to have them, rather than as they really are; and our great anxiety to accomplish an object may sometimes diminish the obstacles below their real measure.

The little knowledge which I have as yet of the doctrine, order or practice of the Church,leaves me under the necessity of acting in all this matter as a stranger, though, as I sincerely hope, as a friend, for such, I assure you I feel myself to be, both towards you collectively, as a people, and individually as sufferers. If it should not be convenient for any one to come up about the 7th or 8th of March, please write me by the mail. Say to Mr. Rigdon, that I regret that I was absent when he was at my house. I cannot visit Quincy until after my return from Burlington, when, I think if it is thought necessary, I can.

Accept, dear sir, for yourself and in behalf of the Church and people, assurance of my sincere sympathy in your sufferings and wrongs, and deep solicitude for your immediate relief from present distress, and future triumphant conquest over every enemy.

Yours truly,

ISAAC GALLAND.

Minutes of the Meeting of the Democratic Association of Quincy.

Wednesday, February 27, 1839, six o'clock p. m.

The members of the Democratic Association and the citizens of Quincy generally, assembled in the court house, to take into consideration the state and condition of the people called the "Latter-day Saints," and organized the meeting by appointing General Leach chairman, and James D. Morgan secretary. Mr. Whitney, from the committee appointed at a former meeting, submitted the following:

The select committee to whom the subject was referred of inquiring into and reporting the situation of the persons who have recently arrived here from Missouri, and whether their circumstances are such as that they would need the aid of the citizens of Quincy and its vicinity, to be guided by what they might deem the principles of an expanded benevolence, have attended to the duties assigned them, and have concluded on the following:

REPORT.

"The first idea that occurred to your committee was, to obtain correctly the facts of the case, for without them the committee could come to no conclusion as to what it might be proper for us to do. Without the facts they could form no basis upon which the committee might recommend to this association what would be proper for us to do, or what measures to adopt. The committee, soon after their appointment, sent invitations to Mr. Rigdon and several others to meet the committee and give them a statement of the facts, and to disclose their situation. Those individuals accordingly met the committe and entered into a free conversation and disclosure of the facts of their situation; and after some time spent therein, the committee concluded to adjourn and report to this meeting, but not without first requesting those individuals to draw up and send us in writing, a condensed statement of the facts relative to the subject in charge of your committee, which those individuals engaged to do, and which the committee request may be taken as part of their report.

"That statement is herewith lettered A.

"The committee believe that our duties at this time, and on this occasion, are all included within the limits of an expanded benevolence and humanity, and which are guided and directed by that charity which never faileth.

"From the facts already disclosed, independent of the statement furnished to the committee, we feel it our duty to recommend to this association that they adopt the following resolutions:

"Resolved, That the strangers recently arrived here from the state of Missouri, known by the name of the 'Latter-day Saints,' are entitled to our sympathy and kindest regard, and that we recommend to the citizens of Quincy to extend all the kindness in their power to bestow on the persons who are in affliction.

"Resolved, That a numerous committee be raised, composed of some individuals in every quarter of the town and its vicinity, whose duty it shall be to explain to our misguided fellow citizens, if any such there be, who are disposed to excite prejudices and circulate unfounded rumors; and particularly to explain to them that these people have no design to lower the wages of the laboring class, but to procure something to save them from starving.

"Resolved, That a standing committee be raised and be composed of individuals who shall immediately inform Mr. Rigdon and others, as many as they may think proper, of their appointment, and who shall be authorized to obtain information from time to time; and should they [the committee] be of opinion that any individuals, either from destitution or sickness, or if they find them houseless, that they appeal directly and promptly to the citizens of Quincy to furnish them with the means to relieve all such cases.

"Resolved, That the committee last aforesaid be instructed to use their utmost endeavors to obtain employment for all these people, who are able and willing to labor; and also to afford them all needful, suitable and proper encouragement.

"Resolved, That we recommend to all the citizens of Quincy, that in all their intercourse with the strangers, they use and observe a becoming decorum and delicacy, and be particularly careful not to indulge in any conversation or expressions calculated to wound their feelings, or in any way to reflect upon those, who by every law of humanity, are entitled to our sympathy and commiseration.

"All which is submitted,

"J. W. WHITNEY, Chairman.

"QUINCY, February 27, 1839."

Document A.

"This, gentlemen, is a brief outline of the difficulties that we have labored under, in consequence of the repeated persecutions that have been heaped upon us; and as the governor's exterminating order has not been rescinded, we as a people were obliged to leave the state of Missouri, and with it our lands, corn, wheat, pork, etc., that we had provided for ourselves and families, together with our fodder, which we have collected for our cattle, horses, etc., those of them that we have been able to preserve from the wreck of that desolation which has spread itself over Daviess and Caldwell counties. In consequence of our brethren being obliged to leave the state, and as a sympathy and friendly spirit has been manifested by the citizens of Quincy, numbers of our brethren, glad to obtain an asylum from the hand of persecution, have come to this place.

"We cannot but express our feelings of gratitude to the inhabitants of this place, for the friendly feelings which have been manifested, and the benevolent hand which has been stretched out to a poor, oppressed, injured, and persecuted people. And as you, gentlemen of the Democratic Association, have felt interested in our welfare, and have desired to be put in possession of a knowledge of our situation, our present wants, and what would be most conducive to our present good, together with what led to those difficulties, we thought that those documents [Memorial, Order of Extermination, and General Clark's Address] would furnish you with as correct information of our difficulties, and what led to them, as anything we are in possession of.

"If we should say what our present wants are, it would be beyond all calculation; as we have been robbed of our corn, wheat, horses, cattle, cows, hogs, wearing apparel, houses and homes, and, indeed, of all that renders life tolerable. We do not, we cannot expect to be placed in the situation that we once were in; nor are we capable of ourselves of supplying the many wants of those of our poor brethren, who are daily crowding here and looking to us for relief, in consequence of our property, as well as theirs, being in the hands of a ruthless and desolating mob.

"It is impossible to give an exact account of the widows, and those that are entirely destitute, as there are so many coming here daily; but from inquiry, the probable amount will be something near twenty; besides numbers of others who are able bodied men, both able and willing to work, to obtain a subsistence: yet owing to their peculiar situation, are destitute of means to supply the immediate wants that the necesssities of their families call for.

"We would not propose, gentlemen, what you shall do; but after making these statements, shall leave it to your own judgment and generosity. As to what we think would be the best means to promote our permanent good, we think that to give us employment, rent us farms, and allow us the protection and privileges of other citizens, would raise us from a state of dependence, liberate us from the iron grasp of poverty, put us in possession of a competency, and deliver us from the ruinous effects of persecution, despotism, and tyranny.

"Written in behalf of a committee of the Latter-day Saints.

"ELIAS HIGBEE, President,
"JOHN P. GREENE, Clerk.

"To the Quincy Democratic Association."

Statement of Sidney Rigdon.

Mr. Rigdon then made a statement of the wrongs received by the Mormons, from a portion of the people of Missouri, and of their present suffering condition.

On motion of Mr. Bushnell, the report and resolutions were laid upon the table until tomorrow evening.

On motion of Mr. Bushnell, the meeting adjourned to meet at this place tomorrow evening at seven o'clock.

Stephen Markham left Far West [on the 27th of February] for Illinois, to fulfill his appointment of the 21st instant.

Minutes of the Adjourned Meeting of the Democratic Association of Quincy.

Thursday evening, February 28th. Met pursuant to adjournment. The meeting was called to order by the chairman.

On motion of Mr. Morris, a committee of three was appointed to take up a collection; Messrs. J. T. Holmes, Whitney and Morris were appointed. The committee subsequently reported that $48.25 had been collected. On motion the amount was paid over to the committee on behalf of the Mormons. On motion of Mr. Holmes, a committee of three, consisting of S. Holmes, Bushnell and Morris, was appointed to draw up subscription papers and circulate them among the citizens, for the purpose of receiving contributions in clothing and provisions. On motion six were added to that committee.

On motion of J. T. Holmes, J. D. Morgan was appointed a committee to wait upon the Quincy Grays [militia company] for the purpose of receiving subscriptions. Mr. Morgan subsequently reported that twenty dollars had been subscribed by that company.

The following resolutions were then offered by Mr. J. T. Holmes:

Resolved, That we regard the rights of conscience as natural and inalienable, and the most sacred guaranteed by the Constitution of our free government.

Resolved, That we regard the acts of all mobs as flagrant violations of law; and those who compose them, individually responsible, both to the laws of God and man, for every depredation committed upon the property, rights, or life of any citizen.

Resolved, that the inhabitants upon the western frontier of the state of Missouri, in their late persecutions of the class of people denominated Mormons, have violated the sacred rights of conscience, and every law of justice and humanity.

Resolved, That the governor of Missouri, in refusing protection to this class of people, when pressed upon by a heartless mob, and turning upon them a band of unprincipled militia, with orders encouraging their extermination, has brought a lasting disgrace upon the state over which he presides.

The resolutions were supported in a spirited manner by Messrs. Holmes, Morris and Whitney.

On motion, the resolutions were adopted.

On motion the meeting then adjourned.

Samuel Leach, Chairman,
J. D. Morgan, Secretary.

CHAPTER XIX.

LETTERS TO THE PROPHET—AFFAIRS IN ENGLAND—PETITIONS.

Tuesday, March 5.—

Edward Partridge's Letter to Joseph Smith, Jun., and Others, Confined in Liberty Jail, Missouri.

QUINCY, ILLINOIS.

BELOVED BRETHREN:—Having an opportunity to send direct to you by Brother Rogers, I feel to write a few lines to you.

President Rigdon, Judge Higbee, Israel Barlow, and myself went to see Dr. Isaac Galland week before last. Brothers Rigdon, Higbee and myself are of the opinion that it is not wisdom to make a trade with the Doctor at present; possibly it may be wisdom to effect a trade hereafter.

The people here receive us kindly; they have contributed near $100 cash, besides other property, for the relief of the suffering among our people. Brother Joseph's wife lives at Judge Cleveland's; I have not seen her, but I sent her word of this opportunity to send to you. Brother Hyrum's wife lives not far from me. I have been to see her a number of times; her health was very poor when she arrived, but she has been getting better; she knows of this opportunity to send. I saw Sister Wight soon after her arrival here; all were well; I understand she has moved about two miles with father and John Higbee, who are fishing this spring. Sister McRae is here, living with Brother Henderson, and is well; I believe she knows of this opportunity to send. Brother Baldwin's family I have not seen, and do not know that she has got here as yet. She, however, may be upon the other side of the river; the ice has run these three days past, so that there has been no crossing; the weather is now moderating, and the crossing will soon commence again.

This place is full of our people, yet they are scattering off nearly all the while. I expect to start tomorrow for Pittsfield, Pike county, Illinois, about forty-five miles southeast from this place. Brother George W. Robinson told me this morning that he expected that his father-in-law, Judge Higbee, and himself would go on a farm about twenty miles northeast from this place. Some of the leading men have given us [that is the Saints] an invitation to settle in and about this place. Many no doubt will stay here.

Brethren, I hope that you will bear patiently the privations that you are called to endure; the Lord will deliver you in His own due time.

Your letter respecting the trade with Galland was not received here until after our return from his residence, at the head of the shoals or rapids. If Brother Rigdon were not here, we might, after receiving your letter, come to a different conclusion respecting that trade. There are some here that are sanguine that we ought to trade with the Doctor. Bishops Whitney and Knight are not here, and have not been, as I know of. Brothers Morley and Billings have settled some twenty or twenty-five miles north of this place, for the present. A Brother Lee, who lived near Haun's Mill, died on the opposite side of the river a few days since. Brother Rigdon preached his funeral sermon in the court-house. It is a general time of health here.

We greatly desire to see you and to have you enjoy your freedom. The citizens here are willing that we should enjoy the privileges guaranteed to all civil people without molestation.

I remain your brother in the Lord,

EDWARD PARTRIDGE.

Don Carlos Smith to Joseph Smith, Jun., and Others Confined in Liberty Jail, Missouri.

QUINCY, ILLINOIS, March 6, 1839.

BROTHERS HYRUM AND JOSEPH:—Having an opportunity to send a line to you, I do not feel disposed to let it slip unnoticed. Father's family have all arrived in this state except you two; and could I but see your faces this side of the Mississippi, and know and realize that you had been delivered from your enemies, it would certainly light up a new gleam of hope in our bosoms; nothing could be more satisfactory, nothing could give us more joy.

Emma and the children are well; they live three miles from here, and have a tolerably good place. Hyrum's children and mother Grinold's are living at present with father; they are all well. Mary [wife of Hyrum Smith] has not got her health yet, but I think it increases slowly. She lives in the house with old Father Dixon; likewise Brother Robert T. Thompson and family; they are probably a half mile from father's. We are trying to get a house, and to get the family together; we shall do the best we can for them, and that which we consider to be most in accordance with Hyrum's feelings.

Father and mother stood their journey remarkably well. They are in tolerable health. Samuel's wife has been sick ever since they arrived. William has removed forty miles from here, but is here now, and says he is anxious to have you liberated, and see you enjoy liberty once more. My family is well; my health has not been good for about two weeks; and for two or three days the toothache has been my tormentor. It all originated with a severe cold.

Dear brethren, we just heard that the governor says that he is going to set you all at liberty; I hope it is true; other letters that you will probably receive will give you information concerning the warm feeling of the people here towards us.

After writing these hurried lines in misery, I close by leaving the blessings of God with you, and praying for your health, prosperity and restitution to liberty.

This from a true friend and brother,

DON C. SMITH.

William Smith to Joseph and Hyrum Smith.

BROTHERS HYRUM AND JOSEPH:—I should have called down to Liberty to have seen you had it not been for the multiplicity of business that was on my hands; and again, I thought that perhaps the people might think that the "Mormons" would rise up to liberate you; consequently too many going to see you might make it worse for you; but we all long to see you and have you come out of that lonesome place. I hope you will be permitted to come to your families before long. Do not worry about them, for they will be taken care of. All we can do will be done; further than this, we can only wish, hope, desire, and pray for your deliverance.

WILLIAM SMITH.

To Joseph Smith, Jun., and Hyrum Smith.

Friday, March 8.—

Minutes of a Meeting of the Committee on Removal.

The committee met at Theodore Turley's, William Huntington in the chair.

Alanson Ripley made a report of his journey to Liberty, and said that President Joseph Smith, Jun., counseled to sell all the land in Jackson county, and all other lands in the state whatsoever.

Resolved, That the names of those of the brethren who have subscribed to our covenant and have done nothing, be sought for, and a record made of them, that they may be had in remembrance.

Resolved, That an extra exertion be made to procure money for removing the poor, by visiting those who have money, and laying the necessities of the committee, in their business of removing the poor out of the state, before them, and solicit their assistance.

Voted that the clerk write a letter to Bishop Partridge, laying before him the advice of President Joseph Smith, Jun., concerning selling the Jackson county lands, and requesting a power of attorney to sell them.

Saturday, 9.—

Minutes of the Adjourned Meeting of the Democratic Association of Quincy.

At a meeting held at the committee room in the city of Quincy, Illinois, at two o'clock, p. m., on the 9th March, 1839, pursuant to previous appointment, it was moved by President Rigdon, and seconded, that Judge Elias Higbee be called to the chair, and he was unanimously appointed. James Sloan was then appointed clerk by vote.

President Rigdon spoke as to the members of the committee being absent who had called the meeting, and proposed that other business be proceeded with in the meantime, and left it to the chair to decide on the propriety thereof. The chair assented to the suggestion of President Rigdon.

President Rigdon then applied for a paper which had been prepared, and signed by several of the citizens of Quincy, describing our situation as a people and calling upon the humane in St. Louis and elsewhere to assist them in affording us relief. The paper, being presented by Brother Ephraim Owen, was then read, and President Rigdon spoke at length upon the subject, and proposed that a committee of two of the brethren be appointed by the voice of the meeting to go to St. Louis on such business. The motion was then put and carried, and Brother Mace was appointed as one of said committee, and Brother Ephraim Owen the other. It was proposed that Brother Orson Pratt (who is now in St. Louis) be appointed an assistant.

After the motion was made, and before it was seconded, President Rigdon spoke of its inconsistency, and stated, as a better mode, that all the Saints in St. Louis, or such of them as the committee may think proper, be called upon to assist them. The motion was withdrawn, and this business closed.

Some of the committee who called this meeting, being now present, President Rigdon spoke of two letters which had been received here by the brethren, from Iowa Territory, respecting lands in said place, and containing sentiments of sympathy on occount of our grievances and distressed situation. One of these letters has been mislaid, and the other, from Isaac Galland to Brother Rogers, was read. It was then proposed that a committee be appointed to visit the lands, and confer with the gentlemen who had so written, and declared themselves interested for our welfare.

Elder John P. Greene moved that a committee be appointed for that purpose, which was seconded, and adopted unanimously President

Rigdon moved that the committe shall select the land, if it can be safely occupied. Seconded by Elder Greene, and carried that the committee be composed of five, viz.: President Rigdon, Elder Greene, Judge Higbee, Brother Benson and Brother Israel Barlow.

It was moved, seconded and adopted, that if any one or more of the committee be unable to go, the remainder of the committee are to appoint others in their stead.

The chairman now produced a power of attorney, sent here from the committee at Far West, to be executed by such of the brethren here who had lands in Caldwell county, and were willing to have them sold, to enable the families who are in distress at that place to get here, say about one hundred families.

Power of attorney was read. Moved, seconded and adopted, that the clerk of this meeting do make out a copy of the minutes of this meeting, to be sent to the committee at Far West.

JAMES SLOAN, Clerk.

Condition of Affairs in England.

While the persecutions were progressing against us in Missouri, the enemy of all righteousness was no less busy with the Saints in England, according to the length of time the Gospel had been preached in that kingdom. Temptation followed temptation, and being young in the cause, the Saints suffered themselves to be buffeted by their adversary. From the time that Elder Willard Richards was called to the apostleship, in July, 1838, the devil seemed to take a great dislike to him, and strove to stir up the minds of many against him. Elder Richards was afflicted with sickness, and several times was brought to the borders of the grave, and many were tempted to believe that he was under transgression, or he would not be thus afflicted. Some were tried and tempted because Elder Richards took to himself a wife; they thought he should have given himself wholly to the ministry, and followed Paul's advice to the letter. Some were tried because his wife wore a veil, and others because she carried a muff to keep herself warm when she walked out in cold weather; and even the President of the Church [Joseph Fielding] there, thought "she had better done without it;" she had nothing ever purchased by the Church; and to gratify their feelings, wore the poorest clothes she had, and they were too good, so hard was it to buffet the storm of feeling that arose from such foolish causes. Sister Richards was very sick for some time, and some were dissatisfied because her husband did not neglect her entirely and go out preaching; and others, that she did not go to meeting when she was not able to go so far.

From such little things arose a spirit of jealousy, tattling, evil speaking, surmising, covetousness, and rebellion, until the Church but too generally harbored more or less of those unpleasant feelings: and this evening [March 9th] Elder Halsal came out openly in council against Elder Richards, and preferred some heavy charges, none of which he was able to substantiate. Most of the Elders in Preston were against Elder Richards for a season, except James Whitehead, who proved himself true in the hour of trial.

Charges of Elder Halsal Against Elder Willard Richards.

Sunday, 10.—When Elder Richards made proclamation from the pulpit, that if anyone had aught against him, or his wife Jennetta, he wished they would come to him and state their grievances, and if he had erred in anything, he would acknowledge his fault, one only of the brethren came to him, and that to acknowledge his own fault to Elder Richards in harboring unpleasant feelings without a cause.

The Cause of Elder Richards' Troubles.

Sister Richards bore all these trials and persecutions with patience. Elder Richards knew the cause of these unpleasantries, his call [to the apostolate] having been made known to him by revelation; but he told no one of it. The work continued to spread in Manchester and vicinity, among the Staffordshire potteries, and other places in England.

Friday, 15.—I made the following petition:

The Petition of the Prophet et al. to Judge Tompkins et al.

To the Honorable Judge Tompkins, or either of the Judges of the Supreme Court of the State of Missouri:

Your petitioners, Alanson Ripley, Heber C. Kimball, Joseph B. Noble,

William Huntington, and Joseph Smith, Jun., beg leave respectfully to represent to your honor, that Joseph Smith, Jun., is now unlawfully confined and restrained of his liberty in Liberty jail, Clay county, Missouri; that he has been restrained of his liberty nearly five months. Your petitioners claim that the whole transaction which has been the cause of his confinement, is unlawful from the first to the last. He was taken from his house by a fraud being practiced upon him by a man of the name of George M. Hinkle, and one or two others; thereby your petitioners respectfully show, that he was forced, contrary to his wishes, and without knowing the cause, into the camp, which was commanded by General Lucas of Jackson county, and thence sent to Ray county, sleeping on the ground, and suffering many insults and injuries, and deprivations, which were calculated in their nature to break down the spirit and constitution of the most robust and hardy of mankind.

He was put in chains immediately on his being landed at Richmond, and there underwent a long and tedious *ex parte* examination.

Your petitioners show that the said Joseph Smith, Jun., was deprived of the privileges of being examined before the court as the law directs; that the witnesses on the part of the state were taken by force of arms, threatened with extermination or immediate death, and were brought without subpoena or warrant, under the awful and glaring anticipation of being exterminated if they did not swear something against him to please the mob or his persecutors; and those witnesses were compelled to swear at the muzzle of the gun, and some of them have acknowledged since, which your petitioners do testify, and are able to prove, that they did swear falsely, and that they did it in order to save their lives.

And your petitioners testify that all the testimony that had any tendency or bearing of criminality against said Joseph Smith, Jun., is false. We are personally acquainted with the circumstances, and being with him most of the time, and being present at the time spoken of by them, therefore we know that their testimony was false; and if he could have had a fair trial, and impartial, and lawful examination before the court, and could have been allowed the privilege of introducing his witnesses, he could have disproved everything that was against him; but the court suffered them to be intimidated, some of them in the presence of the court, and they were driven also and hunted, and some of them driven entirely out of the state.

And thus he was not able to have a fair trial; that the spirit of the court was tyrannical and overbearing, and the whole transaction of his treatment during the examination was calculated to convince your petitioners that it was a religious persecution, proscribing him in the liberty of conscience which is guaranteed to him by the Constitution of the

United States, and the state of Missouri; that a long catalogue of garbled testimony was permitted by the court, purporting to be the religious sentiment of the said Joseph Smith, Jun., which testimony was false, and your petitioners know that it was false, and can prove that it was false; because the witnesses testified that those sentiments were promulgated on certain days, and in the presence of large congregations; and your petitioners can prove, by those congregations, that the said Joseph Smith, Jun., did not promulgate such ridiculous and absurd sentiments for his religion as were testified of and admitted before the Honorable Austin A. King; and at the same time those things had no bearing on the offenses that the said Joseph Smith, Jun., was charged with; and after the examination the said prisoner was committed to the jail for treason against the state of Missouri; whereas the said Joseph Smith, Jun., did not levy war against the state of Missouri; neither did he commit any overt acts; neither did he aid or abet an enemy against the state of Missouri during the time he is charged with having done so.

And further, your petitioners have yet to learn that the state has an enemy; neither is the proof evident, nor the presumption great, in its most malignant form, upon the testimony on the part of the state, exparte as it is in its nature, that the said prisoner has committed the slightest degree of treason, or any other act of transgression against the laws of the state of Missouri; and yet said prisoner has been committed to Liberty jail, Clay county, Missouri, for treason. He has continually offered bail to any amount that could be required, notwithstanding your petitioners allege that he ought to have been acquitted.

Your petitioners also allege, that the commitment was an illegal commitment, for the law requires that a copy of the testimony should be put in the hands of the jailer, which was not done.

Your petitioners allege, that the prisoner has been denied the privilege of the law in a writ of habeas corpus, by the judge of this county. Whether they have prejudged the case of the prisoner, or whether they are not willing to administer law and justice to the prisoner, or that they are intimidated by the high office of Judge King, who only acted in the case of the prisoner as a committing magistrate, a conservator of the peace, or by the threats of a lawless mob, your petitioners are not able to say; but it is a fact that they do not come forward boldly and administer the law to the relief of the prisoner.

And further, your petitioners allege that immediately after the prisoner was taken, his family were frightened and driven out of their house, and that too, by the witnesses on the part of the state, and plundered of their goods; that the prisoner was robbed of a very fine horse, saddle and bridle, and other property of considerable amount;

that they (the witnesses) in connection with the mob, have finally succeeded, by vile threatening and foul abuse, in driving the family of the prisoner out of the state, with little or no means; and without a protector, and their very subsistence depends upon the liberty of the prisoner. And your petitioners allege, that he is not guilty of any crime, whereby he should be restrained of his liberty, from a personal knowledge, having been with him, and being personally acquainted with the whole of the difficulties between the "Mormons" and their persecutors; and that he has never acted at any time, only in his own defense, and that too on his own ground, property and possessions. That the prisoner has never commanded any military company, nor held any military authority, neither any other office, real or pretended in the state of Missouri, except that of a religious instructor; that he never has borne arms in the military rank; and in all such cases has acted as a private character and as an individual.

How, then, your petitioners would ask, can it be possible that the prisoner has committed treason? The prisoner has had nothing to do in Daviess county, only on his own business as an individual.

The testimony of Dr. Avard concerning a council held at James Sloan's was false. Your petitioners do solemnly declare, that there was no such council; that your petitioners were with the prisoner, and there was no such vote or conversation as Dr. Avard swore to. That Dr. Avard also swore falsely concerning a constitution, as he said was introduced among the Danites; that the prisoner had nothing to do with burning in Daviess county; that the prisoner made public proclamation against such things; that the prisoner did oppose Dr. Avard and George M. Hinkle against vile measures with the mob, but was threatened by them if he did not let them alone. That the prisoner did not have anything to do with what is called Bogart's battle, for he knew nothing of it until it was over; that he was at home, in the bosom of his own family, during the time of that whole transaction.

And, in fine, your petitioners allege, that he is held in confinement without cause, and under an unlawful and tyrannical oppression, and that his health, and constitution, and life depend on being liberated from his confinement.

Your petitioners aver that they can disprove every item of testimony that has any tendency of criminality against the prisoner; for they know the facts themselves, and can bring many others also to prove the same.

Therefore your petitioners pray your honor to grant to him the state's writ of habeas corpus, directed to the jailer of Clay county, Missouri, commanding him forthwith to bring before you the body of the prisoner, so that his case may be heard before your honor, and the situation of the prisoner be considered and adjusted according to law and justice, as it shall be presented before your honor, and, as in duty bound, your petitioners will ever pray.

And further, your petitioners testify that the said Joseph Smith, Jun., did make a public proclamation in Far West, in favor of the militia of the state of Missouri, and of its laws and also of the Constitution of the United States; and that he has ever been a warm friend to his country, and did use all his influence for peace; that he is a peaceable and quiet citizen, and is not worthy of death, of stripes, bond, or imprisonment.

The above mentioned speech was delivered on the day before the surrender of Far West,

ALANSON RIPLEY,
HEBER C. KIMBALL,
WILLIAM HUNTINGTON,
JOSEPH B. NOBLE,
JOSEPH SMITH, JUN.

STATE OF MISSOURI, }
COUNTY OF CLAY. } ss.

This day personally appeared before me, Abraham Shafer, a justic of the peace within and for the aforesaid county, Alanson Ripley, Heber C. Kimball, William Huntington, Joseph B. Noble and Joseph Smith, Jun., who being duly sworn, do depose and say that the matters and things set forth in the foregoing petition, upon their own knowledge, are true in substance and in fact; and so far as set forth upon the information of others, they believe to be true.

ALANSON RIPLEY,
HEBER C. KIMBALL,
WILLIAM HUNTINGTON,
JOSEPH B. NOBLE,
JOSEPH SMITH, JUN.

Sworn and subscribed to before me, this 15th day of March, 1839.

ABRHAM SHAFER, J. P.

We, the undersigned, being many of us personally acquainted with the said Joseph Smith, Jun., and the circumstances connected with his imprisonment, do concur in the petition and testimony of the abovenamed individuals, as most of the transactions therein mentioned we know from personal knowledge to be correctly set forth; and from information of others, believe the remainder to be true.

AMASA LYMAN,
H. G. SHERWOOD,
JAMES NEWBERRY,
CYRUS DANIELS,
ERASTUS SNOW,
ELIAS SMITH.

The same day Caleb Baldwin, Lyman Wight, Alexander McRae, and Hyrum Smith, my fellow prisoners, made each a similar petition.

CHAPTER XX.

SUNDRY MOVEMENTS IN THE INTEREST OF THE EXILED SAINTS—PROPHET'S LETTERS FROM LIBERTY PRISON.

Sunday, 17.—I here give an extract from the minutes of a conference of the Church of Jesus Christ of Latter-day Saints, held this day in Quincy; Brigham Young by a unanimous vote was called to the chair, and Robert B. Thompson chosen clerk.

Minutes of the Conference at Quincy, Illinois.

Elder Young arose and gave a statement of the circumstances of the Church at Far West, and his feelings in regard to the scattering of the brethren, believing it to be wisdom to unite together as much as possible in extending the hand of charity for the relief of the poor, who were suffering for the Gospel's sake, under the hand of persecution in Missouri, and to pursue that course which would prove for the general good of the whole Church. He would advise the Saints to settle (if possible) in companies, or in a situation so as to be organized into branches of the Church, that they might be nourished and fed by the shepherds; for without, the sheep would be scattered; and he also impressed it upon the minds of the Saints to give heed to the revelations of God; the Elders especially should be careful to depart from all iniquity, and to remember the counsel given by those whom God hath placed as counselors in His Church; that they may become as wise stewards in the vineyard of the Lord, that every man may know and act in his own place; for there is order in the kingdom of God, and we must regard that order if we expect to be blessed.

Elder Young also stated that Elder Jonathan Dunham had received previous instructions not to call any conferences in this state, or elsewhere; but to go forth and preach repentance, this was his calling; but contrary to those instructions, he called a conference in Springfield, Illinois, and presided there, and brought forth the business which he had to transact; and his proceeding in many respects during the conference was contrary to the feelings of Elder Wilford Woodruff and other official members who were present. They considered his proceedings contrary to the will and order of God.

The conference then voted that Elder Dunham be reproved for his improper course, and that he be advised to adhere to the counsel given him.

After the conference had transacted various other business, Elder George W. Harris made some remarks relative to those who had left us in the time of our perils, persecutions and dangers, and were acting against the interests of the Church; he said that the Church could no longer hold them in fellowship unless they repented of their sins, and turned unto God.

After the conference had fully expressed their feelings upon the subject it was unanimously voted that the following persons be excommunicated from the Church of Jesus Christ of Latter-day Saints, viz.: George M. Hinkle, Sampson Avard, John Corrill, Reed Peck, William W. Phelps, Frederick G. Williams, Thomas B. Marsh, Burr Riggs, and several others. After which the conference closed by prayer.

BRIGHAM YOUNG, President.
ROBERT B. THOMPSON, Clerk.

Departure of Mrs. Pratt.

This day, 17th of March, Parley P. Pratt's wife left the prison house, where she had voluntarily been with her husband most of the winter, and returned to Far West, to get passage with some of the brethren for Illinois.

Action of the Committee of Removal.

The committee met at the house of Daniel Shearer, Far West, William Huntington in the chair.

Present—Brother Daniel W. Rogers, from Quincy, Illinois. Brother Rogers made known the proceedings of the brethren in Quincy, in relation to locating in the Iowa territory, and read a private letter from Dr. Isaac Galland to him on the same subject, and presented a power of attorney from Bishop Partridge to dispose of the lands of the Church in Jackson county, and also some lots in Far West. He then presented a copy of the proceedings of a council held in Quincy on the 9th instant, which was read; after which Brother Rogers explained some things relative to said meeting, and the proceedings thereof.

A bill of articles wanted by the prisoners in Liberty jail, was presented by Elder Heber C. Kimball, and accepted. Charles Bird was appointed to accompany Brother Rogers to Jackson county to assist him in the sale of the Jackson county lands.

On motion, resolved: That we will not patronize Brother Lamb in his market shaving [extortion] shop, or any other of the kind in this place.

A petition of Alanson Ripley and others to the Honorable Judge Thompkins, of the Supreme Court of the State of Missouri, praying for a writ of habeas corpus for Joseph, Smith, Jun., was read by Elder Ripley.

Monday, 18.—The committee met in the course of the day, and appointed Theodore Turley to go to Jefferson City with Elder Heber C. Kimball to carry the petitions of the prisoners in Liberty and Richmond jails.

*Letter of the Prophet to Mrs. Norman Bull.**

LIBERTY JAIL, March 15, 1839.

Dear Sister:

My heart rejoices at the friendship you manifest in requesting to have a conversation with us, but the jailer is a very jealous man, fearing some one will leave tools for us to get out with. He is under the eye of the mob continually, and his life is at stake if he grants us any privileges. He will not let us converse with any one alone. Oh, what joy it would be to us to see our friends! It would have gladdened my heart to have had the privilege of conversing with you, but the hand of tyranny is upon us; thanks be to God, it cannot last always; and He that sitteth in the heaven will laugh at their calamity, and mock when their fear cometh. We feel, dear sister, that our bondage is not of long duration. I trust that I shall have the chance to give such instructions as are communicated to us before long. I suppose you want some instruction for yourself, and also to give us some information and administer consolation to us, and to find out what is best for you to do. I think that many of the brethren, if they will be pretty still, can stay in this country until the indignation is over and past; but I think it would be better for Brother Bull to leave and go with the rest of the brethren, if he keep the faith, and at any rate, thus speaketh the Spirit concerning him. I want him and you to know that I am your true friend. I was glad to see you. No tongue can tell what inexpressible

*Among others who called to see the Prophet in prison about this time was Mrs. Norman Bull; but apparently she was not allowed to have the coveted interview, and hence the prophet wrote to her. The letter here inserted appears in the manuscript history of the Church, but not until now has it been published. It is important as showing the frame of mind the Prophet was in, and his anxiety to administer comfort, and give helpful counsel to the Saints.

joy it gives a man, after having been enclosed in the walls of a prison for five months, to see the face of one who has been a friend. It seems to me that my heart will always be more tender after this than ever it was before. My heart bleeds continually when I contemplate the distress of the Church. O, that I could be with them! I would not shrink at toil and hardship to render them comfort and consolation. I want the blessing once more of lifting my voice in the midst of the Saints. I would pour out my soul to God for their instruction. It has been the plan of the devil to hamper me and distress me from the beginning, to keep me from explaining myself to them; and I never have had opportunity to give them the plan that God has revealed to me; for many have run without being sent, crying "Tidings, my Lord," and have done much injury to the Church, giving the devil more power over those that walk by sight and not by faith. But trials will only give us the knowledge necessary to understand the minds of the ancients. For my part, I think I never could have felt as I now do, if I had not suffered the wrongs that I have suffered. All things shall work together for good to them that love God. Beloved sister, we see that perilous times have truly come, and the things which we have so long expected have at last began to usher in; but when you see the fig tree begin to put forth its leaves, you may know that the summer is nigh at hand. There will be a short work on the earth. It has now commenced. I suppose there will soon be perplexity all over the earth. Do not let our hearts faint when these things come upon us, for they must come, or the word cannot be fulfilled. I know that something will soon take place to stir up this generation to see what they have been doing, and that their fathers have inherited lies and they have been led captive by the devil, to no profit; but they know not what they do. Do not have any feelings of enmity towards any son or daughter of Adam. I believe I shall be let out of their hands some way or another, and shall see good days. We cannot do anything only stand still and see the salvation of God. He must do His own work, or it must fall to the ground. We must not take it in our hands to avenge our wrongs. Vengeance is mine, saith the Lord, and I will repay. I have no fears. I shall stand unto death, God being my helper. I wanted to communicate something, and I wrote this.

Write to us if you can.

(Signed) JOSEPH SMITH, JUN.

To Mrs. Norman Bull, Clay Co., Mo.

While I was in jail, the following statements were made by the witnesses, and sent to Colonel Price, namely:

William E. McLellin is guilty of entering the house of Joseph Smith,

Jun., in the city of Far West, and plundering it of the following articles, viz.—one roll of linen cloth, a quantity of valuable buttons, one piece of cashmere, a number of very valuable books of great variety, a number of vestings, with various other articles of value.

Said McLellin was aided and assisted in the above transactions by Harvey Green, Burr Riggs and Harlow Redfield.*

The above mentioned William E. McLellin also came to and took away from the stable of the said above mentioned Joseph Smith, Jun.,

*When the History of Joseph Smith was being published in the *Deseret News*, and the above part of the History was reached, Harlow Redfield sent the following communications to the Editors vindicating himself from the charge of aiding McLellin in his robberies. It appears in the *News* of March 16, 1854.

To the Editor of The Deseret News:

SIR—In the History of Joseph Smith, published February 2, *News* No. 5, I find my name associated with others, as aiding McLellin and others in plundering the house of Joseph Smith while in prison. This is incorrect. The excitement of those times was sufficient reason for the rumor going abroad incorrectly:

I was at Hyrum Smith's house, rather by accident than design, in company with McLellin and Burr Riggs, at a time when they took some books, etc., but was not with them when they went to Joseph's. Soon after the rumor got afloat; I explained the matter before the Council in Missouri satisfactorily, as I supposed, but some time after, an enemy, in my absence, again agitated the subject before the Conference in Nauvoo, which led to an inquiry before the High Council in presence of Joseph and Hyrum, and the subject appearing in its true light, Joseph instructed the Council to give me a certificate of acquittal, that would close every man's mouth.

The following is the certificate, viz:—

"The High Council of the Church of Jesus Christ of Latter-day Saints met at Nauvoo, 20th October, 1840, to consider the case of Harlow Redfield, against whom certain accusations were brought at our last conference, in consequence of which, he was suspended, and his case referred to the High Council for decision. We being organized to investigate his case, when no charge was brought against him, nor did an implication appear, nor do we believe that a charge could be sustained against Elder Redfield. He volunteered confession of certain inadvertent, imprudent, [but] no evil meaning acts, that he greatly sorrowed for, and asked forgiveness for his folly in such acts. This Council voted that Elder Redfield be forgiven, and restored to his former official state and standing, and to be in full fellowship, the same as if no evil insinuation had ever been brought against him; and that he take a transcript of these proceedings, to be signed by the Clerk of this meeting.

"I hereby certify that the above is a true transcript of the proceedings and decision of the aforesaid case.

"H. G. SHERWOOD."

I will only add that I had before heard how that "poor Tray" got whipped for being in bad company, and it ought to have been a sufficient warning for me, and I trust it will be for the future.

I remain your humble servant,

HARLOW REDFIELD.

Provo, Feb. 7. 1854.

one gig and harness, with some other articles which cannot now be called to mind, aided and assisted by Burr Riggs—which can be proven by the following witnesses—

CAROLINE CLARK,
JAMES MULHOLLAND,
MRS. SALLY HINKLE,
JOANNA CARTER.

J. Stollins is guilty of entering the house of Joseph Smith, Jun., in the city of Far West, in company with Sashiel Woods and another man not known, and taking from a trunk, the property of James Mulholland, an inmate of said house, one gold ring, which they carried away; also of breaking open a sealed letter, which was in said trunk inside a pocket book, in which was the ring above mentioned; besides tossing and abusing the rest of the contents of said trunk; which can be proven by the following persons—

MRS. EMMA SMITH,
MRS. SALLY HINKLE,
CAROLINE CLARK,
JAMES MULHOLLAND.

Monday, March 25.—About this time, Elders Kimball and Turley started on their mission to see the governor. They called on the sheriff of Ray county and the jailer for a copy of the mittimus, by which the prisoners were held in custody, but they confessed they had none. They went to Judge King, and he made out a kind of mittimus. At this time we had been in prison several months without even a mittimus; and that too for crimes said to have been committed in another county.

The Mission of Kimball and Turley to Governor Boggs.

Elders Kimball and Turley took all the papers by which we were held, or which were then made out for them, with our petition to the supreme judges, and went to Jefferson City.

The governor was absent. The secretary of state treated them very kindly; and when he saw the papers, could hardly believe those were all the documents by which the prisoners were held in custody, for they were illegal.

Lawyer Doniphan had also deceived them in his papers and sent them off with such documents, that a change of venue could not be effected in time. The secretary was astonished at Judge King acting as he did, but said he could do nothing in the premises, and if the governor were present, he could do nothing. But the secretary wrote a letter to Judge King.

The Faulty Mittimus.

The brethren then started to find the supreme judges, and get writs of habeas corpus; and after riding hundreds of miles to effect this object, returned to Liberty on the 30th of March, having seen Matthias McGirk, George Thompkins and John C. Edwards, the supreme judges, but did not obtain the writ of habeas corpus in consequence of a lack in the order of commitment, although the judges seemed to be friendly.

We were informed that Judge King said, that there was nothing against my brother Hyrum, only that he was a friend to the Prophet. He also said there was nothing against Caleb Baldwin, and Alexander McRae.

Brother Horace Cowan was put into Liberty jail today for debt, in consequence of the persecution of the mob.

*The Prophet's Epistle to the Church, Written in Liberty Prison.**

LIBERTY JAIL, CLAY COUNTY, MISSOURI,
March 25, 1839.

To the Church of Latter-day Saints at Quincy, Illinois, and Scattered Abroad, and to Bishop Partridge in Particular:

Your humble servant, Joseph Smith, Jun., prisoner for the Lord Jesus Christ's sake, and for the Saints, taken and held by the power of mobocracy, under the exterminating reign of his excellency, the governor, Lilburn W. Boggs, in company with his fellow prisoners and be-

* The following important communication of the Prophet and his fellow prisoners to the Church at large, and to Bishop Edward Partridge in particular, was written between the 20th and 25th of March. In the Prophet's history as published many years ago in current issues of the *Deseret News* and *Millennial Star* the communication is divided near the middle of it by reciting the few incidents happening between the 20th and 25th of March—the former being the date on which the letter was begun, the latter the date on which it was completed; but in this publication it is thought desirable that the letter be given without this division, and hence it appears under the date on which it was completed, *viz*, the 25th of March, 1839. The parts of the communication enclosed in brackets and double leaded were regarded of such special value that they were taken from this communication and placed in the Doctrine and Covenants and comprise sections cxxi, cxxii, cxxiii of that work.

loved brethren, Caleb Baldwin, Lyman Wight, Hyrum Smith, and Alexander McRae, send unto you all greeting. May the grace of God the Father, and of our Lord and Savior Jesus Christ, rest upon you all, and abide with you forever. May knowledge be multiplied unto you by the mercy of God. And may faith and virtue, and knowledge and temperance, and patience and godliness, and brotherly kindness and charity be in you and abound, that you may not be barren in anything, nor unfruitful.

For inasmuch as we know that the most of you are well acquainted with the wrongs and the high-handed injustice and cruelty that are practiced upon us; whereas we have been taken prisoners charged falsely with every kind of evil, and thrown into prison, enclosed with strong walls, surrounded with a strong guard, who continually watch day and night as indefatigable as the devil does in tempting and laying snares for the people of God:

Therefore, dearly beloved brethren, we are the more ready and willing to lay claim to your fellowship and love. For our circumstances are calculated to awaken our spirits to a sacred remembrance of everything, and we think that yours are also, and that nothing therefore can separate us from the love of God and fellowship one with another; and that every species of wickedness and cruelty practiced upon us will only tend to bind our hearts together and seal them together in love. We have no need to say to you that we are held in bonds without cause, neither is it needful that you say unto us, We are driven from our homes and smitten without cause. We mutually understand that if the inhabitants of the state of Missouri had let the Saints alone, and had been as desirable of peace as they were, there would have been nothing but peace and quietude in the state unto this day; we should not have been in this hell, surrounded with demons (if not those who are damned, they are those who shall be damned) and where we are compelled to hear nothing but blasphemous oaths, and witness a scene of blasphemy, and drunkenness and hypocrisy, and debaucheries of every description.

And again, the cries of orphans and widows would not have ascended up to God against them. Nor would innocent blood have stained the soil of Missouri. But oh! the unrelenting hand! The inhumanity and murderous disposition of this people! It shocks all nature; it beggars and defies all description; it is a tale of woe; a lamentable tale; yea a sorrowful tale; too much to tell; too much for contemplation; too much for human beings; it cannot be found among the heathens; it cannot be found among the nations where kings and tyrants are enthroned; it cannot be found among the savages of the wilderness; yea, and I think it cannot be found among the wild and ferocious beasts of the forest—

that a man should be mangled for sport! women be robbed of all that they have—their last morsel for subsistence, and then be violated to gratify the hellish desires of the mob, and finally left to perish with their helpless offspring clinging around their necks.

But this is not all. After a man is dead, he must be dug up from his grave and mangled to pieces, for no other purpose than to gratify their spleen against the religion of God.

They practice these things upon the Saints, who have done them no wrong, who are innocent and virtuous; who loved the Lord their God, and were willing to forsake all things for Christ's sake. These things are awful to relate, but they are verily true. It must needs be that offenses come, but woe unto them by whom they come.

[Oh God! where art Thou? And where is the pavilion that covereth Thy hiding place? How long shall Thy hand be stayed, and Thine eye, yea Thy pure eye, behold from the eternal heavens, the wrongs of Thy people, and of Thy servants, and Thy ear be penetrated with their cries? Yea, O Lord, how long shall they suffer these wrongs and unlawful oppressions, before Thine heart shall be softened towards them, and Thy bowels be moved with compassion towards them?

O Lord God Almighty, Maker of Heaven, Earth and Seas, and of all things that in them are, and who controllest and subjectest the devil, and the dark and benighted dominion of Sheol! Stretch forth Thy hand, let Thine eye pierce; let Thy pavilion be taken up; let Thy hiding place no longer be covered; let Thine ear be inclined; let Thine heart be softened,and Thy bowels moved with compassion towards us, Let Thine anger be kindled against our enemies; and in the fury of Thine heart, with Thy sword avenge us of our wrongs; remember Thy suffering Saints, O our God! and Thy servants will rejoice in Thy name forever.]

Dearly and beloved brethren, we see that perilous times have come, as was testified of. We may look, then, with most perfect assurance, for the fulfillment of all those things that have been written, and with more confidence than ever before, lift up our eyes to the luminary of day, and say in our hearts, Soon thou wilt veil thy blushing face. He that said "Let there be light," and there was light, hath spoken this word. And again, Thou moon, thou dimmer light, thou luminary of night, shalt turn to blood.

We see that everything is being fulfilled; and that the time shall soon come when the Son of Man shall descend in the clouds of heaven. Our hearts do not shrink, neither are our spirits altogether broken by the grievous yoke which is put upon us. We know that God will have our oppressors in derision; that He will laugh at their calamity, and mock when their fear cometh.

O that we could be with you, brethren, and unbosom our feelings to you! We would tell, that we should have been liberated at the time Elder Rigdon was, on the writ of habeas corpus, had not our own lawyers interpreted the law, contrary to what it reads, against us; which prevented us from introducing our evidence before the mock court.

They have done us much harm from the beginning. They have of late acknowledged that the law was misconstrued, and tantalized our feelings with it, and have entirely forsaken us, and have forfeited their oaths and their bonds; and we have a come-back on them, for they are co-workers with the mob.

As nigh as we can learn, the public mind has been for a long time turning in our favor, and the majority is now friendly; and the lawyers can no longer browbeat us by saying that this or that is a matter of public opinion, for public opinion is not willing to brook it; for it is beginning to look with feelings of indignation against our oppressors, and to say that the "Mormons" were not in the fault in the least. We think that truth, honor, virtue and innocence will eventually come out triumphant. We should have taken a habeas corpus before the high judge and escaped the mob in a summary way; but unfortunately for us, the timber of the wall being very hard, our auger handles gave out, and hindered us longer than we expected; we applied to a friend, and a very slight incautious act gave rise to some suspicions, and before we could fully succeed, our plan was discovered; we had everything in readiness, but the last stone, and we could have made our escape in one minute, and should have succeeded admirably, had it not been for a little imprudence or over-anxiety on the part of our friend.*

The sheriff and jailer did not blame us for our attempt; it was a fine breach, and cost the county a round sum; but public opinion says that we ought to have been permitted to have made our escape; that then the disgrace would have been on us, but now it must come on the state; that there cannot be any charge sustained against us; and that the conduct of the mob, the murders committed at Haun's Mills, and the exterminating order of the governor, and the one-sided, rascally proceedings of the legislature, have damned the state of Missouai to all eternity. I would just name also that General Atchison has proved himself as contemptible as any of them.

We have tried for a long time to get our lawyers to draw us some

This alludes to another effort to escape from prison besides the one related by Alexander McRae at pp. 257-8.

petitions to the supreme judges of this state. but they utterly refused. We have examined the law, and drawn the petitions ourselves, and have obtained abundance of proof to counteract all the testimony that was against us, so that if the supreme judge does not grant us our liberty, he has to act without cause, contrary to honor, evidence, law or justice, sheerly to please the devil, but we hope better things and trust before many days God will so order our case, that we shall be set at liberty and take up our habitation with the Saints.

We received some letters last evening—one from Emma, one from Don C. Smith, and one from Bishop Partridge—all breathing a kind and consoling spirit. We were much gratified with their contents. We had been a long time without information; and when we read those letters they were to our souls as the gentle air is refreshing, but our joy was mingled with grief, because of the sufferings of the poor and much injured Saints. And we need not say to you that the floodgates of our hearts were lifted and our eyes were a fountain of tears, but those who have not been enclosed in the walls of prison without cause or provocation, can have but little idea how sweet the voice of a friend is; one token of friendship from any source whatever awakens and calls into action every sympathetic feeling; it brings up in an instant everything that is passed; it seizes the present with the avidity of lightning; it grasps after the future with the fierceness of a tiger; it moves the mind backwark and forward, from one thing to another, until finally all enmity, malice and hatred, and past differences, misunderstandings and mismanagements are slain victorious at the feet of hope; and when the heart is sufficiently contrite, then the voice of inspiration steals along and whispers, [My son, peace be unto thy soul; thine adversity and thine afflictions shall be but a small moment; and then if thou endure it well, God shall exalt thee on high; thou shalt triumph over all thy foes; thy friends do stand by thee, and they shall hail thee again, with warm hearts and friendly hands; thou art not yet as Job; thy friends do not contend against thee, neither charge thee with transgression, as they did Job; and they who do charge thee with transgression, their hope shall be blasted and their prospects shall melt away as the hoar frost melteth before the burning rays of the rising sun; and also that God hath set His hand and seal to change the times and seasons, and to blind their minds, that they may not understand His marvelous workings, that He may prove them also and take them in their own craftiness; also because their hearts are corrupted, and the things which they are willing to bring upon others, and love to have others suffer, may come upon themselves to the very uttermost; that they may be disappointed also, and their hopes may be cut off; and not many years hence, that they and their posterity shall be swept from under heaven, saith God, that not one of them is left to stand by the wall. Cursed are all those that shall lift up the heel against mine anointed, saith the Lord, and cry they have sinned when they have not sinned before me, saith the Lord, but have done that which was meet in mine eyes, and which I commanded them; but those who cry transgression do it because they are the servants of sin and are the children of disobedience themselves; and those who swear falsely against my servants, that they might bring them into bondage and death; wo unto them; because they have offended my little ones; they shall be severed from the ordinances of mine house; their basket shall not be full, and their houses and their barns shall perish, and they themselves shall be despised by those that flattered them; they shall not have right to the Priesthood, nor their posterity after them, from generation to generation; it had been better for them that a millstone had been hanged about their necks, and they drowned in the depth of the sea.

Wo unto all those that discomfort my people, and drive and murder, and testify against them, saith the Lord of Hosts; a generation of vipers shall not escape the damnation of hell. Behold mine eyes see and know all their works, and I have in reserve a swift judgment in the season thereof, for them all; for there is a time appointed for every man according as his work shall be.]

And now, beloved brethren, we say unto you, that inasmuch as God hath said that He would have a tried people, that He would purge them as gold, now we think that this time He has chosen His own crucible, wherein we have been tried; and we think if we get through with any degree of safety, and shall have kept the faith, that it will be a sign to this generation, altogether sufficient to leave them without excuse; and we think also, it will be a trial of our faith equal to that of Abraham, and that the ancients will not have whereof to boast over us in the day of judgment, as being called to pass through heavier afflictions; that we may hold an even weight in the balance with them; but now, after having suffered so great sacrifice and having passed through so great a season of sorrow, we trust that a ram may be caught in the thicket speedily, to relieve the sons and daughters of Abraham from their great anxiety, and to light up the lamp of salvation upon their countenances, that they may hold on now, after having gone so far unto everlasting life.

Now, brethren, concerning the places for the location of the Saints, we cannot counsel you as we could if we were present with you; and as to the things that were written heretofore, we did not consider them anything very binding, therefore we now say once for all, that we think it most proper that the general affairs of the Church, which are necessary to be considered, while your humble servant remains in bondage, should be transacted by a general conference of the most faithful and the most respectable of the authorities of the Church, and a minute of those transactions may be kept, and forwarded from time to time. to your humble servant; and if there should be any corrections by the word of the Lord, they shall be freely transmitted, and your humble servant will approve all things whatsoever is acceptable unto God. If anything should have been suggested by us, or any names mentioned, except by commandment, or thus saith the Lord, we do not consider it binding; therefore our hearts shall not be grieved if different arrangements should be entered into. Nevertheless we would suggest the propriety of being aware of an aspiring spirit, which spirit has oftentimes urged men forward to make foul speeches, and influence the Church to reject milder counsels, and has eventually been the means of bringing much death and sorrow upon the Church.

We would say, beware of pride also; for well and truly hath the wise man said, that pride goeth before destruction, and a haughty spirit before a fall. And again, outward appearance is not always a criterion by which to judge our fellow man; but the lips betray the haughty and overbearing imaginations of the heart; by his words and his deeds let him be judged. Flattery also is a deadly poison. A frank and open rebuke provoketh a good man to emulation; and in the hour of trouble he will be your best friend; but on the other hand, it will draw out all the corruptions of corrupt hearts, and lying and the poison of asps is under their tongues; and they do cause the pure in heart to be cast into prison, because they want them out of their way.

A fanciful and flowery and heated imagination beware of; because the things of God are of deep import; and time, and experience, and careful and ponderous and solemn thoughts can only find them out. Thy mind, O man! if thou wilt lead a soul unto salvation, must stretch as high as the utmost heavens, and search into and contemplate the darkest abyss, and the broad expanse of eternity—thou must commune with God. How much more dignified and noble are the thoughts of God, than the vain imaginations of the human heart! None but fools will trifle with the souls of men.

How vain and trifling have been our spirits, our conferences, our councils, our meetings, our private as well as public conversations—too low, too mean, too vulgar, too condescending for the dignified characters of the called and chosen of God, according to the purposes of His will, from before the foundation of the world! We are called to hold the keys of the mysteries of those things that have been kept hid from the foundation of the world until now. Some have tasted a little of these things, many of which are to be poured down from heaven upon the heads of babes; yea, upon the weak, obscure and despised ones of the earth. Therefore we beseech of you, brethren, that you bear with those who do not feel themselves more worthy than yourselves, while we exhort one another to a reformation with one and all, both old and young, teachers and taught, both high and low, rich and poor, bond and free, male and female; let honesty, and sobriety, and candor, and solemnity, and virtue, and pureness, and meekness, and simplicity crown our heads in every place; and in fine, become as little children, without malice, guile or hypocrisy.

And now, brethren, after your tribulations, if you do these things, and exercise fervent prayer and faith in the sight of God always, [He shall give unto you knowledge by His Holy Spirit, yea by the unspeakable gift of the Holy Ghost, that has not been revealed since the world was until now; which our forefathers have waited with anxious expectation to be revealed in the last times, which their minds were pointed to by the angels, as held in reserve for the fullness of their glory; a time to come in the which nothing shall be withheld, whether there be one God or many Gods, they shall be manifest; all thrones and dominions, principalities and powers, shall be revealed and set forth upon all who have endured valiantly for the Gospel of Jesus Christ; and also if there be bounds set to the heavens, or to the seas; or to the dry land, or to the sun, moon or stars; all the times of their revolutions; all the appointed days, months and years, and all the days of their days, months and years, and all their glories, laws, and set times, shall be revealed, in the days of the dispensation of the fullness of times, according to that which was ordained in the midst of the Council of the Eternal God of all other Gods, before this world was, that should be reserved unto the finishing and the end thereof, when every man shall enter into His eternal presence, and into His immortal rest].

But I beg leave to say unto you, brethren, that ignorance, superstition and bigotry placing itself where it ought not, is oftentimes in the way of the prosperity of this Church; like the torrent of rain from the mountains, that floods the most pure and crystal stream with mire, and dirt, and filthiness, and obscures everything that was clear before, and all rushes along in one general deluge; but time weathers tide; and notwithstanding we are rolled in the mire of the flood for the time being, the next surge peradventure, as time rolls on, may bring to us the fountain as clear as crystal, and as pure as snow; while the filthiness, flood-wood and rubbish is left and purged out by the way.

[How long can rolling water remain impure? What power shall stay the heavens? As well might man stretch forth his puny arm to stop the Missouri river in its decreed course, or to turn it up stream, as to hinder the Almighty from pouring down knowledge from heaven, upon the heads of the Latter-day Saints].

What is Boggs or his murderous party, but wimbling willows upon the shore to catch the flood-wood? As well might we argue that water is not water, because the mountain torrents send down mire and roil the crystal stream, although afterwards render it more pure than before; or that fire is not fire, because it is of a quenchable nature, by pouring on the flood; as to say that our cause is down because renegados, liars, priests, thieves and murderers, who are all alike tenacious of their crafts and creeds, have poured down, from their spiritual wickedness in high places, and from their strongholds of the devil, a flood of dirt and mire and filthiness and vomit upon our heads.

No! God forbid. Hell may pour forth its rage like the burning lava of mount Vesuvius, or of Etna, or of the most terrible of the burning mountains; and yet shall "Mormonism" stand. Water, fire, truth and God are all realities. Truth is "Mormonism." God is the author of it. He is our shield. It is by Him we received our birth. It was by His voice that we were called to a dispensation of His Gospel in the beginning of the fullness of times. It was by Him we received the Book of Mormon; and it is by Him that we remain unto this day; and by Him we shall remain, if it shall be for our glory; and in His Almighty name we are determined to endure tribulation as good soldiers unto the end.

But, brethren, we shall continue to offer further reflections in our next epistle. You will learn by the time you have read this, and if you do not learn it, you may learn it, that walls and irons, doors and creaking hinges, and half-scared-to-death guards and jailers, grinning like some damned spirits, lest an innocent man should make his escape to bring to light the damnable deeds of a murderous mob, are calculated in their very nature to make the soul of an honest man feel stronger than the powers of hell.

But we must bring our epistle to a close. We send our respects to fathers, mothers, wives and children, brothers and sisters; we hold them in the most sacred remembrance.

We feel to inquire after Elder Rigdon; if he has not forgotten us, it has not been signified to us by his writing. Brother George W. Robinson also; and Elder Cahoon, we remember him, but would like to jog his memory a little on the fable of the bear and the two friends who mutually agreed to stand by each other. And perhaps it would not be amiss to mention uncle John [Smith], and various others. A word of consolation and a blessing would not come amiss from anybody, while we are being so closely whispered by the bear. But we feel to excuse everybody and everything, yea the more readily when we contemplate that we are in the hands of persons worse that a bear, for the bear would not prey upon a dead carcass.

Our respects and love and fellowship to all the virtuous Saints. We are your brethren and fellow-sufferers, and prisoners of Jesus Christ for the Gospel's sake, and for the hope of glory which is in us. Amen.

We continue to offer further reflections to Bishop Partridge, and to the Church of Jesus Christ of Latter-day Saints, whom we love with a fervent love, and do always bear them in mind in all our prayers to the throne of God.

It still seems to bear heavily on our minds that the Church would do well to secure to themselves the contract of the land which is proposed to them by Mr. Isaac Galland, and to cultivate the friendly feelings of that gentleman, inasmuch as he shall prove himself to be a man of honor and a friend to humanity; also Isaac Van Allen, Esq., the attorney-general of Iowa Territory, and Governor Lucas, that peradventure such men may be wrought upon by the providence of God, to do good unto His people. We really think that Mr. Galland's letter breathes that kind of a spirit, if we may judge correctly. Governor Lucas also. We suggest the idea of praying fervently for all men who manifest any degree of sympathy for the suffering children of God.

We think that the United States Surveyor of the Iowa Territory may be of great benefit to the Church, if it be the will of God to this end; and righteousness should be manifested as the girdle of our loins.

It seems to be deeply impressed upon our minds that the Saints ought to lay hold of every door that shall seem to be opened unto them, to obtain foothold on the earth, and be making all the preparation that is within their power for the terrible storms that are now gathering in the heavens, "a day of clouds, with darkness and gloominess, and of thick darkness," as spoken of by the Prophets, which cannot be now of a long time lingering, for there seems to be a whispering that the angels of heaven who have been entrusted with the counsel of these matters for the last days, have taken counsel together; and among the rest of the general affairs that have to be transacted in their honorable council, they have taken cognizance of the testimony of those who were murdered at Haun's Mills, and also those who were martyred with David W. Patten, and elsewhere, and have passed some decisions peradventure in favor of the Saints, and those who were called to suffer without cause.

These decisions will be made known in their time; and the council will take into consideration all those things that offend.

We have a fervent desire that in your general conferences everything should be discussed with a great deal of care and propriety, lest you grieve the Holy Spirit, which shall be poured out at all times upon your heads, when you are exercised with those principles of righteousness that are agreeable to the mind of God, and are properly affected one toward another, and are careful by all means to remember, those who are in bondage, and in heaviness, and in deep affliction far your sakes. And if there are any among you who aspire after their own aggrandizement, and seek their own opulence, while their brethren are groaning in poverty, and are under sore trials and temptations, they cannot be benefited by the intercession of the Holy Spirit, which maketh intercession for us day and night with groanings that cannot be uttered.

We ought at all times to be very careful that such high-mindedness shall never have place in our hearts; but condescend to men of low estate, and with all long-suffering bear the infirmities of the weak.

[Behold, there are many called, but few are chosen. And why are they not chosen? Because their hearts are set so much upon the things of this world, and aspire to the honors of men, that they do not learn this one lesson—that the rights of the Priesthood are inseparably connected with the powers of heaven, and that the powers of heaven cannot be controlled nor handled only upon the principles of righteousness. That they may be conferred upon us, it is true; but when we undertake to cover our sins, or to gratify our pride, our vain ambition, or to exercise control, or dominion, or compulsion, upon the souls of the children of men, in any degree of unrighteousness, behold, the heavens withdraw themselves; the Spirit of the Lord is grieved; and when it is withdrawn, *Amen to the Priesthood*, or the authority of that man. Behold! ere he is aware, he is left unto himself, to kick against the pricks; to persecute the Saints, and to fight against God.

We have learned by sad experience that it is the nature and disposition of almost all men, as soon as they get a little authority, as they suppose, they will immediately begin to exercise unrighteous dominion. Hence many are called, but few are chosen.

No power or influence can or ought to be maintained by virtue of the Priesthood, only by persuasion, by long-suffering, by gentleness, and meekness, and by love unfeigned; by kindness, and pure knowledge, which shall greatly enlarge the soul without hypocrisy, and without guile, reproving betimes with sharpness, when moved upon by the Holy Ghost, and then showing forth afterwards an increase of love toward him whom thou hast reproved, lest he esteem thee to be his enemy; that he may know that thy faithfulness is stronger than the cords of death; let thy bowels also be full of charity towards all men, and to the household of faith, and virtue garnish thy thoughts unceasingly, then shall thy confidence wax strong in the presence of God, and the doctrine of the Priesthood shall distill upon thy soul as the dews from heaven. The Holy Ghost shall be thy constant companion, and thy sceptre an unchanging sceptre of righteousness and truth, and thy dominion shall be an everlasting dominion, and without compulsory means it shall flow unto thee forever and ever].

[The ends of the earth shall inquire after thy name, and fools shall have thee in derision, and hell shall rage against thee, while the pure in heart, and the wise, and the noble, and the virtuous, shall seek counsel, and authority and blessings constantly from under thy hand, and thy people shall never be turned against thee by the testimony of traitors; and although their influence shall cast thee into trouble, and into bars and walls, thou shalt be had in honor, and but for a small moment and thy voice shall be more terrible in the midst of thine enemies, than the fierce lion, because of thy righteousness; and thy God shall stand by thee forever and ever.

If thou art called to pass through tribulations; if thou art in perils among false brethren; if thou art in perils among robbers; if thou art in perils by land or by sea; if thou art accused with all manner of false accusations; if thine enemies fall upon thee; if they tear thee from the society of thy father and mother and brethren and sisters; and if with a drawn sword thine enemies tear thee from the bosom of thy wife, and of thine offspring, and thine elder son, although but six years of age, shall cling to thy garments, and shall say, My father, my father, why can't you stay with us? O, my father, what are the men going to do with you? and if then he shall be thrust from thee by the sword, and thou be dragged to prison, and thine enemies prowl around thee like wolves for the blood of the lamb; and if thou shouldst be cast into the pit, or into the hands of murderers, and the sentence of death passed upon thee; if thou be cast into the deep; if the billowing surge conspire against thee; if fierce winds become thine enemy; if the heavens gather blackness, and all the elements combine to hedge up the way; and above all, if the very jaws of hell shall gape open the mouth wide after thee, know thou, my son, that all these things shall give thee experience, and shall be for thy good. The Son of Man hath descended below them all; art thou greater than he?

Therefore, hold on thy way, and the Priesthood shall remain with thee, for their bounds are set, they cannot pass. Thy days are known, and thy years shall not be numbered less; therefore, fear not what man can do, for God shall be with you forever and ever].

Now, brethren, I would suggest for the consideration of the conference, its being carefully and wisely understoood by the council or conferences that our brethren scattered abroad, who understand the spirit of the gathering, that they fall into the places and refuge of safety that God shall open unto them, between Kirtland and Far West. Those from the east and from the west, and from far countries, let them fall in somewhere between those two boundaries, in the most safe and quiet places they can find; and let this be the present understanding, until God shall open a more effectual door for us for further considerations.

And again, we further suggest for the considerations of the Council, that there be no organization of large bodies upon common stock principles, in property, or of large companies of firms, until the Lord shall signify it in a proper manner, as it opens such a dreadful field for the avaricious, the indolent, and the corrupt hearted to prey upon the innocent and virtuous, and honest.

We have reason to believe that many things were introduced among the Saints before God had signified the times; and notwithstanding the principles and plans may have been good, yet aspiring men, or in other words, men who had not the substance of godliness about them, perhaps undertook to handle edged tools. Children, you know, are fond of tools, while they are not yet able to use them.

Time and experience, however, are the only safe remedies against such evils. There are many teachers, but, perhaps, not many fathers. There are times coming when God will signify many things which are expedient for the well-being of the Saints; but the times have not yet come, but will come, as fast as there can be found place and reception for them.

[And again, we would suggest for your consideration the propriety of all the Saints gathering up a knowledge of all the facts and sufferings and abuses put upon them by the people of this state; and also of all the property and amount of damages which they have sustained, both of character and personal injuries, as well as real property; and also the names of all persons that have had a hand in their oppressions, as far as they can get hold of them and find them out; and perhaps a committee can be appointed to find out these things, and to take statements, and affidavits, and also to gather up the libelous publications that are afloat, and all that are in the magazines, and in the encyclopædias, and all the libelous histories that are published, and are writing, and by whom, and present the whole concatenation of diabolical rascality, and nefarious and murderous impositions that have been practiced upon this people, that we may not only publish to all the world, but present them to the heads of government in all their dark and hellish hue, as the last effort which is enjoined on us by our Heavenly Father, before we can fully and completely claim that promise which shall call Him forth from His hiding place, and also that the whole nation may be left without excuse before He can send forth the power of His mighty arm.

It is an imperative duty that we owe to God, to angels, with whom we shall be brought to stand, and also to ourselves, to our wives and children, who have been made to bow down with grief, sorrow, and care, under the most damning hand of murder, tyranny, and oppression, supported and urged on and upheld by the influence of that spirit which hath so strongly riveted the creeds of the fathers, who have inherited lies, upon the hearts of the children, and filled the world with confusion, and has been growing stronger and stronger, and is now the very main-spring of all corruption, and the whole earth groans under the weight of its iniquity.

It is an iron yoke, it is a strong band; they are the very hand-cuffs, and chains, and shackles, and fetters of hell.

Therefore it is an imperative duty that we owe, not only to our own wives and children, but to the widows and fatherless, whose husbands and fathers have been murdered under its iron hand; which dark and blackening deeds are enough to make hell itself shudder, and to stand aghast and pale, and the hands of the very devil to tremble and palsy. And also it is an imperative duty that we owe to all the rising generation, and to all the pure in heart, (for there are many yet on the earth among all sects, parties, denominations, who are blinded by the subtle craftiness of men, whereby they lie in wait to deceive, and who are only kept from the truth because they know not where to find it); therefore, that we should waste and wear out our lives in bringing to light all the hidden things of darkness, wherein we know them; and they are truly manifest from heaven.

These should then be attended to with great earnestness. Let no man count them as small things; for there is much which lieth in futurity, pertaining to the Saints, which depends upon these things. You know, brethren, that a very large ship is benefited very much by a very small helm in the time of a storm, by being kept workways with the wind and the waves.

Therefore, dearly beloved brethren, let us cheerfully do all things that lie in our power, and then may we stand still with the utmost assurance, to see the salvation of God, and for His arm to be revealed].

And again, I would further suggest the impropriety of the organization of bands or companies, by covenant or oaths, by penalties or secrecies; but let the time past of our experience and sufferings by the wickedness of Doctor Avard suffice and let our covenant be that of the Everlasting Covenant, as is contained in the Holy Writ and the things that God hath revealed unto us. Pure friendship always becomes weakened the very moment you undertake to make it stronger by penal oaths and secrecy.

Your humble servant or servants, intend from henceforth to disapprobate everything that is not in accordance with the fullness of the Gospel of Jesus Christ, and is not of a bold, and frank, and upright nature. They will not hold their peace—as in times past when they see iniquity beginning to rear its head—for fear of traitors, or the consequences that shall follow by reproving those who creep in unawares, that they may get something with which to destroy the flock. We believe that the experience of the Saints in times past has been sufficient, that they will from henceforth be always ready to obey the truth without having men's persons in admiration because of advantage. It is expedient that we should be aware of such things; and we ought always to be aware of those prejudices which sometimes so strangely present themselves, and are so congenial to human nature, against our friends, neighbors, and brethren of the world, who choose to differ from us in opinion and in matters of faith. Our religion is between us and our God. Their religion is between them and their God.

There is a love from God that should be exercised toward those of our faith, who walk uprightly, which is peculiar to itself, but it is without prejudice; it also gives scope to the mind, which enables us to conduct ourselves with greater liberality towards all that are not of our faith, than what they exercise towards one another. These principles approximate nearer to the mind of God, because it is like God, or Godlike.

Here is a principle also, which we are bound to be exercised with, that is, in common with all men, such as governments, and laws, and regulations in the civil concerns of life. This principle guarantees to all parties, sects, and denominations, and classes of religion, equal, coherent, and indefeasible rights; they are things that pertain to this life; therefore all are alike interested; they make our responsibilities one towards another in matters of corruptible things, while the former principles do not destroy the latter, but bind us stronger, and make our responsibilities not only one to another, but unto God also. Hence we say, that the Constitution of the United States is a glorious standard; it is founded in the wisdom of God. It is a heavenly banner; it is to all those who are privileged with the sweets of its liberty, like the cooling shades and refreshing waters of a great rock in a thirsty and weary land. It is like a great tree under whose branches men from every clime can be shielded from the burning rays of the sun.

We, brethren, are deprived of the protection of its glorious principles, by the cruelty of the cruel, by those who only look for the time being, for pasturage like the beasts of the field, only to fill themselves; and forget that the "Mormons," as well as the Presbyterians, and those of every other class and description, have equal rights to partake of the fruits of the great tree of our national liberty. But notwithstanding we see what we see, and feel what we feel, and know what we know, yet that fruit is no less precious and delicious to our taste; we cannot be weaned from the milk, neither can we be driven from the breast; neither will we deny our religion because of the hand of oppression; but we will hold on until death.

We say that God is true; that the Constitution of the United States is true; that the Bible is true; that the Book of Mormon is true; that the Book of Covenants is true; that Christ is true; that the ministering angels sent forth from God are true, and that we know that we have an house not made with hands eternal in the heavens, whose builder and maker is God; a consolation which our oppressors cannot feel, when fortune, or fate, shall lay its iron hand on them as it has on us. Now, we ask, what is man? Remember, brethren, that time and chance happen to all men.

We shall continue our reflections in our next.

We subscribe ourselves, your sincere friends and brethren in the bonds of the everlasting Gospel, prisoners of Jesus Christ, for the sake of the Gospel and the Saints.

We pronounce the blessings of heaven upon the heads of the Saints who seek to serve God with undivided hearts, in the name of Jesus Christ. Amen.

JOSEPH SMITH, JUN.,
HYRUM SMITH,
LYMAN WIGHT,
CALEB BALDWIN,
ALEXANDER MCRAE.

CHAPTER XXI.

STIRRING SCENES ABOUT FAR WEST—THE ESCAPE OF THE PROPHET AND HIS FELLOW PRISONERS.

Thursday, April 4.—Brothers Kimball and Turley called on Judge King, who was angry at their having reported the case to the governor, and, said he, "I could have done all the business for you properly, if you had come to me; and I would have signed the petition for all except Joe, and he is not fit to live." I bid Brothers Kimball and Turley to be of good cheer, "for we shall be delivered; but no arm but God's can deliver us now. Tell the brethren to be of good cheer and get the Saints away as fast as possible."

Judge King's Anger.

Brothers Kimball and Turley were not permitted to enter the prison, and all the communication we had with them was through the grate of the dungeon. The brethren left Liberty on their return to Far West.

Friday, April 5.—Brothers Kimball and Turley arrived at Far West.

This day a company of about fifty men in Daviess county swore that they would never eat or drink, until they had murdered "Joe Smith." Their captain, William Bowman, swore, in the presence of Theodore Turley, that he would "never eat or drink, after he had seen Joe Smith, until he had murdered him."

Plot Against the Prophet's Life.

Also eight men—Captain Bogart, who was the county judge, Dr. Laffity, John Whitmer, and five others—came into the committee's room [i.e. the room or office of the committee on removal] and presented to Theodore Turley the paper containing the revelation of July 8, 1838,* to Joseph Smith, directing the Twelve to take their leave of the Saints in

The Truth of a Revelation Questioned.

* See Doctrine and Covenants, sec. cxviii.

Far West on the building site of the Lords House on the 26th of April, to go to the isles of the sea, and then asked him to read it. Turley said, "Gentlemen, I am well acquainted with it." They said, "Then you, as a rational man, will give up Joseph Smith's being a prophet and an inspired man? He and the Twelve are now scattered all over creation; let them come here if they dare; if they do, they will be murdered. As that revelation cannot be fulfilled, you will now give up your faith."

Turley jumped up and said, "In the name of God that revelation will be fulfilled." They laughed him to scorn. John Whitmer hung down his head. They said, "If they (the Twelve) come, they will get murdered; they dare not come to take their leave here; that is like all the rest of Joe Smith's d——n prophecies." They commenced on Turley and said, he had better do as John Corrill had done; "he is going to publish a book called 'Mormonism Fairly Delineated;' he is a sensible man, and you had better assist him."

Turley's Defense of the Prophet.

Turley said, "Gentlemen, I presume there are men here who have heard Corrill say, that 'Mormonism' was true, that Joseph Smith was a prophet, and inspired of God. I now call upon you, John Whitmer: you say Corrill is a moral and a good man; do you believe him when he says the Book of Mormon is true, or when he says it is not true? There are many things published that they say are true, and again turn around and say they are false?" Whitmer asked, "Do you hint at me?" Turley replied, "If the cap fits you, wear it; all I know is that you have published to the world that an angel did present those plates to Joseph Smith." Whitmer replied: "I now say, I handled those plates; there were fine engravings on both sides. I handled them;" and he described how they were hung, and "they were shown to me by a supernatural power;" he acknowledged all.

Colloquy between Turley and John Whitmer.

Turley asked him, "Why is not the translation now

true?" He said, "I could not read it [in the original] and I do not know whether it [i. e., the translation] is true or not." Whitmer testified all this in the presence of eight men.

The committee [on removal of the Saints from Missouri] met, and Brother William Huntington made report of his journey to Liberty on business of the committee.

Land Sales and the Clothing of Prisoners.

The subject of providing some clothing for the prisoners at Richmond was discussed, and the propriety of sending two brethren to Liberty, to make sales of some lands, was taken up, and Elders H. G. Sherwood and Theodore Turley were appointed.

A bill of clothing for the Richmond prisoners having been made up, was presented and given to those appointed to go to Liberty, that they might procure the goods on the sales of land.

The Prisoners Hurried into Daviess County.

Saturday, April 6.—Judge King evidently fearing a change of venue, or some movement on our part to escape his unhallowed persecution (and most probably expecting that we would be murdered on the way) hurried myself and fellow prisoners off to Daviess county, under a guard of about ten men, commanded by Samuel Tillery, deputy jailer of Clay county. We were promised that we should go through Far West, which was directly on our route, which our friends at that place knew, and expected us; but instead of fulfilling their promise, they took us around the city, and out of the direct course some eighteen miles; far from habitations, where every opportunity presented for a general massacre.

Peremptory Orders Considered.

This evening the committee (i. e. on removal) met in council. Prayer by Elder Kimball. The business of the council was the consideration of the order of the leaders of the Daviess mob, delivered this day to the Saints in Caldwell county, to leave before Friday next.

Resolved: To hire all teams that can be hired, to move the families of the Saints out of the county, to Tenny's Grove.

Resolved: To send Henry G. Sherwood immediately to Illinois for assistance, in teams from the Saints there.

The mission of Elders Sherwood and Turley to Liberty was deferred for the present.

Sunday, April 7.—The committee met in council at Brother Turley's. Brother Erastus Snow made a report of his visit to the judges at Jefferson city. A letter from the prisoners at Liberty was read and Daniel Shearer and Heber C. Kimball were appointed to see Mr. Hughes and get him to go to Daviess county and attend the sitting of the court there.

Actions of the Committee.

We continued our travels across the prairie, while the brethren at Far West, anxious for our welfare, gave a man thirty dollars to convey a letter to us in Daviess county, and return an answer.

Monday, April 8.—After a tedious journey—for our long confinement had enfeebled our bodily powers—we arrived in Daviess county, about a mile from Gallatin, where we were delivered into the hands of William Morgan, sheriff of Daviess county, with his guard, William Bowman, John Brassfield and John Pogue. The Liberty guard returned immediately, but became divided, or got lost on their way; a part of them arrived in Far West after dark, and got caught in the fence; and calling for help, Elder Markham went to their assistance and took them to the tavern. From them he got a letter I had written to the committee, informing them of our arrival in Daviess county.

Arrival of the Prisoners in Daviess County.

Tuesday, April 9.—Our trial commenced before a drunken grand jury, Austin A. King, presiding judge, as drunk as the jury; for they were all drunk together. Elder Stephen Markham had been dispatched by the committee to visit us, and bring a hundred dollars that was sent by Elder Kimball, as we were destitute of means at that time. He left Far

Arrival of Stephen Markham in Gallatin.

West this morning, and swimming several streams he arrived among us in the afternoon, and spent the evening in our company. Brother Markham brought us a written copy of a statute which had passed the legislature, giving us the privilege of a change of venue on our own affidavit.

Judge Morin Favors the Prophet's Escape.

Judge Morin arrived from Mill Port, and was favorable to our escape from the persecution we were enduring, and spent the evening with us in prison, and we had as pleasant a time as such circumstances would permit, for we were as happy as the happiest; the Spirit buoyed us above our trials, and we rejoiced in each other's society.

The Examination of Witnesses.

Wednesday, April 10.—The day was spent in the examination of witnesses before the grand jury. Dr. Sampson Avard was one of the witnesses. Brother Markham was not permitted to give his testimony.

Our guard went home, and Colonel William P. Peniston, Blakely, and others took their place.

Letter of Sidney Rigdon to the Prophet. Rigdon's Plans for the Impeachment of Missouri.

QUINCY, ILLINOIS, April 10, 1839.

To the Saints in Prison, Greeting:

In the midst of a crowd of business, I haste to send a few lines by the hand of Brother Mace, our messenger. We wish you to know that our friendship is unabating, and our exertions for your delivery, and that of the Church unceasing. For this purpose we have labored to secure the friendship of the governor of this state, with all the principal men in this place. In this we have succeeded beyond our highest anticipations. Governor Carlin assured us last evening, that he would lay our case before the legislature of this state, and have the action of that body upon it; and he would use all his influence to have an action which should be favorable to our people. He is also getting papers prepared signed by all the noted men in this part of the country, to give us a favorable reception at Washington, whither we shall repair forthwith, after having visited the Governor of Iowa, of whose frienship we have the strongest testimonies. We leave Quincy this day to visit him. Our plan of operation is to impeach the state of Missouri on an item of the Constitution of the United States; that the general government shall give to each state a Republican form of government. Such a form of government does not exist in Missouri, and we can prove it.

Governor Carlin and his lady enter with all the enthusiasm of their natures into this work, having no doubt but that we can accomplish this object.

Our plan of operation in this work is, to get all the governors, in their next messages, to have the subject brought before the legislatures; and we will have a man at the capital of each state to furnish them with the testimony on the subject; and we design to be at Washington to wait upon Congress, and have the action of that body on it also; all this going on at the same time, and have the action of the whole during one session.

Brother George W. Robinson will be engaged all the time between this and the next sitting of the legislatures, in taking affidavits, and preparing for the tug of war; while we will be going from state to state, visiting the respective governors, to get the case mentioned in their respective messages to legislatures, so as to have the whole going on at once. You will see by this that our time is engrossed to overflowing.

The Bishops of the Church are required to ride and visit all scattered abroad, and to collect money to carry on this great work.

Be assured, brethren, that operations of an all-important character are under motion, and will come to an issue as soon as possible. Be assured that our friendship is unabated for you, and our desires for your deliverance intense. May God hasten it speedily, is our prayer day and night.

Yours in the bonds of affliction,

SIDNEY RIGDON.

To Joseph Smith, Jun., Hyrum Smith, Caleb Baldwin, Lyman Wight, Alexander McRae.

*Letter of Alanson Ripley to the Prophet.**

QUINCY, ILLINOIS, April 10, 1839.

Dear Brethren in Christ Jesus:

It is with feelings of no small moment that I take pen in hand to address you, the prisoners of Jesus Christ, and in the same faith of the

*It must be remembered that this letter was written under very great stress of feeling, and that accounts for its general harshness. It should also be remembered that as Edmund Burke said a long while ago—and it is now accepted as a trueism—"It is not fair to judge of the temper or disposition of any man, or any set of men when they are composed and at rest, from their conduct or their expressions in a state of disturbance and irritation."

Gospel with myself—who are holden by the cords of malice and of hellish plottings against the just, and through the lifting up the heel against the Lord's anointed; but they shall soon fall and not rise again, for their destruction is sure; and no power beneath the heavens can save them.

President Rigdon is wielding a mighty shaft against the whole host of foul calumniators and mobocrats of Missouri. Yesterday he spent a part of the day with Governor Carlin of this state. President Rigdon told him that he was informed that Governor Boggs was calculating to take out a bench warrant for himself and others, and then make a demand of his excellency for them to be given up, to be taken back to Missouri for trial; and he was assured by that noble-minded hero, that if Mr. Boggs undertook the thing, he would get himself insulted. He also assured him that the people called "Mormons" should find a permanent protection in this state. He also solicited our people, one and all, to settle in this state, and if there could be a tract of country that would suit our convenience, he would use his influence for Congress to make a grant of it to us, to redress our wrongs, and make up our losses.

We met last night in council of the whole, and passed some resolutions with respect to sending to the city of Washington. We are making every exertion possible that lies in our power, to accomplish that grand object upon which hangs our temporal salvation; and interwoven with this, our eternal salvation; and so closely allied to each other are they, that I want to see the head connected with the body again; and while we are enjoying one, let us be ripening for the other. But my heart says, Where is he whose lips used to whisper the words of life to us? Alas! he is in the hands of Zion's enemies. O Lord! crieth my heart, will not heaven hear our prayers, and witness our tears! Yes, saith the the Spirit, thy tears are all remembered, and shall speedily be rewarded with the deliverance of thy dearly beloved brethren.

But when I see the fearful apprehensions of some of our brethren, it causes me to mourn. One instance I will mention. When I arrived at Far West I made my mind known to some of the community, and told them that I wanted they should send a messenger to the jail to communicate with you; but my request was denied. They said that the Presidency was so anxious to be free once more, that they would not consider the danger the Church was in.

They met in council and passed resolutions that myself, Amasa Lyman, and Watson Barlow, should leave Far West for Quincy forthwith. My spirit has been grieved ever since, so that I can hardly hold my peace; but there is a God in Israel that can blast the hellish desires and designs of that infernal banditti, whose hands have been imbrued in the blood of the martyrs and Saints. They wish to destroy the Church of

God; but their chain is short; there is just enough left to bind their own hands with.

Dear brethren, I am at your service, and I await your counsel at Quincy, and shall be happy to grant you the desire of your hearts. I am ready to act. Please to give me all the intelligence that is in your power. If you take a change of venue, let me know what county you will come to, and when, as near as possible, and what road you will come; for I shall be an adder in the path.

Yes, my dear brethren, God Almighty will deliver you. Fear not, for your redemption draweth near; the day of your deliverance is at hand.

Dear brethren, I have it in my heart to lay my body in the sand, or deliver you from your bonds; and my mind is intensely fixed on the latter.

Dear brethren, you will be able to judge of the spirit that actuates my breast; for when I realize your sufferings, my heart is like wax before the fire; but when I reflect upon the cause of your afflictions, it is like fire in my bones, and burns against your enemies, and I never can be satisfied, while there is one of them to stand against a wall, or draw a sword, or pull a trigger. My sword has never been sheathed in peace, for the blood of David W. Patten and those who were butchered at Haun's Mill, crieth for vengeance from the ground.

Therefore, hear O ye heavens! and write it, O ye recording angels! bear the tidings ye flaming seraphs! that I from this day declare myself the avenger of the blood of those innocent men, and of the innocent cause of Zion, and of her prisoners; and I will not rest until they are as free, who are in prison, as I am.

Your families are all well and in good spirits. May the Lord bless you all. Amen.

Brother Amasa Lyman and Watson Barlow join in saying, Our hearts are as thy heart. Brother Joseph, if my spirit is wrong, for God's sake correct it. Brethren, be of good cheer, for we are determined, as God liveth, to rescue you from that hellish crowd, or die in the furrow. We shall come face foremost.

ALANSON RIPLEY.

N. B.—S. B. Crockett says he has been once driven but not whipped; Brother Brigham Young sends his best respects to you all.

A. R.

Thursday April 11.—

Letter of Don Carlos Smith to His Brother, Hyrum Smith.

Brother Hyrum:

After reading a line from you to myself, and one to father, which awakens all the feelings of tenderness and brotherly affection that one heart is capable of containing, I sit down in haste to answer it. My health and that of my family is good; mother and Lucy have been very sick, but are getting better. Your families are in better health now than at any other period since your confinement.

Brother Hyrum, I am in hopes that my letter did not increase your trouble, for I know that your affliction is too great for human nature to bear; and if I did not know that there was a God in heaven, and that His promises are sure and faithful, and that He is your friend in the midst of all your trouble, I would fly to your relief, and either be with you in prison, or see you breathe free air—air too that had not been inhaled and corrupted by a pack of ruffians, who trample upon virtue and innocence with impunity; and are not even satisfied with the property and blood of the Saints, but must exult over the dead. You both have my prayers, my influence and warmest feelings, with a *fixed determination*, if it should so be that you should be destroyed, to *avenge* your blood four fold.

Joseph must excuse me for not writing to him at this time. Give my love to all the prisoners. Write to me as often as you can, and do not be worried about your families. Yours in affliction as well as in peace.

DON C. SMITH.

Letter of Agnes Smith to Hyrum and Joseph Smith.

Beloved Brothers, Hyrum and Joseph:

By the permit of my companion, I write a line to show that I have not forgotten you; neither do I forget you; for my prayer is to my Heavenly Father for your deliverance. It seems as though the Lord is slow to hear the prayers of the Saints. But the Lord's ways are not like our ways; therefore He can do better than we ourselves. You must be comforted, Brothers Hyrum and Joseph, and look forward for better days. Your little ones are as playful as little lambs; be comforted concerning them, for they are not cast down and sorrowful as we are; their sorrows are only momentary but ours continual.

May the Lord bless, protect, and deliver you from all your enemies and restore you to the bosom of your families, is the prayer of

AGNES M. SMITH.

To Hyrum and Joseph Smith, Liberty, Missouri.

The examination of witnesses was continued, and Elder Markham was permitted to give his testimony. After he had closed, Blakely, one of the guard, came in and said to Markham, that he wanted to speak to him. Brother

Markham walked out with him, and around the end of the house when Blakely called out, "—— —— you —— old Mormon; I'll kill you;" and struck at Markham with his fist and then with a club. Markham took the club from him and threw it over the fence.

Attempt upon the Life of Stephen Markham.

There were ten of the mob who immediately rushed upon Markham to kill him, Colonel William P. Peniston, captain of the guard, being one of the number. But Markham told them he could kill the whole of them at one blow apiece, and drove them off. The court and grand jury stood and saw the affray, and heard the mob threaten Markham's life, by all the oaths they could invent, but they took no cognizance of it.

The ten mobbers went home after their guns to shoot Markham, and the grand jury brought in a bill for "murder, treason, burglary, arson, larceny, theft, and stealing," against Lyman Wight, Alexander McRae, Caleb Baldwin, Hyrum Smith and myself.

A "True Bill" Found against the Prisoners.

This evening the committee [on removal] assembled at Daniel Shearer's. After prayer by Brother James Newberry, he was ordained an Elder on the recommendation of Elder Heber C. Kimball, under the hands of Hiram Clark and William Huntington.

Meeting of the Committee on Removal.

Elder Kimball reported that Jessie P. Maupin, the thirty-dollar messenger they had sent to us, had returned; that the prisoners were well and in good spirits.

Brother Rogers who had returned from Jackson county, reported that he had sold all the lands in Jackson. Elder Kimball was requested to attend a meeting of the Daviess county officials tomorrow, and as an individual, mention the case of the committee [on removal] and the brethren generally, and learn their feelings, whether they would protect the brethren from the abuse of the mob, in case they came im-

Sale of Jackson County Lands.

mediately to drive them out, as they had recently threatened.

During this night the visions of the future were opened to my understanding; when I saw the ways and means and near approach of my escape from imprisonment, and the danger that my beloved Brother Markham was in. I awoke Brother Markham, and told him if he would rise very early and not wait for the judge and lawyers, as he had contemplated doing, but rise briskly, he would get safe home, almost before he was aware of it; and if he did not the mob would shoot him on the way; and I told him to tell the brethren to be of good cheer, but lose no time in removing from the country.

Vision of the Prophet for Markham's safety

Friday, April 12.—This morning Brother Markham arose at dawn of day, and rode rapidly towards Far West, where he arrived before nine a. m. The mobbers pursued to shoot him, but did not overtake him.

Escape of Markham.

This day I received the following letter:

Jacob Stollings' Communication to the Prophet.

DEAR SIR:—Enclosed I send you the receipt which I promised; and if you will pay the necessary attention to it, it will be a benefit to the Church and to me; and I think with a little attention on your part, they can be produced; and any person who will deliver them at any point in the state, so I can get them, I will compensate them well, as I know you feel deeply interested in the welfare of the Church; and when you consider it will add to their character, and look upon it in a proper light, you will spare no pains in assisting me in the recovery of those books.

Yours, etc., in haste,

JACOB STOLLINGS.

To Joseph Smith, Jun., Diahman.

GALLATIN, DAVIESS COUNTY, MISSOURI,
April 12, 1839.

Know all men by these presents—That I, Jacob Stollings, have this day agreed with Joseph Smith, Jun., to release all members of the Mormon Church, from any and all debts due to me from them for goods sold to them by me at Gallatin during the year 1838, on the following condition, viz.: That said Joseph Smith, Jun., return or cause to be returned to me the following books—one ledger, three day books, and one day book of groceries, which was taken from my store in Gallatin when said store was burned. And if said books are returned to me within four months, this shall be a receipt in full, to all intents and purposes, against any debt or debts due from said Mormons to me on said books; but if not returned, this is to be null and void.

Given under my hand this day and date before written.

JACOB STOLLINGS.

Attest, J. Lynch.

The Prophet's Comments.

A curious idea, that I who had been a prisoner many months should be called upon to hunt up lost property, or property most likely destroyed by the mob; but it is no more curious than a thousand other things that have happened; and I feel to do all I can to oblige any of my fellow creatures.

Isaac Galland's Communication to the Quincy Argus.

COMMERCE, ILLINOIS, April 12, 1839.

MESSRS. EDITORS:—Enclosed I send you a communication from Governor Lucas of Iowa territory. If you think the publication thereof will in any way promote the cause of justice, by vindicating the slandered reputation of the people called "Mormons," from the ridiculous falsehoods which the malice, cupidity and envy of their murderers in Missouri have endeavored to heap upon them, you are respectfully solicited to publish it in the *Argus*. The testimony of Governor Lucas as to the good moral character of these people, I think will have its deserved influence upon the people of Illinois, in encouraging our citizens in their humane and benevolent exertions to relieve this distressed people, who are now wandering in our neighborhoods without comfortable food, raiment, or a shelter from the pelting storm.

I am, gentlemen, very respectfully,
Your obedient servant,
ISAAC GALLAND.

Letter of Robert Lucas, Governor of the Territory of Iowa, Respecting the Manner in Which the Saints Might Hope to be Received and Treated in Iowa.

EXECUTIVE OFFICE, IOWA, BURLINGTON,
March, 1839.

DEAR SIR:—On my return to this city, after a few weeks' absence in the interior of the territory, I received your letter of the 25th ultimo, in which you give a short account of the sufferings of the people called Mormons and ask "whether they could be permitted to purchase lands and settle upon them, in the territory of Iowa, and there worship Almighty God according to the dictates of their own consciences, secure from oppression," etc.

In answer to your inquiry, I would say that I know of no authority that can constitutionally deprive them of this right. They are citizens of the United States, and are entitled to all the rights and privileges of other citizens. The 2nd section of the 4th Article of the Constitution of the United States (which all are solemnly bound to support) declares that "the citizens of each state shall be entitled to all the privileges and immunities of citizens of the several states." This privilege extends in full force to the territories of the United States. The first amendment to the Constitution of the United States, declares that "Congress shall make no law respecting an establishment of religion, or prohibiting the free exercise thereof."

The ordinance of Congress of the 13th July, 1787, for the government of the territory northwest of the river Ohio, secures to the citizens of said territory, and the citizens of the states thereafter to be formed therein, certain privileges which were by the late Act of Congress organizing the territory of Iowa, extended to the citizens of this territory.

The first fundamental Article in the Ordinance, which is declared to be forever unalterable, except by common consent, reads as follows, to wit: "No person demeaning himself in a peaceable and orderly manner, shall ever be molested on account of his mode of worship or religious sentiment in said territory."

These principles I trust will ever be adhered to in the territory of Iowa. They make no distinction between religious sects. They extend equal privileges and protection to all; each must rest upon its own merits, and will prosper in proportion to the purity of its principles, and the fruit of holiness and piety produced thereby.

With regard to the peculiar people mentioned in your letter, I know but little. They had a community in the northern part of Ohio for several years; and I have no recollection of ever having heard in that state of any complaints against them for violating the laws of the country. Their religious opinions I consider have nothing to do with our political transactions. They are citizens of the United States, and are entitled to the same political rights and legal protection that other citizens are entitled to.

The foregoing are briefly my views on the subject of your inquiries.

With sincere respect,

I am your obedient servant,

ROBERT LUCAS.

To Isaac Galland, Esq., Commerce, Illinois.

Saturday, April 13.—Elder Markham went to Independence to close the business of the Church in that region.

Sunday, April 14.—The committee [on removal] in council resolved to send Sisters Fosdick and Meeks, and Brother William Monjar and another family, with Brothers Jones, Burton, and Barlow's teams. which had recently arrived at Quincy.

Activity of the Committee on Removal.

The committee moved thirty-six families into Tenney's Grove, about twenty-five miles from Far West; and a few men were appointed to chop wood for them, while Brother Turley was to furnish them with meal and meat, until they could be removed to Quincy. The corn was ground at the committee's horse mill, in Far West. Elder Kimball was obliged to secrete himself in the cornfields during the day, and was in at night counseling the committee and brethren.

Monday, April 15.—Having procured a change of venue we started for Boone county, and were conducted to that place by a strong guard.

The Prophet and Fellow Prisoners Start for Boone county.

This evening the committee [on removal] met to make arrangements concerning teams and the moving of the few families who yet remained at Far West.

Letter of Elias Higbee to Joseph Smith, Jun., and Fellow Prisoners.

TUESDAY, QUINCY, April 16, 1839.

To Joseph Smith, Jun., and others, Prisoners in Liberty or Elsewhere, Greeting:

DEAR BRETHREN IN AFFLICTION:—Through the mercy and providence of God, I am here alive, and in tolerable health, as also are all of your families, as far as I know, having heard from them lately, and having seen Sister Emma yesterday.

Brethren, I have sorrow of heart when I think of your great sufferings by that ungodly mob which has spread such desolation and caused so much suffering among us. I often reflect on the scenes which we passed through together; the course we pursued; the counselings we had; the results which followed, when harassed, pressed on every side insulted and abused by that lawless banditti; and I am decidedly of opinion that the hand of the Great God hath controlled the whole business for purposes of His own, which will eventually work out good for the Saints (I mean those who are worthy of the name). I know that your intentions, and the intentions of all the worthy Saints, have been pure, and tending to do good to all men, and to injure no man in person or property, except we were forced to it in defense of our lives.

Brethren, I am aware that I cannot wholly realize your sufferings; neither can any other person who has not experienced the like afflictions; but I doubt not for a moment, neither have I ever doubted for a moment, that the same God which delivered me from their grasp (though narrowly) will deliver you. I staid near Far West for about three weeks, being hunted by them almost every day; and as I learned, they did not intend to give me the chance of a trial, but put an end to me forthwith, I went for my horse and left the wicked clan and came off. Francis* is with his uncle in Ohio. I received a letter lately from him; he is strong in the faith. I now live in the Big-Neck-Prairie, on the same farm with President Rigdon, who is here with me and waiting for me with his riding dress on, to go home. So I must necessarily close, praying God to speedily deliver you, and bless you.

From yours in the bonds of the everlasting love,

ELIAS HIGBEE.

The Prophet's Reasons for Escaping from the Officers of the Law.

This evening our guard got intoxicated. We thought it a favorable opportunity to make our escape; knowing that the only object of our enemies was our destruction; and likewise knowing that a number of our brethren had been massacred by them on Shoal Creek, amongst whom were two children; and that they sought every opportunity to abuse others who were left in that state; and that they were never brought to an account for their barbarous proceedings, which were winked at and encouraged by those in authority. We thought that it was necessary for us, inasmuch as we loved our lives, and did not wish to die by the hand of murderers and assassins; and inasmuch as we loved our families and friends, to deliver ourselves from our enemies, and from that land of tyranny and oppression, and again take our stand among a people

* This refers to Francis M. Higbee, son of Elias Higbee

in whose bosoms dwell those feelings of republicanism and liberty which gave rise to our nation: feelings which the inhabitants of the State of Missouri were strangers to. Accordingly, we took advantage of the situation of our guard and departed, and that night we traveled a considerable distance.*

*Undoubtedly the guards, and for matter of that Judge Birch himself, and also the ex-sheriff of Daviess county, William Bowman, connived at the escape of the prisoners. The story of the escape was afterwards told in detail by Hyrum Smith, as follows: "They got us a change of venue from Daviess to Boone county, and a mittimus was made out by the pretended Judge Birch, without date, name, or place. They [the court officials at Gallatin] fitted us out with a two horse wagon, a horse and four men, besides the sheriff, to be our guard. There were five of us that started from Gallatin, the sun about two hours high, and went as far as Diahman that evening, and stayed till morning. There we bought two horses of the guard, and paid for one of them in our clothing which we had with us, and for the other we gave our note. We went down that day as far as Judge Morin's, a distance of some four or five miles. There we stayed until the next morning, when we started on our journey to Boone county, and traveled on the road about twenty miles distance. There we bought a jug of whisky, with which we treated the company, and while there the sheriff showed us the mittimus before referred to, without date or signature, and said that Judge Birch told him never to carry us to Boone county, and never to show the mittimus; and, said he, I shall take a good drink of grog, and go to bed, and you may do as you have a mind to. Three others of the guards drank pretty freely of the whisky, sweetened with honey. They also went to bed, and were soon asleep and the other guard went along with us, and helped to saddle the horses. Two of us mounted the horses, and the other three started on foot, and we took our change of venue for the State of Illinois; and in the course of nine or ten days arrived safely at Quincy, Adams county, where we found our families in a state of poverty, although in good health." (From the affidavit of Hyrum Smith before the municipal court of Nauvoo, given July 1, 1843.)

The name of the sheriff in charge of the prisoners was William Morgan, and upon his return to Gallatin both he and the ex-sheriff, William Bowman, who was suspected of complicity in the escape of the prisoners, received harsh treatment at the hands of the citizens of that place. The story is told in the "History of Daviess County," published by Birdsall & Dean, 1882, as follows: "The prisoners took change of venue to Boone county, and the Daviess county officers started with the prisoners to their destination in Boone county. Some of the prisoners having no horses, William Bowman, the first sheriff of Daviess county, [and now ex-sheriff], furnished the prisoners three horses, and they left in charge of William Morgan, the sheriff of the county. The sheriff alone returned on horseback, the guard who accompanied him returning on foot, or riding and tying by turns. The sheriff reported that the prisoners had all escaped in the night, taking the horses with them, and that a search made for them proved unavailing. The people of Gallatin were greatly exercised, and they disgraced themselves by very ruffianly conduct. They rode the sheriff on a rail, and Bowman was dragged over the square by the hair of the head. The men guilty of these dastardly acts, accused sheriff Morgan and ex-Sheriff Bowman of complicity in the escape of the Mormon leaders; that Bowman furnished the horses, and that Morgan allowed them to escape, and both got well paid for their treachery. The truth of history compels us

Wednesday, April 17.—We prosecuted our journey towards Illinois, keeping off from the main road as much as possible, which impeded our progress.

Thursday, April 18.—This morning Elder Kimball went into the committee room and told the committee [on removal] to wind up their affairs and be off, or their lives would be taken. Stephen Markham had gone over the Missouri river on business. Elders Turley and Shearer were at Far West.

Elder Kimball's Warning to the Committee.

Twelve men went to Elder Turley's with loaded rifles to shoot him. They broke seventeen clocks into match wood. They broke tables, smashed in the windows; while Bogart (the county judge) looked on and laughed. One Whitaker threw iron pots at Turley, one of which hit him on the shoulder, at which Whitaker jumped and laughed like a madman. The mob shot down cows while the girls were milking them. The mob threatened to send the committee "to hell jumping," and "put daylight through them."

Attack on Theodore Turley.

The same day, previous to the breaking of the clocks, some of the same company met Elder Kimball on the public square in Far West, and asked him if he was a "—— Mormon;" he replied, "I am a Mormon." "Well, —— —— you, we'll blow your brains out, you —— —— Mormon," and tried to ride over him with their horses. This was in the presence of Elias Smith, Theodore Turley, and others of the committee.

The Mob's Assault on Elder Kimball.

The brethren gathered up what they could and left Far West in one hour; and the mob staid until they left, then plundered thousands of dollars' worth of property which had been left by the exiled brethren and sisters to help the poor to remove.

The Mob Loots Far West.

One mobber rode up, and finding no convenient place

to state that the charges were never sustained by any evidence adduced by the persons who committed this flagrant act of mob law."—See above named history, page 206.

to fasten his horse, shot a cow that was standing near, and while the poor animal was yet struggling in death, he cut a strip of her hide from her nose to the tip of her tail, this he tied round a stump, to which he fastened his halter.

During the commotion this day, a great portion of the records of the committee, accounts, history, etc., were destroyed or lost, so that but few definite items can be registered in their place.

The Loss of Records, Accounts, etc.

When the Saints commenced removing from Far West they shipped as many families and goods as possible at Richmond to go down the Missouri river to Quincy, Illinois. This mission was in charge of Elder Levi Richards and Reuben Hedlock, who were appointed by the committee.

Flight of the Saints *via* Missouri River.

I continued on my journey with my brethren towards Quincy.

Elder David W. Rogers made a donation of money to remove the poor from Missouri.

Assistance for the Poor.

The brethren and sisters who had arrived in Illinois were beginning to write of their sufferings and losses in Missouri. The statement of Sister Amanda Smith, written by her own hand, I will here insert:

Narrative of Amanda Smith Respecting the Massacre at Haun's Mills.

To whom this may come:

I do hereby certify that my husband, Warren Smith, in company with several other families, was moving [in 1838] from Ohio to Missouri. We came to Caldwell county. Whilst we were traveling, minding our own business, we were stopped by a mob; they told us that if we went another step, they would kill us all. They took our guns from us (as we were going into a new country, we took guns along with us); they took us back five miles, placed a guard around us, kept us three days, and then let us go.

I thought—Is this our boasted land of liberty? for some said we must deny our faith, or they would kill us; others said, we should die at any rate.

The names of this mob, or the heads, were Thomas O'Brien, county clerk; Jefferson Brien, William Ewell, Esq., and James Austin, all of Livingston county. After they let us go we traveled ten miles, came to a small town composed of one grist mill, one saw mill, and eight or ten houses belonging to our brethren; there we stopped for the night.

A little before sunset a mob of three hundred came upon us. The men hallooed for the women and children to run for the woods; and they ran into an old blacksmith's shop, for they feared, if we all ran together, they would rush upon us and kill the women and children. The mob fired before we had time to start from our camp. Our men took off their hats and swung them, and cried "quarters" until they were shot. The mob paid no attention to their cries nor entreaties, but fired alternately.

I took my little girls, my boy I could not find, and started for the woods. The mob encircled us on all sides but the brook. I ran down the bank, across the mill-pond on a plank, up the hill into the bushes. The bullets whistled around me all the way like hail, and cut down the bushes on all sides of us. One girl was wounded by my side, and fell over a log, and her clothes hung across the log; and they shot at them, expecting they were hitting her; and our people afterwards cut out of that log twenty bullets.

I sat down and witnessed the dreadful scene. When they had done firing, they began to howl, and one would have thought that all the infernals had come from the lower regions. They plundered the principal part of our goods, took our horses and wagons, and ran off howling like demons.

I came down to view the awful sight. Oh horrible! My husband, and one son ten years old, lay lifeless upon the ground, and one son seven years old, wounded very badly. The ground was covered with the dead. These little boys crept under the bellows in the shop; one little boy of ten years had three wounds in him; he lived five weeks and died; he was not mine.

Realize for a moment the scene! It was sunset; nothing but horror and distress; the dogs filled with rage, howling over their dead masters; the cattle caught the scent of the innocent blood, and bellowed; a dozen helpless widows, thirty or forty fatherless children, crying and moaning for the loss of their fathers and husbands; the groans of the wounded and dying were enough to have melted the heart of anything but a Missouri mob.

There were fifteen dead, and ten wounded; two died the next day. There were no men, or not enough to bury the dead; so they were thrown into a dry well and covered with dirt. The next day the mob came back. They told us we must leave the state forthwith, or be killed. It was cold weather, and they had our teams and clothes, our husbands were dead or wounded. I told them they might kill me and my children, and welcome. They sent word to us from time to time that if we did not leave the state, they would come and kill us. We had little prayer meetings. They said if we did not stop them they would kill every man, woman and child. We had spelling schools for our little children; they said if we did not stop them they would kill every man, woman and child. We did our own milking, got our own wood; no man to help us.

I started the first of February for Illinois, without money, (mob all the way), drove my own team, slept out of doors. I had five small children; we suffered hunger, fatigue and cold; for what? For our religion, where, in a boasted land of liberty, "Deny your faith or die," was the cry.

I will mention some of the names of the heads of the mob: two brothers by the name of Comstock, William Mann, Benjamin Ashley, Robert White, one by the name of Rogers, who took an old scythe and cut an old white-headed man all to pieces. [Thomas McBride.]

I wish further also to state, that when the mob came upon us (as I was told by one of them afterwards), their intention was to kill everything belonging to us, that had life; and that after our men were shot down by them, they went around and shot all the dead men over again, to make sure of their death.

I now leave it with this Honorable Government [the United States] to say what my damages may be, or what they would be willing to see their wives and children slaughtered for, as I have seen my husband, son and others.

I lost in property by the mob—to goods stolen, fifty dollars; one pocketbook, and fifty dollars cash notes; damage of horses and time, one hundred dollars; one gun, ten dollars; in short, my all. Whole damages are more than the State of Missouri is worth.

Written by my own hand, this 18th day of April, 1839.

AMANDA SMITH.

Quincy, Adams County, Illinois.

Thus are the cries of the widows and the fatherless ascending to heaven. How long, O Lord, wilt thou not avenge the blood of the Saints?*

Friday, April 19.—Elders Turley and Clark had traveled but a few miles from Far West when an axle-tree broke,

* The number of killed and wounded in the tragedy at Haun's Mills, [according to information supplied by the late Church Historian, Franklin D. Richards, to the "National Historical Company," St. Louis, Missouri, which issued a history of

and Brother Clark had to go to Richmond after some boxes, which delayed them some days.

Saturday, April 20.—The last of the Saints left Far West.

Sunday, April 21.—I had still continued my journey.

Caldwell and Livingston counties, in 1886], are seventeen of the former and thirteen of the latter; and their names are given as follows:

KILLED.

Thomas McBride,	Simon Cox,
Levi N. Merrick,	Hiram Abbott,
Elias Benner,	John York,
Josiah Fuller,	John Lee,
Benjamin Lewis,	Jchn Myers,
Alexander Campbell,	Warren Smith,
George S. Richards,	Sardius Smith, aged 10,
William Napier,	Charles Merrick, aged 9.
Augustine Harner,	

WOUNDED.

Isaac Laney,	Jacob Haun, (founder of the Mills),
Nathan K. Knight,	Jacob Foutz,
Jacob Myers,	Jacob Potts,
George Myers,	Charles Jimison,
William Yokum,	John Walker,
Tarlton Lewis,	Alma Smith, aged 7 years.

A young Mormon woman, Miss Mary Stedwell, was shot through the hand, as she was running to the woods.

Following this statement concerning the killed and wounded among the Saints, the history above referred to, also says: "The militia, or Jennings' men, had but three men wounded, and none killed. John Renfrow, now [1886] living in Ray county, had a thumb shot off. Allen England, a Daviess county man, was severely wounded in the thigh, and the other wounded man was named Hart.

"*Dies irae!* What a woeful day this had been to Haun's Mills! What a pitiful scene was there when the militia rode away upon the conclusion of their bloody work! The wounded men had been given no attention, and the bodies of the slain were left to fester and putrify in the Indian summer temperature, warm and mellowing. The widows and orphans of the dead came timidly and warily forth from their hiding places as soon as the troops left, and as they recognized one a husband, another a father, another a son, another a brother among the bloody corpses, the wailings of grief and terror that went up were pitiful and agonizing. All that night they were alone with their dead. A return visit of Jennings' men to complete the work of 'extermination' had been threatened and was expected. Verily, the experience of the poor survivors of the Haun's Mills affair was terrible; no wonder that they long remember it."—History of Caldwell and Livingston Counties, Missouri. National Historical Company, 1886.

CHAPTER XXII.

THE PROPHET'S ACCOUNT OF HIS EXPERIENCES IN MISSOURI —FULFILLMENT OF A PROPHETIC REVELATION—COMPLETE EXODUS OF THE SAINTS FROM MISSOURI.

Monday, April 22.—We continued on our journey, both by night and by day; and after suffering much fatigue and hunger, I arrived in Quincy, Illinois, amidst the congratulations of my friends, and the embraces of my family, whom I found as well as could be expected, considering what they had been called to endure. Before leaving Missouri I had paid the lawyers at Richmond thirty-four thousand dollars in cash, lands, etc.; one lot which I let them have, in Jackson county, for seven thousand dollars, they were soon offered ten thousand dollars for it, but would not accept it. For other vexatious suits which I had to contend against the few months I was in this state, I paid lawyers' fees to the amount of about sixteen thousand dollars, making in all about fifty thousand dollars, for which I received very little in return; for sometimes they were afraid to act on account of the mob, and sometimes they were so drunk as to incapacitate them for business. But there were a few honorable exceptions.

The Prophet and Companions Continue their Flight.

Among those who have been the chief instruments and leading characters in the cruel persecutions against the Church of Latter-day Saints, the following stand conspicuous, viz.: Generals Clark, Wilson and Lucas, Colonel Price, and Cornelius Gillium; Captain Bogart also, whose zeal in the cause of oppression and injustice was unequalled, and whose delight has been to rob, murder, and

The Leading Characters in the Persecutions of the Saints.

spread devastation among the Saints. He stole a valuable horse, saddle, and bridle from me, which cost two hundred dollars, and then sold the same to General Wilson. On understanding this, I applied to General Wilson for the horse, who assured me, upon the honor of a gentleman and an officer, that I should have the horse returned to me; but this promise has not been fulfilled.

Part of Governor Boggs in the Persecutions.

All the threats, murders, and robberies, which these officers have been guilty of, are entirely overlooked by the executive of the state; who, to hide his own iniquity, must of course shield and protect those whom he employed to carry into effect his murderous purposes.

Treatment of the Prophet by the Mob.

I was in their hands, as a prisoner, about six months; but notwithstanding their determination to destroy me, with the rest of my brethren who were with me, and although at three different times (as I was informed) we were sentenced to be shot, without the least shadow of law (as we were not military men), and had the time and place appointed for that purpose, yet through the mercy of God, in answer to the prayers of the Saints, I have been preserved and delivered out of their hands, and can again enjoy the society of my friends and brethren, whom I love, and to whom I feel united in bonds that are stronger than death; and in a state where I believe the laws are respected, and whose citizens are humane and charitable.

Calm Assurance of the Prophet Respecting his own Safety.

During the time I was in the hands of my enemies, I must say, that although I felt great anxiety respecting my family and friends, who were so inhumanly treated and abused, and who had to mourn the loss of their husbands and children who had been slain, and, after having been robbed of nearly all that they possessed, were driven from their homes, and forced to wander as strangers in a strange country, in order that they might save themselves and their little ones from the destruction they were threatened with in Missouri, yet as far as I was concerned, I felt perfectly calm, and resigned to the will of my Heavenly Father. I knew my innocence as well as that of the Saints, and that we had done nothing to deserve such treatment from the hands of our oppressors. Consequently, I could look to that God who has the lives of all men in His hands, and who had saved me frequently from the gates of death, for deliverance; and notwithstanding that every avenue of escape seemed to be entirely closed, and death stared me in the face, and that my destruction was determined upon, as far as man was concerned, yet, from my first entrance into the camp, I felt an assurance that I, with my brethren and our families, should be delivered. Yes, that still small voice, which has so often whispered consolation to my soul, in the depths of sorrow and distress, bade me be of good cheer, and promised deliverance, which gave me great comfort.* And although the heathen raged, and the people imagined vain things, yet the Lord of Hosts, the God of Jacob was my refuge; and when I cried unto Him in the day of trouble, He de livered me; for which I call upon my soul, and all that is within me, to bless and praise His holy name. For although I was "troubled on every side, yet not distressed; perplexed, but not in despair; persecuted, but not forsaken; cast down, but not destroyed."

Deportment of the Saints.

The conduct of the Saints, under their accumulated wrongs and sufferings, has been praiseworthy; their courage in defending their brethren from the ravages of the mobs; their attachment to the cause of truth, under circumstances the most trying and distressing which humanity can possibly endure; their love to each other; their readiness to afford assistance to me and my brethren who were confined in a dungeon; their sacrifices in leaving Missouri, and assisting the poor widows and orphans, and securing them houses in a more hospitable

* See the prediction of the Prophet on the safety of himself and fellow prisoners, this volume, p. 200, note.

land; all conspire to raise them in the estimation of all good and virtuous men, and has secured them the favor and approbation of Jehovah, and a name as imperishable as eternity. And their virtuous deeds and heroic actions, while in defense of truth and their brethren, will be fresh and blooming when the names of their oppressors shall be either entirely forgotten, or only remembered for their barbarity and cruelty.

Their attention and affection to me, while in prison, will ever be remembered by me; and when I have seen them thrust away and abused by the jailer and guard, when they came to do any kind offices, and to cheer our minds while we were in the gloomy prison-house, gave me feelings which I cannot describe; while those who wished to insult and abuse us by their threats and blasphemous language, were applauded, and had every encouragement given them.

Sure Reward of the Faithful Saints.

However, thank God, we have been delivered. And although some of our beloved brethren have had to seal their testimony with their blood, and have died martyrs to the cause of truth—

> Short though bitter was their pain,
> Everlasting is their joy.

Let us not sorrow as "those without hope;" the time is fast approaching when we shall see them again and rejoice together, without being afraid of wicked men. Yes, those who have slept in Christ, shall He bring with Him, when He shall come to be glorified in His Saints, and admired by all those who believe, but to take vengeance upon His enemies and all those who obey not the Gospel.

At that time the hearts of the widows and fatherless shall be comforted, and every tear shall be wiped from their faces. The trials they have had to pass through shall work together for their good, and prepare them for the society of those who have come up out of great tribulation, and have washed their robes and made them white in the blood of the Lamb.

The Saints not to Marvel at Persecution.

Marvel not, then, if you are persecuted; but remember the words of the Savior: "The servant is not above his Lord; if they have persecuted me, they will persecute you also;" and that all the afflictions through which the Saints have to pass, are the fulfillment of the words of the Prophets which have spoken since the world began.

We shall therefore do well to discern the signs of the times as we pass along, that the day of the Lord may not "overtake us as a thief in the night." Afflictions, persecutions, imprisonments, and death, we must expect, according to the scriptures, which tell us that the blood of those whose souls were under the altar could not be avenged on them that dwell on the earth, until their brethren should be slain as they were.

The Crime of Missouri to be Viewed in the Light of the Civilized Age in which it was Committed.

If these transactions had taken place among barbarians, under the authority of a despot, or in a nation where a certain religion is established according to law, and all others proscribed, then there might have been some shadow of defense offered. But can we realize that in a land which is the cradle of liberty and equal rights, and where the voice of the conquerors who had vanquished our foes had scarcely died away upon our ears, where we frequently mingled with those who had stood amidst "the battle and the breeze," and whose arms have been nerved in the defense of their country and liberty, whose institutions are the theme of philosophers and poets, and held up to the admiration of the whole civilized world—in the midst of all these scenes, with which we were surrounded, a persecution the most unwarrantable was commenced, and a tragedy the most dreadful was enacted, by a large portion of the inhabitants of one of those free and sovereign states which comprise this vast Republic; and a deadly blow was struck at the institutions for which our fathers had fought many a hard battle, and for which many a patriot had shed his blood. Suddenly was heard, amidst the voice of joy and gratitude for our national liberty, the voice of mourning, lamentation and woe. Yes! in this land, a mob, regardless of those laws for which so much blood had been spilled, dead to every feeling of virtue and patriotism which animated the bosom of freemen, fell upon a people whose religious faith was different from their own, and not only destroyed their homes, drove them away, and carried off their property, but murdered many a free-born son of America—a tragedy which has no parallel in modern, and hardly in ancient, times; even the face of the red man would be ready to turn pale at the recital of it. It would have been some consolation, if the authorities of the state had been innocent in this affair; but they are involved in the guilt thereof, and the blood of innocence, even of children, cry for vengeance upon them.

I ask the citizens of this Republic whether such a state of things is to be suffered to pass unnoticed, and the hearts of widows, orphans, and patriots to be broken, and their wrongs left without redress? No! I invoke the genius of our Constitution. I appeal to the patriotism of Americans to stop this unlawful and unholy procedure; and pray that God may defend this nation from the dreadful effects of such outrages.

The Appeal of the Prophet to the People of the United States.

Is there no virtue in the body politic? Will not the people rise up in their majesty, and with that promptitude and zeal which are so characteristic of them, discountenance such proceedings, by bringing the offenders to that punishment which they so richly deserve, and save the nation from that disgrace and ultimate ruin, which otherwise must inevitably fall upon it?

Pursuit of Elder Markham.

Elder Markham had closed his business in Jackson county and returned to Far West, having been chased as far as the river by the mob on horses at full speed, for the purpose of shooting him. Brother Markham tarried in and near Far West until the 24th of April.

On my arrival at Quincy I found the brethren had been diligent in preparing for an investigation of their wrongs in Missouri, as the following letters will show.

Letter of Governor Lucas of Iowa to Elder Rigdon.

BURLINGTON, IOWA TERRITORY,
April 22, 1839.

DEAR SIR:—I herewith enclose two letters, one addressed to the President of the United States, and one to Governor Shannon, of Ohio. As the object sought by you is an investigation into the facts connected with your misfortunes, I have thought it the most prudent course to refrain from an expression of an individual opinion in the matter, relative to the merits or demerits of the controversy. I sincerely hope that you may succeed in obtaining a general investigation into the cause and extent of your sufferings, and that you may obtain from the government that attention which is your due as citizens of the United States.

Very respectfully your obedient servant,
ROBERT LUCAS.

Doctor Sidney Rigdon.

Letter of Governor Lucas to President Martin Van Buren, Respecting the Latter-day Saints.

BURLINGTON, IOWA TERRITORY,
April 22, 1839.

To His Excellency, Martin Van Buren, President of the United States:

SIR:—I have the honor to introduce to your acquaintance, the bearer, Doctor Sidney Rigdon, who was for many years a citizen of the State of Ohio, and a firm supporter of the administration of the General Government.

Doctor Rigdon visits Washington (as I am informed) as the representative of a community of people called Mormons, to solicit from the Government of the United States, an investigation into the cause that led to their expulsion from the State of Missouri: together with the various circumstances connected with that extraordinary affair.

I think it due to that people to state, that they had for a number of years a community established in Ohio, and that while in that state they were (as far as I ever heard) believed to be an industrious, inoffensive people; and I have no recollection of having ever heard of any of them being charged in that state as violators of the laws.

With sincere respect, I am your obedient servant,

ROBERT LUCAS.

Letter of Governor Lucas to the Governor of Ohio Introducing President Rigdon.

BURLINGTON, IOWA TERRITORY,
April 22, 1839.

To His Excellency Wilson Shannon, Governor of the State of Ohio:

SIR:—I have the honor to introduce to your acquaintance, Doctor Sidney Rigdon, who was for many years a citizen of Ohio. Doctor Rigdon wishes to obtain from the General Government of the United States, an investigation into the causes that led to the expulsion of the people called Mormons from the State of Missouri; together with all the facts connected with that extraordinary affair. This investigation, it appears to me, is due them as citizens of the United States, as well as to the nation at large.

Any assistance that you can render the Doctor, towards accomplishing that desirable object, will be gratefully received and duly appreciated by your sincere friend and humble servant,

ROBERT LUCAS.

Letter of W. W. Phelps to John P. Greene.

FAR WEST, MISSOURI, April 23, 1839.

SIR:—The summit end of Mr. Benson's mill-dam was carried away by the late freshet, and, unless repaired, it will all go the next.

The committee have gone, and if Father Smith would send me a power of attorney, in connection with Mr. Benson's and Corrill's, I have a chance to sell it before it is all lost. Maybe I might save the old gentleman something, which I promised Hyrum I would do if possible, because they have now need. Will you have them do so?

W. W. PHELPS.

To John P. Greene, Quincy, Illinois.

All this day I spent in greeting and receiving visits from my brethren and friends, and truly it was a joyful time.

Wednesday, April 24.—Elder Parley P. Pratt and his fellow prisoners were brought before the grand jury of Ray county at Richmond, and Darwin Chase and Norman

Shearer were dismissed, after being imprisoned about six months. Mrs. Morris Phelps, who had been with her husband in prison some days, hoping he would be released, now parted from him, and, with her little infant, started for Illinois. The number of prisoners at Richmond was now reduced to four. King Follett having been added about the middle of April: he was dragged from his distressed family just as they were leaving the state. Thus of all the prisoners which were taken at an expense of two hundred thousand dollars, only two of the original ones who belonged to the Church, now remained (Luman Gibbs having denied the faith to try to save his life); these were Morris Phelps and Parley P. Pratt. All who were let to bail were banished from the state, together with those who bailed them.

Parley P. Pratt *et al.* Before the Grand Jury at Richmond.

Thus none are like to have a trial by law but Brothers Pratt and Phelps, and they are without friends or witnesses in the state.

Elders Clark and Turley met Alpheus Cutler, Brigham Young, Orson Pratt, George A. Smith, John Taylor, Wilford Woodruff, John E. Page, Daniel Shearer, and others, going up from Quincy to Far West, to fulfill the revelation on the 26th of April, and Clark and Turley turned and went back with them.

The Twelve en route for Far West,

Elder Markham visited at Tenney's Grove.

This evening I met the Church in council.

Minutes of a Council Meeting Held at Quincy, Illinois.

Minutes of a council held in Quincy on the 24th day of April, A. D. 1839, when President Joseph Smith, Jun., was called to the chair, and Brother Alanson Ripley chosen Clerk.

After prayer by the chairman, Elder John P. Greene arose and explained the object of the meeting. A document intended for publication was handed in, touching certain things relative to disorderly persons, who have represented or may represent themselves as belonging to our Church; which document was approved by the council. After which it was

Resolved first: That President Joseph Smith, Jun., Bishop Knight, and Brother Alanson Ripley, visit Iowa Territory immediately, for the purpose of making a location for the Church.

Resolved second: That the advice of the conference to the brethren in general is, that as many of them as are able, move north to Commerce, as soon as they possibly can.

Resolved third: That all the prisoners be received into fellowship.

Resolved fourth: That Brother Mulholland be appointed clerk *pro tem.*

Resolved fifth: That Father Smith's case relative to his circumstances, be referred to the Bishops.

Resolved sixth: That Brother Rogers receive some money to remunerate him for his services in transacting business for the Church in Missouri.

ALANSON RIPLEY, Clerk.

Seeking a New Location

Thursday, April 25.—I accompanied the committee to Iowa to select a location for the Saints. Elder Markham returned from Tenney's Grove to Far West, waiting the arrival of the brethren from Quincy.

Arrival of the Twelve at Far West.

Friday, April 26.—Early this morning, soon after midnight, the brethren arrived at Far West, and proceeded to transact the business of their mission according to the following minutes:

Minutes of the Meeting of the Twelve Apostles at Far West, April 26, 1839.

At a conference held at Far West by the Twelve, High Priests, Elders, and Priests, on the 26th day of April, 1839, the following resolution was adopted:

Resolved: That the following persons be no more fellowshiped in the Church of Jesus Christ of Latter-day Saints, but excommunicated from the same, viz.: Isaac Russell, Mary Russell, John Goodson and wife, Jacob Scott, Sen., and wife, Isaac Scott, Jacob Scott, Jun., Ann Scott, Sister Walton, Robert Walton, Sister Cavanaugh, Ann Wanlass, William Dawson, Jun., and wife, William Dawson, Sen., and wife, George Nelson, Joseph Nelson and wife and mother, William Warnock and wife, Jonathan Maynard, Nelson Maynard, George Miller, John Grigg and wife, Luman Gibbs, Simeon Gardner, and Freeborn Gardner.

The council then proceeded to the building spot of the Lord's House; when the following business was transacted: Part of a hymn was sung, on the mission of the Twelve.

Elder Alpheus Cutler, the master workman of the house, then recommenced laying the foundation of the Lord's House, agreeably to revelation, by rolling up a large stone near the southeast corner.

The following of the Twelve were present: Brigham Young, Heber C. Kimball, Orson Pratt, John E. Page, and John Taylor, who proceeded to ordain Wilford Woodruff,* and George A. Smith, (who had

*Wilford Woodruff was born March 1, 1807, at Farmington (now called Avon), Hartford County, Connecticut. He was the son of Aphek and Beulah Thompson Woodruff. His father, his grandfather, Eldad Woodruff, and his great-grandfather, Josiah Woodruff, were men of strong constitutions, and were noted for their arduous manual labors. His great-grandfather was nearly one hundred years old when he died, and was able to work until shortly before his decease. At an early age Wilford assisted his father on the Farmington mills, and when 20 years of age, took charge of a flouring mill belonging to his aunt, Helen Wheeler, holding the position of manager for three years, when he was placed in charge of the Collins flouring mills at South Canton, Connecticut, and subsequently of the flouring mill owned by Richard B. Cowles, of New Hartford, Connecticut. In the spring of 1832 in company with his brother Azmon Woodruff, he went to Richland, Oswego county, New York, purchased a farm and sawmill, and settled down to business on his own account. On December 29, 1833, he and his brother Azmon heard the Gospel preached by Elders Zera Pulsipher and Elijah Cheney, and they both believed at once, entertained the Elders, offered themselves for baptism, read the Book of Mormon, and received the divine testimony of its truth. He was baptized and confirmed by Elder Zera Pulsipher, December 31, 1833. At a very early age Wilford Woodruff was imbued with religious sentiments, but never allied himself with any of the various sects. He received much information from Robert Mason, who resided at Simsbury, Connecticut, and was called "the old Prophet Mason." He taught that no man had authority to administer in the things of God without revelation from God; that the modern religious societies were without that authority; that the time would come when the true Church would be established with all its gifts and graces and manifestations, and that the same blessings enjoyed in the early Christian Church could be obtained in this age through faith. This led the youthful Wilford to hold aloof from the churches of the day, and to desire and pray for the coming of an Apostle or other inspired man to show the way of life. For three years previous to receiving the everlasting Gospel, he was impressed with the conviction that God was about to set up His Church and kingdom on the earth in the last days, and for the last time, hence, he was prepared to receive the truth when it was presented to him by the Elders. On January 2, 1834, he was ordained a Teacher, and on February 1st, being visited by Elder Parley P. Pratt, he was instructed to prepare himself to join the body of the Church at Kirtland. He immediately commenced to settle up his business, and started with wagon and horses, and arrived in Kirtland April 25, 1834. There he met with the Prophet Joseph Smith, and many leading Elders, and received much light and knowledge. A week later he went to New Portage, where he joined the company of volunteers which was organized by the Prophet Joseph Smith, and known as "Zion's Camp," to go into Missouri for the relief of the suffering Saints in that state. He remained with the camp through all its travels and trials, until it was dispersed in Clay county, Missouri. * * * At a meeting of the High Council in Lyman Wight's house, November 5, 1834, Brother Woodruff was ordained a Priest by Elder Simeon Carter, and was shortly afterwards sent on a mission to the Southern States. * * * On April 13, 1837. he married Phebe W. Carter.

been previously nominated by the First Presidency, accepted by the Twelve, and acknowledged by the Church), to the office of Apostles and members of the quorum of the Twelve, to fill the places of those who are fallen. Darwin Chase and Norman Shearer (who had just been liberated from the Richmond prison, where they had been confined for the cause of Jesus Christ) were then ordained to the office of the Seventies.

The Twelve then offered up vocal prayer in the following order: Brigham Young, Heber C. Kimball, Orson Pratt, John E. Page, John Taylor, Wilford Woodruff, and George A. Smith.* After which we

* * * In July of the same year, when enroute for a mission to the Fox Islands, he preached at Farmington, Connecticut, and converted several members of his father's house. In August he arrived in Fox Islands. (For an account of his success in that mission see volume 2, page 507, and note). In July, 1838, he again visited Farmington, Connecticut, and resumed his labors in the ministry, succeeding in converting his father and step-mother; his sister Eunice, and several other relatives. Meantime, he had been called by revelation (see Doctrine and Covenants, section cxviii) to fill a vacancy in the quorum of the Twelve Apostles, and was ordained under the circumstances given in the minutes of the meeting of the Twelve Apostles at Far West, April 26, 1839. (The foregoing account of Wilford Woodruff's life is taken mainly from a sketch written by Franklin D. Richards, historian of the Church, at the request of Wilford Woodruff.)

* Following is the prophet's account of George A. Smith:—

"George A. Smith, son of John and Clarissa Smith, was born June 26, 1817, in Potsdam, St. Lawrence county, New York. When nine years old he received a blow on the head which deprived him of his senses about three weeks. Five noted physicians decided that he must be trepanned, or he would not recover. His father dismissed them on this decision, believing that God would heal his son; and he firmly believes that He did heal him in answer to the prayer of faith. He was early trained by his parents, who were Presbyterians, to religious habits, and to a regular attendance in the Sabbath school. Hence he had early and anxious desires to know the way of life; but was not satisfied with the sects.

"In the summer of 1830, when my father and my brother Don Carlos visited relatives in St. Lawrence county, George A. became convinced of the truth of the Book of Mormon, and from that time defended the cause against those who opposed it.

"His mother was baptized in August, 1831. His father was baptized on the ninth of January, 1832, and ordained an Elder. He had been given up by the doctors to die of consumption. The weather was extremely cold, and the ice had to be cut. From that time he gained health and strength. George A. was baptized on the 10th of September, 1832, and on the 1st of May, 1833, his father and family took leave of their old home and removed to Kirtland, Ohio. George A. spent the season in laboring on the Temple, although much afflicted with inflammation of the eyes.

"On the 5th of May, 1834, he started for Zion, in the camp, and acted his part well as my armor-bearer although still much afflicted with sore eyes. On the twenty-eighth he was attacked by the cholera, but was delivered by faith. He was ordained into the first Seventy under my hands on the 1st of March, 1835, being seventeen years old. He left on the 5th of June, in company with Lyman Smith, for the State of New York, to preach the Gospel without purse or scrip. Traveled two thousand miles, baptized eight, held eighty meetings, and returned on the

sung Adam-ondi-Ahman, and then the Twelve took their leave of the following Saints, agreeable to the revelation, viz.: Alpheus Cutler, Elias Smith, Norman Shearer, William Burton, Stephen Markham, Shadrach Roundy, William O. Clark, John W. Clark, Hezekiah Peck, Darwin Chase, Richard Howard, Mary Ann Peck, Artimesa Grainger, Martha Peck, Sarah Grainger, Theodore Turley, Hyrum Clark, and Daniel Shearer.

Elder Alpheus Cutler then placed the stone before alluded to in its regular position, after which, in consequence of the peculiar situation of the Saints, he thought it wisdom to adjourn until some future time, when the Lord shall open the way; expressing his determination then to proceed with the building; whereupon the conference adjourned.

BRIGHAM YOUNG, President.
JOHN TAYLOR, Clerk.

The Revelation of April 8, 1838, Fulfilled.

Thus was fulfilled a revelation of July 8, 1838, which our enemies had said could not be fulfilled, as no "Mormon" would be permitted to be in the state.

As the Saints were passing away from the meeting, Brother Turley said to Elders Page and Woodruff, "Stop a bit, while I bid Isaac Russell good bye;" and knocking at the door, called Brother Russell. His wife answered, "Come in, it is Brother Turley." Russell replied, "It is not; he left here two weeks ago;" and appeared quite alarmed; but on finding it was Brother Turley, asked him to sit down; but the latter replied, "I cannot, I shall lose my company." "Who is your company?" enquired Russell. "The Twelve." "*The Twelve!*" "Yes, don't you know that this is the twenty-sixth, and

2nd of November. Spent the winter in school, much afflicted with the rheumatism. In the spring, summer, and fall of 1836, he preached in different parts of Ohio with good success. Returned and went to school in the winter. On the 6th of June, 1837, he took leave of me and started with my blessing for the South. After a successful mission of ten months, mostly in Virginia, he returned and assisted his father in moving to Far West, Missouri. He was ordained a High Councilor at Adam-ondi-Ahman, and sent on a mission to the South in company with Don Carlos Smith; returned about the 25th of December.

"He visited me while in Liberty jail, when I made known to him that he was appointed to fill the place of Thomas B. Marsh in the quorum of the Twelve Apostles. He assisted in moving the Saints out of Far West, and returned with the twelve to fulfill the revelation concerning the Twelve taking their leave of the Saints on the building site of the Temple at Far West."

the day the Twelve were to take leave of their friends on the foundation of the Lord's House, to go to the islands of the sea? The revelation is now fulfilled, and I am going with them.'' Russell was speechless, and Turley bid him farewell.

The brethren immediately returned to Quincy, taking with them the families from Tenney's Grove.

CHAPTER XXIII.

SETTLEMENT AT COMMERCE, ILLINOIS.

THE committee continued to look at the different locations which were presented in Lee county, Iowa, and about Commerce, in Hancock county, Illinois.

Seeking a New Location.

Wednesday, May 1.—The following letter was communicated to the *Quincy Argus*, a weekly newspaper, published at Quincy:

Elder Taylor's Warning to the People of Quincy Against Impostors.

To the Editor of the Argus:

SIR:—In consequence of so great an influx of strangers arriving in this place daily, owing to their late expulsion from the State of Missouri, there must of necessity be, and we wish to state to the citizens of Quincy and the vicinity, through the medium of your columns, that there are many individuals amongst the number who have already arrived, as well as among those who are now on their way here, who never did belong to our Church, and others who once did, but who, for various reasons, have been expelled from our fellowship. Amongst these there are some who have contracted habits which are at variance with the principles of moral rectitude, (such as swearing, dram-drinking, etc.,) which immoralities the Church of Latter-day Saints is liable to be charged with, owing to our amalgamation [with them] under our late existing circumstances. And as we as a people do not wish to lie under any such imputation, we would also state, that such individuals do not hold a name nor a place amongst us; that we altogether discountenance everything of the kind; that every person belonging to our community, contracting or persisting in such immoral habits, has hitherto been expelled from our society; and that we will hold no communion with all such as we may hereafter be informed of, but will withdraw our fellowship from them.

We wish further to state, that we feel ourselves laid under peculiar obligations to the citizens of this place, for the patriotic feeling which has been manifested, and for the hand of liberality and friendship which has been extended to us in our late difficulties; and should feel sorry to see that philanthropy and benevolence abused by wicked and designing people, who under pretense of poverty and distress, would try to work upon the feelings of the charitable and humane, get into their debt without any prospect or intention of paying, and finally, perhaps, we as a people be charged with dishonesty.

We say that we altogether disapprove of such practices, and we warn the citizens of Quincy against such individuals, who may pretend to belong to our community.

By inserting this in your columns, you, sir, will confer upon us a very peculiar favor.

Written and signed in behalf of the Church of Latter-day Saints, by your very humble servant,

JOHN TAYLOR.

Land Purchases.

I this day purchased, in connection with others of the committee, a farm of Hugh White, consisting of one hundred and thirty-five acres, for the sum of five thousand dollars; also a farm of Dr. Isaac Galland, lying west of the White purchase, for the sum of nine thousand dollars; both of which were to be deeded to Alanson Ripley, according to the counsel of the committee; but Sidney Rigdon declared that "no committee should control any property which he had anything to do with;" consequently the Galland purchase was deeded to George W. Robinson, Rigdon's son-in-law, with the express understanding that he should deed it to the Church, when the Church had paid for it according to their obligation in the contract.

The English Saints Warned against Isaac Russell.

A letter was received by the Presidency of the Church in England, then at Preston, from President Heber C. Kimball, stating that Isaac Russell had apostatized, and styled himself the Prophet; and that Joseph had fallen. Elder Kimball said the Spirit signified to him that Russell was secretly trying to lead away the Church at Alston, England, and wished the Elders to see to it. The Spirit had manifested the same thing to Elder Richards, and he was deputed by a council of the Presidency to visit the Alston branch.

Friday, 3.—I returned to Quincy.

Elder Richards left Preston for Alston.

Saturday, 4.—Elder Richards arrived at Alston and discovered by stratagem that a letter had been received from Isaac Russell, as follows:

Isaac Russell's Letter to the Saints in England.

FAR WEST, January 30, 1839.

To the Faithful Brethren and Sisters of the Church of Latter-day Saints in Alston:

DEAR BRETHREN:—Inasmuch as wisdom is only to be spoken amongst those who are wise, I charge you to read this letter to none but those who enter into a covenant with you to keep those things that are revealed in this letter from all the world, and from all the churches, except the churches to whom I myself have ministered, viz.—the church in Alston and the branches round about, to whom I ministered. and to none else; and to none but the faithful amongst you; and wo be to the man or woman that breaketh this covenant.

Now the Indians, who are the children of the Nephites and the Lamanites, who are spoken of in the Book of Mormon, have all been driven to the western boundaries of the States of America, by the Gentiles, as I told you; they have now to be visited by the gospel, for the day of their redemption is come, and the Gentiles have now well nigh filled up the measure of their wickedness, and will soon be cut off, for they have slain many of the people of the Lord, and scattered the rest; and for the sins of God's people, the Gentiles will now be suffered to scourge them from city to city, and from place to place, and few of all the thousands of the Church of Latter-day Saints will stand to receive an inheritance in the land of promise, which is now in the hands of our enemies. But a few will remain and be purified as gold seven times refined; and they will return to Zion with songs of everlasting joy, to build up the old waste places that are now left desolate.

Now the thing that I have to reveal to you is sacred, and must be kept with care; for I am not suffered to reveal it at all to the churches in this land, because of their wickedness and unbelief—for they have almost cast me out from amongst them, because I have testified of their sins to them, and warned them of the judgments that have yet to come upon them; and this thing that I now tell you, will not come to the knowledge of the churches until they are purified.

Now the thing is as follows—The Lord has directed me, with a few others, whose hearts the Lord has touched, to go into the wilderness, where we shall be fed and directed by the hand of the Lord until we are purified and prepared to minister to the Lamanites, and with us the Lord will send those three who are spoken of in the Book of Mormon, who were with Jesus after His resurrection, and have tarried on the earth to minister to their brethren in the last days.

Thus God is sending us before to prepare a place for you and for the remnant who will survive the judgments which are now coming on the Church of Latter-day Saints, to purify them, for we are sent to prepare a Zion, (as Joseph was before sent into Egypt), a city of Peace, a place of Refuge, that you may hide yourselves with us and all the Saints in the due time of the Lord, before His indignation shall sweep away the nations.

These things are marvelous in our eyes, for great is the work of the Lord that He is going to accomplish. All this land will be redeemed by the hands of the Lamanites, and room made for you, when you hear again from me. Abide where you are, and be subject to the powers that be amongst you in the church. Keep diligently the things I taught you, and when you read this, be comforted concerning me, for though you may not see me for some few years, yet as many of you as continue faithful, will see me again, and it will be in the day of your deliverance. Pray for me always, and be assured that I will not forget you. To the grace of God I commend you in Christ. Amen.

ISAAC RUSSELL.

P. S.—We have not yet gone in the wilderness, but we shall go when the Lord appoints the time. If you should hear that I have apostatized, believe it not, for I am doing the work of the Lord. I. R.

Russell's Efforts Counteracted.

Elder Richards being led by the Spirit of God, soon unfolded the sophistry and falsehood of this letter to the convincing of the Saints at Alston and Brampton, so as to entirely destroy their confidence in the apostate Russell, although they had loved him as a father.

Minutes of a General Conference of the Church Held near Quincy, Illinois, May 4th, 5th and 6th, 1839.

Minutes of a general conference held by the Church of Latter-day Saints at the Presbyterian camp ground, near Quincy, Adams county, Illinois, on Saturday, the 4th of May, 1839.

At a quarter past eleven o'clock meeting was called to order and President Joseph Smith, Jun., appointed chairman.

A hymn was then sung, when President Smith made a few observations on the state of his peculiar feelings, after having been separated from the brethren so long, etc., and then proceeded to open the meeting by prayer.

After some preliminary observations by Elder J. P. Greene and President Rigdon, concerning a certain purchase of land in the Iowa Territory, made for the Church by the Presidency, the following resolutions were unanimously adopted:

Resolved 1st: That Almon W. Babbitt, Erastus Snow and Robert B. Thompson be appointed a traveling committee to gather up and obtain all the libelous reports and publications which have been circulated against our Church, as well as other historical matter connected with said Church, that they possibly can obtain.

Resolved 2nd: That Bishop Vinson Knight be appointed, or received into the Church in full bishopric.

Resolved 3rd: That this conference do entirely sanction the purchase lately made for the Church in the Iowa Territory, and also the agency thereof.

Resolved 4th: That Elder Grainger be appointed to go to Kirtland and take the charge and oversight of the House of the Lord, and preside over the general affairs of the Church in that place.

Resolved 5th: That the advice of this conference to the brethren living in the Eastern States is, for them to move to Kirtland and the vicinity thereof, and again settle that place as a Stake of Zion; provided they feel so inclined, in preference to their moving farther west.

Resolved 6th: That George A. Smith be acknowledged one of the Twelve Apostles.

Resolved 7th: That this conference are entirely satisfied with, and give their sanction to the proceedings of the conference of the Twelve and their friends, held on the Temple site at Far West, Missouri, on Friday, the 26th of April last.

Resolved 8th: That they also sanction the act of the council held the same date and same place, in cutting off from the communion of said Church, certain persons mentioned in the minutes thereof.

Resolved 9th: That Elders Orson Hyde and William Smith be allowed the privilege of appearing personally before the next general conference of the Church, to give an account of their conduct; and that in the meantime they be both suspended from exercising the functions of their office.

Resolved 10th: That the conference do sanction the mission intended for the Twelve to Europe, and that they will do all in their power to enable them to go.

Resolved 11th: That the subject of Elder Rigdon's going to Washington be adjourned until tomorrow.

Resolved 12th: That the next general conference be held on the first Saturday in October next, at Commerce, at the house of Elder Rigdon.

Resolved 13th: That we now adjourn until tomorrow at ten o'clock a. m.

JOSEPH SMITH, JUN., President.
J. MULHOLLAND, Clerk.

Certificate of Appointment.

This is to certify that at a general conference held at Quincy, Adams county, Illinois, by the Church of Jesus Christ of Latter-day Saints, on Saturday, the 4th day of May, 1839, President Joseph Smith, Jun., presiding, it was resolved: That Almon W. Babbitt, Erastus Snow, and Robert B. Thompson be appointed a traveling committee to gather up and obtain all the libelous reports and publications which have been circulated against the Church of Jesus Christ of Latter-day Saints, as well as other historical matter connected with said Church, which they can possibly obtain.

JOSEPH SMITH, JUN., President.
JAMES MULHOLLAND, Clerk.

Minutes of the 5th.

Sunday, 5th, 10 a. m.—Conference opened pursuant to adjournment as usual, by prayer and singing; when it was unanimously resolved: That this conference send a delegate to the City of Washington, to lay our case before the General Government; and that President Rigdon be the delegate.

Resolved 2nd: That Almon W. Babbitt be sent to Springfield, Illinois, clothed with authority, and required to set to rights the Church in that place in every way which may become necessary according to the order of the Church of Jesus Christ.

Resolved 3rd: That Colonel Lyman Wight be appointed to receive the affidavits which are to be sent to the City of Washington; after which the afternoon was spent in receiving instructions from the Presidency and those of the Twelve who were present.

At 5 o'clock p. m. conference adjourned.

JOSEPH SMITH, JUN., President.
JAMES MULHOLLAND, Clerk.

Minutes of the 6th.

Monday, 6th.—At a conference held at Quincy, Illinois, on the 6th of

May, 1839, President Joseph Smith, Jun., presiding, the following resolutions were unanimously agreed to:

Resolved 1st: That the families of Elder Marks, Elder Grainger, and Bishop N. K. Whitney, be kept here amongst us for the time being.

Resolved 2nd: That Elder Marks be hereby appointed to preside over the Church at Commerce, Illinois.

Resolved 3rd: That Bishop Whitney also go to Commerce, and there act in unison with the other Bishops of the Church.

Resolved 4th: That Brother Turley's gunsmith tools shall remain for the general use of the Church, until his return from Europe.

Resolved 5th: That the following of the Seventies have the sanction of this council that they accompany the Twelve to Europe, namely. Theodore Turley, George Pitkin, Joseph Bates Noble, Charles Hubbard, John Scott, Lorenzo D. Young, Samuel Mulliner, Willard Snow, John Snider, William Burton, Lorenzo D. Barnes, Milton Holmes. Abram O. Smoot, Elias Smith; also the following High Priests: Henry G. Sherwood, John Murdock, Winslow Farr, William Snow, Hiram Clark.

Resolved 6th: That it be observed as a general rule, that those of the Seventies who have not yet preached, shall not for the future be sent on foreign missions.

Resolved 7th: That Elder John P. Greene be appointed to go to the City of New York and preside over the churches there and in the regions round about.

I also gave the following letter to John P. Greene:

John P. Greene's Letter of Appointment.

At a conference meeting held by the Church of Jesus Christ of Latter-day Saints, in the town of Quincy, Adams county, Illinois, on Monday, the 6th day of May, 1839, Joseph Smith, Jun., presiding, it was unanimously resolved: That Elder John P. Greene be appointed to go to the City of New York, and preside over the Saints in that place and in the regions round about, and regulate the affairs of the Church according to the laws and doctrines of said Church; and he is fully authorized to receive donations by the liberality of the Saints for the assistance of the poor among us. who have been persecuted and driven from their homes in the State of Missouri; and from our long acquaintance with Elder Greene, and with his experience and knowledge of the laws of the Kingdom of God, we do not hesitate to recommend him to the Saints as one in whom they may place the fullest confidence, both as to their spiritual welfare, as well as to the strictest integrity in all temporal concerns with which he may be entrusted.

And we beseech the brethren, in the name of the Lord Jesus, to receive this brother in behalf of the poor with readiness, and to abound unto him in a liberal manner; for "inasmuch as ye have done it unto the least of these, ye have done it unto me."

Yours in the bonds of the everlasting Gospel, though no longer a prisoner in the hands of the Missourians, and still faithful with the Saints.

JOSEPH SMITH, JUN., Chairman.

Tuesday, 7.—I was in council with the Twelve and others at Quincy.

Wednesday, 8.—I was preparing to remove to Commerce, and engaged in counseling the brethren, etc.

Letter of Recommendation to Elder John P. Greene from Certain Citizens of Quincy.

QUINCY, ILLINOIS, May 8, 1839.

To All Whom it May Concern:

The undersigned citizens of Quincy, Illinois, take great pleasure in recommending to the favorable notice of the public, the bearer of this, John P. Greene. Mr. Greene is connected with the Church of "Mormons" or "Latter-day Saints," and makes a tour to the east for the purpose of raising means to relieve the sufferings of this unfortunate people, stripped as they have been of their all, and now scattered throughout this part of the state.

We say to the charitable and benevolent, you need have no fear but your contributions in aid of humanity will be properly applied if entrusted to the hands of Mr. Greene. He is authorized by his Church to act in the premises; and we most cordially bear testimony to his piety and worth as a citizen.

Very respectfully yours,

SAMUEL HOLMES, Merchant.
I. N. MORRIS, Attorney at Law, and Editor of *Argus*.
THOMAS CARLIN, Governor State of Illinois.
RICHARD M. YOUNG, U. S. Senator.
L. V. RALSTON, M. D.
SAMUEL LEACH, Receiver of Public Moneys
HIRAM ROGERS, M. D.
J. T. HOLMES, Merchant.
NICHOLAS WREN, County Clerk.
C. M. WOODS, Clerk of Circuit Court, Adams Co., Ill.

Sidney Rigdon's Letter of Introduction to the President of the United States, et al.

QUINCY, ILLINOIS, May 8, 1839.

To His Excellency the President of the United States, the Heads of Departments, and all to whom this may be shown:

The undersigned citizens of Quincy, Illinois, beg leave to introduce to you the bearer, Rev. Sidney Rigdon. Mr. Rigdon is a divine, connected with the Church of Latter-day Saints, and having enjoyed his acquaintance for some time past, we take great pleasure in recommending him to your favorable notice as a man of piety and a valuable citizen.

Any representation he may make, touching the object of his mission to your city, may be implicitly relied on.

Very respectfully yours,

SAMUEL HOLMES,
THOMAS CARLIN,
RICHARD M. YOUNG,
I. N. MORRIS,
HIRAM ROGERS,
J. T. HOLMES,
NICHOLAS WREN,
C. M. WOODS.

The Prophet Settles at Commerce.

Thursday, 9.—I started with my family for Commerce, Hancock county, and stayed this night at Uncle John Smith's, at Green Plains, where we were most cordially received.

Friday, 10.—I arrived with my family at the White purchase and took up my residence in a small log house on the bank of the river, about one mile south of Commerce City, hoping that I and my friends may here find a resting place for a little season at least.

Sidney Rigdon's General Letter of Introduction.

QUINCY, ILLINOIS, 10th May, 1839.

The bearer, Rev. Sidney Rigdon, is a member of a society of people called "Mormons," or "Latter-day Saints," who have been driven from the State of Missouri, by order of the executive of that state, and who have taken up their residence in and about this place in large numbers. I have no hesitation in saying that this people have been most shamefully persecuted and cruelly treated by the people of Missouri.

Mr. Rigdon has resided in and near this place for three or four months, during which time his conduct has been that of a gentleman and a moral and worthy citizen.

SAMUEL LEECH.

Monday, May 13.—I was engaged in general business at home and in transacting a variety of business with Brother Oliver Granger, and gave him the following letter:

A Letter of Recommendation to Oliver Granger from the First Presidency.

COMMERCE, ILLINOIS, 13th May, 1839.

Joseph Smith, Jun., Sidney Rigdon, and Hyrum Smith, presiding Elders of the Church of Jesus Christ of Latter-day Saints, do hereby certify and solemnly declare unto all the Saints scattered abroad, and send unto them greeting: That we have always found President Oliver Granger to be a man of the most strict integrity and moral virtue; and in fine, to be a man of God.

We have had long experience and acquaintance with Brother Granger. We have entrusted vast business concerns to him, which have been managed skilfully to the support of our characters and interest as well as that of the Church; and he is now authorized by a general conference to go forth and engage in vast and important concerns as an agent for the Church, that he may fill a station of usefulness in obedience to the commandment of God, which was given unto him July 8, 1838, which says, "Let him (meaning Brother Granger) contend earnestly for the redemption of the First Presidency of my Church, saith the Lord."

We earnestly solicit the Saints scattered abroad to strengthen his hands with all their might, and to put such means into his hands as shall enable him to accomplish his lawful designs and purposes, according to the commandments, and according to the instructions which he shall give unto them. And that they entrust him with moneys, lands, chattels, and goods, to assist him in this work; and it shall redound greatly to the interest and welfare, peace and satisfaction of my Saints, saith the Lord God, for this is an honorable agency which I have appointed unto him, saith the Lord. And again, verily, thus saith the Lord, I will lift up my servant Oliver, and beget for him a great name on the earth, and among my people, because of the integrity of his soul: therefore, let all my Saints abound unto him, with all liberality and long suffering, and it shall be a blessing on their heads.

We would say unto the Saints abroad, let our hearts abound with grateful acknowledgements unto God our Heavenly Father, who hath called us unto His holy calling by the revelation of Jesus Christ, in these last days, and has so mercifully stood by us, and delivered us out of the seventh trouble, which happened unto us in the State of Missouri. May God reward our enemies according to their works. We request the prayers of all the Saints, subscribing ourselves their humble brethren in tribulations, in the bonds of the everlasting Gospel.

JOSEPH SMITH, JUN.,
SIDNEY RIGDON,
HYRUM SMITH.

Letter of R. B. Thompson to the First Presidency Complaining of the Conduct of Lyman Wight.

To the Presidency of the Church of Jesus Christ of Latter-day Saints, Greeting:

I beg leave to call your attention to a subject of considerable importance to our Church, and which if not attended to is calculated (in my humble opinion) to raise a prejudice in a considerable portion of the community, and destroy those benevolent and philanthropic feelings which have been manifested towards us as a people by a large portion of this community: I have reference to the letters of Brother Lyman Wight, which have been inserted in the *Quincy Whig*. I am aware that upon a cursory view of these, nothing very objectionable may appear; yet, if they are attentively considered, there will be found very great objections to them indeed; for instance, in condemning the Democracy of Missouri, why condemn that of the whole Union? and why use such epithets as "Demagogue" to Thomas H. Benton, for not answering his letter, when it is very probable that he had not received it?

Yesterday I was waited on by Mr. Morris, who asked me what was intended by such publications, and why we should come out against the Democracy of the nation, when they were doing all in their power to assist us; it was something which he could not understand, and wished to know if we as a people countenanced such proceedings. I told him for my part I was sorry that these letters had ever made their appearance, and believed that such a course was at variance with the sentiments of the greater part of our people.

Yesterday I brought the subject before the authorities of the Church who are here, where it was manifest that his conduct was not fellowshiped, and the brethren wished to disavow all connection with such proceedings, and appointed a committee to wait on Brother Wight, to beg of him not to persist in the course, which, if not nipped in the bud, will probably bring persecution with all its horrors upon an innocent people, by the folly and imprudence of one individual.

From information I understand that the feelings of the governor are very much hurt by the course which is pursued. I think we ought to correct the public mind on this subject, and, as a Church, disavow all connection with politics. By such a procedure we may in some measure counteract the baneful influence which his letters have occasioned. But if such a course which he (Brother Wight) has adopted, be continued, (as I understand that he intends to do), it will block up our way, and we can have no reasonable prospect of obtaining justice from the authorities of the Union, whom we wantonly condemn before we have made application. The same feelings are beginning to be manifested in Springfield by those who have been our friends there.

The Whigs are glad of such weapons, and make the most of them. You will probably think I am a little too officious, but I feel impressed with the subject; I feel for my brethren. The tears of widows, the cries of orphans, and the moans of the distressed, are continually present in my mind; and I want to adopt and continue a course which shall be beneficial to us; but if through the imprudence and conduct of isolated individuals, three, four, or five years hence, our altars should be thrown down, our houses destroyed, our brethren slain, our wives widowed, and our children made orphans, your unworthy brother wishes to lift up his hands before God and appeal to Him and say, Thou who knowest all things, knowest that I am innocent in this matter.

I am with great respect, gentlemen, yours in the bonds of Christ,

R. B. THOMPSON.

P. S.—If you do not intend to be in Quincy this week, would you favor us with your opinion on this subject?

R. B. THOMPSON

Quincy, Monday morning, 13th May, 1839.

Letter of Elder Parley P. Pratt to Judge Austin A. King.

STATE OF MISSOURI, RICHMOND,
RAY COUNTY, May 13, 1839.

To the Honorable Austin A. King, Judge of the Court of this and the adjoining counties:

HONORABLE SIR:—Having been confined in prison near seven months, and the time having now arrived when a change of venue can be taken in order for the further prosecution of our trials, and the time having come when I can speak my mind freely, without endangering the lives of any but myself, I now take the liberty of seriously objecting to a trial anywhere within the bounds of the state, and of earnestly praying to your honor and to all the authorities, civil and military, that my case may come within the law of banishment, which has been so rigorously enforced upon near ten thousand of our society, including my wife and little ones, with all my witnesses and friends.

My reasons are obvious, and founded upon notorious facts, which are known to you, sir, and to the people in general of this Republic, and therefore need no proof. They are as follows: First, I have never received any protection by law, either of my person, property, or family, while residing in this state, to which I first emigrated in 1831. Secondly, I was driven by force of arms from Jackson county, wounded and bleeding, in 1833, while my house was burned, my crops and provision, robbed from me or destroyed, and my land kept from me until now, while my family was driven out without shelter, at the approach of winter. Thirdly, these crimes still go unpunished, notwithstanding I made oath before the Honorable Judge Ryland, then Circuit Judge of that district, to the foregoing outrages; and I also applied in person to His Excellency Daniel Dunklin, then Governor of the state, for redress and protection, and a restoration of myself and about 1,200 of my fellow-sufferers, to our rights—but all in vain.

Fourthly, my wife and children have now been driven from our home and improvements in Caldwell county, and banished from the state on pain of death, together with about ten thousand of our society, including all my friends and witnesses; and this by the express orders of His Excellency Lilburn W. Boggs, Governor of the state of Missouri, and by the vigorous execution of his order, by Generals Lucas and Clark, and followed up by murders, rapes, plunderings, thefts and robberies of the most inhuman character by a lawless mob, who have from time to time for more than five years past, trampled upon all law and authority, and upon all the rights of man.

Fifthly, all these inhuman outrages and crimes go unpunished, and are unnoticed by you, sir, and by all the authorities of the state.

Sixthly, the legislature of the state has approved of and sanctioned this act of banishment, with all the crimes connected with it, by voting some two hundred thousand dollars for the payment of troops engaged in this unlawful, unconstitutional, and treasonable enterprise. In monarchial governments the banishment of criminals after their trial and legal condemnation, has been frequently resorted to—but the banishment of innocent women and children from house and home and country, to wander in a land of strangers, unprotected and unprovided for, while their husbands and fathers are retained in dungeons, to be tried by some other law, is an act unknown in the annals of history, except in this single instance in the nineteenth century, when it has actually transpired in a republican state, where the Constitution guarantees to every man the protection of life and property, and the rights of trial by jury. These are outrages which would put monarchy to the blush, and from which the most despotic tyrants of the dark ages would turn away with shame and disgust. In these proceedings, Missouri has enrolled her name on the list of immortal fame—her transactions will be handed down the stream of time to the latest posterity, who will read with wonder and astonishment the history of proceedings which are without a parallel in the annals of time. Why should the authorities of the state strain at a gnat and swallow a camel? Why be so strictly legal as to compel me to go through all the forms of a slow and legal prosecution previous to my enlargement, [being set free] out of a pretense of respect to laws of the state, which have been openly trampled upon and disregarded towards us from the first to the last? Why not include me in the general wholesale banishment of our society, that I may support my family which are now reduced to beggary, in a land of strangers? But when the authorities of the state shall redress all these wrongs; shall punish the guilty according to law; and shall restore my family and friends to all the rights of which we have been unlawfully deprived, both in Jackson and all other counties; and shall pay all the damages which we as a people have sustained; then I shall believe them sincere in their professed zeal for law and justice; then shall I be convinced that I can have a fair trial in the state. But until then, I hereby solemnly protest against being tried in this state, with the full and conscientious conviction that I have no just grounds to expect a fair and impartial trial.

I therefore most sincerely pray your honor, and all the authorities of the state, to either banish me without further prosecution; or I freely consent to a trial before a judiciary of the United States.

With sentiments of high consideration and due respect, I have the honor to subscribe myself, your honor's most humble and obedient; etc.

PARLEY P. PRATT.

To Austin A. King.

Tuesday, May 14.—I returned to Quincy.

Wednesday and Thursday, 15th and 16th. Was engaged in a variety of business relating to the general welfare of the Church.

Letter of the First Presidency to the Quincy Whig, Disclaiming the Attitude of Lyman Wight.

COMMERCE, May 17, 1839.

To the Editors of the Quincy Whig:

GENTLEMEN:—Some letters in your paper have appeared over the signature of Lyman Wight in relation to our affairs with Missouri. We consider it is Mr. Wight's privilege to express his opinion in relation to political or religious matters, and we profess no authority in the case whatever, but we have thought, and do still think, that it is not doing our cause justice to make a political question of it in any manner whatever.

We have not at any time thought there was any political party, as such, chargeable with the Missouri barbarities, neither any religious society, as such. They were committed by a mob composed of all parties, regardless of all differences of opinion either political or religious.

The determined stand in this state, and by the people of Quincy in particular, made against the lawless outrages of the Missouri mobbers by all parties in politics and religion, have entitled them equally to our thanks and our profoundest regards, and such, gentlemen, we hope they will always receive from us. Favors of this kind ought to be engraven on the rock, to last forever.

We wish to say to the public, through your paper, that we disclaim any intention of making a political question of our difficulties with Missouri, believing that we are not justified in so doing.

We ask the aid of all parties, both in politics and religion, to have justice done us and obtain redress. We think, gentlemen, in so saying, we have the feelings of [i. e. represent] our people generally, however, individuals may differ; and we wish you to consider the letters of Lyman Wight as the feelings and views of an individual, but not of the society as such. We are satisfied that our people as a body disclaim all such sentiments and feel themselves equally bound to both parties in this state, as far as kindness is concerned, and good will; and also believe that all political parties in Missouri are equally guilty.

Should this note meet the public eye through the medium of your paper, it will much oblige your humble servants.

JOSEPH SMITH, JUN.,
SIDNEY RIGDON,
HYRUM SMITH.

CHAPTER XXIV.

ADVENTURES OF THE PRISONERS REMAINING IN MISSOURI—THE PROPHET'S NARRATIVE OF PERSONAL EXPERIENCES IN MISSOURI.

Saturday, May 18.—Finished my business at Quincy for the present.

Sunday, 19.—I arrived at home [Commerce] this evening.

Monday 20.—At home attending to a variety of business.

Tuesday, 21.—To show the feelings of that long scattered branch of the house of Israel, the Jews, I here quote a letter written by one of their number, on hearing that his son had embraced Christianity:

Rabbi Landau's Letter to his Son.

BRESLAU, May 21st, 1839.

My Dear Son—I received the letter of the Berlin Rabbi, and when I read it there ran tears out of my eyes in torrents; my inward parts shook, my heart became as a stone! Now do you not know that the Lord sent me already many hard tribulations? That many sorrows do vex me? But this new harm which you are about to inflict, makes me forget all the former, does horribly surpass them; as well respecting its sharpness, as its stings! I write you this lying on my bed, because my body is afflicted not less than my soul, at the report that you were about to do something which I had not expected from you. I fainted; my nerves and feelings sank, and only by the help of a physician, for whom I sent immediately, I am able to write these lines to you with a trembling hand.

Alas! you, my son, whom I have bred, nourished and fostered; whom I have strengthened spiritually as well as bodily, you will commit a crime on me! Do not shed the innocent blood of your parents for no harm have we inflicted upon you; we are not conscious of any guilt against you, but at all times we thought it our duty to show to you, our first born, all love and goodness. I thought I should have some cheering account of you, but, alas! how terribly I have been disappointed!

But to be short; your outward circumstances are such that you may finish your study or [suffer] pain. Do you think that the Christians, to whom you will go over by changing your religion, will support you and fill up the place of our fellow believers? Do not imagine that your outward reasons, therefore, if you have any, are nothing. But out of true persuasion, you will, as I think, not change our true and holy doctrine, for that deceitful, untrue and perverse doctrine of Christianity.

What! will you give up a pearl for that which is nothing, which is of no value in itself? But you are light-minded; think of the last judgment; of that day when the books will be opened and hidden things will be made manifest; of that day when death will approach you in a narrow pass; when you cannot go out of the way! Think of your death bed, from which you will not rise any more, but from which you will be called before the judgment seat of the Lord!

Do you not know, have you not heard, that there is over you an all-hearing ear and an all-seeing eye? That all your deeds will be written in a book and judged hereafter? Who shall then assist you when the Lord will ask you with a thundering voice, Why hast thou forsaken that holy law which shall have an eternal value; which was given by my servant Moses, and no man shall change it? Why hast thou forsaken that law, and accepted instead of it lying and vanity?

Come, therefore, again to yourself, my son! remove your bad and wicked counselors; follow my advice, and the Lord will be with you! Your tender father must conclude because of weeping.

A. L. Landau, Rabbi.*

*This letter was written, it will be observed in 1839. It cannot fail to be of interest to all to see the marked change which in more recent years has come over Jewish thought concerning Jesus of Nazareth. Nephi prophesied over five hundred years B.C. that in the latter days the Jews would begin to believe in Christ, and should begin to gather in upon the face of the land given to their fathers. In the year 1901 Dr. Isaac K. Funk, for Funk and Wagnalls, published an editon of Dr. George Croly's work entitled, "Salathiel the Immortal," or "The Wandering Jew." This work was first published in 1827. Dr. Funk gave the book the title, "Tarry Thou Till I Come," and in the appendix of the work he published some twenty-seven letters received from distinguished Jews in response to his question, "What is the Jewish thought today of Jesus of Nazareth?" From this great number of answers to this question, the following represent the general trend of the whole collection.

"I regard Jesus of Nazareth as a Jew of the Jews, one whom all Jewish people are learning to love. His teaching has been an immense service to the world in bringing Israel's God to the knowledge of hundreds of millions of mankind. The great change in Jewish thought concerning Jesus of Nazareth, I cannot better illustrate than by this fact:

"When I was a boy, had my father, who was a very pious man, heard the name of Jesus uttered from the pulpit of our synagogue, he and every other man in the congregation would have left the building, and the rabbi would have been dismissed at once.

The Prophet's Letter to W. W Phelps.

COMMERCE, ILLINOIS, May 22, 1839.

Sir:—In answer to yours of the 23rd of April, to John P. Greene, we have to say that we shall feel obliged by your not making yourself officious concerning any part of our business in future. We shall be glad if you can make a living by minding your own affairs; and we desire (so far as you are concerned) to be left to manage ours as well as we can. We would much rather lose our properties than to be molested by

"Now, it is not strange in many synagogues, to hear sermons preached eulogistic of this Jesus, and nobody thinks of protesting—in fact, we are all glad to claim Jesus as one of our people."

"ISADORE SINGER."

New York, March 25, 1901.

"The Jew of today beholds in Jesus an inspiring ideal of matchless beauty. While He lacks the element of stern justice expressed so forcibly in the law and in the Old Testament characters, the firmness of self-assertion so necessary to the full development of manhood, all those social qualities which build up the home and society, industry and worldly progress, He is the unique exponent of the principle of redeeming love. His name as helper of the poor, as sympathizing friend of the fallen, as brother of every fellow sufferer, as lover of man and redeemer of woman, has become the inspiration, the symbol and the watchword for the world's greatest achievements in the field of benevolence. While continuing the work of the synagogue, the Christian Church with the larger means at her disposal created those institutions of charity and redeeming love that accomplished wondrous things. The very sign of the cross has lent a new meaning, a holier pathos to suffering, sickness and sin, so as to offer new practical solutions for the great problems of evil which fill the human heart with new joys of self-sacrificing love."

KAUFMAN KOHLER, Ph. D.,
Rabbi of Temple Beth-El.

New York, August 23, 1904.

"If the Jews up to the present time have not publicly rendered homage to the sublime beauty of the figure of Jesus, it is because their tormentors have always persecuted, tortured, assassinated them in His name. The Jews have drawn their conclusions from the disciples as to the Master, which was wrong, a wrong pardonable in the eternal victims of the implacable, cruel hatred of those who called themselves Christians. Every time that a Jew mounted to the sources and contemplated Christ alone, without His pretended faithful, he cried, with tenderness and admiration: "Putting aside the Messianic mission, this man is ours. He honors our race and we claim Him as we claim the gospels—flowers of Jewish literature and only Jewish."

MAX NORDAU, M. D.,
Critic and Philosopher.

Paris, France.

"The Jews of every shade of religious belief do not regard Jesus in the light of Paul's theology. But the gospel of Jesus, the Jesus who teaches so superbly the principles of Jewish ethics, is revered by all the expounders of Judaism. His words are studied; the New Testament forms a part of Jewish literature. Among the great preceptors that have worded the truths of which Judaism is the historical

such interference; and, as we consider that we have already experienced much over-officiousness at your hands, concerning men and things pertaining to our concerns, we now request, once for all, that you will avoid all interference in our business or affairs from this time henceforth and forever. Amen.*

JOSEPH SMITH, JUN,

guardian, none in our estimation and esteem, takes precedence of the rabbi of Nazareth. To impute to us suspicious sentiments concerning Him does us gross injustice. We know Him to be among our greatest and purest.

EMIL G. HIRSCH, Ph. D., LL. D., L. H. D.,
Rabbi of Sinai Congregation, Professor of Rabbinical Literature in Chicago University, Chicago, Ill., January 26, 1901.

Again, in 1905, the New York *Sun* published a symposium compiled by Dr. Isadore Singer, editor of the "Jewish Encyclopedia," on the same subject, in which he quotes some of the most eminent contemporary Jewish theologians, historians and orientalists. The following is typical of the whole collection.

"If He has added to their [the Jewish prophet's] spiritual bequests new jewels of religious truth, and spoken words which are words of life because they touch the deepest springs of the human heart, why should we Jews not glory in Him? The crown of thorns on His head makes Him only the more our brother, for to this day it is borne by His people. Were He alive today who, think you, would be nearer His heart,—the persecuted or the persecutors?"

DR. GUSTAV GOTTHELL.

* It will be remembered that William W. Phelps, with Oliver Cowdery and the Whitmers, left the Church in 1838, and was among the most bitter enemies of the Prophet; he was also among those who testified against the Prophet and his fellow prisoners before Judge Austin A. King at Richmond. (See report of Missouri Legislature on Mormon Difficulties, pp. 120-5). He also joined with others in whitewashing the proceedings of General Clark and his troops in their treatment of the citizens of Far West. Following is the document as it appears in the report of the Missouri Legislature p. 87:

"*Certificate of Mormons as to the conduct of Gen. Clark and his troops.*

"Richmond, November 23, 1838.

"Understanding that Maj. Gen. Clark is about to return with the whole of his command from the scene of difficulty, we avail ourselves of this occasion to state that we were present when the "Mormons" surrendered to Maj. Gen. Lucas at Far West, and remained there until Maj. Gen. Clark arrived; and we are happy to have an opportunity as well as the satisfaction of stating that the course of him [Clark] and his troops while at Far West was of the most respectful kind and obliging character towards the said Mormons; and that the destitute among that people are much indebted to him for sustenance during his stay. The modification of the terms upon which the "Mormons" surrendered, by permitting them to remain until they could safely go in the spring, was also an act that gave general satisfaction to the Mormons. We have no hesitation in saying that the course taken by Gen. Clark with the Mormons was necessary for the public peace, and that the "Mormons" are generally satisfied with his course, and feel in duty bound to say that the conduct of the General, his staff officers and troops, was highly honorable as soldiers and citizens, so far as our knowledge extends; and

A bill of indictment having been found by a grand jury of the mob in Ray county, against Parley P. Pratt, Morris Phelps and Luman Gibbs, for murder, and against King Follet for robbery, and having obtained a change of venue to Boone county, they were handcuffed together two by two on the morning of the twenty-second, [of May] with irons around the wrists of each, and in this condition they were taken from prison and placed in a carriage. The people of Richmond gathered around them to see them depart, but none seemed to feel for them except two persons. One of these (General Parks' lady) bowed to them through the window, and looked as if touched with pity. The other was a Mr. Hugins, merchant of Richmond, who bowed with some feeling as they passed.

Indictment of Parley P. Pratt *et al.*

They then took leave of Richmond, accompanied by Sheriff Brown, and four guards with drawn pistols, and moved towards Columbia. It had been thundering and raining for some days, and the thunder storm lasted with but short cessations from the time they started till they arrived at the place of destination, which took five days. The small streams were swollen, making it very difficult to cross them.

Thursday, May 23.—The prisoners came to a creek which was several rods across, with a strong current and very deep. It was towards evening, and far from any house, and they had received no refreshments through the day. Here the company halted, and knew not what to do; they waited awhile for the water

An Adventure by the Way.

we have heard nothing derogatory to the dignity of the state in the treatment of the prisoners."

Respectfully, &c.

[Signed] W. W. Phelps, Geo Walter, John Cleminson, G. M. Hinkle, John Corrill.

In view of these proceedings on the part of W. W. Phelps it is no matter of astonishment, when he began to show activity respecting the affairs of the Saints, that the Prophet wrote him the curt letter of the text.

to fall, but it fell slowly. All hands were hungry and impatient, and a lowery night seemed to threaten that the creek would rise before morning by the falling of additional rains.

In this dilemma some counseled one thing and some another. At last Mr. Pratt proposed to the sheriff, that if he would take off his irons, he would go into the water to bathe, and by that means ascertain the depths and bottom. This the sheriff consented to after some hesitation. Brother Pratt then plunged into the stream and swam across, and attempted to wade back; he found it to be a hard bottom, and the water about up to his chin, but a very stiff current.

After this, Mr. Brown, the sheriff, undertook to cross on his horse, but was thrown off and buried in the stream. This accident decided the fate of the day Being now completely wet, the sheriff resolved to effect the crossing of the whole company bag and baggage. Accordingly several stripped off their clothes and mounted on the bare backs of the horses, and taking their clothing, saddles and arms, together with one trunk, and bedding, upon their shoulders, they bore them across in safety, without wetting. This was done by riding backwards and forwards across the stream several times. In this sport and labor prisoners, guards and all mingled in mutual exertion All was now safe but the carriage. Brother Phelps then proposed to swim that across, by hitching two horses before it; and he mounted on one of their backs, while Brother Pratt and one of the guards swam by the side of the carriage to keep it from upsetting by the force of the current; and thus they all got safe to land. Everything was soon replaced; prisoners in the carriage and the suite on horseback, moving swiftly on, and at dark arrived at a house of entertainment, amid a terrible thunder storm.

I was busy in counseling, writing letters and attending to general business of the Church this week.

The Prophet's Letter to E. W. Harris.

COMMERCE, ILLINOIS, May 24, 1839.

Dear Sir:—I write you to say that I have selected a town lot for you just across the street from my own, and immediately beside yours, one for Mr. Cleveland. As to getting the temporary house erected which you desired, I have not been able to find any person willing to take hold of the job, and have thought that perhaps you may meet with some person at Quincy who could take it in hand.

Business goes on with us in quite a lively manner, and we hope soon to have Brother Harris and family, with other friends, to assist us in our arduous, but glorious undertaking.

Our families are all well, as far as we have knowledge, all things are going on quietly and smoothly.

Yours, etc.
JOSEPH SMITH, JUN.

Letter of The Prophet and Emma Smith to Judge Cleveland.

COMMERCE, ILLINOIS, May 24th, 1839.

Dear Mr. and Mrs. Cleveland:—We write you in order to redeem our pledge, which we would have done before now, but that we have been in the midst of the bustle of business of various kinds ever since our arrival here. We, however, beg to assure you and your family that we have not forgotten you, but remember you all, as well as the great kindness and friendship which we have experienced at your hands.

We have selected a lot for you, just across the street from our own, beside Mr. Harris; and in the orchard, according to the desire of Sister Cleveland, and also on the river, adapted to Mr. Cleveland's trade.

The various [lines of] business attendant on settling a new place, go on here at present briskly; while all around and concerning us, goes on quietly and smoothly, as far as we have knowledge. It would give us great pleasure to have you all here along with us, and this we hope to enjoy in a short time. I have also remembered Rufus Cleveland to the surveyor, and am happy to be able to say that the land in Iowa far exceeds my expectations both as to richness of soil, and beauty of location, more so than any part of Missouri which I have seen.

We desire to have Mr. Cleveland and his brother come up here as soon as convenient, and see our situation, when they can judge for themselves, and we shall be happy to see them and give them all information in our power. Father Smith and family arrived here yesterday; his health rather improves. We all join in sending our sincere respects to each and every one of you, and remain your very sincere friends,

JOSEPH SMITH, JUN.,
EMMA SMITH.

Addressed to Judge Cleveland and Lady, Quincy, Illinois.

The Prophet's letter to Bishop Whitney, Asking him to Settle at Commerce.

COMMERCE, ILLINOIS, 24th May, 1839.

DEAR SIR:—This is to inform you that Elder Granger has succeeded in obtaining the house which he had in contemplation when he left here; and as we feel very anxious to have the society of Bishop Whitney and his family here, we hope that he will use every exertion consistent with his own business and convenience to come up to us at Commerce as soon as it is in his power.

JOSEPH SMITH, JUN.

Bishop N. K. Whitney.

Friday, May 24.—The Twelve made a report of the proceedings of the Seventies, which I sanctioned. I also approved of the Twelve going to England.

The Twelve to go to England.

This day the Missouri prisoners crossed the Missouri river at "Arrow Rock," so called from the Lamanites coming from all quarters to get a hard rock from the bluff out of which to make arrow points. During this journey the prisoners had slept each night on their backs on the floor; being all four of them ironed together with hand and ankle irons made for the purpose. This being done the windows and doors were all fastened, and then five guards with their loaded pistols staid in the room, and one at a time sat up and watched during the night. This cruelty was inflicted on them more to gratify a wicked disposition than anything else: for it was vain for them to have tried to escape, without any irons being put on them; and had they wished to escape, they had a tolerably good opportunity at the creek.

Cruel Treatment of Parley P. Pratt and Companions.

Answer of the First Presidency to R. B. Thompson on the Lyman Wight Affair.

COMMERCE, HANCOCK CO., ILLINOIS, 25th May, 1839.

DEAR SIR:—In answer to yours of the 13th instant, to us, concerning the writings of Colonel Lyman Wight, on the subject of our late sufferings in the state of Missouri, we wish to say, that as to a statement of our persecutions being brought before the world as a political question, we entirely disapprove of it. Having, however, great confidence in Colonel Wight's good intentions, and considering it to be the indefeasible right of every free man to hold his own opinion in politics as well as religion, we will only say that we consider it to be unwise, as it is unfair, to charge any one party in politics or any sect of religionists with having been our oppressors, since we so well know that our persecutors in the state of Missouri were of every sect, and of all parties, both religious and political; and as Brother Wight disclaims having spoken evil of any administration, save that of Missouri, we presume that it need not be feared that men of sense will now suppose him wishful to implicate any other.

We consider that in making these remarks we express the sentiments of the Church in general, as well as our own individually, and also when we say in conclusion, that we feel the fullest confidence, that when the subject of our wrongs has been fully investigated by the authorities of the United States, we shall receive the most perfect justice at their hands; whilst our unfeeling oppressors shall be brought to condign punishment, with the approbation of a free and enlightened people, without respect to sect or party.

We desire that you may make whatever use you may think proper of this letter, and remain your sincere friends and brethren.

JOSEPH SMITH, JUN.,
HYRUM SMITH,
SYDNEY RIGDON.

Elder Robert B. Thompson.

Case of Wm. Smith.

Saturday, May 25.—This day I met the Twelve in council. The case of Brother William Smith came up for investigation and was disposed of.*

Sunday, 26.—I spent the day at home. Elders Orson Pratt and John Taylor preached.

Parley P. Pratt and Fellow Prisoners Arrive at Columbia.

As the prisoners in Missouri arrived at their new house in Boone county, I will give a sketch of their experience from Elder Pratt's testimony:

When we arrived within four miles of Columbia the bridge had been destroyed from over a large and rapid

* That is, Elder Smith who had been guilty of some wilful and irregular conduct while in the state of Missouri, was permitted to retain his standing in the quorum of the Twelve.

river; and here we were some hours in crossing over in a tottlish canoe having to leave our carriage, together with our bedding, clothing, our trunk of clothing, books, papers, etc.; but all came to us in safety after two days. After we had crossed the river, our guards having swam their horses,mounted them, and we proceeded towards Columbia, the prisoners walking on foot, being fastened together two by two by the wrists. After walking two or three miles, Mr. Brown hired a carriage and we rode into Columbia. It was about sunset on Sunday evening, and as the carriage and our armed attendants drove through the streets we were gazed upon with astonishment by hundreds of spectators, who thronged the streets and looked out at the windows, doors, etc., anxious to get a glimpse of the strange beings called "Mormons."

On our arrival we were immediately hurried to the prison, without going to a tavern for refreshment, although we had traveled a long summer day without anything to eat. When unloosed from our fetters we were ushered immediately into the jail, and next moment a huge trap door was opened and down we went into a most dismal dungeon, which was full of cobwebs and filth above, below,and all around the walls, having stood empty for nearly two years. Here was neither beds,nor chairs, nor water, nor food, nor friends, nor any one on whom we might call, even for a drink of cold water; for Brown and all the others had withdrawn to go where they could refresh themselves. When thrust into this dungeon, we were nearly ready to faint of hunger and thirst and weariness.

We walked the room for a few moments, and then sank down upon the floor in despondency and wished to die; for like Elijah of old, if the Lord had enquired "What dost thou here?" we could have replied, "Lord, they have killed thy prophets, and thrown down thine altars and have driven out all Thy Saints from the land, and we only are left to tell Thee; and they seek our lives, to take them away; and now, therefore, let us die."

When we had been in the dungeon some time, our new jailer handed down some provisions, but by this time I was too faint to eat; I tasted a few mouthfulls, and then suddenly the trap door opened, and some chairs were handed to us, and the new sheriff, Mr. Martin, and his deputy, Mr. Hamilton, entered our dungeon and talked so kindly to us, that our spirits again revived in some measure. This night we slept cold and uncomfortable, having but little bedding. Next morning we were suffered to come out of the dungeon, and the liberty of the upper room was given us through the day ever afterwards.

We now began to receive kind treatment from our jailer and from our new sheriff; for it was Mr. Brown that had caused all our neglect and sufferings the previous evening. Our jail in Columbia was a large wooden block building with two apartments; one was occupied by the jailer and his family and the other by the prisoners.

Monday, *27*.—I was at home.

The Prophet and Vinson Knight's Letter to Mark Bigler.

COMMERCE, HANCOCK COUNTY, ILLINOIS, May 27, 1839.

Father Bigler:

DEAR SIR:—We have thought well to write you by Brother Markham on the subject of our purchase of lands here, in order to stir up your pure mind to a remembrance of the situation in which we have been placed by the act of the councils of the Church having appointed us a committee to transact business here for the Church. We have, as is known to the Church in general, made purchases and entered into contracts and promised payments of moneys, for all of which we now stand responsible.

Now as money seems to come in too slowly, in order that we may be able to meet our engagements, we have determined to call upon the liberality of Father Bigler, through the agency of Brother Markham, and request that he will place in his hands for us, the sum of five or six hundred dollars, for which he shall have the security of said committee, also through the agency of Brother Markham, and the thanks of the Church besides.

JOSEPH SMITH, JUN.,
VINSON KNIGHT.

To Mark Bigler, Quincy, Illinois.

The Prophet's Letter to Lyman Wight, on the Matter of R. B. Thompson's Complaint.

COMMERCE, ILLINOIS, MAY 27, 1839.

DEAR SIR:—Having last week received a letter from Brother Robert B. Thompson, concerning your late writings in the *Quincy Whig*, and understanding thereby that the Church in general in Quincy were rather uneasy concerning these matters, we have thought best to consider the matter, of course, and accordingly being in council on Saturday last, the subject was introduced, and discussed at some length, when an answer to Brother Thompson's letter was agreed to and sanctioned by the Council, which answer I expect will be published, and of course you will have an opportunity to see it.

It will be seen by that letter that we do not at all approve of the course which you have thought proper to take, in making the subject of our sufferings a political question. At the same time you will perceive that we there express what we really feel: that is, a confidence in your good intentions. And (as I took occasion to state to the Council) knowing your integrity of principle, and steadfastness in the cause of Christ, I feel not to exercise even the privilege of counsel on the subject, save only to request that you will endeavor to bear in mind the importance of the subject, and how easy it might be to get into a misunderstanding with the brethren concerning it; and though last, not least, that whilst you continue to go upon your own credit you will also steer clear of making the Church appear as either supporting or opposing you in your politics lest such a course may have a tendency to bring about persecution on the Church, where a little wisdom and caution may avoid it.

I do not know that there is any occasion for my thus cautioning you in this thing, but having done so, I hope it will be well taken, and that all things shall eventually be found to work together for the good of the Saints.

I should be happy to have you here to dwell amongst us and am in hopes soon to have that pleasure. I was happy to receive your favor of the 20th instant, and to observe the contents; and beg to say in reply that I shall attend to what you therein suggest, and shall feel pleasure at all times to answer any requests of yours, and attend to them also in the best manner possible.

With every possible feeling of love and friendship, for an old fellow prisoner and brother in the Lord, I remain, sir, your sincere friend,

JOSEPH SMITH, JUN.

To Lyman Wight, Quincy, Illinois.

Letter of Appointment to Stephen Markham.

To the Church of Jesus Christ of Latter-day Saints, Greeting:

From our knowledge of the good sacrifices made by the bearer, Brother Stephen Markham, in behalf of the welfare of us, and the Church generally, and from the great trust which we have oftentimes reposed in him, and as often found him trustworthy, not seeking his own aggrandizement, but rather that of the community, we feel warranted in commissioning him to go forth among the faithful, as our agent to gather up and receive such means in money or otherwise, as shall enable us to meet our engagements which are now about to devolve upon us in consequence of our purchases here for the Church; and we humbly trust that our brethren generally will enable him to come to our assistance before our credit shall suffer on this account.

JOSEPH SMITH, JUN., Presiding Elder.

Thursday, May 28.—I was at home.

Parley P. Pratt *et al* Seek a Trial.

When the Missouri prisoners arrived at Columbia they applied to Judge Reynolds for a special term of court to be holden for their trials. The petition was granted and July 1st was appointed for the sitting of the court.

Monday May 29.—I was about home until the latter part of the week, when I went to Quincy in company with my Counselors. I continued to assist in making preparations to lay our grievances before the general government, and many of the brethren were making their reports of damages sustained in Missouri. I wrote as follows:

June 4, 1839.

The Prophet's Narration of his Personal Experiences in Missouri 1838-9, Which he Calls "A Bill of Damages Against the State of Missouri on Account of the Suffering and Losses Sustained Therein."

March 12, 1838. With my family I arrived at Far West, Caldwell county, after a journey of one thousand miles, being eight weeks on my journey, enduring great affliction in consequence of persecution and expending two or three hundred dollars.

Soon after my arrival at that place, I was informed that a number of men living in Daviess county (on the Grinstone Forks) had offered the sum of one thousand dollars for my scalp: persons to whom I was an entire stranger, and of whom I had no knowledge. In order to attain their end, the roads were frequently waylaid for me. At one time in particular, when watering my horse on Shoal Creek, I distinctly heard three or four guns snapped at me. I was credibly informed also, that Judge King, of the Fifth Judicial Circuit, gave encouragement to individuals to carry into effect their diabolical designs, and has frequently stated that I ought to be beheaded on account of my religion.

In consequence of such expressions from Judge King and others in authority, my enemies endeavored to take every advantage of me, and heaping up abuse, getting up vexatious lawsuits, and stirring up the minds of the people against me and the people with whom I was connected, although we had done nothing [on our part] to deserve such treatment, but were busily engaged in our several vocations, and desirous to live on peaceable and friendly terms with all men. In consequence of such threats and abuse which I was continually subject to, my family were kept in a continual state of alarm, not knowing any morning what would befall me from day to day, particularly when I went from home.

In the latter part of September, 1838, I went to the lower part of the county of Caldwell for the purpose of selecting a location for a town. When on my journey I was met by one of our friends with a message from De Witt, in Carrol county, stating that our brethren who had settled in that place, were, and had for some time been, surrounded by a mob, who had threatened their lives, and had shot several times at them. Immediately on hearing this strange intelligence, I made preparations to start, in order if possible to allay the feeling of opposition, if not to make arrangements with those individuals of whom we had made purchases, and to whom I was responsible and holden for part of the purchase money.

I arrived there on the — day of September, and found the account which I heard was correct. Our people were surrounded by a mob, and their provisions nearly exhausted. Messengers were immediately sent to the Governor, requesting protection; but instead of lending any assistance to the oppressed, he stated that the quarrel was between the "Mormons" and the mob, and they must fight it out.

Being now almost destitute of provisions, and having suffered great distress, and some of the brethren having died in consequence of their privations and sufferings—I had then the pain of beholding some of my fellow-creatures perish in a strange land, from the cruelty of a mob—and seeing no prospect of relief, the brethren agreed to leave that place and seek a shelter elsewhere, after having their houses burnt down, their cattle driven away, and much of their property destroyed.

Judge King was also petitioned to afford us some assistance. He sent a company of about one hundred men; but instead of affording us any relief, we were told by General Parks [who commanded them] that he could afford none, in consequence of the greater part of his company, under their officer, Captain Samuel Bogart, having mutinied. About seventy wagons left De Witt for Caldwell, and during their journey were continually insulted by the mob, who threatened to destroy us, and shot at us. In our journey several of our friends died and had to be interred without a coffin, and under such circumstances, this was extremely distressing. Immediately on my arrival at Caldwell, I was informed by General Doniphan, of Clay county, that a company of about eight hundred were marching towards a settlement of our brethren in Daviess county, and he advised one of the officers that we should immediately go to protect our brethren in Daviess county, (in what he called Whit's Town,) until he should get the militia to put them down. A company of militia, to the number of sixty, who were on their route to that place, he ordered back, believing, as he said, that they were not to be depended upon; and to use his own language were "damned rotten hearted."

Lieut.-Colonel Hinkle, agreeably to the advice of General Doniphan, and a number of our brethren, volunteered to go to Daviess county to render what assistance they could. My labors having been principally expended in Daviess county, where I intended to take up my residence; and having a house in building, and having other property there, I hastened up to that place; and while I was there, a number of houses belonging to the brethren were burnt, and depredations were continually committed, such as driving off horses, cattle, sheep, etc., etc.

Being deprived of shelter, and others having no safety in their houses—because of their being scattered—and being alarmed at the approach of the mob, they had to flock together; their sufferings were very great in consequence of their defenseless situation—being exposed to the weather, which was extremely cold, a large snow storm having just fallen.

In this state of affairs, General Parks arrived in Daviess county, and was at the house of Colonel Wight when the intelligence was brought that the mob were burning houses, etc.; and also that men, women, and children were flocking into the village for safety. Colonel Wight, who held a commission in the fifty-ninth regiment under his [Parks] command, asked him what stepss hould be taken. General Parks told him that he must immediately call out his men, and go and put the mob down.

Preparations were made at once to raise a force to quell the mob, who, on ascertaining that we were determined to bear such treatment no longer, but to make a vigorous effort to subdue them, and likewise being informed of the orders of General Parks, broke up their encampment and fled.

Some of the inhabitants in the immediate neighborhood, who seeing no prospects of driving us by force, resorted to stratagem, and actually set fire to their own houses (miserable log houses, after having removed their property and effects) and then sent information to the Governor, stating that our brethren were committing depredations and destroying their property, burning houses, etc.

On the retreat of the mob from Daviess county, I returned home to Caldwell. On my arrival there, I understood that a mob had commenced hostilities in the borders of Caldwell; had taken some of our people prisoners; burnt some houses, and had done considerable damage. Immediately Captain Patten was ordered out by Lieut.-Col. Hinkle to go against them, and about daylight next morning came up with them. Upon the approach of our people the mob fired upon them, and after discharging their pieces, fled with great precipitation.

In this affray, Captain Patten, along with two others, fell a victim to that spirit of mobocracy which has prevailed to such an extent; others were severely wounded. On the day after this affray, Captain Patten sent for me to pray for him, which request I complied with, and then returned to my home.

There continued to be great commotion in the county, caused by the conduct of the mob, who were continually burning houses, driving off horses, cattle, etc., and taking prisoners, and threatening death to all the "Mormons." Amongst the cattle driven off were two cows of mine.

On the 28th of October, a large company of armed soldiers were seen approaching Far West, and encamped about one mile from the town. The next day I was waited upon by Lieutenant-Colonel Hinkle, who stated that the officers of the militia requested an interview with us in order to come to some amicable settlement of the difficulties which then existed; they, the officers, not wishing, under the present circumstances, to carry into effect the exterminating orders they had received. I immediately complied with the request, and in company with Messieurs Rigdon, Robinson, Wight, and Pratt, proceeded to meet the officers of the militia, but instead of treating us with respect, and as persons desirous to accommodate matters, to our astonishment we were delivered up as prisoners of war, and taken into their camp as such. It would be in vain for me to give any idea of the scene which now presented itself in the camp. The hideous yells of more than a thousand infuriated beings, whose desire was to wreak their vengeance upon me and the rest of my friends, was truly awful, and enough to appall the stoutest heart.

In the evening we had to lie down on the cold ground, surrounded by a strong guard. We petitioned the officers to know why we were thus treated; but they utterly refused to hold any conversation with us. The next day they held a court martial upon us and sentenced me, with the rest of the prisoners, to be shot; which sentence was to be carried into effect on Friday morning in the public square, as they said as an ensample to the rest of the members; but through the kind providence of God, their murderous sentence was not carried into execution. The militia then went to my house and drove my family out of doors under sanction of General Lucas, and carried away all my property.

I had an opportunity of speaking to General Wilson, and on asking him the cause of such strange proceedings, I told him that I was a democrat, and had always been a supporter of the Constitution. He answered, "I know that, and that is the reason why I want to kill you, or have you killed."

We were led into the public square, and after considerable entreaty, we were permitted to see our families, being attended by a strong guard. I found my family in tears, they having believed that the mob had carried into effect their sentence; they clung to my garments weeping. I requested to have a private interview with my wife in an adjoining room, but was refused; when taking my departure from my family, it was almost too painful for me. My children clung to me, and were thrust away at the point of the swords of the soldiery. We were then removed to Jackson county, under the care of General Wilson; and during our stay there, we had to sleep on the floor, with nothing but a mantle for our covering, and a stick of wood for our pillow, and had to pay for our own board.

While we were in Jackson county, General Clark with his troops arrived in Caldwell, and sent an order for our return, holding out the inducement that we were to be reinstated to our former privileges; but instead of being taken to Caldwell county, we were taken to Richmond, Ray county, where we were immured in prison and bound in chains. After we were thus situated, we were under the charge of Colonel Price, of Chariton county, who suffered us to be abused in every manner which the people thought proper.

Our situation at this time was truly painful. We were taken before a court of inquiry; but in consequence of the proceedings of the mob, and their threats, we were not able to get such witnesses as would have been serviceable; even those we had were abused by the State's Attorney, and the court, and were not permitted to be examined by the court as the law directs. We were committed to Liberty jail, and petitioned Judge Turnham for a writ of habeas corpus; but owing to the prejudice of the jailer, all communication was entirely cut off. However, at length we succeeded in getting a petition conveyed to the judge, but he neglected to pay any attention to it for fourteen days, and kept us in suspense. He then ordered us to appear before him; but he utterly refused to hear any of our witnesses, which we had been at a great trouble in providing. Our lawyer also refused to act, being afraid of the people.

We likewise petitioned Judge King and the judges of the Supreme Court, but they utterly refused. Our victuals were of the coarsest kind, and served up in a manner which was disgusting. After bearing up under repeated injuries, we were moved to Daviess county under a strong guard. We were then arraigned before the Grand Jury, who were mostly intoxicated, who indicted me and the rest of my companions for treason. We then got a change of venue to Boone county, and when on our way to that place, on the second evening after our departure, our guards getting intoxicated, I thought it a favorable time to effect our escape from such men, whose aim was only to destroy our life and to abuse us in every manner that wicked men could invent. Accordingly we took advantage of their situation, and made our escape; and after enduring considerable fatigue, and suffering hunger and weariness, expecting that our enemies would be in pursuit, we arrived in the town of Quincy, Illinois, amidst the congratulations of our friends, and the joy of our families. I have been here for several weeks, as it is known to the people of the state of Missouri; but they, knowing they had no justice in their crusade against me, have not to my knowledge taken the first step to have me arrested.

The loss of property which I have sustained is as follows:—Losses sustained in Jackson county, Daviess county, Caldwell county, including lands, houses, harness, hogs, cattle, etc.; books and store goods, expenses while in bonds, of moneys paid out, expenses of moving out of the State, and damages sustained by false imprisonments, threatenings, intimidations, exposure, etc., etc., one hundred thousand dollars.

My brother Hyrum Smith wrote the following—

Hyrum Smith's Statement of sufferings and damages sustained in Missouri, and of being driven therefrom.

I left Kirtland, Ohio, in the spring of 1838, having the charge of a family of ten individuals; the weather was very unfavorable, and the roads worse than I had ever seen, which materially increased my expenses, on account of such long delays upon the road. However, after suffering many privations, I reached my destination in safety, and intended to make my permanent residence in the state of Missouri. I sent on by water all my household furniture and a number of farming implements, amounting to several hundred dollars, having made purchases of lands of several hundreds of acres, upon which I intended to settle.

In the meantime, I took a house in Far West, until I could make further arrangements. I had not been there but a few weeks, before the report of mobs, whose intention was to drive us from our homes, was heard from every quarter. I thought that the reports were false, inasmuch as I know that as a people we had done nothing to merit any such treatment as was threatened. However, at length, from false and wicked reports, circulated for the worst of purposes, the inhabitants of the upper counties of Missouri commenced hostilities, threatened to burn our dwellings, and even menaced the lives of our people, if we did not move away; and afterwards, horrid to relate, they put their threats into execution.

Our people endeavored to calm the fury of our enemies, but in vain; for they carried on their depredations to a greater extent than ever, until most of our people who lived in places at a distance from the towns had collected together, so that they might be the better able to escape from the fury of our enemies, and be in better condition to defend their lives and the little property they had been able to save. It is probable that our persecutors might have been deterred from their purposes, had not wicked and shameful reports been sent to the Governor of the state, who ordered out a very large force to exterminate us. When they arrived at Far West, we were told what were their orders. However, they did not fall upon us, but took several of my friends and made them prisoners; and the day after, a company of the militia came to my house and ordered me to go with them into the camp. My family at that time particularly needed my assistance, being much afflicted. I told them my situation, but remonstrance was in vain, and I was hurried into the camp, and was subject to the most cruel treatment.

Along with the rest of the prisoners, I was ordered to be shot; but it was providentially overruled. We were then ordered to Jackson county, where our bitterest persecutors resided. Before we started, after much entreaty, I was privileged to visit my family, accompanied with a strong guard. I had only time to get a change of linen, &c., and was hurried to where the teams were waiting to convey us to the city of Independence, in Jackson county. While there I was subjected to continued insult from the people who visited us. I had likewise to lie on the floor, and had to cover myself with my mantle; after remaining there for some time we were ordered to Richmond, in Ray county, where our enemies expected to shoot us; but finding no law to support them in carrying into effect so strange an act, we were delivered up to the civil law. As soon as we were so, we were thrust into a dungeon, and our legs were chained together. In this situation we remained until called before the court, who ordered us to be sent to Liberty in Clay county, where I was confined for more than four months, and endured almost everything but death, from the nauseous cell, and the wretched food we were obliged to eat.

In the meantime, my family were suffering every privation. Our enemies carried off nearly everything of value, until my family were left almost destitute. My wife had been but recently confined and had to suffer more than tongue can describe; and then in common with the rest of the people, had to move, in the month of February, a distance of two hundred miles, in order to escape further persecutions and injury.

Since I have obtained my liberty, I feel my body broken down and my health very much impaired, from the fatigue and afflictions which I have undergone, so that I have not been able to perform any labor since I have escaped from my oppressors. The loss of property which I sustained in the state of Missouri would amount to several thousand dollars; and one hundred thousand dollars would be no consideration for what I have suffered from privations—from my life being continually sought—and all the accumulated sufferings I have been subjected to.

HYRUM SMITH.

CHAPTER XXV.

COMMERCE—THE PROPHET'S HISTORY—DOCTRINAL DEVELOPMENT.

Wednesday, June 5.—I returnd to Commerce and spent the remainder of the week at home.

Sunday, 9.—I attended meeting with my wife and family at Brother Bosiers. Elder John E. Page preached.

Monday, 10.—Elder Page baptized one woman. I was engaged in study preparatory to writing my history.

Tuesday, 11.—I commenced dictating my history for my clerk, James Mulholland, to write. About this time Elder Theodore Turley raised the first house built by the Saints in this place [Commerce]; it was built of logs, about twenty-five or thirty rods north north-east of my dwelling, on the north-east corner of lot 4, block 147, of the White purchase.

First House Built by the Saints at Commerce.

When I made the purchase of White and Galland, there were one stone house, three frame houses, and two block houses, which constituted the whole city of Commerce. Between Commerce and Mr. Davidson Hibbard's, there was one stone house and three log houses, including the one that I live in, and these were all the houses in this vicinity, and the place was literally a wilderness. The land was mostly covered with trees and bushes, and much of it so wet that it was with the utmost difficulty a footman could get through, and totally impossible for teams. Commerce was so unhealthful, very few could live there; but believing that it might become a healthful place by the blessing of heaven to the Saints, and no more eligible place presenting itself, I considered it wisdom to make an attempt to build up a city.

Description of Commerce.

Wednesday and Thusday, 12 and 13.—I continued to dictate my history.

Letter of Edward Partridge to the Prophet.

QUINCY, June 13, 1839.

President Smith:

SIR:—Your letter in answer to my note to Bishop Knight, I received by the hand of Brother Harris. Respecting the cattle, I had promised three or four yoke to Father Myers. I did expect Brother Shearer would have sent the cattle down immediately, or I should not have been quite so willing to accommodate him with some to move with.

Some of our poor brethren wished me to furnish them teams to move up to town with, and I promised them that when the teams returned, I would. They were very anxious to get up in time to get in a little garden; and were not my plans frustrated, I could have accommodated them greatly to their satisfaction.

The brethren that I allude to are the blind brethren, who say that they had as lief live in tents there as here. It is now too late to think of making gardens, and what is best for them to do, I know not. I had promised some money as soon as I could sell a yoke of cattle. I know of nothing else I have that I can raise money with at this time; and they are getting to be dull sale to what they were.

Sister Meeks has been quite sick, but she is getting better. She has nothing to eat only what she is helped to. A number of other poor here, I think, need assistance; widow Sherman for one; but if you think that all the means should be kept up there [at Commerce], I have nothing to say, only that I do not believe it to be my duty to stay here living on expense, where I can earn nothing for myself, nor do anything to benefit others.

As I before stated, I have promised some money as soon as I can raise it. I have not at this time two dollars in the world, one dollar and forty-four cents is all. I owe for my rent, and for making clothes for some of the poor, and some other things. I am going into the room Brother Harris leaves, to save rent. What is best for me to do, I hardly know. Hard labor I cannot perform; light labor I can; but I know of no chance to earn anything, at anything that I can stand to do. It is quite sickly here. Five were buried in four days—Brother Moses' child, Sister Louisa P. and Brother Pettigrew's son Hiram, eighteen or nineteen years of age; the other two were children of the world.

I spoke to Brother Isaac Higbee about his seine; he said that he would speak to his brother about it. He said he thought they would sell it, or they would come up in the fall and fish a while, but to lend it, he thought it would not be best, as those unaccustomed to fish in the rivers would be apt to tear it to pieces. You perceive that I have not means to get you twine at present; therefore I presume that you will not blame me for not doing it.

Were I well, I would go up to Commerce with Brother Whitney and settle with the committee and Brother Rogers, and see what is best to do; probably may come next week. If Brother Markham could sell one yoke of cattle and let me have the avails of them, I should be glad; and I think it best to let two yoke, that are up there, go to Father Myers. As to teams to move up some of the poor, do as you think best.

EDWARD PARTRIDGE.

President Joseph Smith, Jun., Commerce.

Friday, 14.—Continued writing history. This evening there was a great excitement about the jail of Columbia, Missouri. Several individuals went and called for the jailer, but he was absent. They next called for the jailer's wife, and offered her money to let the prisoners go, which she declined, and becoming alarmed, raised a cry which brought the whole village together, armed with bowie knives, guns, pistols, etc.; but finding no one there, they soon returned home, except a few to guard the prison. This now brought different individuals to see the prisoners, and by acquaintance those feelings were softened towards the Saints.

Excitement at Columbia Prison, Mo.

Saturday, 15.—I started with my family to visit Brother Don Carlos Smith. We met Brother William on the prairie, about four miles west of Carthage; found him in good spirits, and went with him to his house in Plymouth; found his family well. Staid over night, and had a very satisfactory visit.

Visit of the Prophet with Wm. Smith.

Sunday, 16.—We went to Brother Don Carlos Smith's, in McDonough county, near the village of Macombe, where we spent the remainder of the day.

Visit with Don Carlos.

Monday, 17.—Bishops Whitney and Knight arrived at Commerce. I staid at Brother Don Carlos' this day, and my brother Samuel H. Smith came in; I had not seen him before, since my deliverance from prison. Bishop Knight returned to Quincy.

Tuesday, 18.—I went to the house of a man by the name of Matthews. During the evening the neighbors came in and I gave them a short discourse.

Thursday, 20.—Visited at Elder Zebedee Coltrin's. From thence we were invited to visit at Brother Vance's, which we did, and there gave to the brethren and friends of the neighborhood a brief history of the coming forth of the Book of Mormon.

Ministry of the Prophet.

Saturday, 22.—We returned to Brother Don Carlos' place.

Sunday, 23.—Went to Brother Wilcox's and preached to a very crowded congregation; and so eager were they to hear, that a part of them stood out in the rain during the sermon. In general they expressed good satisfaction as to what they heard.

Monday, 24.—We started for home, and went to Brother Perkins, near Fountain Green, in Hancock county, where they insisted we should tarry, and we complied. This day the Church purchased the town of Nashville, in Lee county, Iowa Territory, together with twenty thousand acres of land adjoining it.

Purchase of Lands in Iowa.

Tuesday, 25.—We held a meeting, at which I spoke with considerable liberty to a large congregation.

Wednesday, 26.—I with my family returned to our home at Commerce.

Return of the Prophet to Commerce.

Thursday, 27.—

The Prophet's Answer to Jacob Stollings.

COMMERCE, ILLINOIS, June 27, 1839.

SIR:—In answer to yours concerning those books, I have to say that I have made inquiry concerning them, as far as I consider there is any prospect of obtaining them for you; and not having been able to trace them in the least degree, I have determined to give up the pursuit. I would recommend you to inquire after them of Dr. Avard, as the only chance I know of at present.

Yours, etc.,

JOSEPH SMITH, JUN.

P. S.—Since writing the above, I have ascertained of one man (who told me) that he saw Dr. Avard have the books; but what he did with them, he knows not.

J. S.

To Mr. Jacob Stollings.

I attended a conference of the Twelve, at which time Brother Orson Hyde made his confession, and was restored to the Priesthood again. Restoration of Orson Hyde.

At this time I taught the brethren at considerable length on the following subjects:

The Prophet's Instruction on Various Doctrines.

FAITH comes by hearing the word of God, through the testimony of the servants of God; that testimony is always attended by the Spirit of prophecy and revelation.

REPENTANCE is a thing that cannot be trifled with every day. Daily transgression and daily repentance is not that which is pleasing in the sight of God.

BAPTISM is a holy ordinance preparatory to the reception of the Holy Ghost; it is the channel and key by which the Holy Ghost will be administered.

THE GIFT OF THE HOLY GHOST by the laying on of hands, cannot be received through the medium of any other principle than the principle of righteousness, for if the proposals are not complied with, it is of no use, but withdraws.

TONGUES were given for the purpose of preaching among those whose language is not understood; as on the day of Pentecost, etc., and it is not necessary for tongues to be taught to the Church particularly, for any man that has the Holy Ghost, can speak of the things of God in his own tongue as well as to speak in another; for faith comes not by signs, but by hearing the word of God.

THE DOCTRINE OF THE RESURRECTION OF THE DEAD AND THE ETERNAL JUDGMENT are necessary to preach among the first principles of the Gospel of Jesus Christ.

THE DOCTRINE OF ELECTION. St. Paul exhorts us to make our calling and election sure. This is the sealing power spoken of by Paul in other places.

"13. In whom ye also trusted, that after ye heard the word of truth, the

Gospel of your salvation: in whom also after that ye believed, ye were sealed with that Holy Spirit of promise,

"14. Which is the earnest of our inheritance until the redemption of the purchased possession, unto the praise of His glory, that we may be sealed up unto the day of redemption."—Ephesians, 1st chapter.

This principle ought (in its proper place) to be taught, for God hath not revealed anything to Joseph, but what He will make known unto the Twelve, and even the least Saint may know all things as fast as he is able to bear them, for the day must come when no man need say to his neighbor, Know ye the Lord; for all shall know Him (*who remain*) from the least to the greatest. How is this to be done? It is to be done by this sealing power, and the other Comforter spoken of, which will be manifest by revelation.

There are two Comforters spoken of. One is the Holy Ghost, the same as given on the day of Pentecost, and that all Saints receive after faith, repentance, and baptism. This first Comforter or Holy Ghost has no other effect than pure intelligence. It is more powerful in expanding the mind, enlightening the understanding, and storing the intellect with present knowledge, of a man who is of the literal seed of Abraham, than one that is a Gentile, though it may not have half as much visible effect upon the body; for as the Holy Ghost falls upon one of the literal seed of Abraham, it is calm and serene; and his whole soul and body are only exercised by the pure spirit of intelligence; while the effect of the Holy Ghost upon a Gentile, is to purge out the old blood, and make him actually of the seed of Abraham. That man that has none of the blood of Abraham (naturally) must have a new creation by the Holy Ghost. In such a case, there may be more of a powerful effect upon the body, and visible to the eye, than upon an Israelite, while the Israelite at first might be far before the Gentile in pure intelligence.

The other Comforter spoken of is a subject of great interest, and perhaps understood by few of this generation. After a person has faith in Christ, repents of his sins, and is baptized for the remission of his sins and receives the Holy Ghost, (by the laying on of hands), which is the first Comforter, then let him continue to humble himself before God, hungering and thirsting after righteousness, and living by every word of God, and the Lord will soon say unto him, Son, thou shalt be exalted. When the Lord has thoroughly proved him, and finds that the man is determined to serve Him at all hazards, then the man will find his calling and his election made sure, then it will be his privilege to receive the other Comforter, which the Lord hath promised the Saints, as is recorded in the testimony of St. John, in the 14th chapter, from the 12th to the 27th verses.

Note the 16, 17, 18, 21, 23 verses:

"16. And I will pray the Father, and He shall give you another Comforter, that he may abide with you forever;

"17. Even the Spirit of Truth; whom the world cannot receive, because it seeth him not, neither knoweth him; but ye know him; for he dwelleth with you, and shall be in you.

"18. I will not leave you comfortless: I will come to you. * * *

"21. He that hath my commandments, and keepeth them, he it is that loveth me: and he that loveth me shall be loved of my Father, and I will love him, and will manifest myself to him.

"23. If a man love me, he will keep my words: and my Father will love him, and we will come unto him, and make our abode with him."

Now what is this other Comforter? It is no more nor less that the Lord Jesus Christ Himself; and this is the sum and substance of the whole matter; that when any man obtains this last Comforter, he will have the personage of Jesus Christ to attend him, or appear unto him from time to time, and even He will manifest the Father unto him, and they will take up their abode with him, and the visions of the heavens will be opened unto him, and the Lord will teach him face to face, and he may have a perfect knowledge of the mysteries of the Kingdom of God; and this is the state and place the ancient Saints arrived at when they had such glorious visions—Isaiah, Ezekiel, John upon the Isle of Patmos, St. Paul in the three heavens, and all the Saints who held communion with the general assembly and Church of the First Born.

THE SPIRIT OF REVELATION is in connection with these blessings. A person may profit by noticing the first intimation of the spirit of revelation; for instance, when you feel pure intelligence flowing into you, it may give you sudden strokes of ideas, so that by noticing it, you may find it fulfilled the same day or soon; (i. e.) those things that were presented unto your minds by the Spirit of God, will come to pass; and thus by learning the Spirit of God and understanding it, you may grow into the principle of revelation, until you become perfect in Christ Jesus.

AN EVENGELIST is a Patriarch, even the oldest man of the blood of Joseph or of the seed of Abraham. Wherever the Church of Christ is established in the earth, there should be a Patriarch for the benefit of the posterity of the Saints, as it was with Jacob in giving his patriarchal blessing unto his sons, etc.

CHAPTER XXVI.

THE PROPHET'S MINISTRY IN THE VICINITY OF COMMERCE—ADDRESS TO THE TWELVE.

Friday, 28.—I was transacting business of various kinds; counseling, consulting the brethren, etc., etc.

Saturday 29.—I was mostly at home.

Sunday 30.—I attended meeting at Brother Bosier's. There was a crowded audience, and I bore testimony concerning the truth of the work, and also of the truth of the Book of Mormon.

The Prophet Testifies to the Book of Mormon.

This day Sister Morris Phelps, who had traveled one hundred and fifty miles, in company with her brother, John W. Clark, to see her husband, arrived at Columbia jail.

Monday, July 1, 1839.—I spent the day principally in counseling the brethren.

The Missouri Prisoners.

This day also the court was called for the trial of Parley P. Pratt, and brethren in prison in Boone county; but as they were not ready for trial, (all their witnesses had been banished the state), the court was adjourned to the 23rd of September.

Tuesday 2.—Spent the forenoon of this day on the Iowa side of the river. Went, in company with Elders Sidney Rigdon, Hyrum Smith, and Bishops Whitney and Knight, and others, to visit a purchase lately made by Bishop Knight as a location for a town, and advised that a town be built there, and called Zarahemla.

Founding of Zarahemla.

In the afternoon met with the Twelve and some of the Seventies who are about to proceed on their mission to Europe, and the nations of the earth, and islands of the sea.

The Prophet with the Twelve and the Seventies.

The meeting was opened by singing and prayer, after which the Presidency proceeded to bless two of the Twelve who had lately been ordained into the quorum, namely, Wilford Woodruff and George A. Smith; and one of the Seventies, namely, Theodore Turley; after which, blessings were also pronounced by them [the Presidency] on the heads of the wives of some of those about to go abroad.

Hyrum Smith's Admonition to the Twelve.

The meeting was then addressed by President Hyrum Smith, by way of advice to the Twelve, chiefly concerning the nature of their mission; their practicing prudence and humility in their plans or subjects for preaching; necessity of their not trifling with their office, and of holding on strictly to the importance of their mission, and the authority of the Priesthood.

I then addressed them and gave much instruction calculated to guard them against self-sufficiency, self-righteousness, and self-importance; touching upon many subjects of importance and value to all who wish to walk humbly before the Lord, and especially teaching them to observe charity, wisdom and fellow-feeling, with love one towards another in all things, and under all circumstances, in substance as follows:

The Prophet's Address to the Twelve.

Mercy and Forgiveness.

Ever keep in exercise the principle of mercy, and be ready to forgive our brother on the first intimations of repentance, and asking forgiveness; and should we even forgive our brother, or even our enemy, before he repent or ask forgiveness, our heavenly Father would be equally as merciful unto us.

Humility and Brotherhood of the Twelve.

Again, let the Twelve and all Saints be willing to confess all their sins, and not keep back a part; and let the Twelve be humble, and not be exalted, and beware of pride, and not seek to excel one above another, but act for each other's good, and pray for one another, and honor our brother or make honorable mention of his name, and not backbite and devour our brother. Why will not man learn wisdom by precept at this late age of the world, when we have such a cloud of witnesses and examples before us, and not be obliged to learn by sad experience everything we know? Must the new ones that are chosen to fill the places of those that are fallen, of the quorum of the Twelve, begin to exalt themselves, until they exalt themselves so high that they will soon tumble over and have a great fall, and go wallowing through the mud and mire and darkness, Judas like, to the buffetings of Satan, as several of the quorum have done, or will they learn wisdom and be wise? O God! give them wisdom, and keep them humble, I pray.

Avoid Vain-glory.

When the Twelve or any other witnesses stand before the congregations of the earth, and they preach in the power and demonstration of the Spirit of God, and the people are astonished and confounded at the doctrine, and say, "That man has preached a powerful discourse, a great sermon," then let that man or those men take care that they do not ascribe the glory unto themselves, but be careful that they are humble, and ascribe the praise and glory to God and the Lamb; for it is by the power of the Holy Priesthood and the Holy Ghost that they have power thus to speak. What art thou, O man, but dust? And from whom receivest thou thy power and blessings, but from God?

Be Honest, Sober, Vigilant.

Then, O ye Twelve! notice this *Key*, and be wise for Christ's sake, and your own soul's sake. Ye are not sent out to be taught, but to teach. Let every word be seasoned with grace. Be vigilant; be sober. It is a day of warning, and not of many words. Act honestly before God and man. Beware of Gentile sophistry; such as bowing and scraping unto men in whom you have no confidence. Be honest, open, and frank in all your intercourse with mankind.

O ye Twelve! and all Saints! profit by this important *Key*—that in all your trials, troubles, temptations, afflictions, bonds, imprisonments and death, see to it, that you do not betray heaven; that you do not betray Jesus Christ; that you do not betray the brethren; that you do not betray the revelations of God, whether in the Bible, Book of Mormon, or Doctrine and Covenants, or any other that ever was or ever will be given and revealed unto man in this world or that which is to come. Yea, in all your kicking and flounderings, see to it that you do not this thing, lest innocent blood be found upon your skirts, and you go down to hell. All other sins are not to be compared to sinning against the Holy Ghost, and proving a traitor to the brethren.

Beware of Treason.

I will give you one of the *Keys* of the mysteries of the Kingdom. It is an eternal principle, that has existed with God from all eternity: That man who rises up to condemn others, finding fault with the Church, saying that they are out of the way, while he himself is righteous, then know assuredly, that that man is in the high road to apostasy; and if he does not repent, will apostatize, as God lives. The principle is as correct as the one that Jesus put forth in saying that he who seeketh a sign is an adulterous person; and that principle is eternal, undeviating, and firm as the pillars of heaven; for whenever you see a man seeking after a sign, you may set it down that he is an adulterous man.

The sign of Apostasy.

About this time, in reply to many inquiries, I also gave an explanation of the Priesthood, and many principles connected therewith, of which the following is a brief synopsis:

The Prophet on Priesthood.

The Priesthood was first given to Adam; he obtained the First Presidency, and held the keys of it from generation to generation. He obtained it in the Creation, before the world was formed, as in Gen. i: 26, 27, 28.* He had dominon given him over every living creature. He is Michael the Archangel, spoken of in the Scriptures. Then to Noah, who is Gabriel; he stands next in authority to Adam in the Priesthood; he was called of God to this office, and was the father of all living in his day, and to him was given the dominion. These men held keys first on earth, and then in heaven.

Adam and the Presidency of the Priesthood.

The Priesthood is an everlasting principle, and existed with God from eternity, and will to eternity, without beginning of days or end of years. The keys have to be brought from heaven whenever the Gospel is sent. When they are revealed from heaven, it is by Adam's authority.

Eternity of the Priesthood.

Daniel in his seventh chapter speaks of the Ancient of Days; he means the oldest man, our Father Adam, Michael,† he will call his children together and hold a council with them to prepare them for the coming of the Son of Man. He (Adam) is the

Adam's Place in the Order of the Worthies.

"* And God said, Let us make man in our image, after our likeness: and let them have dominion over the fish of the sea, and over the fowl of the air, and over the cattle, and over all the earth, and over every creeping thing that creepeth upon the earth. So God created man in his own image, in the image of God created he him; male and female created he them. And God blessed them, and God said unto them, Be fruitful, and multiply, and replenish the earth, and subdue it: and have dominion over the fish of the sea, and over the fowl of the air, and over every living thing that moveth upon the earth.—Gen. I: 26-28.

† The reader will better understand the Prophet's exposition of the 7th chapter of Daniel if those parts of it with which he deals are before him, hence the following quotation:

"I beheld till the thrones were cast down, and the Ancient of Days did sit, whose garment was white as snow, and the hair of his head like the pure wool: his throne was like the fiery flame, and his wheels as burning fire. A fiery stream issued and came forth from before him: thousand thousands ministered unto him and ten thousand times ten thousand stood before him: the judgment was set, and the books were opened. * * * * I saw in the night visions, and, behold, one like the Son of Man came with the clouds of heaven, and came to the Ancient of Days, and they brought him near before him. And there was given him dominion, and glory, and a kingdom, that all people, nations, and languages, should serve him: his dominion is an everlasting dominion, which shall not pass away, and his kingdom that which shall not be destroyed."

The Prophet Daniel saw an earth-power arise and make war upon the Saints and prevail against them until—

father of the human family, and presides over the spirits of all men, and all that have had the keys must stand before him in this grand council. This may take place before some of us leave this stage of action. The Son of Man stands before him, and there is given him glory and dominion. Adam delivers up his stewardship to Christ, that which was delivered to him as holding the keys of the universe, but retains his standing as head of the human family.

The Spirit of Man Eternal.

The spirit of man is not a created being; it existed from eternity, and will exist to eternity. Anything created cannot be eternal; and earth, water, etc., had their existence in an elementary state, from eternity. Our Savior speaks of children and says, Their angels always stand before my Father. The Father called all spirits before Him at the creation of man, and organized them. He (Adam) is the head, and was told to multiply. The keys were first given to him, and by him to others. He will have to give an account of his stewardship, and they to him.

The Nature of the Priesthood.

The Priesthood is everlasting. The Savior, Moses, and Elias, gave the keys to Peter, James, and John, on the mount, when they were transfigured before him. The Priesthood is everlasting—without beginning of days or end of years; without father, mother, etc. If there is no change of ordinances, there is no change of Priesthood. Wherever the ordinances of the Gospel are administered, there is the Priesthood.

The Restoration of the Priesthood.

How have we come at the Priesthood in the last days? It came down, down, in regular succession. Peter, James, and John had it given to them and they gave it to others. Christ is the

"The Ancient of Days came, and judgment was given to the Saints of the Most High; and the time came that the Saints possessed the kingdom. * * * * And the kingdom and dominion, and the greatness of the kingdom under the whole heavens, shall be given to the people of the Saints of the Most High, whose kingdom is an everlasting kingdom, and all dominions shall serve and obey him."

Great High Priest; Adam next.* Paul speaks of the Church coming to an innumerable company of angels—to God the Judge of all—the spirits of just men made perfect; to Jesus the Mediator of the new covenant.—Heb. xii: 23.

Adam in the Valley of Adam-ondi-Ahman.

I saw Adam in the valley of Adam-ondi-Ahman. He called together his children and blessed them with a patriarchal blessing. The Lord appeared in their midst, and he (Adam) blessed them all, and foretold what should befall them to the latest generation.†

Labors of the Patriarchs and Moses.

This is why Adam blessed his posterity; he wanted to bring them into the presence of God. They looked for a city, etc., ["whose builder and maker is God."—Heb. xi: 10]. Moses sought to bring the children of Israel into the presence of God, through the power of the Priesthood, but he could not. In the first ages of the world they tried to establish the same thing; and there were Eliases raised up who tried to restore these very glories, but did not obtain them; but they prophesied of a day when this glory would be revealed. Paul spoke of the dispensation of the fullness of times, when God would gather together all things in one, etc.; and those men to whom these keys have been given,

* This is in keeping with the word of the Lord in a revelation given March, 1832, where the Lord, in speaking to the Saints, said that it was His desire—

"That you may come up unto the crown prepared for you, and be made rulers over many kingdoms, saith the Lord God, the Holy One of Zion, who hath established the foundations of Adam-ondi-Ahman; who hath appointed Michael [Adam] your prince, and established his feet, and set him upon high, and given unto him the keys of salvation under the counsel and direction of the Holy One, who is without beginning of days or end of life."

It is generally supposed that Brigham Young was the author of the doctrine which places Adam as the patriarchal head of the human race, and ascribes to him the dignity of future presidency over this earth and its inhabitants, when the work of redemption shall have been completed. Those who read the Prophet's treatise on the Priesthood in the text above will have their opinions corrected upon this subject; for clearly it is the word of the Lord through the Prophet Joseph Smith which established that docrine. The utterances of President Brigham Young but repeat and expound the doctrine which the Prophet here sets forth.

† Doctrine and Covenants, sec. cvii: 53-57.

will have to be there; and they without us cannot be made perfect.

These men are in heaven, but their children are on the earth. Their bowels yearn over us. God sends down men for this reason. "And the Son of Man shall send forth His angels, and they shall gather out of His kingdom all things that give offense and them that do iniquity."—(Matt. xiii: 41). All these authoritative characters will come down and join hand in hand in bringing about this work.

Angels to Have Part in the Work.

The Kingdom of Heaven is like a grain of mustard seed. The mustard seed is small, but brings forth a large tree, and the fowls lodge in the branches. The fowls are the angels. Thus angels come down, combine together to gather their children, and gather them. We cannot be made perfect without them, nor they without us; when these things are done, the Son of Man will descend, the Ancient of Days sit; we may come to an innumerable company of angels, have communion with and receive instructions from them. Paul told about Moses' proceedings; spoke of the children of Israel being baptized.—(I Cor. x: 1-4). He knew this, and that all the ordinances and blessings were in the Church. Paul had these things, and we may have the fowls of heaven lodge in the branches, etc.

The Kingdom of Heaven.

The "Horn" made war with the Saints and overcame them, until the Ancient of Days came; judgment was given to the Saints of the Most High from the Ancient of Days; the time came that the Saints possessed the Kingdom. This not only makes us ministers here, but in eternity.

Future Deliverance of the Saints.

Salvation cannot come without revelation; it is in vain for anyone to minister without it. No man is a minister of Jesus Christ without being a Prophet. No man can be a minister of Jesus Christ except he has the testimony of Jesus; and this is the spirit of prophecy. Whenever salvation has been administered,

Importance of Revelation.

it has been by testimony. Men of the present time testify of heaven and hell, and have never seen either; and I will say that no man knows these things without this.

A Vision and Prophecy.

Men profess to prophesy. I will prophesy that the signs of the coming of the Son of Man are already commenced. One pestilence will desolate after another. We shall soon have war and bloodshed. The moon will be turned into blood. I testify of these things, and that the coming of the Son of Man is nigh, even at your doors. If our souls and our bodies are not looking forth for the coming of the Son of Man; and after we are dead, if we are not looking forth, we shall be among those who are calling for the rocks to fall upon them.

The Mission of Elijah.

The hearts of the children of men will have to be turned to the fathers, and the fathers to the children, living or dead, to prepare them for the coming of the Son of Man. If Elijah did not come, the whole earth would be smitten.

Blessings for the Saints in Stakes of Zion.

There will be here and there a Stake [of Zion] for the gathering of the Saints. Some may have cried peace, but the Saints and the world will have little peace from henceforth. Let this not hinder us from going to the Stakes; for God has told us to flee, not dallying, or we shall be scattered, one here, and another there. There your children shall be blessed, and you in the midst of friends where you may be blessed. The Gospel net gathers of every kind.

Haste to Build up Zion.

I prophesy, that that man who tarries after he has an opportunity of going, will be afflicted by the devil. Wars are at hand; we must not delay; but are not required to sacrifice. We ought to have the building up of Zion as our greatest object. When wars come, we shall have to flee to Zion. The cry is to make haste. The last revelation says, Ye shall not have time to have gone over the earth, until these things come. It will come as did the cholera, war, fires, and earthquakes;

one pestilence after another, until the Ancient of Days comes, then judgment will be given to the Saints.

Peace in Zion and Her Stakes.

Whatever you may hear about me or Kirtland, take no notice of it; for if it be a place of refuge, the devil will use his greatest efforts to trap the Saints. You must make yourselves acquainted with those men who like Daniel pray three times a day toward the House of the Lord. Look to the Presidency and receive instruction. Every man who is afraid, covetous, will be taken in a snare. The time is soon coming, when no man will have any peace but in Zion and her stakes.

The Prophet's Vision of Judgment.

I saw men hunting the lives of their own sons, and brother murdering brother, women killing their own daughters, and daughters seeking the lives of their mothers. I saw armies arrayed against armies. I saw blood, desolation, fires. The Son of Man has said that the mother shall be against the daughter, and the daughter against the mother. These things are at our doors. They will follow the Saints of God from city to city. Satan will rage, and the spirit of the devil is now enraged. I know not how soon these things will take place; but with a view of them, shall I cry peace? No! I will lift up my voice and testify of them. How long you will have good crops, and the famine be kept off, I do not know; when the fig tree leaves, know then that the summer is nigh at hand.

Visions.

We may look for angels and receive their ministrations, but we are to try the spirits and prove them, for it is often the case that men make a mistake in regard to these things. God has so ordained that when He has communicated, no vision is to be taken but what you see by the seeing of the eye, or what you hear by the hearing of the ear. When you see a vision, pray for the interpretation; if you get not this, shut it up; there must be certainty in this matter. An open vision will manifest that which is more important. Lying spirits are going forth in the earth. There will be great manifestations of spirits, both false and true.

Being born again, comes by the Spirit of God through ordinances. An angel of God never has wings. Some will say that they have seen a spirit; that he offered them his hand, but they did not touch it. This is a lie. First, it is contrary to the plan of God: a spirit cannot come but in glory; an angel has flesh and bones; we see not their glory. The devil may appear as an angel of light. Ask God to reveal it; if it be of the devil, he will flee from you; if of God, He will manifest Himself, or make it manifest. We may come to Jesus and ask Him; He will know all about it; if He comes to a little child, He will adapt himself to the language and capacity of a little child.

Angels.

Every spirit, or vision, or singing, is not of God. The devil is an orator; he is powerful; he took our Savior on to a pinnacle of the Temple, and kept Him in the wilderness for forty days. The gift of discerning spirits will be given to the Presiding Elder. Pray for him that he may have this gift. Speak not in the gift of tongues without understanding it, or without interpretation. The devil can speak in tongues; the adversary will come with his work; he can tempt all classes; can speak in English or Dutch. Let no one speak in tongues unless he interpret, except by the consent of the one who is placed to preside; then he may discern or interpret, or another may. Let us seek for the glory of Abraham, Noah, Adam, the Apostles, who have communion with [knowledge of] these things, and then we shall be among that number when Christ comes.

Powers of the Devil.

The Gift of Tongues.

CHAPTER XXVII.

BAPTISM OF ISAAC GALLAND—EPISTLE OF THE TWELVE TO THE CHURCH.

Wednesday, July 3, 1839.—I baptized Dr. Isaac Galland, and confirmed him at the water's edge; and about two hours afterwards I ordained him to the office of an Elder.

Afternoon. I was engaged in dictating my history.

About this time the Twelve wrote the following epistle:

Epistle of the Twelve.

To the Elders of the Church of Jesus Christ of Latter-day Saints, to the Churches Scattered Abroad and to All the Saints:

We, the undersigned, feeling deeply interested in the welfare of Zion, the upbuilding of the Church of Christ, and the welfare of the Saints in general, send unto you greeting, and pray that "grace, mercy and peace may rest upon you from God our Father and the Lord Jesus Christ." But, brethren, the situation of things as they have of late existed has been to us of a peculiarly trying nature.

Many of you have been driven from your homes, robbed of your possessions, and deprived of the liberty of conscience. You have been stripped of your clothing, plundered of your furniture, robbed of your horses, your cattle, your sheep, your hogs, and refused the protection of law; you have been subject to insult and abuse, from a set of lawless miscreants; you have had to endure cold, nakedness, peril and sword; your wives and your children have been deprived of the comforts ot life; you have been subject to bonds, to imprisonment, to banishment, and many to death, "for the testimony of Jesus, and for the word of God." Many of your brethren, with those whose souls are now under the altar, are crying for the vengeance of heaven to rest upon the heads of their devoted murderers, and saying, "How long, O Lord, holy and true, dost Thou not judge and avenge our blood on them that dwell on the earth?" But it was said to them, that they should rest yet for a little season, until their fellow servants also and their brethren that should be killed, as *they were*, should be fulfilled.

Dear brethren, we would remind you of this thing; and although you have had indignities, insults and injuries heaped upon you till further suffering would seem to be no longer a virtue; we would say, be patient, dear brethren, for as saith the apostle, "Ye have need of patience, that after being tried, ye may inherit the promise." You have been tried in the furnace of affliction; the time to exercise patience is now come; and we shall reap, brethren, in due time, if we faint not. Do not breathe vengeance upon your oppressors, but leave the case in the hands of God; "for vengeance is mine, saith the Lord, and I will repay."

We would say to the widow and the orphan, to the destitute and to the diseased, who have been made so through persecution, be patient; you are not forgotten; the God of Jacob has His eye upon you; the heavens have been witness to your sufferings, and these are registered on high; angels have gazed upon the scene, and your tears, your groans, your sorrows, and anguish of heart, are had in remembrance before God; they have entered into the sympathies of one whose bosom is "touched with the feelings of our infirmities," and who was "tempted in all points like unto you;" they have entered into the ears of the Lord of Sabaoth; be patient, then, until the words of God be fulfilled and His design accomplished; and then shall He pour out His vengeance upon the devoted heads of your murderers; and then shall they know that He is God, and that you are His people.

And we would say to all the Saints who have made a covenant with the Lord by sacrifice, that, inasmuch as you are faithful, you shall not lose your reward, although not numbered among those who were in the late difficulties in the west.

We wish to stimulate all the brethren to faithfulness; you have been tried, you are now being tried; and those trials, if you are not watchful, will corrode the mind, and produce unpleasant feelings; but recollect that now is the time of trial; soon the victory will be ours; now may be a day of lamentation—then will be a day of rejoicing; now may be a day of sorrow—but by and by we shall see the Lord; our sorrow will be turned into joy, and our joy no man taketh from us. Be honest; be men of truth and integrity; let your word be your bond; be diligent, be prayerful; pray for and with your families; train up your children in the fear of the Lord; cultivate a meek, a quiet spirit; clothe the naked, feed the hungry, help the destitute, be merciful to the widow and orphan, be merciful to your brethren, and to all men; bear with one another's infirmities, considering your own weakness; bring no railing accusations against your brethren, especially take care that you do not against the authorities or Elders of the Church, for that principle is of the devil; he is called the accuser of the brethren; and Michael, the archangel, dared not bring a railing accusation against the devil, but said, "The Lord rebuke thee, Satan;" and any man who pursues this course of accusation and murmuring, will fall into the snare of the devil, and apostatize, except he repent.

Jude, in the eighth verse, says, "These filthy dreamers defile the flesh, despise dominion, and speak evil of dignities;" and, says he, "Behold, the Lord cometh with ten thousands of His Saints, to execute judgment upon all, and to convince all that are ungodly among them of all their ungodly deeds which they have ungodly committed, and of all their hard speeches which ungodly sinners have spoken against him."

Peter, speaking on the same principle, says: "The Lord knoweth how to deliver the godly out of temptations, and to reserve the unjust unto the day of judgment to be punished: but chiefly them that walk after the flesh in the lust of uncleanness, and despise government. Presumptuous are they, self-willed, they are not afraid to speak evil of dignities. Whereas angels, which are greater in power and might, bring not railing accusation against them before the Lord."

If a man sin, let him be dealt with according to the law of God in the Bible, the Book of Mormon and Doctrine and Covenants; and then leave him in the hands of God to rebuke, as Michael left the devil. Gird yourselves with righteousness, and let truth, eternal truth, be written indelibly on your hearts. Pray for the prosperity of Zion, for the Prophet and his counselors, for the Twelve, the High Council, the High Priests, the Seventies, the Elders, the Bishops, and all Saints—that God may bless them, and preserve His people in righteousness, and grant unto them wisdom and intelligence; that His kingdom may roll forth.

We would say to the Elders, that God has called you to an important office; He has laid upon you an onerous duty; He has called you to an holy calling, even to be the priests of the Most High God, messengers to the nations of the earth; and upon your diligence, your perseverance and faithfulness, the soundness of the doctrines which you preach, the moral precepts that you advance and practice, and upon the sound principles that you inculcate, while you hold that priesthood, hang the destinies of the human family. You are the men that God has called to spread forth His kingdom; He has committed the care of souls to your charge, and when you received this priesthood, you became the legates of heaven; and the Great God demands it of you, that you should be faithful; and inasmuch as you are not, you will not be chosen; but it will be said unto you, "Stand by and let a more honorable man than thou art take thy place, and receive thy crown."

Be careful that you teach not for the word of God the commandments of men, nor the doctrines of men, nor the ordinances of men, inasmuch as you are God's messengers. Study the word of God, and preach it and not your opinions, for no man's opinion is worth a straw. Advance no principle but what you can prove, for one scriptural proof is worth ten thousand opinions. We would moreover say, abide by that revelation which says "Preach nothing but repentance to this generation," and leave the further mysteries of the kingdom till God shall tell you to preach them, which is not now.

The horns of the beast, the toes of the image, the frogs, and the beast mentioned by John, are not going to save this generation; for if a man does not become acquainted with the first principles of the Gospel, how shall he understand those greater mysteries, which the most wise cannot understand without revelation? These things, therefore, have nothing to do with your mission.

We have heard of some foolish vagaries, and wild speculations, originating only in a disordered imagination, which are set forth by some, telling what occupation they had before they came into this world, and what they would be employed with after they leave this state of existence; those and other vain imaginations we would warn the Elders against, because if they listen to such things, they will fall into the snare of the devil; and when the trying time comes, they will be overthrown.

We would also warn the Elders, according to previous counsel, not to go on to another's ground without invitation, to interfere with another's privilege, for your mission is to the world, and not to the churches.

We would also remark, that no man has a right to usurp authority or power over any church, nor has any man power to preside over any church, unless he is solicited and received by the voice of that church to preside.

Preach the first principles of the doctrine of Christ—faith in the Lord Jesus Christ, repentance towards God, baptism in the name of Jesus for the remission of sins, laying on of hands for the gift of the Holy Ghost, the resurrection of the dead, and eternal judgment.

When you go forth to preach, and the Spirit of God rests upon you, giving you wisdom and utterance, and enlightening your understanding, be careful that you ascribe the glory to God, and not to yourselves. Boast not of intelligence, of wisdom, or of power; for it is only that which God has imparted unto you; but be humble, be meek, be patient and give glory to God.

We would counsel all who have not received a recommend since the difficulties in Missouri, to obtain one from the authorities of the Church if they wish to be accounted as wise stewards.

We are glad, dear brethren, to see that spirit of enterprise and perseverance which is manifested by you in regard to preaching the Gospel;

and rejoice to know that neither bonds nor imprisonment, banishment nor exile, poverty or contempt, nor all the combined powers of earth and hell, hinder you from delivering your testimony to the world, and publishing those glad tidings which have been revealed from heaven by the ministering of angels, by the gift of the Holy Ghost, and by the power of God, for the salvation of the world in these last days. And we would say to you that the hearts of the Twelve are with you, and they, with you, are determined to fulfill their mission, to clear their garments of the blood of this generation, to introduce the Gospel to foreign nations, and to make known to the world these great things which God has developed. They are now on the eve of their departure for England, and will start in a few days. They feel to pray for you and to solicit an interest in your prayers and in the prayers of the Church, that God may sustain them in their arduous undertaking, grant them success in their mission, deliver them from the powers of darkness, and stratagem of wicked men, and all the combined powers of earth and hell. And if you unitedly seek after unity of purpose and design: if you are men of humility and of faithfulness, of integrity and perseverance; if you submit yourselves to the teachings of heaven, and are guided by the Spirit of God; if you at all times seek the glory of God and the salvation of men, and lay your honor prostrate in the dust, if need be, and are willing to fulfill the purposes of God in all things, the power of the Priesthood will rest upon you, and you will become mighty in testimony; the widow and the orphan will be made glad and the poor among men rejoice in the Holy One of Israel. Princes will listen to the things that you proclaim, and the nobles of the earth will attend with deference to your words; queens will rejoice in the glad tidings of salvation, and kings bow to the sceptre of Immanuel; light will burst forth as the morning, and intelligence spread itself as the rays of the sun; the cringing sycophant will be ashamed, and the traitor flee from your presence; superstition will hide its hoary head, and infidelity be ashamed. And amid the clamor of men, the din of war, the rage of pestilence, the commotion of nations, the overthrow of kingdoms, and the dissolution of empires, Truth shall walk forth with mighty power, guided by the arm of Omnipotence, and lay hold of the honest in heart among all nations; Zion shall blossom as a rose, and the nations flock to her standard, and the kingdoms of this world shall soon become the kingdoms of our God and of His Christ, and He shall reign for ever and ever. Amen.

Brigham Young,
Heber C. Kimball,
John E. Page,
Wilford Woodruff,
John Taylor,
Geo. A. Smith.

N. B.—We have heard that a man by the name of John M. Hinkle is preaching in the Iowa territory. We would remark to the public, that we have withdrawn our fellowship from him, and will not stand accountable for any doctrines held forth by him; nor will we be amenable for his conduct. The minutes of a conference will be published, mentioning the names of others from whom we have withdrawn our fellowship.

CHAPTER XXVIII.

THE ESCAPE OF PARLEY P. PRATT AND HIS FELLOW PRISONERS FROM MISSOURI—THE CLOSE OF AN EPOCH.

Thursday, July 4, 1839.—I dictated history.

To show the situation of the prisoners at Columbia, Missouri, I quote from Elder Pratt's "Persecution of the Saints"—

Parley P. Pratt's Account of His Escape from Missouri.

Sister Phelps, Orson Pratt, and Sister Phelps' brother came from Illinois on horseback and visited with us for several days.* On the fourth of July we felt desirous as usual to celebrate the anniversary of American liberty; we accordingly manufactured a white flag, consisting of the half of a shirt, on which was inscribed the word "Liberty," in large letters, and also a large American eagle was put on in red; we then obtained a pole from our jailer, and on the morning of the fourth, this flag was suspended from the front window of our prison, overhanging the public square, and floating triumphantly in the air to the full view of the citizens who assembled by hundreds to celebrate the National Jubilee.

With this the citizens seemed highly pleased, and sent a portion of

* This was really a rescuing party as the subsequent events clearly disclose. The plan of escape was as follows: Orson Pratt waited on the district judge and district attorney and obtained various papers and arranged for summoning witnesses from Illinois to attend a trial which had just been adjourned for some months. He was to procure an order from the court to take affidavits in Illinois in case the witnesses should object to come to the state from which they had been banished to attend the trial. This activity on the part of the prisoners for a trial, and their engaging a lawyer or two and paying part of their fees in advance to defend their case, served as a sufficient covering for the real intentions of the rescuing party. The papers were all prepared and placed in the hands of Orson Pratt, but the company of visitors were to remain until after the 4th of July celebration. Arrangements were also made by which Mrs. Phelps was to stay with her husband a few weeks in prison, engaging her board in the meantime in the family of the jailer who occupied part of the prison as a residence. When Orson Pratt and Mr. Clark, brother of Mrs. Phelps, departed, apparently on their mission to secure witnesses, they took Sister Phelps' horse with them as if to take it back to Illinois, all of which, of course, served stillmore to conceal the real plot that was laid for the escape of the prisoners. (See Autobiography of Parley P. Pratt p. 268).

the public dinner to us and our friends, who partook with us in prison with merry hearts, as we intended to gain our liberties or be in paradise before the close of that eventful day.

While we were thus employed in prison, the town was alive with troops parading, guns firing, music sounding, and shouts of joy resounding on every side. In the meantime we wrote the following toast, which was read at their public dinner, with many and long cheers—

"The patriotic and hospitable citizens of Boone county: opposed to tyranny and oppression, and firm to the original principles of republican liberty; may they, in common with every part of our wide spreading country, long enjoy the blessings which flow from the fountain of American Independence."

Our dinner being ended, our two brethren took leave of us and started for Illinois, (leaving Mrs. Phelps to still visit with her husband;) they had proceeded a mile or two on the road and then took into the woods, and finally placed their three horses in a thicket within one-third of a mile of the prison, and there they waited in anxious suspense until sundown. In the meantime we put on our coats and hats and waited for the setting sun.

With prayer and supplication for deliverance from this long and tedious bondage, and for a restoration to the society of our friends and families, we then sung the following lines—

Lord cause their foolish plans to fail,
And let them faint or die;
Our souls would quit this loathsome jail,
And fly to Illinois.

To join with the embodied Saints,
Who are with freedom blessed—
That only bliss for which we pant—
With them a while to rest.

Give joy for grief—give ease for pain;
Take all our foes away;
But let us find our friends again,
In this eventful day.

Thus ended the celebration of our National Liberty; but the gaining of our own was the grand achievement now before us. In the meantime, the sun was setting; the moment arrived—the footsteps of the jailer were heard on the stairs; every man flew to his feet, and stood near the door. The great door was opened, and our supper handed in through a small hole in the inner door, which still remained locked; but at length the key was turned in order to hand in the pot of coffee. No sooner was the key turned than the door was jerked open, and in a moment all three of us were out—and rushing down the stairs, through the entry, and out into the door yard, when Phelps cleared himself without injuring the jailor, and all of us leaped several fences, ran through the fields towards the thicket, where we expected to find our friends and horses.

In the meantime the town was alarmed; and many were seen rushing after us, some on horseback, and some on foot, prepared with dogs, guns, and whatever came to hand. But the flag of Liberty, with its eagle, still floated on high in the distance: and under that banner, our nerves seemed to strengthen at every step.

We gained the horses, mounted, and dashed into the wilderness, each his own way. After a few jumps of my horse, I was hailed by an armed man at pistol shot distance, crying, "d—— you, stop, or I'll shoot you!" I rushed onward deeper into the forest, while the cry was repeated in close pursuit, "d—— you, stop, or I'll shoot you," at every step, till at length it died away in the distance. I plunged a mile into the forest—came to a halt—tied my horse in a thicket—went a distance, and climbed a tree, to await the approaching darkness.

Being so little used to exercise, I fainted through over-exertion, and remained so faint for nearly an hour that I could not get down from the tree; but calling on the Lord, He strengthened me, and I came down from the tree. But my horse had got loose and gone. I then made my way on foot for several days and nights, principally without food, and scarcely suffering myself to be seen.

After five days of dreadful suffering, with fatigue and hunger, I crossed the Mississippi, and found myself once more in a land of freedom. Mr. Phelps made his escape also;* but King Follet was retaken

* The account of Phelp's escape is thus given by Parley P. Pratt: "Mr. Phelps made his escape much in the same manner as myself. He was at first closely pursued, but at length he out-distanced them all, and, once out of their sight, he struck directly into the road, and rode on toward Illinois. He had proceeded but a few miles on his way, when he was suddenly surrounded in the darkness of the night by a company of horsemen who were out in pursuit of the prisoners. They immediately hailed him, and cried out, 'Say, stranger, G—d d—— you, what is your name?' He replied in the same rough and careless manner, 'You d——d rascals, what is yours?' On finding that he could 'damn' as well as themselves, they concluded he could not be a Mormon, while his bold and fearless manner convinced them that he was not a man who was fleeing for his life. They then begged his pardon for the rough manner in which they had accosted him, 'Oh, you are one of the real breed. By G—d, no d——d Mormon could counterfeit that language, you swear real natteral; hurrah for old Kentuck. But whar mout you live, stranger?" He replied, "just up here; you mout a kno'd me, and then agin you moun't. I think I've seed you all a heap o' times, but I've been so d——d drunk at the fourth of Independence, I hardly know myself or anybody else, but hurrah for old Kentuck; and what about the d——d Mormons?' 'What about

and carried back.* Luman Gibbs continued in the prison; he had apostatized and turned traitor to the others."

'em? egad, you'd a know'd that without axin', if you'd a seed 'em run.' 'What! they are not out of prison, are they?' 'Out of prison! yes, the d——d rascals raised a flag of liberty in open day, and burst out, and down stairs right into the midst of the public celebration, out-wrestling the d——d jailer, and outrunning the whole town in a fair foot race. They reached the timber jist as they war overtaken, but afore we could cotch 'em they mounted their nags, and the way they cleared was a caution to Crockett. We tuk one on 'em, and seed the other two a few feet distant, rushin' their nags at full speed, but we couldn't cotch 'em nor shoot 'em either; I raised my new Kentucky rifle, fresh loaded and primed, with a good percussion, and taking fair aim at one of their heads only a few yards distant, I fired, but the d——d cap burst, and the powder wouldn't burn.' 'Well, now, stranger, that's a mighty big story, and seems enemost impossible. Did you say you cotched one on 'em? Why I'd a tho't you'd a kilt him on the spot; what have you done with him?' 'They tuk him back to prison, I suppose, but it was only the old one. If it had been one o' them tother chaps we would a skinn'd 'em as quick as Crockett would a coon, and then eat 'em alive without leaving a grease spot.'

"This interview over, the horsemen withdrew and left Phelps to pursue his way in peace; * * * * and he finally arrived in Illinois in safety, having reached the ferry before his pursuers, and before the news of the escape had spread so far." (Autobiography of Parley P. Pratt pp. 282-4).

* What befell Brother King Follet after he was captured, and his final escape from Missouri is thus related by Parley P. Pratt:

"He had been surrounded, overpowered and taken at the time we were each separated from the others. He was finally rescued from the mob, and thrust alive into the lower dungeon and chained down to the floor. He remained in this doleful situation for a few days, till the wrath of the multitude had time to cool a little, and then he was unchained by the Sheriff and again brought into the upper apartment and treated with some degree of kindness. They now laughed with him about his adventure, praised him for his bravery, and called him a good fellow. The truth of the matter was, they had no great desire to take the lives of any but those whom they had considered leaders; and since they had discovered that Mr. Follett and Mr. Phelps were not considered religious leaders among our society, they were in no great danger, except they should happen to be killed in the heat of excitement or passion. * * * * * Mr. Follet remained in confinement for several months, and finally was dismissed and sent home to Illinois, where he met his family, who had been expelled from the State of Missouri, in common with others, during his confinement." (Autobiography of Parley P. Pratt, pp. 288-9).

The escape of these prisoners from Missouri completed the expulsion of the Latter-day Saints from that state, and closed a great epoch in the history of the Church.

APPENDIX TO VOLUME III.

AFFIDAVITS OF HYRUM SMITH *et al.* ON AFFAIRS IN MISSOURI, 1831-39; OFFICIALLY SUBSCRIBED TO BEFORE THE MUNICIPAL COURT OF NAUVOO THE FIRST DAY OF JULY, 1843.

Explanatory Note.

[In the month of June, 1843, a desperate effort was made to drag the Prophet Joseph Smith back to the state of Missouri, on a charge of treason against that state; and also alleging that because of his escape from Liberty prison in Clay county, Missouri, he had become a fugitive from justice. A process was issued by Thomas Reynolds, governor of the state of Missouri, and placed in the hands of Joseph H. Reynolds, appointed the agent of that state to receive the Prophet from the hands of the Illinois authorities who were to make the arrest. Thomas Ford, governor of Illinois, issued the necessary papers for the arrest, and placed them in the hands of Harmon T. Wilson, who, in company with Reynolds, the Missouri agent, arrested the Prophet near Dixon in Lee county, Illinois, something more than two hundred miles north and east of Nauvoo. The Prophet managed with the assistance of his friends in Illinois, to be returned to Nauvoo, where he succeeded in getting out a writ of *habeas corpus* before the municipal court of that place, by which he was delivered from the hands of the Missouri agent. In the course of the *ex parte* hearing the following witnesses were examined, *viz.*, Hyrum Smith, Parley P. Pratt, Brigham Young, George W. Pitkin, Lyman Wight, and Sidney Rigdon. In the course of the examination of these witnesses by affidavit the story of the persecutions of the Latter-day Saints is related at length. It cannot be said that anything new is added to the Missouri period of the Church history by these affidavits, but they are statements made officially before a court of inquiry and therefore have a value of their own on that account, and as this is a documentary history of the Church, these volumes would be incomplete without them. A desire to group all events closelyrelated has in duced the Editors to take these affidavits out of the place where they were given, in 1843, and place them in this volume, which is so largely devoted to the Missouri period of the Church history.

The municipal court of Nauvoo sat on the first day of July, 1843, at eight o'clock a. m., William Marks acting as chief justice, Daniel H. Wells, Newel K. Whitney, George W. Harris, Gustavus Hills and Hiram Kimball associate justices and the witnesses were examined in the order in which their affidavits are here published.

I.

THE TESTIMONY OF HYRUM SMITH.

Hyrum Smith sworn, said that the defendant now in court is his brother, and that his name is not Joseph Smith, Jun., but Joseph Smith, Sen., and has been for more than two years past.* I have been acquainted with him ever since he was born, which was thirty-seven years in December last; and I have not been absent from him at any one time not even for the space of six months, since his birth, to my recollection, and have been intimately acquainted with all his sayings, doings, business transactions and movements, as much as any one man could be acquainted with another man's business, up to the present time, and do know that he has not committed treason against any state in the Union, by any overt act, or by levying war, or by aiding, abetting or assisting an enemy in any state in the Union; and that the said Joseph Smith, Sen., has not committed treason in the state of Missouri, or violated any law or rule of said state; I being personally acquainted with the transactions and doings of said Smith whilst he resided in said state, which was for about six months in the year 1838; I being also a resident in said state during the same period of time; and I do know that said Joseph Smith, Sen., never was subject to military duty in any state, neither was he in the state of Missouri, he being exempt by the amputation or extraction of a bone from his leg, and by having a license to preach the Gospel, or being, in other words, a minister of the Gospel; and I do know that said Smith never bore arms, as a military man, in any capacity whatever, whilst in the state of Missouri, or previous to that time; neither has he given any orders or assumed any command in any capacity whatever. But I do know that whilst he was in the state of Missouri, the people commonly called "Mormons" were threatened with violence and extermination; and on or about the first

* Joseph Smith, the father of the prophet, died on September 14th, 1840, and hence at the time these warrants were issued against the prophet in June, 1843, he was no longer Joseph Smith, Junior, but Joseph Smith, Senior.

Monday in August, 1838, at the election in Gallatin, the county seat in Daviess county, the citizens who were commonly called "Mormons" were forbidden to exercise the rights of franchise; and from that circumstance an affray commenced and a fight ensued among the citizens of that place; and from that time a mob commenced gathering in that county, threatening the extermination of the "Mormons." The said Smith and myself, upon hearing the mobs were collecting together, and that they also murdered two of the citizens of the same place, [Gallatin] and would not suffer them to be buried, the said Smith and myself went over to Daviess county to learn the particulars of the affray; but upon our arrival at Diahman we learned that none was killed, but several were wounded. We tarried all night at Colonel Lyman Wight's. The next morning, the weather being very warm, and having been very dry, for some time previously, the springs and wells in the region were dried up. On mounting our horses to return, we rode up to Mr. Black's who was then an acting justice of the peace, to obtain some water for ourselves and horses. Some few of the citizens accompanied us there; and, after obtaining water, Mr. Black was asked by said Joseph Smith, Sen., if he would use his influence to see that the laws were faithfully executed, and to put down mob violence; and he gave us a paper written by his own hand, stating that he would do so. He [Joseph Smith, Sen.] also requested him to call together the most influential men of the county on the next day, that we might have an interview with them. To this he acquiesced, and, accordingly, the next day they assembled at the house of Colonel Wight, and entered into a mutual covenant of peace to put down mob violence and protect each other in the enjoyment of their rights. After this, we all parted with the best of feelings, and each man returned to his own home.

This mutual agreement of peace, however, did not last long; for, but a few days afterwards, the mob began to collect again, until several hundreds rendezvoused at Millport, a few miles distant from Diahman. They immediately commenced making aggressions upon the citizens called "Mormons," taking away their hogs and cattle and threatening them with extermination or utter extinction, saying that they had a cannon, and there should be no compromise only at its mouth. They frequently took men, women and children prisoners, whipping them and lacerating their bodies with hickory withes, and tying them to trees and depriving them of food until they were compelled to gnaw the bark from the trees to which they were bound, in order to sustain life; treating them in the most cruel manner they could invent or think of, and doing everything they could to excite the indignation of the "Mormon" people to rescue them, in order that they might make that a pretext for an accusation for the breach of the law, and that they might the better excite the prejudice of the populace, and thereby get aid and assistance to carry out their hellish purposes of extermination.

Immediately on the authentication of these facts, messengers were despatched from Far West to Austin A. King, judge of the fifth judicial district of the state of Missouri, and also to Major-General Atchison, commander-in-chief of that division, and Brigadier-General Doniphan, giving them information of the existing facts, and demanding immediate assistance.

General Atchison returned with the messengers, and went immediately to Diahman, and from thence to Millport, and he found that the facts were true as reported to him—that the citizens of that county were assembled together in a hostile attitude, to the number of two or three hundred men, threatening the utter extermination of the "Mormons." He at once returned to Clay county, and ordered out a sufficient military force to quell the mob.

Immediately after, they were dispersed, and the army returned. The mob commenced collecting again soon after. We again applied for military aid, when General Doniphan came out with a force of sixty armed men to Far West; but they were in such a state of insubordination that he said he could not control them, and it was thought advisable by Col. Hinkle, Mr. Rigdon and others, that they should return home. General Doniphan ordered Colonel Hinkle to call out the militia of Caldwell and defend the town against the mob; for, said he, you have great reason to be alarmed. He said Neil Gillium, from the Platte county, had come down with two hundred armed men, and had taken up their station at Hunter's Mill, a place distant about seventeen or eighteen miles northwest of the town of Far West, and also that an armed force had collected again at Millport, in Daviess county, consisting of several hundred men; and that another armed force had collected at De Witt, in Carroll county, about fifty miles southeast of Far West, where about seventy families of the "Mormon" people had settled upon the banks of the Missouri river, at a little town called De Witt.

Immediately, whilst he was yet talking, a messenger came in from De Witt, stating that three or four hundred men had assembled together at that place, armed *cap-a-pie*, and that they had threatened the utter extinction of the citizens of De Witt, if they did not leave the place immediately; and that they had also surrounded the town and cut off all supplies of food, so that many of the inhabitants were suffering from hunger.

General Doniphan seemed to be very much alarmed, and appeared to be willing to do all he could to assist and to relieve the sufferings of the "Mormon" people. He advised that a petition be gotten up at once and sent to the Governor. A petition was accordingly prepared, and a messenger despatched to the governor, and another petition was sent to Judge King.

The "Mormon" people throughout the country were in a great state of alarm and also in great distress. They saw themselves completely surrounded by armed forces on the north, and on the northwest and on the south. Bogart, who was a Methodist preacher and a captain over a militia company of fifty soldiers, but who had added to this number out of the surrounding counties about one hundred more, which made his force about one hundred and fifty strong, was stationed at Crooked creek, sending out his scouting parties, taking men, women and children prisoners, driving off cattle, hogs and horses, entering into every house on Log and Long creeks, rifling their houses of their most precious articles, such as money, bedding and clothing, taking all their old muskets and their rifles, or military implements, threatening the people with instant death, if they did not deliver up all their precious things and enter into a covenant to leave the state or go into the city of Far West by the next morning, saying that they "calculated to drive the people into Far West, and then drive them to hell." Gillium also was doing the same on the northwest side of Far West; and Sashiel Woods, a Presbyterian minister, was the leader of the mob in Daviess county; and a very noted man of the same society was the leader of the mob in Carroll county. And they were also sending out their scouting parties, robbing and pillaging houses, driving away hogs, horses and cattle, taking men, women and children and carrying them off, threatening their lives, and subjecting them to all manner of abuses that they could invent or think of.

Under this state of alarm, excitement and distress, the messengers returned from the governor and from the other authorities, bringing the startling news that the "Mormons" could have no assistance. They stated that the governor said the "Mormons" had got into a difficulty with the citizens, and they might fight it out, for all he cared. He could not render them any assistance.

The people of De Wit were obliged to leave their homes and go into Far West, but did not do so until after many of them had starved to death for want of proper sustenance, and several died on the road there, and were buried by the wayside, without a coffin or a funeral ceremony; and the distress, sufferings, and privations of the people cannot be expressed.

All the scattered families of the "Mormon" people, with but few exceptions, in all the counties, except Daviess, were driven into Far West.

This only increased their distress, for many thousands who were driven there had no habitations or houses to shelter them, and were huddled together, some in tents and others under blankets, while others had no shelter from the inclemency of the weather. Nearly two months the people had been in this awful state of consternation; many of them had been killed, whilst others had been whipped until they had to swathe up their bowels to prevent them from falling out.

About this time General Parks came out from Richmond, Ray county. He was one of the commissioned officers sent out at the time the mob was first quelled, and went out to Diahman. My brother, Joseph Smith, Sen., and I went out at the same time.

On the evening that General Parks arrived at Diahman, the wife of my brother, the late Don Carlos Smith, came into Colonel Wight's about 11 o'clock at night, bringing her two children along with her, one about two and a half years old, the other a babe in her arms.

She came on foot, a distance of three miles, and waded Grand river. The water was then waist deep, and the snow three inches deep. She stated that a party of the mob—a gang of ruffians—had turned her out of doors and taken her household goods, and had burnt up her house, and she had escaped by the skin of her teeth. Her husband at that time was in Tennessee, [on a mission] and she was living alone.

This cruel transaction excited the feelings of the people of Diahman, especially of Colonel Wight and he asked General Parks in my hearing *how long we had got to suffer such base treatment*. General Parks said he did not know how long.

Colonel Wight then asked him what should be done? General Parks told him "he should take a company of men, well armed, and go and disperse the mob wherever he should find any collected together, and take away their arms." Colonel Wight did so precisely according to the orders of General Parks. And my brother, Joseph Smith, Sen., made no order about it.

And after Col. Wight had dispersed the mob, and put a stop to their burning houses belonging to the "Mormon" people, and turning women and children out of doors, which they had done up to that time to the number of eight or ten houses, which houses were consumed to ashes. After being cut short in their intended designs, the mob started up a new plan. They went to work and moved their families out of the county and set fire to their houses; and not being able to incense the "Mormons" to commit crimes, they had recourse to this stratagem to set their houses on fire, and send runners into all the counties adjacent to declare to the people that the "Mormons" had burnt up their houses and destroyed their fields; and if the people would not believe them, they would tell them to go and see if what they had said was not true.

Many people came to see. They saw the houses burning; and, being filled with prejudice, they could not be made to believe but that the

"Mormons" set them on fire; which deed was most diabolical and of the blackest kind; for indeed the "Mormons" did not set them on fire, nor meddle with their houses or their fields.

And the houses that were burnt, had all been previously purchased by the "Mormons" of the people, together with the pre-emption rights and the corn in the fields, and paid for in money, and with wagons and horses, and with other property, about two weeks before; but they had not taken possession of the premises. This wicked transaction was for the purpose of clandestinely exciting the minds of a prejudiced populace and the executive, that they might get an order that they could the more easily carry out their hellish purposes, in expulsion, or extermination, or utter extinction of the "Mormon" people.

After witnessing the distressed situation of the people in Diahman, my brother, Joseph Smith, Sen., and myself returned to the city of Far West, and immediately dispatched a messenger, with written documents, to General Atchison, stating the facts as they did then exist, praying for assistance, if possible, and requesting the editor of the *Far West* to insert the same in his newspaper. But he utterly refused to do so.

We still believed that we should get assistance from the Governor, and again petitioned him, praying for assistance, setting forth our distressed situation. And in the meantime the presiding judge of the county court issued orders, upon affidavits made to him by the citizens, to the sheriff of the county, to order out the militia of the county to stand in constant readiness, night and day, to prevent the citizens from being massacred, which fearful situation they were in every moment.

Everything was very portentous and alarming. Notwithstanding all this, there was a ray of hope yet existing in the minds of the people that the governor would render us assistance; and whilst the people were waiting anxiously for deliverance—men, women, and children frightened, praying, and weeping, we beheld at a distance, crossing the prairies and approaching the town, a large army in military array, brandishing their glittering swords in the sunshine; and we could not but feel joyful for a moment, thinking that probably the governor had sent an armed force to our relief, notwithstanding the awful forebodings that pervaded our breasts.

But, to our great surprise, when the army arrived, they came up and formed a line in double file within one-half mile on the south of the city of Far West, and despatched three messengers with a white flag to the city. They were met by Captain Morey, with a few other individuals, whose names I do not now recollect. I was myself standing close by, and could very distinctly hear every word they said.

Being filled with anxiety, I rushed forward to the spot, expecting to hear good news. But, alas! and heart-thrilling to every soul that heard them, they demanded three persons to be brought out of the city before they should massacre the rest.

The names of the persons they demanded were Adam Lightner, John Cleminson, and his wife. Immediately the three persons were brought forth to hold an interview with the officers who had made the demand, and the officers told them they had now a chance to save their lives, for they intended to destroy the people and lay the city in ashes. They replied to the officers, if the people must be destroyed and the city burned to ashes, they would remain in the city and die with them.

The officers immediately returned, and the army retreated and encamped about a mile and a half from the city.

A messenger was at once dispatched with a white flag from the colonel of the militia of Far West, requesting an interview with General Atchison and General Doniphan; but as the messenger approached the camp, he was shot at by Bogart, the Methodist preacher.

The name of the messenger was Charles C. Rich, who is now [1843] Brigadier-General in the Nauvoo Legion. However, he gained permission to see General Doniphan; he also requested an interview with General Atchison.

General Doniphan said that General Atchison had been dismounted a few miles back, by a special order of the Governor, and had been sent back to Liberty, Clay county. He also stated that the reason was, that he (Atchison) was too merciful unto the "Mormons," and Boggs would not let him have the command, but had given it to General Lucas, who was from Jackson county, and whose heart had become hardened by his former acts of rapine and bloodshed, he being one of the leaders in murdering, driving, and plundering the "Mormon" people in that county, and burning some two or three hundred of their houses, in the years 1833 and 1834.

Mr. Rich requested General Doniphan to spare the people, and not suffer them to be massacred until the next morning, it then being evening. He coolly agreed that he would not, and also said that he had not as yet received the Governor's order, but expected it every hour, and should not make any further move until he had received it; but he would not make any promises so far as regarded Neil Gillium's army, it having arrived a few minutes previously and joined the main body of the army, he [Gillium] knowing well at what hour to form a junction with the main body.

Mr. Rich then returned to the city, giving this information. The Colonel [G. M. Hinkle] immediately dispatched a second messenger with a white flag, to request another interview with General Doniphan, in order to touch his sympathy and compassion, and, if it were possible for him to use his best endeavors to preserve the lives of the people.

On the return of this messenger, we learned that several persons had been killed by some of the soldiers who were under the command of General Lucas.

One Mr. Carey had his brains knocked out by the breech of a gun, and he lay bleeding several hours; but his family were not permitted to approach him, nor any one else allowed to administer relief to him whilst he lay upon the ground in the agonies of death.

Mr. Carey had just arrived in the country, from the State of Ohio, only a few hours previous to the arrival of the army. He had a family, consisting of a wife and several small children. He was buried by Lucius N. Scovil, who is now [1843] the senior Warden of the Nauvoo [Masonic] lodge.

Another man, of the name of John Tanner, was knocked on the head at the same time, and his skull laid bare to the width of a man's hand; and he lay, to all appearances, in the agonies of death for several hours; but by the permission of General Doniphan, his friends brought him out of the camp; and with good nursing, he slowly recovered, and is now living.

There was another man, whose name is Powell, who was beat on the head with the breech of a gun until his skull was fractured, and his brains ran out in two or three places. He is now alive and resides in this [Hancock] county, but has lost the use of his senses. Several persons of his family were also left for dead, but have since recovered.

These acts of barbarity were also committed by the soldiers under the command of General Lucas, previous to having received the Governor's order of extermination.

It was on the evening of the 30th October, according to the best of my recollections, that the army arrived at Far West, the sun about half-an-hour high. In a few moments afterwards, Cornelius Gillium arrived with his army and formed a junction.

This Gillium had been stationed at Hunter's Mills for about two months previous to that time, committing depredations upon the inhabitants, capturing men, women, and children carrying them off as prisoners and lacerating their bodies with hickory withes.

The army of Gillium were painted like Indians: some, more conspicuous than others, were designated by red spots; and he also was painted in a similar manner with red spots marked on his face, and styled himself the "DELAWARE CHIEF." They would whoop and halloo, and yell as nearly like Indians as they could, and continued to do so all that night.

In the morning, early, the colonel of militia [G. M, Hinkle] sent a messenger into the camp with a white flag, to have another interview with General Doniphan. On his return, he informed us that the governor's order had arrived.

General Doniphan said that the order of the governor was, to exterminate the Mormons, by God; but *he* would be *damned* if *he* obeyed *that order*, but General Lucas might do what he pleased.

We immediately learned from General Doniphan, that "the Governor's order that had arrived was only a copy of the original, and that the original order was in the hands of Major-General Clark, who was on his way to Far West with an additional army of 6,000 men."

Immediately after this, there came into the city a messenger from Haun's Mills, bringing the intelligence of an awful massacre of the people who were residing in that place, and that a force of two or three hundred detached from the main body of the army, under the superior command of Colonel Ashley, but under the immediate command of Captain Nehemiah Comstock, who, the day previous, had promised them peace and protection; but on receiving a copy of the Governor's order "to *exterminate or to expel*" from the hands of Colonel Ashley, he returned upon them the following day and surprised and massacred nearly the whole population of the place, and then came on to the town of Far West, and entered into conjunction with the main body of the army.

The messenger informed us that he himself, with a few others, fled into the thickets, which preserved them from the massacre; and on the following morning they returned and collected the dead bodies of the people, and cast them into a well; and there were upwards of 20 who were dead or mortally wounded; and there are several of the wounded now [1843] living in this city [Nauvoo].

One, of the name of Yocum, has lately had his leg amputated, in consequence of wounds he then received. He had a ball shot through his head, which entered near his eye and came out at the back part of his head, and another ball passed through one of his arms.

The army, during all the while they had been encamped at Far West, continued to lay waste fields of corn, making hogs, sheep, and cattle common plunder, and shooting them down for sport.

One man shot a cow and took a strip of her skin, the width of his hand, from her head to her tail, and tied it around a tree to slip his halter into to tie his horse with.

The city was surrounded with a strong guard; and no man, woman or child was permitted to go out or to come in, under penalty of death. Many of the citizens were shot at in attempting to go out to obtain sustenance for themselves and families.

There was one field fenced in, consisting of 1,200 acres, mostly covered with corn. It was entirely laid waste by the hands of the army. The next day after the arrival of the army, towards evening, Colonel Hinkle came up from the camp, requesting to see my brother Joseph, Parley P. Pratt, Sidney Rigdon, Lyman Wight, and George W. Robinson, stating that the officers of the army wanted a mutual consultation with those men; Hinkle also assured them that these generals—Doniphan, Lucas, Wilson, and Graham—(however, General Graham is an honorable exception; he did all he could to preserve the lives of the people, contrary to the order of the governor);—had pledged their sacred honor that they should not be abused or insulted, but should be guarded back in safety in the morning, or as soon as the consultation was over.

My brother Joseph replied that he did not know what good he could do in any consultation, as he was only a private individual. However, he said he was always willing to do all the good he could, and would obey every law of the land, and then leave the event with God.

They immediately started with Colonel Hinkle to go down into the camp. As they were going down, about half way to the camp, they met General Lucas with a phalanx of men, with a wing to the right and to the left, and a four-pounder [cannon] in the center. They supposed he was coming with this strong force to guard them into the camp in safety; but, to their surprise, when they came up to General Lucas, he ordered his men to surround them, and Hinkle stepped up to the general and said, "These are the prisoners I agreed to deliver up." General Lucas drew his sword and said, "Gentlemen, you are my prisoners," and about that time the main army were on their march to meet them.

They came up in two divisions, and opened to the right and left, and my brother and his friends were marched down through their lines, with a strong guard in front, and the cannon in the rear, to the camp, amidst the whoopings, howlings, yellings, and shoutings of the army, which were so horrid and terrific that it frightened the inhabitants of the city.

It is impossible to describe the feelings of horror and distress of the people.

After being thus betrayed, they [the prisoners] were placed under a strong guard of thirty men, armed *cap-a-pie*, who were relieved every two hours. They were compelled to lie on the cold ground that night, and were told in plain language that they need never to expect their liberties again. So far for their honor pledged! However, this was as much as could be expected from a mob under the garb of military and executive authority in the state of Missouri.

On the next day, the soldiers were permitted to patrol the streets, of Far West to abuse and insult the people at their leisure, and enter into houses and pillage them, and ravish the women, taking away every gun and every other kind of arms or military implements. About twelve o'clock on that day, Colonel Hinkle came to my house with an armed force, opened the door, and called me out of doors and delivered me up as a prisoner unto that force. They surrounded me and commanded me to march into the camp. I told them that I could not go; my family were sick, and I was sick myself, and could not leave home. They said they did not care for that—I must and should go. I asked when they would permit me to return. They made me no answer, but forced me along with the point of the bayonent into the camp, and put me under the same guard with my brother Joseph; and within about half an hour afterwards, Amasa Lyman was also brought and placed under the same guard. There we were compelled to stay all that night and lie on the ground. But some time in the same night, Colonel Hinkle came to me and told me that he had been pleading my case before the court-martial, but he was afraid he would not succeed.

He said there was a court-martial then in session, consisting of thirteen or fourteen officers; Circuit Judge Austin A. King, and Mr. Birch, district attorney; also Sashiel Woods, Presbyterian priest, and about twenty other priests of the different religious denominations in that country. He said they were determined to shoot us on the next morning in the public square in Far West. I made him no reply.

On the next morning, about sunrise, General Doniphan ordered his brigade to take up the line of march and leave the camp. He came to us where we were under guard, to shake hands with us, and bid us farewell. His first salutation was, "By God, you have been sentenced by the court-martial to be shot this morning; but I will be damned if I will have any of the honor of it, or any of the disgrace of it; therefore I have ordered my brigade to take up the line of march and to leave the camp, for I consider it to be cold-blooded murder, and I bid you farewell;" and he went away.

This movement of Colonel Doniphan made considerable excitement in the army, and there was considerable whisperings amongst the officers. We listened very attentively, and frequently heard it mentioned by the guard that "the damned Mormons would not be shot this time."

In a few moments the guard was relieved by a new set. One of those new guards said that "the damned Mormons would not be shot this time," for the movement of General Doniphan had frustrated the whole plan, and that the officers had called another court-martial, and had ordered us to be taken to Jackson county, and there to be executed; and in a few moments two large wagons drove up, and we were ordered to get into them; and while we were getting into them, there came up four or five men armed with guns, who drew up and snapped their guns at us, in order to kill us; some flashed in the pan, and others only snapped, but none of their guns went off. They were immediately arrested by several officers, and their guns taken from them, and the drivers drove off.

We requested General Lucas to let us go to our houses and get some clothing. In order to do this, we had to be driven up into the city. It was with much difficulty that we could get his permission to go and see our families and get some clothing; but, after considerable consultation, we were permitted to go under a strong guard of five or six men to each of us, and we were not permitted to speak to any one of our families, under the pain of death. The guard that went with me ordered my wife to get me some clothes immediately, within two minutes; and if she did not do it, I should go off without them.

I was obliged to submit to their tyrannical orders, however painful it was, with my wife and children clinging to my arms and to the skirts of my garments, and was not permitted to utter to them a word of consolation, and in a moment was hurried away from them at the point of the bayonet.

We were hurried back into the wagons and ordered into them, all in about the same space of time. In the meanwhile our father and mother and sisters had forced their way to the wagons to get permission to see us, but were forbidden to speak to us; and they [the guard] immediately drove off for Jackson county. We traveled about twelve miles that evening, and encamped for the night.

The same strong guard was kept around us, and were relieved every two hours, and we were permitted to sleep on the ground. The nights were then cold, with considerable snow on the ground; and for want of covering and clothing, we suffered extremely with the cold. That night was the commencement of a fit of sickness, from which I have not wholly recovered unto this day, in consequence of my exposure to the inclemency of the weather.

Our provision was fresh beef roasted in the fire on a stick, the army having no bread, in consequence of the want of mills to grind the grain.

In the morning, at the dawn of day, we were forced on our journey, and were exhibited to the inhabitants along the road, the same as they exhibit a caravan of elephants and camels. We were examined from head to foot by men, women and children, only I believe they did not make us open our mouths to look at our teeth. This treatment was continued incessantly until we arrived at Independence, in Jackson county.

After our arrival at Independence, we were driven all through the town for inspection, and then we were ordered into an old log house, and there kept under guard as usual, until supper, which was served up to us as we sat upon the floor, or on billets of wood, and we were compelled to stay in that house all that night and the next day.

They continued to exhibit us to the public, by letting the people come in and examine us, and then go away and give place for others, alternately, all that day and the next night. But on the morning of the following day, we were all permitted to go to the tavern to eat and to sleep; but afterward they made us pay our own expenses for board, lodging, and attendance, and for which they made a most exorbitant charge.

We remained in the tavern about two days and two nights, when an officer arrived with authority from General Clark to take us back to Richmond, Ray county, where the general had arrived with his army to await our arrival. But on the morning of our start for Richmond, we were informed, by General Wilson, that it was expected by the soldiers that we would be hung up by the necks on the road, while on the march to that place, and that it was prevented by a demand made for us by General Clark, who had the command in consequence of seniority; and that it was his prerogative to execute us himself; and he should give us up into the hands of the officer, who would take us to General Clark, and he might do with us as he pleased.

During our stay at Independence, the officers informed us that there were eight or ten horses in that place belonging to the Mormon people, which had been stolen by the soldiers, and that we might have two of them to ride upon, if we would cause them to be sent back to the owners after our arrival at Richmond.

We accepted them, and they were ridden to Richmond, and the owners came there and got them.

We started in the morning under our new officer, Colonel Price, of Keytsville, Chariton county, with several other men to guard us.

We arrived there on Friday evening, the 9th day of November, and were thrust into an old log house, with a strong guard placed over us.

After we had been there for the space of half an hour, there came in a man who was said to have some notoriety in the penitentiary, bringing in his hands a quantity of chains and padlocks. He said he was commanded by General Clark to put us in chains.

Immediately the soldiers rose up, and pointing their guns at us, placed their thumb on the cock, and their finger on the trigger; and the state's prison-keeper went to work, putting a chain around the leg of each man, and fastening it on with a padlock, until we were all chained together—seven of us.

In a few moments General Clark came in. We requested to know of him what was the cause of all this harsh and cruel treatment. He refused to give us any information at that time, but said he would in a few days; so we were compelled to continue in that situation camping on the floor, all chained together, without any chance or means to be made comfortable, having to eat our victuals as it was served up to us, using our fingers and teeth instead of knives and forks.

Whilst we were in this situation, a young man of the name of Jedediah M. Grant, brother-in-law to my brother William Smith, came to see us, and put up at the tavern where General Clark made his quarters. He happened to come in time to see General Clark make choice of his men to shoot us on Monday morning, the 12th day of November. He saw them make choice of their rifles, and load them with two balls in each; and after they had prepared their guns, General Clark saluted them by saying, "*Gentlemen, you shall have the honor of shooting the Mormon leaders on Monday morning at eight o'clock!*"

But in consequence of the influence of our friend, the inhuman general was intimidated, so that he dared not carry his murderous designs into execution, and sent a messenger immediately to Fort Leavenworth to obtain the military code of laws.

After the messenger's return the general was employed nearly a whole week examining the laws; so Monday passed away without our being shot. However, it seemed like foolishness to me that so great a man as General Clark pretended to be should have to search the military law to find out whether preachers of the Gospel, who never did military duty, could be subject to court-martial.

However, the general seemed to learn that fact after searching the military code, and came into the old log cabin where we were under guard and in chains, and told us he had concluded to deliver us over to the civil authorities as persons guilty of "treason, murder, arson, larceny, theft, and stealing." The poor deluded general did not know the difference between theft, larceny, and stealing.

Accordingly, we were handed over to the pretended civil authorities, and the next morning our chains were taken off, and we were guarded to the court-house, where there was a pretended court in session, Austin A. King being the judge, and Mr. Birch the district attorney—the two extremely and very honorable gentlemen who sat on the court-martial when we were sentenced to be shot!

Witnesses were called up and sworn at the point of the bayonet; and if they would not swear to the things they were told to do, they were threatened with instant death; and I do know positively that the evidence given in by those men whilst under duress was false.

This state of things continued twelve or fourteen days; and after that time, we were ordered by the judge to introduce some rebutting evidence—saying that, if we did not do it, we should be thrust into prison.

I could hardly understand what the judge meant, for I considered we were in prison already, and could not think of anything but the persecutions of the days of Nero, knowing that it was a religious persecution, and the court an inquisition. However, we gave him the names of forty persons who were acquainted with all the persecutions and sufferings of the people.

The judge made out a subpoena and inserted the names of those men, and caused it to be placed in the hands of Bogart, the notorious Methodist minister; and he took fifty armed soldiers and started for Far West. I saw the subpoenas given to him and his company, when they started.

In the course of a few days they returned with almost all those forty men whose names were inserted in the subpoenas, and thrust them into jail, and we were not permitted to bring one of them before the court. But the judge turned upon us with an air of indignation and said, "Gentlemen, you must get your witnesses, or you shall be committed to jail immediately; for we are not going to hold the court open on expense much longer for you anyhow."

We felt very much distressed and oppressed at that time. Colonel Wight said, "What shall we do? Our witnesses are all thrust into prison, and probably will be; and we have no power to do anything. Of course, we must submit to this tyranny and oppression: we cannot help ourselves."

Several others made similar expressions in the agony of their souls; but my brother Joseph did not say anything, he being sick at that time with the toothache and pain in his face, in consequence of a severe cold brought on by being exposed to the severity of the weather.

However, it was considered best by General Doniphan and lawyer Rees that we should try to get some witnesses before the pretended court.

Accordingly, I gave the names of about twenty other persons. The Judge inserted them in a subpœna, and caused it to be placed into the hands of Bogart, the Methodist priest; and he again started off with his fifty soldiers to take those men prisoners, as he had done the forty others.

The Judge sat and laughed at the good opportunity of getting the names, that they might the more easily capture them, and so bring them down to be thrust into prison, in order to prevent us from getting the truth before the pretended court, of which he was the chief inquisitor or conspirator. Bogart returned from his second expedition with one witness only, whom he also thrust into prison.

The people at Far West had learned the intrigue, and had left the state, having been made acquainted with the treatment of the former witnesses.

But we, on learning that we could not obtain witnesses, whilst privately consulting with each other what we should do, discovered a Mr. Allen standing by the window on the outside of the house. We beckoned to him as though we would have him come in. He immediately came in.

At that time Judge King retorted upon us again, saying, "Gentlemen, are you not going to introduce some witnesses?"—also saying it was the last day he should hold court open for us; and that if we did not rebutt the testimony that had been given against us, he should have to commit us to jail.

I had then got Mr. Allen into the house and before the court (so called). I told the Judge we had one witness, if he would be so good as to put him under oath. He seemed unwilling to do so; but after a few moments consultation, the State's Attorney arose and said he should object to that witness being sworn, and that he should object to that witness giving in his evidence at all, stating that this was not a court to try the case, but only a court of investigation on the part of the state.

Upon this, General Doniphan arose and said, "He would be —— —— if the witness should not be sworn, and that it was a damned shame that these defendants should be treated in this manner,—that they could not be permitted to get one witness before the court, whilst all their witnesses, even forty at a time, have been taken by force of arms and thrust into that damned 'bull pen,' in order to prevent them from giving their testimony."

After Doniphan sat down, the Judge permitted the witness to be sworn and enter upon his testimony, but as soon as he began to speak, a man by the name of Cook, who was a brother-in-law to priest Bogart, the Methodist, and who was a lieutenant, [in the state militia] and whose duty at that time was to superintend the guard, stepped in before the pretended court, and took him by the nape of his neck and jammed his head down under the pole, or log of wood, that was around the place where the inquisition was sitting to keep the bystanders from intruding upon the majesty of the inquisitors, and jammed him along to the door, and kicked him out of doors. He instantly turned to some soldiers who were standing by him, and said to them, "Go and shoot him, damn him; shoot him, damn him."

The soldiers ran after the man to shoot him. He fled for his life, and with great difficulty made his escape. The pretended court immediately arose, and we were ordered to be carried to Liberty, Clay county, and there to be thrust into jail. We endeavored to find out for what cause; but all we could learn was, that it was because we were "Mormons."

The next morning a large wagon drove up to the door, and a blacksmith came into the house with some chains and handcuffs. He said his orders were from the Judge to handcuff us and chain us together. He informed us that the Judge had made out a mittimus and sentenced us to jail for treason. He also said the Judge had done this that we might not get bail. He also said the Judge declared his intention to keep us in jail until all the "Mormons" were driven out of the state. He also said that the Judge had further declared that if he let us out before the "Mormons" had left the state, we would not let them leave, and there would be another damned fuss kicked up. I also heard the Judge say, whilst he was sitting in his pretended court, that there was no law for us, nor for the "Mormons" in the state of Missouri; that he had sworn to see them exterminated and to see the Governor's order executed to the very letter; and that he would do so. However, the blacksmith proceeded and put the irons upon us, and we were ordered into the wagon, and they drove off for Clay county. As we journeyed along on the road, we were exhibited to the inhabitants, and this course was adopted all the way, thus making a public exhibition of us, until we arrived at Liberty, Clay county.

There we were thrust into prison again, and locked up, and were held there in close confinement for the space of six months; and our place of lodging [bed] was the square side of a hewed white oak log, and our food was anything but good and decent. Poison was administered to us three or four times. The effect it had upon our system was, that it vomited us almost to death; and then we would lie some two or three days in a torpid, stupid state, not even caring or wishing for life,—the poison being administered in too large doses, or it would inevitably have proved fatal, had not the power of Jehovah interposed in our behalf, to save us from their wicked purpose.

We were also subjected to the necessity of eating human flesh for the space of five days or go without food, except a little coffee or a little corn-bread. The latter I chose in preference to the former. We none of us partook of the flesh, except Lyman Wight. We also heard the guard which was placed over us making sport of us, saying they had fed us on "Mormon" beef. I have described the appearance of this flesh to several experienced physicians and they have decided that it was human flesh. We learned afterwards, by one of the guard, that it was supposed that that act of savage cannibalism in feeding us with human flesh would be considered a popular deed of notoriety: but the people, on learning that it would not take, tried to keep it secret; but the fact was noised abroad before they took that precaution.

Whilst we were incarcerated in prison we petitioned the Supreme Court of the state of Missouri for [a writ of] habeas corpus twice but were refused both times by Judge Reynolds, who is now [1843] the Governor of that state. We also petitioned one of the county Judges for a writ of habeas corpus, which was granted in about three weeks afterwards, but were not permitted to have any trial. We were only taken out of jail and kept out for a few hours, and then remanded back again.

In the course of three or four days after that time, Judge Turnham came into the jail in the evening, and said he had permitted Mr. Rigdon to get bail, but said he had to do it in the night, and had also to get away in the night and unknown to any of the citizens, or they would kill him; for they had sworn to kill him, if they could find him. And as to the rest of us, he dared not let us go, for fear of his own life as well as ours. He said it was damned hard to be confined under such circumstances, for he knew we were innocent men; and he said *the people also knew it*; and that it was only a persecution, and treachery, and the scenes of Jackson county acted over again, for fear that we should become too numerous in that upper country. He said that the plan was concocted from the governor down to the lowest judge and that damned Baptist priest, Riley, who was riding into town every day to watch the people, stirring up the minds of the people against us all he could, exciting them and stirring up their religious prejudices against us, for fear they would let us go. Mr. Rigdon, however, got bail and made his escape into Illinois.

The jailer, Samuel Tillery, Esq., told us also that the whole plan was concocted by the governor down to the lowest judge in that upper country early in the previous spring, and that the plan was more fully carried out at the time that General Atchison went down to Jefferson city with Generals Wilson, Lucas, and Gillium, the self-styled Delaware Chief. This was sometime in the month of September, when the mob were collected at De Witt, in Carroll county. He also told us that the governor was now ashamed enough of the whole transaction, and would be glad to set us at liberty, if he dared do it. "But," said he, "you need not be concerned, for the governor has laid a plan for your release." He also said that Squire Birch, the state's attorney, was appointed to be circuit judge on the circuit passing through Daviess county, and that he (Birch) was instructed to fix the papers, so that we should be sure to be clear from any incumbrance in a very short time.

Some time in April we were taken to Daviess county, as they said, to have a trial. But when we arrived at that place, instead of finding a court or jury, we found another inquisition; and Birch, who was the district attorney, the same man who had been one of the court-martial when we were sentenced to death, was now the circuit judge of that pretended court; and the grand jury that were empannelled were all at the massacre at Haun's Mills and lively actors in that awful, solemn, disgraceful, cool-blooded murder; and all the pretense they made of excuse was, they had done it because the governor ordered them to do it.

The same men sat as a jury in the day time, and were placed over us as a guard in the night time. They tantalized us and boasted of their great achievments at Haun's Mills and at other places, telling us how many houses they had burned, and how many sheep, cattle, and hogs they had driven off belonging to the "Mormons," and how many rapes they had committed, and what squealing and kicking there was among the d—— b——s, saying that they lashed one woman upon one of the damned "Mormon" meeting benches, tying her hands and her feet fast, and sixteen of them abused her as much as they had a mind to, and then left her bound and exposed in that distressed condition. These fiends of the lower regions boasted of these acts of barbarity, and tantalized our feelings with them for ten days. We had heard of these acts of cruelty previous to this time, but we were slow to believe that such acts had been perpetrated. The lady who was the subject of this brutality did not recover her health to be able to help herself for more than three months afterwards.

This grand jury constantly celebrated their achievements with grog and glass in hand, like the Indian warriors at their war dances, singing and telling each other of their exploits in murdering the "Mormons," in plundering their houses and carrying off their property. At the end of every song they would bring in the chorus, "G— d—, G— d—, G — d—, Jesus Christ, G— d— the Presbyterians, G— d— the Baptists, G— d— the Methodists," reitering one sect after another in the same manner, until they came to the "Mormons." To them it was, G— d— the G— d— Mormons, we have sent them to hell." Then they would slap their hands and shout, Hosanna! Hosanna! Glory to God! and fall down on their backs and kick with their feet a few moments. Then they would pretend to have swooned away into a glorious trance, in order to imitate some of the transactions at camp meetings. Then they would pretend to come out of the trance, and would shout and again slap their hands and jump up, while one would take a bottle of whisky and a tumbler, and turn it out full of whisky, and pour down each other's necks, crying, "Damn it, take it; you must take it!" And if anyone refused to drink the whisky, others would clinch him and hold him, whilst another poured it down his neck; and what did not go down the inside went down the outside. This is a part of the farce acted out by the grand jury of Daviess county, whilst they stood over us as guards for ten nights successively. And all this in the presence of the *great Judge Birch*, who had previously said, in our hearing, that there was no law for the "Mormons" in the state of Missouri. His brother was there acting as district attorney in that circuit, and, if anything, was a greater ruffian than the judge.

After all their ten days of drunkenness, we were informed that we were indicted for "*treason, murder, arson, larceny, theft, and stealing.*" We asked for a change of venue from that county to Marion county; they would not grant it; but they gave us a change of venue from Daviess to Boone county, and a mittimus was made out by Judge Birch, without date, name, or place.

They fitted us out with a two-horse wagon, and horses, and four men, besides the sheriff, to be our guard. There were five of us. We started from Gallatin in the afternoon, the sun about two hours high, and went as far as Diahman that evening and stayed till morning. There we bought two horses of the guard, and paid for one of them in clothing, which we had with us; and for the other we gave our note.

We went down that day as far as Judge Morin's—a distance of some four or five miles. There we stayed until the next morning, when we started on our journey to Boone county, and traveled on the road about twenty miles distance. There we bought a jug of whisky, with which we treated the company; and while there the sheriff showed us the mittimus before referred to, without date or signature, and said that Judge Birch told him never to carry us to Boone county, and never to show the mittimus; and, said he, I shall take a good drink of grog and go to bed, and you may do as you have a mind to.

Three others of the guard drank pretty freely of whisky, sweetened with honey. They also went to bed, and were soon asleep, and the other guard went along with us, and helped to saddle the horses.

Two of us mounted the horses, and the other three started on foot, and we took our change of venue for the state of Illinois, and in the course of nine or ten days arrived safe at Quincy, Adams county, where we found our families in a state of poverty, although in good health, they having been driven out of the state previously by the murderous militia, under the exterminating order of the executive of Missouri; and now [1843] the people of that state, a portion of them, would be glad to make the people of this state [Illinois] believe that my brother Joseph had committed treason, for the purpose of keeping up their murderous and hellish persecution; and they seem to be unrelenting and thirsting for the blood of innocence; for I do know most positively that my brother Joseph has not committed treason, nor violated one solitary item of law or rule in the state of Missouri.

But I do know that the "Mormon" people, *en masse*, were driven out of that state, after being robbed of all they had; and they barely escaped with their lives, as also my brother Joseph, who barely escaped with his life. His family also were robbed of all they had, and barely escaped with the skin of their teeth, and all this in consequence of the exterminating order of Governor Boggs, the same being sanctioned by the legislature of the state.

And I do know, so does this court, and every rational man who is acquainted with the circumstances, and every man who shall hereafter become acquainted with the particulars thereof, will know that Governor Boggs and Generals Clark, Lucas, Wilson, and Gillium, also Austin A. King, have committed treason upon the citizens of Missouri, and did violate the Constitution of the United States, and also the constitution and laws of the state of Missouri, and did exile and expel, at the point of the bayonet, some twelve or fourteen thousand inhabitants from the state, and did murder a large number of men, women and children in cold blood, and in the most horrid and cruel manner possible; and the whole of it was caused by religious bigotry and persecution, because the "Mormons" dared to worship Almighty God according to the dictates of their own consciences, and agreeable to His divine will as revealed in the scriptures of eternal truth, and had turned away from following the vain traditions of their fathers, and would not worship according to the dogmas and commandments of those men who preach for hire and divine for money, and teach for doctrine the precepts of men; the Saints expecting that the Constitution of the United States would have protected them therein.

But notwithstanding the "Mormon" people had purchased upwards of *two hundred thousand dollars' worth of land*, most of which was entered and paid for at the land office of the United States, in the state of Missouri; and although the President of the United States has been made acquainted with these facts and the particulars of our persecutions and oppressions, by petition to him and to Congress, yet they have not even attempted to restore the "Mormons" to their rights, or given any assurance that we may hereafter expect redress from them. And I do also know most positively and assuredly that my brother Joseph Smith, Sen., has not been in the state of Missouri since the spring of the year 1839. And further this deponent saith not.

[Signed] HYRUM SMITH.

II

TESTIMONY OF PARLEY P. PRATT.

Parley P. Pratt, sworn, says that he fully concurs in the testimony of the preceding witness, so far as he is acquainted with the same; and that Joseph Smith has not been known as Joseph Smith, Jun., for the time stated by Hyrum Smith. He was an eye-witness of most of the scenes testified to by said Hyrum Smith, during the persecutions of our people in Missouri. That during the latter part of summer and fall of the year 1838, there were large bodies of the mob assembled in various places for the avowed object of driving, robbing, plundering, killing, and exterminating the "Mormons," and they actually committed many murders and other depredations, as related by the preceding witness.

The Governor was frequently petitioned, as also the other authorities, for redress and protection. At length, Austin A. King, the Judge of the Circuit court of the Fifth Judicial District, ordered out somewhere near a thousand men, for the avowed purpose of quelling the mob and protecting the "Mormons." These being under arms for several weeks, did in some measure prevent the mob's proceedings for some time. After which, Judge King* withdrew the force, refusing to put the State to further expense for our protection without orders from the Governor.

The mobs then again collected in great numbers, in Carroll, Daviess, and Caldwell counties, and expressed their determination to drive the "Mormons" from the State or kill them. They did actually drive them from De Witt, firing upon some, and taking other prisoners.

They turned a man by the name of Smith Humphrey and family out of doors, when sick, and plundered his house and burned it before his eyes. They also plundered the citizens generally, taking their lands, houses, and property.

Those whose lives were spared, precipitately fled to Far West in the utmost distress and consternation. Some of them actually died on the way, through exposure, suffering and destitution. Other parties of the mob were plundering and burning houses in Daviess county, and another party of the mob were ravaging the south part of Caldwell county in a similar manner.

The Governor was again and again petitioned for redress and protection, but utterly refused to render us any assistance whatever. Under these painful and distressing circumstances, we had the advice of Generals Atchison, Doniphan and Parks to call out the militia of Caldwell and Daviess counties, which was mostly composed of "Mormons" and to make a general defense.

The presiding Judge of Caldwell county, Elias Higbee, gave orders to the sheriff of said county to call out the militia. They were called out under the command of Colonel Hinkle, who held a commission from the Governor, and was the highest military officer in the county. This force effectually dispersed the mob in several places, and a portion of

* For explanation of how it was that the militia was under direction of the Judge, a civil officer, see testimony of Sidney Rigdon.

them were so organized in the city of Far West, that they could assemble themselves upon the shortest notice, and were frequently ordered to assemble in the public square of said city, in cases of emergency.

These proceedings against the mob being misrepresented by designing men, both to the Governor and other authorities and people of the State, caused great excitement against the "Mormons." Many tried to have it understood that the "Mormons" were in open rebellion, and making war upon the State.

With these pretenses, Governor Boggs issued the following:—

Exterminating Order.

HEADQUARTERS OF THE MILITIA,
CITY OF JEFFERSON, October 27, 1838.

Gen. John B. Clark.

SIR:—Since the order of the morning to you, directing you to come with 400 mounted men to be raised within your division, I have received, by Amos Rees, Esq., of Ray county, and Wiley C. Williams, Esq., one of my aides, information of the most appalling character, which entirely changes the face of things, and places the "Mormons" in the attitude of an open and avowed defiance of the laws, and of having made war upon the people of this State.

Your orders are, therefore, to hasten your operations with all possible speed. The "Mormons" must be treated as enemies, and must be exterminated or driven from the State, if necessary, for the public peace.

Their outrages are beyond all descriptions. If you can increase your force, you are authorized to do so to any extent you may consider necessary. I have just issued orders to Major-General Willock, of Marion county, to raise 500 men, and to march them to the northern part of Daviess [county], and there unite with General Doniphan, of Clay, who has been ordered with 500 men to proceed to the same point for the purpose of intercepting the retreat of the "Mormons" to the north. They have been directed to communicate with you by express. You can also communicate with them, if you find it necessary.

Instead, therefore, of proceeding as at first directed, to reinstate the citizens of Daviess, in their homes, you will proceed immediately to Richmond, and there operate against the "Mormons."

Brigadier General Parks, of Ray, has been ordered to have 400 of his brigade in readiness to join you at Richmond. The whole force will be placed under your command.

I am very respectfully your ob't Serv't,
L. W. BOGGS,
Commander-in-chief.*

* The above now celebrated "*Exterminating order*" is copied from the collection of Documents published by order of the "General Assembly" of Missouri (the state legislature), 1841.

In the meantime Major-General Lucas and Brigadier-General Wilson, both of Jackson county, (who had, five years previously, assisted in driving about 1,200 "Mormon" citizens from that county, besides burning 203 houses, and assisted in murdering several, and plundering the rest), raised forces to the amount of several thousand men, and appeared before the city of Far West in battle array.

A few of the militia then paraded in front of the city, which caused the cowardly assailants to come to a halt at about a mile distant, in full view of the town.

A messenger arrived from them and demanded three persons before they massacred the rest and laid the town in ashes. The names of the persons demanded were Adam Lightner, John Clemenson, and his wife. They gave no information who this army were, nor by what authority they came; neither had we at that time any knowledge of the governor's order, nor any of these movements, the mail having been designedly stopped by our enemies for three weeks previously. We had supposed, on their first appearance, that they were friendly troops sent for our protection; but on receiving this alarming information of their wicked intentions, we were much surprised, and sent a messenger with a white flag to inquire of them who they were, and what they wanted of us, and by whose authority they came.

This flag was fired upon by Captain Bogart, the Methodist priest, who afterwards told me the same with his own mouth. After several attempts, however, we got an interview, by which we learned who they were, and that they pretended to have been sent by the governor to exterminate our people.

Upon learning this fact no resistance was offered to their will or wishes. They demanded the arms of the militia, and forcibly took them away. They requested that Mr. Joseph Smith and other leaders of the Church should come into their camp for consultation, giving them a sacred promise of protection and safe return. Accordingly, Messrs. Joseph Smith, Sidney Rigdon, Lyman Wight, George W. Robinson, and myself started in company with Colonel Hinkle to their camp when we were soon abruptly met by General Lucas with several hundred of his soldiers, in a hostile manner, who immediately surrounded us, and set up the most hideous yells that might have been supposed to have proceeded from the mouths of demons, and marched us as prisoners within their lines.

There we were detained for two days and nights, and had to sleep on the ground, in the cold month of November, in the midst of rain and mud, and were continually surrounded with a strong guard, whose mouths were filled with cursing and bitterness, blackguardism and blasphemy—who offered us every abuse and insult in their power, both by night and day; and many individuals of the army cocked their rifles and, taking deadly aim at our heads, swore they would shoot us.

While under these circumstances, our ears were continually shocked with the relation of the horrid deeds they had committed and which they boasted of. They related the circumstance in detail of having, the previous day, disarmed a certain man in his own house, and took him prisoner, and afterwards *beat out his brains with his own gun*, in presence of their officers. They told of other individuals lying here and there in the brush, whom they had shot down without resistance, and who were lying unburied for the hogs to feed upon.

They also named one or two individual females of our society, whom they had forcibly bound, and twenty or thirty of them, one after another, committed rape upon them. One of these females was a daughter of a respectable family with whom I have been long acquainted, and with whom I have since conversed and learned that it was truly the case. Delicacy at present forbids my mentioning the names. I also heard several of the soldiers acknowledge and boast of having stolen money in one place, clothing and bedding in another, and horses in another, whilst corn, pork, and beef were taken by the whole army to support the men and horses; and in many cases cattle, hogs, and sheep were shot down, and only a small portion of them used—the rest left to waste. Of these crimes, of which the soldiers boasted, the general officers freely conversed and corroborated the same. And even General Doniphan, who professed to be opposed to such proceedings, acknowledged the truth of them, and gave us several particulars in detail.

I believe the name of the man whose brains they knocked out was Carey, Another individual had his money chest broken open and several hundred dollars in specie taken out. He was the same Smith Humphrey whose house the mob burned at De Witt.

After the "Mormons" were all disarmed, General Lucas gave a compulsory order for men, women, and children to leave the state forthwith, without any exceptions, counting it a mercy to spare their lives on these conditions. Whilst these things were proceeding, instead of releasing us from confinement, Hyrum Smith and Amasa Lyman were forcibly added to our number as prisoners; and under a large military escort, commanded by General Wilson before mentioned, we were all marched to Jackson county, a distance of between fifty and sixty miles, leaving our families and our friends at the mob's mercy, in a destitute condition, to prepare for a journey of more than two hundred miles, at the approach of winter, without our protection, and every moment exposed to robbery, ravishment, and other insults, their personal property robbed and their houses and lands already wrested from them.

We were exhibited like a caravan of wild animals on the way and in the streets of Independence, and were also kept prisoners for a show for several days.

In the meantime, General Clark had been sent by Governor Boggs with an additional force of 6,000 men from the lower country, to join General Lucas in his operations against the "Mormons." He soon arrived before Far West with his army, and confirmed all Lucas had done, and highly commended them for their virtue, forbearance, and other deeds in *bringing about so peaceable and amicable an adjustment of affairs.* He kept up the same scene of ravage, plunder, ravishment, and depredation, for the support and enrichment of his army, even burning the houses and fences for fuel.

He also insisted that every man, woman, and child of the "Mormon" society should leave the state, except such as he detained as prisoners, stating that *the governor had sent him to exterminate them*, but that *he* would, as a *mercy*, *spare* their *lives*, and gave them until the first of April following to get out of the state.

He also compelled them, at the point of the bayonet, to sign a deed of trust of all their real estate, to defray the expenses of what *he* called "*The Mormon War.*"

After arranging all these matters to *his* satisfaction, he returned to Richmond, thirty miles distant, taking about sixty men, heads of families, with him, and marching them through a severe snowstorm on foot, as prisoners, leaving their families in a perishing condition.

Having established his headquarters at Richmond, Ray county, he sent to General Lucas and demanded us to be given up to him. We were accordingly transported some thirty or forty miles, delivered over to him, and put in close confinement in chains, under a strong guard.

At length we obtained an interview with him, and inquired why we were detained as prisoners. I said to him, "Sir, we have now been prisoners, under the most aggravating circumstances, for two or three weeks, during which time we have received no information as to why we are prisoners, or for what object, and no writ has been served upon us. We are not detained by the civil law; and as ministers of the Gospel in time of peace, *who never bear arms*, we cannot be considered prisoners of war, especially as there has been no war; and from present appearances, we can hardly be considered prisoners of hope. Why, then, these bonds?"

Said he, "You were taken to be tried." "Tried by what authority?" said I. "By court-martial," replied he. "By court-martial?" said I. "Yes," said he. "How," said I, "can men who are not military men, but ministers of the Gospel, be tried by court-martial in this country, where every man has a right to be tried by a jury?" He replied, it was according to the treaty with General Lucas, on the part of the state of Missouri, and Colonel Hinkle, the commanding officer of the fortress of Far West, on the part of the "Mormons," and in accordance with the governor's order. "And," said he, "I approve of all that Lucas has done, and am determined to see it fulfilled." Said I, "Colonel Hinkle was but a colonel of the Caldwell county militia, and commissioned by the governor, and the 'Mormons' had no fortress, but were, in common with others, citizens of Missouri; and therefore we recognize no authority in Colonel Hinkle to sell our liberties or make treaties for us."

Several days afterwards, General Clark again entered our prison, and said he had concluded to deliver us over to the civil authorities. Accordingly, we were soon brought before Austin A. King, judge of the Fifth Judicial Circuit, where an examination was commenced, and witnesses sworn, at the point of the bayonet, and threatened on pain of death, if they did not swear to that which would suit the court.

During this examination, I heard Judge King ask one of the witnesses, who was a "Mormon," if he and his friends intended to live on their lands any longer than April, and to plant crops? Witness replied, "Why not?" The judge replied, "If you once think to plant crops or to occupy your lands any longer than the first of April, the citizens will be upon you; they will kill you every one—men, women and children, and leave you to manure the ground without a burial. They have been mercifully withheld from doing this on the present occasion, but will not be restrained for the future."

On examining a "Mormon" witness, for the purpose of substantiating the charge of treason against Mr. Joseph Smith, he questioned him concerning our religious faith:—1st. Do the Mormons send missionaries to foreign nations? The witness answered in the affirmative. 2nd. Do the Mormons believe in a certain passage in the Book of Daniel (naming the passage) which reads as follows:—"And the kingdom and dominion, and the greatness of the kingdom under the whole heaven, shall be given to the people of the Saints of the Most High, whose kingdom is an everlasting kingdom, and all dominions shall serve and obey him?" (Dan. 7: 27.) On being answered in the affirmative, the judge ordered the scribe to put it down as a strong point for treason; but this was *too* much for even a Missouri lawyer to bear. He remonstrated against such a course of procedure, but in vain. Said he, "Judge, you had better make the Bible treason."

After an examination of this kind for many days, some were set at liberty, others [were] admitted to bail, and themselves and [those who went their] bail [were] expelled from the state forthwith, with the rest of the "Mormon" citizens, and Joseph Smith, Hyrum Smith, Sidney

Rigdon, Lyman Wight, and others, were committed to the Clay county jail for further trial. Two or three others and myself were put into the jail at Ray county for the same purpose.

The "Mormon" people now began to leave the state, agreeably to the exterminating order of Governor Boggs. Ten or twelve thousand left the state during the winter, and fled to the state of Illinois.

A small number of the widows and the poor, together with my family and some of the friends of the other prisoners, still lingered in Far West, when a small band of armed men entered the town and committed many depredations and threatened life; and swore that if my wife and children, and others whom they named, were not out of the state in so many days, they would kill them, as the time now drew near for the completion of the exterminating order of Governor Boggs.

Accordingly, my wife and children and others left the state as best they could, wandered to the state of Illinois, there to get a living among strangers, without a husband, father or protector. Myself and party still remained in prison, after all the other "Mormons" had left the state; and even Mr. Smith and his party had escaped.

In June, by change of venue, we were removed from Ray county to Columbia, Boone county, upwards of one hundred miles towards the state of Illinois; and by our request a special court was called for final trial. But notwithstanding we were removed more than one hundred miles from the scenes of the depredations of the mob, yet such was the fact, that neither our friends nor witnesses dare come into that state to attend our trial, as they had been banished from the state by the governor's order of extermination, executed to the very letter by the principal officers of the state, civil and military.

On these grounds, and having had all these opportunities to know, I testify that neither Mr. Smith nor any other "Mormon" has the least prospect for justice, or to receive a fair and impartial trial in the state of Missouri.

If tried at all, they must be tried by authorities who have trampled all law under their feet, and who have assisted in committing murder, robbery, treason, arson, rape, burglary and felony, and who have made a law of banishment, contrary to the laws of all nations, and executed this barbarous law with the utmost rigor and severity.

Therefore, Mr. Smith, and the "Mormons" generally, having suffered without regard to law, having been expelled from the state, Missouri has no further claims whatever upon any of them.

I furthermore testify that the authorities of other states who would assist Missouri to wreak further vengeance upon any individual of the persecuted "Mormons," are either ignorantly or willfully aiding and abetting in all these crimes.

Cross-examined he stated that he was very intimate with Mr. Smith all the time he resided in the state of Missouri, and was with him almost daily; and that he knows positively that Mr. Smith held no office, either civil or military, either real or pretended, in that state; and that he never bore arms or did military duty, not even in self-defense; but that he was a peaceable, law-abiding and faithful citizen, and a preacher of the Gospel, and exhorted all the citizens to be peaceable, long-suffering and slow to act even in self-defense.

He further stated that there was no fortress in Far West, but a temporary fence made of rails, house logs, floor planks, wagons, carts, etc., hastily thrown together, after being told by General Lucas that they were to be massacred the following morning, and the town burnt to ashes, without giving any information by what authority. And he further states that he only escaped himself from that state by walking out of the jail when the door was open to put in food, and came out in obedience to the governor's order of banishment, and to fulfill the same.

PARLEY P. PRATT.

III.

TESTIMONY OF GEORGE W. PITKIN.

George W. Pitkin sworn. Says that he concurs with the preceding witnesses, Hyrum Smith and Parley P. Pratt, in all the facts with which he is acquainted; that in the summer of 1838 he was elected Sheriff of the county of Caldwell and State of Missouri. That in the fall of the same year, while the county was threatened and infested with mobs, he received an order from Judge Higbee, the presiding Judge of said county, to call out the Militia, and he executed the same.

The said order was presented by Joseph Smith, Sen., who showed the witness a letter from General Atchison, giving such advice as was necessary for the protection of the citizens of said county. Reports of the mobs destroying property were daily received. Has no knowledge that Joseph Smith was concerned in organizing or commanding said Militia in any capacity whatever.

About this time he received information that about forty or fifty "Yauger rifles" and a quantity of ammunition were being conveyed through Caldwell to Daviess county, for the use of the mob, upon which he deputized William Allred to go with a company of men and intercept them, if possible. He did so, and brought the said arms and ammunition into Far West, which were afterwards delivered up to the order of Austin A. King, Judge of the Fifth, Circuit in Missouri.

It was generally understood at that time that said arms had been stolen by Neil Gillum and his company of volunteers, who had been upon a six months' tour of service in the war between the United States and the Florida Indians. They were supposed to have been taken from the Fort at Tampa Bay, and brought to Richmond, Clay county, and that Captain Pollard or some other person loaned them to the mob.

He further says that whilst in office as Sheriff, he was forcibly and illegally compelled by Lieutenant Cook, the son-in-law or brother-in-law of Bogart, the Methodist priest, to start for Richmond; and when he demanded of him by what authority he acted, he was shown a bowie-knife and a brace of pistols; and when he asked what they wanted of him, he said they would let him know when he got to Richmond. Many of the citizens of Caldwell county were taken in the same manner, without any legal process whatever, and thrust into prison.

GEORGE W. PITKIN.

IV.

TESTIMONY OF BRIGHAM YOUNG.

Brigham Young sworn. Says that so far as he was acquainted with the facts stated by the previous witnesses, he concurs with them, and that he accompanied Mr. Joseph Smith, Sen., into the State of Missouri, and arrived at Far West on the 14th day of March, 1838, and was neighbor to Mr. Smith until he was taken by Governor Boggs' Militia a prisoner of war, as they said, and that he was knowing to his character whilst in the State of Missouri; and that he, Mr. Smith, was in no way connected with the Militia of that state, neither did he bear arms at all, nor give advice, but was a peaceable, law-abiding, good citizen, and a true Republican in every sense of the word.

He was with Mr. Smith a great share of the time, until driven out of Missouri by an armed force, under the exterminating order of Governor Boggs.

He heard the most of Mr. Smith's public addresses, and never did he hear him give advice or encourage anything contrary to the laws of the State of Missouri; but, to the contrary, always instructing the people to be peaceable, quiet, and law-abiding; and if necessity should compel them to withstand their enemies, by whom they were daily threatened in mobs at various points, that they, the "Mormons," should attend to their business strictly, and not regard reports; and if the mob did come upon them, to contend with them by the strong arm of the law; and if that should fail, our only relief would be self-defense; and be sure and act only upon the defensive. And there were no operations against the mob by the Militia of Caldwell county, only by the advice of Generals Atchison, Doniphan, and Parks.

At the time that the army came in sight of Far West, he observed their approach, and thought some of the Militia of the state had come to the relief of the citizens; but, to his great surprise, he found that they were come to strengthen the hands of the mobs that were around and which immediately joined the army.

A part of these mobs were painted like Indians; and Gillum, their leader, was also painted in a similar manner, and styled himself the "Delaware Chief;" and afterwards he and the rest of the mob claimed and obtained pay as Militia from the state for all the time they were engaged as a mob, as will be seen by reference to the acts of the Legislature.

That there were "Mormon" citizens wounded and murdered by the army under the command of General Lucas; and he verily believes that several women were ravished to death by the soldiery of Lucas and Clark.

He also stated that he saw Joseph Smith, Sidney Rigdon, Parley P. Pratt, Lyman Wight, and George W. Robinson delivered up by Colonel Hinkle to General Lucas, but expected that they would have returned to the city that evening or the next morning, according to agreement, and the pledge of the sacred honor of the officers that they should be allowed to do so; but they did not return at all.

The next morning, General Lucas demanded and took away the arms of the Militia of Caldwell county, (which arms have never been returned), assuring them that they should be protected. But as soon as they obtained possession of the arms, they commenced their ravages by plundering the citizens of their bedding, clothing, money, wearing apparel, and everything of value they could lay their hands upon; and also attempting to violate the chastity of the women in sight of their husbands and friends, under the pretence of hunting for prisoners and arms.

The soldiers shot down our oxen, cows, hogs, and fowls at our own doors, taking part away and leaving the rest to rot in the streets. The soldiers also turned their horses into our fields of corn.

Here the witness was shown General Clark's speech, which is as follows, viz.:—

"Gentlemen,—You, whose names are not attached to this list of names, will now have the privilege of going to your fields, and of providing corn, wood, etc., for your families.

"Those that are now taken will go from this to prison, be tried, and receive the due demerit of their crimes; but you (except such as charges may hereafter be preferred against,) are at liberty as soon as the troops are removed that now guard the place, which I shall cause to be done immediately.

"It now devolves upon you to fulfill the treaty that you have entered into, the leading items of which I shall now lay before you.

"The first requires that your leading men be given up to be tried according to law. This you have complied with. The second is, that you deliver up your arms. This has also been attended to. The third stipulation is, that you sign over your properties to defray the expenses that have been incurred on your account. This you have also done.

"Another article yet remains for you to comply with, and that is, that you leave the State forthwith. And whatever may be your feelings concerning this, or whatever your innocence is, it is nothing to me.

"General Lucas (whose military rank is equal with mine,) has made this treaty with you. I approve of it. I should have done the same, had I been here, and am therefore determined to see it executed.

"The character of this state has suffered almost beyond redemption, from the character, conduct, and influence that you have exerted; and we deem it an act of justice to restore her character by every proper means.

"The order of the Governor to me was, that you should be exterminated, and not allowed to remain in the state. And had not your leaders been given up and the terms of the treaty complied with before this time, your families would have been *destroyed* and your houses in *ashes.*

"There is a discretionary power vested in my hands, which, considering your circumstances, I shall exercise for a season. You are indebted to me for this clemency.

"I do not say that you shall go now, but you must not think of staying here another season, or of putting in crops; for the moment you do this, the citizens will be upon you. And if I am called here again, in case of non-compliance with the treaty made, do not think that I shall act as I have done now.

"You need not expect any mercy, but *extermination;* for I am determined the Governor's order shall be executed.

"As for your leaders, do not think—do not imagine for a moment—do not let it enter into your minds that they will be delivered and restored to you again; for their *fate* is fixed—the DIE is cast—their doom is *sealed.*

"I am sorry, gentlemen, to see so many apparently intelligent men found in the situation that you are; and oh! if I could invoke that great Spirit of the unknown God to rest upon and deliver you from that awful chain of superstition and liberate you from those fetters of fanaticism with which you are bound—that you no longer do homage to a man! I would advise you to scatter abroad, and never again organize yourselves with Bishops, Priests, etc., lest you excite the jealousies of the people and subject yourselves to the same calamities that have now come upon you.

"You have always been the aggressors. You have brought upon yourselves these difficulties by being disaffected, and not being subject to rule. And my advice is, that you become as other citizens, lest by a recurrence of these events you bring upon yourselves irretrievable ruin."

When asked by the Court if it was correct, and after reading it, he [Brigham Young] replied:—

Yes, as far as it goes; for, continued he, I was present when that speech was delivered, and when fifty-seven of our brethren were betrayed into the hands of our enemies, as prisoners, which was done at the instigation of our open and avowed enemies, such as William E. M'Lellin and others, and the treachery of Colonel Hinkle. In addition to the speech referred to, General Clark said that we must not be seen as many as five together. If you are, said he, the citizens will be upon you and destroy you, but flee immediately out of the state. There was no alternative for them but to flee; that they need not expect any redress, for there was none for them.

With respect to the treaty, the witness further says that there never was any treaty proposed or entered into on the part of the "Mormons," or even thought of. As to the leaders being given up, there was no such contract entered into or thought of by the "Mormons," or any one called a "Mormon," except by Colonel Hinkle. And with respect to the trial of the prisoners at Richmond, I do not consider that tribunal a legal court, but an inquisition, for the following reasons: That Mr. Smith was not allowed any evidence whatever on his part; for the conduct of the Court, as well as the Judge's own words, affirmed that there was no law for "Mormons" in the state of Missouri. He also knew that when Mr. Smith left the state of Missouri, he did not flee from justice, for the plain reason that the officers and the people manifested by their works and their words that there was *no law nor justice* for the people called "Mormons." And further, he knows that Mr. Smith has ever been a strong advocate for the laws and constitutions of his country, and that there was no act of his life while in the state of Missouri, according to his knowledge, that could be implied or construed in any way whatever to prove him a fugitive from justice, or that he has been guilty of "murder, treason, arson, larceny, theft, and stealing,"—the crimes he was charged with by General Clark, when he delivered him over to the civil authorities; and he supposes that the learned General did not know but that there was a difference between "larceny, theft, and stealing."

The witness also says that they compelled the brethren to sign away their property by executing a Deed of Trust at the point of the bayonet; and that Judge Cameron stood and saw the "Mormons" sign away their property; and then he and others would run and kick up their heels, and said they were glad of it, and "we have nothing to trouble us now." This Judge also said, "G—— d—— them, see how well they feel now." General Clark also said he had authority to make what treaties he pleased, and the Governor would sanction it.

The witness also stated that he never transgressed any of the laws of Missouri, and he never knew a Latter-day Saint break a law while there. He also said that if they would search the records of Clay, Caldwell, or Daviess counties, they could not find one record of crime against a Latter-day Saint, or even in Jackson county, so far as witness knew.

BRIGHAM YOUNG.

V.

TESTIMONY OF LYMAN WIGHT.

Lyman Wight sworn, saith that he has been acquainted with Joseph Smith, Sen., for the last twelve years, and that he removed to the state of Missouri in the year 1831, when the Church of Jesus Christ of Latter-day Saints was organized agreeable to the law of the land. No particular difficulty took place until after some hundreds had assembled in that land who believed in the Book of Mormon and revelations which were given through said Joseph Smith, Sen. After nearly two years of peace had elapsed, a strong prejudice among the various sects arose, declaring that Joseph Smith was a false prophet, and ought to die; and I heard hundreds say they had never known the man; but, if they could come across him, they would kill him as soon as they would a rattlesnake. Frequently heard them say of those who believed in the doctrine he promulgated, that, if they did not renounce it, they would exterminate or drive them from the county in which they lived. On inquiring of them if they had any prejudice against us, they said "No: but Joe Smith ought to die; and if ever he comes to this county we will kill him, G— d— him."

Matters went on thus until some time in the summer of 1833, when mobs assembled in considerable bodies, frequently visiting private houses, threatening the inmates with death and destruction instantly, if they did not renounce Joe Smith as a prophet, and the Book of Mormon. Sometime towards the last of the summer of 1833, they commenced their operations of mobocracy. On account of their priests, by uniting in their prejudices against Joseph Smith, Sen., as I believe, gangs of them thirty to sixty, visited the house of George Bebee, called him out of his house at the hour of midnight, with many guns and pistols pointed at his breast, beat him most inhumanly with clubs and whips; and the same night or night afterwards, this gang unroofed thirteen houses in what was called the Whitmer Branch of the Church in Jackson county. These scenes of mobocracy continued to exist with unabated fury.

Mobs went from house to house, thrusting poles and rails in at the windows and doors of the houses of the Saints, tearing down a number of houses, turning hogs and horses into corn fields, and burning fences. Some time in the month of October they broke into the store of A. S. Gilbert & Co., and I marched up with thirty or forty men to witness the scene, and found a man by the name of McCarty, brickbatting the store door with all fury, the silks, calicos, and other fine goods entwined about his feet, reaching within the door of the store-house. McCarty was arrested and taken before Squire Weston; and although seven persons testified against him, he was acquitted without delay. The next day the witnesses were taken before the same man for false imprisonment, and by the testimony of this one burglar were found guilty and committed to jail.

This so exasperated my feelings that I went with 200 men to inquire into the affair, when I was promptly met by the colonel of the militia, who stated to me that the whole had been a religious farce, and had grown out of a prejudice they had imbibed against said Joseph Smith —a man with whom they were not acquainted. I here agreed that the Church would give up their arms, provided the said Colonel Pitcher would take the arms from the mob. To this the colonel cheerfully agreed, and pledged his honor with that of Lieutenant-Governor Boggs, Samuel C. Owen, and others. This treaty entered into, we returned home, resting assured on their honor that we should not be farther molested. But this solemn contract was violated in every sense of the word.

The arms of the mob were never taken away, and the majority of the militia, to my certain knowledge, were engaged the next day with the mob, (Colonel Pitcher and Boggs not excepted), going from house to house in gangs from sixty to seventy in number, threatening the lives of women and children, if they did not leave forthwith. In this diabolical scene men were chased from their houses and homes without any preparation for themselves or families. I was chased by one of these gangs across an open prairie five miles, without being overtaken, and lay three weeks in the woods, and was three days and three nights without food.

In the meantime my wife and three small children, in a skiff, passed down Big Blue river, a distance of fourteen miles, and crossed over the Missouri river, and there borrowed a rag carpet of one of her friends and made a tent of the same, which was the only shield from the inclemency of the weather during the three weeks of my expulsion from home. Having found my family in this situation, and making some inquiry, I was informed I had been hunted throughout Jackson,

Lafayette, and Clay counties, and also the Indian Territory. Having made the inquiry of my family why it was they had so much against me, the answer was, "He believes in Joe Smith and the Book of Mormon, G— d— him; and we believe Joe Smith to be a —— rascal!"

Here, on the banks of the Missouri river, were eight families, exiled from plenteous homes, without one particle of provisions or any other means under the heavens to get any, only by hunting in the forest.

I here built a camp, twelve feet square, against a sycamore log, in which my wife bore me a fine son on the 27th of December. The camp having neither chimney nor floor, nor covering sufficient to shield them from the inclemency of the weather, rendered it intolerable.

In this doleful condition I left my family for the express purpose of making an appeal to the American people to know something of the toleration of such vile and inhuman conduct, and traveled one thousand and three hundred miles through the interior of the United States, and was frequently answered, "that such conduct was not justifiable in a Republican government; yet we feel to say that we fear that Joe Smith is a very bad man, and circumstances alter cases. We would not wish to prejudice a man, but in some circumstances the voice of the people ought to rule."

The most of these expressions were from professors of religion; and in the aforesaid persecution, I saw one hundred and ninety women and children driven thirty miles across the prairie, with three decrepit men only in their company, in the month of November, the ground thinly crusted with sleet; and I could easily follow on their trail by the *blood that flowed from their lacerated feet* on the stubble of the burnt prairie!

This company, not knowing the situation of the country or the extent of Jackson county, built quite a number of cabins, that proved to be in the borders of Jackson county. The mob, infuriated at this, rushed on them in the month of January, 1834, burned these scanty cabins, and scattered the inhabitants to the four winds; from which cause many were taken suddenly ill, and of this illness died. In the meantime, they burned two hundred and three houses and one grist mill, these being the only residences of the Saints in Jackson county.

The most part of one thousand and two hundred Saints who resided in Jackson county, made their escape to Clay county. I would here remark that among one of the companies that went to Clay county was a woman named Sarah Ann Higbee, who had been sick of chills and fever for many months, and another of the name of Keziah Higbee, who, under the most delicate circumstances, lay on the banks of the river, without shelter, during one of the most stormy nights I ever witnessed, while torrents of rain poured down during the whole night, and streams of the smallest size were magnified into rivers. The former was carried across the river, apparently a lifeless corpse. The latter was delivered of a fine son on the banks, within twenty minutes after being carried across the river, under the open conopy of heaven; and from which cause I have every reason to believe she died a premature death.

The only consolation they received from the mob, under these circumstances, was, "G— d— you, do you believe in Joe Smith now?" During this whole time, the said Joseph Smith, Sen., lived in Ohio, in the town of Kirtland, according to the best of my knowledge and belief, a distance of eleven hundred miles from Jackson county, and I think that the Church in Missouri had but little correspondence with him during that time.

We now found ourselves mostly in Clay county—some in negro cabins, some in gentlemen's kitchens, some in old cabins that had been out of use for years, and others in the open air, without anything to shelter them from the dreary storms of a cold and severe winter.

Thus, like men of servitude, we went to work to obtain a scanty living among the inhabitants of Clay county. Every advantage which could be taken of a people under these circumstances was not neglected by the people of Clay county. A great degree of friendship prevailed between the Saints and the people, under these circumstances, for the space of two years, when the Saints commenced purchasing some small possessions for themselves. This, together with the immigration, created a jealousy on the part of the old citizens that we were to be their servants no longer.

This raised an apparent indignation, and the first thing expressed in this excitement was, "You believe too much in Joe Smith." Consequently, they commenced catching the Saints in the streets, whipping some of them until their bowels gushed out, and leaving others for dead in the streets.

This so exasperated the Saints that they mutually agreed with the citizens of Clay county that they would purchase an entire new county north of Ray and cornering on Clay. There being not more than forty or fifty inhabitants in this new county, they frankly sold out their possessions to the Saints, who immediately set in to enter the entire county from the general government.

The county having been settled, the governor issued an order for the organization of the county and of a regiment of militia; and an election being called for a colonel of said regiment, I was elected unanimously, receiving 236 votes in August, 1837; we then organized with subaltern officers, according to the statutes of the state, and received legal and lawful commissions from Governor Boggs for the same.

I think, some time in the latter part of the winter, said Joseph Smith moved to the district of country the Saints had purchased, and he settled down like other citizens of a new county, and was appointed the first Elder in the Church of Jesus Christ of Latter-day Saints, holding no office in the county, either civil or military. I declare that I never knew said Joseph Smith to dictate, by his influence or otherwise, any of the officers, either civil or military; he himself being exempt from military duty from the amputation, from his leg, of a part of a bone, on account of a fever sore.

I removed from Caldwell to Daviess county, purchased a pre-emption right, for which I gave seven hundred and fifty dollars, gained another by the side thereof, put in a large crop, and became acquainted with the citizens of Daviess, who appeared very friendly.

In the month of June or July there was a town laid off, partly on my pre-emption and partly on lands belonging to government. The immigration commenced flowing to this newly laid off town very rapidly. This excited a prejudice in the minds of some of the old citizens, who were an ignorant set, and not very far advanced before the aborigines of the country in civilization or cultivated minds. They feared that this rapid tide of immigration should deprive them of office, of which they were dear lovers. This was more plainly exhibited at the August election in the year 1838. The old settlers then swore that not one "Mormon" should vote at that election; accordingly they commenced operations by fist and skull. This terminated in the loss of some teeth, some flesh, and some blood. The combat being very strongly contested on both sides, many Mormons were deprived of their votes, and I was followed to the polls by three ruffians with stones in their hands, swearing they would kill me if I voted.

A false rumor was immediately sent to Far West, such as that two or three "Mormons" were killed and were not suffered to be buried. The next day a considerable number of the Saints came out to my house. Said Joseph Smith came with them. He inquired of me concerning the difficulty. The answer was, political difficulties. He then asked if there was anything serious. The answer was, No, I think not. We then all mounted our horses and rode on to the prairie, a short distance from my house, to a cool spring near the house of Esquire Black, where the greater number stopped for refreshments, whilst a few waited on Esquire Black. He was interrogated to know whether he justified the course of conduct at the late election, or not. He said he did not, and was willing to give his protest in writing; which he did, and also desired that there should be a public meeting called; which, I think, was done on the next day.

Said Joseph Smith was not addressed on the subject, but I was, who, in behalf of the Saints, entered into an agreement with the other citizens of the county that we would live in peace, enjoying those blessings fought for by our forefathers. But while some of their leading men were entering into this contract, others were raising mobs; and in a short time the mob increased to two hundred and five, rank and file, and they encamped within six miles of Adam-ondi-Ahman.

In the meantime, Joseph Smith and those who came with him from Far West returned to their homes in peace, suspecting nothing. But I, seeing the rage of the mob and their full determination to drive the Church from Daviess county, sent to General Atchison (major-general of the division in which we lived). He immediately sent Brigadier-General Doniphan with between two and three hundred men. General Doniphan moved his troops near the mob force, and came up and conversed with me on the subject. After conversing some time on the subject, Major Hughes came and informed General Doniphan that his men were mutinying, and the mob were determined to fall on the Saints in Adam-ondi-Ahman. Having a colonel's commission under Doniphan I was commanded to call out my troops forthwith, and, to use Doniphan's own language, "kill every G— d—— mobocrat you can find in the county, or make them prisoners; and if they come upon you give them hell." He then returned to his troops and gave them an address, stating the interview he had with me; and he also said to the mob, that if they were so disposed, they could go on with their measures; that he considered that Colonel Wight, with the militia under his command all sufficient to quell every G— d—— mobocrat in the county; and if they did not feel disposed so to do, to go home or G— d—— them, he would kill every one of them. The mob then dispersed.

During these movements, neither Joseph Smith nor any of those of Far West were at Adam-ondi-Ahman, only those who were settlers and legal citizens of the place.

The mob again assembled and went to De Witt, Carroll county, there being a small branch of the Church at that place. But of the transactions at this place I have no personal knowledge. They succeded in driving the Church twice from that place, some to the east and some to the west. This increased their ardor, and, with redoubled forces from several counties of the state, they returned to Daviess county to renew the attack. Many wanton attacks and violations of the rights of citizens took place at this time from the hands of this hellish band.

Believing forbearance no longer to be a virtue I again sent to the Major-General for military aid, who ordered out Brigadier-General Parks. Parks came part of the way, but fearing his men would mutiny and join the mob, he came on ahead and conversed with me a considerable time.

The night previous to his arrival, the wife of Don Carlos Smith was driven from her house by this ruthless mob, and came into Adam-ondi-Ahman—a distance of three miles, carrying her two children on her hips, one of which was then rising of two years old, the other six or eight months old, the snow being over shoemouth deep, and she having to wade Grand river, which was at this time waist deep. The mob burnt the house and everything they had in it. General Parks passing the ruins thereof seemed fired with indignation at their hellish conduct and said he had hitherto thought it imprudent to call upon the militia under my command, in consequence of popular opinion; but he now considered it no more than justice that I should have command of my own troops, and said to me, "I therefore command you forthwith to raise your companies immediately, and take such course as you may deem best in order to disperse the mob from this county."

I then called out sixty men, and placed them under the command of Captain David W. Patten, and I also took about the same number. Captain Patten was ordered to Gallatin, where a party of the mob was located, and I went to Millport where another party was located. Captain Patten and I formed the troops under our command and General Parks addressed them as follows:

"Gentlemen, I deplore your situation. I regret that transactions of this nature should have transpired in our once happy state. Your condition is certainly not an enviable one, surrounded by mobs on one side and popular opinion and prejudice on the other. Gladly would I fly to your relief with my troops, but I fear it would be worse for you. Most of them have relations living in this county, and will not fight against them.

"One of my principal captains (namely Samuel Bogart) and his men have already mutinied and have refused to obey my command.

"I can only say to you, gentlemen, follow the command of Colonel Wight, whom I have commanded to disperse all mobs found in Daviess county, or to make them prisoners and bring them before the civil authorities forthwith.

"I wish to be distinctly understood that Colonel Wight is vested with power and authority from me to disperse from your midst all who may be found on the side of mobocracy in the county of Daviess.

"I deeply regret, gentlemen, (knowing as I do, the vigilance and perseverance of Colonel Wight in the cause of freedom and rights of man) that I could not even be a soldier under his command in quelling the hellish outrages I have witnessed.

"In conclusion, gentlemen, be vigilant, and persevere, and allay every excitement of mobocracy. I have visited your place frequently, find you to be an industrious and thriving people, willing to abide the laws of the land; and I deeply regret that you could not live in peace and enjoy the privileges of freedom. I shall now, gentlemen, return and dismiss my troops, and put Captain Bogart under arrest, leave the sole charge with Colonel Wight, whom I deem sufficiently qualified to perform according to law, in all military operations necessary."

Captain Patten then went to Gallatin. When coming in sight of Gallatin, he discovered about one hundred of the mob holding some of the Saints in bondage, and tantalizing others in the most scandalous manner. At the sight of Captain Patten and company the mob took fright and such was their hurry to get away, some cut their bridle reins, and some pulled the bridles from their horses' heads and went off with all speed.

I went to Millport, and on my way discovered the inhabitants had become enraged at the orders of Generals Doniphan and Parks, and that they had sworn vengeance, not only against the Church, but also against the two generals, together with General Atchison; and to carry out their plans, they entered into one of the most diabolical schemes ever entered into by man, and these hellish schemes were ingeniously carried out.

Namely, by loading their families and goods in covered wagons, setting fire to their houses, moving into the midst of the mob, and crying out, "The Mormons have driven us and burnt our houses." In this situation I found the country between my house and Millport, and also found Millport evacuated and burnt.

Runners were immediately sent to the governor with the news that the "Mormons" were killing and burning everything before them, and that great fears were entertained that they would reach Jefferson City before the runners could bring the news.

This was not known by the Church of Latter-day Saints until two thousand two hundred of the militia had arrived within half a mile of Far West; and they then supposed the militia to be a mob.

I was sent for from Adam-ondi-Ahman to Far West; reached there, the sun about one hour high, in the morning of the 29th of October, 1838; called upon Joseph Smith, and inquired the cause of the great uproar. He declared he did not know, but feared the mob had increased their numbers, and were endeavoring to destroy us.

I inquired of him if he had had any conversation with any one concerning the matter. He said he had not, as he was only a private citizen of the county—that he did not interfere with any such matters.

He told me there had been an order, either from General Atchison or Doniphan, to the sheriff to call out the militia in order to quell the riots, and to go to him; he could give me any information on this subject. On inquiring for the sheriff, I found him not. That between three and four p. m. George M. Hinkle, colonel of the militia in that place, called on me, in company with Joseph Smith, and said Hinkle said he had been in the camp in order to learn the intention of the same. He said they greatly desired to see Joseph Smith, Lyman Wight, Sidney Rigdon, Parley P. Pratt, and George, W. Robinson.

Joseph Smith first inquired why they should desire to see him, as he held no office, either civil or military. I next inquired why it was they should desire to see a man out of his own county.

Colonel Hinkle here observed, There is no time for controversy. If you go not into the camp immediately, they are determined to come upon Far West before the setting of the sun; and said they did not consider us as military leaders, but religious leaders. He said that if the aforesaid persons went into the camp, they would be liberated that night or very early next morning; that there should be no harm done.

We consulted together and agreed to go down. On going about half the distance from the camp, I observed it would be well for Generals Lucas, Doniphan and others, to meet us, and not have us go in so large a crowd of soldiers. Accordingly, the generals moved onwards, followed by fifty artillerymen, with a four-pounder. The whole twenty-two hundred moved in steady pace on the right and left, keeping about even with the former.

General Lucas approached the aforesaid designated persons with a vile, base and treacherous look in his countenance. I shook hands with him and saluted him thus: "We understand, general, you wish to confer with us a few moments. Will not tomorrow morning do as well."

At this moment George M. Hinkle spake and said, "Here, general are the prisoners I agreed to deliver to you." General Lucas then brandished his sword with a most hideous look and said, "You are my prisoners, and there is no time for talking at the present. You will march into the camp."

At this moment I believe that there were five hundred guns cocked, and not less than twenty caps bursted; and more hideous yells were never heard, even if the description of the yells of the damned in hell is true, as given by the modern sects of the day.

The aforesaid designated persons were then introduced into the midst of twenty-two hundred mob militia. They then called out a guard of ninety men, placing thirty around the prisoners, who were on duty two hours and off four. The prisoners were placed on the ground, with nothing to cover them but the heavens, and they were over-shadowed by clouds that moistened them before morning.

Sidney Rigdon, who was of a delicate constitution, received a slight shock of apoplectic fits, which excited great laughter and much ridicule in the guard and mob militia. Thus the prisoners spent a doleful night in the midst of a prejudiced and diabolical community.

Next day Hyrum Smith and Amasa Lyman were dragged from their families and brought prisoners into the camp, they alleging no other reason for taking Hyrum Smith than that he was a brother to Joe Smith the Prophet, and one of his counselors as President of the Church.

The prisoners spent this day as comfortably as could be expected under the existing circumstances. Night came on, and under the dark shadows of the night, General Wilson, subaltern of General Lucas, took me on one side and said; "We do not wish to hurt you nor kill you, neither shall you be, by G——; but we have one thing against you, and that is, you are too friendly to Joe Smith, and we believe him to be a G—— d—— rascal, and, Wight, you know all about his character." I said, "I do, sir." "Will you swear all you know concerning him?" said Wilson. "I will, sir" was the answer I gave. "Give us the outlines," said Wilson. I then told Wilson I believed said Joseph Smith to be the most philanthropic man he ever saw, and possessed of the most pure and republican principles—a friend to mankind, a maker of peace; "and sir, had it not been that I had given heed to his counsel, I would have given you hell before this time, with all your mob forces."

He then observed, "Wight, I fear your life is in danger, for there is no end to the prejudice against Joe Smith." "Kill and be damned sir," was my answer. He answered and said "There is to be a court-martial held this night; and will you attend, sir." "I will not, unless compelled by force," was my reply.

He returned about eleven o'clock that night, and took me aside and said: "I regret to tell you your die is cast; your doom is fixed; you are sentenced to be shot tomorrow morning on the public square in Far West, at eight o'clock." I answered, "Shoot, and be damned."

"We were in hopes," said he, "you would come out against Joe Smith; but as you have not, you will have to share the same fate with him." I answered "You may thank Joe Smith that you are not in hell this night; for, had it not been for him, I would have put you there." Somewhere about this time General Doniphan came up, and said to me, "Colonel the decision is a d—— hard one, and I have washed my hands against such cool and deliberate murder." He further told me that General Graham and several others (names not recollected) were with him in the decision and opposed it with all their power; and he should move his soldiers away by daylight in the morning, that they should not witness a heartless murder. "Colonel, I wish you well."

I then returned to my fellow-prisoners, to spend another night on the cold, damp earth, and the canopy of heaven to cover us. The night again proved a damp one.

At the removal of General Doniphan's part of the army, the camp was thrown into the utmost confusion and consternation. General Lucas, fearing the consequence of such hasty and inconsiderate measures, revoked the decree of shooting the prisoners, and determined to take them to Jackson county. Consequently, he delivered the prisoners over to General Wilson, ordering him to see them safe to Independence, Jackson county.

About the hour the prisoners were to have been shot on the public square in Far West, they were exhibited in a wagon in the town, all of them having families there but myself; and it would have broken the heart of any person possessing an ordinary share of humanity to have seen the separation. The aged father and mother of Joseph Smith were not permitted to see his face, but to reach their hands through the cover of the wagon, and thus take leave of him. When passing his own house, he was taken out of the wagon and permitted to go into the house, but not without a strong guard, and not permitted to speak with his family but in the presence of his guard; and his eldest son, Joseph, about six or eight years old, hanging to the tail of his coat, crying, "Father, is the mob going to kill you?" The guard said to him, "You d—— little brat, go back; you will see your father no more."

The prisoners then set out for Jackson county, accompanied by Generals Lucas and Wilson, and about three hundred troops for a guard. We remained in Jackson county three or four days and nights, during most of which time the prisoners were treated in a gentlemanly manner and boarded at a hotel, for which they had afterwards, when confined in Liberty jail, to pay the most extravagant price, or have their property, if any they had, attached for the same.

At this time General Clark had arrived at Richmond, and, by orders from the Governor, took on himself the command of the whole of the militia, notwithstanding General Atchison's commission was the oldest; but he was supposed to be too friendly to the "Mormons," and therefore dismounted; and General Clark sanctioned the measures of General Lucas, however cruel, and said he should have done the same, had he been there himself.

Accordingly, he remanded the prisoners from Jackson county, and they were taken and escorted by a strong guard to Richmond; threatened several times on the way with violence and death. They were met five miles before they reached Richmond by about one hundred armed men; and when they arrived in town, they were thrust into an old cabin under a strong guard. I was informed by one of the guards that, two nights previous to their arrival, General Clark held a court-martial, and the prisoners were again sentenced to be shot; but he being a little doubtful of his authority, sent immediately to Fort Leavenworth for the military law and a decision from the United States' officers, where he was duly informed that any such proceedings would be a cool-blooded and heartless murder. On the arrival of the prisoners at Richmond, Joseph Smith and myself sent for General Clark, to be informed by him what crimes were alleged against us. He came in and said he would see us again in a few minutes. Shortly he returned and said he would inform us of the crimes alleged against us by the state of Missouri.

"Gentlemen, you are charged with treason, murder, arson, burglary, larceny, theft, and stealing, and various other charges too tedious to mention at this time;" and he immediately left the room. In about twenty minutes, there came in a strong guard, together with the keeper of the penitentiary of the state, who brought with him three common trace chains, noozed together by putting the small end through the ring, and commenced chaining us up, one by one, and fastening us with padlocks about two feet apart.

In this uncomfortable situation the prisoners remained fifteen days, and in this situation General Clark delivered us to the professed civil authorities of the state, without any legal process being served on us at all during the whole time we were kept in chains, with nothing but *ex parte* evidence, and that given either by the vilest apostates or by the mob who had committed murder in the state of Missouri. Notwithstanding all this *ex parte* evidence, Judge King did inform our lawyer, ten days previous to the termination of the trial, whom he should commit and whom he should not; and I heard Judge King say on his bench, in the presence of hundreds of witnesses, that there was no law for the "Mormons," and they need not expect any. Said he, "If the Governor's exterminating order had been directed to me, I would have seen it fulfilled to the very letter ere this time."

After a tedious trial of fifteen days, with no other witnesses but *ex parte* ones, the witnesses for the prisoners were either kicked out of doors or put on trial themselves. The prisoners were now committed to Liberty jail, under the care and direction of Samuel Tillery, jailer. Here we were received with a shout of indignation and scorn by the prejudiced populace.

Prisoners were here thrust into jail without a regular mittimus, the jailer having to send for one some days after. The mercies of the jailer were intolerable, feeding us with a scanty allowance on the dregs of coffee and tea from his own table, and fetching the provisions in a basket, without being cleaned, on which the chickens had roosted the night before. Five days he fed the prisoners on human flesh, and from extreme hunger I was compelled to eat it. In this situation we were kept until about the month of April, when we were remanded to Daviess county for trial before the grand jury. We were kept under the most loathsome and despotic guard they could produce in that county of lawless mobs. After six or eight days, the grand jury (most of whom, by-the-bye, were so drunk that they had to be carried out and into their rooms as though they were lifeless,) formed a fictitious indictment, which was sanctioned by Judge Birch, who was the State's Attorney under Judge King at our *ex parte* trial, and who at that time stated that the "Mormons" ought to be hung without judge or jury. He, the said Judge, made out a mittimus, without day or date, ordering the Sheriff to take us to Columbia. The Sheriff selected four men to guard five of us.

We then took a circuitous route, crossing prairies sixteen miles without houses; and after traveling three days, the Sheriff and I were together by ourselves five miles from any of the rest of the company for sixteen miles at a stretch. The Sheriff here observed to me that he wished to God he was at home, and your friends and you also. The Sheriff then showed me the mittimus, and he found it had neither day nor date to it, and said the inhabitants of Daviess county would be surprised that the prisoners had not left them sooner; and, said he, "By G——, I shall not go much further."

We were then near Yellow Creek, and there were no houses nearer than sixteen miles one way, and eleven another way, except right on the creek. Here a part of the guard took a spree, while the balance helped us to mount our horses, which we purchased of them, and for which they were paid. Here we took a change of venue, and went to Quincy without difficulty, where we found our families, who had been driven out of the State under the exterminating order of Governor Boggs. I never knew of Joseph Smith's holding any office, civil or military, or using any undue influence in religious matters during the whole time of which I have been speaking.

LYMAN WIGHT.

VI.

TESTIMONY OF SIDNEY RIGDON.

Sidney Rigdon sworn, says I arrived in Far West, Caldwell county, Missouri, on the 4th of April, 1838, and enjoyed peace and quietness, in common with the rest of the citizens, until the August following, when great excitement was created by the office-seekers. Attempts were made to prevent the citizens of Daviess from voting. Soon after the election, which took place in the early part of August, the citizens of Caldwell were threatened with violence from those of Daviess county and other counties adjacent to Caldwell.

This, the August of 1838, I may date as the time of the beginning of all the troubles of our people in Caldwell county and in all the counties in the state where our people were living. We had lived in peace from the April previous until this time; but from this time till we were all out of the state, it was one scene of violence following another in quick succession.

There were at this time settlements in Clay, Ray, Carroll, Caldwell, and Daviess counties, as well as some families living in other counties. A simultaneous movement was made in all the counties and in every part of the state, where settlements were made, this soon became violent; and threatenings were heard from every quarter. Public meetings were held, and the most inflammatory speeches made, and resolutions passed, which denounced all the "Mormons" in the most bitter and rancorous manner. These resolutions were published in the papers, and the most extensive circulation given to them that the press of the country was capable of giving.

The first regular mob that assembled was in Daviess county, and their efforts were directed against the settlements made in that county, declaring their determination to drive out of the county all the citizens who were of our religion, and that indiscriminately, without regard to anything else but their religion.

The only evidence necessary to dispossess any individual or family, or all the evidence required, would be that they were "Mormons," as we were called, or rather that they were of the "Mormon" religion. This was considered of itself crime enough to cause any individual or family to be driven from their homes, and their property made common plunder. Resolutions to this effect were made at public meetings held for the purpose, and made public through the papers of the state, in the face of all law and all authority.

I will now give a history of the settlement in Carroll county. In the preceding April, as myself and family were on our way to Far West, we put up at a house in Carroll county, on a stream called Turkey Creek, to tarry for the night. Soon after we stopped, a young man came riding up, who also stopped and stayed through the night. Hearing my name mentioned, he introduced himself to me as Henry Root; said he lived in that county at a little town called De Witt, on the Missouri river, and had been at Far West to get some of those who were coming into that place to form a settlement at De Witt. Speaking highly of the advantages of the situation, and soliciting my interference in his behalf to obtain a number of families to commence at that place, as he was a large proprietor in the town plat, he offered a liberal share in all the profits which might arise from the sale of property there to those who would aid him in getting the place settled. In the morning we proceeded on our journey.

Some few weeks after my arrival, the said Henry Root, in company with a man by the name of David Thomas, came to Far West on the same business; and after much solicitation on their part, it was agreed that a settlement should be made in that place; and in the July following the first families removed there, and the settlement soon increased, until in the October following it consisted of some seventy families. By this time a regular mob had collected, strongly armed, and had obtained possession of a cannon, and stationed themselves a mile or two from the town. The citizens, being nearly all new comers, had to live in their tents and wagons, and were exerting themselves to the uttermost to get houses for the approaching winter. The mob commenced committing their depredations on the citizens, by not suffering them to procure the materials for building, keeping them shut up in the town, not allowing them to go out to get provisions, driving off their cattle, and preventing the owners from going in search of them. In this way the citizens were driven to the greatest extremities, actually suffering for food and every comfort of life; in consequence of which, there was much sickness, and many died. Females gave birth to children, without a house to shelter them; and in consequence of the exposure, many suffered great afflictions, and many died.

Hearing of their great sufferings, a number of the men of Far West determined on going to see what was doing there. Accordingly we started, eluded the vigilance of the mob, and, notwithstanding they had sentinels placed on all the principal roads, to prevent relief from being sent to the citizens, we safely arrived in De Witt, and found the people as above stated.

During the time we were there, every effort that could be was made to get the authorities of the county to interfere and scatter the mob. The judge of the circuit court was petitioned, but without success; and after that, the governor of the state, who returned for answer that the citizens of De Witt had got into a difficulty with the surrounding country, and they might get out of it, for he would have nothing to do with it; or this was the answer the messenger brought, when he returned.

The messenger was a Mr. Caldwell, who owned a ferry on Grand river, about three miles from De Witt, and was an old settler in the place.

The citizens were completely besieged by the mob: no man was at liberty to go out, nor any to come in. The extremities to which the people were driven were very great, suffering with much sickness, without shelter, and deprived of all aid, either medical or any other kind, and being without food or the privilege of getting it, and betrayed by every man who made the least pretension to friendship; a notable instance of which I will here give as a sample of many others of a similar kind.

There was neither bread nor flour to be had in the place. A steamboat landed there, and application was made to get flour; but the captain said there was none on board.

A man then offered his services to get flour for the place, knowing, he said, where there was a quantity. Money was given to him for that purpose. He got on the boat and went off, and that was the last we heard of the man or the money. This was a man who had been frequently in De Witt during the siege, and professed great friendship.

In this time of extremity, a man who had a short time before moved into De Witt, bringing with him a fine yoke of cattle, started out to hunt his cattle, in order to butcher them, to keep the citizens from actual starvation; but before he got far from the town, he was fired upon by the mob, and narrowly escaped with his life, and had to return; or, at least, such was his report when he returned.

Being now completely enclosed on every side, we could plainly see many men on the opposite side of the river, and it was supposed that they were there to prevent the citizens from crossing; and, indeed, a small craft crossed from them, and three men in it, who said that that was the object for which they had assembled.

At this critical moment, with death staring us in the face, in its worst form, cut off from all communication with the surrounding country, and all our provisions exhausted, we were sustained as the children of Israel in the desert, only by different animals,—they by quails, and we by cattle and hogs, which came walking into the camp; for such it truly was, as the people were living in tents and wagons, not being privileged with building houses.

What was to be done in this extremity? Why, recourse was had to the only means of subsistence left, and that was to butcher the cattle and hogs which came into the place, without asking who was the owner, or without knowing; and what to me is remarkable is, that a sufficient number of animals came into the camp to sustain life during the time in which the citizens were besieged by the mob. This, indeed, was but coarse living; but such as it was, it sustained life.

From this circumstance the cry went out that the citizens of De Witt were thieves and plunderers, and were stealing cattle and hogs. During this time, the mob of Carroll county said that all they wanted was that the citizens of De Witt should leave Carroll county and go to Caldwell and Daviess counties.

The citizens, finding that they must leave De Witt or eventually starve, finally agreed to leave; and accordingly preparations were made, and De Witt was vacated.

The first evening after we left, we put up for the night in a grove of timber. Soon after our arrival in the grove, a female who a short time before had given birth to a child, in consequence of exposure, died.

A grave was dug in the grove, and the next morning the body was deposited in it without a coffin, and the company proceeded on their journey, part of them going to Daviess county, and part into Caldwell. This was in the month of October, 1838.

In a short time after their arrival in Daviess and Caldwell counties, messengers arrived, informing the new citizens of Caldwell and Daviess that the mob, with their cannon, was marching to Daviess county, threatening death to the citizens, or else that they should all leave Daviess county. This caused other efforts to be made to get the authorities to interfere. I wrote two memorials, one to the governor and one to Austin A. King, circuit judge, imploring their assistance and intervention to protect the citizens of Daviess against the threatened violence of the mob.

These memorials were accompanied with affidavits, which could leave no doubt on the mind of the governor or judge that the citizens before mentioned were in imminent danger.

At this time things began to assume an alarming aspect both to the citizens of Daviess and Caldwell counties. Mobs were forming all around the country, declaring that they would drive the people out of the state.

This made our appeals to the authorities more deeply solicitous as the danger increased, and very soon after this the mobs commenced their depredations, which was a general system of plunder, tearing down fences, exposing all within the field to destruction, and driving off every animal they could find.

Some time previous to this, in consequence of the threatenings which were made by mobs, or those who were being formed into mobs, and the abuses committed by them on the persons and property of the citizens, an association was formed, called the Danite Band.

This, as far as I was acquainted with it, (not being myself one of the number, neither was Joseph Smith, Sen.,) was for mutual protection against the bands that were forming and threatened to be formed for the professed object of committing violence on the property and persons of the citizens of Daviess and Caldwell counties. They had certain signs and words by which they could know one another, either by day or night. They were bound to keep these signs and words secret, so that no other person or persons than themselves could know them. When any of these persons were assailed by any lawless band, he would make it known to others, who would flee to his relief at the risk of life.

In this way they sought to defend each other's lives and property; but they were strictly enjoined not to touch any person, only those who were engaged in acts of violence against the persons or property of one of their own number, or one of those whose life and property they had bound themselves to defend.

This organization was in existence when the mobs commenced their most violent attempts upon the citizens of the before-mentioned counties; and from this association arose all the horror afterwards expressed by the mob at some secret clan known as Danites.

The efforts made to get the authorities to interfere at this time was attended with some success. The militia was ordered out under the command of Major-General Atchison of Clay county, Brigadier-Generals Doniphan of Clay, and Parks of Ray county, who marched their troops to Daviess county, where they found a large mob; and General Atchison said, in my presence, that he took the following singular method to disperse them.

He organized them with his troops as part of the militia called out to suppress and arrest the mob. After having thus organized them, he discharged them and all the rest of the troops, as having no further need for their services, and all returned home.

This, however, only seemed to give the mob more courage to increase their exertion with redoubled vigor. They boasted, after that, that the authorities would not punish them, and they would do as they pleased.

In a very short time their efforts were renewed with a determination not to cease until they had driven the citizens of Caldwell, and such of the citizens of Daviess as they had marked out as victims, from the state.

A man by the name of Cornelius Gillum, who resided in Clay county, and formerly sheriff of said county, organized a band, who painted themselves like Indians, and had a place of rendezvous at Hunter's Mills, on a stream called Grindstone. I think it was in Clinton county, the county west of Caldwell, and between it and the west line of the state.

From this place they would sally out and commit their depredations. Efforts were again made to get the authorities to put a stop to these renewed outrages, and again General Doniphan and General Parks were called out with such portions of their respective brigades as they might deem necessary to suppress the mob, or rather mobs, for by this time there were a number of them.

General Doniphan came to Far West; and, while there, recommended to the authorities of Caldwell to have the militia of said county called out as a necessary measure of defense, assuring us that Gillum had a large mob on Grindstone Creek, and his object was to make a descent upon Far West, burn the town and kill or disperse the inhabitants; and that it was very necessary that an effective force should be ready to oppose him, or he would accomplish his object.

The militia were accordingly called out. He also said that there had better be a strong force sent to Daviess county to guard the citizens there. He recommended that, to avoid any difficulties which might arise, they had better go in very small parties without arms, so that no legal advantage could be taken of them. I will here give a short account of the courts and internal affairs of Missouri, for the information of those who are not acquainted with the same.

Missouri has three courts of law peculiar to that state—the supreme court, the circuit court, and the county court; the two former about the same as in many other states of the Union. The county court is composed of three judges, elected by the people of the respective counties. This court is in some respects like the court of probate in Illinois, or the surrogate's court of New York; but the powers of this court are more extensive than the courts of Illinois or New York.

The judges (or any one of them of the county court of Missouri) have the power of issuing habeas corpus in all cases where arrests are made within the county where they preside. They have also all power of justices of the peace in civil as well as criminal cases. For instance, a warrant may be obtained from one of these judges by affidavit, and a person arrested under such warrant.

From another of these judges, a habeas corpus may issue, and the person arrested be ordered before him, and the character of the arrest be inquired into; and if, in the opinion of the judge, the person ought not to be holden by virtue of said process, he has power to discharge him. They are considered conservators of the peace, and act as such.

In the internal regulations of the affairs of Missouri, the counties in some respects are nearly as independent of each other as the several states of the Union. No considerable number of men armed can pass out of one county into or through another county, without first obtaining the permission of the judges of the county court, or some one of them; otherwise they are liable to be arrested by the order of said judges; and if in their judgment they ought not thus to pass, they are ordered back from whence they came; and, in case of refusal, are subject to be arrested or even shot down in case of resistance.

The judges of the county court (or any one of them) have the power to call out the militia of said county, upon affidavit being made to them for that purpose by any of the citizens of said county, showing it just, in the judgment of such judge or judges, why said militia should be called out to defend any portion of the citizens of said county.

The following is the course of procedure: Affidavit is made before one or any number of the judges, setting forth that the county (or any particular portion of it) is either invaded or threatened with invasion by some unlawful assembly, whereby the liberties, lives, or property of the citizens may be unlawfully taken.

When such affidavit is made to any one of the judges, or all of them, it is the duty of him or them before whom such affidavit is made to issue an order to the sheriff of the county, to make requisition upon the commanding officer of the militia of said county to have immediately put under military order such portion of the militia under his command as may be necessary for the defense of the citizens of said county.

In this way the militia of any county may be called out at any time deemed necessary by the county judges, independently of any other civil authority of the state.

In case that the militia of the county is insufficient to quell the rioters and secure the citizens against the invaders, then recourse can be had to the judge of the circuit court, who has the same power over the militia of his judicial district as the county judges have over the militia of the county. And in case of insufficiency in the militia of the judicial district of the circuit judge, recourse can be had to the Governor of the state, and all the militia of the state called out; and if this should fail, then the Governor can call on the President of the United States.

I have given this explanation of the internal regulation of the affairs of Missouri, in order that the court may clearly understand what I have before said on this subject, and what I may hereafter say on it.

It was in view of this order of things that General Doniphan, who is a lawyer of some celebrity in Missouri, gave the recommendation he did at Far West, when passing into Daviess county with his troops, for the defense of the citizens of said county.

It was in consequence of this that he said that those of Caldwell county who went into Daviess county should go in small parties and unarmed; in which condition they were not subject to any arrest from any authority whatever.

In obedience to these recommendations the militia of Caldwell county was called out, affidavits having been made to one of the judges of the county, setting forth the danger which it was believed the citizens were in from a large marauding party assembled under the command of one Cornelius Gillum, on a stream called Grindstone.

When affidavit was made to this effect, the judge issued his order to the sheriff of the county, and the sheriff to the commanding officer, who was Colonel George M. Hinkle; and thus were the militia of the county of Caldwell put under orders.

General Doniphan, however, instead of going into Daviess county, soon after he left Far West returned to Clay county with all his troops, giving as his reason the mutinous character of his troops, who he believed would join the mob, instead of acting against them, and that he had not power to restrain them.

In a day or two afterwards, General Parks, of Ray county, also came to Far West, and said that he had sent on a number of troops to Daviess county, to act in concert with General Doniphan. He also made the same complaint concerning the troops that Doniphan had, doubting greatly whether they would render any service to those in

Daviess, who were threatened with violence by the mobs assembling; but on hearing that Doniphan, instead of going to Daviess county, had returned to Clay, followed his example and ordered his troops back to Ray county; and thus were the citizens of Caldwell county and those of Daviess county, who were marked out as victims by the mob, left to defend themselves the best way they could.

What I have here stated in relation to Generals Doniphan and Parks, was learned in conversations had between myself and them, about which I cannot be mistaken, unless my memory has betrayed me.

The militia of the county of Caldwell were now all under requisition, armed and equipped according to law. The mob, after all the authority of the state had been recalled except from the force of Caldwell county, commenced the work of destruction in earnest, showing a determination to accomplish their object.

Far West, where I resided, which was the shire town of Caldwell county, was placed under the charge of a captain by the name of John Killian, who made my house his headquarters. Other portions of the troops were distributed in different portions of the county, wherever danger was apprehended. In consequence of Captain Killian making my house his headquarters, I was put in possession of all that was going on, as all intelligence in relation to the operations of the mob was communicated to him. Intelligence was received daily of depredations being committed not only against the property of the citizens, but their persons; many of whom, when attending to their business, would be surprised and taken by marauding parties, tied up, and whipped in a most desperate manner.

Such outrages were common during the progress of these extraordinary scenes, and all kinds of depredations were committed. Men driving their teams to and from the mills where they got their grinding done, would be surprised and taken, their persons abused, and their teams, wagons and loading all taken as booty by the plunderers. Fields were thrown open, and all within exposed to the destruction of such animals as chose to enter. Cattle, horses, hogs and sheep were driven off, and a general system of plunder and destruction of all kinds of property carried on, to the great annoyance of the citizens of Caldwell and that portion of the citizens of Daviess marked as victims by the mob.

One afternoon a messenger arrived at Far West calling for help, saying that a banditti had crossed the south line of Caldwell and were engaged in threatening the citizens with death, if they did not leave their homes and go out of the state within a very short time—the time not precisely recollected; but I think it was the next day by ten o'clock, but of this I am not certain. He said they were setting fire to the prairies, in view of burning houses and desolating farms; that they had set fire to a wagon loaded with goods, and they were all consumed; that they had also set fire to a house, and when he left it was burning down.

Such was the situation of affairs at Far West at that time, that Captain Killian could not spare any of his forces, as an attack was hourly expected at Far West.

The messenger went off, and I heard no more about it till some time the night following, when I was awakened from sleep by the voice of some man apparently giving command to a military body. Being somewhat unwell, I did not get up. Some time after I got up in the morning the sheriff of the county stopped at the door and said that David W. Patten had had a battle with the mob last night at Crooked River, and that several were killed and a number wounded; that Patten was among the number of the wounded, and his wound supposed to be mortal. After I had taken breakfast, another gentleman called, giving me the same account, and asking me if I would not take my horse and ride out with him and see what was done. I agreed to do so, and we started, and after going three or four miles, met a company coming into Far West. We turned and went back with them.

The mob proved to be that headed by the Reverend Samuel Bogart, a Methodist preacher; and the battle was called the Bogart Battle. After this battle there was a short season of quiet; the mobs disappeared, and the militia returned to Far West, though they were not discharged, but remained under orders until it should be known how the matter would turn.

In the space of a few days, it was said that a large body of armed men were entering the south part of Caldwell county. The county court ordered the militia to go and inquire what was their object in thus coming into the county without permission.

The militia started as commanded, and little or no information was received at Far West about their movements until late the next afternoon, when a large army was descried making their way towards Far West. Far West being an elevated situation, the army was discovered while a number of miles from the place.

Their object was entirely unknown to the citizens as far as I had any knowledge on the subject; and every man I heard speak of their object expressed as great ignorance as myself. They reached a small stream on the south side of the town, which was studded with timber on its banks, and for perhaps from half a mile to a mile on the south side of the stream, an hour before sundown.

There the main body halted; and soon after a detachment under the command of Brigadier-General Doniphan, marched towards the town in line of battle. This body was preceded probably three-fourths of a mile in advance of them by a man carrying a white flag, who approached within a few rods of the eastern boundary of the town and demanded three persons who were in the town, to be sent to their camp; after which, the whole town, he said, would be massacred. When the persons who were inquired for were informed, they refused to go, determined to share the common fate of the citizens. One of those persons did not belong to the Church of Latter-day Saints. His name is Adam Lightner, a merchant in that city.

The white flag returned to the camp. To the force of General Doniphan was opposed the small force of Caldwell militia, under Colonel Hinkle, who also marched in line of battle to the southern line of the town. The whole force of Colonel Hinkle did not exceed three hundred men; that of Doniphan perhaps three times that number. I was in no way connected with the militia, being over age, neither was Joseph Smith, Sen.

I went into the line formed by Colonel Hinkle, though unarmed, and stood among the rest to await the result, and had a full view of both forces. The armies were within rifle shot of each other.

About the setting of the sun, Doniphan ordered his army to return to the camp at the creek. They wheeled and marched off. After they had retired a consultation was held as to what was best to do. By what authority the army was there, no one could tell, as far as I knew. It was agreed to build, through the night, a sort of fortification, and, if we must fight, sell our lives as dearly as we could. Accordingly, all hands went to work; rails, house-logs and wagons were all put in requisition, and the south line of the town as well secured as could be done by the men and means, and the short time allowed; we expected an attack in the morning.

The morning at length came, and that day passed away, and still nothing was done but plundering the cornfields, shooting cattle and hogs, stealing horses and robbing houses, and carrying off potatoes, turnips, and all such things as the army of General Lucas could get, for such they proved to be; for the main body was commanded by Samuel D. Lucas, a deacon in the Presbyterian church. The next day came, and then it was ascertained that they were there by order of the governor.

A demand was made for Joseph Smith, Sen., Lyman Wight, George W. Robinson, Parley P. Pratt and myself to go into their camp. With this command we instantly complied, and accordingly started.

When we came in sight of their camp, the whole army was on parade marching towards the town. We approached and met them, and were informed by Lucas that we were prisoners of war. A scene followed that would defy any mortal to describe; a howling was set up that would put anything I ever heard before or since at defiance. I thought at the time it had no parallel except it might be the perdition of ungodly men. They had a cannon.

I could distinctly hear the guns as the locks were sprung, which appeared, from the sound, to be in every part of the army. General Doniphan came riding up where we were, and swore by his Maker that he would hew the first man down that cocked a gun. One or two other officers on horseback also rode up, ordering those who had cocked their guns to uncock them, or they would be hewed down with their swords. We ware conducted into their camp and made to lie on the ground through the night.

This was late in October. We were kept here for two days and two nights. It commenced raining and snowing until we were completely drenched; and being compelled to lie on the ground, which had become very wet, the water was running around us and under us. What consultation the officers and others had in relation to the disposition that was to be made of us, I am entirely indebted to the report made to me by General Doniphan, as none of us was put on any trial.

General Doniphan gave an account, of which the following is the substance, as far as my memory serves me: That they held a court-martial and sentenced us to be shot at eight o'clock the next morning, after the court-martial was holden, in the public square in the presence of our families; that this court-martial was composed of seventeen preachers and some of the principal officers of the army. Samuel D. Lucas presided. Doniphan arose and said that neither himself nor his brigade should have any hand in the shooting, that it was nothing short of cold-blooded murder; and left the court-martial and ordered his brigade to prepare and march off the ground.

This was probably the reason why they did not carry the decision of the court-martial into effect. It was finally agreed that we should be carried into Jackson county. Accordingly, on the third day after our arrest, the army was all paraded; we were put into wagons and taken into the town, our families having heard that we were to be brought to town that morning to be shot. When we arrived a scene ensued such as might be expected under the circumstances.

I was permitted to go alone with my family into the house. There I found my family so completely plundered of all kinds of food, that they had nothing to eat but parched corn, which they ground with a handmill and thus were they sustaining life.

I soon pacified my family and allayed their feelings by assuring them that the ruffians dared not kill me. I gave them strong assurances that they dared not do it, and that I would return to them again. After this interview I took my leave of them and returned to the wagons, got in, and we were all started off to Jackson county.

Before we reached the Missouri river, a man came riding along the line apparently in great haste. I did not know his business. When we got to the river, Lucas came to me and told me that he wanted us to hurry, as Jacob Stolling had arrived from Far West with a message from General John C. Clark, ordering him to return with us to Far West, as he was there with a large army. He said he would not comply with the demand, but did not know but Clark might send an army to take us by force. We were hurried over the river as fast as possible, with as many of Lucas' army as could be sent over at one time, and sent hastily on, and thus we were taken to Independence, the shire town of Jackson county, and put into an old house, and a strong guard placed over us.

In a day or two they relaxed their severity. We were taken to the best tavern in town, and there boarded and treated with kindness. We were permitted to go and come at our pleasure without any guard. After some days Colonel Sterling G. Price arrived from Clark's army with a demand to have us taken to Richmond, Ray county. It was difficult to get a guard to go with us. Indeed, we solicited them to send one with us, and finally got a few men to go, and we started. After we had crossed the Missouri, on our way to Richmond, we met a number of very rough-looking fellows, and as rough-acting as they were looking. They threatened our lives. We solicited our guard to send to Richmond for a stronger force to guard us there, as we considered our lives in danger. Sterling G. Price met us with a strong force, and conducted us to Richmond, where we were put in close confinement.

One thing I will here mention, which I forgot. While we were at Independence, I was introduced to Burrell Hicks, a lawyer of some note in the country. In speaking on the subject of our arrest and being torn from our families, he said he presumed it was another Jackson county scrape. He said the Mormons had been driven from that county and that without any offense on their part. He said he knew all about it; they were driven off because the people feared their political influence. And what was said about the Mormons was only to justify the mob in the eyes of the world for the course they had taken. He said this was another scrape of the same kind.

This Burrell Hicks, by his own confession, was one of the principal leaders in the Jackson county mob.

After this digression, I will resume. The same day that we arrived at Richmond, Price came into the place where we were, with a number of armed men, who immediately on entering the room cocked their guns; another followed with chains in his hands, and we were ordered to be chained together. A strong guard was placed in and around the house, and thus we were secured. The next day General Clark came in, and we were introduced to him. The awkward manner in which he entered and his apparent embarrassment were such as to force a smile from me.

He was then asked for what he had thus cast us into prison? To this question he could not or did not give a direct answer. He said he would let us know in a few days; and after a few more awkward and uncouth movements he withdrew. After he went out, I asked some of the guard what was the matter with General Clark, that made him appear so ridiculous? They said he was near-sighted. I replied that I was mistaken if he were not as near-witted as he was near-sighted.

We were now left with our guards, without knowing for what we had been arrested, as no civil process had issued against us. For what followed until General Clark came in again to tell us that we were to be delivered into the hands of the civil authorities, I am entirely indebted to what I heard the guards say. I heard them say that General Clark had promised them before leaving Coles county, that they should have the privilege of shooting Joseph Smith, Jun., and myself; and that General Clark was engaged in searching the military law to find authority for so doing, but found it difficult, as we were not military men and did not belong to the militia; but he had sent to Fort Leavenworth for the military code of law, to find law to justify him in shooting us.

I must here again digress to relate a circumstance which I forgot in its place. I had heard that Clark had given a military order to some persons who had applied to him for it, to go to my house and take such goods as they claimed. The goods claimed were goods sold by the sheriff of Caldwell county on an execution, which I had purchased at the sale.

The man against whom the execution was issued availed himself of that time of trouble to go and take the goods wherever he could find them.

I asked General Clark if he had given any such authority. He said that an application had been made to him for such an order, but he said, "Your lady wrote me a letter requesting me not to do it, telling me that the goods had been purchased at the sheriff's sale; and I would not grant the order."

I did not, at the time, suppose that Clark in this had barefacedly lied; but the sequel proved he had; for, some time afterwards, behold there comes a man to Richmond with the order, and showed it to me, signed by Clark. The man said he had been at our house and taken all the goods he could find. So much for a lawyer, a Methodist, and a very pious man at that time in religion, and a major-general of Missouri.

During the time that Clark was examining the military law, there was something took place which may be proper to relate in this place. I heard a plan laying among a number of those who belonged to Clark's army, and some of them officers of high rank, to go to Far West and commit violence on the persons of Joseph Smith, Sen's wife and my wife and daughter.

This gave me some uneasiness. I got an opportunity to send my family word of their design and to make such arrangements as they could to guard against their vile purpose. The time at last arrived, and the party started for Far West. I waited with painful anxiety for their return. After a number of days, they returned. I listened to all they said, to find out, if possible, what they had done. One night—I think the very night after their return—I heard them relating to some of those who had not been with them the events of their adventure. Inquiry was made about their success in the particular object of their visit to Far West. The substance of what they said in answer was that they had passed and repassed both houses, and saw the females; but there were so many men about the town, that they dare not venture, for fear of being detected; and their numbers were not sufficient to acomplish anything, if they made the attempt; and they came off without trying.

No civil process of any kind had been issued against us. We were then held in duress, without knowing what for or what charges were to be preferred against us. At last, after long suspense, General Clark came into the prison, presenting himself about as awkwardly as at the first, and informed us that we would be put into the hands of the civil authorities. He said he did not know precisely what crimes would be charged against us, but they would be within the range of treason, murder, burglary, arson, larceny, theft, and stealing. Here, again, another smile was forced, and I could not refrain from smiling at the expense of this would-be great man, in whom, he said, "the faith of Missouri was pledged." After long and awful suspense, the notable Austin A. King, judge of the circuit court, took the seat, and we were ordered before him for trial; Thomas Birch, Esq., prosecuting attorney. All things being arranged, the trial opened. No papers were read to us, no charges of any kind preferred, nor did we know against what we had to plead. Our crimes had yet to be found out.

At the commencement we requested that we might be tried separately; but this was refused, and we were all put on our trial together. Witnesses appeared, and the swearing commenced. It was so plainly manifested by the judge that he wanted the witnesses to prove us guilty of treason, that no person could avoid seeing it. The same feelings were also visible in the state's attorney. Judge King made an observation something to this effect, as he was giving directions to the scribe who was employed to write down the testimony, that he wanted all the testimony directed to certain points. Being taken sick at an early stage of the trial, I had not the opportunity of hearing but a small part of the testimony when it was delivered before the court.

During the progress of the trial, after the adjournment of the court in the evening, our lawyers would come into the prison, and there the matters would be talked over.

The propriety of our sending for witnesses was also discussed. Our attorneys said that they would recommend us not to introduce any evidence at that trial. Doniphan said it would avail us nothing, for the judge would put us in prison, if a cohort of angels were to come and swear we were innocent. And besides that, he said that if we were to give the court the names of our witnesses, there was a band there ready to go, and they would go and drive them out of the country, or arrest them and have them cast into prison, or else kill them, to prevent them from swearing. It was finally concluded to let the matter be so for the present.

During the progress of the trial, and while I was lying sick in prison, I had an opportunity of hearing a great deal said by those who would come in. The subject was the all-absorbing one. I heard them say that we must be put to death—that the character of the state required it; the state must justify herself in the course she had taken, and nothing but punishing us with death could save the credit of the state; and it must therefore be done.

I heard a party of them, one night, telling about some female whose person they had violated; and this language was used by one of them: "The d— b—, how she yelled!" Who this person was, I did not know; but before I got out of prison I heard that a widow, whose husband had died some few months before, with consumption, had been brutally violated by a gang of them, and died in their hands, leaving three little children, in whose presence the scene of brutality took place.

After I got out of prison and had arrived in Quincy, Illinois, I met a strange man in the street who inquired of me respecting a circumstance of this kind, saying that he had heard of it, and was on his way going to Missouri to get the children if he could find them. He said the woman thus murdered was his sister, or his wife's sister, I am not positive which. The man was in great agitation. What success he had, I know not.

The trial at last ended, and Lyman Wight, Joseph Smith, Sen., Hyrum Smith, Caleb Baldwin, Alexander McRae, and myself were sent to jail in the village of Liberty, Clay county, Missouri.

We were kept there from three to four months; after which time we were brought out on habeas corpus before one of the county judges. During the hearing under the habeas corpus, I had, for the first time, an opportunity of hearing the evidence, as it was all written and read before the court.

It appeared from the evidence that they attempted to prove us guilty of treason in consequence of the militia of Caldwell county being under arms at the time that General Lucas' army came to Far West. This calling out of the militia was what they founded the charge of treason upon, an account of which I have given above. The charge of murder was founded on the fact that a man of their number, they said, had been killed in the Bogart battle.

The other charges were founded on things which took place in Daviess county. As I was not in Daviess county at that time, I cannot testify anything about them.

A few words about this written testimony:

I do not now recollect one single point about which testimony was given, with which I was acquainted, but was misrepresented, nor one solitary witness whose testimony was there written, that did not swear falsely; and in many instances I cannot see how it could avoid being intentional on the part of those who testified, for all of them did swear to things that I am satisfied they knew to be false at the time, and it would be hard to persuade me to the contrary.

There were things there said so utterly without foundation in truth—so much so, that the persons swearing must at the time of swearing have known it. The best construction I can ever put upon it is that they swore things to be true which they did not know to be so; and this, to me, is wilful perjury.

This trial lasted for a long time, the result of which was that I was ordered to be discharged from prison, and the rest remanded back. But I was told by those who professed to be my friends that it would not do for me to go out of jail at that time, as the mob were watching and would most certainly take my life; and when I got out, that I must leave the state, for the mob, availing themselves of the exterminating order of Governor Boggs, would, if I were found in the state, surely take my life; that I had no way to escape them but to flee with all speed from the state. It was some ten days after this before I dared leave the jail. At last, the evening came in which I was to leave the jail. Every preparation was made that could be made for my escape. There was a carriage ready to take me in and carry me off with all speed. A pilot was ready—one who was well acquainted with the country—to pilot me through the country, so that I might not go on any of the public roads. My wife came to the jail to accompany me, of whose society I had been deprived for four months. Just at dark, the sheriff and jailer came to the jail with our supper. I sat down and ate. There were a number watching. After I had supped, I whispered to the jailer to blow out all the candles but one, and step away from the door with that one. All this was done. The sheriff then took me by the arm, and an apparent scuffle ensued,—so much so, that those who were watching did not know who it was the sheriff was scuffling with. The sheriff kept pushing me towards the door, and I apparently resisting until we reached the door, which was quickly opened, and we both reached the street. He took me by the hand and bade me farewell, telling me to make my escape, which I did with all possible speed. The night was dark. After I had gone probably one hundred rods, I heard some person coming after me. I drew a pistol and cocked it, determined not to be taken alive. When the person approaching me spoke, I knew his voice, and he speedily came to me. In a few moments I heard a horse coming. I again sprung my pistol cock. Again a voice saluted my ears that I was acquainted with. The man came speedily up and said he had come to pilot me through the country. I now recollected I had left my wife in jail. I mentioned it to them, and one of them returned, and the other and myself pursued our journey as swiftly as we could. After I had gone about three miles, my wife overtook me in a carriage, into which I got and rode all night. It was an open carriage, and in the month of February, 1839. We got to the house of an acquaintance just as day appeared. There I put up until the next morning, when I started again and reached a place called Tenney's Grove; and, to my great surprise, I here found my family, and was again united with them, after an absence of four months, under the most painful circumstances. From thence I made my way to Illinois, where I now am. My wife, after I left her, went directly to Far West and got the family under way, and all unexpectedly met at Tenney's Grove.

SIDNEY RIGDON.

[END OF VOLUME III.]

INDEX TO VOLUME III.

A

B

D

M

O

P

S

T

V

W

Y

HISTORY

OF THE

CHURCH OF JESUS CHRIST

OF

LATTER-DAY SAINTS

PERIOD I.

History of Joseph Smith, the Prophet

BY HIMSELF

VOLUME IV

AN INTRODUCTION AND NOTES

BY

B. H. ROBERTS

PUBLISHED FOR THE CHURCH
Second Edition Revised

THE DESERET BOOK COMPANY

Salt Lake City, Utah

1976

TABLE OF CONTENTS.

VOLUME IV.

CHAPTER I.

THE DEPARTURE OF THE TWELVE FOR ENGLAND — MANIFESTATION OF GOD'S POWER IN HEALING THE SICK AT COMMERCE.

CHAPTER II.

THE PROPHET'S JOURNEY TO WASHINGTON—THE PETITION OF THE SAINTS TO THE CONGRESS OF THE UNITED STATES FOR REDRESS OF THE WRONGS INFLICTED UPON THEM IN MISSOURI.

CONTENTS.

CHAPTER III.

THE PROPHET'S EFFORTS AT WASHINGTON TO OBTAIN REDRESS OF GRIEVANCES FOR THE SAINTS—AFFIDAVITS ON MISSOURI AFFAIRS.

CHAPTER IV.

DEPARTURE OF THE PROPHET FROM WASHINGTON—LABORS OF ELIAS HIGBEE BEFORE THE SENATE JUDICIARY COMMITTEE—REPORT OF THE COMMITTEE.

CHAPTER V.

AFFAIRS OF THE SAINTS BEFORE UNITED STATES SENATE—GENERAL CONFERENCE OF THE CHURCH AT NAUVOO—ACTION OF THE CHURCH WITH REFERENCE TO SENATE COMMITTEE'S REPORT—MISSION TO PALESTINE.

CHAPTER VI.

DEVELOPMENT OF THE WORK IN ENGLAND—THE PALESTINE MISSION—POSTOFFICE NAME CHANGED FROM COMMERCE TO NAUVOO.

CHAPTER VII.

FIRST FOREIGN PERIODICAL OF THE CHURCH—THE "MILLENNIAL STAR"—THE PROPHET SEEKS RELEASE FROM SECULAR RESPONSIBILITIES.

CHAPTER VIII.

IMPORTANT CONFERENCE OF THE CHURCH IN ENGLAND—KIDNAPPING OF BROWN AND BOYCE BY MISSOURIANS—ACTION OF THE CITIZENS OF NAUVOO.

CHAPTER IX.

THE RETURN OF A PRODIGAL—CONDITIONS IN KIRTLAND—PROGRESS OF THE WORK IN GREAT BRITAIN—THE COMING OF JOHN C. BENNETT—AUSTRALIAN MISSION.

CHAPTER X.

A MISSOURI KIDNAPPING—CONTINUED DEVELOPMENT OF THE WORK IN GREAT BRITAIN—THE DEATH OF JOSEPH SMITH, SEN., FIRST PATRIARCH OF THE CHURCH.

CHAPTER XI.

THREATENING PORTENTS IN THE ACTIONS OF MISSOURI—GENERAL CONFERENCES IN NAUVOO AND ENGLAND—THE DOCTRINE OF PRIESTHOOD.

CHAPTER XII.

PROGRESS OF THE WORK IN GREAT BRITAIN—THE SAINTS AT KIRTLAND REPROVED FOR THEIR COURSE DURING THE MISSOURI PERSECUTIONS—THE PROPHET'S ADDRESS TO THE TWELVE AND SAINTS IN GREAT BRITAIN.

CHAPTER XIII.

INTRODUCTION OF THE GOSPEL IN THE ISLE OF MAN—THE NAUVOO CHARTER.

CHAPTER XIV.

VALE 1840—ENTER 1841—LIST OF PUBLICATIONS FOR AND AGAINST THE CHURCH—WHEREABOUTS OF THE TWELVE APOSTLES—"ELECTION AND REPROBATION"—PROCLAMATION TO THE SAINTS.

CHAPTER XV.

RECONSTRUCTION OF CHURCH AFFAIRS AT NAUVOO—REVELATION—MUNICIPAL ORGANIZATION OF NAUVOO—INSTALLATION OF CIVIC AND MILITARY OFFICERS.

CHAPTER XVI.

THE FIRST FOREIGN MISSION OF THE CHURCH, 1837-1841.

CHAPTER XVII.

CELEBRATION OF THE TWELFTH ANNIVERSARY OF THE ORGANIZATION OF THE CHURCH—ORDER OF LAYING CORNER-STONES OF TEMPLES —COUNCIL MEETINGS OF THE TWELVE IN ENGLAND.

CHAPTER XVIII.

GENERAL CONFERENCE AT NAUVOO—EPISTLE OF THE TWELVE TO THE SAINTS IN ENGLAND—DIFFERENCE BETWEEN BAPTISTS AND LATTER-DAY SAINTS.

CHAPTER XIX.

ORGANIZATION OF THE NAUVOO LEGION—NOTABLE PERSONS AT NAUVOO—THE PROPHET'S SERMON ON INDIVIDUAL RESPONSIBILITY FOR SIN AND THE DOCTRINE OF ELECTION.

CHAPTER XX.

ARREST OF THE PROPHET ON DEMAND OF MISSOURI—TRIAL AT MONMOUTH—THE ACQUITTAL.

CHAPTER XXI.

THE MISSION TO JERUSALEM—PROGRESS OF ORSON HYDE IN HIS JOURNEY.

CHAPTER XXII.

SUNDRY EVENTS AT NAUVOO AND THROUGHOUT THE WORLD—THE MISSION OF THE TWELVE NOTED BY THE PROPHET.

CHAPTER XXIII.

THE DEATH OF DON CARLOS SMITH—HIS LIFE AND LABORS—SPECIAL CONFERENCE AT NAUVOO.

CHAPTER XXIV.

HOTCHKISS LAND PURCHASE TROUBLE—DEATH'S HARVEST, OLIVER GRANGER, ROBERT B. THOMPSON—IMPORTANT ACTION RELATING TO THE TWELVE—THE MISSION IN FOX ISLAND.

CHAPTER XXV.

THE GENERAL CONFERENCE OF THE CHURCH AT NAUVOO—DOCTRINAL SERMON BY THE PROPHET—BAPTISM FOR THE DEAD—ANGELS AND MINISTERING SPIRITS—EPISTLE OF THE TWELVE REVIEWING STATUS OF THE CHURCH.

CHAPTER XXVI.

AFFAIRS IN KIRTLAND AND NAUVOO—EPISTLE OF THE TWELVE TO THE SAINTS IN THE BRITISH ISLANDS—ORSON HYDE'S PRAYER ON THE MOUNT OF OLIVES, DEDICATING THE HOLY LAND PREPARATORY TO THE RETURN OF THE TRIBES OF ISRAEL.

CHAPTER XXVII.

OFFICIAL DENUNCIATION OF THIEVES AT NAUVOO—THE MORAL LAW OF THE CHURCH—ABANDONMENT OF RAMUS AS A STAKE OF ZION—BAPTISM FOR THE DEAD, AN EPISTLE.

CHAPTER XXVIII.

KIRTLAND VS. NAUVOO—POLITICAL ATTITUDE OF THE PEOPLE OF NAUVOO DECLARED—PUBLICATIONS MORMON AND ANTI-MORMON FOR 1841—CLOSE OF THE YEAR.

CHAPTER XXIX

THE OPENING OF THE YEAR 1842—WHEREABOUTS OF THE TWELVE APOSTLES—CORRESPONDENCE OF ELDER HYDE FROM TRIESTE—REPORT OF HIGH COUNCIL ON AFFAIRS IN NAUVOO—EVENTS AND CONDITIONS IN THE BRITISH MISSION.

CHAPTER XXX.

EMIGRATION OF THE SAINTS FROM ENGLAND TO NAUVOO—THE BOOK OF ABRAHAM.

CHAPTER XXXI

THE WENTWORTH LETTER.

CHAPTER XXXII.

THE BENNETT-DYER CORRESPONDENCE—THE PROPHET'S DISCOURSE ON THE SUBJECT OF THE RESURRECTION, AND THE SALVATION OF CHILDREN—EPISTLE OF THE TWELVE TO THE SAINTS IN ENGLAND CONCERNING THEIR EMIGRATION TO AMERICA.

CHAPTER XXXIII.

A MASON'S ESTIMATE OF NAUVOO AND THE PROPHET—ORGANIZATION OF THE FEMALE RELIEF SOCIETY—"TRY THE SPIRITS"—THE PROPHET'S EDITORIAL.

CHAPTER XXXIV.

SPECIAL CONFERENCE OF THE CHURCH AT NAUVOO—THE PROPHET'S REPROOF OF THE WICKED—EPISTLE OF THE TWELVE TO THE SAINTS IN KIRTLAND—STATUS OF THE CHURCH.

CHAPTER XXXV.

THE GENERAL BANKRUPT LAW—THE DOCTRINE OF BAPTISM FOR THE DEAD—THE PROPHET'S ADDRESS TO THE FEMALE RELIEF SOCIETY—THE KEYS OF THE PRIESTHOOD AND THE NAUVOO TEMPLE.

INTRODUCTION TO VOLUME IV.

FIVE subjects may be said to form the outline of the chief events detailed in this volume of the HISTORY OF THE CHURCH *the Founding of Nauvoo; the Appeal of the Church to the National Government for redress of wrongs suffered in Missouri; the Mission of the Twelve Apostles to the British Isles; the Mission of Orson Hyde to Palestine; and the Doctrinal Development of the Church.*

Preliminary Considerations.

Preliminary to a brief consideration of these several subjects, I desire to say a word as to the reception of the Latter-day Saints by the people of Illinois, and the conditions prevailing in that state at the time of their arrival. A knowledge of these conditions is necessary to the understanding of this whole Illinois period of the History of the Church.

Much has been made of the hospitality which the people of Illinois extended to the Latter-day Saints at the time of their expulsion from Missouri. A writer in the *American Historical Magazine* for July, 1906, says: "To the latter state [Illinois] they [the Saints] went in 1839, and were received with such open-armed hospitality as only a very generous and liberty-loving people can extend to those whom they honestly believe to be suffering from a wrongful oppression. The conduct of the Saints in five years turned this feeling of extraordinarily deep-seated sympathy, inducing great practical charities, into a feeling of very bitter hatred, threatening to break into mob violence." Far be it from me me to depreciate the kindness of those who extended a helping hand to the Saints in the hour of their distress. Stripped and sorely wounded they fled from the violence of Missouri militia-mobs, and found for a time a peaceful asylum in Illinois. Many were the acts of disinterested kindness extended to them by the people in the western part of that state; and every such act I am sure was and is remembered, both by those who were the direct recipients of such acts of kindness and by their grateful descendants. But is responding to the calls of humanity so rare a thing in a Christian state, that it must needs be regarded as so exceptional in this case? Such was the condition of the Saints as they fled from Missouri, such the injustice to which they had been subjected in that state, that their situation would have appealed to the generosity of savages, how much more, then, to a civilized and Christian community! And then, speaking of this reception of the Saints *en masse*, by Illinois, and leaving out of consideration for the moment—since they have already been acknowledged—the individual acts of kindness bestowed upon the exiles, was this reception of the Saints by Illinois wholly disinterested? Were there not benefits which the Saints could bestow upon the state in return for the heartiness of the reception given? Would it not have been, under all the circumstances, the gravest of blunders for Illinois to have refused asylum to these exiles? Is it to be presumed that the public men of western Illinois were so blind to their own interests as not to see in these twelve or fifteen thousand people a mighty advantage to the state? It is true they were poor in this world's goods; but they were rich in labor-power, and their reputation for habits of sobriety and of industry had preceded them. Here were thousands of husbandmen seeking lands. Illinois had thousands of acres of unoccupied lands awaiting husbandmen. How shortsighted and unstatesman-like it would have been for the men of Illinois not to have welcomed these settlers into their state? With half an eye it is easy to see that the benefits of this reception of the exiled Mormons by Illinois is not by any means a one-sided affair; and it would be doing an injustice to the intelligence of the people of that state to suppose they were blind to these advantages. This will more fully appear when other conditions are taken into account. Illinois has an area of 56,650 square miles; and at the time of the advent of the Saints in that state a white population of less than four hundred thousand,* as against a present population of five and a half millions.† It will be seen, then, that in 1839, the year of the advent of the Saints into that state, Illinois was very sparsely settled, and needed above all things for her development and prosperity, people to subdue her wilderness and cultivate her rich lands, especially people desirous of making homes, and becoming permanent citizens. Moreover, Illinois had recently launched an extensive system of internal improvements by state aid. This system included the construction of 1,300 miles of railroads in the state, besides provisions for the improvement of the navigation of the Kaskaskia, Illinois, Great and Little Wabash, and Rock rivers. Also the construction of a canal from Lake Michigan to the navigable waters of the Illinois river, a distance of more than one hundred miles (from Chicago to Peru). To carry out this system of internal improvements the state legislature of 1836-7 had appropriated the sum of $12,000,000; and to raise the money state bonds were placed on the stock markets of the eastern states and in England. It is not my province here even to note the wisdom or unwisdom of this policy of wholesale state aid for these internal improvements; let the wisdom

* The population in 1830 was but 155,061; and in 1840, 472,254.

† The population of Illinois in 1900 was 4,821,550—nearly five millions: the estimated population for 1908 is 5,590,000.

or unwisdom be what it may, these conditions emphasized Illinois' demand for population, and again makes it evident that it would have been the height of folly for the people of that state to do other than give hearty welcome to this body of population so rich in labor-power; so potent in wealth producing energy.

Another thing to be noted is the fact that about the time of the advent of the Saints into Illinois, political parties were just taking form in that state, and it is within the record of facts in the case, as well as of great likelihood, that a desire for obtaining political advantage was at least in the background of motives prompting the heartiness of the reception given to the Saints.

Illinois was admitted into the Union in 1818, but it is a matter of common knowledge that in the early years of her history as a state, her officers were elected not on any well defined political party principles, but chiefly on the strength of the personality of the candidates and the special things for which they individually stood. Indeed, it was not until 1830 that anything like party lines were drawn in the state, and that it became a battle ground for the two great national parties, Whigs and Democrats. It was a committee from a Democratic party organization in Quincy, Illinois, that took the initiative in welcoming the Saints into the state, and strive how one may, it is difficult to think there was not some political advantage sought through this action. On the other hand, the Whigs were not slow to urge upon the incoming exiles that it was a Democratic state and a Democratic administration in that state which had not only permitted, but had really ordered their expulsion from Missouri, and that doubtless the injustice they had suffered was owing to Democratic ideas of the administration of government. Nor were there wanting those among the Saints who were willing to believe that such was the case. Indeed, Joseph Smith, the Prophet, found it necessary to gently reprove some of his people who were rapidly making the question of their expulsion from Missouri a political party question in Illinois. This effort to win the Saints to one political party or the other, continued to be a factor in their affairs so long as they remained at Nauvoo. It was owing to this rivalry for their support that doubtless made it possible for the Saints to obtain larger grants of power for their city government, and greater polical privileges and influence in the State than otherwise could have been obtained by them. It also was this rivalry for their favor, as the events in this, but more especially in the succeeding volume will prove, that made them alternately fulsomely flattered and heartily disliked; fawningly courted, and viciously betrayed.

A knowledge of these circumstances, I say, is essential to the right understanding of the Nauvoo period of the Church's history.

The Founding of Nauvoo.

The founding of the city of Nauvoo was an event, the interest of which extends beyond the people immediately concerned in it. It was a unique movement in its way, and may yet suggest a policy in reference to the government of large cities from which great benefits may arise. Very naturally after the experiences of the Mormon people in Missouri, the Prophet was anxious to environ them with conditions that would insure protection to the community, hence for Nauvoo he secured as large concessions of political power as it was possible to obtain, and an examination of the Nauvoo charter proper with its attendant charters providing as they did for an independent educational system, from common schools to a University; an independent military organization with a lieutenant-general as its commander;* a large grant of commercial as well as municipal power, demonstrates how well he succeeded. Commenting upon the charter immediately after its passage by the state legislature had been formally announced, he said: "The City Charter of Nauvoo is of my own plan and device. I concocted it for the salvation of the Church, and on principles so broad, that every honest man might dwell secure under its protective influence without distinction of sect or party."† On another occasion when defending the right of the city to issue writs of habeas corpus, even against proceesses of the state, he held: "If there is not power in our charter and courts, then there is not power in the State of Illinois nor in the Congress or Constitution of the United States; for the United States gave unto Illinois her Constitution or Charter, and Illinois gave unto Nauvoo her charters conceding unto us our vested rights which she has no right or power to take from us. All the power there was in Illinois she gave to Nauvoo. * * * The municipal court has all the power to issue and determine writs of habeas corpus within the limits of this state that the

* Commenting once in a half humorous way upon his "exalted" military rank, the Prophet said to Josiah Quincy, who remarks that the Prophet at the time of his visit to Nauvoo (May, 1843), was at the head of 3,000 men equipped by the state of Illinois, represents him as having said:

"I decided that the commander of my troops ought to be a lieutenant-general, and I was, of course, chosen to that position. I sent my certificate of election to Governor Ford, and received in return a commission of lieutenant-general of the Nauvoo Legion of the militia of the State of Illinois. Now, on examining the constitution of the United States, I find that an officer must be tried by a court martial composed of his equals in rank; and as I am the only lieutenant-general in the country, I think they will find it pretty hard to try me."—*Figures of the Past*, p. 383.

† This volume, p. 249.

Legislature can confer. This city has all the power that the State courts have, and was given by the same authority—the legislature. * * * The charter says that the City Council shall have power and authority to make, ordain, establish, and execute such ordinances not repugnant to the Constitution of the United States, or of this State, as they may deem necessary for the peace, benefit and safety of the inhabitants of said city.* And also that the Municipal Court shall have power to grant writs of habeas corpus in all cases arising under the ordinances of the City Council. The City Council have passed an ordinance 'that no citizen of this city shall be taken out of this city by any writ without the privilege of a writ of habeas corpus.' There is nothing but what we have power over, except where restricted by the Constitution of the United States. 'But,' says the mob, 'what dangerous powers!' Yes—dangerous, because they will protect the innocent and put down mobocrats. There is nothing but what we have power over, except where restricted by the Constitution of the United States. * * * If these powers are dangerous, then the Constitution of the United States, and of this State are dangerous; but they are not dangerous to good men; they are only so to bad men who are breakers of the laws. * * * The lawyers themselves acknowledge that we have all power granted us in our charters, that we could ask for—that we had more power than any other court in the State; for all other courts were restricted while ours was not."

Such views in relation to an ordinary municipal government would unquestionably be stamped as preposterous. No such powers as are here claimed are accorded to ordinary city governments in Illinois or any other of the states of the American Union. What then may be said of the Prophet's claims in respect to the municipal powers of Nauvoo? Nothing in way of defense, except that Nauvoo was *not* an ordinary municipality; that Joseph Smith had sought for extraordinary grants of power for the city of Nauvoo and had obtained them; that his personal experiences and the experiences of his people, both in Ohio and Missouri, had taught him the necessity of having officers charged with the duty of administering government wherein his people were concerned, who were friendly disposed and whose interests were largely identical with those of the Saints; that the things which both the Prophet and his people had suffered justified both him and them in seeking for and obtaining such power as had been conferred by charters upon the city of Nauvoo; that the Prophet was wholly within the lines of right conduct when he invoked the municipal powers in his own protection

* Section 11, this volume, p. 241. The Prophet quoted from memory, and is not exact; the exact language is—"As they deem necessary for the peace, benefit, good order, regulation, convenience and cleanliness of said city."

against the aggressions of his old enemies in Missouri and his new betrayers in Illinois. But whether the legislature of Illinois was fully aware of the extraordinary powers they were conferring upon the city of Nauvoo, or being aware of the import of their action the party in control of the legislature was willing to grant the extraordinary powers in the hope of currying political favor with the Saints, may not now be determined; but in any event these extraordinary powers were granted; and wittingly or unwittingly a "city-state" had practically been established within the state of Illinois. Nothing short of this descriptive term can adequately set forth the municipal government of Nauvoo. It seems to be an unconscious reversion, in an incipient way, to the "city-states" or "city-republics" of the old Greek confederations; or the "free-towns" of medieval times, when the cities were more potent than nations in commerce and even in politics. Whether or not the state courts of Illinois and United States courts would have sustained the Nauvoo charters if the matter of their validity had been referred to them for adjudication, may not be determined; but one can scarcely suppress the thought that the likelihood is that they would not have been sustained; on the contrary they would have been most likely declared anomalous to our system of government as it then stood, and now stands. But certainly if the experiment of such a municipal government had not been interrupted in its progress, it might have been an instructive object lesson in the government of cities; and even as it is, the founding of Nauvoo, the "city-state," suggests an important idea which may work out great practical reforms in municipal government in our country.

The founders of our Government dealt with condititions that were very simple in comparison with the complexity of the conditions which government in its various forms, municipal, state and national, is confronted with today. The Municipal problems which now vex the people had not then arisen above the horizon of their experience. The American commonwealths of the early decades of the nineteenth century were practically rural commonwealths. At the time of Washington's inauguration (1789) the population of New York was but thirty-three thousand; Philadelphia forty-two thousand; Boston but eighteen thousand; Baltimore thirteen thousand; Brooklyn one thousand six hundred, and more village than town. Now compare these cities with their present population. New York has a population of over four millions;* Philadelphia a population of one and a half millions;† Boston more than half

* The official census of 1905 gives the population of New York at 4,014,304. The estimated population on January 1, 1908, is 4,285,435.

† Official returns for 1900 give Philadelphia a population of 1,293,697. The estimated population for Jan. 1, 1908, is 1,491,161.

a million;* Baltimore over five hundred thousand;† Brooklyn is absorbed in New York, but as a borough of the larger city it has a population of nearly one and a half millions;‡ Chicago, which in 1840 had but four thousand inhabitants, much smaller than Nauvoo, has now a population of more than two millions;§ St. Louis which in 1840 had a population of but 16,469, has now a population of three quarters of a million.‖ Nothing like the growth of urban population within the United States during the last fifty years has been known in the history of the world, and it has brought to the inhabitants of these cities problems undreamed of by the founders of our government. Every year discloses more and more distinctly the fact that between these condensed communities and the town, village, and rural population of the states in which they are located, there are very distinct interests and governmental problems of widely differing character. The differences which justify distinct local governments in the state of New York and the peninsula of Florida are not more insistent than the differences between the great commercial city of New York and the state of the same name. Without entering upon elaborate discussion of these questions (a discussion which is foreign to the character of this writing) I venture the suggestion that separate and complete state governments for our large cities, or the elevation of them into what I have called "city-states," such as Nauvoo was, in an incipient way, will be the solution to most of the problems of municipal government in our very large cities. It would greatly enlarge in them the governmental powers essential to their more perfect peace, security, and prosperity. Also it would separate them from embroilment in those questions of the state governments under which they are now located, and in which they have so little interest—often indeed, there is even sharp conflict of interests, engendering bitterness and strife which hinders progress for both city and state. Besides, granting complete statehood to our larger cities would be but a proper recognition of the right of those great aggregations of citizens with their varied industries, their immense wealth and distinct interests, to that measure of influence in our national affairs which their numbers and intelligence and interests justly demand.

* Official statistics for 1905 give Boston a population of 595,083. The estimated population for Jan. 1, 1908, is 607,340.

† Official returns for 1900 give Baltimore a population of 508,957. The estimated population for Jan. 1, 1908, is 567,000.

‡ The estimated population of Brooklyn as a borough of greater New York is given on Jan. 1, 1908, as 1,448,095.

§ Official statistics for 1900 give Chicago a population of 1,698,575. The estimated population for Jan. 1, 1908, is 2,483,641.

‖ Official statistics for 1900 give St. Louis a population of 575,238. The estimated population on Jan. 1, 1908, is 50,000.

The Appeal of the Church to the National Government for Redress of Wrongs Suffered in Missouri.

The Prophet Joseph Smith, Sidney Rigdon, and Judge Elias Higbee were chosen as the committee to present to the National Congress the petition of the Saints for a redress of their grievances, suffered in Missouri. This journey to the nation's Capital was of importance quite apart from the immediate purpose for which it was undertaken; namely, it brought the Prophet in contact with the leading statesmen of the United States. While in Washington, he was brought in contact with and interviewed such men as Henry Clay, John C. Calhoun, President Martin Van Buren, different members of the Cabinet, Senators, and Representatives. Such contact enabled him to take new measurements, not only of a different class of men from those with whom he had been accustomed to associate, but new measurements of himself by comparison and contrast of himself with those leading spirits of the nation. Comparisons which could not result otherwise than in advantage to him; and I think it must be conceded by all students of the Prophet's character, especially to those who have been at all close observers of its development, that after this trip to Washington, which afforded the above noted opportunities of comparison and contrast, the Prophet's growth was immeasurably greater than at any time before that journey.

In some respects however it was unfortunate that the Prophet was not more cosmopolitan in his training and in his views of life on the occasion of this visit to the nation's capital; for lack of such training and views of life led him to the formation of rather hasty judgments as to the character of our nation's public men at that time. He undoubtedly had sticking to him as yet, some of the prejudices of his New England and New York sectional training; and at the time of his visit the spirit of the public men of the nation at Washington was largely influenced by the Southern character and spirit. Bourbon Democracy was at its height. The gentlemen of the South with their extreme notions of chivalry and polite deportment, predominated. In those days men were held to strict account for their manner of address one to another. An improper word, a slight, magnified into an insult, meant a challenge to mortal combat on "the field of honor," and this sense of personal responsibility for utterances begot, no doubt, an extreme politeness in personal deportment which seemed puerile to those reared in another atmosphere and influenced by other sentiments than those which resulted from education in the South. Joseph Smith's judgment upon manners and customs in Washington, was doubtless New England's judgment upon Southern customs with which it had no patience, much less sympathy. It is only from these considerations that the rather harsh judgment of the Prophet in relation to conditions in Washington can be properly understood.

Relative to the business upon which this committee visited Washington, it should be said that Sidney Rigdon failed to participate in it at all, in consequence of an illness which befell him on his journey, and hindered him from reaching Washington until the business was practically settled. A short stay in Washington convinced the Prophet that nothing was to be expected in the way of obtaining a redress of grievances for his people from the very cautious politicians then in control of the government, all of whom were anxious, apparently, to palliate the actions of Missouri with reference to the Saints, for the sake of retaining her political influence on their side; and also because of a prevailing inclination to a strict construction of the powers of the general government in its relations to the states. The Prophet therefore left Washington to preach the Gospel for a short time in New Jersey and Philadelphia, after which he returned to Nauvoo, leaving Judge Elias Higbee to urge consideration of the petition of the Saints which had been referred to the Senate committee on Judiciary, with what result is made known in detail in the body of this volume of the history. It is sufficient here to say that the net result of the Committee's deliberations was simply to recommend that the Saints appeal for a redress of their wrongs to the United States District Court having jurisdiction in Missouri, or they could, if they saw proper, "apply to the justice and magnanimity of the State of Missouri—an appeal which the committee feel justified in believing will never be made in vain by the injured or oppressed."—(Sic!)

This suggestion to take their case to the United States Courts was never acted upon by the Saints, nor does it appear in what manner it would have been practicable for them to do so. True it is expressly provided in the Constitution that "The Judicial power of the United States shall extend to all cases in law and equity, arising under this Constitution, the laws of the United States, and treaties made, or which shall be made, under their authority; to controversies between two or more states; between a state and citizens of another state; between citizens of different states; between citizens of the same state," etc.* The case of the Saints would fall either under the clauses in the above quotation respecting controversies arising between a state (Missouri) and citizens of another state (the Saints, now citizens, of Illinois); or "between citizens of different states," the Saints, citizens of Illinois, and their former persecutors, citizens of Missouri. In considering the question under the first clause it must be remembered that the eleventh amendment to the Constitution (declared in force 1798) provides that

* Art. 111 Const. U. S., Sec. ii.

"The Judicial power of the United States shall not be construed to extend to any suit in law or equity, commenced or prosecuted against one of the United States by citizens of another state, or by citizens or subjects of any foreign state." It is held that "the power as well as the dignity of a state would be gone if it could be dragged into court by a private plaintiff."*

The Supreme Court in the case Chisholm *vs.* the State of Georgia, had decided (1793) that an action did lie against the State of Georgia at a suit of a private plaintiff. The state however refused to appear, whereupon the Supreme Court proceeded, a year later, to give judgment against her by default in case she should not appear and plead before a day; whereupon there arose such a storm of protest, not only in Georgia, but in the other states as well, that the eleventh amendment was adopted exempting a state from being sued in the courts of the United States by citizens of another state, or by citizens subjects of any foreign state. Moreover, states are not suable in any event except with their consent;† and if a state waive its immunity, it may attach any conditions it pleases to its consent.‡ Under these circumstances it is not surprising that the Saints never attempted to bring Missouri before the United States courts. They could only have planted suit against the state by its consent, and if she consented, then under such conditions as she might be pleased to attach to that consent. Moreover, the Saints had the best of reasons for believing that Missouri would never consent.

As to suing their persecutors as individuals before the United States courts, as citizens of one state suing citizens of another, it is only necessary to remind the reader of the insuperable difficulties attending upon that procedure to convince him of the futility of such action, The expensiveness of the undertaking, and the extreme poverty of the exiles alone would be sufficient to bar such an undertaking; for every one knows how bitterly hard it is for the poor to set the judicial machinery of organized society in motion in their favor. Then there was the evident conspiracy entered into by the mobs of Missouri to defeat the ends of justice in respect of the Saints: mobs which an unfriendly governor had converted into a state militia; to which that same governor gave an order to expel from the state or exterminate the entire people; under which order said mob-militia did expel from the state some twelve thousand citizens, depriving them of their property and liberty without due process of law; and afterwards the state through its legislature sanctioned and applauded the actions of this mob-militia for the part it had taken in causing said expulsion—though attended by acts of un-

* Am. Commonwealth (Bryce) Vol. I p. 231.

† Railroad Co. v. Tennessee, U. S. Reports 101, 337.

‡ Clark v. Barnard U. S. 108, 436, and Green v. State 73 Cal. 29 et seq.

speakable atrocity—by appropriating 200,000 dollars to meet the expenses of the mob-militia in carrying out the governor's illegal orders. After these crimes against the Constitution and laws of the state, against American institutions and the civilization of the age—after all this, I say, it is not difficult to understand how farcical would be any procedure before either the state or the federal courts in Missouri. By acts of perjury, in order to still further defeat the ends of justice and protect each other from the penalties due to their crimes, it would have been easy for the people of Missouri to defeat the ends of justice. And after having committed the crimes of murder and robbery; after having unlawfully expelled a whole people, numbering thousands, from their homes—of which the despoilers were then possessed—it is not to be believed that such characters would hesitate to subborn witnesses, commit perjury, or hesitate to do any other thing, however criminal, in order to escape the just punishment for their crimes.

The offense of the State of Missouri against the Saints was a denial of political as well as of civil rights. She had in her treatment of the Saints abdicated republican government. Her officers, including the chief executive of the state had violated the Constitution of the state in that they had entered into a wide-spread conspiracy to deprive the Saints of their liberty and property without due process of law; and in fact had deprived them of those rights by expelling them by force of arms from the state.

These were the wrongs the Saints had endured; this the nature of the crime of the state of Missouri against them, and it seems that for these things which they suffered there could be found no remedy; for, as already explained, a state could not be made party to a suit before the courts, either state or federal, without her consent; and it is a well settled principle of American law that "a suit nominally against an officer but really against a state to enforce performance of its obligation in its political capacity, will not lie." A state, therefore, could not be directly arraigned before the courts or any kind of tribunal for failure to enforce its political obligations; nor could it be indirectly so arraigned through its officers since such an arraignment would undoubtedly have been held to be but "nominally against the officers and really against the state;" hence void. The only arraignment of the state that could be made was evidently at the bar of public opinion and sentiment, and this sentiment, unfortunately viciated by misrepresentations, was against the Saints. All things considered, then, there was little wisdom behind the recommendation of the Senate Judiciary Committee for the Saints to prosecute their case before the Federal courts having jurisdiction in Missouri; and

* See Cooler's Constitutional Limitations, chapter ii, also Louisiana v. Jumel 107 U. S. Reports, p. 711, 2 sup. ct. rep. 128.

the suggestion that they apply to the justice and magnanimity of the state of the Missouri, borders upon mockery. However, Missouri did not escape the chastisement due to her many acts of predatory injustice upon the Saints; there was measured out to her more than four fold of that sorrow and affliction which she had perpetraded upon the Saints. She sowed to the wind in her conduct towards the Mormon people, she reaped the whirl-wind in the terrible experiences of more then ten years of border warfare, banditti rule, and her enormous sacrifice of blood and treasure in the Civil War; all of which is abundantly set forth in the Introduction to Volume III of this work.

The Mission of the Twelve to England.

The mission of the Twelve to England marks an epoch in the missionary experience of the Church. They undertook this mission in fulfillment of a commandment received of the Lord on the 8th of July, 1838, at Far West, Missouri, which revelation was given in answer to the question of the Prophet: "Show us thy will, O Lord, concerning the Twelve." In answer to that question the Lord directed that the several vacancies then existing in the quorum should be filled by the appointment of John Taylor, John E. Page, Wilford Woodruff, and Willard Richards. "And next spring," said the revelation, "let them [the Twelve] depart to go over the great waters and there promulgate my gospel, the fullness thereof, and bear record of my name. Let them take leave of my Saints in the City Far West on the 26th day of April next, on the building spot of my house saith the Lord."*

Notwithstanding the fact that the Church had been expelled from the state of Missouri before the 26th day of April, 1839, a number of the Twelve accompanied by several of those who had been appointed to fill vacancies in the quorum, returned to Far West, held a meeting on the site of the Lord's house in the public square of that place, on the date appointed, sung some hymns, ordained those present who had been appointed to fill vacancies in the quorum, laid a corner stone of the Lord's house, took leave of a few of the brethren who were there, and thence started for foreign lands, stopping for a time *en route* at Nauvoo. Late in the summer of 1839 the Twelve began their departure, usually in pairs, for foreign lands. The work had already been introduced into England by the labors of Elder Heber C. Kimball and associates, Elder Orson Hyde of the quorum of the Twelve; also Elders Willard Richards, Isaac Russell, John Goodson, John Snyder; and Joseph Fielding, a priest. The mission of the Twelve to England as a quorum, however, established the work in the British Isles on a broader and more perma-

III, p. 46.

nent basis, and thence forward the body religious was strengthened from this mission; and as much from the character as from the numbers of the British Saints.

The Mission of Orson Hyde to Palestine.

The mission appointed to Elders Orson Hyde and John E. Page, of the quorum of the Twelve, to Jerusalem, was second in importance only to that appointed to the rest of the Twelve to Great Britain. John E. Page utterly failed to fulfill his appointment, notwithstanding the frequent urging and reproofs of the Prophet. He never left the shores of America, and finally returned to Nauvoo to be serverly censured for his lack of faith and energy. Orson Hyde, on the contrary, in the midst of many hardships, persevered in his journey to the Holy Land, until he succeeded in accomplishing that which had been appointed unto him. Elder Hyde it appears, was a descendant of the tribe of Judah;* and sometime after the Prophet had become acquainted with him, most probably in the year 1832, in the course of pronouncing a blessing upon him, said: "In due time thou shalt go to Jerusalem, the land of thy fathers, and be a watchman unto the house of Israel; and by thy hand shall the Most High do a great work, which shall prepare the way and greatly facilitate the gathering together of that people."† It was in fulfillment of this prediction upon his head that he had been called upon this mission to Jerusalem, to dedicate the land of Palestine by apostolic authority, preparatory to the return of the Jews and other of the tribes of Israel to that land of promise. This mission he fully accomplished. An account of his journey and of his beautiful and powerful prayer of dedication will be found in his letters published in this volume.‡

The question will be asked, Has anything resulted from this mission to dedicate the land of Palestine to the return of the Jews and other tribes of Israel? The only answer is an appeal to facts, to events that have taken place since that prayer of consecration was offered up by this Apostle of the new dispensation of the Gospel, on the 24th of October, 1841.

At the time of Elder Hyde's visit and the ceremonies of dedication he performed on the Mount of Olives, there were comparatively but few Jews at Jerusalem. As late as 1876 the British Consul Reports show that there were but from fifteen to twenty thousand Jews in Judea. But twenty years later the same authority declared the number of Jews at sixty to seventy thousand; and, what was of more importance than

* See this Volume, p. 375.

† *Ibid.*

‡ The prayer of Dedication will be found at pp. 456-459.

the numbers announced, these reports represented that the new Jewish population was turning its attention to the cultivation of the soil, which but requires the blessings of God upon it to restore it to its ancient fruitfulness, and which will make it possible for it to sustain once more a numerous population. The St. Louis *Globe-Democrat* commenting on these Consular Reports of 1896, said:

"Only two decades ago there were not more than fifteen or twenty thousand Jews in Jerusalem. At that time no houses were to be found outside the walls of the city. Since then many changes have taken place and the Hebrew population—mainly on account of the increase of the Jewish immigration from Russia—now stands at between sixty and seventy thousand. Whole streets of houses have been built outside the walls on the site of the ancient suburban districts, which for hundreds of years have remained deserted. It is not, however, only in Jerusalem itself that the Jews abound, but throughout Palestine they are buying farms and establishing themselves in a surprisingly rapid manner. In Jerusalem they form at present a larger community than either the Christian or the Mohammedan."

Also in 1896 that racial movement among the Jews known as "Zionism" took definite form. This movement was really the federation of all the Jewish societies that have cherished the hope of seeing Israel restored to his promised possessions in Palestine. That year the first international conference of Zionists was held in Basel, Switzerland, and since then under the leadership of the late Dr. Herzel of Austria, and since his death under the leadership of Israel Zangwill, and by reason of its annual conferences constantly increasing in interest and attendance, "Zionism" has taken on all the aspects of one of the world's great movements. It is not so much a religious movement as a racial one; for prominent Jews of all shades of both political and religious opinions have participated in it.

After saying through so many centuries at the feast of the Passover, "May we celebrate the next Passover in Jerusalem," the thought seems to have occurred to some Jewish minds that if that hope is ever to be realized some practical steps must be taken looking to the actual achievement of the possibility—hence the "Zionite Movement." The keynotes of that movement are heard in the following utterances of some of the Jewish leaders in explanation of it: "We want to resume the broken thread of our national existence; we want to show to the wor d the moral strength, the intellectual power of the Jewish people. We want a place where the race can be centralized."—(Leon Zoltokoff). "It is for these Jews (of Russia, Roumania and Galicia) that the name of their country (Palestine) spells 'Hope.' I should not be a man if I did not realize that for these persecuted Jews, Jerusalem spells reason, justice, manhood and liberty."—(Rabbi Emil G. Hirsch). "Jewish nationalism on a modern basis in Palestine, the old home of the people." —(Max Nordau). Palestine needs a people, Israel needs a country. Give the country without a people to the people without a country."—(Israel Zangwill). In a word it is the purpose of "Zionism" to redeem Palestine, and give it back to Jewish control, create, in fact, a Jewish state in the land promised to their fathers.

The age has come when the promises of the Lord to Israel must be fulfilled; and hence an apostle of the new dispensation of the Gospel is sent by divine authority to dedicate the land of Palestine preparatory to the return of Israel to his promised inheritance. After which follows this strange and world-wide movement among the Jews looking to the re-establishment of "Jewish nationalism on a modern basis in Palestine." What other relationship can exist between the mission of the Apostle Orson Hyde and this world-wide movement among the Jews for the re-establishment of Israel in Palestine, but the relationship of cause to effect—under, of course, the larger fact that the set time for the restoration of Israel has come? The apostle's mission to Jerusalem for the purpose of dedicating that land, preparatory to the return of Israel, was without doubt part of the general program for the restoration of Israel to their lands and to the favor and blessing of God.

The Doctrinal Development of the Church.

The doctrinal development in this period of the dispensation of the fullness of times, namely, between July, 1839, and the month of May, 1842, about three years, was chiefly in relation to salvation for the dead, and the sacred ritual of the Temple. The foundation for this doctrinal development in relation to salvation for the dead, was laid in the very inception of the work. On the occasion of the first visit of the angel Moroni to the Prophet, on the night of the 21st of September, 1823, among other ancient prophecies quoted by him, and which he declared was soon to be fulfilled, was the prophecy in the fourth chapter of Malachi in relation to the future coming of Elijah the prophet, "before the coming of the great and dreadful day of the Lord." As quoted by the angel there was a slight variation in the language from King James' version, as follows: "Behold, I will reveal unto you the Priesthood by the hand of Elijah the prophet, before the coming of the great and dreadful day of the Lord. And he shall plant in the hearts of the children the promises made to the fathers, and the hearts of the children shall turn to their fathers; if it were not so, the whole world would be wasted at his coming."*

* HISTORY OF THE CHURCH, Vol. I, p. 12.

Here the promise is made, that in consequence of the restoration of a certain Priesthood,or special keys of authority held by Elijah, the promises made to the fathers shall be planted in the hearts of the children, "and the hearts of the children shall turn to their fathers." Why? For a complete answer to that question the Church waited some years. Again, and still early in the history of the work, namely, March, 1830, the Lord in a revelation to Martin Harris through the Prophet Joseph, added another line or two of knowledge to this doctrine; knowledge which pushed out of the horizon of men's conceptions the terrible and unjust doctrine respecting the eternal punishment which God is supposed to inflict upon those who fail to obey the Gospel in this life, and also those who died in ignorance of it. In explanation of the terms, "eternal punishment," and "everlasting punishment," sometimes found in Holy Writ, the Lord said to the Prophet: "Behold, I am endless, and the punishment which is given from my hand is endless, for endless is my name. Wherefore—

"Eternal punishment is God's punishment.

"Endless punishment is God's punishment."

That is to say, the punishment takes the name of Him in whose name it is inflicted; as if it were written, "Eternal's punishment," "Endless's punishment." And also, it must be understood, that the punishment itself is endless. That is, penalties always attend upon law, and follow its violation. That is an eternal principle. Law is inconceivable without accompanying penalties. But it does not follow that those who fall into the transgression of law, and therefore under sentence of Eternal's justice, will have to endure affliction of the penalty eternally. Justice can be satisfied. Mercy must be accorded her claims, and the culprit having been brought to repentance and taught obedience to law through the things which he has suffered, must go free. But only to suffer again the penalties of the law, if he again violates it; for laws and their penalties are eternal. Hence eternal punishment, hence endless punishment administered to the violator of the law, until he learns to live in harmony with law. For, on the one hand, as "that which is governed by law is also preserved by law, and perfected and sanctified by the same;* so "that which breaketh a law and abideth not by the law, but seeketh to become a law unto itself, and willeth to abide in sin and altogether abideth in sin, cannot be sanctified by law, neither by mercy, justice, nor judgment. Therefore they must remain filthy still."† Thus obedience to law becomes a savor of life unto life; while disobedience to law equally becomes a savor of death unto death.

In February, 1832, still further light was shed upon the subject of

* Doctrine and Covenants, Sec. lxxxviii, 34. † *Ibid*, verse 35.

the different states or degrees of glory in which men will live in the future, by the revelation known as "The Vision." This revelation is one of the sublimest ever given to man. It utterly discredits and displaces the dogmas about the future of man held by Christendom, or at least by Protestant Christendom. The orthodox, Protestant view of man's future is that there are two states in one or the other of which man will spend eternity—in heaven or in hell. If one shall gain heaven, even by ever so small a margin, he will enter immediately upon a complete possession of all its unspeakable joys, equally with the angels and the holiest of Saints. Not only in the "Shorter Catechisms," but in nearly all orthodox creeds the accepted doctrine was: "The souls of believers are at their death made perfect in holiness." On the other hand,if one shall miss heaven, even by ever so small a margin, he is doomed to everlasting torment equally with the wickedest of men and vilest of devils, and there is no deliverance for him through all the countless ages of eternity! It will be noted that I have excepted out of participating in the above view of man's future, the Catholic church, by ascribing these views only to orthodox Protestant Christendom. This is because the Catholic church doctrine slightly differs from the doctrine of the Protestants on this subject. That is Catholics do not believe that all Christians at death go immediately into heaven, but on the contrary "believe that a Christian who dies after the guilt and everlasting punishment of mortal sins have been forgiven him, but who, either from want of opportunity, or through his negligence has not discharged the debt of temporal punishment due to his sin, will have to discharge that debt to the justice of God in purgatory." "Purgatory is a state of suffering after this life, in which those souls are for a time detained, which depart this life after their deadly sins have been remitted as to the stain and guilt, and as to the everlasting pain that was due to them, but which souls have on account of those sins still some temporal punishment to pay; as also those souls which leave this world guilty only of venial (that is pardonable) sins. In purgatory these souls are purified and rendered fit to enter into heaven, where nothing defiled enters."* As all works of the Catholic church accessible to me have nothing on the different degrees of glory in which men shall subsist in eternity, I conclude that Catholic teaching is that they who finally attain unto heaven are all equal in glory. So that in the last analysis of the matter, Catholic doctrine falls as far below the great truth that God has revealed upon the subject of the future estate of man, as the doctrine of orthodox Protestant Christendom.

Here is not the place for an extended exposition of the doctrine in

* The quotations in the above are from "Catholic Belief," by Bruno, D.D. of the Catholic church.

relation to the future state of man as revealed to Joseph Smith in the revelation called "The Vision."* It must suffice here to say that its central principle is resident in the justice and the mercy of God, that requires that every man shall be judged according to his works, considered in the light of his intelligence, his consciousness of right and wrong, and the moral law under which he lived. If he lived in the earth when the Gospel of Jesus Christ was not in the world, or if he lived at places or in circumstances where he did not learn of its existence, much less come to a knowledge of its truths, then the plain dictates of justice demand that some means must exist by which its sanctifying powers may be applied to him in the future; so also as to those who have even once rejected the truth (as in the case of the antediluvians who rejected the teaching of righteous Noah, and were disobedient,† when once the long suffering of God waited in vain in those days for their repentance); having paid the just penalty of their disobedience, then justice would demand that some means must exist by which the saving principles of the Gospel of Jesus Christ may be applied to them; for only by the acceptance of the principles of the Gospel, and by the application of its laws and ordinances as the means by which the grace of God is applied to man, can the sons of men hope for salvation. Then as men differ in degree of intelligence; in the intensity of their faith; in the hartiness of their obedience; in the steadiness of their fidelity; and in as much as there is the stern fact of human freedom and responsibility, and the possibility of a short or long resistance to the will of God, even up to eternal resistance to that will, there is an infinitude of states of glory, of so called rewards and punishments, in which man will live in the future. There is one glory of which the sun in heaven is spoken of as being typical; another of which the inferior light of the moon is typical; and another of which the varying light of the stars is typical. And even as one star differs from another star in glory, in light, so differ those states of existence in which men will live in the future, but each assigned to a place, to an environment, that corresponds to the status of his development; which is only the modern way of saying he shall be judged according to his works. These, in brief, are the underlying principles of this remarkable revelation; a revelation which in every way is worthy the encomium that the Prophet Joseph himself bestowed upon it at the time of its inception: "Nothing could be more pleasing to the Saints upon the order of the Kingdom of the Lord, than the light which burst upon the world through the foregoing Vision. Every law, every commandment, every promise, every truth, and every point touching the destiny of man, from Genesis to Revelation, where the purity of the

* Doctrine and Covenants, Sec. lxxvi, and HISTORY OF THE CHURCH Vol. I, 245 *et seq.*

† I Peter iii, 18-22.

Scriptures remains unsullied by the folly of men, go to show the perfection of the theory [of different degrees of glory in the future life] and witnesses the fact that *that document is a transcript from the records of the eternal world*."

In June, 1836, while attending to washings and anointings in the Kirtland Temple, previous to its dedication, the Prophet received still further knowledge as to the future state of man. This also was by means of a vision. He says: "The heavens were opened upon us, and I beheld the celestial kingdom of God, and the glory thereof, whether in the body or out, I cannot tell. I saw the transcendent beauty of the gate through which the heirs of that kingdom will enter,which was like unto circling flames of fire; also the blazing throne of God, whereon was seated the Father and the Son. I saw the beautiful streets of that kingdom, which had the appearnce of being paved with gold. I saw Fathers Adam and Abraham, and my father and mother, my brother, Alvin, that has long since slept, and marveled how it was that he had obtained an inheritance in that kingdom, seeing that he had departed this life before the Lord had set His hand to gather Israel the second time, and had not been baptized for the remission of sins. Thus came the voice of the Lord unto me saying—

"*All who have died without a knowledge of this Gospel,who would have received it if they had been permitted to tarry, shall be heirs of the celestial kingdom of God; also all that shall die henceforth without a knowledge of it, who would have received it with all their hearts, shall be heirs of that kingdom, for I, the Lord, will judge all men according to their works, according to the desire of their hearts.*

"And I also beheld that all children who die before they arrive at the years of accountability, are saved in the celestial kingdom of heaven.

The next step in the development of this doctrine of salvation for the dead was the coming of Elijah to "turn the heart of the fathers to the children, and the heart of the children to the fathers," according to Malachi; to restore the priesthood and "plant in the hearts of the children the promises made to the fathers," by which "the hearts of the children shall be turned to the fathers," according to Moroni. And Elijah committed the keys of this dispensation of turning the hearts of the fathers and children towards each other to Joseph Smith and to Oliver Cowdery. This took place in the Kirtland Temple on the 3rd of April, 1836.*

It was not, however, until the Nauvoo period that the doctrine of salvation for the dead was fully developed and active steps taken looking to the actual performance of ordinances in their behalf. In the revelation that was given on the 19th of January, 1841, the Saints

* See History of the Church, Vol. II, p. 435-436. Also Doc. and Cov. Sec. cx.

were commanded to build a house unto the Lord, a Holy Temple unto the Most High. "For," said this revelation, "there is not a place found on earth that He may come to and restore again that which was lost unto you, or which He hath taken away, even the fullness of the Priesthood; for a baptismal font there is not upon the earth, that they, my Saints, may be baptized for those who are dead; for this ordinance belongeth to my house, and cannot be acceptable to me, only in the days of your poverty, wherein ye are not able to build a house unto me. But I command you, all ye my Saints, to build a house unto me; and I grant unto you a sufficient time to build a house unto me, and during this time your baptisms shall be acceptable unto me." That is, the baptisms for the dead should be acceptable unto the Lord in other places than the temple, until the temple should be prepared for that ordinance, if the Saints would be dillgent and build it according to the Lord's appointment. Moreover, the information is imparted in the revelation that, it is "in Zion, and in her stakes, and in Jerusalem, those places which I [the Lord] have appointed for refuge, shall be the places for your baptisms for your dead."

After this revelation was given to the Church baptism for the dead was a subject frequently expounded in Nauvoo, both by the Prophet and other leading elders. It was a theme upon which the Twelve Apostles dwelt in their Epistles to the Church both in America and in Great Britain. Baptisms for the dead were performed for some time in the Mississippi river, and later, in the latter part of November, 1841, in the baptismal font erected in the basement of the Temple, and dedicated for that sacred purpose. For a time some irregularities obtained in relation to this ordinance owing to the fact that the perfect knowledge of the order of it had not then been obtained, but was developed later in this Nauvoo period of the History of the Church, as will appear in Volume V of this work.

It was a mighty stride forward in the doctrinal development of the Church, this idea of the possibility of salvation for the dead through the administration of the ordinances of the Gospel for and in their behalf by their kindred on earth; and greatly enlarged the views of the Saints in relation to the importance and wide spread effects of their work. The ends of the earth indeed converged in the labors of the Saints henceforth, for their activities in the administrations of the holy ordinances of the Gospel would affect all past generations as well as affect all generations to come. It was a bringing into view the full half of the work which up to this time had lain hidden behind the horizon of men's conceptions of that "great and marvelous work" which God from the beginning declared was about to be brought forth among the children of men.*

* See Doc. and Cov. the opening paragraph of Sections iv, vi, xi, xii, xiv, all iven in the year 1829.

Other Doctrines of the Prophet's Teaching.

Other doctrines taught by the Prophet within the period covered by this volume, relate to the Priesthood; to the Status of Translated Persons; to Man's Personal Responsibility for his own conduct, to Election and Reprobation. A word in relation to each of these doctrines must suffice here since they do not reach their full development in the teachings of the Prophet until the last two years of his eventful life, and must therefore receive fuller treatment in the Introduction of Volume V.

Relative to the Priesthood, the most important items advanced by the Prophet in this volume, are, first, the unity of all Priesthood, and second, the place and power assigned to Adam in the order of the dispensations of the Gospel granted to our earth. Treating on the unity of the Priesthood, the Prophet said: "There are two Priesthoods spoken of in the Scriptures, viz., the Melchisedek and the Aaronic or Levitical. Although there are two Priesthoods, yet the Melchisedek Priesthood comprehends the Aaronic or Levitical Priesthood, and is the grand head, and holds the highest authority which pertains to the Priesthood, and the keys of the kingdom of God in all ages of the world to the latest posterity on the earth, and is the channel through which all knowledge, doctrine, the plan of salvation, and every important matter is revealed from heaven. Its institution was prior to 'the foundation of this earth, or the morning stars sang together, or the Sons of God shouted for joy,' and is the highest and holiest Priesthood, and is after the order of the Son of God, and all other Priesthoods are only parts, ramifications, powers and blessings belonging to the same, and are held, controlled, and directed by it. It is the channel through which the Almighty commenced revealing His glory at the beginning of the creation of this earth, and through which He has continued to reveal Himself to the children of men to the present time, and through which He will make known His purposes to the end of time."

Respecting the place of Adam in the Priesthood and his relationship to the dispensations of that Priesthood to our earth, the Prophet said: "Commencing with Adam, who was the first man, who is spoken of in Daniel as being the 'Ancient of Days,' or in other words, the first and oldest of all, the great, grand progenitor of whom it is said in another place he is Michael, because he was the first and father of all, not only by progeny, but the first to hold the spiritual blessings, to whom was made known the plan of ordinances for the salvation of his posterity unto the end, and to whom Christ was first revealed, and through whom Christ has been revealed from heaven, and will continue to be revealed from henceforth. Adam holds the keys of the dispensation of the fullness of times; i. e., the dispensation of all the times have been and will be revealed through him from the beginning to Christ, and from Christ to the end of all the dispensations that are to be revealed. 'Having made known unto us the mystery of His will, according to His good pleasure which He hath purposed in Himself: that in the dispensation of the fullness of times He might gather together in one all things in Christ, both which are in heaven, and which are on earth; even in him· (Ephesians, 1st chap., 9th and 10th verses). Now the purpose in Himself in the winding up scene of the last dispensation is that all things pertaining to that dispensation should be conducted precisely in accordance with the preceding dispensations. And again. God purposed in Himself that there should not be an eternal fullness until every dispensation should be fulfilled and gathered together in one, and that all things whatsoever, that should be gathered together in one in those dispensations unto the same fullness and eternal glory, should be in Christ Jesus; therefore He set the ordinances to be the same forever and ever, and set Adam to watch over them, to reveal them from heaven to man, or to send angels to reveal them. * * * * These angels are under the direction of Michael or Adam, who acts under the direction of the Lord. * * * * There are many things which belong to the powers of the Priesthood and the keys thereof, that have been kept hid from before the foundation of the world; they are hid from the wise and prudent to be revealed in the last times."

That it was the design of the Lord in building the Temple at Nauvoo, that there should be other ordinances revealed besides "baptism for the dead," is clearly manifested in the revelation itself, for it says: "And again, verily I say unto you, how shall your washings be acceptable unto me, except ye perform them in a house which you have built to my name. * * * * Therefore, verily I say unto you, that your anointings, and your washings, and your baptisms for the dead, and your solemn assemblies, and your memorials for your sacrifices, by the sons of Levi and for your oracles in your most holy places wherein you receive conversations, and your statutes and judgments, for the beginning of the revelations and foundation of Zion, and for the glory, honor, and endowment of all her municipals, are ordained by the ordinance of my holy house which my people are always commanded to build unto my holy name. And verily I say unto you, let this house be built unto my name, that I may reveal mine ordinances therein, unto my people; for I deign to reveal unto my Church things which have been kept hid from before the foundation of the word, things that pertain to the dispensation of the fullness of times."

The ordinances here mentioned in addition to baptism for the dead are chiefly connected with the Priesthood of the Church, and were fully developed in the teachings of the Prophet before the close of his eventful career.

As to the status of translated personages, he said: "Many have supposed that the doctrine of translation was a doctrine whereby men were taken immediately into the presence of God, and into an eternal fulness, but this is a mistaken idea. Their place of habitation is that of the terrestrial order, and a place prepared for such characters He held in reserve to be ministering angels unto many planets, and who as yet have not entered into as great a fullness as those who are resurrected from the dead."

Of man being personally responsible for his own conduct, he is reported by the Editor of the *Times and Seasons* as saying: "He [the Prophet] then observed that Satan was generally blamed for the evils which we did, but if he was the cause of all our wickedness, men could not be condemned. The devil could not compel mankind to do evil; all was voluntary. Those who resisted the Spirit of God, would be liable to be led into temptation, and then the association of heaven would be withdrawn from those who refused to be made partakers of such great glory. God *would not* exert any compulsory means, and the devil *could not*; and such ideas as were entertained [on these subjects] by many were absurd." What beautiful harmony between the Prophet's doctrine here and that of the Apostle James: "Let no man say when he is tempted, I am tempted of God: for God cannot be tempted with evil, neither tempteth he any man: But every man is tempted, when he is drawn away of his own lusts, and enticed. Then when lust hath conceived, it bringing forth sin: and sin when it is finished, bringeth forth death."*

Of election, a term used generally in connection with reprobation, when commenting on the 9th Chapter of Romans,—wherein Paul is supposed to teach the doctrine of election,—the Prophet is represented as saying: "He then spoke on the subject of election, and read the 9th chapter of Romans, from which it was evident that the election there spoken of was pertaining to the flesh, and had reference to the seed of Abraham, according to the promise God made to Abraham, saying, "In thee, and in thy seed, all the families of the earth shall be blessed. * * * The whole of the chapter had reference to the Priesthood and the house of Israel: and unconditional election of individuals to eternal life was not taught by the Apostles. God did elect or predestinate, that all those who would be saved, should be saved in Christ Jesus, and through obedience to the Gospel, but He passes over no man's sins, but visits them with correction, and if His children will not repent of their sins He will discard them."

These several doctrines mark rapid development in the Prophet's work as an instructor in sacred things, and clearly indicate his increasing capacity and power as Prophet, Seer and Teacher.

* James 1, 13-15.

HISTORY

OF THE

CHURCH OF JESUS CHRIST OF LATTER-DAY SAINTS.

VOL. IV.

HISTORY

OF THE

CHURCH OF JESUS CHRIST

OF

LATTER-DAY SAINTS.

PERIOD I.

HISTORY OF JOSEPH SMITH, THE PROPHET.

CHAPTER I.

THE DEPARTURE OF THE TWELVE FOR ENGLAND—MANIFESTATION OF GOD'S POWER IN HEALING THE SICK AT COMMERCE.

Friday, July 5, 1839.—I was dictating history, I say dictating, for I seldom use the pen myself. I always dictate all my communications, but employ a scribe to write them.

The Prophet's Literary Methods.

Saturday, 6.—I was at home reviewing the Church records.

Sunday, 7.—I was at the meeting held in the open air, at which a large assemblage was expected to listen to the farewell addresses of the Twelve, who were then about to take their departure on a most important mission, namely to the nations of the earth and the islands of the sea.

Farewell to the Twelve.

Elder John E. Page being the first of the Twelve present, opened the meeting by addressing a few words of an introductory nature; after singing and prayer, Elder Page delivered a very interesting discourse on the subject of the Book of Mormon, recapitulating, in short terms, the principles of a former discourse on the same subject, and afterwards proceeded to read portions from the Bible and Book of Mormon concerning the best criterions whereby to judge of the authenticity of the latter; and then went on to show in a very satisfactory manner, that no impostor would ever attempt to make such promises as are contained on pages five hundred forty-one,* and five hundred and thirty-four.† He then bore testimony.

After noon the meeting was again opened by prayer. Elder John Taylor spoke on the subject of this dispensation; the other angel which John saw, having the everlasting Gospel to preach, he then bore testimony of the truth of the Book of Mormon.

Elder Woodruff's address went chiefly to exhortation to the Saints; after which he also bore his testimony.

Elder Orson Hyde next came forward, and having alluded to his own late fall,‡ exhorted all to perseverance in the things of God, expressed himself one with his brethren, and bore testimony to his knowledge of the truth, and the misery of falling from it.

Elder Brigham Young made some very appropriate remarks, and also bore testimony to the truth of these things, and gave an invitation to come forward and be baptized, when three manifested their determination to renounce the world and take upon themselves the name of Jesus Christ. One brother was then confirmed; after which President Sidney Rigdon addressed the meeting in a very feeling manner. He showed that it must be no small matter which could induce men to leave their families and their homes to travel over all the earth amidst persecutions and trials, such as always followed the preaching of this Gospel. He then addressed himself to

* See pp. 573-4, current edition.

† See pp. 565-567, current edition.

‡ See History of the Church, Vol. III, pp. 167-8.

the Twelve and gave them some counsel and consolation as far as lay in his power; after which I requested their prayers, and promised to pray for them.

The meeting was large and respectable; a great number were present who did not belong to the Church. The most perfect order prevailed throughout. The meeting was dismissed about half-past five, when we repaired to the water, and the three candidates were baptized and confirmed.

Monday, Tuesday and Wednesday, 8th, 9th and 10th of July.—I was with the Twelve selecting hymns, for the purpose of compiling a hymn book.

The L. D. S. Hymn Book.

About this time much sickness began to manifest itself among the brethren, as well as among the inhabitants of the place, so that this week and the following were generally spent in visiting the sick and administering to them; some had faith enough and were healed; others had not.

Sunday, 21. — There was no meeting on account of much rain and much sickness; however many of the sick were this day raised up by the power of God, through the instrumentality of the Elders of Israel ministering unto them in the name of Jesus Christ.

Administration to the sick.

Monday and Tuesday, 22nd and 23rd.—The sick were administered unto with great success,* but many remain sick, and new cases are occurring daily.

* "In consequence of the persecutions of the Saints in Missouri, and the exposures to which they were subjected, many of them were taken sick soon after their arrival at Commerce, afterwards called Nauvoo; and as there was but a small number of dwellings for them to occupy, Joseph had filled his house and tent with them, and through constantly attending to their wants, he soon fell sick himself. After being confined to his house several days, and while meditating upon his situation, he had a great desire to attend to the duties of his office. On the morning of the 22nd of July, 1839, he arose from his bed and commenced to administer to the sick in his own house and door-yard, and he commanded them in the name of the Lord Jesus Christ to arise and be made whole; and the sick were healed upon every side of him.

"Many lay sick along the bank of the river; Joseph walked along up to the lower stone house, occupied by Sidney Rigdon, and he healed all the sick that lay in his

Sunday 28.—Meeting was held as usual. Elder Parley P. Pratt preached on the gathering of Israel. In the afternoon Orson Pratt addressed the Church on the necessity of keeping the commandments of God. I spoke, and admonished the members of the Church individually to set their houses in order, to make clean the inside of the platter, and to

Discourses by the Brothers Pratt.

path. Among the number was Henry G. Sherwood, who was nigh unto death. Joseph stood in the door of his tent and commanded him in the name of Jesus Christ to arise and come out of his tent, and he obeyed him and was healed. Brother Benjamin Brown and his family also lay sick, the former appearing to be in a dying condition. Joseph healed them in the name of the Lord. After healing all that lay sick upon the bank of the river as far as the stone house, he called upon Elder Kimball and some others to accompany him across the river to visit the sick at Montrose. Many of the Saints were living at the old military barracks. Among the number were several of the Twelve. On his arrival the first house he visited was that occupied by Elder Brigham Young, the President of the Quorum of the Twelve, who lay sick. Joseph healed him, then he arose and accompanied the Prophet on his visit to others who were in the same condition. They visited Elder Wilford Woodruff, also Elders Orson Pratt, and John Taylor, all of whom were living in Montrose. They also accompanied him.

"The next place they visited was the home of Elijah Fordham, who was supposed to be about breathing his last. When the company entered the room, the Prophet of God walked up to the dying man and took hold of his right hand and spoke to him; but Brother Fordham was unable to speak, his eyes were set in his head like glass, and he seemed entirely unconscious of all around him. Joseph held his hand and looked into his eyes in silence for a length of time. A change in the countenance of Brother Fordham was soon perceptible to all present. His sight returned, and upon Joseph asking him if he knew him, he, in a low whisper, answered 'Yes.' Joseph asked him if he had faith to be healed. He answered, 'I fear it is too late; if you had come sooner I think I would have been healed.' The Prophet said 'Do you believe in Jesus Christ?' He answered in a feeble voice, 'I do.' Joseph then stood erect, still holding his hand in silence several moments; Then he spoke in a very loud voice, saying, 'Brother Fordham, I command you, in the name of Jesus Christ, to arise from this bed and be made whole.' His voice was like the voice of God, and not of man. It seemed as though the house shook to its very foundations. Brother Fordham arose from his bed, and was immediately made whole. His feet were bound in poultices which he kicked off; then putting on his clothes he ate a bowl of bread and milk and followed the Prophet into the street.

"The company next visited Brother Joseph Bates Noble, who lay very sick. He also was healed by the Prophet. By this time the wicked became alarmed and followed the company into Brother Noble's house. After Noble was healed, all kneeled down to pray. Brother Fordham was mouth, and while praying he fell to the floor. The Prophet arose, and on looking around he saw quite a number of unbelievers in the house, whom he ordered out. When the room was cleared of the wicked, Brother Fordham came to and finished his prayer.

"After healing the sick in Montrose, all the company followed Joseph to the bank of the river, where he was going to take the boat to return home. While waiting

meet on the next Sabbath to partake of the Sacrament, in order that by our obedience to the ordinances, we might be enabled to prevail with God against the destroyer, and that the sick might be healed.

All this week chiefly spent among the sick, who in general are gaining strength, and recovering health.

Sunday, August 4.—The Church came together for prayer meeting and Sacrament. I exhorted the Church at length, concerning the necessity of being righteous, and clean at heart before the Lord. Many others also spoke; especially some of the Twelve, who were present, professed their willingness to proceed on their mission to Europe, without either purse or scrip. The Sacrament was administered; a spirit of humility and harmony prevailed, and the Church passed a resolution that the Twelve proceed on their mission as soon as possible, and that the Saints provide for their families during their absence.

Prayer Meeting for the Sick.

Letter to Isaac Russell, reproving him for issuing pretended revelations to the Saints.

COMMERCE, HANCOCK COUNTY, ILLINOIS, 5th August, 1839.

DEAR SIR.—I have been requested to write you on behalf of the Twelve, who are just on the eve of their departure for England, and

for the boat, a man from the West, who had seen that the sick and dying were healed, asked Joseph if he would not go to his house and heal two of his children who were very sick. They were twins and were three months old. Joseph told the man he could not go, but he would send some one to heal them. He told Elder Woodruff to go with the man and heal his children. At the same time he took from his pocket a silk bandanna handkerchief, and gave to Brother Woodruff, telling him to wipe the faces of the children with it, and they should be healed; and remarked at the same time: 'As long as you keep that handkerchief it shall remain a league between you and me.' Elder Woodruff did as he was commanded, and the children were healed, and he keeps the handkerchief to this day.

"There were many sick whom Joseph could not visit, so he counseled the Twelve to go and visit and heal them, and many were healed under their hands. On the day following that upon which the above-described events took place, Joseph sent Elders George A. and Don Carlos Smith up the river to heal the sick. They went up as far as Ebenezer Robinson's—one or two miles—and did as they were commanded, and the sick were healed." *Leaves from my Journal*, (Wilford Woodruff) Ch. XIX.

inform you, that "this thing" which you have thought proper to write as a revelation "to the Church in Alston and the branches round about," to which you yourself administered, has "already come to the knowledge of the Churches" both here and elsewhere, and lest you should have any doubt concerning the fact, we send you a copy of your revelation to that Church.

I am sir, with all respect,

Yours truly,

JAMES MULHOLLAND.

P. S.—Isaiah chap. L, 10th and 11th verses.* In my own behalf I wish to state that I sincerely wish that it may soon come to pass that you, sir, and all our friends at Far West may perceive that you are walking in the light of a fire, and sparks that you have yourselves kindled; and that you may turn around and fear the Lord, obey the voice of His servant, and thereby escape the sentence, "Ye shall lie down in sorrow."

J. M.

To Mr. Isaac Russell, Far West, Missouri.

Conference in New Jersey.

Friday, 9.—A Conference was held at Brother Caleb Bennett's Monmouth County, New Jersey, Elder John P. Greene presiding. The New York and Brooklyn branches were represented by the President as being in good fellowship. There were represented at this conference the following branches, by Elder Ball, Shrewsbury, New Jersey, numbering twenty members; Montage, three; Minissink, New Hampshire, two; Albany, eight; Holliston, Massachusetts, sixteen; Elder Dunham represented Hamilton, Madison County, forty-six; Samuel James, Leechburg, Pennsylvania, forty.

Sunday, 11.—I attended meeting in the forenoon and heard a sermon by Parley P. Pratt. In the afternoon there was one baptized, and four were confirmed, namely,

*"Who is among you that feareth the Lord, that obeyeth the voice of His servant, that walketh in darkness, and hath no light? Let him trust in the name of the Lord, and stay upon his God.

"Behold, all ye that kindle a fire, that compass yourselves about with sparks. walk in the light of your fire, and in the sparks that ye have kindled. This shall ye have of mine hand; ye shall lie down in sorrow."

Brother Hibbard, his wife, little son, and daughter. The Sacrament was administered.

This week I spent chiefly in visiting the sick; sickness much decreased.

Sunday, 18.—Rode out in the forenoon. Orson Pratt preached upon the order and plan of creation. Three were baptized.

Afternoon: Three confirmed and one ordained an Elder.

This week I spent chiefly among the sick. The Church made a purchase of eighty acres from William White for four thousand dollars, lying directly north of the Hugh White purchase.

Sunday, 25.—I attended meeting. Sickness decreasing.

Thursday, 29.—Elders Parley P. Pratt and family, Orson Pratt and Hiram Clark, started on their mission to England, in their own two-horse carriage—their route lying through Illinois, Indiana, and to Detroit, the capital of Michigan, situated near the head of Lake Erie, about five hundred and eighty miles distant.

Progress of the Work in England.

Saturday, 31.—The work is spreading in England. Elder Richards went to the Staffordshire potteries this day, and Presidents Joseph Fielding and William Clayton were visiting and setting in order many of the branches, and ordaining many to the ministry who are diligent in preaching as they have opportunity on the Sabbath in the surrounding villages.

Sunday, September 1.—I attended meeting, and spoke concerning some errors in Parley P. Pratt's writings. This week sickness much decreased.

Monday, 9, and the greater part of the week.—I spent in visiting the sick, and attending to to the settlement of our new town.*

* This has reference to the Hotchkiss purchase which had just recently been laid out as part of the rapidly growing town of Nauvoo. It constituted the north west part of the city, extending some distance along the river front, and back on to the height of land overlooking the river bottom.

The Prophet's Letter to Isaac Galland.—Nauvoo Affairs.

COMMERCE, ILLINOIS, 11th September, 1839.

DEAR BROTHER GALLAND:—We have had the great pleasure of receiving your favor of the 24th July; and learning thereby that you and your family had arrived at Chillicothe in safety and in health. We perceive that you have had a rather narrow escape from a serious accident; and doubtless the hand of the Lord is to be acknowledged in the matter, although unperceived by mortal eye. Time and experience will teach us more and more how easily falsehood gains credence with mankind in general, rather than the truth; but especially in taking into consideration the plan of salvation. The plain simple order of the Gospel of Jesus Christ never has been discerned or acknowledged as the truth, except by a few—among whom were "not many wise men after the flesh, not many mighty, not many noble;" whilst the majority have contented themselves with their own private opinions, or have adopted those of others, according to their address, their philosophy, their formula, their policy, or their fineness may have attracted their attention, or pleased their taste. But, sir, of all the other criterions whereby we may judge of the vanity of these things, one will be always found true, namely, that we will always find such characters glorying in their own wisdom and their own works; whilst the humble Saint gives all the glory to God the Father, and to His Son Jesus Christ, whose yoke is easy and whose burden is light, and who told His disciples that unless they became like little children they could not enter the Kingdom of Heaven.

As to the situation of the Church here, matters go with us as well as can reasonably be expected; we have had considerable sickness amongst us, but very few deaths; and as the greater part are now recovering, we yet hope to have shelters provided before the winter shall set in.

Since you left here, we have purchased out all Mr. Hotchkiss' interest hereabouts. His farm we have laid out as an addition to our town, Nauvoo, and the town of Commerce we also hope to build up.

Some of the Twelve and others have already started for Europe, and the remainder of that mission we expect will go now in a few days. According to intelligence received since you left, the work of the Lord rolls on in a very pleasing manner, both in this and in the old country. In England many hundreds have of late been added to our numbers; but so, even so, it must be, for "Ephraim he hath mixed himself among the people." And the Savior He hath said, "My sheep hear my voice;" and also, "He that heareth you, heareth me;" and, "Behold I will bring them again from the north country, and gather them from the coasts of the earth." And as John heard the voice saying, "Come out of her, my people,'' even so must all be fulfilled; that the people of the Lord may live when "Babylon the great is fallen, is fallen."

There has quite a number of families gathered up here already; and we anticipate a continuance, especially as upon inquiry we have found that we have not had more than [the usual] ratio of sickness here, notwithstanding the trials we have had, and the hardships to which we have been exposed. Calculating as we do, upon the mercy and power of God in our behalf, we hope to persevere on in every good and useful work, even unto the end, that when we come to be tried in the balance we may not be found wanting.

With all good wishes and prayers for the temporal and eternal salvation of yourself and your family, as well as of all the honest in heart over the face of the earth,

We remain, sir, with sincerity,

Your friend and brother,

JOSEPH SMITH, Jun.

Addressed to Isaac Galland, Esq., Kirtland, Geauga, County, Ohio.

Friday, 13.—I left home for Brother William Smith's place.

Saturday, 14.—President Brigham Young started from his home at Montrose, for England. His health was very poor; he was unable to go thirty rods to the river without assistance. After he had crossed the ferry he got Brother Israel Barlow to carry him on his horse behind him to Heber C. Kimball's where he remained sick until the 18th. He left his wife sick with a babe only ten days old, and all his children sick, unable to wait upon each other. I returned home this evening.

Brigham Young Starts on his Mission.

Sunday, 15.—I was visiting the sick.

Monday and Tuesday, 16 and 17.—Was engaged in arranging the town lots.

Wednesday, 18.—Went to Burlington, Iowa Territory. Elders Young and Kimball left Sister Kimball and all her children sick, except little Heber;* went thirteen miles on their journey towards England, and were left at Brother Osmon M. Duel's, who

Departure of Elders Young and Kimball from Nauvoo.

* The departure of these two Elders upon their mission to England is worthy of a more extended notice. A brother by the name of Charles Hubbard sent a boy

lived in a small cabin near the railway between Commerce and Warsaw. They were so feeble as to be unable to carry their trunks into the house without the assistance of Sister Duel, who received them kindly, prepared a bed for them to lie on, and made them a cup of tea.

Thursday, *19*.—I Returned this evening from Burlington.

Brother Duel carried Elders Young and Kimball in his wagon to Lima, sixteen miles, where another brother received them and carried them to Father Mikesell's near Quincy, about twenty miles; the fatigue of this day was too much for their feeble health; they were prostrated, and obliged to tarry a few days to recruit.

Friday and Saturday, *20 and 21*.—At home attending to domestic and Church business.

Elders George A. Smith, Reuben Hedlock, and Theodore Turley started for England, and upset their wagon on the bank of the river, before they got out of sight of Commerce. Elders Smith and Turley were so weak they could not get up, and Brother Hedlock had to lift them in again. Soon after, some gentlemen met them and asked who had been robbing the burying ground—so miserable was their appearance through sickness.

Sunday, *22*.—I presided at the meeting, and spoke concerning the "other Comforter," as I had previously taught the Twelve.*

with a team to take them a day's journey on their way. Elder Kimball left his wife in bed shaking with ague, and all his children sick It was only by the assistance of some of the brethren that Heber himself could climb into the wagon. "It seemed to me," he remarked afterwards in relating the circumstance, "as though my very inmost parts would melt within me at the thought of leaving my family in such a condition, as it were, almost in the arms of death. I felt as though I could scarcely endure it." "Hold up!" said he to the teamster, who had just started, "Brother Brigham, this is pretty tough, but let us rise and give them a cheer." Brigham, with much difficulty, rose to his feet, and joined Elder Kimball in swinging his hat and shouting, "Hurrah, hurrah, hurrah, for Israel!" The two sisters, hearing the cheer came to the door—Sister Kimball with great difficulty—and waved a farewell; and the two apostles continued their journey, without purse, without scrip, for England.

* See Vol. III, pp. 379-381.

This week I spent in transacting various business at home, except when visiting the sick, who are in general recovering, though some of them but slowly.

Wednesday, 25.—President Young went to Charles C. Rich's; 26th, to Brother Wilber's; 27th, Brother Wilber carried Elders Young and Kimball to Pittsfield.

Sunday, 29.—Held meeting at my own house. After others had spoken I spoke and explained concerning the uselessness of preaching to the world about great judgments, but rather to preach the simple Gospel. Explained concerning the coming of the Son of Man; also that it is a false idea that the Saints will escape all the judgments, whilst the wicked suffer; for all flesh is subject to suffer, and "the righteous shall hardly escape;" still many of the Saints will escape, for the just shall live by faith; yet many of the righteous shall fall a prey to disease, to pestilence, etc., by reason of the weakness of the flesh, and yet be saved in the Kingdom of God. So that it is an unhallowed principle to say that such and such have transgressed because they have been preyed upon by disease or death, for all flesh is subject to death; and the Savior has said, "Judge not, lest ye be judged."

Items of Doctrine—the Prophet.

Monday, 30.—The fore part of this week I was at home preparing for Conference. Elders Young and Kimball went to Brother Decker's and Mr. Murray's, Sister Kimball's father.

Tuesday, October 1.—Elders Young and Kimball went to Brother Lorenzo Young's.

Thursday, 3.—I was in counsel with the brethren.

Friday, 4.—Lorenzo Young carried Elders Young and Kimball to Jacksonville.

Saturday, 5.—The friends and brethren conveyed the Elders of the British Mission to Springfield, where they were kindly treated and nursed, for they were yet very feeble.

I attended a general conference of the Church of Jesus

Christ of Latter-day Saints at Commerce, Hancock County, Illinois, of which the following are the minutes:

Minutes of Conference at Commerce, Illinois, October 6th, 7th and 8th, 1839.

The meeting was opened by prayer by President Joseph Smith, Jun., after which he was appointed President, and James Sloan Clerk of the conference, by a unanimous voice of the meeting. The President then spoke at some length upon the situation of the Church; the difficulties they have had to contend with; and the manner in which they had been led to this place; and wanted to know the views of the brethren, whether they wished to appoint this a stake of Zion or not; stating that he believed it to be a good place, and suited for the Saints. It was then unanimously agreed upon that it should be appointed a stake and a place of gathering for the Saints.

The following officers were then appointed—namely, William Marks to be President; Bishop Whitney to be Bishop of middle ward; Bishop Partridge to be Bishop of upper ward; Bishop Knight to be Bishop of lower ward; George W. Harris, Samuel Bent, Henry G. Sherwood, David Fullmer, Alpheus Cutler, William Huntington, Thomas Grover, Newel Knight, Charles C. Rich, David Dort, Seymour Brunson, Lewis D. Wilson, to be the High Council; who being respectfully called upon accepted their appointment.

It was then voted that a stake of the Church be established on the west side of the river, in Iowa Territory; over which Elder John Smith was appointed President; Alanson Ripley, Bishop; and Asahel Smith, John M. Burk, Abraham O. Smoot, Richard Howard, Willard Snow, Erastus Snow, David Pettigrew, Elijah Fordham, Edward Fisher, Elias Smith, John Patten, Stephen Chase, were elected High Council. Don C. Smith was elected to be continued as President of the High Priesthood [High Priest's quorum]. Orson Hyde to stand in his former office, [an Apostle] and William Smith to be continued in his standing, [in the quorum of the Twelve.]

Letters were then read respecting the absence of members on account of ill health. It was voted that Harlow Redfield be suspended until he can have a trial; and in the meantime that he should not act as president of a branch, or preach.

Voted that John Daley, James Daley, and Milo Andrus retain their station in the Church. Voted that Ephraim Owen's confession for disobeying the Word of Wisdom be accepted.

Brothers Edward Johnston, Benjamin Johnston, Samuel Musick, John S. Fullmer, Jabez Lake, Benjamin Jones, Henry Our Bough, Reddin A. Allred, George W. Gee, Jesse McIntyre, James

Brown, Henry Miller, Artemas Johnson, Joseph G. Hovey, Robert D. Foster, Fields B. Jacaway, Zadok Bethers, William Allred, William B. Simmons, William W. Edwards, Sen., William H. Edwards, Jun., Hosea Stout, Thomas Rich, Allen J. Stout, Esaias Edwards, John Adams, Daniel Miller, Simeon J. Comfort, Graham Coltrin, William Hyde, Andrew Henry, Reddick N. Allred, Eli Lee, Hiram W. Mikesell and Thomas S. Edwards were appointed Elders of the Church, who all accepted of their appointment, with the exception of Thomas S. Edwards.

John Gaylord was admitted into the Church upon his confession. Abel Casto was confirmed by the laying on of hands.

The meeting then adjourned until Sunday morning; after which six were baptized by Joseph Smith, Jun. The assembly was very large.

The conference met on Sunday morning, the 6th, pursuant to adjournment at eight o'clock a. m., when Samuel Williams, Reuben Foot, Orlando D. Hovey, Tunis Rappleyee, Sheffield Daniels, Albert Milner, David B. Smith, Ebenezer Richardson, Pleasant Ewell, and William Helm were appointed Elders of the Church, and were ordained under the hands of Reynolds Cahoon, Seymour Brunson, Samuel Bent and Alpheus Cutler.

After some remarks from the President respecting order, and decorum during conference, Elder Lyman Wight spoke concerning the duties of Priests and Teachers. President Joseph Smith, Jun., then addressed the conference, in relation to appointing a Patriarch, and other matters connected with the well being of the Church.

Having now got through the business matters, the President proceeded to give instruction to the Elders respecting preaching the Gospel, and pressed upon them the necessity of getting the Spirit, so that they might preach with the Holy Ghost sent down from heaven; to be careful in speaking on those subjects which are not clearly pointed out in the word of God, which lead to speculation and strife.

Those persons who had been baptized, were then confirmed, and several children received blessings by Elders Cutler, Bent, and Brunson. Elder Lyman Wight then addressed the meeting on the subject of raising funds by contribution, towards paying for the lands which had been contracted for as a settlement for the Church, after which contributions were received for that purpose.

Judge Elias Higbee was appointed to acompany Presidents Joseph Smith, Jun., and Sidney Rigdon to the city of Washington.

The meeting then adjourned until Monday morning.

Conference met on Monday morning, October 7th, pursuant to adjournment.

The President spoke at some length to the Elders, and explained many passages of Scripture. Elder Lyman Wight spoke on the subject of the resurrection, and other important subjects; when he offered the following resolution, which passed unanimously;

Resolved: That a new edition of Hymn Books be printed immediately, and that the one published by D. W. Rogers be utterly discarded by the Church.

Elder Ezra Hayes was then put upon trial for teaching doctrine injurious to the Church, and for falsehoods, which were proven against him; his license was taken from him, and he required to give satisfaction to those whom he had offended.

Charges having been preferred against Brother Rogers, it was agreed that the case be handed over to the High Council.

Asahel Perry made application to be received into fellowship, and was voted into his former standing.

After having referred the business not gone into, to the High Council, the President then returned thanks to the conference for their good attention and liberality, and having blessed them in the name of the Lord, the conference was dismissed.

The next conference was appointed to be held on the sixth day of April next.

Tuesday, 8.—After conference, this week I was mostly engaged in attending to the general affairs of the Church, and principally about home.

Friday, 11.—This evening, Elders Young, Kimball, George A. Smith, Hedlock, and Turley started from Springfield, traveled eight miles on their journey, and stayed with Father Draper.

Saturday, 12.—The Elders of the British Mission left Father Draper's and pursued their journey toward Terre Haute.

Death of John Young, Brigham Young's Father.

This day President Brigham Young's father, John Young, Sen., died at Quincy, Adams County, Illinois. He was in his seventy-seventh year, and a soldier of the Revolution. He was also a firm believer in the everlasting Gospel of Jesus Christ; and fell asleep under the influence of that faith that buoyed up his soul, in the pangs of death, to a glorious hope of immortality; fully testifying to all, that the religion he enjoyed in life was able to support him in death. He was driven from Missouri with the Saints in the latter part of last year. He died a martyr to the religion of Jesus, for his death was caused by his sufferings in the cruel persecution.

Sunday, 13.—I attended meeting in the grove. The assembly was small on account of the cold weather.

Tuesday, 15.—In the afternoon I went to Quincy in company with Brother Hyrum Smith, John S. Fullmer, and Bishop Knight. Quite a number of families moving into Commerce.

Thursday, 17.—The brethren arrived at Terre Haute. Brothers Smith, Hedlock, and Turley stopped at Brother Nahum Milton Stow's.

Hardships of the Elders of the British Mission.

In the evening Doctor Modisett went down to see the brethren, and appeared to be very much affected to see them so sick, and having to lie upon the floor on a straw bed that had been put into the wagon at Springfield, by the brethren, for Elder Young to lie on, as he was not able to sit up when he left there. When the doctor returned home, he told Elders Young and Kimball, he could not refrain from shedding tears to see the brethren going upon such a long mission, and in such suffering circumstances. Elders Young and Kimball said they thought the doctor might have relieved them from "their suffering and indigent circumstances upon their long mission," for he told them in the course of the evening, that his taxes in that place amounted to over four hundred dollars, besides having other property to a great amount.

Elder Kimball was very sick; he stopped with Brother Young at Doctor Modisett's. In the evening Doctor Modisett gave Elder Kimball about forty drops of morphine, saying it would relieve him of his distress, and probably he would get a nap. In about fifteen minutes Brother Kimball complained of feeling very strange; he rose from his seat and would have fallen, but Brother Young caught him and gently eased him to the floor, where he lay for some time; and it was by faith and the close attention of Brother Young and the family that his life was preserved through the night.

Friday, 18.—Brothers Smith, Hedlock, and Turley went on their journey.

Saturday, 19.—The High Council appointed for the Stake of the Church in Iowa, met at Asahel Smith's, Nashville, and organized; John Smith, President; Elias Smith, Clerk; Reynolds Cahoon and Lyman Wight were chosen Counselors to President John Smith, and approved by the Council. Council organized according to number.*

Minutes of the Nauvoo High Council, 20th October, 1839.

The members of the High Council elected at the October conference, met and organized at W. D. Huntington's, where Harlow Redfield was restored to fellowship; and voted that this High Council disfellowship any and all persons that shall hereafter carry over or ferry across the river, any people or freight to the injury of said ferry from Commerce to Montrose.

Voted that the Horse Boat be repaired from the moneys received on sale of lots in Nauvoo, and that D. C. Davis be master of said ferry boat for the ensuing year.

Voted that Joseph Smith, Jun., and his family be exempt from receiving in future such crowds of visitors as have formerly thronged his house; and that the same be published in the *Times and Seasons*.

Voted, that this Council disfellowship any and all persons who shall knowingly suffer and allow any animal (subject to their control) to destroy the crops, fruit, or plants of the earth belonging to any other person or persons, and to their injury, and that this resolution be published in the *Times and Seasons*.

Adjourned until tomorrow evening.

High Council met pursuant to adojurnment, and voted that President Joseph Smith, Jun., go as a delegate to Washington; and that if he went he should have a recommend from the Council.

Voted that James Mulholland be Clerk for the land contracts, when needed by President Smith; that Joseph Smith, Jun., be treasurer of said Church, and James Mulholland sub-treasurer.

* That is to say, to quote from the revelation establishing the High Council—"Whenever an High Council of the Church is regularly organized, * * * it shall be the duty of the Twelve Counselors to cast lots by numbers and thereby ascertain, who of the Twelve shall speak first, commencing with number one, and so in succession to number twelve."—*Doctrine and Covenants, Section cii.*

Voted that Henry G. Sherwood should set the price upon, exhibit, contract and sell town lots in Nauvoo, when needed, and report his doings to Presidents Joseph Smith and Hyrum Smith, for their approval, and that five hundred dollars be the average price of lots, i. e., none less than two hundred dollars, nor more than eight hundred dollars.

Voted that the High Council meet every Sunday evening at Dimick Huntington's; that D. C. Davis have thirty dollars per month for his services as ferryman; and that these proceedings be published in the *Times and Seasons*.

[Signed] HENRY G. SHERWOOD, Clerk.

Tuesday, 22.—Brother James Modisett took Elders Young and Kimball in his father's carriage and carried them twenty miles to the house of Brother Addison Pratt; from thence they were carried by Elder Almon W. Babbitt to Pleasant Garden, and put up with Brother Jonathan Crosby. Elder Almon Babbitt was preaching in that region with good success; he had baptized five.

Saturday, 26.—Brother Babbitt took Elders Young and Kimball ten miles on their way to Father Scott's.

King Follett, the last of the brethren in bonds in Missouri, had his trial and was set free some time previous to this day.

Sunday, 27.—John Scott took Elders Young and Kimball on their way fifteen miles, some part of it in the rain; they were yet very feeble, and put up at a tavern in Belville, and when the stage coach came along, took passage, and rode night and day to Willowby, near Kirtland.

The High Council of Nauvoo voted that the Clerk's fees of James Mulholland be thirty dollars per month; that the treasurer pay Vinson Knight one hundred and fifty dollars, for the Iowa side of the ferry at Montrose as per charter.

Voted, that Sister Emma Smith select and publish a hymn-book for the use of the Church, and that Brigham Young be informed of this action and he not publish the hymns taken by him from Commerce; and that the

Council assist in publishing a hymn-book and the *Times and Seasons*.

Monday, 28.—The High Council voted to build a stone house at Upper Commerce, to be used for boarding; that Elder Oliver Granger be requested to assist with funds to print the hymn-book; that Samuel Dent, Davison Hibbard, and David Dort be trustees for building the stone schoolhouse in contemplation; and that Alpheus Cutler and Jabez Durphy be the architects and building committee for said house.

Voted, to finish the office of President Joseph Smith, Jun.

Voted, that the recommends drawn by Elder Sherwood, recommending, constituting, and appointing Joseph Smith, Jun., Sidney Rigdon, and Elias Higbee, delegates for the Church, to importune the President and Congress of the United States for redress of grievances, be signed by this Council.

CHAPTER II.

THE PROPHET'S JOURNEY TO WASHINGTON—THE PETITION OF THE SANTS TO THE CONGRESS OF THE UNITED STATES FOR REDRESS OF THE WRONGS INFLICTED UPON THEM IN MISSOURI.

Tuesday, 29.—I left Nauvoo accompanied by Sidney Rigdon, Elias Higbee, and Orrin P. Rockwell, in a two-horse carriage for the city of Washington, to lay before the Congress of the United States, the grievances of the Saints while in Missouri. We passed through Carthage, and stayed at Judge Higbee's over night, and the next day we arrived at Quincy.

Departure of the Prophet for Washington.

Thursday, 31.—We tarried at Quincy to complete the necessary papers for our mission. Elder Rigdon was sick.

Friday, November 1.—We pursued our journey towards Springfield, Illinois, and put up with Brother Wilber, where we found Doctor Robert D. Foster, who administered to Elder Rigdon.

Saturday, 2.—Continued our journey, and during the day put up with a friend on the bank of the Illinois river, so that Dr. Foster, who had accompanied us so far for that purpose, might administer medicine to Elder Rigdon again.

Sunday, 3.—Continued our journey and staid with a friend over night. Dr. Foster continued to accompany us.

Elders Young and Kimball arrived at Cleveland, Ohio,

about 1 o'clock in the morning; and while waiting for the stage until about noon, Elders Smith, Turley, and Hedlock, who left them at Terre Haute, drove up, having picked up Elder Taylor by the way, he having been left sick by his company in the east part of Indiana. They were in good health, compared with what they had been, and in fine spirits. George A. Smith tarried in Cleveland till the next day, to visit his relatives. Brothers Young, Kimball, Taylor, and Turley rode in the stage, and Brother Hedlock and Mr. Murray in their wagon to Willoughby, and from thence they all rode into Kirtland together.

Progress of the Twelve towards England.

Monday, *4*.—We arrived at Springfield, and put up with Brother John Snider. When within one mile of the city, we met William Law* and company with seven wagons from Canada, who returned with us to Springfield, and tarried while we did, until the 8th. I preached several times while here. General James Adams,† judge of probate, heard of me, sought me out, and took me home with him, and treated me like a father.

Canadian Saints En Route for Nauvoo.

President Brigham Young and his brother John visited their sister, Mrs. Kent.

There was some division of sentiment among the Kirtland brethren.

* William Law was born September 8th, 1809, and was converted to the gospel through the preaching of Elder John Taylor and Almon W. Babbitt. He lived in Canada some twenty-five miles south of Toronto, and was now leading a company of Saints from Canada to Nauvoo.

† Concerning the antecedent of James Adams nothing can be learned from our Church annals. This is unfortunate, since he was truly a noble character, and remained until his death (1843) a most faithful friend of the Prophet's. In a book of Patriarchal blessings, given by Hyrum Smith, is recorded a blessing upon the head of a James Adams, who in every way would be such a man as the James Adams mentioned in the text—I mean as to age, and character indicated in the blessing. This James Adams of the blessing, and who I am personally convinced was the Prophet's friend of the text, was the son of Parmenio and Chloe Adams, born at Limsbury Township, Hartford county, Connecticut, 24th of January, 1783. He is declared by the Patriarch to be of the tribe of Judah. The blesssing was given the 2nd October, 1841.

Thursday, 7.—The High Council of Iowa completed their organization at Elijah Fordham's, at Montrose.

Friday, 8.—We started from Springfield. Dr. Foster having concluded to continue on the journey on account of Elder Rigdon's health, which was still quite poor. We pursued our journey through Indiana towards Columbus, Ohio. The traveling was bad, and our progress slow.

Sunday, 10.—Elder Taylor preached in the forenoon, and Elder Kimball in the afternoon, in the House of the Lord at Kirtland.

Thursday, 14.—Elder Orson Hyde left Commerce, Illinois, intending to go east as far as Philadelphia. He had just begun to recover from a four months' illness of fever and ague.

Elder Taylor Anointed in the Kirtland Temple.

Sunday, 17.—President Young preached in the House of the Lord in the forenoon, and John Taylor in the afternoon. In the evening, President Brigham Young anointed Elder John Taylor in the House of the Lord, and Elder Daniel S. Miles anointed Theodore Turley, all of which was sealed with the shout of Hosanna.

Monday, 18.—President Young visited Brother R. Potter at Newbury, and returned on Tuesday to Kirtland.

About this time we had arrived near Columbus, where the roads were so bad, Elder Rigdon's health so poor, and the time so fast approaching when it was necessary for the committee to be in Washington, that I started in the stage with Judge Higbee on the most expeditious route to Washington City, leaving Brothers Rockwell, Rigdon, and Foster, to come on at their leisure in the carriage.

Elder Brigham Young and company went to Fairport, where they waited for a steamboat until Tuesday.

Elder Parley P. Pratt and company sold their horses and carriage at Detroit, and went on to New York City by steamboats, the canal and railway.

From New York, Elder Parley P. Pratt wrote me on

the 22nd, directed to Commerce, from which I quote the following:

Excerpt from Parley P. Pratt's Letter to the Prophet.

The churches in these parts are prospering greatly, and are firm in the faith, and increasing in numbers continually. The Church in New York and Brooklyn now numbers from one hundred and fifty to two hundred members, and additions are being made every week. A general conference was held in this city on Tuesday and Wednesday of this week. Elders present: Orson Pratt, Wilford Woodruff, Samuel James, Benjamin Winchester, Elders Foster, Layne, Jenks, Brown, Benedict, and myself. Priests present: Addison Everett, Birge, and Vanvelver. Many branches of the Church in the region round about were represented; several hundred members in all, and the numbers still increasing. Great opportunities are open for preaching, and crowded houses are the order of the day.

I have also received letters from Maine and from Michigan, with joyful accounts of the spread of the work of the Lord. You would now find churches of the Saints in Philadelphia, in Albany, in Brooklyn, in New York, in Jersey, in Pennsylvania, on Long Island, and in various other places all around us. Our New York meetings are now held three times every Sabbath in Columbia Hall, Grand Street, a few doors east of the Bowery; it is very central, and one of the best places in the city; it will hold nearly a thousand people, and is well filled with attentive hearers. Brother Winchester has a good hall well fitted up in Philadelphia, where stated meetings are held—several every week, with crowded audiences.

In short the truth is spreading more rapidly than ever before, in every direction, far and near. There is a great call for our books. I am now reprinting the Voice of Warning, The History of the Missouri Persecution, and my Poems. There is a great call for hymn-books, but none to be had. I wish Sister Smith would add to the old collection such new ones as is best, and republish them immediately. If means and facilities are lacking in the west, send it here, and it shall be nicely done for her; and at least one thousand would immediately sell in these parts wholesale and retail. The Book of Mormon is not to be had in this part of the vineyard for love or money; hundreds are wanting in various parts hereabouts, but there is truly a famine in that respect.

The conference took into consideration the pressing calls for this book, and have appointed a committee to raise means for the publication of the same, and also to publish it if we can obtain leave from you, who hold the copyright. Any hymn-book which Sister Smith or the Church will favor us with, shall also be published on similar conditions.

PARLEY P. PRATT.

Some time this month the first number of the *Times and Seasons*, a monthly religious paper, in pamphlet form, was published at Commerce, Hancock County, Illinois, by my brother Don Carlos Smith and Ebenezer Robinson, under the firm name of Robinson & Smith, Publishers.

First Issue of the "Times and Seasons"

Tuesday, *26*.—At one in the afternoon, Elder Brigham Young and company went on board the steamer *Columbus*, at Fairport, and went on towards Buffalo.

Wednesday, *27*.—About 1 o'clock this morning the wind arose, when Elder Brigham Young went on deck, prayed to the Father in the name of Jesus, when he felt to command the wind and the waves to cease, and permit them to proceed on their journey in safety. The winds abated, and he gave glory, honor, and praise to the God who rules all things. Arriving in Buffalo in the morning, they took the stage for Batavia.

The Elements Obey.

While on the mountains some distance from Washington, our coachman stepped into a public house to take his grog, when the horses took fright and ran down the hill at full speed. I persuaded my fellow travelers to be quiet and retain their seats, but had to hold one woman to prevent her throwing her infant out of the coach. The passengers were exceedingly agitated, but I used every persuasion to calm their feelings; and opening the door, I secured my hold on the side of the coach the best way I could, and succeeded in placing myself in the coachman's seat, and reining up the horses, after they had run some two or three miles, and neither coach, horses, or passengers received any injury. My course was spoken of in the highest terms of commendation, as being one of the most daring and heroic deeds, and no language could express the gratitude of the passengers, when they found themselves safe, and the horses quiet. There were some members of Congress with us, who proposed naming the incident to that body, believing they would reward such

The Prophet's Adventure En Route to Washington.

conduct by some public act; but on inquiring my name, to mention as the author of their safety, and finding it to be Joseph Smith the "Mormon Prophet," as they called me, I heard no more of their praise, gratitude, or reward.

Thursday, 28.—I arrived in Washington City this morning, and put up at the corner of Missouri and Third streets.

This evening, Elder Brigham Young and company (except Elder Kimball, who stopped at Byron to visit his sister) rode to Rochester in the steam cars, and from thence rode all night in a horse coach, and arrived at ten in the morning on Friday, 29th, at Auburn, New York. Elders Taylor and Turley proceeded on their way to New York.

The following is a copy of our petition to Congress for redress of our Missouri grievances:

THE SAINT'S PETITION TO CONGRESS.

To the Honorable the Senate aud House of Representatives of the United States of America, in Congress assembled:

Your petitioners, Joseph Smith, Sidney Rigdon, and Elias Higbee, would most respectfully represent, that they have been delegated, by their brethren and fellow-citizens, known as "Latter-day Saints" (commonly called Mormons), to prepare and present to you a statement of their wrongs, and a prayer for their relief, which they now have the honor to submit to the consideration of your Honorable Body.

In the summer of 1831, a portion of the society above-named commenced a settlement in the county of Jackson, in the state of Missouri. The individuals making that settlement had emigrated from almost every state in the Union to the lovely spot in the Far West, with the hope of improving their condition, of building houses for themselves and posterity, and of erecting temples, where they and theirs might worship their Creator according to the dictates of their conscience. Though they had wandered far from the homes of their childhood, still they had been taught to believe, that a citizen born in any one state in this great Republic, might remove to another and enjoy all the rights and immunities of citizens of the state of his adoption—that wherever waved the American flag, beneath its stars and stripes an American citizen might look for protection and justice, for liberty in person and in conscience.

They bought farms, built houses, and erected churches. Some tilled the earth, others bought and sold merchandise, and others again toiled as mechanics. They were industrious and moral, and they prospered, and though often persecuted and vilified for their difference in religious opinion from their fellow citizens, they were happy; they saw their society increasing in numbers, their farms teemed with plenty, and they fondly looked forward to a future, big with hope. That there was prejudice against them, they knew; that slanders were propagated against them, they deplored; yet they felt that these were unjust; and hoped that time, and uprightness of life, would enable them to outlive them. While the summer of peace, happiness, and hope shone over the infant settlement of the Saints, the cloud was gathering, unseen by them, that bore in its bosom the thunderbolt of destruction.

On the 20th of July, 1833, around their peaceful village a mob gathered, to the surprise and terror of the quiet "Mormons"—why, they knew not; they had broken no law, they had harmed no man, in deed or thought. Why they were thus threatened, they knew not. Soon a committee from the mob called upon the leading "Mormons" of the place; they announced that the store, the printing office, and the shops must be closed, and that forthwith every "Mormon" must leave the county. The message was so terrible, so unexpected, that the "Mormons" asked time for deliberation and consultation, which being refused, the brethren were severally asked, "Are you willing to abandon your home?" The reply was, "We will not go;" which determination being reported to the committee of the mob, one of them replied that he was sorry, for said he, "The work of destruction must now begin." No sooner said than it was done. The printing office, a two story brick building, was assailed by the mob and torn down, and, with its valuable appurtenances, destroyed. They next proceeded to the store with a like purpose. Its owner in part, Mr. Gilbert, agreed to close it, and they delayed their purpose.

They then proceeded to the dwelling of Mr. Partridge, the beloved Bishop of the Church there, dragged him and his family to the public square, where, surrounded by hundreds, they partly stripped him of his clothing, and tarred and feathered him from head to foot. A man by the name of Allen was at the same time treated in a similar manner. The mob then dispersed with an agreement to meet again on the next Tuesday, the above outrages having been committed on Saturday.

Tuesday came, and with it came the mob, bearing a red flag, in token of *blood*. They proceeded to the houses of Isaac Morley, and others of the leading men, and seized them, telling them to bid their families farewell, that they would never see them again. They were then driven at the point of the bayonet to the jail, and there, amid the jeers and insults of the crowd, they were thrust into prison, to be kept as hostages; in case any of the mob should be killed, they were to die to pay for it. Here some two or three of the "Mormons" offered to surrender up their lives, if that would satisty the fury of the mob, and purchase peace and security for their unoffending brethren, their helpless wives and children. The reply of the mob was, that the "Mormons" must leave the county *en masse*, or that every man should be put to death.

The "Mormons," terrified and defenseless, then entered into an agreement to leave the county—one half by the first of January, the other half by the first of April next ensuing. This treaty being made and ratified, the mob dipersed. Again, for a time, the persecuted "Mormons" enjoyed a respite from their persecutions; but not long was the repose permitted them.

Some time in the month of October, a meeting was held at Independence, at which it was determined to remove the "Mormons" or die. Inflammatory speeches were made, and one of the speakers swore he would remove the "Mormons" from the county if he had to wade up to his neck in blood.

Be it remarked that up to this time, the "Mormons" had faithfully observed the treaty, and were guilty of no offense against the laws of the land, or of society, but were peaceably following the routine of their daily duties.

Shortly after the meeting above referred to, another persecution commenced; some of the "Mormons" were shot at, others were whipped, their houses were assailed with brickbats, broken open, and thrown down; their women and children were insulted; and thus for many weeks, without offense, without resistance, by night and by day, were they harassed, insulted, and oppressed.

There is a point beyond which endurance ceases to be a virtue. The worm when trampled upon will turn upon its oppressor. A company of about thirty "Mormons" fell in with twice that number of the mob engaged in the destruction of "Mormon" property, when a battle ensued, in which one "Mormon" was killed, and two or three of the mob; acting in concert with the officer who commanded the mob, was Lilburn W. Boggs, Lieutenant-Governor of the state of Missouri. When the noise of the battle was spread abroad, the public mind became much inflamed. The militia collected in arms from all quarters, and in great numbers, inflamed to fury. They demanded that the "Mormons" should surrender up all their arms, and immediately quit the county. Compelled by overpowering numbers, the "Mormons" submitted. They surrendered up fifty-one guns, which have never been returned, or paid for.

The next day, parties of the mob went from house to house, threatening women and children with death, if they did not immediately leave their homes. Imagination cannot paint the terror which now pervaded the "Mormon" community. The weather was intensely cold, and women and children abandoned their homes and fled in every direction without sufficient clothing to protect them from the piercing cold. Women gave birth to children in the woods and on the prairies. One hundred and twenty women and children, for the space of ten days, with only three or four men in the company, concealed themselves in the woods in hourly expectation and fear of massacre, until they finally escaped into Clay county. The society of "Mormons" after the above disturbances, removed to the county of Clay, where they were kindly received by the inhabitants, and their wants administered to by their charity.

In the meantime the houses of the "Mormons" in the county of Jackson, amounting to about two hundred, were burned down or otherwise destroyed by the mob, as well as much of their crops, furniture, and stock.

The damage done to the property of the "Mormons" by the mob in the county of Jackson as above related, as near as they can ascertain, would amount to the sum of one hundred and seventy-five thousand dollars. The number of "Mormons" thus driven from the county of Jackson amounted to about twelve hundred souls. For the property thus destroyed they have never been paid.

After the expulsion of the "Mormons" from the county of Jackson as above related, they removed to and settled in the county of Clay. They there purchased out some of the former inhabitants, and entered at the land office wild lands offered for sale by the General Government. The most of them became freeholders, owning each an eighty or more of land.

The "Mormons" lived peaceably in the county of Clay for about three years, and all that time increased rapidly in numbers, by emigration, and also in wealth by their industry. After they had resided in that county about three years, the citizens not connected with them began to look upon them with jealousy and alarm. Reports were again put in circulation against them: public meetings were held in the counties of Clay and Jackson, at which violent resolutions were passed against the "Mormons," and rumors of mobs began again to spread alarm among the "Mormons." At this juncture the "Mormons" desirous of avoiding all conflict with their fellow-citizens, and anxious to preserve the peace and harmony of the society around them, as well as their own, deputized a committee of their leading men to make terms of peace with their fellow-citizens of Clay county. An interview took place between them and a committee of citizens, at which it was agreed that the "Mormons" should leave the county of Clay, and that the citizens of Clay county should buy their lands.

These terms were complied with. The "Mormons" removed to and settled in the county of Caldwell, and the citizens never paid them value for their lands. Many received nothing at all for their land. The "Mormons," by this removal, sacrificed much both of money and feeling, but the sacrifice was made upon the altar of duty, for the peace of the community.

Your Memorialists would beg here to give what they believe a just explanation of the causes of the prejudice and persecution against the "Mormons" related above, and which will follow. That there might have been some unworthy members among them, cannot be denied; but many aver that as a community they were as moral, as upright, and as observant of the laws of the land as any body of people in the world. Why then this prejudice and persecution? An answer they trust will be found in the fact that they were a body of people distinct from their fellow-citizens, in religious opinions, in their habits, and in their associations. They were numerous enough to make the power of their numerical and moral force a matter of anxiety and dread to the political and religious parties by which they were surrounded; which arose not from what the "Mormons" had done, but from the fear of what they might do.

In addition, the "Mormons" have purchased of the settlers, or of the Government, or obtained by pre-emption, the best lands in all those regions of the state; and at the times of speculation, the cupidity of many was aroused to possess those lands by driving off the "Mormons," and taking forcible possession, or constraining them to sell, through fear and coercion, at a price merely nominal.

After the "Mormons" removed from Clay county, they settled in the county of Caldwell as aforesaid.

Your Memorialists do not deem it necessary for their purpose, to detail the history of the progress, the cares, and anxieties of the "Mormons," from the time they settled in Caldwell in the year 1836 until the fall of the year 1838. They would, however, state, that during all that time they deported themselves as good citizens, obeying the laws of the land, and the moral and religious duties enjoined by their faith. That there might have been some faithless among the faithful is possible. They would not deny that there might have been some who were a scandal to their brethren; and what society, they would ask, has not some unworthy members? Where is the sect, where the community, in which there cannot be found some who trample under foot the laws of God and man? They believe the "Mormon" community to have as few such as any other association, religious or political. Within the above period the "Mormons" continued to increase in wealth and numbers, until in the fall of the year 1838 they numbered about fifteen thousand souls.

They purchased of the Government, or of the citizens, or held by preemption, almost all the lands in the county of Caldwell, and a portion of the lands in Daviess and Carroll. The county of Caldwell was settled almost entirely by "Mormons," and "Mormons" were rapidly filling up the counties of Daviess and Caldwell. When they first commenced settling in those counties, there were but few settlements made there; the lands were wild and uncultivated. In the fall of 1838 large farms had been made, well improved and stocked. Lands had risen in value, and sold for from ten dollars to twenty-five dollars [per acre], The improvement and settlement had been such that it was a common remark that the county of Caldwell would soon be the wealthiest in the state.

Thus stood their affairs in the fall of 1838, when the storm of persecution again raged over the heads of the "Mormons," and the fierce demon of the mob drove them forth houseless and homeless, and penniless, upon the charities of the world, which to them, thank God! have been like angels' visits, but not few, or far between. This last persecution began at an election, which was held in Daviess county on the first Monday of August, 1838. A "Mormon" went to the polls to vote. One of the mob standing by, opposed his voting, contending that a "Mormon" had no more right to vote than a negro; one angry word brought on another, and blows followed. They are, however, happy to state that the "Mormon" was not the aggressor, but was on the defensive; others interfered, not one alone, but many assailed the "Mormon." His brethren, seeing him thus assailed by numbers, rushed to the rescue; then came others of the mob, until finally a general row commenced. The "Mormons" were victorious. The next day, a rumor reached the "Mormons" of Caldwell, that two of their brethren had been killed in this fight, and a refusal had been made to surrender their bodies for burial. Not knowing at the time that this rumor was false, they became much excited, and several of them started for Daviess county, where they arrived next morning, with a view of giving the brethren, whom they supposed to have been killed, a decent interment. Among the citizens this fight produced a great excitement. They held a public meeting and resolved to drive the "Mormons" from the county. Individuals began also to threaten the "Mormons" as a body, and swear that they should leave the county in three days. When the "Mormons" who had gone from Caldwell to Daviess, aforesaid, arrived there, they found this state of excitement to exist. They also heard that a large mob was collecting against them, headed by Adam Black one of the judges of the county court of Daviess county.

Under these circumstances, and with a view to allay the excitement, they called on Mr. Black, and inquired of him whether the reports they had heard in relation to him were true. Upon his denying them to be true, they then requested him to give that denial in writing, which he freely did. This writing they published with a view of calming the public mind, and allaying the excitement. Having done this, they rested in quiet for some time after, hoping that their efforts would produce the desired effect. Their surprise can, under these circumstances, be easily imagined, when a short time after, they learned that said Black had gone before Judge King, and made oath that he was forced to sign the instrument, by armed "Mormons," and procured a warrant for the arrest of Joseph Smith, Jun., and Lyman Wight, which was placed in the hands of the sheriff. It was also reported that the said individuals had refused to surrender themselves, and that an armed force was collecting to come and take them.

Your Memoralists aver that the sheriff had never made any efforts to serve the writ, and that the said Smith and Wight, so far from making any resistance, did not know that such a writ had been issued, until they learned it first by report as above related. In the meantime the rumor had run over the whole country, that the "Mormons" were compelling individuals to sign certain instruments in writing, and that they were resisting the process of the law. The public mind became much inflamed, and the mob began to collect from all quarters and in large numbers, with pretensions of assisting the sheriff to serve the process; and here let it be observed in passing, that Adam Black had sold the improvement and pre-emption claim on which he then resided, to the "Mormons," received his pay for the same, and that through his instrumentality the "Mormons" were driven off, and he now retains both their money and the improvement.

As soon as the above reports reached the ears of the said Smith and Wight, they determined immediately upon the course they ought to pursue, which was to submit to the laws. They both surrendered themselves up to Judge King, underwent a trial, and in the absence of all sufficient testimony they were discharged. They hoped that this voluntary submission of theirs to the law, and their triumphant vindication of the charge, would allay the excitement of the community. But not so; the long-desired opportunity had arrived when the oppression and extermination of the "Mormons" might be made to assume the form of legal proceeding. The mob that had assembled for the pretended purpose of assisting the officers in the execution of process, did not disperse upon the acquittal of Smith and Wight, but continued embodied with the encampments and forms of a military force, and committing depredations upon "Mormon" property. The "Mormons" in this extremity called upon the laws of the land, and the officers of the law, for protection. After much delay, the militia under Generals Atchison, Doniphan, and Parks, were sent to their relief. They arrived on the 13th of September, and encamped between the "Mormons and the mob.

The above officers made no attempt to disperse the mob, excusing themselves by saying, "that their own men had sympathies with the mob." After remaining there for several days, those officers adopted the following expedient of settling the difficulties—they mustered the mob, and enrolled them with their own troops, and then disbanded the whole, with orders to seek their several homes. The officers went home, excepting Parks, who remained for their protection, with his men.

The "Mormons" made an agreement with the citizens of Daviess, to buy out their lands and pre-emption rights, and appointed a committee to make the purchase, and to go on buying till they had purchased to the amount of twenty-five thousand dollars. While these purchases were going on, the citizens were heard to say, that as soon as they had sold out to the "Mormons" and received their pay, they would drive the "Mormons" off, and keep both their lands and the money.

The mob, when disbanded in Daviess by the generals as aforesaid, instead of repairing to their homes as commanded, proceeded in a body to the adjoining county of Carroll, and encamped around Dewitt, a village built and inhabited by "Mormons;" while thus encamped around Dewitt, they sent to the county of Jackson, and procured a cannon. They invested the place so closely, that no person could leave the town in safety; when they did so, they were fired upon by the mob. The horses of the "Mormons" were stolen, and their cattle killed. The citizens of Dewitt, amounting to about seventy families, were in great extremity, and worn out by want and sickness. In their extremity they made application to Governor Boggs for protection and relief; but no protection, no relief was granted them. When reduced to the last extremity, no alternative was left them, but to seek protection by flight, and the abandonment of their homes. Accordingly, on the evening of the 11th of October, 1838, they retreated from Dewitt, and made their way to the counties of Daviess and Caldwell, leaving many of their effects in the possession of the mob.

Your Memorialists will not detail the horrors and sufferings of such a flight, when shared with women and children. They might detail many. One lady, who had given birth to a child just before the flight commenced, died on the road and was buried without a coffin. Many others, sick, worn out, starved, deprived of medical aid, died upon the road. The remnant of "Mormons" from Dewitt arrived in Daviess and Caldwell, and found a short relief and supply of their wants from their friends and brethren there.

After the abandonment of Dewitt, and the flight of the "Mormons" from Carroll, one Sashiel Woods addressed the mob, advising them to take their cannon and march to the county of Daviess, and drive the "Mormons" from that county, and seize upon their lands and other property, saying that the "Mormons" could get no benefit of the law, as they had recently seen. They then commenced their march from Carroll to Daviess, carrying with them the cannon which they had received from Jackson. On their way they captured two 'Mormons," made them ride on the cannon, and taunted them as they went along, telling them that they were going to drive the "Mormons" from Daviess to Caldwell, and from Caldwell to hell; and that they should find no quarters but at the cannon's mouth. The mob at this time was reported to number about four hundred strong.

The "Mormons" in these distresses, in pursuance of the laws of Missouri, made application to Judge King, the circuit judge of that circuit, for protection, and for the aid of the officers of the law to protect them. Judge King, as they have been informed, and believe, gave an order to Major General David R. Atchison to call out the militia to protect the "Mormons" against the fury of the mob. General Atchison thereupon gave orders to Brigadiers Parks and Doniphan. In pursuance of these orders issued as aforesaid, on the 18th of October, 1838, General Doniphan arrived at Far West, a "Mormon" village in the county of Caldwell, with a small company of militia. After he had been at Far West two days, General Doniphan disbanded his company, alleging to the "Mormons," as his reason for so doing, that his company had the same feelings as the mob, and that he could not rely upon them. In a short time General Parks arrived at Far West, and also disbanded his company. At this time the mob was marching from Carroll to Daviess. General Doniphan, while at Far West, directed the "Mormons" to raise a company to protect themselves, telling them that one Cornelius Gilliam was raising a mob to destroy their town, and also advising them to place out guards to watch the motions of the mob. He also directed them to raise a company and send them to Daviess, to aid their brethren there against the mob which was marching down upon them from Carroll. This the "Mormons" did; they mustered a company of about sixty men, who proceeded to Diahman. When General Parks arrived at Far West as aforesaid, and learned that General Doniphan had disbanded his men he expressed great dissatisfaction. The same evening on which General Parks disbanded his company as aforesaid, he proceeded to Diahman, in order to learn what the mob were doing there, and if possible to protect the "Mormons."

When General Parks had arrived in Daviess, he found that the mob had commenced its operations there, which was on the 20th of October, 1838.

They commenced by burning the house of a man [Don Carlos Smith] who had gone to Tennessee on business, and left his wife at home with two small children. When the house was burned down, the wife and two small children were left in the snow, and she had to walk three miles before she could find a shelter, carrying her two children all that distance, and had to wade Grand River, which was three feet deep. The mob on the same evening burned seven other houses, burning and destroying all the property that they thought proper. The next morning, Colonel Lyman Wight, an officer in the militia, inquired of General Parks, what was to be done, as he now saw the course the mob was determined to pursue. General Parks replied that he (Wight) should take a company of men and give the mob battle, and that he would be responsible for the act, saying that they could have no peace with the mob, until they had given them a scourging.

On the next morning, in obedience to this order, David W. Patten was despatched with one hundred men under his command to meet the mob as they were advancing from Carroll, with directions to protect the citizens, and collect and bring into Far West such of the "Mormons" as were scattered through the county, and unprotected, and if the mob interfered, he must fight them. The company under the command of Patten was the same, in part, that had gone from Far West by the order of General Doniphan to protect the citizens of Daviess. As Patten went in the direction of the mob, they fled before him, leaving their cannon, which Patten took possession of. The mob dispered. Patten with his men then returned to Daviess county. Patten in a few days after returned to Far West. It was now supposed that the difficulties were at an end. But contrary to expectation, on the evening of the 23rd of October, messengers arrived at Far West and informed the citizens that a body of armed men had made their appearance in the south part of the county, and that they were burning houses, destroying property, and threatening the "Mormon" citizens with death, unless they left the county the next morning by 10 o'clock, or renounced their religion.

About midnight another messenger arrived with news of the like tenor. Patten collected about sixty men and proceeded to the scene of the disturbance, to protect if possible the lives and property of the "Mormon" citizens. On his arrival at the neighborhood where the first disturbance had commenced, he found that the mob had gone to another neighborhood to prosecute their acts of plunder and outrage. He marched a short distance and unexpectedly came upon the encampment of the mob. The guards of the mob fired upon him and killed one of his men. Patten then charged the mob, and after a few fires, the mob dispersed and fled, but Patten was killed and another of his men. After the fight and dispersion of the mob, Patten's company returned to Far West. The report of the proceedings created much excitement. The community was made to believe that the "Mormons" were in rebellion against the law; whereas the above facts show they were an injured people, standing up in the defense of their persons and their property.

At this time the governor of the state issued an order to General Clark to raise several thousand men and march against the "Mormons," and drive them from the state, or "exterminate them." Major-General Lucas and Brigadier-General Wilson collected three or four thousand men; and with this formidable force, commenced their march and arrived at Far West. In their rear marched General Clark with another formidable force.

In the meantime the "Mormons" had not heard of these immense preparations, and so far from expecting an armed force under the orders of the state to war against them, were daily expecting a force from the governor to protect their lives and their property from the mob.

When this formidable array first made its appearance, intent upon peace, the "Mormons sent a white flag several miles to meet them, to ascertain the reason why an armed force was marching against them, and what we might expect at their hands. They gave us no satisfaction, but continued marching towards Far West. Immediately on their arrival, a man came bearing a white flag from their camp. He was interrogated about his business; he answered the interrogations, saying they wanted three persons out of Far West, before they massacred the rest. Those persons refused to go, and he returned back to the camp. He was closely followed by General Doniphan and his whole brigade marching to the city of Far West in line of battle. The citizens also of Far West formed a line of battle in full front of Doniphan's army: upon this Doniphan ordered a halt, and then a retreat. Night closed upon both parties without any collision.

On the next day, towards evening, the "Mormons" were officially informed that the governor of the state had sent this immense force against them to massacre them, or drive them from the state. As soon as the "Mormons" learned that this order had the sanction of the governor of the state, they determined to make no resistance; to submit themselves to the authorities of the state, how tyrannical and unjust soever the exercise of that authority might be.

The commanders of the Missouri militia before Far West sent a messenger into the town, requesting an interview in their camp with five of the principal citizens among the "Mormons," pledging their faith for their safe return on the following morning at eight o'clock. Invited, as they supposed, to propose and receive terms of peace, and under the pledge of a safe conduct, Lyman Wight, George W. Robinson, Joseph Smith, Jun., Parley P. Pratt, and Sidney Rigdon, went towards the camp of the militia. Before they arrived at the camp, they were surrounded by the whole army; and by order of General Lucas put under guard, and marched to the camp, and were told that they were prisoners of war. A court martial was held that night, and they, without being heard, and in the absence of all proof, were condemned to be shot next morning.

The execution of this bloody order, was prevented by the manly protest of General Doniphan. He denounced the act as cold blooded murder, and withdrew his brigade. This noble stand taken by General Doniphan, prevented the murder of the prisoners. It is here worthy of note, that seventeen preachers of the gospel were on this court martial, and were in favor of the sentence.

The next morning the prisoners were marched under a strong guard to Independence, in Jackson county, and after being detained there for a week, they were marched to Richmond, where General Clark then was with his troops. Here a court of inquiry was held before Judge King; this continued from the 11th until the 28th of November; while the five prisoners were kept in chains, and about fifty other "Mormons," taken at Far West, were penned up in an open, unfinished court house. In this mock court of inquiry the defendants were prevented from giving any testimony on their part, by an armed force at the court house; they were advised by their lawyers not to bring any [witnesses], as they would be in danger of their lives, or be driven out of the county; so there was no testimony examined only against them.

In this inquiry a great many questions were asked relative to religious opinions.* The conclusion of the court of inquiry was to send the prisoners to jail upon a charge of treason.

They do not deem it necessary to detail their sufferings while in prison, the horrors of a prison for four long months, in darkness, in want, alone, and during the cold of winter, can better be conceived than expressed. In the following April the prisoners were sent to the county of Daviess for trial; they were then indicted for treason, and a change of venue was taken to Boone county. The prisoners were sent to the county of Boone, and while on their way made their escape, and fled to the state of Illinois.

That they were suffered to escape admits of no doubt. The truth is, the state of Missouri had become ashamed of their proceedings against the "Mormons," and as the best means of getting out of the scrape, gave the prisoners an opportunity to escape. In proof of this, the prisoners have ever since been living publicly in the state of Illinois,

* See Vol. III., page 212.

and the executive of Missouri has made no demand upon the executive of Illinois. Can it be supposed that the people of Missouri would thus tamely submit to the commission of treason by a portion of their citizens, and make no effort to punish the guilty, when they were thus publicly living in an adjoining state? Is not this passiveness evidence? They knew the "Mormons" were innocent, and the citizens of Missouri wrong?

But to return to the operations of General Lucas before Far West: We need only say that the exterminating order of Governor Boggs was carried into full effect. After the above-named individuals were taken prisoners, all the "Mormons" in Far West, about five hundred in number, surrendered up their arms to the militia without any resistance. The "Mormons" now fled in every direction—women and children, through the dead of winter, marked their footsteps with blood, as they fled from the state of Missouri.

The orders of the governor were, that they should be driven from the state or destroyed. About fifteen thousand souls, between the sacking of Far West and spring, abandoned their homes, their property, their all, hurried by the terrors of their armed pursuers, in want of every necessary of life, with bleeding hearts sought refuge in the state of Illinois, where they now reside.

We cannot trespass upon your time by the relation of cases of individual suffering; they would fill a volume. We forbear for our regard to humanity, to detail the particulars of the conduct of the Missouri militia. We could relate instances of house-burnings, destruction of property, robbings, rapes, and murder, that would shame humanity. One instance as a sample of many scenes which they enacted: Two hundred of the militia came suddenly upon some "Mormon" families emigrating to the state, and then encamped at Haun's mill in Caldwell county. The "Mormon" men and children took refuge in an old log house which had been used as a blacksmith's shop. On seeing the militia approach, the "Mormons" cried for quarters, but in vain; they were instantly fired upon; eighteen fell dead; and their murderers, putting the muzzle of their guns between the logs, fired indiscriminately upon children, upon the dead and dying. One little boy, whose father (Warren Smith) had just been shot dead, cried piteously to the militia to spare his life. The reply was, "Kill him, kill him (with an oath), he is a son of a damned Mormon." At this they shot his head all open, and left him dead by the side of his father. About the same time an old man by the name of McBride, a soldier of the Revolution, came up to them and begged his life; but they hewed him to pieces with an old corn cutter. They then loaded themselves with plunder and departed.

Your petitioners have thus given a brief outline of the history of the

"Mormon" persecutions in Missouri—all which they can prove to be true, if an opportunity be given them. It will be seen from this their brief statement, that neither the "Mormons" as a body, nor individuals of that body, have been guilty of any offense against the laws of Missouri, or of the United States; but their only offense has been their religious opinion.

The above statement will also show, that the "Mormons" on all occasions submitted to the law of the land, and yielded to its authority in every extremity, and at every hazard, at the risk of life and property. The above statement will illustrate another truth: that wherever the "Mormons" made any resistance to the mob, it was in self defense; and for these acts of self defense they always had the authority and sanction of the officers of the law for so doing. Yet they, to the number of about fifteen thousand souls, have been driven from their homes in Missouri. Their property, to the amount of two millions of dollars, has been taken from them, or destroyed. Some of them have been murdered, beaten, bruised, or lamed and have all been driven forth, wandering over the world without homes, without property.

But the loss of property does not comprise half their sufferings. They were human beings, possessed of human feelings and human sympathies. Their agony of soul was the bitterest drop in the cup of their sorrows.

For these wrongs, the "Mormons" ought to have some redress; yet how and where shall they seek and obtain it? Your constitution guarantees to every citizen, even the humblest, the enjoyment of life, liberty, and property. It promises to all, religious freedom, the right to all to worship God beneath their own vine and fig tree, according to the dictates of their conscience. It guarantees to all the citizens of the several states the right to become citizens of any one of the states, and to enjoy all the rights and immunities of the citizens of the state of his adoption. Yet of all these rights have the "Mormons" been deprived. They have, without a cause, without a trial, been deprived of life, liberty and property. They have been persecuted for their religious opinions. They have been driven from the state of Missouri, at the point of the bayonet, and prevented from enjoying and exercising the rights of citizens of the state of Missouri. It is the theory of our laws, that for the protection of every legal right, there is provided a legal remedy. What, then, we would respectfully ask, is the remedy of the "Mormons?" Shall they apply to the legislature of the state of Missouri for redress? They have done so. They have petitioned, and these petitions have been treated with silence and contempt. Shall they apply to the federal courts? They were, at the time of the injury, citizens of the state of Missouri. Shall they apply to the court of the state of Missouri? Whom shall they sue? The order for their destruction, then extermination, was granted by the executive of the state of Missouri. Is not this a plea of justification for the loss of individuals, done in pursuance of that order? If not, before whom shall the "Mormons" institute a trial? Shall they summon a jury of the individuals who composed the mob? An appeal to them were in vain. They dare not go to Missouri to institute a suit; their lives would be in danger.

For ourselves we see no redress, unless it is awarded by the Congress of the United States. And here we make our appeal as *American Citizens*, as *Christians*, and as *Men*—believing that the high sense of justice which exists in your honorable body, will not allow such oppression to be practiced upon any portion of the citizens of this vast republic with impunity; but that some measures which your wisdom may dictate, may be taken, so that the great body of people who have been thus abused, may have redress for the wrongs which they have suffered. And to your decision they look with confidence; hoping it may be such as shall tend to dry up the tear of the widow and orphan, and again place in situations of peace, those who have been driven from their homes, and have had to wade through scenes of sorrow and distress.

And your Memoralists, as in duty bound, will ever pray.

CHAPTER III.

THE PROPHET'S EFFORTS AT WASHINGTON TO OBTAIN REDRESS OF GRIEVANCES FOR THE SAINTS—AFFIDAVITS ON MISSOURI AFFAIRS.

Saturday, November 30, 1839.—Elders Young and George A. Smith went to Brother Isaac Haight's at Moravia.

Sunday, December 1, 1839.—The High Council at Nauvoo met at Oliver Granger's, and voted that Hyrum Smith, George W. Harris, and Oliver Granger, be a committee to send a petition to the legislature to define new boundary lines of the city of Nauvoo, and also of Commerce, and do all other needful acts relative to those cities; that Hyrum Smith furnish the maps and plats for the alteration, and that Seymour Brunson circulate the petition for signatures.

Voted that Bishop Edward Partridge publish a piece in the *Times and Seasons*, informing the brethren in the west, that it is improper to remove from the west for the purpose of locating in Kirtland, Ohio, and that those who do thus remove, will be disfellowshiped by the council.

The Prophet's Letter to Hyrum Smith—Reporting State of Affairs at Washington.

WASHINGTON CITY, CORNER MISSOURI AND 3RD STS.,
December 5th, 1839.

Dear Brother Hyrum, President, and to the Honorable High Council of the Church of Jesus Christ of Latter-day Saints—to whom be fellowship, love, and the peace of Almighty God extended, and the prayer of faith forever and ever. Amen.

Your fellow laborers, Joseph Smith, Jun., Elias Higbee, and agents as well as the servants that are sent by you, to perform one of the most arduous and responsible duties, and also to labor in the most honorable cause that ever graced the pages of human existence, respectfully show by these lines, that we have taken up our cross thus far, and that we arrived in this city on the morning of the 28th November, and spent the most of that day in looking up a boarding house, which we succeeded in finding. We found as cheap boarding as can be had in this city.

On Friday morning, 29th, we proceeded to the house of the President. We found a very large and splendid palace, surrounded with a splendid enclosure, decorated with all the fineries and elegancies of this world. We went to the door and requested to see the President, when we were immediately introduced into an upper apartment, where we met the President, and were introduced into his parlor, where we presented him with our letters of introduction. As soon as he had read one of them, he looked upon us with a kind of half frown, and said, "What can I do? I can do nothing for you! If I do anything, I shall come in contact with the whole state of Missouri."

But we were not to be intimidated; and demanded a hearing, and constitutional rights. Before we left him he promised to reconsider what he had said, and observed that he felt to sympathize with us, on account of our sufferings.

We have spent the remainder of our time in hunting up the Representatives in order to get our case brought before the House; in giving them letters of introduction, etc., and in getting acquainted. A meeting of the delegation of the state of Illinois was appointed today, to consult for bringing our case before Congress. The gentlemen from Illinois are worthy men, and have treated us with the greatest kindness, and are ready to do all that is in their power; but you are aware, brethren, that they with us have all the prejudices, superstition, and bigotry of an ignorant generation to contend with; nevertheless we believe our case will be brought before the House, and we will leave the event with God; He is our Judge, and the Avenger of our wrongs.

For a general thing there is but little solidity and honorable deportment among those who are sent here to represent the people; but a great deal of pomposity and show.

We left President Rigdon and others on the road, and received a letter from them this day. They were, at the date of the letter, on the 20th of November, near Washington, in Pennsylvania, expecting to stop a day or two at his brother's on account of his ill health. He has occasionally a chill yet, but his illness is not dangerous. We expect him here soon.

We have already commenced forming some very honorable acquaintances, and have thus far been prospered as much as we had anticipated, if not more. We have had a pleasing interview with Judge Young, who proposed to furnish us with expense money. We can draw on him for funds to publish our book, and we want you to raise some more money for us, and deposit it in the Branch Bank in Quincy, to be drawn to the order of Judge Young. Send us the amount of your deposit, taking a receipt of the same. You need not be afraid to do this. We think from the proceeds of the sale of books, we can make it all straight. Do therefore be punctual, as much depends upon it. We cannot accomplish the things for which we were sent without some funds. You very well know, brethren, we were contented to start, trusting in God, with little or nothing. We have met with but one accident since we started. The lock of our trunk was broken off, and Brother Lyman Wight's petition is missing; but we trust there is a copy of it preserved; if there is, you will please forward it immediately, with the name and affidavit to it.

For God's sake, brethren, be wide awake, and arm us with all the power possible, for now is the time or never. We want you should get all the influential men you can of that section of country, of Iowa, and of every other quarter, to write letters to the members of Congress, using their influence in our behalf, and to keep their minds constantly upon the subject.

Please to forward this to our wives.

Yours in the bonds of the Everlasting Covenant,

JOSEPH SMITH, JUN.,
ELIAS HIGBEE.

P. S.—Congress has been in session for four days, and the House of Representatives is not yet organized, in consequence of some seats being contested in the New Jersey delegation. They have this day succeeded in electing John Q. Adams to the chair *pro tem.;* but whether they will get their Speaker and Clerk chosen is yet unknown, as there is a great deal of wind blown off on the occasion on each day. There is such an itching disposition to display their oratory on the most trivial occasions, and so much etiquette, bowing and scraping, twisting and turning, to make a display of their witticism, that it seems to us rather a display of folly and show, more than substance and gravity, such as becomes a great nation like ours. (However there are some exceptions).

A warm feeling has been manifested in the discussion of the House today, and it seems as much confusion as though the nation had already began to be vexed. We came with one of the Missouri members from Wheeling to this place, who was drunk but once, and that however was most of the time; there was but one day but what he could navigate, and that day he was keeled over, so he could eat no dinner. The horses ran away with the stage; they ran about three miles;

Brother Joseph climbed out of the stage, got the lines, and stopped the horses, and also saved the life of a lady and child. He was highly commended by the whole company for his great exertions and presence of mind through the whole affair. Elias Higbee jumped out of the stage at a favorable moment, just before they stopped, with a view to assist in stopping them, and was but slightly injured. We were not known to the stage company until after our arrival.

In our interview with the President, he interrogated us wherein we differed in our religion from the other religions of the day. Brother Joseph said we differed in mode of baptism, and the gift of the Holy Ghost by the laying on of hands. We considered that all other considerations were contained in the gift of the Holy Ghost, and we deemed it unnecessary to make many words in preaching the Gospel to him. Suffice it to say he has got our testimony. We watch the postoffice, but have received no letters from our sections of the country. Write instantly.

Yours with respect,

J. S. Jun.,
E. H.

Tuesday, *3*.—High Council of Iowa met at Elijah Fordham's and voted to come up to the law of tithing, so far as circumstances would permit, for the benefit of the poor, and that Alanson Ripley remove to Iowa; and he was ordained Bishop by the Presidency of the Council.

Affairs in Iowa.

Elder Daniel Avery was instructed to call the Elders together and organize the Elder's Quorum.

Saturday, *7*.—The President of the High Council of Iowa proposed the following questions—Have the brethren a right to exact the payment of debts which were due them from others, and were consecrated to the Bishop in the state of Missouri? Six Counselors spoke. The President decided that all such debts ought not to be called for, and that persons making such demands shall be disfellowshiped by the Church; which was approved by the Council. Also that all those who sold goods in Missouri, and were calling for their pay, should be considered as acting in unrighteousness, and ought to be disfellowshiped;

as the property of the Saints had been confiscated by Missouri.

Letter of the Prophet and Elias Higbee to the High Council at Nauvoo—Preliminary Hearing of Grievances.

WASHINGTON CITY, CORNER OF MISSOURI AND 3RD STS.,
December 7th, 1839.

To Seymour Brunson and the Honorable High Council of the Church of Jesus Christ of Latter-day Saints:

Your humble servants, Joseph Smith, Jun., and Elias Higbee, again address you for the purpose of informing you of our proceedings here in relation to our business and prospects of success. We deem it unimportant to say anything in relation to our journey, arrival, and interview with his Excellency, the President of these United States; as they were mentioned in a letter lately addressed to President Hyrum Smith and the High Council. We mentioned in that letter the appointment of a meeting to be held by the Illinois delegation, to consult upon the best measures of getting our business brought before Congress. They met yesterday in one of the committee rooms of the Capitol. All the delegation were present except ex-Governor Reynolds—who is now one of the Representatives in Congress—and on account of whose absence, the meeting was adjourned until today at eleven o'clock; however the subject was partially introduced, and Mr. Robinson took a stand against us, so far as concerned our presenting claims to be liquidated by the United States.

We took a stand against him, asserting our constitutional rights. Brother Joseph maintained the ground in argument against him firmly and respectfully, setting forth the injuries that we have received, and the appeals that we have made to the judiciary of Missouri, and also the governor; their refusals from time to time to do us justice; also the impracticability of doing anything in the judiciary courts of Missouri—which tribunal Mr. Robinson thought was the only proper place for our claims; but he finally said it was his first impression on the subject, not having considered the matter, but would take it into further consideration.

Judge Young of the Senate made some remarks in our favor, saying he would get the opinion of some of the prominent members of the Senate, who were also lawyers, and would report to us the next meeting. We met this day according to appointment, and very friendly feelings were manifested on the occasion. Our business was taken up, and

Judge Young stated that he had asked the opinion of Judge White of Tennessee, of Mr. Wright, and several other members whose names we do not recollect, but were prominent members of the Senate. They all declined giving an opinion at present, as it was a matter that they had not considered sufficiently to decide upon at this time. The meeting then, after some deliberations, decided in our favor, which decision was that a Memorial and Petition be drawn up in a concise manner, (our Representatives promising so to do), and Judge Young present them to the Senate, that they might thereby refer it to the proper committee, with all the accompanying documents, and order the same to be printed.

We want you to assist us now; and also to forward us your certificates, that you hold for your lands in Missouri: your claims to preemption rights, and affidavits to prove that soldiers were quartered on us and in our houses without our consent, or any special act of law for that purpose; contrary to the Constitution of the United States. We think Brother Ripley and others will recollect the circumstances and facts relative to this matter. You will also recollect the circumstances of Brother Joseph and others being refused the privilege of *habeas corpus* by the authorities of Missouri.

These facts must be authenticated by affidavits. Let any particular ransaction of the outrages in Missouri that can be sworn to by the sufferers, or those who were eye-witnesses to the facts, be sent, specifying the particulars. Have the evidence *bona fide* to the point.

The House of Representatives is not organized. Much feeling and confusion have prevailed in the House for a few days past. The House succeeded in electing John Q. Adams chairman *pro tem.* on the 5th instant. They have not yet elected their Speaker or Clerk. The Senate can do nothing of consequence until the House is organized; neither can the President's message until then be received. We design taking a paper and forwarding it to you.

Your brethren in the bonds of the everlasting covenant,

JOSEPH SMITH, JUN.,
ELIAS HIGBEE.

Brigham Young in New York.

Brother Isaac Haight took Elders Young and George A. Smith to Brother Joseph Murdock's, Hamilton, Madison county, New York, where Elder Young preached on Sunday, 8th, and spent the week in preaching, and visiting the brethren. Elder George A. Smith was confined to his room, sick.

This day, the High Council of Nauvoo issued an Epistle

to the Saints west of Kirtland not to return thither. (See *Times and Seasons*, page 29).*

Elders Hiram Clark, Alexander Wright, and Samuel Mulliner arrived in Preston from America. Their licenses were mislaid on their journey, and they had some difficulty in making themselves known.

* This epistle is of interest as showing the spirit of the Church government at that time, (1839) and the recognition of the rights of individuals. For these reasons it is quoted here:

To the Saints scattered abroad, in the region westward from Kirtland, Ohio:

Beloved Brethren:—Feeling that it is our duty, as the servants of God, to instruct the Saints from time to time, in those things which to us appear to be wise and proper—therefore we freely give you a few words of advice at this time.

We have heard it rumored abroad, that some at least, and probably many, are making their calculations to remove back to Kirtland next season.

Now brethren, this being the case, we advise you to abandon such an idea; yea, we warn you, in the name of the Lord, not to remove back there, unless you are counseled so to do by the First Presidency, and the High Council of Nauvoo. We do not wish by this to take your agency from you; but we feel to be plain, and pointed in our advice for we wish to do our duty, that your sins may not be found in our skirts. All persons are entitled to their agency, for God has so ordained it. He has constituted mankind moral agents, and given them power to choose good or evil; to seek after that which is good, by pursuing the pathway of holiness in this life, which brings peace of mind, and joy in the Holy Ghost here, and a fulness of joy and happiness at His right hand hereafter; or to pursue an evil course, going on in sin and rebellion against God, thereby bringing condemnation to their souls in this world, and an eternal loss in the world to come. Since the God of heaven has left these things optional with every individual, we do not wish to deprive them of it. We only wish to act the part of a faithful watchman, agreeably to the word of the Lord to Ezekiel the prophet, (Ezekiel 33 chap , 2, 3, 4, 5, verses,) and leave it for others to do as seemeth them good.

Now for persons to do things, merely because they are advised to do them, and yet murmur all the time they are doing them, is of no use at all; they might as well not do them. There are those who profess to be Saints who are too apt to murmur, and find fault, when any advice is given, which comes in opposition to their feelings, even when they, themselves, ask for counsel; much more so when counsel is given unasked for, which does not agree with their notion of things; but brethren, we hope for better things from the most of you; we trust that you desire counsel, from time to time, and that you will cheerfully conform to it, whenever you receive it from a proper source.

It is very probable, that it may be considered wisdom for some of us, [i. e. at Nauvoo], and perhaps others, to move back to Kirtland, to attend to important business there: but notwithstanding that, after what we have written, should any be so unwise as to move back there, without being first counseled so to do, their conduct will be highly disapprobated.

Done by order and vote of the First Presidency and High Council for the Church of Jesus Christ of Latter-day Saints, at Nauvoo, December 8, 1839.

H. G. Sherwood, Clerk.

Times and Seasons, Vol. 1, p. 29.

Some time this month, Brother Hyrum Smith wrote a long Epistle "To the Saints scattered abroad, Greeting," setting forth his sufferings, etc., in the State of Missouri, and published the same in the *Times and Seasons*, on page 20 and onward.*

Sunday, 15.—President Young preached at Brother Gifford's, in Waterville.

The High Council at Nauvoo voted that Bishop Knight provide for the families of Joseph Smith, Jun., Sidney Rigdon, and Orrin Porter Rockwell, during their absence at Washington.

Elder James Mulholland, my scribe, having died, it was voted that debts contracted for building his house be settled. Also approved of Brothers Annis, Bozier, and Edmunds building a water mill adjoining the city.

Monday 16.—President Young returned to Hamilton.

Wednesday, 18.—Elders Woodruff, John Taylor, and Theodore Turley sailed from New York for England.

Friday, 20.—President Young went to Eaton, to see his cousins Fitch, Salmon, and Phinehas Brigham.

* This communication of Hyrum Smith's adds nothing to his very elaborate statement of the wrongs suffered by himself and the Saints in Missouri already published in Volume III, pp. 403-424, except his testimony to the truth of the Book of Mormon; and as he was one of the Eight Witnesses to the fact of the existence of the Nephite plates from which the record was translated, the paragraphs relating to that testimony are given here:

"Having given my testimony to the world of the truth of the Book of Mormon, the renewal of the everlasting covenant, and the establishment of the kingdom of heaven, in these last days; and having been brought into great afflictions and distresses for the same, I thought that it might be strengthening to my beloved brethren, to give them a short account of my sufferings, for the truth's sake, and the state of my mind and feelings, while under circumstances of the most trying and afflicting nature. * * * * I had been abused and thrust into a dungeon, and confined for months on account of my faith, and the testimony of Jesus Christ. However I thank God that I felt a determination to die, rather than deny the things which my eyes had seen, which my hands had handled, and which I had borne testimony to, [all in plain allusion to his testimony to the existence of the plates from which the Book of Mormon was translated] wherever my lot had been cast; and I can assure my beloved brethren that I was enabled to bear as strong a testimony, when nothing but death presented itself, as ever I did in my life. My confidence in God, was likewise unshaken. I knew that He who suffered me, along with my brethren, to be thus tried, that He could and that He would deliver us out of the hands of our enemies; and in His own due time He did so, for which I desire to bless and praise His holy name."—*Times and Seasons*, Vol. 1, pp. 20 and 23.

For particulars of our proceedings while at Washington, see my letters and Judge Higbee's to friends at Commerce, or Nauvoo, as the place is now frequently called.

Saturday, 21.—I arrived in Philadelphia, direct from Washington City, by the railroad, where I spent several days preaching and visiting from house to house, among the brethren and others.

Letter of Hyrum Smith to Parley P. Pratt—On Printing the Book of Mormon in New York.

NAUVOO, HANCOCK COUNTY, ILLINOIS,
December 22nd, 1839.

DEAR BROTHER PARLEY:—In consequence of the absence of my brother Joseph, your letter has come into my hands, to which I intend to reply, and give such instructions, and advise you respecting the matters and things of which you write, as I feel led by the Spirit of the Lord [to give].

I was truly glad to hear of the prosperity of the churches in and about the vicinity of New York. Truly these things are pleasing to the Saints, and I presume to none more so than yourself, who was the instrument in the hands of God in planting the standard of truth in those regions, around which so many are now rallying.

You express a desire to have the Book of Mormon, etc., printed in New York, etc., etc., and have taken some steps towards accomplishing that object. As respects this matter I would say, that it is one of great importance, and should be properly considered. Not only is the city of New York destitute of this book, but there is truly a famine throughout the Union, and another large edition is certainly required. But at the same time I cannot give any encouragement for the publication of the same, other than at this place, or where it can come out under the immediate inspection of Joseph and his Counselors, so that no one may be chargeable with any mistakes that may occur. I want the books we print here should be a standard to all nations in which they may be printed, and to all tongues into which the same may be translated.

Again, as this place is appointed a Stake and a place of gathering for the Saints, I think that every facility should be rendered it, in order that the Saints may be able to accomplish the great works which have to be performed in this generation. I should therefore strongly advise, yea, urge you and all the Elders of Israel, when they meet with those who have means, and a disposition to forward this work, to send them to this place, where they may receive counsel from time to time.

If when Brothers Joseph and Rigdon return, we should deem it prudent to avail ourselves of the facilities offered in New York for re-printing the Book of Mormon, it is probable that a delegation will be sent to accomplish that object. In the meantime you will be at liberty to go to Europe, for thereunto are you sent.

The above observations will apply to the book of Doctrine and Covenants, Hymn Book, etc., which publications I long to see flowing through the land like a stream, imparting knowledge, intelligence, and joy to all who shall drink at the stream. As to publishing the Book of Mormon in Europe and other nations, I should entirely acquiesce to your proposition. I do not know of any more suitable persons for attending to that business than the Twelve. If it should be deemed wisdom to have the same published in England or elsewhere soon, you will be further advised on the subject, and full powers given you immediately on the return of Joseph, who is at present in the city of Washington, in company with Elder Rigdon and Judge Higbee, endeavoring to get the subject of our late persecutions brought before the councils of the nation.

The families of the Twelve are generally well, but not altogether so comfortably situated as I could wish, owing to the poverty of the Church. I think it would be well for those who have means to spare, to forward the same to their families.

My love to all the brethren. I am your affectionate brother in the bonds of the covenant, HYRUM SMITH.

Addressed to Elder P. P. Pratt, New York City.

Monday, *23*.—President Young went to Waterville with Brother Gifford. About this time Brothers Rockwell and Higbee arrived at Philadelphia with my carriage from Washington, where they had been some time, leaving Elder Rigdon there sick, and Dr. Robert E. Foster to take care of him.

Wednesday, *25*.—Elders Wright and Mulliner left Preston for Scotland, and soon commenced preaching and baptising in Paisley and vicinity.

President Young went six miles north of Rome [New York] to see Brother Blakesly; returned on the 27th to Waterville, and on the 28th went to Hamilton.

Saturday, *28*.—Heber John, son of Willard and Jennetta Richards, died at Preston, England, aged five months and nine days. He had been sick nine days with the small-pox, and was buried in Elswick Chapel yard.

Sunday, 29.—The High Council of Nauvoo voted to print ten thousand copies of the hymn-books, and an edition of the Book of Mormon, under the inspection of the First Presidency at Nauvoo, so soon as means can be obtained.

Monday, 30.—About this time I left Philadelphia with Brother Orson Pratt, and visited a branch of the Church in Monmouth county, New Jersey, where I spent several days, and returned to Philadelphia.

The Prophet in New Jersey

The High Council of Nauvoo voted that a committee be appointed to transact the business relating to the request of the brethren at Washington as follows—Alanson Ripley, in Iowa; Seymour Brunson and Charles C. Rich, at Quincy; Zenas H. Gurley, at Macomb; and that President Hyrum Smith, and Bishops Edward Partridge and Vinson Knight give the committee their instructions.

Wednesday, January 1, 1840.—George A. Smith (who had partially recovered from his illness) and Elder Brigham Young left Hamilton. The brethren helped them on their way, and gave them considerable clothing.

Thursday, 2.—Brother James Gifford brought them to Utica.

As more positive and official testimony was wanted by the authorities at Washington, many of the brethren made affidavits concerning their sufferings in, and expulsion from, Missouri, a few of which I will insert in my history:

Affidavit of Simeon Carter on his Sufferings in Missouri.

I, Simeon Carter, certify that I have been a resident of the state of Missouri for six years and upwards, and that I have suffered many things by a lawless mob; both myself and my family have been driven from place to place, and suffered the loss of much property, and finally were expelled from the state. I further certify, that I belong to the Church of the Latter-day Saints, commonly called "Mormons." And I certify that in the year eighteen hundred and thirty-eight, both I and my people suffered much, by the people of the state of Missouri. And I further certify, that in this same year, in the month of November, between the first and sixth, we were surrounded by a soldiery of the state of

Missouri, in the city of Far West, in Caldwell county, both myself and many of my "Mormon" brethren, and were compelled by the soldiery—which were armed with all the implements of war to shed blood—under a public declaration for our entire extermination, to sign away our all, our property, personal and real estate, and to leave the state of Missouri immediately.

I certify that I had at that time one hundred and sixty-two acres of land, the same which I held the certificate for. I further certify that I was obliged to give up my duplicates to help me to a small sum to carry me out of the state. I further certify not.

SIMEON CARTER.

Territory of Iowa, Lee County.

Sworn to and subscribed before me, a justice of the peace for said county, this 2nd day of January, 1840.

D. W. KILBOURN, J. P.

Letter of Hyrum Smith to the Prophet and Judge Higbee.

NAUVOO. HANCOCK COUNTY, ILLINOIS,
January 3rd, 1840.

To President Joseph Smith, Jun., and Judge Higbee:

DEAR BRETHREN:—It is with feelings of no ordinary kind, that I write you at this time, in answer to the letters with which we were favored. Your letters were truly interesting, and were read with great interest by the brethren here, as well as myself.

We were truly glad to hear of your safe arrival in the city of Washington, your interview with His Excellency the President, and the steps you have since taken for the furtherance of the object you have undertaken to accomplish, and for which you have left the endearments of home, and the society of your friends. The mission on which you are engaged is certainly an important one, and one which every Saint of God, as well as everyone whose breast beats high with those patriotic feelings which purchased our national freedom, must take a deep interest in. And although there may be many who do not value your labors—their sectarian prejudices being greater than their love for truth and the Constitution of our country; yet there are many who will undoubtedly appreciate your services, and will feel it a pleasure to assist you all that they possibly can. Conscious of the righteousness of your cause—having the prayer of the Saints. (amongst whom are many who have shared with you the trials, persecutions, and imprisonments which have been heaped upon the Saints in Missouri), and having the approval of heaven, I would say, go on, dear brethren, in the name of the Lord; and while you are pleading the cause of the widow and the fatherless, may

He who has promised to be a father to the fatherless and a husband to the widow, bless you in your undertakings, and arm you with sufficient strength for the herculean task in which you are engaged. Your exertions will be seconded by the brethren in this region, who are disposed to do all they possibly can.

I had just got ready to start for Springfield when I received your letter. I no sooner read it than I abandoned the idea of going there. I then made exertion to obtain funds for you in this place; but not being able to get any, and hearing that there were brethren in Quincy lately from New York, I started off the following day and succeeded in obtaining from Brother Herringshaw three hundred dollars, which I deposited with Messrs. Holmes & Co., merchants in Quincy, subject to the order of Judge Young. The reason why I deposited it with them was in consequence of the banks not doing any business and refusing to take deposits, etc. I hope that we shall be able to raise you some more soon. Brother William Law has promised to let us have one hundred dollars as soon as he gets a remittance from the east, which he expects daily.

We have not been able to get much on the city lots since you left; not more than enough to pay some wages for surveying, and a few debts. Brother Lyman Wight returned the subscription paper a few days ago, stating that he had not collected anything since you left. In consequence of my health, which has been poor, and the coldness of the weather, I have not been able to attend to it myself. I hardly think we shall be able to raise the one thousand dollars for Mr. William White by the time he will expect it. Elder Granger is yet in Commerce, not being able to move in consequence of the low stage of water in the Ohio river.

I received a letter lately from Parley P. Pratt, stating that he was in the City of New York, and had published another edition of his book, and wanted permission to print an edition of the Book of Mormon and Doctrine and Covenants, with a periodical similar to the *Times and Seasons*, stating that there were men who had means, that would assist in these things. He likewise wanted to get the privilege for the Twelve to print the Book of Mormon in Europe. I wrote in reply, that if there were any of the brethren disposed to aid, and had means to spare for such purposes, to send them to this place, so that not only this place might be benefitted, but that the books might come out under your immediate inspection. I am afraid some have been induced to tarry and assist Parley in these undertakings; and had made arrangements with Elder Granger to assist in liquidating the New York debts.

I want a letter from you, Brother Joseph, as soon as possible, giving me all the instructions you think necessary. I feel the burden in your absence is great. Father expresses a great desire to go to Kirtland, along with Brother Granger, who has promised to pay his and mother's expenses; would you think it advisable for them to go or not?

The High Council met a few days ago, and took your second letter into consideration, and passed some resolutions on the subject; appointed committees to get certificates for land, and to get all other information they could. Some have gone to Quincy, and others to different places. We shall forward from time to time the information you desire.

You will receive enclosed in this a number of duplicates for land from Bishop Partridge and others. The Mississippi is frozen up. The weather is very cold, and a great quantity of snow is on the ground, and has been for some time. Your family is in tolerable good health, excepting one or two having the chills occasionally.

Bishop Knight desires me to inform you, that Brothers Granger and Haws have driven into Commerce a large number of hogs. They are now engaged in slaughtering them. I think there will be a good deal of trade carried on in this line another year.

You may expect to hear from us soon again. I sent you a copy of the deposit I made in Holmes & Co., which I hope you will receive safe.

I am very affectionately,

HYRUM SMITH.

P. S.—We have concluded not to send any duplicates in this letter. The packages of duplicates will be directed to Judge Higbee, thinking they will come more safe to his address.

Friday, *3*.—Elders Brigham Young and George A. Smith went from Utica to Albany, on the railway, and put up at the Railroad House.

Affidavit of William F. Cahoon—Missouri Wrongs.

I hereby certify that in the year 1838 I was residing in Daviess county, Missouri, and while from home I was taken prisoner in Far West by the militia, and kept under guard for six or eight days, in which time I was forced to sign a deed of trust, after which I was permitted to return home to my family in Daviess county, and found them surrounded by an armed force, with the rest of my neighbors, who were much frightened. The order from the militia was to leave the county within ten days, in which time my house was broken open, and many goods taken out by the militia. We were not permitted to go from place to place without a pass from the general, and on leaving the county, I received a pass as follows:

"I permit William F. Cahoon to pass from Daviess to Caldwell county, and there remain during the winter, and thence to pass out of the state of Missouri.

"Signed November 10th, 1838.

"REEVES, a Brigadier-General."

During this time both myself and my family suffered much on account of cold and hunger because we were not permitted to go outside of the guard to obtain wood and provision; and according to orders of the militia, in the spring following, I took my family and left the state with the loss of much property.

WILLIAM F. CAHOON.

Territory of Iowa, Lee county, subscribed and sworn before

D. W. KILBOURN, J. P.

Letter of C. Adams to the Prophet—Cause of the Saints before the Illinois Legislature.

SPRINGFIELD, 4th January, 1840.

RESPECTED SIR:—I had the gratification of the receipt of yours of the 16th December, which gave me pleasure to learn that your prospects were, at that early period, in a measure flattering. I also saw yours of the 19th December to Mr. Weber. We are now consulting and feeling the pulsations relative to your case being brought before the legislature, now in session, by a series of resolutions, instructing our senators, and requesting our representatives to urge relief in your case.

What will be done, remains yet uncertain; still it is my strongest impression, it will be found prudent to get the matter before our legislature, for their action thereon. I am happy to learn that all our delegation are friendly to your intended application for relief in some shape; and it strikes me that the views of the President at this period may be the best, and perhaps the only way that relief could at this time be obtained; and in that event, be no injury to a future application to be restored to all your rights, when prejudice shall in a measure have subsided and the true state of the matter be more readily received, even by those whose prejudices may have closed the avenues to reason and justice in a matter identified with the odium so commonly attached to the sound of "Mormons." This odium will naturally wear off when they have time to learn that "Mormons" are neither anthropophagi or cannibals.

Your friends are generally well.

I am, etc.,

C. ADAMS.

To Joseph Smith, Jun.

Saturday, *4*.—The High Council at Montrose voted to utterly discard the practice of suing brethren at the law, and that such as do it, shall be disfellowshiped by this branch of the Church; that Abraham O. Smoot ordain Daniel Avery President of the Elders' Quorum; and that the sixth instant be devoted to taking affidavits concerning Missouri.

Law Suits to be Abandoned

Elder Young found the brethren in Albany; went to Troy, and Lansingburg, where he heard Elder Phinehas Richards preach.

Sunday, *5*.—Elder Young preached at Lansingburg, and returned to Troy and held a meeting with the brethren.

Monday, *6*.—Elder Young returned to Albany.

Extract from Elder Orson Pratt's Letter to his wife—Reporting Movements of the Brethren in the Eastern States.

January 6th, 1840.

I am well and hearty. After mailing the last letter to you in Pennsylvania, I went to Philadelphia on Saturday, the 21st of December; there I found President Joseph Smith, Jun.; he had just arrived from Washington City, where he had been about three weeks. Four or five days after, Judge Higbee, with Porter Rockwell, came to Philadelphia; they are well. I wrote to Parley P. Pratt to come and see President Smith; he did so, and probably will go to Washington with him in a few days. I stayed with Brother Smith, in Philadelphia, about eight days; we then took the railroad and went some 35 or 40 miles, to a large branch of the Church in Monmouth county, New Jersey, which numbers ninety members; there I left him [President Smith] on New Year's day, and came to New York, where I am at present.

Elder Benjamin Winchester had, when I left Philadelphia, baptized forty-five in that city, and several more had given in their names for baptism, and scores believing. I preached in Chester county, Pennsylvania, about two weeks, and I think I may safely say there are hundreds believing. The work is prospering throughout all this region.

Elders Taylor, Woodruff, and Turley sailed for Liverpool, December 18th, while I was in Pennsylvania. None of the rest of the Twelve have yet arrived. Parley P. Pratt has another book printed, larger than the Voice of Warning, entitled "The Millennium and other Poems," and a piece on the "Eternal Duration of Matter."*

* This treatise on the "Regeneration and Eternal Duration of Matter," was written by Elder Pratt while in Columbia prison, Missouri. He explains that it "was

Letter from John B. Weber to the Prophet—On Supplementing the Latter's Effort to Obtain Redreses from Congress.

SPRINGFIELD, January 6, 1840.

GENTLEMEN:—Your letter of the 19th ult. came to hand ten days after date, immediately after which I called upon many of the prominent members of the Democratic party, with a view to unite them in their influence in your behalf; all of whom expressed a willingness to aid in bringing about justice. But I regret to inform you that but few have exhibited that energy in the matter which might reasonably be expected from all lovers of liberty and advocates of equal rights.

Your energetic friends were first of the opinion that an effort ought to be made by our legislature to memoralize our representatives in Con-

more calculated to comfort and console myself and friends when death stared me in the face, than as an argumentative or philosophical production." This article has for some time been out of print, yet it has much that is instructive in it. The author states as a basic principle in his treatise the following: "Matter and spirit are the two great principles of all existence. Everything animate and inanimate is composed of one or the other, or both of these eternal principles. I say eternal, because the elements are as durable as the quickening power which exists in them. Matter and spirit are of equal duration; both are self-existent,—they never began to exist, and they never can be annihilated. * * * * Matter as well as spirit is eternal, uncreated, self-existing. However infinite the variety of its changes, forms and shapes;—however vast and varying the parts it has to act in the great theater of the universe;—whatever sphere its several parts may be destined to fill in the boundless organization of infinite wisdom, yet it is there, durable as the throne of Jehovah. And eternity is inscribed in indelible characters on every particle. Revolution may succeed revolution;—vegetation may bloom and flourish, generation upon generation may pass away and others still succeed—empires may fall to ruin, and moulder to the dust and be forgotten—the marble monuments of antiquity may crumble to atoms and mingle in the common ruin—the mightiest works of art, with all their glory, may sink in oblivion and be remembered no more—worlds may startle from their orbits, and hurling from their spheres, run lawless on each other in conceivable confusion—element may war with element in awful majesty, while thunders roll from sky to sky, and arrows of lightning break the mountains asunder—scatter the rocks like hailstones—set worlds on fire, and melt the elements with fervent heat, and yet not one grain can be lost—not one particle can be anihilated. All these revolutions and convulsions of nature will only serve to refine, purify, and finally restore and renew the elements upon which they act. And like the sunshine after a storm, or like gold seven times tried in the fire, they will shine forth with additional luster as they roll in their eternal spheres, in their glory, in the midst of the power of God." On this theory of the indestructibility of matter the author proceeds to consider the reality of the resurrection from the dead and the future life of man in a sentient, tangible existence. "The resurrection of the body is a complete restoration and reorganization of the physical system of man; * * * * the elements of which his body is composed are eternal in their duration; * * * * they form the tabernacle—the everlasting habitation of that spirit which animated them in this life; * * * * the spirits and bodies of men are of equal importance and destined to form an eternal and inseparable union with each other."

gress, to use all honorable means to accomplish your desires; but after holding a consultation it was believed that such a course would create a party strife here, and consequently operate against you in Congress. Therefore it was agreed that as many as had friends in Congress should write to them immediately, desiring their aid in your behalf.

If convenient you will please write again. Any information respecting your mission will be thankfully received, and made known to your people here.

Very respectfully yours,

JOHN B. WEBER.

To the Rev. Joseph Smith and his Associates.

Affidavit of John M. Burk—Missouri Outrages.

I hereby certify that General John Clark and his Aid, on their arrival at Far West in Caldwell county, Missouri, came to my tavern stand, and without my leave, pitched their marquees in my yard and did take my wood and hay to furnish the same, and did bring their horses in also, and without my leave, took hay for them, and did take possession of my house, and used it for a council house, and did place a strong guard around it, so as to hinder any person from going in or out, and I myself was not permitted to go in and out; for all this I have received no remuneration, and was not even permitted to pass out of town to water travelers' horses without a permit. The above took place in the first part of November, 1838.

I also certify that Caleb Baldwin, Lyman Wight, Hyrum Smith, Joseph Smith, Jun., and Mr. Alexander McRae, in Clay county, Missouri, did apply for a writ of *habeas corpus* and did not get it.

JOHN M. BURK.

Sworn before D. W. Kilbourn, J. P.

Affidavit of John Lowry—Ditto.

I certify that I saw General John Clark and his Aid, on their arrival at Far West, Caldwell county, Missouri, in the yard of John M. Burk, and gave orders to their waiters to pitch their marquees in his yard, and to take of his wood for fire.

I also saw Captain Samuel Bogart, with his men, come near my dwelling, and did pitch their camp, and took my house logs without my leave, and did burn them. I also saw him with the horse of Joseph Smith, Jun., in his possession.

JOHN LOWRY.

Sworn before D. W. Kilbourn, J. P.

Affidavit of Jedediah Owen—Ditto.

To whom it may concern—This is to certify, that on the day following on which the troops arrived at Far West, that two men of said troops came to my house, broke open my trunk, and took therefrom both money and clothing, and also a number of papers, among which were deeds and notes, and also a number of cooking utensils, and in consequence of the cruel and inhuman treatment which I and others have received from those troops, we are reduced to a state of almost absolute starvation; and Daniel Avery and myself were appointed as a committee to go out and beg corn and meal, or anything we might obtain, that would render assistance or relieve us in our suffering condition.

JEDEDIAH OWEN.

Sworn before D. W. Kilbourn, J. P.

Affidavit of T. Alvord—Ditto.

I removed my family from the state of Michigan to Clay county, Missouri, in the year 1835, where I lived in peace with the people, on my own land, eighteen months or more, when the people began to be excited in consequence of the emigration of our people to that county. The excitement became so great that I was obliged to sell my place at half price, and removed to the county of Caldwell, where I purchased me a farm, and settled my family, and made a good improvement, and was in a good situation to support my family, and there lived in peace with the people until the summer and fall of 1838, when the mob began to rise, and we were obliged to fly to arms in self defense; but notwithstanding our exertion, they murdered and massacred many of our people. We applied to the governor for assistance, and his reply to us was, "If you have got into a scrape with the mob, you must fight it out yourselves, for I cannot help you." The mob still increased, until I was obliged to remove my family to Far West, and there remained, surrounded with mobs of murderers, until General Clark arrived with his army, with the governor's exterminating order. Then we were all taken prisoners; our arms taken away; they then treated us with all the cruelty they were masters of, and took possession of whatever they pleased, burnt timber, and laid waste town and country.

I heard General Clark say that he would execute the Governor's order; "but [said he] notwithstanding, I will vary so much as to give some lenity for the removal of this people, and you must leave the state immediately, for you need not expect to raise another crop here." Those who were not taken to prison, were permitted to return to their homes to make preparations to leave the state. Finding I had no safety for myself and family in Missouri, I fled to Illinois for safety.

T. ALVORD.

Sworn to before D. W. Kilbourn, J. P.

Tuesday, January 7.—Elder Young took stage for Richmond, Massachusetts.

Affidavit of William Hawk—Missouri Affairs.

MONTROSE, LEE COUNTY, IOWA, January 7, 1840.

I hereby certify, that some time in the month of October, 1838, an armed force collected in the county of Carroll, near De Witt, and in open daylight, drove a man by the name of Humphrey out of his house, and set fire to it, and burnt it to ashes, and then sent an express ordering all the "Mormons" to leave the place as soon as the next day. The next day they sent another express ordering them to leave in six hours, or they would be massacred upon the ground. They also fired their guns at different persons traveling the road near the town. The "Mormons" were at length compelled to leave their possessions, and all removed to Caldwell, consisting of seventy and perhaps one hundred families, many of whom were in want of the sustenance of life, sick, and some died upon the way.

About two weeks after this, another armed force invaded Far West, took my gun, and compelled me to sign away my property, both real and personal, and leave the state forthwith.

WILLIAM HAWK.

Sworn to before D. W. Kilbourn, J. P.

Affidavit of Timothy B. Clark—Ditto.

MONTROSE, LEE COUNTY, IOWA TERRITORY, January 7, 1840.

This is to certify that I was at work on my farm on the last of October, 1838, when an armed company under General Lucas, came and took myself and my three sons prisoners, and threw down my fences, and opened my gates, and left them open, and left my crops to be destroyed, and while I was a prisoner, they declared that they had made clean work in destroying the crops as they passed through the country, and they took from me two yoke of oxen, and three horses and two wagons, and compelled me and my sons to drive them loaded with produce of my own farm, to supply their army.

I had in possession at the time, four hundred and eighty acres of land, and rising of a hundred acres improved, with a small orchard and nursery, the necessary buildings of a farm, etc.; and in consequence of my imprisonment my fences remained down, and most of my crops were destroyed; and further this deponent saith not.

TIMOTHY B. CLARK.

Sworn to before D. W. Kilbourn, J. P.

Affidavit of Urban V. Stewart—Ditto.

MONTROSE, LEE COUNTY, IOWA TERRITORY, January 7, 1840.

This is to certify that about the middle of October, I was driven, by the threats of the Daviess county armed force, to leave my possessions, consisting of preemption right to a quarter section of land with thirty acres under improvement, and a good house. I went to Di-Ahman and remained until about the 1st of November, when I was driven from there by an armed force under General Wilson. I then went to Far West. While at Ondi-Ahman the armed force took from me one cow and calf, and a yoke of oxen, one horse and five sheep; they also took from me fifteen hogs. While at Far West, they took two cows belonging to me, and I saw the soldiery killing the live stock of the inhabitants without leave or remuneration, and burning building timbers, fences, etc.

URBAN V. STEWART.

Sworn to before D. W. Kilbourn, J. P.

Affidavit of John Smith—Ditto.

LEE COUNTY, IOWA TERRITORY.

This day personally appeared before me, D. W. Kilbourn, an acting Justice of the Peace in and for said county, John Smith, and after having been duly sworn, desposeth and saith, "That in the months of October and November, 1838, I resided in the town of Adam-ondi-Ahman. Daviess county, Missouri, and whilst being peaceably engaged in the ordinary vocations of life, that in the early part of November my house was entered by a body of armed men painted after the manner or customs of the Indians of North America, and proceeded to search my house for fire arms, stating that they understood the Mormons knew how to hide their guns, and in their search of a bed in which lay an aged, sick female, they threw [her] to and fro in a very rough manner, without regard to humanity or decency. Finding no arms, they went off without further violence.

"Shortly after this above described outrage, there was a number of armed men, say about twenty, rode into my yard and inquired for horses which they said they had lost, and stated, under confirmation of an oath, that they would have the heads of twenty 'Mormons,' if they did not find their horses. These last were painted in like manner as the first. These transactions took place when the citizens of the village and its vicinity were engaged in a peaceable manner in the ordinary pursuits of life."

This deponent further saith, "That the mob took possessson of a store of dry goods belonging to the Church of Latter-day Saints, over which they placed a guard. I went into the store to get some articles to distribute to the suffering poor, and the officer who had the charge of the store ordered me out peremptorily, stating it was too cold to wait on me, that I must come the next morning; and returning the next morning, I found the store almost entirely stripped of its contents.

Thereupon we as a Church were ordered to depart the county and state, under the pains and penalty of death or a total extermination of our society. Having no alternative, (having my wagon stolen), I was compelled to abandon my property, except a few movables which I got off with in the best way that I could, and on receiving a permit or pass which is hereto appended. I then proceeded to depart the state.

" 'I permit John Smith to remove from Daviess to Caldwell county, there remain during the winter, or remove out of the state unmolested.

" 'Daviess county, November 9th, 1838.

" 'R. Wilson, Brigadier-General. By F.G. Cochnu.'

"I accordingly left the state in the month of February following in a destitute condition."

JOHN SMITH.

Sworn to before D. W. Kilbourn, J. P.

Affidavit of Samuel Smith—Ditto.

MONTROSE, LEE COUNTY, IOWA, January 7, 1840.

I do hereby certify, that I, Samuel Smith, made an improvement and obtained a preemption right upon one hundred and sixty acres of land in Daviess county, Missouri, in 1837. On the first of November, 1838, I was compelled to leave the county, by order of General Wilson, in ten days. They took without my consent, two horses, which have never been returned, nor remunerated for; also destroyed my crop of corn, drove off four head of cattle.

SAMUEL SMITH.

Sworn to before D. W. Kilbourn, J. P.

Affidavit of Daniel Avery—Ditto.

LEE COUNTY, IOWA TERRITORY, March 5th, 1840.*

I, Daniel Avery, do hereby certify that the following scenes transpired in the state of Missouri to my personal knowledge—First, in the year 1838, some time in the fall, I was called on by the martial law of the state of Missouri, to aid and assist to rescue women and children from the hands of a mob, from the waters of Grand river, whose husbands and fathers had been driven off. We found the house invested by the mob, some of whom were in the house threatening the lives of the women and children, if they did not leave their property and effects immediately and follow their husbands and fathers. One family lost a

* This affidavit, it will be observed, was given some time after the others of this group, and appears in the Ms. of the Prophet's History under date of March the 5th, but it is brought forward here, with all those that follow in this chapter, that it may appear in connection with the others of its kind.

child while in this situation, for the want of care; the women being compelled, by these monsters, to provide and cook them food. This company of the mob was commanded by James Weldin.

I also saw about seventy families driven from De Witt by a mob commanded by Sashiel Wood. I helped to bury one woman the first night, who had been confined in childbed a night or two before, and could not endure the sufferings.

The next scene I saw I was peaceably traveling the road; a man by the name of Patrick O'Banion was shot dead at my feet. We advanced a little further, when two men were killed and several wounded. I afterwards learned that this gang of mobbers was commanded by Samuel Bogart.

In consequence of being pursued out of the state, by this lawless mob, I was not an eye witness to the many thousand wicked acts committed by the Governor's exterminating militia.

DANIEL AVERY.

Sworn to before D. W. Kilbourn, J. P.

Wednesday, March 11.

Affidavit of James Powell—Ditto.

ILLINOIS, ADAMS COUNTY, March 11, 1840.

I, James Powell, do certify, that I was a citizen of the state of Missouri in 1838. I solemnly declare that while I was peaceably traveling to one of my nearest neighbors, I was assaulted by a company of men, to the number of five—Autherston Wrathey, John Gardner, Philomen Ellis, Jesse Clark, and Ariel Sanders. First they threw a stone and hit me between the shoulders, which very much disabled me; they then shot at me, but did not hit me. One of them then struck me with his gun, and broke my skull about six inches—a part of my brain ran out. I have had fourteen pieces of bone taken out of my skull. My system is so reduced that I have not done a day's work since.

I know no reason why they should have done [this act], as I did not belong to the Mormon Church, neither had I ever heard one preach. In this situation I was forced to leave the state forthwith. I was carried three days without having my head dressed. When I arrived at Huntsville, Doctor Head offered me assistance. I refer to him for further testimony.

JAMES POWELL.

Attest, John Smith.

We certify that the foregoing affidavit of James Powell's is true and correct, as we stood by and saw it with our eyes. We also heard them say they would kill the Mormons, if they did not clear out. We carried the wounded man in our wagon, till he was out of reach of the mob.

PETER WIMMER,
SUSAN WIMMER,
ELLEN WIMMER.

Sworn to before William Oglesby, J. P.

Affidavit of John Smith—Ditto.

ILLINOIS, COLUMBUS, ADAMS COUNTY, March 11, 1840.

I, John Smith, certify that I was a resident in the state of Missouri in 1838, when I was driven from my house, and a pre-emption right, and forbid to stay in the state, [the mob] threatening me if I did not go forthwith. I took my family and pursued my journey one hundred miles. In consequence of cold, snow, water and ice at the inclement season in which I was driven, I fell sick, and for four weeks I was unable to travel; during which time I was threatened daily; yet I was so sick it was considered by many that I could not live, and was compelled to start when I was not able to sit up through the day. I landed in Illinois; the long and fatiguing journey, lying out in the cold, open air, proved too much for my companion; it threw her into a violent fever, with which she died. Many others in the company took sick and died with the same hard fare.

JOHN SMITH.

Sworn to before William Oglesby, J. P.

Affidavit of Smith Humphrey—Ditto.

ILLINOIS, ADAMS COUNTY, March 16, 1840.

I, Smith Humphrey, certify that I was a citizen of Missouri in eighteen hundred and thirty-eight; and some time in the month of October, of the same year, I was fallen upon by a mob commanded by Hyrum Standley. He took my goods out of my house; and said Standley set fire to my house, and burnt it before my eyes, and ordered me to leave the place forthwith. I removed from De Witt to Caldwell county, where I was again assailed by Governor Bogg's exterminating militia. They took me prisoner, and robbed my wagon of four hundred dollars in cash, and one thousand dollars' worth of goods, and drove me out of the state.

SMITH HUMPHREY.

Sworn to before C. M. Woods, Clerk of Circuit Court.

Affidavit of Henry Root—Ditto.

QUINCY, ILLINOIS, 16th March, 1840.

This is to certify that I, Henry Root, am, and was a citizen of De

Witt, Carroll county, Missouri, at the time of the persecutions (known by the name of the "Mormon War") commenced and terminated between the citizens of said state of Missouri and the Mormons; that in the fall of 1838, in the month of September, a mob (under no regular authority) headed by William W. Austin, Sen., consisting of from one hundred to one hundred and fifty men, came into De Witt and ordered the Mormons to leave that place within ten days from that time; that if they did not leave, they would be driven from there by force.

The Mormons did not leave; the appointed time came, and the mob came, armed and equipped for war. The Mormon citizens petitioned to the governor of the state, but no relief came. They sent to the general of the brigade [in that locality], who ordered the militia to repair to De Witt to disperse the mob. On the arrival of the militia, Brigadier-General Parks told me the Mormons had better leave their property and go off, as his men were prejudiced against them, and he could do them no good, nor relieve them. With that the Mormons left.

HENRY ROOT.

Sworn to before C. M. Woods, Clerk of Circuit Court, Adams county, Illinois.

Affidavit of Joseph Clark—Ditto.

QUINCY, ILLINOIS, March 16, 1840.

I, Joseph Clark, certify that I was a citizen of the state of Missouri in 1838; and when peaceably traveling the highway, I was shot at twice by Governor Boggs' exterminating militia, commanded by Major-General John B. Clark.

JOSEPH CLARK.

Sworn to before C. M. Woods, Clerk of Circuit Court, Adams County, Illinois.

Affidavit of Thomas D. Casper—Ditto.

QUINCY, ILLINOIS, March 16th, 1840.

This is to certify that I, Thomas D. Casper, was a resident of the state of Missouri in the year 1838. I was not a member of the Church of Mormons or Latter-day Saints; but witnessed the following acts of distress: As I was on business, I inquired for Perry Moppin, and learned that he, with Samuel Snowden, Esq., had gone after Mr. Wilson, a Mormon, and had threatened and sworn to take his life if he did not tell his name; and they swore they had the tool to take his life if he had not told them his name.

Further they agreed that the Mormons should leave the country of Missouri except they would deny the faith, or their religion. And I heard Anthony McCustian say that he would head a mob in any case, to prevent the lawyers from attending to any case of their (the Mormons') grievances; and he was a postmaster. And I saw two men that said they had been at Haun's mill at the murder; and one by the name of White, and the other Moppin stated that he had slain three Mormons. And I, Thomas D. Casper, witnessed other things too tedious to mention; and solemnly swear, before God and men, that what is here written is a true statement of facts relative to the suffering of the Mormons in the state of Missouri.

THOMAS D. CASPER.

Affidavit of Jesse W. Johnston—Ditto.

QUINCY, ILLINOIS, March 16, 1840.

I, Jesse W. Johnston, certify that the following circumstances took place in the State of Missouri, while I was a resident of that state, viz: I was taken prisoner by Governor Boggs' exterminating militia. I saw one man killed belonging to the Mormon Church, and was forced by them to take corn out of the fields of the Mormon Church without leave. This was in the fall of 1838.

JESSE W. JOHNSTON.

Sworn to before C. M. Woods, Clerk of the Circuit Court, Adams County, Illinois.

Affidavit of Owen Cole—Ditto.

QUINCY, ILLINOIS, March 17, 1840.

This is to certify that I, Owen Cole, was a resident of Caldwell county, state of Missouri, and while residing at my dwelling house, the militia under Governor Boggs, and by his orders, plundered my house, and shot me through my thigh. My damage sustained by the militia, by being driven from the state, besides my wound, was five hundred dollars. The militia men were quartered on the lands of the people called Mormons, contrary to the laws and Constitution of the state. I hereby certify this to be a true statement.

OWEN COLE.

Sworn to before C. M. Woods, Clerk Circuit Court.

Affidavi of Ezekiel Maginn—Ditto.

QUINCY, ILLINOIS, March 17, 1840.

I, Ezekiel Maginn, certify that I was a citizen of the state of Missouri in the year 1838, and was an eye witness to the following facts—First, I saw the militia, called for by Governor Boggs' exterminating order, enter the house of Lyman Wight, and take from it a bed and bedding, pillows, and dishes, personally known to me to be his property.

EZEKIEL MAGINN.

Sworn to before C. M. Woods, Clerk Circuit Court, Adams County.

Affidavit of Addison Green—Ditto.

QUINCY, March 17, 1840.

I, Addison Green, do certify that in the month of October, one thousand eight hundred and thirty-eight, when I was peaceably walking the highroad in Ray county, state of Missouri, I was molested and taken prisoner by ten armed men, who took from me one double-barrel fowling piece and equipage, threatening to blow out my brains and swore that if I was a Mormon they would hang me without further ceremony. They had previously been to my lodging and taken my horse, saddle, and bridle. All was then taken into the woods about one mile to Bogart's camp.

I was kept a prisoner until the next morning, when I was let go; but have not obtained any part of my property, which was worth about one hundred and fifty dollars.

A. GREEN.

Sworn to before John H. Holton, notary public.

Affidavit of John P. Greene—Ditto.

I, John P. Greene, was in company with several of my neighbors walking the road in peace, when one of our company, a young man, by name of O'Banion, was shot down at my side, being shot by a company of mobbers; and soon after this we were fired upon again, and two more were killed and several others wounded. This was about the 25th day of October, one thousand eight hundred and thirty-eight, in the state of Missouri, and I do hereby certify the above to be true according to the best of my knowledge.

JOHN P. GREENE

Sworn to before John H. Holton, notary public.

Affidavit of Asahel A. Lathrop—Ditto.

This is to certify that I, Asahel A. Lathrop, was a citizen of the state of Missouri, at the time the difficulty originated between the people called Mormons and the [other] inhabitants of the aforesaid state, and herein give a statement of the transactions that came under my observation, according to the best of my recollection.

I settled in Missouri in the summer of 1838, in Caldwell county, where I purchased land and erected buildings. The said land I now have a deed of; and in the fall I purchased a claim on what is called the East Fork of Grand River, together with a large stock of cattle and horses, sheep and hogs; it being some sixty miles from the aforesaid county where I first located; and moved on to the latter place, supposing that I was at peace with all men; but I found by sad experience that I was surrounded by enemies; for in the fall of 1838, whilst at home with my family, I was notified by a man by the name of James Welden, that the people of Livingston county, had met at the house of one Doctor William P. Thompson, then living in the attached part of said county, for the purpose of entering into measures respecting the people called Mormons; and the same Welden was a member of the same, and also the aforesaid William P. Thompson was a justice of the peace; and they all jointly agreed to drive every Mormon from the state; and notified me that I must leave immediately, or I would be in danger of losing my life.

All this time some of my family were sick; but after listening to the entreaties of my wife to flee for safety, I committed them into the hands of God and left them, it being on Monday morning; and in a short time after I left, there came some ten or fifteen men to my house, and took possession of the same, and compelled my wife to cook for them, and also made free to take such things as they saw fit; and whilst in this situation, my child died, which I have no reason to doubt was for the want of care; which, owing to the abuse she received, and being deprived of rendering that care she would, had she been otherwise situated. My boy was buried by the mob, my wife not being able to pay the last respects to her child.

I went from my home into Daviess county and applied to Austin A. King and General Atchison for advice, as they were acting officers in the state of Missouri. There were men called out to go and liberate my family, which I had been absent from some ten or fifteen days; and on my return I found the remainder of my family confined to their beds, not being able the one to assist the other, and my house guarded by an armed force.

I was compelled to remove my family in this situation, on a bed to a place of safety. This, together with all the trouble, and for the want of care, was the cause of the death of the residue of my family, as I have no doubt; which consisted of a wife and two more children; as they died a few days after their arrival at my friend's. Such was my situation, that I was obliged to assist in making their coffins.

I will give the names of some of the men that have driven me from my house and abused my family; those that I found at my house on my return were Samuel Law, Calvin Hatfield, Stanley Hatfield, Andy Hatfield; and those that were leading men were James Welden, Doctor William P. Thompson, a justice of the peace, and William Cochran, and many others, the names I do not recollect.

I have also seen men abused in various ways; and that whilst they were considered prisoners; such as the mob cocking their guns and swearing that they would shoot, with their guns to their face, and the officers of the militia, so called, standing by without uttering a word; and in these councils they have said if a Missourian should kill a Mormon he should draw a pension, same as a soldier of the Revolution.

I was also compelled to give up my gun, and the terms were, I was to leave the aforesaid state of Missouri, or be exterminated. My property is yet remaining in said state, whilst I am deprived of the control of the same.

Written this 17th day of March, 1840.

ASAHEL A. LATHROP.

Sworn to before D. W. Kilburn, J. P., Lee county, Iowa Territory.

Affidavit of Burr Riggs.

I, Burr Riggs, of the town of Quincy, and state of Illinois, do hereby certify that in the year 1836, when moving to the state of Missouri, with my family and others, we were met in Ray county, in said state, by a mob of one hundred and fourteen armed men, who commanded us not to proceed any further, but to return, or they would take our lives; and the leader stepped forward at the same time, and cocked his piece. We turned round with our team; and the mob followed us about six miles and left us.

Some time after this I moved to Caldwell county, in said state, and purchased about two hundred acres of land, and a village lot, on which I erected a dwelling house, staked, and commenced improving my land, and had, at the time I was driven away, about forty acres of corn, vegetables, etc.; and in the year 1838, in the month of November, was compelled to leave my house and possessions in consequence of Governor Boggs' exterminating order, without means sufficient to bear my expense out of the state.

Given under my hand at Quincy, Illinois, 17th March, 1840.

BURR RIGGS.

Sworn to before C. M. Woods, Clerk of the Circuit Court, Adams county, Illinois.

Affidavit of Simons P. Curtis.

I, Simons P. Curtis, a resident of Quincy, Adams county, Illinois, certify that in the year 1838, I was a citizen of Caldwell county, Missouri, residing in the city of Far West. Also that I went in search of a lost steer; and passing by Captain Bogart's camp, while he was guarding the city, I saw the hide and feet of said steer, which I knew to be mine; the flesh of which I suppose they applied to their own use.

I also certify that Wiley E. Williams, one of the Governor's aids, who was gunkeeper, caused me to pay thirty-seven and a half cents to him. I also paid twenty-five cents to a justice of the peace to qualify me to testify that the gun was mine. The said Wiley E. Williams is said to be the one that carried the story to Governor Boggs, which story was the cause of the exterminating order being issued, as stated by the Governor in said order.

SIMONS P. CURTIS.

Sworn to before C. M. Woods, Clerk Circuit Court, Adams County, Illinois.

Affidavit of Elisha H. Groves.

I, Elisha H. Groves, of the town of Quincy, and state of Illinois, upon oath say, that I was a resident of Daviess county, in the state of Missouri, and that on the 16th day of November, in the year of our Lord, 1838, Judge Vinson Smith and others came to my house and ordered myself and family, Levi Taylor, David Osborn and others, to leave our possessions which we had bought of Government and paid our money for the same, saying we must within three days leave the county or they would take our lives, for there was no law to save us after that time. In consequence of those proceedings, together with Governor Boggs' exterminating order, we were compelled to leave the state of Missouri. Furthermore this deponent saith not.

Given under my hand at Quincy, the 17th day of March, A. D. 1840.

ELISHA H. GROVES.

Sworn to before C. M. Woods, Clerk Circuit Court.

Affidavit of Jacob Foutz.

QUINCY, ILLINOIS, March 17, A. D. 1840.

This is to certify that I was a citizen, resident of Caldwell county, Missouri, at the time Governor Boggs' exterminating order was issued; and that I was quartered on by the mob militia, without my leave or consent at different times, and at one time by William Mann, Hiram Cumstock, and brother, who professed to be the captain; also Robert White; and that I was at the murder at Haun's mill, and was wounded; and that I was driven from the state, to my inconvenience, and deprived of my freedom, as well as to my loss of at least four hundred dollars.

JACOB FOUTZ.

Sworn to before C. M. Woods, Clerk Circuit Court.

Affidavit of Frederick G. Williams.

I do certify that I was a resident of Caldwell county, in the State of Missouri, in the year of our Lord 1838, and owned land to a considerable amount, building lots, etc., in the village of Far West; and in consequence of mobocracy, together with Governor Boggs' exterminating order, was compelled to leave the state under great sacrifice of real and personal property, which has reduced and left myself and family in a state of poverty, with a delicate state of health, in an advanced stage of life. Furthermore this deponent saith not.

Given under my hand at Quincy, Illinois, March 17, 1840.

FREDERICK G. WILLIAMS.

Sworn to before C. M. Woods, Clerk Adams county, Illinois.

Statement of James Sloan.

James Sloan made affidavit at Quincy, that the officers of the militia under the exterminating order of Governor Boggs in Missouri in 1838, took possession, carried off and destroyed a store of goods, of several hundred dollars' value, belonging to the people called "Mormons," in Daviess county; that his life was threatened, his property taken, and he was obliged to flee the state with his family, greatly to his disadvantage.

Affidavit of David Shumaker.

QUINCY, ILLINOIS, ADAMS COUNTY, March 18, 1840.

I, Jacob Shumaker,do certify that I went back to the state of Missouri about the first of October last, with the calculation to live with my family, but finding it impossible, as the mob, say to the amount of twenty or thirty of them, surrounded my house, and whilst they were quarreling about me, what they should do, and in what way they should dispose of me, I crept out of the back window and made my escape; and leaving my family to their most scandalous abuses; my wife and oldest daughter barely escaping from their unholy designs.

I was thus a second time obliged to leave the state, or remain at the risk of my life. The former alternative I chose. My loss sustained by the above-mentioned abuses was not less than three hundred dollars. A lot of land containing forty acres, for which I paid four dollars per acre, situated in Caldwell county, was unjustly and unlawfully taken from me, and is still retained by some person or persons to me unknown. I hereby certify that the above is a true statement.

JACOB SHUMAKER.

Sworn to before C. M. Woods.

Affidavit of Levi Richards.

I, Levi Richards, a resident of Quincy, Adams county Illinois, practitioner of medicine, certify that in the year one thousand eight hundred and thirty-eight, I was a citizen of Far West, Caldwell county, Missouri, and that in the fall of said year, I saw the city invaded by a numerous armed soldiery, who compelled its inhabitants to surrender, give up their firearms, and submit to their dictation. They then set a strong guard round the city, thereby preventing egress or ingress, without special permission. Then they collected the citizens together upon the public square, formed around them a strong guard of soldiers, and then at the mouths of their rifles, compelled them to sign what was termed a deed of trust, thereby depriving them of all their property and civil rights.

This occupied several days of most inclement weather, when they were brought to the same order by General Clark, and I judge some forty or fifty were made special prisoners by him. At this time he delivered his speech to the "Mormons," which has been published, and which is substantially correct. I was compelled by a company of men armed with rifles, to leave my house, and go to captain Bogart's camp, (he commanded, as I understood, a part of the guard which surrounded the city,) upon an indirect charge or insinuation; was detained a prisoner two days, examined, and liberated. I then asked the clerk of the company, who had been my keeper, the following questions, which he readily answered:

Were those men who massacred the "Mormons" at Haun's mill, out under the Governor's order, or were they mobbers?

A. Mobbers.

Are Captain Cornelius Gilliam and his company out by legal authority, or are they mobbers?

A. Mobbers.

Where are those mobbers now?

A. They have joined the army.

This company [Gilliam's] at the surrender of Far West were painted like Indians. The army wore a badge of red (blood). I saw a large amount of lumber and timber destroyed, and used for fuel by the soldiers. The destruction of cattle, hogs, etc., seemed to be their sport, as their camp and the fields testified when they withdrew. An excellent gun was taken from me, which I have never seen or heard of since. A gun that was left in my care was taken at the same time, which I afterwards found with Wiley E. Williams of Richmond, (reputed one of the Governor's aids,) to obtain which I had to prove property, affirm before a magistrate and pay said Williams fifty cents.

I was called to extract lead, dress the wounds, etc., for several persons (Saints) who were shot in the above siege, two of whom died. Immediately previous to the above transactions, and for a long time before, the citizens of Caldwell, and particularly Far West, were called upon to watch for mobs by day and guard against them by night, till it became a burden almost intolerable.

LEVI RICHARDS.

Sworn to before C. M. Woods. Clerk Circuit Court, Adams county, Illinois.

Affidavit of Gibson Gates.

I, Gibson Gates, do hereby certify that I was residing in Jackson county, Missouri, in the fall of the year, 1833, and had been for the space of about one year. I was at a meeting one day for worship, when a man by the name of Masters came to us, stating that he was sent by the mob to inform us that if we would forsake our religion, they were willing to be our brethren and fight for us; "but if not," said he, "our young men are ready, and we can scarce constrain them from falling upon you and cutting you to pieces."

Soon after this there came a large company of men,armed,to my place, and with much threatening and profane words, ordered me to be gone by the next day, or they would kill me and my family; in consequence of which threatening, we quit our house in the month of November, leaving most of our effects; suffering very much with cold, fatigue and hunger, we took [set out] on the prairie, and went southward twenty miles or more, where we stayed a few weeks. But still being threatened by the mob, we removed to Clay county, where we lived in peace until the fall of 1838, when a mob arose against the people of the Church of Latter-day Saints, when we were again obliged to leave our home, and seek safety in another place for a few weeks. When we returned our house had been broken open, and the lock of a trunk broken open, and the most valuable contents thereof taken away; the most of our bedding and furniture was either stolen or destroyed; and we were then ordered to leave the state.

GIBSON GATES.

Sworn to before David W. Kilbourn, J P.

Affidavit of David Pettigrew.

This is to certify, that I, David Pettigrew, was a citizen of Jackson county, Missouri, and owned a good farm, lying on the Blue river, six miles west of Independence, and lived in peace with the inhabitants until the summer and fall of 1833, when the inhabitants began to threaten us with destruction. I was at work in my field, and a man by the name of Allen, and others with him, came along and cried out, "Mr. Pettigrew, you are at work as though you were determined to stay here, but we are determined that you shall leave the county immediately." I replied that I was a free born citizen of the United States, and had done harm to no man. "I therefore claim protection by the law of the land," and that the law and the Constitution of the land would not suffer them to commit so horrid a crime. They then replied that "the old law and Constitution is worn out, and we are about to make a new one."

I was at a meeting where we had met for prayer, and a man by the name of Masters came and desired an interview with us; he then stated that he was sent by the mob to inform us, that if we would forsake our "Mormon" and Prophet religion, and become of their religion, they, the mob, would be our brothers, and would fight for us; "but if you will not, we are ready and will drive you from the county."

A few days after this, a large mob came to my house, commanded by General Moses Wilson, Hugh Braziel and Lewis Franklin, and broke down my door, and burst into my house, armed with guns, clubs and knives; some of them were painted red and black. This was in the night, and my family was much frightened. They threatened me with immediate death if I did not leave the place. After much abuse they left us for the night, but in a few days they returned and drove me and my family into the street, not suffering us to take anything with us. I saw that we must go or die; we went south to Van Buren county, in company with eighty or ninety others. In a short time after, I returned to my farm and found my house plundered, my grain and crop, stock, and all my farm and farming tools laid waste and destroyed; and shortly after my house was burned to ashes.

I called on Esquire Western, of Independence, and inquired of him if he could inform me what all this mobbing and riot meant, informing him of the destruction and plundering of my house; to which he gave me no satisfaction, but insulted me and treated me roughly. Governor Boggs lived in the county, and I have seen him passing through among us in our great distress, and gave no attention to our distresses. He was then Lieutenant-Governor of the state. On my return to my family in Van Buren county, I was much abused by a man by the name of Brady; he said he would kill me if I ever attempted to go to my farm, or if he saw me passing that way again. I returned to my family, and in a few days after, a company of men came where we lived and said they would spill my blood if I did not leave the place immediately. The leaders of this company were John Cornet, Thomas Langley, and Hezekiah Warden; they lived in Jackson county.

This was in the cold winter, and our sufferings were great. I fled across the Missouri river to Clay county, where I lived three years; in which time I often heard Judge Cameron and others say, that "you Mormons cannot get your rights in any of the courts of the upper country;" and I had not the privilege of voting as a free citizen.

I moved to Caldwell county, bought land and opened a good farm, and lived in peace until the summer and fall of 1838, when mobs arose in the counties round about, and I with the rest was obliged to take up arms in self defense; for the cry was, that mob law should prevail, if we stood against them, until the army came and took us all prisoners of war. I with the rest was obliged to sign a deed of trust at the point of the sword, I with sixty others was selected out and marched to Richmond, in Ray county, by the command of General Clark, where they kept us a number of weeks, pretending to try us as treasoners and murderers. At length I obtained my liberty, and returned to my family in Caldwell county: and I found that there was no safety there, for there was no law, but all a scene of robbing, and plundering, and stealing. They were about to take me again, and I was obliged to leave my family and flee to Illinois. In about two months my family arrived, having suffered much abuse and loss of health and property. Soon after the arrival of my family my son, a young man, died; and I attribute his death to the cruel barbarity of the mob of Missouri, he being a prisoner among them, and having suffered much because of them.

My father was a soldier, and served in the Revolutionary War, under the great Washington, but I have not had protection on my own lands; and I have not been permitted to see my farm in Jackson county, Missouri, in seven years. Soldiers were stationed or quartered in different parts of Far West; and they treated us roughly, threatening to shoot us, and making use of anything they pleased, such as burning house, timber, and rails, and garden fences, and stealing and plundering what they pleased.

When I was at Richmond, a prisoner before Judge King, we sent for many witnesses; and when they came, they were taken and cast into prison with us, and we were not permitted to have any witnesses. The day I came out of prison, they compelled me to sign a writing which was not true or remain in prison.

DAVID PETTIGREW.

Sworn to before D. W. Kilbourn, J. P.

Comment of the Prophet on the Foregoing Affidavits.

Thus I have given a few of the multitude of affidavits which might be given to substantiate the facts of our persecutions and deaths in Missouri. When the brethren left Missouri, they were poor, having been plundered of everything valued by mobs. Much of the plundering was done under the eye of the government officers, according to the foregoing affidavits; and all by the sanction of the state of Missouri, as the acts of her legislature testify.* The Saints, being so numerous, were obliged to scatter over the state of Illinois and different states to get bread and clothing—so that but few accounts against Missouri could be collected without unreasonable exertions. About 491 individuals gave in their claims against Missouri, which I presented to Congress—amounting to about $1,381,044.00; leaving a multitude more of similar bills hereafter to be presented, which, if not settled immediately, will ere long amount to a handsome sum, increasing by compound interest.

* That is to say, the legislature had appropriated two hundred thousand dollars to meet the expenses of the mob-militia in unlawfully dispossessing the Saints of their lands and other property, and then expelling them from the state. While on the other hand, it refused to give any consideration worthy of the name to the petition of the Saints for redress of their grievances; and so far was the legislature from giving the Saints any assurance of re-instatement in the rightful possession of their lands and other property and maintaining them in peaceful possession of them, that it finally refused even to investigate the justice of their claims. Under these circumstances the Prophet is undoubtedly justified in using the language of the text. (See Vol. III, chaps. xv, xvi.)

CHAPTER IV.

DEPARTURE OF THE PROPHET FROM WASHINGTON—LABORS OF ELIAS HIGBEE BEFORE THE SENATE JUDICIARY COMMITTEE—REPORT OF THE COMMITTEE.

Wednesday, *8*.—The High Council at Nauvoo voted to loan all the moneys possible for the relief of the poor Saints.

This evening President Young preached at a school house in the south west part of Richmond,* when the people present commenced making a noise and disturbing the meeting, and when President Young was reproving them for their disgraceful conduct, some of those present fired lucifer matches. President Young rebuked them severely, and taught them better manners, and proposed to send them some Indians from the West to civilize them.

Ministry of Brigham Young and Geo. A. Smith at Richmond, New York.

Thursday, *9*.—About this time I returned to Philadelphia, where I continued to preach and visit for a little season.

George A. Smith preached at Richmond this evening. His health is still very poor, and he is almost blind. President Young also was very feeble. While they were opening the meeting, some one threw a quantity of brimstone in the fire, which nearly suffocated them. As soon as the fumes of brimstone would pemit, Brother Smith told them he thought he should be in no danger of catching the itch in Massachusetts, for the smell of brimstone indicated that it was thoroughly cured.

Sunday, *12*.—Elders Young and Smith held a meeting

* Richmond is in Schoharie county, about seventy miles west of Albany, N. Y.

at William Pierson's, Richmond. After preaching, Elder Smith had a severe shake of the ague, which lasted some hours. The weather was extremely cold, but by the kind attention of Mr. Pierson's family, and William Richards, he was in some measure relieved of his ague before he left Richmond. President Young wore a cradle bed quilt from Far West to Richmond, where Rhoda Richards lined Doctor Richard's old worn out plaid cloak with President Young's quilt, with flannel between, which made him very comfortable.

Monday, *13*.—Elders Wilford Woodruff, John Taylor, and Theodore Turley arrived at Preston, England.

Tuesday, *14*.—About this time Elder Rigdon and Doctor Foster arrived at Philadelphia.

Appointments in the British Mission.

Friday, *17*.—A special council was held at the house of Elder Willard Richards, in Preston, Joseph Fielding, president, Theodore Turley, scribe. Present, Wilford Woodruff, John Taylor, Hiram Clark, and Willard Richards. Council decided that Elders Woodruff and Turley should go to the Staffordshire potteries; Elders Taylor and Fielding, to Liverpool; Elder Clark, to Manchester, with Elder William Clayton; and Elder Willard Richards to go where the Spirit directs; that the Elders of the council communicate with the presidency at Preston once a month; and Elder Richards write to Brothers Alexander Wright and Samuel Mulliner in Scotland, and hold no general conference until more of the Twelve arrive.

Elders Brigham Young and George A. Smith went to Canaan, Connecticut, with Edwin D. Pierson, Elder Smith shaking very severely with the ague in the evening.

Saturday, *18*.—Elders Woodruff and Turley started for the Potteries.

Sunday, *19*.—The High Council at Nauvoo voted to donate a city lot to Brother James Hendrix, who was shot in Missouri; also voted to build him a house; also donated a house and lot to Father Joseph Knight.

Elder Brigham Young preached at Sheffield mills, where he stayed till the twenty-sixth.

Wednesday, 22.—Elders Fielding and Taylor went to Liverpool and commenced their mission.

Saturday, 25.—About this time I visited the Saints at Brandywine, where I spent some days, and returned to Philadelphia.

Monday, 27.—Brothers Gibson Smith and Peter French conveyed Elders Brigham Young and George A. Smith to New Haven, where they tarried until the 31st.

About the last of this month, I left Philadelphia for Washington, in company with Brothers Rockwell, Higbee, and Doctor Foster, traveling by railroad, having sold my carriage, and having left Elder Rigdon sick in Philadelphia.

Friday, 31.—Elders Brigham Young and George A. Smith took steamboat from New Haven for New York City. When within eighteen miles of the city, they took the stage, and arrived at their destination about ten o'clock at night. When they alighted from the carriage they had no funds to pay their fare, and Elder Young asked Captain Stone to pay their bill, fifty cents, which he very readily did; and they found Elder Parley P. Pratt's house in about five minutes, where they stayed Saturday, February 1st.

Sunday, February 2.—Elders Brigham Young and George A. Smith preached in the Columbia Hall. Elder Young preached every evening during the week, till Saturday, three times in the Columbia Hall; by which he injured himself so much, that he was not able to dress himself for four or five days.

On Monday George A. Smith went to Philadelphia.

Thursday, 6.—I had previously preached in Washington, and one of my sermons I find reported in synopsis, by a member of Congress; which I will insert entire.

Mathew S. Davis' Description of the Prophet, and a Report of his Washington Discourse.

WASHINGTON, 6th February, 1840.

MY DEAR MARY:—I went last evening to hear "Joe Smith," the celebrated Mormon, expound his doctrine. I, with several others, had a desire to understand his tenets as explained by himself. He is not an educated man; but he is a plain, sensible, strong minded man. Everything he says, is said in a manner to leave an impression that he is sincere. There is no levity, no fanaticism, no want of dignity in his deportment. He is apparently from forty to forty-five years of age, rather above the middle stature, and what you ladies would call a very good looking man. In his garb there are no peculiarities; his dress being that of a plain, unpretending citizen. He is by profession a farmer, but is evidently well read.

He commenced by saying, that he knew the prejudices which were abroad in the world against him, but requested us to pay no respect to the rumors which were in circulation respecting him or his doctrines. He was accompanied by three or four of his followers. He said, "I will state to you our belief, so far as time will permit." "I believe," said he, "that there is a God, possessing all the attributes ascribed to Him by all Christians of all denominations; that He reigns over all things in heaven and on earth, and that all are subject to His power." He then spoke rationally of the attributes of Divinity, such as foreknowledge, mercy &c., &c. He then took up the Bible. "I believe," said he, "in this sacred volume. In it the 'Mormon' faith is to be found. We teach nothing but what the Bible teaches. We believe nothing, but what is to be found in this book. I believe in the fall of man, as recorded in the Bible; I believe that God foreknew everything, but did not foreordain everything; I deny that foreordain and foreknow is the same thing. He foreordained the fall of man; but all merciful as He is, He foreordained at the same time, a plan of redemption for all mankind. I believe in the Divinity of Jesus Christ, and that He died for the sins of all men, who in Adam had fallen." He then entered into some details, the result of which tended to show his total unbelief of what is termed *original sin*. He believes that it is washed away by the blood of Christ, and that it no longer exists. As a necessary consequence, he believes that we are all born pure and undefiled. That *all* children dying at an early age (say *eight* years) not knowing good from evil, were incapable of sinning; and that all such assuredly go to heaven. "I believe," said he, "that a man is a moral, responsible, free agent; that although it was foreordained he should fall, and be redeemed, yet after the redemption it was not foreordained that he should again sin. In the Bible a rule of conduct is laid down for him; in the Old and New

Testaments the law by which he is to be governed, may be found. If he violates that law, he is to be punished for the deeds done in the body.

I believe that God is eternal. That He had no beginning, and can have no end. Eternity means that which is without beginning or end. I believe that the *soul* is eternal; and had no beginning; it can have no end. Here he entered into some explanations, which were so brief that I could not perfectly comprehend him. But the idea seemed to be that the soul of man, the spirit, had existed from eternity in the bosom of Divinity; and so far as he was intelligible to me, must ultimately return from whence it came. He said very little of rewards and punishments; but one conclusion, from what he did say, was irresistible—he contended throughout, that everything which had a *beginning* must have an *ending;* and consequently if the punishment of man *commenced* in the next world, it must, according to his logic and belief have an *end.*

During the whole of his address, and it occupied more than two hours, there was no opinion or belief that he expressed, that was calculated, in the slightest degree, to impair the morals of society, or in any manner to degrade and brutalize the human species. There was much in his precepts, if they were followed, that would soften the asperities of man towards man, and that would tend to make him a more rational being than he is generally found to be. There was no violence, no fury, no denunciation. His religion appears to be the religion of meekness, lowliness, and mild persuasion.

Towards the close of his address, he remarked that he had been represented as pretending to be a Savior, a worker of miracles, etc. All this was false. He made no such pretensions. He was but a man, he said; a plain, untutored man; seeking what he should do to be saved. He performed no miracles. He did not pretend to possess any such power. He closed by referring to the Mormon Bible, which he said, contained nothing inconsistent or conflicting with the Christian Bible, and he again repeated that all who would follow the precepts of the Bible, whether Mormon or not, would assuredly be saved.

Throughout his whole address, he displayed strongly a spirit of charity and forbearance. The Mormon Bible, he said, was communicated to him, *direct from heaven.* If there was such a thing on earth, as the author of it, then he (Smith) was the author; but the idea that he wished to impress was, that he had penned it as dictated by God.

I have taken some pains to explain this man's belief, as he himself explained it. I have done so because it might satisfy your curiosity, and might be interesting to you, and some of your friends. *I have changed my opinion of the Mormons.* They are an injured and much-abused people. Of matters of *faith*, you know I express no opinion. have only room to add—let William, if you cannot do it, acknwledge the receipt of this, with the enclosure.

Remember me to Sarah and the boys. Kiss the dear baby for me.

Affectionately your husband,
M. L. DAVIS.

P. S.—I omitted to say, he does not believe in infant baptism, *sprinkling*, but in *immersion*, after *eight* years of age.

To Mrs. Mathew L. Davis, 107 Henry Street, New York.

The Prophet's Interview with Van Buren and Calhoun.

During my stay I had an interview with Martin Van Buren, the President, who treated me very insolently, and it was with great reluctance he listened to our message, which, when he had heard, he said: "*Gentlemen, your cause is just, but I can do nothing for you;*" and "*If I take up for you I shall lose the vote of Missouri.*" His whole course went to show that he was an office-seeker, that self-aggrandizement was his ruling passion, and that justice and righteousness were no part of his composition. I found him such a man as I could not conscientiously support at the head of our noble Republic. I also had an interview with Mr. John C. Calhoun, whose conduct towards me very ill became his station. I became satisfied there was little use for me to tarry, to press the just claims of the Saints on the consideration of the President or Congress, and stayed but a few days, taking passage in company with Porter Rockwell and Dr. Foster on the railroad and stages back to Dayton, Ohio.

Friday, 7.—High Council at Montrose voted to disfellowship all brethren who should persist in keeping tippling shops in that branch of the Church.

Sunday, 16.—Elder Brigham Young tarried at Elder Parley P. Pratt's, 58 Mott Street, N. Y., and Elder Heber C. Kimball arrived there this morning.

Thursday, 20.—Judge Higbee I left at Washington, and he wrote me as follows:

Elias Higbee's Letter to the Prophet, Reporting Progress of the Cause of the Saints Before the Senate Committee.

WASHINGTON CITY, Feb. 20th, 1840.

DEAR BROTHER:—I have just returned from the Committee Room, wherein I spoke about one hour and a half. There were but three of the committee present, for which I am very sorry. I think they will be obliged to acknowledge the justice of our cause. They paid good attention; and I think my remarks were well received. It was a special meeting appointed to hear me by my request. The Missouri Senators and Representatives were invited to attend. Dr. Linn, and Mr. Jamieson attended, and God gave me courage, so that I was not intimidated by them. Dr. Linn, I thought, felt a little uneasy at times; but manifested a much better spirit afterwards than Mr. Jamieson.

I told them first, that I represented a suffering people, who had been deprived, together with myself, of their rights in Missouri; who numbered something like fifteen thousand souls; and not only they, but many others were deprived of the rights guaranteed to them by the Constitution of the United States. At least the amount of one hundred and fifty thousand free-born citizens are deprived the enjoyment of citizenship in each and every state; that we had no ingress in the state of Missouri; nor could any of us have, only at the expense of our lives; and this by the order of the executive.

I then took their own declaration of the cause of our expulsion; referred them to Parley P. Pratt's pamphlet, which I held in my hand; then showed that the first accusation therein contained, was on account of our religious tenets; furthermore, that the others were utterly groundless. I went on to prove that the whole persecution, from beginning to end, was grounded on our religious faith. For evidence of this, I referred them to Porter Rockwell's testimony, and P. Powell's. I stated that there was abundant testimony to prove this to be a fact, among the documents.

I then gave a brief history of the persecutions, from the first settlement in the state to our final expulsion. I also stated that the society were industrious, inoffensive, and innocent of crime; had the *Times and Seasons*, from which I read Governor Lucas's letter to Alanson Ripley. I also referred to Judge Young's letter from Pike county, the clerk's and others, respecting our character in their section of the country. I gave them some hints of the Haun's mill massacre, and the murder of the two little boys, but referred them more particularly to the documents for information concerning those things; and furthermore that I had not come here to instruct them in what they were to do in the case, but to present them with the facts—having all confidence in this honorable body (the Congress), believing them to be honorable men.

I demanded from them a restitution of all our rights and privileges as citizens of the United States, and damages for all the losses we had sustained in consequence of our persecutions and expulsion from the state; and told them we could have recourse no where else on earth that I knew of; that we could not sue an army of soldiers, neither could we go into the state to sue anyone else. I told them that I knew not how far Congress had jurisdiction in this case, or how far they had not; but as far as they had, we claimed the exercise of it for our relief; for we were an injured people.

These and some others were the principal subjects of my speech; after which Mr. Jamieson said he was once in the "Mormons'" favor; but afterwards learned that it was impossible to live among them, for they stole their neighbors' hogs; and there being so much testimony, he believed it, etc., etc. I replied something like this: making statements was one thing, and proving them was another. Mr Linn then said he wished me to answer one thing, viz.: If the legislature of Missouri did not refuse to investigate the subject of our difficulties solely on account of the trials then pending. In reply I assured him that I knew they had refused us an investigation; but as to that being the cause, I did not know, but told him they might have done it when those trials were discharged. He seemed to think it an injustice for Congress to take it up before the legislature had acted on it.

I occupied all but a few minutes of the time when the Senate was to go into session, so they adjourned until tomorrow at ten o'clock, when the Missourians are to reply. Mr. Linn observed, that there was a gentleman whom he would have before the committee on the morrow, who lived in the upper part of Missouri, that knew everything relative to the affair. I presume *he* is to put in his gab. I suppose I must attend the committee, as I am solicited by the chairman; but I would rather take a flogging; because I must sit still, and hear a volubility of lies concerning myself and brethren. *Lies* I say, for they have nothing but *lies* to tell, that will in the least degree justify their conduct in Missouri. Mr. Linn said he had written to Missouri, to get all the evidence taken before Judge King; so that if the thing must come up, he would be prepared to have a full investigation of the matter, and that the committee should have power to send for persons, papers, &c,. &c.

In my remarks I stated that an article of the Constitution was violated in not granting compulsory process for witnesses in behalf of the prisoners; and that the main evidence adduced, upon which they were committed, (as I understood), was from Dr. Avard, who once belonged to our society, and was compelled to swear as suited them best, in order to save his life; that I knew him to be a man whose character was the worst I ever knew in all my associations or intercourse with mankind; and that I had evidence by affidavits before them, of five or six respectable men, to prove that all he swore to was false.

Brethren and sisters, I want your especial prayers, that God may give me wisdom to manage this case according to His will, and that He will protect me from our foes, both publicly and privately.

Yours in the bonds of love,

ELIAS HIGBEE.

Second letter of Elias Higbee to the Prophet—Cause of the Saints before the Senate Committee.

WASHINGTON CITY, February 21st, 1840.

DEAR BROTHER.—I have just returned again from the Committee Room. Mr. Linn and Mr. Jamieson made some remarks, to which I replied. Mr. Linn is much more mild and reasonable (mostly perhaps from policy) than Mr. Jamieson, who related a long lingo of stuff, which he said was proven before the legislature in Missouri, which amounted to about this: that Joseph Smith gave the "Mormons" liberty to trespass on their neighbors' property; also told them, that it all belonged to them; as they were Israelites. Upon the strength of this they became the agressors. I replied that the Jackson county people in their declaration of causes that induced them to unite in order to drive the "Mormons," the crime of stealing, or trespassing, was not mentioned; and there was no docket, either clerk's or justice's, that could show it, in Jackson, Clay, Caldwell, or in Daviess counties; and that no man ever heard such teaching or doctrine from Joseph Smith, or any other "Mormon;" that we held to no such doctrine, neither believed in any such thing.

I mentioned some things contained in our Book of Doctrine and Covenants; Government and Laws in general. I told them we had published long ago our belief on that subject. Some things I recollected, which were that all persons should obey the laws of the government under which they lived, and that ecclesiastical power should not be exercised to control our civil rights in any way; particularly that ecclesiastical power should only be used in the Church; and then no further than fellowship was concerned. I think they injured their cause to-day. There is another appointment for them on the morrow, at 10 o'clock. Their friend they said was sick, consequently could not attend to-day. Mr. Linn said he thought it would be time enough to take it up in Congress when they [the Saints] could not get justice from the State; and that he was confident there was a disposition in the state of Missouri to do us justice, should we apply; that the reason of their refusing to investigate before was, the trials of the prisoners were pending; and further said, (when speaking of the trials before Judge King,) that he understood from gentlemen that the prisoners commended the Judge for his clemency and fair dealing towards them; and acknowledged they were guilty in part of the charge preferred against them. Mr. Linn said he presumed I was not present, when said men were tried. I replied in the negative, that I was not there, neither any body else that could be a witness in their favor. The lawyers advised them to keep away if they desired the salvation of their lives. I observed that I had read the proceedings of the legislature, but did not now recollect them; but since yesterday I have been reflecting on the subject, and recollect a conversation I had with Mr. Harvey Redfield, who was the bearer of the petition to Jefferson City, and he informed me that the reasons why they refused an investigation, was on account of the Upper Missouri members being so violently opposed to it, that they used their utmost exertions, and finally succeeded in getting a majority against it; and the reason of their taking this course was, in consequence of one of their members being in the massacre at Haun's mill, viz., Mr. Ashley; and Cornelius Gilliam was a leader of the first mob in Daviess county, which the militia were called out to suppress.

Mr. Linn said if it must come out in Congress, it should be fully investigated, and they, the Committee, should have power to send for persons and papers; for if we have a right to claim damages of the United States, so had they, if all were true concerning the acts alleged against the "Mormons;" that they had a right to ask the Government to pay the war against the "Mormons;" but finally seemed to disapprove of the exterminating order, which was admitted to have existed by Mr. Jamieson, or was issued by their legislature, but that no one ever thought of carrying it into effect. He said that General Clark merely advised the "Mormons" to leave the State. To which I replied, General Clark's speech was before them; that I had stated some of its contents yesterday; and if it were necessary, I could prove it by four or five hundred affidavits.

Then Mr. Jamieson stated something about the prisoners making their escape, and that he had no doubt but that they could have a fair trial in Missouri, for the legislature, to his certain knowledge, passed a law whereby they had a right to choose any county in the State to be tried in. To which I replied, that I understood such a law was passed; but notwithstanding, they could not get their trials in the county wherein they desired; for they were forced to go to Boone, whereas they desired to have their trials in Palmyra, where they could get their witnesses, as that was only sixteen miles from the river, and the other was a great distance. He said that Judge King certainly would not go contrary to law. I told him there were some affidavits in those documents that would tell him some things very strange concerning Judge

King. Mr. Linn then wished to know if the affidavits were from anybody else save "Mormons." I replied that there were some others; but how many I knew not. He then wanted to know how they were certified; whether any clerk's name was attached in the business. I told him they were well authenticated by the Courts of Record, with the Clerk's name attached thereto.

After these things and some others were said, the committee refused to consult on the subject. Only the same three attended that were in yesterday. The Chairman observed that they had not expressed any opinion relative to the subject: but observed his mind was made up in ralation to the matter. I think, from all I have discovered, Mr. Smith of Indiana will be on the side of justice; but how the thing will terminate I cannot tell. Mr. Crittenden and Mr. Strange are the two absent members of the Committee.

Yours in the bond of love,

ELIAS HIGBEE.

Third Letter of Elias Higbee to the Prophet—Cause of the Saints before the Senate Committee.

WASHINGTON, February 22nd, 1840.

DEAR BROTHER.—I have just returned from the Committee Room. The Committee being present to-day, a Mr. Corwin of St. Louis, formerly a democratic editor, emptied his budget; which was as great a bundle of nonsense and stuff as could be thought of; I suppose not what he knew, but what gentlemen had told him; for instance, the religious General Clark and others. I confess I had hard work to restrain my feeling some of the time, but I did succeed in keeping silence tolerably well. Himself, Mr. Jamieson, and Mr. Linn summoned all the energies of their minds to impress upon the assembly that "Joe Smith," as he called him, led the people altogether by Revelation, in their temporal, civil, and political matters, and by this means caused all the "Mormons" to vote the "whole-hog" ticket on one side, except two persons. But when I got an opportunity of speaking, I observed that Joseph Smith never led any of the Church in these matters; as we considered him to have no authority, neither did he presume to exercise any of that nature; that Revelations were only concerning spiritual things in the Church; and the Bible being our standard, we received no Revelations contrary to it. I also observed that we were not such ignoramuses, perhaps, as he fain would have people believe us to be; and some other things on this subject. I then told him that every man exercised the right of suffrage according to his better judgment, and without any ecclesiastical restraint being put upon him; that it was all false about a Revelation on voting; and the reason of our voting that ticket was in consequence of the Democratic principles having been taught us from our infancy, and that they ever extended equal rights to all; and further we had been much persecuted previous to that time—many threatenings being made from the counties round about, as well as among us, by those who took the lead in political affairs. It was true we advised our brethren to vote this ticket, telling them we thought that party would protect our rights, and not suffer us to be driven from our lands, as we had hitherto been; believing it to be by far the most liberal party; but in that we were mistaken, because when it came to the test, there were as many Democrats turned against us as Whigs; and indeed less liberality and political freedom were manifested by them; for one Whig paper came out decidedly in our favor.

I made these remarks partly from motives which I may at another time explain to you. He laid great stress on the trials at Richmond, and a constitution, that he said Avard and others (who were in good standing in the "Mormon" Church at this time) swore to; then went on to relate what it contained, and that it was written by Sidney Rigdon.

I flatly denied it, and I could bring all the "Mormons," both men, women, and children, besides myself, that would swear before all the world, that no such thing ever existed, nor was thought of among the "Mormons."

He then related some things which he said John Corril had told him at the legislature, in Missouri; which were to the effect that the "Mormons" had burnt a number of houses in Daviess county, and that for himself, if he could not get to heaven by being an honest man, he would never go there. Then, I, speaking of some of the dissenters, told him Corril was anxious to get into the Church again, and that it was the fact in regard to damages having been done, after we had been driven from Jackson and Clay—relating the De Witt scrape, and calling of the militia, and the mob's marching to Daviess and saying they would drive the "Mormons" from there to Caldwell, and then to hell; their burning our houses; that small parties on both sides were on the alert, and probably did some damages; though I was not personally knowing to [it], as I was not there. I told him Joseph Smith held no office in the country, neither was he a military man, and did not take gun in hand in the affair to my knowledge. I then stated that John Corril's affidavit, which contained some important facts, was before them,—which facts I forgot to mention yesterday,—importing that he (John Corril) was convinced we would get no redress in Missouri (he being a member of the legislature, ought to know). I saw the Chairman of the Committee not long since, who informed me that the Committee had not come to a final conclusion on this matter as yet.

I saw Mr. Jamieson on the walk, who said the first thing the Committee would do was to decide whether they would take it up and consider it or not; and if they do take it up according to request, the Senate will grant the Committee power to send for persons and papers. The Committee made some inquiries respecting our religion, and I answered them, as a matter of course, as well as I was able.

They inquired very particularly concerning how much land we had entered there, and how much of it yet remained unsold; when Mr. Corwin observed that we had never entered much land there, but were squatters. I then described the size of Caldwell and Daviess counties, giving an explanation on these matters.

I suppose perhaps on Monday or Tuesday, we shall know something relative to this matter. Whether power be given them to send for persons and papers, [or not] you may see where they depend to rally their forces, viz., by endeavoring to make us treasonable characters, by the constitution, said to govern us,and that everything both civil and political among us is done by revelation. These points I desire to blow to the four winds, and that you will select a number of firm brethren, possessing good understanding, who will tell the truth, and willingly send me their names when they know they are wanted. Send plenty of them. They will get two dollars per day, and ten cents a mile to and from, [as] expense money. Do not send them until their subpœnas get there, for they will not draw expense money only for going home.

I will suggest a few names—Alanson Ripley, King Follett, Amasa Lyman, Francis M. Higbee, as they know concerning the De Witt scrape; also send Charles C. Rich, Seymour Brunson, and others. You will know whom to send better than myself.

If the Missourians should send for you, I would say consult God about going.

ELIAS HIGBEE.

P. S.—Mr. Jamieson stated to me this evening, if the "Mormons" could make it appear that they had been wronged, they would use their influence in having them redressed, so the shame should not fall on the whole state, but on those which had been guilty. I then observed that there was a minority in the legislature, much in our favor, which seemed to please him, as they alluded several times to it. The cause of my being so particular, is to show you the whole ground I have taken in this matter. that there may be no inconsistency. If I have erred in this matter, it is my head and not my heart.

ELIAS HIGBEE.

Sunday, 23.—Elder Brigham Young had so far recovered as to be able to attend preaching by Parley P. Pratt, at Columbia Hall, New York.

The High Council of Nauvoo voted, that the notes given into the hands of Bishop Partridge, by certain individuals, as consecrations for building the Lord's House in Far West, be returned to the same by him.

Tuesday, 25.—Elders Brigham Young and Reuben Hedlock went to Hampstead, on Long Island, and preached at Rockaway and the neighborhood till the fourth of March, and baptized nine.

The Fourth Letter of Elias Higbee to the Prophet—Announces that the Senate Committee's Report will be Adverse to the Saints.

WASHINGTON, February 26th, 1840.

DEAR BROTHER.—I am just informed, by General Wall (the Chairman of the Committee), before whom, or to whom, our business is referred, that the decision is against us, or in other words unfavorable, that they believe redress can only be had in Missouri, the courts and legislature. He says, they will report this week. I desire to get a copy of it, and also the papers. I feel a conscience void of offense towards God and man in this matter; that I have discharged my duty here; and as I wish not to be on expense, as soon as I can write to President Rigdon, get my papers, and draw some money to bear my expenses, I shall bid adieu to this city, to return to my family and friends.

I feel now that we have made our last appeal to all earthly tribunals; that we should now put our whole trust in the God of Abraham, Isaac, and Jacob. We have a right now which we could not heretofore so fully claim—that is, of asking God for redress and redemption, as they have been refused us by man.

ELIAS HIGBEE.

To Joseph Smith, Junior.

The Prophet *en route* for Nauvoo.

When I had returned as far as Dayton, Ohio, I found the horses which we left on our journey out, and from thence I pursued my journey through Indiania on horseback, in company with Dr. Foster, leaving Brother Porter Rockwell at Dayton; the traveling being exceedingly bad, my progress was slow and wearisome.

My clerk, James Mulholland, while I was absent, died

on November 3rd, 1839, aged thirty-five years. He was a man of fine education, and a faithful scribe and Elder in the Church.*

Death of James Mulholland.

Wednesday, March 4, 1840. I arrived safely at Nauvoo, after a wearisome journey, through alternate snow and mud, having witnessed many vexatious movements in government officers, whose sole object should be the peace and prosperity and happiness of the whole people; but instead of this, I discovered that popular clamor and personal aggrandizement were the ruling principles of those in authority; and my heart faints within me when I see, by the visions of the Almighty, the end of this nation, if she continues to disregard the cries and petitions of her virtuous citizens, as she has done, and is now doing.

I have also enjoyed many precious moments with the Saints during my journey.

On my way home I did not fail to proclaim the iniquity and insolence of Martin Van Buren, toward myself and an injured people, which will have its effect upon the public mind; and may he never be elected again to any office of trust or power,† by which he may abuse the innocent and let the guilty go free.

I depended on Dr. Foster to keep my daily journal during this journey, but he has failed me.

Elders Brigham Young and Reuben Hedlock returned to New York, and held a conference, when many Elders were ordained.

* Mulholland street in Nauvoo was named in honor of this worthy man. It ran east and west on the south side of the Temple block, and became the principal business street of the city. It was to him that the Prophet dictated a considerable part of his history. See History of the Church, Vol. III, p. 375.

† He never was. In the Presidential election of 1840, Van Buren was renominated by the Democratic Party, but was defeated by William Henry Harrison, the Whig candidate. Harrison received two hundred and thirty-four electoral votes to sixty for Van Buren. In 1848 Van Buren was again a candidate for President being the nominee of the Free Soil Party. Lewis Cass was the nominee of the Democrats, and Zachary Taylor of the Whigs. Taylor was elected, and Van Buren did not receive a single electoral vote.

Report of the Senate Judiciary Committee on the Case of the Saints vs. Missouri.

Twenty-sixth Congress—First Session.—In the Senate of the United States, March 4th, 1840. Submitted, laid on the table, and ordered to be printed, the following Report, made by Mr. Wall—

The Committee on the Judiciary to whom was referred the Memorial of a Delegation of the Latter-day Saints, report—

The Petition of the Memoralists sets forth, in substance, that a portion of their sect commenced a settlement in the county of Jackson, in the state of Missouri, in the summer of 1831; that they bought lands, built houses, erected churches, and established their homes, and engaged in all the various occupations of life; that they were expelled from that county in 1833 by a mob, under circumstances of great outrage, cruelty, and oppression, and against all law, and without any offense committed on their part, and to the destruction of property to the amount of 120,000 dollars; that the society thus expelled amounted to about 1,200 souls; that no compensation was ever made for the destruction of their property in Jackson; that after their expulsion from Jackson county, they settled in Clay county, on the opposite side of the Missouri river, where they purchased lands, and entered others at the land office; where they resided peaceably for three years, engaged in cultivation, and other useful and active employments, when the mob again threatened their peace, lives, and property; and they became alarmed, and finally made a treaty with the citizens of Clay county, that they should purchase their lands, and the Saints should remove; which was complied with on their part, and the Saints removed to the county of Caldwell, where they took up their abode and re-established their settlement, not without heavy pecuniary losses and other inconveniences; that the citizens of Clay county never paid them for their lands, except for a small part; they remained in Caldwell from 1836 until the fall of 1838, and during that time had acquired, by purchase from the Government, the settlers, and pre-emptioners, almost all the lands in the county of Caldwell, and a portion of the lands in Daviess and Carrol counties—the former county being almost entirely settled by the Saints, and they were rapidly filling up the two latter counties.

Those counties, when the Saints first commenced their settlement, were for the most part wild and uncultivated, and they had converted them into large and well improved farms, well stocked. Land had risen in value to ten or even twenty-five dollars per acre, and these counties were rapidly advancing in cultivation and wealth.

That in August, 1838, a riot commenced, growing out of an attempt of a Saint to vote, which resulted in creating great excitement, and the perpetration of many scenes of lawless outrage, which are set forth in the Petition. That they were finally compelled to fly from those counties, and on the 11th October, 1838, they sought safety by that means, with their families, leaving many of their effects behind. That they had previously applied to the constituted authorities of Missouri for protection, but in vain. They allege, that they were pursued by the mob; that conflicts ensued; deaths occurred on each side; and finally a force was organized under the authority of the Governor of the state of Missouri, with orders to drive the Saints from the state, or exterminate them. The Saints thereupon determined to make no further resistance, but to submit themselves to the authorities of the state.

Several of the Saints were arrested and imprisoned on a charge of treason against the state, and the rest, amounting to about 15,000 souls, fled into other states, principally into Illinois, where they now reside.

The petition is drawn up at great length, and sets forth, with feeling and eloquence, the wrongs of which they complain; justifies their own conduct, and aggravates that of those whom they call their persecutors, and concludes by saying they see no redress, unless it be obtained of the Congress of the United States, to whom they make their solemn, last appeal, as American citizens, as Christians, and as men; to which decision they say they will submit.

The committee have examined the case presented by the petition, and heard the views urged by their agent, with care and attention; and after full examination and consideration, unanimously concur in the opinion—

That the case presented for their investigation is not such a one as will justify or authorize any interposition by this government.

The wrongs complained of are not alleged to be committed by any of the officers of the United States, or under the authority of its government in any manner whatever. The allegations in the petition relate to the acts of its citizens, and inhabitants and authorities of the state of Missouri, of which state the petitioners were at the time citizens, or inhabitants.

The grievances complained of in the petition are alleged to have been done within the territory of the state of Missouri. The committee, under these circumstances, have not considered themselves justified in inquiring into the truth or falsehood of the facts charged in the petition. If they are true, the petitioners must seek relief in the courts of judicature of the state of Missouri, or of the United States, which has the appropriate jurisdiction to administer full and adequate redress for the wrongs complained of, and doubless will do so fairly and impartially;*

* The Saints never acted upon the suggestion of the judiciary committee of the Senate, that they take their case before the Federal courts. The reasons why are considered at length in the introduction of this volume which see.

or the petitioners may, if they see proper, apply to the justice and magnanimity of the state of Missouri—an appeal which the committee feel justified in believing will never be made in vain by the injured or oppressed.

It can never be presumed that a state either wants the power or lacks the disposition to redress the wrongs of its own citizens, committed within her own territory, whether they proceed from the lawless acts of her officers or any other persons. The committee therefore report that they recommend the passage of the following resolution:

Resolved, That the committee on the judiciary be discharged from the further consideration of the memorial in this case; and that the memorialists have leave to withdraw the papers which accompany their memorial.

CHAPTER V.

AFFAIRS OF THE SAINTS BEFORE UNITED STATES SENATE—GENERAL CONFERENCE OF THE CHURCH AT NAUVOO—ACTION OF THE CHURCH WITH REFERENCE TO SENATE COMMITTEE'S REPORT—MISSION TO PALESTINE.

Friday, *6*.—Attended the meeting of the High Council of Iowa, at Brother Elijah Fordham's, Montrose.

Extract from the Minutes of the Iowa High Council.

President Joseph Jmith, Jun., addressed the Council on various subjects, and in particular the consecration law; stating that the affairs now before Congress was the only thing that ought to interest the Saints at present; and till it was ascertained how it would terminate, no person ought to be brought to account before the constituted authorities of the Church for any offense whatever; and [he] was determined that no man should be brought before the Council in Nauvoo till that time, etc., etc. The law of consecration could not be kept here, and that it was the will of the Lord that we should desist from trying to keep it; and if persisted in, it would produce a perfect defeat of its object, and that he assumed the whole responsibility of not keeping it until proposed by himself.*

* This is the record of a very important action. The law of consecration and stewardship, with which the action deals, was given to the Church by revelation (Doc. and Cov. sec. xlii). Its fundamental principle is the recognition of God as the possessor of all things, the earth and the fullness thereof. It is His by right of proprietorship. He created it and sustains it by His power. This recognized, it follows that whatsoever man possesses in it, he holds as a stewardship merely. These principles the Saints were called upon to recognize and act under in the establishment of Zion in Missouri; and apparently the Saints in Iowa were disposed to undertake the same order of things in the settlement they were then making, until stopped by the Prophet. The action of the Prophet in this instance demonstrates the elasticity in Church government, and law. The Lord, who commanded to move forward, may also command a halt. He who said take neither purse nor scrip when going to preach the Gospel (Matt. x: 10) may later say, under other circumstances, "He that hath a purse let him take it, and likewise his scrip" (Luke xxii: 35, 36). So, too, in other matters. The Lord commanded the colony of Lehi that there should no man among them "have save it be but one wife, and concubines ye shall have none;" yet reserved the right to command His people otherwise should the accomplishment of His purposes require it. (Book of Mormon, Jacob ii: 24-30.)

He requested every exertion to be made to forward affidavits to Washington, and also letters to members of Congress. The following votes were then passed:

First—That this Council will coincide with President Joseph Smith, Jun.'s decision concerning the consecration law, on the principle of its being the will of the Lord, and of President Smith's taking the responsibility on himself.

Second—That a committee of three be appointed, consisting of Wheeler Baldwin, Lyman Wight, and Abraham O. Smoot, to obtain affidavits and other documents to be forwarded to the city of Washington.

Third—That the clerk of this Council be directed to inform Judge Higbee, that it is the wish of this Council that he should not, upon any consideration, consent to accept of anything of Congress short of our just rights and demands for our losses and damages in Missouri.

Sunday, 8.—I attended the Council of Nauvoo, at Brother Granger's.

President Brigham Young preached in Columbia Hall, New York.

Monday, 9.—Elders Brigham Young, Heber C. Kimball, Parley P. Pratt, Orson Pratt, George A. Smith, and Reuben Hedlock, sailed from New York on the *Patrick Henry* for Liverpool.

Fifth Letter of Elias Higbee to the Prophet—the Affairs of the Saints at Washington.

WASHINGTON, March 9th, 1840.

DEAR BROTHER:—I expected, by this time, that we would be through with our business, but the chairman of the committee gave notice last week, he should call it [the committee's Report] up today in the Senate; through Mr. Young's having gone to Philadelphia, it will not be called up until his return, which will be on next Thursday, according to the information that I have obtained relative to this matter. If the resolution is passed, as annexed to the Report, I shall get my papers and leave the city.

I have written some letters to Brother Rigdon, which it seems he did not get. Brother Samuel Bennett writes that Brother Rigdon left Philadelphia for the Jerseys on the 5th instant. He [Rigdon] stated that he expects me to come there to go with him home, and that he would write me soon on the subject. I shall write for him to make the necessary arrangements. He says Dr. Ell's family left about a week ago for Commerce. Also that the Church there numbers about one hundred; and Parley P. Pratt, Orson Pratt, Brother Kimball, Brother Brigham

Young, George A. Smith, and Brother Hedlock were to sail from New York to England on the 7th instant.

As I have lately written several letters to you, I shall bid adieu, not to write again until after the Senate acts upon our business. Mr. Robinson says he has sent you a report; notwithstanding, I shall enclose another for you.

I have changed my place of boarding in consequence of Mrs. Richey's breaking up house-keeping, and going to Baltimore. I am busy here at chimney corner preaching.

Yours as ever in the bonds of everlasting love,

ELIAS HIGBEE.

To President Joseph Smith, Jun., Commerce, Illinois.

P. S.—Lest my previous letters should not come to hand, I merely say that I have been before the committee three days, and done all in my power to effect the object of our mission; have spoken my mind freely on the subject; and feel to have a conscience void of offense towards God in this matter. The subscription of which the report makes mention, was on condition that they could not lawfully do anything for us; after examination we were to submit and wait until the Great Disposer of human events shall adjust these things, in that place where the wicked cease from troubling and the weary are at rest (this I think is nearly the sentiment though perhaps not the very words); and I for one hope and pray the time will soon come when they will not trouble us in the west, as they have hitherto done.

There is a man here on whom I occasionally call, who owns two printing presses and much type, reading our books, I will with the assistance of God, get him to come to the west as soon as possible with his press, that you may set him to printing the truth. He told me, if we had any printing to do, he would do it cheap, and even go to the west if necessary.

Give my respects to Porter Rockwell, Dr. Foster, and also all the household of faith. E. H.

Friday, 13.—Jacob K. Potts and Levi Stilley made affidavit before William Oglesby, J. P., that they witnessed the massacre at Haun's mill on the 30th of October, 1838, confirming the statements already written in this History. Potts had two balls shot into his right leg.

Sunday, 15.—The High Council of the Church at Nauvoo voted that the First Presidency superintend the affairs of the ferry between Nauvoo and Montrose.

Monday, *16*.—Elder John Taylor wrote from Liverpool:

Extract from Elder John Taylor's Letter—Affairs in British Mission.

I told you about our coming to Liverpool. The first time I preached n came forward [for baptism]. We have been baptizing since; last week we baptized nine, we are to baptize tomorrow, but how many I know not. The little stone is rolling forth. One of the brethren dreamed he saw two men come to Liverpool; they cast a net into the sea and pulled it out full of fishes; he was surprised to see them pick the small fish out first and then the large. Well, if we get all the fish I shall be satisfied.

Brother Woodruff has lately left the Potteries and has gone to another neighborhood, and is making Methodist preachers scarce. He baptized 32 persons in one week—13 of them were Methodist preachers. Elder Clark is preaching and baptizing in and about Manchester. The latest account from Elder Turley, he was well, preaching and baptizing in the Potteries. Elder Willard Richards is very busy at this period, in visiting and setting in order the branches of the Church in Preston, Clithero, and all the regions round about, and holding correspondence with the Elders abroad.

Judge Elias Higbee's Course at Washington Approved.

The High Council met at my house in Nauvoo, and resolved that Robert B. Thompson write a letter to Judge Higbee at Washington, approving his course, and giving him certain names (for which see Thompson's letter), that he may order subpœnas for them as witnesses in the suit now before Congress, namely, the Latter-day Saints *versus* the State of Missouri, for redress of grievances.

Letter of R. B. Thompson to Elias Higbee, Announcing the Approval of the Church Authorities of the Latter's Course at Washington.

NAUVOO, HANCOCK COUNTY, ILLINOIS,
March 17th, 1840.

Elias Higbee, Esq.

DEAR AND HONORED SIR:—It is with the greatest pleasure I sit down to write to you at this time, to inform you of the situation and state of the Church as regards the object of your mission.

Since President Joseph Smith returned we have been favored with several communications from you, giving a statement of the proceedings before the committee, etc. On Monday evening last, your letters were read to a large concourse of our brethren, and other persons who were assembled to hear the same; and I must say that the greatest satisfaction was manifested by the assembled multitude, with the noble stand and straightforward and honorable course which you had pursued; and before the assembly separated, a vote of thanks to you was unanimously agreed upon. I can assure you that, from the feelings there, as well as upon other occasions, [expressed] there is not only a disposition, but a fixed determination, to uphold you in your righteous cause and sustain you in your efforts to obtain redress for the injuries which the Saints have borne from their unfeeling oppressors, and in bringing their case before the authorities of the nation.

In the evening the High Council assembled at the house of President Joseph Smith, Jun., and took your letters into consideration, when it was unanimously resolved that a letter should be written to you approving the measures which you were taking. The High Council likewise send you a list of the names of such persons as they think will testify to such facts as you want to substantiate. The names are as follows:

Alanson Ripley,	William Chapplin,
Francis Higbee,	Ira Mills,
Lyman Wight,	Oliver Olney,
Tarlton Lewis,	Hyrum Smith,
Edward Partridge,	Seymour Brunson,
Parley P. Pratt,	Samuel Bent,
Thorit Parsons,	Porter Rockwell,
King Follett,	George A. Smith,
Isaac Laney,	Stephen Markham,
Harvey Redfield,	Thomas Grover,
Ellis Eames,	Amanda Smith,
Chapman Duncan,	Lyman Leonard,
Smith Humphrey,	Alma Smith,
Erastus Snow,	Zebediah Robinson,
John M. Burk,	Orson Hyde,
Rebecca Judd,	Charles C. Rich,
Heber C. Kimball,	Henry G. Sherwood,
William Seyley,	Elias Smith,
Dr. Isaac Galland,	Sidney Rigdon.

There probably may be others, who may occur to your mind, whom you can send for if you think necessary. We should feel glad if you had the assistance of Presidents Smith and Rigdon at this critical time, while you have to contend with Jamieson, Linn [and others]. However I hope you will go forth in the strength of the Lord, and that truth will prevail. And I would say, "Twice is he armed who hath his quarrel just." The principles, sir, for which you contend are true; they are principles of justice, of humanity, of the Constitution, and the eternal principles of righteousness.

Although mankind may depart from those principles and be swayed by popular prejudices, and undue influences; yet at the same time, that man who contends for the same, although he cannot always carry his point, or convince at all times partial and interested judges—the gem or light of truth may be darkened, and its brilliancy for a while hid—yet when the Son of Righteousness shall arise, and disperse the darkness and mist of superstition and bigotry; when the true light shines, then shall it shine with all its glorious splendor and shed forth its luster with a brilliancy upon its advocates as shall altogether surpass the equipage and glories of those who are now in power.

ROBERT B. THOMPSON.

Letter of Horace R. Hotchkiss to Sidney Rigdon and Joseph Smith, Jun. —Inquiring Concerning the Progress Made Before Congress.

FAIR HAVEN, March 17th, 1840,

Reverends Sidney Rigdon and Joseph Smith, Jun.:

GENTLEMEN:—I some time since addressed a letter to Mr. [Joseph] Smith at Philadelphia, to which I have received no reply; and was in that city two or three weeks ago, but not being able to hear anything of Mr. Smith, I suppose he must of course have left; and with the hope of still reaching you, I now send to Washington. I should have written you long before, and indeed very often this winter, but my health has been miserable; and since my return from Philadelphia, I have been confined to my house.

I beg you to inform me how you are progressing with your petition before Congress, and its probable result; whether you have any friends in the House or in the Senate, who will bring forward your case, and advocate it in sincerity, and persevere in your behalf with skill and ability until something is accomplished. Milk and water friends in Congress are good for nothing. They must be true, have talents, be zealous, or else they will be detrimental rather than advantageous to you.

Should you, gentlemen, and Judge Higbee, come as far east as this, it will afford [me] much gratification to have you take up your quarters at my house. I did intend to see you at Washington, but my health will not now permit.

With much respect, yours,

HORACE R. HOTCHKISS.

Sixth Letter of Elias Higbee to the Prophet—Affairs of the Saints at Washington—Papers Withdrawn.

WASHINGTON CITY, March 24th, 1840.

DEAR BROTHER:—Our business is at last ended here. Yesterday a resolution passed the Senate, that the committee should be discharged; and that we might withdraw the accompanying papers, which I have done. I have also taken a copy of the memorial, and want to be off for the west immediately. I have not gotten a letter from President Rigdon, although I have frequently written to him. I have received a letter from Brother Bennett, stating that he was in the Jerseys, and that he was calculating to have me come that way and go home with him; and also that he had business which he wanted me to attend to at the office here. When he last wrote, he stated that as yet he had no money to get home with, and I hardly know what course to take in regard to the matter. If I do not receive a letter in two or three days, I design leaving for Philadelphia or the west.

There is one honest Quaker-looking sort of a man here, by the name of William Green, (instead of John Green, as I stated in a letter to Brother Robinson), who has two iron printing presses, with other things necessary, that would come to Commerce, provided you could find work for him, and inform him of the same. How much work there is to do I know not; therefore merely write that if such a man and establishment are wanted, you could easily obtain them, or would know where they could be obtained. He believes as much in our religion as any other, but not much in any.

Yours in the Lord,

ELIAS HIGBEE.

P. S.—I would just observe, that information has reached this place, through some of the newspapers, that you have come out for Harrison. It is said that the information came by some gentlemen who obtained it from you, whilst in your company in passing through the state of Indiana. Another paper states that 1,000 houses are to be built in Commerce this season, which I hope is the truth.

I would just observe (on the subject of our business) I am sorry Judge Young had not insisted on the motion to print our papers, as it would have been opposed; then a speech from Clay and Mr. Preston would have been brought forth, as I have since learned; but I think it was a trick of the Missouri Senators to slide it along without making a noise, by its going to the committee as it did. Judge Young says he was anxious to have it brought before the committee, but seemed disposed to let it slide along easily, rather than run the risk of its being refused.

If he had let those speeches been made, almost every one would have read them; which would have shamed Missouri, (if there is any shame in her), and waked up the whole country, so that by another year Congress would do something for us. But there is no need of crying for spilt milk. I have done all I could in this matter, depending on the good judgment of Judge Young to legislate for us to the best advantage. I am inclined, however, to think if it was an error, it was one of the head, and not of the heart.

Mr. Hotchkiss, of Fair Haven, Connecticut, has addressed a letter to yourself, Brother Rigdon and myself, which seems to be written with much good feeling. He desires to know concerning our business here, inviting us to make his house our home, should we travel in that region. He writes that his health is very bad. I have been talking with Mr. Steward concerning a memorial, requesting him to bring it before the House; he has promised to do so if he can. He says he will talk with some of the members respecting it. I have answered Mr. Hotchkiss' letter this day, and sent him the report of the committee.

E. H.

At this time the work of the Lord is spreading rapidly in the United States and England—Elders are traveling in almost every direction, and multitudes are being baptized.

Letter of Horace R. Hotchkiss to Joseph Smith, Jun.—Offering Tract of Land for Sale.

FAIR HAVEN, 1st April, 1840.

Reverend Joseph Smith, Jun.:

MY DEAR SIR:—After writing you at, and then going to, Philadelphia, and not finding you, I addressed a letter to Washington City, and received a reply from Judge Higbee, by which I first learned of your return to Illinois; and at the same time I got the committee's report upon your application to Congress for redress of the outrages perpetrated upon your people by the Missourians. I am not, I must confess, much disappointed in the result; as I know the vacillating, fawning character of many in both houses of Congress; and these are not their worst traits either, for they not only lack the moral courage to do right, but will do what they know to be positively wrong, if they can make political capital by it; and will abandon you, me, or any one else, with perfect indifference, and heartless treachery, if by doing it they can obtain governmental favor, or political preferment. If we should not put our faith in princes, it appears most emphatically true that we should repose no confidence in politicians. The idea conveyed in the report, that exact justice will be meted to you by the judicial tribunals of Missouri, is too preposterous to require comment. It is indeed a new doctrine, that we should apply to robbers, or their supporters, to condemn themselves, to restore the valuables they have stolen, and to betray each other for the murders they have committed.

I do not believe (though I am sorry to say it) that you will ever receive a just or honorable remuneration for your losses of property, or any reparation for the personal indignities, privations and sufferings which your people have sustained in Missouri. The greatest reliance you have for regaining your wealth is in the honorable conduct of your people—their pure morals—their correct habits—their indefatigable industry—their untiring perseverance—and their well-directed enterprise. These constitute a capital which can never be shaken by man, and form the basis of all that is great in commercial influence, or in the attainment of pecuniary power.

Judge Higbee informs me that Mr. Rigdon is probably in New Jersey. It would have afforded me much pleasure to have seen you all at my house, and it was my intention to spend some time at Washington while you were there; but my health has been so very infirm, that it has prevented me from executing nearly all the arrangements I had proposed for myself for the last eight months.

Knowing the additions constantly joining your society, it has occurred to me that some of them may be unprovided with farming lands, and I mention at this time, that I am interested in a tract of about 12,000 acres of very choice lands, consisting of timber and prairie, fifteen or twenty miles from Springfield, upon which Mr. Gillett and several other families are settled and cultivating most excellent farms. It is one of the best neighborhoods in the state.

I do not know what my co-partners in this tract would say about disposing of what remains unsold of the tract, (say eight to nine thousand acres,) but I should be disposed to sell upon reasonable terms, provided from twenty to forty families, valuable for their prudence, industry, and good habits, from your society, can be found to form a small colony of practical farmers. I am also interested with the same gentlemen in lands near Rock River, in Henry and Mercer counties, and believe this would, on many accounts, be another extremely desirable place or location for a colony of your people. I have said nothing to those owning with me relative to this subject, but suppose they would be governed materially by two considerations; namely, the characters of the purchasers, and the fact of their being actual settlers or not.

If you think two small colonies of the right sort can be formed from your society, you will oblige by informing me at your earliest opportunity. The price of the balance in the tract near Springfield, including an average proportion of timber, and an average proportion of prairie, I should think $4.50 per acre. None of the prairie alone has been sold for less than three dollars, and some at three and a half; and I am confident that four and a half dollars for timber and prairie is very low, and especially as a credit, except for a small amount, would be extended to purchasers. The other tract is nearly all prairie, but the finest selection of that region. It is probably worth three and a half dollars per acre.

As my paper is out, I have only room to request my respects presented to all friends at Commerce. I beg you to tell the editor of the *Times and Seasons*, that as soon as my health allows me to go to the bank, I shall send him $10.

Your obedient servant,
HORACE R. HOTCHKISS.

Letter of Sidney Rigdon to the Prophet.

AT JAMES IVANS', NEW JERSEY,
April 3rd, 1840.

Brother Joseph Smith, Jun.

DEAR SIR.—I thought I would occupy a portion of this morning in writing to you. By a letter received from Brother Higbee yesterday, I have learned that the Senate has decided that they have no constitutional right to interfere in the case between us and the people of Missouri; and refer us to the courts for redress; either those of Missouri or the United States. Now I am confident, that there is but one person in Missouri that we can sue with safety, and that is Boggs, and he is known to be a bankrupt, and unable to pay his debts; that if we should sue him, we will have the cost to pay, as he has nothing to pay it with. We are therefore left to bear the loss without redress, at present.

Judge Higbee is on the way home, and has been for ten days. He obtained money from Judge Young, to what amount I cannot say, but he will be able to tell you when he gets home. The Judge continues his friendship, and is ready to accommodate with money, whenever called for. Surely he is a friend indeed, and ought never to be forgotten.

I am up to this time without means to get home, but I have no uneasiness about it. I shall doubtless get means as soon as my health will admit of my going. My health is slowly improving, and I think if I have no relapse, I will be able to leave for home some time in the month of May, &c.

SIDNEY RIGDON.

Arrival of Brigham Young and Associates in England.

Monday, April 6.—Elders Young, Kimball, Pratt, Smith, and Hedlock landed in Liverpool, on the first day of the eleventh year of the Church, after a tedious passage of twenty-eight days, during sixteen of which they encountered head winds, and one severe storm of three or four days; and a great portion of the time the decks were covered with water—all of which tended to increase sea-sickness and suffering.

At the time of sailing President Young's and Elder Kimball's health was very poor. George A. Smith had the ague for six days in succession. When the ship left her moorings the shore resounded with the songs of the Saints, who had come down to bid them farewell; they unitedly sang "The gallant ship is under weigh," * until

* The hymn was composed by W. W. Phelps, and is worthy of reproduction in extenso.

The gallant ship is under weigh
    To bear me off to sea,
And yonder floats the streamer gay
    That says she waits for me.
The seamen dip the ready oar,
    As rippled waves oft tell,
They bear me swiftly from the shore;
    My native land, farewell!

I go, but not to plough the main,
    To ease a restless mind,
Nor yet to toil on battle's plain,
    The victor's wreath to find.
'Tis not for treasures that are hid
    In mountain or in dell,
'Tis not for joys like these I bid
    My native land, farewell!

I go to break the fowler's snare,
    To gather Israel home;
I go the name of Christ to bear
    In lands and isles unknown.
And soon my pilgrim feet shall tread
    On land where errors dwell,
Whence light and truth have long since fled,
    My native land, farewell!

I go, an erring child of dust,
    Ten thousand foes among,
Yet on His mighty arm I trust,
    Who makes the feeble strong.
My sun, my shield, forever nigh.
    He will my fears dispel,
This hope supports me when I sigh,
    My native land, farewell!

I go devoted to His cause,
    And to His will resigned;
His presence will supply the loss
    Of all I leave behind.

out of hearing. The brethren occupied three berths in the forecastle, taking what was called a steerage passage. With the exception of Elder Kimball, not one of them had ever been to sea, and the sailors called them "land lubbers." The ship being loaded with flour and cotton, they were packed in a small compartment with about 100 or 120 passengers, being a motley mixture of English, Welsh, Irish, and Scotch, who were returning home from America to visit their friends, or had got sick of "Yankeedom" and were leaving for "sweet home."

They had scarcely been at sea twelve hours before the whole of them were prostrated by sea-sickness. George A. Smith vomited up his ague.* Brother Brigham Young, although confined to his berth by sea-sickness during the entire journey, was unable to vomit.

On coming into the Mersey the ship cast anchor in order to wait for the tide, when a small boat put off from the shore. Brothers Young, Kimball, and Parley P. Pratt went in it to the landing. On reaching the quay, Brother Young shouted hosannah three times, which he had promised to do whenever he should land on the shores of Old England. The brethren then went to No. 8 Union Street, Liverpool, where they procured bread and wine in order to partake of the Sacrament.

Elders Orson Pratt and George A. Smith, and Reuben Hedlock stayed on board to look after the baggage. About

His promise cheers the sinking heart
And lights the darkest cell,
To exiled pilgrims grace imparts;
My native land, farewell!

I go, it is my Master's call,
He's made my duty plain,
No danger can the heart appall
When Jesus stoops to reign.
And now the vessel's side we've made,
The sails their bosoms swell,
Thy beauties in the distance fade,
My native land, farewell!

* It is said that he never had the ague afterwards.

three p. m., Brother Young sent a small boat for them, and the boatmen piloted them to the same place, where they all met together, partook of the Sacrament, and returned thanks for their safe deliverance.

When they landed they were almost penniless. Two or three of them had sufficient to buy hats for those who needed them the worst.

Minutes of the General Conference of the Church.

At a General Conference of the Church of Jesus Christ of Latter-day Saints, held in Nauvoo, Hancock County, Illinois, on the sixth day of April, A.D. 1840, agreeable to previous appointment, Joseph Smith, Jun., was called upon to preside over the meeting, and Robert B. Thompson was chosen clerk.

The Conference was then opened by prayer by Elder John E. Page.

The President rose, made some observations on the business of the Conference, exhorted the brethren who had charges to make against individuals, and made some very appropriate remarks respecting the pulling the beam out of their own eye, that they may see more clearly the mote which was in their brother's eye.

A letter was read from presidents of the Seventies, wishing for an explanation of the steps, which the High Council had taken, in removing Elder F. G. Bishop from the quorum of the Seventies to that of the High Priests, without any other ordination than he had when in the Seventies, and wished to know whether those ordained into the Seventies at the same time F. G. Bishop was, had a right to the High Priesthood,* or not. After observations on the case by different individuals, the president gave a statement of the authority of the Seventies, and stated that they were Elders and not High Priests, and consequently Brother F. G. Bishop had no claim to that office. It was then unanimously resolved that Elder F. G. Bishop be placed back again into the quorum of the Seventies.

On motion, resolved that the Conference adjourn until two o'clock.

Conference met pursuant to adjournment. Prayer by Elder Joseph Young.

Elder Thomas Grover presented charges against Brother D.W. Rogers for compiling a hymn-book, and selling it as the one compiled and published by Sister Emma Smith; secondly, for writing a private letter to New York City, casting reflections on the character of Elder John P. Greene; and thirdly, for administering medicine unskilfully, which had a bad effect.

* To the office of High Priest is what is meant; Seventies, of course, hold the Melchisedek or High Priesthood.

On motion, resolved, that, as Brother Rogers is not present, his case be laid over until tomorrow.

Elder John Lawson then came forward and stated, that in consequence of some difficulty existing in the branch of the Church where he resided, respecting the Word of Wisdom, fellowship had been withdrawn from him, and also from Brother Thomas S. Edwards. After hearing the particulars, on motion, resolved, that John Lawson and Thomas S. Edwards be restored to fellowship.

Elder Orson Hyde addressed the Conference at some length, and stated that it had been prophesied, some years ago, that he had a great work to perform among the Jews; and that he had recently been moved upon by the Spirit of the Lord to visit that people, and gather up all the information he could respecting their movements, expectations, &c., and communicate the same to this Church, and to the nation at large; stating that he intended to visit the Jews in New York, London, and Amsterdam, and then visit Constantinople and the Holy Land.

On motion, resolved, that Elder Orson Hyde proceed on his mission to the Jews, and that letters of recommendation be given him, signed by the President and Clerk of the Conference.

Elder John E. Page then arose, and spoke with much force on the subject of Elder Hyde's mission, the gathering of the Jews, and the restoration of the house of Israel; proving, in a brief but convincing manner, from the Bible, Book of Mormon, and the Book of Doctrine and Covenants, that these things must take place, and that the time had nearly arrived for their accomplishment.

Adjourned until tomorrow morning, nine o'clock.

Tuesday morning, April 7.

Conference met pursuant to adjournment. A hymn was sung by the choir, and the throne of grace was addressed by Elder Caleb Baldwin.

Brother D. W. Rogers' case was then called up, and after many observations and explanations, it was on motion resolved, that D. W. Rogers be forgiven, and the hand of fellowship be continued towards him.

Conference adjourned for one hour, and met pursuant to adjournment. A hymn was sung by the choir, followed by prayer by Elder Reynolds Cahoon.

The President called upon the Clerk to read the report of the First Presidency and High Council, with regard to their proceedings in purchasing lands, and securing a place of gathering for the Saints. The report having been read, the President made some observations respecting the pecuniary affairs of the Church, and requested the brethren to step forward, and assist in liquidating the debts on the town plot, so that the poor might have an inheritance.

The President then gave an account of their mission to Washington City, the treatment they received, and the action of the Senate on the Memorial which was presented before them. The meeting then called for the reading of the Memorial, and the report of the Committee on Judiciary, to whom the same was referred, which were read.

On motion, resolved that a committee of five be appointed to draft resolutions expressive of the sentiments of this Conference in reference to the report. On motion it was resolved. that Robert D. Foster, Orson Hyde, John E. Page, Joseph Wood, and Robert B. Thompson compose said committee, and report to this Conference.

Resolved, that this meeting adjourn until tomorrow morning.

Wednesday morning, April 8.

Conference met pursuant to adjournment. A number were confirmed who had been baptized the previous evening. Prayer by Elder Marks.

The Committee appointed to draft resolutions on the report of the Senate Committee of the Judiciary were then called upon to make their report. Robert B. Thompson of the Committee then read the

Resolutions:

Whereas, we learn, with deep sorrow, regret, and disappointment, that the Committee on the Judiciary to whom was referred the Memorial of the members of the Church of Jesus Christ of Latter-day Saints (commonly called "Mormons"), complaining of the grievances suffered by them in the state of Missouri, have reported unfavorably to our cause, to justice, and humanity;

Therefore Resolved 1st: That we consider the report of the Committee on Judiciary, unconstitutional, and subversive to the rights of a free people, and justly calls for the disapprobation of all the supporters and lovers of good government and republican principles.

Resolved, 2ndly: That the Committee state, in their report, that our Memorial *aggravates* the case of our oppressors, and at the same time say, that they have not examined into the truth or falsehood of the facts mentioned in said Memorial.

Resolved, 3rdly: That the Memorial does not aggravate the conduct of our oppressors, as every statement set forth in said Memorial was substantiated by indubitable testimony; therefore we consider the statements of the Committee, in regard to that part, as false and ungenerous.

Resolved, 4thly: That that part of the report referring us to the justice and magnanimity of the state of Missouri for redress, we deem it a great insult to our good sense, better judgment, and intelligence, when numerous affidavits, which were laid before the Committee, prove that we could only go into the state of Missouri contrary to the exterminating order of the Governor, and consequently at the risk of our lives.

Resolved, 5thly: That after repeated appeals to the constituted authorities of the state of Missouri for redress, which were in vain, we fondly hoped that in the Congress of the United States, ample justice would have been rendered us; and upon that consideration alone, we pledged ourselves to abide their decision.

Resolved, 6thly: That the exterminating order of Governor Boggs is a direct infraction of the Constitution of the United States, and of the state of Missouri; and the committee in refusing to investigate the proceedings of the Executive and others of the state of Missouri, and turning a deaf ear to the cries of widows, orphans, and innocent blood, we deem no less than seconding the proceeding of that murderous clan, whose deeds are recorded in heaven, and justly call down upon their heads the righteous judgments of an offended God.

Resolved, 7thly: That the thanks of this meeting be tendered to the citizens of the state of Illinois, for their kind, liberal, and generous conduct towards us; and that we call upon them, as well as every patriot in this vast Republic, to aid us in all lawful endeavors to obtain redress for the injuries we have sustained.

Resolved, 8thly: That the thanks of this meeting be tendered to the delegation of Illinois, for the bold, manly, noble, and independent course they have taken in presenting our case before the nation, amid misrepresentation, contumely, and abuse, which were heaped upon us in our suffering condition.

Resolved, 9thly: That the thanks of this meeting be tendered to Governor Carlin of Illinois, Governor Lucas of Iowa Territory, for their sympathy, aid, and protection; and to all other honorable gentlemen who have assisted us in our endeavors to obtain redress.

Resolved, 10thly: That Joseph Smith, Jun., Sidney Rigdon, and Elias Higbee, the Delegates appointed by this Church to visit the City of Washington, to present our sufferings before the authorities of the nation, be tendered the thanks of this meeting for the prompt and efficient manner in which they have discharged their duty; and that they be requested, in behalf of the Church of Jesus Christ of Latter-day Saints throughout the world, to continue to use their endeavors to obtain redress for a suffering people. And if all hopes of obtaining satisfaction for the injuries done us be entirely blasted, that they then appeal our case to the Court of Heaven, believing that the Great Jehovah, who rules over the destiny of nations, and who notices the falling sparrows, will undoubtedly redress our wrongs, and ere long avenge us of our adversaries.*

On motion, *Resolved*, That the report of the committee on the Judici-

* See Introduction to Volume III History of the Church, where retribution on Missouri is considered at length.

ary, as well as the foregoing Preamble and Resolutions, be published in the Quincy papers.

On motion, *Resolved*, That a committee of three be appointed to investigate the recommendations of those persons who wish to obtain an ordination to the ministry, and ordain such as are thought worthy; and that Elders Bent, Wood, and Hyde compose said committee.

Resolved, That this meeting feel satisfied with the proceeding of the Presidency with regard to the sales of town property, &c., and that they are requested to continue in their agency.

Resolved, That this meeting adjourn for one hour.

Conference met pursuant to adjournment.

After singing the President arose and read the 3rd chapter of John's Gospel, after which, prayer was offered by Elder Erastus Snow.

The President commenced making observations on the different subjects embraced in the chapter [previously read] particularly the 3rd, 4th, and 5th verses, illustrating them with a very beautiful and striking figure, and throwing a flood of light on the subjects brought up to review. He then spoke to the Elders respecting their mission, and advised those who went into the world to preach the Gospel, to leave their families provided with the necessaries of life; and to teach the gathering as set forth in the Holy Scripture. That it had been wisdom for the most of the Church to keep on this side of the river, that a foundation might be established in this place; but that now it was the privilege of the Saints to occupy the lands in Iowa, or wherever the Spirit might lead them. That he did not wish to have any political influence, but wished the Saints to use their political franchise to the best of their knowledge.

He then stated that since Elder Hyde had been appointed to visit the Jews, he had felt an impression that it would be well for Elder John E. Page to accompany him on his mission. It was resolved that Elder John E. Page be appointed to accompany Elder Orson Hyde on his mission, and that he have proper credentials given him.

It was then resolved, that as a great part of the time of the Conference had been taken up with charges against individuals, which might have been settled by the different authorities of the Church, that in future no such cases be brought before the Conferences.

The Committee on ordinations reported that they had ordained thirty-one persons to be Elders in the Church, who were ordained under the hands of Alpheus Gifford * and Stephen Perry, which report was accepted.

* Alpheus Gifford was born in Adams township, Berkshire County, Massachusetts, August 28, 1793. At the age of eighteen, having scarcely sufficient learning to enable him to read the Bible, he commenced preaching the Gospel, not for hire, but for the salvation of souls. In 1817, he married Anna Nash, who bore him seven sons and three daughters. In the spring of 1831, hearing of the doctrines taught

Fredrick G. Williams presented himself on the stand, and humbly asked forgiveness for his conduct, [while in Missouri], and expressed his determination to do the will of God in the future. His case was presented to the Conference by President Hyrum Smith, when it was unanimously

Resolved,

That Fredrick G. Williams be forgiven, and be received into the fellowship of the Church.

It was reported that seventy-five persons had been baptized during the Conference, and that upwards of fifty had been received into the quorum of Seventies.

President Hyrum Smith dismissed the assembly. After he had made a few observations, the Conference was closed, under the blessings of the Presidency, until the first Friday in October next.

JOSEPH SMITH, JUN.,
President.

by Joseph Smith he made diligent inquiry and found they were scriptural and was baptized and ordained a priest; he brought home five books of Mormon which he distributed among his friends; he was then living in Tioga County, Pennsylvania. Soon after he went to Kirtland, Ohio, to see the Prophet Joseph Smith and the brethren, when he was ordained an elder; he was accompanied by his brother Levi, Elial Strong, Eleazer Miller, Enos Curtis, and Abraham Brown, who were baptized. On returning to Pennsylvania he preached and baptized many, among whom was Heber C. Kimball. The gifts of the Gospel were enjoyed by many, signs followed those who believed; devils were cast out; the sick were healed; many prophesied; some spake with new tongues; while others interpreted the same. Mr. Calvin Gilmour, with whom Brother Gifford had previously been associated in preaching, heard him speak in tongues and interpret. Gilmour declared he undestood the languages and that they were interpreted correctly, and that he knew Gifford had no classical learning; but that he would rather be damned than believe in Mormonism.

In June 1832, Brother Gifford started for Missouri; traveled to Cincinnati and wintered there with a few Saints who had been baptized by Lyman Wight. He arrived in Jackson county, Missouri, in March, 1833, where he preached extensively; he was driven with the Saints from that county in the fall of that year. He removed to Clay county, enduring the persecution incident upon settling in, and final expulsion from, the same. He went to Kirtland, Ohio, and attended the dedication of the Temple and received the ordinances there administered. He returned to Missouri and was driven with the Saints to Far West, Caldwell county. In the winter of 1839, he was driven from Missouri. He located in the Morley settlement near Lima, Illinois, and subsequently five miles above Nauvoo, where he died December 25, 1841.

(*Addenda*, Ms. Church History, Book "C" 2. Also page 404.)

CHAPTER VI.

DEVELOPMENT OF THE WORK IN ENGLAND—THE PALESTINE MISSION—POST-OFFICE NAME CHANGED FROM COMMERCE TO NAUVOO.

April 7.—The brethren [President Brigham Young, *et al.*] found Elder John Taylor, who, in company with Joseph Fielding, had recently built up a branch of twenty-eight members in Liverpool.

April 8.—President Brigham Young and company went to Elder Richards', at Preston, by railway; when they arrived there, they had not a single sixpence left. So emaciated was President Young at this time from his long sickness, and journey, that when Elder Richards returned home this day from a mission to Clitheroe, and found him in his room, he did not know him.

Letter of Hon. Richard M. Young to Elias Higbee.

WASHINGTON CITY, April 9, 1840.

Judge Elias Higbee:

DEAR SIR.—Having a private opportunity, by Judge Snow, of Quincy, I have sent you two receipts, one for $50, and the other for $90, making together $140, to Mr. E. I. Philips, cashier of the branch of the State Bank of Illinois, at Quincy. When it is convenient for you to make payment, will you have the goodness to send the money to Mr. Philips, who is instructed to receive it, and apply it towards the payment of a note of mine in that bank.

I received a letter from Mr. Rigdon a few days ago. It was mailed in Philadelphia, but was dated on the inside in New Jersey. His health is gradually but slowly improving, and he thinks he will set out for home some time in May. He wished a small sum of money, $40, deposited in one of the banks here, for a gentleman in Buffalo, New York, which I have attended to according to his direction and request. I also informed him, if he stood in need of more, to call on me and it would give me pleasure to accommodate him; so you need not be uneasy on that score.

Nothing new has transpired since you left us, with the exception of the death of one of the Connecticut Senators, Mr. Thadeus Betts, who died yesterday. His funeral took place today, hence no business was transacted in the Senate. We have also lost the Cumberland Road Bill by a final vote in the Senate, 20 voting for and 22 against it; one single vote from the majority would have saved it, by making a tie. The Vice-President was exceedingly anxious for the opportunity of getting the casting vote in its favor. Mr. Clay, of Kentucky, made a speech against and voted throughout against it. Grundy, of Tennessee, Wright of New York, and Buchanan of Pennsylvania, three of the leading Democrats in the Senate voted for it. There were but seven Whigs who voted for it, and thirteen Democrats. I think we will adjourn about the first or second Monday in June.

I received from Mr. Rigdon the Petition and papers in relation to a change of postmaster at Commerce, with an affidavit from Doctor Galland, all of which have been laid before the proper department. As soon as I get an answer, it shall be communicated to you. Don't forget to have the *Times and Seasons* sent to me. Give my respects to Rev. Joseph Smith, and accept for yourself my best wishes for your happiness.

Yours, etc.,

RICHARD M. YOUNG.

The News.

In the *Times and Seasons* of this month is a prospectus for publishing at Nauvoo, a weekly paper, to be called *The News.**

Orson Hyde's Credentials as a Missionary to Palestine.

To all people unto whom these presents shall come, Greeting—

Be it known that we, the constituted authorities of the Church of Jesus Christ of Latter-day Saints, assembled in Conference at Nauvoo, Hancock county, and state of Illinois, on the sixth day of April, in the year of our Lord, one thousand eight hundred and forty, considering an important event at hand, an event involving the interest and fate of the Gentile nations throughout the world—from the signs of the times and from declarations contained in the oracles of God, we are forced to come to this conclusion. The Jewish nations have been scattered abroad among the Gentiles for a long period; and in our estimation, the

* It was announced in the Prospectus that the *News* would "take perfectly neutral ground, in regard to politics, and it is the fixed determination of the publishers to studiously avoid all party strife, and political wranglings which are so prevalent at the present time." The *News*, however, never materialized.

time of the commencement of their return to the Holy Land has already arrived. As this scattered and persecuted people are set among the Gentiles as a sign unto them of the second coming of the Messiah, and also of the overthrow of the present kingdoms and governments of the earth, by the potency of His Almighty arm in scattering famine and pestilence like the frosts and snows of winter, and sending the sword with nation against nation to bathe it in each other's blood; it is highly important, in our opinion, that the present views and movements of the Jewish people be sought after and laid before the American people, for their consideration, their profit and their learning.

And feeling it to be our duty to employ the most efficient means in our power to save the children of men from "the abomination that maketh desolate," we have, by the counsel of the Holy Spirit, appointed Elder Orson Hyde, the bearer of these presents, a faithful and worthy minister of Jesus Christ, to be our Agent and Representative in foreign lands, to visit the cities of London, Amsterdam, Constantinople, and Jerusalem; and also other places that he may deem expedient; and converse with the priests, rulers, and elders of the Jews, and obtain from them all the information possible, and communicate the same to some principal paper for publication, that it may have a general circulation throughout the United States.

As Mr. Hyde has willingly and cheerfully accepted the appointment to become our servant and the servant of the public in distant and foreign countries, for Christ's sake, we do confidently recommend him to all religious and Christian people, and to gentlemen and ladies making no profession, as a worthy member of society, possessing much zeal to promote the happiness of mankind, fully believing that they will be forward to render him all the pecuniary aid he needs to accomplish this laborious and hazardous mission for the general good of the human family.

Ministers of every denomination upon whom Mr. Hyde shall call, are requested to hold up his hands, and aid him by their influence, with an assurance that such as do this shall have the prayers and blessings of a poor and afflicted people, whose blood has flowed to test the depths of their sincerity and to crimson the face of freedom's soil with martyr's blood.

Mr. Hyde is instructed by this Conference to transmit to this country nothing but simple facts for publication, entirely disconnected with any peculiar views of theology, leaving each class to make their own comments and draw their own inferences.

Given under our hands at the time and place before mentioned.

JOSEPH SMITH, Jun., Chairman.
ROBERT B. THOMPSON, Clerk.

Sunday, *12*.—Several of the Twelve bore their public testimony to the Gospel in the Cock Pit, Preston.

The High Council of Nauvoo met at my house, when I proposed that Brother Hyrum Smith go east with Oliver Granger to settle some business transactions of the Church which the Council sanctioned; and voted, "that President Joseph Smith, Jun., make the necessary credentials for Oliver Granger and Hyrum Smith."

Monday, *13*.—From the second of October, 1839, to this date, there have been one hundred and forty-five shocks of earthquake in Scotland, reported by Mr. Milne to the Royal Society of Edinburgh. Some of these shocks were sufficient to alter the natural levels of the ground more than two degrees, and some witnesses thought four degrees, and caused houses to rock like boats on the sea.

Earthquakes.

Tuesday, *14*.—A council of the Twelve, namely, Brigham Young, Heber C. Kimball, Parley P. Pratt, Orson Pratt, Wilford Woodruff, George A. Smith and John Taylor, was held at the house of Elder Willard Richards, in Preston, England, when the latter was ordained to the Apostleship,—agreeably to the revelation,—by President Young, under the hands of the quorum present. Other business was transacted, as also on the following days, all of which may be seen by reference to President Young's letter of the 17th instant.

Ordination of Willard Richards to the Apostleship.

Wednesday, *15*.—Elder Orson Hyde left Commerce for Jerusalem.

Thursday, *16*.—Elder Orson Hyde met with John E. Page at Lima.

Letter of Brigham Young to the Saints of the United States—Affairs of the British Mission.

PRESTON, ENGLAND, April 17, 1840.

To the Saints in the United States of America: For the comfort of the Church in general, in that country, I attempt to address a few lines to you, to let you know where we are, and what we are doing in this country.

The work of the Lord is progressing here, and has been ever since Elders Orson Hyde and H. C. Kimball left this country. According to the account that the Elders give of their labors, there have been about eight or nine hundred persons baptized since they left. The Gospel is spreading, the devils are roaring. As nigh as I can learn, the priests are howling, the tares are binding up, the wheat is gathering, nations are trembling, and kingdoms tottering; "men's hearts failing them for fear, and for looking for those things that are coming on the earth." The poor among men are rejoicing in the Lord, and the meek do increase their joy. The hearts of the wicked do wax worse and worse, deceiving and being deceived.

But I rejoice that I am counted worthy to be one of the number to carry salvation to the poor and meek of the earth. Brethren, I want to say many things, but I shall not have room on this paper, as I design giving the minutes of our conference below.

After a long and tedious voyage of 28 days on the water, we landed in Liverpool, Elders Heber C. Kimball, Parley P. Pratt, Orson Pratt, George A. Smith, Reuben Hedlock and myself, were in the company. We rejoiced in the Lord, and when we cast our minds upon the Saints in that country, [the United States] we could, by faith participate in their joys, realizing they were met in conference, it being the 6th day of April. We soon found a room that we could have to ourselves, which made our solemn assembly glorious. We blest each other and prepared for our labor. The next day we found Elder Taylor in the city. There had been about thirty baptized. On Wednesday went to Preston; met with the church on Sunday, and bore testimony to the things the Lord is doing in these last days. President Joseph Fielding gave out an appointment for a conference for the church on Wednesday, the 15th.

At a council of the Twelve, held in Preston, England, on the 14th of April, 1840, it being the 9th day of the 1st month of the 11th year of the rise of the Church of Jesus Christ, Elders Brigham Young, Heber C. Kimball, Parley P. Pratt, Orson Pratt, Wilford Woodruff, John Taylor, and George A. Smith, being present, Elder Brigham Young was called to preside, and Elder John Taylor chosen secretary.

The council was opened by prayer by Elder Brigham Young. Elder Willard Richards was ordained to the office of an Apostle, and received into the quorum of the Twelve by unanimous vote, according to previous revelation. Elder Brigham Young was unanimously chosen as the President of the Twelve.*

* President Young was also President of the Twelve by virtue of seniority of ordination into the quorum. When the quorum of the Twelve was first organized

Resolved, that he who acts as the secretary of the quorum, shall prepare the minutes of the conference of the quorum, and deposit them in the hands of the president for keeping.

Moved by Elder Kimball, and seconded by Elder Richards, that twenty of the Seventies be sent for, and that it be left discretionary with the President of the Twelve to send for more if he think proper. Conference adjourned. Benediction by Elder Kimball.

At a general conference of the Church of Jesus Christ of Latter-day Saints, held in the Temperance Hall, Preston, Lancashire, England, on the 15th of April, 1840, President Joseph Fielding called upon Elder Kimball to preside, and Elder William Clayton was chosen clerk, it being the 10th day of the 1st month of the 11th year of the rise of the Church

The meeting was opened by singing, and prayer by Elder Kimball. Elder Kimball then called upon the Elders to represent the different branches of the Church. Elder Joseph Fielding represented the church in Preston, consisting of about three hundred members, seven Elders, eight Priests, six Teachers, and two Deacons. Elder Peter Melling represented the church in Penworthan, consisting of seventy-three members, three Elders, one Priest, two Teachers. John Jackson represented the church at Southport, consisting of twenty members, one Priest, and one Teacher. Elder John Moon represented the church at Danbers Lane, and neighborhood—members generally in good standing, consisting of fifty-four members, one Elder, two Priests, three Teachers. Richard Benson, represented the church at Hunter's Hill and neighborhood, consisting of seventeen members, one Elder, one Priest, one Teacher.

Elder Amos Fielding, represented the church at Bolton, consisting of sixty members, one Elder, two Priests, two Teachers. Elder Amos Fielding represented the church at Heskin, consisting of three members, one Elder. Elder Amos Fielding represented the Church at Radcliff, consisting of ten members. Elder Withnal represented the

the members took their place according to age. This arrangement brought Thomas B. Marsh to the head of the quorum, and made him President. After this first arrangement, however, the members of the quorum took their place in it according to seniority of ordination, not of age. (See Volume II this work, pp. 219, 220, and notes). Brigham Young was the second man ordained into the quorum, Lyman E. Johnson being the first. As Lyman E. Johnson was excommunicated from the Church at Far West in 1838, Brigham Young was President of the Twelve by virtue of his seniority of ordination as well as by the choice of his brethren. Indeed the choice of the brethren mentioned in the text can only be regarded as an act recognizing the fact of his presidency by virtue of his seniority of ordination. It may be of interest to remark also, that at the time there was but one man in the quorum President Young's senior by age, namely, John E. Page, born in 1799, and ordained an Apostle in 1838.

church at Whittle, consisting of eighteen members, one Elder, four Priests. Elder Francis Clark represented the church at Ribchester, consisting of twenty-five members, two Elders, one Priest. Elder Thomas Richardson represented the church at Burnley, consisting of twenty four members, generally in good standing, one Priest, one Teacher. Elder Francis Moon represented the church at Blackburn, consisting of fifteen members, one Priest. Elder James Smithies represented the church at Chardgley and Thornley, consisting of twenty-nine members, two Elders, one Priest, one Teacher, one Deacon.

Priest John Ellison represented the church at Waddington, consisting of fifty members, two Priests, two Teachers, one Deacon. Elder Thomas Smith represented the church at Clitheroe, consisting of twenty-seven members, one Elder, three Priests. Elder Thomas Smith represented the church at Catburn, consisting of eighty-four members, one Elder, two Priests, two Teachers, one Deacon. Elder Thomas Smith represented the church at Downham, consisting of twenty members, one Teacher, one Deacon.

Elder Thomas Smith represented the church at Gridleton, consisting of five members. Elder William Clayton represented the church at Manchester, consisting of two hundred and forty member, three Elders, five Priests, four Teachers, one Deacon. Elder William Clayton represented the church at Stockport, consisting of forty members, one Priest, two Teachers, one Deacon. Elder William Clayton represented the church at Peover and Macclesfield, consisting of thirty members, three Priests. Elder William Clayton represented the church at Duckinfield, consisting of thirty members, one Priest. Elder William Clayton represented the church at Altrincham, consisting of eight members, one Priest, one Teacher. Elder William Clayton represented the church at Middlewich, consisting of six members.

Elder David Wilding represented the church at Bury and Elton, consisting of twelve members. Elder Wilford Woodruff represented the church in the Potteries, consisting of one hundred and one members, one Elder, two Priests, four Teachers, one Deacon. Elder Wilford Woodruff represented the church at Herefordshire, consisting of one hundred and sixty members, one Elder, two Priests; about forty of them were Methodist preachers of the United Brethren.

Elder John Taylor represented the church at Liverpool, consisting of twenty-eight members. Elder Joseph Fielding represented the church at Alston, Cumberland, consisting of forty members, two Elders, two Priests, two Teachers. Elder Willard Richards represented the church at Brampton, consisting of thirty members, one Elder, one Priest. Elder Willard Richards represented the church at Bedford, consisting of forty members, one Elder, one Priest. Elder Willard Richards represented the church at Scotland, consisting of twenty-one members, three Elders.

The meeting was then adjourned for one hour. The conference again assembled at half-past one o'clock. Meeting opened by prayer, and business commenced.

Elder John Moon represented the church at Layland Moss, consisting of six members, one Priest.

Elder Willard Richards having been previously ordained into the quorum of the Twelve, according to previous revelation, it was moved by Elder Young, and seconded by Elder Taylor, that Elder Hyrum Clark be appointed as a counselor to Elder Fielding, in the place of Elder Richards; carried unanimously.

Moved by Elder Fielding, seconded by Elder Young, that a hymn-book should be published; carried. Moved and seconded, that the publishing of the hymn-book shall be done by the direction of the Twelve; carried.

Moved and seconded that a monthly periodical shall be published under the direction and superintendence of the Twelve, for the benefit and information of the Church, as soon as a sufficient number of subscribers shall be obtained; carried.

Moved and seconded that Brother John Blazard, of Samsbury, be ordained to the office of a Priest; carried.

Moved and seconded that Brother James Cobridge, of Thornley, be ordained to the office of Priest; carried.

Elder Kimball then laid before the conference the importance and propriety of ordaining a Patriarch to bestow patriarchal blessings on the fatherless, &c.; referred to the Twelve, whose business it is to select one, and ordain him according to the directions of the Spirit.

After various remarks and addresses given by the Elders, President Fielding and his counselors proceeded to ordain Brothers Blazard and Cobridge to their offices, as stated above.

Elder Kimball then called upon the clerk to read over the minutes of the conference, which being done, they were received by the unanimous voice of the conference.

Moved by Elder Young, and seconded by Elder Parley P. Pratt, that this conference be adjourned until the 6th of July next, to be held in Preston, at 10 o'clock a. m.; carried. Meeting then adjourned.

H. C. KIMBALL, President.
WM. CLAYTON, Clerk.

Council Meeting of the Twelve in England—Hymn-Book and the "Millennial Star" Projected.

The Council met pursuant to adjournment, April 16th, 1840. The number of the quorum the same as on the 14th.

Moved by Elder Young, seconded by Elder Taylor, that Elder Parley P. Pratt be chosen as the editor of the monthly periodical for the Church.

Moved by Elder Kimball, seconded by Parley P. Pratt, that a committee of three be appointed to make a selection of hymns.

Moved by Elder Orson Pratt, and seconded by Elder Wilford Woodruff, that Elders Brigham Young, Parley P. Pratt, and John Taylor form the committee for that purpose.

Moved by Elder Willard Richards, seconded by Elder George A. Smith, that the name of the paper or periodical be the *Latter-day Saints Millennial Star.*

Moved by Elder Brigham Young, seconded by Elder Orson Pratt, that the size of the paper, its plan, and price be left at the disposal of the editor.

Moved by Elder Brigham Young, seconded by Elder Heber C. Kimball, that the Saints receive a recommend to the Church in America to move in small or large bodies, inasmuch as they desire to emigrate to that new country.

Moved by Elder Brigham Young, seconded by Parley P. Pratt, that we recommend no one to go to America that has money, without assisting the poor according to our counsel from time to time.

Moved by Elder John Taylor, seconded by Elder Parley P. Pratt, that the copyright of the Book of Doctrine and Covenants and the Book of Mormon be secured as quick as possible.

Moved by Elder Woodruff, seconded by Elder Willard Richards, that Elders Brigham Young, Heber C. Kimball, and Parley P. Pratt be the committee to secure the copyright.

Moved by Elder Heber C. Kimball, and seconded by Elder Willard Richards, that Elder Peter Melling be ordained an evangelical minister [Patriarch] in Preston.

Moved by Elder Heber C. Kimball, that the Twelve meet here on the 6th of July next, seconded by Elder Wilford Woodruff; and carried.

Moved by Elder Willard Richards, and seconded by Elder Wilford Woodruff, that the editor of the periodical keep an account of all the receipts and expenditures connected with the printing, general expense, &c., and the books at all times be open for the inspection of the Council.

The above resolutions were unanimously adopted. The conference closed by prayer.

JOHN TAYLOR, Clerk.

Letter of Brigham Young to the Prophet.

To President Joseph Smith and Counselors:

DEAR BRETHREN:—You no doubt will have the perusal of this letter, and minutes of our conference; this will give you an idea of what we are doing in this country. If you see anything in or about the whole affair, that is not right, I ask, in the name of the Lord Jesus Christ, that you would make known unto us the mind of the Lord, and His will concerning us. I believe that I am as willing to do the will of the Lord, and take counsel of my brethren, and be a servant of the Church, as ever I was in my life; but I can tell you, I would like to be with my old friends; I like new friends, but I cannot part with my old ones for them.

Concerning the hymn-book—when we arrived here, we found the brethren had laid by their old hymn-books, and they wanted new ones; for the Bible, religion, and all is new to them. When I came to learn more about carrying books into the states, or bringing them here, I found the duties were so high that we never should want to bring books from the states.

I request one favor of you, that is, a letter from you, that I may hear from my friends. I trust that I will remain your friend through life and in eternity. As ever. BRIGHAM YOUNG.

April 17.—This day the Twelve blessed and drank a bottle of wine at Penworthan, made by Mother Moon forty years before. Held a Council at her house in the evening, and ordained Peter Melling, Patriarch.*

The following is the aggregate number of churches, official and private members represented at the above Conferences, held in Preston, England: Elders, 36; Priests, 54; Teachers, 36; Deacons, 11; members, 1,686; all contained in 34 branches.

Saturday, 18.—Elders Young, Woodruff, and George A. Smith went to Burslem, and Elders Kimball and Richards to Chaidgley.

Sunday, 19.—The High Council voted to meet at my office every Saturday at two in the afternoon.

Mission Opened in Scotland—Orson Pratt.

Monday, 20.—Elders Young and Woodruff went to Wolverhampton. About this time Elder Orson Pratt went to Edinburgh, Scotland. Elder Taylor returned to Liverpool.

* Peter Melling was the first patriarch ordained in a foreign land, that is, a foreign land from America where the latter-day dispensation of the Gospel was opened. He was the son of Peter Melling, born in Preston, England, on the 14th day of February, 1787. He was, therefore, in his 64th year. He was evidently a man of great force of character, for he proceeded at once with great diligence and ability to fulfill the duties of his high office, all of which is evidenced by the record of the Patriarchial blessings given under his hands, and now in the Historian's office.

Letter of Robert Johnstone to Senator Young — Postoffice Name Changed from Commerce to Nauvoo.

POSTOFFICE DEPARTMENT, APPOINTMENT OFFICE,
21st April, 1840.

SIR:—I have the honor to inform you, that the Postmaster General has this day changed the name of the postoffice at Commerce, Hancock county, Illinois, to "Nauvoo," and appointed George W. Robinson postmaster thereof.

Very respectfully, your obedient servant,
ROBERT JOHNSTONE,
Second Assistant Postmaster General.

To the Hon. Richard M. Young, U. S. Senate.

Elders Young and Woodruff visited the old cathedral at Worcester on their way to Ledbury, where they arrived this night.

Letter of Senator Young to Judge Elias Higbee—Postoffice Name, etc.

WASHINGTON CITY, April 22, 1840.

DEAR SIR:—After your departure from this city, I received, under cover from the Reverend Sidney Rigdon, the petition mentioned by you, for the appointment of George W. Robinson as postmaster at Commerce. This petition I laid before the Honorable Robert Johstone, second assistant postmaster general, who has appointed Mr. Robinson as requested.

We found, on examination of the papers, and a letter from Dr. Galland, that there was a request that the name of the postoffice should be changed to that of Nauvoo, a Hebrew term, signifying a beautiful place. Mr. Johnstone, at my instance, has changed the name accordingly, in the supposition that it would be agreeable to the citizens concerned. Will you please advise with the Rev. Joseph Smith and others most immediately interested, and if the change of the name to Nauvoo should not be acceptable, it can on application be restored to that of Commerce.

I received a letter from Malcolm McGregor, Esq., postmaster at Carthage, a few days ago, in which he urges the necessity of having the mail carried twice a week, between Carthage and Nauvoo, and expresses the opinion that the additional expenses would not exceed one hundred and fifty dollars, as the mail is carried on horseback. I have brought the subject before the proper department as requested by Mr. McGregor, and hope to be able to succeed; although the Postoffice Department, owing to pecuniary embarrassment, is not in a situation to extend facilities at the present time.

Please present my respects to Mr. Smith, and accept for yourself my kindest regards.

Very respectfully, &c.,

RICHARD M. YOUNG.

To Judge Elias Higbee.

Wednesday, *22*.—Elders Young and Woodruff organized a branch of the Church at Frooms Hill, Herefordshire.

Thursday, *23*.—Elders Kimball and Richards returned to Preston. Elder Young visited at Moor Ends Cross, and 24th preached at Malvern Hill. Elder Kimball went to Eccleston and continued some days visiting the churches around Preston.

Saturday, *25*.—Elder Richards went to Manchester, found the *Prospectus* for the *Millennial Star* ready. Elder Young returned to Frooms Hill, and stayed at Brother John Benbow's till the 30th, preaching, and writing letters to his friends in America.

Wednesday, *29*.—Elders Hyde and Page were at Quincy, Illinois.

Elder Woodruff wrote as follows:

Letter of Wilford Woodruff to Don Carlos Smith—Success of Woodruff's Ministry.

LEDBURY, HEREFORDSHIRE, ENGLAND,
April 29, 1840.

Elders Ebenezer Robinson and Don Carlos Smith:

BRETHREN:—As Elder Young is writing, I am privileged with a space of a few lines: knowing that our friends are desirous to hear of the work of the Lord in this land, I make the following remarks concerning the mercy of God and my labors.

Since I last wrote you, (I wrote you a lengthy letter, dated February 27th, in which I gave you an account of my travels, voyage, and labors, from the time I left Montrose unto the date of my letter, which I trust you have received,) I continued laboring in Staffordshire until the first of March, when I felt it to be the will of the Lord that I should go more to the south part of England. I left the care of the Staffordshire church in the hands of Elder Turley, and traveled eighty miles south, in a region where the word had not been preached. I commenced preaching near Ledbury, Herefordshire; this is about forty miles from Bristol, forty from Birmingham, fourteen from Worcester, one hundred and twenty from London. As soon as I began to teach, many received my testimony. I there preached one month and five days, and baptized the superintendent of the church of the United Brethren, a branch of the Methodist church, and with him 45 preachers, mostly of the same order; and about 114 members, making 160 in all. This put into my hands, or under my care, more than forty established places of preaching, licensed according to law, including one or two chapels. This opened a large field for the spread of the work in this country.

Among the number baptized are some of most all churches and classes as well as preachers. There is one constable, and one clerk of the Church of England, with numbers of their members. But in the midst of my labors I received a letter stating that the Twelve had just arrived and wished me to come to Preston, and meet with them in conference. Consequently I traveled 160 miles to Preston, and was once more permitted to strike hands with my brethren from America, and sit in conference with them, the minutes of which you have.

After conference I returned to Herefordshire in company with Elder Brigham Young. We have again commenced our labors here, and there will be many baptized in this region. I have now more than 200 on my list, and scores are now waiting for an opportunity to receive the ordinance of baptism; and the work is progressing in all parts of this country where it is faithfully proclaimed. I understand that Elders Wright and Mulliner are opening some permanent doors in Scotland; and we have many calls through many parts of this country, even more than we are able to fill.

I desire the prayers of the Saints; that I may have wisdom and grace according to my day, and do the work of God in meekness and humility.

WILFORD WOODRUFF.

Thursday, 30.—Elders Young, Woodruff, and Richards met at Elder Kington's, at Dymock.

Letter of Elders Hyde and Page to the Prophet—Plans for the Palestine Mission.

COLUMBUS, May 1, 1840.

President Smith:

SIR:—The mission upon which we are sent swells greater and greater. As there is a great work to be done in Germany, as manifested to us by the Spirit, the following plan has been suggested to us; viz., to write a set of lectures upon the faith and doctrine of our Church, giving a brief history of the coming forth of the Book of Mormon, and an account of its contents in as clear and plain a style as possible; together with the outlines and organization and government of the Church of Latter-day Saints, drawn from the Doctrine and Covenants with all the wisdom and care possible; and get the same translated into German, and publish it when we arrive in Germany, and scatter it through the German empire. Is this correct? Should we consider it necessary to translate the entire Book of Mormon into German, and Doctrine and Covenants too, are we or are we not at liberty to do so? Should we deem it necessary to publish an edition of hymn-books in any country, are we at liberty to do it? The fact is, we need such works, and we cannot get them from the church here; and if we could, we could not well carry them with us, at least in any quantity.

We feel that we are acting under the direction of the Presidency of the Church; and the reason that we make these inquiries, is, that we do not wish to step beyond our limits, or bring ourselves into a snare and dishonor by taking liberties that are not ours. We feel that all our exertions and interests shall become subservient to building up the Kingdom of God. We wish to be co-workers with you and with the Spirit of the Lord. We did not converse so much upon these literary works as we should have done before we left. The fact is, we did not begin to see the greatness of our mission before we left home; our minds were in a nutshell.

It seems to us that we should spread this work among all people, languages and tongues, so far as possible; and gather up all jewels among the Jews besides. Who is sufficient for these things?

As agents for the Church abroad, and as co-workers with yourself, in spreading this kingdom to the remotest corners of the earth, are we at liberty to translate and publish any works that we may think necessary, or that the circumstances in which we are placed seem to require whether original, or works published by the Church? If we are not at liberty to take this wide range, please tell us how far we may go.

We are setting this great work before the people as an inducement to them to help us. If we are setting our standard too high, a word from you will bring it down. We have held a two days' meeting in this place; but in consequence of continual rains, which swelled the creeks so high, the people could not get to us. The meeting was four miles from Columbus; one only baptized.

We have now an opportunity to ride as far east as Indiana, beyond the metropolis, and have the privilege to stop and preach by the way. Will you write to us at Cincinnati, and much oblige

Your brethren in the Kingdom of God,

ORSON HYDE,
JOHN E. PAGE.

P. S.—Will you please send word to Marinda, that I want her to write to me at Cincinnati, Ohio. Please bear it in mind and oblige thy friend.

O. H.

Friday, May 1.—The town of Baji, in the county of Baes, on the river Danube, was almost totally destroyed by fire; about two thousand houses were burnt, with the palace, several churches, and all the great corn magazines; leaving about sixteen thousand inhabitants destitute. The plague is raging in the East—at Silistria, Broussa, Alexandria, Aleppo, &c.; and wars and rumors of wars in Spain, Mexico and South American governments; French and Arabs in Africa, Russia and Circassia, Egypt, England and the East Indies, and the Canada Revolution; all betoken the fulfillment of prophecy.

Commotions in the World.

Thursday, 7.—The city of Natchez was this day to a great extent destroyed, almost in a moment, by a whirlwind, storm and tempest. It is reported that sixty boats sunk, houses and churches blown to atoms, more than three hundred persons killed, and $5,000,000 of property destroyed; nearly the whole country on the Mississippi for 1,100 miles from its mouth is under water.

Letter of Brigham Young to the Prophet—Affairs of the British Mission.

LUGWARDINE, HEREFORDSHIRE, ENGLAND,
May 7, 1840.

BROTHER JOSEPH SMITH: — Through the mercy of our heavenly Father, I am alive and in pretty good health; better than I should have been, had I remained in America. I trust that you and family are well, and I ask my heavenly Father that we may live forever; but not to be chased about by mobs, but live to enjoy each other's society in peace. I long to see the faces of my friends again in that country once more. It is better for me to be here, because the Lord has called me to this great work, but it is hard for me to be parted from my old friends whom I have proved to be willing to lay down their lives for each other. I feel as though the Lord would grant me the privilege of sometime seeing my old friends in America. Give my best wishes to your wife. I remember her in my prayers, and also Father and Mother Smith. I remember the time when I first saw Mother Smith, and the trials she had when the work of the Lord first commenced in her family. I beg to be remembered to Brother Rigdon and family, also to Brother Hyrum and family, and to all the faithful in Christ.

The brethren that have come from America are all well and doing well. I want to ask some questions. Shall we print the Book of of Mormon in this country immediately? They are calling for it from every quarter. The duties are so high on books, we need not think of bringing them from America. Another question, is the Book of Doctrine and Covenants to be printed just as it is now, to go to the nations of the earth; and shall we give it to them as quickly as we can? Or what shall be do? Will the Twelve have to be together to do business as a quorum? Or shall they do business in the name of the Church? Why I ask this is for my own satisfaction; if the Lord has a word for us, for one I am willing to receive it.

I wish you to write as soon as you receive this, and let me know about the Book of Mormon, whether we shall proceed to publish it immediately or not, or whether we shall do according to our feelings. If I should act according to my feelings, I should hand the Book of Mormon to this people as quickly as I could. The people are very different in this country from what the Americans are. They say it cannot be possible that men should leave their homes and come so far, unless they were truly the servants of the Lord; they do not seem to understand argument; simple testimony is enough for them; they beg and plead for the Book of Mormon, and were it not for the priests, the people would follow after the servants of the Lord and inquire what they should do to be saved. The priests feel just as they did in the days of the Savior. If they let "this sect alone, all men will believe on them, and the Romans will come and take away our place and nation."

I wish you would tell me how Cousin Lemuel gets along with his business, and all the boys on the half-breed track, and the whole breed. I think a great deal about our friends, families, and possessions. I look for the time when the Lord will speak so that the hearts of the rebellious will be pierced. You will remember the words of the Savior to His disciples; He says, to you is given to know the mysteries of the kingdom of heaven, but to them that are without, all things are in parables.

The brethren here are very anxious to emigrate to that country; some want to come this fall: where shall they go? Their customs are different from ours, and it would be more pleasant for them to settle by themselves. Almost without exception it is the poor that receive the Gospel. I think there will be some [who will go] over this fall. My counsel to such as intend to go is, that they go to the western states, where they can live among the farmers and wait for orders from the authorities of the Church, and all will be well.

You must excuse my bad writing. I have only caught at ideas. I want to know about the brethren's coming over this fall. I think some of us will come. We shall send our papers to you, and to a number of the rest of the brethren. I wish you would have the goodness to give me a pretty general knowledge of the Church, for I feel for them, and pray for them continually. We need help very much in this country. One American can do more here than a number of Elders who are raised up here by the preaching of the Gospel. We have sent for some to come. I wish you would encourage them to come as quickly as they can.

If we could go four ways at a time, we could not fill all the calls we have for preaching. I shall expect such counsel from you about the Elders coming as you shall think necessary for us and them to have. I wish to know what the prospect is about the government's doing anything for us. When we left New York I thought there was but a poor chance for us.

Concerning calling Seventies and sending them to other countries, I should like to know whether it would be proper to ordain them to that office or not while here. Had any of us better come back this fall? I suppose that some that come over with us will return; Brothers Clark and Hedlock, and Brother Turley if the latter gets at liberty. I suppose you have heard that he is in prison. He has been there ever since my arrival in England, and how long he will remain the the Lord only knows. He was put there through the influence of a priest, as nigh as I can learn, for some old pretended claim, but no one can find out what that claim is.

I have just met with Brother Woodruff; he tells me that the Church in this region of country numbers between three and four hundred; it is only about three months since Brother Woodruff commenced to labor here. I have just received a letter from Brother Turley, which states he expects to leave his place the next day. Brother Woodruff sends his respects.

I am as ever,

BRIGHAM YOUNG.

Release of Elder Turley from prison.

Saturday, 9.—Elder Theodore Turley was released from Stafford jail, where he had been confined since his arrest on the 16th of March last, at the instigation of John Jones, a Methodist preacher, on the pretense of a claim arising under a partnership with another man fifteen years ago, before he left England; but the real object was to stop his preaching. He was without provisions for several days, but the poor Saints in the Potteries, on learning his condition, supplied his wants, some of the sisters actually walking upwards of twenty miles to relieve him. He preached several times to the debtors, was visited by Elders Woodruff, Richards, George A. Smith, A. Cordon, and others, and was dismissed from prison on his persecutors ascertaining their conduct was about to be exposed. This rather encouraged than disheartened the Elders, as I had told them on their leaving Nauvoo, to be of good courage, for some of them would have to look through grates before their return.

Thursday, *14*.—The papers of this date report that the island of Ternate* was nearly ruined by earthquakes on the 14th and 15th February, 1840.

Letter of the Prophet to Elders Hyde and Page—Palestine Mission Considered.

NAUVOO, HANCOCK COUNTY, ILLINOIS,
May 14th, 1840.

To Orson Hyde and John E. Page:

DEAR BRETHREN:—I am happy in being informed by your letter that your mission swells "larger and larger." It is a great and important mission, and one that is worthy those intelligences who surround the throne of Jehovah to be engaged in. Although it appears great at present, yet you have but just begun to realize the greatness, the extent and glory of the same. If there is anything calculated to interest the mind of the Saints, to awaken in them the finest sensibilities, and arouse them to enterprise and exertion, surely it is the great and precious promises made by our heavenly Father to the children of Abraham; and those engaged in seeking the outcasts of Israel, and the dispersed of Judah, cannot fail to enjoy the Spirit of the Lord and have the choicest blessings of Heaven rest upon them in copious effusions.

Brethren, you are in the pathway to eternal fame, and immortal glory: and inasmuch as you feel interested for the covenant people of the Lord, the God of their fathers shall bless you. Do not be discouraged on ac-

*Ternate is a small island in the Moluccas, west of Jilolo, in the Dutch East Indies.

count of the greatness of the work; only be humble and faithful, and then you can say, "What art thou, O great mountain! before Zerubbabel shalt thou be brought down." He who scattered Israel has promised to gather them; therefore inasmuch as you are to be instrumental in this great work, He will endow you with power, wisdom, might, and intelligence, and every qualification necessary; while your minds will expand wider and wider, until you can circumscribe the earth and the heavens, reach forth into eternity, and contemplate the mighty acts of Jehovah in all their variety and glory.

In answer to your inquiries respecting the translation and publication of the Book of Mormon, hymn-book, history of the Church, &c., &c., I would say that I entirely approve of the same, and give my consent, with the exception of the hymn-book, as a new edition, containing a greater variety of hymns, will be shortly published or printed in this place, which I think will be a standard work. As soon as it is printed, you shall have some sent to you, which you may get translated, and printed into any language you please.

Should we not be able to send some to you, and there should be a great call for hymn books where you may be, then I should have no objection to your publishing the present one. Were you to publish the Book of Mormon, Doctrine and Covenants, or hymn-book, I desire the copyrights of the same to be secured in my name.

With respect to publishing any other work, either original, or those which have been published before, you will be governed by circumstances; if you think necessary to do so, I shall have no objection whatever. It will be well to study plainness and simplicity in whatever you publish, "for my soul delighteth in plainness."

I feel much pleased with the spirit of your letter—and be assured, dear brethren, of my hearty co-operation, and my prayers for your welfare and success. In answer to your inquiry in a former letter, relative to the duty of the Seventies in regulating churches, &c., I say that the duties of the Seventies are more particularly to preach the Gospel, and build up churches, rather than regulate them, that a High Priest may take charge of them. If a High Priest should be remiss in his duty, and should lead, or suffer the church to be led astray, depart from the ordinances of the Lord, then it is the duty of one of the Seventies, acting under the special direction of the Twelve, being duly commissioned by them with their delegated authority, to go to the church, and if agreeable to a majority of the members of said church, to proceed to regulate and put in order the same; otherwise, he can have no authority to act.

JOSEPH SMITH, JUN.

Friday, 15.

Letter of Willard Richards to the Editor of the Millennial Star—Reporting Labors.

LEDBURY, HEREFORDSHIRE, May 15th, 1840.

To the Editor of the Millennial Star:

BELOVED BROTHER:—Two weeks ago this day, I parted with Brothers Young and Woodruff in this place, taking different locations in this part of the vineyard, originally opened by Brother Woodruff, and after visiting various places in Herefordshire, Worcestershire, and Gloucestershire, preaching daily, talking night and day, and administering the ordinances of the Gospel as directed by the Spirit, we have again this day found ourselves together, and Elder Kington in our midst (he is devoted wholly to the ministry). By comparing minutes we find there have been in these two weeks about 112 baptized; 200 confirmed; 2 Elders, about 20 Priests, and 1 Teacher ordained; and the Church in these regions now numbers about 320. The branches are small, the brethren much scattered; consequently the field is so large that the reapers cannot call to each other from side to side, neither can they often see each other without a telescope.

There are many doors open which we cannot fill; calls for preaching on almost every hand, which we cannot answer. Oh! that the Saints would pray to the Lord of the harvest to send forth laborers!

I have this day received a letter from my sister in Massachusetts, giving me the intelligence of the death of my aged father. The work of the Lord is rolling forth in that part of the land, such intelligence as this from our native land makes our hearts rejoice, even in affliction.

Your brother in the everlasting covenant,

WILLARD RICHARDS.

CHAPTER VII.

FIRST FOREIGN PERIODICAL OF THE CHURCH, "THE MILLENNIAL STAR"—THE PROPHET SEEKS RELEASE FROM SECULAR RESPONSIBILITIES.

Sunday, May 17.—Elders Young, Woodruff, and Richards held conference with the Saints at Gadfield Elm Chapel.

Monday, 18.—The above Elders met the brethren at Elder Kington's, where they had a tea party, praying, singing, confirming, ordaining, and about twenty were baptized; thus they continued their labors from place to place, until Wednesday 20th, when they found themselves with one accord on the top of "the Herefordshire Beacon,"* and within the old fortification, when after prayer they expressed their feelings concerning the business of the Church, which were (as they had obtained money from Brother John Benbow, and other brethren for printing the hymn-book, and in part sufficient for the Book of Mormon) that Elder Young repair immediately to Manchester, and join his brethren previously appointed with him on a committee, for the printing of the hymn-book, and cause 3,000 copies to be issued without delay. Also that the same committee cause 3,000 copies of the Book of Mormon to be printed and completed with as little delay as possible, with an index affixed to the same, the form of the book to be determined by the committee. Their views were written and signed by Elder Willard Richards and Wilford Woodruff, when President Young left direct for Manchester. He saw George A. Smith, at the Potteries, who approved the "Beacon Conference."

The Beacon Hill Conference.

* One of the noted heights of the Black Mountains, running through the west part of Herefordshire.

Sunday, 24.—President Young met with the Church, and on Monday, 25th, visited the printers to inquire their prices, etc.

A Letter of Heber C. Kimball, et al., Recommending English Saints to the Bishop of the Church.

PRESTON, May 25, 1840.

To the Presidency, High Council and Bishop of the Church of Jesus Christ of Latter-day Saints at Commerce. We commend to your notice the brethren and sisters that have commendatory letters from us of this date, that you will do all that you consistently can for them, for I verily believe they have utmost confidence in you, and will receive with gratitude your advice and instruction, and cheerfully submit to the rules and regulations of the Church. They have our blessings, and we trust their subsequent conduct will entitle them to your blessings also, and the Church generally. We rejoice that we can say the work of God here is in a prosperous way. Yea, we rejoice greatly at the aspect of the times, expecting the time to be not far distant when the standard of truth will be conspicuously raised throughout this land. We have witnessed the flowing of the Saints towards Zion; the stream has begun, and we expect to see it continue running until it shall have drained the salt, or the light, from Babylon, when we hope to shout hosanna home.

Dear brethren, accept our love, and present it to the Church.

Your brethren in the new and everlasting covenant,

HEBER C. KIMBALL,
JOSEPH FIELDING,
WILLIAM CLAYTON.

Tuesday, 26.—Elder John Taylor arrived at Manchester, and on the 27th, Elder Kimball arrived. The committee on the hymn-book commenced and continued selecting hymns until the 30th, when Elders Young, Kimball and Taylor went to Liverpool, and preached on Sunday the 31st.

Death of Bishop Partridge.

Wednesday, 27.—Bishop Edward Partridge* died at Nauvoo, aged forty-six years. He lost his life in consequence of the Missouri persecutions, and he is one of that number whose blood will be required at their hands. His daughter, Harriet Pamela, died on the 16th of May, aged nineteen years.

* See Biographical Note, Vol. I, pp. 128-9.

The first number of *The Latter-day Saints' Millennial Star** was issued at Manchester, in pamphlet form of twenty-four pages. Edited by Parley P. Pratt. Price sixpence. Office 149 Oldham Road.

First Number of the *Millennial Star.*

Monday, June 1, 1840.—The Saints have already erected about two hundred and fifty-houses at Nauvoo, mostly block houses, a few framed, and many more are in course of construction.

The Gospel is spreading through the States, Canada, England, Scotland, and other places, with great rapidity.

* The *Millennial Star* was the first foreign publication of the Church. It was issued as a monthly, but afterwards more frequently, semi-monthly, and finally, and now for many years, a weekly. Its publication has been continuous from the time it was started until the present—1907. Also the *Star* has retained the general character imparted to it by its first publishers. "The *Millennial Star,*" said its Prospectus, "will stand aloof from the common political and commercial news of the day. Its columns will be devoted to the spread of the fulness of the Gospel—the restoration of the ancient principles of Christianity—the gathering of Israel—the rolling forth of the kingdom of God among the nations—the signs of the times—the fulfillment of prophecy—recording the judgments of God as they befall the nations whether signs in the heavens or in the earth, blood fire or vapor of smoke—in short, whatever is shown forth indicative of the coming of the 'Son of Man' and ushering in of his universal reign upon the earth. It will also contain letters from our numerous Elders who are abroad, preaching the word both in America and Europe containing news of their success in ministering the blessings of the glorious Gospel."

As an explanation of its title and mission, the editor in its first number also said: "The word *Millennium* signifies a thousand years, and in this sense of the word, may be applied to any [period of a] thousand years, whether under the reign of wickedness or righteousness. But the term *the Millennium,* is generally understood to apply to the particular thousand years which is mentioned in the Scriptures as the reign of peace—the great sabbath of creation, of which all the other sabbaths or jubilees seem to be but types. It is written that a 'thousand years is as one day, and one day as a thousand years with the Lord.' This being the case, then seven thousand years are seven days with the Lord, and the seventh, or last thousand years would, of course, be a sabbath or jubilee; a rest, a grand release from servitude and woe. * * * The curse will be taken from off the earth, and it will cease to bring forth thorns and thistles, and become fertile as it were a paradise, while sickness, premature death, and all their attendant train of pains and sorrows will scarce be known upon its face; thus peace, and joy, and truth, and love, and knowledge, and plenty, and glory, will cover the face of the earth as the waters do the sea. The tabernacle of God and his sanctuary will be with man, in the midst of the holy cities; and joy and gladness will fill the measure of their cup. Such then, is the *Great Millennium* of which our little '*Star*' would fain announce the dawn."

Elders Young and Kimball were engaged in blessing the brethren who were about to sail for America.

Wednesday, 3.—Elders Young and Taylor visited the printers in Liverpool and Elder Young preached on the Sunday following.

The First Company of Saints from England.

Saturday, 6.—Elder John Moon and a company of forty Saints, to wit., Hugh Moon, his mother and seven others of her family, Henry Moon (uncle of John Moon), Henry Moon, Francis Moon, William Sutton, William Sitgraves, Richard Eaves, Thomas Moss, Henry Moore, Nancy Ashworth, Richard Ainscough, and families, sailed in the ship *Britannia* from Liverpool for New York, being the first Saints that have sailed from England for Zion.

Monday, 8.—Elders Young and Taylor visited Cheshire, and on Tuesday, Manchester, and continued to select hymns.

Brigham Young's Dreams.

Elder Young dreamed of his family in health and want, also of the Church and people, and of a contention between two small companies in the west, one north, the other south—the north prevailing from time to time.

Minutes of the Conference Held at Gadfield Elm Chapel, in Worcestershire, England, June 14th, 1840.

The preachers and members of the Bran Green and Gadfield Elm Branch of the Froomes Hill Circuit, of the United Brethren met at the Gadfield Elm Chapel, Worcestershire, June 14th, 1840, pursuant to previous notice, when the meeting was called to order by Elder Thomas Kington. Elder Willard Richards was chosen president, and Elder Daniel Browett clerk for the meeting. The meeting was opened by prayer by Elder Wilford Woodruff. Remarks were then made by the president respecting the business of the day, and the necessary changes which must take place.

It was then moved by Elder Thomas Kington, seconded by Elder Daniel Browett that this meeting be hereafter known by the name of the "Bran Green and Gadfield Elm Conference of the Church of Jesus Christ of Latter-day Saints," organized and established by the will and commandment of God in the United States of America, on the 6th day of April,

A. D. 1830, this being the eighth day of the third month of the eleventh year of the rise of the Church. Carried unanimously.

[This motion was permitted to accommodate the feelings of the conference, who had all recently been baptized, but there is no such principle in existence, as to transform a church or conference of the world into a church or conference of Christ's fold by vote.]*

Moved by Elder Wilford Woodruff, seconded by Elder T. Kington, that William Jenkins be ordained an Elder; and William Coleman, Joseph Firkins, William Pitt and Robert Harris be ordained to the office of Priest; and that George Burton, James Palmer, and William Loveridge, be ordained Teachers; carried unanimously. Ordained under the hands of Elders Richards and Woodruff.

Moved by Elder Kington, seconded by Elder Woodruff, that Robert Clift, Priest, have the care of the church at Dymock; James Palmer, Priest, have the care of the church at Kilcott; John Hill, Priest, have the care of the church at Twigworth; William Coleman, Priest, have the care of the church at Bran Green; Thomas Brooks, Priest, have the care of the church at Ryton; John Smith, Priest, have the care of the church at Lime Street; Charles Hayes, Priest have the care of the church at Deerhurst; Thomas Smith, Priest, Assistant, have the care of the church at Deerhurst; John Vernon, Priest, have the care of the church at Apperley; William Bayliss, Priest, Assistant, have the care of the church at Apperley; John Arlick, Priest, have the care of the church at Norton; John Spires, Priest, have the care of the church at Leigh; John Davis, Priest, assistant, have the care of the church at Leigh; Thomas Oakley, Priest, have the care of the church at Gadfield Elm.

And that Elder Daniel Browett take charge of the churches on the south, and Elder William Jenkins on the north side, of the river Severn. Carried unanimously.

Moved by Elder Woodruff, and seconded by Elder Richards, that Elder Thomas Kington be the Presiding Elder over the Conference; carried. Meeting adjourned until two o'clock.

Conference met at two o'clock according to adjournment, and administered the sacrament to a large congregation of Saints, accompanied by many observations on many subjects by the President. Ten members were confirmed under the hands of Elders Woodruff and Kington. Remarks were made by the President respecting the "blessing of children." Seven children were then blessed under the hands of Elders Woodruff and Kington.

* The matter in brackets occurs in the Ms. History as also in the History as published in the *Millennial Star*, but it is evidently the comment of the Church Historians.

Moved by Elder Kington, seconded by Elder Woodruff, that Elder Daniel Browett represent this Conference to the general conference, at Manchester, on the 6th day of July next; carried. Moved and carried that the Clerk present to the Presiding Elder, T. Kington, also to the general conference, for safe keeping, a copy of the minutes of this conference.

The above minutes were then read and adopted, article by article, when it was moved by the President, and seconded by Elder Woodruff, that this conference be adjourned to the 13th day of September next at this place; carried unanimously.

Conference closed by prayer; after which the Elders and officers present met in council, and voted unanimously to establish a weekly council of the officers of said conference to be held alternately on the south and north sides of the river Severn, to commence at Leigh on the 25th inst.; and organized the same by appointing Elder Daniel Browett, president and John Hill, Priest, clerk, on the south side of the river; and also on the north side, by appointing Elder William Jenkins, president and John Smith, Priest, clerk; to assemble on the 3rd of July next, at Turkey Hall.

After passing many other votes of minor importance, accompanied by much instruction from Elders Richards and Woodruff, touching the duties of the several officers in their relations to each other, and the Church, the council adjourned. And it is worthy of remark, that no dissenting vote or voice was seen or heard during the day, either in conference or council.

WILLARD RICHARDS, President.
DANIEL BROWETT, Clerk.

Memorial of Joseph Smith, Jun., to the High Council of the Church of Jesus Christ of Latter-day Saints, June 18th, 1840.

The Memorial of Joseph Smith, Jun., respectfully represents—That after the members of the Church of Jesus Christ had been inhumanly as well as unconstitutionally expelled from their homes which they had secured to themselves in the state of Missouri, and although very much scattered and at considerable distance from each other, they found a resting place in the state of Illinois:—That after the escape of your Memorialist from his enemies, he (under the direction of the authorities of the Church) took such steps as has secured to the Church the present locations, viz., the town plot of Nauvoo and lands in the Iowa territory:—That in order to secure said locations, your Memorialist had to become responsible for the payment of the same, and had to use considerable exertion in order to commence a settlement, and a place of gathering for the Saints; and knowing from the genius of the constitution of the Church, and for the well-being of the Saints, that it was necessary that the constituted authorities of the Church might assemble together to act or to legislate for the good of the whole society and that the Saints might enjoy those privileges which they could not enjoy by being scattered so widely apart—your Memorialist was induced to exert himself to the utmost in order to bring about objects so necessary and so desirable to the Saints at large:—Under the then existing circumstances, your Memorialist had necessarily to engage in the temporalities of the Church, which he has had to attend to until the present time:—That your Memorialist feels it a duty which he owes to God, as well as to the Church, to give his attention more particularly to those things connected with the spiritual welfare of the Saints, (which have now become a great people,) so that they may be built up in their most holy faith, and go on to perfection:—That the Church have erected an office where he can attend to the affairs of the Church without distraction, he thinks, and verily believes, that the time has now come, when he should devote himself exclusively to those things which relate to the spiritualities of the Church, and commence the work of translating the Egyptian records, the Bible, and wait upon the Lord for such revelations as may be suited to the conditions and circumstances of the Church. And in order that he may be enabled to attend to those things, he prays your honorable body will relieve him from the anxiety and trouble necessarily attendant on business transactions, by appointing some one to take charge of the city plot, and attend to the business transactions which have heretofore rested upon your Memorialist: That should your Honors deem it proper to do so, your Memorialist would respectfully suggest that he would have no means of support whatever, and therefore would request that some one might be appointed to see that all his necessary wants may be provided for, as well as sufficient means or appropriations for a clerk or clerks, which he may require to aid him in his important work.

Your Memorialist would further represent, that as Elder H. G. Sherwood is conversant with the affairs of the city plot, he would be a suitable person to act as clerk in that business, and attend to the disposing of the remaining lots, &c.

Your Memorialist would take this opportunity of congratulating your honorable body on the peace and harmony which exist in the Church, and for the good feelings which seem to be manifested by all the Saints, and hopes that inasmuch as we devote ourselves for the good of the Church, and the spread of the kingdom, that the choicest blessings of heaven will be poured upon us, and that the glory of the Lord will overshadow the inheritances of the Saints.

JOSEPH SMITH, JUN.

Proceedings of the High Council on the Foregoing Memorial, June 20th, 1840.

The Council relieved President Joseph Smith, Jun., according to his request in the memorial, and appointed H. G. Sherwood to take charge of the city plot and to act as clerk in that business, and also to attend to the disposing of the remaining lots, and the business transactions which have rested upon him [Joseph Smith]. Alanson Ripley was appointed steward to see that all the necessary wants of the First Presidency be supplied, as well as to provide sufficient means or appropriations for a clerk or clerks to aid President Joseph Smith, Jun., in his important work.

HOSEA STOUT, Clerk.

Minutes of the Conference held at Stanley Hill, Castle Froome, Herefordshire, England, June 21st, 1840.

The preachers and members of the Froome's Hill Circuit of the United Brethren met at the house of Elder John Cheese, on Stanley Hill, Herefordshire, England, June 21, A. D. 1840, at ten a. m., according to previous notice; the meeting was called to order by Elder Thomas Kington; Elder Wilford Woodruff was chosen president, and Elder John Benbow, clerk of the meeting.

After prayer by Elder Richards, and remarks by the president concerning the business of the day, it was moved by Elder Thomas Kington, and seconded by Elder John Benbow, that [the several districts represented at] this meeting be hereafter known by the name of the "Froome's Hill Conference of the Church of Jesus Christ of Latter-day Saints," organized and established by the will and commandment of God, in the United States of America, on the 6th day of April, 1830, this being the 15th day of the third month of the eleventh year of the rise of the Church. Carried unanimously.

Moved by Elder Richards, seconded by Elder Kington, that Thomas Clark, Charles Price, James Hill, and Samuel Jones be ordained Elders; also that John James, Joseph Skinn, Henry Jones, James Baldwin, John Morgan, Samuel Badham, and John Dyer, be ordained Priests; also that Robert Hill, George Brooks, James Skinn, and James Watkins be ordained Teachers; carried unanimously; and they were ordained under the hands of Elders Woodruff and Richards.

Moved by Elder Kington, and seconded by Elders Woodruff and Richards, that John James, Priest, have the care of the church at Froome's Hill; John Parry, Priest, have the care of the church at Stanley Hill; James Burns, Priest, have the care of the church at Ridgway Cross; William Possons, Priest, have the care of the church at Moor-end Cross; Jonathan Lucy, Priest, have the care of the church at Caldwell; Thomas Jones, Priest, have the care of the church at Pale House; John Preece,

Priest, have the care of the church at Ledbury; Samuel Warren, Priest, have the care of the church at Keysend Street; James Baldwin, Priest, have the care of the church at Wind Point; George Allen, Priest, have the care of the church at Woferwood Common.

Rough Leasow, Birchwood, Tunbridge, and Dunsclose will all be united in one branch, called Dunsclose.

Samuel Badham, Priest, to have the care of the church at Dunsclose; Edward Phillips, Priest, to have care of the church at Ashfield and Crowcut; John Meeks, Priest, to have care of the church at Old Starridge; John Galley, Priest, to have care of the church at Hope Rough; Benj. Williams, Priest, to have care of the church at Shucknell Hill; John Powell, Priest, to have care of the church at Lugwardine; John Dyer, Priest, to have care of the church at Marden; William Evans, Priest, to have care of the church at Stokes Lane; John Fidoe, Priest, to have care of the church at Bishop Froome. Carried unanimously.

Moved by Elder Richards, and seconded by Elder Kington, that Elder Thomas Clark have charge of the churches at Dunsclose, Old Starridge, Ashfield, and Crowcut; that Elder Samuel Jones have charge of the churches at Keys-end Street, Wind Point, Colwell, Pale House, and Malvern Hill; that Elder Philip Green have charge of the churches at Shucknall Hill, Lugwardine, and Marden; that Elder John Cheese have charge of the churches at Stokes Lane, Woferwood Common, and Bishop Froome; that Elder Charles Price have charge of the churches at Ledbury, Moor-end Cross, and Ridgway Cross; that Elder James Hill have charge of the churches at Hope Rough and Stanley Hill; that Elder John Benbow have charge of the church at Froome's Hill. Carried unanimously.

Moved by the president, seconded by Elder Richards, that Elder Thomas Kington be the Presiding Elder over this conference.

After remarks by the president, the meeting adjourned till 2 o'clock p. m. During the recess ten persons were baptized.

Assembled at 2 o'clock according to adjournment, and administered the sacrament to several hundred Saints; after which twenty were confirmed, and twenty children blessed under the hands of Elders Woodruff and Richards, accompanied with instructions by the president, explanatory of the ordinance.

Moved by Elder Richards, seconded by the president, that Elder Thomas Kington represent this Conference to the general conference at Manchester on the 6th of July; carried. Moved and carried that the clerk of the conference present to the Presiding Elder, T. Lington, a copy of the minutes of this conference for safe keeping; also a copy to present to the general conference at Manchester. The minutes were then read and accepted. The president, followed by Elder Richards, then proceeded to give such instruction to the Saints concerning the order of the Church, and the several duties of the members, as the Spirit directed; and bore testimony to the multitude of the truth of the work; followed by Elder Kington; when it was moved by Elder Richards, seconded by the president, that this conference adjourn to the 21st September next, 10 o'clock a. m., at this place; carried.

After prayer and singing, the assembly dispersed, the Elders and officers went into council, when it was moved by Elder Richards, and seconded by Elder Kington, that we proceed to establish and organize monthly councils of the officers of the Froome's Hill Conference, to commence on Friday, the 3rd of July next, at half-past seven o'clock p. m., in the several divisions, respectively assigned to the different Elders, viz.—

Elder Thomas Clark, president, and James Meeks, clerk, Dunsclose; Elder Charles Price, president, Thomas Jenkins, clerk, Moor-end Cross; Samuel Jones, president, William Williams, clerk, Wind Point; James Hill, president, Joseph Pullen, clerk, Stanley Hill; Philip Green, president, Francis Burnett, clerk, Lugwardine; John Benbow, president, John Morgan, clerk, Froome's Hill; John Cheese, president, George Allen, clerk, Stoke's Lane. Carried.

Moved by Elder Richards, and seconded by Elder Kington, that a monthly general council of the officers of this conference be held at Stanley Hill, to commence on Friday, the 17th of July next, at half-past seven o'clock, p. m. Elder Thomas Kington, president, and Elder John Benbow, clerk. Carried unanimously.

The president then proceeded to explain the nature of the Priesthood, and the duties and privileges of the several officers, and gave such instruction as their situation required, followed by Elder Richards, who explained many important principles connected with the building up of the Kingdom.

The minutes of the council were then read and accepted when the council adjourned; and after singing "The Spirit of God," &c., the brethren separated, with feelings of gratitude and thanksgiving, that God had been with His people, and that the spirit of union and love had prevailed in all the deliberations of the day.

WILFORD WOODRUFF, President.
JOHN BENBOW, Clerk.

REMARKS—The different branches in this region are so scattered, that it has not been possible to ascertain the number of members connected with each individual church; but connected with the Bran Green and Gadfield Elm, and the Froome's Hill conferences, together with a small branch of Little Garway of twelve members, one Priest, and one Teacher, are thirty-three churches, five hundred and thirty-four members, seventy-five officers, viz., ten Elders, fifty-two priests, and thirteen teachers. And for the comforting of the Saints, and with heart-felt gratitude to our heavenly Father, we would say that it is less than four months since the fulness of the Gospel was first preached in this region; which is a proof that God is beginning to make a short work in these last days.

WILFORD WOODRUFF.

June 21.—The Saints hired the Carpenters' Hall in Manchester, which is large enough to accommodate ten or fifteen hundred hearers, for five hundred dollars a year, payable by contribution, and Elders Young and Pratt preached therein this day for the first time.

Carpenters' Hall.

Monday, 22.—Elder Young went to Liverpool to see about printing the Book of Mormon, and returned to Manchester on the 26th; and on Sunday, 28th, preached in Carpenters' Hall.

June 27.—High Council met at my office.

Minutes of the High Council.

Alanson Ripley states to the council that he was authorized to inform them that President Joseph Smith, Jun., had vetoed* the proceedings of the Council of the 20th June, in relation to his Memorial. Laid over for hearing until Friday next.

HOSEA STOUT, Clerk.

Letter of William W. Phelps—Confessing Errors committed in Missouri.

DAYTON, OHIO, June 29, 1840.

BROTHER JOSEPH:—I am alive, and with the help of God I mean to live still. I am as the prodigal son, though I never doubt or disbelieve the fulness of the Gospel. I have been greatly abused and humbled, and I blessed the God of Israel when I lately read your prophetic blessing on my head, as follows:

"The Lord will chasten him because he taketh honor to himself, and when his soul is greatly humbled he will forsake the evil. Then shall

*By reference to the minutes of the High Council which took into consideration the Prophet's "Memorial" it is evident that they failed to grasp the importance of the subjects presented to them, and made such disposition of them as was neither in keeping with the dignity of the Prophet or the weight of the matters on which they acted—hence the "veto," or dissatisfaction with the Council's action—See p. 144 for the conclusion of the matter.

the light of the Lord break upon him as at noonday and in him shall be no darkness," &c.

I have seen the folly of my way, and I tremble at the gulf I have passed. So it is, and why I know not. I prayed and God answered, but what could I do? Says I, "I will repent and live, and ask my old brethren to forgive me, and though they chasten me to death, yet I will die with them, for their God is my God. The least place with them is enough for me, yea, it is bigger and better than all Babylon." Then I dreamed that I was in a large house with many mansions, with you and Hyrum and Sidney, and when it was said, "Supper must be made ready," by one of the cooks, I saw no meat, but you said there was pleanty, and you showed me much, and as good as I ever saw; and while cutting to cook, your heart and mine beat within us, and we took each other's hand and cried for joy, and I awoke and took courage.

I know my situation, you know it, and God knows it, and I want to be saved if my friends will help me. Like the captain that was cast away on a desert island; when he got off he went to sea again, and made his fortune the next time, so let my lot be. I have done wrong and I am sorry. The beam is in my own eye. I have not walked along with my friends according to my holy anointing. I ask forgiveness in the name of Jesus Christ of all the Saints, for I will do right, God helping me. I want your fellowship; if you cannot grant that, grant me your peace and friendship, for we are brethren, and our communion used to be sweet, and whenever the Lord brings us together again, I will make all the satisfaction on every point that Saints or God can require. Amen.*

W. W. PHELPS.

Letter of Elders Orson Hyde and John E. Page to Presidents Joseph Smith, Hyrum Smith, Sidney Rigdon, Pleading for William W. Phelps.

DEAR BROTHER:—We have been in this place a few days, and have preached faithfully, a very great prospect of some able and influential men embracing the faith in this place. We have moved along slowly, but have left a sealing testimony. Baptized a considerable number. We shall write again more particularly as soon as we learn the result of our labors here. We are well and in good spirits through the favor of the Lord.

Brother Phelps requests us to write a few lines in his letter, and we cheerfully embrace the opportunity. Brother Phelps says he wants to

* For William W. Phelps' troubles in the Church, which brought him to this great sorrow and repentance, see Vol. III, pp. 3, 7, 56, 358, 359, 360 and notes.

live, but we do not feel ourselves authorized to act upon his case, but have recommended him to you; but he says his poverty will not allow him to visit you in person, at this time, and we think he tells the truth. We therefore advise him to write, which he has done.

He tells us verbally that he is willing to make any sacrifice to procure your fellowship, life not excepted, yet reposing that confidence in your magnanimity that you will take no advantage of this open and frank confession. If he can obtain your fellowship he wants to come to Commerce as soon as he can. But if he cannot be received into the fellowship of the Church, he must do the best he can in banishment and exile.

Brethren, with you are the keys of the Kingdom; to you is power given to "exert your clemency, or display your vengeance." By the former you will save a soul from death, and hide a multitude of sins; by the latter, you will forever discourage a returning prodigal cause sorrow without benefit, pain without pleasure, [and the] ending [of Brother Phelps] in wretchedness and despair. But former experience teaches [us] that you are workmen in the art of saving souls; therefore with greater confidence do we recommend to your clemency and favorable consideration,the author [of the foregoing] and subject of this communication. "Whosoever will, let him take of the waters of life freely." Brother Phelps says he will, and so far as we are concerned we say he may.

In the bonds of the covenant,

ORSON HYDE,
JOHN E. PAGE.

The Committee of the Twelve in England finished the collection of hymns and prepared the index for the press; and on the 30th Elders Kimball and Richards arrived at Manchester.

Wednesday, July 1, 1840.—Elders Wilford Woodruff and George A. Smith arrived at Manchester from the Potteries.

July 2.

Minutes of a meeting of the Crooked Creek Branch of the Church.

At a meeting of the Saints of Crooked Creek Branch, on the 2nd of July, 1840, to take into consideration the propriety of having a Stake of Zion appointed or located somewhere in the bounds of this branch, Brother John Hicks was called to the chair. Meeting was opened by prayer, after which several remarks were made, and the following resolutions were passed:

Resolved: That it be our wishes that a Stake of Zion be appointed or located within the bounds of this Branch, provided it should meet the minds of the First Presidency of this Church.

Resolved: That a committee of three be appointed to ascertain the mind of the First Presidency and report to the Branch.

Resolved: That Joseph Holebrook, Nathaniel Frampton, and John Hicks compose said committee.

It was ascertained that there were about 2,525 acres of land owned by the brethren, and wherever the Stake should be appointed the lands should be donated or purchased for a very small compensation, and that there are one hundred and twelve members belonging to this Branch.

Resolved: That we meet on Thursday next, at one o'clock, p. m., to receive the report of the committee,

Resolved: That the proceedings of this meeting be signed by the president and clerk.

JOHN A. HICKS, President.
WILLIAM WHITEMAN, Clerk.

Friday, 3.—High Council met at my office.

Minutes of High Council at Nauvoo.

The subject of the Memorial of President Joseph Smith, Jun., was brought up for a rehearing, according to the decision of the last Council (June 27) when the following resolutions were entered into:

1st. *Resolved:* That we feel perfectly satisfied with the course taken by Joseph Smith, Jun., and feel a disposition, as far as it is in our power, to assist him, so as to relieve him from the temporalities of the Church, in order that he may devote his time more particularly to the spiritualities of the same, believing by so doing we shall promote the good of the whole Church. But as he (Joseph Smith, Jun.) is held responsible for the payment of the city plot, and knowing no way to relieve him from the responsibility at present, we would request of him to act as treasurer for the city plot and to whom [i.e., President Smith] those persons whom we may appoint to make sales of lots and attend to the business affairs of the Church may at all times be responsible, and make true and correct returns of all their proceedings, as well as to account for all monies, properties, etc., which may come into their hands. Therefore

Resolved: That Elder Henry G. Sherwood act as Clerk for the same. That Bishop Alanson Ripley be appointed to provide for the wants of the Presidency, and make such appropriations to them, and to their clerk or clerks, which they may require.

Resolved: That the funds of the city plot shall not be taken to provide for the Presidency or clerks, but that the Bishops be instructed to raise funds from other sources to meet calls made on them; and monies received for lots shall be deposited in the hands of the Treasurer to liquidate the debts of the city plot.

The resolutions of the Crooked Creek Branch of the 2nd inst., were taken into consideration by President Joseph Smith, Jun., and it was thought proper to establish a Stake on Crooked Creek, agreeably to the request of said Branch, and a letter was written to the brethren to that effect.

ROBERT B. THOMPSON, Scribe.

Reflections of the Prophet on the Action of Congress.

Since Congress has decided against us, the Lord has begun to vex this nation, and He will continue to do so except they repent; for they now stand guilty of murder, robbery and plunder, as a nation, because they have refused to protect their citizens, and to execute justice according to their own Constitution. A hailstorm has visited South Carolina; some of the stones are said to have measured nine inches in circumference, which swept the crops, killing some cattle. Insects are devouring crops on the high lands, where the floods of the country have not reached, and great commercial distress prevails everywhere.

CHAPTER VII.

IMPORTANT CONFERENCE OF THE CHURCH IN ENGLAND—KIDNAPPING OF BROWN AND BOYCE BY MISSOURIANS—ACTION OF THE CITIZENS OF NAUVOO.

Monday, July 6, 1840.

Conference of the Church in England.

A General Conference of the Church of Jesus Christ of Latter-day Saints was held in the Carpenter's Hall, Manchester, on the 6th day of July, 1840, it being the 1st day of the 4th month of the eleventh year of the Church, when the following officers of the traveling High Council were present, viz.: Elders Brigham Young, Parley P. Pratt, Wilford Woodruff, John Taylor, Willard Richards, Heber C. Kimball, and George A. Smith; other officers, viz.: High Priests 5, Elders 19, Priests 15, Teachers 11, and Deacons 3.

The meeting being called to order, a little after ten o'clock, by Elder William Clayton, it was moved by Elder Brigham Young, seconded by Elder Wilford Woodruff, that Elder Parley P. Pratt be chosen President of the conference,* which was carried unanimously. Elder William

* At the present time the above arrangement by which Elder Parley P. Pratt was chosen president of the conference, while Elder Brigham Young was his senior in the quorum of the Twelve Apostles, will seem somewhat out of order. Such procedure is recorded a number of times in the minutes of conferences and other gatherings in the early years of the Church's history; it is therefore proper to say that in those days the right to presidency by reason of seniority of standing in quorums and councils was not as well settled as it is now. Presidency throughout the councils and quorums of the Church is determined by well settled principles of seniority of ordination, and as soon as any of these organizations are called to order for business the president of the council or conference is determined by the seniority of standing in said organization without any formal action. In the above case the brethren may have been influenced by the fact that Elder Pratt was an older member of the Church than President Young. Also it appears in a subsequent paragraph that some charges were preferred by President Young against one of the Elders in the conference. This course may have been decided upon by the Apostles, who probably thought that it would not be best for the presiding officer over the conference to make such charges, hence Elder Pratt was chosen to preside and Elder Young left free to make the charges aforesaid.

Clayton was chosen clerk. The meeting was opened by singing, and prayer by the President.

Elder Brigham Young then proceeded to prefer charges against Elder T. Green, viz., first, for giving way to a false spirit; second, for abusing a young female, by accusing her, in a public meeting, of things which he could not prove; and third, for abuse to the house and congregation at Duckinfield, June 28th, 1840. The president then proceeded to ask Elder Green whether he was guilty of these charges, or not. He immediately pleaded guilty. After Elder Young had made extended remarks to the meeting, touching the conduct of Elder Green, he proposed that Elder Green go to those characters whom he had abused and insulted, and make confession to them as far as the offense extended, and then to be suspended from office for a season. The President then made remarks to the same effect, and put it to the vote of the meeting, viz., that Elder Green shall make confession, as stated above, and be suspended from office for a season. Carried.

The President then asked Elder Green if he was willing to make confession, he immediately agreed to do it the first opportunity. The meeting adjourned a little after twelve o'clock.

At two o'clock business commenced by singing and prayer, when the President called upon the officers to represent the different branches of the Church, which was done in the following order, viz.—

Branches Represented, &c.	Members.	Elders.	Priests.	Teachers.	Deacons.
The branch at Manchester represented by Elder William Clayton	280	3	5	5	1
" Preston " " Joseph Fielding	354	6	8	4	2
Elders Kington and Browett presented the minutes of the conference held in Herefordshire, which were read by Elder Wilford Woodruff, representing 33 branches of the Church	534	10	52	13	—
Elder Alfred Cordon read the minutes of the conference held at Hanley, Staffordshire, representing 7 branches of the Church .	168	4	13	6	2
The branch at Liverpool, represented by Elder John Taylor	78	1	3	2	—
Elder Joseph Fielding read the minutes of the Thornley conference					
The branches at Chaighley and Thornley, represented by Elder William Kay	30	3	2	1	1
The Branch at Ribchester, represented by Elder Francis Clark	22	2	—	1	—
" Waddington " John Ellison	58	—	2	2	1
" Clitheroe " Brother Lofthouse	35	1	3	1	—
" Chatburn " Elder John Bond	91	2	2	2	—
" Downham " John Spencer	25	—	1	—	—
" Grindleton " Elder Joseph Fielding	5	—	1	—	—
" Whitmore " J. Spencer	3	—	—	—	—
" Burnley " Elder H. C. Kimball	27	1	1	1	—
" Blackburn " "	17	—	1	-	—
Elder Reuben Hedlock read the minutes of the conference held at Paisley, Scotland, representing 5 branches of the Church .	106	6	5	3	2

Branches Represented, &c.		Members.	Elders.	Priests.	Teachers.	Deacons.
The Branch at Alston, represented by	Elder John Sanders	36	2	2	2	—
" Brampton "	"	36	1	1	—	—
" Longton "	Elder Bradshaw	54	2	4	2	—
" Penwortham "	Elder P. Melling	77	4	1	1	1
" Whittle "	Elder Richard Withnall	16	1	4	—	—
" Southport "	R. McBride	19	1	—	2	—
" Daubers Lane & Eccleston "	Elder Richard Withnall	42	—	1	3	—
" Hunter's Hill "	Richard Benson	26	1	1	1	—
" Bolton "	Elder David Wilding	61	1	2	2	—
" Bury and Elton "	"	12	—	—	—	—
" Ratcliff "	Elder Amos Fielding	11	—	—	—	—
" Bedford, &c. "	Elder Willard Richards	40	1	1	—	—
" Stockport "	Elder M. Littlewood	85	2	1	2	1
" Duckinfield "	Elder Henry Royle	41	1	1	—	—
" Macclesfield "	Samuel Heath	14	—	2	—	—
" Middlewich "	"	20	—	1	1	1
" Plover "	"	24	—	1	1	1
" Northwich "	William Berry	14	—	1	—	—
" Altrincham "	"	4	—	—	1	—
" Whitfield "	Walker Johnson	14	—	1	—	—
" Pendlebury "	Elder William Clayton	13	—	1	1	—
" Eccles "	"	5	—	—	—	—
" West Bromwich "	Elder Theodore Turley	16	—	1	1	—

After the officers had got through the representations, the President introduced the new hymn-book; and after suitable remarks had been made by him and Elders Young and Thomas Kington, the President asked the conference if they were satisfied with the labors of those who had made the selection, and if they received the book. The unanimous approbation of the meeting was immediately manifested.

By unanimous vote, Thomas Kington, Alfred Cordon, and Thomas Smith were ordained High Priests; John Albison, John Blezzard, William Berry, John Sanders, John Parkinson, James Worsley, and John Allen were ordained Elders; and Joseph Slinger, George Walker, John Smith, Robert Williams, William Black, John Melling, and John Swindlehurst were ordained Priests.

Elder Brigham Young then called upon those officers, whose circumstances would permit them to devote themselves entirely to the work of the ministry, and would volunteer so to do, to stand up—when the following names were taken, viz.: of the traveling High Council, Brigham Young, Heber C. Kimball, John Taylor, Wilford Woodruff, Willard Richards, and George A. Smith; other officers, namely, William Clayton, Reuben Hedlock, Hiram Clark, Theodore Turley, Joseph Fielding, Thomas Richardson, Amos Fielding, John Parkinson, John Wych, John Needham, Henry Royle, John Blezzard, D. Wilding, Charles Price, Joseph Knowles, Wm. Kay, Samuel Heath, Wm. Parr, R. McBride, and James Morgan.

Moved by Elder Richards, seconded by Elder Kimball, that Elder Peter Melling be appointed to preside over the following branches of the Church, namely—Preston, Longton, Penwortham, North Meols, and Southport: carried.

Moved by Elder Kimball, seconded by Elder Young, that Elder Richard Withnall be appointed to preside over the branches of the Church at Whittle, Daubers Lane, Chorley, Hunter's Hill, and Euxtonburgh: carried.

Moved by Elder Kimball, seconded by Elder Young, that Elder Thomas Smith be appointed to preside over the branches of the Church at Clitheroe, Chatburn, Downham, Chaighley, Grindleton, Whitmore, Burnley, Blackburn, Ribchester, and Thornley: carried.

Moved and seconded, that President Fielding and his counselors be set at liberty from the charge which they have sustained as a presidency, that they may have the privilege of more fully entering into the field of labor; and that their labors be accepted: carried.

Elders Young and Richards then proceeded to ordain those who had been nominated to their respective offices, after which the minutes were read and accepted.

The conference adjourned to the sixth of October next, to be held in the Carpenter's Hall, Manchester, at 10 o'clock, a. m.

Tuesday, 7.

A council of Church Officers, held at Manchester, England.

Pursuant to previous notice, a general council of the Church officers was held in the council room at the *Star* office, Manchester, on the 7th day of July, 1840. The meeting being opened by prayer by Elder Kimball, Elder Young began to speak concerning those officers who had volunteered to devote themselves wholly to the ministry; when it was moved and seconded that Brothers William Kay and Thomas Richardson go to Herefordshire, to labor in that region with Elder Kington: carried.

Moved by Elder Kimball, seconded by Elder Young, that Brothers Hiram Clark and Joseph Knowles go with Elder Hedlock to Scotland: carried.

Moved by Elder Kimball, seconded by Elder Young, that Brother Joseph Fielding go to Bedford: carried.

Moved by Elder Richards, seconded by Elder Kimball, that Brothers Amos Fielding and John Wych go to Newcastle-upon-Tyne: carried.

Moved by Elder Kimball, seconded by Elder Woodruff, that Brother David Wilding go to Garway, Herefordshire: carried.

Moved by Elder Young, seconded by Elder Woodruff, that Brothers William Clayton and John Needham go to Birmingham: carried.

Moved by Elder Richards, seconded by Elder Young, that Brother Henry Royle go to Sheffield: carried.

Moved by Elder Clayton, seconded by Elder Young, that Brother John Albiston take charge of the following Branches of the Church, namely—Duckinfield, Hyde, Woolley Hill, Ashton, and Staley Bridge: carried.

Moved by Elder Pratt, seconded by Elder Woodruff, that Brother William Parr go to Sandbach and Congleton: carried.

Moved by Elder Richards, seconded by Elder Pratt, that Brother Heath continue his labors in Macclesfield: carried.

Moved by Elder Richards, seconded by Elder Woodruff, that Brother John Blezzard go to Cornshaw: carried.

Moved by Elder Kimball, seconded by Elder Richards, that Brother Robert McBride go to Lancaster: carried.

Moved by Elder Richards, seconded by Elder Woodruff, that Brother James Morgan abide in his own neighborhood to labor with Elder David Wilding: carried.

Moved by Elder Pratt, seconded by Elder Woodruff, that Brother Price give up his business, and labor under the advice of Elder Kington as the way opens: carried.

Moved by Elder Richards, seconded by Elder Kimball, that Brother William Black go to Lisburn, Ireland, as the way opens: carried.

Moved by Elder Richards, seconded by Elder Smith, that Brother John Parkinson have a roving commission, so long as he keeps busy, and doing good: carried.

After Elder Young had addressed the meeting upon several important items, the meeting dismissed by blessing from Elder Young.

PARLEY P. PRATT, President.
WILLIAM CLAYTON, Clerk.

At this time Elders Orson Hyde and John E. Page were laboring in Ohio.

Thursday, 9.

Extract from Elder Woodruff's Letter to the Editor of the Millennial Star —Detailing Incidents of his Ministry.

I arrived at Froome's Hill, Castle Froome, Herefordshire, on the 4th of March, and was kindly entertained for the night by Mr. John Benbow, who received my testimony, and opened his door for meeting; and on the evening following, the 5th of March, for the first time I preached the fullness of the Gospel in that place to a small congregation, who manifested much interest in what they heard, and desired to inquire further into those things; and on the evening following I met a large number at Mr. Benbow's, and preached unto them the principles of the Gospel, namely, faith in Christ, repentance, and baptism for the remission of sins and the gift of the Holy Ghost by the laying on of hands; after which I administered the ordinance of baptism unto six persons, Mr. and Mrs. Benbow among the number. I also preached on Sunday the 8th and baptized seven, confirmed thirteen, and broke bread unto them. Several of those who were baptized were preachers of the order called the United Brethren.

The United Brethren formerly belonged to the Primitive Methodists, but had separated themselves from the body, and chose the name of the United Brethren. They had from forty to fifty preachers and about the same number of established places of meeting, including two chapels.

Mr. Thomas Kington was the superintendent of the church of the United Brethren, whose members numbered about four hundred in all, divided into small branches and scattered over an extent of country from fifteen to twenty miles. This people almost universally appeared willing to give heed to the exhortation of Solomon, to hear a matter before they judged or condemned. They opened their doors for me to preach, and searched the Scriptures daily to see if the things which I taught were true; and on finding that the word and spirit agreed and bore record of the truth of the fullness of the Everlasting Gospel, they embraced it with all their hearts, which has brought great joy and satisfaction to many souls in that region.

I continued preaching and baptizing daily; the congregations were large and generally attentive. I was soon privileged with an interview with Mr. Thomas Kington, the superintendent of the United Brethren, before whom I gave an account of the rise and progress of the Church of the Latter-day Saints, and bore testimony of the truth of the great work which God had set His hand to accomplish in these last days.

Mr. Kington received my testimony and sayings with candor; and carried the case before the Lord, made it a subject of prayer, and asked the Father in the name of Jesus Christ, if these things were true; and the Lord manifested the truth of it unto him, and he went forth and was baptized, he and all his household. I ordained him an Elder, and he went forth and began to preach the fullness of the Gospel.

I also baptized about forty preachers of the same order, and several others belonging unto other churches, and about one hundred and twenty members of the United Brethren, which opened about forty doors or preaching places, where the fullness of the Gospel would meet a welcome reception, and all this during the term of one month and five days.

On the 10th of April I took my departure from the Saints in Herefordshire and adjoining country, numbering about one hundred and sixty;

whom I left rejoicing in the fullness of the Gospel, and hundreds of others who were ready to be baptized as soon as a proper time and opportunity arrived. I arrived in Preston on the 13th, by way of Worcester, Wolverhampton, Burslem, and Manchester, a distance of about one hundred and seventy miles, visiting the churches by the way.

On my arrival in Preston, I was blessed with the happy privilege of once more greeting my brethren of the Traveling High Council and other Elders, and of sitting with them on the 14th, 15th, and 16th of April in the first council and general conference which they had ever held, as a quorum, in a foreign nation. After spending several days together, (during which time much business of importance was transacted for the Church,) it became necessary for us again to separate, in order to labor in different parts of the vineyard which were now open before us. I left Preston on the 17th, accompanied by Elder Brigham Young, and visited the churches by the way, until we arrived among the Saints in Herefordshire, who were anxiously looking for my return. In a few days we were joined in our labors by Elder Willard Richards. We took locations in different parts of this new field of labor, which extended through various places in Herefordshire, Worcestershire, and Gloucestershire.

We continued preaching, and baptizing, and administering in the ordinances of the Gospel daily, unto such as would receive our testimony, and obey the Gospel of Jesus Christ. Truth was mighty and prevailed; the work prospered, and multiplied on every hand, until several hundreds, including more than fifty preachers of various sects, were rejoicing in the fullness of the everlasting Gospel, and felt to praise God that they had lived to behold the day when the Lord had set His hand to prune His vineyard once more with a mighty pruning, and to establish the Gospel in its ancient purity again upon the face of the earth; and in many instances signs followed the believer, according to the promise of the Savior. The Spirit of God accompanied the preaching of the word to the hearts of men. Whole households, on hearing the word, have received it into good and honest hearts, and gone forth and received the ordinances of the Gospel; and frequently we have baptized from eight to twelve the first time of meeting with the people in new places, and preaching the word of God to them.

Elder Young labored with us about one month, during which time many were baptized, confirmed, and numbers ordained to preach the Gospel—and while the Saints were much edified, and their hearts made glad with the teaching and instruction by Elder Young, I also obtained much benefit myself by enjoying his society, sitting under his instruction, and sharing in his counsel.

As it became necessary for Elder Young to return to Manchester, to assist in preparing a collection of hymns, and other matters, he took the parting hand with us on the 20th of May; and Elders Richards and myself continued our labors in the vineyard, in connection with Elder Kington, who had given himself wholly to the work of the ministry.

The Lord still continued to bless our labors, and added daily unto the Church. New doors were opening on every hand; and multiplicity of calls constantly reached our ears, many of which we could not answer for the want of laborers. Notwithstanding there were about fifty ordained Elders and Priests in this part of the vineyard, yet there were equally as many places for preaching to be attended to upon the Sabbath day. Thus we continued our labors in this region until the time drew near for the general conference in Manchester on the 6th of July.

But before leaving the Saints, we considered it wisdom to set in order the church, and organize them into branches and conferences, that they might be properly represented before the general conference. Therefore we held two conferences with the Saints before we took our departure from them. The first was held at the Gadfield Elm Chapel, Worcestershire, on the 14th of June, at which time we organized twelve branches, and transacted such business as the occasion required. The second conference was held at Stanley Hill, Herefordshire, on the 21st of June, twenty branches of the Church were organized. The minutes of the above-named conferences I present you for publication, if you think proper.

On the day following, Elder Richards and myself took our leave of the Saints at Froome's Hill, Herefordshire; but before leaving we repaired to a pool three times to baptize and confirm numbers that came to us and requested these ordinances at our hands.

Elder Richards labored in this part of the vineyard about two months, during which time he traveled extensively, preached night and day, gave much instruction to the Saints generally, and had many souls as seals to his ministry. I received much benefit from the counsel which he gave in the organization of the churches, and it was manifest that he had passed through a profitable school of experience during the three years of his travels in England; and the interesting seasons we have enjoyed together during these two months, will not be easily erased from my memory.

It was with no ordinary fellings that we took our departure from the Saints in Herefordshire on this occasion; for, less than four months since, I proclaimed the fullness of the Gospel in this region for the first time; but now, we were leaving between five and six hundred Saints, who were rejoicing in the new and everlasting covenant, and hundreds of others who were wishing to hear and obey. I parted from Elder Richards at Birmingham, who went direct to Manchester, while I visited

West Bromwich, and preached several times to a small branch of the Church which had been raised up in that place by Elder Turley, who baptized several while I was there. I also attended a conference on the 29th June, at Hanley, in the Staffordshire Potteries, in company with Elder George A. Smith and others, after which I arrived in Manchester.

WILFORD WOODRUFF.

Manchester, July 9, 1840.

Saturday, 11.—The High Council met at my office, when I taught them principles relating to their duty as a Council, and that they might be guided by the same in future, I ordered it to be recorded as follows: "That the Council should try no case without both parties being present, or having had an opportunity to be present; neither should they hear one person's complaint before his case is brought up for trial; neither should they suffer the character of any one to be exposed before the High Council without the person being present and ready to defend him or herself; that the minds of the councilors be not prejudiced for or against any one whose case they may possibly have to act upon."

Special Instructions for High Councils.

William Barrett, aged 17, was ordained an Elder in Hanley, Staffordshire, England, by Elders George A. Smith and Alfred Cordon, and took leave for South Australia, being the first Elder who went on a mission to that country.

The First Missionary for Australia.

Sunday, 12—Elias Smith was appointed Bishop by the High Council of Iowa, in place of Alanson Ripley, removed to Nauvoo.

Monday, 13.

*Kidnapping of Alanson Brown and Benjamin Boyce—Affidavit of Daniel H. Wells.**

STATE OF ILLINOIS, HANCOCK COUNTY.

This day personally appeared before the undersigned, an acting justice of the peace, in the aforesaid county, Alanson Brown, who, first

* Daniel Hanmer Wells was the son of Daniel Wells by his second wife Catherine Chapin. He was born at Trenton, Oneida county, New York, October 27, 1814.

being duly sworn according to law, deposes and says, that on the 7th day of July, A. D. 1840, and in the county of Hancock, in said state, William Allensworth, H. M. Woodyard, William Martin, John H. Owsley, John Bain, Light T. Tait, and Halsay White, in company with several other persons, to this affiant unknown, forcibly arrested this affiant, and one Benjamin Boyce, whilst affiant and said Boyce, were quietly pursuing their own lawful business; and that immediately after said arrest, the said Allensworth, Woodyard, Martin, Owsley, Bain, Tait, and White, did illegally and forcibly take, kidnap, and carry this affiant and said Boyce, bound with cords, from the said county of Hancock, in said state, on the day and year above set forth, in the county of Lewis, in the state of Missouri, without having established a claim for such a procedure, according to the laws of the United States.

Affiant states that in a short time after he was taken into the state of Missouri, he was put into a room with said Boyce, and there kept until about eleven o'clock the following night; when they were taken out of the room where they had been confined, into the woods, near at hand, by said Tait, a man by the name of Huner, and another by the name of Monday, and some others, whose name affiant did not learn; they previously placed a rope about the neck of the affiant; Huner and Monday then proceeded to hang the affiant, and did hang him for some time upon a tree, until affiant was nearly strangled, after which they let him down and loosened the rope. Shortly after this, affiant heard repeated blows, which others—belonging to the same gang of Huner—were inflicting upon Boyce, and he could hear also the cries of Boyce, under the pain arising from the blows; after which affiant and Boyce were taken back to the room where they had been confined, in which they found a man by the name of Rogers, and another by the name of Allred.

Affiant further states that he was kept in imprisonment by the per-

His father was a descendant of Thomas Wells, the fourth governor of Connecticut, while his mother was descended from David Chapin, a veteran of the Revolution, who served under Washington, and was a descendant of one of the oldest and most distinguished families of New England. The father of Daniel H. Wells died when the son was but 12 years old, which threw upon him, at this early age, the care of his mother and younger sister. At the age of 16 he migrated with his mother and sister to Marietta, Ohio, where Daniel H. taught school during the winter, and in the spring moved to Illinois, settling at Commerce, where he made extensive purchases of land. One farm of eighty acres was in the very heart of what became the city of Nauvoo, in fact he platted his farm into city lots which he sold at very reasonable prices to the Saints. The Temple site was selected from the western range of blocks in this addition. In 1835 he married Eliza Robison, and a son was born to them a year later. Mr. Wells served a term as constable in the district in which Commerce was situated, and was now a justice of the peace and familiarly called "Squire Wells." He was a stalwart Whig in politics; a man of high character and great courage.

sons heretofore named, and others to him unknown, until Friday evening next ensuing the Tuesday on which Boyce and himself were kidnapped, when he escaped out of their hands and returned into the state of Illinois. Affiant had learned that the name of the place in said county of Lewis, state of Missouri, to which he was taken from the state of Illinois, is called Tully, to which the said Allensworth, Woodyard, Martin, Owsley, Bain, Tait and White, have fled as fugitives from justice, and at which they are now to be found.

I hereby certify that the foregoing affidavit was this day subscribed and duly sworn to before me, by said Alanson Brown.

DANIEL H. WELLS.

Justice of the Peace, July 13, 1840.

Statement of James Allred.

STATE OF ILLINOIS, HANCOCK COUNTY.

This day personally appeared before the undersigned, an acting Justice of the Peace, in and for said county, James Allred, a credible witness, who first being duly sworn according to law, deposes and says that William Allensworth, John H. Owsley, and William Martin, on the 7th day of July, 1840, within the limits of said county of Hancock, aided by several other persons, to this affiant unknown, forcibly arrested this affiant and one Noah Rogers, whilst the affiant and said Rogers were peaceably pursuing their own lawful business; and that the said Allensworth, Owsley and Martin, after said arrest, aided by sundry persons, to affiant unknown, did forcibly take, kidnap and carry this affiant and said Rogers from the said county of Hancock in the state of Illinois, on the day and year above mentioned into the state of Missouri, without having established a claim for such procedure according to the laws of the United States.

Affiant further states, that in a short time after he had been so taken into the state of Missouri, he was put into a room with said Rogers, and there kept until some time during the following night, when they were taken out of the room where they were confined, into the woods near by, and this affiant was bound by the persons conducting him, to a tree, he having been first forcibly stripped by them of every particle of clothing. Those having him in charge then told affiant that they would whip him; one of them, by the name of Monday, saying to this affiant, 'G— d—n you, I'll cut you to the hollow." They, however, at last unbound the affiant without whipping him.

Affiant states that said Rogers was taken just beyond the place where affiant was bound with a rope around his neck, and he heard a great number of blows, which he then supposed, and has since learned were inflicted upon said Rogers, and heard him cry out several times as if in great agony; after which affiant, together with Rogers, was taken back and placed in the room from which they were taken, together with one Boyce and Brown, and detained until Monday next succeeding the day on which he was kidnapped; at which time he received from one of the company, who had imprisoned him, a passport, of which the following is a copy—

"Tully, Missouri, July 12, 1840. The people of Tully, having taken up Mr. Allred, with some others, and having examined into the offenses committed, find nothing to justify his detention any longer, and have released him. By order of the committe.

"H. M. WOODWARD."

And then this affiant was permitted to return home into the state of Illinois. This place in Missouri, to which affiant and said Rogers were taken, he has learned is called Tully, and is situated in the county of Lewis, and at which place the said Allensworth, Owsley and Martin are now living.

I hereby certify that the forgoing affidavit was this day subscribed, and duly sworn to before me, by the said James Allred.

DANIEL H. WELLS,
Justice of the Peace.

Action of the Citizens of Nauvoo in the Matter of the Kidnapping of Brown and Boyce by the Missourians.

At a meeting of the citizens of Nauvoo, Hancock county, Illinois, 13th July, 1840, Judge Elias Higbee was called to the chair, and Robert B. Thompson was appointed Secretary.

On motion a committee was appointed to report resolutions, expressive of the sense of this meeting, consisting of the following persons, to wit.—Isaac Galland, Robert B. Thompson, Sidney Rigdon, and Daniel H. Wells, who retired, and after a short absence, reported the following preamble and resolutions, which were unanimously adopted—

Report of the Committee on Resolutions.

PREAMBLE—The committee appointed to express the sense of this meeting, in relation to the recent acts of abduction, and other deeds of cruelty and inhumanity committed upon our citizens by [some of] the citizens of the state of Missouri, beg leave respectfully to report:

That having under consideration the principal matters involve in the discharge of their duty, they have been forced to arrive at the following conclusions:

First—That the people of Missouri, not having sufficiently slacked their thirst for blood and plunder, are now disposed to pursue us with a repetition of the scenes of brutality which marked their whole course of conduct towards us during our unhappy residence among them.

Second—That notwithstanding they have already robbed us of our homes, murdered our families, stolen and carried away our property; and to complete the measure of their infamy as a state, their executive caused unoffending thousands to be banished from the state, without even the form of a trial, or the slightest evidence of crime; they are now sending their gangs of murdering banditti, and thieving brigands, to wreak further vengeance, and satisfy their insatiable cupidity in the state of Illinois, and that too before we have even had time to erect shelters for our families.

Third—That for the purpose of giving a semblance of justification to their most unhallowed conduct, the people of Missouri have again commenced concealing goods within the limits of our settlements, as they had done before in the state of Missouri, in order to raise a charge of stealing against our citizens, and under this guise they have within a few days kidnapped, and carried away, several honest and worthy citizens of this county.

Fourth—Under these circumstances the first duty and the only redress which seems to offer itself to our consideration is an appeal to the executive of the state of Illinois, for redress, and protection from further injuries, with a confident assurance that he, unlike the governor of Missouri, will extend the executive arm to protect from lawless outrage, unoffending citizens. Therefore,

Resolved 1st: That we view, with no ordinary feelings, the approaching danger as a necessary consequence following the lawless and outrageous conduct of the citizens of Missouri, in setting at defiance the laws of this, as well as of all other states in this Union, by forcing from their homes, and from the state, civil citizens of Illinois, and taking them into the state of Missouri, without any legal process whatever, and there inflicting upon them base cruelties in order to extort false confessions from them, to give a coloring to their (the Missourians') iniquities, and screen themselves from the just indignation of an incensed public.

Resolved 2ndly: That while we deeply deplore the cause which has brought us together on this occasion, we cannot refrain from expressing our most unqualified disapprobation at the infringement of the laws of this state, as set forth in the above Preamble, and strongest indignation at the manner in which the people of Missouri treated those whom they had thus inhumanly taken from among us.

Resolved 3rdly: That inasmuch as we are conscious of our honest and upright intentions, and are at all times ready and willing to submit to the just requirements of the laws, we claim of the citizens and authorities of this state, protection from such unjust and, before, unheard of oppressions.

Resolved 4thly: That the forcible abduction of our citizens by the citizens of Missouri, is a violation of the laws regulating the federal compact, subversive to the rights of freemen, and contrary to our free institutions, and republican principles.

Resolved, 5thly: That the cruelties practiced upon our citizens, since their abduction, is disgraceful to humanity; the height of injustice and oppression, and would disgrace the annals of the most barbarous nations, in either ancient or modern times; and can only find its parallel in the "*Auto da Fe*"—the inquisitions in Spain.

Resolved, 6thly: That such unconstitutional and unhallowed proceedings on the part of the citizens of Missouri, ought to arouse every patriot to exertion and diligence to put a stop to such procedure, and use all constitutional means to bring the offenders to justice.

Resolved, 7thly: That we memorialize the Executive of this state, of the gross outrage which has been committed on our citizens; and pledge ourselves to aid him in such measures as may be deemed necessary to restore our citizens to freedom, and have satisfaction for the wrongs we have suffered.

ELIAS HIGBEE, Chairman,
R. B. THOMPSON, Secretary.

Memorial to Governor Carlin.

To his Excellency Governor Carlin:—The undersigned being a committee to draft a Memorial to your Excellency relative to the recent outrages, would respectfully represent; that after being driven from our homes, and pleasant places of abode, in the state of Missouri, by the authorities of said state, Illinois seemed to be the first shelter or asylum which presented itself to our view; that having left the state of Missouri, your memorialists found an asylum in the state of Illinois; and notwithstanding the false reports which were circulated to our prejudice, we were received with kindness by the noble hearted citizens of Illinois; who relieved our necessities, and bade us welcome; for which kindness we feel thankful.

That under your Excellency's administration, we have had every encouragement given us, and have every reason, from the kindness and sympathy which you have ever manifested towards us in our sufferings, to feel confident that your aid will ever be offered to us in common with the rest of the citizens of the state. That feeling ourselves so happy and secure, and beginning again to enjoy the comforts of life, we are sorry to say that our quiet has been disturbed, our fears alarmed, and our families annoyed by the citizens of Missouri; who, with malice and hatred, which is characteristic of them, have unconstitutionally sent an armed force and abducted some of our friends, namely, James Allred,

Noah Rogers, Alanson Brown, and one Boyce, and carried them into the state of Missouri, and treated them with the greatest barbarity and cruelty; even now their wives and children, as well as their friends, are alarmed for the safety of their lives.

Therefore we have felt it our duty to place the circumstances of this unheard-of outrage before you, and appeal to your Excellency for protection from such marauders, and take such measures as you may deem proper, that our friends may be again restored to the bosom of their families, and the offenders punished for their crimes.

We have the greatest confidence in your Excellency, that every constitutional means will be resorted to, to restore our friends to the society of their families, &c., that we, in common with other citizens of the state of Illinois, may enjoy all the rights and privileges of freemen.

Your memorialists have under all circumstances paid the greatest respect to the laws of the country, and if any should break the same, they have never felt a disposition to screen such from justice, but when under false pretenses, to gratify and satiate a revengeful disposition—for the citizens of another state, regardless of both the laws of God and man, to come and kidnap our friends, to carry off our citizens to cruelly treat our brethren; such offenders, we think, should be brought to an account, to be dealt with according to their merit or demerit; that we may enjoy the privileges guaranteed to us by the Constitution of the United States.

We therefore humbly pray that your Excellency will satisfy yourself of the gross outrage which has been committed on the citizens of the state, and with that energy which is so characteristic of your Exellency's administration, take such steps as you may deem best calculated to repair the injuries which your memorialists have sustained; that you will vindicate the injured laws of the state.

In conclusion, we beg leave to assure your Excellency, that in the discharge of this, as well as every other constitutional movement, you may rely upon the hearty co-operation of your memorialists, who respectfully submit to your Excellency the accompanying Resolutions, which were passed at a large meeting held in this place on this day, and also the affidavit of one of those persons who was kidnapped, but fortunately has made his escape.

CHAPTER IX.

THE RETURN OF A PRODIGAL—CONDITIONS IN KIRTLAND—PROGRESS OF THE WORK IN GREAT BRITAIN—THE COMING OF JOHN C. BENNETT.

AUSTRALIAN MISSION.

Extract of a Letter from Elder William Barratt.

DEPTFORD,* July 15, 1840.

DEAR BROTHER IN CHRIST:—I write to inform you of my arrival in the metropolis this morning, after a tedious journey in the midst of much profaneness and swearing, such as I never heard in my life before. I feel, as the Apostle expresses it, like a lamb among wolves, going into a land of strangers to preach the Gospel; therefore I desire your prayers in my behalf. I have witnessed much of the spirit of revelation since Sunday; in fact, I only thought it a mere thought, when the Elders testified that they were called by revelation; but now I know the truth of the assertion, which proves to me who ought to preach, and that none ought, without they are called by revelation.

Give my love to all the Saints, and tell them that as many as remain faithful I will meet in Zion, bringing my sheaves with me. Tell them my faith is fixed, and my resolution is strong to meet you all there, whom I love in the Lord. Pray that a door may be opened, and that a gift of utterance may be given unto me in a foreign land to preach the Gospel. Brethren, sorrow not for me, as those that have no hope, for we have a hope of living and eating together in the kingdom of our God.

Friday, 17.—By my suggestion, High Council voted that Samuel Bent and George W. Harris go on a mission to procure money for printing certain books.

Saturday, 18.—Elias Smith was ordained a Bishop.

Sunday, 19.—An answer to Brigham Young's letter of the 17th of May was sent by Lorenzo Snow,† which gave

* Formerly a town in Kent and Surrey, England, on the Thames, noted for its dock yards, now part of London.

† Lorenzo Snow was born April 30, 1814, in Mantua, Portage county, Ohio. He

the Twelve permission to publish the Book of Mormon, Doctrine and Covenants, and hymn-book, but not to ordain any into the quorum of the Seventies; and likewise some general instructions.

Monday, 20.—Elder John Moon and company arrived in New Yorkbeing the first arrival of Saints in America.

Wednesday, 22.

*The Prophet's Letter to William W. Phelps—Welcoming him back into the Church.**

NAUVOO, HANCOCK COUNTY, ILLINOIS, July 22, 1840.

DEAR BROTHER PHELPS:—I must say that it is with no ordinary feelings I endeavor to write a few lines to you in answer to yours of the 29th ultimo; at the same time I am rejoiced at the privilege granted me.

was the eldest son of Oliver Snow and Rosetta L. Pettibone. The early years of his life were spent upon his father's farm. Later he entered Oberlin College, a Presbyterian institution, in the town of Oberlin, in Lorain county, Ohio, about sixty miles southwest of Kirtland. In June, 1836, he visited Kirtland and attended the Hebrew classes, then being taught in the Temple. While in Kirtland he became a convert to the faith of the Latter-day Saints and was baptized by Elder John Boynton, one of the Twelve Apostles. The following year he did some missionary work among his relatives and friends in Ohio, and in 1836, with his parents, who in the meantime joined the Church, he moved to Missouri, and shortly afterwards went upon a preaching mission through the states of Kentucky and Illinois. A few days before starting upon this mission mentioned in the text, namely, 17th of July, 1840, he was ordained a Seventy by President Joseph Young, and the day following was made a High Priest under the hands of Don Carlos Smith. The testimony which this man received of the truth of the Gospel is very interesting, and seems to have remained with him throughout his long life, in all the freshness of its first impression upon him. Having received the usual promise of a testimony of the truth of the work if he obeyed the Gospel, he sought that testimony most earnestly in prayer with the following result as stated by himself:

"I had no sooner opened my lips in an effort to pray than I heard a sound just above my head like the rushing of silken robes; and immediately the Spirit of God descended upon me, completely enveloping my whole person, filling me from the crown of my head to the soles of my feet, and oh, the joyful happiness I felt! No language can describe the almost instantaneous transition from a dense cloud of spiritual darkness into a refulgence of light and knowledge, as it was at that time imparted to my understanding. I received a perfect knowledge that God lives, that Jesus Christ is the Son of God, and of the restoration of the Holy Priesthood, and the fullness of the Gospel. It was a complete baptism—a tangible immersion in the heavenly principle or element, the Holy Ghost; and even more physical in its effects upon every part of my system than the immersion by water."

* When the great offense of Elder William W. Phelps is taken into account—amounting as it did to a betrayal of the Prophet and the Church in Missouri, dur-

You may in some measure realize what my feelings, as well as Elder Rigdon's and Brother Hyrum's were, when we read your letter—truly our hearts were melted into tenderness and compassion when we ascertained your resolves, &c. I can assure you I feel a disposition to act on your case in a manner that will meet the approbation of Jehovah, (whose servant I am), and agreeable to the principles of truth and righteousness which have been revealed; and inasmuch as long-suffering, patience, and mercy have ever characterized the dealings of our heavenly Father towards the humble and penitent, I feel disposed to copy the example, cherish the same principles, and by so doing be a savior of my fellow men.

It is true, that we have suffered much in consequence of your behavior—the cup of gall, already full enough for mortals to drink, was indeed filled to overflowing when you turned against us. One with whom we had oft taken sweet counsel together, and enjoyed many refreshing seasons from the Lord—"had it been an enemy, we could have borne it." "In the day that thou stoodest on the other side, in the day when strangers carried away captive his forces, and foreigners entered into his gates, and cast lots upon [Far West], even thou wast as one of them; but thou shouldest not have looked on the day of thy brother, in the day that he became a stranger, neither shouldst thou have spoken proudly in the day of distress."

However, the cup has been drunk, the will of our Father has been done, and we are yet alive, for which we thank the Lord. And having been delivered from the hands of wicked men by the mercy of our God, we say it is your privilege to be delivered from the powers of the adversary, be brought into the liberty of God's dear children, and again take your stand among the Saints of the Most High, and by diligence, humility, and love unfeigned, commend yourself to our God, and your God, and to the Church of Jesus Christ.

Believing your confession to be real, and your repentance genuine, I shall be happy once again to give you the right hand of fellowship, and rejoice over the returning prodigal.

Your letter was read to the Saints last Sunday, and an expression of their feeling was taken, when it was unanimously

ing the troubles of the Saints in that state—this letter is remarkable. The Prophet's frank forgiveness of his erring brother, gently chiding his wrong-doing, but at the same time remembering in a large way that brother's former devotion and labors; the Prophet's willingness to have the prodigal return and occupy his former high standing among the Saints—all this exhibits a broad-mindedness and generosity that can come only from a great soul, influenced by the spirit of charity enjoined upon his disciples by the teachings of the Son of God. One of the surest evidences of Joseph Smith's greatness of mind and of the inspiration of God upon him is to be seen in his treatment of those who had fallen but were willing to and did repent of their sins. His capacity to forgive under these circumstances seemed boundless.

Resolved, That W. W. Phelps should be received into fellowship.

"Come on, dear brother, since the war is past,
For friends at first, are friends again at last."

Yours as ever,
JOSEPH SMITH, JUN.

Credentials of Elders Samuel Bent and George W. Harris.

To all whom it may concern:—This is to certify that Elders Samuel Bent and George W. Harris are authorized agents of the Church of Jesus Christ of Latter-day Saints, being appointed by the First Presidency and High Council of said Church to visit the branches of the Church in the east, or wherever they may be led in the providence of God, to obtain donations and subscriptions for the purpose of printing the Book of Mormon, Doctrine and Covenants, hymn-books, the new translation of the Scriptures. They are likewise instructed and authorized to procure loans in behalf of the Church, for carrying into operation the above and other important works necessary to the well being of said Church.

From our long acquaintance with these our beloved brethren, their long, tried friendship under circumstances the most trying and painful, their zeal for the cause of truth, and their strict morality and honesty, we most cheerfully recommend them to the Saints of the Most High. Any statements they may make relative to their mission may be implicitly relied upon, and any loans which they may obtain, will be considered binding on the Church. And we do hope the Saints will do all in their power to effect the object proposed, and lift up the hands of our beloved brethren who have cheerfully come forward to engage in a work so great and important.

Joseph Smith, Jun., President.
William Marks,
Elias Higbee,
David Dort,
Charles C. Rich,
Seymour Brunson,
William Huntington,
Hyrum Smith,
Newel Knight,
Alpheus Cutler.
Henry G. Sherwood,
David Fullmer,
Thomas Grover,
Lewis D. Wilson.

The Prophet's Letter to Oliver Granger—Dealing Chiefly with Affairs at Kirtland.

Brother Granger:

DEAR SIR:—It was with great pleasure I received your and Brother Richards' letter, dated New York, June 23, 1840, and was very happy to be informed of your safe arrival in that place, and your probability of success; and I do hope that your anticipations will be realized, and that you will be enabled to free the Lord's House from all incumbrances, and be prospered in all your undertakings for the benefit of the Church; and pray that while you are exerting your influence to bring about an object so desirable, that the choicest blessings of heaven may rest down upon you, while you are endeavoring to do so, and attending to the duties laid upon you by the authorities of the Church in this place.

I am sorry to be informed not only in your letter, but from other respectable sources, of the strange conduct pursued in Kirtland by Elder Almon W. Babbitt. I am indeed surprised that a man having the experience which Brother Babbitt has had, should take any steps whatever, calculated to destroy the confidence of the brethren in the Presidency or any of the authorities of the Church.

In order to conduct the affairs of the Kingdom in righteousness, it is all important that the most perfect harmony, kind feeling, good understanding, and confidence should exist in the hearts of all the brethren; and that true charity, love one towards another, should characterize all their proceedings. If there are any uncharitable feelings, any lack of confidence, then pride, arrogance and envy will soon be manifested; confusion must inevitably prevail, and the authorities of the Church set at naught; and under such circumstances, Kirtland cannot rise and free herself from the captivity in which she is held, and become a place of safety for the Saints, nor can the blessings of Jehovah rest upon her,

If the Saints in Kirtland deem me unworthy of their prayers when they assemble together, and neglect to bear me up at the throne of heavenly grace, it is a strong and convincing proof to me that they have not the Spirit of God. If the revelations we have received are true, who is to lead the people? If the keys of the Kingdom have been committed to my hands, who shall open out the mysteries thereof?

As long as my brethren stand by me and encourage me, I can combat the prejudices of the world, and can bear the contumely and abuse with joy; but when my brethren stand aloof, when they begin to faint, and endeavor to retard my progress and enterprise, then I feel to mourn, but am no less determined to prosecute my task, being confident that although my earthly friends may fail, and even turn against me, yet my heavenly Father will bear me off triumphant.

However, I hope that even in Kirtland there are some who do not make a man an offender for a word, but are disposed to stand forth in defense of righteousness and truth, and attend to every duty enjoined upon them; and who will have wisdom to direct them against any movement or influence calculated to bring confusion and discord into the camp of Israel, and to discern between the spirit of truth and the spirit of error.

It would be gratifying to my mind to see the Saints in Kirtland flourish, but think the time is not yet come; and I assure you it never will until a different order of things be established and a different spirit manifested. When confidence is restored, when pride shall fall, and every aspiring mind be clothed with humility as with a garment, and selfishness give place to benevolence and charity, and a united determination to live by every word which proceedeth out of the mouth of the Lord is observable, then, and not till then, can peace, order and love prevail.

It is in consequence of aspiring men that Kirtland has been forsaken. How frequently has your humble servant been envied in his office by such characters, who endeavored to raise themselves to power at his expense, and seeing it impossible to do so, resorted to foul slander and abuse, and other means to effect his overthrow. Such characters have ever been the first to cry out against the Presidency, and publish their faults and foibles to the four winds of heaven.

I cannot forget the treatment I received in the house of my friends. These things continually roll across my mind, and cause me much sorrow of heart; and when I think that others who have lately come into the Church should be led to Kirtland instead of to this place, by Elder Babbitt; and having their confidence in the authorities lessened by such observations as he (Elder Babbitt) has thought proper to make, as well as hearing all the false reports and exaggerated accounts of our enemies—I must say that I feel grieved in spirit, and cannot tolerate such proceedings—neither will I; but will endeavor to disabuse the minds of the Saints, and break down all such unhallowed proceedings.

It was something new to me when I heard there had been secret meetings held in the Lord's House, and that some of my friends—faithful brethren—men enjoying the confidence of the Church, should be locked out. Such proceedings are not calculated to promote union, or peace, but to engender strife; and will be a curse instead of a blessing. To those who are young in the work, I know they are calculated to be, and must be, injurious. Those who have had experience, and who should know better than to reflect on their brethren—there is no excuse for them.

If Brother Babbitt and the other brethren wish to reform the Church, and come out and make a stand against sin and speculation, &c., they must use other weapons than lies, or their object can never be effected;

and their labors will be given to the house of the stranger, rather than to the House of the Lord.

The proceedings of Brother Babbitt were taken into consideration at a meeting of the Church at this place, when it was unanimously resolved, that fellowship should be withdrawn from him until he make satisfaction for the course he has pursued: of which circumstance I wish you to apprise him without delay, and demand his license.

Dear sir, I wish you to stand in your lot, and keep the station which was given you by revelation and the authorities of the Church. Attend to the affairs of the Church with diligence, and then rest assured of the blessings of heaven. It is binding on you to act as president of the Church in Kirtland, until you are removed by the same authority which put you in; and I do hope there will be no cause for opposition, but that good feeling will be manifested in future by all the brethren.

Brother Burdick's letter to Brother Hyrum was duly received, for which he has our best thanks; it was indeed an admirable letter, and worthy of its author. The sentiments expressed were in accordance with the spirit of the Gospel, and the principles are correct.

I am glad that Brother Richards has continued with you, and hope he has been of some service to you. Give my love to him.

Our prospects in this place continue good. Considerable numbers have come in this spring. There were some bickerings respecting your conduct soon after your departure, but they have all blown over, and I hope there will never be any occasion for any more; but that you will commend yourself to God and to the Saints by a virtuous walk and holy conversation.

I had a letter from William W. Phelps a few days ago, informing me of his desire to come back to the Church, if we would accept of him. He appears very humble, and is willing to make every satisfaction that Saints or God may require.

We expect to have an edition of the Book of Mormon printed by the first of September; it is now being stereotyped in Cincinnati.

I am, &c., &c.,

JOSEPH SMITH, JUN.

A Jew's Memorial.

An interesting memorial concerning the Jews, "To the Protestant Powers of Europe and America," signed and sealed in London, the 8th of January, 1839, may be found in the *Millennial Star*, Vol. I, No. 6.*

* The article which appeared first in a periodical, entitled "Memorial Concerning God's Ancient People of Israel," and then in the *London Times*, seems to have

Sunday, 24.—Elder William Donaldson, member of the British army bound for the East Indies, writes from Chatham, 24th of July, "We go on board tomorrow. I have had a glorious vision about going into the land of Egypt."

Saturday, 25.

Letter of John C. Bennett to Joseph Smith and Sidney Rigdon—Announcing His Intention to Join the Saints.

FAIRFIELD, ILLINOIS, July 25, 1840.

REVEREND AND DEAR FRIENDS:—The last time I wrote you was during the pendency of your difficulties with the Missourians. You are aware that at that time I held the office of "Brigadier-General of the Invincible Dragoons" of this state, and proffered you my entire energies for your deliverance from a ruthless and savage, though cowardly foe; but the Lord came to your rescue, and saved you with a powerful arm. I am happy to find that you are now in a civilized land, and in the enjoyment of peace and happiness.

Some months ago I resigned my office with an intention of removing to your town, and joining your people; but hitherto I have been prevented. I hope, however, to remove to Commerce, and unite with your Church next spring. I believe I should be much happier with you. I have many things to communicate which I would prefer doing orally; and I propose to meet you in Springfield on the first Monday in December next, as I shall be there at the time on state and United States business.

If I remove to Commerce, I expect to follow my profession, and to that end I enclose you a slip from the *Louisville Journal*, to give you an idea of my professional standing.

On the first of this month I was appointed to the office of "Quarter-

been written by a Christian Jew. It deals largely with the promises of God to ancient Israel, especially as to their return as a people to Palestine. The closing paragraph is an appeal to the Protestant powers of the north of Europe and America to assist in this restoration: "As the spirit of Cyrus, king of Persia, was stirred up to build the Lord a temple, which was in Jerusalem (II Chron., xxxvi: 22, 23), who is there among you, high and mighty ones of all the nations, to fulfill the good pleasure of the holy will of the Lord of heaven, saying to Jerusalem, 'Thou shalt be built,' and to the temple, 'Thy foundation shall be laid?' (Isa. xliv: 28). The Lord God of Israel be with such. Great grace, mercy and peace shall descend upon the people who offer themselves willingly; and the free offerings of their hearts and hands shall be those of a sweet smelling savor unto him who hath said, 'I will bless thee (Gen. xii: 3), and contend with him that contendeth with thee.'" (Isa. xlix: 25).

master-General of the State of Illinois," which office I expect to hold some years.

I hope you are all quite well. In haste. Write me immediately.

Yours respectfully,

JOHN C. BENNETT.*

To Messrs. Smith and Rigdon.

Monday, 27.

Letter of John C. Bennett to Messrs. Smith and Rigdon—Making Further Tender of his Services to the Church.

QUARTERMASTER-GENERAL'S OFFICE,
FAIRFIELD, ILLINOIS, July 27, 1840.

To the Reverends Sidney Rigdon and Joseph Smith, Jun.:

RESPECTED FRIENDS:—I wrote you a few days ago from this place, but my great desire to be with you and your people prompts me to write again at this time; and I hope it will not be considered obtrusive by friends whom I have always so highly esteemed as yourselves.

At the last District and Circuit Court of the United States, holden at Springfield, in June last, I had the honor of being on the grand inquest of the United States for the District of Illinois, and hoped to have seen you there; but was quite disappointed. I attended the meeting of your people opposite Mr. Lowry's hotel, but did not make myself known, as I had no personal acquaintance in the congregation.

It would be my deliberate advice to you to concentrate all of your Church at one point. If Hancock county, with Commerce for its commercial emporium, is to be that point, well; fix upon it, and let us co-operate with a general concerted action. You can rely upon me in any event. I am with you in spirit, and will be in person as soon as circumstances permit, and immediately if it is your desire. Wealth is no material object with me. I desire to be happy, and am fully satisfied that I can enjoy myself better with your people, with my present views and feelings, than with any other. I hope that time will soon come when your people will become my people, and your God my God.

At the time of your peril and bitter persecution in Missouri, you are

* "This was a Dr. John C. Bennett, a man who seems to have been without any moral character, but who had filled positions of importance. Born in Massachusetts in 1804, he practiced as a physician in Ohio, and later in Illinois, holding a professorship in Willoughby University, Ohio, and taking with him to Illinois testimonials as to his professional skill. In the latter state he showed a taste for military affairs, and after being elected brigadier-general of the Invincible Dragoons, he was appointed quartermaster-general of the state in 1840, and held that position at the state capital when the Mormons applied to the legislature for a charter for Nauvoo." ("The Story of the Mormons," Linn, 1901).

aware I proffered you my utmost energies, and had not the conflict terminated so speedily, I should have been with you then. God be thanked for your rescue from the hand of a savage, but cowardly foe!

I do not expect to resign my office of "Quartermaster-General of the State of Illinois" in the event of my removal to Commerce, unless you advise otherwise. I shall likewise expect to practice my profession; but at the same time your people shall have all the benefit of my speaking powers, and my untiring energies in behalf of the good and holy faith. *Un necessariis unitas, in non necessariis libertas, in omnibus charitas,** shall be my motto with—*Suaviter in modo, fortiter in re.*†

Be so good as to inform me substantially of the population of Commerce and Hancock county, the face of the country, climate, soil, health, &c., &c. How many of your people are concentrated there? Please to write me in full immediately. Louisville paper will accompany this; please inquire for it.

With sentiments of profound respect and esteem, suffer me to subscribe myself,

Yours respectfully,

JOHN C. BENNETT.

Elder John Taylor sailed for Ireland from Liverpool.‡

Tuesday, 28.

Letter of the Prophet to Horace R. Hotchkiss—Rock River Lands and the White Purchase.

NAUVOO, July 28, 1840.

Horace R. Hotchkiss, Esq.:

DEAR SIR:—I acknowledge the receipt of yours of last month, giving me the numbers of the land on Rock River, which you felt disposed to sell. In reply to which I have to say, that we have not yet examined the land, and consequently have not arrived at any conclusion respect-

*Translation: In essentials, unity; in non-essentials, liberty; in all things, charity.

† Gently in the manner, firmly in the act.

‡ Elder John Taylor was accompanied on this mission by Brothers McGuffie and William Black. Elder Taylor had baptized Brother McGuffie while laboring in Liverpool; and as the new convert had some acquaintances in Newry, county Down, Ireland, he thought it advisable to take him along. A large company of Saints went with them to see them off. The day after sailing, Elder Taylor and companions arrived in Newry, a beautiful Irish village nestling among rolling hills, characteristic of that part of Ireland. Brother McGuffie obtained the court house to hold a meeting in, and sent around the bell-man to give notice of it. A congregation of six or seven hundred gathered in at seven o'clock in the evening, and Elder Taylor preached to them. This was the introduction of the Gospel into Ireland.

ing it; but it is probable that some of my friends will visit it this fall, and if we should think it wisdom to locate there, or on the other tract, you will be informed of the same, and arrangements entered into.

I am sorry that your health has been so poor, but hope, ere this, you are perfectly recovered. It would afford me great pleasure indeed, could I hold out any prospect of the two notes due next month being met at maturity, or even this fall. Having had considerable difficulty (necessarily consequent on a new settlement) to contend with, as well as poverty and considerable sickness, our first payment will be probably somewhat delayed, until we again get a good start in the world; and I am happy to say, the prospect is indeed favorable. Under these circumstances we shall have to claim your indulgence, which I have no doubt will be extended. However, every exertion on our part shall be made to meet the demands against us, so that if we cannot accomplish all we wish to, it will be our misfortune, and not our fault. Notwithstanding the impoverished condition of our people, and the adverse circumstances under which we have had to labor, I hope we shall eventually rise above them, and again enjoy the blessings of health, peace, and plenty.

You were informed in a former letter that we had paid Mr. William White the one thousand dollars specified in your bond; a few days ago he called at this place and agreed to give us a deed for the ninety acres, (less one-half acre), providing I would give him an indemnifying bond, and pay the interest due from you to him on the one thousand dollars, which I agreed to do. I have therefore got the deed for the land, and paid him the interest. My reasons for so doing were these: there are some who wish to purchase lots, providing they can get a good title deed for the same, and who would be induced to make purchases and make an effort to raise money, for the sake of getting a deed; which effort they would not be so likely to make if we could only give them a bond. This I think will work both to your advantage and ours, and hope that we shall be able by and by to make some cash sales.

I hope this arrangement with Mr. White will meet your approbation, although it is a departure from the common rules of business; but was induced to do so from the advantages which will result from it, which I hope will be mutual. The amount of interest paid to Mr. White, after deducting $61.50, which was coming from him to you for rents, was eighty-four dollars and forty cents. Mr. White told us that you agreed to pay him as much interest for the money as he could get elsewhere. We accordingly (in good faith) allowed him at the rate of ten per cent. Hoping the course pursued will meet your approbation.

I am, respectfully, your obedient servant,

JOSEPH SMITH, JUN.

P. S.—You will recollect the verbal agreement entered into by us, that the notes for the interest would not be exacted for at least five years. Notwithstanding which, we use our endeavors to meet them as fast as possible, and think that when I have the pleasure of seeing you again, you will be fully satisfied with the course we have taken, and our endeavors to meet all our engagements.

J. S., JUN.

Thursday, 30.

Letter of John C. Bennett to Messrs. Smith and Rigdon—Expressing Anxiety to be with the Saints.

FAIRFIELD, WAYNE COUNTY, ILLINOIS,
July 30th, 1840.

To Reverends Sidney Rigdon, and Joseph Smith, Jun.

RESPECTED FRIENDS:—It is with difficulty that I can forego the felicity of an immediate immersion into the true faith of your beloved people. I have written you several letters, and forwarded you several newspapers to Commerce, which I hope will be duly received, as they contain some matters of importance.

Is Nauvoo, or Commerce, to be the general point of concentration for the Mormon people? For at that point I desire to locate, and ever remain. My anxiety to be with you is daily increasing, and I shall wind up my professional business immediately, and proceed to your blissful abode, if you think it best.

Look at all my letters and papers and write me forthwith. You are aware that at the time of your most bitter persecutions, I was with you in feeling, and proffered you my military knowledge and prowess. My faith is still strong. I believe the God of the whole earth will avenge your wrong in time as well as in eternity.

O my friends, go on and prosper; and may the God of all grace save you with an everlasting salvation.

Yours respectfully,
J. C. BENNETT.

Saturday, August 1.—In the *Times and Seasons* of this month I find the following:

A voice from the holy city—rebuilding of the temple of Solomon—Recall of the people of God to the land of Judah.

We have received by the last packet from England, a copy of a very extraordinary "Circular" issued by the Jews, now residing at Jerusaem, and addressed to all the descendants of Abraham to the uttermost ends of the earth. It is written in the pure Hebrew character, and accompanied with an English translation, which we annex as matter of the deepest curiosity to the people of this country. Next week, if we possibly can, we shall publish the original Hebrew in a double sheet, but at present we must content ourselves with the translation.—*Morning Herald.*

CIRCULAR.

"*To our Brethren the Israelites of Europe and America:*

"The liberal and benevolent contributors towards every holy and pious purpose—ready to stand in the breach and evince their love for the Land of Promise: to the well-wishers of Jerusalem, and friends of Zion (dearer to us than life) who extend their bounteous aid to this Holy City, and devote their best means, in love and affection, 'to take pity on her stones, and show mercy to her dust.' To the illustrious and excellent Rabbies—to their worthy and distinguished Assessors—to the noble Chiefs and faithful Leaders of Israel; to all congregations devoted to the Lord, and to every member thereof—health, life, and prosperity. May the Lord vouchsafe His protection unto them; may they rejoice and be exceedingly glad; and with their own eyes may they behold when the Lord restoreth Zion. Such be His gracious will. Amen.

"It is a fact well known throughout Judah and Israel, that 'the glory altogether departed from the daughter of Zion,' since upwards of one hundred years ago, the congregation of German Jews in this Holy City were forcibly deprived of their homes and inheritance. Dreadful and grievous was the yoke under which the despots of this land oppressed them. Tyranny and cruel usage ground them to the dust, and forced them to forsake their habitations, to abandon their houses and all their property, and to seek safety in flight. Thus the large court they inherited from their ancestors remained deserted and uninhabited, until it was seized upon and possessed by aliens. The sacred edifices it contained, namely, the Synagogue and Medrash, were by them demolished, the whole of the property utterly ruined, and possessions, lawfully ours, devastated before our eyes. Then did our souls refuse all consolation! For how could we bear to witness the evil which befell our people!

"As the light gleams forth from a spark, so did our congregation take heart and return again to form their establishments, and to take root on the Holy Mount. But we could find no rest for our wearied feet—no place consecrated and appointed for our prayer and instruction. Our aching eyes beheld how every nation and tongue, even from the most distant isles of the ocean, is here possessed of structures defended by walls, gates, and portcullis, whilst the people of the Lord, forcibly expelled from their inheritances by rapacious barbarians, were covered with obloquy, scorn, and disgrace.

"The cries of the people ascended unto the Lord who dwelleth in Zion. He looked down, and in pity beheld their sufferings and oppression. And ever since the ruler of Egypt first assumed the government of the Holy Land—a ruler who maintains justice throughout his dominions—an edict was issued permitting Jews to do whatsoever they deemed right and expedient, with respect to the rebuilding of their demolished synagogues and colleges. Us, likewise, the Lord in His mercy vouchsafed to remember, and caused us to be reinstated into the heritage of our fathers, even to the aforementioned court, which is called the Ruin of R. Jehudah the Pious (of blessed memory).

"Blessed be the Lord our God, the God of our fathers, who inspired the heart of the ruler of Egypt to restore unto us the possessions of our ancestors. Nor did we delay or lose time in the matter, but exerted ourselves to rebuild Jerusalem.

"'We fenced it, and gathered up the stones thereof,' and the sacred undertaking prospered in our hands, so that we have completed the Medrash, and 'great is the glory of the house;' and also houses for the teachers of the law, and for the hospitable reception and entertainment of strangers, which were indispensably necessary to accommodate the many pious Israelites who visit the Holy City during the festivals. And on *Rosh Hodesh Shebath* last we joyfully placed a Sepher Torah in the Medrash, which we consecrated by the name of '*Menahem Zion*,' for the Lord has vouchsafed to comfort His people.

"But although we have thus, under the blessings of Providence, retrieved from devastation a part of the possessions bequeathed unto us by our pious ancestors, yet our hearts are afflicted and our eyes are dimmed when we behold the sanctuary of our Lord, the Synagogue, which still lies in ruins; nor is it in the power of all of us (the German Congregation) to rebuild it; for alas! great is the number of our poor who stand in need of bread, and the debts we contracted in building the Medrash are large, and weigh heavily upon us.

"The cause of our grief is thus ever present to our eyes—the ruins of the Synagogue are heaped in the middle of the court, and rank weeds spread over the consecrated pile. We therefore deem it our bounden duty to dispatch a messenger unto our brethren, the children of Israel, who are dispersed and in exile, in order to acquaint them with 'the salvation of the Lord in the land,' so that they may arise and take pity on Zion, for it is time to show mercy unto her.

"To undertake this laborious duty was the voluntary offer of our dearly beloved friend, that profound and renowned Rabbi, the zealous and honorable *Aaron Selig Ashkenazi*. He is a man confirmed in the fear of the Lord, of a faithful stock; and him we depute as our messenger, worthy of all trust, to make proclamation unto the communities of Israel 'according to the sight which he has seen in the Holy Mount,' and to him we have given letters of authorization, containing full particulars as to his pious mission, and every necessary information relating thereto.

"Now, therefore, let the righteous behold and rejoice. Let the pious exult and triumph in gladness. The day ye have so long hoped for is come, and ye see it. The crown of holiness will again adorn its former abode. Therefore, arise, and take upon yourselves, according to the words of this letter, to devote a portion of your wealth as a sacred tribute towards erecting 'the Temple of the Most Holy King on the mountain of the Lord'—that ye may have a portion and a righteous record in Jerusalem.

"Let no one among you refuse his aid, but let the poor man contribute his mite for himself and his household freely, as the rich dispenses the bounty wherewith the Lord hath blessed him. Let fathers and their offspring, the aged and the youthful, alike arise in mercy to Zion at this propitious season.

"Let each man encourage his neighbor and say, 'We will be zealous and persevering for our people and the City of our God. And for the love of Zion, and the sake of Jerusalem, we will not rest nor be easy until Jerusalem is praised throughout the earth, and foremost in our joys, even as we have vowed:—If I forget thee, Jerusalem, let my right hand forget her cunning; if I prefer not Jerusalem above my chief joy.'

"Such are the words of your brethren who address you for the glory of God, and for the honor of His land, His people and His inheritance—continually praying for our exiled brethren, and offering up our orisons on holy ground and particularly near the *Western Wall*, that it may be well with you everlastingly as you yourself desire, and we most sincerely wish.

"Signed at Jerusalem, the 18th day of year 5597 a. m., by the Wardens of the Medrash, and members of the Building Committee, on behalf of the Congregation of German Jews in this Holy City.

["Signed] HIRSH JOSEPH,
"DAVID REUBEN,
"NATHAN SADDIS,
"ABRAHAM S. SALMONS,
"MORDECAI AVIGDOR,
"URIAH S. HYAM.

The undersigned Assessors of the Bethdin, by the direction of the

Rev. Chief Rabbi, hereby certify that Rev. Aaron Selig Ashkenazi is actually deputed for the purpose mentioned in the above circular.

"London, the 7th Tebath,
"24 Dec. 5599.

"ISRAEL LEVY,
"AARON LEVY,
"A. L. BARNETT."

Monday, August 3.—Elders Wilford Woodruff and George A. Smith are at Ledbury, Herefordshire.

Tuesday, 4.—Elder Heber C. Kimball left Manchester for Herefordshire, and Joseph Fielding is at Bedford.

Wednesday, 5.

Extract of a Letter from Wilford Woodruff to the Editor of the Millennial Star—Reporting Labors.

BELOVED BRETHREN:—Since Elder George A. Smith and myself left Manchester for the purpose of going to the south of England, we have visited the churches which lay in our route, and found them universally prospering and receiving additions.

We preached in Leek on Sunday, July 10th, and Elder Smith baptized six persons after meeting: and numbers were also baptized in the churches at the Staffordshire Potteries while we were there. We passed through West Bromwich and Birmingham, and found numbers who were anxiously wishing for some of the Elders to visit that region and labor among them. We arrived in Ludbury, Herefordshire, July 22nd, and here spent about two weeks in visiting the churches through this region, and I am happy to inform you, that we have found the Saints universally rejoicing in the truth, and the work progressing upon every hand.

Elder Thomas Richardson has baptized about forty since he came, and Elder William Kay about twenty; they are both much blessed in their labors. Elder Kington is laboring constantly in this wide field, which is under his care; and he with the Elders and Priests generally throughout this region are blessed with many souls as seals of their ministry. We baptized forty on Sunday last in this region, making 250 since the conference. The churches here now number about 800 members and appear [to be] in a very prosperous state. We are expecting Elder Kimball every hour, and soon after his arrival we shall leave the Saints in this region, for the purpose of visiting the city of London and warning the inhabitants thereof.

WILFORD WOODRUFF.

Saturday, 8.—Soon after the July conference at Manchester, Elder Parley P. Pratt started for America for the purpose of getting his family and taking them to England, meantime leaving the *Star* in charge of President Brigham Young, assisted by Elder Willard Richards.

The Prophet's Letter to John C. Bennett—Bidding Him Welcome to Nauvoo, to partake of—its Poverty.

NAUVOO, HANCOCK COUNTY, ILLINOIS,
August 8th, 1840.

DEAR SIR:—Yours of the 25th ultimo, addressed to Elder Rigdon and myself, is received, for which you have our thanks, and to which I shall feel great pleasure in replying.

Although I have not the pleasure of your acquaintance, yet from the kindness manifested towards our people when in bondage and oppression, and from the frank and noble mindedness breathed in your letter, I am brought to the conclusion that you are a friend to suffering humanity and truth.

To those who have suffered so much abuse, and borne the cruelties and insults of wicked men so long, on account of those principles which we have been instructed to teach to the world, a feeling of sympathy and kindness is something like the refreshing breeze and cooling stream at the present season of the year, and are, I assure you, duly appreciated by us.

It would afford me much pleasure to see you at this place, and from the desire you express in your letter to move to this place, I hope I shall soon have that satisfaction.

I have no doubt you would be of great service to this community in practicing your profession, as well as those other abilities of which you are in possession. Since to devote your time and abilities in the cause of truth and a suffering people may not be the means of exalting you in the eyes of this generation, or securing you the riches of the world, yet by so doing you may rely on the approval of Jehovah, "that blessing which maketh rich and addeth no sorrow." Through the tender mercies of our God we have escaped the hands of those who sought our overthrow, and have secure locations in this state, and in the territory of Iowa. Our principal location is at this place, Nauvoo, (formerly Commerce), which is beautifully situated on the banks of the Mississippi, immediately above the lower rapids, and is probably the best and most beautiful site for a city on the river. It has a gradual ascent from the river nearly a mile, then a fine, level, and fertile prairie—a situation in every respect adapted to commercial and agricultural pursuits, but like all other places on the river, is sickly in summer.

The number of inhabitants is nearly three thousand, and is fast increasing. If we are suffered to remain,* there is every prospect of its becoming one of the largest cities on the river, if not in the western world. Numbers have moved in from the seaboard, and a few from the islands of the sea (Great Britain).

It is our intention to commence the erection of some public buildings next spring. We have purchased twenty thousand acres in the Iowa Territory opposite this place, which is fast filling up with our people. I desire all the Saints, as well as all lovers of truth and correct principles, to come to this place as fast as possible, or [as rapidly as] their circumstances will permit, and endeavor, by energy of action and concentration of talent, &c., &c., to effect those objects, that are so dear to us. Therefore my general invitation is, Let all that will, come, and partake of the poverty of Nauvoo freely.

I should be disposed to give you a special invitation to come as early as possible, believing you will be of great service to us; however, you must make arrangements according to your circumstances. Were it possible for you to come here this season to suffer affliction with the people of God, no one will be more pleased to give you a more cordial welcome than myself.

A charter has been obtained from the legislature for a railroad from Warsaw, being immediately below the rapids of the Mississippi, to this place—a distance of about twenty miles, which if carried into operation will be of incalculable advantage to this place, as steamboats can only ascend the rapids at a high stage of water. The soil is good, and I think not inferior to any in the state. Crops are abundant in this section of country—and I think provisions will be reasonable.

I should be very happy could I make arrangements to meet you in Springfield at the time you mention—but cannot promise myself that pleasure. If I should not, probably you can make it convenient to come and pay us a visit here, prior to your removal.

Elder Rigdon is very sick, and has been for nearly twelve months with the fever and ague, which disease is very prevalent here at this time. At present he is not able to leave his room.

Yours, &c.,

JOSEPH SMITH, JUN.

To J. C. Bennett, M. D.

P. S.—Yours of the 30th is just received, in which I am glad to learn that your increasing desire to unite yourself with a people "that are

* "If we are suffered to remain" sounds somewhat prophetic and ominous.

everywhere spoken against," and the anxiety you feel for our welfare—for which you have my best feelings; and I pray that my heavenly Father will pour out His choicest blessings in this world, and enable you by His grace to overcome the evils which are in the world, that you may secure a blissful immortality in the world that is to come.

J. S., Jun.

August 10.—Colonel Seymour Brunson, aged forty years, ten months and twenty-three days, died at Nauvoo. Colonel Brunson was among the first settlers of this place. He has always been a lively stone in the building of God and was much respected by his friends and acquaintances. He died in the triumph of faith, and in his dying moments bore testimony to the Gospel that he had embraced.

Saturday, 15.

Letter of John C. Bennett to Messrs. Smith and Rigdon—Announcing that he will soon be in Nauvoo.

Wayne County Illinois, August 15, 1840.

Reverends Joseph Smith, Jun., and Sidney Rigdon.

Respected Friends:—I have written you several communications to Commerce and Nauvoo, supposing they were different places, but a brother to a lady in your community, now in this place, informs me that they are one and the same.

I have received no reply to my letters, and attribute the delay to a press of business or professional absence. I have come to the conclusion to join your people immediately, and take up my abode with you. Let us adopt as our motto—*Licut partribus sit Deus nobius*—(as God was with our fathers, so may He be with us), and adapt the means to the end, and the victory is ours. The winged warrior of the air will not cease to be our proud emblem of liberty, and the dogs of war will be forever chained.

I shall be with you in about two weeks, and shall devote my time and energies to the advancement of the cause of truth and virtue, and the advocacy of the holy religion which you have so nobly defended, and so honorably sustained.

My love to all the brethren.

With sentiments of fraternal regard.

Yours respectfully,

J. C. Bennett.

CHAPTER X.

A MISSOURI KIDNAPPING—CONTINUED DEVELOPMENT OF THE WORK IN GREAT BRITAIN—THE DEATH OF JOSEPH SMITH, SEN., FIRST PATRIARCH OF THE CHURCH.

Monday, 17.—Met with the High Council of Nauvoo at my office, also the High Council of Iowa. John Batten preferred many charges against Elijah Fordham. After the testimony, and the councillors had spoken, I addressed the Council at some length, showing the situation of the contending parties, that there was in reality no cause of difference; that they had better be reconciled without an action, or vote of the Council, and henceforth live as brethren, and never more mention their former difficulties. They settled accordingly.

Settlement of a Difficulty.

Tuesday, 18.—Elders Kimball, Woodruff, and George A. Smith left Cheltenham for London, one hundred and ten miles, where they arrived in seven and a half hours, at William Allgood's, No. 19 King Street, Borough, and were kindly received by Mrs. Allgood, who took them to the King's Arms Inn.

Great distress is prevailing in Ireland; no work, and provisions very scarce.

The truth is spreading rapidly in England and Scotland.

Friday, 21—Testimony of Benjamin Boyce:

The Kidnapping of Benjamin Boyce, Mr. Brown, et al.

left my home in Nauvoo to go to Adams county, where I had lived the summer before, for the purpose of meeting some debts. I fell in company with a Mr. Brown, who stated to me that he was in search of some horses that had strayed from him. We had not proceeded far together, before we were hailed by twelve armed men, who demanded of us where we were going. I stated to them where I was going, and likewise Mr. Brown stated his business. They then asked if we were "Mormons;" we said we were; they then said that we could go no further; they said they were sworn to kill all the damned "Mormons" that they could find, and took us prisoners, tied us with ropes, and took us to a boat, and four of the company (one by the name of Martin, the others not known) took us to Missouri, to a little town called Tully, where we were put under guard, and kept till 11 o'clock in the evening, when three men came to us with a long rope, and tied it round each of our necks. I asked them what they were going to do with us; one said they were going to take us to the river, kill us, and make catfish bait of us, his name was Uno. They then led us to the woods, I should think about three-quarters of a mile distant; they then parted us, took and stripped me naked, and tied me fast to a tree; one of the company cocked a pistol and placed it close to my ear, and swore, if I attempted to get away, that he would blow out my brains. They then commenced to whip me with large gads which they had for the purpose, and literally mangled me from my shoulders to my knees.

There were in the company, as near as I could recollect, twelve or fourteen; they were stripped of their hats and coats, with their sleeves rolled up, and collars open, which made them look like murderers and robbers. The names, as far as I can recollect, Monday, Uno, and Martin; the others I do not recollect. After keeping me tied in this condition I should think an hour and a half, they then brought Mr. Brown to me, and after some consultation, loosed me from the tree where I was tied, and led us back to the town, put us in a room where I saw Noah Rogers and James Allred. They then tied them about the neck, and led them out, and in the course of the night, they brought them back to the room where we were.

Brother Rogers said they stripped him, and whipped him very badly. This was on the seventh of July. The next day Rogers and myself were taken before a magistrate; nothing proven against us, only that we were "Mormons;" and we were ordered to prison. Brown and Allred, by some means, were liberated, but we (Rogers and myself) were put in jail and put in irons until the 21st of August, when through the kindness of God we made our escape and returned to Nauvoo.

BENJAMIN BOYCE.

Sunday, 23.—Ten persons who had been baptized were confirmed at Carpenter's Hall, Manchester.*

* The entry of the text is the only one made in the Prophet's manuscript history for the 23rd of August, but "Uncle" John Smith, brother of the Prophet's father,

Saturday, 29—Elder Kimball writes: "The brethren are beginning to excite attention in some of the public grounds in London." Out-door preaching is common in England.

Sunday, 30.—Twenty were confirmed at the hall in Manchester.*

The Beginning of Open-air Meetings.

Elders Kimball, Woodruff, and George A. Smith, after having spent ten days visiting the clergymen and preachers and others of the several denominations, asking the privilege of preaching in their chapels, and being continually refused by them in a contemptuous manner, they determined to preach in the open air, Jonah-like; and accordingly went to Smithfield Market† (to the spot where John Rogers‡ was burnt at the stake), for the purpose of preaching at 10 a. m.,

and formerly president of Adam-ondi-Ahman Stake of Zion, in Missouri, makes the following entry in his journal:

"Attended meeting at Nashville. Joseph and Hyrum Smith present and a large assembly of Saints, who voted to commence building a city at Nashville and a place of worship." Nashville, by the way, was situated in Lee county, Iowa, on the Mississippi river, at the head of the Des Moines Rapids, about three miles southeast of Montrose, eight miles north of Keokuk. The Church had purchased twenty thousand acres of land in this vicinity and surveyed out of it a townsite on which a number of Saints located.

* Again from the journal of "Uncle" John Smith we learn that on the 30th day of August, the Prophet Joseph was in Nashville and preached on "Eternal Judgment and the Eternal Duration of Matter."

† Smithfield is noted for other historical incidents than being the scene of John Rogers' martyrdom. It is an open space of nearly six acres in London, England. It was formerly used as a market place, but is now partially laid out in gardens. It was the scene of Bartholomew Fair; William Wallace was executed there; it was the place of the meeting of Wat Tyler and King Richard II, in 1380, when the former was stabbed by the Mayor of London, and then dispatched by the King's attendants. It was the scene of many martyrdoms.

‡ John Rogers suffered martyrdom by being burnt at the stake in Smithfield, on he 4th of February, 1555. He was the first victim of what is known in histoy as the "Marian Persecution;" and which conferred on England's Catholic queen the title of "Bloody Mary." Archbishop Gardiner, however, is usually credited with being the prime instigator of that persecution, though he died before it reached its height, and not before he had shown symptoms of relenting. Cardinal Pole though "naturally humane and gentle," shares the guilt of sanctioning it; "but the chief agent was Bonner, bishop of London, in whose diocese the majority of all the executions took place. * * * * The total number of men, women and children who were burnt—for even children were thrown into the flames and some at the very moment of their birth"—is computed as follows:

where they were notified by the police, that the Lord Mayor had issued orders prohibiting street preaching in the city. A Mr. Connor stepped up and said, "I will show you a place outside of his jurisdiction," and guided them to "Tabernacle Square," where they found an assembly of about 400 people listening to a preacher who was standing on a chair. When he got through another preacher arose to speak. Elder Kimball stated to the first clergyman, "There is a man present from America who would like to preach;" which was granted; when Elder George A. Smith delivered a discourse of about twenty minutes, on the first principles of the Gospel, taking for his text, Mark xvi: 16; after which Elder Kimball asked the preacher to give out another appointment at the same place for the American Elder to preach; when he jumped up and said, "I have just learned that the gentleman who has addressed you is a Latter-day Saint; I know them—they are a very bad people; they have split up many churches, and have done a great deal of hurt." He spoke all manner of evil, and gave the Latter-day Saints a very bad character, and commanded the people not to hear the Elders, "as we have got the Gospel, and can save the people, without infidelity, socialism, or Latter-day Saints."

Elder Kimball asked the privilege of standing on the chair to give out an appointment himself. The preacher said, "You shall not do it; you have no right to preach here;" jerked the chair away from him, and ran away with it. Several of the crowd said, "You have as much right to preach here as he has, and give out your appointment;" whereupon Elder Kimball gave out an appoint-

1555, from February—72; 1556—94; 1557,—79; 1558, from February to September—(when the persecution closed), 39; making a total of 284. It was during this persecution that Ridley and Latimer suffered. On the way to the execution the latter, it is said, "with a keen quaintness which adorns his sermons," uttered the words which fortunately became prophetic—addressing himself to his companion—"Be of good comfort, Master Ridley; play the man; we shall this day light such a candle, by God's grace, in England, as I trust shall never be put out." (History of England, by William Smith, p. 156).

ment for 3 o'clock p. m.; at which time a large congregation was gathered.

After opening the meeting by singing and prayer, Elder Woodruff spoke about thirty minutes, from Gal. i: 8, 9, upon the first principles of the Gospel. Elder Kimball followed upon the same subjects. The people gave good attention, and seemed much interested in what they had heard. The inhabitants who lived around the square opened their windows to four stories high; the most of them were crowded with anxious listeners, which is an uncommon occurrence. The meeting was dismissed in the midst of good feeling.

Mr. Henry Connor invited the Elders to his house. Soon after they arrived here, Elder Kimball felt impressed to return to the place of preaching. When he got there he found a large company talking about the things which they had heard in the afternoon, and they wished him to speak to them again. He did so, when several persons invited him home with them. While Elder Kimball was preaching, several persons came to Brothers Woodruff and Smith to converse on doctrine, when Mr. Connor offered himself for baptism.

Monday, *31*.—Elder Kimball baptized Henry Connor, watchmaker, 52 Ironmonger's Row, London, in Peerless Pool, being the first baptized in that place, and confirmed him the same evening.

The Electric Telegraph.

The electric telegraph is beginning to be used on the Great Western Railroad in England, between Drayton and Paddington, by which intelligence is communicated at the rate of two hundred thousand miles per second.

An Address by the First Presidency to the Church.

To the Saints Scattered Abroad:

BELOVED BRETHREN:—We address a few lines to the members of the Church of Jesus Christ, who have obeyed from the heart that form of doctrine which has been delivered to them by the servants of the Lord, and who are desirous to go forward in the ways of truth and righteousness, and by obedience to the heavenly command, escape the things which are coming on the earth, and secure to themselves an inheritance among the sanctified in the world to come.

Having been placed in a very responsible station in the Church, we at all times feel interested in the welfare of the Saints, and make mention of them continually in our prayers to our heavenly Father, that they may be kept from the evils which are in the world, and ever be found walking in the path of truth.

The work of the Lord in these last days, is one of vast magnitude and almost beyond the comprehension of mortals. Its glories are past description, and its grandeur unsurpassable. It is the theme which has animated the bosom of prophets and righteous men from the creation of the world down through every succeeding generation to the present time; and it is truly the dispensation of the fullness of times, when all things which are in Christ Jesus, whether in heaven or on the earth, shall be gathered together in Him, and when all things shall be restored, as spoken of by all the holy prophets since the world began; for in it will take place the glorious fulfilment of the promises made to the fathers, while the manifestations of the power of the Most High will be great, glorious, and sublime.

The purposes of our God are great, His love unfathomable, His wisdom infinite, and His power unlimited; therefore, the Saints have cause to rejoice and be glad, knowing that "this God is our God forever and ever, and He will be our Guide until death." Having confidence in the power, wisdom, and love of God, the Saints have been enabled to go forward through the most adverse circumstances, and frequently, when to all human appearances, nothing but death presented itself, and destruction inevitable, has the power of God been manifest, His glory revealed, and deliverance effected; and the Saints, like the children of Israel, who came out of the land of Egypt, and through the Red Sea, have sung an anthem of praise to his holy name. This has not only been the case in former days, but in our days, and within a few months, have we seen this fully verified.

Having through the kindness of our God been delivered from destruction, and having secured a location upon which we have again commenced operations for the good of His people, we feel disposed to go forward and unite our energies for the upbuilding of the Kingdom, and establishing the Priesthood in their fullness and glory. The work which has to be accomplished in the last days is one of vast importance, and will call into action the energy, skill, talent, and ability of the Saints, so that it may roll forth with that glory and majesty described by the prophet; and will consequently require the concentration of the Saints, to accomplish works of such magnitude and grandeur.

The work of the gathering spoken of in the Scriptures will be necessary to bring about the glories of the last dispensation It is probably unnecessary to press this subject on the Saints, as we believe the spirit of it is manifest, and its necessity obvious to every considerate mind; and everyone zealous for the promotion of truth and righteousness, is equally so for the gathering of the Saints.

Dear brethren, feeling desirous to carry out the purposes of God to which work we have been called; and to be co-workers with Him in this last dispensation; we feel the necessity of having the hearty cooperation of the Saints throughout this land, and upon the islands of the sea. It will be necessary for the Saints to hearken to counsel and turn their attention to the Church, the establishment of the Kingdom, and lay aside every selfish principle, everything low and groveling; and stand forward in the cause of truth, and assist to the utmost of their power, those to whom has been given the pattern and design. Like those who held up the hands of Moses, so let us hold up the hands of those who are appointed to direct the affairs of the Kingdom, so that they may be strengthened, and be enabled to prosecute their great designs, and be instrumental in effecting the great work of the last days.

Believing the time has now come, when it is necessary to erect a house of prayer, a house of order, a house for the worship of our God, where the ordinances can be attended to agreeably to His divine will, in this region of country—to accomplish which, considerable exertion must be made, and means will be required—and as the work must be hastened in righteousness, it behooves the Saints to weigh the importance of these things, in their minds, in all their bearings, and then take such steps as are necessary to carry them into operation; and arming themselves with courage, resolve to do all they can, and feel themselves as much interested as though the whole labor depended on themselves alone. By so doing they will emulate the glorious deeds of the fathers, and secure the blessings of heaven upon themselves and their posterity to the latest generation.

To those who feel thus interested, and can assist in this great work, we say, let them come to this place; by so doing they will not only assist in the rolling on of the Kingdom, but be in a situation where they can have the advantages of instruction from the Presidency and other authorities of the Church, and rise higher and higher in the scale of intelligence until they can "comprehend with all Saints what is the breadth and length, and depth and heighth; and to know the love of Christ which passeth knowledge."

Connected with the building up of the Kingdom, is the printing and circulation of the Book of Mormon, Doctrine and Covenants, hymn-book, and the new translation of the Scriptures. It is unnecessary to say anything respecting these works; those who have read them, and who have drunk of the stream of knowledge which they convey, know how to appreciate them; and although fools may have them in derision, yet they are calculated to make men wise unto salvation, and sweep away the cobwebs of superstition of ages, throw a light on the proceedings of Jehovah which have already been accomplished, and mark out the future in all its dreadful and glorious realities. Those who have tasted the benefit derived from a study of those works, will undoubtedly vie with each other in their zeal for sending them abroad throughout the world, that every son of Adam may enjoy the same privileges, and rejoice in the same truths.

Here, then, beloved brethren, is a work to engage in worthy of archangels—a work which will cast into the shade the things which have been heretofore accomplished; a work which kings and prophets and righteous men in former ages have sought, expected, and earnestly desired to see, but died without the sight; and well will it be for those who shall aid in carrying into effect the mighty operations of Jehovah.

By order of the First Presidency,

ROBERT B. THOMPSON, Scribe.

Saturday, September 5.—Elders Young and Richards went from Manchester to Liverpool, and in the evening organized a company of Saints bound for New York, by choosing Elder Theodore Turley to preside, with six counselors.

Minutes of the High Council Meeting, at the Office of Joseph Smith, Jun., Nauvoo, September 5th, 1840.

Joseph Smith, Jun., preferred charges against Elder Almon W. Babbitt, predicated on the authority of two letters, one from Thomas Burdick, the other from Oliver Granger and Levi Richards, accusing Elder Babbitt as follows:

First. For stating that Joseph Smith, Jun., had extravagantly purchased three suits of clothes while he was at Washington City, and that Sidney Rigdon had purchased four suits while at the same place, besides dresses in profusion for their families

Second. For having stated that Joseph Smith, Jun., Sidney Rigdon and Elias Higbee had said that they were worth one hundred thousand dollars each, while they were at Washington, and that Joseph Smith,

Jun., had repeated the same statement while in Philadelphia, and for saying that Oliver Granger had stated that he also was worth as much as they (that is, one hundred thousand dollars).

Third. For holding secret councils in the Lord's House, in Kirtland, and for locking the doors of the house, for the purpose of prohibiting certain brethren in good standing in the Church, from being in the Council, thereby depriving them of the use of the house.

Two were appointed to speak on the case, namely, Thomas Grover, Austin Cowles.

Council adjourned till the 6th September, at 2 o'clock, when Council met according to adjournment, the evidences were all heard on the case pending, and the councilors closed on both sides. The parties spoke at length, after which, Joseph Smith withdrew the charge, and both parties were reconciled to each other, things being adjusted to their satisfacion.

Sunday 6.—Elder Young preached.

Monday 7.—This evening, Elders Kimball, Woodruff and George A. Smith, preached in the south Temperance Hall, London.

On Monday night, Elders Brigham Young and Willard Richards, stayed on board the *North America* with the Saints, and on Tuesday morning, about nine o'clock, the vessel went out with a steamer. The Elders accompanied them fifteen or twenty miles, and left them in good spirits. Elder Richards returned to Manchester the same evening and Elder Young on the 10th.

The Generosity of John Benbow.

Elder John Benbow, who had previously furnished two hundred and fifty pounds towards printing the hymn-book, Book of Mormon, etc., relinquished all claim to said money, except such assistance as his friends, who might wish to emigrate to America the next season, might need, leaving the remainder to the disposal of Brigham Young, Willard Richards, and Wilford Woodruff, who borrowed said moneys for the benefit of the Church of Jesus Christ of Latter-day Saints, forever, also the avails of the Gadfield Elm Chapel, when sold.

Wednesday, 9.—There was a terrific storm on the North of Scotland.

Friday, 11.—There was a terrible earthquake at Mount Ararat, which destroyed the town of Makitchevan, damaged all the buildings at Erivan, and devastated the two districts of Sharour and Sourmate in Armenia. A considerable mass was loosened from Mount Ararat and destroyed everything in its way for nearly five miles. The village of Akhouli was buried, with one thousand inhabitants.

Earthquake at Mount Ararat.

Sunday, 13.—Elder Kimball baptized four in London.

Monday, 14.—My father, Joseph Smith, Sen., Patriarch of the whole Church of Jesus Christ of Latter-day Saints, died at Nauvoo.

The Death of Joseph, Sen.

Biography of Joseph Smith, Sen., Presiding Patriarch of the Church, by the Prophet Joseph, his Son.

Joseph Smith, Sen., was born on the 12th day of July, 1771, in Topsfield, Essex county, Massachusetts; he was the second of the seven sons of Asahel and Mary Smith. Asahel was born in Topsfield, March 7th, 1744. He was the youngest son of Samuel and Priscilla Smith. Samuel was born January 26th, 1714, in Topsfield; he was the eldest son of Samuel and Rebecca Smith. Samuel was born in Topsfield, January 20, 1666, and was the son of Robert and Mary Smith, who emigrated from Old England.

My father removed with his father to Tunbridge, Orange county, Vermont, in 1791, and assisted in clearing a large farm of a heavy growth of timber. He married Lucy, daughter of Solomon and Lydia Mack, on the 14th of January, 1796, by whom he had

Alvin Smith, born February 11th, 1798, died November 19th, 1824.
Hyrum, born February 9th, 1800.
Sophronia, born May 16th, 1803.
Joseph, born December 23rd, 1805.
Samuel Harrison, born March 13th, 1808.
Ephraim, born March 13th, 1810, died March 24th, 1810.
William, born March 13th, 1811.
Catherine, born July 28th, 1812.
Don Carlos, born March 25th, 1816.
Lucy, born July 18th, 1824.

At his marriage he owned a handsome farm in Tunbridge. In 1802, he rented it and engaged in mercantile business, and soon after embarked in a venture of [raising] ginseng * to send to China, and was swindled out of the entire proceeds by the shipmaster and agent, he was consequently obliged to sell his farm and all of his effects to pay his debts.

About the year 1816 he removed to Palmyra, Wayne county, New York, bought a farm and cleared two hundred acres, which he lost in consequence of not being able to pay the last installment of the purchase money at the time it was due. This was the case with a great number of farmers in New York, who had cleared land under similar contracts. He afterwards moved to Manchester, Ontario county, New York, procured a comfortable home with sixteen acres of land, where he lived until he removed to Kirtland, Ohio.

He was the first person who received my testimony after I had seen the angel, and exhorted me to be faithful and diligent to the message I had received.† He was baptized April 6th, 1830.

In August, 1830, in company with my brother Don Carlos, he took a mission to St. Lawrence county, New York, touching on his route at several of the Canadian ports, where he distributed a few copies of the Book of Mormon. He also visited his father, brothers and sister residing in St. Lawrence county, bore testimony to the truth which resulted eventually in all the family coming into the Church, excepting his brother Jesse and sister Susan.

He removed with his family to Kirtland in 1831; was ordained Patriarch and President of the High Priesthood [in Kirtland]‡ under the hands of Oliver Cowdery, Sidney Rigdon, Frederick G. Williams and myself, on the 18th of December, 1833; was a member of the First High Council, organized on the 17th of February, 1834, (when he conferred on me and my brother Samuel H., a father's blessing

* Ginseng is a plant, the roots of which are highly esteemed as medicine, being quite generally regarded as possessing the most extraordinary virtues, and as a remedy for almost all diseases, but particularly for exhaustion of body or mind. In China ginseng is sometimes sold for its weight in gold. It was once introduced in Europe, but was soon forgotten. It is a native plant of Chinese Tartary, and grows from one to two feet in height. Its leaves are five fingered and almost smooth. It is doubted by many botanists if this species is really distinct from *phanx quinquefolium*, a common North American plant, doubtless the species referred to in the text, the root of which is now an article of export from North America to China, and is used to some extent as a domestic medicine in the states west of the Alleghanies, but which European and American medical practitioners generally regard as almost worthless.

† From that time on the Prophet of the Dispensation of the Fullness of Times had no truer or more constant or faithful friend than his father.

‡ This term, "High Priesthood," is oftenused in these annals—as it is above—for High Priest. The intent of the above statement is to say that "Father Smith,"—for

In 1836 he traveled in company with his brother John two thousand four hundred miles in Ohio, New York, Pennsylvania, Vermont, and New Hampshire, visiting the branches of the Church in those states and bestowing patriarchal blessings on several hundred persons, preaching the Gospel to all who would hear, and baptizing many. They returned to Kirtland on the 2nd of October, 1836.

During the persecutions in Kirtland in 1837, he was made a prisoner, but fortunately obtained his liberty, and after a very tedious journey in the spring and summer of 1838, he arrived at Far West, Missouri. After I and my brother Hyrum were thrown into the Missouri jails by the mob, he fled from under the exterminating order of Governor Lilburn W. Boggs, and made his escape in midwinter to Quincy, Illinois, from whence he removed to Commerce in the spring of 1839.

The exposures he suffered brought on consumption, of which he died on this 14th day or September, 1840, aged sixty-nine years, two months, and two days. He was six feet, two inches high, was very straight, and remarkably well proportioned. His ordinary weight was about two hundred pounds, and he was very strong and active. In his younger days he was famed as a wrestler, and, Jacob like, he never wrestled with but one man whom he could not throw. He was one of the most benevolent of men; opening his house to all who were destitute. While at Quincy, Illinois, he fed hundreds of the poor Saints who were flying from the Missouri persecutions, although he had arrived there penniless himself.

Tuesday, 15.--The funeral of Joseph Smith, Sen., took place this day, when the following address was delivered by Elder Robert B. Thompson:

The Discourse of Elder Thompson at the Funeral of Joseph Smith, Sen.

The occasion which has brought us together this day, is one of no

so he was affectionately called by the Saints—was ordained Patriarch and the President of the High Priests in Kirtland. That he was not made President of the High Priesthood is evident from the fact that the Prophet Joseph himself at that time was President of the High Priesthood of the Church, a position to which he was ordained at a Conference of High Priests in Amherst, Loraine county, Ohio, in 1832 (see Church History, Vol. I, p. 243 and note.) The Presidency of the High Priesthood carries with it the office of President of the Church: "And again, the duty of the President of the office of the High Priesthood is to preside over the whole Church, and to be like unto Moses. Behold, here is wisdom, yea, to be a seer, a revelator, a translator, and a Prophet, having all the gifts of God which He bestows upon the head of the Church.." (Doc. and Cov. sec. 107, verses 91-9

ordinary importance: for not only has a single family to mourn and sorrow on account of the death of the individual, whose funeral obsequies we this day celebrate; but a whole society; yes, thousands will this day have to say, *a Father in Israel is gone.*

The man whom we have been accustomed to look up to as a *Patriarch*, a Father, and a Counselor is no more an inhabitant of mortality; he has dropped his clay tenement, bid adieu to terrestial scenes, and his spirit now free and unencumbered, roams and expatiates in that world where the spirits of just men made perfect dwell, and where pain and sickness, tribulation and death cannot come.

The friends we have lost prior to our late venerable and lamented Father, were such as rendered life sweet, and in whose society we took great pleasure, and who shed a lustre in the several walks of life in which they moved, and to whom we feel endeared by friendship's sacred ties. Their virtues and kindnesses will long be remembered by the sorrowing widow, the disconsolate husband, the weeping children, the almost distracted and heart-broken parent, and by a large circle of acquaintances and friends. These, like the stars in yonder firmament, shone in their several spheres, and filled that station to which they had been called by the providence of God, with honor to themselves and to the Church; and we feel to mingle our tears with their surviving relatives.

But on this occasion we realize that we have suffered more than an ordinary bereavement, and consequently we feel the more interested If ever there was a man who had claims on the affections of the community, it was our beloved but now deceased Patriarch. If ever there was an event calculated to raise the feelings of sorrow in the human breast, and cause us to drop the sympathetic tear, it certainly is the present; for truly we can say with the king of Israel, "A prince and a great man has fallen in Israel." A man endeared to us by every feeling calculated to entwine around and adhere to the human heart, by almost indissoluble bonds. A man faithful to his God and to the Church in every situation and under all circumstances through which he was called to pass.

Whether in prosperity, surrounded by the comforts of life, a smiling progeny, and all the enjoyments of a domestic circle; or when called upon, like the Patriarchs of old, to leave the land of his nativity, to journey in strange lands, and become subject to all the trials and persecutions that have been heaped upon the Saints with a liberal hand, by characters destitute of every principle of morality or religion, alike regardless of the tender offspring and the aged sire, whose silvery locks and furrowed cheeks ought to have been a sufficient shield from their cruelty; still, like the Apostle Paul he could exclaim, (and his life and conduct have fully borne out the sentiment) "None of these things move me; neither count I my life dear, so that I may finish my course with joy."

The principles of the Gospel were too well established in that breast, and had got too sure a footing there, ever to be torn down, or prostrated by the fierce winds of persecution, the blasts of poverty, or the swollen waves of distress and tribulation. No; thank God, his house was built upon a *rock*—consequently it stood amid the contending elements, firm and unshaken.

The life of our departed father has indeed been an eventful one, having to take a conspicuous part in the great work of the last days; being designated by the ancient prophets who once dwelt on this continent, as the father of him whom the Lord had promised to raise up in the last days, to lead His people Israel; and by a uniform consistent, and a virtuous course, for a long series of years, he has proved himself worthy of such a son, and such a family by whom he had the happiness of being surrounded in his dying moments; most of whom had the satisfaction of receiving his dying benediction.

He was already in the wane of life, when the light of truth broke in upon the world, and with pleasure he hailed its benign and enlightening rays, and was chosen by the Almighty to be one of the witnesses to the Book of Mormon. From that time, his only aim was the promotion of truth—his soul was taken up with the things of the Kingdom; his bowels yearned over the children of men; and it was more than his meat and his drink to do the will of his Father, who is in heaven.

By unceasing industry of himself and family, he had secured a home in the state of New York, where he no doubt expected, with every honest, industrious citizen, to enjoy the blessings of peace and liberty. But when the principles of truth were introduced and the Gospel of Jesus Christ was promulgated by himself and family, friends forsook, enemies raged, and persecution was resorted to by wicked and ungodly men, insomuch that he was obliged to flee from that place, and seek a home in a more hospitable land.

In Ohio he met with many kind and generous friends, and was kindly welcomed by the Saints; many of whom continue to this day, and can call to mind the various scenes which there transpired; many of which were of such a nature as not to be easily obliterated.

While the House of the Lord was building he took great interest in its erection, and daily watched its progress, and had the pleasure of taking a part at the opening, and seeing it crowded by hundreds of pious worshipers. As the King of Israel longed for and desired to see the completion of the House of the Lord, so did he; and with him he could exclaim, "O Lord, I love the habitation of thine house, and the place where thine honor dwelleth." To dwell in the house of the Lord, and to inquire in his temple, was his dailydelight; and in it he enjoyed many blessings, and spent many hours in sweet communion with his heavenly Father. He has trod its sacred aisles, solitary and alone from mankind, long before the king of day has gilded the eastern horizon; and he has uttered his aspirations within its walls, when nature has been asleep. In its holy enclosures have the visions of heaven been opened to his mind, and his soul has feasted on the riches of eternity; and there under his teachings have the meek and humble been instructed, while the widow and the orphan have received his patriarchal blessings.

There he saw the work spreading far and wide; saw the Elders of Israel go forth under his blessing—bore them up by the prayer of faith, and hailed them welcome when they again returned bringing their sheaves with them. There with his aged partner, he spent many happy days in the bosom of his family, whom he loved with all the tenderness of parental affection.

Here I might enlarge, and expatiate on the "scenes of joy and scenes of gladness" which were enjoyed by our beloved Patriarch, but I shall pass on to an event which was truly painful and trying.

The delightful scene soon vanished; the calm was soon succeeded by a storm and the frail bark was driven by the tempest and foaming ocean, for many who had once been proud to acknowledge him a father and a friend, and who sought counsel at his hands, joined with the enemies of truth, and sought his destruction; and would have rejoiced to see his aged and venerable form immured in a dungeon; but, thank God, this they were not suffered to do; he providentially made his escape, and after evading his enemies for some time, he undertook and accomplished a journey of a thousand miles, and bore up under the fatigue and suffering necessarily attendant on such a journey with patient resignation. After a journey of several weeks, he arrived in safety at Far West, in the bosom of the Church, and was cordially welcomed by the Saints, who had found an asylum in the rich and fertile county of Caldwell.

There he, in common with the rest of the Saints, hoped to enjoy the privileges and blessings of peace. There, from the fertile soil and flowery meads, which well repaid the labor of the husbandman, and poured forth abundance for the support of the numerous herds which decked those lovely and wide-spread prairies, he hoped to enjoy uninterrupted, the comforts of domestic life.

But he had not long indulged these pleasing anticipations before the delightful prospect again vanished; the cup of blessing which he began again to enjoy, was dashed from his aged lips; and the cup of sorrow filled to overflowing, was given him instead; and surely he drank it to the very dregs; for not only did he see the Saints in bondage, treated with cruelty, and some of them murdered; but the kind and affectionate parent saw—and ah! how painful was the sight—two of his sons to whom he looked for protection, torn away from their domestic circles, from their weeping and distracted families, by monsters in the shape of men, who swore and threatened to kill them, and who had every disposition to imbrue their hands in their blood. This circumstance was too much for his agitated and now sinking frame to bear up under; and although his confidence in his God was great, and his conduct was that of a Christian and a Saint, yet he felt like a man and a parent. At that time his constitution received a shock from which it never recovered. Ah! yes, there were feelings agitated in the bosom of our deceased friend at that time of no ordinary kind; feelings of painful anxiety, and emotion too great for his earthly tabernacle to contain without suffering a great and a sensible injury; and which from that time began to manifest itself.

It would be unnecessary to trace him and his aged partner (who shared in all his sorrows and afflictions) from such a scene, as many of the Saints are knowing to the privations and sufferings which they, in common with the Church, endured while moving from that land of oppression; suffice it to say, he arrived in safety in Illinois, broken down in constitution and in health, and since then he has labored under severe afflictions and pain, while disease has been slowly but surely undermining his system.

Whenever he had a short respite from pain, he felt a pleasure in atttending to his patriarchal duties, and with cheerfulness he performed them; and frequently his labors have been more than his strength would admit of; but having great zeal for the cause of truth, he felt willing to be spent in the service of his God.

For some time past he has been confined to his bed, and the time of his departure was near at hand. On Saturday evening last, a rupture of a blood vessel took place, when he vomited a large quantity of blood. His family were summoned to his bedside, it being now evident that he could not long survive.

On Sunday he called his children and grandchildren around him, and like the ancient patriarchs gave them his final benediction. Although his strength was far gone, and he was obliged to rest at intervals, yet his mind was clear, perfectly collected, and calm as the gentle zephyrs. The love of God was in his heart, the peace of God rested upon him, and his soul was full of compassion and blessing.

All the circumstances connected with his death, were calculated to lead the mind back to the time when an Abraham, an Isaac and a Jacob bid adieu to mortality, and entered into rest.

His death, like theirs, was sweet, and it certainly was a privilege indeed to witness such a scene; and I was forcibly reminded of the sentiment of the poet:

> The chamber where the good man meets his fate,
> Is privileged beyond the common walk of virtuous life.

There were no reflections of a misspent life—no fearful forebodings of a gloomy nature in relation to the future; the realities of eternity were dawning, the shades of time were lowering; but there was nothing to terrify, to alarm or disturb his mind; no, the principles of the Gospel, which, "bring life and immortality to light," nobly triumphed in nature's final hour. These principles so long taught and cherished by our lamented friend, were honorably maintained to the last; which is not only a consolation to the immediate relatives, but to the Church at large.

The instructions imparted by him will long be remembered by his numerous progeny, who will undoubtedly profit by the same, and strive to render themselves worthy of such a sire; and the whole Church will copy his examples, walk in his footsteps, and emulate his faith and virtuous actions, and commend themselves to his God and to their God.

Notwithstanding his enemies frequently "shot at him, yet his bow abode in strength, and the arms of his hands were made strong by the hands of the mighty God of Jacob," and his courage and resolution never forsook him.

His anxiety for the spread of truth was great, and he lived to see great and important things accomplished. He saw the commencement of the work, small as a mustard seed, and with attention and deep interest he watched its progress; and he had the satisfaction of beholding thousands on this Continent, rejoicing in its truth, and heard the glorious tidings, that other lands were becoming heirs to the richest blessings.

Under these circumstances, he could exclaim, like pious Simeon of old, "Lord, now lettest thou thy servant depart in peace, for mine eyes have seen thy salvation."

Although his spirit has taken its flight and his remains will soon mingle with their mother earth, yet his memory will long be cherished by all who had the pleasure of his acquaintance, and will be fresh and blooming when those of his enemies shall be blotted out from under heaven.

May we, beloved friends, who survive our venerable Patriarch, study to prosecute those things which were so dear to his aged heart, and pray that a double portion of his spirit may be bestowed on us, that we may be the humble instruments in aiding the consummation of the great work which he saw so happily begun; that when we have to stand before the bar of Christ, we may with our departed friend hear the welcome plaudit, "Come up hither, ye blessed of my Father, inherit the kingdom prepared for you from the foundation of the world. Amen.

CHAPTER XI.

THREATENING PORTENTS IN THE ACTIONS OF MISSOURI—GENERAL CONFERENCES IN NAUVOO AND ENGLAND—THE DOCTRINE OF PRIESTHOOD.

Tuesday, September 15, 1840.

"The governor of Missouri, after a silence of about two years, has at last made a demand on Governor Carlin of Illinois, for Joseph Smith, Jun., Sidney Rigdon, Lyman Wight, Parley P. Pratt, Caleb Baldwin, and Alanson Brown, as fugitives from justice.

"The demand it seems has been complied with by Governor Carlin, and an order issued for their apprehension; accordingly our place has recently received a visit from the sheriff for these men; but through the tender mercies of a kind Providence, who by His power has sustained, and once delivered them from the hands of the blood-thirsty and savage race of beings in the shape of men that tread Missouri's delightful soil; they were not to be found—as the Lord would have it, they were gone from home, and the sheriff returned, of course without them.

"These men do not feel disposed to again try the solemn realities of mob law in that state; and a free and enlightened republic should respond against it, for Missouri has no claim on them, but they have claim on Missouri.

"What right have they to demand of Governor Carlin, as fugitives from justice, men against whom no process had ever been found in that state—no, not so much as the form of a process? They were taken by a mob militia, and dragged from everything that was dear and sacred, and tried (without their knowledge) by a court martial, condemned to be shot, but this failing, they were forced into confinement, galled with chains, deprived of the comforts of life, and even that which was necessary to save life, then brought to a pretended trial, without even having a legal process served, and then deprived of the privilege of defense. They were taken by a mob, tried, condemned and imprisoned by the same, and this Missouri cannot deny.

"What a beautiful picture Governor Boggs has presented to the world, after driving twelve or fifteen thousand inhabitants from their homes, forcing them to leave the state under the pain of extermination, and confiscating their property, and murdering innocent men, women and children; then, because that a few made their escape from his murdering hand, and have found protection in a land of equal rights, so that his plans and designs have all been unfruitful, to that extent that he has caused 'Mormonism' to spread with double vigor; he now has the presumption to demand them back, in order that his thirst for innocent blood may yet be satiated.

"He has no business with them; they have not escaped from justice, but from the hands of a cursed, infuriated, inhuman set, or race of beings who are enemies to their country, to their God, to themselves, and to every principle of righteousness and humanity. They loathe Christianity, and despise the people of God; they war against truth, and inherit lies; virtue they tread under their feet; while vice (with her ten thousand offspring) is their welcome associate; therefore, men on whom Missouri has no claim, she cannot, no, she never shall have."*

Sunday, 20.—Elder Willard Richards went to Preston, held a conference, ordained five Elders, eleven Priests, eight Teachers, one Deacon, and returned to Manchester same day.

Letter of Samuel Bent and George W. Harris to the Presidency—Reporting Labors.

CINCINNATI, Sept. 23, 1840.

To the First Presidency and High Council of the Church of Jesus Christ of Latter-day Saints:

We gladly embrace this opportunity of conveying a few lines to you by Ebenezer Robinson, who we expect will leave this place for Nauvoo in a few days.

Brother George W. Harris and myself have visited the several branches of the Church in Adams county, Pike county, Jacksonville, and Springfield. On our way we stopped at Terre Haute, and Pleasant Garden, Indiana. We found the brethren generally very willing and anxious to do all in their power to assist the Church in the great and glorious cause that we have engaged in respecting the printing of the several books in contemplation, but I am sorry to say I found them destitute of the means to relieve our present necessity.

However, we have succeeded in obtaining several notes of hand from

* The foregoing is an editorial in the *Times and Seasons* for September, 1840.

different brethren in the state of Illinois, to the amount of about eighty-three dollars, which will come due on the first day of October next, and we have handed them over to Ebenezer Robinson, to be delivered to Joseph Smith, Jun., for collection. We expect Brother Robinson will arrive with them at the time they become due.

We have obtained some money, which we have paid over to Brother Ebenezer Robinson. We have also given our obligations as agents for the Church, to Shepherd and Stearns to the amount of three hundred dollars, two hundred of which becomes due on the twenty-sixth day of November next, and the other one hundred on the twenty sixth day of December next, being the amount due Shepherd and Stearns for the stereotype plates.

We have taken up the bond that Brother Brown gave for the wagon or carriage which he let Joseph Smith, Jun., have, and we have succeeded in procuring a horse and harness to put alongside of the other horse to make it easier for him. We got said horse and harness by contributions from the brethren at Dayton and West Milton, Ohio.

Brother Ebenezer Robinson (we think) has been very economical, diligent, and persevering, and successful in the business whereupon he was sent. He has gained the confidence of the gentlemen with whom he has been transacting business in the city, and has done honor to the cause of Christ and His Church of Latter-day Saints. We can further say to you brethren, we think the course he has taken, and our united exertions with him, have established the credit of the Church of Jesus Christ of Latter-day Saints in this place (I mean as to business transactions), to that extent that we can obtain any amount of paper, type, and other materials requisite to carry on the printing business to a large extent, and upon terms that will warrant our success.

We therefore shall go on with renewed courage and zeal, trusting in the Lord to prepare the way before us, and we feel to ask your prayers that God may peradventure expand the minds of the Saints abroad, that they may be able to comprehend the magnitude of the work we so much desire to accomplish, which in all probability will induce them to donate with alacrity.

Brother John E. Page is preaching with the manifestations of the Spirit and power in this place, and with considerable success. We think when Brother Page leaves the city of Cincinnati, the inhabitants thereof will be left without excuse for not receiving the Gospel of Jesus Christ, and his garments clear from their blood in the day of judgment.

Accept our love and best wishes.

Yours in the bonds of the New and Everlasting Covenant,

SAMUEL BENT,
GEORGE W. HARRIS.

Letter of John E. Page to the Presidency—Reporting Progress of Palestine Mission.

CINCINNATI, September 23, 1840.

To the President and Council of the Church of Jesus Christ of Latter-day Saints, and also to all the Saints Assembled in General Conference:

Your humble servant embraces with pleasure this opportunity to pen for your edification a few lines. I congratulate you upon the steady march and advancement of the cause of Christ, as [it] has fallen under my observation. Elder Hyde and myself have been treated with respect, and had the greatest attention paid us by the brethren and sisters; and by gentlemen and ladies of the first class in society, we have been made welcome very heartily to their dwellings and comforts of life. When we separate from them they grip our hands with tears standing full in their eyes, bidding farewell, and often leave something noble with us to help us on our mission; and a firm promise that they will duly reflect on the great things which we have told them. They ardently request us to send them some competent Elder to preach to them.

Yes, dear brethren, the cause of truth is marching onward with unparalleled rapidity, and victory! Victory! will soon be the shout of all the faithful in Christ; and thank the Lord, thank the Lord, is the language of unworthy me, that I have lived to see 1840, with all its attendant evidences of the truth of the Book of Mormon, and the Book of Doctrine and Covenants.

I must save a place in this communication to make some remarks concerning Brother Ebenezer Robinson. I can say, in truth and soberness, that he merits the esteem and confidence of the Saints and all good men for his diligence and economy while getting the Book of Mormon stereotyped, &c., here. The honest and frank course he has pursued towards the gentlemen with whom he has been concerned in business (viz., Messrs. Shepherd, Stearns, and others), has won their everlasting respect and esteem, judging from their own manifestations to me.

Dear brethren and sisters, your humble servants, Orson Hyde and myself, sincerely solicit your special prayers, sealed with a hearty amen.

Elder Hyde is truly a humble servant of the Lord, and a very agreeable companion in the ministry. Our hearts are one, our faith is one, and the strongholds of Satan quake before us. We desire to have grace to perform our mission, that we may return to our families and brethren with triumph and joy.

I anticipate that Elder Hyde is in New York City. I am waiting to obtain a few copies of the third edition of the Book of Mormon. To raise means is hard, yet we trust in the Lord. I shall go to Philadelphia as soon as possible.

I have baptized thirteen in this city; many are believing, and some halting between two opinions; and have baptized in all since I started, eighty-four.

I have had a vision from the Lord, which manifested the present state of the world respecting the Jews, Jerusalem, the remnant of Israel, and also the Gentile world. As hasty summer fruit, so is this nation; as a vineyard of grapes fully ripe, ready to be gathered for the press, so are all the nations of the earth.

I want the conference to send some faithful and competent Elder to this place, to nurse the seed or word that has been sown here, and shall leave this matter with Ebenezer Robinson to lay before the conference.

Elders Bent and Harris are here, and are using all their energies, both of mind and body, to fill their calling. I deem them amply qualified to discharge the function of their office, provided they keep humble.

Dear brethren, remember me to my family, and pray for them; remember me to Sister Hyde, and also all of the wives of the Elders in particular, whose husbands are in the field. Tell them to pray for us. I hope the authorities of the Church will see that they are provided with food and raiment, that they may enjoy life with you.

Yours in the bonds of the Covenant,

JOHN E. PAGE.

Monday, 28.

Extracts from Orson Hyde's Letter—Signs in the Heavens.

BURLINGTON COUNTY, NEW JERSEY.

I left Elder Page at Cincinnati the latter part of August, and came on up the Ohio river as far as Wellsburgh, Virginia. I stopped with Father James. Here I preached twice, and baptized three persons; came on by stage and steamboats to Pittsburg; from thence took the canal to Leechburgh, where I stopped and preached to a small number of Saints, raised up by the instrumentality of Father Nickerson— in good spirits.

As I left this place about nine o'clock in the morning, the most remarkable phenomenon occurred in the heavens that I ever witnessed. There appeared two bright and luminous bodies, one on the north and the other on the south of the sun; in length about ten yards, inclining to a circle resembling a rainbow, about fifty yards distant from the sun; apparently east about twenty-five yards, was a body of light as brilliant almost as the sun itself; and on the west, a great distance from the sun, appeared a white semi-circle passing half way round the horizon, and another crossing it at right angles, exhibiting a scene of the sublimest kind. It was a great wonder to the passengers on board the boat. Put this with the fact that the Jews are gathering home, and that all Europe is in commotion and on the eve of breaking out in open hostilities; and also that the tree of liberty, which has long flourished in the republican soil of America, has been girdled, and her green foliage, which has shielded and protected the sons of oppression from the scorching rays of despotic power, already begins to wither like the accursed fig tree—and what language do these speak to the Saints! "Lift up your heads, for your redemption draweth near!" * * * * * *

I came on, and met with the Saints in Chester county, Pennsylvania, laboring there about one week with Brother Barnes, where we added six to their number. I preached about one week in Philadelphia, and baptized twelve; came on to this place with Brothers Snow and Barnes, and held a two-days' meeting, at which sixteen were baptized. I shall return to Philadelphia in a few days, where I expect to meet Brother Page, and then, if the Lord will, after holding a few meetings in this country, we shall proceed on to New York, there to take ship and sail over the seas.

Orson Hyde.

On the night of the 28th, Elder Heber C. Kimball had the following dream, as related by himself:

Elder Heber C. Kimball's Dream.

Having great anxiety for the welfare of the small branch which we had raised in London, I retired to rest and had the following dream. I thought that we dug a well on high ground in order to obtain water, and after digging some considerable time, we came to an excellent spring; we then commenced to back it up, but before it was finished, we had occasion to leave for a short time and when we returned to complete it, we found it carefully filled up with sand, and all attempts to remove it proved unavailing, we thought it better to choose another spot on lower ground, where we were successful. When we returned to London, we experienced a perfect fulfillment of my dream—having to open a new preaching place at Barrett's Academy, King Square, Goswell Road, our former place being closed against us.

Tuesday, *29.*—Elders Heber C. Kimball and George A. Smith left London for the Manchester conference.

Saturday, *October 3.*

Minutes of the General Conference of the Church of Jesus Christ of Latter-day Saints, held in Nauvoo, Hancock County, Illinois, Beginning October 3, 1840.

The conference was opened with prayer by President William Marks. President Joseph Smith was then unanimously called to the chair, and Robert B. Thompson appointed clerk.

A letter from Elders Bent and Harris, and one from Elder John E. Page were then read by the clerk, which gave very satisfactory accounts of their mission.

On motion, Resolved: That a committee be appointed to ordain such as have recommends to this conference for ordination, and that Jonathan H. Hale, Elisha H. Groves, Charles C. Rich, John Murdock, and Simeon Carter, compose said committee, and report their proceedings before the conference closes.

The President arose and stated that there had been several depredations committed on the citizens of Nauvoo, and thought it expedient that a committee be appointed to search out the offenders, and bring them to justice.

Whereupon it was Resolved: That Joseph Smith, Elias Higbee, William Marks, Vinson Knight, William Law, Charles C. Rich, and Dimick B. Huntington, compose said committee.

On motion, Resolved: That Robert B. Thompson be appointed the General Church Clerk, in the room of George W. Robinson, who intends to remove to Iowa.

It having been requested by Elder Page, that the conference would appoint an Elder to take charge of the church which he and Elder Hyde had raised up in Cincinnati, on motion, Resolved: That Elder Samuel Bennett be appointed to preside there.

The president then arose and stated that it was necessary that something should be done with regard to Kirtland, so that it might be built up; and gave it as his opinion, that the brethren from the east might gather there, and also that it was necessary that some one should be appointed from this conference to preside over that stake. On motion, Resolved: That Elder Almon W. Babbitt be appointed to preside over the church in Kirtland, and that he choose his own counselors.

Conference adjourned for one hour.

One o'clock p. m. Conference met pursuant to adjournment. An opportunity was given to the brethren who had any remarks to make on suitable locations for stakes of Zion. Elder H. W. Miller stated that it was the desire of a number of the brethren residing in Adams county, to have a stake appointed at Mount Ephrain in that county, and stated the advantages of the place for agricultural purposes.

On motion, Resolved: That a stake be appointed at Mount Ephraim, in Adams county.

There being several applications for the appointment of stakes, it was Resolved: That a committee be appointed to organize stakes between this place and Kirtland, and that Hyrum Smith, Lyman Wight, and Almon W. Babbitt, compose said committee.

The President then spoke of the necessity of building a "House of the Lord" in this place. Whereupon it was Resolved: That the Saints build a house for the worship of God, and that Reynolds Cahoon, Elias Higbee, and Alpheus Cutler be appointed a committee to build the same.

On motion, Resolved: That a commencement be made ten days from this date, and that every tenth day be appropriated for the building of the house.

President Hyrum Smith arose and stated that there were several individuals who, on moving to this place, had not settled with their creditors, and had no recommend from the branches of the churches where they had resided. On motion, Resolved: That those persons moving to this place, who do not bring a recommend, be disfellowshiped.

John C. Bennett, M. D., then spoke at some length, on the oppression to which the Church had been subjected, and remarked that it was necessary for the brethren to stand by each other, and resist every unlawful attempt at persecution.

Elder Lyman Wight then addressed the meeting. Adjourned till tomorrow morning.

Sunday morning, October 4.

Conference met pursuant to adjournment, and was opened with prayer by Elder Almon W. Babbitt.

The clerk was then called upon to read the report of the Presidency in relation to the city plat, after which the President made some observations on the status of the debts on the city plat, which will appear at the close of these conference minutes, and advised that a committee be appointed to raise funds to liquidated the same. On motion, Resolved: That William Marks and Hyrum Smith compose said committee.

On motion, Resolved: That a committee be appointed to draft a bill for the incorporation of the town of Nauvoo, and other purposes.

Resolved: That Joseph Smith, John C. Bennett, and Robert B. Thompson be said committee.

Resolved: That John C. Bennett be appointed delegate, to urge the passage of said bill through the legislature.

President Hyrum Smith then rose and gave some general instructions to the Church. Conference adjourned for one hour.

One o'clock p. m. Conference met pursuant to adjournment, and was opened with prayer by Elder John P. Greene.

President Joseph Smith then rose and delivered a discourse on the subject of baptism for the dead, which was listened to with considerable interest, by the vast multitude assembled.

Dr. John C. Bennett from the committee to draft a charter for the city, and for other purposes, reported the outlines thereof. On motion, Resolved: That the same be adopted.

Elder Ebenezer Robinson then rose and gave an account of the printing of another edition of the Book of Mormon, and stated that it was now nearly completed, and that arrangements had been made for the printing of the hymn-book, Book of Doctrine and Covenants, &c.

Conference adjourned to Monday morning.

Monday morning, October 5.

Conference met pursuant to adjournment, and was opened with prayer by Elder Lyman Wight.

Elder Robert B. Thompson, after a few preliminary remarks, read an article on the Priesthood, composed by President Joseph Smith, which will appear at the close of the conference minutes; after which Elder Babbitt delivered an excellent discourse on the same subject, at considerable length.

Conference adjourned for one hour. During the intermission a large number was baptized.

Two o'clock p. m. Conference met pursuant to adjournment. Elder Lyman Wight addressed the congregation on the subject of baptism for the dead, and other subjects of interest to the Church.

The President then made some observations and pronounced his benediction on the assembly.

Dr. John C. Bennett said that many persons had been accused of crime, and been looked upon as guilty, when on investigation it has been ascertained that nothing could be proved against them. Whereupon, on motion, it was Resolved: That no person be considered guilty of crime, unless proved so by the testimony of two or three witnesses.

He next brought before the conference the treatment the Saints had experienced in Missouri, and wished to know whether the conference would take any further steps in relation to obtaining redress. On motion, resolved: That Elias Higbee and Robert B. Thompson be appointed a committee to obtain redress for the wrongs sustained in Missouri.

The committee on ordinations reported that they had ordained thirty-nine to the ministry.

On motion, Resolved: That this conference be dismissed, and that the next conference be held on the 6th day of April next.

JOSEPH SMITH, President.
ROBERT B. THOMPSON, Clerk.

The following is the article on Priesthood referred to in the conference minutes:

PRIESTHOOD.

In order to investigated the subject of the Priesthood, so important to this, as well as every succeeding generation, I shall proceed to trace the subject as far as I possibly can from the Old and New Testaments.

There are two Priesthoods spoken of in the Scriptures, viz., the Melchisedek and the Aaronic or Levitical. Although there are two Priesthoods, yet the Melchisedek Priesthood comprehends the Aaronic or Levitical Priesthood, and is the grand head, and holds the highest authority which pertains to the Priesthood, and the keys of the Kingdom of God in all ages of the world to the latest posterity on the earth, and is the channel through which all knowledge, doctrine, the plan of salvation, and every important matter is revealed from heaven.

Its institution was prior to "the foundation of this earth, or the morning stars sang together, or the Sons of God shouted for joy," and is the highest and holiest Priesthood, and is after the order of the Son of God, and all other Priesthoods are only parts, ramifications, powers and blessings belonging to the same, and are held, controlled, and directed by it. It is the channel through which the Almighty commenced revealing His glory at the beginning of the creation of this earth, and through which He has continued to reveal Himself to the children of men to the present time, and through which He will make known His purposes to the end of time.

Commencing with Adam, who was the first man, who is spoken of in Daniel as being the "Ancient of Days," or in other words, the first and oldest of all, the great, grand progenitor of whom it is said in another place he is Michael, because he was the first and father of all, not only by progeny, but the first to hold the spiritual blessings, to whom was made known the plan of ordinances for the salvation of his posterity unto the end, and to whom Christ was first revealed, and through whom Christ has been revealed from heaven, and will continue to be revealed from henceforth. Adam holds the keys of the dispensation of the fullness of times; i. e., the dispensation of all the times have been and will be revealed through him from the beginning to Christ, and from Christ to the end of all the dispensations that are to be revealed. "Having made known unto us the mystery of His will, according to His good pleasure which He hath purposed in Himself: that in the dispensation of the fullness of times He might gather together in one all things in Christ, both which are in heaven, and which are on earth; even in him." (Ephesians, 1st chap., 9th and 10 verses).

Now the purpose in Himself in the winding up scene of the last dispensation is that all things pertaining to that dispensation should be conducted precisely in accordance with the preceding dispensations.

And again. God purposed in Himself that there should not be an eternal fullness until every dispensation should be fulfilled and gathered together in one, and that all things whatsoever, that should be gathered together in one in those dispensations unto the same fullness and eternal glory, should be in Christ Jesus; therefore He set the ordinances to be the same forever and ever, and set Adam to watch over them, to reveal them from heaven to man, or to send angels to reveal them. "Are they not all ministering spirits, sent forth to minister for them who shall be heirs of salvation?" (Hebrews, i, 14).

These angels are under the direction of Michael or Adam, who acts under the direction of the Lord. From the above quotation we learn that Paul perfectly understood the purposes of God in relation to His connection with man, and that glorious and perfect order which He established in Himself, whereby he sent forth power, revelations, and glory.

God will not acknowledge that which He has not called, ordained, and chosen. In the beginning God called Adam by His own voice. "And the Lord called unto Adam and said unto him, Where art thou? And he said, I heard thy voice in the garden, and I was afraid because I was naked, and hid myself." (See Genesis 3rd chap., 9, 10.) Adam received commandments and instructions from God: this was the order from the beginning.

That he received revelations, commandments and ordinances at the beginning is beyond the power of controversy; else how did they begin to offer sacrifices to God in an acceptable manner? And if they offered sacrifices they must be authorized by ordination. We read in Genesis, (4th chap., 4th), that Abel brought of the firstlings of the flock and the fat thereof, and the Lord had respect to Abel and to his offering. And, again, "By faith Abel offered unto God a more excellent sacrifice than Cain, by which he obtained witness that he was righteous, God testifying of his gifts; and by it he being dead, yet speaketh." (Hebrews xi; 4). How doth he yet speak? Why he magnified the Priesthood which was conferred upon him, and died a righteous man, and therefore has become an angel of God by receiving his body from the dead, holding still the keys of his dispensation; and was sent down from heaven unto

Paul to minister consoling words, and to commit unto him a knowledge of the mysteries of godliness.

And if this was not the case, I would ask, how did Paul know so much about Abel, and why should he talk about his speaking after he was dead? Hence, that he spoke after he was dead must be by being sent down out of heaven to administer.

This, then, is the nature of the Priesthood; every man holding the Presidency of his dispensation, and one man holding the Presidency of them all, even Adam; and Adam receiving his Presidency and authority from the Lord, but cannot receive a fullness until Christ shall present the Kingdom to the Father, which shall be at the end of the last dispensation.

The power, glory and blessings of the Priesthood could not continue with those who received ordination only as their righteousness continued; for Cain also being authorized to offer sacrifice, but not offering it in righteousness, was cursed. It signifies, then, that the ordinances must be kept in the very way God has appointed; otherwise their Priesthood will prove a cursing instead of a blessing.

If Cain had fulfilled the law of righteousness as did Enoch, he could have walked with God all the days of his life, and never failed of a blessing. "And Enoch walked with God after he begat Methuselah 300 years, and begat sons and daughters, and all the days of Enoch were 365 years; and Enoch walked with God, and he was not, for God took him." (Gen. 5th chap., 22nd ver.) Now this Enoch God reserved unt Himself, that he should not die at that time, and appointed unto him a ministry unto terrestrial bodies, of whom there has been but little revealed. He is reserved also unto the Presidency of a dispensation, and more shall be said of him and terrestrial bodies in another treatise. He is a ministering angel, to minister to those who shall be heirs of salvation, and appeared unto Jude as Abel did unto Paul; therefore Jude spoke of him (14, 15 verses). And Enoch, the seventh from Adam, revealed these sayings: "Behold, the Lord cometh with ten thousand of His Saints."

Paul was also acquainted with this character, and received instructions from him. "By faith Enoch was translated, that he should not see death, and was not found, because God had translated him: for before his translation he had this testimony, that he pleased God; but without faith, it is impossible to please Him, for he that cometh to God must believe that He is, and that he is a revealer to those who diligently seek him." (Heb. 11, 5).

Now the doctrine of translation is a power which belongs to this Priesthood. There are many things which belong to the powers of the Priesthood and the keys thereof, that have been kept hid from before the foundation of the world; they are hid from the wise and prudent to be revealed in the last times.

Many have supposed that the doctrine of translation was a doctrine whereby men were taken immediately into the presence of God, and into an eternal fullnes, but this is a mistaken idea. Their place of habitation is that of the terrestrial order, and a place prepared for such characters He held in reserve to be ministering angels unto many planets, and who as yet have not entered into so great a fullness as those who are resurrected from the dead. "Others were tortured, not accepting deliverance, that they might obtain a better resurrection." (See Heb. 11th chap., part of the 35th verse.)

Now it was evident that there was a better resurrection, or else God would not have revealed it unto Paul. Wherein then, can it be said a better resurrection. This distinction is made between the doctrine of the actual resurrection and translation: translation obtains deliverance from the tortures and sufferings of the body, but their existence will prolong as to the labors and toils of the ministry, before they can enter into so great a rest and glory.

On the other hand, those who were tortured, not accepting deliverance, received an immediate rest from their labors. "And I heard a voice from heaven, saying, Blessed are the dead who die in the Lord, for from henceforth they do rest from their labors and their works do follow them." (See Revelation, 14th chap., 13th verse).

They rest from their labors for a long time, and yet their work is held in reserve for them, that they are permitted to do the same work, after they receive a resurrection for their bodies. But we shall leave this subject and the subject of the terrestrial bodies for another time, in order to treat upon them more fully.

The next great, grand Patriarch [after Enoch] who held the keys of the Priesthood was Lamech. "And Lamech lived one hundred and eighty-two years and begat a son, and he called his name Noah, saying, this same shall comfort us concerning our work and the toil of our hands because of the ground which the Lord has cursed." (See Gen. 5th chap., 28th and 29th verses.) The Priesthood continued from Lamech to Noah: "And God said unto Noah, The end of all flesh is before me, for the earth is filled with violence through them, and behold I will destroy them with the earth." (Gen. 6: 13.)

Thus we behold the keys of this Priesthood consisted in obtaining the voice of Jehovah that He talked with him [Noah] in a familiar and friendly manner, that He continued to him the keys, the covenants, the power and the glory, with which he blessed Adam at the beginning; and the offering of sacrifice, which also shall be continued at the last time; for all the ordinances and duties that ever have been required by the Priesthood, under the directions and commandments of the Almighty in any of the dispensations, shall all be had in the last dispensation, therefore all things had under the authority of the Priesthood at any former period, shall be had again, bringing to pass the restoration spoken of by the mouth of all the Holy Prophets; then shall the sons of Levi offer an acceptable offering to the Lord. "And he shall sit as a refiner and purifier of silver: and he shall purify the sons of Levi, and purge them as gold and silver, that they may offer unto the Lord. (See Malachi 3: 3).

It will be necessary here to make a few observations on the doctrine set forth in the above quotation, and it is generally supposed that sacrifice was entirely done away when the Great Sacrifice [*i. e.*, the sacrifice of the Lord Jesus] was offered up, and that there will be no necessity for the ordinance of sacrifice in future: but those who assert this are certainly not acquainted with the duties, privileges and authority of the priesthood, or with the Prophets.

The offering of sacrifice has ever been connected and forms a part of the duties of the Priesthood. It began with the Priesthood, and will be continued until after the coming of Christ, from generation to generation. We frequently have mention made of the offering of sacrifice by the servants of the Most High in ancient days, prior to the law of Moses; which ordinances will be continued when the Priesthood is restored with all its authority, power and blessings.

Elijah was the last Prophet that held the keys of the Priesthood, and who will, before the last dispensation, restore the authority and deliver the keys of the Priesthood, in order that all the ordinances may be attended to in righteousness. It is true that the Savior had authority and power to bestow this blessing; but the sons of Levi were too prejudiced. "And I will send Elijah the Prophet before the great and terrible day of the Lord," etc., etc. Why send Elijah? Because he holds the keys of the authority to administer in all the ordinances of the Priesthood; and without the authority is given, the ordinances could not be administered in righteousness.

It is a very prevalent opinion that the sacrifices which were offered were entirely consumed. This was not the case; if you read Leviticus, second chap., second and third verses, you will observe that the priests took a part as a memorial and offered it up before the Lord, while the remainder was kept for the maintenance of the priests; so that the offerings and sacrifices are not all consumed upon the altar—but the blood is sprinkled, and the fat and certain other portions are consumed.

These sacrifices, as well as every ordinance belonging to the Priesthood, will, when the Temple of the Lord shall be built, and the sons of Levi be purified, be fully restored and attended to in all their powers, ramifications, and blessings. This ever did and ever will exist when the powers of the Melchisedic Priesthood are sufficiently manifest; else how can the restitution of all things spoken of by the holy Prophets be brought to pass? It is not to be understood that the law of Moses will be established again with all its rites and variety of ceremonies; this has never been spoken of by the Prophets; but those things which existed prior to Moses' day, namely, sacrifice, will be continued.

It may be asked by some, what necessity for sacrifice, since the Great Sacrifice was offered? In answer to which, if repentance, baptism, and faith existed prior to the days of Christ, what necessity for them since that time? The Priesthood has descended in a regular line from father to son, through their succeeding generations. (See Book of Doctrine and Covenants).*

REPORT OF THE PRESIDENCY.†

The First Presidency of the Church of Jesus Christ of Latter-day Saints would respectfully report—

That they feel rejoiced to meet the Saints at another General Conference, and under circumstances as favorable as the present. Since our settlement in Illinois we have for the most part been treated with courtesy and respect, and a feeling of kindness and of sympathy has generally been manifested by all classes of the community, who, with us, deprecate the conduct of those men whose dark and blackening deeds are stamped with everlasting infamy and disgrace. The contrast between our past and present situation is great. Two years ago mobs were threatening, plundering, driving and murdering the Saints. Our burning houses lighted up the canopy of heaven. Our women and children, houseless and destitute, had to wander from place to place to seek a shelter from the rage of persecuting foes. Now we enjoy peace, and can worship the God of heaven and earth without molestation, and expect to be able to go forward and accomplish the great and glorious work to which we have been called.

Under these circumstances we feel to congratulate the Saints of the Most High, on the happy and pleasing change in their circumstances, condition and prospects, and which those who shared in the perils and distress, undoubtedly appreciate; while prayers and thanksgivings daily ascend to that God who looked upon our distresses and delivered us from danger and death, and whose hand is over us for good.

From the unpropitious nature of the weather, we hardly expected to behold so many of our friends on this occasion; in this, however, we are agreeably disappointed, which gives us strong assurance that the Saints are as zealous, untiring, and energetic as ever, in the great work of the last days; and gives us joy and consolation, and greatly encour-

* A discourse on the same subject to the Twelve will be found in vol. iii, p. 385, *et seq*.

† This is the report referred to in the conference minutes.

ages us, while contending with the difficulties which necessarily lie in our way. Let the brethren ever manifest such a spirit, and hold up our hands, and we must, we will go forward; the work of the Lord shall roll forth, the Temple of the Lord be reared, the Elders of Israel be encouraged, Zion be built up, and become the praise, the joy, and the glory of the whole earth, and the song of praise, glory, honor, and majesty to Him that sitteth upon the throne, and to the Lamb for ever and ever, shall reverberate from hill to hill, from mountain to mountain, from island to island, and from continent to continent, and the kingdoms of this world become the kingdom of our God and His Christ.

We are glad indeed to know that there is such a spirit of union existing throughout the churches, at home and abroad, on this continent, as well as on the islands of the sea; for by this principle, and by a concentration of action, shall we be able to carry into effect the purposes of our God.

From the Elders abroad we receive the most cheering accounts. Wherever the faithful laborer has gone forth weeping, sowing the seed of truth, he has returned with joy, bringing his sheaves with him; and the information we receive from all quarters is that the laborers are few and that the harvest is great. Many wealthy and influential people have embraced the Gospel, so that not only will the poor rejoice in that they are exalted, but the rich in that they are made low. The calls to the Southern States are indeed great; many places which a short time ago would think it a disgrace to give shelter to a "Mormon," on account of the many misrepresentations which were abroad, now desire to hear an Elder of the Church of the Latter-day Saints.

On the islands of the sea, namely, Great Britain, there continues to be a steady flow of souls into the Church. Branches have been organized in many large and populous cities, and the whole land appears to be thirsting for the pure streams of knowledge and salvation.

The Twelve have already printed a new edition of the hymn-book, and they issue a monthly periodical in that land. Several families have already arrived here from England, and a number more are on their way to this place, and are expected this fall.

If the work rolls forth with the same rapidity it has heretofore done, we may soon expect to see flocking to this place, people from every land and from every nation; the polished European, the degraded Hottentot, and the shivering Laplander; persons of all languages, and of every tongue, and of every color; who shall with us worship the Lord of Hosts in His holy temple and offer up their orisons in His sanctuary.

It was in consideration of these things, and that a home might be provided for the Saints, that induced us to purchase the present city for a place of gathering for the Saints, and the extensive tract of land on the opposite side of the Mississippi. Although the purchase at the time, and under the peculiar circumstances of the Church, appeared to many to be large and uncalled for; yet from what we now see, it is apparent to all that we shall soon have to say, "This place is too straight, give us room that we may dwell." We therefore hope that the brethren who feel interested in the cause of truth, and desire to see the work of the gathering of Israel roll forth with power, will aid us in liquidating the debts which are now owing, so that the inheritances may be secured to the Church, and which eventually will be of great value.

The good spirit which is manifested on this occasion, the desire to do good, and the zeal for the honor of the Church, inspires us with confidence that we shall not appeal in vain, but that funds will be forthcoming on this occasion, sufficient to meet the necessities of the case.

It is with great pleasure that we have to inform the Church that another edition of the Book of Mormon has been printed, and which is expected on from Cincinnati in a short time; and that arrangements are making for printing the Book of Doctrine and Covenants, hymn-book, &c.; so that the demand which may exist for these works will soon be supplied.

In conclusion we would say, brethren and sisters, be faithful, be diligent, contend earnestly for the faith once delivered to the Saints; let every man, woman and child realize the importance of the work, and act as if success depended on his individual exertion alone; let all feel an interest in it, and then consider they live in a day, the contemplation of which animated the bosoms of kings, Prophets, and righteous men thousands of years ago—the prospect of which inspired their sweetest notes, and most exalted lays, and caused them to break out in such rapturous strains as are recorded in the Scriptures; and by and by we will have to exclaim, in the language of inspiration—

> The Lord has brought again Zion,
> The Lord hath redeemed His people Israel.

Tuesday, October 6.

Minutes of a General Conference in England.

Minutes of a general conference of the Church of Jesus Christ of Latter-day Saints, held at Carpenter's Hall, Manchester, Tuesday, the 6th day of October, 1840, it being the first day of the seventh month of the eleventh year of the Church; when the following officers of the Traveling High Council were present, viz.: Elders Brigham Young, Heber C. Kimball, Orson Pratt, Willard Richards, Wilford Woodruff, and George A. Smith; other officers: High Priests 5, Elders 19, Priests 28, Teachers 4, and Deacons 2.

The meeting being called to order at 10 o'clock by Elder Brigham

Young, it was moved by Elder Young, seconded by Elder Woodruff, that Elder Orson Pratt be president of the conference, which was carried unanimously. Elder George Walker was chosen clerk.

After singing, and prayer by the president, the following statistical report was read:

Conferences and Branches.		Members.	Elders.	Priests.	Teachers.	Deacons.
Preston Conference (including all the branches in the care of Elders Melling and Withnall) as represented by	Elder Melling.	665	18	23	11	2
Potteries were represented by	Elder Alfred Cordon	248	9	32	9	9
Birmingham Branch, represented by	Elder Alfred Cordon	4	—	—	—	—
West Bromwich, represented by	Elder Alfred Cordon	21	—	3	1	—
Clitheroe Conference "	Thomas Smith	295	10	11	9	3
Herefordshire, &c., represented by	Wilford Woodruff	1007	19	78	15	1
Glasgow, and regions round about, represented by	Samuel Mulliner	493	8	7	5	3
Hilsboro Branch, Ireland, represented by	Theodore Curtis	5	—	—	—	—
Isle of Man Branch, represented by	Hiram Clark	6	—	—	—	—
Liverpool Conference, represented by	Priest William Mitchell	100	3	4	2	1
London Branch, represented by	Elder Heber C. Kimball	11	—	2	—	—
Macclesfield, represented by	Priest I. Brown	71	—	6	2	2
Altrincham Conference, (including Middlewich, Nortwich, and Peover,) represented by	Elder William Berry	82	1	3	3	3
Bedford Branch, represented by	Elder Brigham Young	36	1	1	—	—
Stockport, represented by	Elder Martin Littlewood	140	2	5	2	1
Bolton, represented by	Priest Barroes	61	—	2	1	—
Duckinfield, represented by	Elder Albiston	76	1	3	1	—
Edinburg Conference, represented by	Orson Pratt	43	—	2	—	—
Pendlebury Branch, represented by	Henry Royle	36	—	2	—	—
Eccles, represented by	Brother E. Leather	13	—	3	—	—
Whitefield, represented by	Elder Walker Johnson	39	1	2	3	—
Ratcliffe, represented by	John Allen	16	1	2	—	—
Brampton, represented by	Thomas Tweddle	40	1	1	1	—
Alston, represented by	John Sanders	39	2	1	2	—
Newcastle-upon-Tyne, represented by	Amos Fielding	6	—	2	1	—
Manchester, represented by	Brigham Young	364	4	27	6	1
Ancrum, represented by	Orson Pratt	9	—	—	—	—

The president brought before the conference the subject of ordinations, and after various observations thereon, it was proposed by Elder George A. Smith, that for the future, ordinations be not attended to, except by the Traveling High Council or under such restrictions as they may adopt in reference thereto. Elder Young spoke on the subject of conferences, and also with respect of restricting ordination; and after taking into consideration the great expense attendant upon holding general conferences, and the inconvenience experienced by members attending them, suggested, that for the future, general conferences should in a great measure be done away with, or restricted to the Traveling High Council to hold conferences at such places and times as they may think proper.

The meeting adjourned at 12 o'clock.

At 2 o'clock the meeting opened with prayer, after which Elder Kimball spoke on the subject of Elders taking upon themselves the responsibility of ordaining officers in this Church; after pointing out the evils that might result therefrom, he proceeded to treat upon the duty of members towards those who preside over them in the Lord, and respecting the members administering to the temporal necessities of those whose calling it is to labor amongst them in spiritual things.

Moved by Elder Willard Richards, seconded by Elder Thomas Smith, and carried unanimously, that all ordinations be confined to or under the regulations of the Traveling High Council.

Elder Young called the attention of the conference to the case of Emma Bolton, a sister from the Potteries, who had conducted herself disorderly. Elder Johnson and others spoke of several cases of improper conduct on her part; after which it was moved by Elder Young, seconded by Elder Kimball, and carried unanimously, that Emma Bolton be cut off from the Church.

The president [of the conference, Elder Orson Pratt], then called the attention of the conference to a letter from Isaac Brown and other officers of the Church at Macclesfield, concerning Elder Heath, and also to some half a dozen charges preferred by the said Isaac Brown, James Galley, Edward Horrocks, and John Horrocks, against the said Samuel Heath, for several items of misconduct, and neglecting the duties of his office; to all of which charges Elder Heath pleaded not guilty. The complainants then entered into proof of the several items, to which Elder Heath replied by stating that the charges against him were in consequence of a misunderstanding, &c. The proceedings opened a wide field for instruction from Elder Young, followed by the president, who recommended the parties to become reconciled to each other, stating that he did not consider the charges preferred against Elder Heath sufficiently substantiated to withdraw fellowship from him; when it was moved and seconded, that no further proceeding be taken on this subject; carried unanimously.

The conference then adjourned till 7 o'clock, p. m.

At 7 o'clock the meeting was opened with prayer.

The president having made such preliminary remarks as the importance of the subject called forth, proceeded to call upon those who were willing to volunteer their services to labor in the vineyard of the Lord, when the officers gave their names as follows:

High Priests—Hiram Clark, Thomas Smith, Alfred Cordon, Thomas Kington, Orson Pratt, Brigham Young, Heber C. Kimball, Willard Richards, Wilford Woodruff, George A. Smith.

Elders—George D. Watt, John Parkinson, David Moss, Martin Littlewood, William Parr, Samuel Heath, John Sanders, Theodore Curtis, Henry Royle, Thomas Tweddle, John Leigh, Amos Fielding, Thomas Richardson.

Priests—William Snailam, William Speakman, John Needham, James Mahon, Frederick Cook, Robert Crooks, William Mitchell, William Black, Robert Williams, William Jones, Thomas Pollitt, Richard Steele, John Burns, Joseph Knowles, Richard Benson, John Wyche, William Roylance, Joseph Street, Joseph White.

Moved, seconded, and carried, that Elder George D. Watt go to Edinburgh; Elder Alfred Cordon to Birmingham, and also take charge of the Staffordshire Potteries Conference, and that John Burns, Priest, go with him.

Elder Thomas Kington to take charge of the Herefordshire Conferences as heretofore, also Garway; and William Snailam and Joseph Knowles, Priests, to accompany him.

Robert Crooks, Priest, to go to Bolton; Thomas Richardson, Elder, and John Needham, Priest, to go to Herefordshire; Elder Hiram Clark to go to the Isle of Man; Elder Thomas Tweddle to Glasgow; Elder John Sanders to labor at Alston, and go to Carlisle as soon as practicable.

Elder Amos Fielding to go to Newcastle-upon-Tyne; Elder John Parkinson to Greenock; Elder Henry Royle and Frederick Cook, Priest, to Cly in Flintshire; William Mitchell, Priest, to Leeds; Elder Thomas Smith to remain at Clitheroe; Elder John Leigh, and James Mahon, Priest, to go to Arden, Cheshire, and Joseph White and Richard Steele, Priests, to labor under the direction of Elder Cordon.

Elder John Smith to be ordained High Priest, to take charge of the church in Manchester and the regions round about: Elder Peter Melling to take charge of the church as heretofore, in connection with Elder H. Withnall; and John Wyche, Priest, to go into Staffordshire, and labor under the direction of Alfred Cordon.

Moved and seconded, that the remainder of the officers who have volunteered, be left to the Traveling High Council to dispose of, and appoint to such places as they may judge expedient; carried.

Moved and seconded, that in consequence of there not being time to transact all the business of this conference, the ordination of officers be left to the Traveling High Council to ordain from time to time such members as they may consider requisite; carried.

Elder Young then addressed the meeting on the propriety of establishing a fund for the support and clothing of such members as may from time to time be called out to labor in the vineyard, and whose circumstances may require that their necessities may be administered unto. The president then addressed the meeting on the same subject, and pointed out the difference between preaching for money and the Elders having their necessities ministered unto, while they are called to labor "without taking thought for the morrow." Elder Richards followed upon the same subject; also Elder Kimball; after which Elder Young moved, that wherever a branch of the Church is established, two members be appointed to receive the weekly voluntary contributions of the members, for promoting the spread of the Gospel, and the same to be disposed of by the vote of the church in council with the Twelve Apostles; seconded by Elder George A. Smith, and carried.

The minutes were then read and accepted, and the conference adjourned *sine die*.

ORSON PRATT, President,
GEORGE WALKER, Secretary.

Thursday, 8.

Minutes of Council of the Twelve in England.

Minutes of a Council of the Twelve, viz., Brigham Young, Heber C. Kimball, Orson Pratt, Wilford Woodruff, George A. Smith, and Willard Richards; also Hiram Clark, and Reuben Hedlock, High Priests, at the house of Willard Richards, No. 1, Chapman Street, Manchester; Brigham Young presiding.

Moved by Elder Kimball, that Elder Willard Richards take charge of the *Millennial Star*, seconded and carried. Voted that our publishing office be removed to London as soon as circumstances will permit; and that Elders Hedlock and Curtis go where they please to labor.

WILLARD RICHARDS, Clerk.

CHAPTER XII.

PROGRESS OF THE WORK IN GREAT BRITAIN—THE SAINTS AT KIRTLAND REPROVED FOR THEIR COURSE DURING THE MISSOURI PERSECUTIONS—THE PROPHET'S ADDRESS TO THE TWELVE AND SAINTS IN GREAT BRITAIN.

Saturday, October 10.—Elder George A. Smith returned to London, and was soon followed by Elder Woodruff.

Charge against Oliver Walker.

David Fulmer preferred a charge against Oliver Walker "for reporting certain slanderous stories of a fallacious and calumniating nature, calculated to stigmatize, and raise a persecution against the Church and individuals in it, in this place, [Nauvoo], and for other acts of unchristianlike conduct," before the High Council at Nauvoo. The defendant pleaded that "he was not prepared to meet the charge, it being too indefinite." Council adjourned till next day.

Sunday, 11.—High Council met according to adjournment. The charge against Oliver Walker was taken up, and the following substituted for the first charge:

Minutes of the High Council.

To the High Council of the Church of Jesus Christ at Nauvoo:

For and in behalf of said Church, I prefer a charge against Elder Oliver Walker, for several different offenses hereinafter set forth, as said to be by him done, performed, said, and committed, as well as various duties omitted, all of which was done at different times, periods, places, and seasons, subsequent to September 1st, A. D. 1838, to-wit.:

For a general course of procedure, of acts, doings, and words, and suggestions by him, the said Elder Oliver Walker, done, performed, said, spoken, hinted at, and suggested, both directly and indirectly, and as calculated to be derogatory to the character of the heads and leaders of the Church, and extremely injurious and hurtful to the upbuilding, welfare, being, and advancement of the same, namely, for fleeing from, quitting, and deserting the society, ranks, and needs of his brethren, in times of difficulty with, and danger from their enemies, "the mob;" restraining from the use of his brethren, his influence, efforts, and needful assistance, at such times of need; as also for joining with, and strengthening the hands, will, evil pursuits, and designs of the mob, and Gentile enemies of the Church, by expressions, hints, and suggestions of wavering and dubious nature, respecting the faith and order of the Church, and of the professed calling, qualifications, proceedings, &c., of Joseph Smith, Jun., as a Seer, Prophet, and one called to bring to light the fullness of the Gospel, &c., in these last days.

Likewise for advancing ideas, notions, or opinions, that the different orders or sects, namely, Methodists and others, could by a pursuit in their faith, order, and pursuits, as readily obtain every celestial attainment and Gospel advantage, as they could by embracing and pursuing the system brought forth by Joseph Smith, Jun., in these last days.

And moreover for suggesting within the last six months, at Alton, Nauvoo, intermediate and adjacent places, that in the Church at Nauvoo there did exist a set of pilferers, who were actually thieving, robbing, plundering, taking and unlawfully carrying away from Missouri, certain goods and chattels, wares and property; and that the act and acts of such supposed thieving, &c., was fostered and conducted by the knowledge and approbation of the heads and leaders of the Church, viz., by the Presidency and High Council; all of which items set forth as aforesaid, together with any and all corroborating acts, doings, hints, expressions, and suggestions in any way belonging to, or connected with, any or all of the aforesaid accusations, he, the said Oliver Walker, is hereby notified to prepare to defend in said trial.

Dated October 11, 1840, Nauvoo.

DAVID FULMER.

Walker pleaded that he was not prepared to defend himself, and the trial was deferred at his request till April conference.

Letter of Heber C. Kimball et al. to Messrs. Ebenezer Robinson and Don Carlos Smith—Reporting Affairs in the British Mission.

MANCHESTER, ENGLAND, October 12, 1840.

Messrs. Ebenezer Robinson, and Don Carlos Smith:

DEAR BRETHREN:—We left Manchester immediately after the July conference, for the purpose of visiting the city of London. We visited the churches which lay on our route through Staffordshire, Herefordshire, Worcestershire, and Gloucestershire; and we had many interesting meetings, baptizing and confirming daily, as we passed along. We baptized forty in one day; many new doors were opening, and all things indicated a short work in England.

The last meeting we held among the Saints while on this journey, was in a field in Leigh, Gloucestershire, on the 16th of August. We had an interesting time; we baptized fifteen, and ordained one Elder and two Priests. Two Methodist priests came twelve miles to hear; we baptized them after the first sermon, and confirmed and ordained them at the same time, and sent them to preach the Gospel. We parted with the Saints there on the 17th, went to Cheltenham, (five miles), and spent the night. There were several Saints in that place.

On the 18th we took coach and rode forty miles, through a level farming country, something like Illinois prairie; we passed through Oxfordshire, leaving the Oxford University a little upon our left. This university consists of twenty colleges endowed, and five halls not endowed; and is considered the largest and most noted university in the world. We then took the railroad and traveled seventy miles, had a splendid view of Windsor Castle as we passed along. We landed at the London terminus of the Great Western Railway at 4 o'clock in the evening. From thence we took coach and rode a few miles into the city; we walked over London Bridge, and called upon Mr. Allgood, 19 King Street, Borough. Mrs. Allgood is sister to Elder Theodore Turley's wife; she treated us kindly, gave us such refreshments as we needed, and directed us to lodgings in the neighborhood, where we spent the night.

After which we immediately commenced our researches through this great metropolis, for the honest in heart and the meek of the earth. We first commenced by visiting the ministers and preachers of the various orders, and requested the privilege of delivering our message unto the people in their churches and chapels; but of course you will not be astonished when we inform you that they denied us this privilege, and rejected our testimony.

We went to and fro through the city of London, from day to day, endeavoring to get some door open whereby we could warn the people and search out the honest in heart; when on diligent search we found the whole city given to covetousness, (which is idolatry), priestcraft, tradition, superstition, and all manner of abominations, wickedness and uncleanness; and all doors closed against us.

We did not hesitate to stand in the midst of the streets, and, Jonah like, cry repentance unto the inhabitants of that mighty city—the metropolis of England—the pride and glory of Britain—the boast of the Gentiles, and the largest commercial city in the world—containing over one million five hundred thousand souls, who are ripening in iniquity, and preparing for the wrath of God; and like the ox going to the slaughter, know not the day of their visitation.

We shall long remember standing together in the midst of that people, and bearing a message which will prove a savor of life unto life, or of death unto death, not only unto them, but unto all those unto whom the sound of the everlasting Gospel shall come; even unto the whole world; and the judgment of the great day shall manifest the truth of it unto all nations. And it will ever sweeten the memory of that eventful period of our lives, to know that our labors, on that occasion, were not in vain; but we were enabled through toil, labor, diligent search, perseverane, and the great mercy of God, to find some of the blood of Ephraim—a few honest souls who were willing to receive and obey the Gospel; and that we were enabled to lay the foundation of a work in the city of London, which will not be removed until the city is warned, so that they will be left without excuse; and the Saints gathered out to stand in holy places, while judgment works. Until that time, the seed which we have sown there, will bring forth fruit, and the fruit will redound to the honor and glory of God.

We have baptized eleven only, in the city of London, but through the faith and the mercy of God, we ere long expect a harvest of souls in that place; but we are willing to acknowledge, that in our travels, either in America or Europe, we have never before found a people, from whose minds we have had to remove a greater multiplicity of objections, or combination of obstacles, in order to excite an interest in the subject and prepare the heart for the reception of the word of God, than in the city of London.

While conversing with the common people concerning the Gospel, we found their highest attainments to be, "Why, I go to church or chapel and get my children christened, what more is necessary?" When we conversed with the learned, we found them too wise to be taught, and too much established in the traditions of their fathers to expect any change in the last days. While conversing with the ministers of the various orders of the day, upon the principles of the Gospel, they would inform us that the ancient order of things was done away, and no longer needed; and some of them had preached forty years the good old religion, and God was with them, and they needed no more revelation, or healing the sick, or anything as manifest in the days of the Apostles, for we can get along without them in this day of refinement, light and knowledge.

When we arose to preach unto the people repentance, and baptism for the remission of sins, the cry of "Baptist, Baptist," would be rung in our ears. If we spoke of the Church and body of Christ being composed of Prophets, and Apostles; as well as other members, "Irvingites, Irvingites," would immediately dash into the mind. If in the midst of our remarks, we even for once suffered the saying to drop from our lips, "The testimony of Jesus is the spirit of prophecy," "O, you belong to Johanna Southcote," would be heard from several places at once. If we spoke of the second coming of Christ, the cry would be, "Aitkenites." If we made mention of the Priesthood, they would call us "Catholics." If we testified of the ministering of angels, the people would reply, "The Irvingites have their angels, and even the Duke of Normandy is ready to swear that he has the administering of angels every night."

These salutations, in connection with a multitude of others, of a similar nature, continued to salute our ears from day to day, until we were about ready to conclude that London had been such a perfect depot of the systems of the nineteenth century, that it contained six hundred three score and six different gods, gospels, redeemers, plans of salvation, religions, churches, commandments, (essential and non-essential), orders of preaching, roads to heaven and to hell; and that this order of things had so affected the minds of the people, that it almost required a horn to be blown from the highest heavens, in order to awaken the attention of the people, and prepare their minds to candidly hear and receive the doctrine of one Gospel, one faith, one baptism, one Holy Ghost, one God, and one plan of salvation, and that, such as Christ and the Apostles preached.

But notwithstanding this, we do not feel discouraged concerning a work being perfected in London, but firmly believe that many souls will embrace the fullness of the Gospel there, though it will be through faith, diligence, perseverance, and prayer.

Having spent twenty-three days together in this first mission in the metropolis, and the time drawing near for our October conference, Elder Woodruff left the city on the 10th of September for the purpose of attending several conferences. He attended the Bran Green and Gadfield Elm conference, held in Worcester on the 14th of September, and also the Froomes Hill conference, held in Herefordshire on the 21st of September. At these two conferences, he heard represented, 40 branches of the Church, containing 1,007 members, and 113 officers, viz., 19 Elders, 78 Priests, 15 Teachers, and 1 Deacon; the whole of whom had received the fullness of the Everlasting Gospel, and been baptized in less than seven months in that part of the vineyard which he first opened in the month of March; and the work is still progressing very rapidly throughout that region; and among the number baptized there have not been much less than one hundred preachers of various sects.

He also attended the conference in the Staffordshire Potteries, which met at Hanley on the 28th of September; where were represented 231 members, 9 Elders, 32 Priests, 9 Teachers, and 9 Deacons; most of whom received the work since our arrival there last winter and spring. While he was attending these conferences, Elders Kimball and George A. Smith continued their labors in London until the first of October, at which time we met together again in Staffordshire, and enjoyed each other's company while journeying together to Manchester, where the quorum of the Traveling High Council, with many Elders and Saints had the privilege of once more sitting in a general conference together, on the 6th of October in the Carpenter's Hall, where we heard represented 3,636 Saints, and 383 official members.

At the July conference there were 2,513 Saints, and 256 official members, making an increase in three months of 1,113 Saints and 127 official members, besides over 200 Saints, including many Elders, Priests, Teachers and Deacons, who have emigrated to America; which would make over 1,300 additions to the Church in Europe during the last three months, and over two thousand since our conference held in Preston on the 15th of April; which representation at that time was 1,671 Saints, and 132 official members.

Thus you see the Lord hath given us an increase, and blessed the labors of the servants of God universally in this land, for which we feel thankful; and our constant prayer to God is that His kingdom may roll forth, that the messengers bearing the everlasting Gospel may be diligent, meek, and humble, not weary in well doing, but waiting with patience for their reward, which lies at the end of the race, that their joy may be full.

HEBER C. KIMBALL,
WILFORD WOODRUFF,
GEORGE A. SMITH.

Saturday, *17*.—A conference was held in Philadelphia, Elder Orson Hyde presiding; 896 members were represented, including 24 Elders, 11 Priests, 6 Teachers, 5 Deacons, in Pennsylvania, New York City, New Jersey, and vicinity.

Parley P. Pratt and family arrived in Manchester, and resumed the editorial labors of the *Star*.

Remarkable Visions by Orson Pratt.

Brother Orson Pratt has recently published a pamphlet, entitled "An interesting account of several Remarkable Visions, and of the late Discovery of Ancient American Records,'' comprising 31 pages giving a brief sketch of the rise of the Church.

Monday, 19.

Letter of Joseph and Hyrum Smith to the Saints in Kirtland—Reproving the Saints for Neglect of their Brethren and Sisters During the Missouri Persecutions.

NAUVOO, HANCOCK COUNTY, ILLINOIS,
October 19th, 1840.

To the Saints in Kirtland, Ohio:

Dear beloved brethren in the kingdom and patience of Jesus Christ—We take this opportunity of informing you that we yet remember the Saints scattered abroad in the regions of Kirtland, and feel interested in their welfare as well as in that of the Saints at large. We have beheld with feelings peculiar to ourselves the situation of things in Kirtland and the numerous difficulties to which the Saints have been subjected, by false friends as well as open enemies.

All these circumstances have more or less engaged our attention from time to time. We likewise must complain of the brethren who are in office and authority in the stake of Kirtland, for not writing to us, and making known their difficulties and their affairs from time to time, so that they might be advised in matters of importance to the well being of said stake; but above all, for not sending one word of consolation to us while we were in the hands of our enemies, and thrust into dungeons. Some of our friends from various sections sent us letters which breathed a kind and sympathetic spirit, and which made our afflictions and sufferings endurable. All was silent as the grave [from Kirtland]; no feelings of sorrow, sympathy, or affection [was expressed] to cheer the heart under the gloomy shades of affliction and trouble through which we had to pass.

Dear brethren, could you realize that your brethren were thus circumstanced, and were to bear up under the weight of affliction and woe which was heaped upon them by their enemies, and you stand unmoved and unconcerned! Where were the bowels of compassion? Where was the love which ought to characterize the Saints of the Most High? Did those high born and noble feelings lie dormant, or were you insensible to the treatment we received? However, we are disposed to leave these things to God, and to futurity, and feel disposed to forget this coldness on the part of the Saints in Kirtland, and to look to the future with more pleasure than while we contemplated the past; and shall by the assistance of our heavenly Father, take such steps as we think best calculated to promote the interests of the Saints, and for the promotion of truth and righteousness, and the building up of the kingdom in these last days.

The situation of Kirtland was brought before the general conference, held at this place on the 3rd instant, when it was resolved that Elder Almon W. Babbitt should be appointed to preside over the stake of Kirtland, and that he be privileged to choose his own counselors. We therefore hope that the Saints will hold up the hands of our beloved brother, and unite with him in endeavoring to promote the interests of the kingdom.

It has been deemed prudent to advise the eastern brethren who desire to locate in Kirtland, to do so; consequently you may expect an increase of members in your stake, who probably will be but young in the faith, and who will require kind treatment. We therefore hope the brethren will feel interested in the welfare of the Saints, and will use all their endeavors to promote the welfare of the brethren who may think proper to take up their residence in that place.

If you will put away from your midst all evil speaking, backbiting, and ungenerous thoughts and feelings: humble yourselves, and cultivate every principle of virtue and love, then will the blessings of Jehovah rest upon you, and you will yet see good and glorious days; peace will be within your gates, and prosperity in your borders; which may our heavenly Father grant in the name of Jesus Christ, is the prayer of yours in the bonds of the covenant,

JOSEPH SMITH,
HYRUM SMITH.

AN EPISTLE OF THE PROPHET TO THE TWELVE.

To the Traveling High Council and Elders of the Church of Jesus Christ of Latter-day Saints in Great Britain:

BELOVED BRETHREN:—May grace, mercy, and peace rest upon you from God the Father and the Lord Jesus Christ. Having several communications lying before me from my brethren the Twelve, some of which ere this have merited a reply, but from the multiplicity of business which necessarily engages my attention, I have delayed communicating with you to the present time.

Be assured, beloved brethren, that I am no disinterested observer of the things which are transpiring on the face of the whole earth; and amidst the general movements which are in progress, none is of more importance than the glorious work in which you are now engaged; consequently I feel some anxiety on your account, that you may by your virtue, faith, diligence and charity commend yourselves to one another, to the Church of Christ, and to your Father who is in heaven; by whose grace you have been called to so holy a calling; and be enabled to perform the great and responsible duties which rest upon you. And I can assure you, that from the information I have received, I feel satisfied that you have not been remiss in your duty; but that your diligence and faithfulness have been such as must secure you the smiles of that God whose servant you are, and also the good will of the Saints throughout the world.

The spread of the Gospel throughout England is certainly pleasing; the contemplation of which cannot but afford feelings of no ordinary kind, in the bosom of those who have borne the heat and burden of the day; and who were its firm supporters and strenuous advocates in infancy, while surrounded with circumstances the most unpropitious, and its destruction threatened on all hands; like the gallant bark that has braved the storm unhurt, spreads her canvas to the breeze, and nobly cuts her way through the yielding wave, more conscious than ever of the strength of her timbers, and the experience and capability of her captain, pilot, and crew.

It is likewise very satisfactory to my mind, that there has been such a good understanding between you, and that the Saints have so cheerfully hearkened to council, and vied with each other in this labor of love, and in the promotion of truth and righteousness. This is as it should be in the Church of Jesus Christ; unity is strength. "How pleasing it is for brethren to dwell together in unity!" Let the Saints of the Most High ever cultivate this principle, and the most glorious blessings must result, not only to them individually, but to the whole Church—the order of the kingdom will be maintained, its officers respected, and its requirements readily and cheerfully obeyed.

Love is one of the chief characteristics of Deity, and ought to be manifested by those who aspire to be the sons of God. A man filled with the love of God, is not content with blessing his family alone, but ranges through the whole world, anxious to bless the whole human race. This has been your feeling, and caused you to forego the pleasures of home, that you might be a blessing to others, who are candidates for immortality, but strangers to truth; and for so doing, I pray that heaven's choicest blessings may rest upon you.

Being requested to give my advice respecting the propriety of your returning in the spring, I will do so willingly. I have reflected on the subject some time, and am of the opinion that it would be wisdom in you to make preparations to leave the scene of your labors in the spring. Having carried the testimony to that land, and numbers having received it, the leaven can now spread without your being obliged to stay.

Another thing—there have been whisperings of the Spirit that there will be some agitations, excitements, and trouble in the land in which you are now laboring. I would therefore say, in the meantime be diligent: organize the churches, and let everyone stand in his proper place, so that those who cannot come with you in the spring, may not be left as sheep without a shepherd.

I would likewise observe, that inasmuch as this place has been appointed for the gathering of the Saints, it is necessary that it should be attended to in the order that the Lord intends it should. To this end I would say, that as there are great numbers of the Saints in England who are extremely poor, and not accustomed to the farming business, who must have certain preparations made for them before they can support themselves in this country, therefore to prevent confusion and disappointment when they arrive here, let those men who are accustomed to make machinery, and those who can command capital, though it be small, come here as soon as convenient, and put up machinery, and make such other preparations as may be necessary, so that when the poor come on, they may have employment to come to. This place has advantages for manufacturing and commercial purposes, which but very few can boast of; and the establishing of cotton factories, foundries, potteries, &c., would be the means of bringing in wealth, and raising it to a very important elevation.

I need not occupy more space on this subject, as its reasonableness must be obvious to every mind.

In my former epistle I told you my mind respecting the printing of the Book of Mormon, hymn-book, &c. I have been favored by receiving a hymn-book from you, and as far as I have examined it, I highly approve of it, and think it to be a very valuable collection. I am informed that the Book of Mormon is likewise printed, which I am glad to hear, and should be pleased to hear that it was printed in all the different languages of the earth. You can use your own pleasure respecting the printing of the Doctrine and Covenants. If there is a great demand for it, I have no objections, but would rather encourage it.

I can say, that as far as I have been made acquainted with your movements, I am perfectly satisfied that they have been in wisdom; and I have no doubt, but that the Spirit of the Lord has directed you; and this proves to my mind that you have been humble, and your desires have been for the salvation of your fellow man, and not for your own aggrandisement, and selfish interests. As long as the Saints manifest such a disposition, their counsels will be approved of, and their exertions crowned with success.

There are many things of much importance, on which you ask counsel, but which I think you will be perfectly able to decide upon, as you are more conversant with the peculiar circumstances than I am; and I feel great confidence in your united wisdom; therefore you will excuse me for not entering into detail. If I should see anything that is wrong, I would take the privilege of making known my mind to you, and pointing out the evil.

If Elder Parley P. Pratt should wish to remain in England some time longer than the rest of the Twelve, he will feel himself at liberty to do so, as his family are with him, consequently his circumstances are somewhat different from the rest; and likewise it is necessary that someone should remain who is conversant with the rules and regulations of the Church, and continue the paper which is published. Consequently, taking all these things into consideration, I would not press it upon Brother Pratt to return in the spring.

I am happy to inform you that we are prospering in this place, and that the Saints are more healthy than formerly; and from the decrease of sickness this season, when compared with the last, I am led to the conclusion that this must eventually become a healthy place. There are at present about 3,000 inhabitants in Nauvoo, and numbers are flocking in daily. Several stakes have been set off in different parts of the country, which are in prosperous circumstances.

Provisions are much lower than when you left. Flour is about $4 per barrel. Corn and potatoes about 25 cents per bushel; and other things in proportion. There has been a very plentiful harvest throughout the Union.

You will observe, by the *Times and Seasons*, that we are about building a temple for the worship of our God in this place. Preparations are now making; every tenth day is devoted by the brethren for quarrying rock, &c. We have secured one of the most lovely situations for it in this region of country. It is expected to be considerably larger than the one in Kirtland, and on a more magnificent scale, and which will undoubtedly attract the attention of the great men of the earth.

We have a bill before the legislature for the incorporation of the city of Nauvoo, and for the establishment of a seminary of learning, and other purposes—which I expect will pass in a short time.

You will also receive intelligence of the death of my father; which event, although painful to the family and to the Church generally, yet the sealing testimony of the truth of the work of the Lord was indeed satisfactory. Brother Hyrum succeeds him as Patriarch of the Church, according to his last directions and benedictions.*

* The last "directions and benedictions" of the Patriarch Joseph Smith, Sen., here referred to, are stated by "Mother Lucy Smith" in her book, "History of the Prophet Joseph," as follows:

"My son Hyrum, I seal upon your head your patriarchal blessing, which I placed upon your head before, for that shall be verified. In addition to this, I now give you my dying blessing. You shall have a season of peace, so that you shall have

Several persons of eminence and distinction in society have joined the Church and become obedient to the faith; and I am happy to inform you that the work is spreading very fast upon this continent. Some of the brethren are now in New Orleans, and we expect a large gathering from the south. I have had the pleasure of welcoming about one hundred brethren who came with Brother Turley; the remainder I am informed stayed in Kirtland, not having means to get any further. I think that those who came here this fall, did not take the best possible route, or the least expensive. Most of the brethren have obtained employment of one kind or another, and appear tolerably well contented, and seem disposed to hearken to counsel.

Brothers Robinson and Smith lately had a letter from Elders Kimball, Smith and Woodruff, which gave us information of the commencement of the work of the Lord in the city of London, which I was glad to hear. I am likewise informed that Elders have gone to Australia and to the East Indies. I feel desirous that every providential opening of the kind should be filled, and that you should, prior to your leaving England, send the Gospel into as many parts as you possibly can.

Beloved brethren, you must be aware in some measure of my feelings, when I contemplate the great work which is now rolling on, and the relationship which I sustain to it, while it is extending to distant lands, and thousands are embracing it. I realize in some measure my responsibility, and the need I have of support from above, and wisdom from on high, that I may be able to teach this people, which have now become a great people, the principles of righteousness, and lead them agreeably to the will of Heaven; so that they may be perfected, and prepared to meet the Lord Jesus Christ when He shall appear in great glory. Can I rely on your prayers to our heavenly Father on my behalf, and on all the prayers of all my brethren and sisters in England, (whom having not seen, yet I love), that I may be enabled to escape every stratagem of Satan, surmount every difficulty, and bring this people to the enjoyment of those blessings which are reserved for the righteous? I ask this at your hands in the name of the Lord Jesus Christ.

Let the Saints remember that great things depend on their individual exertion, and that they are called to be co-workers with us and the Holy Spirit in accomplishing the great work of the last days; and in consideration of the extent, the blessings and glories of the same, let

sufficient rest to accomplish the work which God has given you to do. You shall be as firm as the pillars of heaven unto the end of your days. I now seal upon your head the patriarchal power, and you shall bless the people. This is my dying blessing upon your head in the name of Jesus. Amen."—*History of the Prophet Joseph Smith*, p. 266.

every selfish feeling be not only buried, but annihilated; and let love to God and man predominate, and reign triumphant in every mind, that their hearts may become like unto Enoch's of old, and comprehend all things, present, past and future, and come behind in no gift, waiting for the coming of the Lord Jesus Christ.

The work in which we are unitedly engaged is one of no ordinary kind. The enemies we have to contend against are subtle and well skilled in manœuvering; it behooves us to be on the alert to concentrate our energies, and that the best feelings should exist in our midst; and then, by the help of the Almight, we shall go on from victory to victory, and from conquest to conquest; our evil passions will be subdued, our prejudices depart; we shall find no room in our bosoms for hatred; vice will hide its deformed head, and we shall stand approved in the sight of heaven, and be acknowledged the sons of God.

Let us realize that we are not to live to ourselves, but to God; by so doing the greatest blessings will rest upon us both in time and in eternity.

I presume the doctrine of "baptism for the dead" has ere this reached your ears, and may have raised some inquiries in your minds respecting the same. I cannot in this letter give you all the information you may desire on the subject; but aside from knowledge independent of the Bible, I would say that it was certainly practiced by the ancient churches; and St. Paul endeavors to prove the doctrine of the resurrection from the same, and says, "Else what shall they do which are baptized for the dead, if the dead rise not at all? Why are they then baptized for the dead?"

I first mentioned the doctrine in public when preaching the funeral sermon of Brother Seymour Brunson; and have since then given general instructions in the Church on the subject. The Saints have the privilege of being baptized for those of their relatives who are dead, whom they believe would have embraced the Gospel, if they had been privileged with hearing it, and who have received the Gospel in the spirt, through the instrumentality of those who have been commissioned to preach to them while in prison.

Without enlarging on the subject, you will undoubtedly see its consistency and reasonableness; and it presents the Gospel of Christ in probably a more enlarged scale than some have imagined it. But as the performance of this rite is more particularly confined to this place, it will not be necessary to enter into particulars; at the same time I always feel glad to give all the information in my power, but my space will not allow me to do it.

We had a letter from Elder Hyde, a few days ago, who is in New Jersey, and is expecting to leave for England as soon as Elder Page reaches him. He requested to know if converted Jews are to go to Jerusalem or to come to Zion. I therefore wish you to inform him that converted Jews must come here.

Give my kind love to all the brethren and sisters, and tell them I should have been pleased to come over to England to see them, but I am afraid that I shall be under the necessity of remaining here for some time; therefore I give them a pressing invitation to come and see me.

I remain, dear brethren, yours affectionately,

JOSEPH SMITH.

CHAPTER XIII.

INTRODUCTION OF THE GOSPEL IN THE ISLE OF MAN—THE NAUVOO CHARTER.

Wednesday, October 21, 1840.—Elder Lorenzo Snow arrived in Manchester, England, from Nauvoo.

Thursday, 22.—The committee appointed by the general conference of the Church at Nauvoo on the 3rd inst., (my brother Hyrum presiding) organized a Stake at Lima this evening, by appointing Isaac Morley, president; John Murdock and Walter Cox, his counselors; also a Bishop's Court composed of Gardner Snow, Clark Hulet and Henry Dean, with James C. Snow, clerk.

Friday, 23.—Gardner Snow was ordained Bishop under the hands of Hyrum Smith.

Sunday, 25.—The committee organized a Stake at Quincy. The presidency were Daniel Stanton, Stephen Jones and Ezra T. Benson; the latter was ordained a High Priest; also bishop and counselors, George W. Crouse, Azariah Dustin, and Sylvester B. Stoddard.

Tuesday, 27.—The committee organized a Stake called Mount Hope, at the steam mills, Columbus, Adams county. President and counselors were Abel Lamb, Sherman Gilbert and John Smith. Bishop and counselors, were Daniel A. Miller, Isaac Clark, and John Allen; Simeon J. Comfort, clerk.

At Freedom Stake, near Payson, Adams county, Henry W. Miller, Duncan McArthur, and William Tenney were appointed to preside. Bishop and counselors, Matthew Leach, Horra Kimball, and Jacob Foutz.

Wednesday 28.—[On this date a long communication

was sent to the editors of the *Times and Seasons* signed by Heber C. Kimball, Wilford Woodruff and George A. Smith, detailing their visit to various places in London, but as the communication does not in any way bear upon the incidents of the history of the Church, it is thought unnecessary to publish the letter *in extenso*. The following paragraph from the letter, however, it is thought should be preserved, because it refers to the liberty the Elders of the Church incidentally enjoyed while engaged in the ministry; and also because it breathes that spirit of liberty in the pursuit of knowledge characteristic of the work of God in the last days.—EDITORS.]

We consider it perfectly consistent with our calling, with reason and revelation that we should form a knowledge of kingdoms and countries whether at home or abroad, whether ancient or modern, whether of things past or present or to come; whether it be in heaven, earth or hell, air or seas; or whether we obtain this knowledge by being local or traveling, by study or by faith, by dreams or by visions, by revelation or by prophecy, it mattereth not unto us; if we can but obtain a correct [view of] principles, and knowledge of things as they are, in their true light, past, present and to come. It is under such a view of things that we are endeavoring to avail ourselves of every opportunity in our travels among the nations of the earth, to record an account of things as they pass under our observation.

Thursday, 29.—Elder Woodruff preached twice in London, and baptized three.

Friday, 30.—Elder Lorenzo Snow had a discussion with Mr. Barker, a Methodist minister, at Hill Top, near Birmingham, and baptized two.

Sunday, 31.—I copy the following from the *Manx Liberal* of this date:

MORMONISM IN THE ISLE OF MAN.

To the Editor of the Manx Liberal:

SIR—I feel rather surprised and chagrined that the modern delusion, viz., "Mormonism," should have made such rapid strides in this town, hitherto considered exempt from the many systems of irreligious creeds which abound in England, America, and elsewhere. I had thought that the powerful and argumentative addresses of the dissenting ministers would have checked such a gross piece of imposition in its infancy, and thus prevented the great mass of our town's people from becoming dupes of designing knaves, "and being led away by every wind of doctrine." Above all, I imagined the two pamphlets issued by that holy, religious and devout man of God, Mr. Hays, Wesleyan minister, (to which connection I have the happiness and honor to belong) would have been quite sufficient to prove the fallacy of such a system, and prevent its further spread. But, sir, alas! alas! the case is quite the reverse; numbers continually flock to the Wellington room, and listen with eagerness to the principles there advocated. The members of our society (Methodists) seem to be most conspicuous in sanctioning and promoting this vile and abominable doctrine.

Oh, sir, the result to our connection will be dreadful! the havoc tremendous; just think of the majority of our *leading* and intelligent men aiding and abetting a cause of this description! Oh, sir, lamentable and heart-rending to witness the beaming countenances, and smiles of approbation displayed recently at Taylor's meeting! I could enumerate a host of our members who regularly attend those anti-Christian meetings; but I will just mention, with your permission, the names of a few who attended one of the last meetings. (Here followed a list of names.)

O! Mr. Editor! I quake for the consequence; such a wholesale conversion to Mormonism was never before witnessed in any town or country. What will become of our society? What will become of our class meetings? What will become of our brethren in the faith? And above all, what will become of poor Mr. Hays* that nice and humble man, who so nobly stood forward to expose the errors of the Mormon system; God bless him and preserve him from want! But, Mr. Editor, what makes the case worse is, that a rumor is prevalent that all these pious men are to be baptized! That is duly immersed in the salt water of Douglas Bay, by that abominable creature, Taylor! Surely, there must be something enchanting about the vile man. Immersion! (my hand shakes while I write) and in winter, too! Oh, sir! the thought chills my very soul; surely this American dipper intends to drown them; he can have no other object in view, therefore, brethren of the Methodist society, beware! Drowning is not to be envied, and that too in your sins. Besides, what would the venerable John Wesley, (if he

* Elder Taylor was also opposed by Rev. Thomas Hamilton, whom he met in a public debate and easily vanquished. "No great honor, however," says Elder Taylor in his account of the affair, "as he was a very ignorant man." Elder Taylor secured for his meeting place the Wellington rooms, and from the platform he answered all who opposed him, and succeeded. despite all oppositon, in organzing a branch of the Church in Douglas.

were alive) say to such conduct? What will the conference say? And what will the world say? I leave these questions to yourselves to answer. In conclusion, brethren, I recommend you to read, mark, learn and inwardly digest the things which belong to your eternal peace, and listen no longer to the follies of men.

A STAUNCH WESLEYAN.

Duke Street, Douglas, 29th Oct.

Sunday, November 1, 1840.—The committee organized a Stake, Geneva, Morgan county, Illinois, and called it Geneva Stake; presidents—William Bosley, Howard S. Smith, and Samuel Fowler. Bishop's Court—Gardner Clark, Moses Clare, and David Orton.

Elder Levi Richards arrived in Manchester.

Tuesday, 3.—The English bombarded St. Jean D'Acre, during which a powder magazine exploded, killing over two thousand men.

Thursday, 5.—The committee organized a Stake of the Church at Springfield; presidents—Edwin P. Merriam, Isaac H. Bishop, and Arnold Stephens. Bishop's Court Abraham Palmer, Henry Stephens, and Jonathan Palmer.

Monday, 9.—Elder George A. Smith received counsel to leave London and go to Staffordshire for his health, as he had injured his lungs by preaching in the streets, so that he discharged considerable blood from them.

Tuesday, 10.—Elder Smith took leave of Elder Woodruff and traveled to Birmingham, met Elder Alfred Cordon, preached and baptized five in the evening.

Opposition to the Work in England.

Thursday, 12.—The *Weekly Dispatch*, England, having published a sarcastic article against the Saints in that country, and blaming the Bishop of Gloucester, and his tithe-fattened clergy for allowing the "Mormons" to delude and baptize five hundred in his Diocese, Elder Wilford Woodruff replied to this, but the *Dispatch* refused to publish his reply.

Saturday, 21.—Elders Young, Kimball and Richards, visited the Church at Bolton.

Thursday, 26.—Elders Brigham Young, Heber C. Kimball, and George A. Smith preached to the Saints in Hanley this day, and on the 27th at Stoke-upon-Trent.

Saturday, 28.—Elders Young and Kimball left for London.

Elders Elias Higbee and Robert B. Thompson, the committee appointed at the October Conference, wrote a petition to Congress for the redress of the grievances of the Latter-day Saints in Missouri, setting forth their wrongs and sufferings, in substance the same as my petition in connection with Elias Higbee and Sidney Rigdon, of the 28th day of November, 1839.

Thursday, December 3.—Elders Young, Kimball and Wooodruff visited the tower of London, the Horse Armory, Jewel Room and the Thames Tunnel.

Friday, 4.—Elders Young and Woodruff visited Buckingham Palace and Westminster Abbey.

Excommunication of Sidney Roberts.

There was a conference in New York City, Elder Orson Hyde presiding. The revelations of Elder Sidney Roberts were objected to, which were that a certain brother must give him a suit of clothes, and a gold watch, the best that could be had, also his saluting the sisters with what he calls a holy kiss. Elder Roberts justified himself in these things. Much good counsel was given him, but he said he knew the revelations he had received were from God, and would make no confession; consequently the conference cut him off, and demanded his license, which he refused to give up.

Elder John Taylor has been preaching and baptizing for some time in the Isle of Man, where the work is now progressing.

Saturday, 5.—Elder Brigham Young writes as follows:

Letter of Brigham Young to the Presidency, Detailing Movements of the Mission in England.

No. 40, Ironmonger Row, St. Luke's, December 5th, 1840.

Beloved Brethren—I have just returned from a walk with Brothers Kimball and Woodruff. We have only been as far as St. Paul's and returned by Smithfield Market about three miles. Brother Kimball and myself had fine weather for our journey here; it was a beautiful day that we left Macclesfield for Burslem. We found the brethren in Macclesfield in good spirits, and in a good state as to appearance. They appear to be well suited with Brother James Galley; I think he will be a useful man in this kingdom. We found Brother George A. Smith in Burslem, not in the best of health. He is like the rest of us, the climate does not agree with him; he is affected with a bleeding at the lungs. We stayed with him at the Potteries. I preached two evenings. The Church is in a good state; some of the members have a pretty hard time of it. Brother Smith will stay there for the present.

Saturday, 28th, left for the next stopping place in Grets Green, where we spent the Sabbath. On Saturday evening we called to see Sister Roden, Father Patrick's daughter; she was very glad to see us, and wanted we should stay all night. Her husband was very kind to us, and bid us or other Elders welcome to his house at any time. We could not stay; took tea with them, and agreed to send Elder Lorenzo Snow there if he could come; blessed them, and left them. I preached in the morning to the Saints in Grets Green, stayed afternoon meeting, and then walked to Birmingham; was very tired; heard Elder Snow preach; he is a nice young man, I think. Brother Kimball also spoke to the people after Brother Snow had got through. We found Brother Robert Williams here; he opened the meeting; he seems to be full of the Spirit.

On Monday at 12 o'clock, Brother Kimball and myself took the railway. Brother Williams started on foot for London. We arrived here on Monday evening about six o'clock; found Brother Woodruff well and in good spirits. We have been pretty busy since we have been here.

BRIGHAM YOUNG.

A great part of the city of Messina, Sicily, was this day destroyed by an earthquake. Such was the force of the first shock that the inhabitants of the town were buried in an instant beneath the ruins.

Sunday, *6*.—Elders Young and Kimball preached in Barratt's Academy, London, and administered the sacrament in the evening.

Monday, *7*.—Elder John Taylor issued his third pamphlet in defense of the truth, against the attacks of the Rev. Robert Hays, Wesleyan Minister, Douglas, Isle of Man; the three containing thirty-five pages of closely printed matter,

Elder Taylor's Defense of the Work.

which are a complete expose of the corruptions of the Wesleyan priesthood, and a clear illustration of the truth of the Latter-day work.

Elders Brigham Young, Heber C. Kimball, and Wilford Woodruff, visited the Anatomical Department of the College of Surgeons, London.

Wednesday, 9.—Elders Young and Kimball visited St. Paul's Cathedral, the Monument, London and Southwark Bridges and also the British Museum.

Thursday, 10.—Elder Levi Richards left Manchester for Herefordshire.

Sunday, 13.—I attended the High Council at my office. Robert D. Foster was on trial for lying, slandering the authorities of the Church, profane swearing, etc. Witness was examined in part and trial adjourned to the 20th.

Monday, 14.—Ebenezer Robinson and Don Carlos Smith dissolved co-partnership. The *Times and Seasons* is to be continued by Don Carlos Smith.

Wednesday, 16.—This day the act chartering the "City of Nauvoo," the "Nauvoo Legion," and the "University of the City of Nauvoo," was signed by the Governor, having previously passed the House and Senate. Following is the act *in extenso.*

AN ACT TO INCORPORATE THE CITY OF NAUVOO.

Section 1. Be it enacted by the people of the State of Illinois, represented in the General Assembly, that all that district of country embraced within the following boundaries, to wit: beginning at the north east corner of section thirty-one in Township seven, north of range eight, west of the fourth principal meridian, in the county of Hancock, and running thence west to the northwest corner of said section, thence north to the Mississippi river, thence west to the middle of the main channel of the said river; thence down the middle of said channel to a point due west of the southeast corner of fractional section number twelve in township six, north of range nine, west of the fourth principal meridian, thence east to the southeast corner of said section twelve, thence north on the range line between township six north, and range eight and nine west, to the southwest corner of section six in township six north of range eight west, thence east to the southeast corner of said section, thence north to the place of beginning, including the town plats of Commerce and Nauvoo, shall hereafter be called and known by the name of the "City of Nauvoo," and the inhabitants thereof are hereby constituted a body corporate and politic by the name aforesaid, and shall have perpetual succession, and may have and use a common seal which they may change and alter at pleasure.

Sec. 2. Whenever any tract of land adjoining the "City of Nauvoo" shall have been laid out into town lots, and duly recorded according to law, the same shall form a part of the "City of Nauvoo."

Sec. 3. The inhabitants of said city, by the name and style aforesaid, shall have power to sue and be sued, to plead and be impleaded, defend and be defended, in all courts of law and equity, and all actions whatsoever; to purchase, receive and hold property, real and personal, in said city, to purchase, receive, and hold real property beyond the city, for burying grounds, or for other public purposes, for the use of the inhabitants of said city, to sell, lease,convey or dispose of property,real or personal, for the benefit of the city, to improve and protect such property, and to do all other things in relation thereto as natural persons.

Sec. 4. There shall be a City Council, to consist of a Mayor, four Aldermen, and nine Councillors, who shall have the qualifications of electors of said city, and shall be chosen by the qualified voters thereof, and shall hold their offices for two years, and until their successors shall be elected and qualified. The City Council shall judge of the qualifications, elections and returns of their own members, and a majority of them shall form a quorum to do business, but a smaller number may adjourn from day to day, and compel the attendance of absent members, under such penalties as may be prescribed by ordinance.

Sec. 5. The Mayor, Aldermen and Councillors, before entering upon the duties of their office, shall take and subscribe an oath or affirmation that they will support the Constitution of the United States, and of this State and that they will well and truly perform the duties of their offices to the best of their skill and abilities.

Sec. 6. On the first Monday of February next, and every two years thereafter, an election shall be held for the election of one Mayor, four Aldermen, and nine Councillors; and at the first election under the Act, three Judges shall be chosen *viva voce* by the electors present. The said Judges shall choose two Clerks, and the Judges and Clerks, before entering upon their duties, shall take and subscribe an oath or affirmation such as is now required by law to be taken by Judges or Clerks of other elections; and at all subsequent elections,the necessary number of Judges and Clerks shall be appointed by the City Council. At the first election thus held, the polls shall be opened at 9 o'clock a. m. and closed at 6 o'clock p. m,; at the close of the polls the votes shall be counted and a statement thereof proclaimed at the front door of the house at which said election shall be held; and the Clerks shall leave with each person elected, or at his place of residence, within five days after the election, a written notice of his election; and each person so notified shall within ten days after the election take the oath or affirmation hereinbefore mentioned, a certificate of which oath shall be deposited with the Recorder, whose appointment is hereafter provided for, and be by him preserved; and subsequent elections shall be held, conducted and returns thereof made as may be provided for by ordinance of the City Council.

Sec. 7. All free white male inhabitans, who are of the age of twenty one years, who are entitled to vote for State Officers, and who shall have been actual residents of the city sixty days next preceding said election, shall be entitled to vote for City Officers.

Sec. 8. The City Council shall have authority to levy and collect taxes, for city purposes, upon all property, real and personal, within the limits of the city, one-half per cent per annum, upon the assessed value thereof, and may enforce payment of the same in any manner, to be provided by ordinanee, not repugnant to the Constitution of the United States or of this State.

Sec. 9. The City Council shall have power to appoint a Recorder, Treasurer, Assessor, Marshal, Supervisor of streets, and all such other officers as may be necessary, and to prescribe their duties and remove them from office at pleasure.

Sec. 10. The City Council shall have power to require, of all officers appointed in pursuance of this Act, bonds, with penalty and security, for the faithful performance of their respective duties, such as may be deemed expedient; and also to require all officers appointed as aforesaid, to take an oath for the faithful performance of the duties of their respective offices.

Sec. 11. The City Council shall have power and authority to make, ordain, establish and execute all such ordinances, not repugnant to the Constitution of the United States or of this State, as they may deem necessary for the peace, benefit, good order, regulation, convenience, and cleanliness of said city: for the protection of property therein from destruction by fire, or otherwise, and for the health and happiness thereof: they shall have power to fill all vacancies that may happen by death, resignation, or removal, in any of the offices herein made elective; to fix and establish all the fees of the office of said corporation not herein established; to impose such fines, not exceeding one hundred dollars, for each offense, as they may deem just, for refusing to accept any office under the corporation, or for misconduct therein; to divide the city into wards; to add to the number of Aldermen and Councillors, and apportion them among the several wards as may be most just and conducive to the interests of the city.

Sec. 12. To license, tax, and regulate auctions, merchants, retailers, grocers, hawkers, peddlers, butchers, pawnbrokers, and money-changers.

Sec. 13. The City Council shall have exclusive power within the city, by ordinance, to license, regulate, and restrain the keeping of ferries; to regulate the police of the city; to impose fines, forfeitures, and penalties for the breach of any ordinance, and provide for the recovery of such fines and forfeitures, and the enforcement of such penalties; and to pass such ordinances, as may be necessary and proper for carrying into execution the powers specified in this Act; provided such ordinances are not repugnant to the Constitution of the United States or of this State, and in fine to exercise such other legislative powers as are conferred on the City Council of the City of Springfield, by an Act entitled an Act to Incorporate the City of Springfield, approved February 3rd, 1840.

Sec. 14. All ordinances passed by the City Council shall, within one month after they shall have been passed, be published in some newspaper printed in the city, or certified copies thereof be posted up in three of the most public places in the city.

Sec. 15. All ordinances of the city may be proven by the seal of the corporation, and when printed or published in book or pamphlet form, purporting to be printed or published by authority of the corporation, the same shall be received in evidence in all courts or places without further proof.

Sec. 16. The Mayor and Aldermen shall be conservators of the peace within the limits of said city, and shall have all the powers of Justices of the Peace therein, both in civil and criminal cases, arising under the laws of the State; they shall, as Justices of the Peace, within the limits of said city, perform the same duties, be governed by the same laws, give the same bonds and security, as other Justices of the Peace, and be commissioned as Justices of the Peace in and for said city by the Governor.

Sec. 17. The Mayor shall have exclusive jurisdiction in all cases arising under the ordinances of the corporation, and shall issue such process as may be necessary to carry such ordinances into execution and effect; appeals may be had from any decision or judgment of said Mayor or Aldermen, arising under the city ordinances, to the Municipal Court, under such regulations as may be presented by ordinance; which court shall be composed of the Mayor as Chief Justice, and the Aldermen as Associate Justices, and from the final judgment of the Municipal Court to the Circuit Court of Hancock county, in the same manner of appeals are taken from judgments of the Justices of the Peace; provided that the parties litigant shall have a right to a trial by a jury of twelve men in all cases before the Municipal Court. The Municipal Court shall have power to grant writs of habeas corpus in all cases arising under the ordinances of the City Council.

Sec. 18. The Municipal Court shall sit on the first Monday of every month, and the City Council at such times and place as may be prescribed by city ordinance; special meetings of which may at any time be called by the Mayor or any two Aldermen.

Sec. 19. All process issued by the Mayor, Aldermen, or Municipal Court, shall be directed to the Marshal, and, in the execution thereof, he shall be governed by the same laws as are or may be prescribed for the direction and compensation of constables in similar cases. The Marshal shall also perform such other duties as may be required of him under the ordinances of said city, and shall be the principal ministerial officer.

Sec. 20. It shall be the duty of the Recorder to make and keep accurate records of all ordinances made by the City Council, and of all their proceedings in their corporate capacity, which record shall at all times be open to the inspection of the electors of said city, and shall perform such other duties as may be required of him by the ordinances of the City Council, and shall serve as Clerk of the Municipal Court.

Sec 21. When it shall be necessary to take private property for the opening, widening, or altering any public street, lane, avenue, or alley, the corporation shall make a just compensation therefor to the person whose property is to be taken, and if the amount of such compensation cannot be agreed upon, the Mayor shall cause the same to be ascertained by a jury of six disinterested freeholders of the city.

Sec. 22. All jurors compelled to inquire into the amount of benefits or damages that shall happen to the owners of property so proposed to be taken, shall first be sworn to that effect, and shall return to the Mayor their inquest in writing, signed by each juror.

Sec. 23. In case the Mayor shall at any time be guilty of a palpable omission of duty, or shall wilfully, and corruptly be guilty of oppression, mal conduct, or partiality, in the discharge of the duties of his office, he shall be liable to be indicted in the Circuit Court of Hancock county, and on conviction he shall be fined not more than two hundred dollars, and the Court shall have power on the recommendation of the jury to add to the judgment of the Court that he be removed from office.

Sec. 24. The City Council may establish and organize an institution of learning within the limits of the city, for the teaching of the Arts, Sciences, and Learned Professions, to be called the "University of the City of Nauvoo," which institution shall be under the control and management of a Board of Trustees, consisting of a Chancellor, Registrar, and twenty-three Regents, which Board shall thereafter be a body corporate and politic, with perpetual succession by the name of the "Chancellor and Regents of the University of the City of Nauvoo," and shall have full power to pass, ordain, establish, and execute, all such laws and ordinances as they may consider necessary for the welfare and prosperity of said University, its officers and students; provided that the said laws and ordinances shall not be repugnant to the Constitution of the United States, or of this State; and provided also, that the Trustees shall at all times be appointed by the City Council, and shall have all the powers and privileges for the advancement of the cause of education which appertain to the Trustees of any other College or University of this State.

Sec. 25. The City Council may organize the inhabitants of said city, subject to military duty, into a body of independent military men, to be called the "Nauvoo Legion," the Court Martial of which shall be composed of the commissioned officers of said Legion, and constitute the law-making department, with full power and authority to make, ordain, establish, and execute all such laws and ordinances as may be considered necessary for the benefit, government, and regulation of said Legion; provided said Court Martial shall pass no law or act, repugnant to, or inconsistent with, the Constitution of the United States, or of this State; and provided also that the officers of the Legion shall be commissioned by the Governor of the State. The said Legion shall perform the same amount of military duty as is now or may be hereafter required of the regular militia of the State, and shall be at the disposal of the Mayor in executing the laws and ordinances of the city corporation, and the laws of the State, and at the disposal of the Governor for the public defense, and the execution of the laws of the State or of the United States, and shall be entitled to their proportion of the public arms; and provided also, that said Legion shall be exempt from all other military duty.

Sec. 26. The inhabitants of the city of Nauvoo are hereby exempted from working on any road beyond the limits of the city, and for the purpose of keeping the streets, lanes, avenues, and alleys in repair, to require of the male inhabitants of said city, over the age of twenty-one, and under fifty years, to labor on said streets, lanes, avenues, and alleys, not exceeding three days in each year; any person failing to perform such labor, when duly notified by the Supervisor, shall forfeit and pay the sum of one dollar per day for each day so neglected or refused.

Sec. 27. The City Council shall have power to provide for the punishment of offenders by imprisonment in the county or city jail, in all cases when such offenders shall fail or refuse to pay the fines and forfeitures, which may be recovered against them.

Sec. 28. This Act is hereby declared to be a public Act, and shall take effect on the first Monday of February next.

WM. L. D. EWING,
Speaker of the House of Representatives.
S. H. ANDERSON,
Speaker of the Senate.

Approved Dec. 16, 1840.

THOS. CARLIN.

State of Illinois, Office of Secretary of State.

I, Stephen A. Douglas, Secretary of State, do hereby certify that the foregoing is a true and perfect copy of the enrolled law now on file in my office.

Witness my hand, and Seal of State, at Springfield, this 18th day of December, 1840.

[L. S.]

S. A. DOUGLAS.
Secretary of State.

The following are the Legislative powers alluded to in the 13th section of the foregoing Act, as pertaining to the City Council of the City of Springfield, and which consequently became a part of the Charter of the City of Nauvoo, to wit:

OF THE LEGISLATIVE POWERS OF THE CITY COUNCIL.

Sec. 1. The City Council shall have powers and authority to levy and collect taxes upon all property, real and personal, within the city, not exceeding one-half per cent., per annum, upon the assessed valuation thereof, and may enforce the payment of the same in any manner prescribed by ordinance, not repugnant to the Constitution of the United States and of this State.

Sec. 2. The City Council shall have power to require of all officers appointed in pursuance of the Charters, bonds with penalty and security for the faithful performance of their respective duties as may be deemed expedient, and also to require all officers appointed as aforesaid, to take an oath for the faithful performance of the duties of their respective offices upon entering upon the discharge of the same.

Sec. 3. To establish, support, and regulate common schools, to borrow money on the credit of the city: provided, that no sum or sums of money shall be borrowed at a greater interest than six per cent per annum, nor shall the interest on the aggregate of all the sums borrowed and outstanding ever exceed one half of the city revenue, arising for taxes assessed on real property within the corporation.

Sec. 4. To make regulations to prevent the introduction of contagious diseases into the city, to make Quarantine Laws for that purpose, and enforce the same.

Sec. 5. To appropriate and provide for the payment of the debt and expenses of the city.

Sec. 6. To establish hospitals, and make regulations for the government of the same.

Sec. 7. To make regulations to secure the general health of the inhabitants, to declare what shall be a nuisance, and to prevent and remove the same.

Sec. 8. To provide the city with water, to dig wells and erect pumps in the streets for the extinguishment of fires, and convenience of the inhabitants.

Sec. 9. To open, alter, widen, extend, establish, grade, pave, or otherwise improve and keep in repair streets, avenues, lanes, and alleys.

Sec. 10. To establish, erect, and keep in repair bridges.

Sec. 11. To divide the city into wards, and specify the boundaries thereof, and create additional wards, as the occasion may require.

Sec. 12. To provide for lighting the streets and erecting lamp posts.

Sec. 13. To establish, support, and regulate night watches.

Sec. 14. To erect market houses, establish markets, and market places, and provide for the government and regulation thereof.

Sec. 15. To provide for erecting all needful buildings for the use of the city.

Sec. 16. To provide for enclosing, improving, and regulating all public grounds belonging to the city.

Sec. 17. To license, tax, and regulate auctioneers, merchants, and retailers, grocers, taverns ordinaries, hawkers, peddlers, brokers, pawnbrokers, and money changers.

Sec. 18. To license, tax, and regulate hackney carriages, wagons, carts and drays, and fix the rates to be charged for the carriage of persons, and for the wagonage, cartage and drayage of property.

Sec. 19. To license and regulate porters and fix the rates of porterage.

Sec. 20. To license and regulate theatrical and other exhibitions, shows and amusements.

Sec. 21. To tax, restrain, prohibit, and suppress, tippling houses, dram shops, gaming houses, bawdy and other disorderly houses.

Sec. 22. To provide for the prevention and extinguishment of fires, and to organize and establish fire companies.

Sec. 23. To regulate the fixing of chimneys, and the flues thereof, and stove pipes.

Sec. 24. To regulate the storage of gunpowder, tar, pitch, rosin, and other combustible materials.

Sec. 25. To regulate and order parapet walls, and partition fences.

Sec. 26. To establish standard weights and measures, and regulate the weights and measures to be used in the city in all other cases not provided for by law.

Sec. 27. To provide for the inspection and measuring of lumber and other building materials, and for the measurement of all kinds of mechanical work.

Sec. 28. To provide for the inspection and weighing of hay, lime, and stone coal, the measuring of charcoal, firewood, and other fuel, to be sold or used within the city.

Sec. 29. To provide for and regulate the inspection of tobacco, and of beef, pork, flour, meal, and whiskey in barrels.

Sec. 30. To regulate the weight, quality, and price of bread, sold, and used in the city.

Sec. 31. To provide for taking the enumeration of the inhabitants of the city.

Sec. 32. To regulate the election of city officers, and provide for removing from office any person holding an office created by ordinance.

Sec. 33. To fix the compensation of all city officers, and regulate the fees of jurors, witnesses, and others, for services rendered under this Act or any ordinance.

Sec. 34. To regulate the police of the city, to impose fines, and forfeitures, and penalties, for the breach of any ordinance, and provide for the recovery and appropriation of such fines and forfeitures, and the enforcement of such penalties.

Sec. 35. The City Council shall have exclusive power within the city by ordinance, to license, regulate, and suppress, and restrain, billiard tables, and from one to twenty pin alleys, and every other description of gaming or gambling.

Sec. 36. The City Council shall have power to make all ordinances which shall be necessary and proper for carrying into execution the powers specified in this Act, so that such ordinances be not repugnant to nor inconsistent with, the constitution of the United States or of this state

Sec. 37. The style of the ordinances of the city shall be—"Be it ordained by the city council of the city of Springfield—[Nauvoo]."

Sec. 38. All ordinances passed by the city council shall, within one month after they shall have been passed, be published in some newspaper published in the city, and shall not be in force until they shall have been published as aforesaid.

Sec. 39. All ordinances of the city may be proven by the seal of the corporation, and when printed and published by authority of the corporation, the same shall be received in evidence in all courts and places without fourther proof.

John C. Bennett who had been delegated to Springfield to carry our petition for a City Charter, announced the passage of the bill, as follows—

Letter of John C. Bennett to the "Times and Seasons"—Announcing the passage of the act incorporating Nauvoo.

CITY OF SPRINGFIELD, December 16, 1840.

Editors of the Times and Seasons:

The act incorporating the city of Nauvoo has just passed the council of revision, and is now a law of the land, to take effect and be in force from and after the first Monday in February next. The aforesaid act contains two additional charters—one incorporating the "Nauvoo Legion," the other the "University of the city of Nauvoo."

All these charters are very broad and liberal, conferring the most plenary powers on the corporators. Illinois has acquitted herself with honor, and her state legislators shall never be forgotten. Every power we asked has been granted, every request gratified, every desire fulfilled. In the senate Mr. Little cancelled every obligation to our people, and faithfully, and honestly, and with untiring diligence, discharged every obligation devolving upon him as our immediate representative in the Upper House. Mark well that man, and do him honor. Snyder, and Ralston, and Moore, and Ross, and Stapp, and numerous others, likewise in that branch of our state government, rendered us very essential services; and the act passed that body without a dissenting voice.

In the House of Representatives, Charles, our immediate Representative in the Lower House, was at his post and discharged his duty as a faithful representative; he is an acting, and not a talking man, and has fulfilled all his obligations to us. Many members in this house, likewise, were warmly in our favor; and with only one or two dissenting voices, every representative appeared inclined to extend to us all such powers as they considered us justly entitled to, and voted for the law; and here I should not forget to mention, that Lincoln,* whose name we erased from the electoral ticket in November (not however on account of any dislike to him as a man, but simply because his was the last name on the ticket, and we desired to show our friendship to the Democratic

* This doubtless refers to Abraham Lincoln who was then a member of the legislature. See Nicolay and Hay's *Abraham Lincoln*, Vol. I, p. 42 *et seq.*

party by substituting the name of Ralston for some one of the Whigs) had the magnanimity to vote for our act, and came forward, after the final vote to the bar of the house, and cordially congratulated me on its passage.

Our worthy governor is certainly disposed to do us ample justice in every respect, and to extend to us every facility for our future happiness and prosperity.

Illinois has certainly done her duty, and her whole duty; and now it becomes us to show ourselves upright, honest, just, worthy of the favors bestowed by noble, generous, and magnanimous statesmen, I have said that we are a law-abiding people, and we must now show it. The state has washed her hands in granting all our petitions, and if we do not now show ourselves approved, the curse must fall upon our own heads. Justice, equal justice, should be our fixed object and purpose, and the Great God will prosper us; length of days will be in our right hand, and in our left, glory and honor.

Yours, &c.,

JOHN C. BENNETT.

The City Charter of Nauvoo is of my own plan and device. I concocted it for the salvation of the Church, and on principles so broad, that every honest man might dwell secure under its protective influence without distinction of sect or party.

CHAPTER XIV.

VALE 1840—ENTER 1841—LIST OF PUBLICATIONS FOR AND AGAINST THE CHURCH—WHEREABOUTS OF THE TWELVE APOSTLES—"ELECTION AND REPROBATION"—PROCLAMATION TO THE SAINTS.

Sunday, December 20, 1840.—I was called upon by the High Council to decide the adjourned case of Robert D. Foster. Having heard the witnesses, I decided that he be acquitted of the charges against him, which decision the Council approved.*

The acquittal of R. D. Foster.

This is a fair specimen of the wisdom of the nineteenth century that opposes itself to the work of the Most High God.

An Objector Put Down.

"Your preacher preaches false doctrine," exclaimed a sectarian in Manchester to one of the Saints. "Ah!" inquired the other, "wherein does he teach false doctrine?" "Why, in telling the people to go to America, to be sure," said the sectarian; "and" continued he, "there is nothing in the Bible that commands people to go to America." "Ah!" replied the other, "and there is nothing in the Bible that commands people to stop in Manchester; so I wonder how you dare stay in so unscriptural a place another night; for certainly no one ought to live in England unless they can find scripture for it, any more than in America."

Monday, 21.—The petition of Elias Higbee, and Robert B. Thompson, under date of 28th November, 1840, was presented to the House of Representatives of the United

* For the nature of the charges see ch. xiii.

States, referred to the Committee on the Judiciary, and ordered to be printed.

Friday, 25.—Elders Brigham Young and George A. Smith attended a conference at Hanley, Staffordshire Potteries, at which was represented an increase of six Elders, twenty-six Priests, ten Teachers, nine deacons, and three hundred and fifty-six members, since last July Conference; and also ordained six Elders, six Priests, four Teachers, and three Deacons.

Sunday, 27.—Elders Kimball and Woodruff occupied a chapel belonging to the Independents in London. Elder Woodruff preached.

Monday, 28.—There are ninety-five Saints in Edinburgh, Scotland, raised up by Elder Orson Pratt. Elder George D. Watt is now laboring in that place.

Wednesday, 30.—Elder Brigham Young writes from Liverpool:

Brigham Young's Letter to the Prophet Reporting Labors in England.

BELOVED BROTHER:—I write to inform you of a few particulars of my journey to London. I left Manchester November 25th, in company with Elder Kimball; we visited the following places, viz., Macclesfield, Burslem, Hanley, Lane End, West Bromwich, and Birmingham. We traveled by coach and railway, and arrived in London on Monday 30th: found Elder Woodruff in good health. He had baptized three or four persons the day before we arrived. I stayed in London till the 11th December, when I left for Herefordshire. Brothers Woodruff and Williams came with me to the railway station. Elder Kimball stayed in London.

The prospect for the spread of the Gospel brightened up while we were there. Our feelings were very clear and decisive that Elder Kimball had better stay with Elder Woodruff. I was much interested while there with my brethren. I pray the Lord to roll on His work in that great city. I feel much for the people in that place! yea my feelings are exquisite, for why, God knows; but I believe it is for the glory of God, and the good of souls. May His name be glorified.

I arrived in Cheltenham the same day I left London—only about seven and a half hours going one hundred and one miles, thirty-eight of it by coach. I stayed over the Sabbath there; preached twice to a very attentive congregation. In the afternoon the house was full to overflowing. Elder Henry Glover is preaching in this place, and in the region around with much success. I think he is a humble, good man, and will do much good. I attended the Gadfield Elm conference. The minutes of the Garway conference were read, which had been held on the 8th. After this I visited the brethren till the Stanley Hill conference, which was held on the 21st. The church in Garway numbers ninety-five members, one Elder, seven Priests, three Teachers and one Deacon. At Gadfield Elm conference there were seventeen branches represented, three hundred and twenty-seven members, thirteen Elders, thirty-one Priests, nine Teachers. The Stanley Hill conference contains twenty-five branches, which represented eight hundred and thirty-nine members, seventeen Elders, fifty-seven Priests, sixteen Teachers and one Deacon. Including officers there are in these three conferences twelve hundred and sixty-one members, thirty-one Elders, ninety-five Priests, twenty-eight Teachers and two Deacons; making two hundred and fifty-five added since the October conference.

I attended the conference in the Staffordshire Potteries on the 25th; we had a good meeting; but I have not the minutes before me, so I cannot give a particular statement of the church there, yet I can say they are prospering.

In my travels and at the conferences, there were some baptized and many ordained. We can say truly, that the Lord is doing a great work in the land. The Gospel is preached to the poor, and signs follow them that believe. I arrived in Liverpool last evening and expect to tarry here till the Book of Mormon is completed.

I am as ever, your brother in the Kingdom of Patience,

BRIGHAM YOUNG.

About this time, immense quantities of rain fell which produced a flood in the east and south of France, doing immense damage, carrying with it buildings, bridges and everything in its way. Earthquakes have been felt in divers places the past year; and fearful sights and bloody signs have been witnessed in the heavens, fulfilling the words of the ancient Prophets concerning the last days.

I copy the following from a printed sheet:

SIGNS IN THE SKY.

A most wonderful phenomenon was observed last week by the inhabitants of Hull and the neighborhood. A perfectly blood red flag was seen flying in the heavens, which illuminated the horizon for many miles around. At intervals it changed its form, assuming that of a cross, sword and many other shapes. At one o'clock on Friday morning, the town was nearly as light as noon-day; the inhabitant were parading the streets; fear and dismay pictured in their countenances. This wonder continued until near three o'clock, when it gradually went to the westward, illuminating the Humber as it seemed to sink in her waters. Then for a few seconds all became total darkness, when from the northwest by north, arose the most beautiful light, which shot away towards the western hemisphere, leaving in its train the most beautiful and varigated colors, and which the eye might readily form into armies drawn up in the order of battle, charging and retreating alternately, and then again all was wrapped in the sable curtain of night. It appears that many signs were seen on the same night in different parts of the kingdom.

List of Books.

The following is a list of books, pamphlets, and letters published for and against the Latter-day Saints during the past year, so far as such have come under my observation:

Fourteen numbers of the *Times and Seasons* have been issued from the office in Nauvoo, containing two hundred and twenty-four pages, edited by Ebenezer Robinson and Don Carlos Smith, three numbers having been issued during 1839.

Eight numbers of the *Millennial Star* have been published at 149 Oldham Road, Manchester, England, containing two hundred and sixteen pages, edited by Elder Parley P. Pratt.

A selection of hymns was published about the first of July, in England, by Brigham Young, John Taylor, and Parley P. Pratt, for the use of the Saints in Europe.

The Rev. Robert Hays, Wesleyan minister, Douglas, Isle of Man, published three addresses in pamphlet form, against the Latter-day Saints, which were replied to in the following order:

"An Answer to Some False Statements and Misrepresentations," published by the Rev. Robert Hays, Wesleyan minister, in an address to his society in Douglas, and its vicinity on the subject of Mormonism, by John Taylor, October 7th, 1840.

"Calumny Refuted, and the Truth Defended," being a reply to the second address of the Rev. Robert Hays, by John Taylor, Douglas, October 29, 1840.

"Truth Defended and Methodism Weighed in the Balances and Found Wanting," being a reply to the third address of the Rev. Robert Hays against the Latter-day Saints and also an "Exposure of the Principles of Methodism," by John Taylor, Liverpool, December 7, 1840.

"The Latter-day Saints and the Book of Mormon;" being a few words of warning against the Latter-day Saints, from a minister to his flock. W. J. Morrish, Ledbury, Herefordshire, September.

A second warning by the same W. J. Morrish, October 15th.

"A Few More Facts Relating to the Self-styled 'Latter-day Saints,' " by John Simmons, Church of England minister, Dymock, Herefordshire, September 14th.

Several letters written by Mr. Curran, and published in the *Manx Liberal*, Isle of Man, in October, were replied to by John Taylor.

"Mormonism Weighed in the Balances of the Sanctuary and Found Wanting;" the substance of four lectures by Samuel Haining, published in Douglas, Isle of Man; a tract of sixty-six pages.

Interesting account of several remarkable visions, and of the late discovery of ancient American Records giving an account of the commencement of the work of the Lord in this generation, by Elder Orson Pratt, Edinburgh, September.

The Word of the Lord to the Citizens of London, of every sect and denomination; and to every individual into whose hands it may fall; showing forth the plan of salvation as laid down in the New Testament; namely, faith in our Lord Jesus Christ—Repentance—Baptism for the remission of sins—and the Gift of the Holy Ghost, by the laying on of hands, presented by Heber C. Kimball and Wilford Woodruff, Elders of the Church of Jesus Christ of Latter-day Saints.

An exposure of the errors and fallacies of the self-named "Latter-day Saints." By William Hewitt, of Lane End, Staffordshire, Potteries.

An answer to Mr. William Hewitt's tract against the Latter-day Saints. By Elder Parley P. Pratt.

Plain Facts; showing the falsehood and folly of the Rev. C. Bush(the Church of England minister, of the parish ot Peover, Cheshire); being a reply to his tract against the Latter-day Saints by Parley P. Pratt.

A few remarks by way of reply to an annonymous scribbler, calling himself "a Philanthropist," disabusing the Church of Jesus Christ of Latter-day Saints, of the slanders and falsehoods which he has attempted to fasten upon it. By Samuel Bennett, Philadelphia.

Mormonism unmasked, and Mr. Bennett's reply answered and refuted. By a Philanthropist of Chester County. Published in Philadelphia.

An Appeal to the American People; being an account of the persecutions of the Church of Jesus Christ of Latter-day Saints, and the barbarities inflicted on them by the inhabitants of the State of Missouri, sixty closely printed pages second edition revised by authority of said Church, Joseph Smith, Jun., Sidney Rigdon, Hyrum Smith, Presidency.

A reply to Mr. Thomas Taylor's Pamphlet, entitled "Complete Failure," etc., and also to Mr. Richard Livesey's tract, "Mormonism Exposed" by Parley P. Pratt.

The editor of the *London Dispatch*, published an article on November 8th, against the Latter-day Saints, containing some of the false statements of Captain D. L. St. Clair, in his tract against them, which was replied to by Elder Parley P. Pratt, in the November number of the *Millennial Star*.

"The Millennium, and other Poems:" to which is annexed, "A Treatise on the Regeneration and Eternal

Duration of Matter," by Parley P. Pratt, New York.

January 1, 1841.—Elders Brigham Young, Parley P. Pratt, and John Taylor attended a conference in Liverpool.

Elders Heber C. Kimball, and Wilford Woodruff are in London.

Elder Orson Pratt in Edinburgh.

Elder George A. Smith in Burslem.

Elder Willard Richards in Preston.

Elders Orson Hyde and J. E. Page are *en route* for Jerusalem.

Elder William Smith, at Plymouth, Hancock county, Illinois.

The *Millennial Star* [No. 9, Vol. I] contains the following communication, which I have read several times. It is one of the sweetest pieces that has been written in these last days. I therefore insert it entire.

Election and Reprobation—by Brigham Young and Willard Richards.

Do you believe in election and reprobation? To prevent the necessity of repeating a thousand times what may be said at once, we purpose to answer this oft-asked question in writing, so that the Saints may learn doctrine, and all who will may understand that such election and reprobation as is taught in the Old and New Testaments, and other revelations from God, we fully believe, in connection with every other principle of righteousness; and we ask this favor of all into whose hands our answer may come, that they will not condemn until they have read it through, in the spirit of meekness and prayer.

The Lord (Jehovah) hath spoken through Isaiah (xiii: 1), saying, "Behold my servant whom I uphold—mine elect in whom my soul delighteth;" evidently referring to the Lord Jesus Christ, the Son of God, chosen, or elected by the Father. (I Peter i: 20). "Who verily was foreordained before the foundation of the world, but was manifest in these last times for you, who by Him do believe in God to serve Him in the redemption of the world, to be a covenant of the people (Isaiah xlii: 6), for a light to the Gentiles, and the glory of His people Israel, having ordained Him to be the judge of the quick and dead (Acts x: 42), that through Him forgiveness of sins might be preached (Acts xiii: 38), unto all who would be obedient unto His Gospel." (Mark xvi: 16, 17).

Every High Priest must be ordained (Heb. v: 1), and if Christ had not received ordination, He would not have had power to ordain others, as He did when He ordained the Twelve (Mark iii: 14), to take part in the ministry which He had received of His Father; also, (John xv: 16): "Ye have not chosen me, but I have chosen you, and ordained you, that ye should go and bring forth fruit; (Heb. v: 4), for no man taketh this honor unto himself, but he that is called of God, as was Aaron (v: 5), so also Christ glorified not Himself to be made an High Priest; but He that said unto Him, Thou art my Son, today have I begotten Thee." No being can give that which he does not possess; consequently, no man can confer the Priesthood on another, if he has not himself first received it; and the Priesthood is of such a nature that it is impossible to investigate the principles of election, reprobation, &c., without touching upon the Priesthood also; and although some may say that Christ, as God, needed no ordination, having possessed it eternally, yet Christ says, (Matt. xxviii: 18), "All power is *given* unto me in heaven and in earth;" which could not have been if He was in eternal possession; and in the previously quoted verse we discover that He that said unto Him [*i. e.* His Father] glorified Him to be made an High Priest, or ordained Him to the work of creating the world and all things upon it, (Col. i: 16), "For by Him were all things created that are in heaven, and that are in earth," &c., and of redeeming the same from the fall, and to the judging of the quick and dead, for the right of judging rests in the Priesthood, and it is through this medium that the Father hath committed all judgment unto the Son (John v: 22), referring to His administration on earth. It was necessary that Christ should receive the Priesthood to qualify Him to minister before His Father, unto the children of men, so as to redeem and save them. Does it seem reasonable that any man should take it upon him to do a part of the same work, or to assist in the same Priesthood, who has not been called by the spirit of prophecy or revelation as was Aaron, and ordained accordingly? And can it be expected that a man will be called by revelation who does not believe in revelation? Or will any man submit to ordination for the fulfillment of a revelation or call, in which he hath no faith? We think not.

That we may learn still further that God calls or elects particular men to perform particular works, or on whom to confer special blessings, we read, (Isaiah xlv: 4), "For Jacob my servant's sake, and Israel mine elect, I have even called thee [Cyrus] by thy name," to be a deliverer to my people Israel, and help to plant them on my holy mountain, (Isaiah lxv: 9, see connection) "for mine elect shall inherit it, and my servants shall dwell there," even on the mountains of Palestine, the land of Canaan which God had before promised to Abraham and his seed; (Gen. xvii: 8), and the particular reason why Abraham was chosen or elected to be the father of this blessed nation, is clearly told by the Lord, (Gen. xviii: 19), "For I know him, that he will command his children and his household after him, and they shall keep the way of the Lord, to do justice and judgment; that the Lord may bring upon Abraham that which he hath spoken of him;" and this includes the general principle of election, *i. e* that God chose, elected, or ordained Jesus Christ, His Son, to be the creator, governor, savior, and judge of the world; and Abraham to be the father of the faithful, on account of His foreknowledge of their obedience to His will and commandments, which agrees with the saying in II Tim. ii: 21, "If a man therefore purge himself from these [i. e. iniquities], he shall be a vessel unto honor, sanctified, and meet for the master's use,and prepared unto every good work."

Thus it appears that God has chosen or elected certain individuals to certain blessings, or to the performance of certain works; and that we may more fully understand the movements of the Supreme Governor of the universe, in the order of election, we proceed to quote the sacred writers, (Rom. viii: 29, 30), "For whom He did foreknow, He also did predestinate to be conformed to the image of His Son, that He might be the firstborn among many brethren. Moreover, whom He did predestinate, them He also called: and whom He called, them He also justified: and whom He justified, them He also glorified." And whom did He foreknow? Those that loved Him, as we find in the 28th verse of the same chapter—"And we know that all things work together for good to them that love God, to them who are the called according to His purpose." And "who are the called according to His purpose?" Those whom He foreknew, for He foreknew that those who loved Him would do His will and work righteousness; and it is vain for men to say they love God, if they do not keep His commandments. Cain found it so when he presented an unrighteous offering, for God said unto him, (Gen. iv: 7), "If thou dost well, shalt thou not be accepted?" And yet he was not accepted. "But whoso keepeth his word, in him verily is the love of God perfected; and hereby know we that we are in Him," (I John ii: 5), or, that we "are the called according to his purpose."

The principles of God's kingdom are perfect and harmonious, and the Scriptures of truth must also agree in all their parts, so that one sentiment thereof shall not destroy another, and when we read that, "whom He did foreknow, He also did predestinate;" and that "known unto God are all His works;" so that it might appear from an abstract view thereof, that God foreknew all, and consequently predestinated all "to be conformed to the image of His Son;" we ought also to read, (Mark xvi: 16), "He that believeth not shall be damned;" and (John viii: 14), "If ye believe not that I am he, ye shall die in your sins;" also (Matt. xxv: 41), "Depart from me, ye cursed, * * * for I was an hungered, and ye gave me no meat," &c.

Paul, referring to the Saints, (Rom. 1: 7), calls them beloved of God, called to be Saints; and says, (Rom. viii: 1), "There is no condemnation to them which are in Christ Jesus, who walk not after the flesh, but after the Spirit," and goes on to show in his epistle to the Romans, that the law (the law of carnal commandments given to the children of Israel, the covenant people), could not make the comers thereunto perfect (see also Heb. x: 1), but was given for a schoolmaster to bring us unto Christ (Gal. iii: 24); so that when He had come and offered Himself without spot unto God (Heb. ix: 14), the sacrifice of the law should be done away in him, that the honest in heart all might come unto the perfect law of liberty (James i: 25); or the Gospel of Christ, walking no longer after the flesh but after the spirit, and be of that number who love God and keep His commandments, that they might be called according to His purpose (Rom. viii: 28); and these were the individuals referred to, whom God foreknew; such as Abel, Seth, Enoch, Noah, Melchisedek, Abraham, Lot, Isaac, Jacob, Joseph, Moses, Caleb, Joshua, the harlot Rahab, who wrought righteousness by hiding the servants of God, when their lives were sought by their enemies, Gideon, Barak, Sampson, Jeptha, David, Samuel, and the Prophets; (Heb. xi), "Who through faith, subdued kingdoms, wrought righteousness, obtained promises, stopped the mouths of lions, quenched the violence of fire, escaped the edge of the sword, out of weakness were made strong, waxed valiant in fight, and turned to flight the armies of the aliens." These all died in faith, having kept the commandments of the Most High, having obtained the promise of a glorious inheritance, and are waiting the fulfillment of the promise which they obtained; (Heb. xi: 40), "God having provided some better things for us, that they without us should not be made perfect."

The Prophet Alma bears a similar testimony to the other Prophets concerning election, in his 9th chapter [Book of Mormon] saying, "This is the manner after which they were ordained: being called and prepared from the foundation of the world, according to the foreknowledge of God, on account of their exceeding faith and good works; in the first place being left to choose good or evil; therefore they have chosen good, and exercising exceeding great faith, are called with a holy calling, yea, with that holy calling which was prepared with, and according to, a preparatory redemption for such; and thus they have been called to this holy calling on account of their faith, while others would reject the Spirit of God on account of the hardness of their hearts and blindness of their minds, while, if it had not been for this, they might have had as great privilege as their brethren. Or in fine, in the first place, they were on the same standing with their brethren; thus, this holy calling being prepared from the foundation of the world for such as would not harden their hearts, being in and through the atonement of the only begotten Son, who was prepared; and thus being called by this holy calling, and ordained unto the high priesthood of the holy order of God, to teach His commandments unto the children of men, that they also might enter into His rest: this high priesthood being after the order of His Son, which order was from the foundation of the world: or, in other words, being without beginning of days or end of years, being prepared from eternity to all eternity, according to his foreknowledge of all things." (Rom. ix: 11, 12), "For the children being not yet born, neither having done any good or evil, that the purpose of God according to election might stand, not of works, but of Him that calleth; it was said unto her, The elder shall serve the younger." As we have before shown why God chose Abraham to be the father of the faithful, viz., because He knew Abraham would command his children and his household after him; so now we see, by this, why the purposes of God, according to election, should stand, and that for His oath's sake. (Gen. xxii: 16, 17, 18), "By myself have I sworn, saith the Lord, for because thou hast done this thing, and hast not withheld thy son, thine only son, that in blessing I will bless thee, and in multiplying I will multiply thy seed as the stars of heaven, and as the sand which is upon the sea shore; and thy seed shall possess the gate of his enemies, and in thy seed shall all the nations of the earth be blessed because thou hast obeyed my voice." Here the Lord Jesus, coming through the seed of Abraham, is again referred to, through whose sufferings and death, or in whom all the nations of the earth were to be blessed, or made alive, as they had died in Adam. (1 Cor. xv: 22). In this, election is made manifest, for God elected or chose the children of Israel to be His peculiar people, and to them belong the covenants and promises, and the blessings received by the Gentiles come through the covenants to Abraham and his seed; for through the unbelief of the Jews (Rom. xi: 17) they were broken off, and the Gentiles were grafted in; but they stand by faith (Rom. xi: 20), and not by the oath of election; therefore it becometh them to fear lest they cease quickly to bear fruit and be broken off (verse 21) that the Jews may be grafted in again; for they shall be grafted in again (verse 23), if they abide not in unbelief.

The Gentiles became partakers of the blessings of election and promises, through faith and obedience, as Peter says, writing to the strangers scattered abroad (1 Peter, 1st chap.), who were the Gentiles, the "elect according to the foreknowledge of God the Father, through sanctification of the spirit unto obedience;" (1 Peter, ii: 9) for "ye are a chosen generation, a royal prirsthood, an holy nation, a peculiar people; that ye should show forth the praises of Him who hath called you out of darkness into His marvelous light, (verse 10) which in time past were not a people, but now are the people of God: which had not obtained mercy, but now have obtained mercy."

Why were they a peculiar people? Because God had chosen that generation of Gentiles, and conferred on them the blessings which descended through the Priesthood, and the covenants unto the house of Israel, or grafted them into the good olive tree (Rom. xi: 17); and thus the house of Israel became the ministers of salvation to the Gentiles; and this is what the house of Israel was elected unto, not only their own salvation, but through them salvation unto all others; (John iv: 22) "For salvation is of the Jews," (Rom. xi: 11) and "through their fall salvation is come unto the Gentiles."

Among the promised seed we find Jesus Christ neither last nor least, but the Great High Priest and head of all, who was chosen to lay down His life for the redemption of the world, for without the shedding of blood there could be no remission of sins (Heb. ix: 22). (Deut. vii: 6, 7, 8, 9,) Moses bears a similar testimony with Peter and Paul to the principles of election—"For thou art an holy people unto the Lord thy God: the Lord thy God hath chosen thee to be a special people unto Himself, above all people that are upon the face of the earth. The Lord did not set His love upon you, nor choose you, because ye were more in number than any people; for ye were the fewest of all people: but because the Lord loved you, and because He would keep the oath which He had sworn unto your fathers, hath the Lord brought you out with a mighty hand, and redeemed you out of the house of bondmen, from the hand of Pharoah, king of Egypt. Know therefore that the Lord thy God, He is God, the faithful God, which keepeth covenant and mercy with them that love Him and keep His commandments to a thousand generations;" which proves the long continuance of the blessings of this highly favored people.

And the Lord said unto her, (Rebecca, Gen. xxv: 23) "The elder shall serve the younger." And why? Because that Isaac, the father of Esau and Jacob, the husband of Rebecca, and the son of promise to Abraham, was the heir; and as Esau was the elder son of his father Isaac, he had a legal claim to the heirship; but through unbelief, hardness of heart, and hunger, he sold his birthright to his younger brother Jacob (Gen. xxv: 33); and God knowing beforehand that he would do this of his own free will and choice, or acting upon that agency which God has delegated to all men, said to his mother, "The elder shall serve the younger;" for as the elder son Esau, has sold his birthright, and by that means lost all claim to the blessings promised to Abraham; those blessings and promises must have failed, if they had not descended with the purchased birthright unto the younger son, Jacob, for there was no other heir in Abraham's family; and if those blessings had failed, the purposes of God according to election must have failed in relation to the posterity of Israel, and the oath of Jehovah would have been broken, which could not be though heaven and earth were to pass away. (Rom. ix: 13) "As it is written, Jacob have I loved, but Esau have I hated." Where is it written? (Mal. i: 1, 2). When was it written? About 397 years before Christ, and Esau and Jacob were born about 1,773 years before Christ, (according to the computation of time in Scripture margin), so Esau and Jacob lived about 1,376 years before the Lord spoke by Malachi, saying, "Jacob have I loved, but Esau have I hated," as quoted by Paul. This text is often brought forward to prove that God loved Jacob and hated Esau before they were born, or before they had done good or evil; but if God did love one and hate the other before they had done good or evil, He has not seen fit to tell us of it, either in the Old or New Testament, or any other revelation: but this only we learn that 1,376 years after Esau and Jacob were born, God said by Malachi—"Jacob have I loved, and Esau have I hated;" and surely that was time sufficient to prove their works, and ascertain whether they were worthy to be loved or hated.

And why did He love the one and hate the other? For the same reason that He accepted the offering of Abel and rejected Cain's offering. Because Jacob's works had been righteous, and Esau's wicked, and where is there a righteous father who would not do the same thing? Who would not love an affectionate and obedient son more than one who was disobedient, and sought to injure Him and overthrow the order of His house? (Objection). But God seeth not as man seeth, and He is no respecter of persons. (Acts x: 34). True, but what saith the next verse, "He that feareth God and worketh righteousness is accepted of Him;" but it does not say that he that worketh wickedness is accepted, and this is a proof that God has respect to the actions of persons; and if He did not, why should He commend obedience to His law? For if he had no respect to the actions of men, He would be just as well pleased with a wicked man for breaking His law as a righteous man for keeping it; and if Cain had done well, he would have been accepted as well as Abel (Gen. iv: 7), and Esau as well as Jacob, which proves that God does not respect persons, only in relation to their acts, (see Matt. xxv: 34 to the end) "Come, ye blessed of my Father, inherit the kingdom prepared for you from the foundation of the world: for I was an hungered, and ye gave me meat," &c.; and because that God blessed Abel and Jacob, this would not have hindered His blessing Cain and Esau, if their works had been righteous like unto their brethren; so God's choosing one nation to blessing does not doom another to cursing or make them reprobate, according to the reprobation of God, as some suppose; "But by resisting the truth they became reprobate concerning the faith" (II Tim. iii: 8); and are "abomninable, and disobedient, and unto every good work reprobate" (Titus i: 16); consequently, are not fit subjects for the blessings of election.

Rom. ix: 15, "For He saith to Moses, I will have mercy on whom I will have mercy, and I will have compassion on whom I will have compassion." (See Exod. xxxiii: 13 to the 19) "My presence shall go with thee, and I will give thee rest, * * * for thou hast found grace in my sight, and I know thee by name, and I will make all my goodness to pass before thee, * * * and I will proclaim the name of the Lord before thee; and I will be gracious to whom I will be gracious, and will show mercy on whom I will show mercy." (Rom. ix: 16) "So then it is not of him that willeth, nor of him that runneth, but of God that showeth mercy;" having His eye at the same time directed towards His covenant people in Egyptian bondage. For the Scripture saith unto Pharoah (Exod. ix: 16, 17), "And in very deed for this cause have I raised thee up, for to show in thee my power; and that my name may be declared throughout all the earth. As yet exaltest thou thyself, against my people, that thou wilt not let them go?"

God has promised to bring the house of Israel up out of the land of Egypt at his own appointed time; and with a mighty hand and an outstretched arm, and great terribleness (Deut. xxvi, 8.) He chose to do this thing that His power might be known and his name declared throughout all the earth, so that all nations might have the God of heaven in remembrance, and reverence his holy name; and to accomplish this it was needful that He should meet with opposition to give Him an opportunity to manifest His power; therefore He raised up a man, even Pharaoh, who, He foreknew, would harden his heart against God of his own free will and choice, and would withstand the Almighty in His attempt to deliver His chosen people, and that to the utmost of his ability; and he proved himself worthy of the choice, for he left no means unimproved which his wicked heart could devise to vex the sons of Abraham, and defeat the purposes of the Most High, which gave the God of Abraham an opportunity to magnify his name in the ears of the nations, and in sight of this wicked king, by many mighty signs and wonders, sometimes even to the convincing of the wicked king of his wickedness, and of the power of God, (Exod. viii: 28, etc.) and yet he would continue to rebel and hold the Israelites in bondage; and this is what it meant by God's hardening Pharaoh's heart. He manifested Himself in so many glorious and mighty ways, that Pharaoh could not resist the truth without becoming harder; so that at last, in his madness, to stay the people of God, he rushed his hosts into the Red Sea and they were covered with the floods.

Had not the power of God been exerted in a remarkable manner, it would seem as though the house of Israel must have become extinct, for Pharaoh commanded the midwives to destroy the sons of the Israelitish women as soon as they were born (Exod. i: 15, 16), and called them to account for saving the men children alive (verse 18), and charged all his people saying, "Every son that is born, ye shall cast into the river" (verse 22), and yet God would have mercy on whom He would have mercy (Rom. ix: 18); for he would have mercy on the goodly child, Moses, when he was hid and laid in the flags (Exod. xi: 3) by his mother to save him from Pharaoh's cruel order, and caused that he should be preserved as a Prophet and deliverer to lead His people up to their own country; and whom He would He hardened, for He hardened Pharaoh by passing before him in mighty power and withdrawing His Spirit, and leaving him to his own inclination, for he had set taskmasters over the Israelites to afflict them with their burdens, and caused them to build treasure cities for Pharaoh, and made them to serve with rigor; and made their lives bitter with hard bondage, in mortar and brick and all manner of service in the field (Exod. 1st chap.); besides destroying the men children, thus proving to the God of heaven and all men that he had hardened his own hard heart, until he became a vessel of wrath fitted for destruction (Rom, ix: 22); all this long before God said unto Moses, "I will harden his (Pharaoh's) heart" (Exod. iv: 21).

Are men, then, to be saved by works? Nay, verily, "By grace are ye saved through faith, and that not of yourselves, it is the gift of God" (Eph. ii: 8); "Not of works, lest any man should boast" (v. 9); "Not by works of righteousness which we have done, but according to His mercy He saved us" (Titus iii: 5); and yet faith without works is dead, being alone (James ii: 17). Was not Abraham, our father, justified by works (v. 21)? Shall we then be saved by faith? Nay, neither by faith nor works, but by works is faith made perfect (v. 22); but "by grace are ye saved" (Eph. ii: 8); "And if by grace, then it is no more of works, otherwise grace is no more grace; and if it be of works, then it is no more grace; otherwise works is no works" (Rom. xi: 6); "Ye see then how that a man is justified by works, and not by faith only" (James ii: 24).

Rom. x: 3,4, "For they (Israel) being ignorant of God's righteousness and going about to establish their own righteousness, have not submitted themselves unto the righteousness of God; for Christ is the end of the law for righteousness to every one that believeth." Thus the righteousness of God is made manifest in the plan of salvation by His crucified son; for there is none other name under heaven given among men whereby we must be saved," but the name of Jesus Christ of Nazareth (Acts iv: 10, 12); but of this the Jews were ignorant, although they themselves crucified Him; and they have been going about wandering among all the nations of the earth ever since, for the space of eighteen hundred years, trying to establish their own righteousness, which is of the law of Moses, which law can never make the comers thereto perfect (Heb. x: i.); yet notwithstanding their darkness and long dispersion, there is a remnant, according to the election of grace (Rom. xi: 5); whom God will gather from among all people whither they are scattered and will be sanctified in them in the sight of the heathen; then shall they dwell in their land which God gave to His servant Jacob, and they shall dwell safely therein, and shall build houses and plant vineyards; "Yea, they shall dwell with confidence when I have executed judgments upon all those that despise them round about; and they shall know that I am the Lord their God" (Ezek. xxviii: 25, 26; Is. xi: 11 to 16); and when this gathering shall be completed, "It shall no more be said, The Lord liveth, that brought up the children of Israel out of the land of Egypt, but the Lord liveth that brought up the children of Israel from the land of the north, and from all the lands whither he had driven them: and I will bring them again into their land that I gave unto their fathers" (Jer. xvi: 14 to the end).

Rom. xi: 7. "What then? Israel hath not obtained that which he seeketh for; but the election hath obtained it." And why have they not obtained it? Because they sought it not by faith, but as it were by the works of the law, for they stumbled at the stumbling stone; as it is written, "Behold, I lay in Zion a stumbling stone and rock of offense" (Rom. ix: 32, 33); "to both the houses of Israel, for a gin and for a snare to the inhabitants of Jerusalem. And many among them shall stumble" (Isaiah viii: 14, 15); but "have they stumbled that they should fall? God forbid; but rather through their fall, salvation is come unto the Gentiles" (Rom. xi: 11). "And Jerusalem shall be trodden down by the Gentiles, until the times of the Gentiles be fulfilled (Luke xxi: 24); and when the house of Israel shall be restored to their possessions in Canaan, it may truly be said, the election hath obtained it; for the fulfillment of God's oath of election to Abraham as the father of the faithful, and the promises to His children will obtain that for Israel, which he has sought for in vain by the law of Moses.

This is the election that we believe in, viz., such as we find in the Prophets and Apostles, and the word of the Lord Himself, and as we have not room to give all the quotations in full, in relation to election in this epistle, we would invite the Saints to examine the Scriptures, in connection with these quoted; and whenever they find election, or any other principle or blesssing, given or applied to the house of Israel, let those principles continue with the house of Israel, and not apply that to Esau which belongs to Jacob; or to the churches of modern times which belong to the ancient covenant people; and always ascertain how the Lord, the Apostles and Prophets have applied their words, and ever continue the same application, and knowledge and wisdom will be added unto you; and in the words of the beloved Peter and Paul, we would exhort you to "work out your own salvation with fear and trembling, for it is God which worketh in you both to will and to do of His good pleasure" (Phil. ii: 12, 13); "Giving all diligence to make your calling and election sure" (2 Peter i: 10); for this is that sealing power spoken of in Ephesians (i: 13, 14)—"in whom ye also trusted, after that ye heard the word of truth; the gospel of your salvation, in whom also, after that ye believed ye were sealed with that Holy Spirit of promise, which is the earnest of our inheritance, until the redemption of the purchased possession, until the praise of His glory" (2 Peter i: 11); "For so an entrance shall be ministered unto you abundantly into the everlasting kingdom of our Lord and Savior Jesus Christ." Amen.

Friday, January 8.—Elder Parley P. Pratt wrote President Sidney Rigdon, from Manchester, England, in part as follows:

* * * * * As to the progress of the work of God in this county, it is increasing at every step. It is now prospering in Ireland and in Wales, as well as in Scotland and England. It is spreading into various new places in England. We have several hundred faithful preachers, and the spirit of inquiry seems to be more generally awakened. The clergy of the Church of England, the Methodist priests, the Baptist ministers, and Unitarians, are all in arms, as it were, against the Saints.

The country is flooded with pamphlets, tracts, papers, &c., published against us. * * * * * I must now inform you of the fact that we have reaped the first fruits of Campbellism in England, at a place called Nottingham.

A Proclamation of the First Presidency of the Church to the Saints Scattered Abroad, Greeting:

BELOVED BRETHREN:—The relationship which we sustain to the Church of Jesus Christ of Latter-day Saints, renders it necessary that we should make known from time to time, the circumstances, situation, and prospects of the Church, and give such instructions as may be necessary for the well being of the Saints, and for the promotion of those objects calculated to further their present and everlasting happiness.

We have to congratulate the Saints on the progress of the great work of the "last days," for not only has it spread through the length and breadth of this vast continent, but on the continent of Europe, and on the islands of the sea, it is spreading in a manner entirely unprecedented in the annals of time. This appears the more pleasing when we consider, that but a short time has elapsed since we were unmercifully driven from the state of Missouri, after suffering cruelties and persecutions in various and horrid forms. Then our overthrow, to many, seemed inevitable, while the enemies of truth triumphed over us, and by their cruel reproaches endeavored to aggravate our sufferings. But the Lord of Hosts was with us, the God of Jacob was our refuge, and we were delivered from the hands of bloody and deceitful men; and in the state of Illinois we found an asylum, and were kindly welcomed by persons worthy the character of freemen.

It would be inpossible to enumerate all those who, in our time of deep distress, nobly came forward to our relief, and, like the good Samaritan, poured oil into our wounds, and contributed liberally to our necessities, and the citizens of Quincy *en masse*, and the people of Illinois, generally, seemed to emulate each other in this labor of love. We would, however, make honorable mention of Governor Carlin, Judge Young, General Leech, Judge Ralston, Rev. Mr. Young, Col. Henry, N. Bushnell, John Wood, J. N. Morris, S. M. Bartlett, Samuel Holmes, and J. T. Holmes, Esquires, who will long be remembered, by a grateful community, for their philanthropy to a suffering people, and whose kindness, on that occasion, is indelibly engraved on the tablets of our hearts in golden letters of love.

We would likewise make mention of the legislators of this state, who, without respect to parties, without reluctance, freely, openly, boldly, and nobly, have come forth to our assistance, owned us as citizens and friends, and took us by the hand, and extended to us all the blessings of civil, political, and religious liberty, by granting us, under date of December 16, 1840, one of the most liberal charters, with the most plenary powers ever conferred by a legislative assembly on free citizens, "The City of Nauvoo," the "Nauvoo Legion," and the "University of the City of Nauvoo."

The first of these charters (that for the "City of Nauvoo") secures to us, in all time to come, irrevocably, all those great blessings of civil liberty which of right appertain to all the free citizens of a great civilized republic; it is all we ever claimed. What a contrast does the proceedings of the legislators of this state present when compared with those of Missouri, whose bigotry, jealousy, and superstition, prevailed to such an extent as to deny us our liberty and our sacred rights. Illinois has set a glorious example to the whole United States, and to the world at large, and has nobly carried out the principles of her Constitution, and the Constitution of these United States, and while she requires of us implicit obedience to the laws, (which we hope ever to see observed) she affords us the protection of law, the security of life, liberty, and the peaceable pursuit of happiness.

The name of our city (Nauvoo) is of Hebrew origin, and signifies a beautiful situation, or place, carrying with it, also, the idea of rest; and is truly descriptive of the most delightful location. It is situated on the east bank of the Mississippi river, at the head of the Des Moines Rapids, in Hancock county, bounded on the east by an extensive prairie of surpassing beauty, and on the north, west, and south, by the Mississippi. This place has been objected to by some on account of the sickness which has prevailed in the summer months, but it is the opinion of Doctor Bennett, that Hancock county, and all the eastern and southern portions of the City of Nauvoo, are as healthful as any other portions of the western country, to acclimatized citizens; whilst the northwestern portion of the city has experienced much affliction from fever and ague, which, however, Doctor Bennett thinks can be easily remedied by draining the sloughs on the adjacent islands in the Mississippi.

The population of our city is increasing with unparalleled rapidity, numbering more than 3,000 inhabitants. Every facility is afforded, in the city and adjacent country, in Hancock county, for the successful prosecution of the mechanical arts and the pleasing pursuits of agriculture. The waters of the Mississippi can be successfully used for manufacturing purposes to almost an unlimited extent.

Having been instrumental, in the hands of our heavenly Father, in laying a foundation for the gathering of Zion, we would say, let all those who appreciate the blessings of the Gospel, and realize the importance of obeying the commandments of heaven, who have been blessed of heaven with the possession of this world's goods, first prepare for the general gathering; let them dispose of their effects as fast as circumstances will possibly admit, without making too great sacrifices, and remove to our city and county; establish and build up manufactures in the city, purchase and cultivate farms in the county. This will secure our permanent inheritance, and prepare the way for the gathering of the poor. This is agreeable to the order of heaven, and the only principle on which the gathering can be effected. Let the rich, then, and all who can assist in establishing this place, make every preparation to come on without delay, and strengthen our hands, and assist in promoting the happiness of the Saints. This cannot be too forcibly impressed on the minds of all, and the Elders are hereby instructed to proclaim this word in all places where the Saints reside, in their public administrations, for this is according to the instructions we have received from the Lord.

The Temple of the Lord is in process of erection here, where the Saints will come to worship the God of their fathers, according to the order of His house and the powers of the Holy Priesthood, and will be so constructed as to enable all the functions of the Priesthood to be duly exercised, and where instructions from the Most High will be received, and from this place go forth to distant lands. Let us then concentrate all our powers, under the provisions of our *magna charta* granted by the Illinois legislature, at the "City of Nauvoo" and surrounding country, and strive to emulate the action of the ancient covenant fathers and patriarchs, in those things which are of such vast importance to this and every succeeding generation.

The "Nauvoo Legion" embraces all our military power, and will enable us to perform our military duty by ourselves, and thus afford us the power and privilege of avoiding one of the most fruitful sources of strife, oppression, and collision with the world. It will enable us to show our attachment to the state and nation, as a people, whenever the public service requires our aid, thus proving ourselves obedient to the paramount laws of the land, and ready at all times to sustain and execute them.

The "University of the City of Nauvoo" will enable us to teach our children wisdom, to instruct them in all the knowledge and learning, in the arts, sciences, and learned professions. We hope to make this institution one of the great lights of the world, and by and through it to diffuse that kind of knowledge which will be of practicable utility, and for the public good, and also for private and individual happiness. The Regents of the University will take the general supervision of all matters appertaining to education, from common schools up to the highest branches of a most liberal collegiate course. They will establish a regular system of education, and hand over the pupil from teacher to professor, until the regular gradation is consummated and the education finished.

This corporation contains all the powers and prerogatives of any other college or university in this state. The charters for the University and Legion are *addenda* to the city charter, making the whole perfect and complete.

Not only has the Lord given us favor in the eyes of the community, who are happy to see us in the enjoyment of all the rights and privileges of freemen, but we are happy to state that several of the principal men in Illinois, who have listened to the doctrines we promulgate, have become obedient to the faith, and are rejoicing in the same; among whom is John C. Bennett, M. D., Quartermaster-General of Illinois. We mention this gentleman first, because, that during our persecutions in Missouri, he became acquainted with the violence we were suffering while in that state, on account of our religion; his sympathy for us was aroused, and his indignation kindled against our persecutors, for the cruelties practiced upon us, and their flagrant violation of both the law and the Constitution. Amidst their heated zeal to put down the truth, he addressed us a letter, tendering to us his assistance in delivering us out of the hands of our enemies, and restoring us again to our privileges, and only required at our hands to point out the way and he would be forthcoming, with all the forces he could raise for the purpose. He has been one of the instruments in effecting or safety and deliverance, from the unjust persecutions and demands of the authorities of Missouri, and also in procuring the city charter. He is a man of enterprise, extensive acquirements, and of independent mind, and is calculated to be a great blessing to our community.

Dr. Isaac Galland also, who is one of our benefactors, having under his control a large quantity of land, in the immediate vicinity of our city, and a considerable portion of the city plat, opened both his heart and his hands, and "when we were strangers, took us in," and bade us welcome to share with him in his abundance, leaving his dwelling house, the most splendid edifice in the vicinity, for our accommodation, and partook himself to a small, uncomfortable dwelling. He sold us his large estates on very reasonable terms, and on long credit, so that we might have an opportunity of paying for them without being distressed, and has since taken our lands in Missouri in payment for the whole amount, and has given us a clear and indisputable title for the same. And in addition to the first purchase, we have exchanged lands with him in Missouri to the amount of eighty thousand dollars. He is the honored instrument the Lord used to prepare a home for us, when we were driven from our inheritances, having given him control of vast bodies of land, and prepared his heart to make the use of it the Lord intended he should. Being a man of extensive information, great talents, and high literary fame, he devoted all his powers and influence to give us a standing.

After having thus exerted himself for our salvation and comfort, and formed an intimate acquaintance with many of our people, his mind became wrought up to the greatest feelings, being convinced that our persecutions were like those of the ancient Saints, and, after investigating the doctrines we proclaimed, he became convinced of the truth and of the necessity of obedience thereto, and, to the great joy and satisfaction of the Church, he yielded himself to the waters of baptism, and became a partaker with us in our sufferings, "Choosing rather to suffer afflictions with the people of God than enjoy the pleasures of sin for a season."

In connection with these, we would mention the names of General James Adams, judge of probate, of Sangamon county; Dr. Green of Shelby county, R. D. Foster, and Sidney Knowlton, of Hancock county; Dr. Knight, of Putnam county, Indiana; many others of respectability and high standing in society, and nearly all the old settlers in our immediate neighborhood. We make mention of this that the Saints may be encouraged, and also that they may see that the persecutions we suffered in Missouri were but the prelude to a far more glorious display of the power of truth, and of the religion we have espoused.

From the kind, uniform, and consistent course pursued by the citizens of Illinois, and the great success which has attended us while here, the natural advantages of this place for every purpose we require, and the necessity of the gathering of the Saints of the Most High, we would say—let the brethren who love the prosperity of Zion, who are anxious that her stakes should be strengthened and her cords lengthened, and who prefer her prosperity to their chief joy, come and cast in their lots with us, and cheerfully engage in a work so glorious and sublime, and say with Nehemiah, "We, His servants, will arise and build." It probably would hardly be necessary to enforce this important subject on the attention of the Saints, as its necessity is obvious, and is a subject of paramount importance; but as watchmen to the house of Israel—as shepherds over the flock which is now scattered over a vast extent of country, and the anxiety we feel for their prosperity and everlasting welfare, and for the carrying out the great and glorious purposes of our God, to which we have been called, we feel to urge its necessity, and say—Let the Saints come here; this is the word of the Lord, and in accordance with the great work of the last days. It is true, the idea of a general gathering has heretofore been associated with the most cruel and oppressing scenes, owing to our unrelenting persecutions at the hands of wicked and unjust men; but we hope that those days of darkness and gloom have gone by, and, from the liberal policy of our state government, we may expect a scene of peace and prosperity we have never before witnessed since the rise of our Church, and the happiness and prosperity which now await us, is, in all human probability, incalculably great. By a concentration of action, and a unity of effort, we can only accomplish the great work of the last days which we could not do in our remote and scattered condition, while our interests, both temporal and spiritual, will be greatly enhanced, and the blessings of heaven must flow unto us in an uninterrupted stream; of this, we think there can be no question.

The greatest temporal and spiritual blessings which always flow from faithfulness and concerted effort, never attended individual exertion or enterprise. The history of all past ages abundantly attests this fact. In addition to all temporal blessings, there is no other way for the Saints to be saved in these last days, [than by the gathering] as the concurrent testimony of all the holy Prophets clearly proves, for it is written—"They shall come from the east, and be gathered from the west; the north shall give up, and the south shall keep not back." "The sons of God shall be gathered from far, and His daughters from the ends of the earth."

It is also the concurrent testimony of all the Prophets, that this gathering together of all the Saints, must take place before the Lord comes to "take vengeance upon the ungodly," and "to be glorified and admired by all those who obey the Gospel." The fiftieth Psalm, from the first to the fifth verse inclusive, describes the glory and majesty of that event.

"The mighty God, and even the Lord hath spoken, and called the earth from the rising of the sun unto the going down thereof. Out of Zion, the perfection of beauty, God hath shined. Our God shall come, and shall not keep silence; a fire shall devour before Him, and it shall be very tempestuous round about Him. He shall call to the heavens from above, and to the earth (that He may judge the people). Gather my Saints together unto me; those that have made covenant with me by sacrifice."

We might offer many other quotations from the Scriptures, but believing them to be familiar to the Saints, we forbear.

We would wish the Saints to understand that, when they come here, they must not expect perfection, or that all will be harmony, peace, and love; if they indulge these ideas, they will undoubtedly be deceived, for here there are persons, not only from different states, but from different nations, who, although they feel a great attachment to the cause of truth, have their prejudices of education, and, consequently, it requires some time before these things can be overcome. Again, there are many that creep in unawares, and endeavor to sow discord, strife, and animosity in our midst, and by so doing, bring evil upon the Saints. These things we have to bear with, and these things will prevail either to a greater or less extent until "the floor be thoroughly purged," and "the chaff be burnt up." Therefore, let those who come up to this place be determined to keep the commandments of God, and not be discouraged by those things we have enumerated, and then they will be prospered—the intelligence of heaven will be communicated to them, and they will, eventually, see eye to eye, and rejoice in the full fruition of that glory which is reserved for the righteous.

In order to erect the Temple of the Lord, great exertions will be required on the part of the Saints, so that they may build a house which shall be accepted by the Almighty, and in which His power and glory shall be manifested. Therefore let those who can freely make a sacrifice of their time, their talents, and their property, for the prosperity of the kingdom, and for the love they have to the cause of truth, bid adieu to their homes and pleasant places of abode, and unite with us in the great work of the last days, and share in the tribulation, that they may ultimately share in the glory and triumph.

We wish it likewise to be distinctly understood, that we claim no privilege but what we feel cheerfully disposed to share with our fellow citizens of every denomination, and every sentiment of religion; and therefore say, that so far from being restricted to our own faith, let all those who desire to locate themselves in this place, or the vicinity, come, and we will hail them as citizens and friends, and shall feel it not only a duty, but a privilege, to reciprocate the kindness we have received from the benevolent and kind-hearted citizens of the state of Illinois.

JOSEPH SMITH,
SIDNEY RIGDON,
HYRUM SMITH,
Presidents of the Church.

Nauvoo, January 15th, 1841.

CHAPTER XV.

RECONSTRUCTION OF CHURCH AFFAIRS AT NAUVOO—REVELATION—MUNICIPAL ORGANIZATION OF NAUVOO—INSTALLATION OF CIVIC AND MILITARY OFFICERS.

Friday, January 15, 1841.—I published the following in the *Times and Seasons*—

Reproof of John E. Page and Orson Hyde.

Elders Orson Hyde and John E. Page are informed that the Lord is not well pleased with them, in consequence of delaying their mission, (John E. Page in particular) and they are requested, by the First Presidency, to hasten their journey towards their destination.

Sunday, 17.—Elder Brigham Young preached twice in the Music Hall, Liverpool.

Monday, 18.—Elders Brigham Young and Willard Richards commenced reading the Book of Mormon, and writing an index to the English edition.

Tuesday, 19.—Elder Amos Fielding has baptized twenty-nine at Newcastle-upon-Tyne, England.

I received the following revelation:*

Revelation Given to Joseph Smith at Nauvoo, January 19th, 1841.

Verily, thus saith the Lord unto you, my servant Joseph Smith, I am well pleased with your offering and acknowledgments, which you have made, for unto this end have I raised you up, that I might show forth my wisdom through the weak things of the earth.

Your prayers are acceptable before me, and in answer to them I say unto you, that you are now called immediately to make a solemn proclamation of my Gospel, and of this Stake which I have planted to be a

* See Doctrine and Covenants, section cxxiv.

corner-stone of Zion, which shall be polished with the refinement which is after the similitude of a palace.

This proclamation shall be made to all the kings of the world, to the four corners thereof; to the honorable President elect, and the high-minded Governors of the nation in which you live, and to all the nations of the earth, scattered abroad.

Let it be written in the spirit of meekness and by the power of the Holy Ghost, which shall be in you at the time of the writing of the same;

For it shall be given you by the Holy Ghost to know my will concerning those kings and authorities,even what shall befall them in a time to come.

For, behold! I am about to call upon them to give heed to the light and glory of Zion, for the set time has come to favor her.

Call ye, therefore, upon them with loud proclamation, and with your testimony, fearing them not, for they are as grass, and all their glory as the flower thereof which soon falleth, that they may be left also without excuse,

And that I may visit them in the day of visitation, when I shall unveil the face of my covering, to appoint the portion of the oppressor among hypocrites, where there is gnashing of teeth, if they reject my servants and my testimony which I have revealed unto them.

And again, I will visit and soften their hearts, many of them for your good, that ye may find grace in their eyes, that they may come to the light of truth, and the Gentiles to the exaltation or lifting up of Zion.

For the day of my visitation cometh speedily, in an hour when ye think not of, and where shall be the safety of my people, and refuge for those who shall be left of them?

Awake, O kings of the earth! Come ye, O, come ye, with your gold and your silver, to the help of my people, to the house of the daughters of Zion.

And again, verily I say unto you, let my servant Robert B. Thompson help you to write this proclamation, for I am well pleased with him, and that he should be with you;

Let him, therefore, hearken to your counsel, and I will bless him with a multiplicity of blessings; let him be faithful and true in all things from henceforth, and he shall be great in mine eyes;

But let him remember that his stewardship will I require at his hands.

And again, verily I say unto you, blessed is my servant Hyrum Smith, for I, the Lord, love him because of the integrity of his heart, and because he loveth that which is right before me, saith the Lord.

Again, let my servant John C. Bennett, help you in your labor in sending my word to the kings and people of the earth, and stand by you, even you my servant Joseph Smith, in the hour of affliction, and his reward shall not fail, if he receive counsel;

And for his love he shall be great, for he shall be mine if he do this, saith the Lord. I have seen the work which he hath done, which I accept, if he continue, and will crown him with blessings and great glory.

And again, I say unto you, that it is my will that my servant Lyman Wight should continue in preaching for Zion, in the spirit of meekness, confessing me before the world, and I will bear him up as on eagle's wings, and he shall beget glory and honor to himself, and unto my name.

That when he shall finish his work, that I may receive him unto myself, even as I did my servant David Patten, who is with me at this time, and also my servant Edward Partridge, and also my aged servant Joseph Smith, Sen., who sitteth with Abraham at his right hand, and blessed and holy is he, for he is mine.

And again, verily I say unto you, my servant George Miller is without guile: he may be trusted because of the integrity of his heart; and for the love which he has to my testimony I, the Lord, love him;

I therefore say unto you, I seal upon his head the office of a bishopric, like unto my servant Edward Partridge, that he may receive the consecrations of mine house, that he may administer blessing upon the heads of the poor of my people, saith the Lord. Let no man despise my servant George, for he shall honor me.

Let my servant George, and my servant Lyman, and my servant John Snider, and others, build a house unto my name, such an one as my servant Joseph shall show unto them; upon the place which he shall show unto them also.

And it shall be for a house for boarding, a house that strangers may come from afar to lodge therein; therefore let it be a good house, worthy of all acceptation, that the weary traveler may find health and safety while he shall contemplate the word of the Lord; and the cornerstone I have appointed for Zion.

This house shall be a healthy habitation if it be built unto my name, and if the governor which shall be appointed unto it shall not suffer any pollution to come upon it. It shall be holy, or the Lord your God will not dwell therein.

And again, verily I say unto you, let all my Saints come from afar;

And send ye swift messengers, yea, chosen messengers, and say unto them: Come ye, with all your gold, and your silver, and your precious stones, and with all your antiquities; and with all who have knowledge of antiquities, that will come, may come, and bring the box-tree, and the fir-tree, and the pine-tree, together with all the precious trees of the earth;

And with iron, with copper, and with brass, and with zinc, and with all your precious things of the earth, and build a house to my name for the Most High to dwell therein;

For there is not a place found on earth that He may come and restore again that which was lost unto you, or which He hath taken away, even the fullness of the Priesthood;

For a baptismal font there is not upon the earth, that they, my Saints, may be baptized for those who are dead;

For this ordinance belongeth to my house, and cannot be acceptable to me, only in the days of your poverty, wherein ye are not able to build a house unto me.

But I command you, all ye my Saints, to build a house unto me; and I grant unto you a sufficient time to build a house unto me, and during this time your baptisms shall be acceptable unto me.

But behold, at the end of this appointment, your baptisms for your dead shall not be acceptable unto me; and if you do not these things at the end of the appointment, ye shall be rejected as a church, with your dead, saith the Lord your God.

For verily I say unto you, that after you have had sufficient time to build a house to me, wherein the ordinance of baptizing for the dead belongeth,and for which the same was instituted from before the foundation of the world, your baptisms for your dead cannot be acceptable unto me,

For therein are the keys of the holy Priesthood, ordained that you may receive honor and glory.

And after this time, your baptisms for the dead, by those who are scattered abroad, are not acceptable unto me, saith the Lord;

For it is ordained that in Zion, and in her stakes, and in Jerusalem, those places which I have appointed for refuge, shall be the places for your baptisms for your dead.

And again, verily I say unto you, how shall your washings be acceptable unto me,except ye perform them in a house which you have built to my name? For, for this cause I commanded Moses that he should build a tabernacle, that they should bear it with them in the wilderness, and to build a house in the land of promise, that those ordinances might be revealed which had been hid from before the world was;

Therefore, verily I say unto you, that your anointings,and your washings, and your baptisms for the dead, and your solemn assemblies, and your memorials for your sacrifices, by the sons of Levi, and for your oracles in your most holy places, wherein you receive conversations, and your statutes and judgments, for the beginning of the revelations and foundation of Zion, and for the glory, honor, and endowment of all her municipals, are ordained by the ordinance of my holy house which my people are always commanded to build unto my holy name.

And verily I say unto you, let this house be built unto my name, that I may reveal mine ordinances therein, unto my people;

For I deign to reveal unto my Church things which have been kept hid from before the foundation of the world, things that pertain to the dispensation of the fullness of times;

And I will show unto my servant Joseph all things pertaining to this house, and the Priesthood thereof; and the place whereon it shall be built;

And ye shall build it on the place where you have contemplated building it, for that is the spot which I have chosen for you to build it;

If ye labor with all your might, I will consecrate that spot that it shall be made holy;

And if my people will hearken unto my voice, and unto the voice of my servants whom I have appointed to lead my people, behold, verily I say unto you, they shall not be moved out of their place.

But if they will not hearken to my voice, nor unto the voice of these men whom I have appointed, they shall not be blest, because they pollute mine holy grounds, and mine holy ordinances, and charters, and my holy words which I give unto them.

And it shall come to pass, that if you build a house unto my name, and do not do the things that I say, I will not perform the oath which I make unto you, neither fulfill the promises which ye expect at my hands, saith the Lord;

For instead of blessings, ye, by your own works, bring cursings, wrath, indignation, and judgments upon your own heads, by your follies, and by all your abominations, which you practice before me, saith the Lord.

Verily, verily I say unto you, that when I give a commandment to any of the sons of men, to do a work unto my name, and those sons of men go with all their might, and with all they have, to perform that work, and cease not their diligence, and their enemies come upon them, and hinder them from performing that work; behold, it behooveth me to require that work no more at the hands of those sons of men, but to accept of their offerings;

And the iniquity and transgression of my holy laws and commandments, I will visit upon the heads of those who hindered my work, unto the third and fourth generation, so long as they repent not, and hate me, saith the Lord God.

Therefore for this cause have I accepted the offerings of those whom I commanded to build up a city and a house unto my name, in Jackson county, Missouri, and were hindered by their enemies, saith the Lord your God.

And I will answer judgment, wrath, and indignation, wailing, and anguish, and gnashing of teeth upon their heads, unto the third and fourth generation, so long as they repent not and hate me, saith the Lord your God.

And this I make an example unto you, for your consolation concerning all those who have been commanded to do a work, and have been hindered by the hands of their enemies, and by oppression, saith the Lord your God;

For I am the Lord your God, and will save all those of your brethren who have been pure in heart, and have been slain in the land of Missouri, saith the Lord.

And again, verily I say unto you, I command you again to build a house to my name, even in this place that you may prove yourselves unto me that ye are faithful in all things whatsoever I command you, that I may bless you, and crown you with honor, immortality, and eternal life.

And now I say unto you, as pertaining to my boarding house which I have commanded you to build for the boarding of strangers, let it be built unto my name, and let my name be named upon it, and let my servant Joseph, and his house have place therein, from generation to generation;

For this anointing have I put upon his head, that his blessing shall also be put upon the head of his posterity after him,

And as I said unto Abraham concerning the kindreds of the earth, even so I say unto my servant Joseph, in thee and in thy seed, shall the kindred of the earth be blessed.

Therefore, let my servant Joseph and his seed after him have place in that house, from generation to generation, for ever and ever, saith the Lord.

And let the name of that house be called Nauvoo House, and let it be a delightful habitation for man, and a resting place for the weary traveler, that he may contemplate the glory of Zion, and the glory of this, the corner-stone thereof;

That he may receive also the counsel from those whom I have set to be as plants of renown, and as watchmen upon her walls.

Behold, verily I say unto you, let my servant George Miller, and my servant Lyman Wight, and my servant John Snider, and my servant Peter Haws, organize themselves, and appoint one of them to be a president over their quorum for the purpose of building that house.

And they shall form a constitution whereby they may receive stock for the building of that house.

And they shall not receive less than fifty dollars for a share of stock in that house, and they shall be permitted to receive fifteen thousand dollars from any one man for stock in that house;

But they shall not be permitted to receive over fifteen thousand dollars stock from any one man;

And they shall not be permitted to receive under fifty dollars for a share of stock from any one man in that house;

And they shall not be permitted to receive any man as a stockholder in this house, except the same shall pay his stock into their hands at the time he receives stock;

And in proportion to the amount of stock he pays into their hands, he shall receive stock in that house; but if he pays nothing into their hands, he shall not receive any stock in that house.

And if any pay stock into their hands, it shall be for stock in that house, for himself, and for his generation after him, from generation to generation, so long as he and his heirs shall hold that stock, and do not sell or convey the stock away out of their hands by their own free will and act, if you will do my will, saith the Lord your God.

And again, verily I say unto you, if my servant George Miller, and my servant Lyman Wight, and my servant John Snider, and my servant Peter Haws, receive any stock into their hands, in moneys or in properties, wherein they receive the real value of moneys, they shall not appropriate any portion of that stock to any other purpose, only in that house;

And if they do appropriate any portion of that stock anywhere else, only in that house, without the consent of the stockholder, and do not repay fourfold for the stock which they appropriate anywhere else, only in that house, they shall be accursed, and shall be moved out of their place, saith the Lord God, for I, the Lord, am God, and cannot be mocked in any of these things.

Verily I say unto you, let my servant Joseph pay stock into their hands for the building of that house, as seemeth him good; but my servant Joseph cannot pay over fifteen thousand dollars stock in that house, nor under fifty dollars; neither can any other man, saith the Lord.

And there are others also who wish to know my will concerning them, for they have asked it at my hands.

Therefore I say unto you concerning my servant Vinson Knight, if he will do my will, let him put stock into that house for himself, and for his generation after him, from generation to generation,

And let him lift up his voice long and loud, in the midst of the people, to plead the cause of the poor and the needy, and let him not fail, neither let his heart faint, and I will accept of his offerings, for they shall not be unto me as the offerings of Cain, for he shall be mine, saith the Lord.

Let his family rejoice, and turn away their hearts from affliction, for I have chosen him and anointed him, and he shall be honored in the midst of his house, for I will forgive all his sins, saith the Lord. Amen.

Verily I say unto you, let my servant Hyrum put stock into that house as seemeth him good, for himself and his generation after him, from generation to generation.

Let my servant Isaac Galland put stock into that house, for I, the Lord, love him for the work he hath done, and will forgive all his sins; therefore, let him be remembered for an interest in that house from generation to generation.

Let my servant Isaac Galland be appointed among you, and be ordained by my servant William Marks, and be blessed of him, to go with my servant Hyrum, to accomplish the work that my servant Joseph shall point out to them, and they shall be greatly blessed.

Let my servant William Marks pay stock into that house, as seemeth him good, for himself and his generation, from generation to generation.

Let my servant Henry G. Sherwood pay stock into that house, as seemeth him good, for himself and his seed after him from generation to generation.

Let my servant William Law pay stock into that house, for himself and his seed after him, from generation to generation.

If he will do my will, let him not take his family unto the eastern lands, even unto Kirtland; nevertheless, I, the Lord, will build up Kirtland, but I. the Lord, have a scourge prepared for the inhabitants thereof.

And with my servant Almon Babbitt, there are many things with which I am not pleased; behold, he aspireth to establish his council instead of the council which I have ordained, even the Presidency of my Church, and he setteth up a golden calf for the worship of my people.

Let no man go from this place who has come here essaying to keep my commandments.

If they live here let them live unto me; and if they die, let them die unto me; for they shall rest from all their labors here, and shall continue their works.

Therefore let my servant William put his trust in me, and cease to fear concerning his family, because of the sickness of the land. If ye love me, keep my commandments, and the sickness of the land shall redound to your glory.

Let my servant William go and proclaim my everlasting Gospel with a loud voice, and with great joy, as he shall be moved upon by my Spirit, unto the inhabitants of Warsaw, and also unto the inhabitants of Carthage, and also unto the inhabitants of Burlington, and also unto the inhabitants of Madison, and await patiently and diligently for further instructions at my general conference, saith the Lord.

If he will do my will, let him from henceforth hearken to the counsel of my servant Joseph, and with his interest support the cause of the poor,and publish the new translation of my holy word unto the inhabitants of the earth;

And if he will do this, I will bless him with a multiplicity of blessings, that he shall not be forsaken, nor his seed be found begging bread.

And again, verily I say unto you, let my servant William be appointed, ordained, and anointed as a counselor unto my servant Joseph, in the room of my servant Hyrum; that my servant Hyrum may take the office of Priesthood and Patriarch which was appointed unto him by his father, by blessing and also by right,

That from henceforth he shall hold the keys of the Patriarchal blessings upon the heads of all my people,

That whomsoever he blesses shall be blessed, and whomsoever he curses shall be cursed; that whatsoever he shall bind on earth shall be bound in heaven; and whatsoever he shall loose on earth shall be loosed in heaven;

And from this time forth I appoint unto him that he may be a prophet, and a seer and a revelator unto my Church, as well as my servant Joseph.

That he may act in concert also with my servant Joseph, and that he shall receive counsel from my servant Joseph, who shall show unto him the keys whereby he may ask and receive, and be crowned with the same blessing, and glory, and honor, and Priesthood, and gifts of the Priesthood, that once were put upon him that was my servant Oliver Cowdery;

That my servant Hyrum may bear record of the things which I shall show unto him, that his name may be had in honorable remembrance from generation to generation forever and ever.

Let my servant William Law also receive the keys by which he may ask and receive blessings; let him be humble before me, and be without guile, and he shall receive of my Spirit, even the Comforter, which shall manifest unto him the truth of all things, and shall give him in the very hour what he shall say.

And these signs shall follow him; he shall heal the sick, he shall cast out devils, and shall be delivered from those who would administer unto him deadly poison;

And he shall be led in paths where the poisonous serpent cannot lay hold upon his heel, and he shall mount up in the imagination of his thoughts as upon eagle's wings;

And what if I will that he should raise the dead, let him not withhold his voice.

Therefore, let my servant William cry aloud and spare not, with joy and rejoicing, and with hosannas to Him that sitteth upon the throne forever and ever, saith the Lord your God.

Behold I say unto you, I have a mission in store for my servant William and my servant Hyrum, and for them alone; and let my servant Joseph tarry at home, for he is needed; the remainder I will show unto you hereafter. Even so. Amen.

And again, verily I say unto you, if my servant Sidney will serve me and be counselor unto my servant Joseph, let him arise and come up and stand in the office of his calling, and humble himself before me;

And if he will offer unto me an acceptable offering, and acknowledgments, and remain with my people, behold, I, the Lord your God, will heal him that he shall be healed; and he shall lift up his voice again on the mountains, and be a spokesman before my face.

Let him come and locate his family in the neighborhood in which my servant Joseph resides,

And in all his journeyings let him lift up his voice as with the sound of a trump, and warn the inhabitants of the earth to flee the wrath to come;

Let him assist my servant Joseph; and also let my servant William Law assist my servant Joseph, in making a solem proclamation unto the kings of the earth, even as I have before said unto you;

If my servant Sidney will do my will, let him not remove his family unto the eastern lands, but let him change their habitation even as I have said.

Behold, it is not my will that he shall seek to find safety and refuge out of the city which I have appointed unto you, even the city of Nauvoo.

Verily I say unto you, even now, if he will hearken unto my voice, it shall be well with him. Even so. Amen.

And again, verily I say unto you, let my servant Amos Davis pay stock into the hands of those whom I have appointed to build a house for boarding, even the Nauvoo House;

This let him do if he will have an interest, and let him hearken unto the counsel of my servant Joseph, and labor with his own hands that he may obtain the confidence of men;

And when he shall prove himself faithful in all things that shall be entrusted unto his care, yea, even a few things, he shall be made ruler over many;

Let him therefore abase himself that he may be exalted. Even so. Amen.

And again, verily I say unto you, if my seivant Robert D. Foster will obey my voice, let him build a house for my servant Joseph, according to the contract which he has made with him, as the door shall be open to him from time to time.

And let him repent of all his folly, and clothe himself with charity, and cease to do evil, and lay aside all his hard speeches,

And pay stock also into the hands of the quorum of the Nauvoo House for himself and for his generation after him, from generation to generation,

And hearken unto the counsel of my servants Joseph and Hyrum and William Law, and unto the authorities which I have called to lay the foundation of Zion, and it shall be well with him for ever and ever, Even so. Amen.

And again, verily I say unto you, let no man pay stock to the quorum of the Nauvoo House, unless he shall be a believer in the Book of Mormon, and the revelations I have given unto you, saith the Lord your God;

For that which is more or less than this cometh of evil, and shall be attended with cursings and not blessings, saith the Lord your God. Even so. Amen

And again, verily I say unto you, let the the quorum of the Nauvoo House have a just recompense of wages for all their labors which they do in building the Nauvoo House, and let their wages be as shall be agreed among themselves, as pertaining to the price thereof;

And let every man who pays stock bear his proportion of their wages, if it must needs be, for their support, saith the Lord; otherwise, their labors shall be accounted unto them for stock in that house. Even so. Amen.

Verily I say unto you, I now give unto you the officers belonging to my Priesthood, that ye may hold the keys thereof, even the Priesthood which is after the order of Melchisedek, which is after the order of my Only Begotten Son.

First, I give unto you Hyrum Smith, to be a Patriarch unto you, to hold the sealing blessings of my church, even the Holy Spirit of promise, whereby ye are sealed up unto the day of redemption, that ye may not fall, notwithstanding the hour of temptation that may come upon you.

I give unto you my servant Joseph, to be a presiding elder over all my church, to be a translator, a revelator, a seer, and prophet.

I give unto him for counselors my servant Sidney Rigdon, and my servant William Law, that these may constitute a quorum and First Presidency, to receive the oracles for the whole church.

I give unto you my servant Brigham Young, to be a President over Twelve traveling Council;

Which Twelve hold the keys to open up the authority of my kingdom upon the four corners of the earth, and after that to send my word to every creature.

They are Heber C. Kimball, Parley P. Pratt, Orson Pratt, Orson Hyde, William Smith, John Taylor, John E. Page, Wilford Woodruff, Willard Richards, George A. Smith;

David Patten I have taken unto myself; behold, his Priesthood no man taketh from him; but verily I say unto you, another may be appointed unto the same calling.

And again, I say unto you, I give unto you a High Council, for the corner stone of Zion;

Viz., Samuel Bent, Henry G. Sherwood, George W. Harris, Charles C. Rich, Thomas Grover, Newel Knight, David Dort, Dunbar Wilson; (Seymour Brunson I have taken unto myself, no man taketh his Priesthood, but another may be appointed unto the same Priesthood in his stead; and verily I say unto you, let my servant Aaron Johnson be ordained unto this calling in his stead); David Fullmer,Alpheus Cutler, William Huntington.

And again, I give unto you Don C. Smith, to be a president over a quorum of High Priests;

Which ordinance is instituted for the purpose of qualifying those who shall be appointed standing presidents or servants over different Stakes scattered abroad,

And they may travel also if they choose, but rather be ordained for standing presidents, this is the office of their calling, saith the Lord your God.

I give unto him Amasa Lyman, and Noah Packard, for Counselors, that they may preside over the quorum of High Priests of my Church, saith the Lord.

And again, I say unto you, I give unto you John A. Hicks, Samuel Williams, and Jesse Baker, which Priesthood is to preside over the quorum of elders, which quorum is instituted for standing ministers, nevertheless they may travel, yet they are ordained to be standing ministers to my Church, saith the Lord.

And again, I give unto you, Joseph Young, Josiah Butterfield, Daniel Miles, Henry Harriman, Zera Pulsipher, Levi Hancock, James Foster, to preside over the quorum of seventies,

Which quorum is instituted for traveling elders to bear record of my name in all the world, wherever the traveling High Council, my apostles, shall send them to prepare a way before my face.

The difference between this quorum and the quorum of elders is.

that one is to travel continually, and the other is to preside over the churches from time to time; the one has the responsibility of presiding from time to time, and the other has no responsibility of presiding, saith the Lord your God.

And again, I say unto you, I give unto you Vinson Knight, Samuel H. Smith and Shadrach Roundy, if he will receive it, to preside over the bishopric; a knowledge of said bishopric is given unto you in the book of Doctrine and Covenants.

And again, I say unto you, Samuel Rolfe and his counselors for priests, and the president of the teachers and his counselors, and also the president of the deacons and his counselors, and also the president of the stake and his counselors;

The above offices I have given unto you, and the keys thereof, for helps and for governments, for the work of the ministry, and the perfecting of my Saints;

And a commandment I give unto you that you should fill all these offices and approve of those names which I have mentioned, or else disapprove of them at my general conference;

And that ye should prepare rooms for all these offices in my house when you build it unto my name, saith the Lord your God. Even so. Amen.

Thursday, *21*.—Elders Brigham Young and Willard Richards completed the index to the Book of Mormon, and it was immediately put in type, which closed the printing of the first English edition.

Sunday, *24*.—Elder Brigham Young preached twice at Liverpool on election and reprobation.

Hyrum Smith Installed as Patriarch.

Hyrum Smith, who received the office of Patriarch in the Church, in place of Joseph Smith, Sen., deceased, has by revelation been appointed a Prophet and Revelator. William Law has by revelation been appointed one of the First Presidency, in place of Hyrum Smith, appointed Patriarch. George Miller has been appointed, by revelation, Bishop in place of Edward Partridge, deceased.

Saturday, *30*.—At a special conference of the Church of Jesus Christ of Latter-day Saints, held at Nauvoo pursuant to public notice, I was unanimously elected sole Trustee-in-Trust for the Church of Jesus Christ of Latter-day Saints.

Also Saturday the 30th and Sunday 31st, a Conference was held at Walnut Grove, Knox county, Illinois; Elder William Smith presiding; 113 members, 14 Elders were present; several branches were represented, and several persons baptized.

Monday, *1*.—The first election in Nauvoo, for members of the City Council took place, and the following persons were elected by majorities varying from 330 to 337 votes; to wit, for Mayor, John C. Bennett; Aldermen, William Marks, Samuel H. Smith, Daniel H. Wells, Newel K. Whitney; Councilors, Joseph Smith Hyrum Smith, Sidney Rigdon, Charles C. Rich, John T. Barnett, Wilson Law, Don Carlos Smith, John P. Greene, Vinson Knight.

First Election of Municipal Officers in Nauvoo.

CITY OF NAUVOO, HANCOCK COUNTY, ILLINOIS, Feb. 1, A. D. 1841.

To the County Recorder of the County of Hancock:

DEAR SIR:—At a meeting of the Church of Jesus Christ of Latter-day Saints, at this place on Saturday, the 30th day of January, A. D. 1841, I was elected sole Trustee for said Church, to hold my office during life (my successors to be the First Presidency of said Church) and vested with plenary powers, as sole Trustee in Trust for the Church of Jesus Christ of Latter-day Saints, to receive, acquire, manage or convey property, real, personal, or mixed, for the sole use and benefit of said Church, agreeably to the provisions of an act entitled, "An Act Concerning Religious Societies," approved February 6, 1835.

JOSEPH SMITH, (L. S.)

STATE OF ILLINOIS HANCOCK CO., ss.

This day personally appeared before me, Daniel H. Wells, a justice of the peace, within and for the county of Hancock, County aforesaid, Isaac Galland, Robert B. Thompson, and John C. Bennett, who being duly sworn, depose and say that the foregoing certificate of Joseph Smith is true.

ISAAC GALLAND,
ROBERT B. THOMPSON
JOHN C. BENNETT.

Sworn to and subscribed this third day of February in the year of our Lord one thousand eight hundred and forty-one before me,

DANIEL H. WELLS,
Justice of the Peace.

The above is recorded in the county records at Carthage, in book No. 1, of Bonds and Mortgages, page 95, No. 87.

Wednesday 3.—Elder Taylor reports 160 baptized in Liverpool, England; in Ireland about 25; in the Isle of Man, 70; Hawarden, 30. Elder Lorenzo Snow is laboring in London.

Nauvoo City Council Organized.

The City Council of Nauvoo was organized; the opening prayer was offered by myself, after which the Mayor-elect delivered his inaugural address as published in the *Times and Seasons*, page 316, as follows:

INAUGURAL ADDRESS.

CITY OF NAUVOO, ILLINOIS, Feb. 3rd, 1841.

Gentlemen of the City Council, Aldermen and Councillors:

Having been elected to the Mayoralty of this city by the unanimous suffrage of all parties and interests, I now enter upon the duties devolving upon me as your Chief Magistrate under a deep sense of the responsibilities of the station. I trust that the confidence reposed in me, by my fellow citizens, has not been misplaced, and for the honor conferred they will accept my warmest sentiments of gratitude. By the munificence and wise legislation of noble, high-minded, and patriotic statesmen, and the grace of God, we have been blessed with one of the most liberal corporate acts ever granted by a legislative assembly. As the presiding officer of the law-making department of the municipal government, it will be expected that I communicate to you, from time to time, by oral or written messages, for your deliberative consideration and action, such matters as may suggest themselves to me in relation to the public weal; and upon this occasion I beg leave to present the following as matters of paramount importance:

The 21st section of the addenda to the 13th section of the City Charter, concedes to you plenary power "to tax, restrain, prohibit and suppress, tippling houses, dram shops," etc., etc., and I now recommend, in the strongest possible terms, that you take prompt, strong, and decisive measures to "prohibit and suppress" all such establishments. It is true you have the power "to tax," or license and tolerate, them, and thus add to the city finances; but I consider it much better to raise revenue by an advalorem tax on the property of sober men, than by licensing dram shops, or taxing the signs of the inebriated worshipers at the shrine of Bacchus. The revels of bacchanalians in the houses of blasphemy and noise will always prove a disgrace to a moral people. Public sentiment will do much to suppress the vice of intemperance, and its concomitant evil results; but ample experience has incontrovertibly proven that it cannot do all—the law must be brought to the rescue, and an effective prohibitory ordinance enacted. This cannot be done at a better time than at the present. Let us commence correctly, and the great work of reform, at least so far as our peaceful city is concerned, can be summarily consummated. It would be difficult to calculate the vast amount of evil and crime that would be prevented, and the great good that would accrue to the public at large by fostering the cause of temperance; but suffice it to say that the one would be commensurate to the other. No sales of spirituous liquors whatever, in a less quantity than a quart, except in cases of sickness on the recommendation of a physician or surgeon duly accredited by the Chancellor and Regents of the University, should be tolerated. The liberty of selling the intoxicating cup is a false liberty—it enslaves, degrades, destroys; and wretchedness and want are attendant on every step,—its touch, like that of the poison upas, is death. Liberty to do good should be cheerfully and freely accorded to every man; but liberty to do evil, which is licentiousness, should be peremptorily prohibited. The public good imperiously demands it—and the cause of humanity pleads for help. The protecting ægis of the corporation should be thrown around every moral and religious institution of the day, which is in any way calculated to ennoble, or ameliorate the condition of the human family.

The immediate organization of the University, as contemplated in the 24th section of the act incorporating our city, cannot be too forcibly impressed upon you at this time. As all matters in relation to mental culture, and public instruction, from common schools up to the highest branches of a full collegiate course in the arts, sciences, and learned professions, will devolve upon the Chancellor and Regents of the University, they should be speedily elected, and instructed to perfect their plan, and enter upon its execution with as little delay as possible. The wheels of education should never be clogged, or retrograde, but roll progressively from the Alpha to the Omega of a most perfect, liberal, and thorough course of university attainments. The following observations in relation to false education, from Alexander's Messenger, so perfectly accords with my feelings and views on this highly important subject, that I cannot do better than incorporate them in this message.

"Among the changes for the worse, which the world has witnessed within the last century, we include that specious, superficial, incomplete way of doing certain things, which were formerly thought to be deserving of care, labor and attention. It would seem that appearance is now considered of more moment than reality. The modern mode of education is an example in point. Children are so instructed as to acquire a smattering of everything, and as a matter of consequence, they know nothing properly. Seminaries and academies deal out their moral and natural philosophy, their geometry, trigonometry, and astronomy, their chemistry, botany, and mineralogy, until the mind of the pupil becomes a chaos; and, like the stomach when it is overloaded with a variety of food, it digests nothing, but converts the superabundant nutriment to poison. This mode of education answers one purpose—it enables people to seem learned; and seemingly, by a great many, is thought all sufficient. Thus we are schooled in quackery, and are early taught to regard showy and superficial attainments as most desirable. Every boarding school Miss is a Plato in petticoats, without an ounce of that genuine knowledge, that true philosophy, which would enable her to be useful in the world, and to escape those perils with which she must necessarily be encompassed. Young people are taught to use a variety of hard terms, which they understand but imperfectly—to repeat lessons which they are unable to apply—to astonish their grandmothers with a display of their parrot-like acquisitions; but their mental energies are clogged and torpified with a variety of learned lumber, most of which is discarded from the brain long before its possessor knows how to use it. This is the quackery of education.

"The effects of the erring system are not easily obliterated. The habit of using words without thought, sticks to the unfortunate student through life, and should he ever learn to think, he cannot express his ideas without the most tedious and perplexing verbosity. This is, more or less, the fault of every writer in the nineteenth century. The sense is encumbered with sound. The scribbler appears to imagine that if he puts a sufficient number of words together he has done his part; and, alas! how many books are written on this principle. Thus literature, and even science itself, is overloaded with froth and flummery. Verbalizing has become fashionable and indispensable, and one line from an ancient author will furnish the materials for a modern treatise."

Our University should be a "utilitarian" institution—and competent, industrious teachers and professors should be immediately elected for the several departments. "Knowledge is power,"—foster education and we are forever free! Nothing can be done which is more certainly calculated to perpetuate the free institutions of our common country, for which our progenitors "fought and bled, and died," than the general diffusion of useful knowledge amongst the people. Education should always be of a purely practical character, for such, and such alone, is calculated to perfect the happiness and prosperity of our fellow-citizens—ignorance, impudence, and false knowledge, are equally detestible,—shame and confusion follow in their train. As you now possess the power, afford the most ample facilities to the Regents to make their plans complete; and thus enable them to set a glorious example to the world at large. The most liberal policy should attend the organization of the University, and equal honors and privileges should be extended to all classes of the community.

In order to carry out the provisions of the 25th section of the act incorporating our city, I would recommend the immediate organization of the Legion. Comprising, as it does, the entire military power of our city, with a provision allowing any citizen of Hancock county to unite by voluntary enrollment, early facilities should be afforded the court martial for perfecting their plans of drill, rules, and regulations. Nothing is more necessary to the preservation of order and the supremacy of the laws, than the perfect organization of our military forces, under a uniform and rigid discpline and approved judicious drill; and to this end I desire to see all the departments and cohorts of the Legion put in immediate requisition. The Legion should be all powerful, panoplied with justice and equity, to consummate the designs of its projectors—at all times ready, as minute men, to serve the state in such way and manner as may, from time to time, be pointed out by the Governor. You have long sought an opportunity of showing your attachment to the state government of Illinois—it is now afforded; the Legion should maintain the constitution and the laws, and be ready at all times for the public defense. The winged warrior of the air perches upon the pole of American liberty, and the beast that has the temerity to ruffle her feathers should be made to feel the power of her talons; and until she ceases to be our proud national emblem we should not cease to show our attachment to Illinois. Should the tocsin of alarm ever be sounded, and the Legion called to the tented field by our Executive, I hope to see it able, under one of the proudest mottoes that ever blazed upon a warrior's shield—*Sicut patribus sit Deus nobis;* "as God was with our fathers, so may He be with us"—to fight the battles of our country, as victors, and as freemen; the juice of the uva, or the spirit of insubordination should never enter our camp,—but we should stand, ever stand, as a united people—one and indivisible.

I would earnestly recommend the construction of a wing-dam in the Mississippi, at the mouth of the ravine at or near the head of Main street, and the excavation of a ship canal from that point to a point terminating in a grand reservoir on the bank of said river, east of the foot of said street, a distance of about two miles. This would afford, at the various outlets, the most ample water power for propelling any amount of machinery for mill and manufacturing purposes, so essentially necessary to the building up of a great commercial city in the heart of one of the most productive and delightful countries on earth. I would advise that an agent be immediately appointed on behalf of the city corporation, to negotiate with eastern capitalists for the completion of this great work, on the most advantageous terms, even to the conveyance of the privilege for a term of years. This work finished, and the future greatness of this city is placed upon an imperishable basis. In addition to the great advantages that will otherwise accrue to the city and country by the construction of this noble work, it would afford the best harbor for steamboats, for winter quarters, on this magnificent stream.

The public health requires that the low lands, bordering on the Mississippi, should be immediately drained, and the entire timber removed. This can and will be one of the most healthful cities in the west, provided you take prompt and decisive action in the premises. A board of health should be appointed and vested with the usual powers and prerogatives.

The Governor, council of revision, and legislature of Illinois, should be held in everlasting remembrance by our people—they burst the chains of slavery and proclaimed us forever free! A vote of thanks, couched in the strongest language possible, should be tendered them in our corporate capacity; and, when this is done, Quincy, our first noble city of refuge, when we came from the slaughter in Missouri with our garments stained with blood, should not be forgotten.

As the Chief Magistrate of your city I am determined to execute all state laws and city ordinances passed in pursuance to law, to the very letter, should it require the strong arm of military power to enable me to do so. As an officer I know no man; the peaceful, unoffending citizen shall be protected in the full exercise of all his civil, political, and religious rights, and the guilty violator of law shall be punished, without respect to persons.

All of which is respectfully submitted.* JOHN C. BENNETT.

The following persons were elected by the council to their offices, to-wit—Henry G. Sherwood, marshal; James Sloan, recorder; Robert B. Thompson, treasurer; James Robinson, assessor; Austin Cowles, supervisor of streets. I presented to the city council the following resolution, which was unanimously adopted:

* The foregoing speech is not printed in the "History of Joseph Smith" as published in the *Deseret News* and *Millennial Star*, but such is the prominence of John C. Bennett in the period of the history now reached, and such the dispicable part he later plays, that, as affording an insight into his character, the speech becomes important, hence given here *in extenso*, as it was published in the *Times and Seasons*, Vol. II, No. 8.

Resolved by the City Council of the City of Nauvoo, that the unfeigned thanks of this community be respectfully tendered to the Governor, Council of Revision, and Legislature of the state of Illinois, as a feeble testimonial of their respect and esteem for noble, high-minded, and patriotic statesmen; and as an evidence of gratitude for the signal powers recently conferred; also that the citizens of Quincy be held in everlasting remembrance, for their unparalleled liberality and marked kindness to our people, when in their greatest state of suffering and want.

I presented a bill for an ordinance concerning the University of Nauvoo, which passed as follows:

Sec. 1. Be it ordained by the City Council of the City of Nauvoo, that the "University of the City of Nauvoo," be, and the same is hereby organized by the appointment of the following Board of Trustees, to-wit—John C. Bennett, chancellor; William Law, registrar; and Joseph Smith, Sidney Rigdon, Hyrum Smith, William Marks, Samuel H. Smith, Daniel H. Wells, Newel K. Whitney, Charles C. Rich, John T. Barnett, Wilson Law, Don Carlos Smith, John P. Greene, Vinson Knight, Isaac Galland, Elias Higbee, Robert D. Foster, James Adams, Robert B. Thompson, Samuel Bennett, Ebenezer Robinson, John Snider, George Miller, and Lenos M. Knight, Regents of the "University of the City of Nauvoo;" as contemplated in the 24th section of "An Act to incorporate the City of Nauvoo," approved December 16, 1840.

Sec. 2. The board named in the first section of this ordinance, shall hold its first meeting at the office of Joseph Smith, on Tuesday, the 9th day of February, 1841, at 2 o'clock p. m.

Passed February 3, 1841. JOHN C. BENNETT, Mayor.
JAMES SLOAN, Recorder.

I also presented a bill for an ordinance organizing the Nauvoo Legion, which passed the same day, as follows:

Sec. 1. Be it ordained by the City Council of the City of Nauvoo, that the inhabitants of the City of Nauvoo, and such citizens of Hancock county as may unite by voluntary enrollment, be, and they are hereby organized into a body of independent military men, to be called the "Nauvoo Legion," as contemplated in the 25th section of "An Act to incorporate the City of Nauvoo," approved December 16, 1840.

Sec. 2. The Legion shall be, and is hereby divided into two cohorts; the horse troops to constitute the first cohort, and the foot troops to constitute the second cohort.

Sec. 3. The general officers of the Legion shall consist of a lieutenant-general, as the chief commanding and reviewing officer, and president of the court martial and Legion; a major-general, as the second in command in the Legion, the secretary of the court martial and Legion, and adjutant and inspector-general; a brigadier-general, as the commander of the first cohort; and brigadier-general, as commander of the second cohort.

Sec. 4. The staff of the lieutenant-general shall consist of two principal aids-de-camp, with the rank of colonels of cavalry; and a guard of twelve aids-de-camp, with the rank of captain of infantry; and a drill officer, with the rank of colonel of dragoons, who shall likewise be the chief officer of the guard.

Sec. 5. The staff of the major-general shall consist of an adjutant, a surgeon-in-chief, a cornet, a quarter-master, a paymaster, a commissary, and a chaplain, with the rank of colonels of infantry; a surgeon for each cohort, a quarter-master-sergeant, sergeant-major, and chief musician, with the rank of captains of light infantry, and two musicians, with the rank of captains of infantry.

Sec. 6. The staff of each brigadier-general shall consist of one aid-de-camp, with the rank of lieutenant-colonel of infantry, provided that the said brigadiers shall have access to the staff of the major-general, when not otherwise in service.

Sec. 7. No officer shall hereafter be elected by the various companies of the Legion, except upon the nomination of the court-martial; and it is hereby made the duty of the court-martial to nominate at least two candidates for each vacant office, whenever such vacancies occur.

Sec. 8. The court-martial shall fill and supply all offices ranking between captains and brigadier-generals by granting brevet commissions to the most worthy company officers of the line, who shall thereafter take rank, and command according to the date of their brevets, provided that their original place in the line shall not thereby be vacated.

Sec. 9. The court-martial, consisting of all the military officers, commissioned or entitled to commissions, within the limits of the city corporation, shall meet at the office of Joseph Smith, on Thursday, the 4th day of February, 1841, at 10 o'clock a.m.; and then and there proceed to elect the general officers of the Legion, as contemplated in the 3rd section of this ordinance.

Sec. 10. The court-martial shall adopt for the Legion, as nearly as may be, and so far as applicable, the discipline, drill, uniform, rules, and regulations of the United States army.

Passed February 8, 1841.

JOHN C. BENNETT, Mayor.
JAMES SLOAN, Recorder.

Joseph Smith, Hyrum Smith, Don C. Smith, and Charles C. Rich were duly sworn as members of the City Council.*

The following addition has been made to the Charter of the Nauvoo Legion by the legislature—

Any citizen of Hancock county may, by voluntary enrollment, attach himself to the Nauvoo Legion, with all the privileges, which appertain to that independent military body.

I gave a general invitation to my friends to enroll themselves, so as to have a perfect organization by the fourth of July. I was appointed chairman of several committees, viz: "On the Canal," "For Vacating the Town of Commerce," "Vending Spirituous Liquors," "Code of City Ordinances," "Board of Health," &c. Council adjourned to the 8th.

Thursday, 4.

Minutes of the Meeting which Organized the Nauvoo Legion.

Pursuant to an ordinance of the City Council of the City of Nauvoo, entitled, "An ordinance organizing the Nauvoo Legion," passed February 3, 1841, a court-martial, composed of the commissioned officers of the militia of the state of Illinois, within the city of Nauvoo, assembled at the office of Joseph Smith, on Thursday at 10 o'clock a. m., the 4th day of February, 1841: present—John C. Bennett, quarter-master-general of the state of Illinois; Lieutenant-Colonel Don Carlos Smith; Captains Charles C. Rich, Wilson Law, Albert P. Rockwood, William Law, Titus Billings, Stephen Markham; first lieutenants, Francis M. Higbee, John T. Barnett, John D. Parker, Benjamin S. Wilber, Amos Davis; second lieutenants, Chancy L. Higbee, Nelson Higgins, David H. Redfield, Hosea Stout, Stephen Winchester, Thomas Rich; third lieutenants, John C. Annis, and Alexander Badlam. The court was

* Following is the form of oath taken:

We, Joseph Smith, Hyrum Smith, Don C. Smith, and Charles C. Rich, do solemnly swear in the presence of Almighty God that we will support the Constitution of the United States, and of the State of Illinois, and that we will well and truly perform the duties of councilors of the City of Nauvoo, according to law, and the best of our abilities.

JOSEPH SMITH,
HYRUM SMITH,
DON C. SMITH,
CHARLES C. RICH.

December 3, 1841.

called to order by General Bennett. On motion, Joseph Smith and Hugh McFall were requested to sit in the court. The court-martial then proceeded to the election of the general officers of the Legion; whereupon Joseph Smith was duly elected lieutenant-general of the Nauvoo Legion, and John C. Bennett, major-general. Colonel Wilson Law was elected brigadier-general of the first cohort, and Lieutenant-Colonel Don Carlos Smith brigadier-general of the second cohort, by unanimous vote of the court-martial. Lieutenant-general Joseph Smith, after being duly sworn into office, appointed the following named persons for his staff, to-wit—Captain A. P. Rockwood to be drill officer; Captains William Law and Robert B. Thompson, aids-de-camp; and James Allred, Thomas Grover, C. M. Kreymeyer, John L. Butler, John Snider, Alpheus Cutler, Reynolds Cahoon, Elias Higbee, Henry G. Sherwood, Shadrack Roundy, Samuel H. Smith, and Vinson Knight, guards, and assistant aids-de-camp. The Legion, at its organization, was composed of six companies.

Friday, 5.—Elder Reuben Hedlock is laboring in Glasgow, Scotland. The Church in that place numbers 55, and the spirit of enquiry increases.

Saturday, 6.

Minutes of a Council at Brother Richard Harrison's, 72 Burlington Street, Liverpool, for organizing a company of Saints going to New Orleans on the ship "Sheffield," Captain Porter.

Elders Brigham Young, Willard Richards, John Tayor, and other officers, present. Elder Hyrum Clark was chosen president, and Thomas Walmsley, Miles Romney, Edward Martin, John Taylor, Francis Clark, and John Riley, counselors to President Clark. Edward Martin, clerk and historian. Peter Maughan and John Taylor were ordained Elders. President Clark and his counselors were blessed and set apart for their mission.

Sunday, 7.—Ship *Sheffield* sailed from Liverpool with 235 Saints.

Monday, 8.—Levi Richards writes from Lugwardine—

To the Editor of the Star:

Since Stanley Hill conference, I have attended about thirty council meetings of Church officers, in eleven different places in Herefordshire, Gloucestershire, and Worcestershire, making a circuit of nearly one hundred miles. Union and harmony prevail among them, and a disposition to add to their faith. New places are frequently opened for preaching, which is generally supplied. Many are baptized every week, although the ice has to yield its natural claims, and be put aside. The gift of healing is manifested to quite an extent in this region. The gift of tongues is received in most of the branches where I am acquainted. The spirit of persecution is not yet wholly cast out of the world: for recently preaching was held for the first time in Pendock parish, eight miles from Ledbury, when a congregation, respectable in numbers and appearance, were compelled to retire prematurely, in consequence of the quantity of gravel thrown upon the roof and against the windows. The mob were numerous, and pelted the Saints on their way home with mud. The meeting was held at the shop of a tradesman, who had been clerk of the parish, but was so fortunate as to obey the Gospel, and be turned out of his stewardship; and his wife was dismissed from her school, for the same reason, by the parson of the parish. More or less of the Saints are turned out of employ, and out of their houses, for obeying the Gospel.

Nauvoo Council Opened by Prayer.

City Council met according to adjournment and opened by prayer, which was made a standing rule of the council. I reported a bill for the survey of a canal through the city, which was accepted; and I was appointed to contract for its survey. I also reported a bill for an ordinance on temperance, which was read and laid over.

Wednesday, 10.—Elder James Burnham writes from Overton, Flintshire, North Wales—

I have organized two branches, with about 150 members; and we are continually baptizing, whether it be cold or hot. There is great opposition.

The *Echo* Company.

Thursday, 11.—Elders Young, Richards, and Taylor, in council at 72 Burlington Street, Liverpool, set apart, by the laying on of hands, Elder Daniel Browett, to take charge of a company of Saints, about to sail for New Orleans on ship *Echo*, Captain Wood; and John Cheese, David Wilding, James Lavender, William Jenkins, Robert Harris, and John Ellison, to be his counselors. Robert Harris was ordained an Elder, and Elder Browett was appointed clerk and historian of the company.

Saturday, *13*.—Elder Orson Hyde sailed from New York for Liverpool, on his way to Jerusalem, accompanied by Elder George J. Adams.

Sunday, *14*.

Minutes of the London Conference.

A conference of the Church of Jesus Christ of Latter-day Saints was held at Barrett's Academy, 57 King Square, Goswell Road, London, on Sunday, the 14th of February, 1841, there being present—Elders Heber C. Kimball, Wilford Woodruff, Lorenzo Snow, William Pitt, and four Priests. The meeting was called to order by Elder Kimball at 2 o'clock p. m. Moved by Elder Kimball, seconded by Elder Pitt, that Elder Woodruff be president of this conference; carried unanimously. Moved by Elder Kimball, seconded by Elder Woodruff, that Dr. W. Copeland be clerk; carried unanimously. The meeting opened by Elder Kimball with prayer and singing. The president then called upon the official members to represent their respective branches. The church at Ipswich was represented by Elder Pitt, as consisting of twelve members, one Elder, one Priest, and one Teacher. The church at Bedford was represented by Robert Williams, Priest, as consisting of forty-two members, one Priest, seven moved, two died. The church at Woolwich was represented by John Griffith, Priest, as consisting of six members, one Priest. The church in London was represented by Elder Kimball as consisting of forty-six members, one Elder, two Priests: excellent prospects of a continued increase. James Allen was ordained an Elder, and Thomas Barnes a Priest. Robert Williams was ordained an Elder, to preside over the branch at Bedford; and William Smith and John Sheffield were ordained Priests. Richard Bates was ordained a Priest, in the branch of Woolwich, and A. Painter a Teacher—all under the hands of Elders Kimball, Woodruff and Snow. It was then moved by Elder Kimball, seconded by Elder Woodruff, that Elder Snow be appointed president of this [the Woolwich] conference, also to take the superintendency of the branch in London. Much valuable instruction was given by Elders Kimball and Woodruff in relation to the duties of the official members. It was then moved by Elder Kimball, and seconded by Elder Snow, that this conference be adjourned to Sunday, 16th of May, 1841. The conference was then closed at half-past five, by singing and prayer.

DR. W. COPELAND, Clerk.

Monday, *15*.—As chairman of the committee [on the vending of spirituous liquors] I reported a bill to the City

Council, which, after a long discussion, passed into "An ordinance in relation to temperance."

ORDINANCE.

Sec. 1. Be it ordained by the City Council of the City of Nauvoo, that all persons and establishments whatever, in this city, are prohibited from vending whisky in a less quantity than a gallon, or other spirituous liquors in a less quantity than a quart, to any person whatever, excepting on the recommendation of a physician, duly accredited in writing, by the Chancellor and Regents of the University of the City of Nauvoo; and any person guilty of any act contrary to the prohibition contained in this ordinance, shall, on conviction thereof before the Mayor or municipal court, be fined in any sum not exceeding twenty-five dollars, at the discretion of said Mayor or municipal court; and any person or persons who shall attempt to evade this ordinance by giving away liquor, or by any other means, shall be considered alike amenable, and fined as aforesaid.

Passed February 15, 1841.

JOHN C. BENNETT, Mayor.
JAMES SLOAN, Recorder.

In the discussion of the foregoing bill, I spoke at great length on the use of liquors, and showed that they were unnecessary, and operate as a poison in the stomach, and that roots and herbs can be found to effect all necessary purposes.

Tuesday, 16.

Missouri's "White-washing."

Resolved by the Senate [of the state of Missouri], the House of Representatives concurring, that two thousand copies of the evidence taken before the examining court in relation to "Mormon" difficulties, and such of the letters, orders, and correspondence on that subject, on file in the office of the secretary of state, as may be selected by a joint committee of the two houses, shall be published in pamphlet form, under the direction of the secretary of state; that one copy, in lieu of the manuscript copies, heretofore ordered, be sent to our delegation in Congress, to be laid before the House to which they respectively belong, one to each member of Congress, and the residue be distributed among the Mormons of the general assembly.

Approved February 16, 1841.*

* For a proper characterization of this document see Vol. III, this History, p. 256

Is this Missouri's last struggle to retrieve her lost character to publish to the world a one-sided statement of her robberies, murders, and extermination which she had committed without provocation, at a time when not one Saint was left in Missouri to tell the truth about them?

The ship *Echo* sailed from Liverpool for New Orleans, with 109 Saints, led by Daniel Browett.

Saturday, 20.—Elder Brigham Young went to Harwarden and preached twice on Sunday.

Elders William Kay and Thomas Richardson introduced the Gospel into the City of Hereford.

The court-martial of the Nauvoo Legion, by a unanimous vote, adopted the following resolutions, to-wit —

Legion Resolutions.

That no person whatever, residing within the limits of the City of Nauvoo, betweent the ages of 18 and 45 years, excepting such as are exempted by the laws of the United States, shall be exempt from military duty, unless exempted by a special act of this court; and the fines for neglecting or refusing to appear on the days of general parade were fixed at the following rates: for generals, $25; colonels, $20; captains, $15; lieutenants, $10; and musicians and privates, $5; and for company parade at the following rates—for commissioned officers, $5; non-commissioned officers, $3; musicians and privates, $2. The 1st and 6th of April, and the 3rd of July, were fixed upon as days for general parade for this year.

Ordered that Edward P. Duzette enlist and organize a band of music, not exceeding twenty men. It was also reported that John Scott had been elected captain in the place of William Law, and Lieutenant Hosea Stout in the place of Albert P. Rockwood, who has been promoted.

Monday, 22.—I laid before the City Council the following—

RESOLUTION.

Resolved by the City Council of the City of Nauvoo, that the freedom of the city be, and the same hereby is, conferred on the present Governor, lieutenant-governor, council of revision, and members of both houses of the general assembly, of the state of Illinois, as an evidence of our gratitude for their great liberality and kindness to this community, during the present winter, which was adopted unanimously.

I also presented the following bill for "An ordinance in relation to the University."

ORDINANCE.

Sec. 1. Be it ordained by the City Council of the City of Nauvoo, that all matters and powers whatever in relation to common schools, and all other institutions of learning within the City of Nauvoo be, and the same hereby are transferred from the City Council of the City of Nauvoo, to the chancellor and regents of the University of the City of Nauvoo.

Passed February 22, 1841.

JOHN C. BENNETT, Mayor.
JAMES SLOAN, Recorder.

Tuesday, *23*.—Elder Kington writes from Bristol, England, that eight have been baptized in that place.

AN ACT TO INCORPORATE THE NAUVOO HOUSE ASSOCIATION.

Sec. 1. Be it enacted by the people of the state of Illinois, represented in the general assembly, that George Miller, Lyman Wight, John Snider, and Peter Haws, and their associates, are hereby declared a body corporate, under the name and style of the "Nauvoo House Association;" and they are hereby authorized to erect and furnish a public house of entertainment, to be called the "Nauvoo House."

Sec. 2. The above-named George Miller, Lyman Wight, John Snider, and Peter Haws, and their associates, are hereby declared to be the trustees of the association, with full power and authority to hold in joint tenancy, by themselves and their successors in office, a certain lot in the City of Nauvoo, in the county of Hancock, and state of Illinois, known and designated on the plat of said city, as the south half of lot numbered fifty-six, for the purpose of erecting thereon the house contemplated in the first section of this act.

Sec. 3. The said trustees are further authorized and empowered to obtain by stock subscription, by themselves or their duly authorized agents, the sum of one hundred and fifty thousand dollars, which shall be divided into shares of fifty dollars each.

Sec. 4. No individual shall be permitted to hold more than three hundred, nor less than one share of stock, and certificates of stock shall be delivered to subscribers, so soon as their subscriptions are paid in and not before.

Sec. 5. As soon as the contemplated house shall have been completed and furnished, the stockholders shall appoint such agents as the trustees may deem necessary in the management of the affairs of said association.

Sec. 6. The trustees shall have power to sue and be sued, plead and be impleaded in any court in this state, in the name and style of the "Trustees of the Nauvoo House Association."

Sec. 7. They shall also take the general care and supervision in procuring materials for said house, and constructing and erecting the same, and further to superintend its general management, and to do and perform all matters and things which may be necessary to be done, in order to secure the interest and promote the objects of this association.

Sec. 8. This association shall continue twenty years from the passage of this act, and the house herein provided for shall be kept for the accommodation of strangers, travelers, and all other persons who may resort therein for rest and refreshment.

Sec. 9. It is moreover established as a perpetual rule of said house, to be observed by all persons who may keep or occupy the same, that spirituous liquors of every description are prohibited, and that such liquor shall never be vended as a beverage, or introduced into common use, in said house.

Sec. 10. And whereas Joseph Smith has furnished the said association with the ground whereon to erect said house, it is further declared that the said Smith and his heirs shall hold, by perpetual succession, a suite of rooms in the said house, to be set apart and conveyed in due form of law to him and his heirs by the said trustees, as soon as the same are completed.

Sec. 11. The Board of Trustees shall appoint one of their number as president thereof.

Approved February 23, 1841.

THOMAS CARLIN,
Governor.

W. L. D. EWING,
Speaker of the House of Representatives.

S. H. ANDERSON,
Speaker of the Senate.

State of Illinois,
Office of Secretary of State, } s.s.

I, Stephen A. Douglas, Secretary of State, do hereby certify the foregoing to be a true and perfect copy of the enrolled law on file in my office.

Witness my hand and the seal of State.

Springfield, February 24, A. D. 1841.

[SEAL.] S. A. DOUGLAS,
Secretary of State.

AN ACT TO INCORPORATE THE NAUVOO AGRICULTURAL AND MANUFACTURING ASSOCIATION IN THE COUNTY OF HANCOCK.

Sec. 1. Be it enacted by the people of the state of Illinois, represented in the general assembly, that Sidney Rigdon, George W. Robinson, Samuel James, Wilson Law, Daniel H. Wells, Hyrum Smith, George Miller, William Marks, Peter Haws, Vinson Knight, John Scott, Don Carlos Smith, William Huntington, Sen., Ebenezer Robinson, Robert B. Thompson, William Law, James Allred, John T. Barnett, Theodore Turley, John C. Bennett, Elias Higbee, Isaac Higbee, Joseph Smith, Alpheus Cutler, Israel Barlow, R. D. Foster, John F. Olney, John Snider, Leonard Soby, Orson Pratt, James Kelley, Sidney A. Knowlton, John P. Greene, John F. Weld, and their associates and successors, are hereby constituted a body corporate and politic, by the name of "The Nauvoo Agricultural and Manufacturing Association," and by that name shall be capable of suing and being sued, pleading and being impleaded, answering and being answered, in all courts and places, and may have a common seal, and may alter the same at pleasure.

Sec. 2. The sole object and purpose of said association shall be for the promotion of agriculture and husbandry in all its branches, and for the manufacture of flour, lumber, and such other useful articles as are necessary for the ordinary purposes of life.

Sec. 3. The capital stock of said association shall be one hundred thousand dollars, with the privilege of increasing it to the sum of three hundred thousand dollars, to be divided into shares of fifty dollars, which shall be considered personal property, and be assignable in such manner as the said corporation may, by its by-laws, provide; which capital stock shall be exclusively devoted to the object and purposes set forth in the second section of this act, and to no other object and purposes, and to the same end the said corporation shall have power to purchase, hold, and convey real estate, and other property, to the amount of its capital.

Sec. 4. Said corporation shall have power, by the trustees, or a majority of them present at any regularly called meeting, to make by-laws for its own government, for the purpose of carrying out the objects of this association, provided the same are not repugnant to the laws and constitution of this state, or of the United States.

Sec. 5. Joseph Smith, Sidney Rigdon, and William Law shall be commissioners to receive subscriptions for, and distribute said capital stock for said corporation; said commissioners, or a majority of them, shall, within six months after the passage of this act, either by themselves or their duly appointed agents, open a subscription book for said stock at such times and places as they shall appoint, and at the time of subscription for such stock, at least ten per cent upon each share subscribed for, shall be paid to said commissioners, or their duly appointed agents; and the remainder of said stock, so subscribed for, shall be paid in such sums, and at such times, as shall be provided for by the by-laws of said corporation.

Sec. 6. In case the stock of said corporation shall not all be taken up within one year from the passage of this act, the duties of said commissioners shall cease, and the trustees of said corporation, or a quorum thereof, may thereafter receive subscriptions to said stock, from time to time, until the whole shall be subscribed.

Sec. 7. The stock, property, and concerns of said corporation shall be managed by twenty trustees, who shall be stockholders of said corporation, any five of whom, to be designated by a majority of the trustees, shall form a quorum for the transaction of all ordinary business of said corporation, the election of which trustees shall be annual. The first mentioned twenty persons, whose names are recited in the first section of this act, shall be the first trustees of said corporation, and shall hold their offices until the first Monday in September, A. D. 1841, and until others shall be elected in their places.

Sec. 8. The trustees of said corporation for every subsequent year shall be elected on the first Monday in September, in each and every year, at such place as the trustees for the time being shall appoint, and of which election they shall give at least fifteen days previous notice by advertisement in some newspaper, in or near the City of Nauvoo. At every election of trustees, each stockholder shall be entitled to one vote on each share of stock owned by him: provided that no stockholder shall be entitled to more than twenty votes, and said stockholders, may vote either in person or by proxy. The election for trustees shall be conducted in such manner as shall be pointed out by the by-laws of said corporation, and whenever a vacancy shall happen by death, resignation, or otherwise, among the trustees, the remaining trustees shall have power to fill such vacancy, until the next general election for trustees.

Sec. 9. The trustees of said corporation, as soon as may be, after their appointment or election under this act, shall proceed to elect, out of their number, a president, treasurer, and secretary, who shall respectively hold their offices during one year, and until others shall be elected to fill their places, and whose duties shall be defined and prescribed by the by-laws of the corporation; and said trustees shall also appoint such agents and other persons as may be necessary to conduct the proper business, and accomplish the declared objects of said corporation, and shall likewise have power to fill any vacancy occasioned by the death, resignation, or removal of any officer of said corporation.

Sec. 10. This act shall be construed as a public act, and continue in force for the period of twenty years. And the trustees appointed under the provisions of this act, shall hold their first meeting at the City of Nauvoo, on the first Monday of April, A. D. 1841.

Approved February 27, 1841.

THOMAS CARLIN,
Governor.

W. L. D. EWING,
Speaker of the House of Representatives.

S. H. ANDERSON,
Speaker of the Senate.

State of Illinois, Office of Secretary of State.

I, Lyman Trumbull, Secretary of State, do hereby certify the foregoing to be a true and perfect copy of the enrolled law on the file in my office.

Given under my hand and seal of State, Springfield, March 10, 1841.

LYMAN TRUMBULL,
Secretary of State.

Wednesday, 24.—Elder Brigham Young returned to Liverpool, and on the 25th attended a patriarchal blessing meeting at Brother Dumville's. Father Melling officiated; Elder James Whitehead, scribe.

Suturday, 27.—President Brigham Young went to Manchester, and preached in Lombard Street room on Sunday, the 28th.

Monday, March 1.—The City Council divided the city into four wards, at my suggestion, to-wit: all the district of country within the city limits, north of the center of Knight street, and west of the center of Wells street, shall constitute the first ward. North of the center of Knight street and east of the center of Wells street, the second ward. South

Division of Nauvoo into Municipal Wards.

of the center of Knight street, and east of the center of Wells street, the third ward. South of the center of Knight street, and west of the center of Wells street, the fourth ward.

I attended the City Council, and presented a bill for "An ordinance in relation to Religious Societies."

Ordinance on Religious Liberty in Nauvoo.

Sec. 1. Be it ordained by the City Council of the City of Nauvoo, that the Catholics, Presbyterians, Methodists, Baptists, Latter-day Saints, Quakers, Episcopals, Universalists, Unitarians, Mohammedans, and all other religious sects and denominations whatever, shall have free toleration, and equal privileges, in this city; and should any person be guilty of ridiculing, and abusing or otherwise depreciating another in consequence of his religion, or of disturbing or interrupting any religious meeting within the limits of this city, he shall, on conviction thereof before the Mayor or Municipal Court, be considered a disturber of the public peace, and fined in any sum not exceeding five hundred dollars, or imprisoned not exceeding six months, or both, at the discretion of said Mayor or Court.

Sec. 2. It is hereby made the duty of all Municipal officers to notice and report to the Mayor any breach or violation of this, or any other ordinance of this city, that may come within their knowledge, or of which they may be advised; and any officer aforesaid, is hereby fully authorized to arrest all such violators of rule, law and order, either with or without process.

Passed March 1, 1841.

JOHN C. BENNETT, Mayor.
JAMES SLOAN, Recorder.

I also presented a bill as follows:

An Ordinance in Relation to Public Meetings.

Sec. 1. Be it ordained by the City Council of the City of Nauvoo, that in order to guarantee the constitutional right of free discussion upon all subjects, the citizens of this city, may from time to time peaceably assemble themselves together for all peaceable or lawful purposes whatever; and should any person be guilty of disturbing or interrupting any such meeting or assemblage, he shall on conviction thereof before the Mayor or Municipal Court, be considered a disturber of the public peace, and fined in any sum not exceeding five hundred dollars, or imprisoned not exceeding six months, or both, at the discretion of said mayor or court.

Sec. 2. Should any person be guilty of exciting the people to riot or rebellion, or of participating in a mob, or any other unlawful riotous or tumultuous assemblage of the people, or of refusing to obey any civil officer, executing the ordinances of the city, or the general laws of the state or United States, or of neglecting or refusing to obey promptly, any military order for the due execution of said law or ordinances, he shall, on conviction thereof as aforesaid, be fined or imprisoned, or both, as aforesaid.

Passed March 1, 1841.

JOHN C. BENNETT, Mayor.
JAMES SLOAN, Recorder.

I also offered a bill for "An ordinance, creating certain additional City Officers."

ORDINANCE.

Sec. 1. Be it ordained by the City Council of the City of Nauvoo, that in addition to the city officers heretofore elected, there shall be elected by the City Council, one high constable for each ward; one surveyor and engineer, one market master, one weigher and sealer, and one collector for the city, whose duties shall hereafter be defined by ordinance.

Passed March 1, 1841. JOHN C. BENNETT, Mayor.
JAMES SLOAN, Recorder.

I presented the following report:

COMMITTE'S REPORT.

Your committee, to whom was referred that portion of the address of his honor, the Mayor, which recommended the propriety of vacating the town plats, Commerce, and the City of Commerce, and incorporating them with the city plat of Nauvoo, would respectfully report—That they consider the recommendation contained in the address as one of great importance to the future welfare and prosperity of this city, and if carried into effect would make the streets regular and uniform, and materially tend to beautify this city. We would therefore respectfully recommend that the survey of the City of Nauvoo be carried through the town plats of Commerce and the City of Commerce, as soon as it may be practicable.

We would therefore recommend to the council the passage of the following resolution—That the town plats of Commerce, and Commerce City be vacated, and that the same stand vacated from this time forth, and forever; and that the same be incorporated with the City of Nauvoo, from this time henceforth and forever.

All of which is respectfully submitted.

JOSEPH SMITH, Chairman.

The report was received and adopted, and an ordinance passed accordingly.

A vote of thanks, and the freedom of the city were conferred on the Honorable Richard M. Young, United States Senator for Illinois.

Tuesday, 2.—Elder Brigham Young visited Oldham, and returned on Wednesday, 3rd, to Manchester. Elders Orson Hyde and George J. Adams arrived in Liverpool.

Thursday, 4.—Elder Willard Richards left Liverpool for Preston, and was followed by Elders Hyde, Adams, and Fielding on the 5th.

General William Henry Harrison was inaugurated President of the United States.

Friday, 5.—Elder Parley P. Pratt removed the *Star* office to 47 Oxford Road, Manchester.

Sunday, 7.—Elders Young and Kimball preached at the Carpenter's Hall, Manchester.

Appointment of City Officers.

Monday, 8.—I attended the City Council. The following appointments were made, viz: Alanson Ripley, city surveyor; Theodore Turley, weigher and sealer; James Robinson, assessor; Stephen Markham, market master; James Allred was sworn supervisor of streets, and James Allred, Dimick B. Huntington, and George Morey, high constables.

I gave my views on several local measures proposed by the council.

Wednesday, 10.

Letter of Brigham Young to the Editor of the Star—On Family Prayer.

LIVERPOOL, March 10, 1841.

To the Editor of the Star:

DEAR BROTHER:—I feel anxious to address a few lines to you, on the subject of family prayer (and shall feel obliged by your inserting the same in your next *Star*), for the purpose of imparting instruction to the brethren in general. Having traveled through many branches of the Church in England, I have found it to be a general custom among the brethren I visited, that when any of the Traveling Elders are present, they wait for the Elder to go forward in family prayer, instead of attending to that duty themselves. That is not right; and I would say to them that it would be better for them to understand their duty on this subject. My dear brethren, remember that the Lord holds all of us responsible for our conduct here. He held our father Adam responsible for his conduct, but no more than He does us, in proportion to the station we hold. The kings of the earth will have to give an account to God, for their conduct in a kingly capacity. Kings are heads of nations, governors are heads of provinces; so are fathers or husbands governors of their own houses, and should act accordingly. Heads of families should always take the charge of family worship, and call their family together at a seasonable hour, and not wait for every person to get through with all they may have to say or do. If it were my prerogative to adopt a plan for family prayer, it would be the following: Call your family or household together every morning and evening, previous to coming to the table, and bow before the Lord to offer up your thanksgiving for His mercies and providential care of you. Let the head of the family dictate; I mean the man, not the woman. If an Elder should happen to be present, the head of the house can call upon him, if he choses so to do, and not wait for a stranger to take the lead at such times; by so doing we shall obtain the favor of our Heavenly Father, and it will have a tendency to teach our children to walk in the way they should go, which may God grant for Christ's sake. Amen.

BRIGHAM YOUNG.

Governor Carlin issued the following Commission—

APPOINTMENT OF JOSEPH SMITH LIEUTENANT-GENERAL OF THE NAUVOO LEGION.

Thomas Carlin, Governor of the State of Illinois, to all to whom these presents shall come: Greeting—

Know ye that Joseph Smith, having been duly elected to the office of lieutenant-general, Nauvoo Legion, of the militia of the State of Illinois, I, Thomas Carlin, governor of said state, do commission him lieutenant-general of the Nauvoo Legion, to take rank from the fifth day of February, 1841. He is, therefore, carefully and diligently to discharge the duties of said office, by doing and performing all manner of things thereunto belonging; and I do strictly require all officers and soldiers under his command to be obedient to his orders: and he is to obey such orders and directions as he shall receive, from time to time, from the commander-in-chief or his superior officer.

In testimony whereof, I have hereunto set my hand, and caused the great seal of state to be hereunto affixed. Done at Springfield, this tenth day of March, in the year of our Lord one thousand eight hundred and forty-one, and of the independence of the United States the sixty-fifth.

By the Governor,

[SEAL] THOMAS CARLIN.

LYMAN TRUMBALL,
Secretary of State.

The commission was endorsed on the back as follows—

Headquarters, Nauvoo Legion, City of Nauvoo, Illinois, March 15, 1841—Oath of office administered by me, the day and year above written.

JOHN C. BENNETT,
Major-General of the Nauvoo Legion.

Thursday, 11.—Elders Young, Kimball, Richards, and Taylor met in Liverpool.

Monday, 15.—I attended the City Council, and took part in the discussion concerning Mr. Annis' mill, in the southwest part of the city.

Elder Wilford Woodruff attended a conference at Gadfield Elm; 408 members in eighteen branches represented.

Thursday, 16.—Elder George A. Smith attended a conference at Macclesfield, which branch contains ninety-one members, one Elder, six Priests, five Teachers, and three Deacons. In consequence of incessant preaching, his lungs are much affected.

Wednesday, 17.—Ship *Alesto* sailed from Liverpool for New Orleans, with 54 Saints, led by Elders Thomas Smith and William Moss.

Elders Heber C. Kimball, Willard Richards, and Father Melling went to Preston; Elders Young and Hedlock to Hawarden, and George A. Smith to Leek.

Thursday, 18.—Elder George A. Smith attended a council of the officers and members of the Church at Leek, numbering sixty-three members, one Elder, six Priests, two Teachers, and two Deacons. Stephen Nixon was ordained an Elder; and John Hudson, Jacob Gibson, and Joseph Knight, Priests; and Frederick Rushton and Edwin Rushton, Teachers.

Saturday, *20*.

An Inquiry.

CITY OF NAUVOO, March 20, 1841.

Brother William Allred, Bishop of the stake at Pleasant Vale, and also Brother Henry W. Miller, president of the stake at Freedom, desire President Joseph Smith to inquire of the Lord His will concerning them.

I inquired of the Lord concerning the foregoing question, and received the following answer—

Revelation.

Let my servants, William Allred and Henry W. Miller, have an agency for the selling of stock for the Nauvoo House, and assist my servants Lyman Wight, Peter Haws, George Miller, and John Snider, in building said house; and let my servants William Allred and Henry W. Miller take stock in the house, that the poor of my people may have employment, and that accommodations may be made for the strangers who shall come to visit this place, and for this purpose let them devote all their properties, saith the Lord.

About this time I received a revelation, given in the City of Nauvoo, in answer to the following interrogatory—"What is the will of the Lord, concerning the Saints in the Territory of Iowa?"*

Revelation.

"Verily, thus saith the Lord, I say unto you, if those who call themselves by my name, and are essaying to be my Saints, if they will do my will and keep my commandments concerning them; let them gather themselves together, unto the place which I shall appoint unto them by my servant Joseph, and build up cities unto my name, that they may be prepared for that which is in store for a time to come. Let them build up a city unto my name upon the land opposite to the City of

* See Doctrine and Covenants, section cxxv.

Nauvoo, and let the name of Zarahemla be named upon it. And let all those who come from the east, and the west, and the north, and the south, that have desires to dwell therein, take up their inheritances in the same, as well as in the City of Nashville, or in the City of Nauvoo, and in all the stakes which I have appointed, saith the Lord.

Sunday, 21.—Elder George A. Smith preached at Leek, and confirmed one.

Organization of the Lesser Priesthood at Nauvoo.

The Lesser Priesthood was organized in the City of Nauvoo, March 21, 1841, by Bishops Whitney, Miller, Higbee, and Knight. Samuel Rolf was chosen president of the Priests' quorum, and Stephen Markham and Hezekiah Peck, his counselors. Elisha Everett was chosen president of Teachers, and James W. Huntsman and James Hendricks, counselors. Phinehas R. Bird was chosen president of Deacons, and David Wood and William W. Lane counselors.

CHAPTER XVI.

THE FIRST FOREIGN MISSION OF THE CHURCH 1837-1841

Tuesday, March 23, 1841.—Elder Young returned to Liverpool, and Elder Richards wrote the following history of the "Mission to England, or the first foreign mission of the Latter-day Saints."

History of the British Mission.

About the first of June, 1837, Elder Heber C. Kimball was called by the Spirit of Revelation, and set apart by the First Presidency of the Church of Jesus Christ of Latter-day Saints, then at Kirtland, Ohio, North America, to preside over a mission to England, accompanied by Elder Orson Hyde, who was set apart for the same work at the same time. In a few days Brother Joseph Fielding, Priest, was set apart; and on the eve of the 12th, Elder Willard Richards, (having been absent several months on a long journey, and having returned the day previous) was called and set apart for the same mission.

The following morning, Tuesday, 13th, these brethren gave the parting hand, bid farewell to home, and, without purse or scrip, started for England. They were accompanied twelve miles to Fairport on Lake Erie by Elders Brigham Young, John P. Greene and Brother Levi Richards, and Sisters Kimball, Greene and Fielding (Brother R. B. Thompson and wife accompanied the mission to Buffalo, and Brother Fitch Brigham to Utica) and others with whom they parted in the afternoon, and went on board a steamer for Buffalo; where they arrived next day.

At this place the brethren expected to receive some means from Canada, to assist them on their journey, but they were disappointed. In the evening they took passage on a canal boat, and arrived in Albany on the 19th (Elder Hyde having gone forward to New York from Rochester.) Brother Fielding proceeded to New York, and on the 20th Elder Kimball accompanied Elder Richards to his father's house in Richmond, Massachusetts, thirty miles east, where they spent one day, and having received some assistance from his friends, bade them farewell for the last time (his father and mother having since died, also a sister whom he had left in Kirtland) and on the 21st returned to Albany, and arrived in New York on the 22nd, where they found Brothers Orson Hyde and Fielding, also Elders John Goodson and Isaac Russell, John Snider, Priest, (who had come from Canada to join the mission) anxiously awaiting their arrival, so that they might take passage on the *United States*, which was to sail next day, but they arrived too late.

In New York Elder Richards received some further means, quite providentially, and on the 23rd the brethren engaged passage to Liverpool, on board the *Garrick*, which was to sail on the 1st of July.

In the meantime the brethren received every possible assistance from Elder Elijah Fordham. At that time he was the only member of the Church residing in the city [New York], and having no house of his own, he procured his father's storehouse for the use of the brethren, where they lodged on the floor, amid straw and blankets, one week, eating their cold morsel, and conversing with the people as they had opportunity; for no place could be procured to preach in, and there was no one to receive them into their houses.

Sunday, the 25th, the brethren held a council at their lodgings (Mr. Fordham's store), and organized ready for taking their departure.

On the 29th the brethren sealed, superscribed, and forwarded one hundred and eighty of Elder Orson Hyde's "Timely Warnings" to the ministers of the different denominations in the city, and went on board the *Garrick*, which hauled out into the river and cast anchor.

July 1st, the ship weighed anchor and was towed to Sandy Hook by a steamer, where she spread sail, and in four hours and a half was out of sight of land. With the exception of a strong wind on the 12th, there was generally a gentle breeze from the northwest during the voyage. On the 16th, Elder Orson Hyde preached on the aft quarter deck. On the 18th Cape Clear was visible (eighteen days out of sight of land;) and on the morning of the 20th, the brethren landed in Liverpool twenty days from New York. Here Elders Kimball, Hyde, and Richards found themselves on a foreign shore, surrounded by strangers, without the first farthing in their possession; but the brethren unitedly took lodgings in a private house in Union Street, till after the inspection of the ship; and on Saturday, the 22nd, took coach for Preston. When they had alighted from the coach, and were standing by their trunks in front of the hotel in Preston, a large flag was unfurled over their heads on which was printed in golden letters, "*Truth will prevail;*" at the sight of which their hearts rejoiced, and they cried aloud, "Amen, thanks be unto God, TRUTH WILL PREVAIL."

Brother Joseph Fielding lodged with his brother, Rev. James Fielding, then a preacher in Vauxhall-road Chapel, and the remainder of the brethren took lodgings in St. Wilford Street, Fox Street. The same evening the Elders visited the Rev. Mr. Fielding, by his request at his lodgings. He had previously been apprized of the coming forth of this work in America, through the medium of letters from his relatives and others and had requested his church to pray that God would send them His servants, and exhorted his people to receive their message when they should come.

Sunday the 28th. As they had no place in which to preach, the seven brethren went to Vauxhall Chapel to hear the Rev. Mr. Fielding; and at the close of the morning service, Mr. Fielding gave public notice that an Elder of the Latter-day Saints would preach in the afternoon in his pulpit. This was voluntary with Mr. Fielding as no one had requested the privilege; and in the afternoon, according to the notice, Elder Kimball gave a brief history of the rise of the Church and the first principles of the Gospel, and Elder Hyde bore testimony; after which the Rev. Mr. Fielding requested the brethren to give out an appointment for the evening, when Elder Goodson preached, and Elder Joseph Fielding bore testimony.

At the close Mr. Fielding again gave leave for preaching at the same place on Wednesday evening, when Elder Hyde preached and Elder Richards bore testimony; and from that time the Rev. Mr. Fielding closed his doors against the Elders and began to oppose the work, and stated that the Elders promised to say nothing about baptism in their preaching before he ever consented to let them preach in his pulpit; whereas the subject of the Elders preaching in his chapel had not been named between the parties, before Mr. Fielding gave out the public appointment before referred to: much less (if possible) that they would "say nothing about baptism."

Nine of Mr. Fielding's members offered themselves for baptism; and Mr. Fielding presented himself before the Elders, and forbade their baptizing them, but he received for answer, that "they were of age and could act for themselves." On Sunday, the 30th, they were baptized under the hands of Elder Kimball; Brother George D. Watt being the first who offered himself for baptism in England, and is now an Elder laboring in Edinburgh, Scotland.

Elder Russell preached in the market place in the afternoon,and from that day the doors of private houses were opened on almost every hand for the Elders.

July 31st, a council of the Elders decided that Elders Goodson and Richards should go on a mission to Bedford, and Elder Russell and Priest Snider on a mission to Alston, Cumberland; and after a night of prayer, praise and thanksgiving, the brethren took their departure on the morning of the first of August for their several stations.

The Rev. Mr. Fielding continued to oppose the doctrine of baptism for a season; but finding that he was likely to lose all his "best members," he offered to baptize them himself; but they being aware that he had no authority, declined his friendly offer, whereupon he engaged the Rev. Mr. Giles, a Baptist minister in Preston, of as little authority as himself, to do the baptizing for his flock; but this iniquitous scheme succeeded little better than the other—only one coming forward to his baptism, so far as we have heard. Mr. Fielding's people also stated that he acted the part of a hypocrite and deceived them, when he read the letters to them in public, which he received from America, by keeping back that part which treated on baptism, which, since the foregoing failure he has opposed.

Elders Kimball and Hyde, and Priest Fielding continued to preach daily in different parts of Preston, and on Wednesday and Thursday (August 2nd and 3rd), the meetings were attended by Miss Jeanetta Richards who was visiting her friends in Preston, and on Friday she requested baptism, which was attended to by Elder Kimball, after which she was confirmed at the water side by Elders Kimball and Hyde, it being the first confirmation in a foreign land in these last days.

The day following Sister Richards returned home to her friends, and informed her father, the Rev. Joseph Richards, an Independent minister at Walker-fold, Chaidgely, whom she had found at Preston, what she had done, and requested him to send for Elder Kimball to preach in his chapel. Mr. Richards complied with his daughter's request. Elder Kimball arrived at Walker-fold Saturday eve, August 12, and the day following preached three times in Mr. Richards' pulpit, to crowded assemblies; also twice during the week, and twice the Sunday following, being most kindly and cordially entertained by Mr. and Mrs. Richards for nine days, during which time Elder Kimball baptized several in the neighborhood.

After a short visit to Preston, where Elder Hyde continued to preach and baptize, Elder Kimball returned to Walker-fold, and continued to receive the hospitality of Mr. Richards' house for some days, while the work spread in the neighborhood; and from thence the work went forth to Clitheroe, Waddington, Downham, Cathburn, Thornley, and Ribchester, through the labors of Brothers Kimball and Fielding.

Elders Goodson and Richards arrived in Bedford on the 2nd of August, and having letters of introduction to the Rev. Timothy R. Matthews from Brother Joseph Fielding (Mrs. Matthew's brother), they immediately waited on Mr. Matthews, who expressed great joy at their arrival, and manifested his sincerity by walking arm in arm with the

Elders through the streets of Bedford, calling on the members of his church, and inviting them to attend the lectures of the Elders at his chapel vestry that evening. Mr. Matthews had previously been apprized of the Saints in America through the medium of the Rev. James Fielding of Preston and the letters from America, before referred to. In the evening, his church assembled in the vestry, and Elders Goodson and Richards continued to lecture and testify of the work of God, on that and the three following evenings in the same place, with the entire approbation of Mr. Matthews, who, at the close of the lectures, publicly bore testimony to the truths advanced, and called upon his people to know why they did not come forward for baptism; while they in return wished to know why he did not set them the example.

After this Mr. Matthews engaged another house in the neighborhood for the Elders to preach in, under the pretense that some of the proprietors of the chapel might not be pleased with the Elders occupying the vestry, and Mr. Matthews continued to attend the preaching of the Elders, and also spent a great share of his time, from day to day, in conversation with them.

Mr. Matthews told the Elders that he had received two ordinations, one from Bishop West, whom he had proved to be an impostor, and another from the Church of England, which he acknowledged to be descended from the Church of Rome, and he further acknowledged that he had no authority from God for administering in the ordinances of God's house.

On the 10th Mrs. Braddock and four others were baptized by Elder Goodson. Soon after this, Mr. Joseph Saville, member of Mr. Matthews' church, being very desirous of receiving baptism at the same time with Mr. Matthews, waited on him at his house, in company with Elders Goodson and Richards and Mr. Matthews, and Mr. Saville mutually agreed to meet the Elders on the bank of the river Ouse at a specified hour in the afternoon, and attend to the ordinance of baptism. At the hour appointed Mr. Saville met the Elders at the place previously designated by Mr. Matthews; but as he (the latter) did not make his appearance according to promise, after waiting for him an hour, Mr. Saville was baptized, when the Elders repaired to Mr. Matthews' to learn the cause of his not fulfilling his engagement, and were informed by Mr. Matthews' family that he had gone out into the country to preach.

In a day or two it was currently rumored that Mr. Matthews had baptized himself, and this rumor was afterwards confirmed by Mrs. Matthews, who stated to Elder Kimball at Preston, that Mr. Matthews had baptized himself, reasoning upon this principle within himself: "If I have authority to administer the sacrament to my people, why not have authority to baptize myself," &c.—and all this after Mr. Matthews had acknowledged to Elders Goodson and Richards that he had no authority to administer in the ordinances of God's house; and altogether regardless of the words of the Apostles (Heb. v: 4), "No man taketh this honor unto himself but he that is called of God as was Aaron."

By the foregoing it is plainly to be seen, that Mr. Matthews has attempted to take that upon himself which was never conferred upon him by the spirit of revelation, either by God, His angels, or His servants; viz., the holy Priesthood; and from that period, Mr. Matthews began to preach baptism, and baptized those who felt it their duty to be baptized, and then invited them to the penitent form to get remission of their sins; but finding that would not answer all the design which he intended, he afterwards began to baptize for the remission of sins.

Mr. Matthews appears to have well understood that counterfeit coin is more current the nearer it approximates to the true, and governed himself accordingly; for he continued to preach faith, repentance, baptism for the remission of sins, the second coming of Christ, &c., &c., adding one thing to another in imitation of truth, as fast as it answered his purpose, from those doctrines which he had heard from the Latter-day Saints; but it was some time before he arrived at that heaven-daring conscience-seared hardihood, to lay hands on those whom he had baptized for the reception of the Holy Ghost, and at the same time he acknowledged that he had not got the Holy Ghost himself, by praying that he might receive it—(Query. How can a man communicate that which he is not in possession of?) and he now calls his church "The Church of Latter-day Saints."

Thus has Mr. Matthews been running about from Bedford to Liverpool, from Liverpool to Northampton, from Northampton to Bedford, and other places, crying aloud in public and private, that the Latter-day Saints and their doctrines came from hell; at the same time he has been preaching the same doctrines, calls his church by the same name, is administering in the same ordinances, just as though he fully believed that the doctrines and sacraments of hell would be sanctified and made holy and heavenly, when administered by the tongue and hands of an impostor.

About the time that Mr. Matthews rejected the truth in Bedford, his son (as Mr. Matthews called him), the Rev. Robert Aitkin, commenced his attack on the principles of righteousness in Preston; and while furiously pounding his pulpit with the Book of Mormon, and warning his people to beware of the Latter-day Saints and their doctrines, saying, that they and their record came from hell; called upon his people to use all their efforts to put down the work of God, or stop the progress of the

Latter-day Saints; and, if it could not be put down without, prayed that God would smite the leaders; and from that time to the present, his prayer has been answered on his own head.

After Mr. Aitkin had preached against the corruptions of the Church of England for years, and established many flourishing chapels in Liverpool, Preston, Manchester, Burslem, London, &c.; after he had been visited by the Elders of the Church of Latter-day Saints, and acknowledged to them at one time that baptism was right, but he could find no man who had authority to baptize; and at another time, that he was afraid of them, and rejected their testimony; and last of all would not receive the Elders into his house; after all this, and deserted by a part of his flock, he has fled from the remainder because he was an hireling, and cared not for the sheep; yes, he has deserted his "Christian Society"—ceased to be an Aitkenite, and dissolved his co-partnership with Father Matthews, as may well be supposed, returned, and taken "holy order" in "Mother Church," against the corruptions of which he testified so diligently from year to year, and is now about to enter on his parochial duties in St. John the Evangelist's Church, Hope street, Liverpool, for no other reason, that the writer knows of, only that he could find no one who had authority to baptize for the remission of sins, and not possessing the faith of his father, Matthews, to believe that the doctrines of the pit would become holy and gospel doctrines when taught by the tongue of wickedness and imposture, he has concluded thus publicly to acknowledge himself a servant of those very errors he has so long contended against, for the sake of filthy lucre.

About the 12th of September, Elder Goodson and Priest Snider returned to Preston, and soon after sailed for America.

Some years previously, the principles of the Temperance Society (originally established in America), were introduced into England, and Preston was the first town to receive them. Among the many interesting and valuable items held forth by the Temperance people, it was often remarked by them that Temperance was the fore-runner of the Gospel, which prophecy proved true; for when the fullness of the Gospel came from America to England, it was first preached in Preston, and through the influence of the Temperance Society, the Latter-day Saints procured the use of the Temperance Hall in Preston (a commodious building, originally erected for cock fighting) for their chapel, and commenced meeting therein on the 3rd of September, 1837, and continued until they were ejected through the influence of others, the Temperance Society not having it entirely at their control. Similar favors have been received from several other Temperance Societies in England, for which the Lord reward them.

Elder Richards continued to labor against much opposition in Bedford, and the region round about, until the 7th of March, 1838, when he returned to Preston, leaving about forty members in charge of Elder James Lavender. Elder Russell continued to labor in Alston, Brampton, &c , and returned to Preston near the same time, leaving about sixty member in the care of Elder Jacob Peart.

At Christmas, 1837, Priest Joseph Fielding was ordained Elder, and several were ordained Teachers, &c., at Preston; and in March, 1838, the Church had extended from Preston to Penwortham, Longton, Southport, Eccleston Whittle, Hunter's Hill, Chorley, and the intermediate region, through the labors of Elders Hyde, Kimball, and Fielding, and the members amounted to several hundreds in the regions of Preston and Clitheroe. During this month, Elders Kimball and Hyde were diligently engaged in organizing the different branches; and on the first of April a general conference was called at Preston, when the organization of the churches was completed, and many were ordained, among whom were Elders Joseph Fielding, Willard Richards, and William Clayton to the High Priesthood, [*i. e.* they were ordained High Priests], and set apart by Elders Kimball and Hyde to preside over all the churches in Elgland.

On the 9th, Elders Kimball, Hyde and Russell took leave of the Saints in Preston, and went to Liverpool, where they were visited by Elders Fielding, Richards, Clayton, and others, and on the 20th of April, sailed for New York, on board the *Garrick*, the same ship they came out on to England.

When Elders Fielding and Richards had returned to Longton, they found a pamphlet, purporting to be written by the Rev. Richard Livesey, a Methodist minister, who had spent some time on a mission to the United States, as he says, and having nothing more important to attend to during his mission, it appears that he spent his time in gathering up a heap of lies and filth from the American papers, and imported them to England on his return; and finding that the work of God had commenced in his native land, and was likely to destroy his craft, set himself at work to condense his heterogeneous mass of trans-Atlantic lies, and form the wonderful production of the Rev. Richard Livesey's tract against the Latter-day Saints; it being the first thing of the kind that the enemy of all righteousness had found means to export from America, and circulate in England; but since which he has found servants in abundance, to assist in this nefarious merchandise of his heart's delight.

The Church at this time was in its infancy, and needed much instruction, which necessarily occupied the attention of the presiding Elders to a great extent; and as there were few laborers in the field, the spread of the work was not very rapid for some time.

Sister Alice Hodgin died at Preston on the 2nd of September, 1838; and it was such a wonderful thing for a Latter-day Saint to die in England, that Elder Richards was arraigned before the Mayor's Court at Preston, on the 3rd of October, charged with "killing and slaying" the said Alice with a "black stick," &c., but was discharged without being permitted to make his defense, as soon as it was discoved that the iniquity of his accusers was about to be made manifest.

October 19, 1838, Elder Clayton gave himself wholly to the work, and soon after commenced preaching and baptizing in Manchester, and from thence the work spread into Stockport, and other places in the neighborhood, through the labors of Elders Clayton, Fielding, John Moon, and David Wilding. A small church had previously sprung up in Bolton, through the labors of Elder David Wilding, and was continued by Elder Amos Fielding.

In the summer of 1839 Elders Clayton Richards, and John Moon, labored in Burslem, with some success, and a small church was planted in Burnley by Elder Thomas Richardson, besides many who were added in the older branches, through the instrumentality of the local Elders and Priests, who were generally very faithful.

December 8, 1839, Elders Hiram Clark, Alexander Wright, and Samuel Mulliner arrived in Preston from America; and on the 25th, Brothers Wright and Mulliner started for Scotland and soon commenced preaching and baptizing in Paisley and vicinity.

January 13, 1840, Elders Wilford Woodruff, John Taylor, and Theodore Turley arrived in Preston, from America; and on the 18th Brothers Woodruff and Turley started for the Potteries in Staffordshire, passing through Manchester; and on the 22nd, Elder Taylor left for Liverpool.

April 6, 1840, just ten years from the organization of the Church, Elders Brigham Young, Heber C. Kimball, Parley P. Pratt, Orson Pratt, George A. Smith, and Reuben Hedlock, landed in Liverpool from New York; and on the 9th Elder Kimball arrived in Preston, just two years from the day he left for America.

The arrival of the Elders caused the Saints to rejoice exceedingly, for it had been prophesied by many (not of the Church), that they would never come, and that Elders Kimball and Hyde would never return, but they are both now in England, Elder Orson Hyde having arrived in Liverpool on the 3rd instant from New York.

HEBER C. KIMBALL,
ORSON HYDE,
WILLARD RICHARDS.

Preston, March 24, 1841.

CHAPTER XVII.

CELEBRATION OF THE TWELFTH ANNIVERSARY OF THE ORGANIZATION OF THE CHURCH—ORDER OF LAYING CORNER-STONES OF TEMPLES—COUNCIL MEETINGS OF THE TWELVE IN ENGLAND.

March, 25, 26 and 27, 1841.—Elders Young and Richards were detained at the Liverpool post office, as witnesses in the case of "The Queen vs. Joseph Holloway," for detaining letters.

Saturday, 27.—Elders Wilford Woodruff, and Geo. A. Smith attended a council of the official members of the Staffordshire Conference, at Hanley.

Staffordshire Conference.

Sunday, 28.—Elders Wilford Woodruff and George A. Smith attended a general meeting of the Staffordshire Conference at Hanley, when 13 branches were represented, containing 1 High Priest, 17 Elders, 55 Priests, 25 Teachers, 14 Deacons, and 663 members. Thomas J. Filcher, J. Taylor, Osmond Shaw, W. Ridge, and H. Ridge were ordained Elders, also 8 Priests, 7 Teachers, and 2 Deacons, under the hands of Wilford Woodruff, Geo. A. Smith, and Alfred Cordon. There have been 141 baptized during the past three months.

Union of Commerce and Nauvoo Plats.

Monday, 29.—I attended city council, and moved that the city surveyor be ordered to survey Commerce, and plat the same so as to correspond with the city plat of Nauvoo, and make out a map to be recorded, which was carried by the Council. Much was said in council about fining the owners of dogs, and I contended that it was right to fine individuals who would keep unruly dogs, to worry cattle, sheep, or the citizens, and an ordinance was passed to that effect.

William Marks, president of the stake at Nauvoo, made choice of Charles C. Rich and Austin Cowles as his counselors.

Elders Young and Richards were at Liverpool packing Books of Mormon, to pay off those who had loaned them money in order to carry forward the printing and binding.

The following are extracts from Elder Woodruff's letter.

Letter of Wilford Woodruff to Don C. Smith—Relating to Affairs in England.

BURSLEM, March 29, 1841.

BROTHER DON CARLOS SMITH:—The following is a brief sketch of my journey from London to this place. Elder Kimball left London on the 19th February. I left on the 26th, and arrived at Bristol on the same day, where I found Elder Kington, who was busily engaged in the work of the Lord in that city, and had established a small branch of fourteen members. I tarried there a short time and preached three times in a theatre, had large congregations, good attention, and baptized one, and there appears a good prospect of a work being done in that city. Population of Bristol, 200,000. While there I visited the suspension bridge, now erecting across the river Avon, at St. Vincent's Rocks, Clifton; which bridge is one hundred feet in height above the river, and seven hundred in length. I spent one evening in Monmouth, on the borders of Wales; preached to a large congregation; several applied for baptism after meeting. On the 8th of March I attended a conference in Garway; Elder Levi Richards was chosen president, and James Morgan, clerk; heard four branches represented, containing one hundred and thirty-four members; three were ordained to the ministry. I also preached at Lugwardine, Shucknall Hill, Ledbury, Dymock, and Turkey Hall to large congregations, and find the work of the Lord still progressing throughout that region, The excitement upon the subject in the city of Hereford has been so great, that it has assembled together in the market place three thousand persons at a time to hear something upon the cause of the Latter-day Saints. On the 15th of March I attended the Gadfield Elm conference, which met at the Gadfield Elm Chapel. Elder Wilford Woodruff was chosen president; John Hill, clerk; 18 branches represented, containing 408 members, 8 Elders, 32 Priests, 11 Teacher and 1 Deacon; when such business was transacted as was deemed necessary. I also met large congregations at Keysend street, Coldville, Browcut; Dunclose, Froom's Hill, and Stanley Hill, and left many churches on the right and left, which time would not permit me to visit. I also met with the Froom's Hill conference, on the 22nd March, at Stanley Hill, Herefordshire, there being present one of the traveling High Council, 2 High Priests, 20 Elders, 30 Priests, 9 Teachers, two Deacons. Elder Levi Richards was chosen president, and Elder Woodruff, clerk. On this occasion I heard represented 30 branches, containing 997 members, 24 Elders, 66 Priests, 27 Teachers, 7 Deacons, and 6 were ordained to the ministry. The sum total represented at these conferences was 1,539 members, 36 Elders, 103 Priests, 41 Teachers, 7 Deacons; all of whom have embraced the work in that part of the vineyard in one year, besides many members and officers who have emigrated to America; and I am happy to say that the officers and members, have universally been ready to hearken to counsel, and give heed to our instructions, and it was with no ordinary feelings that I took my farewell of those churches who have been so ready to receive and embrace the truth. I called upon the Saints in Birmingham and Gret's Green, but had not time to hold any meetings among them. I arrived in Hanley on the 25th, where I had the privilege of again meeting with Elder Geo. A. Smith, and was rejoiced to find the churches universally prospering in Staffordshire. I spent one evening with the church at Longton, and baptized seven.

Tuesday, *30.*—Elders Woodruff and Geo. A. Smith arrived in Manchester, after a ride of forty miles.

Wednesday, *31.*—Elders Young and Richards attended conference in Liverpool.

Thursday, *April 1*, *1841.*—Elders Young and Richards went to Manchester, where they found Elders Kimball, Hyde ,Woodruff and Smith, and had a happy meeting.

Friday, *2.*—Elders Orson Pratt and John Taylor arrived at Manchester and went into council.

Minutes of a Council Meeting of the Twelve.

MANCHESTER, ENGLAND, April 2, 1841.

This day Elders Brigham Young, Heber C. Kimball, Orson Hyde, Parley P. Pratt, Orson Pratt, Willard Richards, Wilford Woodruff, John Taylor and Geo. A. Smith, of the quorum of the Twelve, met together at the house of Brother James Bushaw, coachman No. 4, Gray Street, near Oxford road, in this city, in council, after having been separated and sent into various counties. To meet once more in council after a long separation, and having passed through many sore and grievous trials, exposing our lives and our characters to the slanders and violence of wicked and murderous men, caused our hearts to swell with gratitude to God for His providential care over us. Elder Young opened the council by prayer. Elders Brigham Young, Heber C. Kimball, and Parley P. Pratt, the committee appointed about a year ago to secure a copyright for the Book of Mormon, in the name of Joseph Smith, Jun., presented the following certificate:

"Feb. 8, 1841. Then entered for his copy—the property of Joseph Smith, Jun.,—'The Book of Mormon; an account written by the hand of Mormon, upon plates taken from the plates of Nephi; translated by Joseph Smith, Jun. First European, from the second American edition. Received five copies.

"GEORGE GREENHILL."

"The above is a true copy of an entry in the register book of the Company of Stationers kept, at the hall of the said company. Witness my hand, this 17th day of February, 1841.

"GEORGE GREENHILL,
Warehouse-keeper of the Company of Stationers."

The quorum voted that they accepted the labors of said Committee.

Resolved: That as the quorum of the Twelve have had nothing to do with the printing of the Book of Mormon, they will not now interfere with it, but that the said Committee settle the financial or business matters thereof with Joseph Smith, Jun., to whom the profits rightly belong.

Resolved: That Elder Amos Fielding be appointed to superintend fitting out the Saints from Liverpool to America, under the instruction of Parley P. Pratt.

Resolved: That Brother Geo. J. Adams go to Bedford and Northampton and labor in that region.

Adjourned till tomorrow at 10 o'clock, a. m.; Elder Kimball closed by prayer.

ORSON HYDE, Clerk.

Council Meeting of the Twelve—Continued.

MANCHESTER, April 3, 1841.

This day the quorum of the Twelve met pursuant to adjournment. The president called upon Elder Hyde to open by prayer. The quorum then signed a letter of commendation to the churches in England for Elder Hyde.

The business of publishing the *Star* and hymn-book was then taken into consideration. Brother John Taylor moved that those who have had the care and superintendence of publishing the *Star* and hymn-book, should dispose of them according to their own wishes, and dispose of the proceeds in the same way; seconded by Elder Orson Pratt, and carried by unanimous vote. Moved by Elder Young, and seconded by Elder Kimball, that Elder Parley P. Pratt conduct the publication of the *Millennial Star* as editor of the same, after the close of the present volume. *Resolved*, that Elder Parley P. Pratt reprint the hymn-book if he deem it expedient. The hymn-book is not to be altered, except the typographical errors. The above resolution was moved by Elder Geo. A. Smith, and seconded by Elder Wilford Woodruff; carried unanimously. Conference adjourned.

ORSON HYDE, Clerk.

Sunday, 4.—The President of the United States, William Henry Harrison died at Washington of the pleurisy.

Nine of the Twelve at Manchester attended meeting at Carpenter's hall, and individually bore testimony of the fulness of the everlasting Gospel.

Council Meeting of the Twelve—Continued.

MANCHESTER, April 5, 1841.

Met pursuant to adjournment. Elder Orson Pratt opened the council by prayer. It was resolved that the 17th day of April be the day appointed for the Twelve who are going to America, to set sail from Liverpool. Moved by Elder Kimball and seconded by Elder Woodruff that the Twelve do business at the conference as a quorum, and call upon the Church or conference to sanction it. Adjourned till the 6th instant, to meet in general conference at Carpenter's Hall, at 10 o'clock a. m.

O. HYDE, Clerk.

Twelfth Anniversary of the Organization of the Church.

April 6, 1841.—The first day of the twelfth year of the Church of Jesus Christ of Latter-day Saints! At an early hour the several companies comprising the "Nauvoo Legion," with two volunteer companies from Iowa Territory, making sixteen companies in all, assembled at their several places of rendezvous, and were conducted in due order to the ground assigned for general review. The appearance, order and movements of the Legion, were chaste, grand and imposing, and reflected great credit upon the taste, skill and tact of the men comprising said Legion. We doubt whether the like can be presented in any other city in the western country. At half-past seven o'clock a. m., the fire of artillery announced the arrival of Brigadier-Generals Law and Don Carlos Smith, at the front of their respective cohorts; and at 8 o'clock Major-General Bennett was conducted to his post, under the discharge of cannon, and took command of the Legion.

At half-past nine o'clock a. m., Lieutenant-General Smith, with his guard, staff and field officers arrived at the ground, and were presented with a beautiful silk national flag by the ladies of Nauvoo, which was respectfully received and hailed by the firing of cannon, and borne off by Colonel Robinson, the cornet, to the appropriate position in the line; after which the Lieutenant-General with his suite passed the lines in review.

At twelve m., the procession arrived upon the Temple ground, enclosing the same in a hollow square, with Lieutenant-General Smith, Major-General Bennett, Brigadier-Generals Wilson Law and Don Carlos Smith, their respective staffs, guard, field officers, distinguished visitors, choir, band, &c., in the centre, and the ladies and gentlemen, citizens, surrounding in the interior. The superior officers, together with the banner, architects, principal speaker, &c., were duly conducted to the stand at the principal corner stone, and the religious services were commenced by singing from page 65 of the new hymn book.

Sidney Rigdon's Speech.

President Sidney Rigdon then addressed the assembly, and remarked the circumstances under which he addressed the people were of no ordinary character, but of peculiar and indescribable interest, that it was the third occasion of a similar nature, wherein he had been called upon to address the people, and to assist in laying the corner stones of houses to be erected in honor of the God of the Saints. Various scenes had transpired since the first was laid—he with some who were with him on that occasion, had waded through scenes that no other people had ever seen—not cursed, but blessed with. They had seen the blood of the innocent flow, and heard the groans of those dying for the witness of Jesus; in all those scenes of tribulation, his confidence, his courage and his joy had been increasing instead of diminishing. Now the scene had changed; persecution had in a measure subsided; peace and safety, friendship and joy crowned their assembling; and their endeavors to serve God were respected and viewed with interest. The Saints had assembled, not to violate law and trample upon equity and good social order; not to devaste and destroy; but to lift up the standard of liberty and law, to stand in defense of civil and religious, rights, to protect the innocent, to save mankind, and to obey the will and mandate of the Lord of glory; to call up to remembrance the once crucified, but now exalted and glorified Savior; to say that He is again revealed, that He speaks from the heavens, that He reigns; in honor of Him to tell the world that He lives, and speaks, and reigns and dictates—that not every people can build a house to Him, but that people whom He Himself directs—that the present military display is not to usurp authority, but to obey as they are commanded and directed; to honor, not the world, but Him that is alive and reigns, the all in all, the invisible, but beholding, and guiding and directing—that the Saints boast of their King; of His wisdom, His understanding, His power and His goodness—that they honor a God of unbounded power and glory—that He is the chief corner stone in Zion, also the top stone—that He cannot be conquered—that He is working in the world to guide, to conquer, and to subdue—that as formerly, so now He works by revelation—that this is the reason why we are here, and why we are thus—that the Saints have sacrificed all things for the testimony of Jesus Christ—that some from different parts of Europe and from Canada, as well as the different parts of the United States, are present, and among all, a unanimity of purpose and feeling prevails—and why? Because the same God over all had spoken from the heavens and again revealed Himself. He remarked that he defied the devil to collect such an assembly; none but Jesus would or could accomplish such things as we are about to behold; the devil will not build up, but tear down and destroy; the work of Jesus is like Himself in all ages—that as light shines from the east, and spreads itself to the west, so is the progress of spiritual light and truth—that Jesus is a God of order, regularity and uniformity—that he works now by revelation and by messengers as anciently—shows Himself—lifts the veil; that such things are marvelous, but nevertheless true—that the order of laying the corner stones was expressive of the order of the kingdom—that the minutiæ were subject matter of revelation, and all the scenery, acts of obedience are understood by the Saints—that the ancient Prophets beheld and rejoiced at this scene, and are near to witness the fulfillment of their predictions—that we are highly favored of God, and brought near to the spirits of just men made perfect. He then closed by exhortation, first to the multitude, and lastly to the Church. The speaker then gave out a hymn, page 205, and closed by prayer.

The architects then, by the direction of the First Presidency, lowered the first (the south-east corner) stone to its place, and President Joseph Smith pronounced the benediction as follows:

This principal corner stone in representation of the First Presidency, is now duly laid in honor of the Great God; and may it there remain until the whole fabric is completed; and may the same be accomplished speedily; that the Saints may have a place to worship God, and the Son of Man have where to lay His head.

President Sidney Rigdon then pronounced the following:

May the persons employed in the erection of this house be preserved from all harm while engaged in its construction, till the whole is completed, in the name of the Father, and of the Son, and of the Holy Ghost. Even so. Amen.

Adjourned for one hour.

Assembled according to adjournment, and proceeded to lay the remaining corner stones, according to previous order.

The second (south-west corner) stone, by the direction of the president of the High Priesthood, with his council and President Marks, was lowered to its place, when the president of the High Priesthood pronounced the followng:

The second corner stone of the Temple now building by the Church of Jesus Christ of Latter-day Saints, in honor of the Great God, is duly laid, and may the same unanimity, that has been manifested on this occasion continue till the whole is completed; that peace may rest upon it to the laying of the top stone thereof, and the turning of the key thereof; that the Saints may participate in the blessings of Israel's God, within its walls, and the glory of God rest upon the same. Amen.

The third (the north-west corner) stone, superintended by the High Council, was then lowered to its place, with the benediction of Elias Higbee, as follows:

The third corner stone is now duly laid; may this stone be a firm support to the building that the whole may be completed as before proposed.

The fourth (the north-east corner) stone, superintended by the Bishops, was then lowered to its place, and Bishop Whitney pronounced the following:

The fourth and last corner stone, expressive of the Lesser Priesthood, is now duly laid, and may the blessings before pronounced, with all others desirable, rest upon the same forever. Amen.

The services were then declared closed, and the military retired to the parade ground and were dismissed with the approbation and thanks of the commanding officer. The military band, under the command of Captain Duzette, made a conspicuous and dignified appearance, and performed their part honorably. Their soul-stirring strains met harmoniously the rising emotions that swelled each bosom, and stimulated us onward to the arduous but pleasing and honorable duties of the day. The choir also, under the direction of B. S. Wilber, deserve commendation.

What added greatly to the happiness we experienced on this interesting occasion, is the fact that we heard no bscene or profane language; neither saw we any one intoxicated. Can the same be said of a similar assemblage in any other city in the Union? Thank God that the intoxicating beverage, the bane of humanity in these last days, is becoming a stranger in Nauvoo.

Conduct of the People.

In conclusion, we will say we never witnessed a more imposing spectacle than was presented on this occasion, and during the sessions of the conference. Such a multitude of people moving in harmony, in friendship, in dignity, told in a voice not easily misunderstood, that they were a people of intelligence, and virtue and order; in short, that they were *Saints;* and that the God of love, purity and light, was their God, their Examplar, and Director; and that they were blessed and happy.

If the strict order of the Priesthood were carried out in the building of Temples, the first stone would be laid at the south-east corner, by the First Presidency of the Church. The south-west corner should be laid next. The third, or north-west corner next; and the fourth, or north-east corner last. The first Presidency should lay the south-east corner stone and dictate who are the proper persons to lay the other corner stones.

Order of Laying Corner Stones of Temples.

If a Temple is built at a distance, and the First Presidency are not present, then the Quorum of the Twelve Apostles are the persons to dictate the order for that Temple; and in the absence of the Twelve Apostles, then the Presidency of the Stake will lay the south-east corner stone; the Melchisedec Priesthood laying the corner stones on the east side of the Temple, and the Lesser Priesthood those on the west side.

A Conference was held at Philadelphia; President Hyrum Smith presiding; many branches were represented and the branch at Philadelphia was organized by electing Benjamin Winchester, President, and Edson Whipple, and William Wharnot, his Counselors. Jacob Syphret was elected Bishop, and Jesse Prince and James Nicholson his Counselors.

Conference at Philadelphia.

Meeting of the Council of the Twelve in Manchester.

The Council of the Twelve assembled at Manchester, in Carpenter's Hall, on the 6th day of April, 1841, for the first time to transact business as a quorum in the presence of the Church, in a foreign land; being the first day of the 12th year of the rise of the Church of Jesus Christ of Latter-day Saints. Nine of the quorum were present; viz., Brigham Young, Heber C. Kimball, Orson Hyde, Parley P. Pratt, Orson Pratt, Wilford Woodruff, Willard Richards, John Taylor and Geo. A. Smith, President Young having called the meeting to order, and organized, the conference then opened by prayer. Elder Thomas Ward was chosen Clerk. The President then made some introductory remarks relative to the organization of the Church in the House of the Lord in America, in reference to the different quorums in their respective orders and authorities in the Church.

The representation of the churches and conferences throughout the kingdom was then called for.

LOCATION.	BY WHOM REPRESENTED.	MEMBERS.	ELDERS.	PRIESTS.	TEACHERS.	DEACONS.
Manchester	Parley P. Pratt.	443	7	15	9	0
Clitheroe Conference	Heber C. Kimball.	318	6	12	13	3
Preston Conference	Peter Melling.	675	11	15	13	3
Liverpool.	John Taylor.	190	9	8	4	3
Isle of Man	John Taylor.	90	2	4	2	0
London Conference	Lorenzo Snow.	137	3	8	4	2
Birmingham Conference	Alfred Cordon.	110	4	13	4	1
Staffordshire Conference	Alfred Cordon.	574	19	49	28	16
Garway Conference.	Wilford Woodruff.	134	5	6	4	1
Gadfield Elm Conference.	Wilford Woodruff.	408	8	33	11	1
Froom's Hill Conference	Wilford Woodruff.	1008	27	67	27	8
Edingburgh	Orson Pratt	203	6	9	6	2
Glasgow, Paisley, Johnstone, Bridge of Weir. and Thorney Bank	Reuben Hedlock.	368	12	15	13	11
Ireland	Theodore Curtis.	35	2	0	1	0
Wales	James Burnham.	170	2	5	3	3
Newcastle-upon-Tyne	Amos Fielding.	23	1	3	1	0
Alston.	John Sanders.	26	1	0	1	0
Brampton.	John Sanders.	46	0	1	0	0
Carlisle	John Sanders.	43	1	0	0	0
Bolton	Robert Crooks.	189	1	11	8	1
Dukinfield	John Albertson.	120	2	4	3	2
Northwich, Middlewich, &c	Samuel Heath.	112	2	6	6	6
Oldham	William Black.	86	1	4	1	2
Stockport	Elder Magan.	161	1	5	2	2
Eccles	Elder Magan.	24	1	3	1	0
Pendlebury	Elder Magan.	62	0	2	1	1
Whitefield	Elder Magan.	41	1	2	3	0
Radcliffe Bridge	Elder Magan.	18	1	3	0	0
	Total	5814	136	304	169	68

Nearly eight hundred Saints have emigrated to America during the past season. These are not included in this representation.

Conference adjourned till 2 p. m.

Conference met pursuant to adjournment; opened by prayer.

Scattering members were then represented, consisting of nearly fifty, not included in any of the above branches.

President Young then proceeded to make some remarks on the office of Patriarch, and concluded by moving that Elder John Albertson * be ordained to that office. Seconded by Elder Kimball, and carried unanimously.

Resolved: That George D. Watt, George J. Adams, Amos Fielding, William Kay, John Sanders, Thomas Richardson, James Whitehead, Thomas Domville, James Galley and George Simpson be ordained High Priests.

Resolved: That the following persons be ordained Elders—William Miller, William Leach, John Sands, William Moon, William Hardman, William Black, John Goodfellow, Joseph Brotherton, Richard Benson, Theophilus Brotherton, John McIlwick, and William Green.

Resolved: That Manchester, Stockport, Dukinfield, Oldham, Bolton, and all the neighboring branches be organized into one conference, to be called the Manchester Conference.

That the Church in Brampton, Alston, and Carlisle be included in one conference.

That the churches of Liverpool, Isles of Man, Wales, viz., Overton, Harding and Ellsmere, be organized into one conference, to be called the Liverpool conference.

Resolved: That the Macclesfield Conference include Macclesfield, Northwich, Middlewich, and Lostock.

That Edinburgh Conference include Glasgow, Paisley, Bridge of Weir, Johnstone and Thorney Bank.

That George D. Watt preside over the Edinburgh Conference.

That John Greenhow preside over the Liverpool Conference.

That Thomas Ward preside over the Clitheroe Conference.

That Lorenzo Snow preside over the London Conference.

That James Galley preside over the Macclesfield Conference.

That Alfred Cordon preside over the Staffordshire Conference.

That James Riley be ordained a High Priest, and preside over the Birmingham Conference.

That James McAnley preside over the Glasgow Conference.

That Thomas Richardson preside over the Gadfield Elm Conference.

That William Kay preside over the Froom's Hill Conference.

That Levi Richards have the superintendence of the Garway Conference.

* John Albertson was the second Patriarch ordained in England, Peter Melling being the first, he was ordained the 17th of April, 1840.

That Peter Melling preside over the Preston Conference.

That John Sanders preside over the Brampton Conference.

Adjourned till seven o'clock, p. m.

Met pursuant to adjournment; commenced by singing, "When shall we all meet again," and prayer.

The Patriarch Peter Melling, was then called upon to pronounce a patriarchal blessing upon the head of John Albertson, previous to his being ordained to the office of Patriarch. Laying his hands upon him he blessed him in the following words:

"John, I lay my hands upon thy head, in the name of Jesus Christ; and by the authority of the Holy Priesthood committed unto me, I pronounce upon thy head the blessings of Abraham, Isaac and Jacob; and I say unto thee, that, inasmuch as it is in thy heart to do the will of the Lord, thou shalt be blessed, and the desires of thy heart shall be granted thee; and the Lord God will enlarge thy heart; and, inasmuch as thou wilt be humble and faithful before the Lord in thy calling, even that of a Patriarch, thou shalt be blessed, strengthened, and have great wisdom and understanding; thy bowels shall be filled with compassion for the widow and fatherless; and I pray that our Father in Heaven will take thee into His own care, and as He feels for thy welfare, thou shalt be made strong in faith, and the Lord shall bless thee and open thy understanding. Thou shalt know the doctrine of Jesus Christ, and the mysteries of heaven shall be opened to thy mind. Thou shalt also have the gift of prophecy and revelation, and thou shalt predict those things that shall take place to the latest generation. I pray that our Father in heaven may confer these blessings upon thy head; yea, thou shalt be a mighty man, if thou wilt be a faithful man, and a humble man, so that thou mayst be an ornament to thy calling, and a blessing to thy posterity; yea, thy posterity shall be blessed, and they shall become mighty upon the earth, and become blessed inasmuch as thou wilt be faithful in all things, and watch unto prayer. Thou shalt finally overcome, and be lifted up on high, and inherit the mansions prepared for thee in the kingdom of our God. Thou art of the blood of Ephraim; and I seal these blessings upon thy head in the name of Jesus Christ. Amen, and amen."

The Apostles then laid hands on John Albertson, and ordained him to the office of Patriarch.

The ordinations of the High Priests then took place; but, from the pressure of business, it was directed that the High Priests who were present should retire to the vestry, with those who were to be ordained Elders, and there ordain them at the same time that the ordinations of the High Priests were proceeding.

Several appropriate discourses were delivered by different members of the Twelve Apostles in relation to the duties of the officers in their respective callings, and the duties and privileges of the members; also on the prosperity of the work in general.

A very richly ornamented cake, a present from New York, from Elder George J. Adams' wife to the Twelve, was then exhibited to the meeting. This was blessed by them and distributed to all the officers and members, and the whole congregation, consisting, perhaps, of seven hundred people; a large fragment was still preserved for some who were not present. During the distribution several appropriate hymns were sung, and a powerful and general feeling of delight universally pervaded the meeting.

While this was proceeding, Elder Parley P. Pratt composed, and handed over to the clerk, the following lines, which the clerk then read to the meeting:

When in far distant regions,
As strangers we roam,
Far away from our country,
Our friends and our home:

When sinking in sorrow,
Fresh courage we'll take,
As we think of our friends,
And remember the *cake*.

Elder Orson Hyde appealed powerfully to the meeting, and covenanted with the Saints present, in a bond of mutual prayer, during his mission to Jerusalem and the East, which was sustained on the part of the hearers with a hearty amen.

Elder Fielding remarked respecting the rich cake of which they had been partaking, that he considered it a type of the good things of that land from whence it came, and from which they had received the fullness of the Gospel.

The number of official members present at this conference was then taken, viz., quorum of the Twelve Apostles, 9; Patriarchs, 2; High Priests, 16; quorum of the Seventies, 2; Elders, 31; Priests, 28; Teachers, 17; Deacons, 2.

Elders Brigham Young and William Miller then sang the hymn "Adieu, my dear brethren," &c., and President Young blessed the congregation and dismissed them.

BRIGHAM YOUNG, Chairman.
THOMAS WARD, Clerk.

CHAPTER XVIII.

GENERAL CONFERENCE AT NAUVOO—EPISTLE OF THE TWELVE TO THE SAINTS IN ENGLAND—DIFFERENCE BETWEEN BAPTISTS AND LATTER-DAY SAINTS.

Minutes of the General Conference of the Church of Jesus Christ of Latter-day Saints, held in Nauvoo, Illinois, on the 7th day of April, one thousand eight hundred and forty-one.

The names of the presidents of the several quorums were called, and they took their seats on the stand, with their counselors in front. The meeting was called to order. Choir sang a hymn; prayer by William Law.

The clerk then read the report of the First Presidency, as follows—

REPORT OF THE FIRST PRESIDENCY.

The Presidency of the Church of Jesus Christ of Latter-day Saints, feel great pleasure in assembling with the Saints at another general conference, under circumstances so auspicious and cheering; and with greatful hearts to Almighty God for His providential regard, they cordially unite with the Saints, on this occasion, in ascribing honor, glory, and blessing to His Holy name.

It is with unfeigned pleasure that they have to make known the steady and rapid increase of the Church in this state, the United States, and Europe. The anxiety to become acquainted with the principles of the Gospel, on every hand is intense, and the cry of "come over and help us," is reaching the Elders on the wings of every wind; while thousands who have heard the Gospel have become obedient thereto, and are rejoicing in its gifts and blessings. Prejudice, with its attendant train of evil, is giving way before the force of truth, whose benign rays are penetrating the nations afar off.

The reports from the Twelve Apostles in Europe are very satisfactory, and state that the work continues to progress with unparalleled rapidity, and that the harvest is truly great. In the Eastern States the faithful laborers are successful, and many are flocking to the standard of truth

Nor is the South keeping back. Churches have been raised up in the Southern and Western States, and a very pressing invitation has been received from New Orleans, for some of the Elders to visit that city; which has been complied with. In our own state and immediate neighborhood, many are avowing their attachment to the principles of our holy religion, and have become obedient to the faith.

Peace and prosperity attend us; and we have favor in the sight of God and virtuous men. The time was, when we were looked upon as deceivers, and that "Mormonism" would soon pass away, come to nought, and be forgotten. But the time has gone by when it is looked upon as a transient matter, or a bubble on the wave, and it is now taking a deep hold in the hearts and affections of all those who are noble-minded enough to lay aside the prejudice of education, and investigate the subject with candor and honesty. The truth, like the sturdy oak, has stood unhurt amid the contending elements, which have beat upon it with tremendous force. The floods have rolled, wave after wave, in quick succession, and have not swallowed it up. "They have lifted up their voice, O Lord; the floods have lifted up their voice; but the Lord of Hosts is mightier than the mighty waves of the sea;" nor have the flames of persecution, with all the influence of mobs, been able to destroy it; but like Moses' bush, it has stood unconsumed, and now at this moment presents an important spectacle both to men and angels. Where can we turn our eyes to behold such another? We contemplate a people who have embraced a system of religion, unpopular, and the adherence to which has brought upon them repeated persecutions. A people who, for their love to God, and attachment to His cause, have suffered hunger, nakedness, perils, and almost every privation. A people who, for the sake of their religion, have had to mourn the premature death of parents, husbands, wives, and children. A people, who have preferred death to slavery and hypocrisy, and have honorably maintained their characters, and stood firm and immovable, in times that have tried men's souls. Stand fast, ye Saints of God, hold on a little while longer, and the storm of life will be past, and you will be rewarded by that God whose servants you are, and who will duly appreciate all your toils and afflictions for Christ's sake and the Gospel's. Your names will be handed down to posterity as Saints of God and virtuous men.

But we hope that those scenes of blood will never more occur, but that many, very many, such scenes as the present will be witnessed by the Saints, and that in the Temple, the foundation of which has been so happily laid, will the Saints of the Most High continue to congregate from year to year in peace and safety.

From the kind and generous feelings, manifested by the citizens of this state, since our sojourn among them, we may continue to expect the enjoyment of all the blessings of civil and religious liberty, guaranteed by the Constitution. The citizens of Illinois have done themselves honor, in throwing the mantle of the Constitution over a persecuted and afflicted people: and have given evident proof that they are not only in the enjoyment of the privileges of freemen themselves, but also that they willingly and cheerfully extend that invaluable blessing to others, and that they freely award to faithfuless and virtue their due.

The proceedings of the legislature, in regard to the citizens of this place, have been marked with philanthropy and benevolence; and they have laid us under great and lasting obligations, in granting us the several liberal charters we now enjoy, and by which we hope to prosper until our city becomes the most splendid, our University the most learned, and our Legion the most effective of any in the Union. In the language of one of our own poets, we would say—

In Illinois we've found a safe retreat,
A home, a shelter from oppression dire;
Where we can worship God as we think right,
And mobbers come not to disturb our peace;
Where we can live and hope for better days,
Enjoy again our liberty, our rights:
That social intercourse which freedom grants,
And charity requires of man to man.
And long may charity pervade each breast,
And long may Illinois remain the scene
Of rich prosperity, by *peace secured.*

In consequence of the impoverished condition of the Saints, the buildings which are in course of erection do not progress as fast as could be desired; but from the interest which is generally manifested by the Saints at large, we hope to accomplish much by a combination of effort, and a concentration of action, and erect the Temple and other public buildings, which we so much need for our mutual instruction and the education of our children.

From the reports which have been received, we may expect a large emigration this season. The proclamation which was sent, some time ago, to the churches abroad, has been responded to, and great numbers are making preparations to come and locate themselves in this city and vicinity.

From what we now witness, we are led to look forward with pleasing anticipation to the future, and soon expect to see the thousands of Israel flocking to this region in obedience to the heavenly command; numerous inhabitants—Saints—thickly studding the flowery and wide-spread prairies of Illinois; temples for the worship of our God erecting in various parts, and great peace resting upon Israel.

We would call the attention of the Saints more particularly to the building of the Temple, for on its speedy erection great blessings depend. The zeal which is manifested by the Saints in this city is, indeed, praiseworthy, and, we hope will be imitated by the Saints in the various stakes and branches of the Church, and that those who cannot contribute labor will bring their gold and their silver, their brass and their iron, with the pine tree, and box tree, to beautify the same.

We are glad to hear of the organization of the different quorums in this city, and hope that their organization will be attended to in every stake and branch of the Church, for the Almighty is a lover of order and good government.

From the faith and enterprise of the Saints generally, we feel greatly encouraged and cheerfully attend to the important duties devolving upon us, knowing that we not only have the approval of heaven, but also that our efforts for the establishment of Zion and the spread of truth, are cheerfully seconded by the thousands of Israel.

In conclusion we would say, brethren, be faithful, let your love and moderation be known unto all men; be patient, be mindful to observe all the commandments of your Heavenly Father, and the God of all grace shall bless you. Even so, Amen.

JOSEPH SMITH, President,
ROBERT B. THOMPSON, Clerk.

On motion, Resolved that the report be printed in the *Times and Seasons*.

President Rigdon arose and stated that, in consequence of weakness from his labors of yesterday, he would call upon General John C. Bennett to officiate in his place.

General Bennett then read the revelations from "The Book of the Law of the Lord," which had been received since the last general conference, in relation to writing a proclamation to the kings of the earth, building a temple in Nauvoo, the organization of the Church, &c.*

President Joseph Smith rose, and made some observations in explanation of the same; and likewise of the necessity which existed of building the Temple, that the Saints might have a suitable place for worshiping the Almighty; and also the building of the Nauvoo Boarding House, that suitable accommodations may be afforded for the strangers who visit this city.

The choir sung a hymn, and the meeting adjourned for one hour.

* This is the revelation of 19th January, 1841, now section cxxi, Doctrine and Covenants.

Conference met pursuant to adjournment, and was called to order by William Law.

Choir sung a hymn, and President William Marks addressed the throne of grace.

General Bennett read the charters granted by the legislature of this state, for incorporating "the City of Nauvoo," "the Nauvoo Legion," "the University of the City of Nauvoo," "the Agricultural and Manufacturing Association," and "the Nauvoo House Association."

On motion, Resolved that the charters now read be received by the Church.

President Don Carlos Smith arose, and gave an exhortation to the assembly.

General John C. Bennett then spoke at some length on the present situation, prospects, and condition of the Church, and remarked that the hand of God must indeed be visible, in accomplishing the great blessings and prosperity of the Church, and called upon the Saints to be faithful and obedient in all things, and likewise forcibly and eloquently urged the necessity of being united in all their movements; and before he sat down, he wished to know how many of the Saints who were present felt disposed to continue to act in concert and follow the instructions of the First Presidency; and called upon all those who did so, to arise on their feet—when immediately the Saints, almost without exception, arose.

The choir sung a hymn, and the meeting, after prayer, adjourned until tomorrow morning.

Thursday, 8th.

Thursday morning, April 8. At an early hour this morning the different quorums, who had previously been organized, came to the ground and took their seats as follows: The First Presidency, with the presidents of the quorums on the stand, the High Council on the front of the stand, the High Priests on the front to the right of the stand, the Seventies immediately behind the High Priests, the Elders in the front to the left, the Lesser Priesthood on the right.

On motion, Resolved, that this conference continue until Sunday evening.

President Joseph Smith declared the rule of voting to be, a majority in each quorum; exhorted them to deliberation, faith, and prayer; and that they should be strict and impartial in their examinations. He then old them that the presidents of the different quorums would be presented before them for their acceptance or rejection.

Bishop Whitney then presented the First Presidency to the Lesser

Priesthood. President John A. Hicks presented them to the Elders' quorum. President Joseph Young presented them to the quorums of the Seventies. President Don Carlos Smith presented them to the High Priests' quorum. Counselor Elias Higbee presented them to the High Council; and the clerk then presented them to the presidents of all the quorums on the stand, and they were unanimously accepted. John C. Bennett was presented, with the First Presidency, as Assistant President until President Rigdon's health should be restored.

The presidents and counselors belonging to the several quorums were then presented to each quorum separately, for approval or rejection, when the following persons were objected to, viz., John A. Hicks, president of the Elders' quorum; Alanson Ripley, Bishop; Elder John E. Page, one of the Twelve Apostles; and Noah Packard, High Priest. Bishop Newel K. Whitney moved their cases be laid over, to be tried before the several quorums.

President Joseph Smith presented the building committee of the "House of the Lord," viz., Alpheus Cutler, Reynolds Cahoon, and Elias Higbee, to the several quorums collectively, and they were unanimously received.

President Smith observed that it was necessary that someone should be appointed to fill the Quorum of the Twelve Apostles, in the room of the late Elder David W. Patten; whereupon President Rigdon nominated Elder Lyman Wight to that office; and he was unanimously accepted. Elder Wight stated that it was an office of great honor and responsibility, and he felt inadequate to the task; but, inasmuch as it was the wish of the authorities of the Church that he should take that office, he would endeavor to magnify it.

Resolved: That James Allred be appointed to the office of High Councilor, in the place of Charles C. Rich, who had been chosen a counselor to the president of this stake, and that Leonard Soby be appointed one of the High Council, in the room of David Dort, deceased.

The choir sung a hymn, and after prayer by President Rigdon, the meeting adjourned for two hours.

Conference met pursuant to adjournment. A hymn was sung by the choir.

President Rigdon delivered an interesting discourse on the subject of "Baptism for the dead."

President Joseph Smith followed on the same subject; and threw considerable light on the doctrine which had been presented.

The choir then sung a hymn; and after prayer by Elder William Smith, conference adjourned until tomorrow morning at 10 o'clock.

Friday morning, the 9th, conference met pursuant to adjournment.

The quorums reported that they had investigated the conduct of the persons who had been objected to, and that they had rejected Alanson Ripley and James Foster. Leave was given to James Foster to make a few remarks respecting the charges preferred against him: after which it was resolved that Elder James Foster continue his standing in the Church. *Resolved:* That, as Alanson Ripley has not appeared to answer the charges preferred against him, that his Bishopric be taken from him.

President Joseph Smith made some observations respecting the duty of the several quorums, in sending their members into the vineyard, and also stated that labor on the Temple would be as acceptable to the Lord, as preaching in the world, and that it was necessary that some agents should be appointed to collect funds for building the Temple.

Resolved: That John Murdoch, Lyman Wight, William Smith, Henry William Miller, Amasa Lyman, Leonard Soby, Gehiel Savage, and Zenos H. Gurley be appointed to travel and collect funds for the same.

A hymn was then sung by the choir. Prayer by President Don Carlos Smith.

President Joseph Smith then stated that he should resign the meeting to the presidency of the stake, and the president of the High Priests' quorum.

The building committee were called upon to address the assembly. Elder Cahoon spoke at length on the importance of building the Temple, and called upon the Saints to assist them in their great undertaking. Elder Alpheus Cutler made some very appropriate remarks.

Conference adjourned one hour.

Conference met pursuant to adjournment.

Elias Higbee spoke on the same subject [*i. e.* importance of building the Temple]. Elder Lyman Wight then came forward and addressed the meeting at considerable length.

The clerk read a letter from Elder John Taylor in England, to President Joseph Smith, which gave an account of the prosperity of the work of the Lord in that land.

On motion, adjourned until tomorrow morning at 10 o'clock.

Saturday, 10th The weather was unfavorable, consequently no business was transacted.

Sunday, 11th. The conference again met.

Elder Zenos H. Gurley preached on the literal fulfillment of prophecy.

President Rigdon made some observations on baptism for the remission of sins.

Conference adjourned for one hour.

Conference met, and was addressed by the Bishops of the stake, who stated the situation of the poor who had to be supported, and called upon the Saints to assist in relieving the necessities of the widows and fatherless.

Elder Lyman Wight made some observations on the subject.

President Joseph Smith then addressed the assembly, and stated that in consequence of the severity of the weather the Saints had not received as much instruction as he desired, and that some things would have to be laid over until the next conference. As there were many who wished to be baptized, they would now go to the water, and give them opportunity.

The procession was then organized, and proceeded to the Mississippi.

After the baptisms were over, the conference adjourned to the first of October next.

JOSEPH SMITH, President.
R. B. THOMPSON, Clerk.

On the 7th of April, 1841, the Twelve Apostles were in England and were busy in council, visiting the Saints in Manchester, and in the evening supped at "Mother Miller's." On the 9th, they visited the Zoological Gardens, Manchester, England. Elder W. J. Barratt writes from Australia, "he had arrived safe at Adelaide after a rough passage, but had not baptized any persons. Obstacles to the introduction of the work of the Lord are very great."

Letter of George A. Smith to the Star—Report of Labors.

BOLTON, April 11, 1841.

Elder P. P. Pratt:

I thought good to give your readers (through the medium of the *Star*) a short account of my labors in England. I landed in Liverpool on the 6th of April, 1840; and, after attending the Preston conference, I went to the Staffordshire Potteries, where there were about 100 Saints; I remained there three months. The work continued to prosper, and 80 were added to the church in that time. I then left the church there to the care of Elder Alfred Cordon, and, in company with Elders Kimball and Woodruff, visited the churches in Herefordshire and vicinity. Hundreds received our testimony, and were baptized. From thence we proceeded to London, where we met with much difficulty in introducing the fullness of the Gospel; the hearts of the people were barred against the truth, but the Lord blessed our labors, and we succeeded in establishing a branch of the Church there. My health being poor, I was counseled by my brethren of the Twelve Apostles to return to the field of my former labors in Staffordshire; which I did, leaving in London but eleven members. Since that time, my labors have been chiefly confined to the limits of the Staffordshire conference, which has, until lately, included Birmingham and Macclesfield, containing eighteen branches of the Church, 580 members having been added since the time I commenced laboring there. Many have been called to the ministry, who are faithful men, and willing to receive counsel. Although I have suffered much bodily affliction during the past year, the Lord has blessed my labors abundantly, and I can say I never enjoyed myself better in the discharge of my duty, than I have on this mission. Among the greatest blessings I have enjoyed, has been the privilege of attending four general conferences, and meeting in council with the Twelve Apostles. I can assure you that a meeting with those in whose company I have suffered so much tribulation for the Gospel's sake, both at home and abroad, by land and sea, is to me a privilege indeed. I am now preparing to return home with my brethren, according to the instructions of the First Presidency of the Church; and, as I take my leave of the Saints in this land, my prayer to God is that He will preserve His people from the hand of Satan, and prepare them for the coming Redeemer, who is near at hand.

I remain your servant for the Gospel's sake,

GEORGE A. SMITH.

Tuesday, 13.—Elder Heber C. Kimball left Manchester for Preston.

Thursday 15.

Conference in New York City.

A conference of the Church was held in New York City. Elder George W. Harris, of Nauvoo, chairman. Lucien R. Foster was elected president of the branch, and Addison Everett and George Holmes, his counselors. John M. Bernhisel was elected Bishop, and Richard Burge and William Acker his counselors. These six, having been chosen, were ordained and set apart to the several offices under the direction of Elder Harris, he having been specially appointed and authorized by President Hyrum Smith, at the Philadelphia conference, to organize more perfectly the branch in New York.

LUCIEN R. FOSTER, Secretary.

An Epistle of the Twelve Apostles to the Church of Jesus Christ of Latter-day Saints in England, Scotland, Ireland, Wales, and the Isle of Man, Greeting:

BELOVED BRETHREN:—Inasmuch as we have been laboring for some time in this country, and most of us are about to depart for the land of our nativity; and, feeling anxious for your welfare and happiness in time and in eternity, we cheerfully offer you our counsel in the closing number of the first volume of the *Star*, hoping you will peruse it when we are far away, and profit by the same.

First of all, we would express our joy and thanksgiving to Him who rules, and knows the hearts of men, for the heed and diligence with which the Saints in this county have hearkened to the counsel of those whom God has seen fit to send among them, and who hold the keys of this ministry. By this means a spirit of union, and, consequently, of power, has been generally cultivated among you. And now let the Saints remember that which we have ever taught them, both by precept and example, viz., to beware of an aspiring spirit, which would lift you up, one above another, to seek to be the greatest in the kingdom of God. This is that spirit which hurled down the angels. It is that spirit which actuates all the churches of the sectarian world, and most of the civil and military movements of the men of the world. It is that spirit which introduces rebellion, confusion, misrule, and disunion, and would, if suffered to exist among us, destroy our union, and, consequently, our power, which flows from the Spirit, through the Priesthood; which Spirit, and power, and Priesthood, can only exist with the humble and meek of the earth. Therefore, beware, O ye Priests of the Most High! lest ye are overcome by that spirit which would exalt you above your fellow-laborers, and thus hurl you down to perdition, or do much injury to the cause of God.

Be careful to respect, not the eloquence, not the smooth speeches, not the multitude of words, not the talents of men, but the offices which God has placed in the Church. Let the members hearken to their officers, let the Priests, Teachers, and Deacons hearken to the Elders, and let the Elders hearken to the presiding officers of each church or conference, and let all the churches and conferences hearken to the counsel of those who are still left in this country to superintend the affairs of the Church; and, by so doing, a spirit of union will be preserved, and peace and prosperity will attend the people of God.

We have seen fit to appoint our beloved brethren and fellow-laborers, Levi Richards and Lorenzo Snow to travel from conference to conference, and to assist Brother Pratt in the general superintendency of the Church in this country. These are men of experience and soundness of principle, in whose counsel the Church may place entire confidence, as long as they uphold them by the prayer of faith.

The spirit of emigration has actuated the children of men, from the time our first parents were expelled from the garden until now. It was this spirit that first peopled the plains of Shinar, and all other places; yes, it was emigration that first broke upon the death-like silence and loneliness of an empty earth, and caused the desolate land to teem with life, and the desert to smile with joy. It was emigration that first peopled England, once a desolate island, on which the foot of man had never trod, but now abounding in towns and cities. It was emigration that turned the wilds of America into a fruitful field, and besprinkled the wilderness with flourishing towns and cities, where a few years since the war hoop of the savage, or the howl of the wild beasts was heard in the distance. In short, it is emigration that is the only effectual remedy for the evils which now afflict the over-peopled countries of Europe. With this view of the subject, the Saints, as well as thousands of others, seem to be actuated with the spirit of enterprise and emigration, and as some of them are calculating to emigrate to America, and settle in the colonies of our brethren, we would here impart a few words of counsel on the subject of emigration.

It will be necessary, in the first place, for men of capital to go on first and make large purchases of land, and erect mills, machinery, manufactories, &c., so that the poor who go from this country can find employment. Therefore, it is not wisdom for the poor to flock to that place extensively, until the necessary preparations are made. Neither is it wisdom for those who feel a spirit of benevolence to expend all their means in helping others to emigrate, and thus all arrive in a new country empty-handed. In all settlements there must be capital and labor united, in order to flourish. The brethren will recollect that they are not going to enter upon cities already built up, but are going to "build cities and inhabit them." Building cities cannot be done without means and labor. On this subject we would call the particular attention of the Saints to the Epistle, and also to the proclamation signed by the First Presidency of the Church, published in the eleventh number of this work (the *Star*), and would earnestly exhort them to observe the order and instructions there given.

We would also exhort the Saints not to go in haste, nor by flight, but to prepare all things in a proper manner before they emigrate; and especially in regard to their dealings with the world, let them be careful to settle everything honestly, as becometh Saints, as far as lies in their power, and not go away in debt, so far as they have the means to pay. And if any go away in debt, because they have not the means to pay, let it be with the design of paying as industry shall put it in their power, so that the cause of truth be not evil spoken of.

We have found that there are so many "pick-pockets," and so many that will take every possible advantage of strangers in Liverpool, that we have appointed Elder Amos Fielding as the agent of the Church, to superintend the fitting out of the Saints from Liverpool to America.

Whatever information the Saints may want about the preparation for a voyage, they are advised to call on Elder Fielding at Liverpool, as their first movement when they arrive there as emigrants. There are some brethren who have felt themselves competent to do their own business in these matters and, rather despising the counsel of their friends, have been robbed and cheated out of nearly all they had. A word of caution to the wise is sufficient. It is also a great saving to go in companies, instead of going individually.

First, a company can charter a vessel, so as to make the passage much cheaper than otherwise.

Secondly, provisions can be purchased at wholesale, for a company, much cheaper than otherwise.

Thirdly, this will avoid bad company on the passage.

Fourthly, when a company arrives at New Orleans they can charter a steamboat, so as to reduce the passage near one-half. This measure will save some hundreds of pounds on each ship load.

Fifthly, a man of experience can go as leader of each company, who will know how to avoid rogues and knaves.

Sovereigns are more profitable than silver or any other money, in emigrating to America; and the brethren are also cautioned against the American money, when they arrive in that country. Let them not venture to take paper money of that country, until they become well informed in regard to the different banks, for very few of them will pass current very far from the place where they are issued, and banks are breaking almost daily.

It is much cheaper going by New Orleans than by New York; but it will never do for emigrants to go by New Orleans in the summer, on account of the heat and sickness of the climate. It is, therefore, advisable for the Saints to emigrate in autumn, winter, or spring.

Let the Saints be careful also to obtain a letter of recommendation, from the Elders where they are acquainted, to the brethren where they are going, certifying their membership; and let the Elders be careful not to recommend any who do not conduct themselves as Saints; and especially those who would go with a design to defraud their creditors.

In regard to ordaining and licensing officers, each conference is now organized under the care of their respective presidents, who, with the voice of the Church, may ordain, according to the gifts and callings of God, by the Holy Spirit, and under the general superintendence of Elders Pratt, Richards, and Snow. Licenses should be signed by the presiding officers.

There are many other items of importance, which we would gladly mention, had we time and space sufficient; but this must suffice for the present; and may the God of our fathers bless you all with wisdom and grace to act each your part in the great work which lies before you, that the world may be warned, and thousands brought to the knowledge of the truth; and may He bless and preserve you blameless until the day of His coming. Brethren and sisters, pray for us.

We remain, your brethren in the new and everlasting covenant,

BRIGHAM YOUNG,
HEBER C. KIMBALL,
ORSON HYDE,
PARLEY P. PRATT,
ORSON PRATT,
WILLARD RICHARDS,
WILFORD WOODRUFF,
JOHN TAYLOR,
GEO. A. SMITH.

Manchester, April 15, 1841.

Elders Brigham Young, Orson Pratt, Wilford Woodruff, George A. Smith, and Levi Richards went from Manchester to Liverpool to attend a tea-party at the Music Hall.

DIFFERENCE BETWEEN THE BAPTIST AND LATTER-DAY SAINTS, FROM THE "NORTH STAFFORDSHIRE MERCURY."

SIR:—In a late publication, you reported the case of some persons who were taken before T. B. Ross, Esq., for disturbing a congregation of Latter-day Saints, or believers in the "Book of Mormon." A teacher of that sect,on being asked by the magistrate wherein they differed from the Baptists, replied, "In the laying on of hands;" but declined making an honest confession of those peculiarities which separate them as widely from the Baptists, as from every other denomination of the Christian church. This was certainly prudent; but as the Baptists feel themselves dishonored by such an alliance, they would be unjust to themselves were they to leave unanswered such a libel upon their denomination. the following very prominent marks of difference will enable your readers to judge for themselves.

1. The Saints admit all persons indiscriminately to baptism, encouraging them to pass through that rite, with the promise that great spiritual improvement will follow. They baptize for remission of sins, without waiting for creditable evidence of repentance for sin. But the Baptists admit none to that ordinance who do not exhibit this qualification in the most satisfactory manner; and if they found a candidate looking to the water of baptism as having virtue to cleanse him from sin, he would be put back until better instructed.

2. After baptism the Saints kneel down, and their Priest, laying on his hands, professes to give them the Holy Ghost. If effects similar to those produced by the laying on of the Apostles' hands were seen to follow, scepticism must yield to the force of such evidence; but in their case no such effects are produced; the baptized sinner is a sinner still, though flattered and deluded with the epithet "Latter-day Saint." The Baptists regard such mummery with as much disgust as all Christians do.

3. Having, as they suppose, the extraordinary gifts of the Spirit, the Saints consistently pretend to have the power of working wonders, and profess to heal the sick with holy oil; also to the power of prophecy. As most moral evils bring with them their own remedy, these lofty pretensions will ruin them in due time, by opening the eyes of the most deluded, as in the case of the countless sects of impostors who have appeared upon the stage before them. It need not be added, that the Baptists stand far removed from such conceits, and have no part in them.

4. Not satisfied with the Bible as a complete revelation from God, the "Latter-day Saints" have adopted a romance, written in America, as a fresh revelation, and have added a trashy volume of 600 pages to that book, which we are forbidden to add to, or take from, under the most awful penalties! But even this is not enough for their impious presumption. They have published a monthly magazine, in which "new revelations" are served up fresh, as they arrive, for the use of all who can swallow them. The disgust with which the Baptists regard such a melancholy exhibition of human folly and wickedness, separates them to an impassable distance from such people.

5. In order to carry on this order of things, the Latter-day Saints have appointed two Priesthoods. "The Lesser, or Aaronic Priesthood, is to hold the keys of the ministering of angels, and to administer in outward ordinances. The power and authority of the higher, or Melchisedek Priesthood, is to hold the keys of all the spiritual blessings of the Church—to have the privilege of receiving the mysteries of the kingdom of heaven—to have the heavens opened to them—to commune with the general assembly and Church of the First-born; and to enjoy the communion and presence of God the Father, and of Jesus the Mediator of the new covenant," (see page 13). So that, in this wonderful Priesthood, they have provided for an ample supply of new things, in endless variety, and without end, from the hands of wretched men, who blasphemously aspire to a dignity which belongs alone to Him who is the only "Priest forever after the order of Melchisedek."

The fear of trespassing upon your valuable columns, Mr. Editor, prevents my enlarging upon these and very many other points of difference; but enough has been done to show your readers, that no two sects can differ more widely from each other, than the Baptists and the Latter day Saints; and that to confound them in any way together is not only unjust to the former, but involves them in the disgrace of being partakers in a bold imposition, or a pitiable delusion, which they regard with equal abhorrence and disgust.

A BAPTIST.

Hanley, Feb. 16, 1841.

The foregoing article attempts to show the difference between the Baptists and Latter-day Saints. We will now attempt to show the difference between the Baptists and Former-day Saints.

THE DIFFERENCE BETWEEN THE BAPTISTS AND THE FORMER-DAY SAINTS.

1st. The Former-day Saints baptized *for remission of sins*, Acts ii: 38. The Baptists baptize those only who are supposed to have their sins forgiven before they are baptized.

2nd. The Former-day Saints admitted all persons indiscriminately to baptism, as soon as they professed faith and repentance, encouraging them to pass through that rite, with the promise that great spiritual improvement would follow, Acts ii: 38-41 inclusive. But if the Baptists found the penitent believer looking for remission of sins through that rite, they would be put back to "get religion" where they could find it.

3rd. After baptism, the Former-day Saints prayed for, and laid hands on the disciples in the name of Jesus, and professed to give them the Holy Ghost, Acts viii: 17, also Acts xix: 6. The Baptists say, "They regard such mummery with as much disgust as all Christians do."

4th. Having, as they supposed, the extraordinary gifts of the Spirit, the Former-day Saints consistently pretended to have the power of working wonders, and professed to heal the sick with holy oil; James v: 14, 15. Also to the power of prophecy; First Corinthians from 12th to 14th chapter. It need not be added that the Baptists stand far removed from "such conceits," and have no part in them; nor in anything partaining to the gifts and power of God: or, to use the Apostle's own words, "they have a form of godliness, denying the power."

5th. Not satisfied with the Bible as a complete revelation from God, the Former-day Saints have added a volume of several hundred pages (the New Testament), to that book, which (according to Baptist logic)

Moses forbid them to add to, or take from; but new revelations were served up almost daily, fresh as they arrived, for all those who could swallow them. "The disgust with which the Baptists regard such things, considering them but a melancholy exhibition of human folly and wickedness," separates them to an impassable distance from the Former-day Saints; and how, with all these differences, the Baptists should ever have been thought, by themselves, or anybody else, to be the Church of Christ, is difficult to imagine!

6th. In order to carry on their strange work, or order of things, the Former-day Saints had two Priesthoods. The Aaronic Priesthood administered in outward ordinances, as in the case of John the Baptist. The power and authority of the higher, or Melchisedek Priesthood, was to hold the keys of all the spiritual blessing of the Church, as Jesus said, "I give unto thee the keys of the kingdom of heaven—whatsoever thou shalt bind on earth shall be bound in heaven," &c. They were to have the privilege of knowing the mysteries of the kingdom of heaven. "To you it is given to know the mysteries of the kingdom"—to have the heavens opened unto them—to commune with the general assembly and Church of the First born; and to enjoy the communion and presence of God the Father, and of Jesus the Mediator of the new covenant; Heb. xii: 22, 23, 24. So that in this wonderful Priesthood, they have provided for an ample supply of new things, in endless variety, and without end, from those who are and were counted the off-scouring of all things; and who, as the Baptists would insinuate, "did aspire to a dignity," which they say, "Belongs alone to Him who is the only Priest forever after the order of Melchisedek."

The fear of trespassing upon the time and patience of our readers, prevents our enlarging upon these and many other points of difference; but enough has been said to show, that no two sects can possibly differ more widely from each other than do the Baptists and Former-day Saints, and to amalgamate the two systems in any way is not only an act of injustice—but would involve the Baptists, who by the way are an honorable body, in the disgrace of that sect which was "everywhere spoken against." See Acts 28:23.

CHAPTER XIX.

ORGANIZATION OF THE NAUVOO LEGION—NOTABLE PERSONS AT NAUVOO—THE PROPHET'S SERMON ON INDIVIDUAL RESPONSIBILITY FOR SIN AND THE DOCTRINE OF ELECTION.

Tuesday, 20.—Elders Brigham Young, Heber C. Kimball, Orson Pratt, Wilford Woodruff, John Taylor, George A. Smith and Willard Richards and family, went on board of the ship *Rochester*, at Liverpool, Captain Woodhouse (who delayed his sailing two days, to accommodate the Elders), bound for New York with a company of 130 Saints.

The Twelve Embark for Home.

Elder Parley P. Pratt tarried in England to preside over the Church, and continue the publication of the *Millennial Star*, and Elder Hyde to pursue his mission to Jerusalem.

Mr. James Robinson, Assessor for the City of Nauvoo, died, aged 30. He had resided in this county many years, and for his business habits and kind disposition, he was highly respected.

Wednesday, 21.—The *Rochester* sailed.

Saturday, 24.—The High Council of Iowa selected David Pettigrew and Moses Nickerson Counselors to President John Smith, in place of Reynolds Cahoon and Lyman Wight, removed by appointment; James Emmett in the place of David Pettigrew in the High Council, Joseph C. Kingsbury in place of George W. Pitkin, removed to Nauvoo, and William Clayton in place of Erastus Snow, absent.

Changes in the Iowa Stake.

Monday, 26.—I attended the City Council. Several members being absent, I moved that the Marshall be ordered to enforce the attendance of Aldermen and Councillors, at one o'clock on Saturday next, and Council adjourned.

Wednesday, 28.—The ship *Rochester* encountered a tempest, shipped a heavy sea, Wilford Woodruff got thoroughly drenched; Willard Richards escaped under the bulwarks.

Saturday, May 1.—Elder Robert B. Thompson became associate editor of the *Times and Seasons.*

The first Regiment, first cohort of the Nauvoo Legion, consisting of four companies, was organized, and Captain George Miller was elected colonel; Captain Stephen Markham, lieutenant-colonel, and Captain William Wightman, major.

Organization of the Legion.

The first regiment, second cohort, consisting of four companies, was also organized, and Captain Charles C. Rich was elected colonel, Captain Titus Billings, lieutenant-colonel, and Captain John Scott, major.

Also the second regiment, second cohort, consisting of four companies, was organized, and Captain Francis M. Higbee was elected colonel; Captain Nelson Higgins, lieutenant-colonel, and Aaron H. Golden, major.

I attended the City Council, and moved that the sympathies of the Council be tendered to the relatives of James Robinson, deceased, the late assessor and collector for the city, which was carried.

I also moved that a new burying ground be procured, outside the city limits, and purchased at the expense of the corporation; which was carried; and Alderman Daniel H. Wells, and Councillors Wilson Law and John T. Barnett were appointed a committee, and ten acres were ordered to be purchased.

New Burying Ground for Nauvoo.

I spoke at length on the rights and privileges of the owners of the ferry, showing that the City Council has no right to take away ferry privileges, once granted, without damages being paid to the proprietor; and also moved that an ordinance be passed to protect citizens killing dogs running at large, which were set upon cattle or hogs, or molest individuals. And also spoke on other subjects before the council.

Sunday, 2.—The Teachers' quorum was organized in Nauvoo, Elisha Averett, President, James Hendricks and James W. Huntsman, Counselors.

Tuesday, 4.—

Nauvoo Legion Affairs.

HEADQUARTERS, NAUVOO LEGION, CITY OF NAUVOO, ILLINOIS, May 4, 1841.

General Orders. Pursuant to an act of the Court Martial, the troops attached or belonging to the Legion will parade at the place of general rendezvous, in the City of Nauvoo, for drill, review and inspection, on Saturday, the 3rd day of July, at half-past nine o'clock a. m., armed and equipped according to law. At ten o'clock the line will be formed and the general officers conducted to their posts, under a fire of artillery. The commandants of the 1st and 2nd companies, 2nd battalion, 1st regiment, 2nd cohort, are directed to enroll every man residing within the bounds of their respective commands, and not attached to any other company of the Legion, between the ages of eighteen and forty-five years, and notify them of their attachment to the service, and their legal liabilities.

As will be seen by the following legal opinion of Judge Douglas, of the Supreme Court of the State of Illinois, than whom no man stands more deservedly high in the public estimation, as an able and profound jurist, politician and statesman; the officers and privates, belonging to the Legion, are exempt from all military duty, not required by the legally constituted authorities thereof. They are, therefore, expressly inhibited from performing any military services, not ordered by the general officers, or directed by the court martial:

CITY OF NAUVOO, ILLINOIS, May 3, 1841.

General Bennett:

DEAR SIR.—In reply to your request, I have examined so much of the Nauvoo City Charter, and Legislative Acts, as relate to the "Nauvoo Legion," and am clearly of opinion, that any citizen of Hancock county, who may attach himself to the Nauvoo Legion, has all the privileges that appertain to which independent military body, and is exempt from all other military duty, as provided in the 25th section of the City Charter; and cannot, therefore, be fined by any military or civil court, for neglecting or refusing to parade with any other military body, or under the command of any officers who are not attached to said Legion. The language of the laws upon this subject, is so plain and specific as to admit of no doubt as to its true meaning and intent. I do not consider it necessary, therefore, to enter into an argument to prove a position which is evident from an inspection of the laws themselves.

I am very respectfully, your friend,

S. A. DOUGLAS.

The Legion is not, as has been falsely represented by its enemies, exclusively a "Mormon" military association, but a body of citizen soldiers, organized (without regard to political preferences or religious sentiments) for the public defense, the general good, and the preservation of law and order—to save the innocent, unoffending citizens from the iron grasp of the oppressor and perpetuate and sustain our free institutions against misrule, anarchy, and mob violence; no other views are entertained or tolerated. The general parades of the Legion will be in the City of Nauvoo, but all other musters will be within the bounds of the respective companies, battalions, regiments and cohorts.

The 8th section of "An Act for the Organization and Government of the Militia of this State," in force July 2, 1833, provides that "when any person shall enroll himself in a volunteer company, he shall forthwith give notice in writing to the commanding officer of the company in which he was enrolled," &c., and that the commanding officer of a regiment or battalion, may, in a certain contingency, "dissolve such company;" and some of the petty, ignorant, and imprudent militia officers maintain that such is still the law; but those blind leaders of the blind are informed that the 11th section of "An Act Encouraging Volunteer Companies," approved March 2, 1837, reads as follows: "So much of the 8th section of an Act entitled, "An Act for the Organization and Government of the Militia of this State," in force July 2, 1833, as requires a volunteer to give notice in writing to the commanding officer of the company in which he was enrolled, and authorizes commandants of regiments to disband independent companies, be and the same is hereby repealed."

If officers act upon the obsolete laws of the "little book" which have been repealed, years since, it will be sweet to the taste, but "make the belly bitter;" and should any civil or military officer attempt to enforce the collection of any military fines upon the members of the Legion, excepting when such fines are assessed by the court martial of the Legion, such persons are directed to apply to the master in chancery, for Hancock county, for an injunction to stay the illegal proceedings.

The militia companies of Hancock county, and citizens generally, are respectfully invited to unite with the Legion, and partake of its privileges.

All officers are required to enforce the most rigid discipline on all days of public parade.

Persons holding enrolling orders are directed to act with energy; consummate their trust, and make prompt returns to the office of the Major-General.

The Lieutenant-General desires that all his friends should attach themselves to some company, either in the first or second cohort. This will enable them to receive correct military instruction, under the teachings of experienced officers, according to the drill and discipline of the United States army—and qualify them for efficient service in the cause of their beloved country and state, in the hour of peril.

The eleven companies of minute men will, at all times, hold themselves in readiness to execute the laws, as originally instructed by the general officers.

The officers and troops of the Legion are directed to treat with proper respect and decorum, all other officers and troops in the service of this state, or of the United States.

Officers are ordered to treat their troops with marked respect; and, while they discharge their duties with promptitude and boldness as officers, they must not forget or neglect to observe the requisites of gentlemen.

The second company (light infantry), 1st battalion, 1st regiment, 2nd cohort; and the 1st company (lancers), 1st battalion, 3rd regiment, 2nd cohort of the Legion, will act as an escort for the reception of such visiting companies from Illinois and Iowa, as may be present. Should the Governor be present, it will be announced by a fire of artillery, by the 1st and 2nd companies, 1st battalion, 1st regiment, 1st cohort, and the 1st company, 1st battalion, 1st regiment, 2nd cohort, when he will be received by the entire Legion, with the honors due so conspicuous a personage as the Commander-in-Chief of the forces of the state.

Officers, receiving copies of these orders, will promulgate the same without delay, throughout the bounds of their respective commands.

JOSEPH SMITH, Lieutenant-General.

Letter of the Prophet to the "Times and Seasons"—Visit of Notable Persons to Nauvoo.

CITY OF NAUVOO, May 6, 1841.

To the Editors of the "Times and Seasons:"

GENTLEMEN:—I wish, through the medium of your paper, to make known that, on Sunday last, I had the honor of receiving a visit from the Hon. Stephen A. Douglas, Justice of the Supreme Court, and Judge of the Fifth Judicial Circuit of the state of Illinois, and Cyrus Walker,

Esq., of Macomb, who expressed great pleasure in visiting our city, and were astonished at the improvements which were made. They were officially introduced to the congregation who had assembled on the meeting ground, by the mayor; and they severally addressed the assembly.

Judge Douglas expressed his satisfaction of what he had seen and heard respecting our people, and took that opportunity of returning thanks to the citizens of Nauvoo, for conferring upon him the freedom of the city; stating that he was not aware of rendering us any service sufficiently important to deserve such marked honor; and likewise spoke in high terms of our location and the improvements we had made, and that our enterprise and industry were highly creditable to us, indeed.

Mr. Walker spoke much in favor of the place, the industry of the citizens, &c.,and hoped they would continue to enjoy all the blessings and privileges of our free and glorious Constitution, and, as a patriot and a freeman, he was willing, at all times, to stand boldly in defense of liberty and law.

It must indeed be satisfactory to this community to know that kind and generous feelings exist in the hearts of men of such high reputation and moral and intellectual worth.

Judge Douglas has ever proved himself friendly to this people, and interested himself to obtain for us our several chartes, holding at that time the office of Secretary of State.

Mr. Walker also ranks high, and has long held a standing at the bar, which few attain, and is considered one of the most able and profound jurists in the state.

The sentiments they expressed on the occasion were highly honorable to them as American citizens, and as gentlemen. How different their conduct from that of the official characters in the state of Missouri, whose minds were prejudiced to such an extent that, instead of mingling in our midst and ascertaining for themselves our character, kept entirely aloof, but were ready, at all times, to listen to those who had the "poison of adders under their tongues," and who sought our overthrow.

Let every person who may have imbibed sentiments prejudicial to us, imitate the honorable example of our distinguished visitors (Douglas and Walker), and I believe they will find much less to condemn than they anticipated, and probably a great deal to commend.

What makes the late visit more pleasing, is the fact that Messrs. Douglas and Walker have long been held in high estimation as politicians, being champions of the two great parties that exist in the state; but laying aside all party strife, like brothers, citizens, and friends, they mingle with us, mutually disposed to extend to us that courtesy, respect, and friendship, which I hope we shall ever be proud to reciprocate.

I am, very respectfully, yours, &c.,

JOSEPH SMITH.

Saturday, 8.—Brother William Smith is preaching in Pennsylvania.

Accounts of the progress of the Gospel from the Elders abroad are very encouraging.

A magazine of 300 barrels of gunpowder, at Fort Moultrie, South Carolina, exploded, blowing the fort, seven other buildings, and forty persons to atoms.

Wednesday, 12.—The *Rochester*, with the Elders, came in sight of Cape Sable, Nova Scotia.

Saturday, 15.—Good news has recently reached us from Tennessee, New York, Upper Canada, and New Orleans. The Elders are baptizing in all directions.

Sunday, 16.—I addressed the Saints. The following is a sketch of my sermon by the editor of the *Times and Seasons:*

THE PROPHET'S DISCOURSE.

At 10 o'clock a. m., a large concourse of the Saints assembled on the meeting ground, and were addressed by President Joseph Smith, who spoke at considerable length.

He commenced his observations by remarking that the kindness of our Heavenly Father called for our heartfelt gratitude. He then observed that Satan was generally blamed for the evils which we did, but if he was the cause of all our wickedness, men could not be condemned. The devil could not compel mankind to do evil; all was voluntary. Those who resisted the Spirit of God, would be liable to be led into temptation, and then the association of heaven would be withdrawn from those who refused to be made partakers of such great glory. God would not exert any compulsory means, and the devil could not; and such ideas as were entertained [on these subjects] by many were absurd. The creature was made subject to vanity, not willingly, but Christ subjected the same in hope—all are subjected to vanity while they travel through the crooked paths and difficulties which surround them. Where is the man that is free from vanity? None ever were perfect but Jesus; and why was He perfect? Because He was the Son of God, and had the fullness of the Spirit, and greater power than any man. But notwithstanding their vanity, men look forward with hope (because they are "subjected in hope") to the time of their deliverance.

The speaker then made some observations on the first principles of the Gospel, observing, that many of the Saints who had come from different states and nations had only a very superficial knowledge of these principles, not having heard them fully investigated.

He then briefly stated the principles of faith, repentance, and baptism for the remission of sins, these were believed by some of the righteous societies of the day, but the doctrine of laying on of hands for the gift of the Holy Ghost was discarded by them.

The speaker then referred to the 6th capter of Hebrews, 1st and 2nd verses. "Not laying again the foundation of repentance from dead works," &c., but of the doctrines of baptisms, laying on of hands, the resurrection, and eternal judgment, &c. That the doctrine of eternal judgment was perfectly understood by the Apostles, is evident from several passages of Scripture. Peter preached repentance and baptism for the remission of sins to the Jews who had been led to acts of violence and blood by their leaders; but to the rulers he said, "I would that through ignorance ye did it, as did also those ye ruled." "Repent, therefore, and be converted, that your sins may be blotted out, when the times of refreshing (redemption) shall come from the presence of the Lord, for He shall send Jesus Christ, who before was preached unto you," &c. The time of redemption here had reference to the time when Christ should come; then, and not till then, would their sins be blotted out. Why? Because they were murderers, and no murderer hath eternal life. Even David must wait for those times of refreshing, before he can come forth and his sins be blotted out. For Peter, speaking of him says, "David hath not yet ascended into heaven, for his sepulchre is with us to this day." His remains were then in the tomb. Now, we read that many bodies of the Saints arose at Christ's resurrection, probably all the Saints, but it seems that David did not. Why? Because he had been a murderer. If the ministers of religion had a proper understanding of the doctrine of eternal judgment, they would not be found attending the man who forfeited his life to the injured laws of his country, by shedding innocent blood; for such characters cannot be forgiven, until they have paid the last farthing. The prayers of all the ministers in the world can never close the gates of hell against a murderer.

He then spoke on the subject of election, and read the 9th chapter of Romans, from which it was evident that the election there spoken of was pertaining to the flesh, and had reference to the seed of Abraham, according to the promise God made to Abraham, saying, "In thee, and in thy seed, all the families of the earth shall be blessed." To them belonged the adoption and the covenants, &c. Paul said, when he saw their unbelief, "I wish myself accursed"—according to the flesh—not according to the spirit. Why did God say to Pharaoh, "For this cause have I raised thee up"? Because Pharaoh was a fit instrument—a wicked man, and had committed acts of cruelty of the most atrocious nature. The election of the promised seed still continues, and in the last day, they shall have the Priesthood restored unto them, and they shall be the "saviors on Mount Zion," the ministers of our God; if it were not for the remnant which was left, then might men now be as Sodom and Gomorrah. The whole of the chapter had reference to the Priesthood and the house of Israel; and unconditional election of individuals to eternal life was not taught by the Apostles. God did elect or predestinate, that all those who would be saved, should be saved in Christ Jesus, and through obedience to the Gospel; but He passes over no man's sins, but visits them with correction, and if His children will not repent of their sins He will discard them.

This is an imperfect sketch of a very interesting discourse, which occupied more than two hours in delivery, and was listened to with marked attention, by the vast assembly present.

In the afternoon the assembly was addressed by President Hyrum Smith.

Minutes of a Conference in London.

Conference met in London pursuant to adjournment.

Elder Orson Hyde (of the Twelve Apostles) Lorenzo Snow, George J. Adams (High Priest), two Elders, several Priests, Teachers, and Deacons, with a respectable company of members present.

Elder Snow represented the London branch, consisting of 74 members, and good prospect for increase. The branch at Bedford, represented by George J. Adams, consisted of 68 member, 8 Priests, 1 Teacher. John Griffith, Priest, represented the branch at Woolwich, consisted of 6 members. Elder John Bourne, who was sent to labor at Ipswich, was obliged to leave, there being no prospect of success, and the brethren refusing to entertain him, so that he had to sleep on the ground. In consequence of this the conference passed a resolution condemnatory of their conduct.

Arrival of *Rochester* at New York.

Wednesday, 19.—The *Rochester* arrived at quarantine ground, New York, after a toilsome passage. At one time they were beset with head winds and a tedious storm, when the Twelve Apostles united in prayer, the storm abated, the sea became calm, and they went on their way rejoicing.

The following is copied from the *Times and Seasons:*

THE HEALING OF ONE WHO WAS DEAF.

BATAVIA, N. Y., May 19, 1841.

To the Saints scattered abroad, and to all whom it may concern, greeting:

Be it known that on or about the first of December last, we, J. Shamp and Margaret Shamp, of the town of Batavia, Gennesee county, N. Y., had a daughter that had been deaf and dumb four and a half years, and was restored to her hearing, the time aforesaid, by the laying on of the hands of the Elders (Nathan R. Knight and Charles Thompson) of the Church of Jesus Christ of Latter-day Saints, commonly called Mormons, through the power of Almighty God, and faith in the Lord Jesus Christ, as believed and practiced by them in these last days.

[Signed] J. SHAMP,
M. SHAMP.

Several other instances of healing are mentioned by Brother Shamp; and such things are common in the Church at this day, according to the faith of the Saints.

Rowdyism in New York Harbor.

Thursday, 20.—The Twelve Apostles arrived at the dock in New York about four o'clock p. m., but were prevented from landing by the carters and rowdies, until late in the evening. Such is the confusion in New York on the arrival of a ship, steamboat, or coach, that strangers may well suppose the city is without mayor, marshal, police, or any other officer, to keep the peace.

Mob Violence in England.

Elder A. Cordon attempted to speak several times at Swan Village, near Birmingham, England, but was interrupted by a mob. Several of the Saints were struck with stones, but none of them seriously hurt.

Friday, 21.—I attended City Council, and moved that Parley Street be opened and improved to the state road.

Conference in Kirtland.

Saturday, 22.—A conference was held at Kirtland, Ohio, Elder Almon W. Babbitt presiding. Elder Babbitt was elected president of that stake, and Lester Brooks and Zebedee Coltrin his counselors. Thomas Burdick was elected Bishop of Kirtland, and Hiram Winters and Reuben McBride his counselors. Hiram Kellogg was elected president of the High Priests' quorum, and Amos Babcock, president of the Elders' quorum. By-laws were adopted for the preservation of the Lord's House.

Sunday, *23*.—The Twelve addressed the Saints at the Columbian Hall, Grand Street, New York.

Monday, *24*.

LETTER OF THE PRESIDENCY TO THE SAINTS—CONCENTRATION AT NAUVOO.

To the Saints abroad—

The First Presidency of the Church of Jesus Christ of Latter-day Saints, anxious to promote the prosperity of said Church, feel it their duty to call upon the Saints who reside out of this county [Hancock], to make preparations to come in without delay. This is important, and should be attended to by all who feel an interest in the prosperity of this corner-stone of Zion. Here the Temple must be raised, the University built, and other edifices erected which are necessary for the great work of the last days, and which can only be done by a concentration of energy and enterprise. Let it, therefore, be understood, that all the stakes, excepting those in this county, and in Lee county, Iowa, are discontinued, and the Saints instructed to settle in this county as soon as circumstances will permit.

JOSEPH SMITH, President.

City of Nauvoo, Hancock county,
Illinois, May 24, 1841.

Tuesday, *25*.

Legion Affairs.

HEADQUARTERS NAUVOO LEGION,
CITY OF NAUVOO, ILLINOIS, May 25, 1841.

General Orders—The 1st company (riflemen) 1st battalion, 2nd regiment, 2nd cohort, will be attached to the escort, contemplated in the general orders of the 4th inst., for the 3rd of July next. See p. 354.

In forming the Legion, the adjutant will observe the rank of companies in the order they are named, to-wit—1st cohort; flying artillery lancers, visiting companies of dragoons, cavalry, lancers, riflemen. Second cohort: artillery, lancers, riflemen, light infantry, infantry. Visiting companies in their appropriate places on the right of the troops of their own grade.

The ranking company of the 1st cohort will be formed on the right of said cohort; and the ranking company of the 2nd cohort will be formed on the left of said cohort; the next on the left of the right, the next on the right of the left, and so on to the center.

The escort will be formed on the right of the forces.

JOSEPH SMITH, Lieutenant-General.

Wednesday, *26*.—Elder Lorenzo Snow writes from London, that the Church there numbers 74 members, having baptized 18 since his return from Manchester conference, and that Elder Orson Hyde was at the London conference on the 16th instant.

Elder Joseph Fielding was at the Isle of Man.

Thursday, *27*.—Elders Willard Richards, Wilford Woodruff, George A. Smith, and John M. Bernhisel visited the shipping and principal buildings in New York.

Sir Hugh Gough being about to storm Canton with the British forces, the Chinese agreed to pay a ransom of $6,000,000.

Monday, *31*.—Elder Brigham Young visited the Saints on Long Island.

CHAPTER XX.

ARREST OF THE PROPHET ON DEMAND OF MISSOURI—TRIAL AT MONMOUTH THE ACQUITTAL.

Tuesday, June 1, 1841.—I accompanied my brother Hyrum and William Law, as far as Quincy, on their mission to the East.

Elder Sidney Rigdon has been ordained a Prophet, Seer, and Revelator.

Elder Brigham Young returned from Long Island to New York, Elder Willard Richards started to Richmond, Massachusetts with his family and Elder Wilford Woodruff to Portland, Maine.

Friday, 4.—Elders Young, Kimball and Taylor left New York for Nauvoo, by way of Philadelphia, Pittsburgh, and St. Louis. Geo. A. Smith, and Reuben Hedlock started at the same time, and went to New Egypt, New Jersey.

I called on Governor Carlin, at his residence in Quincy.

The Prophet's Visit with Governor Carlin.

During my visit with the Governor, I was treated with the greatest kindness and respect; nothing was said about any requisition having come from the Governor of Missouri for my arrest. In a very few hours after I had left the Governor's residence he sent Thomas King, Sheriff of Adams county, Thomas Jasper, a constable of Quincy, and some others as a posse, with an officer from Missouri, to arrest me and deliver me up to the authorities of Missouri.

Saturday, 5.—While I was staying at Heberlin's Hotel,

Bear Creek, about twenty-eight miles south of Nauvoo, Sheriff King and posse arrested me. Some of the posse on learning the spirit of the officer from Missouri, left the company in disgust and returned to their own homes. I accordingly returned to Quincy and obtained a writ of *habeas corpus* from Charles A. Warren, Esq., Master in Chancery; and Judge Stephen A. Douglas happening to come to Quincy that evening, he appointed to give a hearing on the writ on the Tuesday following, in Monmouth, Warren county, where the court would then commence a regular term.

The Arrest of the Prophet

Elders William Smith, and George A. Smith attended a meeting in the woods near New Egypt, New Jersey, and preached to a large assembly; also preached on Sunday 6th, and three were baptized; and after preaching on the 7th four more were baptized.

Apostles in New Jersey.

Sunday, *6*.—News of my arrest having arrived in Nauvoo last night, and being circulated through the city, Hosea Stout, Tarleton Lewis, William A. Hickman, John S. Higbee, Elijah Able, Uriel C. Nickerson, and George W. Clyde started from the Nauvoo landing, in a skiff in order to overtake me and rescue me, if necessary. They had a heavy head wind, but arrived in Quincy at dusk; went up to Benjamin Jones's house, and found that I had gone to Nauvoo in charge of two officers.

News of the Prophet's Arrest Reaches Nauvoo.

I returned to Nauvoo in charge of the officers (Sheriff King had been suddenly seized with sickness; I nursed and waited upon him in my own house, so that he might be able to go to Monmouth), and notified several of my friends to get ready and accompany me the next morning.

Monday, *7*.—I started very early for Monmouth, seventy-five miles distant (taking Mr. King along with me and attending him during his sickness), accompanied by Charles C. Rich, Amasa Lyman, Shadrack Roundy, Reynolds Cahoon, Charles Hopkins, Alfred Randall, Elias Higbee, Morris Phelps, John P. Greene, Henry G. Sherwood, Joseph Younger, Darwin Chase, Ira Miles, Joel S. Miles, Lucien Woodworth, Vinson Knight, Robert B. Thompson, George Miller and others. We traveled very late, camping about midnight in the road.

The Prophet at Monmouth.

Tuesday, 8.—Arrived at Monmouth and procured breakfast at the tavern; found great excitement prevailing in the public mind, and great curiosity was manifested by the citizens who were extremely anxious to obtain a sight of the Prophet, expecting to see me in chains. Mr. King, (whose health was now partly restored) had considerable difficulty in protecting me from the mob that had gathered there. Mr. Sidney A. Little, for the defense, moved "That the case of Mr. Smith should be taken up," but was objected to by the States' Attorney, *pro tem.*, on account of his not being prepared, not having had sufficient notice of the trial. By mutual consent it was accordingly postponed until Wednesday morning.

In the evening, great excitement prevailed, and the citizens employed several attorneys to plead against me.

I was requested to preach to the citizens of Monmouth; but as I was a prisoner, I kept closeted in my room, for I could not even come down stairs to my meals, but the people would be crowding the windows to get a peep at me, and therefore appointed Elder Amasa Lyman to preach in the Court House on Wednesday evening.

The Trial.

Wednesday, 9.—At an early hour the Court House was filled with spectators desirous to hear the proceedings.

Mr. Morrison, on behalf of the people, wished for time to send to Springfield for the indictment, it not being found with the rest of the papers. This course would have delayed the proceedings, and, as it was not important to the issue, the attorneys for the defense admitted that there was an indictment, so that the investigation might proceed.

Mr. Warren, for the defense, then read the petition, which stated that I was unlawfully held in custody, and that the indictment, in Missouri, was obtained by fraud, bribery and duress, all of which I was prepared to prove.

Mr. Little then called upon the following witnesses, viz.,—Morris Phelps, Elias Higbee, Reynolds Cahoon and George W. Robinson, who were sworn. The counsel on the opposite side objected to hearing evidence on the merits of the case, as they could not go beyond the indictment. Upon this a warm and long discussion occurred, which occupied the attention of the court during the entire day.

All the lawyers on the opposite side, excepting two, viz. Messrs. Knowlton and Jennings, confined themselves to the merits of the case, and conducted themselves as gentlemen; but it was plainly evident that the design of Messrs. Knowlton and Jennings was to excite the public mind still more on the subject and inflame the passions of the people against me and my religion.

Honorable Conduct of Counsel.

The counsel on behalf of the defense, Messrs. Charles A. Warren, Sidney H. Little, O. H. Browning, James H. Ralston, Cyrus Walker, and Archibald Williams, acted nobly and honorably, and stood up in the defense of the persecuted, in a manner worthy of high-minded and honorable gentlemen.

Some had even been told that if they engaged on the side of the defense, they need never look to the citizens of that county for any political favors. But they were not to be overawed by the popular clamor or deterred from an act of public duty by any insinuations or threats whatever, and stated, that if they had not before determined to take a part in the defense, they, after hearing the threats of the community, were now fully determined to discharge their duty. The counsel for the defense spoke well without exception; and strongly urged the legality of the court examining the testimony to prove that the whole proceedings on the part of Missouri, were base and illegal, and that the indictment was obtained through fraud, bribery and corruption.

The court, after hearing the counsel, adjourned about half past six p. m.

When I was at dinner, a man rushed in and said, "Which is Jo Smith? I have got a five dollar Kirtland bill, and I'll be damned if he don't take it back I'll sue him, for his name is to it." I replied, "I am the man;" took the bill and paid him the specie, which he took very reluctantly, being anxious to kick up a fuss.

Judge Douglas.

The crowd in the court was so intense that Judge Douglas ordered the sheriff of Warren county to keep the spectators back; but he neglected doing so, when the judge fined him ten dollars. In a few minutes he again ordered the sheriff to keep the men back from crowding the prisoner and witnesses. He replied, "I have told a constable to do it," when the judge immediately said, "Clerk, add ten dollars more to that fine." The sheriff, finding neglect rather expensive, then attended to his duty.

A young lawyer from Missouri volunteered to plead against me; he tried his utmost to convict me, but was so high with liquor, and chewed so much tobacco, that he often called for cold water. Before he had spoken many minutes, he turned sick, requested to be excused by the court and went out of the court house, puking all the way down stairs. As the Illinoians call the Missouri people "pukes," this circumstance caused considerable amusement to the members of the bar. During his plea, his language was so outrageous that the judge was twice under the necessity of ordering him to be silent.

Mr. O. H. Browning then commenced his plea, and in a short time the puking lawyer returned, and requested the privilege of finishing his plea, which was allowed.

Afterwards Mr. Browning resumed his pleadings which were powerful; and when he gave a recitation of what he himself had seen at Quincy, and on the banks of the Mississippi river' when the Saints were "exterminated from Missouri," where he tracked the persecuted women and children by their bloody footmarks in the snow, they were so affecting that the spectators were often dissolved in tears. Judge Douglas himself and most of the officers also wept.

Elder Amasa Lyman during the evening, preached a brilliant discourse in the Court House, on the first principles of the Gospel, which changed the feelings of the people very materially.

*A Letter from the Editor * of the Times and Seasons to that Journal Giving an Account of the Trial at Monmouth.*

AMERICAN HOTEL, MONMOUTH, WARREN COUNTY, ILLINOIS,
June 9, 1841. Wednesday Evening.

We have just returned from the Court House, where we have listened to one of the most eloquent speeches ever uttered by mortal man, in favor of justice and liberty, by O. H. Browning, Esq., who has done himself immortal honor in the sight of all patriotic citizens who listened to the same. He occupied the attention of the court for more than two hours, and showed the falsity of the arguments of the opposite counsel, and laid down principles in a lucid and able manner which ought to guide the court in admitting testimony for the defendant, Joseph Smith. We have heard Browning on former occasions, when he has frequently delighted his audience by his eloquence; but on this occasion he exceeded our most sanguine expectations. The sentiments he advanced were just, generous and exalted; he soared above the petty quibbles which the opposite counsel urged, and triumphantly, in a manner and eloquence peculiar to himself, avowed himself the friend of humanity, and boldly, nobly and independently stood up for the rights of those who had waded through seas of oppression and floods of injustice, and had sought a shelter in the State of Illinois. It was an effort worthy of a high-minded and honorable gentleman, such as we ever considered him to be, since we have had the pleasure of his acquaintance. Soon after we came out of Missouri, he sympathized with us in our afflictions, and we are indeed rejoiced to know that he

* Don Carlos Smith and Robert B. Thompson were at this time editors and publishers of the *Times and Seasons*, and the above letter was doubtless written by Thompson as he is named as among those who accompanied the Prophet to Monmouth, while Don Carlos Smith is not named as being in the company.

yet maintains the same principles of benevolence. His was not an effort of a lawyer anxious to earn his fee, but the pure and patriotic feelings of Christian benevolence, and a sense of justice and of right. While he was answering the monstrous and ridiculous arguments urged by the opposing counsel, that Joseph Smith might go to Missouri and have his trial; he stated the circumstances of our being driven from that State, and feelingly and emphatically pointed out the impossibility of our obtaining justice there. There we were forbidden to enter in consequence of the order of the Executive, and that injustice and cruelties of the most barbarous and atrocious character had been practiced upon us, until the streams of Missouri had run with blood, and that he had seen women and children, barefoot and houseless crossing the Mississippi to seek refuge from ruthless mobs. He concluded his remarks by saying that to tell us to go to Missonri for a trial was adding insult to injury; and then he said: "*Great God! have I not seen it? Yes, my eyes have beheld the blood-stained traces of innocent women and children, in the drear winter, who had traveled hundreds of miles barefoot, through frost and snow, to seek a refuge from their savage pursuers. 'Twas a scene of horror sufficient to enlist sympathy from an adamantine heart. And shall this unfortunate man, whom their fury has seen proper to select for sacrifice, be driven into such a savage land and none dare to enlist in the cause of Justice? If there was no other voice under heaven ever to be heard in this cause, gladly would I stand alone, and proudly spend my latest breath in defense of an oppressed American citizen.*"

Thursday, 10.—The court was opened about 8 o'clock a. m. when Judge Douglas delivered his opinion on the case. He said:

That the writ being once returned to the Executive by the sheriff of Hancock county was dead, and stood in the same relationship as any other writ which might issue from the Circuit Court, and consequently the defendant could not be held in custody on that writ. The other point, whether evidence in the case was admissible or not, he would not at that time decide, as it involved great and important considerations relative to the future conduct of the different states. There being no precedent, as far as they had access to authorities to guide them, but he would endeavor to examine the subject, and avail himself of all the authorities which could be obtained on the subject, before he would decide that point. But on the other, the defendant must be liberated.

This decision was received with satisfaction by myself and the brethren, and all those whose minds were free from prejudice. It is now decided that before another writ can issue, a new demand must be made by the Governor of Missouri. Thus have I been once more delivered from the fangs of my cruel persecutors, for which I thank God, my Heavenly Father.

The Prophet Set Free.

I was discharged about 11 a. m., when I ordered dinner for my company now increased to about sixty men; and when I called for the bill, the unconscionable fellow replied, "Only one hundred and sixty dollars."

About 2 p. m., the company commenced their return, traveled about twenty miles, and camped by the wayside.

Friday, 11.—Started very early, arrived at La Harpe for dinner and returned safely to Nauvoo by 4 p. m., where I was met by the acclamation of the Saints.

CHAPTER XXI.

THE MISSION TO JERUSALEM—PROGRESS OF ORSON HYDE IN HIS JOURNEY.

ELDER GEORGE A. SMITH met Elder John E. Page at Philadelphia, and advised him to take up contributions to enable him to sail within three days in the *Garrick* for England, and overtake Elder Orson Hyde and accompany him to Jerusalem, promising to use all the influence and exertion in his power to assist him. Elder Page rejected the proposition. Elder Smith subsequently learned that Elder Page had sufficient money, without collections to have taken him through to England.

Elder John E. Page—a Laggard.

Tuesday, 15.

Letter from Elder Orson Hyde to President Joseph Smith—Recounting Incidents of his Journey en Route for Jerusalem.

LONDON, June 15, 1841.

President Smith:

SIR—With pleasure I take my pen to write you at this time, and through you to the *Times and Seasons*, and through it to the Saints at large, and to all whom it may concern. May grace, mercy, and peace from God our Father, and from the Lord Jesus Christ, rest upon you abundantly, and enable you to serve Him acceptably, secure to yourself that honor which cometh from above, guide the counsels of the Saints in wisdom, that peace and good will may reign predominant in Zion, and joy and gladness swell every grateful heart. Most gladly would I embrace an opportunity of a personal interview with you, did one offer, but such a favor is beyond my reach at this time. I have just seen the 12th number of the *Times and Seasons*, containing the minutes of your conference, the report of the Presidency, the celebration of the anniversary of the Church and the laying of the foundation of the Temple. This, to me was a precious gem; it brought tidings from my own country, and from the place rendered doubly endearing from the fact that there is the home of my wife and children.

I was sorry that Elder Page had been so tardy in his movements that objections were made to him. Most gladly would I have hailed him as a companion to the oriental continent; but my hopes of that are fled. I shall go alone or find some other person, in all probability, to go with me.

I have written a book to publish in the German language, setting forth our doctrine and principles in as clear and concise a manner as I possibly could. After giving a history of the rise of the Church, in something the manner that Brother Orson Pratt did, I have written a snug little article on every point of doctrine believed by the Saints; I began with the Priesthood and showed that the Saints were not under the necessity of tracing back the dark and bloody stream of papal superstition to find their authority; neither were they compelled to seek for it among the floating and transient notions of Protestant reformers; but God has sent His holy angel directly from heaven with this seal and authority, and conferred it upon men with His own hands—quoting the letter and testimony of Oliver Cowdery; next was on the use and validity of the holy scriptures in the Church; next on faith, set forth from the scriptures and the Book of Covenants; then on repentance, baptism; laying on of hands; then the different offices of the Church; next the power and authority of each one; and, in fine, the whole order, doctrine and government of the Church. I have not written it as a law binding on the *German Saints;* but have taken this course to illustrate and set forth the true principles of our doctrine to them, fully believing that it would meet with the cordial approbation of those whom I have the distinguished honor to represent, could they but see it. I have written a lengthy preface and introduction to it. I here copy an extract from the introduction: "When in the course of divine Providence it becomes our duty to record one of those remarkable events which gives birth to a new era, and lays the foundation for the renovation of the moral world, it fills the mind with wonder, astonishment and admiration. How welcome are the rays of the morning light, after the shades of darkness have clothed the earth in gloom! So after a long and tedious night of moral darkness under which the earth has rolled, and her inhabitants groaned for the last fourteen hundred years, an angel commissioned from the Almighty, descended and rolled back the curtains of night from the minds of some and caused the sunbeams of truth to enlighten, cheer, and warm the hearts of many. Welcome, welcome to our earth, thou messenger of the Most High! and thrice welcome the tidings which thou hast borne! O Gracious Father! I ask Thee, in the name of Thy holy child, Jesus, to bless with Thy royal favor, the weak exertions of Thy humble servant, and make this production a blessing to all people who may be favored with a perusal of its pages. Wherever it shall go let it be a messenger of conviction to the wicked, and a harbinger of peace to the righteous. Let its contents be borne upon every breeze, and wafted to the remotest climes. Let the angel of the covenant go before it, and prepare its way. Let its heavenly influence be distilled upon the rich and fertile soil of humble and honest hearts. Go forth, therefore, little volume to other nations and tongues, and may the Almighty speed your way, and like a sharp, two-edged sword cut the way through the prejudices of this generation; encamp with all thy virtues in the hearts of the people, and there let thy principles be enthroned."

One thing I was pleased with, which I noticed in the *Times and Seasons*—the remarks made on the use of intoxicating spirits. In my heart they found a corresponding echo. I should not be willing to indulge the thought for a moment that the Saints in Nauvoo would quietly stand by and see a brother gorge himself with that strong drink which makes a hell of his home, and rolls the fiery flood of ruin over the affections of his once happy family. No! they will dash from his lips the cup of wretchedness, and sharply rebuke the homicide that sells to him the wine of wrath, and measures to him his wife's tears. * * * May the lightnings of heaven forever blast (I had almost said) those brewers of strong drink which send forth their corrupt and poisonous streams to sweep down in their filthy current men of sterling talents to an untimely grave. May the Saints of God stand as far from them as Lot stood from Sodom in its evil day. This dizzy flood has sometimes entered the house of worship, invaded the sacred desk, and hushed in death forever the voice that could plead like an angel, the cause of God and man.

I havs just received a note from Dr. S. Hirschell, President Rabbi of the Hebrew community of this country, in reply to a very polite note which I sent him, requesting the indulgence of a personal interview with him. But in consequence of a very severe accident which befell him he is confined to his room, and unable at this time to grant the asked indulgence. (His leg is broken.)

I have addressed to him a communication upon the subject of my mission, a copy of which I transmit to you. It may not be altogether uninteresting to the Saints and friends in America.

Elder Hyde's Letter to Rabbi Hirschell.

REV. SIR:—I cannot but express my sorrow and regret at the misfortune under which you labor, in consequence of the severe accident which befell you, and by which you are confined to your room. Please accept, sir, the sincere wishes of a stranger, that you may speedily recover from the injury you sustained in consequence of the accident, and resume the labors which your high and responsible station calls you to perform.

Feeling that I may not enjoy the privilege and happiness of a personal interview with you, I hope you will indulge the liberty which I now presume to take, in addressing a written communication to you, embracing some of those things which I had fondly hoped would have been the foundation of a mutual interchange of thought between us. But as Providence has laid an embargo upon that distinguished privilege, I must forego, at this time, the pleasure of a verbal relation of those things pertaining to your nation, with which my mind is deeply affected.

Since I have arrived to years of more mature reflection, and become religiously inclined, the writings of the Jewish Prophets have won my affections; and the scattered and oppressed condition of that people has enlisted the finest sympathies of my heart. Believing, therefore, that the words of Hosea, the Prophet, ii; 23, connected with your magnanimity, will prohibit the indulgence of any prejudices in your feelings against the author of this production, in consequence of his not being able by any existing document or record, to identify himself with your nation.

"About nine years ago, a young man with whom I had had a short acquaintance, and one, too, in whom dwelt much wisdom and knowledge—in whose bosom the Almighty had deposited many secrets, laid his hand upon my head and pronounced these remarkable words—'in due time thou shalt go to Jerusalem, the land of thy fathers, and be a watchman unto the house of Israel; and by thy hands shall the Most High do a great work, which shall prepare the way and greatly facilitate the gathering together of that people.' Many other particulars were told me by him at that time, which I do not write in this letter. But sufficient is written to show that divine appointment is claimed as the mainspring that has sent me forth from the embraces of an affectionate family and kind friends, as well as from the land that gave me birth.

My labors since that period have been bestowed upon the Gentiles in various countries, and on both sides of the Atlantic, until in the early part of March, 1840, I retired to my bed one night as usual; and while meditating and contemplating the field of my future labors, the vision of the Lord, like clouds of light, burst into my view (see Joel ii: 28).

The cities of London, Amsterdam, Constantinople and Jerusalem, all appeared in succession before me, and the Spirit said unto me, "Here are many of the children of Abraham whom I will gather to the land that I gave to their fathers; and here also is the field of your labors. Take, therefore, proper credentials from my people, your brethren, and also from the Governor of your state, with the seal of authority thereon, and go ye forth to the cities which have been shown you, and declare these words unto Judah, and say, "blow ye the trumpet in the land; cry, gather together, and say, assemble yourselves, and let us go into the defensed cities. Set up the standard towards Zion—retire, stay not, for I will bring evil from the north and a great destruction. The lion is come up from his thicket, and the destroyer of the Gentiles is on his way—he is gone forth from his place to make thy land desolate, and thy cities shall be laid waste, without an inhabitant. Speak ye comfortably to Jerusalem, and cry unto her, that her warfare is accomplished—that her iniquity is pardoned, for she hath received of the Lord's hand doubly for all her sins. Let your warning voice be heard among the Gentiles as you pass; and call yet upon them in my name for aid and for assistance. With you it mattereth not whether it be little or much; but to me it belongeth to show favor unto them who show favor unto you." The vision continued open about six hours, that I did not close my eyes in sleep. In this time many things were shown unto me which I have never written; neither shall I write them until they are fulfilled in Jerusalem.

It appears from the Prophets, that Jerusalem has none to guide—none to take her by the hand among all the sons whom she hath brought forth and reared. But these two sons are come unto thee! the sons of strangers shall build up thy walls.

Permit me now, Rev. Sir, to trouble you with the reflections of a mind that feels completely untrammelled from every party interest, and from every sectarian influence.

When I look at the condition of your fathers in the days of David and Solomon, and contrast that with the present condition of their descendants, I am led to exclaim, "How are the mighty fallen." Then they possessed a kingdom—a land flowing with milk and honey—then the strong arm of Jehovah taught the surrounding nations to pay tribute and homage to them—then their standard was raised high, their banner floated on every breeze; and under its shade the sons and daughters of Israel reposed in perfect safety; and the golden letters of light and knowledge were inscribed on its folds. But now, no kingdom—no country—no tribute of gain or honor—no standard—no security: Their sceptre has departed! and instead of that light and knowledge which once gave them a transient elevation above other nations, the height of their ambition is now (with some honorable exceptions) the accumulation of sordid gain, by buying and selling the stale refuse with which their fathers would never have defiled their hands.

Why this wonderful change? Is the God of Abraham, Isaac and Jacob a just God? Most certaily He is. If, then, He is a just God, of course He will mete out and apportion the chastisement or penalty to the magnitude of the offense or crime committed. Allowing, then, the law of Moses to be the standard by which actions are weighed: were not idolatry and the shedding of innocent blood the greatest sins which your fathers committed? And was not the penalty inflicted upon them for that transgression, captivity in Babylon seventy years? Have they ever been guilty of idolatry at all since their return from Babylon? No! Have they been guilty of shedding innocent blood, to that extent since their return, that they were before they were taken captive by Nebuchadnezzar? The Jew says, No! Very well; there will none deny, with any claim upon your credulity, but that the disaster and overthrow that befell the Jewish nation in the days of Vespasian,very far exceeded in severity, in almost every particular, the disaster and overthrow that befell them in the days of Nebuchadnezzar.

Now, then, if God be just and mete out and apportion the chastisement or penalty to the magnitude of the offense or crime committed, it follows, of course, that your fathers committed some far greater crime subsequent to their return to Babylon, than ever they before committed. Be that crime whatever it may; know ye that for it, or because of it, the Roman armies were permitted to crowd their conquests to the heart of your city—burn your temple—kill your men, women and children, and disperse your remnant to the four quarters of the earth. The fiery storm that burst upon your nation at that time, and the traces of blood which they have ever since left behind them in their flight and dispersion, together with the recent cursed cruelties inflicted upon them in Damascus and Rhodes, but too plainly declare that the strong imprecation which they uttered on a certain occasion has been fulfilled upon them to the letter. "Let his blood be on us and on our children." If condemning and crucifying Jesus of Nazareth was not the cause of this great evil, what was the cause of it?

Aware that I have written very plainly upon these points, that have come within my notice, you believe me, sir, when I assure you, that my pen is pointed with friendship, and dipped in the fountain of love and good will toward your nation. The thoughts which it records have proceeded from a heart grateful to the Almighty, that the time has arrived when the day-star of your freedom already begins to dispel the dark and gloomy clouds which have separated you from the favor of your God. Ere long it will be said to you, "Arise, shine, for thy light has

has come, and the glory of the Lord has risen upon thee."

The morning breaks, the shadows flee,
Lo! Zion's standard is unfurled;
The dawning of a brighter day
Majestic rises on the world.

The Gentile fulness now comes in,
And Israel's blessings are at hand:
Lo! Judah's remnant, cleansed from sin,
Shall in their promised Canaan stand.

Now, therefore, O ye children of the covenant, repent of all your backslidings, and begin, as in days of old, to turn to the Lord your God. Arise! arise! and go out from among the Gentiles; for destruction is coming from the north to lay their cities waste. Jerusalem is thy home. There the God of Abraham will deliver thee (Joel ii: 32.) There the bending heavens shall reveal thy long looked-for Messiah in fleecy clouds of light and glory, to execute vengeance upon thine enemies; and lead thee and thy brethren of the ten tribes to sure conquest and certain victory. Then shall thrones be cast down, and the kingdoms of this world become the kingdoms of our God. Then will they come from the east, west, north, south, and sit down in the kingdom of God with Abraham, Isaac and Jacob. But the children of the kingdom (Gentiles) shall be cast out, and the kingdom restored to Israel.

With sentiments of distinguished consideration, I have the honor, sir, to subscribe myself,

Your most obedient servant,

ORSON HYDE.

Rev. Dr. Solomon Hirschell, President Rabbi of the Hebrew Society in England.

Conclusion of Elder Hyde's Letter to the Prophet.

It is very hard times in England. Thousands have nothing to do, and are literally starving. Trade of all sorts is at the lowest ebb. Very cold and dry. No harvest unless rain come soon. You will discover that the greater part of the English brethren have always worked under masters; and they have not so much notion of planning and shifting for themselves, particularly in a a strange country, as the Americans. They want some one to be a kind of father to them, to give them plenty of work, and plenty to eat; and they will be content. They are a very industrious people whenever they can get employment: and by a little fatherly care, they will soon get way-wised to the country, and be enabled to shift for themselves. I trust that exertions are made to give employment to as many as possible. You know the reasons there better than I do, and you have received a specimen of the English Saints. Now if you have any counsel to give concerning the gathering, in addition to that already given, I shall be happy to receive and execute it, as far as opportunity offers.

I shall not remain here long, it is true; but Brother Pratt is here, and I shall return here some time if the Lord will.

I must now close by saying for one and all, God bless Zion for ever and ever.

Your brother in Christ,
ORSON HYDE.

CHAPTER XXII.

SUNDRY EVENTS AT NAUVOO AND THROUGHOUT THE WORLD—THE MISSION OF THE TWELVE NOTED BY THE PROPHET.

Press Misrepresentations.

THE newspapers of the United States are teeming with all manner of lies, abusing the Saints of the Most High, and striving to call down the wrath of the people upon His servants.

Wednesday, 16.—Elder Brigham Young and company arrived at Wheeling at 4 p. m., and Sunday, 29th, visited the brethren at Cincinnati.

Monday, 21.—Hyrum Smith and William Law visited the Saints in Chester county, Pennsylvania, on their mission east; and there met Elder George A. Smith on his return home.

Imprisonment of Theodore Curtis.

Tuesday, 22.—Elder Theodore Curtis, having previously been arraigned before a magistrate, and bound over in the sum of forty pounds, for "blasphemy," *i. e.*, preaching the Gospel, appeared at the Court of Sessions, at Gloucester, England, and after remaining five days [in prison], was informed on inquiry, that no bill was found against him, and he was suffered to go at large again after paying one pound and one shilling cost. Thus we see that the same opposition to truth prevails in other countries, as well as in this.

Extract from a Letter in the "Juliet Courier"—Describing the Prophet's Trial at Monmouth, and Affairs at Nauvoo.

MONMOUTH, June, 1841.

MY DEAR SIR.—Before this reaches you, I have no doubt you will have heard of the trial of Joseph Smith, familiarly known as the Mormon Prophet. As some misrepresentations have already gone abroad, in relation to Judge Douglas' decision, and the merits of the question decided by the judge; permit me to say, the only question decided, though many were debated, was the validity of the executive writ which had once been sent out, I think in September, 1840, and a return on it that Mr. Smith could not be found. The same writ was issued in June, 1841. There can really be no great difficulty about this matter, under this state of facts.

The judge acquitted himself handsomely, and silenced clamors that had been raised against the defendant.

Since the trial I have been at Nauvoo, on the Mississippi, in Hancock county, Illinois; and have seen the manner in which things are conducted among the Mormons. In the first place, I cannot help noticing the plain hospitality of the Prophet, Smith, to all strangers visiting the town, aided as he is, in making the stranger comfortable by his excellent wife, a woman of superior ability. The people of the town appear to be honest and industrious, engaged in their usual vocations of building up a town, and making all things around them comfortable. On Sunday I attended one of their meetings, in front of the Temple now building, and one of the largest buildings in the state. There could not have been less than 2,500 people present, and as well appearing as any number that could be found in this or any state. Mr. Smith preached in the morning, and one could have readily learned, then, the magic by which he has built up this society, because, as we say in Illinois, "they believe in him," and in his honesty. It has been a matter of astonishment to me, after seeing the Prophet, as he is called, Elder Rigdon, and many other gentlemanly men anyone may see at Nauvoo, who will visit there—why it is, that so many professing Christianity, and so many professing to reverence the sacred principles of our Constitution (which gives free religious toleration to all), have slandered, and persecuted this sect of Christians.

Saturday, 26.—Elder Young and company arrived on the steamer *Mermaid*, at the mouth of the Ohio river.

Thursday, July 1.—Elders Young, Kimball, and Taylor arrived at Nauvoo, after an interesting mission to England. The accounts of their missions are highly satisfactory.

During a heavy thunderstorm at Derby, England, hundreds of small fish and frogs descended, and were picked up alive by the people.

Saturday, *3.*—The following is an extract from the

Legion Minutes:

The second regiment, first cohort, consisting of four companies, was organized, and Captain George Coulson was elected colonel, Josiah Ells lieutenant-colonel, and Hyrum Kimball major. On the same day, the third regiment, second cohort, consisting of four companies, was organized; Samuel Bent was elected colonel, George Morey, lieutenant-colonel, and William Niswanger, major; and the Legion was called out to celebrate our National Independence (the 4th being Sunday), and was reviewed by Lieutenant-General Joseph Smith, who made an eloquent and patriotic speech to the troops, and strongly testified of his regard for our national welfare, and his willingness to lay down his life in defense of his country, and closed with these remarkable words, "I would ask no greater boon, than to lay down my life for my country."

An elaborate dinner was got up in the grove, of which I partook, in company with the officers of the Legion, President Rigdon and many others, with their ladies.

Elder Willard Richards left his family with his sisters at Richmond, Massachusetts, and started for Nauvoo.

Elder Orson Pratt has published in New York an edition of his History of the Coming Forth of the Book of Mormon, first printed in Edinburgh.

*Revelation given to Joseph Smith, in the house of Brigham Young, in Nauvoo City, July 9, 1841.**

Dear and well beloved Brother Brigham Young, verily thus saith the Lord unto you, my servant Brigham, it is no more required at your hands to leave your family as in times past, for your offering is acceptable to me; I have seen your labor and toil in journeyings for my name. I therefore command you to send my word abroad, and take special care of your family from this time, henceforth and forever. Amen.

Monday, *12.*—Elder William Clayton was appointed clerk of the High Council of Iowa, and John Patton recorder of baptisms for the dead in Iowa.

At the urgent solicitations of the brethren at Zarahemla,

* Doctrine and Covenants, sec. cxxvi.

I had consented, at a previous date, that they might baptize for the dead on the Iowa side of the river.

I was in the City Council, and moved that any person in the City of Nauvoo be at liberty to sell vinous liquors in any quantity, subject to the city ordinances.

Liquor Selling Licensed in Nauvoo.

Tuesday, *13*.—Elder George A. Smith returned from his mission in England.

A treaty was signed between Turkey, Russia, England, France, Austria, and Prussia, whereby the Dardanelles are closed to all foreign ships of war, as long as the Ottoman Porte enjoys peace.

Wednesday, *14*.—The following is translated from the Arabic, in the *Malta Times*—"Aleppo, 3rd May. A great famine has happened in Aleppo, Malitia, and Karbat, insomuch that many people died with hunger, and others sold their sons and daughters to get bread to eat. But the Almighty God rained upon them seed (manna), and fed them withal." "Of the veracity of these words," adds the *Malta Times*, "extracted from an Arabic letter, we are perfectly satisfied. The seed alluded to is known in Malta, being nearly like 'hab' or 'dazz,' and which being kept a little while becomes white, like 'semola' (very fine wheaten flour)."

Manna Rain in Aleppo.

Immense quantities of locusts have appeared in Spain this year, devouring everything in their way; and a shower of flesh and blood is reported in the southern part of the United States.

Thursday, *15*.—Many of the newspapers are publishing lies about me by the wholesale; should I attempt to enumerate them, I could write nothing else; suffice it to say, every falsehood wicked men can invent, assisted by their father the devil, is trumpeted to the world as sound doctrine, which proves the words of Jesus, "They have persecuted me, they will persecute you also."

Press Falsehoods.

I spent considerable part of the day with several of the Twelve Apostles.

Letter of Elder Orson Hyde to President Smith—Detailing Events while en Route to Jerusalem.

RATISBON ON THE DANUBE, July 17, 1841.

Dear Brother Josph, and all whom it may concern: With pleasure I take my pen to write to you at this time, hoping this communication may find you as it leaves me, in good health and enjoying a comfortable measure of the Holy Spirit.

On the twentieth of June last, I left London for Rotterdam in Holland, after writing a lengthy epistle to you, and also the copy of a letter addressed to the Rev. Dr. S. Hirschell, President Rabbi of the Hebrews in London; which I hope you have received ere this; the work of the Lord is steadily advancing in London under the efficient and zealous labors of our worthy brother, Elder Lorenzo Snow.

The fine steamer *Batavier* brought me safely over the billows of a tremendous rough sea in about thirty hours. Never did I suffer more from sea sickness, than during this short voyage; but it was soon over, and we landed safely in Rotterdam. I took my lodgings at the London Hotel, at two florins per diem, about three shillings and five pence sterling, or seventy-five cents. Here I called on the Hebrew Rabbi, and proposed certain questions to him; but as he did not understand a word of English, it was hard for me to enter into particulars with him; I asked, him, however, whether he expected his Messiah to come directly from heaven, or whether he expected Him to be born of a woman on earth? He replied that he expected Him to be born of a woman of the seed and lineage of David. At what period do you look for this event? Answer. "We have been looking a long time, and are now living in constant expectation of His coming." Do you believe in the restitution of your nation to the land of your fathers, called the land of *promise*? "We hope it will be so," was the reply. He then added, "We believe that many Jews will return to Jerusalem and rebuild the city—rear a temple to the name of the Most High, and restore our ancient worship; Jerusalem shall be the capital of our nation—the centre of our union and the standard and ensign of our national existence. But we do not believe that all the Jews will go there, for the place is not large enough to contain them. They are now gathering there," continued he, "almost continually." I told him I had written an address to the Hebrews, and was about procuring its publication in his own language (Dutch), and when completed I would leave him a copy. He thanked me for this token of respect, and I bade him adieu. I soon obtained the publication of five hundred copies of the address, and left one at the house of the Rabbi—he being absent from home, I did not see him.

After remaining here about one week, I took the coach for Amsterdam, distance seven hours or about thirty English miles. Rotterdam is a fine town of about eighty thousand inhabitants. The cleanliness of its streets, the antique order of its architecture, the extreme height of its buildings, the numerous shade trees with which it is beautified, and the great number of canals, through almost every part of the town, filled with ships of various sizes from different parts of the world; all these, with many other things not mentioned, contributed to give this place a peculiarity resembled no where else in the course of my travels, except in Amsterdam. Most of the business men here speak a little English—some speak it very well.

In ascending the waters of the Rhine from the sea to Rotterdam, the numerous windmills which I beheld in constant operation, led me to think, almost, that all Europe came here for their grinding. But I ascertained that they were grinding for distilleries, where the floods of gin are made, which not only deluge our beloved country, with fatal consequences, but many others. Gin is one of the principal articles of exportation from this country.

In going to Amsterdam, I passed through a very beautiful town called "The Hague," the residence of the King of Holland. I saw his palace, which was guarded by soldiers both horse and foot. For grandeur it bore here a faint resemblance to Buckingham Palace, in London. But the beautiful parks and picturesque scenery in and about the Hague, I have never seen equalled in any country.

I remained in Amsterdam only one night and a part of two days. I called on the President Rabbi here, but he was gone from home. I left at his house a large number of the addresses for himself and his people, and took coach for Arnhem on the Rhine. Took boat the same evening for Mainz. Traveling by coach and steam is rather cheaper in this country than in the United States. We were three days in going up the river to Mainz.

Holland and the lower part of Prussia are very low, flat countries. The French and German languages are spoken all along the Rhine; but little or no English. The Rhine is about like the Ohio for size, near its mouth where it empties into the Mississippi. Its waters resemble the Mississippi waters, dark and muddy. The scenery and landscapes along this river have been endowed with art and nature's choicest gifts.

I have been made acquainted with Europe in America, by books, to a certain extent; yet now my eyes behold! It is impossible for a written description of a stranger's beauty to leave the same impression upon the mind, as is made by an ocular view of the lovely object. This is the difference between reading of and seeing the countries of Europe. From Mainz I came to Frankfort on the Maine by railroad—distance seven hours. From Frankfort I came to this place—distance about thirty hours, where Napoleon gained a celebrated victory over the Prussians and Austrians. The very ground on which I now write this letter was covered by about sixty thousand slain in that battle. It is called the battle of Ackeynaeal.

It was my intention to have gone directly down the Danube to Constantinople, but having neglected to get my passport vised by the Austrian Ambassador at Frankfort, I had to forward it to the Austrian Ambassador at Munich and procure his permission, signature and seal before I could enter the Austrian dominions. This detained me five days, during which time I conceived the idea of sitting down and learning the German language scientifically. I became acquainted with a lady here who speaks French and German to admiration, and she was very anxious to speak the English—she proposed giving me instruction in the German, if I would instruct her in English. I accepted her proposal. I have been engaged eight days in this task. I have read one book through and part of another, and translated and written considerable. I can speak and write considerable German already, and the lady tells me that I make astonishing progress. From the past experience I know that the keen edge of any work translated by a stranger, in whose heart the spirit of the matter does not dwell, is lost—the life and animation thereof die away into a cold monotony, and it becomes almost entirely another thing. This step is according to the best light I can get, and hope and trust that it is according to the mind of the Lord. The people will hardly believe but that I have spoken German before; but I tell them *nein* (no). The German is spoken in Prussia, Bavaria, and all the states of Germany, Austria, the south of Russia, and in fine, more or less all over Europe. It appears to me, therefore, that some person of some little experience ought to know this language so as to translate himself, without being dependent on strangers. If I am wrong in my movement pray that the Spirit of the Lord may direct me aright. If I am right, pray that heaven may speedily give me this language.

It is very sickly in Constantinople and Syria and Alexandria at present. I would rather, therefore, wait until cool weather before I go there. I might have written most of this letter in German, but as you would more readily understand it in English, I have written it in English.

With pleasure I leave the historical part of my letter to touch a softer note, and give vent to the feelings of my heart. I hope and trust that the cause which you so fearlessly advocate, is rolling forth in America, with that firm and steady motion which characterizes the work of Jehovah. The enemies which we are forced to encounter are numerous, strong, shrewd and cunning. Their leader transfuses into them his own spirit, and brings them into close alliance with the numerous hosts of precious immortals who have been earlier taken captives by the haughty tyrant, and sacrificed upon the altar of iniquity, transgression and sin. May it please our Father in heaven to throw around thee his protecting arms, to place beneath thee almighty strength ever buoy thy head above the raging waves of tribulation, through which the chart of destiny has evidently marked thy course. I am happy in the enjoyment of the distinguished consideration with which heaven's favor alone has endowed me, of bearing with you some humble part in laying the foundation of the glorious kingdom of Messiah, which is destined in its onward course to break in pieces and destroy all others, and stand for ever. The friendship and good will which are breathed towards me through all your letters, are received as the legacy which noble minds and generous hearts are ever anxious to bequeath. They soften the hard and rugged path in which heaven has directed my course. They are buoyancy in depression—joy in sorrow; and when the dark clouds of despondency are gathering thick around the mental horizon, like kind angels from the fountain of mercy, they dispel the gloom, dry the tear of sorrow, and pour humanity's healing balm into my grieved and sorrowful heart. Be assured, therefore, Brother Joseph, that effusions from the altar of a grateful heart, are smoking to heaven daily in thy behalf; and not only in thine, but in behalf of all Zion's suffering sons and daughters. Though now far separated from you, and also from her, who, with me, has suffered the chilling blasts of adversity, yet hope lingers in this bosom, brightened almost into certainty by the implicit confidence reposed in the virtue of that call which was born on the gentle breeze of the Spirit of God, through the dark shades of midnight gloom, till it found a mansion in my anxious and inquiring heart, that my feet shall once more press the American soil; and under the shade of her streaming banner, embrace again the friends I love.

I never knew that I was in reality an American, until I walked out one fine morning in Rotterdam along the wharf where many ships lay in the waters of the Rhine. Suddenly my eye caught a broad pendant floating in a gentle breeze over the stern of a fine ship at mizzen half mast; and when I saw the wide spread eagle perched on her banner with the stripes and stars under which our fathers were led to conquest and victory, my heart leaped into my mouth, a flood of tears burst from my eyes, and before reflection could mature a sentence, my mouth involuntarily gave birth to these words, "I am an American." To see the flag of one's country in a strange land, and floating upon strange waters, produces feelings which none can know except those who experience them. I can now say that I am an American. While at home the warmth and fire of the American spirit lay in silent slumber in my bosom; but the winds of foreign climes have fanned it into a flame.

I have seen some of the finest specimens of painting and sculpture of both ancient and modern times. The vast varieties of curiosities, also, from every country on the globe, together with every novelty that genius could invent or imagination conceive, which I have been compelled to witness in the course of my travels, would be too heavy a tax upon my time to describe, and upon your patience to read. I have witnessed the wealth and splendor of many of the towns in Europe—have gazed with admiration upon the widely-extended plains, her lofty mountains, her mouldering castles, and her extensive vineyards: for at this season nature is clad in her bridal robes, and smiles under the benign jurisprudence of her Author. I have also listened to the blandishments, gazed upon the pride and fashion of a world grown old in luxury and refinement, viewed the pageantry of kings, queens, lords, and nobles; and am now where military honor, and princely dignity, must bow at the shrine of clearical superiority. In fine, my mind has become cloyed with novelty, pomp, and show; and turns with disgust from the glare of fashion to commune with itself in retired meditation.

Were it consistent with the will of Deity, and consonant with the convictions of my own bosom, most gladly would I retreat from the oppressing heat of public life, and seek repose in the cool and refreshing shades of domestic endearments, and bask in the affections of my own little family circle. But the will of God be done! Can the Messiah's kingdom but be advanced through my toil, privation, and excessive labors, and at last sanctify my work through the effusion of my blood! I yield, O Lord! I yield to thy righteous mandate! Imploring help from thee in the hour of trial, and strength in the day of weakness to faithfully endure until my immortal spirit shall be driven from its earthly mansion to find a refuge in the bosom of its God.

If the friends in America shall be edified in reading this letter from Brother Hyde, I hope they will remember one thing; and that is this, that he hopes he has a wife and two children living there; but the distance is so great between him and them, that his arm is not long enough to administer to their wants. I have said enough. Lord, bless my wife and children, and the hand that ministers good to them, in the name of Jesus Christ. Amen. Adieu for the present.

Good rest on all the Saints throughout the world.

ORSON HYDE.

A violent and destructive hurricane swept over portions of France, Germany, and Switzerland.

Sunday, 18.—This day was observed as a day of fasting and prayer by the Saints in Nauvoo, that they might mourn with them that mourn, "and weep with them that weep," on account of the death of Honorable Sidney H Little of the Senate, who was killed by jumping from a wagon last Sunday, while his horse was unmanageable. Mr. Little was a patriot, statesman, and lawyer.

Death of Senator Little.

Meeting was held in the grove, west of the Temple; Elders Sidney Rigdon, John Taylor, and Geo. A. Smith preached.

Monday, 19.—Council of the Twelve, viz.—Brigham Young, Heber C. Kimball, John Taylor, Orson Pratt, and George A. Smith met at Elder Young's house, conversing with Lyman E. Johnson, who formerly belonged to the quorum. President Rigdon and myself were with them part of the time.

Sunday, 25.—Attended meeting in the grove. Elders Orson Pratt and George A. Smith preached in the forenoon. In the afternoon Elder Sidney Rigdon preached a general funeral sermon, designed to comfort and instruct the Saints, especially those who had been called to mourn the loss of relatives and friends. I followed him, illustrating the subject of the resurrection by some familiar figures.

General Funeral Sermon.

Elder George A. Smith married Bathsheba W. Bigler. Don Carlos Smith performed the ceremony, which was the last official act of his life,he being very feeble at the time.

Brother William Yokum had his leg amputated by Dr. John F. Weld, who operated free of charge; he was wounded in the massacre at Haun's Mill, October 30th, 1838, and had lain on his back ever since; and now it was found the only chance to save his life was to have his leg cut off. He was also shot through the head at the same massacre.

Wednesday, 28.—The Jewish quarter of Smyrna was burned. Three thousand houses and eight synagogues were destroyed.

The Prophet's Account of the Mission of the Twelve.

Sunday, August 1.—All the Quorum of the Twelve Apostles who were expected here this season, with the exception of Elders Willard Richards and Wilford Woodruff, have arrived. We have listened to the accounts which they give of their success, and the prosperity of the work of the Lord in Great Britain with pleasure. They certainly have been the instruments in the hands of God of accomplishing much, and must have the satisfaction of knowing that they have done their duty. Perhaps no men ever undertook such an important mission under such peculiarly distressing and unpropitious circumstances. Most of them when they left this place, nearly two years ago, were worn down with sickness and disease, or were taken sick on the road. Several of their families were also afflicted and needed their aid and support. But knowing that they had been called by the God of Heaven to preach the Gospel to other nations, they conferred not with flesh and blood, but obedient to the heavenly mandate, without purse or scrip, they commenced a journey of five thousand miles entirely dependent on the providence of that God who had called them to such a holy calling. While journeying to the sea board they were brought into many trying circumstances; after a short recovery from severe sickness, they would be taken with a relapse, and have to stop among strangers, without money and without friends. Their lives were several times despaired of, and they have taken each other by the hand, expecting it would be the last time they should behold one another in the flesh. However, notwithstanding their afflictions and trials, the Lord always interposed in their behalf, and did not suffer them to sink in the arms of death. Some way or other was made for their escape—friends rose up when they most needed them, and relieved their necessities; and thus they were enabled to pursue their journey and rejoice in the Holy One of Israel. They, truly, "went forth weeping, bearing precious seed," but have "returned with rejoicing, bearing their sheaves with them."

The minds of thousands are already prepared to hear of the sacking of cities—the marching and countermarching of armies—the burning of towns and villages—the flight of citizens—the rising of the Indians—the commotion in Illinois—the distress in Iowa—the consternation and flight of the Missourians, the exploits of mighty chieftains, &c.—on account of the fooleries and lies which have been trumpeted forth from the press in the United States.

Thursday, 5.—Letters from London, state that there are a number—more or less—baptized every week.

There was a general election of members of Parliament last month. Serious riots occurred in different parts of the kingdom between the Whigs and Tories.

Letter of William Smith to President Smith—Land Transactions.

CHESTER COUNTY, PENNSYLVANIA,
August 5th, 1841.

BROTHER JOSEPH:—I expect to leave here for the Jersey country next week. Doctor Galland left for Nauvoo last week. In the Hotchkiss business, Hyrum requested me to do all I could. Brother James Ivins has received orders on you from Doctor Galland to the amount of twenty-five hundred dollars. The property that he has given these orders for, is well worth the money. I expect Mr. Hotchkiss in new Jersey in a few days to receive this property, which is Cook's Mills Tavern stand, attached to six acres of ground with all the appurtenances. Some of the Jersey people think it worth three thousand dollars. Now the question is, shall I let Mr. Hotchkiss have this property for less than twenty-five hundred, since that is the price you will have to pay at Nauvoo. Why I ask this question is—I have understood that Hotchkiss has said that he would not allow over twenty-two hundred dollars. I got hold of another small piece of land, worth five hundred; and if Hotchkiss will take all at a fair price, I shall be enabled to settle the amount of three thousand dollars soon. Please write me an answer to the above question. The cause in these eastern lands is flourishing, and we want more laborers; fifty doors opened for preaching where there is but one laborer. I wish you would send us help.

Yours in the bonds of the covenant,

WILLIAM SMITH.

CHAPTER XXIII.

THE DEATH OF DON CARLOS SMITH—HIS LIFE AND LABORS—SPECIAL CONFERENCE AT NAUVOO.

Saturday, August 7.—My youngest brother, Don Carlos Smith, died at his residence in Nauvoo this morning, at twenty minutes past two o'clock, in the 26th year of his age. He was born 25th March, 1816, was one of the first to receive my testimony, and was ordained to the Priesthood when only 14 years of age. The evening after the plates of the Book of Mormon were shown to the eight witnesses, a meeting was held, when all the witnesses, as also Don Carlos bore testimony to the truth of the latter-day dispensation. He accompanied father to visit grandfather, Asael Smith, and relatives in St. Lawrence county, New York, in August, 1830. During that mission he convinced Solomon Humphrey, a licentiate of the Baptist order, of the truth of the work. He was one of the 24 Elders who laid the corner stones of the Kirtland Temple. In the fall of 1833, he entered the office of Oliver Cowdery to learn the art of printing. On the 30th July, 1835, he married Agnes Coolbrith, in Kirtland, Ohio. On the 15th January, 1836, he was ordained President of the High Priests' quorum. He took a mission with Wilber Denton in the spring and summer of 1836, in Pennsylvania and New York. On the commencement of the publication of the *Elders' Journal* in Kirtland, he took the control of the establishment until the office was destroyed by fire in December, 1837, when, in consequence of persecution, he moved his family to

The Death of Don Carlos Smith.

New Portage. Early in the spring of 1838 he took a mission through the states of Virginia, Pennsylvania and Ohio, and raised means to assist his father; and immediately after his return he started to Missouri with his family, in company with father and family, and purchased a farm in Daviess county. On the 26th September he started on a mission to the states of Tennessee and Kentucky, to collect means to buy out the claims and property of the mobbers in Daviess county, Missouri. During his absence, his wife and two little children were driven by the mob from his habitation, and she was compelled to carry her children three miles, through snow three inches deep, and wade through Grand river, which was waist deep, during the inclement weather. He returned about the 25th of December, after a very tedious mission, having traveled 1,500 miles, 650 of which were on foot.

I extract the following from his journal—

On the 30th of September, 1838, in company with George A. Smith, Lorenzo D. Barnes, and Harrison Sagers, I went on board the *Kansas* (which had one wheel broken); the Missouri river was very low, and full of snags and sand bars. General Samuel Lucas and Moses Wilson, of Jackson county, Colonel Thompson, from Platt Purchase, and many others of the active mobbers were on board, as also General David R. Atchison. On touching at De Witt, on 1st October, for wood, we found about seventy of the brethren, with their families, surrounded by an armed mob of upwards of two hundred. The women and children there were much frightened, expecting it was a boat loaded with mobbers. We would have stopped and assisted them, but being unarmed, we thought it best to fulfill our mission. From this onward the "Mormons" were the only subject of conversation, and nothing was heard but the most bitter imprecations against them. General Wilson related many of his deeds of noble daring in the Jackson mob, one of which was the following: "I went, in company with forty others, to the house of Hiram Page, a Mormon, in Jackson county. We got logs and broke in every door and window at the same instant; and pointing our rifles at the family, we told them, we would be d—d if we didn't shoot every one of them, if Page didn't come out. At that, a tall woman made her appearance, with a child in her arms. I told the boys she was too d—d tall. In a moment the boys stripped her, and found it was Page. I told them to give him a d—d good one. We gave him sixty or seventy blows with hickory withes which we had prepard. Then after pulling the roof off the house, we went to the next d—d Mormon's house, and whipped him in like manner. We continued until we whipped ten or fifteen of the d—d Mormons, and demolished their houses that night. If the Carroll boys would do that way they might conquer; but it is no use to think of driving them without four or five to one. I wish I could stay, I would help drive the d—d Mormons to hell, Old Joe, and all the rest." At this I looked the General sternly in the face, and told him, that he was neither a republican nor a gentleman, but a savage, without a single principle of honor, or humanity. "If," said I, "the 'Mormons' have broken the law, let it be strictly executed against them; but such anti-republican, and unconstitutional acts as these, related by you, are beneath the brutes." We were upon the hurricane deck, and a large company present were listening to the conversation. While I was speaking, Wilson placed his hand upon his pistol, which was belted under the skirt of his coat; but Cousin George stood by his side, watching every move of his hand, and would have knocked him into the river instantly, had he attempted to draw a deadly weapon. But General Atchison saved him the trouble, by saying, "I'll be d—d to hell if Smith ain't right." At this, Wilson left the company crest-fallen. In the course of the conversation, Wilson said that the best plan was to rush into the Mormon settlements, murder the men, make slaves of the children, take possession of the property, and use the women as they pleased.

A gentleman, present from Baltimore, Maryland, said he never was among such a pack of d—d savages before: he had passed through Far West, and saw nothing among the "Mormons" but good order. Then drawing his pistols, he discharged them, and re-loading, said, "If God spares my life till I get out of Upper Missouri, I will never be found associating with such devils again."

Shortly after this we were invited to preach on board, Elder Barnes and I preached. The rest of the way we were treated more civilly; but being deck passengers, and having very little money, we suffered much for food.

We continued our journey together through every species of hardship and fatigue, until the 11th of October, when Elders Barnes and Harrison Sagers left us at Paducah, after our giving them all the money we had, they starting up the Ohio river, and we to visit the churches in west Tennessee and Kentucky. Soon after this, Julian Moses gave us a five-franc piece, and bade us farewell.

We soon found that the mob spirit was in Kentucky, as well as in Missouri; we preached in a small branch of the Church in Calloway county, and stayed at the house of Sister Selah Parker, which was surrounded in the night by about twenty armed men, led by John McCartney, a Campbellite priest, who had sworn to kill the first "Mormon" Elder who should dare to preach in that place. The family were very much terrified. After trying the doors, the mobbers finally went away. We visited a number of small branches in Tennessee; the brethren generally arranged to be on hand with their money, or lands for exchange in the spring. Brother Samuel West gave us twenty-eight dollars to help defray our traveling expenses. We also received acts of kindness from others, which will never be forgotten.

About this time our minds were seized with an awful foreboding—horror seemed to have laid his grasp upon us—we lay awake night after night for we could not sleep. Our forebodings increased, and we felt sure that all was not right; yet we continued preaching until the Lord showed us that the Saints would be driven from Missouri. We then started home, and, on arriving at Wyatt's Mills, we were told that if we preached there it would cost us our lives. We had given out an appointment at the house of Mrs. Foster, a wealthy widow. She also advised us to give it up; but, as she had no fears for herself, her property or family, we concluded to fill our appointment. The hour of meeting came, and many attended. George A. preached about an hour; during which time Captain Fitch came in at the head of twelve other mobbers, who had large hickory clubs, and they sat down with their hats on. When George A. took his seat, I arose and addressed them for an hour and a half, during which time, I told them that I was a patriot—that I was free—that I loved my country—that I loved liberty—that I despised both mobs and mobbers—that no gentleman, or Christian at heart would ever be guilty of such things, or countenance them. Whereupon the mob pulled off their hats, laid down their clubs, and listened with almost breathless attention.

After meeting Mr. Fitch came to us and said that he was ashamed of his conduct, and would never do the like again; that he had been misinformed about us by some religious bigots, and begged of us to forgive him, which we did.

We continued our journey to Columbus, Hickman county, Kentucky, and put up with Captain Robinson, formerly an officer in the army, who treated us very kindly, assuring us that we were welcome to stay at his house until a boat should come, if it were three months. We stayed nine days, during which a company of thirteen hundred Cherokee Indians were ferried over the river.

We went on board the steamer *Louisville*, and had to pay all our money for a deck passage. About ninety miles from St. Louis our boat got aground, where it lay three days. We had nothing to eat but a little parched corn. We then went on board of a little boat, *The Return*, which landed us in St. Louis the next morning. Here we found Elder Orson Pratt, and learned that Joseph was a prisoner with many others, and that David Patten was killed, and of the sufferings of the Saints, which filled our hearts with sorrow.

The next morning we started on foot for home; at Huntsville, about 200 miles, we stopped at the house of George Lyman to rest. George A.'s feet had now become very sore from walking.

We had not been long in Huntsville before the mob made a rally to use us up, as they said, with the rest of the Smiths: and, at the earnest request of our friends, we thought best to push on, and started about ten at night. The wind was in our faces, the ground slippery, and the night very dark; nevertheless we proceeded on our journey. Traveling twenty-two miles, we came to the Chariton river, which we found frozen over, but the ice too weak to bear us, and the boat on the west side of the river. We went to the next ferry, but finding there was no boat, and knowing that in the next neighborhood a man's brains were beaten out for being a "Mormon," we returned to the first ferry, and tried by hallowing to raise the ferryman on the opposite side of the river, but were not able to awake him. We were almost benumbed with the cold, and to warm ourselves we commenced scuffling and jumping; we then beat our feet upon the logs and stumps, in order to start a circulation of blood; but at last George A. became so cold and sleepy, that he could not stand it any longer, and lay down. I told him he was freezing to death; I rolled him on the ground, pounded and thumped him; I then cut a stick and said I would thrash him. At this he got up, and undertook to thrash me; this stirred his blood a little, but he soon lay down again. By this time the ferryman came over, and set us across the river, where we warmed ourselves a little, and pursued our journey until about breakfast time, when we stopped at the house of a man, who we afterwards learned was a leader of the mob at Haun's Mill massacre. The next morning we started without breakfast. Our route lay through a wild prairie, where there was but very little track, and only one house in forty miles The northwest wind blew fiercely in our faces, and the ground was so slippery that we could scarcely keep our feet, and when the night came on, to add to our perplexity, we lost our way; soon after which, I became so cold that it was with great difficulty I could keep from freezing. We also became extremely thirsty; however, we found a remedy for this by cutting through ice three inches thick with a penknife. While we were drinking, we heard a cowbell; this caused our hearts to leap for joy, and we arose and steered our course towards the sound. We soon entered Tenny's Grove, which sheltered us from the wind, and we felt more comfortable. In a short time we came to the house of Whitford G. Wilson, where we were made welcome and kindly entertained. We lay down to rest about two o'clock in the morning, after having traveled one hundred and ten miles in two days and two nights. After breakfast I set out for Far West, leaving George A. sick, with our hospitable friends. When I arrived on the evening of December 25th, I was fortunate enough to find my family alive, and in tolerable health, which was more than I could have expected, considering the scenes of persecution through which they had passed.

The Visits of Don Carlos to Liberty Prison.

Don Carlos visited us several times while we were in Liberty jail, and brought our wives to see us, and some money and articles to relieve our necessities. He took charge of father's family in his flight from Missouri, and saw them removed to Quincy, Illinois.

In June, 1839, he commenced making preparations for printing the *Times and Seasons*. The press and type had been resurrected by Elias Smith, Hyrum Clark, and others, from its grave in Dawson's yard, Far West, where it was buried for safety the night that General Lucas surrounded the city with the mob militia. The form for a number of the *Elders' Journal* was buried with the ink on it. The types were considerably injured by the damp; it was therefore necessary to get them into use as soon as possible, and in order to do this, Don Carlos was under the necessity of cleaning out a cellar through which a spring was constanty flowing, as the only place where he could put up the press. Ebenezer Robinson and wife being sick, threw the entire burden on him.

His Ministrations to the Sick.

As a great number of brethren lay sick in the town, on Tuesday, 23rd July, 1839, I told Don Carlos and George A. Smith to go and visit all the sick, exercise mighty faith, and administer to them in the name of Jesus Christ, commanding the destroyer to depart, and the people to arise and walk; and not leave a single person on the bed between my house and Ebenezer Robinson's, two miles distant; they administered to over sixty persons, many of whom thought they would never sit up again; but they were healed, arose from their beds, and gave glory to God; some of them assisted in visiting and administering to others who were sick.

Working in the damp cellar, and administering to the sick impaired his health so that the first number of the *Times and Seasons* was not issued until November. He edited thirty-one numbers.

He was elected major in the Hancock county militia, and on the death of Seymour Brunson, was made lieutenant-colonel.

He was elected on 1st February, 1841, a member of the City Council of Nauvoo, and took the necessary oath on 3rd February, and on the fourth he was elected brigadier-general of the second cohort of the Nauvoo Legion.

Personal Appearance of Don Carlos Smith.

He was six feet four inches high, was very straight and well made, had light hair, and was very strong and active. His usual weight when in health was 200 pounds. He was universally beloved by the Saints.

He left three daughters, namely, Agnes C., Sophronia C., and Josephine D.

The Iowa Stake of Zion.

President John Smith was unanimously acknowledged as the president of the stake in Iowa, David Pettigrew, M. C. Nickerson, counselors. Elias Smith was sustained as Bishop, and Joseph B. Noble and Joseph Mecham as his counselors.

A conference of the Church was held at Zarahemla, and the branches in Iowa, so far as represented, consisted of 750 members.

Shocks of an earthquake felt at several places in Spain.

Sunday, 8.—A water-spout destroyed twenty houses of Portpatrick, Scotland.

The funeral of Brother Don Carlos was attended by a vast concourse of friends and relatives; he was buried with military honors.

The Zarahemla conference appointed George W. Gee, Church Recorder, and was addressed by Elders John Taylor and George A. Smith, on building the Temple, and on temperance.

Monday, 9.—The steamboat *Erie* was burned on Lake Erie, thirty miles from Buffalo, and eight from the shore, two hundred persons on board, of whom one hundred and seventy-five perished.

Tuesday, *10*—I spent the day in council with Brigham Young, Heber C. Kimball, John Taylor, Orson Pratt, and George A. Smith, and appointed a special conference for the 16th instant. I directed them to send missionaries to New Orleans; Charleston, South Carolina; Salem, Massachusetts; Baltimore, Maryland; and Washington, District of Columbia. I also requested the Twelve to take the burthen of the business of the Church in Nauvoo, and especially as pertaining to the selling of Church lands.

New Mission Movement Planned.

The department of English literature and mathematics, of the University of the City of Nauvoo, is in operation under the tuition of Professor Orson Pratt.

General Orders, Nauvoo Legion.

HEADQUARTERS, NAUVOO LEGION,
CITY OF NAUVOO, Aug. 10, 1841.

It becomes our painful duty to officially notify the troops of our command of the untimely decease of that noble chief, Brigadier-General Don Carlos Smith—he fell, but not in battle—he perished, but not by the weapons of war—at his burial you paid him honor, but he is gathered to his fathers to receive greater honor.

In consequence of this afflicting dispensation of Divine Providence, the commissioned officers of the staff and line will wear crape on the left arm for thirty days. The commissioned officers of the second cohort will convene at General Smith's office, on Saturday, the 4th day of September, at 10 o'clock a. m., for the purpose of electing a brigadier-general, at which time and place the court of appeals will sit.

The legion will assemble at the usual place of rendezvous, in the city of Nauvoo, on Saturday, the 11th day of September, at 10 o'clock a.m., for the purpose of general parade. The militia officers of the county of

Hancock, Illinois; and the county of Lee, Iowa, are respectfully invited to attend. The adjutants of regiments will form their respective regiments at 9 o'clock and at 10 o'clock; the adjutant of the Legion will form the line by regiments, and not by companies as heretofore. A special court-martial will convene at the usual place, on Saturday, the 28th day of August, at 10 o'clock a. m., for the transaction of business.

JOSEPH SMITH, Lieutenant-General.

A shower of meteoric stones fell at Iwan in Hungary.

Depression of the Times.

Letters from various parts of England and Scotland show that numbers are daily added to the Church; while shipwrecks, floods, houses and workshops falling, great and destructive fires, sudden deaths, banks breaking, men's hearts failing them for fear, shop-keepers and manufacturers failing, because no man buyeth their merchandise, many accidents on the railways, etc., betoken the coming of the Son of Man.

Visit of the Sac and Fox Indians to Nauvoo.

Thursday, 12.—A considerable number of the Sac and Fox Indians have been for several days encamped in the neighborhood of Montrose. The ferryman brought over a great number on the ferry-boat and two flat boats for the purpose of visiting me. The military band and a detachment of Invincibles [part of the Legion] were on shore ready to receive and escort them to the grove, but they refused to come on shore until I went down. I accordingly went down, and met Keokuk, Kis-ku-kosh, Appenoose, and about one hundred chiefs and braves of those tribes, with their families. At the landing, I was introduced by Brother Hyrum to them; and after salutations, I conducted them to the meeting grounds in the grove, and instructed them in many things which the Lord had revealed unto me concerning their fathers, and the promises that were made concerning them in the Book of Mormon. I advised them to cease killing each other and warring with other tribes; also to keep peace with the whites; all of which was interpreted to them.

Keokuk replied that he had a Book of Mormon at his

wigwam which I had given him some years before. "I believe," said he, "you are a great and good man; I look rough, but I also am a son of the Great Spirit. I have heard your advice—we intend to quit fighting, and follow the good talk you have given us."

After the conversation they were feasted on the green with good food, dainties, and melons by the brethren; and they entertained the spectators with a specimen of their dancing.

Saturday, 14.—Sir J. M. Brunel, the engineer, with fifty ladies and gentlemen, made the first passage under the river Thames, England.

Sunday, 15.—My infant son, Don Carlos, died, aged 14 months, 2 days.

Conference met in Zarahemla, and was addressed by Elders Brigham Young and George Miller on building the Temple in Nauvoo.

Monday, 16.—Elder Willard Richards arrived at Nauvoo this morning.

Ebenezer Robinson succeeded Brother Don Carlos as editor of the *Times and Seasons*, with Elder Robert B. Thompson assistant editor.

Minutes of a Special Conference at Nauvoo—Important Action in Relation to the Twelve.

At a special conference of the Church of Jesus Christ of Latter-day Saints, held in the city of Nauvoo, August 16, 1841, Elder Brigham Young was unanimously appointed to preside over the conference, and Elias Smith and Lorenzo D. Barnes were appointed clerks.

Singing by the choir; conference opened by prayer, by the president.

The object of the conference was then presented by the president, who stated that President Joseph Smith (who was then absent on account of the death of his child) had called a special conference to transact certain items of business necessary to be done previous to the October conference—such as to select men of experience to send forth into the vineyard, take measures to assist emigrants who may arrive at the places of gathering, and prevent impositions being practiced upon them by unprincipled speculators. The speaker hoped that no one would view him and his brethren as aspiring, because they had come forward to take part in the proceedings before the conference; he could assure the brethren that nothing could be further from his wishes, and those of his quorum, than to interfere with Church affairs in Zion and her stakes. He had been in the vineyard so long, he had become attached to foreign missions, and nothing could induce him to retire therefrom and attend to the affairs of the Church at home but a sense of duty, the requirements of heaven, or the revelations of God; to which he would always submit, be the consequence what it might; and the brethren of his quorum responded, Amen.

A list of names of Elders and cities were read by the president, and a few were selected by nomination, and designated as follows: Voted that Elders Henry G. Sherwood go to New Orleans; Abraham O. Smoot to Charleston, South Carolina; Erastus Snow and Benjamin Winchester to Salem, Massachusetts; John Murdock to Baltimore, Maryland; and Samuel James to Washington, D. C.

On motion of Vinson Knight, seconded by Samuel Bent, resolved: that the quorum of the Twelve select the individuals to go and preach in such places as they may judge expedient, and present the same to the conference, with a view of expediting the business of the day.

The situation of the poor of Nauvoo City was then presented by Bishops Knight and Miller, and a collection taken for their benefit.

After singing, conference adjournd until 2 o'clock p. m.

All of the Twelve present at the conference went and visited President Joseph Smith to comfort him in his affliction.

Conference assembled at 2 p. m., and was addressed by Elders Lorenzo D. Barnes and Henry G. Sherwood, concerning the spread of the Gospel and the building up of the kingdom of God in these last days.

President Joseph Smith now arriving, proceeded to state to the conference at considerable length, the object of their present meeting, and, in addition to what President Young had stated in the morning, said that the time had come when the Twelve should be called upon to stand in their place next to the First Presidency, and attend to the settling of emigrants and the business of the Church at the stakes, and assist to bear off the kingdom victoriously to the nations, and as they had been faithful, and had borne the burden in the heat of the day, that it was right that they should have an opportunity of providing something for themselves and families, and at the same time relieve him, so that he might attend to the business of translating.

Moved, seconded and carried, that the conference approve of the instructions of President Smith in relation to the Twelve, and that they proceed accordingly to attend to the duties of their office.

Moved, seconded and carried unanimously, that every individual who shall hereafter be found trying to influence any emigrants belonging to the Church, either to buy of them (except provisions) or sell to them (except the Church agents), shall be immediately tried for fellowship, and dealt with as offenders, and unless they repent shall be cut off from the Church.

President Rigdon then made some appropriate remarks on speculation.

Moved, that the conference accept the doings of the Twelve, in designating certain individuals to certain cities, &c.; when President Smith remarked that the conference had already sanctioned the doings of the Twelve; and it belonged to their office to transact such business, with the approbation of the First Presidency; and he would then state what cities should now be built up—viz., Nauvoo, Zarahemla, Warren, Nashville, and Ramus.

Resolved: That this conference adjourn to the general conference in October next.

Closed with prayer by President Young.

BRIGHAM YOUNG, President.

ELIAS SMITH,
LORENZO BARNES,
Clerks.

CHAPTER XXIV.

HOTCHKISS LAND PURCHASE TROUBLES—DEATH'S HARVEST, OLIVER GRANGER, ROBERT B. THOMPSON—IMPORTANT ACTION RELATING TO THE TWELVE—THE MISSION IN FOX ISLAND.

Thursday, August 19, 1841.—Elders Young, Kimball and Richards went to Warsaw, and examined the town plat of Warren which is situated about a mile south of the village of Warsaw, and made some arrangements with the proprietors for building up the place.

The Founding of Warren.

The plat designed for the city of Warren is the school section, No. 16, and opposite the first permanent and good landing place on the Mississippi River below the falls; which is about two miles below the Warsaw landing, which is filling up with sand bars.

The brethren returned about eleven p. m., quite exhausted.

Sunday, 22.—I preached at the stand, on wars and desolations that await the nations.

Wednesday, 25.—I received the following letter:

Letter of Horace R. Hotchkiss to Joseph Smith—Land Affairs in Nauvoo.

FAIR HAVEN, 24th July, 1841.

Rev. Joseph Smith:

DEAR SIR:—I have this moment received a letter from Dr. Galland, dated yesterday, at New York, in which he states his intention of leaving for the west.

It certainly was my expectation that I should again see him before his departure, and be able to make some arrangement with him respecting the interest due to myself, Mr. Tuttle and Mr. Gillet. In this I am disappointed, and considering that a proposition for effecting this object emanated from your brother Hyrum and the doctor, [Isaac Galland] to which no allusion has since been made by them or anybody else, I and Mr. Tuttle think that we have much reason to be dissatisfied at this silence and apparent neglect.

Now, all the transactions relating to Nauvoo have by me and my friends been entered into in the most perfect good faith, and will continue to be conducted on the most honorable principles.

Permit me to ask whether this is a proper return for the confidence we have bestowed, and for the indulgence we have extended?

If you have not already requested your brother Hyrum to call on me when he arrives east, will you write him immediately, and say that it is my urgent wish?

Relative to the Ivins note the Doctor has written me, and referred to Mr. William Smith at New Egypt, on whom I shall call next week.

Your obedient servant,
HORACE R. HOTCHKISS.

I wrote the following answer:

Letter of the Prophet to Horace R. Hotchkiss—Nauvoo Land Transactions.

NAUVOO, August 25, 1841.

To Horace R. Hotchkiss, Esq., New Haven, Connecticut:

DEAR SIR:—Yours of the 24th ultimo came to hand this day, the contents of which I duly appreciate. I presume you are well aware of the difficulties that occurred before, and at the execution of the writings in regard to the land transaction between us, touching the annual payment of interest: if you have forgotten, I will here remind you, you verbally agreed on our refusal and hesitancy to execute the notes for the payment of the land, that you would not exact the payment of the interest that would accrue on them under five years, and that you would not coerce the payment even then; to all this you pledged your honor; and upon an after arrangement you verbally agreed to take land in some one of the Atlantic States, that would yield six per cent interest (to you) both for the principal and interest, and in view of that matter, I delegated my brother Hyrum and Dr. Isaac Galland to go east and negotiate for lands with our friends, and pay you off for the whole purchase that we made of you; but upon an interview with you, they learned that you were unwilling to enter into an arrangement according to the powers that I had delegated to them; that you would not receive any of the principal at all, but the interest alone, which we never considered ourselves in honor or in justice bound to pay under the expiration of five years. I presume you are no stranger to the part of the city plat we bought of you being a deathly sickly hole, and that we have not been able in consequence to realize any valuable consideration from it, although we have been keeping up appearances, and holding out inducements to encourage immigration, that we scarcely think justifiable in consequence of the mortality that almost invariably awaits those who come from far distant parts (and that with a view to enable us to meet our engagements), and now to be goaded by you, for a breach of good faith, and neglect and dishonorable conduct, seems to me to be almost beyond endurance.

You are aware that we came from Missouri destitute of everything but physical force, had nothing but our energies and perseverance to rely upon to meet the payment of the extortionate sum that you exacted for the land we had of you. Have you no feelings of commiseration? Or is it your design to crush us with a ponderous load before we are able to walk? Or can you better dispose of the property than we are doing for your interest? If so, to the alternative.

I therefore propose, in order to avoid the perplexity and annoyance that has hitherto attended the transaction, that you come and take the premises, and make the best you can of it, or stand off and give us an opportunity that we may manage the concern, and enable ourselves by the management thereof to meet our engagements, as was originally contemplated.

We have taken a city plat at Warsaw (at the head of navigation for vessels of heavy tonnage) on the most advantageous terms: the proprietors waiting upon us for the payment of the plat, until we can realize the money from the sales, leaving to ourselves a large and liberal net profit. We have been making every exertion, and used all the means at our command to lay a foundation that will now begin to enable us to meet our pecuniary engagements, and no doubt in our minds to the entire satisfaction of all those concerned, if they will but exercise a small degree of patience, and stay a resort to coercive measures which would kill us in the germ, even before we can (by reason of the season) begin to bud and blossom in order to bring forth a plentiful yield of fruit.

I am, with considerations of high respect,

Your obedient servant,

JOSEPH SMITH.

The Hotchkiss purchase, to which the foregoing letters relate includes all the land lying north of the White purchase to the river and thence on the river south, including the best steamboat landing, but is the most sickly part of Nauvoo.

Location and Character of the Hotchkiss Lands.

Elder Oliver Granger died at Kirtland, Lake county, Ohio, aged forty-nine years. He was the son of Pierce and Clarissa Granger, born in the town of Phelps, Ontario county, New York, 7th February, 1794; received a common school education, was two years a member of the Methodist Church and was a licensed exhorter. On the 8th September, 1813, he married Lydia Dibble; in the year 1827, he in a great measure lost his sight by cold and exposure; he was sheriff of Ontario county, and colonel of the militia. He received the Gospel on reading the Book of Mormon, which he providentially obtained, and was baptized at Sodus, Wayne county, and ordained an Elder by Brigham and Joseph Young, they being the first Elders he saw, and immediately devoted his time to preaching and warning the people.

Death of Oliver Granger.

In the year 1833 he moved to Kirtland, and then took a mission to the east with Elder Samuel Newcomb; returned and was ordained a High Priest; took another mission in the spring of 1836 to New York with John P. Greene; and after his return built up a branch at Huntsburg, Geauga county, Ohio; also a branch at Perry, Richfield county, where he baptized Bradley Wilson and his seven sons and their wives. When the Church left Kirtland he was appointed to settle the Church business.

In June, 1838, he went to Far West, and returned in August of same year; in October he again started, taking his family; he went seventy miles into Missouri, and was driven back by the mob; in the spring of 1839 he went to Nauvoo; in 1840 removed to Kirtland with his family, where he remained until his death.

He was a man of good business qualifications, but had been for many years nearly blind. His funeral was attended by a vast concourse of people from the neighboring towns, although there were but few Saints in the country.

Character.

Thursday, 26.

An Epistle of the Twelve Apostles to the Saints Scattered Abroad Among the Nations, Greeting.

NAUVOO, August 26, 1841.

BELOVED BRETHREN:—You will perceive by the minutes of a conference, held in this city, on the 16th instant, that we have returned from a mission which was required of us by the Lord, and have now been called upon to assist in building up the stakes of Zion, and of planting the Saints upon the lot of their inheritance; and feeling as we do a humble reliance upon divine aid at all times, in our unremitting desire to be useful to our fellow men, and especially to the household of faith, that they may be prepared for the great things which God is about to reveal, and which speedily await this generation, we feel anxious to improve the earliest opportunity to make known unto you the mind of the Spirit concerning those things which require your more immediate attention.

It will be discovered, in the minutes before referred to, that we have already begun to select such individuals as have been with the Church and have had the opportunity of becoming acquainted with the principles thereof to some extent; and to designate certain towns and cities where they will locate themselves and build up churches, inasmuch as the people are willing to receive them. These generally will not take their departure from this to their several stations, until after the October conference, previous to which they will have the opportunity of receiving particular instructions in relation to their mission, and of becoming more perfectly acquainted with those principles which are necessary to be acted upon in order that they may become highly useful in helping to roll forth the kingdom of God in these last days.

All those Elders and Priests who are now in the vineyard, will communicate with us immediately, and inform us of their situations, designs, and all things relating to their ministry, and improve the earliest opportunity of repairing hither, where they will have the privilege of instruction from the First Presidency, and thereby understanding principle and doctrine, not to be learned elsewhere, and which is necessary for them to know, that they may become wise stewards in their Master's house.

We are engaged in a great work, and but little comparatively can be known of the magnitude thereof, of the revelations of heaven, and the order of the kingdom by the Saints, while they are scattered to the four winds; and this being well understood by the ancient prophets and apostles, was the reason why they so often spoke of the gathering in the last days, and as this is the place where the Elders are to receive instruction concerning their ministry, so as to become successful ministers of the dispensation of the fulness of times, so also this is the place where the brethren may receive such instructions as are necessary to constitute them a righteous and holy people, prepared for the reception of the Lord Jesus; therefore, we say to all Saints who desire to do the will of heaven, Arise, and tarry not, but come up hither to the places of gathering as speedily as possible, for the time is rapidly approaching when the Saints will have occasion to regret that they have so long neglected to assemble themselves together and stand in holy places, awaiting those tremendous events which are so rapidly approaching the nations of the earth.

It will be recollected that in a recent communication from the First Presidency, all places of gathering are discontinued, excepting Hancock county, Illinois, and Zarahemla, in Lee county, Iowa territory, opposite Nauvoo, and we would suggest to those coming up the Mississippi particularly, and all others who are disposed, to look at Warsaw, a beautifully located village about twenty miles below Nauvoo, consisting of about five hundred inhabitants, a steam flour and lumber mill; one mile below is a section already surveyed, on which the town of Warren is to be built, and every facility is now offered to the brethren, for the immediate erection of houses, the location being very desirable at the lowest point of the DesMoines rapids.

As we have been called upon to act as agents for the Church, it may be expected that some one or more of our quorum may be found at Nauvoo, Zarahemla, and Warren, ready to render every assistance in our power, towards the location of immigrants; and that we shall occasionally visit the other places of gathering, as necessity requires.

We recommend to the brethren in England to emigrate in the fall or winter; by so doing they will be likely to spare themselves much affliction in becoming accustomed to this climate.

Further communications may be expected from the Twelve.

BRIGHAM YOUNG,
HEBER C. KIMBALL.
ORSON PRATT,
WILLARD RICHARDS,
JOHN TAYLOR,
GEO. A. SMITH.

Friday, 27.—Elder Robert Blashel Thompson died at his residence in Nauvoo, in the 30th year of his age, in the full hope of a glorious resurrection. He was associate editor of the *Times and Seasons*, colonel in the Nauvoo Legion, and had done much writing for myself and the Church.

Death of Robert B. Thompson.

The following synopsis of his life is from the pen of his widow:

Biography of Robert Blashel Thompson.

Robert Blashel Thompson was born October 1st, 1811, in Great Driffield, Yorkshire, England, was educated at Dunnington, in the same county. He united with the Methodists at an early age and preached what he believed to be the Gospel in connection with that sect for a number of years. Emigrated to Upper Canada in 1834. Embraced the Gospel there; being baptized and confirmed by Elder Parley P. Pratt in May, 1836. Was ordained an Elder by Elder John Taylor, at a conference held in Upper Canada, July 22nd, 1836. Removed to Kirtland in May, 1837, where he married Mercy Rachel Fielding, June 4th, 1837, and being appointed to take a mission to Upper Canada, he returned the same month, and commenced preaching in Churchville and the villages adjacent, baptized a considerable number, continued his labors there until he was called upon to remove to Missouri.

He arrived at Kirtland in March, and started from thence in company with Hyrum Smith and family, arrived in Far West June 3rd, where his daughter, Mary Jane, was born on the 14th of June. He remained there until November, when he, with many of the brethren had to flee into the wilderness to escape the fury of the mob, who swore they would kill every man who had been engaged in the Crooked River battle.

He stood near to Brother Patten when he [Patten] fell. With the rest of the brethren he suffered much from exposure and lack of food. He arrived at Quincy, I believe, in December, where he engaged as clerk in the court house, and remained there until the liberation of Joseph and Hyrum from prison; when the Saints settled in Commerce, he removed there, and was engaged as a scribe to Brother Joseph; he was also Church clerk.

When the Nauvoo Legion was formed, he received the office of colonel and also aid-de-camp. In May, 1841, he became associated with Don Carlos Smith in the editing of the *Times and Seasons*. On the 16th of August he was seized with the same disease of which Don Carlos had died on the 7th. The attachment between them was so strong, it seemed as though they could not long be separated. He died on the 27th, leaving one child; was interred in the burying ground on the 29th. By his special request no military procession was formed at his funeral.

Saturday, *28*.—At a conference held at Attica, New York, six branches, ten Elders, seven Priests, five Teachers, two Deacons and one hundred and forty-six members were represented.

Tuesday, *21*.

Minutes of a Council Meeting of the Twelve Apostles at the House of Brigham Young, Nauvoo.

At a council of the Quorum of the Twelve Apostles at the house of President Brigham Young, Nauvoo, August 31, 1841, for the purpose of taking into consideration the situation of the Church, it was resolved unanimously, that as we [the Twelve] have been called upon by the voice of the conference to attend to the business of the Church, assist the Trustee in Trust in his arduous duties, attend to the settling of immigrants, &c.; we sensibly feel the great responsibility that is resting upon us, and will do all in our power to carry out the wishes of the Church, and prove ourselves worthy of the trust imposed in us by the brethren.

Resolved unanimously, that, so far as may be practicable, we will attend to the counseling and locating of immigrants in person, and at present we will appoint no agents for that purpose out of our own body.

Voted, that Elder Willard Richards be requested to locate himself for a season at Warsaw, or vicinity, for the purpose of selling lots on the town plat of Warren, counseling the brethren, and attending to such other business as may be necessary relating to the Church. The foregoing vote was taken after hearing a favorable report from Elders Young, Kimball, and Richards, of the quorum, for building the town called Warren, they having visited the location, accompanied by Mr. Mark Aldrich and other proprietors of the plat.

Resolved, unanimously, that we deeply feel for our beloved President Joseph Smith, and his father's family, on account of the great losses they have sustained in property by the unparalleled persecutions in Missouri, as well as the other many persecutions they have sustained since the rise of the Church, which has brought them to their present destitute situation. Therefore, voted unanimously, that we for ourselves, and the Church we represent, approve of the proceedings of President Smith, so far as he has gone, in making over certain properties to his wife, children, and friends for their support, and that he continue to deed and make over certain portions of Church property which now exist, or which may be obtained by exchange, as in his wisdom he shall judge expedient, till his own, and his father's household, shall have an inheritance secured to them in our midst, agreeably to the vote of the general conference of the Church held at Commerce in October, 1839.

Resolved: that on account of the peculiar situation of the Church hitherto, it has been expedient and necessary, that the deeds, bonds, and properties of the Church should be, and have been taken and holden by committees of the Church, and private individuals; but that we now have a trustee-in-trust, viz., President Joseph Smith, appointed according to the laws of the land. Therefore, voted unanimously, that we advise the trustee-in-trust to gather up all deeds, bonds, and properties belonging to the Church, and which are now held either by committees or individuals, and take the same in his own name as trustee-in-trust for the Church of Jesus Christ of Latter-day Saints, as soon as such arrangements can be made consistently with his various and multiplied cares and business; and that we individually and collectively will use all diligence to render him every assistance possible to accomplish this desirable object.

Voted, that Elder Lorenzo D. Barnes proceed on his mission to England without delay.

Voted, that Elder Harrison Sagers proceed immediately on his mission to Jamaica, West Indies; and Elder Joseph Ball to South America, according to their appointment on the 16th, and that they accompany each other to New Orleans.

It was proposed, that Elder Simeon Carter go on a mission to Germany; but the vote being taken, it was decided that his mission be suspended for the present.

After much deliberation on the situation of the Church at home and abroad, temporarily and spiritually, and in view of the poverty and distress of many who had been robbed of all by unrelenting mobbers, and of others who have sacrificed all they possessed to assist those who had thus been robbed, and others who had borne the burden in the heat of the day; it was voted unanimously, that President Smith, as trustee-in-trust, be requested and instructed by this conference in behalf of the Church, to extend relief to such indigent suffering brethren, either by land or goods, as the properties of the Church will admit, and his wisdom shall judge expedient; so that no one shall be denied the privilege of remaining in our midst and enjoying the necessaries of life, who has been faithful in his duties to God and the Church.

BRIGHAM YOUNG, President.
WILLARD RICHARDS, Clerk.

Wednesday, Sept. 1.—The *New York Sun* contains an account of some singular phenomena; viz., a shower of flesh and blood, a pillar of smoke, and a shower of manna.

Thursday, 2.—The town of Cartago, on the isthmus of Darien, containing 10,000 inhabitants, destroyed by an earthquake.

Changes of Officers in the Legion.

Saturday, 4.—Colonel Charles C. Rich was elected brigadier-general of the second cohort, to fill the vacancy of General Don Carlos Smith, deceased, and Lieutenant-Colonel Titus Billings was elected colonel in the place of Colonel Rich, promoted, and Major John Scott was elected lieutenant-colonel in his place, and Captain Hosea Stout was elected major in his place.

Changes Among the Civil Officers of Nauvoo.

The City Council elected Brigham Young councilor in place of Don Carlos Smith, deceased; and John Taylor and Heber C. Kimball were elected regents of the University, in place of Don Carlos Smith and Robert B. Thompson, deceased.

Orson Pratt was elected professor of mathematics in the University of the City of Nauvoo, and the degree of master of arts conferred on him by the chancellor and board of regents.

A committee was instructed to purchase two blocks for a burying ground; and the city recorder was instructed to procure a seal for the corporation.

Elder Orson Spencer arrived in the city.

The Prophet on Medicine.

Sunday, 5.—I preached to a large congregation at the stand, on the science and practice of medicine, desiring to persuade the Saints to trust in God when sick, and not in an arm of flesh, and live by faith and not by medicine, or poison; and when they were sick, and had called for the Elders to pray for them, and they were not healed, to use herbs and mild food.

Tuesday, 7.—Another shower of flesh and blood is reported in the Boston papers to have fallen in Kensington. "There had been a drizzling rain during a great part of the day, until about 4 o'clock in the afternoon, when the rain stopped and the dark clouds began gradually to assume a brassy hue, until the whole heavens above seemed a sea of fire. The sky continued to grow more bright until about a quarter past five, when almost instantly it became of burnished red, and in a few moments it rained moderately a thick liquid of the appearance of blood, clothing fields and roads for two miles in circumference in a blood-stained garment. The bloody rain continued for about ten minutes, when it suddenly cleared away, and the atmosphere became so intensely cold that overcoats were needed."

A Shower of "Flesh."

Elder Willard Richards went to Warsaw, and located himself, for the purpose of counseling the Saints, and settling the town of Warren, and the day following made sale of three city lots.

The war between England and China continues. The English have fitted out a new expedition to proceed against China with the utmost rigor, and his celestial majesty on the other hand has issued orders for the raising of a "grand army," and the extermination of the English.

British-Chinese War.

Wednesday, 8.—Wars and rumors of wars, earthquakes, tempests, pestilence, and great fires, connected with every kind of wickedness, distress and destruction of property are heard in almost every land and nation.

Sunday, 11.

Extracts from Legion Minutes.

The Legion was out for general parade, in conformity with a special act of the court martial, and was reviewed by Lieutenant-General Joseph Smith, who delivered a military speech to the troops in his usual energetic style. The official returns of the Legion show the aggregate to be 1,490 men.

HOSEA STOUT, Clerk.

Monday, 13.—Brother Edward Hunter, Sen,* of Chester county, Pennsylvania, visited Nauvoo, and invested $4,500 in town lots and farming land; paid me $2,000 in cash, and made arrangements to pay the balance in two months.

The Coming of Edward Hunter to Nauvoo.

Received an invitation from Brigadier-General Ezekiel W. Swazey, and Colonel Amos B. Fuller, of the militia of Lee county, Iowa, to attend the military parade tomorrow, at Montrose, as visitor. Generals Hyrum Smith and John C. Bennett received a similar invitation.

Tuesday, 14.—Went over to Montrose, accompanied by Brothers Edward Hunter and William A. Gheen. I was very courteously received by General Swazey, the officers and militia.

Mr. D. W. Kilbourn attempted to get up an ill feeling by reading the following proclamation at noon, during the recess of exercise, to a considerable number of persons collected round his store, which I insert verbatim—

Bitterness of D. W. Kilbourn.

* Edward Hunter was the second son and seventh child of Edward and Hannah Hunter. He was born in Newtown Township, Delaware county, Pennsylvania. June 22, 1793. His paternal ancestors were from the north of England, and on his mother's side he was of Welsh extraction. John Hunter, his great-grandfather, passed over to Ire and some time in the seventeenth century and served as a lieutenant of cavalry under William of Orange at the battle of the Boyne, where he was wounded. He afterwards came to America and settled in Delaware county, Pennsylvania, about twelve miles from Philadelphia. Edward Hunter, Esq., the Bishop's father, was justice of the peace in Delaware county for forty years. On his mother's side three generations back was Robert Owen of North Wales, a man of wealth and character, a firm sympathizer with Cromwell and the Protectorate, who on the restoration of Charles the Second,refused to take the oath of allegiance, and was imprisoned for five years. After his release he emigrated to America and purchased property near the "City of Brotherly Love." Like the founder of that city, Robert Owen was a Quaker. His son George sat in the state legislature and held various positions of public trust (Whitney).

Edward Hunter finally settled in Chester county, Pennsylvania, where he purchased an extensive farm, and married Ann Standley, daugher of Jacob and Martha Standley. Here Mormonism found him in 1839, through the preaching of some of the Elders laboring in that vicinity, and Mr. Hunter extended to them the hospitality of his home. En route from Washington to Nauvoo, in the winter of 1839-40, the Prophet Joseph visited him, and for several days preached in the vicinity of the Hunter homestead. Other prominent Elders of the Church also visited the Hunter home, among them the Prophet's brother, Hyrum. Finally on the 8th of

Citizens of Iowa:—The laws of Iowa do not require you to muster under, or be *reviewed* by *Joe Smith* or *General Bennett*, and should they have the impudence to attempt it, it is hoped that every person having a proper respect for himself, will at once leave the ranks.

This, however, had no effect whatever on the people.

Myself and brother were not in military uniform, but were treated with every respect that visiting officers of our rank could be, through the entire day. At the dismissal of the military, I went to Mr. Kilbourn's store, and desired to have some conversation with him, but was peremptorily ordered out of doors. This conduct greatly disgusted his few friends, who upbraided Kilbourn with his ungentlemanly conduct, and accompanied me to the ferry, where I left them, showing me every manifestation of friendship.

Tuesday, 21.—The ship *Tyrean* sailed from Liverpool to New Orleans, with 204 Saints, bound for Nauvoo.

Her British Majesty's war steamer *Madagascar*, totally destroyed by fire in the Chinese seas, and fifty-seven lives lost.

Wednesday, 22.—The High Council of Nauvoo adopted the following preamble and resolution—

High Council Resolution.

Whereas this High Council in times past, had of necessity, and by the advice and instruction of the First Presidency, to transact business of a temporal nature for the Church, and thereby involve itself with debts and other temporal burdens which, under other circumstances would not have devolved upon it; and as the proper authorities to which such temporalities belong are now organized and acting in their proper places; therefore, be it

Resolved, that this High Council is prepared to transfer all debts and temporal business; and that all business of a temporal nature, be, and the same is in readiness to be transferred to the proper authorities.

Alpheus Cutler stated [to the council] that he was going to the pineries the ensuing winter, and nominated Elias Higbee, counselor *pro tem.*

October, 1841, Edward Hunter was baptized by Elder Orson Hyde, then on his way to Jerusalem. This brings the biography of the future Bishop of the Church up to the time of his first appearance in Nauvoo, on the 13th of September, 1841, and henceforth the events of his life will be closely interwoven in the history of the Church.

A company of the brethren started for the pinery, some five or six hundred miles north, on the river, for the purpose of procuring lumber for the Temple and Nauvoo House.

Lumber for the Temple.

The Jews in Smyrna are suffering great persecutions on account of their religion—"one was thrown into prison because a cat was missing"—say the journals.

Saturday 25.—Hyrum Smith, son of Hyrum and Jerusha Smith, died, aged seven years, four months, and twenty-eight days.

A conference was held at Vinal Haven, Fox Island; eight Elders, one Priest, two Teachers, one Deacon, and one hundred and forty members were represented, and the work is progressing.

I extract the following from Elder Wilford Woodruff's journal—

The Work on Fox Island.

We left Manitou Island, Lake Michigan, at 4 o'clock p. m., on the steamer *Chesapeake*, which contained 300 passengers, six of whom were members of the Church; a large quantity of freight and coal, eighty cords of wood, eighty mules, besides pigs, chickens, geese, ducks, &c.

We continued our journey towards Chicago without any interruption, until half-past eleven p. m., when we were overtaken by a tremendous storm of wind and rain; it blew a hurricane, and the lake became as rough as it could be by the force of wind, and such a scene as quickly followed I never before witnessed in my travels, either by land or sea. The captain, officers, hands, and most of the passengers expected to go to the bottom of the lake. To have judged from outward appearances I should think there were twenty chances of being lost to one of being saved, yet I did not once expect to be lost, for I believed the Lord would by some means save me and my wife and child, who were with me, from a watery grave.

We were some forty miles from land when the gale struck us, and I was awakened from a sound sleep by the cry, "We are all lost." The first thought that entered my mind was, "No, we shall not be lost."

I immediately leaped out of my berth and went on to the upper deck. I saw we were in imminent danger of being wrecked; the bow of the boat was heavily laden, and frequently engulfed by the heavy waves that washed over her; there were judged to be fifty tons of water at a time on her bow; at one time her bow ran under water, and some thought she would never rise; the water set the mules and all the live stock afloat; washed away the partition; and the mules, pigs, chickens, ducks, and geese, were all hurled in one mass down into the steerage cabin, mixed pell mell with sixty Irish passengers, men, women, and children; at that moment the roaring of the wind, the rush of the waters, the peals of thunder, the flashes of lightning, the braying of asses, the squealing of pigs, the quacking of ducks, geese and chickens, the praying, swearing and screaming of men, women and children, created a confusion of sounds which rent the air, and sent a gloomy thrill through the heart.

We immediately went to work, and helped all the passengers out of the water, and from among the beasts, upon the deck, so their lives were preserved, while all the fowls, pigs, and part of the mules were drowned or killed; many tons of water rushed through the boat, until the water stood nearly to the boilers; it drove the firemen from their places.

About this time when the boat was laboring against wind and tide one of the wheel chains broke, and the boat rolled over on to one side. I again heard the cry that "all was lost," but about thirty of us caught hold of the two detached pieces of chain, and held them together until the engineer mended them with wire.

It took three strong men to manage the wheel; while the boat lay upon her side, it washed away a part of the state rooms; orders were given to clear the boat of everything that was movable; all the wood was fastened with stanchions, on the side that was down, the stanchions were knocked out by the passengers, and forty cords of wood tumbled into the sea at one surge; this caused the boat to right up, and we expected every moment our state room would be washed away. I left it three times with my wife and child, and stepped upon the main deck, expecting to see it washed away; and to add to the horror of the situation, we were wrapped in darkness, as all the lanterns were dashed to pieces.

The men at the wheel labored hard for five hours to turn the boat round, before they accomplished it, so that they could run before the storm. At length daylight appeared, and with it a cessation of the storm in a measure. We returned to Manitou Island at 4 o'clock, being twenty-fours hours out, mostly in the storm.

Thursday, *30*.—The following is a copy of a statement of expenses consequent upon the arrest of Joseph Smith, upon demand from Governor Boggs, and sent to the deputy sheriff of Adams county, he having officiated June, 1841.

NAUVOO, September 30, 1841.

The Deputy Sheriff of Adams County:

The following is a statement of my expenses, costs, and liabilities, consequent upon my arrest and trial while in your custody, to-wit—

To amount of fees in Esquires Ralston, Warren, and Co.	$250.00
To Esquires Little, Williams, Walker, and Browning	100.00
To seven days for self, horse, and carriage, at $5.00	35.00
To money expended during that time, consequent upon the arrest	60.00
To twelve witnesses, to-wit: Elias Higbee, John P. Greene, Amasa Lyman, Darwin Chase, Francis Higbee, Chauncy Higbee, Reynolds Cahoon, George W. Rohinson, J. Younger, L. Woodworth, Vinson Knight, and Robert B. Thompson, four days each; their time, carriages, horses and expenses, at $5.00 each day.......................	240.00
	$685.00

DEAR SIR:—You will please take such measures as to put me in possession of the above amount, which is justly due me as above stated; to say nothing of false imprisonment and other expenses. This would have been presented earlier, but for the sickness and death of Robert B. Thompson, my clerk.

Receive my respects, &c.,

JOSEPH SMITH.

Per JOHN S. FULLMER.

Friday, October 1.—Among the interesting relics of antiquity which have been brought to light in these days, is the following sentence from the *Courier des Etats Unis:*

Sentence Rendered by Pontius Pilate, Acting Governor of Lower Galilee, Stating that Jesus of Nazareth shall Suffer Death on the Cross.

In the year seventeen of the Emperor Tiberius Cæsar, and the 25th day of March, the city of the Holy Jerusalem, Anna and Caiaphas being priests, sacrificators of the people of God, Pontius Pilate, governor of Lower Galilee, sitting on the presidential chair of the Prætory, condemns Jesus of Nazareth to die on the cross between two thieves—the great and notorious evidence of the people saying—1. Jesus is a seducer. 2. He is seditious. 3. He is an enemy of the law. 4. He calls himself falsely the Son of God. 5. He calls himself falsely the King of Israel. 6. He entered into the temple, followed by a multitude bearing palm branches in their hands. Order the first centurion, Quills Cornelius, to lead him to the place of execution. Forbid to any person whomsoever, either poor or rich, to oppose the death of Jesus.

The witnesses who signed the condemnation of Jesus are, viz.—1. Daniel Robani. 2. Raphel Robani. 3. Capet, a citizen. Jesus shall go out of the city of Jerusalem by the gate of Struenus.

The above sentence is engraved on a copper plate; on one side are written these words—"A similar plate is sent to each tribe." It was found in an antique vase of white marble, while excavating in the ancient city of Aquilla, in the kingdom of Naples, in the year 1820, and was discovered by the Commissaries of Arts attached to the French armies. At the expedition of Naples, it was found enclosed in a box of ebony, in the Sacristy of the Chartrem. The vase in the Chapel of Caserta. The French translation was made by the members of the Commission of Arts. The original is in the Hebrew language. The Chartrem requested earnestly that the plate should not be taken away from them. The request was granted as a reward for the sacrifice they had made for the army. M. Denon, one of the Savans, caused a plate to be made of the same model, on which he had engraved the above sentence. At the sale of his collection of antiquities, &c., it was bought by Lord Howard for 2,890 francs. Its intrinsic value and interest are much greater.

A few years ago, there was found at Catskill, in New York, a shekel of Israel, of the time of our Savior. On one side was the representation of a palm leaf, on the other a picture of the temple, with the words underneath, "Holy Jerusalem," in the Hebrew tongue.

Relics like these, properly authenticated, have about them an inexpressible sacredness.*

* To the sentiment here expressed by the Prophet, no one will withhold his assent, but he will need to emphasize the phrase "properly authenticated," because it is unquestionably the case that many alleged early Christian documents of the character of the above are spurious; and whether the above alleged formal sentence was really rendered by Pontius Pilate or not, may not be determined. As remarked by nearly all authorities upon this subject, it is probable that Pilate made an official report to Tiberius of both the condemnation and punishment of Jesus Christ. Rev. J. R. Beard, D.D., member of the Historico-Theological Society of Liepzig, and author of the article "Pilate," in Kitto's Biblical Literature, says: "The voice of antiquity intimates that Pilate did make such a report; the words of Justin Martyr are: [second century] 'That these things were so done you may know from the 'Acts' made in the time of Pontius Pilate.' A similar passage is found a little

further on in the same work [i. e. Justin's apology]. Now when it is considered that Justin's Apology was a set defense of Christianity, in the shape of an appeal to the heathen world through the persons of its highest functionaries, it must seem very unlikely that the words would have been used had no such document existed; and nearly as improbable that these 'Acts' [of Pilate] would have been referred to had they not been genuine." Dr. Lardner, who has, perhaps, more fully discussed the subject than any other writer upon it, decides that, "It must be allowed by all that Pontius Pilate composed some memoirs concerning our Savior, and sent them to the emperor." (See Lardner, Vol. vi, p. 610.) And yet this very author says that the Acts of Pontius Pilate, "and his letter to Tiberius which we now have, are not genuine, but manifestly spurious."

In Smith's Dictionary of the Bible, it is stated that "We learn from Justin Martyr, Tertullian, Eusebius and others, that Pilate made an official report to Tiberius of our Lord's trial and condemnation, and in a homily ascribed to, though marked as spurious by his Benedictine editors, certain 'acts' or 'comments' of Pilate, are spoken of as well known documents in common circulation." (Article Pilate.) Then the author of this article on Pilate—Rev. Henry Wright Phillott, student of Christ Church, Oxford, adds: "That he, (Pilate) made such a report is highly probable, and it may have been in existence in Chrysostom's time; but the 'Acts of Pilate,' (Acta Pilati,) now extant in Greek, and two Latin epistles from him to the emperor, are certainly spurious;" and it is further said, "The number of extant 'Acta Pilati,' in various forms, is so large as to show that very early the demand created a supply of documents manifestly spurious, and we have no reason for looking on any one of those that remain as more authentic than the others."

Whether or not the above document in the text, purported to be Pilate's formal sentence of death upon Jesus is among the early Christian documents that are spurious, I am not able to determine by any works at my command, and the modification in the sentence of the Prophet above, which states, that "relics like these, *properly authenticated*, have about them an inexpressible sacredness," would rather indicate the existence of doubt in his own mind as to the absolute certainty of the above document being genuine; and I by no means consider that he commits himself to the genuineness of the document by publishing it in the annals of the Church. Such documents are only inexpressibly sacred if the authentication is beyond question; and he does not here discuss that question.

CHAPTER XXV.

THE GENERAL CONFERENCE OF THE CHURCH AT NAUVOO—DOCTRINAL SERMON BY THE PROPHET—BAPTISM FOR THE DEAD—ANGELS AND MINISTERING SPIRITS—EPISTLE OF THE TWELVE REVIEWING STATUS OF THE CHURCH.

GEORGE M. HINCKLE, who robbed my house in Far West while I was in prison, passing down the river with a flat boat, I commenced suit against him before the District Court, now sitting at Burlington, Iowa. I sent Elias Smith, and Geo. W. Gee to attend to the suit; but Hinckle gave security, and got it put off till spring.

Suit Against Geo.M.Hinckle.

Day stormy and cold, a few assembled, but conference did not organize.

I received a letter from Benjamin Winchester, requesting to be excused from accompanying Elder Erastus Snow on his mission to Salem, Massachusetts, on account of ill health and pecuniary embarrassments, and expressing his conviction that Elder John E. Page had means enough to accompany Elder Orson Hyde to Jerusalem.

Saturday, October 2, 1841.

Minutes of the General Conference of the Church Held at Nauvoo.

Conference met in the Grove. The Presidency being absent laying the corner stone of the Nauvoo House, the meeting was called to order by President Brigham Young; the several quorums were arranged and seated in order.

President Brigham Young opened conference by prayer.

The conference then made choice of President Joseph Smith to preside, and Elias Smith and Gustavus Hills, Clerks. Meeting adjourned until 2 p. m.

Prayer by Orson Pratt.

2 p. m., President Joseph Smith opened the meeting. Choir sung the 18th hymn.

The President then read a letter from Elder Orson Hyde, dated Ratisbon, July 17, 1841, giving an account of his journey and success in his mission, which was listened to with intense interest; and the conference by vote, expressed their approbation of the style and spirit of said letter. The President then made remarks on the inclemency of the weather, and the uncomfortable situation of the Saints with regard to a place of worship, and a place of public entertainment.

The conference was then called upon by the President, to elect a general Church clerk, in place of Robert B. Thompson, deceased. James Sloan was nominated and elected.

Elder Lyman Wight nominated Bishop George Miller to preside over the High Priests' quorum in place of Don Carlos Smith, deceased. He was duly elected.

President Brigham Young then presented the business commenced at the late special conference of the 16th of August with regard to the appointment of suitable and faithful men to the several important stations of labor in this and other countries.

Elder Lyman Wight addressed the conference on the importance of order, uniformity of instruction, and unanimity of effort to spread the work of the kingdom.

President Joseph Smith made some corrections of doctrine, quoting I Cor. xii:28, showing the principle of order and unity in the offices of the Priesthood.

The Patriarch Hyrum Smith made remarks disapproving of the course pursued by some Elders in counteracting the efforts of the presidency to gather the Saints, and in enticing them to stop in places not appointed for the gathering, particularly referring to the conduct of Elder Almon W. Babbitt of Kirtland.

Elders Lyman Wight, and Henry W. Miller testified that they had traveled in places where Elder Babbitt had been, on his return from his visit to Nauvoo, [he had] taught doctrine contrary to the revelations of God, and detrimental to the interests of the Church.

Moved and carried that Elder Almon W. Babbitt be disfellowshiped until he shall make satisfaction.

Choir sang Hymn 124. Prayer by Elder George A. Smith.

Conference adjourned until tomorrow at nine o'clock.

Sunday, 3.

Conference assembled in Nauvoo according to adjournment; prayer by Elder Heber C. Kimball.

President Joseph Smith, by request of the Twelve Apostles, gave instructions on the doctrine of baptism for the dead, which were listened to with intense interest by the large assembly. He presented baptism for the dead as the only way that men can appear as saviors on Mount Zion.

The proclamation of the first principles of the Gospel was a means of salvation to men individually; and it was the truth, not men, that saved them; but men, by actively engaging in rites of salvation substitutionally became instrumental in bringing multitudes of their kindred into the kingdom of God.

He explained the difference between an angel and a ministering spirit; the one a resurrected or translated body, with its spirit ministering to embodied spirits—the other a disembodied spirit, visiting and ministering to disembodied spirits. Jesus Christ became a ministering spirit (while His body was lying in the sepulchre) to the spirits in prison, to fulfill an important part of His mission, without which He could not have perfected His work, or entered into His rest. After His resurrection He appeared as an angel to His disciples.

Translated bodies cannot enter into rest until they have undergone a change equivalent to death. Translated bodies are designed for future missions.

The angel that appeared to John on the Isle of Patmos was a translated or resurrected body [i. e. personage], Jesus Christ went in body after His resurrection, to minister to resurrected bodies. There has been a chain of authority and power from Adam down to the present time.

The best way to obtain truth and wisdom is not to ask it from books, but to go to God in prayer, and obtain divine teaching. It is no more incredible that God should *save* the dead, than that he should *raise* the dead.

There is never a time when the spirit is too old to approach God. All are within the reach of pardoning mercy, who have not committed the unpardonable sin, which hath no forgiveness, neither in this world, nor in the world to come. There is a way to release the spirits of the dead; that is by the power and authority of the Priesthood—by binding and loosing on earth. This doctrine appears glorious, inasmuch as it exhibits the greatness of divine compassion and benevolence in the extent of the plan of human salvation.

This glorious truth is well calculated to enlarge the understanding, and to sustain the soul under troubles, difficulties and distresses. For illustration, suppose the case of two men, brothers, equally intelligent, learned, virtuous and lovely, walking in uprightness and in all good conscience, so far as they have been able to discern duty from the muddy stream of tradition, or from the blotted page of the book of nature.

One dies and is buried, having never heard the Gospel of reconciliation; to the other the message of salvation is sent, he hears and embraces it, and is made the heir of eternal life. Shall the one become the partaker of glory and the other be consigned to hopeless perdition? Is there no chance for his escape? Sectarianism answers "none." Such an idea is worse than atheism. The truth shall break down and dash in pieces all such bigoted Pharisaism; the sects shall be sifted, the honest in heart brought out, and their priests left in the midst of their corruption.

Many objections are urged against the Latter-day Saints for not admitting the validity of sectarian baptism, and for withholding fellowship from sectarian churches. Yet to do otherwise would be like putting new wine into old bottles, and putting old wine into new bottles. What! new revelations in the old churches? New revelations would knock out the bottom of their bottomless pit. New wine into old bottles! The bottles burst and the wine runs out! What! Sadducees in the new church! Old wine in new leathern bottles will leak through the pores and escape. So the Sadducee saints mock at authority, kick out of the traces, and run to the mountains of perdition, leaving the long echo of their braying behind them.

He then referred to the [lack of] charity of the sects, in denouncing all who disagree with them in opinion, and in joining in persecuting the Saints, who believe that even such may be saved, in this world and in the world to come (murderers and apostates excepted).

This doctrine presents in a clear light the wisdom and mercy of God in preparing an ordinance for the salvation of the dead, being baptized by proxy, their names recorded in heaven and they judged according to the deeds done in the body. This doctrine was the burden of the scriptures. Those Saints who neglect it in behalf of their decased relatives, do it at the peril of their own salvation. The dispensation of the fullness of times will bring to light the things that have been revealed in all former dispensations; also other things that have not been before revealed. He shall send Elijah, the Prophet, &c., and restore all things in Christ.

President Joseph Smith then announced: "There shall be no more baptisms for the dead, until the ordinance can be attended to in the Lord's House; and the Church shall not hold another General Conference, until they can meet in said house. *For thus saith the Lord!*"

Prayer by President Hyrum Smith.

Adjourned for one hour.

Afternoon conference opened by the choir singing hymn 105, and prayer by Elder Lyman Wight.

President Brigham Young addressed the Elders at some length, on the importance of teaching abroad the first principles of the Gospel, leaving the mysteries of the kingdom to be taught among the Saints, also on the propriety of many of the Elders remaining at home, and working on the Lord's House; and that their labors will be as acceptable to the Lord as their going abroad, and more profitable for the Church. That those who go abroad must take a recommend from the proper authorities, without which they will not be fellowshiped; and that those who go, and those who remain make consecrations more abundantly than heretofore.

Elder Lyman Wight followed with remarks of a similar purport; resigning his mission of gathering means for the Temple and Nauvoo House.

The conference appointed Elias Higbee, John Taylor, and Elias Smith, to petition Congress for redress of wrongs sustained in Missouri; and Elder John Taylor to present the petition.

Closed by the choir singing hymn 125, and prayer by President John Smith.

Conference assembled on the morning of Monday, the 4th.

Prayer by Elder George A. Smith.

President Joseph Smith made a lengthy exposition of the condition of the temporal affairs of the Church, the agency of which had been committed to him at a general conference in Quincy—explaining the manner that he had discharged the duties involved in the agency, and the conditions of the lands and other property of the Church.

On motion, resolved: that Elder Reuben McBride be invested with power of attorney to settle the business at Kirtland, left in an uncertain condition by Elder Oliver Grange, deceased.

Prayer by Elder Lyman Wight.

Adjourned for one hour.

Afternoon conference opened. Prayer by President John Smith.

Elder Lyman Wight spoke at some length on the subject introduced in the former part of the day, and on the old debts and obligations that are frequently brought up from Kirtland and Missouri; one of which, in the form of a $50 note, he held in his hand, and proclaimed it as his text.

On motion, voted unanimously, that the trustee-in-trust be instructed not to appropriate Church property to liquidate old claims that may be brought forward from Kirtland and Missouri.

President Hyrum Smith presented to the notice of the conference some embarrassment growing out of his signing as security, a certain obligation in Kirtland in favor of Mr. Eaton.

Voted, that Church property here shall not be appropriated to liquidate said claim.

President Brigham Young made some appropriate and weighty remarks on the importance of more liberal consecrations and more energetic efforts to forward the work of building the Temple and Nauvoo House; and after purchasing Elder Wight's text, by paying him fifty cents, tore it in pieces and gave it to the winds, saying, "Go ye and do likewise, with all old claims against the Church."

Choir sang hymn 104, and President Hyrum Smith closed by prayer.

Tuesday, 5th. Conference opened by the choir singing hymn 274, and prayer by Elder Orson Pratt.

Elder Orson Pratt, by request of President Joseph Smith, read a letter from Smith Tuttle, Esq., one of the proprietors of the Hotchkiss purchase, in reference to some misunderstanding in the adjustment of their claims, and conciliatory of any hard feelings growing out of such misunderstanding.

President Brigham Young spoke on the contents of the letter, and expressed his earnest desire that the business might be speedily adjusted, and a proper title obtained by the Church.

Elders Lyman Wight and Hyrum Smith followed with appropriate remarks.

On motion, voted, That President Joseph Smith write to Mr. Hotchkiss on the subject.

On motion by President Joseph Smith, voted, that the Twelve write an epistle to the Saints abroad, to use their influence and exertions to secure by exchange, purchase, donation, &c., a title to the Hotchkiss purchase.

President Brigham Young presented an appeal from the decision of the Elders' quorum on a charge made against Elder John A. Hicks by Dimick B. Huntington for a breach of the ordinances of the city, for falsehood and schismatical conversation. After hearing the testimony in the case it was voted that Elder John A. Hicks be cut off from the Church.

Closed by the choir singing hymn 275; prayer by President Brigham Young.

Adjourned for one hour.

Afternoon conference opened by the choir singing hymn 104, and prayer by Elder Orson Pratt, who then read the minutes of a special conference held in Nauvoo, August 16, 1841.

President Joseph Smith made remarks explanatory of the importance of the resolutions and votes passed at that time.

On motion, voted, that this conference sanction the doings of said special conference.

President Brigham Young proposed to the congregation, that those who would take laborers on the Lord's House to board, while thus laboring, should manifest their willingness by rising and giving their names. About sixty persons arose.

Conference closed by the choir singing hymn 284, and prayer by President Brigham Young.

Conference adjourned *sine die.*

Although the conference commenced under discouraging circumstances owing to the inclemency of the weather, yet a vast number of the brethren and visitors from abroad were present, and on Saturday and Sunday, the weather having become favorable, the congregation was immense. The greatest unanimity prevailed; business was conducted with the most perfect harmony and good feelings, and the assembly dispersed with new confidence in the great work of the last days.

JOSEPH SMITH, President.

ELIAS SMITH,
GUSTAVUS HILLS,
Clerks.

An earthquake at Constantinople, occasioning extensive destruction of property.

Elder Joseph Beebee writes from New York that he has been preaching in that city, and has baptized twenty-nine.

Wednesday, 6.—Elder Woodruff arrived in Nauvoo.

Elders Kimball, Richards, and Woodruff laid hands on President Young, who was very sick, and he recovered.

Thursday, 7.

Minutes of a Meeting of the Council of the Twelve.

Elders Brigham Young, Heber C. Kimball, Orson Pratt, Lyman Wight, John Taylor, Wilford Woodruff, and Willard Richards, of the quorum of the Twelve Apostles, assembled in council at the house of Elder John Taylor. Voted, that

Elder John D. Lee go on a mission to Jackson and Rutherford counties, Tennessee.

Elder David Evans, to Augusta, Iowa Territory.

Elder Elisha H. Groves, to Iowa county, Wisconsin.

Elder Hiram Clark, to Pike, Brown, and Adams counties, Illinois.

Elder Joseph Ball, to South America.

Elder Harrison Sagers, to Jamaica.

Elder William Bosley, to Utica, New York.

Elder Amasa Lyman, to New York City.

Elder Arza Adams to Kingston, Canada.

Elder Lyman Stoddard, to go with Elisha H. Groves to Wisconsin.

Elder Phinehas H. Young, to Cincinnati, Ohio.

Elder Abraham Palmer, to Chicago, Illinois.

Elder George W. Gee, to Pittsburg, Pennsylvania.

Elder James Blakesley, to Nauvoo, Illinois.

Elder John D. Parker, to New Orleans, Louisiana.

Voted, that Phinehas H. Young be ordained to a High Priest and recommended accordingly.

That Daniel Garns be nominated for president of the Elders' quorum.

That a conference be held at Father Morley's, at Lima, on Saturday and Sunday, the 23rd and 24th instant.

That a committee of three, namely, Brigham Young, Willard Richards, and John Taylor be a committee to draft an address to the eastern churches, as directed by the general conference.

Adjourned to Bishop Miller's tomorrow evening at 6 o'clock.

BRIGHAM YOUNG, President.
WILLARD RICHARDS, Clerk.

Saturday, 9.

Copy of a Letter to Smith Tuttle, Esq.—The Hotchkiss Land Troubles.

DEAR SIR:—Your kind letter of September was received during our conference, which is just over, containing a full and particular explanation of everything which gave rise to some feelings of disappointment in relation to our business transactions; and I will assure you it has allayed on our part every prejudice. It breathes the spirit of kindness and truth. I will assure you that we exceedingly regret that there has been any ground for hardness and disappointment. But as far as I am concerned, I must plead innocent, and you will consider me so, when you come to know all the facts. I have done all that I could on my part. I will still do all that I can. I will not leave one stone unturned.

Now the facts are these: I sent my brother Hyrum, and Doctor Galland with means in their hands—say not money—but with power to obtain either property or money which was necessary to enable them to fulfill the contract I made with Mr. Hotchkiss. My brother Hyrum was under the necessity of returning to this place on account of his ill health, leaving the business in the hands of Dr. Galland, with the fullest expectation that he would make over the property or money to Mr. Hotchkiss, and make everything square so far as the interest is concerned, if not the principal. He was instructed to pay the interest that had accrued, and should accrue up to the fall of 1842, so as to be in advance of our indebtedness.

I had also made arrangements with the eastern churches, and had it in my power to deed over lands for the whole debt, and had expected that an arrangement of that kind would have been entered into.

I am well assured that Dr. Galland did not look for any means whatever, to pay the interest at any rate, if not the principal; and, why he has not done according to my instructions, God only knows. I do not feel to charge him with having done wrong, until I can investigate the matter, and ascertain to a certainty where the fault lies. It may be through sickness or disaster, this strange neglect has happened. I would to God the thing had not happened.

When I read Mr. Hotchkiss' letter, I learned that he was dissatisfied. I thought that he meant to oppress me, and felt accordingly mortified and sorrowful in the midst of affliction, to think that he should distrust me for a moment that I would not do all that was within my power.

But upon having an explanation of the whole matter, my feelings are changed, and I think that you all have had cause for complaining. But you will in the magnanimity of your good feelings, certainly not blame me when you find that I have discharged an honorable duty on my part.

I regret exceedingly that I did not know some time since what I now know, that I might have made another effort before it got so late. Cold weather is now rolling in upon us. I have been confined here this season by sickness, and various other things that were beyond my control; such as having been demanded by the governor of Missouri, of the governor of this state, and he did not have moral courage enough to resist the demand, although it was founded in injustic and cruelty. I accordingly was taken prisoner, and they put me to some ten or eleven hundred dollars' expense and trouble, such as lawyer's fees, witnesses, &c., &c., before I could be redeemed from under the difficulty. But I am now clear of them once more.

And now in contemplating the face of the whole subject, I find that I am under the necessity of asking a little further indulgence—say, till next spring, so that I may be enabled to recover myself, and then, if God spares my life, and gives me power to do so, I will come in person to your country, and will never cease my labors until the whole matter is completely adjusted to the full satisfaction of all of you. The subject of your debt was fairly presented before our general conference held on the first of this month, consisting of ten thousand people for their decision on the wisest and best course in relation to meeting your demands.

The Twelve, as they are denominated in the *Times and Seasons* were ordered by the conference to make arrangements in the Eastern branches of the Church, ordering them to go to you and turn over their property as you and they might agree, and take up our obligations and bring them here, and receive property here for them; and I have been ordered by the conference to write this letter to you, informing you of the measures which are about to be taken to make all things right.

I would inform you that Dr. Galland has not returned to the western country as yet. He has a considerable amount of money in his hands, which was to have been paid to you, as we intended. He is on his way, for aught we know, and is retarded in his journey by some misfortune or other. He may return, however, as yet, and give a just and honorable account of himself. We hope this may be the case. I am sorrowful on account of your disappointments. It is a great disappointment to me, as well as to yourselves.

As to the growth of our place, it is very rapid, and it would be more so, were it not for sickness and death. There have been many deaths, which leaves a melancholy reflection, but we cannot help it. When God speaks from the heavens to call us hence, we must submit to His mandates.

And as for your sincerity and friendship, gentlemen, we have not the most distant doubt of it. We will not have any. We know it is for your interest to do us good, and for our welfare and happiness to be punctual in fulfillment of all our vows, and we think for the future you will have no cause for complaint. We intend to struggle with all our misfortunes in life, and shoulder them up handsomely, like men.

We ask nothing, therefore, but what ought to be required between man and man, and by those principles which bind man to man, by kindred blood, in bearing our own part in everything which duty calls us to do, as not inferior to any of the human race; and we will be treated as such, although we differ with some in matters of opinion in things (viz., religious matters), for which we only feel ourselves amenable to the Eternal God. And may God forbid that pride, ambition, a want of humanity, in any degree of importance, should have any unjust dominion in our bosoms.

We are the sons of Adam. We are the free born sons of America, and having been trampled upon, and our rights taken from us—even our constitutional rights, by a good many who boast themselves of being valiant in freedom's cause, while their hearts possess not a spark of its benign and enlightening influence—will afford a sufficient excuse, we hope, for any harsh remarks that may have been dropped by us, when we thought there was an assumption of superiority designed to gall our feelings.

We are very sensitive as a people—we confess it: but we want to be pardoned for our sins, if any we have committed. With regard to the time when the first payment of interest should be called for, it appears we misunderstood each other, but suffice it to say, that it shall not prevent our making arrangements concerning the whole matter. It is still, however, my firm conviction that my understanding concerning the interest was correct.

I remain, gentlemen, with sentiments of respect, yours, &c.,

JOSEPH SMITH.

Monday, 10.—The Twelve met for the purpose of counsel, and spent most of the day in visiting the sick.

Elder Erastus Snow writes from Northbridge, Massachusetts. He had been laboring in Salem and vicinity four weeks, organized a branch of thirty members, and the prospects are flattering.

Tuesday, 12.

An Epistle of the Twelve Apostles, to the Brethren Scattered Abroad on the Continent of America, Greeting:

BELOVED BRETHREN:—It seemeth good to us to write unto you at this time concerning the great things of the kingdom of our God, and more especially as we have been called upon by the late general conference so to do, that the work may not be hindered, but that all may understand their privilege and duty in this day of glorious events, so that by exercising themselves therein, they may attain unto those blessings which God has in store for His people in the last days.

We have abundant occasion, and we rejoice exceedingly at the privilege we have had of beholding so many thousands of our brethren and sisters as were assembled at the late conference; and for the perfect harmony and good feeling which prevailed throughout all their deliberations; for the great amount of valuable instructions by President Joseph Smith and others; and for the disposition which we have seen manifested, by all who were present, to carry into effect all those noble plans and principles which were derived from heaven, and have been handed down to earth to carry forward the great and glorious work which is already commenced, and which must be consummated to secure the salvation of Israel.

While the minutes of the general conference are before you, which will be read with interest by every lover of Zion, we shall recapitulate some items, and detail more particularly to the understanding of those who had not the privilege of being present on that interesting occasion, the past, present and future situation and prospects of the Church, and the stakes, and those things which immediately concern their best interests.

A short time since, and the Saints were fleeing from their enemies. Whippings, imprisonments, tortures, and death stared them in the face, and they were compelled to seek an asylum in a land of strangers. They sought, they found it within the peaceful bosom of Illinois—a state whose citizens are inspired with a love of liberty, whose souls are endowed with those noble principles of charity and benevolence which ever bid the stranger welcome, and minister to his wants; in this state, whose soil is vieing with its citizens in all that is good and lovely, the Saints have found a resting place where, freed from tyranny and mobs, they are beginning to realize the fulfillment of the ancient prophets—"They shall build houses and inhabit them, plant vineyards and eat the fruit thereof, having none to molest or make afraid."

In this city, the Church has succeeded in securing several extensive plats of land, which have been laid out in city lots, a part of which have been sold, a part has been distributed to the widow and orphan, and a part remains for sale. These lots are for the inheritance of the Saints, a resting place for the Church, a habitation for the God of Jacob; for here He has commanded a house to be built unto His name where He may manifest Himself unto His people as in former times, when He caused the ark, the tabernacle, and the temple to be reared, and the cloud, and the fire to rest down thereon; and not that the temple be built only, but that it be completed quickly, and that no more general conference be held, till it shall be held therein; and that the Nauvoo House be finished for the accommodation of the brethren from afar, and the stranger who shall come up hither to inquire after the work of the Lord, and worship in His temple.

Scores of brethren in this city have offered to board one and two laborers each, till the temple is completed, many have volunteered to labor continually, and the brethren generally are giving one-tenth part of their time, or one-tenth part or their income, according to circumstances; while those sisters who can do nothing more, are knitting socks and mittens, and preparing garments for the laborers, so that they may be made as comfortable as possible during the coming winter. In view of these things we would invite our brethren for many miles distant around us, to send in their teams for drawing stone, lumber, and materials for the building; and at the same time load their wagons with all kinds of grain and meat, provisions, and clothing, and hay, and provender in abundance, that the laborer faint not, and the teams be made strong; also that journeymen stonecutters, &c., come, bringing their tools with them, and enlist in the glorious enterprise.

Most of the plats in this city before referred to, as well as several farms and large lots of land in this, and adjoining counties are paid for, and secured to the Church by good and sufficient titles; while the town plat for the town of Warren, near Warsaw, is secured on such conditions that the brethren can be accommodated with lots on very reasonable terms; but the large plat in Nauvoo, purchased of Messrs. Hotchkiss, Tuttle & Co., of New Haven, Connecticut, remains unpaid for, and the time has now arrived, when it is very desirable on the part of the Church, as well as on the part of the gentlemen of whom it was purchased, that payment should be made, and a warrantee title secured: to accomplish which we have been called upon by the united voice of the general conference to address the churches in the eastern states, to advise with the brethren in those regions, and devise ways and means whereby this debt may be liquidated, Hotchkiss & Co. satisfied, the plat secured to the Church, and the brethren in the East at the same time transfer their real estate from the place where it now is, to this city or region of country, according to their desire.

The contract for the "Hotchkiss purchase" in Nauvoo, consisting of upwards of five hundred acres, was entered into on or about the 9th of August, 1839, for the specified sum of fifty-three thousand five hundred dollars, and security was given to Messrs. Horace R. Hotchkiss, Smith Tuttle and John Gillet, for the amount of the same, in two notes of equal amount, one payable in ten years, and the other in twenty years from the date thereof; signed by Messrs. Hyrum Smith, Joseph Smith and Sidney Rigdon. In August last interest to the amount of six thousand dollars or upwards had accumulated on said notes, which it has not been in the power of the Church to pay up to the present time. The nature of this purchase and the situation of the Church is such, that it is necessary that the notes should be taken up, the interest stopped, and a warrantee title secured immediately; a correspondence is now in progress with Messrs. Hotchkiss and Co., to effect this thing, and bring forward a final settlement.

But, say you, what can we do to accomplish this great and desirable object? Let the brethren in the eastern states who have lands which they wish to dispose of, so that they may remove hither, and secure to themselves an inheritance among the Saints either in the cities or farms in the vicinity, and are willing to have their lands in the East made over to Messrs. Hotchkiss and Co. towards the payment of the foregoing notes, communicate with us immediately, at this place, stating to us the extent and value of their property.

Then, as soon as we shall have received communications concerning property, sufficient to cancel the obligations, and the necessary preliminaries are understood with Messrs. Hotchkiss and Co., we will dispatch an agent to New Haven to complete the negotiation, transfer your property, take up the notes and secure a deed; and those whose property is thus transferred can have the value thereof here in city lots or lands in the vicinity; and thus your property will prove to you as good as money, inasmuch as you desire to emigrate; and you will no longer be obliged to tarry afar off because that money is so scarce you cannot sell and get your pay. If there are those among you to whom God has given in abundance, and they desire to appropriate some portion thereof for the benefit of His people, for the redemption of Zion, for a blessing to the widows of those who have been slain for the word of God,—and been buried in a well,—for a sustenance to their fatherless children, and provide for them a habitation, they cannot do it more effectually than by devoting a portion of their sustenance toward liquidating this claim.

To those brethren who live so far distant that they cannot send in their loaded teams, and yet desire to assist in building the Lord's house, we would say, gather yourselves together and bring of your substance, your silver, and gold, and apparel, and of your superabundance cast into the treasury of the Lord, and see if He will not pour you out a blessing till there is not room enough to receive it.

Brethren, the blessings of the kingdom are for you, for the body of Christ, for all the members, and God will help those who will help themselves, and bless those who will bless each other, and do as they would be done unto. The gold and the silver is the Lord's; all the treasures of the earth, the flocks and the herds of the fields, and the cattle on the thousand hills are His; if He were hungry, would He crave thy food, or thirsty, would He ask thy drink? Nay! He would only ask that which was His own, He would feast on His own flocks and quench His thirst at His own springs. This God is the God of the Saints, He is your God and He has made you stewards of all that has been committed to you, and will require His own with usury, and will you not be faithful in a little, that you may be made rulers over many cities? Yes, you will, we know you will.

The journeyings, and gatherings and buildings of the Saints are nothing new, and as they are expecting, looking and praying for the completion of the dispensation of the fullness of times, they must also expect that their progress will be onward, or they will be of no avail, for what is not of faith is sin, and can you believe that God will hear your prayers and bring you on your journey, gather you and build your houses, and you not put forth your hand or make one exertion to help yourselves? No. Therefore, inasmuch as the Saints believe that Father Abraham journed to a distant land at the command of the Highest, where himself and household, (whose household we are if we keep the commandments) might enjoy the fruits of their labors unmolested, and worship the God of heaven according to the dictates of their own conscience and His law; that his seed afterwards gathered to Canaan, the land of promise; that the people of God were commanded to build a house where the Son of Man might have a place to lay his head, and the disciples be endowed with power from on high, and were with one accord in one place; they must also believe that this dispensation comprehends all the great works of all former dispensations; and that the children must gather as did the fathers, must build a house where they may be endowed, and be found together worshiping and doing as their fathers did when Jehovah spake, and the angels of heaven ministered unto them; and if these things are not in this generation, then we have not arrived at the dispensation of the fullness of times as we anticipate, and our faith and prayers are vain.

Is it possible that we labor in vain and toil for nought, and that we shall be disappointed at the last? No! We know assuredly that the set time to favor Zion has come, and her sons and daughters shall rejoice in her glory. The time has come when the great Jehovah would have a resting place on earth, a habitation for His chosen where His law shall be revealed, and His servants be endowed from on high, to bring together the honest in heart from the four winds; where the Saints may enter the baptismal font for their dead relatives, so that they may be judged according to men in the flesh, and live according to God in the spirit, and come forth in the celestial kingdom; a place over which the heavenly messengers may watch and trouble the waters as in days of old, so that when the sick are put therein, they shall be made whole: a place wherein all the ordinances shall be made manifest, and the Saints shall unite in the songs of Zion, even praise, thanksgiving and hallelujahs to God and the Lamb, that He has wrought out their deliverance, and bound Satan fast in chains.

What then shall we do? Let us all arise, and with one united and mighty exertion, by the strength of Israel's God, oppose the powers of darkness, and every being and principle that may rise up against us and complete the work already commenced. Let us not for a moment lend an ear to evil and designing men who would subvert the truth and blacken the character of the servant of the Most High God, by publishing abroad that the Prophet is enriching himself on the spoils of the brethren.

When Brother Joseph stated to the general conference the amount and situation of the property of the Church, of which he is Trustee-in-Trust by the united voice of the Church, he also stated the amount of his own possessions on earth; and what do you think it was? We will tell you: his old Charley (a horse) given him in Kirtland, two pet deer, two old turkeys and four young ones, the old cow given him by a brother in Missouri, his old Major, (a dog) his wife, children and a little household furniture; and this is the amount of the great possessions of that man whom God has called to lead His people in these last days, this is the sum total of the great estates, the splendid mansions and noble living of him who has spent a life of toil and suffering, of privation and hardships, of imprisonments and chains, of dungeons and vexatious lawsuits, and every kind of contumely and contempt ungodly men could heap upon him, and last of all report him as rolling in wealth and luxury which he had plundered from the spoils of those for whose good he had thus toiled and suffered. Who would be willing to suffer what he has suffered, and labor near twenty years, as he has done, for the wealth he is in possession of?

Brethren, in view of all these things, let us be up and doing. Let those in the eastern states use all diligence in communicating to us their ability to assist in the Hotchkiss payment, being assured that no exertion they can make will equal what has already been made for them and the Church generally; and let all the Saints come up to the places of gathering, and with their mites and their abundance as God has given them in trust, help to build up the old waste places which have been thrown down for many generations, knowing that when they are completed they will belong unto the people of the Most High God, even the meek, the honest in heart, they shall possess all things, in the due time of the Lord. Be not covetous, but deal in righteonsness, for what the Saints shall not possess by purchase and in righteousness they shall not possess, for no unrighteous thing can enter into the kingdom; therefore beloved brethren, deal gently, love mercy, walk humbly before God, and whatever your hands find to do, do it with your might, keeping all the commandments, and then, whether in life or in death, all things will be yours, whether they be temples or lands, houses or vineyards, baptisms or endowments, revelations or healings, all things will be yours, for you will be Christ's and Christ is God's.

Brigham Young,
Heber C. Kimball,
Orson Pratt,
Lyman Wight,
John Taylor,
Wilford Woodruff,
George A. Smith,
Willard Richards.

Nauvoo, October 12, 1841.

CHAPTER XXVI.

AFFAIRS IN KIRTLAND AND NAUVOO—EPISTLE OF THE TWELVE TO THE SAINTS IN THE BRITISH ISLANDS—ORSON HYDE'S PRAYER ON THE MOUNT OF OLIVES, DEDICATING THE HOLY LAND PREPARATORY TO THE RETURN OF THE TRIBES OF ISRAEL.

Wednesday, October 20, 1841.—The following extract of a letter from Elder Hyde, dated Jaffa, October 20, 1841, on his way to Jerusalem.

Extract from Orson Hyde's Letter.

On my passage from Beyrut to this place (Jaffa) night before last, at one o'clock, as I was meditating on the deck of the vessel, as she was beating down against a sultry wind, a very bright glittering sword appeared in the heavens, about six feet in length, with a beautiful hilt, as plain and complete as any cut you ever saw; and what is still more remarkable, an arm with a perfect hand stretched itself out,and took hold of the hilt of the sword. The appearance really made my hair rise, and the flesh, as it were, crawl on my bones. The Arabs made a wonderful outcry at the sight. Allah! Allah! Allah! [O Lord, O Lord, O Lord] was their exclamation all over the vessel. I mention this because you know there is a commandment of God for me, which says, "Unto you it shall be given to know the signs of the times, and the sign of the coming of the Son of Man."

Yours in Christ,

ORSON HYDE.

Saturday, 23.—I attended the city council.

Minutes of Conference held at Lima.

Lima [Adams county, Illinois] conference convened pursuant to previous appointment. Elders Brigham Young, John Taylor, and Willard

Richards, of the Twelve Apostles, were in attendance. Elder Brigham Young was unanimously chosen president, and James C. Snow, clerk of the conference.

President Young then made some preliminary remarks, setting forth and explaining the object of the meeting; followed by President Isaac Morley. Elder James C. Snow then represented the branch of the Church at Lima, consisting of 424 members, including 9 High Priests, 32 Elders, 4 Priests, 5 Teachers, and 4 Deacons, mostly in good standing.

President Young, Elders Taylor and Richards, then made some very appropriate remarks, showing and proving the absolute necessity of finishing and completing the House of the Lord now building in Nauvoo, in preference to anything else that can be done, either by mental or physical exertion, in spreading light, knowledge,and intelligence among the nations of the earth.

Conference adjourned till tomorrow, ten o'clock.

In the evening President Morley met with his counselors together with President Young, Elders Taylor, and Richards, and brethren of the Lima branch, for the purpose of entering into certain resolutions necessary, in order to become more active in forwarding the work on the House of the Lord.

After much deliberation, it was moved and seconded, that all those who are willing to consecrate one tenth of their time and property to the building of the temple at Nauvoo, under the superintendence of President Morley and counselors, to signify it by the uplifted hands; when the motion was carried unanimously.

Sunday morning, at ten o'clock conference met pursuant to adjournment.

Elder John Taylor delivered an address, upon the object of Christ's mission into this world, the resurrection and redemption of the Saints, and pointed out very clearly the course to be pursued in order to become the sons of God, through the ordinances of the gospel, that the Saints may, at last, be exalted at the right hand of God, to dwell with Him eternally in the heavens.

After an intermission of one hour, the sacrament was administered by President Young and Elder Richards. The minutes of the conference were then read and accepted.

President Young made some very just remarks on the priesthood, authority, and calling.

Conference adjourned *sine die*.

Benediction by President Morley.

BRIGHAM YOUNG, President,
JAMES C. SNOW, Clerk.

Extract of a Letter from Parley P. Pratt—Emigration of Saints, and Status of the Work in England.

MANCHESTER, ENGLAND.

On the 20th of September, the ship *Tyrean* sailed from Liverpool for New Orleans, under a charter of the Latter-day Saints; she had upwards of two hundred Saints on board, with Elder Joseph Fielding at their head. By chartering [the vessel] we saved the company [of Saints] at least 500 or 600 dollars. The splendid new ship *Chaos*, 1,200 tons burthen, will sail on the 5th of November, under our charter. She will have from one to two hundred Saints on board, with Patriarch Peter Melling at their head.

The Saints in this country are generally rejoicing, and filled with the testimony of Jesus. Great zeal is manifested by the officers in general, of whom there are probably more than a thousand. We are increasing in numbers, and in gifts and blessings. New branches of the Church are rising in many places, and great additions made to the old ones. Manchester and vicinity has poured forth a stream of emigration for the last eighteen months, and still we numbered at our conference, two weeks ago, nearly sixteen hundred members, and between one and two hundred officers; all these within one hour's journey of Manchester.

There has been a general time of pruning; we have cut off upwards of one hundred members from this conference in a few months; this causes the young and tender branches to grow with double vigor.

Thursday, 28.

Copy of a Letter of Attorney from Joseph Smith, "Sole Trustee in Trust for the Church of Jesus Christ of Latter-day Saints," to Reuben McBride, of Kirtland, Ohio.

Know all men by these presents, that I, Joseph Smith, of Nauvoo, Hancock county, and State of Illinois, "sole trustee in trust for the Church of Jesus Christ of Latter-day Saints," have made, constituted and appointed, and by these presents do make, constitute, and appoint, Reuben McBride, of Kirtland, Lake county, and state of Ohio, my true and lawful attorney for me and in my name, and for my use as "sole trustee in trust for the Church of Jesus Christ of Latter-day Saints," to ask, demand, sue for, recover, and receive all such sum or sums of money, debts, goods, wares, and other demands which are or shall be due, owing, payable, or belonging to me, as trustee in trust as aforesaid, by any manner or means whatsoever; also, to dispose of in my name, to grant, bargain, sell, release, and confirm all or any part of my real estate as trustee in trust as aforesaid, in and about Kirtland, Lake county, and state of Ohio, and throughout any of the northern and eastern states, and to receive all such sum or sums of money accruing therefrom, for me and for my use as sole trustee in trust for the Church of Jesus Christ of Latter-day Saints, and to take up the power of attorney which I gave to Oliver Granger, and all the papers and obligations of every description specified therein, or in his possession by virtue thereof, and to settle the same in my name, for me and for my use as above described; and I, as trustee in trust as aforesaid, hereby give and grant unto the said Reuben McBride, my attorney, full power and authority in and about the premises, to have, use, and take all lawful ways and means in my name for the purposes aforesaid, and upon the receipt of any such debts, dues, or sums of money (as the case may be), acquittances,or other sufficient discharges, for me and in my name as aforesaid Trustee, to make and give, and generally to do all other acts and things in the law whatsoever needful and necessary to be done, in the before mentioned places, for me and in my name as aforesaid Trustee, to do, execute, and perform,as fully and to all intents and purposes, as I might or could do, if personally present. Hereby ratifying all and whatsoever my said attorney shall, in the place above specified, by virtue hereof.

In witness whereof I have hereunto set my hand and seal this 28th day of October, 1841.

JOSEPH SMITH, (L.S.)

Witness: John Taylor, John S. Fullmer.

Friday, *29.*—Those of the Twelve Apostles who were in Nauvoo, met in council.

Saturday, *30.*—I attended the city council, and spoke against the council remitting a fine assessed against John Eagle by a jury of twelve men, considering that the jury might be as sensible men as any of the city council, and I asked the council not to remit the fine.

Lyman Wight, Willard Richards, and Wilford Woodruff were elected councilors, and Hiram Kimball and George W. Harris, Aldermen.

In obedience to an order from the mayor, I called out two companies of the Nauvoo Legion,and removed a grog shop kept by Pulaski S. Cahoon, which had been declared a nuisance by the city council.

Sunday, *31.*—I was in council with the brethren at brother Hyrum's office.

Attended a council with the Twelve Apostles. Benjamin Winchester being present, complained that he had been neglected and misrepresented by the Elders, and manifested a contentious spirit. I gave him a severe reproof, telling him of his folly and vanity, and showing him that the principles which he suffered to control him would lead him to destruction. I counseled him to change his course, govern his disposition, and quit his tale-bearing and slandering his brethren.

I instructed the council on many principles pertaining to the gathering of the nations, the wickedness and downfall of this generation, &c.

After having received the following minutes—"A conference was held at Kirtland, Ohio, Oct. 2, 1841. Almon W. Babbitt, president, and William W. Phelps, clerk. Resolved, that Thomas Burdick, Bishop of Kirtland, and his counselors, be constituted a company to establish a press in Kirtland, and publish a religious paper, entitled *The Olive Leaf*, and that the Saints adjacent be solicited to carry the above resolution into effect"—my brother Hyrum wrote to the brethren in Kirtland, of which the following is an extract—

Excerpt of Hyrum Smith's Letter to the Saints in Kirtland—Disapproving of Certain Plans for Building up Kirtland.

All the Saints that dwell in that land are commanded to come away, for this is "Thus saith the Lord;" therefore pay out no moneys, nor properties for houses, nor lands in that country, for if you do you will lose them, for the time shall come, that you shall not possess them in peace, but shall be scourged with a sore scourge; yet your children may possess them, but not until many years shall pass away; and as to the organization of that branch of the Church, it is not according to the Spirit and will of God; and as to the designs of the leading members of that branch relative to the printing press, and the ordaining of Elders, and sending out Elders to beg for the poor, are not according to the will of God; and in these things they shall not prosper, for they have neglected the House of the Lord, the baptismal font, in this place, wherein their dead may be redeemed, and the key of knowledge that unfolds the dispensation of the fullness of times may be turned, and the mysteries of God be unfolded, upon which their salvation, and the salvation of the world, and the redemption of their dead depends; for "thus saith the Lord," there shall not be a general assembly for a general conference assembled together until the House of the Lord and the baptismal font shall be finished; and if we are not diligent the Church shall be rejected, and their dead also, saith the Lord." Therefore, dear brethren, any proceedings of the Saints otherwise than to put forth their hands with their might to do this work, is not according to the will of God, and shall not prosper; therefore, tarry not in any place whatever, but come forth unto this place from all the world, until it is filled up, and polished, and sanctified according to my word, saith the Lord. Come ye forth from the ends of the earth, that I may hide you from mine indignation that shall scourge the wicked, and then I will send forth and build up Kirtland, and it shall be polished and refined according to my word; therefore your doings and your organizations and designs in printing, or any of your councils, are not of me, saith the Lord, even so. Amen.

HYRUM SMITH,
Patriarch for the whole Church.

Monday, November 1.—I attended the city council, spoke and acted on many local matters, and contended at great length against paying the owner of a city nuisance, damages sustained by the removal of that nuisance.*

* The circumstance of removing the nuisance here referred to, for which damages were demanded, is related in an editorial note in the *Times and Seasons* as follows: The "Mr. Kilbourn," referred to in the editorial, was a very bitter anti-Mormon, and became one of the Prophet's most deadly enemies.

THE NUISANCE.

"It is known to many of our patrons, that a certain young man very injudiciously, and contrary to the remonstrances of his friends, and in violation of the ordinances of this city, not long since erected a small building, near the Temple square avowedly for the purpose of transacting the business of a grocer. Said building was for a short time occupied for that purpose; but so heavy did the frown of public disapprobation rest upon it, that it was finally vacated, and stood some time, a lonely wreck of folly. In the meantime, the very sanctimonious and extremely unfortunate Mr. Kilbourn of Montrose, throw out to the public, ungentlemanly and slanderous imputations concerning the matter, saying that the Presidency of the Church abetted and approbated the concern, etc., and the building having become a monument for every fool to write upon and exhibit his folly, to the annoyance of the citizens, the city council very judiciously ordered the building removed as a nuisance. Some opposition to the execution of this order was exhibited, and the authorities called out a few of the military and demolished the building. The city authorities manifest a determination to carry out strictly the temper-

Sidney Rigdon resigned his seat in the city council, on account of ill health.

Tuesday, 2.—I executed letters today revoking the power of attorney given to Almon W. Babbitt.

Saturday, 6.—Wilford Woodruff took the oath as a councilor in the city council.

Sunday, 7.—Elder William O. Clark preached about two hours, reproving the Saints for a lack of sanctity, and a want of holy living, enjoining sanctity, solemnity, and temperance in the extreme, in the rigid sectarian style.

Reproof of William O. Clark.

I reproved him as Pharisaical and hypocritical and not edifying the people; and showed the Saints what temperance, faith, virtue, charity, and truth were. I charged the Saints not to follow the example of the adversary in accusing the brethren, and said, "If you do not accuse each other, God will not accuse you. If you have no accuser you will enter heaven, and if you will follow the revelations and instructions which God gives you through me, I will take you into heaven as my back load. If you will not accuse me, I will not accuse you. If you will throw a cloak of charity over my sins, I will over yours—for charity covereth a multitude of sins. What many people call sin is not sin; I do many things to break down superstition, and I will break it down;" I referred to the curse of Ham for laughing at Noah, while in his wine, but doing no harm. Noah was a righteous man, and yet he drank wine and became intoxicated; the Lord did not forsake him in consequence thereof, for he retained all the power of his priesthood, and when he was accused by Canaan, he cursed him by the priesthood which he held, and the Lord had respect

ance ordinances of the city, and in this we wish them 'God speed.' We suppose, however, that Kilbourn and his junto will bray worse than ever, and 'Mormonism' be adjudged by 'witch law.' 'Take the accused, bind him head and foot, and cast him into the pool; if he sinks and drowns he is innocent, if he floats take him out and hang him or burn him with fire.' We say, let the poor fools judge till they themselves are overtaken by judgment, and let them bray till they burst their wind chests." (*Times and Seasons*, Vol. III, pp. 559-560).

to his word, and the priesthood which he held, notwithstanding he was drunk, and the curse remains upon the posterity of Canaan until the present day.

In the p. m., I attended a council of the Elders at my council room, relative to some affairs in which my brother William was interested.

Monday, 8.—At five o'clock p. m., I attended the dedication of the baptismal font in the Lord's House. President Brigham Young was spokesman.

Dedication of the Baptismal Font.

The baptismal font is situated in the center of the basement room, under the main hall of the Temple; it is constructed of pine timber, and put together of staves tongued and grooved, oval shaped, sixteen feet long east and west, and twelve feet wide, seven feet high from the foundation, the basin four feet deep, the moulding of the cap and base are formed of beautiful carved work in antique style. The sides are finished with panel work. A flight of stairs in the north and south sides lead up and down into the basin, guarded by side railing.

The font stands upon twelve oxen, four on each side, and two at each end, their heads, shoulders, and fore legs projecting out from under the font; they are carved out of pine plank, glued together, and copied after the most beautiful five-year-old steer that could be found in the country, and they are an excellent striking likeness of the original; the horns were formed after the most perfect horn that could be procured.

The oxen and ornamental mouldings of the font were carved by Elder Elijah Fordham, from the city of New York, which occupied eight months of time. The font was enclosed by a temporary frame building sided up with split oak clapboards, with a roof of the same material, and was so low that the timbers of the first story were laid above it. The water was supplied from a well thirty feet deep in the east end of the basement.

This font was built for the baptisms for the dead until

the Temple shall be finished, when a more durable one will supply its place.

I received a letter from N. K. Whitney, stating that he had purchased $5,000 worth of goods for me; and that he should visit Kirtland before his return home.

Up to this period a series of storms and earthquakes have desolated parts of the two Sicilies.

A second English edition of the Saints' hymn book has been issued by Elder Parley P. Pratt.

A great part of Vicksburg, Mississippi, has been consumed by fire.

Saturday, 13.—I attended the city council, and moved that the mayor and recorder of the city receive each one hundred dollars per annum for their services, which became a law.

I also presented a bill for "An ordinance concerning vagrants and disorderly persons," which passed into an ordinance as follows—

An Ordinance Concerning Vagrants and Disorderly Persons.

Be it ordained by the city council of the city of Nauvoo, that all vagrants, idle, or disorderly persons; persons found drunk in or about the streets; all suspicious persons; persons who have no fixed place of residence, or visible means of support, or cannot give a good account of themselves; persons guilty of profane and indecent language or behavior; persons guilty of using indecent, impertinent, or unbecoming language towards any city officer when in the discharge of his duty, or of menacing, threatening or otherwise obstructing said officer, shall on conviction thereof before the mayor or municipal court, be required to enter into security for good behavior for a reasonable time, and indemnify the corporation against any charge, and in case of refusal or inability to give security, they shall be confined to labor for a time not exceeding ninety days, or be fined in any sum not exceeding five hundred dollars, or be imprisoned not exceeding six months or all, [i.e. or both imprisonment and fine] at the discretion of said mayor or court.

I also presented a bill for "An ordinance in relation to appeals," which passed unanimously.

I also argued before the council the right of taxation, but

that the expense of the city did not require it at present.

Sunday, 14.—I preached to a large congregation at the Temple.

Nine of the Twelve Apostles met in council, to prepare an epistle to the Saints in Europe.

Monday, 15.

An Epistle of the Twelve Apostles to the Saints Scattered Abroad in England, Scotland, Ireland, Wales, the Isle of Man, and the Eastern Continent, Greeting:

BELOVED BRETHREN:—We rejoice and thank our Heavenly Father daily in your behalf, that we hear of your faithfulness and diligence in the great work unto which you have been called, by the Holy Spirit, through the voice of the servants of the Most High, who have been, and are now amongst you, for the purpose of instructing you in those principles which are calculated to prepare the children of men for the renovation of the earth, and the restitution of all things spoken by the Prophets.

Several months have passed away, since we bid adieu to our brethren and sisters on the islands of the sea, and passed over the great deep to our homes, our kindred, the bosom of the Church, and the stakes of Zion: but neither time nor distance can efface from our memories the many expressions of kindness which we have heard from your lips and experienced from your hands, which have so often ministered to our necessities, while we were wandering in your midst, like our Master, having no place to lay our heads, only as furnished by your liberality and benevolence; and it is a subject of no small consolation to us that we have this testimony of so many of you, that you are the disciples of the Lord Jesus;* and we give you our warmest thanks, and our blessing, that you have not only ministered unto us, but that you continue to minister to our brethren who are still laboring amongst you, for which an hundred fold shall be returned unto your bosoms.

After parting with the Saints in Liverpool, and sailing thirty days, much of the time against head winds, with rough seas, which produced much sea sickness among the brethren and sisters who accompanied us, we arrived in the city of New York, where we were received by the brethren with open hearts, and by whom we were entertained most cordially some days, till we were rested from the fatigues of the ship: we were then assisted on our journey, and taking different routes, and

* "Whoso receiveth you receiveth me, and the same will clothe you and give you money. And he who feeds you, or clothes you or gives you money, shall in no wise lose his reward: And he who doeth not these things is not my disciple; by this you may know my disciples." (Doc. & Cov., sec. lxxxiv.)

visiting many of the churches in different states, we have all safely arrived in this city.

In our travels in this land, we have discovered a growing interest among the people generally, in the great work of the Lord. Prejudice is giving way to intelligence; darkness to light; and multitudes are making the important discovery that error is abroad in the earth, and that the signs of the times proclaim some mighty revolution among the nations. The cry is from all quarters, send us Elders to instruct us in the principles of your religion, that we may know why it is that you are had in derision by the multitude, more than other professors are. Teach us of your principles and your doctrines, and if we find them true we will embrace them.

The Saints are growing in faith, and the intelligence of heaven is flowing into their understanding, for the Spirit of the Lord is with them, and the Holy Ghost is instructing them in things to come. The spirit of union is increasing, and they are exerting themselves to come up to the gathering of the faithful, to build up the waste places and establish the stakes of Zion.

Since our arrival in this place there has been one special and one general conference of the Church, and the Twelve have been called to tarry at home for a season, and stand in their lot next to the First Presidency, and assist in counseling the brethren, and in the settling of immigrants, &c.; and the first great object before us, and the Saints generally, is to help forward the completion of the Temple and the Nauvoo House—buildings which are now in progress according to the revelations, and which must be completed to secure the salvation of the Church in the last days; for God requires of His Saints to build Him a house wherein His servants may be instructed, and endowed with power from on high, to prepare them to go forth among the nations, and proclaim the fullness of the Gospel for the last time, and bind up the law, and seal up the testimony, leaving this generation without excuse, and the earth prepared for the judgments which will follow. In this house all the ordinances will be made manifest, and many things will be shown forth, which have been hid from generation to generation.

The set time to favor the stakes of Zion is at hand, and soon the kings and the queens, the princes and the nobles, the rich and the honorable of the earth will come up hither to visit the Temple of our God, and to inquire concerning His strange work; and as kings are to become nursing fathers, and queens nursing mothers in the habitations of the righteous, it is right to render honor to whom honor is due; and therefore expedient that such, as well as the Saints, should have a comfortable house for boarding and lodging when they come hither, and it is according to the revelations that such a house should be built.

The foundations of this house, and also of the Temple, are laid; and the walls of the basement stories of each nearly completed; and the finishing of the whole is depending on the exertions of the Saints. Every Saint on earth is equally interested in these things, and all are under equal obligations to do all in their power to complete the buildings by their faith, and by their prayers, with their thousands and their mites, their gold and their silver, their copper and their zinc, their goods and their labors, until the top stone is laid with shoutings, and the place is prepared to be filled with the glory of the Highest; and if there are those among you who have more than they need for the gathering, and for assisting the destitute who desire to gather with them, they cannot make a more acceptable offering unto the Lord, than by appropriating towards the building of His Temple.

He that believeth shall not make haste, but let all the Saints who desire to keep the commandments of heaven and work righteousness, come to the place of gathering as soon as circumstances will permit. It is by united efforts that great things are accomplished, and while the Saints are scattered to the four winds, they cannot be united in action, if they are in spirit; they cannot all build at one city, or lift at one stone of the great Temple, though their hearts may all desire the same thing. We would not press the subject of the gathering upon you, for we know your hearts, and your means; and so far as means fail, let patience have its perfect work in your souls, for in due time you shall be delivered, if you faint not.

We are not altogether ignorant of the increase of difficulty among the laboring classes in England since our departure through the stoppage of factories and similar occurrences, and we would counsel those who have, to impart unto those who have not, and cannot obtain; remembering that he who giveth unto the poor lendeth unto the Lord, and he shall receive in return four fold.

The idler shall not eat the bread of the laborer; neither must he starve who would [labor] but cannot find employment. Inasmuch as ye desire the fullness of the earth, let not the cries of the widow, the fatherless and the beggar ascend to heaven, or salute your ears in vain, but follow the example we have set before you, and give liberally of your abundance, even if it be but a penny, and it shall be returned unto you. Good measure pressed down and running over, shall the Lord return into your store house.

Cultivate the spirit of patience, long-suffering, forbearance and charity among yourselves, and ever be as unwilling to believe an evil report about a brother or a sister as if it were about yourself, and as you dislike to be accused, be slow to accuse the brethren, for the measure you mete shall be measured to you again, and the Judge condemneth no man who is not accused.

Keep all the commandments, nothing fearing, nothing doubting, for this is virtue, this is wisdom, and the wise, the virtuous and the meek shall inherit the earth and the fullness thereof. In all things follow the counsel which you shall receive from the president and council who are among you; and inasmuch as you uphold Elders Pratt, Richards and Snow by the prayer of faith, you shall receive right counsel.

Remember that those whom John saw on Mount Zion were such as had come up through great tribulation; and do not imagine that you can ever constitute a part of that number without sharing a part of their trials. You must necessarily pass through perils and trials, and temptations and afflictions by sea and land in your journeyings hither, and if you cannot settle it in your hearts to endure unto the end as good soldiers, you may as well remain where you are to be destroyed, as to suffer all the privations and hardships you will be obliged to suffer before the walls of Zion shall be built, no more to be thrown down, and after all to turn away and be destroyed.

The ancient prophet has said, they shall wear out the Saints of the Most High. This has already been fulfilled to some extent, for many through the abundance of their persecutions have become exhausted, and laid their bodies down to rest, to rise no more till the morn of the first resurrection; and although the people of these states are at peace with us, yet there are those who would gladly wear out and destroy the weak in faith, through the influence of their foolish lies. When you arrive on our shores, and while sailing up our rivers, you need not be surprised if your ears are saluted by the false and filthy language of wicked and designing men who are ever ready to speak evil of the things they understand not, and who would gladly blast the character of the Prophet of the Most High God, and all connected with him, with their foul anathemas, beyond anything you ever thought of. We would not dishearten you, neither would we have you ignorant of the worst that awaits the righteous.

If the Saints are not prepared to rejoice and be glad when they hear the name of the Prophet and their own name cast out as evil, as gluttonous, wine-bibber, friend of publicans and sinners, Beelzebub, thief, robber and murderer, they are not prepared for the gathering. The wheat and tares must grow together till the harvest; at the harvest the wheat is gathered together into the threshing floor, so with the Saints—the stakes are the threshing floor. Here they will be threshed with all sorts of difficulties, trials, afflictions and everything to mar their peace, which they can imagine, and thousands which they cannot imagine, but he that endures the threshing till all the chaff, superstition, folly and unbelief are pounded out of him, and does not suffer himself to be blown away as chaff by the foul blast of slander, but endures faithfully to the end, shall be saved. If you are prepared for all these things; if you choose rather to suffer afflictions with the people of God, than to enjoy the pleasures of sin for a little moment, come up hither; come direct to New Orleans, and up the Mississippi river, for the expense is so much less, and the convenience of water navigation is so much greater than it is by Montreal, New York or Philadelphia, that it is wisdom for the Saints to make New Orleans their general established port, and be sure to start at such times that they may arrive here during the cold months, for the change from the cold climate of England to this place in the hot season, is too great for the health of immigrants, till there is more faith in the Church.

In this region of country there are thousands and millions of acres of beautiful prairie unoccupied, which can be procured on reasonable terms, and we will hail the time with joy when these unoccupied lands shall be turned into fruitful fields, and the hands of those who are now idle for want of employment shall be engaged in the cultivation of the soil.

When the brethren arrive they will do well to call on some of the Twelve, inasmuch as they desire counsel, for by so doing they may escape the influence of designing men who have crept in unawares, and would willingly subvert the truth by conniving to their own advantage, if they have the opportunity.

The Church has commenced a new city twenty miles below this, and one mile below Warsaw, called Warren, where many city lots and farms in the vicinity can be had on reasonable terms; and it will be wisdom for many of the brethren to stop at that place, for the opportunity for erecting temporary buildings will be greater than at this place, also the chance for providing food will be superior to those who wish to labor for it.

Warsaw is at the foot of the Des Moines Rapids, and one of the best locations for mercantile purposes there is in this western country.

So far as the brethren have the means they will do well to come prepared with a variety of mechanical tools according to their professions, such as carpenters, joiners, cabinet-makers, hatters, coopers, masons, printers, binders, tanners, curriers, &c., and all sorts of manufactory and foundry implements convenient for transportation, so that when they arrive they may be prepared to establish themselves in business, and give employment to spinners, weavers, moulders, smelters and journeymen of every description; for all sorts of woollens, cottons, hardware, &c., will find a ready market in new countries, and a great field is now open to the capitalists in this vicinity, even though the capital be small, and we would urge the importance of the immediate establishment of all kinds of manufactories among us, as well for the best interests of the individuals concerned, as for the Church generally.

Cities cannot be built without houses, houses cannot be built without materials, or occupied without inhabitants, the inhabitants cannot exist without food and clothing; food and clothing cannot be had without planting, sowing, and manufacturing, so that Zion and her stores cannot be built without means, without industry, without manufacturing establishments unless the windows of heaven were opened, and cities and their appendages were rained down among us. But this we do not expect until the new Jerusalem descends, and that will be some time hence; therefore it is necessary and according to godliness and the plan of salvation in these last days, that the brethren should see to all these things, and clothe and adorn themselves with the labor of their own hands, build houses and inhabit them, plant vineyards and eat the fruit thereof.

Brethren, pray for us and the First Presidency, the leader of the people, even Joseph, that his life and health may be precious in the sight of heaven, till he has finished the work which he has commenced: and for the Elders of Israel, that every man may be faithful in his calling, the whole household of faith, and all subjects of prayer.

Brethren, farewell; may the blessings of heaven and earth be multiplied unto you in spirit and in body, in basket and in store, in the field and in the shop, on the land and on the sea, in the house and by the way, and in all situations and circumstances, until you shall stand on Mount Zion, and enter the celestial city; in the name of Jesus Christ. Amen.

BRIGHAM YOUNG,
HEBER C. KIMBALL.
ORSON PRATT,
WILLIAM SMITH,
LYMAN WIGHT,
WILFORD WOODRUFF,
JOHN TAYLOR,
GEO. A. SMITH.
WILLARD RICHARDS,

Nauvoo, Hancock County, Illinois, Nov. 15, 1841.

The greater part of the city of St. John's, New Brunswick, and a large quantity of shipping, destroyed by fire.

Wednesday, 17.—Elders Brigham Young and Willard Richards went to La Harpe.

Thursday, 18.

Minutes of a Meeting at Ramus, Illinois—Alanson Brown, et al. Disfellowshiped.

Proceedings of a meeting of the Church of Jesus Christ of Latter-day

Saints, held at Ramus, November 18, 1841, opened by singing and prayer by Elder Brigham Young. The object of the meeting was then stated by the president, which was for the purpose of taking into consideration the cases of Alanson Brown, James B. T. Page and William H. Edwards, who stand indicted for larceny, &c.

After the evidence was brought forward, it was unanimously resolved, that said persons be expelled from the Church. Appropriate remarks for the occasion were then made by Elders Young, Richards, Savage, Gurley, and others.

A charge was then preferred against Thomas S. Edwards for assault and battery, with evidence that a warrant was issued for his apprehension, and against William W. Edwards for being accessory to the same. Unanimously resolved, that Thomas S. Edwards also be expelled from the Church; and that the proceedings of this meeting be published in the *Times and Seasons.*

JOEL H. JOHNSON, President.
JOSEPH E. JOHNSON, Church Recorder.

Saturday, 20.—Seven of the Twelve Apostles met in council at the house of President Young, on the subject of the *Times and Seasons;* they not being satisfied with the manner in which Gustavus Hills had conducted the editorial department since the death of Robert B. Thompson.

Sunday, 21.—My brother Hyrum and Elder John Taylor preached.

Baptisms for the Dead.

The Twelve met in council at President Young's, and at four o'clock, repaired to the baptismal font in the basement of the Temple. Elders Brigham Young, Heber C. Kimball and John Taylor baptized about forty persons for the dead. Elder Willard Richards, Wilford Woodruff and George A. Smith confirming. These were the first baptisms for the dead in the font.

Monday, 22.—The following letter from Elder Orson Hyde, is from the *Millennial Star:*

Elder Orson Hyde's Letter—His Prayer of Dedication on the Mount of Olives.

ALEXANDRIA, Nov. 22, 1841.

DEAR BROTHER PRATT:—A few minutes now offer for me to write, and I improve them in writing to you.

I have only time to say that I have seen Jerusalem precisely according to the vision which I had. I saw no one with me in the vision; and although Elder Page was appointed to accompany me there, yet I found myself there alone.

The Lord knows that I have had a hard time, and suffered much, but I have great reason to thank Him that I enjoy good health at present, and have a prospect before me of soon going to a civilized country, where I shall see no more turbans or camels. The heat is most oppressive, and has been all through Syria.

I have not time to tell you how many days I have been at sea, without food, or how many snails I have eaten; but if I had had plenty of them, I should have done very well. All this is contained in a former letter to you written from Jaffa.

I have been at Cairo, on the Nile, because I could not get a passage direct. Syria is in a dreadful state—a war of extermination is going on between the Druses and Catholics. At the time I was at Beyroot, a battle was fought in the mountains of Lebanon, near that place, and about 800 killed. Robberies, thefts and murders are daily being committed. It is no uncommon thing to find persons in the streets without heads. An English officer, in going from St. Jean D'Acre to Beyroot, found ten persons murdered in the street, and was himself taken prisoner, but was rescued by the timely interference of the pasha. The particulars of all these things are contained in a former letter.

An American traveler, by the name of Gager, who was a licensed minister of the Congregational or Presbyterian church, left Jerusalem in company with me. He was very unwell with the jaundice when we left, and at Damietta, we had to perform six days quarantine before we ascended the Nile. On our passage up, he was taken very ill with a fever, and became helpless. I waited and tended upon him as well as our circumstances would allow; and when we landed at Bulack, I got four men to take him to the American consuls at Cairo, on a litter; I also took all his baggage there, and assisted in putting him upon a good bed—employed a good faithful Arabian nurse, and the English doctor. After the physician had examined him, he told me that he was very low with a typhus fever, and that it would be doubtful whether he recovered. Under these circumstances I left him to obtain a passage to this place. After I had gone on board a boat, and was just about pushing off, a letter came from the doctor, stating that poor Mr. Gager died in about two hours after I left him. He told me before we arrived at Cairo that he was twenty-seven years of age, and his friends lived in Norwich, Connecticut, near New London, I think. There are many particulars concerning his death, which would be interesting to his friends, but I have no time to write them now.

On Sunday morning, October 24, a good while before day, I arose from sleep, and went out of the city as soon as the gates were opened, crossed the brook Kedron, and went upon the Mount of Olives, and there, in solemn silence, with pen, ink, and paper, just as I saw in the vision, offered up the following prayer to Him who lives forever and ever—

Prayer of Orson Hyde on the Mount of Olives.

"O Thou! who art from everlasting to everlasting, eternally and unchangeably the same, even the God who rules in the heavens above, and controls the destinies of men on the earth, wilt Thou not condescend, through thine infinite goodness and royal favor, to listen to the prayer of Thy servant which he this day offers up unto Thee in the name of Thy holy child Jesus, upon this land, where the Sun of Righteousness set in blood, and thine Anointed One expired.

"Be pleased, O Lord, to forgive all the follies, weaknesses, vanities, and sins of Thy servant, and strengthen him to resist all future temptations. Give him prudence and discernment that he may avoid the evil, and a heart to choose the good; give him fortitude to bear up under trying and adverse circumstances, and grace to endure all things for Thy name's sake, until the end shall come, when all the Saints shall rest in peace.

"Now, O Lord! Thy servant has been obedient to the heavenly vision which Thou gavest him in his native land; and under the shadow of Thine outstretched arm, he has safely arrived in this place to dedicate and consecrate this land unto Thee, for the gathering together of Judah's scattered remnants, according to the predictions of the holy Prophets—for the building up of Jerusalem again after it has been trodden down by the Gentiles so long, and for rearing a Temple in honor of Thy name. Everlasting thanks be ascribed unto Thee, O Father, Lord of heaven and earth, that Thou hast preserved Thy servant from the dangers of the seas, and from the plague and pestilence which have caused the land to mourn. The violence of man has also been restrained, and Thy providential care by night and by day has been exercised over Thine unworthy servant. Accept, therefore, O Lord, the tribute of a grateful heart for all past favors, and be pleased to continue Thy kindness and mercy towards a needy worm of the dust.

"O Thou, Who didst covenant with Abraham, Thy friend, and Who didst renew that covenant with Isaac, and confirm the same with Jacob with an oath, that Thou wouldst not only give them this land for an everlasting inheritance, but that Thou wouldst also remember their seed forever. Abraham, Isaac, and Jacob have long since closed their eyes in death, and made the grave their mansion. Their children are scattered and dispersed abroad among the nations of the Gentiles like sheep that have no shepherd, and are still looking forward for the fulfillment of those promises which Thou didst make concerning them; and even this land, which once poured forth nature's richest bounty, and flowed, as it were, with milk and honey, has, to a certain extent, been smitten with barrenness and sterility since it drank from murderous hands the blood of Him who never sinned.

"Grant, therefore, O Lord, in the name of Thy well-beloved Son, Jesus Christ, to remove the barrenness and sterility of this land, and let springs of living water break forth to water its thirsty soil. Let the vine and olive produce in their strength, and the fig-tree bloom and flourish. Let the land become abundantly fruitful when possessed by its rightful heirs; let it again flow with plenty to feed the returning prodigals who come home with a spirit of grace and supplication; upon it let the clouds distil virtue and richness, and let the fields smile with plenty. Let the flocks and the herds greatly increase and multiply upon the mountains and the hills; and let Thy great kindness conquer and subdue the unbelief of Thy people. Do Thou take from them their stony heart, and give them a heart of flesh; and may the Sun of Thy favor dispel the cold mists of darkness which have beclouded their atmosphere. Incline them to gather in upon this land according to Thy word. Let them come like clouds and like doves to their windows. Let the large ships of the nations bring them from the distant isles; and let kings become their nursing fathers, and queens with motherly fondness wipe the tear of sorrow from their eye.

"Thou, O Lord, did once move upon the heart of Cyrus to show favor unto Jerusalem and her children. Do Thou now also be pleased to inspire the hearts of kings and the powers of the earth to look with a friendly eye towards this place, and with a desire to see Thy righteous purposes executed in relation thereto. Let them know that it is Thy good pleasure to restore the kingdom unto Israel—raise up Jerusalem as its capital, and constitute her people a distinct nation and government, with David Thy servant, even a descendant from the loins of ancient David to be their king.

"Let that nation or that people who shall take an active part in behalf of Abraham's children, and in the raising up of Jerusalem, find favor in Thy sight. Let not their enemies prevail against them, neither let pestilence or famine overcome them, but let the glory of Israel overshadow them, and the power of the Highest protect them; while that nation or kingdom that will not serve Thee in this glorious work must perish, according to Thy word—'Yea, those nations shall be utterly wasted.'

"Though Thy servant is now far from his home, and from the land bedewed with his earliest tear, yet he remembers, O Lord, his friends who are there, and family, whom for Thy sake he has left. Though poverty and privation be our earthly lot, yet ah! do Thou richly endow us with an inheritance where moth and rust do not corrupt, and where thieves do not break through and steal.

"The hands that have fed, clothed, or shown favor unto the family of Thy servant in his absence,or that shall hereafter do so, let them not lose their reward, but let a special blessing rest upon them, and in Thy kingdom let them have an inheritance when Thou shalt come to be glorified in this society.

"Do Thou also look with favor upon all those through whose liberality I have been enabled to come to this land; and in the day when Thou shalt reward all people according to their works, let these also not be passed by or forgotten, but in time let them be in readiness to enjoy the glory of those mansions which Jesus has gone to prepare. Particularly do Thou bless the stranger in Philadelphia, whom I never saw, but who sent me gold, with a request that I should pray for him in Jerusalem. Now, O Lord, let blessings come upon him from an unexpected quarter, and let his basket be filled, and his storehouse abound with plenty, and let not the good things *of* the earth be his only portion, but let him be found among those to whom it shall be said, 'Thou hast been faithful over a few things, and I will make thee ruler over many.'

"O my Father in heaven! I now ask Thee in the name of Jesus to remember Zion, with all her Stakes, and with all her assemblies. She has been grievously afflicted and smitten; she has mourned; she has wept; her enemies have triumphed, and have said, 'Ah, where is thy God?' Her Priests and Prophets have groaned in chains and fetters within the gloomy walls of prisons, while many were slain, and now sleep in the arms of death. How long, O Lord, shall iniquity triumph, and sin go unpunished?

"Do Thou arise in the majesty of Thy strength, and make bare Thine arm in behalf of Thy people. Redress their wrongs, and turn their sorrow into joy. Pour the spirit of light and knowledge, grace and wisdom, into the hearts of her Prophets, and clothe her Priests with salvation. Let light and knowledge march forth through the empire of darkness, and may the honest in heart flow to their standard, and join in the march to go forth to meet the Bridegroom.

"Let a peculiar blessing rest upon the Presidency of Thy Church, for at them are the arrows of the enemy directed. Be Thou to them a sun and a shield, their strong tower and hiding place; and in the time of distress or danger be Thou near to deliver. Also the quorum of the Twelve, do Thou be pleased to stand by them for Thou knowest the obstacles which they have to encounter, the temptations to which they are exposed, and the privations which they must suffer. Give us, [the Twelve] therefore, strength according to our day, and help us to bear a faithful testimony of Jesus and His Gospel, to finish with fidelity and honor the work which Thou hast given us to do, and then give us a place in Thy glorious kingdom. And let this blessing rest upon every faithful officer and member in Thy Church. And all the glory and honor will we ascribe unto God and the Lamb forever and ever. Amen."

On the top of Mount Olives I erected a pile of stones as a witness according to ancient custom. On what was anciently called Mount Zion, [Moriah?] where the Temple stood, I erected another, and used the rod according to the prediction upon my head.

I have found many Jews who listened with intense interest. The idea of the Jews being restored to Palestine is gaining ground in Europe almost every day. Jerusalem is strongly fortified with many cannon upon its walls. The wall is ten feet thick on the sides that would be most exposed, and four or five feet where the descent from the wall is almost perpendicular. The number of inhabitants within the walls is about twenty thousand. About seven thousand of this number are Jews, the balance being mostly Turks and Armenians. Many of the Jews who are old go to this place to die, and many are coming from Europe into this eastern world. The great wheel is unquestionably in motion, and the word of the Almighty has declared that it shall roll.

I have not time to write particulars now, but suffice it to say that my mission has been quite as prosperous as I could expect.

I am now about to go on board a fine ship for Trieste, and from thence I intend to proceed to Regensburg and there publish our faith in the German language. There are those who are ready and willing to assist me.

I send you this letter by Captain Withers, an English gentleman, who goes direct to England, on board the Oriental steamer. He has come with me from Jerusalem. If I had money sufficient I should be almost tempted to take passage on board of her to England, but this I cannot do.

On receipt of this, I wish you to write to me immediately, and direct to Regensburg, on the Danube, Bayern, or Bavaria. If you know anything of my family tell me.

My best respects to yourself and your family, to Brothers Adams and Snow, and to all the Saints in England.

May grace, mercy and peace, from God our Father, and from the Lord Jesus Christ, rest upon you all from this time, henceforth and for ever. Amen.

Your brother in Christ,

ORSON HYDE.

CHAPTER XXVII.

OFFICIAL DENUNCIATION OF THIEVES AT NAUVOO—THE MORAL LAW OF THE CHURCH—ABANDONMENT OF RAMUS AS A STAKE OF ZION—BAPTISM FOR THE DEAD, AN EPISTLE.

Wednesday, 24.—Elder Joseph Fielding, who sailed from Liverpool, on the *Tyrean*, with 204 Saints, arrived at Warsaw with his company; and Elders Willard Richards and John Taylor went to meet them and to give such counsel as their situation required.

Friday, 26.

Affiidavit of Hyrum Smith—Denouncing Theft.

Whereas it hath been intimated to me by persons of credibility that there are persons in the surrounding country, who profess to be members of the Church of Jesus Christ of Latter-day Saints, who have been using their influence and endeavors to instil into the minds of good and worthy citizens in the state of Illinois. and the adjoining states, that the First Presidency, and others in authority and high standing in said Church, do sanction and approbate the members of said Church in stealing property from those persons who do not belong to said Church, and thereby to induce persons to aid and abet them in the act of stealing, and other evil practices; I therefore, hereby disavow any sanction or approbation by me, of the crime of theft, or any other evil practice, in any person or persons whatever, whereby either the lives or property of our fellow men may be unlawfully taken or molested; neither are such things sanctioned or approbated by the First Presidency, or any other person in authority or good standing in said Church, but such acts are altogether in violation of the rules, order, and regulations of the Church, contrary to the teachings given in said Church, and the laws of both God and man. I caution the unwary, who belong to the aforesaid Church, and all other persons, against being duped or led into any act or scheme which may endanger their character, lives, or property, or bring reproach upon the Church; and I certify that I hold my person and property ready to support the laws of the land, in the detection of any person or persons who may commit any breach of the same. To which I subscribe my name, and testify, this 26th day of November, 1841.

HYRUM SMITH.

Sworn to and subscribed before me this 26th day of November, 1841.
EBENEZER ROBINSON, J.P.

I attended city council and presented a bill for "an Ordinance in relation to Hawkers, Pedlars, Public Shows, and Exhibitions, in order to prevent any immoral or obscene exhibition," which passed the council by unanimous vote.

Sunday, 28.—I spent the day in the council with the Twelve Apostles at the house of President Young, conversing with them upon a variety of subjects. Brother Joseph Fielding was present, having been absent four years on a mission to England. I told the brethren that the Book of Mormon was the most correct of any book on earth, and the keystone of our religion, and a man would get nearer to God by abiding by its precepts, than by any other book.

The Prophet's Estimate of the Book of Mormon.

Monday, 29.—I gave the following affidavit, and published it in the *Times and Seasons.*

The Prophet's Denunciation of Thieves.

CITY OF NAUVOO, ILLINOIS, November 29, A.D. 1841.

TO THE PUBLIC.

The occurrence of recent events makes it criminal for me to remain longer silent. The tongue of the vile yet speaks, and sends forth the poison of asps, the ears of the spoiler yet hear, and he puts forth his hands to iniquity. It has been proclaimed upon the house top and in the secret chamber, in the public walks and private circle, throughout the length and breadth of this vast continent, that stealing by the Latter-day Saints has received my approval; nay, that I have taught the doctrine, encouraged them in plunder, and led on the van—than which nothing is more foreign from my heart. I disfellowship the perpetrators of all such abominations—they are devils and not Saints, totally unfit for the society of Christians or men. It is true that some professing to be Latter-day Saints have taught such vile heresies, but all are not Israel that are of Israel; and I wish it to be distinctly understood in all coming time, that the Church, over which I have the honor of presiding, will ever set its brows like brass, and its face like steel, against all such abominable acts of villainy and crime; and to this end I append my affidavit of disavowal, taken this day before General Bennet, that there may be no mistake hereafter as to my real sentiments, or those of the leaders of the Church, in relation to this important matter.

STATE OF ILLINOIS, HANCOCK COUNTY.

Before me, John C. Bennett, Mayor of the City of Nauvoo, personally came Joseph Smith, President of the Church of Jesus Christ of Latter-day Saints (commonly called the Mormon Church), who being duly sworn according to law, deposeth and saith, that he has never directly or indirectly encouraged the purloining of property, or taught the doctrine of stealing, or any other evil practice, and that all such vile and unlawful acts will ever receive his unreserved and unqualified disapproval, and the most vigorous opposition of the Church over which he presides; and further this deponent saith not.

JOSEPH SMITH,
President of the Church of Jesus Christ
of Latter-day Saints.

Sworn to and subscribed before me, at my office, in the city of Nauvoo, this 29th day of November, A.D. 1841.

JOHN C. BENNETT,
L. S. Mayor of the City of Nauvoo.

Now it is to be hoped that none will hereafter be so reckless as to state that I, or the Church to which I belong, approve of thieving—but that all the friends of law and order will join in ferreting out thieves wherever and whenever they may be found, and assist in bringing them to that condign punishment which such infamous crimes so richly merit.

JOSEPH SMITH,
President of the Church of Jesus Christ
of Latter-day Saints.

Conference in New York.

A conference was held in New York City, Elder John E. Page presiding; in which were represented New York City, 17 Elders, 2 Priests, 1 Teacher, 2 Deacons, 179 members. Five branches were represented, including 5 Elders, 6 Priests, 3 Teachers, 3 Deacons, 149 members. 3 Elders, 2 Priests, 1 Teacher, were ordained. There were present at the conference, 1 Apostle, 6 High Priests, 16 Elders, 3 Priests, 2 Teachers, 2 Deacons.

Tuesday, 30.—Attended a council of the Twelve Apostles at President Brigham Young's home. President Brigham Young, Heber C. Kimball, Willard Richards, Orson Pratt, Lyman Wight, John Taylor, and Wilford Woodruff were present.

It was voted that Ebenezer Robinson be solicited to give up the department of printing the *Times and Seasons* to Elder Willard Richards.

Voted, that if Brother Robinson does not comply with this solicitation, Elder Richards be instructed to procure a press and type, and publish a paper for the Church.

Moved by Elder Young, and seconded by Elder Woodruff, that Lyman Wight and John Taylor present these resolutions to Brother Robinson.

Wednesday, December 1.—In view of the proceedings of the meeting of the Church at Ramus, on the 18th November, when certain individuals were cut off from the Church for stealing, the Twelve issued the following epistle:

Warning of the Twelve Apostles Against Thieves.

We are glad that the perpetrators of the above crime have been caught in their iniquitous practices; and we are only sorry that anybody should be found who would bail them out of prison, for such individuals, if the charges are true, ought to be made an example of, and not be suffered to run at large.

We have been informed that some of them have been talking of moving into this place, but we would here inform them that persons whose conduct has exposed them to the just censure of an indignant public, can have no fellowship amongst us, as we cannot, and will not countenance rogues, thieves, and scoundrels knowingly; and, we hereby warn them that the law will be as rigorously enforced against them in this place as in any other, as we consider such characters a curse to society, whose pestilential breath withers the morals, and blasts the fame and reputation of any people among whom they may sojourn. There is no person that is, and ought to be despised more than the thief, by any respectable community; yet more especially ought such persons to be abhorred who have taken upon them the name of Christ, and thus with the pretext of religion, and garb of sanctity, cloak their nefarious practices.

We have been told that some individual or individuals have, under false pretenses, been wishing to palm their wicked and devilish principles upon the authorities of the Church, stating that it was part and parcel of the Gospel which God had revealed, and that it is one of the mysteries which the initiated only are acquainted with. We know not how to express our abhorrence at such an idea, and can only say that it is engendered in hell, founded in falsehood, and is the offspring of the devil; and it is at variance with every principle of righteousness and truth, and will damn all that are connected with it, for all mysteries are only such to the ignorant, and vanish as soon as men have sufficient intelligence to comprehend them; and there are no mysteries connected with godliness and our holy religion, but what are pure, innocent, virtuous, just, and righteous. If this [the foregoing practice of thieving] is a mystery, it is the "mystery of iniquity." We are at a loss to know who could be vile enough to propagate such base and unfounded statements, and we would say to the Church, beware of such men! Set them down as the worst of scoundrels, and reject their foul insinuations with the indignation and disgust that such unhallowed and vile insinuations deserve; for such men are either avowed apostates, or on the eve of apostasy, or have only taken the name of religion to cloak their hypocrisy; we fear the latter, in some instances is the case, and that Mississippi scoundrels* palm themselves upon us to cover their guilt. We fur-

* This has reference to the blacklegs that infested the upper Mississippi region, and who plied their trade in disposing of counterfeit money and stolen goods along the river. The character of the old inhabitants in Northern Illinois at this time, (1840-44), Governor Ford describes in his "*History of Illinois*" as follows: "Then, again, the northern part of the State was not destitute of its organized bands of rogues, engaged in murders, robberies, horse-stealing, and in making and passing counterfeit money. These rogues were scattered all over the north; but the most of them were located in the counties of Ogle, Winnebago, Lee, and De-Kalb. In the county of Ogle, they were so numerous, strong, and well-organized, that they could not be convicted for their crimes. By getting some of their numbers on the juries, by producing hosts of witnesses to sustain their defense by perjured evidence, and by changing the venue from one county to another, and by continuances from term to term, and by the inability of witnesses to attend from time to time at a distant and foreign county, they most generally managed to be acquitted."

ther call upon the Church to bring all such characters before the authorities, that they may be tried, and dealt with according to the law of God, and delivered up unto the laws of the land.

It is scarcely possible that any virtuous man could be made to believe any such statements, however ignorant; yet lest through false pretenses the innocent might be drawn into a snare, we would quote the following from the Book of Doctrine and Covenants, section 42, paragraph 84, 85, "And if any man or woman shall rob, he or she shall be delivered up unto the law of the land. And if he or she shall steal, he or she shall be delivered up unto the law of the land." Again, section 42, paragraph 20,* "Thou shalt not steal, and he that stealeth and will not repent shall be cast out." The broad law of God is, "Thou shalt not steal," and thieves, together with "liars and whoremongers," will eventually be found without the city, with dogs and sorcerers. We need only say that if we find such characters engaged in their nefarious practices, whether in or out of the Church, we shall take them up, and deal with them according to the law of God and man; and we wish the Church to inform us of such delinquents, or the sin will lie at their own door.

As there are gangs of robbers up and down this river, from whom we have suffered much, having had many horses, cattle and other property stolen, we purpose instituting a police for the protection of our property, and the rigorous enforcement of the laws of our country; and should any, who call themselves Latter-day Saints, be found in their midst, they will be cut off from the Church, and handed over to the law of the land.

We hope that what we have written may suffice, and take this opportunity of expressing our decided and unqualified disapprobation of anything like theft in all its bearings, as being calculated to destroy the peace of society, to injure the Church of Jesus Christ, to wound the character of the people of God, and to stamp with eternal infamy all

* The above references are published to correspond in current editions of the Doctrine and Covenants. The revelation quoted was given as a law to the Church, February 9, 1831. It was given in the presence of twelve Elders, at Kirtland, in fulfillment of the promise that the Lord made to the Church while yet located in New York, in a revelation commanding them to move from the eastern countries to the Ohio; "And there," said the Lord, "I will give unto you my law, and there you shall be endowed with power from on high." (Doctrine and Covenants, section 38: 32.) As introductory to the revelation the Prophet said under date of February 9: "According to the promise heretofore made, the Lord gave the following revelation embracing the Law of the Church;" and indeed, it is appropriately so called, for it embraces well nigh every moral law of the Gospel, and is a most valuable chapter of divine instructions to the Church.

who follow such diabolical practices; to blast their character on earth, and to consign them to eternal perdition.

BRIGHAM YOUNG,
HEBER C. KIMBALL,
PARLEY P. PRATT,
ORSON HYDE,
WILLIAM SMITH,
ORSON PRATT,
JOHN E. PAGE,
WILLARD RICHARDS,
LYMAN WIGHT,
WILFORD WOODRUFF,
JOHN TAYLOR,
GEORGE A. SMITH.

Nauvoo, Illinois, December 1, 1841.*

*About this time there were gangs of robbers operating up and down the Mississippi River, from which the Saints suffered, as many of their horses and cattle were stolen, but more serious injury arose from the fact that the acts of these robbers were attributed to the Saints themselves, and did much to prejudice the minds of the public against them. Governor Ford in his "History of Illinois," from 1814 to 1847 in referring to these charges against the Saints, and speaking of events taking place about this time in Nauvoo, said: "It was a fact also, that some larcenies and robberies had been committed, and that Mormons had been convicted of the crimes, and that other larcenies had been committed by persons unknown, but suspected to be Mormons. Justice, however, requires me here to say, that upon such investigation as I then could make, the charge of promiscuous stealing appeared to be exaggerated." (History of Illinois, Ford, p. 329.)

The practice of charging these robberies upon members of the Church continued through the next three or four years. Speaking of the time somewhat later than the period with which our annals above deal, the Governor said: "On my late visit to Hancock county, I was informed by some of their violent enemies, that the larcenies of the Mormons had become unusually numerous and insufferable. They indeed admitted that but little had been done in this way in their immediate vicinity. But they insisted that sixteen horses had been stolen by the Mormons in one night, near Lima in the county of Adams. At the close of the expedition, I called at this same town of Lima, and upon inquiry was told that no horses had been stolen in that neighborhood, but that sixteen horses had been stolen in one night in Hancock county. This last informant being told of the Hancock story, again changed the venue to another distant settlement in the northern edge of Adams." (History of Illinois, p. 331.)

And thus sensational reports of "Mormon stealings" were made the shuttle-cock between the battle-doors of various neighborhoods.

In addition to the very emphatic utterances of the Prophet Joseph, his brother Hyrum, and the Twelve, the *Times and Seasons* editorally said:

"THIEVES.

"We are highly pleased to see the very energetic measures taken by our citizens to suppress thieving. It has been a source of grief unto us that there were any in our midst who would wilfully take property from any person which did not belong

Thursday, 2.—I received the following revelation to Nancy Marinda Hyde—

Revelation.

Verily thus saith the Lord unto you my servant Joseph, that inasmuch as you have called upon me to know my will concerning my handmaid Nancy Marinda Hyde—behold it is my will that she should have a better place prepared for her, than that in which she now lives, in order that her life may be spared unto her; therefore go and say unto my servant, Ebenezer Robinson, and to my handmaid his wife—Let them open their doors and take her and her children into their house and take care of them faithfully and kindly until my servant Orson Hyde returns from his mission, or until some other provision can be made for her welfare and safety. Let them do these things and spare not, and I the Lord will bless them and heal them if they do it not grudgingly, saith the Lord God; and she shall be a blessing unto them; and let my handmaid Nancy Marinda Hyde hearken to the counsel of my servant Joseph in all things whatsoever he shall teach unto her, and it shall be a blessing upon her and upon her children after her, unto her justification, saith the Lord.

Saturday, 4.—I attended the city council, and spoke in defense of the marshal, in his not serving a warrant, when his life would have been endangered.

Conference at Ramus.

A conference was held at Ramus on the 4th and 5th of December, 1841, over which the Patriarch of the Church, Hyrum Smith, presided; Joseph Johnson acted as clerk; Brigham Young, Heber C. Kimball, Willard Richards and John Taylor, of the

to them, knowing that if any person, who does, or ever did belong to this Church, should steal, the whole Church would have to bear the stigma, and the sound goes abroad that the Mormons are a set of thieves and robbers, a charge which we unequivocally deny, and pronounce a falsehood of the basest kind. That there are some amongst us base enough to commit such acts we do not pretend to deny, but whether they are all members of this Church or not, we do not know; but some who are have been caught in their iniquity, and one was among the missing after a warrant was out for him; circumstantial proof is so strong against him, that his guilt is established without a doubt. We have heard that some of those characters have said that such things are sanctioned by the authorities of the Church, this is the most base of all lies: and we would here warn all well disposed persons, to be aware of such characters, and if any such thing is ever intimated to them, to heed it not, unless it be to report such persons to the proper authorities so that they can be brought to condign punishment; for know assuredly that if you listen to them, they will prove an adder in your path, and eventually lead you down to destruction."—*Times and Seasons*, p. 615.

quorum of the Twelve Apostles were present. It was unanimously resolved by the conference that the organization of the Church at Ramus as a Stake be discontinued and that John Lawson be presiding Elder over the branch at Ramus, and Joseph Johnson, clerk; and that William Wightman, the Bishop, transfer all the Church property in Ramus to the sole Trustee in Trust, Joseph Smith, President of the whole Church.

Prophet Proof Reads Book of Mormon.

Sunday, 5. I commenced to proof read the Book of Mormon, previous to its being stereotyped; read sixty pages.

In the evening Brother Wilford Woodruff and wife visited me. We conversed about the Missouri troubles, and the death of David W. Patten; also his last request.*

Tuesday, 7.—The following is a copy of a letter to Lawyers Bushnell and Browning of Quincy:

Letter of the Prophet to Esquires Browning and Bushnell—Payment of Notes.

Esquires Browning and Bushnell:

GENTLEMEN:—Your letter of the 23rd ultimo, concerning two notes placed in your hands by Messrs. Halsted, Haines and Co., against myself and thirty-one others, for collection, was duly received. In reply, I must inform you, that I am not in possession of means, belonging to me individually to liquidate those notes at present; the reason is apparent to every one; I need not relate to you the persecution I have suffered, and the loss and confiscation of all my effects at various times as a reason of my inability; you know it all, and so do the gentlemen whose notes you hold for collection. But I wish you to say to them that if they will give me my time (and no more than I must necessarily have), they shall have their pay in some way or other. I have the means at command in the East, which, with a sufficient indulgence, will enable me to pay them every whit, but unless this is granted me, it will be impossible for me to do so. All I ask of those gentlemen and this generation is that they should not tie up my hands, nor thwart me in my operations. If this is granted me, I pledge my word, yea, my sacred honor, that all that can in fairness be demanded at my hands, either now or at any time shall ultimately be adjusted to the satisfaction of all concerned. This is all that I can say at this time, or do,

* See Vol. III., p. 171.

hoping that you will communicate to Messrs. Holsted, Haines and Co. the contents, or at all events the purport of this letter, together with my sincere regard for their welfare, and as regards you, gentlemen,

I remain very respectfully,

Your obedient servant,

JOSEPH SMITH.

Wednesday, 8.—The Twelve who attended the Ramus conference on the 4th instant returned with nearly a thousand dollars worth of property, consisting of horses, wagons, provisions, clothing, etc., for the Temple, which had been donated by the Saints at Ramus.

Friday 10.—I wrote to Horace R. Hotchkiss, Esq.

The Prophet's Letter to Mr. Hotchkiss—Commerce Lands.

DEAR SIR;—Your letters, dated October, 11th and November 9th, 1841, have both been received, and that of the 9th of November is now before me. I am glad that you are pleased with the proceedings of our last conference relative to "Mr. Hotchkiss purchase," concerning which there had been some unpleasant feeling which had originated partly from a misunderstanding between us, and partly through the inefficiency, neglect or sickness of Dr. Galland. I wrote a letter to your friend and partner, Esquire Tuttle, some time since, which no doubt you have seen before now, and with which I hope you are also satisfied. I have handed your request to the editor of the *Times and Seasons*, who will forward you the desired papers. I am glad that James Ivins settled with you the $2,500 note, but sorry that you suffered yourself to lose in the sale of the land you had of him. As regards the Cook's Mill Tavern stand, and the one hundred and thirty-seven acres of pine land, which you propose to allow the Church three thousand dollars for, I have to say in reply, that I have consulted, not only my own feelings as sole Trustee in Trust for the Church; but also the feelings of those of the Church whose opinions I can always rely upon in such matters, and the conclusion is that thirty-two hundred dollars is the least the property ought to be sold for. You can, therefore, have it for three thousand two hundred, which is considerably less than it cost the Church; we are willing to make a partial sacrifice in the property, but under the circumstances, think that you can afford to give us two hundred dollars more than you proposed. The health of our place is at this time pretty good, and we hope it may continue to improve, with the improvements of the city.

I remain very respectfully yours, &c.,

JOSEPH SMITH.

Saturday, 11.—Late this evening, while sitting in council with the Twelve in my new store on Water street, I directed Brigham Young, President of the Twelve Apostles, to go immediately and instruct the building committee in their duty, and forbid them receiving any more property for the building of the Temple, until they received it from the Trustee in Trust, and if the committee did not give heed to the instruction, and attend to their duty, to put them in the way so to do.

Elder Willard Richards has left Warsaw for Nauvoo, it being considered unnecessary for him to tarry there any longer.

The Prophet's Difficulties in Writing the Annals of the Church.

Since I have been engaged in laying the foundation of the Church of Jesus Christ of Latter-day Saints, I have been prevented in various ways from continuing my journal and history in a manner satisfactory to myself or in justice to the cause. Long imprisonments, vexatious and long-continued law-suits, the treachery of some of my clerks, the death of others, and the poverty of myself and brethren from continued plunder and driving, have prevented my handing down to posterity a connected memorandum of events desirable to all lovers of truth; yet I have continued to keep up a journal in the best manner my circumstances would allow, and dictate for my history from time to time, as I have had opportunity so that the labors and suffering of the first Elders and Saints of this last kingdom might not wholly be lost to the world.

Sunday, 12.—I preached in the morning at Snyder's Hotel.

In the evening, the Twelve met in council at Brother Heber C. Kimball's.

Monday, 13.—I appointed Willard Richards recorder for the Temple, and my private Secretary and general Clerk, and he commenced his labors in my new office in the brick store.

Some time in the fall of 1839, Daniel S. Witter, of the

steam mill at Warsaw, solicited the First Presidency of the Church to make a settlement on the school section No. 16, one mile south of Warsaw, and the solicitations were continued by Daniel S. Witter, Mark Aldrich and others, from time to time, till the spring or summer of 1841, when articles of agreement were entered into between Calvin A. Warren, Esq., Witter, Aldrich and others, owners of the school section and the First Presidency, giving the Saints the privilege of settling on the school section, which had been surveyed and laid out in town lots, and called *Warren*, on certain conditions, and Willard Richards went to Warsaw on the 8th of September, and spent several weeks to prepare for the reception of immigrants. In the meantime the inhabitants of Warsaw attempted to form an anti-Mormon society, and were much enraged because Esquire Davis (who had spoken favorably of the Saints) was appointed clerk of the county by Judge Stephen A. Douglas.

Anti Mormonism at Warsaw.

In November two hundred and four Saints arrived at Warsaw, from England, led by Joseph Fielding, and were visited on the 24th of November by Elders Willard Richards, and John Taylor of the Twelve, and counseled to tarry at Warsaw according to the instruction of the First Presidency.

December 13.—Isaac Decker, presiding Elder at Warsaw, stated to the Presidency of Nauvoo, that Mr. Witter had raised one dollar per barrel on flour, and sold the sweepings of his mill to the Saints at $2.25 per hundred; and that Witter and Aldrich had forbidden the brethren the privilege of getting the old wood on the school section, which they had full liberty to get; that the price of wood on the wharf had fallen twenty-five cents per cord since the arrival of the Saints; that the citizens had raised their rent, &c.; and the First Presidency decided that the Saints should remove from

Further Trouble at Warsaw.

Warsaw to Nauvoo immediately; and that the proceedings at Warsaw be published in the *Times and Seasons*.

This morning President Young delivered the message I gave him on Saturday evening to Reynolds Cahoon and Elias Higbee, the Temple Committe, in presence of Elders Kimball, Woodruff, and Richards.

Elder Richards by letter instructed the Saints at Warsaw to remove to Nauvoo.

BAPTISM FOR THE DEAD.

An Epistle of the Twelve Apostles to the Saints of the Last Days.

The building of the Temple of the Lord in the city of Nauvoo, is occupying the first place in the exertions and prayers of many of the Saints at the present time, knowing, as they do, that if this building is not completed speedily, "we shall be rejected as a Church with our dead;" for the Lord our God hath spoken it.

But while many are thus engaged in laboring and watching and praying for this all important object, there are many, very many more, who do not thus come up to their privilege and their duty in this thing, and in many instances we are confident that their neglect arises from a want of proper understanding of the principles upon which this building is founded, and by which it must be completed.

The children of Israel were commanded to build a house in the land of promise; and so are the Saints of the last days, as you will see in the Revelation given to Joseph the Seer, January 19, 1841, wherein those ordinances may be revealed which have been hid for ages, even their anointings and washings, and baptisms for the dead; wherein they may meet in solemn assemblies for their memorials, sacrifices, and oracles in their most holy places; and wherein they may receive conversations and statutes, and judgments, for the beginning of the revelations and foundations of Zion, and the glory and honor and adornment of all her municipals through the medium which God has ordained.

In the same revelation the command is to "all the Saints from afar," as well as those already gathered to this place: to arise with one consent and build the Temple; to prepare a place where the Most High may manifest Himself to His people. No one is excepted who hath aught in his possession, for what have ye that ye have not received? And I will require mine own with usury, saith the Lord; so that those who live thousands of miles from this place, come under the same law, and are entitled to the same blessings and privileges as those who have already gathered. But some may say, how can this be, I am not there, therefore I cannot meet in the Temple, cannot be baptized in the font? The command of heaven is to you, to all, gather; and when you arrive here, if it is found that you have previously sent of your gold, or your silver, or your substance, the tithing and consecrations which are required of you for this building, you will find your names, tithings and consecrations written in the Book of the Law of the Lord, to be kept in the Temple, as a witness in your favor, showing that you are a proprietor in that building, and are entitled to your share of the privileges thereunto belonging.

One of those privileges which is particularly attracting the notice of the Saints at the present moment, is baptism for the dead, in the font which is so far completed as to be dedicated, and several have already attended to this ordinance by which the sick have been made whole, and the prisoner set free; but while we have been called to administer this ordinance, we have been led to inquire into the propriety of baptizing those who have not been obedient, and assisted to build the place for baptism; and it seems to us unreasonable to expect that the Great Jehovah will approbate such administration; for if the Church must be brought under condemnation, and rejected with her dead, if she fail to build the house and its appurtenances, why should not individuals of the Church, who thus neglect, come under the same condemnation? For if they are to be rejected, they may as well be rejected without baptism as with it; for their baptism can be of no avail before God, and the time to baptize them may be appropriated to building the walls of the house, and this is according to the understanding which we have received from him who is our spokesman.

Let it not be supposed that the sick and the destitute are to be denied the blessings of the Lord's house; God forbid; His eye is ever over them for good. He that hath not, and cannot obtain, but saith in his heart, if I had, I would give freely, is accepted as freely as he that gives of his abundance. The Temple is to be built by tithing and consecration, and every one is at liberty to consecrate all they find in their hearts so to do; but the tithings required, is one-tenth of all anyone possessed at the commencement of the building, and one-tenth part of all his increase from that time until the completion of the same, whether it be money, or whatever he may be blessed with.

Many in this place are laboring every tenth day for the house, and this is the tithing of their income, for they have nothing else; others would labor the same, but they are sick, therefore excusable; when they get well, let them begin; while there are others who appear to think their own business of more importance than the Lord's. Of such we would ask, who gave you your time, health, strength, and put you into business? And will you not begin quickly to return with usury that which you have received? Our God will not wait always.

We would remind some two or three hundred Elders, who offered to go on missions, some six months, others one year, and some two years, and had their missions assigned them at the general conference to labor on the Temple, that most of their names are still with us, and we wish them to call and take their names away, and give them up to the building committee.

Brethren, you have as great an interest at stake in this thing as we have, but as our Master, even the Master-builder of the Temple, whose throne is on high, has seen fit to constitute us stewards in some parts of His household; we feel it important for us to see to it that our Master is not defrauded, and especially by those who have pledged their word, their time, their talents, to His services; and we hope this gentle hint will suffice, that we may not be compelled to publish the names of those referred to.

Probably some may think they could have gone on a mission, but cannot labor, as they have no means of boarding themselves, but let such remember that several score of brethren and sisters in this city, offered at the general conference, to board one or more laborers on the Temple till the same should be completed, and but few of those as yet have had the opportunity of boarding any one. To all such we would say, you are not forgotten, we have your names also, and we expect soon to send someone to your table, therefore put your houses in order and never be ready to refuse the first offer of a guest.

Large stores of provisions will be required to complete the work, and now is the time for securing it, while meat is plenty and can be had for one half the value that it can at other seasons of the year, and the weather is cool and suitable for packing. Let the brethren for two hundred miles around drive their fat cattle and hogs to this place, where they may be preserved, and there will be a supply till another favorable season rolls around, or till the end of the labor.

Now is the time to secure food, now is the time that the trustee is ready to receive your droves. Not the maimed, the lean, the halt, and the blind, and such that you cannot use; it is for the Lord, and He wants no such offering; but if you want His blessing, give Him the best, give Him as good as He has given you. Beds and bedding, socks, mittens, shoes, clothing of every description, and store goods are needed for the comfort of the laborers this winter; journeymen, stone cutters, quarrymen, teams and teamsters for drawing stone and all kinds of provision for men and beast, are needed in abundance.

There are individuals who have given nothing as yet, either as tithing or consecration, thinking that they shall be able to do a great deal some time hence if they continue their present income to their own use, but this is a mistaken idea. Suppose that all should act upon this principle, no one would do ought at present, consequently the building must cease, and this generation remain without a house, and the Church be rejected; then suppose the next generation labor upon the same principle, and the same in all succeeding generations, the Son of God would never have a place on earth to lay His head.

Let every individual remember that their tithings and consecrations are required from what they have, and not what they expect to have some time hence, and are wanted for immediate use. All money and other property designed for tithing and consecrations to the building of the Temple must hereafter be presented to the Trustee in Trust, President Joseph Smith, and entered at the recorder's office, in the book before referred to; and all receipts now holden by individuals, which they have received of the building committee for property delivered to them, must also be forwarded to the recorder's office for entry, to secure the appropriation of said property according to the original design.

The Elders everywhere will instruct the brethren both in public and in private, in the principles and doctrines set forth in this Epistle, so that every individual in the Church may have a perfect understanding of his duty and privileges.

BRIGHAM YOUNG,
HEBER C. KIMBALL,
ORSON PRATT,
WILLIAM SMITH,
LYMAN WIGHT.
WILFORD WOODRUFF
JOHN TAYLOR,
GEO. A. SMITH,
WILLARD RICHARDS.

Nauvoo, Illinois, December 13, 1841.

CHAPTER XXVIII.

KIRTLAND *vs.* NAUVOO—POLITICAL ATTITUDE OF THE PEOPLE OF NAUVOO DECLARED—PUBLICATIONS MORMON AND ANTI-MORMON FOR 1841—CLOSE OF THE YEAR.

Tuesday, December 14, 1841.—I commenced opening, unpacking, and assorting a lot of dry goods in the second story of my new store, situate on the northwest corner of block 155.* The joiners and masons are yet at work in the lower part of the building.

Wednesday, 15.—In reply to inquiries concerning Almon W. Babbitt, and the printing press at Kirtland, contained in a letter written at Kirtland, November 16, 1841, by Lester Brooks and Zebedee Coltrin, acting presidents, and Thomas Burdick, Bishop and council, to President Joseph Smith and Brigham Young, it was decided as follows:

Decision in the Case of Almon W. Babbitt and Kirtland.

It remains for Almon W. Babbitt to offer satisfaction, if he wishes so to do, according to the minutes of the conference. You are doubtless all well aware that all the stakes, except those in Hancock county, Illinois, and Lee county, Iowa, were discontinued some time since by the First Presidency, as published in the *Times and Seasons*; but as it appears that there are many in Kirtland who desire to remain there, and build up that place, and as you have made great exertions according to your letter, to establish a printing press, and take care of the poor, &c., since that period, you may as well continue operations according to your designs, and go on with your printing, and do what you can in righteousness to build up Kirtland, but do not suffer yourselves to harbor the idea that Kirtland will rise on the ruins of Nauvoo. It is the privilege of brethren emigrating from any quarter to come to this place, and it is not right to attempt to persuade those who desire it, to stop short.

The foregoing is an extract from my letter in reply.

* On the corner of Granger and Water streets, in the southwest part of the city.

The Twelve Apostles were in council at Elder Kimball's.

Tuesday, 16.—William Wightman of Ramus, delivered to President Joseph Smith, sole trustee-in-trust, the deed to the unsold and bonded lots of land in the town of Ramus, bearing date December 8, 1841; also the plat of the "first addition to Ramus," and the notes which have been received of individuals who have purchased lots, and the bonds of William Miller, September 21, 1840, and of Ute Perkins, November 26, 1840, and of William J. Perkins, November 7, 1840, and of John F. Charles, November 16, 1841, for lots of land adjoining Ramus, and which may hereafter be added to the town plats (a part of the land included in William Miller's bond is included in the first addition to Ramus, and the notes were transferred to the sole trustee-in-trust, for the benefit of the whole Church, by a vote of the Ramus conference, December 4 and 5, 1841), after applying sufficient of said property to liquidate the claims of those from whom the town was purchased, and also paying two notes given by William Wightman for money borrowed to pay for the above property, viz., to Lyman Prentice $11.45, and James Cummins $50.00, and some other small demands against said Wightman which have been contracted for the benefit of the Church in Ramus.

Affairs at Ramus.

Saturday, 18.—I attended the city council, and stated circumstances which I had heard concerning mobocracy, from a person late from Macombe, and requested an ordinance passed, so that persons ordering any person to leave their peaceful homes could be dealt with rigorously; also presented the following—

Expressions of Gratitude to James Gordon Bennett and the New York Herald.

Resolved by the city council of the city of Nauvoo, that the high-minded and honorable editor of the *New York Weekly Herald*, James Gordon Bennett, Esq., is deserving of the lasting gratitude of this community, for his very liberal and unprejudiced course towards us as a people, in giving us a fair hearing in his paper, thus enabling us to reach the ears of a portion of the community, who, otherwise would ever have remained ignorant of our principles and practices.

Resolved, That we recommend our fellow citizens to subscribe for the *New York Weekly Herald*, and thus be found patronizing true merit, industry, and enterprise.

Sunday, 19.—The Twelve were in council at Elder Brigham Young's—morning.

Meeting at my house in the evening.

The subjoined minutes are from Elder Wilford Woodruff's journal—

Minutes of a Meeting of the Twelve in the House of the Prophet.

Elder Heber C. Kimball preached at the house of President Joseph Smith, on the parable in the 18th chapter of Jeremiah, of the clay in the hands of the potter, that when it marred in the hands of the potter it was cut off the wheel and then thrown back again into the mill, to go into the next batch, and was a vessel of dishonor; but all clay that formed well in the hands of the potter, and was pliable, was a vessel of honor; and thus it was with the human family, and ever will be: all that are pliable in the hands of God and are obedient to His commands, are vessels of honor, and God will receive them.

President Joseph arose and said—"Brother Kimball has given you a true explanation of the parable," and then read the parable of the vine and its branches, and explained it, and said, "if we keep the commandments of God, we should bring forth fruit and be the friends of God, and know what our Lord did.

"Some people say I am a fallen Prophet, because I do not bring forth more of the word of the Lord. Why do I not do it? Are we able to receive it? No! not one in this room. He then chastened the congregation for their wickedness and unbelief, 'for whom the Lord loveth he chasteneth, and scourgeth every son and daughter whom he receiveth,' and if we do not receive chastisements then we are bastards and not sons."

On the subject of revelation, he said, a man would command his son to dig potatoes and saddle his horse, but before he had done either he would tell him to do something else. This is all considered right; but as soon as the Lord gives a commandment and revokes that decree and commands something else, then the Prophet is considered fallen. Because we will not receive chastisement at the hand of the Prophet and

Apostles, the Lord chastiseth us with sickness and death. Let not any man publish his own righteousness, for others can see that for him; sooner let him confess his sins, and then he will be forgiven, and he will bring forth more fruit. When a corrupt man is chastised he gets angry and will not endure it. The reason we do not have the secrets of the Lord revealed unto us,is because we do not keep them but reveal them; we do not keep our own secrets, but reveal our difficulties to the world, even to our enemies, then how would we keep the secrets of the Lord? I can keep a secret till Doomsday. What greater love hath any man than that he lay down his life for his friend; then why not fight for our friend until we die?

Elder Brigham Young said—one thing lay with weight on his mind; that is, that we should be prepared to keep each commandment as it came from the Lord by the mouth of the Prophet, and as the Lord had commanded us to build a temple, we should do it speedily.

Monday, 20.—I communicated to the *Times and Seasons*, as follows—

The Prophet on the Attitude of the Saints in Politics.

TO MY FRIENDS IN ILLINOIS—The Gubernatorial Convention of the state of Illinois has nominated Colonel Adam W. Snyder* for Governor, and Colonel John Moore for Lieutenant-Governor,of the state of Illinois, election to take place in August next.

Colonel Moore, like Judge Douglas and Esquire Warren, was an intimate friend of General Bennett long before that gentleman became a member of our community; and General Bennett informs us that no men were

* Governor Ford, in his "History of Illinois," gives the following biographical information about Adam W. Snyder, and as I can find nothing concerning him elsewhere, I quote Ford:—

"In December, 1841, a State Democratic convention assembled at Springfield, and nominated Adam W. Snyder as the Democratic candidate for governor, to be elected in August, 1842. Mr. Snyder was a native of Pennsylvania, and a distant relative of Gov. Snyder of that State. In his early youth, he learned the trade of a fuller and woolcarder. He came to Illinois when he was about eighteen years old; settled in the French village of Cahokia: followed his trade for several years: studied law; removed to the county seat, where he commenced his profession, in which he was successful in getting practice. In 1830 he was elected to the State Senate, and was afterwards elected to Congress, from his district; and was again elected to the State Senate in 1840. Mr. Snyder was a very showy, plausible and agreeable man in conversation, and was gifted with a popular eloquence,which was considerably effective. He was a member of the Senate when the Mormon charters were passed, and had taken an active part in furthering their passage." In fact Mr. Snyder was chairman of the Judiciary committee, to which the charters were referred,and he reported them to the Senate with a recommendation that they pass.

more efficient in assisting him to procure our great chartered privileges, than were Colonel Snyder, and Colonel Moore. They are sterling men, and friends of equal rights, opposed to the oppressor's grasp, and the tyrant's rod. With such men at the head of our State, government will have nothing to fear. In the next canvass, we shall be influenced by no party consideration, and no Carthagenian coalescence or collusion with our people will be suffered to effect, or operate against General Bennett, or any other of our tried friends, already semi-officially in the field; so the partizans in this county, who expect to divide the friends of humanity and equal rights, will find themselves mistaken—we care not a fig for Whig or Democrat; they are both alike to us, but we shall go for our friends, our tried friends, and the cause of human liberty, which is the cause of God. We are aware that "divide and conquer" is the watchword with many, but with us it cannot be done—we love liberty too well—we have suffered too much to be easily duped—we have no catspaws amongst us. We voted for General Harrison because we loved him—he was a gallant officer and a tried statesman; but this is no reason why we should always be governored by his friends. He is now dead, and all of his friends are not ours. We claim the privilege of freemen, and shall act accordingly. Douglas is a master spirit, and his friends are our friends—we are willing to cast our banners in the air, and fight by his side in the cause of humanity and equal rights—the cause of liberty and the law. Snyder and Moore are his friends—they are ours. These men are free from the prejudices and superstitions of the age, and such men we love, and such men will ever receive our support, be their political predilections what they may. Snyder and Moore are known to be our friends; their friendship is vouched for by those whom we have tried. We will never be justly charged with the sin of ingratitude—they have served us, and we will serve them.*

JOSEPH SMITH.
Lieutenant-General of the Nauvoo Legion.

* For some time there had been an agitation going on in respect of the Saints and their relationship to the politics of the State; and political capital was sought to be made by manifestations of friendliness or of hostility towards them. Although, in the main, the people of Nauvoo had sustained the Whig candidates, both locally and nationally, in the preceding election, including the Whig candidate for Congress, Mr. John J. Stuart, yet there were outbreaks against them both among the Whig politicians and in the Whig press of Illinois. "The Whig newspapers," writes Governor Ford, in his "History of Illinois," "teemed with accounts of the wonders and enormities of Nauvoo, and of the awful wickedness of a party which could consent to receive the support of such miscreants. Governor Duncan, [nominated in opposition to Snyder] who was really a brave, honest man, and who had nothing to do with getting the Mormon charters passed through the legislature, took the stump on this subject in good earnest, and expected to be elected governor almost on this question alone." (History of Illinois, Ford, p. 269.)

Tuesday, 21.—I received from Edward Hunter a letter on business, to which I wrote the following reply—

The Prophet's Letter to Edward Hunter—Business Affairs at Nauvoo.

NAUVOO, Dec. 21, 1841.

Mr. Edward Hunter,

BELOVED BROTHER:—Yours of the 27th of October came to hand at a late date, but I am now able to say to you that the power of attorney is executed and sent up to the clerk's office for the seal of the state, and

The position of the Saints in their relation to the political parties in the state of Illinois is tersely set forth by the late President John Taylor in his review of affairs at Nauvoo, leading up to the martyrdom of the Prophet; which document was prepared at the request of the Historians of the Church, and filed in the archives of the Church as the testimony of an eye witness and participant in those events. The document, under the title of "The Martyrdom of Joseph Smith," was published by permission of the author in Tyler's "History of the Mormon Battalion." Of the political situation at Nauvoo—which was forming at the period to which the political announcement of the text above belongs—President Taylor says:

"There were always two parties, the Whigs and Democrats, and we could not vote for one without offending the other; and it not unfrequently happened that candidates for office would place the issue of their election upon opposition to the 'Mormons,' in order to gain political influence from religious prejudice, in which case the 'Mormons' were compelled, in self-defense, to vote against them, which resulted almost invariably against our opponents. This made them angry; and although it was of their own making, and the 'Mormons' could not be expected to do otherwise, yet they raged on account of their discomfiture, and sought to wreak their fury on the 'Mormons.' As an instance of the above, when Joseph Duncan was candidate for the office of governor of Illinois, [in the campaign to which the document in the body of the text above relates] he pledged himself to his party that, if he could be elected, he would exterminate or drive the 'Mormons' from the State. The consequence was that Governor Ford was elected." (History of the Mormon Battalion, Introduction, pp. 12 and 13.)

It cannot in truth be claimed that any favor shown by the Democratic party, as such, to the Mormon people was the cause of the announcement of the above independent attitude in politics. For while Judge Douglas, a leading Democrat, had recently rendered a decision favorable to the Prophet, liberating him from the clutches of Missouri, it should be remembered that the Judge had but pronounced upon the course of the officers of the states of Missouri and Illinois and found that course at variance with the law,and there was no alternative but to set the Prophet free. But it was the law that vindicated Joseph Smith, not the favor of Judge Douglas. And then,if a Democratic Judge had decided a case in favor of the Prophet, it should be remembered that it was the act, and I might say the unwarranted, the illegal act, of a Democrat, Governor Carlin, which had put the life and liberty of the Prophet in jeopardy by issuing an illegal requisition for his arrest and deliverance to Missouri. This to show that it was not any favor that had been shown by the Democratic party, as such, that prompted the assumption of an independent attitude in politics by the Prophet; but that for weal or woe, the attitude was taken as a measure of self-defense, and for the protection of the people in whose interest it was announced.

will be forwarded direct from them; it is now on the way most probably.

Your letter did not arrive till after Mr. Potter returned with the goods, which I received in safety; and Brother Potter has started on a mission to the inhabitants of Jamaica, one of the West India isles.

I will accept the goods as you propose, on your debt, so far as it goes, and answer the remainder on the payments which you mention, as they become due.

I have purchased ninety acres of timber land in the vicinity of Nauvoo, a little up the river, and have made proposals to McFall, but as yet, am waiting for him to receive answers from his correspondent in the east. I shall be able to purchase all the wood land you will want, in a little time.

As respects steam engines and mills, my opinion is, we cannot have too many of them. This place has suffered exceedingly from the want of such mills in our midst, and neither one nor two can do the business of this place another season. We have no good grain or board mill in this place; and most of our flour and lumber has to be brought twenty miles; which subjects us to great inconvenience.

The city is rapidly advancing, many new buildings have been erected since you left us, and many more would have arisen, if brick and lumber could have been obtained. There is scarcely any limits which can be imagined to the mills and machinery and manufacturing of all kinds which might be put into profitable operation in this city, and even if others should raise a mill before you get here, it need be no discouragement either to you or Brother Buckwalter, for it will be difficult for the mills to keep pace with the growth of the place, and you will do well to bring the engine. If you can persuade any of the brethren who are manufacturers of woollens or cottons to come on and establish their business, do so.

I have not ascertained definitely as yet how far the goods will go towards liquidating Dr. Fosters's note, or finishing your house; but this I can say, I will make the most of it, and benefit you every possible way.

Your message is delivered to Mrs. Smith, and she will be glad to have returns on her letter of attorney, as speedily as circumstances will permit, according to the understanding thereof.

I am happy to hear of your welfare, and the health of your family; and also to inform you that the health of Nauvoo has much improved since last summer, and considering the very mild state of the weather most of the time, it is excellent.

Myself and family are in health, and our enemies are at peace with us, as much as can be expected in this generation. Should anything new occur, which may be for our advantage, you will please write, and I will do the same. I remain, yours in the Gospel of Christ,

JOSEPH SMITH.

P.S.—You will endeavor to have the money on your letter of attorney from Mrs. Smith, ready to furnish a fresh supply of goods early in the spring.

J. S.

Wednesday, 22.

NAUVOO, December 22, 1841.

Revelation to John Snyder and Amos B. Fuller.

The word of the Lord came unto Joseph the Seer, verily thus saith the Lord, let my servant John Snyder take a mission to the eastern continent, unto all the conferences now sitting in that region; and let him carry a package of epistles, that shall be written by my servants the Twelve making known unto them their duties concerning the building of my houses which I have appointed unto you, saith the Lord, that they may bring their gold and their silver, and their precious stones, and the box-tree, and the fir-tree,and all fine wood to beautify the place of my sanctuary, saith the Lord; and let him return speedily with all means which shall be put into his hands, even so. Amen.

Elder Amos B. Fuller, of Zarahemla, stated to me that he had settled all his debts, made all necessary provision for his family, and desired to know the will of God concerning him.

Revelation.

"Verily thus saith the Lord unto my servants the Twelve, let them appoint unto my servant A. B. Fuller a mission to preach my Gospel unto the children of men, as it shall be manifested unto them by my Holy Spirit. Amen."

This day I commenced receiving the first supply of groceries at the new store. Thirteen wagons arrived from Warsaw, loaded with sugar, molasses, glass, salt, tea, coffee, &c., purchased in St. Louis. The original stock purchased in New Orleans having been detained at St. Louis by one Holbrook, innkeeper, under false pretenses.

Work on Proclamation to Kings of the Earth.

This evening I commenced giving instructions to the scribe concerning writing the proclamation to the kings of the earth, mentioned in the revelation given January 19, 1841.

Friday, 24.—This evening I had a consultation with President Young and Bishop Whitney about establishing an agency in England for the cheap and expeditious conveyance of the Saints to Nauvoo. and for our convenience in merchandise; and I said, "in the name of the Lord we will prosper, if we will go forward in this thing."

Immigration Agency in England.

Elder Truman Gillett, Jun., returned from a short mission to Van Buren county, Iowa, where he baptized fourteen, bringing $20 as a donation to the building of the Temple, from Samuel Moore.

Saturday, 25.—Being Christmas, Brigham Young, Heber C. Kimball, Orson Pratt, Wilford Woodruff, John Taylor, and their wives, and Willard Richards spent the evening at Hiram Kimball's; and after supper, Mr. Kimball gave each of the Twelve Apostles a fractional lot of land lying on the west side of his second addition to Nauvoo.

Xmas at Nauvoo, 1841.

Alpheus Gifford, a member of the Church since 1831, and a faithful Elder in the Church [it was he who baptized Heber C. Kimball] died at his home some five miles above Nauvoo.*

Conference Minutes—New York and Maine.

At a conference held in Batavia, Genessee county, New York, 11 branches, comprising 15 Elders, 7 Priests, 7 Teachers, 4 Deacons, and 207 members were represented.

A conference met in the Universalist Church, in Hope, Waldo

* Alpheus Gifford was born in Adams township, Berkshire county, Massachusetts, August 28, 1793. At the age of eighteen, having scarcely sufficient learning to enable him to read the Bible, he commenced preaching the Gospel, not for hire, but for the salvation of souls.

In 1817, he married Anna Nash, who bore him seven sons and three daughters. In the spring of 1831, hearing of the doctrines taught by Joseph Smith, he made diligent inquiry, and found they were scriptural, and was baptized and ordained a

county, Maine, when Fox Islands, with five Elders, 1 Priest, 2 Teachers, 1 Deacon, and 100 members, also the Main Land, with 6 Elders, 2 Priests, 3 Teachers, 1 Deacon, and 68 members were represented; Otis Shaw, president, and Calvin C. Pendleton, clerk.

Sunday, *26*.—The public meeting of the Saints was at my house this evening, and after Patriarch Hyrum Smith and Elder Brigham Young had spoken on the principles of faith, and the gifts of the Spirit, I read the 13th chapter of First Corinthians, also a part of the 14th chapter, and remarked that the gift of tongues was necessary in the Church; but that if Satan could not speak in tongues, he could not tempt a Dutchman, or any other nation, but the English, for he can tempt the Englishman, for he has tempted me, and I am an Englishman; but the gift of tongues by the power of the Holy Ghost in the Church, is for the benefit of the servants of God to preach to unbelievers, as on the day of Pentecost. When devout men from every nation

Purpose of the Gift of Tongues.

priest; he brought home five Books of Mormon which he distributed among his friends; he was then living in Tioga county, Pennsylvania. Soon after he went to Kirtland, Ohio, to see the Prophet Joseph Smith and the brethren, when he was ordained an Elder; he was accompanied by his brother Levi, Elial Strong, Eleazar Miller, Enos Curtis and Abraham Brown, who were baptized. On returning to Pennsylvania he preached and baptized many, among whom was Heber C. Kimball. The gifts of the Gospel were enjoyed by many; signs following those that believed, devils were cast out; the sick were healed; many prophesied; some spake with new tongues; while others interpreted the same. Mr. Calvin Gilmour, with whom Brother Gifford had previously been associated in preaching, heard him speak in tongues and interpret. Gilmour declared he understood the languages and that they were interpreted correctly, but that he would rather be damned than believe in Mormonism.

In June, 1832, Brother Gifford started for Missouri; traveled to Cincinnatti and wintered there with a few Saints, who had been baptized by Lyman Wight. He arrived in Jackson county, Mo., in March, 1833, where he preached much. He was driven with the Saints in the fall of that year. He removed to Clay county, and subsequently went to Kirtland, Ohio, and attended the dedication of the Temple and received the ordinances there administered. He returned to Missouri, and removed with the Saints to Far West, Caldwell county. In the winter of 1839 he was driven from Missouri. He located in the Morley settlement near Lima, Illinois, and subsequently removed five miles above Nauvoo, where he died December 25, 1841. (The above is taken from a sketch of his father's life by Samuel K. Gifford, furnished the Church Historian in November, 1861, and filed in the History of the Church under date of December, 1841.)

shall assemble to hear the things of God, let the Elders preach to them in their own mother tongue, whether it is German, French, Spanish or "Irish," or any other, and let those interpret who understand the language spoken, in their own mother tongue, and this is what the Apostle meant in First Corinthians xiv: 27.*

Monday, 27.—I was in council with Brothers Brigham Young, Heber C. Kimball, Willard Richards and John Taylor, at my office, instructing them in the principles of the kingdom, and what the Twelve should do in relation to the mission of John Snyder, and the European conferences, so as to forward the gathering of means for building the Temple and Nauvoo House; that Brigham might go with John Snyder on his mission if he chose, but the object of the mission could be accomplished without.

Instructions to the Twelve.

Tuesday, 28.—I baptized Sidney Rigdon in the font, for and in behalf of his parents; also baptized Reynolds Cahoon and others.

Thursday and Friday, December 30th and 31st—Calvin A. Warren, Esq., Mark Aldrich and Daniel S. Witter, visited me at my office, and after much explanation and conversation concerning Warren and Warsaw, in which Esquire Warren manifested the kindest and most confidential feelings and Aldrich and Witter expressed their entire approbation of past proceedings of the Presidency, they all agreed that if I did not succeed in the next attempt to establish and build up Warren, that they would fully excuse me from all censure, and would feel satisfied that I had done all that could reasonably be required of any man in a like case, be the consequence what it might to themselves; and Esquire Warren frankly acknowledged that his temporal salvation depended on the success of the enterprise, and

Warren and Warsaw Affairs.

"* If any man speak in an unknown tongue, let it be by two, at the most by three, and that by course, and let one interpret. But if there be no interpreter, let him keep silence in the Church; and let him speak to himself and to God."

made liberal proposals for the benefit of the brethren, to help forward the undertaking. The party retired manifesting the best of feeling, and expressing the most perfect satisfaction with their visit, with me and all concerned.

Thursday evening at the office, while conversing with Calvin A. Warren, Esq., about the proceedings at Warsaw, I prophesied in the name of the Lord, that the first thing toward building up Warsaw was to break it down, to break down them that are there, that it never would be built up till it was broken down, and after that keep them entirely in the dark concerning our movements; and it is best to let Sharp* publish what he pleases and go to the devil, and the more lies he prints the sooner he will get through; not buy him out or hinder him; and after they have been in the dark long enough, let a certain set of men go there who will do as I tell them, a certain kind of men, some of those capitalists from the Eastern States, say from Pennsylvania; wise men who will take the lead of business, and go ahead of those that are there before they know what we are about, and the place will prosper, and not till then.

A Prophecy Respecting Warsaw.

The following list shows some of the books, pamphlets, letters, &c., published for and against the Latter-day Saints in 1841.

Mormon Literature, (pro et con) 1841.

"A Proclamation to the Saints Scattered Abroad:" January 15, by Joseph Smith, Sidney Rigdon, Hyrum Smith.

Twenty-three numbers of the "Times and Seasons," published at Nauvoo.

Twelve numbers of the "Millennial Star," published in England by Parley P. Pratt.

First European edition of the Book of Mormon, published in England, 21st January, by Elders Brigham Young, and Willard Richards.

* This reference is to Thomas Sharp, editor of the Warsaw *Signal*, a bitter anti-Mormon, and described by the late President John Taylor, as "a violent and unprincipled man, who shrank not from any enormity."

A third edition of the "Voice of Warning" was published in Manchester, England, by Parley P. Pratt.

"A Letter to Queen Victoria of England, Touching the Signs of the Times, and the Political Destiny of the World:" in pamphlet form, by Parley P. Pratt, Manchester, England.

Five hundred copies of "An Address to the Hebrews," in the Dutch language, by Orson Hyde. Published in Rotterdam, Holland, in July; being the first pamphlet pertaining to the Church of Jesus Christ of Latter-day Saints, written in a foreign language.

A pamphlet containing 116 pages, 8vo., by Orson Hyde, containing "A Synopsis of the Faith of the Church of Jesus Christ of Latter-day Saints:" addressed to the German nation in their own language.

A Small Collection of Hymns, by Christopher Merkley.

"Evidences in Proof of the Book of Mormon:" a work of 256 pages, 32 mo. Published at Batavia, New York, by Charles Thompson.

A lengthy "Address to the Citizens of Salem, Massachusetts, and Vicinity," by Erastus Snow, and Benjamin Winchester, October.

"Gospel Reflector," a monthly periodical, by Benjamin Winchester. published in Philadelphia.

"Proclamation and Warning to the Inhabitants of America," by Charles Thompson.

The editor of the "Times and Seasons" noticed the following "From the 'Upper Mississippian,' a series of letters, entitled 'Nauvoo Mormon Religion,' &c., the writer no doubt intended to give a fair statement, and in the main did so; but respecting our faith (on some points), the Book of Mormon, &c., he is wide of the mark."

An article published in the "North Staffordshire Mercury," showing the difference between the Baptists and Latter-day Saints. Hanley, February, 16, signed "A Baptist." Replied to by Parley P. Pratt, who showed the difference between the Baptists and Former-day Saints.

A severe article against the Latter-day Saints, which filled several columns of fine print, was published in "Edinburgh Intelligencer" of April 7th, taken from the "Athenæum" on the subject of the "Book of Mormon and the Latter-day Saints." Replied to by Parley P. Pratt. May.

Mr. J. B. Rollo, of Edinburgh, Scotland, published a pamphlet entitled "Mormonism Exposed." Replied to by Parley P. Pratt, July 10.

The "Preston Chronicle" of April 24, published a long article against the Latter-day Saints, which was replied to by Parley P. Pratt, in the "Millennial Star," July 10.

A bitter article was published in the "Cheltenham Free Press" of

August 23rd, headed "Latter-day Saints' Swindle," replied to by Parley P. Pratt in the "Star" of October.

"A Few Plain Facts, Showing the Folly, Wickedness and Imposition of the Rev. Timothy R. Matthews." By George J. Adams, Bedford, England.

The St. Louis, Missouri, "Atlas" published a favorable article entitled, "The Latter-day Saints."

The "Juliet Courier" published a favorable account of the late trial of Joseph Smith. Monmouth, June.

The "Philadelphia Saturday Courier" and the "Public Ledger" on July 10, published several articles anathematizing the Latter-day Saints.

A slanderous pamphlet entitled "Mormonism Unmasked," by A. Gardner, of Rochdale, England.

"The Mormons—Arrest of Joe Smith" was the heading of an article published in the "New York Herald of Commerce," and copied in many of the Eastern papers.

"The Christian Messenger and Reformer" published an account of the Latter-day Saints, collected from the book of Edward D. Howe, of Painsville, Ohio.

Thomas Sharp, editor of the "Warsaw Signal," devoted his entire time to slandering, to lying against and misrepresenting the Latter-day Saints.

CHAPTER XXIX.

THE OPENING OF THE YEAR 1842—WHEREABOUTS OF THE TWELVE APOSTLES—CORRESPONDENCE OF ELDER HYDE FROM TRIESTE—REPORT OF HIGH COUNCIL ON AFFAIRS IN NAUVOO—EVENTS AND CONDITIONS IN BRITISH MISSION.

Saturday, January 1, 1842.—I again have the pleasure to report the location of the Twelve Apostles. Brigham Young, Heber C. Kimball, Orson Pratt, John Taylor, Wilford Woodruff and Willard Richards are in Nauvoo. George A. Smith, in Zarahemla, Ohio. Orson Hyde in quarantine at Trieste, Italy. Parley P. Pratt in Liverpool. Lyman Wight in Ohio. William Smith in New Jersey. John E. Page somewhere in the Eastern States.

Sundry Labors of the Prophet.

I commenced placing goods on the shelves of my new store, assisted by Bishop Newel K. Whitney and others; and in the evening attended city council.

Five hundred and twelve Saints were reported at the Glasgow Conference of this date.

Several of the Twelve spent the day at Sylvester B. Stoddard's and in the city council, which lasted from 6 p.m. until midnight, on the trial of Gustavus Hills.

Sunday, 2.—Meeting at my house, day and evening; Brother Hyrum and Elder Woodruff preached.

Tuesday, 4.—I wrote Dr. John M. Bernhisel, of New York, on business.

Joseph Duncan, candidate for Governor of Illinois, made an inflammatory speech against the Saints at Edwardsville, a mass of falsehoods.

Wednesday, 5.—William Wightman signed over and delivered the town plat of Ramus to me, as sole Trustee in Trust for the Church of Jesus Christ of Latter-day Saints.

My new store was opened for business this day for the first time, it was filled with customers, and I was almost continually behind the counter, as clerk, waiting on my friends.

I dictated a letter to Edward Hunter, West Nantmeal, Pennsylvania, as follows:

The Prophet's Letter to Edward Hunter—Reports Opening of the New Store.

NAUVOO, January 5, 1842.

Mr. Edward Hunter.

BELOVED BROTHER:—I am happy that it is my privilege to say to you that the large new building which I had commenced when you were here is now completed, and the doors are opened this day for the sale of goods for the first time. The foundation of the building is somewhat spacious (as you will doubtless recollect) for a country store.

The principal part of the building below, which is ten feet high, is devoted exclusively to shelves and drawers, except one door opening back into the space, on the left of which are the cellar and chamber stairs, and on the right the counting room; from the space at the top of the chamber stairs opens a door into the large front room of the same size with the one below, the walls lined with counters, covered with reserved goods.

In front of the stairs opens the door to my private office, or where I keep the sacred writings, with a window to the south, overlooking the river below, and the opposite shore for a great distance, which, together with the passage of boats in the season thereof, constitutes a peculiarly interesting situation, in prospect, and no less interesting from its retirement from the bustle and confusion of the neighborhood and city, and altogether is a place the Lord is pleased to bless.

The painting of the store has been executed by Edward Martin, one of our English brethren; and the counters, drawers, and pillars present a very respectable representation of oak, mahogany and marble for a backwoods establishment.

The Lord has blessed our exertions in a wonderful manner, and although some individuals have succeeded in detaining goods to a considable amount for the time being, yet we have been enabled to secure goods in the building sufficient to fill all the shelves as soon as they were completed, and have some in reserve, both in loft and cellar.

Our assortment is tolerably good—very good, considering the different purchases made by different individuals at different times, and under circumstances which controlled their choice to some extent; but I rejoice that we have been enabled to do as well as we have, for the hearts of many of the poor brethren and sisters will be made glad with those comforts which are now within their reach.

The store has been filled to overflowing, and I have stood behind the counter all day, dealing out goods as steady as any clerk you ever saw, to oblige those who were compelled to go without their usual Christmas and New Year's dinners, for the want of a little sugar, molasses, raisins, &c., &c; and to please myself also, for I love to wait upon the Saints, and be a servant to all, hoping that I may be exalted in the due time of the Lord.

With sentiments of high consideration, I remain your brother in Christ.

JOSEPH SMITH.

Rejoicing of the Prophet.

Thursday, *6*.—The new year has been ushered in and continued thus far under the most favorable auspices, and the Saints seem to be influenced by a kind and indulgent Providence in their dispositions and [blessed with] means to rear the Temple of the Most High God, anxiously looking forth to the completion thereof as an event of the greatest importance to the Church and the world, making the Saints in Zion to rejoice, and the hypocrite and sinner to tremble. Truly this is a day long to be remembered by the Saints of the last days,—a day in which the God of heaven has begun to restore the ancient order of His kingdom unto His servants and His people,—a day in which all things are concurring to bring about the completion of the fullness of the Gospel, a fullness of the dispensation of dispensations, even the fullness of times; a day in which God has begun to make manifest and set in order in His Church those things which have been, and those things which the ancient prophets and wise men desired to see but died without beholding them; a day in which those things begin to be made manifest, which have been hid from before the foundation of the world, and which Jehovah has promised should be made known in His own due time unto His servants, to prepare the earth for the return of His glory, even a celestial glory, and a kingdom of Priests and kings to God and the Lamb, forever, on Mount Zion, and with him the hundred and forty and four thousand whom John the Revelator saw, all of which is to come to pass in the restitution of all things.

Conference held at Zarahemla, at which that stake was discontinued; a branch was organized in place thereof, and John Smith appointed president.

Wednesday, 12.—The ship *Tremont* sailed from Liverpool for New Orleans with the Saints, about this time.

The following notice was published in the *Times and Seasons:*

Tithings and Consecrations for the Temple of the Lord.

From this time the Recorder's Office will be opened on the Saturday of each week for the reception of the tithings and consecrations of the brethren, and closed on every other day of the week. This regulation is necessary, to give the Trustee and Recorder time to arrange the Book of Mormon, translation of the Bible, Hymn Book, and Doctrine and Covenants for the press, all of which the brethren are anxious to see in their most perfect form, consequently the Saints should be particular to bring their offerings on the day specified, until further notice, but not relax their exertions to carry on the work.

The Elders will please give the above notice in all public meetings, until the plan is understood.

WILLARD RICHARDS,
Recorder for the Temple.

NAUVOO, Jannary 12, 1842.

I rode south about seven miles to my wood land, accompanied by Brother John Sanders and Peter Maughan,*

* Peter Maughan was born May 7, 1811, at Breckenridge, in the parish of Parley, county of Cumberland, England. He married Miss Ruth Harrison in 1829. He was baptized into the Church by Elder Isaac Russell in 1838, and emigrated to Nauvoo with his family of six children, now motherless, his wife having died in 1841. He came on ths ship *Rochester*, in company with Brigham Young and several other members of the quorum of the Twelve on their return home. He was a man of keen intelligence and commanding personal influence.

and found a vein of coal about eighteen inches thick, apparently of good quality for the western country.

Elder Benjamin Winchester was suspended by the quorum of the Twelve until he made satisfaction for disobedience to the First Presidency.

Thursday, *13*.—My clerk, Willard Richards, commenced boarding with me.

The British forces having evacuated Cabul,* they were attacked in the Pass, a few miles from the city, and after three days' fighting; they were nearly all slaughtered.

Book of Mormon Corrections.

Saturday, *15*.—I commenced reading the Book of Mormon, at page 54, American stereotype edition (the previous pages having been corrected), for the purpose of correcting the stereotype plates of some errors which escaped notice in the first edition.

Attended city council, and was appointed on committee of ways and means and municipal laws.

Sunday, *16*.—I preached at my house, morning and evening, illustrating the nature of sin, and showing that it is not right to sin that grace may abound.

Monday, *17*.—Transacted a variety of business in the city. Myself and Brother Willard Richards dined with Sister Agnes M. Smith.†

Meeting with the Twelve.

In the evening I attended a council of the Twelve at my office; present, Elders Young, Kimball, Orson Pratt, Taylor, Woodruff, George A. Smith and Richards—appointed Elder Amos B. Fuller a mission to Chicago, according to the revelation of the 22nd of December, and Elder Henry Jacobs to accompany him. The council were unanimously opposed to Robin-

* Cabul is the capital of Afghanistan, situated on the river Kabul. It is noted as a commercial and strategic center, and the event named in the text above is an incident in what is usually called the first Afghan War. While the British were compelled to evacuate the place, as stated in the text, they re-took it in September following.

† Widow of the late Don Carlos Smith, the Prophet's brother.

son's publishing the Book of Mormon and other books.

Tuesday, 18.—This day revoked my power of attorney given to Dr. Isaac Galland to transact business for the Church.

After transacting a variety of business, sleeping an hour from bodily infirmities, I read for correction in the Book of Mormon, and debated in the evening with the mayor [John C. Bennett] concerning the Lamanites and Negroes.

For an extract of a letter from Elder Orson Hyde, "Trieste, January 1 and 18, 1842," see *Millennial Star*, vol. II, pages 166-169.*

HIGHLY INTERESTING FROM JERUSALEM.

We have lately received two lengthy and highly interesting communications from Elder Orson Hyde, dated at Trieste, January 1st, and 18th, containing a sketch of his voyages and travels in the East, his visit to Jerusalem, a description of ancient Zion, the pool of Siloam, and many other places famous in holy writ, with several illustrations of the manners and customs of the East,as applicable to Scripture texts, and several conversations held between himself and some of the Jews, missionaries, etc., in Jerusalem, together with a masterly description of a terrible tempest and thunder storm at sea, with a variety of miscellaneous reflections and remarks, all written in an easy, elegant, and masterly style, partaking of the eloquent and sublime, and breathing a tone of that deep feeling, tenderness, and affection so characteristic of his mission and the spirit of his holy and sacred office.

Elder Hyde has by the grace of God been the first proclaimer of the fullness of the Gospel both on the continent of Europe and in far off Asia, among the nations of the East. In Germany, Turkey (Constantinople), Egypt, and Jerusalem. He has reared as it were the ensign of the latter-day glory, and sounded the trump of truth, calling upon the people of those regions to awake from their thousand years' slumber, and to make ready for their returning Lord.

* The article from the *Star* here referred to is inserted *in extenso*, and that for the reason that so many letters of Elder Hyde's concerning his journey to Jerusalem have already appeared in this volume, that this one seems necessary to the completion of the history of that mission, which must be regarded as an important movement on the part of the Church at this period.

In his travels he has suffered much, and has been exposed to toils and dangers, to hunger, pestilence and war. He has been in perils by land and sea, in perils among robbers,in perils among heathens, Turks, Arabs, and Egyptians; but out of all these things the Lord hath delivered him, and hath restored him in safety to the shores of Europe, where he is tarrying for a little season, for the purpose of publishing the Truth in the German language, having already published it in French and English in the various countries of the East,and we humbly trust that his labors will be a lasting blessing to Jew and Gentile.

We publish the following extract of his communication, and we shall soon issue the whole from the press in pamphlet form. It will, no doubt, meet with a ready sale; and we purpose devoting the profits to his benefit, to assist him in his mission.

Excerpts from Elder Hyde's Letters.

"Summoning up, therefore, what little address I had, I procured a *valet d'place*, or lackey, and proceeded to the house of Mr. Simons, a very respectable Jew, who with some of his family had lately been converted and joined the English Church. I entered their dwelling. They had just sat down to enjoy a dish of coffee, but immediately arose from the table to meet me. I spoke to them in German and asked them if they spoke English. They immediately replied 'Yes,' which was a very agreeable sound to my ear. They asked me in German if I spoke English; I replied, 'Ya, mein Herr.' I then introduced myself to them, and with a little apology it passed off as well as though I had been introduced by the pasha. With that glow of warmth and familiarity which is a peculiar trait in the German character,they would have me sit down and take a dish with them; and as I began to relate some things relative to my mission, the smiles of joy which sat upon their countenances bespoke hearts not altogether indifferent. There were two ministers of the Church of England there. One was confined to his bed by sickness, and the other, a German, and a Jew by birth, soon came in. After an introduction, I took the liberty to lay open to him some of our principles, and gave him a copy of the communication to the Jews in Constantinople to read. After he had it, he said that my motives were undoubtedly very good. but questioned the propriety of my undertaking from the fact that I claimed God had sent me. If, indeed, I had gone to Jerusalem under the direction of some missionary board or society, and left God out of the question altogether, I should have been received as a celestial messenger. How truly did our Savior speak, when He said, 'I am come in my Father's name, and ye receive me not; but if another were to come in his own name, him ye would receive.' I replied, however, that so far as I could know my own heart, my motives were most certainly good; yet, said I, no better than the cause which has brought me here. But he, like all others who worship a God 'without body or parts,' said that miracles, visions, and prophecy had ceased.

"The course which the popular clergy pursue at this time in relation to the Divine economy looks to me as though they would say, 'O Lord, we will worship Thee with all our hearts, serve Thee with all our souls, and be very pious and holy; we will even gather Israel, convert the heathen, and bring in the millennium, if Thou wilt only let us alone that we may do it in our own way, and according to our own will; but if Thou speakest from heaven to interfere with our plan, or cause any to see visions or dreams, or prophesy, whereby we are disturbed or interrupted in our worship, we will exert all our strength and skill to deny what Thou sayest, and charge it home upon the devil or some wild, fanatic spirit, as being its author.'

"That which was looked upon by the ancient saints as among the greatest favors and blessings, viz., revelation from God and communion with Him by dreams and by visions, is now looked upon by the religious world as the height of presumption and folly. The ancient saints considered their condition most deplorable when Jehovah would not speak to them; but the most orthodox religionists of this age deem it quite heterodox to even admit the probability that He ever will speak again. O my soul! language fails to paint the absurdity and abomination of such heaven-opposing and truth-excluding dogmas; and were it possible for those bright seraphs that surround the throne above, and bask in the sunbeams of immortality, to weep over the inconsistency and irrationality of mortals, the earth must be bedewed with celestial tears. My humble advice to all such is, that they repent and cast far from them these wicked traditions, and be baptized into the new and everlasting covenant,lest the Lord speak to them in His wrath,and vex them in His sore displeasure.

"After some considerable conversation upon the priesthood and the renewal of the covenant, I called upon him [i. e. the aforesaid German-Jew church of England minister] to be baptized for the remission of his sins, that he might receive the gift of the Holy Ghost. 'What' said he, 'I be baptized?' 'Yes,' said I, 'you be baptized.' 'Why,' saith he, 'I have been baptized already.' I replied something after the following: 'You have probably been sprinkled, but that has no more to do with baptism than any other ordinance of man's device; and even if you had been immersed, you would not have bettered your condition, for your priesthood is without power. If, indeed, the Catholic church has power to give you an ordination, and by that ordination confer the priesthood upon you, they certainly had power to nullify that act, and take the priesthood from you; and this power they exercised when you dissented from their communion, by excluding you from their church. But, if the Catholic church possessed not the priesthood, of course your claims to it are as groundless as the airy phantoms of heathen mythology. So, view the question on which side you may, there is no possible chance of admitting the validity of your claims to it. Be it known, therefore, that ordinances performed under the administration of such a priesthood, though they may even be correct in form, will be found destitute of the seal of that authority by which heaven will recognize His [own] in the day when every man's work shall be tried. Though a priesthood may be clothed with the wealth and honors of a great and powerful nation and command the respect and veneration of multitudes whose eyes are blinded by the thick veil of popular opinion, and whose powers of reflection and deep thought are confused and lost in the general cry of 'Great is Diana of the Ephesians,' yet all this does not impart to it the Divine sanction, or animate it with the spirit of life and power from the bosom of the living God; and there is a period in future time when, in the smoking ruins of Babel's pride and glory, it must fall and retire to the shades of forgetfulness, to the grief and mortification of its unfortunate votaries.'

"In consequence of his great volubility, I was under the disagreeable necessity of tuning my voice to a pretty high key, and of spacing short between words, determining that neither his greatness or learning should shield him from the shafts of a faithful testimony. But there is more hope of those Jews receiving the fullness of the gospel, whose minds have never been poisoned by the bane of modern sectarianism, which closes the mouth of Deity and shuts up in heaven all the angels, visions, and prophesyings. Mrs. Whiting told me that there had been four Jewish people in Jerusalem converted and baptized by the English minister, and four only; and that a part of the ground for an English church had been purchased there. It was by political power and influence that the Jewish nation was broken down, and her subjects dispersed abroad; and I will here hazard the opinion, that by political power and influence they will be gathered and built up; and further, that England is destined in the wisdom and economy of heaven to stretch forth the arm of political power, and advance in the front ranks of this glorious enterprise. The Lord once raised up a Cyrus to restore the Jews, but that was not evidence that He owned the religion of the Persians. This opinion I submit, however, to your superior wisdom to correct if you shall find it wrong.

"There is an increasing anxiety in Europe for the restoration of that people [the Jews]; and this anxiety is not confined to the pale of any religious community, but it has found its way to the courts of kings. Special ambassadors have been sent, and consuls and consular agents have been appointed. The rigorous policy which has hitherto characterized the course of other nations towards them now begins to be softened by the oil of friendship, and modified by the balm of humanity. The sufferings and privations under which they have groaned for so many centuries have at length touched the main-springs of Gentile power and sympathy; and may the God of their fathers, Abraham, Isaac, and Jacob, fan the flame by celestial breezes, until Israel's banner, sanctified by a Savior's blood, shall float on the walls of old Jerusalem, and the mountains and valleys of Judea reverberate with their songs of praise and thanksgiving to the Lamb that was slain.

"The imperial consul of Austria, at Galatz, near the mouth of the Danube, to whom I had a letter of introduction from his cousin in Vienna, told me that in consequence of so many of their Jewish subjects being inclined, of late, to remove to Syria and Palestine, his government had established a general consul at Beyroot for their protection. There are many Jews who care nothing about Jerusalem, and have no regard for God. Their money is the god they worship, yet there are many of the most pious and devout among them who look towards Jerusalem as the tender and affectionate mother looks upon the home where she left her lovely little babe."

Wednesday, 19.—I wrote Dr. Galland as follows:

The Prophet's Letter to Isaac Galland—On Settlement of Accounts.

DEAR SIR:—By your reply of the 18th instant to my note of the 17th, I am led to conclude that you received my communication in a manner altogether unintended by me, and that there may be no misunderstanding between us, and that you may be satisfied that I did not intend, and that I do not now intend anything,only upon the principles of the strictest integrity and uprightness before God, and to do as I would be done unto, I will state I have become embarrassed in my operations to a certain extent, and partly from a presentation of notes, which you, as my agent, had given for lands purchased in the eastern states, they having been sent to me. I have been obliged to cash them, and having no returns from you to meet those demands, or even the trifling expenses of your outfit, it has placed me in rather an unpleasant situation,and having a considerable amount of your scrip on hand, enough, as I suppose, to counterbalance the debts due you, and leave a balance in my favor, to some extent,even if it were small; and as I was pressed for funds, from the causes above mentioned, as well as others, I had hoped it would be convenient for you to lend me some assistance at the present time, and this was the reason why I sent a messenger to you as I did.

And now, sir, that we may have no misunderstanding in this matter, I think we had better have a settlement, and if I am owing you, I will pay you as soon as I can, and if you owe me, I shall only expect the same in return, for it is an old and trite maxim, that short reckonings make long friends. With this view of the matter, I would request you to call as soon as you possibly can make it convenient, and compare accounts, so that all things may be understood most perfectly between us in future time, and that all occasion for unpleasant feelings, if any such there be, may be entirely obliterated.

I remain, sir, most respectfully yours, &c.,

JOSEPH SMITH.

Read in the Book of Mormon, and in the evening visited Bishop Miller's wife, who was very sick, and the Bishop absent, collecting the funds for building the Temple and Nauvoo House.

Isaac Galland Affair.

Thursday, 20.—I attended a special conference of the Church at 10 o'clock a. m., concerning Dr. Galland. The conference voted to sanction the revocation of Dr. Galland's agency, dated the 18th of January, as published in the *Times and Seasons*, and also instructed the trustee-in-trust to proceed with Dr. Galland's affairs in relation to the Church, as he shall judge most expedient.

Six o'clock evening, attended a special council in the upper room of the new store.

George Washington Gee died today.*

* George W. Gee was the first son of Solomon and Sarah W. Gee, born in Rome, Ashtabula county, Ohio, August 13, 1815. Was baptized at Kirtland, Geauga countb, Ohio, February 17, 1833. Married Mary Jane Smith in Kirtland, February 5, 1838, by whom he had two sons named Elias S. and George W. Went to Caldwell county, Missouri, 1838. Was driven out by a mob in the spring of 1839. Went to Nauvoo, and was ordained an Elder in the Church of Jesus Christ of Latter-day Saints, at the first conference held at Nauvoo, in October, 1839. Removed to Ambrosa, Lee county, Iowa, where he was appointed postmaster and deputy county surveyor; he surveyed the city plats of Nashville and Zarahemla, under the direction of President Joseph Smith. Was sent by the fall conference in 1841, to Pittsburg, Pennsylvania, where he died, January 20, 1842, while in discharge of his duties, having won the affections of all the Saints with whom he had become acquainted, by his integrity and perseverance. His opportunity for schooling had been limited, but by his own exertion he attained to an excellent education, and collected quite a respectable library.

Friday, 21.—I read the Book of Mormon, transacted a variety of business in the store and city, and spent the evening in the office with Elders Taylor and Richards, interpreting dreams, &c.

The presidents of the different quorums met with the High Council at Brother Hyrum's office, to receive instructions, according to appointment of the council on the 18th.

Seventies' Quorum Affairs

President Joseph Young stated the reasons why the quorum of Seventies had granted licenses; that he applied to President Joseph Smith for permission, on the solicitations of the quorums; that their reasons for so doing were because licenses could not be obtained from the Church clerk. President Joseph Butterfield testified to the same, and the council was satisfied with the testimony. The council was then addressed by President Hyrum Smith on the Word of Wisdom.

Saturday, 22.—I was very busy in appraising tithing property, and in the evening revised the rules of the city council, attended council, and spoke on their adoption, and was elected mayor, *pro tem.* of the city of Nauvoo.

Sunday, 23.—Spent the day mostly at the office, and on the presentation of charges by Elder William Draper, Jun., silenced Elder Daniel Wood, of Pleasant Vale, for preaching that the Church ought to unsheath the sword, and Elder A. Litz for preaching that the authorities of the Church were done away, &c., and cited him to appear before the High Council of Nauvoo for trial.

Monday, 24.—Reckoned with William and Wilson Law in the counting room, and examined the lots on which they are about to build a steam, grain, and sawmill.

Tuesday, 25.—Signed deeds for lots, to Law; transacted a variety of business in the city and office. In the evening debated with John C. Bennett and others to show that the Indians have greater cause to complain of the treatment of the whites, than the negroes, or sons of Cain.

NAUVOO LEGION HEADQUARTERS,
NAUVOO LEGION, CITY OF NAUVOO, ILLINOIS,
January 23rd, 1842.

General Orders. All the public arms will be required to be in the best possible condition, at the general inspection and parade, on the 7th of May proximo, and no deficiency whatever will be countenanced, overlooked, or suffered to pass without fine, on that occasion. All persons, therefore, holding said arms, will take notice, and govern themselves accordingly; and in order that the general inspection may pass off in a truly military style, alike honorable to the Legion, and creditable to the citizen soldiers, the brigadiers are required to attend the battalion parades within their respective commands, and inspect said arms in *propria personæ*, prior to the general parade. Persons disregarding these general orders, whether officers or privates, will find themselves in the *vocative*. The invincibles (Captain Hunter's company of light infantry), will be detailed for fatigue duty, on escorts and special service, and will take post by assignment, and receive their orders direct from the major general, through his herald and armor bearer. His Excellency the Governor of Illinois, the circuit judge of the judicial circuit, and the members of the bar, the officers of Hancock county, Colonel Williams and Colonel Deming, with their respective field and staff officers of the Illinois militia, and General Swazey and Colonel Fuller, with their respective field and staff officers, and Captain Davis and Avery's companies of cavalry of Iowa militia, are respectfully invited to attend and participate in the general parade on the 7th May.

JOSEPH SMITH, Lieutenant General.

Wednesday, 26.—Rode out to borrow money, to refund for money borrowed of John Benbow, as outfit for Dr. Galland in his agency. Transacted a variety of business, explained scripture to Elder Orson Spencer in my office, read in the Book of Mormon in the evening. Wrote a long letter to Edward Hunter, West Nantmeal, on temporal business.

The Church is in a prosperous condition, and the Saints are exerting themselves to build the Temple. The health of the city is good.

Upwards of twenty-three vessels wrecked on different parts of the British coast.

Thursday, 27.—Attended to baptism in general; in the afternoon, in council with the recorder, and gave some particular instructions concerning the order of the kingdom, and the management of business; placed the carpet given by Carlos Granger on the floor of my office; and spent the evening in general council in the upper room.

In the course of the day, Brigam Young, and James Ivins returned, and gave a favorable report from Dr. Galland, with his letter of attorney, letters and papers which he had received of me and the Church.

Friday, 28.—While I was at my office, Emma and Sister Whitney came in and spent an hour.

I received the following revelation to the Twelve concerning the *Times and Seasons*, given January 28, 1842—

Revelation.

Verily thus saith the Lord unto you, my servant Joseph, go and say unto the Twelve, that it is my will to have them take in hand the editorial department of the *Times and Seasons*, according to that manifestation which shall be given unto them by the power of my Holy Spirit in the midst of their counsel, saith the Lord. Amen.

I also decided that Elder John Snyder should go out on a mission, and if necessary some one go with him and raise up a church, and get means to go to England, and carry the epistle required in the revelation of December 22nd; and instructed the Twelve, Brigham Young, Heber C. Kimball, Wilford Woodruff and Willard Richards being present, to call Elder Snyder into their council and instruct him in these things, and if he will not do these things he shall be cut off from the Church, and be damned.

Elias Higbee, of the temple committee, came into my office, and I said unto him: The Lord is not well pleased with you; and you must straighten up your loins and do better, and your family also; for you have not been as diligent as you ought to have been, and as spring is approaching, you must arise and shake yourself, and be active, and make your children industrious, and help build the Temple.

Elder Snyder had appeared very backward about fulfilling the revelation concerning him, and felt that he could not do it unless the Twelve would furnish him means, when he was more able to furnish his own means, as all the Elders were obliged to do when they went on missions, or go without.

The High Council heard and accepted the report of their committee of the 18th instant, as follows—

Report of High Council Committee.

The High Council of the Church of Jesus Christ to the Saints of Nauvoo, greeting—

DEAR BRETHREN:—As watchmen upon the walls of Zion, we feel it to be our duty to stir up your minds, by way of remembrance, of things which we conceive to be of the utmost importance to the Saints.

While we rejoice at the health and prosperity of the Saints, and the good feeling which seems to prevail among them generally, and their willingness to aid in the building of the "House of the Lord," we are grieved at the conduct of some, who seem to have forgotten the purpose for which they have gathered.

Instead of promoting union, they have appeared to be engaged in sowing strifes and animosities among their brethren, spreading evil reports, brother going to law with brother for trivial causes, which we consider a great evil, and altogether unjustifiable, except in extreme cases, and then not before the world.

We feel to advise taking the word of God for our guide, and exhort you not to forget that you have come up as saviors upon Mount Zion, consequently to seek each other's good—to become one, inasmuch as the Lord has said, "Except ye become one, ye are not mine."

Let us always remember the admonition of the Apostle—"Dare any of you, having a matter against another, go to law before the unjust, and not before the Saints? Do ye not know the Saints shall judge the world? and if the world shall be judged by you, are ye unworthy to judge the smallest matters? Know ye not that we shall judge angels? how much more things that pertain to this life? If, then, ye have judgments of things pertaining to this life, set them to judge who are least esteemed in the Church. I speak to your shame. Is it so, that there is not a wise man among you? no, not one that shall be able to judge between his brethren. But brother goeth to law with brother, and that before the unbelievers. Now therefore there is utterly a fault among you, because ye go to law one with another. Why do ye not rather take wrong?

why do ye not rather suffer yourselves to be defrauded? Nay, ye do wrong, and defraud, and that your brethren. Know ye not that the unrighteous shall not inherit the kingdom of God? Be not deceived; neither fornicators, nor idolaters, nor adulterers, nor effeminate, nor abusers of themselves with mankind, nor thieves, nor covetous, nor drunkards, nor revilers, nor extortioners, shall inherit the kingdom of God" (I Cor. 6:1-10). Who, observing these things, would go to law distressing his brother, thereby giving rise to hardness, evil speaking, strifes and animosities among those who have covenanted to keep the commandments of God—who have taken upon them the name of Saints, and if Saints are to judge angels, and also to judge the world—why then are they not competent to judge in temporal matters, especially in trivial cases, taking the law of the Lord for their guide, brotherly kindness, charity, &c., as well as the law of the land? Brethren, these are evils which ought not to exist among us. We hope the time will speedily arrive when these things will be done away, and everyone stand in the office of his calling, as a faithful servant of God. building each other up, bearing each other's infirmities, and so fulfill the law of Christ.

William Marks, President; Samuel Bent, Lewis D. Wilson, David Fullmer, Thomas Grover, Newel Knight, Leonard Soby, James Allred, Elias Higbee, George W. Harris, Aaron Johnson, William Huntington, Sen., Daniel Carrier, Austin Cowles, Charles C. Rich, Counselors.

Attest: Hosea Stout, Clerk.

Sir Robert Sale [commander of the British forces in Afghanistan] received a letter from Sha-Shoojah, requiring him to evacuate Jellalabad, with which he refused to comply.

Saturday,29.—I was much engaged with the tithings; in the afternoon in my office, counseling various individuals: and in the evening in council with Brothers Young, Kimball, Richards and others, showing forth the Kingdom and the order thereof concerning many things, and the will of God concerning His servants.

Letter of G. Walker to Elder Brigham Young et al.—Affairs in England since Departure of the Apostles.

MANCHESTER, ENGLAND, Jan. 29, 1842.

To President Young, Elders Kimball and Richards.

BELOVED BRETHREN—Soon after your departure, a clergyman of the church of England called upon my employer, to request that he might have an interview with me, as he had a wish to propound certain questions to me; upon his request being complied with, we retired to a private room, when he produced a long list of questions, written down, opposite to which he wrote my answers. The rise of the Church, Priesthood, doctrines offices, sacraments, &c., were the principal queries he advanced. When he demurred to any of our principles I was proceeding to explain, he cut my discourse short by saying he would not hold any controversy, his object being only to obtain information. After the disposal of his queries, he wished to be informed where he could obtain the whole of the publications of the Latter-day Saints, as he wished to be in possession of them; I informed him at 47 Oxford street, Manchester, and he promised to send for them.

Soon after the visit of this reverend gentleman, I had reason to suspect that undermining operations were in progress against me, I therefore tendered my resignation to the directors, but they would not accept it; and very soon after a public accountant was employed by them to investigate their accounts for several years back, and I was happy to be able to answer satisfactorily every question that was asked of me respecting them.

After this another minister sent a lengthy article extracted from an American paper, purporting to be the production of a Mr. Anthon, with a request that I would "read, mark, learn, and inwardly digest" the same. I replied to the statements of Mr. Anthon, and after disposing of them paragraph for paragraph, I told him that I was obliged by his favoring me with it, inasmuch as it satisfied my mind, and was confirmatory of the prediction of Isaiah being fulfilled, seeing that Mr. Anthon admitted that "the words of the book were delivered to the learned," &c. I then proceeded to contrast the church of England with churches established by the Apostles; but he has not acknowledged the receipt of my letter as yet. The clergy are building ten new churches in this town and neighborhood, and are employing additional curates to go round to the houses of their parishoners, to coerce or intimidate them into an attendance upon their services in fulfillment of the words of Paul, In the last days perilous times will come, &c., that they would have a form of godliness, but deny the power, and would creep into houses to lead captive silly women," &c. (See II Timothy, 1st chapter, 1st to 8th verses.) These curates make repeated visits, generally when the heads of families are from home, and take special care to enquire where the family are employed, and what place of worship they attend, &c., and leave tracts for the family to read.

One of the Rev. Hugh Stowell's curates has paid several visits to my house, but always in my absence, although he was requested to call when I was at home, and informed of the time when he might meet with me.

The following discourse took place in our own neighborhood: Curate: What religion may you be, my good woman? I am a churchwoman, sir. What church do you usually attend? I never attend any, sir.

After reprimanding the woman for pretending to be one of his flock, while she absented herself from the fold, he went to the house of a poor woman who had lately joined the Saints. I am a minister of the Church of Jesus Christ in England, and have called to inquire what school you send your children to, and what religion you profess? The woman replied she was a "Latter-day Saint." "Oh! delusion, delusion!" he rejoined, and began to rail against the Saints, whereupon she handed him the Bible, and requested him to read the place where she casually opened to, namely the third chapter of Micah, and to preach a discourse from that part of the Bible; but he retreated from before her and has not troubled her since.

The Lord Bishop of Chester and the Protestant clergymen, have hired a person of the name of Brindley to go about lecturing against the Saints, and have commenced a monthly periodical in which the foul slanders heaped upon the Saints in America and elsewhere are retailed out to satisfy the malice of the enemies of truth. The *Manchester Courier* has had several articles against our society and principles, and the old Spaulding romance has been resuscitated for the occasion. The Rev. Charles Burton, Doctor of Laws, minister of "All Saints," has been several times to see me lately, and upon one occasion invited me to his house, where I went and discussed our principles for several hours, until he was glad to withdraw from the contest; I found him ignorant in a great measure of what the Bible contains respecting the latter-days. He admitted that the Saints would reign on earth.

The great work of the Lord is still progressing in spite of all the opposition of lying priests and their auxiliaries of the newspaper press. I baptized Elizabeth Smith, who resided with us when you were in England, and she purposes coming out to America along with us.

There is very great distress among the operatives and the poor generally, and great excitement respecting the agitation of the repeal of the corn laws. Great fires have frequently occurred at the commencement of this year; a large carrier's warehouse was consumed by fire, about from £200,000 to £300,000 ($1,000,000 to $1,500,000) worth of cotton and grain, &c., destroyed. It was the Union Company's carrying ware house, Piccadilly. There is great depression in almost every branch of manufactures, and great perplexity; and I am daily more and more convinced that the time is not far distant when Babylon the great will be fallen and become a desolation, and the kings and the merchants of the earth will weep and mourn over her, and she will be cast down, even as a great mill-stone cast into the sea, and will be found no more at all.

I opened a place for preaching at Blakesley, about six week's ago; and there were three baptized and confirmed there last week. I was with Elder John Brotherton at Middleton on Sunday last, where he and Elder Hardman had obtained a room to preach to the Chartists.* We have also a place opened at Disbury and Heaton.

About three weeks ago there was a letter inserted in the *Manchester Courier*, by a writer who signs himself R P., calling upon the clergymen of the church of England, and the respectable inhabitants, and the most respectable and intelligent of the police, to attend our meetings at the Carpenters' Hall, as they had fondly hoped that the system would have fallen to the ground by the weight of its own absurdity; but they found that there was method and consistency in the apparent madness of these deluded people, and that experience had taught them that such expectations were vain; as they had observed that there was considerable consistency displayed, and method attending our arrangements, there being an emigration office established in this town, &c. The writer suspected there was a genuine American trick being practiced by the interested parties at the head of the system, to decoy the ignorant and unwary to perish in the swamps of New Orleans, and that they were draining the country of their best artists; and it was high time some steps were taken to put a stop to such practices.

We have since discovered that the writer is no other than Robert

* "Chartism" and the "Chartists," may be said to have come into existence early in the reign of Queen Victoria, in consequence of the formal declarations of the leaders of the Liberal party in parliament not to proceed further in the reforms to which it was generally understood they were pledged. "Quietly studied now," says Justin McCarthy (1878) "the people's charter does not seem a very formidable document. There is so little smell of gun-powder about it. Its 'points' as they were called were six:" Manhood suffrage; annual parliaments; vote by ballot; abolition of the "property qualification" for members of parliament; payment of the members of parliament; and the division of the country into equal electoral districts. "There's your charter," said Daniel O'Connel, to the secretary of the Workingmen's Association—"There's your charter, agitate for it, and never be content with anything less." It was this circumstance that gave to the movement and to its supporters the name "chartism" and "chartists." "Nothing," to again quote McCarthy, "can be more unjust than to represent the leaders and promoters of the movement as mere factions and self-seeking demagogues. Some of them were impassioned young poets drawn from the class whom Kingsley has described in 'Alton Locke;' some were men of education; many were earnest and devoted fanatics; and so far as we can judge, all, or nearly all, were sincere." *History of Our Own Times*, Vol. I. Chapter V. This to show that the preaching of the Elders of the Church to the "Chartists," was no effort to unite Church work with any wild and disorderly political movement in England.

Philips, Esq., an extensive manufacturer and merchant, brother to Mark Philips, Esq., another great manufacturer and member of parliament for the Borough of Manchester. The editor of the *Courier* has been playing upou the same string for several weeks since, and feels satisfied that from the exposure he has given the whole system, it must inevitably die away. He was therefore satisfied with having done his duty, and could safely leave them to the management of the proper parties, and recommend the police to do their duty. It appears that the gallant officer at the head of the police (Sir Charles Shaw), has too much discretion and good sense to be set on like a dog to worry out a society of Christians, because the editor of the Puseyite Oracle pointed the finger of scorn at them, because they dared to worship God according to the dictates of their own consciences. I should have liked very well for the police to have been there on Sunday last, for three persons had to be put out by the brethren for disturbing the meeting in the sacrament services.

I remain, beloved brethren, your brother and fellow laborer,

G. WALKER.

P. S.—I omitted to say that the writer in the paper alluded to, informed the public that he was endeavoring to obtain information respecting the movements of the people. He had previously sent a person to Elder Pratt to get him to state something in writing respecting emigration, and after the publication of the letter before referred to, he again sent to Elder Pratt for additional information in writing. I happened to be at Elder Pratt's when he made the second application, and I told Elder Pratt that he was the individual who had published the letter in the *Courier*. Elder Pratt sent him another letter containing the required information; and also stated that he had no objection to submit to him, or to the government of this country, or any of its departments, the religious principles of our society, our place of emigration, and indeed the whole of our movements in this and other countries, for the strictest investigation.

The manufacturers are evidently beginning to be jealous of the mechanics and workmen emigrating with people having so systematic an organization as the Latter-day Saints display in their arrangements in this town.

I remain yours, &c. G. W.

CHAPTER XXX.

EMIGRATION OF THE SAINTS FROM ENGLAND TO NAUVOO—THE BOOK OF ABRAHAM.

Sunday, January 30, 1842.—I preached at my house morning and evening, concerning the different spirits, their operations, designs, &c.

Monday, 31.—Assisted in appraising the tithings of Saturday with Emma. Received many calls. Read in the Book of Mormon. After dinner visited Brother Chase who was very sick, and in the evening was in council with Brigham Young, Heber C. Kimball, Orson Pratt, Wilford Woodruff, and Willard Richards concerning Brother Snyder and the printing office; spent the evening very cheerfully, and retired about ten o'clock.

Tuesday, February 1.—Two large stones, for door sills, for the Nauvoo House, were landed.

The following article is from the *Millennial Star* of this date:

EMIGRATION.

In the midst of the general distress which prevails in this country on account of the want of employment, the high price of provisions, the oppression, priestcraft, and iniquity of the land, it is pleasing to the household of faith to contemplate a country reserved by the Almighty as a sure asylum for the poor and oppressed,—a country every way adapted to their wants and conditions—and still more pleasing to think that thousands of the Saints have already made their escape from this country, and all its abuses and distress, and that they have found a home, where, by persevering industry, they may enjoy all the blessings of liberty, peace and plenty.

It is not yet two years since the Saints in England, in obedience to the command of their heavenly Father, commenced a general plan of emigration to the land of Zion.

They were few in number, generally poor, and had every opposition to encounter, both from a want of means and from the enemies of truth, who circulated every falsehood calculated to hinder or discourage them. Newspapers and tracts were put in circulation, sermons and public speeches were delivered in abundance, to warn the people that Nauvoo was a barren waste on the sea shore—that it was a wild and uninhabited swamp—that it was full of savages, wild beasts and serpents—that all the English Saints who should go there would be immediately sold for slaves by the leaders of the Church—that there was nothing to eat, no water, and no way possible to obtain a living; that all who went there would have their money taken from them, and themselves imprisoned, &c. But notwithstanding all these things, thousands have emigrated from this country, and now find themselves comfortably situated, and in the enjoyment of the comforts of life, and in the midst of society where God is worshiped in the spirit of truth and union, and where nearly all are agreed in religious principles. They all find plenty of employment and good wages, while the expense of living is about one-eighth of what it costs in this country. For instance —beef and pork costs about one penny per pound, flour from 2s to 3s for forty pounds, and Indian meal about one shilling for sixty pounds; butter from 4d to 6d per pound, while milch cows are to be had in plenty for about £3 per head, and other things in proportion. Millions on millions of acres of land lie before them unoccupied, with a soil as rich as Eden, and a surface as smooth, clear, and ready for the plough as the park scenery of England.

Instead of a lonely swamp or dense forest filled with savages, wild beasts and serpents, large cities and villages are springing up in their midst, with schools, colleges, and temples. The mingled noise of mechanism, the bustle of trade, the song of devotion, are heard in the distance, while thousands of flocks and herds are seen grazing peacefully on the plains, and the fields and gardens smile with plenty, and the wild red men of the forest are only seen as they come on a friendly visit to the Saints and to learn the way of the Lord.

Several large ships have been chartered by the Saints during the present fall and winter, and have been filled with emigrants, who have gone forth with songs of joy; and some of them have already arrived safely in the promised land, while others are, doubtless, still tossing upon the ocean.

The expense of passage and provisions to New Orleans has, at no time this season, exceeded £4, and it is generally as low as three pounds fifteen shillings. This is remarkable when we reflect that each passenger has provisions and water provided in plenty for ten weeks. But it is obtained at this low price by a union of effort among the Saints, and by the faithful and persevering exertions of their agents. For instance they purchase provisions by the quantity, and duty free, and the moment they bid farewell to their native shores they hoist the *Flag of Liberty*—the Ensign of Zion—the stars and stripes of the American Union; and under its protection they completely and practically nullify the bread tax. They eat free bread, free tea, free sugar, free everything, and thus accomplish a journey of five thousand miles on the same money that is would cost to feed them for the same length of time in England.

Who that has a heart to feel, or a soul to rejoice, will not be glad at so glorious a plan of deliverance? Who will not hail the messengers of the Latter-day Saints as the friends of humanity—the benefactors of mankind.

> Thousands have gone, and millions more must go,
> The Gentiles as a stream to Zion flow.

Yes, friends, this glorious work has but just commenced; and we now call upon the Saints to come forward with united effort, with persevering exertion, and with union of action, and help yourselves and one another to emigrate to the Land of Promise.

In this way we shall not only bring about the deliverance of tens of thousands, who must otherwise suffer in this country, but we shall add to the strength of Zion, and help to rear her cities and temples—"to make her wilderness like Eden, and her desert like the garden of the Lord," while the young men and the middle aged will serve to increase her legions—to strengthen her bulwarks—that the enemies of law and order who have sought her destruction, may stand afar off and tremble, and her banner become terrible to the wicked.

Ye children of Zion, once more we say, in the name of Israel's God, arise, break off your shackles, loose yourselves from the bands of your neck, and go forth to inherit the earth, and to build up waste places of many generations.

All who would go before September next, should go in the early part of March, as it is as late as is advisable to venture by way of New Orleans, on account of the extreme heat of summer; and to go by New York or Quebec, will be double the expense. Experience has taught us that an emigrant can go from Liverpool to New Orleans, and from thence 1,500 miles up the river to Nauvoo for something like £5 per head, including all provisions and expenses; while by way of New York or Quebec it will cost from ten to thirteen pounds; and besides there is another consideration, and that is, goods will cost but a trifle for freight up the Mississippi on a steamer, while the expense would be immense the other way.

Therefore the Saints will please take notice, that after the 10th of March next, emigration had better entirely cease, till about the 20th of

September following. If thousands should wish to go between this time and the 10th of March, they have only to furnish us with their names and about £4 per head (children under fourteen years half price), and we will provide them passage and provisions, for the voyage, and return the overplus, if any, at Liverpool.

We would again urge upon emigrants the important fact that if they make known to us their intentions, and send their money and names some weeks beforehand, it will be a great convenience, and save confusion, trouble and expense. All applications should be addressed to Messrs. Pratt and Fielding, 36 Chapel street, Liverpool, or to the *Star* office, 47 Oxford street, Manchester.

We do not wish to confine the benefit of our emigration plan to the Saints, but are willing to grant all industrious, honest, and well-disposed persons who may apply to us the same information and assistance as emigrants to the western states, there being abundant room for more than a hundred millions of inhabitants.

Death of Laura Phelps.

Wednesday, 2.—Sister Laura Phelps, wife of Morris Phelps, died, aged 36 years. She was driven from Jackson county in 1833, was in the persecution of Missouri, in 1838, and went from Iowa to Missouri to assist in liberating her husband, and was left in the prison yard when he made his escape, willing to suffer all the abuses a savage horde could inflict upon her to set her companion free from the grasp of his murderous enemies. Her rest is glorious.

I spent the day in council with Dr. Isaac Galland and Calvin A. Warren, Esq.

Thursday, 3.—In council with Calvin A. Warren, Esq., concerning a settlement with the estate of Oliver Granger, and delivered him the necessary papers.

Elder Woodruff took the superintendence of the printing office, and Elder Taylor the editorial department of the *Times and Seasons*; and he commenced by taking an inventory of the establishment this day.

Friday, 4.—Instructed that an invoice of Dr. Galland's scrip be made.

Closed a contract with Ebenezer Robinson for the printing office on the corner of Bain and Water streets, also the paper fixtures, bookbindery, and stereotype foundry, by proxy, namely, Willard Richards, cost between 7,000 and 8,000 dollars. In the evening attended a debate. At this time debates were held weekly, and entered into by men of the first talents in the city, young and old, for the purpose of eliciting truth, acquiring knowledge, and improving in public speaking.

Debates in Nauvoo.

Saturday, 5.—Elder Daniel Wood, who had been silenced by Presidents Smith and Young, on a complaint for teaching false doctrine, came before the High Council at Nauvoo, and proved that he had not taught false doctrine, but had been complained of by those who had prejudice and hardness against him, and was restored to his former standing in the Church.

Vindication of Daniel Wood.

This being Tithing Day, upwards of $1,000 worth of property was received.

The ship *Hope* sailed from Liverpool for New Orleans with 270 Saints.

Sunday, 6.—Elders Brigham Young and Heber C. Kimball went to La Harpe to hold a two-days meeting.

From this time I was engaged in counseling the brethren and attending to the common vocations of life and my calling, reading the Book of Mormon, &c.

Thursday, 10.—I was sick and kept my bed.

The war continues to rage between England and China.

Friday, 11.—I was convalescent, and walked twice to the store.

Saturday, 12.—An ordinance regulating weights and measures was passed, also an ordinance regulating auctions, by the city council which I attended. During the sitting of the council the subject of our chartered rights was discussed.

In the afternoon, plead in an action of slander before the mayor, in behalf of the city against Lyman O. Littlefield, and obtained judgment of $500 bonds to keep the peace.

Sunday, 13—In council with the mayor, Brother Hyrum and Elder Willard Richards, and visited Samuel Bennett (who was sick) in company with William Law and wife.

Monday, 14.—Spent the day at my office, transacting a variety of business, and continued to do the same from day to day till the 17th.

Thursday, 17.—I attended a special session of the city council, when an ordinance was passed authorizing and regulating marriages in the city of Nauvoo.

Letter of Alfred Cordon to Joseph Smith—Reporting Affairs in England.

HANLEY, STAFFORD COUNTY, ENGLAND, February 17, 1842.

PRESIDENT JOSEPH SMITH:—The work in which we are engaged rolls on in this lands and in spite of all its enemies, moves onward in majesty and power; there are many who devote all their time and talent in endeavoring to overthrow it; but I discover that they can "do nothing against the truth but for the truth." Many tracts have been published against us, containing all manner of lies, but in the end good will be the result. "He that knoweth God, heareth us." Some of the tools of Satan are doing more in spreading the truth than we are able to do; one in particular, a Mr. Brindley, is publishing a periodical showing the "errors and blasphemies" of "Mormonism;" and in order to do this, he publishes many of the revelations of God given to us, and through this means, the testimony is visiting the mansions of the high and mighty ones—the "reverends, right reverends" and all the noble champions of sectarians receive them as a precious morsel; and they are read with much interest; whereas, if we had sent them, they would have been spurned from their dwellings, and would not have been considered worth reading.

The state of this country is very awful, and is, according to prospects, on the eve of a mighty revolution; all confidence is gone between master and man, and men are afraid of each other; peace is fast removing from this land; in the course of the last few days, in many parts of this isle, they have been burning the effigy of the great men of this nation—poverty, distress and starvation abound on every hand. The groans, and tears and wretchedness of the thousands of people are enough to rend the hearts of demons; many of the Saints are suffering much through hunger and nakedness; many with large families can scarcely get bread and water enough to hold the spirit in the tabernacle; many, very many, are out of employment, and cannot get work to do, and others that do work hard fourteen or fifteen hours per day, can scarcely earn enough to enable them to live upon the earth. Surely there is need of deliverance in Zion, and I am ready to exclaim, thanks be to Thy name, O Lord, for remembering Thy covenants! and that the "set time to favor Zion has come," and that He has chosen the west for a refuge for His people.

Wishing you all success, I remain, yours in the new and everlasting covenant.

ALFRED CORDON.

Friday, 18.—I attended an adjourned city council, and spoke at considerable length in committee of the whole on the great privileges of the Nauvoo Charter, and especially on the registry of deeds for Nauvoo, and prophesied in the name of the Lord God, that Judge Douglas and no other judge of the Circuit Court will ever set aside a law of the city council, establishing a registry of deeds in the city of Nauvoo.

Confidence in the Nauvoo Charter.

Saturday, 19.—I was engaged in the Recorder's Office (in the first story of the Brick Store), on the tithings, and in council in my office with Elders Brigham Young, Heber C. Kimball and others.

A severe shock of an earthquake threw down all the parapets, bastions, and guard houses constructed by Sir Robert Sale, and demolished a third part of the town of Jellalabad, India.

Sunday, 20.—I attended the meeting on the hill. About this time the ship *John Cummins* sailed from Liverpool for New Orleans with Saints. The *Tremont* sailed on the 12th of January with 143 passengers, mostly Saints. The expenses of passage from Liverpool to New Orleans averages from £3, 15s to £4, including provisions.

Monday, 21.—I was visiting in the city in the morning, and transacting a variety of business at the office in the afternoon and evening.

Announcement of the Trustee in Trust for the Church Respecting Work on the Temple.

TO THE BRETHREN IN NAUVOO CITY: GREETING—It is highly important for the forwarding of the Temple, that an equal distribution of labor should be made in relation to time; as a superabundance of hands one week, and none the next, tends to retard the progress of the work: therefore every brother is requested to be particular to labor on the day set apart for the same, in his ward; and to remember that he that sows sparingly, shall also reap sparingly, so that if the brethren want a plentiful harvest, they will do well to be at the place of labor in good season in the morning, bringing all necessary tools, according to their occupation, and those who have teams bring them also, unless otherwise advised by the Temple Committee. Should any one be detained from his labor by unavoidable circumstances on the day appointed, let him labor the next day, or the first day possible.

N.B —The captains of the respective wards are particularly requested to be at the place of labor on their respective days, and keep an accurate account of each man's work, and be ready to exhibit a list of the same when called for.

The heart of the Trustee is daily made to rejoice in the good feelings of the brethren, made manifest in their exertion to carry forward the work of the Lord, and rear His Temple; and it is hoped that neither planting, sowing, or reaping will hereafter be made to interfere with the regulations hinted at above.

JOSEPH SMITH, Trustee in Trust.

An Additional Word from the Twelve.

RECORDER'S OFFICE, Febr. 21, 1842.

We would also say to all the churches, that inasmuch as they want the blessings of God and angels, as also of the Church of Jesus Christ, and wish to see it spread and prosper through the world, and Zion built up and truth and righteousness prevail,—let all the different branches of the Church of Jesus Christ of Latter-day Saints in all the world, call meetings in their respective places and tithe themselves and send up to this place to the Trustee in Trust, so that his hands may be loosed, and the Temple go on, and other works be done, such as the new translation of the Bible, and the record of Father Abraham published to the world.

Beloved brethren, we as the messengers of the Lord feel to call upon you to help roll on the mighty work, it is our duty so to do, and it is your reasonable service—and the Lord will bless you in so doing.

We subscribe ourselves your humble servants, and standard bearers to the world.

BRIGHAM YOUNG, President,
WILLARD RICHARDS, Clerk of the Twelve.

Tuesday, 22.—Attended to a variety of business as usual.

Wednesday, 23.—Settled with and paid Brother Chase, and assisted in the counting room in settling with Ebenezer Robinson, visiting the printing office, and gave Reuben Hedlock instruction concerning the cut for the altar and gods in the Records of Abraham, as designed for the *Times and Seasons*.

Thursday, 24.—Engaged in council with the brethren, attended to business at the general office. In the afternoon explained the records of Abraham to the recorder. Sisters Marinda, Mary, and others present to hear the explanations.

Letter of the Prophet's to an Unknown Brother on Tithing.

NAUVOO, Feb. 24, 1842.

BELOVED BROTHER—Yours of the 24th ult. is received, in relation to certain tithings of your neighborhood being transferred to your account, which you hold against the Church to the amount of $305, including $150 of your own.

There are no receipts issued for property received on tithing; but an entry is made in the Book of the Law of the Lord, and parties living at a distance notified of the same.

If the parties named will pay you the sum specified in your letter, and you will endorse the same, i. e. $305, on the obligation you hold against the Church, and give me notice accordingly, with a schedule of individuals' names and payments, the same shall be entered to their credit on tithing.

Yours, &c.

JOSEPH SMITH,
WILLARD RICHARDS, Scribe.

Friday, 25.—Engaged in counseling and general business.

Saturday, 26.—At the recorder's office engaged in the tithing, and at the court at the office of the Patriarch.

Sunday, 27.—Engaged in counseling the Saints.

Monday, 28.—I offered a settlement to Father Snow by

Jenkins' notes, which he declined, choosing to take land in Ramus; paid Brother Robert Pierce $2,700, the balance due him for a farm Dr. Galland bought of Brother Pierce in Brandywine Township, Chester county, Pennsylvania, for $5,000, namely a deed for lot 2, block 94, $1,100, and lot 1, block 95, $800, and lot 4, block 78, $806, the remainder having been previously paid. The bond was cancelled and given up, and Brother Pierce expressed his satisfaction of the whole, in the *Times and Seasons*, as follows—

Note of Robert Pierce—Expressing Satisfaction at Financial Settlement.

NAUVOO, Feb. 28, 1842.

President Joseph Smith.

DEAR SIR—I feel anxious to express my feelings concerning the business transactions between the Church and myself; as it is well known to many, that Dr. Galland, as agent for the Church, purchased my farm while I was living in Brandywine Township, Chester county, Pennsylvania, and many supposed, or pretended to suppose, I would get nothing in return; but I wish to say to all my old friends and enemies in Pennsylvania, through the medium of the *Times and Seasons*, that I have received my pay in full from the Church of Jesus Christ of Latter-day Saints, through yourself, sir, as their trustee in trust, according to the original contract; and that from my acquaintance with yourself, and those brethren who are assisting you in the great and increasing business of the Church, I have the fullest confidence in all the transactions of the Church, and I request those papers in Philadelphia, who published concerning my sale and loss, with such bitter lamentations, to publish this also.

I am, sir, your brother and well-wisher,

ROBERT PIERCE.

Thursday, March 1, 1842.—During the forenoon I was at my office and the printing office, correcting the first plate or cut of the records of Father Abraham, prepared by Reuben Hedlock, for the *Times and Seasons*, and in council in my office, in the afternoon; and in the evening with the Twelve and their wives at Elder Woodruff's, at which time I explained many important principles in relation to progressive improvement in the scale of intelligent existence.

I commenced publishing my translations of the Book of Abraham in the *Times and Seasons* as follows—

FAC-SIMILE FROM THE BOOK OF ABRAHAM—NO. 1.

EXPLANATION OF THE ABOVE CUT.

Fig. 1. The angel of the Lord.

Fig. 2. Abraham fastened upon an altar.

Fig. 3. The idolatrous priest of Elkenah attempting to offer up Abraham as a sacrifice.

Fig. 4. The altar for sacrifice, by the idolatrous priests, standing before the gods of Elkenah, Libnah, Mahmackrah, Korash, and Pharaoh.

Fig. 5. The idolatrous god of Elkenah.

Fig. 6. The idolatrous god of Libnah.

Fig. 7. The idolatrous god of Mahmackrah.

Fig. 8. The idolatrous god of Korash.

Fig 9. The idolatrous god of Pharaoh.

Fig. 10. Abraham in Egypt.

Fig. 11. Designed to represent the pillars of Heaven, as understood by the Egyptians.

Fig. 12. Raukeeyang, signifying expanse, or the firmament over our heads; but in this case in relation to this subject, the Egyptians meant it to signify Shauman, to be high, or the heavens; answering to the Hebrew word, Shaumahyeem.

FAC-SIMILE FROM THE BOOK OF ABRAHAM—NO. 2.

EXPLANATION OF THE ABOVE CUT.

Fig. 1. Kolob, signifying the first creation, nearest to the celestial, or the residence of God. First in government, the last pertaining to the measurement of time. The measurement, according to celestial time; which celestial time signifies one day to a cubit. One day in Kolob is equal to a thousand years, according to the measurement of this earth, which is called by the Egyptians Jah-oh-eh.

Fig 2 Stands next to Kolob, called by the Egyptians Oliblish, which is the next grand governing creation near to the celestial, or the place where God resides; holding the key of power also, perta ning to other planets; as revealed from God to Abraham, as he offered sacrifice upon an altar which he had built unto the Lord.

Fig. 3. Is made to represent God, sitting upon His throne clothed with power and authority, with a crown of eternal light upon His head; representing, also, the grand key words of the Holy Priesthood, as reavealed to Adam in the Garden of Eden, as also to Seth, Noah, Melchisedek, Abraham, and all to whom the Priesthood was revealed.

Fig. 4. Answers to the Hebrew word Raukeeyang, signifying expanse or the firmament of the heavens; also a numerical figure in Egyptian, signifying one thousand; answering to the measuring of the time of Oliblish, which is equal with Kolob in its revolution and in its measuring of time.

Fig. 5. Is called in Egyptian Enish-go-on-dosh; this is one of the governing planets also, and is said by the Egyptians to be the Sun, and to borrow its light from Kolob, through the medium of Kae-e-vanrash, which is the grand Key, or in other words, the governing power, which governs fifteen other fixed planets or stars, as also Floeese or the Moon, the Earth and the Sun, in their annual revolutions. This planet received its power through the medium of Kli-flos-is-es, or Hah-ko-kau-beam, the stars represented by numbers 22, and 23, receiving light from the revolutions of Kolob.

Fig. 6. Represents the earth in four quarters.

Fig. 7. Represents God sitting upon His throne, revealing through the heavens the grand Key Words of the Priesthood; as also the sign of the Holy Ghost unto Abraham, in the form of a dove.

Fig. 8. Contains writing that cannot be revealed unto the world; but is to be had in the Holy Temple of God.

Fig. 9. Ought not to be revealed at the present time.

Fig. 10. Also.

Fig. 11. Also.—If the world can find out these numbers, so let it be. Amen.

Figures 12, 13, 14, 15, 16, 17, 18, 19, and 20, will be given in the own due time of the Lord.

The above translation is given as far as we have any right to give at the present time.

EXPLANATION OF CUT NO. 3.

Fig. 1. Abraham sitting upon Pharaoh's throne, by the politeness of the king, with a crown upon his head, representing the Priesthood, as emblematical of the grand Presidency in Heaven, with the sceptre of justice and judgment in his hand.

Fig. 2. King Pharaoh, whose name is given in the characters above his head.

Fig. 3. Signifies Abraham in Egypt; referring to Abraham, as given in the ninth number of the Times and Seasons. (Also as given in the first fac-simile of this book.)

Fig. 4. Prince of Pharaoh, King of Egypt, as written above the hand.

Fig. 5. Shulem, one of the king's principal waiters, as represented by the characters above his hand.

Fig. 6. Olimlah, a slave belonging to the prince.

Abraham is reasoning upon the principles of astronomy, in the king's court.

FAC-SIMILE FROM THE BOOK OF ABRAHAM—NO 3.

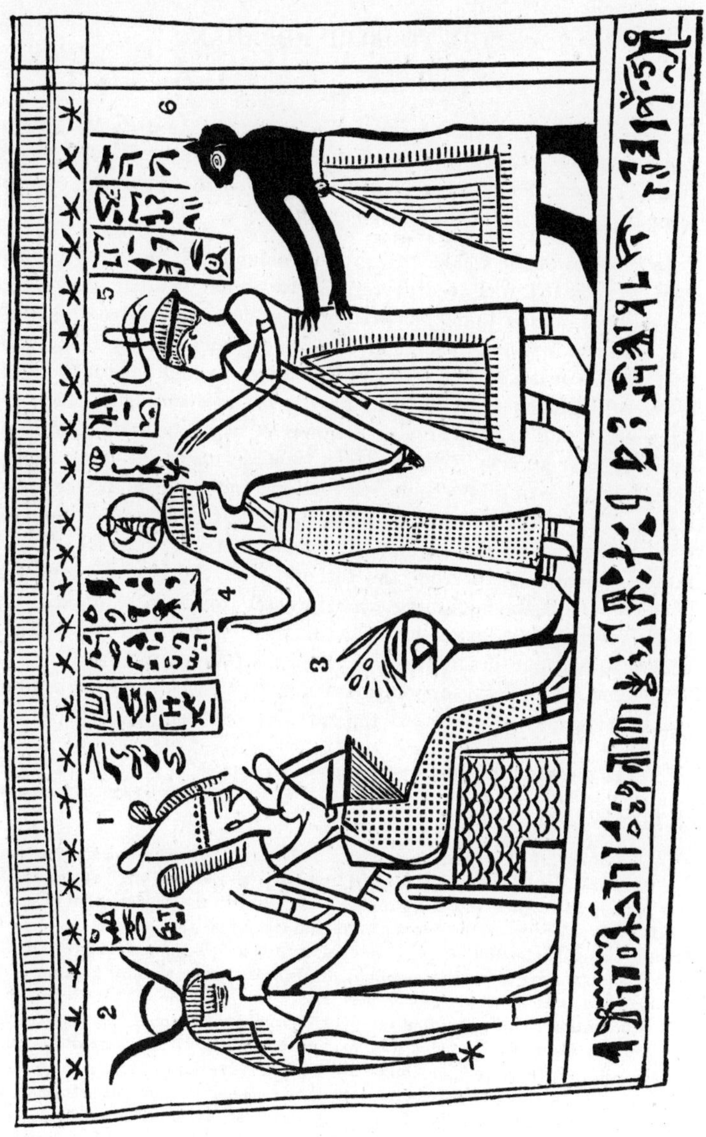

THE BOOK OF ABRAHAM.*

TRANSLATED FROM THE PAPYRUS, BY JOSEPH SMITH.†

A Translation of some Ancient Records that have fallen into our hands, from the Catacombs of Egypt, purporting to be the writings of Abraham, while he was in Egypt, called the Book of Abraham, written by his own hand upon papyrus.

In the land of the Chaldeans, at the residence of my father, I Abraham, saw that it was needful for me to obtain another place of residence, and finding there was greater happiness, and peace and rest for me, I sought for the blessings of the fathers, and the right whereunto I should be ordained to administer the same; having been myself a follower of righteousness, desiring also to be one who possessed great knowledge, and to be a greater follower of righteousness, and to possess a greater knowledge, and to be a father of many nations, a prince of peace; and desiring to receive instructions and to keep the commandments of God, I became a rightful heir, a High Priest, holding the right belonging to the fathers; it was conferred upon me from the fathers; it came down from the fathers, from the beginning of time, yea, even from the beginning, or before the foundations of the earth, to the present time, even the right of the first born, or the first man, who is Adam, our first Father, through the fathers, unto me.

2. I sought for mine appointment unto the Priesthood according to the appointment of God unto the fathers, concerning the seed. My

* For an account of how the Prophet came into possession of the Book of Abraham see this History Vol. II, pp. 235, 6, 8; also 286, and more especially pp. 349—50, and *note* p. 350.

† The Book of Abraham was first published in the *Times and Seasons* in two numbers, Vol. III, Nos. 9 and 10, March 1 and March 15, 1842, respectively. In this form it was copied into the Prophet's history with the several historical items which occurred between the dates of the publication of the two parts, and in this form is found in the *Millennial Star*, Vol. XIX, pp. 100-103 and 164-168; but it is now thought proper to publish the Book of Abraham entire without dividing it into two articles, as in the above named periodicals.

It is important to note also that the Book of Abaham was published in the *Times and Seasons* when the Prophet was responsible editor of the periodical (he announces his editorial responsibility in No. 9 of Vol. III, p. 710). Attention is called to this fact, in passing, because it is contended on the part of some, that the doctrine of the plurality of divine personages, as now understood by the Church, was not a doctrine taught by Joseph Smith; whereas it is a doctrine of the Book of Abraham, as will be seen by reference to it, published by him in a periodical of which he was the responsible editor; and, moreover, the Book of Abraham was often referred to by the Prophet in approving terms.

fathers having turned from their righteousness, and from the holy commandments which the Lord their God had given unto them, unto the worshiping of the gods of the heathen, utterly refused to hearken to my voice; for their hearts were set to do evil, and were wholly turned to the god of Elkenah, and the god of Libnah, and the god of Mahmackrah, and the god of Korash, and the god of Pharaoh, king of Egypt, therefore they turned their hearts to the sacrifice of the heathen in offering up their children unto their dumb idols, and hearkened not unto my voice, but endeavored to take away my life by the hand of the priest of Elkenah—the priest of Elkenah was also the priest of Pharaoh.

3. Now at this time it was the custom of the priest of Pharaoh, the king of Egypt, to offer up upon the altar which was built in the land of Chaldea, for the offering unto these strange gods, men, women and children. And it came to pass that the priest made an offering unto the god of Pharaoh, and also unto the god of Shagreel, even after the manner of the Egyptians. Now the god of Shagreel was the Sun. Even the thank-offering of a child did the priest of Pharaoh offer upon this altar, which stood by the hill called Potiphar's hill, at the head of the plain of Olishem. Now, this priest had offered upon the altar three virgins at one time, who were the daughters of Onitah, one of the royal descent, directly from the loins of Ham. These virgins were offered up because of their virtue; they would not bow down to worship gods of wood, or of stone, therefore they were killed upon this altar, and it was done after the manner of the Egyptians.

4. And it came to pass that the priests laid violence upon me, that they might slay me also, as they did those virgins, upon this altar; and that you may have a knowledge of this altar, I will refer you to the representation at the commencement of this record. It was made after the form of a bedstead, such as was had among the Chaldeans, and it stood before the gods of Elkenah, Libna, Mahmackrah, Korash, and also a god like unto that of Pharaoh, king of Egypt. That you may have an understanding of these gods, I have given you the fashion of them in the figures at the beginning, which manner of the figures is called by the Chaldeans Rahleenos, which signifies hieroglyphics.

5. And as they lifted up their hands upon me, that they might offer me up and take away my life, behold I lifted up my voice unto the Lord my God; and the Lord hearkened and heard, and he filled me with a vision of the Almighty, and the angel of his presence stood by me, and immediately unloosed my bands, and his voice was unto me, Abraham! Abraham! behold my name is JEHOVAH, and I have heard thee, and have come down to deliver thee, and to take thee away from thy father's house, and from all thy kinsfolk, into a strange land that thou knowest

not of, and this because they have turned their hearts away from me, to worship the god of Elkenah, and the god of Libnah, and the god of Mahmackrah, and the god of Korash, and the god of Pharaoh, king of Egypt; therefore I have come down to visit them, and to destroy him who hath lifted up his hand against thee, Abraham my son, to take away thy life. Behold I will lead thee by my hand, and I will take thee to put upon thee my name, even the Priesthood of thy father; and my power shall be over thee; as it was with Noah so shall it be with thee, but through thy ministry my name shall be known in the earth for ever, for I am thy God.

6. Behold Potiphar's Hill was in the land of Ur, of Chaldea; and the Lord broke down the altar of Elkenah, and of the gods of the land, and utterly destroyed them, and smote the priest that he died; and there was great mourning in Chaldea, and also in the court of Pharaoh, which Pharaoh signifies king by royal blood. Now this king of Egypt was a descendant from the loins of Ham, and was a partaker of the blood of the Canaanites by birth. From this descent sprang all the Egyptians, and thus the blood of the Canaanites was preserved in the land.

7. The land of Egypt being first discovered by a woman, who was the daughter of Ham, and the daughter of Egyptus, which, in the Chaldean, signifies Egypt, which signifies, that which is forbidden. When this woman discovered the land it was under water, who afterwards settled her sons in it: and thus from Ham, sprang that race which preserved the curse in the land. Now the first government of Egypt was established by Pharaoh, the eldest son of Egyptus, the daughter of Ham, and it was after the manner of the government of Ham, which was patriarchal. Pharaoh being a righteous man, established his kingdom and judged his people wisely and justly all his days, seeking earnestly to imitate that order established by the fathers in the first generations, in the days of the first partriarchal reign, even in the reign of Adam, and also of Noah, his father, who blessed him with the blessings of the earth, and with the blessings of wisdom, but cursed him as pertaining to the Priesthood.

8. Now Pharaoh being of that lineage by which he could not have the right of Priesthood, notwithstanding the Pharaohs would fain claim it from Noah, through Ham, therefore my father was led away by their idolatry; but I shall endeavor hereafter to delineate the chronology, running back from myself to the beginning of the creation, for the records have come into my hands which I hold unto this present time.

9. Now, after the priest of Elkenah was smitten, that he died, there came a fulfillment of those things which were said unto me concerning the land of Chaldea, that there should be a famine in the land. Accordingly a famine prevailed throughout all the land of Chaldea, and my

father was sorely tormented because of the famine, and he repented of the evil which he had determined against me, to take away my life. But the records of the fathers, even the patriarchs, concerning the right of Priesthood, the Lord my God preserved in mine own hands, therefore a knowledge of the beginning of the creation, and also of the planets, and of the stars, as they were made known unto the fathers, have I kept even unto this day, and I shall endeavor to write some of these things upon this record, for the benefit of my posterity that shall come after me.

10. Now, the Lord God caused the famine to wax sore in the land of Ur, insomuch that Haran, my brother died, but Terah, my father, yet lived in the land of Ur of the Chaldees. And it came to pass that I, Abraham, took Sarai to wife, and Nehor,my brother,took Milcah to wife, who were the daughters of Haran. Now the Lord said unto me,Abraham, get thee out of thy country, and from thy kindred and from thy father's house unto a land that I will show thee. Therefore I left the land of Ur, of the Chaldees, to go into the land of Canaan; and I took Lot, my brother's son, and his wife, and Sarai, my wife, and also my father followed after me, unto the land which we denominated Haran. And the famine abated; and my father tarried in Haran and dwelt there, as there were many flocks in Haran; and my father turned again unto his idolatry, therefore he continued in Haran.

11. But I,Abraham, and Lot, my brother's son, prayed unto the Lord, and the Lord appeared unto me, and said unto me, arise, and take Lot with thee, for I have purposed to take thee away out of Haran, and to make of thee a minister, to bear my name in a strange land which I will give unto thy seed after thee for an everlasting possession, when they hearken to my voice, for I am the Lord thy God; I dwell in heaven, the earth is my footstool; I stretch my hand over the sea, and it obeys my voice; I cause the wind and the fire to be my chariot; I say to the mountains depart hence, and behold they are taken away by a whirlwind, in an instant, suddenly. My name is Jehovah, and I know the end from the beginning, therefore, my hand shall be over thee, and I will make of thee a great nation, and I will bless thee above measure; and make thy name great among all nations, and thou shalt be a blessing unto thy seed after thee, that in their hands they shall bear this ministry and Priesthood unto all nations; and I will bless them through thy name; for as many as receive this Gospel shall be called after thy name, and shall be accounted thy seed, and shall rise up and bless thee, as their father, and I will bless them that bless thee, and curse them that curse thee, and in thee (that is, in thy Priesthood), and in thy seed (that is thy Priesthood), for I give unto thee a promise that this right shall continue in thee, and in thy seed after thee (that is to say, the

literal seed, or the seed of the body) shall all the families of the earth be blessed, even with the blessings of the Gospel, which are the blessings of salvation, even of life eternal.

12. Now, after the Lord had withdrawn from speaking to me, and withdrawn his face from me, I said in my heart, thy servant has sought thee earnestly, now I have found thee. Thou didst send thine angel to deliver me from the gods of Elkenah,and I will do well to hearken unto thy voice, therefore let thy servant rise up and depart in peace. So I, Abraham, departed as the Lord had said unto me, and Lot with me, and I, Abraham,was sixty and two years old when I departed out of Haran. And I took Sarai, whom I took to wife when I was in Ur in Chaldea, and Lot, my brother's son, and all our substance that we had gathered, and the souls that we had won in Haran, and came forth in the way to the land of Canaan, and dwelt in tents, as we came on our way: therefore, eternity was our covering, and our rock, and our salvation, as we journeyed from Haran by the way of Jershon, to come to the land of Canaan.

13. Now I, Abraham, built an altar in the land of Jershon, and made an offering unto the Lord, and prayed that the famine might be turned away from my father's house, that they might not perish; and then we passed from Jershon through the land, unto the place of Sechem. It was situated in the plains of Moreh, and we had already come into the borders of the land of the Canaanites, and I offered sacrifice there in the plains of Moreh, and called on the Lord devoutly, because we had already come into the land of this idolatrous nation.

14. And the Lord appeared unto me in answer to my prayers, and said unto me, unto thy seed will I give this land. And I, Abraham, arose from the place of the altar which I had built unto the Lord, and removed from thence unto a mountain on the east of Bethel, and pitched my tent there; Bethel on the west, and Hai on the east; and there I built another altar unto the Lord, and called again upon the name of the Lord.

15. And I, Abraham, journeyed, going on still towards the south; and there was a continuation of a famine in the land, and I, Abraham, concluded to go down into Egypt, to sojourn there, for the famine became very grievous. And it came to pass when I was come near to enter into Egypt, the Lord said unto me, behold Sarai, thy wife, is a very fair woman to look upon, therefore it shall come to pass, when the Egyptians shall see her they will say, she is his wife; and they will kill you, but they will save her alive: therefore, see that ye do on this wise, let her say unto the Egyptians she is thy sister, and thy soul shall live. And it came to pass that I, Abraham, told Sarai, my wife, all that the Lord had said unto me; therefore, say unto them, I pray thee, thou art

my sister, that it may be well with me for thy sake, and my soul shall live because of thee.

16. And I, Abraham, had the Urim and Thummim, which the Lord my God had given unto me, in Ur of the Chaldees; and I saw the stars, that they were very great, and that one of them was nearest unto the throne of God: and there were many great ones which were near unto it; and the Lord said unto me, these are the governing ones; and the name of the great one is Kolob, because it is near unto me; for I am the Lord thy God. I have set this one to govern all those which belong to the same order as that upon which thou standest. And the Lord said unto me, by the Urim and Thummim, that Kolob was after the manner of the Lord, according to its times and seasons in the revolutions thereof, that one revolution was a day unto the Lord, after His manner of reckoning, it being one thousand years according to the time appointed unto that whereon thou standest; this is the reckoning of the Lord's time, according to the reckoning of Kolob.

17. And the Lord said unto me, the planet which is the lesser light, lesser than that which is to rule the day, even the night, is above, or greater than that upon which thou standest in point of reckoning, for it moveth in order more slow; this is in order, because it standeth above the earth upon which thou standest, therefore the reckoning of its time is not so many as to its number of days, and of months and of years. And the Lord said unto me, Now Abraham, these two facts exist, behold thine eyes see it; it is given unto thee to know the times of reckoning, and the set time, yea, the set time of the earth upon which thou standest, and the set time of the greater light, which is set to rule the day, and the set time of the lesser light, which is set to rule the night.

18. Now the set time of the lesser light, is a longer time as to its reckoning than the reckoning of the time of the earth upon which thou standest; and where these two facts exist, there shall be another fact above them; that is, there shall be another planet whose reckoning of time shall be longer still; and thus there shall be the reckoning of the time of one planet above another, until thou come nigh unto Kolob, which Kolob is after the reckoning of the Lord's time; which Kolob is set nigh unto the throne of God, to govern all those planets which belong to the same order as that upon which thou standest. And it is given unto thee to know the set time of all the stars, that are set to give light, until thou come near unto the throne of God.

19. Thus I, Abraham, talked with the Lord face to face, as one man talketh with another; and He told me of the works which His hands had made; and He said unto me, My son, my son, (and His hand was stretched out,) behold, I will show you all these. And He put His hand upon mine eyes, and I saw those things which His hands had made,

which were many; and they multiplied before mine eyes, and I could not see the end thereof; and He said unto me this is Shinehah which is the sun. And He said unto me, Kokob, which is star. And He said unto me, Olea, which is the moon. And He said unto me, Kokaubeam, which signifies stars, or all the great lights which were in the firmament of heaven. And it was in the night time when the Lord spake these words unto me: I will multiply thee and thy seed after thee, like unto these; and if thou canst count the number of sands so shall be the number of thy seeds.

20. And the Lord said unto me, Abraham, I show these things unto thee, before ye go into Egypt, that ye may declare all these words. If two things exist, and there be one above the other, there shall be greater things above them; therefore Kolob is the greatest of all the Kokaubeam that thou hast seen, because it is nearest unto me; now if there be two things, one above the other, and the moon be above the earth, then it may be that a planet, or a star may exist above it, (and there is nothing that the Lord thy God shall take in His heart to do, but what He will do it;) howbeit that He made the greater star; as, also, if there be two spirits, and one shall be more intelligent than the other, yet these two spirits, notwithstanding one is more intelligent than the other, have no beginning, they existed before; they shall have no end, they shall exist after, for they are gnolaum or eternal.

21. And the Lord said unto me, these two facts do exist, that there are two spirits, one being more intelligent than the other, there shall be another more intelligent than they: I am the Lord thy God, I am more intelligent than they all. The Lord thy God sent His angel to deliver thee from the hands of the priest of Elkenah. I dwell in the midst of them all; I, now, therefore, have come down unto thee, to deliver unto thee the works which my hands have made, wherein my wisdom excelleth them all, for I rule in the heavens above, and in the earth beneath, in all wisdom and prudence, over all the intelligences thine eyes have seen from the beginning; I came down in the beginning in the midst of all the intelligences thou hast seen.

22. Now the Lord had shown unto me, Abraham, the intelligences that were organized before the world was; and among all these there were many of the noble and great ones, and God saw these souls that they were good, and He stood in the midst of them, and He said, These I will make my rulers; for He stood among those that were spirits, and he saw that they were good; and He said unto me, Abraham, thou art one of them, thou wast chosen before thou wast born. And there stood one among them that was like unto God, and he said unto those who were with Him, We will go down, for there is space there, and we will take of these materials, and we will make an earth whereon these may

dwell; and we will prove them herewith, to see if they will do all things whatsoever the Lord their God shall command them; and they who keep their first estate, shall be added upon; and they who keep not their first estate shall not have glory in the same kingdom with those who keep their first estate; and they who keep their second estate, shall have glory added upon their heads for ever and ever.

23. And the Lord said: Whom shall I send? And one answered like unto the Son of Man: Here am I, send me. And another answered and said: Here am I, send me. And the Lord said: I will send the first. And the second was angry, and kept not his first estate, and at that day many followed after him. And then the Lord said: Let us go down; and they went down at the beginning, and they (that is, the Gods), organized and formed the heavens and the earth. And the earth, after it was formed, was empty and desolate; because they had not formed anything but the earth; and darkness reigned upon the face of the deep, and the Spirit of the Gods was brooding upon the face of the waters.

24. And they (the Gods), said: Let there be light, and there was light. And they, the Gods, comprehended the light for it was bright; and they divided the light, or caused it to be divided from the darkness, and the Gods called the light day, and the darkness they called night. And it came to pass that from the evening until morning they called night; and from the morning until the evening they called day; and this was the first, or the beginning of that which they called day and night.

25. And the Gods also said: Let there be an expanse in the midst of the waters and it shall divide the waters from the waters. And the Gods ordered the expanse, so that it divided the waters which were under the expanse, from the waters which were above the expanse, and it was so, even as they ordered. And the Gods called the expanse heaven. And it came to pass that it was from evening until morning that they called night; and it came to pass that it was from morning until evening that they called day; and this was the second time that they called night and day.

26. And the Gods ordered, saying: Let the waters under the heaven be gathered together unto one place, and let the earth come up dry, and it was so, as they ordered; and the Gods pronounced the dry land earth. and the gathering together of the waters, pronounced they great waters; and the Gods saw that they were obeyed. And the Gods said: Let us prepare the earth to bring forth grass; the herb yielding seed; the fruit tree yielding fruit after his kind, whose seed in itself yieldeth its own likeness upon the earth; and it was so, even as they ordered. And the Gods organized the earth to bring forth grass from its own seed, and the herb to bring forth herb from its own seed, yielding seed

after his kind, and the earth to bring forth the tree from its own seed, yielding fruit, whose seed could only bring forth the same, in itself after his kind; and the Gods saw that they were obeyed. And it came to pass that they numbered the days: from the evening until the morning they called night. And it came to pass from the morning until the evening they called day; and it was the third time.

27. And the Gods organized the lights in the expanse of the heavens, and caused them to divide the day from the night; and organized them to be for signs, and for seasons, and for days, and for years and organized them to be for lights in the expanse of the heaven, to give light upon the earth; and it was so. And the Gods organized the two great lights, the greater light to rule the day, and the lesser light to rule the night, with the lesser light they set the stars, also; and the Gods set them in the expanse of the heavens, to give light upon the earth, and to rule over the day and over the night, and to cause to divide the light from the darkness. And the Gods watched those things which they had ordered, until they obeyed. And it came to pass that it was from evening until morning that it was night; and it came to pass that it was from morning until evening that it was day; and it was the fourth time.

28. And the Gods said, Let us prepare the waters to bring forth abundantly the moving creatures that have life; and the fowl that they may fly above the earth, in the open expanse of heaven. And the Gods prepared the waters that they might bring forth great whales, and every living creature that moveth, which the waters were to bring forth abundantly after their kind; and every winged fowl after their kind; and the Gods saw that they would be obeyed, and that their plan was good. And the Gods said, We will bless them and cause them to be fruitful and multiply, and fill the waters in the seas, or great waters; and cause the fowl to multiply in the earth. And it came to pass that it was from evening until morning that they called night; and it came to pass that it was from morning until evening that they called day; and it was the fifth time.

29. And the Gods prepared the earth to bring forth the living creature after his kind, cattle, and creeping things, and beasts of the earth after their kind; and it was so as they had said. And the Gods organized the earth to bring forth the beasts after their kind, and cattle after their kind, and everything that creepeth upon the earth after its kind; and the Gods saw they would obey. And the Gods took counsel among themselves, and said: Let us go down, and form man in our image, after our likeness, and we will give them dominion over the fish of the sea, and over the fowl of the air, and over the cattle, and over all the earth, and over every creeping thing, that creepeth upon the earth. So the Gods went down

to organize man in their own image, in the image of the Gods, to form they him male and female, to form they them; and the Gods said We will bless them. And the Gods said, We will cause them to be fruitful, and multiply and replenish the earth, and subdue it, and to have dominion over the fish of the sea, and over the fowl of the air, and over every living thing that moveth upon the earth. And the Gods said, Behold, we will give them every herb bearing seed that shall come upon the face of all the earth, and every tree which shall have fruit upon it, yea the fruit of the tree, yielding seed to them we will give it, it shall be for their meat; and to every beast of the earth, and to every fowl of the air, and to everything that creepeth upon the earth, behold we will give them life, and also we will give to them every green herb for meat, and all these things shall be thus organized. And the Gods said, We will do everything that we have said, and organize them; and behold, they shall be very obedient. And it came to pass that it was from evening until morning that they called night; and it came to pass that it was from morning until evening that they called day, and they numbered the sixth time.

30. And thus we will finish the heavens and the earth, and all the hosts of them. And the Gods said among themselves, On the seventh time, we will end our work, which we have counseled; and we will rest on the seventh time from all our work which we have counseled. And the Gods concluded upon the seventh time, because that on the seventh time they would rest from all their works, which they, the Gods, counseled among themselves to form, and sanctified it. And thus were their decisions, at the time that they counseled among themselves to form the heavens and the earth. And the Gods came down and formed these, the generations of the heavens and of the earth, when they were formed, in the day that the Gods formed the earth and the heavens, according to all that which they had said, concerning every plant of the field, before it was in the earth, and every herb of the field, before it grew; for the Gods had not caused it to rain upon the earth, when they counseled to do them; and had not formed a man to till the ground; but there went up a mist from the earth, and watered the whole face of the ground. And the Gods formed man from the dust of the ground, and took his spirit, that is the man's spirit, and put it into him, and breathed into his nostrils the breath of life, and man became a living soul.

31. And the Gods planted a garden, eastward in Eden, and there they put the man, whose spirit they had put into the body, which they had formed. And out of the ground made the Gods to grow every tree that is pleasant to the sight, and good for food; the tree of life also, in the midst of the garden, and the tree of knowledge of good

and evil. There was a river running out of Eden, to water the garden, and from thence it was parted and became into four heads. And the Gods took the man and put him in the garden of Eden, to dress it and to keep it; and the Gods commanded the man, saying: Of every tree of the garden thou mayest freely eat, but of the tree of knowledge of good and evil, thou shalt not eat of it; for in the time that thou eatest thereof, thou shalt surely die. Now I, Abraham, saw that it was after the Lord's time, which was after the time of Kolob; for as yet, the Gods had not appointed unto Adam his reckoning.

32. And the Gods said, Let us make an helpmeet for the man, for it is not good that the man should be alone, therefore we will form an helpmeet for him. And the Gods caused a deep sleep to fall upon Adam; and he slept, and they took one of his ribs, and closed up the flesh in the stead thereof, and of the rib which the Gods had taken from man, formed they a woman, and brought her unto the man. And Adam said this was bone of my bones, and flesh of my flesh, now she shall be called woman, because she was taken out of man; therefore shall a man leave his father and his mother and shall cleve unto his wife, and they shall be one flesh. And they were both naked, the man and his wife, and were not ashamed. And out of the ground the Gods formed every beast of the field, and every fowl of the air, and brought them unto Adam to see what he would call them, and whatsoever Adam called every living creature, that should be the name thereof. And Adam gave names to all cattle, to the fowl of the air, to every beast of the field; and for Adam, there was found an helpmeet for him.

CHAPTER XXXI.

THE WENTWORTH LETTER.*

March 1, 1842.—At the request of Mr. John Wentworth, Editor and Proprietor of the *Chicago Democrat*, I have written the following sketch of the rise, progress, persecution, and faith of the Latter-day Saints, of which I have the honor, under God, of being the founder. Mr. Wentworth says that he wishes to furnish Mr. Bastow, a friend of his, who is writing the history of New Hampshire, with this document. As Mr. Bastow has

* The "Wentworth Letter" is one of the choicest documents in our Church literature; as also it is the earliest published document by the Prophet making any pretension to consecutive narrative of those events in which the great latter-day work had its origin. It was published in number 9 of Volume III of the "Times and Seasons," March 1st, 1842; while the publication of that more pretentious History of the Church under the title "History of Joseph Smith," of which these volumes are but a reproduction, was not commenced until number 10, Volume III, of the "Times and Seasons," March 15th, 1842. Introducing this "History of Joseph Smith" in the "Times and Seasons" (Vol. III, p. 726) is the following note referring to the Wentworh Letter and the more pretentious "History."

"In the last number I gave a brief history of the rise and progress of the Church, I now enter more particularly into that history, and extract from my journal."

Referring again to this Wentworth Letter, I may say that for combining conciseness of statement with comprehensiveness of treatment of the subject with which it deals, it has few equals among historical documents, and certainly none that excel it in our Church literature. In it one has in a few pages (less than six of these pages) a remarkably full history of the leading events in the Church, and an epitome of her doctrines, from the beginning (the birth of the Prophet, 1805) up to the date of publication, March, 1842, a period of thirty-six years. The epitome of the doctrines of the Church, since called "The Articles of Faith," and published by millions, has been carried to all the nations of the earth and tribes of men where the gospel has been preached. These Articles of Faith were not produced by the labored efforts and harmonized contentions of scholastics, but were struck off by one inspired mind at a single effort to make a declaration of that which is most assuredly believed by the Church, for one making earnest inquiry about the truth. The combined directness, perspicuity, simplicity and comprehensiveness of this statement of the principles of our religion may be relied upon as strong evidence of a divine inspiration resting upon the Prophet, Joseph Smith.

taken the proper steps to obtain correct information, all that I shall ask at his hands, is, that he publish the account entire, ungarnished, and without misrepresentation.

I was born in the town of Sharon, Windsor County, Vermont, on the 23rd of December, A.D. 1805. When ten years old, my parents removed to Palmyra, New York, where we resided about four years, and from thence we removed to the town of Manchester. My father was a farmer and taught me the art of husbandry. When about fourteen years of age, I began to reflect upon the importance of being prepared for a future state, and upon inquiring [about] the plan of salvation, I found that there was a great clash in religious sentiment; if I went to one society they referred me to one plan, and another to another; each one pointing to his own particular creed as the *summum bonum* of perfection. Considering that all could not be right, and that God could not be the author of so much confusion, I determined to investigate the subject more fully, believing that if God had a Church it would not be split up into factions, and that if He taught one society to worship one way, and administer in one set of ordinances, He would not teach another, principles which were diametrically opposed.

Believing the word of God, I had confidence in the declaration of James—"If any of you lack wisdom, let him ask of God, that giveth to all men liberally, and upbraideth not; and it shall be given him." I retired to a secret place in a grove, and began to call upon the Lord; while fervently engaged in supplication, my mind was taken away from the objects with which I was surrounded, and I was enwrapped in a heavenly vision, and saw two glorious personages, who exactly resembled each other in features and likeness, surrounded with a brilliant light which eclipsed the sun at noon day. They told me that all religious denominations were believing in incorrect doctrines, and that none of them was acknowledged of God as His Church and kingdom: and I was expressly commanded "to go not after them," at the same time receiving a promise that the fullness of the Gospel should at some future time be made known unto me.

On the evening on the 21st of September, A.D. 1823, while I was praying unto God, and endeavoring to exercise faith in the precious promises of Scripture, on a sudden a light like that of day, only of a far purer and more glorious appearance and brightness, burst into the room, indeed the first sight was as though the house was filled with consuming fire; the appearance produced a shock that affected the whole body; in a moment a personage stood before me surrounded with a glory yet greater than that with which I was already surrounded. This messenger proclaimed himself to be an angel of God, sent to bring the joyful tidings that the covenant which God made with ancient Israel was at hand to be fulfilled, that the preparatory work for the second coming of the Messiah was speedily to commence; that the time was at hand for the Gospel in all its fullness to be preached in power, unto all nations that a people might be prepared for the Millennial reign. I was informed that I was chosen to be an instrument in the hands of God to bring about some of His purposes in this glorious dispensation.

I was also informed concerning the aboriginal inhabitants of this country and shown who they were, and from whence they came; a brief sketch of their origin, progress, civilization, laws, governments, of their righteousness and iniquity, and the blessings of God being finally withdrawn from them as a people, was made known unto me; I was also told where were deposited some plates on which were engraven an abridgment of the records of the ancient Prophets that had existed on this continent. The angel appeared to me three times the same night and unfolded the same things. After having received many visits from the angels of God unfolding the majesty and glory of the events that should transpire in the last days, on the morning of the 22nd of September, A.D. 1827, the angel of the Lord delivered the records into my hands.

These records were engraven on plates which had the appearance of gold, each plate was six inches wide and eight inches long, and not quite so thick as common tin. They were filled with engravings, in Egyptian characters, and bound together in a volume as the leaves of a book, with three rings running through the whole. The volume was something near six inches in thickness, a part of which was sealed. The characters on the unsealed part were small, and beautifully engraved. The whole book exhibited many marks of antiquity in its construction, and much skill in the art of engraving. With the records was found a curious instrument, which the ancients called "Urim and Thummim," which consisted of two transparent stones set in the rim of a bow fastened to a breast plate. Through the medium of the Urim and Thummim I translated the record by the gift and power of God.

In this important and interesting book the history of ancient America is unfolded, from its first settlement by a colony that came from the Tower of Babel, at the confusion of languages to the beginning of the fifth century of the Christian Era. We are informed by these records that America in ancient times has been inhabited by two distinct races of people. The first were called Jaredites, and came directly from the Tower of Babel. The second race came directly from the city of Jerusalem, about six hundred years before Christ. They were principally Israelites, of the descendants of Joseph. The Jaredites were destroyed about the time that the Israelites came from Jesusalem, who succeeded them in the inheritance of the country. The principal nation of the second race fell in battle towards the close of the fourth century. The remnant are the Indians that now inhabit this country. This book also tells us that our Savior made His appearance upon this continent after His resurrection; that He planted the Gospel here in all its fulness, and richness, and power, and blessing; that they had Apostles, Prophets, Pastors, Teachers, and Evangelists; the same order, the same priesthood, the same ordinances, gifts, powers, and blessings, as were enjoyed on the eastern continent, that the people were cut off in consequence of their transgressions, that the last of their prophets who existed among them was commanded to write an abridgment of their prophecies, history,&c, and to hide it up in the earth, and that it should come forth and be united with the Bible for the accomplishment of the purposes of God in the last days. For a more particular account I would refer to the Book of Mormon, which can be purchased at Nauvoo, or from any of our Traveling Elders.

As soon as the news of this discovery was made known, false reports, misrepresentation and slander flew, as on the wings of the wind, in every direction; the house was frequently beset by mobs and evil designing persons. Several times I was shot at, and very narrowly escaped, and every device was made use of to get the plates away from me; but the power and blessing of God attended me, and several began to believe my testimony.

On the 6th of April, 1830, the "Church of Jesus Christ of Latter-day Saints" was first organized in the town of Fayette, Seneca county, state of New York. Some few were called and ordained by the Spirit of revelation and prophecy, and began to preach as the Spirit gave them utterance, and though weak, yet were they strengthened by the power of God, and many were brought to repentance, were immersed in the water, and were filled with the Holy Ghost by the laying on of hands. They saw visions and prophesied, devils were cast out, and the sick healed by the laying on of hands. From that time the work rolled forth with astonishing rapidity, and churches were soon formed in the states of New York, Pennsylvania Ohio, Indiana, Illinois, and Missouri; in the last named state a considerable settlement was formed in Jackson county: numbers joined the Church and we were increasing rapidly; we made large purchases of land, our farms teemed with plenty, and peace and happiness were enjoyed in our domestic circle, and throughout our neighborhood; but as we could not associate with our neighbors (who were, many of them, of the basest of men, and had fled from the face of civilized society, to the frontier country to escape the hand of justice,) in their midnight revels, their Sabbath breaking, horse racing and gambling; they commenced at first to ridicule, then to persecute, and finally an organized mob assembled and burned our houses, tarred and feathered and whipped many of our brethren, and finally, contrary to law, justice and humanity, drove them from their habitations; who, houseless and homeless, had to wander on the bleak prairies till the children left the tracks of their blood on the prairie. This took place in the month of November, and they had no other covering but the canopy of heaven, in this inclement season of the year; this proceeding was winked at by the government, and although we had warantee deeds for our land, and had violated no law, we could obtain no redress.

There were many sick, who were thus inhumanly driven from their houses, and had to endure all this abuse and to seek homes where they could be found. The result was, that a great many of them being deprived of the comforts of life, and the necessary attendances, died; many children were left orphans, wives, widows and husbands, widowers; our farms were taken possession of by the mob, many thousands of cattle, sheep, horses and hogs were taken, and our household goods, store goods, and printing press and type were broken, taken, or otherwise destroyed.

Many of our brethren removed to Clay county, where they continued until 1836, three years; there was no violence offered, but there were threatenings of violence. But in the summer of 1836 these threatenings began to assume a more serious form, from threats, public meetings were called, resolutions were passed, vengeance and destruction were threatened, and affairs again assumed a fearful attitude, Jackson county was a sufficient precedent, and as the authorities in that county did not interfere they boasted that they would not in this; which on application to the authorities we found to be too true, and after much privation and loss of property, we were again driven from our homes.

We next settled in Caldwell and Daviess counties, where we made large and extensive settlements, thinking to free ourselves from the power of oppression, by settling in new counties, with very few inhabitants in them; but here we were not allowed to live in peace, but in 1838 we were again attacked by mobs, an exterminating order was issued by Governor Boggs, and under the sanction of law, an organized banditti ranged through the country, robbed us of our cattle, sheep, hogs, &c., many of our people were murdered in cold blood, the chastity of our women was violated, and we were forced to sign away our property at the point of the sword; and after enduring every indignity that could be heaped upon us by an inhuman, ungodly band of marauders, from twelve to fifteen thousand souls, men women, and children were driven from their own firesides, and from lands to which they had warantee deeds, houseless, friendless, and homeless (in the depths of winter) to wander as exiles on the earth, or to seek an asylum in a more genial clime, and among a less barbarous people. Many sickened and died in consequence of the cold and hardships they had to endure; many wives were left widows, and children, orphans, and destitute. It would take more time than is allotted me here to describe the injustice, the wrongs, the murders the bloodshed, the theft, misery and woe that have been caused by the barbarous, inhuman, and lawless proceedings of the state of Missouri.

In the situation before alluded to, we arrived in the state of Illinois in 1839, where we found a hospitable people and a friendly home: a people who were willing to be governed by the principles of law and humanity. We have commenced to build a city called "Nauvoo," in Hancock county. We number from six to eight thousand here, besides vast numbers in the county around, and in almost every county of the state. We have a city charter granted us, and charter for a Legion, the troops of which now number 1,500. We have also a charter for a University, for an Agricultural and Manufacturing Society, have our own laws and administrators, and possess all the privileges that other free and enlightened citizens enjoy.

Persecution has not stopped the progress of truth, but has only added fuel to the flame, it has spread with increasing rapidity. Proud of the cause which they have espoused, and conscious of our innocence, and of the truth of their system, amidst calumny and reproach, have the Elders of this Church gone forth, and planted the Gospel in almost every state in the Union; it has penetrated our cities, it has spread over our villages, and has caused thousands of our intelligent, noble, and patriotic citizens to obey its divine mandates, and be governed by its sacred truths. It has also spread into England, Ireland, Scotland, and Wales, where, in the year 1840, a few of our missionaries were sent, and over five thousand joined the Standard of Truth; there are numbers now joining in every land.

Our missionaries are going forth to different nations, and in Germany, Palestine, New Holland, Australia, the East Indies, and other places, the Standard of Truth has been erected; no unhallowed hand can stop the work from progressing; persecutions may rage, mobs may combine, armies may assemble, calumny may defame, but the truth of God will go forth boldly, nobly, and independent, till it has penetrated every continent, visited every clime, swept every country, and sounded in every ear, till the purposes of God shall be accomplished, and the Great Jehovah shall say the work is done.

We believe in God the eternal Father, and in His Son Jesus Christ, and in the Holy Ghost.

We believe that men will be punished for their own sins, and not for Adam's transgression.

We believe that through the atonement of Christ all mankind may be saved by obedience to the laws and ordinances of the Gospel.

We believe that the first principle and ordinances of the Gospel are: (1) Faith in the Lord Jesus Christ; (2) Repentance; (3) Baptism by immersion for the remission of sins; (4) Laying on of hands for the gift of the Holy Ghost.

We believe that a man must be called of God by prophecy and by the laying on hands, by those who are in authority, to preach the Gospel and administer in the ordinances thereof.

We believe in the same organization that existed in the primitive Church, viz: apostles, prophets, pastors, teachers, evangelists, etc.

We believe in the gift of tongues, prophecy, revelation, visions, healing, interpretation of tongues, etc.

We believe the Bible to be the word of God, as far as it is translated correctly; we also believe the Book of Mormon to be the word of God.

We believe all that God has revealed, all that He does now reveal, and we believe that He will yet reveal many great and important things pertaining to the kingdom of God.

We believe in the literal gathering of Israel and in the restoration of the Ten Tribes; that Zion will be built upon this [the American] continent; that Christ will reign personally upon the earth; and that the earth will be renewed and receive its paradisiacal glory.

We claim the privilege of worshiping Almighty God according to the dictates of our own conscience, and allow all men the same privilege, let them worship how, where, or what they may.

We believe in being subject to kings, presidents, rulers and magistrates, in obeying honoring, and sustaining the law.

We believe in being honest, true, chaste, benevolent, virtuous, and in doing good to *all men;* indeed we may say that we follow the admonition of Paul, "We believe all thing, we hope all things, we have endured many things, and hope to be able to endure all things. If there is anything virtuous, lovely, or of good report, or praiseworthy, we seek after these things.

Respectfully, &c.,

JOSEPH SMITH.

CHAPTER XXXII.

THE BENNETT-DYER CORRESPONDENCE—THE PROPHET'S DISCOURSE ON THE SUBJECT OF THE RESURRECTION, AND THE SALVATION OF CHILDREN—EPISTLE OF THE TWELVE TO THE SAINTS IN ENGLAND CONCERNING THEIR EMIGRATION TO AMERICA.

Wednesday, March 2.—I read the proof of the *Times and Seasons*, as editor for the first time, No. 9, Vol. III, in which is the commencement of the Book of Abraham;* paid taxes to Mr. Bagby, in the general business office, for county and state purposes, but refused to pay the taxes in the city and town of Commerce, as the demand was illegal, there being no such place known in law, the city and town of Commerce having been included in the city plat of Nauvoo, but continued by our enemies on the tax list for the purpose of getting more money from the Saints; I commenced a settlement with Gilbert Granger on the estate [Kirtland] of his father, Oliver Granger; and continued in my office till nine in the evening, having received a visit from General Dudley of Connecticut.

Tax Controversy.

Thursday, 3.—I attended council in the general business office (over the store) at nine o'clock a. m.

In the afternoon, continued the settlement with Gilbert Granger, but finally failed to effect anything, except to get Newel's note.† Granger refused to give up the papers to me, which he had received of his father, the same being Church property, although I presented him deeds, mort-

Attempted Settlement with Hilbert Granger.

* No. 9 of the *Times and Seasons* was evidently not published on time, since it is supposed to have been published on March the first, and here is an account of the proofs being read on the second of March.

† This refers doubtless to Bishop Newel K. Whitney.

gages and paper to the amount of some thousands against his father, more than he had against the Church.

I also wrote Hiram Barney, Esq., of New York, in reply to his letter of the 24th of January, offering him one hundred dollars per acre, for his twenty acres of land in this city, lying somewhere between the Hotchkiss purchase on the north, and Galland's purchase on the south, or to take an agency to sell the same.

Friday, 4.—At my office exhibiting the Book of Abraham in the original to Brother Reuben Hedlock, so that he might take the size of the several plates or cuts, and prepare the blocks for the *Times and Seasons;* and also gave instruction concerning the arrangement of the writing on the large cut,* illustrating the principles of astronomy, with other general business.

Book of Abraham Fac-similes.

Attended city council, and moved "that when property is sold at sheriff's, marshal's or constable's sale under ordinance of this city, the persons having their property sold shall have the privilege of redeeming the same, by paying the principal and fifteen per cent on principal, with cost and charges, within thirty days after sale."

Saturday, 5.—Attended the city council, and spoke at considerable length on the powers and privileges of our city charter; among other business of importance, the office of registrar of deeds was established in the city of Nauvoo, and I was chosen registrar by the city council.

Sunday, 6.—I preached at Elder Orson Spencer's near the Temple.

Monday, 7.—At the general business office. Peter Melling, the Patriarch from England, brought to the office cash $13.47½, and clothing $65 from Parley P. Pratt and Amos Fielding, of England; I transacted much general business and wrote the mayor as follows:

* This refers to Fac-simile No. 2, p. 521, which was published in the *Times and Seasons* in double page size.

Letter of the Prophet to John C. Bennett—on Bennett's Correspondence Anent Slavery.

EDITOR'S OFFICE, NAUVOO, ILLINOIS, March 7, 1842.

General Bennett:

RESPECTED BROTHER:—I have just been perusing your correspondence with Doctor Dyer, on the subject of American slavery, and the students of the Quincy Mission Institute, and it makes my blood boil within me to reflect upon the injustice, cruelty, and oppression of the rulers of the people. When will these things cease to be, and the Constitution and the laws again bear rule? I fear for my beloved country —mob violence, injustice and cruelty appear to be the darling attributes of Missouri, and no man taketh it to heart! *O tempora! O mores!* What think you should be done?

Your friend,

JOSEPH SMITH.

*Correspondence between Dr. C. V. Dyer and General J. C. Bennett.**

CHICAGO, January 3, 1842.

DEAR SIR:—I am not sure that I am not indebted to you for your last letter, not having answered it, as I remember. But as I have been very sick during the long interval of my silence, you will readily excuse any apparent neglect on my part. I thank you for your paper sent me, the *Times and Seasons*, and have got much information from it, and since that, from other sources, in relation to the outrages committed upon the Latter-day Saints by the authorities as well as the people of the state of Missouri; and my blood boiled with indignation to see the whole Christian world—and the whole political world, too, look tamely on, and never raise a warning voice— a voice of expostulation, nor even giving the facts in the case! O what outrages will not be allowed or winked at by those in authority, and the people generally, if they happen to be inflicted upon those who bear an

* The correspondence between Dr. Dyer, Chicago, and Dr. John C. Bennett, referred to in the Prophet's letter above, is thought to be of sufficient importance to be inserted in the body of the History, though heretofore, when the history of the Prophet has been published, it has been omitted. The case of the three men from the Quincy Mission Institute being imprisoned for twelve years in the Missouri penitentiary "for no crime at all, or only as such as God would regard as a virtue" —"for barely teaching a fellow being," as Dr. Dyer naively put it, "how to go to a place where he may learn the sciences, have his own wages, aye, and his own person. This case was one in which the three men had violated some local law of the state of Missouri against encouraging slaves to leave their masters for the purpose of going into free states as the national fugitive slave law was not then in existence, and was not enacted until 1850.

unpopular name, espouse an unpopular cause, and are poor and obscure! It seems as if we had again fallen upon the middle ages, when the privileged classes could pour out their sympathies by the hour, and the very circumstantial and minute details of the loss of the life, or any other serious evil that befel one of their own number; but they could write [of] or hear without emotion, and even with satisfaction and joy, the history of the massacre of a thousand defenseless women and children, if they belonged to the common sort of people. Just read, for example, Madame de Sevigne's account in a letter to her daughter, dated "Aux Rochers," 30 Oct., 1675, in the second volume of De Toquerville's Democracy in America. What, my dear sir, do you think of the treatment which the subject of American slavery receives at the hands of the American press—amongst the people generally, and especially in the halls of Congress? What think you of the sentencing of three men from the Quincy Mission Institute in this state, a short time since, to twelve years confinement in the penitentiary of Missouri, for no crime at all, or only such as God would regard as a virtue? Please look into this matter, and see if you cannot join with the benevolent and fearless, and call the attention of the nation or the state, to these outrages of Missouri, I send you a paper, and mark one of the pieces for your perusal. Read it. I do not know whether you have examined the whole subject of American slavery; but if you have not, I beseech you to do so, and let me hear from you. Is it not sin? Yes. Then is it not right to repent of it? Yes. When? God allows not a moment. Is not repentance and abandonment of sin safe, so long as God commands, and stands ready to look after the consequences? Certainly so. Well, can any court, either state or national, rob me of liberty for twelve years (even against their own state laws),for acting precisely in accordance with the letter and spirit of the Constitution of the United States, and the precepts of Jesus Christ? Is it to be submitted to tamely, that three men shall be immured in a dungeon for twelve years, torn from their families and friends, and from society and usefulness, for barely teaching a fellow being how to go to a place where he may learn the sciences—have his own wages, aye, and his own person? Let me hear from you. Have we not a right to sympathize with each other?

I am, very sincerely, your friend and obedient servant,

CHARLES V. DYER.

Gen. John C. Bennett.

Nauvoo, Hancock county, Illinois.

NAUVOO, ILL., January 20th, A. D. 1842.

DEAR SIR:—Yours of the 3rd inst., accompanied by the *Genius of Liberty*, containing the address of Alvin Stewart, Esq., is before me, and I seize upon this, the first, opportunity to reply. You refer me to Madame de Sevigne's letter to her daughter, dated "Aux Rochers," 30th Oct., A. D. 1675, in the second volume of De Toquerville's Democracy in America; and ask me to examine the subject of American slavery. I have done so: I gave it a full and fair investigation years ago—I swore in my youth that my hands should never be bound nor my feet fettered, nor my tongue palsied—I am the friend of liberty, "Universal liberty," both civil and religious. I ever detested servile bondage. I wish to see the shackles fall from the feet of the oppressed, and the chains of slavery broken. I hate the oppressor's grasp, and the tyrant's rod; against them I set my brows like brass, and my face like steel; and my arm is nerved for the conflict. Let the sons of thunder speak, achieve victories before the cannon's mouth, and beard the lion in his den; till then the cry of the oppressed will not be heard; till then the wicked will not cease to trouble, nor the weary bondman be at rest. Great God, has it come to this—that the free citizens of the sovereign state of Illinois can be taken and immured within the walls of a Missouri penitentiary for twelve long years, for such a crime as God would regard as a virtue! simply for pointing bondsmen to a state of liberty and law! and no man take it to heart? Never, no never, no never! Let the friends of freedom arise and utter their voice, like the voice of ten thousand thunders—let them take every constitutional means to procure a redress of grievances—let there be a concerted effort, and the victory is ours. Let the broad banners of freedom be unfurled, and soon the prison doors will be opened, the captive set at liberty, and the oppressed go free. Missouri will then remember the unoffending Mormons in the days of their captivity and bondage—when murder and rapine were her darling attribute,—why, my heart is filled with indignation, and my blood boils within me, when I contemplate the vast injustice and cruelty which Missouri has meted out to that great philanthropist and devout Christian, General Joseph Smith, and his honest and faithful adherents—the Latter-day Saints, or Mormons; but the time has passed, and God will avenge their wrongs in His own good time. Dr. Dyer, put your hand upon your heart, and remember Zion. Just investigate the wrongs which our people have suffered in their unprecedented privations, the confiscation of their property, and the murder of their friends—the persecutions of the Waldenses in former ages were not to be compared to it, and history affords not a parallel. Now let us make a strong, concerted, and vigorous effort, for Universal Liberty, to every soul of man—civil, religious and political. With high considerations of respect and esteem, suffer me to subscribe myself,

Yours respectfully,

Charles V. Dyer, M. D. JOHN C. BENNETT.

P. S. Gen. Smith informs me that there are white slaves in Missouri* (Mormons) in as abject servitude as the blacks, and we have, as yet, no means of redress! God grant that the day of righteous retribution may not be procrastinated.

J. C. B.

Letter of John C. Bennett to Joseph Smith—Anent the Dyer-Bennett Correspondence.†

MAYOR'S OFFICE, CITY OF NAUVOO, ILLINOIS,
March 8, A. D., 1842.

Esteemed Friend:

Yours of the 7th inst. has been received, and I proceed to reply, without undue emotion or perturbation. You ask, "When will these things cease to be, and the Constitution and the laws again bear rule?" I reply—once that noble bird of Jove, our grand national emblem, soared aloft, bearing in her proud beak the words "Liberty and Law," and that man that had the temerity to ruffle her feathers, was made to feel the power of her talons; but a wily archer came, and with his venomed arrow dipped in Upas' richest sap, shot the flowing label from the eagle's bill—it fell inverted, and the bird was sick, and is—the label soon was trampled in the dust—the eagle bound and caged. The picture is now before you in bold relief. What think you should be done? The master spirits of the age must rise and break the cage, restore the label, unbind the bird, and let her tower unfettered in the air—then will the nation have repose, and the present minions of power hide their faces in the dust. Many of Missouri's noble sons detest her acts of cruelty and crime, and gladly would they wipe them from the escutcheon of her fame, and will; yes they will lend a helping hand—and all must help, for the time is at hand—and if man, rebellious, cowardly, faltering man, will not do the work, the thunderings of Sinai will wind up the scene—the blood of the murdered Mormons cries aloud for help, and the restoration of the inheritances of the Saints; and God has

* The "slaves" here referred to are explained in an editorial note in the *Times and Seasons* in which the above correspondence appears (Vol. III, No. 10) to mean children of Mormon parentage still in Missouri—"the children of murdered parents; others of Mormon parents now in this city"—Nauvoo. The charge of their being "slaves" is far-fetched and was made only because of the severe stress of feeling experienced by the Saints when contemplating things that related to Missouri, and some allowance must be made for the bombast, bragadocio and hypocrisy of John C. Bennett.

† Because of its bearing upon the character of John C. Bennett, as also to complete this Dyer-Bennett correspondence, the letter of John C. Bennett to the Prophet in answer to the note of the latter, introducing this whole correspondence, the following communication is inserted.

heard the cry—and the moral battle must be fought, and the victory won, he who answers by fire will cause sword and flame to do their office, and again make the Constitution and the laws paramount to every other consideration—and I swear by the Lord God of Israel, that the sword shall not depart from my thigh, nor the buckler from my arm, until the trust is consummated, and the hydra-headed, fiery dragon slain. This done the proud southron will no longer boast of ill-gotten gain, or wash his hands in the blood of the innocent, or immure the freemen of the prairie State within Missouri's sullied, poisoned, deathly prison walls. Let us always take refuge under the broad folds of the Constitution and the laws, and fear no danger, for the day of vengeance will assuredly come when the Omnipotent hand of the Great God will effect the restitution of the trophies of the brigand victories of Missouri, and again place the Saints on high.

Yours respectfully,
JOHN C. BENNETT.

General Joseph Smith.

Tuesday, 8.—Recommenced translating from the Records of Abraham for the tenth number of the *Times and Seasons*, and was engaged at my office day and evening.

Wednesday, 9.—Examining copy for the *Times and Seasons*, presented by Messrs. Taylor and Bennett, and a variety of other business in my office, in the morning; in the afternoon continued the translation of the Book of Abraham, called at Bishop Knight's and Mr. Davis', with the recorder, and continued translating and revising, and reading letters in the evening, Sister Emma being present in the office.

I also wrote Edward Hunter, as follows—

Letter of the Prophet to Edward Hunter—Business Transactions.

DEAR SIR:—I yesterday had the pleasure of receiving your letter of February 10. Am much pleased that you have effected a sale, and are so soon to be with us, &c.

I have purchased the lands you desired, and will use my influence to have the improvements made which you wish. Brother Weiler received your letter and says he will do what he can to have all done.

The eight hundred dollars for the Temple and Nauvoo House, I wish you to bring in goods, for which I will give you stock and credit as soon as received.

I wish you to invest as much money as you possibly can in goods, to bring here, and I will purchase them of you when you come, if we can agree on terms; or you can have my new brick store to rent. I wish the business kept up by some one in the building, as it is a very fine house, and cost me a handsome amount to build it. Some eight or ten thousand dollars worth of goods would be an advantage to this place; therefore, if you or some of the brethren, would bring them on, I have no doubt but that I can arrange for them in some way to your or their advantage.

As to money matters here, the State Bank is down, and we cannot tell you what bank would be safe a month hence. I would say that gold and silver is the only safe money a man can keep these times, you can sell specie here for more premium than you have to give; therefore there would be no loss and it would be safe. The bank you deposit in might fail before you had time to draw out again.

I am now very busily engaged in translating, and therefore cannot give as much time to public matters as I could wish, but will nevertheless do what I can to forward your affairs. I will send you a memorandum of such goods as will suit this market.

Yours affectionately,

JOSEPH SMITH.

Thursday, *10*.—Gave instructions concerning a deed to Stephen Markham, Shadrack Roundy, and Hiram Clark, and letter of attorney from Miss Smith to Edward Hunter, and did a great variety of business; rode out; and in the evening attended trial at Brother Hyrum's office, the City of Nauvoo *versus* Amos Davis, for indecent and abusive language about me while at Mr. Davis' the day previous. The charges were clearly substantiated by the testimony of Dr. Foster, Mr. and Mrs.. Hibbard, and others. Mr. Davis was found guilty by the jury, and by the municipal court, bound over to keep the peace six months, under $100 bond; after which I retired to the printing office with Emma, and supped with the Twelve and their wives, who were spending the evening with Sister Hyde.

Friday, *11*.

Extract from the Legion Minutes.

The Nauvoo Legion was on parade, commanded by Lieutenant-General Joseph Smith in person. Several of the Twelve Apostles rode in the general staff as Chaplains. The line was formed at ten o'clock, a. m., and soon the Legion marched from their usual place of parade, below the Temple, to Water-street, in front of General Smith's house, where the troops were inspected, and after a recess marched west on the bank of the river, and taking a circuitous route, resumed their usual post on the parade ground, and closed the day in good order and with good feelings, and to the full satisfaction of the Commander-in-Chief.

Extract of High Council Minutes.

In the evening President Smith attended the trial of Elder Francis Gladden Bishop, at his (the president's) house. Elder Bishop appeared before the High Council of Nauvoo on complaint of having received, written, and published or taught certain "revelations" and doctrines not consistent with the Doctrine and Covenants of the Church. Mr. Bishop refusing to present the written "revelation" the Mayor, (John C. Bennett) issued his warrant and brought them before the council, when parts of the same were read by Mr. Bishop himself to council, the whole mass of which appeared to be the extreme of folly, nonsense, absurdity, falsehood and bombastic egotism—so much so as to keep the Saints laughing, when not overcome by sorrow and shame. President Joseph explained the nature of the case and gave a very clear elucidation of the tendency of such prophets and prophesyings, and gave Mr. Bishop over to the buffetings of Satan until he shall learn wisdom. After a few appropriate observations from Patriarch Hyrum and some of the council, the council voted unanimously that Francis Gladden Bishop be removed from the fellowship of the Church; President Joseph having previously committed the "revelation" above referred to, to the flames.

Saturday, 12.—I presided over a court-martial of the officers of the Nauvoo Legion at my own house, for the purpose of deciding upon the rank and station of the several officers, and the more perfect organization of the Legion.

Sunday, 13.—I was with my family.

Monday, 14.—Transacted a great variety of business at the office.

Tuesday, 15.—I officiated as grand chaplain at the installation of the Nauvoo Lodge of Free Masons, at the Grove near the Temple. Grand Master Jonas, of Columbus, being present, a large number of people assembled on the occasion. The day was exceedingly fine; all things were done in order, and universal satisfaction was manifested. In the evening I received the first degree in Free Masonry in the Nauvoo Lodge, assembled in my general business office.

Some time previous to this [March 15th] Sister Elizabeth Morgan died at London without medical aid, after calling for the Elders, &c., which created much excitement, and a coroner's inquest was called by Mr. Baker, who brought in a verdict of "natural death."

The Prophet Becomes Editor of the Times and Seasons.

This paper commences my editorial career; I alone stand responsible for it, and shall do for all papers [i.e. Nos. of the *Times and Seasons*,] having my signature henceforward. I am not responsible for the publication or arrangement of the former paper; the matter did not come under my supervision.

JOSEPH SMITH.

We extract the following from the New York *Tribune:*

Honor Among Thieves.

"The paymaster of the Missouri Militia, called out to put down the Mormons some two years since, was supplied with money some time since, and started for Western Missouri, but has not yet arrived there. It is feared he has taken the Saline slope."

We are not surprised that persons who could wantonly, barbarously, and without shadow of law, drive fifteen thousand men, women and children from their homes, should have among them a man who was so lost to every sense of justice, as to run away with the wages for this infamous deed; it is not very difficult for men who can blow out the brains of children; who can shoot down and hew to pieces our ancient veterans who fought in defense of our country, and delivered it from the oppressor's grasp; who could deliberately and in cold blood, murder men and rob them of their boots, watches, &c., and whilst their victims were yet weltering in their blood, and grappling with death, proceed to rob the widows' houses. Men who can deliberately do this, and steal nearly all the horses, cattle, sheep, hogs, and property of a whole community, and drive them from their homes *en masse*, in an inclement season of the year, will not find many qualms of conscience in stealing the pay of his brother thieves, and taking the "Saline slope." The very idea of Government paying these men for their bloody deeds, must cause the sons of liberty to blush, and to hang their harps upon the willow, and make the blood of every patriot run chill.

The proceedings of that state have been so barbarous and inhuman that our indignation is aroused when we reflect upon the scene. We are here reminded of one of the patriotic deeds of the government of that state, who after they had robbed us of everything we had in the world, and taken from us many hundred thousand dollars' worth of property, had their sympathies so far touched (*alias* their good name) that they voted two thousand dollars to the relief of the "*suffering Mormons*," and choosing two or three of her noblest sons, to carry their heavenly boon, these angels of salvation came in the plentitude of their mercy and in the dignity of their office to Far West. To do what? To feed its hungry and clothe its naked with the $2,000? Verily nay! but to go into Daviess county and steal the Mormons' hogs (which they were prohibited themselves from obtaining under penalty of death) to distribute among the destitute, and to sell where they could obtain the money. These hogs thus obtained were shot down in their blood and not otherwise bled; they were filthy to a degree. These, the Mormons' own hogs, and a few goods, the sweepings of an old store in Liberty, were what these patriotic and noble-minded men gave to the "poor Mormons," and then circulated to the world how sympathetic, benevolent, kind and merciful the Legislature of the State of Missouri was, in giving two thousand dollars to the "suffering Mormons." Surely "the tender mercies of the wicked are cruel."

Wednesday, March 16.—I was with the Masonic Lodge and rose to the sublime degree.

Thursday, 17.—The High Council withdrew the hand of fellowship from Elder Oliver Olney for setting himself up as a prophet, and took his license.

I assisted in commencing the organization of "The Female Relief Society of Nauvoo" in the Lodge Room.

Origin of the Female Relief Society.

Sister Emma Smith, President, and Sister Elizabeth Ann Whitney and Sarah M. Cleveland, Counselors. I gave much instruction, read in the New Testament, and Book of Doctrine and Covenants, concerning the Elect Lady, and showed that the elect meant to be elected to a certain work, &c., and that the revelation was then fulfilled by Sister Emma's election to the Presidency of the Society, she having previously been ordained to expound the Scriptures. Emma was blessed, and her counselors were ordained by Elder John Taylor.

Friday, 18 and Saturday 19.—At home and at my office engaged in business, temporal and spiritual.

Sunday, 20.—I preached to a large assembly in the grove, near the Temple on the west. The body of a deceased child of Mr. Windsor P. Lyon being before the assembly, changed my design in the order of my remarks.

[The following is a brief synopsis of the Prophet's remarks, by Elder Wilford Woodruff:]

The Prophet's Sermon on Life and Death; the Resurrection and the Salvation of Children.

President Smith read the 14th chapter of Revelation, and said—We have again the warning voice sounded in our midst, which shows the uncertainty of human life; and in my leisure moments I have meditated upon the subject, and asked the question, why it is that infants, innocent children, are taken away from us, especially those that seem to be the most intelligent and interesting. The strongest reasons that present themselves to my mind are these: This world is a very wicked world; and it is a proverb that the "world grows weaker and wiser;" if that is the case, the world grows more wicked and corrupt. In the earlier ages of the world a righteous man,and a man of God and of intelligence, had a better chance to do good, to be believed and received than at the present day: but in these days such a man is much opposed and persecuted by most of the inhabitants of the earth, and he has much sorrow to pass through here. The Lord takes many away, even in infancy, that they may escape the envy of man, and the sorrows and evils of this present world; they were too pure, too lovely, to live on earth; therefore, if rightly considered, instead of mourning we have reason to rejoice as they are delivered from evil, and we shall soon have them again.

What chance is there for infidelity when we are parting with our friends almost daily? None at all. The infidel will grasp at every straw for help until death stares him in the face, and then his infidelity takes its flight, for the realities of the eternal world are resting upon him in mighty power; and when every earthly support and prop fails him, he then sensibly feels the eternal truths of the immortality of the soul. We should take warning and not wait for the death-bed to repent, as we see the infant taken away by death, so may the youth and middle aged, as well as the infant be suddenly called into eternity. Let this, then, prove as a warning to all not to procrastinate repentance, or wait till a death-bed, for it is the will of God that man should repent and serve Him in health, and in the strength and power of his mind, in order to secure His blessing, and not wait until he is called to die.

The doctrine of baptizing children, or sprinkling them, or they must welter in hell, is a doctrine not true, not supported in Holy Writ, and is not consistent with the character of God. All children are redeemed by the blood of Jesus Christ,and the moment that children leave this world, they are taken to the bosom of Abraham. The only difference between the old and young dying is, one lives longer in heaven and eternal light and glory than the other, and is freed a little sooner from this miserable, wicked world. Notwithstanding all this glory, we for a moment lose sight of it, and mourn the loss, but we do not mourn as those without hope.

My intention was to have spoken on the subject of baptism, but having a case of death before us, I thought proper to refer to that subject. I will now, however say a few words upon baptism, as I intended.

God has made certain decrees which are fixed and immovable; for instance,—God set the sun, the moon, and the stars in the heavens, and gave them their laws, conditions and bounds, which they cannot pass, except by His commandments; they all move in perfect harmony in their sphere and order, and are as lights, wonders and signs unto us. The sea also has its bounds which it cannot pass. God has set many signs on the earth, as well as in the heavens; for instance, the oak of the forest, the fruit of the tree, the herb of the field—all bear a sign that seed hath been planted there; for it is a decree of the Lord that every tree, plant, and herb bearing seed should bring forth of its kind, and cannot come forth after any other law or principle. Upon the same principle do I contend that baptism is a sign ordained of God, for the believer in Christ to take upon himself in order to enter into the kingdom of God, "for except ye are born of water and of the Spirit ye cannot enter into the kingdom of God," said the Savior. It is a sign and a commandment which God has set for man to enter into His kingdom. Those who seek to enter in any other way will seek in vain; for God will not receive them,neither will the angels acknowledge their works as accepted, for they have not obeyed the ordinances,nor attended to the signs which God ordained for the salvation of man,to prepare him for, and give him a title to, a celestial glory; and God had decreed that all who will not obey His voice shall not escape the damnation of hell. What is the damnation of hell? To go with that society who have not obeyed His commands.

Baptism is a sign to God, to angels, and to heaven that we do the will of God, and there is no other way beneath the heavens whereby God hath ordained for man to come to Him to be saved, and enter into the kingdom of God, except faith in Jesus Christ, repentance, and baptism for the remission of sins, and any other course is in vain; then you have the promise of the gift of the Holy Ghost.

What is the sign of the healing of the sick? The laying on of hands is the sign or way marked out by James, and the custom of the ancient Saints as ordered by the Lord, and we cannot obtain the blessing by pursuing any other course except the way marked out by the Lord. What if we should attempt to get the gift of the Holy Ghost through any other means except the signs or way which God hath appointed—would we obtain it? Certainly not; all other means would fail. The Lord says do so and so, and I will bless you.

There are certain key words and signs belonging to the Priesthood which must be observed in order to obtain the blessing. The sign of Peter was to repent and be baptized for the remission of sins, with the promise of the gift of the Holy Ghost; and in no other way is the gift of the Holy Ghost obtained.

There is a difference between the Holy Ghost and the gift of the Holy Ghost. Cornelius received the Holy Ghost before he was baptized, which was the convincing power of God unto him of the truth of the Gospel, but he could not receive the gift of the Holy Ghost until after he was baptized. Had he not taken this sign or ordinance upon him, the Holy Ghost which convinced him of the truth of God, would have left him. Until he obeyed these ordinances and received the gift of the Holy Ghost, by the laying on of hands, according to the order of God, he could not have healed the sick or commanded an evil spirit to come out of a man, and it obey him; for the spirits might say unto him, as they did to the sons of Sceva: "Paul we know and Jesus we know, but who are ye?" It mattereth not whether we live long or short on the earth after we come to a knowledge of these principles and obey them unto the end. I know that all men will be damned if they do not come in the way which He hath opened, and this is the way marked out by the word of the Lord.

As concerning the resurrection, I will merely say that all men will come from the grave as they lie down, whether old or young; there will not be "added unto their stature one cubit," neither taken from it; all will be raised by the power of God, having spirit in their bodies, and not blood. Children will be enthroned in the presence of God and the

Lamb with bodies of the same stature* that they had on earth, having been redeemed by the blood of the Lamb; they will there enjoy the fullness of that light, glory and intelligence, which is prepared in the celestial kingdom. "Blessed are the dead who die in the Lord, for they rest from their labors and their works do follow them."

The speaker, before closing, called upon the assembly before him to humble themselves in faith before God, and in mighty prayer and fast-

* It must be remembered that the above report of the Prophet's remarks, as also the report of the King Follett sermon (preached in April, 1844, and which will appear in Volume V of this history), where the same matter of infants being enthroned in power while remaining of the same stature as when on earth, and at the time of their death, is mentioned—were reported in long hand and from memory, so that they are very likely to contain inaccuracies and convey wrong impressions. This matter of children after the resurrection remaining of the same stature as at their death is well known to be such an error. The writer of this note distinctly remembers to have heard the late President Wilford Woodruff, who reported the above sermon, say, that the Prophet corrected the impression that had been made by his King Follett sermon, that children and infants would remain fixed in the stature of their infancy and childhood in and after the resurrection. President Woodruff very emphatically said on the occasion of the subject being agitated about 1888-9, that the prophet taught subsequently to his King Follett sermon that children while resurrected in the stature at which they died would develope to the full stature of men and women after the resurrection; and that the contrary impression created by the report of the Prophet's King Follett sermon was due to a misunderstanding of his remarks and erroneous reporting. In addition to this personal recollection of the writer as to the testimony of the late President Wilford Woodruff, the following testimony of Elder Joseph Horne and his wife, M. Isabella Horne, on the same subject is important. The statements here copied were delivered in the presence of President Angus M. Cannon, of the Salt Lake Stake of Zion, and Elder Arthur Winter, at the residence of Brother Horne, in Salt Lake City, on November 19, 1896, and were reported stenographically by Arthur Winter, the Church official reporter.

Sister M. Isabella Horne said:

"In conversation with the Prophet Joseph Smith once in Nauvoo, the subject of children in the resurrection was broached. I believe it was in Sister Leonora Cannon Taylor's house. She had just lost one of her children, and I had also lost one previously. The Prophet wanted to comfort us, and he told us that we should receive those children in the morning of the resurrection just as we laid them down, in purity and innocence, and we should nourish and care for them as their mothers. He said that children would be raised in the resurrection just as they were laid down, and that they would obtain all the intelligence necessary to occupy thrones, principalities and powers. The idea that I got from what he said was that the children would grow and develop in the Millennium, and that the mothers would have the pleasure of training and caring for them, which they had been deprived of in this life.

"This was sometime after the King Follett funeral, at which I was present."

Brother Joseph Horne said:

"I heard the Prophet Joseph Smith say that mothers should receive their children just as they laid them down, and that they would have the privilege of doing for them what they could not do here, the Prophet remarked: "How would you know them if you did not receive them as you laid them down?" I also got the idea that

ing to call upon the name of the Lord, until the elements were purified over our heads, and the earth sanctified under our feet, that the inhabitants of this city may escape the power of disease and pestilence, and the destroyer that rideth upon the face of the earth, and that the Holy Spirit of God may rest upon this vast multitude.

At the close of the meeting, President Smith said he should attend to the ordinance of baptism in the river, near his house, at two o'clock, and at the appointed hour, the bank of the Mississippi was lined with a multitude of people, and President Joseph Smith went into the river and baptized eighty persons for the remission of their sins, and what added joy to the scene was, that the first person baptized was M. L. D. Wasson, a nephew of Mrs. Emma Smith—the first of her kindred that has embraced the fullness of the Gospel.

At the close of this interesting scene, the administrator lifted up his hands towards heaven, and implored the blessing of God to rest upon the people; and truly the Spirit of God did rest upon the multitude, to the joy and consolation of our hearts.

After baptism, the congregation again repaired to the grove, near the Temple, to attend to the ordinance of confirmation, and, notwithstanding President Smith had spoken in the open air to the people, and stood in the water and baptized about eighty persons, about fifty of those baptized received their confirmation under his hands in the after part of the day.

While this was progressing, great numbers were being baptized in the font.

children would grow and develop after the resurrection,and that the mothers would care for them and train them."

We hereby certify that the foregoing is a full, true and correct account of the statements made by Joseph and M. Isabella Horne on the subject mentioned.

Angus M. Cannon.
Arthur Winter.

We have read the foregoing, and certify that it is correct.

Joseph Horne.
M. Isabella Horne.

In the Improvement Era for June, 1904, President Joseph F. Smith in an editorial on the Resurrection said:

"The body will come forth as it is laid to rest, for there is no growth or development in the grave. As it is laid down, so will it arise, and changes to perfection will come by the law of restitution. But the spirit will continue to expand and develop, and the body, after the resurrection will develop to the full stature of man."

This may be accepted as the doctrine of the Church in respect to the resurrection of children and their future development to the full stature of men and women; and it is alike conformable to that which will be regarded as both reasonable and desirable.

After this, I baptized a large number in the font myself.

An Epistle of the Twelve to the Church of Jesus Christ of Latter-day Saints in its Various Branches and Conferences in Europe. Greeting:

BELOVED BRETHREN.—We feel it our privilege and a duty we owe to the great and glorious cause in which we have enlisted, to communicate to you at this time, some principles which if carried into effect, will facilitate the gathering of the Saints, and tend to ameliorate the condition of those who are struggling with poverty and distress, in this day when the usual means of support seem to be cut short to the laboring classes, through the depression that everywhere prevails in the general business mart of the civilized world. Our situation is such in these last days, and our salvation spiritually is so connected with our salvation temporally, that if one fail, the other necessarily must be seriously affected, if not wholly destroyed. God has made us social beings; He has endowed us with capacities for enjoying each other's society, and it is our duty to bring those powers and privileges into exercise, so far as we can, and for this it is our duty to strive by all lawful and expedient measures within our reach.

While we remain in this state of existence, we need food and raiment, habitations and society, and without these our enjoyments must be greatly limited, and the real object of our existence diminished, if not wholly destroyed. Though the Saints should possess all the common gifts of the Spirit of God, and yet remain destitute of those comforts so much needed for the sustenance of their bodies, they would be comparatively miserable; but when they arrive at that state of perfection, and are clothed upon with the more special gifts and power of increasing the widow's oil and meal, or if receiving their food from the ravens, like Elijah, they will not need to bestow so much attention on every trifle of the passing moments, as they now do; and until that period arrives they will recollect that to be in the exercise of the fullness of spiritual blessings they must be watchful and careful to provide things honest in the sight of all men for the sustenance and comfort of all these frail, perishable bodies. That we may be instruments in the hands of God of thus promoting your present and future temporal and spiritual welfare, we write you at the present time.

Many of you are desirous of emigrating to this country, and many have not the means to accomplish their wishes, and if we can assist you by our prayers and our counsels to accomplish the desires of your hearts in this thing, so far we will rejoice and be satisfied. You not only wish to emigrate to this section of the earth, but you desire also to have some laudable means of comfortable subsistence after you arrive here, and this also is important. How then, shall these things be accomplished and your souls be satisfied? We answer, by united understanding and concert of action.

You all, or most of you, have trades or different kinds of business, with which you have been long familiarized, and in which you would like to continue for the purpose of procuring a subsistence; and a great proportion of your occupation is such that no employment can be had in this city or vicinity; for instance: there are no cotton manufactories established here, and many of you know no other business. You want to come here, and when here, want to continue your labors in your accustomed branches of business; but you have no means to get here, and when here there are no factories, and yet factories are needed here, and there would be a ready market for all the fabrics which could be manufactured.

Now comes the concert of action; if the Church will arise unitedly; if the brethren will individually feel that the great work of the Lord is depending on themselves as instruments to assist in carrying it forward; and will unite all their means, faith and energy, in one grand mass, all that you desire can speedily be accomplished. A short time only will elapse before you yourselves will be astonished at the result, and you will feel that your desires are more than realized.

While the Saints are united, no power on the earth, or under the earth can prevail against them; but while each one acts for himself, many, very many, are in danger of being overthrown. God has promised all things to those who love Him and keep His commandments; then why be afraid that one should get a little more than another, or that one should gain, for a little moment, what another might lose; when Jesus has promised that the faithful shall be one with Him, as He is one with the Father, and shall possess all things in the due time of the Lord; not by stealth, not by force, not by the sword, but by the gift of the Father, through faithfulness to His commands; and the more they shall suffer, while they work in righteousness on the earth, the greater will be their reward, the more glorious their kingdom, the more extended their power, when they shall arrive in the celestial paradise.

Knowing and feeling these things as we do, and having respect unto the recompense of reward to be revealed hereafter, regardless of all necessary privation and labor to accomplish what our Master has given us to do, and desiring not to possess the kingdom alone, but that all the honest in heart should be united with us in the great and glorious work of building up Zion and her stakes, we will call upon you, dear brethren, to unite with us, all with one accord, to do what? To do the very things you desire should be done; to convey you to the place where you are, and then put you in possession of all the means you may need for your support; so that you may enjoy the fullness of the blessings belonging to the sons and daughters of Zion's King.

Had we means we would not ask your aid; we would gladly send the ships of Tarshish to bear you across the great waters, we would bring you to our homes, to our firesides; we would provide you habitations, lands and food, when you arrive among us. Our hearts are large enough to do all this, and a great deal more; but we have not the means; we have to labor for our own subsistence, as well as attend to those things which are laid upon us of the Lord, and which concern the whole Church as much as ourselves.

It is not the will of heaven that any one should be put in possession of all things without striving for them. Where much is given, much is required; and he who has but one talent, must be as diligent in the use thereof as he that has ten, or he will lose his talent and his blessing; and it becometh him who hath but one, five or ten, to use them in the most economical manner possible, or he will not have enough to bring him hither; and that he who hath five pounds may have enough and to spare to him who hath but one, or in other words to help the brethren to accomplish with a little what otherwise would require much more than they can command, is the object of this Epistle.

Had we the means we would send vessels of our own, laden with flour, meats, fruits, and all sea stores nesessary for the comfort of the brethren on the water, so that they would have nothing more to do than go on shipboard, and land at New Orleans; from thence we would take them on our steamers, and bring them to this place, for this is the best place for the Saints to stop at for the present.

There may be other places where individuals might have the prospect of adding at once, more rapidly to their pecuniary interest, than they could here; but we can only say, it is the will of the Lord that the Saints build Nauvoo, and settle therein or in the vicinity; and we know assuredly that those who give heed to every word that proceedeth out of the mouth of the Lord, will be richer eventually—and not far distant—than those who may seem to prosper more by following their own inclinations.

Brethren, we wish not to control you or your means; it is not for our peace or interest; nay, rather, it is a source of labor, trouble and anxiety to have ought to do with the pecuniary business of the Church, which we would gladly avoid, could we do it, and do our duty—could we do it, and the things desired be accomplished, and we stand guiltless where God hath placed us—and for this reason we desire to make such arrangements as will most tend to leave the business in your own hands, or in the hands of those whom you shall select; men of your own acquaintance, in whom you can repose confidence that they will execute their trust in righteousness. And that our plans may be understood by you, and carried into execution, we have sent unto you our beloved brother, Elder John Snyder, the bearer of this Epistle, and other Epistles also, previously written by us to you; and we beseech you, brethren, to receive him as a servant of the Most High, authorized according to the order of the kingdom of heaven, and assist him by all lawful means in your power,to execute the mission entrusted to him; for great events depend upon his success; but to none will they be greater than to yourselves.

Our authority for thus sending Brother Snyder to you, is found in the "Book of the Law of the Lord," page 36, as follows—

"Nauvoo, December 22, 1841. The word of the Lord came unto Joseph the Seer; verily thus saith the Lord—Let my servant John Snyder take a mission to the Eastern continent, unto all the conferences now sitting in that region, and let him carry a package of epistles that shall be written by my servants the Twelve, making known unto the Saints their duties concerning the building of my houses, which I have appointed unto you, saith the Lord, that they may bring their gold, and their silver, and their precious stones, and the box tree, and the fir tree, and all fine wood to beautify the place of my sanctuary, saith the Lord, and let him return speedily, with all means which shall be put into his hands: even so. Amen.

In this revelation, the brethren will discover their duty in relation to the building of the Temple of the Lord in Nauvoo, and the Nauvoo House; and we call upon them with united cry to give heed unto the things written, and help to build the houses which God has commanded, so that Brother Snyder may speedily return with means to strengthen the hands of the laborers, and adorn and beautify the Tabernacle of Jehovah.

Brethren, while you are thus preparing to send up your offerings to this place, if you will act in concert with our well beloved brother,Elder Parley P. Pratt, and the regularly constituted authorities of the Church in England; and collect as great an amount of cotton, linen, and woollen goods, silks, cutlery, and hardware, &c., even all the varieties of goods which might be useful in this country, and which can be obtained by the brethren in this time of monied scarcity, and forward the same to us by Brother Snyder, or your own agent, in company with him, or otherwise, and at other times, we will pay you for those goods, in lands, in or out of the city, in houses, cattle, and such kind of property as you may need; and with those goods we will purchase lands, &c., flour, meat, and all things necessary for a sea voyage, which can be had cheaper here than in England, and charter ships, and forward the same to England, or such places as emigration may require, and bring back in return a ship load of emigrants, at a cheaper rate than they can now emigrate; while, at the same time, those who remain can continue to collect and forward merchandize as before, which will give us the means of continuing our purchases here, of keeping ships passing and repassing, and of building manufacturing establishments ready for the brethren when they arrive in our midst.

While the great depression of the moneyed institutions continues as it now is, the people are compelled to resort to all laudable measures to effect those exchanges of property which are necessary to accomplish their designs in removing from one place to another, and from one kingdom to another; and by a faithful execution of the plans proposed above, much, very much, may be effected in emigration without the aid of cash, or with very little, at the most; and goods may be obtained to advantage for houses and lands which the brethren may have to dispose of, and in payment of debts due them, when it would be impossible for them to sell for cash at any price, or get their pay for debts due them even at a great discount, and thus thousands and tens of thousands may be made to rejoice in this land of plenty, while, were it not for a concert of action, they might remain where they are for years, or never have the opportunity of appearing among us on this side the great waters, until the morning of the first resurrection.

But, brethren, we want to see you here. We long to see all here who want to be here, and none others, for we desire the increase of those who love God and work righteousness, that Zion's cords may be lengthened, and her stakes strengthened; though the country is free to all who will abide her laws, and we have no disposition to cast out any from our midst who will submit thereto.

For many particulars in relation to the times and course of emigration, and many other important items connected with the general and particular interest of the Church, we would refer you to our former epistles, as to enter into a particular and minute detail of all items referred to in this epistle, would be impossible. Brother Snyder will enter into the subject more minutely, and with the assistance of the presidency among you, will unfold the same, so that no one need misunderstand.

The brethren need not suppose that this thing is of our own imagination, simply; or that the result thereof, if fully carried into execution, will be of doubtful character. We have been guided by the Spirit of the Lord in our deliberations concerning the matter; and have been instructed by the Prophet of the Most High, even Joseph, the Seer and Revelator, for the Church, whose instructions to us are as the voice of the Lord, and whose admonitions we ever regard as true and faithful, and worthy the confidence of all who profess the Gospel of Jesus Christ.

We have been with him in prosperity and adversity, in sickness and health, in public and private, in all situations where men may reasonably associate with each other, and know that his words are true, his teachings sacred, his character unsullied among men of truth, and that he is what the Church acknowledge him to be, a man of God, and the spokesman of the Most High unto His people; and we bear this testimony unto the world, calling on all the honest in heart to uphold him by their faith and prayers, that he may live long, enjoy much, and accomplish great things for the kingdom which he has been the honored instrument of establishing on the earth in these last days, even that he may lead a great multitude into the celestial kingdom.

That the Saints may enjoy the teachings of the Prophet; those teachings which can be had only at this place, so that they may go on from knowledge to knowledge even to perfection, they want to come up hither; and that the plans before suggested may by facilitated, let some individuals with capital come immediately and build factories—individuals who have the means, understand the business, and are capable of superintending the concerns thereof.

There is every natural advantage at this place for facilitating such an order of things; water, wood, and coal in abundance, and it only wants the hand of the laborer to bring them forth in form suited to their several uses; and, while the gold and the silver are secreted by the hands of unprincipled speculators, let us go forward and accomplish without gold or silver, that which might be more easily and expeditiously done with it.

Let the brethren ever remember the admonitions we have so often given, that Zion is not to be built up without labor, fatigue, and trial of the faith of many; that when John saw the great company on Mount Zion, he saw those who had come up through great tribulation; he also saw those who had endured great tribulation after they had arrived,and before the kingdom was completed.

The Saints of this day are of the number John saw, and those—and those only who are willing to endure tribulation, as good soldiers, without murmuring—will eventually find their names enrolled in the Lamb's Book of Life, and obtain an inheritance in the holy city.

To all those who are desirous of sharing in the poverty and sufferings incident to new countries and the children of the kingdom, we would say, come up hither, and help us to bear the burden, and you shall share the riches, glory and honors of the kingdom. And those who are not willing to suffer afflictions, losses, crosses, and disappointments with the people of God, may as well stay away and be destroyed, as to come here and perish, for perish they must who cannot abide a celestial law, and endure to the end in all meekness, patience, and faithfulness.

Inasmuch as Elder Levi Richards has asked for counsel, we would recommend him to return to Nauvoo, as soon as circumstances shall permit.

Praying that you may be blessed with wisdom, intelligence, and perseverance, in every good word and work, so that you may accomplish your desires, and help to roll on the great work in which you have enlisted, we subscribe ourselves your brethren and fellow laborers in the kingdom of patience. Amen.

BRIGHAM YOUNG, President.
HEBER C. KIMBALL,
WILLIAM SMITH,
ORSON PRATT,
JOHN E. PAGE,
LYMAN WIGHT,
WILFORD WOODRUFF,
JOHN TAYLOR,
GEO. A. SMITH,
WILLARD RICHARDS, Clerk.

City of Nauvoo, Hancock County, Illinois, March 20, 1842.

CHAPTER XXXIII.

A MASON'S ESTIMATE OF NAUVOO AND THE PROPHET—ORGANIZATION OF THE FEMALE RELIEF SOCIETY—"TRY THE SPIRITS"—THE PROPHET'S EDITORIAL.

Monday, March 21, 1842.—I commenced a settlement with William Marks, who had loaned money and property to the Church at various times.

Tuesday, 22.—I was at the general business office through the day, and at home in the evening.

The following is from the *Advocate*, printed at Columbus, the residence of Grand Master [i. e. grand master mason] Jonas:

NAUVOO AND THE MORMONS.

MR. EDITOR.—Having recently had occasion to visit the city of Nauvoo, I cannot permit the opportunity to pass without expressing the agreeable disappointment that awaited me there. I had supposed, from what I had previously heard, that I should witness an impoverished, ignorant and bigotted population, completely priest-ridden, and tyrannized over by Joseph Smith, the great prophet of these people.

On the contrary, to my surprise, I saw a people apparently happy, prosperous and intelligent. Every man appeared to be employed in some business or occupation. I saw no idleness, no intemperance, no noise, no riot—all appeared to be contented, with no desire to trouble themselves with anything except their own affairs. With the religion of these people I have nothing to do; if they can be satisfied with the doctrines of their new revelation, they have a right to be so. The Constitution of the country guarantees to them the right of worshiping God according to the dictates of their own conscience, and if that can be so easily satisfied, why should we who differ from them complain?

But I protest against the slanders and persecutions that are continually heaped upon these people. I could see no disposition on their part to be otherwise than a peaceable and law-abiding people, and all they ask of the country is to permit them to live under the protection of the laws, and to be made amenable for their violations. They may have among them bad and desperate characters, and what community has not? But I am satisfied the Mormon people, as a body, will never be the aggressors or violators of the law.

While at Nauvoo I had a fine opportunity of seeing the people in a body. There was a Masonic celebration, and the Grand Master of the state was present for the purpose of publicly installing the officers of a new lodge. An immense number of persons assembled on the occasion, variously estimated from five to ten thousand persons, and never in my life did I wittness a better-dressed or a more orderly and well-behaved assemblage: not a drunken or disorderly person to be seen, and the display of taste and beauty among the females could not well be surpassed anywhere.

During my stay of three days, I became well acquainted with their principal men, and more particularly with their Prophet, the celebrated "Old Joe Smith." I found them hospitable, polite, well-informed and liberal. With Joseph Smith, the hospitality of whose house I kindly received, I was well pleased; of course on the subject of religion, we widely differed, but he appeared to be quite as willing to permit me to enjoy my right of opinion, as I think we all ought to be to let the Mormons enjoy theirs; but instead of the ignorant and tyrannical upstart, judge my surprise at finding him a sensible, intelligent, companionable and gentlemanly man. In frequent conversations with him he gave me every information that I desired, and appeared to be only pleased at being able to do so. He appears to be much respected by all the people about him, and has their entire confidence. He is a fine looking man about thirty-six years of age, and has an interesting family.

The incorporated limits of Nauvoo contains, it is said, about seven thousand persons; the buildings are generally small and much scattered. The Temple and Nauvoo House, now building, will probably, in beauty of design, extent and durability, excel any public building in the state, and will both be enclosed before winter.

From all I saw and heard, I am led to believe that, before many years, the city of Nauvoo will be the largest and most beautiful city of the west, provided the Mormons are unmolested in the peaceable enjoyment of their rights and privileges, and why they should be troubled while acting as good citizens, I cannot imagine; and I hope and trust that the people of Illinois have no disposition to disturb unoffending people who have no disposition but to live peaceably under the laws of the country, and to worship God under their own vine and fig tree.—AN OBSERVER, Adams County.

Extract from a Letter from Elder E. P. Maginn, Salem, Massachusetts.

I am on a visit to assist Elder Erastus Snow in his successful and extended field of labor in this branch. Sixty-five have been obedient to the faith of the Gospel, and hundreds of others almost persuaded. In Boston near forty have obeyed through the faithful labors of Elder Freeman Nickerson. I have been absent from Peterborough two weeks; have preached three or four times in Boston, Salem, Marblehead, Chelsea, &c., and purpose returning to Peterborough next Sunday, where I have been laboring with good success, thirty-six have obeyed since last fall; at New Salem, Massachusetts, thirty-five to forty have obeyed since August last; Leverett, eighteen or twenty; Gilsum, New Hampshire, twenty to thirty. I have preached from one to three times every day, and cannot fill one in twenty of the calls for preaching; there is the greatest excitement in this country that I ever beheld during my travels since I left Nauvoo—a period of near three years, in which I have traveled through eighteen states and British provinces.

Wednesday, 23.—In council with Heber C. Kimball, Willard Richards and others at my office.

Thursday, 24.—I attended by request, the Female Relief Society, whose object is the relief of the poor, the destitute, the widow and the orphan, and for the exercise of all benevolent purposes. Its organization was completed this day. Mrs. Emma Smith takes the presidential chair; Mrs. Elizabeth Ann Whitney and Sarah M. Cleveland are her counselors; Miss Elvira Cole is treasurer, and our well-known and talented poetess, Miss Eliza R. Snow, secretary. There was a very numerous attendance at the organization of the society, and also at the subsequent meetings, of some of our most intelligent, humane, philanthropic and respectable ladies; and we are well assured from a knowledge of those pure principles of benevolence that flow spontaneously from their humane and philanthropic bosoms, that with the resources they will have at command, they will fly to the relief of the stranger; they will pour in oil and wine to the wounded heart of the distressed; they will dry up the tears of the orphan and make the widow's heart to rejoice.

Organization of the Relief Society.

Our women have always been signalized for their acts of benevolence and kindness; but the cruel usage that they received from the barbarians of Missouri, has hitherto prevented their extending the hand of charity in a conspicuous manner; yet in the midst of their persecution, when the bread has been torn from their helpless offspring by their cruel oppressors, they have always been ready to open their doors to the weary traveler, to divide their scant pittance with the hungry, and from their robbed and impoverished wardrobes, to divide with the more needy and destitute; and now that they are living upon a more genial soil, and among a less barbarous people, and possess facilities that they have not heretofore enjoyed, we feel convinced that with their concentrated efforts, the condition of the suffering poor, of the stranger and the fatherless will be ameliorated.

Character of the Mormon Women.

We had the privilege of being present at their organization, and were much pleased with their *modus operandi*, and the good order that prevailed. They are strictly parliamentary in their proceedings.

An earthquake at Falmouth this morning.

Friday, *25*.—Attending to a variety of business; counseling, &c.

Saturday, *26*.—Elder John Snyder received his final instructions from the President, and received his blessing from Elder Brigham Young, with the laying on of the hands of President Joseph Smith, John E. Page and Willard Richards, and started for England this day.

Mission of John Snyder.

Sunday, *27*.—After speaking to the Saints for some time on the subject of baptism for the dead, I baptized one hundred and seven individuals.

[The following brief extract is from Elder Woodruff's journal.]

Synopsis of the Prophet's Sermon on Baptism for the Dead.

This was an interesting day. A large assembly met in the grove near the Temple. Brother Amasa Lyman addressed the people in a very interesting manner. He was followed by Joseph, the Seer, who made some highly edifying and instructive remarks concerning baptism for the dead. He said the Bible supported the doctrine, quoting 1 Cor., xv: 29: "Else what shall they do which are baptized for the dead, if the dead rise not at all, why are they then baptized for the dead?" If there is one word of the Lord that supports the doctrine of baptism for the dead, it is enough to establish it as a true doctrine. Again; if we can, by the authority of the Priesthood of the Son of God, baptize a man in the name of the Father, of the Son, and of the Holy Ghost, for the remission of sins, it is just as much our privilege to act as an agent, and be baptized for the remission of sins for and in behalf of our dead kindred, who have not heard the Gospel, or the fullness of it.

After meeting closed, the congregation again assembled upon the banks of the river, and Joseph, the Seer, went into the river, and baptized all that came unto him.

I also witnessed the landing of 170 English brethren from the steamer *Ariel*, under the presidency of Elder Lyman Wight; also about $3,000 worth of goods for the Temple and Nauvoo House.

Monday, 28.—I was at the office. Received Parley P. Pratt's donations from England, and attended to a variety of business; as also on the 29th and 30th.

The following extract is from a letter received from Elder Lorenzo D. Barnes—

BRISTOL, March 28, 1842.

Letter of Lorenzo D. Barnes to Parley P. Pratt—Reporting Labors.

Elder Pratt.

MUCH ESTEEMED BROTHER:—I am happy to be able to state to you that I arrived here in safety and in health on Saturday, the 26th instant, after making a tour through a number of churches on my way from Cheltenham, which place I left in the evening of the 14th; visited the church at Lea; in the neighborhood of which I preached twice. I then went to Garway, where I preached five times to overflowing congregations; from thence visited Abergavenny, and preached three times. The work appears to be upon the onward march in all these places. Many are inquiring after truth and embracing it. The brethren and friends appeared very anxious for me to tarry longer, but being desirous to commence my labors in this city, I took my leave on Saturday, the 26th, and came *via* Newport, by the packet to this city, and preached three times yesterday. There appears to be a good feeling manifested here at present. In the evening our hall was quite full, and the people listened very attentively; persons of respectable appearance were present. We intend getting a large hall, and putting out bills shortly. Enclosed is an order for ten shillings, it being a donation for the building of the Temple at Nauvoo, mostly from the branch of the Church at Frogmarsh.

Yours in the bonds of the new covenant,

LORENZO D. BARNES.

Wednesday, 30.—I met with the Female Relief Society, and gave them some instructions, of which the following brief sketch was reported by Miss Eliza R. Snow—

Synopsis of the Prophet's Remarks to the Female Relief Society.

President Joseph Smith arose. Spoke of the organization of the Female Relief Society; said he was deeply interested, that it might be built up to the Most High in an acceptable manner; that its rules must be observed; that none should be received into it but those who were worthy; proposed a close examination of every candidate; that the society was growing too fast. It should grow up by degrees, should commence with a few individuals, thus have a select society of the virtuous, and those who would walk circumspectly; commended them for their zeal, but said sometimes their zeal was not according to knowledge. One principal object of the institution was to purge out iniquity; said they must be extremely careful in all their examinations, or the consequences would be serious.

All difficulties which might and would cross our way must be surmounted. Though the soul be tried, the heart faint, and the hands hang down, we must not retrace our steps; there must be decision of character, aside from sympathy. When instructed, we must obey that voice, observe the laws of the kingdom of God, that the blessing of heaven may rest down upon us. All must act in concert, or nothing can be done, and should move according to the ancient Priesthood; hence the Saints should be a select people, separate from all the evils of the world—choice, virtuous, and holy. The Lord was going to make of the Church of Jesus Christ a kingdom of Priests, a holy people, a chosen generation, as in Enoch's day, having all the gifts as illustrated to the Church in Paul's epistles and teachings to the churches in his day—that it is the privilege of each member to live long and enjoy health. He then blessed the Saints.

Monday, 31.—In council at my office with Elders

Brigham Young, John Taylor, Willard Richards,&c., and wrote an epistle to the Female Relief Society, and spoke to the society in the afternoon.

Friday, April 1, 1842.—I was engaged in the general business office.

"Try the Spirits"—The Prophet's Editorial in the Times and Seasons.

Recent occurrences that have transpired amongst us render it an imperative duty devolving upon me to say something in relation to the spirits by which men are actuated.

It is evident from the Apostles' writings, that many false spirits existed in their day, and had "gone forth into the world," and that it needed intelligence which God alone could impart to detect false spirits, and to prove what spirits were of God. The world in general have been grossly ignorant in regard to this one thing, and why should they be otherwise—"for no man knows the things of God, but by the Spirit of God."

The Egyptians were not able to discover the difference between the miracles of Moses and those of the magicians until they came to be tested together; and if Moses had not appeared in their midst, they would unquestionably have thought that the miracles of the magicians were performed through the mighty power of God, for they were great miracles that were performed by them—a supernatural agency was developed, and great power manifested.

The witch of Endor is a no less singular personage; clothed with a powerful agency she raised the Prophet Samuel from his grave, and he appeared before the astonished king, and revealed unto him his future destiny. Who is to tell whether this woman is of God, and a righteous woman—or whether the power she possessed was of the devil, and she a witch as represented by the Bible? It is easy for us to say now, but if we had lived in her day, which of us could have unravelled the mystery?

It would have been equally as difficult for us to tell by what spirit the Apostles prophesied, or by what power the Apostles spoke and worked miracles. Who could have told whether the power of Simon, the sorcerer, was of God or of the devil?

There always did, in every age, seem to be a lack of intelligence pertaining to this subject. Spirits of all kinds have been manifested, in every age, and almost amongst all people. If we go among the pagans, they have their spirits; the Mohammedans, the Jews, the Christians, the Indians—all have their spirits, all have a supernatural agency, and all contend that their spirits are of God. Who shall solve the mystery? "Try the spirits," says John, but who is to do it? The learned, the eloquent, the philosopher, the sage, the divine—all are ignorant. The heathens will boast of their gods, and of the great things that have been unfolded by their oracles. The Mussulman will boast of his Koran, and of the divine communications that his progenitors have received. The Jews have had numerous instances, both ancient and modern, among them of men who have professed to be inspired, and sent to bring about great events, and the Christian world has not been slow in making up the number.

"Try the spirits," but what by? Are we to try them by the creeds of men? What preposterous folly—what sheer ignorance—what madness! Try the motions and actions of an eternal being (for I contend that all spirits are such) by a thing that was conceived in ignorance, and brought forth in folly—a cobweb of yesterday! Angels would hide their faces, and devils would be ashamed and insulted, and would say, "Paul we know, and Jesus we know, but who are ye?" Let each man of society make a creed and try evil spirits by it, and the devil would shake his sides; it is all that he would ask—all that he would desire. Yet many of them do this, and hence "many spirits are abroad in the world."

One great evil is, that men are ignorant of the nature of spirits; their power, laws, government, intelligence, &c., and imagine that when there is anything like power, revelation, or vision manifested, that it must be of God. Hence the Methodists, Presbyterians, and others frequently possess a spirit that will cause them to lie down, and during its operation, animation is frequently entirely suspended; they consider it to be the power of God, and a glorious manifestation from God—a manifestation of what? Is there any intelligence communicated? Are the curtains of heaven withdrawn, or the purposes of God developed? Have they seen and conversed with an angel—or have the glories of futurity burst upon their view? No! but their body has been inanimate, the operation of their spirit suspended, and all the intelligence that can be obtained from them when they arise, is a shout of "glory," or "hallelujah," or some incoherent expression; but they have had "the power."

The Shaker will whirl around on his heel, impelled by a supernatural agency or spirit, and think that he is governed by the Spirit of God; and the Jumper will jump and enter into all kinds of extravagances. A Primitive Methodist will shout under the influence of that spirit, until he will rend the heavens with his cries; while the Quakers (or Friends) moved as they think, by the Spirit of God, will sit still and say nothing. Is God the author of all this? If not of all of it, which does He recognize? Surely, such a heterogeneous mass of confusion never can enter into the kingdom of heaven.

Every one of these professes to be competent to try his neighbor's spirit, but no one can try his own, and what is the reason? Because they have not a key to unlock, no rule wherewith to measure, and no criterion whereby they can test it. Could any one tell the length, breadth or height of a building without a rule? test the quality of metals without a criterion, or point out the movements of the planetary systems, without a knowledge of astronomy? Certainly not; and if such ignorance as this is manifested about a spirit of this kind, who can describe an angel of light? If Satan should appear as one in glory, who can tell his color, his signs, his appearance, his glory?—or what is the manner of his manifestation? Who can detect the spirit of the French prophets with their revelations and their visions, and power of manifestations? Or who can point out the spirit of the Irvingites, with their apostles and prophets, and visions and tongues, and interpretations, &c., &c. Or who can drag into daylight and develop the hidden mysteries of the false spirits that so frequently are made manifest among the Latter-day Saints? We answer that no man can do this without the Priesthood, and having a knowledge of the laws by which spirits are governed; for as "no man knows the things of God, but by the Spirit of God," so no man knows the spirit of the devil, and his power and influence, but by possessing intelligence which is more than human, and having unfolded through the medium of the Priesthood the mysterious operations of his devices; without knowing the angelic form, the sanctified look and gesture, and the zeal that is frequently manifested by him for the glory of God, together with the prophetic spirit, the gracious influence, the godly appearance, and the holy garb, which are so characteristic of his proceedings and his mysterious windings.

A man must have the discerning of spirits before he can drag into daylight this hellish influence and unfold it unto the world in all its soul-destroying, diabolical, and horrid colors; for nothing is a greater injury to the children of men than to be under the influence of a false spirit when they think they have the Spirit of God. Thousands have felt the influence of its terrible power and baneful effects. Long pilgrimages have been undertaken, penances endured, and pain, misery and ruin have followed in their train; nations have been convulsed, kingdoms overthrown, provinces laid waste, and blood, carnage and desolation are habiliaments in which it has been clothed.

The Turks, the Hindoos, the Jews, the Christians, the Indian; in fact all nations have been deceived, imposed upon and injured through the mischievous effects of false spirits.

As we have noticed before, the great difficulty lies in the ignorance of the nature of spirits, of the laws by which they are governed, and the signs by which they may be known; if it requires the Spirit of God to know the things of God; and the spirit of the devil can only be unmasked through that medium, then it follows as a natural consequence that unless some person or persons have a communication, or revelation from God, unfolding to them the operation of the spirit, they must eternally remain ignorant of these principles; for I contend that if one man cannot understand these things but by the Spirit of God, ten thousand men cannot; it is alike out of the reach of the wisdom of the learned, the tongue of the eloquent, the power of the mighty. And we shall at last have to come to this conclusion, whatever we may think of revelation, that without it we can neither know nor understand anything of God, or the devil; and however unwilling the world may be to acknowledge this principle, it is evident from the multifarious creeds and notions concerning this matter that they understand nothing of this principle, and it is equally as plain that without a divine communication they must remain in ignorance. The world always mistook false prophets for true ones, and those that were sent of God, they considered to be false prophets, and hence they killed, stoned, punished and imprisoned the true prophets, and these had to hide themselves "in deserts and dens, and caves of the earth," and though the most honorable men of the earth, they banished them from their society as vagabonds, whilst they cherished, honored and supported knaves, vagabonds, hypocrites, impostors, and the bas est of men.

A man must have the discerning of spirits, as we before stated, to understand these things, and how is he to obtain this gift if there are no gifts of the Spirit? And how can these gifts be obtained without revelation? "Christ ascended into heaven, and gave gifts to men; and He gave some Apostles, and some Prophets, and some Evangelists, and some Pastors and Teachers. And how were Apostles, Prophets, Pastors, Teachers and Evangelists chosen? By prophecy (revelation) and by laying on of hands:—by a divine communication, and a divinely appointed ordinance—through the medium of the Priesthood, organized according to the order of God, by divine appointment. The Apostles in ancient times held the keys of this Priesthood—of the mysteries of the kingdom of God, and consequently were enabled to unlock and unravel all things pertaining to the government of the Church, the welfare of society, the future destiny of men, and the agency, power and influence of spirits; for they could control them at pleasure, bid them depart in the name of Jesus, and detect their mischievous and mysterious operations when trying to palm themselves upon the Church in a religious garb, and militate against the interest of the Church and spread of truth. We read that they "cast out devils in the name of Jesus," and when a woman possessing the spirit of divination, cried before Paul and Silas, "these are the servants of the Most High God that show unto us the way of salvation," they detected the spirit. And although she spake favorably of them, Paul commanded the spirit to come out of her, and saved themselves from the opprobrium that might have been heaped upon their heads, through an alliance with her, in the development of her wicked principles, which they certainly would have been charged with, if they had not rebuked the evil spirit.

A power similar to this existed through the medium of the Priesthood in different ages. Moses could detect the magician's power, and show that he [himself] was God's servant—he knew when he was upon the mountain (through revelation) that Israel was engaged in idolatry; he could develop the sin of Korah, Dathan and Abiram, detect witches and wizards in their proceedings, and point out the true prophets of the Lord. Joshua knew how to detect the man who had stolen the wedge of gold and the Babylonish garment. Michaiah could point out the false spirit by which the four hundred prophets were governed; and if his advice had been taken, many lives would have been spared, (II Chronicles xviii) Elijah, Elisha, Isaiah, Jeremiah, Ezekiel, and many other prophets possessed this power. Our Savior, the Apostles, and even the members of the Church were endowed with this gift, for, says Paul, (I Corinthians xii), "To one is given the gift of tongues, to another the interpretation of tongues, to another the working of miracles, to another prophecy, to another the discerning of spirits." All these proceeded from the same Spirit of God, and were the gifts of God. The Ephesian church were enabled by this principle, "to try those that said they were apostles, and were not, and found them liars," (Revelation ii: 2.)

In tracing the thing to the foundation, and looking at it philosophically, we shall find a very material difference between the body and the spirit; the body is supposed to be organized matter, and the spirit, by many, is thought to be immaterial, without substance. With this latter statement we should beg leave to differ, and state that spirit is a substance; that it is material, but that it is more pure, elastic and refined matter than the body; that it existed before the body, can exist in the body; and will exist separate from the body, when the body will be mouldering in the dust; and will in the resurrection, be again united with it.

Without attempting to describe this mysterious connection, and the laws that govern the body and the spirit of man, their relationship to each other, and the design of God in relation to the human body and spirit, I would just remark, that the spirits of men are eternal, that they are governed by the same Priesthood that Abraham, Melchisedek, and the Apostles were: that they are organized according to that Priesthood which is everlasting, "without beginning of days or end of years,"—that they all move in their respective spheres, and are governed by the law of God; that when they appear upon the earth they are in a probationary state, and are preparing, if righteous, for a future and greater glory; that the spirits of good men cannot interfere with the wicked beyond their prescribed bounds, for "Michael, the Archangel, dared not bring a railing accusation against the devil, but said, "The Lord rebuke thee, Satan."

It would seem also, that wicked spirits have their bounds, limits, and laws by which they are governed or controlled, and know their future destiny; hence, those that were in the maniac said to our Savior, "Art thou come to torment us before the time," and when Satan presented himself before the Lord, among the sons of God, he said that he came "from going to and fro in the earth, and from wandering up and down in it;" and he is emphatically called the prince of the power of the air; and, it is very evident that they possess a power that none but those who have the Priesthood can control, as we have before adverted to, in the case of the sons of Sceva.

Having said so much upon general principles, without referring to the peculiar situation, power, and influence of the magicians of Egypt, the wizards and witches of the Jews, the oracles of the heathen, their necromancers, soothsayers, and astrologers, the maniacs or those possessed of devils in the Apostles' days, we will notice, and try to detect (so far as we have the Scriptures for our aid) some few instances of the development of false spirits in more modern times, and in this our day.

The "French Prophets" were possessed of a spirit that deceived; they existed in Vivaris and Dauphany, in great numbers in the year 1688; there were many boys and girls from seven to twenty-five; they had strange fits, as in tremblings and faintings, which made them stretch out their legs and arms, as in a swoon; they remained awhile in trances, and coming out of them,uttered all that came in their mouths [see Buck's Theological Dictionary].

Now God never had any prophets that acted in this way; there was nothing indecorous in the proceeding of the Lord's prophets in any age; neither had the apostles, nor prophets in the apostles's day anything of this kind. Paul says, "Ye may all prophesy, one by one; and if anything be revealed to another let the first hold his peace, for the spirit of the prophets is subject to the prophets;" but here we find that the prophets are subject to the spirit, and falling down, have twitchings, tumblings, and faintings through the influence of that spirit, being entirely under its control. Paul says, "Let everything be done decently and in order," but here we find the greatest disorder and indecency in the conduct of both men and women, as above described. The same rule would apply to the fallings, twitchings, swoonings, shaking, and trances of many of our modern revivalists.

Johanna Southcott professed to be a prophetess, and wrote a book of prophecies in 1804, she became the founder of a people that are still extant. She was to bring forth, in a place appointed, a son, that was to be the Messiah, which thing has failed. Independent of this, however, where do we read of a woman that was the founder of a church, in the word of God? Paul told the women in his day, "To keep silence in the church, and that if they wished to know anything to ask their husbands at home;" he would not suffer a woman "to rule, or to usurp authority in the church;" but here we find a woman the founder of a church, the revelator and guide, the Alpha and Omega, contrary to all acknowledged rule, principle, and order.

Jemimah Wilkinson was another prophetess that figured largely in America, in the last century. She stated that she was taken sick and died, and that her soul went to heaven, where it still continues. Soon after, her body was reanimated with the spirit and power of Christ, upon which she set up as a public teacher, and declared that she had an immediate revelation. Now the Scriptures positively assert that "Christ is the first fruit, afterwards those that are Christ's at His coming, then cometh the end." But Jemimah, according to her testimony, died, and rose again before the time mentioned in the Scriptures. The idea of her soul being in heaven while her body was [living] on earth, is also preposterous. When God breathed into man's nostrils, he became a living soul, before that he did not live, and when that was taken away his body died; and so did our Savior when the spirit left the body, nor did His body live until His spirit returned in the power of His resurrection. But Mrs. Wilkinson's soul [life] was in heaven, and her body without the soul [or life] on earth, living [without the soul, or] without life!

The Irvingites, are a people that have counterfeited the truth, perhaps the nearest of any of our modern sectarians. They commenced about ten years ago in the city of London, in England; they have churches formed in various parts of England and Scotland, and some few in Upper Canada. Mr. Irving, their founder, was a learned and talented minister of the Church of Scotland, he was a great logician, and a powerful orator, but withal wild and enthusiastic in his views. Moving in the higher circles, and possessing talent and zeal, placed him in a situation to become a conspicuous character, and to raise up a society similar to that which is called after his name.

The Irvingites have apostles, prophets, pastors, teachers, evangelists, and angels. They profess to have the gift of tongues, and the interpretation of tongues, and, in some few instances, to have the gift of healing.

The first prophetic spirit that was manifested was in some Misses

Campbell that Mr. Irving met with, while on a journey in Scotland; they had [what is termed among their sect] "utterances," which were evidently of a supernatural agency. Mr. Irving, falling into the common error of considering all supernatural manifestations to be of God, took them to London with him, and introduced them into his church.

They were there honored as the prophetesses of God, and when they spoke, Mr. Irving or any of his ministers had to keep silence. They were peculiarly wrought upon before the congregation, and had strange utterances, uttered with an unnatural, shrill voice, and with thrilling intonations they frequently made use of a few broken, unconnected sentences, that were ambiguous, incoherent, and incomprehensible; at other times they were more clearly understood. They would frequently cry out, "There is iniquity! There is iniquity!" And Mr. Irving has been led, under the influence of this charge, to fall down upon his knees before the public congregation, and to confess his sin, not knowing whether he had sinned, nor wherein, nor whether the thing referred to him, or somebody else. During these operations, the bodies of the persons speaking were powerfully wrought upon, their countenances were distorted, they had frequent twitchings in their hands, and the whole system was powerfully convulsed at intervals; they sometimes, however, (it is supposed) spoke in correct tongues, and had true interpretations.

Under the influence of this spirit the church was organized by these women; apostles, prophets, &c. were soon called, and a systematic order of things introduced, as above mentioned. A Mr. Baxter (afterwards one of their principal prophets) upon going into one of their meetings, says, "I saw a power manifested, and thought that was the power of God, and asked that it might fall upon me, and it did so,and I began to prophesy." Eight or nine years ago they had about sixty preachers going through the streets of London, testifying that London was to be the place where the "two witnesses" spoken of by John, were to prophesy; that (they) "the church and the spirit were the witnesses, and that at the end of three years and a half there was to be an earthquake and great destruction, and our Savior was to come. Their apostles were collected together at the appointed time watching the event, but Jesus did not come, and the prophecy was then ambiguously explained away. They frequently had signs given them by the spirit to prove to them that what was manifested to them should take place. Mr. Baxter related an impression that he had concerning a child. It was manifested to him that he should visit the child, and lay hands upon it, and that it should be healed; and to prove to him that this was of God, he should meet his brother in a certain place, who should speak unto him certain words. His brother addressed him precisely in the way and manner that the manifestation designated. The sign took place, but when he laid his hands upon the child it did not recover. I cannot vouch for the authority of the last statement, as Mr. Baxter at that time had left the Irvingites, but it is in accordance with many of their proceedings, and the thing never has been attempted to be denied.

It may be asked, where is there anything in all this that is wrong?

1st. The church was organized by women, and "God placed in the Church (first apostles, secondarily prophets), and not first women; but Mr. Irving placed in his church first women (secondarily apostles, and the church was founded and organized by them. A woman has no right to found or organize a church—God never sent them to do it.

2nd. Those women would speak in the midst of a meeting, and rebuke Mr. Irving or any of the church. Now the Scripture positively says, "Thou shalt not rebuke an Elder, but entreat him as a father:" not only this, but they frequently accused the brethren, thus placing themselves in the seat of Satan, who is emphatically called "the accuser of the brethren."

3rd. Mr. Baxter received the spirit on asking for it, without attending to the ordinances, and began to prophesy, whereas the scriptural way of attaining the gift of the Holy Ghost is by baptism, and by laying on of hands.

4th. As we have stated in regard to others, the spirit of the prophets is subject to the prophets; but those prophets were subject to the spirits, the spirits controlling their bodies at pleasure.

But it may be asked how Mr. Baxter could get a sign from a second person? To this we would answer, that Mr. Baxter's brother was under the influence of the same spirit as himself, and being subject to that spirit he could be easily made to speak to Mr. Baxter whatever the spirit should dictate; but there was not power in the spirit to heal the child.

Again it may be asked, how it was that they could speak in tongues if they were of the devil! We would answer that they could be made to speak in another tongue, as well as their own, as they were under the control of that spirit, and the devil can tempt the Hottentot, the Turk, the Jew, or any other nation; and if these men were under the influence of his spirt, they of course could speak Hebrew, Latin, Greek, Italian, Dutch, or any other language that the devil knew.

Some will say, "try the spirits" by the word. "Every spirit that confesseth that Jesus Christ is come in the flesh is of God, and every spirit that confesseth not that Jesus Christ is come in the flesh is not of God." John 4:2, 3. One of the Irvingites once quoted this passage whilst under the influence of a spirit, and then said, "I confess that Jesus Christ is come in the flesh." And yet these prophecies failed, their Messiah did not come; and the great things spoken of by them have fallen to the ground. What is the matter here? Did not the Apostle speak the truth? Certainly he did—but he spoke to a people who were under the penalty of death, the moment they embraced Christianity; and no one without a knowledge of the fact would confess it, and expose themselves to death, and this was consequently given as a criterion to the church or churches to which John wrote. But the devil on a certain occasion cried out, "I know thee, who thou art, the Holy One of God!" Here was a frank acknowledgment under other circumstances that "Jesus had come in the flesh." On another occasion the devil said, "Paul we know, and Jesus we know"—of course, "come in the flesh." No man nor set of men without the regular constituted authorities, the Priesthood and discerning of spirits, can tell true from false spirits. This power they possessed in the Apostles' day, but it has departed from the world for ages.

The Church of Jesus Christ of Latter-day Saints has also had its false spirits; and as it is made up of all those different sects professing every variety of opinion, and having been under the influence of so many kinds of spirits, it is not to be wondered at if there should be found among us false spirits.

Soon after the Gospel was established in Kirtland, and during the absence of the authorities of the Church, many false spirits were introduced, many strange visions were seen, and wild, enthusiastic notions were entertained; men ran out of doors under the influence of this spirit, and some of them got upon the stumps of trees and shouted, and all kinds of extravagances were entered into by them; one man pursued a ball that he said he saw flying in the air, until he came to a precipice, when he jumped into the top of a tree, which saved his life; and many ridiculous things were entered into, calculated to bring disgrace upon the Church of God, to cause the Spirit of God to be withdrawn, and to uproot and destroy those glorious principles which had been developed for the salvation of the human family. But when the authorities returned, the spirit was made manifest, those members that were exercised with it were tried for their fellowship, and those that would not repent and forsake it were cut off.

At a subsequent period a Shaker spirit was on the point of being introduced, and at another time the Methodist and Presbyterian falling down power, but the spirit was rebuked and put down, and those who would not submit to rule and good order were disfellowshiped. We have also had brethren and sisters who have had the gift of tongues falsely; they would speak in a muttering unnatural voice, and their bodies be distorted like the Irvingites before alluded to; whereas, there is nothing unnatural in the Spirit of God. A circumstance of this kind took place in Upper Canada, but was rebuked by the presiding Elder; another, a woman near the same place, professed to have the discerning of spirits, and began to *accuse* another sister of things that she was not guilty of, which she said she knew was so by the spirit, but was afterwards proven to be false; she placed herself in the capacity of the "*accuser* of the brethren," and no person through the discerning of spirits can bring a charge against another, they must be proven guilty by positive evidence, or they stand clear.

There have also been ministering angels in the Church which were of Satan appearing as an angel of light. A sister in the state of New York had a vision,who said it was told her that if she would go to a certain place in the woods, an angel would appear to her. She went at the appointed time, and saw a glorious personage descending, arrayed in white, with sandy colored hair; he commenced and told her to fear God, and said that her husband was called to do great things, but that he must not go more than one hundred miles from home, or he would not return; whereas God had called him to go to the ends of the earth, and he has since been more than one thousand miles from home, and is yet alive. Many true things were spoken by this personage, and many things that were false. How, it may be asked, was this known to be a bad angel? By the color of his hair; that is one of the signs that he can be known by, and by his contradicting a former revelation.

We have also had brethren and sisters who have written revelations, and who have started forward to lead this Church. Such was a young boy in Kirtland, Isaac Russel, of Missouri, and Gladden Bishop, and Oliver Olney of Nauvoo. The boy is now living with his parents who have submitted to the laws of the Church. Mr. Russell stayed in Far West, from whence he was to go to the Rocky Mountains, led by three Nephites; but the Nephites never came, and his friends forsook him, all but some of the blood relations, who have since been nearly destroyed by the mob. Mr. Bishop was tried by the High Council, his papers examined, condemned and burned, and he cut off the Church. He acknowledged the justice of the decision, and said "that he now saw his error, for if he had been governed by the revelations given before, he might have known that no man was to write revelations for the Church, but Joseph Smith," and begged to be prayed for, and forgiven by the brethren. Mr. Olney has also been tried by the High Council and disfellowshiped, because he would not have his writings tested by the word of God; evidently proving that he loves darkness rather than light, because his deeds are evil.

CHAPTER XXXIV.

SPECIAL CONFERENCE OF THE CHURCH AT NAUVOO—THE PROPHET'S REPROOF OF THE WICKED—EPISTLE OF THE TWELVE TO THE SAINTS IN KIRTLAND—STATUS OF THE CHURCH.

Saturday, April 2.—I paid Hugh Rhodes $1,150 for a farm.

The fourth regiment of the second cohort of the Nauvoo Legion, consisting of four companies, was organized, Jonathan Dunham was elected colonel, James Brown, lieutenant-colonel, and Jesse P. Harmon, major of the same.

Monday, 4.—Transacted business at my house with Josiah Butterfield, concerning the Lawrence estates; and closed a settlement with William Marks in the counting room, and paid him off, principal and interest to the last farthing, for all that myself or the Church had had of him.

Tuesday, 5.—Settled with Brother Niswanger.

The Thirteenth Anniversary of the Organization of the Church.

Wednesday, 6.—The first day of the thirteenth year of the rise of the Church of Jesus Christ of Latter-day Saints. A special conference had been appointed at the city of Nauvoo, but it was so wet and cold, that it was not prudent for me to go out, as my health was not good, and I spent the day with my family. Brother Hyrum and Elders Brigham Young, Heber C. Kimball, and Willard Richards called on me in the morning, and I gave them instructions how to organize and adjourn the conference. Before they left, Brother Hyrum and the Twelve present bore testimony that they had never heard me teach any principles but those of the strictest virtue, either in public or private.

CONFERENCE MINUTES.

Special Conference of the Church of Jesus Christ of Latter-day Saints. City of Nauvoo, April 6, 1842.

The day being wet, the First Presidency did not attend, and Elder Page addressed those present upon the subject of the charges against him, and said he would be happy to have an opportunity of laying his statement before the conference at a convenient time. President William Law, General Bennett, president *pro tem*, and President Hyrum Smith all spoke upon the subject of military affairs, showing the necessity of a well organized and efficient force; that as we were bound to serve our country, if required, in common with all good citizens, we ought not to be behind any of our neighbors in point of good order, neat uniforms and equipments, and a well organized and thoroughly disciplined legion.

Thursday, April 7. Conference met. President Joseph Smith had the several quorums put in order and seated. He then made some very appropriate remarks concerning the duties of the Church, the necessity of unity of purpose in regard to the building of the houses, and the blessings connected with doing the will of God, and the inconsistency, folly, and danger of murmuring against the dispensations of Jehovah.

He said that the principal object of the meeting was, to bring the case of Elder Page before them; and that another object was, to choose young men and ordain them, and send them out to preach, that they may have an opportunity of proving themselves, and of enduring the tarring and feathering, and such things as those of us who have gone before them have had to endure.

Elder Page, having arrived, was called upon, and addressed the congregation in relation to the non-performance of his mission to Jerusalem. He said that when he started with Elder Hyde, joy filled their hearts, and they were aware of the responsibility of their mission. Elder Hyde's vision was that he should be in Jerusalem alone, Elder Page considered Elder Hyde to be his father and guide in the mission, and felt it his duty to submit to Elder Hyde's opinion in all things; no Elders ever were more in concert on a mission than they were while together. They made a covenant in Quincy to stand by each other while on the mission, and if they were insulted or imposed upon they would stand by each other, even unto death, and not separate unless to go a few miles to preach a sermon, that all moneys should go into one purse, and it did so.

Elder Hyde, in Indiana, first said he would go to visit Brother Knight, and that Elder Page should stay and preach; he assented, and went and returned to Indianapolis. Elder Page had a mare given him on account of both. Elder Hyde then took the mare, went on, left his luggage with Elder Page; while away he sold the mare for $40, and received $60 more as a donation from the man to whom he had sold the mare; he returned, they preached at Dayton and received a handsome contribution. Elder Page preached sixteen miles off, and raised a branch. Elder Hyde went to Cincinnati, revised the "Missouri Persecutions," got 2,000 copies printed, paid for them, and took part of them with him, and left a large box full, and about 150 loose copies with Elder Page. Elder Hyde started for Philadelphia, purposing to visit churches on the way; he left Elder Page $23.31. Elder Page returned to Dayton and Milton, and sold books, with the intention of following Elder Hyde as soon as practicable; but he stayed a day or two too long, and the river closed by the frost, from one to two weeks earlier than usual. Elder Hyde told him that it was possible they might be from one to two years before they would leave America, as it would take upwards of $1,000 each to take them to Jerusalem and back, that it would be slow gleaning in England, and assigned this as a reason for not immediately following Elder Hyde, thinking that he would be sure of seeing him in the spring. Elder Page accused himself of not using better economy in proceeding on his journey.

There came out a piece in the paper, stating the displeasure of the Lord respecting Elder Hyde and Elder Page, he sat down and wrote a piece to put in the paper, acknowledging the justice of the charge, but wisdom prevented its being published; preached about Washington, &c., gathered funds for the mission in Westchester and in Philadelphia.

Elder Hyde raised funds on behalf of the mission, by applauding Elder Page's talents, wisdom, &c., but they were disappointed in him when they saw him; he raised funds for the mission, the most liberal was in Philadelphia. He intended to sail on the 25th of July, but the brethren said that if he would remain two weeks, they would raise funds for him; they found that it would take longer, and he decided to stay a month, he then received a command through a letter from President Hyrum Smith to an official character in Philadelphia, requesting him to return; he wrote to ascertain the reason but did not get an answer, he was then called in by President Joseph Smith and Elder Brigham Young.

Elder Hyde would often renew the covenant between them to never part with each other in that mission. Elder Page had no blame to attach to Elder Hyde; he supposed he had done right, but if he had been in his place, he would have tarried for him until the spring. The reports of his having apostatized, &c., returned even from this place to New York. Many reproved him for leaving Cincinnati for Dayton.

President Joseph Smith then arose and stated that it was wrong to make the covenant referred to by him; that it created a lack of confidence for two men to covenant to reveal all acts of secrecy or otherwise, to each other, and Elder Page showed a little grannyism. He said that no two men, when they agreed to go together ought to separate, that the Prophets of old would not, and quoted the circumstance of Elijah and Elisha, 2 Kings ii., when about to go to Gilgal, also when about to go to Jericho, and to Jordan, that Elisha could not get clear of Elijah, that he clung to his garment until he was taken to heaven; and that Elder Page should have stuck by Elder Hyde, and he might have gone to Jerusalem, that there is nothing very bad in it, but by the experience let us profit; again the Lord made use of Elder Page as a scape goat to procure funds for Elder Hyde. When Elder Hyde returns, we will reconsider the matter, and perhaps send them back to Jerusalem; we will fellowship Elder Page until Elder Hyde comes, and we will then weld them together and make them one. A vote was then put and carried that we hold Elder Page in full fellowship.

Voted that Elder Page be sent to Pittsburgh.

Sung a hymn—adjourned for one hour and a half, at one o'clock.

Met agreeable to adjournment—choir sung a hymn—prayer by Elder H. C. Kimball.

Elder Lyman Wight called to know if there were any present of the rough and weak things, who wished to be ordained, and go and preach, who have not been before ordained. Elder Lyman Wight then addressed those who intended to be ordained, on the subject of their duty and requirements to go and preach.

President Hyrum Smith spoke concerning the Elders who went forth to preach from Kirtland, and were afterwards called in for the washing and anointing at the dedication of the House, and those who go now will be called in also, when this Temple is about to be dedicated, and will then be endowed to go forth with mighty power, having the same anointing, that all may go forth and have the same power, the first, second, and so on, of the Seventies, and all those formerly ordained. This will be an important and beneficial mission, and not many years until those now sent will be called in again. He then spoke in contradiction of a report in circulation about Elders Heber C. Kimball, Brigham Young, himself, and others of the Twelve, alleging that a sister had been shut in a room for several days, and that they had endeavored to induce her to believe in having two wives. Also cautioned the sisters against going to the steamboats.

President Joseph Smith spoke upon the subject of the stories respecting Elders Kimball and others, showing the folly and inconsistency of spending any time in conversing about such stories, or hearkening to them, for there is no person that is acquainted with our principles who would believe such lies, except Sharp, the editor of the *Warsaw Signal*.

Baptisms for the dead, and for the healing of the body must be in the font, those coming into the Church, and those re-baptized may be baptized in the river. A box should be prepared for the use of the font, that the clerk may be paid, and a book procured by the moneys to be put therein, by those baptized, the remainder to go to the use of the Temple.

Sung a hymn.

Ordinations to take place tomorrow morning. Baptisms in the font also.

There were 275 ordained to the office of Elder, under the hands of the Twelve, during the Conference.

Friday 8. Conference assembled. Sung a hymn. Prayer by Elder Heber C. Kimball.

Elder Page then addressed the assembly upon several subjects; made many interesting remarks concerning being called to the ministry, labor in the vineyard, &c. Spoke of his own travels and the fruits of his labors as an encouragement to the young Elders who were going into the vineyard.

President Joseph Smith said the baptisms would be attended to, also the ordinations.

Sung a hymn.

Elder John Taylor preached a sermon while the ordinations and baptisms were going on, on the subject of infidelity, showing that the arguments used against the Bible were rationally, scientifically, and philosophically false.

The stand was occupied in the afternoon by Elder Amasa M. Lyman, who was followed by Elder William Smith; then the Conference closed by the benediction of President Joseph Smith.

JAMES SLOAN, Clerk.

Saturday, *9.*—In the morning I attended the funeral of Brother Ephraim Marks, and in the evening attended city council.

[The following brief synopsis of President Smith's remarks is from Elder Wilford Woodruff's journal:]

Remarks of the Prophet at the Funeral of Ephraim Marks.

The Saints in Nauvoo assembled at the house of President Marks, at an early hour in the morning, to pay their last respects to the body of Ephraim Marks, son of President William Marks, who died on the evening of the 7th. A large procession formed and walked to the Grove, where a numerous congregation had assembled. President Joseph Smith spoke upon the occasion with much feeling and interest. Among his remarks he said, "It is a very solemn and awful time. I never felt more solemn; it calls to mind the death of my oldest brother, Alvin, who died in New York, and my youngest brother, Don Carlos Smith, who died in Nauvoo. It has been hard for me to live on earth and see these young men upon whom we have leaned for support and comfort taken from us in the midst of their youth. Yes, it has been hard to be reconciled to these things. I have sometimes thought that I should have felt more reconciled to have been called away myself if it had been the will of God; yet I know we ought to be still and know it is of God, and be reconciled to His will; all is right. It will be but a short time before we shall all in like manner be called: it may be the case with me as well as you. Some have supposed that Brother Joseph could not die; but this is a mistake: it is true there have been times when I have had the promise of my life to accomplish such and such things, but, having now accomplished those things, I have not at present any lease of my life, I am as liable to die as other men.

I can say in my heart, that I have not done anything against Ephraim Marks that I am sorry for, and I would ask any of his companions if they have done anything against him that they are sorry for, or that they would not like to meet and answer for at the bar of God, if so, let it prove as a warning to all to deal justly before God, and with all mankind, then we shall be clear in the day of judgment.

When we lose a near and dear friend, upon whom we have set our hearts, it should be a caution unto us not to set our affections too firmly upon others, knowing that they may in like manner be taken from us. Our affections should be placed upon God and His work, more intensely than upon our fellow beings.

Sunday, April 10.—I preached in the Grove, and pronounced a curse upon all adulterers, and fornicators, and unvirtuous persons, and those who have made use of my name to carry on their iniquitous designs.

[The following brief synopsis of the Prophet's remarks is from the journal of Elder Wilford Woodruff:]

Synopsis of Remarks of the Prophet—Reproof of all Wickedness.

Joseph the Seer arose in the power of God; reproved and rebuked wickedness before the people, in the name of the Lord God. He wished to say a few words to suit the condition of the general mass, and then said: I shall speak with authority of the Priesthood in the name of the Lord God, which shall prove a savor of life unto life, or of death unto death. Notwithstanding this congregation profess to be Saints, yet I stand in the midst of all [kinds of] characters and classes of men. If you wish to go where God is, you must be like God, or possess the principles which God possesses, for if we are not drawing towards God in principle, we are going from Him and drawing towards the devil. Yes, I am standing in the midst of all kinds of people.

Search your hearts, and see if you are like God. I have searched mine, and feel to repent of all my sins.

We have thieves among us, adulterers, liars, hypocrites. If God should speak from heaven, he would command you not to steal, not to commit adultery, not to covet, nor deceive, but be faithful over a few things. As far as we degenerate from God, we descend to the devil and lose knowledge, and without knowledge we cannot be saved, and while our hearts are filled with evil, and we are studying evil, there is no room in our hearts for good, or studying good. Is not God good? Then you be good; if He is faithful, then you be faithful. Add to your faith virtue, to virtue knowledge, and seek for every good thing.

The Church must be cleansed, and I proclaim against all iniquity. A man is saved no faster than he gets knowledge, for if he does not get knowledge, he will be brought into captivity by some evil power in the other world, as evil spirits will have more knowledge, and consequently more power than many men who are on the earth. Hence it needs revelation to assist us, and give us knowledge of the things of God.

What is the reason that the Priests of the day do not get revelation? They ask only to consume it upon their lust. Their hearts are corrupt, and they cloak their iniquity by saying there are no more revelations. But if any revelations are given of God, they are universally opposed by the priests and Christendom at large; for they reveal their wickedness and abominations.

Many other remarks of interest were made.

Monday, 11.—I was at the lodge and at home.

The following is from the *West Messenger.*

A METEOR FALLS.

Mr. Horace Palmer who was on his way from Dunkirk to Westfield, about three o'clock this morning, states that when about three miles from Dunkirk, he was suddenly surrounded by a painful vivid light proceeding from a quantity of jelly-like substance, which fell on and about him, producing a sulphurous smell, a difficulty of breathing and a severe sensation of heat. As soon as he could so far recover from his astonishment as to look up, he saw the body of a terrific meteor passing above him, and appearing to be about a mile high. Its size appeared to be three or four feet in diameter, and nearly a mile in length. Its dimensions soon varied, becoming at first broader, and then diminishing to one fourth less than its former size, when it apparently separated in pieces, and fell to the earth; and immediately after he heard the explosion, which he says was tremendous.

When Mr. Palmer arrived at Westfield, his face had the appearance of being severely scorched, and his eyes were much affected, and he did not recover for two or three days. Mr. Palmer is reputed to be a man of integrity and temperate habits; and his story, though marvelous, is generally believed.

The meteor was seen by several other people, who speak of luminous bodies being detached from it. Its progress was attended by a noise similar to that of a train of cars on a railroad.

A man who saw it from Salem represents it to have been of dimensions much larger than described by Mr. Palmer. The report of the explosion was heard also at Buffalo.

Tuesday, 12.—I attended the meeting of the lodge. The Twelve, namely Brigham Young, Heber C. Kimball, Orson Pratt, William Smith, Wilford Woodruff, John Taylor, John E. Page, and Willard Richards, clerk, assembled in the lodge room at four o'clock p. m., and appointed John Taylor, Brigham Young and Heber C. Kimball a committee to make arrangements for the payments due from President Smith as Trustee in Trust, to Mr. Wilkie, and voted that Randolph Alexander go on a mission south to preach the Gospel. Also voted that the Twelve unite their influence to persuade the brethren to consecrate all the old notes, deeds, and obligations which they hold against each other to the building of the Temple in Nauvoo, and that Willard Richards write an epistle in the name of the Twelve on that subject, and publish it in the *Times and Seasons*, which he did as follows:

Council Meeting with the Twelve.

An Epistle of the Twelve to the Saints in America, Greeting.

BELOVED BRETHREN: We have whereof to congratulate you at the present time, as we have the opportunity from day to day to witness the progress of the building of the Temple of the Lord in this city, and which is and must be accomplished by the united exertions of the labors of the brethren who reside here, and the tithings and contributions of those who are scattered abroad in the different states.

In this glorious object the hearts of all the faithful are united, the hands of the laborer are made strong continually, and the purse strings of the more opulent are unloosed from time to time, to supply those things which are necessary for upraising the stones of this noble edifice; and it may truly be said that the blessing of the Lord is upon His people; we have peace without and love within the borders of our beautiful city; beautiful, indeed, for situation is Nauvoo; the crown of the great valley of the Mississippi, the joy of every honest heart.

Although all things are more prosperous concerning the Temple than at any former period, yet the Saints must not suppose that all is done, or that they can relax their exertions and the work go on. It is a great work that God has required of His people, and it will require long and unwearied diligence to accomplish it; and redoubled diligence will be necessary with all, to get the building enclosed before another winter, so that the joiner can be employed during the cold weather; and we would again call upon all the Saints abroad to unite in making their deposits in banks known to be good and safe, and forward their certificate to the Trustee in Trust, as speedily as possible; when trusty men are not coming immediately to this place who can bring your offerings. All will want the privileges and blessings of the sanctuary, when it is completed; and all can have their wishes; but they can obtain them only by faithfulness and diligence in striving to build.

We praise our God for the liberality that has hitherto been manifested; many have given more than was required of them, many have given their all, but they have done it cheerfully; they have done it voluntarily; and they shall have a great reward; for the blessings of heaven and earth shall be multiplied unto such; even the blessings of that Priesthood which hath neither beginning of days nor end of life.

While there are those who of their abundance have built unto themselves fine houses, and who ride in fine carriages and on horseback, and regale themselves with the good things of the land, and at the same time they have left the Lord's house untouched, or, if touched at all, have touched it so lightly as scarce to leave the print of their little finger: their reward will be according to their deeds, and unless they speedily repent, and come up with their abundance to the help of the Lord, they will find in the end that they have no part nor lot in this matter; their gold and silver will become cankered, their garments moth eaten, and they will perish in their own slothfulness and idolatry, leaving none to mourn their absence.

But, brethren, the Temple will be built. There are hundreds and thousands who stand ready to sacrifice the last farthing they possess on the earth rather than have the building of the Lord's house delayed, and while this spirit prevails no power beneath the heavens can hinder its progress: but we desire you all to help with the ability which God has given you; that you may all share the blessings which will distil from heaven to earth through this consecrated channel.

This is not all. It will be in vain for us to build a place where the Son of Man may lay his head, and leave the cries of the widow and the fatherless, unheard by us, ascending up to the orphan's God and widow's Friend. It is in vain, we cry Lord,Lord. and do not the things our Lord hath commanded; to visit the widow, the fatherless, the sick, the lame, the blind, the destitute, and minister to their necessities; and it is but reasonable that such cases should be found among a people who have but recently escaped the fury of a relentless mob on the one hand, and gathered from the half-starved population of the scattered nations on the other.

Neither is this all. It is not sufficient that the poor be fed and clothed, the sick ministered unto, the Temple built—no, when all this is accomplished, there must be a year of Jubilee: there must be a day of rejoicing· there must be a time of release to Zion's sons, or our offerings, our exertions, our hopes, and our prayers will be in vain, and God will not accept of the doings of His people.

On these days of darkness which overspread our horizon; when the wolf was howling for his prey around the streets of Kirtland; when the burglar was committing his midnight and midday depredations in Jackson county; when the heartless politician was thrusting his envious darts in Clay county—and when the savage war whoop, echoed and reechoed through Far West, and Zion's noblest sons were chained in dungeons, and her defenseless daughters driven by a horde of savages, from their once peaceful homes,to seek a shelter in a far distant land—many of the brethren stepped forward to their rescue, and not only expended all they possessed for the relief of suffering innocence, but gave their notes and bonds to "obtain more means, with which to help those who could not escape the overwhelming surge of banishment from all that they possessed on earth."

Death, wounds, and sickness, from the mob, and the cold and shelterless situation of the brethren, followed in quick succession; and all the means which could possibly be obtained from each other, in addition to the noble charities of the citizens of Illinois, were brought into requisition to sustain a remnant of the Saints, who now mostly inhabit this place.

To accomplish this, the President and Bishops loaned money and such things as could be obtained, and gave their obligations in good faith for the payment of the same; and many of the brethren signed with them at different times and in different places, to strengthen their hands and help them carry out their designs; fully expecting, that, at some future day, they would be enabled to liquidate all such claims, to the satisfaction of all parties.

Many of these claims have already been settled; many have been given up as cancelled by those who held them, and many yet remain unsettled. The Saints have had many difficulties to encounter since they arrived at this place. In a new country, destitute of houses, food, clothing, and nearly all the necessaries of life, which were rent from them by an unfeeling mob—having to encounter disease and difficulties unnumbered, it is not surprising that the Church has not been able to liquidate all such claims, or that many individuals should yet remain involved, from the foregoing circumstances; and while things remain as they are, and men remain subject to the temptations of evil as they now are, the day of release, and year of jubilee cannot be; and we write you especially at this time, brethren, for the purpose of making a final settlement of all such claims, of brother against brother; of the brethren against the Presidency and Bishops, &c.; claims which have originated out of the difficulties and calamities the Church has had to encounter, and which are of long standing, so that when the Temple is completed, there will be nothing from this source to produce jars, and discords, strifes and animosities, so as to prevent the blessings of heaven descending upon us as a people.

To accomplish this most desirable object, we call on all the brethren who hold such claims, to bring them forward for a final settlement; and also those brethren who have individual claims against each other, of long standing, and the property of the debtor has been wrested from him by violence, or he has been unfortunate, and languished on a bed of sickness till his means are exhausted; and all claims whatsoever between brother and brother, where there is no reasonable prospect of a just and equitable settlement possible, that they also by some means, either by giving up their obligations, or destroying them, see that all such old affairs be adjusted, so that it shall not give occasion for difficulties to arise hereafter. Yes, brethren, bring all such old accounts, notes, bonds, etc., and make a consecration of them to the building of the Temple, and if anything can be obtained on them, it will be obtained; and if nothing can be obtained, when the Temple is completed, we will make a burnt-offering of them, even a peace-offering, which shall bind the brethren together in the bonds of eternal peace, and love and union; and joy and salvation shall flow forth into your souls, and you shall rejoice and say it is good that we have harkened unto counsel, and set our brethren free, for God hath blessed us.

How can we prosper while the Church, while the Presidency, while the Bishops, while those who have sacrificed everything but life, in this thing, for our salvation, are thus encumbered? It cannot be. Arise, then, brethren, set them free, and set each other free, and we will all be free together, we will be free indeed.

Let nothing in this epistle be so construed as to destroy the validity of contracts, or give any one license not to pay his debts. The commandment is to pay every man his dues, and no man can get to heaven who justly owes his brother or his neighbor, who has or can get the means and will not pay it; it is dishonest, and no dishonest man can enter where God is.

We remain, your brethren in the Gospel of Peace,

BRIGHAM YOUNG, President,
HEBER C. KIMBALL,
ORSON PRATT,
WILLIAM SMITH,
JOHN E. PAGE,
LYMAN WIGHT,
WILFORD WOODRUFF,
JOHN TAYLOR,
GEO. A. SMITH,
WILLARD RICHARDS, Clerk.

Military Appointments.

James Arlington Bennett, of Arlington House, Long Island, is hereby appointed Inspector-General of the Nauvoo-Legion, with the rank and title of Major-General; his place to be supplied when absent, by the Major-General of the Legion.

JOSEPH SMITH, Lieutenant-General.

City of Nauvoo, Illinois, April 12th, A. D. 1842.

CHAPTER XXXV.

THE GENERAL BANKRUPT LAW—THE DOCTRINE OF BAPTISM FOR THE DEAD—THE PROPHET'S ADDRESS TO THE FEMALE RELIEF SOCIETY—THE KEYS OF THE PRIESTHOOD AND THE NAUVOO TEMPLE.

Wednesday, April 13.—I introduced Messrs. Backenstos, Stiles, and Robinson into the Lodge Room in the morning, and Samuel H. Smith, William Smith, and Vinson Knight in the evening.

About 150 Saints, from England landed in Nauvoo from the steamer *Louisa*, and about 60 from the *Amaranth*.

Thursday, 14.—Calvin A. Warren, Esq., lawyer, from Quincy, arrived, and commenced an investigation of the principles of general insolvency in my behalf according to the statutes; for the United States Congress had previously instituted a general bankrupt law, by which any individual who was owing to a certain amount more than he was able to pay, could make out a schedule of his property, and of debts due from himself, and by a specified process, pass the same in the hands of a commissioner, government agent, or "assignee," who could make a dividend of all his effects, and pay his creditors whatever percentage his property amounted to, and then the individual was at liberty to start anew in the world, and was not subject to liquidate any claims which were held against him previous to his insolvency, although his property might not have paid but the least percentage, or none at all.

The Bankrupt Law.

The justice or injustice of such a principle in law, I leave for them who made it, the United States. Suffice it to say, the law was as good for the Saints as for the Gentiles, and whether I would or not, I was forced into the measure by having been robbed, mobbed, plundered, and wasted of all my property, time after time, in various places, by the very ones who made the law, namely, the people of the United State, thereby having been obliged to contract heavy debts to prevent the utter destruction of myself, family and friends, and by those who were justly and legally owing me, taking the advantage of the same act of bankruptcy, so that I could not collect my just dues, thus leaving me no alternative but to become subject again to stripping, wasting, and destitution, by vexatious writs, and law suits, and imprisonments, or take that course to extricate myself, which the law had pointed out.

The Prophet Forced into Bankruptcy.

Friday, *15.*—Editorial from the *Times and Seasons:*

BAPTISM FOR THE DEAD.

The great designs of God in relation to the salvation of the human family, are very little understood by the professedly wise and intelligent generation in which we live. Various and conflicting are the opinions of men concerning the plan of salvation, the requisitions of the Almighty, the necessary preparations for heaven, the state and condition of departed spirits, and the happiness or misery that is consequent upon the practice of righteousness and iniquity according to their several notions of virtue and vice.

The Mussulman condemns the heathen, the Jew, and the Christian, and the whole world of mankind that reject his Koran, as infidels, and consigns the whole of them to perdition. The Jew believes that the whole world that rejects his faith and are not circumcised, are Gentile dogs, and will be damned. The heathen is equally as tenacious about his principles, and the Christian consigns all to perdition who cannot bow to his creed, and submit to his *ipse dixit*.

But while one portion of the human race is judging and condemning the other without mercy, the Great Parent of the universe looks upon the whole of the human family with a fatherly care and paternal regard; He views them as His offspring, and without any of those contracted feelings that influence the children of men, causes "His sun to rise on the evil and on the good, and sendeth rain on the just and on the unjust." He holds the reins of judgment in His hands; He is a wise Lawgiver, and will judge all men, not according to the narrow, contracted notions of men, but, "according to the deeds done in the body whether they be good or evil," or whether these deeds were done in England, America, Spain, Turkey, or India. He will judge them, "not according to what they have not, but according to what they have," those who have lived without law, will be judged without law, and those who have a law, will by judged by that law. We need not doubt the wisdom and intelligence of the Great Jehovah; He will award judgment or mercy to all nations according to their several deserts, their means of obtaining intelligence, the laws by which they are governed, the facilities afforded them of obtaining correct information, and His inscrutable designs in relation to the human family; and when the designs of God shall be made manifest, and the curtain of futurity be withdrawn, we shall all of us eventually have to confess that the Judge of all the earth has done right.

The situation of the Christian nations after death, is a subject that has called forth all the wisdom and talent of the philosopher and the divine, and it is an opinion which is generally received, that the destiny of man is irretrievably fixed at his death, and that he is made either eternally happy, or eternally miserable; that if a man dies without a knowledge of God, he must be eternally damned, without any mitigation of his punishment, alleviation of his pain, or the most latent hope of a deliverance while endless ages shall roll along. However orthodox this principle may be, we shall find that it is at variance with the testimony of Holy Writ, for our Savior says, that all manner of sin and blasphemy shall be forgiven men wherewith they shall blaspheme; but the blasphemy against the Holy Ghost shall not be forgiven, neither in this world, nor in the world to come, evidently showing that there are sins which may be forgiven in the world to come, although the sin of blasphemy [against the Holy Ghost] cannot be forgiven. Peter, also, in speaking concerning our Savior, says, that "He went and preached unto the spirits in prison, which sometimes were disobedient, when once the long suffering of God waited in the days of Noah," (I Peter iii: 19, 20). Here then we have an account of our Savior preaching to the spirits in prison, to spirits that had been imprisoned from the days of Noah; and what did He preach to them? That they were to stay there?. Certainly not! Let His own declaration testify. "He hath sent me to heal the broken hearted, to preach deliverance to the captives, and recovering of sight to the blind, to set at liberty them that are bruised." (Luke iv: 18. Isaiah has it—"To bring out the prisoners from the prison, and them that sit in darkness from the prison house." (Isaiah xlii: 7. It is very evident from this that He not only went to preach to them, but to deliver, or bring them out of the prison house. Isaiah, in testifying concerning the calamities that will overtake the inhabitants of the earth, says, "The earth shall reel to and fro like a drunkard, and shall be removed like a cottage; and the transgression thereof shall be heavy upon it; and it shall fall and not rise again. And it shall come to pass in that day, that the Lord shall punish the host of the high ones that are on high, and the kings of the earth upon the earth. And they shall be gathered together, as prisoners are gathered in the pit, and shall be shut up in the prison, and after many days shall they be visited." Thus we find that God will deal with all the human family equally, and that as the antediluvians had their day of visitation, so will those characters referred to by Isaiah, have their time of visitation and deliverance, after having been many days in prison.

The great Jehovah contemplated the whole of the events connected with the earth, pertaining to the plan of salvation, before it rolled into existence, or ever "the morning stars sang together" for joy; the past, the present, and the future were and are, with Him, one eternal "now;" He knew of the fall of Adam, the iniquities of the antediluvians, of the depth of iniquity that would be connected with the human family, their weakness and strength, their power and glory, apostasies, their crimes, their righteousness and iniquity; He comprehended the fall of man, and his redemption; He knew the plan of salvation and pointed it out; He was acquainted with the situation of all nations and with their destiny; He ordered all things according to the council of His own will; He knows the situation of both the living and the dead, and has made ample provision for their redemption, according to their several circumstances, and the laws of the kingdom of God, whether in this world, or in the world to come.

The idea that some men form of the justice, judgment, and mercy of God, is too foolish for an intelligent man to think of: for instance, it is common for many of our orthodox preachers to suppose that if a man is not what they call converted, if he dies in that state he must remain eternally in hell without any hope. Infinite years in torment must he spend, and never, never, never have an end; and yet this eternal misery is made frequently to rest upon the merest casualty. The breaking of a shoe-string, the tearing of a coat of those officiating, or the peculiar location in which a person lives, may be the means, indirectly of his damnation, or the cause of his not being saved. I will suppose a case which is not extraordinary: Two men, who have been equally wicked, who have neglected religion, are both of them taken sick at the same time; one of them has the good fortune to be visited by a praying man, and he gets converted a few minutes before he dies; the other sends for three different praying men, a tailor, a shoemaker, and a tinman; the tinman has a handle to solder to a can, the tailor has a button-hole to work on some coat that he needed in a hurry, and the shoemaker has a patch to put on somebody's boot; they none of them can go in time, the man dies, and goes to hell: one of these is exalted to Abraham's bosom, he sits down in the presence of God and enjoys eternal, uninterrupted happiness, while the other, equally as good as he, sinks to eternal damnation, irretrievable misery and hopeless despair, because a man had a boot to mend, the button-hole of a coat to work, or a handle to solder on to a saucepan.

The plans of Jehovah are not so unjust, the statements of holy writ so visionary, nor the plan of salvation for the human family so incompatible with common sense; at such proceedings God would frown with indignance, angels would hide their heads in shame, and every virtuous, intelligent man would recoil.

If human laws award to each man his deserts, and punish all delinquents according to their several crimes, surely the Lord will not be more cruel than man, for He is a wise legislator, and His laws are more equitable, His enactments more just, and His decisions more perfect than those of man; and as man judges his fellow man by law, and punishes him according to the penalty of the law, so does God of heaven judge "according to the deeds done in the body." To say that the heathens would be damned because they did not believe the Gospel would be preposterous, and to say that the Jews would all be damned that do not believe in Jesus would be equally absurd; for "how can they believe on him of whom they have not heard, and how can they hear without a preacher, and how can he preach except he be sent;" consequently neither Jew nor heathen can be culpable for rejecting the conflicting opinions of sectarianism, nor for rejecting any testimony but that which is sent of God, for as the preacher cannot preach except he be sent, so the hearer cannot believe without he hear a "sent" preacher, and cannot be condemned for what he has not heard, and being without law, will have to be judged without law.

When speaking about the blessings pertaining to the Gospel, and the consequences connected with disobedience to the requirements, we are frequently asked the question, what has become of our fathers? Will they all be damned for not obeying the Gospel, when they never heard it? Certainly not. But they will possess the same privilege that we here enjoy, through the medium of the everlasting priesthood, which not only administers on earth, but also in heaven, and the wise dispensations of the great Jehovah; hence those characters referred to by Isaiah will be visited by the Priesthood, and come out of their prison upon the same principle as those who were disobedient in the days of Noah were visited by our Savior [who possessed the everlasting Melchisedek Priesthood] and had the Gospel preached to them, by Him in prison;

and in order that they might fulfill all the requisitions of God, living friends were baptized for their dead friends, and thus fulfilled the requirement of God, which says, "Except a man be born of water and of the Spirit, he cannot enter into the kingdom of God," they were baptized of course, not for themselves, but for their dead.

Chrysostum says that the Marchionites practiced baptism for their dead. "After a catechumen was dead, they had a living man under the bed of the deceased; then coming to the dead man, they asked him whether he would receive baptism, and he making no answer, the other answered for him, and said that he would be baptized in his stead; and so they baptized the living for the dead." The church of course at that time was degenerate, and the particular form might be incorrect, but the thing is sufficiently plain in the Scriptures, hence Paul, in speaking of the doctrine, says, "Else what shall they do which are baptized for the dead, if the dead rise not at all? Why are they then baptized for the dead?" (1 Cor. xv: 29). Hence it was that so great a responsibility rested upon the generation in which our Savior lived, for, says he, "That upon you may come all the righteous blood shed upon the earth, from the blood of righteous Abel unto the blood of Zacharias, son of Barachias, whom ye slew between the temple and the altar. Verily I say unto you,all these things shall come upon this generation." (Matthew xxiii: 35, 36). Hence as they possessed greater privileges than any other generation, not only pertaining to themselve, but to their dead, their sin was greater, as they not only neglected their own salvation but that of their progenitors, and hence their blood was required at their hands.

And now as the great purposes of God are hastening to their accomplishment, and the things spoken of in the Prophets are fulfilling, as the kingdom of God is establised on the earth, and the ancient order of things restored, the Lord has manifested to us this day and privilege, and we are commanded to be baptized for our dead, thus fulfilling the words of Obadiah, when speaking of the glory of the latter-day: "And saviors shall come upon Mount Zion to judge the remnant of Esau, and the kingdom shall be the Lord's." A view of these things reconciles the Scriptures of truth, justifies the ways of God to man, places the human family upon an equal footing, and harmonizes with every principle of righteousness, justice and truth. We will conclude with the words of Peter: "For the time past of our life may suffice us to have wrought the will of the Gentiles." "For, for this cause was the Gospel preached also to them that are dead, that they might be judged according to men in the flesh, but live according to God in the spirit."

I continued busily engaged in making out a list of

debtors and an invoice of my property to be passed into the hands of the assignee, until—

Saturday evening the 16th.—On this day the first number of *The Wasp*, a miscellaneous weekly newspaper was first published at my office, William Smith, editor, devoted to the arts, sciences, literature, agriculture, manufacture, trade, commerce, and the general news of the day, on a small sheet, at $1.50 per annum.

Sunday, 17.—Spent the day with my family at home.

Monday, 18.—In consequence of the utter annihilation of our property by mob violence in the state of Missouri, and the immense expenses which we were compelled to incur, to defend ourselves from the cruel persecutions of that state, we were reduced to the necessity of availing ourselves of the privileges of the general bankrupt law; therefore I went to Carthage with my brothers Hyrum and Samuel H. Smith, and severally testified to our list of insolvency before the clerk of the county commissioners' court. Sidney Rigdon and many more brethren were at Carthage the same day on business. My clerk, Dr. Richards, went with us.

Causes of the Prophet's Insolvency.

About this time a disturbance broke out in Rhode Island by a part of the inhabitants, wishing to change their Constitution, and make it like those of other states in the Union, which created much confusion and angry feeling in that state, and excitement in other states.

Tuesday, 19.—Rode out and examined some land near the northern limits of the city, &c.

Wednesday, 20.—Assisted in surveying some land in section 25, which I sold to William Cross.

Thursday, 21.—Friday and Saturday was engaged in temporal and spiritual affairs at home, the office, &c.

Friday, 22.—

James Arlington Bennett Honored.

Honorary Degree. Ordered by the chancellor and regents of the University of the City of Nauvoo, that the honorary degree of L. L.

D. be, and the same hereby is, conferred on General James Arlington Bennett, of Arlington House, New York.

Passed April 22, 1842.

JOHN C. BENNETT, Chancellor,
WILLIAM LAW, Registrar.

Sunday, 24.—Preached on the hill near the Temple, concerning the building of the Temple, and reproved the merchants and the rich who would not assist in building it.

Monday, 25, Tuesday, 26 and Wednesday, 27.—I was engaged in reading, meditation, &c., mostly with my family.

Thursday, 28.—

"*Repast Militaire.*"

General Joseph Smith and lady, present their compliments to the officers (and their respective ladies) of the consolidated General Staff of the Nauvoo Legion, that is to say, his personal staff, Major-General Bennett's staff, including the band, Brigadier-General Law's staff, and Brigadier-General Rich's staff, and respectfully solicit their company at a *Repast Militaire,* at his quarters on the 7th day of May *proximo,* at one o'clock p. m.

General Bennett has been ordered to issue a programme of the operations and field exercises of the day, which will appear in ample form, and due season.

April 28, A. D. 1842.

HEADQUARTERS, NAUVOO LEGION,
CITY OF NAUVOO, ILLINOIS, April 28, 1842.

General Orders—

The Lieutenant-General directs that a *programme militaire* issue from the office of his commanding general for the 7th of May *proximo,* which I now proceed to consummate.

1st. The Adjutants will form the lines of their respective regiments, and the Colonels of the line assume command at nine o'clock, a. m.

2nd. The Adjutant-General will form the line of the Legion, and the Brigadier-Generals assume the command of their respective cohorts at half-past nine o'clock a. m,

3rd. The Major-General will assume the command of the Legion at ten o'clock a. m.

4th. At a quarter past ten o'clock a. m., the Lieutenant-General will be escorted to the field at the review station.

5th. General review and inspection will follow, accompanied by such evolutions and exercises as the time will admit of.

6th. At half-past twelve o'clock p. m. the forces will be dismissed until a quarter before two o'clock p. m.

7th. At two o'clock p. m. the Major-General will resume the command and perform such military movements and field exercises as the Lieutenant-General may direct.

8th. At three o'clock p. m. the cohorts will separate and form the line of battle, the Brigadiers assume their respective commands and General Law's command will make a descent upon that of General Rich's in order of sham battle.

9th. At half-past three o'clock p. m. the cohorts will resume their positions in the line of the Legion, and a sham battle will be fought between the mounted riflemen under the immediate command of Lieutenant General Smith and the Invincibles under the immediate command of Major-General Bennett.

10th. At half-past four o'clock p. m. the forces will be dismissed for the day.

11. Every officer, musician and private will be required to be at their respective posts at the hours specified throughout the day, under the most severe penalties of the law.

JOHN C. BENNETT.
Major-General.

The Rights and Privileges of Women in the Church.

At two o'clock I met the members of the "Female Relief Society," and after presiding at the admission of many new members, gave a lecture on the Priesthood, showing how the sisters would come in possession of the privileges, blessings and gifts of the Priesthood, and that the signs should follow them, such as healing the sick, casting out devils, &c., and that they might attain unto these blessings by a virtuous life, and conversation, and diligence in keeping all the commandments; a synopsis of which was reported by Miss Eliza R. Snow, as follows:

Remarks of the Prophet to the Relief Society.

President Smith arose and called the attention of the meeting to the 12th chapter 1st Corinthians—"Now concerning spiritual gifts, I would not have you ignorant." Said that the passage in the third verse, which reads, "No man can say that Jesus is the Lord, but by the Holy Ghost,' should be translated "no man can *know* that Jesus is the Lord, but by the Holy Ghost." He continued to read the chapter, and give instructions respecting the different offices, and the necessity of every individual acting in the sphere allotted him or her, and filling the several offices to which they are appointed. He spoke of the disposition of many men to consider the lower offices in the Church dishonorable, and to look with jealous eyes upon the standing of others who are called to preside over them; that it was the folly and nonsense of the human heart for a person to be aspiring to other stations than those to which they are appointed of God for them to occupy; that it was better for individuals to magnify their respective callings, and wait patiently till God shall say to them, "Come up higher."

He said the reason of these remarks being made was, that some little foolish things were circulating in the society, against some sisters not doing right in laying hands on the sick. Said that if the people had common sympathies they would rejoice that the sick could be healed; that the time had not been before that these things could be in their proper order; that the Church is not fully organized, in its proper order, and cannot be, until the Temple is completed, where places will be provided for the administration of the ordinances of the Priesthood.

President Smith continued the subject, by quoting the commission given to the ancient Apostles in Mark, 16th chapter, 15th, 16th, 17th, 18th verses, "Go ye into all the world, and preach the Gospel to every creature. He that believeth and is baptized shall be saved; but he that believed not shall be damned. And these signs shall follow them that believe: In my name shall they cast out devils; they shall speak with new tongues; they shall take up serpents; and if they drink any deadly thing, it shall not hurt them; they shall lay hands on the sick, and they shall recover."

No matter who believeth, these signs, such as healing the sick, casting out devils, &c., should follow all that believe, whether male or female. He asked the Society if they could not see by this sweeping promise, that wherein they are ordained, it is the privilege of those set apart to administer in that authority, which is conferred on them; and if the sisters should have faith to heal the sick, let all hold their tongues, and let everything roll on.

He said, if God has appointed him, and chosen him as an instrument to lead the Church, why not let him lead it through? Why stand in the way when he is appointed to do a thing? Who knows the mind of God? Does He not reveal things differently from what we expect? He remarked that he was continually rising, although he had everything bearing him down, standing in his way, and opposing; notwithstanding all this opposition, he always comes out right in the end.

Respecting females administering for the healing of the sick, he further remarked, there could be no devil in it, if God gave His sanction by healing; that there could be no more sin in any female laying hands on and praying for the sick, than in wetting the face with water; it is no sin for anybody to administer that has faith, or if the sick have faith to be healed by their administration.

He reproved those that were disposed to find fault with the management of the concerns of the Church, saying God had called him to lead the Church, and he would lead it right; those that undertake to interfere will be ashamed when their own folly is made manifest; that he calculates to organize the Church in its proper order as soon as the Temple is completed.

President Smith continued by speaking of the difficulties he had to surmount ever since the commencement of the work, in consequence of aspiring men. "Great big Elders," as he called them, who had caused him much trouble; to whom he had taught the things of the kingdom in private councils, they would then go forth into the world and proclaim the things he had taught them, as their own revelations; said the same aspiring disposition will be in this Society, and must be guarded against; that every person should stand, and act in the place appointed, and thus sanctify the Society and get it pure. He said he had been trampled under foot by aspiring Elders, for all were infected with that spirit; for instance, John E. Page and others had been aspiring; they could not be exalted, but must run away as though the care and authority of the Church were vested with them. He said he had a subtle devil to deal with, and could only curb him by being humble.

As he had this opportunity, he was going to instruct the ladies of this Society, and point out the way for them to conduct themselves, that they might act according to the will of God; that he did not know that he should have many opportunities of teaching them, as they were going to be left to themselves; they would not long have him to instruct them; that the Church would not have his instructions long, and the world would not be troubled with him a great while, and would not have his teachings [in person].

He spoke of delivering the keys of the Priesthood to the Church, and said that the faithful members of the Relief Society should receive them in connection with their husbands, that the Saints whose integrity has been tried and proved faithful, might know how to ask the Lord and receive an answer; for according to his prayers, God had appointed him elsewhere.

He exhorted the sisters always to concentrate their faith and prayers for, and place confidence in their husbands, whom God has appointed for them to honor, and in those faithful men whom God has placed at the head of the Church to lead His people; that we should arm and sustain them with our prayers; for the keys of the kingdom are about to be given to them, that they may be able to detect everything false; as well as to all the Elders who shall prove their integrity in due season.

He said if one member becomes corrupt, and you know it, you must immediately put it away, or it will either injure or destroy the whole body. The sympathies of the heads of the Church have induced them to bear a long time with those who were corrupt until they are obliged to cut them off, lest all become contaminated; you must put down iniquity, and by your good examples, stimulate the Elders to good works; if you do right, there is no danger of your going too fast.

He said he did not care how fast we run in the path of virtue; resist evil, and there is no danger; God, men, and angels will not condemn those that resist everything that is evil, and devils cannot; as well might the devil seek to dethrone Jehovah, as overthrow an innocent soul that resists everything which is evil.

This is a charitable Society, and according to your natures; it is natural for females to have feelings of charity and benevolence. You are now placed in a situation in which you can act according to those sympathies which God has planted in your bosoms.

If you live up to these principles, how great and glorious will be your reward in the celestial kingdom! If you live up to your privileges, the angels cannot be restrained from being your associates. Females, if they are pure and innocent, can come in the presence of God; for what is more pleasing to God than innocence; you must be innocent, or you cannot come up before God: if we would come before God, we must keep ourselves pure, as He is pure.

The devil has great power to deceive; he will so transform things as to make one gape at those who are doing the will of God. You need not be teazing your husbands because of their deeds, but let the weight of your innocence, kindness and affection be felt, which is more mighty than a millstone hung about the neck; not war, not jangle, not contradiction, or dispute, but meekness, love, purity—these are the things that should magnify you in the eyes of all good men. Achan [see Joshua vii.] must be brought to light, iniquity must be purged out from the midst of the Saints; then the veil will be rent, and the blessings of heaven will flow down—they will roll down like the Mississippi river.

If this Society listen to the counsel of the Almighty, through the heads of the Church, they shall have power to command queens in their midst.

I now deliver it as a prophecy, if the inhabitants of this state, with the people of the surrounding country, will turn unto the Lord with all their hearts, ten years will not roll round before the kings and queens of the earth will come unto Zion, and pay their respects to the leaders of this people; they shall come with their millions, and shall contribute of their abundance for the relief of the poor, and the building up and beautifying of Zion.

After this instruction, you will be responsible for your own sins; it is a desirable honor that you should so walk before our heavenly Father as to save yourselves; we are all responsible to God for the manner we improve the light and wisdom given by our Lord to enable us to save ourselves.

President Smith continued reading from the above-mentioned chapter, and to give instructions respecting the order of God, as established in the Church, saying everyone should aspire only to magnify his own office and calling.

He then commenced reading the 13th chapter—"Though I speak with the tongues of men and angels, and have no charity, I am become as sounding brass, or a tinkling cymbal;" and said, don't be limited in your views with regard to your neighbor's virtue, but beware of self-righteousness, and be limited in the estimate of your own virtues, and not think yourselves more righteous than others; you must enlarge your souls towards each other, if you would do like Jesus, and carry your fellow-creatures to Abraham's bosom. He said he had manifested long-suffering, forbearance and patience towards the Church, and also to his enemies; and we must bear with each other's failings, as an indulgent parent bears with the foibles of his children.

President Smith then read the 2nd verse—"Though I have the gift of prophecy, and understand all mysteries, and all knowledge; and though I have all faith, so that I could remove mountains, and have not charity, I am nothing." He then said, though a man should become mighty, do great things, overturn mountains, perform mighty works, and should then turn from his high station to do evil, to eat and drink with the drunken, all his former deeds would not save him, but he would go to destruction! As you increase in innocence and virtue, as you increase in goodness, let your hearts expand, let them be enlarged towards others; you must be long-suffering, and bear with the faults and errors of mankind.

How precious are the souls of men! The female part of the community are apt to be contracted in their views. You must not be contracted, but you must be liberal in your feelings. Let this Society teach women how to behave towards their husbands, to treat them with mildness and affection. When a man is borne down with trouble, when he is perplexed with care and difficulty, if he can meet a smile instead of an argument or a murmur—if he can meet with mildness, it will calm down his soul and soothe his feelings; when the mind is going to despair, it needs a solace of affection and kindness.

You will receive instructions through the order of the Priesthood which God has established, through the medium of those appointed to lead, guide and direct the affairs of the Church in this last dispensation; and I now turn the key in your behalf in the name of the Lord, and this Society shall rejoice, and knowledge and intelligence shall flow down from this time henceforth; this is the beginning of better days to the poor and needy, who shall be made to rejoice and pour forth blessings on your heads.

When you go home, never give a cross or unkind word to your husbands, but let kindness, charity and love crown your works henceforward; don't envy the finery and fleeting show of sinners, for they are in a miserable situation; but as far as you can, have mercy on them, for in a short time God will destroy them, if they will not repent and turn unto him.

Let your labors be mostly confined to those around you, in the circle of your own acquaintance, as far as knowledge is concerned, it may extend to all the world; but your administering should be confined to the circle of your immediate acquaintance, and more especially to the members of the Relief Society. Those ordained to preside over and lead you, are authorized to appoint the different officers, as the circumstances shall require.

If you have a matter to reveal, let it be in your own tongue; do not indulge too much in the exercise of the gift of tongues, or the devil will take advantage of the innocent and unwary. You may speak in tongues for your own comfort, but I lay this down for a rule, that if anything is taught by the gift of tongues, it is not to be received for doctrine.

President Smith then gave instruction respecting the propriety of females administering to the sick by the prayer of faith, the laying on hands, or the anointing with oil; and said it was according to revelation that the sick should be nursed with herbs and mild food, and not by the hand of an enemy. Who are better qualified to administer than our faithful and zealous sisters, whose hearts are full of faith, tenderness, sympathy and compassion. No one. Said he was never placed in similar circumstances before, and never had given the same instruction; and closed his instructions by expressing his heart-felt satisfaction in improving this opportunity.

The Spirit of the Lord was poured out in a very powerful manner, never to be forgotten by those present on this interesting occasion.

Friday, *29*.—A conspiracy against the peace of my household was made manifest, and it gave me some trouble to counteract the design of certain base individuals, and restore peace. The Lord makes manifest to me many things, which it is not wisdom for me to make public, until others can witness the proof of them.

Saturday, 30.—I received a visit from Judge James Adams, of Springfield, and spent most of the day with him and my family. Signed deeds to James and Charles Ivins, and many others.

Sunday, May 1, 1842.—I preached in the grove, on the keys of the kingdom, charity, &c. The keys are certain signs and words by which false spirits and personages may be detected from true, which cannot be revealed to the Elders till the Temple is completed. The rich can only get them in the Temple, the poor may get them on the mountain top as did Moses. The rich cannot be saved without charity, giving to feed the poor when and how God requires, as well as building. There are signs in heaven, earth and hell; the Elders must know them all, to be endowed with power, to finish their work and prevent imposition. The devil knows many signs, but does not know the sign of the Son of Man, or Jesus. No one can truly say he knows God until he has handled something, and this can only be in the holiest of holies.

Monday, 2.—The following Editorial appeared in the *Times and Seasons:*

THE TEMPLE.

This noble edifice is progressing with great rapidity; strenuous exertions are being made on every hand to facilitate its erection, and materials of all kinds are in a great state of forwardness, and by next fall we expect to see the building enclosed; if not the top stone raised with "shouting of grace—grace unto it." There have been frequently, during the winter, as many as one hundred hands quarrying rock, while at the same time multitudes of others have been engaged in hauling, and in other kinds of labor.

A company was formed last fall to go up to the pine country to purchase mills, and prepare and saw lumber for the Temple and the Nauvoo House, and the reports from them are very favorable: another company has started, this last week, to take their place and to relieve those that are already there: on their return they are to bring a very large raft of lumber, for the use of the above-named houses.

While the busy multitudes have thus been engaged in their several vocations performing their daily labor, and working one-tenth of their time, others have not been less forward in bringing in their tithings and consecrations for the same great object. Never since the foundation of this Church was laid, have we seen manifested a greater willingness to comply with the requisitions of Jehovah, a more ardent desire to do the will of God, more strenuous exertions used, or greater sacrifices made than there have been since the Lord said, "Let the Temple be built by the tithing of my people." It seemed as though the spirit of enterprise, philanthropy and obedience rested simultaneously upon old and young, and brethren and sisters, boys and girls, and even strangers, who were not in the Church, united with an unprecedented liberality in the accomplishment of this great work; nor could the widow, in many instances, be prevented, out of her scanty pittance from throwing in her two mites.

We feel at this time to tender to all, old and young, both in the Church and out of it, our unfeigned thanks for their unprecedented liberality, kindness, diligence, and obedience which they have so opportunely manifested on the present occasion. Not that we are personally or individually benefitted in a pecuniary point of view, but when the brethren, as in this instance, show a unity of purpose and design, and all put their shoulder to the wheel, our care, labor, toil and anxiety is materially diminished, our yoke is made easy and our burden is light.

The cause of God is one common cause, in which the Saints are alike all interested; we are all members of the one common body, and all partake of the same spirit, and are baptized into one baptism and possess alike the same glorious hope. The advancement of the cause of God and the building up of Zion is as much one man's business as another's. The only difference is, that one is called to fulfill one duty, and another another duty; "but if one member suffers, all the members suffer with it, and if one member is honored all the rest rejoice with it, and the eye cannot say to the ear, I have no need of thee, nor the head to the foot, I have no need of thee;" party feelings, separate interests, exclusive designs should be lost sight of in the one common cause, in the interest of the whole.

The building up of Zion is a cause that has interested the people of God in every age; it is a theme upon which prophets, priests and kings have dwelt with peculiar delight; they have looked forward with joyful anticipation to the day in which we live; and fired with heavenly and joyful anticipations they have sung and written and prophesied of this our day; but they died without the sight; we are the favored people that God has made choice of to bring about the Latter-day glory; it is left for us to see, participate in and help to roll forward the Latter-day glory, "the dispensation of the fullness of times, when God will gather together all things that are in heaven, and all things that are upon the earth, "even in one," when the Saints of God will be gathered in one from every nation, and kindred, and people, and tongue, when the Jews will be gathered together into one, the wicked will also be gathered together to be destroyed, as spoken of by the prophets; the Spirit of God will also dwell with His people, and be withdrawn from the rest of the nations, and all things whether in heaven or on earth will be in one, even in Christ. The heavenly Priesthood will unite with the earthly, to bring about those great purposes; and whilst we are thus united in the one common cause, to roll forth the kingdom of God, the heavenly Priesthood are not idle spectators, the Spirit of God will be showered down from above, and it will dwell in our midst. The blessings of the Most High will rest upon our tabernacles, and our name will be handed down to future ages; our children will rise up and call us blessed; and generations yet unborn will dwell with peculiar delight upon the scenes that we have passed through, the privations that we have endured; the untiring zeal that we have manifested; the all but insurmountable difficulties that we have overcome in laying the foundation of a work that brought about the glory and blessing which they will realize; a work that God and angels have contemplated with delight for generations past; that fired the souls of the ancient patriarchs and prophets; a work that is destined to bring about the destruction of the powers of darkness, the renovation of the earth, the glory of God, and the salvation of the human family.

END OF VOLUME IV.

INDEX TO VOLUME IV.

M

N

O

P

Z

HISTORY

OF THE

CHURCH OF JESUS CHRIST

OF

LATTER-DAY SAINTS.

PERIOD I.

History of Joseph Smith, the Prophet.

BY HIMSELF.

VOLUME V.

AN INTRODUCTION AND NOTES
BY
B. H. ROBERTS.

PUBLISHED BY THE CHURCH.

BY

DESERET BOOK COMPANY
SALT LAKE CITY, UTAH

1980

Lithographed by
DESERET PRESS
in the United States of America

TABLE OF CONTENTS.

VOLUME V.

INTRODUCTION.

CHAPTER I.

INAUGURATION OF ENDOWMENT CEREMONIES—PERFIDY AND EXPOSURE OF JOHN C. BENNETT—HIS RESIGNATION AS MAYOR OF NAUVOO—EPISTLE OF THE HIGH COUNCIL TO THE SAINTS.

CHAPTER II.

ACTIONS IN RELATION TO JOHN C. BENNETT, *et al.*—THE PROPHET'S INSTRUCTIONS TO THE RELIEF SOCIETY—TREATISE ON THE HOLY GHOST—WILLIAM LAW'S DEFENSE OF THE SAINTS—THE PROPHET'S ADDRESS TO THE CHURCH.

CHAPTER III.

CORRESPONDENCE BETWEEN THE PROPHET AND GOVERNOR THOMAS CARLIN—ANENT JOHN C. BENNETT'S CHARACTER—PHRENOLOGICAL CHARTS OF THE PROPHET *et al.*—THE GOVENMENT OF GOD.

CHAPTER IV.

THE PROPHET CHARGED WITH BEING ACCESSORY TO THE ASSAULT ON EX-GOVERNOR BOGGS OF MISSOURI—CORRESPONDENCE WITH GOVERNOR CARLIN—THE CHARACTER OF JOHN C. BENNETT—PROPHECY THAT THE SAINTS WOULD BE DRIVEN TO THE ROCKY MOUNTAINS.

CHAPTER V.

THE PROPHET IN SECLUSION—CORRESPONDENCE WITH WILSON LAW—COMPANIONSHIP OF THE PROPHET AND HIS WIFE, EMMA SMITH—THE PROPHET'S APPRECIATION OF HIS FRIENDS.

CHAPTER VI.

CORRESPONDENCE BETWEEN JOSEPH SMITH AND WILSON LAW, *et al.*—THE PROPHET ON THE ATTITUDE OF GOVERNOR CARLIN TOWARDS HIMSELF AND THE SAINTS—REVIVAL OF THE ZEAL OF SIDNEY RIGDON—THE PROPHET'S BLESSINGS UPON HIS FRIENDS.

CHAPTER VII.

EFFORTS TO COUNTERACT THE WICKED INFLUENCE OF JOHN C. BENNETT —THE PROPHET'S REAPPEARANCE AMONG THE PEOPLE— HIS DISCOURSE AT THE SPECIAL CONFERENCE AND BEFORE THE RELIEF SOCIETY AT NAUVOO.

CHAPTER VIII.

INSTRUCTIONS ON BAPTISM FOR THE DEAD—CORRESPONDENCE BETWEEN EMMA SMITH AND GOVERNOR CARLIN—THE PROPHET'S FIRST LETTER TO JAMES ARLINGTON BENNETT.

CHAPTER IX.

CORRESPONDENCE OF THE PROPHET WITH JAMES ARLINGTON BENNETT—EMMA'S ILLNESS—PLOTS TO ENTRAP THE PROPHET—LEGAL OPINION OF JUSTIN BUTTERFIELD ON MISSOURI PROCEDURE.

CHAPTER X.

TEMPLE AFFAIRS—THE PROPHET'S ADDRESS TO "NEW-COMERS"—CITY COUNCIL'S ACTIONS AS TO WRITS OF HABEAS CORPUS.

CHAPTER XI.

PROPHET'S RETIREMENT FROM EDITORSHIP OF "TIMES AND SEASONS"—PROGRESS OF WORK ON TEMPLE—DIVISION OF NAUVOO INTO TEN WARDS—WILLIAM SMITH IN THE ILLINOIS LEGISLATURE—GOVERNOR FORD OF MISSOURI'S DEMAND FOR THE PROPHET.

CHAPTER XII.

THE PROPHET AT SPRINGFIELD, ILLINOIS—HIS CONVERSATIONS AND INTERVIEWS—PROCEEDINGS ON WRIT OF HABEAS CORPUS BEFORE JUDGE POPE—RELEASE OF THE PROPHET BY ORDER OF THE COURT AND THE EXECUTIVE ORDER OF GOVERNOR FORD—OFFICIAL PAPERS IN THE CASE.

CHAPTER XIII.

THE PROPHET AGAIN IN NAUVOO—CELEBRATION OF HIS RELEASE FROM OPPRESSION—"VADE MECUM"—REINSTATEMENT OF ORSON PRATT—DISCOURSES OF THE PROPHET "THE KINGDOM OF GOD"—"THE MISSION AND GREATNESS OF JOHN THE BAPTIST"—INTERPRETATION OF SCRIPTURES.

CHAPTER XIV.

PROVISIONS FOR THE ENLARGEMENT OF THE MUNICIPAL GOVERNMENT OF NAUVOO—SUNDRY ACTIVITIES OF THE PROPHET—KEYS OF KNOWLEDGE BY WHICH ANGELIC ADMINISTRATIONS MAY BE KNOWN—THE PROPHET'S PARABLE, "THE LIONS OF THE PRESS."

CHAPTER XV.

VISIT OF THE PROPHET TO SHOKOQUON—WOOD CUTTING BEE—THE PROPHET'S SPEECH ON CONDITIONS AT NAUVOO—ON THE COMING OF THE SON OF MAN.

CHAPTER XVI.

ATTEMPT TO REPEAL PARTS OF THE NAUVOO CHARTER—GOLD AND SILVER ALONE MADE LEGAL TENDER IN NAUVOO—SIGNS IN THE HEAVENS—"THE WASP" CHANGED INTO THE "NAUVOO NEIGHBOR"—SUSPICIONS OF THE PROPHET AGAINST SIDNEY RIGDON.

CHAPTER XVII.

EULOGY OF LORENZO D. BARNES—THE BEGINNING OF AUXILIARY ORGANIZATIONS IN THE CHURCH—IMPORTANT ITEMS OF DOCTRINE PROCLAIMED AT RAMUS—THE GENERAL CONFERENCE OF APRIL 6TH, 1843.

CHAPTER XVIII.

A GREAT MISSIONARY MOVEMENT—SPECIAL INSTRUCTIONS TO ELDERS UNDERTAKING MISSIONS—IMPRISONMENT OF ORRIN P. ROCKWELL—ARRIVAL OF SAINTS FROM ENGLAND—SPEECH OF THE PROPHET—INDIAN ELOQUENCE.

CHAPTER XIX.

THE PROPHET ON THE RESURRECTION—DIRECTIONS GIVEN AS TO THE LABORS OF THE TWELVE ET AL.—THE KINDERHOOK PLATES—FIRST ISSUE OF THE "NAUVOO NEIGHBOR"—NEW MISSION APPOINTMENTS.

CHAPTER XX.

IMPORTANT DOCTRINAL ITEMS: SALVATION THROUGH KNOWLEDGE—AGED MEN IN COUNCILS—IMPORTANCE OF THE DOCTRINE OF THE ETERNITY OF THE MARRIAGE COVENANT—THE NATURE OF MATTER—THE PROPHECY ON THE HEAD OF STEPHEN A. DOUGLAS—THE WORK AMONG THE SCANDINAVIANS IN ILLINOIS.

CHAPTER XXI.

DEFINITION OF THE WORD "MORMON"—DISCOURSE ON MAKING "CALLING" AND "ELECTION" SURE—MISSION TO THE SOCIETY ISLANDS OPENED—CHARACTER SKETCH OF THE PROPHET, "BOSTON BEE"—TRIAL OF BENJAMIN WINCHESTER.

CHAPTER XXII.

FORMS OF CREDENTIALS OF THE TWELVE—CONFERENCE AT MANCHESTER, ENGLAND—DEATH OF JUDGE ELIAS HIGBEE—"THE PURPOSE OF GATHERING"—A DISCOURSE BY THE PROPHET.

CHAPTER XXIII.

THE PROPHET'S VISIT TO DIXON, LEE CO.—CONDITIONS IN NAUVOO—SALEM ARGUS—SUMMARY OF THE WORLD'S EVENTS FOR THE YEAR 1843, UP TO JUNE—NEWS OF THE IMPENDING ARREST OF THE PROPHET RECEIVED AT NAUVOO—EXPEDITIONS FOR HIS PROTECTION—THE ARREST—TURNING THE TABLES —RETURN TO NAUVOO

CHAPTER XXIV.

APPLICATION TO THE MUNICIPAL COURT OF NAUVOO FOR WRIT OF HABEAS CORPUS—THE PROPHET'S SPEECH AT NAUVOO—PROCEEDINGS BEFORE THE MUNICIPAL COURT—THE PRISONER DISCHARGED FROM CUSTODY.

CHAPTER XXV.

AFTERMATH OF THE PROPHET'S RELEASE FROM ARREST—FOURTH OF JULY CELEBRATION AT NAUVOO—APPEALS TO GOVERNOR FORD FOR EMPLOYMENT OF MILITARY FORCE—SUPPLEMENTARY AFFIDAVITS ON AFFAIRS IN MISSOURI.

CHAPTER XXVI.

DISCOURSE OF THE PROPHET—HIS LOVE FOR MANKIND—PRESENTATION OF THE DOCUMENTS OF THE LATE TRIAL TO GOVERNOR FORD—REVELATION ON THE ETERNITY OF THE MARRIAGE COVENANT AND PLURALITY OF WIVES.

CHAPTER XXVII.

STATE OF AFFAIRS IN NAUVOO—WILLARD RICHARDS—A POLITICAL TRICK—ILLINOIS STATE REGISTER—BURDEN OF THE PROPHET'S MINISTRY—DISCOURSE—ENLARGEMENT OF MORMONISM—"BOSTON BEE"—THE PROPHET ON POLITICS—DISCOURSE—MOVEMENTS OF THE APOSTLES.

CHAPTER XXVIII.

THE PROPHET ON THE LIFE AND CHARACTER OF JUDGE ELIAS HIGBEE—LIFE AND RESURRECTION—EXPLANATION OF ELECTION DAY TROUBLES—GOVERNOR FORD'S REFUSAL TO PLAY INTO THE HANDS OF MISSOURI—ANTI-MORMON AGITATION AT CARTHAGE—ELDER JONATHAN DUNHAM'S REPORT OF HIS WESTERN EXPLORATIONS.

INTRODUCTION TO VOLUME V.

This volume deals with the History of the Church from May 3, 1842, to 31st of August, 1843. It, therefore, covers a period of about sixteen months. The main external events may be set down as follows: First, exposure of the wickedness of John C. Bennett, and his departure from Nauvoo; (2) the charge against the Prophet Joseph of complicity in an attempted assassination of Ex-governor Lilburn W. Boggs, under whose celebrated exterminating order the body of the Church was driven from Missouri; (3) the attempt of the state of Missouri to extradite the Prophet from the state of Illinois, to be tried as an accessory before the fact to an assault on ex-Governor Boggs; (4) a second attempt on the part of Missouri to extradite the Prophet from the state of Illinois on the old charge of "murder, treason, burglary, arson, larceny, theft and stealing," first brought against him in the year 1838; (5) a preliminary prospecting of the West, doubtless with a view to the contemplated removal of the Saints to the Rocky Mountains.

Of events that relate more nearly to the Church as an organization there should be mentioned: (1) the introduction of the endowment ceremonies and enlarged instruction on the subject of baptism for the dead; (2) an extension of auxiliary organization by bringing into existence the Young Men's and Women's Society.

Another item of great interest in this volume is the manifest development of the character and spiritual strength of the Prophet during this period. The trying experiences through which he passed seemed to discover new qualities of soul power within him, and to emphasize those which he was known to have possessed.

The doctrinal development of the period covered by this volume deals with several items which may be regarded as preliminary to that richer unfolding of philosophical thought to which the last year of the Prophet's teaching was so largely devoted. Let us now consider these several items more in detail.

Dr. John C. Bennett.

At the first glance it may be difficult to comprehend how a character like John C. Bennett could find favor and place with the Church of

Christ. There is a strong temptation, when the whole truth about this man is known, to regard him as an adventurer and a wicked man from the beginning. But those who had, perhaps, the best opportunity to know him held that his motives for coming to Nauvoo were honest, that his intentions in life at that time were honorable, but that he fell into transgression and would not repent. Such were the views of John Taylor, who was closely associated with Bennett in affairs at Nauvoo (see foot note, pages 80 and 81 this volume); and the Lord in the revelation given on the 19th of January, 1841, accepts of him and speaks approvingly of Bennett's love for the work: "And for his love he shall be great. * * * * * I have seen the work which he hath done, which I accept, *if he continue*, and will crown him with blessings and great glory." (Doc. and Cov., Sec. 124; 17.)

It cannot be otherwise, then, but that John C. Bennett in coming to the Saints did so out of love for the work, had a desire to work righteousness but was among those who failed—he did not "continue" in his right intentions. It is possible even for men whose lives are not above reproach to feel indignation at acts of injustice, such as was perpetrated upon the Latter-day Saints by the state of Missouri; and sure it is that John C. Bennett expressed himself very pronouncedly against the injustice suffered by the Church at the hands of the officers and people of that state, and he "proffered his military knowledge and prowess" to the Saints while the latter were yet in Missouri, but undergoing expulsion. His proposal was to go to their assistance with all the forces he could raise in Illinois, as "his bosom swelled with indignation" at the treatment the Saints were receiving at the hands of the cruel and cowardly Missourians. That proffered service, however, was not accepted; doubtless because the Saints depended for vindication of their reputation, and redress of their wrongs upon the officers of the state and nation, rather than upon incensed persons, however sincere and well meaning, who offered their service to wage war upon their enemies. But after the Saints bagan gathering at Commerce, Bennett again expressed a desire to connect his fortunes with them. When he contemplated removing to Commerce, he held the position of quartermaster-general in the militia of the state of Illinois, a position he did not wish to resign. Indeed he expressed a desire to hold the position for a number of years. He was also a physician with an extensive practice, and forwarded extracts to the Prophet from the *Louisville Courier-Journal* which gave evidence of high standing in his profession. Writing of these things to Joseph, he said:

I do not expect to resign my office of quartermaster-general of the state of Illinois, in the event of my removal to Commerce, unless you advise otherwise. I shall likewise expect to practice my profession, but at the same time your people shall have all the benefit of my speaking powers, and my untiring energies in behalf of the good and holy faith.

In a communication following the one from which I make the above quotation he said:

You are aware that at the time of your most bitter persecution, I was with you in feeling, and proffered you my military knowledge and powers.

While Joseph extended a hearty welcome to the Doctor to come to Commerce, he by no means held out any very flattering inducements to him, as may be seen by his letters in answer to Bennett's expressing his determination to join the Saints. The Prophet said:

I have no doubt that you would be of great service to this community in practicing your profession, as well as those other abilities of which you are in possession. Though to devote your time and abilities in the cause of truth and a suffering people, may not be the means of exalting you in the eyes of this generation, or securing you the riches of this world, yet by so doing you may rely on the approval of Jehovah, "that blessing which maketh rich and addeth no sorrow." * * * * * * Therefore, my general invitation is, let all who will come, come and partake of the poverty of Nauvoo, freely. I should be disposed to give you a special invitation to come as early as possible, believing you will be of great service to us. However, you must make your own arrangements according to your circumstances. Were it possible for you to come here this season to suffer affliction with the people of God, no one will be more pleased to give you a cordial welcome than myself.

Surely this was frank enough, and ought to have dispelled from the Doctor's mind all thoughts of winning worldly fame, or gratifying vain ambition, by linking his fortunes with those of the Church of Jesus Christ. The whole course of the Prophet here outlined, and as further set forth in the parts of this volume dealing with the case of John C. Bennett, vindicates him and the Church from any complicity with the wickedness and vileness of that man.

Bennett's attempted vindication of his course of procedure, and his defense against the action of the Church in exposing his wickedness and excommunicating him is, that from the beginning he came amongst the Saints as a spy, to become acquainted with their alleged treasonable designs against several of the western states, for the purpose of exposing them; all which is set forth in a note at pp. 79, 80 of this volume. All this was ridiculous; and the whole presentation of this view of the matter in his book under the pompous title, *The History of the Saints; or An Expose of Joe Smith and Mormonism*,* convinced nobody, since Bennett's insincerity and putridity of mind is evidenced upon

* Published in Boston, 1842.

every page of his repulsive book. "The role of traitor," says H. H. Bancroft, in his history of Utah, dealing with John C. Bennett:—

The role of traitor is not one which in any wise brings credit to the performer, either from one side or the other. However great the service he may render us, we cannot but feel that he is false hearted and vile. Many of the apostates, though they may not have written books, declare that they joined the sect only to learn their secrets and then expose them. These are the most contemptible of all. There may be cases, where a young or inexperienced person, through ignorance or susceptibility, has been carried away for a time contrary to the dictates of cooler judgment; but the statements of such persons are justly regarded with more or less suspicion. Far better is it, far more honest and praiseworthy, for him who, having unwittingly made a mistake, seeks to rectify it, to go his way and say nothing about it; for if he talks of writing a book for the good of others, as a warning, and that they may avoid his errors, few will believe him. "If he has proved traitor once," they say, "he will deceive again; and if he is sincere, we cannot more than half believe him, for such an individual is never sure of himself." John C. Bennett, general, doctor, methodist preacher, and quack, is from his own showing a bad man. He devotes some fifty pages to the vindication of his character, which would not be necessary were he honest; other fifty are given to defaming his late worshipful patron Joseph Smith, which would never have been written were he true. When a man thrusts in your face three-score certificates of his good character, each signed by from one to a dozen persons, you may know that he is a very great rascal. Nor are we disappointed here. This author is a charlatan, pure and simple; such was he when he joined the Mormons, and before and after. We may credit him fully when he says, "I never believed in them or their doctrines;" although in a letter to Dr. Dyer, dated Nauvoo, Jan. 20, 1842, he declares: "My heart is filled with indignation, and my blood boils within me, when I contemplate the vast injustice and cruelty which Missouri has meted out to the great philanthropist and devout Christian, General Joseph Smith, and his honest and faithful adherents." When, however, he affects patriotism and lofty devotion to the welfare of his fellow-men, pretending to have joined the society in order to frustrate "a daring and colossal scheme of rebellion and usurpation throughout the north-western states, ... a despotic military and religious empire, the head of which, as emperor and pope, was to be Joseph Smith," we know that the writer is well aware that it is all nonsense. Nor do we believe that he was induced to print his book "by a desire to expose the enormous iniquities which have been perpetrated by one of the grossest and most infamous impostors that ever appeared upon the face of the earth." We have heard and are still hearing so much of that kind of talk from some of the worst men in the community that it is becoming somewhat stale, and if the general really does not know better than this why he wrote his book, perhaps he will excuse me for telling him that it was, first, for notoriety; second, for money; and third, in order to make people think him a better and greater man than he is. When a man's ambition is pitched so low, it is a pity that he should not have the gratification of success. Bravely, then, the general proceeded to offer himself on the altar of his country, "to overthrow the impostor and expose his iniquity" by "professing himself a convert to his doctrines;" for "the fruition of his hopeful project would, of course, have been preceded by plunder, devastation, and bloodshed, and by all the countless horrors which invariably accompany civil war." We are still more impressed when we read: "I was quite aware of the danger I ran"—that of being kicked out of some back door—"but none of these things deterred me." Without wasting more time and space upon the man, we are well enough prepared to place a proper estimate upon his statements, particularly when we take into account that, in May of the very year in which his book was published, he went before Alderman Wells and made affidavit that Joseph Smith was an honest, virtuous, sincere, high-minded, and patriotic man. He says himself that he solemnly swore to be true to the Mormons and not reveal their secrets, and now in breaking that oath he has the audacity to ask us to regard him as an honest and truthful man! In some measure, at least, the statements of such men as this, taken up by the press and people, and reiterated throughout the land, have given the Latter-day Saints a worse name than they deserve. Some of his charges are too coarse and filthy for repetition." *

The only description I have seen of Dr. Bennett is given in the *Essex County Washingtonian*, published in Salem, Massachusetts, and that is contained in the issue of the fifteenth of September, 1842. According to that description he was a man of about five feet nine inches high, well formed, black hair sprinkled with gray, dark complexion, a rather thin face, and black restless eyes.

He finally died in obscurity, and also, it is said, in poverty, (Cannon's Life of Joseph Smith, p. 377).

The Attempted Assassination of Ex-Governor Boggs of Missouri.

When an attempt was made to assassinate ex-Governor Boggs of Missouri it was perhaps to be expected that suspicion would fall upon the Mormon people and upon the head of Joseph Smith especially. Surely Boggs had given sufficient provocation to that people to make it probable that some fanatic of their number might undertake in misguided zeal, the act of revenge; and surely there would not be wanting those who would say that Joseph Smith in his capacity as Prophet had predicted the violent taking off of the ex-governor. Joseph Smith, however, in his communication to the *Quincy Whig*, in which appeared the first account of the rumored assassination of Boggs, promptly denied making the alleged prediction, and also denied any complicity whatsoever in the wretched business. It is only just to his memory to say that in all the investigation had upon the subject, historically, or judicially, his denial is not controverted. Even in the case of Orrin Porter Rock-

* Bancroft's History of Utah, pp. 150, 151 *note*.

well who was charged directly with the attempted assassination and taken to Jackson county, Missouri, for trial, it had to be admitted that "there was not sufficient proof adduced against him to justify an indictment for shooting at ex-Governor Boggs, and the grand jury therefore did not indict him for that offense." (*Independent Expositor*, *Nile's Register*, Sept. 30, 1843.)

John C. Bennett labors hard to prove by statements alleged to have been made to him by the Prophet, and subsequently by Rockwell, that they were jointly guilty of this attempted assassination; but there is no weight of evidence in his presentation of the case; nor is there any evidence that the Mormon people or the officials of the Mormon Church approved of revenge by acts of assassination. Bennett in his book "The History of the Saints," (p. 282) makes a quotation from the *Nauvoo Wasp* in which he charges editorial expressions of approval of the deed, as follows:

> The *Nauvoo Wasp* of May 28, A. D., 1842, a paper edited by William Smith, one of the Twelve Mormon Apostles, and brother of the Prophet, declared, ["Boggs is undoubtedly killed according to report, but]* Who did the Noble Deed remains to be found out."

This, however, is not an editorial expression of the *Wasp*; but is found in a communication, on the editorial page, it is true, signed by a now unknown writer under the non de plume, "Vortex," who is indignantly taking to task a correspodent in the *Hawk Eye*, a paper published in Keokuk, Iowa, for charging the supposed assassination of Boggs upon some Mormon. It is "Vortex" in the *Wasp* that refers to the then supposed assassination of Boggs as a "noble deed," not the editor. The editorial comment of the *Wasp* on this communication from "Vortex" is as follows: "We admit the foregoing communication to please our correspondent, not that we have any faith that any one has killed Governor Boggs. The last account we have received is that he is still living and likely to live." On the same page of the *Wasp* is published Joseph Smith's denial of complicity in the then supposed assassination of Boggs and also the prediction of his violent death.

The First Attempt of Missouri to Extradite the Prophet.

That Joseph Smith should be accused of the crime of being accessory before the fact to the attempted assassination of ex-Governor Boggs, was perhaps to be expected as soon as a Mormon was charged with the assault. But that his extradition should be demanded by Missouri on the ground that he was "a fugitive from justice from that State" is something at which to be astonished, even when the

* The words in brackets are in the *Wasp* communication, but not in Bennett's book. They are inserted here for clearness.

action is by the officials of Missouri of the period of which I am writing. For surely it must be a true principle of law—since it is a plain deduction from common sense principles—that the alleged fugitive from justice must be such in connection with and in consequence of the crime with which he is charged. It was matter of common knowledge both in Missouri and in Illinois, that Joseph Smith had not been in Missouri for more than three years preceding the assault upon Boggs, nor since the time of the assault; and that on the day the assault was made he was in attendance upon an officer's drill. Finally, then, he was not a fugitive from the State of Missouri in respect of this particular crime, therefore not extraditable under such charge. If, then, Joseph Smith had committed the crime of being accessory before the fact, to the assault upon Boggs at all, it must have been a crime committed in the state of Illinois and not in the state of Missouri. Therefore he was not extraditable for the offense at all, but he must be tried, if tried at all, in the state where the crime was committed, *viz.*, in Illinois. But if astonishment is due that even Missouri should make such palpable blunders in legal procedure in moving for the extradition of the Prophet, astonishment changes to amazement when Governor Carlin of Illinois becomes a party to the attempted illegal extradition. The whole procedure up to the close of Carlin's administration (which went out of existence on the 8th of December 1842), warrants the conclusion that a conspiracy existed between the high state officials of both Missouri and Illinois against Joseph Smith, and that it was the intent of that conspiracy to encompass his destruction. When the Prophet and Orrin Porter Rockwell were arrested (8th of August, 1842) by the deputy sheriff of Adams county, they made no attempt to evade the officer, but immediately applied to the municipal court of Nauvoo for a writ of *habeas corpus*, which was granted, but the deputy sheriff refused to recognize the authority of the municipal court in this case, and leaving his prisoner in the hands of the city marshal, withdrew from Nauvoo. He returned two days later, however, determined to take the Prophet from Nauvoo and deliver him to the agents of the state of Missouri. The Prophet, however, avoided arrest and went into retirement, where he remained—with now and then an occasional appearance among the people—throughout the summer of 1842. In the early days of December, Governor Carlin's administration came to an end and Ford's began,and the Prophet at once petitioned the new executive to rescind Carlin's order for his arrest. Ford referred the matter to the judges of the Supreme Court, who were unanimously of the opinion that the requisition from Missouri was illegal, but advised that the matter be settled in the courts rather than by executive action. The Governor suggested that if the Prophet found it necessary to repair to

Springfield, the state capital, for a judicial investigation of his rights, he did not think there would be any disposition to use illegal violence against him; and the governor pledged himself to protect the Prophet if necessary with any amount of force from mob violence while asserting his rights before the courts, as well as when going to and returning from them. This advice was supplemented by the advice of his eminent counsel, Justin Bntterfield; also by his very dear and trusted friend, General James Adams. The Prophet accordingly submitted to arrest and immediately set out for Springfield with a company of his friends.

The matter once before the Circuit Court of the United States for the district of Illinois, Judge Pope presiding, the matter was soon disposed of by declaring the procedure of Missouri and the executive of Illinois, (Carlin) illegal, and ordering that the Prophet be discharged from his arrest, as set forth in detail in the body of this volume.

The Second Attempt of Missouri to Extradite the Prophet.

A second attempt of Missouri to drag the Prophet from the state of Illinois by extradition procedure, was even more infamous than the first. No sooner was Joseph released from arrest and departed from Springfield than John C. Bennett arrived there and wrote some of his friends in Nauvoo his intention to leave immediately for Missouri and obtain a new indictment by a grand jury on the old charge of "murder, treason, burglary, theft," etc., brought against the Prophet, Hyrum Smith, Lyman Wight, Parley P. Pratt *et al.*, in 1838, hoping that upon this charge he might succeed in getting out extradition papers on the ground that the Prophet was a fugitive from the justice of the state of Missouri. It will be remembered that a former attempt was made under this same charge, in June, 1841, when the Prophet was tried on writ of *habeas corpus* at Monmouth, Warren county, Illinois, before Judge Douglas and set at liberty. It was on this occasion that Esquire O. H. Browning declared that to ask Joseph Smith "to go to Missouri for a trial was adding insult to injury" (Vol. IV, chapter XX).

An indictment on these old charges was finally obtained, supposedly at the instance of Bennett and the Prophet's old Missouri enemies, at a special term of the Circuit Court of Daviess county, Missouri, on the 5th of June, 1843. Governor Reynolds, of Missouri issued a requisition on Governor Ford for Joseph Smith, and appointed J. H. Reynolds as agent of Missouri to receive the Prophet from the authorities of Illinois. The story of the arrest and the incidents thereto are given in great detail in the body of this volume, and need not be dwelt upon here. It will be sufficient to say that Joseph finally succeeded in bringing his captors to Nauvoo where he obtained a writ of *habeas corpus* from the municipal court of Nauvoo by which the validity of the procedure of Missouri might be tested. When Joseph was on trial upon these same charges before Judge Douglas on a writ of *habeas corpus* in 1841, the Monmouth court refused to enter into a consideration of the merits of the case, as the judge doubted whether on the writ of *habeas corpus* he had a right to go beyond the writ and inquire into the merits of the ease, but ordered the release of the prisoner on the ground of some defect in the writ under which he was held. The same point was avoided by Judge Pope in the hearing at Springfield on the charge against the Prophet for complicity in the assault upon ex-Governor Boggs. But the Nauvoo municipal court had no such scruples, and at once proceeded to try the case *exparte* on its merits, and Hyrum Smith, P. P. Pratt, Brigham Young, Geo. W. Pitkin, Lyman Wight, and Sidney Rigdon were examined as witnesses. Their affidavits before the court concerning events that happened to the Saints in Missouri, afford the most circumstantial, reliable and exhaustive data for the history of the Church while in that state. They will be found in the Appendix to Vol. III of this history. After hearing the testimony of these witnesses and the pleading of counsel the court ordered that Joseph Smith be released from the arrest and imprisonment of which he complained for want of substance in the warrant by which he was held, as well as upon the merits of the case. A copy of the proceedings before the municipal court at Nauvoo and all the papers connected with the case were immediately sent to Governor Ford, as also were affidavits from leading counsel and gentlemen from outside places. I may anticipate a little by saying that about a year later a jury in Lee county, Illinois, awarded $40.00 damages and costs against Wilson, a sheriff in the state of Illinois, and Reynolds, the Missouri agent, for false imprisonment and abuse of the Prophet, a verdict, which while it confirms the unlawful course of those officers, and the fact that their prisoner was abused, insults justice by awarding such an amount for damages.

At the time of the action by the municipal court of Nauvoo, ordering the Prophet's release from arrest, it was a question in Illinois whether said court had the authority to hear and determine writs of *habeas corpus* arising from arrests made by virtue of warrants issued by the courts of the state or of the governor, as in the foregoing case; or whether the clause in the city charter granting the right of issuing writs of *habeas corpus* was not confined to cases arising strictly from arrests made on account of the violation of some city ordinance. The clause in the charter, giving to the municipal court the power to issue writs of *habeas corpus* was as follows:

The municipal court shall have power to grant writs of *habeas corpus* in all cases arising under the ordinances of the city council.

And in addition there was the general welfare provision, which provided that the

City council shall have power and authority to make,ordain, establish and execute such ordinances not repugnant to the constitution of the United States or of this state, as they may deem necessary for the peace, benefit and safety of the inhabitants of said city.

It was maintained on the part of those who believed that the municipal court had the right to issue writs of *habeas corpus* against process issued from the state courts that all the power there was in Illinois she gave to Nauvoo, and that the municipal court had all the power within the limits of the city that the state courts had, and that power was given by the same authority—the legislature. A number of lawyers of more or less prominence in the state professed to hold these views; but little reliance can be put in the support they bring to the case, since all of them were seeking political preferment, immediately or remotely, and would and did in their interpretation of the powers granted by the charter, favor that side of the controversy most likely to please the citizens of Nauvoo. Governor Ford, too, at the time, gave a tacit approval of the course taken by the municipal court in issuing the writ of *habeas corpus*, though he afterwards became very pronounced in his opposition to the exercise of such powers. His acquiescence appears in this, that as soon as Joseph was liberated, sheriff Reynolds applied to Governor Ford for a *posse* to retake him, representing that the Prophet had been unlawfully taken out of his hands by the municipal court of Nauvoo: whereupon the governor refused to grant the petition. Subsequently the governor of Missouri asked Governor Ford to call out the militia to retake Joseph,but this he also refused to do,and gave as a reason that "no process, officer, or authority of the state had been resisted or interfered with;" and recited how the prisoner had been released on *habeas corpus* by the municipal court of Nauvoo. The governor acted in this instance with perfect knowledge of what had taken place, for the petition and statement of Reynolds were in his possession, as were also complete copies of all the documents which contained the proceedings before the municipal court of Nauvoo; and in addition to these sources of information, the governor had dispatched a trusted secret agent, a Mr. Brayman, to Nauvoo, who investigated the case and reported the result to him. It must be held, however, both as a matter of fact and of law, that the grant in the Nauvoo city charter was intended by the legislature only to give power to the municipal court to issue writs of *habeas corpus* in cases of arrest for violation of city ordinances; and that giving power to the municipal court to test the warrants or processes issued from the state courts was never contemplated by the legislature, and that the passage of any ordinance by the city council that would bring about or authorize any such unusual proceeding was an unwarranted assumption of power, utterly wrong in principle and consequenly subversive of government. But whatever opinion may be entertained on the legal point under consideration, there can be no question but what upon the broad principles of justice the Prophet Joseph ought to have been set free. The state of Missouri had no just claims upon him. He had been arrested and several times examined on these old charges now revived by the personal malice of John C. Bennett, and after being held a prisoner awaiting indictment and trial for five months in Missouri in the winter of 1838-9, so conscious were the officers of the state that they had no case against him, that they themselves connived at his escape. After such proceedings to demand that he be dragged again into Missouri, among his old enemies for a trial on these old and time-worn charges, was an outrage against every principle of justice, and was a course prompted solely by malice.

Prospecting the West with a View to Removal of the Saints.

It may be that what is here set down with reference to prospecting the west with a view to the ultimate removal of the Saints, can reach no higher from the data supplied by this volume than conjecture; but taken in connection with the well-known projects of the last year of the Prophet's life—upon which now our history, even in this volume, has entered—and the facts to which attention is called appear quite significant. These facts are: The Prophet's remarkable and well attested prediction of 6th of August, 1843, that the Saints would yet be driven to the Rocky mountains where they would become a great people (p. 85 and note;) the several visits of delegations of Pottawattamie Indian chiefs to the Prophet, the body of their people being then settled on the Missouri river nearly due west some three hundred miles from Nauvoo; the appointment of Elder Jonathan Dunham, a man of character and judgment, to visit this tribe of Indians, under the Pottawattamie guide Neotanah; and the incorporation of the journal of Elder Dunham within the narrative of the Prophet's autobiographical journal. The concluding paragraph of Dunham's journal expresses disappointment with his explorations,* the object of which since his journey covered something like six hundred miles, and was attended by Indian guides both

*"I have seen much delightful country, but the prospect for bee hunting is not as good as I could wish."

going and returning, was not "bee hunting;" but most probably prospecting a possible trail and locating resting places for the Saints when engaged in a great westward movement.

Development of the Prophet's Character.

During the trying events of the fifteen months of which this volume is a history, the nature of the Prophet underwent a remarkable development. There never was, of course, any doubt as to the physical courage of the Prophet. From boyhood he had been noted for his fearlessness under trying circumstances, but during the period here considered he was the constant object of assault, both by legal processes, under the leadership of cunning, malicious men, and the physical brutality of officials charged with the execution of the law; and both when facing the maliciously skillful in their proceedings under the color of law, and the threats of physical force from brutal captors, the conduct of the Prophet was most admirable. Also in seclusion, when others were easily excited and manifested symptoms of panic under the ciruumstances of conflicting rumors of impending dangers, it is refreshing to see how calmly the Prophet keeps his balance and rightly judges the true status of many trying situations. But what is most pleasing to record of this period of enforced seclusion while avoiding his enemies, is the development of that tenderness of soul manifested in his reflections upon the friends who had stood by him from the commencement of his public career: for his father and mother, for his brother Alvin, for Emma, his wife, for his brother Hyrum, the Knights,who were his friends even before the Book of Mormon was translated, and especially for the friends who received him and ministered unto him during his retirement from public ministry. No act of kindness seems to go unmentioned. No risk run for him that is not appreciated. Indeed he gathers much benefit from those trials, since their effect upon his nature seems to be a softening rather than a hardening influence; and the trials of life are always beneficial where they do not harden and brutalize men's souls; and every day under his trials the Prophet seems to have grown more tender-hearted, more universal in his sympathies; his moments of spiritual exaltation are superb. No one can read them and doubt that the inspiration of God was giving this man's spirit understanding.

Doctrinal Development.

The doctrinal development of the Church for the period covered by this volume covers a wide range of subjects; the Prophet's definition of the "Kingdom of God," meaning in its narrowest as in its broadest sense, the "government of God, whether represented by a single individual, an institution or a great and complex organization (p. 256); the keys by which angelic administrations may be known (p. 267); the virtue of Blood Atonement (p. 296); the physical nature of God, the Father, the Son, and the Holy Spirit (p. 323, 325, 426); the earth becoming a Urim and Thummim to those who shall inherit it in its glorified and perfected state; the coming of the Son of Man; the persistence of acquired knowledge; the impossibility of being saved in ignorance (pp. 323-5). But the climax in doctrine as in moral daring is reached in this volume by the Prophet committing to writing the revelation on the eternity of the marriage covenant, and, under special circumstances and divine sanction the rightfulness, of a plurality of wives. As the time at which this revelation was given has been questioned, and also the authorship of it, extended consideration is given to both these matters in the following treatise:

The Time When the Revelation on the Eternity of the Marriage Covenant, Including a Plurality of Wives, Was Given, and its Authorship.

I.

The Date of the Revelation.

The date in the heading of the Revelation on the Eternity of the Marriage Covenant, Including the Plurality of Wives, notes the time at which the revelation was committed to writing, not the time at which the principles set forth in the revelation were first made known to the Prophet. This is evident from the written revelation itself which discloses the fact that Joseph Smith was already in the relationship of plural marriage, as the following passage witnesses:

"And let mine handmaid, Emma Smith, receive all those that have been given unto my servant Joseph, and who are virtuous and pure before me."

There is indisputable evidence that the revelation making known this marriage law was given to the Prophet as early as 1831. In that year, and thence intermittently up to 1833, the Prophet was engaged in a revision of the English Bible text under the inspiration of God, Sidney Rigdon in the main acting as his scribe. As he began his revision with the Old Testament, he would be dealing with the age of the Patriarchs in 1831. He was doubtless struck with the favor in which the Lord held the several Bible Patriarchs of that period, notwithstanding they had a plurality of wives. What more natural than that he should inquire of the Lord at that time, when his mind must have been impressed with the fact—Why, O Lord, didst Thou justify Thy servants, Abraham, Isaac and Jacob; as also Moses, David, and Solomon, in the matter of their having many wives and concubines (see opening paragraph of the Revelation)? In answer to that inquiry came the revelation, though not then committed to writing.

Corroborative evidences of the fact of the revelation having been given thus early in the Prophet's career are to be found in the early charges against the Church about its belief in "polygamy." For example: When the Book of Doctrine and Covenants was presented to the several quorums of the priesthood of the Church for acceptance in the general assembly of that body, the 17th of August, 1835, an article on "Marriage" was presented by W. W. Phelps, which for many years was published in the Doctrine and Covenants. It was not a revelation, nor was it presented as such to the general assembly of the priesthood. It was an article, however, that represented the views of the assembly on the subject of marriage at that time, unenlightened as they were by the revelation already given to the Prophet on the subject. What the Prophet Joseph's connection was with this article cannot be learned. Whether he approved it or not is uncertain, since he was absent from Kirtland at the time of the general assembly of the priesthood which accepted it, on a visit to the Saints in Michigan (see HISTORY OF THE CHURCH, Vol. I, pp. 243-53).

In this article on marriage the following sentence occurs:

"Inasmuch as this Church of Christ has been reproached with the crime of fornication and polygamy, we declare that we believe that one man should have one wife, and one woman but one husband, except in case of death, when either is at liberty to marry again."

From this it is evident that as early at least as 1835 a charge of polygamy was made against the Church. Why was that the case unless the subject of "polygamy" had been mooted within the Church? Is it not evident that some one to whom the Prophet had confided the knowledge of the revelation he had received concerning the rightfulness of plural marriage—under certain circumstances—had unwisely made some statement concerning the matter?

Again, in May, 1836, in Missouri, in a series of questions asked and answered through the *Elder's Journal*, the following occurs:

"Do the Mormons believe in having more wives than one?"

To which the answer is given;

"No, not at the same time."

This again represents the belief of the Saints at that time, unenlightened as they then were by the revelation received by their Prophet. But again, why this question unless there had been some agitation of the subject? Had some one before the time had come for making known this doctrine to the Church, again unwisely referred to the knowledge which had been revealed to the Prophet some seven years earlier?

All these incidents blend together and make it clearly evident that the revelation on marriage was given long before the 12th of July, 1843. Doubtless as early as 1831.

In addition to these indirect evidences is the direct testimony of the late Elder Orson Pratt, of the council of the Twelve Apostles. In 1878, in company with President Joseph F. Smith, Elder Pratt visited several states east of the Mississippi in the capacity of a missionary; and at Plano, Illinois, at a meeting of the so-called Reorganized Church of the Latter-day Saints, he was invited by the presiding officer, a Mr. Dille, and the meeting, to occupy the time, which he did. In his remarks, according to his own and his companion's report of the meeting—

"Elder Pratt gave a plain, simple narration of his early experience in the Church, relating many interesting incidents connected with its rise; explained the circumstances under which several revelations were received by Joseph, the Prophet, and the manner in which he received them, he being present on several occasions of the kind. Declared [that] at such times Joseph used the Seerstone when inquiring of the Lord, and receiving revelation, but that he was so thoroughly endowed with the inspiration of the Almighty and the spirit of revelation that he often received them without any instrument, or other means than the operation of the spirit upon his mind. Referred to the testimony which he received of the truth of the great latter-day work while yet a boy. Testified that these things were not matters of belief only with him, but of actual knowledge. He explained the circumstances connected with the coming forth of the revelation on plural marriage. Refuted the statement and belief of those present that Brigham Young was the author of that revelation; showed that Joseph Smith the Prophet had not only commenced the practice himself,and taught it to others, before President Young and the Twelve had returned from their mission in Europe, in 1841, but that Joseph actually received revelations upon that principle as early as 1831. Said: 'Lyman Johnson, who was very familiar with Joseph at this early date, Joseph living at his father's house, and who was also very intimate with me, we having traveled on several missions together, told me himself that Joseph had made known to him as early as 1831, that plural marriage was a correct principle. Joseph declared to Lyman that God had revealed it to him, but that the time had not come to teach or practice it in the Church, but that the time would come.' To this statement Elder Pratt bore his testimony. He cited several instances of Joseph having had wives sealed to him, one at least as early as April 5th, 1841, which was some time prior to the return of the Twelve from England. Referred to his own trial in regard to this matter in Nauvoo, and said it was because he got his information from a wicked source, from those disaffected, but as soon as he learned the truth, he was satisfied.

(Signed) "ORSON PRATT,
(Signed) "JOSEPH F. Smith."

(The above is taken from a signed report of Elders Orson Pratt and Joseph F. Smith of the Council of the Twelve on the occasion of their visit to the East in 1878, and is to be found in the *Millennial Star*, Vol. 40, Nos. 49 and 50.)

Relative to committing the revelation to writing on the 12th of July, 1843, that can best be told by the man who wrote the revelation as the Prophet Joseph dictated it to him, William Clayton; and the man who copied it the day following, Joseph Kingsbury; and from which copy the revelation was afterwards printed as it now stands in the current edition of the Doctrine and Covenants. In a sworn statement before John T. Caine, a notary public in Salt Lake City, on February 16th, 1874, William Clayton said:

"On the 7th of October, 1842, in the presence of Bishop Newel K. Whitney and his wife, Elizabeth Ann, President Joseph Smith appointed me Temple Recorder, and also his private clerk, placing all records, books papers, etc., in my care, and requiring me to take charge of and preserve them, his closing words being, 'when I have any revelations to write, you are the one to write them.' * * * On the morning of the 12th of July, 1843; Joseph and Hyrum Smith came into the office in the upper story of the brick store, on the bank of the Mississippi river. They were talking on the subject of plural marriage. Hyrum said to Joseph, 'If you will write the revelation on celestial marriage, I will take it and read it to Emma, and I believe I can convince her of its truth, and you will hereafter have peace.' Joseph smiled and remarked, 'You do not know Emma as well as I do.' Hyrum repeated his opinion, and further remarked, 'The doctrine is so plain, I can convince any reasonable man or woman of its truth, purity and heavenly origin,' or words to that effect. Joseph then said, 'Well, I will write the revelation and we will see.' He then requested me to get paper and prepare to write. Hyrum very urgently requested Joseph to write the revelation by means of the Urim and Thummim, but Joseph in reply, said he did not need to, for he knew the revelation perfectly from beginning to end.

"Joseph and Hyrum then sat down and Joseph commenced to dictate the revelation on celestial marriage, and I wrote it, sentence by sentence, as he dictated. After the whole was written, Joseph asked me to read it through, slowly and carefully, which I did, and he pronounced it correct. He then remarked that there was much more that he could write on the same subject, but what was written was sufficient for the present.

"Hyrum then took the revelation to read to Emma. Joseph remained with me in the office until Hyrum returned. When he came back, Joseph asked him how he had succeeded. Hyrum replied that he had never received a more severe talking to in his life, that Emma was very bitter and full of resentment and anger.

"Joseph quietly remarked, 'I told you you did not know Emma as well as I did.' Joseph then put the revelation in his pocket, and they both left the office.

"The revelation was read to several of the authorities during the day. Towards evening Bishop Newel K. Whitney asked Joseph if he had any objections to his taking a copy of the revelation; Joseph replied that he had not, and handed it to him. It was carefully copied the following day by Joseph C. Kingsbury. Two or three days after the revelation was written Joseph related to me and several others that Emma had so teased, and urgently entreated him for the privilege of destroying it, that he became so weary of her teasing, and to get rid of her annoyance, he told her she might destroy it and she had done so, but he had consented to her wish in this matter to pacify her, realizing that he knew the revelation perfectly, and could rewrite it at any time if necessary.

"The copy made by Joseph C. Kingsbury is a true and correct copy of the original in every respect. The copy was carefully preserved by Bishop Whitney, and but few knew of its existence until the temporary location of the Camps of Israel at Winter Quarters, on the Missouri River, in 1846. * * * * *

(signed) "WM. CLAYTON.

"Salt Lake City, Feb. 16th, 1874."

On May 22, 1886, Joseph C. Kingsbury made the following statement before Charles W. Stayner, a notary public, in Salt Lake City:

"In reference to the affidavit of Elder William Clayton, on the subject of the celestial order of patriarchal marriage, published in the *Deseret Evening News* of May 20th, 1886, and particularly as to the statement made therein concerning myself, as having copied the original revelation written by Brother Clayton at the dictation of the Prophet Joseph, I will say that Bishop Newel K. Whitney, handed me the revelation above referred to either on the day it was written or the day following, and stating what it was, asked me to take a copy of it. I did so, and then read my copy of it to Bishop Whitney, we compared it with the original which he held in his hand while I read to him. When I had finished reading, Bishop Whitney pronounced the copy correct, and Hyrum Smith coming into the room at the time to fetch the original, Bishop Whitney handed it to him. I will also state that this copy, as also the original are identically the same as that published in the present edition [1886] of the Book of Doctrine and Covenants.

"I will add that I also knew that the Prophet Joseph Smith had married other women besides his first wife, Emma; I was well aware of the fact of his having married Sarah Ann Whitney, the eldest daughter of Bishop Newel K. Whitney and Elizabeth Ann Whitney, his wife. And the Prophet Joseph told me personally that he had married other women, in accordance with the revealed will of God, and spoke concerning the principle as being a command of God for holy purposes.

(Signed) "JOSEPH C. KINGSBURY."

II.

Authorship of the Revelation.

In addition to the testimony of these affidavits as to the authorship of the revelation, and many more on file in the Church Historian's office, equally positive and unimpeachable, which might be quoted, there is another sort of evidence as to the authorship, not before used, so far as I know, to which I desire to appeal, and which is even more certain and convincing on this subject than the testimony of any affidavit by whomsoever given. I refer to the internal evidence that Joseph Smith, under the inspiration of God, of course, is the author of it. The revelation carries with it so many characteristics of his style found in other revelations given through him, that to doubt his authorship of it is impossible. Let us consider these characteristics.

1. *The Revelation Was Given in Answer to the Prophet's Inquiry—A Characteristic of Nearly All His Revelations.*

The revelation was given in answer to the Prophet's inquiries upon one branch of the subject of which it treats, *viz.*, the justification of some of the Bible Patriarchs and Prophets in having a plurality of wives. It is so generally the case that the revelations the Prophet received came in response to inquiries either by himself or by those who sought to learn their duty or to know some truth, that such inquiries may be considered as a condition precedent to his receiving revelations; at any rate it is plainly a characteristic of the whole volume of revelations which Joseph Smith gave to the world.

The Prophet's first revelation, the one respecting the errancy of the religious world, accompanied as it was by a full view of God the Father, and God the Son, was received in answer to a most earnest inquiry to know what course he should pursue in the midst of the religious confusion then existing—which church should he join. (History of the Church, Vol. I, chapt. 1.)

The first of that series of meetings with the angel Moroni, which finally resulted in the coming forth of the Book of Mormon, was brought about through the Prophet asking for a spiritual manifestation from the Lord, that he might know of his "state and standing before Him." (History of the Church, Vol. I, chapt. 2).

The series of revelations given during the time the Book of Mormon was in course of translation were chiefly given in response to inquiries on the part of the persons who came to the Prophet seeking to know the will of the Lord with reference to the relationship they should assume towards the work then coming forth. See Doc. and Cov., Sec. 10; History of the Church, Vol. I, p. 23, also pp. 28-33, 36, 45, 48, 49, 51, 53. These revelations are found in the Doc. and Cov., Sec. 3, 4, 5, 6, 7, 8, 10, 11, 12, 14, 15, 16, 17.)

The revelation authorizing the organization of the Church and outlining that organization and some of the fundamental doctrines of the Church (Doc. and Cov., Sec. 20), was given in answer to most earnest inquiry as to how the Prophet and his associates should proceed with the work of organization. "We had for some time made this matter a subject of humble prayer," writes the Prophet, "and at length we got together in the chamber of Mr. Whitmer's house, in order more particularly to seek of the Lord what we now so earnestly desired; and here to our unspeakable satisfaction, did we realize the truth of the Savior's promise, 'ask, and it shall be given you; seek, and ye shall find; knock, and it shall be opened unto you'—for we had not long been engaged in solemn and fervent prayer, when the word of the Lord came to us in the chamber." (History of the Church, chapt. 7.) Then follows the revelation on Church organization and doctrine.

I may say that all the great revelations of the Church, as well as those which might be regarded as merely personal, were received in response to earnest inquiries of the Lord. Thus the revelation which in 1831 was regarded as making known the moral law of the Gospel was received after earnest inquiry. (History of the Church, Vol. I, p. 148; Doc. and Cov., Sec. 42, par. 3.) So also the great revelation on priesthood. (History of the Church, Vol. I, p. 287; Doc. and Cov., Sec. 84.) The great revelation on the order of the priesthood and the relations of the quorums to each other was given in response to a formal and very earnest petitition on the part of the quorum of the Twelve Apostles. (History of the Church, Vol. II, pp. 219, 220; Doc. and Cov., Sec. 107.) So also as to the revelation on tithing and the disposition of it. (Doc. and Cov., Sec. 119, 120; History of the Church, Vol. III, p. 44.) So the great revelation setting in order the affairs of the Church at Nauvoo, given January 19, 1841. "Your prayers are acceptable before me," said the Lord to the Prophet, "and in answer to them I say unto you," then continues that great revelation. (Doc. and Cov., Sec. 124: 2.) In fact, to particularize no further, it may be said that by far the greater number of the revelations received by the Prophet were in response to his petitions and inquiries of the Lord; and therefore the fact that this revelation on marriage was given in response to inquiries by the Prophet, to know why the Lord justified the worthy patriarchs named, and some of the prophets, in their plural marriage relations, is characteristic of practically all the revelations received by him.

2. *It Possesses the Characteristic of Frankness in Reproving the Prophet.*

Another characteristic of the Prophet Joseph's revelations is the frankness with which the Prophet himself is reproved for his follies and transgressions of the counsels of the Lord. He is never shielded; never justified when he steps aside from the path direct; reproof, chastisement and warnings are administered to him. God in these revelations deals with him indeed as with a son whom he loves, if it be true—and we have warrant of holy writ that it is—that God chasteneth whom he loveth, and scourgeth every son whom he receiveth. (Heb. 12: 6-8.) The following quotations from the revelations will illustrate what I mean. The Lord thus reproved the Prophet in 1829: "And behold, how oft you have transgressed the commandments and the laws of God, and have gone on in the persuasions of men. * * * * You should not have feared man more than God. * * * * Thou wast chosen to do the work of the Lord, but because of transgression, if thou art not aware, thou wilt fall. * * * Repent. * * * Except thou do this, thou shalt be delivered up and become as other men, and have no more gift. * * * Thou hast suffered the counsel of thy director to be trampled upon from the beginning. (Doc. and Cov., Sec. 3.)

Again in 1829 this: "I command you my servant Joseph to repent and walk more uprightly before me, and yield to the persuasions of men no more. (Doc. and Cov., Sec. 5.)

This was said of the Prophet in a revelation given in 1830: "After it was truly manifested unto this first elder (Joseph Smith) that he had received a remission of his sins, he was entangled again in the vanities of the world. But after repenting and humbling himself sincerely, through faith, God ministered unto him by an holy angel," etc. that is, took him again into divine favor. (See Doc. and Cov., Sec. 20.)

Again in 1830: "Thou art not excusable in thy transgressions; nevertheless, go thy way and sin no more." (Doc. and Cov., Sec. 24.)

In 1831 this was said of the Prophet: "There are those who have sought occasion against him without cause; nevertheless he has sinned, but verily I say unto you, I the Lord, forgive sins unto those who confess their sins before me and ask forgiveness, who have not sinned unto death." (Doc. and Coy., Sec. 64.)

In 1833, this: "Verily, I say unto you, my son, thy sins are forgiven thee, according to thy petition, for thy prayers, and the prayers of thy brethren, have come up into my ears." (Doc. and Cov., Sec. 90.)

In the same year this: "Verily, I say unto Joseph Smith, Jr., you have not kept the commandments, and must needs stand rebuked before the Lord." (Doc. and Cov., Sec. 93.)

In 1841 this was said to the Prophet: "Verily thus saith the Lord unto you my servant Joseph Smith, I am well pleased with your offering and acknowledgments, which you have made, for unto this end have I raised you up, that I might show forth my wisdom through the weak things of the earth." (Doc. and Cov., Sec. 124.)

It is but in harmony then with the whole course of God with this man that in this revelation on marriage his sins should be referred too. It is particularly Joseph Smith-like that it should be done, and it is done: "Let my handmaid forgive my servant Joseph his trespasses; and then shall she be forgiven her trespasses wherein she has trespassed against me. * * * * * * Let no one, therefore, set on my servant Joseph; for I will justify him; for he shall do the sacrifice which I require at his hands, for his transgressions, saith the Lord your God." (Doc. and Cov., Sec. 132: 56-60).

Thus it will appear that all the frankness with which the Prophet was reproved in other revelations is manifested in this revelation on marriage; and hence, to the extent of that characteristic, identifies this revelation on the marriage covenant with the other revelations received by the Prophet.

3. *The Evidence of the Largeness of Range in the Revelation on Marriage.*

The next characteristic to be noted is the largeness of range in this revelation so characteristic of all the Prophet's revelations. His main inquiry was why God justified the ancient patriarchs in having many wives. The answer went far beyond the inquiry, and there was given to the Prophet a new marriage law, so far transcending the conceptions of men concerning marriage, as the thoughts of God transcend the thoughts of men on all subjects. The marriage covenant must be an eternal one, not marriage "until death does you part." The marriage relation will exist in heaven. Pro-creation within the marriage covenant of man is to be an eternal, creative power. It shall people the increasing heavens as it has the multiplying worlds with offspring of the Sons of God. It is to be of the things that shall not pass away, but a means of perpetuating the lives and all their purifying, and uplifting relationships. And the power to establish these relationships is in the Priesthood of God, the keys of which were restored through Joseph Smith.

4. The Evidence of Identical Phraseology in This and Other Revelations.

The recurrence and peculiar use of certain phrases to be found in both this revelation on Marriage and the other revelations given out by Joseph Smith, establish clearly the authorship to be the same. Such, for example, as the peculiar use of "*mine*" instead of "my." In the revelation on marriage we have this: "Behold! *mine* house is a house of order" (v.8); "If a man be called of my Father, * * * by *mine* own voice," etc., (v. 59). "Through the medium of *mine* anointed, whom I have appointed," etc., (v. 7); and are sealed * * * according to *mine* appointment (v. 26); and let *mine* handmaid Emma Smith, (v. 54); "verily I say, let *mine* handmaid forgive my servant Joseph," etc., (v. 56).

Let these expressions be compared with the following phrases from various revelations: "Behold this is *mine* authority and the authority of my servants" (Doc. and Cov. sec. 1: 6); "They have strayed from *mine* ordinances (v. 15); "that *mine* everlasting covenant be established," etc., (v. 22); "shall all be fulfilled, whether by *mine* own voice or the voice of my servants" (v. 38); "it is meet unto you to know even as *mine* apostles" (sec. 19:8); "ye are called to bring to pass the gathering of *mine* elect for *mine* elect hear my voice" (sec. 29: 7); "it hath gone forth * * * that *mine* apostles, the Twelve," etc. (v. 12); "it is the workmanship of *mine* hand" (v. 25); "Michael, *mine* archangel, shall sound his trump" (v. 26); "through faith on the name of *mine* Only Begotten Son" (v. 42); "from the foundation of the world through *mine* Only Begotten" (v. 46); "according to *mine* own pleasure" (v. 48). And so on throughout the revelations this phrase occurs. It is used eight times in the revelation on marriage and runs through nearly all the revelations sometimes fewer, sometimes more than this. In section 101 it occurs eleven times, in section 103 six times. But it is always used sufficiently to make it a characteristic of the revelations received by Joseph Smith.

(2) The phrase "as touching," is used several times in this revelation on marriage; "as touching the principle and doctrine,"etc., (v. 1); "will answer thee as touching this matter" (v. 2); "and as touching Abraham and his seed" (v. 30); "as touching the law of the priesthood," etc., (v. 5). The same expression is found in Sec. 42—"As ye * * * are agreed as touching this one thing" (v. 3). Also in the Book of Mormon: "He spake as touching all things concerning my people."

(3) Such phrases as "I am the Lord thy God, and will answer thee," etc., are frequent in this revelation. The above is in verse 2; then again, "I am the Lord thy God, and will give unto thee the law," etc., (v. 28); "I am the Lord thy God, and I gave unto thee an appointment (v. 40); the same in verse 57; indeed it comes in almost as a re-

frain of poetic emphasis at about equal distances throughout the revelation, giving them in places almost rhythmic effect. This will be found characteristic of several other revelations, notably section 1: The Lord speaking of His servants says: "I, the Lord, have commanded them" (v. 5); "Wherefore I, the Lord, knowing the calamity which should come," etc., (v. 17); "for, I, the Lord, cannot look upon sin," etc., (v. 31.)

So also in slightly different form the peculiarity will be found in section 12: "Behold, I am God and give heed, etc., (v. 2); "behold, I speak unto you," etc., (v. 7); "behold, I am the light and life of the world," etc., (v. 9). Also in section 29: "Thus did I the Lord God appoint unto man" (v. 43); "wherefore I, the Lord God, will send forth flies" (v. 18); "wherefore I, the Lord God, caused that he should be cast out," (v. 41); "and thus did I, the Lord God, appoint unto man the days," etc., (v. 43). Again in section 50: "Behold, I, the Lord. have looked upon you" (v. 4); wherefore I, the Lord, ask you this question" (v. 13). Also section 52; "Behold, thus saith the Lord unto the Elders," etc., (v. 1); "I, the Lord, will make known unto you" (v. 2); "behold I, the Lord, will hasten the city," etc., (v. 43.)

The peculiar use of "none other," in place of "no other," and of "none" instead of "no one," is an expression both in the revelation on marriage and a number of other revelations about which there is no question of the authorship being Joseph Smith's. In the revelation on marriage we have this: "Abraham * * * abode in my law, as Isaac also, and Jacob did *none other* things than that which they were commanded; and because they did *none other* things than that which they were commanded, they have entered into their exaltation (v. 37). In section 43 we have the same phrase: "There is *none other* appointed unto you," etc., (v.3); "I say unto you that *none else* shall be appointed unto this gift" (v. 4); also in Section 61, the following: "It shall be said in days to come that *none* is able to go up to the land" (v. 16); also Section 82, "and *none* doeth good, for all have gone out of the way (v. 6); and they * * * shall find *none* inheritance in that day," etc., (Sec. 85:9).

The use of the plural "*Gods*" in the revelation on marriage and in other revelations, tends to prove common authorship. In the revelation on marriage we have the following: "And henceforth are not *Gods*, but are angels of God forever and ever" (v. 17); "it cannot be received there because the angels and the *Gods* are appointed there, by whom they cannot pass" etc. (v. 18); "then shall they be *Gods* because they have no end; then shall they be *Gods* because they have all power (v. 20); and sit upon thrones, and are not angels, but are *Gods* (v. 36); in the revelation called the Vision, Doc. and Cov. Sec. 76, which revelation was given in February, 1832, and first published in the *Eveneng and Morning Star* of July, 1833, (vol. 1, number 2, p. 28) occurs the following: "And are priests of the most high, * * * wherefore, as it is written, they are *Gods* even the Sons of God (v. 58) also in Sec. 121; "Nothing shall be withhheld, whether there be one God or many *Gods*, they shall be manifest (v. 28); according to that which was ordained in the midst of the Council of the Eternal God of all other *Gods*, before this world was" (v. 32).

The phrase, "My house is a house of order," is used in the revelation on marriage (v. 18), also in Doc. and Cov., section 88, the phrase occurs, "a house of glory, a house of order, a house of God" (v. 119); "this shall be the order of the house of the presidency" (v. 128).

In closing the revelation on marriage the paragraph reads as follows: "And now, as pertaining to this law, verily, verily I say unto you, I will reveal more unto you hereafter; therefore let this suffice for the present. Behold, I am Alpha and Omega. Amen." This is somewhat characteristic of the closing of a number of revelations in the Doctrine and Covenants. The revelation in section 60 closes with—'Behold, this is sufficient for you * * * the residue hereafter. Even so. Amen." Section 84 closes, "I am Alpha and Omega, the beginning and the end. Amen" (v. 120). Section 94 closes: "And now I give you no more at this time (v. 17). Section 95 closes "Let the higher part of the inner court be dedicated unto me for the school of mine apostles, saith Son Ahman; or in other words, Alphus, or in other words, Omegus, even Jesus Christ your Lord. Amen" (v. 17).

In other revelations the expression Alpha and Omega comes in the body of the revelation as for instance in section 45, "Verily I say unto you that I am Alpha and Omega, the beginning and the end, the light and life of the world" (v. 7). The same phraseology is used in the body of section 63, v. 60.

In section 19 it opens the revelation, "I am Alpha and Omega, Christ the Lord, yea even I am He, the beginning and the end, the Redeemer of the world" (v. 1). "Behold, and hearken unto the voice of Him who has all power, who is from everlasting to everlasting, even Alpha and Omega, the beginning and the end" (section 61, v. 1).

Other revelations close in the same impressive manner and with the somewhat equivalent expressions in English, instead of the use of the Greek terms, Alpha and Omega. Thus section 18 closes: "Behold, I, Jesus Christ, your Lord and your God and your Redeemer by the power of my spirit have spoken it" (v. 47). Section 1 ends, "For behold and lo, the Lord is God and the Spirit beareth record, and the record is true, and the truth abideth forever and ever. Amen" (v. 39).

The same occurs in section 75 and 14; but whether the phrase occurs in the opening of the revelation or the middle of it, or in the closing paragraph, it occurs with sufficient frequency to be noted as a peculiarity of the Prophet's phraseology, and aids in the identification of his inspired style.

The term "forgiveness of sin" occurs in the revelation on marriage as follows: "Behold, I have seen your sacrifices [Joseph's], and will forgive all your sins." This is both a principle and phraseology frequent in the revelations, as an example, section 64: "There are those who have sought occasion against him (Joseph) without cause; nevertheless he has sinned, but verily I say unto you, I, the Lord, forgive sins unto those who confess their sins before me" (v. 7). Let the spirit of this be compared with the following from the revelation on marriage: "Let no one, therefore, set on my servant Joseph, for I will justify him, for he shall do the sacrifices which I require at his hands for his transgressions, saith the Lord your God" (v. 60). "Again, verily I say, let mine handmaid forgive my servant Joseph his trespasses, and then shall she be forgiven her trespasses wherein she has trespassed against me" (v. 56).

In the revelation on marriage occurs the following phraseology: "Verily, verily, I say unto you, that whatsoever you seal on earth, shall be sealed in heaven; and whatsoever you bind on earth, in my name, and by my word, saith the Lord, it shall be eternally bound in the heavens" (v. 46). The same phraseology is used in section 124 in speaking of Hyrum Smith, who was appointed to hold the keys of the patriarchal blessings upon the heads of God's people; namely, "Whosoever he blesses shall be blessed, and whosoever he curses shall be cursed; and whatsoever he shall bind on earth shall be bound in heaven; and whatsoever he shall loose on earth shall be loosed in heaven" (v. 93). In section 128 the same phraseology is used in describing the power of the priesthood (v. 8). And again in v. 10, quoting it from the New Testament (Matt. 16: 18, 19).

In verse 26 on the revelation on marriage, this phraseology is found: "They shall be destroyed in the flesh and shall be delivered unto the buffetings of Satan, unto the day of redemption, saith the Lord God." The same phraseology occurs in section 82. "The soul that sins * * * shall be delivered over to the buffeting of Satan until the day of redemption" (v. 21). The same phraseology occurs in section 78, v. 12; section 104, v. 9, 10. In the revelation on marriage this passage occurs: "I give unto my servant Joseph, that he shall be made ruler over many things, for he hath been faithful over a few things." Section 117 practically the some phraseology occurs with reference to William Marks, "Let my servant, William Marks, be faithful over a few things, and he shall be a ruler over many."

Again it is said: "and if they commit no murder, wherein they shed innocent blood—yet they shall come forth in the first resurrection and enter into their exaltation; but they shall be destroyed in the flesh, and shall be delivered unto the buffetings of Satan unto the day of redemption, saith the Lord God (v. 26). "The blasphemy against the Holy Ghost, which shall not be forgiven in the world, nor out of the world is in that ye commit murder, wherein ye shed innocent blood, and assent unto my death after ye have received my new and everlasting covenant (v. 27). That is to say, the doctrine is here set forth that the murderer hath not eternal life abiding in him (I Jno. 1: 15). There is no forgiveness for him in this world or in the world to come. The same idea is to be found in other revelations of Joseph Smith. Notably in section 42: "Behold, I speak unto the Church. Thou shalt not kill; and he that kills shall not have forgiveness in this world nor in the world to come" (v. 18); "if any persons among you shall kill, they shall be delivered up and dealt with according to the law of the land; for remember, that he hath no forgiveness" (v. 79); then again and in connection with breaking covenant, note the following expression: "And this is all according to the oath and covenant of the priesthood. * * * But whoso breaketh this covenant, after he hath received it, and altogether turned therefrom, shall not have forgiveness in this world or in the world to come (v. 39-40.)

The expression "new and everlasting covenant" (v. 4) occurs several times in the revelation on marriage: "as pertaining to the new and everlasting covenant it was instituted," etc. (v. 6); "if a man marry a wife * * * * * by the new and everlasting covenant, and it is sealed, etc. (v. 19). The phrase occurs a number of other times in the revelation, viz., in verses 26, 27, 41 and 42. It occurs also in many other revelations by Joseph Smith: In section 1—"That mine everlasting covenant might be established" (v. 22); "this is a new and ever lasting covenant" (Sec. 22, 1); "I have sent mine everlasting covenant into the world" (Sec. 45: 9); same in Sec. 49, 9; 66, 2; 76, 101; 78: 11, and in at least a score of other sections

5. The Evidence of Recurrence of Principles in the Revelation on Marriage That are Found in Other Revelations Through Joseph Smith.

Principles that appear in previous revelations reappear in this revelation on marriage: for example, it is said in Sec. 130: "There is a law irrevocably decreed in heaven, before the foundations of this world, upon which all blessings are predicated; and when we obtain any blessing from God it is by obedience to that law upon which it is predicated." In Sec. 88, occurs the following: "All kingdoms have a law given: and there are many kingdoms; and unto every kingdom is given a law; and unto every law there are certain bounds also and conditions. All beings who abide not in those conditions are not justified," verse

36 to 38. In the revelation on marriage this doctrine is set forth in the following passage: "No one can reject this covenant and be permitted to enter into my glory; for all who will have a blessing at my hands shall abide the law which was appointed for that blessing, and the conditions thereof, as were instituted from before the foundation of the world. * * * * * * * * * And will I appoint unto you, saith the Lord, except it be by law, even as I and my Father ordained unto you, before the world was! * * * * * * * * * * * I am the Lord thy God, and will give unto thee the law of my Holy Priesthood, as was ordained by me, and my Father, before the world was," verses 4, 5, 11, 28. The identity of the principle is complete, and tends to establish identity of authorship.

6. The Evidence of the Particularization of Ideas.

In the revelation on marriage there is a singularity of expression, which, for want of a better term, I will call a particularization of ideas, that is decidedly peculiar to the Prophet, for example: "And verily I say unto you, that the conditions of this law are these: All covenants, contracts, bonds, obligations, oaths, vows, performances, connections, associations, or expectations, that are not made, and entered into, and sealed, by the Holy Spirit of promise, of him who is anointed, both as well for time and for all eternity, and that too most holy, by revelation and commandment through the medium of mine anointed, whom I have appointed on the earth to hold this power, (and I have appointed unto my servant Joseph to hold this power in the last days, and there is never but one on the earth, at a time, on whom this power and the keys of this Priesthood are conferred,) are of no efficacy, virtue or force, in and after the resurrection from the dead; for all contracts that are not made unto this end, have an end when men are dead. * * * * And everything that is in the world, whether it be ordained of men, by thrones, or principalities, or powers, or things of name, whatsoever they may be, that are not by me, or by my word, saith the Lord, shall be thrown down, and shall not remain after men are dead, neither in nor after the resurrection, saith the Lord your God!" (verses 7, 13).

A similar particularization of things is found in verses 15, 18, 19, 26, 30, 59, 61, of the revelation on marriage.

With the above quoted passage compare the following: "Whoso receiveth you receiveth me, and the same will feed you, and clothe you and give you money. And he who feeds you, or clothes you or gives you money, shall in no wise loose his reward: And he that doeth not these things is not my disciple; by this you may know my disciples. He that receiveth you not, go away from him alone by yourselves, and cleanse your feet even with water, pure water, whether in heat or in cold, and bear testimony of it unto your Father which is in heaven, and return not again unto that man. And in whatsoever village or city ye enter, do likewise. Nevertheless, search diligently and spare not; and wo unto that house, or that village or city that rejecteth you, or your words, or your testimony concerning me. Wo, I say again, unto that house, or that village or city that rejecteth you, or your words, or your testimony of me." Sec. 84: 89-95. Similar passages of particularizationfrequently occur in other revelations. The following is a notable example:

"All thrones and dominions, principalities and powers, shall be revealed and set forth upon all who have endured valiantly for the Gospel of Jesus Christ; and also if there be bounds set to the heavens or to the seas; or to the dry land, or to the sun, moon, or stars; all the times of their revolutions; all the appointed days, months and years, and all the days of their months and years, and all their glories, laws and set times, shall be revealed in the days of the dispensation of the fullness of times, according to that which was ordained in the midst of the council of the eternal God of all other Gods, before the world was" (Doc. and Cov., Sec. 121: 29-31).

7. *The Evidences of Identity in Grandeur of Style.*

One other pecularity in the inspired style of the Prophet is seen in a certain growing grandeur in statement, by means of repetitions—repetitions, too, that make a paragraph fairly scintillate with prismatic hues as well as giving to it a *crescendo* of emphasis: for example, in speaking of the glory that shall come to those who keep covenant with the Lord, it is written in this revelation on marriage:

"And they shall pass by the angels, and the Gods which are set there, to their exaltation and glory in all things, as hath been sealed upon their heads, which glory shall be a fullness and a continuation of the seeds for ever and ever.

Then shall they be Gods, because they have no end;

Therefore shall they be from everlasting to everlasting, because they continue;

Then shall they be above all, because all things are subject unto them.

Then shall they be Gods, because they have all power, and the angels are subject unto them" * (verses 19-21).

With this compare the following:

* I have taken liberty of placing the lines in poetic form, to which they so readily lend themselves, that they may be the more readily compared with the verses from another revelation which follows from Doc. and Cov., sec. 84.

"The power and authority of the Higher or Melchisedek, Priesthood, is to hold the keys of all the spiritual blessings of the Church—to have the privilege of receiving the mysteries of the kingdom of heaven—to have the heavens opened unto them—to commune with the general assembly and church of the first born, and to enjoy the communion and presence of God the Father, and Jesus the Mediator of the new covenant" (Sec. 107: 18, 19). Also this:

"And if thou shouldst be cast into the pit, or into the hands of murderers, and the sentence of death passed upon thee; if thou be cast into the deep; if the billowing surge conspire against thee; if fierce winds become thine enemy; if the heavens gather blackness, and all the elements combine to hedge up the way; and above all, if the very jaws of hell shall gape open the mouth wide after thee, know thou, my son, that all these things shall give thee experience, and shall be for thy good. The Son of Man hath descended below them all; art thou greater than he?"

And as covering both the two last peculiarities—particularization of things and a growing grandeur in statement by repetition, consider the following passage:

"I the Almighty have laid my hands upon the nations, to scourge them for their wickedness: and plagues shall go forth, and they shall not be taken from the earth until I have completed my work which shall be cut short in righteousness, until all shall know me, who remain, even from the least unto the greatest, and shall be filled with the knowledge of the Lord, and shall see eye to eye, and shall lift up their voice, and with the voice together sing this new song, saying—

The Lord hath brought again Zion;
The Lord hath redeemed His people, Israel,
According to the election of grace,
Which was brought to pass by the faith
And covenant of their fathers.

The Lord hath redeemed His people,
And Satan is bound and time is no longer:
The Lord hath gathered all things in one:
The Lord hath brought down Zion from above.
The Lord hath brought up Zion from beneath.

The earth hath travailed and brought forth her strength:
And truth is established in her bowels:
And the heavens have smiled upon her:
And she is clothed with the glory of her God:
For He stands in the midst of His people:

Glory, and honor, and power, and might,
Be ascribed to our God; for He is full of mercy,
Justice, grace and truth, and peace,
For ever and ever. Amen.

It should be remarked, in conclusion,that these peculiarities of scope, structure, phraseology, re-appearance of principles, texture of composition and the like, which identify this revelation on marriage as the composition of Joseph Smith (under the inspiration of the Lord, of course) are not forced into the revelation. Its composition gives no evidence of being a conglomerate of Joseph Smith's thought-gems held together by some one else's clay. It is all of one piece, it is not patch work. Unity above all things is characteristic of it. Words, phrases, sentences, ideas all blend together, preserving strict unity of style and that style Joseph Smith's. No one else could have written it. The literary peculiarities of that revelation as readily proclaim it to be Joseph Smith's composition to those familiar with his literary style,as the contour of his face, the form of his features, the color of his hair and eyes, the tint of his complexion, the intonation of his voice, together with his form and bearing would reveal his physical personality to those who familiarly knew him in life. There will be no doubt whatever as to Joseph Smith being the author of it in the minds of those who will give it literary analysis. Whatever has come of it, or whatever may come of it in the future, Joseph Smith is the author of that revelation, and is responsible before God and the world for the introduction of that marriage law into the Church—the law that contemplates marriage as an eternal union, and the rightfulness of a plurality of wives under certain conditions and divine sanctions, when permissible under the laws of the land and the law of the Church.

HISTORY

OF THE

CHURCH OF JESUS CHRIST OF LATTER-DAY SAINTS.

VOL. V.

HISTORY
OF THE
CHURCH OF JESUS CHRIST
OF
LATTER-DAY SAINTS.

PERIOD I.
HISTORY OF JOSEPH SMITH, THE PROPHET.

CHAPTER I.

INAUGURATION OF ENDOWMENT CEREMONIES—PERFIDY AND EXPOSURE OF JOHN C. BENNETT—HIS RESIGNATION AS MAYOR OF NAUVOO—EPISTLE OF THE HIGH COUNCIL TO THE SAINTS.

Tuesday, May 3, 1842.—Passed the day mostly with my family.

Wednesday, 4.—I spent the day in the upper part of the store, that is in my private office (so called because in that room I keep my sacred writings, translate ancient records, and receive revelations) and in my general business office, or lodge room (that is where the Masonic fraternity meet occasionally, for want of a better place) in council with General James Adams, of Springfield, Patriarch Hyrum Smith, Bishops Newel K. Whitney and George Miller, and President

Inauguration of Endowment Ceremonies.

Brigham Young and Elders Heber C. Kimball and Willard Richards, instructing them in the principles and order of the Priesthood, attending to washings, anointings, endowments and the communication of keys pertaining to the Aaronic Priesthood, and so on to the highest order of the Melchisedek Priesthood, setting forth the order pertaining to the Ancient of Days, and all those plans and principles by which any one is enabled to secure the fullness of those blessings which have been prepared for the Church of the First Born, and come up and abide in the presence of the Eloheim in the eternal worlds. In this council was instituted the ancient order of things for the first time in these last days. And the communications I made to this council were of things spiritual, and to be received only by the spiritual minded: and there was nothing made known to these men but what will be made known to all the Saints of the last days, so soon as they are prepared to receive, and a proper place is prepared to communicate them, even to the weakest of the Saints; therefore let the Saints be diligent in building the Temple, and all houses which they have been, or shall hereafter be, commanded of God to build; and wait their time with patience in all meekness, faith, perseverance unto the end, knowing assuredly that all these things referred to in this council are always governed by the principle of revelation.*

Thursday, 5.—General Adams started for Springfield,

* This is the Prophet's account of the introduction of the Endowment ceremonies in this dispensation, and is the foundation of the sacred ritual of the temples. There has been some controversies as to the time when these ceremonies were introduced into the Church. A sect styling itself the "Re-organized Church," even goes so far as to claim that these ceremonies were not introduced into the Church by the Prophet Joseph Smith at all, but on the contrary claim that they had their origin with Brigham Young and the Apostles who followed him in the migration from Nauvoo to Great Salt Lake Valley in Utah. The evidence, however, against such claims, is overwhelming. First, the statement of the Prophet in the text above. Second, a previous allusion to the same thing in his remarks at Nauvoo, on the 6th of January, 1842. (See HISTORY OF THE CHURCH, Vol. IV. p. 492.) Third, the same ceremonies are referred to in the Revelation of Jan. 19, 1841, in which washings, anointings, conversations, statutes, judgments, etc., are explicitly referred to. (HISTORY OF THE CHURCH. Vol. IV, p. 277.) In addition to this evi-

and the remainder of the council of yesterday continued their meeting at the same place, and myself and Brother Hyrum received in turn from the others, the same that I had communicated to them the day previous.

The city of Hamburg, the commercial emporium of Germany, was destroyed by fire, about this time.

Friday, *6*.—I attended the Legion officers' drill in the morning, and visited Lyman Wight, who was sick.

Saturday, *7*.—

Legion History.

The Nauvoo Legion was on parade by virtue of an order of the 25th of January, 1842, and was reviewed by Lieutenant-General Joseph Smith, who commanded through the day. One year since, the Legion consisted of six companies; today of twenty-six companies, amounting to about two thousand troops.

The consolidated staff of the Legion with their ladies, partook of a sumptuous dinner at the house of the commander-in-chief, between one and three o'clock, p. m. The weather was very fine.

In the afternoon the Legion was separated into cohorts,and fought an animated sham battle; the first cohort under the command of General Wilson Law, the second under General Charles C. Rich. At the close of the parade, Lieutenant-General Joseph Smith delivered a most animated and appropriate address, in which he remarked "that his soul was never better satisfied than on this occasion." Such was the curious and interesting excitement which prevailed at the time, in the surrounding country, about the Legion, that Judge Douglas adjourned the circuit court, then in session at Carthage, and came with some of the principal lawyers, to see the splendid military parade of the Legion; upon notice of which being given to General Smith, he immediately invited them to partake of the repast prepared as above.

dence also, Ebenezer Robinson, associate editor of the *Times and Seasons* when that periodical was founded by Don Carlos Smith and himself, and who at the death of Don Carlos Smith, 1841, became editor-in-chief of that periodical, and so continued until the 15th of March, 1842—declares that such ceremonies as are alluded to in the text were inaugurated by special action of the Prophet as early as 1843. Mr. Robinson subsequently left the Church, but when in 1890, the aforesaid self-styled "Re-organized Church" persisted in claiming that Joseph Smith the Prophet did not inaugurate these Temple ceremonies, he published an article in the magazine he was then conducting, called *The Return*, in which he bears emphatic testimony to the effect above stated,namely,that all these ceremonies were introduced into the Church by the Prophet Joseph Smith at least as early as 1843. [See *The Return*, Vol. II, No. 4, p. 252.]

In addition to this quotation, I would remark that the day passed very harmoniously, without drunkenness, noise or confusion. There was an immense congregation of spectators, and many distinguished strangers expressed much satisfaction. But one thing I will notice: I was solicited by General Bennett to take command of the first cohort during the sham battle; this I declined. General Bennett next requested me to take my station in the rear of the cavalry, without my staff, during the engagement; but this was counteracted by Captain A. P. Rockwood, commander of my life guards, who kept close to my side, and I chose my own position. And if General Bennett's true feelings toward me are not made manifest to the world in a very short time, then it may be possible that the gentle breathings of that Spirit, which whispered me on parade, that there was mischief concealed in that sham battle, were false; a short time will determine the point. Let John C. Bennett answer at the day of judgment, "Why did you request me to command one of the cohorts, and also to take my position without my staff, during the sham battle, on the 7th of May, 1842, where my life might have been the forfeit, and no man have known who did the deed?

General John C. Bennett's Perfidy.

The following diagram shows the position in which the Legion was drawn up:

Lieutenant-General Joseph Smith, Staff, Guard, and Ladies on horseback.

Band of Music.

Major-General J. C. Bennett and Staff.

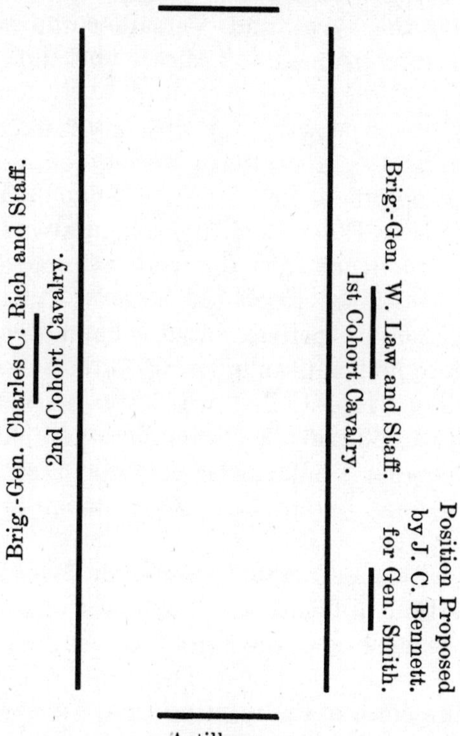

Artillery.

A violent shock of an earthquake is reported to have been experienced at the island of St. Domingo, at twenty minutes past seven, p. m. It was also felt at St. Marc, Gonaives, and Cape Haytien, and at various places from Port-au-Prince, to the base of the Rocky Mountains, comprising a distance of 1,500 miles. At Santiago de Cuba the cathedral and several extensive buildings were prostrated. About ten thousand persons were killed at Cape Haytien.

Earthquake in St. Domingo.

Sunday, 8.— Attended meeting at the grove, and heard Elder Rigdon preach.

After meeting many persons were baptized, some in the font, others in the river.

Eighty persons killed and as many wounded, by an accident on the Paris and Versailles railroad, the carriages being consumed by fire, and their passengers roasted alive.

Monday, 9.—Spent the day with my family.

Tuesday, 10.—Transacted a variety of business at the store, printing office, &c.

By letter from Elder Levi Richards, dated at Liverpool, we learn that the work is progressing in the north of England, namely, Carlisle, Brampton, Burnstones, Alstone, and Newcastle-upon-Tyne, where he has been laboring for a few weeks.

The Work in England.

Wednesday, 11.—Called with my clerk at Brother Joseph W. Coolidge's to examine a new cabinet for the Temple Recorder's office; also called at Bishop Knight's; dictated several letters and other items of a business nature.

Thursday, 12.—Dictated a letter to Elder Rigdon concerning certain difficulties, or surmises which existed and attended the meeting of the Female Relief Society, the house being filled to overflowing. There was a heavy thunderstorm at the close of the meeting.

Friday, 13.—Received a letter from Sidney Rigdon in reply to mine of yesterday.

Spent most of the day in my garden and with my family.

Dictated the following letter to Horace R. Hotchkiss, Esq.

The Prophet's Letter to Horace R. Hotchkiss.—Explaining why the Former had taken Advantage of the Bankrupt Law.

DEAR SIR—I proceed without delay to give a hasty reply to yours of the 12th ultimo, just received. My engagements will not admit of a lengthy datail of events and circumstances which have transpired to bring about that state of things which now exists in this place, as before you receive this you will probably be apprised of the failure of myself and brethren to execute our designs in paying off our contracts, or in other words, that we have been compelled to pay our debts by the most popular method; that is by petitioning for the privilege of general bankruptcy, a principle so popular at the present moment throughout the Union.

A pressure of business has been sufficient excuse for not giving you earlier notice, although it could have been of no real use to you, yet I wish you to understand our intentions to you and your company, and why we have taken the course we have. You are aware, sir, in some measure of the embarrassment under which we have labored through the influence of mobs and designing men, and the disadvantageous circumstances under which we have been compelled to contract debts in order to our existence, both as individuals and as a society, and it is on account of this as well as a pressure on us for debts absolutely unjust in themselves, that we have been compelled to resort to the course we have [taken] to make a general settlement, and this we deferred to the last moment, hoping that something would turn in our favor, so that we might be saved the painful necessity of resorting to such measures,to accomplish which,justice demanded a very different course from those who are justly our debtors, but demanded in vain.

We have been compelled to the course we have pursued, and you are aware, sir, that all have to fare alike in such cases. But, sir, you have one, yea, two things to comfort you; our faith, intention and good feeling remain the same to all our creditors, and to none more than yourself; and secondly, there is property sufficent in the inventory to pay every debt, and some to spare, according to the testimony of our solicitors, and the good judgment of others; and if the court will allow us some one for assignee, who will do justice to the cause, we confidently believe that yourself and all others will get their compensation in full,and we have enough left for one loaf more for each of our families. Yes,and I have no doubt you will yet,and in a short time,be enabled to have your pay in full, in the way I have before proposed, or some other equally advantageous, but money is out of sight, it might as well be out of mind, for it cannot be had.

Rest assured, dear sir, that no influence or exertion I can yet make shall be wanting to give you satisfaction, and liquidate your claims, but for a little season you are aware that all proceedings are staid; but I will seek the earliest moment to acquaint you with anything new in this matter.

I remain, sir, with sentiments of respect, your friend and well-wisher,

JOSEPH SMITH.

In the evening I walked with Elder Richards to the post office, and had an interview with Elder Rigdon, concerning certain evil reports put in circulation by Francis M. Higbee, about some of Elder Rigdon's family, and others; much apparent satisfaction was manifested at the conversation, by Elder Rigdon; and Elder Richards returned with me to my house.

Interview With Sidney Rigdon.

Saturday, 14.—I attended city council in the morning, and advocated strongly the necessity of some active measures being taken to suppress houses and acts of infamy in the city; for the protection of the innocent and virtuous, and the good of public morals; showing clearly that there were certain characters in the place, who were disposed to corrupt the morals and chastity of our citizens, and that houses of infamy did exist, upon which a city ordinance concerning brothels and disorderly characters was passed, to prohibit such things. It was published in this day's *Wasp.*

Moral Improvement of Nauvoo.

I also spoke at length for the repeal of the ordinance of the city licensing merchants, hawkers, taverns, and ordinaries, desiring that this might be a free people, and enjoy equal rights and privileges, and the ordinances were repealed.

After council, I worked in my garden, walked out in the city, and borrowed two sovereigns to make a payment.

Brother Amos Fielding arrived from Liverpool.

It was reported in Nauvoo, that ex-Governor Boggs of Missouri had been shot.

I granted the petition of J. B. Nicholson, and about seventy other members of the Church in Philadelphia, for the organization of a branch of the Church in the north part of the city, dated April 22nd, and my doings were sanctioned by the Twelve, who at the same time silenced

Branch Organization for Philadelphia Authorized.

Elder Benjamin Winchester for not following counsel.

Sunday, 15.—Attended meeting at the stand.

News of the attempted assassination of Governor Boggs was confirmed by general report, and was mentioned on the stand.

General Conference in England.

A general conference was held in the new Corn Exchange, Manchester, England, President Parley P. Pratt presiding. There were present at the opening of the conference, High Priests, 14; Elders, 50; Priests, 64; Teachers, 37; Deacons, 8. The representation of the Church was as follows:

Manchester Conference represented by Charles Miller, consists of 1,531 members, 36 Elders, 79 Priests, 50 Teachers, 19 Deacons, and includes the branches of Manchester, Duckinfield, Bolton, Stockport, Pendlebury, Whitefield, Heatons, Eccles, Oldham, Rochdale, Leeds, Radcliffe, Bridge and Blakely.

Liverpool Conference, represented by John Greenhow, consists of 570 members, 23 Elders, 26 Priests, 21 Teachers, 10 Deacons, and includes the branches of Liverpool, Warrington and Newton, St. Helens, Isle of Man, Wales, and York.

Preston Conference, represented by Elder Struthars, consists of 665 members, 16 Elders, 22 Priests, 15 Teachers, 3 Deacons, and includes the branches of Preston, Penworthen, Longton, Southport, Farrington, Hunter's Hill, Kendal, Brigsteer, Holme, Lancaster, and Euxton Birth.

Clitheroe Conference represented by Thomas Ward, consists of 325 members, 15 Elders, 23 Priests, 17 Teachers, 6 Deacons, and includes the branches of Clitheroe, Chatburn, Waddington, Downham, Blackburn, Burnley, Accrington, Ribchester, Chaidgley, and Grindleton.

London Conference, represented by Lorenzo Snow, consists of 400 members, 14 Elders, 32 Priests, 7 Teachers, 8 Deacons, and includes the branches of London, Woolwich, Bedford, Wybosson, Thorncut, Honeydon, Irchester, and Waddon.

Macclesfield Conference, represented by James Galley, consists of 238 members, 8 Elders, 23 Priests, 14 Teachers, 9 Deacons, and includes the branches of Macclesfield, Congleton, Bollington, Middlewich, Northwich and Plumbley.

Birmingham Conference, represented by J. Riley, consists of 309 members, 11 Elders, 18 Priests, 12 Teachers, 5 Deacons, and includes the branches of Birmingham, Great's Green, West Broomwich,Oldbury, Allchurch, Dudley, Wolverhampton, and Ashby Wolds.

Staffordshire Conference, represented by Alfred Cordon, consists of 507 members, 25 Elders, 54 Priests, 23 Teachers, 14 Deacons, and includes the branches of Hanley, Burslem, Stoke, Newcastle, Baddaley Edge, Bradley Green, Knutton Heath, Lane End, Audlem, Prees, Tunstall, Leek, Longport, Tittensor Heath, Doncaster, Sheffield and Brampton.

Garway Conference, represented by John Needham, consists of 197 members, 2 Elders, 12 Priests, 7 Teachers, 2 Deacons, and includes the branches of Garway, Abergavenny, Monmouth, Keven, Orcop, and Euyasharrold.

Cheltenham Conference, represented by Theodore Curtis, consists of 540 members, 8 Elders, 22 Priests, 12 Teachers, 4 Deacons, and includes the branches of Newbury Hill, Rock Hill, Earl's Common, Pinvin, Dounton Beaucamp, Edge Hills, Little Dean, Woodside, Ponsett, Killcott, Frogsmarsh, Red Marley, Bran Green, Apperley, Deerhurst, Cheltenham, Norton, and Bristol.

Froom's Hill Conference, represented by William Kay, consists of 1,101 members, 24 Elders, 56 Priests, 24 Teachers, 12 Deacons, and includes the branches of Moor End's Cross,Ridgway Cross,Dun's Close, Old Storridge, Broomyard's Downs, Clifton, Widbourn, Brinesteed, Woofren Common, Ashfield, Malvern Hill, Palle House, Callwell, Ledbury, Shaken Hill, Lugwardine, Marden, Bushbank, Leominster, Ball Gate, Coom's Move, Stoke's Lane, Froom's Hill, Stanley Hill, Easthampton, and Worcester Broad Heath.

Edinburgh Conference, represented by George D. Watt, consists of 271 members, 13 Elders, 19 Priests, 7 Teachers, 3 Deacons, and includes the branches of Edinburgh, Wemyss, and Sterling.

Glasgow Conference represented by John McAuley, consists of 564 members, 22 Elders, 30 Priests, 26 Teachers, 15 Deacons, and includes the branches of Glasgow, Thorny Bank, Shaw, Toll Cross, Airdrie, Renfrew, Paisley, Johnson, Bridge of Weir, Kilbirnie, Bonshill, Greenock, Brechenney, Nelson, Campsie and Ayr.

Brampton Conference, represented by Richard Benson, consists of 171 members, 6 Elders, 11 Priests, 7 Teachers, 2 Deacons, and includes the branches of Carlisle, Brampton, Alston, and Newcastle-upon-Tyne.

Irish Conference, represented by David Wilkie, consists of 71 members, 1 Elder, 1 Priest, 2 Teachers, 1 Deacon, and includes the branches of Hillsborough, and Crawfoot's Burn.

Bradford and York, represented by Henry Cuerden, consists of 54 members, 1 Elder, 4 Priests. 2 Teachers, 1 Deacon.

Total connected with the Church at the present time, in England,

Ireland, and Scotland, members, 7,514; Elders, 220, Priests, 421; Teachers, 110.

Monday, 16.—I was transacting business at the store until 10 o'clock a. m. Then at home. In the afternoon at the printing office, in council with Brothers Young, Kimball and Richards and others.

I published in this day's *Times and Seasons* the following *fac-simile* from the Book of Abraham.*

Attitude of the Press.

Several of the most widely circulated papers are beginning to exhibit "Mormonism" in its true light. The first out of a *fac-simile* from the Book of Abraham, has been republished both in the New York *Herald* and in the *Dollar Week Bostonian*, as well as in the *Boston Daily Ledger*, edited by Mr. Bartlett; together with the translation from the Book of Abraham.

Tuesday, 17.—I was about home, and at the office through the day. In the evening went to Brother John Snyder's to see Clark Leal, of Fountain Green, concerning a quarter section of land.

Affidavit of John C. Bennett.

State of Illinois, city of Nauvoo, personally appeared before me, Daniel H. Wells, an Alderman of the said city of Nauvoo, John C. Bennett, who being duly sworn, according to law, desposeth and sayeth, that he was never taught anything in the least contrary to the strictest principles of the Gospel, or of virtue or of the laws of God or man, under any circumstances, or upon any occasion, either directly or indirectly, in word or deed, by Joseph Smith, and that he never knew the said Smith to countenance any improper conduct whatever either in public or private; and that he never did teach to me in private that an illegal, illicit intercourse with females, was under any circumstance justifiable, and that I never knew him to so teach others.

JOHN C. BENNETT.

Sworn to and subscribed before me, this 17th day of May, A. D. 1842.
DANIEL H. WELLS, Alderman.

* The *fac-simile* referred to will be found on page 523 of Vol. IV of this History, where it is published in connection with an explanation of the various figures on the plate and preceding the Prophet's translation of the Book of Abraham, taken from the *Times and Seasons*.

John C. Bennett resigned the office of mayor of Nauvoo.

Wednesday, *18*.—Rode on horseback, accompanied by Dr. Richards and Clark Leal, to John Benbow's, and searched out the N. E. quarter of section 15, 6 N. 8 W. and contracted for the refusal of the same, at three dollars per acre; dined at Brother Benbow's, visited Brother Sayer's, &c., which, with business at the different offices, closed the day.

There was a general representation of the branches in the Eastern States, at a conference of the Church at New York.

Thursday, *19*.—It rained, and I was at home until one o'clock; when I attended a special session of the city council. John C. Bennett having discovered that his whoredoms and abominations were fast coming to light, and that the indignation of an insulted and abused people were rising rapidly against him, thought best to make a virtue of necessity, and try to make it appear that he was innocent, by resigning his office of mayor, which the council most gladly accepted; and Joseph Smith was elected mayor of the city of Nauvoo by the council, and Hyrum Smith vice-mayor.

Resignation of Bennett as Mayor of Nauvoo.

While the election was going forward, I received and wrote the following revelation:

Revelation.

Verily thus saith the Lord unto you, my servant Joseph, by the voice of my Spirit, Hiram Kimball has been insinuating evil, and forming evil opinions against you, with others; and if he continue in them, he and they shall be accursed, for I am the Lord thy God, and will stand by thee and bless thee. Amen.

This I threw across the room to Hiram Kimball, one of the councillors. After the election, I spoke at some length concerning the evil reports which were abroad in the city concerning myself, and the necessity of counteracting the designs of our enemies, establishing a night watch, &c., whereupon the council resolved that the mayor be authorized to establish a night watch, and control the same.

William Smith was elected councilor in place of Joseph Smith, elected mayor; George A. Smith councilor, in place of Hugh McFall, removed from the city.

On account of the reports in circulation in the city this day, concerning the ex-mayor, and to quiet the public mind, before the council closed, I asked John C. Bennett if he had aught against me, when Dr. Bennett arose, before the council and a house filled with spectators, and replied:

Statement of John C. Bennett before the City Council.

I know what I am about, and the heads of the Church know what they are about, I expect; I have no difficulty with the heads of the Church. I publicly avow that any one who has said that I have stated that General Joseph Smith has given me authority to hold illicit intercourse with women is a liar in the face of God. Those who have said it are damned liars; they are infernal liars. He never either in public or private gave me any such authority or license, and any person who states it is a scoundrel and a liar. I have heard it said, that I would become a second Avard, by withdrawing from the Church, and that I was at variance with the heads, and would use an influence against them, because I resigned the office of mayor. This is false, I have no difficulty with the heads of the Church, and I intend to continue with you, and hope the time may come when I may be restored to full confidence, fellowship, and my former standing in the Church, and that my conduct may be such as to warrant my restoration, and should the time ever come that I may have the opportunity to test my faith, it will then be known whether I am a traitor or true man.

I then said to him, "Will you please state definitely whether you know anything against my character, either in public or private?" General Bennett replied, "I do not. In all my intercourse with General Smith, in public and in private, he has been strictly virtuous."

I then made some pertinent remarks before the council, concerning those who had been guilty of circulating false reports, &c., and said:

Let one twelve months see if Brother Joseph is not called for, to go to every part of the city to keep them out of their graves; and I turn the keys upon them from this hour, if they will not repent and stop their lyings and surmisings, let God curse them, and let their tongues cleave to the roofs of their mouths.

Friday, *20*.—Charges having been preferred against Robert D. Foster, by Samuel H. Smith before a special council, for abusive language towards Samuel H. Smith; also for abusing the marshal of the city, I spent the day in council, and such was the proof against Foster, I had considerable labor to get him clear, even after his confession, which I desired to do, hoping he would amend.

Charge Against Robert D. Foster.

Saturday, *21*.—I spent the day with the High Council of Nauvoo, investigating the case of Robert D. Foster, Chauncey L. Higbee and others.

Sunday, *22*.—I spent the day mostly at home. In looking at the papers, I discovered the following in the Quincy *Whig:*

ASSASSINATION OF EX-GOVERNOR BOGGS OF MISSOURI.

Lilburn W. Boggs, late governor of Missouri, was assassinated at his residence in Independence, Missouri, by an unknown hand, on the 6th instant. He was sitting in a room by himself, when some person discharged a pistol loaded with buckshot, through an adjoining window, three of the shots took effect in his head, one of which penetrated the brain. His son, a boy, hearing the report of the pistol, ran into the room in which his father was seated, and found him in a helpless situation, upon which he gave the alarm. Footprints were found beneath the window, and the pistol which gave the fatal shot. The governor was alive on the seventh, but no hopes are entertained of his recovery. A man was suspected, and is probably arrested before this. There are several rumors in circulation in regard to the horrid affair; one of which throws the crime upon the Mormons, from the fact, we suppose, that Mr. Boggs was governor at the time, and in no small degree instrumental in driving them from the state. Smith, too, the Mormon Prophet, as we understand, prophesied, a year or so ago, his death by violent means. Hence, there is plenty of foundation for rumor. The citizens of Independence had offered a reward of $500 for the murderer.

I went to the editor's office, and inserted the following in the *Wasp:*

NAUVOO, ILLINOIS, May 22, 1842.

Mr. Bartlett:

DEAR SIR:—In your paper (the *Quincy Whig*) of the 21st instant, you have done me manifest injustice in ascribing to me a prediction of the demise of Lilburn W. Boggs, Esq., ex-governor of Missouri, by violent hands. Boggs was a candidate for the state senate, and, I presume, fell by the hand of a political opponent, with "his hands and face yet dripping with the blood of murder;" but he died not through my instrumentality. My hands are clean, and my heart pure, from the blood of all men. I am tired of the misrepresentation, calumny and detraction, heaped upon me by wicked men; and desire and claim, only those principles guaranteed to all men by the Constitution and laws of the United States and of Illinois. Will you do me the justice to publish this communication? and oblige,

Yours respectfully,

[Signed] JOSEPH SMITH.

An Epistle of the High Council of the Church of Jesus Christ of Latter-day Saints in Nauvoo, to the Saints scattered abroad, Greeting:

DEAR BRETHREN:—Inasmuch as the Lord hath spoken, and the commandment hath gone forth for the gathering together of His people from Babylon, that "they partake not of her sins, and receive not of her plagues;" it seemeth, "good unto us, and also to the Holy Ghost" to write somewhat for your instruction, in obeying that commandment. That you have no need that we exhort you to the observance of this commandment, is evident; for you yourselves know that this is that which was spoken by the Lord, in the parable of the tares of the field, who promised, that in the harvest he would say to the servant "gather the wheat into my barn;" the signs of the times proclaim this—the end of the world; and thus admonish us to the performance of this duty. "Yet notwithstanding the Spirit testifieth of these things, and you desire with great anxiety to gather with the Saints; yet are many of you hindered even to this day;" so that *to will* to obey the commandment is present; but how to perform, you find not. Feeling, therefore, the responsibility binding on you to observe the statutes and commandments of the Lord, and living in the midst of a generation that are ignorant of what the mind of the Lord is concerning His people, and of the things that belong to their peace; we are well aware of the embarrassments under which many of you labor in endeavoring to obey the laws pertaining to your salvation. It is then no marvel that in this day when darkness covers the earth, and gross darkness the people, that this generation who know not the day of their visitation, nor the dispensation of the fullness of times in which they live, should mock at the gathering together of the Saints for salvation, as did the antediluvians at the mighty work of righteous Noah, in building an ark in the midst of the land, for the salvation of his home by water; seeing then that such "blindness hath happened to the Gentile world, which to them is an evident token of perdition, but to you of salvation," and that of God, think it not strange that you should have to pass through the like afflictions which all your brethren the saints in all ages have done before you; to be reviled, persecuted, and hated of all men, for the name of Christ and the Gospel's sake, is the portion which all saints have had to partake, who have gone before you. You then can expect no better things than that there be men of corrupt minds, reprobate concerning the truth, who will evil entreat you, and unjustly despoil you of your property and embarrass you in pecuniary matters, and render it the more difficult to obey the command to gather with the Saints; pretending to do God's service, "whose judgment now lingereth not, and their damnation slumbereth not."

But, brethren, with all these considerations before you, in relation to your afflictions, we think it expedient to admonish you, that you bear, and forbear, as becometh Saints, and having done all that is lawful and right, to obtain justice of those that injure you, wherein you come short of obtaining it, commit the residue to the just judgment of God, and shake off the dust of your feet as a testimony of having done so.

Finally, brethren, as it is reported unto us, that there be some who have not done that which is lawful and right, but have designedly done injury to their neighbor or creditor by fraud, or otherwise, thinking to find protection with us in such iniquity; let all such be warned and certified, that with them we have no fellowship, when known to be such, until all reasonable measures are taken to make just restitution to those unjustly injured. Now, therefore, let this epistle be read in all the branches of the Church, as testimony, that as representatives thereof, we have taken righteousness for the girdle of our loins, and faithfulness for the girdle of our reins, "and that for Zion's sake we will not rest; and for Jerusalem's sake we will not hold our peace, until the righteousness thereof go forth as brightness, and the salvation thereof, as a lamp that burneth."

Your brethren and servants in the kingdom and patience of Jesus.

William Marks,
Austin Cowles, } Presidents.
Charles C. Rich,
James Allred,
Elias Higbee,
George W. Harris,
Aaron Johnson,
William Huntington, Sen.,
Henry G. Sherwood,
Samuel E. Bent,
Lewis D. Wilson,
David Fullmer,
Thomas Grover,
Newel Knight,
Leonard Soby.

Attest: Hosea Stout, Clerk.
May 22, 1842.

CHAPTER II.

ACTIONS IN RELATION TO JOHN C. BENNETT ET AL.—THE PROPHET'S INSTRUCTIONS TO THE RELIEF SOCIETY—TREATISE ON THE "HOLY GHOST"—WILLIAM LAW'S DEFENSE OF THE SAINTS—THE PROPHET'S ADDRESS TO THE CHURCH.

Monday, May 23, 1842.—I called a special session of the city council, at which Dimick B. Huntington was elected coroner of the city of Nauvoo.

Tuesday, 24.—Chauncey L. Higbee was cut off from the Church by the High Council, for unchaste and unvirtuous conduct towards certain females, and for teaching it was right, if kept secret, &c. He was also put under $200 bonds to keep the peace, on my complaint against him for slander, before Ebenezer Robinson, justice of the peace.

The Fall of Chauncey L. Higbee.

Wednesday, 25.—I spent the day in counseling the Bishops, and assisting them to expose iniquity.

Notice was this day given to John C. Bennett, that the First Presidency, Twelve, and Bishops had withdrawn fellowship from him, and were about to publish him in the paper, but on his humbling himself, and begging we would spare him from the paper, for his mother's sake, the notice was withdrawn from the paper.

Thursday, 26.—This forenoon I attended a meeting of nearly a hundred of the brethren in the Lodge Room, to whom John C. Bennett acknowledged his wicked and licentious conduct toward certain females in Nauvoo, and that he was worthy of the severest chastisements, and cried like a

Confessions of John C. Bennett.

child, and begged that he might be spared, in any possible way; so deep was his apparent sense of his guilt and unfitness for respectable society; so deeply did he feign, or really feel contrition for the moment, that he was forgiven still. I plead for mercy for him.

At one p. m. I attended a large and respectable meeting of the citizens of Nauvoo, near the Temple, and addressed them on the principles of government, at considerable length, showing that I did not intend to vote the Whig or Democratic ticket as such, but would go for those who would support good order, &c.

The Prophet's Political Attitude.

The meeting nominated candidates for senators, representatives, and other officers, and expressed their entire disapprobation of the *Quincy Whig*, relative to my being concerned against Governor Boggs.

I met with the Ladies' Relief Society, and gave them a short address; a synopsis was reported by Miss E. R. Snow.

Address of the Prophet to the Relief Society.

President Joseph Smith read the 14th chapter of Ezekiel—said the Lord had declared by the Prophet, that the people should each one stand for himself, and depend on no man or men in that state of corruption of the Jewish church—that righteous persons could only deliver their own souls—applied it to the present state of the Church of Jesus Christ of Latter-day Saints—said if the people departed from the Lord, they must fall—that they were depending on the Prophet, hence were darkened in their minds, in consequence of neglecting the duties devolving upon themselves, envious towards the innocent, while they afflict the virtuous with their shafts of envy.

There is another error which opens a door for the adversary to enter. As females possess refined feelings and sensitiveness, they are also subject to overmuch zeal, which must ever prove dangerous, and cause them to be rigid in a religious capacity—[they] should be armed with mercy, notwithstanding the iniquity among us.

Said he had been instrumental in bringing iniquity to light—it was a melancholy thought and awful that so many should place themselves under the condemnation of the devil, and going to perdition. With deep feeling he said that they are fellow mortals, we loved them once, shall we not encourage them to reformation? We have not [yet] forgiven them seventy times seven, as our Savior directed; perhaps we have not forgiven them once. There is now a day of salvation to such as repent and reform;—and they who repent not should be cast out from this society; yet we should woo them to return to God, lest they escape not the damnation of hell! Where there is a mountain top, there is also a valley—we should act in all things on a proper medium to every immortal spirit. Notwithstanding the unworthy are among us, the virtuous should not, from self importance, grieve and oppress needlessly, those unfortunate ones—even these should be encouraged to hereafter live to be honored by this society, who are the best portions of the community. Said he had two things to recommend to the members of this society, to put a double watch over the tongue: no organized body can exist without this at all. All organized bodies have their peculiar evils, weaknesses and difficulties, the object is to make those not so good reform and return to the path of virtue that they may be numbered with the good, and even hold the keys of power, which will influence to virtue and goodness—should chasten and reprove, and keep it all in silence, not even mention them again; then you will be established in power, virtue, and holiness, and the wrath of God will be turned away.

I have one request to make of the President and members of the society, that you search yourselves—the tongue is an unruly member—hold your tongues about things of no moment—a little tale will set the world on fire. At this time, the truth on the guilty should not be told openly, strange as this may seem, yet this is policy. We must use precaution in bringing sinners to justice, lest in exposing these heinous sins we draw the indignation of a Gentile world upon us (and, to their imagination, justly too). It is necessary to hold an influence in the world, and thus spare ourselves an extermination; and also accomplish our end in spreading the Gospel, or holiness, in the earth. If we were brought to desolation, the disobedient would find no help. There are some who are obedient, yet men cannot steady the ark—my arm cannot do it—God must steady it. To the iniquitous show yourselves merciful.

I am advised by some of the heads of the Church to tell the Relief Society to be virtuous, but to save the Church from desolation and the sword; beware, be still, be prudent, repent, reform, but do it in a way not to destroy all around you. I do not want to cloak iniquity—all things contrary to the will of God, should be cast from us, but don't do more hurt than good, with your tongues—be pure in heart. Jesus designs to save the people out of their sins. Said Jesus, "Ye shall do the work, which ye see me do." These are the grand key-words for the society to act upon. If I were not in your midst to aid and counsel you, the devil would overcome you. I want the innocent to go free—rather spare ten iniquitous among you, than condemn one innocent one. "Fret not thyself because of evil doers." God will see to it.

Friday, 27.—Had an attack of a bilious nature, stayed at home, took some medicine.

Saturday, 28.—Convalescent. Walked to the store with Emma, transacted some business in the city. At eight in the evening, called at the printing office, with the night watch, to see the *Wasp.*

Violent shocks of earthquakes were experienced in Greece about this time.

The High Council were in session, as they had been from day to day through the week, investigating charges against various individuals for unvirtuous conduct, committed through the teachings and influence of John C. Bennett; several were cut off, and some were forgiven on confession.

Sunday, 29.—I was at home; and about the city engaged in counselling the brethren, &c., and also on Monday and Tuesday, the 30th, and 31st.

Wednesday, June 1.—I attended a political meeting in the grove, for the nomination of county officers, for the county at large, in which I concurred, with the exception of the candidate for the sheriffalty, and spoke in favor of the proceedings.

A general conference was held in the Exchange, Manchester, England, Elder Parley P. Pratt, presiding, at which 16 conferences were represented, comprising 7,514 members, 220 Elders, 421 Priests, and 110 Teachers.

Thursday, 2.—Rode out with Brother Bowen and my clerk, and sold lot 1 in block 143.

The State of Michigan repudiated its debt for $2,350,000.

Friday, 3.—In the forenoon I rode out in the city, and sold to Brother Harmer lot 1 in block 123, and in the afternoon rode to Brother John Benbow's, on horseback, accompanied by Emma and others.

Saturday, 4.—At the printing office in the morning, and heard letters read from Grand Master Jonas, Dr. King and Mr. Helme, concerning John C. Bennett's expulsion from the Masonic Lodge in Ohio.

In the afternoon paid E. B. Nourn $505 for land bought of Hugh McFall, and settled with the heirs of Edward Lawrence at my house, assisted by Newel K. Whitney and my clerk.

Sunday, 5.—I preached this morning to a large congregation. The subject matter of my discourse was drawn from 32nd and 33rd chapters of Ezekiel, wherein it was shown that old Pharaoh was comforted and greatly rejoiced that he was honored as a kind of king devil over those uncircumcised nations that go down to hell for rejecting the word of the Lord, notwithstanding His mighty miracles, and fighting the Saints; the whole exhibited as a pattern to this generation, and the nations now rolling in splendor over the globe, if they do not repent, that they shall go down to the pit also and be rejoiced over, and ruled over by old Pharaoh, king-devil of mobocrats, miracle-rejecters, Saint-killers, hypocritical priests, and all other fit subjects to fester in their own infamy.

Discoure by the Prophet.

Monday, 6.—I rode on the prairie to view some land, accompanied by Brother Yearsley and my clerk; dined at Brother Lot's, and returned home; when I approved of a series of resolutions passed by a court martial of the Nauvoo Legion.

Tuesday, 7.—Sold David D. Yearsley a quarter section of land. Quite a snowstorm is reported in many parts of the New England and Middle States.

Wednesday, 8.—I was about home. Sent Dr. Richards to Carthage on business. On his return, old Charley, while on a gallop, struck his knees and breast instead of his feet, fell in the street, and rolled over in an instant, and the doctor narrowly escaped with his life. It was a trick of the devil to kill my clerk. Similar attacks have been made on myself of late, and Satan is seeking our destruction on every hand.

Thursday, *9*.—At home, and about the neighborhood, attending to domestic affairs, and the business of the Church.

Minutes of Meeting of the Female Relief Society, at the Grove, Nauvoo, June 9, 1842, (Reported by Miss E. R. Snow.)

President Joseph Smith opened the meeting by prayer, and then addressed the congregation on the design of the institution. Said it is no matter how fast the society increases, if all the members are virtuous; that we must be as particular with regard to the character of members now, as when the society was first started; that sometimes persons wish to crowd themselves into a society of this kind when they do not intend to pursue the ways of purity and righteousness, as if the society would be a shelter to them in their iniquity.

He said that henceforth no person shall be admitted, but by presenting regular petitions, signed by two or three members in good standing in the society, and whoever comes in must be of good report.

Objections having been previously made against Mahala Overton, they were now removed; after which President Joseph Smith continued his address; said he was going to preach mercy. Suppose that Jesus Christ and holy angels should object to us on frivolous things, what would become of us? We must be merciful to one another, and overlook small things.

Respecting the reception of Sister Overton, President Joseph Smith said: It grieves me that there is no fuller fellowship; if one member suffer all feel it; by union of feeling we obtain power with God. Christ said He came to call sinners to repentance, to save them. Christ was condemned by the self-righteous Jews because He took sinners into His society; He took them upon the principle that they repented of their sins. It is the object of this society to reform persons, not to take those that are corrupt and foster them in their wickedness; but if they repent, we are bound to take them, and by kindness sanctify and cleanse them from all unrighteousness by our influence in watching over them. Nothing will have such influence over people as the fear of being disfellowshiped by so goodly a society as this. Then take Sister Overton, as Jesus received sinners into His bosom. Sister Overton, in the name of the Lord, I now make you free. Nothing is so much calculated to lead people to forsake sin as to take them by the hand, and watch over them with tenderness. When persons manifest the least kindness and love to me, O what power it has over my mind, while the opposite course has a tendency to harrow up all the harsh feelings and depress the human mind.

It is one evidence that men are unacquainted with the principles of godliness to behold the contraction of affectionate feelings and lack of charity in the world. The power and glory of godliness is spread out on a broad principle to throw out the mantle of charity. God does not look on sin with allowance, but when men have sinned, there must be allowance made for them.

All the religious world is boasting of righteousness: it is the doctrine of the devil to retard the human mind, and hinder our progress, by filling us with self-righteousness. The nearer we get to our heavenly Father, the more we are disposed to look with compassion on perishing souls; we feel that we want to take them upon our shoulders, and cast their sins behind our backs. My talk is intended for all this society; if you would have God have mercy on you, have mercy on one another.

President Smith then referred them to the conduct of the Savior, when He was taken and crucified, &c.

He then made a promise in the name of the Lord, saying that that soul who has righteousness enough to ask God in the secret place for life, every day of their lives, shall live to three score years and ten. We must walk uprightly all the day long. How glorious are the principles of righteousness! We are full of selfishness; the devil flatters us that we are very righteous, when we are feeding on the faults of others. We can only live by worshiping our God; all must do it for themselves; none can do it for another. How mild the Savior dealt with Peter, saying, "When thou art converted, strengthen thy brethren." At another time, He said to him, "Lovest thou me?" and having received Peter's reply, He said, "Feed my sheep." If the sisters loved the Lord, let them feed the sheep, and not destroy them. How oft have wise men and women sought to dictate Brother Joseph by saying, "O, if I were Brother Joseph, I would do this and that;" but if they were in Brother Joseph's shoes they would find that men or women could not be compelled into the kingdom of God, but must be dealt with in long-suffering, and at last we shall save them. The way to keep all the Saints together, and keep the work rolling, is to wait with all long-suffering, till God shall bring such characters to justice. There should be no license for sin, but mercy should go hand in hand with reproof.

Sisters of the society, shall there be strife among you? I will not have it. You must repent, and get the love of God. Away with self-righteousness. The best measure or principle to bring the poor to repentance is to administer to their wants. The Ladies' Relief Society is not only to relieve the poor, but to save souls.

President Smith then said that he would give a lot of land to the society by deeding to the treasurer, that the society may build houses for the poor. He also said he would give a house, frame not finished, and that Brother Cahoon will move it on to the aforesaid lot, and the society can pay him by giving orders on the store; that it was a good plan to set those to work who are owing widows, and thus make an offset, &c.

Friday, 10.—Went to Brother Hibbard's with my clerk, to purchase some land.

Saturday, 11.—Presided in city council. Council resolved to publish the city charter, ordinances of the city council, and Nauvoo Legion, before the first day of next July. Also resolved that the bond given by William Marks, binding him to make a deed for the land purchased of him for a burying ground, for the use of the city, be put on record in the office for the registry of deeds in the city of Nauvoo.

Riots and mobs are multiplying in the land.

Sunday, 12.—Mostly at home. Called at the printing office for some papers.

Monday, 13.—Attended a general council in the lodge room to devise ways and means to furnish the poor with labor. Many of the English Saints have gathered to Nauvoo, most of whom are unacquainted with any kind of labor, except spinning, weaving, &c.; and having no factories in this place, they are troubled to know what to do. Those who have funds have more generally neglected to gather, and left the poor to build up the city and the kingdom of God in these last days.

Conditions of English Saints in Nauvoo.

Tuesday, 14.—Rode to the big mound on the La Harpe road, accompanied by Emma, Hiram Kimball, and Dr. Richards, and purchased a three-quarter section of land of Kimball, including the mound.

The Twelve—namely, President Brigham Young, Heber

C. Kimball, Wilford Woodruff, John Taylor, and Willard Richards, Bishop George Miller, and Hiram Clark, of the High Priest's quorum, in council at the printing office.

Hyrum Clark Sent to England.

Voted that Hiram Clark go immediately to England, take a letter to gather means of the churches to go on his journey and take charge of the emigration in England, instead of Amos Fielding; also collect means for building the Temple, purchase goods, &c., and that letters be given him to Brother Parley P. Pratt to this effect. Voted that Brother Fielding come immediately to this place with his family after his return from England.

John C. Bennett's defense of the proceedings at Nauvoo, &c., may be seen on the 37th, 38th, and 39th pages of the *Wasp*.

Wednesday, 15.—Visited at different places in the city, and my farm on the prairie, accompanied by my clerk and Orrin Porter Rockwell, and supped at Hiram Kimball's.

Issued an editorial on the Gift of the Holy Ghost, as follows:—

The Gift of the Holy Ghost.

Various and conflicting are the opinions of men in regard to the gift of the Holy Ghost. Some people have been in the habit of calling every supernatural manifestation the effects of the Spirit of God, whilst there are others that think there is no manifestation connected with it at all; and that it is nothing but a mere impulse of the mind, or an inward feeling, impression, or secret testimony or evidence, which men possess, and that there is no such a thing as an outward manifestation.

It is not to be wondered at that men should be ignorant, in a great measure, of the principles of salvation, and more especially of the nature, office, power, influence, gifts, and blessings of the gift of the Holy Ghost; when we consider that the human family have been enveloped in gross darkness and ignorance for many centuries past, without revelation, or any just criterion [by which] to arrive at a knowledge of the things of God, which can only be known by the Spirit of God. Hence it not infrequently occurs, that when the Elders of this Church preach to the inhabitants of the world, that if they obey the Gospel they shall receive the gift of the Holy Ghost, that the people expect to see some wonderful manifestation, some great display of power, or some extraordinary miracle performed; and it is often the case that young members of this Church for want of better information, carry along with them their old notions of things, and sometimes fall into egregious errors. We have lately had some information concerning a few members that are in this dilemma, and for their information make a few remarks upon the subject.

We believe in the gift of the Holy Ghost being enjoyed now, as much as it was in the Apostles' days; we believe that it [the gift of the Holy Ghost] is necessary to make and to organize the Priesthood, that no man can be called to fill any office in the ministry without it; we also believe in prophecy, in tongues, in visions, and in revelations, in gifts, and in healings; and that these things cannot be enjoyed without the gift of the Holy Ghost. We believe that the holy men of old spake as they were moved by the Holy Ghost, and that holy men in these days speak by the same principle; we believe in its being a comforter and a witness bearer, that it brings things past to our remembrance, leads us into all truth, and shows us of things to come; be believe that "no man can know that Jesus is the Christ, but by the Holy Ghost." We believe in it [this gift of the Holy Ghost] in all its fullness, and power, and greatness, and glory; but whilst we do this, we believe in it rationally, consistently, and scripturally, and not according to the wild vagaries, foolish notions and traditions of men.

The human family are very apt to run to extremes, especially in religious matters, and hence people in general, either want some miraculous display, or they will not believe in the gift of the Holy Ghost at all. If an Elder lays his hands upon a person, it is thought by many that the person must immediately rise and speak in tongues and prophesy; this idea is gathered from the circumstance of Paul laying his hands upon certain individuals who had been previously (as they stated) baptized unto John's baptism; which when he had done, they "spake in tongues and prophesied." Phillip also, when he had preached the Gospel to the inhabitants of the city of Samaria, sent for Peter and John, who when they came laid their hands upon them for the gift of the Holy Ghost; for as yet he was fallen upon none of them; and when Simon Magus saw that through the laying on of the Apostles' hands the Holy Ghost was given, he offered them money that he might possess the same power. (Acts viii.) These passages are considered by many as affording sufficient evidence for some miraculous, visible manifestation, whenever hands are laid on for the gift of the Holy Ghost.

We believe that the Holy Ghost is imparted by the laying on of hands of those in authority, and that the gift of tongues, and also the gift of prophecy are gifts of the Spirit, and are obtained through that medium; but then to say that men always prophesied and spoke in tongues when they had the imposition of hands, would be to state that which is untrue, contrary to the practice of the Apostles, and at variance with holy writ; for Paul says, "To one is given the gift of tongues, to another the gift of prophecy, and to another the gift of healing;" and again: "Do all prophesy? do all speak with tongues? do all interpret?" evidently showing that all did not possess these several gifts; but that one received one gift, and another received another gift—all did not phophesy, all did not speak in tongues, all did not work miracles; but all did receive the gift of the Holy Ghost; sometimes they spake in tongues and prophesied in the Apostles' days, and sometimes they did not. The same is the case with us also in our administrations, while more frequently there is no manifestation at all; that is visible to the surrounding multitude; this will appear plain when we consult the writings of the Apostles, and notice their proceedings in relation to this matter. Paul, in 1st Cor. xii, says, "Now concerning spiritual gifts, brethren, I would not have you ignorant;" it is evident from this, that some of them were ignorant in relation to these matters, or they would not need instruction.

Again, in chapter xiv, he says, "Follow after charity and desire spiritual gifts, but rather that ye may prophesy." It is very evident from these Scriptures that many of them had not spiritual gifts, for if they had spiritual gifts where was the necessity of Paul telling them to follow after them, and it is as evident that they did not all receive those gifts by the imposition of the hands; for they as a Church had been baptized and confirmed by the laying on of hands—and yet to a Church of this kind, under the immediate inspection and superintendency of the Apostles, it was necessary for Paul to say, "Follow after charity, and desire spiritual gifts, but rather that ye may prophesy," evidently showing that those gifts were in the Church, but not enjoyed by all in their outward manifestations.

But suppose the gifts of the Spirit were immediately, upon the imposition of hands, enjoyed by all, in all their fullness and power; the skeptic would still be as far from receiving any testimony except upon a mere casualty as before, for all the gifts of the Spirit are not visible to the natual vision, or understanding of man; indeed very few of them are. We read that "Christ ascended into heaven and gave gifts unto men; and He gave some Apostles, and some Prophets, and some Evangelists, and some Pastors and Teachers." (Eph. iv).

The Church is a compact body composed of different members, and is strictly analogous to the human system, and Paul, after speaking of the different gifts, says, "Now ye are the body of Christ and members in particular; and God hath set some in the Church, first Apostles, secondarily Prophets, thirdly Teachers, after that miracles, then gifts of healing, helps, governments, diversities of tongues. Are all Teachers? Are all workers of miracles? Do all speak with tongues? Do all interpret?" It is evident that they do not; yet are they all members of one body. All members of the natural body are not the eye, the ear, the head or the hand—yet the eye cannot say to the ear I have no need of thee, nor the head to the foot, I have no need of thee; they are all so many component parts in the perfect machine—the one body; and if one member suffer, the whole of the members suffer with it: and if one member rejoice, all the rest are honored with it.

These, then, are all gifts; they come from God; they are of God; they are all the gifts of the Holy Ghost; they are what Christ ascended into heaven to impart; and yet how few of them could be known by the generality of men. Peter and John were Apostles, yet the Jewish court scourged them as impostors. Paul was both an Apostle and Prophet, yet they stoned him and put him into prison. The people knew nothing about it, although he had in his possession the gift of the Holy Ghost. Our Savior was "anointed with the oil of gladness above his fellows," yet so far from the people knowing Him, they said He was Beelzebub, and crucified Him as an impostor. Who could point out a Pastor, a Teacher, or an Evangelist by their appearance, yet had they the gift of the Holy Ghost?

But to come to the other members of the Church, and examine the gifts as spoken of by Paul, and we shall find that the world can in general know nothing about them, and that there is but one or two that could be immediately known, if they were all poured out immediately upon the imposition of hands. In I. Cor. xii., Paul says, "There are diversities of gifts yet the same spirit, and there are differences of administrations but the same Lord; and there are diversities of operations, but it is the same God which worketh all in all. But the manifestations of the Spirit is given unto every man to profit withal. For to one is given, by the Spirit, the word of wisdom, to another, the word of knowledge by the same Spirit; to another faith, by the same Spirit; to another the gifts of healing, by the same Spirit; to another the working of miracles; to another prophecy; to another the discerning of spirits; to another divers kinds of tongues; to another the interpretation of tongues. But all these worketh that one and the self same spirit, dividing to each man severally as he will."

There are several gifts mentioned here, yet which of them all could be known by an observer at the imposition of hands? The word of wisdom, and the word of knowledge, are as much gifts as any other, yet if a person possessed both of these gifts, or received them by the imposition of hands, who would know it? Another might receive the gift of faith, and they would be as ignorant of it. Or suppose a man had the gift of healing or power to work miracles, that would not then be known; it would require time and circumstances to call these gifts into operation. Suppose a man had the discerning of spirits, who would be the wiser for it? Or if he had the interpretation of tongues, unless someone spoke in an unknown tongue, he of course would have to be silent; there are only two gifts that could be made visible—the gift of tongues and the gift of prophecy. These are things that are the most talked about, and yet if a person spoke in an unknown tongue, according to Paul's testimony, he would be a barbarian to those present. They would say that it was gibberish; and if he prophesied they would call it nonsense. The gift of tongues is the smallest gift perhaps of the whole, and yet it is one that is the most sought after.

So that according to the testimony of Scripture and the manifestations of the Spirit in ancient days, very little could be known about it by the surrounding multitude, except on some extraordinary occasion, as on the day of Pentecost.

The greatest, the best, and the most useful gifts would be known nothing about by an observer. It is true that a man might prophesy, which is a great gift, and one that Paul told the people—the Church—to seek after and to covet, rather than to speak in tongues; but what does the world know about prophesying? Paul says that it "serveth only to those that believe." But does not the Scriptures say that they spake in tongues and prophesied? Yes; but who is it that writes these Scriptures? Not the men of the world or mere casual observers, but the Apostles—men who knew one gift from another, and of course were capable of writing about it; if we had the testimony of the Scribes and Pharisees concerning the outpouring of the Spirit on the day of Pentecost, they would have told us that it was no gift, but that the people were "drunken with new wine," and we shall finally have to come to the same conclusion that Paul did—"No man knows the things of God but by the Spirit of God;" for with the great revelations of Paul when he was caught up into the third heaven and saw things that were not lawful to utter, no man was apprised of it until he mentioned it himself fourteen years after; and when John had the curtains of heaven withdrawn, and by vision looked through the dark vista of future ages, and contemplated events that should transpire throughout every subsequent period of time, until the final winding up scene—while he gazed upon the glories of the eternal world, saw an innumerable company of angels and heard the voice of God—it was in the Spirit, on the Lord's day, unnoticed and unobserved by the world.

The manifestations of the gift of the Holy Ghost, the ministering of angels, or the development of the power, majesty or glory of God were very seldom manifested publicly, and that generally to the people of God, as to the Israelites; but most generally when angels have come, or God has revealed Himself, it has been to individuals in private, in their chamber; in the wilderness or fields, and that generally without noise or tumult. The angel delivered Peter out of prison in the dead of night; came to Paul unobserved by the rest of the crew; appeared to Mary and Elizabeth without the knowledge of others; spoke to John the Baptist whilst the people around were ignorant of it.

When Elisha saw the chariots of Israel and the horsemen thereof, it was unknown to others. When the Lord appeared to Abraham it was at his tent door; when the angels went to Lot, no person knew them but himself, which was the case probably with Abraham and his wife; when the Lord appeared to Moses, it was in the burning bush, in the tabernacle, or in the mountain top; when Elijah was taken in a chariot of fire, it was unobserved by the world; and when he was in a cleft of a rock, there was loud thunder, but the Lord was not in the thunder; there was an earthquake, but the Lord was not in the earthquake; and then there was a still small voice, which was the voice of the Lord, saying, "What doest thou hear, Elijah?"

The Lord cannot always be known by the thunder of His voice, by the display of His glory or by the manifestation of His power; and those that are the most anxious to see these things, are the least prepared to meet them, and were the Lord to manifest His power as He did to the children of Israel, such characters would be the first to say, "Let not the Lord speak any more, lest we His people die."

We would say to the brethren, seek to know God in your closets, call upon him in the fields. Follow the directions of the Book of Mormon, and pray over, and for your families, your cattle, your flocks, your herds, your corn, and all things that you possess; ask the blessing of God upon all your labors, and everything that you engage in. Be virtuous and pure; be men of integrity and truth; keep the commandments of God; and then you will be able more perfectly to understand the difference between right and wrong—between the things of God and the things of men; and your path will be like that of the just, which shineth brighter and brighter unto the perfect day."

Be not so curious about tongues, do not speak in tongues except there be an interpreter present; the ultimate design of tongues is to speak to foreigners, and if persons are very anxious to display their intelligence, let them speak to such in their own tongues. The gifts of God are all useful in their place, but when they are applied to that which God does not intend, they prove an injury, a snare and a curse instead of a blessing. We may some future time enter more fully into this subject, but shall let this suffice for the present.

Thursday, 16.—The following notice was published by the Nauvoo [Masonic] lodge:

NOTICE.

To all whom it may concern, *greeting:*—Whereas, John Cook Bennett, in the organization of the Nauvoo Lodge, under dispensation palmed himself upon the fraternity as a regular mason, in good standing: and satisfactory testimony having been produced before said lodge, that he, said Bennett, was an expelled mason, we therefore publish to all the masonic world the above facts that he, the said Bennett, may not impose himself again upon the fraternity of masons. All editors who are friendly to the fraternity of free and accepted ancient York masons will please insert the above.

GEORGE MILLER,
Master of Nauvoo Lodge under Dispensation.

The British forces captured the Chinese fortifications on the Yang-tse-Kiang river with 364 pieces of artillery.

Friday, 17.—

Defense of the Saints in Nauvoo by William Law.

What have the Mormons done to Illinois? is the question which I have frequently asked of those who are busy with the tongue of slander in calumniating the Latter-day Saints, but as yet I have found none who are willing to answer me honestly or correctly. Perhaps many judge from rumor, not having investigated the matter for themselves. I have, therefore, thought it might be well to lay before the public some facts in relation to the case, believing that there is a respectable portion of the community, who, after having received correct information, will frown with indignation upon the conduct of those who are endeavoring to raise a persecution against our people.

In the first place, we would say, that where a crime is committed there is a law broken, for if no law has been violated, there cannot have been a crime committed; if, then, our people have broken the law is there not power in those laws to vindicate themselves, or to redress the wrongs of those who are injured? We say there is; neither would we cast any aspersion upon the characters of the administrators of the laws, as though they were not vigilant in the discharge of their duty; we believe, with very few exceptions, they have been vigilant.

With these facts before us, there is then no difficulty in obtaining correct information as to the amount of crime committed by the Mormons throughout the state. You have only to refer to the various dockets kept by the administrators of law, from the highest court to the lowest, throughout the length and breadth of the land, and there you will find recorded the crimes of the Mormons, if it so be that they have committed any.

We say their faults are few compared to the population. Where is there a record of murder committed by any of our people? None in the State. Where is there a record against any of our people for a penitentiary crime?—Not in the State. Where is there a record of fine or county imprisonment (for any breach of law) against any of the Latter-day Saints? I know of none in the State. If, then, they have broken no law, they consequently have taken away no man's rights—they have infringed upon no man's liberties.

We have been three years in this State, and have not asked for any county or state office. Laws have been administered by those not of our persuasion; administered rigorously, even against the appearance of crime, and yet there has been no conviction of which I have heard. Where is there another community in any state, against none of whom there is a record of conviction for crime in any court during the space of three years? And yet there are those who cry out "Treason! murder! bigamy! burglary! arson! and everything that is evil, without being able to refer to a single case that has ever been proved against the Mormons.

This, then, must be the "head and front of our offending," that by industry in both spiritual and temporal things, we are becoming a great and numerous people; we convert our thousands and tens of thousands yearly to the light of truth—to the glorious liberty of the Gospel of Christ; we bring thousands from foreign lands, from under the yoke of oppression and the iron hand of poverty, and we place them in a situation where they can sustain themselves, which is the highest act of charity toward the poor. We dry the widow's tear, we fill the orphan's hand with bread, and clothe the naked; we teach them principles of morality and righteousness, and they rejoice in the God of Abraham and in the Holy One of Israel, and are happy.

Thus it is with the honest in heart: but when the wicked creep in amongst us for evil, to trample upon the most holy and virtuous precepts, and find our moral and religious laws too strict for them, they cry out, "Delusion, false prophets, speculation, oppression, illegal ordinances, usurpation of power, treason against the government, &c. You must have your charters taken away; you have dared to pass an ordinance against fornicators and adulterers; you have forbidden the vending of spirituous liquors within your city; you have passed an ordinance against vagrants and disorderly persons; with many other high-handed acts! You even threaten to vote at the next election, and may be, (at least we fear) you will send a member to the legislature; none of which doings we, the good mobocrats and anti-Mormon politicians (and some priests as well) are willing to bear."

This is the cry of the base and the vile, the priest and the speculator, but the noble, the high-minded, the patriotic and the virtuous breathe no such sentiment; neither will those who feel an interest in the welfare of the state, for who does not know that to increase the population ten thousand a year with the most industrious people in the world, to pay thousands of dollars of taxes, to bring into the state immense sums of gold and silver, from all countries; to establish the greatest manufacturing city in America (which Nauvoo will be in a few years,) and to create the best produce market in the west,—is for the good and prosperity of the community at large, and of the state of Illinois in particular. As to the city ordinances we have passed all such as we deemed necessary for the peace, welfare and happiness of the inhabitants, whether Jew or Greek, Mohammedan, Roman Catholic, Latter-day Saint or any other; that they all worship God according to their own conscience, and enjoy the rights of American freemen.

WILLIAM LAW.

Nauvoo, June 17, 1842.

The above are plain matters of fact, that every one may become acquainted with by reference to the county and state records. We might add that in regard to moral principles, there is no city either in this state, or in the United States that can compare with the city of Nauvoo. You may live in our city for a month, and not hear an oath sworn; you may be here as long and not see one person intoxicated. So notorious are we for sobriety, that at the time the Washington convention passed through our city a meeting was called for them, but they expressed themselves at a loss what to say, as there were no drunkards to speak to.

The Prophet's Confirmation of Wm. Law's Defense of the Saints.

Saturday, 18.—The following brief extract is from the journal of Elder Wilford Woodruff:

Minutes of a Public Meeting in Nauvoo.

The citizens of Nauvoo, both male and female, assembled near the Temple for a general meeting; many thousands were assembled.

Joseph the Seer arose and spoke his mind in great plainness concerning the iniquity, hypocrisy, wickedness and corruption of General John Cook Bennett. He also prophesied in the name of the Lord, concerning the merchants in the city, that if they and the rich did not open their hearts and contribute to the poor, they would be cursed by the hand of God, and be cut off from the land of the living.

The main part of the day was taken up upon the business of the Agricultural and Manufacturing Society. Arrangements were entered into to commence operations immediately, under the charter granted by the legislature.

Also Joseph commanded the Twelve to organize the Church more according to the law of God; that is to require of those that come in to be settled according to their counsel, and also to appoint a committee to wait upon all who arrive, make them welcome and counsel them what to do. Brigham Young, Heber C. Kimball, George A. Smith and Hyrum Smith were the committee appointed to wait upon emigrants and settle them.

Tuesday, 21.—I attended a large assembly of the Saints, at the stand near the Temple, and addressed them on the subject of agriculture, manufacture, and trade, and was followed by the Twelve and others on the same subject.

Wednesday, 22.—There was a special session of the city council held, when was passed "an ordinance repealing all ordinances and resolutions relative to the changing of the names of streets" in the city of Nauvoo.

Thursday, 23.—I published the following:

An Address to the Church of Jesus Christ of Latter-day Saints and to all the Honorable Part of the Community.

It becomes my duty to lay before the Church of Jesus Christ of Latter-day Saints and the public generally, some important facts relative to the conduct and character of Dr. John C. Bennett, who has lately been expelled from the aforesaid Church and the honorable part of the community may be aware of his proceedings, and be ready to treat him, and regard him as he ought to be regarded, viz., as an impostor and base adulterer.

It is a matter of notoriety that the said Dr. John C. Bennett became favorable to the doctrines taught by the Elders of the Church of Jesus Christ of Latter-day Saints, and located himself in the city of Nauvoo, about the month of August, 1840, and soon after joined the Church.

Soon after it was known that he had become a member of said Church, a communication was received at Nauvoo from a person of respectable character and residing in the vicinity where Bennett had lived. This letter cautioned us against him, setting forth that he was a very mean man, and had a wife and two or three children in McConnellsvill, Morgan county, Ohio; but knowing that it is no uncommon thing for good men to be evil spoken against, the above letter was kept quiet, but held in reserve.

He had not been long in Nauvoo before he began to keep company with a young lady, one of our citizens; and she, being ignorant of his having a wife living, gave way to his addresses, and became confident from his behavior towards her, that he intended to marry her; and this he gave her to understand he would do. I, seeing the folly of such an acquaintance, persuaded him to desist, and on account of his continuing his course, finally threatened to expose him if he did not desist. This, to outward appearance, had the desired effect, and the acquaintance between them was broken off.

But, like one of the most abominable and depraved beings which could possibly exist, he only broke off his publicly wicked actions to sink deeper into iniquity and hypocrisy. When he saw that I would not submit to any such conduct, he went to some of the females in the city who knew nothing of him but as an honorable man, and began to teach them that promiscuous intercourse between the sexes was a doctrine believed in by the Latter-day Saints, and that there was no harm in it, but this failing, he had recourse to a more influential and desperately wicked course, and that was to persuade them that myself and others of the authorities of the Church, not only sanctioned but practiced the same wicked acts, and when asked why I publicly preached so much against it, said that it was because of the prejudice of the public, and that it would cause trouble in my own house. He was well aware of the consequence of such wilful and base falsehoods, if they should come to my knowledge, and consequently endeavored to persuade his dupes to keep it a matter of secrecy, persuading them there would be no harm if they did not make it known. This proceeding on his part answered the desired end; he accomplished his wicked purposes; he seduced an innocent female by his lying, and subjected her character to public disgrace, should it ever be known.

But his depraved heart would not suffer him to stop here. Not being contented with having disgraced one female, he made an attempt upon others; and by the same plausible tale overcame them also, evidently not caring whose character was ruined, so that his wicked, lustful appetites might be gratified.

Some time, about the early part of July, 1841, I received a letter from Elders Hyrum Smith and William Law, who were then in Pittsburgh, Pennsylvania. This letter was dated June 15th, and contained the particulars of a conversation betwixt them and a respectable gentleman from the neighborhood where Bennett's wife and children resided. He stated to them that it was a fact that Bennett had a wife and children living, and that she had left him because of his ill treatment toward her. This letter was read to Bennett, which he did not attempt to deny, but candidly acknowledged the fact.

Soon after this information reached our ears, Dr. Bennett made an attempt at suicide by taking poison, but he being discovered before it took effect, and the proper antidote being administered, he recovered; but he very much resisted when an attempt was made to save him. The public impression was that he was so much ashamed of his base and wicked conduct, that he had recourse to the above deed to escape the censures of an indignant community.

It might have been supposed that these circumstances, transpiring in the manner they did, would have produced a thorough reformation in his conduct; but, alas! like a being totally destitute of common decency, and without any government over his passions, he was soon busily engaged in the same wicked career, and continued until a knowledge of the same reached my ears. I immediately charged him with it, and he admitted that it was true; but in order to put a stop to all such proceedings for the future, I publicly proclaimed against it, and had those females notified to appear before the proper officers, that the whole subject might be investigated and thoroughly exposed.

During the course of investigation, the foregoing facts were proved by credible witnesses, and were sworn and subscribed to before an alderman of the city, on the 15th ultimo. The documents containing the evidence are now in my possession.

We also ascertained by the above investigation that others had been led by his conduct to pursue the same adulterous practice, and in order to accomplish their detestible designs made use of the same language insinuated by Bennett, with this difference, that they did not hear me say anything of the kind, but Bennett was one of the heads of the Church, and he had informed them that such was the fact and they credited his testimony.

The public will perceive the aggravating nature of this case, and will see the propriety of this exposure. Had he only been guilty of adultery, that was sufficient to stamp disgrace upon him, because he is a man of better information, and has been held high in the estimation of many. But, when it is considered that his mind was so intent upon his cruel and abominable deeds, and his own reputation not being sufficient to enable him to do it, he must needs make use of my name in order to effect his purposes,an enlightened public will not be astonished at the course I have pursued.

In order that it may be distinctly understood that he willfully and knowingly lied in the above insinuations, I will lay before my readers an affidavit taken before an alderman of the city, after I had charged him with these things:—

State of Illinois,
City of Nauvoo.

Personally appeared before me, Daniel H. Wells, an alderman of said city of Nauvoo, John C. Bennett, who being duly sworn according to law, deposeth and saith,—that he never was taught anything in the least contrary to the strictest principles of the Gospel, or of virtue, or of the laws of God or man, under any circumstances, or upon any occasion, either directly or indirectly, in word or deed, by Joseph Smith, and that he never knew the said Smith to countenance any improper conduct whatever, either in public or private; and that he never did teach me in private that an illegal, illicit intercourse with females was, under any circumstances justifiable, and that I never knew him so to teach others.

JOHN C. BENNETT.

Sworn to, and subscribed before me, this 17th day of May, A. D. 1842.

DANIEL H. WELLS, Alderman.

The following conversation took place in the City Council, and was elicited in consequence of its being reported that the doctor had stated that I had acted in an indecorous manner, and given countenance to vices practiced by the doctor and others:—

Dr. John C. Bennett, ex-mayor, was then called upon by the mayor to state if he knew aught against him [i.e.,Joseph Smith], when Mr. Bennet replied: I know what I am about, and the heads of the Church know what they are about, I expect. I have no difficulty with the heads of the Church. I publicly avow that any one who has said that I have stated that General Joseph Smith has given me authority to hold illicit intercourse with women, is a liar in the face of God; those who have said it are damned liars; they are infernal liars. He never, either in public or private, gave me any such authority or license, and any person who states it, is a scoundrel and a liar. I have heard it said that I would become a second Avard by withdrawing from the Church, and that I was at variance with the heads, and would use an influence against them, because I resigned the office of mayor; this is false. I have no difficulty with the heads of the Church, and I intend to continue with you, and hope the time may come when I may be restored to full confidence and fellowship, and my former standing in the Church; and that my conduct may be such as to warrant my restoration; and should the time ever come that I may have the opportunity to test my faith, it will then be known whether I am a traitor or a true man.

Joseph Smith then asked: "Will you please state definitely whether you know anything against my character either in public or private?"

General Bennett answered: "I do not; in all my intercourse with General Smith, in public and in private, he has been strictly virtuous."

WILSON LAW,
HIRAM KIMBALL,
BRIGHAM YOUNG,
WILLARD RICHARDS,
HEBER C. KIMBALL,
WILFORD WOODRUFF,
GEO. A. SMITH,
NEWEL K. WHITNEY,
ORSON SPENCER,
JOHN TAYLOR,
JOHN P. GREENE,
GUSTAVE HILLS,
GEORGE W. HARRIS,
JAMES SLOAN, City Recorder.

May 19, 1842.

After I had done all in my power to persuade him to amend his conduct, and these facts were fully established (not only by testimony, but by his own confessions) he having acknowledged that they were true, and seeing no prospects of any satisfaction from his future life, the hand of fellowship was withdrawn from him as a member of the Church by the officers; but on account of his earnest requesting that we would not publish him to the world, we concluded not to do so at that time, but would let the matter rest until we saw the effect of what we had already done.

It appears evident that as soon as he perceived that he could no longer maintain his standing as a member of the Church, nor his respectability as a citizen, he came to the conclusion to leave the place, which he has done, and that very abruptly; and had he done so quietly, and not attempted to deceive the people around him, his case would not have excited the indignation of the citizens so much as his real conduct has done. In order to make his case look plausible, he has reported that he had withdrawn from the Church because we were not worthy of his society; thus, instead of manifesting a spirit of repentance, he has to the last proved himself to be unworthy the confidence or regard of any upright person, by lying to deceive the innocent, and committing adultery in the most abominable and degraded manner.

We are credibly informed that he has colleagued with some of our former wicked persecutors, the Missourians, and has threatened destruction upon us; but we should naturally suppose that he would be so much ashamed of himself at the injury he has already done to those who never injured him, but befriended him in every possible manner, that he could never dare to lift up his head before an enlightened public with the design either to misrepresent or persecute; but be that as it may, we neither dread him nor his influence, but this much we believe, that unless he is determined to fill up the measure of his iniquity, and bring sudden destruction upon himself from the hand of the Almighty, he will be silent, and never more attempt to injure those concerning whom he has testified upon oath he knows nothing but that which is good and virtuous.

Thus I have laid before the Church of Latter-day Saints, and before the public, the character and conduct of a man who has stood high in the estimation of many; but from the foregoing facts, it will be seen that he is not entitled to any credit, but rather to be stamped with indignity and disgrace so far as he may be known. What I have stated, I am prepared to prove, having all the documents concerning the matter in my possession, but I think that to say further is unnecessary, as the subject is so plain that no one can mistake the true nature of the case.

I remain, yours respectfully,

JOSEPH SMITH.

Nauvoo, June 23, 1842.

I have been engaged in domestic affairs and counseling the brethren the last week.

I addressed the following letter to Richmond, Massachusetts:

The Prophet's Letter to Jennetta Richards.

NAUVOO, June 23, 1842.

SISTER JENNETTA RICHARDS:—Agreeable to your request in the midst of the bustle and business of the day, and the care of all the churches both at home and abroad, I now embrace a moment to address a few words to you, thinking peradventure it may be a consolation to you to know that you, too, are remembered by me, as well as all the Saints.

My heart's desire and prayer to God is all the day long for all the Saints, and in an especial and particular manner for those whom He hath chosen and anointed to bear the heaviest burthens in the heat of the day, among which number is your husband received—a man in whom I have the most implicit confidence and trust. You say I have got him; so I have, in the which I rejoice, for he has done me a great good, and taken a great burthen off my shoulders since his arrival in Nauvoo. Never did I have a greater intimacy with any man than with him. May the blessings of Elijah crown his head for ever and ever. We are about to send him in a few days after his dear family; he shall have our prayers fervently for his safe arrival in their embraces; and may God speed his journey, and return him quickly to our society; and I want you, beloved sister, to be a general in this matter, in helping him along, which I know you will. He will be able to teach you many things which you never have heard; you may have implicit confidence in the same.

I have heard much about you by the Twelve, and in consequence of the great friendship that exists between your husband and me, and the information they all have given me of your virtue and strong attachment to the truth of the work of God in the last days, I have formed a very strong brotherly friendship and attachment for you in the bonds of the Gospel. Although I never saw you, I shall be exceedingly glad to see you face to face, and be able to administer in the name of the Lord, some of the words of life to your consolation, and I hope that you may be kept steadfast in the faith, even unto the end.

I want you should give my love and tender regard to Brother Richards' family, and those who are friendly enough to me to inquire after me in that region of the country, not having but very little time to apportion to any one, and having stolen this opportunity, I therefore subscribe myself, in haste, your most obedient brother in the fullness of the Gospel,

JOSEPH SMITH.

P. S.—Brother Richards having been with me for a long time, can give you any information which you need, and will tell you all about me. I shall be very anxious for his return; he is a great prop to me in my labors.

J. S.

The Afghan war has cost great Britain $15,000,000 per annum since its commencement.

Friday, 24.—Called St. John's day. I rode in Masonic procession to the grove where a large assembly of masons and others listened to an address from President Rigdon.

Dined at the Masonic Hall Hotel, kept by Brother Alexander Mills.

Wrote Governor Carlin as follows:

The Prophet's Letter to Governor Carlin on John C. Bennett Affairs.

NAUVOO, June 24, 1842.

Thomas Carlin, Governor of the State of Illinois:

DEAR SIR:—It becomes my duty to lay before you some facts relative to the conduct of our major-general, John C. Bennett, which have been proven beyond the possibility of a dispute, and which he himself has admitted to be true in my presence.

It is evident that his general character is that of an adulterer of the worst kind, and although he has a wife and children living, circumstances which have transpired in Nauvoo, have proven to a demonstration that he cares not whose character is disgraced, whose honor is destroyed, nor who suffers, so that his lustful appetite may be gratified; and further, he cares not how many or how abominable the falsehoods he has to make use of to accomplish his wicked purposes, even should it be that he brings disgrace upon a whole community.

Some time ago it having been reported to me that some of the most aggravated cases of adultery had been committed upon some previously respectable females in our city, I took proper methods to ascertain the truth of the report, and was soon enabled to bring sufficient witnesses before proper authority to establish the following facts:

More than twenty months ago Bennett went to a lady in the city and began to teach her that promiscuous intercourse between the sexes was lawful and no harm in it, and requested the privilege of gratifying his passions; but she refused in the strongest terms, saying that it was very wrong to do so, and it would bring a disgrace on the Church.

Finding this argument ineffectual, he told her that men in higher standing in the Church than himself not only sanctioned, but practiced the same deeds; and in order to finish the controversy, said and affirmed that I both taught and acted in the same manner, but publicly proclaimed against in consequence of the prejudice of the people, and for fear of trouble in my own house. By this means he accomplished his designs; he seduced a respectable female with lying, and subjected her to public infamy and disgrace.

Not contented with what he had already done, he made the attempt on others, and by using the same language, seduced them also.

About the early part of July, 1841, I received a letter from Pittsburg, Pennsylvania; in it was contained information setting forth that said Bennett had a wife and two or three children then living. This I read to him, and he acknowledged it was true.

A very short time after this, he attempted to destroy himself by taking poison; but being discovered before it had taken sufficient effect, and proper antidotes being administered, he recovered.

The impression made upon the minds of the public by this event, was that he was so ashamed of his base conduct, that he took this course to escape the censure of a justly indignant community. It might have been supposed that after this he would have broken off his adulterous proceedings; but to the contrary, the public consternation had scarcely ceased, before he was again deeply involved in the same wicked proceedings and continued until a knowledge of the fact reached my ears. I immediately charged him with the whole circumstance, and he candidly acknowledged the truth of the whole.

The foregoing facts were established on oath before an alderman of the city; the affidavits are now in my possession.

In order that the truth might be fully established, I asked Bennett to testify before an alderman, whether I had given him any cause for such aggravating conduct. He testified that I never taught him that illicit intercourse with females was under any circumstances justifiable, neither did he ever hear me teach anything but the strictest principles of righteousness and virtue. This affidavit is also in my possession. I have also a similar affidavit taken before the City Council, and signed by the members of the Council.

After these things transpired, and finding that I should resist all such wicked conduct, and knowing that he could no longer maintain himself as a respectable citizen, he has seen fit to leave Nauvoo, and that very abruptly.

I have been credibly informed that he is colleaguing with some of our former cruel persecutors, the Missourians, and that he is threatening destruction upon us; and under these circumstance I consider it my duty to give you information on the subject, that a knowledge of his proceedings may be before you in due season.

It can be proven by hundreds of witnesses that he is one of the basest of liars, and that his whole routine of proceedings, while among us, has been of the basest kind.

He also stated that he had resigned his commission as major-general to the Governor, whether this be true or not, I have no knowledge. I wish to be informed on the subject, that we may know how to act in regard to the Legion.

A short time ago, I was told by a friend of mine (not a member of the Church) that some of the Missourians were conspiring to come up to Nauvoo and kidnap me, and not doubting but that it might be true,

I consulted with General Bennett upon the most proper course to be pursued. We concluded to write to you on the subject, and I requested him to do so. I understand he has written to you, but I know not in what manner, and I should be very much pleased if you would write to me on receipt of this, giving me the contents of his communication.

I have also heard that you have entertained of late very unfavorable feelings towards us as a people, and especially so with regard to myself, and that you have said that I ought to be shot, &c. If this be true, I should be pleased to know from yourself the reason of such hostile feelings, for I know of no cause which can possibly exist that might produce such feelings in your breast.

It is rumored, and strong evidence exists, that Dr. Bennett and David and Edward Kilbourn have posted bills in Galena, calling upon the people to hold meetings, and have themselves in readiness at a moment's warning to be assembled and come here and mob us out of the place, and try to kidnap me; we know not as to the truth of this report, but we have conversed with some transient persons who had the report from a gentleman who lately came from there, and had seen those hand bills posted in Galena.

In case of any mob coming upon us, I wish to be informed by the Governor what will be the best course for us to pursue, and how he wishes us to act in regard to this matter.

JOSEPH SMITH.
Lieutenant-General Nauvoo Legion.

There was a severe shock of an earthquake at Antigua.

Saturday, *25*.—Transacted business with Brother Hunter, and Mr. Babbitt, and sat for a drawing of my profile to be placed on a lithograph of the map of the city of Nauvoo.

The Work of Stephens and Catherwood.

Messrs. Stephens and Catherwood have succeeded in collecting in the interior of America a large amount of relics of the Nephites, or the ancient inhabitants of America treated of in the Book of Mormon, which relics have recently been landed in New York.

Sunday, *26*.—President Young preached on the law of consecration, and union of action in building up the city and providing labor and food for the poor.

I attended meeting and council at my house at six

o'clock p. m.; present Hyrum Smith, George Miller, Newel K. Whitney, William Marks, Brigham Young, Heber C. Kimball, and Willard Richards, to take into consideration the situation of the Pine country, and lumbering business, and other subjects of importance to the Church; after consultation thereon the brethren united in solemn prayer that God would make known His will concerning the Pine country, and that He would deliver His anointed, His people, from all the evil designs of Governor Boggs, and the powers of the state of Missouri, and of Governor Carlin and the authorities of Illinois, and of all Presidents, Governors, Judges, Legislators, and all in authority, and of John C. Bennett, and all mobs and evil designing persons, so that His people might continue in peace and build up the city of Nauvoo, and that His chosen might be blessed and live to man's appointed age, and that their households, and the household of faith might continually be blest with the fostering care of heaven, and enjoy the good things of the earth abundantly. Adjourned to Monday evening.

Council meetings at the Prophet's Home.

Monday, 27.—Transacted a variety of business. Borrowed money of Brothers Woolley, Spencer, &c., and paid Hiram Kimball for the mound.

When the council assembled in the evening, Brothers Hunter, Ivins, Woolley, Pierce and others being present, the adjourned council was postponed till Tuesday evening, and I proceeded to lecture at length on the importance of uniting the means of the brethren for the purpose of establishing manufactories of all kinds, furnishing labor for the poor, &c. Brothers Hunter and Woolley offered their goods towards a general fund, and good feelings were generally manifested.

This morning little Frederick G. W. Smith told his dream to all the house, that "the Missourians had got their heads knocked off."

Tuesday, 28.– Paid Brothers Woolley and Spencer.

Brother Hunter's goods were received at the store, and Brother Robins consecrated his goods and money to the general fund.

The adjourned council of Sunday evening met in my upper room, and were agreed that a reinforcement go immediately to the Pine country, led by Brother Ezra Chase. The council dispersed after uniting in solemn prayer to God for a blessing on themselves and families, and the Church in general, and for the building up of the Temple and Nauvoo House and city; for deliverance from their enemies, and the spread of the work of righteousness: and that Brother Richards (who was expected to go East tomorrow for his family) might have a prosperous journey, have power over the winds and elements, and all opposition and dangers, his life and health be preserved, and be speedily returned to this place with his family, that their lives and health might be preserved, and that they might come up in peace to this place, and that Brother Richards might be prospered according to the desire of his heart, in all things in relation to his household, and the Church, and that the Spirit of God might rest upon him continually, so that he may act according to the wisdom of heaven.

Previous to the council, in company with Bishop Miller, I visited Elder Rigdon and his family, and had much conversation about John C. Bennett, and others, much unpleasant feeling was manifested by Elder Rigdon's family, who were confounded and put to silence by the truth.

George Miller's Letter to Governor Reynolds of Missouri.

To his Excellency Governor Reynolds, of Missouri.

DEAR SIR:—You will permit me to ask you to peruse this letter and the accompanying newspaper, relative to the character and conduct of John Cook Bennett, who associated himself with our religious community nearly two years ago, he being a man of respectable talents and moderately good literary attainments.

In the judicial organization of our city under the charter granted by the legislature of Illinois, said Bennett was elected mayor; and continued to hold said office of mayor until within the last two months or less. He having learned that he could no longer maintain a standing as an honorable man in our society, he tendered his resignation, which was accepted.

The object of this communication is, therefore, to inform you of the true character of said John C. Bennett, that he may not injure the innocent by gaining credence with you, or those over whom your Excellency is placed to govern.

We have learned from respectable sources that John Cook Bennett has entered into a conspiracy with some of the citizens of your state, to bring a mob upon us, and thereby disturb our peaceful vocations of life, and destroy and drive us from our homes and firesides.

Believing that your Excellency cannot be influenced by the popular prejudice, almost everywhere entertained against us, on account of our peculiar tenets, I am the more free to write to you without reserve, knowing that the high-toned and honorable men of the earth will not be easily carried away by popular opinion or vulgar prejudice; but will always be found on the side of the law-abiding portion of the community, and will suppress, so far as in them lies, every movement that tends to abridge the rights, or mar the peace and happiness of any portion of the citizens of the common country.

I have resided in this city nearly three years, and have attached myself to the Church of Jesus Christ of Latter-day Saints, soon after their location here; and have had a good opportunity of learning the feelings of the leading members of the said Church in regard to the citizens of Missouri which are of the most friendly nature, ever desiring to live in peace and cultivate friendship with all the citizens of your state, as also all the states, and all mankind generally; it being a principle of our faith to cultivate friendship and live in peace with all mankind; and if Dr. John Cook Bennett, or any other person, may conspire with citizens of your state to bring upon us mob violence, we confide in you as one who will under all circumstances, interpose the strong arm of the law in the suppression of conspiracy or mobs, or any other violation of law. As citizens of the United States we claim the protection of the several states and the United States in all our constitutional rights; and having learned something of your character, we, the more confidently, expect your protection against all lawless aggressions by any of the citizens of your state.

Whatever may be reported concerning us, we assure your Excellency that our feelings are, as I have before stated, of the most friendly nature, and should Bennett or any other person report anything contrary, your Excellency need pay no attention to it; for it is not the truth, and is only designed by wicked men to cause the overthrow of the innocent.

Should any report have already reached your ears, I would esteem it as a great favor, if you would give me information of the same by letter mmediately on receipt of this.

I am, yours respectfully,

GEORGE MILLER.

CHAPTER III.

CORRESPONDENCE BETWEEN THE PROPHET AND GOVERNOR THOMAS CARLIN—ANENT JOHN C. BENNETT'S CHARACTER —PHRENOLOGICAL CHARTS OF THE PROPHET ET AL.—THE GOVERNMENT OF GOD.

Wednesday, 29.—I held a long conversation with Francis M. Higbee. Francis found fault with being exposed, but I told him I spoke of him in self defense. Francis was, or appeared, humble, and promised to reform.

Heard the recorder read in the Law of the Lord; paid taxes; rode out in the city on business, with Brigham Young.

My clerk, Willard Richards, being about to leave me for a season, committed the business of my office to Elder William Clayton, who had been engaged with him for a few weeks past.

Thursday, 30.—In the forenoon, spent some time with C. A. Warren, Esq., from Quincy, and others, in the private office, and in the afternoon was in the court martial, giving testimony concerning John C. Bennett, who was cashiered.

Letter of Governor Thomas Carlin to Joseph Smith—Anent John C. Bennett.

QUINCY, June 30, 1842.

DEAR SIR:—I received by the last mail, your letter of the 24th instant, in which you have thought proper to give me a statement of charges against the conduct and character of General John C. Bennett; I can say that I regret that any individual should so far disregard his obligations to his God, and to his fellow man, as to condescend to the commission of the crimes alleged in your letter to have been perpetrated by General Bennett. It is, however, in accordance with representations of his character, made to me more than two years since, and which I then felt constrained to believe were true, since which time I have desired to have as little intercourse with him as possible. No resignation of his commission as major-general of the Nauvoo Legion has reached me.

Some weeks since I read a short note from him, stating that you had reason to believe that a conspiracy is getting up in the state of Missouri, for the purpose of mobbing the Mormons at Nauvoo, and kidnapping you, and take you to that state, and requested to be informed in case of such mob, whether you would be protected by the authorities of this state, etc. To which I replied; that as all men were held amenable to the laws, so in like manner the rights of all would be protected, and the dignity of the state maintained, to the letter of the constitution and laws. The above is, in substance, the contents of his note to me, and my reply to him, having destroyed his letter, as I considered it of no use, should it be retained.

You state that you have heard that I have of late entertained unfavorable feelings towards you (the Mormons) as a people, and especially so with regards to yourself, &c., &c. If this should be true, you would be pleased to know from me the reasons of such hostile feelings.

In reply, I can in truth say that I do not entertain or cherish hostile or revengeful feelings towards any man or set of men on earth; but that I may have used strong expressions in reference to yourself, at times when my indignation has been somewhat aroused by repeated admonitions of my friends (both before and since the attempt to assassinate Ex-Governor Boggs) to be upon my guard; that you had prophesied that Boggs should die a violent death, and that I should die in a ditch, all this, however, if true, I looked upon as idle boasting until since the assassination of Boggs, and even since then, in reference to myself, I cannot view it in any other light, because whatever your feelings may have been towards Boggs, the mere discharge of an official duty on my part, enjoined upon me by the constitution and laws of this state, and of the United States, could not possibly engender feelings of such deep malignity. Be assured that this matter gives me no uneasiness, nor would the subject now have been mentioned, had you not requested a reply to your inquiries.

I have seen your denial published in the *Wasp*, of the prediction, attributed to you, of the death (or assassination) of Governor Boggs; be that true or false, nothing has contributed more towards fixing the belief upon the public mind, that you had made such prediction, than the repeated statements of a portion of your followers, that the manner of his death had been revealed to you, and their exultation that it needs must be fulfilled.

In reference to your request, to be advised how you should act, in case a mob should come upon you, I should feel very much at a loss to recommend any course for you to adopt, other than the resort to the first law of nature, namely, to defend your own rights; because, were I to advise a quiet submission on your part, I could not expect that you would fold your arms, and silently look on, whilst those rights were violated and outraged, as long as you have the power to protect them. I, however, have not the most distant thought that there exists, at present, any real cause for the apprehension of a mob coming upon you, otherwise I should feel it my duty to endeavor to arrest it.

Very respectfully, your obedient servant,

THOMAS CARLIN.

To General Joseph Smith.

I received a letter from Horace R. Hotchkiss, of which the following is a copy:—

Letter of Horace R. Hotchkiss to Joseph Smith—On the Prophet taking Advantage of the Bankrupt Act.

FAIR HAVEN, May 27, 1842.

Rev. Joseph Smith:

DEAR SIR:—Yours, notifying me of your application for the benefit of the bankrupt act, is at hand. I regret very much the step you have taken, as I am fearful it will have a most disastrous influence upon your society, both commercially and religiously; you have, however, probably weighed the subject with sufficient care to arrive at a correct decision.

You will oblige me by stating, immediately upon the receipt of this letter, your precise meaning, in saying, that "all your creditors would fare alike." It is, as you will see, important for me to know the course taken with my notes, and also the position in which we stand to each other.

You have my bond for certain lands, or rather you have my bond that you shall have a deed to certain lands upon the payment of notes specified in said bond. I wish to know exactly how this bond stands in your inventory. Of course, it cannot stand as a title to the property; but I want to know the disposition which is to be made of it.

Possibly some arrangement might be made between us at once; still I do not know how Mr. Tuttle and Mr. Gillet will view the subject.

Yours, &c.,

HORACE R. HOTCHKISS.

To which I wrote the following answer:—

Letter of Joseph Smith to H. R. Hotchkiss—Reply to Above.

NAUVOO, June 30, 1842.

H. R. Hotchkiss, Esq.:

DEAR SIR:—Yours of the 27th May has been received, which I shall now briefly answer. In regard to my application for the benefit of the bankrupt act, there was no other course for me to pursue than the one I have already taken; and, as I have said before, all my creditors will have to fare alike. Your papers are inventoried along with all the other property.

The influence this step may have upon our society, either commercially or religiously, is a matter we cannot stop to consult, as we had no alternative left. We have been compelled to pursue this course on account of the extreme pressure of the times, which continued to bear harder upon us, until we took the step we have.

A great pressure of business prevents writing more at the present, you will, therefore, excuse a short communication.

I remain yours respectfully,

JOSEPH SMITH.

Friday, July 1.—Elder Willard Richards left Nauvoo for New England.

Saturday, 2.—Rode out in the city with my clerk, Mr. Clayton, to look at some lots; afterwards rode to Hezekiah Peck's, accompanied by Emma and others.

In this day's *Wasp*, I find the following:—

Mr. Editor:

SIR:—I take the liberty to inform you that a large number of persons in different places have manifested a desire to know the phrenological development of Joseph Smith's head. I have examined the Prophet's head, and he is perfectly willing to have the chart published. You will please publish in your paper such portions of it as I have marked, showing the development of his much-talked-of brain, and let the public judge for themselves whether phrenology proves the reports against him true or false. Time will prove all things, and a "word to the wise is sufficient."

Yours respectfully,

A. CRANE.

A Phrenological Chart of Joseph Smith the Prophet by A. Crane, M. D., Professor of Phrenology.

Propensities.

Amativeness—11, L. Extreme susceptibility; passionately fond of the company of the other sex.

Philoprogenitiveness—9, L. Strong parental affection, great solicitude for their happiness.

Inhabitiveness—5, F. Attached to place of long residence; no desire to change residence.

Adhesiveness—8, F. Solicitous for the happiness of friends, and ardent attachments for the other sex.

Combativeness—8, L. Indomitable perseverance, great courage; force, ability to overpower.

Destructiveness—6, M. Ability to control the passions, and is not disposed to extreme measures.

Secretiveness—10, L. Great propensity and ability to conceal feelings, plans, &c.

Acquisitiveness—9, L. Strong love of riches, desire to make and save money.

Alimentativeness—9, L. Strong relish for food; keen and severe appetite.

Vitativeness—4, M. or S. Indifference to life; views the approach of death without fear.

Feelings.

Cautiousness—7, F. Provision against prospective dangers and ills, without hesitation or irresolution.

Approbativeness—10, L. Ambition for distinction; sense of character; sensibility to reproach, fear of scandal.

Self-esteem—10, L. High-mindedness, independence, self-confidence, dignity, aspiration for greatness.

Concentrativeness—7, F. Can dwell on a subject without fatigue, and control the imagination.

Sentiments.

Benevolence—10, L. Kindness, goodness, tenderness, sympathy.

Veneration—6, F. Religion, without great awe or enthusiasm; reasonable deference to superiority.

Firmness—10, L. Stability and decison of charcter and purpose.

Conscientiousness—8, L. High regard for duty, integrity, moral principle, justice, obligation, truth, &c.

Hope—10, L. Cheerfulness, sanguine expectation of success and enjoyment.

Marvelousness—10 L. Wonder, credulity, belief in the supernatural.

Imitation—5, M. Inferior imitative powers; failure to copy, describe, relate stories, &c.

Prepossession—8, L. or F. Attached to certain notions; not disposed to change them, &c.

Ideality—9, L. Lively imagination; fancy, taste, love of poetry, elegance, eloquence, excellence, &c.

Perceptives.

Admonition—8, F. or M. Desirous to know what others are doing; ready to counsel, and give hints of a fault or duty, &c.

Constructiveness—7, F. Respectable ingenuity, without uncommon skill, tact or facility in making, &c.

Tune—5, F. or M. Love of music, without quickness to catch or learn tunes by the ear.

Time—11, V. L. Distinct impressions as to the time when, how long, &c.

Locality—11, V. L. or L. Great memory of place and position.

Eventuality—11, V. L. Extraordinary recollection of minute circumstances.

Individuality—10, L. Great desire to see; power of observation.

Form—10, F. Cognizance, and distinct recollection of shapes, countenances, &c.

Size—11, N. L. or F. Ability to judge of proportionate size, &c.

Weight—9, V. L., L. F. Knowledge of gravitation, momentum, &c.

Color—9, F. or M. Moderate skill in judging of colors, comparing and arranging them.

Language—6, F. Freedom of expression, without fluency or verbosity; no great loquacity.

Order—9, L. Love of arrangement, everything in its particular place.

Number—7. Respectable aptness in arithmetical calculations, without extraordinary talent.

Reflectives.

Mirthfulness—10, L. Wit, fun, mirth, perception and love of the ludicrous.

Causality—9, L. Ability to think and reason clearly, and perceive the relation of cause and effect.

Comparison—11, V. L. Extraordinary critical acumen; great power of analysis.

There are four temperaments. The lymphatic or phlegmatic, in which the secreting glands are the most active portion of the system, produces both corporeal and mental langour, dullness, and inactivity. The sanguine in which the arterial portion of the system is most active, gives strong feelings and passions, and more ardor, zeal, and activity, than of strength or power. The bilious, in which the muscular portion predominates in activity, produces strength, power, and edurance of body, with great force and energy of mind and character. The nervous, in which the brain and nervous system are most active, gives the highest degree of activity, with clearness of perception and of thought, but less endurance. Sharp and prominent organs denote activity; smooth and broad ones intensity and strength.

Explanation of the Chart.

The written figures opposite the organs and ranging in a scale from 1 to 12, indicate the various degrees in which the respective organs are developed in the head of the individual examined; thus 1, 2 indicate that the organ is very small or almost wholly wanting; 3, 4 means small, or feeble, and inactive; 5, 6 moderate or active only in a subordinate degree; 7, 8, full or fair, and a little above par; 9, 10, large, or quite energetic, and having a marked influence upon the character; 11, 12, mean very large, or giving a controlling influence, and extreme liability to perversion. The size of the brain, combinations of the faculties and temperament of the individual, may be indicated in the same manner as the degrees of the faculties or organs.

The initials V. L. denote very large, L. large, F. full, M. moderate, S. small, V. S. very small.

I give the foregoing a place in my history for the gratification of the curious, and not for [any] respect [I entertain for] phrenology.

The following communication was sent to the *Wasp:*

TO THE CITIZENS OF HANCOCK COUNTY.

As a people, the Church of Jesus Christ of Latter-day Saints are found "more sinned against than sinning." In political affairs we are ever ready to yield to our fellow citizens of the county equal participation in the selection of candidates for office.

We have been disappointed in our hopes of being met with the same disposition on the part of some of the old citizens of the county—they indeed seem to manifest a spirit of intolerance and exclusion incompatible with the liberal doctrines of true republicanism.

At the late anti-Mormon convention, a complete set of candidates, pledged to a man to receive no support from, and to yield no quarters to, "Mormons," are commended to all the citizens of this county for their suffrages!

As a portion of the said citizens of Hancock, we embrace the opportunity to decline this ticket for the want of reciprocity in its terms, and honesty and intelligence in the character of some of its candidates.

If the old citizens of the county are still desirous of equal participations with us in the choice of candidates, we are ready to co-operate with them. If independent gentlemen possessing the requisite qualities, capacity and integrity, will announce themselves, they will receive the united support of our people in the county.

The time for holding a convention seems to have already gone by—there is time enough for the friends of justice and fair play to elect a ticket to be announced in the independent manner we have suggested· Let the gentlemen who have the courage to oppose the spirit of dictation, which governed the anti-Mormon convention candidates show themselves, and we will exercise enough, on the terms proposed in this article, to ensure complete success. JOSEPH SMITH.

Sunday, 3.—This morning I preached at the grove to about 8,000 people. The subject matter of my discourse was from the Prophet Daniel's saying, that in the last days the God of heaven would set up a kingdom, &c.

In the afternoon I heard Brother Hyrum preach at the grove.

The steamer *Edna* collapsed her flues at the mouth of the Missouri river; more than sixty persons were badly scalded. A proof among many similar that the waters of the West are cursed, as saith the Lord in a revelation.*

Monday, 4.—The Legion appeared on parade under command of Brigadier-General Wilson Law, ranking officer of the line. Lieutenant-General Smith reviewed the Legion at 11 a. m., and continued in command through the day, which was somewhat unpleasant, yet an immense number of spectators were present, including the passengers of three steamers from the neighboring cities and villages.

Parade of the Legion.

* See Doctrine and Covenants sec. lxi: 14-29. Also see an article in the *Improvement Era*, September number, 1903, "The Fulfillment of Prophecy, the Testimony of the Floods."

At the close of the day General Smith expressed his entire satisfaction in an animated speech, in which he illustrated the design of the organization of the Legion, viz., to yield obedience to the institutions of our country, and protect the Saints from mobs, after which leave was given for strangers to address the Legion, when General Swanzey, of Iowa, expressed his friendly feelings towards Nauvoo, and his gratification at the good discipline of the Legion.

Mrs. Emma Smith and the ladies of other distinguished officers accompanied their companions on the parade. A few Lamanites were present, and there was but little drinking. Two individuals were fined $10.25 for offering whisky for sale.

Tuesday, 5.—Attended court-martial and city council; an ordinance in relation to public shows and exhibitions was passed.

The following was also passed:—

An Ordinance in Relation to Writs of Habeas Corpus.

Sec. 1. Be it, and it is hereby ordained by the city council of the city of Nauvoo, that no citizen of this city shall be taken out of the city by any writs without the privilege of investigation before the municipal court, and the benefit of a writ of habeas corpus, as granted in the 17th section of the Charter of this city. Be it understood that this ordinance is enacted for the protection of the citizens of this city, that they may in all cases have the right of trial in this city, and not be subjected to illegal process by their enemies.

JOSEPH SMITH, Mayor.

Passed July 5, 1842.

JAMES SLOAN, Recorder.

Wednesday, 6.—Transacted business in the city, and rode to La Harpe with Emma.

Expedition to the Pineries.

Two keel boats, sloop-rigged, and laden with provisions and apparatus necessary for the occasion, and manned with fifty of the brethren, started this morning on an expedition to the upper Mississippi, among the pineries, where they can join those already there, and erect mills, saw boards and plank, make shingles, hew timber, and return next spring with rafts, for the Temple of God, Nauvoo House, &c., to beautify the city of Nauvoo, according to the Prophets.

Thursday, 7.—Weather very cool at Nauvoo, thermometer at six degrees.

Saturday, 9.—I rode on the prairie with Brothers Clayton and Gheen to look at some land. Dined on my farm; hoed potatoes, &c., and in the afternoon returned to the city and transacted a variety of business.

I find the following phrenological chart of my clerk, Elder Willard Richards, of the quorum of the Twelve, by A. Crane, M. D.:—

Phrenological Chart of Willard Richards.

Propensities.

Amitiveness—8, F. Very partial to the opposite sex; generally reciprocated by them.

Philoprogenitiveness—7, F. Interested in the happiness of children; fond of their company.

Inhabitiveness—7, F. Attached to place of long residence; no desire to change residence.

Adhesiveness—11, V. L. Passionately and devotedly attached to lovers and friends.

Combativeness—7, F. Great powers of exertion and sustaining under opposition and difficulties.

Destructiveness—6, M. Ability to control the passions, and is not disposed to extreme measures.

Secretiveness—10, L. Great propensity and ability to conceal feelings, plans, &c.

Acquisitiveness—8, F. Frugality and industry, without much of the miserly, penurious, or stingy feeling.

Alimentativeness—8, F. A good appetite, but not excessive, partiality for a variety of rich hearty dishes.

Vitativeness—7, L. Strong desire to exist; contemplates death as the greatest misfortune.

Feelings.

Cautiousness—Discretion, carefulness, anxiety, apprehension, &c.

Approbativeness—10, L. Ambition for distinction; sense of character, sensibility to reproach, fear of scandal.

Self-esteem—10, L. High-mindedness, independence, self-confidence, dignity; aspiration for greatness.

Concentrativeness—7, F. Can dwell on a subject without fatigue, and control the imagination.

Sentiments.

Benevolence—9, L. Kindness, goodness, tenderness, sympathy.

Veneration, 7, F. Religion without great awe or enthusiasm; reasonable deference to superiority.

Firmness—9, L. Stability and decision of character and purpose.

Conscientiousness—8, L. High regard for duty, integrity, moral principle, justice, obligation, truth, &c.

Hope—7, F. Reasonable hopes, a fine flow of spirits; anticipation of what is to be realized.

Marvelousness—6, F. Openness to conviction without blind credulity; tolerably good degree of faith.

Imitation—10, F. A disposition and respectable ability to imitate, but not to mimic or to act out.

Prepossession—8, L. or F. Attached to certain notions; not disposed to change them, &c.

Ideality—10, L. Lively imagination; fancy, taste, love of poetry; elegance, eloquence, excellence, &c.

Perceptives.

Admonition—9, F, or M. Desirous to know what others are doing; ready to counsel and give hints of a fault or duty, &c.

Constructiveness—8, L. Great mechanical ingenuity, talent and skill.

Tune—8, F. or M. Love of music, without quickness to catch or learn tunes by the ear.

Time—8, F. or M. Indistinct notions of the lapse of time, of ages dates and events, &c.

Locality—11, V. L. or L. Great memory of places and position.

Eventuality—9, L. Retentive memory of events and particulars.

Individuality—10, L. Great desire to see; power of observation.

Form—8, F. Cognizance and distinct recollection of shapes, countenances, &c.

Size—11, V. L., L. or F. Ability to judge of proportionate size, &c.

Weight—6, M. S. or V. S. Deficient balancing power; failure in equilibrium.

Color—11, V. L. or L. Great power of recollecting and comparing colors.

Language—7, F. Freedom of expression, without fluency or verbosity; no great loquacity.

Order—10, L. Love of arrangement; everything in its particular place.

Number—9, L. Quickness, facility, and correctness in calculating figures.

Reflectives.

Mirthfulness—10, L. Wit, fun, mirth; perception and love of the ludicrous.

Causality—11, L. Ability to think and reason clearly, and perceive the relations of cause and effect.

Comparison—10, L. A discrimination; power of illustration, ability to perceive and apply analogies, &c.—[See explanation of numbers, etc. to my chart].

Sunday, 10.—Attended meeting at the stand. Elder Woodruff preached. My health was not good. At home in the afternoon.

Monday, 11.—In the morning, transacting business with Mr. Hunter. In the afternoon, at the printing office reading the papers, and bought a horse of Harmon T. Wilson, which I named Joe Duncan.

Tuesday, 12.—At the court room in consultation about Bennett.

Bishop Miller and Erastus Derby started for Quincy and Missouri.

Attended city council. An ordinance was passed regulating auctions; also provision was made for publishing the Legion laws, &c., &c.

Mobs, riots, earthquakes, tumults and distress of nations, are common. In England the manufacturers are reducing the wages of the laborers, and turn-outs and starvation follow.

The Asiatic cholera has appeared again in India.

Friday, 15.—It was reported early in the morning that Elder Orson Pratt was missing. I caused the Temple hands and the principal men of the city to make search for him. After which, a meeting was called at the Grove, and I gave the public a general outline of John C. Bennett's conduct.

The people met again in the afternoon, and were addressed on the same subject by Brother Hyrum and Elder Kimball. I then stated that I had heard that Edward and D. Kilbourn were engaged with John C. Bennet to bring a mob on the city, from Galena, and asked Edward Kilbourn, who was present, if it was so? To which Mr. Kilbourn replied at some length, and denied the charge.

Elder Pratt returned in the evening.

I find an editorial, in the *Times and Seasons*, on the government of God as follows:—

The Government of God.

The government of the Almighty has always been very dissimilar to the governments of men, whether we refer to His religious government, or to the government of nations. The government of God has always tended to promote peace, unity, harmony, strength, and happiness; while that of man has been productive of confusion, disorder, weakness, and misery.

The geatest acts of the mighty men have been to depopulate nations and to overthrow kingdoms; and whilst they have exalted themselves and become glorious, it has been at the expense of the lives of the innocent, the blood of the oppressed, the moans of the widow, and the tears of the orphan.

Egypt, Babylon, Greece, Persia, Carthage, Rome—each was raised to dignity amidst the clash of arms and the din of war; and whilst their triumphant leaders led forth their victorious armies to glory and victory, their ears were saluted with the groans of the dying and the misery and distress of the human family; before them the earth was a paradise, and behind them a desolate wilderness; their kingdoms were founded in carnage and bloodshed, and sustained by oppression, tyranny, and despotism. The designs of God, on the other hand, have been to promote the universal good of the universal world; to establish peace and good will among men; to promote the principles of eternal truth; to bring about a state of things that shall unite man to his fellow man; cause the world to "beat their swords into plowshares, and their spears into pruning hooks," make the nations of the earth dwell in peace, and to bring about the millennial glory, when "the earth shall yield its increase, resume its paradisean glory, and become as the garden of the Lord."

The great and wise of ancient days have failed in all their attempts to promote eternal power, peace and happiness. Their nations have crumbled to pieces; their thrones have been cast down in their turn, and their cities, and their mightiest works of art have been annihilated; or their dilapidated towers, of time-worn monuments have left us but feeble traces of their former magnificence and ancient grandeur. They proclaim as with a voice of thunder, those imperishable truths—that man's strength is weakness, his wisdom is folly, his glory is his shame.

Monarchial, aristocratical, and republican governments of their various kinds and grades, have, in their turn, been raised to dignity, and prostrated in the dust. The plans of the greatest politicians, the wisest senators, and most profound statesmen have been exploded; and the proceedings of the greatest chieftains, the bravest generals, and the wisest kings have fallen to the ground. Nation has succeeded nation, and we have inherited nothing but their folly. History records their puerile plans, their short-lived glory, their feeble intellect and their ignoble deeds.

Have we increased in knowledge or intelligence? Where is there a man that can step forth and alter the destiny of nations and promote the happiness of the world? Or where is there a kingdom or nation that can promote the universal happiness of its own subjects, or even their general well being? Our nation, which possesses greater resources than any other, is rent, from center to circumference, with party strife, political intrigues, and sectional interest; our counselors are panic stricken, our legislators are astonished, and our senators are confounded, our merchants are paralyzed, our tradesmen are disheartened, our mechanics out of employ, our farmers distressed, and our poor crying for bread, our banks are broken, our credit ruined, and our states overwhelmed in debt, yet we are, and have been in peace.

What is the matter? Are we alone in this thing? Verily no. With all our evils we are better situated than any other nation. Let Egypt, Turkey, Spain, France, Italy, Portugal, Germany, England, China, or any other nation, speak, and tell the tale of their trouble, their perplexity, and distress, and we should find that their cup was full, and that they were preparing to drink the dregs of sorrow. England, that boasts of her literature, her science, commerce, &c., has her hands reeking with the blood of the innocent abroad, and she is saluted with the cries of the oppressed at home. Chartism, O'Connelism, and radicalism are gnawing her vitals at home; and Ireland, Scotland, Canada, and the east are threatening her destruction abroad. France is rent to the core, intrigue, treachery, and treason lurk in the dark, and murder, and assassination stalk forth at noonday. Turkey, once the dread of European nations, has been shorn of her strength, has dwindled into her dotage, and has been obliged to ask her allies to propose to her tributary terms of peace; and Russia and Egypt are each of them opening their jaws to devour her. Spain has been the theater of bloodshed, of misery and woe for years past. Syria is now convulsed with war and bloodshed. The great and powerful empire of China, which has, for centuries resisted the attacks of barbarians, has become tributary to a foreign foe, her batteries thrown down, many of her cities destroyed, and her villages deserted. We might mention the Eastern Rajahs, the miseries and oppressions of the Irish; the convulsed state of Central America; the situation of Texas and Mexico; the state of Greece, Switzerland and Poland; nay, the world itself presents one great theater of misery, woe, and "distress of nations with perplexity." All, all, speak with a voice of thunder, that man is not able to govern himself, to legislate for himself, to protect himself, to promote his own good, nor the good of the world.

It has been the design of Jehovah, from the commencement of the world, and is His purpose now, to regulate the affairs of the world in His own time, to stand as a head of the universe, and take the reins of government in His own hand. When that is done, judgment will be administered in righteousness; anarchy and confusion will be destroyed, and "nations will learn war no more." It is for want of this great governing principle, that all this confusion has existed; "for it is not in man that walketh, to direct his steps;" this we have fully shown.

If there was anything great or good in the world, it came from God. The construction of the first vessel was given to Noah, by revelation. The design of the ark was given by God, "a pattern of heavenly things." The learning of the Egyptians, and their knowledge of astronomy was no doubt taught them by Abraham and Joseph, as their records testify, who received it from the Lord. The art of working in brass, silver, gold, and precious stones, was taught by revelation, in the wilderness. The architectural designs of the Temple at Jerusalem, together with its ornaments and beauty, were given of God. Wisdom to govern the house of Israel was given to Solomon, and to the judges of Israel; and if he had always been their king, and they subject to his mandate, and obedient to his laws, they would still have been a great and mighty people—the rulers of the universe, and the wonder of the world.

If Nebuchadnezzar, or Darius, or Cyrus, or any other king possessed knowledge or power, it was from the same source, as the Scriptures abundantly testify. If, then, God puts up one, and sets down another at His pleasure, and made instruments of kings, unknown to themselves, to fulfill His prophecies, how much more was He able, if man would have been subject to His mandate to regulate the affairs of this world, and promote peace and happiness among the human family!

The Lord has at various times commenced this kind of government, and tendered His services to the human family. He selected Enoch, whom He directed, and gave His law unto, and to the people who were with him; and when the world in general would not obey the commands of God, after walking with God, he translated Enoch and his church, and the Priesthood or government of heaven was taken away.

Abraham was guided in all his family affairs by the Lord; was conversed with by angels, and by the Lord; was told where to go, and when to stop; and prospered exceedingly in all that he put his hand unto; it was because he and his family obeyed the counsel of the Lord.

When Egypt was under the superintendence of Joseph it prospered, because he was taught of God; when they oppressed the Israelites, destruction came upon them. When the children of Israel were chosen with Moses at their head, they were to be a peculiar people, among whom God should place His name; their motto was: "The Lord is our lawgiver; the Lord is our Judge; the Lord is our King, and He shall reign over us." While in this state they might truly say, "Happy is that people, whose God is the Lord." Their government was a theocracy; they had God to make their laws, and men chosen by Him to administer them; He was their God, and they were His people. Moses received the word of the Lord from God Himself; he was the mouth of God to Aaron, and Aaron taught the people, in both civil and ecclesiastical affairs; they were both one, there was no distinction; so will it be when the purposes of God shall be accomplished: when "the Lord shall be King over the whole earth," and "Jerusalem His throne." "The law shall go forth from Zion, and the word of the Lord from Jerusalem."

This is the only thing that can bring about the "restitution of all things spoken of by all the holy Prophets since the world was"—"the dispensation of the fullness of times, when God shall gather together all things in one." Other attempts to promote universal peace and happiness in the human family have proved abortive; every effort has failed; every plan and design has fallen to the ground; it needs the wisdom of God, the intelligence of God, and the power of God to accomplish this. The world has had a fair trial for six thousand years; the Lord will try the seventh thousand Himself; "He whose right it is, will possess the kingdom, and reign until He has put all things under His feet;" iniquity will hide its hoary head, Satan will be bound, and the works of darkness destroyed; righteousness will be put to the line, and judgment to the plummet, and "he that fears the Lord will alone be exalted in that day." To bring about this state of things, there must of necessity be great confusion among the nations of the earth; "distress of nations with perplexity." Am I asked what is the cause of the present distress? I would answer, "Shall there be evil in a city and the Lord hath not done it?"

The earth is groaning under corruption, oppression, tyranny and bloodshed; and God is coming out of His hiding place, as He said He would do, to vex the nations of the earth. Daniel, in his vision, saw convulsion upon convulsion; he "beheld till the thrones were cast down, and the Ancient of Days did sit;" and one was brought before him like unto the Son of Man; and all nations, kindred, tongues, and people, did serve and obey Him. It is for us to be righteous, that we may be wise and understand; for none of the wicked shall understand; but the wise shall understand, and they that turn many to righteousness shall shine as the stars for ever and ever.

As a Church and a people it behooves us to be wise, and to seek to know the will of God, and then be willing to do it; for "blessed is he that heareth the word of the Lord, and keepeth it," say the Scriptures. "Watch and pray always," says our Savior, "that ye may be accounted worthy to escape the things that are to come on the earth, and to stand before the Son of Man." If Enoch, Abraham, Moses, and the children of Israel, and all God's people were saved by keeping the commandments of God, we, if saved at all, shall be saved upon the same principle. As God governed Abraham, Isaac and Jacob as families, and the children of Israel as a nation; so we, as a Church, must be under His guidance if we are prospered, preserved and sustained. Our only confidence can be in God; our only wisdom obtained from Him: and He alone must be our protector and safeguard, spiritually and temporally, or we fall.

We have been chastened by the hand of God heretofore for not obeying His commands, although we never violated any human law, or transgressed any human precept; yet we have treated lightly His commands, and departed from His ordinances, and the Lord has chastened us sore, and we have felt His arm and kissed the rod; let us be wise in time to come and ever remember that "to obey is better than sacrifice, and to hearken than the fat of rams." The Lord has told us to build the Temple and the Nauvoo House; and that command is as binding upon us as any other; and that man who engages not in these things is as much a transgressor as though he broke any other commandment; he is not a doer of God's will, not a fulfiller of His laws.

In regard to the building up of Zion, it has to be done by the counsel of Jehovah, by the revelations of heaven; and we should feel to say, "if the Lord go not with us, carry us not up hence." We would say to the Saints that come here, we have laid the foundation for the gathering of God's people to this place, and they expect that when the Saints do come, they will be under the counsel that God has appointed. The Twelve are set apart to counsel the Saints pertaining to this matter; and we expect that those who come here will send before them their wise men according to revelation; or if not practicable, be subject to the counsel that God has given, or they cannot receive an inheritance among the Saints, or be considered as God's people, and they will be dealt with as transgressors of the laws of God. We are trying here to gird up our loins, and purge from our midst the workers of iniquity; and we hope that when our brethren arrive from abroad, they will assist us to roll forth this good work, and to accomplish this great design, that "Zion may be built up in righteousness; and all nations flock to her standard;" that as God's people, under His direction, and obedient to His law, we may grow up in righteousness and truth; that when His purposes shall be accomplished, we may receive an inheritance among those that are sanctified.

Saturday, 16.—Rode on the prairie with my clerk, to show some land to Brother Russell from New York; dined with my farmer, Brother Cornelius P. Lott, and hoed potatoes.

CHAPTER IV.

THE PROPHET CHARGED WITH BEING ACCESSORY TO THE ASSAULT ON EX-GOVERNOR BOGGS OF MISSOURI—CORRESPONDENCE WITH GOVERNOR CARLIN—THE CHARACTER OF JOHN C. BENNETT—PROPHECY THAT THE SAINTS WOULD BE DRIVEN TO THE ROCKY MOUNTAINS.

Sunday Morning, July 17, 1842.—Attended meeting at the Grove; was sick and tarried at home the remainder of the day.

Monday, 18.—Rode out to Brother Kearns and the farm.

Tuesday 19.—Rode with Dr. Foster, Henry Kearns and others to examine some timber lands, &c.

Wednesday, 20.—

Affidavit of Lilburn W. Boggs, Ex-Governor of Missouri.

State of Missouri, county of Jackson: This day personally appeared before me, Samuel Weston, a justice of the peace, within and for the county of Jackson, the subscriber, Lilburn W. Boggs, who being duly sworn doth depose and say that on the night of the 6th day of May, while sitting in his dwelling, in the town of Independence, in the county of Jackson, he was shot with intent to kill, and that his life was despaired of for several days, and that he believes and has good reason to believe from evidence and information now in his possession, that O. P. Rockwell, a citizen or resident of the state of Illinois, is the person who shot him on the night aforesaid, and the said deponent hereby applies to the Governor of the State of Illinois, to deliver the said O. P. Rockwell to some person authorized to receive him and convey him to the county aforesaid, there to be dealt with according to law.

LILBURN W. BOGGS.

Sworn to and subscribed before me, this 20th day of July, 1842.

SAMUEL WESTON, J. P.

Affidavit of the City Council anent John C. Bennett.

We, the undersigned, members of the city council, of the city of

Nauvoo, testify that John C. Bennett was not under duress at the time he testified before the city council, May 19, 1842, concerning Joseph Smith's innocence, virtue and pure teaching. His statements that he has lately made concerning this matter are false; there was no excitement at the time, nor was he in anywise threatened, menaced or intimidated. His appearance at the city council was voluntary; he asked the privilege of speaking, which was granted. After speaking for some time on the city affairs, Joseph Smith asked him if he knew anything bad concerning his public or private character. He then delivered those statements contained in the testimony voluntarily, and of his own free will, and went of his own accord, as free as any member of the council. We further testify that there is no such thing as a Danite Society in the city, nor any combination, other than the Masonic Lodge of which we have any knowledge.

WILSON LAW,	GEO. A. SMITH,
JOHN TAYLOR,	GEO. W. HARRIS,
WILFORD WOODRUFF,	NEWEL K. WHITNEY,
VINSON KNIGHT,	BRIGHAM YOUNG,
HEBER C. KIMBALL,	CHARLES C. RICH,
JOHN P. GREENE,	ORSON SPENCER.
WILLIAM MARKS,	

Subscribed and sworn to by the persons whose names appear to the foregoing affidavit, the 20th day of July, A. D. 1842, except Newel K. Whitney, who subscribed and affirmed to the foregoing this day [July 21st] before me.

DANIEL H. WELLS,
Justice of the peace within and for Hancock county, Illinois.

Friday, *22*.—A special session of the city council was called at eight o'clock this morning; the Vice-Mayor presiding, when the following petition was written:

Petition of the Nauvoo City Council to Governor Carlin.

To His Excellency, Thomas Carlin, Governor of the State of Illinois:

We, the undersigned citizens of the State of Illinois, having heard that many reports are in circulation prejudicial to the interest, happiness, peace, well being and safety of the inhabitants of the city of Nauvoo and vicinity have thought proper to lay before your Excellency the following statement:

Whereas, the Latter-day Saints having suffered much in the state of Missouri, in time past through the hand of oppression, brought upon them by the falsehoods and misrepresentations of wicked and designing men, whose hands are yet dripping with the blood of the innocent, and whose fiendish rage has sent many a patriot to his long home, leaving in our midst many widows and orphans whose sorrows and tears even time cannot wipe away:

We would represent to your Excellency that we broke no law, violated no constitutional rights, nor trampled upon the privileges of any other people in Missouri; yet we had to suffer banishment, exile, the confiscation of our properties, and have diseases, distress and misery entailed upon us and our children, the effects of which we bear about in our bodies, and are indelibly engraven on our minds, and we appeal to your Excellency at the present time, that you will not suffer an occurrence of such heart-rending scenes to take place under your administration.

Whilst we have been in this state we have behaved as good, peaceable citizens; we have availed ourselves of no privileges but what are strictly constitutional, and such as have been guaranteed by the authority of this state; we have always held ourselves amenable to the laws of the land; we have not violated any law, nor taken from any their rights.

Your Excellency must be acquainted with the false statements and seditious designs of John Cook Bennett, with other political demagogues, pertaining to us as a people. We presume, sir, that you are acquainted with the infamous character of that individual, from certain statements made to us by yourself pertaining to him, but lest you should not be we forward to you documents pertaining to the affair, which will fully show the darkness of his character, and the infamous course that he has taken.

Concerning those statements made by him against Joseph Smith, we know that they are false. Joseph Smith has our entire confidence; we know that he has violated no law, nor has he in anywise promoted sedition or rebellion; nor has he sought the injury of any citizen of this or any other place. We are perfectly assured that he is as loyal, patriotic and virtuous a man, as there is in the state of Illinois, and we appeal to your Excellency, if in three years acquaintance with him you have seen anything to the contrary?

Inasmuch as this is the case, we your petitioners, knowing that Joseph Smith could not have justice done him in the state of Missouri—that he has suffered enough in that state unjustly already, and that if he goes there it is only to be murdered—pray your Excellency not to issue a writ for him to be given up to the authorities of Missouri; but if your Excellency thinks that he has violated any law, we request that he may be tried by the authorities of this state, for he shrinks not from investigation.

We furthermore pray that our lives and the lives of our wives and children may be precious in your sight and that we may have the privilege of following our avocations, of living on our farms, and by our own firesides in peace, and that neither said John C. Bennett, nor any other person may be able to influence your Excellency, either by intrigue or falsehood, to suffer us as a people to be injured by mob violence, but if, in the estimation of your Excellency, we have done wrong, we appeal to the laws of this state.

Having heard a report that your Excellency had called upon several companies of militia, to prepare themselves and be in readiness in case of emergency, we would further ask of your Excellency, that if the state or country should be in danger, that the Nauvoo Legion may have the privilege of showing their loyalty in the defense thereof.

We have the fullest confidence in the honor, justice and integrity of your Excellency, and feel confident that we have only to present our case before you to insure protection, believing that the cries of so many peaceable and patriotic citizens will not be disregarded by your Excellency.

We therefore ask you as the chief magistrate of this state to grant us our requests, and we, as in duty bound, will ever pray.

Signed by the Vice-Mayor and City Council.

This forenoon I attended a general meeting of the citizens at the stand; Orson Spencer, Esq., presiding. The object of the meeting was to correct the public mind relative to false reports put in circulation by Bennett and others, and General Wilson Law presented the following:

Resolution of a Nauvoo Mass Meeting.

Resolved, That having heard that John C. Bennett was circulating many base falsehoods respecting a number of the citizens of Nauvoo, and especially against our worthy and respected Mayor, Joseph Smith, we do hereby manifest to the world, that so far as we are acquainted with Joseph Smith, we know him to be a good, moral, virtuous, peaceable and patriotic man, and a firm supporter of law, justice and equal rights; that he at all times upholds and keeps inviolate the constitution of this state and the United States.

This resolution was adopted unanimously by the numerous assembly.

The assembly came together in the afternoon, and

about eight hundred signed the foregoing petition presented by the city council to Governor Carlin.

The "Ladies Relief Society" also drew up a petition signed by about one thousand ladies, speaking in the highest terms of the virtue, philanthropy and benevolence of Joseph Smith, begging that he might not be injured, and that they and their families might have the privilege of enjoying their peaceable rights.

A petition was also drawn up by many citizens in and near Nauvoo, who were not "Mormons" setting forth the same things. (See affidavits of Hyrum Smith and William Law *Times and Seasons*, Vol. III, page 870, &c. Also certificates of Elias Higbee and Francis M. Higbee, *Times and Seasons*, Vol. III, page 874.)*

Affidavit of Hyrum Smith.

On the seventeenth day of May, 1842, having been made acquainted with some of the conduct of John C. Bennett, which was given in testimony, under oath before Alderman G. W. Harris, by several females who testified that John C. Bennett endeavored to seduce them, and accomplished his designs by saying it was right; that it was one of the mysteries of God, which was to be revealed when the people was strong enough in faith to bear such mysteries—that it was perfectly right to have illicit intercourse with females, providing no one knew it but themselves, vehemently trying them from day to day, to yield to his passions, bringing witnesses of his own clan to testify that there were such revelations and such commandments, and that they were of God; also stating that he would be responsible for their sins, if there were any, and that he would give them medicine to produce abortions, provided they should become pregnant. One of these witnesses, a married woman that he attended upon in his professional capacity whilst she was sick, stated that he made proposals to her of a similar nature; he told her that he wished her husband was dead, and that if he was dead, he would marry her and clear out with her; he also begged her permission to give

*The matters of which these affidavits treat are of such importance in the CHURCH HISTORY, since they establish the villainy of John C. Bennett and prove the Prophet to be innocent of those things charged against him by Bennett that it is thought proper to give them here *in extenso*, as also an extract from an editorial from the *Times and Seasons*, explaining the long forbearance with this arch-apostate and traitor.

him [her husband] medicine to that effect; he did try to give him medicine, but he would not take it. On interrogating her what she thought of such teaching, she replied she was sick at the time, and had to be lifted in and out of her bed like a child. Many other acts as criminal were reported to me at the time. On becoming acquainted with these facts, I was determined to prosecute him, and bring him to justice. Some person knowing my determination, having informed him of it, he sent to me William Law and Brigham Young, to request an interview with me, and to see if there could not be a reconciliation made. I told them I thought there could not be, his crimes were so heinous; but told them I was willing to see him; he immediately came to see me; he begged on me to forgive him this once, and not prosecute him and expose him; he said he was guilty, and did acknowledge the crimes that were alleged against him; he seemed to be sorry that he had committed such acts, and wept much and desired that it might not be made public, for it would ruin him forever; he wished me to wait, but I was determined to bring him to justice, and declined listening to his entreaties; he then wished me to wait until he could have an interview with the Masonic fraternity; he also wanted an interview with Brother Joseph; he wished to know of me if I would forgive him, and desist from my intentions, if he could obtain their forgiveness; and requested the privilege of an interview immediately. I granted him that privilege as I was acting as master *pro tem* at that time; he also wished an interview first with Brother Joseph; at that time Brother Joseph was crossing the yard from the house to the store, he immediately came to the store and met Dr. Bennett on the way; he reached out his hand to Brother Joseph and said, Will you forgive me? weeping at the time; he said, Brother Joseph, I am guilty, I acknowledge it, and I beg of you not to expose me, for it will ruin me; Joseph replied, Doctor! why are you using my name to carry on your hellish wickedness? Have I ever taught you that fornication and adultery were right, or polygamy or any such practice? He said, You never did. Did I ever teach you anything that was not virtuous—that was iniquitous, either in public or private? He said, You never did. Did you ever know anything unvirtuous or unrighteous in my conduct or action at any time, either in public or private? He said, I did not. Are vou willing to make oath to this before an alderman of the city? He said I am willing to do so. Joseph said, Doctor, go into my office and write what you can in conscience subscribe your name to, and I will be satisfied. I will, he said, and went into the office, and I went with him, and he requested pen, ink and paper of Mr. Clayton, who was acting clerk in that office, and was also secretary *pro tem.* for the Nauvoo Lodge, U. D. William Clayton gave him paper, pen and ink, and he stood at the desk and wrote the following article which was published in the 11th No. of the *Wasp;* sworn to and subscribed before Daniel H. Wells, Alderman, 17th day of May, A. D. 1842. He called in Brother Joseph and read it to him, and asked him if that would do; he said it would; he then swore to it as before mentioned, the article was as follows:

STATE OF ILLINOIS, CITY OF NAUVOO.

Personally appeared before me, Daniel H. Wells, an alderman of said city of Nauvoo, John C. Bennett, who being duly sworn, according to law, deposeth and saith: that he never was taught anything in the least contrary to the strictest principles of the Gospel, or of virtue, or of the laws of God, or man, under any occasion, either directly or indirectly, in word or deed by Joseph Smith: and that he never knew the said Smith to countenance any improper conduct whatever, either in public or private; and that he never did teach to me in private that an illegal, illicit intercourse with females was, under any circumstances, justifiable, and that I never knew him so to teach others.

JOHN C. BENNETT.

Sworn to and subscribed before me, this 17th day of May, 1842.

DANIEL H. WELLS,
Alderman.

During all this intercourse I was present with him, and there was no threats used nor harshness, everything was as pacific as could be under existing circumstances. I then immediately convened the Masonic Lodge, it being about 4 o'clock p. m. He then came into the lodge and charges of a similar nature were preferred against him. He admitted they were true, in the presence of about sixty in number. He arose and begged the privilege of speaking to the brethren; he acknowledged his wickedness; and begged for the brethren to forgive him still longer, and he called God and angels to witness that he never would be guilty of the like crimes again—he would lay his hand on the Bible and swear that he would not be guilty of such crimes. He seemed to be very penitent and wept much; his penitence excited sympathy in the minds of the brethren, and they withdrew the charge for the time being until he could be heard on other charges which had been preferred against him by members of the Pickaway Lodge of Ohio, through the communications of the Grand Master, A. Jones. After this we found him to be an expelled Mason, in consequence of his rascally conduct, from the Pickaway Lodge, in Ohio; the circumstances and documents were mentioned in the 11th number of the *Wasp*, signed by George Miller, Master of Nauvoo Lodge, under dispensation, and reads as follows:

NOTICE.

To All Whom it May Concern, Greeting:

Whereas John Cook Bennett, in the organization of the Nauvoo Lodge, under dispensation, palmed himself upon the fraternity as a regular Mason in good standing; and satisfactory testimony having been produced before said Lodge, that he, said Bennett, was an expelled Mason, we therefore publish to all the Masonic world, the above facts, that he, the said Bennett may not impose himself upon the fraterns of Masons.

All editors who are friendly to the fraternity of free and accepted ancient York Masons will please insert the above.

GEORGE MILLER,
Master of Nauvoo Lodge under dispensation.

Still after all this we found him guilty of similar crimes again, and it was found to our satisfaction that he was conspiring against the peace and safety of the citizens of this state—after learning these facts we exposed him to the public; he then immediately left the place abruptly; threatening to drink the hearts blood of many citizens of this place. Previous to this last disclosure, the hand of fellowship was withdrawn from him, May 11, 1842, by the First Presidency, six days previous to the time he pretended to withdraw from the Church, which you will see published in the *Times and Seasons*, June 15, 1842. I was also present at the time when he gave this testimony before the city council, as printed in the *Times and Seasons*, July 1, 1842, on page 841, which reads as follows:

Dr. John C. Bennett, ex-Mayor, was then called upon by the Mayor to state if he knew aught against him; when Mr. Bennett replied: "I know what I am about,and the heads of the Church know what they are about, I expect. I have no difficulty with the heads of the Church. I publicly avow that any one who has said that I have stated that General Joseph Smith has given me authority to hold illicit intercourse with women, is a liar in the face of God, those who have said it are damned liars; they are infernal liars. He never either in public or private gave me any such authority or license,and any person who states it is a scoundrel and a liar. I have heard it said that I should become a second Avard by withdrawing from the Church, and that I was at variance with the heads and should use an influence against them because I resigned the office of mayor; this is false. I have no difficulty with the heads of the Church, and I intend to continue with you, and hope the time may come when I may be restored to full confidence, and fellowship, and my former standing in the Church, and that my conduct may be such as to warrant my restoration—and should the time ever come that I may have an opportunity to test my faith, it will then be known whether I am a traitor or a true man."

Joseph Smith then asked: "Will you please state definitely whether you know anything against my character either in public or private?"

General Bennett answered: "I do not; in all my intercourse with Gen. Smith, in public and in private, he has been strictly virtuous."

ALDERMEN.	COUNCILLORS.
NEWEL K. WHITNEY,	WILLARD RICHARDS,
HIRAM KIMBALL,	WILSON LAW,
ORSON SPENCER,	JOHN TAYLOR,
GUST. HILLS,	BRIGHAM YOUNG,
G. W. HARRIS,	JOHN P. GREENE,
	HEBER C. KIMBALL,
JAMES SLOAN, recorder.	WILFORD WOODRUFF,
MAY 19th, 1842.	GEORGE A. SMITH.

I know he was not under duress at the time, for his testimony was given free and voluntarily, after requesting the privilege of the council to speak (which was granted him) on matters pertaining to the city ordinances, while speaking, or before he took his seat, he was requested by the mayor of the city, Joseph Smith, to state to the council if he knew aught against him, and he replied according to the above.

I also know that he had no private intercourse with Joseph in the preparation room on the 17th day, as he stated in his letter as printed in the *Sangamo Journal*, for the lodge was convened on that day, and I had the keys of the doors in my possession from 7 o'clock a. m. until 6 o'clock p. m., and it was when the lodge called off for refreshment during recess, that I had the interview with him, at which time he wrote the affidavit and subscribed it in my presence, and I was with him during the whole time from his first coming to me, until he signed it and until the lodge convened again at 4 o'clock.

HYRUM SMITH.

Sworn to and subscribed before me, July 23, 1842.

GEORGE W. HARRIS,
Alderman of the city of Nauvoo.

Affidavit of Wm. Law.

As John C. Bennett has become our open enemy, and is engaged in circulating falsehoods of the blackest character, I deem it a duty to make the following statement of facts:

John C. Bennett states in the *Sangamo Journal* that the withdrawal of the hand of fellowship by the First Presidency, and the Twelve was after he had withdrawn from the Church. I presume the notice of our withdrawal was not published till after he withdrew, but that does not prove his statement true, for I hereby testify that I signed the article in question several days before he withdrew. I believe it was on the evening of the 11th day of May, some four or five days afterwards I had some conversation with John C. Bennett and intimated to him that such a thing was concluded upon, which intimation, I presume led him to withdraw immediately. I told him we could not bear with his conduct any longer—that there were many witnesses against him, and that they stated that he gave Joseph Smith as authority for his illicit intercourse with females. John C. Bennett declared to me before God that Joseph Smith had never taught him such doctrines, and that he never told any one that he (Joseph Smith) had taught any such things, and that any one who said so told base lies; nevertheless he said he had done wrong, that he would not deny, but he would deny that he had used Joseph Smith's name to accomplish his designs on any one; stating that he had no need of that, for that he could succeed without telling them that Joseph approbated such conduct.

These statements he made to me of his own free will, in a private conversation which we had on the subject; there was no compulsion or threats used on my part; we had always been on good terms, and I regretted exceedingly that he had taken such a course. He plead with me to intercede for him, assuring me that he would turn from his iniquity, and never would be guilty of such crimes again. He said that if he were exposed it would break his mother's heart—that she was old, and if such things reached her ears it would bring her down with sorrow to the grave. I accordingly went to Joseph Smith and plead with him to spare Bennett from public exposure, on account of his mother. On many occasions I heard him acknowledge his guilt, and beg not to be destroyed in the eyes of the public, and that he would never act so again, so "help him God." From such promises and oaths I was induced to bear with him longer than I should have done.

On one occasion I heard him state before the city council that Joseph Smith had never taught him any unrighteous principles, of any kind, and that if any one says that he ever said that Joseph taught such things they are base liars, or words to that effect. This statement he made voluntarily; he came into the council room about an hour after the council opened, and made the statement, not under duress, but of his own free will, as many witnesses can testify.

On a former occasion he came to me and told me that a friend of his was about to be tried by the High Council, for the crime of adultery, and that he feared his name would be brought into question. He entreated me to go to the council and prevent his name from being brought forward, as, said he, "I am not on trial, and I do not want my mother to hear of these things, for she is a good woman."

I would further state that I do know from the amount of evidence which stands against John C. Bennett, and from his own acknowledgments, that he is a most corrupt, base, and vile man; and that he has published many base falsehoods since we withdrew the hand of fellowship from him.

About the time that John C. Bennett was brought before the Masonic Lodge he came to me and desired that I would go in company with Brigham Young to Hyrum Smith, and entreat of him to spare him—that he wished not to be exposed—that he wanted to live as a private citizen, and would cease from all his folly, etc. I advised him to go to Texas, and when he returned, if he would behave well we would reinstate him. He said he had no means to take him to Texas, and still insisted on Brigham Young and myself to intercede for him.

WILLIAM LAW.

Sworn to, and subscribed before me a justice of the peace, within and for the county of Hancock, state of Illinois, July 20th, 1842.

DANIEL H. WELLS.

Certificate of Elias and Francis M. Higbee.

Mr. Editor:

Sir, from a perusal of the St. Louis papers, I find from an article signed J. C. Bennett, stating that all who are friends to Mr. Joseph Smith he considers his enemies—as a matter of course, then, I must be one, for I am, and have been for a long time the personal friend of Joseph Smith; and I will here say that I have never yet seen or known anything against him that I should change my mind. It is true many reports have been and are put in circulation by his enemies for political or religious effect, that upon investigation are like the dew before the morning sun, vanish away, because there is no real substance in them.

Could Dr. Bennett expect any man acquainted with all the circumstances, and matters of fact which were developed both here and from abroad, respecting his conduct and character, previous to his leaving this place, for one moment to believe him—I answer, *No!* he could not. And all his affidavits, that came from any person entitled to credit, (I say entitled to credit, because some there are who are not entitled to credit; as Dr. Bennett very well knows) are in amount nothing at all, when summed up, and render no person worthy of death or bonds.

Francis M. Higbee's knowledge concerning the murder of a prisoner in Missouri, I am authorized to say, by Francis M. Higbee that he knows of no such thing—that no prisoner was ever killed in Missouri, to the best of his knowledge. And I also bear the same testimony that there never was any prisoner killed there, neither were we ever charged with any such thing, according to the best of my recollection.

ELIAS HIGBEE.

July 22, 1842.

This is to certify that I do not know of the murder of any prisoner in Missouri, as above alluded to.

FRANCIS M. HIGBEE.

July 22, 1842.

[The following is the excerpt from the *Times and Seasons* alluded to in the foot note at page 71:]

JOHN C. BENNETT.

In the state of Missouri we had our Hinckle, our Avard, Marsh, McLellin, and others who were the first to flee in time of danger—the first to tell of things that they never knew, and swear to things that they never before had heard of They were more violent in their persecutions, more relentless and sanguinary in their proceedings, and sought with greater fury the destruction and overthrow of the Saints of God who had never injured them, but whose virtue made them blush for their crimes. All that were there remember that they were the stoutest and the loudest in proclaiming against oppression; they protested vehemently against mob and misrule, but were the first in robbing, spoiling, and plundering their brethren. Such things we have always expected; we know that the "net will gather together of every kind, good and bad," that "the wheat and tares must grow together until the harvest," and that even at the last there will be five foolish as well as five wise virgins. Daniel, in referring to the last days says, in speaking concerning the "Holy Covenant," that many shall have indignation against it, and shall obtain information from those that forsake the Holy Covenant, "and the robbers of thy people shall seek to exalt themselves, but they shall fall." This we have fully proven—we have seen them try to exalt themselves, and we have seen their fall. He goes on further to state, that "many shall cleve unto them by flatteries." Such was Dr. Avard, and John C. Bennett—with the latter we have to do at the present time, and in many of the foregoing statements and prophecies we shall see his character and conduct exemplified. He professed the greatest fidelity, and eternal friendship, yet was he an adder in the path, and a viper in the bosom. He professed to be virtuous and chaste, yet did he pierce the heart of the innocent, introduce misery and infamy into families, reveled in voluptuousness and crime, and led the youth that he had influence over to tread in his unhallowed steps; he professed to fear God, yet did he desecrate His name, and prostitute his authority to the most unhallowed and diabolical purposes; even to the seduction of the virtuous, and the defiling of his neighbor's bed. He professed indignation against Missouri, saying, "My hand shall avenge the blood of the innocent;" yet now he calls upon Missouri to come out against the Saints, and he "will lead them on to glory and to victory."

It may be asked why it was that we would countenance him so long after being apprised of his iniquities, and why he was not dealt with long ago. To this we would answer, that he has been dealt with from time to time; when he would acknowledge his iniquity, ask and pray for forgiveness, beg that he might not be exposed, on account of his mother, and other reasons, saying, he should be ruined and undone. He frequently wept like a child, and begged like a culprit for forgiveness, at the same time promising before God and angels to amend his life, if he could be forgiven. He was in this way borne with from time to time, until forbearance was no longer a virtue, and then the First Presidency, the Twelve, and the Bishops withdrew their fellowship from him, as published in the 16th number of this paper. The Church afterwards publicly withdrew their fellowship from him, and his character was published in the 17th number of this paper; since that time he has published that the conduct of the Saints was bad—that Joseph Smith and many others were adulterers, murderers, etc., that there was a secret band of men that would kill people, etc., called Danites—that he was in duress when he gave his affidavit, and testified that Joseph Smith was a virtuous man—that we believed in and practiced polygamy,* that we believed in secret murders, and aimed to destroy the government, etc., etc. As he has made his statements very public, and industriously circulated them through the country, we shall content ourselves with answering his base falsehoods and misrepresentations, without giving publicity to them, as the public is generally acquainted with them already."†

*A distinction here must be kept in mind between the "polygamy" charged against the Saints by Bennett and plurality of wives allowed under certain restrictions by the revelation on the Eternity of the Marriage Covenant. It was the vicious, promiscuous polygamous associations charged by Bennett that belief in and practice of by the Saints that is here denied, not the plural relations under the seal and covenant of the marriage law in the aforesaid revelation. See Bennett's "History of the Saints," (1842), pp. 217-260.

†According to Bennett's own statement concerning himself, he joined the Church for the purpose of exposing the alleged treasonable designs of the Mormon people against several of the western states. In his book, entitled "The History of the Saints," (Leland & Whitney, Boston, 1842), he says:

"I find that it is almost universally the opinion of those who have heard of me

Affidavit of Daniel H. Wells Anent John C. Bennett.

STATE OF ILLINOIS, COUNTY OF HANCOCK.

I hereby certify that on the 17th day of May last, John C. Bennett subscribed and swore to the affidavit over my signature of that date and published in the *Wasp*, after writing the same in my presence, in the office where I was employed in taking depositions of witnesses. The door of the room was open and free for all, or any person to pass or repass. After signing and being qualified to the affidavit aforesaid,

in the eastern part of the United States, that I united myself to the Mormons from a conviction of the truth of their doctrines, and that I was, at least for some time, a convert to their pretended religion. This, however, is a very gross error. I never believed in them or their doctrines. This is, and indeed was, from the first, well known to my friends and acquaintances in the western country, who were well aware of my reasons for connecting myself with the Prophet; which reasons I will now proceed to state. My attention had been long turned towards the movements and designs of the Mormons, with whom I had become pretty well acquainted, years before, in the state of Ohio; and after the formation of their establishment at Nauvoo, in 1839, the facts and reports respecting them, which I continually heard, led me to suspect, and, indeed, believe, that their leaders had formed, and were preparing to execute, a daring and colossal scheme of rebellion and usurpation throughout the Northwestern States of the Union. It was to me evident that temporal, as well as spiritual, empire was the aim and expectation of the Prophet and his cabinet. The documents that will hereafter be introduced, will clearly show the existence of a vast and deep-laid scheme, upon their part, for conquering the states of Ohio, Indiana, Illinois, Iowa, and Missouri, and erecting upon the ruin of their present governments a despotic military and religious empire, the head of which, as emperor and pope, was to be Joseph Smith, the Prophet of the Lord, and his ministers and viceroys, the apostles, high priests, elders, and bishops, of the Mormon Church. The fruition of this hopeful project would, of course, have been preceded by plunder, devastation, and bloodshed, and by all the countless horrors which invariably accompany civil war. American citizens could not be expected to stand quietly by, and suffer their governments to be overthrown, their religion subverted, their wives and children converted into instruments for a despot's lust and ambition, and their property forcibly appropriated to the use and furtherance of a base imposture. The Mormons would, of course, meet with resistance as soon as their intentions became evident; and so great was already their power, and so rapidly did their numbers increase, that the most frightful consequences might naturally be expected to ensue, from an armed collision between them and the citizens who still remained faithful to the God and the laws of their fathers. These reflections continually occurred to me, as I observed the proceedings of the Mormons, and, at length, determined me to make an attempt to detect and expose the movers and machinery of the plot.

The promised documentary proofs of the alleged scheme to overthrow government in the states named, and establish on their ruins a despotic military government, etc., did not appear in the book compiled by Bennett, nor can his statement be true that he joined the Church for the purpose of exposing a secret plot on the part of Joseph Smith and his associates against government in the United States. The most probable and most charitable view in relation to Bennett's actions and character is that expressed by the late President John Taylor in his public dishe requested to speak to me at the door. I followed him out; he told me some persons had been lying about him, and showed me a writing granting him the privilege to withdraw from the Church, and remarked that the matter was perfectly understood between him and the heads of the Church; and that he had resigned the mayor's office, and should resign the office he held in the Legion; but as there was a court-martial to be held in a few days Joseph Smith desired that he would wait until that was over.

I was in the city council on the 19th day of May last. I there heard him say what has been published concerning the teachings of Joseph Smith, and of his own course. I afterwards met him in company with Colonel Francis M. Higbee. He then stated that he was going to be the candidate, (meaning the candidate for the legislature) and Joseph and Hyrum Smith were going in for him. Said: "You know it will be better for me not to be bothered with the mayor's office, Legion, 'Mormon,' or anything else."

During all this time, if he was under duress or fear, he must have a good faculty for concealing it, for he was at liberty to go and come when and where he pleased, so far as I am capable of judging.

I know that I saw him in different parts of the city even after he had made these statements, transacting business as usual, and said he was going to complete some business pertaining to the mayor's office; and I think did attend to work on the streets.

I was always personally friendly with him, after I became acquainted

cussion with a number of Protestant ministers in France, 1850, who relied on Bennett's "disclosures" concerning Joseph Smith and the Mormon people for the data of their arguments. Of Bennett, with whom he was well and intimately acquainted, the late President John Taylor said:

"Respecting John C. Bennett: I was well acquainted with him. At one time he was a good man, but fell into adultery, and was cut off from the Church for his iniquity; and so bad was his conduct, that he was also expelled from the municipal courts, of which he was a member. He then went lecturing through the country, and commenced writing pamphlets for the sake of making money, charging so much for admittance to his lectures, and selling his slanders. His remarks, however, were so bad, and his statements so obscene and disgraceful, that respectable people were disgusted."

Elder Taylor's opponents regarded this as an attack upon Bennett's character, to which Elder Taylor answered: "Mr. Carter * * tells us that it is now too late to attack John C. Bennett's motives for joining the Church. Did I ever attack John C. Bennett's motives for joining the Church? * * * * I stated concerning John C. Bennett, that at one time he was a good man, but that he fell into iniquity and was cut off from the Church for adultery, and then commenced his persecutions. If I had my books here I could have shown an affidavit made before the city council about the time he was cut off, stating that he knew nothing evil or bad of Joseph Smith, an affidavit that I heard him make himself." (Public discussion between Reverends Cleeve, Robinson, Carter, and Elder John Taylor at Boulogne-Sur-Mer, France, 1850.)

with him. I never heard him say anything derogatory to the character of Joseph Smith, until after he had been exposed by said Smith, on the public stand in Nauvoo.

DANIEL H. WELLS.

July 22nd, A. D. 1842.

Sworn to and subscribed before me, a justice of the peace, in and for the city of Nauvoo, in said county, this 22nd day of July, 1842.

GUSTAVUS HILLS,
[L. S.] J. P. and Alderman.

Times and Seasons Editor's Note.—"Daniel H. Wells, Esq., is an old resident in this place, and not a Mormon."

Sunday, 24.—This morning at home sick. Attended meeting at the Grove in the afternoon, and spoke of Brother Miller's having returned with the good news that Bennett would not be able to accomplish his designs.

Tuesday, 26.—Sick this morning. Rode to my farm in the afternoon.

Wednesday, 27—Attended meeting at the Grove and listened to the electioneering candidates, and spoke at the close of the meeting.

Letter of Governor Carlin to Joseph Smith, Anent the Foregoing Resolution and Petition.

QUINCY, July 27, 1842.

DEAR SIR:—Your communication of the 25th instant, together with the petitions of the citizens of the city of Nauvoo, both male and female, were delivered to me last evening by Brevet-Major-General Wilson Law; also a report of James Sloan, Esq., Secretary of Nauvoo Legion, of the proceedings of a Court Martial of Brevet-Major-General had upon charges preferred against Major-General John C. Bennett; upon which trial the court found the defendant guilty, and sentenced him to be cashiered; all of which have been considered.

In reply to your expressed apprehensions of "the possibility of an attack upon the peaceable inhabitants of the city of Nauvoo and vicinity, through the intrigues and false representations of John C. Bennett and others," and your request that I would issue official orders to you to have the Nauvoo Legion in readiness to be called out at a moment's warning in defense of the peaceable citizens, &c., I must say that I cannot conceive of the least probability, or scarcely possibility, of an attack of violence upon the citizens of Nauvoo from any quarter whatever, and as utterly impossible that such attack is contemplated by any sufficient number of persons to excite the least apprehension of danger or injury,and whilst I should consider it my imperative duty to promptly take measures to suppress and repel any invasion, by violence of the people's rights, I nevertheless think that it is not in my province to interpose my official authority gratuitously when no such exigency exists.

From the late exposure, as made by General Bennett it is not strange that the apprehensions of the citizens of Nauvoo are excited, but so far as I can learn from the expression of public opinion, the excitement is confined to the Mormons themselves, and only extends to the community at large as a matter of curiosity and wonder.

Very respectfully,

Your obedient servant,

To General Joseph Smith. THOMAS CARLIN.

Elder W. Woodruff started for St. Louis, to procure printing paper for the *Times and Seasons*.

Saturday, 30.—I wrote to Thomas Carlin, Governor of the state of Illinois as follows:

Letter of the Prophet to Governor Carlin—Satisfied with the Governor's Attitude.

NAUVOO, July 30, 1842.

ESTEEMED SIR:—Your favor of the 27th instant per Brevet Major-General Wilson Law is before me. I cannot let this opportunity pass without tendering to you my warmest thanks for the friendly treatment my lady as well as those with her received at your hands during the late visit,and also for the friendly feelings breathed forth in your letter. Your Excellency may be assured that they are duly appreciated by me, and shall be reciprocated.

I am perfectly satisfied with regard to the subject under consideration, and with your remarks. I shall consider myself and our citizens secure from harm under the broad canopy of the law under your administration. We look to you for protection in the event of any violence being used towards us, knowing that our innocence with regard to all the accusations in circulation will be duly evidenced before an enlightened public.

Any service we can do the state at any time will be cheerfully done, for our ambition is to be serviceable to our country.

With sentiments of respect and esteem, I remain your humble servant,

JOSEPH SMITH.

My wife's nephew, L. D. Wasson, who had gone out on

a preaching mission, wrote us this day from Philadelphia —(see *Times and Seasons*, Vol. III, pages 891 and 892.)

Death of Bishop Vinson Knight.

Sunday, *31*.—In council with Bishops Miller and Whitney, Brigham Young, John Taylor, &c., concerning Bishop Vinson Knight's sickness. Brother Knight has been sick about a week, and this morning he began to sink very fast until twelve o'clock when death put a period to his sufferings.

Requirements of High Priests.

The High Priests' Quorum met in council, and instructed their clerk to publish in the *Times and Seasons* that it is the duty of the High Priests to have their names enrolled on the records of the quorums when they arrive at Nauvoo. The members, when they spoke in turns, were required to state whether they had any hardness with the brethren, kept the Word of Wisdom, had family prayers, &c.,

An earthquake was recently felt in Dublane Cathedral, near Comrie Scotland.

Monday, *August 1*, *1842*.—A most disgraceful riot is reported to have commenced in Philadelphia, between the colored and white people, which continued three or four days.

Wednesday, *3*.—In the city transacting a variety of business in company with General James Adams, and others. Brigadier-General Wilson Law elected Major-General of the Nauvoo Legion (by a small majority over Lyman Wight) in place of John C. Bennett, cashiered.

Thursday, *4*.—In company with fifteen others learning sword exercise with Colonel Brewer, and attending to a variety of business.

Friday, *5*.—Engaged in a variety of business, and at six in the evening presided in the city council; Councilor Taylor brought forward a bill to regulate proceedings in the Municipal Court under habeas corpus—the bill was read the first time, and upon motion for a second reading it was referred to a select committee, namely Alderman Spencer, and Councilors Taylor and William Law, to report thereon at the next sitting of council.

Saturday, 6.—Passed over the river to Montrose, Iowa, in company with General Adams, Colonel Brewer, and others, and witnessed the installation of the officers of the Rising Sun Lodge Ancient York Masons, at Montrose, by General James Adams, Deputy Grand-Master of Illinois. While the Deputy Grand-Master was engaged in giving the requisite instructions to the Master-elect, I had a conversation with a number of brethren in the shade of the building on the subject of our persecutions in Missouri and the constant annoyance which has followed us since we were driven from that state. I prophesied that the Saints would continue to suffer much affliction and would be driven to the Rocky Mountains, many would apostatize, others would be put to death by our persecutors or lose their lives in consequence of exposure or disease, and some of you will live to go and assist in making settlements and build cities and see the Saints become a mighty people in the midst of the Rocky Mountains.*

Prophecy that the Saints Would be Driven to the Rocky Mountains.

* It is thought important that the following statement from a biography of Anson Call, by Edward Tullidge, should be made part of the history of this prophetic incident, as doubtless the testimony of Brother Call relates to the same incident as that described in the Prophet's text of the History, notwithstanding some confusion of dates that exists in the Call testimony. It will be seen that the Prophet fixes the date of his prophecy on Saturday, the 6th of August, 1842. In Whitney's History of Utah, Vol. IV.—(Biographical section of the history, p. 143), the date on which Call heard the prophecy, is given as the 8th of August, 1842. While in Tullidge's biography of Call the date is given as the 14th of July, 1843, evidently an error. There is no entry in the Prophet's journal for the 8th of August, 1842, and the entries for the 8th of August, 1843, and the 14th of July, 1843, relate to matters of quite a different character. Tullidge, in relating Anson Call's recollection of the incident also says that J. C. Bennett was present on the occasion, which must also be an error, as the rupture between Bennett and the Church and its authorities occurred and he had left Nauvoo previous to the 6th of August, 1842. In the Call statement as published by Tullidge, the name of Mr. Adams, the Deputy Grand Master Mason in charge of the ceremonies, is given as George, it should be James.

Statement of Anson Call.

"On the 14th of July, 1843, with quite a number of his brethren, he crossed the Mississippi river to the town of Montrose, to be present at the installment of the Masonic Lodge of the "Rising Sun." A block schoolhouse had been prepared with shade in front, under which was a barrel of ice water. Judge George [James] Adams was the highest masonic authority in the state of Illinois, and had been sent there

Sunday, 7. -At home through the day.

Monday, 8—This forenoon I was arrested by the deputy sheriff of Adams county, and two assistants, on a warrant issued by Governor Carlin, founded on a requisition from Governor Reynolds of Missouri, upon the affidavit of ex-Governor Boggs, complaining of the said Smith as "being an accessory before the fact, to an assault with intent to kill made by one Orrin P. Rockwell on Lilburn W. Boggs," on the night of the sixth of May, A. D. 1842. Brother Rockwell was arrested at the same time as principal.

Arrest of the Prophet on a Requisition of Missouri.

to organize this lodge. He, Hyrum Smith, and J. C. Bennett. being high Masons, went into the house to perform some ceremonies which the others were not entitled to witness. These, including Joseph Smith, remained under the bowery. Joseph, as he was tasting the cold water, warned the brethren not to be too free with it. With the tumbler still in his hand he prophesied that the Saints would yet go to the Rocky Mountains; and, said he, this water tastes much like that of the crystal streams that are running from the snow-capped mountains. We will let Mr. Call describe this prophetic scene: "I had before seen him in a vision, and now saw while he was talking his countenance change to white; not the deadly white of a bloodless face, but a living brilliant white. He seemed absorbed in gazing at something at a great distance, and said: 'I am gazing upon the valleys of those mountains.' This was followed by a vivid description of the scenery of these mountains, as I have since become acquainted with it. Pointing to Shadrach Roundy and others, he said: 'There are some men here who shall do a great work in that land.' Pointing to me, he said: 'There is Anson, he shall go and shall assist in building up cities from one end of the country to the other, and you, rather extending the idea to all those he had spoken of, shall perform as great a work as has been done by man, so that the nations of the earth shall be astonished, and many of them will be gathered in that land and assist in building cities and temples, and Israel shall be made to rejoice.'

"It is impossible to represent in words this scene which is still vivid in my mind, of the grandeur of Joseph's appearance, his beautiful descriptions of this land, and his wonderful prophetic utterances as they emanated from the glorious inspirations that overshadowed him. There was a force and power in his exclamations of which the following is but a faint echo: 'Oh the beauty of those snow-capped mountains! The cool refreshing streams that are running down through those mountain gorges!' Then gazing in another direction, as if there was a change of locality: 'Oh the scenes that this people will pass through! The dead that will lay between here and there.' Then turning in another direction as if the scene had again changed: 'Oh the apostasy that will take place before my brethren reach that land!' 'But,' he continued, 'The priesthood shall prevail over its enemies, triumph over the devil and be established upon the earth, never more to be thrown down!' He then charged us with great force and power, to be faithful to those things that had been and should be committed to our charge, with the promise of all the blessings that the Priesthood could bestow. 'Remember these things and treasure them up. Amen.'" (Tullidge's Histories, Vol. II. History of Northern Utah, and Southern Idaho.—Biographical Supplement, p. 271 *et seq.*)

There was no evasion of the officers, though the municipal court issued a writ of habeas corpus according to the constitution of the state, Article 8, and Section 13. This writ demanded the bodies of Messrs. Smith and Rockwell to be brought before the aforesaid court; but these officers refused to do so, and finally without complying, they left us in the care of the marshal, without the original writ by which we were arrested, and by which only we could be retained, and returned to Governor Carlin for further instructions, and myself and Rockwell went about our business.

The Prophet's Comments on His Arrest.

I have yet to learn by what rule of right I was arrested to be transported to Missouri for a trial of the kind stated. "An accessory to an assault with intent to kill," does not come under the provision of the *fugitive* act, when the person charged has not been out of Illinois, &c. An accessory before the fact to manslaughter is something of an anomaly. The isolated affidavit of ex-Governor Boggs is no more than any other man's, and the constitution says, "that no person shall be liable to be transported out of the state, for an offense committed within the same." The whole is another Missouri farce. In fact, implied power, and constructive guilt, as a *dernier resort*, may answer the purpose of despotic governments, but are beneath the dignity of the Sons of Liberty, and would be a blot on our judicial escutcheon.

I received a letter from the postoffice, which had been broken open, and I was grieved at the meanness of its contents.

The city council passed the following "Ordinance regulating the mode of proceeding in cases of habeas corpus before the municipal court:"

Ordinance on Habeas Corpus Procedure.

Sec. 1. Be it ordained by the city council of the city of Nauvoo, that in all cases where any person or persons, shall at any time hereafter, be arrested or under arrest in this city, under any writ or process, and shall be brought before the municipal court of this city, by virtue of a writ of habeas corpus, the court shall in every such case have power and authority, and are hereby required to examine into the origin, validity and legality of the writ of process, under which such arrest was made, and if it shall appear to the court, upon sufficient testimony that said writ or process was illegal, or not legally issued, or did not proceed from proper authority, then the court shall discharge the prisoner from under said arrest; but if it shall appear to the court that said writ or process had issued from proper authority, and was a legal process, the court shall then proceed and fully hear the merits of the case, upon which said arrest was made, upon such evidence as may be produced and sworn before said court, and shall have power to adjourn the hearing, and also issue process from time to time, in their discretion, in order to procure the attendance of witnesses, so that a fair and impartial trial and decision may be obtained in every such case.

Sec. 2. And be it further ordained that if upon investigation it shall be proven before the municipal court, that the writ or process has been issued, either through private pique, malicious intent, or religious or other persecution, falsehood or misrepresentation, contrary to the constitution of this state, or the Constitution of the United States, the said writ or process shall be quashed and considered of no force or effect, and the prisoner or prisoners shall be released and discharged therefrom.

Sec. 3. And be it also further ordained that in the absence, sickness, debility, or other circumstances disqualifying or preventing the mayor from officiating in his court, as chief justice of the municipal court, the aldermen present shall appoint one from amongst them to act as chief justice, or president pro tempore.

Sec. 4. This ordinance to take effect and be in force from and after its passage.

Passed August 8, 1842.

HYRUM SMITH,
Vice-Mayor and President Pro Tempore.
JAMES SLOAN, Recorder.

A disgraceful and bloody riot occurred in Cincinnati this evening, in and about the "Sans Souci House."

CHAPTER V.

THE PROPHET IN SECLUSION—CORRESPONDENCE WITH WILSON LAW—COMPANIONSHIP OF THE PROPHET AND HIS WIFE, EMMA SMITH—THE PROPHET'S APPRECIATION OF HIS FRIENDS.

Tuesday, *August 9.*—In company with Judge Ralston and Lawyer Powers, preparing for the return of the sheriff; prepared a writ of habeas corpus for the master in chancery.

Wednesday, *10.*—The deputy sheriff returned to Nauvoo, but I was absent and he did not see me, nor Brother Rockwell. He endeavored to alarm my wife and the brethren with his threats, if I was not forthcoming, but they understood the law in such cases, and his threats proved harmless.

Thursday, *11.*—This forenoon Brother William Law entered into conversation with the sheriff on the illegality of the whole proceedings in reference to the arrest, when the sheriff acknowledged that he believed Joseph was innocent, and that Governor Carlin's course which he had pursued, was unjustifiable and illegal.

Meeting of the Prophet with Confidential Friends.

I spent the day at Uncle John Smith's in Zarahemla, and sent word that I wished to see Emma, Brothers Hyrum Smith, William Law and others, with instructions to meet me on the island between Nauvoo and Montrose. After dark, Emma, Hyrum, William Law, Newel K. Whitney, George Miller William Clayton, and Dimick Huntington, met at the waterside near the brick store, and proceeded in a skiff between the islands until they arrived near the lower end; and then hailed to shore. After waiting a very little while, the skiff arrived from the opposite shore, and in it were myself, and Brother Erastus H. Derby. A council was then held in the skiffs, and various statements set forth in regard to the state of things. It was reported that the governor of Iowa had issued a warrant for my apprehension, and that of Orrin P. Rockwell, and that the sheriff of Lee county was expected down immediately; very strong evidence was also manifested that Governor Reynolds of Missouri was not acquainted with these proceedings; that ex-Governor Boggs had made oath before a justice of the peace or a judge, and that the judge had made the requisition, and not Governor Reynolds, also that the writ issued by Carlin was illegal and unjustifiable. It is absolutely certain that the whole business is another glaring instance of the effects of prejudice against me as a religious teacher, and that it proceeds from a persecuting spirit, the parties have signified their determination to have me taken to Missouri, whether by legal or illegal means. It was finally concluded that I should be taken up the river in a skiff, and be landed below Wiggan's farm, so called, and that I should proceed from thence to Brother Edward Sayers, and there abide for a season.

This being concluded upon, we separated, myself and Brother Derby being rowed up the river by Brother Dunham, and the remainder crossed over to Nauvoo. It was agreed that Brother Albert P. Rockwood should proceed up the river on shore to the place where the skiff should stop, and there light up two fires as a signal for a stopping place. After the boat had proceeded some distance above the city, a fire was discovered on shore. We concluded that it was the signal and immediately rowed towards shore. When near the shore one of the company hailed a person on the banks, but received a very unsatisfactory answer, whereupon we turned about and put to the channel, and upon coming near the middle of the river, discovered two fires a little higher up the stream. We immediately steered towards the fires and were happy to find Brother Rockwood awaiting our arrival. We then proceeded through the timber to Brother Sayers' house, where we were very kindly received and made welcome.

Judge Ralston and Lawyer Powers departed, each for home, expressing their perfect willingness to aid us in every possible manner. Judge Ralston also promised to ascertain the state of affairs in Quincy, and give us the earliest information.

State of Things in Iowa.

Friday, 12.—This forenoon it appeared still more evident that the whole course of proceedings by Governor Carlin and others was illegal. After some consultation with Brother William Law, Emma concluded to dispatch a messenger with a letter to Lawyer Powers, of Keokuk, to request him to go to Burlington, Iowa Territory, and there see the governor of Iowa, and endeavor to ascertain whether Governor Reynolds had made any requisition on him for myself and Rockwell. William Walker proceeded to cross the river on my horse, "Joe Duncan," in sight of a number of persons—one chief design in this movement was to draw the attention of the sheriffs and public from all idea that I was on the Nauvoo side of the river.

At night William Clayton and John D. Parker, left Nauvoo after dark, and came to see me, and found me cheerful and in good spirits.

Efforts to Throw the Prophet off his Guard.

Saturday, 13.—This forenoon Brother Hyrum received a letter from Elder Hollister at Quincy, stating that Governor Carlin had said that his proceedings were illegal and he should not pursue the subject any further. The letter also stated that Ford (the agent to receive me from the hands of the sheriff and carry me to Missouri) had concluded to take the first boat and start home; and that he was going to fetch a force from Missouri. All this, my friends thought, was only a scheme got up for the purpose of throwing us off our guard, that they might come unexpectedly, kidnap, and carry me to Missouri.

Visit of Emma to the Prophet

I had sent a request to Emma to come to see me, and she concluded to start in the carriage, but while it was preparing, it attracted the attention of the sheriff, who kept a close watch of all movements. To avoid suspicion, Emma walked to Sister Durphy's and waited the arrival of the carriage which passed off down the river with William Clayton and Lorin Walker, with raised curtains, receiving Emma by the way, without any discovery by the sheriff; when about four miles down the river, the carriage turned on the prairie and passing around the city, turned into the timber opposite Wiggan's farm, when Emma alighted and walked to Brother Sayers', and the carriage returned. I was in good spirits, although somewhat afflicted in body, and was much rejoiced to meet my dear wife once more.

A report came over the river to the following effect:

> There are several small companies of men in Montrose, Nashville, Keokuk, &c., in search of Joseph, they saw his horse go down the river yesterday, and were confident he was on that side. They swear they will have him. It is said there is a reward of thirteen hundred dollars offered for the apprehension and delivery of Joseph and Rockwell, and this is supposed to have induced them to make search. The sheriff and deputy have uttered heavy threats several times; saying that if they could not find Joseph they would lay the city in ashes. They say they will tarry in the city a month, but what they will find him.

Great freshet in Virginia, Indian murders in Florida, and riots in Canada are reported in this day's *Wasp*.

Sunday, 14.—Spent the forenoon chiefly in conversation with Emma on various subjects, and in reading my history with her—both felt in good spirits and very cheerful. Wrote the following letter to Wilson Law (who was officially reported to have been duly elected to the office of major-general of the Nauvoo Legion) as follows:

Letter of the Prophet to Wilson Law—Directing the Latter How to Proceed on Certain Contingencies Arising.

HEADQUARTERS OF NAUVOO LEGION, August 14, 1842.

Major-General Law:

DEAR GENERAL:—I take this opportunity to give you some instructions how I wish you to act in case our persecutors should carry their pursuits so far as to tread upon our rights as free-born American citizens. The orders which I am about to give you, are the result of a long series of contemplations since I saw you. I have come fully to the conclusion both since this last difficulty commenced as well as before, that I never would suffer myself to go into the hands of the Missourians alive, and to go into the hands of the officers of this state is nothing more or less than to go into the hands of the Missourians; for the whole farce has been gotten up unlawfully and unconstitutionally, as well on the part of the Governor as others, by a mob spirit, for the purpose of carrying out mob violence, to carry on mob intolerance in a religious persecution. I am determined, therefore, to keep out of their hands, and thwart their designs, if possible, that perhaps they may not urge the necessity of force and bloodshed against their own fellow citizens, and loyal subjects [of the state], and become ashamed and withdraw their pursuits. But if they should not do this, and shall urge the necessity of force; and if I by any means should be taken, these are therefore to command you forthwith, without delay, regardless of life or death, to rescue me out of their hands. And further, to treat any pretensions to the contrary, unlawful and unconstitutional, and as a mob got up for the purpose of a religious persecution to take away the rights of men.

And further that our chartered rights and privileges shall be considered by us as holding the supremacy in the premises, and shall be maintained. Nothing short of the Supreme Court of this State having authority to disannul them; and the Municipal Court having jurisdiction in my case. You will see, therefore, that the peace of the city of Nauvoo is kept, let who will endeavor to disturb it. You will also see, that whenever any mob force, or violence is used on any citizen thereof, or that belongeth thereunto, you will see that that force or violence, is immediately dispersed and brought to punishment; or meet it, or contest it, at the point of the sword with firm, undaunted and unyielding valor; and let them know that the spirit of old Seventy-Six and of Washington yet lives, and is contained in the bosoms and blood of the children of the fathers. If there are any threats in the city, let legal steps be taken against them; and let no man, woman or child be intimidated, or suffer it to be done. Nevertherless, as I said in the first place, we will take every measure that lays in our power, and make every sacrifice that God or man could require at our hands to preserve the peace and safety of the people without collision. And if sacrificing my own liberty for months and years without stooping to the disgrace of Missouri persecutions and violence, and Carlin's misrule and corruption, I bow to my fate with cheerfulness, and all due deference in consideration of the lives, safety and welfare of others. But if this policy cannot accomplish the desired object let our charter and municipality, free trade, and sailor's rights be our motto, and go-ahead David Crocket like, and lay down our lives like men, and defend ourselves to the best advantage we can to the very last. You are therefore hereby authorized and commanded by virtue of the authority which I hold, and commission granted me by the executive of this state, to maintain the very letter and spirit of the above contents of this letter to the very best of your ability; to the extent of our lives and our fortunes, and to the lives and fortunes of the Legion; as also all those who may volunteer their lives and fortunes with ours; for the defense of our wives and children, our fathers and our mothers; our homes, our grave yards and our tombs; and our dead and their tombstones, and our dear bought American liberties, with the blood of our fathers and all that is dear and sacred to men.

Shall we shrink at the onset? No! Let every man's brow be as the face of a lion; let his breast be as unshaken as the mighty oak, and his knee confirmed as the sapling of the forest: and by the voice and loud roar of the cannon; and the loud peals and thundering of artillery; and by the voice of the thunderings of heaven as upon Mount Sinai; and by the voice of the heavenly hosts; and by the voice of the eternal God; and by the voice of innocent blood; and by the voice of innocence; and by the voice of all that is sacred and dear to man, let us plead the justice of our cause; trusting in the arm of Jehovah, the Eloheim, who sits enthroned in the heavens; that peradventure He may give us the victory; and if we bleed, we shall bleed in a good cause, in the cause of innocence and truth; and from henceforth will there not be a crown of glory for us? And will not those who come after hold our names in sacred remembrance? And will our enemies dare to brand us with cowardly reproach?

With these considerations, I subscribe myself, yours most faithfully and respectfully, with acknowledgments of your high and honored trusts as Major-General of the Nauvoo Legion.

JOSEPH SMITH,

Mayor of the City of Nauvoo, and Lieutenant-General of the Nauvoo Legion, of Illinois Militia.

P. S.—I want you to communicate all the information to me of all the transactions as they are going on daily, in writing, by the hands of my aides-de-camp. As I am not willing that anything that goes from my hand to you should be made a public matter, I enjoin you to keep all things in your own bosom; and I want everything that comes from you to come through my aides. The bearer of this will be able to pilot them in a way that will not be prejudicial to my safety.

JOSEPH SMITH.

I gave the foregoing letter to Emma with a charge to deliver it to General Law tomorrow. After considerable conversation on various subjects, and partaking of dinner Emma, accompanied by Brothers Derby and Clayton started for Nauvoo. The morning had been very wet, and the roads were very muddy. It was difficult walking—they proceeded to the river and entered a skiff, in which they proceeded across the river, and then down the side of the islands—soon after they got on the water, the wind began to blow very hard, and it was with much difficulty and apparent danger that they could proceed; but they continued on, and after considerable toil arrived opposite the city of Nauvoo—they went between the islands and crossed over the river to Montrose. As soon as they landed the wind abated, and was nearly calm. Brother Derby wanted to return up the river without the additional toil of crossing to Nauvoo—they met with Brother Ivins' skiff just about to go over to Nauvoo, they got into that skiff and left Brother Derby to return at his own leisure. Before they could get over the wind arose again considerably, but they arrived safe home about six o'clock in the evening, where they found Mr. Powers from Keokuk, who had just returned from Burlington. While there he ascertained that there was no writ issued in Iowa for me.

The Departure of Emma for Nauvoo.

The people inquired "if it was not true that Joseph had been commissioned by the United States to visit the Indians and negotiate with them for a tract of land," such being the report in circulation. Mr. Powers answered that he "was not authorized to assert that the report was true, but he thought that it was not only possible, but probable;" but in this Mr. Powers was mistaken.

Monday, 15.—This forenoon several reports were in circulation in the city, that the militia are on their way here, and the same is said to have been stated by the stage driver, but it is supposed that it is only a scheme to alarm the citizens. Emma presented the foregoing letter to Major-General Law, to which he responded as follows:

Letter of Wilson Law to the Prophet, Expressing Willingness to Carry out the Latter's Instructions.

NAUVOO CITY, ILLINOIS, August 15, Afternoon, 1842.

Lieutenant-General Joseph Smith:

DEAR FRIEND.—I this morning received a line from you, by the young man (Walker) respecting the guns, &c. One of them is in the stone shop by the Nauvoo house. One I expect to get put into Mr. Ivins' barn, and the other I cannot get under lock and key in any place I know of yet, but I will have them taken the best care of that I can.

I have also received from the hand of your lady your orders at length respecting matters and things, and I am happy indeed to receive such orders from you, for your views on these subjects are precisely my own. I do respond with my whole heart to every sentiment you have so nobly and so feelingly expressed, and while my heart beats, or this hand which now writes is able to write and wield a sword, you may depend on it being at your service in the glorious cause of liberty and truth, and ready in a moment's warning to defend the rights of man, both civil and religious. Our common rights and peace is all we ask, and we will use every peaceable means in our power to enjoy these; our rights we must have, peace we must have if we have to fight for it.

There has nothing worthy of notice come to my knowledge today, the gentlemen officers are seemingly very unhappy and out of humor with themselves more than with anybody else. They see we have the advantage of them and that they cannot provoke us to break the law; and I think they know if they do that, we will use them up the right way. I guess they see that in our patience we possess our souls, and I know that if they shed, or cause to be shed, a drop of blood, of one of the least amongst us, that the lives of the transgressers shall atone for it, with the help of our God.

I send you the ordinance that was passed by the court martial on

Saturday last, for your approval or otherwise, as it cannot become a law without your approbation. I also send you the returns of the election for Major-General, as you ordered the election, you will please order the war secretary of the Legion (Colonel Sloan) to send for a commission.

With the warmest feelings of my heart, I remain most respectfully yours,

WILSON LAW.

P. S.—Afternoon, 6 o'clock, I have just learned that Mr. Pitman got a letter about noon and got ready immediately, and started off, as he said for Carthage, but I think for Quincy, giving it up for a bad job.

W. L.

Unfriendly Spirit at Carthage.

About dark Brother Woolley returned from Carthage and stated that he had conversed with Chauncey Robinson, who informed him that he had ascertained that the sheriffs were determined to have me, and if they could not succeed themselves they would bring a force sufficient to search every house in the city, and if they could not find me there, they would search the state, &c.

As before stated, the sheriffs left the city, about four o'clock, saying they were going to Carthage, but Brother Woolley did not meet them on the road. It is believed they are gone to Quincy.

Calmness and Courage of the Prophet.

In consequence of these reports it was considered wisdom that some of the brethren should go and inform me. Accordingly about nine o'clock Hyrum Smith, George Miller, William Law, Amasa Lyman, John D. Parker, Newel K. Whitney and William Clayton started by different routes on foot and came to the place where I was. When the statement was made to me I proposed to leave the city, suspecting I was no longer safe, but upon hearing the whole statement from those present I said I should not leave my present retreat yet, I did not think I was discovered, neither did I think I was any more unsafe than before. I discovered a degree of excitement and agitation manifested in those who brought the report, and I took occasion to gently reprove all present for letting report excite them, and advised them not to suffer themselves to be wrought upon by any report, but to maintain an even, undaunted mind. Each one began to gather courage, and all fears were soon subsided, and the greatest union and good feeling prevailed amongst all present. Various subjects then were conversed upon, and counsel given which was felt to be most seasonable and salutary. After conversing awhile in the grove the company retired into the house and sat and conversed until about two o'clock, at which time they departed, evidently satisfied and much encouraged by the interview.

A great whirlwind at Chauffailes, France. Thirty houses were carried away, and over twenty persons killed. Six hundred houses with all they contained were burned at Ursel, Russia.

The following editorial appeared in the *Times and Seasons*:

PERSECUTION.

"If ye will live godly in Christ Jesus, ye shall suffer persecution," was the solemn proclamation made by one of the ancient servants of God; a prophecy that has received its fulfillment in all ages, that has been known and understood by all Saints, and that has been engraven upon the memories of all the faithful; for while blood, and fire, and sword, and torture, have been brought into requisition against the Saints; whilst chains, and fetters and death have been employed, and their sighings and mournings have been wafted on the wings of the wind; their solitary hours and midnight cries; their distress and calamity have been disregarded. This eternal truth has re-echoed in their ears; it has touched their inmost soul; has been written on the tablet of their hearts—"if ye will live godly in Christ Jesus, ye shall suffer persecution."

Ever since the formation of the Church of Jesus Christ of Latter-day Saints, calumny, reproach and persecution have flown plentifully into their lap—detraction, slander, falsehood, and misrepresentation have been gratuitously heaped upon them; they have been assailed by vexatious law suits, organized mobs, and illegally treated by militia; they have been imprisoned, whipped, tarred and feathered, and driven from their homes; they have had their property confiscated, and have suffered banishment, exile and death for their religion.

Missouri has been one of the principal actors in the scene; she has made many a wife a widow, and many a child an orphan. The tears of the oppressed have plentifully watered her soil; the cries of her robbed and spoiled have rung through her valleys, and been re-echoed from hill to hill; many a weary pilgrim borne down with oppression and weary of life has laid himself down to sleep in the arms of death, while the blood of the innocent has drenched her soil. And never till the trump of God shall sound, the sleeping dead shall arise, the books be opened and the secret history of peoples and nations be unfolded, will the amount of their sufferings be fully known. That day will unfold scenes of wickedness, misery and oppression, and deeds of inhumanity and blood that the most eloquent cannot portray, the pencil of the limner depict; and that is beyond the power of language to unfold—scenes of misery, of woe, and human suffering. Dipped in the malice of the most fiendish hate, the cup of misery has been wrung out, and they have drunk it to the very dregs.

Missouri, frantic with rage, and not yet filled with blood, wishes now to follow her bleeding victims to their exile, and satiate herself with blood. And not satisfied with staining her own escutcheon, she wishes to decoy the noble, generous and patriotic sons of Illinois—to deceive them with appearances—to draw them into her snare, that they may be sharer in her crimes, and participate in her guilt and stamp with eternal infamy their character. We have already to blush for the gullibility of many of her [Illinois] editors who feel desirous to fan the deadly flame, and stain their hands with her [Missouri's] foul deeds. We would advise such to halt, to pause for a moment—to reflect upon what they are doing. Have they not witnessed Missouri's wanton persecution; her cruel oppression; her deadly hate? Have they not loudly exclaimed against such proceedings; stood forth in defense of republicanism—and as true patriots defended the rights of man? And can they now advocate a cause that would attempt to make an innocent, virtuous people "tremble at the sight of gathering hosts!" or even moot the question.

Who is it that has made his affidavit that Joseph Smith has been accessory to shooting him? Governor Boggs of Missouri, a man, who, three years ago, issued an order to exterminate fifteen thousand men, women and children in republican America; a man who sanctioned mobocracy, and raised militia for that effect; a man who has been the cause of the death of scores of innocent people, and has actually been a wholesale murderer. This is the man who prefers the charge; a man who has long ago violated his constitutional oath. We deprecate at all times the commission of so diabolical a crime as that of murder if committed upon our greatest enemies; and would content ourselves with letting the Lord take vengeance into His own hands. Moreover we would seriously ask if his [Governor Boggs'] statement concerning Joseph Smith is probable, or even possible, under the circumstances mentioned by him? Could Governor Boggs swear that Joseph Smith was accessory before the fact, when he has not seen him for three years? and when Joseph Smith has not been in the state of Missouri for that length of time? Whatever his belief might be about his being engaged in the plot, he could not swear to it. Concerning Rockwell, he was in Missouri, and it is reported that he is gone there to prove himself clear, but we should think that Missouri is the last place to go for *justice;* we don't think that she is capable of administering it to the Mormons; she must, however, first atone for her bloody deeds, and refund to them what she has robbed them of before their confidence can be restored in her justice, or righteousness. But we would ask, is there no one to murder men but Mormons? Are not assassins stalking through her streets daily? Let the history of the frequent murders in St. Louis and other places in Missouri answer. But again, who does not know that Boggs has been in frequent difficulties with other people; that he has been on the point of duelling with senators, and that his life has been frequently threatened, and that not by Mormons: this we are prepared to prove. Without saying more upon this subject we will proceed to give a history of the arrest.

On Monday the 8th instant General Smith was arrested upon a warrant under the signature of Governor Carlin, in accordance, as stated, with a call from Governor Reynolds of Missouri, upon the affidavit of ex-Governor Boggs. Mr. Rockwell was arrested at the same time as the principal. There was no evasion of this call for the persons of Messrs. Smith and Rockwell. The Municipal Court, however, issued a writ of habeas corpus, according to the constitution and city charter. This writ demanded the bodies of Smith and Rockwell to be brought before the said court, but the officers in charge of these men refused to obey its call; though after some deliberation, they left them in charge of the city marshal, without the original writ by which they were arrested, and by which only they could be retained, and returned back to Governor Carlin for further instruction. Thus Messrs. Smith and Rockwell were free from the arrest, as the marshal had no authority to hold them in custody. Some two or three days after, the aforesaid officers returned, for the purpose of executing the Governor's order, without paying attention to the writ of habeas corpus issued by the Municipal Court; but Messrs. Smith and Rockwell were absent.

In a free government every person's rights and privileges are the same; no extraordinary process can issue legally, nor no extra-judicial act be required; justice, like her representative goddess, is blind to appearances, and favors no one. In this point of view, then, let us legally examine the case in question:—Mr. Boggs makes an affidavit in Missouri, and charges one O. P. Rockwell with "shooting Lilburn W. Boggs with intent to kill," on the night of the 6th of May, 1842, and that the said Rockwell had fled from justice to the state of Illinois. Shooting with intent to kill, and Mr. Boggs alive two or three months after to swear to it may be set down as insufficient grounds for writ from the governor of one state, to demand a person as a fugitive from justice in another state. For aught that appears to the contrary, he might have shot in his own defense and been justifiable; as the charge is not grounded on the wilful, malicious, or felonious intent, without the fear of God before his eyes, to murder. The affidavit is therefore not sufficient for the apprehension, detention and transportation of the said Rockwell to the courts of Missouri. Here we deny that the Orrin P. Rockwell arrested is the one intended in the writ, this Rockwell being not guilty.

If Mr. Boggs *knew*, of himself, the fact that Mr. Rockwell shot at him with intent to kill, why did he delay the prosecution some two or three months? If he obtained his knowledge from a second or third person, why not avail himself of their affidavits in the body of the writ?

Again, Mr. Boggs charges one Mr. Joseph Smith with being "accessory before the fact to an assault with intent to kill," on the night of the sixth of May, 1842. This must allude to some other Joseph Smith, as the Joseph Smith of this city, was in Nauvoo on the aforesaid sixth of May, 1842, and on the next day he was at his post as Lieut. Gen. of the Nauvoo Legion. Nor can it be proved that he has been in the state of Missouri for the last three years.

But for the sake of argument admit the language of the writ, and Joseph Smith as an accessory before the fact, with intent to kill, must have aided or abetted by words, or by means, while in the state of Illinois, and cannot come under the purview of the fugitive act. Having not fled from justice from another state; and, according to the express language of the constitution; "he could not be liable to be transported out of the state for an offense committed within the same."

An accessory before the fact in man-slaughter is an anomaly—and now if *the* Joseph Smith of Nauvoo, has committed a crime of the nature charged in the writ, which we deny *in toto*, he should he held amenable to the laws of Illinois, and in the ordinary course of procedure by indictment, in accordance with the right of the constitution, which says that he should have a "speedy public trial by an impartial jury of the vicinage."

Judging now from all the facts of the case, taking the two affidavits together, we must say that the whole forms but a poor excuse for executive interference, and when properly weighed by good judges of law in criminal jurisprudence, will be found wanting in all the important counts which constitute a fair case.

As to the writ of habeas corpus, issued by the Municipal Court of the city of Nauvoo, it was not acted upon, though we believe that so long as it was not incompatible with the spirit and meaning of the constitution of the state, and of the constitution of the United States, its power was sovereign, as to the rights and privileges of citizens, granted to them by the City Charter, having these express privileges, in words as follows: "To make, ordain, establish and execute all such ordinances, not repugnant to the constitution of the United States and of this state, as they may deem necessary for the peace, benefit, good order, regulation, convenience and cleanliness of the city"—*and* "the Municipal Court shall have power to grant writs of habeas corpus in all cases arising under the ordinance of the city council."

Now, it is well known that if this court exceeded the bounds of the chartered power, or transcended the limits of the constitution of the state, or United States, it could be made to respond in a writ of *quo warranto;* and, as a writ of habeas corpus can only test the *validity*, not the virtue of a process (as testimony to prove the *guilt* or *innocence* of a person—under an investigation by habeas corpus, is inadmissible), we believe, that judges, lawyers, and jurors, will not be very apprehensive that the law of the land, or the rights of the people, will *suffer violence* on this account.

Under the existing animosity of the inhabitants of the state of Missouri, manifested towards the Church of Latter-day Saints, prudence would dictate great caution, and forbearance in the proceedings of public functionaries, relative to claims for persons or property in favor of either party, holding sacred the old maxim: "That it would be better to let ninety and nine guilty persons go unpunished, than to punish one innocent person unjustly."

Concerning the whole matter, we believe that the parties are entirely innocent of the charges alleged against them; and that the whole of it is a wicked and malicious persecution. But it may here be asked by some, if they are innocent, why did they not apply to the master in chancery for a writ of habeas corpus, present themselves before the judge of the District Court, and prove themselves clear?

First, we would answer, that the writ of our Municipal Court was treated with contempt by the officers, and it would have been dishonoring our municipal authorities to have acknowledged the insufficiency of their writ, and to have let our city charter be wantonly trodden under foot; and that could not have been enforced without coersion, and perhaps employing military force, which under the present excited state of society might have been construed to treason.

In the second place, if they appealed to the District Court it might have availed them nothing, even if the judge felt disposed to do justice (which we certainly believe he would have done) as their dismissal would rest upon some technicalities of law, rather than upon the merits of the case; as testimony to prove the guilt or innocence of the persons charged, could not be admitted on the investigation on a writ of habeas corpus, the question not being whether the persons are guilty or not guilty; but merely to test the validity of the writ; which if proved to be issued in due form of law, however innocent the parties might be, would subject them to be transported to Missouri—to be murdered.

Upon the whole we think that they have taken the wisest course; we have no reflections to make upon their conduct, and shall maintain unshaken our opinions unless we have more light on the subject than we now possess.

Tuesday, August 16.—Wrote as follows:—

The Prophet's Letter to Emma Smith—Detailing Prospective Movements.

NAUVOO, August 16, 1842.

MY DEAR EMMA:—I embrace this opportunity to express to you some of my feelings this morning. First of all, I take the liberty to tender you my sincere thanks for the two interesting and consoling visits that you have made me during my almost exiled situation. Tongue cannot express the gratitude of my heart, for the warm and true-hearted friendship you have manifested in these things towards me. The time has passed away, since you left me, very agreeably thus far; my mind being perfectly reconciled to my fate, let it be what it may. I have been kept from melancholy and dumps, by the kind-heartedness of Brother Derby, and his interesting chit-chat from time to time, which has called my mind from the more strong contemplation of things and subjects that would have preyed more earnestly upon my feelings.

Last night Brothers Hyrum, Miller, Law, and others came to see us. They seemed much agitated, and expressed some fears in consequence of some maneuverings and some flying reports which they had heard in relation to our safety; but, after relating what it was, I was able to comprehend the whole matter to my entire satisfaction, and did not feel at all alarmed or uneasy. They think, however, that the militia will be called out to search the city; and if this should be the case, I would be much safer for the time being at a little distance off, until Governor Carlin could get weary, and be made ashamed of his corrupt and unhallowed proceedings. I had supposed, however, that if there were any serious operations taken by the governor, that Judge Ralston, or Brother Hollister would have notified us; and cannot believe that anything very serious is to be apprehended, until we obtain information from a source that can be relied upon.

I have consulted whether it is best for you to go to Quincy and see the Governor; but, on the whole, he is a fool; and the impressions that are suggested to my mind are, that it will be of no use; and the more we notice him and flatter him, the more eager he will be for our destruction. You may write to him whatever you see proper, but to go and see him, I do not give my consent at present.

Brother Miller again suggested to me the propriety of my accompanying him to the Pine Woods, and then he return, and bring you and the children. My mind will eternally revolt at every suggestion of that kind, more especially since the dream and vision that was manifested to me on the last night. My safety is with you, if you want to have it so. Anything more or less than this cometh of evil. My feelings and counsel I think ought to be abided. If I go to the Pine country, you shall go along with me, and the children; and if you and the children go not with me, I don't go. I do not wish to exile myself for the sake of my own life, I would rather fight it out. It is for your sakes, therefore, that I would do such a thing. I will go with you, then, in the same carriage, and on horseback from time to time as occasion may require; for I am not willing to trust you in the hands of those who cannot feel the same interest for you that I feel; to be subject to the caprice, temptations, or notions of anybody whatever. And I must say that I am prepossessed somewhat with the notion of going to the Pine country anyhow; for I am tired of the mean, low, and unhallowed vulgarity of some portions of the society in which we live; and I think if I could have a respite of about six months with my family, it would be a savor of life unto life, with my house. Nevertheless, if it were possible, I would like to live here in peace and wind up my business; but if it should be ascertained to a dead certainty that there is no other remedy, then we will round up our shoulders and cheerfully endure it; and this will be the plan: Let my horse, saddle, saddle-bags, and valise to put some shirts and clothing in, be sent to me. Let Brothers Derby and Miller take a horse and put it into my buggy, with a trunk containing my heavier clothes, shoes, boots,&c.; and let Brother Taylor accompany us to his father's, and there we will tarry, taking every precaution to keep out of the hands of the enemy, until you can arrive with the children. Let Brother Hyrum bring you. Let Lorin Farr and Brother Clayton come along, and bring all the writings, and papers, books, and histories, for we shall want a scribe in order that we may pour upon the world the truth, like the lava from Mount Vesuvius. Then, let all the goods, household furniture, clothes, and store goods that can be procured be put on the boat, and let twenty or thirty of the best men that we can find be put on board to man it, and let them meet us at Prairie-du-Chien; and from thence we will wend our way like larks up the Mississippi, until the towering mountains and rocks shall remind us of the places of our nativity, and shall look like safety and home; and then we will bid defiance to the world, to Carlin, Boggs, Bennett, and all their whorish whores and motly clan, that follow in their wake, Missouri not excepted, and until the damnation of hell rolls upon them, by the voice, and dread thunders, and trump of the eternal God. Then in that day will we not shout in the victory, and be crowned with eternal joys, for the battles we have fought, having kept the faith and overcome the world?

Tell the children it is well with their father as yet; and that he remains in fervent prayer to Almighty God for the safety of himself, and for you, and for them.

Tell Mother Smith that it shall be well with her son, whether in life or in death; for thus saith the Lord God. Tell her that I remember her all the while, as well as Lucy, and all the rest. They all must be of good cheer.

Tell Hyrum to be sure and not fail to carry out my instructions; but, at the same time if the militia does not come, and we should get any favorable information, all may be well yet.

Yours in haste, your affectionate husband until death, through all eternity; for evermore.

JOSEPH SMITH.

P. S.—I want you to write to Lorenzo D. Wasson, and get him to make affidavit to all he knows about Bennett, and forward it. I also want you to ascertain from Hyrum whether he will conform to what I have requested; and you must write me an answer per bearer, giving me all the news you have, and what is the appearance of things this morning.

J. S.

I also wrote General Law as follows:—

Joseph Smith's Letter to Wilson Law—Concerning Probable Movements of the Prophet.

HEADQUARTERS NAUVOO LEGION, August 16, 1842.

Major-General Law:

BELOVED BROTHER AND FRIEND:—Those few lines which I received from you, written on the 15th, were to me like apples of gold in pictures of silver. I rejoice with exceeding great joy to be associated in the high and responsible stations which we hold, [with one] whose mind and feelings and heart are so congenial with my own. I love that soul that is so nobly entabernacled in that clay of yours. May God Almighty grant that it may be satiated with seeing a fulfillment of every virtuous and manly desire that you possess! May we be able to triumph gloriously over those who seek our destruction and overthrow, which I believe we shall.

The news you wrote me is more favorable than that which was communicated by the brethren. They seemed a little agitated for my safety, and advised me for the Pine Woods country, but I succeeded admirably in calming all their fears; but, nevertheless, as I said in my former letter, I was willing to exile myself for months and years, if it would be for the welfare and safety of the people; and I do not know but it would be as well for me to take a trip to the Pine countries, and remain until arrangements can be made for my most perfect safety when I return. These are, therefore, to confer with you on this subject, as I want to have a concert of action in everything I do. If I knew that they would oppress me alone, and let the rest of you dwell peaceably and quietly, I think it would be the wisest plan to absent myself for a little season, if by that means we could prevent the effusion of blood.

Please write and give me your mind on that subject, and all other information that has come to hand today, and what are the signs of the times. I have no news, for I am where I cannot get much. All is quiet and peaceable around. I therefore wait with earnest expectation for your advices. I am anxious to know your opinion on any course that I may see proper to take, for in the multitude of counsel there is safety.

I add no more, but subscribe myself your faithful and most obedient servant, friend, and brother,

JOSEPH SMITH,
Lieut.-General of the Nauvoo Legion of Illinois Militia.

The foregoing letters were delivered to Brother Derby, who proceeded immediatedly to the city.

Brother Derby has taken the greatest interest in my welfare, and I feel to bless him.

Blessing of the Prophet upon Erastus H. Derby.

Blessed is Brother Erastus H. Derby, and he shall be blessed of the Lord. He possesses a sober mind, and a faithful heart. The snares therefore that will subsequently befall other men, who are treacherous and rotten hearted, shall not come nigh unto his doors, but shall be far from the path of his feet. He loveth wisdom and shall be found possessed of her. Let there be a crown of glory and a diadem upon his head. Let the light of eternal truth shine forth upon his understanding; let his name be had in everlasting remembrance; let the blessings of Jehovah be crowned upon his posterity after him, for he rendered me consolation in the lonely places of my retreat. How good and glorious it has seemed unto me, to find pure and holy friends, who are faithful, just, and true, and whose hearts fail not; and whose knees are confirmed and do not falter, while they wait upon the Lord, in administering to my necessities, in the day when the wrath of mine enemies was poured out upon me.

In the name of the Lord, I feel in my heart to bless them, and to say in the name of Jesus Christ of Nazareth, that these are the ones that shall inherit eternal life. I say it by virtue of the Holy Priesthood, and by the ministering of holy angels, and by the gift and power of the Holy Ghost.

Sentiments of the Prophet Towards His Wife Emma.

How glorious were my feelings when I met that faithful and friendly band, on the night of the eleventh, on Thursday, on the island at the mouth of the slough, between Zarahemla and Nauvoo: with what unspeakable delight, and what transports of joy swelled my bosom, when I took by the hand, on that night, my beloved Emma—she that was my wife, even the wife of my youth, and the choice of my heart. Many were the reverberations of my mind when I contemplated for a moment the many scenes we had been called to pass through, the fatigues and the toils, the sorrows and sufferings, and the joys and consolations, from time to time, which had strewed our paths and crowned our board. Oh what a commingling of thought filled my mind for the moment, again she is here, even in the seventh trouble—undaunted, firm, and unwavering—unchangeable, affectionate Emma!

The Prophet's Love for His Brother Hyrum.

There was Brother Hyrum who next took me by the hand—a natural brother. Thought I to myself, Brother Hyrum, what a faithful heart you have got! Oh may the Eternal Jehovah crown eternal blessings upon your head, as a reward for the care you have had for my soul! O how many are the sorrows we have shared together; and again we find ourselves shackled with the unrelenting hand of oppression. Hyrum, thy name shall be written in the book of the law of the Lord, for those who come after thee to look upon, that they may pattern after thy works.

Said I to myself, Here is Brother Newel K. Whitney also. How many scenes of sorrows have strewed our paths together; and yet we meet once more to share again. Thou art a faithful friend in whom the afflicted sons of men can confide, with the most perfect safety. Let the blessings of the Eternal also be crowned upon his head. How warm that heart! how anxious that soul! for the welfare of one who has been cast out, and hated of almost all men. Brother Whitney, thou knowest not how strong those ties are that bind my soul and heart to thee.

The Band Between the Prophet and Newel K. Whitney.

My heart was overjoyed as I took the faithful band by the hand, that stood upon the shore, one by one. William Law, William Clayton, Dimick B. Huntington, George Miller, were there. The above names constituted the little group.

I do not think to mention the particulars of the history of that sacred night, which shall forever be remembered by me; but the names of the faithful are what I wish to record in this place. These I have met in prosperity, and they were my friends; and I now meet them in adversity, and they are still my warmer friends. These love the God that I serve; they love the truths that I promulgate; they love those virtuous, and those holy doctrines that I cherish in my bosom with the warmest feelings of my heart, and with that zeal which cannot be denied. I love friendship and truth; I love virtue and law; I love the God of Abraham, of Isaac, and of Jacob; and they are my brethren, and I shall live;

The Prophet's Exaltation of Spirit.

and because I live they shall live also. These are not the only ones who have administered to my necessity and whom the Lord will bless. There is Brother John D. Parker and Brother Amasa Lyman, and Brother Wilson Law, and Brother Henry G. Sherwood. My heart feels to reciprocate the unwearied kindnesses that have been bestowed upon me by these men. They are men of noble stature, of noble hands, and of noble deeds; possessing noble, and daring, and giant hearts and souls. There is Brother Joseph B. Noble also, I would call up in remembrance before the Lord. There is Brother Samuel H. Smith, a natural brother—he is even as Hyrum. There is Brother Arthur Millikin also, who married my youngest sister, Lucy: he is a faithful, an honest, and an upright man.

The Prophet's Gratitude.

While I call up in remembrance before the Lord these men, I would be doing injustice to those who rowed me in the skiff up the river that night, after I parted with the lovely group—who brought me to this my safe, and lonely, and private retreat—Brother Jonathan Dunham, and the other, whose name I do not know. Many were the thoughts that swelled my aching heart, while they were toiling faithfully with their oars. They complained not of hardship and fatigue to secure my safety. My heart would have been harder than an adamantine stone, if I had not prayed for them with anxious and fervent desire. I did so, and the still small voice whispered to my soul: These, that share your toils with such faithful hearts, shall reign with you in the kingdom of their God; but I parted with them in silence, and came to my retreat. I hope I shall see them again, that I may toil for them, and administer to their comfort also. They shall not want a friend while I live; my heart shall love those, and my hands shall toil for those, who love and toil for me, and shall ever be found faithful to my friends. Shall I be ungrateful? Verily no! God forbid!

I design to continue this subject at a future time.

CHAPTER VI.

CORRESPONDENCE BETWEEN JOSEPH SMITH AND WILSON LAW, ET AL.—THE PROPHET ON THE ATTITUDE OF GOVERNOR CARLIN TOWARDS HIMSELF AND THE SAINTS—REVIVAL OF THE ZEAL OF SIDNEY RIGDON—THE PROPHET'S BLESSINGS UPON HIS FRIENDS.

Tuesday, August 16, 1842.—Brother Derby returned in the evening, bringing the following letter:

Letter of Emma Smith to Joseph Smith, Relating to the Future Movements of the Prophet, and Items of Business.

DEAR HUSBAND:—I am ready to go with you if you are obliged to leave; and Hyrum says he will go with me. I shall make the best arrangements I can and be as well prepared as possible. But still I feel good confidence that you can be protected without leaving this country. There are more ways than one to take care of you, and I believe that you can still direct in your business concerns if we are all of us prudent in the matter. If it was pleasant weather I should contrive to see you this evening, but I dare not run too much of a risk, on account of so many going to see you.

General Adams sends the propositions concerning his land, two dollars an acre, payments as follows: Assumption of mortgage, say about fourteen hundred, interest included. Taxes due, supposed about thirty dollars. Town property one thousand dollars. Balance, money payable in one, two, three or four years.

Brother Derby will tell you all the information we have on hand. I think we will have news from Quincy as soon as tomorrow.

Yours affectionately forever,

EMMA SMITH.

Letter of Wilson Law to Joseph Smith—Advises Retirement of the Prophet from Nauvoo until Next Governor Takes his Seat of Office.

NAUVOO CITY, ILLINOIS, 1 o'clock, afternoon, August 16, 1842.

Lieutenant-General Joseph Smith:

MY DEAR FRIEND.—I have just received and read yours of today, and hasten to reply.

There is no movement of any kind going on today amongst the enemy, as far as I can see, which helps to strengthen me in my opinion of yesterday; but still it might be a calm before a storm,and if so we will meet it when it comes. You wish my opinion respecting your absenting yourself for some time from those friends that are dear to you as life, and to whom you are also as dear, and from the place and station to which you are called by Him who ruleth in the armies of heaven and amongst the inhabitants of the earth.

I must confess that I feel almost unworthy to give an opinion on the subject, knowing that your own judgment is far superior to mine; but nevertheless you shall have it freely. It is this: I think that if they cannot get you peaceably according to the forms of law, that they will not dare to attempt violence of any kind upon the inhabitants of the city; for they are well aware that they cannot insult us with impunity, neither use violence, only at the risk of their lives; and there are but few men who are willing to risk their lives in a bad cause. It is the principles and spirit of liberty, of truth, of virtue, and of religion, and equal rights, that make men courageous, and valiant and fearless in the day of battle and of strife, and just the contrary with the oppressor; for nine times out of ten, a bad cause will make a man a coward, and he will flee when no man pursueth.

Now if I am right in thinking that it is you alone they seek to destroy, as soon as they find they cannot get you, they will cease to trouble the city except with spies; and if we knew that you were completely out of their reach, we could either laugh at their folly, or whip them for impertinence or anything else, as the case may be; for we would feel so happy in your safety, that we could meet them in any shape.

On the whole, I think it would be better for you to absent yourself till the next governor takes the chair, for I do think if you are not here they will not attempt any violence on the city; and if they should, they will disgrace themselves in the eyes of the world, and the world will justify us in fighting for our rights, and then you can come out like a lion, and lead your people to victory and to glory in the name of the Lord of Hosts.

I know the sacrifice you must make in taking this course. I know it will grieve your noble spirit to do so; for when I think of it myself, I feel no desire in life but to fight, and to cut off from the earth all who oppress, and to establish that true form of government at once, which would guarantee to every man equal rights. I know we have justice on our side in respect of city laws, and that the acts of the Municipal Court are legal; but the question is, are we now able to assert them? or had we better wait till we are more able? The latter course will give us peace a little while, by sacrificing your liberty, and the feelings of your family and friends,and depriving us all of your society and governing wisdom.

I will only add I am ready for either course; and may God direct us to do that that is best. If you should conclude to go for awhile, I must see you before you go; and for the present, I will bid you be cheerful, and make yourself as happy as you can, for the right side of the wheel will soon be up again.

And till then and forever, I remain under every circumstance, your friend and obedient servant,

WILSON LAW.

General James Arlington Bennett wrote me from New York as follows:

Letter of James Arlington Bennett to Joseph Smith, Anent John C. Bennet and his Forthcoming Anti-Mormon Book.

ARLINGTON HOUSE, August 16, 1842.

DEAR SIR.—Your polite and friendly note was handed to me a few days since by Dr. Willard Richard's, who I must say, is a very fine specimen of the Mormon people, if they are all like him; and indeed I think him a very excellent representative of yourself, as I find he is your most devoted admirer and true disciple. He spent two days with me, and from his arguments, and from his mild and gentlemanly demeanor, almost made me a Mormon.

You have another representative here (who spent a day with me some time since) of the name of Foster, who is, I think, president of the Church in New York, and most unquestionably a most excellent and good man, and would be so if he were Turk, Jew or Saint. He is *ab initio*, a good man, and to you a most true, enthusiastic and devoted disciple. He has no guile. Dr. Bernhisel, of New York, too, is a most excellent man and true Christian. These are men with whom I could associate forever, even if I never joined their Church or acknowledged their faith.

General John C. Bennett called on me last Friday and spent just two hours, when he left, he said for the Eastern States. Being aware that Elder Richards is here, he had very little to say. He, however, proposed to me to aid him, whether serious or not, in arranging materials for publishing "An Exposition of Mormon Secrets and Practices," which I promptly refused, on two grounds:

1st. That I had nothing to do with any quarrel that might arise between you and him, as I could not be a judge of the merits or demerits of the matter: and

2nd. That inasmuch as he himself had proposed to you and your council to confer on me honors which I never sought, yet which I highly prize, it would be the height of ingratitude, as well as inconsistent with every principle of common honesty and propriety, for me to join him in an effort to lower my own honors by attempting to lower in public estimation the people from whom those honors emanated.

He gave Bennett of the *Herald* his commission, which I opposed from the very first; and you now see, by that paper, the sport which that man has made of it. I tell you there is no dependence on the friendship of that editor, when his interest is at issue. I am assured that James Gordon Bennett is going to publish, conjointly with John C. Bennett, on half profit, the exposition against you and your people, which is going to contain a great number of scandalous cuts and plates. But don't be concerned; you will receive no injury whatever from any thing any man or set of men may say against you. The whole of this muss is only extending your fame, and will increase your numbers tenfold.

You have nothing to expect from that part of the community who are bigotedly attached to other churches. They have always believed and still believe everything said to your disadvantage; and what General John C. Bennett is now saying in the papers is nothing more than what was common report before, throughout this whole community, insomuch that I had to contradict it in the *Herald* under the signature of "Cincinnatus"—and even requested the Elders of the Mormon Church to do so long ago. You, therefore have lost not a whit of ground by it. I must in charity forbear commenting on the course of General Bennett in this matter. Considering all things delicacy forbids such a course.

There are some things, however, I feel very sorely, and could wish they had not transpired. He and the *Herald* will make money out of the book, and there the matter will end, as you will find that the *Herald* will puff it to the skies.*

The books which I sent you you will retain in your hands for the present.

* Bennett's book, "The History of the Saints, or an Exposure of Joseph Smith and Mormonism," was not published by the New York *Herald*, but by a Boston publishing house, Leland & Whiting, 71 Washington St. The book was a failure from every point of view, in structure, literary merit and convincing power. The insincerity and the corrupt-mindedness of the author is loudly proclaimed by the ribald spirit that pervades the whole work.

My respects to your amiable lady and all friends; and believe me as ever, though not a Mormon, your sincere friend,

JAMES ARLINGTON BENNETT.

P. S.—I know of no reason why the *Wasp* was not continued to be sent to me. I don't like the name. Mildness should characterize everything that comes from Nauvoo; and even a name, as Peleg says in his ethics, has much influence on one side or the other. My respects to your brother, its editor. I would just say that General John C. Bennett appeared to me to be in very low spirits, and I find that many communications intended for you from me have never reached you. Those books were made over to John C. Bennett, on the presumption that he would, in his own name, present them for the benefit of the Temple.

J. A. B.

Wednesday, August 17.—I walked out into the woods for exercise in company with Brother Derby where we were accidentally discovered by a young man. We asked him various questions concerning the public feeling and situation of matters around, to all which he answered promptly. On being requested not to make it known where we were, he promised faithfully he would not, and said time would tell whether he did or no.

The Prophet's Place of Retirement Discovered.

Letter of Wilson Law to Joseph Smith—Advising that the Prophet Secrete Himself in Nauvoo.

NAUVOO CITY, ILLINOIS, August 17, 1842.

Lieutenant-General Joseph Smith:

DEAR FRIEND:—Everything is moving along in the city in the usual tranquil and industrious manner. There is no change in the appearance of things that a common observer could see, although to one who knows and is acquainted with the countenances of the thinking few, it is evident that their minds are troubled more than common; and I know by myself that they cannot help it. And why should it be otherwise, when the Lord's anointed is hunted like a lion of the forest, by the most wicked and oppressive generation that has ever been since the days of our Savior. Indeed, every movement of this generation reminds me of the history of the people who crucified Christ. It was nothing but mob law, mob rule, and mob violence all the time. The only difference is that the governors then were more just than the governors now; they were willing to acquit innocent men, but our governors now despise justice, garble and pervert the law, and join in with the mob in pursuit of innocent blood.

I have been meditating on your communication of yesterday, and will just add a thought or so on the subject, respecting particularly your going to the Pine country. I think I would not go there for some time, if at all. do not believe that an armed force will come upon us at all unless they get hold of you first; and then we rescue you, which we would do under any circumstances, with the help of God; but I would rather do it within the limits of the city, under the laws of the city. Therefore I would think it better to quarter in the city and not long in one place at once. I see no reason why you might not stay in safety within the city for months without any knowing it, only those who ought, and that as few as is necessary.

I must close for the present, remaining as ever, your affectionate friend and obedient servant,

WILSON LAW.

Letter of Emma Smith to Governor Carlin—Pleading the Cause of the Prophet and the People of Nauvoo Before his Excellency.

NAUVOO, August 17, 1842.

To his Excellency Governor Carlin:

SIR:—It is with feeling of no ordinary cast that I have retired, after the business of the day, and evening too, to address your honor. I am at a loss how to commence; my mind is crowded with subjects too numerous to be contained in one letter. I find myself almost destitute of that confidence, necessary to address a person holding the authority of your dignified and responsible office; and I would now offer, as an excuse for intruding upon your time and attention, the justice of my cause.

Was my cause the interest of an individual, or of a number of individuals, then, perhaps, I might be justified in remaining silent. But it is not. Nor is it the pecuniary interest of a whole community alone that prompts me again to appeal to your Excellency. But, dear Sir, it is for the peace and safety of hundreds, I may safely say, of this community, who are not guilty of any offense against the laws of the country; and also the life of my husband, who has not committed any crime whatever; neither has he transgressed any of the laws, or any part of the Constitution of the United States; neither has he at any time infringed upon the rights of any man, or of any class of men, or community of any description. Need I say he is not guilty of the crime alleged against him by Governor Boggs? Indeed it does seem entirely superfluous for me, or any one of his friends in this place, to testify his innocence of that crime, when so many of the citizens of your place, and of many other places in this state, as well as in the Territory, [of Iowa] do know positively that the statement of Governor Boggs is without the least shadow of truth: and we do know, and so do many others, that the prosecution against him has been conducted in an illegal manner; and every act demonstrates the fact that all the design of the prosecution is to throw him into the power of his enemies, without the least ray of hope that he would ever be allowed to obtain a fair trial: and that he would be inhumanly and ferociously murdered, no person, having a knowledge of the existing circumstances, has one remaining doubt: and your honor will recollect that you said to me that you would not advise Mr. Smith ever to trust himself in Missouri.

And, dear Sir, you cannot for one moment indulge unfriendly feeling towards him, if he abides by your counsel. Then, Sir, why is it that he should be thus cruelly pursued? Why not give him the privilege of the laws of this state? When I reflect upon the many cruel and illegal operations of Lilburn W. Boggs, and the consequent suffering of myself and family, and the incalculable losses and sufferings of many hundreds who survived, and the many precious lives that were lost,—all the effect of unjust prejudice and misguided ambition, produced by misrepresentation and calumny, my bosom heaves with unutterable anguish. And who, that is as well acquainted with the facts as the people at the city of Quincy, would censure me, if I should say that my heart burned with just indignation towards our calumniators as well as the perpetrators of those horrid crimes?

But happy would I now be to pour out my heart in gratitude to Governor Boggs, if he had rose up with the dignity and authority of the chief executive of the state, and put down every illegal transaction, and protected the peaceable citizens and enterprising immigrants from the violence of plundering outlaws, who have ever been a disgrace to the state, and always will, so long as they go unpunished. Yes, I say, how happy would I be to render him not only the gratitude of my own heart, but the cheering effusions of the joyous souls of fathers and mothers, of brothers and sisters, widows and orphans, whom he might have saved, by such a course, from now drooping under the withering hand of adversity, brought upon them by the persecutions of wicked and corrupt men.

And now may I entreat your Excellency to lighten the hand of oppression and persecution which is laid upon me and my family, which materially affect the peace and welfare of this whole community; for let me assure you that there are many whole families that are entirely dependent upon the prosecution and success of Mr. Smith's temporal business for their support; and, if he is prevented from attending to the common vocations of life, who will employ those innocent, industrious, poor people, and provide for their wants?

But, my dear Sir, when I recollect the interesting interview I and my friends had with you, when at your place, and the warm assurances you gave us of your friendship and legal protection, I cannot doubt for a moment your honorable sincerity; but do still expect you to consider our claims upon your protection from every encroachment upon our legal rights as loyal citizens, as we always have been, still are, and are determined always to be a law-abiding people; and I still assure myself that, when you are fully acquainted with the illegal proceedings practiced against us in the suit of Governor Boggs, you will recall those writs which have been issued against Mr. Smith and Rockwell, as you must be aware that Mr. Smith was not in Missouri, and of course he could not have left there; with many other considerations, which, if duly considered, will justify Mr. Smith in the course he has taken.

And now I appeal to your Excellency, as I would unto a father, who is not only able but willing to shield me and mine from every unjust prosecution. I appeal to your sympathies, and beg you to spare me and my helpless children. I beg you to spare my innocent children the heart-rending sorrow of again seeing their father unjustly dragged to prison, or to death. I appeal to your affections as a son, and beg you to spare our aged mother—the only surviving parent we have left—the unsupportable affliction of seeing her son, whom she knows to be innocent of the crimes laid to his charge, thrown again into the hands of his enemies, who have so long sought for his life; in whose life and prosperity she only looks for the few remaining comforts she can enjoy. I entreat of your Excellency to spare us these afflictions and many sufferings which cannot be uttered, and secure to yourself the pleasure of doing good, and vastly increasing human happiness—secure to yourself the benediction of the aged, and the gratitude of the young, and the blessing and the veneration of the rising generation.

Respectfully, your most obedient,

EMMA SMITH.

P. S.—Sir, I hope you will favor me with an answer.

E. S.

Several rumors were afloat in the city, intimating that my retreat had been discovered, and that it was no longer safe for me to remain at Brother Sayers'; consequently

Emma came to see me at night, and informed me of the report. It was considered wisdom that I should remove immediately, and accordingly I departed in company with Emma and Brother Derby, and went to Carlos Granger's, who lived in the north-east part of the city. Here we were kindly received and well treated.

The Prophet's Removal to Carlos Granger's in Nauvoo.

Friday morning, 19. William Clayton presented Emma's letter of the 17th to Governor Carlin at Quincy, in presence of Judge Ralston. The governor read the letter with much attention, apparently; and when he got through, he passed high encomiums on Emma Smith, and expressed astonishment at the judgment and talent manifest in the manner of her address. He presented the letter to Judge Ralston, requesting him to read it. Governor Carlin then proceeded to reiterate the same language as on a former occasion, viz., that he was satisfied there was "no excitement anywhere but in Nauvoo, amongst the 'Mormons' themselves;" all was quiet, and no apprehension of trouble in other places, so far as he was able to ascertain.

Governor Carlin's Views of Affairs in Nauvoo.

He afterwards stated, when conversing on another subject, that "persons were offering their services every day, either in person or by letter, and held themselves in readiness to go against the 'Mormons' whenever he should call upon them; but he never had the least idea of calling out the militia, neither had he thought it necessary."

There was evidently a contradiction in his assertions in the above instances; and, although he said "there was no excitement but amongst the Mormons," it is evident he knew better. He also said that it was his opinion that, if Joseph would give himself up to the sheriff, he would be honorably acquitted, and the matter would be ended; but, on Judge Ralston asking how he thought Mr. Smith could go through the midst of his enemies, without violence being used towards him; and, if acquitted, how he was to get back; the governor was evidently at a loss what to say, but made light of the matter, as though he thought it might be easily done. He took great care to state that it was not his advice that Mr. Smith should give himself up, but thought it would be soonest decided. It appeared evident, by the conversation, that Governor Carlin was no friend to the Saints, and they could expect no good things from him. He explicitly acknowledged his ignorance of the law touching the case in question.

The Prophet's Return to His Home.

After spending the day in conversation and reading, in the evening I received a visit from my aunt Temperance Mack, and at night went to the city and concluded to tarry at home until something further transpired relative to the designs of my persecutors.

Saturday, 20.—Spent the day in my general business office, otherwise called the Lodge, or Assembly Room, or Council Chamber, which is over my store, and the place where most of the business of the city and Church is transacted: my health very indifferent. In the evening had an interview with my Brother Hyrum, William Law, Wilson Law, Newel K. Whitney and George Miller, on the illegality of the proceedings of our persecutors.

Minutes of the Nauvoo High Council Meeting, August 20th, 1842.

The High Council, in session, "Resolved that the city of Nauvoo be divided into ten [ecclesiastical] wards, according to the division made by the temple committee; and that there be a bishop appointed over each ward; and also that other bishops be appointed over such districts immediately out of the city and adjoining thereto as shall be considered necessary. Resolved that Samuel H. Smith be appointed bishop in the place of Bishop Vinson Knight, deceased; also that Tarleton Lewis be appointed bishop of the 4th ward; John Murdock, of the 5th ward; Daniel Garn, of the 6th ward; Newel K. Whitney, of the 7th ward; Jacob Foutz, of the 8th ward; Jonathan H. Hale, of the 9th ward; Hezekiah Peck, of the 10th ward; David Evans, of the district south of the city, called the 11th ward; Israel Calkins, of the district east of the city, and south of Knight street; William W. Spencer, of the district east of the city and north of Knight street." *

The city council instructed the sexton to report weekly to the editor of some newspaper published in this city, the names and ages of persons deceased, and the nature of their disease, or cause of their death.

Ordination of Amasa M. Lyman to the Apostleship.

The Twelve met in council, and ordained Amasa Lyman to be one of the Twelve Apostles. Amasa Lyman was born in Lyman, Grafton county, N. H., 30th March, 1813, where he received the gospel through the ministry of Elder Orson Pratt, 27th April, 1832; ordained an elder under my hands, 23rd August, 1832, in Hiram, Portage county, Ohio. He was one of my fellow-prisoners, bound with the same chain in Richmond jail, Missouri.

John C. Bennett Deposed as Chancellor of Nauvoo University.

John C. Bennett was declared unworthy to hold the office of chancellor of the University, and was discharged; and Orson Spencer was elected in his stead, and received the oath of office. Amasa Lyman was elected regent of the University, in place of Vinson Knight, deceased.

* On March 1st, 1842, Nauvoo was divided into four ecclesiastical wards, (CHURCH HISTORY, Vol. IV, pp. 305-6), and four bishops were set to preside over them, viz.: Newel K. Whitney, George Miller, Isaac Higbee, and Vinson Knight, (See "History of the Aaronic Priesthood"—Orson F. Whitney—*Contributor*, Vol. VI, p. 405). There is, however, some uncertainty as to the respective wards over which these bishops presided. Previous to this division of Nauvoo into four wards, there had been but three wards, known as the middle, upper and lower wards, which division was recognized at the October conference held at Commerce (afterwards Nauvoo) on the 6th, 7th and 8th of October, 1839. Edward Partridge was made bishop of the upper ward; Newel K. Whitney of the middle ward; and Vinson Knight of the lower ward, (see HISTORY OF THE CHURCH, Vol. IV, p. 12). When the division of the city into four wards was made on the 1st of March, 1842, Isaac Higbee, was made bishop of the 2nd ward (see autobiographical sketch of Isaac Higbee in Jenson's "Biographical Encyclopedia," p. 480). In what wards the other bishops presided cannot be determined with certainty. But as matters stood after the division of the city into ten wards, with the assignments of the text made—with Tarleton Lewis as bishop of the 4th ward, and Newel K. Whitney as bishop of the 7th ward—the bishops of the 1st and 3rd wards would be Samuel H. Smith and George Miller, but which presided over the 1st and which over the 3rd cannot be ascertained. The reason for mentioning the fact that Newel K. Whitney was bishop of the 7th ward, is because in all other publications of the text above, the 7th ward and who was bishop of it is omitted.

This day Sidney Rigdon went to the meeting near the Temple, and stated to the congregation, that he was not upon the stand to renounce his faith in Mormonism, as had been variously stated by enemies and licentious presses, but appeared to bear his testimony of its truth, and add another to the many miraculous evidences of the power of God; neither did he rise to deliver any regular discourse, but to unfold to the audience a scene of deep interest which had occurred in his own family. He had witnessed many instances of the power of God in this Church, but never before had he seen the dead raised; yet this was a thing that had actually taken place in his own family.

Sidney Rigdon's Re-affirmation of his Faith.

His daughter Eliza was dead. The doctor told him that she was gone; when, after a considerable length of time, she rose up in the bed and spoke in a very powerful tone to the following effect, in a supernatural manner:—She said to the family that she was going to leave them (being impressed with the idea herself that she had only come back to deliver her message, and then depart again), saying the Lord had said to her the very words she should relate; and so particular was she in her relation, that she would not suffer any person to leave out a word or add one. She called the family around her, and bade them all farewell, with a composure and calmness that defies all description, still impressed with the idea that she was to go back.

The Strange Experience of Eliza Rigdon.

Up to the time of her death, she expressed a great unwillingness to die; but, after her return, she expressed equally as strong a desire to go back. She said to her elder sister, Nancy, "It is in your heart to deny this work; and if you do, the Lord says it will be the damnation of your soul." In speaking to her sister Sarah, she said, "Sarah, we have but once to die, and I would rather die now, than wait for another time." She said to her sisters that the Lord had great blessings in store for them, if they continued in the faith; and after delivering her message, she swooned, but recovered again.

During this time, she was as cold as she will be when laid in the grave, and all the appearance of life was the power of speech. She thus continued till the following evening, for the space of thirty-six hours, when she called her father unto her bed, and said to him that the Lord had said to her, if he would cease weeping for his sick daughter, and dry up his tears, that he should have all the desires of his heart; and that if he would go to bed and rest, he should be comforted over his sick daughter, for in the morning she should be getting better, and should get well: that the Lord had said unto her, because that her father had dedicated her to God, and prayed to Him for her, that He would restore her back to him again.

This ceremony of dedicating and praying took place when she was struggling in death, and continued to the very moment of her departure; and she says the Lord told her that it was because of this that she must go back to her father again, though she herself desired to stay.

She said concerning George W. Robinson, as he had denied the faith, the Lord had taken away one of his eyeteeth, and unless he repented he would take away another; and concerning Dr. Bennett that he was a wicked man and that the Lord would tread him under his feet. Such is a small portion of what she related.

Elder Rigdon's Attitude Towards the Prophet.

Elder Rigdon observed that there had been many idle tales and reports abroad concerning him, stating that he had denied the faith; but he would take the opportunity to state that his faith was, and had been, unshaken in the truth. It has also been rumored that I believe that Joseph Smith is a fallen prophet. In regard to this I unequivocally state that I never thought so, but declare that I know he is a prophet of the Lord, called and chosen in this last dispensation, to roll on the kingdom of God for the last time. He closed by saying, as it regards his religion, he had no controversy with the world, having an incontrovertible evidence that, through obedience to the ordinances of the religion, he now believes the Lord had actually given back his daughter from the dead. No person need, therefore come to reason with him, to convince him of error, or make him believe another religion, unless those who profess it can show, through obedience to its laws, the dead have been, and can be, raised; if it has no such power, it would be insulting his feelings to ask him to reason about it; and if it had, it would be no better than the one he had; and so he had done with controversy; wherefore he dealt in facts and not in theory.

Remarks of Hyrum Smith.

President Hyrum Smith spoke at great length and with great power. He cited Elder Rigdon's mind back to the revelation concerning him, that if he would move into the midst of the city and defend the truth, he should be healed, &c.; and showed that what Elder Rigdon felt in regard to the improvement in his health was a fulfillment of the revelation.

He then proceeded to show the folly of any person's attempting to overthrow or destroy Joseph, and read from the Book of Mormon in various places concerning the Prophet who, it was prophesied, should be raised up in the last days, setting forth the work he was destined to accomplish, and that he had only just commenced; but inasmuch as we could plainly see that the former part of the prophecy had been literally fulfilled, we might be assured that the latter part would also be fulfilled, and that Joseph would live to accomplish the great things concerning him, &c.

Hyrum Smith's Admonition.

He concluded his address by calling upon the Saints to take courage and fear not, and also told Elder Rigdon that inasmuch as he had seen the mercy of the Lord exerted in his behalf, it was his duty to arise and stand in the defense of the truth and innocence, and of those who were being persecuted innocently; and finally called for all those who were willing to support and uphold Joseph, and who believed that he was doing his duty and was innocent of the charges alleged against him by our enemies, to hold up their right hands; when almost every hand was raised and no opposite vote was called for.

Effect of the Meeting.

The meeting was productive of great good by inspiring the Saints with new zeal and courage, and weakening the hands and hearts of the treacherous, and of evil and designing persons disposed to secret combinations against the truth. Elder Rigdon visited Brother Hyrum in the course of the day, and manifested a determination to arouse his [Rigdon's] energies in defense of the truth.

The Prophet's Blessing on Joseph Knight, Sen.

Tuesday, *22*.—I find my feelings of the 16th inst. towards my friends revived,*while I contemplate the virtues and the good qualities and characteristics of the faithful few, which I am now recording in the Book of the Law of the Lord,—of such as have stood by me in every hour of peril, for these fifteen long years past,—say, for instance, my aged and beloved brother, Joseph Knight, Sen., who was among the number of the first to administer to my necessities, while I was laboring in the commencement of the bringing forth of the work of the Lord, and of laying the foundation of the Church of Jesus Christ of Latter-day Saints. For fifteen years he has been faithful and true, and even-handed and exemplary, and virtuous and kind, never deviating to the right hand or to the left. Behold he is a righteous man, may God Almighty lengthen out the old man's days; and may his trembling, tortured, and broken body be renewed, and in the vigor of health turn upon him, if it be Thy will, consistently, O God; and it shall be said of him, by the sons of Zion, while there is one of them re-

* See closing pages of chapter V.

maining, that this man was a faithful man in Israel; therefore his name shall never be forgotten.

Newel Knight and Joseph Knight, Jun., the Prophet's Friends.

There are his sons, Newel Knight and Joseph Knight, Jun., whose names I record in the Book of the Law of the Lord with unspeakable delight, for they are my friends.

The Prophet's Feelings Towards Orrin Porter Rockwell.

There is a numerous host of faithful souls, whose names I could wish to record in the Book of the Law of the Lord; but time and chance would fail. I will mention, therefore, only a few of them as emblematical of those who are too numerous to be written. But there is one man I would mention, namely Orrin Porter Rockwell, who is now a fellow-wanderer with myself, an exile from his home, because of the murderous deeds, and infernal, fiendish dispositions of the indefatigable and unrelenting hand of the Missourians. He is an innocent and a noble boy. May God Almighty deliver him from the hands of his pursuers. He was an innocent and a noble child and my soul loves him. Let this be recorded for ever and ever. Let the blessings of salvation and honor be his portion.

The Prophet's Testimony of his Father.

But, as I said before, so say I again, while I remember the faithful few who are now living, I would remember also the faithful of my friends who are dead, for they are many; and many are the acts of kindness—paternal and brotherly kindnesses—which they have bestowed upon me; and since I have been hunted by the Missourians, many are the scenes which have been called to my mind. I have remembered scenes of my childhood. I have thought of my father who is dead, who died by disease which was brought upon him through suffering by the hands of ruthless mobs. He was a great and a good man. The envy of knaves and fools was heaped upon him, and this was his lot and portion all the days of his life. He was of noble stature and possessed a high, and holy, and exalted, and virtuous mind. His soul soared above all those mean and groveling principles that are so congenial to the human heart. I now say that he never did a mean act, that might be said was ungenerous in his life, to my knowledge. I love my father and his memory; and the memory of his noble deeds rests with ponderous weight upon my mind, and many of his kind and parental words to me are written on the tablet of my heart.

Sacred to me are the thoughts which I cherish of the history of his life, that have rolled through my mind, and have been implanted there by my own observation, since I was born. Sacred to me is his dust, and the spot where he is laid. Sacred to me is the tomb I have made to encircle o'er his head. Let the memory of my father eternally live. Let his soul, or the spirit, my follies forgive. With him may I reign one day in the mansions above, and tune up the lyre of anthems, of the eternal Jove. May the God that I love look down from above and save me from my enemies here, and take me by the hand that on Mount Zion I may stand, and with my father crown me eternally there.

Words and language are inadequate to express the gratitude that I owe to God for having given me so honorable a parentage.

The Prophet's Characterization of his Mother.

My mother also is one of the noblest and the best of all women. May God grant to prolong her days and mine, that we may live to enjoy each other's society long, yet in the enjoyment of liberty, and to breathe the free air.

The Prophet's Description of his Brother Alvin.

Alvin, my oldest brother—I remember well the pangs of sorrow that swelled my youthful bosom and almost burst my tender heart when he died. He was the oldest and the noblest of my father's family. He was one of the noblest of the sons of men. Shall his name not be recorded in this book? Yes, Alvin, let it be had here and be handed down upon these sacred pages for ever and ever. In him there was no guile. He lived without spot from the time he was a child. From the time of his birth he never knew mirth. He was candid and sober and never would play; and minded his father and mother in toiling all day. He was one of the soberest of men, and when he died the angel of the Lord visited him in his last moments.

These childish lines I record in remembrance of my childish scenes.

My brother Don Carlos Smith, whose name I desire to record, also was a noble boy; I never knew any fault in him; I never saw the first immoral act, or the first irreligious or ignoble disposition in the child from the time that he was born till the time of his death. He was a lovely, a good-natured, a kind-hearted and a virtuous and a faithful, upright child; and where his soul goes, let mine go also. He lies by the side of my father.

The Character of Don Carlos.

Let my father, Don Carlos and Alvin and children that I have buried be brought and laid in the tomb I have built. Let my mother and my brethren and my sisters be laid there also; and let it be called the tomb of Joseph, a descendant of Jacob; and when I die let me be gathered to the tomb of my father.

There are many souls whom I have loved stronger than death. To them I have proved faithful—to them I am determined to prove faithful, until God calls me to resign up my breath. O Thou, who seest and knowest the hearts of all men—Thou eternal, omnipotent, omniscient, and omnipresent Jehovah—God —Thou Eloheim, that sittest, as saith the Psalmist, "enthroned in heaven," look down upon Thy servant Joseph at this time; and let faith on the name of Thy Son Jesus Christ, to a greater degree than Thy servant ever yet has enjoyed, be conferred upon him, even the faith of Elijah; and let the lamp of eternal life be lit up in his heart, never to be taken away; and let the words of eternal life be poured upon the soul of Thy servant, that he may know

The Prophet's Prayer.

Thy will, Thy statutes, and Thy commandments, and Thy judgments, to do them.

As the dews upon Mount Hermon, may the distillations of Thy divine grace, glory, and honor, in the plenitude of Thy mercy, and power, and goodness, be poured down upon the head of Thy servant. O Lord, God, my heavenly Father, shall it be in vain, that Thy servant must needs be exiled from the midst of his friends, or be dragged from their bosoms, to clank in cold and iron chains; to be thrust within the dreary prison walls; to spend days of sorrow, and of grief, and misery there, by the hand of an infuriated, incensed, and infatuated foe; to glut their infernal and insatiable desire upon innocent blood; and for no other cause, on the part of Thy servant, than for the defense of innocence; and Thou a just God will not hear his cry? Oh, no; Thou wilt hear me—a child of woe, pertaining to this mortal life, because of sufferings here, but not for condemnation that shall come upon him in eternity; for Thou knowest, O God, the integrity of his heart. Thou hearest me, and I knew that Thou wouldst hear me, and mine enemies shall not prevail; they all shall melt like wax before Thy face, and, as the mighty floods and waters roar, or as the bellowing earthquake's devouring gulf, or rolling thunder's loudest peal, or vivid forked lightning's flash, or sound of the archangel's trump, or voice of the Eternal God,—so shall the souls of my enemies be made to feel in an instant, suddenly, and shall be taken, and ensnared, and fall backwards, and stumble in the ditch they have dug for my feet, and the feet of my friends, and perish in their own infamy and shame, be thrust down to an eternal hell, for their murderous and hellish deeds!

I design to renew this subject at a future time.

Received an interesting visit from mother and aunt Temperance Mack. My health and spirits good.

This afternoon received a few lines from Emma, informing me that she would expect me home this evening, believing that she could take care of me better at home than elsewhere. Accordingly, soon after dark, I started for home, and arrived safe, without being noticed by any person. All is quiet in the city.

CHAPTER VII.

EFFORTS TO COUNTERACT THE WICKED INFLUENCE OF JOHN C. BENNETT—THE PROPHET'S REAPPEARANCE AMONG THE PEOPLE—HIS DISCOURSE AT THE SPECIAL CONFERENCE AND BEFORE THE RELIEF SOCIETY AT NAUVOO.

Wednesday, August 24.—At home all day; received a visit from Brothers Newel K. Whitney and Isaac Morley.

Letter of Governor Carlin to Emma Smith, anent the Prophet's Difficulties in Missouri.

QUINCY, August 24, 1842.

DEAR MADAM.—Your letter of this date has just been handed to me, which recalls to my mind your great solicitude in reference to the security and welfare of your husband; but I need not say it recalls to my mind the subject matter of your solicitude, because that subject, except at short intervals, has not been absent from my mind. I can scarcely furnish you a justifiable apology for delaying a reply so long; but, be assured, madam, it is not for want of regard for you and your peace of mind that I have postponed, but a crowd of public business which has required my whole time, together with very ill health, since the receipt of your former letter; and it would be most gratifying to my feelings now if due regard to public duty would enable me to furnish such a reply as would fully conform to your wishes; but my duty in reference to all demands made by executives of other states for the surrender of fugitives from justice appears to be plain and simple, consisting entirely of an executive, and not a judicial character, leaving me no discretion or adjudication as to the innocence or guilt of persons so demanded and charged with crime; and it is plain that the Constitution and laws of the United States, in reference to fugitives from justice, presumes and contemplates that the laws of the several states are ample to do justice to all who may be charged with crime; and the statute of this state simply requires, "That whenever the executive of any other state, or of any territory of the United States, shall demand of the executive of this state any person as a fugitive from justice, and shall have complied with the requisitions of the Act of Congress in that case made and provided, it shall be the duty of the executive of this state to issue his warrant under the seal of the state to apprehend the said fugitive," &c.

With the constitution and laws before me, my duty is so plainly marked out that it would be impossible to err, so long as I abstain from usurping the right of adjudication. I am aware that a strict enforcement of the laws by an executive, or a rigid administration of them by a judicial tribunal, often results in hardships to those involved; and to you it doubtless appears peculiarly so, in the present case of Mr. Smith.

If, however, as you allege, he is innocent of any crime, and the proceedings are illegal, it would be the more easy for him to procure an acquittal. In reference to the remark you attribute to me that I "would not advise Mr. Smith ever to trust himself in Missouri," I can only say, as I have heretofore said on many occasions, that I never have entertained a doubt that, if Mr. Smith should submit to the laws of Missouri, the utmost latitude would be allowed him in his defense, and the fullest justice done him; and I only intended to refer, (in the remark made to you, when at my house) to the rabble, and not to the laws of Missouri.

Very much has been attributed to me, in reference to General Smith, that is without foundation in truth: a knowledge of which fact enables me to receive what I hear, as coming from him, with great allowance.

In conclusion, dear madam, I feel conscious when I assure you that all my official acts in reference to Mr. Smith have been prompted by a strict sense of duty, and in discharge of that duty, have studiously pursued that course least likely to produce excitement and alarm, both in your community and the surrounding public; and I will here add that I much regret being called upon to act at all and that I hope he will submit to the laws and that justice will ultimately be done.

Be pleased to present my best respects to Mrs. Smith and Miss Snow, your companions when at Quincy, and accept of my highest regard for yourself and best wishes for your prosperity and happiness.

Your obedient servant,

THOS. CARLIN.

To Mrs. Emma Smith:

Friday, August 26.—At home all day. In the evening, in council with some of the Twelve and others. I gave some important instructions upon the situation of the Church, showing that it was necessary that the officers who could should go abroad through the states; and inasmuch as a great

Plans for the Defense of the Church.

excitement had been raised, through the community at large, by the falsehoods put in circulation by John C. Bennett and others, it was wisdom in God that the Elders should go forth and deluge the state with a flood of truth, setting forth the mean, contemptible persecuting conduct of ex-Governor Boggs of Missouri, and those connected with him in his mean and corrupt proceedings, in plain terms, so that the world might understand the abusive conduct of our enemies, and stamp it with indignation.

I advised the Twelve to call a special conference on Monday next to give instructions to the Elders, and call upon them to go forth upon this important mission; meantime that all the affidavits concerning Bennett's conduct be taken and printed, so that each Elder could be properly furnished with correct and weighty testimony to lay before the public.

Great distress prevails in England on account of the dull state of trade.

Saturday, *27*.—In the assembly room with some of the Twelve and others, who were preparing affidavits for the press.

Emma Smith's Letter to Governor Carlin.—Defense of the Prophet, Arraignment of Missouri.

NAUVOO, August 27, 1842.

To his Excellency Governor Carlin:

DEAR SIR:—I received your letter of the 24th in due time, and now tender you the sincere gratitude of my heart for the interest which you have felt in my peace and prosperity; and I assure you that every act of kindness and every word of consolation have been thankfully received and duly appreciated by me and my friends also; and I much regret your ill health, but still hope that you will avail yourself of sufficient time to investigate our cause, and thoroughly acquaint yourself with the illegality of the prosecution instituted against Mr. Smith. And I now certify that Mr. Smith, myself nor any other person, to my knowledge, has ever, nor do we, at this time, wish your honor to swerve from your duty as an executive in the least.

But we do believe that it is your duty to allow us, in this place, the privileges and advantages guaranteed to us by the laws of this state and the United States. This is all we ask; and if we can enjoy these rights unmolested, it will be the ultimate end of all our ambition; and the result will be peace and prosperity to us, and all the surrounding country, so far as we are concerned. Nor do we wish to take any undue advantage of any intricate technicalities of law, but honorably and honestly to fulfil all of the laws of this state and of the United States; and then, in turn to have the benefits resulting from an honorable execution of those laws.

And now, your excellency will not consider me assuming any unbecoming dictation; but recollect that the many persecutions that have been got up unjustly and pursued illegally against Mr. Smith, instigated by selfish and irreligious motives, have obliged me to know something for myself. Therefore, let me refer you to the eleventh section of our city charter—"All power is granted to the city council to make, ordain, establish and execute all ordinances, not repugnant to the Constitution of the State, or of the United States, or, as they may deem necessary, for the peace and safety of said city." Accordingly there is an ordinance passed by the city council to prevent our people from being carried off by an illegal process; and if any one thinks he is illegally seized, under this ordinance, he claims the right of habeas corpus, under section 17 of the charter, to try the question of identity, which is strictly constitutional.

These powers are positively granted in the charter over your own signature. And now, dear sir, where can be the justice in depriving us of these rights which are lawfully ours, as well as they are the lawful rights of the inhabitants of Quincy, and Springfield and many other places, where the citizens enjoy the advantages of such ordinances without controversy?

With these considerations, and many more which might be adduced, give us the privilege, and we will show your honor, and the world besides, if required, that the Mr. Smith referred to in the demand from Missouri, is not the Joseph Smith of Nauvoo, for he was not in Missouri; neither is he described in the writ according as the law requires; and that he is not a fugitive from justice. Why, then, be so strenuous to have my husband taken, when you know him to be innocent of an attempt on the life of Governor Boggs, and that he is not a fugutive from justice?

It is not the fear of a just decision against him that deters Mr. Smith from going into Missouri, but it is an actual knowledge that it was never intended he should have a fair trial.

And now, sir, if you were not aware of the fact, I will acquaint you with it now, that there were lying in wait, between this place and Warsaw, twelve men from Jackson county, Missouri, for the purpose of taking Mr. Smith out of the hands of the officers who might have him in custody. Also those two men from Missouri that were here with Messrs. King and Pitman divulged the most illegal and infernal calculations concerning taking Mr. Smith into Missouri, the evidence of which we can furnish you at any time, if required.

And, dear sir, our good feelings revolt at the suggestion that your excellency is acquainted with the unlawful measures taken by those engaged in the prosecution—measures, which, if justice was done to others, as it would be done to us, were we to commit as great errors in our proceedings, would subject all concerned in the prosecution to the penalty of the law, and that without mercy.

I admit, sir, that it is next to an impossibility for any one to know the extent of the tyranny, treachery and knavery of a great portion of the leading characters of the state of Missouri; yet it only requires a knowledge of the Constitution of the United States and statutes of the state of Missouri, and a knowledge of the outrage committed by some of the inhabitants of that state upon the people called "Mormons," and that passed unpunished by the administrators of the law, to know that there is not the least confidence to be placed in any of those men that were engaged in those disgraceful transactions.

If the law was made for the lawless and disobedient, and punishment instituted for the guilty, why not execute the law upon those that have transgressed it, and punish those who have committed crime, and grant encouragement to the innocent, and liberality to the industrious and peaceable?

And now I entreat your honor to bear with me patiently while I ask what good can accrue to this state or the United States, or any part of this state, or the United States, or to yourself, or to any other individual, to continue this persecution upon this people, or upon Mr. Smith—a persecution that you are well aware, is entirely without any just foundation or excuse?

With sentiments of due respect, I am your most obedient servant,

EMMA SMITH.

*Happiness.**

Happiness is the object and design of our existence; and will be the end thereof, if we pursue the path that leads to it; and this path is vir-

* It is not positively known what occasioned the writing of this essay; but when it is borne in mind that at this time the new law of marriage for the Church—marriage for eternity, including plurity of wives under some circumstances—was being introduced by the Prophet, it is very likely that the article was written with a view of applying the principles here expounded to the conditions created by introducing said marriage system.

tue, uprightness, faithfulness, holiness, and keeping all the commandments of God. But we cannot keep all the commandments without first knowing them, and we cannot expect to know all, or more than we now know unless we comply with or keep those we have already received. That which is wrong under one circumstance, may be, and often is, right under another.

God said, "Thou shalt not kill;" at another time He said "Thou shalt utterly destroy." This is the principle on which the government of heaven is conducted—by revelation adapted to the circumstances in which the children of the kingdom are placed. Whatever God requires is right, no matter what it is, although we may not see the reason thereof till long after the events transpire. If we seek first the kingdom of God, all good things will be added. So with Solomon: first he asked wisdom, and God gave it him, and with it every desire of his heart, even things which might be considered abominable to all who understand the order of heaven only in part, but which in reality were right because God gave and sanctioned by special revelation.

A parent may whip a child, and justly, too, because he stole an apple; whereas if the child had asked for the apple, and the parent had given it, the child would have eaten it with a better appetite; there would have been no stripes; all the pleasure of the apple would have been secured, all the misery of stealing lost.

This principle will justly apply to all of God's dealings with His children. Everything that God gives us is lawful and right; and it is proper that we should enjoy His gifts and blessings whenever and wherever He is disposed to bestow; but if we should seize upon those same blessings and enjoyments without law, without revelation, without conmandment, those blessings and enjoyments would prove cursings and vexations in the end, and we should have to lie down in sorrow and wailings of everlasting regret. But in obedience there is joy and peace unspotted, unalloyed; and as God has designed our happiness—and the happiness of all His creatures, he never has—He never will institute an ordinance or give a commandment to His people that is not calculated in its nature to promote that happiness which He has designed, and which will not end in the greatest amount of good and glory to those who become the recipients of his law and ordinances. Blessings offered, but rejected, are no longer blessings, but become like the talent hid in the earth by the wicked and slothful servant; the proffered good returns to the giver; the blessing is bestowed on those who will receive and occupy; for unto him that hath shall be given, and he shall have abundantly, but unto him that hath not or will not receive, shall be taken away that which he hath, or might have had.

Be wise today; 'tis madness to defer:
Next day the fatal precedent may plead.
Thus on till wisdom is pushed out of time
Into eternity.

Our heavenly Father is more liberal in His views, and boundless in His mercies and blessings, than we are ready to believe or receive; and, at the same time, is more terrible to the workers of iniquity, more awful in the executions of His punishments, and more ready to detect every false way, than we are apt to suppose Him to be. He will be inquired of by His children. He says: "Ask and ye shall receive, seek and ye shall find;" but, if you will take that which is not your own, or which I have not given you, you shall be rewarded according to your deeds; but no good thing will I withhold from them who walk uprightly before me, and do my will in all things—who will listen to my voice and to the voice of my servant whom I have sent; for I delight in those who seek diligently to know my precepts, and abide by the law of my kingdom; for all things shall be made known unto them in mine own due time, and in the end they shall have joy.

Sunday, 28.—At home. James Whitehead, Peter Melling, Tarleton Lewis, and Ezra Strong were received into the High Priests' quorum at Nauvoo.

The British convict ship, *Waterloo*, was wrecked at Cape Town, during a gale. Two hundred lives lost.

Monday, 29.—

Minutes of a Special Conference, held at Nauvoo.

This being the day appointed for the conference referred to on the 26th instant, the elders assembled in the Grove near the Temple. About 10 o'clock in the forenoon, President Hyrum Smith introduced the object of the conference by stating that the people abroad had been excited by John C. Bennett's false statements, and that letters had frequently been received inquiring concerning the true nature of said reports; in consequence of which it is thought wisdom in God that every elder who can, should go forth to every part of the United States, and take proper documents with them, setting forth the truth as it is, and also preach the gospel, repentance, baptism, and salvation, and tarry preaching until they shall be called home. They must go wisely, humbly setting forth the truth as it is in God, and our persecutions, by which the tide of public opinion will be turned. There are many elders here doing little, and many people in the world who want to hear the truth. We want the official members to take their staff and go east (not west); and if a mob should come here, they will only have women and children to fight with. When you raise churches, send the means you get to build the Temple, and get the people to take stock in the Nauvoo House. It is important that the Nauvoo House should be finished, that we may have a suitable place wherein to entertain the great ones of the earth, and teach them the truth. We want the Temple built, that we may offer our oblations, and where we can ask forgiveness of our sins every week, and forgive one another, and offer up our offering, and get our endowment. The gospel will be turned from the Gentiles to the Jews. Sometime ago, almost every person was ordained, the purpose was to have you tried and ready to receive your blessings. Every one is wanted to be ready in two or three days, and I expect there will be a liberal turn out.

Return of the Prophet to the People.

Near the close of Hyrum's remarks, I went upon the stand. I was rejoiced to look upon the Saints once more, whom I have not seen for about three weeks. They also were rejoiced to see me, and we all rejoiced together. My sudden appearance on the stand, under the circumstances which surrounded us, caused great animation and cheerfulness in the assembly. Some had supposed that I had gone to Washington, and some that I had gone to Europe, while some thought I was in the city; but whatever difference of opinion had prevailed on this point, we were now all filled with thanksgiving and rejoicing.

When Hyrum had done speaking, I arose and congratulated the brethren and sisters on the victory I had once more gained over the Missourians. I had told them formerly about fighting the Missourians, and about fighting alone. I had not fought them with the sword, or by carnal weapons; I had done it by stratagem, by outwitting them; and there had been no lives lost, and there would be no lives lost, if they would hearken to my counsel.

Up to this day God had given me wisdom to save the people who took counsel. None had ever been killed who abode by my counsel. At Hauns' Mill the brethren went contrary to my counsel; if they had not, their lives would have been spared.

I had been in Nauvoo all the while, and outwitted Bennett's associates, and attended to my own business in the city all the time. We want to whip the world mentally, and they will whip themselves physically. The brethren cannot have the tricks played upon them that were played at Kirtland and Far West. They have seen enough of the tricks of their enemies, and know better. Orson Pratt has attempted to destroy himself, and caused almost all the city to go in search of him. Is it not enough to put down all the infernal influences of the devil, what we have felt and seen, handled and evidenced, of this work of God? But the devil had influence among the Jews, after all the great things they had witnessed, to cause the death of Jesus Christ, by hanging Him between heaven and earth. They would deliver me up, Judas like; but a small band of us shall overcome.

The Saints' Weapons of Warfare.

We don't want or mean to fight with the sword of the flesh, but we will fight with the broad sword of the Spirit. Our enemies say our charter and writs of habeas corpus are worth nothing. We say they came from the highest authority in the state, and we will hold to them. They cannot be disannulled or taken away.

I then told the brethren I was going to send all the elders away, and when the mob came there would only be women and children to fight, and they would be ashamed. I don't want you to fight, but go and gather tens, hundreds, and thousands to fight for you. If oppression comes, I will then show them that there is a Moses and a Joshua amongst us; and I will fight them, if they don't take off oppression from me. I will do as I have done this time, I will run into the woods, I will fight them in my own way. I will send Brother Hyrum to call conferences everywhere throughout the states, and let documents be taken along and show to the world the corrupt and oppressive conduct of Boggs,

The Prophet's Plan of Campaign.

Carlin, and others, that the public may have the truth laid before them.

Let the Twelve send all who will support the character of the Prophet, the Lord's anointed; and if all who go will support my character, I prophesy in the name of the Lord Jesus, whose servant I am, that you will prosper in your missions. I have the whole plan of the kingdom before me, and no other person has. And as to all that Orson Pratt, Sidney Rigdon, or George W. Robinson can do to prevent me, I can kick them off my heels, as many as you can name; I know what will become of them.

I concluded my remarks by saying I have the best of feelings towards my brethren, since this trouble began; but to the apostates and enemies, I will give a lashing every opportunity, and I will curse them.

During the address, an indescribable transport of good feeling was manifested by the assembly, and about 380 elders volunteered to go immediately on the proposed mission.

Treaty signed between Great Britain and China, Chinese to pay $31,000,000, throw open five ports for trade, and cede Hong Kong to Great Britain.

Tuesday, *30*.—At home through the day.

Wednesday, *31*.—At home in the forenoon; afternoon rode to the Grove with Emma, and attended the Female Relief Society's meeting.

The following minutes were reported by Miss E. R. Snow:—

Minutes of the Female Relief Society's Meeting—Remarks of the Prophet.

President Joseph Smith arose and said, "I am happy and thankful for the privilege of being present on this occasion. Great exertions have been made on the part of our enemies to carry me to Missouri and destroy my life; but the Lord has hedged up their way, and they have not, as yet, accomplished their purpose. God has enabled me to keep out of their hands. I have warred a good warfare, insomuch as I have out-generalled or whipped out all Bennett's corrupt host.

My feelings at the present time are that, inasmuch as the Lord Almighty has preserved me until today, He will continue to preserve me, by the united faith and prayers of the Saints, until I have fully accomplished my mission in this life, and so firmly established the dispensation of the fullness of the priesthood in the last days, that all the powers of earth and hell can never prevail against it.

This constant persecution reminds me of the words of the Savior, when He said to the Pharisees, "Go ye, and tell that fox, Behold, I cast out devils, and I do cures today and tomorrow, and the third day I shall be perfected." I suspect that my Heavenly Father has decreed that the Missourians shall not get me into their power; if they do, it will be because I do not keep out of their way.

I shall triumph over my enemies: I have begun to triumph over them at home, and I shall do it abroad. All those that rise up against me will surely feel the weight of their iniquity upon their own heads. Those that speak evil of me and the Saints are ignorant or abominable characters, and full of iniquity. All the fuss, and all the stir, and all the charges got up against me are like the jack-a-lantern, which cannot be found.

Although I do wrong, I do not the wrongs that I am charged with doing: the wrong that I do is through the frailty of human nature, like other men. No man lives without fault. Do you think that even Jesus, if He were here, would be without fault in your eyes? His enemies said all manner of evil against Him—they all watched for iniquity in Him. How easy it was for Jesus to call out all the iniquity of the hearts of those whom He was among!

The servants of the Lord are required to guard against those things that are calculated to do the most evil. The little foxes spoil the vines—little evils do the most injury to the Church. If you have evil feelings, and speak of them to one another, it has a tendency to do mischief. These things result in those evils which are calculated to cut the throats of the heads of the Church.

When I do the best I can—when I am accomplishing the greatest good, then the most evils and wicked surmisings are got up against me. I would to God that you would be wise. I now counsel you, that if you know anything calculated to disturb the peace or injure the feelings of your brother or sister, hold your tongues, and the least harm will be done.

The Female Relief Society have taken a most active part in my welfare against my enemies, in petitioning to the governor in my behalf. These measures were all necessary. Do you not see that I foresaw what was coming, beforehand, by the spirit of prophecy? All these movements had an influence in my redemption from the hand of my enemies. If these measures had not been taken, more serious consequences would have resulted. I have come here to bless you. The Society have done well: their principles are to practice holiness. God loves you, and your prayers in my behalf shall avail much: let them not cease to ascend to God continually in my behalf. The enemies of this people will never get weary of their persecution against the Church, until they are overcome. I expect they will array everything against me that is in their power to control, and that we shall have a long and tremendous warfare. He that will war the true Christian warfare against the corruptions of these last days will have wicked men and angels of devils, and all the infernal powers of darkness continually arrayed against him. When wicked and corrupt men oppose, it is a criterion to judge if a man is warring the Christian warfare. When all men speak evil of you falsely, blessed are ye, &c. Shall a man be considered bad, when men speak evil of him? No. If a man stands and opposes the world of sin, he may expect to have all wicked and corrupt spirits arrayed against him. But it will be but a little season, and all these afflictions will be turned away from us, inasmuch as we are faithful, and are not overcome by these evils. By seeing the blessings of the endowment rolling on, and the kingdom increasing and spreading from sea to sea, we shall rejoice that we were not overcome by these foolish things.

A few very important things have been manifested to me in my absence respecting the doctrine of baptism for the death, which I shall communicate to the Saints next Sabbath, if nothing should occur to prevent me.

President Smith then addressed the throne of grace in fervent prayer.

The prayers of the society were requested in behalf of Mr. Repshaw.

President Joseph Smith remarked that Mrs. Repshaw had long since been advised to return to her husband. It has been ascertained, by good evidence, that she left her husband without just cause—that he is a moral man and a gentleman. She has got into a way of having revelations, but not the revelations of God. If she will go home and do her duty, we will pray for her; but, if not, our prayers will do her no good.

President Smith said, "I have one remark to make respecting the baptism for the dead to suffice for the time being, until I have opportunity to discuss the subject at greater length—all persons baptized for the dead must have a recorder present, that he may be an eyewitness to record and testify of the truth and validity of his record. It will be necessary, in the Grand Council, that these things be testified to by competent witnesses. Therefore let the recording and witnessing of baptisms for the dead be carefully attended to from this time forth. If there is any lack, it may be at the expense of our friends; they may not come forth."

Closed with prayer by Elder Derby.

CHAPTER VIII.

INSTRUCTIONS ON BAPTISM FOR THE DEAD—CORRESPONDENCE BETWEEN EMMA SMITH AND GOVERNOR CARLIN—THE PROPHET'S FIRST LETTER TO JAMES ARLINGTON BENNETT.

Hyde's Pamphlet.

Some time this month [August, 1842] Elder Hyde published a pamphlet in the German language, in Germay, entitled "A Cry out of the Wilderness," &c., of about 120 pages, setting forth the rise, progress and doctrines of the Church of Jesus Christ of Latter-day Saints.

About this time, while I was crossing from Montrose to Nauvoo in a boat in company with Brother Hyrum, we passed through an immense shoal of fish of considerable size. Hundreds jumped in and over the boat; but we succeeded in catching about sixteen, which we brought to shore.

Thursday, *September 1*, *1842*.—During the forenoon in the Assembly Room, and in the afternoon at home, attending to business. wrote the following:

*A Letter from the Prophet to the Saints at Nauvoo—Directions on Baptism for the Dead.**

To all the Saints in Nauvoo.—Forasmuch as the Lord has revealed unto me that my enemies, both in Missouri and this state, were again in the pursuit of me; and inasmuch as they pursue me without a cause, and have not the least shadow or coloring of justice or right on their side, in the getting up of their prosecutions against me; and inasmuch as their pretensions are all founded in falsehood of the blackest dye, I have thought it expedient and wisdom in me to leave the place for a short season, for my own safety and the safety of this people.

I would say to all those with whom I have business, that I have left my affairs with agents and clerks, who will transact all business in a

* See Doc. and Cov. cxxvii. See also *Times and Seasons* vol. III, page 919.

prompt and proper manner, and will see that all my debts are cancelled in due time, by turning out property, or otherwise, as the case may require, or as the circumstances may admit of. When I learn that the storm is fully blown over, then I will return to you again.

2. And as for the perils which I am called to pass through, they seem but a small thing to me, as the envy and wrath of man have been my common lot all the days of my life; and for what cause it seems mysterious, unless I was ordained from before the foundation of the world, for some good end, or bad, as you may choose to call it. Judge ye for yourselves. God knoweth all these things, whether it be good or bad.

But, nevertheless,deep water is what I am wont to swim in; it all has become second nature to me. And I feel, like Paul, to glory in tribulation: for to this day has the God of my fathers delivered me out of them all, and will deliver me from henceforth; for behold, and lo, I shall triumph over all my enemies, for the Lord God hath spoken it.

3. Let all the Saints rejoice, therefore, and be exceedingly glad, for Israel's God is their God; and he will mete out a just recompense of reward upon the heads of all your oppressors.

4. And again, verily, thus saith the Lord, let the work of my Temple, and all the works which I have appointed unto you, be continued on and not cease; and let your diligence and your perseverance, and patience, and your works be redoubled; and you shall in no wise lose your reward, saith the Lord of Hosts; and if they persecute you, so persecuted they the prophets and righteous men that were before you. For all this there is a reward in heaven.

5. And again I give unto you a word in relation to the baptism for your dead.

6. Verily thus saith the Lord unto you concerning your dead: when any of you are baptized for your dead, let there be a recorder; and let him be eyewitness of your baptisms; let him hear with his ears, that he may testify of a truth, saith the Lord.

7. That in all your recordings it may be recorded in heaven; whatsoever you bind on earth may be bound in heaven; whatever you loose on earth shall be loosed in heaven.

8. For I am about to restore many things to the earth pertaining to the Priesthood, saith the Lord of Hosts.

9. And again, let all the records be had in order, that they may be put in the archives of my Holy Temple, to be held in remembrance from generation to generation, saith the Lord of Hosts.

10. I will say to all the Saints, that I desired with exceedingly great desire to have addressed them from the stand on the subject of baptism for the dead, on the following Sabbath. But inasmuch as it is out of

my power to do so, I will write the word of the Lord from time to time, on that subject and send it you by mail, as well as many other things.

11. And now I close my letter for the present, for the want of more time; for the enemy is on the alert; and, as the Savior said, the prince of this world cometh, but he hath nothing in me.

12. Behold my prayer to God is, that you all may be saved: and I subscribe myself your servant in the Lord, Prophet and Seer of the Church of Jesus Christ of Latter-day Saints.

JOSEPH SMITH,

The following is from the *Times and Seasons* of September 1st.

Excerpt from a Communication from William Law.

Let none suppose that God is angry with His Saints because He suffers the hand of persecution to come upon them. He chasteneth those whom He loveth, and trieth and proveth every son and daughter, that they may be as gold seven times purified. Rejoice then, ye Saints of the Most High; for the God of Abraham is your God, and He will deliver you from all your enemies. Seek diligently to know His will, and observe to do it. Be zealous in the cause of truth, in building up the kingdom of Christ upon the earth, in rearing up the Temple of God at Nauvoo, and in all works of righteousness. And say not "The Lord delayeth His coming;" for behold the day draweth near; the hour approacheth; be ye ready.

Be virtuous, be just, be honorable, be full of faith, love and charity; pray much and be patient; wait a little season and the voice of God shall thunder from the heavens His voice shall be very terrible; then the wicked shall tremble and fall back; they shall be taken in their own snares, and fall into the pit that they have digged for others; but the just shall live by faith, and shall shine forth as the stars in the firmament; their glory shall be as the brightness of the sun; for they are God's.

WILLIAM LAW.

Friday, 2.—Spent the day at home. A report reached the city this afternoon that the sheriff was on his way to Nauvoo with an armed force.

Saturday, 3.—In the morning at home, in company with John F. Boynton.*

* John F. Boynton, as will be remembered, was at one time a member of the quorum of the Twelve Apostles in the Kirtland period of Church history; see Vol. II, pp. 187 and 191.

[Under this date, the Prophet's secretary wrote the following:]

An Attempt to Arrest the Prophet.

A letter was received from Brother Hollister to the effect that the Missourians were again on the move, and that two requisitions were issued, one on the governor of this state,and the other on the governor of Iowa. Their movements were represented as being very secret and resolute. Soon after 12 o'clock, Pitman, the deputy sheriff, and two other men came into the house. It appears that they had come up the riverside, and hitched their horses below the Nauvoo House, and then proceeded on foot undiscovered, until they got into the house. When they arrived, President Joseph Smith was in another apartment of the house, eating dinner with his family. John Boynton happened to be the first person discovered by the sheriffs, and they began to ask him where Mr. Smith was. He answered that he saw him early in the morning; but did not say that he had seen him since.

While this conversation was going on, President Joseph Smith passed out of the back door, and through the corn in his garden to Brother Newel K. Whitney's. He went up stairs undiscovered. Meantime Sister Emma went and conversed with the sheriffs. Pitman said he wanted to search the house for Mr. Smith. In answer to a question by Sister Emma, he said he had no warrant authorizing him to search, but insisted upon searching the house. She did not refuse, and accordingly they searched through, but to no effect.

This is another testimony and evidence of the mean, corrupt, illegal proceedings of our enemies, notwithstanding the Constitution of the United States says, Article 4th, "The right of the people to be secure in their persons, houses, papers and effects against unreasonable searches and seizures shall not be violated, and no warrants shall issue but upon probable cause, supported by oath or affirmation, and particularly describing the place to be searched and the persons or things to be seized."

Yet these men audaciously, impudently and altogether illegally searched the house of President Joseph Smith even without any warrant or authority whatever. Being satisfied that he was not in the house, they departed. They appeared to be well armed, and no doubt intended to take him either dead or alive; which we afterwards heard they had said they would do; but the Almighty again delivered His servant from their bloodthirsty grasp.

It is rumored that there are fifteen men in the city along with the sheriffs, and that they dined together today at Amos Davis's. Soon after sundown, Thomas King and another person arrived at the house and demanded to search, which they immediately did; but, finding nothing they also went towards Davis's. Some of them were seen about afterwards; but at about ten o'clock all was quiet.

It is said that they started from Quincy yesterday, expecting and fully determined to reach Nauvoo in the night, and fall upon the house unawares; but report says they lost the road, and got scattered away one from another, and could not get along until daylight. This, in all probability, is true, as they appeared much fatigued, and complained of being weary and sore from riding.

President Smith, accompanied by Brother Erastus Derby, left Brother Whitney's about nine o'clock, and went to Brother Edward Hunter's, where he was welcomed, and made comfortable by the family, and where he can be kept safe from the hands of his enemies.

Sunday, 4.—Hyrum Smith and William Law left for the Eastern States.

Monday, 5.—The sisters wrote as follows:

Petition of the Female Relief Society to Governor Carlin.

To his Excellency Thomas Carlin, Governor of the State of Illinois:

We, the undersigned members of the Nauvoo Relief Society, and Ladies of Nauvoo, hearing many reports concerning mobs, threats of extermination, and other excitement, set on foot by John C. Bennett, calculated to disturb the peace, happiness and well-being of this community, have taken the liberty to petition your Excellency for protection.

It may be considered irrelevant for ladies to petition your Excellency on the above-named subject, and may be thought by you, Sir, to be officious, and that it would be more becoming for our husbands, fathers, brothers and sons to engage in this work, and in our defense. This, Sir, we will admit, in ordinary cases is right, and that it would be more consistent with the delicacy of the female character to be silent; but on occasions like the present, our desires for the peace of society, the happiness of our friends, the desire to save the lives of our husbands, our fathers, our brothers, our children, and our own lives, will be a sufficient palliation, in the estimation of your Excellency, for the step we have taken in presenting this petition, in support of the one already sent your Excellency by the male inhabitants of this city.

We would respectfully represent to your Excellency that we have not yet forgotten the scenes of grief, misery and woe that we had to experience from the hands of ruthless and bloodthirsty mobs in the state of Missouri. The cup of misery was prepared by lying, slander and misrepresentation. It was wrung out and filled by tyranny and oppression, and by a ruthless, inhuman mob. We had to drink it to the dregs.

Your Excellency will bear with us if we remind you of the cold-blooded atrocities that we witnessed in that state. Our bosoms heave with horror, our eyes are dim, our knees tremble, our hearts are faint, when we think of their horrid deeds; and if the petitions of our husbands, brothers, fathers, and sons will not answer with your Excellency, we beseech you to remember that of their wives, mothers, sisters and daughters. Let the voice of injured innocence in Missouri speak; let the blood of our fathers, our brothers, our sons and our daughters speak; let the tears of the widows and orphans, the maimed and impoverished speak; and let the injuries sustained by fifteen thousand innocent, robbed, spoiled, persecuted, and injured people speak; let the tale of woe be told; let it be told without embellishment, prejudice or color; and we are persuaded there is no heart but will be softened, no feelings but will be affected, and no person, but will flee to our relief.

Far be it from us to accuse your Excellency of obduracy or injustice. We believe you to be a humane, feeling, benevolent and patriotic man; and therefore we appeal to you.

Concerning John C. Bennett who is trying with other political demagogues, to disturb our peace, we believe him to be an unvirtuous man and a most consummate scoundrel, a stirrer up of sedition, and a vile wretch unworthy the attention or notice of any virtuous man; and his published statements concerning Joseph Smith are bare-faced, unblushing falsehoods.

We would further recommend to your Excellency, concerning Joseph Smith, that we have the utmost confidence in him, as being a man of integrity, honesty, truth, and patriotism. We have never, either in public or private, heard him teach any principles but the principles of virtue and righteousness. And so we have knowledge, and we know him to be a pure, chaste, virtuous and godly man.

Under these circumstances, we would petition your Excellency to exert your privilege in an official capacity, and not to suffer him (should he be demanded) to go into the state of Missouri; for we know that, if he should, it would be the delivering up the innocent to be murdered. We would represent to your Excellency that we are a law-abiding people, a virtuous people, and we would respectfully refer your Excellency to the official documents of the state during our three years' residence in it, in proof of this. If we transgress laws, we are willing to be tried by those laws, but we dread mobs, we dread illegal process; we dread fermentation, calumny and lies, knowing that our difficulties in Missouri first commenced with these things.

We pray that we may not be delivered into the hands of mobs, or subjected to illegal proceedings of the militia, but that we may have the privilege of self-defense, in case of attack, without having to contend with legalized mobs as in Missouri; and we therefore appeal to the honor, philanthropy, justice, benevolence and patriotism of your Excellency, to afford us all legal protection and to grant us our request; and we, as in duty bound, will ever pray.

Tuesday, September 6, 1842.—I wrote as follows:

*Letter of the Prophet to the Church—Further Directions on Baptism for the Dead.**

NAUVOO, September 6, 1842.

To the Church of Jesus Christ of Latter-day Saints, greeting:—

1. As I stated to you in my letter, before I left my place, that I would write to you from time to time, and give you information in relation to many subjects, I now resume the subject of the baptism for the dead, as that subject seems to occupy my mind, and press itself upon my feelings the strongest, since I have been pursued by my enemies.

2. I wrote a few words of revelation to you concerning a recorder. I have had a few additional views in relation to this matter, which I now certify. That is, it was declared in my former letter that there should be a recorder who should be eye-witness, and also to hear with his ears, that he might make a record of a truth before the Lord.

3. Now, in relation to this matter, it would be very difficult for one recorder to be present at all times, and to do all the business. To obviate this difficulty, there can be a recorder appointed in each ward of the city, who is well qualified for taking accurate minutes; and let him be very particular and precise in taking the whole proceedings, certifying in his record that he saw with his eyes and heard with his ears, giving the date, and names, &c., and the history of the whole transaction; naming also, some three individuals that are present, if there be any present, who can at any time, when called upon, certify to the same, that in the mouth of two or three witnesses every word may be established.

4. Then let there be a general recorder, to whom these other records can be handed, being attended with certificates over their own signatures, certifying that the record they have made is true. Then the general church recorder can enter the record on the general church book, with the certificates and all the attending witnesses, with his own statement that he verily believes the above statement and records to be true, from his knowledge of the general character and appointment of those

* See Doc. and Cov. sec. cxxviii.

men by the Church. And when this is done on the general church book, the record shall be just as holy, and shall answer the ordinance just the same as if he had seen with his eyes, and heard with his ears, and made a record of the same on the general church book.

5. You may think this order of things to be very particular; but let me tell you that it is only to answer the will of God, by conforming to the ordinance and preparation that the Lord ordained and prepared before the foundation of the world, for the salvation of the dead who should die without a knowledge of the gospel.

6. And further, I want you to remember that John the Revelator was contemplating this very subject in relation to the dead, when he declared, as you will find recorded in Revelation xx, 12: "And I saw the dead, small and great, stand before God; and the books were opened; and another book was opened, which was the book of life; and the dead were judged out of those things which were written in the books, according to their works."

7. You will discover, in this quotation, that the books were opened; and another book was opened, which was the book of life; but the dead were judged out of those things which were written in the books; according to their works: consequently, the books spoken of must be the books which contained the record of their works; and refer to the records which are kept on the earth. And the book which was the book of life is the record which is kept in heaven; the principle agreeing precisely with the doctrine which is commanded you in the revelation contained in the letter which I wrote to you previously to my leaving my place, that in all your recordings it may be recorded in heaven.

8. Now, the nature of this ordinance consists in the power of the priesthood, by the revelation of Jesus Christ; wherein it is granted that whatsoever you bind on earth shall be bound in heaven, and whatsoever you loose on earth shall be loosed in heaven. Or in other words, taking a different view of the translation, whatsoever you record on earth shall be recorded in heaven, and whatsoever you do not record on earth shall not be recorded in heaven; for out of the books shall your dead be judged, according to their own works, whether they themselves have attended to the ordinances in their own *propria persona* or by the means of their own agents, according to the ordinance which God has prepared for their salvation from before the foundation of the world, according to the records which they have kept concerning their dead.

9. It may seem to some to be a very bold doctrine that we talk of—a power which records or binds on earth, and binds in heaven: nevertheless, in all ages of the world, whenever the Lord has given a dispensation of the priesthood to any man by actual revelation, or any set of men, this power has always been given. Hence, whatsoever those men

did in authority, in the name of the Lord, and did it truly and faithfully, and kept a proper and faithful record of the same, it became a law on earth and in heaven, and could not be annulled, according to the decrees of the great Jehovah. This is a faithful saying—who can hear it?

10. And again, for a precedent, Matthew xvi: 18, 19. "And I also say unto thee, that thou art Peter; and upon this rock I will build my church, and the gates of hell shall not prevail against it: and I will give unto thee the keys of the kingdom of heaven; and whatsoever thou shalt bind on earth shall be bound in heaven, and whatsoever thou shalt loose on earth shall be loosed in heaven."

11. Now the great and grand secret of the whole matter, and the *summum bonum* of the whole subject that is lying before us, consists in obtaining the powers of the holy priesthood; for him to whom these keys are given, there is no difficulty in obtaining a knowledge of facts in relation to the salvation of the children of men, both as well for the dead as for the living.

12. Herein is glory, and honor, and immortality, and eternal life: The ordinance of baptism by water, to be immersed therein in order to answer to the likeness of the dead, that one principle might accord with the other. To be immersed in the water and come forth out of the water is in the likeness of the resurrection of the dead, in coming forth out of their graves. Hence, this ordinance was instituted to form a relationship with the ordinance of baptism for the dead, being in likeness of the dead.

13. Consequently, the baptismal font was instituted as a simile of the grave, and was commanded to be in a place underneath where the living are wont to assemble, to show forth the living and the dead, and that all things may have their likeness, and that they may accord one with another,—that which is earthly conforming to that which is heavenly, as Paul hath declared, I Cor, xv: 46, 47, and 48.

14. "Howbeit that was not first which is spiritual, but that which is natural, and afterwards that which is spiritual. The first man is of the earth, earthy; the second man is the Lord from heaven. As is the earthy, such are they also that are earthy; and as is the heavenly, such are they also that are heavenly." And as are the records on the earth in relation to your dead, which are truly made out, so also are the records in heaven. This, therefore, is the sealing and binding power, and, in one sense of the word, the keys of the kingdom, which consist in the key of knowledge.

15. And now, my dearly beloved brethren and sisters, let me assure you that these are principles, in relation to the dead and the living, that cannot be lightly passed over, as pertaining to our salvation. For their

salvation is necessary and essential to our salvation, as Paul says concerning the fathers, "that they without us cannot be made perfect;" neither can we without our dead be made perfect.

16. And now, in relation to the baptism for the dead, I will give you another quotation of Paul, I Corinthians xv: 29: "Else what shall they do which are baptized for the dead, if the dead rise not at all? why are they then baptized for the dead?"

17. And again, in connection with this quotation, I will give you a quotation from one of the prophets, who had his eye fixed on the restoration of the priesthood, the glories to be revealed in the last days, and in an especial manner this most glorious of all subjects belonging to the everlasting gospel, viz., the baptism for the dead; for Malachi says, last chapter, verses 5th and 6th, "Behold I will send you Elijah the prophet before the coming of the great and dreadful day of the Lord; and he shall turn the heart of the fathers to the children, and the heart of the children to their fathers, lest I come and smite the earth with a curse."

18. I might have rendered a plainer translation to this, but it is sufficiently plain to suit my purpose as it stands. It is sufficient to know, in this case, that the earth will be smitten with a curse, unless there is a welding link of some kind or other between the fathers and the children, upon some subject or other: and behold, what is that subject? It is the baptism for the dead. For we without them cannot be made perfect; neither can they without us be made perfect. Neither can they nor we be made perfect without those who have died in the gospel also; for it is necessary, in the ushering in of the dispensation of the fullness of times, which dispensation is now beginning to usher in, that a whole, and complete, and perfect union, and welding together of dispensations, and keys, and powers, and glories should take place, and be revealed, from the days of Adam even to the present time; and not only this, but those things which never have been revealed from the foundation of the world, but have been kept hid from the wise and prudent, shall be revealed unto babes and sucklings in this the dispensation of the fullness of times.

19. Now, what do we hear in the gospel which we have received? "A voice of gladness! A voice of mercy from heaven, and a voice of truth out of the earth; glad tidings for the dead; a voice of gladness for the living and the dead; glad tidings of great joy. How beautiful upon the mountains are the feet of those that bring glad tidings of good things, and that say unto Zion, Behold! thy God reigneth. As the dews of Carmel, so shall the knowledge of God descend upon them."

20. And again, what do we hear? Glad tidings from Cumorah! Moroni, an angel from heaven, declaring the fulfillment of the prophets

—the book to be revealed. A voice of the Lord in the wilderness of Fayette, Seneca county, declaring the three witnesses to bear record of the book. The voice of Michael on the banks of the Susquehanna, detecting the devil when he appeared as an angel of light. The voice of Peter, James, and John, in the wilderness between Harmony, Susquehanna county, and Colesville, Broome county, on the Susquehanna river, declaring themselves as possessing the keys of the kingdom and of the dispensation of the fullness of times.

21. And again, the voice of God in the chamber of old Father Whitmer in Fayette, Seneca county, and at sundry times and in divers places, through all the travels and tribulations of this Church of Jesus Christ of Latter-day Saints. And the voice of Michael, the Archangel, the voice of Gabriel and of Raphael, and of divers angels from Michael or Adam down to the present time, all declaring their dispensation, their rights, their keys, their honors, their majesty and glory, and the power of their Priesthood; giving line upon line, precept upon precept; here a little, and there a little; giving us consolation by holding forth that which is to come, confirming our hopes.

22. Brethren, shall we not go on in so great a cause? Go forward and not backward? Courage, brethren, and on, on to the victory! Let your hearts rejoice, and be exceeding glad. Let the earth break forth into singing. Let the dead speak forth anthems of eternal praise to the King Immanuel, who hath ordained before the world was, that which would enable us to redeem them out of their prisons; for the prisoners shall go free.

23. Let the mountains shout for joy, and all ye valleys cry aloud; and all ye seas and dry lands tell the wonders of your eternal King. And ye rivers, and brooks, and rills flow down with gladness. Let the woods and all the trees of the field praise the Lord; and ye solid rocks weep for joy. And let the sun, moon, and the morning stars sing together, and let all the sons of God shout for joy. And let the eternal creation declare His name for ever and ever. And again I say, how glorious is the voice we hear from heaven, proclaiming in our ears, glory, and salvation, and honor, and immortality and eternal life, kingdoms, principalities and powers.

24. Behold the great day of the Lord is at hand; and who can abide the day of His coming, and who can stand when He appeareth? For He is like a refiner's fire, and like fuller's soap; and He shall sit as a refiner and purifier of silver, and He shall purify the sons of Levi, and purge them as gold and silver, that they may offer unto the Lord an offering in righteousness. Let us, therefore, as a Church and a people, and as Latter-day Saints, offer unto the Lord an offering in righteousness, and let us present, in His holy Temple, when it is finished, a

book containing the records of our dead, which shall be worthy of all acceptation.

25. Brethren, I have many things to say to you on the subject, but shall now close for the present, and continue the subject another time.

I am, as ever, your humble servant, and never deviating friend,

JOSEPH SMITH.

The important instructions contained in the foregoing letter made a deep and solemn impression on the minds of the Saints; and they manifested their intentions to obey the instructions to the letter.

The Letter's Effect

In the evening, William Clayton and Bishop Whitney called to see me concerning a settlement with Edward Hunter. Also Brigham Young, Heber C. Kimball, and Amasa Lyman, called to counsel concerning their mission to the branches and people abroad.

Wednesday, September 7.—Early this morning Elders Adams and Rogers, of New York, brought me several letters —one from Dr. Willard Richards, who, referring to his visit with James Arlington Bennett, Esq., of Arlington House, says, he "would be pleased to receive a letter of President Joseph's own dictation, signed by his own hand;" which request I was disposed to comply with, but deferred it till the next day.

Governor Carlin wrote as follows:

Governor Carlin's Letter to Emma Smith—Nauvoo's Charter and the Writ of Habeas Corpus.

QUINCY, September 7, 1842.

DEAR MADAM.—Your letter of the 27th ultimo was delivered to me on Monday, the 5th instant, and I have not had time to answer it until this evening; and I now appropriate a few moments to the difficult task of replying satisfactorily to its contents, every word of which evinces your devotedness to the interest of your husband, and pouring forth the effusions of a heart wholly his. I am thus admonished that I can say nothing, that does not subserve his interest that can possibly be satisfactory to you; and before I proceed, I will here repeat my great regret that I have been officially called upon to act in reference to Mr. Smith in any manner whatever.

I doubt not your candor when you say you do not desire me "to swerve from my duty as executive in the least," and all you ask is to be allowed the privileges and advantages guaranteed to you by the Constitution and laws. You then refer me to the 11th Section of the Charter of the city of Nauvoo, and claim for Mr. Smith the right to be heard by the Municipal Court of said city, under a writ of habeas corpus emanating from said court, when he was held in custody under an executive warrant.

The Charter of the city of Nauvoo is not before me at this time; but I have examined both the Charters and city ordinances upon the subject and must express my surprise at the extraordinary assumption of power by the board of aldermen as contained in said ordinance! From my recollection of the Charter it authorizes the Municipal Court to issue writs of habeas corpus in all cases of imprisonment or custody arising from the authority of the ordinances of said city, but that the power was granted, or intended to be granted, to release persons held in custody under the authority of writs issued by the courts or the executive of the state, is most absurd and ridiculous; and to attempt to exercise it is a gross usurpation of power that cannot be tolerated.

I have always expected and desired that Mr. Smith should avail himself of the benefits of the laws of this state, and, of course, that he would be entitled to a writ of habeas corpus issued by the Circuit Court, and entitled to a hearing before said court; but to claim the right of a hearing before the Municipal Court of the city of Nauvoo is a burlesque upon the city Charter itself.

As to Mr. Smith's guilt or innocence of the crime charged upon him, it is not my province to investigate or determine; nor has any court on earth jurisdiction of his case, but the courts of the state of Missouri; and as stated in my former letter, both the Constitution and laws presume that each and every state in this Union are competent to do justice to all who may be charged with crime committed in said state.

Your information that twelve men from Jackson county, Missouri, were lying in wait for Mr. Smith between Nauvoo and Warsaw, for the purpose of taking him out of the hands of the officers who might have him in custody, and murdering him, is like many other marvelous stories that you hear in reference to him—not one word of it true; but I doubt not that your mind has been continually harrowed up with fears produced by that and other equally groundless stories. That that statement is true is next to impossible; and your own judgment, if you will but give it scope, will soon set you right in reference to it.

If any of the citizens of Jackson county had designed to murder Mr. Smith, they would not have been so simple as to perpetrate the crime in Illinois, when he would necessarily be required to pass through to the interior of the state of Missouri, where the opportunity would have been so much better, and the prospect of escape much more certain. That is like the statement made by Mr. Smith's first messenger, after his arrest, to Messrs. Ralston and Warren, saying that I had stated that Mr. Smith should be surrendered to the anthorities of Missouri, dead or alive; not one word of which was true. I have not the most distant thought that any person in Illinois or Missouri contemplated personal injury to Mr. Smith by violence in any manner whatever.

I regret that I did not see General Law when last at Quincy. A previous engagement upon business that could not be dispensed with prevented, and occupied my attention that evening until dark. At half-past one o'clock p. m., I came home, and learned that the General had called to see me; but the hurry of business only allowed me about ten minutes time to eat my dinner, and presuming, if he had business of any importance, that he would remain in the city until I returned.

It may be proper here, in order to afford you all the satisfaction in my power, to reply to a question propounded to my wife by General Law, in reference to Mr. Smith,—viz., whether any other or additional demand had been made upon me by the Governor of Missouri for the surrender of Mr. Smith. I answer, none. No change whatever has been made in the proceedings. Mr. Smith has been held accountable only for the charge as set forth in my warrant under which he was arrested.

In conclusion you presume upon my own knowledge of Mr. Smith's innocence; and ask why the prosecution is continued against him. Here I must again appeal to your own good judgment; and you will be compelled to answer that it is impossible I could know him to be innocent; and, as before stated, it is not my province to investigate as to his guilt or innocence. But could I know him innocent, and were he my own son, I would nevertheless, (and the more readily) surrender him to the legally constituted authority to pronounce him innocent.

With sentiments of high regard and esteem, your obedient servant,

THOMAS CARLIN.

To Mrs. Emma Smith.

Brothers Adams and Rogers called again this afternoon, and I related to them many interpositions of Divine Providence in my favor, &c.

Thursday, 8.—I dictated the following:

The Prophet's Letter to James Arlington Bennett—The Forthcoming Book of John C. Bennett.

NAUVOO, September 8, 1842.

I have just received your very consoling letter, dated August 16, 1842, which is, I think, the first letter you ever addressed to me, in which you speak of the arrival of Dr. Willard Richards, and of his personality very respectfully. In this I rejoice, for I am as warm a friend to Dr. Richards as he possibly can be to me. And in relation to his almost making a "Mormon" of yourself, it puts me in mind of the saying of Paul in his reply to Agrippa, Acts xxvi: 29, "I would to God that not only thou, but also all that hear me this day, were both almost and altogether such as I am, except these bonds." And I will here remark, my dear sir, that "Mormonism" is the pure doctrine of Jesus Christ; of which I myself am not ashamed.

You speak also of Elder Foster, President of the Church in New York, in high terms; and of Dr. Bernhisel, in New York. These men I am acquainted with by information; and it warms my heart to know that you speak well of them, and, as you say, could be willing to associate with them for ever, if you never joined their Church or acknowledged their faith. This is a good principle; for when we see virtuous qualities in men, we should always acknowledge them, let their understanding be what it may in relation to creeds and doctrine; for all men are, or ought to be free, possessing unalienable rights,and the high and noble qualifications of the laws of nature and of self-preservation, to think, and act, and say as they please, while they maintain a due respect to the rights and privileges of all other creatures, infringing upon none.

This doctrine I do most heartily subscribe to and practice, the testimony of mean men to the contrary notwithstanding. But, sir, I will assure you that my soul soars far above all the mean and groveling dispositions of men that are disposed to abuse me and my character, I therefore shall not dwell upon that subject.

In relation to those men you speak of referred to above, I will only say that there are thousands of such men in this Church, who, if a man is found worthy to associate with, will call down the envy of a mean world, because of their high and noble demeanor; and it is with unspeakable delight that I contemplate them as my friends and brethren. I love them with a perfect love; and I hope they love me, and have no reason to doubt that they do.

The next in consideration is John C. Bennett. I was his friend; I am yet his friend, as I feel myself bound to be a friend to all the sons of Adam. Whether they are just or unjust, they have a degree of my compassion and sympathy. If he is my enemy, it is his own fault; and the responsibility rests upon his own head; and instead of arraigning his character before you, suffice it to say that his own conduct, wherever he goes, will be sufficient to recommend him to an enlightened public, whether for a bad man or a good one.

Therefore whosoever will associate themselves with him, may be assured that I will not persecute them; but I do not wish their association, and what I have said may suffice on that subject, so far as his character is concerned. Now, in relation to his book that he may write. I will venture to prophesy that whoever has any hand in the matter, will find themselves in a poor fix in relation to the money matters; and as to my having any fears of the influence that he or any other man or set of men may have against me—I will say this is most foreign from my heart; for I never knew what it was, as yet, to fear the face of clay, or the influence of man. My fear, sir, is before God. I fear to offend Him, and strive to keep His commandments. I am really glad that you did not join John C. Bennett in relation to his book, from the assurances which I have that it will prove a curse to all those who touch it.

In relation to the honor that you speak of, both for yourself and James Gordon Bennett, of the *Herald*, you are both strangers to me; and as John C. Bennett kept all his letters which he received from you entirely to himself, and there was no correspondence between you and me, that I know of, I had no opportunity to share very largely in the getting up of any of those matters. I could not, as I had not sufficient knowledge to enable me to do so. The whole, therefore, was at the instigation of John C. Bennett, and a quiet submission on the part of the rest, out of the best of feelings; but as for myself, it was all done at a time when I was overwhelmed with a great many business cares, as well as the care of all the churches. must be excused, therefore, for any wrongs that may have taken place in relation to this matter; and so far as I obtain a knowledge of that which is right, it shall meet with my hearty approval.

I feel to tender you my most hearty and sincere thanks for every expression of kindness you have tendered towards me or my brethren, and would beg the privilege of intruding myself a little while upon your patience, in offering a short relation of my circumstances. I am at this time persecuted the worst of any man on the earth, as well as this people, here in this place, and all our sacred rights are trampled under the feet of the mob. I am now hunted as a hart by the mob, under the pretense or shadow of law, to cover their abominable deeds. * * * * * * * *

I now appeal to you, sir, inasmuch as you have subscribed yourself our friend: Will you lift your voice and your arm with indignation against such unhallowed oppression? I must say, sir, that my bosom swells with unutterable anguish when I contemplate the scenes of horror that we have passed through in the state of Missouri, and then look, and behold, and see the storm and cloud gathering ten times blacker, ready to burst upon the heads of this innocent people. Would to God that I were able to throw off the yoke. Shall we bow down and be slaves? Are there no friends of humanity in a nation that boasts itself so much? Will not the nation rise up and defend us? If they will not defend us, will they not grant to lend a voice of indignation against such unhallowed oppression? Must the tens of thousands bow down to slavery and degradation? Let the pride of the nation arise and wrench these shackles from the feet of their fellow citizens, and their quiet, and peaceable, and innocent and loyal subjects. But I must forbear, for I cannot express my feelings.

The legion would all willingly die in the defense of their rights; but what would this accomplish? I have kept down their indignation, and kept a quiet submission on all hands, and am determined to do so at all hazards. Our enemies shall not have it to say that we rebel against government or commit treason. However much they may lift their hands in oppression and tyranny, when it comes in the form of government we tamely submit, although it lead us to the slaughter and to beggary; but our blood be upon their garments: and those who look tamely on and boast of patriotism shall not be without their condemnation.

And if men are such fools as to let once the precedent be established, and through their prejudices give assent to such abominations, then let the oppressor's hand lay heavily throughout the world, until all flesh shall feel it together, and until they may know that the Almighty takes cognizance of such things. And then shall church rise up against church, and party against party, mob against mob, oppressor against oppressor, army against army, kingdom against kingdom, and people against people, and kindred against kindred.

And where, sir, will be your safety or the safety of your children, if my children can be led to the slaughter with impunity by the hand of murderous rebels? Will they not lead yours to the slaughter with the same impunity? Ought not, then, this oppression, sir, to be checked in the bud, and to be looked down [upon] with just indignation by an enlightened world, before the flame become unextinguishable, and the fire devours the stubble?

But again I say I must forbear, and leave this painful subject. I wish you would write to me in answer to this, and let me know your views.

On my part, I am ready to be offered up a sacrifice in that way that can bring to pass the greatest benefit and good to those who must necessarily be interested in this important matter. I would to God that you could know all my feelings on this subject, and the real facts in relation to this people, and their unrelenting persecution. And if any man feels an interest in the welfare of their fellow-beings, and would think of saying or doing anything in this matter, I would suggest the propriety of a committee of wise men being sent to ascertain the justice or injustice of our cause, to get in possession of all the facts, and then make report to an enlightened world whether we, individually or collectively, are deserving such high-handed treatment.

In relation to the books that you sent here, John C. Bennett put them into my store, to be sold on commission, saying that, when I was able, the money must be remitted to yourself. Nothing was said about any consecration to the Temple.

Another calamity has befallen us. Our post office in this place is exceedingly corrupt. It is with great difficulty that we can get our letters to or from our friends. Our papers that we send to our subscribers are embezzled and burned, or wasted. We get no money from our subscribers, and very little information from abroad; and what little we do get, we get by private means, in consequence of these things: and I am sorry to say, that this robbing of the post office of money was carried on by John C. Bennett; and since he left here, it is carried on by the means of his confederates.

I now subscribe myself your friend, and a patriot and lover of my country, pleading at their feet for protection and deliverance, by the justice of their Constitution,

I add no more. Your most obedient servant,

JOSEPH SMITH.

CHAPTER IX.

LETTER OF JAMES ARLINGTON BENNETT TO THE PROPHET AND THE N. Y. "HERALD"—EMMA'S ILLNESS—PLOTS TO ENTRAP THE PROPHET—LEGAL OPINION OF JUSTIN BUTTERFIELD ON THE MISSOURI PROCEDURE.

Friday, September 9, 1842.—At 10 p. m. I received a very interesting visit from Emma, Amasa Lyman, George A. Smith and Wilson Law.

I counseled George A. Smith and Amasa Lyman to stay in Illinois and preach in the principal cities against mobocracy, and to notify the Twelve that it was my wish that they should also labor in Illinois. After a conversation of two hours, I accompanied the brethren and Emma to my house, remaining there a few minutes to offer a blessing upon the heads of my sleeping children; then called a few minutes at the house of my cousin George A. Smith, on my way to my retreat at Edward Hunter's. John D. Parker accompanied me as guard.

Movements of the Prophet in Nauvoo.

Brigham Young, Heber C. Kimball, Amasa Lyman, George A. Smith, and Charles C. Rich declared to the city council their intention of absence for three months or more, and others were appointed to fill their places during their absence. John P. Greene, Lyman Wight, and William Law were absent, and their places were filled. The object of the absence of these brethren was to preach the gospel in different states, and show up the wickedness and falsehood of the apostate John C. Bennett.

An ordinance relative to the returns of writs of habeas corpus was passed by the city council as follows:

An ordinance relative to the return of writs of Habeas Corpus.

Sec. 1, Be it, and it is hereby ordained by the city council of the city of Nauvoo, that the Municipal Court, in issuing writs of Habeas Corpus, may make the same returnable forthwith.

Sec. 2. This ordinance to take effect, and be in force from, and after its passage, passed September 9th, 1842.

GEO. W. HARRIS,
President pro tem.

JAMES SLOAN, Recorder.

President Young started on his mission.

Saturday, 10.—Heber C. Kimball, George A. Smith, and Amasa Lyman started on their mission, and proceeded as far as Lima, where they met Brigham Young, who was preaching to a congregation. This was the day for the training of the companies of the Nauvoo Legion; and, lest I should be observed by the multitude passing and repassing, I kept very still. After dark, my wife sent a messenger and requested me to return home, as she thought I would be as safe there as anywhere; and I went safely home undiscovered.

Sunday, 11.—I was at home all day. My letter of the 6th of September was read to the Saints, at the grove near the temple. The High Priests' quorum met. Several had gone on missions; others were preparing to go, but few were present, and the meeting adjourned *sine die*.

Elders Brigham Young, Heber C. Kimball, George A. Smith and Amasa Lyman addressed a large assembly in the grove in Lima, in relation to the slanderous reports of John C. Bennett.

Monday, 12.—

Letter from Brigham Young and Heber C. Kimball—Reporting their Movements.

To the Editor of the Times and Seasons:

DEAR BROTHER:—Having commenced our mission yesterday, we held our first conference at Brother Isaac Morley's. We had a good time. The brethren here are in good spirits. We ordained nineteen elders, and baptized twelve. We expect next Saturday and Sunday to hold a two days' meeting in Quincy, being the 17th and 18th instant; on the 24th and 25th, at Payson; the 1st and 2nd of October, at Pleasant Vale; the 8th and 11th October, at Pittsfield, the 15th and 16th October, at Apple Creek in Green county. From thence we shall proceed to Jacksonville and Springfield.

If you please, notice the above in your paper for the benefit of those friends scattered abroad.

Yours in the everlasting covenant,

BRIGHAM YOUNG,
HEBER C. KIMBALL.

Morley Settlement, September 12, 1842.

I was at home all day in company with Brothers Adams and Rogers, and counseled Brother Adams to write a letter to the governor. In the evening, Emma received governor Carlin's letter of the 7th instant.

Tuesday, 13.—At home all day. Settled with Edward Hunter.

Wednesday, 14.—At home. Mr. Remmick gave me a deed of one half his landed property in Keokuk, though it will be a long time, if ever, before it will be of any benefit to me. Had a consultation with Calvin A. Warren, Esq. In the evening I received the following letter from General James Arlington Bennett:

Letter of James Arlington Bennett—Treating Chiefly of John C. Bennett and his Book.

ARLINGTON HOUSE, September 1, 1842.

Lieutenant General Smith:

DEAR SIR:—Mrs. Smith's letter to Mrs. Bennett, containing a very lucid account of Dr. John C. Bennett, has been received; and the only thing concerning him that I regard of importance is that you found it necessary to expose him. I wish most ardently that you had let him depart in peace, because the public generally think no better of either the one party or the other, in consequence of the pretended exposures with which the newspapers have teemed. But then, in the long run, you will have the advantage, inasmuch as the universal notoriety which you are now acquiring will be the means of adding to Nauvoo three hundred fold.

That you ought to be given up to the tender mercies of Missouri no man in his senses will allow, as you would be convicted on the shadow of evidence when the people's passions and prejudices are so strongly enlisted against you; and, under such a state of things, how easily it would be to suborn witnesses against you, who would seal your fate! Add to this, too, the great difficulty under which an impartial jury, if such could be found, would labor in their attempt to render an honest verdict, being coerced by surrounding public prejudice and malice. And yet, as you are now circumstanced, it will not do to oppose force to force for your protection, as this in the present case would be treason against the state, and would ultimately bring to ruin all those concerned.

Your only plan, I think, will be to keep out of the way until this excitement shall have subsided, as, from all I can understand, even from the Dr. himself, there is no evidence on which an honest jury could find a verdict against you; and this opinion I have expressed to him.

I most ardently wish that you had one hundred thousand *true* men at Nauvoo, and that I had the command of them, *times and things would soon alter.* I hope to see the day, before I die, that such an army will dictate terms from Nauuoo to the enemies of the Mormon people. I say this in the most perfect candor, as I have nothing to gain by the Mormons, nor am I a Mormon in creed; yet I regard them in as favorable a light (and a little more so,) as I do any other sect. In fact, I am a philosophical Christian, and wish to see an entire change in the religious world.

I have been long a Mormon in sympathy alone, and probably can never be one in any other way; yet I feel that I am a friend of the people, as I think them honest and sincere in their faith; and those I know [are] as good and honorable men as any other professing Christians.

Dr. Bennett has been the means of bringing me before your people, you will therefore see, for *this act*, I am in honor bound to say, "*Peace to his manes.*" To act otherwise would be ungrateful and dishonorable, both of which qualities are strangers to my nature: nevertheless, by leaving him as he is, I can still be your friend; for be assured that nothing I have seen yet from his pen has in the least altered my opinion of you. I well know what allowances to make in such cases.

Dr. Bennett and Bachelor are now delivering lectures in New York against you and your doctrines and asserted practices at Nauvoo.

Elder Foster told me, this forenoon, that the seats have been torn to pieces out of his church in Canal-street, and that the congregation had to move to another place.

I intimated to you, in my last, that Bennett of the *Herald* was about to publish, conjointly with the Doctor, his Book of Exposures; but since, have learned that it is about to come out in Boston. He expects to make a fortune out of it, and I presume he needs it; but I feel sure that it will make converts to the Mormon faith. He has borrowed largely from Com. Morris' lascivious poems.

A general order, signed by Hugh McFall, Adjutant-General, and authorized by you, has appeared in the *Herald*, ordering me to repair to Nauvoo, to take command of the Legion, and to bring with me Brig.-Gen. J. G. Bennett, which states that, if the requisition be persisted in, blood must be shed. I have assured Bennett of the *Herald* that I deem it a *hoax*, but he insists upon it that it is genuine. My reply to it has appeared to day in that paper. I have there stated that I have written to Gov. Carlin for instructions. This is not so: it is only a *rub*.

On the whole, you will only be made a greater prophet and a greater man—a great *Emperor*, by the affliction and consideration of your good friends.

My respects, with those of Mrs. B., to your lady.

I am, dear sir, your sincere friend,

JAMES ARLINGTON BENNETT.

This letter was placed in the hands of General Hugh McFall, who immediately wrote a refutation of the clause concerning himself to Governor Carlin, and also one for the *Wasp*. The general order was not written by McFall, neither had he a knowledge of its existence until shown to him in the letter. It was evidently got up by our enemies to increase excitement and anger, and is barely another addition to the many slanderous reports put in circulation by evil and designing men.

Thursday, 15.—In council with C. A. Warren, Esq. Also counseled Uncle John Smith and Brother Daniel C. Davis to move immediately to Keokuk, and help to build up a city.

Friday, 16.—At home with Brother Rogers, who was painting my likeness.

Saturday, 17.—I was at home with Brother Rogers, who continued painting my portrait. Elder William Clayton wrote Governor Carlin a long letter, showing up the Missouri persecution and my sufferings in their true colors.

Ship *Sidney* sailed from Liverpool for New Orleans with 180 Saints.

Sunday, 18.—At home. In the evening, received a visit from my mother.

Monday, 19, and *Tuesday, 20.*—With Brother Rogers, painting at my house.

Wednesday, 21.—In the large room over the store. In the evening had a visit from Elder John Taylor, who is just recovering from a long and very severe attack of sickness. I counseled Elder Taylor concerning the printing office, removing one press to Keokuk, &c.

Thursday, 22.—At home, arranging with Remmick concerning moving printing press to Keokuk, buying paper, &c.

Friday, 23.—At home. Visited by Elder Taylor.

Colonel George Miller was elected Bigadier-General of the 1st Cohort, Nauvoo Legion, to fill the vacancy of General Wilson Law, promoted.

Saturday, 24.—The legion was called out for general parade, and reviewed by General Law. In the evening, Lieutenant-Colonel Stephen Markham was elected Colonel of the 1st Regiment, 1st Cohort, to fill the place of Colonel George Miller, promoted; and Captain John D. Parker elected to fill his place; and Captain Thomas Rich to fill the place of Major Wightman, deceased.

At home. Had a visit from Mr. Joseph Murdock, Sen., and lady concerning some land, &c., at St. Joseph.

Sunday, 25.—At the Grove. Spoke more than two hours, chiefly on the subject of persecution.

Ship *Medford* sailed from Liverpool for New Orleans with 214 Saints.

Monday, 26.—The office of Notary Public for the city of Nauvoo was created by the city council, and James Sloan was elected. A seal for the Municipal Court was ordered by the council.

Tuesday, 27, and *Wednesday, 28.*—At home. Nothing of importance transpired. 28.—Ship *Henry* sailed from Liverpool for New Orleans with 157 Saints.

September 28, 1841:

A Baptist Excommunication.

Resolved, that William Seichrist be excluded from the fellowship of this [the first regular Baptist] church [of the city of Alleghany, Alleghany county, Pennsylvania,] for embracing and maintaining a heresy,—to *wit*, doctrines peculiar to a late sect called Mormons or Latter-day Saints, that miracles can be wrought through the instrumentality of faith; that special revelations from God are now given to men; and that godly men are now endowed with the gift of prophecy, such as to foretell future events. William Benson, Church Clerk. Deacon John Beck was moderator of the meeting.

Thursday, 29.—This day, Emma began to be sick with fever; consequently I kept in the house with her all day.

Friday, 30.—Emma is no better. I was with her all day.

Saturday, October 1.—This morning I had a very severe pain in my left side, and was not able to be about. Emma sick as usual. I had previously sent for the Temple committee to balance their accounts and ascertain how the Temple business was going on. Some reports had been circulated that the committee was not making a righteous disposition of property consecrated for the building of the Temple, and there appeared to be some dissatisfaction amongst the laborers. After carefully examining the accounts and enquiring into the manner of the proceedings of the committee, I expressed myself perfectly satisfied with them and their works. The books were balanced between the trustee and committee, and the wages of all agreed upon.

Temple Committe Affairs.

I said to the brethren that I was amenable to the state for the faithful discharge of my duties as trustee-in-trust, and that the Temple committee were accountable to me, and to no other authority; and they must not take notice of any complaints from any source, but let the complaints be made to me, if any were needed, and I would make things right. The parties separated perfectly satisfied, and I remarked that I would have a notice published, stating that I had examined their accounts and was satisfied,

&c. It was also agreed that the recorder's office should be moved to the Temple, for the convenience of all.

In this day's *Wasp* I noticed the following letter from Elder Pratt:

Letter of Elder Orson Pratt—Denying any Relations with John C. Bennett.

CITY OF NAUVOO, ILLINOIS, September 26, 1842.

Mr. Editor:

DEAR SIR:—I noticed in the last week's *Wasp* a letter from Dr. R. D. Foster, written from New York city, which states that Dr. John C. Bennett had declared in said city that he had received a letter from me and from my wife, and that we were preparing to leave and expose Mormonism.

I wish through the medium of your paper to say to the public that said statements are entirely false. We have never at any time written any letter or letters to Dr. J. C. Bennett, on any subject whatever. Neither are we "preparing to leave and expose Mormonism," but intend to make Nauvoo our residence, and Mormonism our motto.

Respectfully,

ORSON PRATT.

Sunday, 2.—About ten o'clock in the forenoon, a messenger arrived from Quincy, stating that the governor had offered a reward of $200 for Joseph Smith, Jun., and also $200 for Orrin P. Rockwell. This report was fully established on receipt of the mail papers. The *Quincy Whig* also stated that Governor Reynolds has offered a reward, and published the governor's proclamation offering a reward of $300 for Joseph Smith, Jun., and $300 for Orrin P. Rockwell. It is not expected that much will be effected by the rewards.

Reward offered for the Arrest of the Prophet.

Emma continued very sick. I was with her all day.

Monday, 3.—Emma was a little better. I was with her all day.

Tuesday, 4.—Emma is very sick again. I attended with her all the day, being somewhat poorly myself.

Wednesday, 5.—My dear Emma was worse. Many fears were entertained that she would not recover. She was baptized twice in the river, which evidently did her much good. She grew worse again at night, and continued very sick indeed. I was unwell, and much troubled on account of Emma's sickness.

The illness of Emma Smith.

Elder Rigdon called Elder William Clayton into his office, and said he had some matters to make known. He had been at Carthage and had conversation with Judge Douglas concerning Governor Carlin's proceedings, &c., and had ascertained that Carlin had intentionally issued an illegal writ, expecting thereby to draw President Joseph to Carthage to get acquitted by habeas corpus before Douglas, and having men there waiting with a legal writ to serve on Joseph as soon as he was released under the other one, and bear him away to Missouri, without further ceremony. Elder Rigdon asked what power the governor's proclamation gave to any man or set of men who might be disposed to take President Joseph. He was answered, "Just the same power and authority which a legal warrant gave to an officer."

Rigdon's Reports of Plots.

It is more and more evident that Carlin is determined to have me taken to Missouri, if he can. But may the Almighty Jehovah shield and defend me from all their power, and prolong my days in peace, that I may guide His people in righteousness, until my head is white with old age. Amen.

Thursday, *6*.—Emma is better; and although it is the day on which she generally grows worse, yet she appears considerably easier. May the Lord speedily raise her to the bosom of her family, that the heart of His servant may be comforted again. Amen. My health is comfortable.

Friday, *7*.—This morning Elder Elias Higbee states about the same things as were stated by Elder Rigdon two days ago, and also that he had been informed that many of the Missourians are coming to unite with the militia of this state voluntarily, and at their own expense; so that after the court rises at Carthage, if

More Missouri Plots.

they don't take me there, they will come and search the city, &c. It is likely that this is *only* report.

Emma is somewhat better. I am cheerful and well.

From the situation and appearance of things abroad, I concluded to leave home foı a short season, until there should be some change in the proceedings of my enemies. Accordingly, at twenty minutes after eight o'clock in the evening, I started away in company with Brothers John Taylor, Wilson Law, and John D. Parker, and traveled through the night and part of next day; and, after a tedious journey, arrived at Father James Taylor's well and in good spirits.

The Prophet's Removal to Father Taylor's.

This day the teachers met in Nauvoo, and organized into a quorum, by appointing Elisha Averett, president; James Huntsman and Elijah Averett, counselors; Samuel Eggleston, scribe; and eleven members.

Monday, 10.—Elder Taylor returned to Nauvoo and found Emma gaining slowly. My health and spirits are good.

Tuesday, 11.—From the *Times and Seasons*:—

Announcement Concerning Temple Committee Affairs.

To the Saints at Nauvoo and Scattered Abroad:

This may certify that President Joseph Smith, the trustee-in-trust for the Temple, called upon the Temple committee on the 1st instant to present their books and accounts for examination, and to give account of their work at the temple. After carefully and attentively examining and comparing their books and accounts, the trustee expressed himself well satisfied with the proceedings and labors of the committee, and ordered that this be published in the *Times and Seasons*, that the Saints may know the facts, and be thereby encourged to double their exertions and forward means to roll on the building of the Temple in Nauvoo. It was also ordered that the recorder's office be henceforth removed to the committee house near the Temple. All property and means must therefore be brought to that place, where it will be recorded in due form.

WILLIAM CLAYTON.
Clerk and Recorder of the Temple.

NAUVOO, October 11, 1842.

Thursday, 13.—The brethren arrived from Wisconsin

with a raft of about 90,000 feet of boards and 24,000 cubic feet of timber for the Temple and Nauvoo House.

Saturday 15.—Brother John D. Parker returned to Nauvoo and informed my friends that I was well.

Sunday, 16.—I copy the following from the *New York Herald:*

THE MORMONS.

ARLINGTON HOUSE, October 16, 1841.

General J. G. Bennett·

SIR:—Some time since I addressed a letter to Joseph Smith, the Mormon Prophet, in answer to a letter of his introducing to "my kind attention," a friend of his from the holy city of Nauvoo.

In this letter I expressed my regret that the quarrel between him and John C. Bennett should have at all found its way to the public eye, this being the sole cause of placing him in his present awkward situation. I likewise commiserated with him in his affliction, and signed myself at the conclusion of my letter, as his friend, which I really am, and the friend of all good Mormons, as well as other good men.

Why should I not be Joseph Smith's friend? He has done nothing to injure me, nor do I believe he has done anything to injure ex-Governor Boggs, of Missouri. The governor, no doubt, under strong feelings, may have thought and believed that Smith had preconcerted the plan for his assassination; but there is no legal evidence whatever of that fact—none by which an unprejudiced jury would convict any man; yet to send this man into Missouri, under the present requisition, would be an act of great injustice, as his ruin would be certain.

How could any man, against whom there is a bitter religious prejudice escape ruin, being in the circumstances of Smith? Look at the history of past ages—see the force of fanaticism and bigotry in bringing to the stake some of the best of men; and in all these cases the persecutors had their pretexts, as well as in the case of the Mormon chief. Nothing follows its victim with such deadly aim as religious zeal, and therefore nothing should be so much guarded against by the civil power.

Smith, I conceive, has just as good a right to establish a church, if he can do it, as Luther, Calvin, Wesley, Fox, or even King Henry the Eighth. All these chiefs in religion had their opponents, and their people their persecutors. Henry the Eighth was excommunicated, body and bones, soul and all, by his holiness, the Pope; still the church of England has lived as well as all the other sects.

Just so it will be with the Mormons. They may kill one prophet and confine in chains half his followers, but another will take his place, and the Mormons will still go ahead. One of their Elders said to me, when conversing on this subject, that they were like a mustard plant, —"If you don't disturb it, the seed will fall and multiply; and if you kick it about, you only give the seed more soil, and it will multiply the more."

Undertake to convince them that they are wrong, and that Smith is an impostor, and the answer is, laying the hand on the heart, "I know in my own soul that it is true, and want no better evidence: I feel happy in my faith; and why should I be disturbed?"

Now, I cannot see but what this is the sentiment that governs all religiously disposed persons, their object being heaven and happiness, no matter what their church and creed. They, therefore, cannot be put down while the Constitution of the United States offers them protection in common with all other sects, and while they believe that their eternal salvation is at stake. From what I know of the people, I fully believe that all the real, sincere Mormons would die sooner than abandon their faith and their religion.

General John C. Bennett has stated that to conquer the Mormon Legion it would require five to one against them, all things taken into consideration, and that they will die to a man sooner than give up their Prophet.

Now, is the arrest of this man worth such a sacrifice of life as must necessarily follow an open war with his people? The loss of from one to three thousand lives will, no doubt, follow in an attempt to accomplish an object not in the end worth a button. Persecute them, and you are sure to multiply them. This is fully proved since the Missouri persecution, as since that affair they have increased one hundred fold.

It is the best policy, both of Missouri and Illinois, to let them alone; for if they are drove farther west, they may set up an independent government, under which they can worship the Almighty as may suit their taste. Indeed, I would recommend to the Prophet to pull up stakes and take possession of the Oregon territory in his own right, and establish an independent empire. In one hundred years from this time, no nation on earth could conquer such a people. Let not the history of David be forgotten. If the Prophet Joseph would do this, millions would flock to his standard and join his cause. He could then make his own laws by the voice of revelation, and have them executed like the act of one man.

With respect to myself, I would just repeat that I am the Prophet's friend, and the friend of his people, merely from sympathy, as my arm has ever been lifted on the side of the persecuted and oppressed. I have never in my life followed the fat ox, nor bowed for a favor on my own account to mortal man. While I despise the purse-proud man, I am proud to the proud man, and humble to the humble; and where men were contending, have ever thrown myself on the weakest side.

By inserting this communication, it is presumed that no one will hold the *Herald* responsible for the sentiments it contains; yet I have no doubt that there are thousands of independent, liberal-minded men in this country who think as I do. Neither the Mormon Prophet nor his people can add anything to my fortune or reputation. I expect nothing from them; they are a poor and industrious people, and have nothing to give. I am influenced in my conduct towards them by a spirit of benevolence and mercy, and hope the governor and state of Illinois will act in the like manner. It is true I was commissioned in their Legion, through the instrumentality of their enemy, General John C. Bennett, an act entirely of their own, without my agency; but I was as much their friend before as since.

The Missouri persecution fixed my attention and commiseration on the people. It must be recollected, too, that the Mormon Prophet and his people are the most ardent friends and promoters of literature and science. These are elementary principles in their social system, and this certainly is contrary to everything like despotism.

I hope, therefore, and with great deference express that hope, that ex-Governor Boggs will withdraw his demand for the Prophet, and let those poor people rest in peace. Both he and Governor Carlin will feel much more at peace with themselves by quashing the whole proceedings.

Most respectfully,
Your humble servant,
JAMES ARLINGTON BENNETT.
Counselor at Law, &c.

By this I discover a spark of liberty burning in the bosom of the writer. May it continue to burn and burn, till it once more fires the whole land with its heavenly influence.

Thursday, 20.—Early this morning I arrived at home on a visit to my family. During the day I was visited by several of the brethren, who rejoiced to see me once more. Emma is still getting better, and is able to attend to a little business, having this day closed contract and received pay for a quarter section of land of Brother Job V. Barnum.

Justin Butterfield's Legal Opinion on the Efforts to Drag Joseph Smith into Missouri.

CHICAGO, October 20, 1842.

Sidney Rigdon, Esq.

DEAR SIR:—In answer to your favors of the 17th instant, Mr. Warren was correct in the information he gave you of my opinion of the illegality of the requisition made by the governor of Missouri upon the governor of this state for the surrender of Joseph Smith, and that the governor of this state should cause him to be arrested for the purpose of being surrendered. I had no doubt but the supreme court of this state would discharge him upon habeas corpus. Subsequent examination has confirmed me in that opinion.

I understand from your letter, and from the statement of facts made to me by Mr. Warren, that the requisition of the governor of Missouri is accompanied by an affidavit of ex-Governor Boggs, stating in substance that on the 6th day of May last he was shot while sitting in his house, with intent to kill; and, as he verily believes, the act was committed by O. P. Rockwell; and that Joseph Smith was accessory to the crime before its commission; and that he has *fled* from justice. That it can be proved that Joseph Smith was not in the state of Missouri at the time the crime was committed, but was in this state; that it is untrue that he was in the state of Missouri at the time of the commission of the said crime, or has been there at any time since. He could not, therefore, have *fled* from that state since the commission of said crime.

The right on the part of the governor of Missouri to demand Smith, and the duty on the part of the governor of this state to deliver him up, if they exist, are given and imposed by that clause of the Constitution of the United States which declares "that a person charged in any state with treason, felony, or other crime, who *shall flee* from justice and be found in another state, shall, on demand of the executive authority of the state from which he fled, be delivered up, to be removed to the state having jurisdiction of the crimes.

It is unnecessary to refer to the act of Congress in relation to the delivery up of fugitives from justice, as Congress has just so much power, and *no more,* than is expressly given by the said clause in the Constitution. The Constitution is the best exponent of itself. What persons, then, can be surrendered up by the governor of one state to the governor of another?

First. He must be a person charged with treason, felony, or other crime. "It is sufficient if he be *charged* with the commission of crime, either by indictment found or by affidavit. Second. He must be a person who shall flee from justice and be found in another state."

It is not sufficient to satisfy this branch of the Constitution, that he should be "charged" with having fled from justice. Unless he has actually *fled* from the state where the offense was committed, to *another state*, the governor of this state has no jurisdiction over his person, and cannot deliver him up,

When Mr. Smith is brought up on a habeas corpus, he will have a right, under the 3rd section of our habeas corpus act, to introduce testimony, and show that the process upon which he is arrested was obtained by *false pretense;* that it is untrue that he fled from the state of Missouri, to evade being brought to justice there, for the crime of which he is charged. He will have the right to place himself upon the platform of the Constitution of the United States, and say, I am a citizen of the state of Illinois; I have not fled from the state of Missouri, or from the "justice" of that state, on account of the commission of the crime with which I am charged. I am ready to prove that the charge of having fled from that state is false, and I am not, therefore, subject under the Constitution of the United States, to be delivered up to that state for trial.

You say, in your letter to me, that you doubt whether on a habeas corpus the court would have a right to try the question, whether Smith was in Missouri at the time of the commission of the crime of which he is charged. To this I answer, that upon a habeas corpus, the court would be bound to try the question, whether Smith fled from justice from Missouri to this state. The affidavit of Mr. Boggs is not conclusive on this point. It may be rebutted. Unless Smith is a person who has fled from justice, he is not subject to be delivered up, under the express provisions of our own habeas corpus act. He has a right to show that the affidavit is false, and that the order for his arrest was obtained by false pretenses. Again, the affidavit on its face was not sufficient to authorize the arrest of Smith. It is evasive and deceptive. It does not show that he fled from the state of Missouri to evade justice for the commission of the crime of which he is charged by Governor Boggs.

Robert G. Williams, in the year 1835, was indicted in the state of Alabama for attempting to incite rebellion and insurrection in that state. He was demanded by the governor of that state of the governor of New York, and the requisition stated that he had fled from justice. The governor of the state of New York (Marcy) took notice that the said Williams was a citizen of the state of New York, and had not fled from justice from Alabama, and on *that ground alone* refused to surrender him up. This was a stronger case than that of Smith, as an *indictment had been found.* Governor Marcy puts his refusal upon the express ground that, by the Constitution of the United States, the governor of one state had no right to demand, nor the governor of another state a right to surrender up, one of his citizens, unless he had fled from justice; and it was the right and duty of the governor upon whom the demand was made to inquire into the fact whether he had fled from justice before he made the surrender.

I have the book containing all the proceedings in this case of Williams. There are several other cases equal in point, and they proceed upon the ground that a governor of a state has no jurisdiction over the body of a citizen to arrest and surrender him up to a foreign state, unless he is a fugitive from that state, unless he has fled from the state to evade "justice," or, in other words, to evade being tried for the offense with which he is charged.

In a despotic form of government, the sovereign power is the will of the monarch, who can act in every instance as may suit his pleasure. But can the governor of one of our states, of his own mere will, without any authority from the Constitution, or the legislative power of the state, arrest and deliver up to a foreign government any person whatever? If he can do this, then is the liberty of the citizen wholly at his disposal.

The writ of habeas corpus is a suit which every person imprisoned or unlawfully detained has a right to prosecute for the recovery of his liberty; and, if he is in custody by process from a competent power, he is entitled to his discharge when the jurisdiction has been executed.

The government of this state has no power or jurisdiction over the person of a citizen of this state to arrest and cause him to be delivered up and transported to another state, except the power is expressly given to him by the Constitution of the United States. And what is that power? It only authorizes the governor of one state to surrender up a fugitive from justice, to return him back to the state from whence he has fled.

First, The person to be surrendered up must be a fugitive from the state to which it is attempted to surrender him.

Second. He must be a fugitive *from justice;* in other words, he must have been in the state when and where the crime was committed, and have fled from the state to evade being apprehended and tried for that crime.

Third. Unless he is, in fact, such a fugitive from justice, the governor has no power, by the laws and Constitution, to deliver him up.

Fourth. If he is charged with being a fugitive from justice, and the governor cause him to be apprehended on that charge, he has a right to sue out a habeas corpus; and when brought up on that writ, he has the undoubted right of showing that the governor has no constitutional power to deliver him up to another state; that he has not "fled from justice into this state,'' and is not such a person as the Constitution authorizes the governor to deliver up; and that it would be an excess of jurisdiction on the part of the governor to deliver him up.

The question to be examined into, upon the return of the habeas corpus, would be a mere question of locality. The question would be was Smith in this state, or not, at the time the crime was committed in Missouri? If he was in this state at that time, then he could not be a fugitive from justice from Missouri, in the sense of the Constitution; and the governor would have no power to deliver him up.

The argument that because Governor Boggs has made affidavit that Smith has fled from justice, his affidavit is to be taken as conclusive on that point, and that upon the return of a habeas corpus, Smith would be precluded from controverting or showing the falsity of that affidavit, is too absurd to require a serious answer.

The liberties of the citizens of this state are not held on quite so feeble a tenure, nor does the Constitution authorize the governor to transport the citizens of this state upon a mere ''charge'' made by a citizen of another state. Such is not the reading of the Constitution. That instrument only authorizes the delivery up of such persons, ''who shall flee,'' upon the demand of the executive authority of the state from which they ''fled.'' There must have been a ''flight'' in *fact and in deed* from the state where the offense was committed, or the governor has no jurisdiction to ''deliver up.''

If the charge of having ''fled'' is made and the governor acting in *pais** is attempting to deliver up upon that charge, the person attempted to be made the victim has a clear, undoubted, constitutional right by means of a writ of habeas corpus, to test its truth before a judicial tribunal of the country; and, if the charge is proven to be false, the governor is ousted of his jurisdiction over the person of the prisoner, and he is restored to his liberty before he has undergone the penalty of the transportation to a foreign country upon the mere charge of an interested or partial witness.

The power of the executive of a state to surrender up a citizen to be transported to a foreign state for trial, is a most tremendous power, which might be greatly abused, were it not limited by constitutional checks, and the citizens secured against its despotic exercise by the writ of habeas corpus.

In the case of Williams, the governor of New York, in his reply to the governor of Alabama, says, ''What occurs daily in the ordinary course of criminal proceedings, may take place in regard to persons transported to a distant jurisdiction for trial. It may happen that an innocent man will be accused; and, if demanded, he must be delivered

* A judicial act outside of court and not recorded.—Century Dictionary.

up, should your exposition of the Constitution be sanctioned. Under these circumstances, his condition would be perilous indeed,—dragged from his home, far removed from friends, borne down by the weight of imputed guilt, and unable, probably, to obtain the evidence by which he might vindicate his innocence. If appearances were against him, he could scarcely hope to escape unmerited condemnation."

The American colonists regard the exercise of this power as an act of revolting tyranny, and assigned it in the Declaration of Independence as one of the prominent causes that impelled them to a separation from the British Empire. A power which may be thus oppressively used should be resorted to with the greatest caution. When its exercise is invoked, it is not sufficient that the case may apparently come within the letter of the Constitution. It is the duty of the Executive before yielding a blind obedience to the letter of the law, to see that the case comes within the spirit and meaning of the Constitution.

It may be pleasing as well as instructive to look into the proceedings of the executive of our sister state, and witness that, by faithfully administering the law in relation to the delivering up of fugitives from justice, according to its spirit and meaning, they have saved at least two of the citizens of Illinois from becoming victims to its abuse. In the year 1839, the governor of the state of New York was presented with the copy of an indictment by a grand jury in the city of New York against John and Nathan Aldrich, for fraud in obtaining goods by false pretenses, and was requested to make a requisition upon the governor of Illinois to surrender them up as fugitives from justice.

Now, here was a case which came exactly within the letter of the law of Congress in relation to fugitives from justice. An indictment *had been found* charging them with having *committed a crime*. But did the governor of New York make the "requisition?" No; he referred the application to the Hon. John C. Spencer, now Secretary of War, and one of the most enlightened lawyers of the age.

Extract of Mr. Spencer's Opinion upon the Case.

The constitutional provision under which requisitions may be made by the governor of one state upon the governor of another was a substitute for the principle recognized by the law of nations, by which one sovereign is bound to deliver to another fugitives who have committed certain offenses. These offenses are of the deepest grade of criminality, and robbers, murderers and incendiaries, and those enumerated as proper to be surrendered. Following the analogy thus suggested, the provisions in our Constitution, it would seem, should be construed to embrace similar cases only, except, perhaps, those offenses which arise from an abuse of the same constitutional provision. That provision must be guarded with the utmost care, or it will become intolerable. I do not think the circumstances of the case before me are of such grave import, or the offense itself of such high grade, as to justify the requisition desired. The power given by the Constitution ought not to be cheapened or applied to trifling offenses, or indeed to any that was not originally contemplated.

For the reasons stated in Mr. Spencer's opinion, the governor of New York refused to make the requisition upon the governor of Illinois. The case certainly came within the letter of the law, but not within the spirit and meaning. So with the affidavit of Governor Boggs, when he swears that Smith has fled from justice. It may come within the letter of the Constitution; but does it come within its spirit and meaning? Does it show that Smith was in Missouri at the time of the commission of the crime,and that he fled from that state to evade being brought to justice for that crime? Or does it refer to the flight of Smith and the Mormons from Missouri some years since?

I will refer to one more case of a similar nature. Lord Campbell, formerly attorney-general of England, in a recent debate in Parliament upon the subject of the Creole, made the following remarks:

"To show how cautious states should be in making such concessions one to the other reciprocally, he would mention a case that occurred when he was attorney-general. A treaty had been agreed upon between the state of New York and the province of Canada, by which the government of each agreed reciprocally to deliver up the citizens or subjects of the other against whom grand juries had found a bill, and who had sought refuge within the territories of the other. It happened that a slave had escaped from his master in New York, and had got to Canada. To facilitate his escape,he rode a horse of his master's for a part of the way, but turned him back on reaching the frontier. The authorities of New York well knew that England would not give up a runaway slave, and that as they could not claim him under the treaty, they therefore had a bill of indictment against him, before a New York grand jury for stealing the horse, though it was clear the *animus furandi* was wanting. The grand jury, however, found a true bill against him for the felony, and he was claimed under the treaty. The governor, under such circumstances refused to give him up until he had consulted the government in England. He (Lord Campbell) was consulted, and gave it as his opinion that the man ought not to be given up, as the true bill, where no felony had been committed, did not bring the case within the treaty. The man was not given up, and there the matter rested. This, he repeated, showed the necessity of the greatest caution where reciprocal rights of surrender were granted between states.

It is not to be presumed that the executive of this state would knowingly, lend his aid in dragging one of our citizens, who is not a fugitive from justice, into a foreign state for trial. The governor has undoubtedly been misled by the evasive affidavit which accompanied the requisition.

I would advise that Mr. Smith procure respectable and sufficient affidavits to prove beyond all question, that he was in the state and not in Missouri, at the time the crime with which he is charged was committed, and upon these affidavits, apply to the governor to countermand the warrant he has issued for his arrest.

If he should refuse so to do, I am clearly of the opinion that, upon the above state of facts, the supreme court will discharge him upon habeas corpus.

Respectfully your obedient servant,
JUSTIN BUTTERFIELD.

The foregoing letter of Mr. Butterfield (United States' attorney for the district of Illinois,) shows, in a very lucid manner, what our rights and privileges are, pertaining to the habeas corpus, and accords with the opinion of every intelligent man,—the opinions of ex-Governor Boggs, Governor Reynolds, of Missouri, and Governor Carlin, to the contrary, notwithstanding.

CHAPTER X.

TEMPLE AFFAIRS—THE PROPHET'S ADDRESS TO "NEW-COMERS"—CITY COUNCIL'S ACTIONS AS TO WRITS OF HABEAS CORPUS.

Friday, October 21, 1842.—This evening I returned, in company with John D. Parker, to Father Taylor's, judging it wisdom to keep out of the way of my enemies a while longer at least, although all is peace and quiet, and a prospect that my enemies will not trouble me much more at present.

Temporary Floor in the Temple.

Sunday, 23.—This day the Temple committee laid before the Saints the propriety and advantages of laying a temporary floor in the Temple, that the brethren might henceforth meet in the Temple to worship, instead of meeting in the Grove. This was my instructions, and the Saints seemed to rejoice at this privilege very much.

Monday, 24.—Printing office took fire, which was extinguished with difficulty.

Tuesday, 25.—Ship *Emerald* sailed from Liverpool with 250 Saints for New Orleans.

Friday, 28.—Soon after daylight this morning, I returned home again to visit my family. I found Emma worse; the remainder of the family well. In the afternoon I rode out into the city and took a little exercise. From the appearance of things abroad, we are encouraged to believe that my enemies will not trouble me much more at present.

This day the brethren finished laying the temporary floor, and seats in the Temple, and its appearance is truly pleasant and cheering. The exertions of the brethren during the past week to accomplish this thing are truly praiseworthy.

Saturday, 29.—About ten in the forenoon I rode up and viewed the Temple. I expressed my satisfaction at the arrangements, and was pleased with the progress made in the sacred edifice. After conversing with several of the brethren, and shaking hands with numbers who were very much rejoiced to see their Prophet again, I returned home; but soon afterwards went over to the store, where a number of brethren and sisters were assembled, who had arrived this morning from the neighborhood of New York, Long Island, &c. After Elders Taylor, Woodruff, and Samuel Bennett had addressed the brethren and sisters, I spoke to them at considerable length, showing them the proper course to pursue, and how to act in regard to making purchases of land, &c.

The Prophet at the Temple.

I showed them that it was generally in consequence of the brethren disregarding or disobeying counsel that they became dissatisfied and murmured; and many when they arrived here, were dissatisfied with the conduct of some of the Saints, because everything was not done perfectly right, and they get angry, and thus the devil gets advantage over them to destroy them. I told them I was but a man, and they must not expect me to be perfect; if they expected perfection from me, I should expect it from them; but if they would bear with my infirmities and the infirmities of the brethren, I would likewise bear with their infirmities.

The Prophet's Advice to New-comers.

I told them it was likely I would have again to hide up in the woods, but they must not be discouraged, but build up the city, the Temple, &c. When my enemies take away my rights, I will bear it and keep out of the way; but if they take away your rights, I will fight for you. I blessed them and departed.

Dr. Willard Richards returned to Nauvoo with his family, having visited most of the churches in the Eastern States, and preached to them the necessity of building the Temple and gathering to this place, in obedience to the commandment of God to His people.

Return of Dr. Richards to Nauvoo.

Sunday, 30.—The Saints met to worship on a temporary floor, in the Temple, the walls of which were about four feet high above the basement; and notwithstanding its size, it was well filled. It had been expected that I would address them, but I sent word that I was so sick that I could not meet with them; consequently Elder John Taylor delivered a discourse. In the evening I went to visit the sick, &c.

Monday, 31.—I rode out to my farm with my children, and did not return until after dark.

Tuesday, Nov. 1, 1842.—I rode with Emma to the Temple for the benefit of her health. She is rapidly gaining. In the afternoon went to see Dr. Willard Richards, who was very sick at Elder Woodruff's; afterwards, accompanied by my children and William Clayton, rode out towards the farm. When going down the hill, near Casper's the carriage got over-balanced and upset. I was thrown some distance from the carriage, and all three of the children almost under it. I arose and enquired if any of the children were killed; but upon examination, there was no one seriously hurt. Frederick G. Williams had his cheek bruised, which was the worst injury received.

Accident to the Prophet's Carriage.

It seemed miraculous how we escaped serious injury from this accident; and our escape could not be attributed to any other power than that of Divine Providence. I feel thankful to God for this instance of His kind and watchful care over His servant and family.

The carriage was so much broken, we left it, and putting the children in Brother Stoddard's buggy, returned. In the evening I rode to the Temple with two of my children.

Wednesday, *2*.—Spent this forenoon in removing the books, desk, &c., from my store over to my house. In the afternoon rode out to my farm, and spent the time plowing, &c.

Thursday, *3*.—Rode out with Emma to the Temple.

Friday, *4*.—Rode out with Lorin Walker to examine his timber north of the city.

Return of Hyrum Smith and William Law.

Brothers Hyrum Smith and William Law returned from their mission to the East. They bring very good reports concerning the public feeling, and say that John C. Bennett's *expose* has done no hurt, but much good.

Return of Brigham Young, et al.

President Brigham Young, Heber C. Kimball George A. Smith and Amasa Lyman, of the Twelve, also returned from their missions, and brought a similar report. They had visited the conferences according to the notice which they had published on September 12th, and had also visited many of the principal places in the state, delivered addresses to the people, and found a friendly feeling in most cases.

Saturday, *5*.—I tarried at home on account of the rain. I received a visit from some Indians, who were accompanied by a negro interpreter. They expressed great friendship for the Mormon people, and said they were their friends. After considerable conversation and partaking of victuals, they departed, evidently highly gratified with their visit.

I told Dr. Richards the Mississippi would be frozen over in less than a month, although the weather was then warm and pleasant.

Sunday, *6*.—At home all day. My brother Hyrum preached. Afternoon received a visit from Dr. Willard Richards.

Monday, *7*.—Spent the forenoon in council with Brother Hyrum Smith and some of the Twelve, and in giving instructions concerning the contemplated journey to Springfield on the 15th December next, and what course ought to be pursued in reference to the case of bankruptcy. In the afternoon Calvin A. Warren, Esq., arrived, and I called upon some of the Twelve and others to testify before Squire Warren what they knew in reference to the appointment of trustee-in-trust, &c., showing also from the records that I was authorized by the Church to purchase and hold property in the name of the Church, and that I had acted in all things according to the counsel given to me.

The Prophet's Consultation with Calvin A. Warren.

Tuesday, *8*. -This afternoon called upon Windsor P. Lyons and others to make affidavits concerning the frauds and irregularities practiced in the post office in Nauvoo. A petition was drawn and signed by many, and sent by Squire Warren to Judge Young, [U. S. senator from Illinois] with a request that the latter should present the same to the postmaster general, and use his influence to have the present postmaster removed, and a new one appointed. I was recommended for the appointment. In the afternoon officiated in court as mayor at my house.

Post Office Affairs at Nauvoo.

Wednesday, *9*.—Paid E. Rhodes $436.93, it being the amount of three notes due for the north-west quarter of Sec. 9, 6 N. 8 W., and presided in city council, a special meeting to investigate the writ of habeas corpus.

Thursday, *Friday*, *and Saturday*, *10*, *11*, *12*.—Presided at adjourned session of the city council at my house.

Sunday, *13*.—I was at home through the day.

Letter of George D. Watt, Reporting Arrival of Emigrants.

SHIP SIDNEY, NEW ORLEANS, November 13, 1842.

DEAR BROTHER.—We have had a passage of fifty-six days—fine weather—with a kind captain and crew, who allowed us every reasonable privilege. There have been five deaths out of the company, and one sailor who fell from the yard arm and was killed. Brother Yates' eldest child, Sister Cannon, Brother Browne's child, and two children belonging to a man not in the Church.

We stuck upon the bar at the mouth of the river, thirty-four hours. About two hours after we got off, the *Medford* came on the bar, where she stuck thirty hours. We landed here on the 11th instant, and the *Medford* arrived today, 13th. She lies about ten yards from us. They have had two deaths. Upon the whole, a good passage.

We have taken one of the largest and best steamboats in this port. We pay two and a half dollars per head, and twenty-five cents per cwt. above the weight allowed each person, which is one hundred pounds. We are all going up together.

Yours truly,
GEORGE D. WATT.

Monday, 14.—Presided at city council, when was passed the following "Ordinance regulating the proceedings on writs of habeas corpus."

Writ of Habeas Corpus.

Sec. 1. Be it ordained by the city council of the city of Nauvoo, that if any person or persons shall be or stand committed or detained for any criminal or supposed criminal matter, it shall and may be lawful for him, her, or them to apply to the municipal court, when in session, or to the clerk thereof in vacation, for a writ of habeas corpus; which application shall be in writing and signed by the prisoner, or some person on his, her, or their behalf, setting forth the facts concerning his, her, or their imprisonment, and in whose custody he, she, or they are detained; and shall be accompanied by a copy of the warrant, or warrants of commitments, or an affidavit that the said copy had been demanded of the person or persons in whose custody the prisoner or prisoners are detained, and by him or them refused or neglected to be given. The said court or clerk to whom the application shall be made, shall forthwith award the said writ of habeas corpus, unless it shall appear from the petition itself, or from the documents annexed, that the party can neither be discharged nor admitted to bail, nor in any other manner relieved, which said writ shall be issued under the hand of the clerk, and the seal of the court; which seal may be a written one, until another shall be obtained, and shall be in the following words, to wit: "Seal of the Municipal Court of the city of Nauvoo."

STATE OF ILLINOIS, } ss.
City of Nauvoo, }

To the People of the State of Illinois, to the Marshal of said City, Greeting:

Whereas application has been made before the municipal court of said city that the body (or bodies) of A B, &c., is or are in the custody of C D, &c., of &c., these are therefore to command, the said C D, &., of &c., to safely have the body (or bodies) of said A B, &c., in his custody, detained, as it is said, together with the day and cause of his (her or their) caption and detention by whatsoever name the said A, B,&c., may be known or called, before the municipal court of said city, forthwith to abide such order as the said court shall make in his behalf; and further, if the said C D, &c., or other person or persons having said A B, &c., in custody shall refuse, or neglect to comply with the provisions of this writ, you, the marshal of said city, or other person authorized to serve the same, are hereby required to arrest the person or persons so refusing or neglecting to comply as aforesaid, and bring him or them, together with the person or persons in his or their custody, forthwith before the municipal court aforesaid, to be dealt with according to law; and herein fail not to bring this writ with you.

Witness, J. S,, clerk of the municipal court at Nauvoo, this......day of.........in the year of our Lord one thousand eight hundred and forty..........

J. S., Clerk.

And [this shall] be directed to the city marshal, and shall be served by delivering a copy thereof to the person or persons in whose custody the prisoner or prisoners are detained, and said writ shall be made returnable forthwith, and the form and substance thereof, as herein set forth, and be taken and considered as part and parcel of this ordinance. To the intent that no officer, sheriff, jailer, keeper, or other person, or persons, upon whom such writ shall be served, may pretend ignorance thereof, every such writ and copy thereof served shall be endorsed with these words, "By the Habeas Corpus Act;" and whenever the said writ shall by any person be served upon the sheriff, jailor, keeper, or other person or persons whomsoever, holding said prisoner or prisoners, or being brought to him or them, or being served upon any of his or their under-officers or deputies at the jail, or place where the prisoner or prisoners are detained, he or they, or some of his or their under-officers or deputies shall, upon payment or tender of the charges of bringing the said prisoner or prisoners, to be ascertained by the court awarding the said writ, and endorsed thereon, not exceeding ten cents per mile; and upon sufficient security given to pay the charges of carrying him, her, or them back, if he, she, or they shall be remanded, make return of such writ, and bring or cause to be brought, the body or bodies of the prisoner or prisoners before the municipal court forthwith, and certify the true cause of his, her, or their imprisonment, unless the commitment of such person or persons shall be to the county jail in Hancock county, in which case the time shall be prolonged till five days, after the delivery of the writ as aforesaid, and not longer.

Provided, nevertheless, that in case any person or persons may at any time hereafter be taken and lodged in the city or county jail, under any writ or process, as provided by the city charter of the city of Nauvoo, and shall require a writ of habeas corpus to issue to bring him, her, or them before the municipal court of said city, said writ shall issue to bring him, her, or them before said court, and be directed to the city marshal to be served upon the person or persons in whose custody such prisoner or prisoners may then be detained.

Sec. 2. Where any person or persons not being committed or detained for any criminal or supposed criminal matter shall be confined or restrained of his, her, or their liberty, under any color or pretense whatever, he, she, or they may apply for a writ of habeas corpus, as aforesaid, which application shall be in writing, signed by the party, or some person on his, her, or their behalf, setting forth the facts concerning his, her, or their imprisonment, and wherein the illegality of such imprisonment consists, and in whose custody he, she or they are detained; which application or petition shall be verified by the oath or affirmation of the party applying, or some other person on his, her, or their behalf. If the confinement or restraint is by virtue of any judicial writ or process, or order, a copy thereof shall be annexed thereto, or an affidavit made that the same had been demanded and refused: the same proceedings shall thereupon be had in all respects, as are directed in the preceding section, and any officer, person, or persons, knowing that he or they have an illegal writ, or not having any writ, who shall attempt through any false pretext to take or intimidate any of the inhabitants of this city, through such pretext, shall forfeit for every such offense a sum not exceeding one thousand dollars, nor less than five hundred dollars, or in case of failure to pay such forfeiture, to be imprisoned not more than twelve months nor less than six months.

Sec. 3. Upon the return of the writ of habeas corpus, a day shall be set for the hearing of the cause of imprisonment or detainer, not exceeding five days thereafter, unless the prisoner or prisoners shall request a longer time. The said prisoner or prisoners may deny any of the material facts set forth in the return, or may allege any fact to show either that the imprisonment or detention is unlawful, or that he, she, or they, is or are then entitled to his, her, or their discharge, which allegations or denials shall be made on oath. The said return may be amended, by leave of the court, before or after the same is filed, as also may all suggestions made against it, that thereby material facts may be ascertained. The said court shall proceed in a summary way to settle the said facts, by hearing the testimony and arguments, as well of all parties interested civilly, if any there be, as of the prisoner or prisoners, and the persons or person who holds him, her, or them in custody, and shall dispose of the prisoner or prisoners as the case may require. If it appear that the prisoner or prisoners are in custody by virtue of process from any court, legally constituted, he, she, or they can be discharged for the following causes:—First, where the court has exceeded the limits of its jurisdiction, either as to the matter, place, sum, person, or persons; second, where, though the original imprisonment was lawful, yet by some act, omission, or event which has subsequently taken place, the party has become entitled to his, her, or their discharge; third, where the process is defective in some substantial form required by law; fourth, where the process though in proper form has been issued in a case, or under circumstances where the law does not allow process, or orders for imprisonment or arrest, to issue; fifth, where although in proper form the process has been issued or executed by a person or persons, either unauthorized to issue or execute the same, or where the person or persons having the custody of the prisoner or prisoners under such process is not the person or persons empowered by law to detain him, her, or them; sixth, where the process appears to have been obtained by false pretense or bribery; seventh, where there is no general law, nor any judgment, order, or decree of a court, to authorize the process, if in a civil suit, nor any conviction, if in a criminal proceeding. In all cases where the imprisonment is for a criminal or supposed criminal matter, if it shall appear to the said court that there is sufficient legal cause for the commitment of the prisoner or prisoners, although such commitment may have been informally made, or without due authority, or the process may have been executed by a person or persons not duly authorized, the court shall make a new commitment, in proper form, and directed to the proper officer or officers, or admit the party to bail, if the case be bailable.

Sec. 4. When any person or persons shall be admitted to bail on habeas corpus, he, she, or they shall enter into recognizance with one or more securities in such sum as the court shall direct, having regard to the circumstances of the prisoner or prisoners, and the nature of the offense, conditioned for his, her, or their appearance at the next circuit court to be holden in and for the county where the offense was committed, or where the same is to be tried. Where the court shall admit to bail, or remand any prisoner or prisoners brought before the court, on any writ of habeas corpus, it shall be the duty of said court to bind all such persons as to declare any thing material to prove the offense, with which the prisoner or prisoners are charged by recognizance to appear at the proper court having cognizance of the offense, on the first day of the next term thereof, to give evidence thereof touching the said offense, and not to depart the said court without leave; which recognizance so taken, together with the recognizance entered into by the prisoner or prisoners, when he, she, or they are admitted to bail, shall be certified and returned to the proper court, on the first day of the next succeeding term thereof. If any such witness or witnesses shall neglect or refuse to enter into a recognizance as aforefaid, when thereunto required, it shall be lawful for the court to commit him, her, or them to jail until he, she, or they shall enter into such recognizance, or be otherwise discharged by due course of law. If the court shall neglect or refuse to bind any such witness or witnesses, prisoner or prisoners, by recognizance as aforesaid, or to return any such recognizance, when taken as aforesaid, the court shall be deemed guilty of a misdemeanor in office, and be proceeded against accordingly.

Sec. 5. Where any prisoner or prisoners brought up on a habeas corpus shall be remanded to prison, it shall be the duty of the municipal court remanding him, her, or them to make out and deliver to the sheriff, or other person or persons to whose custody he, she, or they shall be remanded, an order in writing, stating the cause or causes of remanding him, her, or them. If such prisoner or prisoners shall obtain a second writ of habeas corpus, it shall be the duty of such sheriff or other person or persons upon whom the same shall be served, to return therewith the order aforesaid; and if it shall appear that the said prisoner or prisoners were remanded for an offense adjudged not bailable, it shall be taken and received as conclusive, and the prisoner or prisoners shall be remanded without further proceedings.

Sec. 6. It shall not be lawful for the municipal court, on a second writ of habeas corpus obtained by such prisoner or prisoners, to discharge the said prisoner or prisoners, if he, she, or they are proven guilty of the charges clearly and specifically charged in the warrant of commitment with a criminal offense; but if the prisoner or prisoners shall be found guilty, the municipal court shall only admit such prisoner or prisoners to bail, where the offense is bailable by law or ordinance, or remand him, her, or them to prison, where the offense is not bailable; or being bailable, if such prisoner or prisoners shall fail to give the bail required.

Sec. 7. No person or persons who have been discharged by order of the municipal court on a habeas corpus, shall be again imprisoned, restrained, or kept in custody for the same cause, unless he, she, or they, be afterwards indicted for the same offense, or unless by the legal order or process of the municipal court wherein he, she, or they are bound by recognizance to appear, the following shall not be deemed to be the same cause. First, if after a discharge for defect of proof, or any material defect in the commitment in a criminal case, the prisoner or prisoners should be again arrested upon sufficient proof and committed by legal process, for the same offense; second, if in a civil suit the party or parties have been discharged for any illegality in the judgment or process, and are afterwards imprisoned by legal process, for the same cause of action; third, generally whenever the discharge has been ordered on account of the non-observance of any of the forms required by law, the party or parties may be a second time imprisoned, if the cause be legal and the forms required by law observed.

Sec. 8. If any person or persons shall be committed for a criminal matter, in case of the absence of a witness or witnesses whose testimony may be considered to be of importance in behalf of the people, the municipal court may adjourn from time to time at its discretion, provided they decide upon the case within thirty days, if it shall appear by oath or affirmation that the witness or witnesses for the people of the state are absent, such witness or witnesses being mentioned by name, and the court shown wherein their testimony is material.

Sec. 9. Any person or persons being committed to the city or county jail, as provided in the Charter in the City of Nauvoo, or in the custody of an officer, sheriff, jailer, keeper, or other person or persons, or his or their under-officer or deputy, for any criminal or supposed criminal matter, shall not be removed from said prison or custody into any prison or custody, unless it be by habeas corpus, or by an order of the municipal court, or in case of sudden fire, infection, or other necessities; if any person or persons shall, after such commitment as aforesaid, make out, sign, or countersign any warrant or warrants for such removal, then he or they shall forfeit to the prisoner or prisoners aggrieved a sum not exceeding five hundred dollars, to be recovered by the prisoner or prisoners aggrieved, in the manner hereinafter mentioned.

Sec. 10. If any member of the municipal court, or the clerk of said court shall corruptly refuse or neglect to issue writ or writs of habeas corpus when legally applied to in a case where such writ or writs may lawfully issue, or who shall for the purpose of oppression unreasonably delay the issuing of such writ or writs, shall for every such offense forfeit to the prisoner or prisoners, party or parties aggrieved, a sum not less than five hundred dollars and not exceeding one thousand dollars, and be imprisoned for six months.

Sec. 11. If any officer, sheriff, jailer, keeper, or other person or persons upon whom any such writ shall be served, shall neglect or refuse to make the returns as aforesaid, or to bring the body of the prisoner or prisoners according to the command of the said writ within the time required by this ordinance, all and every such officer, sheriff, jailer, keeper, or other person or persons shall be guilty of a contempt of the municipal court who issued said writ: whereupon the said court may and shall issue an attachment against said officer, sheriff, jailer, keeper, or other person or persons, and cause him or them to be committed to the city or county jail as provided for by the city charter of the city of Nauvoo, there to remain without bail or mainprize, until he or they shall obey the said writ; such officer, sheriff, jailer, keeper, or other person or persons shall also forfeit to the prisoner or prisoners, party or parties aggrieved, a sum not exceeding one thousand dollars, and not less than five hundred dollars.

Sec. 12. Any person or persons having a prisoner or prisoners in his or their custody, or under his or their restraint, power, or control, for whose relief a writ or writs of habeas corpus is issued, who, with intent to avoid the effect of such writ or writs, shall transfer such person or persons to the custody of, or place him, her, or them under the control of any other person or persons, or shall conceal him, her, or them, or change the place of his, her, or their confinement, with intent to avoid the operation of such writ or writs, or with intent to remove him, her, or them out of the state, shall forfeit for every such offense one thousand dollars, and may be imprisoned not less than one year, nor more than five years. In any prosecution for the penalty incurred under this section, it shall not be necessary to show that the writ or writs of habeas corpus had issued at the time of the removal, transfer, or concealment therein mentioned, if it be proven that the acts therein forbidden were done with the intent to avoid the operation of such writ or writs.

Sec. 13. Any sheriff, or his deputy, any jailer or coroner having custody of any prisoner or prisoners committed on any civil or criminal process, of any court or magistrate, who shall neglect to give such prisoner or prisoners a copy of the process, order, or commitment, by virtue of which he, she, or they are imprisoned, within six hours after demand made by said prisoner or prisoners, or any one on his, her, or their behalf, shall forfeit five hundred dollars.

Sec. 14. Any person, knowing that another has been discharged, by order of the municipal court, on a habeas corpus, shall, contrary to the provisions of this ordinance, arrest or detain him or her again for the same cause which was shown on return of such writ, shall forfeit one thousand dollars for the first offense, and two thousand dollars for every subsequent one.

Sec. 15. All the pecuniary forfeitures incurred under this ordinance shall be and inure to the use of the party for whose benefit the writ of habeas corpus was issued, and shall be sued for and recovered with costs by the city attorney, in the name of the city by information, and the amount when recovered shall, without any deduction, be paid to the parties entitled thereto.

Sec. 16. In any action or suit for any offense against the provisions of this ordinance, the defendant or defendants may plead the general issue, and give the special matter in evidence.

Sec. 17. The recovery of said penalties shall be no bar to a civil suit for damages.

Sec. 18. The municipal court, upon issuing a writ of habeas corpus, may appoint any suitable person to serve the same, other than the marshal, and shall endorse the appointment on the back of said writ.

Sec. 19. This ordinance to take effect and be in force from and after its passage, any act heretofore to the contrary thereof in any wise notwithstanding. Passed November 14, 1842.

JOSEPH SMITH, Mayor.

JAMES SLOAN, Recorder.

Many other bills were discussed on this and previous days.

CHAPTER XI.

PROPHET'S RETIREMENT FROM EDITORSHIP OF "TIMES AND SEASONS"—PROGRESS OF WORK ON THE TEMPLE—DIVISION OF NAUVOO INTO TEN WARDS—WM. SMITH IN THE ILLINOIS LEGISLATURE—GOVERNOR FORD ON MISSOURI'S DEMAND FOR THE PROPHET.

Tuesday, November 15, 1842.—About home. Wrote for the *Times and Seasons* the following:

VALEDICTORY.

I beg leave to inform the subscribers of the *Times and Seasons* that it is impossible for me to fulfill the arduous duties of the editorial department any longer. The multiplicity of other business that daily devolves upon me renders it impossible for me to do justice to a paper so widely circulated as the *Times and Seasons.* I have appointed Elder John Taylor, who is less encumbered and fully competent to assume the responsibilities of that office, and I doubt not that he will give satisfaction to the patrons of the paper. As this number commences a new volume, it also commences his editorial career.

JOSEPH SMITH.

Elder Taylor proceeded to his duties as editor.

Elder Bradley Wilson died suddenly in his 74th year. He received the gospel in Ohio, removed his family to Missouri, and was driven to Nauvoo in 1839. He has left seven sons and thirty-nine grand-children residing in Nauvoo.

Wednesday, 16.—About home. In the evening started on a journey to the counties north, in company with John D. Parker.

Thursday, 17.—There was a severe snow storm, and Elder Alpheus Harmon (who was just returning from a mission), and another man, were frozen to death on the prairie between Nauvoo and Carthage. The Mississippi was frozen over, which fulfilled my prophecy of the 5th instant.

Monday, *21.*—A Council of the Twelve, namely, Brigham Young, Heber C. Kimball, Wilford Woodruff, John Taylor, George A. Smith, Amasa Lyman, and Willard Richards, assembled at the house of Elder Heber C. Kimball, in Nauvoo, and decided by unanimous acclamation that the printing of the *Millennial Star* and all other publications in England relating to the Church of Jesus Christ of Latter-day Saints be suspended, on the return of Elder Parley P. Pratt from that country, until further instruction from the quorum; and that the foregoing minutes be forwarded to Elder Pratt or to the editor of the *Star*, which was done by letter from the president and clerk of the council.

Vote to Suspend the *Millennial Star*.

Tuesday, *22.*—I arrived at home, after a pleasant outing, in good health and spirits.

Wednesday, *23.*—At home all day.

Thursday, *24.*—By report of the papers, the island of Madeira was visited by a dreadful storm. The summer was hot and weather fine till the 15th, when the rain commenced falling heavily and continued to the 24th. At one o'clock in the afternoon the water fell in torrents, the sky became dark, the streets in the capital became inundated, and the affrighted inhabitants in town and country fled to the mountains. Upwards of two hundred houses were destroyed at Funchal, and much corn and wine. The damage to lives, houses, and crops on the island, and boats in the harbors was incalculable.

Disaster on the Island of Madeira.

Saturday, *26.*—At home in the morning. At ten, met in city council, which resolved that the inscription for the seal to be procured for the municipal court of this city shall consist of a circle, including the words "Municipal Court, City of Nauvoo," within which is to be a book circled with rays, on which is to be inscribed the words "Constitution and Charter."

Wrote as follow:—

Letter of the Prophet to H. R. Hotchkiss—Land Purchase Contract Considered.

NAUVOO, November 26, 1842.

Horace R. Hotchkiss, Esq.

DEAR SIR:—Yours of the 8th instant to Sidney Rigdon has been received; and, in consequence of his not knowing anything concerning the matters therein mentioned, or being in any way connected or interested in my affairs, he of course, has handed the letter to me, which I shall proceed to answer.

And, sir, permit me to say, on the subject of the deal between myself, as Trustee-in-Trust for the Church of Latter-day Saints, and you, that I am as anxious as ever to have the contract continue good between us, and to meet the obligations specified in the contract. I am not, neither have I ever been, wishful to shrink from it in any manner whatever, but intend to make payments as fast as my circumstances will admit.

But, sir, you are not unacquainted with the extreme hardness of the times and the great scarcity of money, which put it out of my power to meet all the payments as they fell due, and which has been the only cause of any failure on my part; and should you feel disposed not to press the payments, but offer a lenity equivalent to the state of the times, then, sir, I shall yet endeavor to make up the payments as fast as possible, and consider the contract as still good between us.

I would here say that when I found it necessary to avail myself of the benefits of the bankrupt law, I knew not but that the law required of me to include you amongst the list of my creditors, notwithstanding the nature of the contract between us. This explains the reason of my doing so.

I have since learned, from a decision of the judge of the supreme court, that it was not necessary, and that the [bankrupt] law has no jurisdiction over such a contract. Consequently, as I have before stated, I am disposed to hold it, provided you will not press the payments. Under these circumstances, I consider it necessary to give you the information required in your letter, in regard to the number and kind of houses on the land, &c.

I shall expect to hear from you again soon. In regard to your having written to me some few weeks ago, I will observe that I have received no communication from you for some months back. If you wrote to me, the letter has been broken open and detained, no doubt, as has been the case with a great number of letters from my friends of late, and especially within the last three months.

Few if any letters for me can get through the post office in this place, and more particularly letters containing money, and matters of much importance. I am satisfied that Sidney Rigdon and others connected with him have been the means of doing incalculable injury, not only to myself, but to the citizens in general; and, sir, under such a state of things, you will have some idea of the difficulties I have to encounter, and the censure I have to bear through the unjust conduct of that man and others, whom he permits to interfere with the post office business. Having said so much, I must close for the present.

You will hereby understand my feelings upon the subject and the reasons of the course I have hitherto pursued.

With sentiments of due respect, I remain, as ever, yours respectfully,

JOSEPH SMITH.

P. S.—Should it suit you better, I am ready on my part to renew the contract, and would prefer it.

J. S.

Sudden Illness of Brigham Young.

In the evening went to see Brigham Young, in company with Dr. Richards. He was suddenly and severely attacked by disease, with strong symptoms of apoplexy. We immediately administered to him by laying on of hands and prayer, accompanied with the use of herbs. Profuse vomiting and purging followed, which were favorable indications. Although few so violently attacked ever survive long, yet the brethren were united in faith, and we had firm hopes of his recovery.

Sunday, 27.—At home, except visiting President Young, who remained extremely sick.

Temple Structure Difficulties.

Monday, 28.—At home all day. Charges of an unequal distribution of provisions, giving more iron and steel tools to Reynolds Cahoon's sons than to others, giving short measure of wood to Father Huntington, also letting the first course of stone around the Temple to the man who would do it for the least price, &c., having been instituted by the stonecutters against the Temple committee,—viz., Cahoon and Higbee, I requested the parties to appear at my house this day to have the difficulties settled by an investigation before myself and Counselor William Law. President Hyrum Smith acted as counsel for the defendants, and Elder Henry G. Sherwood for the accusers. The hearing of testimony lasted until four o'clock, at which time the meeting adjourned for half an hour. On coming together again, President Hyrum addressed the brethren at some length, showing the important responsibility of the committee, also the many difficulties they had to contend with. He advised the brethren to have charity one with another, and be united, &c., &c. Elder Sherwood replied to President Hyrum's remarks. President Hyrum explained some remarks before made. Elder William Law made a few pointed remarks, after which I gave my decision, which was that the committee stand in their place as before. I likewise showed the brethren that I was responsible to the state for a faithful performance of my office as sole trustee-in-trust, &c., and the Temple committee were responsible to me and had given bonds to me, to the amount of $12,000, for a faithful discharge of all duties devolving upon them as a committee, &c. The trial did not conclude until about nine o'clock in the evening.

Tuesday, *29*.—In council with Brother Hyrum, Willard Richards, and others, concerning bankruptcy. Afternoon, attended court at the house of Mr. Hunter, grocer, before Alderman Spencer, for slander. I forgave Hunter the judgment, but he was fined $10 for contempt of court.

Wednesday, *30*.—Morning, in counsel in the large assembly room preparing evidence in the case of bankruptcy. Afternoon, had Amos Davis brought before the municipal court for slander; but, in consequence of the informality of the writ drawn by Squire Daniel H. Wells, I was nonsuited.

A severe storm of snow, rain and wind is reported to have been experienced at Boston this day and evening, doing much damage to the ships and wharves.

Thursday, *December 1*, *1842*.—Emma was sick, attendance upon her occupied some of my time. Visited George A. Smith and Brigham Young, who were sick. Called at Mr. Angel's, in company with Elder Richards, to give some counsel concerning a sick sister. Called on William W. Phelps to get the historical documents, &c.; after which I commenced reading and revising history.

Extract of a Letter from Orrin Porter Rockwell, superscribed to Newel K. Whitney, dated Philadelphia, December 1, 1842, whither he had gone to escape the hands of those who sought his life in Missouri.

DEAR BROTHER JOSEPH SMITH:—I am requested by our friend Orrin Porter [Rockwell] to drop a few lines informing you that he is in this place. His health is good, but his spirits are depressed, caused by his being unable to obtain employment of any kind. He has applied in different parts of the city and country, but all without success, as farmers can get persons to work from sunrise till dark for merely what they eat. He is most anxious to hear from you, and wishes you to see his mother and the children and write all the particulars, how matters and things are, and what the prospects are. I pity him from the bottom of my heart. His lot in life seems marked with sorrow, bitterness and care. He is a noble, generous friend. But you know his worth: any comments from me would be superfluous. He will wait in this place until he hears from you. Please write immediately, as it will be a source of great comfort to him to hear [from you].

If Joseph is not at home, Brother Whitney will be kind enough to write. He says every other one he has come across has been afraid of their shadows, but he watches them well. He comes to see me every day, and I keep him a close prisoner! But he does not complain of my cruelty, or being hard-hearted, but, when with me, seems resigned to whatever punishment I may see proper to inflict: but he takes it in good part. Answer this as soon as received.

Yours truly,

S. ARMSTRONG,

for Orrin Porter [Rockwell].

Friday, 2.—Sat as Mayor on trial of Amos Davis, who was fined in the sum of $25 for breach of city ordinance for selling spirits by the small quantity. In the evening, called on Elder Richards, and Bishop Whitney to take an appraisal of the printing office establishment, preparatory to a lease to Elders Taylor and Woodruff for the term of five years.

Saturday, 3.—Called at the printing office several times. In the afternoon, attended the municipal court in the case of Amos Davis, for breach of city ordinance, &c.

Sunday, 4.—The weather being very wet, I remained at home all day.

The High Council of Nauvoo met, heard, accepted, and adopted the report of their committee for dividing the city into ten wards, as follows:—

The First Ward is bounded on the north by the city boundary line, and on the south by Brattle street.

The Second Ward is bounded on the north by Brattle street or the First Ward, and on the south by Carlos street or the Third Ward.

The Third Ward is bounded on the north by Carlos street or the Second Ward, and on the south by Joseph street or the Fourth Ward.

The Fourth Ward is bounded on the north by Joseph street or the Third Ward, and on the south by Cutler street or the Fifth Ward.

The Fifth Ward is bounded on the north by Cutler street or the Fourth Ward, and on the south by Mulholland street.

The Sixth Ward is bounded on the west by the Missis sippi river, and on the east by Main street or the Seventh Ward.

The Seventh Ward is bounded on the west by Main street or the Sixth Ward, and on the east by Durfee street or the Eight Ward.

The Eight Ward is bounded on the west by Durfee street or the Seventh Ward, and on the east by Robinson street or the Ninth Ward.

The Ninth Ward is bounded on the west by Robinson street or the Eight Ward, and on the east by Green street or the Tenth Ward.

The Tenth Ward is bounded on the west by Green street or the Ninth Ward, and on the east by the city boundary line.

Monday, 5.--In the morning, attended in council with Brother Hyrum and others on bankruptcy, making an inventory of our property, and schedule of our liabilities, that we might be prepared to avail ourselves of the laws of the land as did others. Afternoon, had conversation with Brother Green. In the evening, attended the Masonic Lodge.

Tuesday, 6.—Attended the trial of an appealed case of Amos Davis before the municipal court. Judgment confirmed.

Wednesday, 7.—Dined with Elder Orson Hyde and family. Elder Hyde has this day returned home from his mission to Jerusalem. His presence was truly gratifying. Spent the day with Elder Hyde and drawing wood.

Thursday, 8.—Spent the day at home. Received a visit from Elder Hyde and wife.

Inaugural Address of Governor Ford.

This day, Thomas Ford, governor of Illinois, in his inaugural address to the Senate and House of Representatives, remarked that a great deal has been said about certain charters granted to the people of Nauvoo. These charters are objectionable on many accounts, but particularly on account of the powers granted. The people of the state have become aroused to the subject, and anxiously desire that these charters should be modified so as to give the inhabitants of Nauvoo no greater privileges than those enjoyed by others of our fellow citizens.

Friday, 9.—I chopped wood all day. My Brother Hyrum started for Springfield to attend to his case of bankruptcy, with Benjamin Covey as witness. Willard Richards, William Clayton, Henry G. Sherwood, Peter Haws, Heber C. Kimball, Alpheus Cutler, and Reynolds Cahoon accompanied them to attend to my case, present testimony to the government that I was in Illinois at the time Boggs was shot—consequently could not have been a fugitive from the justice of Missouri, and thus procure a discharge from Governor Ford, on Governor Carlin's writ for my arrest. The weather was very cold, and the traveling tedious; yet my messengers traveled thirty-four miles, and stayed with my Brother Samuel Smith, who kept a public-house at Plymouth.

Agitation as to Nauvoo Charters.

Mr. Davis, of Bond county, introduced a resolution to the house of Representatives at Springfield, concerning the charter of Nauvoo, and urged its repeal.

Mr. Hicks was in favor of having the state arms taken from the Mormons.

Mr. Owen thought they had no more than their quota.

[The arms referred to consisted of three cannon, six-pounders, and a few score of muskets, swords, and pistols, which were furnished by the United States to Illinois, for the supply of her militia for common defense, of which the Nauvoo Legion had received but a small portion of that to which it was entitled.]

My Brother, William Smith, representative of Hancock county, colleague with Mr. Owen, made the following speech in the House, in reply to Mr. Davis:—

Speech of William Smith, Brother of the Prophet, on the Chartered Rights of Nauvoo.

MR. SPEAKER.—I beg the privilege of making a few remarks on this subject. This, sir, seems to be a question which has excited, to a very considerable extent, the attention of members who compose this honorable body. But, Mr. Speaker, it does really appear to me that this is a question that has been gotten up quite prematurely; for I doubt not many members here have not yet had the opportunity of learning what privileges are granted in the Nauvoo City Charter.

The subject which the gentleman has raised is only an assumption. I doubt not that if the subject had been fairly investigated, and weighed equally in the balance by every candid individual in the community, that prejudices of this kind would not have obtained such a hold upon the public mind. In the estimation of genuine democracy, the rights of the people of Nauvoo are just as sacred as those of any other people. The people that live there should have just the same privileges extended to them as are awarded to Springfield, Chicago, Quincy, or any other city in the state.

It is true, indeed, that they have labored under many embarrassments. The public mind has been heated in regard to what was supposed to be their chartered privileges. But you, Mr. Speaker, are well aware that all the corporate privileges that they enjoy have been granted to them by a previous Legislature. Upon that occasion all that was done was not considered, by any, more than an act of justice towards them. They had no greater rights or privileges given them than were already enjoyed by the citizens of Quincy or Springfield. The people had chartered privileges in both of those cities, and we have the same in Nauvoo. Our condition in that respect is not at all different from Chicago, Alton, and many other chartered cities in this state. It would be hardly worth while, Mr. Speaker, to detain either you or this honorable body by making many preliminary remarks in respect to our religion. This is a matter that cannot at all come under the purview of this legislature.

I do not fancy myself placed here before a body of sectarians invested, in their own estimation, with authority to enact rules for the government or regulation of any sect upon matters of religion. I do not suppose that I stand in the presence of persons disposed to take away one single religious right pertaining to the people among whom I dwell.

But what could legislation in regard to the matter effect? What would it prove? It would neither prove Joseph Smith to be a Christian nor that Tom Thumb came from the moon. It would prove nothing in reference to the principles of any body of religionists. But I do not feel it my prerogative to enter into a discussion of religious principles here. I know very well that the people called "Mormons" are thought to be a very strange people. I come right from among them, and you can all judge whether or not they seem to have the appearance of a strange animal of seven heads and ten horns. You can all decide for yourselves whether, from the appearance I present, I should be numbered among outcasts, or be ranked among human beings.

One word further as to the chartered privileges. They have, as this honorable body is well aware, assembled a population of from five to ten or fifteen thousand inhabitants. It is in consequence of the privileges granted in their Charter that they have been induced to do this. Nauvoo is not, as some may erroneously suppose—a city composed entirely of Mormons. I can inform gentlemen that Methodists, Presbyterians, Baptists, Universalians, in short, many of the different kinds of religion, and even infidels may be found there; and all these are tolerated there just as in any other community. A great many persons have gone to Nauvoo, and there invested their property. They are now engaged in the erection of buildings, which, when consummated will cost enormous sums of money. But should the Charter of that city be repealed, individuals who now consider themselves rising to wealth, in consequence of what has been done by a former legislature of this state, will be reduced to wretchedness and want. In that event property now worth three to ten thousand dollars will not be worth five hundred, or nothing in comparison to that amount.

There is another point, Mr. Speaker, to which I would call your attention, and that is to the observations which have been made in regard to taking away from the city of Nauvoo the state arms. Well suppose that should be done, would that effect anything? They are now organized, and have, under existing laws drawn a certain portion of the public arms. In that wherein are they acting differently from any other citizens? They have not even that equal proportion of arms that they are entitled to by law. What would be the object in taking away the public arms from the militia of this state? It surely cannot be believed that there is any danger of the Mormons breaking out and killing the people. There is no more danger of that than there is that five, six or a dozen old women and a few boys should do the same thing. Is this state to be carried by a hue-and-cry of that kind raised by politicians? I own that it is not the design of that people even so much as to molest a hair on the head of a single individual; but that, on the contrary, it is their intention in all things to conform to the Constitution and laws of the land. If prejudices have been accumulating upon the public mind calculated to produce the expression that they are villains, such prejudices are entirely unfounded. And it is a great mistake to suppose the contrary. Those people consider themselves bound by the laws, and endeavor to obey them. Have they not, I would ask, contributed their portion towards replenishing your county and state revenues? Have they ever refused to pay their taxes? Have they not always been both ready and willing to obey both the civil and military laws of this state? Where, then, is the necessity, that this honorable body should enact a law taking away from them their chartered privileges?

I will not, Mr. Speaker, detain you or this honorable body much longer. I am heartily sorry that a blow has been aimed at the chartered privileges of Nauvoo. I speak in defense of my constituents upon this occasion, feeling myself bound to do so, not by any former pledges, but by principle. I believe in defending the cause of the defenseless, as has already been remarked. All that we claim is equal rights and equal provisions. I would remark, for the satisfaction of my own feelings in this matter, that I was some little interested in the event of the last election. I then was engaged in the cause of Democracy, enlisted in the campaign of canvassing my county, and in consequence of the many prejudices, that were excited against the "Mormons," as they are called, I was placed under circumstances of most unparalleled embarrassment; but still I thought it a favorable opportunity to unite the Democracy of the county.

I know that considerable political capital has been made by the question of Mormonism and anti-Mormonism. Perhaps one thing that now contributes to that result is, that there are hints in the governor's message in regard to a repeal of the Nauvoo Charter. It is a circumstance within my own knowledge that, previous to the last election in Hancock connty, some few individuals there made strong efforts to get our votes for the governor's election. By exertions made there, more than a thousand votes were cast for the governor by Mormon influence; and since I have been here, a gentleman of opposite politics has said to me, "Now your governor is paying you off."

I do not allude to this to wound the feelings of any person whatever. I do not consider that the recommendation of the governor was designed to effect the repeal of our Charter. All that we have to say is that we throw ourselves upon your mercy. As Democrats we ask for equal justice and equal rights. Give us those rights, and we are content; without them we are deprived of that which was purchased by the blood of our fathers.

Saturday, 10.—In this day's paper, William Smith gave his valedictory, resigning the editorship of the *Wasp* to Elder John Taylor.

Tuesday, 13.—I continued to chop and haul wood, and attend to my domestic concerns. My delegation arrived at Springfield about three o'clock this afternoon, and found the question of the repeal of the Nauvoo Charter in a high state of agitation in the legislature.

Wednesday, 14.—My delegation at Springfield having made affidavit that I was in Illinois on the 6th of May last, and consequently could not have been concerned in the attempted assassination of ex-Governor Boggs, and also having prepared a petition to Governor Ford to revoke the writ and proclamation of Governor Carlin for my arrest, they called on Governor Ford at four in the afternoon, there were present by their selection: Dr.

Richards, Brother Hyrum, Elders Sherwood and Clayton, in company with Mr. Butterfield, United States district attorney, who read his communication to Sidney Rigdon, Esq., of the 20th October, my petition to revoke and countermand Governor Carlin's writ and proclamation, and the affidavit of Lilburn W. Boggs.

Governor Ford, in reply, stated that he had no doubt but that the writ of Governor Carlin was illegal; but he doubted as to his authority to interfere with the acts of his predecessor. He finally concluded that he would state the case before the judges of the supreme court at their council next day, and whatever they decided on shall be his decision. He then stated his reasons for recommending a repeal of the Charter, and said that he regretted that he had not recommended a repeal of all the charters in the state.

Thursday, 15.—My delegates at Springfield continued to prosecute my discharge. On the 16th, Brother Hyrum received his discharge in case of bankruptcy; every arrangement was made with Mr. Butterfield, whereby I was equally entitled to a discharge, but was put off with a plea that he must write to the office at Washington before it could be granted.

Saturday, 17.—

Governor Ford to Joseph Smith—on the Missouri Requisition.

SPRINGFIELD, December 17, 1842.

DEAR SIR:—Your petition requesting me to rescind Governor Carlin's proclamation and recall the writ issued against you has been received and duly considered. I submitted your case and all the papers relating thereto to the judges of the Supreme Court, or at least to six of them who happened to be present. They were unanimous in the opinion that the requisition from Missouri was illegal and insufficient to cause your arrest, but were equally divided as to the propriety and justice of my interference with the acts of Governor Carlin. It being, therefore, a case of great doubt as to my power, and I not wishing, even in an official station, to assume the exercise of doubtful powers, and inasmuch as you have a sure and effectual remedy in the courts, I have decided to decline interfering. I can only advise that you submit to the laws and have a judicial investigation of your rights. If it should become necessary, for this purpose, to repair to Springfield, I do not believe that there will be any disposition to use illegal violence towards you; and I would feel it my duty in your case, as in the case of any other person, to protect you with any necessary amount of force from mob violence whilst asserting your rights before the courts, going to and returning.

I am most respectfully yours,

THOMAS FORD.

Letter of Justin Butterfield—Opinion on Governor Ford's Action.

SPRINGFIELD, December 17, 1842.

Joseph Smith, Esq.

DEAR SIR:—I have heard the letter read which Governor Ford has written to you, and his statements are correct in relation to the opinion of the judges of the Supreme Court. The judges were unanimously of the opinion that you would be entitled to your discharge under a habeas corpus to be issued by the Supreme Court, but felt some delicacy in advising Governor Ford to revoke the order issued by Governor Carlin. My advice is, that you come here without delay, and you do not run the least risk of not being protected while here, and of being discharged by the Supreme Court by habeas corpus. I have also the right to bring the case before the U. S. Court, now in session here; and there you are certain of obtaining your discharge. I will stand by you, and see you safely delivered from your arrest.

Yours truly,

J. BUTTERFIELD.

Letter from James Adams, Advising the Prophet to Appear for Trial.

CITY OF SPRINGFIELD, December 17, 1842.

General J. Smith.

MY SON:—It is useless for me to detail facts that the bearer can tell. But I will say that it appears to my judgment that you had best make no delay in coming before the court at this place for a discharge under a habeas corpus.

I am, &c.,

J. ADAMS.

On receiving the foregoing letters, and Dr. Richards having entered for the copyright of a map of the city of Nauvoo for Joseph Smith, in the clerk's office of the

District of Illinois, the brethren left Springfield for Nauvoo.

Tuesday, 20.—Chopping and drawing wood with my own hands and team, as I had done mostly since the 9th. President Young continued very sick. This afternoon the brethren arrived from Springfield and presented me with Messrs. Ford, Butterfield and Adams' letters, and general history of their proceedings, which was highly satisfactory.

The First Elder to Die in a Foreign Land.

Elder Lorenzo D. Barnes died this morning at a quarter past three o'clock, at Bradford, England. He is the first Elder who has fallen in a foreign land in these last days. He had been long connected with the Church, and had been distinguished, both in his native land and in Great Britain, for his piety, and virtue. Read correspondence between Dr. Richards and General James Arlington Bennett, and read German with Elder Orson Hyde. Brother Shearer inquired the meaning of the "little leaven which a woman hid in three measures of meal." I replied, it alluded expressly to the last days, when there should be but little faith on the earth, and it should leaven the whole world; also there shall be safety in Zion and Jerusalem, and in the remnants whom the Lord our God shall call. The three measures refer directly to the Priesthood, truth springing up on a fixed principle, to the three in the Grand Presidency, confining the oracles to a certain head on the principle of three.

Friday, 23.—Wrote R. M. Young, Esq., U. S. Senator from Illinois, Washington City, that I would accept the proposals of John C. Walsh, and give him $2,500 for the north-west quarter of section 8, 6 north, 8 west, said land lying between my farm and the city.

Saturday, 24.—At home afternoon. Read and revised my history with Secretary Richards, and walked with him to see Sister Lyon, who was sick. Her babe died a few minutes before our arrival. From there we went to

Brother Sabine's to compute expense money for our journey to Springfield, having just borrowed $100 for that purpose. While there, Brother Richards asked if I wanted a wicked man to pray for me? I replied, Yes; if the fervent, affectionate prayer of the righteous man availeth much, a wicked man may avail a little when praying for a righteous man. There is none good but One. The better a man is, the more his prayer will avail. Like the publican and the Pharisee, one was justified rather than the other, showing that both were justified in a degree. The prayer of a wicked man may do a righteous man good, when it does the one who prays no good.

Sunday, 25.—I wrote to Orrin Wright, Jun., Philadelphia.

The Manchester, (England) conference met, numbering 1,507 members, including thirty-three Elders, eighty-seven Priests, fifty-three Teachers, and nineteen Deacons under the presidency of Elder Thomas Ward.

CHAPTER XII.

THE PROPHET AT SPRINGFIELD, ILLINOIS—HIS CONVERSATIONS AND INTERVIEWS—PROCEEDINGS ON WRIT OF HABEAS CORPUS BEFORE JUDGE POPE—RELEASE OF THE PROPHET BY ORDER OF THE COURT AND THE EXECUTIVE ORDER OF GOVERNOR FORD—OFFICIAL PAPERS IN THE CASE.

Monday, December 26, 1842.—In the morning, held court, and I was afterwards arrested by General Wilson Law, on the proclamation of Governor Carlin, and Elders Henry G. Sherwood; and William Clayton went to Carthage to obtain a writ of habeas corpus to take me before the court at Springfield. General Law gave me into the custody of Dr. Richards, with whom I visited Sister Morey, who was severely afflicted. We prescribed *lobelia* for her, among other things, which is excellent in its place. I have learned the value of it by my own experience. It is one of the works of God, but, like the power of God, or any other good, it becomes an evil when improperly used. Brother Morey gave me a walking stick, the body of which was from the tooth of the sperm whale, and the top of whale ivory, with an interstice of mahogany. On my return home, I found my wife Emma sick. She was delivered of a son, which did not survive its birth.

Second Arrest of the Prophet on the Boggs Affair.

The Herefordshire conference (England) under the presidency of Elder William Kay, met at Colwall, numbering eight hundred and forty-four members, including twenty elders, fifty-three priests, twenty-two teachers, and ten deacons.

Tuesday, 27.—At nine in the morning, started in custody of Wilson Law for Springfield, in company with Hyrum

Smith, Willard Richards, John Taylor, William Marks, Levi Moffit, Peter Haws, Lorin Walker and Orson Hyde. On our way to Carthage, we met William Clayton and Henry G. Sherwood, who had obtained an order for a writ of habeas corpus from the master in chancery, as no writ could issue, the clerk of court having been elected to the State Senate.

The Prophet's Start for Springfield.

There was considerable snow, and the traveling heavy; but we arrived at my Brother Samuel's, in Plymouth, a little after sunset, and we were soon joined by Edward Hunter, Theodore Turley, Dr. Tate, and Shadrach Roundy.

The Prophet's Dream.

I supped with Brother William Smith's family, who lived under the same roof, slept with Dr. Willard Richards on a buffalo skin spread upon the floor, and dreamed that I was by a beautiful stream of water and saw a noble fish, which I threw out. Soon after, I saw a number more, and threw them out. I afterwards saw a multitude of fish, and threw out a great abundance, and sent for salt and salted them.

Wednesday, *28*.—The morning was wet. We started about eight o'clock, and arrived at Mr. Stevenson's tavern, in Rushville, at three in the afternoon, about twenty miles. Brother William's wife, who was sick, went with us, accompanied by Sister Durphy, who went with us from Nauvoo to take care of her. I spent a part of the evening with Mr. Uriah Brown and family and a part of my company. In conversation respecting the repeal of charters, I told them that to touch the Nauvoo Charter was no better than highway robbery; and that I never would consent to lowering our charter, but they might bring other charters up to it. On my return to the tavern, the brethren took my height, which was six feet, and my Brother Hyrum's the same.

Thursday, *29*.—Started early; crossed the Illinois river at eleven, and arrived at Captain Dutche's before five in the evening, about thirty-two miles: the weather extremely cold. General Law asked why the sun was called by a masculine name and the moon by a feminine one. I replied that the root of masculine is stronger, and of feminine weaker. The sun is a governing planet to certain planets, while the moon borrows her light from the sun, and is less or weaker.

Let the government of Missouri redress the wrongs she has done to the Saints, or let the curse follow them from generation to generation until they do.

A Missouri Reminiscence.

When I was going up to Missouri, in company with Elder Rigdon and our families, on an extreme cold day, to go forward was fourteen miles to a house, and backward nearly as far. We applied to all the taverns for admission in vain: we were "Mormons," and could not be received. Such was the extreme cold that in one hour we must have perished. We pleaded for our women and children in vain. We counseled together, and the brethren agreed to stand by me, and we concluded that we might as well die fighting as to freeze to death.

I went into a tavern and pleaded our cause to get admission. The landlord said he could not keep us for love or money. I told him we must and would stay, let the consequence be what it might; for we must stay or perish. The landlord replied, "We have heard the Mormons are very bad people; and the inhabitants of Paris have combined not to have anything to do with them, or you might stay." I said to him, "We will stay; but no thanks to you. I have men enough to take the town; and if we must freeze, we will freeze by the burning of these houses." The taverns were then opened, and we were accommodated, and received many apologies in the morning from the inhabitants for their abusive treatment.

The Prophet Meets Justin Butterfield *et al.*

Friday, *30*.—Started at eight this morning, and arrived at Judge Adams', in Springfield, at half past two o'clock in the afternoon, where I saw Justin Butterfield, Esq., United States district attorney, who told me that Judge Pope had continued the court two or three days on account of my case, and would close on the morrow, and that he should try my case on its merits, and not on any technicality.

Sheriff Pitman, of Adams county, was in the place, but would not say whether he had the original writ which had previously been demanded of the officers of Adams county, King and Pitman. I gave Mr. Butterfield a general history of my Missouri persecution, and it was agreed by him that I should be arrested on the writ. Had an interview with my Brother, William Smith, who was a member of the Legislature at the time, and spent the evening with Judge Adams and the brethren from Nauvoo. We all lodged at Judge Adams'.

The Reign of Christ on Earth Expounded.

While in conversation at Judge Adams' during the evening, I said, Christ and the resurrected Saints will reign over the earth during the thousand years. They will not probably dwell upon the earth, but will visit it when they please, or when it is necessary to govern it. There will be wicked men on the earth during the thousand years. The heathen nations who will not come up to worship will be visited with the judgments of God, and must eventually be destroyed from the earth.

The Prophet's Trial Before Judge Pope.

Saturday, 31.—At nine in the morning, Mr. Butterfield called and informed me that King had the original writ, and I signed a petition to Governor Ford to issue a new writ, that my case may be tried thereon, as well as on the proclamation. My petition was granted, and at eleven o'clock I was arrested thereon by a deputy, Mr. Maxey, in presence of Mr. Butterfield, my attorney, who immediately wrote a petition to Judge Pope for a writ of habeas corpus, which I signed, and at half-past eleven in the morning went before Judge Pope.

Mr. Butterfield read my petition, and stated that the writ and warrant were different from the requisition of the governor of Missouri. He then read Governor Ford's warrant, Watson's affidavit; Governor Reynolds' requisition on the governor of Illinois, and the proclamation of Governor Carlin, showing that Reynolds had made a false statement, as nothing appeared in the affidavits to show that Smith was in Missouri. He also stated that all the authority for transportation of persons from one state to another rests on the Constitution and the law of Congress. We ask for habeas corpus because the papers are false, and because that we can prove that Joseph Smith was in this state at the time of the commission of the crime.

The writ was granted, returned, and served in one minute, and I walked up to the bar. Mr. Butterfield read the habeas corpus, and moved the court to take bail till I could have a hearing,—which was granted; and although it was only a case of misdemeanor, Generals James Adams and Wilson Law were bailed for me in the sum of $2,000 each, and Monday was set for trial.

A Disturbance Threatened.

The court-room was crowded; and, on our returning, as General Law came to the top of the stairs, one of the crowd observed, "There goes Smith the Prophet, and a good looking man he is;" "And [said another] as damned a rascal as ever lived." Hyrum replied, "And a good many ditto." "Yes, [said the man,] ditto, ditto, G— d— you; and every one that takes his part is as damned a rascal as he is."

When at the foot of the stairs, General Law said, "I am the man, and I'll take his part." Said the man, "You are a damned rascal too." "You are a lying scoundrel," replied Law; and the man began to strip off his clothes and ran out in the street, cursing and swearing, and raising a tumult, when Mr. Prentice, the marshal, interfered, and with great exertions quelled the mob. Much credit is due Mr. Prentice for his zeal to keep the peace.

The Prophet's Interview with Governor Ford.

When the rowdies had dispersed, I went with Mr. Butterfield and Dr. Richards to see Governor Ford, who was sick. He told me he had a requisition from the governor for a renewal of persecution in the old case of treason against Missouri; but he happened to know that it was all dead. We dined with Mr. Butterfield at the American House, where the governor quartered, after which we returned to the general's room. In course of conversation he remarked he was no religionist. I told him I had no creed to circumscribe my mind; therefore the people did not like me. "Well, [said the general,] from reports, we had reason to think the Mormons were a peculiar people, different from other people, having horns or something of the kind; but I find they look like other people: indeed, I think Mr. Smith a very good-looking man."

At two in the afternoon, I returned to Judge Adams', and appointed Elders Hyde and Taylor to preach in the Representatives' Hall on the morrow.

Judge Douglas stated that it was possible to revoke political charters, but not company charters. I argued that if a legislature has power to grant a charter for ten years, it has no power to revoke it until after the expiration thereof. The same principle will hold good for twenty or one hundred years, and also for a perpetual charter: it cannot be revoked in time.

A Discussion with Judge Douglas.

John Darby came in and said he was going to California with Brewster. I told him I would say, as the Prophet said to Hezekiah, "Go, and prosper; but ye shall not return in peace." Brewster may set out for California, but he will not get there unless somebody shall pick him up by the way, feed him and help him along. Brewster showed me the manuscript he had been writing. I inquired of the Lord, and the Lord told me the book was not true—it was not of Him. If God ever called me, or spake by my mouth, or gave me a revelation, he never gave revelations to that Brewster boy* or any of the Brewster race.

The Brewster Movement.

* James Collins Brewster, the person mentioned by the Prophet in the text, was a boy about sixteen years of age, having been born as nearly as may be ascertained, in the year 1827. He claimed several years previous to this time to have had revela-

This afternoon, a team ran away, and went past the State House, when the hue-and-cry was raised, "Joe Smith is running away!" which produced great excitement and a sudden adjournment of the House of Representatives.

Sunday morning, January 1, 1843.—The speaker of the House of Representatives called on me to say we might have the hall for preaching this day. Had a pleasant interview with Mr. Butterfield, Judge Douglas, Senator Gillespie, and others. In reply to Mr. Butterfield, I stated that the most prominent difference in sentiment between the Latter-day Saints and sectarians was, that the latter were all circumscribed by some peculiar creed, which deprived its members the privilege of believing anything not contained therein, whereas the Latter-day Saints have no creed, but are ready to believe all true principles that exist, as they are made manifest from time to time.

Chief Distinction between the Saints and Sectarians.

At the suggestion of the company, I explained the nature of a prophet.

If any person should ask me if I were a prophet, I should not deny it, as that would give me the lie; for, according to John, the testimony of Jesus is the spirit of prophecy; therefore, if I profess to be a witness or teacher, and have not the spirit of prophecy, which is the testimony of Jesus, I must be a false witness; but if I be a true teacher and witness, I must possess the spirit of prophecy, and that constitutes a prophet; and any man who says he is a teacher or preacher of righteousness, and denies the spirit of prophecy, is a liar,

A Prophet Defined.

tions while in Kirtland, by which he translated the so-called "Book of Esdras' which in some way, not altogether clear, was interpreted to be a guide for the Latter-day Saints. He succeeded in converting his parents and a small number of people to the genuineness of his prophetic powers and gift of translation; and was now contemplating a removal of those who believed in him to California. After the death of the Prophet, in connection with one Hazen Aldridch, he succeeded in holding together a following for a few years, but in the end the Brewster-Aldridch movement was a flat failure, and the organization ceased to exist.

and the truth is not in him; and by this key false teachers and imposters may be detected.

At half-past eleven a. m., we repaired to the Representatives' Hall, where Elder Orson Hyde read the hymn "Rejoice ye Saints of Latter Days." Elder Taylor followed in prayer. The Saints then sang "The Spirit of God like a fire is burning." Elder Hyde then preached from the 3rd chapter of Malachi. Most of the members of the Legislature and the various departments of the state were in attendance.

Mormon Service at Springfield.

I dined with Judge Adams at one p. m., and at half-past two returned to the hall, and heard Elder Taylor preach from Revelation 14th chapter, 6th and 7th verses, on the first principles of the Gospel. There was a respectable congregation, who listened with good attention, notwithstanding the great anxiety to "see the Prophet."

I supped at Brother Bowman's, where I saw Sister Lucy Stringham (who was one of the first fruits of the Church at Colesville, New York,) and many more of the Saints. At seven I returned to Judge Adams'.

A Prophecy.

Monday, 2.—After breakfasting with Judge Adams, I prophesied, in the name of the Lord, that I should not go to Missouri dead or alive. At half-past nine a. m., repaired to the court-room; and at ten, Judge Pope took his seat on the bench, accompanied by several ladies.

My case was called up, when Mr. Lamborn, the attorney-general of Illinois, requested the case to be continued till the next day, and Wednesday morning was set for my trial. My attorney, Mr. Butterfield, filed some objections to points referred to in the habeas corpus, and, half-past ten, I repaired to the Senate lobby, and had conversation with several gentlemen. Dined at the American House. As we rose from table, Judge Brown invited me to his room, and informed me he was about publishing a history of Illinois, and wished me to furnish a history of the rise and progress of the Church of Latter-day Saints to add to it.

At half-past one p. m. returned to General Adams. A gentleman from St. Louis told General Law that the general impression was that Smith was innocent, and it would be a kind of murder to give him up—that "he ought to be whipped a little and let go." It was evident that prejudice was giving way in the public mind.

General Sentiment of the Prophet's Innocence.

At four, Mr. Lamborn, Mr. Prentice, the marshal, and some half dozen others called to see me. The marshal said it was the first time during his administration that the ladies had attended court on a trial. A peculiarly pleasant and conciliatory feeling prevailed in the company, and the marshal invited me to a family dinner, when I should be freed.

At five went to Mr. Sollars' with Elders Hyde and Richards. Elder Hyde inquired the situation of the negro. I replied, they came into the world slaves, mentally and physically. Change their situation with the whites, and they would be like them. They have souls, and are subjects of salvation. Go into Cincinnati or any city, and find an educated negro, who rides in his carriage, and you will see a man who has risen by the powers of his own mind to his exalted state of respectability. The slaves in Washington are more refined than many in high places, and the black boys will take the shine off many of those they brush and wait on.

The Prophet's View of the Negro Race.

Elder Hyde remarked, "Put them on the level, and they will rise above me." I replied, if I raised you to be my equal, and then attempted to oppress you, would you not be indignant and try to rise above me, as did Oliver Cowdery, Peter Whitmer, and many others, who said I was a fallen Prophet, and they were capable of leading the people, although I never attempted to oppress them, but had always been lifting them up? Had I anything to do with the negro, I would confine them by strict law to their own species, and put them on a national equalization.

The World's Lack of Faith.

Because faith is wanting, the fruits are. No man since the world was had faith without having something along with it. The ancients quenched the violence of fire, escaped the edge of the sword, women received their dead, &c. By faith the worlds were made. A man who has none of the gifts has no faith; and he deceives himself, if he supposes he has. Faith has been wanting, not only among the heathen, but in professed Christendom also, so that tongues, healings, prophecy, and prophets and apostles, and all the gifts and blessings have been wanting.

The Meekness of a Prophet.

Some of the company thought I was not a very meek Prophet; so I told them: "I am meek and lowly in heart," and will personify Jesus for a moment, to illustrate the principle, and cried out with a loud voice, "Woe unto you, ye doctors; woe unto you, ye lawyers; woe unto you, ye scribes, Pharisees, and hypocrites!" &c. But you cannot find the place where I ever went that I found fault with their food, their drink, their house, their lodgings; no, never; and this is what is meant by the meekness and lowliness of Jesus.

A Sample of Folly.

Mr. Sollars stated that James Mullone, of Springfield, told him as follows:—"I have been to Nauvoo, and seen Joe Smith, the Prophet: he had a gray horse, and I asked him where he got it; and Joe said, "You see that white cloud." "Yes." "Well, as it came along, I got the horse from that cloud." This is a fair specimen of the ten thousand foolish lies circulated by this generation to bring the truth and its advocates into dispute.

The Prophet's Illustration.

What is it that inspires professors of Christianity generally with a hope of salvation? It is that smooth, sophisticated influence of the devil, by which he deceives the whole world. But, said Mr. Sollars, "May I not repent and be baptized, and not pay any attention to dreams, visions, and other gifts of the Spirit?" I replied: "Suppose I am traveling and am hungry, and meet with a man and tell him I am hungry, and he tells me to go yonder, there is a house of entertainment, go and knock, and you must conform to all the rules of the house, or you cannot satisfy your hunger; knock, call for food, sit down and eat;—and I go and knock, and ask for food, and sit down to the table, but do not eat, shall I satisfy my hunger? No. I must eat. The gifts are the food; and the graces of the Spirit are the gifts of the Spirit. When I first commenced this work, and had got two or three individuals to believe, I went about thirty miles with Oliver Cowdery, to see them. We had only one horse between us. When we arrived, a mob of about one hundred men came upon us before we had time to eat, and chased us all night; and we arrived back again a little after daylight, having traveled about sixty miles in all, and without food. I have often traveled all night to see the brethren; and, when traveling to preach the Gospel among strangers, have frequently been turned away without food."

Thus the evening was spent in conversation and teaching, and closed by singing and prayer, when we parted, and Elders Hyde, Richards and myself lay down upon a bed on the floor, and enjoyed refreshing rest till morning.

Tuesday, 3.—After breakfast, called on Sister Crane, and blessed her little baby, Joseph Smith Crane, and returned to Judge Adams', where we conversed with Messrs. Trobridge, Jonas, Browning, and others, on my old Missouri case of treason. At half-past nine, went to the court-room, and had conversation with Messrs. Butterfield, Owen, Pope, Prentice, and others.

Conversations with Prominent Men.

At twelve, returned and spent the afternoon at Judge Adams'. At dusk, the marshal called with subpoenas for my witnesses. Spent the evening with the brethren at Judge Adams' in a very social manner, and prophesied in the name of the Lord that no very formidable opposition would be raised at my trial on the morrow. Slept on a sofa as usual while at Springfield.

Procedure of Trial.

Wednesday, *4*.—At nine o'clock a. m., repaired to the court-room, Judge Pope on the bench, and ten ladies by his side, when Josiah Lamborn, attorney-general of the state of Illinois, appeared and moved to dismiss the proceedings, and filed the following objections to the jurisdiction of the court, —viz.:

Objection of Jurisdiction.

1. The arrest and the detention of Smith was not under or by color of authority of the United States, or of any officer of the United States, but under and by color of authority of the State of Illinois, by the officers of Illinois.

2. When a fugitive from justice is arrested by authority of the governor of any state upon the requisition of the governor of another state, the courts of justice, neither state nor federal, have any authority or jurisdiction to enquire into any facts behind the writ.

My counsel then offered to read, in evidence, affidavits of several persons, showing conclusively that I was at Nauvoo, in the county of Hancock, and state of Illinois, on the whole of the 6th and 7th days of May, in the year 1842, and on the evenings of those days more than three hundred miles distant from Jackson county, in the state of Missouri, where it is alleged that the said Boggs was shot; and that I had not been in the state of Missouri at any time between the 10th day of February and the 1st day of July, 1842, the said persons having been with me during the whole of that period. That on the 6th day of May aforesaid, I attended an officer's drill at Nauvoo aforesaid, in the presence of a large number of people; and on the 7th day of May aforesaid I reviewed the Nauvoo Legion in presence of many thousand people.

The reading of these affidavits was objected to by the attorney-general of the state of Illinois, on the grounds that it was not competent for Smith to impeach or contradict the return of the habeas corpus. It was contended by my counsel, 1st, that I had a right to prove that the return was untrue. 2nd, that the said affidavits did not contradict the said return, as there was no averment under the oath in said return that I was in Missouri at the time of the commission of the alleged crime, or had fled from the justice of that state. The court decided that the said affidavits should be read in evidence, subject to all objections; and they were read accordingly, all of which will appear on my discharge. B. S. Edwards, Esq., opened the defense in an animated speech, and made some very pathetic allusions to our sufferings in Missouri, followed by Mr. Butterfield, who made the following points:—

Summary of Counsel Butterfield's Argument.

1. This court has jurisdiction. The requisition purports on its face to be made, and the warrant to be issued, under the constitution and laws of the United States regulating the surrender of fugitives from justice, 2nd sec., 4th article Constitution of the United States, 1st sec. of the Act of Congress of 12th Feb., 1793. When a person's rights are invaded under a law of the United States, he has no remedy except in the courts of the United States, 2nd sec., 3rd article Constitution United States, 12th Wendall, 325—16 Peters, 543.

The whole power in relation to the delivering up of fugitives from justice and labor has been delegated to the United States, and Congress has regulated the manner and form in which it shall be exercised. The power is exclusive. The State Legislatures have no right to interfere; and if they do, their acts are void, 2nd and 3rd clause of 2nd sec., 4th article Constitution United States, 2nd vol. Laws United States 331—16 Peters, 617, 618, 623; 4th Wheaton's Reports, 122, 193-12; Wendall, 312.

All courts of the United States are authorized to issue writs of habeas corpus when the prisoner is confined under or by color of authority of the United States, Act of Congress of Sept. 24th, 1789, sec. 14; 2nd Condensed 33; 3rd Cranch, 447; 3rd Peters, 193.

2. The return to the habeas corpus is not certain and sufficient to warrant the arrest and transportation of Smith. In all cases on habeas corpus previous to indictment, the court will look into the depositions before the magistrate; and though the commitment be full and in form, yet, if the testimony prove no crime, the court will discharge *ex-parte;*

Taylor 5th; Cowen 50. The affidavit of Boggs does not show that Smith was charged with any crime committed by him in Mo., nor that he was a fugitive from justice. If the commitment be for a matter for which by law the prisoner is not liable to be punished, the court must discharge him; 3rd Bacon, 434. The executive of this state has no jurisdiction over the person of Smith to transport him to Missouri, unless he has fled from that state.

3. The prisoner has a right to prove facts not repugnant to the return, and even to go behind the return and contradict it, unless committed under a judgment of a court of competent jurisdiction; 3rd Bacon, 435, 438; 3rd Peters, 202; Gale's revised laws of Illinois, 323. The testimony introduced by Smith at the hearing, showing conclusively that he was not a fugitive from justice, is not repugnant to the return.

J. Lamborn, attorney-general of the state of Illinois, in support of the points made by him, cited 2nd Condensed Reports, 37; Gordon's Digest, 73; Gale's Statutes of Illinois, 318; Conkling, 85; 9th Wendall, 212.

The Plea of Mr. Butterfield.

In the course of his plea, Mr. Butterfield showed that Governor Reynolds had subscribed to a lie in his demand for me, as will appear in the papers, [published in this chapter]; and said that Governor Carlin would not have given up his dog on such a requisition. That an attempt should be made to deliver up a man who has never been out of the state, strikes at all the liberty of our institutions. His fate today may be yours tomorrow. I do not think the defendant ought, under any circumstances, to be given up to Missouri. It is a matter of history that he and his people have been murdered or driven from the state. If he goes there, it is only to be murdered, and he had better be sent to the gallows. He is an innocent and unoffending man. If there is a difference between him and other men, it is that this people believe in prophecy, and others do not; the old prophets prophesied in poetry and the modern in prose.

Esquire Butterfield managed the case very judiciously. The court-room was crowded during the whole trial; the utmost decorum and good feeling prevailed, and much prejudice was allayed. Esquire Lamborn was not severe, apparently saying little more than his relation to the case demanded.

Court adjourned till tomorrow nine a. m., for the making up of opinion. After an introduction to several persons, I retired to Judge Adams', and after dinner spent some time in conversation with Brother Hyrum and Theodore Turley. At half-past five o'clock I rode in Mr. Prentice's carriage to his house, accompanied by General Law and Elder Orson Hyde, where I had a very interesting visit with Mr. Prentice and family, Judge Douglas, Esquires Butterfield, Lamborn and Edwards, Judge Pope's son, and many others; partook of a splendid supper; there were many interesting anecdotes, and everything to render the repast and visit agreeable; and returned to Judge Adams' about eleven o'clock.

The Treatment of the Prophet at Springfield.

Thursday, 5.—At nine a. m., repaired to the court-room, which was crowded with spectators anxious to "behold the Prophet," and hear the decision of Judge Pope, who soon took his seat, accompanied by half-a-dozen ladies, and gave the following:

Opinion of Judge Pope.

The importance of this case, and the consequences which may flow from an erroneous precedent, affecting the lives and liberties of our citizens, have impelled the court to bestow upon it the most anxious consideration. The able arguments of the counsel for the respective parties have been of great assistance in the examination of the important question arising in this cause.

When the patriots and wise men who framed our Constitution were in anxious deliberation to form a perfect union among the states of the confederacy, two great sources of discord presented themselves to their consideration—the commerce between the states and fugitives from justice and labor.

The border collisions in other countries have been seen to be a fruitful source of war and bloodshed, and most wisely did the constitution confer upon the national government the regulation of those matters, because of its exemption from the excited passions awakened by conflicts between neighboring states, and its ability alone to adopt a uniform rule, and establish uniform laws among all the states in those cases.

This case presents the important question arising under the Constitution and laws of the United States, whether a citizen of the state of Illinois can be transported from his own state to the state of Missouri, to be there tried for a crime, which, if he ever committed, was committed in the state of Illinois; whether he can be transported to Missouri, as a fugitive from justice, when he has never fled from that state.

Joseph Smith is before the court on habeas corpus, directed to the sheriff of Sangamon county, state of Illinois. The return shows that he is in custody under a warrant from the executive of Illinois, professedly issued in pursuance of the Constitution and laws of the United States and of the state of Illinois, ordering said Smith to be delivered to the agent of the executive of Missouri, who had demanded him as a fugitive from justice, under the 2nd section, 4th article of the Constitution of the United States, and the act of Congress passed to carry into effect that article.

The article is in these words, viz.:—"A person charged in any state with treason, felony, or other crime, who shall flee from justice, and be found in another state, shall, on demand of the executive authority of the state from which he fled, be delivered up to be removed to the state having jurisdiction of the crime."

The act of Congress made to carry into effect this article directs that the demand be made on the executive of the state where the offender is found, and prescribes the proof to support the demand,—viz., indictment or affidavit.

The court deemed it respectful to inform the governor and attorney-general of the state of Illinois of the action upon the habeas corpus. On the day appointed for the hearing, the attorney-general for the state of Illinois appeared and denied the jurisdiction of the court to grant the habeas corpus. 1st. Because the warrant was not issued under color or by authority of the United States, but by the state of Illinois. 2nd. Because no habeas corpus can issue in this case from either the Federal or State Courts to inquire into facts behind the writ.

In support of the first point, a law of Illinois was read, declaring that whenever the executive of any other state shall demand of the executive of this state any person as a fugitive from justice, and shall have complied with the requisition of the act of Congress in that case made and provided, it shall be the duty of the executive of this state to issue his warrant to apprehend the said fugitive, &c. It would seem that this act does not purport to confer any additional power upon the executive of this state independent of the power conferred by the Constitution and laws of the United States, but to make it the duty of the executive to obey and carry into effect the act of Congress.

The warrant on its face purports to be issued in pursuance of the Constitution and laws of the United States, as well as of the state of Illinois. To maintain the position that this warrant was not issued under color or by authority of the laws of the United States, it must be proved that the United States could not confer the power on the executive of Illinois; because if Congress could and did confer it, no act of Illinois could take it away, for the reason that the Constitution and laws of the United States, passed in pursuance of it, and treaties, are the supreme law of the land, and the judges in every state shall be bound thereby, anything in the Constitution or laws of any state to the contrary notwithstanding. This is enough to dispose of that point.

If the Legislature of Illinois, as is probable, intended to make it the *duty* of the governor to exercise the power granted by Congress, and no more, the executive would be acting by authority of the United States. It may be that the Legislature of Illinois, appreciating the importance of the proper execution of those laws, and doubting whether the governor could be punished for refusing to carry them into effect, deemed it prudent to impose it as a duty, the neglect of which would expose him to impeachment. If it intended more, the law is unconstitutional and void—16 Peters, 617 Prigg *versus* Pennsylvania.

In supporting the second point, the attorney-general seemed to urge that there was greater sanctity in a warrant issued by the governor than by an inferior officer. The court cannot assent to this distinction.

This is a government of laws, which prescribes a rule of action as obligatory upon the governor as upon the most obscure officer. The character and purposes of the habeas corpus are greatly misunderstood by those who suppose that it does not review the acts of an executive functionary. All who are familiar with English history must know that it was extorted from an arbitrary monarch, and that it was hailed as a second Magna Charta; and that it was to protect the subject from arbitrary imprisonment by the king and his minions, which brought into existence that great palladium of liberty in the latter part of the reign of Charles the Second. It was indeed a magnificent achievement over arbitrary power. Magna Charta established the principles of liberty—the habeas corpus protected them. It matters not how great or obscure the prisoner, how great or obscure the prison-keeper, this munificent writ, wielded by an independent judge, reaches all. It penetrates alike the royal towers and the local prisons, from the garret to the secret recesses of the dungeon. All doors fly open at its command, and the shackles fall from the limbs of prisoners of state as readily as from those committed by subordinate officers. The warrant of the king and his secretary of state could claim no more exemption from that searching inquiry, "The cause of his caption and detention," than a warrant granted by a justice of the peace. It is contended that the United States is a government of granted powers, and that no department of it can exercise powers not granted. This is true. But the grant is to be found in the second section of the third article of the Constitution of United States:—"The judical power shall extend to all cases in law or equity arising under this Constitution, the laws of the United States, and treaties made, and which shall be made under their authority."

The matter under consideration presents a case arising under the 2nd section, 4th article of the Constitution of the United States; and the act of Congress of February 12th, 1793, to carry it into effect. The judiciary act of 1789 confers on this court (indeed on all the courts of the United States,) power to issue the writ of habeas corpus, when a person is confined, "under color of, or by the authority of the United States." Smith is in custody under color of, and by authority of the 2nd section, 4th article of the Constitution of the United States. As to the instrument employed or authorized to carry into effect that article of the Constitution, (as he derives from it the authority to issue the warrant,) he must be regarded as acting by the authority of the United States. The power is not officially in the governor, but personal. It might have been granted to any one else by name, but considerations of convenience and policy recommended the selection of the executive who never dies. The citizens of the states are citizens of the United States; hence the United States are as much bound to afford them protection in their sphere as the states are in theirs.

This court has jurisdiction. Whether the state courts have jurisdiction or not, this court is not called upon to decide. The return of the sheriff shows that he has arrested and now holds in custody Joseph Smith, in virtue of a warrant issued by the Governor of Illinois, under the 2nd section of the 4th article of the Constitution of the United States, relative to fugitives from justice, and the act of Congress passed to carry it into effect. The article of the Constitution does not designate the person upon whom the demand for the fugitive shall be made, nor does it prescribe the proof upon which he shall act. But Congress has done so. The proof is "an indictment or affidavit," to be certified by the governor demanding. The return brings before the court the warrant, the demand and affidavit. The material part of the latter is in these words, viz.—

"Lilburn W. Boggs, who being duly sworn, doth depose and say that on the night of the 6th day of May, 1842, while sitting in his dwelling, in the town of Independence, in the county of Jackson, he was shot with intent to kill; and that his life was despaired of for several days; and that he believes, and has good reason to believe from evidence and information now in his possession, that Joseph Smith, commonly called the "Mormon Prophet," was accessory before the fact of the intended murder, and that the said Joseph Smith is a citizen or resident of the state of Illinois."

This affidavit is certified by the governor of Missouri to be authentic. The affidavit being thus verified, furnished the only evidence upon which the governor of Illinois could act. Smith presented affidavits proving that he was not in Missouri at the date of the shooting of Boggs.

This testimony was objected to by the attorney-general of Illinois, on the ground that the court could not look behind the return. The court deems it unnecessary to decide that point, inasmuch as it thinks Smith entitled to his discharge for defect in the affidavit.

To authorize the arrest in this case, the affidavit should have stated distinctly—1st, that Smith had committed a crime; 2nd, that he committed it in Missouri.

It must appear that he fled from Missouri to authorize the governor of Missouri to demand him, as none other than the governor of the state from which he *fled* can make the demand. He could not have fled from justice unless he committed a crime, which does not appear. It must appear that the crime was committed in Missouri, to warrant the governor of Illinois in ordering him to be sent to Missouri for trial.

The 2nd section,4th article,declares he "shall be removed to the state having jurisdiction of the crime." As it is not charged that the crime was committed by Smith in Missouri, the governor of Illinois could not cause him to be removed to that state, unless it can be maintained that the state of Missouri can entertain jurisdiction of crimes committed in other states. The affirmative of this proposition was taken in the argument with a zeal indicating sincerity. But no adjudged case or dictum was adduced in support of it. The court conceives that none can be. Let it be tested by principle.

Man, in a state of nature, is a sovereign, with all the prerogatives of king, lords, and commons. He may declare war and make peace, and as nations often do who "feel power and forget right," may oppress, rob, and subjugate his weaker and unoffending neighbors. He unites in his person, the legislative, judicial, and executive power; "can do no wrong," because there is none to hold him to account. But when he unites himself with a community, he lays down all the prerogatives sovereign (except self defense,) and becomes a subject. He owes obedience to its laws and the judgments of its tribunals, which he is supposed to have participated in establishing, either directly or indirectly. He surrenders also the right of self-redress.

In consideration of all which, he is entitled to the *ægis* of that community to defend him from wrongs. He takes upon himself no allegiance to any other community, so owes it no obedience, and therefore cannot disobey it. None other than his own sovereign can prescribe a rule of action to him. Each sovereign regulates the conduct of its subjects, and they may be punished upon the assumption that they have known the rule, and have consented to be governed by it; it would be a gross violation of the social compact if the state were to deliver up one of its citizens to be tried and punished by a foreign state to which he owes no allegiance, and whose laws were never binding on him. No state can or will do it.

In the absence of the constitutional provision, the state of Missouri would stand on this subject in the same relation to the state of Illinois that Spain does to England. In this particular, the states are independent of each other; a criminal fugitive from one state to another could not be claimed as of right to be given up.

It is most true, as mentioned by writers on the laws of nations that every state is responsible to its neighbors for the conduct of its citizens so far as their conduct violates the principles of good neighborhood; so it is among private individuals. But for this, the inviolibility of territory or private dwellings could not be maintained. This obligation creates the right and makes it the duty of the state to impose such restraints upon the citizen as the occasion demands.

It was in the performance of this duty that the United States passed laws to restrain citizens of the United States from setting on foot and fitting out military expeditions against their neighbors. While the violators of this law kept themselves within the United States the conduct was cognizable in the courts of the United States, and not of the offended state, even if the means provided had assisted in the invasion of the foreign state. A demand by the injured state upon the United States for the offenders whose operations were in their own country, would be answered that the United States' laws alone could act upon them, and that as a good neighbor it would punish them.

It is the duty of the state of Illinois to make it criminal in one of its citizens to aid, abet, counsel or advise any person to commit a crime in her sister state. Any one violating the law would be amenable to the laws of Illinois, executed by its own tribunals. Those of Missouri could have no agency in his conviction and punishment. But if he shall go into Missouri he owes obedience to her laws, and is liable before her courts to be tried and punished for any crime he may commit there; and a plea that he was a citizen of another state would not avail him. If he escape, he may be surrendered to Missouri for trial. But when the offense is perpetrated in Illinois, the only right of Missouri is to insist that Illinois compel her citizens to forbear to annoy her. This she has a right to expect. For the neglect of it, nations go to war and violate territory.

The court must hold that where a necessary fact is not stated in the affidavit,it does not exist. It is not averred that Smith was accessory before the fact, in the state of Missouri, nor that he committed a crime in Missouri; therefore he did not commit the crime in Missouri, did not flee from Missouri to avoid punishment.

Again the affidavit charges the shooting on the 6th of May, in the county of Jackson, and state of Missouri, "that he believes, and has good reason to believe from evidence and information now (then) in his possession, that Joseph Smith was accessory before the fact, and is a resident or citizen of Illinois."

There are several objections to this. Mr. Boggs having the "evidence and information in his possession," should have incorporated it in the affidavit, to enable the court to judge of their sufficiency to support his "belief."

Again, he swears to a legal conclusion, when he says that Smith was *accessory before the fact.* What acts constitute a man an accesory in a question of law are not always of easy solution. Mr. Boggs' opinion, then, is not authority. He should have given the facts. He should have shown that they were committed in Missouri, to enable the court to test them by the laws of Missouri,to see if they amounted to a crime.

Again the affidavit is fatally defective in this, that Boggs swears to his *belief.* The language in the Constitution is, "Charged with felony or other crime." Is the Constitution satisfied with a *charge* upon suspicion?

It is to be regretted that no American adjudged case has been cited to guide the court in expounding this article. Language is ever interpreted by the subject matter. If the object were to arrest a man near home, and there were fears of escape if the movement to detain him for examination were known, the word *charged* might warrant the issuing of a capias on *suspicion.* Rudyard (reported in Skinner 676), was committed to Newgate for refusing to give bail for his good behavior, and was brought before common pleas on habeas corpus. The return was that he had been complained of for exciting the subjects to disobedience of the laws against *seditious conventicles;* and upon examination they found *cause* to suspect him. Vaughan, Chief Justice, "Tyrell and Archer against Wild," held the return insufficient; 1st, because it did not appear but that he might abet frequenters of conventicles in the way the law allows; 2nd, to say that he was complained of or was examined is no proof of his guilt. And then to say that he had cause to suspect him is too cautious; for who can tell what they count a cause of *suspicion*, and how can that ever be tried? At this rate they would have arbitrary power upon their own allegation, to commit whom they pleased."

From this case it appears that suspicion does not warrant a commitment, and that all legal intendments are to avail the prisoner: that the return is to be most strictlv construed in favor of liberty. If suspicion in the foregoing case did not warrant a commitment in London by its officers, of a citizen of London, might not the objection be urged with greater force against the commitment of a citizen of our state to be transported to another on *suspicion?*

No case can arise demanding a more searching scrutiny into the evidence, than in cases arising under this part of the Constitution of the United States. It is proposed to deprive a freeman of his liberty; to deliver him into the custody of strangers; to be transported to a foreign state, to be arraigned for trial before a foreign tribunal, governed by laws unknown to him; separated from his friends, his family, and his witnesses, unknown and unknowing.. Had he an immaculate character, it would not avail him with strangers. Such a spectacle is appalling enough to challenge the strictest analysis.

The framers of the Constitution were not insensible of the importance of courts possessing the confidence of the parties. They therefore provided that citizens of different states might resort to the Federal Courts in civil causes. How much more important that the criminal have confidence in his judge and jury. Therefore, before the capias is issued, the officers should see that the case is made out to warrant it. Again, Boggs was shot on the 6th of May, the affidavit was made on the 20th of July following. Here was time for enquiry which would confirm into certainty, or dissipate his suspicions. He had time to collect facts to be had before a grand jury, or be incorporated in his affidavit.

The court is bound to assume that this would have been the course of Mr. Boggs; but that his suspicions were light and unsatisfactory. The affidavit is insufficient, 1st, because it is not positive; 2nd because it charges no crime; 3rd, because it charges no crime committed in the state of Missouri. Therefore,he [Joseph Smith] did not flee from the justice of the state of Missouri,nor has he taken refuge in the state of Illinois.

The proceedings in this affair, from the affidavit to the arrest, afford a lesson to governors and judges whose action may hereafter be invoked in cases of this character. The affidavit simply says that the affiant was shot with intent to kill; and he believes that Smith was accessory before the fact to the intended murder, and is a citizen or resident of the state of Illinois. It is not said who shot him, or that the person was unknown. The governor of Missouri, in his demand, calls Smith a fugitive from justice, charged with being accessory before the fact to an assault with intent to kill, made by one O. P. Rockwell, on Lilburn W. Boggs, in this state (Missouri). This governor expressly refers to the affidavit as his authority for that statement.

Boggs, in his affidavit, does not call Smith a *fugitive from justice*, nor does he state a fact from which the governor had a right to infer it. Neither does the name of O. P. Rockwell appear in the affidavit, nor does Boggs say Smith *fled*. Yet the governor says he *has fled* to the state of Illinois. But Boggs only says he is a *citizen* or *resident* of the state of Illinois. The governor of Illinois responding to the demand of the executive of Missouri for the arrest of Smith, issues his warrant for the arrest of Smith, reciting that "whereas Joseph Smith stands charged by the affidavit of Lilburn W. Boggs with being accessory before the fact to an assault, with intent to kill, made by one O. P. Rockwell, on Lilburn W. Boggs, on the night or the 6th day of May, 1842, at the county of Jackson, in said state of Missouri; and that the said Joseph Smith has fled from the justice of said state, and taken refuge in the state of Illinois."

Those facts do not appear by the affidavit of Boggs. On the contrary, it does not assert that Smith was accessory to O. P. Rockwell, nor that he had fled from the justice of the state of Missouri, and taken refuge in the state of Illinois.

The court can alone regard the facts set forth in the affidavit of Boggs as having any legal existence. The mis-recitals and over-statements in the requisition and warrant are not supported by oath, and cannot be received as evidence to deprive a citizen of his liberty and transport him to a foreign state for trial. For these reasons Smith must be discharged.

At the request of J. Butterfield, counsel for Smith, it is proper to state, in justice to the present executive of the state of Illinois, Governor Ford, that it was admitted on the argument that the warrant which originally issued upon the said requisition was issued by his predecessor; that when Smith came to Springfield to surrender himself up upon that warrant, it was in the hands of the person to whom it had been issued at Quincy, in this state; and that the present warrant which is a copy of the former one, was issued at the request of Smith, to enable him to test its legality by writ of habeas corpus.

Let an order be entered that Smith be discharged from his arrest.

At the close I arose, and bowed to the court, which adjourned to ten o'clock tomorrow. I accepted an invitation to see Judge Pope in his room, and spent an hour in conversation with his honor, in which I explained to him that I did not profess to be a prophet any more than every man ought

The Prophet's Hour with Judge Pope.

to who professes to be a preacher of righteousness; and that the testimony of Jesus is the spirit of prophecy; and gave the judge a brief but general view of my principles. Esquire Butterfield asked me "to prophesy how many inhabitants would come to Nauvoo." I said, I will not tell how many inhabitants will come to Nauvoo; but when I went to Commerce, I told the people I would build up a city, and the old inhabitants replied "We will be damned if you can." So I prophesied that I would build up a city, and the inhabitants prophesied that I could not; and we have now about 12,000 inhabitants. I will prophesy that we will build up a great city; for we have the stakes and have only to fill up the interstices.

The judge was very attentive and agreeable, and requested of me that my secretary, Dr. Richards, would furnish him a copy of his decision for the press. Dined at General Adams', and in the afternoon visited Mr. Butterfield with Brother Clayton. In the evening visited Mr. Groves, and lodged at General Adams' with Dr. Richards.

The Advice of Governor Ford.

Friday, 6.—In the morning went to see Judge Pope with Dr. Richards, who presented the judge with a report of his decision; called on Mr. Butterfield, and gave him two notes of two hundred and thirty dollars each, having paid him forty dollars as fee for his service in my suit. I took certified copies of the doings of the court, and waited on Governor Ford for his certificate thereto, after which he offered me a little advice, which was, that I "should refrain from all political electioneering." I told him that I had always acted upon that principle, and proved it by General Law and Dr. Richards: and that the "Mormons" were driven to union in their elections by persecution, and not by my influence: and that the "Mormons" acted on the most perfect principle of liberty in all their movements.

During the day I had considerable conversation in the

court room with the lawyers and others, on various topics and particularly on religion. Judge Pope's son wished me well, and hoped I would not be persecuted any more, and I blessed him. Mr. Butterfield said I must deposit my discharge and all my papers in the archives of the Temple when it is completed. My discharge, here referred to, commenced with my petition for habeas corpus and closed with the certificate of Thomas Ford, governor of Illinois, including all the documents relating to my trial on separate sheets of paper, attached by a blue ribbon, and secured by the seal of the court, and reads as follows:

Sundry Conversations.

Official Papers Relating to the Prophet's Trial at Springfield, Ill., Before Judge Pope.

I.

Pleas before the Circuit Court of the United States for the district of Illinois, at the December term, A. D., 1842, December 31st.

In the matter of Joseph Smith: Petition for habeas corpus.

Justin Butterfield, attorney for said petitioner, comes and moves the court for the allowance of a writ of habeas corpus, and files the annexed petition and the papers referred to therein.

To the Honorable the Circuit Court of the United States for the district of Illinois:

The petition of Joseph Smith respectfully showeth that he has been arrested, and is detained in custody by William F. Elkin, sheriff of Sangamon county, upon a warrant issued by the governor of the state of Illinois, upon the requisition of the governor of Missouri, as a fugitive from justice, a copy of the said warrant and the requisition and affidavit upon which the same was issued, is hereto annexed. And your petitioner is also arrested by Wilson Law, and by him also held and detained in custody, (jointly with the said sheriff of Sangamon county) upon a proclamation issued by the governor of the state of Illinois, a copy of which proclamation is hereunto annexed. Your petitioner prays that a writ of habeas corpus may be issued by this court, directed to the said William F. Elkin and Wilson Law, commanding them forthwith and without delay to bring your petitioner before this honorable court, to abide such order and direction as the said court may make in these premises. Your petitioner states that he is arrested and detained as aforesaid under color of a law of the United

States, and that his arrest and detention is illegal and in violation of law; and without the authority of law, in this, that your petitioner is not a fugitive from justice, nor has he fled from the state of Missouri. And your petitioner, as in duty bound, will ever pray.

JOSEPH SMITH.

II.

The Governor of the State of Missouri to the Governor of the State of Illinois—greeting:

Whereas it appears by the annexed document, which is hereby certified as authentic, that one Joseph Smith is a fugitive from justice, charged with being accessory before the fact, to an assault with intent to kill, made by one O. P. Rockwell on Lilburn W. Boggs, in this state; and it is represented to the executive department of this state, has fled to the state of Illinois:

Now, therefore, I, Thomas Reynolds, governor of the state of Missouri, by virtue of the authority in me vested by the Constitution and laws of the United States, do, by these presents demand the surrender and delivery of the said Joseph Smith to Edward R. Ford, who is hereby appointed as the agent to receive the said Joseph Smith on the part of this state.

In testimony whereof, I, governor of the state of Missouri, have hereunto set my hand and caused to be affixed the great seal of the state of Missouri.

Done at the city of Jefferson, this 22nd day of July, in the year of our Lord one thousand eight hundred and forty-two; of the Independence of the United States, the sixty-seventh, and of this state the twenty-third.

By the Governor,

[Seal] THOMAS REYNOLDS.

Jas. L. Minor, Secretary of State.

III.

Affidavit of Lilburn W. Boggs.

STATE OF MISSOURI,
County of Jackson, } ss.

This day personally appeared before me, Samuel Weston, a justice of the peace within and for the county of Jackson; the subscriber, Lilburn W. Boggs, who being duly sworn, doth depose and say, that on the night of the sixth day of May, 1842, while sitting in his dwelling, in the town of Independence, in the county of Jackson, he was shot, with intent to kill; and that his life was despaired of for several days, and that he believes, and has good reason to believe, from evidence and information now in his possession, that Joseph Smith, commonly called the Mormon Prophet, was accessory before the fact of the intended murder; and that the said Joseph Smith is a citizen or resident of the state of Illinois, and the said deponent hereby applies to the governor of the state of Missouri to make a demand on the governor of the state of Illinois to deliver the said Joseph Smith, commonly called the Mormon Prophet, to some person authorized to receive and convey him to the state and county aforesaid, there to be dealt with according to law.

LILBURN W. BOGGS.

Sworn to and subscribed before me, this 20th day of July, 1842.

SAMUEL WESTON, J. P.

IV.

Certificate of Secretary of State of Illinois.

STATE OF ILLINOIS,
Office of Secretary of State.

I, Lyman Trumbull, secretary of state, of the state of Illinois, do hereby certify the foregoing to be a true and perfect copy of the demand of the governor of the state of Missouri upon the governor of this state, for the apprehension and surrender of Joseph Smith, who is charged with being a fugitive from justice, and the affidavit of Lilburn W. Boggs attached to the same, which are on file in this office.

In testimony whereof I have hereunto set my hand, and affixed the great seal of state at Springfield, this thirty-first day of December, A. D., one thousand eight hundred and forty-two.

[Seal.] LYMAN TRUMBULL,
Secretary of State.

December 31, 1842.

I do hereby certify the foregoing to be true copies of the demand and affidavit upon which the writ for the apprehension of Joseph Smith was this day issued.

L. TRUMBULL,
Secretary of State.

December 31, 1842.

V.

Governor Ford's Order for the Prophet's Arrest.

The people of the State of Illinois to the Sheriff of Sangamon County, greeting:

Whereas it has been made known to me by the executive authority of the state of Missouri, that one Joseph Smith stands charged by the affidavit of one Lilburn W. Boggs, made on the 20th day of July, 1842, at the county of Jackson, in the state of Missouri, before Samuel Weston, a justice of the peace within and for the county of Jackson aforesaid, with being accessory before the fact to an assault with intent to kill, made by one O. P. Rockwell on Lilburn W. Boggs, on the night of the sixth of May, A.D. 1842, at the county of Jackson, in said state of Missouri; and that the said Joseph Smith has fled from the justice of said state, and taken refuge in the state of Illinois:

Now, therefore, I, Thomas Ford, governor of the state of Illinois, pursuant to the Constitution and laws of the United States, and of this state, do hereby command you to arrest and apprehend the said Joseph Smith, if he be found within the limits of the state aforesaid, and cause him to be safely kept and delivered to the custody of Edward R. Ford, who has been duly constituted the agent of said state of Missouri to receive said fugitive from the justice of said state, he paying all fees and charges for the arrest and apprehension of said Joseph Smith, and make due return to the executive department of this state, the manner in which the writ may be executed.

In testimony whereof, I have hereunto set my hand and caused the great seal of the state to be affixed.

Done at the city of Springfield, this 31st day of December, in the year of our Lord one thousand eight hundred and forty-two; and of the Independence of the United States, the sixty-seventh.

By the Governor,

[Seal.] THOMAS FORD.

LYMAN TRUMBULL, Secretary of State.

VI.

Governor Carlin's Proclamation.

EXECUTIVE DEPARTMENT, ILLINOIS,
September 20, 1842.

Whereas a requisition has been made upon me, as the executive of this state, by the governor of the state of Missouri, for the apprehension and surrender of O. P. Rockwell, who is charged with the crime of shooting Lilburn W. Boggs, with intent to kill, in the county of Jackson and state of Missouri, on the night of the sixth day of May, A. D., 1842:

And whereas a demand has also been made by the governor of Missouri upon me for the apprehension and surrender of Joseph Smith, commonly called the Mormon Prophet, who is charged with the crime of being accessory to the shooting of said Boggs at the time and place aforesaid, with intent to kill:

And whereas, in obedience to the Constitution and laws of the United States, and of this state, executive warrants have been issued, and the said Rockwell and Smith arrested as fugitives from justice from the state of Missouri; and whereas the said Rockwell and Smith resisted the laws by refusing to go with the officers who had them in custody as fugitives from justice, and escaped from the custody of said officers:

Now, therefore, I, Thomas Carlin, governor of the state of Illinois, in conformity to an act entitled "An Act concerning fugitives from justice," approved January 6, 1827, do offer a reward of two hundred dollars to any person or persons for the apprehension and delivery of each or either of the above-named fugitives from justice, viz., O. P. Rockwell and Joseph Smith, to the custody of James M. Pitman and Thomas C. King, or to the sheriff of Adams county, at the city of Quincy.

In testimony whereof, I have hereunto set my hand, and caused the great seal of state to be affixed, the day and the date above mentioned.

By the Governor,

[Seal.] THOMAS CARLIN.

LYMAN TRUMBULL, Secretary of State.

The *Fulton Advocate*, *Quincy Herald*, *Galena Sentinel*, and *Rockford Pilot*, will copy the above for two weeks.

VII.

Petition of the Prophet for Writ of Habeas Corpus.

In the United States' Circuit Court, District of Illinois, of December Term, 1842, December 31st day.

In the matter of Joseph Smith, on petition of Habeas Corpus.

And now at this day comes the said Joseph Smith by Justin Butterfield, his attorney, and presents to the court his petition, setting forth that he has been arrested and is detained in custody by William F. Elkin, Sheriff of Sangamon county, upon a warrant issued by the governor of the state of Illinois, upon the requisition of the governor of Missouri, as a fugitive from justice; and that he is also arrested by Wilson Law, and by him also held and detained in custody (jointly with the sheriff of Sangamon county), upon a proclamation issued by the governor of the state of Illinois; that he is arrested and detained as aforesaid, under color of a law of the United States; and that his arrest and detention is illegal and in violation of law, and without the authority of law in this, that the said petitioner is not a fugitive from justice, nor has he fled from the state of Missouri; and praying that a writ of habeas corpus may be issued by this court, directed to the said William F. Elkin and Wilson Law, commanding them forthwith and without delay to bring the petitioner before this court to abide such order and direction as this court may make in the premises: upon reading and filing of which said petition, it is considered and ordered by the court that a writ of habeas corpus be issued as prayed for in said petition, returnable forthwith.

And thereupon a writ of habeas corpus was issued in the words and figures following,—to wit:

VIII.

Writ of Habeas Corpus.

The United States of America to William F. Elkin, Sheriff of Sangamon county, State of Illinois, and Wilson Law, greeting.

We command you that you do forthwith, without excuse or delay, bring or cause to be brought, before the Circuit Court of the United States for the district of Illinois, at the District Court-room, in the city of Springfield, the body of Joseph Smith, by whatever name or addition he is known or called, and who is unlawfully detained in your custody, as it is said, with the day and cause of his caption and detention, then and there to perform and abide such order and direction as the said court shall make in that behalf. And hereof make due return under the penalty of what the law directs.

Witness, Roger B. Taney, Chief Justice of the Supreme Court of the United States at Springfield, in the district of Illinois, this 31st day of December, A. D., 1842, and of our Independence the sixty-seventh year.

[Seal.] JAMES F. OWINGS, Clerk.

IX.

Returns on the Above Writ of Habeas Corpus.

And afterwards, on the said 31st day of December aforesaid, the said writ of habeas corpus was returned, with returns endorsed thereon in the words and figures following:—

I, William F. Elkin, sheriff of Sangamon county, do hereby return the within writ, that the within named Joseph Smith is in my custody, by virtue of a warrant issued by the governor of the state of Illinois upon the requisition of the governor of the state of Missouri, made on the affidavit of L. W. Boggs, and a copy of the said warrant, requisition, and affidavit is hereunto annexed, dated December 31, 1842.

WM. F. ELKIN,
Sheriff S. C., Illinois.

I, Wilson Law, do return to the within writ that the said Joseph

Smith is in my custody by virtue of an arrest made by me of his body under and by virtue of a proclamation of the governor of the state of Illinois; a copy whereof is hereunto annexed, dated December 31, 1842.

WILSON LAW.

The return to the within writ of habeas corpus appears by the foregoing returns and the schedule hereunto annexed, and the body of the said Joseph Smith is in court.

WM. PRENTISS,
U. S. Marshal, district of Illinois.

December 31, 1842.

IX.

Orders of the Court.

And afterwards, to wit, on the same day aforesaid, upon the return of the said writ of habeas corpus, the following orders were made in this cause:—

In the the matter of Joseph Smith, on Habeas Corpus.

William F. Elkin and Wilson Law having made return to the writ of habeas corpus issued in this cause, and brought the body of the said Joseph Smith into court, on motion of Justin Butterfield, his attorney, it is ordered that the said Joseph Smith be admitted to bail; and thereupon came the said Joseph Smith in proper person, principal, and James Adams and Wilson Law, sureties, and severally acknowledge themselves to owe and be indebted to the United States of America, in the sum of two thousand dollars each, to be levied of their respective goods and chattels, lands and tenements; but to be void on condition that the said Joseph Smith shall be and appear before the Circuit Court of the United States for the district of Illinois, now sitting from day to day, and shall not depart without leave of the court. And thereupon it is ordered that this cause be set for hearing on Monday next; and it is further ordered that the governor of Illinois and the attorney-general be informed by the marshal that Joseph Smith, arrested on a warrant issued for his apprehension by the governor of Illinois, 31st December, 1842, is before this court on habeas corpus, and that the case will be heard on Monday, January 2nd, 1843, and that a copy of this order be handed to each of those officers.

It is ordered that the governor of Illinois and the attorney-general be informed by the marshal that Joseph Smith, arrested on a warrant issued for his apprehension by the governor of Illinois, 31st December, 1842, is before this court on a writ of habeas corpus, and that the case will be heard on Monday, 2nd January, 1843, and that a copy of this order be handed to each of those officers.

UNITED STATES OF AMERICA,
District of Illinois.

I, James F. Owings, clerk of the Circuit Court of the United States for the district aforesaid, do certify that the foregoing is a true copy of an order passed by said court, the 31st day of December, 1842.

In testimony whereof I have hereunto subscribed my name and affixed the seal of said court at Springfield, this 31st day of December, A. D., 1842.

[Seal.] JAMES F. OWINGS, Clerk.

Delivered a copy of the within order to Thomas Ford, governor, and Josiah Lamborn, attorney-general of the state of Illinois, December 31st, 1842.

WM. PRENTISS, Marshal.

In the matter of Joseph Smith on habeas corpus; copy of order, marshal's fees for serving on two, $4.00; returning twelve, $4.12.

X.

Denials of the Prophet.

And afterwards, to-wit, on the 2nd day of January, A. D. 1843, Justin Butterfield, attorney of said petitioner, filed the written denials of the said petitioner of the matters and things set forth, in the return to the said writ of habeas corpus, which denial is in the words and figures following,—viz.:

Circuit Court of the United States, }
District of Illinois, }

In the matter of Joseph Smith upon habeas corpus.

Joseph Smith, being brought up on habeas corpus before this court, comes and denies the matter set forth in the return to the same in this, that he is not a fugitive from the justice of the state of Missouri; but alleges and is ready to prove, that he was not in the state of Missouri at the time of the commission of the alleged crime set forth in the affidavit of L. W. Boggs, nor had he been in said state for more than three years previous to that time, nor has he been in said state since that time; but, on the contrary, at the time the said alleged assault was made upon the said Boggs, as set forth in the affidavit the said Smith was at Nauvoo, in the county of Hancock, in the state of Illinois, and that he has not fled from the justice of the state of Missouri, and taken refuge in the state of Illinois, as is most untruly stated in the warrant upon which he is arrested, and that the matter set forth in the requisition of the governor of Missouri, and in the said warrant, are not supported by oath.

JOSEPH SMITH.

State of Illinois, ss.

Joseph Smith being duly sworn, saith that the matter and things set forth in the foregoing statement are true.

JOSEPH SMITH.

Sworn and subscribed to before me, this second day of January, 1843.

JAMES F. OWINGS, Clerk.

XI.

Procedure of the Court.

And afterwards, to-wit, on the same day and year last aforesaid, the following order was made in this cause,—viz.:

In the matter of Joseph Smith on habeas corpus.

At this day comes the said Joseph Smith, and, by Justin Butterfield, his attorney, files his written denial, verified by affidavit, of the matters and things set forth in the return to the writ of habeas corpus issued in this cause; and at the same time also comes Josiah Lamborn, attorney-general of the state of Illinois, and on his motion it is ordered that this cause be continued for hearing until Wednesday morning next.

And afterwards, to-wit, on the fourth day of January, 1843, Josiah Lamborn, attorney-general of the state of Illinois, filed his objections to the jurisdiction of this court in this cause, and moved to dismiss the proceedings herein, which said motion and objections are in the words and figures following—viz.:

United States of America,
In the Circuit Court of the State of Illinois. }

In the matter of Joseph Smith.

J. Lamborn, attorney-general of Illinois, moves the court to dismiss the proceedings herein, for the reason that this court has no jurisdiction.

1st. The arrest and detention of said Smith was not under or by color of authority of the United States, or any of the officers of the United States, but under and by color of authority of the state of Illinois, and by the officers of Illinois.

2nd. When a fugitive from justice is arrested by authority of the government of any state, upon the requisition of any other governor of another state, the courts of justice, neither state nor federal have any authority or jurisdiction to inquire into any facts behind the writ.

J. LAMBORN,
Attorney-General of Illinois.

And afterwards, to-wit, on the same day and year last aforesaid, the following order was made in this cause,—viz.:

In the matter of Joseph Smith, on habeas corpus.

And now, again, at this day, comes the said Joseph Smith, by Justin Butterfield, his attorney; and at the same time also comes Josiah Lamborn, attorney-general of the state of Illinois, and enters his motion to dismiss the proceedings herein, for want of jurisdiction; and the court having heard the allegations and proofs herein, and the argument of counsel upon the same, and also upon the aforesaid motion, and not being sufficiently advised took time, &c.

XII.

Affidavits of Sundry Witnesses.

And afterwards, to-wit, on the same day and year aforesaid, Justin Butterfield, attorney for said petitioner, filed the affidavits, of which the following are copies:

Circuit Court of the United States, }
District of Illinois. }

In the matter of Joseph Smith, upon habeas corpus.

District of Illinois, ss.

Stephen A. Douglas. James H. Ralston, Almeron Wheat, J. B. Backenstos, being duly sworn,each for himself, says that they were at Nauvoo in the county of Hancock, in this state on the seventh day of May last; that they saw Joseph Smith on that day reviewing the Nauvoo Legion at that place in the presence of several thousand persons.

J. B. Backenstos,
Stephen A. Douglas.

Sworn to and subscribed in open court, this 4th day of January, 1843.

James F. Owings, Clerk.

Circuit Court of the United States,
District of Illinois.

In the matter of Joseph Smith upon habeas corpus.

District of Illinois:—Wilson Law, Henry G. Sherwood, Theodore Turley, Shadrach Roundy, Willard Richards, William Clayton, and Hyrum Smith, being duly sworn, say that they know that Joseph Smith was in Nauvoo, in the county or Hancock, in the state of Illinois, during the whole of the sixth and seventh days of May last; that on the sixth day of May, aforesaid, the said Smith attended an officer-drill at Nauvoo, from ten o'clock in the forenoon to about four o'clock in the afternoon, at which drill the said Joseph Smith was present. And these deponents, Hyrum Smith, Willard Richards, Henry G. Sherwood, John Taylor, and William Clayton, were with the said Smith at Nauvoo aforesaid, during the evening of the sixth day of May last, and sat with the said Joseph Smith in Nauvoo Lodge from six until nine o'clock of said evening. And these deponents, Hyrum Smith, Willard Richards, and William Marks, were with the said Smith at his dwelling house, in Nauvoo, on and during the evening of the fifth day of May last, and conversed with him; and all of the deponents aforesaid do say that, on the seventh day of May aforesaid, the said Smith reviewed the Nauvoo Legion, and was present with the said Legion all that day, in the presence of many thousand people, and it would have been impossible for the said Joseph Smith to have been at any place in the state of Missouri at any time on or between the sixth or seventh days of May aforesaid. And these deponents, Willard Richards, William Clayton, Hyrum Smith, and Lorin Walker, say that they have seen and conversed with the said Smith at Nauvoo, aforesaid, daily, from the tenth of February last, until the first day of July last, and know that he has not been absent from said city of Nauvoo, at any time during that time, long enough to have been in the state of Missouri; that Jackson county in the state of Missouri is about three hundred miles from Nauvoo.

WILSON LAW,
HENRY G. SHERWOOD,
THEODORE TURLEY,
SHADRACH ROUNDY,
WILLARD RICHARDS,
WILLIAM CLAYTON,
JOHN TAYLOR,
WILLIAM MARKS,
LORIN WALKER.

Sworn to and subscribed in open court, this 4th Jauuary, 1843.

OWINGS, Clerk.

XIII.

Denial of the Court to Dismiss the Case.

And afterwards, to wit on the 5th day of January, 1843, the following order was made in this cause,—viz.:

In the matter of Joseph Smith on habeas corpus.

And now, at this day, comes again the said Joseph Smith, by Justin Butterfield, his attorney, and at the same time also comes Josiah Lamborn, attorney-general of the state of Illinois; and the court being now sufficiently advised of and concerning the motion heretofore entered to dismiss the proceedings in this cause, it is considered that said motion be denied; and the court having fully considered the petition of the said Joseph Smith, and the matters and things set forth in the return made to the writ of habeas corpus issued herein, and being now sufficiently advised of and concerning the same, it is considered and adjudged that the matters and things set forth in the return to the said writ of habeas corpus are wholly insufficient in law to authorize the arrest and detention of the said Joseph Smith; and it is further considered, ordered, and adjudged by the court that the said Joseph Smith be fully released and discharged from the custody of William F. Elkin, sheriff of Sangamon county, under the warrant of the governor of the state of Illinois, mentioned in the said return, and also from the custody of Wilson Law, on the proclamation of the said governor mentioned in the said return, and that he go hence without day.

United States of America } ss.
Disirict of Illinois. }

1, James F. Owing, clerk of the United States Circuit Court for the district of Illinois, do certify that the foregoing is a true and correct copy of the record and proceedings before said court, in the matter of Joseph Smith, on petition, to be discharged on habeas corpus, as the same remain on the record and files of said court.

In testimony whereof, I have hereunto subscribed my name, and affixed the seal of said court at Springfield, this sixth day of January, A. D. 1843, and of our independence the 67th year.

[Seal] JAMES F. OWING, Clerk.

XIV.

Executive's Order of Release.

I do hereby certify that I have inspected the foregoing record, and there is now no further cause for arresting or detaining Joseph Smith, therein named, by virtue of any proclamation or executive warrant heretofore issued by the governor of this state; and that since the judgment of the Circuit Court of the United States for the district of Illinois, all such proclamations are inoperative and void.

Witness my hand and seal, at Springfield, this 6th day of January, 1843.

[Seal] THOMAS FORD,
Governor of Illinois.

The Prophet's Comment on Judge Pope's Opinion.

The opinion of Judge Pope as recorded in this history, was copied from the *Sangamon Journal*, and believed to be Judge Pope's opinion, as corrected and altered by him from the report furnished him by my secretary.

In the judge's opinion on the bench, he remarked like this:—"Were it my prerogative to impeach Congress for any one thing, it would be for granting power for the transportation of fugitives on affidavit, and not on indictment alone." He also passed several severe strictures on the actions of different governors and officers concerned in my case, but which I suppose he thought proper to omit in his printed copy.

I received many invitations to visit distinguished gentlemen in Springfield, which time would not permit me to comply with; also a ticket from the manager to attend the theatre this evening; but the play was prevented by the rain.

CHAPTER XIII.

THE PROPHET AGAIN IN NAUVOO—CELEBRATION OF HIS RELEASE FROM OPPRESSION—"VADE MECUM"—REINSTATEMENT OF ORSON PRATT—DISCOURSES OF THE PROPHET, "THE KINGDOM OF GOD;" "THE MISSION AND GREATNESS OF JOHN THE BAPTIST;" "INTERPRETATION OF SCRIPTURES."

Saturday, January 7, 1843.—At half-past eight in the morning, we left Judge Adams' to return to Nauvoo, and arrived at Captain Dutch's at four in the evening. Traveling very bad, with snow and mud, and yet so cold as to whiten the horses with frost. While riding this day, General Law and Dr. Richards composed a *Jubilee Song*, which they wrote and sang in the evening, and "dedicated to all lovers of Illinois' liberties," as printed on the first page of 37th Number of *The Wasp*.

The Start for Nauvoo.

Recent accounts from Alexandria, in Egypt, state the mortality (murrain) among the cattle still continues; and it was estimated that upwards of 200,000 oxen had already died.

Sunday, 8.—At eight in the morning we left Captain Dutch's, and, passing through Geneva and Beardstown, and crossing the Illinois river on the ice, arrived at Rushville at four in the evening. After supper, I went to Mr. Uriah Brown's, with several of the brethren and spent the evening very agreeably, partly in examining drafts of improvements he had made in some operative and defensive machinery.

Monday, 9.—At half-past eight in the morning, started for Plymouth: roads very hard, smooth and icy. When about two miles west of Brooklyn, at half-past twelve p.m., the horses of the large carriage slipped and became unmanageable; and horses and carriage, with Lorin Walker and Dr. Richards in it, went off the embankment some six or eight feet perpendicular, doing no damage except breaking the fore-axletree and top of the carriage. It was a remarkable interposition of Providence that neither of the brethren were injured in the least. The company agreed that Lilburn W. Boggs should pay the damage; cut down a small tree, spliced the axle, drove on, and arrived at Brother Samuel Smith's in Plymouth, about four p. m. After supper, I visited my sister, Catherine Salisbury, accompanied by Dr. Richards and Sister Durphy. This was the first time I had visited my sister in the state of Illinois, and the circumstance brought vividly to my mind many things pertaining to my father's house,* of which I spake freely, and particularly of my brother Alvin. He was a very handsome man, surpassed by none but Adam and Seth, and of great strength. When two Irishmen were fighting, and one was about to gouge the other's eyes, Alvin took him by his collar and breeches, and threw him over the ring, which was composed of men standing around to witness the fight.

An Accident by the Way.

We returned to Brother Samuel's just before the close of the meeting at the schoolhouse, where Elder John Taylor preached. After passing the usual salutations with several who had called to see me, singing the Jubilee Song, etc., retired to rest.

Tuesday, 10.—At half-past eight in the morning, we started for Nauvoo, and, stopping only to water at the public well at Carthage, arrived at my house at half-past two p. m.; found my family well,

Arrival in Nauvoo.

* "While there," said Dr. Richards, "my heart was pained to see a sister of Joseph's almost barefoot, and four lovely children entirely so, in the middle of a severe winter. What has not Joseph and his father's family suffered to bring forth the work of the Lord in these latter days!"

who, with many friends assembled to greet us on our safe return and my freedom. My aged mother came in and got hold of my arm before I saw her, which produced a very agreeable surprise, and she was overjoyed to behold her son free once more.

Wednesday, 11.—I rode out with Emma this morning, designing to go to Brother Daniel Russel's, and apologize for breaking his carriage on our return from Springfield: but broke a sleigh-shoe, and returned home, where I received a visit from a company of gentlemen and ladies from Farmington, on the Des Moines river, who left at half-past two p. m.

I directed letters of invitation to be written from myself and lady for a dinner party at my house on Wednesday next, at ten a. m., to be directed to Brothers Wilson Law, William Law, Hyrum Smith, Samuel Bennett, John Taylor, William Marks, Peter Haws, Orson Hyde, Henry G. Sherwood, William Clayton, Jabez Durphy, H. Tate, Edward Hunter, Theodore Turley, Shadrach Roundy, Willard Richards, Arthur Millikin, Brigham Young, Heber C. Kimball, Wilford Woodruff, George A. Smith, Alpheus Cutler, Reynolds Cahoon, and ladies; also Mr. Levi Moffat, and Carlos Granger, and ladies; my mother, Lucy Smith, and Sisters Eliza R. Snow and Hannah Ells.

A Dinner Party at the Prophet's Home.

On hearing of my invitation for dinner, the Twelve Apostles issued the following

PROCLAMATION.

To the Saints in Nauvoo.

Feeling a deep sense of gratitude to our Heavenly Father for the great blessings which He has conferred on us in the deliverance of our beloved President, Joseph Smith, from the oppression with which he has so long been bound, the Traveling High Council invite the brethren in Nauvoo to unite with them in dedicating Tuesday, the 17th day of January instant, as a day of humiliation, fasting, praise, prayer, and thanksgiving before the great Eloheim, that He will continue the outpouring of His Holy Spirit upon this people, that they may ever walk humbly before Him, seek out and follow the counsels given through His servant, and ever be united, heart and hand, in building up this stake of Zion and the Temple, where God will reveal Himself to this people; that no strife or confusion may ever be found in our midst, but peace and righteousness may be our companions; and as the Lord has hitherto sustained His Prophet in all the difficulties he has had to encounter, so He will continue to do, until the Prophet has finished the great work committed to his charge; and that all those who have been called to his assistance in the holy ministry, may be diligent and faithful in all things, that his hands may be stayed on high, like unto Moses; that our enemies, if such we have, may repent and, turning away from their enmity, get forgiveness and salvation; and that they may have no dominion over the servants of God or His Saints, but that Zion may flourish upon the mountains and be exalted on the hills, and that all nations shall flow unto it and be saved—we will humble ourselves with fasting and supplication and sing praises unto our God with the voice of melody and thanksgiving, for the deliverance He has wrought out for His servant Joseph, through the legally constituted authorities of our government.

The bishops of the several wards are requested to see that meetings are appointed sufficient for the accommodation of the brethren, and make a report unto us immediately of the same; and it may be expected that some one of the brethren who visited Springfield will be present at the different meetings, and give a history of the proceedings.

In our fastings, humiliations and thanksgivings, let us not forget the poor and destitute, to minister to their necessities; and respectfully would we suggest to the consideration of the brethren the situation of our President, who has long had all his business deranged, and has been recently obliged to expend large sums of money in procuring his release from unjust persecution, leaving him destitute of necessaries for his family and of means for prosecuting the History of the Church and the translations which he is anxious should be in the hands of the brethren as speedily as possible. We therefore recommend that collections be taken at the different meetings for his benefit; and such as have not cash will recollect that provisions will be an excellent substitute, whenever it is convenient to bring them in: and we hope our brethren who are farmers in La Harpe, Ramus, Zarahemla, etc., and the region around, will have the opportunity of reading these few hints. A word to the wise is sufficient. The Lord loveth a cheerful and a bountiful giver, and will restore an hundredfold; for the laborer is worthy of his hire.

BRIGHAM YOUNG, President.

W. RICHARDS, Clerk.
Nauvoo, January 11, 1843.

Thursday, 12.—At home all day.

Friday, 13.—At home till near sunset; then went to Brother William Marks with Dr. Richards, to see Sophia Marks, who was sick: heard her relate her vision or dream of a visit from her two brothers who were dead, touching the associations and relations of another world.

Saturday, 14.—Rode out with Emma in the morning. At ten attended city council, and in the evening called the quorum of the Twelve together in my chamber, to pray for Sophia Marks, who was very sick.

Sunday, 15.—I spent at home with my family.

Monday, 16.—I was about home, and directed a letter to be written as follows:—

Letter of the Prophet to Josiah Butterfield—On Bennett's Movements.

NAUVOO, January 16, 1843.

Josiah Butterfield, Esq.

DEAR SIR:—I now sit down to inform you of our safe arrival home on Tuesday last, after a cold and troublesome journey of four days. We found our families well and cheerful. The news of our arrival was soon generally known; and when it was understood that justice had once more triumphed over oppression, and the innocent had been rescued from the power of mobocracy, gladness filled the hearts of the citizens of Nauvoo, and gratitude to those who had so nobly and manfully defended the cause of justice and innocence was universally manifest; and of course I rejoiced with them, and felt like a free man at home.

Yesterday, a letter was received by Sidney Rigdon, Esq., from John C. Bennett, which was handed to me this morning. From that letter, it appears that Bennett was at Springfield a few days after we left there, and that he is determined, if possible, to keep up the persecution against me. I herewith transmit a copy of his letter, and shall rely upon your counsel, in the event of any further attempt to oppress me and deprive me of liberty; but I am in hopes that Governor Ford will not gratify the spirit of oppression and mobocracy so glaringly manifest in the conduct of John C. Bennett.

The following is a copy of his letter:—

Letter of John C. Bennett to Sidney Rigdon and Orson Pratt.

SPRINGFIELD, ILLINOIS, January 10, 1843.

Mr. Sidney Rigdon and Orson Pratt.

DEAR FRIENDS:—It is a long time since I have written to you, and I should now much desire to see you; but I leave to-night for Missouri, to meet the messenger charged with the arrest of Joseph Smith, Hyrum Smith, Lyman Wight, and others, for murder, burglary, treason, &c., &c., who will be demanded, in a few days, on *new* indictments found by the grand jury of a called court on the original evidence, and in relation to which a *nolle prosequi* was entered by the District Attorney.

New proceedings have been gotten up on the *old* charges, and no habeas corpus can then save them. We shall try Smith on the Boggs case, when we get him into Missouri. The war goes bravely on; and, although Smith thinks he is now safe, the enemy is near, even at the door. He has awoke the wrong passenger. The governor will relinquish Joe up at once on the new requisition. There is but one opinion on the case, and that is, nothing can save Joe on a new requisition and demand predicated on the *old* charges on the *institution of new writs*. He must go to Missouri; but he shall not be harmed, if he is not guilty: but he is a *murderer*, and must suffer the penalty of the law. Enough on this subject.

I hope that both of your kind and amiable families are well, and you will please to give them *all* my best respects. I hope to see you all *soon*. When the officer arrives, I shall be near at hand. I shall see you all again. Please to write me at Independence *immediately*.

Yours respectfully,

JOHN C. BENNETT.

P. S. Will Mr. Rigdon please to hand this letter to Mr. Pratt, after reading?

J. C. B.

This is his letter *verbatim et literatim*.

In the foregoing the designs of Bennett are very plainly manifest; and, to see his rascality, you have only to read some articles from his pen, published in the *Times and Seasons* about two years ago, on the subject of the Missouri affair. I shall be happy to hear from you on this subject as soon as convenient; also if you have received any communication from Washington. We are ready to execute the mortgage at any time.

Yours very respectfully,

JOSEPH SMITH.

By WILLIAM CLAYTON, Agent.

P. S. I would just remark, that I am not at all indebted to Sidney Rigdon for this letter, but to Orson Pratt, who, after he had read it, immediately brought it to me.

J. S.

The ship *Swanton* sailed from Liverpool with a company of Saints for New Orleans, led by Elder Lorenzo Snow.

Tuesday, *17*.—This being the time appointed by the Twelve as a day of humiliation, fasting, praise, prayer, and thanksgiving before the great Eloheim, I attended a public meeting in my own house, which was crowded to overflowing. Many other meetings were held in various parts of the city, which were well attended, and there was great joy among the people, that I had once more been delivered from the grasp of my enemies. In the evening I attended a referee case, with six others, on a land case of Dr. Robert D. Foster's.

A Day of Fasting and Prayer.

Wednesday, *18*.—At ten o'clock in the morning, the party invited began to assemble at my house, and before twelve they were all present, except Levi Moffatt and wife, and Brother Hyrum's wife, who was sick. I distributed cards among them, printed for the occasion, containing the Jubilee Song of Brothers Law and Richards; also one by Sister Eliza R. Snow, as printed on the 96th page, 4th volume of *Times and Seasons*, which were sung by the company with the warmest feelings.

I then read John C. Bennett's letter to Messrs. Sidney Rigdon and Orson Pratt, of the 10th instant, and told them that Mr. Pratt showed me the letter. Mr. Rigdon did not want to have it known that he had any hand in showing the letter, but wanted to keep it a secret, as though he were holding a private correspondence with Bennett; but as soon as Mr. Pratt got the letter, he brought it to me, which proves that Mr. Pratt had no correspondence with Bennett, and had no fellowship for his works of darkness. I told them I had sent word to Governor Ford, by Mr. Backenstos, that, before I would be troubled any more by Missouri, I would fight.

Conversation continued on various topics until two o'clock, when twenty-one sat down to the dinner-table, and Emma and myself waited on them, with other assistants. My room was small, so that but few could be accommodated at a time. Twenty sat down to the second table, which was served as the first, and eighteen at the third, among whom were myself and Emma; and fifteen at the fourth table, including children and my household.

Many interesting anecdotes were related by the company, who were very cheerful, and the day passed off very pleasantly. President Brigham Young was present, although very feeble. This was the first time that he had been out of his house since he was taken sick. His fever had been so severe, that he had lain in a log-house, rather open, without fire most of the time, when it was so cold that his attendants, with great coat and mittens on, would freeze their toes and fingers while fanning him. One thing more, which tended to give a zest to the occasion, was, that it was fifteen years this day since I was married to Emma Hale.

The brethren dispersed about six o'clock, with many thanks and expressions of gratitude; and in the evening I attended the Lodge.

Thursday, 19.—I was at home, excepting a short out in the city in the forenoon.

Friday, 20.—Visited at Brother William Marks' this morning; returned at ten a. m., and gave Dr. Richards and W. W. Phelps some instructions about the History, when I received the following communication:—

VADE MECUM.

From W. W. Phelps to Joseph Smith, the Prophet.

Go with me, will you go to the Saints that have died,
  To the next better world, where the righteous reside,
Where the angels and spirits in harmony be,
  In the joys of a vast paradise? Go with me.

Go with me, where the truth and the virtues prevail,
  Where the union is one, and the years never fail:
Not a heart can conceive—not a natural eye see
  What the Lord had prepared for the just. Go with me.

Go with me, where there is no destruction nor war,
Neither tyrants nor mobbers, nor nations ajar,—
Where the system is perfect, and happiness free,
And the life is eternal, with God. Go with me.

Go with me, will you go to the mansions above,
Where the bliss and the knowledge, the light and the love,
And the glory of God do eternally be?
Death, the wages of sin, is not there. Go with me.*

In the afternoon I attended a council of the Twelve, at President Young's. There were present, Brigham Young, Heber C. Kimball, Orson Hyde, Orson Pratt, John Taylor, Wilford Woodruff, George A. Smith, Willard Richards, and Brother Hyrum Smith. We had conversation on a great variety of subjects. I related my dream:—"I dreamed this morning that I was in the lobby of the Representatives' Hall, at Springfield, when some of the members, who did not like my being there, began to mar, and cut, and pound my shins with pieces of iron. I bore it as long as I could, then jumped over the rail into the hall, caught a rod of

Council Meeting of the Twelve.

* After the martyrdom of the Prophet both the title and the phraseology of this hymn were changed by the author of it, to "Come to me, will ye come," etc., as it now stands in the Latter-day Saints hymn book, page 326, *Deseret News* edition of 1905; also the following stanzas were added by Elder Phelps:

Come to me; here are Adam and Eve at the head
Of a multitude quickened and raised from the dead;
Here's the knowledge that was, or that is, or will be,
In the gen'ral assembly of worlds. Come to me.

Come to me; here's the mysteries man hath not seen,
Here's our Father in heaven, and Mother, the Queen;
Here are worlds that have been, and the worlds yet to be,
Here's eternity, endless; amen. Come to me.

Come to me, all ye faithful and blest of Nauvoo,
Come, ye Twelve, and ye High Priests, and Seventies, too,
Come, ye Elders, and all of the great company,
When your work you have finished on the earth, come to me.

Come to me; here's the future, the present and past;
Here is Alpha, Omega, the first and the last,
Here's the "Fountain," the "River of Life," and the "Tree!"
Here's your Prophet and Seer, Joseph Smith. Come to me.

iron, and went at them, cursing and swearing at them in the most awful manner, and drove them all out of the house. I went to the door, and told them to send me a clerk, and I would make some laws that would do good. There was quite a collection around the State House, trying to raise an army to take me, and there were many horses tied round the square. I thought they would not have the privilege of getting me; so I took a rod of iron, and mowed my way through their ranks, looking after their best race-horse, thinking they might catch me where they could find me. Then I awoke." To dream of flying signifies prosperity and deliverance from enemies. To dream of swimming in deep water signifies success among many people, and that the word will be accompanied with power.

I told Elder Hyde that when he spoke in the name of the Lord, it should prove true; but he must not curse the people—rather bless them.

I prophesy, in the name of the Lord God, as soon as we get the Temple built, so that we shall not be obliged to exhaust our means thereon, we will have means to gather the Saints by thousands and tens of thousands.

The Case of Orson Pratt Before the Council.

This council was called to consider the case of Orson Pratt who had previously been cut off from the Church for disobedience, and Amasa Lyman had been ordained an Apostle in his place. I told the quorum: you may receive Orson back into the quorum of the Twelve and I can take Amasa into the First Presidency. President Young said there were but three present when Amasa was ordained, the rest of the Twelve being either on a mission or sick. I told them that was legal when no more could be had. I told the council that from the sixth day of April next, I go in for preparing with all present for a mission through the United States, and when we arrive at Maine we will take ship for England and so on to all countries where we shall have a mind to go. We must send for John E. Page to come home, and have all the quorum to start from this place.

Let the Twelve be called on, on the 6th of April, and a notice be given for a special conference on the platform of the House of the Lord. If I live, I will yet take these brethren through the United States and through the world, and will make just as big a wake as God Almighty will let me. We must send kings and governors to Nauvoo, and we will do it.

At three o'clock, council adjourned to my house; and at four I baptized Orson Pratt and his wife, Sarah Marinda, and Lydia Granger in the Mississippi river, and confirmed them in the Church, ordaining Orson Pratt to his former office in the quorum of the Twelve.

Saturday, 21.—At home, except going out in the city with Elder Orson Hyde to look at some lots.

Sunday, 22.– I preached at the Temple on the setting up of the kingdom of God. The subject arose from two questions proposed at a lyceum meeting.

1st. Did John baptize for the remission of sins?

2nd. Whether the kingdom of God was set up before the day of Pentecost, or not till then?*

[The following is a synopsis of this sermon, as reported by Elder Wilford Woodruff]:

The Kingdom of God.

Some say the kingdom of God was not set up on the earth until the day of Pentecost, and that John did not preach the baptism of repentance for the remission of sins; but I say, in the name of the Lord, that the kingdom of God was set up on the earth from the days of Adam to the present time. Whenever there has been a righteous man on earth unto whom God revealed His word and gave power and authority to administer in His name, and where there is a priest of God—a minister who has power and authority from God to administer in the ordinances of the gospel and officiate in the priesthood of God, there is the kingdom of God; and, in consequence of rejecting the Gospel of Jesus Christ and the Prophets whom God hath sent, the judgments of God have rested upon people, cities, and nations, in various ages of the world, which

* This was the contention of the sect of the Disciples, or Campbellites; especially was it the view of Alexander Campbell, founder of said sect.

was the case with the cities of Sodom and Gomorrah, that were destroyed for rejecting the Prophets.

Now I will give my testimony. I care not for man. I speak boldly and faithfully and with authority. How is it with the kingdom of God? Where did the kingdom of God begin? Where there is no kingdom of God there is no salvation. What constitutes the kingdom of God? Where there is a prophet, a priest, or a righteous man unto whom God gives His oracles, there is the kingdom of God; and where the oracles of God are not, there the kingdom of God is not.

In these remarks, I have no allusion to the kingdoms of the earth. We will keep the laws of the land; we do not speak against them; we never have, and we can hardly make mention of the state of Missouri, of our persecutions there, &c., but what the cry goes forth that we are guilty of larceny, burglary, arson, treason, murder, &c., &c., which is false. We speak of the kingdom of God on the earth, not the kingdoms of men.

The plea of many in this day is, that we have no right to receive revelations; but if we do not get revelations, we do not have the oracles of God; and if they have not the oracles of God, they are not the people of God. But say you, What will become of the world, or the various professors of religion who do not believe in revelation and the oracles of God as continued to His Church in all ages of the world, when He has a people on earth? I tell you, in the name of Jesus Christ, they will be damned; and when you get into the eternal world, you will find it will be so, they cannot escape the damnation of hell.

As touching the Gospel and baptism that John preached, I would say that John came preaching the Gospel for the remission of sins; he had his authority from God, and the oracles of God were with him, and the kingdom of God for a season seemed to rest with John alone. The Lord promised Zacharias that he should have a son who was a descendant of Aaron, the Lord having promised that the priesthood should continue with Aaron and his seed throughout their generations. Let no man take this honor upon himself, except he be called of God, as was Aaron; and Aaron received his call by revelation. An angel of God also appeared unto Zacharias while in the Temple, and told him that he should have a son, whose name should be John, and he should be filled with the Holy Ghost. Zacharias was a priest of God, and officiating in the Temple, and John was a priest after his father, and held the keys of the Aaronic Priesthood, and was called of God to preach the Gospel of the kingdom of God. The Jews, as a nation, having departed from the law of God and the Gospel of the Lord, prepared the way for transferring it to the Gentiles.

But, says one, the kingdom of God could not be set up in the days of John, for John said the kingdom was at hand. But I would ask if it could be any nearer to them than to be in the hands of John. The people need not wait for the days of Pentecost to find the kingdom of God, for John had it with him, and he came forth from the wilderness crying out, "Repent ye, for the kingdom of heaven is nigh at hand," as much as to say, "Out here I have got the kingdom of God and I am coming after you; I have got the kingdom of God, and you can get it, and I am coming after you; and if you don't receive it, you will be damned;" and the scriptures represent that all Jerusalem went out unto John's baptism. There was a legal administrator, and those that were baptized were subjects for a king; and also the laws and oracles of God were there; therefore the kingdom of God was there; for no man could have better authority to administer than John; and our Savior submitted to that authority Himself, by being baptized by John; therefore the kingdom of God was set up on the earth, even in the days of John.

There is a difference between the kingdom of God and the fruits and blessings that flow from the kingdom; because there were more miracles, gifts, visions, healings, tongues, &c., in the days of Jesus Christ and His apostles, and on the day of Pentecost, than under John's administration, it does not prove by any means that John had not the kingdom of God, any more than it would that a woman had not a milk-pan because she had not a pan of milk, for while the pan might be compared to the kingdom, the milk might be compared to the blessings of the kingdom.

John was a priest after the order of Aaron, and had the keys of that priesthood, and came forth preaching repentance and baptism for the remission of sins, but at the same time cries out, "There cometh one mightier than I after me, the latchet of whose shoes I am not worthy to stoop down and unloose," and Christ came according to the words of John, and He was greater than John, because He held the keys of the Melchisedek Priesthood and kingdom of God, and had before revealed the priesthood of Moses, yet Christ was baptized by John to fulfill all righteousness; and Jesus in His teachings says,. "Upon this rock I will build my Church, and the gates of hell shall not prevail against it." What rock? Revelation.

Again he says. "Except a man be born of water and of the Spirit, he cannot enter into the kingdom of God;" and, "heaven and earth shall pass away, but my words shall not pass away. "If a man is born of water and of the Spirit, he can get into the kingdom of God. It is evident the kingdom of God was on the earth, and John prepared subjects for the kingdom, by preaching the Gospel to them and baptizing them, and he prepared the way before the Savior, or came as a forerunner, and prepared subjects for the preaching of Christ; and Christ preached through Jerusalem on the same ground where John had preached; and when the apostles were raised up, they worked in Jerusalem, and Jesus commanded them to tarry there until they were endowed with power from on high. Had they not work to do in Jerusalem? They did work, and prepared a people for the Pentecost. The kingdom of God was with them before the day of Pentecost, as well as afterwards; and it was also with John, and he preached the same Gospel and baptism that Jesus and the apostles preached after him. The endowment was to prepare the disciples for their missions unto the world.

Whenever men can find out the will of God and find an administrator legally authorized from God, there is the kingdom of God; but where these are not, the kingdom of God is not. All the ordinances, systems, and administrations on the earth are of no use to the children of men, unless they are ordained and authorized of God; for nothing will save a man but a legal administrator; for none others will be acknowledged either by God or angels.

I know what I say; I understand my mission and business. God Almighty is my shield; and what can man do if God is my friend? I shall not be sacrificed until my time comes; then I shall be offered freely. All flesh is as grass,and a governor is no better than other men; when he dies he is but a bag of dust. I thank God for preserving me from my enemies; I have no enemies but for the truth's sake. I have no desire but to do all men good. I feel to pray for all men. We don't ask any people to throw away any good they have got; we only ask them to come and get more. What if all the world should embrace this Gospel? They would then see eye to eye, and the blessings of God would be poured out upon the people, which is the desire of my whole soul. Amen.

Monday, 23.—Was at home, and wrote the editor of the *Wasp* as follows:

The Prophet on Participation in Politics.

DEAR SIR:—I have of late had repeated solicitations to have something to do in relation to the political farce about dividing the county; but as my feelings revolt at the idea of having anything to do with politics, I have declined, in every instance, having anything to do on the subject. I think it would be well for politicians to regulate their own affairs. I wish to be let alone, that I may attend strictly to the spiritual welfare of the Church.

Please insert the above, and oblige

Nauvoo, Jan. 23, 1843. JOSEPH SMITH.

In the evening rode with Emma to see Dr. Richards, who was sick, at the old postoffice building, up the river.

Elder John Snyder returned from his mission to England.

Tuesday, *24.*—Was at home till noon, when I rode out with Emma. Evening, attended the Masonic Lodge.

Wednesday, *25.*—Was about home.

Thursday, *26.*—In the afternoon rode to the Temple, and afterwards to William Clayton's.

Friday, *27.*—Rode on the prairie with William Clayton. Dined at Brother Cornelius P. Lott's.

Saturday, *28.*—Played ball with the brethren a short time. Rode round the city with Mr. Taylor, a land agent from New York.

Some snow fell, the ice began to give way in the river, and a steamer that had wintered at Montrose went over the rapids.

Sunday, *29.*—I attended meeting at the Temple. After reading the parable of the prodigal son, and making some preliminary remarks, I stated that there were two questions which had been asked me concerning my subject of the last Sabbath, which I had promised to answer in public, and would improve this opportunity.

The Greatness and Mission of John the Baptist.

The question arose from the saying of Jesus—"Among those that are born of women there is not a greater prophet than John the Baptist; but he that is least in the kingdom of God is greater than he." How is it that John was considered one of the greatest of prophets? His miracles could not have constituted his greatness.

First. He was entrusted with a divine mission of preparing the way before the face of the Lord. Whoever had such a trust committed to him before or since? No man.

Secondly. He was entrusted with the important mission, and it was required at his hands, to baptize the Son of Man. Whoever had the honor of doing that? Whoever had so great a privilege and glory? Whoever led the Son of God into the waters of baptism, and had the privilege of beholding the Holy Ghost descend in the form of a dove, or rather in the *sign* of the dove, in witness of that administration? The sign of the dove was instituted before the creation of the world, a witness for the Holy Ghost, and the devil cannot come in the sign of a dove. The Holy Ghost is a personage, and is in the form of a personage. It does not confine itself to the *form* of the dove, but in *sign* of the dove. The Holy Ghost cannot be transformed into a dove; but the sign of a dove was given to John to signify the truth of the deed, as the dove is an emblem or token of truth and innocence.

Thirdly. John, at that time, was the only legal administrator in the affairs of the kingdom there was then on the earth, and holding the keys of power. The Jews had to obey his instructions or be damned, by their own law; and Christ Himself fulfilled all righteousness in becoming obedient to the law which he had given to Moses on the mount, and thereby magnified it and made it honorable,instead of destroying it. The son of Zacharias wrested the keys, the kingdom, the power, the glory from the Jews, by the holy anointing and decree of heaven, and these three reasons constitute him the greatest prophet born of a woman.

Second question:—How was the least in the kingdom of heaven greater than he?

In reply I asked—Whom did Jesus have reference to as being the least? Jesus was looked upon as having the least claim in God's kingdom, and [seemingly] was least entitled to their credulity as a prophet; as though He had said—"He that is considered the least among you is greater than John—that is I myself."

The Parables of Jesus and the Interpretation of the Scriptures.

In reference to the prodigal son, I said it was a subject I had never dwelt upon; that it was understood by many to be one of the intricate subjects of the scriptures; and even the Elders of this Church have preached largely upon it, without having any rule of interpretation. What is the rule of interpretation? Just no interpretation at all. Understand it precisely as it reads. I have a key by which I understand the scriptures. I enquire, what was the question which drew out the answer, or caused Jesus to utter the parable? It is not national; it does not refer to Abraham, Israel or the Gentiles, in a national capacity, as some suppose. To ascertain ts meaning, we must dig up the root and ascertain what it was that drew the saying out of Jesus.

While Jesus was teaching the people, all the publicans and sinners drew near to hear Him; "and the Pharisees and scribes murmured, saying, This man receiveth sinners, and eateth with them." This is the keyword which unlocks the parable of the prodigal son. It was given to answer the murmurings and questions of the Sadducees and Pharisees, who were querying, finding fault, and saying, "How is it that this man, as great as He pretends to be, eats with publicans and sinners?" Jesus was not put to it so, but He could have found something to illustrate His subject, if He had designed it for a nation or nations; but He did not It was for men in an individual capacity; and all straining on this point is a bubble. "This man receiveth sinners and eateth with them." And he spake this parable unto them—"What man of you, having an hundred sheep, if he lose one of them, doth not leave the ninety-and-nine in the wilderness, and go after that which is lost, until he find it? And when he hath found it, he layeth it on his shoulders, rejoicing. And when he cometh home, he calleth together his friends and neighbors, saying unto them, Rejoice with me; for I have found my sheep which was lost. I say unto you, that likewise joy shall be in heaven over one sinner that repenteth, more than over ninety-and-nine just persons which need no repentance." The hundred sheep represent one hundred Sadduces and Pharisees, as though Jesus had said, "If you Sadducees and Pharisees are in the sheepfold, I have no mission for you; I am sent to look up sheep that are lost; and when I have found them, I will back them up and make joy in heaven." This represents hunting after a few individuals, or one poor publican, which the Pharisees and Sadducees despised.

He also gave them the parable of the woman and her ten pieces of silver, and how she lost one, and searching diligently, found it again, which gave more joy among the friends and neighbors than the nine which were not lost; like I say unto you, there is joy in the presence of the angels of God over one sinner that repenteth, more than over ninety-and-nine just persons that are so righteous; they will be damned anyhow; you cannot save them.

CHAPTER XIV.

PROVISIONS FOR THE ENLARGEMENT OF THE MUNICIPAL GOVERNMENT OF NAUVOO—SUNDRY ACTIVITIES OF THE PROPHET—KEYS OF KNOWLEDGE BY WHICH ANGELIC ADMINISTRATIONS MAY BE KNOWN—THE PROPHET'S PARABLE, "THE LIONS OF THE PRESS."

Monday, January 30, 1843.—Spent the day at home until six in the evening, when I presided in the city council, where much business was transacted, the most important of which was a bill reported by a committee, [providing for the enlargement of the municipal government of Nauvoo.]

[The enactment provided for certain officers in addition to those named in the charter; namely, city engineer, market master, weigher and sealer of weights and measures, a fire warden in each ward of the city, a sexton and police officer to act under the direction of the mayor as captain of the watch, and a supervisor of streets and allies. It also provided for the preservation of good order in the city, keeping clear streets and alleys, defining nuisances and providing against them. Providing for the prevention of fires, defining the duties of the city watch, and providing for a public market place, etc., etc.—EDITORS.]

Tuesday, 31.—At home all day. A severe snowstorm.

Thursday, February 2, 1843.—Spent the day at home. The weather extremely cold.

Towards evening I rode on to the hill to enquire about the caucus which was held there the previous evening, Davidson Hibbard presiding, and Brother Benjamin L. Clapp, chief speaker, reporting that Joseph and Hyrum had attempted to take away the rights of the citizens, referring to the election of the last city council. I corrected the error and returned home.

Scripture Correction.

"The Spirit maketh intercession for us with groanings and cannot be uttered." It would be better thus:—"The Spirit maketh intercession for us with striving which cannot be expressed."

Friday, 3.—This morning, read German; at eleven, walked out in the city: returned at a quarter past twelve; read proof of "Doctrine and Covenants," which is now being stereotyped.

Brother John Mayberry sent me a cow to assist in bearing my expenses at Springfield.

Saturday, 4.—At home till one o'clock in the afternoon, when I attended the general city election caucus at the Temple, where all things were amicably settled and mutual good feelings restored to all parties. Brother Clapp made a public confession for the speech which he made at a former caucus.

I returned home at about four o'clock, and was visited by Amasa M. Lyman. I told him that I had restored Orson Pratt to the quorum of the Twelve Apostles, and that I had concluded to make Brother Amasa a counselor to the First Presidency.

In the evening presided in the municipal court.

Sunday, 5.—At home, reading German.

Result of City Election.

Monday, 6.—Spent the forenoon at the election of mayor, aldermen and councilors for the city, to serve during the next two years, at Brother Hyrum Smith's office. Dined at home. One o'clock, afternoon, Thomas Moore came in and enquired about a home. I blessed him and said, God bless you for ever and ever! May the blessings of Abraham, Isaac and Jacob rest upon you for ever and ever; and may you sit on thrones high and lifted up, in the name of Jesus Christ. Amen.

When I returned to the election, Joseph Smith was elected mayor by unanimous vote. Orson Spencer, Daniel H. Wells, George A. Smith, and Stephen Markham were elected aldermen. Hyrum Smith, John Taylor, Orson Hyde, Orson Pratt, Sylvester Emmons, Heber C. Kimball, Benjamin Warrington, Daniel Spencer, and Brigham Young were elected councilors.

Tuesday, 7.—This forenoon attended a council of the Twelve Apostles at the house of President Brigham Young. This afternoon I sent a search warrant to Hyrum Kimball's for the purpose of obtaining a book of patriarchal blessings given by Father Joseph Smith, which was stolen from Far West. The warrant was issued on the affidavit of Jonathan H. Holmes, and the book obtained. In the evening Hyrum Kimball came to my house for an explanation, and I informed him that the book was the property of the Church; that it had been stolen, and after passing through various hands, had been secured by Oliver Granger, while acting as agent for the Church at Kirtland, and should have been given up by him. I have since been informed that Sister Sarah, Hyrum Kimball's wife, had procured the book of her brother, son of Oliver Granger, for the purpose of returning it to the Church; but, being under a pledge to her brother not to give up the book until he had seen her again, she had neglected to mention it to me.

A Stolen Record Secured.

Elder Parley P. Pratt arrived home from England this evening.

Wednesday, 8.—This morning, I read German, and visited with a brother and sister from Michigan, who thought that "a prophet is always a prophet;" but I told them that a prophet was a prophet only when he was acting as such. After dinner Brother Parley P. Pratt came in: we had conversation on various subjects. At four in the afternoon, I went out with my little Frederick, to exercise myself by sliding on the ice.

A Prophet not Always a Prophet.

The public papers say that Point Petre, in Guadaloupe, was totally destroyed, and ten thousand persons supposed to have been killed by an earthquake.

Thursday, 9.—Part of the forenoon I spent at the Masonic Hall, conversing with Mr. Rennick, of Keokuk, and trying to effect a settlement with him. He promised to let me have some notes on a paper maker in Louisville, towards paying me, and then went off contrary to promise. I also had a conversation with Master Nye, and read several letters, one from Judge Young, and directed the following in reply:

Joseph Smith to Hon. R. M. Young (U. S. Senator)—Payment of Loan, and Nauvoo Postoffice Matters.

Hon. R. M. Young, City of Washington:

DEAR SIR:—I have this day received your favor of the 7th ult., covering one from John C. Walsh, and barely state in this, that I shall despatch a messenger immediately to Quincy, to deposit the $500 in the hands of General Leach, according to your instructions; but seeing that I had little time to lose, I concluded to send this by the first mail to inform you of my intentions. My next, in which I shall enclose General Leach's receipt, together with my obligations, will be mailed at Quincy, and may be expected three days after you receive this.

I shall not be able to obtain George Miller's name as security, he being at this time several hundred miles north of Nauvoo, and is not expected back until spring. I can, however, obtain the signature of Mr. Edward Hunter, late from Chester county, Pennsylvania, who owns about twenty thousand dollars' worth of property in this vicinity, and probably as much more in the east, which I presume will be entirely satisfactory to Mr. Walsh, instead of Mr. Miller. Judge Higbee's name will be on the obligations.

When you receive this, you may expect the other three days later. All the difference will be the time required to go from here to Quincy and do the business.

Some time ago, a petition, signed by the principal inhabitants of this city, praying the postmaster-general to remove the present Nauvoo postmaster and appoint another in his stead, was put in the hands of C. A. Warren, Esq., of Quincy, with a request that he would hand it to you about the time you left for Washington. We have not yet heard whether Mr. Warren handed it to you or neglected to do so, but we feel extremely anxious to learn something on the subject, as the citizens generally are suffering severely from the impositions and dishonest conduct of the postmaster and those connected with the post-office in this city. The petition was accompanied by some affidavits, proving that letters had frequently been broken open, money detained, and letters charged twice over, &c, &c., at this office, the repeated occurrence of which circumstances caused the people to be anxious for an immediate change. It will be seen by the petition, that I was nominated for the office. I can only say that, if I receive the appointment, I shall do my utmost to give general satisfaction. Whoever may be appointed, it is necessary, in my estimation, to have it done as soon as circumstances will possibly admit.

Accept, sir, of my sincere acknowledgments for past favors, which are not forgotten, and accept of the best wishes and sincere thanks of yours respectfully,

JOSEPH SMITH.

By William Clayton, his agent.

Spent most of the day in conversation with Parley P. Pratt and others.

REVELATION.*

Three Grand Keys by which Good or Bad Angels or Spirits may be Known—Revealed to Joseph the Prophet, at Nauvoo, Illinois, February 9, 1843.

There are two kinds of beings in heaven—viz., angels, who are resurrected personages, having bodies of flesh and bones. For instance, Jesus said, "Handle me and see, for a spirit hath not flesh and bones, as ye see me have. 2nd. The spirits of just men made perfect—they who are not resurrected, but inherit the same glory. When a messenger comes, saying he has a message from God, offer him your hand, and request him to shake hands with you. If he be an angel he will do so, and you will feel his hand. If he be the spirit of a just man made perfect, he will come in his glory; for that is the only way he can appear. Ask him to shake hands with you, but he will not move, because it is contrary to the order of heaven for a just mnn to deceive; but he will still deliver his message. If it be the devil as an angel of light, when you ask him to shake hands he will offer you his hand, and you will not feel anything; you may therefore detect him. These are three grand keys whereby you may know whether any administration is from God.

Items of the Prophet's Experience.

A man came to me in Kirtland, and told me he had seen an angel, and described his dress. I told him he had seen no angel, and that there was no such dress in heaven. He grew mad, and went into the street and commanded fire to come

* See Doctrine and Covenants, sec. cxxix.

down out of heaven to consume me. I laughed at him, and said, You are one of Baal's prophets; your God does not hear you; jump up and cut yourself: and he commanded fire from heaven to consume my house.

When I was preaching in Philadelphia, a Quaker called out for a sign. I told him to be still. After the sermon, he again asked for a sign. I told the congregation the man was an adulterer; that a wicked and adulterous generation seeketh after a sign; and that the Lord had said to me in a revelation, that any man who wanted a sign was an adulterous person. "It is true," cried one, "for I caught him in the very act," which the man afterwards confessed, when he was baptized.

Boston Conference.

A conference was held at Boylston Hall, Boston, when fourteen branches of the Church in Boston and the vicinity were represented, comprising seven hundred and ninety-three members, thirty-three elders, forty-three lesser officers, most of whom had been raised up in about fifteen months. Elder George J. Adams, E. P. Maginn, Erastus Snow, Erastus H. Derby, and others, took active parts in the conference.

Interview with John B. Cowan.

Friday, 10.—After conversation with Mr. John B. Cowan, and others, I reviewed the history of the mob in Hiram, Portage county, Ohio, on the 25th of March, 1832, and my first journey to Missouri. At three o'clock, afternoon, attended a council of the Twelve Apostles at my house. Of the Twelve there were present Brigham Young, Heber C. Kimball, Orson Hyde, Parley P. Pratt, Orson Pratt, Wilford Woodruff, John Taylor, George A. Smith and Willard Richards. I requested that all business be presented briefly and without comments, and told the council that I had an interview with Mr. Cowan this morning; that he was delegated by the inhabitants of Shokoquon (which is twenty miles above this place on the river) to come to Nauvoo, and petition that "a talented Mormon preacher take up his residence with them, they would find him a good house and give him support, and with liberty for him to invite as many 'Mormons' to settle in that place as may please so to do.'' Council decided that Brother John Bear go and preach to them.

I suggested that a general meeting be called in the city in relation to the postoffice and other things, and instructed the council to call Elder George J. Adams to Nauvoo, with his family, and to say that he is ordered to come by the First Presidency, and that he preach no more till he comes.

At five o'clock, I opened a mayor's court at my house, when John D. Parker, deputy sheriff, presented Oliver Olney before the court for stealing goods from the store of Moses Smith on the 23rd of January, when Olney declared before the court that he had been visited many times by the Ancient of Days; that he sat with him on the 9th, 10th and 11th of last June, and should sit in counsel again with him on Tuesday next; that he had had a mission from him to the four quarters of the world; that he had been and established the twelve stakes of Zion, and had visited them all, except one in the south; that he had suffered much for two or three years for want of clothing; that he despised a thief, except when he stole to clothe himself; that he opened the store of Moses Smith on the 23rd of January, and took out the goods then present (several hundred pieces) hid them in the cornfield, and carried them home from time to time, under the same roof with Mr. Smith, and that no one knew anything about the robbery but himself.

Case of Oliver Olney.

Olney was once a member of the Church of Jesus Christ of Latter-day Saints, but had been cut off a considerable time previous. He declared that the Church never taught him to steal; and I have written his voluntary confession here, that others may take warning and behave themselves in such a manner that they shall not be cut off the Church; for if they are the Spirit of the living God will depart from them, and they may be left to a worse spirit of delusion and wickedness than even Oliver Olney, who never saw the Ancient of Days nor anything like him. But on the testimony presented, I bound him over to the next circuit court for trial, in the sum of five thousand dollars; and for want of bail, he was committed to Carthage jail.

Saturday 11.—This day had an interview with Elder Rigdon and his family. They expressed a willingness to be saved. Good feelings prevailed, and we again shook hands together.

At ten o'clock attended the city council. I prophesied to James Sloan, city recorder, that it would be better for him ten years hence, not to say anything more about fees; and addressed the new council, urging the necessity of their acting upon the principle of liberality, and of relieving the city from all unnecessary expenses and burdens, and not attempt to improve the city, but enact such ordinances as would promote peace and good order; and the people would improve the city; capitalists would come in from all quarters and build mills, factories, and machinery of all kinds; new buildings would arise on every hand, and Nauvoo would become a great city. I prophesied that if the council would be liberal in their proceedings, they would become rich, and spoke against the principle of pay for every little service rendered, and especially of commitees having extra pay for their services; reproved the judges of the late election for not holding the polls open after six o'clock, when there were many wishing to vote.

The Prophet on Pay for Public Service.

Dr. Robert D. Foster took an active part in electioneering for the opposition ticket and obstructing the passage to the polls. The council elected James Sloan, city recorder; Henry G. Sherwood, marshal; William Clayton, treasurer; approved W. W. Phelps as mayor's clerk; Dimick B. Huntington, William D. Huntington, Lewis Robison and John Barker, constables; Alanson Ripley, surveyor; James Allred, supervisor of streets; Dimick B. Huntington, coroner; James Sloan, notary public; Theodore Turley, weigher and sealer; H. G. Sherwood, market master; W. W. Phelps, fire warden; Sidney Rigdon, city attorney; and Samuel Bennett, market inspector for the city.

A board of health was established, to consist of Joseph Smith, William Law, William Marks and Samuel Bennett.

Nauvoo Market Place Proposed.

The council resolved that a market be established in the city. It was proposed to build two markets. But I told the council that if we began too large, we should do nothing; we had better build a small one at once, to be holden by the corporation; and that if that would support itself, we could go on to build another on a larger scale; that the council should hold an influence over the prices of markets, so that the poor should not be oppressed, and that the mechanic should not oppress the farmer; that the upper part of the town had no right to rival those on the river. Here, on the bank of the river, was where we first pitched our tents; here was where the first sickness and deaths occurred; here has been the greatest suffering in this city. We have been the making of the upper part of the town, We have located the Temple on the hill, and they ought to be satisfied. We began here first; and let the market go out from this part of the city; let the upper part of the town be marketed by wagons, until they can build a market; and let the first market be established on the rising ground on Main Street, about a quarter of a mile north of the river. Council continued through the day.

Mother came to my house to live.

Elders Young and Richards wrote George J. Adams, notifying him to come to Nauvoo, according to the decision of the council, and answer to the charges of adultery which had been preferred against him, before the First Presidency.

Sunday, 12.—Seven or eight young men came to see me, part of them from the city of New York. They treated me with the greatest respect. I showed them the fallacy of Mr. Miller's *data* concerning the coming of Christ and the end of the world, or as it is commonly called, Millerism,* and preached them quite a sermon; that error was in the Bible, or the translation of the Bible; that Miller was in want of correct information upon the subject, and that he was not so much to blame as the translators. I told them the prophecies must all be fulfilled; the sun must be darkened and the moon turned into blood, and many more things take place before Christ would come.

The Prophet on "Millerism."

Monday, 13.—Elder Rigdon came in early in the morning, and gave a brief history of our second visit to Jackson county, Missouri. I then read awhile in German and walked out in the city with Elder Hyde, returning at twelve o'clock. Brother John C. Annis called for counsel. The marshal called, and informed me that Mr. Rollison was trying to get the postoffice, and that Dr. R. D. Foster was the first to sign the petition. I gave instruction about a bond for a part of a lot to Brother John Oakley. A quarter before four, went to the printing office with Brother W. W. Phelps.

I spent the evening at Elder Orson Hyde's. In the course of conversation I remarked that those brethren who came here having money, and purchased without the

* Millerism here referred to is the sum of the doctrines taught by William Miller, an American religious zealot who emphasized in his religious teachings the Millennial Reign of Christ on earth, which reign, he declared, as early as 1831, would commence in the year 1843. His predictions were based largely upon computations of time on the prophecies of Daniel and the Book of Revelation. After the great disappointment which came to his followers in 1843, they abandoned all attempts at fixing the date on which the second advent of Christ would take place, but otherwise continued to believe in the doctrines advocated by Mr. Miller. "There are several divisions or sects of Adventists, the principal of which are: the Advent Christians, the largest; the Seventh-day Adventists, much smaller, but more compactly organized; and the Evangelical Adventists, the smallest. The members of the first two believe in the final annihilation of the wicked, which those of the third reject. The second observe the seventh day as the Sabbath, and believe in the existence of the spirit of prophecy among them; they maintain missions in various parts of the world, and a number of institutions at Battle Creek, Michigan, their headquarters."—*Century Dictionary.*

Church and without counsel, must be cut off. This, with other observations, aroused the feelings of Brother Dixon, from Salem, Massachusetts, who was present, and he appeared in great wrath.

I received the following communication:

Rigdon's Suggested Petition as to Nauvoo Postmaster.

To the Hon. Mr. Bryant, Second Assistant Postmaster-General:

We, your petitioners, respectfully beg leave to submit that as an attempt is now, by certain individuals, being made to place the post-office in this place into the hands of William H. Rollison, a stranger in our place, and one whose conduct since he came here, has been such as to forbid our having confidence in him; and we do hope and pray, both for ourselves, and that of the public, that he may not receive the appointment of postmaster in Nauvoo, Illinois, but that the present postmaster may continue to hold the office.

Brother Joseph Smith, if the foregoing can have a number of respectable subscribers, I believe Rollinson cannot get the office. I should like to have it so as to send it on Sunday's mail. Respectfully,

SIDNEY RIGDON.

Tuesday, 14.—Sent William Clayton to Quincy, and by him deposited five hundred dollars with General Leach, for Mr. Walsh, for land which lies between my farm and the city, agreeable to my letter to Judge Young.

Read proof of the "Doctrine and Covenants" with Brother Phelps. Read in German from half-past nine to eleven, forenoon. Had the stove removed from the large room in my house into a small brick building which was erected for a smoke house, designing to use it for a mayor's office, until I could build a new one. Had much conversation with Mr. Cowan and various individuals.

Sold Dr. Richards a cow.

Wednesday, 15.—This morning I spent some time in changing the top plate of the office stove, which had been put together wrong. Read a libelous letter in the *Alton Telegraph*, written to Mr. Bassett, of Quincy, concerning Judge Pope, Mr. Butterfield, and the ladies attending my late trial at Springfield; and published the following letter in the *Times and Seasons:*

Joseph Smith's Parable—the Lions of the Press.

Mr. Editor:

SIR:—Ever since I gave up the editorial department of the *Times and Seasons*, I have thought of writing a piece for publication, by way of valedictory, as is usual when editors resign the chair editorial. My principal remarks I intend to apply to the gentlemen of the quill, or, if you please, that numerous body of respectable gentlemen who profess to regulate the tone of the public mind in regard to politics, morality, religion, literature, the arts and sciences, &c., &c.,—viz., the editors of the public journals; or, if you please, I will designate them the lions of the forest. This latter cognomen, sir, I consider to be more appropriate because of the tremendous noise that they make when they utter their voice.

It came to pass that, as I went forth like a young fawn, one day, to feed upon the green grass in my pasture, an ass saw me and brayed, and made a great noise, which a neighboring lion hearing, roared, even as a lion roareth when he beholds his prey. At the sound of his voice, the beasts of the field were alarmed, and the lions in the adjoining jungles pricked up their ears and roared in their turn; and behold all the lions of the forest, alarmed by their noise, opened their mouths and uttered forth their voice, which was as the roaring of a cataract, or as the voice of thunder; so tremendous was their roaring, that the trees of the forest shook, as if they were shaken by a mighty wind, and all the beasts of the forest trembled as if a whirlwind were passing.

I lifted up mine eyes with astonishment when I heard the voice of the lions, and saw the fury of their rage. I asked, is it possible that so many lords of the forest, such noble beasts should condescend to notice one solitary fawn that is feeding alone upon his pasture, without attempting to excite either their jealousy or anger? I have not strayed from the fold, nor injured the trees of the forest, nor hurt the beasts of the field, nor trampled upon their pasture, nor drunk of their streams. Why, then, their rage against me? When lo! and behold! they again uttered their voices, as the voice of great thunderings, and there was given unto them the voice of men; but it was difficult for me to distinguish what was said among so many voices; but ever and anon I heard a few broken, incoherent sentences like the following: "Murder! Desolation! Bloodshed! Arson! Treason! Joe Smith and the Mormons! Our nation will be overturned! The impostor should be driven from the state! The fawn will be metamorphosed into a lion—will devour all the beasts of the field, destroy all the trees of the forest, and tread under foot all the rest of the lions!"

I then lifted up my voice and said, Hear me, ye beasts of the forest! and all ye great lions, pay attention! I am innocent of the things whereof ye accuse me. I have not been guilty of violating your laws, nor of trespassing upon your rights. My hands are clean from the blood of all men, and I am at the defiance of the world to substantiate the crimes whereof I am accused; wherefore, then should animals of your noble mien stoop to such little jealousies, such vulgar language, and lay such unfounded charges at the door of the innocent?

It is true that I once suffered an ass to feed in my pasture. He ate at my crib and drank at my waters; but possessing the true nature of an ass, he began to foul the water with his feet, and to trample under foot the green grass and destroy it. I therefore put him out of my pasture, and he began to bray. Many of the lions in the adjoining jungles, mistaking the braying for the roaring of a lion, commenced roaring. When I proclaimed this abroad many of the lions began to enquire into the matter. A few, possessing a more noble nature than many of their fellows, drew near, and viewing the animal found that he was nothing more than a decrepit, broken down, worn out ass, that had scarcely anything left but his ears and voice.

Whereupon many of the lions felt indignant at the lion of Warsaw, the lion of Quincy, the lion of Sangamon, the lion of Alton, and several other lions, for giving a false alarm, for dishonoring their race, and for responding to the voice of so base an animal as an ass. And they felt ashamed of themselves for being decoyed into such base ribaldry and foul-mouthed slander. But there were many that lost sight of their dignity, and continued to roar, although they knew well that they were following the braying of so despicable a creature.

Among these was a great lion, whose den was on the borders of the Eastern Sea. He had waxed great in strength. He had terrible teeth, and his eyes were like balls of fire. His head was large and terrific, and his shaggy mane rolled with majestic grandeur over his terrible neck. His claws were like the claws of a dragon, and his ribs were like those of a Leviathan. When he lifted himself up, all the beasts of the field bowed with respectful deference; and when he spake, the whole universe listened; and the cinders of his power covered creation. His might, his influence, were felt to the ends of the earth. When he lashed his tail, the beasts of the forest trembled; and when he roared, all the great lions and the young lions crouched down at his feet.*

This great lion lifting up himself and beholding the fawn afar off, he opened his mouth, and, joining in the common roar, uttered the following great swelling yelp:—

"*Joe Smith in Trouble.*—By a letter which we published on Sunday,

* This alludes to the New York *Herald*, published by James Gordon Bennett, who had been influenced by the misrepresentation of affairs at Nauvoo, by John C. Bennett.

from Springfield, Illinois, it appears that Joe Smith, the great Mormon Prophet, has at last given himself up to the authorities of Illinois. He is charged with fomenting or conspiring to assassinate Governor Boggs, of Missouri, and is demanded by the functionary of that state of the governor of Illinois. Joe has taken out a writ of habeas corpus, denying the fact, and is now waiting the decision of the court at Springfield. This will bring Joe's troubles to a crisis. In the meantime, why does not Joe try his power at working a miracle or two? Now's the time to prove his mission, besides being very convenient for himself."

When I heard it, I said, "Poor fellow! How has thy dignity fallen! and how has thy glory departed? Thou that once ranked among the foremost of the beasts of the field, as the lord of the forest!—even thou hast condescended to degrade thyself by uniting with the basest of animals, and to join in with the braying of an ass."

And now, friend B., allow me to whisper a word in thine ear. Dost thou not know that there is a God in the heavens that judgeth—that setteth up one and putteth down another, according to the counsel of his own will? That if thou possessest any influence, wisdom, dominion, or power, it comes from God, and to him thou art indebted for it? That he holds the destiny of men in his power, and can as easily put down as he has raised up? Tell me, when hast thou treated a subject of religious and eternal truth with that seriousness and candor that the importance of the subject demands from a man in thy standing, possessing thy calling and influence? As you seem to be quite a theologist, allow me to ask a few questions. Why did not God deliver Micaiah from the hands of his persecutors? Why did not Jeremiah "*work a miracle or two*" to help him out of the dungeon? It would have been "*very convenient.*" Why did not Zachariah, by a miracle, prevent the people from slaying him? Why did not our Savior come down from the cross? The people asked Him to do it; and besides, He had "saved others," and could not save Himself, so said the people. Why did He not prove His mission by working a miracle and coming down? Why did not Paul, by a miracle, prevent the people from stoning and whipping him? It would have been "very convenient." Or why did the Saints of God in every age have to wander about in sheep-skins or goat-skins, being tempted, tried, and sawn asunder, of whom the world was not worthy? I would here advise my worthy friend, before he talks of "proving missions," "working miracles," or any "convenience" of that kind, to read his Bible a little more, and the garbled stories of political demagogues less.

I listened, and lo! I heard a voice, and it was the voice of my Shepherd, saying, Listen, all ye lions of the forest; and all ye beasts of he field, give ear. Ye have sought to injure the innocent, and your hands have been lifted against the weak, the injured, and the oppressed. Ye have pampered the libertine, the calumniator, and the base. Ye have winked at vice, and trodden under foot the virtuous and the pure. Therefore hear, all ye lions of the forest: The Lord God will take from you your teeth, so that you shall no longer devour. He will pluck out your claws, so that you can no longer seize upon your prey. Your strength will fail you in the day of trouble, and your voice will fail, and not be heard afar off; but mine elect will I uphold with mine arm, and my chosen shall be supported by my power. And when mine anointed shall be exalted, and all the lions of the forest have lost their strength, then shall they remember that the Lord he is God.

JOSEPH SMITH.

I copy the following from the public prints:—

Horrors of a British-Chinese War.

An English officer, writing to his friend in England, from Ching Keang Foo, says—"I never saw such loss of life and property as took place here: we lost officers and men enough, but it is impossible even to compute the loss of the Chinese; for when they found they could stand no longer against us, they cut the throats of their wives and children, or drove them into wells and ponds, and then destroyed themselves. In many houses there were from eight to twelve bodies, and I myself have seen a dozen women and children drowning themselves in a small pond the day after the fight. The whole of the city and suburbs are a mass of ruins: whole streets have been burnt down." Oh, the horrors of Christian warfare!

About one o'clock in the afternoon I started for Shokoquon, with Mr. John B. Cowan and Elders Orson Hyde and Parley P. Pratt, in sleighs. When we came on the prairie, it was so extremely cold, I proposed to Mr. Cowan to wait till tomorrow; but he chose to go forward, and we arrived in safety at Mr. Rose's, where we had supper; and in the evening I gave a long exposition of Millerism. That night I slept with Mr. Cowan.

CHAPTER XV.

VISIT OF THE PROPHET TO SHOKOQUON—WOOD CUTTING BEE —THE PROPHET'S SPEECH ON CONDITIONS AT NAUVOO —ON THE COMING OF THE SON OF MAN.

Thursday, February 16, 1843.—After breakfast, we [the Prophet, Mr. Cowan and their party] proceeded towards Shokoquon. After traveling five miles, Brothers Hyde and Pratt's sleigh upset. Brother Hyde hurt his hand; the horse ran away, and we brought it back. After dinner, at McQueen's Mills, we went to Shokoquon, viewed the place and found it a very desirable location for a city, when we returned to the place where we dined. Elder Hyde prayed and I preached to a large and attentive audience two hours (from Rev. xix, 10), and proved to the people that any man that denied himself as being a prophet was not a preacher of righteousness. They opened their eyes, and appeared well pleased. When we had returned as far as McQueen's Mills, Mr. Cowan halted and proposed to call. While waiting a moment, Mr. Crane's horse, (Mr. Crane came with our company,) which was behind us, ran and jumped into our sleigh as we jumped out, and thence over our horse and the fence, sleigh and all, the sleigh being still attached to the horse, and the fence eight rails high; and both horses ran over lots and through the woods, clearing themselves from the sleighs, and had their frolic out without hurting themselves or drivers. It was a truly wonderful feat, and as wonderful a deliverance for the parties. We took supper at Mr. Crane's, and I stayed at Mr. Rose's that night.

The Visit to Shokoquon.

Dr. Richards invited the brethren to come to my house on Monday next to chop and pile up my wood.

Friday, *17*.—Mr. Cowan returned with me to my house, where we arrived about noon; and I enjoyed myself by my own fireside, with many of my friends around me, the remainder of the day. Mr. Cowan proposed to give me one-fourth of the city lots in Shokoquon.

The Prophet at Home.

Saturday, *18*.—Mostly about home and at the office. Several called for counsel on points of law. Esquire Warren, of Quincy, called on me. He had hurt his horse, and said it was not the first time he had missed it by not following my advice. While at dinner, I remarked to my family and friends present, that when the earth was sanctified and became like a sea of glass, it would be one great urim and thummim, and the Saints could look in it and see as they are seen.*

Letter of the Twelve—Calling for Assistance for the Prophet.

The Twelve to the Church of Jesus Christ of Latter-day Saints in La Harpe, greeting:—

Beloved Brethren:—We wish to present, briefly, one important item for your serious consideration. Our beloved President Joseph Smith is now delivered from the prosecution and oppression from without, by which he has been bound, and also by the same process has been relieved of his property; so that he has nothing now to hinder his devoting his time to the History of the Church and the spiritual interest thereof, except he has to spend his time in gathering food for his family.

This is the point, brethren, whether you will do your duty in supplying the President with food, that he may attend to the business of the

* This is the first mention made in the history of the Prophet of this idea which receives its fuller development in "Important Items of Instruction" given by him on the second of April, 1843, and found at length in the Doctrine and Covenants, section 130. In these "Items of Instruction" we learn that the place where God resides is a great urim and thummim, that the earth itself when sanctified and made an immortal sphere will be a urim and thummim to the inhabitants who dwell upon it, whereby all things pertaining to inferior kingdoms will be revealed to them, and to each of such inhabitants an individual urim and thummim will be given through which knowledge pertaining to kingdoms of a higher order will be revealed.

Church, and devote his whole time to the spiritual affairs thereof; or shall he attend to your business [i. e., that which the Saints ought to do for the Prophet] by running here and there for a bushel of wheat or a pound of beef and pork, while the revelations to the Church cease? This question is for the Church to answer. Therefore we call upon the brethren in La Harpe at this time, for immediate relief. You are all well aware that we do not raise wheat, corn, beef, pork, tallow, lard, butter, eggs, and provisions and vegetables in the city, such as you all use, not excepting cotton, or woollen goods, or groceries, [a fact] which you are all well acquainted with. And we are the same kind of beings in Nauvoo as in the country; and what you raise and eat in La Harpe, we would eat in Nauvoo, if we could get it, our President not excepted. And everything which is required to fill a larder in La Harpe is required in this place; and by this you may know what is wanting by our President to prosecute the Lord's work and bring about your salvation.

Brethren, we hope you will give an immediate answer to this by loaded teams or letter.

BRIGHAM YOUNG,
President.

WILLARD RICHARDS, Clerk.
NAUVOO, February 18, 1843.

Sunday, *19*.—Spent the day from nine in the morning till midnight, in the High Council, who were attending to the case of Wilson Law and Uriel C. Nickerson, who were in dispute about the title to certain lands on the Island. After hearing the testimony, I explained the laws of the United States, Iowa, and Illinois, and showed that Nickerson had the oldest claim and best right, and left it for Law to say how much Nickerson should have; and the parties shook hands, in token of a settlement of all difficulties.

Settlement of a Difficulty.

The following is copied from the *Times and Seasons*:—

Letter of Sidney Rigdon to Alfred Stokes—Correcting Misrepresentations of Nauvoo Affairs.

NAUVOO, ILLINOIS, February 19, 1843.

Mr. Alfred Edward Stokes.

DEAR SIR:—In obedience to your request, I send you one number of each of the papers published in this place. I am well aware that designing men, for sinister purposes, have put in circulation reports concerning the people here, which are so monstrous that it is a matter of surprise how any rational being could profess to believe them at all. If I were even to profess to believe such incredible and ridiculous nonsense about any people, I should consider the public would have sufficient cause to scorn me as the mere tool of corrupt and foul slanderers: but anything to stop the progress of that which cannot be stopped by fact and scripture truth. That man must have a large stock of moral courage who dare in anywise profess belief in such outlandish representations as are made in the public papers concerning the people of Nauvoo, and circulated orally by wicked and designing men. The old, stale story about common stock, in defiance of fact and truth, it would appear by your letter and that of your friend Evans, is professedly believed by the people in the vicinity of Waynesville, Ohio. This falsehood was invented by an ignorant blockhead, by the name of Matthew Clapp, who, for want of any other means to stop the progress of truth in its more incipient stages, invented this falsehood, and, finding it took with persons of his own stamp, circulated it with untiring perseverance, in direct opposition to the testimony of his senses, knowing, at the time he commenced circulating it, that it was false. He was a preacher of the Campbellite faith.

It would require the ignorance of barbarians and the credulity of savages to attempt a belief in the falsehoods which are circulated against the Saints with great zeal by many. I have never supposed that the authors of these defamatory tales ever expected the public would believe them; but they expected that men of corrupt minds, like themselves, would profess to believe them; neither do I now believe that those who profess to believe them do actually believe one word of them; but they profess to do it, thinking that, by so doing, they can make some headway against us: but it is a vain attempt; for every attempt of the kind has only excited inquiry, awakened curiosity, and caused investigation, which have, in every instance, resulted in an increase of members to the Church; so that we grant full license to all defamers to do their uttermost.

Our city is a great thoroughfare: people of all classes are crowding into it; multitudes who do not belong to the Church of Latter-day Saints are seeking locations where they can prosecute their respective callings. If you wish the papers, you can put the money into a letter, and the postmaster at your place will send it without expense.

Yours, with respect,

SIDNEY RIGDON, P. M.

Elder William Henshaw having been directed by Elder Lorenzo Snow to go to South Wales, he commenced preaching in the English language privately to several families in Pen y Darren, near Merthyr Tydvil, Glamorganshire. A number of the people believed his testimony, and this day he baptized William Rees Davis, his wife, and two of his sons, and commenced preaching publicly in Brother Davis's house, about one-third of the people only understanding the English language.

Beginning of the Work in South Wales.

Monday, 20.—About seventy of the brethren came together, according to previous notice, and drawed, sawed, chopped, split, moved, and piled up a large lot of wood in my yard. The day was spent by them with much pleasantry, good humor and feeling. A white oak log, measuring five feet four inches in diameter was cut through with a cross-cut saw, in four-and-a-half minutes, by Hyrum Dayton and Brother John Tidwell. This tree had been previously cut and hauled by my own hands and team.

Wood-cutting Bee at the Prophet's Home.

From nine to eleven this morning, I was reading in German; and from eleven to twelve, held mayor's court on assumpsit, Charles R. Dana, *v.* William B. Brink, which was adjourned ten days.

Last night, Arthur Milliken had a number of books stolen, and found them this afternoon in Brother Hyrum's hayloft. Two boys, Thomas Morgan and Robert Taylor, were arrested on suspicion and brought before me for examination. After a brief investigation, the court adjourned until ten o'clock tomorrow morning.

While the court was in session, I saw two boys fighting in the street, near Mills' Tavern. I left the business of the court, ran over immediately, caught one of the boys (who had begun the fight with clubs,) and then the other; and, after giving them proper instruction, I gave the bystanders a lecture for not interfering in such cases, and told them to quell all disturbances in the street at the first onset. I returned to the

The Prophet a Peace Maker.

court, and told them that nobody was allowed to fight in Nauvoo but myself.

In the evening, called at Brother Heber C. Kimball's.

John Quincy Adams presented to the House of Representatives of the United States a petition signed by 51,863 citizens of Massachusetts, praying congress to pass such acts and propose such amendments to the Constitution as would separate the petitioners from all connection with the institution of slavery.*

Tuesday, 21.—Opened mayor's court at ten o'clock forenoon, according to adjournment. Robert Taylor was again brought up for stealing, and Thomas Morgan for receiving the books, [referred to above] and each sentenced to six months imprisonment in Carthage jail.

Temple Workers' Difficulties.

At eleven I went to the Temple, and found a large assembly, and Brother Haws preaching about the Nauvoo House; after which, Mr.

* This was but one of a series of such petitions from New England which Mr. Adams presented to the House of Representatives. In fact upon his entrance as a member of the House, in 1831, (following his term of President of the United States) he had begun an agitation of the slavery question in Congress, but his contention in the main was for the maintenance of the sacred right of petition by the people, which right had undoubtedly been abridged by some unwise resolutions that had been adopted by the Congress of the United States. In 1838 a set of resolutions was adopted in the House by a vote of 146 to 52, in which, among other things, it was "Resolved, that petitions for the abolition of slavery in the District of Columbia and territories of the United States, and against the removal of slaves from one state to another, was part of the plan of operation set on foot to affect the institution of slavery in the southern states and thus tending, indirectly, to destroy that institution within their limits. * * * And that every petition, memorial, resolution, proposition, or paper touching or relating in any way or to any extent whatever to slavery as aforesaid, or the abolition thereof, shall on presentation thereof, without any further question thereon, be laid upon the table without being debated, printed, or referred." In the Congress of 1842, notwithstanding these resolutions, Mr. Adams, in January, presented a petition from the citizens of Haverhill, Massachusetts, "praying the immediate adoption of measures peaceably to desolve the union of these states, signed by Benjamin Emerson and four hundred and fifty-six other persons, in which the reasons of the petition were set forth with instructions to report an answer to the petitioners showing the reasons why the prayer of it ought not to be granted." (Stephens' History of the U. S.) Mr. Adams of course had no sympathy with this and many other petitions that he presented, but he held the right of petition to be sacred, and he continued the fight for it until he saw such changes in the rules of the House of Representatives as allowed petitions on the question of slavery to be received without objection and freely discussed.

Lucian Woodworth, the architect of the house, continued the subject, and said, "When I have had a pound of meat or a quart of meal, I have divided with the workmen. ['Pretty good doctrine for Paganism,' said I. At this time Mr. Woodworth was not baptized, and called himself the Pagan Prophet.] We have had about three hundred men on the job, and some of the best men in the world. Those that have not complained I want to continue with me; and those that hate 'Mormonism' and everything else that's good, I want them to get their pay and run away as quickly as possible." When Mr. Woodworth had done speaking, I addressed the multitude in substance as follows:—

Remarks of the Prophet to Workmen on the Temple.

Well, the Pagan Prophet has preached us a pretty good sermon this morning, and I don't know that I can better it much; but I feel disposed to break off the yoke of oppression, and say what I have a mind to. If the pagans and the Pagan Prophet feel more for our prosperity than we do for ourselves, it is curious; I am almost converted to his doctrine. He has prophesied that if these buildings go down, it will curse the place. I verily know it is true. Let us build the Temple. There may be some speculations about the Nauvoo House, say some. Some say, because we live on the hill, we must build up this part on the hill. Does that coat fit you, Dr. Foster? (Foster: "Pretty well.") Put it on, then. This is the way people swell, like the toad in the fable. They'll come down under the hill among little folks and say, "Brother Joseph, how I love you; can I do anything for you?" and then go away secretly and get up opposition, and sing out our names to strangers and scoundrels with an evil influence. I want all men to feel for me, when I have shook the bush and borne the burden in the heat of the day; and if they do not, I speak in authority, in the name of the Lord God, they shall be damned.

Some say that the people on the flats are aggrandizing themselves by the Nauvoo House. But who laid the foundation of the Temple? Brother Joseph, in the name of the Lord,—not for his aggrandizement, but for the good of the whole of the Saints. Our speculators say, "Poor folks on the flat are down, and keep them down." How the Nauvoo House cheats this man and that man, say the speculators. Those who report such things as facts ought to hide their heads in hollow pumpkins, and never take them out again.

The first principle brought into consideration is aggrandizement. Some think it unlawful; but it is lawful with any man, while he has a disposition to aggrandize all around him. It is a false principle for a man to aggrandize himself at the expense of another. Everything that God does is to aggrandize His kingdom. And how does He lay the foundation? "Build a Temple to my great name, and call the attention of the great, the rich, and the noble." But where shall we lay our heads? In an old log cabin.

I will whip Hirum Kimball and Esquire Wells, and everybody else, over Dr. Foster's head, who, instead of building the Nauvoo House, build a great many little skeletons. See Dr. Foster's mammoth skeletons rising all over the town; but there is no flesh on them; they are all for personal interest and aggrandizement. But I do not care how many bones there are in the city; somebody may come along and clothe them. See the bones of the elephant yonder, (as I pointed to the big house on Mulholland Street, preparing for a tavern, as yet uncovered,) the crocodiles and man-eaters all about the city, such as grog shops, and card shops, and counterfeit shops, &c., got up for their own aggrandizement, and all for speculation, while the Nauvoo House is neglected. Those who live in glass houses should not throw stones. The building of the Nauvoo House is just as sacred in my view as the Temple. I want the Nauvoo House built. It *must* be built. Our salvation [as a city] depends upon it.

When men have done what they can or will do for the Temple, let them do what they can for the Nauvoo House. We never can accomplish one work at the expense of another. There is a great deal of murmuring in the Church about me; but I don't care anything about it. I like to hear it thunder, and I like to hear the Saints grumble; for the growling dog gets the sorest head. If any man is poor and afflicted, let him come and tell of it, and not complain or grumble about it.

The finishing of the Nauvoo House is like a man finishing a fight; if he gives up, he is killed; if he holds out a little longer, he may live. I'll tell you a story: A man who whips his wife is a coward. When I was a boy, I once fought with a man who had whipped his wife. It was a hard contest; but I still remembered that he had whipped his wife; and this encouraged me, and I whipped him till he said he had enough. Brethren, hurry on to the Nauvoo House thus, and you will build it. You will then be on Pisgah's top, and the great men will come from the four quarters of the earth—will pile the gold and silver into it till you are weary of receiving them; and if you are not careful, you will be lifted up, and become full of pride, and will be ready to destroy yourselves, and they will cover up and clothe all your former sins and, according to the scripture, will hide a multitude of sins; and you will shine forth fair as the sun, clear as the moon, and you will become terrible, like an army with banners.

I will say to those who have labored on the Nauvoo House, and cannot get their pay—Be patient; and if any man takes the means which are set apart for the building of that house, and applies it to his own use, let him, for he will destroy himself. If any man is hungry, let him come to me, and I will feed him at my table. If any are hungry or naked, don't take away the brick, timber and materials, that belong to that house, but come and tell me, and I will divide with them to the last morsel; and then if the man is not satisfied, I will kick his backside.

There is a great noise in the city, and many are saying there cannot be so much smoke without some fire. Well, be it so. If the stories about Joe Smith are true, then the stories of John C. Bennett are true about the ladies of Nauvoo; and he says that the Ladies' Relief Society are all organized of those who are to be the wives of Joe Smith. Ladies, you know whether this is true or not. It is no use living among hogs without a snout. This biting and devouring each other I cannot endure. Away with it. For God's sake, stop it.

There is one thing more I wish to speak about, and that is political economy. It is our duty to concentrate all our influence to make popular that which is sound and good, and unpopular that which is unsound. 'Tis right, politically, for a man who has influence to use it, as well as for a man who has no influence to use his. From henceforth I will maintain all the influence I can get. In relation to politics, I will speak as a man; but in relation to religion I will speak in authority. If a man lifts a dagger to kill me, I will lift my tongue.

When I last preached, I heard such a groaning, I thought of the Paddy's eel. When he tried to kill it, he could not contrive any better way to do it, so he put it into the water to drown it; and as it began to come to, "See," said he, "what pain it is in; how it wiggles its tail." So it is with the nation: the banks are failing, and it is our privilege to say what kind of currency we want. We want gold and silver to build the Temple and Nauvoo House: we want your old nose-rings, and finger rings, and brass kettles no longer. If you have old rags, watches guns, &c., go and peddle them off, and bring the hard metal; and if we will do this by popular opinion, we shall have a sound currency. Send home all bank notes, and take no more paper money. Let every man write back to his neighbors before he starts for home to exchange his property for gold and silver, that he may fulfil the scripture, and come up to Zion, bringing his gold and silver with him. I have contemplated these things a long time, but the time had not come for me to speak of them till now. I would not do as the Nauvoo House committee have done—

sell stock for an old store-house, where all the people who tried to live in it died, and put that stock into a man's hands to go east and purchase rags to come here and build mammoth bones with.

As a political man, in the name of old Joe Smith, I command the Nauvoo House committee not to sell stock in the Nauvoo House without the gold or silver. We must excuse Brother Snider, for he was in England when the committee sold stock for the store-house. I leave this subject.

This meeting was got up by the Nauvoo House committee. The pagans, Roman Catholics, Methodists and Baptists shall have place in Nauvoo—only they must be ground in Joe Smith's mill. I have been in their mill. I was ground in Ohio and York States, in a Presbyterian smut machine, and the last machine was in Missouri; and the last of all, I have been through the Illinois smut machine; and those who come here must go through my smut machine, and that is my tongue.

As I closed, Dr. Robert D. Foster remarked to the assembly—"Much good may grow out of a very little, and much good may come out of this. If any man accuses me of exchanging Nauvoo stock for rags, &c., he is mistaken. I gave a thousand dollars to this house, (this he said upon his own responsibility) and fifty dollars to the Relief Society, and some to Fullmer to get stone to build Joseph a house; and I mean to build Joseph a house, and you may build this, and I will help you. I mean to profit by this: and I will divide the mammoth bones with you. I am guilty of all of which I have been charged. I have signed my name to a petition to have William H. Rollison to have the postoffice. I did not then know of a petition for Joseph Smith."

I replied—"I thought I would make a coat; but it don't fit the doctor only in the postoffice. If it does fit any one let him put it on. The doctor's mammoth bones are skeletons, and as old Ezekiel said, I command the flesh and sinews to come upon them, that they may be clothed."

Wednesday, 22.—At nine this morning Brother Abel Owen presented a claim of considerable amount against Carter, Cahoon & Co., Kirtland, and notes of Oliver Granger of about $700 for payment. He said he was poor and unable to labor, and wanted something to live on. I told him to burn the papers, and I would help him. He gave me the papers, and I gave him an order on Mr. Cowan for fifteen dollars worth of provisions. This was a gift, as the Church was not obligated to pay those debts.

I rode about the city with Mr. Cowan during the day, and also read German.

The latest accounts from the East Indies state that the cholera was raging in Burmah, Asia, to a fearful extent, whole villages in the interior had become desolate either by flight or death.

Thursday, *23*.—This morning read German and rode out a few miles, but did not get off my horse.

In the afternoon Mr. Bagby called to collect county and state taxes. Brother Dixon called concerning some lost or stolen property. I burned twenty-three dollars of city scrip, and while it was burning, said, "So may all unsound and uncurrent money go down!" Gave my clerk instructions not to pay any more taxes on the Hotchkiss purchase.

Elder Amasa Lyman started for Shokoquon this morning and commenced preaching in that place.

Filed my bond as mayor of the city of Nauvoo.

Friday, *24*.—Rode out with Elder Brigham Young; dined from home; called on Dr. Foster; had some conversation about the postoffice and several other matters; returned to my office; and at three o'clock walked out with Elder Young.

In reply to W. W. Phelps's *Vade Mecum*, or "Go with me," of 20th of January last, I dictated an answer: [It consisted of the "Revelation known as the Vision of the Three Glories," Doctrine and Covenants, section lxxvi, made into verse.]

Saturday, *25*.—This morning Brother Samuel C. Brown made me a present of a gold watch. Spent the forenoon in the city council. The council passed "An ordinance in relation to interments," "An ordinance in relation to the duties of city attorney," and an ordinance concerning a market on Main Street." Stephen Markham resigned his office as an alderman, and Wilson Law was elected to fill his place.

At three o'clock the council assembled after an adjournment for dinner. The subject of a sound currency for the city having previously arisen, I addressed the council at considerable length, giving, amongst others, the following hints.

Views of the Prophet on Constitutional Powers.

Situated as we are, with a flood of immigration constantly pouring in upon us, I consider that it is not only prudential, but absolutely necessary to protect the inhabitants of this city from being imposed upon by a spurious currency. Many of our eastern and old country friends are altogether unacquainted with the situation of the banks in this region of country; and as they generally bring specie with them, they are perpetually in danger of being gulled by speculators. Besides there is so much uncertainty in the solvency of the best of banks, that I think it much safer to go upon the hard money system altogether. I have examined the Constitution upon this subject and find my doubts removed. The Constitution is not a law, but it empowers the people to make laws. For instance, the Constitution governs the land of Iowa, but it is not a law for the people. The Constitution tells us what shall not be a lawful tender. The 10th section declares that nothing else except gold and silver shall be lawful tender, this is not saying that gold and silver shall be lawful tender. It only provides that the states may make a law to make gold and silver lawful tender. I know of no state in the Union that has passed such a law; and I am sure that Illinois has not. The legislature has ceded up to us the privilege of enacting such laws as are not inconsistent with the Constitution of the United States and the state of Illinois; and we stand in the same relation to the state as the state does to the Union. The clause referred to in the Constitution is for the legislature—it is not a law for the people. The different states, and even Congress itself, have passed many laws diametrically contrary to the Constitution of the United States.

The state of Illinois has passed a stay law making property a lawful tender for the payment of debts; and if we have no law on the subject we must be governed by it. Shall we be such fools as to be governed by its laws, which are unconstitutional? No! We will make a law for gold and silver; and then the state law ceases and we can collect our debts. Powers not delegated to the states or reserved from the states are constitutional. The Constitution acknowledges that the people have all power not reserved to itself. I am a lawyer; I am a big lawyer and comprehend heaven, earth and hell, to bring forth knowledge that shall cover up all lawyers, doctors and other big bodies. This is the doctrine of the Constitution, so help me God. The Constitution is not law to us, but it makes provision for us whereby we can make laws. Where it provides that no one shall be hindered from worshiping God according to his own conscience, is a law. No legislature can enact a law to prohibit it. The Constitution provides to regulate bodies of men and not individuals.

Alderman Wells and Counselor Orson Pratt objected to the ordinance regulating the currency from taking immediate effect. Orson Spencer and Brigham Young spoke in favor of the bill. I invited W. W. Phelps and Dr. Willard Richards, who were present, to give their opinion on the bill. They both spoke in favor of a gold and silver currency, and that it take immediate effect in the city.

The bill was postponed until the next council.

Sunday, 26.—At home all day. My mother was sick with inflammation of the lungs, and I nursed her with my own hands.

Monday, 27.—I nursed my mother most of the day, who continued very sick. I issued a search warrant for Brother Dixon to search ——— Fidler's and John Eagle's houses for a box of stolen shoes.

Tuesday, 28.—Mostly with my mother and family. Mr. John Brassfield, with whom I became acquainted in Missouri, called on me and spent the day and night. In the afternoon, mother was somewhat easier; and at four o'clock I went to Elder Orson Hyde's to dinner.

I saw a notice in the Chicago *Express* that one Hyrum Redding had seen the sign of the Son of Man, &c.; and I wrote to the editor of the *Times and Seasons*, as follows:

The "Sign" of the Son of Man.

SIR:—Among the many signs of the times and other strange things which are continually agitating the minds of men, I notice a small speculation in the *Chicago Express*, upon the certificate of one Hyrum Redding, of Ogle county, Illinois, stating that he has seen the sign of the Son of Man as foretold in the 24th chapter of Matthew.

The slanderous allusion of a "seraglio" like the Grand Turk, which the editor applies to me, he may take to himself, for, "out of the abundance of the heart the mouth speaketh." Every honest man who has visited the city of Nauvoo since it existed, can bear record of better things, and place me in the front ranks of those who are known to do good for the sake of goodness, and show all liars, hypocrites and abominable creatures that, while vice sinks them down to darkness and woe, virtue exalts me and the Saints to light and immortality.

The editor, as well as some others, "thinks that Joe Smith has his match at last," because Mr. Redding thinks that he has seen the sign of the Son of Man. But I shall use my right, and declare that, notwithstanding Mr. Redding may have seen a wonderful appearance in the clouds one morning about sunrise (which is nothing very uncommon in the winter season,) he has not seen the sign of the Son of Man, as foretold by Jesus; neither has any man, nor will any man, until after the sun shall have been darkened and the moon bathed in blood; for the Lord hath not shown me any such sign; and as the prophet saith, so it must be—"Surely the Lord God will do nothing, but He revealeth His secret unto His servants the prophets." (See Amos 3: 7.) Therefore hear this, O earth: The Lord will not come to reign over the righteous, in this world, in 1843, nor until everything for the Bridegroom is ready.

Yours respectfully,

JOSEPH SMITH.

CHAPTER XVI.

ATTEMPT TO REPEAL PARTS OF THE NAUVOO CHARTER—GOLD AND SILVER ALONE MADE LEGAL TENDER IN NAUVOO—SIGNS IN THE HEAVENS—"THE WASP" CHANGED INTO "THE NAUVOO NEIGHBOR"—SUSPICIONS OF THE PROPHET AGAINST SIDNEY RIGDON.

Wednesday, March 1, 1843.—This morning I read and recited in German, went to my office, and reviewed my valedictory letter in the *Times and Seasons*, No. 7, Vol. 4; after which, I went with Marshal Henry G. Sherwood to procure some provisions for Thomas Morgan and Robert Taylor, who, on petition of the inhabitants of the city, I had directed should work out their punishment on the highways of Nauvoo.

The Prophet's Cheerfulness.

Elder Orson Hyde called on me this afternoon to borrow a horse. I instructed my ostler to put the Lieutenant-General's saddle on my horse, "Joe Duncan," and let Elder Hyde ride the "governor" on the Lieutenant-General's saddle.

Signed a power of attorney, dated February 28th, to Amasa Lyman, to sell all the lands in Henderson county, Illlinois, deeded to me by Mr. McQueen.

The Mississippi froze up on the 19th of November last, and still continues so. Wagons and teams constantly pass over on the ice to Montrose.

I am constantly receiving applications from abroad for elders, which were replied to in the *Times and Seasons* of this day—that the conference on the 6th of April next, will attend to as many of the applications as possible.

The council of the Twelve Apostles wrote to Ramus, Lima, Augusta, and other branches, as follows:—

The Twelve to the Church of Jesus Christ of Latter-day Saints, in and about Ramus, greeting:—

BELOVED BRETHREN:—As our beloved President Joseph Smith is now relieved from his bondage and his business, temporarily, and his property, too, he has but one thing to hinder his devoting his time to the spiritual interests of the Church, to the bringing forth of the revelations, translation, and history. And what is that? He has not provision for himself and family, and is obliged to spend his time in providing therefor. His family is large and his company great, and it requires much to furnish his table. And now, brethren, we call on you for immediate relief in this matter; and we invite you to bring our President as many loads of wheat, corn, beef, pork, lard, tallow, eggs, poultry, venison, and everything eatable at your command, (not excepting unfrozen potatoes and vegetables, as soon as the weather will admit,) flour, etc., and thus give him the privilege of attending to your spiritual interest.

The measure you mete shall be measured to you again. If you give liberally to your President in temporal things, God will return to you liberally in spiritual and temporal things too. One or two good new milch cows are much needed also.

Brethren, will you do your work, and let the President do his for you before God? We wish an immediate answer by loaded teams or letter.

Your brethren in Christ, in behalf of the quorum,

BRIGHAM YOUNG, President.

WILLARD RICHARDS, Clerk.

P. S. Brethren, we are not unmindful of the favors our President has received from you in former days. But a man will not cease to be hungry this year because he ate last year.

B. Y.

W. R.

Some thirty inhabitants of Saratogo, New York, have died recently of a disease called the black tongue.

About this time, a slide from Mount Ida, near Troy, New York, took place, burying ten houses and killing thirty or forty persons.

Thursday, 2.—I was engaged in the court-room, sitting on the case of Charles R. Dana *versus* William B. Brink all day. In the evening, examining Blackstone and Phillips on evidence.

I visited with Elders Brigham Young and Orson Hyde, with their wives, at Elder Heber C. Kimball's.

The legislature of Illinois took up the bill to repeal the Nauvoo City Charter.

Nauvoo Charter in the House of the Illinois Legislature.

Mr. Davis, of Bond county, moved to take up the bill to repeal a part of the Nauvoo Charter. Objections being made by several members, it was decided in the affirmative, and placed on the orders of the day; the question being on ordering the bill to a third reading.

Mr. Simms moved the previous question.

Mr. Logan hoped the previous question would not be sustained. Some of the provisions proposed to be repealed are very innocent ones, and he thought the house would be willing to retain them. He wanted to repeal the provisions allowing the writ of habeas corpus and some others. The previous question was then lost.

Mr. Logan denied that any discussion had been had on the provisions of the Charter proposed to be repealed. He wanted the gentlemen interested to have an opportunity to be heard.

Mr. Thomas B. Owen, of Hancock, went into the subject at some length. He compared the Charter of Nauvoo with any other city in the State, and showed that the bill repealed the same powers in the Nauvoo Charter which others contained and are permitted to retain. He thought this unjust, and was opposed to the principle of making such distinctions. He bore testimony to the good order and industry of the Mormons, and he had no doubt but they were much abused.

He alluded to the course of the Whigs during the canvass of the last election, and appealed to his party to sustain the Mormons, as they had so nobly carried the last election. He cautioned them against taking the other course, and predicted, if they did, that they would be the means of electing a Whig to Congress in that district, and at the next gubernatorial election would elect the governor also; that the arms of the Whigs were open to receive them [The "Mormons."]

Friday, 3.—I was again sitting on the case of Dana *versus* Brink until half-past ten p. m. Many witnesses were examined, many lawyers' pleas made, and much law read. It was a very tedious suit, and excited much feeling among the people. When I returned home, I found my mother's health improving. In company with Dr. Willard Richards I visited Sister Durphy, who was sick.

Bishop Newel K. Whitney returned from Ramus this evening, with five teams loaded with provisions and grain, as a present to me, which afforded me very seasonable relief. I pray the Lord to bless those who gave it abundantly; and may it be returned upon their heads an hundred fold!

Action of the House Repealing Part of the Nauvoo Charter.

Mr. William Smith, of Hancock, moved a roll call of the house (some members were leaving).

The bill passed by yeas and nays, as follows:—

Yeas—Messrs. Aldrich, Baillache, Bell, Blakeman, Bone, Brinkley, Brown (of Sangamon), Burklow, Busey, Caldwell, Cloud, Cochran, Compton, Courtright, Danner, Dollins, Douglas, Edwards, Epler, Ervin, Ewing, Ficklin, Flanders, Fowler, Glass, Gobble, Haley, Hambaugh, Hick, Hickman, Hinton, Horney, Howard, Hunsucker, Keorner, Kuykendall, Lawler, Loy, McClernand, Marshall, Menard, Mitchell. Murphy, Nesbit, Norris, Penn, Shurley, Simms, Thomson, Turner, Vance, Vinyard, Weatherford, Wheat, White, Whitten, Wilson and Woodworth—58.

Nays—Messrs. Adams, Ames, Andrus, Arnold, Brown (of Pike), Browning, Collins, Cushman, Dougherty; Dubois, Graves, Hanniford, Hanson, Harper, Hatch, Jackson (of McHenry), Jackson (of Whiteside), Jonas, Kendall, Langworthy, Lockhart, Logan, McDonald (of Calhoun), McDonald (of Joe Davis), Owen, Pickering, Smith (of Crawford), Smith (of Hancock), Spicer, Stewart, Tackerbury, Vandever, Whitcomb, and Mr. Speaker—33.

The Speaker: The bill is passed. The title of the bill:—(The Speaker recited the title of the bill).

Mr. Smith, of Hancock: I wish to amend the title of the bill. (Profound silence.)

The Speaker: The title has passed.

By several members: In time, in time.

Mr. Smith sent his amendment to the chair.

The Speaker: The amendment is not respectful, and not in order.

Great sensation. Several members called for a reading of the amendment.

The amendment was read—"*A bill for an act to humbug the citizens of Nauvoo.*" (Profound sensation.)

Mr. Smith said he considered the amendment as perfectly describing the contents of the bill. He was anxious that things should be called by their right names.

The chair decided that the amendment was not in order.

A member: I wish a vote, to ascertain if the house does not sustain the decision of the chair.

Mr. Smith withdrew his amendment.

The title of the bill then passed.

English papers report an eruption of Mount Etna; considerable torrents of lava flowing towards Bronte, doing immense damage.

Saturday, 4.—In council with Brother Benjamin F. Johnson and others from Ramus, on the subject of building a meetinghouse there, out of Church property. I told them the property of the Church should be disposed of by the direction of the Trustee-in-Trust, appointed by the voice of the whole Church, and made the following comparison:—There is a wheel; Nauvoo is the hub: we will drive the first spoke in Ramus, second in La Harpe, third Shokoquon, fourth in Lima: that is half the wheel. The other half is over the river: we will let that alone at present. We will call the Saints from Iowa to these spokes, then send elders over and convert the whole people.

Manner of Disposing of Church Property.

I agreed to go to Ramus this day week.

At ten o'clock, I attended the city council.

The Questions of "Currency" and Blood Atonement, in the Nauvoo City Council.

Prayer by George A. Smith, when a bill regulating the currency was read; and, as the Legislature of Illinois have long been trying to repeal the charter of Nauvoo, I made some remarks (as I had frequently done on former occasions), to show the council and others that the legislature can not constitutionally repeal a charter where there is no repealing clause. After which, I read a letter from James Arlington Bennett, dated February 1, 1843, which confirms my decision.

In debate, George A. Smith said imprisonment was better than hanging.

I replied, I was opposed to hanging, even if a man kill another, I will shoot him, or cut off his head, spill his blood on the ground, and let the smoke thereof ascend up to God; and if ever I have the privilege of making a law on that subject, I will have it so.

In reply to some of the councilors, who thought it impolitic to stop circulating bank notes as currency *at once*, I replied, I would use a figure, and talk like some foolish fathers do to their children. If you want to kill a serpent, don't cut off his head, for fear he will bite you;

but cut off his tail, piece by piece, and perhaps you won't get bit. It is the same with this bill. I say, if paper currency is an evil, put it down *at once*. When councilors get up here, I want them to speak sense. Great God, where is common sense and reason? Is there none on the earth? Why have the canker remaining any longer to sap our life? If you get hold of a $5 bill, you can get nothing with it. There is no one who dares to touch it, fearing it to be a counterfeit, or the note of a broken bank. I wish you had my soul long enough to know how good it feels. I say it is expedient when you strike at an enemy, to strike the most deadly blow possible.

Councilor Hyde asked me what an editor should do. I told him, advertise in your next paper to your agents to send you gold and silver, as paper will no longer be taken as pay.*

The ordinance regulating currency in the city passed by a unanimous vote, as follows:—

ORDINANCE.

Sec. 1. Be it ordained by the City Council of the city of Nauvoo, that, from and after the passage of this bill, gold and silver coin only can be received a lawful tender in payment of city taxes and of debts, and also of fines imposed under the ordinances of the city.

Sec. 2. That city scrip shall not hereafter be emitted as monied currency; provided, however, that nothing in this bill shall be so construed as to prevent the redemption of previous emissions.

Sec. 3. That any person passing counterfeit gold, or silver, or copper coin, or counterfeit or spurious paper currency, or aiding or abetting therein, or holding the same with intent to pass it, knowing it to be such, shall be liable to a fine not exceeding five thousand dollars, or to imprisonment or hard labor in the city, for a term not exceeding fourteen years, or all these penalties at the discretion of the court.

Sec. 4. That any person passing a paper currency, or aiding and abetting therein, or holding the same with intent to pass it within the bounds of this city corporation, shall be liable to a fine of one dollar for every dollar thus offered or passed, to be recovered as in action of debt; one-half of said fine to be paid to the complainant, the other half to the said corporation.

JOSEPH SMITH, Mayor.

I was re-elected Registrar of Deeds for the city.

Dr. Samuel Bennett was chosen Alderman, and Albert P. Rockwood. Elijah Fordham, and Charles C. Rich, Firewardens in the city.

* These remarks and the passage of the ordinance making gold and silver alone Legal Tender in Nauvoo is further evidence that the Prophet regarded Nauvoo, under her charter as a "city state"—see the subject discussed in *Introduction* to Vol. IV of this HISTORY, pp. xxii-xxv.

By my suggestion, the Committee on Public Works were instructed to prepare an ordinance to provide for the erection of a city prison.

Items of Instruction.

On returning to my office after dinner, I spoke the following proverb: For a man to be great, he must not dwell on small things, though he may enjoy them; this shows that a Prophet cannot well be his own scribe, but must have some one to write for him.

The battle of Gog and Magog will be after the millennium. The remnant of all the nations that fight against Jerusalem were commanded to go up to Jerusalem to worship in the millennium.

I told Dr. Richards that there was one thing he failed in as a historian, and that was noting surrounding objects, weather, etc.

I dictated to my scribe my decision in the case of Brink *versus* Dana, until half-past four p. m.

Repeal of Parts of the Nauvoo Charter Defeated in the Senate.

This day, Mr. Warren, in the State Senate, moved to take from the table the bill to repeal the charter of the city of Nauvoo; but the senate refused to repeal it. Nays, 17; ayes, 16.

Orrin Porter Rockwell was taken prisoner in St. Louis by the Missourians, on an advertisement accusing him of shooting ex-Governor Boggs on the 6th day of May, 1842.

Sunday, *5*.—I stayed at home all day to take care of my mother, who was still sick.

A severe shock of an earthquake felt at Memphis, Tenn.

Monday, *6*.—I read, in the *Boston Bee*, a letter from Elder George J. Adams, and also another communication showing the progress of the truth in Boston and vicinity. At nine o'clock, called in my office, and requested Dr. Richards to write to the *Bee;* after which, I recited in German until dinner, and in the evening rode out to visit the sick.

The Municipal Court was in session to hear any complaints against the city assessment, but none appeared.

In the evening a grand display of burning prairie on the Iowa side of the river.

Tuesday, *7*.—I was in my office at nine a. m., and reviewed my decision in the case of Brink *versus* Dana, and conversing with Dr. Richards on the subject of medicine. After dinner, I executed several deeds for city lots, and settled with the purchasers, assisted by William Clayton.

Brother David Manhard, of Lee county, Iowa, brought me two loads of corn and one hog; for which may the Lord bless him!

East wind through the day. Commenced raining at three p. m.

Wednesday, *8*.—In office at eight a. m., and signed some documents in relation to the Nauvoo Legion, and also settling with William Ford. Rode out with Mr. John B. Cowan in the evening.

In the evening, a meeting was held in the house of Elder Heber C. Kimball, which was crowded. He preached from Jeremiah xviii, 2-5, on the figure of clay in the hands of the potter.

The ship *Yorkshire* left Liverpool, England, with eighty-three Saints on board, under the supervision of Elders Thomas Bullock and Richard Rushton.

A terrible earthquake occurred at Guadeloupe and other West India Islands. Thousands of persons buried under the ruins of the fallen houses.

Thursday, *9*.—Mr. John B. Cowan took the decision of Judge Pope in the United States District Court, on the 5th January last, and other papers relating thereto, also Mr. Butterfield's opinion, to lay before the governor of Iowa, in order to induce him to recall a writ issued on the requisition of the governor of Missouri, for my arrest, in case I should visit my friends in Iowa.

Precaution against Missouri Movements against the Prophet in Iowa.

I told Brother Phelps that he should be a lawyer and understand law, and the time will come when I shall not need say to you, Thus and thus is the law; for you shall know it.

E. H. Mower wrote me from Clinton county, Indiana, that he had recently baptized thirty-two, and a great many were inquiring after the truth.

William O. Clark gave me a load of corn, and Sanford Porter gave me a hog.

Rain and sleet the whole of the day.

Friday, 10.—Clear and cold day.

I opened court at ten a. m. Messrs. Emmons and Skinner, counsel for plaintiff; and Messrs. Marr and Rigdon, counsel for defendant. Parties to the suit present and many spectators.* Court decided after full hearing of the case that plaintiff recover from the defendant the sum of his bill, ninety-nine dollars and cost. After I had delivered my decision, I referred to the threat of the defendant's counsel to intimidate, etc. Counsel explained satisfactorily.

I directed Lucien Woodworth to fix a room to confine the city prisoners in.

I told Theodore Turley that I had no objection to his building a brewery.

PROVERB.

"As finest steel doth show a brighter polish
The more you rub the same,
E'en so in love rebuke will ne'er demolish
A wise man's goodly name."

I issued an execution against Dr. Brink, and a search-warrant on oath of William Law, to search the house of Dial Sherwood. In the evening, the marshal brought two try squares, one padlock, one shirt; also a bit stock, smoothing-plane, and other tools, some of which were claimed as stolen property.

Friday, 10.—With Willard Richards, Wilford Woodruff

* The case was one in which mal-practice was charged against Dr. William B. Brink in a case of accouchement of Charles A. Dana's wife.

and many others, about seven p. m., I discovered a stream of light in the southwest quarter of the heavens. Its pencil rays were in the form of a broad sword, with the hilt downward, the blade raised, pointing from the west, southwest, raised to an angle of forty-five degrees from the horizon, and extending nearly, or within two or three degrees to the zenith of the degree where the sign appeared. This sign gradually disappeared from half-past seven o'clock, and at nine had entirely disappeared. As sure as there is a God who sits enthroned in the heavens, and as sure as He ever spoke by me, so sure will there be a speedy and bloody war; and the broad sword seen this evening is the sure sign thereof.

Signs in the Heavens.

Last night I dreamed that a silver-headed old man came to me and said there was a mob force coming upon him, and he was likely to lose his life. He had heard that I was a lieutenant-general, having the command of a large force, and that I always sought to defend the oppressed, and that I was also a patriot, and disposed to protect the innocent and unoffending; and he wanted that I should protect him, and had come to hear with his own ears what I would say to him. I told him I wanted some written documents to show the facts that they [the mob] were the aggressors, and I would raise a force sufficient to protect him, and would collect the Legion. The old man turned to go from me. When he got a little distance, he suddenly turned again, and said to me, "You must call out the Legion," and he would have the papers ready when I arrived. And, said he, "I have any amount of men, which you can have under your command."

The Prophet's Dream.

A shock of an earthquake felt in Lancashire, England, and on the Isle of Guernsey, produced considerable alarm.

The papers teem with accounts of singular phenomena. Fearful sights are seen in all parts of the world.

Saturday, 11.—Very cold last night. The water froze in the warmest rooms in the city.

At nine a. m., I started in company with Brother Brigham Young, to Ramus, and had a delightful drive. Arrived at Brother McClary's at a quarter to four. Lodged with Brother Benjamin F. Johnson. In the evening, when pulling sticks, I pulled up Justus A. Morse, the strongest man in Ramus, with one hand.

It is reported in the papers that the workmen employed on the *General Pratt* (a steamboat which was burned and sunk last fall near Memphis in the Mississippi,) with a diving bell, on the 3rd of January, found the wreck in about twenty-four feet of water. On that night was an earthquake. Next day the wreck had disappeared, no trace could be found, and the water was from one hundred to one hundred and twenty feet deep, and for about one hundred feet no bottom; and in another place a bar was discovered where previously was deep water.

The *New York Herald* publishes "The Vision" in poetry, &c.; also Miss Eliza R. Snow's Festival Song;—an unusual act of liberality towards the Saints, for a publisher.

The Prophet at Ramus.

Sunday, 12.—I preached to the Saints at Ramus, in the morning, taking for a text 14th chapter of John, 2nd verse:—"In my Father's house are many mansions."

I found the brethren well, and in good spirits. In the afternoon, Brother Brigham preached. Stayed at Brother Benjamin F. Johnson's all night.

Elder George J. Adams having been called to Nauvoo, twelve hundred inhabitants of Boston petitioned for Elders Heber C. Kimball and Orson Hyde to come and labor in that place. A similar petition was also sent from Salem, Massachusetts, by Elder Erastus Snow.

Monday, 13.—I wrestled with William Wall, the most expert wrestler in Ramus, and threw him.

In the afternoon, held a Church meeting. Almon W.

Babbitt was appointed, by the vote of the people, the presiding elder of that place.

In the evening meeting twenty-seven children were blessed, nineteen of whom I blessed myself, with great fervency. Virtue went out of me, and my strength left me, when I gave up the meeting to the brethren.

Mercury was three degrees below zero, at sunrise in Nauvoo.

Mr. Ivins arrived at Nauvoo, and stated that Orrin Porter Rockwell came with him from New Jersey to St. Louis, when Rockwell was arrested by advertisement on the 4th of March, and put in St. Louis jail.

Elder Hyde went to Quincy to preach.

Newspapers report that iron filings and sulphur have fallen in the form of a snow storm in five counties in Missouri.

The Prophet's Explanation of "Virtue Went Out of Me."

Tuesday, 14.—Elder Jedediah M. Grant enquired of me the cause of my turning pale and losing strength last night while blessing children. I told him that I saw that Lucifer would exert his influence to destroy the children that I was blessing, and I strove with all the faith and spirit that I had to seal upon them a blessing that would secure their lives upon the earth; and so much virtue went out of me into the children, that I became weak, from which I have not yet recovered; and I referred to the case of the woman touching the hem of the garment of Jesus. (Luke, 8th chapter). The virtue here referred to is the spirit of life; and a man who exercises great faith in administering to the sick, blessing little children, or confirming, is liable to become weakened.

Elder Brigham Young and myself returned from Ramus, and after a severely cold ride in a heavy snow-storm, arrived in Nauvoo about four p. m.

Mr. Wilson, the assessor for the county of Hancock, assessed a number of lots to Dr. Willard Richards, which he had previously assessed to me as trustee in trust, in order no doubt, to collect taxes twice, for the benefit of his own pocket, or to make trouble to the "Mormons;" about which the following letter was written:

Willard Richards to Mr. Bagby, Anent Taxes.

Mr. Bagby,—Sir:—I received an anonymous letter this morning, which was dated at Warsaw, requesting an immediate answer. I know not to whom to direct the answer; but as it appears to be concerning taxes, I suppose it most probable that you are the person, and direct my answer accordingly.

I received your letter from Carthage, and requested Mr. Clayton to answer it, which he did, stating the facts in the case, which, in substance, I will repeat:

In the year 1842 I had no taxable property in Illinois, real or personal. I never gave Mr. Wilson, the assessor, a list by which to assess lots to me. If ever I gave him any list, it was to assist him in the information what lots to assess to the "trustee in trust," and for no other purpose; which Mr. Wilson very well knew at the time, and now knows it.

You ask, "What shall I do with the lots?" I answer, "They are lots which on another part of your list, are assessed to the trustee in trust, or Mr. Smith; and, doubtless, it would be the most just and equitable course for the assessor to correct his error, and let the matter rest where it was originally. But if this cannot be, you must take your own course. It is not for me to advise you in your duty. But of this I can advise you—that I have not the first farthing of personal property liable to taxation in this county, or to be sold for taxes this side of eternity.

Yours respectfully,

WILLARD RICHARDS.

At half-past seven o'clock in the evening, the sword which had made its appearance [in the heavens] for several evenings past, moved up nearer the moon and formed itself into a large ring round the moon. Two balls immediately appeared in the ring opposite each other, something in the form of sun-dogs.

The *Wasp* Changed to *The Nauvoo Neighbor*.

Wednesday, 15.—I wrote a letter to George J. Adams, and signed several deeds. In the office most of the day. Gave the following name to the *Wasp*, enlarged as is contemplated—

The Nauvoo Neighbor, our motto, "The Saints' Singularity is Union, Liberty, Charity." The following is an extract from the prospectus of this date:

Prospectus of the Nauvoo Neighbor.

We feel pleasure in announcing to our readers and the public generally that we have determined to enlarge the *Wasp* to double its size, as soon as the present volume shall be completed, which will be on the 19th of April.

It made its appearance in the world near twelve months ago, small in stature, dressed in a very humble garb, and under very inauspicious circumstances. It was then thought by many that its days would not be long in the land, and that at any rate it would not survive the sickly season. Many of its elder brethern, who thought that they had attained to the size of manhood, sneered contemptuously at the idea of their smaller and younger brother taking the field; and, like David's brethren, they thought that he was but a stripling, and that he would certainly fall by the hand of some of the great Goliaths. But, on the contrary, while some of advanced years, noble mien, and possessing a more formidable appearance, have given up the ghost, the little *Wasp* has held on in the even tenor of his way, the untiring, unflinching supporter of integrity, righteousness and truth, neither courting the smiles nor fearing the frowns of political demagogues, angry partisans, or fawning sycophants. Partaking so much of the nature of the industrious bee, it has gathered honey from every flower, and its pages are now read with interest by a large and respectable number of subscribers.

As the young gentleman is now nearly a year old, we propose on his birthday to put on him a new dress, and to make him double the size, that he may begin to look up to the world, and not be ashamed of associating with his older brethren. And as he has acted the part of a good Samaritan, we propose giving him a new name. Therefore his name shall no longer be called the "*Wasp*," but the "*Neighbor*."

A Prophecy as to Orrin Porter Rockwell.

I prophesied, in the name of the Lord Jesus Christ, that Orrin Porter Rockwell would get away honorably from the Missourians. I cautioned Peter Hawes to correct his boys: for if he did not curtail them in their wickedness, they would eventually go to prison.

I dreamed last night that I was swimming in a river of pure water, clear as crystal, over a shoal of fish of the largest size I ever saw. They were directly under my belly. I was astonished, and felt afraid that they might drown me or do me injury.

The *Wasp* has the following editorial:—

The Nauvoo Charter—A Guaranteed Perpetual Succession.

What reliance can be placed upon a legislature that will one session grant a charter to a city, with "*perpetual succession*," and another session take it away? We expect, however, that this honorable body believe in the common adage—"Promises and pie-crusts are made to be broken," and we have sometimes ourselves seen boys crying for their marbles again, after they have given them away.

We suppose, however, with them, that the words "*perpetual succession*" do not mean what they say. The house, in the dignity of its standing, passes a bill, at the request of the people, telling them that they shall have a charter granting them several privileges, and telling them that it shall be *perpetual*, without any repealing clause. It is made a law, and the grand seal of state appended to it. The people, on the good faith of the state, go to work and improve under the provisions of that charter. Companies are formed, buildings are erected, and money expended; but by-and-by they find out that they have been leaning upon a broken reed, that there is no dependence to be placed in government, that they [the legislature] have broken their most sacred promises, violated their plighted faith, and wantonly and wickedly sought to injure thousands of men who relied on their promises, by an unprecedented, unconstitutional, and tyrannical law, trampling under foot the faith of the state, and virtually saying that the members of the legislature that granted the charter were all fools or knaves, and that we, the pure representatives of the people, must break the plighted faith of the state to set them right!

The *New York Herald* gives a list of indebtedness of the several states who refuse to pay the same, as follows:—

Indebtedness of the States.

Pennsylvania, $29,129,123; Georgia, $3,184,323; Indiana, $12,129,339; Maryland, $20,901,040; Louisiana, $21,213,000; Mississippi, $5,500,000; Illinois, $13,836,379; Alabama, $9,843,536; Arkansas, $3,900,000; Michigan, $5,611,000; Florida, $3,500,000.

A great fire at Valparaiso, unequalled heretofore in Chili. Damage $2,000,000.

Thursday, 16.—In the office, reading papers, and gave counsel to Brother Hyrum, Dr. Foster, and many others.

Friday, 17.—Part of the day in my office; the remainder at home.

Settled with Father Perry; gave him a deed for eighty acres of land and city lot, and prophesied that it would not be six months before he could sell it for cash.

At four p. m., Newel K. Whitney brought in a letter from R. S. Blennarhassett, Esq., St. Louis, dated 7th instant, concerning Orrin Porter Rockwell; which I immediately answered.

Renewal of Old Missouri Charges.

Reports reached us that new indictments had been found against myself, Brother Hyrum, and some hundred others, on the old Missouri troubles, and that John C. Bennett was making desperate threats.

The Island of Hong-Kong was ceded to Great Britain by the Emperor of China, who opened five ports to the English trade by treaty.

Saturday, 18.—I was most of the forenoon in the office, in cheerful conversation with Dr. Willard Richards and others. Finishing writing a letter to Arlington Bennett.

The Prophet "Studying" Law!

About noon, I lay down on the writing table, with my head on a pile of law books, saying, "Write and tell the world I acknowledge myself a very great lawyer; I am going to study law, and this is the way I study it;" and then fell asleep.

Rode out in the afternoon with William Clayton, looking at lots for Bishop Newel K. Whitney, and afterwards played ball with the boys.

The French seized upon the Society group of Pacific Isles.

Sunday, 19.—Rode out with Emma and visited my farm; returned about eleven, a. m., and spent the remainder of the day at home.

Dimick B. Huntington started for Chicago, with a letter to Mr. Justin Butterfield, U. S. Attorney, concerning Orrin Porter Rockwell.

The Work of Elder Parley P. Pratt in England.

Received a letter from Elder Parley P. Pratt, giving a synopsis of his mission to England since August, 1839, in which I find he has published, since April, 1841, (at which time the remainder of the Twelve returned home,) 1,500 "Hymn Books," 2,500 "Voice of Warning," 3,000 Tracts, entitled "Heaven on Earth," 3,000 copies of "Elder Hyde's Mission to Jerusalem," 10,000 copies of "A Letter to the Queen," and some other works, and continued the *Star* monthly. He left England October 20, 1842, and, after a voyage of ten weeks, arrived in New Orleans, being ice-bound on the river; and having a dislike to the outlaws who govern Missouri, he wintered at Chester, Illinois. On the news of his arrival, he was warmly pressed to preach, which he did several times, and baptized two men in that place.

Scientists on the Comet.

Sir James South, Sir John Herschel, and other astronomers in Europe have published notices of the sword seen in the heavens on the eve of the 10th and several successive evenings. They represent it as the stray tail of a comet, as no nucleus could be discovered with the most powerful instruments. At Paris, M. Arago communicated to the Academy of Sciences, on the subject of the comet, that the observations of the astronomers were not complete, the nucleus not being discovered.

Monday, 20.—I rode out to see Hiram Kimball, with Mrs. Butterfield, about a deed for the Lawrence estate. Settled with Dr. Robert D. Foster, and gave him a note to balance all demands; and afterwards acknowledged about twenty deeds to different individuals, which occupied my time until about three p. m.

A letter appears in the *Millennial Star*, giving particulars of the passage of the ship *Swanton*, from Liverpool, and arrival at New Orleans, loaded with Saints, in which the power of the holy priesthood was manifested in the healing of the sick:—

Excerpt of Letter from Millennial Star.

The stewart of this vessel was so injured by a blow from one of the crew, that his life was despaired of; and I stood over him for some time, and thought that life was gone. The captain had administered to him all that he could think of in the way of medicine, but to no effect; and after they gave up all hopes of his recovery, at twelve o'clock at night, he sent for Elder Lorenzo Snow,* and by anointing him with oil, and the laying on of hands, in the name of the Lord, he was there and then raised up and perfectly healed. For this token of the divine favor we will praise the God of Israel.

Tuesday, *21*.—Was in the office about nine, writing orders. About noon, started with William Clayton for Shokoquon. Dined at Brother Russel's, and then resumed our journey to Libeus T. Coon's, sixteen miles, when I returned.

Wonderful signs have been seen in the heavens during the week.

A Sign in the Heavens.

This night, about twelve o'clock, the pilot and officers of the steamer *William Penn*, on the Ohio river, between Aurora and the rising sun, Indiana, observed a great light in the sky, in the form of a serpent. It turned to a livid, bright red, deep and awful, and remained stationary among the stars for two or three minutes, and then in a gradual manner formed a distinct roman G: in about a minute and a half, it turned into a distinct O, and afterwards changed to a plain D, when it turned into an oblong shape, and gradually disappeared.†

Wednesday, *22*.—Was spent in visiting my friends.

Elder Edwin D. Woolley writes from Westfield, Massachusetts, that he has baptized twenty and organized a branch in Little River village.

Elder James Burnham died in Richmond, Massachu-

* Elder Snow was in charge of this company of Saints.

† This description is condensed from an article in the *Times and Seasons* (Vol. IV, No. 10), quoted from a paper called the *Daily Sun*, but whether a New York or a local Illinois paper cannot be learned.

setts, aged 46. He had been on a mission to England and Wales about two years, and was then on a mission in the Eastern States, and, through excessive labor and exposure, brought on quick consumption. He left a wife and several children to lament his loss.

Thursday, 23.—Spent the day in visiting my friends.

Signs in the Heavens.

At seven-and-a-half, a. m., the heavens exhibited a splendid appearance of circles, accompanied by mock suns. For further particulars, see *Times and Seasons*, page 151.

The sword has been seen for several nights past; also, on the opposite side of the horizon, a black streak about the size of the light one. While the one is as black as darkness, the other has considerably the appearance of the blaze of a comet; but it is not a comet, for it appears about seven o'clock, and disappears about nine.

Friday, 24.—I took a ride to Camp Creek; met Brother Clayton; returned to Libeus T. Coon's, where we warmed for an hour, and then returned home.

In the evening, two teams arrived from Lima, loaded with provisions; also one load from Augusta.

The *St. Louis Republican* says:—

"At Point-a-Pitre, Guadaloupe, one of the West India Islands, 2,000 persons ran together in the public square, when the earth opened and swallowed the whole mass."

The papers report that General Napier, with 3,700 English troops, gained a brilliant victory over the Belochee army of 22,000 men, on the 17th ult.

Saturday, 25.—In the office at eight, a. m.; heard a report from Hyrum Smith concerning thieves; whereupon I issued the following

PROCLAMATION.

To the Citizens of Nauvoo:

Whereas it appears, by the republication of the foregoing proceedings and declaration, that I have not altered my views on the subject of stealing: And

Whereas it is reported that there now exists a band of desperadoes, bound by oaths of secrecy, under severe penalties in case any member of the combination divulges their plans of stealing and conveying properties from station to station, up and down the Mississippi and other routes: And

Whereas it is reported that the fear of the execution of the pains and penalties of their secret oath on their persons prevents some members of said secret association (who have, through falsehood and deceit, been drawn into their snares,) from divulging the same to the legally-constituted authorities of the land:

Know ye, therefore, that I, Joseph Smith, mayor of the city of Nauvoo, will grant and insure protection against all personal mob violence to each and every citizen of this city who will freely and voluntarily come before me and truly make known the names of all such abominable characters as are engaged in said secret combination for stealing, or are accessory thereto, in any manner. And I would respectfully solicit the co-operation of all ministers of justice in this and the neighboring states to ferret out a band of thievish outlaws from our midst.

Given under my hand at Nauvoo City, this 25th day of March, A. D., 1843.

JOSEPH SMITH.
Mayor of said City.

Received a letter from Grand Master A. Jonas, requesting the loan of cannon, to celebrate the organization of the new county of Marquette, which I granted.

Also received a letter from United States Senator Richard M. Young, with a bond for a quarter section of land.

I baptized Mr. Mifflin, of Philadelphia.

Issued a writ for the arrest of A. Fields, for disorderly conduct. He was brought in drunk about noon, and abused the court. I ordered him to be put in irons till he was sober.

Case of Benj. Hoyt Before High Council.

The High Council, with my brother Hyrum presiding, sat on an appeal of Benjamin Hoyt, from the decision of David Evans, bishop; which was, that Brother Hoyt cease to call certain characters witches or wizards, cease to work with the divining rod, and cease burning a board or boards to heal those whom he said were bewitched. On hearing the case, the council decided to confirm the decision of Bishop Evans.

Destructive Tempests.

The *St. Louis Gazette* reports "an awful gale" within the last six weeks. 154 vessels were wrecked on the coast of England, and 190 lives lost; on the coast of Ireland, 5 vessels and 134 lives; on the coast of Scotland, 17 vessels, 39 lives; and on the coast of France, 4 vessels and 100 lives: value of vessels and cargoes, roughly estimated, $4,125,000.

The Thames Tunnel completed and opened for foot passengers, when 30,000 persons passed through the first day.

Opposition to the Work in South Wales.

Elder William Henshaw, who has encountered considerable opposition since he commenced preaching in South Wales, organized the Pen-y-darran branch, and ordained William Rees Davis, priest, who commenced preaching in the Welsh language, which caused opposition to increase and a considerable number to receive the gospel. While he established that branch of the Church, Brother Henshaw supported himself by work in the coal mines.

Sunday, *26*.—At home, the weather being too severe for meeting.

Monday, *27*.—I dictated the following letter to Sidney Rigdon:—

Letter of Joseph Smith to Sidney Rigdon—Expressing Belief in Rigdon's Complicity in Conspiracy, with John C. Bennett et al.

DEAR SIR:—It is with sensations of deep regret and poignant grief that I sit down to dictate a few lines to you this morning, to let you know what my feelings are in relation to youiself, as it is against my principles to act the part of a hypocrite or to dissemble in anywise whatever with any man. I have tried for a long time to smother my feelings and not let you know that I thought that you were secretly and underhandedly doing all you could to take the advantage of and injure me; but whether my feelings are right or wrong remains for eternity to reveal.

I cannot any longer forbear throwing off the mask and letting you know of the secret wranglings of my heart, that you may not be deceived in relation to them, and that you may be prepared, sir, to take whatever course you see proper in the premises.

I am, sir, honest, when I say that I believe and am laboring under the fullest convictions that you are actually practicing deception and wickedness against me and the Church of Jesus Christ of Latter-day Saints; and that you are in connection with John C. Bennett and George W. Robinson in the whole of their abominable practices, in seeking to destroy me and this people; and that Jared Carter is as deep in the mud as you, sir, are in the mire, in your conspiracies; and that you are in the exercise of a traitorous spirit against our lives and interests, by combining with our enemies and the murderous Missourians. My feelings, sir, have been wrought upon to a very great extent, in relation to yourself, ever since soon after the first appearance of John C. Bennett in this place. There has been something dark and mysterious hovering over our business concerns, that are not only palpable but altogether unaccountable, in relation to the post office. And, sir, from the very first of the pretensions of John C. Bennett to secure to me the post office, (which, by-the-bye, I have never desired, if I could have justice done me in that department, without my occupancy,) I have known, sir, that it was a fraud practiced upon me, and of the secret plottings and connivings between him and yourself in relation to the matter the whole time, as well as many other things which I have kept locked up in my own bosom. But I am constrained, at this time, to make known my feelings to you.

I do not write this with the intention of insulting you, or of bearing down upon you, or with a desire to take any advantage of you, or with the intention of laying even one straw in your way detrimental to your character or influence, or to suffer anything whatever that has taken place, which is within my observation or that has come to my knowledge to go abroad, betraying any confidence that has ever been placed in me. But I do assure you, most sincerely, that what I have said I verily believe; and this is the reason why I have said it—that you may know the real convictions of my heart, not because I have any malice or hatred, neither would I injure one hair of your head; and I will assure you that these convictions are attended with the deepest sorrow.

I wish to God it were not so, and that I could get rid of the achings of my heart on that subject; and I now notify you that unless something should take place to restore my mind to its former confidence in you, by some acknowledgments on your part, or some explanations that shall do away my jealousies, I must, as a conscientious man, publish my withdrawal of my fellowship from you to the Church, through the medium of the *Times and Seasons*, and demand of the conference a hearing concerning your case; that, on conviction of justifiable grounds, they will demand your license. I could say much more, but let the above suffice for the present.

Yours, in haste,

JOSEPH SMITH.

I sent the above communication to Elder Rigdon by Dr. Willard Richards; to which I received the following reply.

Sidney Rigdon to Joseph Smith—Denies Existence of Just Cause of the Prophet's Suspicions.

President Joseph Smith.

DEAR SIR:—I received your letter by the hands of Dr. Richards a few minutes since, the contents of which are surprising to me, though I am glad that you have let me know your feelings, so as to give me a chance to reply to them.

Why it is that you have the feelings which you seem to entertain, I know not; and what caused you to think that I had any connection with John C. Bennett at any time is not within my power to say.

As to the post office, I never asked Bennett one word about it when I made application for it. If he ever wrote to the department at Washington anything about it, it was and is without my knowledge; for surely I know of no such thing being done at any time; neither did I know, at the time I applied for the office, that you intended to apply for it; nor did I know of it for some time afterwards. As far as the post office is concerned, these are the facts. I wrote myself to the department, offering myself as an applicant, and referred the department to several members of Congress to ascertain my character. This is all I ever did on the subject. I never wrote but one letter to the department on the subject; neither had I at the time any acquaintance of any amount with Bennett, nor for a very considerable time afterwards. He never was at our house but very little, and then always on business, and always in a hurry, did his business, and went off immediately. I know not that Bennett ever knew that I had applied for the office; and I am quite satisfied he did not till some time after I had written to the department on the subject; and if he ever did anything about it, it was and is to this day without my having any knowledge of it.

As to the difficulties here, I never at any time gave Bennett any countenance in relation to it, and he knows it as well as I do, and feels it keenly. He has threatened me, severely, that he could do with me as he pleased, and that if I did not cease to aid you and quit trying to save "my Prophet," as he calls you, from the punishment of the law, he would turn against me; and while at St. Louis, on his way to Upper Missouri, he, in one of his speeches, made a violent attack on myself, all predicated on the fact that I would not aid him. Such are his feelings on the subject and his threatenings.

As to Jared Carter, if there is anything in his mind unfavorably disposed to you, he has, as far as I know, kept it to himself; for he never said anything to me, nor in my hearing, from which I could draw even an inference of that kind. He was here yesterday, when you came, much dejected in spirit in relation to his temporal affairs, and commenced telling of the great injuries he had received by his son-in-law, and the great losses he had sustained by him, and seemed greatly dejected on account of it; but he never mentioned any other subject.

When I went to La Harpe on Friday, it was purely in relation to temporal matters, making arrangements for provisions for the ensuing season and to regulate some matters in relation to property only. While there, I heard the report of the new indictments; and Mr. Higbee told me, the day before I went out, that I was among the number of those who were to be demanded. In relation to this, I made such inquiry as I thought would enable me to determine the fact, but failed in the attempt. I confess I felt some considerable interest in determining this fact, and felt anxious to know if I could find out how it was.

Now, on the broad scale, I can assert in truth, that with myself and any other person on this globe there never was nor is there now existing anything privately or publicly to injure your character in any respect whatever; neither has any person spoken to me on any such subject. All that has ever been said by me has been said to your face, all of which you know as well as I.

As to your rights in the post office, you have just the same as any other man. In the new case which occurred yesterday, I have examined all the laws and rules in this office, and find but one section in relation to it, and that indirectly, but gives the postmaster no right to abate the postage, nor make any disposition of the letter or letters; but address the department, and they will give such instruction in the case as they may deem correct. I have written on the subject to the department.

I can conclude by only saying that I had hoped that all former difficulties had ceased for ever. On my part they were never mentioned to any person, nor a subject of discourse at any time nor in any place. I was tired hearing of them, and was in hopes that they slumbered for ever. While at La Harpe the subject was never once mentioned. The only thing was the inquiry I made myself to find out, as far as I could, whether the report made to me by Mr. Higbee was correct or no, and this in relation to myself only. If being entirely silent on the subject at all times and in all places is an error, then I am guilty. If evading the subject at all times, whenever introduced by others, be a crime, then I am guilty; for such is my uniform custom.

If this letter is not satisfactory, let me know wherein; for it is peace I want. I have been interrupted a great many times since I began to write, by people calling at the office.

Respectfully,

SIDNEY RIGDON.

P. S.—I do consider it a matter of just offense to me to hear about Bennett's assisting me to office. I shall have a lower opinion of myself than I now have when I think I need his assistance.

S. R.

Opened court to try Field for drunkenness and abusing his wife. I fined him $10 and costs, and required him to find bail of $50 to keep the peace for six months.

A conference held at Hartland, Niagara county, New York. Three elders and one priest were ordained, and five added to the Church.

It is estimated that the Chinese loss, in their recent war with England, was 15,000 men, 1,500 pieces of cannon, and a great portion of their navy.

Tuesday, 28.—I removed my office from the smoke house (which I have been obliged to occupy for some months,) to the small upper room in the new brick store.

Insult Resented.

Josiah Butterfield came to my house and insulted me so outrageously that I kicked him out of the house, across the yard, and into the street.

Elder Brigham Young visited George A. Smith, who was very sick.

Wednesday, 29.—Sat with Orson Spencer on a case of debt, and gave judgment against Dr. Foster, the defendant.

Thursday, 30.—In the office, in relation to a new bond presented to me by Dr. Brink, which I rejected as informal, and told Charles Ivins he might improve my share of the ferry one year, and cautioned him that if he did not consider Brink good for heavy damages, he would be foolish to be his bondsman.

Brink afterwards took an appeal to the Municipal Court, to be tried on the 10th of April.

Elder Hyde returned from Quincy, having delivered ten lectures and baptized three persons.

At half-past one, p. m., I was called to sit as justice of the peace, with Alderman George W. Harris, on the case of Webb *v.* Rigby, for forcible entry and detainer. During the trial the court fined Esquire O. C. Skinner twenty dollars for insulting a witness, and would have fined him ten dollars more for his contempt of court, but let him off on his submissive acknowledgments. The trial closed about one o'clock on Friday morning.

The Prophet as a Justice of the Peace.

Friday, 31.—At ten, a. m., I opened court for trial of Amos Lower, for assaulting John H. Burghard. After hearing testimony, fined Lower $10.

Spent the afternoon at Mr. Lucian Woodworth's in company with Brother Hyrum, Heber C. Kimball, Orson Hyde, Wilford Woodruff, and Brother Chase, with our wives; had a good time, and feasted on a fat turkey.

CHAPTER XVII.

EULOGY OF LORENZO D. BARNES—THE BEGINNING OF AUXILIARY ORGANIZATIONS IN THE CHURCH—IMPORTANT ITEMS OF DOCTRINE PROCLAIMED AT RAMUS—THE GENERAL CONFERENCE OF APRIL 6TH, 1843.

Saturday, April 1, 1843.—Called at the office about ten a. m., for "the Law of the Lord;" and about noon I heard read "Truthiana" No. 3, from the *Boston Bee.* At two p. m., I started in company with Orson Hyde and William Clayton for Ramus. The roads were very muddy. We arrived about half-past six, p. m., and were very joyfully received by Brother Benjamin F. Johnson, where we slept for the night.

Elders Brigham Young and John Taylor went to La Harpe.

The *Times and Seasons* contains a well written editorial upon the signs of the times. (See vol. IV, page 153.)

Minutes of a Conference at Augusta, Lee County, Iowa, April 1st, 1843.

James Brown was appointed the presiding Elder of the Augusta branch, which numbered eighty-four members in good standing, including two high priests, eleven elders, four priests, two teachers and one deacon. Twelve persons united with the branch. Seven elders, two priests and one deacon were ordained. One of the elders was a Lamanite of the Delaware tribe. A resolution was unanimously passed to uphold the first presidency and follow their counsels, and to use their utmost endeavors to build the Nauvoo House as well as the Temple. A number of discourses were preached during the conference, and several persons requested baptism at the close.

Elder P. P. Pratt writes:

Letter of Elder Parley P. Pratt Eulogizing Lorenzo D. Barnes, the First Elder to Die while on a Foreign Mission.

ALTON, April 1, 1842.

DEAR BROTHER:—Brother Lorenzo Snow arrived at St. Louis last Wednesday,from England with about two hundred and fifty emigrants. They are now lying on a boat bound forNauvoo as soon as the river opens. They sailed from England some time in January, and bring a copy of the *Millennial Star* and some private letters, under date of January 1st, 1843. From these we learn the painful fact that our dear brother and fellow-laborer, Elder Lorenzo D. Barnes is gone to be with Christ. He lingered some weeks with a fever,and at length died in the triumphs of faith.

He died on the morning of tho 20th of December last, at Bradford, —the first messenger of this last dispensation, who, for Christ's sake and the Gospel's, has laid down his life in a foreign land.

In this dispensation of Providence, an entire people are called to mourn. Brother Barnes was everywhere known and universally beloved as a meek, humble, and zealous minister of the Gospel, who has labored extensively for many years with great success. Such was his wisdom and prudence, and such his modesty and kindness, that he won the friendship not only of the Saints, but of thousands of various sects, and of those who made no profession. In short, his was the favored portion which falls to the lot of but few men, even among the great and good. He was loved and esteemed by many and hated by few, in all the wide circle of his acquaintance. But in the midst of a useful career on earth, he is suddenly and to us unexpectedly called away to a higher and more glorious field of action, with the spirits of the just, in the high council of the King of Kings. His spirit now justly claims an honored seat; his voice is now heard in the deliberations of the high and mighty ones,who are the principal movers in the great events of the dispensation of the fullness of times, whilst his body lies sleeping far away from his native shore, on a distant island of the sea.

No father or mother, or kindred were near
To receive his last blessing or drop a kind tear,
With heart-broken anguish to weep o'er his tomb,
To adorn it with roses of richest perfume.

Yet he was lamented with many a tear,
By hearts full of sorrow—by soul's as sincere,
Who in solemn procession repaired to the grave,
To mourn for the stranger no kindness could save.

'Twas a tribute from souls he had won for his Lord—
Yea, brothers and sisters made nigh by his word,
Whose love was as strong and whose friendship as pure—
Whose grief was as heart-felt as heart can endure.

His name and memory will be dear to thousands, and will be handed down to all generations, as one who has devoted his time from early youth in the service of his God and of his fellow-creatures, and has laid down his life for Christ's sake and the Gospel's, to find it again, even life eternal.*

The Saints in England seem to be still rejoicing in the truth and increasing in numbers.

The emigration to Nauvoo is gathering as a cloud, yea, they are flocking as doves to their windows from all parts of England and the United States. The ice remaining so late in the river has congregated them in St. Louis in great numbers, some from Ohio and the East, and from various places. I think that thousands will land in Nauvoo in the course of the spring. Yes, as soon as the ice is out, they will throng to Nauvoo in swarms. The people in Missouri are beginning to be more and more astonished, and are expressing great fears that "Joe Smith" will yet prevail, so as to restore the supremacy of the laws in that dark corner of the earth, where a gang of robbers and murderers have so long controlled a state.

I long to be with you on the 6th of April, but fear that the ice will prevent.

I am in haste,
Yours in the new covenant,
PARLEY P. PRATT.

A Short Sketch of the Rise of the "Young Gentlemen and Ladies Relief Society" from in the Times and Seasons.†

In the latter part of January, 1843, a number of young people assembled at the house of Elder Heber C. Kimball, who warned them

* Lorenzo D. Barnes, the subject of the above eulogy, was born in 1812, and ordained a member of the second quorum of Seventy at Kirtland, in 1835. When the Adam-ondi-Ahman stake of Zion was organized in June, 1838, he was made a member of the High Council, and also the secretary of that stake, though continuing to hold the office of Seventy. He was one of the Seventy appointed to accompany the Twelve on their mission to Europe. (See minutes of the general conference of the Church, held in Quincy, Illinois, May 4, 5, 6, 1839. HISTORY OF THE CHURCH, vol. iii, pp. 246-7.) He died December 20, 1842, at Bradford, England. In 1852 his body was brought from England and interred in the Salt Lake City cemetery, where a suitably inscribed monument erected by the second quorum of Seventy Salt Lake City, marks his resting place.

†Vol. iv, p. 154-7. A reading of the above minutes will more clearly describe a Mutual Improvement Association than a Relief Society; and this incident may not

against the various temptations to which youth is exposed, and gave an appointment expressly for the young at the house of Elder Billings; and another meeting was held in the ensuing week, at Brother Farr's school-room, which was filled to overflowing. Elder Kimball delivered addresses, exhorting the young people to study the scriptures, and enable themselves to "give a reason for the hope within them," and to be ready to go on to the stage of action, when their present instructors and leaders had gone behind the scenes; also to keep good company and to keep pure and unspotted from the world.

The next meeting was appointed to be held at my house; and notwithstanding the inclemency of the weather, it was completely filled at an early hour. Elder Kimball, as usual, delivered an address, warning his hearers against giving heed to their youthful passions, and exhorting them to be obedient and to pay strict attention to the advice of their parents, who were better calculated to guide them on the pathway of youth than they themselves. My house being too small the next meeting was appointed to be held in the hall over my store. I addressed the young people for some time, expressing my gratitude to Elder Kimball for having commenced this glorious work, which would be the means of doing a great deal of good, and said the gratitude of all good men and of the youth would follow him through life, and he would always look back upon the winter of 1843 with pleasure. I experienced more embarrassment in standing before them than I should before kings and nobles of the earth; for I knew the crimes of which the latter were guilty, and I knew precisely how to address them; but my young friends were guilty of none of them, and therefore I hardly knew what to say. I advised them to organize themselves into a society for the relief of the poor, and recommended to them a poor lame English brother (Maudesley) who wanted a house built, that he might have a home amongst the Saints; that he had gathered a few materials for the purpose, but was unable to use them, and he has petitioned for aid. I advised them to choose a committee to collect funds for this purpose, and perform this charitable act as soon as the weather permitted. I gave them such advice as I deemed was calculated to guide their conduct through life and prepare them for a glorious eternity.

A meeting was appointed to carry out these suggestions, at which William Cutler was chosen president and Marcellus L. Bates, clerk. Andrew Cahoon, Claudius V. Spencer and Stephen Perry were appointed to draft a constitution for the society and the meeting adjourned to the 28th of March, when the said committee submitted a

improperly be regarded as the first step towards that great movement in the Church which has been such a mighty aid in holding to the faith of their fathers the youth of Israel.

draft of a constitution, consisting of twelve sections. The report was unanimously adopted, and the meeting proceeded to choose their officers, William Walker was chosen president; William Cutler, vice-president; Lorin Walker, treasurer; James M. Monroe, secretary. Stephen Perry, Marcellus L. Bates, Redden A. Allred, William H. Kimball and Garret Ivans were appointed a committee of vigilance. The meeting then adjourned until the next Tuesday evening.

The next meeting was addressed by Elders Brigham Young, Heber C. Kimball and Jedediah M. Grant, whose instructions were listened to with breathless attention.

The *Boston Weekly Bee* has the following:

MORMONISM,

SIR:—On Thursday evening, March 23, agreeable to appointment, Elder George J. Adams addressed a large concourse of people on the Character and Mission of Joseph Smith the Prophet. In speaking of him, he bears a positive and direct testimony to the divinity of his mission. He does this without hesitation, just as if he meant what he said, and said what he meant. He does not say he hopes Joseph Smith is a true prophet, but says he is positive that such is the fact. On the Sabbath, March 26th, during the day, he introduced Elder E. P. Maginn, and gave him a high recommendation as an able minister of the fullness of the Gospel, who is to take his place in Boston for the present. He also spoke of Elder Orson Hyde, one of the Twelve Apostles, that would probably visit them this spring; and, according to Adams' account of him, he must be a perfect Apollo in learning and eloquence. The Boylston hall was a perfect jam during the day and evening. On Tuesday evening he gave his farewell lecture. That was a rich treat indeed, embodying the outline of the faith and doctrine of Latter-day Saints. But on Wednesday evening, at the great tea party, was the time it was clearly manifested that kindest feelings existed in this city towards the Mormons. There were present on that occasion over five hundred people: three hundred and fifty sat down at the first table. After supper, Elder Adams delivered a very appropriate and eloquent address. It was listened to with profound attention, during which time we saw the tear start in many an eye. During his remarks he spoke very beautifully of "the marriage supper of the Lamb," that was to wind up this last dispensation, cause creation to cease to groan, and usher in the long-looked-for period when universal religion, liberty and toleration shall be proclaimed from "mountain-top to mountain-top and every man in every place shall meet a brother and a friend."

Yours truly, (not a Mormon, but) one of the many friends to that much abused people."

D. W. R.

Boston, April 1, 1843.

Sunday, 2.—Wind N. E. Snow fell several inches, but melted more or less.

Orson Hyde Corrected by the Prophet.

At ten a. m. went to meeting. Heard Elder Orson Hyde preach, comparing the sectarian preachers to crows living on carrion, as they were more fond of lies about the Saints than the truth. Alluding to the coming of the Savior, he said, "When He shall appear, we shall be like Him, &c. He will appear on a white horse as a warrior, and maybe we shall have some of the same spirit. Our God is a warrior. (John xiv, 23.) It is our privilege to have the Father and Son dwelling in our hearts, &c."

We dined with my sister Sophronia McCleary, when I told Elder Hyde that I was going to offer some corrections to his sermon this morning. He replied, "They shall be thankfully received."

Important Items of Instruction given by Joseph the Prophet at Ramus, Illinois, April 2nd, 1843.*

When the Savior shall appear, we shall see Him as He is. We shall see that He is a man like ourselves, and that the same sociality which exists among us here will exist among us there, only it will be coupled with eternal glory, which glory we do not now enjoy. (John xiv: 23.) The appearing of the Father and the Son, in that verse, is a personal appearance; and the idea that the Father and the Son dwell in a man's heart is an old sectarian notion, and is false.

In answer to the question, "Is not the reckoning of God's time, angel's time, prophet's time, and man's time according to the planet on which they reside? I answer, yes. But there are no angels who minister to this earth but those who do belong or have belonged to it. The angels do not reside on a planet like this earth; but they reside in the presence of God, on a globe like a sea of glass and fire, where all things for their glory are manifest—past, present, and future, and are continually before the Lord. The place where God resides is a great

* See Doctrine and Covenants, section cxxx.

Urim and Thummim. This earth in its sanctified and immortal state, will be made like unto crystal and will be a Urim and Thummim to the inhabitants who dwell thereon, whereby all things pertaining to an inferior kingdom, or all kingdoms of a lower order, will be manifest to those who dwell on it; and this earth will be Christ's. Then the white stone mentioned in Revelation ii: 17, will become a Urim and Thummim to each individual who receives one, whereby things pertaining to a higher order of kingdoms, will be made known; and a white stone is given to each of those who come into the celestial kingdom, whereon is a new name written, which no man knoweth save he that receiveth it. The new name is the key word.

I prophesy, in the name of the Lord God, that the commencement of the difficulties which will cause much bloodshed previous to the coming of the Son of Man will be in South Carolina. It may probably arise through the slave question. This a voice declared to me while I was praying earnestly on the subject, December 25th, 1832.*

I was once praying very earnestly to know the time of the coming of the Son of Man, when I heard a voice repeat the following: "Joseph, my son, if thou livest until thou art eighty five years old, thou shalt see the face of the Son of Man; therefore let this suffice, and trouble me no more on this matter." I was left thus, without being able to decide whether this coming referred to the beginning of the millennium or to some previous appearing, or whether I should die and thus see His face. I believe the coming of the Son of Man will not be any sooner than that time.

The Prophet Expounds the Scriptures.

At one p. m., attended meeting, I read the 5th chapter of Revelation, referring particularly to the 6th verse, showing from that the actual existence of beasts in heaven. Probably those were beasts which had lived on another planet, and not ours. God never made use of the figure of a beast to represent the kingdom of heaven. When it is made use of, it is to represent an apostate church. This is the first time I have ever taken a text in Revelation; and if the young Elders would let such things alone it would be far better.

Then corrected Elder Hyde's remarks, the same as I had done to him privately.

* See Doctrine and Covenants, section lxxxvii. Also HISTORY OF THE CHURCH vol. I, chapter xxii, where the revelation here alluded to is given *in extenso*.

At the close of the meeting we expected to start for Carthage, but the bad weather prevented; so I called another meeting in the evening.

Between meetings I read in Revelation with Elder Hyde, and expounded the same, during which time several persons came in and expressed their fears that I had come in contact with the old scriptures.

At seven o'clock meeting, I resumed the subject of the beast, and showed very plainly that John's vision was very different from Daniel's prophecy—one referring to things actually existing in heaven; the other being a figure of things which are on earth.

*The Persistence of Intelligence—Blessings Predicated on Law.**

Whatever principle of intelligence we attain unto in this life, it will rise with us in the resurrection; and if a person gains more knowledge and intelligence in this life through his diligence and obedience than another, he will have so much the advantage in the world to come. There is a law irrevocably decreed in heaven before the foundations of this world, upon which all blessings are predicated; and when we obtain any blessing from God, it is by obedience to that law upon which it is predicated.

The Father has a body of flesh and bones as tangible as man's; the Son also; but the Holy Ghost has not a body of flesh and bones, but is a personage of Spirit. Were it not so, the Holy Ghost could not dwell in us. A man may receive the Holy Ghost, and it may descend upon him and not tarry with him.

Questions Submitted to the Prophet.

"What is the meaning of the scripture, 'He that is faithful over a few things shall be made ruler over many; and he that is faithful over many, shall be made ruler over many more'? What is the meaning of the parable of the Ten Talents? Also the conversation with Nicodemus, 'Except a man be born of water and of the Spirit'? " were questions put to me which I shall not answer at present.

I closed by flagellating the audience for their fears, and called upon Elder Hyde to get up and fulfill his

* See Doctrine and Covenants, section cxxx.

covenant to preach three-quarters of an hour, otherwise I would give him a good whipping.

Elder Hyde arose and said "Brothers and sisters, I feel as though all had been said that can be said. I can say nothing, but bless you."

At the close of the meeting, we returned to Benjamin F. Johnson's, where we slept; and I remarked that the hundred and forty-four thousand sealed are the priests who should be anointed to administer in the daily sacrifice.

Dimick B. Huntington returned from Chicago, having had a very cold and severe journey. The ice in Chicago harbor was three feet thick. Brought me a letter from Mr. Justin Butterfield.

Monday, April 3.—Miller's day of judgment has arrived, but it is too pleasant for false prophets.*

At two p. m., started for Carthage, where we arrived about four p. m., and stayed at Jacob B. Backenstos'.

Elders Young and Taylor returned to Nauvoo, having preached four times.

In the evening, reading the Book of Revelation with Elder Hyde and conversing with Esquire Backman.

Upward of $12,000,000 have been recently expended by the French government to fortify the city of Paris.

Tuesday, 4.—Spent five hours preaching to Esquire Backman, Chancery Robinson, and Backenstos. Backman said, "Almost thou persuadest me to be a Christian."

We left Carthage about two p. m., and arrived at Nauvoo, at have-past five.

Wednesday, 5.—Sat with Aldermen Spencer, Wells, Hills, Harris, Whitney and Kimball, associate-justices in the municipal court on a writ of habeas corpus, and discharged Jonathan and Lewis Hoopes from custody.

A branch of the Church organized at Mount Holly, New Jersey, of twenty-five members, by Elder Newton.

* This has reference to William Miller, who predicted that on the 3rd of April, 1843, the Christ would come in glory, and the end of the world would come. See footnote, page 272, this volume.

Thursday, April 6.—I was detained from conference to hear a case of assumpsit, Widow Thompson, *versus* Dixon, until eleven a. m.

The first day of the fourteenth year of the Church of Jesus Christ of Latter-day Saints. Sun shone clear, warm and pleasant. The snow has nearly all disappeared, except a little on the north side of the hill above Zarahemla, Iowa. The ice is about two feet thick on the Mississippi, west of the Temple. A considerable number of the brethren crossed from the Iowa side of the river to the conference, on the ice. The walls of the Temple are from four to twelve feet above the floor.

Minutes of the General Conference, Beginning April 6th, 1843.

An annual conference of the Church of Jesus Christ of Latter-day Saints was convened on the floor of the Temple. There were present—Hyrum Smith, Patriarch; Brigham Young, Heber C. Kimball, Orson Pratt, Wilford Woodruff, John Taylor, George A. Smith, and Willard Richards, of the quorum of the Twelve; Elder Amasa Lyman, and a very large assembly of the elders and Saints.

Elder Brigham Young announced that President Joseph Smith was detained on business, but would be present soon.

Sang a hymn.

Elder Amasa Lyman opened by prayer, and another hymn was sung.

Elder Orson Pratt then read the third chapter of the second epistle of Peter, and spoke upon the subject of the resurrection.

At ten minutes before twelve o'clock, President Joseph Smith and Elders Rigdon and Hyde arrived.

PRESENTATION OF AUTHORITIES.

At twelve o'clock, President Joseph Smith commenced by saying, "We all ought to be thankful for the privilege we enjoy this day of meeting so many of the Saints, and for the warmth and brightness of the heavens over our heads; and it truly makes the countenances of this great multitude to look cheerful and gladdens the hearts of all present." He next stated the object of the meeting, which was—

First. To ascertain the standing of the First Presidency, which he should do by presenting himself before the conference.

Second. To take into consideration the expediency of sending out the

Twelve, or some of them, amongst the branches of the Church, to obtain stock to build the Nauvoo house; for the time has come to build it.

Third. The elders will have the privilege of appeals from the different conferences to this, if any such cases exist.

These are the principal items of business which I have at present to lay before you.

It is necessary that this conference give importance to the Nauvoo House. A prejudice exists against building it, in favor of the Temple; and the conference is required to give stress to the building of the Nauvoo House. This is the most important matter for the time being; for there is no place in this city where men of wealth, character and influence from abroad can go to repose themselves, and it is necessary we should have such a place. The Church must build it or abide the result of not fulfilling the commandment.

President Joseph then asked the conference if they were satisfied with the First Presidency, so far as he was concerned as an individual to preside over the whole Church, or would they have another? If, said he, I have done anything to injure my character, reputation, or standing, or have dishonored our religion by any means in the sight of angels or in the sight of men and women, I am sorry for it; and if you will forgive me, I will endeavor to do so no more. I do not know that I have done anything of the kind. But if I have, come forward and tell me of it. If any one has any objection to me, I want you to come boldly and frankly and tell me of it; and if not, ever after hold your peace.

Motion was made and seconded, that President Joseph Smith continue President of the whole Church. After a few minutes' silence, the motion was put by President Brigham Young, when one vast sea of hands was presented, and the motion was carried unanimously.

President Joseph returned his thanks to the assembly for the manifestation of their confidence, and said he would serve them according to the best ability God should give him.

Elder Brigham Young moved, and Elder Orson Hyde seconded, that Elder Sidney Rigdon be continued in his office as counselor to President Smith.

Elder Rigdon spoke, saying, "The last time I had the privilege of attending conference was at the laying of the corner stones of this Temple; and I have had but poor health since, and have been connected with circumstances the most forbidding, which, doubtless, have produced some feelings. I have never had a doubt of the work. My feelings concerning Bennett were always the same. I told my family to guard against that fellow, for some time he will attempt to make a rupture among this people. I had so little confidence in him that I always felt myself at his defiance. I was once threatened by Warren Parrish, if I would not coincide with his views; and I have just received such a threatening letter from John C. Bennett, that if I did not turn my course I should feel the force of his power. As there is now an increase of my health and strength, I desire to serve you in any way it is possible for me to do. If any one has any feelings against me, I hope they will express them.

Dimick B. Huntington asked him what he meant when he said Bennett was a good man, etc., when he called him a perfect gentleman and he had nothing against him.

Elder Rigdon said he did not recollect it. He did not then know as much about Bennett as he had learned afterwards. I say now, he never offered any abuse in my house. Bennett has never been about my house but little. I never saw anything about the man but what was respectable. He came to Robinson's. I was in debt to him, and consequently boarded him. I think Dimick must be mistaken.

Dimick: I know I am not. I have no private pique against Elder Rigdon.

The vote was then put and carried almost unanimously.

President Joseph Smith presented William Law as his second counselor, who was sustained by unanimous vote.

President Hyrum Smith, patriarch, said he wished to be tried, when it was voted unanimously that he retain his office of patriarch. He then blessed the people and asked the Lord to bless them also.

REMARKS OF THE PROPHET ON COLLECTING FUNDS.

President Joseph Smith said he did not know anything against the Twelve. If he did, he would present them for trial. It is not right that all the burden of the Nauvoo House should rest on a few individuals; and we will now consider the propriety of sending the Twelve to collect means for it. There has been too great a solicitude in individuals for the build- of the Temple to the exclusion of the Nauvoo House. Agents have had too great latitude to practice fraud by receiving donations, and never making report. The Church has suffered loss, and I am opposed to that system of collecting funds when any elder may receive moneys. I am opposed to any man handling the public funds of the Church who is not duly authorized. I advise that some means be devised for transacting business on a sure foundation. The Twelve are the most suitable persons to perform this business, and I want the conference to devise some means to bind them as firm as the pillars of heaven, if possible. The Twelve were always honest, and it will do them no hurt to bind them. It has been reported that they receive wages at two dollars per day for their services. I have never heard this till recently, and I do not believe it. I know the Twelve have never had any wages at all. They have fulfilled their duties; they have always gone where they were sent, and have labored with their hands for their support when at home. If we send them into the world to collect funds, we want them to return those funds to this place, that they may be appropriated to the very purpose for which they were designed. I go in for binding up the Twelve solid, putting them under bonds; and let this conference institute an order to this end, and that the traveling expenses of the agents shall not be borne out of the funds collected for building these houses; and let no man pay money or stock into the hands of the Twelve, except he transmit an account of the same immediately to the Trustee-in-Trust; and let no man but the Twelve have authority to act as agent for the Temple and Nauvoo House. I would suggest the propriety of your saying that no money should ever be sent by any man, except it be by some one whom you have appointed as agent, and stop every other man from receiving moneys. It has been customary for any elder to receive moneys for the Temple when he is traveling. But this system of things opened a wide field for every kind of imposition, as any man can assume the name of a "Mormon" elder and gather his pockets full of money and go to Texas. Many complaints have come to me of money being sent that I have never received. I will mention one case. He is a good man: his name is Daniel Russell, from Akron, New York. His brother Samuel had been east on business for him, and there received twenty or twenty-five dollars as a donation to the Temple, which he put in Daniel Russell's bag, with his money, and forgot to take it out before he returned the bag. Two or three days after his return, he called on his brother for the money belonging to the Church; but Daniel thought Samuel had paid out too much of his money, and he would keep the Church's money to make good his own. I called to see Daniel Russell about the money, and he treated me so very politely, but did not give me to understand he ever meant to pay it. He said he did not know at the time that there was any Church money in the bag,—that he had paid it out, and he had none now.

Samuel Russell, who brought the money from the east, stated to the conference that he did not think it was because his brother was short of funds that he kept it, for he had money enough. He had told him that he should not be out of funds again—that his brother had twenty dollars of the Church funds and some dried fruit for the President.

President Joseph resumed: I give this as a sample of a thousand instances. We cannot give an account to satisfy the people on the Church books unless something is done. I propose that you send your moneys for the Temple by the Twelve or some agent of your own choosing; and if you send by others and the money is lost, it is lost to yourselves; I cannot be responsible for it. Everything that falls into my hands shall be appropriated to the very thing it was designed for. It is wrong for the Church to make a bridge of my nose in appropriating funds for the Temple. The act of incorporation required of me securities, which were lodged in the proper hands, as the law directs; and I am responsible for all that comes into my hands. The Temple committee are bound to me in the sum of $2,000, with good security. If they apply any property where they ought not, they are liable to me for it. Individuals are running to them with funds every day, and thus make a bridge over my nose. I am not responsible for it. If you put it into the hands of the Temple committee, neither I nor my clerk know anything of it. So long as you consider me worthy to hold this office, [Sole Trustee-in-Trust for the Church] it is your duty to attend to the legal forms belonging to the business; and if not, put some other one in my place. My desire is that the conference minutes may go forth in such form that those abroad may learn the order of doing business, and that the Twelve be appointed to this special mission of collecting funds for the Nauvoo House, so that all may know how to send their funds safely, or bring them themselves and deliver them to the Trustee-in-Trust or his clerk, who can always be found in the office. Who are the Temple committee, that they should receive the funds? They are nobody. When I went to the White House at Washington, and presented letters of introduction from Thomas Carlin, governor of Illinois, to Martin Van Buren, he looked at them very contemptuously, and said, "Governor Carlin! Governor Carlin! Who's Governor Carlin? Governor Carlin's nobody." I erred in spirit: I have been sorry for it ever since. I confess my mistake; and I here make my apology to all the world; and let it be recorded on earth and in heaven that I am clear of the sin of being angry with Martin Van Buren for saying, "Governor Carlin's nobody." All property ought to go through the hands of the Trustee-in-Trust. There have been complaints against the Temple committee for appropriating Church funds more freely for the benefit of their own children than to others who need assistance more than they do; and the parties may have till Saturday to prepare for trial.

It was then voted unanimously that the Twelve be appointed a committee to collect funds to build the Nauvoo House and receive moneys for the Temple, with this proviso—That the Twelve give bonds for the safe delivery of all funds coming into their hands belonging to the Nauvoo House and Temple to the Trustee-in-Trust; and that the payer also make immediate report to the Trustee-in-Trust of all moneys paid by him to the Twelve; and that the instructions of President Joseph Smith to the conference be carried into execution.

Elder W. W. Phelps proposed that the Twelve sign triplicate receipts for moneys received, for the benefit of the parties concerned.

Elder Brigham Young objected, and said he should never give receipts for cash, except such as he put into his own pocket for his own use; for it was calculated to make trouble hereafter, and there were better methods of transacting the business and more safe for the parties concerned; that he wished this speculation to stop, and would do all in his power to put it down: to which the Twelve responded, Amen. Elder Young asked if any one knew anything against any one of the Twelve —any dishonesty. If they did, he wanted it exposed. He said he knew of one who was not dishonest. He also referred to muzzling the ox that treadeth out the corn, etc.

President Joseph said, I will answer Brother Brigham. There is no necessity for the Twelve being abroad all the time preaching and gathering funds for the Temple. Spend the time that belongs to preaching abroad, and the rest of the time at home to support themselves. It is no more for the Twelve to go abroad and earn their living in this way than it is for others. The idea of not muzzling the ox is a good old Quaker song; but we will make the ox tread out the corn first, and then feed him. I am bold to declare that I have never taken the first farthing of Church funds for my own use, till I have first consulted the proper authorities. When there was no quorum of the Twelve or High Priests for me to consult, I have asked the Temple committee, who had no particular business with it; but I did it for the sake of peac. (Elder Cutler said it was so.) Let the conference stop all agents from collecting funds, except the Twelve. When a man is sent to preach the first principles of the gospel, he should preach that, and let the rest alone.

Choir sang a hymn.

Elder Orson Hyde prayed; and twelve minutes before two o'clock, p. m., conference adjourned for one hour.

Afternoon Session.

[Conference re-assembled at three o'clock, p. m.]

HYRUM SMITH'S REMARKS ON THIEVES.

Patriarch Hyrum Smith commenced by saying that he had some communication to make to the conference on stealing, and he would do it while waiting for President Joseph Smith, and referred to the article in the last number of the *Wasp*. Said he, I have had an interview with a man who formerly belonged to the Church. He revealed to me that there is a band of men, and some who pretend to be strong in the faith of the doctrine of the Latter-day Saints; but they are hypocrites, and some who do not belong to the Church, who are bound together by secret oaths, obligations, and penalties to keep the secret; and they hold that it is right to steal from any one who does not belong to the

Church, provided they consecrate one-third of it to the building of the Temple. They are also making bogus money.

This man says he has become convinced of the error of his ways and has come away from them to escape their fury. I wish to warn you all not to be duped by such men, [these outlaws] for they are the Gadiantons of the last days.

He then read from the *Wasp*, as republished from the *Times and Seasons*, his own affidavit and the proceedings of the authorities of the Church generally, dated Nov. 26, 1841. The man who told me said, "this secret band refer to the Bible, Book of Doctrine and Covenants, and Book of Mormon to substantiate their doctrines; and if any of them did not remain steadfast, they ripped open their bowels and gave them to the cat-fish." But no such doctrines are taught in those books

They say that it has been taught from this stand that they are the little foxes that spoil the vines, and the First Presidency are the big foxes; and the big foxes wanted the little foxes to get out of the city and spread abroad, so that the big foxes might have a chance; which everybody knows is false. All these things are used to decoy the foolish and unwary.

I will mention two names—David Holman and James Dunn. They were living in my house. I went to them and asked them if they were stealing for a livelihood? Holman confessed that he had stolen from the world, not from the brethren. I told them to get out of my house. David asked me to forgive him, and he lifted his hands towards heaven and swore, if I would forgive him, he would never do so again. Soon after he went to Montrose, where he was found stealing salt. He then stole a skiff and came across the river, stole a barrel of flour that had just been landed from a steamer, rowed down the river to Keokuk and sold the flour for $2.00, saying he had picked it up in the river, and it was likely a little damaged, got his pay, and went his way. Dunn would not promise to quit stealing, but said he would go to St. Louis. I tell you today, the men that steal shall not long after be brought to the penitentiary. They will soon be brought to condign punishment. I demand, in the presence of God, that you will exert your wit and your power to bring such characters to justice. If you do not, the curse of God will rest upon you. Such things would ruin any people. Should I catch a Latter-day Saint stealing, he is the last man to whom I would show mercy.

President Joseph Smith said, I think it best to continue this subject. I want the elders to make honorable proclamation abroad concerning what the feelings of the First Presidency are; for stealing has never been tolerated by them. I despise a thief. He would betray me if he could get the opportunity. I know that he would be a detriment to any cause; and if I were the biggest rogue in the world, he would steal my horse when I wanted to run away.

It has been said that some were afraid to disclose what they knew of these secret combinations; consequently I issued a proclamation, which you may read in the *Wasp*, Number 48. If any man is afraid to disclose what he knows about this gang of thieves, let him come to me and tell me the truth, and I will protect him from violence. Thieving must be stopped.

Opportunity was then offered to the elders to bring forward their appeals from other conferences; but no case was presented.

THE PROPHET'S REMARKS ON CONDITIONS IN IOWA.

President Joseph Smith continued his remarks and said, it is necessary that I make a proclamation concerning Keokuk and also in relation to the economy of the Church on that side of the river.

The governor of Iowa has issued a writ in the same manner that Carlin did, and it is now held in Iowa as a cudgel over my head. I was told by the United States attorney that the governor of Iowa had no jurisdiction after the decision of the Supreme Court, and that all writs thus issued were legally dead. Appeals have been made to Governor Chambers; but although he has no plausible excuse, he is not willing to kill that writ or to take it back. I will therefore advise you to serve them a trick that the devil never did,—*i. e.*, come away and leave them; come into Illinois, pay taxes in Illinois, and let the Iowegians take their own course. I don't care whether you come away or not. I do not wish to control you; but if you wish for my advice, I would say, let every man, as soon as he conveniently can, come over here; for you can live in peace with us. We are all green mountain boys—Southerners, Northerners, Westerners, and every other kind of "ers," and wil treat you well: and let that governor know that we don't like to be imposed upon.

In relation to Keokuk, it has been supposed that I made a great bargain with a certain great man there. In the beginning of August last, a stranger came to my house, put on a very long face, and stated that he was in great distress—that he was a stranger in this city, and having understood that I was benevolent, he had come to me for help. He said that he was about to lose $1,400 of property at sheriff's sale for $300 in cash; that he had money in St. Louis, which he expected in two or three days; that the sale would take place the next day; and that he wanted to hire some money for two or three days. I thought on the subject over night, and he came the next morning for an answer. I did not like the looks of the man; but thought I, he is a stranger. I then reflected upon the situation that I had been frequently placed in, and that I had often been a stranger in a strange land, and whenever I had asked for assistance I had obtained it; and it may be that he is an honest man; and if I turn him away, I shall be guilty of the sin of ingratitude. I therefore concluded to loan him $200 in good faith sooner than be guilty of ingratitude. He gave me his note for the same, and said, "whenever you call on me, you shall have the money." Soon after, when I was taken with Carlin's writ, I asked him for the money; but he answered, "I have not got it from St. Louis, but shall have it in a few days." He then said, "since I saw you, a project has entered my mind, which I think may be profitable both for you and me. I will give you a quit claim deed for all the land you bought of Galland, which is twenty thousand acres. You paid Galland the notes, and ought to have them: they are in my hands as his agent, and I will give them up. I also propose deeding to you one-half of my right to all my land in the Iowa territory; and all I ask is for you to give your influence to help to build up Keokuk." I answered, "I have not asked for your property: I don't want it, and would not give a snap of my finger for it; but I will receive the papers; and if I find it as you say, I will use my influence to help to build up the place; but I won't give you anything for the land," and told him I wanted the $200 which was due me. He made out the deeds and gave them to me, and I got them recorded, and he gave up the notes, except a few. I then said to Uncle John Smith, if you go there with the brethren, I will give you the property. But he would not accept it. I then let the same gentleman have some cloth to the amount of $600 or $700. He began, soon after, to tell the brethren what obligations I was under to him. I then wrote him a letter on the subject; but I have since found that he is swindling, and that there is no prospect of getting anything from him. He is owing me about $1,100; and I thought it my duty to publish his rascality, that the elders might do the same in that territory, and prevent the brethren from being imposed upon. He has got a writing to this effect, that if he owned as much as he pretended and did as he said, I would give my influence to build up Keokuk, and on no other terms. His name is J. G. Remick. He took this plan to swindle me out of money, cloth, lumber, etc. I want all the congregation to know it. I was not going to use any influence to have the brethren go to be swindled. My advice is, if they choose, that they come away from Keokuk, and not go there any more. It is not a good location.

I am not so much a "Christian" as many suppose I am. When a man undertakes to ride me for a horse, I feel disposed to kick up and throw him off, and ride him. David did so, and so did Joshua. My only weapon is my tongue. I would not buy property in Iowa territory: I consider it stooping to accept it as a gift.

In relation to the half-breed land, it is best described by its name—it is half-breed land; and every wise and judicious person as soon as he can dispose of his effects, if he is not a half-breed, will come away. I wish we could exchange some half-breeds and let them go over the river. If there are any that are not good citizens, they will be finding fault tomorrow at my remarks, and that is the key-word whereby you may know them. There is a chance in that place for every abomination to be practiced on the innocent, if they go; and I ask forgiveness of all whom I advised to go there. The men who have possession have the best title; all the rest are forms for swindling. I do not wish for the Saints to have a quarrel there.

President Joseph Smith stated that the next business was to settle difficulties where elders have had their licenses taken away, etc., or their membership. But whilst they were preparing, if there was any such case, he would talk on other subjects.

THE PROPHET ON THE SECOND COMING OF THE CHRIST.

The question has been asked, can a person not belonging to the Church bring a member before the high council for trial? I answer, No. If I had not actually got into this work and been called of God, I would back out. But I cannot back out: I have no doubt of the truth. Were I going to prophesy, I would say the end [of the world] would not come in 1844, 5, or 6, or in forty years. There are those of the rising generation who shall not taste death till Christ comes.

I was once praying earnestly upon this subject, and a voice said unto me, "My son, if thou livest until thou art eighty-five years of age, thou shalt see the face of the Son of Man." I was left to draw my own conclusions concerning this; and I took the liberty to conclude that if I did live to that time, He would make His appearance. But I do not say whether He will make his appearance or I shall go where He is. I prophesy in the name of the Lord God, and let it be written—the Son of Man will not come in the clouds of heaven till I am eighty-five years old. Then read the 14th chapter of Revelation, 6th and 7th verses—"And I saw another angel fly in the midst of heaven, having the everlasting gospel to preach unto them that dwell on the earth, and to every nation, and kindred, and tongue, and people, saying with a loud voice, Fear God and give glory to Him, for the hour of His judgment is come." And Hosea, 6th chapter, After two days, etc.,—2,520 years; which brings it to 1890. The coming of the Son of Man never will be—never can be till the judgments spoken of for this hour are poured out: which judgments are commenced. Paul says, "Ye are the children of the light, and not of the darkness, that that day should overtake you as a thief in the night." It is not the design of the Almighty to come upon the earth and crush it and grind it to powder, but he will reveal it to His servants the prophets.

Judah must return, Jerusalem must be rebuilt, and the temple, and water come out from under the temple, and the waters of the Dead Sea be healed. It will take some time to rebuild the walls of the city and the temple, &c.; and all this must be done before the Son of Man will make His appearance. There will be wars and rumors of wars, signs in the heavens above and on the earth beneath, the sun turned into darkness and the moon to blood, earthquakes in divers places, the seas heaving beyond their bounds; then will appear one grand sign of the Son of Man in heaven. But what will the world do? They will say it is a planet, a comet, &c. But the Son of Man will come as the sign of the coming of the Son of Man, which will be as the light of the morning cometh out of the east.

Choir sang a hymn.

Prayer by W. W. Phelps.

Adjourned at six p. m., until tomorrow morning.

Friday, 7.—

Conference convened at ten a. m.

Singing, prayer by Elder Orson Hyde, and singing.

President Joseph Smith stated that the next business in order was to listen to appeals of elders, &c.; but none appeared. He was rather hoarse from speaking so long yesterday, and therefore said he would use the boys' lungs today.

The next business in order was to appoint some elders on missions.

Voted that Jedediah M. Grant be sent to preside over the church at Philadelphia.

Voted that Joshua Grant be sent to preside over the church at Cincinnati.

Voted that Pelatiah Brown go to the village of Palmyra, in New York, and raise up a branch of the Church,

Complaints Against the Temple Committee.

The Temple committee was called up for trial.

William Clayton said: Some may expect I am going to be a means of the downfall of the Temple committee. It is not so; but I design to show that they have been partial. Elder Higbee has overrun the amount allowed by the trustees about one-fourth. Pretty much all Elder Higbee's son has received has been in money and store pay. Higbee's son has had nothing credited on his tithing. William F. Cahoon has paid all his tenth; the other sons of Cahoon have had nothing to their credit on tithing. The committee have had a great amount of store pay. One man, who is laboring continually, wanted twenty-five cents in store pay when his family were sick; but Higbee said he could not have it. Pulaski S. Cahoon was never appointed boss over the stone-cutting shop, but was requested to keep an account of labor in it. During the last six months very little means have been brought into the Temple committee. There are certain individuals in this city who are watching every man who has anything to give the Temple, to get it from him and pay for the same in his labor.

Alpheus Cutler said he did not know of any wrong he had done. If any one would show it, he would make it right.

The conference voted him clear.

Reynolds Cahoon said: This is not an unexpected matter for me to be called up. I do not want you to think I am perfect. Somehow or other, since Elder Cutler went up into the pine country, I have, from some cause been placed in very peculiar circumstances. I think I never was placed in so critical a position since I was born. When President Smith had goods last summer, we had better property; goods would not buy corn without some cash: instead of horses, &c., we took store pay. I have dealt out meal and flour to the hands to the last ounce, when I had not a morsel of meal, flour or bread left in my house. If the trustee, Brother Hyrum, or the Twelve, or all of them will examine and see if I have too much, it shall go freely. I call upon the brethren, if they have anything against me, to bring it forward and have it adjusted.

Patriarch Hyrum Smith said: I feel it my duty to defend the committee as far as I can; for I would as soon go to hell as be a committee-man. I will make a comparison for the Temple committee. A little boy once told his father he had seen an elephant on a tree; the people did not believe it, but ran out to see what it was: they looked, and it was only an owl.

Reynolds Cahoon said, when Brother Cutler was gone, Brother Higbee kept the books, and they have found as many mistakes against Brother Higbee as in his favor.

The conference then voted Cahoon clear.

Elias Higbee said: I am not afraid or ashamed to appear before you. When I kept the books, I had much other business on my hands and made some mistakes.

The conference voted in favor of Elder Higbee unanimously.

President Joseph Smith stated that the business of the conference had closed, and the remainder would be devoted to instruction. It is an insult to a meeting for persons to leave just before its close. If they must go out, let them go half an hour before. No gentlemen will go out of meeting just at closing.

Singing by the choir.

Prayer by Elder Brigham Young.

The Afternoon Session.

Conference called to order at two-thirty p. m.

Singing. Prayer by Elder Brigham Young. Singing.

Elder Orson Pratt delivered a discourse from the prophecy of Daniel on the Ancient of Days; for a synopsis of which see *Times and Seasons*, page 204.

While the choir was singing, President Joseph remarked to Elder Rigdon: This day is a millennium within these walls, for there is nothing but peace.

To a remark of Elder Orson Pratt's, that a man's body changes every seven years, President Joseph Smith replied: There is no fundamental principle belonging to a human system that ever goes into another in this world or in the world to come; I care not what the theories of men are. We have the testimony that God will raise us up, and he has the power to do it. If any one supposes that any part of our bodies, that is, the fundamental parts thereof, ever goes into another body, he is mistaken.

Singing by the choir. Prayer by Elder John Taylor.

The ice, which had made a bridge across the river since last November, moved away in immense masses.

Morning Session of the Conference, Saturday, April 8th, 1843.

President Joseph Smith addressed the Saints. [The following synopsis was reported by Willard Richards and William Clayton:]

President Joseph Smith called upon the choir to sing a hymn, and remarked that "tenor charms the ear, bass, the heart." After singing, he spoke as follows:

I have three requests to make of the congregation: The first is, that all who have faith will exercise it and pray the Lord to calm the wind; for as it blows now, I cannot speak long without seriously injuring my health; the next is that I may have your prayers that the Lord will strengthen my lungs, so that I may be able to make you all hear; and the third is, that you will pray for the Holy Ghost to rest upon me, so as to enable me to declare those things that are true.

The Prophet Expounds the Scriptures.

The subject I intend to speak upon this morning is one that I have seldom touched upon since I commenced my ministry in the Church. It is a subject of great speculation, as well amongst the elders of this Church, as amongst the divines of the day: it is in relation to the beasts spoken of by John the Revelator. I have seldom spoken from the revelations; but as my subject is a constant source of speculation amongst the elders, causing a division of sentiment and opinion in relation to it, I now do it in order that division and difference of opinion may be done away with, and not that correct knowledge on the subject is so much needed at the present time.

It is not very essential for the elders to have knowledge in relation to the meaning of beasts, and heads and horns, and other figures made use of in the revelations; still, it may be necessary, to prevent contention and division and do away with suspense. If we get puffed up by thinking that we have much knowledge, we are apt to get a contentious spirit, and correct knowledge is necessary to cast out that spirit.

The evil of being puffed up with correct (though useless) knowledge is not so great as the evil of contention. Knowledge does away with darkness, suspense and doubt; for these cannot exist where knowledge is.

There is no pain so awful as that of suspense, This is the punishment of the wicked; their doubt, anxiety and suspense cause weeping, wailing and gnashing of teeth.

In knowledge there is power. God has more power than all other beings, because he has greater knowledge; and hence he knows how to subject all other beings to Him. He has power over all.

I will endeavor to instruct you in relation to the meaning of the beasts and figures spoken of. I should not have called up the subject had it not been for this circumstance. Elder Pelatiah Brown, one of the wisest old heads we have among us, and whom I now see before me, has been preaching concerning the beast which was full of eyes before and behind; and for this he was hauled up for trial before the High Council.

I did not like the old man being called up for erring in doctrine. It looks too much like the Methodist, and not like the Latter-day Saints. Methodists have creeds which a man must believe or be asked out of their church. I want the liberty of thinking and believing as I please. It feels so good not to be trammelled. It does not prove that a man is not a good man because he errs in doctrine.

The High Council undertook to censure and correct Elder Brown, because of his teachings in relation to the beasts. Whether they actually corrected him or not, I am a little doubtful, but don't care. Father Brown came to me to know what he should do about it. The subject particularly referred to was the four beasts and four-and-twenty elders mentioned in Rev. 5: 8—"And when he had taken the book, the four beasts and four-and-twenty elders fell down before the Lamb, having every one of them harps, and golden vials full of odors, which are the prayers of saints."

Father Brown has been to work and confounded all Christendom by making out that the four beasts represented the different kingdoms of God on the earth. The wise men of the day could not do anything with him, and why should we find fault? Anything to whip sectarianism, to put down priestcraft, and bring the human family to a knowledge of the truth. A club is better than no weapon for a poor man to fight with.

Father Brown did whip sectarianism, and so far so good; but I could not help laughing at the idea of God making use of the figure of a *beast* to represent His kingdom on the earth, consisting of men, when He could as well have used a far more noble and consistent figure. What! the Lord make use of the figure of a creature of the brute creation to represent that which is much more noble, glorious, and important—the glories and majesty of His kingdom? By taking a lesser figure to represent a greater, you missed it that time, old gentleman; but the sectarians did not know enough to detect you.

When God made use of the figure of a beast in visions to the prophets He did it to represent those kingdoms which had degenerated and become corrupt, savage and beast-like in their dispositions, even the degenerate kingdoms of the wicked world; but He never made use of the figure of a beast nor any of the brute kind to represent His kingdom.

Daniel says (ch. 7, v. 16) when he saw the vision of the four beasts, "I came near unto one of them that stood by, and asked him the truth of all this," the angel interpreted the vision to Daniel; but we find, by the interpretation that the figures of beasts had no allusion to the kingdom of God. You there see that the beasts are spoken of to represent the kingdoms of the world, the inhabitants whereof were beastly and abominable characters; they were murderers, corrupt, carnivorous, and brutal in their dispositions. The lion, the bear, the leopard, and the ten-horned beast represented the kingdoms of the world, says Daniel; for I refer to the prophets to qualify my observations which I make, so that the young elders who know so much, may not rise up like a flock of hornets and sting me. I want to keep out of such a wasp-nest.

There is a grand difference and distinction between the visions and figures spoken of by the ancient prophets, and those spoken of in the revelations of John. The things which John saw had no allusion to the scenes of the days of Adam, Enoch, Abraham or Jesus, only so far as is plainly represented by John, and clearly set forth by him. John saw that only which was lying in futurity and which was shortly to come to pass. See Rev. i: 1-3, which is a key to the whole subject: "The revelation of Jesus Christ, which God gave unto Him, to show unto his servants things which must shortly come to pass; and He sent and signified it by His angel unto His servant John: who bare record of the word of God, and of the testimony of Jesus Christ, and of all things that he saw. Blessed is he that readeth, and they that hear the words of this prophecy, and keep those things that are written therein: for the time is at hand." Also Rev. iv: 1. "After this I looked, and, behold, a door was opened in heaven; and the first voice which I heard was as it were of a trumpet talking with me; which said, Come up hither, and I will show thee things which must be hereafter."

The four beasts and twenty-four elders were out of every nation; for they sang a new song, saying, "Thou art worthy to take the book, and to open the seal thereof: for thou wast slain, and hast redeemed us to God by thy blood out of every kindred, and tongue, and people, and nation." (See Rev. 5: 9.) It would be great stuffing to crowd all nations into four beasts and twenty-four elders.

Now, I make this declaration, that those things which John saw in heaven had no allusion to anything that had been on the earth previous to that time, because they were the representation of "things which must shortly come to pass," and not of what has already transpired. John saw beasts that had to do with things on the earth, but not in past ages. The beasts which John saw had to devour the inhabitants of the earth in days to come. "And I saw when the Lamb opened one of the seals; and I heard, as it were the noise of thunder, one of the four beasts saying, Come and see. And I saw, and beheld a white horse: and he that sat on him had a bow; and a crown was given unto him: and he went forth conquering, and to conquer. And when he had opened the second seal, I heard the second beast say, Come and see. And there went out another horse that was red: and power was given to him that sat thereon to take peace from the earth, and that they should kill one another: and there was given unto him a great sword." (Rev. 6: 1, 2, 3, 4.) The book of Revelation is one of the plainest books God ever caused to be written.

The revelations do not give us to understand anything of the past in relation to the kingdom of God. What John saw and speaks of were things which he saw in heaven; those which Daniel saw were on and pertaining to the earth.

I am now going to take exceptions to the present translation of the Bible in relation to these matters. Our latitude and longitude can be determined in the original Hebrew with far greater accuracy than in the English version. There is a grand distinction between the actual meaning of the prophets and the present translation. The prophets do not declare that they saw a beast or beasts, but that they saw the *image* or *figure* of a beast. Daniel did not see an actual bear or a lion, but the images or figures of those beasts. The translation should have been rendered "image" instead of "beast," in every instance where beasts are mentioned by the prophets. But John saw the actual beast in heaven, showing to John that beasts did actually exist there, and not to represent figures of things on the earth. When the prophets speak of seeing beasts in their visions, they mean that they saw the images, they being types to represent certain things. At the same time they received the interpretation as to what those images or types were designed to represent.

I make this broad declaration, that whenever God gives a vision of an image, or beast, or figure of any kind, He always holds Himself responsible to give a revelation or interpretation of the meaning thereof, otherwise we are not responsible or accountable for our belief in it. Don't be afraid of being damned for not knowing the meaning of a vision or figure, if God has not given a revelation or interpretation of the subject.

John saw curious looking beasts in heaven; he saw every creature that was in heaven,—all the beasts, fowls and fish in heaven,—actually there, giving glory to God. How do you prove it? (See Rev. 5: 13.) "And every creature which is in heaven, and on the earth, and under the earth, and such as are in the sea, and all that are in them, heard I saying, Blessing, and honor, and glory, and power, be unto Him that sitteth upon the throne, and unto the Lamb for ever and ever."

I suppose John saw beings there of a thousand forms, that had been saved from ten thousand times ten thousand earths like this,—strange beasts of which we have no conception: all might be seen in heaven. The grand secret was to show John what there was in heaven. John learned that God glorified Himself by saving all that His hands had made, whether beasts, fowls, fishes or men; and He will glorify Himself with them.

Says one, "I cannot believe in the salvation of beasts." Any man who would tell you that this could not be, would tell you that the revelations are not true. John heard the words of the beasts giving glory to God, and understood them. God who made the beasts could understand every language spoken by them. The four beasts were four of the most noble animals that had filled the measure of their creation, and had been saved from other worlds, because they were perfect: they were like angels in their sphere. We are not told where they came from, and I do not know; but they were seen and heard by John praising and glorifying God.

The popular religionists of the day tell us, forsooth, that the beasts spoken of in the Revelation represent kingdoms. Very well, on the same principle we can say that the twenty-four elders spoken of represent beasts; for they are all spoken of at the same time, and are represented as all uniting in the same acts of praise and devotion.

This learned interpretation is all as flat as a pancake! "What do you use such vulgar expressions for, being a prophet?" Because the old women understand it—they make pancakes. Deacon Homespun said the earth was flat as a pancake, and ridiculed the science which proved to the contrary. The whole argument is flat, and I don't know of anything better to represent it. The world is full of technicalities and misrepresentation, which I calculate to overthrow, and speak of things as they actually exist.

Again, there is no revelation to prove that things do not exist in heaven as I have set forth, nor yet to show that the beasts meant anything but beasts; and we never can comprehend the things of God and of heaven, but by revelation. We may spiritualize and express opinions to all eternity; but that is no authority.

Oh, ye elders of Israel, harken to my voice; and when you are sent into the world to preach, tell those things you are sent to tell; preach and cry aloud, "Repent ye, for the kingdom of heaven is at hand; repent and believe the Gospel." Declare the first principles, and let mysteries alone, lest ye be overthrown. Never meddle with the visions of beasts and subjects you do not understand. Elder Brown, when you go to Palmyra, say nothing about the four beasts, but preach those things the Lord has told you to preach about—repentance and baptism for the remission of sins.

He then read Rev. 13: 1—8. John says, "And I saw one of his heads as it were wounded to death; and his deadly wound was healed; and all the world wondered after the beast." Some spiritualizers say the beast that received the wound was Nebuchadnezzar, some Constantine, some Mohammed, and others the Roman Catholic Church; but we will look at what John saw in relation to this beast. Now for the wasp's nest. The translators have used the term "dragon" for devil. Now it was a beast that John saw in heaven, and he was then speaking of "things which must shortly come to pass;" and consequently the beast that John saw could not be Nebuchadnezzar. The beast John saw was an actual beast, and an actual intelligent being gives him his power, and his seat, and great authority. It was not to represent a beast in heaven: it was an angel in heaven who has power in the last days to do a work.

"All the world wondered after the beast," Nebuchadnezzar and Constantine the Great not excepted. And if the beast was all the world, how could the world wonder after the beast? It must have been a wonderful beast to cause all human beings to wonder after it; and I will venture to say that when God allows the old devil to give power to the beast to destroy the inhabitants of the earth, all will wonder. Verse 4 reads, "And they worshiped the dragon which gave power unto the beast; and they worshiped the beast, saying, Who is like unto the beast? Who is able to make war with him?

Some say it means the kingdom of the world. One thing is sure, it does not mean the kingdom of the Saints. Suppose we admit that it means the kingdoms of the world, what propriety would there be in saying, Who is able to make war with my great big self? If these spiritualized interpretations are true, the book contradicts itself in almost every verse. But they are not true.

There is a mistranslation of the word dragon in the second verse. The original word signifies the devil, and not dragon, as translated. In chapter 12, verse 9, it reads, "That old serpent, called the devil," and it ought to be translated devil in this case, and not dragon. It is sometimes translated Apollyon. Everything that we have not a key-word to, we will take it as it reads. The beasts which John saw and speaks of as being in heaven, were actually living in heaven, and were actually to have power given to them over the inhabitants of the earth, precisely according to the plain reading of the revelations. I give this as a key to the elders of Israel. The independent beast is a beast that dwells in heaven, abstract [apart] from the human family. The beast that rose up out of the sea should be translated the image of a beast, as I have referred to it in Daniel's vision.

I have said more than I ever did before, except once at Ramus, and then up starts the little fellow (Charles Thompson) and stuffed me like a cock-turkey with the prophesies of Daniel, and crammed it down my throat with his finger.

At half-past eleven o'clock President Smith's lungs failed him, the wind blowing briskly at the time.

Choir sung a hymn.

Elder John Taylor rose and made a few remarks, among which were the following: "I have never said much about the beasts, &c., in my preaching. When I have done it, it has been to attract attention and keep the people from running after a greater fool than myself.

Singing and prayer.

Adjourned till two p. m.

A strong west wind; ice floating down the Mississippi seen from the stand.

Afternoon Session, two p. m.

Conference again opened; but the wind being too strong, the congregation made a temporary stand at the east end of the Temple walls, when Elder Taylor resumed his remarks on the kingdom of God being set up in the last days, which will be like the little stone cut out of the mountain.

Elder Orson Hyde said it was three years since he met with the Saints and was set apart for his mission to Jerusalem. He had traveled in the four quarters of the globe and had been among people speaking fourteen or fifteen different languages, and they all agree that some great event is close at hand.

Singing and prayer.

Sunday, 9th. Conference opened by singing, "The Spirit of God like a fire is burning."

Prayer and singing. In consequence of President Joseph Smith being afflicted in his lungs and breast, he was not able to preach, and called on Elder Joshua Grant to speak, who stated that he had just returned from a mission of three years. He had traveled through several states, and had, in company with his brother, Jedediah M. Grant, raised up a church of two hundred members. For synopsis of discourse, see *Times and Seasons*, vol. iv, page 236-7.

Elder Amasa M. Lyman also preached an eloquent discourse on the Book of Mormon, resurrection of the dead, and eternal judgment. See *Times and Seasons*, vol. iv, pages 218-20.

CHAPTER XVIII.

A GREAT MISSIONARY MOVEMENT—SPECIAL INSTRUCTIONS TO ELDERS UNDERTAKING MISSIONS—IMPRISONMENT OF ORRIN P. ROCKWELL—ARRIVAL OF SAINTS FROM ENGLAND—SPEECH OF THE PROPHET—INDIAN ELOQUENCE.

Monday, April 10, 1843.—At 10 a. m. a special conference of elders convened and continued by adjournment from time to time till the 12th. There were present of the quorum of the Twelve, Brigham Young, president; Heber C. Kimball, William Smith, Orson Hyde, Orson Pratt, Wilford Woodruff, John Taylor, George A. Smith, and Willard Richards.

A Special Conference at Nauvoo.

The object of the conference was to ordain elders and send them forth into the vineyard to build up churches; and the following appointments were made, with united voices by the conference, agreeable to requests which were made by individuals who were acquainted with the several places which they represented:—

Names and Appointments of Elders.

James M. Munroe and Truman Gillet, Auburn, New York.

Dominicus Carter, Lockport, Indiana.

Joshua Holman and John Pierce, Madison, Indiana.

Wandall Mace and Isaac C. Haight, Orange county, New York.

William O. Clark, Richardson Settlement, Iowa.

Benjamin L. Clapp, John Blair, Wilkinson Hewitt, and Lyman O. Littlefield, Alabama.

Alonzo Whitney and J. Goodale, Dublin, Ohio.

William Eaton, Westfield, Sullivan county, New York.

Zebedee Coltrin, Graham Coltrin, and James H. Flanigan, Smith and Tazwell counties, Virginia.

Jonathan Dunham, Laurenceburgh, Indiana.

Lewis Robbins and Jacob Gates have a roving commission in Massachusetts, with leave to take their wives, but to keep out of the churches.

Stephen Markham and Truman Waite, Huron county, Ohio.

John D. Chase and A. M. Harding, Pittsfield, Vermont.

Amos B. Fuller and Cyrus H. Wheelock, Windham county, Vermont.

John S. Gleason and Henry C. Jacobs, west part of the State of New York.

Marcellus L. Bates and Norman B. Shearer, Sackets Harbor, New York.

Samuel Brown, Maryland.

Lemuel Mallory and George Slater, Washtenau county, Michigan.

Moses Wade, some county in New York, where there has not been any preaching by the Saints.

Chillion Daniels and Ebenezar Robinson, St. Lawrence county, New York.

William Brown and Daniel Cathcart, Pensacola, Florida.

Eleazar Willis, go where he likes.

John Zundall, St. Clair county, Illinois.

Crandall Dunn, Michigan.

George Middow, Waterloo, Canada.

Samuel H. Rogers and Harvey Green, Cumberland, New Jersey.

Daniel Spencer, Canada.

Elias Harmar, Chenango county, New York.

Harvey Tate, Fort Wayne, Indiana; Robert D. Foster and Jonathan Allen, Tioga county, New York.

William Wharton, of Philadelphia, Wilmington, Delaware.

Leonard Soby, Peru, Indiana.

Warner Hoops, York county, Pennsylvania.

F. D. Wilson and George W. Brandon, Dyer and Montgomery counties, Tennessee.

Elisha H. Groves and George P. Dykes, from Terre Haute to Shawneetown and Cairo, on both sides of the Wabash.

Perigrine Sessions, Oxford county, Maine.

John L. Butler and David Lewis, Lexington, Kentucky.

Charles C. Rich, Ottowa, Illinois.

William W. Rust, Worcester county, Massachusetts.

Aaron M. York, Maine.

Asaph Rice, Pontiac, Michigan.

Orson Spencer, New Haven, Connecticut.

Lorin Farr, Connecticut.

Stephen Perry, Amos B. Tomlinson, E. G. Terrill, Amos P. Rogers Joseph Outhouse, and William Bird, Connecticut.

Francis Edwards and Charles Ryan, Jackson county, Tennessee.

Benjamin Kempton, Wheeling to Mount Vernon, Ohio.

Peter Hess, of Philadelphia, Lancaster, Pennsylvania.

Noah Curtis and Luman H. Calkins, Wayne county, New York.

Stratton Thornton and Sandford Porter, south-east part of Illinois and Indiana.

Benjamin Leland and Eden Smith Erie county, Pennsylvania.

Samuel Swarner, Orleans county, New York.

Samuel Parker, York county, Maine.

Jacob E. Terry and Err Terry, Niagara district, Upper Canada.

Edward P. Duzette and Elisha Edwards, Loraine and Huron counties, Ohio.

Edwin Williams, Hunterdon county, New Jersey.

Jacob G. Bigler, Lewis county, Virginia.

Orlando Hovey, Franklin county, Indiana.

William B. Brink, some place in the interior of Pennsylvania, where the elders have not been.

F. B. Jacaway and Samuel Rowland, Adams county, Ohio.

Moses Tracy, Perry county Illinois.

Alfred Brown, Chautauque county, New York.

Noah Rogers, Peter Lemons, Joseph Mount, B. W. Wilson, Addison Pratt, and John Brown, Vermont.

Samuel C. Brown to labor on the Temple.

James Caroll, Henry county, Indiana.

Levi Stewart and James Pace, Williamson and Gallatin counties, Illinois.

Edwin Clegg, Rock Island, Illinois.

John Carns, Richmond, Indiana.

Edward Bosley and Rodman Clark, Livingston county, New York.

James Hutchins and Daniel Tyler, Natchez, Mississippi.

George M. Chase, Geauga county, Ohio.

John Royce, Sing Sing, New York.

Lyman Whitney, Franklin county, Vermont.

Charles Ryan, Jacob E. Terry, Henry Moore, Samuel P. Carter, William Isherwood, Samuel Rowland, Dorr P. Curtis, Abraham S. Workman, Jeremiah Hatch, James G. Culberston, Samuel Ferrin, Samuel Crane, David Moore, William Brown, Benjamin Barber, Oliver B. Huntington, Edward Clegg, Daniel McRae, William S. Covert, William B. Brink, James Long, and William Empy were ordained elders, with this express injunction, that they quit the use of tobacco and keep the Word of Wisdom.

Almon W. Babbitt was restored to fellowship by the conference.

Elder Curtis Hodges (who has a wife in this place,) was cut off from the Church for his *anti*-Christian conduct in Warrick county, Indiana.

Elders James Allred, John Snider, and Aaron Johnson were appointed to administer baptism for the dead in the river while the font could not be used.

President Young instructed the elders not to go from church to church for the purpose of living themselves or begging for their families or for preaching, but to go to their places of destination, journeying among the world and preaching by the way as they have opportunity; and if they get anything for themselves, they must do it in those churches they shall build up or from the world, and not enter into other men's labors.

Several elders have been presented to us having traveled extensively the past season, preaching but little or none, living on the brethren and begging for their own emolument. Such elders, be they where they may, far or near, are instructed to repair forthwith to Nauvoo and give an account of their stewardship, and report the amount of leg service performed by them, and on their return be sure to keep out of the churches.

It is wisdom for the elders to leave their families in this place when they have anything to leave with them; and let not the elders go on their missions until they have provided for their families. No man need say again, "I have a call to travel and preach," while he has not a comfortable house for his family, a lot fenced, and one year's provisions in store, or sufficient to last his family during his mission or means to provide it.

The Lord will not condemn any man for following counsel and keeping the commandments; and a faithful man will have dreams about the work he is engaged in. If he is engaged in building the Temple, he will dream about it; and if in preaching, he will dream about that; and not, when he is laboring on the Temple, dream that it is his duty to run off preaching and leave his family to starve. Such dreams are not of God.

When I was sick last winter, some of the sisters came and whispered in my ear, "I have nothing to eat." Where is your husband? "He is gone a preaching." "Who sent him?" said I; "for the Lord never sent him, to leave his family to starve."

When the Twelve went to England, they went on a special mission, by special commandment, and they left their families sick and destitute, God having promised that they should be provided for. But God does not require the same thing of the elders now, neither does He promise to provide for their families when they leave them contrary to counsel. The elders must provide for their families.

I wish to give a word of advice to the sisters, and I will give it to my wife. I have known elders who had by some means got in debt, but had provided well for their families during their contemplated mission; and after they had taken their departure, their creditors would teaze their wives for the pay due from their husbands, till they would give them the last provision they had left them, and they were obliged to subsist on charity or starve till their husbands returned. Such a course of conduct on the part of the creditor is anti-Christian and criminal; and I forbid my wife from paying one cent of my debts while I am absent attending to the things of the kingdom; and I want the sisters to act on the same principle.

Elder Orson Hyde said, if there is an elder who does not provide for his family in the unrighteous mammon, shall we commit to him the true riches, the priesthood, missions, etc.? No!

Elder Wilford Woodruff requested the elders to remember in their travels that there was a printing press in Nauvoo, and that it is in the hands of the Church, and wished the elders would procure subscribers for the papers, collect pay for the same, and forward it to the editor in cash.

Elder Heber C. Kimball instructed the elders that when they found a place where the people wanted preaching, they must stay themselves and preach, and not run away somewhere else and write to Nauvoo to have elders sent to the place they had left.

Elders Wilford Woodruff and John Taylor requested that when the elders had built up a church, they would write a brief statement of facts, unencumbered with useless matter, and forward their communication to the editor of the *Times and Seasons* post paid.

The elders were reminded that they need not expect any attention would be given to unpaid letters directed to the Presidency.

The elders were also reminded that although they were not sent out to be taught, but to teach, yet, if they would prosper in their missions, they must be careful to teach those things alone which would be profitable to their hearers; that they must bear their testimony of the truth of the fullness of the gospel, and preach nothing but faith and repentance to this generation; and that if they presumed to teach to babes those things which belong to men, they might expect to return to Nauvoo as destitute as they went out; but if they adhered closely to the first principles, and taught the "Word of Wisdom" more by example than by precept, walking before God and the world in all meekness and lowliness of heart, living by every word that proceedeth out of the mouth of the Lord, they might expect an abundant harvest; and as doves return to their windows in flocks when they see the storm approaching, so will multitudes, by listening to their voices, learn of the things which await the earth, and arise and flee, and return unto Mount Zion and her stakes with them who shall be seals of their ministry in the day of celestial light and glory.

BRIGHAM YOUNG, President.

W. RICHARDS, Clerk.

I gave a letter of attorney to Benjamin F. Johnson to sell some of the Church property in Macedonia.

A conference was held at Batavia, New York, on the 6th and 7th of April; Elder John P. Greene, president; R. J. Coats, Clerk. Eleven branches, one hundred sixty-seven members, one high priest, forty-eight elders, two priests, and three teachers were represented in good standing; a general spirit of enquiry prevailing. Seven elders were ordained. Elder Greene and others delivered addresses to the elders on the signs of the times, the mission of the Prophet, and the building of the Temple.

Batavia, New York, Conference.

A conference was also held in the House of the Lord at Kirtland, at which was passed a resolution for the removal of all the Saints in that place to Nauvoo. Elder Lyman Wight, the president, preached several times, and about one hundred apostates and a few new members were baptized during the conference.

Kirtland Conference.

J. H. Reynolds wrote to Bishop Newel K. Whitney on the 7th as follows:

Letter of J. H. Reynolds to Newel K. Whitney—Imprisonment of Orrin P. Rockwell.

INDEPENDENCE, MO., April 7, 1843.

SIR:—At the request of Orrin Porter Rockwell, who is now confined in our jail, I write you a few lines concerning his affairs. He is held to bail in the sum of $5,000, and wishes some of his friends to bail him out. He also wishes some friend to bring his clothes to him. He is in good health and pretty good spirits. My own opinion is, after conversing with several persons here, that it would not be safe for any of Mr. Rockwell's friends to come here, notwithstanding I have written the above at his request; neither do I think bail would be taken (unless it was some responsible person well known here as a resident of this state). Any letter to Mr. Rockwell, (post paid,) with authority expressed on the back for me to open it, will be handed to him without delay. In the meantime he will be humanely treated and dealt with kindly until discharged by due course of law.

Yours, etc.,

J. H. REYNOLDS.

Mr. Newel K. Whitney.

The plague appeared at Alexandria, Mansourah, and Damietta, making great ravages.

Tuesday, *11*.—In the office most of the day. Some rain and wind.

A volcano broke out near Konigshutte, in Silesia.

Wednesday, *12*.—In conversation with Mr. Gillet concerning the Hotchkiss purchase.

Overseer of Work on the Temple Appointed.

In consequence of misunderstanding on the part of the Temple committee, and their interference with the business of the architect, I gave a certificate to William Weeks to carry out my designs and the architecture of the Temple in Nauvoo, and that no person or persons shall interfere with him or his plans in the building of the Temple.

Arrival of Saints from England.

Before the elders' conference closed,* the steamer *Amaranth* appeared in sight of the Temple, coming up the river, and about noon landed her passengers at the wharf opposite the old post office building, consisting of about two hundred and forty Saints from England, under the charge of Elder Lorenzo Snow, who left Liverpool last January, after a mission of nearly three years. With a large company of the brethren and sisters I was present to greet the arrival of our friends, and gave notice to the new-comers to meet at the Temple tomorrow morning at ten o'clock, to hear instructions.

After unloading the Saints, the *Amaranth* proceeded up the river, being the first boat up this season.

* The conference of the elders continued from the 10th of April to the 12th, it will be remembered. See page 347.

About five p. m. the steamer *Maid of Iowa* hauled up at the Nauvoo House landing, and disembarked about two hundred Saints, in charge of Elders Parley P. Pratt and Levi Richards. These had been detained at St. Louis, Alton, Chester, etc, through the winter, having left Liverpool last fall. Dan Jones, captain of the *Maid of Iowa*, was baptized a few weeks since: he has been eleven days coming from St. Louis, being detained by ice. I was present at the landing and the first on board the steamer, when I met Sister Mary Ann Pratt (who had been to England with Brother Parley,) and her little daughter, only three or four days old. I could not refrain from shedding tears.

So many of my friends and acqaintances arriving in one day kept me very busy receiving their congratulations and answering their questions. I was rejoiced to meet them in such good health and fine spirits; for they were equal to any that had ever come to Nauvoo.

Thursday, 13.—Municipal Court met at nine a. m. to hear the case of Dana *v.* Brink on appeal, but adjourned the case to the 19th.

At ten a. m. the emigrants and a great multitude of others assembled at the Temple. Choir sung a hymn; prayer by Elder Heber C. Kimball; when I addressed the Saints. [The following synopsis was written by Willard Richards:]

Remarks of the Prophet to the Saints Newly Arrived from England.

I most heartily congratulate you on your safe arrival in Nauvoo, and on your safe deliverance from all the dangers and difficulties you have had to encounter on the way; but you must not think that your tribulations are ended. This day I shall not address you on doctrine, but concerning your temporal welfare.

Inasmuch as you have come up here, essaying to keep the commandments of God, I pronounce the blessings of heaven and earth upon you; and inasmuch as you will follow counsel, act wisely and do right, these blessings shall rest upon you so far as I have power with God to seal them upon you.

I am your servant, and it is only through the Holy Ghost that I can do you good. God is able to do His own work.

We do not present ourselves before you as anything but your humble servants, willing to spend and be spent in your service; and therefore we shall dwell upon your temporal welfare on this occasion.

In the first place, where a crowd is flocking from all parts of the world, of different minds, religions, &c., there will be some who do not live up to the commandments; there will be some designing characters who would turn you aside and lead you astray. You may meet speculators who would get away your property; therefore it is necessary that we should have an order here, and when emigrants arrive, instruct them concerning these things. If the heads of the Church have laid the foundation of this place, and have had the trouble of doing what has been done, are they not better qualified to tell you how to lay out your money than those who have had no interest in the work whatever?

Some start [in faith] on the revelations to come here. Before they arrive, they get turned away, or meet with speculators who get their money for land with bad titles, and lose all their property; then they come and make their complaints to us, when it is too late to do anything for them. The object of this meeting is to tell you these things; and then, if you will pursue the same course, you must bear the consequences of your own folly.

There are several objects in your coming here. One object has been to bring you from sectarian bondage; another object was to bring you from national bondage to where you can be planted in a fertile soil. We have brought you into a free government,—not that you are to consider yourselves outlaws. By free government we do not mean that a man has a right to steal, rob, &c.; but [a government that renders you] free from bondage, unjust taxation, oppression, and everything, if he conduct [himself] honestly and circumspectly with his neighbors,—free [also] in a spiritual capacity. This is the place that is appointed for the oracles of God to be revealed. If you have any darkness, you have only to ask, and the darkness is removed. It is not necessary that miracle should be wrought to remove darkness. Miracles are the fruits of faith.

"How then shall they call on Him in whom they have not believed? And how shall they hear without a preacher? And how shall they preach except they be sent?"

God may translate the scriptures by me if He chooses. Faith comes by hearing the word of God. If a man has not faith enough to do one thing, he may have faith to do another: if he cannot remove a mountain, he may heal the sick. Where faith is there will be some of the fruits: all gifts and power which were sent from heaven, were poured out on the heads of those who had faith.

You must have a oneness of heart in all things, and then you shall be satisfied one way or the other before you have done with us.

There are a great many old huts here, but they are all new; for our city is not six or seven hundred years old, as those you came from. This city is not four years old; it is only a three-year old last fall: there are very few old settlers.

I got away from my keepers in Missouri; and when I came to these shores, I found four or five hundred families who had been driven out of Missouri without houses or food; and I went to work to get meat and flour to feed them. The people were not afraid to trust me, and I went to work and bought all this region of country, and I cried out, "Lord, what wilt Thou have me to do?" And the answer was, "Build up a city and call my Saints to this place;" and our hearts leap with joy to see you coming here. We have been praying for you all winter from the bottom of our hearts, and we are glad to see you. We are poor, and cannot do by you as we would; but we will do for you all we can. It is not expected that all of you can locate in the city. There are some who have money and who will build and hire others. Those who cannot purchase lots can go out into the country; the farmers want your labor. No industrious man need suffer in this land. The claims of the poor on us are such that we have claim on your good feelings, for your money to help the poor; and the Church debts also have their demands to save the credit of the Church. This credit has been obtained to help the poor and keep them from starvation, &c. Those who purchase Church land and pay for it, this shall be their sacrifice.

Men of considerable means who were robbed of everything in the state of Missouri, are laboring in this city for a morsel of bread; and there are those who must have starved, but for the providence of God through me. We can beat all our competitors in lands, price and everything; we have the highest prices and best lands, and do the most good with the money we get. Our system is a real smut machine, a bolting machine; and all the shorts, bran and smut runs away, and all the flour remains with us. Suppose I sell you land for ten dollars an acre, and I gave three, four or five dollars per acre; then some persons may cry out, "You are speculating." Yes. I will tell how: I buy other lands and give them to the widow and the fatherless. If the speculators run against me, they run against the buckler of Jehovah. God did not send me up as he did Joshua. In the former days God sent His servants to fight; but in the last days, He has promised to fight the battle Himself. God will deal with you Himself, and I will bless or curse you as you behave yourselves. I speak to you as one having authority, that you may know when it comes, and that you may have faith and know that God has sent me.

Some persons may perhaps inquire which is the most healthful location. I will tell you. The lower part of the town is most healthful. In the upper part of the town are the merchants, who will say that I am partial, &c.; but the lower part of the town is much the most healthful; and I tell it you in the name of the Lord. I have been out in all parts of the city, and at all hours of the night to learn these things. The doctors in this region don't know much; and the lawyers, when I speak about them, begin to say, "We will denounce you on the stand." But they don't come up; and I take the liberty to say what I have a mind to about them. Doctors won't tell you where to go to be well; they want to kill or cure you, to get your money. Calomel doctors will give you calomel to cure a sliver in the big toe; and they do not stop to know whether the stomach is empty or not; and calomel on an empty stomach will kill the patient. And the lobelia doctors will do the same. Point me out a patient and I will tell you whether calomel or lobelia will kill him or not, if you give it.

The Mississippi water is more healthful to drink than the spring water, but you had better dig wells from fifteen to thirty feet deep, and then the water will be wholesome. There are many sloughs on the islands from whence miasma arises in the summer and is blown over the upper part of the city; but it does not extend over the lower part of the city. All those persons who have not been accustomed to living on a river or lake, or large pond of water, I do not want to stay on the banks of the river. Get away to the lower part of the city, or back to the hill where you can get good well water. If you feel any inconvenience, take some mild physic two or three times, and follow that up with some good bitters. If you cannot get anything else, take a little salts and cayenne pepper. If you cannot get salts, take ipecacuanha, or gnaw down a butternut tree, or use boneset or horehound.

Those who have money, come to me, and I will let you have lands; and those who have no money, if they will look as well as I do, I will give them advice that will do them good. I bless you in the name of Jesus Christ. Amen.

Hyrum Smith made some remarks concerning the prophets. Every report in circulation not congenial to good understanding is false—false as the dark regions of hell.

Closed by singing and prayer.

After meeting, many of the Saints repaired to the landing at the Nauvoo House. The steamer, *Maid of Iowa*, arrived from Keokuk, where it went last night after the freight which it had left to enable it to get over the rapids.

I was among them until about three o'clock. When the boat left, I walked home with Brother Kimball.

Eighteen vessels wrecked on the Irish coast by the easterly winds.

The gunpowder mills at Waltham-Abbey, England, exploded, killing seven persons.

The Siamese twins, Chang and Eng, married the two sisters, Sarah and Adelaide Yates, of Wilkes county, North Carolina.

Friday, *14*.—Rode out to my farm and to the prairie with some of the emigrants; sold twenty acres of land; and when I was again riding out in the evening, broke the carriage on the side hill, when we all returned home on foot.

I give the following speech, entire, copied from the *National Intelligencer*, as a specimen of the way the seed of Joseph are being "wasted before the Gentiles."

Speech of Colonel Cobb, Head Mingo of the Choctaws, East of the Mississippi, in Reply to the Agent of the U. S.

BROTHER:—We have heard you talk as from the lips of our father, the great white chief at Washington, and my people have called upon me to speak to you. The red man has no books; and when he wishes to make known his views like his fathers before him he speaks from his mouth. He is afraid of writing. When he speaks he knows what he says. The Great Spirit hears him. Writing is the invention of the pale faces; it gives birth to error and to feuds. The Great Spirit talks. We hear him in the thunder, in the rushing winds and the mighty waters. But he never writes.

Brother: When you were young, we were strong. We fought by your side, but our arms are now broken. You have grown large. My people have become small.

Brother: My voice is weak: you can scarcely hear me. It is not the shout of a warrior, but the wail of an infant. I have lost it in mourning for the misfortunes of my people. These are their graves, and in those aged pines you hear the ghosts of the departed. Their ashes are here, and we have been left to protect them. Our warriors are nearly all gone to the far country west; but here are our dead. Shall we go, too, and give their bones to the wolves?

Brother: Two sleeps have passed since we heard you talk. We have thought upon it. You ask us to leave our country, and tell us it is our father's wish. We would not desire to displease our father. We respect him, and you, his child. But the Choctaw always thinks. We want time to answer.

Brother: Our hearts are full. Twelve winters ago our chiefs sold our country. Every warrior that you see here was opposed to the treaty. If the dead could have been counted, it would never have been made; but, alas! though they stood around, they could not be seen or heard. Their tears came in the rain drops,and their voices in the wailing wind. But the pale face knew it not, and our land was taken away.

Brother: We do not now complain. The Choctaw suffers, but he never weeps. You have the strong arm, and we cannot resist. But the pale face worships the Great Spirit. So does the red man. The Great Spirit loves truth. When you took our country you promised us land. There is your promise in the book. Twelve times have the trees dropped their leaves, and yet we have received no land. Our houses have been taken from us. The white man's plough turns up the bones of our fathers. We dare not kindle up our fires; and yet you said we might remain, and you would give us land.

Brother: Is this truth? But we believe now our great father knows our condition, he will listen to us. We are as mourning orphans in our country; but our father will take us by the hand. When he fulfills his promise, we will answer his talk. He means well. We know it. But we cannot think now. Grief has made children of us. When our business is settled, we shall be men again, and talk to our great father about what he has promised.

Brother: You stand in the moccasins of a great chief; you speak the words of a mighty nation, and your talk was long. My people are small. Their shadow scarcely reaches to your knee. They are scattered and gone. When I shout, I hear my voice in the depths of the woods, but no answering shouts come back. My words, therefore, are few. I have nothing more to say, but to tell what I have said to the tall chief of the pale faces, whose brother (William Tyler, of Virginia, brother to the president of the United States, recently appointed one of the Choctaw commissioners) stands by your side.

CHAPTER XIX.

THE PROPHET ON THE RESURRECTION—DIRECTIONS GIVEN AS TO THE LABORS OF THE TWELVE ET AL.—THE KINDERHOOK PLATES— FIRST ISSUE OF "THE NAUVOO NEIGHBOR"—NEW MISSION APPOINTMENTS.

Saturday, April 15, 1843.—Attended court-martial which was held at my house.

In the evening rode out in my carriage with Emma.

A conference was held at Vinalhaven, Fox Island, Maine, when four branches, consisting of one hundred and twenty-eight members, four elders, five priests, six teachers and three deacons, were represented. Quite a number have been recently baptized.

Sunday, 16—Meeting at the Temple at 10 a. m. I read Brother Parley P. Pratt's letter to the editor of the *Times and Seasons*, concerning the death of Lorenzo Dow Barnes, who died in England, December 20, 1842; and I remarked that I read it because it was so appropriate to all who had died in the faith. [The following was reported by W. Richards and W. Woodruff.]

Remarks of the Prophet on the Death of Lorenzo D. Barnes—The Resurtion.

Almost all who have fallen in these last days in the Church have fallen in a strange land. This is a strange land to those who have come from a distance.

We should cultivate sympathy for the afflicted among us. If there is a place on earth where men should cultivate the spirit and pour in the oil and wine in the bosoms of the afflicted, it is in this place; and this spirit is manifest here; and although a stranger and afflicted when he arrives, he finds a brother and a friend ready to administer to his necessities.

I would esteem it one of the greatest blessings, if I am to be afflicted in this world to have my lot cast where I can find brothers and friends all around me. But this is not the thing I referred to: it is to have the privilege of having our dead buried on the land where God has appointed to gather His Saints together, and where there will be none but Saints, where they may have the privilege of laying their bodies where the Son of Man will make His appearance, and where they may hear the sound of the trump that shall call them forth to behold Him, that in the morn of the resurrection they may come forth in a body, and come up out of their graves and strike hands immediately in eternal glory and felicity, rather than be scattered thousands of miles apart. There is something good and sacred to me in this thing. The place where a man is buried is sacred to me. This subject is made mention of in the Book of Mormon and other scriptures. Even to the aborigines of this land, the burying places of their fathers are more sacred than anything else.

When I heard of the death of our beloved Brother Barnes, it would not have affected me so much, if I had the opportunity of burying him in the land of Zion.

I believe those who have buried their friends here, their condition is enviable. Look at Jacob and Joseph in Egypt, how they required their friends to bury them in the tomb of their fathers. See the expense which attended the embalming and the going up of the great company to the burial.

It has always been considered a great calamity not to obtain an honorable burial: and one of the greatest curses the ancient prophets could put on any man, was that he should go without a burial.

I have said, Father, I desire to die here among the Saints. But if this is not Thy will, and I go hence and die, wilt thou find some kind friend to bring my body back, and gather my friends who have fallen in foreign lands, and bring them up hither, that we may all lie together.

I will tell you what I want. If tomorrow I shall be called to lie in yonder tomb, in the morning of the resurrection let me strike hands with my father, and cry, "My father," and he will say, "My son, my son," as soon as the rock rends and before we come out of our graves.

And may we contemplate these things so? Yes, if we learn how to live and how to die. When we lie down we contemplate how we may rise in the morning; and it is pleasing for friends to lie down together, locked in the arms of love, to sleep and wake in each other's embrace and renew their conversation.

Would you think it strange if I relate what I have seen in vision in relation to this interesting theme? Those who have died in Jesus Christ may expect to enter into all that fruition of joy when they come forth, which they possessed or anticipated here.

So plain was the vision, that I actually saw men, before they had ascended from the tomb, as though they were getting up slowly. They took each other by the hand and said to each other, "My father, my son, my mother, my daughter, my brother, my sister." And when the voice calls for the dead to arise, suppose I am laid by the side of my father, what would be the first joy of my heart? To meet my father, my mother, my brother, my sister; and when they are by my side, I embrace them and they me.

It is my meditation all the day, and more than my meat and drink, to know how I shall make the Saints of God comprehend the visions that roll like an overflowing surge before my mind.

Oh! how I would delight to bring before you things which you never thought of! But poverty and the cares of the world prevent. But I am glad I have the privilege of communicating to you some things which, if grasped closely, will be a help to you when earthquakes bellow, the clouds gather, the lightnings flash, and the storms are ready to burst upon you like peals of thunder. Lay hold of these things and let not your knees or joints tremble, nor your hearts faint; and then what can earthquakes, wars and tornadoes do? Nothing. All your losses will be made up to you in the resurrection, provided you continue faithful. By the vision of the Almighty I have seen it.

More painful to me are the thoughts of annihilation than death. If I have no expectation of seeing my father, mother, brothers, sisters and friends again, my heart would burst in a moment, and I should go down to my grave.

The expectation of seeing my friends in the morning of the resurrection cheers my soul and makes me bear up against the evils of life. It is like their taking a long journey, and on their return we meet them with increased joy.

God has revealed His Son from the heavens and the doctrine of the resurrection also; and we have a knowledge that those we bury here God will bring up again, clothed upon and quickened by the Spirit of the great God; and what mattereth it whether we lay them down, or we lay down with them, when we can keep them no longer? Let these truths sink down in our hearts, that we may even here begin to enjoy that which shall be in full hereafter.

Hosanna, hosanna, hosanna to Almighty God, that rays of light begin to burst forth upon us even now. I cannot find words in which to express myself. I am not learned, but I have as good feelings as any man.

O that I had the language of the archangel to express my feelings once to my friends! But I never expect to in this life. When others rejoice, I rejoice; when they mourn, I mourn.

To Marcellus Bates let me administer comfort. You shall soon have the company of your companion in a world of glory, and the friends of Brother Barnes and all the Saints who are mourning. This has been a warning voice to us all to be sober and diligent and lay aside mirth, vanity and folly, and to be prepared to die tomorrow. [President Smith preached about two hours]

Erastus Snow said that he was a boarder with President Joseph Smith the first week he was in Nauvoo: he helped to carry the chain for the surveyor, and helped to lay out the first city lot.

President Joseph Smith said: "As president of this house, I forbid any man leaving just as we are going to close the meeting. He is no gentleman who will do it. I don't care who does it, even if it were the king of England. I forbid it.

Dismissed with singing, and prayer by John Taylor.

I received a letter from the postoffice, of which the following is a copy:

A Canard.

WASHINGTON, D. C., March 31, 1841.

SIR:—You stand accused of high treason. You will deliver yourself up to the governor at Springfield, Illinois, in order to be tried before the Supreme Court of the United States next term.

The governor of Illinois will be directed to take you in custody, if you will not deliver yourself up.

The president will issue a proclamation against you, if you obey not this order by May 1, 1843.

Respectfully yours,
HUGH L. LEGARE,
Attorney-General.

Joseph Smith, Esq.

This letter was superscribed, "By order of J. Tyler, President of the United States."

I insert this letter in my history to show a specimen of the many despicable falsehoods resorted to by the enemies of the truth to annoy me and my friends.

Monday, 17.—Rain last night, green grass begins to appear.

Walked out in the city with William Clayton. Visited Elder John Taylor, and gave him some instructions about the letter purporting to come from Attorney-General Legare, also called on Samuel Bennett in relation to the house he lived in, above the old burying ground; returned home, and conversed with Elder Erastus Snow. Received from Parley P. Pratt fifty gold sovereigns for the Temple and Nauvoo House; also received eighty-seven pounds from the English brethren for land. At half-past five p. m., called at the printing office for a short time, when I returned home and listened to the reading of a synopsis of my sermon of last Sabbath.

Sundry Movements of the Prophet.

Advices from Guadeloupe state that up to the 25th of March forty-five hundred bodies had been dug out of the ruins of Point-a-Pitre, and twenty-two hundred of the wounded by the late earthquake were in the hospital at Basse-Terre, and that five other shocks had been subsequently felt.

Elder E. M. Webb writes that he has been laboring with success in several counties in Michigan, when he came to Comstock, in Kalamazoo county, Dr. John C. Bennett was lecturing in Kalamazoo, the shire town, and was told that there was a Mormon Elder in the neighborhood. Bennett said, "That is one of Joe Smith's destroying angels, who is come to kill me;" and he left in such haste that he forgot to pay his tavern bill, also the poor Presbyterians for lighting and warming the house for him. Elder Webb commenced preaching there, baptized twenty-four and organized a branch.

John C. Bennett Lecturing.

One hundred barrels, or ten thousand pounds of gunpowder were deposited in fifteen separate chambers and simultaneously fired, with complete success, in the Abbot's Cliff, Dover, England.

Tuesday, *18*.—Signed an appointment to John F. Cowan of Shokoquon, as one of my aides-de-camp, as a lieutenant-general of the Nauvoo Legion, and conversed with him.

Rode out on the prairie. Sold one hundred and thirty acres of land to the English brethren and took a bond from John T. Barnett for two lots.

Signed a transcript of the mayor's docket, Thompson vs. Dixon.

In the evening had a talk with three Indian chiefs, who had come as a delegation from the Pottawatamie tribe, who complained of having their cattle, horses, &c., stolen. They were much troubled, and wanted to know what they should do. They had borne their grievances patiently.

Visit Pottawatamie Indians.

The quorum of the Twelve met in my office.

Wednesay, 19.—Went to the office at nine o'clock, to attend a municipal court in case of Dana vs. Dr. Brink, on appeal from mayor's decision of March 10.

Mayor's Court at Nauvoo.

At half past nine called to order and issued an attachment against William Marks, George W. Harris, Orson Spencer, Gustavus Hills, Daniel H. Wells, Hiram Kimball, and Newel K. Whitney, associate-justices, to bring them before the court forthwith to answer for contempt. Aldermen Harris, Spencer, Hills and Whitney appeared, and were excused upon condition of their paying the costs of attachment and marshal's fees. Daniel H. Wells was excused on account of absence from the city.

Half-past twelve p. m. court opened, original papers being called for. The clerk (James Sloan) inquired if the execution would issue from the court. "Sit down," said the mayor, "and attend to your own business. If anything is wanted you will be told time enough." Counsel for Brink moved that the case be dismissed for want of jurisdiction in the court below. Much law was quoted on both sides.

The court decided that the mayor had jurisdiction but the municipal court had not, being authorized only by the charter to try appeals in cases arising under the ordinances of the city. The case arose under the statutes of Illinois, and should have been appealed directly to the Circuit Court, and dismissed the appeal accordingly; and then stated that a legal bond for appeal was not presented till after the twenty days had expired, and therefore it could not now be legally appealed to the Circuit Court.

After adjournment, while conversing with Dr. Brink and Mr. Marr, I told them I had been called to thousands of cases in sickness, and I have never failed in administering comfort where the patient has thrown himself unreservedly on me, and the reason is that I never prescribed anything that would injure the patient, if it did him no good.

I have lost a father, brother, and child, because in my anxiety I depended more on the judgment of other men than my own, while I have raised up others who were lower than they were. By-the-by, I will say that that man, (pointing to Levi Richards) is the best physician I have ever been acquainted with. People will seldom die of disease, provided we know it seasonably, and treat it mildly, patiently and perseveringly, and do not use harsh means.

It is like the Irishman's digging down the mountain. He does not put his shoulder to it to push it over, but puts it in his wheelbarrow, and carries it away day after day, and perseveres in it until the whole mountain is removed. So we should persevere in the use of simple remedies, and not push against the constitution of the patient, day after day; and the disease will be removed and the patient saved. It is better to save the life of a man than to raise one from the dead.

At three p. m. I met with Brigham Young, William Smith, Parley P. Pratt, Orson Pratt, Wilford Woodruff, John Taylor, Geo. A. Smith, and Willard Richards, of the quorum of the Twelve, in my office, and told them to go in the name of the Lord God of Israel, and tell Lucien Woodworth to put the hands on the Nauvoo House, and begin the work, and be patient till means can be provided.

Call on the inhabitants of Nauvoo, and get them to bring in their means, then go to La Harpe and serve them the same. Thus commence your career, "and never stand still the Master appears:" for it is necessary the house should be built. Out of the stock that is handed to me, you shall receive as you have need; for the laborer is worthy of his hire.

I hereby command the hands to go to work on the house. Tell Woodworth to put them on and he shall be backed up in it. You must get cash, property, lands, horses, cattle, flour, corn, wheat, &c. The grain can be ground in this place.

If you can get hands onto the Nauvoo House, it will give such an impetus to the work, that it will take all the devils out of hell to stop it.

Let the Twelve Apostles keep together. You will do more good to keep together, not travel together all the time, but meet in conference from place to place, and associate together, and not be found long apart from each other. Then travel from here to Maine, till you make a perfect highway for the Saints.

It is better for you to be together; for it is difficult for a man to have strength of lungs and health to be instant in season and out of season, under all circumstances; and you can assist each other. And when you go to spend a day or two in a place, you will find the people will gather together in great companies. If twelve men cannot build that house, they are poor tools.

President Young asked if any of the Twelve should go to England.

I replied—No! I don't want the Twelve to go to England this year. I have sent them to England, and they have broken the ice, and done well. And now I want to send some of the elders and try them.

Lorenzo Snow may stay at home till he gets rested. The Twelve must travel to save their lives. I feel all the veins and strata necessary for the Twelve to move in to save their lives.

You can never make anything out of Benjamin Winchester if you take him out of the channel he wants to be in. Send Samuel James to England, thus saith the Lord; also Reuben Hedlock; he ought to be a heavenly messenger wherever he goes. You need not be in a hurry. Send these two now; and when you think of some others, send them.

John Taylor, I believe you can do more good in the editorial department than preaching. You can write for thousands to read; while you can preach to but a few at a time. We have no one else we can trust the paper with, and hardly with you, for you suffer the paper to come out with so many mistakes.

Parley may stay at home and build his house.

Brother George A. Smith, I don't know how I can help him to a living, but to let him go and preach. If he will go, his lungs will hold out. The Lord will give him a good pair of lungs yet.

Wilford Woodruff can be spared from the printing office. If you both stay, you will disagree. I want Orson Pratt should go.

Brother Brigham asked if he should go. Yes, go.

I want John E. Page to be called away from Pittsburg, and a good elder sent in his place. If he stays there much longer, he will get so as to sleep with his granny, he is so self-righteous. When he asked to go back there, he was going to tear up all Pittsburg; and he cannot even get money enough to pay postage on his letters, or come and make us a visit.

Orson Hyde can go and travel; and I want you all to meet in Boston.

I want Elder Willard Richards to continue in the History at present. Perhaps he will have to travel some to save his life. The History is going out by little and little, in the papers, and cutting its way; so that, when it is completed, it will not raise a persecution against us.

When Lyman Wight comes home from Kirtland, I intend to send him right back again.

William Smith is going East with his sick wife.

Brother Kimball will also travel.

I want you to cast up a highway for the Saints from here to Maine.

Don't be scared about the Temple. Don't say anything against it, but make all men know that your mission is to build up the Nauvoo House.

It is not necessary that Jedediah and Joshua Grant should be ordained High Priests in order to preside. They are too young. They have got into Zebedee Coltrin's habit of clipping half their words, and I intend to break them of it. If a high priest comes along, and goes to snub either of them in their presidency, because they are Seventies, let them knock the man's teeth down his throat—I mean spiritually. You shall make a mighty wake as you go.

William Clayton, tell the Temple committee to put hands enough on that house (on the diagonal corner from the brick store), and finish it right off. The Lord hath need of other houses as well as a Temple.

I can sell $10,000 worth of property this spring, I will meet you at any conference in Maine, or any conference where you are, and stay as long as it is wisdom.

Take Jacob Zundall and Frederick H. Moeser, and tell them never to drink a drop of ale, wine, or any spirit, only that which flows right out from the presence of God; and send them to Germany; and when you meet with an Arab, send him to Arabia; when you find an Italian, send him to Italy; and a Frenchman, to France; or an Indian, that is suitable, send him among the Indians. Send them to the different places where they belong. Send somebody to Central America and to all Spanish America; and don't let a single corner of the earth go without a mission.

Write to Oliver Cowdery and ask him if he has not eaten husks long enough? If he is not almost ready to return, be clothed with robes of righteousness, and go up to Jerusalem? Orson Hyde hath need of him. (A letter was written accordingly.)

I returned home about half-past four p. m.

This evening located the site for a music hall on lot 4, block 67, on the corner of Woodruff and Young streets.

By a certificate of William Smith, of this date, we learn that Elder Benjamin Winchester has recently published a synopsis of concordance to the scriptures.

Thursday, 20.—I went out with Brother Manhard to show him some lots, and settled with him; and afterwards heard read a proof sheet of the elders' conference.

Elder Rigdon received a letter last Sunday, informing

him that the Nauvoo post office was abolished. He foolishly supposed it genuine, neglected his duty, and started for Carthage to learn more about it, but was met by Mr. Hamilton, an old mail contractor, who satisfied him it was a hoax; and he returned home, and the mail arrived as usual today.

Sidney Rigdon's Alarm.

Friday, 21.—I rode out in the city, and in the afternoon went to my farm.

There was an officer's drill of the Nauvoo legion.

Saturday, 22.—The cohorts of the legion were in exercise this day. My staff came out with me, and spent the day in riding, exercising, and organizing, and sitting in court-martial, to ascertain to what staff Robert D. Foster, Surgeon-General, Hugh McFall, Adjudant-General, and Daniel H. Wells, Commissary-General, belonged.

Nauvoo Legion Drill

Sunday, 23.—Nine to ten a. m. at home; heard read *Truthiana*, No. 6, also the minutes of special conference, which I revised.

Special Conference.

Eleven, a. m., meeting at the Temple-stand; Brigham Young, Parley P. Pratt, Orson Pratt, Orson Hyde, George A. Smith, and Willard Richards present.

Orson Hyde prayed.

President Brigham Young preached on the subject of salvation, and the Twelve commenced their mission to build the Nauvoo House. For the salvation of the Church it was necessary that the public buildings should be erected, etc.

Parley P. Pratt preached in the afternoon, showing the rapid progress of Nauvoo during the past three years.

Peter Haws called for twenty-five hands to go with him to the Pine country, to get lumber for the Nauvoo House.

President Brigham Young instructed the laborers on the Nauvoo House to commence next morning, even if they had to beg food of their neighbors to commence with; and requested families to board hands till means could be procured.

Monday, 24.—In the morning I took my children a pleasure ride in the carriage.

At one p. m. President Brigham Young, Heber C. Kimball, Orson Hyde, John Taylor, George A. Smith, Wilford Woodruff, and Willard Richards met in council in my office, and agreed to go to Augusta, Iowa, to spend the next Sabbath and devise means to secure the property which has been purchased of Moffat by the Nauvoo House trustees, and voted John Cairnes go on a mission to England; Peter Haws and James Brown to Tuscaloosa, Alabama; that Elder Murray Seaman be instructed to return home immediately; and that Mr. Lucien Woodworth be respectfully requested immediately to furnish the Twelve with a draft of the exterior and interior of the Nauvoo House.

Visit of the Twelve to Augusta, Iowa.

Prince Louis Napoleon, claimant of the imperial throne of France, writes from his prison at Ham to the Parisian journals—"I would prefer captivity on the French soil to freedom in exile."

Tuesday, 25.—In the office in the morning, and heard read the proceedings of the Twelve Apostles yesterday.

Lucius N. Scovil and other Masons came to see me concerning Henry G. Sherwood, when I was told that Grand Master G. M. Nye was dead, which caused the following remark:—

The Prophet's Remarks on G. M. Nye.

When Nye was here trying to pull me by the nose and trample on me, I enquired of the Lord if I was to be led by the nose and cuffed about by such a man. I received for answer, "Wait a minute." Nye is dead; and any man or Mason who attempts to ride me down and oppress me will run against the boss of Jehovah's buckler and will be quickly moved out of the way. Nye was a hypocritical Presbyterian preacher, and was known to have committed adultery in this city and violated his oath as a Master Mason. He started an opposition lodge on the hill, called the Nye Lodge; on which subject I said, they will do us all the injury they can; but let them go ahead, although it will result in a division of the lodge. Nye, fearing the penalty of the city ordinances on adultery, speedily fled from Nauvoo, and soon after died suddenly in Iowa.

At three-and-a-quarter p. m. rain fell in torrents, and wind blew strong from the north west. Several barns were blown down. So dark for fifteen minutes, could not see to write. Considerable hail fell. The creeks rose very high. The land covered with water.

Wednesday, *26*.—At home. Squally and cold weather.

Received of Wilford Woodruff a deed of north half of lot 4, block 12, on Kimball's second addition, valued at $50 on tithing.

Thursday, *27*.—At eleven a. m. sat in mayor's court, when Jonathan Ford proved a stolen horse to be his.

Visited at Brother Heber C. Kimball's with William Clayton.

The Nye Lodge was installed on the hill.

English state documents show an annual loss of £3,000,000 and 1,000 lives on the coast of Portsmouth, for want of harbors of refuge.

Friday, *28*.—At home.

Saturday, *29*.—Rode out to the prairie with my brothers, William and Samuel, and John Topham, and apportioned a lot between Sister Mullholland and John Scott.

Elders Brigham Young, Heber C. Kimball, Wilford Woodruff, George A. Smith, Joseph Young, and Peter Haws rode to Augusta, Iowa.

Sunday, *30*.—The brethren held a meeting at Augusta, and had a good time. About 200 Saints were present. Augusta is a flourishing little town. There are three saw mills and two flour mills, having excellent water privileges.

At ten a. m. a trial commenced before the First Presidency, Graham Coltrin *v*. Anson Matthews, being an appeal from the High Council on complaint—

Minutes of a High Council Meeting—Coltrin vs. Matthews.

First, for a failure in refusing to perform according to contract respecting the sale of a piece of land by him [Matthews] sold to me [Coltrin]. Second for transferring his [Matthews] property in a way to enable him to bid defiance to the result and force of law, and to evade the aforesaid contracts, thereby wronging me [Coltrin] out of my just claim to the same; and also for lying, etc.

Witnesses for plaintiff—Henry G. Sherwood, N. G. Blodgett, Zebedee Coltrin, Father Coltrin.

Witnesses for defense—Two affidavits of George Reads, Mrs. Matthews, Brother Browett, Samuel Thompson, Richard Slater.

Decision of the Council is that the charges are not sustained."

Monday, May, 1.—I rode out with Lucien Woodworth, and paid him £20 for the Nauvoo House, which I borrowed of William Allen.

I insert fac-similes of the six brass plates found near Kinderhook, in Pike county, Illinois, on April 23, by Mr. Robert Wiley and others, while excavating a large mound. They found a skeleton about six feet from the surface of the earth, which must have stood nine feet high. The plates were found on the breast of the skeleton and were covered on both sides with ancient characters.

Comment of the Prophet on the Kinderhook Plates.

I have translated a portion of them, and find they contain the history of the person with whom they were found. He was a descendant of Ham, through the loins of Pharaoh, king of Egypt, and that he received his kingdom from the Ruler of heaven and earth.

I quote the following editorial from the *Times and Seasons*:—

ANCIENT RECORDS.

Circumstances are daily transpiring which give additional testimony to the authenticity of the Book of Mormon. A few years ago, although supported by indubitable, unimpeachable testimony, it was looked upon in the same light by the world in general, and by the religious world in particular, as the expedition of Columbus to this continent was by the different courts that he visited, and laid his project before. The literati looked upon his expedition as wild and visionary, they suspected very much the integrity of his pretensions, and looked upon him—to say the least—as a fool, for entertaining such wild and visionary views. The royal courts aided by geographers, thought it was impossible that another continent should or could exist; and they were assisted in their views by the learned clergy, who, to put the matter beyond all doubt, stated that it was contrary to Scripture; that the apostles preached to all the world, and that as they did not come to America, it was impossible that there should be any such place. Thus at variance with the opinions of the great, in opposition to science and religion, he set sail, and actually came to America; it was no dream, no fiction; but a solid reality; and however unphilosophical and infidel the notion might be, men had to believe it; and it was soon found out that it would agree both with religion and philosophy.

So when the Book of Mormon first made its appearance among men, it was looked upon by many as a wild speculation, and that it was dangerous to the interest and happiness of the religious world. But when it was found to teach virtue, honesty, integrity, and pure religion, this objection was laid aside as being untenable.

We were then told that the inhabitants of this continent were and always had been a rude, barbarous race, uncouth, unlettered, and without civilization. But when they were told of the various relics that have been found indicative of civilization, intelligence, and learning,—when they were told of the wealth,architecture, and splendor of ancient Mexico,— when recent developments proved beyond a doubt that there are ancient ruins in Central America, which, in point of magnificence, beauty, strength, and architectural design, vie with any of the most splendid ruins on the Asiatic Continent,—when they could trace the fine delineations of the sculptor's chisel on the beautiful statue, the mysterious hieroglyphic, and the unknown character, they began to believe that a wise, powerful, intelligent, and scientific race had inhabited this continent; but still it was improbable—nay almost impossible, notwithstanding the testimony of history to the contrary, that anything like plates could have been used anciently, particularly among this people.

The following letter and certificate will perhaps have a tendency to convince the sceptical that such things have been used and that even the obnoxious Book of Mormon may be true. And as the people in Columbus' day were obliged to believe that there was such a place as America, so will the people in this day be obliged to believe, however reluctantly, that there may have been such plates as those from which the Book of Mormon was translated.

Mr. Smith has had those plates, what his opinion concerning them is, we have not yet ascertained. The gentleman that owns them has taken them away, or we should have given a fac-simile of the plates and characters in this number. We are informed however, that he purposes returning with them for translation, if so, we may be able yet to furnish our readers with it.

It will be seen by the annexed statement of the *Quincy Whig*, that there are more dreamers and money-diggers than Joseph Smith in the world; and the worthy editor is obliged to acknowledge that this circumstance will go a good way to prove the authenticity of the Book of Mormon. He further states that "if Joseph Smith can decipher the hieroglyphics on the plates, he will do more towards throwing light on the early history of this continent than any man living." We think that he has done that already in translating and publishing the Book of Mormon, and would advise the gentleman and all interested to read for themselves and understand. We have no doubt, however, but Mr. Smith will be able to translate them.

To the Editor of the Times and Seasons.

On the 16th of April last, a respectable merchant, by the name of Robert Wiley, commenced digging in a large mound near this place; he excavated to the depth of ten feet and came to rock. About that time the rain began to fall, and he abandoned the work.

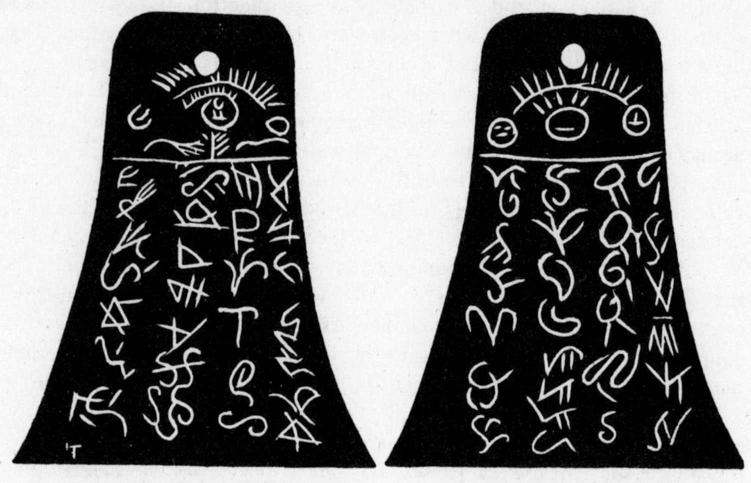

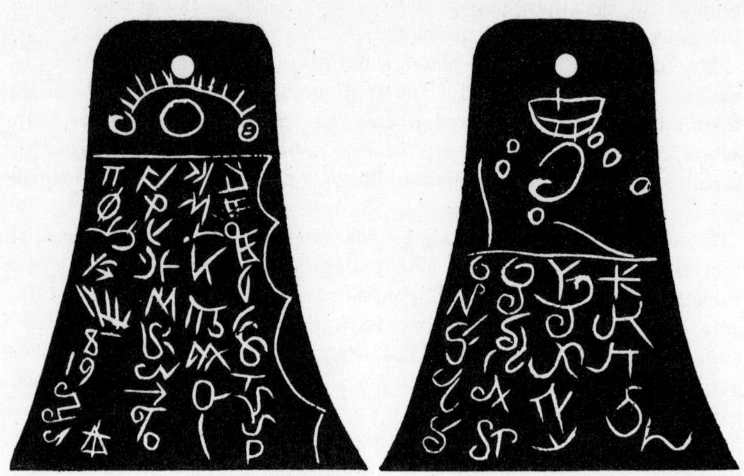

On the 23rd, he and quite a number of the citizens, with myself, repaired to the mound; and after making ample opening, we found plenty of rock, the most of which appeared as though it had been strongly burned; and after removing full two feet of said rock, we found plenty of charcoal and ashes; also human bones that appeared as though they had been burned; and near the encephalon a bundle was found that consisted of six plates of brass of a bell shape, each having a hole near the small end, and a ring through them all, and clasped with two clasps. The rings and clasps appeared to be iron very much oxydated. The

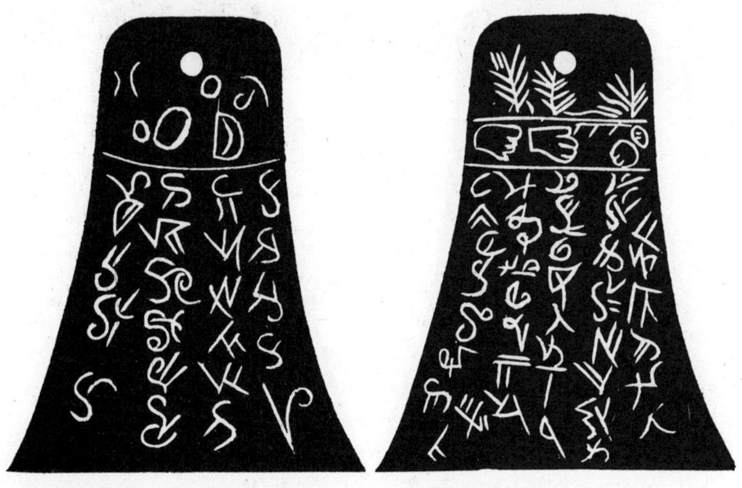

plates appeared first to be copper, and had the appearance of being covered with characters.

It was agreed by the company that I should cleanse the plates. Accordingly I took them to my house, washed them with soap and water and a woolen cloth; but, finding them not yet cleansed, I treated them with dilute sulphuric acid, which made them perfectly clean, on which it appeared that they were completely covered with hieroglyphics that none as yet have been able to read.

Wishing that the world might know the hidden things as fast as they come to light, I was induced to state the facts, hoping that you would give it an insertion in your excellent paper; for we all feel anxious to know the true meaning of the plates, and publishing the facts might lead to the true translation.

They were found, I judged, more than twelve feet below the surface of the top of the mound.

I am, most respectfully, a citizen of Kinderhook,

W. P. HARRIS, M. D.

We, the citizens of Kinderhook, whose names are annexed, do certify and declare that on the 23rd of April, 1843, while excavating a large mound in this vicinity, Mr. R. Wiley took from said mound *six brass plates* of a bell shape, covered with ancient characters. Said plates were very much oxydated. The bands and rings on said plates mouldered into dust on a slight pressure.

ROBERT WILEY,	W. LONGNECKER,	GEO. DECKENSON,
FAYETTE GRUBB,	W. FUGATE.	W. P. HARRIS,
J. R. SHARP,	G. W. F. WARD,	IRA S. CURTIS,

(From the *Quincy Whig.*)

SINGULAR DISCOVERY.—MATERIAL FOR ANOTHER MORMON BOOK.

A Mr. J. Roberts of Pike County, called upon us last Monday with a written description of a discovery which was recently made near Kinderhook, in that county. We have not room for his communication at length, and will give so much of a summary of it, as will enable the reader to form a pretty correct opinion of the discovery made.

It appeared that a young man by the name of Wiley, a resident in Kinderhook, dreamed three nights in succession, that in a certain mound in the vicinity, there were treasures concealed. Impressed with the strange occurrence of dreaming the same dream three nights in succession, he came to the conclusion to satisfy his mind by digging into the mound. For fear of being laughed at, if he made others acquainted with his design he went by himself and labored diligently one day in pursuit of the supposed treasure, by sinking a hole in the centre of a mound.

Finding it quite laborious, he invited others to assist him. A company of ten or twelve repaired to the mound and assisted in digging out the shaft commenced by Wiley. After penetrating the mound about eleven feet, they came to a bed of limestone that had been subjected to the action of fire. They removed the stones, which were small and easy to handle, to the depth of two feet more, when they found *six brass plates*, secured and fastened together by two iron wires, but which were so decayed that they readily crumbled to dust upon being handled.

The plates were so completely covered with rust as almost to obliterate the characters inscribed upon them; but, after undergoing a chemical process, the inscriptions were brought out plain and distinct.

There were six plates, four inches in length, one inch and three-quarters wide at the top, and two inches and three-quarters wide at the bottom, flaring out to points. There are four lines of characters or hieroglyphics on each. On one side of the plates are parallel lines running lengthways.

By whom these plates were deposited there must ever remain a secret, unless some one skilled in deciphering hieroglyphics may be found to unravel the mystery. Some pretend to say that Smith, the Mormon leader, has the ability to read them. If he has, he will confer a great favor on the public by removing the mystery which hangs over them. A person present when the plates were found remarked that it would go to prove the authenticity of the Book of Mormon, which it undoubtedly will.

In the place where these plates were deposited were also found human bones in the last stage of decomposition. There were but few bones found; and it is believed that it was but the burial-place of a person or family of distinction in ages long gone by, and that these plates contain the history of the times, or of a people that existed far, far beyond the memory of the present race. But we will not conjecture anything about this wonderful discovery, as it is one which the plates alone can reveal.

The plates above alluded to were exhibited in this city last week, and are now, we understand, in Nauvoo, subject to the inspection of the Mormon Prophet. The public curiosity is greatly excited; and if Smith can decipher the hieroglyphics on the plates, he will do more towards throwing light on the early history of this continent than any man now living.*

* It is proper here to call attention to the fact that the genuineness of this discovery of the Kinderhook plates is questioned by some anti-Mormon writers, among them Professor William A. Linn in his late work *The Story of Mormonism*. In which, after citing the fact that both John Hyde and T. B. H. Stenhouse—both anti-Mormon authors—accept the genuineness of the discovery of the Kinderhook plates, which led the first in his *Mormonism* to insist that "Smith did have plates of some kind," in connection with the putting forth of the Book of Mormon; and the second to say of the Kinderhook plates that they were "actually and unquestionably discovered by one Mr. R. Wiley"—he says:

"But the true story of the Kinderhook plates was disclosed by an affidavit made by W. Fugate of Mound Station, Brown county, Illinois, before Jay Brown, justice of the peace, on June 30, 1879. In this he stated that the plates were a humbug, gotten up by Robert Wiley, Bridge Whitton, and myself. Whitton (who was a blacksmith) cut the plates out of some pieces of copper; Wiley and I made the hieroglyphics by making impressions on beeswax and filling them with acid, old iron and lead, and bound them with a piece of hoop iron, covering them completely with the rust. He describes the burial of the plates and their digging up, among the spectators of the latter being two Mormon Elders, Marsh and Sharp. Sharp declared that the Lord had directed them to witness the digging. The plates were

Slavery was this day abolished in every part of the British dominions in India, under the administration of Lord Ellenborough.

Tuesday, 2.—Rode out in the forenoon. About three p. m., the *Maid of Iowa* arrived from St. Louis. I was on the bank of the river, awaiting the arrival of my wife, who returned with Lorin Walker.

Elders Brigham Young, Heber C. Kimball, Wilford Woodruff, George A. Smith, and Joseph Young returned from Augusta, Iowa.

John E. Page wrote me a letter, wanting to dispose of Church property and establish a printing press in Pittsburg, on which I directed the Twelve to send him to Liberia, or some other place, in order to save him.

About one p.m., the mate of the ship *Yorkshire* opened

borrowed and shown to Smith, and were finally given to one Professor McDowell of St. Louis, for his museum." (*The Story of the Mormons*, Linn, p. 87.)

Of this presentation of the matter it is only necessary to say that it is a little singular that Mr. Fugate alone out of the three said to be in collusion in perpetrating the fraud should disclose it, and that he should wait from 1843 to 1879—a period of thirty-six years—before doing so, when he and those said to be associated with him had such an excellent opportunity to expose the vain pretensions of the Prophet —if Fugate's tale be true—during his life time. For while the statement in the text of the Prophet's journal to the effect that the find was genuine, and that he had translated some of the characters and learned certain historical facts concerning the person with whose remains the plates were found, may not have been known at the time to the alleged conspiritors to deceive him still it is quite apparent that the editor of the *Times and Seasons*—John Taylor, the close personal friend of the Prophet—took the find seriously, and expressed implicit confidence in his editorial that the Prophet could give a translation of the plates. And this attitude the Church, continued to maintain; for in *The Prophet*, (a Mormon weekly periodical, published in New York) of the 15th of February, 1845, there was published a *fac-simile* of the Kinderhook plates, together with the *Times and Seasons* editorial and all the above matter of the text. How easy to have covered Joseph Smith and his followers with ridicule by proclaiming the hoax as soon as they accepted the Kinderdook plates as genuine! Why was it not done? The fact that Fugate's story was not told until thirty-six years after the event, and that he alone of all those who were connected with the event gives that version of it, is rather strong evidence that his story is the hoax, not the discovery of the plates, nor the engravings upon them.

"The plates," says Professor Linn, "were finally given to one 'Professor' Mc-Dowell of St. Louis, for his museum." This on the authority of *Wyl's Mormon Portraits*, (p. 207). And Professor Linn in a note adds: "The secretary of the Missouri Historical Society writes me that McDowell's museum disappeared some time ago, most of its contents being lost or stolen, and the fate of the Kinderhook plates cannot be ascertained." (*Story of the Mormons*, p. 87 and footnote.)

the Testament at the 27th chapter of Acts, and asked the passengers how they would feel to be shipwrecked like Paul? Elder Thomas Bullock replied instantly, "It is very likely we shall be shipwrecked; but the hull of this old vessel has got to carry us safe into New Orleans." The mate was then called away to hoist the fore-top-royal sail.

A Prophecy.

Between one and two next morning, when off Cape St. Antonio, Cuba, there was much vivid lightning, when a white squall caught the fore-top-royal sail, which careened the vessel, when the foremast, mainmast, and mizzenmast snapped asunder with an awful crash: the whole of the masts above, with the jib and spanker, and sixteen sails and studding poles, were carried overboard with a tremendous splash and surge, when the vessel righted. Daybreak, found the deck all in confusion and a complete wreck. During the day, hoisted a sail from the stump of the mainmast to the bow of the vessel, thus leaving nothing but the hull of the vessel to carry the Saints into New Orleans.

Wednesday, 3.—Called at the office and drank a glass of wine with Sister Jenetta Richards, made by her mother in England, and reviewed a portion of the conference minutes.

Two p. m., mayor's court, "City *versus* A. Gay," on complaint of William Law, for unbecoming language and refusing to leave the store when told to. Fined $5 and costs.

Directed a letter to be written to Gen. James Adams, of Springfield, to have him meet the *Maid of Iowa* on her return from St. Louis, and arrange with the proprietors to turn her into a Nauvoo ferry boat, which letter was written the same hour.

This day the first number of the *Nauvoo Neighbor* was issued by John Taylor and Wilford Woodruff, in place of the *Wasp*, which ceased; and I here insert the first editorial:—

Editorial from the Nauvoo Neighbor.

We now, according to promise, present our young friend before the world in his new dress and with his new name. As the last week has been one of the warm weeks in the spring, when vegetation springs forth and life and animation are given to the vegetable world, so our efforts to cultivate the plant of Intelligence, having been watered by industry, enlivened by perseverance, and warmed by the genial rays of patronage, have not been unsuccessful; for the young gentleman has grown in one short week to double his former size.

Relative to his dress, we have to apologize a little. As we did not live near a store, we could not get all the trimmings which we could have desired, to have made him pass so well with the *elite* in the fashionable world. However, among plain folks, he will now pass very well; and we soon expect to see him in a form that will suit the taste of the most fastidious.

Relative to the course that we shall pursue, we shall endeavor to cultivate a friendly feeling towards all, and not interfere with the rights of others, either politically or religiously. We shall advocate the cause of the innocent and oppressed, uphold the cause of right, sustain the principles of republicanism, and fly to the succor of the helpless and forlorn, pouring in oil and wine to their wounds, and acting in every way to all the human family in the capacity that our name imports—viz., that of a *Neighbor*.

We have had and may have to defend ourselves against the oppressions, persecutions, and innovations of men. And if this should be the case, we shall not shrink from the task, but shall fearlessly and unflinchingly defend our rights, sustaining that liberty which our glorious constitution guarantees to every American citizen, for which our fathers jeopardized their liberty, their lives, and their sacred honor.

Amidst the warring elements that are disturbing the world, we are glad to find so amiable and friendly a spirit manifested to us at the present time by the press; and we can assure them that, so long as they let us alone, we shall not interfere with them.

It has been our study to avoid contention, and we have never interfered with others until they have thrown down the gauntlet; and as we have not been up to the present the aggressors so we are determined for the future not to be the aggressors.

We have always endeavored to cultivate a spirit of friendship, amity, and peace with mankind. If we have not succeeded, the fault has not been with us. Rumor, with her ten thousand tongues, has always been busy circulating falsehood and misrepresentation concerning us; and men have frequently, in the absence of correct information, entertained unfavorable opinions concerning us, and have spoken as they thought: but when they have been better informed, they have regretted their course, and have seen that calumny has been like a viper in our path and has stung like an adder.

In regard to our political rights, our religion has frequently been made use of by political demagogues as a bugbear to deprive us of the free untrammelled rights of American citizens. This is a thing that we have always protested against, and we always shall, so long as that blood that fired the bosoms of our ancestors who fought, bled, and died, in defense of equal rights, flows through our veins.

Concerning religion we consider that all men have a right to worship Almighty God according to the dictates of their own conscience. And while we allow all men freely to enjoy this privilege untrammeled by us, we look upon all men that would abridge us or others in their religious rights as enemies to the constitution, recreant to the principles of republicanism; and whilst they render themselves despicable, they are striking a secret but deadly blow at the freedom of this great republic; and their withering influence, though unseen and unobserved by the many, is like a worm gnawing the very vitals of the tree of liberty. We shall always contend for our religious rights. In short, the liberty of the press, liberty of conscience and of worship, free discussion, sailors' rights, we shall always sustain.

Thursday, 4.—At four p. m., heard read a letter from James Arlington Bennett, showing that he was sick and could not attend the inspection of the Nauvoo Legion, according to his appointment.

Having received a letter from George W. Robinson in relation to his land difficulties, I went to Sidney Rigdon and procured a deed for Carlos Granger's farm, and settled that business.

Friday, 5.—Told the Temple committee that I had a right to take away any property I chose from the Temple office or store, and they had no right to stand in the way. It is the people that are to dictate me, and not the committee. All the property I have belongs to the Temple, and what I do is for the benefit of the Temple; and you have no authority only as you receive it from me.

Received the following:—

Letter of H. R. Hotchkiss to Joseph Smith—Property Titles.

NEW YORK, 7th April, 1843.

Joseph Smith, Esq.

DEAR SIR:—I received on Saturday last a letter from Mr. Catlin, notifying me that the equity of redemption in my Nauvoo property would be sold on the 12th instant, and asking me whether I wished it to be purchased for me. I suppose it is quite immaterial whether I or you hold the right of redeeming; for if it should again come into my possession, I wish it understood distinctly by them who have built upon it that I shall not attempt to take their buildings from them, but shall be ready at any time to give them a lease of their lots for a very long period, at a reasonable rent. My wish, as well as my interest, leads me to conciliate and make them my friends, instead of making them my enemies.

Your obedient servant,
H. R. HOTCHKISS.

Which I recorded in the City Record of Deeds:—

Hotchkiss Letter Recorded.

RECORDER'S OFFICE, May 5, 1843.

State of Illinois,
City of Nauvoo, } ss.

I, Joseph Smith, recorder in and for the said city of Nauvoo, Hancock county, and state aforesaid, do hereby certify that the within letter was duly recorded in Book A, page 140, and numbered 134.

JOSEPH SMITH, Recorder.

By WILLIAM CLAYTON, Clerk.

Saturday, 6.—In the morning, had an interview with a lecturer on Mesmerism and Phrenology. Objected to his performing in the city. Also had an interview with a Methodist preacher, and conversed about his God without body or parts.

At half-past nine a. m., I mounted with my staff, and with the band, and about a dozen ladies, led by Emma, and proceeded to the general parade-ground of the Nauvoo Legion, east of my farm on the prairie. The Legion looked well—better than on any former occasion, and they performed their evolutions in admirable style.

Legion Parade.

The officers did honor to the Legion. Many of them were equipped and armed *cap-a-pie*. The men were in good spirits. They had made great improvements both in uniform and discipline, and we felt proud to be associated with a body of men, which, in point of discipline, uniform, appearance, and a knowledge of military tactics, are the pride of Illinois, one of its strongest defenses, and a great bulwark of the western country.

In the course of my remarks on the prairie, I told the Legion that when we have petitioned those in power for assistance, they have always told us they had no power to help us. Damn such traitors! When they give me the power to protect the innocent, I will never say I can do nothing for their good: I will exercise that power, so help me God. At the close of the address, the Legion marched to the city and disbanded in Main Street, about two p.m., the day being windy and very cold.

There were two United States officers and General Swazey, of Iowa, present, who expressed great satisfaction at our appearance and evolutions.

In the evening, attended Mr. Vicker's performance of wire dancing, legerdemain, magic, etc.

A conference was held at Toulon, Stark county, Illinois: 5 branches, 17 elders, 3 priests, 4 teachers, 2 deacons, and 129 members were represented.

A branch has been recently organized at Lyons, Wayne county, New York, consisting of two elders, 1 priest, 1 teacher, and 22 members.

Sunday, 7.—In the forenoon I was visited by several gentlemen, concerning the plates that were dug out near Kinderhook.

The council of the First Presidency met.

Elder Brigham Young preached at La Harpe.

Monday, 8.—I called at the office at seven a. m., with a supersedeas to stay suit, Thompson *versus* Dixon.

John Scott was unwilling to give Sister Mulholland one-fourth of the lot as directed by me.

Steam Boat Excursion.

Tuesday, 9.—In company with my wife, mother, and my adult family, also Sidney Rigdon, Parley P. Pratt, John Taylor, Wilford Woodruff, and about one hundred gentlemen and ladies, went aboard the *Maid of Iowa*, started at ten minutes before eight a.m., from the Nauvoo dock, under a salute of cannon, having on board a fine band of music.

We had an excellent address from our esteemed friend, Parley P. Pratt. The band performed its part well. Much good humor and hilarity prevailed. The captain and officers on board did all they could to make us comfortable, and we had a very agreeable and pleasant trip.

We started with the intention of visiting Augusta; but, in consequence of the lowness of Shunk river, it was impracticable. We therefore altered our course to Burlington, touching at Fort Madison on our way up, and at Shokoquon on our return.

In consequence of the governor of Iowa having refused to withdraw a writ reported to have been issued on a demand from the executive of Missouri, on the same charge as that for which I had been discharged by Judge Pope, I dispensed with the pleasure of calling upon my friends in Burlington and Fort Madison. During our stay at those places, I kept myself concealed on the boat.

The *Maid of Iowa* did well. Her accomodations are good for the size of the boat, and she performed her trip in less time than we anticipated, and we returned home about eight p. m.

Wednesday, 10.—Directed Dr. Willard Richards never to let the court-room be occupied by any person until he received $2 in advance.

The blossoms on the apple and other trees appeared.

Took my brother William, Elders Jedediah M. Grant, Ebenezer Robinson and Horace K. Whitney in my carriage to the Upper Steam Boat Landing and back, They were intending to start on their missions, but no steamboat came.

A meeting of the Saints was held at Leechburgh, Pennsylvania, numbered 5 elders, 2 priests, 1 teacher, and 50 members.

Thursday, 11.—At six a. m., baptized Louisa Beeman, Sarah Alley, and others.

Eight a. m., went to see the new carriage made by Thomas Moore, which was ready for traveling. Emma went to Quincy in the new carriage. I rode out as far as the prairie.

Ten a. m., Brigham Young, Heber C. Kimball, Parley P. Pratt, Orson Pratt, Orson Hyde, Wilford Woodruff, George A. Smith, John Taylor, and Willard Richards assembled in council, and voted—

Mission Appointments

That Addison Pratt, Noah Rogers, Benjamin F. Grouard, and Knowlton F. Hanks go on a mission to the Pacific Isles; Captain Dan Jones prepare himself to take a mission to Wales; James Sloan go to Ireland; Reuben Hedlock, John Cairnes and Samuel James to England, and that Reuben Hedlock preside over the Church in Great Britain, and be assisted by Elders Hiram Clark and Thomas Ward; that Brother Cairnes go to Scotland, Lucius N. Scovil to England, under the direction of Brother Hedlock; and that Amos Fielding come immediately to Nauvoo, or be cut off from the Church. Also, that this quorum recommend George Walker to President Joseph Smith, as clerk of the Nauvoo House.

President Young stated that Lucien Woodworth had offered the use of his draft for the Nauvoo House, table, etc., if any one would copy it; but he had not time to comply with the request of the quorum to furnish a full draft.

Friday, 12.—Purchased half of the steamer *Maid of Iowa*, from Moffatt; and Captain Dan Jones commenced running her between Nauvoo and Montrose as a ferry-boat.

At sunrise, Bishop George Miller arrived with a raft of 50,000 feet of pine lumber for the Temple and Nauvoo House, from the pinery on Black River, Wisconsin, where the snow was about 2½ feet deep in the winter.

In the council of the Twelve it was agreed to visit Lima, La Harpe, and Ramus, and hold conferences concerning the Nauvoo House.

CHAPTER XX.

IMPORTANT DOCTRINAL ITEMS: SALVATION THROUGH KNOWLEDGE — AGED MEN IN COUNCILS — IMPORTANCE OF THE DOCTRINE OF THE ETERNITY OF THE MARRIAGE COVENANT —THE NATURE OF MATTER. THE PROPHECY ON THE HEAD OF STEPHEN A. DOUGLAS—THE WORK AMONG THE SCANDINAVIANS IN ILLINOIS.

Saturday, May 13, 1843.—I rode to Yelrome, in company with Brothers Wilford Woodruff and George A. Smith, and tarried for the night with Father Morley. Brothers Woodruff and Smith slept at Brother Durfee's. Brother Brigham Young went to La Harpe, and Brothers Heber C. Kimball and Orson Pratt to Ramus.

Sunday, 14.—Meeting at Yelrome, where I preached. [The following is a synopsis, reported by Elder Woodruff.]

Salvation Through Knowledge.

It is not wisdom that we should have all knowledge at once presented before us; but that we should have a little at a time; then we can comprehend it. President Smith then read the 2nd Epistle of Peter, 1st chapter, 16th to last verses, and dwelt upon the 19th verse with some remarks.

Add to your faith knowledge, &c. The principle of knowledge is the principle of salvation. This principle can be comprehended by the faithful and diligent; and every one that does not obtain knowledge sufficient to be saved will be condemned. The principle of salvation is given us through the knowledge of Jesus Christ.

Salvation is nothing more nor less than to triumph over all our enemies and put them under our feet. And when we have power to put all enemies under our feet in this world, and a knowledge to triumph over all evil spirits in the world to come, then we are saved, as in the case of Jesus, who was to reign until He had put all enemies under His feet, and the last enemy was death.*

Perhaps there are principles here that few men have thought of. No person can have this salvation except through a tabernacle.

Now, in this world, mankind are naturally selfish, ambitious and striving to excel one above another; yet some are willing to build up others as well as themselves. So in the other world there are a variety of spirits. Some seek to excel. And this was the case with Lucifer when he fell. He sought for things which were unlawful. Hence he was sent down, and it is said he drew many away with him; and the greatness of his punishment is that he shall not have a tabernacle. This is his punishment. So the devil, thinking to thwart the decree of God, by going up and down in the earth, seeking whom he may destroy—any person that he can find that will yield to him, he will bind him, and take possession of the body and reign there, glorying in it mightily, not caring that he had got merely a stolen body; and by-and-by some one having authority will come along and cast him out and restore the tabernacle to its rightful owner. The devil steals a tabernacle because he has not one of his own: but if he steals one, he is always liable to be turned out of doors.

Now, there is some grand secret here, and keys to unlock the subject. Notwithstanding the apostle exhorts them to add to their faith, virtue, knowledge, temperance, &c., yet he exhorts them to make their calling and election sure. And though they had heard an audible voice from heaven bearing testimony that Jesus was the Son of God, yet he says we have a more sure word of prophecy, whereunto ye do well that ye take heed as unto a light shining in a dark place. Now, wherein could they have a more sure word of prophecy than to hear the voice of God saying, This is my beloved Son, &c.

Now for the secret and grand key. Though they might hear the voice of God and know that Jesus was the Son of God, this would be no evidence that their election and calling was made sure, that they had part with Christ, and were joint heirs with Him. They then would want that more sure word of prophecy, that they were sealed in the heavens and had the promise of eternal life in the kingdom of God. Then, having this promise sealed unto them, it was an anchor to the soul, sure and steadfast. Though the thunders might roll and lightnings flash, and earthquakes bellow, and war gather thick around, yet this hope and knowledge would support the soul in every hour of trial, trouble

* It is evident from this remark, "the last enemy was death," that the prophet in saying that "salvation is * * * to triumph over all our enemies," does not allude alone, or even chiefly, to personal "enemies;" but to evil inclinations, weaknesses, passions, sickness and death, as well.

and tribulation. Then knowledge through our Lord and Savior Jesus Christ is the grand key that unlocks the glories and mysteries of the kingdom of heaven.

Compare this principle once with Christendom at the present day, and where are they, with all their boasted religion, piety and sacredness while at the same time they are crying out against prophets, apostles, angels, revelations, prophesying and visions, &c. Why, they are just ripening for the damnation of hell. They will be damned, for they reject the most glorious principle of the Gospel of Jesus Christ and treat with disdain and trample under foot the key that unlocks the heavens and puts in our possession the glories of the celestial world. Yes, I say, such will be damned, with all their professed godliness. Then I would exhort you to go on and continue to call upon God until you make your calling and election sure for yourselves, by obtaining this more sure word of prophecy, and wait patiently for the promise until you obtain it, &c.

Elders George A. Smith and Wilford Woodruff followed him with a few remarks, and meeting closed for one hour. When we met again, Wilford Woodruff opened meeting and spoke upon revelation and obeying the commandments by building the Nauvoo House, and was followed by George A. Smith upon the same subject. Elder Lorenzo Snow then spoke somewhat at length concerning his mission to England, which was interesting.

After meeting, we rode to Lima, and took supper with Calvin Beebe; and while we were conversing with Brother Joseph and Brother Isaac Morley, Brother Joseph made the following remarks:

The Value of Aged Men in Counsel.

The way to get along in any important matter is to gather unto yourselves wise men, experienced and aged men, to assist in council in all times of trouble. Handsome men are not apt to be wise and strong-minded men; but the strength of a strong-minded man will generally create coarse features, like the rough, strong bough of the oak. You will always discover in the first glance of a man, in the outlines of his features something of his mind.

Excitement has almost become the essence of my life. When that dies away, I feel almost lost. When a man is reined up continually by excitement, he becomes strong and gains power and knowledge; but when he relaxes for a season, he loses much of his power and knowledge. But in all matters, temporal or spiritual, preaching the Gospel of Jesus Christ, or in leading an army to battle, victory almost entirely depends upon good order and moderation. In going to battle, move slowly, dress up into line; and though your enemy rush upon you with fury, meet them slowly but firmly. Let not confusion or terror seize upon you, but meet them firmly and strike a heavy blow and conquer. A man can bear a heavy burthen by practice and continuing to increase it. The inhabitants of this continent anciently were so constituted, and were so determined and persevering, either in righteousness or wickedness, that God visited them immediately either with great judgments or blessings. But the present generation, if they were going to battle, if they got any assistance from God, they would have to obtain it by faith.

President Young preached at La Harpe.

Almon W. Babbitt preached all the afternoon, and prevented Elders Kimball and Orson Pratt from giving instructions regarding their mission to Ramus.

The wind blew terribly from the southwest all day.

A naval action took place between the Texan and Mexican fleets at Campeachy.

Edward Brazier, aged 18, was drowned in the Mississippi river, by the upsetting of a skiff. Samuel Kearns was preserved from a similar fate by Captain Dan Jones.

Monday, 15.—Emma having arrived at Yelrome, last night from Quincy, with the carriage, we rode home together. On our way, we stopped a short time at Brother Perry's. Brothers George A. Smith and Wilford Woodruff rode in my buggy. I was asked if the horse would stand without tying. I answered, "Yes: but never trust property to the mercy or judgment of a horse."

[The following under this date is from the journal of George A. Smith:]

The Love of the Prophet for George A. Smith.

At noon, stopped at the house of Mr. McMahon, a notorious anti-Mormon, at Green Plains, and waited some time for Mac to come in. Joseph and myself spent this time in conversation on the grass-plot south of the house. Joseph asked my opinion of W. W. Phelps as an editor. I told him that I considered Phelps the sixth part of an editor, and that was the satirist. When it came to the cool direction necessarily intrusted to an editor in the control of public opinion—the soothing of enmity, he was deficient, and would always make more enemies than friends; but for my part, if I were able, I would be willing to pay Phelps for editing a paper, providing no body else should have the privilege of reading it but myself. Joseph laughed heartily—said I had the thing just right. Said he, "Brother Phelps makes such a severe use of language as to make enemies all the time."

At the close of the conversation, Joseph wrapped his arms around me, and squeezed me to his bosom and said, "George A., I love you as I do my own life." I felt so affected, I could hardly speak, but replied, "I hope, Brother Joseph, that my whole life and actions will ever prove my feelings, and the depth of my affection towards you."

A great hailstorm in Gettysburg, Penn. The stones were from six to eight inches in circumference. Much damage done.

Visit of the Prophet to Ramus.

Tuesday, 16.—At eleven o'clock, with George Miller, William Clayton, Eliza and Lydia Partridge and J. M. Smith, I started for Carthage, where we tarried about half-an-hour conversing with different individuals, when we started for Ramus; arrived about half-past three, p. m., and stayed at William G. Perkins for the evening; then went to Benjamin F. Johnson's with William Clayton to sleep. Before retiring, I gave Brother and Sister Johnson some instructions on the priesthood; and putting my hand on the knee of William Clayton, I said:

Remarks of the Prophet at Ramus—Lives that are Hid with God in Christ —Importance of the Eternity of the Marriage Covenant.

Your life is hid with Christ in God, and so are many others. Nothing but the unpardonable sin can prevent you from inheriting eternal life for you are sealed up by the power of the Priesthood unto eternal life, having taken the step necessary for that purpose

Except a man and his wife enter into an everlasting covenant and be married for eternity, while in this probation, by the power and authority of the Holy Priesthood, they will cease to increase when they die; that is, they will not have any children after the resurrection. But those who are married by the power and authority of the priesthood in this life, and continue without committing the sin against the Holy Ghost, will continue to increase and have children in the celestial glory. The unpardonable sin is to shed innocent blood,or be accessory thereto. All other sins will be visited with judgment in the flesh, and the spirit being delivered to the buffetings of Satan until the day of the Lord Jesus.

The way I know in whom to confide—God tells me in whom I may place confidence.

In the celestial glory there are three heavens or degrees; and in order to obtain the highest, a man must enter into this order of the priesthood, [meaning the new and everlasting covenant of marriage;] and if he does not, he cannot obtain it. He may enter into the other, but that is the end of his kingdom: he cannot have an increase."*

The Twelve met in the office to see Mr. Brown, but he did not appear; and they voted that John E. Page be requested to repair immediately to Cincinnati and preach till they arrive.

Wednesday, 17.—Partook of breakfast at Brother Perkins'; after which we took a pleasure ride through Fountain Green.

At ten a. m. preached from 2nd Peter, 1st chapter and showed that knowledge is power; and the man who has the most knowledge has the greatest power.

Items of Doctrine by the Prophet.

Salvation means a man's being placed beyond the power of all his enemies.

The more sure word of prophecy means a man's knowing that he is sealed up into eternal life by revelation and the spirit of prophecy, through the power of the holy priesthood. It is impossible for a man to be saved in ignorance.†

Paul saw the third heavens, and I more. Peter penned the most sublime language of any of the apostles.

In the afternoon attended council, and afterwards rode with Benjamin F. Johnson's family.

In the evening went to hear a Methodist preacher lecture. After he got through, offered some corrections as follows:

Items of Doctrine by the Prophet.

The 7th verse of 2nd chapter of Genesis ought to read—God breathed

* The last paragraph is found in the Doctrine and Covenants, section 131: 1-4.

† This paragraph is also included in the Doctrine and Covenants, section 131: 5 6.

into Adam his spirit [i. e. Adam's spirit]* or breath of life; but when the word "rauch" applies to Eve, it should be translated lives.

Speaking of eternal duration of matter, I said:

There is no such thing as immaterial matter. All spirit is matter, but is more fine or pure, and can only be discerned by purer eyes. We cannot see it, but when our bodies are purified, we shall see that it is all matter.

The priest seemed pleased with the correction, and stated his intention to visit Nauvoo.

New York Conference.

A conference was held in the Columbia Hall, Grand Street, New York, where fifteen branches, six high priests, thirty-six elders, nineteen priests, sixteen teachers, five deacons, and three hundred and eighty-seven members were represented. Forty-nine have been baptized since last conference; many have removed to Nauvoo; and twenty-eight have been excommunicated. Four elders and one priest were ordained.

Thursday, 18.—We left Macedonia about half past eight a. m., and arrived at Carthage at ten.

[The following brief account of the prophet's visit with Judge Douglas while at Carthage is from the journal of William Clayton, who was present:]

The Great Prophecy on the Head of Stephen A. Douglas.

Dined with Judge Stephen A. Douglas, who is presiding at court. After dinner Judge Douglas requested President Joseph to give him a history of the Missouri persecution, which he did in a very minute manner, for about three hours. He also gave a relation of his journey to Washington city, and his application in behalf of the Saints to Mr. Van Buren, the President of the United States, for redress and Mr. Van Buren's pusillanimous reply, "Gentlemen, your cause is just, but I can do nothing for you;" and the cold, unfeeling manner in which he was treated by most of the senators and representatives in relation to the subject, Clay saying, "You had better go to Oregon," and Calhoun shaking his head solemnly, saying, "It's a nice question—a critical question, but it will not do to agitate it."

The judge listened with the greatest attention and spoke warmly in

* Doctrine and Covenants, section 131: 7-8. The interpretation implied in the words in brackets is justified by the following from the Book of Abraham: "And the Gods formed man from the dust of the ground, and took his spirit (that is, the man's spirit) and put it into him, and breathed into his nostrils the breath of life, and man became a living soul." Chap. v: 7, 8.

depreciation of the conduct of Governor Boggs and the authorities of Missouri, who had taken part in the extermination, and said that any people that would do as the mobs of Missouri had done ought to be brought to judgment: they ought to be punished.

President Smith, in concluding his remarks, said that if the government, which received into its coffers the money of citizens for its public lands, while its officials are rolling in luxury at the expense of its public treasury, cannot protect such citizens in their lives and property, it is an old granny anyhow; and I prophesy in the name of the Lord God of Israel, unless the United States redress the wrongs committed upon the Saints in the state of Missouri and punish the crimes committed by her officers that in a few years the government will be utterly overthrown and wasted, and there will not be so much as a potsherd left, for their wickedness in permitting the murder of men, women and children, and the wholesale plunder and extermination of thousands of her citizens to go unpunished, thereby perpetrating a foul and corroding blot upon the fair fame of this great republic, the very thought of which would have caused the high-minded and patriotic framers of the Constitution of the United States to hide their faces with shame. Judge, you will aspire to the presidency of the United States; and if ever you turn your hand against me or the Latter-day Saints,you will feel the weight of the hand of Almighty upon you; and you will live to see and know that I have testified the truth to you; for the conversation of this day will stick to you through life.

He [Judge Douglas] appeared very friendly, and acknowledged the truth and propriety of President Smith's remarks.*

We then rode home, where we arrived about half-past five p. m., and found my family all well.

Mr. Joseph H. Jackson, who professed to be a Catholic priest, was at my house awaiting my arrival.

At six p. m., I called at my office for Arlington Bennett's letter.

Friday, *19*.—I borrowed of Orson Hyde fifty dollars, which I paid to Mr. Eric Rhodes, and which he is either to repay in cash or let me have lumber.

I rode out with Mr. Jackson in the afternoon.

Told Brother Phelps a dream that the history must go ahead before anything else.

Elder George P. Dykes writes:

* See note at end of chapter.

The Work Among the Scandinavians of Illinois.

One year since, I visited a settlement of Norwegians in La Salle county, Illinois, and baptized five, and ordained one elder, when I left them for about one month; then returned and organized the branch, and called it the La Salle Branch of the Church of Jesus Christ of Latter-day Saints, and ordained Brother Gudmund Haugaas an elder—a man of strong mind and well skilled in the scriptures. He can preach in Norway, Sweden and Demark, having an understanding of their languages.

I returned to Nauvoo, and in a few days I was appointed by the special conference in August to labor in Illinois. I traveled through eighteen different counties, baptized six in Perry county, and returned home in December.

In January I left again and went to St. Clair county, where I was joined by Brother Henry B. Jacobs, who baptized twelve; and I baptized a German after he left.

I preached in Chester, Sparta and Bellville. From thence returned home, and again visited Ottawa, La Salle county. Spent two weeks, and baptized seven. I found the Church there in good spirits and in the enjoyment of the spiritual gifts.

The La Salle branch now numbers fifty-eight in good standing. Elder Ole Hoier was chosen to preside over them. He is well worthy of the office.

Elder Gudmund Haugaas and Brother J. R. Anderson visited the Norwegian settlement in Lee county, Iowa, in January last. Spent three weeks, baptized ten, ordained one priest, and left them and went home to La Salle county.

From thence Brothers Haugaas and Hoier visited a large body from Norway in Wisconsin Territory, and have laid the foundation of a great work, to all appearance. There are now fifty-seven members of the Church from Norway; and the time is not far distant when the saying of Micah iv, 2 will he fulfilled.

NOTE.

The Prophet Joseph's Prediction Respecting Stephen A. Douglas.

The prediction concerning Stephen A. Douglas in this chapter, is one of the most remarkable prophecies either in ancient or modern times. It was impossible for any merely human sagacity to foresee the events predicted. Stephen A. Douglas was a bright, but comparatively an unknown man, nationally, at the time of the interview, May, 1843, and but thirty years of age. It is a matter of history that Stephen A. Douglas did, however, aspire to the presidency of the United States, and was nominated for that office by the Democratic convention held in Charleston, South Carolina, on the 23rd of June, 1860.

When in the convention he was declared the regular nominee of the Democratic party, "the whole body rose to its feet, hats were waved in the air, and many tossed aloft; shouts, screams and yells, and every boisterous mode of expressing approbation and unanimity, were resorted to."

When Mr. Douglas aspired to the presidency, no man in the history of American politics had more reason to hope for success. The political party of which he was the recognized leader, in the preceding presidential election had polled one hundred and seventy-four electoral votes as against one hundred and twenty-two cast for the other two parties which opposed it; and a popular vote of 1,838,169 as against 1,215,789 votes for the two parties opposing. It is a matter of history, however, that the Democratic party in the election of 1860 was badly divided; and factions of it put candidates into the field with the following results: Mr. Abraham Lincoln, candidate for the Republican party, was triumphantly elected. He received 180 electoral votes; Mr. Breckinridge 72; Mr. Bell 39; and Mr. Douglas 12. "By a plurality count of the popular vote, Mr. Lincoln carried 18 states; Mr. Breckinridge 11; Mr. Bell 3: and Mr. Douglas but one!" Twenty days less than one year after his nomination by the Charleston convention, while yet in the prime of manhood—forty-eight years of age,—Mr. Douglas died at his home in Chicago, a disappointed, not to say heart-broken man.

Let us now search out the cause of his failure. Fourteen years after the interview containing the prophecy recorded in this chapter, and about one year after the prophecy had been published in the *Deseret News*, Mr. Douglas was called upon to deliver a speech in Springfield, the capital of Illinois. His speech was delivered on the 12th of June, 1857, and published in the *Missouri Republican* of June 18, 1857. It was a time of excitement throughout the country concerning the Mormon Church in Utah. Falsehoods upon the posting winds seemed to have filled the air with the most outrageous calumny. Crimes, the most repulsive—murders, robberies, rebellion and high treason—were falsely charged against its leaders. It was well known that Mr. Douglas had been on terms of intimate friendship with the Prophet Joseph Smith; and was well acquainted with the other Church leaders. He was therefore looked upon as one competent to speak upon the "Mormon question," and was invited to do so in the speech to which reference is here made. Mr. Douglas responded to the request. He grouped the charges against the Mormons, then passing current, in the following manner:

"First, that nine-tenths of the inhabitants are aliens by birth who have refused to become naturalized, or to take the oath of allegiance, or do any other act recognizing the goverment of the United States as the paramount authority in that territority [Utah];

"Second, that the inhabitants, whether native or alien born, known as Mormons (and they constitutute the whole people of the territory) are bound by horrible oaths and terrible penalties, to recognize and maintain the authority of Brigham Young, and the government of which he is head, as paramount to that of the United States, in civil as well as religious affairs; and they will in due time, and under the direction of their leaders, use all the means in their power to subvert the government of the United States, and resist its authority.

"Third, that the Mormon government, with Brigham Young at its head, is now forming alliance with Indian tribes in Utah and adjoining territories—stimulating the Indians to acts of hostility and organizing bands of his own followers under the name of Danites or destroying angels, to prosecute a system of robbery and murders upon American citizens who support the authority of the United States, and denounce the infamous and disgusting practices and institutions of the Mormon government."

Mr. Douglas based his remarks upon these rumors against the Saints, in the course of which he said:

"Let us have these facts in an official shape before the president and Congress, and the country will learn that in the performance of the high and solemn duty devolving upon the executive and Congress, there will be no vacillating or hesitating policy. It will be as prompt as the peal that follows the flash—as stern and unyielding as death. Should such a state of things actually exist as we are led to infer from the reports—and such information comes in an official shape—the knife must be applied to this pestiferous, disgusting cancer which is gnawing into the very vitals of the body politic. It must be cut out by the roots, and seared over by the red hot iron of stern, unflinching law. * * * Should all efforts fail to bring them (the Mormons) to a sense of their duty, there is but one remedy left. Repeal the organic law of the territory, on the ground that they are alien enemies and outlaws, unfit to be citizens of a territory, much less ever to become citizens of one of the free and independent states of this confederacy. To protect them further in their treasonable, disgusting and bestial practices would be a disgrace to the country—a disgrace to humanity—a disgrace to civilization, and a disgrace to the spirit of the age. Blot it out of the organized territories of the United States. What then? It will be regulated by the law of 1790, which has exclusive and sole jurisdiction over all the territory not incorporated under any organic or special law. By provisions of this law, all crimes and misdemeanors, committed on its soil can be tried before the legal authorities of any state or territory to which the offenders shall first be brought to trial and punished. Under that law persons have been arrested in Kansas, Nebraska and other territories, prior to their organization as territories, and hanged for their crimes. The law of 1790 has sole and exclusive jurisdiction where no other law of a local character exists, and by repealing the organic law of Utah, you give to the general government of the United States the whole and sole jurisdiction over the territory."

The speech of Mr. Douglas was of great interest and importance to the people or Utah at that juncture. Mr. Douglas had it in his power to do them great good. Because of his personal acquaintance with Joseph Smith and the great body of the Mormon people then in Utah, as well as their leaders (for he had known both leaders and people in Illinois, and those whom he had known in Illinois constituted the great bulk of the people in Utah, when he delivered the Springfield speech), he knew that the reports carried to the East by vicious and corrupt men were not true. He knew that these reports in the main were but a rehash of the old exploded charges made against Joseph Smith and his followers in Missouri; and he knew them to be false by many evidences furnished him by Joseph Smith in the interview of the 18th of May, 1843, and by the Mormon people at sundry times during his association with them at Nauvoo. He had an opportunity to befriend the innocent, to refute the calumny cast upon a virtuous community; to speak a word in behalf of the oppressed; but the demagogue triumphed over the statesman, the politician, over the humanitarian; and to avoid the popular censure which he feared befriending the Mormon people would bring to him, he turned his hand against them with the result that he did not destroy them but sealed his own doom—in fulfillment of the words of the prophet, he felt the weight of the hand of the Almighty upon him.

There is, and can be no question about the prophecy preceding the event. The prophecy was first published in the *Deseret News* of September 24, 1856. It was afterwards published in England in the *Millennial Star*, February, 1859. The publication in the *Deseret News* preceding Douglas' Springfield speech, mentioned above, (June, 1857) by about one year, and about four years before Douglas was nominated for the presidency by the Charleston Democratic convention.

Moreover, a lengthy review of Mr. Douglas' speech was published in the editorial columns of the *Deseret News* in the issue of that paper for September 2nd,

1857, of which the following is the closing paragraph addressed directly to Mr. Douglas:

"In your last paragraph [of the Springfield speech] you say, 'I have thus presented to you plainly and fairly my views of the Utah question;' with at least equal plainness and with far more fairness have your views now been commented upon. And inasmuch as you were well acquainted with Joseph Smith, and this people, also with the character of our maligners, and did know their allegations were false, but must bark with the dogs who were snapping at our heels, to let them know that you were a dog with them; and also that you may have a testimony of the truth of the assertion that you did know Joseph and his people and the character of their enemies (and neither class have changed, only as the Saints have grown better and their enemies worse); and also that you may thoroughly understand that you have voluntarily, knowingly and of choice sealed your damnation, and by your own chosen course have closed your chance for the presidential chair, through disobeying the counsel of Joseph which you formerly sought and prospered by following, and that you in common with us, may testify to all the world that Joseph was a true prophet, the following extract from the History of Joseph Smith is again printed for your benefit, and is kindly recommended to your careful perusal and most candid consideration."

Then follows the interview between Joseph Smith and Mr. Douglas as recorded in the journal of William Clayton, as published in the *News* a year before Mr. Douglas' Springfield speech, and as now given in this chapter of the HISTORY OF THE CHURCH.

This *News* editorial boldly accepted the challenge of Mr. Douglas. He raised his hand against the followers of Joseph Smith, despite the warning of the prophet; and they in the chief organ of the Church, reproduced the prophecy and told Mr. Douglas that he had "sealed his damnation and closed his chance for the presidential chair" through disobeying the counsel of the prophet. The presidential election of 1860, and the death of Mr. Douglas in the prime of life, the year following, tells the rest.

CHAPTER XXI.

DEFINITION OF THE WORD "MORMON"—DISCOURSE ON MAKING "CALLING" AND "ELECTION" SURE—MISSION TO THE SOCIETY ISLANDS OPENED—CHARACTER SKETCH OF THE PROPHET, "BOSTON BEE"—TRIAL OF BENJAMIN WINCHESTER.

Saturday, May 20, 1843.—Received of Ezra Oakley a certificate of deposit in the Fulton Bank, New York, value five hundred dollars, and gave receipt payable in lands or money ten days from date.

At court room, and adjourned the case of Samuel Fuller.

Corrected and sent to the *Times and Seasons* the following:

The Prophet's Definition of the Word "Mormon."

Editor of the Times and Seasons:

SIR:—Through the medium of your paper I wish to correct an error among men that profess to be learned, liberal and wise; and I do it the more cheerfully because I hope sober-thinking and sound-reasoning people will sooner listen to the voice of truth than be led astray by the vain pretensions of the self-wise.

The error I speak of is the definition of the word "Mormon." It has been stated that this word was derived from the Greek word *mormo*. This is not the case. There was no Greek or Latin upon the plates from which I, through the grace of the Lord, translated the Book of Mormon. Let the language of the book speak for itself.

On the 523rd page of the fourth edition, it reads: "And now, behold we have written this record according to our knowledge in the characters which are called among us the Reformed Egyptian, being handed down and altered by us, according to our manner of speech; and if our plates had been sufficiently large, we should have written in Hebrew; but the Hebrew hath been altered by us also; and if we could have written in Hebrew, behold, ye would have had no imperfection in our record. But the Lord knoweth the things which we have written, and also that none other people knoweth our language; therefore He hath prepared means for the interpretation thereof."

Here, then, the subject is put to silence; for "none other people knoweth our language;" therefore the Lord, and not man, had to interpret, after the people were all dead. And, as Paul said, "The world by wisdom know not God;" so the world by speculation are destitute of revelation; and as God in His superior wisdom has always given His Saints, wherever he had any on the earth, the same spirit, and that spirit, as John says, is the true spirit of prophecy, which is the testimony of Jesus. I may safely say that the word "Mormon" stands independent of the wisdom and learning of this generation. * * * *

The word Mormon, means literally, more good.

Yours,

JOSEPH SMITH.

Mr. Joseph H. Jackson representing himself as being out of employment and destitute of funds, he desired I would employ him and relieve his necessities. I took compassion and employed him as a clerk to sell lands, so as to give him a chance in the world.

Sunday, 21. At half-past ten a. m. I arrived at the Temple, and had to press my way throught the crowd in the aisles to get to the stand, when I remarked that there were some people who thought it a terrible thing that anybody should exercise a little power. I thought it a pity that anybody should give occasion to have power exercised, and requested the people to keep out of the aisles; for if they did not, I might some time run up and down and hit some of them; and called on two constables to keep the aisles clear.

The Prophet's Reproof of the People.

After singing and prayer, I read 1st chapter of 2nd Epistle of Peter, and preached thereon. [The following synopsis was written by Dr. Willard Richards.]

The Prophet's Discourse from II Peter, First Chapter—Reproof of Self-Righteousness.

I do not know when I shall have the privilege of speaking in a house large enough to convene the people. I find my lungs are failing with continual preaching in the open air to large assemblies.

I do not think there have been many good men on the earth since the days of Adam; but there was one good man and his name was Jesus. Many persons think a prophet must be a great deal better than anybody else. Suppose I would condescend—yes, I will call it condescend, to be a great deal better than any of you, I would be raised up to the highest heaven; and who should I have to accompany me?

I love that man better who swears a stream as long as my arm yet deals justice to his neighbors and mercifully deals his substance to the poor, than the long, smooth-faced hypocrite.

I do not want you to think that I am very righteous, for I am not. God judges men according to the use they make of the light which He gives them.

"We have a more sure word of prophecy, whereunto you do well to take heed, as unto a light that shineth in a dark place. We were eye witnesses of his majesty and heard the voice of his excellent glory." And what could be more sure? When He was transfigured on the mount, what could be more sure to them? Divines have been quarreling for ages about the meaning of this.

The Prophet's Characterization of Himself.

I am like a huge, rough stone rolling down from a high mountain; and the only polishing I get is when some corner gets rubbed off by coming in contact with something else, striking with accelerated force against religious bigotry, priestcraft, lawyer-craft, doctor-craft, lying editors, suborned judges and jurors, and the authority of perjured executives, backed by mobs, blasphemers, licentious and corrupt men and women—all hell knocking off a corner here and a corner there. Thus I will become a smooth and polished shaft in the quiver of the Almighty, who will give me dominion over all and every one of them, when their refuge of lies shall fail, and their hiding place shall be destroyed, while these smooth-polished stones with which I come in contact become marred.

There are three grand secrets lying in this chapter, [II Peter i.] which no man can dig out, unless by the light of revelation, and which unlocks the whole chapter as the things that are written are only hints of things which existed in the prophet's mind, which are not written concerning eternal glory.

I am going to take up this subject by virtue of the knowledge of God in me, which I have received from heaven. The opinions of men, so far as I am concerned, are to me as the crackling of thorns under the pot, or the whistling of the wind. I break the ground; I lead the way like Columbus when he was invited to a banquet, where he was assigned the most honorable place at the table, and served with the ceremonials which were observed towards sovereigns. A shallow courtier present, who was meanly jealous of him, abruptly asked him whether he thought that in case he had not discovered the Indies, there were not other men in Spain who would have been capable of the enterprise? Columbus made no reply, but took an egg and invited the company to make it stand on end. They all attempted it, but in vain; whereupon he struck it upon the table so as to break one end, and left it standing on the broken part, illustrating that when he had once shown the way to the new world nothing was easier than to follow it.

Paul ascended into the third heavens, and he could understand the three principal rounds of Jacob's ladder—the telestial, the terrestrial, and the celestial glories or kingdoms, where Paul saw and heard things which were not lawful for him to utter. I could explain a hundred fold more than I ever have of the glories of the kingdoms manifested to me in the vision, were I permitted, and were the people prepared to receive them.

The Lord deals with this people as a tender parent with a child, communicating light and intelligence and the knowledge of his ways as they can bear it. The inhabitants of the earth are asleep: they know not the day of their visitation. The Lord hath set the bow in the cloud for a sign that while it shall be seen, seed time and harvest, summer and winter shall not fail; but when it shall disappear, woe to that generation, for behold the end cometh quickly.

Calling and Election to be Made Sure.

Contend earnestly for the like precious faith with the Apostle Peter, "and add to your faith virtue," knowledge, temperance, patience, godliness, brotherly kindness, charity; "for if these things be in you, and abound, they make you that ye shall neither be barren nor unfruitful in the knowledge of our Lord Jesus Christ." Another point, after having all these qualifications, he lays this injunction upon the people "to make your calling and election sure." He is emphatic upon this subject—after adding all this virtue knowledge, &c., "Make your calling and election sure." What is the secret—the starting point? "According as His divine power hath given unto us all things that pertain unto life and godliness." How did he obtain all things? Through the knowledge of Him who hath called him. There could not anything be given, pertaining to life and godliness, without knowledge. Woe! woe! woe to Christendom!—especially the divines and priests if this be true.

Salvation is for a man to be saved from all his enemies; for until a man can triumph over death, he is not saved. A knowledge of the priesthood alone will do this.

The spirits in the eternal world are like the spirits in this world. When those have come into this world and received tabernacles, then died and again have risen and received glorified bodies, they will have an ascendency over the spirits who have received no bodies, or kept not their first estate, like the devil. The punishment of the devil was that he should not have a habitation like men. The devil's retaliation is, he comes into this world, binds up men's bodies, and occupies them himself. When the authorities come along, they eject him from a stolen habitation.

The design of the great God in sending us into this world, and organizing us to prepare us for the eternal worlds, I shall keep in my own bosom at present.

We have no claim in our eternal compact, in relation to eternal things, unless our actions and contracts and all things tend to this end. But after all this, you have got to make your calling and election sure. If this injunction would lie largely on those to whom it was spoken, how much more those of the present generation!

1st key: Knowledge is the power of salvation. 2nd key: Make your calling and election sure. 3rd key: It is one thing to be on the mount and hear the excellent voice, &c., &c., and another to hear the voice declare to you, You have a part and lot in that kingdom.

Judge Adams arrived at my house from Springfield.

Monday, 22.—Called at the office at nine, a m., having received letters from Sisters Armstrong and Nicholson, of Philadelphia, complaining of the slanderous conduct of Benjamin Winchester; and I directed the Twelve Apostles to act upon the matter.

Complaint against Benjamin Winchester.

This morning received a large hickory walking stick having a silver head, with the motto "BEWARE."

Rode out to my farm; dined at Cornelius P. Lott's;

then rode to the Lima road, and returned home at half-past seven, p. m.

Wrote the editor of *Times and Seasons*:

The Prophet on Forming Temperance Societies.

DEAR BROTHER:—In answer to yours of May 4th, concerning the Latter-day Saints' forming a temperance society, we would say, as Paul said—"Be not unequally yoked with unbelievers, but contend for the faith once delivered to the Saints;" and as Peter advises, so say we, "Add to your knowledge, temperance." As Paul said he had to become all things to all men, that he might thereby save some, so must the elders of the last days do; and, being sent out to preach the Gospel and warn the world of the judgments to come, we are sure, when they teach as directed by the Spirit, according to the revelations of Jesus Christ, that they will preach the truth and prosper without complaint. Thus we have no new commandment to give, but admonish elders and members to live by every word that proceedeth forth from the mouth of God, lest they come short of the glory that is reserved for the faithful.

Tuesday, 23—In conversation with Judge Adams and others.

At eight a. m., rode out to visit the sick.

Two p. m. Brigham Young, Heber C. Kimball, Parley P. Pratt, Orson Pratt, Orson Hyde, Wilford Wooodruff, John Taylor, George A. Smith, Willard Richards and others met in the office.

Elder Addison Pratt was ordained a seventy and blessed and set apart to go to the Society Islands, by President Brigham Young, assisted by Heber C. Kimball, Orson Hyde, Parley P. Pratt,—that he should be a swift messenger to the nations of the earth, have power over the elements, and not fear when tempests arise. "Do not be hasty and passionate, but acknowledge goodness in all, where you find it. Hearken ye, they will say, one to another, to this man; and they will carry you and give presents, etc., you shall have power over the ship's course, and shall return again to this land and rejoice with your family, if you are faithful."

Elder Noah Rogers, of the Seventies, was blessed by the same brethren, Elder Kimball being mouth. It was said that he might have power to discern between good and evil, be filled with the power of God, have faith to heal the sick, cast out devils, and cause the lame to walk, and have the heavens opened, and have an appointment from on high, even from God, if he was faithful. "Except thou art willing to be led, thou shalt never lead. Thou shalt return to this place." He was set apart to accompany Brother Addison Pratt to the Pacific Islands.

Elder Benjamin Grouard was ordained a seventy by the same brethren, Orson Hyde mouth. Prayed that the angel of God might watch over him and deliver him from his enemies and the tempests and troubles of the sea, that he might perform the mission with honor to himself, and return in safety.

Elder Knowlton F. Hanks was also set apart to the islands.

Reuben Hedlock, high priest, was blessed and set apart to go to England.

Other Ordinations and Appointments.

Elder John Cairnes was ordained high priest and set apart to accompany Brother Hedlock.

President Young said to Brother Addison Pratt and his associates: We commit the keys of opening the gospel to the Society Islands to you, when all the Twelve said, Aye.

Elder Rogers was appointed president of the mission.

Reuben Hedlock's mission was to preside over the churches in England, over the emigration, and over business in general, by vote of the quorum.

Elder Young said he wanted the funds in Liverpool to pay the passage of those who were expected to be sent for by Brother John Benbow and his wife, on account of moneys lent by him to commence the printing of the Book of Mormon, *Millennial Star*, Hymn Book, etc., and to send the worthy poor to this country, and let Brother Hedlock use what is necessary for his own convenience; and voted unanimously that the foregoing be caried into execution.

Let the Books of Mormon be sold as fast as they can in England, and the avails be retained by Elder Hedlock till further orders.

Voted that Sister Ann Dawson and her family, William Bradbury with his family, Brother Leech, of Preston, and his family, Brother Anderson, of Stoke-upon-Trent, and all the poor Saints be brought over to this country.

Voted on reading Elder Ward's letters of March 4th and 16th to the First Presidency and Twelve, that the printing in England be stopped, according to previous instructions, and Elders Thomas Ward and Amos Fielding come to this place, and the funds referred to in Elder Ward's letter be expended by Elder Hedlock, as before stated.

Wednesday, 24.—Elder Addison Pratt presented the tooth of a whale, coral, bones of an Albatross' wing and skin of a foot, jaw-bone of a porpoise, and tooth of a South Sea seal as the beginning for a museum in Nauvoo.

First Contribution to the Nauvoo Museum.

I bought eleven quarter-sections of land from Judge Adams, and then rode out on the hill.

I find in the *Boston Bee* of this date a letter; and as it is so remarkable that any editor will publish anything in the columns of his paper concerning me or the Saints but slander, I take pleasure in transcribing the following:

A Character Sketch of the Prophet—His Doctrine of Inspiration.

Sir, in bygone years, and long before I heard of the Prophet Joseph Smith, and indeed before he had existence, I had formed some very curious ideas about the ancient prophets. From reading their history in the Bible, I supposed they must have been men of no ordinary proportions; or, if so, that there was something about them different from other men, by which they might be distinguished at sight. As a matter of course, I thought they must have had gray hairs for a covering to make them appear very dignified, and beards as long as a Jew's; for if they shaved, it would show that they were men; and could I have had the privilege of looking at one, I should have expected to have seen him clad in sheep, goat, bear or wolf skin, wandering about on the mountains like the beasts he had robbed of their garment, lodging in the caves and dens of the earth, and subsisting on the fruits and nuts of the forest,—a being too holy, too sanctified, too exalted by his high calling, to appear in the habitations or among the society of men, unless he had some important message to communicate direct from heaven—some revelation or commandment to promulgate to his fellows; and then he would just come forth and cry out, like the beasts in the wilderness, with so much sacred sanctity, that everybody would know he was a prophet,and if by nothing else,when they saw his nails like birds' claws,and his hairs like eagles' feathers and his hands and face as filthy as a baboon; for it never occurred to me that clean hands, in administering before the Lord, as mentioned in the scripture, meant anything more than a good conscience; and I had never supposed but that a man could worship God just as acceptably all covered with dirt, and filth and slime, as though he had bathed in Siloam every hour, until I heard the Mormon prophet lecturing his people on the subject of neatness and cleanliness, teaching them that all was clean in heaven, and that Jesus was going to make the place of His feet glorious; and if the Mormons did not keep their feet out of the ashes, they could not stand with Him on Mount Zion.

I had no thought before but that dirty people could get to heaven as well as clean ones; and that if the priests offered sacrifices with polluted hands, the fire would cleanse both the offering and the hands that offered it. I cannot say how much there may be in scripture to contradict my views, neither can I vouch for it that the churches of the day believe any such doctrine; for I never belonged to any of them, but have rather been called an infidel. As to that, I have not altered much. I like consistency, find it where I may.

With all these curious notions I fell into the Mormon settlement, and saw the prophet; but having never heard a Mormon preach, you can imagine me not quite ready to receive all the impressions incident to an interview with such a distinguished personage. But I will give it as I find it, hit or miss the faith or feelings of any one. I have had an interview since my last, and found anything but the truth in the current reports. "The Prophet Joseph" (as he is called among his people) said in a conversation with a gentleman present, that he no more professed to be a prophet than every man must who professes to be a preacher of righteousness or a minister of the new testament.

To be a minister of Jesus, a man must testify of Jesus; and to testify of Jesus, a man must have the spirit of prophecy; for, according to John, the testimony of Jesus is the spirit of prophecy.

If a man professes to be a minister of Jesus and has not the spirit of prophecy, he must be a false witness, for he is not in possession of that gift which qualifies him for that office; and the difference between him and the clergy of this generation is, he claims to be in possession of that spirit of prophecy which qualifies him to testify of Jesus and the Gospel of salvation; and the clergy deny that spirit, even the spirit of prophecy, which alone could constitute them true witnesses or testators of the Lord Jesus, and yet claim to be true ministers of salvation.

In this, said he, I am honest, and they are dishonest, and that is the difference between us. Were they true and honest witnesses of Jesus Christ, they would acknowledge they have the testimony of Him, and that is the spirit of prophecy; and every man who possesses that spirit is a prophet.

I, said he, claim no more than what every servant of Christ must possess to qualify him for his office, while the clergy of the 19th century deny that which alone could constitute what they profess to be. He said he did not profess to be a very good man, but acknowledged himself a sinner like other men, or, as all men are, imperfect; and it is necessary for all men to grow into the stature of manhood in the Gospel.

I could not help noticing that he dressed, talked and acted like other men, and in every respect exactly the opposite of what I had conjured up in my imagination a prophet.

The Mormons have not yet completed their great Temple, and have no commodious place of worship; but the apostles and elders preach in private houses on the Sabbath and at other times, though I seldom attended these latter meetings. But when the weather will admit they meet in the grove, or on the rough floor of the basement of the Temple, and then the prophet frequently preaches. On one of these occasion I heard him preach concerning the prodigal son.

After naming his text, the prophet remarked that some one had asked him the meaning of the expression of Jesus—"Among those born of women, there has not arisen a greater than John;" and said he had promised to answer it in public, and he would do it then. It could not have been on account of the miracles John performed, for he did no miracles; but it was—First, because he was trusted with a divine mission of preparing the way before the face of the Lord. Who was trusted with such a mission before or since? No man. Second, he was trusted and it was required at his hands to baptize the Son of Man. Who ever did that? Who ever had so great a privilege or glory? Who ever led the Son of God into the waters of baptism, beholding the Holy Ghost descend upon him in the sign of a dove? No man. Third, John at that time was the only legal administrator holding the keys of power there was on earth. The keys, the kingdom, the power, the glory had departed from the Jews; and John, the son of Zachariah, by the holy anointing and decree of heaven, held the keys of power at that time.

Elder H. Tate writes that in Cuba, Illinois, the people were anxious to hear him, when the Rev. John Rigdon, a Campbellite preacher refused to let him preach in the chapel, because Elder Tate was "sent by the authority of Jesus Christ," saying, "That recommend will not do, for the world has condemned it already;" but at Pekin Elder Tate baptized six in twelve days, and many more were favorable.

Labors of Elder H. Tate.

Received a long letter from Thomas Rancliff, complaining of William and Wilson Law and Dr. Foster's swindling him, which is another example that people will not obey counsel, although it was so pointedly made known to the people on the 13th of April last.

Complaints against the Laws and Dr. Foster.

Thursday, *25*.—Sent William Clayton to Carthage to redeem the city lots on the Galland tract, which had been sold for taxes.

Dr. Imbert, Messrs. Chastan and Manlan, missionaries, with seventy Christians were beheaded, and one hundred and eighty strangled in Korea, East Asia.

The town of Tallahassee, Florida, was destroyed by fire.

Friday, *26*.—At five p. m. I met in counsel in the upper room, with my brother Hyrum, Brigham Young, Heber C. Kimball, Willard Richards, Judge James Adams, Bishop Newel K. Whitney and William Law, and gave them their endowments and also instructions in the priesthood on the new and everlasting covenant, &c.

Wrote a letter of instructions to Reuben Hedlock.

Saturday, *27*.—In the morning received visitors.

At two p. m. I met brother Hyrum, the Twelve, Judge Adams, Bishop Whitney and others, in council to investigate the conduct of Benjamin Winchester, charges having been preferred against him by letter from Sybella Armstrong and others in Philadelphia, Sisters Jarman and Adams. George J. Adams and others gave their testimony, when they disfel-

Benjamin Winchester Investigated.

lowshiped Winchester, and took his license until he made satisfaction to the aggrieved parties.

[Extract from Wilford's Woodruff's journal.]

Elder Wilford Woodruff's Minutes of the Investigation of Benjamin Winchester.

A rainy day.

In the afternoon I met in council with the Twelve and First Presidency, when the case of Benjamin Winchester was brought up on trial for improper conduct, slandering the Saints in Philadelphia, for rejecting the counsel of Hyrum, Joseph and the Twelve, and tearing to pieces the Saints instead of building them up.

Hyrum pleaded for mercy, Joseph for justice, and the Twelve decided according to testimony; and in all we had an interesting time. Elder Winchester was refractory and out of order. President Joseph Smith wished the Twelve or president of the quorum to call the house to order.

Several letters were read touching the subject; after which Elder Winchester made a lengthy speech trying to justify himself. Was fol-followed by President Hyrum Smith, who pleaded in behalf of Winchester on the side of mercy.

Elder George J. Adams gave his testimony against Winchester; then Elder Winchester followed Adams, and both spoke several times. Then President Joseph Smith arose and rebuked Elder Winchester in the sharpest manner; said he had a lying spirit and had lied about him, and told him of many of his errors.

After hearing the testimony, Elder Brigham Young, president of the quorum of the Twelve, said he had made up his mind, and his decision was that Elder Winchester should give up his license and cease preaching until he should reform.

President Hyrum Smith said he should not like to have such a decision given without another trial and giving Elder Winchester a chance to get more testimony if he could.

President Brigham Young said he should then prefer to have the case turned over to the high council.

President Joseph Smith said it was not the business of the high council. They could not try him. It belonged to the Twelve, and them alone; for it was concerning matters abroad, and not in Nauvoo. The high council was to try cases that belong to the stake, and the Twelve to regulate the churches and elders abroad in all the world; and Elder Winchester's case comes under the jurisdiction of the Twelve and theirs alone.

President Hyrum Smith urged that the case should be put off until tomorrow. President Joseph Smith said that the case might be put off until tomorrow at ten o'clock, if it would do anybody any good.

President Brigham Young arose and spoke in the majesty of his calling; and among other remarks, said that his mind was made up, and that the remarks of Brother Hyrum or of Brother Joseph had not altered it. As for himself, he would not sit upon the case another day. He considered the course Brother Winchester had taken an insult upon his office and calling as an apostle of Jesus Christ, and he would not bear it. As for the rest of the Twelve, they might do as they pleased. As for himself, he would not submit to it. Benjamin Winchester has despised and rejected the counsel of the Presidency and the Twelve—has said they had no jurisdiction over him in Philadelphia, and to say where he should go, &c. But he and others will find there *is* power in the Twelve. We know through whom we have received our power and who are our benefactors, and we are thankful for it. Benjamin Winchester has never for the first time received our counsel, but has gone contrary to it. No one is safe in his hands. He calls Hyrum an old granny, and slanders everybody. He says there is a contradiction between Hyrum and the Twelve. There is no contradiction between Hyrum and the Twelve—is there, Brother Hyrum? [Hyrum answered "No."]

After Brigham Young closed, President Joseph Smith said he would give us a little counsel, if we saw fit to accept it. He thought it proper for us to silence Elder Winchester, take his license and have him bring his family to Nanvoo; and if he would not do that, let him go out of the Church.

It was then moved and seconded that Elder Winchester be silenced, and give up his license, and come with his family to Nauvoo. The motion was carried unanimously.

Brother Joseph then addressed the Twelve, and said that in all our counsels, especially while on trial of any one, we should see and observe all things appertaining to the subject, and discern the spirit by which either party was governed. We should be in a situation to understand every spirit and judge righteous judgment and not be asleep. We should keep order and not let the council be imposed upon by unruly conduct. The Saints need not think because I am familiar with them and am playful and cheerful, that I am ignorant of what is going on. Iniquity of any kind cannot be sustained in the Church, and it will not fare well where I am; for I am determined while I do lead the Church, to lead it right.

Brother Joseph further remarked, concerning Elder Adams, that he had given satisfaction to him concerning the thing whereof he was accused. He had confessed all wherein he had done wrong, and had asked for mercy, and he had taken the right course to save himself; that he would now begin anew in the Church.

After much instruction was given from Joseph, the council adjourned.

I then instructed the Twelve to investigate the condition of the whole Philadelphia church while in council.

List of Persons to be Helped to Immigrate to Nauvoo.

Voted that the following persons be assisted to emigrate from England—viz., Mr. Elizabeth Pixton, Mrs. Sarah Taylor, Jeremiah Taylor, Mrs. Mary Greenhalgh, Mrs. Elizabeth Clayton and two children, Hugh Patrick and family, Mrs. Ann Farrar and three children, Maria Barrows and children, Alice Bailey and two children, William Player's family, Prudence Parr and six children, Rebecca Partington.

A tremendous rain-storm all day, commencing with thunder in the morning.

A petition for the repeal of the parliamentary union, with England—representing four hundred and fifty thousand persons—was sent from Menagh, Ireland.

Sunday, *28.*—Cold, rainy day.

Endowments at Nauvoo.

At five p. m. I met with brother Hyrum, Brigham Young, Heber C. Kimball, Willard Richards, Newel K. Whitney, and James Adams, in the upper room to attend to ordinances and counseling. Prayed that James Adams might be delivered from his enemies, and that Orrin P. Rockwell might be delivered from prison, and that the Twelve be prospered in collecting means to build the Nauvoo House.

Record of the First Twelve in Relations with the Prophet.

Of the Twelve Apostles chosen in Kirtland, and ordained under the hands of Oliver Cowdery, David Whitmer and myself, there have been but two but what have lifted their heel against me—namely Brigham Young and Heber C. Kimball.

Monday, *29.*—At nine a. m., I met in council with brother Hyrum, Brigham Young, Heber C. Kimball,

Willard Richards, Newel K. Whitney, and James Adams.

Singing, and prayer by Elder Brigham Young. Conversation, instruction and teaching concerning the things of God. Had a pleasant interview.

Two p. m., in mayor's court. Tried a case—"The People vs. Thompson," for assault. Fined Thompson three dollars.

Gave instructions to have the account of the Lawrence estate made out.

Judge James Adams gave a deed of eleven quarter sections of land on the prairie to the trustee-in-trust.

Six p. m., the Twelve Apostles met and directed the following to be published in the *Times and Seasons*.

Special Message to the Saints in Philadelphia.

To the Church in Philadelphia:

All the members of that branch of the Church of Jesus Christ of Latter-day Saints which is located in Philadelphia, Pennsylvania, who are desirous of doing the will of heaven and of working out their own salvation by keeping the laws of the celestial kingdom, are hereby instructed and counseled to remove from thence without delay and locate themselves in the city of Nauvoo, where God has a work for them to accomplish.

Done at Nauvoo the 20th day of May, 1843, agreeable to the instructions of the First Presidency.

By order of the quorum of the Twelve,

BRIGHAM YOUNG,
President of the quorum.

WILLARD RICHARDS, Clerk.

Appointments by the Quorum of the Twelve.

Elder James Sloan, to Ireland. Elder Benjamin Brown, accompanied by Elder Jesse W. Crosby, to the province of Nova Scotia. Elder Edwin W. Webb, to Galena. Elder Issac Chase, to the Eastern States, Elder Stephen Abbott and Charles E. Spencer to Wisconsin territory, Elder Issac Thompson to accompany them.

WILLARD RICHARDS, Clerk.

Pleasant, but cool after the rain.

Tuesday, 30.—In the office from nine till noon examining Nauvoo stock, and transacting business with the Twelve Apostles, and taking bonds from Brigham Young, Heber C. Kimball, Orson Hyde, Orson Pratt, Wilford Woodruff, and George A. Smith, of which I insert one as follows:

Form of Bond Executed by Brigham Young et al. to the Prophet.

Know all men by these presents, that we, Brigham Young and John M. Bernhisel, are held and firmly bound unto Joseph Smith, as sole trustee-in-trust for the Church of Jesus Christ of Latter-day Saints, in the penal sum of two thousand dollars, lawful money of the United States; for the payment of which sum, well and truly to be made, we bind ourselves, our heirs, assigns and administrators firmly by these presents.

Dated at Nauvoo, this 30th day of May, 1843.

The condition of the above obligation is such that the above bounden Brigham Young who has been appointed an agent to collect funds for the Nauvoo House Association and for the Temple now building in the city of Nauvoo, shall faithfully pay to the said truste-in trust as aforesaid, all moneys that he may collect for either house, then this obligation be null and void, otherwise to remain in full force and virtue.

Signed, sealed and delivered the day and year first above written.

BRIGHAM YOUNG, [L. S.]
JOHN M. BERNHISEL, [L. S.]

And directed that receipts be also written for the Nauvoo stock as follows:

Form of Receipt for Stock Certificate.

Received May 30th, 1843, of Joseph Smith, Sole Trustee-in-Trust for the Church of Jesus Christ of Latter-day Saints, three hundred stock certificates of Nauvoo House Association, numbering as follows:

200	numbering	1 to 200	inclusive,	dated	Feb.	8,	1841.
36	"	125 to 160	"	"	"	5,	"
36	"	376 to 411	"	"	"	10,	"
28	"	5 to 32	"	"	"	6,	"
—							

300 shares value $15,000.

BRIGHAM YOUNG.

Afterwards I superintended the preparation of papers to settle the Lawrence business. My brother Hyrum baptized Jonathan C. Wright and ordained him an elder.

Wednesday, 31.—Called at the office and court room before breakfast and conferred with Dr. Richards on business.

City council met at ten a. m. and gave instructions to a committee to draft an ordinance in relation to the ferry.

Rode out in the afternoon on the prairie with Mr. Houston, the Speaker of the House of Representatives for Missouri, Judge Sylvester Emmons, Lawyer Marr and O. C. Skinner, and William Clayton.

At six p. m. met with the city council, when the ordinance in relation to the ferry passed its second reading.

Signed letters of recommendation to James Brown and Peter Haws to collect funds in Mississippi and Alabama.

Elder Brigham Young moved out of his log cabin into a new brick house, small, but comfortable and convenient,

The steamer *Amaranth* landed at Nauvoo the Saints who had left Liverpool in the *Yorkshire* under the care of Elders Thomas Bullock and Richard Rushton, all well; and also some Saints who had left there more recently in the *Swanton.*

News arrived that General Charles Napier gained a brilliant victory near Hyderabad, after a dreadful combat of three hours. The Belochee army of twenty-two thousand men were completely overthrown by twenty-seven hundred English troops, who sustained a loss of only two hundred and fifty killed and wounded, including eighteen officers.

Four hundred and fifty clergymen have lately seceded from the Church of Scotland, being nearly one-half of the whole number.

CHAPTER XXII.

FORMS OF CREDENTIALS OF THE TWELVE—CONFERENCE AT MANCHESTER, ENGLAND—DEATH OF JUDGE ELIAS HIGBEE—"THE PURPOSE OF GATHERING," A DISCOURSE BY THE PROPHET.

Thursday, June 1, 1843.—Presided in the city council, which passed "An ordinance to establish a ferry across the Mississippi river at the city of Nauvoo."

And also passed "An ordinance respecting mad dogs and other animals."

I addressed the council, and criticised James Sloan's account current charging for room, candles, fuel, etc., etc., as extras. Willard Richards, Newel K. Whitney, and William Clayton [were engaged] all day preparing papers for the settlement of the Lawrence estate.

I gave the following recommend to Elder Brigham Young.

Credentials of Brigham Young.

To all Saints and Honorable Men of the Earth, Greeting:

DEAR BRETHREN AND FRIENDS:—I, Joseph Smith, a servant of the Lord, and trustee-in-trust for the Temple of the Lord at Nauvoo, do hereby certify that the bearer hereof, Brigham Young, an elder and one of the Twelve Apostles of the Church of Jesus Christ of Latter-day Saints, has deposited with me his bond and security, to my full satisfaction, according to the resolution of the conference held in this city on the 6th day of April last.

He, therefore, is recommended to all Saints and honorable people as a legal agent to collect funds for the purpose of building the Nauvoo House and Temple of the Lord. Confident that he will honor this high trust, as well as ardently fulfill his commission as a messenger of peace and salvation, as one of the Lord's noble men, I can fervently say, May the Lord clear his way before him and bless him, and bless those that obey his teachings, wherever there are ears to hear and hearts to feel.

He is the friend of Israel, and worthy to be received and entertained as a man of God; yea, he has, as had the ancient apostles, the good word, even the good word that leadeth unto eternal life.

Wherefore, brethren and friends, while you have the assurance of the integrity, fidelity and ability of this servant of the living God, and trusting that your hearts and energies will be enlivened and deeply engaged in the building of those houses directed by revelation for the salvation of all Saints, and that you will not rest where you are until all things are prepared before you, and you are gathered home with the rest of Israel to meet your God, I feel strong in the belief and have a growing expectation that you will not withhold any means in your power that can be used to accomplish this glorious work.

Finally, as one that greatly desires the salvation of men, let me remind you all to strive with godly zeal for virtue, holiness, and the commandments of the Lord. Be good, be wise, be just, be liberal; and above all, be charitable, always abounding in all good works. And may health, peace and the love of God our Father, and the grace of Jesus Christ our Lord be and abide with you all, is the sincere prayer of your devoted brother and friend in the everlasting Gospel,

JOSEPH SMITH.

City of Nauvoo, June 1, 1843.

Similar letters were given to Elders Heber C. Kimball, Orson Pratt, Orson Hyde, Wilford Woodruff and George A. Smith.

Signed a conveyance of Eric Rhodes' bonds to Joseph Smith to William Clayton.

Gave a letter of instruction to George J. Adams, who is to accompany Elder Orson Hyde on his mission to Russia.

Elders Addison Pratt, Benjamin F. Grouard, Knowlton F. Hanks and Noah Rogers started on their mission for the Society Islands at two p. m., on the steamer *Sarah Ann*, for St. Louis.

The quorum of the Twelve Apostles met in council in my office, to make arrangements to start on their mission to collect funds for the Temple and Nauvoo House.

Friday, 2.—Closed the contract whereby I gave two notes for $1,375, and became half owner of the steamboat *Maid of Iowa*. Continued in the office with Captain Dan Jones most of the morning, which was very rainy.

In the afternoon rode out in the city to invite several friends to take an excursion on *Maid of Iowa* tomorrow, and had a long conversation with a Presbyterian minister.

Outrages were committed in Wales on public property, under an organized band called "Rebecca and her daughters."

An Excursion on the Mississippi.

Saturday, *3*.—This morning, I, with my family and a large company of brethren and sisters, started for Quincy, on a pleasure voyage on the steamboat *Maid of Iowa*, had a fine band of music in attendance, and arrived there at about one p. m.

The accounts of the Lawrence estate were presented to the probate judge, to which he made objections, when a new account was made out by William Clayton, which we made oath to, when the accounts were accepted by the probate judge.

At five p. m. started on our return, but tied up at Keokuk, at one a. m. on account of a severe storm until daylight, when we started home and were glad to arrive in Nauvoo at seven a. m. of the 4th.

Sunday, *4*.—At ten a. m. I engaged in conversation with Mr. De Wolf, a clergyman of the Episcopal order, who was much of a gentleman.

Minutes of a Conference Held at Manchester, England, June 4, 1843.

A conference was commenced in the New CornExchange, Manchester, and by adjournment moved into the large room at Hayward's Hotel, Bridge street. The assembly was large, although the weather was unfavorable.

Elder Thomas Ward was president, and William Walker, clerk. President Ward and Elders Hiram Clark and Amos Fielding preached giving excellent teachings on the plan of salvation, and the Lord's Supper. There were present six high priests, fifty-eight elders, sixty-four priests, forty teachers, ten deacons.

The representations of the churches being next called for, the following statements were made:

Conferences	Presidents	Members	High Priests	Elders	Priests	Teachers	Deacons	No. of Branches
Manchester	Charles Miller	1481	...	38	75	54	17	30
Liverpool	Thomas Ward	558	...	31	30	14	10	4
Preston	William Snalem	655	1	18	18	18	2	15
London	William W. Major	...	...	...	...	...	...	...
" West End	...	58	...	3	9	3	...	...
" East End Clerkenwell	...	156	...	3	9	2	2	...
" Newbury	...	22	...	1	2	...		...
" Woolwich	...	30	...	1	..	...	...	...
Macclesfield	James Galley	250	...	11	28	15	9	6
Birmingham	Cooper Royle	509	...	32	32	18	10	16
Staffordshire	...	377	...	38	59	14	10	12
Edinburgh	Henry McEwan	302	.	10	10	8	2	4
Garway	Charles Taysum	176	...	4	5	7	2	5
Glasgow	Peter McCue	721	..	24	32	28	16	14
Froomes' Hill	...	784	1	21	47	21	9	36
Carlisle	John Parker	154	...	8	19	8	3	4
Sheffield	James Carigan	128	...	4	9	3	3	...
Bradford	Robert Parker	240	...	8	15	11	6	7
Bedford	Thomas Margetts	242	...	14	20	8	4	10
Ireland, Hillsborough	...	55	...	3	2	2	1	...
Lincolnshire, Louth	...	14	...	1	2	1	...	...
Wigan	...	5	...	...	...	...	...	...
Nottingham	...	5	...	...	...	...	...	...
Worcestershire	——Smith		...		...	...	...	...
" Earls Common	...	61	..	3	4	1	...	...
" Penvin	...	19	...	1	2	1	...	...
" Broomsgrove	...	36	...	1	3	...	..	...
	Total	7038	2	278	432	237	106	163

The sacrament was administered in the afternoon.

Monday, 5.—The following persons devoted themselves to the work of the ministry—viz., Osmond Shaw, Thomas Shaw, Samuel Downes, Elders William Speakman and George Eyres.

The following persons were then ordained elders—viz., R. Cowen, T. Pratt, Samuel Downe, John Williams, Peter McCue, Joseph Walker, and Levi Rigg.

Priests: J. Flint, Joseph Smith, J. Nightingale, J. Lee, Thomas Jackson, Samuel Wells, Charles Turner, Christopher Riding, George Robinson.

Teachers: George Hewitt, Thomas Jennings.

Elder Barradale was appointed to preside over Cheltenham branch; Elder Rudd, over the Nottingham circuit; Elder Pritchard, to labor in Derbyshire; Elder Speakman, with Elder Robert Parker, in the Bradford conference; Osmond Shaw, Addingham, Yorkshire; Elder George Eyers, in Lincolnshire and Hull, in connection with Elder Henry Cuerdon and Elder Samuel Downes, in Derbyshire, with Elder Hibbert.

Tuesday, 6.—I rode out to the Prairie Farm.

Earthquake occurred in Java, destroying Nias and burying its inhabitants in the ruins.

The total national debt of Europe is estimated at $10,-499,710,000. A century ago the European treasury was comparatively unencumbered.

Wednesday, 7.—Concluded a settlement with J. W. Coolidge. Gave him a deed for city lot.

Visited Elias Higbee, who was very sick.

John Workman and a company of 30 Saints, mostly his own family, arrived from Tennessee.

Thursday, 8.—This morning, about daybreak, Elder Elias Higbee died at his residence near the Temple.*

We copy the following from page 315 of the Law of the Lord—†

* He was son of Isaac and Sophia Higbee, born 23rd October, 1795, in Galloway, Gloucester county, New Jersey. In 1803, removed with his parents to Clermont county, Ohio. At the age of 22 he married Sarah Ward, and removed to Cincinnati. He received the gospel in the spring of 1832, and in the summer of the same year went to Jackson county, Missouri, where he was baptized, and returned to Cincinnati, and was ordained an elder under the hands of his brother, Isaac Higbee, 20th February, 1833. Arrived in Jackson county with his family in March, and was driven by the mob to Clay county in the fall of 1833; ordained a high priest under the hands of Amasa M. Lyman, by order of the high council in Clay county. 26th March, 1835, started on a mission, preaching the gospel through the states of Missouri, Illinois, Indiana, and Ohio. Arriving at Kirtland, he labored on the Temple until it was finished, and received his edowment therein. In the spring of 1836, returned to his family in Missouri; removed them to Caldwell county, where he was appointed County Judge.

Judge Higbee was also appointed to go with the Prophet to Washington to plead the cause of the Saints before congress, and perhaps will be chiefly remembered for his earnest but temperate zeal in their cause; also for the courage and judgment he manifested before the Senate Committee on Judiciary, before which the hearing was had. The case was conducted by Judge Higbee, practically alone. See his reports to the Prophet, Vol. IV, pp. 81-91. His course approved, *Ibid.* p. 96.

† The "Law of the Lord" is a manuscript book kept personally by the Prophet,

JUDGE ELIAS HIGBEE.

He has been sick only five days of cholera morbus and inflammation, which produced mortification, and his death was unexpected by all. His loss will be universally lamented, not only by his family, but by a large circle of brethren who have long witnessed his integrity and uprightness, as well as a life of devotedness to the cause of truth. He has endured a great share of persecution and tribulation for the cause of Christ, both during the Missouri troubles and other times. On the 6th day of October, 1840, he was appointed one of the committee to build the Temple in Nauvoo, which office he maintained during his life. In that station he has shown a disposition to do right at all times, and always manifested a great anxiety for the prosperity of the Temple as well as the work at large. He has left a large family to mourn his departure; but he is gone to his rest for a little season, even until the morning of the resurrection, when he will again come forth and strike hands with the faithful, and share the glory of the kingdom of God for ever and ever.

Emma was sick.

In the afternoon, rode out on horseback; called on Willard Richards, who was at work in his garden; asked him who gave him leave to occupy that lot. He answered, "Your honor?" when I replied, "You are perfectly welcome to it, so far as I am concerned;" then continued my journey to the prairie.

Friday, *9*.—Rode out to show Mr. Lewis some lots in the city.

Continued most of the day with Emma, who was very sick.

Saturday, *10*.—At home. Brothers Livingston and Goodrich, from Peterboro, New Hampshire, visited me about establishing a cotton factory in Nauvoo.

City council met and passed "An ordinance to regulate the rates of toll at the ferry in the city of Nauvoo," which is published in the *Neighbor*.

Several petitions were presented to repeal the hog law, which were rejected.

wherein, with other specially valuable documents, he recorded character sketches and the good deeds of the faithful Saints; also the blessings he pronounced upon them. See this Vol., pp. 108, 124-128.

The court-martial ordered an arsenal to be built in the city of Nauvoo, for the security of the public arms; and also ordered Brigadier-General Charles C. Rich to organize the 2nd battalion, 1st regiment, 2nd cohort, into a regiment of light infantry, to be the 5th regiment, 2nd cohort.

To show the wickedness and rascality of John C. Bennett and the corrupt conspiracy formed against me in Missouri and Illinois, I insert the following under date of the letter:—

Letter of Samuel C. Owens to Governor Ford—Informing the Latter of an Indictment Against Joseph Smith.

INDEPENDENCE, MO., June 10, 1843.

To His Excellency Governor Ford.

SIR:—For the last three months I have been corresponding with Dr. John C. Bennett relative to one certain Joe Smith, Mormon Prophet, etc., of your state. In several of Dr. Bennett's letters to me, he informs me that my name is known to you. Taking this for granted authorizes me without hesitation to write you full upon a subject that the people of this part of our state feel themselves vitally interested in.

At the last term of the Circuit court of Daviess county, an indictment was found by the grand jury of said county against Joseph Smith for treason against this state. The necessary papers are now on their way to Governor Reynolds, who, on the receipt thereof, I have no doubt, will make a requisition on you for the apprehension and delivery of said Smith to the bearer, Mr. Joseph Reynolds, who goes as a special agent to attend to this business; and I am in hopes that, so soon as the proper papers come to hand, you will take that course that will secure this imposter and have him delivered over to Mr. Reynolds.

Dr. Bennett further writes me that he has made an arrangement with Harmon T. Wilson, of Hancock county (Carthage, seat of justice) in whose hands he wishes the writ that shall be issued by you to be put. From the tenor of his letters I am induced to believe that he has made the same suggestions to you. The only wish of the people of this state is, that this man, Joseph Smith, may be brought to that justice which the magnitude of his crime merits.

Respectfully your obedient servant,

SAM. C. OWENS,

[Commander-in-chief of the mob in Jackson county].

A steamship of iron, called the *Great Britain*, was built at Bristol, England, at a cost of 90,000 pounds. She has six masts, and is 320 feet in length on deck, and is said to be the largest vessel that has been built since the days of Noah.

Sunday, *11*.—Ten a. m., meeting at the stand.

The following report is from the journals of Elders Willard Richards and Wilford Woodruff:—

The Prophet's Discourse—The Purpose of the Gathering of Israel.

A large assembly of the Saints met at the Temple stand. Hymn by the choir. Prayer by Elder Parley P. Pratt, and singing.

President Joseph Smith remarked—"I am a rough stone. The sound of the hammer and chisel was never heard on me until the Lord took me in hand. I desire the learning and wisdom of heaven alone. I have not the least idea, if Christ should come to the earth and preach such rough things as He preached to the Jews, but that this generation would reject Him for being so rough."

He then took for his text the 37th verse of 23rd chapter of Matthew—"O Jerusalem, Jerusalem, thou that killest the prophets and stonest them which are sent unto thee; how often would I have gathered thy children together, even as a hen gathereth her chickens under her wings, and ye would not."

This subject was presented to me since I came to the stand. What was the object of gathering the Jews, or the people of God in any age of the world? I can never find much to say in expounding a text. A man never has half so much fuss to unlock a door, if he has a key, as though he had not, and had to cut it open with his jack-knife.

The main object was to build unto the Lord a house whereby He could reveal unto His people the ordinances of His house and the glories of His kingdom, and teach the people the way of salvation; for there are certain ordinances and principles that, when they are taught and practiced, must be done in a place or house built for that purpose.

It was the design of the councils of heaven before the world was, that the principles and laws of the priesthood should be predicated upon the gathering of the people in every age of the world. Jesus did everything to gather the people, and they would not be gathered, and He therefore poured out curses upon them. Ordinances instituted in the heavens before the foundation of the world, in the priesthood, for the salvation of men, are not to be altered or changed. All must be saved on the same principles.

It is for the same purpose that God gathers together His people in the last days, to build unto the Lord a house to prepare them for the ordinances and endowments, washings and anointings, etc. One of the ordinances of the house of the Lord is baptism for the dead. God decreed before the foundation of the world that that ordinance should be administered in a font prepared for that purpose in the house of the Lord. "This is only your opinion, sir," says the sectarian. * * * * *

If a man gets a fullness of the priesthood of God, he has to get it in the same way that Jesus Christ obtained it, and that was by keeping all the commandments and obeying all the ordinances of the house of the Lord.

Where there is no change of priesthood, there is no change of ordinances, says Paul, if God has not changed the ordinances and the priesthood. Howl, ye sectarians! If he has, when and where has He revealed it? Have ye turned revelators? Then why deny revelation?

Many men will say, "I will never forsake you, but will stand by you at all times." But the moment you teach them some of the mysteries of the kingdom of God that are retained in the heavens and are to be revealed to the children of men when they are prepared for them, they will be the first to stone you and put you to death. It was this same principle that crucified the Lord Jesus Christ, and will cause the people to kill the prophets in this generation.

Many things are insoluble to the children of men in the last days: for instance, that God should raise the dead, and forgetting that things have been hid from before the foundation of the world, which are to be revealed to babes in the last days.

There are a great many wise men and women too in our midst who are too wise to be taught; therefore they must die in their ignorance, and in the resurrection they will find their mistake. Many seal up the door of heaven by saying, So far God may reveal and I will believe.

All men who become heirs of God and joint-heirs with Jesus Christ will have to receive the fulness of the ordinances of his kingdom; and those who will not receive all the ordinances will come short of the fullness of that glory, if they do not lose the whole.

I will say something about the spirits in prison. There has been much said by modern divines about the words of Jesus (when on the cross) to the thief, saying, "This day shalt thou be with me in paradise." King James' translators make it out to say paradise. But what is paradise? It is a modern word: it does not answer at all to the original word that Jesus made use of. Find the original of the word paradise. You may as easily find a needle in a haymow. Here is a chance for battle, ye learned men. There is nothing in the original word in Greek from which this was taken that signifies paradise; but it was—This day thou shalt be with me in the world of spirits: then I will teach you all about it and answer your inquiries. And Peter says he went and preached to the world of spirits (spirits in prison, I Peter, 3rd chap., 19th verse), so that they who would receive it could have it answered by proxy by those who live on the earth, etc.

The doctrine of baptism for the dead is clearly shown in the New Testament; and if the doctrine is not good, then throw the New Testament away; but if it is the word of God, then let the doctrine be acknowledged; and it was the reason why Jesus said unto the Jews, "How oft would I have gathered thy children together, even as a hen gathereth her chickens under her wings, and ye would not!"—that they might attend to the ordinances of baptism for the dead as well as other ordinances of the priesthood, and receive revelations from heaven, and be perfected in the things of the kingdom of God—but they would not. This was the case on the day of Pentecost: those blessings were poured out on the disciples on that occasion. God ordained that He would save the dead, and would do it by gathering His people together.

It always has been when a man was sent of God with the priesthood and he began to preach the fullness of the gospel, that he was thrust out by his friends, who are ready to butcher him if he teach things which they imagine to be wrong; and Jesus was crucified upon this principle.

I will now turn linguist. There are many things in the Bible which do not, as they now stand, accord with the revelations of the Holy Ghost to me.

I will criticise a little further. There has been much said about the word hell, and the sectarian world have preached much about it, describing it to be a burning lake of fire and brimstone. But what is hell? It is another modern term, and is taken from hades. I'll hunt after hades as Pat did for the woodchuck.

Hades, the Greek, or Shaole, the Hebrew: these two significations mean a world of spirits. Hades, Shaole, paradise, spirits in prison, are all one: it is a world of spirits.

The righteous and the wicked all go to the same world of spirits until the resurrection. "I do not think so," says one. If you will go to my house any time, I will take my lexicon and prove it to you.

The great misery of departed spirits in the world of spirits, where they go after death. is to know that they come short of the glory that others enjoy and that they might have enjoyed themselves, and they are their own accusers. "But," says one, "I believe in one universal heaven and hell, where all go, and are all alike, and equally miserable or equally happy."

What! where all are huddled together—the honorable, virtuous, and murderers, and whoremongers, when it is written that they shall be judged according to the deeds done in the body? But St. Paul informs us of three glories and three heavens. He knew a man that was caught up to the third heavens. Now, if the doctrine of the sectarian world, that there is but one heaven, is true, Paul, what do you tell that lie for, and say there are three? Jesus said unto His disciples, "In my Father's house are many mansions, if it were not so, I would have told you. I go to prepare a place for you, and I will come and receive you to myself, that where I am ye may be also."

Any man may believe that Jesus Christ is the Son of God, and be happy in that belief, and yet not obey his commandments, and at last be cut down for disobedience to the Lord's righteous requirements.

A man of God should be endowed with wisdom, knowledge, and understanding, in order to teach and lead the people of God. The sectarian priests are blind, and they lead the blind, and they will all fall into the ditch together. They build with hay, wood, and stubble, on the old revelations, without the true priesthood or spirit of revelation. If I had time, I would dig into hell, hades, shaole, and tell what exists there.

There is much said about God and the Godhead. The scriptures say there are Gods many and Lords many, but to us there is but one living and true God, and the heaven of heavens could not contain him; for he took the liberty to go into other heavens. The teachers of the day say that the Father is God, the Son is God, and the Holy Ghost is God, and they are all in one body and one God. Jesus prayed that those that the Father had given him out of the world might be made one in them, as they were one; [one in spirit, in mind, in purpose]. If I were to testify that the Christian world were wrong on this point, my testimony would be true.

Peter and Stephen testify that they saw the Son of Man standing on the right hand of God. Any person that had seen the heavens opened knows that there are three personages in the heavens who hold the keys of power, and one presides over all.

If any man attempts to refute what I am about to say, after I have made it plain, let him beware.

As the Father hath power in Himself, so hath the Son power in Himself, to lay down His life and take it again, so He has a body of His own. The Son doeth what He hath seen the Father do: then the Father hath some day laid down His life and taken it again; so He has a body of His own; each one will be in His own body; and yet the sectarian world believe the body of the Son is identical with the Father's.

Gods have an ascendancy over the angels, who are ministering servants. In the resurrection, some are raised to be angels; others are raised to become Gods.

These things are revealed in the most holy place in a Temple prepared for that purpose. Many of the sects cry out, "Oh, I have the testimony of Jesus; I have the Spirit of God: but away with Joe Smith; he says he is a prophet; but there are to be no prophets or revelators in the last days." Stop, sir! The Revelator says that the testimony of Jesus is the spirit of prophecy; so by your own mouth you are condemned. But to the text. Why gather the people together in this place? For the same purpose that Jesus wanted to gather the Jews—to receive the ordinances, the blessings, and glories that God has in store for His Saints.

I will now ask this assembly and all the Saints if you will now build this house and receive the ordinances and blessings which God has in store for you; or will you not build unto the Lord this house, and let Him pass by and bestow these blessings upon another people? I pause for a reply.

Rev. De Wolf Preaches at Nauvoo.

At half-past two p.m., I introduced to the congregation Mr. De Wolf, a clergyman of the Episcopal church, and requested the attention of the congregation in his behalf. He read the 6th chapter of Hebrews, and then kneeled and prayed, dressed in his black clerical gown, which excited some curiosity among some of the Saints. After the choir sang a hymn, he preached from Hebrews, 6th chapter, 1st and 2nd verses, touching on such principles only that are acknowledged and received by the Church. In his closing remarks he observed—"I may never meet you all again this side of the eternal world; but I will appoint a meeting—i. e. when the Lord Jesus shall descend with his angels to call the dead from their graves, and sit in judgment on all the world."

Conference at Lima.

A conference was held at Lima, and the branch reorganized, under the direction of Elder Heber C. Kimball; Isaac Morley, President; Walter Cox and Edwin Whiting, counselors; Gardiner Snow, bishop; Clark Hallet and Henry Dean, counselors; William Woodland, Solomon Hancock, James C. Snow, James Israel, Edmond Durfee, Daniel Stanton, Moses Clawson,

Joseph S. Allen, Philip Garner, Henry Ettleman, Reuben Daniels, and Horace Rawson, high council; James C. Snow, clerk of the branch.

During the appointing of the high council, Elder Kimball made some general remarks upon the Word of Wisdom.

Heber C. Kimball on the Word of Wisdom.

He commenced by saying that he always despised a penurious principle in any man, and that God despised it also; for he was liberal and did not look at every little thing as we do. He looked at the integrity of the heart of man. He said some would strain, nip and tuck at the Word of Wisdom, and at the same time they would turn away a poor brother from their door when he would ask for a little meal for his breakfast. He compared it to the man that was stretched upon the iron bedstead; if he was too long, they would cut him off; if he was too short, they would stretch him out. And again, he said, it made him think of the old Indian's tree, which stood so straight that it leaned a little the other way, and the best way was to stand erect.

In the after part of the day he renewed the subject by saying that he did not wish to have any one take any advantage of what he had said, for he spoke in general terms; but said he had always obeyed the Word of Wisdom, and wanted every Saint to observe the same. He said that, when he was in England, he only taught it once or twice in public, and the Saints saw his example and followed it. So likewise when the elders go to preach, if they will observe the Word of Wisdom, all of those will whom they bring into the kingdom; but if they do not, they cannot expect their children will, but they will be just like themselves; for every spirit begets its own. Neither will such elders be able to do much good; for the Holy Ghost will not dwell in them, neither will the Father nor the Son; for they will not dwell where the Holy Ghost will not, and neither of them will dwell in unholy temples.

He said that he wanted wise and honorable men to fill responsible offices who were worthy. He then closed his subject by recommending the Saints to observe the counsel of President Morley. He made some very appropriate remarks with regard to the Temple and Nauvoo House.

Elder William Curtis was appointed to go with Elder Aaron M. York to the State of Maine.

CHAPTER XXIII.

THE PROPHET'S VISIT TO DIXON, LEE CO.—CONDITIONS IN NAUVOO—SALEM ARGUS—SUMMARY OF THE WORLD'S EVENTS FOR THE YEAR 1843, UP TO JUNE—NEWS OF THE IMPENDING ARREST OF THE PROPHET RECEIVED AT NAUVOO—EXPEDITIONS FOR HIS PROTECTION—THE ARREST—TURNING THE TABLES—RETURN TO NAUVOO

Monday, June 12, 1843.—At the office morning and afternoon, and approved of the resolutions of a court martial of the Nauvoo Legion, passed June 10, 1843, to the effect

That an arsenal be built in the city of Nauvoo, to be located in any part of the city where the lieutenant and major generals may direct, who are also authorized to make or cause to be made, a draft of the same, and also to purchase any piece of land for the aforesaid purposes which they may deem proper.

That Colonel Jonathan Dunham be and is hereby appointed agent for the Legion to superintend the business of the building of the aforesaid arsenal, and that he be allowed one dollar and forty-cents per day for his services while employed in that business, to be paid out of any money in the treasury not otherwise appropriated; that he be armorer of said arsenal, when completed; and that he be allowed such remuneration for said services as may be hereafter fixed by law; also that he be required to give bonds to the amount of five thousand dollars, with approved securities, before entering upon the duties of said office.

That any constable or collector of fines be and is hereby authorized, if he cannot obtain money, to take property in payment of fines, at a fair valuation at his discretion, and make returns thereof to the proper officers, as in other cases.

That Brigadier-General Rich be and is hereby authorized to organize the second battalion, first regiment second cohort, into a regiment of light infantry, to be called "The Escort Regiment of Light Infantry," to take place in the second cohort, according to assignment, on parade days, and do such duties of escort, &c., as may be necessary; and that he organize the first battalion, first regiment, second cohort, into a regiment of artillery.

About forty Saints arrived from Peterboro, New Hampshire.

Thursday, 13.—I started north with Emma and the children to see her sister, Mrs. Wasson and family, living near Dixon, Lee county Illinois.

Departure of the Prophet for Dixon, Lee Co., Ill.

Elder Wilford Woodruff, when going to the prairie with several brethren to fence his five-acre lot broke the reach of his wagon and it fell into a pile together. The wheel fell on his arm and bruised him considerably; but he was able to mend his wagon and continue his journey. After working hard all day he went to Brother Cheney's house to obtain a drink of water, when an ugly dog bit him through the calf of the leg, which made him very lame.

Wednesday, 14.—Business is progressing. Buildings are going up in every direction, and the citizens manifest a determination that Nauvoo shall be built up. The stones of the Temple begin to rise tier upon tier, and it already presents a stately and noble appearance.

The Mississippi has been rising three or four days, and is now three or four inches above high water mark.

Thursday, 15.—We give the following extract from the *Salem Advertiser and Argus*, being an extract from a lecture delivered in Salem by Mr. J. B. Newhall:

Synopsis of a Lecture Delivered in Salem, on Nauvoo and the Prophet.

The Nauvoo Temple is a very singular and unique structure. It is one hundred and fifty feet in length, ninety-eight feet wide, and when finished will be one hundred and fifty feet high. It is different from anything in ancient or modern history. Everything about it is on a magnificent scale, and when finished and seen from the opposite side of the river, will present one, if not the most beautiful, chaste and noble specimens of architecture to be found in the world.

We should like to be in possession of a model of this building, both on account of its great notoriety as being connected with the Mormon or Latter-day Saints' religion and also a work of art.

Did our limits here permit, we might give a very minute description of the whole order of architecture. The splendid drawing was executed by Mr. Newhall, while in Nauvoo, from a copy in the archives of that city. We wish he had taken it on a large scale, but he probably did not on account of transportation. We regret exceedingly that we did not have the privilege of a near inspection of the map of the city of Nauvoo, the place which for some time past has created more intense interest, perhaps, than any other city, town or village in the country, if not in the world. But on enquiring for it, we found it had been rolled up and packed away.

He gave a very glowing and interesting account of this city. The location is one of the most beautiful upon earth, situated upon the Mississippi river, rising in an inclined plane till it reaches the height where it overlooks an extensive tract of territory, unrivaled in rich and varying scenery.

His account of the military displays in Nauvoo, where Smith's Legion, as it is called, turns out, is very interesting and exciting. He spoke of the six ladies on horses, with white feathers or plumes waving over black velvet, riding up and down in front of the Legion. This must appear singular, at least to a Yankee.

He has had personal interviews with Joseph; and to sum up his character in a word, he is a jolly fellow, and according to his view, he is one of the last persons on earth whom God would have raised up as a prophet or priest, he is so diametrically opposite to that which he ought to be in order to merit the titles or to act in such offices. Among others he is very sociable, cheerful, kind and obliging, and very hospitable.

We have seen Hyrum Smith, a brother of Joseph's, and heard him preach, and conversed with him about his religion, its origin and progress; and we heard him declare in this city, in public, that what is recorded about the plates is God's solemn truth.

He declared to us in the Masonic Hall, in this city, that the statements are true, and called upon God with uplifted hands as a witness. We think it would be very interesting to the good people of Salem, and in fact to the whole Eastern States, to have the prophet come and make us a visit. We very much doubt whether there is a man on earth who would create so much excitement and deep interest at least for the time being, as the prophet.

The *Times and Seasons* of this date has the following:

Calamities of 1843, up to June.

The past year has been distinguished by calamities. In some instances the elements seem to have been commissioned to perform the work of destruction to an awful extent and unprecedented severity.

Three of the greatest calamities that have occurred within a century, happened within the short period of one hundred hours. The terrible fire at Hamburg, which destroyed two thousand houses, and nearly thirty million dollars of property, in the fairest portion of the city, was followed in less than two days by the earthquake at St. Domingo. In this earthquake the towns of Haytien and Santiago, sixty miles apart, were entirely destroyed, and not less than seven thousand five hundred of the inhabitants perished.

On the very next day, while St. Domingo was yet rocking with the shocks of the earthquake, and the ruins of Hamburg were not three days old, a train of cars filled with passengers on the railroad from Paris to Versailles were thrown from the track and set on fire by the engine. Before the passengers, who were locked in, could be removed, seventy of them perished in the flames.

More recently the city of Liverpool has suffered by fire to an extent only surpassed by the fire at Hamburg.

In this country, the cities of Portland, New York, Charleston, and Columbia have suffered severely from the same cause.

At one period of several weeks during the year it was estimated that the loss of steamboats on the western waters averaged one a day. In connection with six of the boats, two hundred lives were lost. If to all this we add the loss of life at sea, which has been unusually great the past year, we must regard it as a year of calamities.

Another Arrest of the Prophet Threatened.

Friday, 16.—Judge James Adams wrote by express from Springfield, at ten p. m., that Governor Thomas Ford had told him that he was going to issue a writ for me on the requisition of the Governor of Missouri, and that it would start tomorrow.

I copy the following from the *Neighbor.*

Proscription Against the Jews.

At the very moment when a spirit of toleration seemed to influence the feelings of society throughout the civilized world, we regret to perceive that the tribunals of the pope are, in June, 1843, reviving at Rome and Ancona, the very worst proscriptions of that fell and sanguinary institute, the Inquisition, as will be seen by a perusal of the following document:

"We, Fra Vincenzo Salina, of the order of Predicatori, Master in Theology, General Inquisitor in Ancona, Singaglia, Jesi, Osino, Cingoli, Macerata, Tolentino, Loreta, Recanati, and other towns and districts,. &c.

"It being deemed necessary to revive the full observance of the disciplinary laws relative to the Israelites residing within our jurisdiction, and having hitherto without effect employed prayers and exhortation to obtain obediedce to those laws in the Ghetti (Jewries) of Ancona and Sinigaglia,authorized by the despatch of the Sacred and Supreme Inquisition of Rome, dated June 10, 1843, expressly enjoining and commanding the observance of the decrees and pontificial constitutions, especially in respect to Christian nurses and domestic servants, or to the sale of property either in town or country districts, purchased and possessed previously to 1827, as well as subsequently to that period, we decree as follows:

"1. From the interval of two months after the date of this day, all gipsy and Christian domestics, male and female, whether employed by day or by night, must be dismissed from service in the said two Ghetti; and all Jews residing within our jurisdiction are expressly prohibited from employing any Christian nurse, or availing themselves of the services of any Christian in any domestic occupation whatever under pain of being immediately punished according to the pontifical constitutions.

"2. That all Jews who may possess property either in town or country permanent or moveable, or rents or interest, or any right involving shares in funded property, or leased landed property, must, within the term of three months from this day dispose of it by a positive and real, and not by any pretended or fictitious contract. Should this not be done within the time specified, the holy office is to sell the same by auction, on proof of the annual harvest being got in.

"3. That no Hebrew nurses, and still less any Hebrew family, shall inhabit the city, or reside in or remove their property into any town or district where there is no Ghetto (place or residence for Jews); and that such as may actually be there in conformity to the laws must return to their respective Ghetto within the peremptory period of six months, otherwise they will be proceeded against according to the tenor of the law.

"4. That especially in any city where there is a Ghetto, no Hebrew must presume to associate at table with Christians, either in public houses or ordinaries, out of the Ghetto.

"5. That in a city which has a Ghetto, no Hebrew shall sleep out of the Israelite quarter, nor make free to enter into familiar conversation in a Christian house.

"6. That no Hebrew shall take the liberty, under any pretext whatever to induce male Christians, and still less female Christians, to sleep within the boundaries of the Ghetto.

"7. That no Hebrews shall hire Christians, even only by the day, to work in their houses in the Ghetto.

"8. That no Hebrew, either male or female, shall frequent the houses of Christians, or maintain friendly relations with Christian men or women.

"9. That the laws shall remain in force respecting the decorum to be observed by the Hebrews who may absent themselves from their Ghetto to travel in the other parts of the state."

After laying down their monstrous rescripts, which we had hoped even the Romish church would not have attempted to revive, and still less reclothe with authority, and arm with tremendous pains and penalties, the savage order is issued that these intolerant laws shall be read in each of the Jewish synagogues. It is added, "They who violate the above articles will incur some or all of the penalties prescribed in the edicts of the Holy Inquisition.

Saturday, 17.—The *Maid of Iowa* went to Shokoquon with the Temple hands on a pleasure excursion. While there, the steamer *Shokoquon* came to port with many citizens from Burlington, when Elder George A. Smith delivered a lecture.

Sunday, 18. Meeting at the Temple. Elder Eli P. Maginn preached in the forepart of the day, to the edification of the Saints. The sacrament was administered in the afternoon.

Markham and Clayton Sent to Warn the Prophet.

Judge Adams' message arrived early in the evening, when my Brother Hyrum sent William Clayton and Stephen Markham as fast as possible to inform me. Markham had two hundred and fifty dollars, and Clayton borrowed two hundred dollars.

They left Nauvoo about half-past twelve at night, and proceeded to La Harpe.

Elder Elijah F. Sheets writes that he and Joseph A. Stratton have been preaching in Illinois, Indiana and Pennsylvania since September 4, 1842; have baptized thirty-two, and many more are convinced of the truth of the work; and that they are continuing their labors.

Monday, 19.—The laborers held a meeting in the grove to investigate the price and principles of labor.

Clayton and Markham arrived at La Harpe at sunrise, tarried about two hours to get a horse shod and take breakfast; started again at seven for Monmouth, where they arrived at three p. m., and put up their horses to feed and rest. They took dinner and slept till seven, when they started again and rode till midnight, when, the horses being tired and weary, they turned them out to feed, and they themselves lay down to sleep about two hours; after which they again resumed their journey and rode one mile north of Hendersonville, where they stopped to feed their horses.

Progress of Markham and Clayton.

Tuesday, 20.—About half-past seven, a. m., Markham and Clayton again started on their journey, and arrived at Andover about ten a. m. They turned out their horses to graze in the woods for about half-an-hour, when they proceeded to Gennesseo, where they arrived at half-past two p. m. They tried to hire a pair of horses to continue their journey, but did not succeed. They left Gennesseo, at six p. m., and traveled to Portland, where they arrived at twelve, put up their horses, and went to bed until four a. m.

Markham and Clayton Arrive at Portland.

The following appears in the *Nauvoo Neighbor*, and serves to illustrate the benefit of chartered rights in Illinois:

Projected Industries at Nauvoo Menaced by Portending Legislation.

SIR:—In obedience to the call made in your paper for information in relation to the affairs of the Agricultural and Manufacturing Association of this city, I give you such facts as I think will be satisfactory.

The first great object of the company was to establish a pottery for the manufacturing of the various kinds of crockery in common use in the country. Persons were deputed to make the necessary search whether suitable materials could be obtained.

The persons who were employed in this service were such as had been employed all their lives in the business. Their report was favorable, having found all the materials of as good a quality as those used in the old world for that purpose, in the immediate vicinity.

Efforts were accordingly made to commence the business with as little delay as possible. An eligible situation was obtained and the work of building commenced.

A stone building of sufficient size was put under construction and progressed with much rapidity. Persons possessing means felt desirous of investing a part of them at least in the business. All was prosperous and all flattering.

A considerable amount of land was obtained for agricultural purposes, it being the wish of the managers to supply all their workmen with all their necessaries as far as could be. Arrangements were making to get stock of the various kinds for this purpose.

The building had progressed nearly to the height of one story, when the electioneering campaign commenced, and it was roundly asserted that if certain persons were elected, all the charters granted by a previous legislature to the citizens of Nauvoo would be repealed.

At first the association supposed that this was merely an electioneering intrigue. But it assumed a formidable appearance, and began to assume the character of a fixed determination to carry the design into execution.

The subsequent acts of the legislature have given but too much evidence that such was the real intention of a very considerable portion of the members of the last legislature, if not a majority of them. This instantly paralyzed the exertions of the company. Many who were about to contribute to the funds of the society paused, not knowing what was best; and in consequence the work stopped.

Not that the company supposed that there was any such power vested in the legislature, either in the constitution or common sense; but they did not know how far a reckless spirit might lead men in the violation of both.

As the matter now stands, those having capital are at a loss whether to invest it in that way or not, lest the same reckless spirit may inevitably carry the proposed design into effect.

The work has not stopped for want of means or materials to carry on the business, as means, materials, and workmen of the first order are all at hand. But where is the safety, while such doctrines are boldly maintained by our legislature?

All the prospects of the company may be blasted at any stage of their business by one single act of men who seem to have no interest in the prosperity of the state or the citizens thereof, apart from their own political preferment.

Pledges can be made, for the sake of preferment, to an ignorant constituency to commit the most flagrant abuses upon the rights of private companies or even individuals, and attempts made with zeal and determination to carry them out to the full extent.

If public confidence be restored, the work can go on more vigorously than ever.

Respectfully,
SIDNEY RIGDON,
President of the Company.

Donations to the Temple.

Elder John Snider reported the names of various persons in Great Britain and Ireland who donated various small sums between May and December, 1842, as contributions for building the Temple, and paid over nine hundred and seventy-five dollars and four cents. The names of the donors and amounts are recorded in the "Law of the Lord."

Generosity of Earl Spencer.

I insert the following as an exception to the general rule:—Earl Spencer keeps all the poor in the parish of Wormleighton, England, and so prevents a poor rate. He allows his laborers nine shillings a week when out of employment, and they pay only a shilling a year as a nominal rent for the house in which they severally reside.

Meeting of the Prophet with Markham and Clayton.

Wednesay, 21.—Markham and Clayton left Portland at four a. m., and traveled to within nine miles of Dixon. They changed their course, and went direct to Inlet Grove, where they arrived at half-past twelve, took dinner and fed their horses. Left Inlet at two p. m., and arrived at Wasson's at four p. m., where they learned that I was gone to Dixon in the carriage; and although their horses were tired down, they started for Dixon, but met me about half way.

They returned with me to Wasson's, and were glad to find a resting place, having ridden two hundred and twelve miles in sixty-six hours and had very little rest on the way; the horses were tired,—their backs very sore. I told them not to be alarmed. "I have no fear. I shall not leave here: I shall find friends, and Missourians cannot hurt me, I tell you in the name of Israel's God."

Thursday, 22.—Another meeting of the laborers in the grove near the temple concerning wages.

Postponement of the Prophet's Appointment at Dixon.

I had previously given out an appointment to preach this day at Dixon, but on account of the change in circumstances, I wrote to Dixon, telling the people there was a writ out for me, and therefore declined preaching; and I kept myself quiet all day, telling my friends that if I started for home I might be arrested where I had no friends and be kidnapped into Missouri, and thought it best to tarry at Inlet and see the result. Many [at Dixon] were desirous to hear me preach, but were disappointed.

Lawyer Edward Southwick, of Dixon, having heard of the writ being out against me, rode twelve miles to inform me. I thanked him for his kindness, paid him twenty-five dollars and introduced him to my friends, Markham and Clayton, showing that I had received previous information.

Friday, 23.—Judge Adams arrived at Nauvoo from Springfield.

At eight a. m. a company of the brethren gathered to remove the timbers from the Temple to the grove.

I sent William Clayton to Dixon at ten a. m., to try and find out what was going on there. He met Mr. Joseph H. Reynolds, the sheriff of Jackson county, Missouri, and Constable Harmon T. Wilson, of Carthage, Illinois, about half way, but they being disguised, they were not known by him; and when at Dixon they represented themselves as Mormon elders who wanted to see the prophet. They hired a man and team to carry them, for they had run their horses almost to death.

They arrived at Mr. Wasson's while the family were at dinner, about two p. m. They came to the door and said they were Mormon elders, and wanted to see Brother Joseph. I was in the yard going to the barn when Wilson stepped to the end of the house and saw me. He accosted me in a very uncouth, ungentlemanly manner, when Reynolds stepped up to me, collared me, then both of them presented cocked pistols to my breast, without showing any writ or serving any process. Reynolds cried out, "G— d— you, if you stir I'll shoot; G— d— if you, stir one inch, I shoot you, be still, or I'll shoot you, by G—." I enquired "What is the meaning of all this?" "I'll show you the meaning, by G—; and if you stir one inch, I'll shoot you, G— d— you." I answered, "I am not afraid of your shooting; I am not afraid to die." I then bared my breast and told them to shoot away. "I have endured so much oppression, I am weary of life; and kill me, if you please. I am a strong man, however, and with my own natural weapons could soon level both of you; but if you have any legal process to serve, I am at all times subject to law, and shall not offer resistance." Reynold replied, "G— d— you, if you say another word I will shoot you, by G—." I answered, "Shoot away; I am not afraid of your pistols."

The Arrest at Dixon.

By this time Stephen Markham walked deliberately towards us. When they saw him coming, they turned their pistols from me to him, and threatened his life if he came any nearer; but he paid no attention to their threats, and continued to advance nearer. They then turned their pistols on me again, jamming them against my side, with their fingers on the triggers, and ordered Markham to stand still or they would shoot me through. As Markham was advancing

Markham's Courage.

rapidly towards me, I said, "You are not going to resist the officers, are you, Brother Markham?" He replied, "No, not if they are officers: I know the law too well for that."

They then hurried me off, put me in a wagon without serving any process, and were for hurrying me off without letting me see or bid farewell to my family or friends, or even allowing me time to get my hat or clothes, or even suffer my wife or children to bring them to me. I then said, "Gentlemen, if you have any legal process, I wish to obtain a writ of habeas corpus," and was answered,—"G— d— you, you shan't have one." They still continued their punching me on both sides with their pistols.

Brutality of the Arrest.

Markham then sprung and seized the horses by the bits, and held them until my wife could bring my hat and coat. Reynolds and Wilson again threatening to shoot Markham, who said, "There is no law on earth that requires a sheriff to take a prisoner without his clothes." Fortunately at this moment I saw a man passing, and said to him, "These men are kidnapping me, and I wish a writ of habeas corpus to deliver myself out of their hands. But as he did not appear to go, I told Markham to go, and he immediately proceeded to Dixon on horseback, where the sheriff also proceeded with me at full speed, without even allowing me to speak to my family or bid them good bye. The officers held their pistols with the muzzles jamming into my side for more than eight miles, and they only desisted on being reproached by Markham for their cowardice in so brutally ill-treating an unarmed, defenseless prisoner. On arriving at the house of Mr. McKennie, the tavern-keeper, I was thrust into a room and guarded there, without being allowed to see anybody; and fresh horses were ordered to be ready in five minutes.

I again stated to Reynolds, "I wish to get counsel," when he answered. G— d— you, you shan't have counsel: one word more, G— d— you, and I'll shoot you."

"What is the use of this so often?" said I. "I have repeatedly told you to shoot; and I now tell you again to shoot away!" I saw a person passing and shouted to him through the window, "I am falsely imprisoned here, and I want a lawyer. Lawyer Edward Southwick came, and had the door banged in his face, with the old threat of shooting him if he came any nearer.

Another lawyer (Mr. Shepherd G. Patrick) afterwards came and received the same treatment, which began to cause considerable excitement in Dixon.

A Mr. Lucien P. Sanger asked Markham what was the matter, when he told him all, and stated that the sheriff intended to drag me away immediately to Missouri, and prevent my taking out a writ of habeas corpus.

The Timely Interference of Mr. Dixon.

Sanger soon made this known to Mr. Dixon, the owner of the house, and his friends, who gathered around the hotel door, and gave Reynolds to understand that if that was their mode of doing business in Missouri, they had another way of doing it in Dixon. They were a law-abiding people and Republicans, and gave Reynolds to understand that he should not take me away without giving me the opportunity of a fair trial, and that I should have justice done me; but that if he persisted in his course, they had a very summary way of dealing with such people.

The Prophet's Appeal to the People of Dixon.

Mr. Reynolds finding further resistance to be useless, allowed Mr. Patrick and Mr. Southwick to come into the room to me, (but Wilson was inside guarding the door, and Reynolds guarded the outside of the door,) when I told them I had been taken prisoner by these men without process; I had been insulted and abused by them. I showed them my flesh, which was black for about eighteen inches in circumference on each side, from their punching me with their pistols; and I wanted them to sue out a writ of habeas corpus, whereupon Reynolds swore he should only wait half-an-hour to give me a chance. A messenger was immediately sent by Mr. Dixon to Mr. Chamberlain, the Master-in-Chancery, who lived six miles distant, and, another message to Cyrus H. Walker, who happened to be near, to have them come down and get out the writ of habeas corpus.

Cyrus H. Walker.

A writ was sued out by Markham before a justice of the peace against Reynolds and Wilson for threatening his life. They were taken into custody by the constable. He sued out another writ for assault and threatening my life, whereupon they were again arrested.

At this time Markham rushed into the room and put a pistol (unobserved) into my pocket, although Reynolds and Wilson had their pistols cocked at the same time and were threatening to shoot him.

About midnight he sued out a writ for a violation of the law in relation to writs of habeas corpus, Wilson having transferred me to the custody of Reynolds, for the purpose of dragging me to Missouri, and thereby avoiding the effect and operation of said writ, contrary to law, which was put over to be heard at ten o'clock tomorrow morning; and I was conducted back to the room and guarded through the night.

The 5th legion, 2nd cohort, Nauvoo Legion, consisting of four companies, organized. Hosea Stout was elected colonel; Theodore Turley, lieutenant-colonel; Jesse D. Hunter, major.

Legion Enlargement.

Saturday, *24*.—As my favorite horse, Jo. Duncan, was somewhat jaded, with being ridden so hastily by Brother Clayton, I hired a man with his horse and buggy to carry Brother Clayton to Rock Island, where the steamer *Amaranth* fortunately came in about fifteen minutes, on which he took passage to Nauvoo, to inform my brother Hyrum of what was being done, and request him to send me some assistance forthwith.

Clayton's Return to Nauvoo.

About eight, the master-in-chancery arrived and issued a writ of habeas corpus returnable before the Hon. John

D. Caton, Judge of the 9th Judicial Circuit at Ottawa, which was duly served on Reynolds and Wilson.

Mr. Cyrus Walker, who was out electioneering to become the representative for Congress, told me that he could not find time to be my lawyer unless I could promise him my vote. He being considered the greatest criminal lawyer in that part of Illinois, I determined to secure his aid, and promised him my vote. He afterwards went to Markham and joyfully said, "I am now sure of my election, as Joseph Smith has promised me his vote, and I am going to defend him."

Cyrus Walker's Terms for Legal Service.

At ten a. m. another writ was issued—this time from the Circuit Court of Lee county, against Reynolds and Wilson. for private damage and for false imprisonment, claiming ten thousand dollars damages upon the ground that the writ issued by the governor of Illinois was a void writ in law; upon which said writ they were held to bail in ten thousand dollars each, and they had to send to Missouri for bondsmen and were placed in the custody of the sheriff of Lee county.

Turning the Tables on Reynolds and Wilson.

Reynolds and Wilson felt bad when these last writs were served on them, and began to cool in their conduct a little; after which they also obtained a writ of habeas corpus, for the purpose of being discharged before Judge Caton.

I was conveyed by Reynolds and Wilson, upon the first writ of habeas corpus, towards Ottawa, as far as Pawpaw Grove, thirty-two miles, where I was again abused by Reynolds and Wilson, which was observed by the landlord.

Arrival at Pawpaw Grove.

Esquire Walker sent Mr. Campbell, sheriff of Lee county, to my assistance, and he came and slept by me. In the morning certain men wished to see me, but I was not allowed to see them.

The news of my arrival had hastily circulated about the neighborhood; and very early in the morning the largest room in the hotel was filled with citizens, who were anxious to hear me preach and requested me to address them.

Sheriff Reynolds entered the room and said, pointing to me, "I wish you to understand this man is my prisoner, and I want you to disperse: you must not gather around here in this way." Upon which Mr. David Town, an aged gentleman, who was lame and carried a large hickory walking-stick, advanced towards Reynolds, bringing his hickory upon the floor, and said:

David Town's Effective Speech.

"You damned infernal puke, we'll learn you to come here and interrupt gentlemen. Sit down there, (pointing to a very low chair,) and sit still. Don't open your head till General Smith gets through talking. If you never learned manners in Missouri, we'll teach you that gentlemen are not to be imposed upon by a nigger-driver. You cannot kidnap men here, if you do in Missouri; and if you attempt it here, there's a commitee in this grove that will sit on your case; and, sir, it is the highest tribunal in the United States, as *from its decision there is no appeal.*"

Reynolds, no doubt aware that the person addressing him was the head of a committee who had prevented the settlers on the public domain from being imposed upon by land speculators, sat down in silence while I addressed the assembly for an hour-and-a-half on the subject of marriage, my visitors having requested me to give them my views of the laws of God respecting marriage. My freedom commenced from that hour.

Departure of Emma Smith from Dixon.

Immediately after I left Dixon, my wife and children started with my carriage from Inlet Grove for Nauvoo being driven by her nephew, Lorenzo D. Wasson.

The quorum of the Twelve received a letter from Asahel Smith, [the prophet's father's brother, and father of the late Judge Elias Smith] of Nashville, Iowa, requesting them to appoint a conference in that place to settle some difficulties existing there.

The free and accepted ancient York Masons met at the lodge room, being the anniversary of St. John's Day; then formed a procession in due masonic form in front of the hall, and walked to Main street, where the corner stone for a Masonic Temple was laid by the Worshipful Master, Hyrum Smith. Two masonic hymns were sung, after which they proceeded to the Grove near the Temple, where an oration was delivered by Brother John Taylor. From thence they proceeded to Mr. Warner's, where about two hundred sat down to an excellent dinner. The company broke up early in the afternoon, highly delighted with the day's proceedings.

A Masonic Temple for Nauvoo.

Sunday, 25.—At Pawpaw Grove it was ascertained that Judge Caton was on a visit to New York, whereupon Reynolds, Wilson, Walker, Southwick, Patrick, Dixon, Stephen Markham and myself, with others, started about eight a. m., and returned to the town of Dixon, arriving about four p. m. when, I was again locked in a room and guarded through the night.

The water has fallen in the Mississippi more than a foot since last Sunday.

At ten a. m., meeting at the Temple. Elder Lyman Wight preached on charity; and in the afternoon, Elder Maginn was preaching, when my brother Hyrum went to the stand and requested the brethren to meet him at the Masonic Hall in thirty minutes.

Excitement at Nauvoo.

The brethren immediately went there in such numbers that one fourth of them could not get into the room; so they adjourned to the green and formed a hollow square, when my brother Hyrum informed them that Elder William Clayton had arrived about two, and told him that Joseph H. Reynolds, sheriff of Jackson county, Missouri, and Harmon T. Wilson, of Carthage, had come upon me by surprise and arrested me, and related the occurrence as far as known, up to my arrival in Dixon. He wanted a company to go up to my assistance and see that I had my rights. He called for volunteers, when upwards of three hundred volunteered, from whom they selected such as were wanted.

Relief Expeditions.

Generals Law and Charles C. Rich started the same evening, with a company of about one hundred and seventy-five men on horseback. Previous to starting, Elder Wilford Woodruff went to the company and donated a barrel of rifle powder, when every man filled his horn or flask.

Wilson Law declared he would not go a step unless he could have money to bear his expenses, upon which Elder Brigham Young said the money should be forthcoming, although he did not know at the time where he could raise a dollar. In about thirty minutes he got on the track, and in the course of two hours he had borrowed seven hundred dollars, and put it in the hands of Hyrum Smith and Wilson Law, to defray the expenses of the expedition. About seventy-five on board the *Maid of Iowa*, with Captain Dan Jones, went up the Illinois river for Peoria, and to examine the steamboats, suspecting I might be a prisoner on board one of them, as they supposed me on the road to Ottawa.

Several of the Pottawatamie Indians called to see the Nauvoo House and Temple. They wanted to talk, but their interpreter could not speak much.

Writ of Habeas Corpus Secured.

The writ of habeas corpus [the one first issued and made returnable before Judge Caton at Ottawa] was returned endorsed thereon, "Judge absent," when another writ of habeas corpus was issued at seven a. m. by the Master-in-Chancery, and was worded at Colonel Markham's request, "Returnable before the nearest tribunal in the Fifth Judicial District authorized to hear and determine writs of habeas corpus;" and the sheriff of Lee county served it on them [Reynolds and Wilson] in a few minutes afterwards. I, my lawyers, Markham, Dixon and other friends held a council and arranged to start before nine a. m., to go before Judge

Stephen A. Douglas, at Quincy, a distance of about two hundred and sixty miles. I employed Mr. Lucien P. Sanger with the stage coach to convey us on our journey towards Quincy.

After these arrangements were made, I sent Markham with a letter to General Wilson Law, directing him to meet me at Monmouth on Wednesday evening, with sufficient force to prevent my being kidnapped into Missouri, as I well knew that the whole country was swarming with men anxious to carry me there and kill me, without any shadow of law or justice, although they well knew that I had not committed any crime worthy of death or bonds.

Monday, 26.—It was reported that there were state writs in Nauvoo to take Lyman Wight, Parley P. Pratt, and Alexander McRae to Missouri, who armed themselves to prevent being kidnapped.

I copy the following from the *Chicago Democrat:*

Account of the Prophet's Arrest in the Chicago Democrat.

Dear Sir:—Our little town has been in an unusual state of excitement for a few days past, originating from the arrest of General Joseph Smith, which took place at the Inlet Grove, while he was on a visit with his family to a sister [an error, his wife's nephew] who resides there. He was arrested on Friday last by an officer from Hancock county, and delivered over to the sheriff of Jackson county, Missouri, in compliance with the orders of the governor.

The officers who took him brought him into town in the evening and confined him closely to his room, refusing admission not only to the citizens whose curiosity had drawn them to the spot, but to counsel whom he had requested to have employed.

Our citizens, conceiving it a violation of right that a man should be deprived of that advice and assistance which is accorded to the most degraded and guilty offender in all civilized countries under such circumstances, expressed themselves in such strong and indignant terms, that the officers finally permitted counsel to have access to him.

He applied for the benefit of the habeas corpus; and while the lawyers were busy drawing up the necessary papers, the officers frequently asserted that they would not wait, but would leave for the Mississippi at all hazards.

They were however, induced, by the force of argument, to desist from their intention and wait until morning, when the habeas corpus was served. After which they stated their determination to go to Rock Island and by steamboat from thence to Galena, before Judge Brown. General Smith justly felt fearful that once on a steamboat, he should hardly reach Galena. The distance from this place to Rock Island is the same as from here to Galena.

General Smith, finding this their determination, commenced suit against the sheriff of Missouri for trespass, and held him to bail, which he was unable to procure, which circumstance lowered his tune a little; and thus finally, today, has left for Quincy in search of Judge Young.

The severe treatment of the general, together with his pleasing deportment and equanimity under all his trials, has made him many friends and created almost universal sympathy. Persecution or oppression always helps the cause of the persecuted or oppressed, whether their cause is right or wrong.

In haste, yours,

G.

From Dixon we traveled about forty miles, and stayed for the night at a farm house. Markham rode to Genesseo with my letter and stayed all night.

Tuesday, 27.—I started with the company, and took dinner at Genesseo. At about two p. m., we resumed our journey. While crossing Fox River, I requested Reynolds to give me the privilege of riding on horseback, which he refused; but, by the intercession of Sheriff Campbell and Mr. Cyrus Walker, Walker took my seat in the stage-coach, and I his in the buggy with Mr. Montgomery, son-in-law and law student of Cyrus Walker. In about two miles we met Peter W. Conover and William L. Cutler, and shook hands with both of them at the same time, and could not refrain from tears at seeing the first of my friends come to meet me, and then said to Mr. Montgomery, "I am not going to Missouri this time. These are my boys."

En route for Quincy.

I next enquired how many were with them, and was answered, There were ten started, but they had sent one with my letter to Wilson Law, and two to Monmouth.

While we were talking, Markham, with Captain Thomas Grover, and the other five brethren, rode up. At the same time, the company who started with me from Dixon rode up. I then said to Reynolds, "Now, Reynolds, I can have the privilege of riding old Joe Duncan," and mounted my favorite horse; and the entire company then rode towards a farm house, where we made a halt.

Reynolds and Wilson, who trembled much, then rode up to Conover, who was an old acquaintance of Wilson's; when Conover asked Wilson, "What is the matter with you? Have you got the ague?" Wilson replied, "No."

Reynolds asked, "Is Jem Flack in the crowd?" and was answered, "He is not now, but you will see him tomorrow about this time." "Then," said Reynolds, "I am a dead man; for I know him of old." Conover told him not to be frightened, for he would not be hurt.

Reynolds stood trembling like an aspen-leaf, when Markham walked up to him and shook hands with him. Reynolds said, "Do I meet you as a friend? I expected to be a dead man when I met you again." Markham replied, "We are friends, except in law: That must have its course."

The company moved on to Andover, where the sheriff of Lee county requested lodgings for the night for all the company. I was put up into a room and locked up with Captain Grover. It was reported to me that some of the brethren had been drinking whisky that day in violation of the Word of Wisdom.

I called the brethren in and investigated the case, and was satisfied that no evil had been done.

Conover's Account of the First Division of the Expedition to Relieve the Prophet.

Peter W. Conover gave me the following relation of the travels of the brethren from Nauvoo to the place where I met them:—

I started with General Wilson Law, William Law, and about 175 men, on Sunday, the 25th of June, at eight p. m., in the direction of

Peoria: traveled part of the night. About one o'clock next morning General Charles C. Rich took 35 of the company and continued towards Peoria. The two Laws, with their company, started up the river road in the direction of Monmouth. We traveled till daylight on Monday morning, crossed Honey Creek, ate a cold breakfast, and fed the horses; then continued on till noon, when a consultation was held, and ten of the best mounted men—viz., Thomas Grover, Peter W. Conover, Zebedee Coltrin, Graham Coltrin, Philemon C. Merrill, Philander Colton, Henry Hoyt, William L. Cutler, Daniel F. Cahoon, and John L. Butler were selected to take the nearest road to Dixon, with instructions to continue until we found you.

We took the middle road between Oquaka and Monmouth, and continued on until Tuesday at two a. m., when we rested for one hour, then passed through Hendersonville on to the prairie, about nine a. m., at which time we met Colonel Stephen Markham with your letter of instructions to General Wilson Law. We read the letter. Philander Colton was sent with the despatch to Wilson Law. We then made a halt at Andover, where the inhabitants refused to sell us food.

Here we held a council, and sent Daniel Cahoon and Henry Hoyt back to Monmouth, with instructions to the brethren to wait there until they got further orders. We then traveled ten miles and obtained some corn at a farm-house. One p. m., left there and traveled on to the prairies until we met you.

Here Conover exchanged with me one of Allen's four-inch barrel six-shooter revolvers for the single shooter which Markham had slipped into my pocket at Dixon.

Reynolds and Wilson's Design of Kidnapping.

About eight p. m., Reynolds, Wilson, and the landlord consulted about sending out to raise a company to take me by force, and run with me to the mouth of Rock River on the Mississippi, as there was a company of men ready to kidnap me over the river. Markham overheard the conversation, and notified the sheriff of Lee county, who immediately ordered a guard placed, so that no one might pass in or out of the house during the night.

Markham started at daybreak, and went about twenty miles, passing through Andover at eight a. m.; and about nine he met Captain Thomas Grover and a company of ten men, to whom he delivered my message. Held a council and forwarded it on to General Law by Philander Colton. Markham turned back with the company.

My wife and children arrived in Nauvoo this evening, having burned off one arm of the carriage going home.

Many strangers reported in the city: the watch was doubled in the night.

Wednesday, 28.—We left Andover about eight o'clock; went to a little grove at the head of Elleston Creek, where we stayed an hour to feed our animals. Reynolds said, "Now, we will go from here to the mouth of Rock River and take steamboat to Quincy." Markham said, "No; for we are prepared to travel, and will go by land."

Wilson and Reynolds both spoke and said, "No, by G—, we won't; we will never go by Nauvoo alive;" and both drew their pistols on Markham, who turned round to Sheriff Campbell, of Lee county, saying, "When these men took Joseph a prisoner, they took his arms from him, even to his pocket-knife. They are now prisoners of yours, and I demand of you to take their arms from them, that is according to law."

Reynolds and Wilson Disarmed.

They refused to give them up, when the sheriff was told, "If you cannot take the arms from them, there are men enough here, and you can summon a posse to do it; for it is plain to be seen that they are dangerous men."

Reynolds and Wilson then reluctantly gave up their arms to the sheriff. The company then started, taking the middle road towards Nauvoo to within six miles of Monmouth, and stopped at a farmhouse, having traveled about forty miles; got there about sundown, and called for supper and lodging.

Peter W. Conover laid down at the S. W. corner of the building outside the house. In about ten minutes, Reynolds and Wilson came out of the house with the son of the landlord. They talked for some time, and came to the conclusion to take the carriage horses, go to Monmouth, raise a mob, and come

Further Plans of Kidnapping.

to the farmhouse in the night, seize Joseph, and convey him to the Mississippi river, and take him to Missouri, as they had a steamboat in readiness at the mouth of Rock River for that purpose.

After completing their plan of operations, Reynolds, Wilson and the boy separated and went towards the stable. Conover, who had heard the plot unobserved, immediately rose and came to me, and told me what he had just heard.

I consulted with Cyrus Walker, the landlord, and Sheriff Campbell, who took Reynolds and Wilson into his custody, and put them in the upper room, placing a guard of two men at the door, with orders not to allow any man to pass in or out of the house, except the landlord, who, as soon as he was told of the attempt to get his son into difficulty, put a stop to his proceedings at once.

Some anxiety at Nauvoo about so many strangers and suspicious characters being in the city.

The *Neighbor* of this day has the following:—

Fourth of July Celebration Appointed for Nauvoo.

By the counsel and advice of President Hyrum Smith, Messrs. O. Hyde and G. J. Adams, who have been appointed to go on a mission to Russia, will deliver two addresses on the 4th July, upon the subject of our holy religion, for the benefit and edification not only of our own citizens, but also for strangers who may be pleased to visit our town on that day. The morning's address by Mr. Hyde, at half past ten o'clock; and the afternoon by Mr. Adams, at two o'clock.

From the circumstances under which we are placed, this course is thought far more advisable for all who wish to be considered Saints to assemble for religious worship and collectively offer up our prayers to Almighty God for peace and prosperity to attend us as a people.

The giddy and unthinking will, no doubt, resort to public dinners, festivals, and perhaps to the ball chamber, to spend their time and money to gratify their appetite and vanity; but no true-hearted Saint at this peculiar moment will do it.

At the close of each address a collection will be taken for the especial purpose of assisting to complete Elder Hyde's house, that he may be the sooner liberated to proceed on his important mission to St. Petersburg.

He who has money to spend on that day can spend it more to the glory of God in the above manner than after the custom and practice of the corrupt age in which we live.

It is hoped that the band and choir will favor us on that occasion.

The lectures will be delivered in the Grove near the Temple where seats are provided.

Thursday, *29*.—Continued our journey this morning, leaving Monmouth on our left, and Oquaka five miles on our right; and after passing Monmouth about three miles, William Empy, Gilbert Rolfe, James Flack, and three others met us.

The Prophet Protects Reynolds Against Flack.

I called Flack to my side and told him not to injure Reynolds, whatever provocation he had previously received from him, as I had pledged myself to protect him, and requested Flack to bury his feelings against Reynolds.

Reynolds then got out of the stage, exchanged seats with one of the horsemen, and Flack and Reynolds rode by themselves about a quarter-of-a-mile, when they again joined the company and rode together. The company continued to Henderson River, and took dinner at a farmhouse owned by Mr. Alanson Hagerman.

While staying at this farmhouse, General Wilson Law, and William Law, and about sixty men came up in several little squads. I walked out several rods to meet the company. William and Wilson Law jumped from their horses, and unitedly hugged and kissed me, when many tears of joy were shed.

I extract from the journal of Albert P. Rockwood, the acting adjutant of the company, some of the movements of the company:—

Rockwood's Account of the Second Division of the Expedition to Relieve the Prophet.

After breakfast at the tavern, on Thursday, 29th, had a few minutes deliberation. It was determined that those who had animals which were able to continue the pursuit, with a reasonable prospect of catching up, should follow at the full speed of their animals. Having heard that the posse had taken a westerly direction, as we believed, designing to cross the Mississippi at Oquaka Ferry, and so through Iowa to Missouri, raised an excitement, and most of us thought we were good for twelve miles an hour.

Several brethren swapped their worn-out animals for fresh ones; others bought; so that, in a few minutes, about two-thirds of the detachment were in swift pursuit.

On arriving near the farmhouse where the posse stayed last night, we learned that they had been gone about two hours. Then General Law said, "Now, boys, comes the tug of war: every man and horse try your best;" and away we went with our blood at fighting heat.

By frequent enquiries we learned that we were gaining upon them. As we approached the river, we quickened our pace, which left some far in the rear.

At a watering-place, about three miles from the river, General Wilson Law and William Law, Elisha Everett, Albert P. Rockwood, and two others took passage in a wagon. Having fresh animals, we left most of the detachment in the rear: yet Brother Follet and from five to ten others were up with us, positively charged with fight.

While in the wagon, Wilson Law remarked, "We must overhaul them before they can get on the ferry-boat to cross the river, and we must take the stand that Joseph should not be taken over the river: therefore prepare yourselves for your best licks; for if Joseph goes into Missouri, they will kill him, and that will break us up, as our property in Nauvoo will become useless or of no value," etc., etc.

During the conversation we emerged from the timber and saw a small village on the bank of the river. We put our animals at their full speed and charged in with drawn swords, our guns and pistols cocked and primed, ready for attack.

Our sudden appearance and hostile movements caused much excitement in the village. General Law forced the contents of a bottle of spirits down his horse. Some of our horses fell to the ground as soon as we halted. All were foaming with sweat and nearly exhausted.

Some of the citizens refused to give us any information. Others declared, "I have done nothing," and expressed their fears and anxieties in various ways. I ran down to the river and down the beach, while William Law ran up, each in search of the ferry-boat, which happened to be on the other side. No tracks or other evidence could be found by us that any persons had passed the river this morning. Wilson Law was at this time making enquiries of the citizens.

Some of the horsemen rode on full speed through the village of Oquaka in search of the Prophet, while others left their exhausted horses standing or lying in the streets, and ran on foot.

As soon as William Law and myself returned to the wagon, we concluded that the posse, knowing that we were near by to rescue, had taken to the woods to secrete themselves or evade us; therefore Brother Follet and such others as they came in were ordered to search the timbers. In a short time a wayfaring man reported he had seen a company passing down the river road below the village, whereupon all hands were ordered to the pursuit, and soon the village was clear of "the destroying angels" (as they called us), and they were left to their own reflections and meditations on the strange scene. My opinion is that we were in the village from thirty to forty minutes, until we were all again on the trail.

Those who were in the rear of our detachment saw the posse who had Joseph traveling down the road. They crossed the prairie and arrived nearly one hour before the advance, who missed the trail about half-a-mile from the village, at the junction of the Monmouth and River Roads. On their arrival Joseph sent a messenger back to notify us where he was, who met us about a mile from the place where he was stopping.

Change of Destination from Quincy to Nauvoo.

I consulted with my lawyers, and told them that Nauvoo was the nearest place where writs of habeas corpus could be heard and determined They examined the subject and decided I was correct, when we turned our steps towards Nauvoo, which gladdened my heart at the prospect of soon being in the midst of my friends again. I sent a messenger to inform the citizens of Nauvoo of the glad change; and I requested Conover to ride ahead to Mr. Michael Crane's, on Honey Creek, and call for supper for one hundred men.

After dinner we traveled about fifteen miles. On arriving at Crane's, I jumped out of the buggy, and instead of going through the gate or climbing the fence, walked up and jumped over the fence without touching it. Mr. Crane ran out and embraced me, and bade me welcome.

A flock of turkeys and chickens were killed, and a substantial supper was provided for all; and the company feasted, sang, and had a happy time that night. I showed my sides to Mr. Crane and the company, which still continued black and blue from the bruises I had received from the pistols of Reynolds and Wilson, while riding from Inlet Grove to Dixon eight days ago.

Nauvoo, an Ordinance Concerning Strangers, etc.

To the Recorder of the City of Nauvoo:

We, your petitioners, aldermen of said city, request you to notify the marshal to call a special meeting of the city council, at the mayor's court-room, this afternoon at two o'clock.

GEO. A. SMITH,
W. W. PHELPS
GEO. W. HARRIS, } Aldermen.

City council accordingly met and passed "An ordinance concerning strangers and contagious diseases, and for other purposes," as follows:—

Sec. 1. Be it ordained by the city council of the city of Nauvoo, for the peace, benefit, good order, convenience, cleanliness, health and happiness of said city, agreeable to the charter of the same, that the city council, marshal, constables, and city watch are hereby authorized, empowered, and required to require all strangers who shall be entering this city, or are already tarrying, or may hereafter be tarrying in said city, in a civil and respectful manner to give their names, former residence, for what intent they have entered or are tarrying in the city, and answer such other questions as the officer shall deem proper or necessary for the good order, health, or convenience of the said city; and for a failure or refusal on the part of strangers to give the desired information, or for giving false names or information, they shall be subject to the penalty of the "ordinance concerning vagrants and disorderly persons."

Sec. 2. And be it further ordained that the aforesaid authorities of the said city are further authorized and empowered, and required to hail and take all persons found strolling about the city at night, after nine o'clock and before sunrise, and to confine them in ward for trial, according to the aforesaid "Ordinance concerning vagrants and disorderly persons," unless they give a good and satisfactory account of themselves, or offer a reasonable excuse for being thus caught out after nine o'clock.

Sec. 3. And be it further ordained that the aforesaid authorities are further authorized, empowered, and required to require all such persons as they may suspect, to give information whether they have recently had or have been exposed to any contagious disease or diseases from whence they come, under the same penalties as are annexed to the two preceding sections of this ordinance.

Sec. 4. And be it further ordained that the aforesaid authorities are further authorized, empowered, and required to enter all hotels, or houses of public entertainment, and such other habitations as they may judge proper, and require the inmates to give immediate iuformation of all persons residing in said hotel or habitation, and their business, occupation, or movements; and for a failure, non-compliance, or false information, their license shall be a forfeit, if it be a public-house, and they and the transient persons subject to the penalties of the three preceding sections.

Sec. 5. And be it further ordained that if any of the aforesaid officers shall refuse or neglect to do their duty as required by this ordinance, they shall be fined $100, and be broke of office.

They also passed "An ordinance concerning confining or keeping animals in the city of Nauvoo;" also "An ordinance concerning bathing and swimming."

Friday, 30.—A messenger started from my company in the night, and arrived in Nauvoo early in the morning, saying that I and the company would be in the city about noon. Dr. Willard Richards and Wilford Woodruff arranged the seats in the court-room, preparatory to my arrival.

Announcement of the Arrival of the Prophet at Nauvoo.

At half-past ten o'clock, the Nauvoo Brass Band and Martial Band started with Emma and my brother Hyrum to meet me; also a train of carriages, containing a number of the principal inhabitants.

At eight a. m., the company with me again started; arrived at the Big Mound about half-past ten, where the brethren decorated the bridles of their horses with the flowers of the prairie, and were met by a number of the citizens. Continued our journey; and at 11:25 a. m., I was gladdened, when opposite my brother Hyrum's farm, about one-and-a-half miles east of the Temple, with seeing the train approaching towards us; and I directed Colonel Rockwood to place my Life Guards in their appropriate position in the procession. I was in a buggy with Mr. Montgomery. Sheriff Reynolds and Wilson, with my three lawyers, Cyrus Walker, Shepherd G. Patrick, and Edward Southwick, were in the stage coach with Lucien P. Sanger, the stage proprietor. Mr. Campbell, the sheriff of Lee county, and a company of about 140 were with me on horseback.

I was a prisoner in the hands of Reynolds, the agent of Missouri, and Wilson, his assistant. They were prisoners in the hands of Sheriff Campbell, who had delivered the whole of us into the hands of Colonel Markham, guarded by my friends, so that none of us could escape.

When the company from the city came up, I said I thought I would now ride a little easier; got out of the buggy; and, after embracing Emma and my brother Hyrum, who wept tears of joy at my return, as did also most of the great company who surrounded us, (it was a solemn, silent meeting,) I mounted my favorite horse, "Old Charley," when the band struck up "Hail Columbia," and proceeded to march slowly towards the city, Emma riding by my side into town.

The Entrance Into Nauvoo.

The carriages having formed in line, the company with me followed next, and the citizens fell in the rear. As we approached the city, the scene continued to grow more interesting; the streets were generally lined on both sides with the brethren and sisters, whose countenances were joyous and full of satisfaction to see me once more safe.

I was greeted with the cheers of the people and firing of guns and cannon. We were obliged to appoint a number of men to keep the streets open for the procession to pass, and arrived at my house about one o'clock, where my aged mother was at the door to embrace me, with tears of joy rolling down her cheeks, and my children clung around me with feelings of enthusiastic and enraptured pleasure. Little Fred. exclaimed, "Pa, the Missourians won't take you away again, will they?" The friends from Dixon gazed with astonishment and rapture to see the enthusiastic attachment of my family and the Saints towards me.

The multitude seemed unwilling to disperse until after I had arisen on the fence and told them, "I am out of the hands of the Missourians again, thank God. I thank you all for your kindness and love to me. I bless you all in the name of Jesus Christ. Amen. I shall address you at the Grove, near the Temple, at four o'clock this afternoon."

When I went to dinner with my family, Reynolds and Wilson were placed at the head of the table, with about 50 of my friends, and were served with the best that the table afforded, by my wife, whom they refused to allow me to see, when they so cruelly arrested and ill-treated me, which contrasted strongly with their treatment to me when I was first arrested by them, and until my friends met me.

CHAPTER XXIV.

APPLICATION TO THE MUNICIPAL COURT OF NAUVOO FOR WRIT OF HABEAS CORPUS—THE PROPHET'S SPEECH AT NAUVOO—PROCEEDINGS BEFORE THE MUNICIPAL COURT—THE PRISONER DISCHARGED FROM CUSTODY.

June 30, 1843 (continued.)—As soon as we arrived in the city, the Municipal Court came together, when I told them, "The writ of habeas corpus granted by the Master in Chancery at Dixon was made returnable to the nearest court having jurisdiction; and you are that court."

A requisition was made on Reynolds to return the writ, who refused, when I signed the following petition:—

The Prophet's Petition to the Municipal Court of Nauvoo, for a Writ of Habeas Corpus.

To the Honorable the Municipal Court of the City of Nauvoo, Hancock County, and State of Illinois:—

Your petitioner, Joseph Smith, Sen., who has been arrested by and under the name of Joseph Smith,Jun., states on oath that he is now detained as a prisoner, and in the custody of Joseph H. Reynolds, in the said city of Nauvoo and state of Illinois, who claims to be the agent of the state of Missouri, and that your petitioner was arrested by one Harmon T. Wilson, by virtue of what purports to be a warrant issued by his Excellency, Thomas Ford, governor of the state of Illinois, in the county of Lee and state of Illinois, and by said Wilson, your petitioner was delivered into the custody of said Joseph H. Reynolds, at and within the county of Lee, aforesaid; that said supposed warrant so issued by his Excellency, Thomas Ford, governor as aforesaid, and the arrest thereupon and the imprisonment consequent thereupon by said Wilson, and afterwards by said Joseph H. Reynolds, is illegal and in violation of law, and without the authority of law, as he is informed and verily believes, for the following, besides other reasons, to wit—

1st. The said supposed warrant so issued by the said governor of the state of Illinois as aforesaid does not confer any authority to arrest your petitioner, for that it commands the officers therein named to arrest one Joseph Smith, Jun.,whereas the name of your petioner is Joseph Smith, Sen.; and your petitioner avers that he is not known and reputed by the name of Joseph Smith, Jun.

2nd. The said supposed warrant is defective and void, for that it does not recite that the Joseph Smith, Jun., mentioned therein, has been demanded by the executive of the state of Missouri of the executive of the state of Illinois.

3rd. Said supposed warrant is defective and void, for that it does not state that said Joseph Smith, Jun., therein named, has been indicted,or that any other legal accusation of any offense has been legally preferred, and is as pending against him in the said state of Missouri.

4th. It is defective and void, for that it does not show that any legal foundation was furnished by the executive of the state of Missouri, upon which to issue the same, and your petitioner avers that the same was issued without due authority of law.

5th. Said supposed warrant is in other respects defective and void.

6th. The said Joseph H. Reynolds has no authority to detain your petitioner in custody, for that he is not an officer of the state of Illinois, nor is he legally authorized by the said governor of the state of Illinois, or otherwise, as the agent of the state of Missouri in the state of Illinois, or in any other character and capacity,to imprison your petitioner within the said state of Illinois.

7th. Your petitioner, before the making of the said arrest upon which he is now detained and imprisoned, had been arrested for the same cause and upon a charge for the same offense for which he is now arrested and imprisoned, by virtue of a warrant issued by the governor of the said state of Illinois, upon a requisition of the executive authority of the said state of Missouri, and was discharged from said arrest and imprisonment by judgment of the circuit court of Warren county, at a court holden in the said county of Warren, in or about the month of June, A. D. 1841, in such manner as not to be liable to the said second arrest for the same cause.

8th. Your petitioner is not a fugitive from justice, and has not fled from the justice of the said state of Missouri, and he is not guilty and has not been guilty of treason in or against the state of Missouri.

9th. Your petitioner was not and has not been within the limits of the said state of Missouri for more than four years next before the making of said arrest and imprisonment whereby he is now detained, nor for or during four years before any indictment or other legal accusation was preferred against him.

10. Your petitioner avers that the said supposed warrant so issued by the said governor of the said state of Illinois, and under color of which your petitioner is now imprisoned, and the document purporting to be an authority to receive the said Joseph Jmith, Jr., are wholly defective and insufficient to legally authorize the arrest and imprisonment of your petitioner; copies of which supposed warrant and the supposed authority from the executive of the state of Missouri are hereunto annexed.

Wherefore, your petitioner prays that a writ of habeas corpus may be awarded, directed to the said Joseph H. Reynolds, commanding him that he bring your petitioner forthwith and without delay before this honorable court, together with the causes of his caption and detention, in order that your petitioner may be dealt with according to law; and your petitioner, as in duty bound, will ever pray.

JOSEPH SMITH, Sen.

Subscribed and sworn to before me this 30th day of June, A. D., 1843, at the city of Nauvoo, Illinois.

JAMES SLOAN,
Clerk of the Municipal Court of the City of Nauvoo.

Whereupon the court issued the following:—

State of Illinois, }
City of Nauvoo. } ss.

The people of the state of Illinois to the marshal of said city, greeting:—

Whereas application has been made before the Municipal Court of said city that the body of one Joseph Smith, Sen., of the said city of Nauvoo, (who is styled in the warrant by which he is held in custody, Joseph Smith, Jun.,) is in the custody of Joseph H. Reynolds: These are therefore to command the said Joseph H. Reynolds to safely have the body of the said Joseph Smith, Sen., who is styled Joseph Smith, Jun., in his custody detained, as it is said, together with the day and cause of his caption and detention, by whatsoever name the said Joseph Smith, Sen., may be known or called, before the Municipal Court of said city, forthwith, to bide such order as the said court shall make in his behalf; and further, if the said Joseph H. Reynolds, or other person or persons having said Joseph Smith, Sen., of said city of Nauvoo, in custody, shall refuse or neglect to comply with the provisions of this writ, you, the marshal of said city, or other person authorized to serve the same, are hereby required to arrest the person or persons so refusing or neglecting to comply as aforesaid, and bring him or them together with the person or persons in his or their custody, forthwith before the Municipal Court aforesaid, to be dealt with according to law: and herein fail not, and bring this writ with you.

Witness, James Sloan, Clerk of the Municipal Court of Nauvoo, this 30th day of June, in the year of our Lord one thousand eight hundred and forty-three.

[Seal.] JAMES SLOAN, Clerk.

Which was endorsed.

I, Joseph H. Reynolds, the within named, do hereby return this writ, with the body of Joseph Smith, with the following cause of caption and detention, to wit—The within named Joseph Smith was arrested on a warrant issued by the governor of the state of Illinois, by one Harmon T. Wilson, a constable of Hancock county, in the state of Illinois, on the 23rd day of June, A. D., 1843, a copy of which warrant is hereunto annexed, and marked letter A, and delivered over to my custody as directed by said writ. The person of said Smith was, on said 23rd of June, in the county of Lee, and state of Illinois, by the said Wilson, delivered over to my custody; and that I received and detained the said Smith in my custody, by virtue of a certain warrant of attorney issued by the governor of the state of Missouri, a copy of which is hereunto annexed and marked letter B, directing me to receive the said Smith, and convey him to and deliver him to the sheriff of Daviess county, in the state of Missouri; and that the within detention referred to is the same referred to, and none other.

JOSEPH H. REYNOLDS.

Nauvoo, June 30, A. D., 1843.

Executive Department,
City of Jefferson.

Know ye that I, Thomas Reynolds, governor of the state of Missouri, having full trust and confidence in the integrity and abilities of Joseph H. Reynolds, do hereby constitute and appoint him as the agent of the said state of Missouri, to proceed to the state of Illinois, for the purpose of receiving from the proper authorities of the state one Joseph Smith, Jun., charged with treason by him committed against the state of Missouri, and as having fled from justice to the state of Illinois; and I do hereby authorize and direct said Joseph H. Reynolds to convey said Joseph Smith, Jun., from the state of Illinois, and deliver him to the custody of the sheriff of Daviess county, in the state of Missouri.

In testimony whereof, I have hereunto set my hand and caused to be affixed the great seal of the state of Missouri.

Done at the city of Jefferson, this 13th day of June, in the year of our Lord one thousand eight hundred and forty-three.

By the Governor,

[Seal.] THOS. REYNOLDS.

JAMES L. MINOR, Secretary of State.

Thomas Ford, governor of the state of Illinois, to all sheriffs and constables of any county of the state, and to Harmon T. Wilson, of the county of Hancock, greeting:—

Whereas it has been made known to me by the executive authority of the state of Missouri, that one Joseph Smith, Jun., stands charged with the crime of treason against the state of Missouri, and alleged that Joseph Smith, Jun., has fled from the justice of the said state of Missouri and taken refuge in the state of Illinois.

Now, therefore, I, Thomas Ford, governor of the state of Illinois, pursuant to the constitution and laws of the United States and of this state, do hereby command you to arrest and apprehend the said Joseph Smith, Jun., if he be found within the limits of the state aforesaid, and cause him to be safely kept and delivered to the custody of Joseph H. Reynolds, Esq , who has been duly constituted the agent of the said state of Missouri to receive the said fugitive from the justice of said state, he paying all fees and charges for the arrest and apprehension of said Joseph Smith, Jun., and make due returns to the executive department of this state, of the manner in which this writ may be executed.

In testimony whereof, I have hereunto set my hand, and caused the great seal of the state to be affixed.

Done at the city of Springfield, this 17th day of June, in the year of our Lord one thousand eight hundred and forty-three, and of the Independence of the United States the sixty-seventh.

By the Governor,

THOMAS FORD.

THOMAS CAMPBELL, Secretary of State.

Mr. Reynolds refused to submit to the writ, but submitted to the attachment, and I was delivered into the hands of the marshal of the city. I told the court I had an appointment to preach to the people, and requested the privilege from the court, which they granted, and adjourned until eight o'clock tomorrow morning.

At five p. m., I went to the grove and delivered an address to the public.

The following is a brief synopsis, as reported by Dr. Willard Richard and Elder Wilford Woodruff:—

The Prophet's Speech at Nauvoo—Relation of his Arrest at Dixon. The Right of Habeas Corpus Proceedings Under Nauvoo Charter Claimed.

The congregation is large. I shall require attention. I discovered what the emotions of the people were on my arrival at this city, and I have come here to say "How do you do?" to all parties; and I do now at this time say to all "How do you do?" I meet you with a heart full of gratitude to Almighty God, and I presume you all feel the same. I am well—I am hearty. I hardly know how to express my feelings. I feel as strong as a giant. I pulled sticks with the men coming along, and I pulled up with one hand the strongest man that could be found. Then two men tried, but they could not pull me up, and I continued to pull, mentally, until I pulled Missouri to Nauvoo. But I will pass from that subject.

There has been great excitement in the country since Joseph H. Reynolds and Harmon T. Wilson took me; but I have been cool and dispassionate through the whole. Thank God, I am now a prisoner in the hands of the municipal court of Nauvoo, and not in the hands of Missourians.

It is not so much my object to tell of my afflictions, trials and troubles as to speak of the writ of habeas corpus, so that the minds of all may be corrected. It has been asserted by the great and wise men, lawyers and others, that our municipal powers and legal tribunals are not to be sanctioned by the authorities of the state; and accordingly they want to make it lawful to drag away innocent men from their families and friends, and have them put to death by ungodly men for their religion!

Relative to our city charter, courts, right of habeas corpus, etc., I wish you to know and publish that we have all power; and if any man from this time forth says anything to the contrary, cast it into his teeth.

There is a secret in this. If there is not power in our charter and courts, then there is not power in the state of Illinois, nor in the congress or constitution of the United States; for the United States gave unto Illinois her constitution or charter, and Illinois gave unto Nauvoo her charters, ceding unto us our vested rights, which she has no right or power to take from us. All the power there was in Illinois she gave to Nauvoo; and any man that says to the contrary is a fool.

The municipal court has all the power to issue and determine writs of habeas corpus within the limits of this city that the legislature can confer. This city has all the power that the state courts have, and was given by the same authority—the legislature.

I want you to hear and learn, O Israel, this day, what is for the happiness and peace of this city and people. If our enemies are determined to oppress us and deprive us of our constitutional rights and privileges as they have done, and if the authorities that are on the earth will not sustain us in our rights, nor give us that protection which the laws and constitution of the United States and of this state guarantee unto us, then we will claim them from a higher power—from heaven—yea, from God Almighty.

I have dragged these men here by my hand, and I will do it again; but I swear I will not deal so mildly with them again, for the time has come when forbearance is no longer a virtue; and if you or I are again taken unlawfully, you are at liberty to give loose to blood and thunder. But be cool, be deliberate, be wise, act with almighty power; and when you pull, do it effectually—make a sweep-stakes for once!

My lot has always been cast among the warmest hearted people. In every time of trouble, friends, even among strangers, have been raised up unto me and assisted me.

The time is come when the vail is torn off from the state of Illinois, and its citizens have delivered me from the state of Missouri. Friends that were raised up unto me would have spilt their life's blood to have torn me from the hands of Reynolds and Wilson, if I had asked them; but I told them no, I would be delivered by the power of God and generalship; and I have brought these men to Nauvoo, and committed them to her from whom I was torn, not as prisoners in chains, but as prisoners of kindness. I have treated them kindly. I have had the privilege of rewarding them good for evil. They took me unlawfully, treated me rigorously, strove to deprive me of my rights, and would have run with me into Missouri to have been murdered, if Providence had not interposed. But now they are in my hands; and I have taken them into my house, set them at the head of my table, and placed before them the best which my house afforded; and they were waited upon by my wife, whom they deprived of seeing me when I was taken.

I have no doubt but I shall be discharged by the municipal court. Were I before any good tribunal, I should be discharged, as the Missouri writs are illegal and good for nothing—they are "without form and void."

But before I will bear this unhallowed persecution any longer—before I will be dragged away again among my enemies for trial, I will spill the last drop of blood in my veins, and will see all my enemies in hell! To bear it any longer would be a sin, and I will not bear it any longer. Shall we bear it any longer? [One universal "No!" ran through all the vast assembly, like a loud peal of thunder.]

I wish the lawyer who says we have no powers in Nauvoo may be choked to death with his own words. Don't employ lawyers, or pay them money for their knowledge, for I have learned that they don't know anything. I know more than they all.

Go ye into all the world and preach the gospel. He that believeth in our chartered rights may come here and be saved; and he that does not shall remain in ignorance. If any lawyer shall say there is more power in other places and charters with respect to habeas corpus than in Nauvoo, believe it not. I have converted this candidate for congress [pointing to Cyrus Walker, Esq.,] that the right of habeas corpus is included in our charter. If he continues converted, I will vote for him.

I have been with these lawyers and they have treated me well; but I am here in Nauvoo, and the Missourians too. I got here by a lawful writ of habeas corpus issued by the master in chancery of Lee county, and made returnable to the nearest tribunal in the fifth judicial district having jurisdiction to try and determine such writs: and here is that tribunal, just as it should be.

However indignant you may feel about the high handed oppression which has been raised against me by these men, use not the hand of violence against them, for they could not be prevailed upon to come here till I pledged my honor and my life that a hair of their heads should not be hurt. Will you all support my pledge, and thus preserve my honor? [One universal "Yes!" burst from the assembled thousands.] This is another proof of your attachment to me. I know how ready you are to do right. You have done great things, and manifested your love towards me in flying to my assistance on this occasion. I bless you, in the name of the Lord, with all the blessings of heaven and earth you are capable of enjoying.

I have learned that we have no need to suffer as we have heretofore: we can call others to our aid. I know the Almighty will bless all good men: he will bless you; and the time has come when there will be such a flocking to the standard of liberty as never has been or shall be hereafter. What an era has commenced! Our enemies have prophesied that we would establish our religion by sword. Is it true? No. But if Missouri will not stay her cruel hand in her unhallowed persecutions against us, I restrain you not any longer. I say in the name of Jesus Christ, by the authority of the holy priesthood, I this day turn the key that opens the heavens to restrain you no longer from this time forth. I will lead you to the battle; and if you are not afraid to die, and feel disposed to spill your blood in your own defense, you will not offend me. Be not the aggressor: bear until they strike you on the one cheek; then offer the other, and they will be sure to strike that; then defend yourselves, and God will bear you off, and you shall stand forth clear before his tribunal.

If any citizens of Illinois say we shall not have our rights, treat them as strangers and not friends, and let them go to hell and be damned! Some say they will mob us. Let them mob and be damned! If we have to give up our chartered rights, privileges, and freedom, which our fathers fought, bled, and died for, and which the constitution of the United States and of this state guarantee unto us, we will do it only at the point of the sword and bayonet.

Many lawyers contend for those things which are against the rights of men, and I can only excuse them because of their ignorance. Go forth and advocate the laws and rights of the people, ye lawyers. If not, don't get into my hands, or under the lash of my tongue.

Lawyers say the powers of the Nauvoo charter are dangerous; but I ask, is the constitution of the United States or of this state dangerous? No. Neither are the charters granted to Nauvoo by the legislature of Illinois dangerous, and those who say they are are fools. We have not enjoyed unmolested those rights which the constitution of the United States of America and our charters grant.

Missouri and all wicked men raise the hue-and-cry against us, and are not satisfied. Some political aspirants of this state also are raising the hue-and-cry that the powers in the charters granted unto the city of Nauvoo are dangerous; and although the general assembly have conferred them upon our city, yet the whine is raised—"Repeal them—take them away." Like the boy who swapped off his jack-knife, and then cried, "Daddy, daddy, I have sold my jack-knife and got sick of my bargain, and I want to get it back again."

But how are they going to help themselves? Raise mobs? And what can mobocrats do in the midst of Kirkpatrickites? No better than a hunter in the claws of a bear. If mobs come upon you any more here, dung your gardens with them. We don't want any excitement; but after we have done all, we will rise up, Washington-like, and break off the hellish yoke that oppresses us, and we will not be mobbed.

The day before I was taken at Inlet Grove, I rode with my wife through Dixon to visit my friends, and I said to her, "here is a good people." I felt this by the Spirit of God. The next day I was a prisoner in their midst, in the hands of Reynolds, of Missouri, and Wilson, of Carthage. As the latter drove up, he exclaimed, "ha, ha, ha! By G—, we have got the Prophet now!" He gloried much in it, but he is now our prisoner. When they came to take me, they held two cocked pistols to my head, and saluted me with—"G— d— you, I'll shoot you! I'll shoot you, G— d— you,"—repeating these threats nearly fifty times, from first to last. I asked them what they wanted to shoot me for. They said they would do it, if I made any resistance.

"Oh, very well," I replied; "I have no resistance to make." They then dragged me away, and I asked them by what authority they did these things. They said, "By a writ from the governors of Missouri and Illinois." I then told them I wanted a writ of habeas corpus. Their reply was, "G— d— you, you shan't have it," I told a man to go to Dixon, and get me a writ of habeas corpus. Wilson then repeated, "G— d— you, you shan't have it: I'll shoot you."

When we arrived at Dixon, I sent for a lawyer, who came; and Reynolds shut the door in his face, and would not let me speak to him, repeating, "G— d— you, I'll shoot you." I turned to him, opened my bosom, and told him to "shoot away. I have endured so much persecution and oppression that I am sick of life. Why, then, don't you shoot and have done with it, instead of talking so much about it?"

This somewhat checked his insolence. I then told him that I would have counsel to consult, and eventually I obtained my wish. The lawyers came to me, and I got a writ of habeas corpus for myself, and also a writ against Reynolds and Wilson for unlawful proceedings and cruel treatment towards me. Thanks to the good citizens of Dixon, who nobly took their stand against such unwarrantable and unlawful oppression, my persecutors could not get out of the town that night, although, when they first arrived, they swore I should not remain in Dixon five minutes, and I found they had ordered horses accordingly to proceed to Rock Island. I pledged my honor to my counsel that the Nauvoo city charter conferred jurisdiction to investigate the subject; so we came to Nauvoo, where I am now a prisoner in the custody of a higher tribunal than the circuit court.

The charter says that "the city council shall have power and authority to make, ordain, establish, and execute such ordinances not repugnant to the constitution of the United States, or of this state, as they may deem necessary, for the peace, benefit, and safety of the inhabitants of said city." And also that "the municipal court shall have power to grant writs of habeas corpus in all cases arising under the ordinances of the city council."

The city council have passed an ordinance "that no citizen of this city shall be taken out of this city by any writ, without the privilege of a writ of habeas corpus." There is nothing but what we have power over, except where restricted by the constitution of the United States. "But," says the mob, "What dangerous powers!" Yes—dangerous, because they will protect the innocent and put down mobocrats. The constitution of the United States declares that the privilege of the writ of habeas corpus shall not be denied. Deny me the writ of habeas corpus, and I will fight with gun, sword, cannon, whirlwind, and thunder, until they are used up like the Kilkenny cats. We have more power than most charters confer, because we have power to go behind the writ and try the merits of the case.

If these powers are dangerous, then the constitution of the United States and of this state are dangerous; but they are not dangerous to good men: they are only so to bad men who are breakers of the laws. So with the laws of the country, and so with the ordinances of Nauvoo: they are dangerous to mobs, but not to good men who wish to keep the laws.

We do not go out of Nauvoo to disturb anybody, or any city, town, or place. Why, then, need they be troubled about us? Let them not meddle with our affairs, but let us alone. After we have been deprived of our rights and privileges of citizenship, driven from town to town, place to place, and state to state, with the sacrifice of our homes and lands, our blood has been shed, many having been murdered, and all this because of our religion—because we worship Almighty God accord-to the dictates of our own conscience, shall we longer bear these cruelties which have been heaped upon us for the last ten years in the face of heaven, and in open violation of the constitution and law of these United States and of this state? God forbid! I will not bear it. If they take away my rights, I will fight for them manfully and righteously until I am used up. We have done nothing against the rights of others.

You speak of lawyers. I am a lawyer too; but the Almighty God has taught me the principle of law; and the true meaning and intent of the writ of habeas corpus is to defend the innocent and investigate the subject. Go behind the writ and if the form of one that is issued against an innocent man is right, he should [nevertheless] not be dragged to another state, and there be put to death, or be in jeopardy of life and limb, because of prejudice, when he is innocent. The benefits of the constitution and laws are alike for all; and the great Eloheim has given me the privilege of having the benefits of the constitution and the writ of habeas corpus; and I am bold to ask for that privilege this day, and I ask in the name of Jesus Christ, and all that is sacred, that I may have your lives and all your energies to carry out the freedom which is chartered to us. Will you all help me? If so make it manifest by raising the right hand (There was a unanimous response, a perfect sea of hands being elevated). Here is truly a committee of the whole.

When at Dixon, a lawyer came to me as counsel. Reynolds and Wilson said I should not speak to any man, and they would shoot any man who should dare to speak to me. An old, gray-headed man came up and said I should have counsel, and he was not afraid of their pistols.

The people of Dixon were ready to take me from my persecutors, and I could have killed them, notwithstanding their pistols; but I had no disposition to kill any man, though my worst enemy,— not even Boggs. In fact, he would have more hell to live in the reflection of his past crimes than to die. After this, I had lawyers enough, and I obtained a writ for Joseph H. Reynolds and Harmon T. Wilson, for damages, assault and battery, as well as the writ of habeas corpus.

We started for Ottawa, and arrived at Pawpaw Grove, 32 miles, where we stopped for the night. Esquire Walker sent Mr. Campbell, sheriff of Lee county, to my assistance, and he came and slept by me. In the morning, certain men wished to see me, but I was not allowed to see them. The news of my arrival had hastily circulated about the neighborhood, and very early in the morning the largest room in the hotel was filled with citizens, who were anxious to hear me preach, and requested me to address them.

Sheriff Reynolds entered the room and said, pointing to me, "I wish you to understand this man is my prisoner, and I want you should disperse. You must not gather round here in this way." Upon which, an aged gentleman, who was lame and carried a large hickory walking-stick, advanced towards Reynolds, bringing his hickory upon the floor and said, "You damned infernal puke! we'll learn you to come here and interrupt gentlemen. Sit down there [pointing to a very low chair] and sit still. Don't open your head till General Smith gets through talking. If you never learned manners in Missouri, we'll teach you that gentlemen are not to be imposed upon by a nigger-driver. You cannot kidnap men here, if you do in Missouri; and if you attempt it here, there is a committee in this grove that will sit on your case. And, sir, it is the highest tribunal in the United States, as from its decision there is no appeal."

Reynolds, no doubt, aware that the person addressing him was at the head of a committee who had prevented the settlers on the public domain from being imposed upon by land speculators, sat down in silence, while I addressed the assembly for an hour and a half on the subject of marriage, my visitors having requested me to give them my views of the law of God respecting marriage.

My freedom commenced from that hour. We came direct from Pawpaw Grove to Nauvoo, having got our writ directed to the nearest court having authority to try the case, which was the municipal court of this city.

It did my soul good to see your feelings and love manifested towards me. I thank God that I have the honor to lead so virtuous and honest a people—to be your leader and lawyer, as was Moses to the children of Israel. Hosannah! Hosannah! Hosannah! to Almighty God, who has delivered us thus from out of the seven troubles. I commend you to His grace; and may the blessings of heaven rest upon you, in the name of Jesus Christ. Amen.

President Smith then introduced Mr. Cyrus Walker to the assembled multitude, and remarked to him: "These are the greatest dupes, as a body of people, that ever lived, or I am not so big a rogue as I am reported to be. I told Mr. Warren that I would not discuss the subject of religion with you. I understand the gospel and you do not. You understand the quackery of law, and I do not." Mr. Walker then addressed the people to the effect that, from what he had seen in the Nauvoo City Charter, it gave the power to try writs of habeas corpus, etc. After which, President Smith continued as follows:—

If the legislature have granted Nauvoo the right of determining cases of habeas corpus, it is no more than they ought to have done, or more than our fathers fought for. Furthermore, if Missouri continues her warfare, and to issue her writs against me and this people unlawfully and unjustly, as she has done, and to take away and trample upon our rights, I swear, in the name of Almighty God, and with uplifted hands to heaven, I will spill my heart's blood in our defense. They shall not take away our rights; and if they don't stop leading me by the nose, I will lead them by the nose; and if they don't let me alone, I will turn up the world—I will make war. When we shake our own bushes, we want to catch our own berries. The lawyers themselves acknowledge that we have all power granted us in our charters that we could ask for—that we had more power than any other court in the state; for all other courts were restricted, while ours was not; and I thank God Almighty for it. I will not be rode down to hell by the Missourians any longer; and it is my privilege to speak in my own defense; and I appeal to your integrity and honor that you will stand by and help me, according to the covenant you have this day made.

While I was speaking, Reynolds and Wilson started for Carthage, in company with Lawyer Davis, of Carthage, threatening to raise the militia and come again and take me out of Nauvoo.

Saturday, July 1.—At eight a. m., the municipal court met in the court-room. Present: William Marks (acting chief justice), Daniel H. Wells, Newel K. Whitney, George W. Harris, Gustavus Hills, and Hiram Kimball, (associate justices,) to investigate the writ of habeas corpus.

The following witnesses were examined—namely: Hyrum Smith, Parley P. Pratt, Brigham Young, George W. Pitkin, Lyman Wight, and Sidney Rigdon.*

Messrs. Walker, Patrick, Southwick, and Backman (the counsel on my behalf), then respectively addressed the court; and they exhorted the "Mormons" to stand for their rights—stand or fall, sink or swim, live or die. Mr. Mason was counselor for Reynolds.

* The affidavits here alluded to, since they refer to events that happened in Missouri from 1831 to 1839, were transfered to the Missouri period of the history and will be found in the Appendix of Vol. III, pp. 403 to 466.

After which the following order was made:—

Order of the Municipal Court of Nauvoo.

This day came the said Joseph Smith, Sen., in proper person; and the said Joseph H. Reynolds having made return of said writ of habeas corpus, and produced the body of said Smith, in pursuance to the mandate of said writ, and after hearing the evidence in support of said petition, it is ordered and considered by the court that the said Joseph Smith, Sen., be discharged from the said arrest and imprisonment complained of in said petition, and that the said Smith be discharged for want of substance in the warrant upon which he was arrested, as well as upon the merits of said case, and that he go hence without delay.

In testimony whereof, I have hereunto set my hand and affixed the seal of said court, at the city of Nauvoo, this second day of July, 1843.

[Seal.] JAMES SLOAN, Clerk.

A Public Meeting in Relation to the late Arrest of General Joseph Smith.

Nauvoo, Illinois, July 1st, 1843. At a meeting of the citizens of Nauvoo, held this day in the Assembly Hall, it was

Resolved unanimously—That Messrs. Sanger and Dixon, of the town of Dixon, and the citizens of Dixon, Pawpaw Grove, and Lee county generally, in this state, receive the warmest thanks of this meeting for the firm patriotism, bold and decided stand taken against lawless outrage and the spirit of mobocracy, as manifested in the arrest or capture of General Joseph Smith, while on a visit to his friends in that district of country, by Harmon T. Wilson and Joseph H. Reynolds pretending to act under authority of a writ obtained from the governor of this state, given in consequence of a pretended requisition made on him from the executive of Missouri, for the arrest and delivery of said Joseph Smith unto the authorities of Missouri. In maintaining the legal rights of persons thus arrested, and seeing the laws of Illinois maintained, and the full benefits of them enjoyed by every citizen of said state, they have shown themselves republicans, patriots, and worthy citizens of this state, and have entitled themselves not only to the thanks of this meeting, but to that of all lovers of law and good order. With such citizens as these, Illinois will long enjoy the benefits of good order and the blessings of a free people.

Resolved unanimously—That the foregoing resolution be published in the newspapers.

[Signed.] SIDNEY RIGDON, Moderator.

WILLARD RICHARDS, Clerk.

A strong wind from the north-west, with thunder and rain in the afternoon.

In consequence of Reynolds and Wilson leaving abruptly last night for Carthage, I sent Colonel Markham to learn what they were doing.

A tremendous shower at Chester, Pennsylvania. Over twenty lives were lost, fifty bridges destroyed, besides many houses and stores. Damage $250,000.

Elders Heber C. Kimball and Orson Pratt started on their mission to the east, for the purpose of attending conferences at Cincinnati and Pittsburgh, where they will wait until the rest of the Twelve arrive.

CHAPTER XXV.

AFTERMATH OF THE PROPHET'S RELEASE FROM ARREST—FOURTH OF JULY CELEBRATION AT NAUVOO—APPEALS TO GOVERNOR FORD FOR EMPLOYMENT OF MILITARY FORCE—SUPPLEMENTARY AFFIDAVITS ON AFFAIRS IN MISSOURI.

Sunday, July 2, 1843.—A large congregation met at the Grove, near the Temple, and heard an interesting address from Elder Orson Hyde. After he closed, Messrs. Walker, Southwick, Patrick, and Wasson spoke on the stand, stating that I had subjected myself to the law in every particular, and had treated my persecutors and kidnappers with courtesy and kindness. They also spoke on the unlawful conduct of my enemies.

Messrs. Patrick, Walker, Southwick, and Harmon Wasson made the following affidavit:—

Affidavit of Attorneys.

Shepherd G. Patrick, Harmon Wasson, Edward Southwick, and Cyrus Walker, being duly sworn, depose and say that they were in company with Joseph H. Reynolds and Harmon T. Wilson, the former acting as agent of the state of Missouri, and having in custody Joseph Smith, who was styled, in the warrant by which he had been arrested. Joseph Smith, Jr.; and who had been delivered into the custody of said Reynolds by said Wilson, who had first, as an officer of the state of Illinois, arrested him, the said Smith, upon a warrant issued by his Excellency Thomas Ford, to apprehend him as a fugitive from the justice of the state of Missouri, when it was alleged he was charged with treason against the said state of Missouri; that the arrest and transfer of the custody of said Smith took place in Lee county, Illinois; and that while said Joseph H. Reynolds was at Dixon, in said county, a writ of habeas corpus was served on him, in behalf of said Smith, commanding him to bring said Smith before the nearest judge or judicial tribunal in the fifth judicial district of the state of Illinois, authorized to hear and determine upon writs of habeas corpus; that said Harmon T. Wilson acted as a guard and assistant under said Joseph H. Reynolds on their journey from Dixon, till they arrived at the city of Nauvoo; that said Smith was allowed by said Reynolds to ride his horse and in a buggy on said journey, while the said Reynolds rode in the coach, upon the assurance and pledge of James Campbell, Esq., the sheriff of Lee county, Illinois, who had said Reynolds and Wilson in custody for want of bail in a civil action, and upon whom they had served habeas corpus, returnable before Judge Young at Quincy, Illinois.

Your affiants as well as others in the company, at the same time gave assurance and pledges to said Reynolds that his prisoner, the said Smith, should not escape from him; and the said Reynolds was satisfied, as he avowed, with the pledges aforesaid, and expressed himself to be so at the time, and fully consented that the said Smith might travel on said journey in the manner he did.

That the friends of said Smith met him in great numbers as he approached the city of Nauvoo, by which place the sheriff, as these affiants believe, voluntarily decided to go at the request of said Smith, and upon representations made to him that it was the best route to Quincy.

That no violence was offered to said Reynolds or Wilson; and that to the best of these affiants' knowledge and belief, no threats or intimidation were made use of to influence and control their conduct, either during the journey to or after their arrival at Nauvoo. Said Reynolds and Wilson dined with said Smith at his own house, and were hospitably entertained; and after dinner, say in two hours after the arrival of the party in said city, a writ of habeas corpus was issued by the municipal court of the said city of Nauvoo in favor of said Smith, which was served upon said Reynolds.

The said Reynolds made return of the writ, together with the body of said Smith, and alleged the causes of his capture and detention, at the same time denying the jurisdiction of the court, and alleging that he had been served with the prior writ of habeas corpus before mentioned. Said Reynolds remained in Nauvoo, and a part of the time in the municipal court-room, and sometime after the examination of the writ of habeas corpus issued by the municipal court had commenced, and, as your affiants believe, during the whole sitting of the court on Friday afternoon, the 30th of June, and then departed for Carthage, after a patient examination of the fact and matter of law set forth in complainant's petition, which said examination lasted from Friday afternoon till the next day, Saturday, at night. The said Smith was discharged as for defects in the warrant under which he had been arrested, and was imprisoned, as upon the merits of the case by the said municipal court; and these affiants further say that said Reynolds and Wilson were, before they arrived at the city of Nauvoo, and while they were there, assured by the said Smith and many of the company who had traveled together from Dixon, (these affiants among the number,) that they should be protected from violence; and that the said Smith did publicly declare in Nauvoo, to the people there assembled, that his honor was pledged that said Reynolds should be protected from violence, and requested every one to preserve his pledge inviolate.

These affiants state further that no violence or threats, to their knowledge or belief, were made use of towards the said Reynolds or the said Wilson, either before or after their arrival at Nauvoo; but the numbers who met and accompanied the said Smith and his escort on the journey, conducted themselves in an orderly and peaceable manner, and manifested only their attachment to said Smith, and joy to find him safe in the custody of the laws of the state of Illinois; all of which facts are true, to the best of the knowledge and recollection of the affiants.

SHEPHERD G. PATRICK,
CYRUS WALKER,
E. SOUTHWICK,
HARMON WASSON.

Sworn to, etc.

Colonel Markham, Mr. Sanger, and myself also made affidavits on the same subject.

Judge Adams came from Carthage and stated that Wilson and Reynolds were inciting the people to mobocracy, and sending a petition to Governor Ford for a posse to retake me.

A petition to the governor, praying him not to issue any more writs, was immediately made out, and signed by about 150 citizens of Nauvoo; and also

A remonstrance against the Carthage proceedings was gotten up. Signed and forwarded the same to Carthage by Messrs. Southwick and Patrick.

I directed the clerk to make a transcript of the proceedings before the municipal court, to forward to the governor, and to which he attached the following certificate:—

Certification of Documents.

I, James Sloan, Clerk of the Municipal Court of the city of Nauvoo, Illinois, do hereby certify that the foregoing hereunto attached papers and documents—to wit, that the foregoing petition of Joseph Smith, Sen., and warrant from the governor of the state of Illinois, and commission issued by Thomas Reynolds, governor of the state of Missouri, to Joseph H. Reynolds, and the writ of habeas corpus, and the return of the said Joseph H. Reynolds thereto, and endorsed thereon, are true copies of the papers and originals filed in this court, in the exparte case of Joseph Smith, Sen., upon the petition of said Smith, for a discharge from arrest on habeas corpus; and that the foregoing is a true copy of the true, full, and perfect record of the proceedings had in said case.

In witness whereof, I have hereunto set my hand, and affixed the seal of said court, at the city of Nauvoo, Illinois, this third day of July, A. D., 1843.

[L. S.]

JAMES SLOAN,
Clerk of the Municipal Court
of the city of Nauvoo, Illinois.

He also made a transcript of the ordinances relating to habeas corpus, and attached the following certificate:—

I, James Sloan, city recorder of the city of Nauvoo, Illinois, and clerk of the city council of said city, do hereby certify that the foregoing hereunto attached are true copies of the ordinances of said city, regulating the proceedings on writs of habeas corpus, the one passed the 8th day of August, A. D., 1842, and the other passed November 14, 1842, both of which said ordinances are unrepealed and now in force in said city.

In witness whereof, I have hereunto set my hand and affixed the corporate seal of said city of Nauvoo at said city, this 3rd day of July, A. D., 1843.

[L. S.]

JAMES SLOAN,
City Recorder and Clerk of the City Concil
of the city of Nauvoo, Illinois.

Which documents were delivered to my lawyers, with instructions to see Governor Ford immediately.

I had an interview with several Pottawattamie chiefs, who came to see me during my absence.

Interview with Pottawattamie Chiefs.

(From Wilford Woodruff's Journal.)

The Indian chiefs remained at Nauvoo until the Prophet returned and had his trial. During their stay they had a talk with Hyrum Smith in the basement of the Nauvoo House. Wilford Woodruff and some others were present. They were not free to talk, and did not wish to communicate their feelings until they could see the great Prophet.

At length, on the 2nd day of July, 1843, President Joseph Smith and several of the Twelve met those chiefs in the court-room, with about twenty of the elders. The following is a synopsis of the conversation which took place as given by the interpreter:—

The Indian orator arose and asked the Prophet if the men who were present were all his friends. Answer—"Yes."

He then said—"We as a people have long been distressed and oppressed. We have been driven from our lands many times. We have been wasted away by wars, until there are but few of us left. The white man has hated us and shed our blood, until it has appeared as though there would soon be no Indians left. We have talked with the Great Spirit, and the Great Spirit has talked with us. We have asked the Great Spirit to save us and let us live; and the Great Spirit has told us that he had raised up a great Prophet, chief, and friend, who would do us great good and tell us what to do; and the Great Spirit has told us that you are the man (pointing to the Prophet Joseph). We have now come a great way to see you, and hear your words, and to have you to tell us what to do. Our horses have become poor traveling, and we are hungry. We will now wait and hear your word."

The Spirit of God rested upon the Lamanites, especially the orator. Joseph was much affected and shed tears. He arose and said unto them: "I have heard your words. They are true. The Great Spirit has told you the truth. Im am your friend and brother, and I wish to do you good. Your fathers were once a great people. They worshiped the Great Spirit. The Great Spirit did them good. He was their friend; but they left the Great Spirit, and would not hear his words or keep them. The Great Spirit left them, and they began to kill one another, and they have been poor and afflicted until now.

The Great Spirit has given me a book, and told me that you will soon be blessed again. The Great Spirit will soon begin to talk with you and your children. This is the book which your fathers made. I wrote upon it (showing them the Book of Mormon). This tells what you will have to do. I now want you to begin to pray to the Great Spirit. I want you to make peace with one another, and do not kill any more Indians: it is not good. Do not kill white men; it is not good; but ask the Great Spirit for what you want, and it will not be long before the Great Spirit will bless you, and you will cultivate the earth and build good houses like white men. We will give you something to eat and to take home with you."

When the Prophet's words were interpreted to the chiefs, they all said it was good. The chief asked, "How many moons would it be before the Great Spirit would bless them?" He [Joseph] told them, Not a great many.

At the close of the interview, Joseph had an ox killed for them, and they were furnished with some more horses, and they went home satisfied and contented.

Return of the *Maid of Iowa* Relief Expedition.

About six p.m., the *Maid of Iowa* returned to her landing at the Nauvoo House. The company who had been on the expedition on board of her formed in a procession and walked up to my office, where they formed a hollow square, and sent in a deputation to me. As soon as I had bid them welcome, I opened the window of my office and requested that no man would leave the ground until I had spoken to them. My brother Hyrum and I went into the hollow sqare and directed them not to allow their ranks to be broken. I then shook hands with each man, blessing them and welcoming them home.

I then took off my hat and related to them how I was brought home to the midst of my friends, and how I regained my liberty. I feel, by the Spirit of the Lord, that if I had fallen into your hands that you would either have brought me safe home, or that we should all have died in a heap together.

At this time, a well dressed man, a stranger, who had a cloak around him, broke through the south line of the ranks, when the orderly sergeant took the stranger by the nape of the neck and kicked him outside the ranks, telling him not to come in again. As soon as quiet was resumed, I continued my address to the company.

About dusk I dismissed the company, blessing them in the name of the Lord.

My brother Hyrum then blessed them also, commending them for their diligence and attention to the instructions given by him before their departure.

The following is the report of their doings, as reported by Daniel M. Burbanks:

Burbanks' Account of the Maid of Iowa Expedition for the Prophet's Relief.

Sunday, June 25.—The brethren were collecting through the night on the *Maid of Iowa*, and commenced making preparations for the trip, all hands uniting in loading the boat with firewood.

26th.—About half-past eight a. m., President Hyrum Smith, in company with Judge Adams, came on board and instructed us to watch for the steamboats that may run up the Illinois river; and if any persons were running Brother Joseph down the river, under any pretext whatever, as the *Amaranth* had carried the news to Missouri that Joseph Smith was going to be tried at Ottawa, and it had been reported that a company of men were armed in St. Louis and had chartered a steamboat to run up to Ottawa, there to seize Joseph and kidnap him to Missouri;—and if we saw such a boat, we were to rescue Joseph, at all hazards and bring him to Nauvoo

President Hyrum then blessed the company in the name of the Lord, and the *Little Maid* started at a quarter-past nine a. m., down the Mississippi river, with the following persons on board—namely, Dan Jones, Captain of boat; Daniel M. Burbanks, first Pilot; Dimick B. Huntington, Mate; Jonathan Dunham, Captain of Company; George W. Langley, Lieutenant; John Taylor, Chaplain; John M. Bernhisel, Surgeon; John S. Higbee, Isaac Higbee, Lucius N. Scovil, Enoch M. King, Lewis Dunbar Wilson, Whitford G. Wilson, Bushrod W. Wilson, John Bair, Ben Rolfe, Sylvester B. Stoddard, James Aikin, Elijah Averett, Levi W. Hancock, William Meeks, Calvin Reed, Robert C. Moore, Levi Stewart, Urban V. Stewart, Allen Stout, Welcome Chapman, William S. Yocum, Thomas Briley, Henry J. Young, James Worthington, George W. Thatcher, H. M. Alexander, Elbridge Tufts, Benjamin L. Clapp, Joseph C. Kingsbury, A. Young, John Fido, John Murdoch, John Lytle, Thomas Carrico, E. J. Sabin, Daniel Avory, H. B. M. Jolley, J. F. Lane, J. H. Holmes, H. P. Palmer, Benjamin Jones, Robert C. Egbert, Tarlton Lewis, R. A. Allred, J. Foutz, H. Permain, John Binby, George W. Rosecran, and about twenty-five others whose names are not reported.

At nine p. m., the boat turned the point of the bend and started up the Illinois river. She did not stop until opposite Diamond Isle, about four o'clock on Tuesday morning, 27th, where the company learned that the *Chicago Belle* had passed up the Illinois river the day previous with a large company of men, having a swivel gun on the forecastle, as they said, with the intention of taking Joseph Smith, at all hazards,and conveying him to Missouri.

The *Maid* next hailed at the Erie landing, five miles above Beardstown, where they were told that the *Belle* was twelve hours ahead, and the company on board had left word that if the *Maid of Iowa* followed, they would send the "Mormon" boat and crew, with Jo Smith, to hell. The people advised the company on the *Maid* to return. Stayed there half-an-hour to take in wood, and then continued our journey.

Wednesday, 28th.—At an hour before daybreak, passed Pekin, and the *Chicago Belle* aground in an island chute. When she saw us coming, she backed her star-board wheel and blocked up the passage.

When the pilot of the *Maid* came near, he stopped his engine and hailed them with his speaking trumpet, requesting a passage. They inquired, "What boat is that?" and were told, the *Maid of Iowa*. They replied, "You cannot pass, and we will see you all d—d and in hell first." The pilot saw a little opening in the willows of about twelve feet wide on her left, and signaled for the engineer to put on all steam, and drove her through this narrow channel and a small tow head about five rods, tearing the willows down on each side with the guards and wheelhouse, the captain crying out all the time, "Stop her!—stop her! For God's sake, stop her! You will smash the boat in pieces!"

When the boat had headed round the *Belle*, and was once more in deep water, the pilot stopped the engine and asked the captain, "What is the matter?" The captain was afraid, and said, "My God, you will smash the boat to pieces," and was answered, "All is safe, and we will go ahead," leaving the *Belle* still aground in the channel.

Then went to Peoria, about ten miles; found Jesse P. Harmon and Alanson Ripley, who had come from the horsemen with an express instructing the company to proceed to the mouth of Fox River. We took them on board and proceeded on our way.

Thursday, 29th.—Arrived at Peru, at ten a. m. There met William F. Lane with an express from Charles C. Rich, reporting that the company who had Joseph in charge had started from Fox River for Shokoquon, destined to run him through the Iowa territory by that route, and then into Missouri, as they had learned their way by the Illinois river was blocked up by the *Maid of Iowa*, and for the boat and company to return to Quincy, and there await further orders. We immediately turned round, and on arriving at the mouth of Spoon River, landed Ripley and Harmon, with instructions to pursue their journey by land to Nauvoo.

About one p. m., again overhauled the *Chicago Belle* at the Grand Pass while they were wooding. They hailed us to inquire "If old Jo was on board," and were answered, "It is none of your business," when another man on the hurricane deck of the *Belle* shouted, "Hurrah, hurrah for old Jo Smith!"

We continued our journey and again arrived at the Mississippi at nine p. m. In rounding to, broke the tiller rope and came to an anchor; repaired the same, and then continued up the Mississippi.

Arrived at the island below Quincy about eight p. m., on Friday, 30th, when John Taylor, Jonathan Dunham, Dan Jones, George W. Langley, and Daniel M. Burbanks took the yawl and went up to Quincy to learn the news and see if there was any excitement. They found all peace, then returned to the boat, got up steam, and went up to Quincy, landing about midnight.

Saturday, July 1st.—About eight a. m., left Quincy, after steaming about eight miles. Sidney Roberts and another messenger came in a skiff with a letter from Hyrum, saying that Joseph had arrived in Nauvoo, and was going to be tried before the municipal court, and for us to hurry home as quick as possible.

On reaching Keokuk, the engineer, Benjamin Orum (who was not a member of the Church) got dead drunk, when the first pilot turned engineer, aud the second pilot took the wheel and run the boat over the rapids to Nauvoo,

Application for Posse to Retake the Prophet.

Colonel Markham returned from Carthage in the evening, and reported that on his arriving at Carthage, he found that Reynolds and Wilson had filed their affidavits, that he (Markham) had with armed force taken Joseph Smith out of their hands at the head of Elleston Grove, and that they had also got up a petition, which was signed by the inhabitants of Carthage, and sent it to Governor Ford by the hands of Reynolds and Wilson, requesting him to raise a posse comitatus, and they would come to Nauvoo and take me. They were to start by the mail early this morning; and Markham requested Jacob Backenstos to go with the mail to Governor Ford and request him to suspend all proceedings until documents would be got to show the true state of the case.

On going to the stage proprietor, he engaged and paid for a passage for one man. On their finding who was going, Reynolds and Wilson objected to his going; and that objection was accepted by the stage proprietor, although he had received the passage money. The proprietor then hired a horse from Mr. Hamilton for him [Markham] to ride.

Monday, July 3.—I directed the Twelve Apostles to call

a special conference to choose elders to go into the different counties of Illinois to preach the gospel and disabuse the public mind with regard to my arrest.

Elders Brigham Young, Orson Hyde, Parley P. Pratt, John Taylor, George A. Smith, Wilford Woodruff, and Willard Richards met at the Grove with the elders, and it was decided that the following elders go on a special mission to the following counties in the state of Illinois:

List of Special Missionaries.

Elijah Reed and Jesse Hitchcock, Adams and Pike; Salmon Warner and Jeremiah Curtis, Calhoun and Jersey; Erastus H. Derby, Orson Hyde, and George J. Adams, Lee; Charles C. Rich and Harvey Green, La Salle and De Calb; Levi Richards, Luther A. Jones, and E. Robinson, Joe Davis; John Murdock, Vermillion; Daniel Avery, Schuyler; Zebedee Coltrin, McDonough; Truman Gillet, Benjamin Brown, and Jesse W. Crosby, Cook; Graham Coltrin, Fulton; John L. Butler, Hamilton; David Lewis, Wayne; James Twist, Bureau; George P. Dykes and Samuel Brown, St. Clair; Pardon Webb, Will; E. M. Webb, Grundy; Simeon Dunn, Warren; H. S. Eldredge, Mason; Thomas Dobson, Tazewell; Cyrus Canfield, Menard; Jared Carter, Morgan; Samuel James and J. C. Wright, Scott; Luman H. Calkins, White; J. M. King, Mercer; Daniel Allen, Rock Island; U. C. Nickerson, Henry; Alfred Brown, Putnam; Priddy Meeks, McCoupin; Abel Butterfield and J. H. Van Natta, Winnebago; William Nelson, Iroquois; Samuel Russell, Boone; Levi Stewart, Franklin; William Meeks, Green; W. B. Brink and George Chamberlin, Sangamon; Jacob Wiley, Edwards; William S. Covert, Stark; M. F. Bartlett and Melvin Wilbur, Bond; John Outhouse, Alexander; Cheney G. Van Buren, Brown; James Carroll, Carroll; David Jones, Fayette; John Lowry, Munroe; Urban V. Stewart, Williamson; James McFate, Montgomery; Lyman O. Littlefield, Clinton; Elisha H. Groves, Madison; Theodore Curtis, Cass; Samuel Keele, Jefferson; James Hale, Washington; George W. Thatcher and John A. Forgeus, Hancock; Jacob H. Butterfield, Henderson; George Middah, Clay; James M. Munroe, Crawford; Ezra Chase, Coles; Jesse Chase, Edgar; Amos Lewell, Clark; John Miller, Whitesides; William Martin, Christian; Reuben Parkhurst, De Witt; John Keele, Perry; George W. Langley, Johnson; James M. Henderson, Gallatin; James W. Cummings, Randolph; John Workman, Shelby; Elijah Fordham, Knox; George W. Pitkin and John Wakefield, Peoria.

BRIGHAM YOUNG, President.

W. RICHARDS, Clerk.

About noon, General Charles C. Rich, with twenty-five men, returned, formed a square in front of my house, and sang a new song. I went out, shook hands with each individual, and blessed them in the name of the Lord. The following is a report of their expedition:

Report of Relief Expedition Led by Charles C. Rich.

The detachment left the main body of the camp and started from McQueen's Mills about one a. m., on Monday, the 26th of June, under the command of General Rich, as follows:—C. C. Rich, Hosea Stout, John Pack, Truman R. Barlow, James W. Cummings, Daniel Carnes, Jesse P. Harmon, Alanson Ripley, Stephen Abbott, Charles W. Hubbard, A. L. Fullmer, Joel E. Terry, Alfred Brown, Dr. Josiah Ells, William Edwards, Thomas Woolsey, Osmon M. Duel, Dr. Samuel Bennett,——Babcock, Isaiah Whitesides, Jesse B.Nichols, Stephen Wilkinson, Samuel Gulley, and four or five others, on horses, with one baggage wagon drawn by two horses, with instructions to proceed to Peoria, there cross the Illinois river, and then proceed up the east side of the river on the main stage road leading from Springfield to Ottawa. We traveled till about three o'clock in the morning, when we halted for about an hour and put out a guard. At daybreak we again took up the line of march, and traveled through the day, mostly without a road, and the following night till near daybreak of the 27th, and again made a halt for an hour and passed through Ellesville before sunrise. When going through that village, the people were opening their shops, and many persons came in their shirts to the windows.

Dr. Ells and J. W. Cummings were behind the company about six rods, when one man came running, full of anxiety, and inquired, "Where in the world are you all going to?" Dr. Ells, who carried a very sanctified face, drawled out, "We're a-hunting a wheelbarrow's nest:" after which, we again resumed the march, about noon halted on the Kic-a-poo creek, and sent Hosea Stout and A. L. Fullmer to Peoria to see Lawyer Charles C. Ballance and obtain what information they could get from him; and about two p. m., crossed the Illinois river at Peoria, where we obtained supplies for our further journey. Here we left Jesse P. Harmon and Alanson Ripley with instructions to hail the steamer *Maid of Iowa*, and procure what information they had of the whereabouts of Brother Joseph Smith.

The company after crossing the river, proceeded nearly due east, till they intersected the stage road running from Springfield to Ottawa, at a small town named Washington, ten miles east of Peoria. There we stopped for about an hour and fed our horses. At dusk we again resumed the march on the stage road towards Ottawa, and traveled about ten miles to Black Partridge Point, and camped for the night.

At daybreak of the 28th, we were on the march, traveled about 35 miles to the little town of Magnolia, and halted for noon, where we fed ourselves and animals at the public house of Captain William Haws (the captain of a company in which Hosea Stout served in the Black Hawk war). We again resumed the march, and about dark camped about two miles below Ottawa, near the Illinois river, having traveled over 200 miles in two days and eighteen hours with the same horses, which had become very tired.

General Rich left the company about an hour before sunset, and about dusk crossed the Illinois river into Ottawa, and put up at Brother Sanger's. There he learned positively that Joseph had come as far as Pawpaw Grove, where he was informed that Judge Caton was absent, and had returned to Dixon and obtained another writ of habeas corpus, and had started in the direction of Quincy, Adams county; and also that Lucien P. Sanger had taken his stage-coach to convey Brother Joseph to Quincy. When he had obtained this information, he left orders for the *Maid of Iowa* to return with all speed to Quincy.

Early on the morning of the 29th, General Rich returned to his company and gave them the information, when the company started on their return for Nauvoo, came as far as Captain Haws', and stayed all night. He gave us the use of the barn to sleep in. In conversing with the citizens of Magnolia, they approbated our course, manifested a warm feeling, and offered to help us with their artillery company, if we needed their assistance.

On the 30th we made a direct course for the Narrows, four miles above Peoria, where we recrossed the Illinois river, and camped near the town.

1st July. We traveled forty miles and camped on a small creek near a farmhouse, where the entire company had an abundance of milk for the night.

July 2nd. Early in the morning, Jesse B. Nichols went into the village of Gallsburg, waked up a blacksmith, and employed him to set a couple of horse-shoes. The blacksmith objected, saying it was Sunday morning, and, being a professor of religion, he would not do it unless for double price, which Nichols consented to give him. He went to the shop; and whilst setting the shoes, the company passed through, exciting considerable curiosity among the villagers. Two of the brethren remained to accompany Nichols. As he was about paying the blacksmith for the work, a Presbyterian minister came up and said to him, "You ought to charge a dollar a shoe. These are Mormons; and you, who are a church member, have been shoeing this Mormon's horse on

Sunday; and you ought to be brought before the church for doing it." Upon which, the blacksmith demanded two dollars for his work instead of one as agreed before. Nichols handed him one dollar, the priest telling the blacksmith he ought not to take it—that Joe Smith was an impostor, and ought to be hung. The son of Vulcan, however, took the dollar, but demanded more; upon which Nichols mounted his horse and left, amid the loud cheers of a number of spectators.

We continued our journey to La Harpe, where we learned the full particulars of Brother Joseph's safe arrival and trial before the municipal court, when we made merry, composed a song, and danced, and proceeded to Nauvoo.

During the entire journey the heat was extremely oppressive; and as the necessity of the case was very urgent, we had not time to sleep. It may be safely said to be one of the most rapid, fatiguing marches that is on record, having traveled with the same horses about 500 miles in seven days.

Another copy of the remonstrance to the governor against his sending an armed force was made out and taken to the porch of the Temple, where it was signed in the course of the day by about 900 persons.

Tuesday, 4.—About one a.m., Messrs. Walker, Patrick, Southwick, Markham, and Lucien Woodworth started for Springfield, carrying with them the affidavits, petition, and the doings of the municipal court.

Fourth of July Celebration at Nauvoo.

At a very early hour people began to assemble at the Grove, and at eleven o'clock near 13,000 persons had congregated, and were addressed in a very able and appropriate manner by Elder Orson Hyde, who has recently been appointed on a mission to St. Petersburg, Russia.

A constant accession of numbers swelled the congregation to 15,000 as near as could be estimated.

At two p. m., they were again addressed by Elder Parley P. Pratt on redemption, in a masterly discourse, when I made some remarks.

The following is the report of the speech by Wilford Woodruff:

The Prophet's Speech—Politics and Military Organization at Nauvoo.

If the people will give ear a moment, I will address them with a few words in my own defense in relation to my arrest. In the first place, I will state to those that can hear me that I never spent more than six months in Missouri, except while in prison. While I was there, I was at work for the support of my family. I never was a prisoner of war during my stay, for I had nothing to do with war. I never took up a pistol, gun or sword: and the most that has been said on this subject by the Missourians is false. I have been willing to go before any governor, judge, or tribunal where justice would be done, and have the subject investigated. I could not have committed treason in that state while I resided there,for treason in Missouri consists in levying war against the state or adhering to her enemies. Missouri was at peace, and had no enemy that I could adhere to, had I been disposed; and I did not make war, as I had no command or authority, either civil or military, but only in spiritual matters, as a minister of the gospel.

This people was driven from that state by force of arms, under the exterminating order of Governor Boggs. I have never committed treason. The people know very well I have been a peaceable citizen; but there has been a great hue and cry about Governor Boggs being shot. No crime can be done, but it is laid to me. Here I was again dragged to the United States Court and acquitted on the merits of the case, and now it comes again. But as often as God sees fit for me to suffer, I am ready; but I am as innocent of the crimes alleged against me as the angels in heaven. I am not an enemy to mankind, I am a friend to mankind. I am not an enemy to Missouri, nor to any governor or people.

As to the military station I hold, the cause of my holding it is as follows: When we came here the state required us to bear arms and do military duty according to law; and as the Church had just been driven from the state of Missouri, and robbed of all their property and arms, they were poor and destitute of arms. They were liable to be fined for not doing duty when they had not arms to do it with. They came to me for advice, and I advised them to organize themselves into independent companies and demand arms of the state. This they did. Again: There were many elders having license to preach,which by law exonerated them from military duty; but the officers would not release them on this ground. I then told the Saints that though I was clear from military duty by law, in consequence of lameness in one of my legs, yet I would set them the example and would do duty myself. They then said they were willing to do duty, if they could be formed into an independent company, and I could be at their head. This is the origin of the Nauvoo Legion and of my holding the office of lieutenant-general.

All the power that I desire or have sought to obtain has been the enjoyment of the constitutional privilege for which my fathers shed their blood, of living in peace in the society of my wife and children, and enjoying the society of my friends and that religious liberty which is the right of every American citizen, of worshiping according to the dictates of his conscience and the revelations of God.

With regard to elections, some say all the Latter-day Saints vote together, and vote as I say. But I never tell any man how to vote or whom to vote for. But I will show you how we have been situated by bringing a comparison. Should there be a Methodist society here and two candidates running for office, one says, "If you will vote for me and put me in governor, I will exterminate the Methodists, take away their charters," &c. The other candidate says, "If I am governor, I will give all an equal privilege." Which would the Methodists vote for? Of course they would vote *en masse* for the candidate that would give them their rights.

Thus it has been with us, Joseph Duncan said if the people would elect him he would exterminate the Mormons, and take away their charters. As to Mr. Ford, he made no such threats, but manifested a spirit in his speeches to give every man his rights; hence the members of the Church universally voted for Mr. Ford and he was elected governor. But he has issued writs against me the first time the Missourians made a demand for me, and this is the second one he has issued for me, which has caused me much trouble and expense.

President Smith also rehearsed the account of his being taken by Reynolds and Wilson, and the unlawful treatment he received at their hands.

The multitude gave good attention and much prejudice seemed to be removed.

Nauvoo's Visitors.

Three steamers arrived in the afternoon; one from St. Louis, one from Quincy and one from Burlington, bringing from eight hundred to a thousand ladies and gentlemen. On the arrival of each boat, the people were escorted by the Nauvoo band to convenient seats provided for them, and were welcomed by the firing of cannon, which brought to our minds the last words of the patriot Jefferson, "Let this day be celebrated by the firing of cannon," &c. The visitors and Saints appeared to be highly gratified.

A collection was taken in the morning to assist Elder Hyde to build his house; and in the afternoon Elder Hyde on his own responsibility, proposed a collection to assist me in bearing the expenses of my persecution.

The meeting closed about 7 p. m. The day was pleasant, sky clear, and nothing tended to disturb the peace.

I extract from the *Quincy Whig:*

Report of the Fourth of July Celebration at Nauvoo—The Quincy Whig.

I left Quincy on the glorious Fourth, on board the splendid steamer *Annawan*, Captain Whitney, in company with a large number of ladies and gentlemen of this city, on a pleasure excursion to the far-famed city of Nauvoo. The kindness of the officers of the boat and the hearty welcome received from the citizens of Nauvoo on our arrival there, induced me to return to each and all of them my own and the thanks of every passenger on board the *Annawan*, and I am sure all alike feel grateful for the pleasure they experienced. We left Quincy at half-past eight, and reached Nauvoo at about two o'clock p. m., where we received an invitation from the Prophet to attend the delivering of an oration, which was accepted; and two companies of the Legion were sent to escort us to the Grove (on the hill near the Temple), where the oration was to be delivered. When we reached the brow of the hill, we received a salute from the artillery there stationed, and proceeded on to the Grove, where we were welcomed in a cordial and happy manner by the Prophet and his people.

The large concourse of people assembled to celebrate the day which gave birth to American independence, convinced me that the Mormons have been most grossly slandered, and that they respect, cherish and love the free institutious of our country, and appreciate the sacrifice and bloodshed of those patriots who established them. I never saw a more orderly, gentlemanly and hospitable people than the Mormons, nor a more interesting population, as the stirring appearance of their city indicates. Nauvoo is destined to be, under the influence and enterprise of such citizens as it now contains, and her natural advantages, a populous, wealthy and manufacturing city.

The services of the day were opened by a chaste and appropriate prayer by an Elder whose name I do not know, which was followed by rich strains of vocal and instrumental music. Then followed the oration which was an elegant, eloquent and pathetic one, as much so as I ever heard on a similar occasion.

We started home about six o'clock, all evidently much pleased with Nauvoo, and gratified by the kind reception of her citizens.

A CITIZEN OF QUINCY.

Wednedsag, 5.—I called in the office and heard the testimony of my brother Hyrum before the municipal court read.

Judge Adams and Esquire Southwick returned from Warsaw; found but little excitement there. Esquire Southwick wrote a piece for the Warsaw paper in my defense, and the justice of the decision of the municipal court.

The remainder of the day I was at home.

Thursday 6.—I remained at home all day.

Governor Ford wrote the following letter:

Letter of Governor Ford to Sheriff Reynolds Replying to a Petition for Military force to Re-arrest the Prophet.

EXECUTIVE DEPARTMENT,
SPRINGFIELD, July 6, 1843.

Joseph H. Reynolds, Esq.:

SIR:—I have received your petition for a detatchment of Illinois Militia to assist you in retaking Joseph Smith, Junior, representing him to have escaped from your custody after having been arrested on a warrant granted for his apprehension. I have also received a remonstrance and some affidavits adverse to the prayer of your petitition. I have also to inform you that I had heard, before your arrival in this city, of the escape of Smith, and rumors that he had been rescued by a military force. Deeming these remarks of sufficient importance to justfy me in so doing, I did, on the 4th day of this present month, dispatch a trusty and competent person as my agent to collect information of the various matters contained in your petition; and you will, I hope, at once see the propriety of all action being suspended on my part until I can receive the most authentic and unquestionable information as to the movements complained of.

I am, most respectfully, your obedient servant,

THOMAS FORD.

And endorsed on the back of it:

MR. BACKENSTOS:—The annexed letter to Joseph H. Reynolds is all the answer which I can at present make to either of the parties touching his application for a detatchment of militia to assist him in retaking Joseph Smith, said to be a fugitive from justice.

I have the honor to be, very respectfully, your obedient servant,

THOMAS FORD.

Friday, 7.—Mr. Braman, a messenger from the governor, arrived in Nauvoo, requesting a copy of all the testimony that was given before the municipal court and other affidavits concerning the expulsion of the Mormons from Missouri.

I therefore employed James Sloan, Samuel Gulley, George Walker and Joseph M. Cole, in addition to my other clerks, who sat up all night to copy the testimony.

In addition to the above I made the following affidavit:

Joseph Smith's Affidavit on the Troubles in Missouri, Sent to Governor Ford.

STATE OF ILLINOIS, }
HANCOCK COUNTY. } ss.

Personally appeared before me, Ebenezer Robinson, a notary public within and for said county, Joseph Smith, senior; who being duly sworn, says that in the year 1838 he removed with his family to the state of Missouri; that he purchased land and became a resident of Caldwell county; that he was an elder and teacher of the Church of Latter-day Saints; that the religious society of which he was an elder numbered several thousand people, who were remarkably industrious in their habits, quiet in their manners and conscientious observers of the laws; that they had been for some years prior to his removal thither purchasing and improving lands, and were possessed of a vast amount of property, probably to the amount of $3,500,000 of real and personal estate; that prejudices had for a long time existed in the minds of the rough and uncultured people by whom his people were surrounded, on account of their peculiar religious views and their different habits of life; that in the summer of 1838 the prejudice of the people against the deponent and his associates became great; that while in the peaceful pursuit of their labors upon their own farms, without any violence or aggression on their part, they were frequently attacked by armed mobs, their houses burned, their cattle stolen, their goods burned and wasted, many innoffensive people murdered, whole families driven out and dispersed over the country at inclement seasons, and every barbarity which the ingenuity and malice of mobs could devise inflicted upon them.

These scenes of violence raged unchecked by the civil authorities, and many officers of the state of Missouri were open leaders of the mob and shared in its crimes. The armed militia of the state were arrayed, without authority of law, for the purpose of driving the deponent and his inoffensive people out of the state, or of exterminating them if they should remain within it. (For proof of this fact see the order of Governor Boggs, dated October 27, 1838, sent herewith). That this deponent and his people received notices, warnings and orders from the civil and military officers of Missouri, as well as from mobs who co-operated with them, to leave the state, and were threatened with death if they refused: that this deponent with others was taken prisoner by an armed mob, and oppressed, imprisoned, and carried from place to place, without authority of law. That his whole people, comprising at least 15,000 people, were driven out like wild beasts, that hundreds were murdered by shooting, stabbing and beating, and having their brains beaten out with clubs. Great numbers were starved to death; many died from fatigue and hardship in the fields; women were ravished, children murdered, and every cruelty inflicted. This deponent with his comrades was imprisoned about six months and until nearly all his people were driven out of the state; that they were then, by order of the officers of the state, set at liberty and ordered to flee from the state. That, after they were released, they were pursued by armed men, who endeavored to shoot them; and they thus were pursued out of the state, and were in peril of their lives as long as they remained within its limits.

And this deponent says that he never committed any crime against the laws of Missouri; that he never commanded or controlled any military or other force; that he never left the state voluntarily, and hoped to be permitted to enjoy his rights, property and liberty, like other peaceable citizens; but that he was driven out by force directed by the officers and approved by the legislature of Missouri; and that the lands and homes which his people had purchased and improved are now in many cases occupied and enjoyed by the very men who composed the mobs who dispossessed them; and he believes that the desire of plunder was one of the inducements which led to the great wrongs which his people have suffered.

And he further says that the recent requisition made upon the governor of Illinois, upon which a warrant for his arrest has been issued, has its origin in the proceedings before recited, in which this deponent, instead of being a "fugitive" from the justice of Missouri, was driven at the point of the bayonet beyond its borders; and that since such expulsion he has not been within the limits of Missouri.

Wherefore he prays that, upon examination of the premises, the governor of Illinois will cause the writ issued by him to be revoked, and this deponent released from further proceedings in the premises.

JOSEPH SMITH.

Sworn to and subscribed before me this 7th day of July, A. D. 1843. Given under my hand and notarial seal, the day and year last written.

[L. S.] EBENEZER ROBINSON,
Notary Public.

Hancock county, Illinois.

Also Caleb Baldwin and Alanson Ripley joined me in the following:

Supplementary Affidavits.

STATE OF ILLINOIS, }
HANCOCK COUNTY. } SS.

Personally came before Ebenezer Robinson, a notary public in and for said county, Caleb Baldwin who being sworn, says that after the arrest of himself and others as mentioned in the foregoing affidavit, he went to Judge Austin A. King, and asked Judge King to grant him a fair trial at law, saying that with the result of such a trial, he would be satisfied. But Judge King answered that "there was no law for the Mormons:" that "they must be exterminated;" that the prisoners, this deponent Smith and others, must die; but that some people, as women and children, would have the privilege of leaving the state, but there was no hope for them.

He told Judge King that his family, composed of helpless females, had been plundered and driven out into the prairie; and asked Judge King what he should do. To which Judge King answered, that if he would renounce his religion and forsake Smith, he would be released and protected. That the same offer was made to the other prisoners; all of whom, however, refused to do so, and were in reply told that they would be put to death.

Alanson Ripley, being in like manner sworn, says that the same offer was made to him by Mr. Birch, the prosecuting attorney, that if he would forsake the Mormons, he should be released and restored to his home, and suffered to remain; to which he returned an answer similar to that of Mr. Baldwin.

Joseph Smith, being in like manner sworn, says that he and Mr. Baldwin were chained together at the time of the conversation above recited by Mr. Balwin; which conversation he heard, and which is correctly stated above; but that no such offer was made to him, it being understood for certain that he was to be shot.

JOSEPH SMITH,
CALEB BALDWIN,
ALANSON RIPLEY.

Sworn to and subscribed before me, this 7th day of July, A. D. 1843. Given under my hand and notarial seal, the day and year last written.

[L. S.] EBENEZER ROBINSON.
Notary Public, Hancock County, Illinois.

Afterwards Caleb Baldwin, Lyman Wight, Parley P. Pratt, Hyrum Smith, James Sloan, Alexander McRae, and Dimick B. Huntington joined me in the following affidavit:

STATE OF ILLINOIS, }
HANCOCK COUNTY. } SS.

Personally appeared before Ebenezer Robinson, a notary public within and for said county, the undersigned citizens of said county; who, being first duly severally sworn according to law upon said oath, depose and say that the said affiants were citizens and residents of Caldwell county and the adjoining counties in the state of Missouri during the years A. D. 1837, 1838, and a part of A. D. 1839. That said affiants were personally conversant with and sufferers in the scenes and troubles usually denominated the Mormon war in Missouri. That Governor Boggs, the acting executive officer of said state, together with Major-General Atchison and Brigadier-General Doniphan, and also the authorities of the counties within which the Mormons resided, repeatedly by direct and public orders and threats commanded every Mormon in the state, Joseph Smith, their leader included, to leave the state, on peril of being exterminated. That the arrest of said Smith in the month of November, A. D. 1838, was made without authority, color, or pretended sanction of law; said arrest having been made by a mob, by which said Smith, among others, was condemned to be shot; but which said sentence was finally revoked. Said mob, resolving itself into a pretended court of justice without the pretended sanction of law, then and there made out the charges and procured the pretended conviction for the same which are mentioned in the indictment against the said Smith; by virtue of which he, the said Smith, on the requisition of the executive of Missouri, has been recently arrested by the order of his excellency, Thomas Ford, governor of the state of Illinois.

Said affiants further state that they were imprisoned with the said

Joseph Smith, when they and the said Smith were delivered into the hands of a guard to be conducted out of the state of Missouri, and by said guard, by the order and direction of the authorities of said counties where said Mormons were arrested and confined, and by order of the governor of the state of Missouri, were set at large, with directions to leave the state without delay. That said Joseph Smith and his affiants were compelled to leave the state for the reasons above mentioned, and would not and did not leave said state for any other cause or reason than that they were ordered and driven from the state of Missouri by the governor and citizens thereof. And further say not.

CALEB BALDWIN,
LYMAN WIGHT,
PARLEY P. PRATT,
HYRUM SMITH,
JAMES SLOAN,
ALEXANDER MCRAE,
DIMICK B. HUNTINGTON.

Sworn to before me, and subscribed in my presence, this 7th day of July, A. D. 1843. In testimony whereof, I hereunto set my hand and affix my notarial seal at my office in Nauvoo, this 7th day of July, A. D. 1843.

EBENEZER ROBINSON,
Notary Public, Hancock County, Illinois.*

About four p. m. Elders Brigham Young, Wilford Woodruff, George A. Smith and Eli P. Maginn, started on the steamer *Rapids* on their eastern mission.

Saturday, 8.—Municipal Court sat and approved of the copies of the evidence heard on the habeas corpus and revised it for the press. In the afternoon Shadrach Roundy started with the affidavits of Hyrum Smith, Parley P. Pratt, Brigham Young, Lyman Wight, and G. W. Pitkin, to carry to the governor.

Bishop Miller arrived from the Pinery with one hundred and fifty-seven thousand feet of lumber, and seventy thousand shingles for the Temple.

Elders Young, Woodruff, and Smith arrived at St. Louis, and reshipped on board the *Lancet* for Cincinnati.

* The affidavits on Missouri troubles supplement those on the same subject published in the Appendix to Volume III of this work. Taken together they comprise a somewhat exhaustive history of the Latter-day Saints in the state of Missouri.

CHAPTER XXVI.

DISCOURSE OF THE PROPHET—HIS LOVE FOR MANKIND—PRESENTATION OF THE DOCUMENTS OF THE LATE TRIAL TO GOVERNOR FORD—REVELATION ON THE ETERNITY OF THE MARRIAGE COVENANT AND PLURALITY OF WIVES.

Sunday, July 9, 1843.—Meeting at the Grove in the morning. I addressed the Saints.

[The following is a brief synopsis, as reported by Dr. Willard Richards:]

The Cause of the Prophet's Success—Love for His Fellow-Man.

Joseph remarked that all was well between him and the heavens: that he had no enmity against any one; and as the prayer of Jesus, or his pattern, so prayed Joseph—"Father, forgive me my trespasses as I forgive those who trespass against me," for I freely forgive all men. If we would secure and cultivate the love of others, we must love others, even our enemies as well as friends.

Sectarian priests cry out concerning me, and ask, "Why is it this babbler gains so many followers, and retains them?" I answer, It is because I possess the principle of love. All I can offer the world is a good heart and a good hand.

The Saints can testify whether I am willing to lay down my life for my brethren. If it has been demonstrated that I have been willing to die for a "Mormon." I am bold to declare before Heaven that I am just as ready to die in defending the rights of a Presbyterian, a Baptist, or a good man of any other denomination; for the same principle which would trample upon the rights of the Latter-day Saints would trample upon the rights of the Roman Catholics, or of any other denomination who may be unpopular and too weak to defend themselves.

It is a love of liberty which inspires my soul—civil and religious liberty to the whole of the human race. Love of liberty was diffused into my soul by my grandfathers* while they dandled me on their knees; and shall I want friends? No.

* Revolutionary ancestors of the Prophet.

The inquiry is frequently made of me, "Wherein do you differ from others in your religious views?" In reality and essence we do not differ so far in our religious views, but that we could all drink into one principle of love. One of the grand fundamental principles of "Mormonism" is to receive truth, let it come from whence it may.

We believe in the Great Eloheim who sits enthroned in yonder heavens. So do the Presbyterians. If a skilful mechanic, in taking a welding heat, uses borax, alum, etc., and succeeds in welding together iron or steel more perfectly then any other mechanic, is he not deserving of praise? And if by the principles of truth I succeed in uniting men of all denominations in the bonds of love, shall I not have attained a good object?

If I esteem mankind to be in error, shall I bear them down? No. I will lift them up, and in their own way too, if I cannot persuade them my way is better; and I will not seek to compel any man to believe as I do, only by the force of reasoning, for truth will cut its own way. Do you believe in Jesus Christ and the Gospel of salvation which He revealed? So do I. Christians should cease wrangling and contending with each other, and cultivate the principles of union and friendship in their midst; and they will do it before the millennium can be ushered in and Christ takes possession of His kingdom.

"Do you believe in the baptism of infants?" asks the Presbyterian. No. "Why?" Because it is nowhere written in the Bible. Circumcision is not baptism, neither was baptism instituted in the place of circumcision. Baptism is for remission of sins. Children have no sins. Jesus blessed them and said, "Do what you have seen me do." Children are all made alive in Christ, and those of riper years through faith and repentance.

So far we are agreed with other Christian denominations. They all preach faith and repentance. The gospel requires baptism by immersion for the remission of sins, which is the meaning of the word in the original language—namely, to bury or immerse.

We ask the sects, Do you believe this? They answer, No. I believe in being converted. I believe in this tenaciously. So did the Apostle Peter and the disciples of Jesus. But I further believe in the gift of the Holy Ghost by the laying on of hands. Evidence by Peter's preaching on the day of Pentecost, Acts 2:38. You might as well baptize a bag of sand as a man, if not done in view of the remission of sins and getting of the Holy Ghost. Baptism by water is but half a baptism, and is good for nothing without the other half—that is, the baptism of the Holy Ghost.

The Savior says, "Except a man be born of water and of the Spirit, he cannot enter into the kingdom of God." "Though we or an angel from heaven, preach any other gospel unto you than that which we have preached unto you, let him be accursed," according to Galatians 1:8.

I am free today. Messengers have returned with offers of peace from the governor.

This morning, [the 9th of July] Esquire Patrick and Colonel Markham returned from Springfield. Markham stated that on the 4th they drove to Beardstown hired fresh horses, and got to Springfield, 124 miles, about seven on the morning of the 5th, about two hours in advance of the Carthage mail, carrying Reynolds and Wilson, and ready with the documents to see the governor. The affidavits were in the possession of Cyrus Walker, who refused to give them up, on account of a political squip in the *State Register*, charging Walker with making capital stock out of my arrest to favor his election to Congress. Markham then demanded them as my agent, telling him that, if he would not give them up, he would take them from him. Walker then turned and said, "I will do my duty, if it takes my head," and then went with Markham and delivered the papers to the governor. When they received the decision of the governor, they started on their return home. When they returned to Rushville, they learned that General Moses Wilson* had been staying there two or three weeks, with ten or twelve men, waiting for an opportunity of transporting me to Jackson county, and had only left there the morning previous, when they learned the decision of Governor Ford.

Markham Outwits Sheriffs Reynolds and Wilson.

In the evening, Shadrach Roundy started for Springfield, to carry further affidavits and see Governor Ford.

Monday, 10.—I rode out with Emma to the farm.

Tuesday, 11.—I rode out with my family in the carriage.

Wednesday, 12.—I received the following revelation in

* This was the Gen. Moses Wilson who was active in the Missouri persecutions of the Saints, see Vol. II, pp. 46, 191. Also Autobiography of Parley P. Pratt. Edition of 1874, chapt. xxi, Affidavit. Hist. of the Church, Vol. III, Appendix.

the presence of my brother Hyrum and Elder William Clayton:—

*Revelation on the Eternity of the Marriage Covenant, including the Plurality of Wives. Given through Joseph, the Seer, in Nauvoo, Hancock County, Illinois, July 12th, 1843.**

Verily thus saith the Lord unto you my servant Joseph, that inasmuch as you have inquired of my hand to know and understand wherein I the Lord justified my servants Abraham, Isaac, and Jacob, as also Moses, David, and Solomon my servants, as touching the principle and doctrine of their having many wives and concubines; behold and lo, I am the Lord thy God, and will answer thee as touching this matter. Therefore prepare thy heart to receive and obey the instructions which I am about to give unto you; for all those who have this law revealed unto them must obey the same; for, behold, I reveal unto you a new and an everlasting covenant; and if ye abide not that covenant, then are ye damned; for no one can reject this covenant and be permitted to enter into my glory; for all who will have a blessing at my hands shall abide the law which was appointed for that blessing and the conditions thereof, as were instituted from before the foundation of the world: and as pertaining to the new and everlasting covenant, it was instituted for the fulness of my glory; and he that receiveth a fulness thereof must and shall abide the law, or he shall be damned, saith the Lord God.

And verily I say unto you, that the conditions of this law are these: All covenants, contracts, bonds, obligations, oaths, vows, performances, connections, associations, or expectations that are not made and entered into and sealed by the Holy Spirit of promise, of him who is anointed, both as well for time and for all eternity, and that too most holy, by revelation and commandment, through the medium of mine anointed, whom I have appointed on the earth to hold this power, (and I have appointed unto my servant Joseph to hold this power in the last days, and there is never but one on the earth at a time on whom this power and the keys of this Priesthood are conferred,) are of no efficacy, virtue, or force in and after the resurrection from the dead; for all contracts that are not made unto this end have an end when men are dead.

Behold, mine house is a house of order, saith the Lord God, and not a house of confusion. Will I accept of an offering, saith the Lord, that is not made in my name? Or will I receive at your hands that which I have not appointed? And will I appoint unto you, saith the Lord, ex-

* Doctrine and Covenants, section 132. For a treatise on the date of publication and authorship of this revelation see Introduction to this volume.

cept it be by law, even as I and my father ordained unto you before the world was? I am the Lord thy God, and I give unto you this commandment, that no man shall come unto the Father but by me, or by my word, which is my law, saith the Lord; and everything that is in the world, whether it be ordained of men, by thrones, or principalities, or powers, or things of name, whatsoever they may be, that are not by me, or by my word, saith the Lord, shall be thrown down, and shall not remain after men are dead, neither in nor after the resurrection, saith the Lord your God; for whatsoever things remain are by me, and whatsoever things are not by me shall be shaken and destroyed.

Therefore, if a man marry him a wife in the world, and he marry her not by me nor by my word, and he covenant with her so long as he is in the world, and she with him, their covenant and marriage are not of force when they are dead and when they are out of the world; therefore they are not bound by any law when they are out of the world: therefore, when they are out of the world, they neither marry nor are given in marriage, but are appointed angels in heaven, which angels are ministering servants, to minister for those who are worthy of a far more and an exceeding and an eternal weight of glory: for these angels did not abide my law; therefore they cannot be enlarged, but remain separately and singly, without exaltation, in their saved condition, to all eternity, and from henceforth are not gods, but are angels of God for ever and ever.

And again, verily I say unto you, If a man marry a wife, and make a covenant with her for time and for all eternity, if that covenant is not by me or by my word, which is my law, and is not sealed by the Holy Spirit of promise, through him whom I have anointed and appointed unto this power, then it is not valid, neither of force, when they are out of the world, because they are not joined by me, saith the Lord, neither by my word. When they are out of the world it cannot be received there, because the angels and the gods are appointed there, by whom they cannot pass: they cannot, therefore, inherit my glory, for my house is a house of order, saith the Lord God.

And again, verily I say unto you, If a man marry a wife by my word, which is my law, and by the new and everlasting covenant, and it is sealed unto them by the Holy Spirit of promise, by him who is anointed, unto whom I have appointed this power and the keys of this Priesthood, and it shall be said unto them, Ye shall come forth in the first resurrection; and if it be after the first resurrection, in the next resurrection; and shall inherit thrones, kingdoms, principalities, and powers, dominions, all heights and depths; then shall it be written in the Lamb's book of life, that he shall commit no murder, whereby to shed innocent blood; and if ye abide in my covenant, and commit no murder whereby to shed innocent blood, it shall be done unto them in all things whatsoever my servant hath put upon them, in time and through all eternity, and shall be of full force when they are out of the world; and they shall pass by the angels and the gods which are set there, to their exaltation and glory in all things, as hath been sealed upon their heads; which glory shall be a fullness and a continuation of the seeds for ever and ever.

Then shall they be gods, because they have no end; therefore shall they be from everlasting to everlasting, because they continue. Then shall they be above all, because all things are subject unto them. Then shall they be gods, because they have all power, and the angels are subject unto them.

Verily, verily, I say unto you, except ye abide my law, ye cannot attain to this glory; for strait is the gate and narrow the way that leadeth unto the exaltation and continuation of the lives, and few there be that find it, because ye receive me not in the world, neither do ye know me But if ye receive me in the world, then shall ye know me, and shall receive your exaltation, that where I am, ye shall be also. This is eternal lives, to know the only wise and true God, and Jesus Christ whom He hath sent. I am He. Receive ye, therefore, my law. Broad is the gate and wide the way that leadeth to the deaths; and many there are that go in thereat, because they receive me not, neither do they abide in my law.

Verily, verily, I say unto you, If a man marry a wife according to my word, and they are sealed by the Holy Spirit of promise, according to mine appointment, and he or she shall commit any sin or transgression of the new and everlasting covenant whatever and all manner of blasphemies, and if they commit no murder, wherein they shed innocent blood,—yet they shall come forth in the first resurrection, and enter into their exaltation; but they shall be destroyed in the flesh, and shall be delivered unto the buffetings of Satan, unto the day of redemption; saith the Lord God.

The blasphemy against the Holy Ghost, which shall not be forgiven in the world, nor out of the world, is in that ye commit murder, wherein ye shed innocent blood, and assent unto my death, after ye have received my new and everlasting covenant, saith the Lord God; and he that abideth not this law can in nowise enter into my glory, but shall be damned, saith the Lord.

I am the Lord thy God, and will give unto thee the law of my Holy Priesthood, as was ordained by me and my Father before the world was. Abraham received all things, whatsoever he received by revelation and commandment, by my word, saith the Lord, and hath entered into his exaltation, and sitteth upon his throne.

Abraham received promises concerning his seed and of the fruit of his loins,—from whose loins ye are—viz., my servant Joseph,—which were to continue so long as they were in the world; and as touching Abraham and his seed out of the world, they should continue: both in the world and out of the world should they continue as innumerable as the stars; or, if ye were to count the sand upon the sea shore, ye could not number them. This promise is yours also, because ye are of Abraham, and the promise was made unto Abraham; and by this law are the continuation of the works of my Father, wherein He glorifieth Himself. Go ye, therefore, and do the works of Abraham; enter ye into my law, and ye shall be saved. But if ye enter not into my law, ye cannot receive the promises of my Father, which He made unto Abraham.

God commanded Abraham, and Sarah gave Hagar to Abraham to wife. And why did she do it? Because this was the law; and from Hagar sprang many people. This, therefore, was fulfilling, among other things, the promises. Was Abraham therefore under condemnation? Verily, I say unto you, Nay; for I the Lord commanded it. Abraham was commanded to offer his son Isaac; nevertheless, it was written, Thou shalt not kill. Abraham, however, did not refuse, and it was accounted unto him for righteousness.

Abraham received concubines, and they bare him children, and it was accounted unto him for righteousness, because they were given unto him, and he abode in my law; as Isaac also and Jacob did none other things than that which they were commanded, they have entered into their exaltation, according to the promises, and sit upon thrones, and are not angels, but are gods.

David also received many wives and concubines, and also Solomon, and Moses my servant, as also many others of my servants, from the beginning of creation until this time; and in nothing did they sin, save in those things which they received not of me.

David's wives and concubines were given unto him of me, by the hand of Nathan my servant, and others of the prophets who had the keys of this power; and in none of these things did he sin against me, save in the case of Uriah and his wife; and therefore he hath fallen from his exaltation and received his portion; and he shall not inherit them out of the world, for I gave them unto another, saith the Lord.

I am the Lord thy God, and I gave unto thee, my servant Joseph, an appointment, and restore all things. Ask what ye will, and it shall be given unto you, according to my word. And as ye have asked concerning adultery, verily, verily, I say unto you, If a man receiveth a wife in the new and everlasting covenant, and if she be with another man, and I have not appointed unto her by the holy anointing, she hath committed adultery, and shall be destroyed. If she be not in the new and everlasting covenant, and she be with another man, she has committed adultery; and if her husband be with another woman, and he was under a vow, he hath broken his vow and hath committed adultery; and if she hath not committed adultery, but is innocent, and hath not broken her vow, and she knoweth it, and I reveal it unto you, my servant Joseph, then shall you have power, by the power of my Holy Priesthood to take her and give her unto him that hath not committed adultery, but hath been faithful; for he shall be made ruler over many; for I have conferred upon you the keys and power of the Priesthood, wherein I restore all things, and make known unto you all things in due time.

And verily, verily, I say unto you, that whatsoever you seal on earth shall be sealed in heaven; and whatsoever you bind on earth, in my name and by my word, saith the Lord, it shall be eternally bound in the heavens; and whosesoever sins you remit on earth shall be remitted eternally in the heavens; and whosesoever sins you retain on earth shall be retained in heaven.

And again, verily I say, Whomsoever you bless I will bless; and whomsoever you curse I will curse, saith the Lord; for I the Lord am thy God.

And again, verily I say unto you, my servant Joseph, that whatsoever you give on earth, and to whomsoever you give any one on earth by my word and according to my law, it shall be visited with blessings, and not cursings, and with my power, saith the Lord, and shall be without condemnation on earth and in heaven; for I am the Lord thy God, and will be with thee, even unto the end of the world and through all eternity; for verily I seal upon you your exaltation, and prepare a throne for you in the kingdom of my Father, with Abraham your father. Behold, I have seen your sacrifices, and will forgive all your sins. I have seen your sacrifices, in obedience to that which I have told you. Go, therefore; and I make a way for your escape, as I accepted the offering of Abraham of his son Isaac.

Verily, I say unto you, A commandment I give unto mine handmaid, Emma Smith, your wife, whom I have given unto you, that she stay herself, and partake not of that which I commanded you to offer unto her; for I did it, saith the Lord, to prove you all, as I did Abraham,and that I might require an offering at your hand, by covenant and sacrifice; and let mine handmaid, Emma Smith, receive all those that have been given unto my servant Joseph, and who are virtuous and pure before me: and those who are not pure, and have said they were pure, shall be destroyed, saith the Lord God; for I am the Lord thy God, and ye shall obey my voice: and I give unto my servant Joseph that he shall be made ruler over many things, for he hath been faithful over a few things; and from henceforth I will strengthen him.

And I command mine handmaid, Emma Smith, to abide and cleave unto my servant Joseph, and to none else. But if she will not abide this commandment, she shall be destroyed, saith the Lord; for I am the Lord thy God, and will destroy her, if she abide not in my law: but if she will not abide this commandment, then shall my servant Joseph do all things for her, even as he hath said; and I will bless him, and multiply him, and give unto him an hundredfold, in this world, of fathers and mothers, brothers and sisters, houses and lands, wives and children, and crowns of eternal lives in the eternal worlds. And again, verily I say, Let mine handmaid forgive my servant Joseph his trespasses, and then shall she be forgiven her trespasses, wherein she has trespassed against me; and I the Lord thy God will bless her, and multiply her, and make her heart to rejoice.

And again, I say, Let not my servant Joseph put his property out of his hands, lest an enemy come and destroy him, for Satan seeketh to destroy; for I am the Lord thy God, and he is my servant; and behold and lo, I am with him, as I was with Abraham thy father, even unto his exaltation and glory.

Now, as touching the law of the Priesthood, there are many things pertaining thereunto. Verily, if a man be called of my Father, as was Aaron, by mine own voice, and by the voice of Him that sent me, and I have endowed him with the keys of the power of this Priesthood, if he do anything in my name, and according to my law, and by my word, he will not commit sin, and I will justify him. Let no one, therefore, set on my servant Joseph; for I will justify him; for he shall do the sacrifice which I require at his hands for his transgressions, saith the Lord your God.

And again, as pertaining to the law of the Priesthood. If any man espouse a virgin, and desire to espouse another, and the first give her consent, and if he espouse the second, and they are virgins, and have vowed to no other man, then is he justified; he cannot commit adultery, for they are given unto him; for he cannot commit adultery with that that belongeth unto him and to no one else: and if he have ten virgins given unto him by this law, he cannot commit adultery, for they belong to him, and they are given unto him: therefore is he justified. But if one or either of the ten virgins, after she is epoused, shall be with another man, she has committed adultery, and shall be destroyed; for they are given unto him to multiply and replenish the earth, according to my commandment, and to fulfill the promise which was given by my Father before the foundation of the world, and for their exaltation in the eternal worlds, that they may bear the souls of men, for herein is the work of my Father continued, that he may be glorified.

And again, verily, verily I say unto you, If any man have a wife who holds the keys of this power, and he teaches unto her the law of my Priesthood as pertaining to these things, then shall she believe and administer unto him, or she shall be destroyed, saith the Lord your God, for I will destroy her; for I will magnify my name upon all those who receive and abide in my law. Therefore, it shall be lawful in me, if she receive not this law, for him to receive all things whatsoever I, the Lord his God, will give unto him, because she did not believe and administer unto him according to my word; and she then becomes the transgressor, and he is exempt from the law of Sarah, who administered unto Abraham according to the law, when I commanded Abraham to take Hagar to wife. And now, as pertaining to this law, verily, verily I say unto you, I will reveal more unto you hereafter; therefore let this suffice for the present. Behold, I am Alpha and Omega. Amen.

Hyrum took the revelation and read it to Emma.

I directed Clayton to make out deeds of certain lots of land to Emma and the children.

I extract from the *Neighbor*:—

Editorial.

Joseph Smith is at Nauvoo in peace, quietly pursuing his own business; where we hope he will long remain free from the power of his inhuman persecutors.

The testimony already given* needs no comment. It shows but too plainly the inhumanity, recklessness, barbarism, and lawlessness of the state of Missouri; and we could wish, for the sake of humanity, for the sake of suffering innocence, and for the sake of our honored institutions, that our nation's escutcheon had never been stained by the inhuman acts and bloody deeds of Missouri, and that the non-efficiency of the nation to execute law had not been so fully developed. But it is too true, we have witnessed most of the things mentioned by Mr. Smith, and we have also witnessed the carelessness and apathy of Congress on this subject, or their inefficiency to remedy the evil; the which, had it been fully investigated, and the perpetrators of those damning crimes brought to condign punishment, it would have exposed a blacker history than ever was written of any pagan, not to say Christian nation, and would have exposed half of that state to the charge of treason, murder robbery, arson, burglary, and extermination.

* This has reference to the testimony of Hyrum Smith published in the same issue of the *Neighbor* in which the Editorial appeared. The late President John Taylor was the editor.

As it is, the blood of the innocent yet cries for vengeance; and if it overtakes them not here, and God spares my breath, if no one else does it, their deeds shall be handed down to posterity, that unborn generations may execrate these anti-republico cannibals, and tell that in the state of Missouri lived a horde of savages, protected and shielded by American republican legislative authority, who, in the face of open day, dragged the innocent to prison, because of their religion,—who murdered the oppressed that they had in their power, and fed the victims with their flesh; that they glutted their diabolical lust on defenseless innocence, and violated female chastity in a manner too horrid to relate; that in their mock tribunals they refused all testimony in favor of the accused, and thrust their witnesses into prison; that, after robbing them of their property, they drove 15,000 persons from the state; that they cried to the authorities of that state for redress, and from them to Congress; but the echo from both was—"We can render you no assistance."

Elders Brigham Young, Wilford Woodruff, and George A. Smith arrived in Louisville, and visited Mr. Porter, the "Kentucky baby!" 7 feet 7 inches high, and weighing 250 lbs.

Sheriff Reynolds, having published a garbled statement of my arrest in *The Old School Democrat*, [St. Louis] it was replied to by Esq. Southwick in the same paper.

CHAPTER XXVII.

STATE OF AFFIRS IN NAUVOO, WILLARD RICHARDS—A POLITICAL TRICK, ILLINOIS STATE REGISTER—BURDEN OF THE PROPHET'S MINISTRY, DISCOURSE—ENLARGEMENT OF MORMONISM, "BOSTON BEE"—THE PROPHET ON POLITICS, DISCOURSE—MOVEMENTS OF THE APOSTLES.

Thursday, July 13, 1843.—I was in conversation with Emma most of the day, and approved of the revised laws of the Legion.

The Legion authorized the issuing of Legion scrip to the amount of $500.

Shadrach Roundy returned from Springfield, and reported that the Governor had gone to Rock River; and he therefore left the affidavits in the care of Judge Adams. Brother Roundy had started with an old decrepit animal, and rode him all the way there and back again. He also reported that General Moses Wilson, of Missouri, had started from Jacksonville for Washington City.

Elders Ezra T. Benson, Q. S. Sparks and Noah Rogers preached at Cabbotville, Mass. While Elder Rogers was preaching, some person threw stones through the windows, and one hit Elder Benson on the thigh. The mob threw stones at them which flew like hail, when they left the room, but did not injure the brethren.

Friday, 14.—Spent the day at home. I was visited by a number of gentlemen and ladies who had arrived from Quincy on a steamboat. They manifested kind feelings.

Elder Jonathan Dunham started on an excursion to the western country.

Saturday, 15.—Spent the day at home. Weather very hot.

A shower this morning wet the ground one inch.

At six p. m. went with my family and about one hundred others on a pleasure excursion on the *Maid of Iowa*, from the Nauvoo House landing to the north part of the city, and returned at dusk.

A theatrical performance in the evening by Mr. Chapman.

Sunday, 16.—Preached in the morning and evening at the stand in the Grove, near the west of the Temple, concerning a man's foes being those of his own household.

"The same spirit that crucified Jesus is in the breast of some who profess to be Saints in Nauvoo. I have secret enemies in the city intermingling with the Saints, etc. Said I would not prophesy any more, and proposed Hyrum to hold the office of prophet to the Church, as it was his birthright.

"I am going to have a reformation, and the Saints must regard Hyrum, for he has the authority, that I might be a Priest of the Most High God; and slightly touched upon the subject of the everlasting covenant, showing that a man and his wife must enter into that covenant in the world, or he will have no claim on her in the next world. But on account of the unbelief of the people, I cannot reveal the fullness of these things at present."

Elders Brigham Young and Wilford Woodruff preached at the house of Father Hewitt in Cincinnati. Afterwards went to Kentucky to attend an appointment at the Licking Branch. Elders Wilford Woodruff and George A. Smith afflicted with the influenza, politically called "the Tyler gripe."

Monday, 17.—At home with my brother Hyrum, conversing on the Priesthood. Called at the office once, and in the evening visited the performance of Mr. Chapman in the court room.

Elders Brigham Young and Wilford Woodruff preached at Collins Pemberton's near Licking River, and blessed eight children.

Tuesday, 18.—I was making hay on my farm.

Elder Willard Richards wrote the following to President Brigham Young:

Letter of Willard Richards to Brigham Young—Detailing Current Events at Nauvoo.

By this time, I suppose you would like to hear a word from the city of the prophets. I forgot to hand you your introduction to General James Arlington Bennett; therefore I enclose it in this. Don't forget to remember me to the General and his delightful family most warmly, together with Mrs. Richards (read, seal and deliver, if it suits you.) As you passed our office on the 7th, I discharged my last charge of powder and ball over your heads: had no occasion to reload since; all is peace.

Saturday, 8. Municipal court session, to compare minutes of the habeas corpus trial and make ready for the press.

Sunday, 9. Beckenstos and Esquire Patrick returned from Springfield, when Reynolds, Mason, &c., started from Carthage for Springfield in the stage. They crowded Beckenstos out, so he borrowed a team, and when they arrived at Springfield, Beckenstos had been there six hours, seen the friends, and Governor, &c. The Governor had sent Mr. Breman, a special agent, to Nauvoo to learn the facts, as reports said, "the Mormons had rescued Jo," &c. Reynolds petitioned for a posse to retake Jo. Governor would not grant it, but waits the return of his agent. Reynolds started for Missouri. At St. Louis, 10th inst. he published a garbled account in the *Old School Democrat*. Esquire Southwick was in St. Louis, and refreshed Reynolds' memory by a reply, on the 12th inst., same paper. Governor manifested every feeling of friendship; wanted affidavits similar to those on trial, and would quash the writ. Joseph gave a sweet conciliatory discourse at the stand, expressive of good feeling to all men. This eve, Shadrach Roundy started for Springfield with affidavits.

Monday, 10. Preparing minutes of trial for publication.

Tuesday, 11. Platted my ground for a house.

Wednesday, 12. Warsaw Message published an extra to circulate correct information concerning the "Mormons" and they have given it correctly. George J. Adams and Hollister returned from Springfield. Popular opinion is going in our favor. General Wilson of Missouri was visiting his brother near Jacksonville, when news of the Governor's inaction to Reynolds arrived, and he started immediately for Washington city (report says). Also that General Clark, or some famous military chief from Missouri, has been taking a survey of Nauvoo City. Do you believe it? *Bah*! It is more generally believed that Ford will quash the writ, issue no more, and Missouri will make no further attempts only by mob. Distance is but short between this and Upper Missouri. Is it? *Bah*!

13th. Roundy returned from Springfield this p. m., less than four days. Governor gone to Rock River visiting; ten days or two weeks absence: left the affidavits with General Adams.

14th-15th. Sun hour high p. m., president and family and private secretary and family, and about one hundred more went on board the steamboat *Maid of Iowa* at Nauvoo House, and went up to north part of city and back. At dusk, evening, a theatre in the store chamber; Mr. Chapman and suite, actors. Rain this morning; wet the ground one inch.

Sunday, 16th. Joseph preached all day; a. m., 27th chap. Matthew &c. Did not hear him. Man's foes, they are of his own house; the spirit that crucified Christ; same spirit in Nauvoo; referred particularly to—I won't say who; was it Brother Marks? Did not say. Brother Cole? Did not hear the sermon; why ask me. Nothing new; same as when you left The spirit was against Christ because of His innocence; so in the present case. Said he would not prophesy any more; Hyrum should be the prophet; (did not tell them he was going to be a priest now, or a king by and by;) told the Elders not to prophesy when they went out preaching.

17th. Theatre again. 18th. And again this eve. I am writing for your eye.

18th. Evening, Bishop Miller arrived with 157,000 feet of lumber, sawed shingles, &c., about 170,000 feet in all. He says it was all sawed in two weeks and brought down in two more; says he has bought all the claims on those mills for $12,000 payable in lumber at the mills in three years, one third already paid for. Two saws did this job. Chance for as many mills as they may have a mind to build, and every saw can run five thousand feet per day, year round. Two saws now running, can deliver 157,000 every fortnight. All that is wanting is hands. I understand the *Maid of Iowa* starts for Black River, Thursday. Bishop feels well. No investigation of Nauvoo House books yet. Clayton tells me today the committee do not want a clerk, and Joseph says little about it. Showers all around us; little rain here. Joseph is on the prairie haying today. Wind blowing from all quarters for four days past. More calm after a shower. Good hay weather. Vegetation is drying with drought—*dying*, Brother Orson, if you want to criticise.

Proceedings of court to the end of Hyrum's affidavit were published in the last *Neighbor* and *Times and Seasons*, to be continued in the next, all in pamphlet when finished. Shall mail paper for you and the brethren in New York, where I will direct this. I have said nothing about Brothers Kimball and Pratt, and Woodruff, and Smith, and Page, &c., &c.; but you will understand this is a kind of family letter, I suppose. Brother Woodruff's paper arrived, but no line, no letter from St. Louis. I have seen most of the widows since you left. Sister Young is well; was afflicted on Saturday with cholera morbus; called the Elders and right up again. Sisters Kimball is well. Sisters Woodruff is well, and I believe all the Sisters be's well; Sisters Pratt and Smith and all.

19th. I send by this mail six papers to Brother Woodruff, same direction. Just met Hyrum in the street; said to him, I am writing to the brethren, has our new prophet anything to say to them? "Give my respects to them." Elders Taylor's and Hyde's best compliments, with success. Great many loves to you all; mine particularly to all the brethren.

Yours for ever,
WILLARD.

A shower of rain in the p. m. The son of James Emmett, aged eight years, killed by lightning while standing in his father's doorway in Bain Street.

To show the spirit of the times, although I do not vouch for the accuracy of the statements, I copy from the *Illinois State Register:*

Was the Arrest of the Prophet a Political Trick?

The public is already aware that a demand was lately made upon the Governor of this State for the arrest of Joseph Smith, and that a writ was accordingly issued against him. We propose now to state some of the facts, furnishing strong ground of suspicion that the demand which was made on the Governor here, was a manœuvre of the Whig party.

1. A letter was shown to a gentleman of this city, by the agent of Missouri, from the notorious John C. Bennett to a gentleman in one of the western counties of that State, urging the importance of getting up an indictment immediately against Smith, for the five or six year old treason of which he was accused several years ago.

2. This charge had been made once before, and afterwards abandoned by Missouri. It is the same charge on which Smith was arrested and carried before Judge Douglas and discharged two years ago. After that decision, the indictment against Smith was dismissed and the charge wholly abandoned.

3. But in the letter alluded to, Bennett says to his Missouri agent, Go to the Judge, and never leave him until he appoints a special term of the court; never suffer the court to adjourn until an indictment is found against Smith for treason. When an indictment shall have been found, get a copy, and go immediately to the governor, and never leave him until you get a demand on the governor of Illinois for Smith's arrest; and then dispatch some active and vigilant person to Illinois for a warrant, and let him never leave the governor until he gets it; and then let him never come back to Missouri without Smith.

4. A special term of the circuit court of Daviess county, Missouri, was accordingly called on the 5th day of June last. An indictment was found against Smith five years old. A demand was made and a writ issued, as anticipated, by the 17th of the month.

5. Bennett, it is well known, has for a year past been a mere tool in the hands of the Whig junto at Springfield. He has been under their absolute subjection and control, and has been a regular correspondent of the *Sangamo Journal*, the principal organ of the Whig party. He has been a great pet of both the *Journal* and the junto, and that paper has regularly announced his removal from place to place, until latterly and within the last year has published more of his writings than of any other person except the editor.

6. Cyrus Walker, a short time after his nomination as the Whig candidate for Congress, in the 6th district, made a pilgrimage to Nauvoo, for the purpose of currying favor with the Mormons and getting their support. But in this he was disappointed, as it appeared that many of the Mormons were disposed to support the Democratic candidate. Cyrus went home disappointed and dejected; and it was generally believed that, failing to get the Mormon vote, he would be beaten by his Democratic opponent.

7. Let it be also borne in mind that the treason of which Smith was accused was five or six years old; that it had been abandoned as a charge by Missouri; that the circuit court of that State sat three times a year; that Smith was permanently settled at Nauvoo, no person dreaming that he would leave there for years to come; that they might have waited in Missouri for a regular term of the court, if the design was simply to revive a charge of treason against Smith, with a perfect assurance that he would always be found at home, and be as subject to arrest at one time as another. But this delay did not suit the conspirators, as it would put off an attempt to arrest Smith until after the August election.

Let it be borne in mind also that the agent of Missouri, after he had obtained the custody of Smith at Dixon, refused to employ a Democratic lawyer, and insisted upon having a Whig lawyer of inferior abilities, simply upon the ground, as he stated, that the Democrats were against him.

Let it also be borne in mind that Cyrus Walker, the Whig candidate for Congress, miraculously *happened* to be within six miles of Dixon when Smith was arrested, ready and convenient to be employed by Smith to get him delivered from custody; and that he was actually employed, and actually did get Smith enlarged from custody; and withal, let it be remembered that John C. Bennett is the pliant tool and pander of the junto at Springfield; and that he was the instigator of an unnecessary special term in Missouri, on the 5th day of June last, for the purpose of getting Smith indicted.

We say, let all these facts be borne in mind, and they produce a strong suspicion, that the whole affair is a Whig conspiracy to compel a Democratic governor to issue a writ against Smith, pending the Congressional election, so as to incense the Mormons, create a necessity for Walker's and perhaps Browning's professional services in favor of Smith, to get him delivered out of the net of their own weaving, and thereby get the everlasting gratitude of the Mormons and their support for the Whig cause.

Thursday, 20.—I furnished Bishop Miller with $290 for the expedition to the Pinery.

Friday, 21.—Rode to the farm with my daughter Julia.

The *Maid of Iowa* sailed for the Pinery in Wisconsin, with Bishop Miller, Lyman Wight and a large company, with their families.

Lieutenant-Colonel John Scott was elected Col. 1st, Reg., 2nd cohort of the Nauvoo Legion, to fill the vacancy of Col. Titus Billings, resigned.

Saturday, 22.—I rode out in my buggy in the evening.

Sister Mary Ann Holmes was brought to my house sick. She has been confined to her bed for upwards of two years.

Elders Brigham Young, Wilford Woodruff, and George A. Smith left Cincinnati at eleven a. m. on board the *Adelaide*, for Pittsburg.

Elder Kimball dreamed that he was at work in a pottery, where there was a large amount of clay drawn together: he examined it and found it to be yellow, rotten stuff of no account; and he thought it was easier to go to the clay bank and get new clay, which would make better vessels; but, after awhile he concluded to work up this clay into vessels, which when made proved to be rotten; which is a representation of the people of Cincinnati.

Sunday, 23.—Meeting at the stand. I preached. I insert a brief synopsis of the discourse, reported by Dr. Willard Richards:

Discourse—Burden of the Prophet's Ministry—Friendship.

I commence my remarks by reading this text—Luke xvi: 16:—"The law and the prophets were until John: since that time the kingdom of God is preached, and every man presseth into it."

I do not know that I shall be able to preach much; but, with the faith of the Saints, may say something instructive. It has gone abroad that I proclaimed myself no longer a prophet. I said it last Sabbath ironically: I supposed you would all understand. It was not that I would renounce the idea of being a prophet, but that I had no disposition to proclaim myself such. But I do say that I bear the testimony of Jesus, which is the spirit of prophecy.

There is no greater love than this, that a man lay down his life for his friends. I discover hundreds and thousands of my brethren ready to sacrifice their lives for me.

The burdens which roll upon me are very great. My persecutors allow me no rest, and I find that in the midst of business and care the spirit is willing, but the flesh is weak. Although I was called of my Heavenly Father to lay the foundation of this great work and kingdom in this dispensation, and testify of His revealed will to scattered Israel, I am subject to like passions as other men, like the prophets of olden times.

Notwithstanding my weaknesses, I am under the necessity of bearing the infirmities of others, who, when they get into difficulty, hang on to me tanaciously to get them out, and wish me to cover their faults. On the other hand, the same characters, when they discover a weakness in Brother Joseph, endeavor to blast his reputation, and publish it to all the world, and thereby aid my enemies in destroying the Saints. Although the law is given through me to the Church, I cannot be borne with a moment by such men. They are ready to destroy me for the least foible, and publish my imaginary failings from Dan to Beersheba, though they are too ignorant of the things of God, which have been revealed to me, to judge of my actions, motives or conduct, in any correct manner whatever.

The only principle upon which they judge me is by comparing my acts with the foolish traditions of their fathers and nonsensical teachings of hireling priests, whose object and aim were to keep the people in ignorance for the sake of filthy lucre; or as the prophet says, to feed themselves, not the flock. Men often come to me with their troubles, and seek my will, crying, Oh, Brother Joseph, help me! help me! But when I am in trouble, few of them sympathize with me, or extend to me relief. I believe in a principle of reciprocity, if we do live in a devilish and wicked world where men busy themselves in watching for iniquity, and lay snares for those who reprove in the gate.

I see no faults in the Church, and therefore let me be resurrected with the Saints, whether I ascend to heaven or descend to hell, or go to any other place. And if we go to hell, we will turn the devils out of doors and make a heaven of it. Where this people are, there is good society. What do we care where we are, if the society be good? I don't care what a man's character is; if he's my friend—a true friend, I will be a friend to him, and preach the Gospel of salvation to him, and give him good counsel, helping him out of his difficulties.

Friendship is one of the grand fundamental principles of "Mormonism"; [it is designed] to revolutionize and civilize the world, and cause wars and contentions to cease and men to become friends and brothers. Even the wolf and the lamb shall dwell together; the leopard shall lie down with the kid, the calf, the young lion and the fatling; and a little child shall lead them; the bear and the cow shall lie down together, and the sucking child shall play on the hole of the asp, and the weaned child shall play on the cockatrice's den; and they shall not hurt or destroy in all my holy mountains, saith the Lord of hosts. (Isaiah.)

It is a time-honored adage that love begets love. Let us pour forth love—show forth our kindness unto all mankind, and the Lord will reward us with everlasting increase; cast our bread upon the waters and we shall receive it after many days, increased to a hundredfold. Friendship is like Brother Turley in his blacksmith shop welding iron to iron; it unites the human family with its happy influence.

I do not dwell upon your faults, and you shall not upon mine. Charity, which is love, covereth a multitude of sins, and I have often covered up all the faults among you; but the prettiest thing is to have no faults at all. We should cultivate a meek, quiet and peaceable spirit.

Have the Presbyterians any truth? Yes. Have the Baptists, Methodists, &c,, any truth? Yes. They all have a little truth mixed with error. We should gather all the good and true principles in the world and treasure them up, or we shall not come out true "Mormons."

Last Monday morning certain brethren came to me and said they could hardly consent to receive Hyrum as a prophet, and for me to resign. But I told them, "I only said it to try your faith; and it is strange, brethren, that you have been in the Church so long, and not yet understand the Melchisedek Priesthood."

I will resume the subject at some future time.

It is contrary to Governor Ford's oath of office, to send a man to Missouri, where he is proscribed in his religious opinions; for he is sworn to support the Constitution of the United States and also of this State, and these constitutions guarantee religious as well as civil liberty to all religious societies whatever.

Monday, *24*.—This morning I had a long conversation with Mr. Hoge, the Democratic candidate for Congress. I showed him the corruption and folly of the governor's sending an armed force to take me, &c., and told him this made the 38th vexatious lawsuit against me for my religion.

The Thirty-eighth Vexatious Lawsuit.

Exhibition of Divine, the Fire King, in the court room.

Settled with William and Wilson Law. They were $167 in my debt, for which William Law gave his note.

Tuesday, *25*.—During this day I signed Nauvoo Legion scrip, a copy of one of which I insert:

NAUVOO LEGION, July 25, 1843.

No. 406. This certificate will be received by the Nanvoo Legion, as one dollar in payment of debts due the Legion, and redeemable by the Paymaster-General on demand, with any moneys in the treasury.

WILSON LAW, Major General,
JOSEPH SMITH, Lieutenant-General.
JOHN S. FULLMER, Paymaster-General.

Being sick, I lay on my bed in the middle of the room: visited by Dr. Willard Richards.

Elder Noah Rogers administered to Sister Webster at Farmington, Connecticut, who had been unable to walk for several years past.

Wednesday, *26*.—Sister Webster arose from her bed this morning and walked.

I copy from the *Boston Bee*:

Prospective Enlargement of Mormonism—Missouri Rapped.

Sir,—In my last I touched upon the vested rights of the city of the

Saints, as they appear upon the face of the charter; and it may be proper hereafter to go into the merits of that document, for I hold the maxim good that the "Union is interested in the Union;" but at the present time I have another subject on the tapis, which more immediately concerns the wise and honest portions of the American people. I reason from facts, no matter who may cry, "hush!" as to "Mormonism" and the "disgrace" which the State of Missouri inherits from her barbarous treatment and unlawful extermination of the Mormon people.

The great day has already been ushered in, and the voice of the Mormon is not only heard setting forth his own rights and preaching the Gospel of the Son of God in power and demonstration incontrovertible from revelation, in every city and hamlet in our wide-spread American Free States; but other realms and kingdoms hear tho same tidings; even the Indians, Australia, Pacific Islands, Great Britain, Ireland, Germany and the Holy Land, where God Himself once spoke, have heard a Mormon; and all this in the short space of twelve or fourteen years; yea, and measures have been taken that Russia may hear the "Watchman cry."

Now, sir, "what has been done can be done." I shall not be surprised if the Mormons undertake to cope with the world. Virtue and truth are twin sisters of such winning charms, that honest men of every nation, kindred and tongue will fall in love with them; and what hinders the Mormons, with the Bible in one hand and humanity in the other, from Mormonizing all honest men? Nothing. The meaning of "Mormon," the Prophet Joe says, is "More good;" and no matter where it is the Mormons will have it; and if they cannot obtain it by exertion in the world, they will merit it by faith and prayer from the "old promise" of "ask and ye shall receive."

But do not think that I, even I, have been Mormonized by what I write for I say nay; though I am willing to admit—and all men of sense will do the same—the more light, the more truth: the more truth, the more love; the more love, the more virtue; the more virtue, the more peace; the more peace, the more heaven—what everybody wants. The Mormons believe rather too much for me. I can't come it.

Another word on Missouri. When her constitution was framed, they commenced the preamble as follows: "We, the people of Missouri, &c., by our representatives in convention assembled at St. Louis on Saturday, the 12th day of June, 1820, do mutually agree to establish a free and independent Republic," &c. *Independent Republic!* Well, some of the subsequent acts prove the truth of it, and as the broad folds of the constitution often conceal more than meets the eye, notwithstanding it is the aegis of the people to keep lawmakers and law-breakers within and without bonds, let us quote from the 13th article of the aforesaid constitution, the 3rd paragraph: "That the people have a right peaceably to assemble for their common good, and to apply to those vested with the powers of government for redress of grievances; and that their right to bear arms in defense of themselves and the state cannot be questioned." This otherwise right of gun-fence was made, as I have earned, for breachy Indians, but was used by Governor Boggs as a *sine quo non*, pointed with steel and burning with brimstone, to exterminate the Mormons. Truly we may ask, what is right and what is law contrary to the constitution? The Legislature of Missouri acknowledged the exterminating order of Boggs as constitutional, and appropriated more than $200,000 to pay the drivers and robbers, and I may as well say, mobbers of the Mormons, for services rendered the State in 1838. *O Gladius! O Crumena! Viator.*

Shower of rain at noon.

Thursday, 27.—I drove through the city with Father Morley in my carriage.

Movements of Brigham Young, et al.

The *Adelaide* run aground on the sand bar. Elders Brigham Young, Wilford Woodruff and George A. Smith were set ashore and each took coach for Pittsburg, where they arrived at six o'clock: went to the Temperance Hall, and unobserved heard Elder John E. Page preach against the sects. Here they met with Elders Heber C. Kimball and Orson Pratt.

Friday, 28.—I was at home sick, and was visited by Father Morley.

At noon James Sloan, the recorder, brought the desk containing city and Church books and papers to the mayor's office, as he was about to go on a missien to Ireland.

The Twelve met at Richard Savary's. Elder Young inquired concerning the proceedings of the Twelve in Cincinnati; found that Elders Kimball, Pratt and Page had held a conference, organized the church, and then left for Pittsburg.

Elder Page stayed a few days and overruled what had been done, and reorganized the church, but the church was left in no better situation. Elder Young reproved Brother Page for undoing alone what three of the quorum had done together. He also alluded to my instructions to be gentle and mild in their teachings, and not to fight the sects any more at present, but to win the affection of the people.

Unwisdom of Elder Page.

In the evening they met at Jeremiah Cooper's house. Elders Young, Kimball and Smith addressed the Saints, numbering seventy-five.

Saturday, 29.—I rode up to the Temple and sent a copy of certificate of trustee, and Granger's power of attorney to Reuben McBride, Kirtland. Walked up to near the lodge room, met my brother Hyrum and had a conversation about Henry G. Sherwood. There was a political meeting at the Temple, when Mr. Joseph P. Hoge, candidate for Congress, addressed the citizens for three hours, and was replied to in short by Mr. Cyrus Walker.

Political Debate, Hoge vs. Walker.

Council of the Twelve met in the evening at Brother Savary's to teach the Elders. Elder Young said:

Views of Brigham Young on Presidency.

A man should, in the first place preside over himself, his passions, his person, and bring himself into subjection to the law of God; then preside over his children and his wife in righteousness; then he will be capable of presiding over a branch of the Church. But many Elders are contending about presiding over churches, when they are not capable of presiding over themselves or the least child they have.

The first principle of our cause and work is to understand that there is a prophet in the Church, and that he is at the head of the Church of Jesus Christ on earth.

Who called Joseph Smith to be a prophet? Did the people or God? God, and not the people called him. Had the people gathered together and appointed one of their number to be a prophet, he would have been accountable to the people; but inasmuch as he was called by God, and not the people, he is accountable to God only and the angel who committed the gospel to him, and not to any man on earth. The Twelve are accountable to the prophet, and not to the Church for the course they pursue; and we have learned to go and do as the prophet tells us.*

Conference met in Utica, New York Elder John P. Greene in the chair. Four branches were represented, containing 7 elders, 5 priests, 6 teachers, 2 deacons, and 159 members; 1 elder, 2 priests, 1 teacher and 1 deacon were ordained.

Illness of the Prophet.

Sunday, *30.*—I was very sick, my lungs oppressed and overheated, through preaching last Sunday; and called for my brother Hyrum and William Law, and Willard Richards to lay on hands and pray for me.

Elder John Taylor preached in the morning. After preaching, President Marks called a special conference to appoint recorders for baptism for the dead. Elder Sloan having started on his mission to Ireland, Willard Richards was appointed General Church Recorder; and Joseph M. Cole, George Walker, Jonathan H. Hale, and J. A. W. Andrews, recorders for the baptisms for the dead. In the afternoon clerks met to organize and prepare for their duties.

* The principle in the above in the main is doubtless correct, but side by side with the principle there set forth should be considered the principle that modifies it somewhat, namely, the principle of common consent and the voice of the people in the government of the Church. The Lord will call whom He sees proper to call to His priesthood; and so far they are amenable to Him alone for the discharge of the duties of the priesthood. But when in the exercise of the functions of the priesthood or its offices it comes to presiding over the Church or any of the branches or departments thereof, that can only be with the consent of those over whom they preside (see Doctrine and Covenents, sec. xx: 65, 66; Ibid sec. xxvi: 2; Ibid. sec. cvii: 22). It is evident and a well settled principle that in these relationships to the Church, the officers of the Church, even the President thereof and the apostles, as well as all others, are amenable to the Church, else why the doctrine of the revelations that there is not any person belonging to the Church who is exempt from the law of the Church, and that inasmuch as even the president of the high priesthood, who is also the president of the Church, (Doc. and Cov. sec. cvii) shall transgress, he shall be had in remembrance before the common council of the Church (Presiding Bishopric) assisted by twelve counselors of the high priesthood; that court is competent to try him, even the president of the Church; "and their decision upon his head shall be an end of controversy concerning him. Thus none shall be exempt from the justice and the law of God." The Church, in other words is greater than any man in it (Doc. and Cov. sec. cvii; 81-84).

Brothers Wilford Woodruff and George A. Smith preached in the morning, John E. Page and Orson Pratt in the afternoon, and Heber C. Kimball and Brigham Young in the evening, in the Temperance Hall in Pittsburg.

Meeting in Pittsburg.

A conference was held in Briton, Michigan, when Mephibosheth Sirine was chosen president. Nine branches were represented, comprising 5 elders, 6 priests, 7 teachers, 1 deacon, and 225 members.

Conference in Michigan.

Monday, 31.—My health improving, I went to the prairie, sold one hundred acres of land, and called at my farm. Wrote to General Adams.

The following is from Elder Woodruff's journal under this date:

Enterprises in Pittsburg, 1843.

Our quorum assembled and walked over Pittsburg. We first visited Mr. Curling's glass works, and saw them at work through each branch. We saw them make pressed, stamped and plain tumblers, large jars, &c. We next went on the bluff above the city, and had a view of the new basin that is to contain the water to be forced into it from the Alleghany river to water the city. From this place we had a fair view of the city below. It truly sends forth its columns of smoke and blackness that arise from the coal fires which propel the numerous engines that are the mainspring of all the foundries, manufactories and works of the great city of Pittsburg.

We then descended the hill and visited the city water works or reservoir. The building is 150 feet long, 110 feet wide, and contains two engines of 200 horse power each, to drive a force pump to force the water from the Alleghany river into the basin on the bluff, to supply the wants of the citizens. The whole cost of this building, reservoir, and basin was $200,000. The building is after the Roman order. The whole architecture, design, making and finishing the building, was executed by Elder Charles Beck, a member of the Church of Jesus Christ of Latter-day Saints. We visited every branch of the Miltonberger's iron works; saw the iron form the keel of an iron steam ship of war, 140 feet long. The vessel is designed to navigate Lake Erie.

Tuesday, August 1, 1843.—I was very sick at home in the morning. At four p. m. I rode up to the Temple and complained to the clerks that Mr. Hamilton had got a tax title from the sheriff on one of my city lots. Mr. Bagby, the collector, came up in the midst of our conversation, and when asked about it denied all knowledge of it. I told him that I had always been ready to pay all my taxes when I was called upon; and I did not think it gentlemanly treatment to sell any of my lots for taxes; and I told him that he was continually abusing the citizens here. Bagby called me a liar, and picked up a stone to throw at me, which so enraged me that I followed him a few steps, and struck him two or three times. Esquire Daniel H. Wells stepped between us and succeeded in separating us. I told the Esquire to assess the fine for the assault, and I was willing to pay it. He not doing it, I rode down to Alderman Whitney, stated the circumstances, and he imposed a fine which I paid, and then returned to the political meeting. Bagby stayed awhile, muttering threats against me. I went home, commenced to work awhile, but soon was very sick.

The Prophet's Altercation with Bagby.

Received a private communication from a Mr, Braman, stating that the writ was returned to the governor and killed.

Hyrum and Hoge called at the office, when Hoge acknowledged the power of the Nauvoo Charter habeas corpus.

Esquire Walker gave a stump speech at the stand until dusk, and was immediately replied to by Esquire Hoge for over two hours, having lit candles for the purpose to hear them politically castigate each other.

The Twelve visited Alleghany City. Elders Young, Page and Kimball preached in the evening.

The Temple is progressing steadily. The walls of the noble edifice continue to rise, and its completion is looked forward to with great interest and anxiety by many.

All kinds of improvements are going on rapidly in Nauvoo and vicinity. Houses are going up in every direction in the city and farms are being inclosed without. "The wilderness" will soon "blossom as the rose."

Elder Luman A. Shurtliff writes that he has traveled in the New England States, and recently baptized twenty persons.

Wednesday, 2.—I was a little easier today and rode out to Jacob Baum's to borrow money. In the evening conversing with Dr. J. M. Bernhisel.

A subscription has been got up to build a house for Elder Willard Richards, to which I subscribed a city lot. The brethren subscribed $25 cash, 10 cords of stone, 30 bushels of lime, 105 days work, $59 in work, 15,900 bricks, glass, lumber and other materials, together with a quantity of produce. I hope the day is not far distant when my clerk will have a comfortable house for his family.

Thursday, 3.—Elder Beck of Pittsburg having paid $48 for the passage of six of the Twelve Apostles to Baltimore, they started this morning and rode all day and night over the Alleghany mountains in the stage

I continued unwell. I received $800 in specie, and a $200 note from Benjamin Meginness for one hundred acres of land.

Friday, 4.—My health improving, I rode out to the farm. In the evening went with Emma to visit Elder Cahoon, where I met my brother Hyrum and his wife.

Saturday, 5.—Elders Brigham Young, Heber C. Kimball, Orson Pratt, John E. Page, Wilford Woodruff and George A. Smith arrived in Philadelphia at 4 a. m., having traveled four hundred and thirty miles in forty-eight hours by stage, railroad and steamboat. A very severe storm of wind and rain raged in Philadelphia in the evening, doing immense damage.

Sunday, 6.—Meeting at the stand. Elder Parley P. Pratt preached on testimony.

When he closed, I told the people I would preach my sermon next Sunday, I was not able today; but I would now speak on another subject—viz., the election.

The Prophet's Attitude on Politics.

I am above the kingdoms of the world, for I have no laws. I am not come to tell you to vote this way, that way or the other. In relation to national matters, I want it to go abroad unto the whole world that every man should stand on his own merits. The Lord has not given me a revelation concerning politics. I have not asked Him for one. I am a third party, and stand independent and alone. I desire to see all parties protected in their rights. As for Mr. Walker, he is the Whig candidate, a high-minded man. He has not hung onto my coat tail to gain his election, as some have said. I am going to give a testimony, but not for electioneering purposes. Before Mr. Walker came to Nauvoo, rumor came up that he might become a candidate. Said I—He is an old friend, and I'll vote for him. When he came to my house, I voluntarily told him I should vote for him. When I made him acquainted with the ordinances of Nauvoo, in relation to writs of habeas corpus, he acted in accordance therewith on my testimony. The rascals (Reynolds and Wilson) took Walker's and Montgomery's security when I was arrested. Walker made Reynolds come to me and beg my pardon for the abuse he gave me; and through his means and influence the pistols were taken from the rascals. He (Walker) withdrew all claim to your vote and influence if it would be detrimental to your interests as a people.

Brother Hyrum tells me this morning that he has had a testimony to the effect it would be better for the people to vote for Hoge; and I never knew Hyrum to say he ever had a revelation and it failed. Let God speak and all men hold their peace. I never authorized Brother Law to tell my private feelings, and I utterly forbid these political demagogues from using my name henceforth and for ever. It is my settled opinion that if Governor Ford erred in granting a writ against me, it is an error of the head, and not of the heart; and I authorize all men to say I am a personal friend of Governor Ford.

The cap to Parley's sermon is this—Every word that proceedeth from the mouth of Jehovah has such an influence over the human mind—the logical mind—that it is convincing without other testimony. Faith cometh by hearing If ten thousand men testify to a truth you *know* would it add to your faith? No. Or will ten thousand testimonies destroy your knowledge of a fact? No. I don't want any one to tell I am a prophet, or attempt to prove my word.

I prophesy in the name of God Almighty, they [the Saints] shall bear off the palm.

Hyrum Smith explained at some length concerning the election.

Emma started to St. Louis to transact some business for me, it not being prudent for me to go to Missouri.

Meeting of the Twelve Apostles in Philadelphia.

The quorum of the Twelve Apostles in Philadelphia held a meeting in the Canaanite Church. About three hundred Saints were present. Meeting was opened by Jedediah M. Grant,and President Brigham Young addressed the congregation at considerable length. He said that a man or woman may ask of God, and get a witness and testimony from God concerning any work or messenger that is sent unto them; but if a person asks for a thing that does not concern him, such as governing the Church, as a member of the Church inquiring concerning the duty of a presiding Elder, what the prophet or the Twelve ought to do, &c. he will not get an snswer. It he does it will not be from God. He also remarked that if any in the Church had the fullness of the Melchisedec Priesthood, he did not know it. For any person to have the fullness of that priesthood, he must be a king and priest. A person may have a portion of that priesthood, the same as governors or judges of England have power from the king to transact business; but that does not make them kings of England. A person may be anointed king and priest long before he receives his kingdom.

In the evening Elder Orson Pratt preached, and was followed by Elder George A. Smith. (*Above from Wilford Woodruff's Journal.*)

Monday, *7*.—Election of Representatives to Congress and state and county officers, the Democratic ticket prevailing in Nauvoo by an overwhelming majority.

Tuesday, *8*.—The Twelve in Philadelphia went out on a pleasure excursion on the Delaware river, with about one hundred and fifty of the Saints. They went down to Glouster Point and spent the day in various innocent amusements.

Wednesday, *9*.—I rode out to my farm with a gentleman.

Thursday, *10*.—Rode through the city with my brother Hyrum.

OBITUARY.

(*From the Times and Seasons.*)

Friday, *11*. It is with regret that we announce the death of our respected brother, General James Adams, of Springfield. He joined the

Church some time ago in the above place, and had come to Nauvoo for the purpose of arranging matters preparatory to his removal to this place. He was attacked by the cholera morbus, and died on Friday night, the 11th instant. He has left an amiable family and a large circle of acquaintances, by whom he was greatly respected, to mourn his loss. Peace to his ashes!

Saturday, 12.—Emma returned from St. Louis. I was sick at home. Robert D. Foster having on Monday last been elected school commissioner, and George W. Thatcher, clerk of county commissioner's court, they went to Carthage to give bonds and take oath of office. When before the court, Harmon T. Wilson, John Wilson, Franklin J. Morrill and Prentice, and twelve or fifteen others, came in armed with hickory clubs, knives, dirks and pistols, and told the court they must not approve the bonds [of the above officers elect] or swear them into office; if they did blood would be spilt; and pledged their word, honor and reputation, to keep them out of office and put down the Mormons. The bonds, however, were accepted, and the mob gave notice of a meeting of the anti-Mormons of Hancock county for Saturday next, to consider about the Mormons retaining their offices.

Elder Willard Richards was sworn into office as recorder of the city of Nauvoo.

CHAPTER XXVIII.

THE PROPHET ON THE LIFE AND CHARACTER OF JUDGE ELIAS HIGBEE—LIFE AND RESURRECTION — EXPLANATION OF ELECTION DAY TROUBLES—GOVERNOR FORD'S REFUSAL TO PLAY INTO THE HANDS OF MISSOURI—ANTI-MORMON AGITATION AT CARTHAGE—ELDER JONATHAN DUNHAM'S REPORT OF HIS WESTERN EXPLORATIONS.

Sunday, August 13, 1843.—I went to the stand on Sunday morning, August 13, 1843, and preached on the death of Judge Higbee, a synopsis of which was reported by my clerk, Dr. Willard Richards.

The Prophet's Remarks at the Funeral of Judge Higbee.

BRETHREN AND SISTERS, you will find these words in II Peter iii, 10, 11:—"But the day of the Lord will come as a thief in the night; in the which the heavens shall pass away with a great noise, and the elements shall melt with fervent heat; the earth also and the works that are therein shall be burned up. Seeing then that all these things shall be dissolved, what manner of persons ought ye to be in all holy conversation and godliness."

I am not like other men. My mind is continually occupied with the business of the day, and I have to depend entirely upon the living God for every thing I say on such occasions as these.

The great thing for us to know is to comprehend what God did institute before the foundation of the world. Who knows it? It is the constitutional disposition of mankind to set up stakes and set bounds to the works and ways of the Almighty.

We are called this morning to mourn the death of a just and good man—a great and mighty man. It is a solemn idea that man has no hope of seeing a friend after he has lost him. But I will give you a more painful thought. It is simple; for I never design to communicate any ideas but what are simple; for to this end I am sent. Suppose you have an idea of a resurrection, etc., etc., and yet know nothing at all of the gospel, nor comprehend one principle of the order of heaven, but find yourselves disappointed—yes, at last find yourselves disappointed in every hope or anticipation, when the decision goes forth from the lips of the Almighty. Would not this be a greater disappointment—a more painful thought than annihilation?

Had I inspiration, revelation, and lungs to communicate what my soul has contemplated in times past, there is not a soul in this congregation but would go to their homes and shut their mouths in everlasting silence on religion till they had learned something.

Why be so certain that you comprehend the things of God, when all things with you are so uncertain. You are welcome to all the knowledge and intelligence I can impart to you. I do not grudge the world all the religion they have got: they are welcome to all the knowledge they possess.

The sound saluted my ears—"Ye are come unto Mount Zion, and unto the city of the living God,the heavenly Jerusalem, and to an innumerable company of angels, to the general assembly and church of the firstborn, which are written in heaven, and to God the Judge of all, and to the spirits of just men made perfect, and to Jesus the Mediator of the new covenant" (Hebrews xii, 22, 23, 24). What would it profit us to come unto the spirits of the just men, but to learn and come up to the standard of their knowledge?

Where has Judge Higbee gone?

Who is there that would not give all his goods to feed the poor, and pour out his gold and silver to the four winds, to go where Judge Higbee has gone?

That which hath been hid from before the foundation of the world is revealed to babes and sucklings in the last days.

The world is reserved unto burning in the last days. He shall send Elijah the prophet, and he shall reveal the covenants of the fathers in relation to the children, and the covenants of the children in relation to the fathers.

Four destroying angels holding power over the four quarters of the earth until the servants of God are sealed in their foreheads, which signifies sealing the blessing upon their heads, meaning the everlasting covenant, thereby making their calling and election sure. When a seal is put upon the father and mother, it secures their posterity, so that they cannot be lost, but will be saved by virtue of the covenant of their father and mother.

To the mourners I would say—Do as the husband and the father would instruct you, and you shall be reunited.

The speaker contined to teach the doctrine of election and the sealing powers and principles, and spoke of the doctrine of election with the seed of Abraham, and the sealing of blessings upon his posterity, and the sealing of the fathers and children, according to the declarations of the prophets. He then spoke of Judge Higbee in the world of spirits, and the blessings which he would obtain, and of the kind spirit and disposition of Judge Higbee while living; none of which was reported.

Remarks by President Joseph Smith, on Sunday afternoon, August 13, 1843, reported by Dr. Willard Richards:

The Prophet's Explanation of Election Day Troubles.

President Joseph Smith complained of the citizens of Nauvoo. He reproved some young men for crowding on to the ladies' seats on the meeting ground, and laughing and mocking during meeting; and, as mayor, he instructed the marshal to keep that portion of the grove clear of young men. "The city is enlarging very fast. We have many professedly learned men in this city, and the height of their knowledge is not to know enough to keep in their place."

He then complained of the treatment he had received from Walter Bagby, the county assessor and collector, who has exercised more despotic power over the inhabitants of the city than any despot of the eastern country over his serfs. I met him, and he gave me some abusive language, taking up a stone to throw at me: I seized him by the throat to choke him off. He then spoke of Esquire Daniel H. Wells interfering when he had no business, and of the abuses he received at the election on the hill. They got a constable by the name of King. I don't know what need there was of a constable. Old Father Perry said, "Why, you can't vote in this precinct."

King took me by the collar and told me to go away. (All our wrongs have arisen under the power and authority of Democracy; and I have sworn that this arm shall fall from my shoulder, and this tongue cleave to the roof of my mouth, before I will vote for them,) unless they make me satisfaction, and I feel it sensibly. I was abused and neglected at the ground, and there was not a man in the crowd to say, "This is Brother Joseph, or this is the Mayor." He then spoke of the grog shops, and the disturbance of the crowd in the street by Mœser's grocery. I have been ferreting out grog shops, groceries, and beer barrels. I have warned the rum and beer dealers to be scarce after this time, and the peace officers to watch the grog shops and give me seasonable notice of any disorder. If they are conducted as they have been, I will rip them up."

He then sat down, but resumed—"I had forgotten one thing. We have had certain traders in this city, who have been writing falsehoods to Missouri; and there is a certain man in this city who has made a covenant to betray and give me up to the Missourians, and that, too, before Governor Carlin commenced his persecutions. That man is no other than Sidney Rigdon. This testimony I have from gentlemen from abroad, whose names I do not wish to give.

I most solemnly proclaim the withdrawal of my fellowship from this man, on condition that the foregoing be true; and let the Saints proclaim it abroad, that he may no longer be acknowledged as my counselor: and all who feel to sanction my proceedings and views will manifest it by uplifted hands.

There was a unanimous vote that Sidney Rigdon be disfellowshiped. and his license demanded.

The Twelve Apostles held meetings in various parts of Philadelphia.

Monday, 14.—Rode out at nine a. m. At home at one p. m. In the evening, attended the funeral of Lydia Walker, who died at my house yesterday.

I copy from the *State Register* as follows:—

A Post-Election Denial of Governor Ford Menacing the Citizens of Nauvoo.

We have seen and heard a statement that Governor Ford had delayed making a decision upon the demand of Missouri for the militia to arrest Joseph Smith, until after the election, so as by intimidation to compel the Mormons to vote the Democratic ticket.

The authors of this desperate and reckless slander take counsel from their own corrupt hearts, and judge others by a knowledge of what they would do in like case. No doubt but that they would do this, and more too, if necessary, to secure the success of their party; and hence their readiness to believe evil of others.

If, however, they had been in the least degree inclined to judge correctly, they would have gone, as we have done, to the records of the secretary's office, where they would have ascertained that all these suspicions were groundless, and that the governor had actually decided not to call out the militia eleven days before the election.

The following letters we copy from the records in the office of the secretary of state:—

[Mentioned in the above article from the *State Register.*]

Official Documents Proving that Governor Ford Decided not to Call out Militia to Arrest Joseph Smith Previous to Late Election.

EXECUTIVE DEPARTMENT, SPRINGFIELD,
ILLINOIS, July 26, 1843.

To his Excellency, Thomas Reynolds, Governor of Missouri:—

SIR,—The demand of Joseph H. Reynolds, Esq., the agent appointed by you to receive Joseph Smith, Jr., for a detachment of militia to assist in retaking said Smith, has been duly considered by me; and I now, at the earliest moment, after coming to a conclusion on the subject, proceed to lay before you the result of my deliberations.

The request for a military force is declined. The reasons which have influenced me in coming to this determination will be furnished to you at large, as soon as I can obtain leisure to do so.

I have the honor to be, very respectfully

Your obedient servant,

THOMAS FORD.

EXECUTIVE DEPARTMENT, SPRINGFIELD,
ILLINOIS, August 14, 1843.

To his Excellency, Thomas Reynolds, Governor of the State of Missouri:

SIR,—On the 26th day of July last, I had the honor to inform you by letter that, after full consideration, I had come to the conclusion to decline ordering out a detachment of the militia to assist in retaking Joseph Smith, Jr., who was said to have escaped from the custody of the Missouri agent; and in that letter I engaged to furnish you with my reasons at large for coming to that determination.

It appears that an indictment was found, at a special term of the Daviess Circuit Court, Missouri, held on the 5th day of June last, against Smith for treason. Upon this indictment, the governor of Missouri issued a requisition to the governor of this state, demanding the arrest and delivery of Smith. A writ was thereupon duly issued by me for the apprehension and delivery of Smith as demanded. This writ was put into the hands of an officer of this state to be executed. The officer to whom it was directed immediately arrested Smith, and delivered him to Joseph H. Reynolds, the agent of Missouri, appointed to receive him. The writ has been returned to me as having been fully executed.

After Smith was delivered into the hands of Mr. Joseph H. Reynolds, it is alleged that he was rescued from his custody by the Municipal Court of the city of Nauvoo.

Affidavits on both sides of the question have been filed before me, and I also have additional information on the subject contained in a report of Mr. Brayman, Esq., a special agent appointed by myself to investigate and collect facts in relation to the whole matter.

The undisputed facts of the case are, that Smith was arrested near Dixon, in Lee county. He was immediately delivered over to Mr. Reynolds. Smith immediately brought an action against Mr. Reynolds for false imprisonment, and held him to bail in the sum of $400. Mr. Reynolds being in a strange country and unable to give bail, was taken into custody by the sheriff of Lee county and held as a prisoner, whilst Reynolds held Smith as his prisoner.

The parties finally concluded to get out writ of habeas corpus, and try the legality of the imprisonment in each case. The writs were accordingly issued, returnable before the nearest judicial tribunal in the circuit in which Quincy is situated; and thereupon all parties proceeded in the direction of Quincy, Smith being in the custody of Reynolds, and Reynolds himself in the custody of the sheriff of Lee county.

On the road, during their progress, they were met by parties of the citizens of Nauvoo, some or most of whom are said to have been members of the Nauvoo Legion, though there is no evidence that they appeared in a military capacity. There was no exhibition of arms of any description, nor was there any military or warlike array, nor was there any actual force used, though Mr. Reynolds testifies that he felt under constraint, and that Smith, soon after meeting the first parties of Mormons, enlarged himself from his custody.

Mr. Reynolds also testifies (and there can be no doubt of the fact) that he was taken to Nauvoo against his will.

But whether he was taken there by the command of Smith and his friends, or by the voluntary act of the sheriff of Lee county, who had him in custody, does not appear by any testimony furnished by Mr. Reynolds. The affidavit of the sheriff has not been obtained, though there is an evidence on the other side to show that the sheriff of Lee county voluntarily carried Mr. Reynolds to the city of Nauvoo, without any coercion on the part of any one.

After arriving at Nauvoo, a writ of habeas corpus was issued by the Municipal Court of that city, and Mr. Reynolds was compelled by the authority of the court to produce Mr. Smith before that tribunal. After hearing the case, the court discharged Smith from arrest.

There is much other evidence submitted; but the foregoing is the material part of it to be considered on the present occasion.

Now, sir, I might safely rest my refusal to order a detachment of militia to assist in retaking Smith upon the ground that the laws of this state have been fully exercised in the matter. A writ has been issued for his apprehension. Smith was apprehended and was duly delivered by the officer of this state to the agent of the state of Missouri appointed to receive him. No process, officer, or authority of this state *has been resisted* or interfered with. I have fully executed the duty which the laws impose on me, and have not been resisted either in the writ issued for the arrest of Smith or in the person of the officer appointed to apprehend him. If there has been any resistance to any one, it has been to the officer of Missouri, after Smith came to his custody; and everything had been done on my part which the law warranted me in doing.

Another objection to ordering a detachment of militia, arises out of the militia laws of this state, the forty-third section of which is as follows:—

"Whenever it may be necessary to call into actual service any part of the militia of this state, on a requisition by the executive of the United States, on an actual or threatened invasion of this state, or any of the neighboring states or territories of the United States, the commander-in-chief shall forthwith demand from each division a detachment in proportion to the strength thereof, except as hereinafter excepted, which order shall be delivered by a special messenger to the several commandants of divisions, specifying the number demanded from each division, the time and place of rendezvous, if ordered to march; and if the same be detached under any particular act of the United States, to endorse the same on such order: Provided that whenever the safety of any of the frontier settlements in this state shall, in the opinion of the governor, require it, he may exempt the militia in such settlements from being called into service, and make such further provision for the defense as the necessity of the case may require; which exemption shall be expressed in his orders to commandants of the divisions, who, together with the commandants of brigades, regiments, battalions, and companies, shall govern themselves accordingly. And provided, also, that such militia men may be required to serve as spies on their own frontiers; and that, on actual invasion *or any extreme emergency*, the commander-in-chief, commandants of divisions, brigades, battalions, and companies, may call on the whole or any part of the militia under their respective commands, as the nature of the case may require; who shall continue in service, if necessary, until the militia can be regularly called out."

The governor has no other authority, in calling out the militia, than that which is contained in this section; by which it appears that there must be either a requisition from the president, an actual or threatened invasion, or some extreme emergency, to warrant the governor in exercising this power. No one of these contingencies has arisen. There has been no requisition from the president; there has been no actual or threatened invasion of the state; nor is this such an extreme emergency as is contemplated by the law.

If we allow that force was exhibited and threatened to compel your agent to carry his prisoner before the municipal court of Nauvoo, that the court there took cognizance of the cause without jurisdiction and against the consent of your agent, it would amount at most to a riot; and to a resistance of authority in a single case, and that, too, under color of law and legal process. To constitute an extreme emergency, so as to justify a call for the militia, there ought, in my opinion, to be something more than a mere illegal act—something more than a design to resist the law in a single instance. The design ought to be general, as in treason, rebellion, or insurrection; in which cases a universality of design is essential to constitute the offense.

If a person resist a constable or sheriff, or other officer charged with the execution of process, with an intention to resist the law in that particular instance, such an act is a misdemeanor at most, is indictable as such, and may be met by the *posse comitatus*. But something more than a mere misdemeanor must have been contemplated by the law. It would seem to me that it could never have been intended that the governor should call out the militia in every case, where a constable or sheriff may be resisted; and even in a case of a riotous resistance it would not be an extreme emergency without some military array, some warlike show, or some threatened resistance to the government itself.

In this case, there has been no warlike array in the proceedings of Smith and his friends, no exhibition of arms, and no actual force of an illegal character. Mr. Reynolds was not subjected to illegal imprisonment. He was arrested on lawful process; and although that process may have been wrongfully obtained, yet his arrest was not riotous or unlawful, but according to the forms of law. Mr. Reynolds continued in the custody of the sheriff, by virtue of that process, until he was taken to Nauvoo; and although he was taken to that city against his will, and was by that means compelled to take his prisoner there, yet was he taken by lawful process, by an authorized officer who acted, so far as I have any evidence, freely and voluntarily, in so doing. In no one aspect of the case can I consider the present an extreme emergency, warranting a call for the militia according to the provisions of law in this state.

Thus, sir, I have stated to you the principal reasons which have influenced me in refusing to order a call of the militia. To my mind they are entirely satisfactory, and I hope they will meet with the approval of your Excellency and the citizens of Missouri.

I have the honor to be
Your Excellency's most obedient servant,
THOMAS FORD.

Tuesday, 15.—Went in the evening to see Mr. La Forest exhibit feats of strength.

Wednesday, 16.—At ten a. m., attended the funeral of General James Adams, who was buried with Masonic honors.

I sent Sidney Rigdon's affidavit to Governor Ford.

Thursday, 17.—I held mayor's court through the day, and tried several suits.

Elders Parley P. Pratt and Orson Hyde started from Nauvoo for Boston, *via* Chicago.

Elder J. M. Grant wrote me a letter reporting the church in Philadelphia to be in a prosperous condition.

Friday, 18.—Conversed with Mr. Swartout, of Quincy, and bought from him thirteen quarter-sections of land. Visited the lumber yard.

Elders Young and Kimball visited Mount Holly, New Jersey.

Saturday, 19.—"*Great Meeting of Anti-Mormons!*" At a public meeting of the citizens of Hancock county, without distinction of party, held at the Court House in Carthage, in pursuance of previous notice, on Saturday, the 19th of August, A. D. 1843.

Anti-Mormon Meeting at Carthage.

Major Reuben Graves was called to the chair, and William D. Abernethy appointed secretary. The object of the meeting was then stated by Valentine Wilson in an animated address. The meeting was afterwards addressed by Walter Bagby and also by Hiram Boyle, of Adams county.

On motion of F. J. Bartlett, a committee of nine was appointed by the chair to draft and report resolutions for the action of the meeting.

F. J. Bartlett, Walter Bagby, Valentine Wilson, G. M. Swope, R. T. Madison, J. A. Beebe, John Wilson, Henry Hunter, and John Cameron were appointed that committee.

After a short absence the committee submitted the following:

REPORT.

Your committee respectfully requests to be excused from making a formal report at this time, owing to the short time allowed them and the importance of the business that has called us together, and ask to be discharged from further duties and recommend that a committee of six be appointed to draft resolutions and make a report to an adjourned meeting.

Whereupon the following gentlemen were appointed to compose that committee,—viz.:

Walter Bagby, F. J. Bartlett, Stephen Owen, Stephen H. Tyler, Valentine Wilson and Joel Weston.

The meeting then adjourned to meet again at this place on the 6th of September next, at one o'clock p. m.

REUBEN GRAVES, Chairman.

W. D. ABERNETHY, Secretary.

Sunday. 20.—I was at home all day. My brother Hyrum preached at the stand, and Sidney Rigdon read a copy of a letter to show the people that he was not guilty of treachery.

Monday 21.—I received a letter from Mr. Patrick, covering one from Mr. J. Hall, of Independence, Missouri, breathing hard things against us as a people. I gave instructions to have them copied with some additional remarks, and sent to Governor Ford. The following is a copy of the letter, with the comments of the *Neighbor* thereon.

Letter of J. Hall, Missouri, on the Recent Arrest and Trial of the Prophet.

INDEPENDENCE, MO., July 23, 1843.

MY DEAR OLD FRIEND:—Your letter dated on the 12th, and mailed on the 14th instant, is just at hand; and not being able to answer your questions correctly or advise you judicially, in relation to the Rockwell case until after I see him and some other of my friends, I will postpone that part of this letter until tomorrow, and in the meantime will say such things as I can write about without much reflection.

Sheriff Reynolds, upon his return gave me his compliments from you and for the first time I learned that you resided in Illinois. He also gave a narrative of his adventures in your state, which was anything but favorable, either to the reputation of your people or yourself, as a law abiding people or a profound or honest lawyer. Certainly there can be but little virtue in the community, and little honesty in the officers or the law, who will trample upon the forms of justice, the laws of the country and bid open defience to both in the manner that Sheriff Reynolds informs us that you acted with him, after his arrest of the Mormon Prophet. That the state courts have a right upon a writ of habeas corpus to investigate the legality of all imprisonment within their respective chartered limits, whether such imprisonment is by the authority of the United States or of a state, no sound lawyer, perhaps, will doubt; but it is equally certain that no court upon such a writ has any right to go beyond the forms and the *prima facia* evidence of the case. If the officers of courts and the community are so corrupt as to disregard their own laws and trample them under their feet, and liberate their criminals in defiance of law, then it appears to me that the power of self government is extinct; if Illinois by her own authority, cannot capture the prophet, it will be but a small matter to raise volunteers enough here to raze the city of Nauvoo to the ground; if Illinois fails to deliver up Jo Smith, there will be something serious between the two states. Missouri will have Jo Smith for trial or impose as powerful restrictions as the Constitution will allow upon the intercourse of the citizens of Illinois in Missouri. If the governor of Illinois is so imbecile as to allow his warrant to be disregarded by the Mormons, and permit the Prophet to go at large, then let him be impeached, and a new, honorable, energetic man be placed in his stead. I have it from a high source that Missouri will hold the whole state responsible for the treatment of our messenger, and for the delivery of the Prophet. Had you liberated the Prophet by a regular writ of habeas corpus without mistreating our Reynolds, I should have gloried in my acquaintance with you; but to have done it in the manner it was done reflects no honor either on yourself, your people, or your government. The Mormons are only a lawless banditti, and I fear the pestilence has contaminated the whole community; and if Reynolds' opinion be correct, yourself among the rest, Holy Jo was not afraid of the "injustice of our people;" it is the just punishment and their violated laws that he fears.

I will now give you an impartial opinion of the prejudices against Rockwell here, and my opinion of his guilt. There is not a man in this community but believes him guilty. There is a chain of circumstances against him so strong that no rational man can doubt his guilt. I was at Boggs' house two minutes after the deed; it is in sight of mine; and the incidiousness of the offense renders it difficult to restrain the citizens from hanging him up without judge or jury. So far, however, we have succeeded in quelling it; but should he be discharged upon trial, the power of man cannot save him. (More tomorrow.)

J. HALL.

*Editorial Comments of the "Nauvoo Neighbor" on the Foregoing Letter.**

The foregoing letter was sent from J. Hall, of Independence, Missouri, to a respectable lawyer of Dixon, Illinois, and by him with an explana-

* The editorial is by John Taylor.

tory letter enclosed and forwarded to General Smith of this city; and after retaining copies, it was thought advisable to forward both the originals to Governor Ford for his consideration. By this proceeding it is not to be understood that the citizens of Nauvoo fear that "*volunteers from Missouri will raze Nauvoo to the ground.*" There is too much honor and patriotism in Illinois to allow such a barbarous and disgraceful transaction; but it was done to apprize his Excellency of the mode and manner of doing business in cases of emergency in Missouri, and to show his Excellency how much responsibility he and the state were under in case the Prophet should not be delivered up on the requisition of Missouri, where, according to the nicest calculations of the famous lawyer Hall, taking Rockwell's case for a sample, if he were discharged upon his trial, "*the power of man could not save him!*"

As to the non-intercourse, or "*restrictions*" which Missouri may assume or *inflict* over the citizens of Illinois, we have nothing to say. The Latter-day Saints have seen Boggs' signature to such a bill as that and many know the penalty.

There is little need of comment on Mr. Hall's famous letter; for to us it seems to be of itself a *comment* that makes honesty, virtue and common sense blush, and law, liberty and republicism shudder! We appeal to the liberal-minded and proud-hearted Americans, whether such a spot upon the withering character of Missouri could be removed, any more than an African could be washed white, or a wolf be possessed of the innocence of a lamb, unless the Lord interfered.

Talk of justice in Missouri! You might as well make a burning lime-kiln or coal-pit an ice-house or hospital! The ice would melt and the sick would suffocate, *the power of man could not save them!* No wonder a negro could be burned alive in Missouri! No wonder a criminal could be taken out of jail and murdered while the sheriff held a respite in his hand, in Missouri; and no wonder that a Mormon will not risk his life in Missouri; *the power of man could not save him*, even if discharged by what is styled *a court of justice.*

To glance at the whole without recurring to the many crimes of the people of the state, officially or unofficially, whether it be feeding prisoners on *human flesh*, or taking them out of jail and *lynching* them without mercy, to help justice beforehand, or whether it be Boggs' exterminating order or even the present hint at *restriction* and assumption of *responsibility*, we are apt to believe that the good sense and virtue of the citizens of Illinois in general and the Mormons *especially* like the *old experienced rat will shun Missouri as a whitened heap under which there is mischief concealed.*

Rode out with Mr. Moore. In the afternoon held mayor's court, and tried Frederick J. Moeser for breach of temperance ordinance. Fined him $3 and costs.

Mary Ann Young, daughter of Elder Brigham Young, died, aged six years and eigth months, of dropsy around the heart.

Elders Brigham Young, Heber C. Kimball and George A. Smith arrived in New York.

Tuesday, 22.—Held mayor's court, and fined Stephen Wilkinson for selling spirits without a license.

We constantly hear rumors that the people of Carthage are determined to raise a mob to drive the Mormons out of the state.

My brother Hyrum has gone to Plymouth.

Wednesday, 23.—I attended mayor's court and tried several suits.

Sent George J. Adams to Augusta to procure some articles for the temple.

Elders Orson Pratt and Wilford Woodruff arrived in New York, accompanied by Elders Jedediah M. Grant and James Sloan.

Thursday, 24.—Engaged in land business, selling and making titles of land and settling with several individuals.

Friday, 25.—My brother Hyrum in the office, conversing with me about the new revelation upon celestial marriage.

Rain in gentle showers through the day, being the first of any amount that has fallen in Nauvoo since the 1st of June. The earth has been exceedingly dry, and the early potatoes nearly destroyed. Corn has been stunted in its growth and even vines much injured by the drouth.

Saturday, 26.—Six hundred houses destroyed by fire in Kingston, Jamaica: estimated damage, $1,500,000.

The U. S. steam frigate *Missouri* destroyed by fire.

Elder Jonathan Dunham returned from his exploring excursion west. The following is extracted from his journal:

*Extracts from Journal of Elder Jonathan Dunham while Engaged on an Exploration in the Western Country.**

Saturday, July 16, 1843.—Stayed all day at Zarahemla; all night at Mr. Hawley's.

Sunday, 17.—Miss Daniels finished my tent, &c. Left Hawley's at twelve o'clock, went fifteen miles and camped for the night. In the morning our horses were gone; we hunted for them some time before we found them.

18th July.—Left the camp at seven o'clock; traveled all day; came within sixteen miles of the agency. Camped on the prairie.

Tuesday, 19.—Left the camp at six o'clock; passed the agent's house, half-past twelve. Came to Sugar Grove creek; stopped, rested our horses, took dinner, &c., at two o'clock p. m.; stopped at dark on Mesquito creek, and stayed all night.

Wednesday, 20.—Started at six o'clock; traveled thirty miles; fell in with the Sac Indians, who had been to the old Sac village after corn. At night they got drunk and fought. We encamped at dark, and stayed all night in the timber, on a bluff bank of the Des Moines river.

Started late in the morning of Thursday, 21st. We traveled until twelve o'clock: stopped in the round flat of the Des Moines river (here another drunken Indian frolic which lasted all the afternoon); left the ground at half-past two p. m. and went thirteen miles; came within twenty miles of the garrison troops, or Sac settlement, and encamped on the edge of the prairie.

Friday, 22nd July.—Left for the Sac village; at noon we got parted from each other, and the Indians got drunk and quarreled; and Captain Joe would not go any further. He lay down, was mad, and I could not get him to go. So I left him and went towards the Sac village. Stayed all night at the trading house.

Saturday morning, 23rd July.—Came to the Sac village, and waited for Captain Joe to arrive with his party.

Sunday, 24.—Stayed at the Sac waiting for my pilot, who was sick and lame in one knee, so that he could not travel.

Monday, 25.—This morning at Wapamuneto's; stayed until noon of Tuesday, 26th; then Neotanah, my guide came, and we started off immediately for Missouri; stayed on the prairie all night.

Wednesday, 27.—Traveled until noon; baited our horses; no water; we had nothing to eat; continued our journey; it rained all the afternoon; stayed all the night in the prairie; lay in the wet grass.

Thursday, 28.—Started on our journey this morning early. Saw in

* See this volume, page 509.

the forenoon a herd of elk. The Indian went up the hollow to shoot one, while I held the horses out of sight of the elk. He crawled in the grass some fifty or sixty rods, and snapped four times at them when they were lying down; he could not get his gun off. The elk ran off a rifle shot and looked at him. He broke his gun to pieces on the ground and threw it away down the hill, and came back to me swearing mad. Went on until three o'clock, then baited our horses and prepared for a shower that was apparently nigh at hand. We went until sundown, then pitched our tents in the grass; and such rain and thunder and lightning I never before witnessed. Lay all night in the rain. Our tent blew over.

Friday, 29th July.—We dried our things by the fire, and then went on about twenty-five miles; came to a village of the Pottawatamies about sunset; found nobody at home; went into the house of my guide; his wife was dead, and his son and wife gone to the north on a buffalo hunt. We made a fire, and got something to eat. Late in the night there came four Indians and one old squaw; they brought some jerked venison and some half-boiled corn.

Saturday morning, 30th July.—We were sent for to the chief's house. We went. The Indians, squaws and children came from every quarter to see the man that had come with Neotanah. Breakfast was ready for us as soon as we came in. This was the first time that I ever ate at a wigwam amongst little and great, when the vituals relished as it did at this time; but this is easily accounted for: hunger will make anything that is eatable taste good. Stayed all day at the chief's house. My rifle seemed to be the great wonder amongst all Indians and squaws; it went the rounds, from one to another, as if it had been one of the seven wonders of the world. This Indian town stands on the creek called the Pottawatamie Tour-se-pas. This creek is from three to eight rods wide, is deep, and often flows its banks. Its length is sixty miles and it enters into the Missouri river, thirty miles from Pottawatamie town.

Sunday, 31.—Nothing this day transpired worth mentioning. About three o'clock p. m. a delegate from the Pottwatamie tribe returned from Iowa river, where he met in council with two of the Sioux and one Winnebago. He said the distance from the Pottawatamies to Galena is five hundred miles.

Monday, 1st August, 1843.—This day I spent in looking up the creek for a mill seat, and found one and two beds of iron ore.

Tuesday, 2.—This morning the chief of the warriors brought me two cat fish, and left them in the wik-a-up where I stayed. I cooked half of one of them, and it eat very good. The Indians all are very kind to me, more so than I could expect. This tribe is somewhat scattered, through the timber up and down the creek; but the main village or town stands on an eminence that overlooks the whole of the rest of the Indian habitations. It appears to be a healthy habitation. The water is good and the climate wholesome. Some considerable timber, though no very great sawing timber, except bass wood, black walnut, some cottonwood. This tribe have been here for six years from Rock river.

The Pottawatamies this side of the Missouri river, they say, will number 2,000 men, women and children. Thirty-four miles from the Pottawatamie town to the Council Bluffs, 200 miles south lies Fort Leavenworth; and about the same distance southeast lies Far West. One hundred miles north is a buffalo country, where the Pottawatamies hunt and catch buffalo.

Wednesday, August 3.—Council met at two o'clock. They own five millions of acres of land. Last annuities, the number was 1,552 souls. Council arose at sunset, when the decision was made that Neotanah should conduct me back again to the agency in Iowa, on the nearest and most convenient route. The head chief was to conduct me home; but in council a messenger arrived and brought news that the superintendent of the annuities had arrived at the garrison, Leavenworth, and the middle of August he would visit the chiefs at Council Bluffs to pay them their money. He said he was very sorry that he could not conduct me to Nauvoo; he wanted to see the place and the people. The interpreter appeared very friendly indeed, and regretted much that he could not go with me home; but said he would visit Nauvoo in the spring, as early as the weather and streams of water would permit.

Thursday, 4.—This morning I discovered a little dissatisfaction in some, which began to cause a division, that the same Indian that conducted me to their nation should conduct me back again.

The Pawnees on the head of the Big Platte, 150 miles from Council Bluffs.

About the 7th of July, (1843) the Sacs, 600 men, came against the Pawnees, 160. They fought from daylight until noon, killed sixty Sioux and about sixty-two of the Pawnees. The missionary went upon the bluff and saw the battle. They offered no abuse to the whites.

Friday, 5.—Nothing of note passed.

Saturday, 6.—This day I took dinner with a friend, who had just come from the buffalo hunt. His daughter cooked a johnny cake and got some tea; had sugar a plenty, and buffalo meat. This, for the first time that I had seen any corn meal, was pounded in a mortar, and the finest sorted out and baked; but the manner in which it was wet up and shortened was a caution to the hogs. But this all passed over very well. I have no reason to complain, for they did the best they knew how. Severe hunger made all things relish well that was eatable for dogs.

Sunday, 7.—Went down the creek to make some arrangements about returning home. Saw some new Indians, and had to go and dine with them; then, after dinner, went up town and stayed all night.

Monday, 8.—Went about eight or ten miles after wild honey; found two trees, got the honey, and returned home by dark the same day.

Tuesday, 9.—This morning had breakfast of honey, and buffalo meat dried and smoked; then, in about one hour and a half, boiled corn and elk bone broth was served up. This was a great dish amongst the Lamanites; but not so good a dish for me as I have seen in past days in my own land and amongst my own people.

On the 8th instant a great feast was held at the Black Chief's, called the buffalo feast, or after the buffalo hunt was over; and all returned in safety and all their labors crowned with success. An address was delivered by a subordinate speaker because the chief was very ill. This address or sermon was lengthy and delivered in great oratorical style. At the end of the last sentence the congregation responded a loud amen; then they commenced eating as the feast was prepared already. After the feast the singers commenced to sing, and sang three songs, the dances commenced at a loud whoop from the war chief. After dancing was passed off the priest offered up a prayer to the Great Spirit for giving them good hunting. The congregation then dispersed.

Wednesday, 10.—Another feast was prepared for the lower town, who were absent at the first feast. This last feast held all night, or the dance continued all night.

Thursday, 11.—I went to the lower town and visited them: they also were very friendly. The town is situated on the east bank of the river, about three miles below the middle town, and the middle town about one mile below the upper town. The head chief lives in the middle town and one chief in each of the other towns.

Friday, 12.—All was still and quiet, nothing going on worthy of notice; all busy about their employment. The old men were lying on their couches and smoking their pipes; the old women were making sacks in which to gather their corn and beans and potatoes: the young women were making mats to sleep on and weaving wampum belts for the warriors; the young men were constantly riding from town to town visiting and playing cards and gambling continually after the return from their buffalo hunt, which lasted fourteen days.

When a hunter rides out for elk or deer, and returns with the spoils, he rides to the door of his wigwam, where he finds his wife sitting at work, and a kettle of corn and beans and a little buffalo meat or bones broken, or elk meat, all ready for him. If not quite done, she steps to the next door and returns with his wooden bowl and ladle full. The Indian throws off at the door his meat in a great hurry, unharnesses his horse, lies down on some skins or blankets and eats his food prepared for him, enough for four white men.

The meat is left in charge with the squaw. He has no more care of it. He has done his part in getting the meat and bringing it to his house. The squaws then prepare and dry or smoke the meat. This they call jerking the meat, so that it will not spoil. Meat prepared this way is dried in the blood, and will keep year after year if not eaten before. Nothing of notice occurred through the day.

I spent the forenoon in the town. In the afternoon I went to see the Indian who was appointed by the council to conduct me home. He was gone to the lower town on a drunken frolic. I stayed until he came home, which was a little before sunset. I then returned to my place of lodging. Soon after I had got to bed or laid down upon my blanket, I heard the beating of a drum. An Indian came in, or came to the door and said that we must all attend the feast or dance. At an instant each one caught a bowl and ladle, and ran for the place of gathering. I went with the crowd, though not equipped. I had no bowl or ladle, but was made welcome as though I was an Indian with the rest. A place was prepared for me to sit or lie down as I chose; and as they all lay down, I laid down with the rest, between two large warriors, who soon commenced smoking their pipes. The music was continually playing. After smoking was past, the war chief began to dance, and was followed by his braves with a hideous yell as each fell into the dance. They passed around the room three or four times, and then they were joined by the squaws. They all and each one performed their parts well that was assigned them, from the least to the greatest; and I think better time kept by those that danced I never saw before. All was solemn and silent as though they were going to be burnt at the stake,—except, when the chief gave the whoop, they all answered with a yell that would reach the very heavens. This dance continued about one hour while the supper was preparing. They then all took supper; and after supper, commenced dancing again as usual. This performance lasted until about three o'clock in the morning when all went quietly to their homes.

The next morning, the chief sent for me to take breakfast with him. I immediately went. The two little girls were cooking, frying flour pancakes. The chief's wife was busily engaged attending on her sick child in a small booth built for that purpose out at the door. These cakes above mentioned, fried by those little girls, were just scorched a little on either side, and the middle was dough. As it was those cakes and sweetened water was a good breakfast.

Saturday morning, 13.—This morning the chief told me that in consequence of being used in the manner I was, in coming to visit them. they had come to the conclusion that they would not let the same Indian go back with me that came with me, and that they had selected in the first council, but after more investigation, they concluded to make a new selection of men that would be more respectable and could do honor to their nation, and have authority to act for the tribe; and it would be satisfactory to the whole nation, as the nation was much displeased with the conduct of Neotanah, and in council gave him a severe flogging, and said that he was not fit to go anywhere amongst the whites. They seemed to express much regret and feeling of sorrow that I had received such treatment from one that pretended to be a friend and an honorable man of the Pottawatomies, for they consider themselves honorable men.

While I now write, I have seven of the most honorable in the tribe around me—the head chief and his counselors. One of them is aged, his head is silvered o'er with age; while in his prime none could endure more fatigue, none whose constitution was stronger than his: but now he says, he is soon to go and shake hands with the great Shaminyto (that is, God) that had made him, and had given him strength to hunt, and in war to fight his enemies. Here the old man would show the wounds received in battle, in fighting for his nation, his wife and little ones. He said he had never fought but on the defensive. Ninety-eight years, as near as he can remember, he has seen; and now, he says, he wants to know how the Mormons worship the great Shaminyto different from what he did; if the best way, he wanted to get into it before he went on his journey to see the great Shaminyto.

Sunday, 14.—There is no day known amongst these Indians. Every day is alike unto them. They have no day of the month, neither day of the week. All things move on one day after another. They count their months by moons, and twelve moons make a year. They can tell how many years they have lived in the west, and most of them can tell how old they are, &c.

Monday, 15.—This morning the Indians arrived from Missouri, and brought an interpreter, and one to go to the East or to the Mississippi, to conduct me home and to see the big chief. Council is to sit at nine o'clock this morning; but in consequence of the head chief's child to be buried this morning, council will be called immediately after dinner. The afternoon was spent in business matters, writing, preparing for the journey to Nauvoo.

Tuesday, 16.—This morning I went to see a squaw that was bitten last night by a rattlesnake twice upon the top of her left foot. She was in great pain all night, her foot and leg very much swollen. In the afternoon the Indians all met for worship and to prepare for drawing the blankets and money. They were as merry as bees in a hive, old and young, from the grey head to the suckling on a board. They had their meeting until one o'clock in the morning. Danced and prayed and preached some.

Wednesday, 17.—They commenced again the worship about sunrise, dressed in the richest and best style possible,except some few who were employed in cooking for the rest. Here I will notice that the most profound silence and good order that I ever saw in any congregation whatever, small or great, was observed. All that is wanting to make them the happiest people in the world is the Gospel, a perfect knowledge of it, and to feel its power. Their sectarian creeds and ceremonies would go to the moles and bats soon. Although they labor with as much energy of body and mind, and have as much zeal as the shaking Quakers, yet it is heathen worship, like all other sectarian societies. Their idea of the Supreme Being is much more consistent than many of the holy enlightened sectarians; for the Indians believe in the Great Shaminyto as having body and parts like unto a man.

Thursday, 18.—This morning, we started for Nauvoo. A long and tedious journey to perform lay before us. We had no compass to steer our course by: the sun rising in the morning was our principal guide. Our course was due east. This course we intended to follow as near as we could.

The place we left, Belle Vue, or Mosquito Creek, is in the same latitude as Nauvoo. Therefore on our return, our course must be east; and this direction we followed until we came to the Keosoqua, on the Des Moines river. We traveled fifteen miles unto another Indian village, stayed all night; and in the morning a council was called, and we stayed all day.

Friday, 19.—At the village we got some provisions cooked, and the chief's brother was sent as a delegate from the band. Our company now consisted of four Indians, one squaw, one interpreter, and myself, seven in number. The interpreter was a white man, half English and half French, formerly from Canada; and since the last war has lived with the Pottawatamies; married a squaw, sister to the chief where we now are. We came to the conclusion to stay all day on Friday, because two of our horses went back to where we first started.

Saturday, 20th of August.—Left the village at ten o'clock. Traveled all day until dark. Encamped on the battle-ground where the Sioux and Pottawattamies and sixteen of the Oneidas fought. I took up one of their blankets to ride on. We started this morning as soon as it was light enough to see to follow the trail.

Sunday, 21.—Came to the Naama river, or creek, at twelve o'clock. Stopped and took dinner on a high bank. On this stream, on either side, is a quantity of timber. Where we crossed is a beautiful mill seat, &c. Traveled until dark, and encamped in the weeds all night.

Monday, 22.—We started at daybreak; went until twelve o'clock; stopped on the east bank of White Breast Creek and took dinner. Here we found plenty of red plums, though not fully ripe; but my comrades dined heartily upon them. This was a good hit for me: when we came to eat dinner they could eat but little. By this means I made out to get nearly enough to satisfy hunger, for I had eaten nothing since the night before. We passed on until we came to English creek. Stayed all night.

Tuesday, 23.—Started about sunrise without breakfast. Traveled until two o'clock. Crossed the Des Moines river at Eddyville. There I bought a loaf of wheat bread, a loaf of sweet cake and an apple pie, and went up on the side hill to the Indian Spring, and there we all took dinner. And this was a dinner indeed, good enough for the king. I thought the best that I ever ate in my life; but being so extremely hungry, it was delicious, &c. Came ten miles; stayed all night at Mosquito creek; got two ears of green corn apiece and roasted them.

Wednesday, 24.—This morning we started at daylight, then ten miles from the old agency of the Sacs and Fox. We traveled twenty-five miles beyond the agency, which made thirty-five miles, then encamped for the night. Here we bought some bacon and half a loaf of warm wheat bread.

Thursday, 25.—This morning some rain and lowery. We took a bite and then started for Nauvoo city; traveled until sunset, then camped in the woods about twelve miles from Nauvoo. We killed one grey squirrel, and eat a little dry buffalo meat, and lay down in the rain all night.

In the morning we got a few potatoes and boiled them. I killed two grey squirrels and the squaw burned off the hair and boiled them.

Friday, 26.—We traveled all day in the rain, and at night reached the Mississippi river, and encamped on the bank, above the Potter house.

I have seen much delightful country, but the prospect for bee hunting is not as good as I could wish.

[N. B. The names of places and distances were procured from the Indians and are not accurate.]

August 27.—The Quorum of the Twelve met with

the Saints in the Columbian Hall, Grand Street, New York, in conference.

Minutes of a Meeting of the Twelve in New York City.

Meeting opened by prayer.

President Young arose and addressed the meeting in an interesting manner upon the subject of the gathering, the building of the Nauvoo House and Temple. He spoke of the Priesthood, and said that it was a perfect system of government.

In the afternoon the conference reassembled; and Elder Kimball spoke in parables—Gather in the wheat and the tares, thrash the wheat and the mill will blow away the chaff. He said an elder could get a people together and could get them to receive the work, if he did not whip the sects so much. He compared such elders to a shepherd who would call up a buck and a flock of sheep and hand them a little salt; and just as they begin to eat, hit him with a club across the head, and the sheep will run away.

Elder George A. Smith followed and bore testimony of the work. Spoke of the elders spending their time in speaking about mysteries and speculating about things beyond the grave which they did not understand. Advised them to wait till God revealed hidden mysteries to them before they undertook to preach them to the people. * * * * Elder Smith counseled the elders to be wise enough to let such things alone, in other words to tell the good things of the kingdom which we have received and do understand, and wait patiently until the Lord takes off the veil of darkness. He spoke of the collegiate education he received from President Joseph Smith which was to preach short sermons and make short prayers, which had done him much good in life.

President Brigham Young said the scriptures had been mystified to that degree that the greatest divines of the day are as ignorant as the dumb ass concerning the things of God; comparatively they don't know their right hand from their left. We try to revere the scriptures and to make them so simple that the people can understand them. Place a man in this room who is ignorant of science, and take everything out that he can see and then ask him if there is anything in the room. He will say, No, only we two. I tell him there are millions of live animals in the room—that we even breath them; and I will show him by the aid of the microscope that there are live animals in a drop of water, which appear to be eight feet long; but he won't believe it until he sees it through the magnifying glass. So with the unbeliever in revelation. He does not believe in God, in angels or in spirits, because he cannot see them; but let him have spiritual glasses, or obey the commandments of God, get the Spirit of God, and then he can see the truth.

A hymn was then sung.

Then several questions were asked as follows:

1. Can any officer in any branch of the Church say that his word is law and shall be obeyed?

Answer: He can say that his word is law; but does that make it so? Yes, if he has the law of God and delivers it: otherwise it is not.

2. Is it right for a priest to be appointed to accompany a teacher to the house of each member, when his duty is set forth in the Covenants?

Answer: Yes, any officer from a high priest to a deacon may visit the Church or members, and be set apart for this purpose, if the Church will receive it.

3. Can a branch of the Church make by-laws on the principle of expediency, which are not specified in any revelation?

Answer: Yes, if they wish, they may make laws to stick their fingers into their eyes; but it is like the man who habituated himself to sticking his fingers into a knot-hole in a board partition every morning, until custom compelled him to do it; for having omitted it one morning he felt so curiously at the breakfast table, that he could not eat. He then bethought himself, went and put his finger into the knot-hole and returned with a good appetite, and ate a hearty breakfast.*

Elder Young said that if elders or high priests are so situated that they cannot get word from the Prophet or the Twelve Apostles, they may get a revelation concerning themselves. The Twelve may get a revelation in any part of the world concerning the building up of the kingdom, as they have to establish it in all parts of the world. So any person can ask the Lord for a witness concerning himself, and get an answer, but not to lead the Church: that belongs to the head of the Church.

Conference met at half-past ten o'clock, according to adjournment. Meeting opened by singing. Prayer by Elder Jedediah M. Grant. The congregation was then addressed by Elder Wilford Woodruff from II Peter 1: 20, 21: "Knowing this first, that no prophecy of the scripture is of any private interpretation. For the prophecy came not in old time by the will of man; but holy men of God spake as they were moved by the Holy Ghost.

If the prophecies that had been fulfilled were fulfilled literally, in like manner would those prophecies which are still unfulfilled be ful-

* The answer is not as direct as one might wish it to be, but certainly it is not favorable to the making of by-laws not "specified in any revelation."

filled literally. The gathering of the Saints, the building up of Zion, the gathering of the Jews, the rebuilding of Jerusalem, the establishing of the Church and kingdom of God in the last days, and the preaching of the Gospel to all the world are events looked for by the Latter-day Saints. And notwithstanding these things are unpopular, and not looked for or believed in by the world, yet we feel encouraged to persevere and press forward in assisting to accomplish these great and glorious things, with a firm belief that they will as truly be brought to pass and perfected as those things were which were prophecied in ancient days. He also bore testimony of the truth of the Book of Mormon, Book of Doctrine and Covenants, and of Joseph Smith being a prophet of God.

Elder Kimball gave his testimony, when the meeting took a recess for two hours.

In the afternoon, after Elder John E. Page had addressed the meeting, Elder George T. Leach was appointed to preside over the Church in New York, in place of Elder L. R. Foster, who was about to remove to Nauvoo. After which several children were blessed, and the meeting adjourned until evening; at which time Elder Orson Pratt addressed the people in an edifying manner concerning the Book of Mormon, its history, what it was, &c.; that it was a history of nearly one-half of the globe, and the people that inhabited it; that it gave a history and names of cities that have been of late discovered by Catherwood and Stephens; that it spoke or the establishing of our government; and what is more highly interesting, it reveals its final fate and destiny; so that, by reading the Book of Mormon, you can clearly see what will befall this nation, and what will be its final end.*

* This statement of Elder Orson Pratt's views is doubtless faulty. The Book of Mormon does not predict what will befall our nation, the United States, nor "its final end." But it contains a conditional prophecy in relation to the two American continents. These continents are a promised land. They are given, according to the Book of Mormon, primarily to the descendants of the Patriarch Joseph, son of Jacob, as an inheritance, but the Gentile races are also given an inheritance in them with the descendants of Joseph. The whole land, however, is dedicated to righteousness and liberty and the people who possess it, whether of the house of Israel or Gentile must be a righteous people and worship "the God of the land, who is Jesus Christ." In that event God stands pledged to preserve the land and the people thereof, free from bondage of all other nations, and to bless them with very great and peculiar bressings, guaranteeing to them freedom and peaceful possession of the land forever. If the Gentile races shall observe these conditions they and their children are to share in the blessings of the land in connection with the descendants of the Patriarch Joseph. But if they depart from justice, reject righteousness and Jesus Christ, then judgments of destruction decreed in the Book of Mormon, will overtake them until they are wasted away. This is the de-

In that book you will find recorded the pure principles of the gospel of Jesus Christ, as taught by Himself on the continent of America, so plain that no two persons could disagree as to the points of doctrine set forth. He then bore testimony of the truth of Joseph Smith being a prophet of God, and that the Book of Mormon was true; also that the Church of the Latter-day Saints was the Church of God. He spoke about two hours; and after he closed five children were blessed, and then the people were dismissed.

August 27.—I attended meeting at the stand at ten a. m., and made a few remarks; the following report of which is by Dr. Willard Richards:

Address of the Prophet—Sidney Rigdon's Status—The Priesthood Expounded.

Two weeks ago today something was said about Elder Sidney Rigdon, and a vote was taken to disfellowship him and to demand his license, on account of a report brought by Elder Hyde from Quincy.

He [President Smith] then read a letter from Thomas Carlin to Sidney Rigdon as follows:

QUINCY, ILLINOIS, August 18, 1843.

DEAR SIR:—Yours of the 15th instant was received, but not in time to answer it by return mail. You say that a Mr. Orson Hyde, on board of the steamboat *Anawan* a short time since, was told by an officer of the boat that a Mr. Prentice, in the vicinity of Quincy, said that some person in high standing in the Church of Latter-day Saints in this place (Quincy) had an interview with you (me) said he would use all the influence that his circumstances would admit of to have Joseph Smith arrested and delivered into the hands of the Missourians, &c. This interview is said to have taken place at the time the first warrant was issued against Smith, and since the last warrant was issued, that the same person had written to you, (me) or had an interview with you, giving the same assurances. It has been publicly said in this town that I (Sidney Rigdon) was the person who had this interview or interviews and correspondence with you. Now, sir, it gives me pleas-

cree of God respecting the western hemisphere, and is one of the important messages that the Book of Mormon has to deliver to the present generation. See Book of Mormon II Nephi 1: 5-12; also Ether. 1: 42; III Nephi 20: 14-20; III Nephi 20: 27, 28; III Nephi 21: 11-25; also "New Witness for God Vol. III, pp. 314-323. But it will be seen that these prophecies are conditional, and therefore cannot be held to be predictions of what the final end of our nation, the United States and other nations of the American continents, will be, since it yet remains to be demonstrated whether they will abide or violate the conditions upon which they may possess the continents perpetually.

ure to be perfectly able to disabuse you. I have not seen you to my recollection, nor had any correspondence with you, until the present, since 1839; and in all the intercourse I have had with you I have always looked upon you as one of the most devoted followers of Joseph Smith and one of the pillars of the Church of Latter-day Saints. I never sought through the aid of any person to entrap Joseph Smith. A faithful discharge of my official duties was all that I attempted or desired.

Very respectfully
Your obedient servant,
THOMAS CARLIN.

[He, President Smith] then resumed: The letter is one of the most evasive things, and carries with it a design to hide the truth. Has any man been concerned in a conspiracy to deliver Joseph Smith to Missouri? If so, who?

He then read the 7th chap. Hebrews. Salem is designed for a Hebrew term. It should be Shiloam, which signifies righteousness and peace: as it is, it is nothing—neither Hebrew, Greek, Latin, French, nor any other language.

I say to all those who are disposed to set up stakes for the Almighty, You will come short of the glory of God.

To become a joint heir of the heirship of the Son,one must put away all his false traditions.

I prophesy and bear record this morning that all the combined powers of earth and hell shall not and cannot ever overthrow or overcome this boy, for I have a promise from the eternal God.

If I have sinned, I have sinned outwardly; but surely I have contemplated the things of God.

Respecting the Melchizedek Priesthood, the sectarians never professed to have it; consequently they never could save any one, and would all be damned together. There was an Episcopal priest who said he had the priesthood of Aaron, but had not the priesthood of Melchizedek: and I bear testimony that I never have found the man who claimed the Priesthood of Melchizedek. The power of the Melchizedek priesthood is to have the power of "endless lives;" for the everlasting covenant cannot be broken.

The law was given under Aaron for the purpose of pouring out judgments and destructions.

The sectarian world are going to hell by hundreds, by thousands and by millions.

There are three grand orders of priesthood referred to here.

1st. The King of Shiloam. (Salem) had power and authority over that of Abraham, holding the key and the power of endless life. Angels desire to look into it, but they have set up too many stakes. God cursed the children of Israel because they would not receive the last law from Moses.

The sacrifice required of Abraham in the offering up of Isaac, shows that if a man would attain to the keys of the kingdom of an endless life; he must sacrifice all things. When God offers a blessing or knowlledge to a man, and he refuses to receive it, he will be damned. The Israelites prayed that God would speak to Moses and not to them; in consequence of which he cursed them with a carnal law.

What was the power of Melchizedek? 'Twas not the Priesthood of Aaron which administers in outward ordinances, and the offering of sacrifices. Those holding the fullness of the Melchizedek Priesthood are kings and priests of the Most High God, holding the keys of power and blessings. In fact, that priesthood is a perfect law of theocracy, and stands as God to give laws to the people, adminstering endless lives to the sons and daughters of Adam.

Abraham says to Melchizedek, I believe all that thou hast taught me concerning the priesthood and the coming of the Son of Man; so Melchizedek ordained Abraham and sent him away. Abraham rejoiced, saying, Now I have a priesthood.

Salvation could not come to the world without the mediation of Jesus Christ.

How shall God come to the rescue of this generation? He will send Elijah the prophet. The law revealed to Moses in Horeb never was revealed to the children of Israel as a nation.

Elijah shall reveal the covenants to seal the hearts of the fathers to the children, and the children to the fathers.

The anointing and sealing is to be called, elected and made sure.

"Without father, without mother, without descent, having neither beginning of days nor end of life, but made like unto the Son of God, abideth a priest continually." The Melchizedek Priesthood holds the right from the eternal God, and not by descent from father and mother; and that priesthood is as eternal as God Himself, having neither beginning of days nor end of life.

The 2nd Priesthood is Patriarchal authority. Go to and finish the temple, and God will fill it with power, and you will then receive more knowledge concerning this priesthood.

The 3rd is what is called the Levitical Priesthood, consisting of priests to administer in outward ordinance, made without an oath; but the Priesthood of Melchizedek is by an oath and covenant.

The Holy Ghost is God's messenger to administer in all those priesthoods.

Jesus Christ is the heir of this Kingdom—the only begotten of the Father according to the flesh, and holds the keys over all this world.

Men have to suffer that they may come upon Mount Zion and be exalted above the heavens.

I know a man that has been caught up to the third heavens, and can say, with Paul, that we have seen and heard things that are not lawful to utter.

Fifteen minutes past one, closed my address.

Sidney Rigdon said: "I never saw Governor Carlin but three times, and never exchanged a word with any man living on the subject.* I ask pardon for having done anything which should give occasion to make you think so."

In the evening I attended council and prayer meeting with my brother Hyrum, Newel K. Whitney, Willard Richards, William Law and William Marks.

Monday, *28*.—I was visited by a deputation of Pottawattamie Indians.

Tuesday, *29*.—Elder Brigham Young paid a visit to James Arlington Bennett, Arlington House, Long Island, and baptized and confirmed him next day.

I held a mayor's court and tried several cases. Erastus H. Derby was bound over to keep the peace for six months. Previous to the close of the trial he gave up his license as an elder to the Church Recorder.

Wednesday, *30*.—The *Nauvoo Neighbor* publishes an article from the *Boston Bee*, upholding the chartered rights of Nauvoo.

Thursday, *31*.—I commenced removing into the Nauvoo Mansion.

(END OF VOLUME V.)

* i. e. of betraying Joseph Smith to Missouri.

ERRATUM: At page 504 a line is omitted in the third paragraph, fourth line. This should be inserted after the word "commanded;"—*and because they did none other thing than that which they were commanded*—

INDEX TO VOLUME V.

A

B

C

M

N

O

P

T

W

Y

HISTORY

OF THE

CHURCH OF JESUS CHRIST

OF

LATTER-DAY SAINTS.

PERIOD I.

History of Joseph Smith, the Prophet

BY HIMSELF.

VOLUME VI.

AN INTRODUCTION AND NOTES

BY

B. H ROBERTS

PUBLISHED BY THE CHURCH.

DESERET BOOK COMPANY
44 EAST SOUTH TEMPLE
SALT LAKE CITY, UTAH

1980

Lithographed by

in the United States of America

TABLE OF CONTENTS.

VOLUME VI.

INTRODUCTION.

CHAPTER I.

AN ESTIMATE OF THE PROPHET JOSEPH AS A RELIGIOUS LEADER—ANTI-MORMON MEETING AT CARTHAGE—HISTORICAL SKETCH—IMPORTANT CONFERENCE OF THE TWELVE HELD IN BOSTON.

CHAPTER II.

MOVEMENTS OF APOSTLES IN THE EAST—THE NAUVOO MANSION—ROCKWELL ACQUITTED—SPECIAL CONFERENCE AT NAUVOO—DISCOURSE OF THE PROPHET ON THE DEMISE OF JAMES ADAMS.

CHAPTER III.

ANCIENT RUINS IN AMERICA, BOOK OF MORMON EVIDENCES—THE PROPHET ON THE U. S. CONSTITUTION AND THE BIBLE—MISREPRESENTATIONS CORRECTED—LETTER TO THE U. S. PRESIDENTIAL CANDIDATES—THE PROPHET'S ADDRESS TO THE SAINTS.

CHAPTER IV.

CORRESPONDENCE BETWEEN JAMES ARLINGTON BENNETT AND PRESIDENT JOSEPH SMITH—RENEWAL OF PETITIONS TO CONGRESS FOR REDRESS OF MISSOURI GRIEVANCES—PRESIDENT JOSEPH SMITH'S APPEAL TO THE GREEN MOUNTAIN BOYS, VERMONT—STATUS OF THE NAUVOO LEGION IN ILLINOIS MILITIA.

CHAPTER V.

THE AVERY KIDNAPPING—DEFENSIVE PREPARATIONS AGAINST MISSOURI MOBS—APPEALS TO THE GENERAL GOVERNMENT FOR PROTECTION—NAUVOO LEGION OFFERED AS UNITED STATES TROOPS.

CHAPTER VI.

MEMORIAL OF CITY COUNCIL TO CONGRESS ANENT MISSOURI AFFAIRS—ROCKWELL RETURNS TO NAUVOO—RECITAL OF HIS ADVENTURES—AVERY'S ACQUITTAL BY MISSOURI'S COURTS—NAUVOO'S POLICE FORCE INCREASED PUBLICATION ON MORMONISM, PRO ET CON—1843.

CHAPTER VII.

PRESIDENT SMITH'S CORRESPONDENCE WITH JOHN C. CALHOUN—CARTWRIGHT DROWNING CASE, ENGLAND—CITY GUARDS INCREASED—FEARS OF LAW AND MARKS—INVESTIGATION BY THE CITY COUNCIL—RESISTANCE OF OFFICERS AT CARTHAGE—ANTI-MORMON OBJECTIONS TO CITY ORDINANCES—THE PROPHET'S DIFFICULTIES WITH FRANCIS M. HIGBEE—REGULATIONS FOR THE SALE OF SPIRITUOUS LIQUORS.

CHAPTER VIII.

PRESENTATION OF THE BOOK OF MORMON TO QUEEN VICTORIA—THE SEALING POWERS OF THE PRIESTHOOD—GOVERNOR FORD'S WARNING TO THE PEOPLE OF HANCOCK COUNTY—APOSTROPHE TO MISSOURI—JOSEPH SMITH NOMINATED FOR PRESIDENT OF THE UNITED STATES—HIS VIEWS ON THE POWERS AND POLICY OF THE GOVERNMENT OF THE UNITED STATES.

CHAPTER IX

COMMENTS ON CANDIDACY OF JOSEPH SMITH FOR PRESIDENT OF THE UNITED STATES—TENDERS OF PEACE TO MISSOURI—PRELIMINARY STEPS TO WESTERN MOVEMENT OF THE CHURCH—JAMES A. BENNETT AND VICE-PRESIDENCY.

CHAPTER X.

URGING THE BUILDING OF THE TEMPLE—TENDERS OF PEACE TO MISSOURI—PROPHET'S DISCOURSE ON ELIAS, ELIJAH, MESSIAH—LYMAN WIGHT'S PROPOSAL OF A SOUTHWEST MOVEMENT FOR THE CHURCH.

CHAPTER XI.

ORSON PRATT SENT TO WASHINGTON AS AGENT OF NAUVOO—AMOS FIELDING TO ENGLAND, DITTO—COMMENT ON THE CANDIDACY OF JOSEPH SMITH FOR PRESIDENT OF THE U. S.—CONSPIRACY OF THE LAWS, HIGBEES, FOSTERS ET AL AGAINST JOSEPH SMITH—THE PROPHET'S MEMORIAL TO CONGRESS—OCCUPATION OF THE WEST CONTEMPLATED.

CHAPTER XII.

THE AUTHORITIES OF NAUVOO VS. THE HIGBEES ET AL.—DEDICATION OF THE MASONIC HALL—THE CHURCH CONFERENCE IN APRIL, 1844—ADDRESS OF PRESIDENT SIDNEY RIGDON.

CHAPTER XIII.

CONFERENCE OF THE CHURCH, APRIL, 1844, CONTINUED—ADDRESS OF PATRIARCH HYRUM SMITH—THE BUILDING OF THE TEMPLE.

CHAPTER XIV.

CONFERENCE OF THE CHURCH, APRIL, 1844 (CONTINUED)—THE KING FOLLETT SERMON—THE CHARACTER OF GOD—RELIGIOUS FREEDOM—GOD AN EXALTED MAN—ETERNAL LIFE TO KNOW GOD AND JESUS CHRIST—EVERLASTING BURNINGS—MEANING OF THE HEBREW SCRIPTURES—A COUNCIL OF THE GODS—MEANING OF THE WORD CREATE—THE IMMORTAL INTELLIGENCE—THE RELATION OF MAN TO GOD—OUR GREATEST RESPONSIBILITY—THE UNPARDONABLE SIN—THE FORGIVENESS OF SIN—THE SECOND DEATH.

CHAPTER XV.

GENERAL CONFERENCE FOR APRIL, 1844, (CONCLUDED)—THE ANNOUNCEMENT THAT THE WHOLE LAND OF AMERICA IS ZION—INSTRUCTIONS TO ELDERS SET APART FOR MISSIONS—A GENERAL CONFERENCE IN ENGLAND.

CHAPTER XVI.

DIFFICULTIES WITH THE HIGBEES AND FOSTERS, CONFERENCES APPOINTED BY THE TWELVE THROUGHOUT THE UNITED STATES—INSTRUCTIONS TO REUBEN HEDLOCK, PRESIDENT OF THE BRITISH MISSION—PREPARATIONS FOR ENLARGEMENT OF THE WORK—FRANCIS M. HIGBEE'S SUIT AGAINST PRESIDENT SMITH—THE PROPHET RELEASED.

CHAPTER XVII.

ADDRESS OF THE PROPHET—HIS PROPHETIC CALLING AND THE RESURRECTION—STATUS OF AFFAIRS AT NAUVOO—HYDE'S REPORT FROM WASHINGTON OF THE WESTERN MOVEMENT—OREGON.

CHAPTER XVIII.

THE STATE PRESIDENTIAL CONVENTION AT NAUVOO—THE STATES REPRESENTED—SPEECH OF JOHN S. REID, ESQ.—EARLY DAYS WITH THE PROPHET.

CHAPTER XIX.

CHARGES AGAINST PRESIDENT SMITH BEFORE THE CIRCUIT COURT—HIS VOLUNTARY APPEARANCE AT COURT—TREATMENT—RETURN TO NAUVOO.

CHAPTER XX.

CASE OF JEREMIAH SMITH BEFORE MUNICIPAL COURT AT NAUVOO—AFFIDAVITS OF CRIMES OF CHAUNCEY L. HIGBEE—APPEARANCE OF THE "EXPOSITOR."

CHAPTER XXI.

THE DESTRUCTION OF THE "NAUVOO EXPOSITOR"—PROCEEDINGS OF THE NAUVOO CITY COUNCIL AND MAYOR.

CHAPTER XXII.

PRESIDENT SMITH ARRESTED FOR RIOT IN RELATION TO "EXPOSITOR" AFFAIR—HABEAS CORPUS PROCEEDINGS BEFORE MUNICIPAL COURT—A CALL FROM ARKANSAS—THE PROPHET'S DREAMS — MASS MEETING AT WARSAW — LETTERS TO GOVERNOR FORD ON "EXPOSITOR" AFFAIR.

CHAPTER XXIII.

DISCOURSE OF THE PROPHET—THE GODHEAD—THE MOB UPRISING—ARREST OF PRESIDENT SMITH ET AL. OVER THE "EXPOSITOR" AFFAIR BEFORE ESQUIRE WELLS.

CHAPTER XXIV.

RUMORS OF INVASION FROM MISSOURI—THE LEGION ORDERED TO ASSIST THE CITY MARSHAL—NAUVOO PLACED UNDER MARTIAL LAW—THE MAYOR'S ADDRESS TO THE LEGION.

CHAPTER XXV.

ATTEMPTS TO DRAFT SAINTS INTO MOB SERVICE AGAINST NAUVOO—THREATENED INVASION FROM MISSOURI—JAMES A. BENNETT URGED TO COME TO NAUVOO.

CHAPTER XXVI.

THE TWELVE CALLED FROM EASTERN MISSION—GOVERNOR FORD AT CARTHAGE—NAUVOO DELEGATION TO GOVERNOR—THREATS AND CONSPIRACY AGAINST THE PROPHET'S LIFE — GOVERNOR FORD INVITED TO NAUVOO TO INVESTIGATE CONDITIONS.

CHAPTER XXVII.

PREPARATIONS TO DEFEND NAUVOO—MOB MOVEMENTS ON CARTHAGE ROAD — GOVERNOR FORD'S REVIEW OF HANCOCK COUNTY DIFFICULTIES—JOSEPH SMITH'S ACCOUNT OF THE SAME DIFFICULTIES—DEFENSE OF HIS OWN AND ASSOCIATES' COURSE.

CHAPTER XXVIII.

GOVERNOR FORD'S WRONG VIEWPOINT—ELDER TAYLOR'S ACCOUNT OF THE INTERVIEW WITH THE GOVERNOR AT CARTHAGE—CLOSE OF THE PROPHET'S JOURNAL NARRATIVE OF HIS LIFE.

CHAPTER XXIX

THE PROPHET STARTS FOR THE ROCKY MOUNTAINS—THE COUNSEL OF FALSE BRETHREN—THE RETURN TO NAUVOO—THE SURRENDER AND ARRIVAL AT CARTHAGE.

CHAPTER XXX.

ARREST OF JOSEPH AND HYRUM SMITH ON A CHARGE OF TREASON—FALSE IMPRISONMENT—ELDER TAYLOR'S PROTEST—FALSE IMPRISONMENT.

CHAPTER XXXI.

INTERVIEW IN CARTHAGE PRISON BETWEEN GOVERNOR FORD AND THE PROPHET—TAYLOR'S REPORT OF THE INTERVIEW—TESTIMONY TO THE EXISTENCE OF A CARTHAGE CONSPIRACY AGAINST THE PROPHET'S LIFE.

CHAPTER XXXII.

THE PROPHET IN CARTHAGE PRISON—THE UNION OF JUDICIAL, EXECUTIVE, AND MILITARY AUTHORITY IN DEALING WITH THE PRISONERS—THE LAST NIGHT IN PRISON.

CHAPTER XXXIII.

THE DAY OF THE MARTYRDOM—THREATS—REPEATED WARNINGS OF THE PRISONERS' DANGER GIVEN TO GOVERNOR FORD—THE CARTHAGE GREYS AS GUARDS.

CHAPTER XXXIV.

DEPARTURE OF GOVERNOR FORD FOR NAUVOO—THE AFTERNOON IN CARTHAGE PRISON—THE ASSAULT ON THE PRISON—THE MARTYRDOM OF JOSEPH AND HYRUM SMITH.

CHAPTER XXXV.

GOVERNOR FORD IN NAUVOO—NEWS OF THE MARTYRDOM MESSAGE TO NAUVOO—ARRIVAL OF THE BODIES—SORROWFUL SCENES—THE BURIAL.

INTRODUCTION.

I. The Time Period.

The time-period covered in this sixth volume of the HISTORY OF THE CHURCH is less than one year. Nine months and twenty-eight days, to be exact; or from the 1st of September, 1843, to the 29th of June, 1844. Events within this period are therefore given in elaborate detail. The general reader and the student of our history will find in this volume a larger collection of documents, official and otherwise, covering this period, than will be found elsewhere.

This volume also closes the first Period of our Church History, the period marked off by two events: (1) the birth of the Prophet Joseph Smith; and (2) his martyrdom and that of his brother Hyrum, at Carthage, Illinois.

The Journal History of the Prophet, that great source of historical knowledge concerning the development of the New Dispensation, closes with his entry of the 22nd of June, 1844. After that, for our knowledge of the remaining events of the Prophet's life, we are dependent upon collections of *data* by the Church historians from public and private sources, of which collections there are two: the first extends from the 22nd of June to the 29th of that month, and forms the concluding chapters of this volume; the second begins also with the 22nd of June, and extends to the 8th of August, 1844; at which time the Twelve Apostles were sustained for the time being as the presiding council of the Church. This second collection of *data* by the Church historians will open Volume VII of this HISTORY.

In the present volume we see the Prophet's brave struggle against the overwhelming odds of his foes—foes within the Church, false brethren; and foes without the Church—the combination of political and sectarian enemies fixed in their determination to kill him, destroy Nauvoo, and expel the Saints from Illinois: for all these things were included in the program of the anti-Mormons of Illinois, even before the death of the Prophet was encompassed. Three score and seven years now give perspective to the stirring events in which the really great drama was enacted; and from that vantage ground of perspective said events may be reviewed to the enlightenment of those who seek to know the truth, and the injustice of the things enacted in Illinois during the closing months of the Prophet Joseph's earthly carèer.

II. Why the Latter-day Saints were Welcomed to Illinois.

On the one hand, in the above mentioned struggle, was a people who but a few years before had been welcomed into Illinois as exiles from a neighboring state, the victims of a cruel and ignorant intolerance. They were welcomed, in part, because of the injustice to which they had been subjected in a neighboring state, and because their physical sufferings, arising from want of shelter and food in an inclement season of the year to which they were exposed, was such as to move adamantine hearts to pity. Also they were welcomed because, as pointed out in the Introduction to Volume IV of this HISTORY, the state of Illinois needed augmentation of her population by just such a people as the Latter-day Saints were—industrious, frugal, skilled mechanics, successful farmers, experienced men of affairs, men capable of trade and commerce, enterprising and with a larger proportion of educated men and women among them than was to be found among the people of western Illinois in those days. I do not here employ the language of adulation on the one hand, nor seek to make invidious distinctions upon the other. Either would be vain, since the well-known and accepted facts of history would disprove the declarations made if not founded in truth. The fact is, however, that all that is claimed above for the Missouri exiled Latter-day Saints is true and well-attested by their achievements in settling Nauvoo, which in four years rose from a ware-house or two and a few half tumble-down shacks on the banks of the river, and called "Commerce," to the dignity of being the first city in Illinois in population and commercial enterprise, and also gave promise of developing into a manufacturing center of great importance. This last item was evidenced in the fact that the founder of Nauvoo, President Joseph Smith, and the Nauvoo city council appreciated the possibilities in the water power of the Lower Des Moines Rapids in the Mississippi, at the head of which the city was located. Reference to his journal entry for the 23rd of September (this volume, p. 80) will witness that he suggested that a petition be sent to the national Congress for the construction of a canal around the rapids to overcome the obstruction for the free passage of river craft, which the rapids prevented during the low water period of each year, and thus enhance the value of the great stream to the inland commerce of the west.* Reference again to President Smith's journal

* That the general government of the United States has since constructed such a canal from Keokuk to Montrose, directly opposite Nauvoo on the west, and at a cost of more than four and a half million dollars, completing it in 1877, is noted in this volume, p. 80 and foot note.

entry for the 8th of December, 1843 (this volume, p. 103) will disclose the fact that he gave instruction in the forenoon to his clerk to draw a plan for a dam in the Mississippi; and that in the afternoon of the same day the city council met and passed an ordinance authorizing Joseph Smith to "erect a dam of suitable height to propel mills and machinery from any point within the limits of said city, and below the Nauvoo House;" also in connection with this dam to construct a "harbor or basin for steamboats and other craft;" and to construct docks, wharfs and landings," the wharfage fees to be "regulated by ordinance of said city (this volume p. 106).

III. Nauvoo as a Possible Manufacturing Center.

What further contributed to the promise that Nauvoo would be a great manufacturing center as well as the center of an immense agricultural region with a splendid commercial outlet, was the fact that artisans and tradesmen of the very first order in skill, were rapidly gathering into the city, not only from the New England and other Eastern states of our own country, but also from the British Isles. It was inevitable if let alone that Nauvoo would become the greatest manufacturing center of Illinois, and among the first of such cities in the United States. The Prophet did not live to see even a commencement made upon these large enterprises he had conceived, but subsequently his zealous followers organized a company to carry them to a successful conclusion under the title of "The Nauvoo Water Power Company,"* which began the construction of the dam on the 29th of April, 1845; but which had to be abandoned because of the hostilities that soon after increased and continued until they culminated in the expulsion of the Latter-day Saints from Illinois.†

* See *Nauvoo Neighbor* for March 5th and March 12th. John E. Page was president of the company; and in a communication to the *Neighbor* (March 12, 1845) urging a vigorous prosecution of the enterprise, he said:

"We have commenced active operations for the building of a dam in the river, as noticed in the *Neighbor* of last week. * * *

"Here is the proud and gallant Mississippi, with her rapid current, tumbling to the broad Atlantic, seeming to say (as she quickens her pace over the rugged rocks of the lower rapids just opposite to our beautiful Nauvoo) only improve my shores and banks, ye Saints, as ye improve my neighboring soil; and I will propel your mills, cotton and woollen manufactories, by which your laborers can find employ, and your poor can be clothed and fed."

† As the suggestion of Joseph Smith for building the canal around the Des Moines Rapids by the general government of the United States was carried out; so also is the water power of the Des Moines Rapids being utilized for manufacturing and other purposes, first suggested by the Prophet, but now, of course, in a way and on a larger scale than it was possible even for men to dream of when the

In addition to these measures, manufacturing and agricultural associations were incorporated; also the "Nauvoo House Associations" for the erection of a hotel,ambitious to be known as the finest hostelry in the Upper Mississippi country. One of the agricultural associations, known as the "Big Field Corporation," held six sections, or three thousand eight hundred and forty acres of land east of Nauvoo; and the year following the Prophet's death the company harvested about thirty thousand bushels of corn, nearly the same amount of wheat, besides an "abundance of oats, barley, buckwheat. potatoes and other vegetables.*

IV. Educational Measures at Nauvoo.

And not only in material things was the superior character of Nauvoo's founders and builders proclaimed; but equally broad and comprehensive were their preparations for an educational system. By their city charter they were empowered to establish an institution of learning within the limits of the city for the teaching of the arts and sciences and learned professions, to be called the "University of the City of Nauvoo;" also a common school system for the city, all of which was in course of development even in the early years of Nauvoo's existence. And in addition to these direct educational institutions of common schools and projected university, literary and dramatic associations were organized, as also choral and band organizations for the cultivation of musical talents and to promote the pleasure and refinement of society; while the religious zeal of the community expressed itself in the rapidly rising walls of the splendid temple—soon to be the most solid and pretentious building in the state; and in the tireless missionary enterprise of the dominant Church.

city council of Nauvoo, in 1843, authorized the construction of a dam to harness this power in the Mississippi for the service of man. This, however, is now nearly an accomplished fact through the enterprise of the Keokuk and Hamilton Water Power Company, which, between Hamilton on the Illinois side, and Keokuk on the Iowa side of the Mississippi (eight or nine miles below Nauvoo), has in course of construction a dam which, including abutments, will be 4,700 feet in length, will stand 32 feet above the river bed, and be 42 feet wide at its base, built of solid concrete. In connection with the dam, and incident to it will be wharfage and a large drydock for the construction and repair of floating craft. There will be developed and for sale as the result of this enterprise, 200,000 horsepower for the service of St. Louis and other towns of Missouri, Illinois and Iowa. The dam and power house will be built at a cost of $22,000,000.

* See "History of the Mormon Church," *Americana* magazine, number for January, 1911, Ch. LIX; also Elder John Taylor's Journal entry for 5th of September, 1844.

V. Jealousy of Nauvoo's Promising Greatness.

Nothing was lacking, then, in the promises of constant and rapid growth, of prosperity and future greatness of Nauvoo. Small wonder if the narrow bigotry and jealousy of small-souled men of the time and vicinity—especially those who were inhabitants of rival towns, particularly those of Warsaw and Carthage—were envious of Nauvoo's prosperity and promise of future greatness. Hitherto this element of jealousy of Nauvoo's prosperity and promise of future greatness has not been accorded the importance due to it as a contributing cause to the warfare made upon that city and the Saints. Little doubt, however, can be entertained, now attention has been called to it, but what as a contributing cause jealousy of Nauvoo stood next to religious prejudice and political distrust and hatred.

A correspondent from Fair Haven, Connecticut, to a gentleman in Nauvoo, set forth this matter most convincingly. An excerpt of the letter was published in the *Nauvoo Neighbor* of August 7th, 1844. It is proper to say that the writer was not a member of the Mormon Church; "but," as the editor of the *Neighbor* describes him, "a citizen of Connecticut, loving law and liberty and life;" and now the paragraph dealing with the point under discussion:

"It is now known here that the lazy speculators of Warsaw, and the still lazier office drones at Carthage, cared nothing for Joseph Smith personally, or for his tenets either; but the prosperity of Nauvoo increasing as it did, beyond any former parallel, even in the western world, excited in their bosoms envy, hatred and all ungodliness. This is the true secret of all their barbarous movements against Mormonism—and they supposed by destroying the Smiths they should extinguish their religion, disperse the Mormons—depopulating and desolating Nauvoo."

Also a correspondent to the *State Register* published at Springfield, Illinois, speaking of Thomas C. Sharp, editor of the *Warsaw Signal* and the anti-Mormon disturbances in Hancock county said:

"He [Sharp] is also described as having made himself the 'organ of a gang of town lot speculators at Warsaw,' who are afraid that Nauvoo is about to kill off their town and render speculation abortive."*

Mr. Backenstos in January, 1845, when the repeal of the Nauvoo Charter was under discussion in the Illinois legislature, referred to this same subject in a speech on the floor of the house of representatives, in the course of which he said;

"Town rivalry had also something to do with this opposition to Nauvoo. While Warsaw was on the decline, Nauvoo was rapidly in-

*The *Register* article is copied into the the *Nauvoo Neighbor* for November 13th, 1844.

creasing in wealth and population; a plan to bring about a re-action was soon concocted by the leading men of Warsaw, who made one pilgrimage after another to Nauvoo, imploring the Mormon Prophet to aid them in building up a city adjoining the town of Warsaw, by settling a portion of the Mormon population in and about Warsaw, and commence the building of a new city. The bubble soon exploded, and the speculation failed. This gave rise to dissatisfaction with some who had heretofore been exceedingly polite to '*Lieutenant General Joseph Smith!*' "*

Thus in every way, to refer back to the point of starting the discussion of this subdivision, the Latter-day Saints are proven by their achievements and the foundations they laid for the future greatness of their city, to be a superior people, and hence a desirable addition to the population of the then-young commonwealth of Illinois.

VI. The Character of the People of Western Illinois.

On the other hand there was a population in western Illinois, and perhaps more especially in Hancock county, which had more than its full share of lawless and desperate men; who, as by a law of social gravitation, seek the frontiers of civilization. Moreover it is notorious that the whole upper Mississippi was a rendezvous for gamblers, counterfeiters, horse thieves, murderers and other criminals that infested the great river, which gave easy ingress and egress to a frontier wilderness on the one hand, and to such centers of population and activity, on the other, as New Orleans, St. Louis, and many minor places, besides. "I must give some account of the anti-Mormons," says Governor Ford in his History of Illinois, when referring to the inhabitants of Hancock county. "I had a good opportunity to know the settlers of Hancock county," he continues. "I had attended the circuit courts there as state's attorney, from 1830, when the county was first organized, up to 1834; and to my certain knowledge the early settlers, with some honorable exceptions, were in popular language, hard cases" (page 406). Then for a period of several years to the advent of the "Mormons" he had no means of knowing the character of the people who drifted into the country: "But," he adds, "having passed my whole life on the frontier, on the outer edge of the settlements, I have frequently seen that a few first settlers would fix the character of a settlement for good or for bad, for many years after its commencement. If bad men began the settlement, bad men would be attracted to them, upon the well known principle that birds of a feather will flock together. Rogues will find each other out, and so will honest men. From all which it appears extremely probable, that the later

**Nauvoo Neighbor*, March 12th, 1845.

immigrants were many of them attracted to Hancock by a secret sympathy between them and the early settlers."

Indeed the governor suggests that it may have been "the promptings of a secret instinct," which led the "Mormons" to "discern their fellows" and induced them to settle in Hancock in preference to other localities open to them. All which may be regarded as an ingenious thrust at the Latter-day Saints, but which fails of reaching its mark from the fact that it was the criminal element chiefly in Hancock county's population which arrayed itself in antagonism against the Saints, and against whom they were arrayed in all their conflicts in that county. Whereas, under the governor's theory, this criminal element among the "old citizens" and the Saints should have been as hand in glove in their co-operation of encompassing evil things. But to the contrary; from the time the "Mormons" appeared on the scenes at Commerce, in 1839, until they were expelled, they steadfastly and emphatically set their faces against the evils that cursed that community, and denounced all manner of evil both as manifested in a few of their own delinquent members, apostates and camp followers who trailed after the main body of the Church from Missouri, as well as in others: such as dram-drinking, swearing, Sabbath-breaking, contracting debts under pretense of poverty and distress without any prospects or intention of paying,* and especially did they denounce stealing, under any and all pretexts what soever.†

And as it was largely the criminal element among the "old citizens" that was arrayed against the Saints (with unprincipled politicians and a few bigoted and jealous religious leaders added), so was it the conservative and law-abiding portion of the community among whom they had many friends; and nearly all of whom were at least so far friendly with the Saints that they could not be induced to oppose them, much less join in acts of mob violence to the injury of their persons or property; for which reason this portion of the non-Mormon population were called by the contemptuous name of "Jack-Mormons," which epithet was invented by the editor of the Warsaw *Signal*, Thomas C. Sharp, who also originated the term "Jack-Mason" when editing an anti-Masonic paper in western New York. In all probability it was this second name which suggested the first.

*See John Taylor's communication to the Quincy *Argus*, May 1st, 1839. HISTORY OF THE CHURCH, Vol. III, Chapter XXIII.

†See Denunciation of Thieves, 1844, by Hyrum Smith; by President Smith and the formal action of the Apostles quorum, this HISTORY Vol. IV, Chapter XVII. Also the minutes of the conference held at Nauvoo April, 1843, this HISTORY, Vol V, Chapter XVII.

VII. Educational Status of the People of Western Illinois.

Education among the masses of Hancock's non-Mormon population was of the meagrest kind. Even Mr. Gregg, the historian of the county, who always gives the best report possible of conditions, remarks, when treating of the county's educational status, that "a new country and among pioneers, is not the place where prosperous colleges and seminaries, or even high schools, are actually found. Hence common schools and, in many instances, very 'common' ones at that, were the best means of education in Hancock county in early days," But this is said of the schools of Hancock county; the greater number of the adult population, 1839-1846, which represent the years when the Saints lived in the county, had migrated from states where educational opportunities were even fewer and less advanced than in western Illinois. Even some of the men prominent in political life in the state were men of extremely limited education. Joseph Duncan, elected governor of Illinois in 1834, and who had served four terms in Congress previous to his election as governor, had but a limited education," says Gregg.* And of Thomas Carlin, who was the governor of Illinois when the exiled Saints moved into the state—he had previously held many minor offices—the same authority says: "He had but a meager education."†

But while the above represents the educational conditions both among the masses of Hancock county and western Illinois in general, and of some of the men in public life, it is also true that there were here and there men in Hancock and surrounding counties of good education and enlightened culture, such as Stephen A. Douglas, O. H. Browning, Major Warren, John J. Hardin, General Minor R. Deming, Samuel Marshal, Judge Jesse B. Thomas, Josiah Lamborn, Governor Ford and others.

VIII. The Political Phase.

It has already been observed in these volumes (Vol. IV, Introduction) that in addition to the Latter-day Saints being welcomed into Illinois on account of their economic value in a newly and sparsely settled country, as wealth creators through their industry, frugality and skill in mechanics and husbandry, political parties of Illinois both Whigs and Democrats vied with each other in heartiness of welcome, each hoping to profit by the influx of the new population in both state

*History of Hancock County, p. 158.
†Ibid.

and national elections. Hence it was possible to obtain for Nauvoo the exceptiona powers that constituted her, under the letter of her charter, an autonomy within the limits of her boundaries more akin to a sovereign state than to a municipality within a state and a county. And such were the powers claimed for her by her founders.* Hence also that catering to the misconception and wrong interpretations of the chartered powers of Nauvoo by lawyers and politicians seeking professional and political favors of the people, which encouraged the belief that the city government was the omnipotent political power within the city limits; and that her municipal court was not only equal to, but even superior to the state courts—"for all other courts were restricted," it was contended, while the municipal court of Nauvoo was not restricted! Similar claims of absolutism were made respecting the city council as a law-making power; and thus were the people of Nauvoo misled by their legal and political advisers, who gave false counsel instead of true, and who encouraged the people in their prejudices and flattered their vanity rather than corrected their errors by an appeal to sound judgment and to the law.

IX. Mischief Arising from False Legal and Political Counsel.

Much mischief arose from this source. It was because of these misconceptions in respect of the character of their city government that led to the enactment of those ill advised and unwarranted city ordinances—

That made gold and silver alone legal tender within the city;

That declared Joseph Smith exempt from arrest on requisitions from Missouri founded upon the old difficulties in that state, and providing that persons making an attempt to arrest him might be taken with or without process, imprisoned for life, and might not be pardoned by the governor without consent of the mayor;†

That authorized the city council, marshal, constables and city watch to require all strangers entering the city or already tarrying there to give their names, former residence and for what intent they were tarrying in the city, and answer such other questions as the officers respectively deemed proper to ask; refusal to give the desired information, or giving false names or information subjected them to the same penalties as "vagrants and disorderly persons;"

That further authorized and required the above named officers to

* See this HISTORY Vol. V, Ch. xxiv and Vol. IV. Introduction pp, xxii *et seq.*

† This ordinance about a month after its enactment was repealed at the suggestion of President Smith. See this volume pp. 55-6.

"hail and take all persons found strolling about the city at night after nine o'clock and before sunrise, and to confine them in ward for trial under the ordinances concerning vagrants and disorderly persons, unless they could give a good account of themselves for being out "after nine o'clock;"

That further authorized and required the aforesaid officers to enter all hotels or houses of public entertainment, and such other habitations as they may judge proper, and require the inmates to give immediate information of all persons residing in said hotel or habitation, and their business, occupation or movements, under penalty of forfeiture of license, if a public house, and they and the transient persons subject to the penalties visited upon vagrants for failure to give the information required, or giving false information; while the officer who should "refuse or neglect to perform the above duties should be fined $100, and be broke of his office;"

That forbade the search and seizure of person or property by foreign process [*i. e.* other process than that issuing from the city's authority] within the city of Nauvoo, leading to the widespread belief that the design of said ordinance was "to hinder the execution of the statutes of Illinois" within said city;*

That asked the general government to ratify the Nauvoo Charter, and in addition constitute the city a territorial government, by granting "all rights, powers, privileges and immunities belonging to territories and not repugnant to the constitution of the United States," with power granted to the mayor to call to his aid a sufficient number of the United States troops, in connection with the Nauvoo Legion, to repel the invasion of mobs, keep the public peace, protect the innocent from lawless banditti; the United States officers to obey the requisition of this ordinance; and the Nauvoo Legion, when in service quelling mobs and preserving the public peace, to be under the same regulations, ru es and laws of pay as the troops of the United States; the territorial privileges to continue until the "state of Missouri restores to those exiled citizens [the Latter-day Saints] the lands, rights, privileges, property, and damages for all losses" they had sustained by being banished from that commonwealth;†

And, finally, that asserted the right of the municipal court to arrest

* This alleged "design" of the ordinance President Smith specifically denied in the open session of the city council, and to a committee of lawyers from Carthage, who waited upon the city council to protest against this ordinance; and the ordinance was amended by a third section disclaiming such alleged intention, but still retaining the feature that forced state process to be served through the agency of Nauvoo's city officers. See this vol. pp. 173-4.

† This volume pp. 130-132.

process issued by the state's circuit courts, and even by the United States courts, by *habeas corpus* proceedings; and insisted, not only upon the right to pass judgment upon the sufficiency of writs under which arrests were made, but upon the right also to go behind the writs and try the cases upon their merits.

X. *Subserviency of Politicians and Lawyers.*

Blame for this political subserviency and misleading political and legal advice, may not be charged on one party more than another. If Cyrus Walker, a Whig candidate for congress, assented to the doctrine as understood by Nauvoo's leading men, that the municipal court of Nauvoo held the power under *habeas corpus* procedure to arrest execution of process of the state courts, as he did,* so, too, did Joseph P. Hoge, Democratic nominee; and even Governor Ford, when requested to call out the militia to rearrest Joseph Smith after he had been liberated from the custody of Sheriff Reynolds, agent of Missouri, under *habeas corpus* proceedings, took refuge behind the *habeas corpus* proceedings of the Municipal Court at Nauvoo. In that case the court not only inquired into the sufficiency of the writ of requisition from Missouri, and granted by Governor Ford himself, but also went back of the writ and tried the case *exparte* on its merits, and finally discharged the prisoner, both "for want of substance in the warrant, * * * as well as upon the merits of the case."† When answering the request of Missouri to rearrest Joseph Smith, Governor Ford, I say, at least took refuge behind the aforesaid proceedings of the Municipal Court to the extent of saying, in the face of that procedure, that "no process, officer or authority of Illinois had been resisted or interfered with,"‡ and therefore refused to call out the militia to rearrest President Smith.

It is but fair to Governor Ford, however, to say that in his inaugural speech of December 8th, 1842, he pointed out what he regarded as objectionable features in the Nauvoo charter, and recommended its modification.§ and later censured the lawyers for misleading the Nauvoo city authorities in this matter, in the following passage from a letter to the Mayor and City Council of Nauvoo, under date of June 22nd, 1844.

You have also assumed to yourselves more power than you are entitled to in relation to *habeas corpus* under your charter. I know that you have been told by lawyers, for the purpose of gaining your favor,

* This HISTORY Vol. V, pp. 467-8, 472.

† This HISTORY, Vov. V. pp. 473-4.

‡ See Ford's letter to Thomas Reynolds, Governor of Missouri, under date of August 14, 1843. This HISTORY, Vol. V, pp. 553-6.

§ Ibid p. 200.

that you have this power to any extent. In this they have deceived you for their own base purposes. Your charter supposes that you may pass ordinances, a breach of which will result in the imprisonment of the offender.

For the purpose of giving more speedy relief to such persons authority was given to the Municipal Court to issue writs of *habeas corpus* in all cases arising under the ordinances of the city.

It was never supposed by the Legislature, nor can the language of your charter be tortured to mean that a jurisdiction was intended to be conferred which would apply to all cases of imprisonment under the general laws of the state or of the United States, as well as the city ordinances.

To which President Smith replied:

Whatever power we have exercised in the *habeas corpus* has been done in accordance with the letter of the Charter and Constitution as we confidently understood them; and that, too, with the ablest counsel; but if it be so that we have erred in this thing, let the Supreme Court correct the evil. We have never gone contrary to constitutional law, so far as we have been able to learn it. If lawyers have belied their profession to abuse us the evil be on their heads.*

XI The Fate of a Balance of Power Factor in Politics.

Being misled by false legal and political advice was not the only misfortune of the kind perpetrated upon the Saints, first by the subserviency of, and then the betrayal by, politicians and lawyers. The hope of both parties to secure political advantage by the influx of the new Latter-day Saint population into the state has been already referred to; as also the efforts of both parties to gain their favor by granting exceptional favors to them in founding Nauvoo. When, however, the time for voting came, and the Saints voted according to their convictions of duty, or as their inclinations prompted, the defeated party or candidates blamed them for the defeat, and straightway favored the adoption of an anti-Mormon policy, which found support not only in the defeated party, but also among those who felt a grievance against the Saints on other accounts; some because Nauvoo's prosperity and constantly increasing importance as a center of population and trade and commerce was rapidly eclipsing all other towns of the state; and others, over-anxious to retard, if not destroy, a rival system on account of religious prejudice. When an anti-Mormon party took the field, pledged itself to repeal the Nauvoo charter, and to drive the Mormons from the state—as was the pledge of Joseph Duncan, Whig candidate for Governor of Illinois in 1841,† there was really no other course for the Saints to pursue but to combine solidly for the defeat of the candidate and

* This HISTORY, Vol. VI. Ch. XXVI, where both letters will be found at length.

† See Ford's *History of Illinois*, p. 269; also this HISTORY, Vol IV, pp. 479-481 and footnotes; Vol. V, p. 490.

party making such pledges; the instinct of self-preservation impelled such a course, rather than the prompting of inclination.

For a time, as in all such cases, the party receiving the support of this practically solid Mormon vote could be relied upon to protect and defend those who had made success possible for them; but at the first indication that the hold of the favored party upon such vote is precarious, that there is a possibility that it might go to the other side,* naturally the ardor of their friendship, seldom or never sincere, cools; and they are as ready to combine for the destruction of their former allies as others have been. And when in addition to precariousness of hold upon those who possess the balance of power there stands up in the back ground of things the possibility that the balance of power party may become strong enough in the political subdivision in which they are located to run affairs on their own account, the likelihood of all parties combining against them becomes all the more assured. In Illinois the Latter-day Saints ran the entire political gamut of experience as a "balance of power" factor in the politics of western Illinois. The final phase of that experience had been reached when at a mass meeting held at Carthage on the sixth of September, 1843, it was—

Resolved, That as it has been too common for several years past for politicians of both political parties, not only of this county, but likewise of the state, to go to Nauvoo and truckle to the heads of the Mormon clan for their influence, we pledge ourselves that we will not support any man of either party in the future who shall thus debase himself.†

Politicians still sought Mormon aid to encompass their own political ends, but, as Governor Ford later remarked, '"they were willing and anxious for Mormon voters at elections, but they were unwilling to risk their popularity with the people, by taking part in their favor even when law and justice, and the Constitution, were all on their side;"† and

*Such appeared to be the very great probability in the election of 1843. As will be remembered by the readers of Vol. IV of this HISTORY, Cyrus Walker, Esq., Whig candidate for Congress, rendered valuable service in delivering the Prophet from the hands of those bent upon running him into Missouri for trial on the old complaint against him in that state. That service could only be obtained in that crisis by Joseph Smith pledging himself to vote for Walker, which was interpreted to meam, of course, the Mormon vote; and it was generally conceded that the Whigs receiving the Mormon vote would be successful. Before the day of election, however, there had arisen strong reasons for believing that the arrest of the Prophet and the effort to take him to Missouri, as also Walker's appearance upon the scene to effect his liberation, was itself a political trick to secure the Mormon vote for the Whig party, which was thwarted by the Mormons voting, at the last moment, the Democratic ticket. (See Vol. V, Chapter XXVI).

†Ford's History of Illinois, p. 364.

so finally all parties turned against them, and they were at tne last, as we shall see in a future volume of this history, expelled without mercy from the state.

XII. Joseph Smith's Candidacy for the Presidency.

The mischief that threatened during the Prophet's life time, and which finally befell the Saints, was clearly foreseen by the Church leaders; and the desire to escape from the threatening portents of it prompted the nomination of Joseph Smith for the office of President of the United States, in the general election of 1844. Of course there could be no hope seriously entertained that he would be elected; but, as explained by an editorial in the *Times and Seasons*,* if the Saints could not succeed in electing their candidate, they would have the satisfaction of knowing that they had acted conscientiously; they had used their best judgment, under the circumstances, and if they had to throw away their votes, it was better to do so upon a worthy than upon an unworthy individual who might use the weapon they put into his hand to destroy them. The Prophet himself evidently regarded his nomination humorously rather than seriously, except that it might result in withdrawing the Saints from the position of shuttle-cock between the battle doors of the two old political parties. "I care but little about the presidential chair," he said on one occasion. "I would not give half as much for the office of President of the United States as I would for the one I now hold as Lieutenant General of the Nauvoo Legion." Again he said: "When I get hold of eastern papers, and see how popular I am; I am afraid myself that I shall be elected; but if I should be, I would not say [*i. e.* to the Latter-day Saints] your cause is just but I can do nothing for you."

As a further evidence that Joseph Smith did not regard his candidacy as likely to be successful, he was, at the time of his nomination and afterwards, pushing vigorously his project of a western movement for the Church. He had drawn up a memorial and ordinance to the national congress asking to be authorized by the general government to raise one hundred thousand armed volunteers to police the intermountain and Pacific coast west from Oregon to Texas, for the purpose of assuring Texas her independence, and maintaining the claims of the United States to Oregon, and affording the whole western population of our country protection from Indian depredations; and thus contribute to the rapid settlement and development of that noble extent of country lyıng between the Mississippi and the Pacific Ocean. His agents, Orson Hyde and Orson Pratt, presented the matter to sen-

*See this volume, pp. 214-217, where the editorial is given *in extenso*.

ators and representatives at Washington, and a number favored the project of the removal of the Mormons to the west, but generally urged that Joseph Smith go without seeking special authorization from the government. Reference to Orson Hyde's report of the procedure among congressmen and their views upon the subject will be found in his two important communications to the Prophet from Washington, in chapter XVI of this volume. Mr. John Wentworth, representative to Congress from northern Illinois, introduced President Smith's Memorial and Ordinance into the House on the 25th of May, to be read for the information of the House; but before the reading was concluded, objection was made, and as it required unanimous consent to have it read, further reading was prevented. A vote to suspend the rules in order that Mr. Wentworth might secure the reading of the memorial stood 79 yeas, and 86 nays, which vote gives evidence at least of a wide-spread desire to have the matter presented to the House.*

XIII. Missouri as a Factor in the Affairs of Nauvoo.

In addition to all the Illinois factors that entered into the complex situation confronting the Saints at Nauvoo, at the time of the Prophet's death, and some time previous to his arrest, was the attitude and course pursued by Missouri with reference to Nauvoo and the Saints, Disgraced as a state by her own conduct towards the Latter-day Saints, when they were inhabitants within her borders, her people were all too willing to co-operate with any party or agency that would continue to make war upon them. If the state of Illinois which with open arms had received the people that Missouri exiled from her borders, under such circumstances of cruelty, could also be brought to drive them from that state, it would be regarded, in a way, as a vindication of Missouri and the course she had taken in her treatment of the Saints, since in effect it would say, that the people of Illinois, no less than the people of Missouri, found it impossible to tolerate the "Mormons;" and therefore there must be something fundamentally wrong with them, rather than with the people of these states. Hence the anti-Mormons of Hancock and adjoining counties in Illinois, always found support in whatever of violence or wrong they planned against the Saints. Hence the constant threats of invasion of mobs from Missouri, emphasized by occasional kidnapping expeditions into Hancock county, together with frequent requisitions upon the Illinois authorities for the arrest and extradition of Joseph Smith on the old charges against him in Missouri. And these

*See Chapter XI, this volume, where the memorial itself, Hyde's two letters and the action in the House of Representatives will he found in full.

Missouri threats and outrages were not among the least of the annoyances and anxieties of the Saints; and they make clear tue necessity that was felt for an efficient militia force at Nauvoo. Hence the Nauvoo Legion and the lively interest manifested in its frequent musters and drills, and its thorough equipment; all of which, but for the constant danger of invasion from Missouri mobs, and the co-operation with them of like forces in Illinois, would have been inconsistent with the deportment of a religious community whose mission was one of peace and good will towards men; and who had been especially commanded to "renounce war and proclaim peace" (Doc and Cov. Sec. 98, 16); and commanded also to "sue for peace," both to those who had "smitten" them—the revelation was given after the expulsion from Jackson county, Missouri—and "to all people;" and "lift up an ensign of peace, and make a proclamation of peace unto the ends of the earth" (Doc. and Cov. sec 105: 38-40). But invasions from Missouri constantly menacing them, and the danger of mob violence breaking out in Illinois, justified the organization of the Legion, and the maintenance of its efficiency by full equipment of arms and frequent drills and musters; for the right of self-preservation is not abrogated by any divine law given to the Saints; and duty to protect home and family against the assaults of the evil-disposed, presses as firmly upon the Saints, as upon those who have not definitely pledged themselves to a program of righteousness.

XIV. Apostate Conspirators at Nauvoo.

One other factor only remains to be mentioned of those that enter into that combination of forces that resulted in the death of the Prophet and the Patriarch. That is the conspiracy of apostates within Nauvoo itself.

The apostates and their sympathizers were headed by a coterie of prominent young men: The two Law brothers, William and Wilson; Robert D. and Charles A. Foster, brothers; Francis M. and Chauncey L. Higbee, brothers, and unworthy sons of that most faithful man and the Prophet's devoted friend, Judge Elias Higbee (See Vol. IV pp. 81-100 *passim*); Sylvester Emmons and Joseph H. Jackson. Of these, William Law was counselor in the First Presidency, and Wilson Law was a major general, and commander of one of the cohorts of the Nauvoo Legion, and all were or had been more or less prominent in the public life of Nauvoo.

The cause of their apostasy seems to have been the baneful influence of John C. Bennett's immoralities; for these men were quite generally associates of his before his flight from Nauvoo. They evidently lost the spirit of the gospel, wandered through sin into spiritual darkness, and seemingly were obsessed by a murderous spirit against the Prophet who boldly revealed their wickedness and publicly denounced their conduct; and in retaliation this coterie of apostates entered into conspiracies to encompass President Smith's death, and that of his brother Hyrum. They were in communication with the Prophet's enemies in Missouri, and sought to betray him into their hands. They were among the chief actors in all schemes of opposition and conspiracies against him in the closing year of his life, including those plots which eventuated in the martyrdom of both Prophet and Patriarch at Carthage.

XV. The "Expositor" Affair.

Such are the chief factors that enter into the combination of events detailed in this volume of HISTORY and which have a direct relationship to the martyrdom of the Smith brothers. They existed as combustible matarials awaiting only the spark that would set them aflame to work death and destruction.

The spark came. It came in the destruction of the *Nauvoo Expositor*, published by the above mentioned coterie of apostates. It was the intention of the *Expositor*, as its name would indicate, to make an *expose* of alleged conditions in Nauvoo, in the moral, social, religious and political phase of them. Also to agitate for the "*unconditional repeal of the Nauvoo Charter*." This was a challenge to mortal combat, the issue being the life of the city of Nauvoo; and after that the question of the existence of the Church in Illinois, or even within the confines of the United States; for undoubtedly the city charter once repealed, carrying with it the disorganization of the Legion, protection for the Saints, as matters stood in 1844, both civil and military, would be gone. It was a life and death struggle then that the advent of the *Expositor* inaugurated. The Saints stood at such disadvantage in the proposed contest that if the *Expositor* was allowed to run its course it would inevitably have won its case against the city; and against the Church, so far as the latter continuing in Illinois, and perhaps as far as its continuance in the United States was concerned.

The new marriage system, involving the practice, within certain limitations and under very special conditions, of a plurality of wives, constituted a ground of appeal to popular prejudices and passions that would have been absolutely resistless if the paper had been allowed to proceed. The charter would have been repealed; the city government destroyed, or at the least modified and placed in the hands of an apostate or anti-Mormon minority whose administration would have been intolerable to the large majority of Nauvoo's citizens; and finally the scenes of Missouri would have been re-enacted in an Illinois setting.

In the presence of such difficulties, what was to be done? In addition to declaring the existence of the practice of plural marriage, not yet announced or publicly taught as a doctrine of the Church, and agitating for the unqualified repeal of the Nauvoo charter, gross immoralities were charged against leading citizens which doubtless rendered the paper grossly libelous. In other cities such an avowed enemy as the *Expositor* was, would have been destroyed by a mob. For the people of Nauvoo to have so proceeded would have been a departure from their principles of upholding law and order, and would have brought upon them the people of the surrounding counties, and from Missouri in overwhelming numbers. Mob violence could not be thought of; and yet the safety of the community imperatively demanded the suppression of the *Expositor* at any cost.

Under these circumstances the city council met and took under consideration the *Expositor* and the necessity of destroying it. As their charter conferred upon the city the right to remove nuisances, the city council declared the *Expositor* press a nuisance and directed the Mayor to have it destroyed, which he did by giving an order to that effect, and it was destroyed without riot or tumult.

The legality of the action of the Mayor and City Council was, of course, questionable, though some sought to defend it on legal grounds; but it must be conceded that neither proof nor argument for legality are convincing. On the grounds of expediency or necessity the action is more defensible. The existence of the city, the preservation of the Latter-day Saints until provision could be made for a retreat from Illinois—which retreat was even then being provided for by the Prophet in the projected movement of the Church to the west—demanded the cessation of the publication of the *Expositor*. By proceeding at least under the forms of law, the city council, though they might be conscious of the illegality of their action,avoided the necessity of the people resorting to mob action for self-preservation, and made it possible for the legality of their course to be determined in the courts, and the parties injured to recover compensation for the press and damages by civil process. Meantime the libelous press with its mission of destruction of the Saints at Nauvoo was silenced; and had events taken the course which the action of the city council provided, a respite would have been gained from impending violence, during which arrangements for the retreat of the Saints from Illinois could have been completed and a goal of safety won for them. Under a plea, then, of absolute necessity to self-preservation of a community, and to achieve the retreat here alluded to, and with the certainty that those injured in property by the *Expositor's* destruction would be fully compensated in civil action before the courts—the action of the mayor and city council of Nauvoo is defensible, even if not on the ground of the legality of their procedure.*

XVI. The Appeal to the Mob Spirit.

Events did not take the course planned for them. The uproar that followed the destruction of the *Expositor* press, put all reason at defiance. At Warsaw a mass meeting was held which issued a statement, in connection with the resolutions it passed, that "A mob at Nauvoo, under a city ordinance, has violated the highest privilege in government; and to seek redress in the ordinary way would be utterly ineffectual * * * *Resolved*, that we hold ourselves at all times in readiness to co-operate with our fellow citizens in this state, Missouri, and Iowa, to exterminate, *utterly exterminate* the wicked and abominable Mormon leaders, the authors of our troubles. * * * The time, in our opinion, has arrived when the adherents of Smith as a body should be driven from the surrounding settlements into Nauvoo. That the Prophet and his miscreant adherents should then be demanded at their hands; and, if not surrendered, a war of extermination should be waged to the entire destruction, if necessary for our protection, of his adherents. And we hereby recommend this resolution to the consideration of the several townships, to the mass convention to be held at Carthage."

The Carthage meeting held a few days later embodied the above in their resolutions, as did other mass meetings held at various places. The *Warsaw Signal* in its impression of June 12th, passionately said:†

"We have only to state that this [i. e. The destruction of the *Expositor* press] is sufficient! War and extermination is inevitable! CITIZENS ARISE, ONE and ALL!!! Can you stand by, and suffer such INFERNAL DEVILS! to ROB men of their property rights, without avenging them? We have no time to comment: every man will make his own. LET IT BE MADE WITH POWDER and BALL!!!"

All the combustible material to which attention is called in this Introduction was instantly aflame at the destruction of the *Expositor* press. Every passion was appealed to, jealousy, envy, cupidity, hatred. All the lawless elements of the community were practically invited to

*See Chapter XXX, *passim* this volume for a discussion of the *Expositor*; also Taylor-Colfax Discussion on the "Mormon" Question, p. 20. Also an editorial from the Nauvoo *Neighbor*, see p. 496, this volume.

†I follow the typing and punctuation from the *Signal* as given by the late John Hay, secretary of state, *Atlantic Monthly* of December, 1869.

assemble and run riot in lawless violence, and excess of carnage and destruction of property and life. Nothing but the wholesome fear of the strength and effectiveness of the Nauvoo Legion at that time held this lawless element in check.

It was all in vain that hearings were had before the municipal court of Nauvoo, on the *Expositor* matter; in vain that a subsequent hearing was had before Esquire Wells, then not a Mormon and living outside of Nauvoo limits; in vain that the *Nauvoo Neighbor* sought to conciliate the awakening wrath that was aroused in the community, by pleading that if the city council had "exceeded the law of the land, a higher court could regulate the proceedings;" in vain that President Smith urged Governor Ford to come to Nauvoo to make personal investigation of conditions and take the necessary steps to prevent riot and war—all was in vain; preparations were in the making on all sides for an uprising angainst Nauvoo and the Saints, and there was nothing left but to defend the city by placing it under martial law and calling upon the Legion to resist the threatened assault, which act was made the basis for the subsequent charge of "treason."

Then followed in quick succession the demand of the governor for the Mayor and members of the City Council to come to Carthage and submit to trial under circumstances that inevitably meant death; the inspiration of the Prophet to go to the West and all would be well; the crossing of the Mississippi by the Prophet and a few trusted friends to make preparations for that journey; the accusation by false friends of cowardice on the Prophet's part, the flight as of a false shepherd leaving the flock to be devoured by wolves; the lightning-like retort of the Prophet—"*If my life is of no value to my friends, it is of none to myself;*" the return to Nauvoo; the subsequent going to Carthage to submit to the demands of the governor of Illinois in every particular, and the well-known story of Carthage jail—the martyrdom.

XVII. The Prophet's Nobility in the hour of Trial.

The bearing of the Prophet throughout the closing months with which this volume deals is admirable. There is no faltering or evidence of weakness at any point of his conduct. If criticised at all it would be for over-daring, for over self-confidence, that approached sublimity. Strong men through wickedness fell away from their discipleship, and conspired against him; the Prophet reproved them in the gate, and proclaimed their iniquities in public when hope of reforming them was gone. He saw mobs forming for the destruction of himself and Nauvoo and his people; he calmly prepared to meet force with force, and drilled and prepared his legion for the conflict, entrenched some of the approaches to the city, and picketed them with guards; as mayor of the city he placed the city under martial law; and as lieutenant-general he took personal command of the Nauvoo Legion and stood ready to defend the rights of himself and his people, for which his revolutionary ancestry had fought in the war for American independence. He believed gloriously in the right of self-defense, and **resistance** to oppression by physical force if necessary. To his uncle John Smith at Ramus who had asked for counsel in the disturbed state of things, he wrote ten days before his death:

"I write these few lines to inform you that we feel determined in this place not to be dismayed if hell boils over all at once. We feel to hope for the best, and determined to prepare for the worst, and we want this to be your motto in common with us: *We will never ground our arms until we give them up by death.*"

And from Carthage prison, on the morning of the day of his martyrdom, he wrote to his wife for transmission to his people:

"There is one principle which is eternal: It is the duty of all men to protect their lives and the lives of their household, whenever necessity requires, and no power has a right to forbid it, should the last extreme arrive; but I anticipate no such extreme; *but caution is the parent of safety.*"

When the jail in Carthage was assailed, and the mob was pouring murderous volleys into the room occupied by himself and friends, the Prophet turned from the prostrate form of his murdered brother to face death-dealing guns and bravely returned the fire of his assailants, "bringing his man down every time," and compelling even John Hay, who but reluctantly accords the Prophet any quality of virtue, to confess that he "made a handsome fight" in the jail.*

XVIII. Always the Prophet-Teacher.

But what was more wonderful than the manifestation of moral and physical courage and good generalship during these turbulent months of his career, was the pursuance of his duties as a teacher of religious truth—his calling as a Prophet of God. Notwithstanding he was troubled on every side, he could compose his mind to instruct the

*This is the late Secretary of State John Hay, in the *Atlantic Monthly* for December, 1869; "Joe Smith died bravely, he stood by the jam of the door and fired four shots, bringing his man down every time. He shot an Irishman named Wills, who was in the affair from his congenital love of a brawl, in the arm; Gallagher, a Southerner from the Mississippi bottom, in the face; Voorhees, a half-grown hobbledehoy from Bear Creek, in the shoulder; and another gentleman, whose name I will not mention, as he is prepared to prove an *alibi*, and besides stands six feet two in his moccasins." In a later paragraph he refers to "the handsome fight in the jail."

Church on such doctrines as the complete salvation of their dead; how to proceed with the administration of all ordinances given for and in behalf of the dead; the doctrine of the resurrection and the reality of spiritual existences; the plurality of Divine Intelligences, or Gods; the nature of man's spirit; the doctrine of eternal progress for intelligences who keep the estates through which they are appointed to pass; the nature and character of the Godhead, and the relationship of man to God. All these themes and many more he dwelt upon in public discourse and private interview and written communications. He lived his life, as I have said elsewhere, *in cresendo*, it grew in intensity and volume as he approached its close. Higher and still higher the inspiration of God directed his thoughts; bolder were his conceptions, and clearer his expositions of them. So far was he from being a "fallen prophet" in the closing months of his career, as apostates charged, that he grew stronger with each passing day; more impressive in weight of personal character, and charm of manner; for he preserved amid all the conflicts and trials through which he passed—until the shadows of impending death began to fall upon him in Carthage prison—the natural sweetness of his nature, and the intellectual playfulness characteristic of him from boyhood—*so do not fallen prophets.*

* * * * * * *

Side by side on the banks of the majestic river that half encircles Nauvoo, the "beautiful," carrying with it also the idea of "rest," peacefully sleep the brothers, Joseph and Hyrum Smith, the Prophet and the Patriarch of the Church in the New Dispensation of the Gospel. Their lives were interlaced by almost daily associations from childhood to the last awful scene of martyrdom. It was therefore most fitting that they should be buried beside each other, on the banks of the "Father of Waters" in the city they had founded, where they had toiled and suffered and achieved; where their joys rose to greater heights and their sorrows sounded greater depths than falls to the lot of but few men in this world. Undisturbed may their death slumber be until it shall be ended by the trump of God, calling them forth to a glorious resurrection.

* * * * * * *

Prophet and Patriarch

In the Temple square at Salt Lake City, where tens of thousands, made up of people of nearly every nation in the world view them, stand two bronze statues, life size, on granite bases. They are the statues of the Brothers Smith, the Prophet and the Patriarch of the New Dispensation of the Gospel. On the granite basements, respectively, are bronze tablets on which is engraved the Life Record of these men, and what is characteristic of each.

The text of the bronze plate of Hyrum Smith's statue is as follows:

HYRUM SMITH.

The Patriarch and a witness of the Book of Mormon.

An elder brother, and the steadfast friend and counselor of Joseph Smith, the Prophet.

Born at Tunbridge, Vermont, February 9th, 1800; suffered martyrdom with the Prophet at Carthage, Illinois, on the 27th of June, 1844.

The friendship of the brothers Hyrum and Joseph Smith is foremost among the few great friendships of the world's history. Their names will be classed among the martyrs for religion.

The Book of Mormon—the plates of which Hyrum Smith both saw and handled; the revelations in the Book of Doctrine and Covenants; the Church of Jesus Christ of Latter-day Saints—these, to bring them forth for the salvation of the world, cost the best blood of the 19th century.

"I could pray in my heart that all men were like my brother Hyrum, who possesses the mildness of a lamb and the integrity of Job, and, in short, the meekness and humility of Christ. I love him with that love that is stronger than death."—*Joseph Smith.*

"If ever there was an exemplary, honest and virtuous man, the embodiment of all that is noble in the human form, Hyrum Smith was the representative."—*President John Taylor.*

As he shared in the labors, so does he share in the honor and glory of the New Dispensation with his Prophet Brother.

In life they were not divided; in death they were not separated; in glory they are one.

The text on the west side of the base of Joseph Smith's tablet is:

JOSEPH SMITH.

The Prophet of the New Dispensation of the Gospel of Jesus Christ our Lord. He was born at Sharon, Vermont, on the 23rd of December, 1805; and suffered Martyrdom for the word of God and the testimony of Jesus at Carthage, Illinois, on the 27th of June, 1844.

HIS VISION OF GOD.

I saw two Personages whose glory and brightness defy all description. One of them spake unto me and said:

"*This is my Beloved Son: hear Him.*"

I asked which of all the sects was right, and which I should join. I was answered I must join none of them; they were all wrong; they teach for doctrine the commandments of men; I received a promise that the fulness of the Gospel would at some future time be made known to me.

THE BOOK OF MORMON.

This book was revealed to him, and he translated it by the gift and power of God. It is an inspired history of ancient America, and contains the fullness of the Gospel. It is the American Testament of our Lord and Savior Jesus Christ.

THE ORGANIZATION OF THE CHURCH.

Joseph Smith received divine authority through the ministration of angels to teach the Gospel and administer the ordinances thereof. He established again in the earth the Church of Jesus Christ, organizing it by the will and commandment of God on the 6th day of April, 1830.

He also received commission to gather Israel and establish Zion on this land of America; to erect temples and perform all ordinances therein both for the living and the dead; and prepare the way for the glorious coming of the Lord Jesus Christ to reign on earth.

The contents of the tablet on the east side of the base of the Prophet's statue are these gems from his teachings:

TRUTH GEMS.

The glory of God is intelligence.

It is impossible for a man to be saved in ignorance.

Whatever principles of intelligence we attain unto in this life will rise with us in the resurrection.

There is a law irrevocably decreed in heaven before the foundations of this world upon which all blessings are predicated; and when we obtain any blessing from God it is by obedience to that law on which it is predicated.

This is the work and glory of God: to bring to pass the immortality and eternal life of man.

Adam fell that man might be; and men are that they might have joy.

The intelligence of spirits had no beginning, neither will it have an end. Jesus was in the beginning with the Father: man was also in the beginning with God. Intelligence, or the light of truth, was not created or made, neither indeed can be.

The spirit and body is the soul of man; and the resurrection from the dead is the redemption of the soul.

It is the first principle of the Gospel to know for a certainty the character of God; and to know that man, (as Moses) may converse with Him as one man converses with another.

This message of the Prophet, and these doctrines of the east bronze tablet, together with other doctrines taught by him in this PERIOD I of our CHURCH HISTORY, and to be found scattered through the six volumes now published of that history, await only the mind of some God-inspired Spencer to cast them into synthetical form—to be adequately presented and witnessed—to constitute Mormonism both the Religion and the Philosophy of modern times—to bring to pass and to glorify the Golden Age of the long-promised Millennium of Christian hope.

HISTORY

OF THE

CHURCH OF JESUS CHRIST OF LATTER-DAY SAINTS

VOL. VI

HISTORY

OF THE

CHURCH OF JESUS CHRIST

OF

LATTER-DAY SAINTS.

PERIOD I.

HISTORY OF JOSEPH SMITH, THE PROPHET.

CHAPTER I.

AN ESTIMATE OF THE PROPHET JOSEPH AS A RELIGIOUS LEADER—ANTI-MORMON MEETING AT CARTHAGE—HISTORICAL SKETCH—IMPORTANT CONFERENCE OF THE TWELVE HELD IN BOSTON.

Friday, September 1, 1843.— A conference was held in Buffalo, New York, Elder John P. Greene presiding; Wm. H. Folsom,* clerk: 13 branches, 1 High Priest, 58

* William H. Folsom named above afterward became prominent as an architect in Utah. He was born in Portsmouth, New Hampshire, in March, 1815, and died in Salt Lake City, 1901, at the advanced age of 86 years. When a boy he moved to Buffalo N.Y. with his parents. When in his twenty fifth year he heard a Mormon Elder preach and was converted to the gospel and joined the Church. As a consequence of this act he was ostracised by his people. He took his family and moved to Nauvoo and established himself as an architect and builder, and assisted in the construction of the Nauvoo Temple.

Brother Folsom was expelled from Nauvoo at the time of the general exodus of the Saints and settled for a time at Keokuk. He subsequently moved to Council Bluffs, and in 1860 went on to Salt Lake valley. His ability as an architect and builder was soon required by President Brigham Young. President Young conceived the general plan of the now celebrated "Mormon Tabernacle" at Salt Lake City, but William Folsom took President Young's suggestions and worked out the plans. While others scouted the idea of the structure, Folsom had faith in it, and as a consequence he has associated his name inseparably with the building, that

Elders, 2 Teachers, 1 Deacon, and 247 members were represented.

I attended the meeting of the High Council as a witness in the case of Cowles* vs. George J. Adams. Charges not sustained.

Saturday, *2*. — I was not well, and therefore adjourned Mayor's Court.

Sunday, *3*. — I attended council with my brother Hyrum, Newel K. Whitney, Willard Richards, William Law and William Marks, and gave instructions to the brethren in relation to things in futurity.

A tremendous storm at Chester, Penn. The creek rose twenty-three feet in two hours, and swept away all the bridges, many factories and houses, and upwards of twenty persons drowned.

A conference was held at Hayward's Hotel, Manchester, England.

Minutes of the Manchester Conference, held 3rd of September, 1843.

Charles Miller, President; William Walker, Clerk. Present: 1 Patriarch, 1 High Priest, 25 Elders, 40 Priests, 21 Teachers, and 4 Deacons.

Total number of members represented was as follows: 1,549 members, including 44 Elders, 99 Priests, 56 Teachers, 22 Deacons. Baptized since last general conference, 80; cut off, 29; emigrated, 18; removed, 26; died, 4.

Monday, *4*. — Attended mayor's court and tried three cases—viz.,

City *versus* A. Dodge, S. Dodge, and Luther Purtelow. The two first I fined five dollars, and the last one dollar and costs. One, p. m., called and gave licence for

stands as one of the world's centers of interest and curiosity. He was the architect and superintendent of construction of the Manti Temple, and was an able assistant in the construction of all the Temples in Utah. He was the designer of the Salt Lake Theater, and of many other buildings that are this day admired for their architectural grace and durability.

* This was Austin Cowles, for some time counselor in the Nauvoo stake of Zion (HISTORY OF THE CHURCH, Vol. IV, p. 323) and subsequently a member of the High Council. The nature of the charges made against George J. Adams at this time is not known.

a circus performance, which I attended with my family until five, p. m.

I copy from the *New York Sun* as follows:—

"JOE SMITH, THE MORMON PROPHET."*

This Joe Smith must be set down as an extraordinary character, a prophet-hero, as Carlyle might call him. He is one of the great men of this age, and in future history will rank with those who, in one way or another, have stamped their impress strongly on society.

Nothing can be more plebeian, in seeming, than this Joe Smith. Little of dignity is there in his cognomen; but few in this age have done such deeds, and performed such apparent miracles. It is no small thing, in the blaze of this nineteenth century, to give to men a new revelation, found a new religion, establish new forms of worship, to build a city, with new laws, institutions, and orders of architecture, — to establish ecclesiastic, civil and military jurisdiction, found colleges, send out missionaries, and make proselytes in two hemispheres: yet all this has been done by Joe Smith, and that against every sort of opposition, ridicule and persecution. This sect has its martyrs also; and the spirit in which they were imprisoned and murdered in Missouri, does not appear to have differed much from that which has attended religious persecutions in all ages of the world.

That Joe Smith, the founder of the Mormons, is a man of great talent, a deep thinker, and eloquent speaker, an able writer, and a man of great mental power, no one can doubt who has watched his career. That his followers are deceived, we all believe; but, should the inherent corruptions of Mormonism fail to develop themselves sufficiently to convince its followers of their error, where will the thing end? A great military despotism is growing up in the fertile West, increasing faster in proportion, than the surrounding population, spreading its influence around, and marshalling multitudes under its banners, causing serious alarm to every patriot.

What is the reason that men are so blind that they cannot or will not see the hand of the Lord in His work of the last days!

Tuesday, 5. — Went to the office at nine, a. m., with Mr. Hamilton, of Carthage, who had obtained a deed from

* This article is much of the complexion of one published many years later — 1882 — by Josiah Quincy of Boston, who visited the Prophet about eight or nine months later, and published an account of his visit, and his impression of the Prophet in his "Figures of the Past," under the title "Joseph Smith at Nauvoo."

the sheriff of the county for lot 2, block 103, in the city of Nauvoo, for taxes, although I had previously paid them; which is another specimen of the oppression, injustice, and rascality of Mr. Collector Bagby, who by such foul means robs me and other Saints, and abuses all who come unfortunately in his power.

I requested my clerk to make out a bill of fare for the "Mansion."

The ship *Metoka* sailed from Liverpool with a company of Saints on board.

Wednesday, 6.—I went to the recorder's about half past six, a. m., and found him in bed.

Held mayor's court in the case, "City *versus* Joseph Owen."

*Anti-Mormon Meeting at Carthage, Seat of Hancock, County Illinois.**

Meeting convened pursuant to adjournment. The former chairman † not being present.

EdsonWhitney, Esq., was called to the chair, and the meeting being organized, the following preamble and resolutions were submitted by the committee, and unanimously adopted:—

PREAMBLE AND RESOLUTIONS.

This meeting having convened for the purpose of taking under advisement a subject of vital importance not only to this county, but to all the surrounding counties, regret that we are necessarily and irresistibly forced to the conclusion that a certain class of people have obtruded themselves upon us, calling themselves Mormons, or Latter-day Saints, and under the sacred garb of Christianity, assumed, as we honestly believe, that they may the more easily, under such a cloak, perpetrate the most lawless and diabolical deeds that have ever, in any age of the world, disgraced the human species.

In evidence of the above charge, we find them yielding implicit obedience to the ostensible head and founder of this sect, who is a pretended prophet of the Lord, and under this Heaven-daring assump-

* This was an adjourned meeting from one of the same character which had met at the same place on the 19th of August previous, which after hearing Anti-Mormon addresses and appointing committees to draft resolutions against the Mormons, adjourned to meet again on the above date, 6th of September. (See HISTORY OF THE CHURCH, Vol. IV pp. 537—8).

† The former chairman was Major Reuben Groves. (See minutes of the 19th of August, above note.)

tion claiming to set aside, by his vile and blasphemous lies, all those moral and religious institutions which have been established by the Bible, and which have in all ages been cherished by men as the only means of maintaining those social blessings which are so indispensably necessary for our happiness.

We believe that such an individual, regardless as he must be of his obligations to God, and at the same time entertaining the most absolute contempt for the laws of man, cannot fail to become a most dangerous character, especially when he shall have been able to place himself at the head of a numerous horde, either equally reckless and unprincipled as himself, or else made his pliant tools by the most absurd credulity that has astonished the world since its foundation.

In the opinion of this meeting, a crisis has arrived, when many of the evils to be expected from a state of things so threatening have transpired. We feel convinced that circumstances have even now occurred which prove to us most conclusively that Joseph Smith, the false Prophet before alluded to, has evinced, in many instances, a most shameless disregard for all the forms and restraints of law, by boldly and presumptuously calling in question the acts of certain officers, who had fearlessly discharged the duties absolutely imposed upon them by the laws, particulary when they have come in contact with his own sordid and selfish interests.

He has been heard to threaten—nay, he *has* committed violence upon the person of an officer, because that officer dared honestly to do his duties according to law.

He has caused his city council to pass laws contrary to the laws of the state, and subversive of the rights of citizens of this state.

Citizens have been arrested, tried and punished for breaches of those mock laws, from time to time, in such manner, that they have been compelled to the humiliating necessity of seeking an asylum elsewhere, in order to escape the tyranny and oppression of this modern Caligula.

He has caused the writ of *habeas corpus* to be issued by the municipal court of the city of Nauvoo, in a case not provided for in the charter of this city, and indeed contrary to the letter of that instrument; and, himself a prisoner, arrested under grave charges made by a neighboring state, brought before said court, tried, and acquitted; thereby securing his own rescue from the custody of the law.

Citizens from the adjoining counties have been denied the right to regain property stolen and taken to Nauvoo, even after they have discovered both the thief and the property; and themselves, under the most frivolus pretenses, arrested, fined, and other property rifled from them, to satisfy the mock judgments and costs of his cormorant officers.

Persons upon whom stolen property has been found in the city of Nauvoo, have been brought before this religio-political chief; and he, in the capacity of mayor of the city, has refused to convict, where the cases have been most clear and palpable.

We have had men of the most vicious and abominable habits imposed upon us to fill our most important county offices, by his dictum, in order, as we verily believe, that he may the more certainly control our destinies, and render himself, through the instrumentality of these base creatures of his ill-directed power, as absolutely a despot over the citizens of this county as he now is over the serfs of his own servile clan.

And, to crown all, he claims to merge all religion, all law, and both moral and political justice, in the knavish pretension that he receives fresh from heaven divine instructions in all matters pertaining to these things; thereby making his own depraved will the rule by which he would have all men governed.

He has caused large bodies of his ragamuffin soldiery to arm themselves, and turn out in pursuit of officers legally authorized to arrest himself; he being charged with high crimes and misdemeanors committed in the state of Missouri, and those officers arrested by the vilest hypocrisy, and placed in duress, that he might enable himself to march triumphantly into Nauvoo, and bid defiance to the laws of the land.

In view of the above grievances, this meeting feel that it is their bounden duty to resist, by every laudable means, all such unwarrantable attacks upon their liberties. Therefore—

Resolved, 1st. That inasmuch as we honestly believe that the combination of people calling themselves Mormons, or Latter-day Saints, have given strong indications, in their recent movements, that they are unwilling to submit to the ordinary restraints of law, we are therefore forced to the conclusion that the time is not far distant when the citizens of this country will be compelled to assert their rights in some way.

Resolved, 2nd. That while we would deprecate anything like lawless violence, without justifiable cause, yet we pledge ourselves in the most solemn manner to resist all the wrongs which may be hereafter attempted to be imposed on this community by the Mormons, to the utmost of our ability,—peaceably, if we can, but forcibly, if we must.

Resolved, 3rd. That in the event of our being forced into a collision with that people, we pledge ourselves that we will stand by and support each other in every emergency up to the death.

Resolved, 4th. That we believe that it is also the interest of our friends in the neighboring counties and also neighboring states to begin to take a firm and decided stand against the high pretensions and base designs of this latter-day would-be Mahomet.

Resolved, 5th. That provided we must necessarily, for the well-being of this community, the protection of our dearest rights, and the preservation of our excellent institutions, adopt measures to humble the pride and arrogance of that audacius despot; we therefore call upon all good and honest men, without distinction of party or place, to come to the rescue.

Resolved, 6th. That we pledge ourselves in the most determined manner that if the authorities of the State of Missouri shall make another demand for the body of Joseph Smith, and our Governor shall issue another warrant to stand ready at all times to serve the officer into whose hands such warrant may come, as a *posse*, in order that it may not be said of us, in future, that the most outrageous culprits have been suffered "to go unwhipped of justice."

Resolved, 7th. That a corresponding committee be appointed to communicate with the different parts of this county, and also with other counties; and we would also recommend to all surrounding counties to appoint like committees for the purpose of a mutual interchange of views in regard to the subjects embraced in these proceedings.

Resolved, 8th. That as it has been too common for several years past for politicians of both political parties, not only of this county, but likewise of the state, to go to Nauvoo and truckle to the heads of the Mormon clan for their influence, we pledge ourselves that we will not support any man of either party in future who shall thus debase himself.

Resolved, 9th. That if the Mormons carry out the threats they have made in regards to the lives of several of our citizens, we will, if failing to obtain speedy redress from the laws of the land, take summary and signal vengeance upon them as a people.

Resolved, 10th. That when the Government ceases to afford protection, the citizens of course fall back upon their original inherent right of self-defense.

In pursuance of the 7th resolution, the following gentlemen were appointed to act as a central corresponding committee at Carthage—namely, Captain Robert F. Smith, Major T. J. Bartlet, Harmon T. Wilson, Frank A. Worrel, and Walter Bagby.

On motion of Henry Stevens, it was ordered that committees, consisting of two persons, be appointed in each election precinct of this county, for the purpose of communicating with the central committee at Carthage; and that those two may add to their number at discretion.

On motion of Daniel Beaver, it was made the duty of the person whose name stands first on the list of each committee to act as chairman; and that all communications from the other committees, or from any other source, shall be added.

The following gentlemen were then appointed by the chair as committees in the several precincts, to wit:—

Green Plains—Edson Whitney and Levi Williams.

Bear Creek—William White and Andrew Moore.

Chili—Stephen Owen and Arthur Morgan.

Augusta—William D. Abernethy and Alexander Oliver.

Saint Mary's—Willlam Darnell and Daniel Beaver.

Fountain Green—Thomas Geddis and S. H. Tyler.

La Harpe—Jesse Gilmer and Charles Comstock.

Camp Creek—James Graham and Thomas Harris.

Appanooce—John McCanley and John R. Atherton.

Montebello—Samuel Steel and Benjamin B. Gates.

Warsaw—Thomas C. Sharp and Mark Aldrich.

On motion of Levi Williams, Colonel Root, of McDonough county, was added to the central corresponding committee of Carthage.

On motion of Henry Newton, Esq.,

Resolved, That the central committee of correspondence act as a general committee of supervision; and, in case of a contingency occurring requiring aid, that they immediately call on the precinct committees and upon all others favorable to our cause to furnish such aid as the exigency of the case may require.

On the motion of Charles C. Stevens, the following supplementary resolutions were unanimously adopted:—

Resolved, That the president of this meeting be requested to communicate with the Governor of Missouri, and respectfully request him to make another demand upon the authorities of this state for the body of Joseph Smith, commonly called the Mormon Prophet; and in the event of a requisition and an order for his arrest and delivery to the proper officers of the state of Missouri, we offer our services to enforce said order, and pledge ourselves to sustain the supremacy of the laws at all hazards and under all circumstances.

Resolved, That a copy of the proceedings of this meeting be forwarded to the publisher of the *Warsaw Message*, *Quincy Whig*, and *Quincy Herald*, for publication, with a request to them to add a note, soliciting all editors friendly to our cause in this state, Missouri, and Iowa Territory, to copy.

It was then moved and seconded, That this meeting adjourn, subject to the call of the central corresponding committee.

EDSON WHITNEY, Chairman.

W. D. ABERNETHY, Secretary.

Editors throughout Illinois, Missouri, Iowa Territory, friendly to the Anti-Mormon cause, are requested to publish the proceedings, in today's paper, of a meeting held at Carthage on the 6th instant.

Thursday, 7.— I took home the letter written to Harrisburg* for the Church History, a small fragment of which only has been preserved, and is as follows:—

Historical Sketch of the Church of Jesus Christ of Latter-day Saints.

Messrs. Editors,—The Church of Jesus Christ of Latter-day Saints was founded upon direct revelation, as the true Church of God has ever been, according to the Scriptures (Amos iii: 7, and Acts i: 2); and through the will and blessings of God, I have been an instrument in His hands, thus far, to move forward the cause of Zion: therefore, in order to fulfill the solicitations of your letter of July last, I shall commence with my life.

[Then follows a brief historical sketch of the Church from the birth of the Prophet to the settlement of the Saints at Nauvoo, much in the strain of the "*Wentworth Letter*" already published in this HISTORY, (Vol. IV, Ch. xxxi); and for the reason that all the historical data in this I. Daniel Rupp sketch is contained in the *Wentworth Letter*, it is thought unnecessary to reproduce it here, excepting the closing paragraphs which deal with conditions and prospects at Nauvoo, on the date at which we have arrived in our HISTORY, viz. September, 1843.—Editor.]

Nauvoo, upon every point connected with increase and prosperity has exceeded the most sanguine expectations of thousands. It now contains near 3,500 houses, and more than 15,000 inhabitants. The charter contains, among its important powers, privileges or immunities, a grant for "The University of Nauvoo," with the same liberal powers of the city, where all the arts and sciences will grow with the growth and strengthen the strength of this beloved city of the Saints of the last days.

Another very commendatory provision of the charter is that that portion of the citizens subject to military duty are organized into a body of independent military men, styled the "Nauvoo Legion," whose highest officer holds the rank and is commissioned lieutenant-general. This Legion, like other independent bodies of troops in this Republican Government, is at the disposal of the Governor of the state, and President of the United States. There is also an act of incorporation for an Agricultural and Manufacturing Association, as well as the Nauvoo House Association.

Since the organization of this Church, its progress has been rapid, and its gain in numbers regular. Besides these United States, where

* This was a Brief Historical Account of the Rise and Progress of the Church prepared for one I. Daniel Rupp, of Harrisburg, Penn. It was published in 1844, in a "History of Religious Denominations," p. 409.

nearly every place of notoriety has heard the glad tidings of the Gospel of the Son of God, England, Ireland and Scotland have shared largely in the fullness of the everlasting Gospel, and thousands have already gathered with their kindred Saints to this the corner stone of Zion. Missionaries of this Church have gone to the East Indies, to Australia, Germany, Constantinople, Egypt, Palestine, the islands of the Pacific, and are now preparing to open the door in the extensive dominions of Russia.

There is no correct data by which the exact number of members composing this now extensive and still extending Church of Jesus Christ of Latter-day Saints can be known. Should it be supposed at 150,000,* it might still be short of the truth.

Believing the Bible to say what it means and mean what it says, and guided by revelation, according to the ancient order of the fathers, to whom came what little light we enjoy, and circumscribed only by the eternal limits of truth, this Church must continue the even tenor of its way.

Called at the office, and administered the laying on of hands to Sister Partington and her two children.

Dreadful conflagration at Stuhlweissenburg, in Hungary. About six hundred houses destroyed.

Friday, 8.—My wife being sick, I was at home all day.

Stephen Markham started for Dixon with the court papers in relation to the writ of habeas corpus, and as a witness.

I directed William Clayton to go to Augusta, Iowa, to get a deed signed by Mr. Moffit for the steamer *Maid of Iowa*.

Muster day of the first cohort.

The Twelve held a meeting in Boylston Hall, Boston. Present—Elders Heber C. Kimball, Orson Pratt, George A. Smith, Wilford Woodruff, John E. Page.

Saturday, 9.— My wife a little more comfortable. William Clayton went to Augusta, got the deed signed by Mr. Moffit and his wife, and returned in the evening.

General training of the Nauvoo Legion.

The quorum of the Twelve met the church in Boston, at Boylston Hall, in conference. Sixteen branches were represented, containing 878 members. A great deal of valuable instruction was given by the Twelve, and the hall, a very large one, was crowded. A number were baptized during conference, which lasted three days. The minutes of conference I here insert:—

Important Conference of the Twelve, Held at Boylston Hall, Boston, September 9, 1843.

Present of the Quorum of the Twelve—Elders Brigham Young, Heber C. Kimball, Parley P. Pratt, Orson Pratt, Orson Hyde, John E. Page. Wilford Woodruff, George A. Smith.

[*Reported by Wilford Woodruff.*]

Conference opened with prayer by Elder George A. Smith.

After the various branches in the New England States were represented, Elder P. P. Pratt made a few remarks, of which the following is a synopsis:

Some Elders tell us that they have taught the gathering according to the Scriptures. But it is not sufficient to teach the principle from the Scriptures alone; for if there was no other guide, the people would be left in doubt as to whether they should gather to Jerusalem, Africa, America, or elsewhere. It is right to teach the gathering according to the Scriptures, although some predictions of the Prophets are obscure; but we are not left to them alone. We know and all the Saints ought to know that God has appointed a place and time of gathering and has raised up a Prophet to bring it about, of which we are witnesses. Our message is that we are witnesses of the fulfillment of the predictions of the Prophets.

We have not to lay down a long, round-about [system] of arguments and calculations. The specific time and place are pointed out, the stakes are driven, the foundations of the city and temple are laid, and a people already gathered. We therefore know where to go; and to reject the revelations of God, which have pointed out these things to us, only brings condemnation. If this is not the case, then our faith is vain, and our works and hopes are vain also.

We worship a God who can inspire His servants to tell the people what to do. We have already got the opinions of men enough concerning the coming of Jesus Christ; but we need the voice of a Prophet in such a case and we have it. I am willing to risk my all upon it: and if the Elders understand the principle of gathering, and teach it correctly, the people will have the correct spirit of the gathering.

It is time we come out and declared boldly and definitely what God had for the people. We want more than opinions—we want your works. He has said he would send a Prophet to prepare the way. And let me ask these profound sectarians, why He has not done it? If the angels found a God in heaven able to give instructions, shield them from sword and famine, &c., why have we not found Him? Let the teachers bear the message they are entrusted with; and if the people wish then for Scripture, tell them that their message is in fulfillment of prophecy; but let them have the whole message.

Elder E. P. Maginn said he for one had taught the gathering according to the Scriptures; but he considered all modern revelations Scripture as well as those given anciently.

Elder Brigham Young addressed the meeting on the subject of our faith. We hear the Elders represent the feeling of the brethren concerning the gathering. This is right. The Spirit of the Lord Jesus Christ is a gathering spirit. Its tendency is to gather the virtuous and good, the honest and meek of the earth, and, in fine, the Saints of God. The time has come when the Lord is determined to fulfill his purposes. The people are apt to say that if they had lived in the days of Jesus Christ they would have received His work. But judge ye if the people are better now than then. They are not. When the full, set time was come, the Lord came in the flesh to do His work, whether the people were prepared or not; and He would not have come at all, if He had waited till the people were prepared to receive Him. It was decreed from all eternity that He should come, and He came. The people were not prepared then, nor are they any more prepared now. And now the full set time has come for the Lord God Almighty to set His hand to redeem Israel. We are not bound to make the people believe, but we are bound to preach the Gospel; and having done this, our garments are clear.

The Lord does not require every soul to leave his home as soon as He believes. Some may be wanted to go to the isles of the sea, and some to go north,and some south. But He *does* require them to hearken to counsel, and follow that course which He points out, whether to gather or stay to do some other work.

The Spirit of the Lord and His work are on the alert, and those who keep up with the work must be on the alert also. The Spirit of the Lord will leave them who sit down and refuse to obey. When the Lord says, "Gather yourselves together," why do you ask Him what for? Had you not rather enjoy the society of Saints than sinners whom you cannot love? Is it not the principle of the Saints to mingle together and promote the great cause in which they are engaged?

Perhaps some of you are ready to ask, "Cannot the Lord save us as well where we are as to gather together?" Yes, if the Lord says so. But if He commands us to come out and gather together, He will not save us by staying at home. Have you not received the Gospel? Yes.

Then do you believe what we say? Have you not received the Holy Ghost, by receiving the Gospel which we have brought unto you? Yes. thousands have; and it stands as a testimony that God has got a Prophet on the earth. You might have been baptized seventy times seven in any way except the way God had ordained and pointed out, and you would not have received the Holy Ghost. This also is a testimony to you.

Are you engaged with us in this great work? "Yes, certainly," you answer, "heart and hand." "Can we do any good?" Yes, you can. The sectarian world send the Bible to the nations of the earth. The poor among them put sixpence, fifty cents or a dollar into the box to carry out that object; and can the Latter-day Saints do nothing? Let them do what God requires. He has required that we should build a house unto His name, that the ordinances and blessings of His kingdom may be revealed, and that the Elders may be endowed, go forth and gather together the blood of Ephraim—the people of God, from the ends of the earth.

Can you get an endowment in Boston or anywhere, except where God appoints? No, only in that place which God has pointed out. Now, query—Could Moses have obtained the law if he had stayed in the midst of the children of Israel, instead of going up on to the mountain? The Lord said, "Go and do so and so; stand before Pharaoh; pull off they shoes, for the place is holy." Moses obeyed, and obtained blessings which he would not have received if he had been disobedient.

Has the Lord spoken in these last days, and required us to build Him a house? Then why query about it? If He has spoken, it is enough. I do not care whether the people gather or not, if they don't want to do so. I do not wish to save the people against their will. I want them to choose whether they will gather and be saved with the righteous, or remain with the wicked and be damned. I would like to have all people bow down to the Lord Jesus Christ; but it is one of the decrees of the Lord that all persons shall act upon their agency, which was the case even with the angels who fell from heaven.

Now, will you help us to build the Nauvoo House and Temple? If so, you will be blessed: if not, we will build it without you. And if you don't hearken, you will not have the Spirit of the Lord; for the Spirit of the Lord is on the move.

The Apostles tried to gather the people together in their day. Christ said He would gather the Jews oft as a hen gathereth her chickens under her wings, but they would not. Neither God nor angels care whether men hear or forbear: they will carry on their work; for the full, set time is come for God to set up His kingdom, and we go about it. We must build a house, and get an endowment, preach the gospel, warn the people, gather the Saints, build up Zion, finish our work, and be prepared for the coming of Christ.

Now, we want to send four missionaries to the Pacific Islands, and we want a little clothing, and beds, and money to pay their passage. Can you do something for them? This is not all. We want you to give all you have to spare towards building the Temple. We shall be able to build it, if we have to work with a sword in one hand. But perhaps you are afraid you will not have enough for yourself, when you get there; yet how easy it is for the Lord to take it away from you by fire or otherwise!

Elder Maginn had an ivory cane. I asked him for it, but he declined making me a present of it. Not long after, he had it stolen from him in a crowd, and it now does neither of us any good. Perhaps your purse may slip through your pocket, or you may lose your property; for the Lord can give and take away. Jacob, with his faith, obtained all the best cattle his father-in-law had.

If I had a wife and ten children, I would give all my money to build the Temple and Nauvoo House, and I would trust in God for their support. Yet I will be richer for it; for God would prosper me in business. Men are apt to serve God on Sunday, and neglect Him all the week. Who blesses you and all the people? God. But do the people acknowledge the hand of God in all these things? No; they turn away from Him, and do not acknowledge Him, or realize from whom their blessings flow. They know not who blesses them. It never comes into their hearts. So with the farmer. The blessings are constantly flowing to him, and he considers not whence they come.

Let me tell you a secret. When the Lord shakes the earth, and every valley shall be exalted, and every mountain and hill shall be made low, He will bring gold for brass, silver for iron, brass for wood, and iron for stones. Then you will have no use for gold, for money and gods as you now have. You will not care so much about it; but the Lord will think as much of it then as now.

But now we want some of the gods of the Gentiles—some of the gold and silver to build the Temple and Nauvoo House for the accommodation of the kings, princes and nobles of the earth, when they come to inquire after the wisdom of Zion, that they may have a place for their entertainment, and for the weary traveler to be refreshed. Let us have your gold to take to Nauvoo for this purpose.

Is there wisdom in Zion? We think so, and the world begins to think so. Let the world come forward and translate the plates that have of late come forth,* if they have wisdom to do it. The Lord

* Having reference to certain plates known as the "Kinderhook Plates," found at Kinderhook, Illinois, April, 1843. See this HISTORY, Vol. V., pp. 372-378.

intends to take away the gods of the Gentiles: He pulleth down and He buildeth up at His own pleasure.

Sacrifice your gods for the building up of Zion. Administer of your substance. Send our missionaries to the islands of the seas. Don't be afraid of a dollar, or a hundred dollars, or even a thousand dollars. I would not. I have made a sacrifice of all I possessed a good many times. I am richer the more I give; for the Lord has promised and does reward me a hundredfold; and if I sacrifice all for the cause of God, no good thing will be withheld from me. I have taken this course to get rich. I have given all I had, and God has given many blessings in consequence. If I am too bold in asking, be too bold in giving. I ask, expecting to receive. Put your shoulders to the wheel with all your might. Give your all, and become rich by receiving a hundredfold.

Adjourned until half-past two o'clock. when the meeting was opened by singing.

Prayer by Elder Parley P. Pratt. Singing.

Elder Parley P. Pratt said: I have a few remarks to make concerning the subject spoken of in the forenoon by Elder Brigham Young, who said we wanted all your gold, silver, and precious things. We not only want your all as pertaining to gold, silver, &c., but we want you, your wives and children, and all you have to be engaged in the work of the Lord.

I don't know that I can give you a better pattern of what we want than the case of Joseph in Egypt. Israelites will get all they can. They are very great to go ahead. The Egyptians believed in dreams; and by the peculiar gift of interpretation of dreams, Joseph entered into a great scheme of speculation. He used the gift of interpretation to become great in the eyes of the Egyptians. He obtained great political influence, came out with gold ornaments, and rode in the king's chariot in great splendor. He laid up corn in great abundance during the seven years of plenty; and when the famine came, he got all their gold, silver, cattle, land, property, and, finally their persons. * * *

God is the origin of power—the Sovereign. He made the people and the earth, and He has the right to reign. There will be good times and good government, when the world will acknowledge the God of heaven as the Lawgiver, and not till then; and if I could live under His government, I should be thankful, although I am a real Republican in principle, and would rather live under the voice of the people than the voice of one man. But it will be for the good and happiness of man when that government is established, which we pray for when we say, "Thy kingdom come, Thy will be done on earth as it is in heaven;" and until that time arrives we must pray for it.

This Joseph in Egypt—the speculator—what a great and good man he was! I love him, I admire his course, and I believe a little of his blood is in my veins. But had Joseph been like the religious world at the present day—had he said he had got religion and done with the world, he would not have rode the king's horse, worn his robe, or had to do with gold and silver; and he would have done no good, built no storehouses, and saved no corn, for fear of speculation.

But he acted differently. And there is an ancient prediction respecting our modern prophet, Joseph—namely, that a prophet and seer should be raised up, and those who seek to destroy him shall be confounded. This has proved true. Upwards of thirty law suits have been brought against the Lord's anointed, and his persecutors have as often been confounded. He has been raised and supported according to the prophecy, to do a work on the earth, and the Lord has been with him. Every weapon formed against him has been broken. He has overcome all the lawsuits which have been brought against him, and no accusation has been sustained against him; yet he will lay a plan to speculate as large as ancient Joseph did; he will have power to buy up all the rest of the world.

What Elder Young said is good. We want all he spoke of, and a great deal more, We do not want it for ourselves, but for you. We want you to use it; and we have a Prophet who tells how, when and where to use it. Take your means and unite your exertions in this work. We want you to take that course which will save you. Build up a city and temples, and enjoy them, and do as the Lord tells you, and hearken to counsel.

We have prophets to tell us what to do, and we should get as much wisdom as the world. If they want a railroad built, all they have to do is to open books. The people subscribe stock, a railroad is soon built, and an income is realized. The Saints ought to be as well united as the world, and do the things that God has required, that a great nation may be saved from all nations.

The old gentleman [Satan] that rules the nations has ruled long enough; and if I were an infidel, I would like to have the Lord raise up a Joseph, or a Daniel, or a Mordecai, or an Esther, to obtain political, temporal, and spiritual power, and cause a change for the good of the world. Thank heaven, he has begun to raise them up. He has raised up another Joseph to do the great work of God, and it will continue on until the saying goes forth that the Lord has built up Zion.

The kingdom of God must be established, and it will be. I read that gold, silver, power, thrones, and dominions will be connected with the great work of God in the last days. Then let us wake up to see what God says shall come to pass, and let us enlarge our hearts and prepare for the great and glorious work.

Do the Saints here in Boston know that they are identified with the laying of the foundation, and establishing of a great and mighty kingdom, which is to include all the great and glorious work to be fulfilled in the last dispensation and fullness of times? And I prophesy, in the name of the Lord, that whether the Saints of Boston or any other place, stand for it or rise against it, numberless millions will celebrate that day when the foundation of this work was laid.

Elder George A. Smith said: I am pleased with the many remarks which have been made this day. You can easily see a similarity between the two Josephs, and the revelations that are given for the salvation of the present generation. Joseph in Egypt, a savior of his father's house and the Egyptians: Joseph [Smith] at this day holds the keys of salvation not only to the Gentiles, but also to the house of Israel.

I do not know but some may have reflections different from my own. I will, however, show how the Lord deals with mankind. Some may say, "Who can believe that God who dwells in heaven will condescend to speak to the people about building Him a house in this day of religion and science?

This may be considered simple in the eyes of many; but the day was when the salvation or damnation of the whole world hung upon as small a circumstance. "Noah, by faith, being warned of God of things not seen as yet, moved with fear, prepared an ark to the saving of his house, by which he condemned the world, and became heir of the righteous which is by faith."

Had the editors of this day lived then, I think they would have said and written more against it than they have against Joseph Smith and the revelations he has received and published.

We find God was in the habit of telling men to do many simple things, even to the giving of a law concerning the protection of birds' nests. You talk about God condescending to speak of small things in the last days, but it is only as it was in the days of Moses; for we read in the Bible how God commanded the children of Israel, when they found a bird's nest, (Deut. xxii: 7) not to take the dam with the young: "But thou shalt in any wise let the dam go, and take the young to thee." Why? "That it may be well with thee, and that thou mayst prolong thy days."

We see from this, that however small and simple the commandments of God appear to be, they are great in their results. Connecting this with the law of God to Israel concerning the eating of locusts, beetles and grasshoppers (Leviticus xi: 22). "Even these of them ye may eat; the locust after his kind, and the bald locust after his kind, and the beetle after his kind, and the grasshopper after his kind."

Is this as small business for the Lord to talk about as it is for Him to command the Saints to build a tavern or boarding house for visitors who constantly go to Nauvoo, which, when done, will do much good for the spreading of the work to all nations. What good could arise from a law of God permitting the eating of beetles and grasshoppers, I cannot say.

All the prophecies have aimed at the gathering of the people, and saving them in the last days. But it is better never to have known the Master's will than to know it and not perform it; and my advice is, If you cannot take hold of the work and go through the whole course, stop and go no further. If you have not courage to go on at the expense of all things, it is better to turn back.

We do not want to deceive you. Our traditions have taught us to be very religious, to wear long faces, never to tell an amusing story, nor to laugh, &c. This was the case with the long-faced Christians in Missouri, and they were the first to strike a dagger to our hearts. It is better for a man to act out what he is than to be a hypocrite. "Pure religion and undefiled before God and the Father, is this," says James, "to visit the fatherless and widows in their affliction, and to keep himself unspotted from the world."

I do not like that religion which lies in a man's long face, or his coat or his hat. If I wear a strange hat, it is not because of my religion: for where the religion of a man is in the shape of a hat or coat, it is not very extensive anywhere else.

Some of the Elders want to appear very big, and to be called great preachers; but whenever I have seen them trying to preach something large and mysterious, to get a name, I have concluded they have yet much to learn. I have been eleven years a member of this Church, and was a believer two years before I entered it; and during that time I have seen many Elders who like to preach large and mysterious sermons.

As many are desirous of hearing mysteries, I will rehearse a short sermon of mysteries for their edification. Elder Kimball has had a long standing in the Church. He has preached much, done much good, brought many souls into the kingdom, had great influence, and is considered the most successful minister among us.

Elder Amasa Lyman and myself went into Pike county, Illinois, to preach where the Elders had preached all the mysteries about beasts, heads and horns. They wanted us to preach mysteries. We told them we were not qualified to preach mysteries; but if they would send for Elder Kimball he would preach them. So they sent about forty miles for Elder Kimball, and brought him down, they were so anxious to hear mysteries.

When he came, he had a large congregation assembled. He arose and remarked that he understood they had sent for him to come and preach the mysteries to them. "I am well qualified, and fully competent to do it, and am happy to have the privilege. I want the attention of all." When every mind was stretched and eager to learn these great mysteries he said, "The first mystery I shall present before you is this, "Look at Elder Amasa Lyman; he needs a pair of pantaloons and a new hat. But it appears you do not see it; consequently I want to open your eyes and reveal to you a great mystery; for an Elder in the Church has need of a hat and a pair of breeches as well as yourselves, and *especially* when the Saints *know* he is so much in need of them!" He preached a few more mysteries of the same nature, and the result of this sermon was that Elder Lyman got a pair of pants and a new hat, and Elder Kimball and myself each a barrel of flour for our families.

Elder Brigham Young arose and said: I will make an apology for my remarks in the former part of the day. Some may think I spoke very plainly; but the object I had in view was to teach you your duty, as I am aware the people are not made to feel it; and the apology I have to make is this: I will turn Thomsonian doctor, and give the composition without cream and sugar,—it matters not whether I get friends or foes. If this work does not live, I do not want to live; for it is my life, my joy, my all; and if it sinks, God knows I do not want to swim.

I wish you to understand this—that he that gathereth not with us scattereth, and they have not the Spirit of God. We live in anticipation of the day when mobs cannot harm us, and they who have tasted the bitter cup feel to realize this hope. Wake up, ye Elders of Israel who have sought to build yourselves up, and not the kingdom of God, and put on your sword. Wake up, ye that have daubed with untempered mortar! Hearken and hear me; for I say unto you, in the name of Jesus Christ, that if you do not help us to build the Temple and the Nauvoo House, you shall not inherit the land of Zion.

If you do not help to build up Zion and the cause of God, and help me and my brethren on our way when we want to go on the Lord's business, you shall not partake of the blessings which are laid up in store for the Saints. Many Elders seek to build themselves up, and not the work of the Lord. They will say "Put gold rings on my fingers; give me what I want;" and they care nothing about the Temple. This they should not do. I will not allow myself to do so; and when any one does this, no matter who he may be, even though he was one of the Twelve, he will not prosper. Those of the Twelve and others of the Elders who have apostatized, I have known their hearts and their breathings. I have known their movements although they thought I did not know much. But I knew all about them; and when I see men preaching to build themselves up, and not Zion, I know what it will end in. But you may say you are young. I don't care if you are. Are you old enough to know what you are about? If so, preach and labor for the building up of the city of Zion; concentrate your means and influence there, and not scatter abroad. Instead of which, some of the Elders appear to be dumb and lazy, and care for nothing but themselves.

Now, ye Elders, will you be faithful? If not, you will not be chosen, for the day of choosing is at the door. Why be afraid of a sacrifice? I have given my all many times, and am willing to do it again. I would be glad to hear the Lord say through His servant Joseph, "Let my servant Brigham give again all that he has," I would obey it in a moment, if it took the last coat off my back.

A hymn was sung.

Elder Kimball arose and said: I get up of necessity to say a few words. I am unwell, but I feel the importance of this work. I have been a member of this Church twelve years. I came out of the Baptist church and joined this with all my heart, as I was seeking after truth. I have passed through everything but death; in fact I have been brought into situations even worse than death. It has been my lot and privilege to sacrifice all I possessed from time to time; and we have come here to call for help to build the Temple and Nauvoo House. I have spent thirty dollars to get here, and have collected fifteen and that with much difficulty.

We were commanded of the Lord to come: but it seems as though but few felt interested in it. Here I see four brethren going as missionaries to the Sandwich Islands, and destitute of means to help themselves. I could weep for them. I feel interested in this great work. We are seeking to bring about a work that could never before be performed.

When the time is brought about that we are to receive our inheritances, the more faithful we are, the larger will be our reward. We have come out to reap, but do we have time to reap new grain? No; for it takes all our time to try to save that which is already reaped.

We have reapers in the field, and we are trying to save the wheat. We want to get it on the barn floor, so that we may thrash it. We have come after it to warn you. You think Elder Young put the flail on rather heavy; but it is nothing to be compared with the thrashing you will get in Zion, and those who have the hardest heads will, of course, have to be thrashed the hardest. But don't be troubled about the chaff when it comes to the barn, for God will prepare a great winnowing mill which will blow all the chaff away, and the wheat will be found before the mill: then it has to go through the smut machine, then ground, then put through the bolting machine, and many will bolt in going through. I speak in parables. I compare the Saints to a good cow. When you milk her clean, she will always have an abundance of milk to give; but if you only milk her a little, and don't strip her, she will soon dry up. So with the Saints: if they do but little in building up Zion, they soon have but little to do with. This was the case in Cincinnati.

The night before arriving at Cincinnati, I had a dream while on the steamboat. I dreamt that I had a wagon with a rack on it, and an individual with me. We were going to a field of wheat of mine that had been cut, bound and shocked up, in order to haul into the barn. When we came to the field, I jumped off the wagon, and got over the fence to examine it, pulled off the cap sheaf, and behold it was oats. Pulling the bundles apart, I found there were clusters of rats. On further examination I found clusters of mice, and the oats were all eaten up.

In my dream I was going to haul in wheat, but to my astonishment it was oats, and they were all eaten up by the rats and mice.

I thought these rats and mice were the Elders and official members who had been in and lain on the Church at Cincinnati—lived on the wheat—eaten it up instead of building up new branches; so that when the Twelve came along, they could not get anything for the Temple or Nauvoo House, or hardly a place to stay. The rats had eaten up the wheat, so we had to go to the world for a home to stay while we were there.

We do not profess to be polished stones like Elders Almon W. Babbitt, George J. Adams, James Blakeslee, and Eli P. Maginn, &c., &c.; but we are rough stones out of the mountain; and when we roll through the forest, and knock the bark from the trees, it does not hurt us, even if we should get a corner knocked off occasionally; for the more we roll about, and knock the corners off, the better we are; but if we were polished and smooth when we get the corners knocked off, it would deface us.

Joseph Smith never professed to be a dressed, smooth, polished stone, but to have come rough out of the mountain; and he has been rolling among the rocks and trees, yet it has not hurt him at all: but he will be as smooth and polished in the end as any other stone, while many who were so very polished and smooth in the beginning get badly defaced and spoiled while they are rolling about.

Elder Parley P. Pratt said—Some are going to Zion, and the rest want to know what they shall do. The Lord, through Jeremiah (iii, 14,15) says, "I will take you one of a city, and two of a family, and I will bring you to Zion: and I will give you pastors according to mine heart, which shall feed you with knowledge and understanding." Inasmuch as you hearken to counsel, you will know what the will of the Lord is concerning you in all things. Meet often together to worship God and to speak to each other of the things of God. Gather as soon as you can. Come up to the mountain of the Lord's house, and there learn of these things, that the Scriptures may be fulfilled.

Elder Orson Pratt said—I do not know that I can say anything to impress the subjects which have been spoken upon more fully upon your minds than has been done. There are some things, however, I wish to mention. We have learned from what we have heard this day that great blessings will be given to the faithful when the Temple is finished. I will speak of some of the consequences that will follow, if we do not obey.

When the Temple is reared, God will manifest Himself in a peculiar manner. If we are obedient, He has told us He will make manifest to us things we are ignorant of. He has said He will reveal things which pertain to this dispensation that have been hidden and kept secret from the foundation of the world.

No former age or generation of the world have had the same things revealed: all other dispensations will be swallowed up in this. He declares, in His revelations, the consequences of not building the house unto His name within such a time. The Lord says, If you build the house in that time, you shall be blessed; but if not, you shall be rejected as a church with your dead, saith the Lord. So, if that house is not built, then in vain are all our cares; our faith and works, our meetings and hopes are vain also; our performances and acts will be void.

The servants of God who are faithful and do their duty will get the blessing; and we are determined to do our duty, and lay these principles before the Saints, so that they may have the privilege of contributing. We will turn this responsibility upon the heads of the Saints; then our garments will be clear, and the Lord is able and will be willing to endow all the faithful in some other place.

This Church, in its infancy, was directed to do a certain work, and the consequences pointed out. The Lord gave a revelation several years since to the Church to appoint our wise men, and send up our moneys by them to buy land: if not, we should not have an inheritance, but our enemies should be upon us. We went through and told the Saints these things; but did the churches do as God commanded? No, they did not. But the revelation was fulfilled, and the enemies of the Saints came upon them, and drove them from their houses and homes, and finally from the State of Missouri. This was in consequence of their disobeying the commandments of God through His servant Joseph.

Many suppose they must get direct revelation from God for themselves. Not so. He has a prophet, and he says the Church shall give heed to the words of the Prophet, as he is to hold the keys of the kingdom of God in this life and in the world to come. Then it is of much consequence that you give heed to his word.

Says one, Suppose we are not satisfied that this is the work of God? You can ask God if the work is true, and He will give you a testimony. You can put every confidence in the Book of Mormon and in Joseph, the Prophet; and if you are not satisfied, go to God. I doubt in my own mind if men can stand what they will have to pass through, unless they do get a witnes for themselves; and I pray you to give heed to the words which the Twelve have taught you, and ask God to help you.

The conference was adjourned until ten o'clock tomorrow morning.

Sunday, 10th. Conference met according to adjournment.

Meeting was opened by singing, and prayer by Elder Maginn; after which Elder Wilford Woodruff addressed the assembly from Amos iii:7—"Surely the Lord God will do nothing, but he revealeth his secret unto his servants the prophets?" According to the testimony of the Scriptures in all ages of the world, whenever God was about to bring a judgment upon the world or accomplish any great work, the first thing he did was to raise up a Prophet, and reveal unto him the secret, and send him to warn the people, so that they may be left without excuse. This was the case in the days of Noah and Lot. God was about to bring judgments upon the people, and he raised up those Prophets who warned the people of it: yet they gave no heed to them, but rejected their testimony; and the judgments came upon the people, so that they were destroyed, while the Prophets were saved by pursuing the course marked out by the Lord.

Jesus Christ testified to the Jews of the things that awaited them as a nation, the fall of Jerusalem, and their dispersion among the Gentile world; but they did not believe it. Yet the secret of all these things was revealed to the Prophets and Apostles. They believed it, and looked for its fulfillment; and it came to pass as it was predicted, though contrary to the expectation of the Jewish nation.

In like manner do we look for the certain fulfillment of those tremendous events upon the heads of the Gentile world which have been spoken of and pointed out by all the holy Prophets and Apostles since the world began, they having spoken as they were moved upon by the power of God and the gift of the Holy Ghost, events which more deeply concern the Gentile world than the overthrow of Jerusalem and the dispersion of the Jews did the Jewish nation; for while they stumbled at the stone they were broken; but when it falls upon the heads of the Gentile world, it will grind them to powder.

The full set time is come for the Lord to set His hand to accomplish these mighty events; and as He has done in other ages, so has He done now—He has raised up a Prophet, and is revealing unto him His secrets. Through that Prophet He has brought to light the fullness of the everlasting Gospel to the present generation, and is again once more for the last time establishing His Church upon the foundation of the ancient Apostles and Prophets, which is revelation, Jesus Christ being the chief corner stone.

In the Church is now found judges as at the first, and counselors as at the beginning; also Apostles, Prophets, Evangelists, Pastors, and Teachers, with gifts and graces, for the perfecting of the Saints, the work of the ministry, and the edifying of the body of Christ.

The Lord has raised up His servants, and sent them into the vineyard to prune it once more for the last time, to preach the Gospel of Jesus Christ, and to warn the nations, that they may be left without excuse in the day of their visitation; also to gather the honest in heart and the meek of the earth, that Zion may be built up, and the sayings of the Prophets fulfilled.

One of the secrets that God has revealed unto his Prophet in these days is the Book of Mormon; and it was a secret to the whole world until it was revealed unto Joseph Smith, whom God has raised up as a Prophet, Seer, and Revelator unto His people. This record contains an account of the ancient inhabitants of this continent and of the cities with which they overspread this land from sea to sea, the ruins of which still remain as standing monuments of the arts, science, power, and greatness of their founders. It also points out the establishing of this our own nation, with the conditions for its progress, and those predictions contained in the Book of Mormon—the stick of Joseph in the hand of Ephraim, will as truly be fulfilled as those contained in the Bible—the stick and record of Judah; and both these sticks or records contain prophecies of great import concerning the Gentile nations, and especially this land and nation, which are not yet fulfilled, but must shortly come to pass: yea, their fulfillment is nigh, even at the doors.

Though the secrets which God is revealing through His servant the Prophet in these last days may be unpopular and unbelieved in by the world, yet their unbelief will not make the truth of God of none effect, any more than it did in the days of Lot and Noah, or at the fall of Jerusalem.

When Jesus Christ said there should not be left one stone upon another in the temple that should not be thrown down, the Jewish nation did not believe it, neither would they receive such testimony; but they looked at outward circumstances, and were ready to say, "Who can prevail against us? What nation like unto our nation? We have held the giving of the law, the oracles, and the Urim and Thummim; the lawgiver has never departed from between our feet; we have held the power of government from generation to generation; and what nation hath power now to prevail against us?"

Through this order of reasoning they were blinded, and knew not the day of their visitation: they understood not the things that belonged to their peace; they rejected their Lord and King, contended against the word and testimony, and finally put Him to death on the cross, with many who followed Him. But this did not hinder the fulfillment of His predictions concerning that nation. The words of the Lord had gone forth out of His mouth, and could not return unto Him void. The things that belonged to their peace were hid from their eyes, and they were counted unworthy as a nation. The kingdom was to be rent out of their hands and given to another; the die was cast, and judgment must come.

Jerusalem was soon surrounded by the Roman army, led on by the inspired Titus; and a scene of calamity, judgment, and woe immediately overspread the inhabitants of that city, which was devoted to destruct-ion,—such a calamity as never before rested upon the nation of Israel. Blood flowed through their streets; tens of thousands fell by the edge of the sword, and thousands by famine. Women were evil towards the children of their own bosoms in the straitness of the siege, the spectacle of which shocked the Roman soldiers as they entered the city. The Jews were crucified in such numbers by their enemies that they could find no more wood for crosses, or room for their bodies; and while despair was in every face, and every heart sinking while suffering under the chastening hand of God, their enemies rushed upon them in the city to strike the last fatal blow; and, as their last resort, they rushed for safety into the temple, which was soon on fire, and they sank in the midst of the flames with the cry of their sufferings ascending up on high, accompanied by the smoke of the crackling spires and towers.

The remaining population were sold as slaves, and driven like the dumb ass under his burthen, and scattered, as corn is sifted in a sieve, throughout the Gentile world. Jerusalem was razed from its foundations, the ruins of the temple thrown down, and the foundation thereof ploughed up, that not one stone was left upon another. Christ said that Jerusalem should be trodden down of the Gentiles until the times of the Gentiles be fulfilled, which has been the case to the very letter until the present generation.

Will not God in like manner as truly and faithfully bring to pass those great, important and tremendous events upon the heads of the Gentile world which have been proclaimed by the Prophets Isaiah, Jeremiah, Ezekiel, Daniel, and many other holy Prophets; also by Christ and the Apostles on the continent of Asia, as well as by Lehi, Nephi, Alma, Moroni, and others on this continent—all of whom have proclaimed these things as they were moved upon by the Spirit of inspiration, the power of God, and the gift of the Holy Ghost?

The Apostle says that "No prophecy of the Scripture is of any private interpretation, for the prophecy came not of old time by the will of man: but holy men of God spake as they were moved by the Holy Ghost."

Isaiah's soul seemed to be on fire, and his mind wrapt in the visions of the Almighty, while he declared, in the name of the Lord, that it should come to pass in the last days that God should set His hand again the second time to recover the remnant of His people, assemble the outcasts of Israel, gather together the dispersed of Judah, destroy the tongue of the Egyptian sea and make men go over dry-shod, gather them to Jerusalem on horses, mules, swift beasts, and in chariots, and rebuild Jerusalem upon her own heaps; while, at the same time, the destroyer of the Gentiles will be on his way; and while God was turning the captivity of Israel, he would put all their curses and afflictions upon the heads of the Gentiles, their enemies, who had not sought to recover, but to destroy them, and had trodden them under foot from generation to generation.

At the same time the standard should be lifted up, that the honest in heart, the meek of the earth among the Gentiles, should seek unto it; and that Zion should be redeemed and be built up a holy city, that the glory and power of God should rest upon her, and be seen upon her; that the watchman upon Mount Ephraim might cry— "Arise ye, and let us go up unto Zion, the city of the Lord our God;" that the Gentiles might come to her light, and kings to the brightness of her rising; that the Saints of God may have a place to flee to and stand in holy places while judgment works in the earth; that when the sword of God that is bathed in heaven falls upon Idumea, or the world,—when the Lord pleads with all flesh by sword and by fire, and the slain of the Lord are many, the Saints may escape these calamities by fleeing to the places of refuge, like Lot and Noah.

Isaiah, in his 24th chapter, gives something of an account of the calamities and judgments which shall come upon the heads of the Gentile nations, and this because they have transgressed the laws, changed the ordinance, and broken the everlasting covenant. The Apostle Paul says to his Roman brethren, that if the Gentiles do not continue in the goodnes of God, they, like the house of Israel, should be cut off. Though Babylon says, "I sit as a queen, and am no widow, and shall see no sorrow," the Revelator says, "Therefore shall her plagues come in one day, death and mourning and famine; and she shall be utterly burned with fire, for strong is the Lord God who judgeth her."

Jesus communicated the parable of the fig-tree, which in putting forth its leaves betokens the approach of summer; and so likewise, when we see the signs in the sun, moon, and stars, and in the heavens and the earth of which He spoke, we might know that His coming is near—that the generation in which those signs appeared should not pass away till all should be fulfilled.

These things are about to come to pass upon the heads of the present generation, notwithstanding they are not looking for it, neither do they believe it. Yet their unbelief will not make the truth of God of none effect. The signs are appearing in the heavens and on the earth, and all things indicate the fulfillment of the Prophets. The fig-tree is leafing, summer is nigh, and the Lord has sent his angels to lay the foundation of this great and important work.

Then why should not God reveal His secrets unto His servants the Prophets, that the Saints might be led in paths of safety, and escape those evils which are about to engulf a whole generation in ruin?

Monday, 11. Conference met at Boylston Hall at nine o'clock, a. m. Present of the quorum of the Twelve, Elders Brigham Young, Parley P. Pratt, Orson Pratt, John E. Page, Wilford Woodruff, George A. Smith, Heber C. Kimball, and Orson Hyde.

Opened with prayer by Elder Page.

Elder Brigham Young stated the object of the meeting. The first item of business is the spread of the Gospel of salvation. I want to state what devolves upon the Twelve. Nine years ago a revelation was given which was fulfilled in 1835; and when fulfilled, the Prophet lifted up his head and rejoiced before the Lord. Previously, the responsibility of spreading the Gospel rested on him; now it is on the Twelve. This is the relation we hold between the living and the dead—to direct how you may escape.

Last winter we were directed to send men to the nations of the earth. Elder Addison Pratt had been to the Sandwich Islands, and proffered his services. We have power to ordain them, and call upon the Church to assist in sending them. Here are four men willing to go, and we do not wish them to cease trying, unless it be to die trying. One of them is ill. If he stays, he will die. I would go, or die trying.

We call on the churches to fit out these men with necessaries. Elder Eli P. Maginn and Elder Philip B. Lewis we call on to fit them out. If

Elder Lewis does not, Maginn will do it himself. This takes the responsibility from us.

If the Saints will not help, the curse of God will rest upon them. If the Temple at Nauvoo is not built, we will receive our endowments, if we have to go into the wilderness and build an altar of stone. If a man gives his all, it is all God requires. Brother Kimball has received one dollar since he came to Boston, and seventeen dollars and a half before, towards building the Temple. A book is kept of all sums given. This book will also be opened. All is recorded. I have received twenty-three dollars, and I have spent about forty-five or fifty dollars. I am rich, and expect to be so throughout all eternity, with the help of God and my brethren. I can get home, if I can sell land. Some of the Twelve are more destitute; but they are the best set of boys you ever saw.

During the persecution in Missouri, when the mob came against Far West, Elder Kimball stood near me in one of the companies; and every time they formed, he rammed down another ball into his old musket, until be got five balls in. We are a good-feeling set of men, because of the Spirit which is in us. What produces it? The impulse of the heart. We should feel the same on the desert of Arabia, or on the islands of the sea; we feel happy wherever we are. When we ask for victuals, and get turned away, as we often have been, we feel just as well.

The Spirit which is in me prompts me to look forward to something better. We have a prospect of selling shares of the Nauvoo House, and of obtaining subscriptions for the Temple, and we feel better.

Here are twelwe men, and I defy all creation to bring a charge of dishonesty against them. We had to give security for the faithful performance of our duty as agents for the Nauvoo House and Temple. This has been heretofore unheard of in the Church. I glory in it. The financial affairs of the Church rest on our shoulders, and God is going to whip us into it. When men are in future called to do like Brigham, I will be one to bind them: this is a precedent. We are the only legally authorized agents of the Church to manage affairs, give counsel to emigrants how to dispose of goods, &c.

Some men come into this Church through designing purposes. Mr. Cowen, who lives about 30 miles above Nauvoo, wanted Brother Joseph to make a settlement at Shoquokon. Several of the brethren went there and preached, and some families moved up with the intention of settling. Mr. Cowen was all love—a charming fellow, and calculated to magnetize. He is now in the Eastern country, and going amongst the brethren. He gives one a kiss, and says he, "I am not a Mormon, but expect to be: Brother Joseph and myself are confidential friends. Can't you lend me five hundred dollars? I have got land, and I will give you a mortgage." At the same time, he knew quite well that his land was in a perfect swamp, and that the place was not fit for a settlement. Even the captains of steamers could with difficulty be persuaded upon to call there, either on account of goods or passengers. His name is John F. Cowen, and he stands five feet six inches high. There are others.

I would ask the Latter-day Saints, Do you know your benefactors? Do you know the source from whence you derive your knowledge? Take in the publications and periodicals of the Church. They give you intelligence of all matters pertaining to this dispensation with revelations for the guidance of the Church.

I know that men who go through the world with the truth have not much influence; but let them come with silk velvet lips and sophistry, and they will have an influence. It is your privilege to be discerners of spirits. If you don't know me or the Twelve, walk with us fifty years, and perhaps you will know us then; and if such a man as Cowen comes along, will you trust him or me? No power can hide the heart from the discerning eye. If we are ignorant, what knowledge have the rest of the people? I sit down with all my ignorance, and read people's hearts as I see their faces, and they can't help themselves.

No one has ever stepped aside but I have known it. I know the result of their actions, and they cannot help themselves. If you find out my heart, you are welcome to it. If any of the Twelve take a wrong path, or a course by themselves, I know the path, and know the end of it. They are soon in the ditch, crying for help. I sit down and let others run. I strike with a crooked stick to hit the whole.

Now, the Twelve must be helped home, and there must be something for the Temple and the Nauvoo House. We have got a plot of the city of Nauvoo for lithographing. If any wish to advance the money to lithograph, and have a few thousands struck off, they shall be paid till they are satisfied. There was not wealth enough in New York and the regions round about. [He here exhibited the map of Nauvoo.] He concluded with a few remarks relative to the circumstances of Elder Hyde, who had just returned from his mission to Jerusalem.

Elder Parley P. Pratt spoke as follows:—In the middle of last April I arrived at Nauvoo houseless and with a large family. Brother Joseph said to me, "Brother Parley, stay at home and build a house." I was behindhand in instructions and information, while others had been at home learning the great things of God. I have now come East principally on business, though I always have a mission, wherever I am. I speak for my brethren: they have an absolute claim; it belongs to them, and they want it. It is justly theirs. I ask for nothing for myself.

Elder Heber C. Kimball said, I suppose you all understand what

Elder Young has said, and I consider his counsel good. He is my superior and my head in the council of the Twelve. If I go astray, it will be through ignorance. We must be subject to the powers that be; and there are no powers but what are ordained of God; and if we reject their counsel, we shall be damned. Some of our finest-looking and smartest men have fallen.

I consider those trees in the forest which have the largest and highest tops are in the greatest danger: they are blown down; and there is no way of restoring them but to cut them off. Let the stump go back, and new sprouts come out. Those who have most responsibility are in most danger. We must be careful how we treat God's officers.

No man ever fell, unless it was through rejecting counsel. I as well as my brethren see this. My superior knows more than I, because he is nearer the fountain. To get knowledge, begin at the foot of the stream, and drink all up till you get to the fountain, and then you get all the knowledge.

It is necessary for the people here to obey counsel. God has sent me forth, through his servants, to take my part in this great work, and the work is true. I know there are but few in this Church who will be able to walk in this narrow path. We must keep the celestial law in the flesh. The more simple we teach, the better for us.

It is a wrong idea of Elders whipping sects. Try and win the people; salt both sheep and shepherd too; get them up so that they will lick the salt out of your hands. [An infidel here handed money to Brother Kimball, who prophesied that he would be a Saint and an Elder, and all his family should be Saints.] Give them good salt, gain the affections of the shepherd, and the whole flock will come. Now, we get sheep up to lick; and when the old shepherd of the sheep comes up to lick salt, the Elders will hit him over the head with a cane. Their religion is as dear to them as ours to us. Don't feed too much salt at once, but give a little at a time, or they are cloyed.

Elders of Israel, be wise! Give short discourses, as long ones cloy your hearers, who will say, "A good discourse, but I got tired."

Never infringe on the right of other people, and never tear down other people's houses until you have built a better. We are sent to preach repentance, and let people alone. How do you like to go into other Churches and hear them abuse us? Do as you would be done by. Persuade men, and not compel them, unless the time spoken of by the Savior comes, when the Lord shall say unto His servants "Go out into the highways and hedges, and compel them to come in, that my house may be filled." (Luke 14 ch., 23 v.) Let men be humble, kind and affectionate.

CHAPTER II.

MOVEMENTS OF APOSTLES IN THE EAST—THE NAUVOO MANSION—ROCKWELL ACQUITTED—SPECIAL CONFERENCE AT NAUVOO—DISCOURSE OF THE PROPHET ON THE DEMISE OF JAMES ADAMS.

Sunday, September 10, 1843.—Cold, and considerable rain. Kindled a fire in the office for the first time this fall. This is the first rain of any consequence since the first of June. There have been occasional—say three or four slight showers, but not enough to wet the potatoe hills, and the vegetables in the gardens have generally stopped growing, on account of the drougth. Even corn is seriously injured,—much of it by a worm in the ear. Early potatoes are scarcely worth digging.

The Drought of 1843.

Monday, 11.—Early in the morning a petition was presented to me, as Lieut.-General, to devise means to get the public arms of the State for the Legion; whereupon I appointed William W. Phelps, Henry Miller, and Hosea Stout a committee to wait on Governor Ford on the subject.

Election for probate justice; weather cold; people cold. Greenleaf received most of the votes in Nauvoo—say seven hundred votes.

Six, p. m., I met with my Brother Hyrum, William Law, Newel K. Whitney, and Willard Richards in my private room, where we had a season of prayer for Brother Law's little daughter, who was sick, and Emma, who was somewhat better.

Tuesday, 12.—Rainy day.

Woodruff in a Train Wreck.

Elder Woodruff left Boston for Portland by railroad and while passing through Chester woods, the engine was thrown off the tracks, and with the baggage cars smashed to pieces. Several of the passenger cars mounted the ruins, but none of the passengers were injured, except two very slightly. The engineer, however, was killed instantaneously. Elder Woodruff, with most of the passengers, remained all night in the woods, and found it very cold.

Wednesday, 13.—I attended a lecture at the Grove, by Mr. John Finch, a Socialist, from England, and said a few words in reply.

The following article appears [this day] in the *Neighbor*, copied from *The New Haven*, Conn., *Herald:*—

NAUVOO AND JOSEPH SMITH.

A gentleman of this town, (New Haven, Conn.) of undoubted veracity, who has lately spent several weeks at Nauvoo and among the Mormons, informs us that the general impression abroad in regard to that place and people is very erroneous. During his residence there he became quite familiar with their manners, principles, and habits, and says there is not a more industrious, moral, and well-ordered town in the country. Society is as much diversified there as it is here, the Mormons constituting about two-thirds of the population, while all religious sects are as freely tolerated as in any other part of the State. He was at the late trial and acquittal of Joseph Smith, and says that the charges against him were of the most frivolous and unsubstantial nature. He [Joseph Smith] is an agreeable man in conversation, is respected by those who know him, and is 'as much sinned against as sinning.' He only claims the privilege of exercising and enjoying his own religion,—a privilege which he and his followers cheerfully award to others. They invite immigrants to come among them, and receive those who design to enter into the Mormon community with great attention and kindness. Houses are prepared for their reception, to which they are conducted on their arrival by a committee appointed for that purpose, whose next business is to attend to their immediate wants and see them comfortably situated. Education is by no means neglected, proper schools and teachers being provided, and temperance reigns throughout. It has now about 15,000 to 18,000 inhabitants, and promises to become a place of extensive business, four or five steamboats stopping there every day.

The gentleman remarked to us that he wished he could speak as well of his own native town as he could of Nauvoo. This is news to us, as no doubt it will be to many; but no one who knows him can doubt the integrity of our informant.

Thursday, 14.—I attended a second lecture on Socialism, by Mr. Finch; and after he got through, I made a few remarks, alluding to Sidney Rigdon and Alexander Campbell getting up a community at Kirtland, and of the big fish there eating up all the little fish. *I said I did not believe the doctrine.*

The Prophet on Socialism.

Mr. Finch replied in a few minutes, and said—"I am the voice of one crying in the wilderness. I am the spiritual Prophet—Mr. Smith the temporal."

Elder John Taylor replied to the lecture at some length.

Friday, 15.—I put up a sign,

"NAUVOO MANSION."

In consequence of my house being constantly crowded with strangers and other persons wishing to see me, or who had business in the city, I found myself unable to support so much company free of charge, which I have done from the foundation of the Church. My house has been a home and resting-place for thousands, and my family many times obliged to do without food, after having fed all they had to visitors; and I could have continued the same liberal course, had it not been for the cruel and untiring persecution of my relentless enemies. I have been reduced to the necessity of opening "The Mansion" as a hotel. I have provided the best table accommodations in the city; and the Mansion, being large and convenient, renders travelers more comfortable than any other place on the Upper Mississippi. I have erected a large and commodious brick stable, and it is capable of accommodating seventy-five horses at one time, and storing the requisite amount of forage, and is unsurpassed by any similar establishment in the State.

"Nauvoo Mansion" Made a Hotel.

There was an officers' drill in Nauvoo.

Rhoda Ann, daughter of Willard and Jenetta Richards, was born at fifteen minutes to three, p. m., in Nauvoo.

Legion Parade and Inspection.

Saturday, 16.—General parade of the Nauvoo Legion near my farm. Went in company with my staff to the muster, was met by an escort, and arrived before the Legion about noon. I was received and saluted with military honors. The Legion was dismissed at about one, p. m., for two hours, and I rode home to dinner. I returned about twenty minutes after three, attended the review, and with my staff inspected the Legion; after which, I took my post and gave orders.

After the inspection, I made a speech to the Legion on their increasing prosperity, and requested the officers to increase the Legion in numbers.

I was highly gratified with the officers and soldiers, and I felt extremely well myself.

About sundown the Legion was dismissed. I rode home with my staff, highly delighted with the day's performance, and well paid for my services.

Sunday, 17.—I was at meeting; and while Elder Almon W. Babbitt was preaching, I took my post as Mayor outside the assembly to keep order and set an example to the other officers.

After preaching, I gave some instructions about order in the congregation, men among women, and women among men, horses in the assembly, and men and boys on the stand who do not belong there, &c.

In the evening Mr. Blodgett, a Unitarian minister, preached. I was gratified with his sermon in general, but differed in opinion on some points, on which I freely expressed myself to his great satisfaction,—*viz.*, on persecution making the work spread, like rooting up a flower-garden or kicking back the sun!

Monday, 18.— I received a letter from Governor Ford as follows:—

Letter of Governor Ford to the Prophet.

SPRINGFIELD, September 13, 1843.

DEAR SIR,—In answer to your letter, I have the honor to reply, that I will consider it my duty to prevent the invasion of this State, if in my power, by any persons elsewhere for any hostile purposes whatever.

From information in my possession, I am of opinion that there is but little danger of any such invasion. It is altogether more likely that some other mode of annoyance will be adopted. My enemies here, I think, are endeavoring to put something of the kind on foot.

I am, most respectfully,

Your obedient servant,

THOMAS FORD.

I attended a council at my old house.

Conference in Nova Scotia.

A conference was held at Preston, Halifax County, Nova Scotia. 1 Elder, 1 Teacher, 1 Deacon, and 14 members were represented. Robert Dixon, president; J. Jermen, clerk.

David Greenleaf was elected probate judge for the county of Hancock, by a majority of 598 votes.

Tuesday, 19.—I directed Brother Phelps to answer the letter recently received from the Governor, and to enclose a copy of the resolutions passed at the meeting of the mobocracy at Carthage; which he did.

Wrote a letter to J. B. Backenstos.

A portion of the Twelve were present at a general muster of the independent companies of Boston. Saw a sham battle, in which thirty-five brass cannon were discharged seven times. One party was commanded by the Governor of Mass., and the other by the officer next in rank.

Wednesday, 20.—Visited my farm, accompanied by my Brother Hyrum.

The *Neighbor* has the following:—

PORTER ROCKWELL.

A few short months ago, it was heralded through this State that Porter Rockwell was the individual who attempted to murder ex-Governor Boggs, of Missouri. It was confidently stated that Joseph Smith was accessory before the fact. The thing was swallowed as a precious morsel by the enemies of Mormonism. It was iterated and reiterated by the public journals, and the general expression of a certain class was that Mr. Smith ought to be hung; there was no doubt of his guilt; he was one of the most inhuman, diabolical, dangerous, and malignant persons in the universe; and when a requisition was made for him by the Governor of Missouri, it was considered worse than "arson" or "treason" that he should be acquitted by the legal authorities of this State, under *habeas corpus;* and afterwards, when Porter Rockwell was taken, it was exultingly stated that they had got the scoundrel, and that he would now receive the due demerit of his crime. How stands the matter when it is investigated—investigated by a Missouri court? The following will show:—

The last *Independence Expositor* says:—"Orin Porter Rockwell, the Mormon confined in our county jail, some time since, for the attempted assassination of ex-Governor Boggs, was indicted by our last grand jury for escaping from our county jail some time since, and sent to Clay county for trial. Owing, however, to some informality in the proceedings, he was remanded to this county again for trial. There was not sufficient proof adduced against him to predicate an indictment for shooting ex-Govornor Boggs, and the grand jury therefore did not indict him for that offense."—[*St. Louis New Era.*]

It appears, then, after all the bluster, the hue-and-cry about Mormon outrages, Mormon intrigue, "blood," "arson," and "murder," that "there was not sufficient proof adduced against him to predicate an indictment for shooting ex-Governor Boggs, and the grand jury therefore did not indict him for that offense." This speaks for itself: it needs no comment. We are glad, for the sake of suffering innocence, that Mr. Rockwell stands clear in the eyes of the law. Thus it seeme that after exerting all their malice and hellish rage to implicate the innocent, they can find no proof against him. But yet he must be again incarcerated, without proof, for another hearing. This is Missouri justice. If he was guilty of breaking jail, why not try and punish him for that before that court? Where is the necessity of remanding him to another county for another hearing? It is evident that they wish to immolate him, and, by offering him as a sacrifice, glut their thirst for innocent blood.

I answered Governor Ford's letter received on the 18th.

Pacific Island Mission.

Elder Brigham Young instructed Elder Addison Pratt to go and engage a passage for himself and Elders Noah Rogers, Knowlton F. Hanks, and B. F. Grouard, as missionaries to the Pacific Islands, although they had not one-tenth of the means on hand to pay their passage.

In the evening, Elders Brigham Young, Heber C. Kimball, Orson Pratt, Wilford Woodruff, George A. Smith, and John E. Page visited Mr. O. S. Fowler, the phrenologist, who examined their heads and gave their phrenological charts.

Thursday, *21*.—Made affidavit with Willard Richards and William Clayton to Auditor of State *v.* Walter Bagby.

About eleven, a. m., called with my Brother Samuel H. to see about getting a copy of his blessing, and wished Doctor Richards much joy in his new daughter.

About noon, went on board the *Maid of Iowa*, with William Clayton, clerk of the boat.

One, p. m., the thermometer stood at 100 deg. in the shade.

Friday, *22*.—The Twelve visited the Navy Yard and Harbor of Boston, the *Mississippi* steamship, the rope-walk, the Bunker-hill monument, the State-house, and the State's prison. In the evening they addressed the Saints in Boylston Hall.

Elder Addison Pratt, accompanied by Elder Philip B. Lewis engaged a passage to the Society Islands at $100 each for himself, Noah Rogers, Knowlton F. Hanks, and B. F. Grouard.

Saturday. *23*.—Elder Stephen Markham returned from Dixon, the trial of Reynolds and Wilson being postponed till May next.

Bishop George Miller returned from the Pinery. He reports the water in Black River so low that they could not get their raft into the Mississippi.

Report from the Pinery.

I had an interview with Elder Orson Spencer, from whom I borrowed $75 for the Temple.

Sunday, *24*.—I preached on the stand about one hour on the 2nd chapter of Acts, designing to show the folly of common stock. In Nauvoo every

Stewardship vs. Common Stock.

one is steward over his own. After preaching, I called upon the brethren to draw stone for the Temple, and gave notice for a special conference for the 6th of October next. Adjourned the meeting about one, p. m., on account of the prospect of rain. Judge McBride and a lawyer from Missouri were present at the meeting.

Monday, 25.—Wet day. At home. Held a conversation with the Missouri lawyer.

Tuesday, 26—Held Mayor's Court, and tried the case of "Dana *v.* Leeches." No cause of action. Called at the store about six, p. m., and directed the clerk to issue papers in the case of "Medagh *v.* Hovey."

Wednesday, 27.—The *Neighbor* of this date has the following editorial:-

CONCERNING HORSE THIEVES.

We find that the *Quincy Whig* has some very righteous remarks to make concerning the Mormons, emanating from the purest principles of patriotism. (?) The editor has had some "*private* conversation" with some individual or individuals about certain charges brought against the Mormons, particulary that of screening horse thieves.

We think that the *Whig* has not done itself much credit in advocating the principles contained in those resolutions. We leave that, however, for a discerning public to judge.

Concerning the horse thieves, however, the informant of the *Whig* would have shown himself a better friend to society to have given information to the proper authorities, and had these pests of society brought to condign punishment. And the editor of that paper would have proved himself more patriotic by telling us who these people are that are screened in our midst, than dealing thus in generals and stabbing in the dark.

Come, Mr. *Whig*, out with it, and let us know who it is that is found transgressing. Who knows but that, far fallen as we are, there yet may be virtue enough left to prosecute a horse thief! We have tried this more than once, and prosecuted them as far as Carthage; but no sooner do they arrive in the jail there than we lose all track of them. The lock of the door is so slippery, that it lets them all out. We presume, however, that it is on account of the honesty of the people. (?) We are pleased to find that the *Whig* is in the secret!

Mr. Ivins, of this city, had a horse stolen last week, and we frequently have occurrences of the kind. Will the editor of that paper be so kind as to ask his informant who the thieves are, and where they live, and give us the desired information? and we shall esteem it a peculiar favor.

I was at home all day, and gave Brother Phelps the privilege of occupying the small house near the store.

Thursday, *28*.—At half-past eleven, a. m., a council convened over the store, consisting of myself, my brother Hyrum, Uncle John Smith, Newel K. Whitney, George Miller, Willard Richards, John Taylor, Amasa Lyman, John M. Bernhisel, and Lucien Woodworth; and at seven in the evening we met in the front upper room of the Mansion, with William Law and William Marks. By the common consent and unanimous voice of the council, I was chosen president of the special council.

Meeting of a Special Council.

The president led in prayer that his days might be prolonged until his mission on the earth is accomplished, have dominion over his enemies, all their households be blessed, and all the Church and the world.

Friday, *29*.—Elder Brigham Young started from Boston for Nauvoo. The Twelve were now scattered among the branches in the Eastern States.

Saturday, *30*.—Rainy, and strong west wind.

Elders Young and Woodruff stayed at Elder Forster's, in New York.

Sunday, *October 1*, *1843*.—I copy the following from the *Times and Seasons* of this date:—

WHO SHALL BE OUR NEXT PRESIDENT?

This question we frequently hear asked, and it is a question of no small importance to the Latter-day Saints.

We, as a people, have labored and are still laboring under great injustice from the hands of a neighboring state. The Latter-day Saints have had their property destroyed, and their houses made desolate by the hands of the Missourians; murders have been committed with impunity, and many, in consequence of oppression, barbarism, and cruelty, have slept the sleep of death. They [the Saints] have been obliged to flee from their possessions into a distant land, in the chilling frosts of winter, robbed, spoiled, desolate, houseless, and homeless, without any just pretext or shadow of law, without having violated the laws of that state, or the United States; and have had to wander as exiles in a strange land, without as yet being able to obtain any redress for their grievances.

We have hitherto adopted every legal measure. First, we petitioned the State of Missouri, but in vain. We have memorialized Congress, but they have turned a deaf ear to our supplication, and referred us again to the State and *justice* of Missouri. Doubtless many of the members of that honorable body were not sufficiently informed of the enormity and extent of the crimes of our persecutors, nor of the indelible stain which our national escutcheon has received through their inhuman daring. They have been allowed to revel in blood and luxuriate in the miseries of the oppressed, and no man has laid it to heart.

The fact is that gentlemen of respectability and refinement, who live in a civilized society, find it difficult to believe that such enormities could be practiced in a Republican government. But our wrong cannot slumber. Such tyranny and oppression must not be passed over in silence. Our injuries, though past, are not forgotten by us; they still rankle in our bosoms, and the blood of the innocent yet cries for justice; and as American citizens we have appealed and shall still continue to appeal to the legally-constituted authorities of the land for redress, in the hopes that justice, which has long slumbered, may be aroused in our defense; that the spirit which burned in the bosoms of the patriots of '76 may fire the souls of their descendants; and though slow, that their indignation may yet be aroused at the injustice of the oppressor; and that they may yet mete out justice to our adversaries, and step forward in the defense of the innocent.

We shall ask no one to commit themselves on our account. We want no steps taken but what are legal, constitutional and honorable. But we are *American citizens*; and as American citizens we have rights in common with all that live under the folds of the "star-spangled banner." Our rights have been trampled upon by lawless miscreants. We have been robbed of our liberties by mobocratic influence, and all those honorable ties that ought to govern and characterize Columbia's sons have been trampled in the dust. Still we are *American Citizens*; and as American citizens we claim the privilege of being heard in the councils of our nation. We have been wronged, abused, robbed, and banished; and we seek redress. Such crimes can not slumber in Republican America. The cause of common humanity would revolt at it, and Republicanism would hide its head in disgust.

We make these remarks for the purpose of drawing the attention of our brethren to this subject, both at home and abroad, that we may fix upon the man who will be the most likely to render us assistance in obtaining redress for our grievances; and not only give our own votes, but use our influence to obtain others; and if the voice of suffering innocence will not sufficiently arouse the rulers of our nation to investigate our case, perhaps a vote of from fifty to one hundred thousand may rouse them from their lethargy.

We shall fix upon the man of our choice, and notify our friends duly.

I published the following in the same number of the *Times and Seasons*:—

THE APPOINTMENT OF A MISSION TO RUSSIA.

To all the Saints and honourable men of the earth to whom the Lord has given liberally of this world's goods, *greeting*:

Our worthy Brother, Elder George J. Adams, has been appointed by the First Presidency of the Church of Jesus Christ of Latter-day Saints at Nauvoo to present to them the importance, as well as the things connected with his mission to Russia, to introduce the fullness of the Gospel to the people of that vast empire, and also to which is attached some of the most important things concerning the advancement and building up of the kingdom of God in the last days, which cannot be explained at this time. But as the mission is attended with much expense, all those who feel disposed to bestow according as God has blessed them shall receive the blessings of Israel's God, and tenfold shall be added unto them, as well as the prayers of the Saints of God.

With sentiments of high esteem, we subscribe ourselves your friends and brethren in the now and everlasting covenant,

JOSEPH SMITH,
HYRUM SMITH.

Presidents of the Church of Jesus Christ of Latter-day Saints.*

I attended meeting this morning, and adjourned it in consequence of the cold and rain. The afternoon being more pleasant, the people assembled, and were addressed by Elders Marks, Charles C. Rich and Bishop Jacob Foutz.

Council met in the evening same as on Thursday previous.

Monday, 2.—At home.

Movements of Apostles in the East.

Tuesday, 3.—Elders Brigham Young, Heber C. Kimball, Orson Hyde, George A. Smith, Wilford Woodruff, and Jedediah M. Grant spent the day in visiting the Saints in Philadelphia. In the evening they partook of an oyster supper, on the invitation of Mr. Jeffreys.

* The fact that Sidney Rigdon and Wm. Law did not sign this document as in the First Presidency, should be noted.

The brethren assembled with their wives, to the number of about one hundred couple, and dined at the Mansion as an opening to the house. A very pleasant day, and all things passed off well.

The following is extracted from the *Neighbor* of this date.

PLEASURE PARTY AND DINNER AT THE NAUVOO MANSION.

General Joseph Smith, the proprietor of said house, provided a luxurious feast for a pleasure party; and all having partaken of the luxuries of a well-spread board, the cloth was removed, and a committee appointed to draft resolutions suitable to the occasion. They adjourned for a few moments and returned, when Robert D. Foster was appointed chairman.

The object of the meeting was then briefly stated by the chairman; after which a hymn was sung, and prayer by Elder Taylor. The chairman then arose and made some appropriate remarks for the occasion, touching upon the rise and progress of the city, the varied scenes through which the Saints had to pass, the persecutions and abuses the Prophets had to undergo, &c., &c. After which he read the following resolutions and toast, which were unanimously adopted:—

Resolved, 1st. That a vote of thanks be presented to General Joseph Smith and lady, through the medium of the *Nauvoo Neighbor*, for the very bountiful feast by them provided, for the accommodation of this party of more than one hundred couple at their Mansion.

Resolved, 2nd. General Joseph Smith, whether we view him as a Prophet at the head of the Church, a General at the head of the Legion, a Mayor at the head of the City Council, or as a landlord at the head of his table, if he has equals, he has no superiors.

Resolved, 3rd. Nauvoo, the great emporium of the West, the center of all centers, a city of three years' growth, a population of 15,000 souls congregated from the four quarters of the globe, embracing the intelligence of all nations, with industry, frugality, economy, virtue, and brotherly love, unsurpassed by any age in the world,—a suitable home for the Saints.

Resolved, 4th. Nauvoo Legion, a well disciplined and faithful band of invincibles, ready at all times to defend their country with this motto, "Vive la Republique."

Resolved, 5th. Nauvoo Charter, like the laws of the Medes and Persians, an unalterable decree by a patriotic band of wise legislators for the protection of the innocent.

Resolved, 6th. Thomas Ford, Governor of Illinois, fearless and faithful in the discharge of all official duties,—long may he live, and blessings attend his administration.

Colonel Francis M. Higbee was then called to the stand, who addressed the audience in a very spirited and appropriate manner for the day.

Professor Orson Spencer was then called, who arose, and in his usual easy and eloquent manner highly entertained the company for nearly half-an-hour.

The next called was Elder John Taylor, who alone was capable of putting on the top stone of the entertainment. His address was highly interesting, combining, like a Lacoon, a volume in every gesture.

General Smith then arose, and, in a very touching and suitable manner, tendered his thanks to the company for the encomiums and honors conferred on him. He recited the many woes through which he had passed, the persecutions which he had suffered, and the love he had for the brethren and citizens of Nauvoo. He tendered his gratitude for the pleasing prospects that surrounded him to the great Giver of all good. He said he thought that his case was similar to that of old Job's—that after he had suffered and drank the very dregs of affliction, the Lord had remembered him in mercy, and was about to bless him abundantly.

After he had done, Mrs. Emma Smith presented her thanks, through the chair, to the company present; after which, a motion was made and carried, to adjourn, whereupon the company were called to their feet. Benediction by Elder Taylor, and the party retired with the most perfect satisfaction and good humor as was ever witnessed on such occasions.

ROBERT D. FOSTER, Chairman.

In the evening Mr. William Backenstos and Clara M. Wasson were married at the Mansion. I solemnized the marriage in presence of a select party.

Wednesday, 4.—I extract the following from the *Neighbor* of this date:—

ANTI-MORMONISM.

With respect to the Carthage meeting, I take upon myself to deny the charges *in toto*, and challenge them to the proof. If we harbor horse-thieves among us, as is basely asserted, let the man that has lost his horse publish his name and the name of the villain, or how he knows him to be a Mormon, and where he is harbored, that we may have something more than vague assertions. They well know that no such proof can be produced, but that the charges had their birth in the minds of one or two heartless scoundrels thirsting for revenge for their late disappointments. The whole of the charges are a tissue of falsehoods got up with the idea of intimidating a peaceable body of citizens. But, sir, we set such designing knaves at defiance and laugh at their threats, treating them with utter contempt, but ever ready to abide by the truth.

JOHN GREENHOW.

Elder Reuben Hedlock wrote the following letter:—

Elder Reuben Hedlock to the First Presidency.

LIVERPOOL, October 4, 1843.

To the First Presidency and Quorum of the Twelve Apostles, greeting:—

DEAR AND MUCH ESTEEMED BRETHREN,—I hasten to inform you of my arrival in Liverpool on the 30th day of September, in company with Elders John Cairns, James Sloan and wife, James Houston, and William G. Jermon. We left six of the Twelve in the city of New York, the 2nd day of September, and came on board of the ship *Columbus.* Our passage money was five dollars. We had a very hard passage. We were very much crowded in the steerage. There were 236 persons—Dutch, Irish, English and Scotch, and as dirty as any I ever saw. We were not much sick; the weather was cold. Had it been otherwise, we should have suffered more. A steamer leaves for New York to-day, and I thought I would announce to you my arrival by this opportunity, and such information as I was in possession of up to this date. There is a ship to sail on the 14th instant, by which I shall write you again.

I found Elders Hyrum Clark, Thomas Ward, and Amos Fielding in Liverpool, and they were well; and as far as I was informed by them, the Church is in a good state and on the increase; it numbers somewhere between eight and nine thousand members. There is a great want of laborers in the vineyard. Many of the first Elders have left this for Nauvoo, leaving their places vacant. I presented to the Presidency here your decision relative to the printing. Elders Ward and Fielding received it, and manifested a desire to abide by it. Elder Fielding wept when I showed him your decision concerning him and his coming to Nauvoo by the first ship to see you face to face. The brethren say here that he has been too hasty in some things, and has given some an offense; but I do not as yet know anything derogatory to his character that I could say aught against him. I shall write you all the particulars as fast as I come in possession of them. As regards the printing in this land, we shall stop it after the next number is published. In it we wish to publish the news from Nauvoo for the benefit of the Saints, and to announce our arrival in this country.

Permit me here to give you my opinion as regards the printing in this land, and I will cheerfully abide your advice notwithstanding. After we stop the *Star*, we shall have during the shipping season to advertise and give general information in the emigration business to the Saints scattered abroad. I think it would be best to republish the *Times and Seasons* for the benefit of the Church. The duties on books are £2-10s. per hundredweight; and there are now 1,600 *Stars* circulated here at the present, and the demands of our publications are on the increase. The duties would almost reprint the *Times and Seasons,* and then we could do our advertising on the last page, if thought advisable. We could afford it as cheap as the present *Star*, and pay you something for the privilege of publishing, as well as to pay it to the crown. I have not yet learned the amount of funds remaining here subject to your order. I have not had much time as yet to inquire into those matters, in consequence of the multitude of business in unloading our freight from shipboard.

The brethren that came with me wish to say to those whom it may concern, that they are well, and will in a few days leave for their fields of labor.

I shall write to you once a month, no preventing Providence, and should be glad to have you write to me as often, and give me your advice and counsel relating to those things you,in your wisdom,may think beneficial to the Saints and emigration in this land.

I wish Elder Taylor would forward to me the amount of the number that will make the volume of the *Times and Seasons* complete by the first opportunity. By so doing I can sell the 200 volumes to advantage. I will try to forward to him what I can obtain for the *Times and Seasons* already here. If it should be thought wisdom to reprint the *Times and Seasons* here, I wish Brother Taylor would be particular to send, so that we could obtain them, if possible. I am informed by Elder Ward that they have not received any intelligence from you since last February.

I wish you would write me your mind concerning the printing immediately on the receipt of this sheet, so that our communication with the Saints in England may not be stopped long.

I am, as ever, your humble servant in the bonds of the new and everlasting covenant,

REUBEN HEDLOCK.

The Prophet's visit with Justin Butterfield.

I was at the mansion preparing some legal papers.—Justin Butterfield, Esq., U. S. Attorney for Illinois, arrived this afternoon; and I spent the rest of the day in riding and chatting with him.

Council of the quorum [special council, see p. 39] met and adjourned to Sunday evening; my Brother Hyrum's child being sick.

The quorum of the Twelve started from Philadelphia for Pittsburgh.

Thursday, 5.—This morning I rode out with Esquire Butterfield to the farm.

Instructions Respecting Plurality of Wives.

In the afternoon, rode to the prairie to show some of the brethren some land. Evening, at home, and walked up and down the streets with my scribe. Gave instructions to try those persons who were preaching, teaching, or practicing the doctrine of plurality of wives; for, according to the law, I hold the keys of this power in the last days; for there is never but one on earth at a time on whom the power and its keys are conferred; *and I have constantly said no man shall have but one wife at a time, unless the Lord directs otherwise.*

Friday, 6.—I attended special conference; but as few people were out, in consequence of the weather proving unfavorable, the organization of the conference was adjourned until to morrow, or the first pleasant day.

The Prophet's Dissatisfaction with Sidney Rigdon.

After giving notice that President Rigdon's case would be considered, &c., I walked towards home, and gave instructions to my scribe to cause all the papers relating to my land-claims in the Half Breed Tract in Iowa, to be placed in the hands of Esquire Butterfield.

Saturday, 7.—I attended conference.

Sunday, 8.—Slight frost last night. Conference convened in the morning; but, as it rained, adjourned till Monday at ten, a. m.

Prayer-meeting at my house in the evening. Quorum present; also, in addition, Sisters Adams, Elizabeth Ann Whitney, my aunt Clarissa Smith, and my mother.

My brother Hyrum and his wife were blessed, ordained and anointed.

The Twelve arrived at Pittsburgh at ten, a. m., and again left by the steamer *Raritan*, at eleven, a. m., *en route* for Nauvoo.

Monday, 9.—Attended conference, and preached a funeral sermon on the death of General James Adams; a brief synopsis of which, as reported by Dr. Willard Richards, will be found in the minutes below.

I here insert the conference minutes.

MINUTES OF A SPECIAL CONFERENCE.

The Church of Jesus Christ of Latter-day Saints, in Special Conference, held in the City of Nauvoo, commencing on the 6th of October, 1843.

Friday, October 6, ten o'clock, a. m.

The weather proving unfavorable, the organization of the Conference was postponed until the next day at ten o'clock, a. m.

Saturday, ten o'clock, a. m.

Conference assembled and proceeded to business.

President Joseph Smith was called to the chair, and Gustavus Hills was chosen clerk.

Singing by the choir, and prayer by Elder Almon W. Babbitt.

The president stated the items of business to be brought before the conference to be—

1st. The case and standing of Elder Sidney Rigdon, Counselor in the First Presidency.

2nd. The further progress of the Temple; after which, any miscellaneous business.

Elder Sidney Rigdon addressed the conference on the subject of his situation and circumstances among the Saints.

President Joseph Smith addressed the conference, inviting an expression of any charges or complaints which the conference had to make. He stated his dissatisfaction with Elder Sidney Rigdon as a Counselor, not having received any material benefit from his labors or counsels since their escape from Missouri. Several complaints were then brought forward in reference to his management in the post office; a supposed corespondence and connection with John C. Bennett, with Ex-Governor Carlin, and with the Missourians, of a treacherous character; also his leaguing with dishonest persons in endeavoring to defraud the innocent.

President Joseph Smith related to the conference the detention of a document from Justin Butterfield, Esq., which was designed for the benefit of himself, (President Smith,) but was not handed over for some three or four weeks, greatly to his disadvantage; also, an indirect testimony from Missouri, through the mother of Orrin P. Rockwell, that said Rigdon and others had given information, by letter, of President Smith's visit to Dixon, advising them to proceed to that place and arrest him there. He stated that, in consequence of these and other circumstances, and Elder Rigdon's unprofitableness to him as a Counselor, he did not wish to retain him in that station, unless those difficulties could be removed; but desired his salvation, and expressed his willingness that he should retain a place among the Saints.

Elder Almon W. Babbitt suggested the propriety of limiting the complaints and proofs to circumstances that had transpired since the last conference.

President Joseph Smith replied, and showed the legality and propriety of a thorough investigation, without such limitation.

Elder Sidney Rigdon pleaded, concerning the document from Justin Butterfield, Esq., that he received it in answer to some inquiries which he [Rigdon] had transmitted to him [Butterfield]; that he [Rigdon] received it at a time when he was sick, and unable to examine it; did not know that it was designed for the perusal and benefit of President Joseph Smith; that he had, consequently, ordered it to be laid aside, where it remained until inquired for by Joseph Smith. He had never written to Missouri concerning the visit of Joseph Smith to Dixon, and knew of no other person having done so. That, concerning certain rumors of belligerent operations under Governor Carlin's administration, he had related them, not to alarm or disturb any one; but that he had the rumors from good authorities, and supposed them well founded. That he had never received but one communication from John C. Bennett, and that of a business character, except one addressed to him conjointly with Elder Orson Pratt, which he handed over to President Smith. That he had never written any letters to John C. Bennett.

The weather becoming inclement, conference adjourned until Sunday, ten o'clock, a. m.

Sunday, 8th, ten o'clock, a. m.

Conference assembled agreeably to adjournment.

Singing by the choir, and prayer by Elder William W. Phelps.

Elder Sidney Rigdon resumed his plea of defense. He related the circumstances of his reception in the city of Quincy, after his escape from Missouri,—the cause of his delay in not going to the city of Washington, on an express to which he had been appointed: and closed with a moving appeal to President Joseph Smith, concerning their former friendship, associations, and sufferings; and expressed his willingness to resign his place, though with sorrowful and indescribable feelings. During this address, the sympathies of the congregation were highly excited.

Elder Almon W. Babbitt related a conversation he had had with Esquire Johnson, in which he exonerated Elder Sidney Rigdon from the charge or suspicion of having had a treacherous correspondence with ex-Governor Carlin.

President Joseph Smith arose and explained to the congregation the supposed treacherous correspondence with ex-Governor Carlin, and expressed entire lack of confidence in his integrity and steadfastness, judging from their past intercourse.

Patriarch Hyrum Smith followed with appropriate and impressive remarks on the attributes of mercy in God, as that by which He influences, controls and conquers; and the propriety and importance of the Saints exercising the same attribute towards their fellows, and especially towards their aged companion and fellow-servant in the cause of truth and righteousness.

Elder Almon W. Babbitt and President William Law followed with remarks in defense of Elder Sidney Rigdon.

On motion by President William Marks, and seconded by Patriarch Hyrum Smith, conference voted that Elder Sidney Rigdon be permitted to retain his station as Counselor in the First Presidency.

*President Joseph Smith arose and said, "I have thrown him off my shoulders, and you have again put him on me. You may carry him, but I will not."**

Singing. Prayer by Elder William Law.

Conference adjourned for one hour.

Three, p. m.

Conference assembled; but in consequence of the inclemency of the weather, business was postponed until Monday, ten o'clock, a. m.

Monday, ten o'clock, a. m.

Conference assembled, and resumed business.

Singing by the choir. Prayer by Elder Alpheus Cutler.

The business pertaining to the Temple was then announced by the President as next in order.

Elder Alpheus Cutler, on the part of the Temple Committee, represented the work of the Temple to be retarded for want of team work and provisions—also of iron, steel, blasting powder, and clothing,—giving as his opinion that the walls could easily be completed next season, if these embarrassments were removed, and the brethren would come forward to sustain them in the work with the means that were in their hands.

Elder Reynolds Cahoon followed, seconding the remarks of Elder Cutler, and setting forth the importance of the Saints using their utmost exertions to fulfill the revelation concerning the Temple, earnestly exhorting the Saints here and abroad to roll in the necessary means into the hands of the Trustee, that the work may advance with rapidity.

* This paragraph in Italics appears as footnote in the Ms. History.

President Hyrum Smith followed with pertinent remarks on the importance of the work—the ease with which it might be advanced to its completion,—that it had already become a monument for the people abroad to gaze on with astonishment. He concluded with some advice to parents to restrain their children from vice and folly, and employ them in some business of profit to themselves, to the Temple, or elsewhere.

On motion by Elder William Law, and seconded by President Hyrum Smith, conference voted that we, as a conference and individuals, will use all the means, exertions, and influence in our power to sustain the Temple Committee in advancing the work of the Temple.

Conference adjourned for one hour.

Two o'clock, p. m.

Conference re-assembled, and listened with profound attention to an impressive discourse from President Joseph Smith, commemorative of the decease of James Adams, Esq., late of this city, and an honorable, worthy, useful and esteemed member of the Church of Jesus Christ of Latter-day Saints.

THE PROPHET'S REMARKS ON THE DEMISE OF JAMES ADAMS.

All men know that they must die. And it is important that we should understand the reasons and causes of our exposure to the vicissitudes of life and of death, and the designs and purposes of God in our coming into the world, our sufferings here, and our departure hence. What is the object of our coming into existence, then dying and falling away, to be here no more? It is but reasonable to suppose that God would reveal something in reference to the matter, and it is a subject we ought to study more than any other. We ought to study it day and night, for the world is ignorant in reference to their true condition and relation. If we have any claim on our Heavently Father for anything, it is for knowledge on this important subject. Could we read and comprehend all that has been written from the days of Adam, on the relation of man to God and angels in a future state, we should know very little about it. Reading the experience of others, or the revelation given to *them*, can never give *us* a comprehensive view of our condition and true relation to God. Knowledge of these things can only be obtained by experience through the ordinances of God set forth for that purpose. Could you gaze into heaven five minutes, you would know more than you would by reading all that ever was written on the subject.

We are only capable of comprehending that certain things exist, which we may acquire by certain fixed principles. If men would acquire salvation, they have got to be subject, before they leave this world, to certain rules and principles, which were fixed by an unalterable decree before the world was.

The disappointment of hopes and expectations at the resurrection would be indescribably dreadful.

The organization of the spiritual and heavenly worlds, and of spiritual and heavenly beings, was agreeable to the most perfect order and harmony: their limits and bounds were fixed irrevocably, and voluntarily subscribed to in their heavenly estate by themselves, and were by our first parents subscribed to upon the earth. Hence the importance of embracing and subscribing to principles of eternal truth by all men upon the earth that expect eternal life.

I assure the Saints that truth, in reference to these matters, can and may be known through the revelations of God in the way of His ordinances, and in answer to prayer. The Hebrew Church "came unto the spirits of just men made perfect, and unto an innumerable company of angels, unto God the Father of all, and to Jesus Christ, the Mediator of the new covenant." What did they learn by coming of the spirits of just men made perfect? Is it written? No. What they learned has not been and could not have been written. What object was gained by this communication with the spirits of the just? It was the established order of the kingdom of God: the keys of power and knowledge were with them to communicate to the Saints. Hence the importance of understanding the distinction between the spirits of the just and angels.

Spirits can only be revealed in flaming fire or glory. Angels have advanced further, their light and glory being tabernacled; and hence they appear in bodily shape. The spirits of just men are made ministering servants to those who are sealed unto life eternal, and it is through them that the sealing power comes down.

Patriarch Adams is now one of the spirits of the just men made perfect; and, if revealed now, must be revealed in fire; and the glory could not be endured. Jesus showed Himself to His disciples, and they thought it was His spirit, and they were afraid to approach His spirit. Angels have advanced higher in knowledge and power than spirits.

Concerning Brother James Adams, it should appear strange that so good and so great a man was hated. The deceased ought never to have had an enemy. But so it was. Wherever light shone, it stirred up darkness. Truth and error, good and evil cannot be reconciled. Judge Adams had some enemies, but such a man ought not to have had one. I saw him first at Springfield, when on my way from Missouri to Washington. He sought me out when a stranger, took me to his home, encouraged and cheered me, and gave me money. He has been a most intimate friend. I anointed him to the patriarchal power—to receive the keys of knowledge and power, by revelation to himself. He has had revelations concerning his departure, and has gone to a more important work. When men are prepared, they are better off to go hence. Brother Adams has gone to open up a more effectual door for the dead. The spirits of the just are exalted to a greater and more glorious work; hence they are blessed in their departure to the world of spirits. Enveloped in flaming fire, they are not far from us, and know and understand our thoughts, feelings, and motions, and are often pained therewith.

Flesh and blood cannot go there; but flesh and bones, quickened by the Spirit of God, can.

If we would be sober and watch in fasting and prayer, God would turn away sickness from our midst.

Hasten the work in the Temple, renew your exertions to forward all the work of the last days, and walk before the Lord in soberness and righteousness. Let the Elders and Saints do away with lightmindedness, and be sober.

Such is a faint outline of the discourse of President Joseph Smith, which was delivered with his usual feeling and pathos, and was listened to with the most profound and eager attention by the multitude, who hung upon his instructions, anxious to learn and pursue the path of eternal life.

After singing by the choir, and prayer by the President, Conference adjourned *sine die*, with the benediction of the President.

JOSEPH SMITH, President.

GUSTAVUS HILLS, Clerk.

Pacific Islands Mission Embarks.

The missionaries to the Society Islands went on board the ship *Timoleon*, Captain Plasket, at New Bedford, and got under way. Elder Philip B. Lewis donated $300 towards their passage and fitout. Elder Knowlton F. Hanks' health was very poor.

CHAPTER III.

ANCIENT RUINS IN AMERICA, BOOK OF MORMON EVIDENCE—THE PROPHET ON THE U. S. CONSTITUTION AND THE BIBLE--MISREPRESENTATIONS CORRECTED—LETTER TO THE U. S. PRESIDENTIAL CANDIDATES—THE PROPHET'S ADDRESS TO THE SAINTS.

Tuesday, October 10, 1843.—My brother Hyrum was appointed, by the voice of the Spirit, one of the Temple Committee, in place of Judge Elias Higbee, deceased.

I spent the day in council with J. and O. C. Skinner and the Rhodes' about the sale of land, and appointed William Clayton to buy the property.

Wednesday, 11.—I was at home this morning. In the afternoon I went with my brother Hyrum, William Law, and our wives, to Brother John Benbow's.

The following is from the *Times and Seasons*:—

ANCIENT RUINS—INTRODUCTORY.

Every day adds fresh testimony to the already accumulated evidence on the authenticity of the Book of Mormon. At the time that book was translated, there was very little known about ruined cities and dilapidated buildings. The general presumption was that no people possessing more intelligence than our present race of Indians had ever inhabited this continent; and the accounts given in the Book of Mormon concerning large cities and civilized people having inhabited this land were generally disbelieved and pronounced a humbug. Priest, since then, has thrown some light on this interesting subject. Stephens, in his "Incidents of Travels in Central America," has thrown in a flood of testimony, and from the following statements it is evident that the Book of Mormon does not give a more extensive account of large and populous cities than those discoveries demonstrate to be even now in existence.—Ed.]

(Article from the Texas Telegraph, October 11.)

We have been informed by a gentleman who has traversed a large portion of the Indian country of Northern Texas, and the country lying between Santa Fe and the Pacific, that there are vestiges of ancient cities and ruined castles or temples on the Rio Puerco, and on the Colorado of the West.

He says that on one of the branches of the Rio Puerco, a few days' travel from Santa Fe, there is an immense pile of ruins that appear to belong to an ancient temple. Portions of the walls are still standing, consisting of huge blocks of limestone regularly hewn and laid in cement. The building occupies an extent of more than an acre. It is two or three stories high, has no roof, but contains many rooms, generally of a square form, without windows; and the lower rooms are so dark and gloomy that they resemble caverns rather than the apartments of an edifice built for a human habitation.

Our informant did not give the style of architecture, but he believes it could not be erected by Spaniards or Europeans, as the stones are much worn by the rains, and indicate that the building has stood many hundred years. From his description, we are induced to believe that it resembles the ruins of Palenque or Otulum.

He says there are many similar ruins on the Colorado of the West, which empties in the Californian sea. In one of the valleys of the Cordilleras traversed by this river, and about four hundred miles from its mouth, there is a large temple still standing, its walls and spires presenting scarcely any traces of dilapidation; and were it not for the want of a roof, it might still be rendered habitable. Near it, scattered along the declivity of a mountain, are the ruins of what must have been once a large city.

The traces of a large aqueduct, part of which is, however, in the solid rock, are still visible. Neither the Indians residing in the vicinity nor the oldest Spanish settlers of the nearest settlements can give any account of the origin of these buildings. They merely know that they have stood there from the earliest periods to which their traditions extend.

The antiquarian who is desirous to trace the Aztec or the Toltec races in their migrations from the northern regions of America may find in their ancient edifices many subjects of curious speculation.

Thursday, 12.—Prayer-meeting in my room. We prayed for William Marks, who was sick.

I sent William Clayton to Lathrop, to borrow $50, that I might be able to redeem $5000 worth of property, which was published to be sold to-day at Rhodes'; but Lathrop refused. He also went to Eli Chase's, but was refused by him. I was grieved that the brethren felt so penurious in their spirit, although they professed to be guided by the revelations which the Lord gives through me. On my afterwards giving a pledge that I would repay the $50 in forty-eight hours, Lathrop lent the money and enabled me to redeem the land.

I received the following from H. R. Hotchkiss:

Letter—H. R. Hotchkiss to Joseph Smith.

NEW YORK, 27th September, 1843.

Rev. Joseph Smith.

DEAR SIR,—I see by the newspapers that there has been a meeting of citizens at Carthage relative to the Mormons, and that several severe resolutions have been passed condemning the conduct of the Mormons. Knowing how little I can rely upon public rumor upon such subjects, I have taken the liberty of applying directly to you for correct information, and solicit as a particular favor that you will communicate at your earliest convenience the facts in the case.

Of course I feel an interest in the prosperity of Nauvoo, and an interest also in the success of the Mormon enterprise, and a deep interest in the welfare of your people; and the more so, certainly, as their pecuniary interest is identified with my own. I make this frank acknowledgment, because it is always best for men of sense to talk as they mean. I should, howewer, be solicitous for a successful termination of your great enterprise, had I not one dollar invested in Nauvoo, because the complete triumph of energetic exertions is always gratifying to all business men.

Your obedient servant,

HORACE R. HOTCHKISS.

I wrote this reply:—

Letter—Joseph Smith to H. R. Hotchkiss.

NAUVOO, Ill., Oct. 12, 1843.

DEAR SIR,—Your letter of the 27th ult. is at hand, soliciting information concerning the "Carthage resolutions." In answer to your very candid inquiry and interest relative to our welfare, brevity will suffice. Unprincipled men and disappointed demagogues, with here and there an "untamed sucker," composed that disgraceful and disgracing as well as mobocratic assemblage; and I feel proud to say that patriots and honest men generally frown upon such audacious proceedings as beneath the dignity of freemen. It is to be hoped that public opinion will continue to spurn at such doings, and leave the actors to fester in their own shame.

With the smiling prospects around us at present, success seems certain; and, with the blessings of Jehovah, we shall reap the reward of virtue and goodness. I go for the good of the world; and if all honest men would do so, mean men would be scarce. You are at liberty to use this to counteract falsehoods as you may deem proper.

Respectfully, I am your obedient servant,

JOSEPH SMITH.

Friday, *13*.—First severe frost at Nauvoo this season. Ice on the water.

At home; made arrangements to prepare provisions for the workmen in the pinery. From ten, a. m. to three, p. m., presided in municipal court, on *habeas corpus* in favor of Charles Drown, to be delivered from the custody of Samuel Waterman. The prisoner being sick, adjourned the case to the 16th.

In the afternoon, trying a span of grey horses in the carriage.

Dr. Turner, a phrenologist, came in. I gratified his curiosity for about an hour by allowing him to examine my head.

I was engaged settling accounts with D. S. Hollister.

Location of the mind.

Saturday, *14*.—In the morning, at home, having a long conversation with a physiologist and mesmeriser. I asked them to prove that the mind of man was seated in one part of the brain more than another.

Sat in City Council till one, p. m., which passed "An Ordinance concerning the inspection of flour," and appointed William E. Horner inspector of flour for the city of Nauvoo.

Sunday, *15*.—Cool, calm, and cloudy. At eleven, a. m., I preached at the stand east of the Temple. The following synopsis was reported by Dr. Willard Richards:—

The Prophet on the Constitution of the United States and the Bible—Temporal Economies.

It is one of the first principles of my life, and one that I have cultivated from my childhood, having been taught it by my father, to allow every one the liberty of conscience. I am the greatest advocate of the

Constitution of the United States there is on the earth. In my feelings I am always ready to die for the protection of the weak and oppressed in their just rights. The only fault I find with the Constitution is, it is not broad enough to cover the whole ground.

Although it provides that all men shall enjoy religious freedom, yet it does not provide the manner by which that freedom can be preserved, nor for the punishment of Government officers who refuse to protect the people in their religious rights, or punish those mobs, states, or communities who interfere with the rights of the people on account of their religion. Its sentiments are good, but it provides no means of enforcing them. It has but this one fault. Under its provision, a man or a people who are able to protect themselves can get along well enough; but those who have the misfortune to be weak or unpopular are left to the merciless rage of popular fury.

The Constitution should contain a provision that every officer of the Government who should neglect or refuse to extend the protection guaranteed in the Constitution should be subject to capital punishment; and then the president of the United States would not say, "*Your cause is just, but I can do nothing for you,*" a governor issue exterminating orders, or judges say, "The men ought to have the protection of law, but it won't please the mob; the men must die, anyhow, to satisfy the clamor of the rabble; they must be hung, or Missouri be damned to all eternity." Executive writs could be issued when they ought to be, and not be made instruments of cruelty to oppress the innocent, and persecute men whose religion is unpopular.

I cannot believe in any of the creeds of the different denominations, because they all have some things in them I cannot subscribe to, though all of them have some truth. I want to come up into the presence of God, and learn all things; but the creeds set up stakes, and say, "Hitherto shalt thou come, and no further;" which I cannot subscribe to.

I believe the Bible as it read when it came from the pen of the original writers. Ignorant translators, careless transcribers, or designing and corrupt priests have committed many errors. As it read, Gen. vi. 6, "It repented the Lord that he had made man on the earth;" also, Num. xxiii. 19, "God is not a man, that he should lie; neither the Son of man, that he should repent;" which I do not believe. But it ought to read, "It repented *Noah* that God made man." This I believe, and then the other quotation stands fair. If any man will prove to me, by one passage of Holy Writ, one item I believe to be false, I will renounce and disclaim it as far as I promulged it.

The first principles of the Gospel, as I believe, are, faith, repentance, baptism for the remission of sins, with the promise of the Holy Ghost.

Look at Heb. vi. 1 for contradictions—"Therefore leaving the principles of the doctrine of Christ, let us go on unto perfection." If a man leaves the principles of the doctrine of Christ, how can he be saved in the principles? This is a contradiction. I don't believe it. I will render it as it should be—"Therefore *not* leaving the principles of the doctrine of Christ, let us go on unto perfection, not laying again the foundation of repentance from dead works, and of faith toward God, of the doctrine of baptisms, and of laying on of hands, and of resurrection of the dead, and of eternal judgment."

It is one thing to see the kingdom of God, and another thing to enter into it. We must have a change of heart to see the kingdom of God, and subscribe the articles of adoption to enter therein.

No man can receive the Holy Ghost without receiving revelations. The Holy Ghost is a revelator.

I prophesy, in the name of the Lord God of Israel, anguish and wrath and tribulation and the withdrawing of the Spirit of God from the earth await this generation, until they are visited with utter desolation. This generation is as corrupt as the generation of the Jews that crucified Christ; and if He were here to-day, and should preach the same doctrine He did then, they would put Him to death. I defy all the world to destroy the work of God; and I prophesy they never will have power to kill me till my work is accomplished, and I am ready to die.

I will now speak a little on the economy of this city. I think there are too many merchants among you. I would like to see more wool and raw materials instead of manufactured goods, and the money be brought here to pay the poor for manufacturing goods. Set our women to work, and stop their spinning street yarns and talking about spiritual wives.

Instead of going abroad to buy goods, lay your money out in the country, and buy grain, cattle, flax, wool, and work it up yourselves.

I proclaim, in the name of the Lord God Almighty, that I will fellowship nothing in the Church but virtue, integrity, and uprightness.

We cannot build up a city on merchandise. I would not run after the merchants. I would sow a little flax, if I had but a garden spot, and make clothing of it.

The temporal economy of this people should be to establish and encourage manufactures, and not to take usury for their money. I do not want to bind the poor here to starve. Go out into the country and into the neighbouring cities, and get food, and gird up your loins, and be sober. When you get food, return, if you have a mind to.

Some say it is better to give to the poor than build the Temple. The building of the Temple has sustained the poor who were driven from Missouri, and kept them from starving; and it has been the best means for this object which could be devised.

Oh, all ye rich men of the Latter-dav Saints from abroad, I would invite you to bring up some of your money—your gold, your silver, and your precious things, and give to the Temple. We want iron, steel, spades, and quarrying and mechanical tools.

It would be a good plan to get up a forge to manufacture iron, and bring in raw materials of every variety, and erect manufacturing establishments of all kinds, and surround the rapids with mills and machinery.

I never stole the value of a pin's head, or a picayune in my life; and when you are hungry don't steal. Come to me, and I will feed you.

The secret of masonry is to keep a secret. It is good economy to entertain strangers—to entertain sectarians. Come up to Nauvoo, ye sectarian priests of the everlasting Gospel, as they call it, and you shall have my pulpit all day.

Woe to ye rich men, who refuse to give to the poor, and then come and ask me for bread. Away with all your meanness, and be liberal. We need purging, purifying and cleansing. You that have little faith in your Elders when you are sick, get some little simple remedy in the first stages. If you send for a doctor at all, send in the first stages.

All ye doctors who are fools, not well read, and do not understand the human constitution, stop your practice. And all ye lawyers who have no business, only as you hatch it up, would to God you would go to work or run away!"

Monday, *16*.—At home nearly all day, attending to family concerns.

Went to municipal court, and adjourned hearing of the case* to the 17th.

Tuesday, *17*.—Went to municipal court. The prosecutor not appearing, court ordered that the prisoner be discharged.

Wednesday, *18*.—Pleasant and comfortable day.

Fifteen deaths have occured during the past week in the city.

Thursday, *19*.—Warm and pleasant day. The water has risen about two feet in the Mississippi, and is still rising.

The Prophet's Visit to Macedonia.

About noon, started for Macedonia, in company with Brother William Clayton. Arrived there about

* This was the case of Chas. Drown on *habeas corpus* referred to under date of 13th of October.

sundown, and I stayed at Brother Benjamin F. Johnson's for the night.

Friday, 20.—In the evening I gave instructions to Benjamin F. Johnson and others in relation to the blessings of the everlasting covenant and the sealings of the Priesthood.

Elder John P. Greene returned from a Mission to the State of New York, with about 100 emigrants, some of them from Pennsylvania, who joined his company on the way.

Warm, smoky day, with strong wind, very dark evening.

Saturday, 21.—We left Macedonia, and arrived home about two p. m. Pleasant cool day.

Sunday, 22.—Meeting at the stand. Elder Rigdon preached half-an hour on "Poor Rich Folks."

I remained at home all day, and held a prayer-meeting at my house at two, p. m.; tweuty-four persons present.

Labors of the Apostles in the East.

Elders Young, Kimball, and George A. Smith returned from their mission to the Eastern States, having, in connection with Elders Orson Pratt and Wilford Woodruff, visited the branches in Kentucky, Ohio, Pennsylvania, New Yersey, New York, Connecticut, Massachusetts, Rhode Island, New Hampshire, and Maine; held conferences, set in order the churches, collected tithings for the Temple and subscriptions for the Nauvoo House, baptized many, and stirred up a general system of gathering among the Saints in the Eastern countries. They have been absent nearly four months, and have accomplished a good work. I was very glad to see them, and blessed them in the name of the Lord. Elders Daniel Spencer and Bradford Elliot also returned from their missions, and quite a respectable number of Saints came in their company.

Pleasant, cool day.

Monday, 23.—Those of the Twelve who returned from the East yesterday visited me through the day, and paid over the means they had received for the Temple and the

Nauvoo House. I immediately gave directions to send to St. Louis for groceries and different articles necessary for the Temple and the workmen thereon.

Hyrum Smith Appointed on Temple Committee.

This morning President Hyrum Smith entered upon the duties of his office, having previously been appointed by the voice of the Spirit to supply the place of the late Elias Higbee, deceased, as one of the Temple Committee. On his arrival at the Temple he was greeted by a hearty welcome from those engaged on the works, and the universal feeling is that great good will result from this appointment.

The day cloudy, with strong east wind.

Tuesday, 24.—William W. Phelps and Colonel Dunham started for Springfield to see the Governor, and endeavor to obtain from him the quota of State arms which belong to the Legion.

Morning warm and pleasant; afternoon wind west by north. At four, a little rain, accompanied by snow, for the first time this fall.

Wednesday, 25.—Ice one-third of an inch thick on small bodies of water. Cloudy and cold day.

In the evening settled the taxes for the Temple and Nauvoo House.

Eleven deaths in the city reported this week.

Friday, 27.—I was at home and received a visit from Bishop George Miller and Elder Peter Haws, who have just returned from their trip to Mississippi and Alabama.

Many emigrants have arrived in Nauvoo the last few weeks.

Prayer-meeting at my house in the evening.

Saturday, 28.—Cold east wind. At home all day.

Sunday, 29.—Meeting at the stand, south side of the Temple, from eleven, a. m. to two, p. m. Elders Brigham Young and John Taylor preached. Dr. Willard Richards called for a collection of $8, to buy a new book in which to record history, which sum was made up.

At nine, a. m., Elders Richards, Miller and Haws

ordained William C. Steffey (who was going to Texas on business,) an Elder.

Two, p. m., prayer-meeting in my house; twenty-five present. I gave instructions on the priesthood.

Monday, 30.—At nine, a. m., went to mayor's court, and adjourned it for one week.

Twelve, noon, attended a court in the office, when the parties agreed to leave their difficulty to be settled by the arbitration of Brother Flagg.

I received $300 from Brother Spencer, and immediately paid it to Dr. Robert D. Foster.

On account of the cold weather, most of the masons have discontinued the work on the Temple.

Tuesday, 31.—At nine, a. m., Mr. Moore was brought before me for a breach of city ordinance, which was proved, and I fined him $5.

I rode out with Hyrum in the carriage to the prairie, returning about three, p. m. Snow on the ground this morning; cold east wind, and rain all day.

Wednesday, November 1, 1843.—In the evening there was a prayer-meeting in the mansion; twenty-nine present.

Thursday, 2—Sitting in council with Hyrum, Brigham Young, Heber C. Kimball, Willard Richards, John Taylor, William Law, and William Clayton, at ten, a. m., on the subject of the following letter from Joseph L. Heywood:—

Letter: Joseph L. Heywood to Joseph Smith.

QUINCY, October 23, 1843.

Gen. Joseph Smith.

DEAR SIR,—In a conversation with Colonel Frierson, of this place, a short time since, he expressed, in very warm terms, feelings of sympathy for the wrongs yourself and brethren suffered in Missouri, as well as his sense of the vindictive feelings the authorities of that State still manifest towards you personally.

Mr. F. has not yet had the pleasure of a personal acquaintance with yourself, although he says he had the pleasure of meeting your lady at her sister's residence on Rock River. Mr. F. has been written by the Hon. B. Rhett, of S. Carolina, upon the subject of the *Persecution*: and

Mr. F. thinks, of all men, he would be the best qualified to present a petition in our behalf; and says, should such an arrangement meet your approbation, he will use his influence in favor of a petition; and says he knows of some honorable men in Missouri who, he has no doubt, are anxious to wipe off the stain that rests upon them, by [making] some just reparation.

I submit, by permission of Mr. F., a copy of a letter he has written to a distinguished citizen of South Carolina, together with a circular put out confidentially by the friends of Mr. Calhoun, of S. C., whom with my present feelings I should cheerfully support for our next President, and who, I have no doubt would be preferred, by the brethren to Mr. Van Buren.

If the plan suggested of memorializing Congress should meet your approbation, please inform me. Colonel Frierson promises his aid in such an event, and says he would go to Nauvoo and assist in arranging papers relative to such a step. Please accept my assurances of love and esteem for yourself and family, and a prayer that wisdom from on high may direct you in your deliberations.

I remain your brother in Christ,

JOS. L. HEYWOOD.

Letters to Candidates for Presidency of the U. S. Decided upon

We agreed to write a letter to the five candidates for the Presidency of the United States, to inquire what their feelings were towards us as a people, and what their course of action would be in relation to the cruelty and oppression that we have suffered from the State of Missouri, if they were elected.

The Twelve Apostles published the following in the *Times and Seasons*:—

An Epistle of the Twelve, to the Elders and Churches Abroad.

On our late mission to the Eastern States, we discovered that the publications at Nauvoo were very little patronised by the Saints and branches in the various sections of the country where we passed, while the common newspapers of the day received a liberal support by those who pretend to "hunger and thirst after righteousness." We feel justified, therefore, in reprobating such a course as detrimental to the general good of the whole Church, that shows a lack of charity in the Elders.

"Do men gather grapes of thorns, or figs of thistles?"

Nauvoo at present is the seat of the First Presidency, the place of the gathering for all Saints, and the great center of the world for pure religion, revelation, truth, virtue, knowledge, and everything else preparatory to the coming of the Son of Man. The best news, the best people, and the best plan of salvation must be there. Wherefore,

Resolved unanimously that the traveling Elders are hereby instructed to use due diligence in obtaining subscribers for the *Times and Seasons* and *Nauvoo Neighbor*, and forward the pay by safe hands to the publishers at Nauvoo, that the Saints and the world may receive "line upon line and precept upon precept, here a little and there a little," together with such extracts of translations and revelations as the Presidency of the Church may direct, for the edification of the whole body of the Church in righteousness.

Done in council at Nauvoo, Nov. 2nd, 1843.

BRIGHAM YOUNG,
President of the Twelve.

WILLARD RICHARDS, Clerk.

Friday, 3rd.—I continued in council all day.

Died at sea, Elder Knowlton F. Hanks. The following extract is from a letter of Addison Pratt, one of the Pacific Islands missionaries:—

[Under this date there is inserted in the Prophet's History a long letter from Elder Addison Pratt of the Pacific Island mission, describing in great detail the last illness, death and burial at sea of Elder Knowlton F. Hanks. Elder Hanks died of consumption; and of the death the Prophet remarks: "Elder Hanks is the first Elder who has died at sea while on a foreign mission. He was a faithful Elder, cut off by consumption in the flower of his days."]

Saturday, 4.—Elders Richards and Taylor were with me at the Mansion, assisting writing letters.

Wrote to John C. Calhoun as follows:—

President Smith's Letter to John C. Calhoun, and other Presidential Candidates.

Hon. John C. Calhoun.

DEAR SIR,—As we understand you are a candidate for the Presidency at the next election; and as the Latter-day Saints (sometimes called "Mormons," who now constitute a numerous class in the school politic of this vast republic,) have been robbed of an immense amount of property, and endured nameless sufferings by the State of Missouri, and from her borders have been driven by force of arms, contrary to our national covenants; and as in vain we have sought redress by all constitutional, legal, and honorable means, in her courts, her executive councils, and her legislative halls; and as we have petitioned Congress to take cognizance of our sufferings without effect, we have judged it wisdom to address you this communication, and solicit an immediate, specific, and candid reply to "*What will be your rule of action relative to us as a people*," should fortune favor your ascension to the chief magistracy?

Most respectfully, sir, your friend,
and the friend of peace, good order,
and constitutional rights,
JOSEPH SMITH.
In behalf of the Church of Jesus Christ of Latter-day Saints.

Similar letters were written to Gen. Lewis Cass, Hon. Richard M. Johnson, Hon. Henry Clay, and President Martin Van Buren. To Mr. Van Buren's letter I added the following:—

Post Script to Van Buren.

Also whether your views or feelings have changed since the subject matter of this communication was presented you in your then official capacity at Washington, in the year 1841, and by you treated with a coldness, indifference, and neglect, bordering on contempt.

Elder Wilford Woodruff arrived at Nauvoo with paper for the use of the printing office.

Sunday, 5.—Rode out with mother and others for her health.

The Prophet poisoned.

At dinner I was taken suddenly sick; went to the door and vomited all my dinner, dislocated my jaw, and raised fresh blood, and had many symptoms of being poisoned.

In the evening a prayer-meeting in the hall over the store.

Mr. Cole having kept a school in the hall for some time, the noise proved a nuisance for the clerks in the history office, and I gave Dr. W. Richards orders to tell Mr. Cole he must find some other room in which to teach school, as the room is needed for councils.

Meeting at the stand. Elder Rigdon preached.

Received a letter from Reuben Hedlock, dated Liverpool, October 16. He informs me there is a great call for preaching, and many Elders are wanted throughout the British Isles. Much opposition. The Saints are anxious to have the *Star* continue its publication, as 1,600 copies are circulated.

Work in the British Mission.

Also received a letter from Hyrum Clark, giving a partial account of the business affairs of the emigration and publishing offices.

Monday, 6.—Domestic affairs kept me busy in the morning, and in the afternoon listened to William W. Phelps giving a relation of his visit to the governor, which amused me.

It has been very cool for some days past.

Elder Erastus Snow arrived with a company from Massachusetts.

Tuesday, 7.—Mr. Cole moved the tables back into the hall, when Richards and Phelps called to report that the noise in the school disturbed them in the progress of writing the History. I gave orders that Cole must look out for another place, as the history must continue and not be disturbed, as there are but few subjects that I have felt a greater anxiety about than my history, which has been a very difficult task, on account of the death of my best clerks and the apostasy of others, and the stealing of records by John Whitmer, Cyrus Smalling and others.

The Prophet's Anxiety concerning the History of the Church.

The quorum of the Twelve—viz., President Brigham Young, Parly P. Pratt, Orson Pratt, Wilford Woodruff, John Taylor, George A. Smith, and Willard Richards, assembled in the mayor's office, and voted to raise $500 to get paper, &c., to print the *Doctrine and Covenants.* Also voted that Parley P. Pratt, Wilford Woodruff, and John Taylor be a committee to borrow or get the money, and that President Young go along with them.

Preliminary Steps to Publish in Nauvoo Edition of Doctrine and Covenants.

Wednesday, 8.—From nine to eleven, a. m., had an interview with Richards and Phelps, read and heard read part of my history, then attended to settling some accounts with several individuals. In the afternoon, I examined a sample of fringe designed for the pulpits of the Temple; and from two to three, conversed with Phelps, Lewis, John Butler and others.

The *Neighbor* has the following:—

Misrepresentations Corrected.

We know that statements made by the Carthage mob in their resolutions, as published in the late *Warsaw Message*, were false. We also felt convinced that the parties themselves were apprized of that fact, and that it was a thing generally understood by the public; and therefore we did not trouble ourselves about it. But having the following testimonies and affidavits sent us for publication, we insert them for the information of those who may not have had opportunities of informing themselves relative to this subject.

STATE OF ILLINOIS, }
LEE COUNTY. } ss.

We the undersigned citizens of the town of Dixon, county of Lee, State of Illinois, being duly sworn according to law, depose and say that we have seen the article entitled "Statement of facts connected with the arrest of Joseph Smith and his discharge therefrom," published in the *Warsaw Message* of the date of 15th of July, A.D. 1843; and have also seen an editorial article in the same number of said paper, in which it is stated that said statement of facts was furnished by E. Southwick, one of Mr. Smith's attorneys in said case; and that we know the fact stated in that statement—to wit, that Reynolds, for a considerable length of time immediately after his arrival at Dixon, did peremptorily refuse to allow Smith a private interview with his counsel; and that said Reynolds did expressly state that no conversation could be had with Smith by his attorneys, unless he, Reynolds, was present at such conversation.

The length of time which such refusal to allow said private conversation continued, was, in the belief of these deponents, at least one hour; and that such private conversation was not permitted by Reynolds, until after being informed by at least two of these deponents (Messrs. Dixon and Sanger) that such private interview must be allowed Mr. Smith, as that was a right he had guaranteed to him by law.

JOHN DIXON, J. D. MCCOMSAY,
ISAAC ROBINSON, J. ALBERT HELFENSTEIN,
L. P. SANGER. S. G. PATRICK,
E. SOUTHWICK.

Sworn and subscribed to before me at Dixon, this 29th day of July, 1843.

FREDERICK R. DUTCHER,
Justice of the Peace for Lee County, Ill.

We, the undersigned, state under oath that we traveled in company with Joseph H. Reynolds, the agent of the State of Missouri, from Dixon to Nauvoo, at the time he had Joseph Smith in custody with the intention of taking him to Missouri, between the 26th of June last and the 1st instant; and that the Mormons, friends of Mr. Smith, who met us on said journey, before we arrived at Nauvoo, conducted themselves, so far as we could perceive and were able to judge, with the strictest propriety; and to our knowledge made use of no means of intimidation towards either H. T. Wilson or said Reynolds; but, on the contrary, several of them, and said Smith among that number, pledged themselves that said Wilson and Reynolds should be personally safe; and that said Mormons, none of them as we could perceive, were armed, so far as was discernible; and further, that the statement made in the *Old School Democrat* of the 12th instant, over the signature of T. H. Reynolds, that he and said Wilson were disarmed soon after they were arrested on the trespass suit commenced against them by said Smith, and that their arms were not returned to them until after the said Smith's discharge at Nauvoo, was incorrect. And in relation to this, these deponents say that said Wilson and Raynolds were arrested on said action of trespass at Dixon, on Saturday morning, the 24th of June last. That they were not disarmed by the sheriff of Lee county, who had them in custody, nor by any other person, until the following day, at Paw-paw Grove, thirty-two miles distant from Dixon; and that the arms of said Wilson and Reynolds were restored to them by the said sheriff of Lee county, who had them in custody for default of bail, at their (Wilson and Reynolds') own request, while on the journey from Dixon to Nauvoo, before the company had arrived within at least eigthy miles of Nauvoo.

J. D. MCCOMSAY,
L. P. SANGER,
E. SOUTHWICK,
S. G. PATRICK.

Sworn and subscribed to before my, at Dixon, this 29th day of July, A.D. 1843.

FREDERICK R. DUTCHER,
Justice of the Peace.

To the Editor of the Warsaw Message:

GENTLEMEN:—It appears from an article in your paper of the 15th of July under the editorial head, that there is a question of veracity therein raised, between Mr. H. T. Wilson and myself, relative to the proceed ings had after the late arrest by him of Joseph Smith. Now, in order that the public may no longer be deceived in the premises, be pleased to publish, together with this note, the above affidavits, that the charge of falsehood may attach where it properly belongs.

Very respectfully yours,
E. SOUTHWICK.

DIXON, July 29, 1843.

I wrote to the *Times and Seasons*:—

Communication of President Joseph Smith to the Saints.

Messrs. Taylor and Woodruff:

It has been so long since I addressed the Saints through the medium of the *Times and Seasons*, that I feel confident that a few words from my pen, by way of advice, will be well received, as well as a "way-mark" to guide the "faithful" in future. I was sorry to learn, by your remarks upon the resolutions of the "Twelve" concerning your papers, which appeared not long since, that many of the Saints abroad were more apt to patronize the common newspapers of the day than yours, for the important reason that the Church of Jesus Christ of Latter-day Saints has the words of eternal life, and your paper, as it has hitherto done, must continue to publish such portions of them for the benefit of the Saints and the salvation of mankind as wisdom shall from time to time direct.

Freedom is a sweet blessing. Men have a right to take and read what papers they please; "but do men gather grapes of thorns, or figs of thistles?" It certainly is no more than just to suppose that *charity begins at home*; and if so, what must such as profess to be Saints think, when they patronize the splendor of Babylon and leave the virtue of Zion to linger for want of bread?

Beside which, if virtue is justified rather than vanity, the best of everything calculated to happify man and dignify society will—yea, must be in Nauvoo. And as the new commandment given anciently was *to love one another*, even so the works of the Saints at home and abroad will bear its own testimony whether *they love the brethren.*

In all the world the *Times and Seasons* is the only paper that virtually sustains, according to the forms of Scripture and prophecy, "Apostles, Prophets, Evangelists," and revelations. And what shall be said of him that, like the "Levite," passes on the other side of the way, when we behold men who "have borne the heat and the burden of the day" struggling against the popular opinions of a vain world, the burlesque of a giddy throng, the vulgarity of a self-wise multitude, and the false-hoods of what may justly be termed the "civilized meanness of the age," and not lending a helping hand? The 25th chapter of Matthew contains the simple answer.

Now, let me say once for all, like the Psalmist of old, "How good and how pleasant it is for brethren to dwell together in unity." "As the precious ointment upon the head that ran down upon Aaron's beard, that went down to the skirts of his garments, as the dew of Hermon that descended upon the mountains of Zion," is such unity; for there the Lord commanded the blessing, even life for evermore!" Unity is power; and when the brethren as one man sustain the *Times and Seasons*, they sustain me, by giving a spread to the revelations, faith, works, history and progress of the Church. The brethren who conduct the paper have been appointed to that important station, because they are worthy and well qualified; and what a blessed sign of a faithful friend to God and man is it to see the charity of a brother support his brethren, as an evidence that he means to pass from death into life?

Many of the articles which appear in the *Times and Seasons* are extracts of revelations, translations, or are the united voice of conferences, which, like "apples of gold in pictures of silver," are treasures more than meat for the called, chosen and faithful among the Saints, and should be more than *drink* to those that hunger and thirst after righteousness. As Nauvoo is rising in glory and greatness, so shall I expect to see the *Times and Seasons* increase in circulation by the vigilance of the Elders and Saints, so as to be a herald of truth and a standard of pure and undefiled religion. Finally, men and brethren, when you support my friends, you support me. In the bonds of the new and everlasting covenant,

I am your humble servant,

JOSEPH SMITH.

CHAPTER IV.

CORRESPONDENCE BETWEEN JAMES ARLINGTON BENNETT AND PRESIDENT JOSEPH SMITH—RENEWAL OF PETITIONS TO CONGRESS FOR REDRESS OF MISSOURI GRIEVANCES—PRESIDENT JOSEPH SMITH'S APPEAL TO THE "GREEN MOUNTAIN BOYS"—VERMONT—STATUS OF THE NAUVOO LEGION IN ILLINOIS MILITIA.

Thursday, November, 9, 1843.—At the office, dictating letters and signing deeds.

The missionaries to the Pacific Islands touched at Cape de Verde Islands, and laid in a supply of fruits of various kinds.

Prosperity of the Work in England.

Saturday, 11.—A company of Saints arrived from England. The work is still prospering in that country, poverty and distress are making rapid strides, and the situation of the laboring classes is getting every day more deplorable.

City Council met. Hyrum Smith, president *pro tem.* Albert P. Rockwood assessor and collector for 1st ward; Daniel Hendricks for 2nd ward; Jonathan H. Hale, 3rd ward; and Henry G. Sherwood for 4th ward.

Sunday, 12.—Prayer-meeting in the evening, in the south-east room of my old house.

Clear, cold.

Monday 13.—Having received a letter from James Arlington Bennett, Esq., I copy it:—

Letter: James Arlington Bennett to President Joseph Smith.

ARLINGTON HOUSE, Oct. 24, 1843.

DEAR GENERAL:—I am happy to know that you have taken possession of your new establishment, and presume you will be eminently successful and happy in it, together with your good lady and family.

You are no doubt already aware that I have had a most interesting visit from your most excellent and worthy friend, President B. Young, with whom I have had a glorious frolic in the clear blue ocean; for most assuredly a frolic it was, without a moment's reflection or consideration.

Nothing of this kind would in the least attach me to your person or cause. I am capable of being a most *undeviating friend*, without being governed by the smallest religious influence.

As you have proved yourself to be a philosophical divine, you will excuse me when I say that we must leave their influence to the mass. The boldness of your plans and measures, together with their unparalleled success so far, are calculated to throw a charm over your whole being, and to point you out as the most extraordinary man of the present age.

But my mind is of so mathematical and philosophical a cast, that the divinity of Moses makes no impression on me, and you will not be offended when I say that I rate you higher as a legislator than I do Moses, because we have you present with us for examination, whereas Moses derives his chief authority from prescription and the lapse of time.

I cannot, however, say but you are both right, it being out of the power of man to prove you wrong. It is no mathematical problem, and can therefore get no mathematical solution. I say, therefore, Go a-head: you have my good wishes. You know Mahomet had his "*right hand man.*"

The celebrated Thomas Brown, at New York, is now engaged in cutting your head on a beautiful cornelian stone, as your *private seal*, which will be set in gold to your order, and sent to you. It will be a gem, and just what you want. His sister is a member of your Church. The expense of this seal, set in gold, will be about $40; and Mr. Brown assures me that if he were not so poor a man, he would present it to you free.

You can, however, accept it or not, as he can apply to it another use. I am myself short for cash; for although I had sometime since $2,000 paid me by the Harpers, publishers, as the first instalment on the purchase of my copyright, yet I had got so much behind during the hard times, that it all went to clear up old scores. I expect $38,000 more, however, in semi-annual payments, from those gentlemen, within the limits of ten years; a large portion of which I intend to use in the State of Illinois, in the purchase and conduct of a large tract of land; and therefore should I be compelled to announce in this quarter that I have no connection with the Nauvoo Legion, you will of course remain silent, as I shall do it in such a way as will make all things right.

I may yet run for a high office in your state, when you would be sure of my best services in your behalf; therefore, a known connection with you would be against our mutual interest. It can be shown that a commission in the Legion was a *Herald* hoax, coined for the fun of it by me, as it is not believed even now by the public. In short, I expect to be yet, through your influence, governor of the State of Illinois.

My respects to Brothers Young, Richards, Mrs. Emma, and all friends.

Yours most respectfully,

JAMES ARLINTON BENNETT.

P.S.—As the office of inspector-general confers no command on me. being a mere honorary title,—if, therefore, there is any gentleman in Nauvoo who would like to fill it in a practical way, I shall with great pleasure and good-will resign it to him, by receiving advice from you to that effect. It is an office that should be filled by some scientific officer.

J. A. B.

I insert my reply:—

Letter: President Joseph Smith to James Arlington Bennett.

NAUVOO, ILLINOIS, Nov. 13, 1843.

DEAR SIR:—Your letter of the 24th ult. has been regularly received, its contents duly appreciated, and its whole tenor candidly considered; and, according to my manner of judging all things in righteousness, I proceed to answer you, and shall leave you to meditate whether "mathematical problems," founded upon the truth of revelation, or religion as promulgated by me, or by Moses, can be solved by rules and principles existing in the systems of common knowledge.

How far you are capable of being "a most undeviating friend, without being governed by the smallest religious influence," will best be decided by your survivors, as all past experience most assuredly proves. Without controversy, that friendship which intelligent beings would accept as sincere must arise from love, and that love grow out of virtue, which is as much a part of religion as light is a part of Jehovah. Hence the saying of Jesus, "Greater love hath no man than this, that a man lay down his life for his frieuds."

You observed, "as I have proven myself to be a philosophical divine" I must excuse you when you say that we must leave these *influences* to the mass. The meaning of "philosophical divine" may be taken in various ways. If, as the learned world apply the term, you infer that I have achieved a victory, and been strengthened by a scientific religion, as practiced by the popular sects of the age, through the aid of colleges, seminaries, Bible societies, missionary boards, financial organizations, and gospel money schemes, then you are wrong. Such a combination of men and means shows a form of godliness without the power; for is it not written, "I will destroy the wisdom of the wise." "Beware lest any man spoil you through philosophy and vain deceit, after the rudiments of the world, and not after the doctrines of Christ." But if the inference is that by more love, more light, more virtue, and more truth from the Lord, I have succeeded as a man of God, then you reason truly, though the weight of the sentiment is lost, when the "*influence is left to the mass.*" "Do men gather grapes of thorns, or figs of thistles?"

Of course you follow out the figure, and say, the boldness of my plans and measures, together with their unparalleled success, so far, are calculated to throw a charm over my whole being, and to point me out as the most extraordinary man of the present age! The *boldness of my plans and measures* can readily be tested by the touchstone of all schemes, systems, projects, and adventures—*truth;* for truth is a matter of fact; and the fact is, that by the power of God I translated the Book of Mormon from hieroglyphics, the knowledge of which was lost to the world, in which wonderful event I stood alone. an unlearned youth, to combat the worldly wisdom and multiplied ignorance of eigtheen centuries, with a new revelation, which (if they would receive the everlasting Gospel,) would open the eyes of more than eight hundred millions of people, and make "plain the old paths," wherein if a man walk in all the ordinances of God blameless, he shall inherit eternal life; and Jesus Christ, who was, and is, and is to come, has borne me safely over every snare and plan laid in secret or openly, through priestly hypocrisy, sectarian prejudice, popular philosophy, executive power, or law-defying mobocracy, to destroy me.

If, then, the hand of God in all these things that I have accomplished towards the salvation of a priest-ridden generation, in the short space of twelve years, through the boldness of the plan of preaching the Gospel, and the boldness of the means of declaring repentance and baptism for the remission of sins, and a reception of the Holy Ghost by laying on of the hands, agreeably to the authority of the Priesthood, and the still more bold measures of receiving direct revelation from God, through the Comforter, as promised, and by which means all holy men from ancient times till now have spoken and revealed the will of God to men, with the consequent "success" of the gathering of the Saints, throws any "charm" around my being, and "points me out as the most extraordinary man of the age," it demonstrates the fact that truth is mighty and must prewail, and that one man empowered from Jehovah has more influence with the children of the kingdom than eight hundred millions led by the precepts of men. God exalts the humble, and debases the haughty.

But let me assure you in the name of Jesus, "who spake as never man spake," that the "boldness of the plans and measures," as you term them, but which should be denominated the righteousness of the cause, the truth of the system, and power of God, which "so far" has borne me and the Church, (in which I glory in having the privilege of being a member,) successfully through the storm of reproach, folly, ignorance, malice, persecution, falsehood, sacerdotal wrath, newspaper satire, pamphlet libels, and the combined influence of the powers of earth and hell,—I say these powers of righteousness and truth are not the decrees or rules of an ambitious and aspiring Nimrod, Pharaoh, Nebuchadnezzar, Alexander, Mahomet, Bonaparte, or other great sounding heroes that dazzled forth with a trail of pomp and circumstances for a little season, like a comet, and then disappeared, leaving a wide waste where such an existence once was, with only a name; nor where the glorious results of what you term "boldness of plans and measures," with the attendant "success," matured by the self-aggrandizing wisdom of the priests of Baal, the scribes and Pharisees of the Jews, popes and bishops of Christendom, or pagans of Juggernaut: nor were they extended by the divisions and subdivisions of a Luther or Calvin, a Wesley, or even a Campbell, supported by a galaxy of clergymen and churchmen, of whatever name or nature, bound apart by cast-iron creeds, and fastened to set stakes by chain-cable opinions, without revelation. Nor are they the lions of the land, or the leviathans of the sea, moving among the elements, as distant chimeras to fatten the fancy of the infidel; but they are as the stone cut out of the mountain without hands, and will become a great mountain, and fill the whole earth.* * * * * *

It seems that your mind is of such "a mathematical and philosophical cast," that the divinity of Moses makes no impression upon you, and that I will not be offended when you say that you rate me higher as a legislator than you do Moses, because you have me present with you for examination; that "Moses derives his chief authority from prescription and the lapse of time." You cannot, however, say but we are both right, it being out of the power of man to prove us wrong. "It is no mathematical problem, and can therefore get no mathematical solution."

* The omitted part of the letter is a paragraph in which are quoted a number of foreign phrases from Egyptian, Hebrew, Greek, German, Portuguese and other tongues; which are in no way germane to the subject discussed, but are a mere pedantic display, doubtless admitted, in this instance, in a spirit of humor by President Smith, as an offset to Bennett's assumption of so lofty an intellect—a mind of "so mathematical and philosophical a cast—that the divinity of Moses," etc., made no "impression" on him. The display of foreign phrases was doubtless the work of W. W. Phelps, who had some smattering knowledge of languages, which he was ever fond of displaying. Unfortunately similar displays were injected into President Smith's appeal to his native state—Vermont; and his paper, "Views of the Powers and Policy of the Government of the United States." These injections were also doubtless the work of Elder Phelps, who was one of the Prophet's clerks and amenuenses when the documents named above were prepared. Because these displays of pedantry mar these documents, and are in no way germane to the subjects of which they treat, and are not really the work of President Smith, they are omitted from the papers referred to as published in this HISTORY, the omission being indicated by elipses signs.

Now, sir, to cut the matter short, and not dally with your learned ideas, for fashion's sake you have here given your opinion, without reserve, that revelation, the knowledge of God, prophetic vision, the truth of eternity, cannot be solved as a mathematical problem. The first question then is, What is a mathematical problem? and the natural answer is, A statement, proposition or question that can be solved, ascertained, unfolded or demonstrated by knowledge, facts or figures; for "mathematical" is an adjective derived from *mathesis* (Gr.), meaning, in English, learning or knowledge. "Problem" is derived from *probleme* (French), or *problema* (Italian, or Spanish), and in each language means a question or proposition, whether true or false. "Solve" is derived from the Latin verb "*solvo*," to explain or answer.

One thing more in order to prove the work as we proceed. It is necessary to have witnesses, two or three of whose testimonies, according to the laws or rules of God and man, are sufficient to establish any one point.

Now for the question. How much are one and one? Two. How much is one from two? One. Very well; one question or problem is solved by figures. Now, let me ask one for facts: Was there ever such a place on the earth as Egypt? Geography says yes; ancient history says yes; and the Bible says yes: so three witnesses have solved that question. Again: Lived there ever such a man as Moses in Egypt? The same witnesses reply, *Certainly*. And was he a Prophet? The same witnesses, or a part, have left on record that Moses predicted in Leviticus that if Israel broke the covenant they had made, the Lord would scatter them among the nations, till the land enjoyed her Sabbaths: and, subsequently, these witnesses have testified of their captivity in Babylon and other places, in fulfillment. But to make assurance doubly sure, Moses prays that the ground might open and swallow up Korah and his company for transgression, and it was so: and he endorses the prophecy of Balaam, which said, Out of Jacob shall come he that shall have dominion, and shall destroy him that remaineth of the city: and Jesus Christ, as Him that "had dominion," about fifteen hundred years after, in accordance with this and the prediction of Moses, David, Isaiah, and many others, came, saying, Moses wrote of me, declaring the dispersion of the Jews, and the utter destruction of the city; and the Apostles were his witnesses, unimpeached, especially Jude, who not only endorses the facts of Moses "divinity," but also the events of Balaam and Korah, with many others, *as true*.

Besides these tangible facts, so easily proven and demonstrated by simple rules and testimony unimpeached, the art (now lost,) of embalming human bodies, and preserving them in the catacombs of Egypt, whereby men, women and children, as *mummies*, after a lapse of near three thousand five hundred years, come forth among the living; and although *dead*, the papyrus which has lived in their bosoms, unharmed, speaks for them in language like the sound of an earthquake. *Ecce veritas! Ecce cadaveros!* Behold the truth! Behold the mummies!

Oh, my dear sir, the sunken Tyre and Sidon, the melancholy dust where the city of Jerusalem once was, and the mourning of the Jews among the nations, together with such a cloud of witnesses, if you had been as well acquainted with your God and Bible as with your purse and pence table, the divinity of Moses would have dispelled the fog of five thousand years and filled you with light; for facts, like diamonds, not only cut glass, but they are the most precious jewels on earth. The spirit of prophecy is the testimony of Jesus.

The world at large is ever ready to credit the writings of Homer. Hesiod, Plutarch, Socrates, Pythagoras, Virgil, Josephus, Mahomet, and an hundred others; but where, tell me, where, have they left a line—a simple method of solving the truth of the plan of eternal life? Says the Savior, "If any man will do his [the Father's] will, he shall know of the doctrine, whether it be of God, or whether I speak of myself." Here, then, is a method of solving the divinity of men by the divinity within yourself, that as far exceeds the calculations of numbers as the sun exceeds a candle. Would to God that all men understood it and were willing to be governed by it, that when one had filled the measure of his days, he could exclaim like Jesus, *Veni mori, et reviviscere!*'

Your good wishes to go ahead, coupled with Mahomet and a right hand man, are rather more vain than virtuous. Why, sir, Cæsar had his right hand Brutus, who was his left hand assassin,—not, however, applying the allusion to you.

As to the private seal you mention, if sent to me, I shall receive it with the gratitude of a servant of God, and pray that the donor may receive a reward in the resurrection of the just.

The summit of your future fame seems to be hid in the political policy of a "mathematical problem" for the chief magistracy of this state, which I suppose might be solved by "double position," where the *errors* of the *supposition* are used to produce a true answer.

But, sir, when I leave the dignity and honor I received from heaven, to boost a man into power, through the aid of my friends, where the evil and designing, after the object has been accomplished, can lock up the clemency intended as a reciprocation for such favors, and where the wicked and unprincipled, as a matter of course, would seize the opportunity to flintify the hearts of the nation against me for dabbling at a sly game in politics,—verily I say, when I leave the dignity and honor of heaven, to gratify the ambition and vanity of man or men, may my power cease, like the strength of Samson, when he was shorn of his locks, while asleep in the lap of Delilah. Truly said the Savior, "Cast not your pearls before swine, lest they trample them under their feet, and turn again and rend you."

Shall I, who have witnessed the visions of eternity, and beheld the glorious mansions of bliss, and the regions and the misery of the damned,—shall I turn to be a Judas? Shall I, who have heard the voice of God, and communed with angels, and spake as moved by the Holy Ghost for the renewal of the everlasting covenant, and for the gathering of Israel in the last days,—shall I worm myself into a political hypocrite? Shall I, who hold the keys of the last kingdom, in which is the dispensation of the fullness of all things spoken by the mouths of all the holy Prophets since the world began, under the sealing power of the Melchisedec Priesthood,—shall I stoop from the sublime authority of Almighty God, to be handled as a monkey's cat-paw, and pettify myself into a clown to act the farce of political demagoguery? No—verily no! The whole earth shall bear me witness that I, like the towering rock in the midst of the ocean, which has withstood the mighty surges of the warring waves for centuries, *am impregnable*, and am a faithful friend to virtue, and a fearless foe to vice,—no odds whether the former was sold as a pearl in Asia or hid as a gem in America, and the latter dazzles in palaces or glimmers among the tombs.

I combat the errors of ages; I meet the violence of mobs; I cope with illegal proceedings from executive authority; I cut the gordian knot of powers, and I solve mathematical problems of universities, *with truth—diamond truth; and God is my "right hand man."**

And to close, let me say in the name of Jesus Christ to you, and to presidents, emperors, kings, queens, governors, rulers, nobles, and men in authority everywhere, Do the works of righteousness, execute justice and judgment in the earth, that God may bless you and her inhabitants; and

The laurel that grows on the top of the mountain
Shall green for your fame while the sun sheds a ray;
And the lily that blows by the side of the fountain
Will bloom for your virtue till earth melts away.

With due consideration and respect, I have the honor to be

Your most obedient servant, JOSEPH SMITH.

P.S. The court-martial will attend to your case in the Nauvoo Legion. J. S.

* Not in the blasphemous sense attributed to him by some anti-Mormon writers; namely, that God was subordinate to him—his right hand man (See Riley's "Founder of Mormonism" ch. x); but in the sense of the passage near the close of his address to "The Green Mountain Boys" (this chapter)—"And Jesus Christ, the Son of God, is my Great Counselor"—reverently said.

Tuesday, 14.—In the evening called at the office with Mr. Southwick, of Dixon, and had my letter to James Arlington Bennett read.

Wednesday, 15.—Mayor's court in the office. "Erskine *versus* Pullen." Nonsuit.

P. M. At the office. Suggested the idea ofpreparing a grammar of the Egyptian language.

Grammar for the Egyptian Language Suggested.

Prayer-meeting at the old house. I spoke of a petition to Congress, my letter to Bennett, and intention to write a proclamation to the kings of the earth.

Thursday, 16.—Held a court — "Averett *versus* Bostwick."

At home the remainder of the day. Chilly east wind and foggy.

Friday, 17.—Deeded lot 4, block 135, to Sally Phelps, wife of W. W. Phelps.

About ten, a.m., called in the office with Esquire Southwick, of Dixon.

Thunder, lightning and rain last night. Warm and foggy morning.

Saturday, 18.—Rode out on horseback to the prairie, accompanied by Mr. Southwick.

Conference of the church held at Halifax, Nova Scotia. Robert Dixon, president; Edward Cook, secretary. Two branches were represented, containing 2 Elders, 1 Teacher, 2 Deacons, and 34 members.

Sunday, 19.—Eleven a.m. to two p.m., prayer-meeting at the old house, and fasting.

In the evening, prayer-meeting and breaking of bread, &c.

Meeting at the Prophet's Home.

Monday, 20.—Two gentlemen from Vermont put up at the Mansion. I rode round with them in the afternoon to show them the improvements in the city. In the evening, several of the Twelve and others called to visit me. My family sang hymns, and Elder John Taylor prayed and gave an address, to which they paid great attention, and seemed very much interested.

Tuesday, 21.—Council of the Twelve and others at my old house all day. Dictated to my clerk an appeal to the Green Mountain boys of Vermont, my native State.

Also instructed Elders Richards, Hyde, Taylor and Phelps to write a "Proclamation to the Kings of the Earth."

Wednesday, 22.—Rode out to the prairie with W. Clayton and Lorenzo D. Wasson, and found Arthur Smith cutting timber on my land without my consent, which I objected to.

Prayer-meeting in the evening at the old house.

Five deaths in the city during the past week.

Thursday, 23.—Met in council in the old house; then walked down to the river to look at the stream, rocks, &c., about half-past eleven, a.m. Suggested the idea of petitioning Congress for a grant to make a canal over the falls, or a dam to turn the water to the city, so that we might erect mills and other machinery.*

Canal Around the Rapids.

Issued a writ of habeas corpus, on application of John M. Finch.

Friday, 24.—Attended Municipal Court "on habeas corpus, John M. Finch at suit of Amos Davis." Finch discharged, Davis to pay costs, it being a vexatious and malicious suit.

The young men have established a debating society in Nauvoo, to discuss topics of various descriptions.

* The General Government finally constructed a canal around the rapids at a cost of $4,582,000, completing the work in 1877. The canal is seven and a half miles in length and has in it three locks, overcoming the obstruction in river navigation which the Des Moines rapids in early days presented. It is called the Des Moines Rapids Canal.

Saturday, 25.—Colonel Frierson, United States Surveyor from Quincy, arrived in Nauvoo. In the evening the High Council sat on the case of Harrison Sagers, charged with seduction, and having stated that I had taught it was right. Charge not sustained. I was present with several of the Twelve, and gave an address tending to do away with every evil, and exhorting them to practice virtue and holiness before the Lord; told them that the Church had not received any permission from me to commit fornication, adultery, or any corrupt action; but my every word and action has been to the contrary. If a man commit adultery, he cannot receive the celestial kingdom of God. Even if he is saved in any kingdom, it cannot be the celestial kingdom. I did think that the many examples that have been made manifest, such as John C. Bennett's and others, were sufficient to show the fallacy of such a course of conduct.

The Prophet's Stand on Chastity and General Morality.

I condemned such actions *in toto*, and warned the people present against committing such evils; for it will surely bring a curse upon any person who commits such deeds.

After adjournment, held a council, and agreed to meet Mr. Frierson* at the Mansion to morrow morning.

I received a letter signed by George B. Wallace and six other Elders, requesting permission for Elder John E. Page to remain in Boston the ensuing winter. Also a letter from John E. Page, giving his assent to the petition, to which the Twelve Apostles wrote the following reply:—

Letter: Brigham Young in Behalf of the Twelve to Elder John E. Page, Appointing him to go to Washington.

Elder John E. Page:

BELOVED BROTHER:—Your letter dated at Boston, in connection with

* This Col. Frierson resided at Quincy, was a political representative of John C. Calhoun, then an active aspirant for the presidency of the United States. See letter of Joseph L. Heywood, pp. 62, 63.

some one hundred and fifty of the brethren, is received, and we proceed to reply. Your letter is not before us this moment; consequently you must excuse a reference to dates and names which have escaped our recollection. But the subject is fresh, and the letter was read in a council of Presidents Joseph, Hyrum, and the Twelve, when the word of the Lord came through Joseph the Seer thus:—"Let my servant John E. Page take his departure *speedily* from the city of Boston, and go directly to the city of Washington, and there labor diligently in proclaiming my Gospel to the inhabitants thereof: and if he is humble and faithful, lo! I will be with him, and will give him the hearts of the people, that he may do them good and build up a church unto my name in that city."

Now, Brother Page, if you wish to follow counsel and do the will of the Lord, as we believe you desire to do, call the church at Boston together, *without delay*, and read this letter to them, calling upon them to assist you on your mission, and go thy way speedily unto the place which is appointed unto you by the voice of the Lord, and build up a church in the city of Washington; for it is expedient and absolutely necessary that we have a foothold in that popular city. Let your words be soft unto the people, but full of the spirit and power of the Holy Ghost. *Do not challenge the sects for debate*, but treat them as brethren and friends; and the God of heaven will bless you, and we will bless you in the name of the Lord Jesus, and the people will rise up and bless you, and call you a sweet messenger of peace. You will pardon us for giving you such counsel, for we feel to do it in the name of the Lord.

When you have built a church at Washington so as to warrant the expense. It will be wisdom for you to send or take your wife to Washington; so says President Joseph.

All things go on smoothly here. As to the reports circulated while we were in Boston, there is nothing of them. Brother Joseph has commenced living in his new house, and enjoys himself well. He has raised a sign, entitled "Nauvoo Mansion," and has all the best company in the city. Many strangers from abroad call on him, feeling perfect liberty so to do, since he has made his house public; and it is exerting a blessed influence on the public mind.

The Temple has been progressing rapidly until the recent frosts. The walls are now above the windows of the first story, and some of the circular windows are partly laid. The brethren of the Twelve have all arrived home, are tolerably well, and their families, except Sister Hyde, who has been very sick, and is yet, though at last report rather better. No prospect of any of the Twelve leaving home this winter that we know of. Elder Snow has arrived with his company from Boston, generally in good spirits.

The devil howls some: may be you will hear him as far as Boston, for there cannot a blackleg be guilty of any crime in Nauvoo, but somebody will lay it to the servants of God. We shall give the substance of this communication to your wife same mail.

We remain your brother in the new and everlasting covenant, in behalf of the quorum,

BRIGHAM YOUNG, President.

W. RICHARDS, Clerk.

Sunday, *26*.—I met with Hyrum, the Twelve and others, in council with Colonel Frierson, at the Mansion, concerning petitioning Congress for redress of grievances. Read to him the affidavits of Hyrum Smith, Brigham Young, Parley P. Pratt, Lyman Wight, George W. Pitkin and Sidney Rigdon, taken before the municipal court on *habeas corpus*, and conversed with him thereon.

Renewal of Petitions to Congress.

At eleven, a.m., Elder Orson Pratt preached in the Assembly Room.

In the evening, Elder Parley P. Pratt lectured in the Mansion. Rainy, muddy day.

Monday, *27*.—Wet day. Being quite unwell, I stayed at home.

Tuesday, *28*.—At home. Colonel Frierson wrote a Memorial to Congress.*

Wednesday, *29*.—At home. Clear and cold. Colonel Frierson left for home, taking with him a copy of the Memorial, to get signers in Quincy. I here insert a copy of the—

* The reason Col. John Frierson interested himself in this matter was that Hon. R. B. Rhett a representative in the National Congress from South Carolina, and a political friend of John C. Calhoun, had expressed a willingness to present to Congress a memorial for a redress of grievances suffered by the Saints in Missouri; and of course all this in the interest of Calhoun as candidate for President. See pp. 62,63; also *Nauvoo Neighbor* for the 5th June, 1844.

MEMORIAL.

To the Honorable the Senate and House of Representatives of the United States, in Congress Assembled.

The memorial of the undersigned inhabitants of Hancock county, in the State of Illinois, respectfully showeth—

That they belong to the society of Latter-day Saints, commonly called "Mormons;" that a portion of our people commenced settling in Jackson county, Missousi, in the summer of 1831, where they purchased lands and settled upon them with the intention and expectation of becoming permanent citizens in common with others.

From a very early period after the settlement began, a very unfriendly feeling was manifested by the neighboring people; and as the society increased, this unfriendly spirit also increased, until it degenerated into a cruel and unrelenting persecution, and the society was at last compelled to leave the county. An account of these unprovoked persecutions has been published to the world; yet we deem it not improper to embody a few of the most prominent items in the memorial, and lay them before your honorable body.

On the 20th July, 1833, a mob collected at Independence, a deputation or committee from which called upon a few members of our Church there, and stated to them that the store, printing office, and all mechanic shops belonging to our people must be closed forthwith, and the society leave the county immediately.

These conditions were so unexpected and so hard, that a short time was asked for to consider on the subject before an answer could be given, which was refused; and when some of our men answered that they could not consent to comply with such propositions, the work of destruction commenced.

The printing office—a valuable two-story brick building, was destroyed by the mob, and with it much valuable property. They next went to the store for the same purpose; but one of the owners thereof agreeing to close it, they abandoned their design.

A series of outrages was then commenced by the mob upon individual members of our society. Bishop Partridge was dragged from his house and family, where he was first partially stripped of his clothes, and then tarred and feathered from head to foot. Mr. Charles Allen was also tarred at the same time.

Three days afterwards the mob assembled in great numbers, bearing a red flag, and proclaiming that unless the society would leave *en masse*, every man of them should be killed. Being in a defenseless situation, to avoid a general massacre, a treaty was entered into and ratified, by which it was agreed that one-half of the society should leave the county by the 1st of January, and the remainder by the 1st of April following.

In October, while our people were gathering their crops and otherwise preparing to fulfil their part of the treaty, the mob again collected without any provocation, shot at some of our people, whipped others, threw down their houses, and committed many other depredations. The members of the society were for some time harassed hoth day and night, their houses assailed and broken open, and their women and children insulted and abused.

The store-house of A. S. Gilbert and Company was broken open, ransacked, and some of the goods strewed in the streets. These repeated assaults so aroused the indignant feelings of our people, that a small party thereof, on one occasion, when wantonly abused, resisted the mob. A conflict ensued, in which one of our people and some two or three of their assailants were killed.

This unfortunate event raised the whole county in arms, and we were required forthwith to surrender our arms and leave the county. Fifty-one guns were given up, which have never been returned or paid for to this day.

Parties of the mob, from thirty to seventy in number, then scoured the county in every direction, threatening and abusing women and children, until they were forced first to take shelter in the woods and prairies at a very inclement season of the year, and finally to make their escape to Clay county, where the people permitted them to take refuge for a time.

After the society had left Jackson county, their buildings, amounting to about two hundred, were either burned or otherwise destroyed, with a great portion of their crops, as well as furniture, stock, &c.; for which they have not as yet received any remuneration.

The society remained in Clay county nearly three years, when, in compliance with the demands of the citizens there, it was determined to remove to that section of country known afterwards as Caldwell county.

In order to secure our people from molestation, the members of the society bought out most of the former inhabitants of what is now Caldwell county, and also entered much of the wild land then belonging to the United States in that section of country, fondly hoping that as we were American citizens, obeying the laws and assisting to support the government, we would be protected in the use of homes which we had honestly purchased from the General Government and fully paid for.

Here we were permitted to enjoy peace for a season; but as our society increased in numbers and settlements were made in Daviess and Carrol counties, unfounded jealousies sprang up among our neighbors, and the spirit of the mob was soon manifested again. The people of our Church who had located themselves at De Witt were compelled by the mob to leave the place, notwithstanding the militia were called out for their protection.

From De Witt the mob went to Daviess county, and, while on their way, took some of our people prisoners, and greatly abused and mistreated them. Our people had been driven by force from Jackson county; they had been compelled to leave Clay county, and sell their lands there, for which they have never been paid: they had finally settled in Caldwell county, where they had purchased and paid for nearly all the Government land within its limits, in order to secure homes where they could live and worship in peace; but even here they were soon followed by the mob.

The society remained in Caldwell from 1836 until the fall of 1838, and during that time had acquired by purchase from the Government, the settlers, and preemptioners, almost all the lands in the county of Caldwell, and a portion of those in Daviess and Carrol counties.

Those counties, when our people first commenced their settlements, were for the most part wild and uncultivated, and they had converted them into large and well improved farms, well stocked. Lands had risen in value, from 10 to 25 dollars per acre, and those counties were rapidly advancing in cultivation and wealth.

In August, 1838, a riot commenced, growing out of the attempt of a member of the society to vote, which resulted in creating great excitement and many scenes of lawless outrage. A large mob, under the conduct of Cornelius Gilliam, came into the vicinity of Far West, drove off our stock, and abused our people. Another party came into Caldwell county, took away our horses and cattle, burnt our houses, and ordered the inhabitents to leave their homes immediately.

By order of Brigadier-General Doniphan and Colonel Hinkle, a company of about sixty men, under the command of David W. Patten, went to disperse this mob. A conflict ensued, in which Captain Patten and two of his men were killed, and others wounded.* A mob party, from two to three hundred in number, many of whom are supposed to have come from Chariton county, fell on our people, and, notwithstanding they begged for quarters, shot down and killed eighteen, as they would so many wild beasts.

They were finally compelled to flee from those counties; and on the 11th October, 1838, they sought safety by that means, with their families,

* This is an error. Col. Frierson has confounded two incidents—the "Battle" at Crooked River, and a movement in Daviess county. General Doniphan gave no orders in respect of the skirmish in which David Patten lost his life, usually called the "Battle of Crooked River;" but he and also General Park gave some orders to Col. Wight and Col. Hinkle in relation to movements of militia in Daviess county against Millport and Gallatin. (See Vol. iii, ch. xii.)

leaving many of their effects behind. That they had previously applied to the constituted authorities of Missouri for protection, but in vain.

The society were pursued by the mob, conflicts ensued, deaths occurred on each side, and finally a force was organized under the authority of the Governor of the state of Missouri, with orders to drive us from the State, *or exterminate us.*

Abandoned and attacked by those to whom we had looked for *protection*, we determined to make no further resistance, but submit to the authorities of the State and yield to our fate, however hard it might be. Several members of the society were arrested and imprisoned on a charge of treason against the State: and the rest, amounting to above 14,000 souls, fled into the other States, principally into Illinois, where they now reside.

Your memorialists would further state that they have heretofore petitioned your honorable body, praying redress for the injuries set forth in this memorial; but the committee to whom our petition was referred reported, in substance, that the General Government had no power in the case, and that we must look for relief to the courts and the legislature of Missouri.

In reply, your memorialists would beg leave to state that they have repeatedly appealed to the authorities of Missouri in vain; that though they are American citizens, at all times ready to obey the laws and support the institutions of the country, none of us would dare enter Missouri for any such purpose, or for any purposes whatever.

Our property was seized by the mob or lawlessly confiscated by the State; and we were forced, at the point of the bayonet, to sign deeds of trust relinquishing our property. But the exterminating order of the Governor of Missouri is still in force, and we dare not return to claim our just rights. The widows and orphans of those slain, who could legally sign no deeds of trust, dare not return to claim the inheritance left them by their murdered parents.

It is true the Constitution of the United States gives to us, in common with all other native or adopted citizens, the right to enter and settle in Missouri; but an executive order has been issued to exterminate us if we enter the State, and a part of the Constitution becomes a nullity, so far as we are concerned.

Had any foreign state or power committed a similar outrage upon us, we cannot for a moment doubt that the strong arm of the General Government would have been stretched out to redress our wrongs; and we flatter ourselver that the same power will either redress our grievances or shield us from harm in our efforts to regain our lost property, which we fairly purchased from the General Government.

Finally, your memorialists pray your honorable body to take their wrongs into consideration, receive testimony in the case, and grant such relief as by the Constitution and laws you may have power to give.

And your memorialists will ever pray.

Eleven copies were also made for circulation and signatures by Thomas Bullock, one of my clerks.

Activities in Renewal of Appeals to Congress.

Four, p.m. A meeting of the citizens in the assmbly room, [over President Smith's store] when Brigham Young was chosen chairman of the meeting, and Willard Richards, clerk.

The object of the meeting was briefly explained by the clerk, followed by Judge Phelps, which was to petition Congress for redress of grievances in relation to the Missouri persecutions.

Voted that the chairman appoint a committee to get the names of memorialists in this city.

The chairman appointed the assessors and collectors in their several wards.

Voted that the same committee collect means to purchase paper. President Sidney Rigdon to go to La Harpe, and Elder Heber C. Kimball to Ramus, to procure signers.

The charmain appointed committees to visit other places.

Joseph Smith, the Mayor, made some remarks, and his Appeal to the Green Mountain Boys was read by William W. Phelps, as follows:—

President Smith's Appeal to his Native State—Vermont.

I was born in Sharon, Vermont, in 1805, where the first quarter of my life grew with the growth and strengthened with the strength of that "first-born" State of the "United Thirteen." From the old "French War" to the final consummation of American Independence, my fathers, heart to heart, and shoulder to shoulder, with the noble fathers of our liberty, fought and bled; and with the most of that venerable band of patriots, they have gone to rest, bequeathing a glorious country, with all her inherent rights, to millions of posterity. Like other honest citizens, I not only (when manhood came,) sought my own peace, prosperity, and happiness, but also the peace, prosperity, and happiness of my friends; and, with all the rights and realm before me, and the revelations of Jesus Christ to guide me into all truth, I had good reasons to enter into the blessings and privileges of an American citizen, the rights of a Green Mountain Boy, unmolested, and enjoy life and religion according to the most virtuous and enlightened customs, rules, and etiquette of the nineteenth century. But, to the disgrace of the United States, it is not so. These rights and privileges, together with a large amount of property, have been wrested from me, and thousands of my friends, by lawless mobs in Missouri, supported by executive authority; and the crime of plundering our property, and the unconstitutional and barbarous act of our expulsion, and even the inhumanity of murdering men, women, and children, have received the *pass-word of "justifiable"* by legislative enactments; and the horrid deeds, doleful and disgraceful as they are, have been paid for by Government.

In vain have we sought for redress of grievances and a restoration to our rights in the courts and legislature of Missouri. In vain have we sought for our rights and the remuneration for our property in the halls of Congress and at the hands of the President. The only consolation yet experienced from these highest tribunals and *mercy-seats* of our bleeding country *is that our cause is just, but the Government has no power to redress us.*

Our arms were forcibly taken from us by those Missouri marauders; and, in spite of every effort to have them returned, the State of Missouri still retains them: and the United States militia law, with this fact be fore the Government, still compels us to military duty; and, for a lack of said arms, the law *forces us to pay fines.* As Shakespeare would say *"thereby hangs a tale."*

Several hundred thousand dollars' worth of land in Missouri was purchased at the United States Land Offices in that district of country and the money, without doubt, has been appropriated to strengthen the army and navy, or increase the power and glory of the nation in some other way. And notwithstanding Missouri has robbed and mobbed me and twelve or fifteen thousand innocent inhabitants, murdered hundreds, and expelled the residue, at the point of the bayonet, without law, contrary to the express language of the Constitution of the United States and every State in the Union, and contrary to the custom and usage of civilized nations, and especially one holding up the motto, *"The asylum of the oppressed."* yet the comfort we receive to raise our wounded bodies and invigorate our troubled spirits, on account of such immense sacrifices of life, property, patience, and right, and as an equivalent for the enormous taxes we are compelled to pay to support these functionaries in a dignified manner, after we have petitioned and pleaded with tears, and been showed like a caravan of foreign animals, for the peculiar gratification of connoiseurs in humanity, that flare along in public life like lamps upon lamp-posts, because they are better calculated for the schemes of the night than for the scenes of the day, is, as President Van Buren said, *Your cause is just, but Government has no power to redress you!*

No wonder,after the Pharisee's prayer, the publican smote his breast and said, "*Lord be merciful to me a sinner!*" What must the manacled nations think of freemen's rights in the land of liberty? * * * *

Now, therefore, having failed in every attempt to obtain satisfaction at the tribunals, where all men seek for it, according to the rules of right, I am compelled to appeal to the honor and patriotism of my native State—to the clemency and valor of "Green Mountain Boys;" for throughout the various periods of the world, whenever a nation, kingdom, state, family, or individual has received an insult or an injury from a superior force. (unless satisaction was made,) it has been the custom to call in the aid of friends to assist in obtaining redress. For proof we have only to refer to the recovery of Lot and his effects by Abraham in the days of Sodom and Gomorrah, or to turn to the relief afforded by France and Holland for the achievement of the Independence of these United States, without bringing up the great bulk of historical facts, rules, laws, decrees, and treaties, and Bible records, by which nations have been governed, to show that mutual alliance for the general benefit of mankind to retaliate and repel foreign aggressions. To punish and prevent home wrongs, when the conservators of justice and the laws have failed to afford a remedy, are not only common and in the highest sense justifiable and wise, but they are also proper expedients to promote the enjoyment of equal rights, the pursuit of happiness, the preservation of life, and the benefit of posterity.

With all these facts before me, and a pure desire to ameliorate the condition of the poor and unfortunate among men, and, if possible, to entice all men from evil to good, and with firm reliance that God will reward the just, I have been stimulated to call upon my native State for a "union of all honest men," and to appeal to the valor of the "Green Mountain Boys" by all honorable methods and means to assist me in obtaining justice from Missouri, not only for the property she has stolen and confiscated, the murders she has commited among my friends, and for our expulsion from the State, but also to humble and chastise or abase her for the disgrace she has brought upon constitutional liberty until she atones for her sins.

I appeal also to the fraternity of brethren who are bound by kindred ties to assist a brother in distress in all cases where it can be done ac-

* The omission here indicated is the paragraph of foreign phrases not germane to the matter as explained in the footnote at page 75.

cording to the rules of order, to extend the boon of benevolence and protection in avenging the Lord of His enemies, as if a Solomon, a Hiram, a St. John, or a Washington raised his hands before a wondering world, and exclaimed, "My life for his!" Light, liberty, and virtue forever!

I bring this appeal before my native State, for the solemn reason that an injury has been done, and crimes have been committed, which a sovereign State, of the Federal compact, one of the great family of "*E pluribus unum,*" refuses to compensate, by consent of parties, rules of law, customs of nations, or in any other way. I bring it also because the National Government has fallen short of affording the necessary relief, as before stated, *for want of power*, leaving a large body of her own free citizens, whose wealth went freely into her treasury for lands, and whose gold and silver for taxes still fills the pockets of her dignitaries "in ermine and lace," defrauded, robbed, plundered, ravished, driven, exiled, and banished from the "Independent Republic of Missouri!"

And in the appeal let me say, Raise your towers, pile your monuments to the skies, build your steam frigates, spread yourselves far and wide, and open the iron eyes of your bulwarks by sea and land; and let the towering church steeples marshal the country like the dreadful splendor of an army with bayonets. But remember the flood of Noah; remember the fate of Sodom and Gomorrah; remember the dispersion and confusion at the tower of Babel; remember the destruction of Pharaoh and his hosts; remember the handwriting upon the wall, "*Mene, mene, tekel upharsin;*" remember the angel's visit to Sennacherib, and the one hundred and eighty-five thousand Assyrians; remember the end of the Jews and Jerusalem, and remember the Lord Almighty will avenge the blood of His Saints that now crimsons the skirts of Missouri! Shall wisdom cry aloud, and her speech not be heard?

Has the majesty of American liberty sunk into such vile servitude and oppression, that justice has fled? Have the glory and influence of a Washington, an Adams, a Jefferson, a Lafayette, and a host of others, forever departed; and the wrath of a Cain, a Judas, and a Nero whirled forth in the heraldry of hell, to sprinkle our garments with blood, and lighten the darkness of midnight with the blaze of our dwellings? Where is the patriotism of '76? Where is the virtue of our forefathers? and where is the sacred honor of freemen!

Must we, because we believe in the fulness of the Gospel of Jesus Christ, the administration of angels, and the communion of the Holy Ghost, like the Prophets and Apostles of old,—must we be mobbed with impunity, be exiled from our habitations and property without remedy, murdered without mercy, and Government find the weapons and pay the vagabonds for doing the jobs, and give them the plunder into the bargain? Must we, because we believe in enjoying the constitutional privilege and right of worshiping Almighty God according to the dictates of our own consciences, and because we believe in repentance, and baptism for the remission of sins, the gift of the Holy Ghost by the laying on of hands, the resurrection of the dead, the millennium, the day of judgment, and the Book of Mormon as the history of the aborigines of this continent,—must we be expelled from the institutions of our country, the rights of citizenship and the graves of our friends and brethren, and the Government lock the gate of humanity and shut the door of redress against us? If so, farewell freedom! adieu to personal safety! and let the red hot wrath of an offended God purify the nation of such sinks of corruption; for that realm is hurrying to ruin where vice has the power to expel virtue.

My father, who stood several times in the battles of the American Revolution, till his companions in arms had been shot dead at his feet, was forced from his home in Far West, Missouri, by those civilized—or satanized—savages, in the dreary season of winter, to seek a shelter in another State; and the vicissitudes and sufferings consequent to his flight brought his honored grey head to the grave a few months after. And my youngest brother also, in the vigor and bloom of youth, from his great exposure and fatigue in endeavoring to assist his parents on their journey, (I and my brother Hyrum being in chains, in dungeons, in Missouri, *where they tried to feed us with—human flesh*) was likewise so debilated that he found a premature grave shortly after my father; and my mother, too, though she yet lingers among us, from her extreme exposure in that dreadful tragedy, was filled with rheumatic affections and other diseases, which leave her no enjoyment of health. She is sinking in grief and pain, broken-hearted, from Missouri persecution.

O death! wilt thou not give to every honest man a heated dart to sting those wretches while they pollute the land? And O Grave! wilt thou not *open the trap door* to the pit of ungodly men, that they may stumble in?

I appeal to the "Green Mountain Boys" of my native State to rise in the majesty of virtuous freemen, and by all honorable means help to bring Missouri to the bar of justice. If there is one whisper from the spirit of an Ethen Allen, or a gleam from the shade of a General Stark, let it mingle with our sense of honor and fire our bosoms for the cause of suffering innocence, for the reputation of our disgraced country, and for the glory of God; and may all the earth bear me witness, if Missouri—blood-stained Missouri, escapes the due merit of her crimes—the vengeance she so justly deserves—that Vermont is a hypocrite, a *coward*, and this nation the hotbed of political demagogues!

I make this appeal to the sons of liberty of my native State for help to frustrate the wicked designs of sinful men. I make it to hush the violence of mobs. I make it to cope with the unhallowed influence of wicked men in high places. I make it to resent the insult and injury made to an innocent, unoffending people, by a lawless ruffian State. I make it to obtain justice where law is put at defiance. I make it to wipe off the stain of blood from our nation's escutcheon. I make it to show presidents, governors, and rulers prudence. I make it to fill honorable men with discretion. I make it to teach senators wisdom. I I make it to teach judges justice. I make it to point clergymen to the path of virtue. And I make it to turn the hearts of this nation to the truth and realities of pure and undefiled religion, that they may escape the perdition of ungodly men; and Jesus Christ, the Son of God, is my Great Counselor.

Wherefore let the rich and the learned, the wise and the noble, the poor and the needy, the bond and the free, both black and white, take heed to their ways, and a leave to the knowledge of God, and execute justice and judgment upon the earth in righteousness, and prepare to meet the judge of the quick and the dead, for the hour of His coming is nigh.

And I must go on as the herald of grace,
Till the wide-spreading conflict is over.
And burst through the curtains of tyrannic night;
Yes, I must go on to gather our race,
Till the high blazing flame of Jehovah
Illumines the globe as a triumph of right.

As a friend of equal rights to all men, and a messenger of the everlasting Gospel of Jesus Christ, I have the honor to be,

Your devoted servant,

JOSEPH SMITH.

Sidney Rigdon spoke.

Parley P. Pratt confessed he was wrong in one thing in Missouri; that is, he left alive, and left them alive; and asked forgiveness, and promised never to do so again.

Parley P. Pratt offered to deliver the President's "Appeal to the Green Mountain Boys" to all the large towns in New York, if he could have a copy.

The President offered a copy and it was voted that

Elder Pratt shall have this mission granted him, and voted in addition that he go to all the towns in Vermont.

The Chairman [Brigham Young] spoke.

The Mayor [President Smith] spoke. Said he rose to make a confession, that he used all his influence to prevent the brethren from fighting when mobbed in Missouri. If I did wrong, I will not do so any more. It was a suggestion of the head. He would never do so again; but when the mobs come upon you, kill them. I never will restrain you again, but will go and help you.

The Chairman [Brigham Young] spoke again; acknowledged his wrong; said he would never put his hand on Brother Hosea Stout's shoulder again to hold him back when he was abused.

John Taylor spoke of Missouri; said he would never submit to such treatment again.

Mayor [President Smith] spoke again. If I do not stand with those who will stand by me in the hour of trouble and danger, without faltering, I give you leave to shoot me.*

Mayor read a letter in reply to one he wrote to Henry Clay.

Parley P. Pratt stated that the history of the persecution was put into the hand of Henry Clay.

* Relative to the spirit of this meeting in Nauvoo on the 29th of November, 1843; and also of many of the articles published as Editorials, and letters that were written about this time to public men, the reader should be reminded that these leading brethren of the Church were speaking and writing under a great stress of feeling—under a sense of outraged justice. Their minds had been refreshed and their feelings again wrought up by the detailed recital of the acts of injustice endured in Missouri by the Memorial to congress drawn up by Colonel Frierson; and under such circumstances it is scarcely to be expected that strong men will not give expression to the vehemence they feel. Edmund Burke once said in defense of the rashness expressed in both speech and action of some of the patriots of the American Revolution, that "*It is not fair to judge the temper or the disposition of any man or set of men when they are composed and at rest from their conduct or there expressions in a state of disturbance and irritation.*" The justice of Burke's assertion has never been questioned, and without any wresting whatsoever it may be applied to the prominent Church leaders on the occasion of this meeting at Nauvoo; and, moreover, they saw again forming those mobocratic tendencies in Illinois from which they had suffered in Missouri.

Moved by Joseph Smith, That every man in the meeting who could wield a pen write an address to his mother country. Carried.

Mayor read the Memorial to Congress. The State rights doctrines are what feed mobs. They are a dead carcass —a stink, and they shall ascend up as a stink offering in the nose of the Almighty.

They shall be oppressed as they have oppressed us, not by "Mormons," but by others in power. They shall drink a drink offering, the bitterest dregs, not from the "Mormons," but from a meaner source than themselves. God shall curse them.

Adjourned till next Monday evening, early candle-light.

At ten, a.m., rode out with Mr. Jackson At home most all day.

The "Appeal to the Green Mountain Boys" sent to press.

Severe frost, so that the ice is on the water in the house.

W. L. D. Ewing writes to Major John Bills—

Letter: W. L. D. Ewing, State Auditor, Illinois, to Major John Bills—Legion Affairs.

The foregoing opinions constitute my reason for refusing to issue the warrants in your favor. I am not satisfied myself entirely of the correctness of the opinions of the Attorney-General. If you should be dissatisfied with the decision, I would advise you to raise the question before the Supreme Court, which will be in session on the 2nd Monday of December. I am the more anxious that this should be done because I wish to be satisfied whether I was correct or not in issuing warrants to you in the spring. Be pleased to advise me on the subject.

Respectfully,

W. L. D. EWING, Auditor.

Enclosing the opinion of the Attorney-General, Josiah Lamborn, as follows:—

Letter: J. Lamborn, Attorney General of Illinois—Legal Opinion of Above.

SPRINGFIELD, ILLINOIS, Nov. 30, 1843.

I have examined the claim of J. C. Bennett as brigade-inspector of the Nauvoo Legion, and it is my opinion that the claim should be disallowed.

The Legislature, in giving authority for the organization of a body of "independent military men" at Nauvoo, intended, no doubt, that all expenses, &c., except "their proportion of public arms," should be defrayed by the city and its privileged Legion.

They occupy a novel position, disconnected from the military communities of the whole State, and in no way subject to the regular military officers, possessing an exemption even from subjection to the general military laws, with a law-making power invested in their own Legion. It is not reasonable to suppose that the Legislature would confer so many exclusive favors, and yet pay those who profit by this condition of things as much as is paid to regular militia officers.

In the absence of any express provision by law to authorize the payment of the claim, I can see nothing from which an authority of the kind could be derived, and therefore advise accordingly.

J. LAMBORN, Attorney-General.

And copy of letter from J. N. McDougall to General W. L. D. Ewing:—

Letter: J. N. McDougall to State Auditor.

SPRINGFIELD, ILLINOIS, Nov. 30, 1843.

General W. L. D. Ewing, Auditor, &c.—

I have examined the claim of John Bills, brigade-major of the Nauvoo Legion, for services under the 53rd section of the militia law, and have arrived at the conclusion that the Nauvoo Legion are not to be considered as a part of the regular militia of this State, and that the general law has no further application to them than is expressly provided for in the law authorizing their organization. The law providing for the organization of the Legion making no provision for the payment of its officers by the State, it is my opinion that the above claim ought not to be audited.

The Legion was organized by the City Council, is subject to their control for the purpose of enforcing their ordinances. It is entirely independent of the general military law, may have a different organization, make laws for its own government, and seems evidently designed to sustain the municipal authorities of Nauvoo. If there are expenses to be paid, the municipality of which they form a very important element, must meet them. I am, with great respect,

Your obedient servant,

J. N. McDOUGALL.

Mr. Ewing reported to Major Bills that the returns made

out [for Mr. Bills], and sent to the State Department, were the best reports by any brigade-major in the State, and did him great credit: the refusal to pay him for his services is a mere pretext, as the Nauvoo Charter requires that the Nauvoo Legion shall perform the same amount of duty as is now or may hereafter be required of the regular militia of the State, and shall be at the disposal of the Governor for the public defense and the execution of the laws of the State, and be entitled to their proportion of the State arms; and were it not for the prejudice against us on account of our religion, his claim would have been paid without a word of complaint.

CHAPTER V.

THE AVERY KIDNAPPING—DEFENSIVE PREPARATIONS AGAINST MISSOURI MOBS—APPEALS TO THE GENERAL GOVERNMENT FOR PROTECTION—NAUVOO LEGION OFFERED AS UNITED STATES TROOPS.

Friday, December 1, 1843.—At home. In the evening, walking out and administering to the sick.

At noon, Dr. Willard Richards called on me to get a petition to Congress for an appropriation to improve the Rapids.

Progress of the Work.

I continue to receive letters from Elders in the different States, giving news of the progress of the work.

Clear and cold day. Some ice floating in the river.

Saturday 2.—Prayer-meeting from one to six p. m., in the assembly room over the store. Orson Hyde, Parley P. Pratt, Wilford Woodruff, George A. Smith, and Orson Spencer received their endowments and further instructions in the Priesthood. About thirty-five persons present.

A conference was held at Alexander in Genesee county, New York. Ten branches, containing 44 Elders and 206 members, were represented. Two High Priests, one Seventy, 21 Elders and one Deacon present.

Hyrum Smith Meets with an Accident

Sunday, 3.—I arrived at the assembly room* about noon: found all present, except Hyrum and his wife. He had slipped and turned his knee-joint backward, and sprained the large muscle of his leg, and I had been ministering unto him. Emma had been unwell during the night. After the meeting was organized, William W. Phelps

* This was the upper room of President Smith's brick store.

read my "Appeal to the Green Mountain Boys," which was dedicated by prayer after all had spoken upon it. We also prayed for Nathan Pratt, who was very sick, Hyrum, and others. I afterwards instructed them in the things of the Priesthood.

Monday, 4.—At six in the evening, I attended the adjourned meeting of citizens in the assembly room, which was crowded with a select congregation. Many could not get admission. There were two Missourians present. I made some observations at the opening of the meeting, requested them to be calm and cool, but let the spirit of '76 burn in their bosoms, and when occasion requires, say little, but act; and when the mob comes, mow a hole through them.

My "Appeal to the Green Mountain Boys" was read by W. W. Phelps.

Elder Parley P. Pratt read his "Appeal to the State of New York."

Number of the Prophet's Vexatious Lawsuits

My clerk, Willard Richards, read the memorial to Congress, when the assembly unanimously voted their approbation of the memorial, when I spoke two-and-a-half hours, relating many circumstances which transpired in Missouri, not mentioned in the memorial. I have already had thirty-eight vexatious lawsuits, and have paid Missouri $150,000 for land. I borrowed $500 of Judge Young in Washington, to pay the expenses of the party that accompanied me, and had to borrow of others.

Daniel Avery and his son were kidnapped from the neighborhood of Warsaw by a company of Missourians, assisted by some anti-Mormons of this county, and carried into Missouri.*

Tuesday, 5.—Six p. m., met the Twelve, also Phelps, Clayton, and Turley, in council, in the office, on important business.

* This occurred on the 2nd of December. See Avery's Affidavit, Chapter VI, this volume.

Advised the Twelve to raise money to send to Elder Hyde, who is east, for him to get paper to print the Doctrine and Covenants, and get new type and metal for sterotyping the same.

Wednesday, 6.—At home and took the following affidavit:—

Chapman's Affidavit in the Avery Case.

STATE OF ILLINOIS,
CITY OF NAUVOO. } SS.

On the sixth day of December, in the year of our Lord one thousand eight hundred and forty-three, came Delmore Chapman before me, Joseph Smith, mayor of said city; and after being duly sworn, deposeth and saith that on the nineteenth day of November, 1843, a man named Richardson came to one of his neighbors living in Bear Creek precinct, in the county of Hancock, named Philander Avery, and enticed him to the Mississippi at Warsaw, by false pretenses; and from thence by a company he was forced over the river and taken to Monticello jail; and that on the second day of December, some of the same party and others came to the aforesaid Bear Creek and kidnapped Daniel Avery, the father of the aforesaid Philander Avery, and by force of arms hurried him across the said Mississippi river into the State of Missouri, to aforesaid jail at Monticello, Lewis countv. where your said affiant verily believes they are both now incarcerated illegally and inhumanly in prison; and further report says that some of them are to come to Nauvoo next, to kidnap Nelson Turner; and further your affiant saith not.

DELMORE CHAPMAN.

Subscribed and sworn to before me, this sixth day of December, 1843.

JOSEPH SMITH, Mayor.

Upon which I wrote to his Excellency Thomas Ford:—

LETTER—PRESIDENT JOSEPH SMITH TO GOVERNOR FORD.

NAUVOO, December 6, 1843.

SIR:—The enclosed affidavit is forwarded to your Excellency for instructions to know what shall be done in the premises. I shall act ac cording to the best of my judgment, constitutionally, till I receive your instructions, and in the meantime shall forward, as soon as they can be had, all the facts relative to the case as a suitable person will go immediately to the place and get the necessary affidavits. Send your instructions by the bearer.

Respectfully, I have the honor to be,

Your obedient servant,
JOSEPH SMITH,
Lieutenant-General of N. L.

P. S. Shall any portion of the Legion be called out?

N. B. An express has just reached me that Governor Reynolds will make another demand for me. I rely on the honor of Illinois, for no writ can legally issue against me. I have suffered from their insatiable thirst for my blood long enough, and want the peace of my family to remain undisturbed.

Wednesday, 6.—Esquire Goodwin and others, not members of the Church, petitioned the Governor not to help Missouri to persecute the Saints.

Thursday, 7.—At eleven a. m. a meeting of the citizens of Nauvoo was held. The minutes of which I extract from the *Neighbor* as follows:—

PUBLIC MEETING AT NAUVOO.

At a meeting of the citizens of Nauvoo, held near the Temple, on the 7th day of December, 1843, Alpheus Cutler was called to the chair, and Willard Richards appointed secretary; whereupon, after the object of the meeting was stated, a committee of three—namely, W. W. Phelps, Reynolds Cahoon, and Hosea Stout, were appointed to draft a preamble and resolutions expressive of the sentiments of the people of the city of Nauvoo relative to the repeated unlawful demands by the State of Missouri for the body of General Joseph Smith, as well as the common, cruel practice of kidnapping citizens of Illinois, and forcing them across the Mississippi river, and then incarcerating them in the dungeons or prisons of Missouri. And after a few minutes' absence they returned with the following:—

RESOLUTIONS.

Whereas, the State of Missouri, with the Governor at the head, continues to make demands upon the executive of Illinois for the body of General Joseph Smith, as we verily believe, to keep up a system of persecution against the Church of Latter-day Saints, for the purpose of justifying the said State of Missouri in her diabolical, unheard of, cruel and unconstitutional warfare against said Church of Latter-day Saints, and which she has practiced during the last twelve years, whereby many have been murdered, mobbed and ravished, and the whole community expelled from the State:

And also to heave dust in the eyes of the nation and the world, while she, as a State, with the Government to back her, continues to slip over the river to steal the property of the Latter-day Saints, and kidnap the members of said Church to glut her vengeance, malice, revenge, and avarice, and to make slaves of the said captives or murder them: Therefore,

Resolved unanimously: As we do know that Joseph Smith is not guilty of any charge made against him by the said State of Missouri, but is a good, industrious, well-meaning, and worthy citizen of Illinois, and an officer that does faithfully and impartially administer the laws of the State, that we as citizens of Illinois, crave the protection of the Constitution and laws of the oountry as an *ægis* to shield him, the said General Joseph Smith, from such cruel persecutions, beseeching the Governor of Illinois not to issue any more writs against the said General Joseph Smith, or other Latter-day Saints (unless they are guilty), but to let the Latter-day Saints "breathe awhile like other men," and enjoy the liberty guaranted to every honest citizen by the Magna Charta of our common country.

Resolved, That as citizens of the State of Illinois, we solicit the attention of the Governor and officers generally of the State to take some lawful means and measures to regain the citizens that have been kidnapped by the Missourians, and to prevent the said Missourians and government from committing further violence upon the citizens of Illinois.

Resolved, as the sense of this meeting, That, according to the true meaning of the law, those citizens of any section of country who do not rise up as virtuous freemen (when any portion of inhabitants congregate or combine to injure, slander, or deprive another portion of their rights,) and magnify the law, to clear themselves from such unhallowed attempts to subvert order and law, that they by their silence make themselves accessories of the crime of such unlawful assemblage or outrageous individuals.

Resolved, unimously, That we solicit the Governor by all honorable means to grant us peace, for we will have it.

ALPHEUS CUTLER, Chairman.

WILLARD RICHARDS, Secretary.

In the afternoon, Lucien Woodworth started with the papers to the Governor, and the petition from Goodwin and others, and Delmore Chapman's affidavit.

The German brethren met at the assembly room at six p. m., and choose Bishop Daniel Garn as their Presiding Elder, and organized to have preaching in their native language.

Provision for German Meetings.

Directed copies of my Appeal to the various authorities of Vermont and the United States.

Friday, 8.—At eleven a. m. I went to my office and gave instructions to my clerk for the drawing of a draft of a dam on the Mississippi river, and directed that the city council be called at four this afternoon to make preparations for any invasion from Missouri.

Precautionary Steps against Missouri Invasion

Willard Richards and Philip B. Lewis made an affidavit, which I insert:—

Richards' and Lewis' Affidavit.

STATE OF ILLINOIS, }
CITY OF NAUVOO. } SS.

On the 8th day of December, 1843, came Willard Richards and Philip B. Lewis before me, Joseph Smith, Mayor of said city, and after being duly sworn, depose and say that they have been informed that two men have been kidnapped recently by the Missourians, in connection with some of the lawless inhabitants of the county of Hancock, and that rumors are now afloat that it is the intention of said lawless persons, in connection with the aforesaid Missourians, to kidnap some of the citizens of this city; and further your affiants would state that they are of opinion, to prevent difficulties of such a vexatious nature, that something should be done to secure the peace of this city from being disturbed. And further your affiants say not.

WILLARD RICHARDS,
PHILIP B. LEWIS.

Subecribed and sworn to before me, this 8th day of December, 1843.
W. W. PHELPS, Clerk.

Whereupon I issued the following notification:—

An Order to the City Marshal.

STATE OF ILLINOIS, }
CITY OF NAUVOO. } SS.

To the Marshal of said City, Greeting:—

Whereas complaint has been made to me upon oath, that some persons have been kidnapped by the Missourians, in connection with some of the lawless inhabitants of Hancock county, and that threats have been made that some of the citizens of Nauvoo will be kidnapped or arrested, and forcibly carried away from said city without being allowed the benefit of the writ of *habeas corpus*, according to the ordinance in such case made and provided, you will therefore take the necessary measures to have the rights of the citizens of this city held sacred, and the ordinances of said city duly carried into full force and effect. To which end, should you judge that the peace and safety of the city require it, you are further notified to call for a suitable portion of the Nauvoo Legion to be in complete readiness to compel obedience to the ordinances of the said city.

Given under my hand and seal this 8th day of December, 1843.

JOSEPH SMITH, Mayor,

W. W. PHELPS, Clerk, M. C.

In consequence thereof, I received from the City Marshal:—

The City Marshal's Reply.

CITY OF NAUVOO, December 8, 1843.

SIR:—Your order to have the ordinances of this city fully carried into effect will be duly attended to; but in order so to do, it will be necessary for you as Mayor of the city, to issue orders to Major General Wilson Law for a suitable portion of the Nauvoo Legion to be in readiness to *compel obedience* to said ordinances, if necessary.

Respectfully, &c.,

HENRY G. SHERWOOD, City Marshal.

To Joseph Smith, Mayor.

And I issued:—

Mayor's Order to the Commander of the Nauvoo Legion.

"HEADQUARTERS NAUVOO LEGION,
CITY OF NAUVOO, Dec. 8, 1843.

The Marshal of this city having made a demand of me for a suitable portion of the Nauvoo Legion to protect the rights of the citizens and carry the ordinances of said city into full effect, you are hereby directed and required to hold in readiness such portions of the said Nauvoo Legion, which you have the honor to command, as may be necessary to compel obedience to the ordinances of said city and secure the peace of the citizens, and call them out, if occasion require, without further notice.

With due regard, I have the honor to be

Your obedient servant

JOSEPH SMITH,
Lieutenant-General, N. L.

Major-General Wilson Law,
Commanding Nauvoo Legion.

Four p. m., attended City Council, which passed "An extra ordinance for the extra case of Joseph Smith and others."

Special Ordinance in the Prophet's Case, vs. Missouri.

Whereas, Joseph Smith has been three times arrested and three times acquitted upon writs founded upon supposed crimes or charges preferred by the State of Missouri, which acquittals were made from investigations upon writs of *habeas corpus*—namely one in the United States Court for the district of Illinois, one in the Circuit Court of the State of Illinois, and one in the Municipal Court of Nauvoo:

And whereas, a *nolle prosequi* has once been entered in the courts of Missouri upon all the cases of Missouri against Joseph Smith and others:

And whereas, there appears to be a determined resolution by the State of Missouri to continue these unjust, illegal, and murderous demands for the body of General Joseph Smith:

And whereas,it has become intolerable to be thus continually harassed and robbed of our money to defray the expenses of these prosecutions:

And whereas, according to the Constitution of Illinois, "all men are born equally free and independent, and have certain inherent and indefeasible rights, among which are those of enjoying and defending life and liberty, and of acquiring, possessing, and protecting property and reputation, and pursuing their own happiness:"

And whereas, it is our bounden duty, by all common means, if possible, to put a stop to such vexatious lawsuits and save expense: Therefore—

Section 1. Be it ordained by the City Council of the City of Nauvoo, according to the intent and meaning of the Charter for the "benefit and convenience" of Nauvoo, that hereafter, if any person or persons shall come with process, demand, or requisition, founded upon the aforesaid Missouri difficulties, to arrest said Joseph Smith, he or they so offending shall be subject to be arrested by any officer of the city, with or without process, and tried by the Municipal Court, upon testimony, and, if found guilty, sentenced to imprisonment in the city prison for life; which convict or convicts can only be pardoned by the Governor, with the consent of the Mayor of said city.

Section 2. And be it further ordained that the preceding section shall apply to the case of every and all persons that may be arrested, demanded, or required upon any charge founded in the aforesaid Missouri difficulties.

Section 3. And be it further ordained that the jury that makes the presentment, in any case above specified, shall not, nor either of them, act as jurors on the final trial; but the trial shall be conducted according to the fifth and sixth articles of the amendment to the Constitution of the United States.

Passed December 8, 1843.

JOSEPH SMITH, Mayor.

WILLARD RICHARDS, Recorder.*

The City Council also passed "An ordinance to erect a dam in the Mississippi river, and for other purposes."

Ordinance Providing for the Erection of a Dam in the Mississippi.

Section 1. Be it ordained by the City Council of the City of Nauvoo, that Joseph Smith and his successors for the term of perpetual succession are hereby authorized and empowered to erect a dam, of suitable height to propel mills and machinery, from any point within the limits of said city and below the Nauvoo House, and in a proper direction to reach the island this side of Montrose; but not to interfere with the main channel of the Mississippi river.

Section 2. And be it further ordained that the said Joseph Smith and his successors are further authorized to erect north of the aforesaid island, a dam, pier, or breakwater to intersect the sandbar above.

Section 3. Be it further ordained that said Joseph Smith and his successors are also authorized and have full liberty to use the said dam and water for the purpose of propelling mills and machinery, and shall be governed in their rates of toll and rules of manufactory by ordinance of said city.

Section 4, And be it further ordained that the said Joseph Smith and his successors are further authorized and empowered to use the space within the limits of the said dam as a harbor or basin for steamboats and other water craft; and for which purpose they may construct docks, wharfs, and landings, and receive such fees for wharfage as may be regulated by ordinance of said city.

Section 5. And be it further ordained that said Joseph Smith and his successors are further authorized to build an embankment on the east side of the aforesaid island, to connect the said dam with the pier on the north, and to use the top of said dam for a public road or highway, receiving for compensation from those who cross upon it such rates as may be allowed by ordinance of said city.

Passed December 8, 1843.

JOSEPH SMITH, Mayor.

WILLARD RICHARDS, Recorder.

*The Ordinance was about a month later repealed at the suggestion of President Smith.

I suggested to the Council the idea of petitioning Congress to receive the City of Nauvoo under the protection of the United States Government, to acknowledge the Nauvoo Legion as U. S. troops, and to assist in fortifications and other purposes, and that a messenger be sent to Congress for this purpose at the expense of the city.

Petition for Nauvoo to Be Placed under the General Government

Messrs. John Taylor, Orson Spencer, and Orson Pratt were appointed a committee to draft a memorial according to my suggestions.

Saturday, *9*.—At home.

Prayer-meeting in the assembly room.

I copy from the *Neighbor*.

PUBLIC MEETING AT NAUVOO MAKING AN APPEAL TO THE GENERAL GOVERNMENT ON SUNDRY LOCAL AFFAIRS.

At a very large meeting of the citizens of Nauvoo, held at the corner of Main and Water streets, Mr. Heber C. Kimball was elected chairman, and John M. Bernhisel appointed secretary. Mr. George A. Smith having made a few observations, Mr. John Taylor read the preamble and resolutions of a meeting held at the temple, on the 7th instant; also an ordinance entitled "An extra ordinance for the extra case of Joseph Smith and others," recently passed by the City Council of the City of Nauvoo; likewise the fifth and sixth articles of the amendments of the Constitution of the United States, and the opinion of the Attorney-General of the State of Illinois on the subject of the organization of the Nauvoo Legion, he being of the opinion that said Legion was disconnected from the military communities of the whole State, and in no way subject to the regular military officers, possessing an exemption even from subjection to the general military laws, with a law-making power vested in their own Legion.

After some pertinent remarks by Mr. Taylor, General Joseph Smith briefly addressed the meeting. He dissented entirely from the opinion of the Attorney-General, and observed that it was stated in the Charter that the Legion was a part of the Militia of Illinois, and that his commission declared that he (General Smith) was the Lieutenant-General of the Nauvoo Legion and of the Militia of the State of Illinois; and as such, it was not only his duty to enforce the city ordinance, but the laws of the State, when called on by the Governor. He also stated that he had been informed that the Chief Magistrate of Missouri had it in contemplation to make another requisition on the Governor of Illinois for him (Joseph Smith).

The meeting then adjourned *sine die*.

H. C. KIMBALL, Chairman.

J. M. BERNHISEL, Secretary.

Received the following:—

Letter of Wilson Law to Joseph Smith Anent the Legion.

NAUVOO LEGION, NAUVOO CITY,
December 9, 1843.

Lieutenant-General Joseph Smith.

In consequence of the orders I received from you ' to hold in readiness a sufficient portion of the legion, &c.,—to make said forces efficient,'' it will be necessary to supply them with munitions of war, which of course must be done at the expense of the city. You will therefore please to give orders to the commandants of cohorts on their application to you on the city treasury for whatever amount you may think proper on the present occasion.

Most respectfully your obedient servant,
WILSON LAW,
Major-General, N. L.

Sunday, 10.—Rainy day. I stayed at home.

A prayer-meeting held this evening in the assembly room. I was not present. Brigham Young presided. Several sick persons were prayed for.

Avery Case—a Reminiscence of Missouri Days.

By letter from J. White, deputy sheriff of Clark county, Missouri, I learn that Mr. Daniel Avery is in Marion county prison, without trial. The sheriff requests several men to go there as witnesses. It is evidently a trap to get some more of our people into their power. When I was in prison in Missouri, my witnesses were arrested before they got into court to testify, except one, who was kicked out of the court by an officer, Lieutenant Cook, who damned him, and ordered some of his company to shoot him. After which, the State's attorney, Birch, turned to me tauntingly, saying, ''Why the hell don't you bring on your witnesses?'' and Judge King laughed at my discomfiture. The Saints have had enough of Missouri mob justice.

Monday, 11. The following affidavit will show that some of the citizens of Illinois are so far fallen and so much governed by mobocratic influence as to assist the Missouri wretches in their hellish designs:—

Affidavit of Sission Chase—The Avery Case.

STATE OF ILLINOIS, }
HANCOCK COUNTY. } SS.

On the 11th day of December, 1843, came Sission A. Chase before me Aaron Johnson, a Justice of the Peace of said county; and, after being duly sworn, deposeth and saith that the crime of kidnapping has been committed in Hancock County; and on the 2nd day of this present December, 1843, at the house of Schrench Freeman, about four miles and a half south of Warsaw, in said county, your said affiant heard a man by the name of John Elliot say that he was going a shooting turkeys. When asked what he was going to shoot them with, he showed a brace of pistols and a large hickory cane. Your affiant observed that he thought he could not kill turkeys with such weapons; and the said Elliot said that there was a certain cock he meant to take before night, and they would do for that. He, the said Elliot, went off, and your affiant did not see him till Sunday evening the 3rd, when your affiant asked the said Elliot if he had caught his turkey; and he replied, yes, the one he was after—a Mormon Elder. Your affiant then asked him who he was; and he said, Daniel Avery. Your affiant then asked the said Elliot what had been done with said Avery; and he said we put him on to a horse, tied his legs, and guarded him to the river, from whence, about ten o'clock at night, we took him into Clark county, Missouri, for stealing a horse four years ago, where they would try him; and if found guilty, they would then take him into another county, where there was a jail, as there was none in Clark county. On the 4th day of December, I asked him if they had writs or authority to take Mr. Avery. He replied, we all had writs. On the 5th, said Elliot said he expected to get into difficulty on account of this scrape; but if any Mormon makes any business with me, I will shoot him. And further your affiant says not.

SISSION A. CHASE.

Subscribed and sworn to this 11th day of December, 1843, before me

AARON JOHNSON, J. P.

Which I sent to the Governor, with this letter:—

Letter—Joseph Smith to Governor Ford.

NAUVOO, December 11, 1843.

SIR:—I herewith forward your Excellency another affidavit on the subject of the late kidnapping, and shall continue [to do] the same as they come to hand, expecting your cordial co-operation in the premises that the laws may be magnified and made honorable, and our lives held precious, our friends saved from jeopardy, and the captives freed.

Respectfully, I have the honor to be

Your obedient servant,

JOSEPH SMITH.

Nauvoo's Police Force Enlarged.

Meetings were held and resolutions passed in all the wards of the city, requesting the city council to raise a company of forty men to act as police.

Last night, two ruffians, whose names are unknown, went to the house of Brother Richard Badham—a farmer living on the prairie, robbed the house of $4.50, threatened his life, stabbed him in the abdomen, when part of his caul gushed out. Dr. John M. Bernhisel dressed his wounds today, and he thinks there is a prospect of his recovering.

Tuesday, 12.—In office at nine a. m., and wrote a letter to my uncle:—

Letter—Joseph Smith to John Smith—The Latter Appointed a Patriarch.

President John Smith:—The petition of a special conference at Macedonia of last November for your appointment as Patriarch in the Church has been received, duly considered, and is granted. You have my best wishes in your behalf, as well as my prayers, that you may fill so honorable and exalted a station with the dignity, sobriety, and grace which has hitherto characterized your conduct and communion with men, as a man of God.

Respectfully yours,

JOSEPH SMITH.

At ten, a. m., attended City Council, which passed an ordinance exempting all church property from city tax.

In accordance with the petitions from the several wards, the council passed the following:—"An ordinance for selecting forty policemen and for other purposes.

Ordinance Enlarging Police Force.

"Section 1. Be it ordained by the City Council of the City of Nauvoo that the Mayor of said city be, and is hereby authorized to select and have in readiness for every emergency forty policemen, to be at his disposal in maintaining the peace and dignity of the citizens, and enforcing the ordinances of the said city, for ferreting out thieves and bringing them to justice, and to act as daily and nightly watchmen, and be under the pay of said city.

Passed December 12, 1843.

JOSEPH SMITH, Mayor.

W. RICHARDS, Recorder.

The Council also passed "An ordinance for the health and convenience of travelers and other persons."

Ordinance on the Personal Sale of Liquors.

Section 1. Be it ordained by the City Council of Nauvoo, that the Mayor of the city be and is hereby authorized to sell or give spirits of any quantity as he in his wisdom shall judge to be for the health and comfort, or convenience of such travelers or other persons as shall visit his house from time to time.

Passed December 12, 1843.

JOSEPH SMITH, Mayor.

WILLARD RICHARDS, Recorder.

Wednesday, *13.*—At home.

I insert an editorial from the *Neighbor*:—

PUBLIC MEETING AT NAUVOO—THE AGGRESSIONS OF MISSOURI.

It will be seen in another column that a public meeting was held in this place for the purpose of providing some remedy for the repeated aggressions of the State of Missouri; since which time an ordinance has been passed by the City Council to carry into effect that object, and to prevent the citizens of this place from being any longer imposed upon by the continued illegal proceedings of the state and citizens of Missouri.

We think that it is high time that something should be done to screen ourselves from the continued aggressions of the meddling, troublesome, bloodthirsty herd; and we know of no means that will be more efficient and lawful than the one adopted.

We have done good for evil long enough, in all conscience. We think that we have fulfilled the Scriptures every whit. They have smitten us on the one cheek, and we have turned the other, and they have smitten that also.

We have also fulfilled the law, and more than fulfilled it. And for sake of peace, when we knew that we had violated no law, nor in anywise subjected ourselves to persecutions, we have endured the wrong patiently, without offering violence or in anywise injuring the heartless wretches who could be trusted with such a dishonorable document.

Those vagabonds have been suffered to prowl at large, and boast of their inglorious deeds in our midst; and no man has injured them, or said, Why do you so?

The time, however, is now gone by for this mode of proceeding, and those vagabonds must keep within their own borders and let peaceable citizens alone, or receive the due merit of their crimes. We think that this ordinance passed by the City Council is wise, judicious, and well-timed,and is well calculated to protect peaceable citizens in their rights, and to prevent those lawless vagabonds from interfering with the rights of peaceable citizens.

To those unaquainted with our relationship to Missouri, and the accumulated wrongs and repeated aggressions that we have received from the hands of that State, our language may appear harsh and illtimed; but those who are in possession of those facts know better. Their merciless, unrelenting, inhuman prosecutions and persecutions, from the time of our first settlement in that state until the present, have been wholly and entirely unprovoked and without the shadow of law.

Joseph Smith has been suffered to be taken time and again by them; we say suffered, because he could not be legally and constitutionally taken, Joseph Smith never committed the crimes of which he is charged. He is an innocent man.

But allowing their false, diabolical accusations to be true, what then? Does it follow that he is continually to be followed for the same offense? Verily no. The Constitution of the United States expressly says—"Nor shall any person be subject for the same offense to be *twice* put in jeopardy of life or limb." And yet we find that the State of Missouri has put Joseph Smith in jeopardy no less than four or five times. He was tried once by a military tribunal in Missouri, and sentenced to be shot. He was afterwards tried by a pretended civil (mobocratic) court; and since then he has been several times apprehended, tried, and acquitted for the same offense, in this State, by Missouri requisitions.

Is he still illegally and unconstitutionally to be held in abeyance by these miscreants? or shall we as freeborn American citizens, assert our rights, put the law in force upon those lawless, prowling vagabonds and say that he shall be free?

Shall we suffer our pockets to be picked through the influence of these scoundrels eternally, by defending ourselves against vexatious lawsuits? or shall we take a more summary way, and by a legal course punish the aggressors, proclaim our freedom, and shield ourselves under the broad folds of the Constitution? The latter is the course for us to pursue.

The ordinance passed by the City Council will secure this object;

and we are glad to find that the opinion of J. Lamborn, attorney general, and J. N. McDougall, correspond so much with our own—"That the Nauvoo Legion is an independent military organization, and is by law expressly required to sustain the municipal laws of Nauvoo.

What are we to say about these kidnappers who infest our borders and carry away our citizens—those infernals in human shape?

The whole European world has been engaged in a warfare against those who traffic in human blood. Negotiations have been made, treaties entered into, and fleets have been sent out, through the combined efforts of the nations, to put a stop to this inhuman traffic. But what would those nations think, if they were told the fact that in America—Republican America, the boasted cradle of liberty and land of freedom,—that those dealers in human flesh and blood, negro dealers and drivers, are allowed with impunity to steal white men, and those sons of liberty can obtain no redress.

Great God! has it come to this, that freeborn American citizens must be kidnapped by negro drivers? What are our authorities doing! Why are not these wretches brought to justice? We have heard that one or two of the citizens of Illinois have been engaged in assisting these wretches. We shall try to find out who they are and their whereabouts and make them known; and then, if they are not brought to condign punishment, we shall say that justice has fled from Illinois."

Thursday, 14.—At home.

Philander Avery arrived in Nauvoo, having made his escape from his kidnappers in Missouri.

I received the following milk-and-water letter from Governor Ford:—

Letter—Governor Ford to President Smith.

SPRINGFIELD, December 12, 1843.

General Joseph Smith.

SIR:—I have received your favor of the 6th instant, together with the proceedings of a public meeting of the citizens of Nauvoo, on the subject of the late kidnapping, by the people of Missouri and others, of two citizens of this State.

You request to know if any portion of the Legion shall be called out. My answer is, No. The Militia cannot be called out, except in the cases specified by me in my letter to Governor Reynolds, dated in the month of August last, in which I took the ground that the Militia can only be called out to repel an invasion, suppress an insurrection, or on some extreme emergency; and not to suppress, prevent, or punish individual crimes. I still am of the opinion that the ground assumed by me on that occasion is the true one. The prevention and punishment of individual offenses has been confided by the constitution and laws of this State to the judicial power, and not to the executive.

If a citizen of the State has been kidnapped, or if property has been stolen from this State, and carried to the State of Missouri, those who have done either are guilty of an indictable offense. But the constitution and the laws have provided no means whereby either the person or property taken away can be returned, except by an appeal to the laws of Missouri. The Governor has no legal right to demand the return of either. The only power I would have would be simply this: If any of the guilty persons should be charged with larceny or kidnapping, by indictment or affidavit, duly certified, and with having fled to Missouri, then I would have the power, and it would become my duty to make a demand upon the Governor of Missouri for the surrender of the fugitives, to be tried by the courts of this State. I am fully satisfied that in ordinary cases this is all the power I would possess. It would be simply a power to be exercised in aid of the judicial power. Any other powers to be exercised by the Governor would be to make him a dictator and a despot. It is true that an extraordinary case might arise, in which the inhabitants of one State might arise in warlike and hostile array against those of another; in which case a state of war would exist, and then only could I interfere.

I would advise your citizens to be strictly peaceable towards the people of Missouri. You ought to be aware that in every country individuals are liable to be visited with wrong, which the law is slow to redress, and *some of which are never redressed in this world.* This fact, however, has never been held to be a justification for violence, not warranted by law.

If any of the people of Nauvoo should invade Missouri for the purpose of rescuing persons there in jail, the consequence would be that indictments would be presented against them, and demands made upon me for their arrest and surrender; which demands I would be compelled to obey, and thus they would be harassed by interminable demands and prosecutions; and very likely it would lead to a species of border warfare, which would be exceedingly annoying to a peaceable city,and, if you could be placed in the wrong, might lead to exceedingly unpleasant consequences with reference both to law and public opinion.

You inform me that you are informed that Governor Reynolds is about to make a new demand for you; and you implore my protection from what you term this renewed persecution. In the month of August last, I was furnished by your friends with a very large amount of affidavits and evidence, said to be intended to show cause why no further writs should be issued against you. As they are very voluminous, I have not yet read them, and probably never will, unless a new demand should be made; in which case they will receive a careful perusal; and you may rest assured that no steps will be taken by me but such as the constitution and laws may require.

I am, very respectfully, &c.,
THOMAS FORD.

It appears from this letter, that Governor Ford has never taken pains to examine the evidences placed in his hands, "and probably never will," in relation to the Missouri writs; and evidently as little pains to examine the Constitution of the United States or even reflect upon the ordinary principles of human rights, to suppose that a State, after having, by a union of executive, judicial and military powers, exterminated 15,000 of its innocent inhabitants, who were not even charged with any crime, robbing them of all they possessed on earth, murdering scores of men, women and children, and expelling all the others from the State, among strangers, in mid-winter, destitute of everything upon the face of the earth that could possibly have a tendency to make life desirable, should be constitutionally entitled to demand back from banishment persons who have thus suffered its absolute decrees of exile, to satiate a yet unsatiated thirst for human blood and torture. O reason, where art thou fled! O humanity, where hast thou hidden thyself? Patriots of '76, has your blood been spilt in vain, that in 1843 the Executive of a great Republican State can coolly say, "I have not yet read them, and probably never will?" Is liberty only a name? Is protection of person and property fled from free America? *Let those answer who can.*

Comment of the Prophet on Governor Ford's attitude.

Friday, 15.—I awoke this morning in good health, but was soon suddenly seized with a great dryness of the mouth and throat, sickness of the stomach, and vomited freely. My wife waited on me, assisted by my scribe, Dr. Willard Richards, and his brother Levi, who administered to me herbs and mild

A Sudden Illness of the Prophet.

drinks. I was never prostrated so low, in so short a time, before; but by evening was considerably revived.

Very warm for the season.

Saturday, 16.—This morning I felt considerably better; arose at 10, and sat all day in the City Council, which was held in my house for my accommodation.

The Mayor, Aldermen, and Councilors signed officially the Memorial to Congress for redress of losses and grievances in Missouri. While discussing the petition to Congress, I prophesied, by virtue of the holy Priesthood vested in me, and in the name of the Lord Jesus Christ, that, if Congress will not hear our petition and grant us protection, they shall be broken up as a government.* * * *

Comment on Appeal to the General Government for Protection.

I informed the Council that it was my wish they should ask the privilege of calling on Government for the United States troops to protect us in our privileges, which is not unconstitutional, but lies in the breast of Congress.

Heber C. Kimball was duly elected city auctioneer, in place of Charles Warner, removed.

The Council passed "An ordinance regulating merchants and grocers;" also "An ordinance concerning the landing of steamers;" and Jonathan Dunham was appointed wharf-master for one year.

* This prediction doubtless has reference to the party in power; to the "government" considered as the administration; not to the "government" considered as the country; but the administration party, the Democratic Party, which had controlled the destiny of the country for forty years. It is matter of history that a few years later the party then in power lost control of the national government, followed by the terrible conflict of the Civil War. The Party against which the above prediction was made so far lost its influence that it did not again return to power for a quarter of a century; and when it did return to power it was with such modified views as to many great questions of government, that it could scarcely be regarded as the same party except in name.

Lest it should be urged that the Whig party was in control of the government in 1843, I call attention to the fact that while General Harrison, a Whig, was elected in 1840, he was President only one month, as he died on the 4th of April, 1841. His whole cabinet, excepting Mr. Webster, Secretary of State, resigned, and the Vice President became President. Though elected by the Whigs Mr. Tyler was a Democrat "and the Whig administration had but a month's actual existence.' (See History of the United States, Morris, pp 311, 312).

Heber C. Kimball and George A. Smith were appointed a committee to wait on Mr. Davidson Hibbard, and solicit from him a block of land, whereon to erect a city prison.

After Council, conversed with some of the Twelve, brother Turley and others, till 8 p. m. Prayer meeting in the evening.

Warm, foggy, and muddy day.

Sunday, 17.—At home till 4 p. m.; attended prayer meeting at the assembly room. Samuel Harrison Smith admitted. Returned home at 7.

River clear of ice as far up as the Stone Tavern.

Mr. King Follet, one of the constables of Hancock County, started with ten men this afternoon to arrest John Elliott for kidnapping Daniel Avery, upon a warrant granted by Aaron Johnson, Esq., J. P.

Monday, 18.—After dinner, Constable Follet returned with John Elliott, a schoolmaster, when an examination was had before Esq. Johnson, in the assembly room. Elliott was found guilty of kidnapping Avery, and bound over in the sum of $3,000 to the Circuit court of Carthage for trial. I endeavored to have the court reduce those bonds, as Mr. Elliott was comparatively a stranger in Nauvoo; but did not succeed.

During the investigation, testimony appeared to show that Elliott had threatened my life; and for this I made affidavit and brought him to trial before Robert D. Foster, J. P., immediately after he had been bound over by Esq. Johnson. I extract from the proceedings, in part, from the *Neighbor:*—

THE TRIAL OF JOHN ELLIOTT.

The prisoner was brought forward, and the court said it was his privilege to plead for a change of venue, by paying the costs; but as the costs were not forthcoming, the court proceeded.

Mr. Styles then read the "Act to regulate the apprehension of offenders and for other purposes," p 219, r. s. The act sets forth that the use of threatening language is sufficient to criminate individuals. This we are prepared to prove.

Sisson Chase sworn.

The testimony was similar to that before deliverd, [in Chase affidavit see p. 109] with the following additional items:—

I did ask him if he had authority. In the morning he said that he would not care about shooting some of the Mormons. In conversation with him, he carried the idea that a conspiracy was formed against Joseph Smith and others, and that some of them would be shot. These conversations were had at different times. He thought Mr. Smith was a bad character. He thought they ought to be taken. Question: Who? Joseph Smith and some others.

I told him he had been taken, but had been acquitted. He did not thank the Governor for that. He carried the idea that there was a conspiracy against his life, and said we have a plan in operation that will pop him over.

Mr. Elliott sworn.

By the Court: Is your residence, Mr. Elliott, in this county? Yes.

Messrs. Marr and Styles, attorneys, resident in Nauvoo, made some thrilling remarks pertaining to the outrageous proceedings of Missouri. The diabolical conduct of those wretches who could be engaged in destroying and kidnapping their fellowmen was portrayed in glowing colors.

Judge Phelps and General Smith then followed on the same subject: their language was thrillingly eloquent and powerful. If ever inhumanity and deeds of blood were depicted in their true colors, it was on that occasion: their thoughts flashed as fire, and they spake in "words that burned." We never saw the character of General Smith so clearly developed; for while he abhorred and depicted the fiendish crime that the culprit stood charged with in its true colors, he pitied the poor wretch that then stood before him, and with feelings of commiseration, benevolence, and philanthrophy, withdrew his charge—wished, if it was within the power of the court, that the culprit might be forgiven,—promised to pay all the charges, and invited him and those of his friends who came along with him, to come to his house, and they should be taken care of. It would be superfluous for us to attempt to give even a faint outline of the remarks made by the above-named gentlemen. We hope to have at least a synopsis of their speeches for publication, which we are sure would be highly interesting to our readers. Upon the whole, although a painful, yet it was an interesting occasion and will long be remembered; and unless Mr. Elliott's heart and those of his friends were made of adamant, it must have made an indelible impression on their minds, and almost made them hate themselves.

I received from Aaron Johnson, Esq., the following demand:—

Legion Aid Applied For.

CITY OF NAUVOO, December 18, 1843.

SIR:—I have been informed that a writ issued by me for the body of Levi Williams, for kidnapping Daniel Avery, will be resisted by an armed force: Therefore, according to the provision of the Charter, I wish you to order me a detachment of the Nauvoo Legion—say 100 men, to enforce the law of the State, and bring the said Williams to justice.

AARON JOHNSON, J. P.

Which demand I complied with by writing to Major-General Wilson Law.

Detachment of the Legion Ordered into Service.

CITY OF NAUVOO, Dec. 18, 1843.

SIR;—You will detach 100 men, under the direction of Aaron Johnson, a Justice of the Peace, for the purpose of assisting the constable in executing the law of the State in taking Levi Williams, who is charged with kidnapping Daniel Avery.

Yours,

JOSEPH SMITH, Lieut-Gen., N. L.

TO MAJOR-GEN. WILSON LAW,
Commanding Nauvoo Legion.

Gen. Wilson detached Colonel Stephen Markham with 100 men for that purpose.

Rumors of Mob Risings.

About 10 p. m., two young men arrived as express, stating that a mob was collecting at Warsaw, also at Colonel Levi Williams' house; and messengers had gone to the mob in Missouri to reinforce their number there.

Dr. Richards made the following affidavit:—

Affidavit of Willard Richards that Nauvoo was in Danger.

STATE OF ILLINOIS, CITY OF NAUVOO,
December 18, 1843.

Personally appeared Willard Richards before me, Joseph Smith, Mayor of said city, and upon his oath deposeth and saith that from information he has received, he verily believes that the peace of said city is in danger from a mobocratic assemblage at Warsaw, and a force collected under the command of Colonel Levi Williams in the lower part of the county, and runners having been sent to Missouri to excite the Missourians to join the mobbers in this county, for the purpose of making a descent on said city, or disturbing its peaceable inhabitants; and further your deponent saith not.

WILLARD RICHARDS.

Subscribed and sworn to before me this 18th December, 1843.

W. W. PHELPS,
Clerk of the Mayor's Court.

Whereupon I wrote to Major-General Wilson Law:—

Legion Ordered into Service.

CITY OF NAUVOO, Dec. 18, 1843.

SIR:—I am credibly informed that a warlike force is collecting at or near Warsaw, for the purpose of some violent move towards this city or some of the inhabitants thereof. You will therefore order out such a portion of the Nauvoo Legion as may be necessary to repel any such mobocratic or hostile design of the same unlawful force, and also as may be sufficient to secure the peace of the citizens, according to law.

Yours,
JOSEPH SMITH, Lieut-Gen. N. L.

MAJOR-GEN. WILSON LAW,
Commanding Nauvoo Legion.

I returned home to rest about one o'clock in the morning of the 19th.

Tuesday, 19.—At home. About 9 a. m., a part of the company who went with Hosea Stout returned, and stated that they went within two miles of Colonel Williams', when they were informed that a body of men, armed with rifles, &c., were collected at his house, and he judged it prudent to return for weapons and help; also that Brother Chester Loveland told them that he had seen thirty armed men following Constable King Follett some miles on his way, when he had Elliott in custody.

Moves and Counter Moves of Forces.

Esq. Johnson immediately wrote to Loveland to have him come to Nauvoo and make affidavit of the warlike movements of the mob, that he might send to the Governor.

I directed my clerks to make copies of the affidavits respecting the kidnapping of the Averys to send to Governor Ford, that he might be left without excuse, although he may probably not read them.

Elder William Martindale writes from Washington, Wayne county, Iowa:—

STRANGE CELESTIAL PHENOMENON—1860.

A singular phenomenon was seen in this neighborhood. Jesse Fox, William and Lorenzo Fox, David Bale, James Wilson, and William Cole, with some others, retired to the house of Solomon Mendenhall, at which place they stayed a short time. While there they discovered a ball rising from the east in an oblique line; and as it ascended it moved towards the west with great rapidity until it was high in the heavens, leaving a streak of light behind it, which to the natural eye, had the appearance of being thirty or forty feet in length. This light remained stationary for about one minute. Both ends then coming round, formed a figure 8, which figure also retained its position for the same space of time. It then was transformed into a figure 6, which also remained for about a minute. It then was formed into a cypher or 0, which remained for about three minutes. The figures put together made 1860 in large figures in the heavens. The phenomenon was indeed singular, and has been a matter of great speculation with us.

Legion Parade

At one p. m. I was present when the Legion paraded near the Temple, were inspected by the officers, and instructed to prepare themselves with arms and ammunition and to hold themselves in readiness, for a moment's notice. Brother Henry Boley was shot severely under the arm by the accidental discharge of his gun.

Amos S. Chase made the following affidavit:—

Affidavit of Amos Chase.

STATE OF ILLINOIS, } ss.
CITY OF NAUVOO. }

On the 19th day of December, 1843, came Amos S. Chase before me Joseph Smith, Mayor of said city; and after being duly sworn, deposeth and saith that on the 18th day of December, 1843, he was about four miles below Warsaw, in Hancock County, shortly after the constable arrested John Elliott for being concerned in kidnapping Daniel Avery, not long since, and saw the men of the neighborhood gathering with arms to retake the said John Elliott; and when asked what they would do, if the Governor did not sanction such an unlawful course, several of them replied, "Damn the Governor! If he opens his head, we will punch a hole through him! He dare not open his head! We will serve him the same sauce we will the Mormons." The said mob then went to Warsaw, where your affiant saw them with their arms; and further your affiant saith not.

AMOS S. CHASE,

Subscribed and sworn to before me this 19th day of December, 1843.

W. W. PHELPS, Clerk, M. C.

Wednesday, *20*.—At home, in good health and spirits, counseling and attending to business in general.

The Clerk of the Municipal Court took the following affidavits:—

AFFIDAVITS OF PHILANDER AVERY—MISSOURI KIDNAPPING.

STATE OF ILLINOIS, } ss.
CITY OF NAUVOO. }

On the 20th day of December, 1843, personally appeared before me, Willard Richards, clerk of the Municipal Court of said city Philander Avery, of Bear Creek precinct, in said county, and after being duly sworn, deposeth and saith that on the 19th day of November, 1843, at his house, in the precinct aforesaid, Ebenezer Richardson, of Lee county, Territory of Iowa, by false pretenses, persuaded your affiant to accompany said Richardson to the Missisippi river at Warsaw, where your affiant was seized by one Joseph C. McCoy, of Clark county, Missouri, in connection with the said Richardson, and about one dozen of other individuals, whose names are unknown to your affiant, and by them forced across said Mississippi River, where they bound your affiant; and Mark Childs swore that your affiant had stolen said McCoy's horse and colt, and that his father Daniel Avery had secreted said horse and colt, and said Richardson threatened your affiant with death or seven years' imprisonment, in order to persuade him to make false statements, and testify that his father, Daniel Avery, had stolen said McCoy's horse and colt, which statements your affiant made, and swore to the same, while in duress, with a bowie-knife presented to intimidate. And your affiant further saith that the testimony he gave concerning his father's guilt, was extorted from him through fear, while in duress, and said testimouy was absolutely false, and your affiant fully believes that his father is innocent of the crime of stealing said McCoy's horse and colt; and further your deponent saith not.

PHILANDER AVERY.

[L. S.] Subscribed and sworn to before me; in testimony whereof I have set my hand and affixed the seal of said court at Nauvoo aforesaid, this 20th day of December, A. D. 1843.

WILLARD RICHARDS,
Clerk of the Municipal Court of the City of Nauvoo.

Affidavit of the Hamiltons.

STATE OF ILLINOIS, } ss.
COUNTY OF HANCOCK, }

On the 20th day of December, 1843, personally appeared before me Aaron Johnson, a Justice of the Peace in and for said county, Andrew H. Hamilton, and James B. Hamilton, of Bear Creek precinct, in said county, and, after being duly sworn, depose and say that on the evening of the 2nd day of December, 1843, at Vernon Doty's mill, in said precinct, Colonel Levi Williams, of said Hancock county, as principal, and his son, John Williams, with William Middleton, of the county of Clark and State of Missouri, Captain McCoy, of the said county of Clark and State of Missouri, John Fox of Green Plains precinct, and about a dozen other men, armed with pistols, dirks and bowie knives came forcibly upon Daniel Avery at said Doty's mill, and seized and bound him. The said Avery told them to stand off. They said they had a writ. He observed, he would not resist legal authority. They said they would take said Avery to Warsaw, and there to try him. The said Avery replied, "I understand you: you will take me to Warsaw, and there pass me over the river to Missouri." Some of said gang then shouted, "Lay hold of him; G—d d—n him, lay hold of him: there's no use of parleying;" at which Colonel Levi Williams, with a large bowie-knife in his hand, and others, then forced the said Daniel Avery to submit, telling him (without a writ,) that his life would be taken if he did not submit. They then tied him with silk handkerchiefs. Colonel Levi Williams and another person then led the said Daniel Avery away: and as they passed your affiants within the distance of about four rods, the said Daniel Avery cried out to one of your said affiants, "tell my friends where I am gone." Colonel Williams told said Avery to hold his peace, for it was of no use. William Middleton then got a horse; and after tying him upon said horse, as sworn to before by another witness, they then conveyed him to Missouri without a writ or trial, as your affiants verily believe; and further they say not.

ANDREW M. HAMILTON.
JAMES B. HAMILTON.

Subscribed and sworn to this 20th day of December, 1843, before me.

AARON JOHNSON, J. P.

CHAPTER VI.

MEMORIAL OF CITY COUNCIL TO CONGRESS ANENT MISSOURI AFFAIRS—ROCKWELL'S RETURN TO NAUVOO—RECITAL OF HIS ADVENTURES—AVERY'S ACQUITTAL BY MISSOURI'S COURTS—NAUVOO'S POLICE FORCE INCREASED—PUBLICATIONS ON MORMONISM, PRO ET CON—1843.

Thursday, December 21, 1843.—About one o'clock in the morning I was alarmed by the firing of a gun, got up, and went down to the river bank to see the guard, and inquire the cause of it. To my surprise, they had not heard it, although I felt sure it was fired in Montrose. The morning proved it to be correct, some rowdies in Montrose had been firing in the night.

At noon met with the City Council which voted that Councilor Orson Pratt present the Memorial and Ordinance to Congress.

Passed "An ordinance to prevent unlawful search or seizure of person or property by foreign [i.e. outside] process in the city of Nauvoo."

Heber C. Kimball resigned his office as city auctioneer and Charles Warner was re-elected.

John P. Greene was duly elected city marshal, in the room of Henry G. Sherwood, who expects to leave soon.

The Prophet for a Clean, Orderly City.

I gave instructions to the marshal and policemen to see that all carrion is removed out of the city, and all houses kept in order,—to stop the boys when fighting in the streets, and prevent children from floating off on the ice, and correct anything out of order, like fathers; and I offered to build the city jail, if it was left to my dictation, which the Council authorized me to do.

I insert the Memorial from the City Council to the Congress of the United States for redress of grievances and protection from further persecution, which was signed by them:—

MEMORIAL OF THE CITY COUNCIL TO CONGRESS.

"*To the Honorable Senators and Representatives of the United States of America in Congress assembled,*

We, the undersigned members of the City Council of the City of Nauvoo, citizens of Hancock County, Illinois, and exiles from the State of Missouri, being in council assembled, unanimously and respectfully, for ourselves, and in behalf of many thousands of other exiles, memorialize the honorable Senators and Representatives of our nation upon the subject of the unparalleled persecutions and cruelties inflicted upon us and upon our constituents by the constituted authorities of the State of Missouri, and likewise upon the subject of the present unfortunate circumstances in which we are placed in the land of our exile. As a history of the Missouri outrages has been extensively published, both in this country and in Europe, it is deemed unnecessary to particularize all of the wrongs and grievances inflicted upon us in this memorial. As there is an abundance of well-attested documents to which your honorable body can at any time refer, hence we only embody the following important items for your consideration.

First:—Your memorialists, as freeborn citizens of this great republic, relying with the utmost confidence upon the sacred "articles of the Constitution," by which the several States are bound together, and considering ourselves entitled to all the privileges and immunities of free citizens in what State soever we desired to locate ourselves, commenced a settlement in the county of Jackson, on the western frontiers of the State of Missouri, in the summer of 1831.

There we purchased lands from the Government, erected several hundred houses, made extensive improvements, and shortly the wild and lonely prairies and stately forests were converted into well cultivated and fruitful fields. There we expected to spend our days in the enjoyment of all the rights and liberties bequeathed to us by the sufferings and blood of our noble ancestors. But alas! our expectations were vain.

Two years had scarcely elapsed before we were unlawfully and unconstitutionally assaulted by an organized mob, consisting of the highest officers in the county, both civil and military, who openly and boldly avowed their determination in a written circular to drive us from said county.

As a specimen of their treasonable and cruel designs, your honorable body are referred to said circular, of which the following is but a short extract,—namely: "We the undersigned citizens of Jackson county, believing that an important crisis is at hand, as regards our civil society, in consequence of a pretended religious sect of people that have settled and are still settling in our county, styling themselves Mormons, and intending as we do to rid our society, 'peaceably if we can, forcibly if we must;' and believing as we do that the arm of the civil law does not afford us a guarantee, or at least a sufficient one, against the evils which are now inflicted upon us, and seem to be increasing by the said religious sect, deem it expedient and of the highest importance to form ourselves into a company for the better and easier accomplishment of our purpose."

This document was closed in the following words:—"We therefore agree that, after timely warning, and receiving an adequate compensation for what little property they cannot take with them, they refuse to leave us in peace, as they found us, we agree to use such means as may be sufficient to remove them; and to that end we each pledge to each other our bodily powers, our lives, fortunes, and sacred honors."

To this unconstitutional document were attached the names of nearly every officer in the county, together with the names of hundreds of others.

It was by this band of murderers that your memorialists, in the year 1833, were plundered of their property and robbed of their peaceable homes. It was by them that their fields were laid waste, their houses burned, and their men, women, and children, to the number of about twelve hundred persons, banished as exiles from the county, while others were cruelly murdered by their hands.

Second: After our expulsion from Jackson county, we settled in Clay county, on the opposite side of the Missouri river, where we purchased lands both from the old settlers and from the [U. S.] Land Office: but soon we were again violently threatened by mobs, and obliged to leave our homes, and seek out a new location.

Third: Our next settlement was in Caldwell county, where we purchased the most of the land in said county, beside a part of the lands in Daviess and Carroll counties. These counties were almost entirely in a wild and uncultivated state; but, by the persevering industry of our citizens, large and extensive farms were opened in every direction, well stocked with numerous flocks and herds. We also commenced settlements in several other counties of the state, and once more confidently hoped to enjoy the hard-earned fruits of our labor unmolested.

But our hopes were soon blasted. The cruel and murderous spirit which first began to manifest itself in the constituted authorities and inhabitants of Jackson county, and afterwards in Clay and the surrounding counties, receiving no check either from the civil or military power of the state, had in the meantime taken courage, and boldly and fearlessly spread its contaminating and treasonable influence into every department of the government of said state. Lieutenant-Governor Boggs, a resident of Jackson county, who acted a conspicuous part in our expulsion from said county, instead of being tried for treason and rebellion against the Constitution, and suffering the just penalty of his crimes, was actually elected governor; and placed in the executive chair.

Thus the inhabitants of the State were greatly encouraged to renew with redoubled fury, their unlawful attacks upon our defenseless settlements. Men, women, and children were driven away in every direction before their merciless persecutors, robbed of their possessions, their property, their provisions, and their all, cast forth upon the bleak, snowy prairies, houseless and unprotected. Many sank down and expired under their accumulated sufferings, while others, after enduring hunger and the severities of the season, suffering all but death, arrived in Caldwell county, to which place they were driven from all the surrounding counties, only to witness a still more heart-rending scene.

In vain had we appealed to the constituted authorities of Missouri for protection and redress of our former grievances. In vain we now stretched out our hands and appealed as the citizens of this great republic to the sympathies, to the justice, and magnanimity of those in power. In vain we implored again and again at the feet of Governor Boggs, our former persecutor, for aid and protection against the ravages and murders now inflicted upon our defenseless and unoffending citizens. The cry of American citizens, already twice driven and deprived of liberty, could not penetrate their adamantine hearts.

The Governor, instead of sending us aid, issued a proclamation for our extermination and banishment, ordered out the forces of the State, placed them under the command of General Clark, who, to execute these exterminating orders, marched several thousand troops into our settlements in Caldwell county, where, unrestrained by fear of law or justice, and urged on by the highest authority of the state, they laid waste our fields of corn, shot down our cattle and hogs for sport, burned our dwellings, inhumanly butchered some eighteen or twenty defenseless citizens, dragged from their hiding-places little children, and placing the muzzles of their guns to their heads, shot them [such acts being accompanied] with the most horrid oaths and imprecations.

An aged hero and patriot of the Revolution, who served under General Washington, while in the act of pleading for quarter, was cruelly murdered and hewed in pieces with an old corn cutter; and in addition to all these savage acts of barbarity, they forcibly dragged virtuous and inoffensive females from their dwellings, bound them upon benches used for public worship, where they in great numbers ravished them in the most brutal manner.

Some fifty or sixty of the citizens were thrust into prisons and dungeons, where, bound in chains, they were fed on human flesh, while their families and some fifteen thousand others were at the point of the bayonet, forcibly expelled from the State.

In the meantime, to pay the expenses of these horrid outrages, they confiscated our property, and robbed us of all our possessions.

Before our final expulsion, with a faint and lingering hope we petitioned the State legislature then in session, unwilling to believe that the virtue and patriotism of the venerable fathers of the Revolution had fled from the bosoms of their illustrious descendants—unwilling to believe that American citizens could appeal in vain for a restoration of liberty cruelly wrested from them by cruel tyrants. But in the language of our noble ancestors, "our repeated petitions were only answered by repeated injuries."

The legislature, instead of hearing the cries of 15,000 suffering, bleeding, unoffending citizens, sanctioned and sealed the unconstitutional acts of the governor and his troops, by appropriating 200,000 dollars to defray the expenses of exterminating us from the State. No friendly arm was stretched out to protect us. The last ray of hope for redress in that State was now entirely extinguished. We saw no other alternative but to bow down our necks and wear the cruel yoke of oppression, and quietly and submissively suffer ourselves to be banished as exiles from our possessions, our property, and our sacred homes, or otherwise see our wives and children coldly butchered and murdered by tyrants in power.

Fourth. Our next permanent settlement was in the land of our exile, the State of Illinois, in the spring of 1839; but even here we are not secure from our relentless persecutor, the State of Missouri. Not satisfied in having drenched her soil in the blood of innocence, and expelling us from her borders, she pursues her unfortunate victims into banishment, seizing upon and kidnapping them in their defenseless moments, dragging them across the Mississippi river, upon their inhospitable shores, there they are tortured, whipped, immured in dungeons, and finally hung [as a means of torture, but not unto death] by the neck without any legal process what ever.

We have memorialized the former Executive of this State, Governor Carlin, upon these lawless outrages committed upon our citizens; but he renderd us no protection. Missouri, receiving no check in her murderous career, continues her depredations, again and again kidnapping our citizens and robbing us of our property; while others, who fortunately survived the execution of her bloody edicts, are again and again demanded by the Executive of that State, on pretense of some crime said to have been committed by them during the exterminating expedition against our people.

As an instance, General Joseph Smith, one of your memorialists, has been three times demanded, tried, and acquitted by the courts of this State, upon investigation under writs of *habeas corpus*, once by the United States Court for the District of Illinois, again by the Circuit Court of the State of Illinois, and lastly by the Municipal Court of the City of Nauvoo, when at the same time a *nolle prosequi* had been entered by the courts of Missouri upon all the cases of that State against Joseph Smith and others.

Thus the said Joseph Smith has been several times tried for the same alleged offense, put in jeopardy of life and limb, contrary to the fifth article of the amendments to the Constitution of the United States; and thus we have been continually harassed and robbed of our money to defray the expenses of these vexatious prosecutions. And what at the present time seems to be still more alarming, is the hostility manifested by some of the authorities and citizens of this State [Illinois.] Conventions have been called, inflammatory speeches made, and many unlawful and unconstitutional resolutions adopted to deprive us of our rights, our liberties, and the peaceable enjoyment of our possessions.

From the present hostile aspect, and from bitter experience in the State of Missouri, it is greatly feared lest the barbarous scenes acted in that State will be re-acted in this. If Missouri goes unpunished, others will be greatly encouraged to follow her murderous examples.

The afflictions of your memorialists have already been overwhelming—too much for humanity, too much for American citizens to endure without complaint. We have groaned under the iron hand of tyranny and oppression these many years. We have been robbed of our property to the amount of two millions of dollars. We have been hunted as wild beasts of the forest. We have seen our aged fathers who fought in the Revolution and our innocent children alike slaughtered by our persecutors; we have seen the fair daughters of American citizens insulted and abused in the most inhuman manner; and finally we have seen fifteen thousand souls—men, women and children, driven by force of arms during the severities of the winter from their sacred homes and firesides, penniless and unprotected, to a land of strangers.

Under all these afflicting circumstances, we imploringly stretch forth our hands towards the highest councils of our nation, and humbly appeal to the illustrious Senators and Representatives of a great and free people for redress and protection.

Hear, O hear the petitioning voice of many thousands of American citizens, who now groan in exile on Columbia's free soil! Hear, O hear the weeping and bitter lamentations of widows and orphans, whose husbands and fathers have been cruelly martyred in the land where the proud eagle exulting soars! Let it not be recorded in the archives of the nations that Columbia's exiles sought protection and redress at your hands, but sought it in vain. It is in your power to save us, our wives, and our children from a repetition of the bloodthirsty scenes of Missouri, and greatly relieve the fears of a persecuted and injured people, by ordaining for their protection the following ordinance, namely—

AN ORDINANCE

For the protection of the people styled the Church of Jesus Christ of Latter-day Saints, residing on the western borders of the State of Illinois.

PREAMBLE.

Whereas the State of Missouri at sundry times has unconstitutionally deprived a certain portion of her citizens (called "Mormons,") of their rights, property, lands, and even of their lives:

And whereas, in the years 1838 and 1839 the said State of Missouri with impunity did illegally and inhumanly exile and banish for ever from her limits and jurisdiction all the said citizens (called "Mormons,") that remained alive.

And whereas, after being hospitably received by the citizens of Illinois, the said State of Illinois did grant, enact, and charter for the benefit and convenience of the said exiled "Mormons" as follows:—

[Here in the original document is inserted the city charter of Nauvoo already published, Vol. IV, pp 239-249.]

And whereas, by the 10th article of the Constitution of the United States as amended—"Art. 10. The powers not delegated to the United States by the Constitution, nor prohibited by it to the States, are reserved to the States respectively, or to the people;" and whereas, according to the fourth article and section second, "The citizens of each state shall be entitled to all privileges and immunities of citizens in the several States:" and whereas, according to the second paragraph of the third section of said Constitution, "The Congress shall have power to dispose of and make the needful rules and regulations respecting territory;" and whereas the said Congress has the power to protect each state against invasion and insurrection: and whereas most of the inhabitants of the city of Nauvoo are exiles from the State of Missouri: and whereas most of the lands owned in the State of Missouri were purchased from the United States, and patented by the United States to the amount of more than $200,000 worth: and whereas the United States are bound to clear the title and protect it: and whereas the said exiles or expelled "Mormons" have lost in property and damages about two millions of dollars: and whereas the said State of Missouri continues her ravages, persecutions, and plunderings, by kidnapping said exiles from Illinois, and by other depredations:

Now, therefore, to show the fatherly care of the United States, to ratify the said charter, to protect the said exiles from mob violence, and shield them in their rights:—

Section 1. Be it ordained by the Senate and House of Representatives of the United States of America in Congress assembled, that all the rights, powers, privileges, and immunities belonging to Territories, and not repugnant to the Constitution of the United States, are hereby granted aud secured to the inhabitants of the city of Nauvoo, in addition to the spirit, letter, meaning, and provisions of the afore-mentioned charter, or act of incorporation from the State of Illinois, until the State of Missouri restores to those exiled citizens the lands, rights, privileges, property, and damage for all losses.

Section 2. And be it further ordained, in order to effect the object and further intention of this ordinance, and for the peace, security, happiness, convenience, benefit, and prosperity of the said city of Nauvoo, and for the common weal and honor of our country, that the mayor of Nauvoo be, and he is hereby empowered by this consent of the President of the United States; whenever the actual necessity of the case and the public safety shall require it, to call to his aid a sufficient number of United States forces, in connection with the Nauvoo Legion, to repel the invasion of mobs, keep the public peace, and protect the innocent from the unhallowed ravages of lawless banditti that escape justice on the western frontier; and also to preserve the power and dignity of the Union.

Section 3. And be it further ordained that the officers of the United States army are hereby required to obey the requisitions of this ordinance.

Section 4. And be it further ordained that, for all services rendered in quelling mobs and preserving the public peace the said Nauvoo

Legion shall be under the same regulations, rules, and laws of pay as the troops of the United States.

City of Nauvoo, Illinois, December 21st, 1843.

HYRUM SMITH,
JOHN TAYLOR,
ORSON PRATT,
W. W. PHELPS,
HEBER C. KIMBALL,
BENJAMIN WARRINGTON,
DANIEL SPENCER,
BRIGHAM YOUNG,
ORSON HYDE,

Councilors;

ORSON SPENCER,
DANIEL H. WELLS,
SAMUEL BENNETT,
GEO. A. SMITH,
GEO. W. HARRIS,

Aldermen;

JOSEPH SMITH, Mayor;
WILLARD RICHARDS, Recorder;
JOHN P. GREENE, Marshal. *

Two letters came into the post-office from the sheriff of Clark County, Missouri. From them it appears that that State wishes to continue the old game of seizing witnesses and making prisoners of them, to cover up her mobocracy and kidnapping under a legal form. The following answer was written:—

Letter: W. W. Phelps to J. White, Esq., Anent Avery Affair.

CITY OF NAUVOO, ILL., Dec. 21, 1843.

SIR,—Two letters were put into my hands this morning relative to the witnesses of Mr. Avery's innocence as to being accessory to horse stealing some four years since. In the first place, Mr. Avery was abducted from this State without process, contrary to law. In the second place, the principal for felony by the law of Missouri should be indicted within three years, &c. Again, the revised statutes of Missouri have a wise provision in such cases as Mr. Avery's. If Mr. Avery, therefore, will sue out a commission according to the law con

* There was also a Memorial prepared by the Prophet from the inhabitants of Hancock county generally to the same effect as the above, but it was never extensively signed or presented to Congress.

cerning depositions, (R. S., page 219 to 222,) directed to Alderman Geo. W. Harris, an acting justice of the peace for the city of Nauvoo, and county of Hancock, the necessary testimony to establish Mr. Avery's innocence will be taken according to law, and forwarded to the proper officer in due time.

Respectfully, &c..

W. W. PHELPS.

J. WHITE, ESQ., Dep. Sheriff,
Clark Co., Waterloo, Mo.

P.S. You will have the politeness to show this to Mr. Avery.

In the evening I was visited by several strangers, and had considerable conversation with them.

Friday, *22*.—At home at nine o'clock, a. m., reading a magazine to my children.

Attitude of Prophet on Mobocracy and Politics.

A little after twelve went into the store-room occupied by Butler and Lewis, and commenced a conversation with Dr. John F. Charles, to convince him that mobocracy is not justifiable, and that I did not deal in politics.

David Holman, living about two miles from Ramus, went out in the evening with his family visiting. About ten o'clock he discovered his house on fire. The neigbors had inquired how long he would be gone. A man rode to Carthage. A company went up, secured the provisions to themselves, and fired the house.

Warm and pleasant weather.

Saturday, *23*.—At home, counseling the brethren who called on me, and attending to my domestic duties, making preparations for a Christmas dinner party.

Prayer meeting in the Assembly Room.

Sunday, *24*.—At home. Received a visit from Mr. Richardson, one of the men who assisted in kidnapping Avery. He manifested some repentance and sorrow for his part in that transaction, and promised to use what influence he had with the Missourians to have Avery set at liberty.

Monday, 25.—This morning, about one o'clock, I was aroused by an English sister, Lettice Rushton, widow of Richard Rushton, Senior, (who, ten years ago, lost her sight,) accompanied by three of her sons, with their wives, and her two daughters, with their husbands, and several of her neighbors, singing, "Mortals, awake! with angels join," &c., which caused a thrill of pleasure to run through my soul. All of my family and boarders arose to hear the serenade, and I felt to thank my Heavenly Father for their visit, and blessed them in the name of the Lord. They also visited my brother Hyrum, who was awakened from his sleep. He arose and went out of doors. He shook hands with and blessed each one of them in the name of the Lord, and said that he thought at first that a cohort of angels had come to visit him, it was such heavenly music to him.

A Christmas Serenade.

At home all day. About noon, gave counsel to some brethren who called on me from Morley Settlement, and told them to keep law on their side, and they would come out well enough.

At two o'clock, about fifty couples sat down at my table to dine. While I was eating, my scribe called, requesting me to solemnize the marriage of his brother, Dr. Levi Richards, and Sara Griffiths; but as I could not leave, I referred him to President Brigham Young, who married them.

A large party supped at my house, and spent the evening in music, dancing, &c., in a most cheerful and friendly manner. During the festivities, a man with his hair long and falling over his shoulders, and apparently drunk, came in and acted like a Missourian. I requested the captain of the police to put him out of doors. A scuffle ensued, and I had an opportunity to look him full in the face, when, to my great surprise and joy untold, I discovered it was my long-tried, warm, but cruelly persecuted friend, Orrin

Rockwell's Return to Nauvoo.

Porter Rockwell, just arrived from nearly a year's imprisonment, without conviction, in Missouri.

The following is his statement of his experience and sufferings by that people:—

ROCKWELL'S EXPERIENCE IN MISSOURI.

I, Orrin Porter Rockwell, was on my way from New Jersey to Nauvoo; and while at St. Louis, on the 4th March, 1843, was arrested by a Mr. Fox, on oath of Elias Parker, who swore I was the O. P. Rockwell advertised in the papers as having attempted to assassinate Lilburn W. Boggs, and was taken before a magistrate in St. Louis.

I was then put into the St. Louis county jail, and kept two days with a pair of iron hobbles on my ankles. About midnight, was taken into the stage coach in charge of Fox, and started for Jefferson City. There were nine passengers, two of them women. I sat on the middle seat. One of the men behind me commenced gouging me in the back. I spoke to him, and told him that it was dark, and I could not see him, but that he was no gentleman. One of the ladies whispered to him, and he ceased the operation.

The next night, the driver, being drunk, ran against a tree, and broke the king bolt; and not knowing what to do, ironed as I was, I crawled into the boot, and found an extra bolt, and in the dark fixed the coach, got it off the tree, and we started on. Soon after, ran against a bank, and could not move. I was asleep at the time, but the bustle awoke me, when I told them, if they would take off my irons, I would get off and drive, as the driver was too drunk to manage the horses. They refused. I, however, got hold of the lines, and, by the help of other passengers lifting at the wheels, got it righted, and I drove to the next stand, near the Osage river. The roads were very bad, and the load heavy; so we got along slowly.

There was an officer of the U. S. army in the coach. We were two days and two nights from St. Louis in reaching Jefferson City, where I was lodged in the jail two days and two nights. The U. S. officer went on.

Started on for Independence, still in charge of Fox. At Boonville, overtook the U. S. officer. We three were all that were in the coach all the way from Boonville to Independence. Sheriff Reynolds told me afterwards that when he looked into the stage he took me for the guard, and the officer for the prisoner, for he looked like the guilty one.

Was about four days going to Independence: arrived there just at night. A large crowd gathered around, making many remarks. Some were for hanging me at once. I was then placed in the jail. In two or three days, underwent a sham trial before a justice of the peace. The courthouse was crowded, and the men were armed with hickory clubs. They set on boys from ten to twelve years of age to kick and punch me, which they did repeatedly. While in court, Fox was the main witness introduced, and he swore falsely.

Fox swore that I had stated to him that I had not been in the county for five years. I informed the court that Fox swore falsely, in proof thereof that the people of Independence knew that I had traveled through Independence several times during that time, for the people were all well aware of my having visited this place, which fact alone should satisfy them that Fox was swearing for money, which I afterwards learned that he obtained and divided with Parker.

The magistrate committed me to prison for my safe preservation, as he was afraid the people would kill me; but he could find no crime against me. This I was told by the officer who conveyed me to prison.

I was re-committed to jail, still wearing the iron hobbles, and was kept in the upper part in the day-time, and in the dungeon at night, with a little dirty straw for a bed, without any bedding, no fire, and very cold weather. For eighteen days I was not free from shaking with cold. I then got permission to buy 1½ bushels of charcoal, which I put into an old kettle, and kept a little fire. When that was gone, I could not obtain any more.

After I was arrested at St. Louis, I was visited by Joseph Wood, an apostate "Mormon," who professed to be a lawyer. He was accompanied by Mr. Blanerhasset, who told me that everything I had would be taken from me, and proposed to take charge, keep, and return to me any property I might have with me. I let him have a pair of pistols, a bowie knife, and watch, which he never returned to me.

After the weather got a little warmer, they furnished me with a few old newspapers to read. A family lived at the corner of the jail. The women once in a while used to send out a little negro girl with a small basket of victuals. She handed up to the grate a big Missouri whip-stock, with a piece of twine, which I tied to the pole and drew up the basket, and let it down again.

I made a pin-hook and tied to the twine, and baited with a chunk of corn-dodger hard enough to knock a negro down with, and stuck it out of the grated window and fished for pukes. When passers-by came along, they would stop and gawk at me awhile, and pass on.

A preacher who had a family of girls lived on the opposite side of the street. The girls would watch and laugh at them, and call out and ask me if I got any bites. I replied, No, but some glorious nibbles.

Numbers were put into the jail with me at different times, and taken out again. One of them, who was charged with a fraudulent issue of U. S. Treasury notes, was allowed to have his saddle-bags with him. They contained some fire-steels, gun-flints, and articles of Indian trade. I sawed the irons nearly off with one of the fire-steels. He got the negro girl to get him a knife, and I finished cutting the fetters with it. He would frequently call for a good supper and pay for it, which was allowed him, but not allowed me. He was very anxious to escape, and urged me to undertake it with him. He ordered a good supper, and he ate very heartily. I would not eat, telling him that he could not run if he ate so much. Nearly dusk, as the jailer came in to get the dishes, we sprang to the door, and I locked him in, and threw the key into the garden. In coming down stairs, we met the jailer's wife. I told her that her husband was unharmed; I had only locked him up. We had a board fence to climb over, which was about twelve feet high. I climbed it, and ran about twenty rods, when he called me to come and help him over, which I did. If I had not, I should have escaped. The pure air had so great an effect upon me, that I gave out and slacked my pace, The populace of the place came up, and I told them to run; they would soon catch him; and that I had given out and could not run. They soon returned with him. I fell into the crowd and walked back to the jail yard.

Sheriff J. H. Reynolds laid his hand upon my shoulder, he being the first to approach me. Asked where the key was. I told him, In the garden.

Smallwood Nowlin was the first who proposed to hang me on the spot, when Reynolds gave me a push towards the crowd, and said, "There he is, G— d—n him! Do what you damn please with him." Nowlin's son in-law (by marrying one of his mulatto wenches), a Mexican, stepped up to me to lay hold of me, when I told him to stand off, or I would mash his face. He stepped back.

I then walked up stairs into the jail. Was followed by Reynolds and others, until the room and stairs were full. Reynolds asked me what I had cut my irons off with. I went to the saddle-bags and handed him the knife and fire-steel. While feeling for them, I got hold of a piece of buckskin that had some three or four pounds of bullets tied up in it, which I intended to use in mashing in the head of any one that should attempt to put a rope on my neck. A rope was passed along over the heads of the people into the room to a bald-headed man. About this time pistols could be heard cocking in every part of the room, and bowie-knives were produced as if for fight. In a few minutes the room was clear of all but three or four persons.

I was then put into the dungeon, my feet ironed together, my right hand to my left foot, so close that I could not half straighten myself. The irons, when put on my wrists, were so small that they would hardly go on, and swelled them; but in eighteen days I could slip them up and turn them around my arm at the elbow. I was fed on cold corndodger and meat of the poorest description; and if I did not eat it all up, it was returned the next time.

About a month after the court sat, my irons were taken off, and I was so weak that I had to be led to the court-room by the officer. I was notified that a bill was found against me for breaking jail, and that the grand jury had failed to find a bill against me on the charge of shooting Boggs, as charged in the advertisement offering a reward for my apprehension.

I was taken into court, and was asked by the judge if I had any counsel. I told him I had not. He asked if I had any means to employ a counsel. I answered that I had none with me that I could control. He then said, Here are a number of counselors: if I was acquainted with any of them, I could take my choice. I told him I would make choice of Mr. Doniphan, who arose and made a speech, saying he was crowded with business, but that here are plenty of young lawyers who could plead for me as well as he could. The judge heard his plea, and then told me he did not consider that a sufficient excuse, and I could consider Mr. Doniphan my counsel.

I was then ordered back to jail, and ironed again in the same way. Mr. Doniphan asked for and obtained a change of venue to Clay County, which is in another district.

When the officers came to Independence jail for me, they requested me to get ready in a hurry, as they feared the mob would kill me. I told them I wanted to put on a clean shirt, if it cost me my life, as I had not been permitted to enjoy the luxury of a change of linen since I had boarded at the expense of Jackson County. While I was changing my shirt, the officers several times told me to hurry, or the mob would be on me and kill me.

When I got ready to start, the officers furnished me a very hard-trotting horse, with a miserable poor saddle, tied my feet under the horse with ropes, and my hands behind my back, and started off at a good round trot, in charge of two officers. In a short time a strange gentleman fell into our company, who was also on horseback. It was six miles to the ferry, where we could cross the Missouri river. When we got there, we saw the boat land on the opposite side, when several men got off the boat, and took a course to the woods, through which the road ran. The boat returned. This stranger asked—"Where are those men going?" and was answered—"They are going to the woods to hew timber."

We then crossed, and took our way for Liberty. When we left the boat, we saw no signs of people, nor heard any sound of axes. After traveling some two or three miles, the woods became dense and brushy: we heard the crackling of brush, and the noise of men traveling through it. The officers and stranger appeared frightened, and urged speed, keeping close watch. We came to an opening in the woods, when the noise of crackling of brush ceased. We traveled safely to Liberty, where this stranger told his friends that he overheard several men in Independence planning to waylay me in the thick timber on the Missouri bottom, at the place where we heard the noises; but his being in company counteracted their plot. I was then lodged in Liberty jail. In a few days afterwards I learned that the men who went into the brush told it, that they went into the woods according to agreement to waylay me; but when they saw this stranger, it frustrated their plans.

In about ten days, on pretext of informality in the papers, I was remanded back to Independence jail. It was rumored that I was again going to be waylaid, when the two officers from Clay county took me by a different road, and so I escaped the second time.

When I was put in Independence jail, I was again ironed hand and foot, and put in the dungeon, in which condition I remained about two months. During this time, Joseph H. Reynolds, the sheriff, told me he was going to arrest Joseph Smith, and they had received letters from Nauvoo which satisfied them that Joseph Smith had unlimited confidence in me, that I was capable of toting him in a carriage or on horseback anywhere that I pleased; and if I would only tote him out by riding or any other way, so that they could apprehend him, I might please myself whether I stayed in Illinois or came back to Missouri; they would protect me, and any pile that I would name the citizens of Jackson county would donate, club together, and raise, and that I should never suffer for want afterwards: "you only deliver Joe Smith into our hands, and name your pile." I replied—"I will see you all damned first, and then I won't."

About the time that Joseph was arrested by Reynolds at Dixon, I knew that they were after him,and [yet had] no means under heaven of giving him any information. My anxiety became so intense upon the subject, knowing their determination to kill him, that my flesh twitched on my bones. I could not help it; twitch it would. While undergoing this sensation, I heard a dove alight on the window in the upper room of the jail, and commence cooing, and then went off. In a short time, he came back to the window, where a pane was broken: he crept through between the bars of iron, which were about two and-a-half inches apart.

I saw it fly round the trap-door several times: it did not alight, but continued cooing until it crept through the bars again, and flew out through the broken window.

I relate this, as it was the only occurrence of the kind that happened during my long and weary imprisonment; but it proved a comfort to me: the twitching of my flesh ceased, and I was fully satisfied from that moment that they would not get Joseph into Missouri, and that I should regain my freedom. From the best estimates that can be made, this incident occurred about the time when Joseph was in the custody of Reynolds.

In a few days afterwards, Sheriff Reynolds came into the jail and told me that he had made a failure in the arrest of Joseph.

After the lawyers had been about two months making out fresh papers, I was again conveyed to Liberty jail on a miserable horse, with feet and hands tied as before, but [by] a different road.

In a few days afterwards, my mother found where I was, and she came to see me and brought me $100, whereby I was enabled to fee Mr. Doniphan for his services as counsel.

The time of trial being continually delayed, I began to be uneasy. I was handcuffed in the dungeon, which is the basement story of the prison, and is about nine feet high. I took down the stove-pipe, pushed my clothes up through the stove-pipe hole, and then crawled through the hole in the floor, which was made of logs about fourteen inches thick, into the upper room. The hole was so small that it scratched my flesh, and made me bleed from many wounds. I then examined the inside door, and with the bail of the water pail I unbolted it; but finding I could not get through the outside door, I returned to my dungeon through the same narrow pass.

The following night I made another attempt through the same way; but, failing to get through the outside door, I lay down on the upper floor, where the boys who were bringing my food next morning found me. They made an alarm, when five or six men came and again conveyed me down into the dungeon. It caused quite an excitement.

My mother, learning that Mr. Doniphan had returned home, went to him, and prevailed on him to come and speak to me at the dungeon grate. While he was talking to me, a little boy, the son of a poor widow, about five or six years old, who had previously been to see me, finding I had no fire, had run home and brought some fire and chips to the grate. Mr. Doniphan said—"You little devil you, what are you doing here with this fire?" He replied, "I am going to give it to Mr. Rockwell, so that he can warm him." Doniphan then said—"You little devil you, take this fire and leave;" when the little urchin replied (looking him in the face)—"Mr. Doniphan, you go to hell: I am going to give Mr. Rockwell this fire, so that he can warm him;" and he pushed it through the grate, gave me the chips, and continued to supply my daily wants of chips and fire while I continued in the dungeon.

From Mr. Doniphan I learned that a special term of court was called, and my trial would come on in about fifteen days. The night following this visit, some men came to the grates of my dungeon, and asked if I wanted to get out. I told them, No, as I had been informed that day that I should have a trial in a fortnight. They replied—"Honor bright: if you wish to get out, we'll let you out in a few minutes." I replied that I would rather remain, as my trial would come on so soon. Next morning one of the men came, put some money in the cleft of a stick, and put it through the hole to me. He refused to tell his name; but I knew by his voice that he was one of the men who came to me in the night.

The trial came on according to my last notification. I was tried for breaking Independence jail; and although the law of Missouri reads that, in order to break jail, a man must break a lock, a door, or a wall, still Judge King ruled that it was breaking jail to walk out when the door is open; and under this ruling the jury brought in a verdict of "five minutes' imprisonment in the county jail;" but I was kept there four or five hours, during which time several attempts were made to get up some other charge against me.

About 8 p.m. on December 13th, General Doniphan took me out and told me I must take across the country on foot, and not walk on any traveled road, unless it was during the night, as they would be apt to follow and again take me, as they did not care on what grounds, so they could make me trouble.

I accordingly started, accompanied by my mother, and went to the house of a widow, where I obtained my first supper in freedom for more than nine months. We then traveled two miles and obtained $4.

I then took through the woods to the road, where I heard two men riding on horseback. I hid behind a shady tree, and overheard one of them say, "He has not been gone many minutes: we shall soon overtake him."

I went round the houses and traveled in the fields by the side of the road. The moon was in its first quarter, and I traveled during the night about twenty-five miles. I carried a little food with me, and next day traveled on the road, and walked past Crooked River to a Mr. Taylor's, with all the skin off my feet.

A neighbor offered to take me in for the night, if I would go back two miles. I did so, found his wife very cross with her husband, who said, "Stranger, you see my wife is very cross. I have got some whisky; let's drink: my wife will soon have something to eat." When supper was eaten, she became good tempered. I stayed in peace through the night. Next morning I ate breakfast with them, and gave them fifty cents, when the man brought out a horse, and sent a little boy with me fourteen miles, which was a very great relief to my weary feet.

The next night I stopped near where the Haun's Mill massacre took place.

The third day I walked till noon, and then hired a man to carry me the remainder of the day for seventy-five cents. Stayed at a house where I was well acquainted; but the people did not recognize me, and I did not make myself known. Paid fifty cents for supper, lodging, breakfast, and being sent twelve miles on horseback the next morning.

I then continued my journey about thirty miles, where I rested three days to recruit my feet. I was then carried twenty-five miles on horseback, and walked the same day twenty-five miles. The day following I walked forty miles, and then waited another day and engaged a man to carry me to Montrose, to which place I was three days in going. I immediately crossed the river to Nauvoo in a small boat, and came straight to the Mansion.

Release of Daniel Avery.

Daniel Avery was liberated from his imprisonment in Missouri by *habeas corpus*. This was, no doubt, on account of our vigilance in communicating with the Governor, and endeavoring to prosecute the kidnappers, and continually making public the conduct of Missouri.

Warm day; rain in the evening.

A PLAN FOR WOMEN'S SUBSCRIPTIONS TO THE TEMPLE.

(From the Millenial Star.)

We have much pleasure in publishing and recommending the following plan to be adopted amongst the sisters of the Church of Jesus Christ of Latter-day Saints in England. We believe that the completion of the Temple is as near the hearts of the sisters as to the hearts of the brethren, and that the following proposed [plan] will be responded to on the part of the English sisters in a manner that shall reflect honor upon themselves, and be materially instrumental in forwarding the great work.

NAUVOO, Dec. 25, 1843.

To the Sisters of the Church of Jesus Christ in England, Greeting:—

DEAR SISTERS:—This is to inform you that we have here entered into a small weekly subscription for the benefit of the Temple funds. One thousand have already joined it, while many more are expected, by which we trust to help forward the great work very much. The amount is only one cent or a halfpenny per week.

As Brother Amos Fielding is waiting for this, I cannot enlarge more than to say that myself and Sister Thompson are engaged in collecting the same.

We remain,

Your affectionate sisters in Christ,

MARY SMITH,

M. R. THOMPSON.

NAUVOO, Dec. 25, 1843.

The ladies' subscription for the Temple, of one cent per week, is fully sanctioned by the First Presidency.

HYRUM SMITH.

We feel much to encourage this plan, and trust that the sisters in England will manifest that they will not be behind the sisters in Nauvoo in this laudable work. One thing in connection with this work we would mention, and request that it be attended to with the strictest accuracy; that is, that the name of each individual be recorded, and the amount which they subscribe, in order that such names may be transmitted to Nauvoo, where they will have to be entered in the books of the Lord's House. The sisters or others who may collect the subscriptions will please to be very particular on this point.

Prophet's Joy at the Return of Rockwell and Avery.

Tuesday, 26.—At home. I rejoiced that Rockwell had returned from the clutches of Missouri, and that God had delivered him out of their hands. Brother Daniel Avery also arrived about dusk this evening; and the Missourians have no longer the pleasure of exulting over any Mormon victims for the present; but their blood-thirstiness will not long be satisfied unless they seek out another victim on whom to glut their malice and vengeance.

Wednesday, 27.—Cold: a little ice in the river, which has been clear for some time past.

I received letters from General Lewis Cass, of Michigan, and Hon. John C. Calhoun, of South Carolina, in answer to mine of Nov. 4.

Mr. Keith gave a lecture and concert of music in the assembly room this evening.

MR. ROCKWELL.

(*Editorial From the Neighbor.*)

The name of this individual is, no doubt, familiar to most of our readers. He has obtained some celebrity in the world also, not for his reputed virtue, but for his supposed crimes.

It will be recollected that he is the person who was basely and falsely implicated, along with Joseph Smith, as the reputed [would be] murderer of ex-Governor Boggs, while Mr. Smith was charged with being accessory before the fact. A vexatious lawsuit was instituted against Joseph Smith, wherein he was charged with the above-named crime; and finally, after many attempts of the governor of Missouri to get him into his power, was acquitted by the United States Court for the district of Illinois,

Stories of murder and blood were circulated from Maine to Missouri; they were iterated and reiterated by the newspapers of the whole Union, and painted in the most glowing colors that human ingenuity could invent. Mr. Rockwell was branded as a murderer, and Joseph Smith as accessory before the fact, without any other evidence than a story fabricated by some of our generous politicians, engendered in falsehood by hearts as dark as Erebus for religious and political effect.

This demagoguery and political corruption has caused an innocent man to be immolated in a Missouri dungeon for upwards of eight months, without the slightest evidence of his guilt, or even the most remote evidence of crime leading to his committal. He was taken without process, and committed to jail upon mere supposition, and finally acquitted without any shadow of proof having been adduced from beginning to end. This is the way that Missouri treats free-born American citizens, and they can obtain no redress.

Mr. Rockwell arrived here on Monday night, and has given us some of the details of his history since he was first taken in Missouri to the present time; and we can assure our readers that it will "a tale unfold" relative to that state, which even many of those who have been driven therefrom will find it difficult to believe that there did exist such monsters in human shape.

Thursday, 28.—At home. Elder Orson Hyde returned

from Adams county, having obtained quite a number of signatures to the Memorial to Congress, and made an affidavit of what he learned in Warsaw concerning the mob.

Affidavit of Orson Hyde—Disclosing Plan To Drive the Saints.

STATE OF ILLINOIS, }
CITY OF NAUVOO. } SS.

On the 28th day of December, 1843, came Orson Hyde before me, Joseph Smith, mayor of said city; and after being duly sworn, deposeth and saith that on the 26th instant, as he was passing from Lima to Nauvoo, through that part of Hancock county where Colonel Levi Williams resides, he was credibly informed that on Saturday previous the anti-Mormons held a meeting, drew up an article, and passed several resolutions, among which were these:—"We will revere and hold sacred and inviolate the Constitution of the United States, and also the Constitution of this State. We will visit the Mormons residing in our vicinity and require them to give up their guns; and such as do it shall dwell here in peace; but those who will not do it may have thirteen days to leave in; and if they are not off in that time, we will drive them." The above is the substance, but perhaps not the very words. They also swear that the Mormons shall never raise another crop in that region, &c.; &c., and further this deponent saith not.

ORSON HYDE.

Subscribed and sworn to before me this 28th of December, 1843,

W. W. PHELPS, Clerk, M. C.

Daniel Avery having made affidavit of the cruel treatment he had recently received at the hands of Missourians, I here insert it:-

Affidavit of Daniel Avery—His Treatment in Missouri.

STATE OF ILLINOIS, }
CITY OF NAUVOO. } SS.

On the 28th day of December, 1843, came Daniel Avery before me, Joseph Smith, mayor of the city aforesaid, and after being duly sworn, deposeth and saith that on the second day of December, 1843, he was unlawfully arrested by force and arms, and kidnapped at Doty's Mill in Bear Creek precinct, Hancock county, and State aforesaid, by Colonel Levi Williams, his son John Williams, of Hancock county; John Elliott, a schoolmaster, from four-and-a-half miles below Warsaw; William Middleton and Joseph McCoy, of Clark county, Missouri, and four others. Colonel Williams held his bowie-knife to his breast. Six of the others stood with their pistols cocked and their fingers upon the triggers, muzzles presented at his body, ready to fire; and two stood with clubs, and amidst the most horrid oaths and imprecations, took and bound with silk handkerchiefs your said affiant, and led him away between two men, one holding a savage bowie-knife on one side, and the other a cocked pistol on the other side, (having taken away your said affiant's weapons while binding him in the mill,) and led your affiant about a mile. Your affiant refused to walk any further, and they put him upon a horse, and tied his legs under the horse; and John Elliott, the aforesaid schoolmaster, led the horse as fast as he could make his way, through a thicket and by-way to the house of the aforesaid Colonel Williams. Here the kidnappers ate and drank; and after they had unbound me, (for they had bound me so tight that I was in great pain,) I was also suffered to partake.

They then put me upon the horse again, and bound me, and started for the river, the said schoolmaster Elliott leading the horse. When we came near a schoolhouse where there was a meeting, they came to a halt, sent messengers to the meeting, and in the course of half an hour they returned with an armed mob, with rifles and other weapons, sufficient to make the whole company number about twenty. Being all on horseback, they formed a circle, with your affiant in the center, (who up to that time had acquainted every man he saw that *they were kidnapping him*, and marched in that order to a house on a point below Warsaw; and as I was very cold from being bound, they took me into the house to warm. I now called for a trial, as I had told them all the way that I never resisted legal authority. They said they were hunting a magistrate. Said I, "I understand you; you mean to force me into Missouri." McCoy returned, and said, "We are ready." It was about midnight. We went about three hundred yards up the river to a skiff. I refused to cross as they had promised me a trial. They forced me into a skiff and bound me, and five men put me across. Their names, so far as I could ascertain, are William Middleton, William Clark, Joseph McCoy, John Elliott, and Charles Coolidge. They landed at the tavern on the south side of the Des Moines, and took me into a back room, threw down a buffalo robe for my bed; but as my arms were bound so tight that I could not rest, I complained; told Middleton that was not the way he was used at my house. They felt at my arms and exclaimed, "By God, they are not too tight!" I begged to have one arm liberated, and finally they untied both, and I slept (under guard) on the buffalo robe before the fire.

About noon they got ready and started with me, guarded upon a horse, for McCoy's in Clark county, Missouri, about twelve miles distant. It being night when we arrived, and I unwell through fatigue and confinement and the abuses before received, I went to bed. They had sent runners ahead; and after I had been in bed awhile, the sheriff came up from Waterloo, the county seat, a distance of about two miles, to arrest me and take me before a magistrate that night; but Middleton and McCoy objected, as I was sick. The sheriff, however, executed his writ, and left me in their care till morning. It being late before we breakfasted, he came in the morning and made the second scope of his authority and took me. He quizzed me the night before, to draw something out for testimony; but as innocence cannot be affected by truth, he was as wise at one end of the story as the other.

At Waterloo I was examined by a magistrate, who committed me upon the substance of an affidavit made by my son in duress with a bowie-knife at his breast, and upon a promise that he should be liberated from Monticello jail, where he was confined after being kidnapped some three or four weeks previous. My bonds were fixed at $1000; and as I had no bail in such a strange place, I was started for Palmyra jail, in Marion county. The deputy sheriff took me to Musgrove, the sheriff, a distance of ten miles. Here I sued out a writ of habeas corpus, but the judge remanded me to prison.

At Monticello my chains were taken off, and I was at liberty in the midst of a strong guard to view the town. Here a lawyer agreed to take me and my son through court (as the Missourians say,) for a horse. Saw my son in the prison; said he was forced at the point of a bowie-knife to make an affidavit against me; but he knew I was innocent.

I tried to be left with him in jail; but no, I was compelled to go to Palmyra, where I arrived the next evening. The sheriff thrust me into the dungeon without waiting to eat, warm, or anything else. The next morning the blacksmith came into the jail and ironed me to the middle of a great chain that was fast to the floor, where I remained in the horrid gloom of a Missouri prison two weeks.

From thence the deputy sheriff started, with me chained upon the horse in this wise. He then chained my right leg, and then passed the chain up to my left hand. In this way I traveled nine miles, when we stopped, and he changed the chain from my hand to the horse's neck. We arrived at Monticello, and I was chained all night.

The next day I was conveyed to Waterloo, and delivered into the custody of the sheriff of Clark county. I was kept under a strong guard by day, and at night chained to one of the guards or to the bedpost.

I was informed that Middleton and McCoy procured an indictment against me, by giving bonds to the amount of some two or three hundred dollars, that they would hunt up testimony to the point for next court, there being nothing against me but the affidavit of my son before alluded to; and so the grand jury found a bill.

Ellison, my lawyer, deceived me, and put over my case for six months, because, as I suppose, I, being kidnapped, had no fees for him. I objected to having my trial put off for six months. I did not fancy the dungeon of Palmyra prison. The court concluded to let me to bail under bonds of $1000, but this I could not obtain. Subsequently it was reduced to $500, but all in vain, for I was unaquainted with the people.

This was on Saturday, and I was thus left to meditate on the mischief that may be made out of a little matter by meddlesome men.

On Monday I sued out a writ of habeas corpus; and after a fair hearing of the matter, I received the following order:—

STATE OF MISSOURI, }
COUNTY OF CLARK. } SS.

December, 25, 1843.

Ordered by the Clark County Court that Samuel Musgrove, sheriff of Clark county, discharge Daniel Avery from imprisonment, on an indictment found against him for the alleged crime of stealing a mare of Joseph McCoy.

By order of Court.

[L.S.] Witness—Willis Curd, Clerk of said court, and seal of office this 25th of December, 1843.

Done at office in Waterloo, date above.

WILLIS CURD, Clerk.

HONS. JOHN W. DEWELLIN, }
HENRY SNIVELY, } Judges.

Very early on Tuesday morning your affiant started for Nauvoo and arrived the same evening about sundown, a distance of nearly twenty miles so crippled from the iron bondage and hard usage of Missouri, that he is hardly able to walk. To those who assisted your said affiant to obtain his release from bondage, he tenders his grateful acknowledgements; and further your affiant saith not.

Subscribed and sworn to before me, this 28th day of December, 1843.

DANIEL AVERY.

W. W. PHELPS, Clerk, M. C.

Friday, 29.—At home. In the forenoon, W. W. Phelps called and gave us a lesson on eloquence, and read my Appeal to the Green Mountain Boys, and also a New Year's hymn without rhyme. Three p. m., I related to Dr. Bernhisel and Joseph H. Jackson* my commencement in receiving revelations. Mr. Jackson said he was almost persuaded to be one with me. I replied, I would that he were not only almost, but altogether.

Joseph H. Jackson—Prophet's Interview with.

At four p. m., I met with the city council.

Having selected forty men to act as city policemen, they met with the Council, and were sworn into office to support the Constitution of the United States and the State of Illinois, and obey the ordinances of this city and the instructions of the Mayor, according to the best of their ability.

Police Force of Nauvoo Increased.

Names of police called by Captain Jonathan Dunham:

Jonathan Dunham, High Policeman,
Hosea Stout, 2nd Lieutenant,
John Pack, Ensign,
John D. Lee, 2nd Sergeant,
Josiah Arnold, 4th Sergeant,
Alexander Mills, 2nd Corporal,
William Pace, 4th Corporal,
Levi W. Hancock, Fifer,
Richard D. Sprague, Drummer,
Charles C. Rich, 1st Lieutenant,
Shadrack, Roundy, 3rd Lieut.,
Jesse P. Harmon, Orderly Sergt.
Daniel Carn, 3rd Sergeant,
James Emmett, 1st Corporal,
Steven H. Goddard, 3rd Corporal
Abraham C. Hodge, Pioneer,
Daniel M. Repsher, Fifer.
Samuel Billings, Drummer,

*This man afterwards was discovered to be an adventurer and a most desperate character. Gregg in his Prophet of Palmyra, chapter XXX, speaks of him as "an adventurer of fine appearance and gentlemanly manners, who appeared in the county (Hancock) during the troubles; went to Nauvoo, and became intimate with Smith and the leaders; afterwards turned against them—went to Warsaw and issued a pamphlet—claiming to be an expose of Mormonism and the evil purposes and practices of the Prophet * * * He was an entire stranger to the county and its people; no one knew whence he came or what became of him afterwards, when the excitement was all over. Hence it is just to say, that the equivocal position in which he stood very justly tended to lessen confidence of the public in his statements, and his little book made slight impression. The Mormons charged that he was an adventurer of the worst class—himself a counterfeiter, etc., and that he quarreled with the Prophet and the authorities because he was detected and exposed." Gregg also says that this "Expose was much of the same character as that of General Bennett's." (Ibid).

Abraham O. Smoot,
John Lytle,
Andrew Lytle.
Howard Egan,
Benjamin Boyce,
Lorenzo Clark,
Davies McOlney,
Abram Palmer,
Isaac C. Haight,
John L. Butler,
Elbridge Tufts,
Truman R. Barlow,
Dwight Harding,
Simeon A. Dunn,
Appleton M. Harmon,
James Pace,
Francis M. Edwards.
William H. Edwards,
Moses M. Sanders,
Warren A. Smith,
George W. Clyde,
Vernon H. Bruce,
Armsted Moffet,
Azra Adams.

The Mayor said—

Address of the Mayor to the Nauvoo Police.

It is expected that a part will be on duty while others rest. It might be expected that thieves had crept into the Church for the purpose of concealing their wickedness under the garb of sanctity.

It is an abominable thing to set a thief to catch a thief; and I would look with the utmost contempt upon men who do this as guilty of a mean or cowardly act.

Some city councils have taken thieves out of their prisons, and employed them as policemen, under the old and foolish adage—"Set a rogue to catch a rogue," which is decidedly wrong, and is corrupt in policy.

You will act under the direction of Jonathan Dunham—we will call him High Policeman. In reality he is the captain of the police: but as men are apt to be frightened at a military title, we will use a civil title, as these policemen are all civil officers of the city.

Captain Dunham is the man to send after a thief. He will not come back, after following him a mile, to ask if he may shoot him, if he resists. Some men have strange ears and changeable hearts: they become transformed from their original purity and integrity, and become altogether different from what they were.

If the bloodthirsty hell-hounds of Missouri continue their persecution, we will be forbearing, until we are compelled to strike; then do it decently and in good order, and break the yoke effectually, so that it cannot be mended. The mob have been so repulsed in their last attempt at kidnapping, they may stand in fear, at least for a short time.

We will be in peace with all men, so long as they will mind their own business and let us alone. Even "Peace with Missouri" shall be the motto of the Church of Jesus Christ of Latter-day Saints, from this time forth, if they will stop their persecution and oppressive warfare against us. Let them alone, for they stink in the nostrils of the Almighty: let them alone. Porter Rockwell has come home clear. A Missouri grand jury could not find a bill against him even in Jackson county; and that proves me clear of the charge of being accessory of shooting Lilburn W. Boggs. Many of our difficulties from the State of Missouri are hurled upon us through the influence of some of our near neighbors.

Governor Ford has boasted of being a law-abiding man. A governor certainly should be law-abiding. It is therefore our best policy to acquaint the Executive, by affidavits, of every violation of our rights, so that when the onset comes, he will be obliged by law to send the militia to our support. Let us keep cool as a cucumber on a frosty morning. Do not be excited. Say nothing about Missouri's oppresion. "A soft answer turns away wrath but grievous words stir up anger," therefore we "poor pussy" this generation.

Keep a strict account of the time you serve as policemen. Have the ordinances of the city always in your possession, and study them, and ferret out all grogshops, gambling-houses, brothels, and disorderly conduct; and if a transgressor resists, cuff his ears. If anyone lifts a weapon or presents a pistol at you, take his life, if need be, to preserve your own; but enforce the ordinances, and preserve the peace of the city, and take care of your own lives. Let no horses be taken away out of the city, or anything else stolen, if you can help it.

Let Missouri alone. Keep out of her territory. Don't go over there on any business whatever. Any of this people would be subject to cruel abuse, if found in that State, in the same manner that Porter Rockwell has been. He was seized in St. Louis while attending to his lawful business, picked up and ironed, and thrown in jail without any form of law, conveyed to Independence in the custody of a ruffian who swore falsely in the hope of getting a reward, kept in irons all the way, lodged in Independence jail without even the form of an inquiry, chained double in a filthy, damp, unventilated dungeon,—chained hand and foot, so that he could not straighten for months, till his body was reduced to a mere skeleton, and he unable to walk when the irons were taken off, and he had to be led,—half fed on the refuse of what dogs would not eat: his case presented to a Jackson county grand jury, and not evidence enough to warrant them in even finding an indictment. After which, the Missouri court, in the plenitude of their justice, transmitted the innocent and unindicted man back to the dungeon, without fire, provisions, or any other comfort,—hoping by this torture, no doubt, to produce death, or force him to accede to an infamous proposition, "that whether Jo Smith was guilty or innocent, only come out against him, you shall have your liberty, and receive a liberal reward." After months have passed away, without any shadow of law, the door is opened, and he is told to "slip off privately, or the people will hang you." Keep out of Missouri, if you don't want such treatment as this; for the Averys, Rockwell, and many others have been thankful to get away with their lives.

If any man attempts to bribe you in any way whatever, or persuade you to neglect your duty, tell the same to me. Let us have a reformation.

There are speculators in this State who are wanting to sell revolving pistols to us, in order to fight the Missourians, and at the same time inciting the Missourians to fight us. Don't buy: it would be better to buy ploughshares and raise corn with them.

My life is more in danger from some little dough-head of a fool in this city than from all my numerous and inveterate enemies abroad. I am exposed to far greater danger from traitors among ourselves than from enemies without, although my life has been sought for many years by the civil and military authorities, priests, and people of Missouri; and if I can escape from the ungrateful treachery of assassins, I can live as Cæsar might have lived, were it not for a right-hand Brutus. I have had pretended friends betray me. All the enemies upon the face of the earth may roar and exert all their power to bring about my death, but they can accomplish nothing, unless some who are among us and enjoy our society, have been with us in our councils, participated in our confidence, taken us by the hand, called us brother, saluted us with a kiss, join with our enemies, turn our virtues into faults, and, by falsehood and deceit, stir up their wrath and indignation against us, and bring their united vengeance upon our heads. All the hue-and-cry of the chief priests and elders against the Savior, could not bring down the wrath of the Jewish nation upon His head, and thereby cause the crucifixion of the Son of God, until Judas said unto them, "Whomsoever I shall kiss, he is the man; hold him fast." Judas was one of the Twelve Apostles, even their treasurer, and dipt with their Master in the dish, and through his treachery, the crucifixion was brought about; and *we have a Judas in our midst.*

The Mayor blesses the Police.

It shall be said in time to come, Where are our old policemen? Let us have one of the old policemen, to stand at our window, guard our interest, and protect our families, and we shall be safe.

If you will magnify your office, the full confidence of Israel shall be the blessing that shall be conferred on you in time to come.

Counselor Hyrum Smith spoke of the importance of the police office.

The Mayor said that if any one offered a bribe to a policeman, the city will pay that policeman twice the amount effered for the information, when reported to the Mayor.

Friday, 29.—My clerk made copies of five affidavits made yesterday by Elder Orson Hyde, Mr. Daniel Avery, and others, and sent the same to the Governor, with the following letter:—

Letter to Governor Ford—Accompanying Affidavits.

NAUVOO, December 30, 1843.

SIR:—I forward to your Excellency a number of affidavits relative to the late kidnapping of the Averys, and upon other matters. When the mob made efforts to resist the laws, Joseph Smith, as Mayor, gave notice to Major-General Law to hold a portion of the Nauvoo Legion in readiness; and Aaron Johnson, Esq., called for some troops to maintain the laws: but I am happy to say, none were ordered to march, as it was deemed most advisable to let Colonel Levi Williams and his mob flourish until indictments could be made at the Circuit Court of Hancock county.

We shall continue to keep your Excellency informed upon all matters of moment touching the premises.

Saturday, 30.—At nine, a.m., held Mayor's court. Two boys, Roswell and Evander White, were brought up for stealing six hens and a rooster. They were sentenced to pay for the fowls, and to ten days' hard labor each on the streets.

In the afternoon, met in the assembly room with the quorum. William Law and wife were not present. Warm and rainy.

Sunday, 31st.—At home.

In the afternoon, called with Elder Parley P. Pratt to see his wife.

At early candle-light, went to prayer-meeting; administered the sacrament; after which I retired. At midnight, about fifty musicians and singers sang Phelps' New Year's Hymn under my window.

Warm and rainy. No ice to be seen.

The subjoined list shows a few of the publications for and against the Saints during the year.

Pro et con Mormonism, publications for the year 1843.

The *Alton Telegraph* published several very severe articles against the Church.

Edward Brotherton published a scurrilous pamphlet at Manchester, England, entitled "Mormonism—its Rise and Progress, and the Prophet Joseph Smith."

The *Richmond Palladium* published an amusing and fovorable article on "Mormonism."

The *Boston Bee* published a series of articles favorable to the Saints, which had a beneficial effect in putting down prejudice and misrepresentation.

A favorable account of a visit to Nauvoo was published by Samuel A. Prior, Methodist minister.

The *Morning Star*, a Freewill Baptist paper, published a long and bitter article against the Latter-day Saints, entitled "Mormon Perversion."

A favorable article, entitled "Nauvoo and Mormonism," was published by a Traveler.

The *Quincy Whig* published several bitter articles against me.

The *Warsaw Message*, and subsequently the *Warsaw Signal*, published a continual tirade of abuse, misrepresentation, and lies against the Saints.

The *New Haven* (Con.) *Herald* published a favorable account of the "Mormons" in Nauvoo.

CHAPTER VII.

PRESIDENT SMITH'S CORRESPONDENCE WITH JOHN C. CALHOUN—CARTWRIGHT DROWNING CASE, ENGLAND—CITY GUARDS INCREASED—FEARS OF LAW AND MARKS—INVESTIGATION BY THE CITY COUNCIL—RESISTANCE OF OFFICERS AT CARTHAGE—ANTI-MORMON OBJECTIONS TO CITY ORDINANCES—THE PROPHET'S DIFFICULTIES WITH FRANCIS M. HIGBEE—REGULATIONS FOR THE SALE OF SPIRITUOUS LIQUORS.

Monday, January 1, 1844.—A cold, blustering rainstorm ushered in the new year.

At sunrise, Thomas Miller, James Leach, James Bridges, and John Frodsham were brought before me by the police, charged with disorderly conduct. Fined Miller $5: the others were discharged.

A large party took a new year's supper at my house, and had music and dancing till morning. I was in my private room with my family, Elder John Taylor and other friends.

New Year's at the Mansion.

Tuesday 2.—Two p. m., Hyrum Dayton was brought before Mayor's court for disorderly conduct in resisting and abusing the police: fined $25 and costs. His son, Lysander Dayton, for the same offense, was sentenced to ten days' hard labor, on the public streets; and subsequently, for contempt of court, ten days more.

Snow one inch deep.

I here insert Mr. Calhoun's answer to my letter of inquiry, dated November 4, 1843:—

Letter: John C. Calhoun to Joseph Smith—Defining What Former's Policy would be Towards the Saints if Elected President.

FORT HILL, December 2, 1843.

Sir:—You ask me what would be my rule of action relative the Mormons or Latter-day Saints, should I be elected President; to which I answer, that if I should be elected, I would strive to administer the government according to the Constitution and the laws of the union; and that as they make no distinction between citizens of different religious creeds I should make none. As far as it depends on the Executive department, all should have the full benefit of both, and none should be exempt from their operation

But as you refer to the case of Missouri, candor compels me to repeat what I said to you at Washington, that, according to my views, the case does not come within the jurisdiction of the Federal Government, which is one of limited and specific powers.

With respect, I am, &c,, &c.,

J. C. CALHOUN.

MR. JOSEPH SMITH.

To which I wrote the following reply:—

Letter: Joseph Smith to John C. Calhoun—The Latter's Policy Towards the Latter-day Saints, if Elected President of the U. S. Considered.

NAUVOO, ILLINOIS, January 2, 1844.

Sir:—Your reply to my letter of last November, concerning your rule of action towards the Latter-day Saints, if elected President, is at hand; and that you and your friends of the same opinion relative to the matter in question may not be disappointed as to me or my mind upon so grave a subject, permit me, as a law-abiding man, as a well-wisher to the perpetuity of constitutional rights and liberty, and as a friend to the free worship of Almighty God by all, according to the dictates of every person's own conscience, to say that *I am surprised* that a man or men in the highest stations of public life should have made up such a fragile "view" of a case, than which there is not one on the face of the globe fraught with so much consequence to the happiness of men in this world or the world to come.

To be sure, the first paragraph of your letter appears very complacent and fair on a white sheet of paper. And who, that is ambitious for greatness and power, would not have said the same thing? Your oath binds you to support the Constitution and laws; and as all creeds and religions are alike tolerated, they must, of course, all be justified or condemned according to merit or demerit. But why—tell me why are all the principal men held up for public stations *so cautiously careful* not to publish to the world that they will *judge a righteous judgment, law or no law?* for laws and opinions, like the vanes of steeples, change with the wind.

One Congress passes a law, another repeals it; and one statesman says that the Constitution means this, and another that; and who does not know that all may be wrong? the opinion and pledge, therefore, in the first paragraph of your reply to my question, like the forced steam from the engine of a steam-boat, makes the show of a bright cloud at first; but when it comes in contact with a purer atmosphere, dissolves to common air again.

Your second pargraph leaves you naked before yourself, like a likeness in a mirror, when you say, that according to your *view*, the Federal Government is "one of limited and specific powers," and has no jurisdiction in the case of the "Mormons." So then a State can at any time expel any portion of her citizens with impunity: and, in the language of Mr. Van Buren, frosted over with your gracious "*views of the case*," though the cause is ever so just, Goverment can do nothing for them, because it has no power.

Go on, then, Missouri, after another set of inhabitants (as the Latter-day Saints did,) have entered some two or three hundred thousand dollars' worth of land, and made extensive improvements thereon; go on, then, I say; banish the occupants or owners, or kill them, as the mobbers did many of the Latter-day Saints, and take their land and property as spoil; and let the Legislature, as in the case of the "Mormons," appropriate a couple of hundred thousand dollars to pay the mob for doing that job; for the renowned Senator from South Carolina, Mr. J. C. Calhoun, says the powers of the Federal Government are so *specific and limited that it has no jurisdiction of the case!* O ye people who groan under the oppression of tyrants!—ye exiled Poles, who have felt the iron hand of Russian grasp!—ye poor and unfortunate among all nations! come to the asylum of the oppressed; buy ye lands of the General Government; pay in your money to the treasury to strenghten the army and the navy; worship God according to the dictates of your own consciences; pay in your taxes to support the great heads of a glorious nation: but remember a "*sovereign State*" is so much more powerful than the United States, the parent Government, that it can exile you at pleasure, mob you with impunity, confiscate your lands and property, have the Legislature sanction it,—yea, even murder you as an edict of an emperor, *and it does no wrong;* for the noble Senator of South Carolina says the power of the federal Government is *so limited and specific, that it has no jurisdiction of the case!* What think ye of *imperium in imperio?*

Ye spirits of the blessed of all ages, hark! Ye shades of departed statesmen, listen! Abraham, Moses, Homer, Socrates, Solon, Solomon, and all that ever thought of right and wrong, look down from your exaltations, if you have any; for it is said, "In the midst of counselors there *is safety;*" and when you have learned that fifteen thousand innocent citizens, after having purchased their lands of the United States and paid for them, were expelled from a "sovereign State," by order of the Governor, at the point of the bayonet, their arms taken from them by the same authority, and their right of migration into said State denied, under pain of imprisonment, whipping, robbing, mobbing, and even death, and no justice or recompense allowed; and, from the Legislature with the Governor at the head, down to the Justice of the Peace, with a bottle of whisky in one hand and a bowie-knife in the other, hear them all declare that there is no justice for a "Mormon" in that State; and judge ye a righteous judgment, and tell me when the virtue of the States was stolen, where the honor of the General Government lies hid, and what clothes a senator with wisdom. O nullifying Carolina! O little tempestuous Rhode Island! Would it not be well for the great men of the nation to read the fable of the *partial judge*; and when part of the free citizens of a State had been expelled contrary to the Constitution, mobbed, robbed, plundered, and many murdered, instead of searching into the course taken with Joanna Southcott, Ann Lee, the French Prophets, the Quakers of New England, and rebellious negroes in the slave States, to hear both sides and then judge, rather than have the mortification to say, "Oh, it is *my* bull that has killed *your* ox! That alters the case! I must inquire into it; *and if, and if*—!

If the General Government has no power to reinstate expelled citizens to their rights, there is a monstrous hypocrite fed and fostered from the hard earnings of the people! A real "bull beggar" upheld by sycophants. And although you may wink to the priests to stigmatize, wheedle the drunkards to swear, and raise the hue-and-cry of—"Impostor! false prophet! G— d—n old Joe Smith!" yet remember, if the Latter-day Saints are not restored to all their rights and paid for all their losses, according to the known rules of justice and judgment, reciprocation and common honesty among men, that God will come out of His hiding place, and vex this nation with a sore vexation: yea, the consuming wrath of an offended God shall smoke through the nation with as much distress and woe as independence has blazed through with pleasure and delight. Where is the strength of Government? Where is the patriotism of a Washington, a Warren, and Adams? And where is a spark from the watch-fire of '76, by which one candle might be lit that would glimmer upon the confines of Democracy? Well may it be said that one man is not a state, nor one state the nation.

In the days of General Jackson, when France refused the first instalment for spoliations, there was power, force, and honor enough to resent injustice and insult, and the money came: and shall Missouri, filled with negro-drivers and white men stealers, go "unwhipped of justice" for tenfold greater sins than France? No! verily, no! While

I have powers of body and mind—while water runs and grass grows—while virtue is lovely and vice hateful; and while a stone points out a sacred spot where a fragment of American liberty once was, I or my posterity will plead the cause of injured innocence, until Missouri makes atonement for all her sins, or sinks disgraced, degraded, and damned to hell, "where the worm dieth not, and the fire is not quenched."

Why, sir, the powers not delegated to the United States and the States belong to the people, and Congress sent to do the people's business have all power; and shall fifteen thousand citizens groan in exile? O vain men! will ye not, if ye do not restore them to their rights and $2,000,000 worth of property, relinquish to them, (the Latter-day Saints,) as a body, their portion of power that belongs to them according to the Constitution? Power has its convenience as well as inconvenience. "The world was not made for Cæsar alone, but for Cassius too."

I will give you a parable. A certain lord had a vineyard in a goodly land, which men labored in at their pleasure. A few meek men also went and purchased with money from some of these chief men that labored at pleasure a portion of land in the vineyard, at a very remote part of it, and began to improve it, and to eat and drink the fruit thereof,—when some vile persons, who regarded not man, neither feared the lord of the vineyard, rose up suddenly and robbed these meek men, and drove them from their possessions, killing many.

This barbarous act made no small stir among the men in the vineyard; and all that portion who were attached to that part of the vineyard where the men were robbed rose up in grand council, with their chief man, who had firstly ordered the deed to be done, and made a covenant not to pay for the cruel deed, but to keep the spoil, and never let those meek men set their feet on that soil again, neither recompense them for it.

Now, these meek men, in their distress, wisely sought redress of those wicked men in every possible manner, and got none. They then supplicated the chief men, who held the vineyard at pleasure, and who had the power to sell and defend it, for redress and redemption; and those men, loving the fame and favor of the multitude more than the glory of the lord of the vineyard, answered—"Your cause is just, but we can do nothing for you, because we have no power."

Now, when the lord of the vineyard saw that virtue and innocence were not regarded, and his vineyard occupied by wicked men, he sent men and took the possession of it to himself, and destroyed those unfaithful servants, and appointed them their portion among hypocrites.

And let me say that all men who say that Congress has no power to restore and defend the rights of her citizens have not the love of the truth abiding in them. Congress has power to protect the nation against foreign invasion and internal broil; and whenever that body passes an act to maintain right with any power, or to restore right to any portion of her citizens, it is the *supreme law of the land*; and should a State re fuse submission, that State is guilty of *insurrection or rebellion*, and the President has as much power to repel it as Washington had to march against the "whisky boys at Pittsburg," or General Jackson had to send an armed force to suppress the rebellion of South Carolina.

To close, I would admonish you, before you let your "*candor compel*" you again to write upon a subject great as the salvation of man, consequential as the life of the Savior, broad as the principles of eternal truth, and valuable as the jewels of eternity, to read in the 8th section and 1st article of the Costitution of the United States, the *first*, *fourteenth* and *seventeenth* "specific" and not very "limited powers" of the Federal Government, what can be done to protect the lives, property, and rights of a virtuous people, when the administrators of the law and law-makers are unbought by bribes, uncorrupted by patronage, untempted by gold, unawed by fear, and uncontaminated tangling alliances—even like Cæsar's wife, not only *unspotted, but unsuspected!* And God, who cooled the heat of a Nebuchadnezzar's furnace or shut the mouths of lions for the honor of a Daniel, will raise your mind above the narrow notion that the General Government has no power, to the sublime idea that Congress, with the President as Executor, is as almighty in its sphere as Jehovah is in his.

With great respect, I have the honour to be

Your obedient servant,

JOSEPH SMITH.

HON. ("MR") J. C. CALHOUN,
Fort Hill, S. C.

Release of Pugmire and Cartwright from Prison, England.

Jonathan Pugmire, Senior, and Thomas Cartwright discharged by Judge Whitehead, at Chester, England. The judge would not allow the costs of prosecution or witnesses to be paid by the Crown. It was very evident that the Church of England ministers were at the bottom of the machinations, and were sorely discomfited at the result. I insert the statement of the unfortunate occurrence given by Jonathan Pugmire, Junior:—

Cartwright Drowning—Accident at a Baptism in England.

Thomas Cartwright was baptized November 6, 1843, unknown to his wife, by Elder Jonathan Pugmire, Senior; but she had mistrusted he had gone to the water, and went to Pugmire's house the same evening, and inquired where Tom was, (meaning her husband). Mrs. Pugmire answered she did not know.

After this, Mrs. Cartwright went out and met them returning from the waters of baptism, and shouted—"Damn you, I'll dip ye!" and expressing her determination to have revenge on Pugmire's family, she used a great deal of very bad language.

Some of the neighbors (not belonging to the Church) advised her not to speak too much against the Latter-day Saints, as she might yet become convinced of the truth of their doctrines and be baptized herself. She replied, "I hope to God, if ever I am such a fool, that I'll be drowned in the attempt!"

A short time afterwards, in consequence of her husband talking to her about the truths of the Gospel, she consented to go to Pugmire's house and hear for herself.

After attending a few times, she told her husband she had a dream, in which she saw it was a fearful thing to fall in the hands of the living God, and requested to be baptized.

Mrs. Pugmire talked with her, reminding her of her harsh expression. She confessed all, and said, "I am very sorry; and as my conduct is known to all this neighborhood, I do not wish to have my baptism public, but to have it done privately; and I wish no female to accompany me to the water but you."

On the night of her baptism (November 23, 1843), she was conducted to the water by her husband and Elder Pugmire, witnessed by Mrs. Pugmire and James Moore. Previous to this time, Elder Pugmire had baptized eight or ten persons in the same place.

On arriving at the water, they found the creek had overflowed its banks, in consequence of a heavy rain which had fallen that day. Elder Pugmire examined its banks, and concluded he could attend to the ordinance without going into the regular bed of the creek.

This was done; but on raising Mrs. Cartwright, and as they were walking out, they both went under the water.

It was afterwards discovered that the water had undermined the bank, and it gave way under their feet. Meantime, Thomas Cartwright leaped into the creek and seized hold of his wife's petticoat; but the water carried her off, and left the garment in his hand.

James Moore got hold of Elder Pugmire by the hair of his head, Mrs. Pugmire holding Moore's hand, and thus they dragged him out.

Moore then ran to the village to give the alarm. On his return, he found Cartwright about one hundred yards from where he leaped in, with his head above water, holding on to the stump of a tree. He said he could not have remained in that situation one minute longer.

George Knowlen swam the stream and got him out; but his wife was not found until the day following, when she was found about two hundred yards from where the accident occurred, standing upon her feet, with her head above water, the stream having fallen about two feet.

On Pugmire reaching home, a Church of England minister had him arrested and dragged from his family the same evening, and kept in custody of a constable until a coroner's inquest was held on the body of the deceased.

After she was buried, Cartwright was arrested, and both were sent to Chester jail, to wait their trial befor the judge of assize. They were in confinement six weeks and three days before their trial came on.

The judge (Whitehead) remarked to the jury that baptism was an ordinance of our religion, and that it was a mere accident which had occurred. He advised the jurymen to be very careful how they examined the case before them—that it was an ordinance instituted by God (at that moment the Lord spoke by the voice of thunder, which shook the court house,) and advised the prisoners to be very careful in the future to select a proper place for the performance of that rite. They were then set free.

During their imprisonment, Pugmire had a vision, in which he was informed that they would be liberated; and he told Cartwright to be of good cheer, for they certainly would be acquitted.

Wednesday 3.—At home.

At noon, met with the City Council. The following is a copy of the minutes:—

Difficulty of Wm. Law et al. With the Police.

SPECIAL CITY COUNCIL, Jan. 3, 1844, 12 o'clock.

Names of members called. All present.

The mayor directed the marshal to notify William Law and John Snyder that the council was in session, and informed the council that William Law had said to his brother Hyrum that the police had been sworn by him (the Prophet) secretly to put Law out of the way. [The Prophet said] "I have had no private conversation with any of the police but the high policeman, Jonathan Dunham, and that was to request him to have especial care of my personal safety, as I apprehended attempts to kidnap me by the Missourians." He called on the policemen to say if they had received any private oath from him, when they all said, "No."

Councilor Hyrum Smith said that William Law told him the police had sworn him (Law) to keep the secret, which was that he was to be put out of the way in three months.

The mayor said he wished policemen to understand forever that all he wanted was that they should execute the ordinances of the city and his orders according to law.

Several of the police called for the individual to be named who made the statement to William Law.

The mayor said he thought proper that William Law should come and make his statement to the council on oath.

The mayor then said to the police, "If you see a man stealing, and you have told him three times to stand, and warned him that he is a dead man if he does not stand, and he runs shoot off his legs. The design of the office of the police is to stop thieving; but an enemy should not be harmed until he draws weapons upon you."

William Law came in, and was sworn to tell the whole truth touching the case before the council.

William Law said he had been informed that some of the policemen had had another oath administered besides the one administered to them publicly: that one of them said there was a Judas in General Smith's cabinet,—one who stood next to him; and he must be taken care of, and that he must not be allowed to go into the world, but must be taken care of; and he was not only a dough-head and a traitor like Judas, but an assassin like Brutus: that the idea had been advanced that the scriptures support such a doctrine.

Alderman Harris. Who is the person? and who told you?

Law. I am under obligations *not* to tell.

Alderman Harris. That is immaterial. You are bound to disclose the whole truth here by virtue of your oath.

Law. I am afraid to tell. One oath is as good as another.

The Mayor said he would protect him. He was bound to tell.

Law. Eli Norton told me.

Alderman Harris. Was Eli Norton of the police?

Law. No; but he got his information from Daniel Carn, who is a policeman.

The marshal was sent to bring Eli Norton.

The mayor said to the police—"On conditions I have had no private conversation with any of you, rise up and change the breech of your gun upwards," when all arose and changed the positions of their guns as indicated.

Counselor Hyrum Smith considered the matter very alarming when he heard it. He referred to Dr. Sampson Avard's and John Carl's treachery and false swearing in Missouri, and rehearsed what was said by the mayor to the police in the former council.

The mayor said, "The reason why I made the remarks I did was on account of the reports brought from Missouri jail by O. P. Rockwell, that my enemies were determined to get me into their power and take my life, and thereby thought they would accomplish the overthrow of 'Mormonism.' And to enable them to effect this, they had secured the services of some of my most confidential friends, whom I did not suspect, and who were living in Nauvoo, to deliver me into their hands so that their religious organizations upon their own principles might stand; for they feared that 'Mormonism' would destroy their present religious creeds, organizations, and orthodox systems. They did not design to try me, but hang me, or take my life anyhow: that they had a man in our midst who would fix me out, if they could not get me into their power without." He then referred to his remarks at the previous council.

Minutes of last council being called for, were then read.

Eli Norton sworn.

Question by the Mayor Did Carn say I had administered a private oath?

Norton. No. Did not say much about Law. Did not say you had ever administered any private oath. Carn never intimated to me that Law must be put out of the way. Did not call William Law's name, nor any other name. Did not say the policemen had received a private oath. Understood Carn to say they had received private instructions; and if a man could not keep a secret, he was not worthy of a place in the Church. Did not say the mayor had given him a private charge. Did not tell where the danger was expected to come from. Told me there were dough-heads about. Did not say the dough-heads were in danger, but the mayor was in danger from the dough-heads.

Question by William Law: Did you not understand from Brother Carn that he was suspicious of some person near Joseph being a dough-head, and that that person was myself?

Answer: He mentioned a dough-head as being very near Joseph, and he guessed you was the man; and I thought it might be that Daniteism was not done with.

Mayor: Tell what you know that made you so alarmed about Brcther Law.

Answer: There was no chain to the conversation; but I drew the inference that Brother Law was the dough-head from Carn's conversation; but Carn did not name Law.

Daniel Carn was sworn: Said, "I told Brother Norton that certain men had been counseled by the Prophet to invest their means in publishing the new translation of the Bible; and they instead of obeying that counsel, had used their property for the purpose of building a steam-mill and raising a hundred acres of hemp; and the Lord had not blessed them in the business, but sunk their hemp in the Mississippi river. I told him it was my opinion that Brother Law was the dough-head referred to.

I have had no secret conversation whatever with the mayor, and never received any charge except the one, with the rest of the police, before the city council.

The mayor suggested the propriety, since Rockwell and others are clear, and we have the promise of protection from the governor; and as the police are now well organized, that they put up their guns and that the council pass such an order. The Danite system alluded to by Norton never had any existence. It was a term made use of by some of the brethren in Far West, and grew out of an expression I made use of when the brethren were preparing to defend themselves from the Missouri mob, in reference to the stealing of Macaiah's images (Judges chapter 18)—If the enemy comes, the Danites will be after them, meaning the brethren in self-defense.

The mayor instructed the police to lay up their arms till further orders.

At half past four p. m. council adjourned.

Reconciliation of the Prophet and Wm. Law.

The council spent nearly the whole day in investigating the subject and examining these two witnesses. The police were all sworn and cross-examined by William Law and the aldermen, and the result showed nothing but imagination, having grown out of the surmises of Daniel Carn; upon which Law became satisfied, shook hands with me, declaring he did not believe a word of the story, and said he would stand by me to the death, and called the whole council and the police to witness his declaration.

Thursday 4.—At home.

Repartee of Joseph and Emma Smith

I took dinner in the north room, and was remarking to Brother Phelps what a kind, provident wife I had,—that when I wanted a little bread and milk, she would load the table with so many good things, it would destroy my appetite. At this moment Emma came in, while Phelps, in continuation of the conversation said, "You must do as Bonaparte did—have a little table, just large enough for the victuals you want yourself." Mrs. Smith replied, "Mr. Smith is a bigger man than Bonaparte: he can never eat without his friends." I remarked, "That is the wisest thing I ever heard you say."

Friday 5.—At home.

Last night I dreamed I saw two serpents swallowing each other tail foremost.

Another tempest in a tea-pot, or big fuss about nothing at all. In consequence of the night being severely cold, some persons built a fire on the bank of the river, nearly opposit William Marks' house. He then became afraid, and concluded he must either be the Brutus or the dough-head, and lay awake all night, thinking the police had built the fire to kill him by! In the morning he called on me, reported the circumstances and expressed his fears, when another session of inquiry was held by the city council at his request, and the police sworn and questioned. The following is a synopsis of the minutes:—

Alarm of William Marks.

Special Session o the City Council—Fears of Wm. Law and Marks.

Friday, January 5, 1844, 11 a. m.

Names of members called.

Prayer by O. Spencer.

Minutes of the last two councils read and approved.

Object of the council stated by the mayor, similar to the last council as William Law and William Marks had considered themselves in danger. When he heard the report he was unwilling to believe anything about it, from the course the thing took in the last council; but, for the sake of others, he had called this council.

As Leonard Soby was going home night before last, he was hailed by a supposed policeman with a gun, which frightened him. Soby says that a policeman had told him that Marks and Law must not cross his tracks; that Warren Smith said at another time that William Marks and William Law were enemies to Joseph.

I have never thought even to dream of doing anything against the peace of the inhabitants of this city. Did not know I had any enemies in this city: have stayed at home and heard but little: did not know that there was so much evil surmising among the people. My long forbearance to my enemies ought to be sufficient testimony of my peaceful disposition toward all men. It occurred to my mind that it was not fear, but got up for effect; but I do not know it. I want the council to investigate this matter.

William Marks sworn. Testified that on Monday evening Brother Soby came up and said, "Are you aware of the danger you are in?" Marks replied, "No."

Soby: "Your life is threatened; a policeman stopped me in the dark last night as I was going home; I was alarmed. I supposed the threats were from that policeman, but I was mistaken. Another policeman, Warren Smith, said last Sunday that Joseph had enemies—that Law and myself were Joseph's enemies, and if they came in his way they might be popped over. A fire was kindled in the street near my house, and I thought I was watched. Francis Higbee told me, and a man in the east part of the town told me; and a man came from the other side of the river and told the story to that man, as he said. Yesterday morning, Hyrum Smith, Wilson Law, and William Law met in the street, and I told the story as before related.

Mayor. Did ever anybody tell you I directed you to be watched?

William Marks. No.

Marshal went for Francis M. Higbee and George W. Crouse.

Leonard Soby sworn. On Sunday, 31st December last, I met Warren Smith in Crouse's store; asked him if he knew who the Brutus was. Warren Smith said he believed William Law was one, and Marks another; they had better not come in his way. Did not say he would shoot them, or endanger their life in any way. Did not know whether there were any private instructions, or not. Believed Brother Marks was in danger. Did not think Marks in any danger from Joseph. Thought Warren Smith was under a wrong impression with regard to Marks. Warren Smith said, "He, Marks, had better not cross my path when I am on duty." I gathered the idea there was something wrong with Brother Warren Smith. Do not recollect any person present.

Mayor. Did Warren Smith or any other policeman give you to understand that I had authorized him to believe there was any difficulty between me and Brother Law or Marks?

Soby. No. He did not think Warren Smith would transcend his official duties towards Law or Marks. Felt at the time Marks and Law were in danger. Did not think they were in danger, if they did not rise up against the authorities.

Did not say he had any instruction. Said to Mr. Marks, "You have enemies." My impression was that somebody had been to Joseph to make a bad impression on his mind. Warren Smith did mention brother Marks' name, I think.

Thirty policemen, all who were present, sworn. Testified that General Smith had never given them any private instruction concerning the case before the council.

Warren Smith said Soby asked his opinion who was the Judas. I said, from rumor, I would suspect William Law. Does not believe he mentioned Marks' name. My opinion was founded on rumor. Brother Isaac Hill said Brother Law was in a bad situation—was kicking, and if he did not mind, he wonld go over the board. If he had his property in available means and was away, he would feel better. Have heard it talked of that Brother Law was not going to stand. Hil did not tell what he was kicking at. I understand a Brutus to mean a treacherous man.

George W. Crouse sworn. Does not recollect any conversation between Warren Smith and Leonard Soby, at his store, relative to the case in question. Had a discussion about the duties of policemen.

Councilor John Taylor said it was customary in all cities for policemen to go armed in time of danger.

Councilor Orson Hyde confirmed Councilor Taylor's observation.

Councilor Hyrum Smith spoke. Told a story of the old Dutchman and the ox. Soby makes me think of an old Dutchman that had an ox—the first animal he ever owned in his life, and he broke him to ride; then he filled a sack with rocks and laid it on the ox's back, and got on himself, and told his son to hide by the roadside, and when he came along, to jump out and hollo boo, as he wanted to know how well his ox was broke. The son did accordingly. The ox was frightened, and threw the old man off. "Father," said the son, "I did as you told me." "Yes," said the old man; "but you made too big a boo."

Francis M. Higbee sworn. Have received the impression from rumor that Mr. Law, Mr. Marks and probably one or two others, could not subscribe to all things in the Church, and there were some private matters that might make trouble. Don't know of anyone being in danger. No one told me the police had received any private instruction. Could not tell who he had received these rumors from.

William Law spoke. Said he had no personal feeling against Warren Smith. Some two or three years since, he sued Brother Warren, and stayed the suit, &c. Was suspicious Warren Smith's feelings might have risen from that source.

Councilor Hyrum Smith, Daniel Carn, Warren Smith, Leonard Soby, and William Marks addressed the council.

The mayor spoke. Said no one had come to him with tales about William Marks, to prejudice his mind against him. Was totally ignorant of it. I said to Brother Dunham,—If any man approach my house with arms, or attempted to disturb my house, I wanted the police to take care of that individual, whoever he might be. I repeat the instruction, and am perfectly astonished that Brother Law, Marks, or any other man should entertain such an idea [that they were in danger.] I live above suspicion on this subject from any source whatever. I never could bring my feelings to take revenge on my enemies. The City Council did not concoct the idea of having a police. The several wards petitioned for a police to protect them against invasion—wanted citizens to pass the streets at any time of night without molestation; but if the police see a man breaking in to my house or barn, or anybody's house or barn, tell him to stand, and inquire his business. I think it possible that some person has been practicing fraud on Brother Soby and the police and upon individuals, as the police, according to their instructions, had laid away their guns.

Don't guard Brother Marks' house any more. Men must not pervert the power entrusted to them like ex-Governor Boggs, whose executive oath required him to protect the Saints in Missouri, but perverted his power to enforce their extermination from the State.

Brother Soby does not know that it was a policeman who stopped him. Brother Marks does not know that the police kindled the fire before his house. Let the police have canes. Let the citizens pass and repass at all times of night.

Councilor Taylor spoke. Thought the conclusion drawn up by Brother Soby, that Joseph or somebody was going to get revenged by setting the guard to kill Marks, was the most contemptible that could be imagined; and if Brother Soby had had the respect for Brother Joseph he ought to have had, he could not have formed such a conclusion.

Mayor referred to Francis Higbee's testimony. Thought Francis Higbee had better stay at home and hold his tongue, lest rumor turn upon him and disclose some private matters which he would prefer kept hid. Did not believe there was any rumor of the kind afloat, or he could have told some of the names of his informants. Thought the young men of the city had better withdraw from his society, and let him stand on his own merits. I by no means consider him the standard of the city.

There has been a system of corruption and debauchery, which these rumors have grown out of; and the individuals who are the authors of them are those who do not want a police: they want to prowl in the streets at pleasure without interruption.

Alderman Orson Spencer spoke, approving the conduct of the police.

General Wilson Law said, "I am Joseph's friend: he has no better friend in the world: I am ready to lay down my life for him;" and upon that the mayor and General Wilson Law shook hands.

The ordinance concerning the forty policemen read twice.

The mayor objected to assuming the entire disposal of the police beyond the definition of the ordinance.

Alderman George A. Smith said he could sleep with a fire near his house, if there were some of the police warming themselves by it; and he believed any honest man could do the same.

The police received the thanks of the council.

The cross-examination and speeches are generally omitted.

Council adjourned at dusk for the want of candles.

Reflections of the Prophet as to Traitors in High Places

What can be the matter with these men? Is it that the wicked flee when no man pursueth, that hit pigeons always flutter, that drowning men catch at straws, or that Presidents Law and Marks are absolutely traitors to the Church, that my remarks should produce such an excitement in their minds. Can it be possible that the traitor whom Porter Rockwell reports to me as being in correspondence with my Missouri enemies, is one of my quorum? The people in the town were astonished, almost every man saying to his neighbor, "Is it possible that Brother Law or Brother Marks is a traitor, and would deliver Brother Joseph into the hands of his enemies in Missouri?" If not, what can be the meaning of all this? "The righteous are as bold as a lion."

A number of gentlemen boarding at my house conversed with me on national affairs. I sent for Brother Phelps, who came and read my letter to John C. Calhoun, with which they were highly edified.

Elder Brigham Young went to La Harpe for the purpose of instructing the Saints.

Commenced snowing a little before sunset, and continued all night.

Saturday, 6.—Snow about four inches deep. I rode out with Emma in a sleigh.

The Bishops and lesser Priesthood met at Henry W. Miller's hall.

Sunday, 7.—At home in the morning. In the afternoon, rode out to my farm, and preached in Brother Cornelius P. Lott's house.

The Twelve Apostles attended meetings and preached in different parts of the city.

At six p. m. attended prayer-meeting with the quorum in the assembly room. Law and Marks absent.

Monday, 8.—At home in the morning.

At eleven went to my office to investigate a difficulty between John D. Parker and his wife. After laboring with them about two hours, brought about a reconciliation.

I also had an interview with William Law in the streets.

My uncle, John Smith, from Macedonia, visited me.

Amos Fielding arrived from Liverpool.

Tuesday, 9.—At home.

I insert the following from the *Neighbor*, as a specimen of the respect which the Carthage mob has for law or justice:

DISGRACEFUL AFFAIR AT CARTHAGE—OFFICERS RESISTED.

On Tuesday last Horace S. Eldredge, one of our county officers, went to Carthage for the purpose of arresting Milton Cook, on the charge of bastardy, and bringing him before R. D. Foster, justice of the peace of this county, before whom affidavit had been made to that effect. He found the accused in Bartlett's grocery, (Carthage,) and arrested him.

Cook had a gun that he said he had loaded for the purpose, and would make a hole through the constable if he molested him, and swore he would not be taken.

Harmon T. Wilson and others then stepped forward to his assistance, and said that they had sworn to stand by him, and that he should not go. He [Eldredge] then returned with his process to the justice of the peace, and told him what had occurred.

Mr. R. D. Foster then summoned eleven men to go along with the constable and assist him in bringing the delinquent. They went out and drove to the grocery, where they expected to find him; but he was not there. They then went out for a short time, without making known their business, when they saw an armed force gathering.

They shortly afterwards returned to the grocery, and saw him there where he swore he would not be taken. There was also an armed force standing in the door, who also swore he should not be taken.

The officer having the process, Mr. Markham and Mr. Eagle stepped forward and wished to reason the case with them, the officer at the same time demanding their assistance. They were met with an armed force of about twenty, four of whom stood in the doorway, two with guns and bayonets, and two with pistols.

The two having the bayonets charged directly at Mr. Markham, and swore they would run him through, and rushed upon him with their bayonets. He, however, warded off their blows with his arm, and the bayonet glanced and struck Mr. John Eagle in the abdomen. The bayonet went through his clothes, scratched his body, and glanced off without doing any further injury, other than giving him a slight cut in the hand.

Those having the pistols then attempted to shoot, when Mr.Markham seized the hand of one of them that held the pistol, and prevented him from firing. The other put his pistol to Mr. Eagle's breast, and swore he would shoot him.

The company at that time used all their force, and crowded the officers and their assistants some distance back, and carried off and secreted the prisoner. The officer and his company then went to the tavern to stay all night.

The next morning, about eight o'clock, the constable and Mr. Markham went to the grocery and searched, and Bartlett said that he was gone—that he had taken his horse and gone out of town.

They then saw a company of men gathered at Harmon T. Wilson's store, armed with guns, bayonets, pistols, clubs, and other missiles. Mr. Markham went to the store, where he found the constable and the prisoner. There were fifty in and about the store, all armed.

Mr. Eldredge then told the company present who he was, and demanded all in the house to assist in taking the prisoner, and then seized him. As soon as he laid hold of the prisoner, about six or eight men laid hold of the constable. Mr. Markham assisted the constable. When Mr. Markham had nearly succeeded in liberating the constable, a man who was called Dr. Morrison, drew his pistol and shot at Markham. The ball missed Markham, but came so near Mr. Coltrin's head, who was one of the assistants, as to graze his forehead.

As there were only four of the assistants in the store, they were overpowered by superior numbers, and the prisoner was taken away from them.

They saw that it would be impossible to take him without bloodshed, and consequently returned home. The parties engaged in this affray swore that, regardless of all law, they would defend the prisoner, and he should not be taken.

We have received the above particulars from Mr. Markham, and can consequently rely upon the correctness of the statement, as he is one of the parties mentioned. The woman who was *enciente*, who made the affidavit, is not in the Church, neither is Mr. Eagle—the person who was struck with the bayonet. Mr. Eagle has gone to the governor to make complaint.

We think that it is high time that prompt measures be taken to put a stop to such abominable outrages. If officers can be insulted in this manner and the law violated with impunity, we think that we shall speedily slide back into the barbarous ages.

Some of our mobocratic friends who assembled at a mobocratic meeting some time ago in Carthage, were considerably chagrined at our terming them mobocrats. We wonder whether they now believe that they are, or not? If such proceedings as those are cherished, fare well to our Republican institutions! farewell to law, equity, and justice! and farewell to all those sacred ties that bind men to their fellowmen!

We would here ask where the sheriff was. Why was he not applied to? We merely ask for information. We don't know that he was present or applied to. If he was, it certainly was his duty to see the law magnified.

Wednesday 10.—At home.

John Smith, Uncle of the Prophet, Ordained a Patriarch.

Ordained Uncle John Smith a patriarch. Enjoyed myself well in an interview with the brethren, and concluded to take a ride part way with my uncle on his return to Macedonia.

In consequence of a visit from some gentlemen from Carthage, I called the City Council together at seven p. m. I copy the minutes:—

Special Session of City Council; Complaints of Carthage Citizens Considered.

January 10, 1844, 7. p. m.

Names of members called.

The mayor said:—"Messrs. Backman, Hamilton, and Sherman, lawyers from Carthage, have called on me and told me that the occasion of the excitement at Carthage and the resistance to the law, in the case of the arrest of Cook, was the late ordinance of this council to prevent unlawful search or seizure of person or property by foreign process in the city of Nauvoo; that they considered said ordinance was designed to hinder the execution of the statutes of Illinois within this city; consequently, they, the old citizens, felt disposed to stop the execution of processes issuing from the city precincts. They also raised objections against the process by Justice Foster for the apprehension of Cook, because it was made returnable to him alone, whereas they said the statute required it to be made returnable before himself or some other justice.

I explained to them the nature and reason of the ordinance—that was to prevent kidnapping under the pretense of law or process, and to facilitate the apprehension of thieves, &c., in this city, by throwing all foreign processes into the hands of the marshal, who would be most likely to know the hiding-places of fugitives from justice, who might secrete themselves in our city; and said that if any wrong impression had gone abroad with regard to the motives of the council in passing said ordinance, I would call the council immediately, that they might have the opportunity of giving any explanation necessary, so that the public might understand the ordinance in its true light. I have therefore called the council accordingly. I also referred the lawyers from Carthage to the statute which requires all processes issued in cases of bastardy to be returnable alone to the justice issuing the same, which they doubted until I showed them the law, when they looked a little crest-fallen and foolish."

After deliberation, an additional section relative to the foregoing ordinance was read three times, and passed, by way of amendment:—

"Secttion 3. Be it ordained by the city council of the city of Nauvoo, that nothing in the foreging ordinance shall be so construed as to prevent, hinder, or thwart the designs of justice, or to retard the civil officers of the state or county in the discharge of their official duties, but to aid and assist them within the limits of this city.

"Passed January 10, 1844.

"JOSEPH SMITH, Mayor.

"WILLARD RICHARDS, Recorder."

Council adjourned.

Wrote a letter to Esquire Backman to inform him what the City Council had done.

Complaints of F. M. Higbee against the Prophet.

I received a long equivocating letter from Francis M. Higbee, charging me with having slandered his character and demanding a public trial before the Church. It contains no denial of the charges which he accuses me of having spoken against him, but is full of bombast.

Thursday 11.—At home.

Rode out, ten a. m., and returned at half-past one p. m.

This morning William Jones, who had stayed all night at Wilson's Tavern in Carthage, was arrested without process by Colonel Levi Williams and his company, who kept him in custody until noon without rations.

The Twelve Apostles gave an invitation to the Saints in Nauvoo to cut and draw for me seventy-five or one hundred cords of wood on the 15th and 16th instant.

Friday 12.—Thaw: snow nearly gone.

Conference in Michigan

A conference was held in Brownstown, Main county, Michigan. Elder Mephibosheth Sirrine, president; and Gehiel Savage, clerk. Nine branches were represented, containing 6 elders, 9 priests, 7 teachers, 1 deacon, 136 members, and 45 scattered members; one hundred members having removed from that state to Nauvoo since the conference in July last.

Saturday 13.—At home in the morning.

At ten o'clock, attended City Council, where a bill for an ordinance concerning the recording of deeds in this city was taken under consideration, and read twice. It elicited much discussion.

The ten policemen who were not present at the meeting of the City Council on the 5th instant were sworn in the matter of William Law and William Marks, and testified they had received no private instructions whatever from me.

A discussion took place on the subject of granting licenses for the sale of spirits.

I signed resolutions passed at a court martial held this morning.

Stephen M. Farnsworth was chosen president of the priests' quorum, and William Carmichael and William Box his counselors.

Sunday 14.—At home all day.

A prayer-meeting was held at the assembly room. I did not attend.

Warm and rainy towards evening.

The Twelve Apostles preached at private houses in various parts of the city.

A branch of the Church was organized in New Orleans, with 34 members. T. B. Jackaway, president, and E. L. Brown, clerk.

Monday 15.—At home. Wrote to Sister Maria L. Campbell, Elmira, N. Y.

A Wood Bee.

At nine, a. m., teams began to arrive with wood, according to the appointment of the Twelve Apostles, there being about 200 of the brethren chopping in the woods, and from thirty to forty teams engaged in drawing the wood to my house. About 100 loads were drawn, and as many more chopped, and left to be drawn another day.

Threats of Francis M. Higbee.

At ten, a. m., Dr. Richards called, and told me it was reported that Francis M. Higbee was going to put me under $10,000 bonds for speaking against him. At the same time, Constable Eldredge summoned me to attend a court as witness before Esquire Johnson; and I went accordingly, to give my testimony.

The Twelve Apostles wrote the following letter:—

Letter: The Twelve Apostles to the Saints at Morley Settlement—Material Help Asked for.

NAUVOO, January 15, 1844.

To President Isaac Morley and the Saints at Morley Settlement, the Twelve send greeting:—

BELOVED BRETHREN—While the work of the Lord is great and sought out by all them that have pleasure therein, the Lord of the vineyard has laid special charges upon some of His servants to execute; and while we are striving by all means to raise funds to hasten the Temple the approaching spring, we are not unmindful of the "History of the Church," the "Great Proclamation to the Kings of the Earth," and the "Memorials to Congress," &c., all of which are now before the Church, though their progress is retarded for the want of the necessaries of life, in the families of those who are employed in this business.

Two or three clerks are necessarily employed, and that continually, by our Prophet, who cheerfully devote their time—not a *tenth*, but the *whole*, to roll on these desirable objects; but their hands are palsied and their pens stayed, more or less. Therefore, with the approbation of our President, we again call on you, as those who have ever been ready to listen to the wants of the Church, that you would raise such collections of provisions as you may have at your disposal, and forward the same *without delay* to us, for the special benefit of the clerks of President Smith or the Church. Asking no more, it is right they should not go hungry or naked.

Do you ask what is wanting? We answer, Look to your own households, and say what it requires to make them comfortable, and you will know just what is wanting by these men. *Eatables of every kind*, and even soap to keep their hands clean, is scarce at Nauvoo, and it takes many lights to keep the pen in motion these long evenings.

The President has plenty to do without supporting a number of clerks, whose business as deeply concerns every other individual in the Church as himself, although he has done it to a great extent and with great inconvenience; and we are confident that when you are made acquainted with the facts, you will be unwilling that *Joseph* should *do all, and get all the blessing*. And as you shall continue your liberality in temporal things, God shall pour out upon your heads blessings spiritual and temporal; and *now* is the time for *action*.

All is peace at Nauvoo, and the last report from the Carthagenians was, they were beginning to think it was time to throw down their arms and attempt a compromise. But the "Mormons" can truly say they have had no quarrel with them. It has all been between the citizens and the law, their own officers being the executors thereof; and we feel disposed to let them fight it out among themselves, while we live in peace and laugh at their folly.

With our prayers and blessings, we subscribe ourselves

Your brethren in Christ Jesus.

In behalf of the quorum,

B. YOUNG, President.

W. RICHARDS, Clerk.

The Municipal Court issued a warrant for the arrest of Francis M. Higbee, on affidavit of Orson Pratt.

East wind in forenoon, and some rain. Brisk wind from N.W. in afternoon.

Benjamin Andrews published in the *Times and Seasons* "An Appeal to the people of the State of Maine," setting forth the persecutions, murders, and robberies committed upon the Saints by the people of the State of Missouri, and soliciting the assistance of his native State in procuring redress.

Andrews' Appeal to the State of Maine

Tuesday, *16*.—Cold and windy.

At ten, a.m., Francis M. Higbee was brought up before the Municipal Court, on complaint of Orson Pratt, for absenting himself from City Council without leave, when summoned as a witness, and for slanderous and abusive language towards one of the members of the Council.

Francis M. Higbee on Trial—Reconciliation with Prophet.

The court adjourned, and the City Council commenced their session, continuing till two o'clock, during which time a reconciliation took place with Francis M. Higbee, who had written a slanderous letter concerning me, and said many hard things, which he acknowledged; and I forgave him. I went before the Council and stated that all difficulties between me and F. M. Higbee were eternally buried, and I was to be his friend for ever. To which F. M. Higbee replied, "I will be his friend for ever, and his right-hand man."

A number of the brethren assembled and chopped up the firewood which had been hauled to my house yesterday, and piled it up ready for use.

The following "Ordinance concerning the sale of Spirituous Liquors" was passed by the City Council:

An Ordinance concerning the Sale of Spirituous Liquors.

Whereas, the use and sale of distilled and fermented liquors for all purposes of beverage and drink by persons in health are viewed by this City Council with unqualified disapprobation:

Whereas, nevertheless the aforesaid liquors are considered highly beneficial for medical and mechanical purposes, and may be safely employed for such uses, under the counsel of discreet persons: Therefore,

Sect. 1. Be it ordained by the City Council of the city of Nauvoo, that the Mayor of this city is hereby authorized to sell said liquors in such quantities as he may deem expedient.

Sect. 2. Be it further ordained, that other persons not exceeding one to each ward of the city, may also sell said liquors in like quantities for medical and mechanical purposes by obtaining a license of the Mayor of the city. The above ordinance to be in full force and effect immediately after its passage,—all ordinances to the contrary notwithstanding.

Passed January 16, 1844.

JOSEPH SMITH, Mayor.

W. RICHARDS, Recorder.

An ordinance was also passed, authorizing Henry G. Sherwood to make out a city directory, and to establish an intelligence office in the city. Also the following ordinance:—

An Ordinance concerning Witnesses and Jurors' Fees.

Be it ordained by the City Council of the city of Nauvoo, that hereafter all persons subpœnaed and attending upon courts of trial as witnesses, or as jurors in civil cases, shall not be compelled to testify or be held in attendance either as witness or juror, unless they shall first be tendered the sum of fifty cents per day for each witness and each juror subpœnaed.

Passed January 16, 1844.

JOSEPH SMITH, Mayor.

W. RICHARDS, Recorder.

Wednesday, 17.—At home settling accounts with various individuals. Gave deed of a lot to John Lytle.

The steamer *Shepherdess* sank near St. Louis, drowning forty passengers.

Thursday, 18.—At home, and wrote letters to Reuben McBride and Joseph Coe, Kirtland; Clark Leal, of Fountain Green; and to Justin J. Butterfield, Esq., Chicago.

This afternoon a man called on Brother Nelson Judd, and said he wanted to sell him some wood below Davidson Hibbard's. He went to see the wood, the man saying he would meet him at the place. When below, Hibbard's two

Assault Upon Nelson Judd.

men came up on horseback, and told him they had a warrant for him, for taking away Avery's things from Bear Creek. One shot at him twice and the other snapped at him twice with their pistols. Judd then coolly said, "Now, 'tis my turn," putting his hand into his pocket, although he knew he had no pistols: yet the men fled.

There was a cotillion party at the Mansion this evening.

Friday, 19.—Rode out in the course of the day. In the evening, gave a lecture on the Constitution of the United States, and on the candidates for the Presidency.

Mild weather. Cloudy in the afternoon.

A meeting was held in the assembly room to devise means for the founding of another library institution in Nauvoo.

CHAPTER VIII.

PRESENTATION OF THE BOOK OF MORMON TO QUEEN VICTORIA—THE SEALING POWERS OF THE PRIESTHOOD—GOVERNOR FORD'S WARNING TO THE PEOPLE OF HANCOCK COUNTY—APOSTROPHE TO MISSOURI—JOSEPH SMITH NOMINATED FOR PRESIDENT OF THE UNITED STATES—HIS VIEWS ON THE POWERS AND POLICY OF THE GOVERNMENT OF THE UNITED STATES.

Saturday, January 20th, 1844.—Held Mayor's Court on the case—"City of Nauvoo *versus* Stephen Wilkinson," for breach of ordinance. I discharged the defendant, he paying costs.

At six, p. m., prayer-meeting in the assembly room. I was at home.

The High Council met, but, having no business, adjourned.

"STANZAS"

On the Presentation of the Book of Mormon to Queen Victoria.

BY MISS E. R. SNOW.

Before leaving London, Elder Lorenzo Snow presented to her Majesty Queen Victoria, and his Royal Highness Prince Albert, through the politeness of Sir Henry Wheatly, two neatly bound copies of the Book of Mormon, which had been donated by President Brigham Young, and left in the care of Elder Snow for that purpose; which circumstance suggested the following lines:—

Of all the monarchs of the earth
  That wear the robes of royalty,
She has inherited by birth
  The broadest wreath of majesty.

From her wide territorial wing
  The sun does not withdraw its light,
While earth's diurnal motions bring
  To other nations day and night.

All earthly thrones are tottering things,
  Where lights and shadows intervene;
And regal honor often brings
  The scaffold or the guillotine.

But still her sceptre is appproved;
  All nations deck the wreath she wears:
Yet, like the youth whom Jesus loved,
  One thing is lacking even there.

But lo! a prize possessing more
  Of worth than gems with honor rife—
A herald of salvation bore
  To her the words of endless life.

That GIFT, however fools deride,
  Is worthy of her royal care:
She'd better lay her crown aside
  Than spurn the light reflected there.

Oh would she now her influence bend—
  The influence of royalty,
Messiah's kingdom to extend,
  And Zion's "nursing mother" be.

Thus with the glory of her name
  Inscribed on Zion's lofty spire,
She'd win a wreath of endless fame,
  To last when other wreaths expire.

Though over millions called to reign—
  Herself a powerful nation's boast,
'Twould be her everlasting gain
  To serve the King, the Lord of Hosts.

For there are crowns and thrones on high,
  And kingdoms there to be conferred;
There honors wait that never die;
  There fame's immortal trump is heard.

Truth echoes—'tis Jehovah's word;
  Let kings and queens and princes hear;
In distant isles the sound is heard;
  Ye heavens rejoice! O earth, give ear!

The time, the time is now at hand
  To give a glorious period birth:
The son of God will take command
  And rule the nations of the earth.

Nauvoo, Jan. 20, 1844.

Sunday 21.—Preached at the southeast corner of the temple to several thousand people, although the weather was somewhat unpleasant. My subject was the sealing of the hearts of the fathers to the children, and the hearts of the children to the fathers.

[The following synopsis was reported by Elder Wilford Woodruff:]—

Discourse: The Sealing Power in the Priesthood.

When I consider the surrounding circumstances in which I am placed this day, standing in the open air with weak lungs, and somewhat out of health, I feel that I must have the prayers and faith of my brethren that God may strengthen me and pour out His special blessing upon me, if you get very much from me this day.

There are many people assembled here to-day, and throughout the city, and from various parts of the world, who say that they have received to a certainty a portion of the knowledge from God, by revelation, in the way that He has ordained and pointed out.

I shall take the broad ground, then, that we have received a portion of knowledge from God by immediate revelation, and from the same source we can receive all knowledge.

What shall I talk about to-day? I know what Brother Cahoon wants me to speak about. He wants me to speak about the coming of Elijah in the last days. I can see it in his eye. I will speak upon that subject then.

The Bible says, "I will send you Elijah the Prophet before the coming of the great and dreadful day of the Lord; and he shall turn the hearts of the fathers to the children, and the hearts of the children to the fathers, lest I come and smite the earth with a curse."

Now, the word *turn* here should be translated *bind*, or seal. But what is the object of this important mission? or how is it to be fulfilled? The keys are to be delivered, the spirit of Elijah is to come, the Gospel to be established, the Saints of God gathered, Zion built up, and the Saints to come up as saviors on Mount Zion.

But how are they to become saviors on Mount Zion? By building their temples, erecting their baptismal fonts, and going forth and receiving all the ordinances, baptisms, confirmations, washings, anointings, ordinations and sealing powers upon their heads, in behalf of all their progenitors who are dead, and redeem them that they may come forth in the first resurrection and be exalted to thrones of glory with them; and herein is the chain that binds the hearts of the fathers to the children, and the children to the fathers, which fulfills the mission of Elijah. And I would to God that this temple was now done, that we might go into it, and go to work and improve our time, and make use of the seals while they are on earth.

The Saints have not too much time to save and redeem their dead, and gather together their living relatives, that they may be saved also, before the earth will be smitten, and the consumption decreed falls upon the world.

I would advise all the Saints to go to with their might and gather together all their living relatives to this place, that they may be sealed and saved, that they may be prepared against the day that the destroying angel goes forth; and if the whole Church should go to with all their might to save their dead, seal their posterity, and gather their living friends, and spend none of their time in behalf of the world, they would hardly get through before night would come, when no man can work; and my only trouble at the present time is concerning ourselves, that the Saints *will be divided, broken up, and scattered*, before we get our salvation secure; for there are so many fools in the world for the devil to operate upon, it gives him the advantage oftentimes.

The question is frequently asked "Can we not be saved without going through with all those ordinances, &c.?" I would answer, No, not the fullness of salvation. Jesus said, "There are many mansions in my Father's house, and I will go and prepare a place for you." *House* here named should have been translated kingdom; and any person who is exalted to the highest mansion has to abide a celestial law, and the whole law too.

But there has been a great difficulty in getting anything into the heads of this generation. It has been like splitting hemlock knots with a corn-dodger for a wedge, and a pumpkin for a beetle. Even the Saints are slow to understand.

I have tried for a number of years to get the minds of the Saints prepared to receive the things of God; but we frequently see some of them, after suffering all they have for the work of God, will fly to pieces like glass as soon as anything comes that is contrary to their traditions: they cannot stand the fire at all. How many will be able to abide a celestial law, and go through and receive their exaltation, I am unable to say, as many are called, but few are chosen.

Prayer-meeting in the Assembly Room.

Monday, 22.—Rainy; wind easterly; mud very deep.

Rented the Nauvoo Mansion and stables to Ebenezer Robinson for one thousand dollars per annum and board for myself and family and horses, reserving to myself three rooms in the house.

Nauvoo Mansion Leased.

Prayer-meeting at President Young's; ten present.

Tuesday. 23.—Ebenezer Robinson took possession of the Nauvoo Mansion, to continue it as a public-house. W. W. Phelps, Newel K. Whitney and Willard Richards valued the printing office and lot at $1,500; printing apparatus, $950; bindery, $112; foundry, $270; total, $2,832. I having sold the concern to John Taylor, who in consideration was to assume the responsibility of the Lawrence estate.

Sale of the Printing Establishment to John Taylor

There was a cotillion party in the evening at the Nauvoo Mansion. The night was clear and cold.

The ship *Fanny*, Captain Patterson, sailed from Liverpool with 210 Saints on board.

Wednesday, 24.—Called at my office about one o'clock. I think the appraised valuation of the printing office rather too low.

Weather very cold.

The mob party at Carthage, Warsaw, and Green Plains continued their agitation.

Thursday, 25.—At home.

Prayer-meeting at Brother Brigham's: eight of the Twelve Apostles present. Weather extremely cold.

I approved of the doings of a generel court-martial held January 13th.

Friday, *26.*—I dictated to my clerk an article on the situation of the nation, referring to the President's Message, &c.

Prayer-meeting at Brother Young's: eight of the Twelve Apostles present. Elder Orson Hyde went to Carthage to preach. Weather clear and cool.

Saturday, *27.*—Weather extremely cold and clear.

Prayer-meeting in the assembly room. High Council met, but, having no business, adjourned.

Sunday, *28.*—I had some company in the evening from Warsaw. I conversed with them on politics, religion, &c. Prayer-meeting in the assembly room. Weather very cold.

I insert the following from the *Millennial Star:*—

Importance of Elders Keeping Journals, Case of Healing Recorded.

MR. EDITOR:—The idea has frequently crossed my mind, that were the Elders of the Church of Jesus Christ in this age to keep a journal of their travels and ministry, and record all the healings and miracles they had witnessed from time to time,—that should their separate journals be afterwards collected together and published in a volume, I am inclined to believe that a far greater number of manifest displays of the power of God would be therein recorded than is found in the journals of the Elders of the Church of Jesus Christ in the early ages, at least so far as they are faithfully handed down to us in the New Testament Scriptures.

And although, as in days of old, we are frequently branded with the epithets of "fools, fanatics, religious enthusiasts, dupes, and vile impostors," yet "what we have felt and seen, with confidence we tell."

We have frequently heard from individuals on whose testimony we can rely with the greatest confidence, of extraordinary displays of the power of God in the gift of healing; such, for instance, as the blind receiving their sight, the deaf having their hearing restored, the lame man being made to "leap as an hart," the dumb spirit being cast out, and one instance of the dead being restored to life.

Another instance of the kind last mentioned, with a heart overflowing with gratitude, I desire to record. On the afternoon of yesterday, a child of mine, a girl aged eight years, was sliding on the rails of the staircase, when on a sudden she turned over, and fell from top to bottom with a most tremendous crash, falling on her head, and being completely double when picked up by her mother,—so much so indeed, that her brother, who heard the noise, looked out of the kitchen, and seeing something lying in the passage motionless, concluded that his sister had thrown some dirty linen over the rails, and took no further notice. Her mother, on hearing the noise occasioned by her fall, hastened out of the parlor to the fatal spot, and immediately discovered it was poor Mary Jane, who lay motionless, speechless, senseless, yea, lifeless. She instantly took her up in her arms, and when she beheld her appearance, in an agony she cried out, "My child is dead! she has fallen and killed herself."

By this time I had hastened to the horrid scene, where I beheld my lovely girl stretched on the lap of her disconsolate mother, without the slightest appearance of life. I immediately examined her, and found that she breathed not, and that her pulsation had ceased. Her eyes also were wide open, and quite fixed as in death, and there appeared to be gathering over them the film of dissolution. In fact, if it be true that Eutychus (the young man mentioned in the 20th chapter of the Acts of the Apostles, who fell from an upper story,) was taken up dead, it is equally true that my daugther was taken up dead, for there was not the slightest vestige of life apparent.

At this moment, with heart uplifted to my Heavenly Father, I, in mighty faith, placed my hands upon her and ejaculated, "Lord, heal my child!" when in one moment she shewed signs of life, and attempted to speak.

I immediately gave her to drink a little cold water, and bathed her head with the same. She then sat up and vomited considerably, and she is now so far recovered as this morning to sing a verse of a hymn and walk about as usual.

During my presidency over the Liverpool Conference, which is nearly eighteen months, I have witnessed many cases of healing, but never any so very striking as the one I have just related.

If you deem the narrative worthy of a place in your pages of the *Millennial Star*, you are quite at liberty to insert it.

I remain, dear brother,

Yours sincerely in the Gospel of Jesus,

GEORGE MITCHELSON.

Monday, *29*.—At ten, a.m., the Twelve Apostles, together with Brother Hyrum and John P. Greene, met at the mayor's office, to take into consideration the proper course for this people to pursue in relation to the coming Presidential election.

The Presidential Election Considered.

The candidates for the office of President of the United States at present before the people are Martin Van Buren and Henry Clay. It is morally impossible for this people, in justice to themselves, to vote for the re-election of President Van Buren—a man who criminally neglected his duties as chief magistrate in the cold and unblushing manner which he did, when appealed to for aid in the Missouri difficulties. His heartless reply burns like a firebrand in the breast of every true friend of liberty—"*Your cause is just, but I can do nothing for you.*"

As to Mr. Clay, his sentiments and cool contempt of the people's rights are manifested in his reply—"*You had better go to Oregon for redress,*" which would prohibit any true lover of our constitutional privileges from supporting him at the ballot-box.

It was therefore moved by Willard Richards, and voted unanimously—

That we will have an independent electoral ticket, and that Joseph Smith be a candidate for the next Presidency; and that we use all honorable means in our power to secure his election.

I said—

The Prophet on the Campaign.

If you attempt to accomplish this, you must send every man in the city who is able to speak in public throughout the land to electioneer and make stump speches, advocate the "Mormon" religion, purity of elections, and call upon the people to stand by the law and put down mobocracy. David Yearsly must go,—Parley P. Pratt to New York, Erastus Snow to Vermont, and Sidney Rigdon to Pennsylvania.

After the April Conference we will have General Conferences all over the nation, and I will attend as many as convenient. Tell the people we have had Whig and Democratic Presidents long enough: we want a President of the United States. If I ever get into the presidential chair, I will protect the people in their rights and liberties. I will not electioneer for myself. Hyrum, Brigham, Parley and Taylor must go. Clayton must go, or he will apostatize. The Whigs are striving for a king under the garb of Democracy. There is oratory enough in the Church to carry me into the presidential chair the first slide.

Captain White, of Quincy, was at the Mansion last night,

and this morning drank a toast. * * * "May Nauvoo become the empire seat of government!"

I dictated to Brother Phelps the heads of my pamphlet, entitled, "Views on the Powers and Policy of the Government of the United States."

Commencement of the Prophet's Views on Powers and Policy of U.S.

A Millerite lecturer came into the office with Brother Clayton, about five, p.m. I had some conversation with him about the definition of the Greek word Hades, and the Hebrew word Sheol, &c He lectured in the evening in the hall.

Prayer-meeting at Elder Brigham Young's.

Governor Ford wrote the following expostulatory epistle to the citizens of Hancock County, through the *Warsaw Signal:*—

Governor Ford's Warning to the People of Hancock County.

SPRINGFIELD, January 29, 1844.

DEAR SIR:—I have received the copy of the proceeding and resolutions of a meeting of the citizens of Hancock County, which you did me the honor to send me.

I have observed with regret that occasions have been presented for disturbing the peace of your county; and if I knew what I could legally do to apply a corrective, I would be very ready to do it. But if you are a lawyer, or at all conversant with the law, you will know that I, as a Governor, have no right to interfere in your difficulties.

As yet, I believe that there has been nothing like war among you: and I hope that all of you will have the good sense to see the necessity of preserving peace. If there is anything wrong in the Nauvoo charters, or in the mode of administering them, you will see that nothing short of legislative or judicial power is capable of enforcing a remedy.

I myself had the honor of calling the attention of the Legislature to this subject at the last session; but a large majority of both political parties in that body either did not see the evil which you complain of, or, if they did, they repeatedly refused to correct it. And yet a call is made upon me to do that which all parties refused to do at the last session.

I have also been called upon to take away the arms from the *Mormons*, to raise the militia to arrest a supposed fugitive, and in fact to repeal some of the ordinances of the City of Nauvoo.

Hancock County is justly famed for its intelligence; and I cannot believe that any of its citizens are so ignorant as not to know that I have no power to do these things.

The absurd and preposterous nature of these requests give some color to the charge that they are made for political effect only. I hope that this charge is untrue; for, in all candor, it would be more creditable to those concerned to have their errors attributed to ignorance than to a disposition to embroil the country in the horrors of war for the advancement of party ends.

But if there should be any truth in the charge, (which God forbid.) I affectionately entreat all the good citizens engaged in it to lay aside their designs and yield up their ears to the voice of justice, reason, and humanity. All that I can do at present is to admonish both parties to beware of carrying matters to extremity.

Let it come to this—let a state of war ensue, and I will be compelled to interfere with executive power. In that case also, I wish, in a friendly, affectionate, and candid manner, to tell the citizens o Hancock County, *Mormons* and all, that my interference will be against those who shall be the first transgressors.

I am bound by the laws and Constitution to regard you all as citizens of the State, possessed of equal rights and privileges, and to cherish the rights of one as dearly as the rights of another. I can know no distinction among you except that of assailant and assailed.

I hope, dear sir, you will do me the favor to publish this letter in the papers of your county, for the satisfaction of all persons concerned.

I am, with the highest respect,

Your obedient servant,

THOMAS FORD.

Tuesday 30.—At eleven, a.m., I went into the office with Colonel Jackson.

One, p.m., held mayor's court at my office, on the case "City *versus* Thomas Coates." Fined the defendant $25 and costs for beating John Ellison.

A Millerite preached again in the assembly room, and Elder Rigdon replied to him. There was a full house.

Prayer-meeting at Elder Brigham Young's.

Winchester's Mission to Warsaw.

Wednesday, 31.—Eleven, a. m., I called at the office, and told Benjamin Winchester to go to Warsaw and preach the first principles of the Gospel, get some lexicons, and return home.

Prayer-meeting at Elder Brigham Young's in the evening. There seems to be quite a revival throughout Nauvoo, and an inquiry after the things of God, by all the quorums and the Church in general.

Rigdon's Appeal to Pennsylvania.

Sidney Rigdon published a lengthy appeal to the Legislature of the State of Pennsylvania, setting forth in pathetic style the grievances he had suffered through the persecution against the Church by the State of Missouri, which concludes as follows:—

Peroration of Rigdon's Appeal to Pennsylvania.

In confidence of the purity and patriotism of the representatives of the people of his native state, your memorialist comes to your honorable body, through this his winged messenger, to tell you that the altar which was erected by the blood of your ancestors to civil and religious liberty, from whence ascended up the holy incense of pure patriotism and universal good will to man, into the presence of Jehovah, a savior of life, is thrown down, and the worshipers thereat have been driven away, or else they are lying slain at the place of the altar. He comes to tell your honorable body that the temple your fathers erected to freedom, whither their sons assembled to hear herprecepts and cherish her doctrines in their hearts, has been desecrated—its portals closed, so that those who go up thither are forbidden to enter.

He comes to tell your honorable body that the blood of the heroes and patriots of the revolution, who have been slain by wicked hands for enjoying their religious rights, the boon of Heaven to man, has cried and is crying in the ears of the Lord of Sabaoth, saying, "Redress, redress our wrongs, O Lord God of the whole earth."

He comes to tell your honorable body that the dying groans of infant innocence and the shrieks of insulted and abused females, and many of them widows of revolutionary patriots, have ascended up into the ears of Omnipotence, and are registered in the archives of eternity, to be had in the day of retribution as a testimony against the whole nation, unless their cries and groans are heard by the representatives of the people, and ample redress made, as far as the nation can make it, or else the wrath of the almighty will come down in fury against the whole nation.

Under all these circumstances, your memorialist prays to be heard by your honorable body touching all the matters of his memorial. And as a memorial will be presented to Congress this session for redress of our grievances, he prays your honorable body will instruct the whole delegation of Pennaylvania, in both houses, to use all their influence in the national councils to have redress granted.

And, as in duty bound, your memorialist will ever pray.

SIDNEY RIGDON.

Miss E. R. Snow published the following apostrophe to—

"MISSOURI."

What aileth thee, O Missouri! that thy face should gather blackness? and why are thy features so terribly distorted?

Rottenness has seized upon thy vitals, corruption is preying upon thy inward parts, and the breath of thy lips is full of destructive contagion.

What meaneth thy shaking? and why art thou terrified? Thou hast become like Belshazzar. "*Mene, mene, tekel, upharsin!*" is indeed written against thee; but it is the work of thine own hand; the characters upon thy wall are of thine own inscription; and wherefore dost thou tremble?

Wouldst thou know the interpretation thereof? Hast thou sought for a Daniel to declare it unto thee? Verily one greater than a Daniel was in thy midst; but thou hast butchered the Saints, and hast hunted the Prophets like Ahab of old.

Thou has extinguished the light of thy own glory; thou hast plucked from thy head the crown of honor; thou hast divested thyself of the robe of respectability; thou hast thrust from thine own bosom the veins that flowed with virtue and integrity.

Thou hast violated the laws of our sacred constitution; thou hast unsheathed the sword against thy dearest national rights, by rising up against thine own citizens, and moistening thy soil with the blood of those that legally inherited it.

When thou hadst torn from helpless innocence its rightful protectors thou didst pollute the holy sanctury of female virtue, and barbarously trampled upon the most sacred gems of domestic felicity.

Therefore the daughters of Columbia count thee a reproach, and blush with indignation at the mention of thy name.

Thou hast become an ignominious stain on the escutcheon of a noble, free and independent republic; thou hast become a stink in the nostrils of the Goddess of Liberty.

Thou art fallen—thou art fallen beneath the weight of thine own unhallowed deeds, and thine iniquities are pressing as a heavy load upon thee.

But although thy glory has departed—though thou hast gone down like a star that is set forever, thy memory will not be erased; thou wilt be had in remembrance even until the Saints of God shall forget that the way to the celestial kingdom is "through great tribulation."

Though thou shouldst be severed from the body of the Union, like a mortified member—though the lion from the thicket should devour thee, thy doings will be perpetuated; mention will be made of them by the generations to come.

Thou art already associated with Herod, Nero, and the bloody Inquisition; thy name has become synonymous with oppression, cruelty, treachery, and murder.

Thou wilt rank high with the haters of righteousness and the shedders of innocent blood: the hosts of tyrants are waiting beneath to meet thee at thy coming.

O ye wise legislators! ye executives of the nation! ye distributors of justice! ye advocates of equal rights! arise and redress the wrongs of an innocent people, and redeem the cause of insulted liberty.

Let not the contagious spirit of corruption wither the sacred wreath that encircles you, and spread a cloud of darkness over the glory of your star-spangled banner;

Lest the monarchs of the earth should have you in derision; lest you should be weighed in the balance with the heathen nations, and should be found wanting; lest the arm of the Lord should be revealed in judgment against you; lest an arrow of vengeance from the almighty should pierce the rotten fabric of a once sheltering constitution, and your boasted confidence become like an oak dismembered of its branches, whose shattered trunk is torn piecemeal by the uprising of the tempest!

For the cries of the widow and fatherless, the groans of the oppressed and the prayers of the suffering exile have come up before the God of Hosts, who brought our pilgrim fathers across the boisterous ocean, and raised up a Washington to break the yoke of foreign oppression.

Morley Settlement, January, 1844.

Thursday, February 1.—At home: weather cold.

An Appeal to Massachusetts—Phinehas Richards.

Phinehas Richards published a thrilling appeal to the inhabitants of his native state of Massachusetts, to consider the wrongs sustained in the loss of lives and property, and other damages done to the Church of Jesus Christ of Latter-day Saints, of which he is a member.

Elder Reuben Hedlock wrote to President Brigham Young, giving the names of those who had emigrated at the expense of the office, amounting to $2,378; which is due from the emigrants.

Friday, 2.—Dr. Willard Richards called and read Phinehas Richards' appeal to the inhabitants of Massachusetts, for redress of Missouri grievances.

Prayer-meeting at Elder Brigham Young's. Weather cold.

I went into the assembly room, where I found Elders Wilford Woodruff, Willard Richards, and W. W. Phelps, to whom I related the following dream, which Elder Wilford Woodruff reported:

The Prophet's Dream—Troubled Waters Overcome.

I was standing on a peninsula, in the midst of a vast body of water where there appeared to be a large harbor or pier built out for boats to come to. I was surrounded by my friends, and while looking at this harbor I saw a steamboat approaching the harbor. There were bridges on the pier for persons to cross, and there came up a wind and drove the steamboat under one of the bridges and upset it.

I ran up to the boat, expecting the persons would all drown; and wishing to do something to assist them, I put my hand against the side of the boat,and with one surge I shoved it under the bridge and righted it up, and then told them to take care of themselves. But it was not long before I saw them starting out into the channel or main body of the water again.

The storms were raging and the waters rough. I said to my friends that if they did not understand the signs of the times and the spirit of prophecy, they would be apt to be lost.

It was but a few moments after when we saw the waves break over the boat, and she soon foundered and went down with all on board.

The storm and waters were still very rough; yet I told my friends around me that I believed I could stem those waves and that storm, and swim in the waters better than the steamboat did; at any rate I was determined to try it. But my friends laughed at me, and told me I could not stand at all, but would be drowned.

The waters looked clear and beautiful, though exceedingly rough; and I said I believed I could swim, and I would try it anyhow. They said I would drown. I said I would have a frolic in the water first, if I did; and I drove off in the raging waves.

I had swam but a short distance when a towering wave overwhelmed me for a time; but I soon found myself on the top of it, and soon I met the second wave in the same way; and for a while I struggled hard to live in the midst of the storm and waves, and soon found I gained upon every wave, and skimmed the torrent better; and I soon had power to swim with my head out of water: so the waves did not break over me at all, and I found that I had swam a great distance; and in looking about, I saw my brother Samuel by my side.

I asked him how he liked it. He said, "First rate," and I thought so too. I was soon enabled to swim with my head and shoulders out of water, and I could swim as fast as any steamboat.

In a little time it became calm, and I could rush through the water, and only go in to my loins, and soon I only went in to my knees, and finally could tread on the top of the water, and went almost with the speed of an arrow.

I said to Samuel, See how swift I can go! I thought it was great sport and pleasure to travel with such speed, and I awoke.

Saturday 3.—Prayer-meeting in the assembly room.

The High Council met. Did but little business.

A rather favorable article appears in Niles' *National Register* of this date, noticing the correspondence between myself and John C. Calhoun, a copy of which is contained in the political department of the same number.

It also notices the correspondence between myself and James Arlington Bennett, publishing the same, with some of our city ordinances. The editor also quotes the following from the *Hawk Eye*:—

Mormon Improvements.

Atthough much complaint has been made about the Mormons, we saw on our late trip evidences of improvement on our prairies which we consider highly creditable to the Mormons who made them, without whom we doubt whether they would have been made for many years to come. All those who have traveled over the large prairie between Fort Madison, Warsaw and Carthage, remember how dreary it was a few years since. Now it is studded with houses and good farms. The English, who understand hedging and ditching far better than our people, have gone upon that prairie and have enclosed extensive fields in this manner. Along the old Rock Island tract, which we traveled seven years ago, and which was then a dreary waste, we saw a field enclosed with a good sod fence, six miles long and one wide. We think such enterprise is worthy to be mentioned. As long as the Mormons are harmless, and do not interfere with the rights of our people we think they should be treated well. We shall never convince them that they are a deluded people, as far as their religious notions are concerned, in any other way.

Sunday 4.—I attended prayer-meeting with the quorum in the assembly room, and made some remarks respecting the hundred and forty-four thousand mentioned by John the Revelator, showing that the selection of persons to form that number had already commenced.

The 144,000 Selection Begun.

President Brigham Young held a meeting at Brother Chamberlain's, in the neighborhood north of the city; and Elder Wilford Woodruff, at Thomas Kingston's, six miles east of the city.

Monday 5.—The regular session of the Municipal Court was opened in the Mayor's office. Present, George W. Harris, George A. Smith, and N. K. Whitney. Adjourned to the Nauvoo Mansion, on account of the severity of the weather. I presided as Chief Justice. The assessors of the different wards in the city presented their tax-lists, which occupied nearly all day. The court remitted the taxes of the widows and of the poor who were unable to pay.

City Council.

In the afternoon, Elder William Weeks (whom I had employed as architect of the Temple,) came in for instruction. I instructed him in relation to the circular windows designed to light the offices in the dead work of the arch between stories. He said that round windows in the broad side of a building were a violation of all the known rules of architecture, and contended that they should be semicircular—that the

Architecture of the Nauvoo Temple.

building was too low for round windows. I told him I would have the circles, if he had to make the Temple ten feet higher than it was originally calculated; that one light at the centre of each circular window would be sufficient to light the whole room; that when the whole building was thus illuminated, the effect would be remarkably grand. "I wish you to carry out *my* designs. I have seen in vision the splendid appearance of that building illuminated, and will have it built according to the pattern shown me."

Called at my office in the evening, and revised my "Views of the Powers and Policy of the Government of the United States." I was the first one who publicly proposed a national bank on the principles set forth in that pamphlet.

Originality of Bank Views.

Tuesday, 6.—Very cold day.

I spent the evening with my brother Hyrum, Sidney Rigdon, and the Twelve Apostles and their wives, at Elder John Taylor's; took supper, and had a very pleasant time.

Wednesday, 7.—An exceedingly cold day. In the evening I met with my brother Hyrum and the Twelve Apostles in my office, at their request, to devise means to promote the interests of the General Government. I completed and signed my "Views of the Powers and Policy of the Government of the United States," which I here insert:

Views of the Powers and Policy of the Government of the United States.—Joseph Smith.

Born in a land of liberty, and breathing an air uncorrupted with the sirocco of barbarous climes, I ever feel a double anxiety for the happiness of all men, both in time and in eternity.

My cogitations, like Daniel's, have for a long time troubled me, when I viewed the condition of men throughout the world, and more especially in this boasted realm, where the Declaration of Independence "holds these thruths to be self-evident, that all men are created equal; that they are endowed by their Creator with certain unalienable rights; that among these are life, liberty, and the pursuit of happiness;" but at the same time some two or three millions of people are held as slaves for life, because the spirit in them is covered with a darker skin than ours; and hundreds of our own kindred for an infraction, or supposed infraction, of some over-wise statute, have to be incarcerated in dungeon gloom, or penitentiaries, while the duellist, the debauchee, and the defaulter for millions, and other criminals, take the uppermost rooms at feasts, or, like the bird of passage, find a more congenial clime by flight.

The wisdom which ought to characterize the freest, wisest, and most noble nation of the nineteenth century, should, like the sun in his meridian splendor, warm every object beneath its rays; and the main efforts of her officers, who are nothing more nor less than the servants of the people, ought to be directed to ameliorate the condition of all, black or white, bond or free; for the best of books says, "God hath made of one blood all nations of men for to dwell on all the face of the earth."

Our common country presents to all men the same advantages, the facilities, the same prospects, the same honors, and the same rewards; and without hypocrisy, the Constitution, when it says, "We, the people of the United States, in order to form a more perfect union, establish justice, ensure domestic tranquility, provide for the common defense, promote the general welfare, and secure the blessings of liberty to ourselves and our posterity, do ordain and establish this Constitution for the United States of America," meant just what it said without reference to color or condition, *ad infinitum.*

The aspirations and expectations of a virtuous people, environed with so wise, so liberal, so deep, so broad, and so high a charter of *equal rights* as appears in said Constitution, ought to be treated by those to whom the administration of the laws is entrusted with as much sanctity as the prayers of the Saints are treated in heaven, that love, confidence, and union, like the sun, moon, and stars, should bear witness,

> "For ever singing as they shine,
> The hand that made us is divine!"

Unity is power; and when I reflect on the importance of it to the stability of all governments, I am astounded at the silly moves of persons and parties to foment discord in order to ride into power on the current of popular excitement; nor am I less surprised at the stretches of power or restrictions of right which too often appear as acts of legislators to pave the way to some favorite political scheme as destitute of intrinsic merit as a wolf's heart is of the milk of human kindness. A Frenchman would say, "*Presque tout aimer richesses et pouvoir.*" (Almost all men like wealth and power.)

I must dwell on this subject longer than others; for nearly one hundred years ago that golden patriot, Benjamin Franklin, drew up a plan of union for the then colonies of Great Britain, that *now* are such an independent nation, which, among many wise provisions for obedient children under their father's more rugged hand, had this:—"They have power to make laws, and lay and levy such general duties, imports, or taxes as to them shall appear most equal and just, (considering the ability and other circumstances of the inhabitants in the several colonies,) and such as may be collected with the least inconvenience to the people, rather discouraging luxury than loading industry with unnecessary burthens." Great Britain surely lacked the laudable humanity and fostering clemency to grant such a just plan of union; but the sentiment remains, like the land that honored its birth, as a pattern for wise men *to study the convenience of the people more than the comfort of the cabinet.*

And one of the most noble fathers of our freedom and country's glory, great in war, great in peace, great in the estimation of the world, and great in the hearts of his countrymen, (the illustrious Washington,) said in his first inaugural address to Congress—"I behold the surest pledges that as, on one side, no local prejudices or attachments, no separate views or party animosities will misdirect the comprehensive and equal eye which ought to watch over this great assemblage of communities and interests, so, on another, that the foundations of our national policy will be laid in the pure and immutable principles of private morality, and the pre-eminence of free government be exemplified by all the attributes which can win the affections of its citizens and command the respect of the world."

Verily, here shine the virtue and wisdom of a statesman in such lucid rays, that had every succeeding Congress followed the rich instruction in all their deliberations and enactments, for the benefit and convenience of the whole community and the communities of which it is composed, no sound of a rebellion in South Carolina, no rupture in Rhode Island, no mob in Missouri expelling her citizens by Executive authority, corruption in the ballot-boxes, a border warfare between Ohio and Michigan, hard times and distress, outbreak upon outbreak in the principal cities, murder, robbery, and defalcation, scarcity of money, and a thousand other difficulties, would have torn asunder the bonds of the Union, destroyed the confidence of man with man, and left the great body of the people to mourn over misfortunes in poverty brought on by corrupt legislation in an hour of proud vanity for self-aggrandizement.

The great Washington, soon after the foregoing faithful admonition for the common welfare of his nation, further advised Congress that "among the many interesting objects which will engage your attention, that of providing for the common defense will merit particular regard. To be prepared for war is one of the most effectual means of preserving peace." As the Italian would say—"*Buono aviso.*"

The elder Adams, in his inaugural address, gives national pride such a grand turn of justification, that every honest citizen must look back upon the infancy of the United States with an approving smile, and rejoice that patriotism in their rulers, virtue in the people, and prosperity in the Union once crowded the expectations of hope, unveiled the sophistry of the hypocrite, and silenced the folly of foes. Mr. Adams said, "If national pride is ever justifiable or excusable, it is when it springs not from *power* or riches, grandeur or glory, but from conviction of national innocence, information, and benevolence."

There is no doubt such was actually the case with our young realm at the close of the last century. Peace, prosperity, and union filled the country with religious toleration, temporal enjoyment, and virtuous enterprise; and grandly,too,when the deadly winter of the "StampAct," the "Tea Act," and other close communion acts of Royalty had choked the growth of freedom of speech, liberty of the press, and liberty of conscience—did light, liberty, and loyalty flourish like the cedars of God.

The respected and venerable Thomas Jefferson, in his inaugural address, made more than forty years ago, shows what a beautiful prospect an innocent, virtuous nation presents to the sage's eye,where there is space for enterprise, hands for industry, heads for heroes, and hearts for moral greatness. He said, "A rising nation spread over a wide and fruitful land, traversing all the seas with the rich productions of their industry, engaged in commerce with nations who feel power and forget right, advancing rapidly to destinies beyond the reach of mortal eye,—when I contemplate these transcendent objects, and see the honor, the happiness, and the hopes of this beloved country committed to the issue and the auspices of this day, I shrink from the contemplation, and humble myself before the magnitude of the undertaking."

Such a prospect was truly soul-stirring to a good man. But "since the fathers have fallen asleep," wicked and designing men have unrobed the Government of its glory; and the people, if not in dust and ashes, or in sackcloth, have to lament in poverty her departed greatness, while demagogues build fires in the north and south, east and west, to keep up their spirits *till it is better times*. But year after year has left the people to *hope*, till the very name of *Congress* or *State Legislature* is as horrible to the sensitive friend of his country as the house of "Bluebard" is to children, or "Crockford's" Hell of London to meek men.*

When the people are secure and their rights properly respected, then the four main pillars of prosperity—viz., agriculture, manufactures,

* Reference is had to Crockford's famous gaming club house at No. 50 on the west side of St. James St., London.

navigation, and commerce, need the fostering care of Government; and in so goodly a country as ours, where the soil, the climate, the rivers, the lakes, and the sea coast, the productions, the timber, the minerals, and the inhabitants are so diversified, that a pleasing variety accommodates all tastes, trades, and calculations, it certainly is the highest point of supervision to protect the whole northern and southern, eastern and western, centre and circumference of the realm, by a judicious tariff. It is an old saying and a true one, "If you wish to be *respected*, respect yourselves."

I will adopt in part the language of Mr. Madison's inaugural address, —"To cherish peace and friendly intercourse with all nations, having correspondent dispositions; to maintain sincere neutrality towards belligerent nations; to prefer in all cases amicable discussion and reasonable accommodation of differences to a decision of them by an appeal to arms; to exclude foreign intrigues and foreign partialities, so degrading to all countries, and so baneful to free ones; to foster a spirit of independence too just to invade the rights of others, too proud to surrender our own, too liberal to indulge unworthy prejudices ourselves, and too elevated not to look down upon them in others; to hold the union of the States as the basis of their peace and happiness; to support the Constitution, which is the cement of the Union, as well in its limitations as in its authorities; to respect the rights and authorities reserved to the States and to the people as equally incorporated with and essential to the success of the general system; to avoid the slightest interference with the rights of conscience or the functions of religion, so wisely exempted from civil jurisdiction; to preserve in their full energy the other salutary provisions in behalf of private and personal rights, and of the freedom of the press,—so far as intention aids in the fulfillment of duty, are consummations too big with benefits not to captivate the energies of all honest men to achieve them, when they can be brought to pass by reciprocation, friendly alliances, wise legislation, and honorable treaties."

The Government has once flourished under the guidance of trusty servants; and the Hon. Mr. Monroe, in his day, while speaking of the Constitution, says, "Our commerce has been wisely regulated with foreign nations and between the States. New States have been admitted into our Union. Our Territory has been enlarged by fair and honorable treaty, and with great advantage to the original States; the States respectively protected by the national Government, under a mild paternal system against foreign dangers, and enjoying within their separate spheres, by a wise partition of power, a just proportion of the sovereignty, have improved their police, extended their settlements, and attained a strength and maturity which are the best proofs of wholesome laws well administered. And if we look to the condition of individuals, what a proud spectacle does it exhibit! On whom has oppression fallen in any quarter of our Union? Who has been deprived of any right of person or property?—who restrained from offering his vows in the mode which he prefers to the Divine Author of his being? It is well known that all these blessings have been enjoyed in their fullest extent; and I add, with peculiar satisfaction, that there has been no example of a capital punishment being inflicted on any one for the crime of high treason." What a delightful picture of power, policy, and prosperity! Truly the wise man's proverb is just—Righteousness exalteth a nation, but sin is a reproach to any people.

But this is not all. The same honorable statesman, after having had about forty years' experience in the Government, under the full tide of successful experiment, gives the following commendatory assurance of the efficiency of the *Magna Charta* to answer its great end and aim—*to protect the people in their rights*. "Such, then, is the happy Government under which we live; a Government adequate to every purpose for which the social compact is formed; a Government elective in all its branches, under which every citizen may by his merit obtain the highest trust recognized by the Constitution, which contains within it no cause of discord, none to put at variance one portion of the commuuity with another; a Government which protects every citizen in the full enjoyment of his rights, and is able to protect the nation against injustice from foreign powers."

Again, the younger Adams, in the silver age of our country's advancement to fame, in his inaugural address (1825), thus candidly declares the majesty of the youthful republic in its increasing greatness:—"The year of jubilee, since the first formation of our union, has just elapsed: that of the Declaration of Independence is at hand. The consummation of both was effected by this Constitution. Since that period, a population of four millions has multiplied to twelve. A Territory, bounded by the Mississippi, has been extended from sea to sea. New States have been admitted to the Union, in numbers nearly equal to those of the first confederatiou. Treaties of peace, amity, and commerce have been concluded with the principal dominions of the earth. The people of other nations, the inhabitants of regions acquired, not by conquest, but by compact, have been united with us in the participation of our rights and duties, of our burdens and blessings. The forest has fallen by the ax of our woodsman. The soil has been made to teem by the tillage of our farmers. Our commerce has whitened every ocean. The dominion of man over physical nature has been extended by the invention of our artists. Liberty and law have marched hand in hand. All the purposes of human association have been accomplished as effectively as under any other Government on the globe, and at a cost little exceeding, in a whole generation, the expenditures of other nations in a single year."

In continuation of such noble sentiments, General Jackson, upon his ascension to the great chair of the chief magistracy, said, "As long as our Government is administered for the good of the people, and is regulated by their will, as long as it secures to us the rights of person and property, liberty of conscience, and of the press, it will be worth defending; and so long as it is worth defending, a patriotic militia will cover it with an impenetrable *œgis*."

General Jackson's administration may be denominated the *acme* of American glory, liberty, and prosperity; for the national debt, which in 1815, on account of the late war, was $125,000,000, and being lessened gradually, was paid up in his golden day, and preparations were made to destribute the surplus revenue among the several States; and that august patriot, to use his own words in his farewell address, retired. leaving "a great people prosperous and happy, in the full enjoyment of liberty and peace, honored and respected by every nation of the world."

At the age, then, of sixty years, our blooming Republic began to decline under the withering touch of Martin Van Buren! Disappointed ambition, thirst for power, pride, corruption, party spirit, faction, patronage, perquisites, fame, tangling alliances, priestcraft, and spiritual wickedness in *high places*, struck hands and revelled in midnight splendor.

Trouble, vexation, perplexity, and contention, mingled with hope, fear, and murmuring, rumbled through the Union and agitated the whole nation, as would an earthquake at the centre of the earth, the world heaving the sea beyond its bounds and shaking the everlasting hills; so, in hopes of better times, while jealousy, hypocritical pretensions, and pompous ambition were luxuriating on the ill-gotten spoils of the people, they rose in their majesty like a tornado, and swept through the land, till General Harrison appeared as a star among the storm-clouds for better weather.

The calm came, and the language of that venerable patriot, in his inaugural address, while descanting upon the merits of the Constitution and its framers, thus expressed himself:—"There were in it features which appeared not to be in harmony with their ideas of a simple representative Democracy or Republic. And knowing the tendency of power to increase itself, particularly when executed by a single individual, predictions were made that, at no very remote period, the Government would terminate in virtual monarchy.

"It would not become me to say that the fears of these patriots have been already realized. But as I sincerely believe that the tendency of measures and of men's opinions for some years past has been in that direction, it is, I conceive, strictly proper that I should take this occasion to repeat the assurances I have heretofore given of my determination to arrest the progress of that tendency, if it really exists, and restore the Government to its pristine health and vigor."

This good man died before he had the opportunity of applying one balm to ease the pain of our groaning country, and I am willing the nation should be the judge, whether General Harrison, in his exalted station, upon the eve of his entrance into the world of spirits, told the truth, or not, with acting President Tyler's three years of perplexity, and pseudo-Whig-Democrat reign to heal the breaches or show the wounds, *secundum artem*.

Subsequent events, all things considered, Van Buren's downfall, Harrison's exit, and Tyler's self-sufficient turn to the whole, go to show*— * * * * *certainly there is a God in heaven to reveal secrets*.

No honest man can doubt for a moment but the glory of American liberty is on the wane, and that calamity and confusion will sooner or later destroy the peace of the people. Speculators will urge a national bank as a savior of credit and comfort. A hireling pseudo-priesthood will plausibly push abolition doctrines and doings and "human rights" into Congress, and into every other place where conquest smells of fame, or opposition swells to popularity. Democracy, Whiggery, and cliquery will attract their elements and foment divisions among the people, to accomplish fancied schemes and accumulate power, while poverty, driven to despair, like hunger forcing its way through a wall, will break through the statutes of men to save life, and mend the breach in prison glooms.

A still higher grade of what the "nobility of nations" call "great men" will dally with all rights, in order to smuggle a fortune at "one fell swoop," mortgage Texas, possess Oregon, and claim all the unsettled regions of the world for hunting and trapping; and should an humble, honest man, red, black, or white, exhibit a better title, these gentry have only to clothe the judge with richer ermine, and spangle the lawyer's finger with finer rings, to have the judgment of his peers and the honor of his lords as a pattern of honesty, virtue, and humanity, while the motto hangs on his nation's escutcheon—"*Every man has his price!*"

Now, O people! people! turn unto the Lord and live, and reform this nation. Frustrate the designs of wicked men. Reduce Congress at

* For Explanation of Elipses see footnote p. 75 this volume.

least two-thirds. Two Senators from a State and two members to a million of population will do more business than the army that now occupy the halls of the national Legislature. Pay them two dollars and their board per diem (except Sundays.) That is more than the farmer gets, and he lives honestly. Curtail the officers of Government in pay, number, and power; for the Philistine lords have shorn our nation of its goodly locks in the lap of Delilah.

Petition your State Legislatures to pardon every convict in their several penitentiaries, blessing them as they go, and saying to them, in the name of the Lord, *Go thy way, and sin no more.*

Advise your legislators, when they make laws for larceny, burglary, or any felony, to make the penalty applicable to work upon roads, public works, or any place where the culprit can be taught more wisdom and more virtue, and become more enlightened. Rigor and seclusion will never do as much to reform the propensities of men as reason and friendship. Murder only can claim confinement or death. Let the penitentiaries be turned into seminaries of learning, where intelligence, like the angels of heaven, would banish such fragments of barbarism. Imprisonment for debt is a meaner practice than the savage tolerates, with all his ferocity. "*Amor vincit omnia.*"

Petition, also, ye goodly inhabitants of the slave States, your legislators to abolish slavery by the year 1850, or now, and save the abolitionist from reproach and ruin, infamy and shame.

Pray Congress to pay every man a reasonable price for his slaves out of the surplus revenue arising from the sale of public lands, and from the deduction of pay from the members of Congress.

Break off the shackles from the poor black man, and hire him to labor like other human beings; for "an hour of virtuous liberty on earth is worth a whole etermity of bondage." Abolish the practice in the army and navy of trying men by court-martial for desertion. If a soldier or marine runs away, send him his wages, with this instruction, that his country will never trust him again; he has forfeited his honor.

Make honor the standard with all men. Be sure that good is rendered for evil in all cases; and the whole nation, like a kingdom of kings and priests, will rise up in righteousness, and be respected as wise and worthy on earth, and as just and holy for heaven, by Jehovah, the Author of perfection.

More economy in the national and state governments would make less taxes among the people; more equality through the cities, towns, and country, would make less distinction among the people; and more honesty and familiarity in societies would make less hypocrisy and flattery in all branches of the community; and open, frank, candid decorum to all men, in this boasted land of liberty, would beget esteem, confidence, union, and love; and the neighbor from any state or from any country, of whatever color, clime or tongue, could rejoice when he put his foot on the sacred soil of freedom, and exclaim, The very name of "*American*" is fraught with "*friendship*!" Oh, then, create confidence, restore freedom, break down slavery, banish imprisonment for debt, and be in love, fellowship and peace with all the world! Remember that honesty is not subject to law. The law was made for transgressors. Wherefore a * * * * good name is better than riches.

For the accommodation of the people in every state and territory, let Congress show their wisdom by granting a national bank, with branches in each State and Territory, where the capital stock shall be held by the nation for the Central bank, and by the states and territories for the branches; and whose officers and directors shall be elected yearly by the people, with wages at the rate of two dollars per day for services; which several banks shall never issue any more bills than the amount of capital stock in her vaults and the interest.

The net gain of the Central bank shall be applied to the national revenue, and that of the branches to the states and territories' revenues. And the bills shall be par throughout the nation, which will mercifully cure that fatal disorder known in cities as *brokerage*, and leave the people's money in their own pockets.

Give every man his constitutional freedom and the president full power to send an army to suppress mobs, and the States authority to repeal and impugn that relic of folly which makes it necessary for the governor of a state to make the demand of the President for troops, in case of invasion or rebellion.

The governor himself may be a mobber; and instead of being punished, as he should be, for murder or treason, he may destroy the very lives, rights, and property he should protect. Like the good Samaritan, send every lawyer as soon as he repents and obeys the ordinances of heaven, to preach the Gospel to the destitute, without purse or scrip, pouring in the oil and the wine. A learned Priesthood is certainly more honorable than "*an hireling clergy.*"

As to the contiguous territories to the United States, wisdom would direct no tangling alliance. Oregon belongs to this government honorably; and when we have the red man's consent, let the Union spread from the east to the west sea; and if Texas petitions Congress to be adopted among the sons of liberty, give her the right hand of fellowship, and refuse not the same friendly grip to Canada and Mexico. And when the right arm of freemen is stretched out in the character of a navy for the protection of rights, commerce, and honor, let the iron eyes of power watch from Maine to Mexico, and from California to Columbia. Thus may union be strengthened, and foreign speculation prevented from opposing broadside to broadside.

Seventy years have done much for this goodly land. They have burst the chains of oppression and monarchy, and multiplied its inhabitants from two to twenty millions, with a proportionate share of knowledge keen enough to circumnavigate the globe, draw the lightning from the clouds, and cope with all the crowned heads of the world.

Then why—oh, why will a once flourishing people not arise, phœnix-like over the cinders of Martin Van Buren's power, and over the sinking fragments and smoking ruins of other catamount politicians, and over the windfalls of Benton, Calhoun, Clay, Wright, and a caravan of other equally unfortunate law doctors, and cheerfully help to spread a plaster and bind up the *burnt, bleeding wounds,* of a sore but blessed country?

The Southern people are hospitable and noble. They will help to rid so *free* a country of every vestige of slavery, whenever they are assured of an equivalent for their property. The country will be full of money and confidence when a National Bank of twenty millions, and a State Bank in every state, with a million or more, gives a tone to monetary matters, and make a circulating medium as valuable in the purses of a whole community as in the coffers of a speculating banker or broker.

The people may have faults, but they should never be trifled with. I think Mr. Pitt's quotation in the British Parliament of Mr. Prior's couplet for the husband and wife, to apply to the course which the King and ministry of England should pursue to the then colonies of the *now* United States, might be a genuine rule of action for some of the *breath-made* men in high places to use towards the posterity of this noble, daring people:—

"Be to her faults a little blind;
Be to her virtues very kind."

We have had Democratic Presidents, Whig Presidents, a pseudo-Democratic-Whig President, and now it is time to have a *President of the United States*; and let the people of the whole Union, like the inflexible Romans, whenever they find a *promise* made by a candidate that is not *practiced* as an officer, hurl the miserable sycophant from his exaltation, as God did Nebuchadnezzar, to crop the grass of the field with a beast's heart among the cattle.

Mr. Van Buren said, in his inaugural address, that he went in the Presidential chair the inflexible and uncompromising opponent of every attempt, on the part of Congress, to abolish slavery in the District of Columbia, against the wishes of the slave-holding States, and also with a determination equally decided to resist the slightest interference with it in the States where it exists.

Poor little Matty made this rhapsodical sweep with the fact before his eyes, that the State of New York, his native State, had abolished slavery without a struggle or a groan. Great God, how independent! From henceforth slavery is tolerated where it exists, constitution or no constitution, people or no people, right or wrong: *Vox Matti! Vox Diaboli!* And peradventure, his great "sub-treasury" scheme was a piece of the same mind. But the man and his measures have such a striking resemblance to the anecdote of the Welshman and his cart-tongue, that when the Constitution was so long that it allowed slavery at the capitol of a free people, it could not be cut off; but when it was so short that it needed a *sub-treasury* to save the funds of the nation, it *could be spliced!* Oh, granny, granny, what a long tail our puss has got.* * * * But his mighty whisk through the great national fire, for the presidential chestnuts, *burnt the locks of his glory with the blaze of his folly!*

In the United States the people are the government, and their united voice is the only sovereign that should rule, the only power that should be obeyed, and the only gentlemen that should be honored at home and abroad, on the land and on the sea. Wherefore, were I the president of the United States, by the voice of a virtuous people, I would honor the old paths of the venerated fathers of freedom; I would walk in the tracks of the illustrious patriots who carried the ark of the Government upon their shoulders with an eye single to the glory of the people, and when that people petitioned to abolish slavery in the slave states, I would use all honorable means to have their prayers granted, and, give liberty to the captive by paying the Southern gentlemen a reasonable equivalent for his property, that the whole nation might be free indeed!

When the people petitioned for a National Bank, I would use my best endeavors to have their prayers answered, and establish one on national principles to save taxes, and make them the controllers of its ways and means. And when the people petitioned to possess the territory of Oregon, or any other contiguous territory, I would lend the influence of a Chief Magistrate to grant so reasonable a request, that they might extend the mighty efforts and enterprise of a free people from the east to the west sea, and make the wilderness blossom as the rose. And when a neighboring realm petitioned to join the union of liberty's sons, my voice would be, *Come*—yea, come, Texas; come Mexico, come Canada; and come, all the world: let us be brethren, let us be one great family, and let there be a universal peace. Abolish the cruel custom of prisons (except certain cases), penitentiaries, court-martials for desertion; and let reason and friendship reign over the ruins of ignorance and barbarity; yea, I would, as the universal friend of man, open the prisons, open the eyes, open the ears, and open the hearts of all

* For explanation of Elipses see footnote p. 75 this volume.

people, to behold and enjoy freedom—unadulterated freedom; and God who once cleansed the violence of the earth with a flood, whose Son laid down His life for the salvation of all His Father gave him out of the world, and who has promised that He will come and purify the world again with fire in the last days, should be supplicated by me for the good of all people. With the highest esteem, I am a friend of virtue and of the people,

JOSEPH SMITH,

NAUVOO, ILLINOIS, February 7, 1844.

CHAPTER IX.

COMMENTS ON CANDIDACY OF JOSEPH SMITH FOR PRESIDENT OF THE UNITED STATES—TENDERS OF PEACE TO MISSOURI—PRELIMINARY STEPS TO WESTERN MOVEMENT OF THE CHURCH—JAMES A. BENNETT AND VICE PRESIDENCY.

Wednesday, February 7, 1844.—A piece of doggerel appears in the *Warsaw Message* of this date, entitled "Buckeye's Lamentations for the Want of More Wives," evidently the production of Wilson Law, and breathing a very foul and malicious spirit.

Thursday, 8.—Held Mayor's court, and tried two negroes for attempting to marry white women: fined one $25, and the other $5. In the evening there was a political meeting in the assembly room, when Brother Phelps publicly read for the first time my "Views of the Powers and Policy of the General Government." I addressed the meeting as follows:—

Views of the Prophet on His Candidacy for President of United States.

I would not have suffered my name to have been used by my friends on anywise as President of the United States, or candidate for that office, if I and my friends could have had the privilege of enjoying our religious and civil rights as American citizens, even those rights which the Constitution guarantees unto all her citizens alike. But this as a people we have been denied from the beginning. Persecution has rolled upon our heads from time to time, from portions of the United States, like peals of thunder, because of our religion; and no portion of the Government as yet has stepped forward for our relief. And in view of these things, I feel it to be my right and privilege to obtain what influence and power I can, lawfully, in the United States, for the protection of injured innocence; and if I lose my life in a good cause I am willing to be sacrificed on the altar of virtue, righteousness and truth, in maintaining the laws and Constitution of the United States, if need be, for the general good of mankind.

I was followed by Elders Hyde and Taylor, and a unanimous vote was taken to maintain my political views.

Friday, *9.*—Held Mayor's court in my dining-room on the case, "Nauvoo *versus* William Withers," for assault. Case withdrawn on my recommendation.

This evening a public meeting was held. I extract from the *Neighbor*:—

PUBLIC MEETING.

On Friday, the 9th instant, a public meeting was held in the assembly room, at which a public address of General Joseph Smith's to the citizens of the United States was read by Judge Phelps. The address is certainly an able document, big with meaning and interest, clearly pointing out the way for the temporal salvation of this Union, showing what would be our best policy, pointing out the rocks and quick-sand where the political bark is in danger of being wrecked, and the way to escape it, and evincing a knowledge and foresight of our political economy worthy of the writer.

Appropriate remarks were made by several gentlemen after the reading of the address.

Saturday, *10.*—I instructed the marshal to inform Mr. Cole, who kept a select school in the assembly room, that I must for the future have that room for my own use.

Prayer-meeting in the assembly room. Prayed for Sister Richards and others, who were sick.

A conference was held at Tuscaloosa county, Alabama: Elder John Brown, president; and George W. Stewart, clerk. Three branches were represented, containing nine elders, two priests, three teachers, three deacons, and 123 members.

Sunday, *11.*—Snow on the ground. Thaw commenced in the afternoon. I was at home.

Monday, 12.—I sat in the city council, and recommended the repeal of the ordinances entitled "An extra ordinance for the extra case of Joseph Smith," "An ordinance to prevent unlawful search or seizure of persons or property, by foreign* process, in the city of Nauvoo," and "An ordinance regulating the currency;" and they were repealed accordingly. The Memorial to Congress, passed December 21, 1843, was again read, and signed by the councilors, aldermen, mayor, recorder, and marshal.

I instructed Councilor Orson Pratt to call all the Illinois representatives together, and tell them our sufferings have been such that we must have that document passed, and we *will* have it.

"You must go in for it. Go to John Quincy Adams and ask him to call the delegates from Massachusetts separate from the Illinois delegation, and demand the same. Go to Henry Clay and other prominent men. Call public meetings in the city of Washington. Take the saloon, publish the admittance so much per ticket, invite the members of both houses to come and hear you, and roar upon them. You may take all my writings you think anything of and read to them, &c., and you shall prosper, in the name of God. Amen."

The recorder presented the report of the attendance of the city council, from which it appears that I have sat with them eleven sessions, from the 14th of October, 1843, to the 16th of January, 1844, inclusive.

Councilor Orson Pratt nominated George P. Stiles as councilor during his absence, which was confirmed by the council.

I burned $81 of city scrip according to ordinance.

Thawing. Streets very dirty.

Tuesday, 13.—I was at home. Settled with Theodore Turley, and gave him the deed of a lot.

Having received an invitation from Brother Joseph L. Heywood to visit Quincy, I wrote him in reply:—

*That is, process outside of the city government.

Letter:—Joseph Smith to Joseph L. Heywood—Anent a visit to Quincy.

NAUVOO, February 13, 1844.

DEAR BROTHER HEYWOOD,—I sit down at this time to acknowledge the receipt of, and reciprocate the friendly feelings manifest in yours of the 7th instant; and, although surrounded by a press of business, shall take pleasure in spending a few moments to reply.

I would take the greatest pleasure imaginable in coming down to Quincy on a visit to see you and all my friends in your city, would business and circumstances permit; but it would be a matter of impossibility almost for me to leave home at the present time, in consequence of a multitude of business which I have daily to attend to. Moreover, wisdom and prudence seem to forbid my coming, on account of the bitter feeling which manifests itself in various places between this and Quincy,—not that I have any apprehensions for my personal safety; for the same kind hand which hath hitherto been my shield and support would save me from the power of my wicked persecutors; but something might grow out of it which would prompt my adversaries to get out another illegal writ, and would eventually, probably, cost me some three or four thousand dollars, as in other cases, and under which I have still to labor to disadvantage. Under these considerations, therefore, I am compelled to decline paying you a visit for the present. At the same time, in connection with Mrs. Smith, I tender my warmest acknowledgement for the invitation.

I am pleased to hear of the prosperity of your branch, and hope it will continue; for, although I never feel to force my doctrine upon any person; I rejoice to see prejudice give way to truth, and the traditions of men dispersed by the pure principles of the Gospel of Jesus Christ.

I should be pleased to have the privilege of forming an acquaintance with your partner, Mr. Kimball, and his lady; and should they ever come up this way, I hope they will call and see me.

As respects things in Nauvoo, I have nothing to say but good. Although the mobocrats of this county breathe out their shame with a continual foam, and threaten extermination, &c..the citizens of Nauvoo are at peace; they fear no danger, for the report of mobs has become so common, that the "Mormons" pay no attention to it whatever. Each man minds his own business, and all are making improvements as fast as they can. In fact, things in general seem prosperous and pleasing; and I never saw a better feeling amongst the Saints than at the present time.

My family have been somewhat sick of late, and continue so, especially my youngest boy.

Accept, dear sir, the warmest respects of myself and Mrs. Smith, and please present the same to your lady. In the meantime I remain your friend and brother,

JOSEPH SMITH.

President Brigham Young returned from Bear creek settlements, where he had been preaching for the last few days.

Wednesday, 14.—At home through the day. In the evening the assembly room was filled by the brethren, when my "Views of the Powers and Policy of the Government of the United States" was again read. I afterwards spoke on the same subject at a considerable length.

Thursday, 15.—At home. A beautiful day.

I insert the following article from the *Times and Seasons*:—

WHO SHALL BE OUR NEXT PRESIDENT?

This is an inquiry which to us as a people is a matter of the most paramount importance, and requires our most serious, calm, and dispassionate reflection. Executive power, when correctly wielded, is a great blessing to the people of this great commonwealth, and forms one of the firmest pillars of our confederation. It watches the interests of the whole community with a fatherly care; it wisely balances the other legislative powers when over-heated by party spirit or sectional feeling; it watches with jealous care our interests and commerce with foreign nations, and gives tone and efficacy to legislative enactments.

The President stands at the head of these United States, and is the mouth-piece of this vast republic. If he be a man of an enlightened mind and a capacious soul,—if he be a virtuous man, a statesman, a patriot, and a man of unflinching integrity,—if he possess the same spirit that fired the souls of our venerable sires, who founded this great commonwealth, and wishes to promote the good of the whole republic, he may indeed be made a blessing to the community.

But if he prostrates his high and honorable calling to base and unworthy purposes,— if he make use of the power which the people have placed in his hands for their interests to gratify his ambition, for the purpose of self-aggrandizement or pecuniary interest,—if he meanly pander with demagogues, loses sight of the interest of the nation, and sacrifice the Union on the altar of sectional interests or party views, he renders himself unworthy of the dignified trust reposed in him, debases the nation in the eyes of the civilized world, and produces misery and confusion at home. "When the wicked rule, the people mourn."

There is perhaps no body of people in the United States who are at the present time more interested about the issue of the presidential contest than are the Latter-day Saints. And our situation in regard to the two great political parties is a most novel one. It is a fact well understood that we have suffered great injustice from the State of Missouri, that we have petitioned to the authorities of that state for redress in vain, that we have also memorialized Congress under the late administration, and have obtained the heartless reply that "Congress has no power to redress your grievances."

After having taken all the legal and constitutional steps that we can, we are still groaning under accumulated wrongs. Is there no power anywhere to redress our grievances? Missouri lacks the disposition and Congress lacks both the disposition and power (?); and thus fifteen thousand inhabitants of these United States can with impunity be dispossessed of their property; have their houses burned, their property confiscated, many of their numbers murdered, and the remainder driven from their homes and left to wander as exiles in this boasted land of freedom and equal rights; and after appealing again and again to the legally-constituted authorities of our land for redress, we are coolly told by our highest tribunals, "We can do nothing for you."

We have paid hundreds of thousands of dollars into the coffers of Congress for their lands, and they stand virtually pledged to defend us in our rights, but they have not done it. If a man steals a dollar from his neighbor, or steals a horse or a hog, he [the neighbor] can obtain redress; but we have been robbed by wholesale, the most daring murders have been committed, and we are coolly told that we can obtain no redress. If a steamboat is set on fire on our coast by foreigners, even when she is engaged in aiding and abetting the enemies of that power, it becomes a matter of national interference and legislation; or if a foreigner, as in the case of McLeod, is taken on our land and tried for supposed crimes committed by him against our citizens, his nation interferes, and it becomes a matter of negotiation and legislation. But our authorities can calmly look on and see the citizens of a county butchered with impunity: they can see two counties dispossessed of their inhabitants, their houses burned, and their property confiscated; and when the cries of fifteen thousand men women and children salute their ears, they deliberately tell us that we can obtain no redress.

Hear it, therefore, ye mobbers! Proclaim it to all the scoundrels in the Union! Let a standard be erected around which shall rally all the renegadoes of the land: assemble yourselves and rob at pleasure; murder till you are satiated with blood; drive men, women and children from their homes: there is no law to protect them, and Congress has no power to redress their grievances; and the great father of the Union (the President) has not got an ear to listen to their complaints.

What shall we do under this state of things? In the event of either of the prominent candidates, Van Buren or Clay, obtaining the presidential chair, we should not be placed in any better situation.

In speaking of Mr. Clay, his politics are diametrically opposed to ours. He inclines strongly to the old school of Federalists, and as a matter of course would not favor our cause, neither could we conscientiously vote for him. And we have yet stronger objections to Mr. Van Buren on other grounds. He has sung the old song of Congress—"Congress has no power to redress your grievances."

But did the matter rest here, it would not be so bad. He was in the presidential chair at the time of our former difficulties. We appealed to him on that occasion, but we appealed in vain, and his sentiments are yet *unchanged*.

But all these things are tolerable in comparison to what we have yet to state. We have been informed from a respectable source that there is an understanding between Mr. Benton, of Missouri, and Mr. Van Buren, and a conditional compact entered into, that if Mr. Benton will use his influence to get Mr. Van Buren elected, Van Buren when elected, shall use his executive influence to wipe away the stain from Missouri by a further persecution of the "Mormons," and wreaking out vengeance on their heads, either by extermination or by some other summary process. We could scarcely credit the statement; and we hope yet, for the sake of humanity, that the suggestion is false: but we have too good reason to believe that we are correctly informed.

If, then, this is the case, can we conscientiously vote for a man of this description, and put the weapons into his hands to cut our throat with? We cannot. And however much we might wish to sustain the Democratic nomination, we cannot—we will not vote for Van Buren. Our interests, our property, our lives, and the lives of our families are too dear to us to be sacrificed at the shrine of party spirit and to gratify party feelings. We have been sold once in the State of Missouri, and our liberties bartered away by political demagogues, through executive intrigue, and we wish not to be betrayed again by Benton and Van Buren.

Under these circumstances, the question again arises, Whom shall we support? General Joseph Smith—a man of sterling worth and integrity and of enlarged views—a man who has raised himself from the humblest walks in life to stand at the head of a large, intelligent, respectable, and increasing society, that has spread not only in this land, but in distant nations,—a man whose talents and genius are of an exalted nature, and whose experience has rendered him in every way adequate to the onerous duty. Honorable, fearless, and energetic, he would administer justice with an impartial hand, and magnify and dignify the office of Chief Magistrate of this land; and we feel assured that there is not a man in the United States more competent for the task.

One great reason that we have for pursuing our present course is, that at every election we have been made a political target for the filthy demagogues in the country to shoot their loathsome arrows at. And every story has been put into requisition to blast our fame from the old fabrication of "walk on the water" down to "the murder of ex-Governor Boggs." The journals have teemed with this filthy trash, and even men who ought to have more respect for themselves—men contending for the gubernatorial chair have made use of terms so degrading, so mean, so humiliating, that a Billingsgate fisherwoman would have considered herself disgraced with. We refuse any longer to be thus bedaubed for either party. We tell all such to let their filth flow in its own legitimate channel, for we are sick of the loathsome smell.

Gentlemen, we are not going either to "murder ex-Governor Boggs, nor a Mormon in this state for not giving us his money," nor are we going to "walk on the water," "nor drown a woman," nor "defraud the poor of their property," nor send "destroying angels after General Bennett to kill him," nor "marry spiritual wives," nor commit any other outrageous act this election to help any party with. You must get some other persons to perform these kind offices for you for the future. We withdraw.

Under existing circumstances, we have no other alternative; and if we can accomplish our object, well: if not, we shall have the satisfaction of knowing that we have acted conscientiously, and have used our best judgment. And if we have to throw away our votes, we had better do so upon a worthy rather than upon an unworthy individual, who might make use of the weapon we put in his hand to destroy us with.

Whatever may be the opinions of men in general in regard to Mr. Smith, we know that he needs only to be known to be admired; and that it is the principles of honor, integrity, patriotism, and philanthropy that have elevated him in the minds of his friends; and the same principles, if seen and known, would beget the esteem and confidence of all the patriotic and virtuous throughout the Union.

Whatever, therefore, be the opinions of other men, our course is marked out, and our motto henceforth will be—*General Joseph Smith.*

Friday, 16.—At home. This evening I spent two hours in the office. Settled with Brother Whitney; gave him deed of several town lots, and took his receipt in full.

Saturday, 17.—I wrote the following article:—

PACIFIC INUENDO.

The very candid, pacific, and highly creditable *advice* which Governor Ford has done himself the honor to address to "the citizens of Hancock county, Mormons and all," and which appears in the *Warsaw Signal* of the 14th instant, is like the balm of Gilead, well calculated to ease the pain which has troubled the heads and hearts of the Carthagenians, Warsawvians, and other over-jealous bodies for *weal and woe.*

It certainly must be admitted, on all hands, that Governor Ford has exalted himself as a mediator, patriot, lawyer, governor, peacemaker, and friend of all, not only to magnify the law and make it honorable, but also in pointing out the part of peace.

Such is what the Latter-day Saints have ever sought at the hands of those in authority; and with an approving conscience clear as the crystal spring, and with a laudable intention warm as the summer zephyr, and with a charitable prayer mellow as the morning dew, it is now our highest consolation to hope that all difficulties will cease, and give way to reason, sense, peace, and goodwill.

The Saints, if they will be humble and wise, can now practice what they preach,and soften by good examples, rather than harden by a distant course of conduct, the hearts of the people.

For general information, it may be well to say that there has never been any cause for alarm as to the Latter-day Saints. The legislature of Illinois granted a liberal charter for the City of Nauvoo; and let every honest man in the Union who has any knowledge of her say whether she has not flourished beyond the most sanguine anticipations of all. And while they witness her growing glory, let them solemnly testify whether Nauvoo has willfully injured the country, county, or a single individual one cent.

With the strictest scrutiny publish the facts, whether a particle of law has been evaded or broken: virtue and innocence need no artificial covering. Political views and party distinctions never should disturb the harmony of society; and when the whole truth comes before a virtuous people, we are willing to abide the issue.

We will here refer to the three last dismissals upon writs of *habeas corpus*, of Joseph Smith, when arrested under the requisitions of Missouri.

The first, in June, 1841, was tried at Monmouth, before Judge Douglas, of the fifth judicial circuit: and as no exceptions have been taken to that decision by the state of Missouri—but Missouri previously entered a *nolle prosequi* on all the old indictments against the Mormons in the difficulties of 1838—it is taken and granted that that decision was just!

The second, in December, 1842, was tried at Springfield before Judge Pope in the U. S. District Court; and from that honorable discharge, as no exceptions from any source have been made to those proceedings, it follows as a matter of course that that decision was just!

And the third, in July, 1843, was tried at the city of Nauvoo, before the Municipal Court of said city; and as no exceptions to that discharge have been taken, and as the governor says there is "evidence on the other side to show that the sheriff of Lee county *voluntarily* carried Mr. Reynolds (who had Mr. Smith in custody,) to the city of Nauvoo without any coercion on the part of any one," it must be admitted that that decision was just!

But is any man unconvinced of the justness of these strictures relative to the two last cases, let the astounding fact go forth, that *Orrin Porter Rockwell*, whom Boggs swore was the principal in his [attempted] assassination, and as accessory to which Mr. Smith was arrested, has returned home, "clear of sin." In fact, there was not a witness to get up an indictment against him.

The Messrs. Averys, who were unlawfully transported out of this state, have returned to their families in peace; and there seems to be no ground for contention. no cause for jealousy, and no excuse for a surmise that any man, woman, or child will suffer the least inconvenience from General Smith, the charter of Nauvoo, the city of Nauvoo, or even any of her citizens.

There is nothing for a bone of contention! Even those ordinances which appeared to excite the feeling of some people have recently been repealed; so that if the "intelligent" inhabitants of Hancock county want peace, want to abide by the Governor's advice, want to have a character at home, and really mean to follow the Savior's golden rule, "To do unto others as they would wish others to do unto them," they will be still now, and let their own works praise them in the gates of justice and in the eyes of the surrounding world. Wise men ought to have understanding enough to conquer men with kindness.

"A soft answer turneth away wrath," says the wise man; and it will be greatly to the credit of the Latter-day Saints to show the love of God, by now kindly treating those who may have, in an unconscious moment, done wrong; for truly said Jesus, Pray for thine enemies.

Humanity towards all, reason and refinement to enforce virtue, and good for evil are so eminently designed to cure more disorders of society than an appeal to arms, or even argument untempered with friendship, and the one thing needful that no vision for the future, guide-board for the distant, or expositor for the present, need trouble any one with what he ought to do.

His own good, his family's good, his neighbor's good, his country's good, and all good seem to whisper to every person—The governor has told you what to do. Now do it.

The constitution expects every man to do his duty; and when he fails the law urges him; or should he do too much, the same master rebukes him.

Should reason, liberty, law, light, and philanthropy now guide the destinies of Hancock county with as much sincerity as has been manifested for her notoriety or welfare, there can be no doubt that peace, prosperity, and happiness will prevail, and that future generations as well as the present one will call Governor Ford *a peacemaker*. The Latter-day Saints will, at all events, and profit by the instruction, and call upon honest men to help them cherish all the love, all the friendship, all the courtesy, all the kindly feelings, and all the generosity that ought to characterize clever people in a clever neighborhood, and leave candid men to judge which tree exhibits the best fruit—the one with the most clubs and sticks thrown into its boughs and the grass trodden down under it, or the one with no sticks in it, some dead limbs, and rank grass growing under it; for by their signs ye can know their fruit, and by the fruit ye know the trees.

Our motto, then, is Peace with all! If we have joy in the love of God, let us try to give a reason of that joy, which all the world cannot gainsay or resist. And may be, like as when Paul started with recommendations to Damascus to persecute the Saints, some one who has raised his hand against us with letters to men in high places may see a light at noonday, above the brightness of the sun, and hear the voice of Jesus saying, "It is hard for thee to kick against the pricks."

Intelligence is sometimes the messenger of safety. And, willing to aid the governor in his laudable endeavors to cultivate peace and honor the laws, believing that very few of the citizens of Hancock county will be found in the negative of such a goodly course, and considering his views a kind of manifesto, or olive leaf, which shows that there is rest for the soles of the Saints' feet we give it a place in the *Neighbor*, wishing it God speed, and saying, God bless good men and good measures! And as Nauvoo has been, so it will continue to be, a good city, affording a good market to a good country; and let those who do not mean to try the way of transgressors, say "Amen."

The High Council met and settled several cases of difficulty betwixt brethren.

The Anti-Mormons held a convention at Carthage, the object being to devise ways and means of expelling the Saints from the State. Among other resolutions was one appointing the 9th of March next as the day of fasting and prayer, wherein the pious of all orders are requested to pray to Almighty God that He would speedily bring the false Prophet Joseph Smith to deep repentance, or that He will make a public example of him and his leading accomplices.

Anti-Mormon Convention at Carthage.

The ice broke up in the river.

Sunday, 18.—Beautiful day. Southwest wind.

A very large assembly of the Saints met at the stand, near the Temple, when I preached a lengthy discourse.

Four p. m., went to my office with Hyrum and two gentlemen from St. Louis. Heard Dr. Richards read my correspondence with Senator Calhoun, and Phelps read my "Views of the Power and Policy of the General Government."

At seven, attended prayer-meeting in the assembly room.

Monday, 19.—At nine a. m. went to my office with Dr. Bernhisel, who proposed some alterations in my views of the government. Phelps read the same, and the doctor seemed better pleased with it than before.

To the Editor of the Neighbor:—

SIR,—I wish to say to you, as there seems to be a prospect of peace, that it will be more love-like, more God-like, and man-like, to say nothing about the *Warsaw Signal.*

If the editor breathes out that old sulphurous blast, let him go and besmear his reputation and the reputation of those that uphold him with soot and dirt, but as for us and all honest men, we will act well our part, for there the honor lies.

We will honor the advice of Governor Ford, cultivate peace and friendship with all, mind our own business, and come off with flying colors, respected, because, in respecting others, we respect ourselves.

Respectfully, I am
JOSEPH SMITH.

A conference was held in Halifax, Halifax county,

Nova Scotia, Elder Robert Dickson, president. Two branches were represented, consisting of thirty members, three elders, one priest, one teacher, and two deacons.

The wild geese commenced flying north.

Tuesday, 20.—At ten a. m. went to my office, where the Twelve Apostles and some others met in council with Brothers Mitchell Curtis and Stephen Curtis, who left the pinery on Black river, 1st January. They were sent by Lyman Wight and Bishop Miller to know whether Lyman should preach to the Indians, the Menominees and Chippeways having requested it.

Delegation from Lyman Wight on Indian Affairs

The Chippeways had given Brother Wight some wampum as a token of peace, and the brethren had given them half a barrel of flour and an ox to keep the Indians from starving, and Wight had gone through to Green Bay with them to make a road.

I told them to tell Brother Wight I had no counsel to give him on the subject. He is there on his own ground and must act on his own responsibility, and do what he thinks best in relation to the Indians, understanding the laws and nature of the subject as well as I can here, and he shall never be brought into difficulty about it by us.

I instructed the Twelve Apostles to send out a delegation and investigate the locations of California and Oregon, and hunt out a good location, where we can remove to after the temple is completed, and where we can build a city in a day, and have a government of our own, get up into the mountains, where the devil cannot dig us out, and live in a healthful climate, where we can live as old as we have a mind to.

Western Movement for the Church Contemplated

Warm. The ice floating down the river.

A meeting of the citizens of Hancock county was held at the court-house in Carthage. Passed a resolution that the second Saturday of March be appointed for a general wolf-hunt, being the same day

A Wolf Hunt Called for Hancock Co.

selected by the convention of the 17th instant for a day of fasting and prayer for my destruction.

Wednesday 21.—The Rev. Mr. De Wolfe, Episcopalian, lectured in the assembly room in the evening. I attended and, after the sermon, at his request, spoke to the people, showing them that to get salvation we must not only do some things, but everything which God has commanded. Men may preach and practice everything except those things which God commands us to do, and will be damned at last. We may tithe mint and rue, and all manner of herbs, and still not obey the commandments of God. The object with me is to obey and teach others to obey God in just what He tells us to do. It mattereth not whether the principle is popular or unpopular, I will always maintain a true principle, even if I stand alone in it.

The Prophet on the Necessity of Complete Obedience to God.

My *Pacific Inuendo*, written on the 17th instant, appeared in the *Neighbor* of to-day, in connection with Governor Ford's letter of the 29th of January.

Ice left the west bank of the river, opposite the lower brick house.

Very warm and pleasant.

Council of the Twelve met in my office. I insert the minutes:—

Minutes of a Council Meeting of the Twelve.

At a meeting of the Twelve, at the mayor's office, Nauvoo, February 21, 1844, seven o'clock, p. m., Brigham Young, Parley P. Pratt, Orson Pratt, Wilford Woodruff, John Taylor, George A. Smith, Willard Richards and four others being present, called by previous notice, by instruction of President Joseph Smith on the 20th instant, for the purpose of selecting a company to explore Oregon and California, and select a site for a new city for the Saints.

Jonathan Dunham, Phineas H. Young, David D. Yearsley, and David Fullmer, volunteered to go; and Alphonzo Young, James Emmett, George D. Watt, and Daniel Spencer were requested to go.

Voted the above persons to be notified to meet with the council on Friday evening next, at the assembly room,

WILLARD RICHARDS, Clerk.

Thursday, *22*.—At home.

Ice continues to run in the river. Very pleasant, cool nights.

Friday, *23*.—W. W. Phelps received a letter from John Whitmer in relation to certain records, and a book containing some of the early history of the Church which had been written by my clerks, and was Church property, and which had been fraudulently detained from my possession by John Whitmer; to which Dr. Richards replied.

The Western Exploring Equipment.

Met with the Twelve in the assembly room concerning the Oregon and California Exploring Expedition; Hyrum and Sidney present. I told them I wanted an exploration of all that mountain country. Perhaps it would be best to go direct to Santa Fe. "Send twenty-five men: let them preach the Gospel wherever they go. Let that man go that can raise $500, a good horse and mule, a double barrel gun, one-barrel rifle, and the other smooth bore, a saddle and bridle, a pair of revolving pistols, bowie-knife, and a good sabre. Appoint a leader, and let them beat up for volunteers. I want every man that goes to be a king and a priest. When he gets on the mountains he may want to talk with his God; when with the savage nations have power to govern, &c. If we don't get volunteers, wait till after the election."

George D. Watt said, "Gentlemen, I shall go." Samuel Bent, Joseph A. Kelting, David Fullmer, James Emmett, Daniel Spencer, Samuel Rolfe, Daniel Avery, and Samuel W. Richards, volunteered to go.

Saturday, *24*.—At home. Had an interview with Brother Phelps at nine o'clock.

Seth Palmer, Amos Fielding, Charles Shumway, and John S. Fullmer volunteered to go to Oregon and California.

Fifteen hundred copies of my "Views" out of press.

Very pleasant the past two weeks; the pleasantest February I ever saw.

President Brigham Young went to Knowlton's settlement on Bear creek, and preached.

Sunday, 25.—I preached at the temple block. Hyrum also preached.

Evening, I attended prayer-meeting in the assembly room. We prayed that "General Joseph Smith's Views of the Powers and Policy of the United States," might be spread far and wide, and be the means of opening the hearts of the people. I gave some important instructions, and prophesied that within five years we should be out of the power of our old enemies, whether they were apostates or of the world; and told the brethren to record it, that when it comes to pass they need not say they had forgotten the saying.

A Prophecy of Deliverance of the Saints

Some rain in the evening; cloudy and foggy.

Monday, 26.—At home. A cold wind from the north. Rainy, dull day.

In the afternoon, held court at the Mansion. City of Nauvoo *versus* Orsimus F. Botswick, on complaint of Hyrum Smith for slanderous language concerning him and certain females of Nauvoo. Bostwick was fined $50 and costs. Francis M. Higbee, his attorney, gave notice he should appeal to the municipal court, and then to the circuit court. I told Higbee what I thought of him for trying to carry such a suit to Carthage—it was to stir up the mob and bring them upon us.

The Case of Botswick Slander of Hyrum Smith.

Prayer-meeting in the assembly room in the afternoon. My uncle John Smith and lady were present, were anointed, and received blessings; and in the evening Father Morley was also blessed.

Ira S. Miles volunteered to join the mountain exploring expedition.

Tuesday, 27.—At home. Cool and clear. River clear of ice.

In the afternoon, visited the printing office.

Mailed my "Views of Powers and Policy," &c., to the

President and cabinet, supreme judges, senators, representatives, principal newspapers in the United States, (all the German), and many postmasters and individuals.

Almon L. Fullmer and Hosea Stout volunteered to go on the Western Exploring Expedition.

Wednesday, *28.*—At home. Rainy day.

At four, p. m., steamboat *General Brooke* passed up the river: first boat this season. No ice in sight.

In the evening I sent Brother Coolidge to Brother Phelps, to call the brethren and pray for Brother Coolidge's sick child, as he thought it could not live till morning. Elder John Taylor and others prayed for him.

Dr. Alphonzo Young published an appeal to his native state of Tennessee, giving a history of our Missouri troubles, and asking the influence of that state to obtain redress.

The *Neighbor* of to-day publishes the following:—

FOR PRESIDENT, JOSEPH SMITH.

Having now raised the name of our General and Prophet to the head of our columns, it becomes us, as Latter day Saints, to be prudent and energetic in the cause that we pursue, and not let any secondary influences control our minds or govern our proceedings.

The step that we have taken is a bold one, and requires our united efforts, perseverance, and diligence; but important as it may be, it is no greater than others have taken, and they have conceived that they had a right, without molestation, to pursue that course, and to vote for that man whose election they in their wisdom thought would be most conducive to the public weal.

As American citizens, then we presume that all will concede to us this right; and whatever may be their views respecting the policy of such a step, they will acknowledge that we act legally, justly, and constitutionally in pursuing our present course.

Some have nominated Henry Clay, some Colonel Johnson, others John C. Calhoun, others Daniel Webster, and others Martin Van Buren.

Those several committees, unquestionably thought that they had each of them made the wisest selection in naming the man of their choice. They selected their several candidates because they thought they were the wisest, the greatest statesmen, and the most competent to fill the presidential chair, whilst they severally thought that the other candidates were incompetent.

We have governed by the same principles; and if others think they have made the wisest selection, so do we. If others think they have nominated the greatest statesman, so do we; and while those several committees think that none of the nominations made are so good as their own, we think that the man of our choice is the most able, the most competent, the best qualified, and would fill the Presidential chair with greater dignity to the nation; and that his election would be conducive of more happiness and prosperity at home and abroad than that of any other man in these United States.

This is a thing that we, as Latter-day Saints, know; and it now devolves upon us as an imperative duty to make others acquainted with the same things, and to use all our influence at home and abroad for the accomplishment of this object.

Mr. Smith is not so generally known personally as are several of the above-named candidates; and although he has been much spoken of as a man, he has been a great deal calumniated and misrepresented, and his true character is very little known.

It is for us to take away this false coloring; and by lecturing, by publishing, and circulating his works, his political views, his honor, integrity and virtue, to stop the foul mouth of slander, and present him before the public in his own colors, that he may be known, respected, and supported.

Thomas S. Edwards volunteered to join the exploring expedition to the Rocky Mountains.

Thursday, 29.—Called at my office, and gave Brother Phelps the *Zanesville Gazette* of January 31, containing the speech of Cassius M. Clay, delivered in Scott county, Kentucky, December 30, 1843, on annexing Texas to the United States; and instructed him to reply to the same, and gave him the subject matter, and directed the manner I wished it done; and then rode out with Porter Rockwell.

A Reply Sketched to Cassius M. Clay.

The steamer *Ohio* went up the river.

Moses Smith and Rufus Beach volunteered to join the Oregon exploring expedition.

Friday, March 1.—Very frosty night; showery day, west wind.

Spent the day in counseling.

Letters from the elders show a rapid progress of the work of the Lord in different parts of the Union. Elder John E. Page has gone to Washington for the purpose of proclaiming to the rulers of our nation the principles of eternal truth. By a letter received from him, we learn he has been preaching and baptizing in Boston and vicinity.

The High Council to the Saints in Nauvoo.

The High Council of the Church of Jesus Christ of Latter-day Saints at Nauvoo to the Saints of this [Nauvoo] Stake, greeting.

BELOVED BRETHREN,—Realizing as we do, the importance of the work in which we are engaged, we deem it expedient to lay before you such matters from time to time as in our opinion will be beneficial to the Saints, and the spirit in us may seem to require.

We would remind our brethren, the elders, who have at sundry times been sent forth as flaming heralds, messengers of the everlasting Gospel, who proclaim a message of salvation to their fellow-men, thereby gathering and bringing up to Zion the scattered elect of God, to be taught more perfectly he principles of salvation; that whilst their message is abroad we have had our mission to remain at Nauvoo and to participate with the Saints in the blessing of poverty, if such it may be called; amid sickness and distress, in the vexations and turmoils of the unruly and ungodly, for which no man has paid us, for days, weeks, months, and years; that our time has been spent in endeavoring to settle difficulties, set in order the things needful to salvation; in trying to reconcile and cement the feelings of our brethren to each other in the spirit of the Gospel; whilst at times, circumstances of a more painful nature have been presented.

Individuals have been brought before us charged with high crimes in violation of the laws of heaven, on whom much patient exertion in the labors of love have by us been bestowed, to reclaim them from the error and evil of their doings.

We regret to have it to say that in some instances our efforts have been fruitless; for after we have found in them an obstinate and unyielding spirit to the principles of right, we have (reluctantly) been compelled to sever them from the Church as withered branches.

Such persons not unfrequently manifest their wickedness by their trifling with and bidding defiance to all and every good rule, regulation and law, set forth for the guidance of all Saints.

One single trait of their depravity is frequently manifested by their going to some ignorant elder and getting re-baptized into the Church, not having first made the least satisfaction (as was required) to such as they have injured.

We have to say that baptism in such cases is not valid and cannot profit. We here continue to say; let such expelled person first be reconciled to his injured brother, and bring forth fruit mete for repentance; or, in case of dissatisfaction with our decision, take an appeal and reverse it, if found wrong.

Expelled persons not complying with these rules (which are in accordance with the order of heaven), whom we have been once necessitated to withdraw fellowship from, cannot be restored in any illegal way; and we would say that all such clandestine entering into the Church is climbing up some other way, and that such persons can only be considered as thieves and robbers. We would also remind the elders that it is improper for them to re-baptize any such expelled persons while they remain thus obstinate; and that it will subject them to censure, and bring them to trial before a proper tribunal of the Church.

We therefore hope, for the future, that certain officious, forward-feeling elders will be more prudent in such cases hereafter.

We remain yours in the bonds of the new and everlasting covenant,

WILLIAM MARKS,
CHARLES C. RICH,
Presidents.

SAMUEL BENT,
DAVID FULLMER,
NEWEL KNIGHT,
JAMES ALLRED,
GEORGE W. HARRIS,
WILLIAM HUNTINGTON, SEN.,
L. DUNBAR WILSON,
THOMAS GROVER,
LEONARD SOBY,
ALPHEUS CUTLER,
AARON JOHNSON,
HENRY G. SHERWOOD,
Counselors.

HOSEA STOUT, Clerk.

The *Times and Seasons* of March 1st presents my name to the public as candidate for president of the United States.

Jonathan Dunham filed his bonds with the recorder, and took the oath of office as wharf-master of the city of Nauvoo.

Elder Wilford Woodruff very sick; the 37th anniversary of his birthday.

Saturday, 2.—Ten a. m. held Mayor's court. Reproved Elder S. B. Stoddard for giving appearance of evil in attempting to be bail for Orsimus F. Boswick. Brother Stoddard afterwards explained to my satisfaction.

President Brigham Young visited Macedonia, accompanied by his brother, L. D. Young, and preached there on the Sabbath.

Sunday, 3.—Ground covered with snow. Attended prayer-meeting in the evening.

Monday, 4.—I suggested the name of James Arlington Bennett, of Long Island, as a candidate for Vice-President.

At early candle-light, the First Presidency, Twelve Apostles, temple committee, and others, met in council. I insert the minutes.

Minutes of a Council Meeting—Twelve and Temple Committee.

George Coray came in, and said he was sent by Lyman Wight to get sheep, &c, to carry to the Pine country, to receipt for them, or agree to pay lumber.

President Joseph suggested that it was best to let the Nauvoo House remain as it is until the temple is completed, as we need the temple more than anything else.

Elder Haws said there was some dissatisfaction about being sent from the Pinery without accounts, &c., and could not have credit on tithing, and one month at the Pinery is only called fifteen days here.

President Joseph told them that they should have their number of days in full. "We will let the Nauvoo house stand until the temple is done, and we will put all our forces on the Temple, turn our lumber towards the Temple, and cover it in this fall, and sell the remainder to get blasting powder, fuse, rope, steel, &c.

And when the temple is completed, no man shall pass the threshold till he has paid five dollars; and every stranger shall pay five dollars towards liquidating the cash debts on the Temple, and I will not have the house dirtied.

Let Woodworth go to the pinery, take the things wanted, and bring back the lumber, and his wages go on as usual.

Let a special conference be called on the 6th of April, and all the elders called home who can come. Let the people of this city come together on Thursday, at nine o'clock in the morning. After two or three lectures, we will call on the people to fill up the boxes with liberal contributions, to procure cash materials for the temple.

I instructed a letter to be written to James Arlington

Bennett to consult him on the subject of nominating him for Vice-President. I here insert the letter:—

Letter—Willard Richards to James Arlington Bennett—The Matter of Bennett Becoming Candidate for Vice-President of U. S.

NAUVOO, March 4, 1844.

DEAR GENERAL,—Yours of the 1st of February, was duly received, and produced the most pleasing sensations among your friends here, and especially with the Prophet, who said, "Tell General Bennett I am perfectly satisfied with his explanation; and as to *temper*, I had not even thought of it."

You suggest that Brother Joseph's correspondence with Mr. Calhoun would appear in some degree to contradict the noble sentiments expressed in that able document to yourself; but if you will notice that his communication to you was written as an individual, and that to Mr. Calhoun as the voice of the people he represents, I think you will discover no discrepancy; but if so, tell me particulars without delay, and you shall have an explanation.

I have recently mailed to you General Smith's "Views of the Powers and Policy of the Government of the United States," which were drawn forth in consequence of his friends selecting him as a candidate for the next Presidency, which he very reluctantly acquiesced in, and it seems would not, only to support a favorite maxim—"*The people must govern;*" but having once been prevailed upon to suffer his name to go abroad as a candidate, it is desirable to him of course, as to every patriot, that those who have brought him forward should use all honorable means to sustain him in the canvass; and if I had not felt disposed to uphold him before the people, I never would have been the first to urge his nomination; and during the short space since his name has been published, his friends have been astonished at the flood of influence that is rolling through the Western States in his favor, and in many instances where we might have least expected it.

I need not assert what the wisest of the wise admit without argument—that General Smith is the greatest statesman of the 19th century. Then why should not the nation secure to themselves his superior talents, that they may rise higher and higher in the estimation of the crowned heads of the nations, and exalt themselves through his wisdom?

Your friends here consider your letter about the Governorship of Illinois just like every man in your quarter, mere sport, child's sport; for who would stoop to the play of a single State, when the whole nation was on the board?—a cheaper game!

General Smith says, if he must be President, Arlington Bennett must be Vice-President. To this his friends are agreed—agreed in everything; and in this consists our power: consequently, your name will appear in our next paper as our candidate for Vice-President of the United States. You will receive our undivided support, and we expect the same in return for General Smith for the Presidency; and we will go it with the rush of a whirlwind, so peaceful, so gentle, that it will not be felt by the nation till the battle is won.

Dear General, if glory, honor, force, and power in righteous principles are desired by you, now is your time. You are safe in following the counsel of that man who holds communion with heaven; and I assure you, if you act well your part, victory's the prize.

Brother Arlington, look well to "General Smith's Views," and his letter to Calhoun, and comprehend him fully. Say to the *New York Herald*, now is the time for your exaltation; raise your standard high, sound your trumpet long and loud, support General Smith and myself at the next election; and when we are exalted, you shall not be forgotten.

Hold forth no false shadows to honest men; yet though there is but one best piece to the fatted calf, yet there are many good slices; therefore you will not forget the "*Advertiser*," "*Niles Register*," "*Globe*," &c., &c.

Get up an electoral ticket—New York, New Jersey, Pennsylvania, and any other state within your reach. Open your mouth wide, and God shall fill it. Cut your quill, and the ink shall flow freely.

Commence at your own mansion and stay not, only for electioneering purposes, till by some popular route you reach Nauvoo; and if you preach Mormonism it will help you. At every stage, tavern, boat and company, expose the wickedness of Martinism in saying, if he is elected President, he will annihilate the Mormons, and proclaim the sycophancy of the candidates generally, and uphold Joseph against every aspersion and you shall triumph gloriously.

We have many things to say to you, which we must keep till we see you face to face.

All is right at Nauvoo. We are now fitting out a noble company to explore Oregon and California, and progressing rapidly with the great Temple, which we expect to roof this season, though there is yet a chance at the *eleventh hour* for you to bring in your thousand, and secure your "penny."

On the 6th of April is our special conference at Nauvoo. I wish you could be here on that occasion, but the time is too short. From that period our Elders will go forth by hundreds or thousands and search the land, preaching religion and politics; and if God goes with them, who can withstand their influence?

My words are the words of your friends here—Come and see us.

Brother Joseph's, Young's, and Bernhisel's respects to you. Mrs. Richards' kind respects with mine to yourself and love to all yours.

Most respectfully yours,

WILLARD RICHARDS.

The temple committee proposed to establish a powder manufactory.

CHAPTER X.

URGING THE BUILDING OF THE TEMPLE—TENDERS OF PEACE TO MISSOURI—PROPHET'S DISCOURSE ON ELIAS, ELIJAH, MESSIAH—LYMAN WIGHT'S PROPOSAL OF A SOUTHWEST MOVEMENT FOR THE CHURCH.

Tuesday, March 5, 1844.—I saw Hyrum Kimball at Bryant's store, and gave him a lecture on his resisting the ordinances of the city, by telling the captains of the steamboats they need not pay wharfage, &c.

Rode out with Emma.

At two, p. m., met with the City Council. I copy the minutes:—

Special Session of the City Council.

March 5, 1844, 2 p. m.

Names of members called. Quorum present.

Mayor stated that he had called the council, because that when the wharf-master called on the steamboats for wharfage, the officers of the boats declined paying, assigning as a reason that Hyrum Kimball and —— Morrison had told them that they owned the land, and they need pay no wharfage to the city; and he called the council to know their views on the subject, as he had told Hyrum Kimball that he should see the ordinances executed; and if the boats did not pay, he should blow them up and all those who upheld them in resisting the ordinances. Every measure is taken to palsy the hands of the officers of the city; and I want to know how to remedy the evil, or whether I shall abandon the ordinances, &c.

Alderman Harris said that it was the mayor's duty to enforce the ordinances of the city, and that no man has a right to build a wharf without leave from the city council.

Councilor Phelps suggested the propriety of licensing those who owned wharves to collect a tax for the landing of the boat.

Alderman Wells concurred.

Mayor said the land on the water's edge was a street.

Alderman Wells suggested the propriety of having the street worked as soon as may be.

Councilor Phelps said, if Water street extended round the city, then Kimball had been constructing a nuisance.

Mayor spoke in explanation, and said that Kimball said, if the city would make a wharf, he would give up what he had done.

Councilor Orson Spencer said he wished the mayor to execute the law of the city.

Councilor Brigham Young concurred.

Councilor W. W. Phelps proposed that Water street be worked the whole length.

Councilor Taylor said, "I go in for executing the laws of the city."

Marshal stated that Morrison said he had a bond for a deed to low-water mark, and the city could not take his personal rights, and he objected to the boats paying wharfage.

Councilor Orson Pratt said, if Kimball or Morrison or any one else has built wharves since that street was laid out, they could get no damages.

Councilor Daniel Spencer considered the ordinance passed good, and it ought to be enforced.

Councilor Hyrum Smith, believed it was our duty to stand up to the ordinances.

Moved by Brigham Young that the city council instruct the Mayor to order the supervisor to open Water street from Joseph Smith's store north to the north line of the city.

Councilor Phelps approved of the motion, that the road might be cleared from rafts, and the rafts might also pay license.

Councilor Warrington said the upper stone house was in the street.

Mayor said that was the greatest nuisance there was in the street.

Councilor Orson Spencer was in favor [i.e., of the motion to open Water street.] Motion carried unanimously.

The governor having refused to issue commissions to the aldermen-elect of the city, Councilor Whitney inquired who were aldermen.

The mayor explained that if the governor refuses to grant a commission, it does not disqualify the officer elect from acting in his office; consequently, there is no virtue in the commission, but the virtue of the office consists in the election.

Councilor Young thought they were aldermen all the time or none of the time.

Mayor said he wanted all the aldermen to be added to the city council.

Alderman Wells said he considered the election made the aldermen, and not the commission.

Mayor said if he had been elected alderman and filed his bonds, he would act as councilor and magistrate.

Packard's Memorial to Legislature of Massachusetts

Noah Packard sent a memorial to the governor, senate, and house of representatives of Massachusetts, his native state, setting forth in detail the sufferings of the Saints in Missouri, and their expulsion from that state.

Wednesday, *6* —Went to my office, and thence with Brother Phelps to Mr. Bryant's, to see him about his uniting with Hiram Kimball and others to resist the ordinances of the city.

The *Neighbor* publishes the name of James Arlington Bennett as candidate for Vice-President.

Thursday, *7.*—A splendid day; wind from the south-west.

Minutes of a General Meeting in the Interest of the Temple.

[Reported by Elders Willard Richards and Wilford Woodruff.]

A vast assembly of Saints met at the Temple of the Lord at nine o'clock a. m., by a special appointment of President Joseph Smith, for the purpose of advancing the progress of the Temple, &c.

The Patriarch, Hyrum Smith, was present; also of the Twelve Apostles, Brigham Young, Heber C. Kimball, Parley P. Pratt, Orson Pratt, Willard Richards, Wilford Woodruff, John Taylor, and George A. Smith; also the temple committee and about eight thousand Saints.

A hymn was sung by the choir; prayer by Elder Parley P. Pratt, when another hymn was sung.

Patriarch Hyrum Smith took the stand and said, The object of the meeting is to stir up your minds by way of remembrance. It is necessary to have a starting-point, which is to build the Temple.

With the assistance of the sisters, we expect to get the nails and glass; and with the assistance of the brethren, we expect to do the rest. I will proclaim in public and in private thet the sisters bought the glass and nails by penny subscription. Choose ye this day whom ye will serve.

We shall call upon this vast multitude for a donation to buy powder and fuse-ropes to blast the rocks in the quarry. We want the brethren to at least do as much as the sisters.

We do not intend to finish the Nauvoo House this season, but to take all the hands and finish the Temple this summer, or the walls of it, and get the roof on by December, and do off the inside next winter; and about a year from this spring we will dedicate it.

We can do anything we undertake. We have power, and we can do great things. In five years to come the work will progress more than it has done for ten years past.

Isaiah said we should perform a marvelous work and a wonder. I don't wonder he said so, if he saw this vast multitude; and I think this people is abundantly able to build this temple, and much depends upon it for our endowments and sealing powers; and many blessings depend upon it.

President Joseph Smith then arrived, took the stand, arose, and, after requesting Orson Pratt to come to the stand and take his post, said:—

I do not know whether the object of the meeting has been told you or not. I apologize for not coming sooner.

I have had so much on my mind since I saw you, that I hardly know where to begin or what to say; but one of the grand objects I had in view in calling this meeting was to make a few remarks relative to the laws and ordinances of the city and the building of the temple.

The reason I want to speak of the city ordinances is that the officers have difficulty in administering them.

We are republicans, and wish to have the people rule; but they must rule in righteousness. Some would complain with what God Himself would do.

The laws or ordinances are enacted by the city council on petition of the people; and they can all be repealed, if they wish it, and petition accordingly.

At all events, the people ought not to complain of the officers; but if they are not satisfied, they should complain to the lawmakers by petition.

I am instructed by the city council to tell this people that if there is any law passed by us which you dislike. we will repeal it, for we are your servants. Those who complain of our rights and charters are wicked and corrupt, and the devil is in them.

The reason I called up this subject is, we have a gang of simple fellows here who do not know where their elbows or heads are. If you preach virtue to them, they will oppose that; or if you preach a Methodist God to them, they will oppose that; and the same if you preach anything else; and if there is any case tried by the authorities of Nauvoo, they want it appealed to Carthage to the circuit court. Mr. Orsimus F. Bostwick's case had to go to Carthage. Our lawyers will appeal anything to the circuit court.

I want the people to speak out and say whether such men should be tolerated and supported in our midst; and I want to know if the citizens will sustain me when my hands are raised to heaven for and in behalf of the people.

From this time I design to bring such characters who act against the interests of the city before a committee of the whole; and I will have the voice of the people, which is republican, and is likely to be the voice of God; and as long as I have a tongue to speak, I will expose the iniquity of the lawyers and wicked men.

I fear not their boiling over nor the boiling over of hell, their thunders, nor the lightning of their forked tongues.

If these things cannot be put a stop to, I will give such men into the hands of the Missouri mob. The hands of the officers of the city falter and are palsied by their conduct.

There is another person I will speak about. He is a Mormon—a certain man who lived here before we came here; the two first letters of his name are Hiram Kimball. When a man is baptized and becomes a member of the Church, I have a right to talk about him, and reprove him in public or private, whenever it is necessary, or he deserves it.

When the city passed an ordinance to collect wharfage from steamboats, he goes and tells the captains of the steamboats that he owned the landing, and that they need not pay wharfage.

I espise the man who will betray you with a kiss; and I am determined to use up these men, if they will not stop their operations. If this is not true, let him come forward and throw off the imputation.

When they appeal to Carthage, I will appeal to this people, which is the highest court. I despise the lawyers who haggle on lawsuits, and I would rather die a thousand deaths than appeal to Carthage,

Kimball and Morrison say they own the wharves; but the fact is, the city owns them, sixty-four feet from high water mark. From the printing office to the north limits of the city is public ground, as Water street runs along the beach, and the beach belongs to the city and not to individuals.

Another thing: I want to speak about the lawyers of this city. I have good feelings towards them; nevertheless I will reprove the lawyers and doctors anyhow. Jesus did, and every prophet has; and if I am a prophet, I shall do it: at any rate, I shall do it, for I profess to be a prophet.

The maritime laws of the United States have ceded up the right to regulate all tolls, wharfage, &c., to the respective corporations who have jurisdiction, and not to individuals.

Our lawyers have read so little that they are ignorant of this: they have never stuck their noses into a book on maritime law in their lives, and, as Pope says:—

> Shallow draughts intoxicate the brain;
> Drink deep, or taste not the Pierian Spring.

Our city lawyers are fools to undertake to practice law when they know nothing about it.

I want from this time forth every fool to stay at home and let the steamboats and captains alone. No vessel could land anywhere, if subject to individual laws.

The corporation owns the streets of the city, and has as much right to tax the boats to make wharves as to tax citizens to make roads. Let every man in this city stay at home, and let the boat-captains, peace-officers and everybody alone.

How are we to keep peace in the city, defend ourselves against mobs, and keep innocent blood from being shed? By striking a blow at everything that rises up in disorder.

I will wage an eternal warfare with those that oppose me while I am laboring in behalf of the city. I will disgrace every man by publishing him on the house top, who will not be still and mind his own business. Let them entirely alone, and they will use themselves up.

I was visited by an old gentleman this morning, who told me that the spirit of mobocracy was about subsiding. A couple of merchants in this city (I will not tell their names,) have told the country people not to bring butter, eggs, &c., to Nauvoo for sale; at least, so the people abroad say.

Now, if they will not let the people bring their produce, the people will not buy their goods; and the result will be, the merchants will get a spirit of mobocracy.

Another man (I will not call his name,) has been writing to the *New York Tribune*, some of the most disgraceful things possible to name. He says, in that article, that there are a great many donations to the Temple which have been appropriated to other purposes.

His object evidently was to stigmatize the trustee and excite prejudice against us abroad. But I pledge myself that whoever has contributed any old shoes, harness, horses, wagons, or anything else, if he will come forward, will show that every farthing is on the book and has been appropriated for the building of the Temple.

I pledge myself that if he finds the first farthing that we cannot show where it has been appropriated, I will give him my head for a football.

He also states that the Temple cannot be built, it costs so much. Who does not know that we can put the roof on the building this season, if we have a mind to? By turning all the means from the Nauvoo House and doubling our diligence we can do it.

There are men in our midst who are trying to build up themselves at our expense, and others who are watching for iniquity, and will make a man an offender for a word. The best way for such men is to be still. If I did not love men, I would not reprove them, but would work in the darkness as they do.

As to who is the author of the article in the *Tribune*, read it and you will see for yourselves. He is not a lawyer; he is nearer related to a doctor—a small man. (Mr. McNeil inquired if he was the man.) No; I do not know you: you are a stranger. But I will rest myself and give way for others.

President Hyrum Smith arose and made a few remarks. He compared the lawyers to polliwogs, wigglers, and toads. He said they would dry up next fall. "Those characters, I presume, were made in gizzard making time, when it was cheaper to get gizzards than souls; for if a soul cost $5, a gizzard would cost nothing: like tree toads, they change color to suit the object they are upon. They ought to be ferreted out like rats. You could describe them as you would a hedgehog: they are in every hedge, stinking like the skunk."*

Charles Foster asked if Joseph meant him.

Joseph said, "I will reply by asking you a question."

Foster: "That is no way."

Joseph. "Yes, that is the way the Quakers do. But Jesus said, "Whose image and superscription is this? Why did you apply the remarks to yourself? Why did you ask if we meant you?

Foster. "Then I understand you meant me.

Joseph. "You said it."

Foster. "You shall hear from me."

Joseph. "As Mayor, I fine you $10 for that threat, and for disturbing the meeting."

Doctor Foster spoke in palliation of his brother Charles, and asked Joseph to await, &c. He said, "He has not threatened you." Joseph said, "He has." Doctor Foster said: "No one has heard him threaten you," when hundreds cried, "I have!" Doctor Foster continued to speak, when the Mayor called him to order, or, said he, "I will fine you."

William W. Phelps then read General Smith's "Views of the Powers and Policy of the General Government of the United States;" after which, it was voted, unanimously, with one exception, to uphold General Smith for the Presidency of the United States.

* Nauvoo was unfortunate in being overrun with pettifogging lawyers at this time, and it was to these, doubtless, that the disparaging remarks of both the Prophet and Hyrum, rspecting lawyers referred. It is unfortunate that they did not segregate the pettifoggers from the worthy men of the profession; than whom no class of citizens,and no other profession, render more valuable service to the state.

An article was also read by W. W. Phelps, entitled, "A Voice of Innocence from Nauvoo," and all the assembly said "Amen" twice.

At thirty minutes past twelve, the meeting adjourned till two p. m.

When the people assembled according to adjournment, choir sang a hymn. Prayer by Elder Orson Pratt. Singing.

President Brigham Young addressed the congregation. He said: I wish to speak upon the duty of lawyers, as they have been spoken of this morning. They were first among the children of Israel to explain the laws of Moses to the common people.

I class myself as a lawyer in Israel. My business is to make peace among the people; and when any man who calls himself a lawyer takes a course to break peace instead of making it, he is out of the line of his duty. A lawyer's duty is to read the law well himself, then tell the people what it is, and let them act upon it, and keep peace; and let them receive pay like any laboring man.

It is desirable for justices of the peace, when men call for writs, to inquire into the merits of the case, and tell the parties how to settle it, and thus put down lawsuits. To cure lawing, let us pay attention to our business.

When we hear a story, never tell it again, and it will be a perfect cure. If your brother mistreats you, let him alone; if your enemy cheats you, let it go; cease to deal with men who abuse you. If all men had taken the straightforward course that some have, we should not have such disorderly men in our midst.

I have no objection to any man coming here, but I will have nothing to do with men who will abuse me at midnight and at noonday. Our difficulties and persecutions have always arisen from men right in our midst.

It is the lust of individuals to rob us of everything, and to take advantage of divisions that may arise among us to build themselves up. I feel that I want every man should stay and lift up holy hands without dubiety, wrath or doubting.

To the men who own land here I would say: Do not think you can sell your lands here, and then go off and spend it somewhere else in abusing the Mormons. I tell you nay; for know it, ye people, that Israel is here; and they are the head, and not the tail; and the people must learn it. All those who have gone from us have gone from the head to the tail.

The grand object before us is to build the temple this season.

We have heard the effects of slander, and we want a cure and balm; and I carry one with me all the while, and I want all of you to do the same. I will tell you what it is: it is to mind your own business, and let others alone, and suffer wrong rather than do wrong. If any take your property away, let them alone, and have nothing to do with them.

A spirit has been manifested to divide the Saints. It was manifest in the last election. It was said, if they did not look out, the Saints on the flat would beat the Saints on the hill.

Great God! how such a thing looks, that the Saints should be afraid of beating one another in the election, or being beat? I would ask, who built up this city? Would steamboats have landed here, if the Saints had not come? Or could you, even the speculators, have sold your lands for anything here, if the Saints had not come? They might have sold for a few bear and wolf skins, but not for money.

If any of you wish to know how to have your bread fall butter-side up, butter it on both sides, and then it will fall butter-side up. Oppose this work, and it will roll over you.

When did this work ever stop since it began? Never. The only thing the Saints now want to know is—what does the Lord want of us, and we are ready to do it.

Well, then, build the Temple of the Lord. Keep the law of God, ye Saints, and the hypocrite and scoundrel will flee out of your midst and tremble, for the fire of God will be too hot for them.

I expect the Saints are so anxious to work, and so ready to do right, that God has whispered to the Prophet, "Build the Temple, and let the Nauvoo House alone at present." I would not sue a man, if he owed me five hundred or a thousand dollars, should he come to me and say he would not pay me.

Elder John Taylor remarked that it was said by some discontented persons that the municipal officers of the city were acting in an arbitrary manner, which was false. He then went to explain the principles of Democracy, until it was announced that it would be desirable to set a contribution on foot immediately to get fuse rope and blasting powder, as a boat was coming down the river, and the messenger was waiting to go down to St. Louis.

Elder Taylor paused awhile for this purpose,and a collection amounting to about sixty dollars was made. He then continued his speech: "When society was first organized they found themselves without legislature, congress, house of lords, or anything of the kind, every man was lord over his own house.

Difficulties began to arise, and the people began to contend and combine together in governments. By-and-by, some two or three requested that they might return to their original customs, and the government said they might. This was the situation of this city in the main, when we asked for a charter.

Of General Joseph Smith some are afraid, and think it doubtful about his election; and, like the ostrich, stick their heads under a bush, and leave their bodies out, so that we can all see them; and after this it will be a by-word—"That man is an ostrich who hides his head in this cause." He spoke also on going on with the temple.

President Brigham Young said—"Those who have not paid their property tithing we shall call upon, and take dinner; and we had rather be saved that trouble, and have them come up and pay. You will want a blessing in the temple when it is done."

President Joseph Smith remarked:—In relation to those who give in property for the temple. We want them to bring it to the proper source, and to be careful into whose hands it comes, that it may be entered into the Church books, so that those whose names are found in the Church books shall have the first claim to receive their endowments in the temple. I intend to keep the door at the dedication myself, and not a man shall pass who has not paid his bonus.

As to politics, I care but little about the presidential chair. I would not give half as much for the office of President of the United States as I would for the one I now hold as Lieutenant-General of the Nauvoo Legion.

We have as good a right to make a political party to gain power to defend ourselves, as for demagogues to make use of our religion to get power to destroy us. In other words, as the world has used the power of government to oppress and persecute us, it is right for us to use it for the protection of our rights. We will whip the mob by getting up a candidate for President.

When I get hold of the Eastern papers, and see how popular I am, I am afraid myself that I shall be elected; but if I should be, I would not say, "*Your cause is just, but I can do nothing for you.*"

What I have said in my views in relation to the annexation of Texas is with some unpopular; the people are opposed to it. Some of the Anti-Mormons are good fellows. I say it, however, in anticipation that they will repent. They object to Texas on account of slavery. Why, it is the very reason she ought to be received, so that we may watch over them; for, of the two evils, we should reject the greatest.

Governor Houston of Texas, says—"if you refuse to receive us into the United States, we must go to the British Government for protection."

This would certainly be bad policy for this nation; the British are now throughout that whole country, trying to bribe all they can; and the first thing they would do, if they got possession, would be to set the negroes and the Indians to fight, and they would use us up. British officers are now running all over Texas to establish British influence in that country.

It will be more honorable for us to receive Texas and set the negroes free, and use the negroes and Indians against our foes. Don't let Texas go, lest our mothers and the daughters of the land should laugh us in the teeth; and if these things are not so, God never spoke by any Prophet since the world began.

How much better it is for the nation to bear a little expense than to have the Indians and British upon us and destroy us all. We should grasp all the territory we can. I know much that I do not tell. I have had bribes offered me, but I have rejected them.

The government will not receive any advice or counsel from me: they are self-sufficient. But they must go to hell and work out their own salvation with fear and trembling.

The South holds the balance of power. By annexing Texas, I can do away with this evil. As soon as Texas was annexed, I would liberate the slaves in two or three States, indemnifying their owners, and send the negroes to Texas, and from Texas to Mexico, where all colors are alike. And if that was not sufficient, I would call upon Canada, and annex it.

Singing by the choir. Prayer by President B. Young.

Arrival of Wm. Kay and Company of English Saints.

The barque *Fanny*, Captain Patterson, arrived at New Orleans with 210 souls, led by Elder William Kay. They express, [the opinion] in a letter to the *Millennial Star*, that no people ever had a more prosperous voyage than the Lord has favored this company with; and such a captain and crew, for kindness, could scarcely be met with, the captain frequently administering from the cabin stores unto the necessities of all who required it.

Elder John E. Page published an address to the inhabitants of Washington.

Friday, 8.—Very heavy rain all night, accompanied by thunder.

Bishop Miller arrived from the Pinery.

Jas. A. Bennett Ineligible for Vice-President of U. S.

At ten a. m., my scribe, Willard Richards, called to tell me that James Arlington Bennett was a native of Ireland, and therefore was not constitutionally elegible to be the Vice-President. He wanted to know who should be nominated for Vice-President. I told him to counsel with others upon that point, when he said he would call a council this evening.

At seven p. m., the First Presidency, the Twelve, Bishop Miller, Levi Richards, W. W. Phelps, and Lucian Woodworth assembled in the Mayor's office, when W. W. Phelps read the following pacific communication, which I had previously dictated him to write:—

A Friendly Hint to Missouri.

One of the most pleasing scenes that can occur on earth, when a sin has been committed by one person against another, is, to forgive that sin; and then according to the sublime and perfect pattern of the Savior, pray to our Father in heaven to forgive him also.

Verily, verily, such a friendly rebuke is like the mellow zephyr of summer's eve—it soothes, it cheers and gladdens the heart of the humane and the savage. Well might the wise man exclaim, "A soft answer turneth away wrath;" for men of sense, judgment, and observation, in all the various periods of time, have been witnesses, figuratively speaking, that water, not wood, checks the rage of fire.

Jesus said: "Blessed are the peacemakers, for they shall be called the children of God." Wherefore if the nation, a single State, community, or family ought to be grateful for anything, it is peace.

Peace, lovely child of heaven!—peace like light from the same great parent, gratifies, animates, and happifies the just and the unjust, and is the very essence of happiness below, and bliss above.

He that does not strive with all his powers of body and mind, with all his influence at home and abroad, and to cause others to do so too—to seek peace and maintain it for his own benefit and convenience, and for the honor of his State, nation, and country, has no claim on the clemency of man; nor should he be entitled to the friendship of woman or the protection of government.

He is the canker-worm to gnaw his own vitals; and the vulture to prey upon his own body; and he is, as to his own prospects and prosperity in life, a *felo-de-se* of his own pleasure.

A community of such beings are not far from hell on earth, and should be let alone as unfit for the smiles of the free or praise of the brave.

But the peacemaker, O give ear to him! for the words of his mouth and his doctrine drop like the rain, and distil as the dew. They are like the gentle mist upon the herbs, and as the moderate shower upon the grass.

Animation, virtue, love, contentment, philanthropy, benevolence, compassion, humanity and friendship push life into bliss: and men, a little below the angels, exercising their powers, privileges, and knowledge according to the order, rules, and regulations of revelation, by Jesus Christ, dwell together in unity; and the sweet odor that is wafted by the breath of joy and satisfaction from their righteous communion is like the rich perfume from the consecrated oil that was poured upon the head of Aaron, or like the luscious fragrance that rises from the field of Arabian spices. Yea, more, the voice of the peacemaker—

> It is like the music of the spheres—
> It charms our souls and calms our fears;
> It turns the world to Paradise,
> And men to pearls of greater price.

So much to preface this friendly hint to the state of Missouri: for, notwithstanding some of her private citizens and public officers have committed violence, robbery, and even murder upon the rights and persons of the Church of Jesus Christ of Latter-day Saints, yet compassion, dignity, and a sense of the principles of religion among all classes, and honor and benevolence, mingled with charity by high-minded patriots, lead me to suppose that there are many worthy people in that state who will use their influence and energies to bring about a settlement of all those old difficulties, and use all consistent means to urge the State, for her honor, prosperity, and good name, to restore every person she or her citizens have expelled from her limits, to their rights, and pay them all damage, that the great body of high-minded and well-disposed Southern and Western gentlemen and ladies—the real peace-makers of a western world, will go forth—good Samaritan-like, and pour in the oil and the wine, till all that can be healed are made whole; and after repentance, they shall be forgiven; for verily the Scriptures say, "Joy shall be in heaven over one sinner that repents, more than over ninety-and-nine just persons that need no repentance."

Kowing the fallibility of man, considering the awful responsibility of rejecting the cries of the innocent, confident in the virtue and patriotism of the noble-minded Western men, tenacious of their character and standing, too high to stoop to disgraceful acts, and too proud to tolerate meanness in others; yea, may, I not say, without boasting that the best blood of the West, united with the honor of the illustrious fathers of freedom, will move, as the forest is moved by a mighty wind, to promote peace and friendship in every part of our wide-spread, lovely country.

Filled with a love almost unspeakable, and moved by a desire pleasant as the dew of heaven, I supplicate not only our Father above, but also the civil, the enlightened, the intelligent, the social, and the best inhabitants of Missouri—those that feel bound by principles of honor, justice, moral greatness, and national pride, to arise in the character of virtuous freemen from the disgrace and reproach that might inadvertantly blur their good names, for want of self-preservation.

Now is the time to brush off the monster that, incubus-like, seems hanging upon the reputation of the whole State. A little exertion, and the infamy of the evil will blacken the guilty only, for is it not written, "The tree is known by its fruit?"

The voice of reason, the voice of humanity, the voice of the nation, and the voice of Heaven seem to say to the honest and virtuous throughout the State of Missouri, wash yourselves, make you clean, lest your negligence should be taken by the world, from the mass of facts before it, that you are guilty!

Let there be one unison of hearts for justice; and when you reflect around your own firesides, remember that fifteen thousand once among you, now not, but who are just as much entitled to the privileges and blessings you enjoy as yourselves, like the widow before the unjust judge, are fervently praying for their rights.

When you meditate upon the massacre at Haun's mill, forget not that the Constitution of your State holds this broad truth to the world, that none shall be deprived of life, liberty, or property, but by the judgement of his peers or the law of the land.

And when you assemble together in towns, counties, or districts, whether to petition your legislature to pay the damage the Saints have sustained in your State, by reason of oppression and misguided zeal, or to restore them to their rights according to Republican principles and benevolent designs, reflect, and make honorable, or annihilate, such statute law as was in force in your state in 1838,—*viz*: "If twelve or more persons shall combine to levy war against any part of the people of this state, or to remove [them] forcibly out of the state or from their habitations, evidenced by taking arms and assembling to accomplish such purpose, every person so offending shall be punished by imprisonment in the Penitentiary for a period not exceeding five years, or by a fine not exceeding five thousand dollars and imprisonment in the county jail not exceeding six months.

Finally, if honor dignifies an honest people, if virtue exalts a community, if wisdom guides great men, if principle governs intelligent beings, if humanity spreads comfort among the needy, and if religion affords consolation by showing that charity is the first, best and sweetest token of perfect love, then, O ye good people of Missouri, like the woman in Scripture who had lost one of her ten pieces of silver, arise, search diligently till you find the lost piece, and then make a feast, and call in your friends for joy.

With due consideration, I am the friend of all good men,

JOSEPH SMITH.

NAUVOO, ILL., March 8, 1844.

Brother George A. Smith brought the information that Brother Farnham had just returned from St. Louis, and said the people in that place were saying, "Things have come to a strange pass. If Joe Smith is elected President, he will raise the devil with Missouri; and if he is not elected, he will raise the devil anyhow."

St. Louis Comment on the Prophet's Candidacy.

It was agreed that Colonel Solomon Copeland, living at Paris, Henry county, Tennessee, should be written to on the subject of the Vice-Presidency; and that Elder Wilford Woodruff should write the letter, and invite him to visit us, and see if he would suffer his name to run for that office.

Copeland of Tennessee Considered as Candidate for Vice-President.

Saturday, 9.—Met in the City Council, and gave my reasons in favor of the repeal of the hog law. [The subject was discussed at some length.]

Council adjourned for one hour. In the afternoon City Council rejected the petition to repeal the hog law.

I proposed to license Hiram Kimball and Mr. Morrison, who own the land opposite to the wharf, to make wharves and collect wharfage; then the city can dispense with a wharf-master; that Kimball and Morrison pay a tax for the landing of every boat; and they could tax the boat, or not, as they liked.

Matter of Wharfage.

The Female Relief Society met twice in the assembly room, and sanctioned "The Voice of Innocence From Nauvoo," and then adjourned for one week to accommodate others who could not get into the room at either of the meetings.

Our worthy brother, King Follett, died this morning, occasioned by the accidental breaking of a rope, and the falling of a bucket of rock upon him while engaged in walling up a well, and the men above were in the act of lowering the rock to him.

Death of King Follett.

KING FOLLETT BIOGRAPHY.

Elder Follett was one of those who bore the burden, in common with others of his brethren, in the days when men's faith was put to the test. He was a native of Vermont, and moved many years since into Cuyahoga county, Ohio.

There, for the first time, he heard the Gospel preached, united with the Church of Jesus Christ of Latter-day Saints in the spring of 1831, and has been a sharer in the afflictions through which the Saints have passed from that time until the time of his death.

He shared in the violence of Missouri persecution, was cast into prison, and endured many months' imprisonment; and, after long delay, obtained a trial on the charges preferred against him, and was honorably discharged, being acquitted of all the crimes with which a band of wicked persecutors could ch arge him

All the persecutions he endured only tended to strengthen his faith and confirm his hope; and he died as he had lived, rejoicing in the hope of future felicity.

Having united with the Church in the forty-first year of his age, he filled up the prime of his life in the service of his God, and went to rest in his fifty-sixth year, being fifty-five years, seven months, and fourteen days old when he slept the sleep of death.

So the righteous pass, and so they sleep, until the mandate of Him for whom they suffer and in whom they trust shall call them forth to glory, honor, immortality and eternal life.

Sunday, 10.—Frost in the night; beautiful day. South wind.

Brother King Follett was buried this day with Masonic honors.

I attended meeting at the stand, and preached on the subject of Elias, Elijah, and Messiah. [A sketch of which was reported by Elder Wilford Woodruff, as follows]:—

Discourse of the Prophet.—Elias, Elijah, Messiah.

There is a difference between the spirit and office of Elias and Elijah. It is the spirit of Elias I wish first to speak of; and in order to come at the subject, I will bring some of the testimony from the Scripture and give my own.

In the first place, suffice it to say, I went into the woods to inquire of the Lord, by prayer, His will concerning me, and I saw an angel, and he laid his hands upon my head, and ordained me to a Priest after the order of Aaron, and to hold the keys of this Priesthood, which office was to preach repentance and baptism for the remission of sins, and also to baptize. But I was informed that this office did not extend to the laying on of hands for the giving of the Holy Ghost; that that office was a greater work, and was to be given afterward; but that my ordination was a preparatory work, or a going before, which was the spirit of Elias; for the spirit of Elias was a going before to prepare the way for the greater, which was the case with John the Baptist. He came crying through the wilderness, "Prepare ye the way of the Lord, make his paths straight." And they were informed, if they could receive it, it was the spirit of Elias; and John was very particular to tell the people, he was not that Light, but was sent to bear witness of that Light.

He told the people that his mission was to preach repentance and baptize with water; but it was He that should come after him that should baptize with fire and the Holy Ghost.

If he had been an imposter, he might have gone to work beyond his bounds, and undertook to have performed ordinances which did not belong to that office and calling, under the spirit of Elias.

The spirit of Elias is to prepare the way for a greater revelation of God, which is the Priesthood of Elias, or the Priesthood that Aaron was ordained unto. And when God sends a man into the world to prepare for a greater work, holding the keys of the power of Elias, it was called the doctrine of Elias, even from the early ages of the world.

John's mission was limited to preaching and baptizing; but what he did was legal; and when Jesus Christ came to any of John's disciples, He baptized them with fire and the Holy Ghost.

We find the apostles endowed with greater power than John: their office was more under the spirit and power of Elijah than Elias.

In the case of Phillip when he went down to Samaria, when he was under the spirit of Elias, he baptized both men and women. When Peter and John heard of it, they went down and laid hands upon them, and they received the Holy Ghost. This shows the distinction between the two powers.

When Paul came to certain disciples, he asked if they had received the Holy Ghost? They said, No. Who baptized you, then? We were baptized unto John's baptism. No, you were not baptized unto John's baptism, or you would have been baptized by John. And so Paul went and baptized them, for he knew what the true doctrine was, and he knew that John had not baptized them. And these principles are strange to me, that men who have read the Scriptures of the New Testament are so far from it.

What I want to impress upon your minds is the difference of power in the different parts of the Priesthood, so that when any man comes among you, saying, "I have the spirit of Elias," you can know whether he be true or false; for any man that comes, having the spirit and power of Elias, he will not transcend his bounds.

John did not transcend his bounds, but faithfully performed that part belonging to his office; and every portion of the great building should be prepared right and assigned to its proper place; and it is necessary to know who holds the keys of power, and who does not, or we may be likely to be deceived.

That person who holds the keys of Elias hath a preparatory work. But if I spend much more time in conversing about the spirit of Elias, I shall not have time to do justice to the spirit and power of Elijah.

This is the Elias spoken of in the last days, and here is the rock upon which many split, thinking the time was past in the days of John and Christ, and no more to be. But the spirit of Elias was revealed to me, and I know it is true; therefore I speak with boldness, for I know verily my doctrine is true.

Now for Elijah. The spirit, power, and calling of Elijah is, that ye have power to hold the key of the revelation, ordinances, oracles, powers and endowments of the fullness of the Melchisedeck Priesthood and of the kingdom of God on the earth; and to receive, obtain, and perform all the ordinances belonging to the kingdom of God, even unto the turning of the hearts of the fathers unto the children, and the hearts of the children unto the fathers, even those who are in heaven.

Malachi says, "I will send you Elijah the prophet before the coming of the great and dreadful day of the Lord: and he shall turn the heart of the fathers to the children, and the heart of the children to their fathers, lest I come and smite the earth with a curse."

Now, what I am after is the knowledge of God, and I take my own course to obtain it. What are we to understand by this in the last days?

In the days of Noah, God destroyed the world by a flood, and He has promised to destroy it by fire in the last days: but before it should take place, Elijah should first come and turn the hearts of the fathers to the children, &c.

Now comes the point. What is this office and work of Elijah? It is one of the greatest and most important subjects that God has revealed. He should send Elijah to seal the children to the fathers, and the fathers to the children.

Now was this merely confined to the living, to settle difficulties with families on earth? By no means. It was a far greater work. Elijah! what would you do if you were here? Would you confine your work to the living alone? No: I would refer you to the Scriptures, where the ubject is manifest: that is, without us, they could not be made perfect, nor we without them; the fathers without the children, nor the children without the fathers.

I wish you to understand this subject, for it is important; and if you will receive it, this is the spirit of Elijah, that we redeem our dead, and connect ourselves with our fathers which are in heaven, and seal up our dead to come forth in the first resurrection;and here we want the power of Elijah to seal those who dwell on earth to those who dwell in heaven. This is the power of Elijah and the keys of the kingdom of Jehovah.

Let us suppose a case. Suppose the great God who dwells in heaven should reveal Himself to Father Cutler here, by the opening heavens, and tell him, "I offer up a decree that whatsoever you seal on earth with your decree, I will seal it in heaven; you have the power then; can it be taken off? No. Then what you seal on earth, by the keys of Elijah, is sealed in heaven; and this is the power of Elijah, and this is the difference between the spirit and power of Elias and Elijah; for while the spirit of Elias is a forerunner, the power of Elijah is sufficient to make our calling and election sure; and the same doctrine, where we are exhorted to go on to perfection, not laying again the foundation of repentance from dead works, and of laying on of hands, ressurection of the dead, &c.

We cannot be perfect without the fathers, &c. We must have revelation from them, and we can see that the doctrine of revelation far transcends the doctrine of no revelation; for one truth revealed from heaven is worth all the sectarian notions in existence.

This spirit of Elijah was manifest in the days of the apostles, in delivering certain ones to the buffetings of Satan, that they might be saved in the day of the Lord Jesus. They were sealed by the spirit of Elijah unto the damnation of hell until the day of the Lord, or revelation of Jesus Christ.

Here is the doctrine of election that the world has quarreled so much about; but they do not know anything about it.

The doctrine that the Presbyterians and Methodists have quarreled so much about—once in grace, always in grace, or falling away from grace, I will say a word about. They are both wrong. Truth takes a road between them both, for while the Presbyterian says "once in grace, you cannot fall;" the Methodist says: "You can have grace today, fall from it to-morrow, next day have grace again; and so follow on, changing continually." But the doctrine of the Scriptures and the spirit of Elijah would show them both false, and take a road between them both; for, according to the Scripture, if men have received the good word of God, and tasted of the powers of the world to come, if they shall fall away, it is impossible to renew them again, seeing they have crucified the Son of God afresh, and put Him to an open shame; so there is a possibility of falling away; you could not be renewed again, and the power of Elijah cannot seal against this sin, for this is a reserve made in the seals and power of the Priesthood.

I will make every doctrine plain that I present, and it shall stand upon a firm basis, and I am at the defiance of the world, for I will take shelter under the broad cover of the wings of the work in which I am engaged. It matters not to me if all hell boils over; I regard it only as I would the crackling of the thorns under a pot.

A murderer, for instance, one that sheds innocent blood, cannot have forgiveness. David sought repentance at the hand of God carefully with tears, for the murder of Uriah; but he could only get it through hell: he got a promise that his soul should not be left in hell.

Although David was a king, he never did obtain the spirit and power of Elijah and the fullness of the Priesthood; and the Priesthood that he received, and the throne and kingdom of David is to be taken from him and given to another by the name of David in the last days, raised up out of his lineage.

Peter referred to the same subject on the day of Pentecost, but the multitude did not get the endowment that Peter had; but several days after, the people asked "What shall we do?" Peter says, "I would ye had done it ignorantly," speaking of crucifying the Lord, &c. He did not say to them, "Repent and be baptized, for the remission of your sins;" but he said, "Repent ye therefore, and be converted, that your sins may be blotted out, when the times of refreshing shall come from the presence of the Lord." (Acts iii. 19.)

This is the case with murderers. They could not be baptized for the remission of sins for they had shed innocent blood.

Again: The doctrine or sealing power of Elijah is as follows:—If you have power to seal on earth and in heaven, then we should be wise. The first thing you do, go and seal on earth your sons and daughters unto yourself, and yourself unto your fathers in eternal glory. * * * * * * * * I will walk through the gate of heaven and claim what I seal, and those that follow me and my counsel.

The Lord once told me that what I asked for I should have. I have been afraid to ask God to kill my enemies, lest some of them should, peradventure, repent.

I asked a short time since for the Lord to deliver me out of the hands of the Governor of Missouri, and if it needs must be to accomplish it, to take him away; and the next news that came pouring down from there was, that *Governor Reynolds had shot himself*. And I would now say, "Beware, O earth, how you fight against the Saints of God and shed innocent blood; for in the days of Elijah, his enemies came upon him, and fire was called down from heaven and destroyed them.

The spirit of Elias is first, Elijah second, and Messiah last. Elias is a forerunner to prepare the way, and the spirit and power of Elijah is to come after, holding the keys of power, building the Temple to the capstone, placing the seals of the Melchisedec Priesthood upon the house of Israel, and making all things ready; then Messiah comes to His Temple, which is last of all.

Messiah is above the spirit and power of Elijah, for He made the world, and was that spiritual rock unto Moses in the wilderness. Elijah was to come and prepare the way and build up the kingdom before the coming of the great day of the Lord, although the spirit of Elias might begin it.

I have asked of the Lord concerning His coming; and while asking the Lord, He gave a sign and said, "In the days of Noah I set a bow in the heavens as a sign and token that in any year that the bow should be seen the Lord would not come; but there should be seed time and harvest during that year: but whenever you see the bow withdrawn, it shall be a token that there shall be famine, pestilence, and great distress among the nations, and that the coming of the Messiah is not far distant.

But I will take the responsibility upon myself to prophesy in the name of the Lord, that Christ will not come this year, as Father Miller has prophesied, for we have seen the bow; and I also prophesy, in the name of the Lord, that Christ will not come in forty years; and if God ever spoke by my mouth, He will not come in that length of time. Brethren, when you go home, write this down, that it may be remembered.

Jesus Christ never did reveal to any man the precise time that He would come. Go and read the Scriptures, and you cannot find anything that specifies the exact hour He would come; and all that say so are false teachers.

There are some important things concerning the office of the Messiah in the organization of the world. which I will speak of hereafter, May God Almighty bless you and pour out His Spirit upon you, is the prayer of your unworthy servant. Amen.

At half-past three p. m., I met with the Twelve, Bishop Miller and the Temple Committee, in the Nauvoo Mansion.

The following letter from Lyman Wight and others was read:—

Letter:—Lyman Wight to the First Presidency—Preaching the Gospel to the Indians and Proposing to Migrate to Texas.

BLACK RIVER FALLS, Feb. 15, 1844.

To the First Presidency and the Quorum of the Twelve of the Church of Christ of Latter-day Saints.

DEAR BRETHREN,—Through the goodness and mercy of God, the Eternal Father, and grace of our Lord and Savior Jesus Christ, we are permitted to write and send by a special messenger a concise account of our lumbering operations, together with the apparent prospects of the introduction and spread of the Gospel among the Chippewa and Menomanee Indians, and also the projects of our hearts in regard to future operations in spreading the Gospel south in all the extent of America,and the consequences growing out of the same,all of which we beg leave to submit to your consideration that we may have your concurrence, or such views as shall be in accordance with the mind and will of the Lord, and govern ourselves in accordance therewith.

Since we have been here lumbering, we have had many difficulties to encounter; but the main hindrance to our successful operations was the feeding, clothing, and transporting a great many lazy, idle men, who have not produced anything by their pretended labor, and thus eating up all that the diligent and honest could produce by their unceasing application to labor; and we have not yet got entirely clear of such persons.

But under all these mighty clogs and hindrances, we have been able to accomplish and have in progress, so that we can deliver in Nauvoo about one million feet of lumber by the last of July next, which will be a great deal more than what is necessary to build the Temple and the Nauvoo House. Besides all this, we have made valuable improvements here,—all the result of much labor done under trying circumstances.

We have recently ascertained that the lands from the falls of Black River to its sources are the property of the Menomanee Indians,and the general government having urged them to move off the lands in the vicinity of Green Bay to their own lands. The Indians say they will, provided the Government will remove all strange Indians and trespassing white men off their lands; consequently, the agent and superintendent of Indian Affairs are taking such steps as will stop all further trespassing on the Indian lands, on the Wisconsin, Black and Chippewa rivers, under the penalties of the laws relative to the cases.

We sent Brothers Miller and Daniels, in company with the principal chief of the Menomanee Indians, overland to the Wisconsin river, to ascertain more about the matter. They saw the agent; found him a gruff, austere man, determined to stop all trespassing on Indian lands.

The Indians are willing to sell privileges to individuals for lumbering and cutting timber, as they have hitherto done; but the agent is opposed to it. Thus a difficulty arises between themselves.

Now, as regards the introduction of the Gospel of Christ among the Indians here, it will require more exertion, to all appearances, to check the enthusiastic ardor of these our red brethren, until the full principles of faith in our Lord and Savior Jesus Christ shall be reasoned into their minds, than to urge them on to receive it. They have great confidence in us.

The country belonging to these northern Indians is a dreary, cold region, and to a great extent, cranberry marshes, pine barrens, and swamps, with a small amount of good lands, scarce of game, and only valuable in mill privileges and facilities for lumbering purposes.

As to mineral resources, they have not been fully developed. There is no doubt as to the abundance of iron ore, but uncertain as to quality.

Now, under all these circumstances, a few of us here have arrived at this conclusion in our minds (such as can undergo all things,)—that as the Gospel has not been fully opened in all the South and Southwestern States, as also Texas, Mexico, Brazil, &c., together with the West Indian Islands, having produced lumber enough to build the Temple and Nauvoo House,—also having an influence over the Indians, so as to induce them to sell their lands to the United States, and go to a climate southwest, (all according to the policy of the U. S. Government),—and having also become convinced that the Church at Nauvoo or in the Eastern States will not build the Nauvoo House according to the commandment, neither the Temple in a reasonable time, and that we have, so far as we have made trials, got means in the south,—we have in our minds to go to the table-lands of Texas, to a point we may find to be the most eligible, there locate, and let it be a place of gathering for all the South (they being incumbered with that unfortunate race of beings, the negroes); and for us to employ our time and talents in gathering together means to build according to the commandments of our God, and spread the Gospel to the nations according to the will of our Heavenly Father. We, therefore, our beloved brethren, send our worthy Brother Young, with a few of our thoughts, on paper, that you may take the subject-matter under consideration, and return us such instructions as may be according to the mind and will of the Lord our God.

We have thought it best to sell the mills here, if you think it expedient. We feel greatly encouraged to spend and be spent in the cause of Christ, according to the will of our Heavenly Father.

You will, therefore, after due deliberation, send us, by the hands of Brother Young, such instructions as may be the result of your deliberations.

Holding ourselves ready under all circumstances in life to try to do all things whatsoever commanded or instructed to do by those ordained to direct the officers of the Church of Jesus Christ; subscribing ourselves yours truly, while life shall endure,

LYMAN WIGHT,
GEORGE MILLER,
PHINEAS R. BIRD
PIERCE HAWLEY,
JOHN YOUNG.

Select Committee to write expressly the views of the branch of the Church at Black River Falls.

JOSEPH SMITH, P. C.
BRIGHAM YOUNG, P. T.
WILLARD RICHARDS, Clerk.

Also a letter to myself from Lyman Wight and others—

Letter:—Lyman Wight to President Joseph Smith—Suggesting a South-west Movement for the Church.

BLACK RIVER FALLS, WISCONSIN TERRITORY,
February 15th, 1844.

To Joseph Smith, President of the Church of Jesus Christ of Latter-day Saints, and to the Twelve Apostles, greeting:—

Believing a concert of action in all things in this Church to be highly important, we deem it necessary, under existing circumstances, to make you acquainted with our views, feelings, and temporal and spiritual prospects, as they now exist.

We wrote you last fall a full and complete description of this country as high as the falls on Black River, without exaggeration, giving a slight description of the Pinery.

With the exception of several renegadoes and false brethren, things passed smoothly until some time in the month of January, when we were visited by three different tribes of Lamanites upon the most friendly terms, receiving us as their counselors, both temporal and spiritual.

The names of those tribes are Menomanees, Chippewa, and Winnebagoes. They informed us that all the land above the falls belongs to the Menomanee tribe, and that the agents and the governor, the general agent in the northwest of all the Indian affairs, had agreed with them to remove all the lumbermen from Black River, Chippewa, and Lemanware rivers, by their request; but after a lengthy conversation with them, they felt to treat us as their friends, and not their enemies.

We dispatched two messengers—namely, George Miller and Cyrus Daniels, to go immediately to Wisconsin, where they met with the agent, who gave them to understand we could get the timber, which is already cut, at a reasonable rate, and for any future prospect we will be under the necessity of entering into a contract.

We calculate the present prospect for lumber betwixt this and the last of July next will be from eight to twelve hundred thousand feet, which we deem will be all sufficient to finish the two houses, which will accomplish the mission on which we started to this country.

We, therefore, as a brahch and a member of the body of the Church of Jesus Christ of Latter-day Saints chose the following committee—namely, Lyman Wight, George Miller, Pierce Hawley, Phineas R. Bird and John Young, to correspond with your reverend council, giving you our views concerning matters and things, and requesting your counsel on the same.

This committee views it inexpedient to purchase standing timber on so rapid and unnavigable a stream for the purpose of making lumber to gain wealth.

The Lamanites owning this land, notwithstanding their great anxiety to receive the Gospel and the Book of Mormon, have a strong desire, if counseled by us so to do, to go south-west, where game is more plentiful as their only resource here for a living is the pitiful annuities and proceeds from their pine timber, which timber is the only inducement to the Government to purchase their lands.

This committe is therefore led to take a brief view of the south and western part of North America, together with the Floridas, Texas, West India Islands, and the adjacent islands to the Gulf of Mexico, together with the Lamanites bordering on the United Territories from Green Bay to the Mexican Gulf, all crying with one voice, through the medium of their chiefs, Give us an understanding of your doctrine and principles, for we perceive that your ways are equal, and your righteousness far exceeds the righteousness of all the missionaries that we have yet become acquainted with,—that your conduct with one another is like that of ours, and that all your feasts and attendant ceremonies are precisely like ours.

Your servants. the committee, have viewed the Colorado river, with all its beautiful hills and valleys and fertile soil, with deep regret, when viewing the countless thousands of inhabitants on either side thereof, without the knowledge of God or the doctrine of the Church of Jesus

Christ of Latter-day Saints, and say in their hearts, Would it be expedient to form a mission of those true and full-blooded Ephraimites, who, from principle, and the love of the truth, have borne the most extreme burdens, fatigue, and hunger, to prosecute the mission, to procure lumber sufficient to build the two houses, to open the door to all the regions which we have named, which regions have never yet had an opportunity to hear the Gospel and to be made acquainted with the plan of salvation? or shall they continue to suffer the fatigues of hunger, wet and cold, in a rigid, inclement climate, for the pitiful sum that it shall avail them, after undergoing those hazardous perils? or shall they, like Timothy and Titus, with Paul, hazard the perils of the sea and land through the Southern States and West India Islands,and all the Lamanite world, go forth and proclaim to them the Gospel of our Lord and Savior Jesus Christ, and teach them to build up Zion?

Are there not thousands of the rich planters who would embrace the Gospel, and, if they had a place to plant their slaves, give all the proceeds of their yearly labor, if rightly taught, for building up the kingdom, being directed by the President of the whole Church to make the right application? We answer, Yes, we believe they would.

Your servants, the committee,are of the opinion that a concerted and reciprocity of action between the North and the South would greatly advance the building up of the kingdom.

The committee is well informed of the Cherokee and the Chocktaw nations who live between the state of Arkansas and the Colorado river of the Texans, owning large plantations and thousands of slaves, and that they are also very desirous to have an interview with the Elders of this Church, upon the principles of the Book of Mormon.

This committee is of the opinion that they can choose soldiers for this expedition who are as undeviating in the principles of the doctrine of Christ and the Book of Mormon as the sun in his daily course, and as indefatigable in their exertions in this cause as the earth is in its daily revolution.

This committee views it as a matter of investigation, whether would the Southerner, with his slaves and abundance of wealth, do better to take them to some slave-holding point, keep them in lively exercise according to his former customs and habits turning over his yearly proceeds into the hands of the Trustee-in-Trust for the whole Church, or to abolish slavery and settle himself in a climate uncongenial to his nature and entirely derogatory to his former occupations in life?

After having procured the lumber for those two houses, the committee is of the opinion that the preaching of the Gospel and raising funds in the south would be a far more speedy way of accomplishing the work than any other that could be introduced at the present time.

We, your servants, therefore, will wait patiently the result of your council, and submit ourselves to the same with all cheerfulness, our only object being to advance the cause and kingdom of God, stand ready to take hold wherever your wise council may consider it to be of the most advantage.

This committee view with deep regret the many different teachings this Church has received concerning the distribution of their property, such as raising funds for the printing of tracts, evidences of the Book of Mormon, and pamphlets of various descriptions, which we consider has not advanced the cause in the least degree, but has tended directly to sap the foundation of building the houses.

We therefore believe that no person embracing the doctrine of the Church of Jesus Christ of Latter-day Saints should give any part or parcel of the property without a direct counsel, written or oral, from the First Presidency of the Church.

Whereas the committee having appointed George Miller and Lyman Wight to write the views of the committee, each wrote separate and apart, having laid the same before the committee, the committee resolved that both productions be sent without alterations.

We, the committee, conclude by subscribing ourselves your friends and well-wishers in the Lord, praying a speedy answer from your worthy council, or the word of the Lord.

LYMAN WIGHT,
GEORGE MILLER,
PHINEAS R. BIRD,
PIERCE HAWLEY,
JOHN YOUNG,

Select Committee to write expressing the views of the branch of the Church at Black River Falls.

JOSEPH SMITH, SEN., P. C.
BRIGHAM YOUNG, P. T.
WILLARD RICHARDS, Clerk.

The brethren went into council on the subject matter of the letters during the evening.

Monday 11.—At home till nine; then spent the day in council in the lodge room over Henry Miller's house.

Special Council Meeting on Wight and Miller Letters.

Present—Joseph Smith, Hyrum Smith, Brigham Young, Heber C. Kimball, Willard Richards, Parley P. Pratt, Orson Pratt, John Taylor,

George A. Smith, William W. Phelps, John M. Bernhisel, Lucien Woodworth, George Miller, Alexander Badlam, Peter Haws, Erastus Snow, Reynolds Cahoon, Amos Fielding, Alpheus Cutler, Levi Richards, Newel K. Whitney, Lorenzo D. Wasson, and William Clayton, whom I organized into a special council, to take into consideration the subject matter contained in the above letters, and also the best policy for this people to adopt to obtain their rights from the nation and insure protection for themselves and children; and to secure a resting place in the mountains, or some uninhabited region, where we can enjoy the liberty of conscience guaranteed to us by the Constitution of our country, rendered doubly sacred by the precious blood of our fathers, and denied to us by the present authorities, who have smuggled themselves into power in the States and Nation.

CHAPTER XI.

ORSON PRATT SENT TO WASHINGTON AS AGENT OF NAUVOO—AMOS FIELDING TO ENGLAND, DITTO—COMMENT ON THE CANDIDACY OF JOSEPH SMITH FOR PRESIDENT OF THE U. S.—CONSPIRACIES OF THE LAWS, HIGBEES, FOSTERS, ET AL. AGAINST JOSEPH SMITH—THE PROPHET'S MEMORIAL TO CONGRESS—OCCUPATION OF THE WEST CONTEMPLATED.

Tuesday, March 12, 1844.—At home in the morning. At eleven a. m., I told Brother Cole I wanted the room over the store for more important purposes, and wished him to remove the school to Henry Miller's house immediately; which he did.

The brethren who were in council with me yesterday assembled there in the afternoon and evening.

Gave the following recommend to Elder Orson Pratt.

Credentials of Orson Pratt as Agent for the City of Nauvoo.

CITY OF NAUVOO, ILLINOIS, March 12, 1844.

TO WHOM IT MAY CONCERN:—

We, the mayor and recorder of said city, do hereby certify that Orson Pratt, Esq., the bearer, a councilor in city council of said city, is sent as an agent by the authorities of said city or corporation to transact such business as he may deem expedient and beneficial for the community which he represents; and as such agent and gentleman of principle and character, he by us is recommended to the due consideration of all the executive officers of the government, both houses of Congress, and gentlemen generally of the United States.

In witness whereof we have hereunto set our hands and affixed the seal of said corporation at the time and place aforesaid.

[CORPORATION SEAL.]

JOSEPH SMITH, Mayor.

WILLARD RICHARDS, Recorder.

A dull cloudy day.

A meeting of the inhabitants of the Tenth ward was held this evening at the schoolhouse on the hill, in Parley street, to take into consideration the propriety of establishing a store on the principle of co-operation or reciprocity. The subject was fully investigated, and the benefits of such an institution clearly pointed out.

Co-operative Store Planned.

The plan proposed for carrying out the object of the meeting was by shares of five dollars each.

The leading feature of the institution was to give employment to our own mechanics, by supplying the raw material, and manufacturing all sorts of domestic goods, and furnishing the necessaries and comforts of life on the lowest possible terms.

A committee was appointed to draft a plan for the government of said institute, to be submitted for adoption or amendment at their next meeting; after which an adjournment took place till next Tuesday evening, at half-past six o'clock, at the same place.

Wednesday, 13.—In special council from nine to twelve a. m. Orson Hyde, Wilford Woodruff and James Emmett were present, in addition to those of the preceding day. Willard Richards was appointed historian, and William Clayton clerk of the council.

It was decided that Amos Fielding should return to England, when I and my brother Hyrum gave him the following letter of attorney:—

Credentials of Elder Amos Fielding on Departing for England.

"This is to certify that the bearer thereof, our worthy brother Elder Amos Fielding, hath been appointed by the First Presidency of the Church of Jesus Christ of Latter-day Saints, our agent, to transact such business as may be deemed necessary for the benefit of said Church, and such as he shall see proper throughout the island of Great Britain.

He is hereby authorized to receive moneys for the Temple in Nauvoo, the poor, or for the Church; and the brethren will be safe should they deposit money in his hands for any purpose pertaining to the Church business in this place.

In witness whereof we have hereunto set our hands and placed the corporation seal of City of Nauvoo this 13th day of March, A. D. 1844.

[CORPORATION SEAL.]

JOSEPH SMITH,
HYRUM SMITH,

Presiding Elders of the whole Church of Jesus Christ of Latter-day Saints.

Thursday, 14.—In special council over the store from nine till one.

At two, went to see Brother John Wilkie. He had sent to me to come and see him. He wanted to know what he should do. I told him of the order of tithing, &c., and he wanted I should come again.

At four, went to assembly room again. Lucien Woodworth sent on a mission to Texas. At seven, adjourned to next Tuesday, at nine, a. m.

Friday 15.—Dull, cloudy day, north wind. Frosty night. Spent the day in council.

Being in a strait to raise money to assist the hands in the Pine country, I sent Elders Brigham and Willard Richards to borrow some money from Mr. Orme, who, it is believed, had a large sum of money lying idle, but they did not get any.

I copy from the Law of the Lord:—

John Wilkie. The Blessing of the Prophet upon Him.

"This day President Joseph Smith rode over to Brother John Wilkie's at his special request, to give him some instructions relative to his duty in regard to tithing and consecration.

Brother Wilkie has for a long time back been struggling with his feelings, designing to do right. but laboring under many fears and prejudices, in consequence of having in some degree given way to believe the base reports circulated by individuals for the purpose of injuring the authorities of the Church, and also from various other causes. His faithful companion has persevered diligently, and with fervent prayer has called upon God in his behalf, until she has realized her utmost wishes.

Brother Wilkie now feels anxious to do right in all things, and especially to pay his tithing to the full. President Joseph showed him the principles of consecration and the means whereby he might realize the fullness of the blessings of the celestial kingdom; and as an evidence that he desired to do right, he paid over to the Trustee-in-Trust the sum of three hundred dollars in gold and silver for the benefit of the Temple, and which is now recorded on consecration.

He also signified his intention of paying more as soon as he could get matters properly arranged. The president then pronounced a blessing upon him and his companion, that they should have the blessing of God to attend them in their basket and in their store—that they should have the blessing of health and salvation and long life, inasmuch as they would continue to walk in obedience to the commandments of God.

May the Lord grant his Spirit and peace to abide upon Brother Wilkie and his companion through the remainder of their days; may their hearts expand and become enlarged to receive the fullness of the blessings of the kingdom of heaven; may they have the light of eternal truth continually springing up in them like a well of living water; may they be shielded from the powers of Satan and the influence of designing men, and their faith increase from day to day until they shall have power to lay hold on the blessings of God and the gifts of the Spirit until they are satisfied; and, finally, may they live to a good old age; and when they have lived while they desire life, may they die in peace and be received into the mansions of eternal life, and enjoy a celestial glory forever and ever! Even so, amen.

The editors of the *Times and Seasons* published a short account of "Our City and the Present Aspect of Affairs," which we insert.

STATUS OF NAUVOO IN THE SPRING OF 1844.

Believing that our patrons and friends are pleased to hear of our prosperity, we feel happy in apprising them of the same, through the columns of our paper.

Owing to the scarcity of provision and the pressure in the money market during the past winter, commercial business has been somewhat dull; consequently, those who were not previously prepared have been obliged to employ the principal portion of their time in obtaining the necessary means for the sustenance of their families: therefore little improvement has been made. But old Boreas is now on his receding march, and spring has commenced its return with all its pleasantness.

Navigation is open, and steamboats are almost continually plying up and down our majestic river. They have already brought several families of emigrants to this place, who have cordially joined with their friends and brethren in the great work of the upbuilding of Zion and the rolling forth of the kingdom of God.

The work of improvement is now actively begun, and in every direction may be heard the sound of the mason's trowel, the carpenters's hammer, the teamster's voice, or, in other words, the hum of industry and the voice of merriment. Indeed, to judge from the present appearance, a greater amount of improvement will be done the ensuing summer than in the preceding one.

Almost every stranger that enters our city is excited with astonishment that so much has been done in so short a time; but we flatter ourselves, from the known industry, perseverance, and diligence of the Saints, that by the return of another winter so much more will be accomplished, that his astonishment will be increased to wonder and admiration.

Quite extensive preparations are being made by the farmers in this vicinity for the cultivation of land; and should the season prove favorable, we doubt not that nearly,if not a sufficient amount of produce will be raised to supply the wants of the city and adjacent country.

We are also pleased that we can inform our friends abroad that the Saints here of late have taken hold of the work on the Temple with the zeal and energy that in no small degree excites our admiration. Their united efforts certainly speak to us that it is their determination that this spacious edifice shall be enclosed, if not finished, this season.

And a word we would say to the Saints abroad, which is, that the Temple is being built in compliance with a special commandment of God not to a few individuals, but to all. Therefore we sincerely hope you will contribute of your means as liberally as your circumstances will allow, that the burden of the work may not rest upon a few, but proportionately upon all.

Where is the true-hearted Saint that does not with joy and delight contemplate the endowment of the servants of God and the blessings He has promised to His people on condition that they speedily build the Temple? Certainly you cannot reasonably expect to enjoy these blessings if you refuse to contribute your share towards its erection.

It is a thing of importance, and much depends upon its accomplishment: therefore we wish to forcibly impress the matter upon your minds, hoping you will become aroused to a sense of your duty—that every company of Saints, every Elder that comes here, and every mail may bring money and other property for this important work,—which,

when completed, will stand, in one sense of the word, as a firm pillar in Zion, and which will greatly facilitate the prosperity of the great cause of truth which we all are actively engaged in.

Saturday, 16.—At home. At one p. m., I sat in council with Willard Richards, Orrin P. Rockwell, and Bishop George Miller.

The Female Relief Society had two meetings in the assembly room, as it would not hold all at once, and sanctioned the "Voice of Innocence from Nauvoo."

Sunday, 17.—Last night, Nauvoo was visited by a very strong wind from the west. It blew down a portion of the west wall of the new hall (28 by 40 feet on the ground,) which the Seventies had commenced on Bain street, and they had raised for the roof.

Wind Storm at Nauvoo.

The wind continued very strong all day. In the evening, had a smart snowstorm, which covered the ground, was succeeded by a frosty night.

Attended prayer meeting.

Monday, 18.—The frost of last night was so severe as to form ice inside the houses.

I stayed at home to recite German with Brother Neibaur.

Tuesday, 19.—Met in council in the assembly room. Elder Samuel Bent, Uriah Brown, Samuel James, John D. Parker, Orrin P. Rockwell, Sidney Rigdon, William Marks, and Orson Spencer met in council, in addition to the former names.

In the afternoon, heavy, driving rain. Northwest wind. Dull, cold day.

Wednesday, 20.—Severely cold northwest wind, with a snow and hail storm until ten a. m. Afternoon dull. West wind.

Spent the morning and afternoon in the assembly room, studying the languages.

Elder Woodruff read me a letter which he had written to Colonel Solomon Copeland concerning his nomination to be a candidate for the Vice-President of the United States.

Col. Copeland and the Vice-Presidency.

The *Illinois Springfield Register* has the following:—

GENERAL JOSEPH SMITH A CANDIDATE FOR PRESIDENT.

It appears by the Nauvoo papers that the Mormon Prophet is actually a candidate for the presidency. He has sent us his pamphlet, containing an extract of his principles, from which it appears that he is up to the hub for a United States bank and a protective tariff. On these points he is much more explicit than Mr. Clay, who will not say that he is for a bank, but talks all the time of restoring a national currency. Nor will Mr. Clay say what kind of a tariff he is for. He says to the south that he has not sufficiently examined the present tariff, but thinks very likely it could be amended.

General Smith posesses no such fastidious delicacy. He comes right out in favor of a bank and a tariff, taking the true Whig ground, and ought to be regarded as the real Whig candidate for President, until Mr. Clay can so far recover from his shuffling and dodging as to declare his sentiments like a man.

At present we can form no opinion of Clay's principles, except as they are professed by his friends in these parts.

Clay himself has adopted the notion which was once entertained by an eminent grammarian, who denied that language was intended as a means to express one's ideas, but insisted that it was invented on purpose to aid us in concealing them.

The *Iowa Democrat* publishes the following:—

A New Candidate in the Field.

We see from the *Nauvoo Neighbor* that General Joseph Smith, the great Mormon Prophet, has become a candidate for the next presidency. We do not know whether he intends to submit his claims to the National Convention, or not; but, judging from the language of his own organ, we conclude that he considers himself a full team for all of them.

All that we have to say on this point is, that if superior talent, genius, and intelligence, combined with virtue, integrity, and enlarged views, are any guarantee to General Smith's being elected, we think that he will be a "full team of himself."

The *Missouri Republican* believes that it will be death to Van Buren, and all agree that it must be injurious to the Democratic ranks, inasmuch as it will throw the Mormon vote out of the field.

A traveler, having visited Nauvoo for a few days, wrote to the *Times and Seasons*—

"Mr. Editor,—Before I take my departure, permit me to express my views relative to the leading men of your city, where I have been these few days.

I have been conversant with the great men of the age; and, last of all I feel that I have met with the greatest, in the presence of your esteemed Prophet, General Joseph Smith. From many reports, I had reason to believe him a bigoted religionist, as ignorant of politics as the savages; but, to my utter astonishment, on the short acquaintance, I have found him as familiar in the cabinet of nations as with his Bible and in the knowledge of that book I have not met with his equal in Europe or America. Although I should beg leave to differ with him in some items of faith, his nobleness of soul will not permit him to take offense at me. No, sir; I find him open, frank, and generous,—as willing others should enjoy their opinions as to enjoy his own.

The General appears perfectly at home on every subject, and his familiarity with many languages affords him ample means to become informed concerning all nations and principles, which with his familiar and dignified deportment towards all must secure to his interest the affections of every intelligent and virtuous man that may chance to fall in his way, and I am astonished that so little is known abroad concerning him.

Van Buren was my favorite, and I was astonished to see General Smith's name as a competitor; but, since my late acquaintance, Mr. Van Buren can never re-seat himself in the Presidential chair on my vote while General Smith is in the field. Forming my opinions alone on the talents of the two, and from what I have seen, I have no reason to doubt but General Smith's integrity is equal to any other individual; and I am satisfied he cannot easily be made the pliant tool of any political party. I take him to be a man who stands far aloof from little caucus quibblings and squabblings, while nations, governments, and realms are wielded in his hand as familiarly as the top and hoop in the hands of their little masters.

Free from all bigotry and superstition, he dives into every subject, and it seems as though the world was not large enough to satisfy his capacious soul, and from his conversation one might suppose him as well acquinted with other worlds as this.

So far as I can discover, General Smith is the nation's man, and the man who will exalt the nation, if the people will give him the opportunity; and all parties will find a friend in him so far as right is concerned.

General Smith's movements are perfectly anomalous in the estimation of the public. All other great men have been considered wise in drawing around them wise men; but I have frequently heard the General called a fool because he has gathered the wisest of men to his cabinet, who direct his movements; but this subject is too ridiculous to dwell upon. Suffice it to say, so far as I have seen, he has wise men at his side—superlatively wise, and more capable of managing the affairs of a State than most men now engaged therein, which I consider much to his credit, though I would by no means speak diminutively of my old friend.

From my brief acquaintance, I consider General Smith (independent of his peculiar religious views, in which by-the-by, I have discovered neither vanity nor folly,) the *sine qua non* of the age to our nation's prosperity. He has learned the all-important lesson "to profit by the experience of those who have gone before;" so that, in short, General Smith begins where other men leave off. I am aware this will appear a bold assertion to some; but I would say to such, call, and form your acquaintance, as I have done; then judge.

Thus, sir, you have a few leading items of my views of General Smith, formed from personal acquaintance, which you are at liberty to dispose of as you think proper. I anticipate the pleasure of renewing my acquaintance with your citizens at a future day.

Yours respectfully,
A TRAVELER.

A writer in the *Quincy Herald* reflects very strongly upon the conduct of the *Quincy Whig*, *New York Tribune*, and other newspapers, for publishing slanderous falsehoods against the Saints.

Ten, p. m., commenced snowing again.

Thursday, 21.—A cold snow-storm through the night.

Origin of Memorial to Congress.

In council in the assembly room, discussing the propriety of petitioning Congress for the privilege of raising troops to protect the making of setments in the uncivilized portions of our continent.

Willard Richards was appointed a committee to draw up a memorial to Congress.

Friday, 22.—Snow on the ground; cold, bleak north wind; cloudy.

At ten a. m., held Mayor's court, and afterwards read German in the reading room.

In the afternoon, met with the Twelve in prayer at President Brigham Young's house.

The Seventies' Hall, Instructions on Re-building.

I advised the Seventies to pull down the remainder of the walls and rebuild the Seventies' hall on a permanent basis from the foundation, and not erect for themselves a trap, but build one two stories high. and strong enough to stand for a generation.

Saturday, 23.—Day warmer. Rode out with Clayton to endeavor to raise money to furnish the hands in the Pinery with supplies. Visited the Temple and public works

Also called with William Clayton and Alexander Neibaur at Dr. Foster's. He was gone to Appanoose, and Mrs. Foster was at Mr. Gilman's.

I here extract from William Clayton's journal:—

President Smith's Interview With Mrs. Foster.

We went down there and saw her, [Mrs. Foster]. President Joseph asked Sister Foster if she ever in her life knew him guilty of an immoral or indecent act, She answered, "No." He then explained his reasons for asking; which were, he had been informed that Dr. Foster had stated that Joseph made propositions to his wife calculated to lead her astray from the path of virtue; and then asked if ever he had used any indecent or insulting language to her. She answered, "Never." He further asked if he ever preached anything like the "plurality of wife" doctrine to her other than what he had preached in public? She said, "No." He asked her if he ever proposed to have illicit intercourse with her, and especially when he took dinner during the doctor's absence. She said, "No." After some further conversation on the subject, we left. Mrs. Gillman was present all the time. President Joseph and Neibaur then went on foot to the farm.

Sunday, 24.—At ten, a. m., met at the stand near the

Temple. [The following very brief outline of the speeches is from the journal of Wilford Woodruff]:—

Discourse of President Smith—Conspiracies in Nauvoo.

"President Joseph Smith addressed the people. The following is the substance of what I heard him say:—

I have been informed by two gentlemen that a conspiracy is got up in this place for the purpose of taking the life of President Joseph Smith, his family, and all the Smith family, and the heads of the Church. One of the gentlemen will give his name to the public, and the other wishes it to be hid for the present: they will both testify to it on oath, and make an affidavit upon it. The names of the persons revealed at the head of the conspiracy are as follows:—Chancey L. Higbee, Dr. Robert D. Foster, Mr. Joseph H. Jackson, William and Wilson Law. And the lies that C. L. Higbee has hatched up as a foundation to work upon are—he says that I had men's heads cut off in Missouri, and that I had a sword run through the hearts of the people that I wanted to kill and put out of the way. I won't swear out a warrant against them, for I don't fear any of them: they would not scare off an old setting hen. I intend to publish all the iniquity that I know of them. If I am guilty, I am ready to bear it. There is sometimes honor among enemies. I am willing to do anything for the good of the people. I will give the name of one of the gentlemen who have divulged the plot: his name is M. G. Eaton. He will swear to it: he is a bold fellow. Joseph H. Jackson said a Smith should not be alive in two weeks,—not over two months anyhow. Concerning the character of these men, I will say nothing about it now; but if I hear anything more from them on this subject, I will tell what I know about them.

Elder Orson Spencer addressed the people as follows:—

While listening to President Smith's remarks, I thought of a figure, i.e.,if a physician was going to dissect a body, he would not be likely to begin at the limbs but cut the head off first. So the adversary of the Saints has laid a plan to cut off the head of the Church with the intention of scattering and destroying the whole body. It was so in the days of Jesus Christ; the enemies of the truth sought to kill Him, that the body might be destroyed; which was also the case in the days of Elijah, Daniel, and many of the ancients.

I once heard a man say, who was opposed to this work, "That it might be true, but it gave Joseph Smith power." True, said I; but if his power be subordinate to the power of God, it is right. If a man set up a kingdom by the power of God, then let others seek power from the same source. God sets up kingdoms and pulls down kingdoms:

this makes men mad who will not submit to the kingdom of God. We all know the result of the power of Moses, who was the representative of God.

Judging from what is past, how will it be when God sets up His kingdom in the last days? Whether there is a conspiracy now, or not, I don't know; but no doubt there will be, if not now, for it has always been so. In the days of the Nephites, they had their Gadianton robbers. I have not any doubt but that the apostates will join with the other wicked powers to try to put down the power of God, and I am glad to have the power of the kingdom of God tested; I care not what sacrifice I am called to make for such a kingdom. If it is friends, wealth, or even life, at the purchase of such a kingdom, it is cheap. Did the ancient Apostles, Prophets, or Saints who died pay too much for that kingdom? They did not. It is necessary that men be put in possession of the knowledge and mysteries of the kingdom of God, in order to sin as far as they wish, that they may go to the highest pitch. How often men lay down their lives for their country and other purposes. How much better, then, to die for the cause of Zion! Good and righteous men will administer justice and rebuke evil. The Church should be cleansed from bad men, and the Lord will take His own way to cleanse the Church.

We should lift up our voice against wickedness of all kinds. But will the rulers of our land do it? No, they will not; they will be cowards until there is no man to fight, and then be brave. When Government will not do it, some man should take the helm of government that will do it. Will it be called treason, if the God of heaven should set up a kingdom? May the Lord give you more and more of His Spirit, light and intelligence, until you are cemented together in union and love. Amen.

Elder Sidney Rigdon addressed the meeting.

President Joseph Smith again arose and said—In relation to the power over the minds of mankind which I hold, I would say, It is in consequence of the power of truth in the doctrines which I have been an instrument in the hands of God of presenting unto them, and not because of any compulsion on my part. I wish to ask if ever I got any of it unfairly? if I have not reproved you in the gate? I ask, Did I ever exercise any compulsion over any man? Did I not give him the liberty of disbelieving any doctrine I have preached, if he saw fit? Why do not my enemies strike a blow at the doctrine? They cannot do it: it is truth, and I defy all men to upset it. I am the voice of one crying in the wilderness, "Repent ye of your sins and prepare the way for the coming of the Son of Man; for the kingdom of God has come unto you, and henceforth the ax is laid unto the root of the tree; and every tree that bringeth not forth good fruit, God Almighty (and not Joe Smith) shall hew it down and cast it into the fire."

After meeting, I rode out with Emma. The trees begin to bud forth.

In the evening, held a conversation with a large company of friends at my door.

Elder R. H. Kinnamon writes that during the last 22 months he has baptized over 100 persons while on a mission in Virginia and North Carolina, organized two branches in Virginia, and calls are continually made for preaching in every direction.

Monday, 25.—At home in the morning. After dinner rode up to the upper landing to see the *St. Louis Oak* steamer. Learned that a company of emigrants from England were expected soon. Called at my office on returning, and heard read the draft of a memorial to Congress which my clerk had been writing, as a committee appointed by the council on Thursday last, and was pleased with the instrument.

Progress on Memorial to Congress.

Millions of wild pigeons flying north, and millions of gnats dancing in the air. Dull day. At night thunder, lightning and rain.

Tuesday, 26.—Dull day. From nine to twelve, noon, in council; also from two to five p. m.

The memorial drawn up by Dr. Richards was read, discussed, and approved by the general council.

Started this morning to go to Ramus with Brother Amasa Lyman. Rode as far as the Temple, and found it so muddy that we turned back.

Issued a warrant on the complaint of Vernon H. Bruce, against Ianthus Rolfe, for stealing two stone-cutter's tools.

I wrote the following:—

The Prophet's Memorial to Congress.

To the Honorable the Senate and House of Representatives of the United States of America, in Congress Assembled:

Your memorialist, a free-born citizen of these United States, respectfully showeth that from his infancy his soul has been filled with the most intense and philanthropic interest for the welfare of his native country; and being fired with an ardor which floods cannot quench, crowns cannot conquer, nor diplomatic intrigue corrupt, to see those principles which emanated from the bosoms of the fathers of seventy-six, and which cost the noblest talents and richest blood of the nation, maintained inviolate and perpetuated to future generations; and the proud eagle of American freedom soar triumphant over every party prejudice and local sinistry, and spread her golden pinions over every member of the human family, who shall stretch forth their hands for succor from the lion's paw or the oppressor's grasp; and firmly trusting in the God of liberty, that He has designed universal peace and goodwill, union, and brotherly love to all the great family of man, your memorialist asks your honorable body to pass the following:—

ORDINANCE.

An Ordinance for the Protection of the Citizens of the United States Emigrating to the Territories, and for the Extension of the Principles of Universal Liberty.

PREAMBLE.

Whereas, many of the citizens of these United States have migrated and are migrating to Texas, Oregon, and other lands contiguous to this nation; and whereas, Texas has declared herself free and independent, without the necessary power to protect her rights and liberties; *and whereas* Oregon is without any organized government, and those who emigrate thither are exposed to foreign invasion and domestic feuds; *and whereas* the Oregon, by geographical location and discovery more rightfully belongs to these United States than any other general government; *and whereas* it is necessary that the emigrants of that newly settling territory should receive protection; *and whereas* the Texan Government has petitioned the United States to be received into our Union, but yet retains her national existence; *and whereas* the United States remember with gratitude the seasonable support they received in a like situation from a LaFayette; *and whereas* the United States desire to see the principles of her free institutions extended to all men, especially where it can be done without the loss of blood and treasure to the nation; *and whereas* there is an almost boundless extent of territory on the west and south of these United States, where exists little or no organization of protective Government; *and whereas* the lands thus unknown; unowned, or unoccupied, are among some of the richest and most fertile of the continent; *and whereas* many of the inhabitants of the Union would gladly embrace the opportunity of extending their researches and acquirements so soon as they can receive protection in their enterprise, thereby adding strength, durability, and wealth to the nation; *and whereas* the red man, the robber, and the desperado have frequenty interrupted such research and acquisition without justifiable cause; *and whereas* Joseph Smith has offered and does hereby offer these United States, to show his loyalty to our Confederate Union and the Constitution of our Republic; to prevent quarrel and bloodshed our frontiers; to extend the arm of deliverance to Texas; to on protect the inhabitants of Oregon from foreign aggressions and domestic broils; to prevent the crowned nations from encircling us as a nation on our western and southern borders, and save the eagle's talon from the lion's paw; to still the tongue of slander, and show the world that a Republic can be, and not be ungrateful; to open the vast regions of the unpeopled west and south to our enlightened and enterprising yeomanry; to protect them in their researches; to secure them in their locations, and thus strengthen the Government and enlarge her borders; to extend her influence; to inspire the nations with the spirit of freedom and win them to her standard; to promote intelligence; to cultivate and establish peace among all with whom we may have intercourse as neighbors; to settle all existing difficulties among those not organized into an acknowledged government bordering upon the United States and Territories; to save the national revenue in the nation's coffers; to supercede the necessity of a standing army on our western and southern frontiers; to create and maintain the principles of peace and suppress mobs, insurrections, and oppression in Oregon and all the lands bordering upon the United States and not incorporated into any acknowledged national government; to explore the unexplored regions of our continent; to open new fields for enterprise to our citizens, and protect them therein; to search out the antiquities of the land, and thereby promote the arts and sciences, and general information; to amalgamate the feelings of all with whom he may have intercourse on the principles of equity, liberty, justice, humanity and benevolence; to break down tyranny and oppression and exalt the standard of universal peace, provided he shall be protected in those rights and privileges which constitutionally belong to every citizen of this Republic; therefore, that the said memorialist may have the privilege, and that no citizen of the United States shall obstruct, or attempt to obstruct or hinder, so good,so great,so noble an enterprise to carry out those plans and principles as set forth in this preamble,and be shielded from every opposition by evil and designing men.

Section 1. *Be it ordained by the Senate and House of Representatives of the United States of America, in Congress Assembled*, that Joseph Smith, of the city of Nauvoo, in the State of Illinois, is hereby authorized and empowered to raise a company of one hundred thousand armed volunteers in the United States and Territories, at such times, and places and in such numbers, as he shall find necessary and convenient for the purposes specified in the foregoing preamble, and to execute the same.

Sec. 2. *And be it further ordained* that if any person or persons shall hinder or attempt to hinder or molest the said Joseph Smith from executing his designs in raising said volunteers, and marching and transporting the same to the borders of the United States and Territories, he, or they so hindering, molesting, or offending, shall be punished by a fine not exceeding one thousand dollars each for every offense, or by hard labor on some public work not exceeding two years, or both, at the discretion of the nearest District Court of the United States, where the hindrance or offense shall be committed, having jurisdiction.

See. 3. *And be it further ordained*, the more fully to remove all obstructions and hindrances to the raising, enlisting, and marching the volunteers as aforesaid, the said Joseph Smith is hereby constituted a member of the army of these United States, and is authorized to act as such in the United States and Territories, and on all lands bordering upon the United States and Territories, for the purposes specified in the foregoing preamble,provided said land shall not be within the acknowledged jurisdiction of any acknowledged national government.

Sec. 4. *And be it further ordained* that nothing in this ordinance shall be so construed by any individual or nation to consider the volunteers aforesaid as constituting any part of the army of the United States; neither shall the said Joseph Smith, as a member of the United States army, disturb the peace of any nation or government acknowledged as such, break the faith of treaties between the United States and any other nation, or violate any known law of nations, thereby endangering the peace of the United States.

Sec. 5. *And be it further ordained*, that the said Joseph Smith shall confine his operations to those principles of action specified in the preamble to this ordinance, the perpetuity of which shall be commensurate with the circumstances and specifications which have originated it.

And your memorialist will ever pray, &c.

JOSEPH SMITH.

CITY OF NAUVOO, ILLINOIS, March 26, 1844.

Dr. Willard Richards wrote to the Saints at Augusta, Lee County, Iowa, requesting a brief history of the settling of that branch, and also asking a donation of lumber for his house.

In the afternoon, Abiathar B. Williams made the following affidavit before Daniel H. Wells, Esq:—

Affidavit of Abiathar B. Williams, Concerning a Conspiracy against the Prophet.

STATE OF ILLINOIS, } ss.
HANCOCK COUNTY, }

Personally appeared before me, Daniel H. Wells, Acting Justice of the Peace in and for the said county, Abiathar B. Williams, who, being duly sworn according to law, deposeth and saith that on or about the 15th day of March, A. D., 1844, Joseph H. Jackson came to my house and requested me to walk with him; which I did. During the time we were walking, said Joseph H. Jackson said that he was then coming direct from Mr. Law's; that there was going to be a secret meeting in the city of Nauvoo, probably tomorrow evening: but, as it was not decided, he could not say positively as to the time; but he would inform me in season. The said Joseph H. Jackson said that Doctor Foster, Chauncey L. Higbee, and the Laws were red hot for a conspiracy, and he should not be surprised if in two weeks there should not be one of the Smith family left alive in Nauvoo. After we arrived at Mr. Loomis',near the Masonic hall, in the city of Nauvoo, he related some things which he stated that Dr. Foster had said relative to his family. This he did in the presence of Mr. Eaton and myself, and strongly solicited myself and Mr. Eaton to attend the secret meeting and join them in their intentions. The said Joseph H. Jackson further said that Chauncey Higbee had said that he, the said Chauncey Higbee, had seen men tied hand and foot, and run through the heart with a sword, and their heads taken off, and then buried; and he durst not say a word. This the said Jackson said in Mr. Loomis' room. And further this deponent saith not.

A. B. WILLIAMS.

Sworn to and subscribed before me this 27th day of March, A. D. 1844.

[L. S.] DANIEL H. WELLS, J. P.

Also M. G. Eaton made affidavit as follows:—

Affidavit of M. G. Eaton—A conspiracy Against Joseph Smith.

STATE OF ILLINOIS, } ss.
HANCOCK COUNTY, }

Personally appeared before me, Daniel H. Wells, an acting Justice of the Peace, in and for the said county, M. G. Eaton, who being duly sworn according to law, deposeth and saith that on or about the fifteenth day of March, A. D. 1844, Joseph H. Jackson came to me several times and requested me to go on the hill with him. I finally consented went with him to the Keystone Store, in the city of Nauvoo. Dr. Foster and one of the Higbees (I think Chauncey L. Higbee) were in the store. The said Joseph H. Jackson, together with the said R. D. Foster and said Higbee, went into the back room of the store. They appeared to enter into private council. Soon after they went into the said room, the said Joseph H. Jackson invited me into the room where they were sitting. I immediately complied.

Soon after I went in, the said Higbee commenced talking about the spiritual wife system. He said he had no doubt but some of the Elders had ten or twelve apiece. He said they married them, whether the females were living or not; and they did it by recording the marriage in a large book, which book was sealed up after the record was made, and was not to be opened for a long time,—probably not till many of the husbands of those who were thus married were dead. They would then open the book and break the seals in the presence of those females, and when they saw their names recorded in that book they would believe that the doctrine was true and they must submit. He said this book was kept at Mr. Hyrum Smith's. I asked the Chauncey L Higbee.

* * * * *

[Here follows some expressions too indecent for insertion.]

The aforesaid R. D. Foster then asked me what I would think, if, during my absence from home, a carriage should drive up to my house, a person alight, and the carriage then drive off again; this person should then go into my house and begin to tell my wife a great many things against me to prejudice her mind against me, and use every possible means to do this, and finally would introduce and preach the spiritual wife doctrine to her, and make an attempt to seduce her; and further, this person should sit down to dine with my wife, bless the victuals, &c.; and while they were thus engaged, I should come home and find them thus associated, this person should rise up and say, "How do you do?" and bless me in a very polite manner, &c.; and also if, upon these appearances, I should feel jealous that something was wrong, and when the person was gone I would ask my wife what had been the conversation between her and this person, but she would refuse to tell me; I then draw a pistol and present it to her head and threaten to shoot her if she did not tell me all, but she would still refuse: I then would give her a double-barrelled pistol, and say to her, "Defend yourself; for if you don't tell me, either you or I would shoot:" she would then faint away through fear and excitement, and when she came to again, she would begin and tell how this person had been trying to poison your wife's mind against you, and, by preaching the spiritual wife system to her, had endeavored to seduce her. I replied, I should think he was a rascal: but who has had such a trial as that? The said R. D. Foster answered that he was the man who had had that trial, and who had been thus abused.

The said Dr. Foster, Higbee, and Joseph H. Jackson then remarked that they were about to hold a secret meeting to oppose and try to put a stop to such things. The said Joseph H. Jackson also said that if any person undertook to arrest him, he should begin to cut them.

The said R. D. Foster further said he was afraid of his life, and dared not be out at nights.

The said Higbee said he had not a doubt but there had been men killed in Missouri who had secrets that they were afraid they would divulge. He said he was afraid of his life.

The said Jackson further said he should not be surprised if there should be a real muss and an insurrection in the city in less than two months; and that if a disturbance should take place, the Carthagenians and others would come and help them.

He mentioned some names of persons who would come from Carthage, which names I do not remember. The same day, when in Mr. Loomis' room, I heard the said Jackson say that the Laws were ready to enter into a secret conspiracy, tooth and nails.

The said Higbee also said, while at the Keystone Store, that if ever he was brought before the Mayor's court again, and the Mayor told him to hold his tongue, he should get up and tell him he had a right to speak, and should do so; and then if any man attempted to put him out of court, he would shoot him through. And further this deponent saith not.

M. G. EATON.

Sworn to and subscribed before me, this 27th day of March, A. D., 1844.

[L. S.] DANIEL H. WELLS, J. P.*

*In addition to these affidavits the Prophet was apprised by two young men Dennison L. Harris and Robert Scott, the latter living in the family of William Law, of a secret movement then on foot to take his life, and the lives of several other leading men in the Church, among them the Prophet's brother, Hyrum. These

This evening, Dr. Reynolds, of Iowa City, lectured on astronomy in the assembly room.

Thursday, 28.—Dull day, drizzling rain, cold northeast wind.

Transferred the trial of Ianthus Rolfe to Aaron Johnson, J. P.

This afternoon, had the assembly room and office plastered where the same had been knocked off, &c.

Friday, 29.—Night boisterous: about eight, a. m., hailstorm, northeast wind, nipping frost; frost, hail, and strong wind all day.

Spent the day at home.

Saturday, 30.—This morning I heard there was some disturbance on the hill; I rode up and found it reported that a robbery had been committed at the Keystone Store, kept by Mr. Rollasson, of some $400 or $500, and some goods, and they were suspicious of a certain black man. I issued a search-warrant and returned to my office, where I found the black man, —— Chism, with his back lacerated from his shoulders to his hips, with twenty or more lashes. My clerk, Dr. Richards, kept him secreted, and called Aaron Johnson, a justice of the peace, who issued a warrant for —— ——, a Missourian, who had boarded at my house a few days, and on testimony fined him $5 and costs for whipping —— Chism. One Easton, a witness, said he could not testify without implicating himself, and he was apprehended and held in custody. W. H. J. Marr, Esq., refused to testify, because he was counsel.

The Robbery at Rollasson's Store in Nauvoo.

I got prepared a memorial to his Excellency John Tyler,

young men were invited to the secret meetings by the conspirators, but before going conferred with the Prophet, who told them to go, but to take no part in the proceedings of these wicked men against himself. They carried out his instructions, and at the risk of their lives attended the secret meetings three times, and brought to President Smith a report of what they had witnessed. A full account of this conspiracy written by Horace Cummings—the narrative being detailed to him by Dennison L. Harris—was published in the *Contributor*, for April, 1884.

the President of the United States, embodying in it the same sentiments as are in my Petition to the Senate and House of Representatives of the United States, dated 26th March, 1844, asking the privilege of raising 100,000 men to extend protection to persons wishing to settle Oregon and other portions of the territory of the United States, and extend protection to the people in Texas.

Memorial to the President of the United States.

Sunday, 31.—Cold, fine day.

At home this morning until nine, when I went over to my reading-room, again heard read and signed my memorial to Congress for the privilege of raising 100,000 volunteers to protect Texas, Oregon, &c., dated 26th instant; and also a memorial to the President for the same purpose, if the other fail.

Also signed an introductory letter to Elder Orson Hyde, who is going to carry the memorials* to Washington as follows:—

* President Smith's memorial to Congress, of the 26th of March, asking to be appointed "a member of the army of these United States," to be authorized "to raise 100,000 armed volunteers" to police the inter-mountain and Pacific slope west, was presented to the House of Representatives by Mr. John Wentworth, of Chicago, where the following occurred with reference to it:

MORMONS:

"Mr. Wentworth asked permission to present a memorial from Gen. Joseph Smith, the head of the Mormons, and required that it might be read by the clerk for the information of the House.

"The Clerk commenced the reading of the memorial.

"Before the reading was concluded.

"Mr. J. R. Ingersoll interposed, and objected to the reception at first, and still objected.

"Mr. Weber observed that if memorials of this kind were to be read, he was entrusted with the presentation of one of a peculiar character, from certain citizens of Frederick county, Md.

"Mr. Wentworth said he would move a suspension of the rules to enable him to have the paper read; and he wished to inquire of the chair whether it would be in order for him to assign his reasons for making such a motion.

"Mr. Duncan observed, if the gentleman would yield him the floor, he would move to suspend the rules, to go into committee of the whole on the Oregon bill.

"Mr. Wentworth said that, as he had the floor, he would make the motion. Mr. Wentworth then moved that the rules be suspended, for the purpose of going into committee of the whole on the Oregon Bill.

Credentials of Orson Hyde, Agent to Present the Prophet's Memorial to Congress.

CITY OF NAUVOO, ILLINOIS, March 30, 1844.

To whom it may concern: We, the Mayor and Recorder of said city, do certify that Orson Hyde, Esq., the bearer, a Councilor in the City Council of said city, is sent as our agent, by the authorities of said city, to transact such business as he may deem expedient and beneficial for the party whom he represents; and such agent and gentleman of principle and character, he by us is recommended to the due consideration of all the executive officers of the Government, both houses of Congress, and gentlemen generally of the United States.

In witness whereof, we have hereunto set our hands and affixed the seal of said corporation at the time and place aforesaid.

[CORPORATION SEAL.]

JOSEPH SMITH, Mayor.

WILLARD RICHARDS, Recorder.

About this time, Brother Alexander Mills, one of the police, informed me that Chauncey L. Higbee drew a pistol on him the night before, and threatened to shoot him. I instructed him to make complaint to Esquire Wells, and have him apprehended.

"The Speaker said that the question would be put on suspending the rules to go into committee of the whole. If that motion prevailed, the gentleman could move to take up any bill he pleased.

"Mr. Vance called for the yeas and nays on the question; which were ordered.

"Mr. McKay inquired if the House should refuse to go into committee of the whole, if it could by postponement of the previous orders, take up the naval appropriation bill which had been reported from the committee of the whole.

"The Speaker said a motion to that effect would require a vote of two-thirds.

"The question was put on suspending the rules and rejected—yeas 79, nays 86." ("Congressional Globe" for May 25th, 1844. Vol. 13, No. 39, p 624.)

CHAPTER XII.

THE AUTHORITIES OF NAUVOO VS. THE HIGBEES, ET. AL—DEDICATION OF THE MASONIC HALL—THE CHURCH CONFERENCE OF APRIL, 1844—ADDRESS OF PRESIDENT SIDNEY RIGDON; DITTO PATRIARCH HYRUM SMITH—HISTORICAL RESUME, AND BUILDING THE TEMPLE.

Monday, April 1, 1844.—In the the court-room in the Mansion, Mr. J. Easton was brought up as being accessory to whipping Chism, [a negro]. Referred the case to Alderman Wells. On investigation, it appeared to the satisfaction of the court that he had been on trial for the same offense before Robert D. Foster, and acquitted.

I extract from the *Neighbor*:—

Comment on the Negro Chism's Case.

After the court dismissed the case, General Smith fearlessly stated that he believed that it was a plot on the part of those who were instrumental in getting up the previous trial to thwart the ends of justice and screen the prisoner from the condemnation he justly deserves. Mr. Foster then stated, by way of an apology, that at the time he issued the warrant he did not know that the prisoner was under an arrest, or that there was any process out against him.

We hope, for the honor of such a man as Mr. Foster, that his statement is true. Mr. Foster, however, called upon one of his jurors, Mr. Carn, to corroborate what he had said; but, to our astonishment, he replied that when Mr. Foster summoned him to appear and act as a juryman, he was not informed what case he was to act upon, nor did he learn until he entered the office, where he acted according to the evidence given; but believed then, as well as now, that it was a sham trial, and a mere mockery of justice. We state facts as they are, and let the public judge for themselves.

The statement of the negro was that Messrs. Easton, Townsend, and Lawyer W. H. J. Marr were the persons engaged in this diabolical affair. Mr. Gibbs, one of the witnesses against Townsend, believed the above persons were engaged in it; but as a negro knows nothing in this state, and Mr. Gibbs could not positively swear to it, of course we don't know; but we have our opinion, and so have the public. We don't remember ever having seen more indignation manifest than was manifested on this occasion, and the public mind is not satisfied at the turn affairs have taken. Lynch law will not do in Nauvoo, and those who engage in it must expect to be visited by the wrath of an indignant people, not according to the rule of Judge Lynch, but according to law and equity.

It was thought best to acquit Easton and leave the case to the Circuit Court.

The Higbee Brothers in Trouble.

Francis M. Higbee and Chauncey L. Higbee were brought up before Esquire Wells for assaulting the police, and acquitted. Chauncey L. Higbee a lawyer, was brought before Daniel H. Wells Esq., on the charge of using abusive language to and insulting the city marshal while in the discharge of his official duty. He was fined ten dollars.

Also Robert D. Foster, Esq., was taken before Isaac Higbee, J. P., and fined ten dollars, for a breach of the ordinance pertaining to gambling, &c.

We are sorry to find that our lawyers and magistrates should be taking the lead among gamblers and disorderly persons, and be numbered among the law-breakers, rather than supporting virtue, law, and the dignity of the city.

Counter move of the Higbees.

Tuesday, 2.—At home, somewhat unwell, and kept my house this fine day. John P. Greene, marshal; Andrew Lytle, and John Lytle, policemen, were arrested by a warrant issued by Robert D. Foster, on complaint of Francis M. Higbee, for false imprisonment. As the case was going to trial, the prisoners were taken by John D. Parker, with a writ of *habeas corpus* before the Municipal Court; and tomorrow, at one, p. m., was fixed for trial.

Wednesdey, 3.—At one, p. m., presided in a special session of the Municipal Court, with Aldermen William Marks, Newel K. Whitney, Orson Spencer, George W. Harris, Gustavus Hills, George A. Smith, and Samuel Bennett as Associate-Justices. John P. Greene, Andrew Lytle, and John Lyttle were brought up on *habeas corpus* having been taken from the officer who held them on a writ issued by Robert D. Foster, before whom they had been arraigned on the complaint of Chauncey L. Higbee, charged with false imprisonment.

Joel S. Miles, Andrew Lytle, John Lytle, John P. Greene, and Robert D. Foster were sworn, gave testimony in the case, and the court decided that Greene and the two Lytles be discharged, and that Chauncey L. Higbee is a very disorderly person; that this case on *habeas corpus* originated in a malicious and vexatious suit, instituted by Chauncey L. Higbee against the petitioners now discharged; and that said Higbee pay the costs.

Warm and cloudy.

Conference in New York.

A conference was held in the city of New York; Elder William Smith presiding, and Elder William H. Miles, clerk. Fifteen branches were represented, containing 566 members, including 3 High Priests, 26 Elders, 15 Priests, 16 Teachers, and 9 Deacons.

Thursday, 14.—In a general council in the assembly room from nine to twelve, a. m., and from one to four, p. m.

I was visited by eleven Indians, who wanted counsel, and had an impressive interview.

Elder Orson Hyde was in the council, and left immediately for Washington.*

*The object of his mission was to assist Elders Orson Pratt and John E. Page in getting President Smith's Memorial, asking to be appointed "a member of the U. S. Army" and to be authorized to raise one hundred thousand armed volunteers to police the inter-mountain and Pacific coast west from Oregon to Texas.

A company of Saints arrived on the steamer *St. Croix*. Showery day.

Friday, 5.—Attended the dedication of the Masonic Temple, which was attended by about 550 members of the Masonic fraternity from various parts of the world. A procession was formed at Henry Miller's house, and was accompanied by the Nauvoo Brass Band to the hall. The dedicatory ceremonies were performed by the Worshipful Master Hyrum Smith. Elder Erastus Snow delivered an able Masonic address. Dr. Goforth and I also addressed the assembly. All the visiting Masons were furnished a dinner at the Masonic Hall at the expense of the Nauvoo Lodge. The building is admitted to be the most substantial and best finished Masonic Temple in the Western States. It has been erected under the direction of Mr. Lucius N. Scovil.

Dedication Masonic Temple.

In consequence of ill health, I deferred preaching the funeral sermon of King Follett until Sunday. Elder Amasa Lyman addressed a very large assembly at the stand.

General Conference Minutes of the Church, April, 1844.

Conference met pursuant to adjournment. Present—President Joseph Smith, Hyrum Smith, Sidney Rigdon, and William Marks. Of the Twelve—Brigham Young, Heber C. Kimball, Willard Richards, Wilford Woodruff, John Taylor, and George A. Smith.

The members of the High Council, an immense number of Elders, and a very large concourse of people.

Presidents Joseph and Hyrum Smith came to the stand at a quarter-past ten o'clock, when the meeting was called to order by Elder Brigham Young. The choir sang a hymn, after which

Opening Address of President Joseph Smith.

President Joseph Smith rose to state to the congregation the nature of the business which would have to come before them. He stated that it had been expected by some that the little petty difficulties which have existed would be brought up and investigated before this conference, but it will not be the case: these things are of too trivial a nature to occupy the attention of so large a body. I intend to give you some instruction on the principles of eternal truth, but will defer it until others have spoken, in consequence of the weakness of my lungs. The Elders will give you instruction; and then, if necessary, I will offer such corrections as may be proper to fill up the interstices. Those who feel desirous of sowing the seeds of discord will be disappointed on this occasion. It is our purpose to build up and establish the principles of righteousness, and not to break down and destroy. The Great Jehovah has ever been with me, and the wisdom of God will direct me in the seventh hour. I feel in closer communion and better standing with God than ever I felt before in my life, and I am glad of this opportunity to appear in your midst. I thank God for the glorious day that He has given us. In so large a congregation it is necessary that the greatest order and decorum be observed. I request this at your hands, and believe that you will all keep good order.

Prayer was offered by W. W. Phelps, after which the choir sang a hymn.

Elder Sidney Rigdon.

Elder Sidney Rigdon then rose and said: It is with no ordinary degree of satisfaction I enjoy this privilege this morning. Want of health and other circumstances have kept me in silence for nearly the last five years. It can hardly be expected that when the violence of sickness has used its influence, and the seeds of disease have so long preyed upon me, that I can rise before this congregation, only in weakness. I am now come forth from a bed of sickness, and have enough of strength left to appear here for the first time in my true character. I have not come before a conference for the last five years in my true character. I shall consider this important privilege sacred in my family history during life. I hardly promise myself lungs to make this congregation hear me. I shall do the best I can, and the greatest can do no more.

The circumstance by which we are now surrounded point out the principles of my discourse—the history of this Church, which I have known from its infancy. My text is—"Behold the Church of God of the last days." I do not know that I can find it in the Bible. I do not think it necessary to have Paul to make a text for me; I can make a text for myself. I recollect in the year 1830 I met the whole Church of Christ in a little old log-house about 20 feet square, near Waterloo, N. Y., and we began to talk about the kingdom of God as if we had the world at our command. We talked with great confidence, and talked big things. Although we were not many people, we had big feelings.

We knew fourteen years ago that the Church would become as large as it is today. We were as big then as we ever shall be. We began to talk like men in authority and power. We looked upon the men of the earth as grasshoppers. If we did not see this people, we saw by vision the Church of God, a thousand times larger. And when men would say we wanted to upset the Government, although we were not enough to well man a farm, or meet a woman with a milk-pail, all the Elders, all the members met in conference in a room twenty feet square.

I recollect Elder Phelps being put in jail for reading the Book of Mormon. He came to see us, and expressed great astonishment, and left us, apparently pondering in his heart. He afterwards came to Kirtland, Ohio, and said he was a convert. Many things were taught, believed, and preached then, which have since come to pass. We knew the whole world would laugh at us; so we concealed ourselves, and there was much excitement about our secret meetings, charging us with designs against the Government, and with laying plans to get money, &c., which never existed in the hearts of any one else [*i. e.*, but in the hearts of their accusers]. And if we had talked in public, we should have been ridiculed more than we were. The world, being entirely ignorant of the testimony of the Prophets, and without knowledge of what God was about to do, treated all we said with pretended contempt and much ridicule, and had they heard all we said, it would have made worse for us.

We talked about the people coming as doves to the windows; and that nations should flock unto it; that they should come bending to the standard of Jesus, saying, "Our fathers have taught falsehoods and things in which there is no profit," and of whole nations being born in one day. We talked such big things that men could not bear them, and they not only ridiculed us for what we did say in public, but threatened and inflicted much personal abuse; and if they had heard all we said, their violence would have been insupportable. God had great things to say for the salvation of the world, which, if they had been told the public, would have brought persecution upon us unto death: so we were obliged to retire to our secret chamber and commune ourselves with God. If we had told the people what our eyes behold this day, we should not have been believed; but the rascals would have shed our blood if we had only told them what we believed. There we sat in secret and beheld the glorious visions and powers of the kingdom of heaven pass and repass. We had not a mighty congregation to shelter us. If a mob came upon us, we had to run and hide ourselves to save our lives.

The time has now come to tell why we held secret meetings. We were maturing plans fourteen years ago which we can now tell. Were we maturing plans to corrupt the world, to destroy the peace of society? No. Let fourteen years' experience of the Church tell the story. The Church never would have been here if we had not done as we did in secret. The cry of "False prophet and imposter!" rolled upon us. I do not know that anything has taken place in the history of this Church which we did not then believe. It was written upon our hearts and never could be taken away. It was indelibly engraved; no power beneath yonder heavens could obliterate it. This was the period when God laid the foundation of the Church, and He laid it firmly, truly, and upon eternal truth.

If any man says it is not the work of God, I know he lies. Some of you who know you have a house, how long would it take to make you reason yourselves into a belief that you have no house where you now reside with your family? Neither have we any power whereby we can ever persuade ourselves that this is not the Church of God. We do not care who sinks or swims, or opposes, but we know here is the Church of God, and I have authority before God for saying so. I have the testimony of Jesus, which is the spirit of prophecy. I have slept with it,—I have walked with it. The idea has never been out of my heart for a moment, and I will reap the glory of it when I leave this world. I defy men and hell and devils to put it out of my heart. I defy all, and will triumph in spite of them.

I know God. I have gazed upon the glory of God, the throne, visions and glories of God, and the visions of eternity in days gone by. What is a man of God to do, when he sees all the madness, wrath and follies of our persecutors? He will do as God does—he will sit and laugh. * * * These were the beginning of good days—shut up in a room eating nothing but dry johnny-cake and buttermilk. Every man who had a little farm or clothes, sold them and distributed what he had among the rest, and did the best he could. I had a little to eat—little to wear, and yet it was the beginning of good days.

Some say "I want plenty to eat, plenty to drink, plenty to wear, and a good house to live in; and, say they then I will believe. But God will not give it until you have proved yourselves unto Him.

No wonder, then, that we should be joyful today. If the people will do as they are told, I will tell you what to do. Get the visions of heaven, and seek not what you shall eat or what you shall drink, but seek the will of God. Get into the presence of God, and then you will have johnny-cake and milk-and-water no more. Would you not be astonished if even now we should tell the glories and privileges of the Saints of God to you and to the world? We should be ridiculed; and no wonder we shut it up in secret. If we were to tell you when Jehovah is looked upon, lo it is beauty, it is heaven, it is felicity to look upon Jehovah. I should marvel if it were otherwise. If a man tells you one glory or one message, he is learning another at the same time. Do not be astonished, then, if we even yet have secret meetings, asking God for things for your benefit.

Do not be afraid. Go back to the commencement of this Church, and see what was concocted then. There was no evil concocted when we first held secret meetings, and it is the same now. Has God forgotten to be gracious, to be merciful to mankind? Did He ever concoct anything that was devilish for mankind? He could not do it. I never am afraid of God or man concocting anything to hurt me. I have faith to detect men, even if they did. I would ask God to detect them, and hold them fast before they should do it. I am not afraid of men or devils. I have none of those fears, jealousies, dreads, forebodings, surmisings, &c. I put my trust in God, and whatever God does for me is only for my salvation.

A man is a bad teamster who runs his team in the worst road. What I have already said is only to prepare the way. [Here five of the Pottawattomie tribe appeared with their interpreter, and were assisted to the stand by the President.] I am going to tell of something that surprised me at the beginning of the Church. I have handled, heard, seen and known things which I have not yet told.

After the Church began to grow, it was favored with marvelously wise men. They had so much wisdom that they could dispute what God said, and what His servant said. They were opposed to virtue. They would say they had revelations and visions, and were as certain that the Lord had given it as I was that the devil had.

He referred to the children of Israel who were snivelling and murmuring about their leeks and onions, &c., &c.; and so it is in these last days; some men are always yelling about what the Church believes and opposing every good thing.

I want devils to gratify themselves; and if howling, yelling and yelping will do you any good, do it till you are all damned.

If calling us devils, &c., will do you any good, let us have the whole of it, and you can then go on your way to hell without a grunt.

We hear these things ever since the Church existed. They have come up with us; they have had so much more wisdom, they knew all about the kingdom before God revealed it, and they know all things before they were heard; they understand more than God knows. We gather of all kinds. If we get all nations, we get all wisdom, cunning, and everything else.

The sectarians cannot be as wise as we are, for they have only got man's plans, the devil's plans, and, the best of all, we have God's plan.

I do not know whether there are any of these wise men here this morning or not; I have merely given this as a part of the history of this Church. I am disposed to give some reasons why salvation only belongs to the kingdom of God, and to that alone.

I will endeavor to show why salvation belongs to us more peculiarly, in contradistinction to all other bodies. Will this be clear enough?

I discover one thing: Mankind have labored under one universal mistake about this—viz., salvation was distinct from government; *i. e.*, that I can build a Church without government, and that thing have power to save me!

When God sets up a system of salvation, He sets up a system of government. When I speak of a government, I mean what I say. I mean a government that shall rule over temporal and spiritual affairs.

Every man is a government of himself, and infringes upon no government. A man is not an honorable man, if he is not above all law and above government.

I see in our town we have need of government. Some study law only for the purpose of seeing how many feuds, how many broils they can kick up, how much they can disturb the peace of the public without breaking the law, and then say—"I know my rights, and will have them;" "I did not know it was the marshal, or I would not have done it."

He is no gentleman. Gentlemen would not insult a poor man in the street, but would bow to him, as much as those who appear mor respectable. No marshal or any one else, should pull me up. We ought to live a great way within the circle of the laws of the land. I would live far above all law.

The law of God is far more righteous than the laws of the land. The kingdom of God does not interfere with the laws of the land, but keeps itself by its own laws. (Reported by Elder Thomas Bullock.)

Elder Rigdon stopped to refresh himself. The choir sang hymn 104.

Elder John Taylor, being called upon to address the congregation, said—It gives me pleasure to meet and associate with so large an assemblage of the Saints. I always feel at home among the brethren. I consider them the honorable of the earth; and if I can do anything to conduce to their happiness, or that will in anywise tend to their edification, I am satisfied.

I therefore address this congregation with cheerfulness and pleasure, and if by unfolding any of the principles of truth that I am in possession of, or laying before you anything pertaining to the kingdom—if my ideas will enlarge your minds, or produce beneficial results to any, I shall consider myself on this, as on all other occasions, amply repaid.

Many things have been spoken by Elder Rigdon concerning the early history of this Church. There is no person who has searched the oracles of eternal truth, but his mind will be touched with the remarks made by our venerable friend, which unfold the dispensation of Jehovah, and have a tendency to produce the most thrilling feelings in the bosoms of many who are this day present, and to promote our general edification. He traces with pleasure on the historic page—the rise of nations, kingdoms and empires. Historians dwell with great minuteness on the heroic deeds, the chivalrous acts, the dangers and deliverances, the tact, bravery, and heroism of their chieftains, generals and governments.

We, as Republicans, look back to the time when this nation was under the iron rule of Great Britain, and groaned under the power, tyranny and oppression of that powerful nation. We trace with delight the name of a Washington, a Jefferson, a LaFayette, and an Adams, in whose bosoms burned the spark of liberty. These themes are dwelt upon with delight by our legislators, our governors and presidents; they are subjects which fire our souls with patriotic ardor.

But if these things animate them so much, how much more great, noble and exalted are the things laid before us! They were engaged in founding kingdoms and empires that were destined to dissolution and decay; and although many of them were great, formidable and powerful, they now exist only in name. Their cloud-capped towers, their solemn temples, are dissolved, and nothing now remains of their former magnificence or ancient grandeur but a few dilapidated buildings and broken columns. A few shattered fragments remain to tell to this and to other generations the perishable nature of earthly pomp and worldly glory.

They were engaged in founding empires and establishing kingdoms and powers that had in themselves the seeds of destruction, and were destined to decay. We are laying the foundation of a kingdom that shall last forever—that shall bloom in time and blossom in eternity. We are engaged in a greater work than ever occupied the attention of mortals. We live in a day that prophets and kings desired to see, but died without the sight.

When we hear the history of the rise of this kingdom from one who has been with it from its infancy—from the lips of our venerable friend who has taken an active part in all the history of the Church, can we be surprised if he should feel animated, and that his soul should burn with heavenly zeal? We see in him a man of God who can contemplate the glories of heaven, the visions of eternity, and yet who looks forward to the opening glories which the great Elohim has manifested to him pertaining to righteousness and peace—a man who now beholds the things roll on which he has long since beheld in prophetic vision.

Most men have established themselves in authority by laying desolate other kingdoms and the destruction of other powers. Their kingdoms have been founded in blood, and supported in tyranny and oppression. The greatest chieftains of the earth have obtained their glory—if glory it can be called—by blood, carnage and ruin. One nation has been built up at the expense and ruin of another, and one man has been made at the expense of another; and yet these great men were called honorable for their inglorious deeds of rapine. They have slain their thousands, and caused the orphans to weep and the widows to mourn.

Men did these things because they could do it—because they had power to desolate nations, and spread terror and desolation. They have made themselves immortal as great men. The patriots of this country had indeed a laudable object in view—a plausible excuse for the course they took. They stood in defense of their rights, liberty and freedom. But where are now those principles of freedom? Where are the laws that protect all men in their religious opinions? Where the laws that say, "A man shall worship God according to the dictates of his own conscience? What say ye, ye Saints—ye who are exiles in the land of liberty? How came you here? Can you in this land of equal rights return in safety to your possessions in Missouri? No. You are exiles from thence, and there is no power, no voice, no arm to redress your grievance. Is this the gracious boon for which your fathers fought and struggled and died? Shades of the venerable dead, could you but gaze upon this scene, and witness tens of thousands of Americans in exile on Columbia's soil—if pity could touch your bosoms, how you would mourn for the oppressed! If indignation, how would you curse the heartless wretches that have so desecrated and polluted the temple of liberty? "How has the gold become dim, and the fine gold, how has it changed." Let it not be told among the monarchs of Europe, lest they laugh and say, "Ha; so would we have it."

Ye Saints, never let it go abroad that ye are exiles in the land of liberty, lest ye disgrace your republic in the eyes of the nations of the earth; but tell it to those who robbed and plundered and refused to give you your rights. Tell your rulers that all their deeds of fame are tarnished, and their glory is departed.

Are we now, indeed, in a land of liberty, of freedom, of equal rights? Would to God I could answer, Yes. But no, no, I cannot! They have robbed us, we are stripped of our possessions, many of our friends are slain, and our government says, "Your cause is just, but we can do nothing for you."

Hear it, ye great men, we are here in exile! Here are thousands of men in bondage in a land of liberty—of freedom! If ye have any patriotism, shake off your fetters and come and proclaim us free, and give us our rights. I speak of this government as being one of the best of governments—as one of the greatest and purest; and yet, what a melancholy picture! O ye venerable fathers who fought for your liberty, blush for your children, and mourn, mourn over your country's shame! We are now talking about a government which sets herself up as a pattern for the nations of the earth, and yet, oh, what a picture! If this is the best, the most patriotic, the most free, what is the situation of the rest?

Here we speak with national pride of a Washington, a LaFayette, a Monroe aud a Jefferson, who fought for their liberties, achieved one of the greatest victories ever won; and scarcely has one generation passed away before fifteen thousand citizens petition government for redress of their wrongs, and they turn a deaf ear to their cry.

Let us compare this with the Church of Christ. Fourteen years ago a few men assembled in a log cabin; they saw the visions of heaven, and gazed upon the eternal world; they looked through the rent vista of futurity, and beheld the glories of eternity; they were planting those principles which were concocted in the bosom of Jehovah; they were laying a foundation for the salvation of the world, and those principles which they then planted have not yet begun to dwindle; but the fire still burns in their bones; the principles are planted in different nations and are wafted on every breeze.

When I gaze upon this company of men, I see those who are actuated by patriotic and noble principles, who will stand up in defense of the oppressed, of whatever country, nation, color or clime. I see it in their countenances. It is planted by the Spirit of God. They have received it from the great Elohim, and all the power or influence of mobs, priestcraft or corrupt men cannot quench it. It will burn. It is comprehensive as the designs of God, and as expansive as the universe and reaches to all the world. No matter whether it was an Indian, a negro, or any other man or set of men that are oppressed, you would stand forth in their defense.

I say unto you, continue to cherish those principles. Let them expand. And if the tree of liberty has been blasted in this nation—if it has been gnawed by worms, and already blight has overspread it, we will stand up in defense of our liberties, and proclaim ourselves free in time and in eternity.

The choir, by request, sang, "O stop and tell me, Red Man." After prayer by Elder John P. Greene, the meeting was adjourned for one hour.

CHAPTER XIII.

CONFERENCE OF THE CHURCH, APRIL, 1844, CONTINUED—ADDRESS OF PATRIARCH HYRUM SMITH—THE BUILDING OF THE TEMPLE.

Saturday, April 6, 1844, [*Conference Report Continued.*]

The President arrived at the stand at half-past two o'clock, p. m. The choir sang a hymn; after which prayer by Elder John P. Greene, when the choir sang another hymn.

Elder Rigdon resumed his history of the Church.

A little before five o'clock the assembly was dismissed without ceremony, until next morning, on the appearance of a shower. The people had scarcely time to retire before a heavy shower of rain, wind, thunder and lightning followed. A splendid double rainbow seen in the heavens.

Sunday, 7.

Very pleasant morning. The President arrived at ten o'clock, the largest congregation ever seen in Nauvoo having assembled. The choir sang the hymn, "Ye slumbering nations that have slept."

President Rigdon offered an affectionate appeal for the prayers of the Saints on behalf of the sick, and then prayer by Elder George J. Adams.

Choir sang the hymn, "The Spirit of God like a fire is burning," &c.

President Joseph Smith.

The Mayor requested the people to keep good order, and observed to the police, who were round the outskirts of the congregation to keep order, "Policemen, I want you to exercise your authority; and don't say you can't do anything for us, for the constitutional power calls you to keep good order, and God Almighty calls you, and we command you to do it."

Elder Sidney Rigdon arose and continued his subject of yesterday.

Choir sang. Benediction. Intermission.

During the intermission, thirty-five were baptized in the Mississippi river for the remission of their sins.

Address of Elder Hyrum Smith, Patriarch to the Church.

At 2 o'clock p. m.

Patriarch Hyrum Smith arrived at the stand, and said he wanted to say something about the temple.

"We want 200,000 shingles, as we shall resume the work on the Temple immediately. All who have not paid their tithing, come on and do it. We want provisions, money, boards, planks, and anything that is good; we don't want any more old guns or watches. I thought some time ago I would get up a small subscription, so that the sisters might do something. In consequence of some misunderstanding, it has not gone on as at first. It is a matter of my own; I do not ask it as a tithing. I give a privilege to any one to pay a cent a week, or fifty cents a year. I want it by next fall to buy nails and glass. It is difficult to get money. I know that a small subscription will bring more than a large one. The poor can help in this way. I take the responsibility upon myself, and call again upon the sisters. I call again until I get about $1,000. It only requires two thousand subscribers.

I have sent this subscription plan to England and the branches. I am not to be dictated to by any one except the Prophet and God. I want you to pay in your subscriptions to me, and it shall always be said boldly by me, the sisters bought the glass in that house, and their names shall be written in the Book of the Law of the Lord. It is not a tax, but a free will offering to procure something which shall ever be a monument of your works. No member of the Relief Society got it up. I am the man that did it. They ought not to infringe upon it. I am not a member of the Female Relief Society! I am one of the committee of the Lord's House.

I wish to accomplish something, I wish all the Saints to have an opportunity to do something. I want the poor with the purse of five dollars to have a chance. The widow's two mites were more in the eyes of the Lord than the purse of the rich; and the poor woman shall have a seat in the house of God—she who pays her two mites as well as the rich, because it is all she has. I wish to have a place in that house. I intend to stimulate the brethren. I want to get the roof on this season. I want to get the windows in, in the winter, so that we may be able to dedicate the House of the Lord by this time next year, if nothing more than one room. I will call upon the brethren to do something.

I cannot make a comparison between the House of God and anything now in existence. Great things are to grow out of that house. There is a great and mighty power to grow out of it. There is an endowment. Knowledge is power. We want knowledge. We have frequently difficulties with persons who profess to be Latter-day Saints. When the sacrament will be administered in the Lord's House it will do away with a great deal of difficulty that is now in existence. If we can have a privilege and confess our faults unto God and one another every Sabbath day,it will do away with these. * * * You sisters shall have a seat in that house. I will stand on the top of that pulpit and proclaim to all what the sisters have done. When you offer up your sacraments every Sabbath, you will feel well a whole week; you will get a great portion of the Spirit of God, enough to last you a week—and you will increase. We are now deprived of the privilege of giving the necessary instruction; hence we want a house.

All the money shall be laid out for what you design it. It shall not be paid for anything else. I am one of the committee. The committee tells me the quarry is blockaded; it is filled with rock. The stone cutters are wanting work. Come on with your teams as soon as conference is over. It is not necessary for me to tell who will come and do it. I will prophesy that you will do it. There is not one in the city but what will do right if he knows it, with only one or two exceptions, and they are not worth notice. God will take care of them, and if He doesn't, the devil will. I described them once, and you will always know them while you see them. They will keep hopping till they hop out of town. Some of them are tree toads, who climb the trees and are continually croaking.

We are now the most noble people on the face of the globe, and we have no occasion to fear tadpoles. We are designated by the All-seeing Eye to do good, not to stoop to anything low. We are apt to suffer prejudice to get into our hearts on hearing reports. We never should allow it—never should pass our judgment until we hear both sides.

I will tell a Dutch anecdote: A certain Dutchman had a case brought before him, and heard one side, and he gave in his decision—"Sure you have got the case;" and when the other party brought their witnesses, he said again, "Sure, you have got the case, too." If you hear of any one in high authority, that he is rather inclined to apostasy, don't let prejudice arise, but pray for him. God may feel after him, and he may return. Never speak reproachfully nor disrespectfully; he is in the hands of God. I am one of those peacemakers who take a stand above these little things. It has been intimated we should have investigations this conference. Do you think I would trouble this conference with it? If I have a difficulty with a man, I will go and settle it. Let them settle their difficulties. There is not a man who has had a difficulty who would trouble this congregation about it. We ask no favors; we can settle it ourselves. Don't think anything about persons who are on the eve of apostasy; God is able to take care of them. Let God judge. do your duty and let men alone.

Never undertake to destroy men because they do some evil thing. It is natural for a man to be led, and not driven. Put down iniquity by good works. Many men speak without any contemplation; if they had given the matter a little contemplation it would not have been spoken We ought to be careful what we say, and take the example of Jesus, cast over men the mantle of charity, and try to cover their faults. We are made to enlighten, and not to darken one another; save men, not destroy them. Do unto others what you would have them do unto you. It is well enough to root out conspiracy. Do not fear, but if you are in the right track, having God to guide you, He will save you; for God will save you, if He has to destroy the wicked so as by fire.

I want to put down all false influence. If I thought I should be saved and any in the congregation be lost, I should not be happy. For this purpose Jesus effected a resurrection. Our Savior is competent to save all from death and hell. I can prove it out of the revelation. I would not serve a God that had not all wisdom and all power.

The reason why I feel so good is because I have a big soul. There are men with small bodies who have got souls like Enoch. We have. We have gathered our big souls from the ends of the earth. The Gospel picks the big souls out of all creation, and we will get the big souls out of all the nations, and we shall have the largest city in the world.

We will gather all the big souls out of every nation. As soon as the Gospel catches hold of noble souls, it brings them all right up to Zion. There is a thing called guiding star. The Gospel is similar. We will have a people great enough to be saved.

Popery could not write what Enoch preached. He told the people that the Spirit of God took him up into a high mountain, showed him the distress of the people—the destruction of the world, and he said his heart swelled wide as eternity. But adherents of Popery could not receive anything as large as that, and every man-made society is just like them. Men's souls conform to the society in which they live, with very few exceptions, and when men come to live with the Mormons, their souls swell as if they were going to stride the planets as I stride the Republic of America. I can believe that man can go from planet to planet—a man gets so high in the mansions above.

A certain good sister came to my house, and she was troubled because she heard so many big things. She thought it weakened her faith. I told her she had too much faith. She believed too much. I will tell you how you may know whether the thing is true or not. When any one comes to you with a lie, you feel troubled. God will trouble you, and will not approbate you in such belief. You had better get some antidote to get rid of it. Humble yourself before God, and ask Him for His Spirit and pray to Him to judge it for you. It is better not to have so much faith, than to have so much as to believe all the lies.

Before this conference closes, I want to get all the Elders together.

I shall make a proclamation. I want to take the line and ax and hew you, and make you as straight as possible. I will make you straight as a stretched line. Every Elder that goes from Nauvoo to preach the Gospel, if he preaches anything else, we will silence him through the public print. I want all the Elders to meet and to understand; and if they preach anything but the pure truth, we will call them home.

At a quarter-past three p. m., President Smith having arrived, the choir sang a hymn. Elder Amasa Lyman offered prayer.

President Joseph Smith delivered a discourse before twenty thousand Saints, being the funeral sermon of Elder King Follett.

CHAPTER XIV.

CONFERENCE OF THE CHURCH, APRIL, 1844 (CONTINUED)—THE KING FOLLETT SERMON—THE CHARACTER OF GOD—RELIGIOUS FREEDOM—GOD AN EXALTED MAN—ETERNAL LIFE TO KNOW GOD AND JESUS CHRIST—EVERLASTING BURNINGS—MEANING OF THE HEBREW SCRIPTURES—A COUNCIL OF THE GODS—MEANING OF THE WORD CREATE—THE IMMORTAL INTELLIGENCE — THE RELATION OF MAN TO GOD — OUR GREATEST RESPONSIBILITY—THE UNPARDONABLE SIN—THE FORGIVENESS OF SIN—THE SECOND DEATH.

Sunday, April 7, 1844.—[Conference Report Continued.]

At quarter past three, p.m., the President having arrived, the choir sang a hymn, Elder Amasa Lyman offered prayer.

President Joseph Smith delivered the following discourse before about twenty thousand Saints, being the funeral sermon of Elder King Follett. Reported by Willard Richards, Wilford Woodruff, Thomas Bullock and William Clayton.*

Beloved Saints: I will call [for] the attention of this congregation while I address you on the subject of the dead. The decease of our beloved brother, Elder King Follett, who was crushed in a well by the falling of a tub of rock, has more immediately led me to this subject. I have been requested to speak by his friends and relatives, but inasmuch as there are a great many in this congregation who live in this city as well as elsewhere, who have lost friends, I feel disposed to speak on the subject in general, and offer you my ideas, so far as I have ability, and so far as I shall be inspired by the Holy Spirit to dwell on this subject.

I want your prayers and faith that I may have the instruction of Almighty God and the gift of the Holy Ghost, so that I may set forth things that are true and which can be easily comprehended by you,

* This was not a stenographic report, but a carefully and skillfully prepared one made by these men who were trained in reporting and taking notes. Evidently, there are some imperfections in the report and some thoughts expressed by the Prophet which were not fully rounded out and made complete; nevertheless it contains many wonderful truths pertaining to the subjects discussed and therefore is valuable in giving us a better understanding than we would have without it.

and that the testimony may carry conviction to your hearts and minds of the truth of what I shall say. Pray that the Lord may strengthen my lungs, stay the winds, and let the prayers of the Saints to heaven appear, that they may enter into the ears of the Lord of Sabaoth, for the effectual prayers of the righteous avail much. There is strength here, and I verily believe that your prayers will be heard.

Before I enter fully into the investigation of the subject which is lying before me, I wish to pave the way and bring up the subject from the beginning, that you may understand it. I will make a few preliminaries, in order that you may understand the subject when I come to it. I do not calculate or intend to please your ears with superfluity of words or oratory, or with much learning; but I calculate [intend] to edify you with the simple truths from heaven.

The Character of God

In the first place, I wish to go back to the beginning—to the morn of creation. There is the starting point for us to look to, in order to understand and be fully acquainted with the mind, purposes and decrees of the Great Eloheim, who sits in yonder heavens as he did at the creation of the world. It is necessary for us to have an understanding of God himself in the beginning. If we start right, it is easy to go right all the time; but if we start wrong we may go wrong, and it will be a hard matter to get right.

There are but a very few beings in the world who understand rightly the character of God. The great majority of mankind do not comprehend anything, either that which is past, or that which is to come, as it respects their relationship to God. They do not know, neither do they understand the nature of that relationship; and consequently they know but little above the brute beast, or more than to eat, drink and sleep. This is all man knows about God or His existence, unless it is given by the inspiration of the Almighty.

If a man learns nothing more than to eat, drink and sleep, and does not comprehend any of the designs of God, the beast comprehends the same things. It eats, drinks, sleeps, and knows nothing more about God; yet it knows as much as we, unless we are able to comprehend by the inspiration of Almighty God. If men do not comprehend the character of God, they do not comprehend themselves. I want to go back to the beginning, and so lift your minds into more lofty spheres and a more exalted understanding than what the human mind generally aspires to.

I want to ask this congregation, every man, woman and child, to answer the question in their own hearts, what kind of a being God is? Ask yourselves; turn your thoughts into your hearts, and say if any of you have seen, heard, or communed with Him? This is a question that may occupy your attention for a long time. I again repeat the question—What kind of a being is God? Does any man or woman know? Have any of you seen Him, heard Him, or communed with Him? Here is the question that will, peradventure, from this time henceforth occupy your attention. The scriptures inform us that "This is life eternal that they might know thee, the only true God, and Jesus Christ whom thou hast sent."

If any man does not know God, and inquires what kind of a being He is,—if he will search diligently his own heart—if the declaration of Jesus and the apostles be true, he will realize that he has not eternal life; for there can be eternal life on no other principle.

My first object is to find out the character of the only wise and true, God, and what kind of a being He is; and if I am so fortunate as to be the man to comprehend God, and explain or convey the principles to your hearts, so that the Spirit seals them upon you, then let every man and woman henceforth sit in silence, put their hands on their mouths, and never lift their hands or voices, or say anything against the man of God or the servants of God again. But if I fail to do it, it becomes my duty to renounce all further pretensions to revelations and inspirations, or to be a prophet; and I should be like the rest of the world—a false teacher, be hailed as a friend, and no man would seek my life. But if all religious teachers were honest enough to renounce their pretensions to godliness when their ignorance of the knowledge of God is made manifest, they will all be as badly off as I am, at any rate; and you might just as well take the lives of other false teachers as that of mine. If any man is authorized to take away my life because he thinks and says I am a false teacher, then, upon the same principle, we should be justified in taking away the life of every false teacher, and where would be the end of blood? And who would not be the sufferer?*

The Privilege of Religious Freedom

But meddle not with any man for his religion: all governments ought to permit every man to enjoy his religion unmolested. No man is authorized to take away life in consequence of difference of religion, which all laws and governments ought to tolerate and protect, right or wrong. Every man has a natural, and, in our country, a constitutional right to be a false prophet, as well as a true prophet. If I show, verily, that I have the truth of God, and show that ninety-nine out of every hundred professing religious ministers are false teachers, having no authority, while they pretend to hold the keys of God's kingdom on earth, and was to kill them because they are false teachers, it would deluge the whole world with blood.

* It should be remembered that at the time of this discourse apostates and other enemies of the Prophet were seeking his life, and open threats were being made even in his presence. The forces of evil were determined that the Prophet should be destroyed. It was less than three months following the date of this discourse when he and his brother Hyrum were martyred.

I will prove that the world is wrong, by showing what God is. I am going to inquire after God; for I want you all to know Him, and to be familiar with Him; and if I am bringing you to a knowledge of Him, all persecutions against me ought to cease. You will then know that I am His servant; for I speak as one having authority.

God An Exalted Man

I will go back to the beginning before the world was, to show what kind of a being God is. What sort of a being was God in the beginning? Open your ears and hear, all ye ends of the earth, for I am going to prove it to you by the Bible, and to tell you the designs of God in relation to the human race, and why He interferes with the affairs of man.

God himself was once as we are now, and is an exalted man, and sits enthroned in yonder heavens! That is the great secret. If the veil were rent today, and the great God who holds this world in its orbit, and who upholds all worlds and all things by His power, was to make himself visible,—I say, if you were to see him today, you would see him like a man in form—like yourselves in all the person, image, and very form as a man; for Adam was created in the very fashion, image and likeness of God, and received instruction from, and walked, talked and conversed with Him, as one man talks and communes with another.

In order to understand the subject of the dead, for consolation of those who mourn for the loss of their friends, it is necessary we should understand the character and being of God and how He came to be so; for I am going to tell you how God came to be God. We have imagined and supposed that God was God from all eternity. I will refute that idea, and take away the veil, so that you may see.

These are incomprehensible ideas to some, but they are simple. It is the first principle of the gospel to know for a certainty the character of God, and to know that we may converse with Him as one man converses with another, and that He was once a man like us; yea, that God himself, the Father of us all, dwelt on an earth, the same as Jesus Christ Himself did; and I will show it from the Bible.

Eternal Life to Know God and Jesus Christ

I wish I was in a suitable place to tell it, and that I had the trump of an archangel, so that I could tell the story in such a manner that persecution would cease forever. What did Jesus say? (Mark it, Elder Rigdon!) The scriptures inform us that Jesus said, as the Father hath power in himself, even so hath the Son power— to do what? Why, what the Father did. The answer is obvious—in a manner to lay down his body and take it up again. Jesus, what are you going to do? To lay down my life as my Father did, and take it up again. Do you believe it? If you do not believe it you do not believe the Bible. The scriptures say it, and I defy all the learning and wisdom and all the combined powers of earth and hell together to refute it. Here, then, is eternal life—to know the only wise and true God; and you have got to learn how to be gods yourselves, and to be kings and priests to God, the same as all gods have done before you, namely, by going from one small degree to another, and from a small capacity to a great one; from grace to grace, from exaltation to exaltation, until you attain to the resurrection of the dead, and are able to dwell in everlasting burnings, and to sit in glory, as do those who sit enthroned in everlasting power. And I want you to know that God, in the last days, while certain individuals are proclaiming His name, is not trifling with you or me.*

The Righteous to Dwell in Everlasting Burnings

These are the first principles of consolation. How consoling to the mourners when they are called to part with a husband, wife, father, mother, child, or dear relative, to know that, although the earthly tabernacle is laid down and dissolved, they shall rise again to dwell in everlasting burnings in immortal glory, not to sorrow, suffer, or die any more, but they shall be heirs of God and joint heirs with Jesus Christ. What is it? To inherit the same power, the same glory and the same exaltation, until you arrive at the station of a god, and ascend the throne of eternal power, the same as those who have gone before. What did Jesus do? Why, I do the things I saw my Father do when worlds came rolling into existence. My Father worked out His kingdom with fear and trembling, and I must do the same; and when I get my kingdom, I shall present it to My Father, so that He may obtain kingdom upon kingdom, and it will exalt Him in glory. He will then take a higher exaltation, and I will take His place, and thereby become exalted myself. So that Jesus treads in the tracks of His Father, and inherits what God did before; and God is thus glorified and exalted in the salvation and exaltation of all His children. It is plain beyond disputation, and you thus learn some of the first principles of the gospel, about which so much hath been said.

When you climb up a ladder, you must begin at the bottom, and ascend step by step, until you arrive at the top; and so it is with

* The argument here made by the Prophet is very much strengthened by the following passage: "The Son can do nothing of himself, but what he seeth the Father do; for what things soever he [the Father] doeth, these also doeth the Son likewise. (John 5:19.)

Henry Drummond, for instance (following the Prophet by half a century), in his work, **Natural Law in the Spiritual World,** in his chapter on growth, has said: "The end of salvation is perfection, the Christ-like mind, character and life. * * * Therefore the man who has within himself this great formative agent, Life [spiritual life] is nearer the end than the man who has morality alone. The latter can never reach perfection, the former **must**. For the life must develop out according to its type; and being a germ of the Christ-life, it **must unfold into a Christ.**"

the principles of the gospel—you must begin with the first, and go on until you learn all the principles of exaltation. But it will be a great while after you have passed through the veil before you will have learned them. It is not all to be comprehended in this world; it will be a great work to learn our salvation and exaltation even beyond the grave. I suppose I am not allowed to go into an investigation of anything that is not contained in the Bible. If I do, I think there are so many over-wise men here that they would cry "treason" and put me to death. So I will go to the old Bible and turn commentator today.

I shall comment on the very first Hebrew word in the Bible; I will make a comment on the very first sentence of the history of creation in the Bible—*Berosheit*. I want to analyze the word. *Baith*—in, by, through, and everything else. *Roch*—the head, *Sheit*—grammatical termination. When the inspired man wrote it, he did not put the baith there. An old Jew without any authority added the word; he thought it too bad to begin to talk about the head! It read first, "The head one of the Gods brought forth the Gods." That is the true meaning of the words. *Baurau* signifies to bring forth. If you do not believe it, you do not believe the learned man of God. Learned men can teach you no more than what I have told you. Thus the head God brought forth the Gods in the grand council.

I will transpose and simplify it in the English language. Oh, ye lawyers, ye doctors, and ye priests, who have persecuted me, I want to let you know that the Holy Ghost knows something as well as you do. The head God called together the Gods and sat in grand council to bring forth the world. The grand councilors sat at the head in yonder heavens and contemplated the creation of the worlds which were created at the time. When I say doctors and lawyers, I mean the doctors and lawyers of the scriptures. I have done so hitherto without explanation, to let the lawyers flutter and everybody laugh at them. Some learned doctors might take a notion to say the scriptures say thus and so; and we must believe the scriptures; they are not to be altered. But I am going to show you an error in them.

I have an old edition of the New Testament in the Latin, Hebrew, German and Greek languages. I have been reading the German, and find it to be the most [nearly] correct translation, and to correspond nearest to the revelations which God has given to me for the last fourteen years. It tells about Jacobus, the son of Zebedee. It means Jacob. In the English New Testament it is translated James. Now, if Jacob had the keys, you might talk about James through all eternity and never get the keys. In the 21st. of the fourth chapter of Matthew, my old German edition gives the word Jacob instead of James.

The doctors (I mean doctors of law, not physic) say, "If you preach anything not according to the Bible, we will cry treason." How can we escape the damnation of hell, except God be with us and reveal to us? Men bind us with chains. The Latin says Jacobus, which means Jacob; the Hebrew says Jacob, the Greek says Jacob and the German says Jacob, here we have the testimony of four against one. I thank God that I have got this old book; but I thank him more for the gift of the Holy Ghost. I have got the oldest book in the world; but I have got the oldest book in my heart, even the gift of the Holy Ghost. I have all the four Testaments. Come here, ye learned men, and read, if you can. I should not have introduced this testimony, were it not to back up the word *rosh*—the head, the Father of the Gods. I should not have brought it up, only to show that I am right.

A Council of the Gods

In the beginning, the head of the Gods called a council of the Gods; and they came together and concocted [prepared] a plan to create the world and people it. When we begin to learn this way, we begin to learn the only true God, and what kind of a being we have got to worship. Having a knowledge of God, we begin to know how to approach Him, and how to ask so as to receive an answer.

When we understand the character of God, and know how to come to Him, he begins to unfold the heavens to us, and to tell us all about it. When we are ready to come to him, he is ready to come to us.

Now, I ask all who hear me, why the learned men who are preaching salvation, say that God created the heavens and the earth out of nothing? The reason is, that they are unlearned in the things of God, and have not the gift of the Holy Ghost; they account it blasphemy in any one to contradict their idea. If you tell them that God made the world out of something, they will call you a fool. But I am learned, and know more than all the world put together. The Holy Ghost does, anyhow, and he is within me, and comprehends more than all the world; and I will associate myself with him.

Meaning of the Word Create

You ask the learned doctors why they say the world was made out of nothing, and they will answer, "Doesn't the Bible say He *created* the world?" And they infer, from the word create, that it must have been made out of nothing. Now, the word create came from the word *baurau*, which does not mean to create out of nothing; it means to organize; the same as a man would organize materials and build a ship. Hence we infer that God had materials to organize the world out of chaos—chaotic matter, which is element, and in which dwells all the glory. Element had an existence from the time He had. The pure principles of element are principles which can never be destroyed; they may be organized and re-organized, but not destroyed. They had no beginning and can have no end.*

* The view of the Prophet on this subject of creation is abundantly sustained by men of learning subsequent to his time. The Rev. Baden Powell of Oxford University, for instance, writing for Kitto's **Cyclopedia of Biblical Literature,** says: "The meaning of this word (create) has been commonly associated with the idea of 'making out of nothing.' But when we come to inquire more precisely into the subject, we can of course satisfy ourselves as to the meaning only from an examination of the original phrase." The learned professor then proceeds to say that three distinct Hebrew verbs are in different places employed with reference to the same divine act, and may be translated, respectively, "create," "make," "form or fashion." "Now," continues the professor, "though each of these has its shade of distinction, yet the best critics understand them as so nearly synonymous that, at least in regard to the idea of making out of nothing, little or no foundation for that doctrine can be obtained from the first of these words." And of course, if no foundation for the doctrine can be obtained from the first of these words—**viz.**, the verb translated "create," then the chances are still less for there being any foundation for the doctrine of creation from nothing in the verb translated "made," "formed," or "fashioned."

Professor Powell further says: "The idea of 'creation,' as meaning absolutely 'making out of nothing,' or calling into existence that which did not exist before, in the strictest sense of the term, is not a doctrine of scripture; but it has been held by many on the grounds of natural theology, as enhancing the ideas we form of the divine power, and more especially since the contrary must imply the belief in the eternity and self existence of matter."

Dr. William Smith's great dictionary of the Bible, (Hackett edition, 1894) has no article on the term "create" or "creation," but in the article "earth," we have reference to the subject, and really an implied explanation as to why this work contains no treatise on "create" or "creation." The act of creation itself, as recorded in the first chapter of Genesis, is a subject beyond and above the experience of man, human language, derived, as it originally was, from the sensible and material world, fails to find an adequate term to describe the act; for our word 'create' and the Hebrew **bara**, though most appropriate to express the idea of an original creation, are yet applicable and must necessarily be applicable to other modes of creation; nor does the addition of such expressions as 'out of things that were not,' or 'not from things which appear,' contribute much to the force of the declaration. The absence of a term which shall describe exclusively an original creation is a necessary infirmity of language; as the events occured but once, the corresponding term must, in order to be adequate, have been coined for the occasion and reserved for it alone, which would have been impossible."

The philosophers with equal emphasis sustain the contention of the Prophet. Herbert Spencer, in his **First Principles** (1860), said:

"There was once universally current, a notion that things could vanish into absolute nothing, or arise out of absolute nothing. * * * The current theology, in its teachings respecting the beginning and end of the world, is clearly pervaded by it. * * * The gradual accumulation of experiences, has tended slowly to reverse this conviction; until now, the doctrine that matter is indestructible has become a commonplace. All the apparent proofs that something can come of nothing, a wider knowledge has one by one cancelled. The comet that is suddenly discovered in the heavens and nightly waxes larger, is proved not to be a newly-created body, but a body that was until lately beyond the range of vision. The cloud which in the course of a few minutes forms in the sky, consists not of substance that has begun to be, but of substance that previously existed in a more diffused and transparent form. And similarly with a crystal or precipitate in relation to the fluid depositing it. Conversely, the seeming annihilations of matter turn out, on closer observation, to be only changes of state. It is found that the evaporated water, though it has become invisible, may be brought by condensation to its original shape. The discharged

The Immortal Intelligence

I have another subject to dwell upon, which is calculated to exalt man; but it is impossible for me to say much on this subject. I shall therefore just touch upon it, for time will not permit me to say all. It is associated with the subject of the resurrection of the dead,—namely, the soul—the mind of man—the immortal spirit. Where did it come from? All learned men and doctors of divinity say that God created it in the beginning; but it is not so: the very idea lessens man in my estimation. I do not believe the doctrine; I know better. Hear it, all ye ends of the world; for God has told me so; and if you don't believe me, it will not make the truth without effect. I will make a man appear a fool before I get through; if he does not believe it. I am going to tell of things more noble.

We say that God Himself is a self-existing being. Who told you so? It is correct enough; but how did it get into your heads? Who told you that man did not exist in like manner upon the same principles? Man does exist upon the same principles. God made a tabernacle and put a spirit into it, and it became a living soul. (Refers to the Bible.) How does it read in the Hebrew? It does not say in the Hebrew that God created the spirit of man. It says, "God made man out of the earth and put into him Adam's spirit, and so became a living body."

The mind or the intelligence which man possesses is co-equal [co-eternal] with God himself.* I know that my testimony is true; hence,

fowling-piece gives evidence that though the gunpowder has disappeared, there have appeared in place of it certain gases, which, in assuming a larger volume, have caused the explosion."

Fiske follows Spencer, of course, and in his **Cosmic Philosophy** sums up the matter in these words: "It is now unconceivable that a particle of matter should either come into existence, or lapse into non-existence."

Robert Kennedy Duncan (1905), in his **New Knowledge** says: "Governing matter in all its varied forms, there is one great fundamental law which up to this time has been ironclad in its character. This law, known as the law of the conservation of mass, states that no particle of matter, however small, may be created or destroyed. All the king's horses and all the king's men cannot destroy a pin's head. We may smash that pin's head, dissolve it in acid, burn it in the electric furnace, employ, in a word, every annihilating agency, and yet that pin's head perists in being. Again, it is as uncreatable as it is indestructible. In other words, we cannot create something out of nothing. The material must be furnished for every existent article. The sum of matter in the universe is x **pounds**,—and, while it may be carried through a myriad of forms, when all is said and done, it is just— x **pounds**."

"The elements are eternal, and spirit and element inseparably connected receive a fulness of joy. * * * The elements are the tabernacle of God; yea, man is the tabernacle of God, even temples." (D. & C. Sec. 93:35.) Notes by Elder B. H. Roberts.

*It is obvious that the word "co-equal" should have been written "co-eternal," for we know the doctrines of the Church as revealed to, and taught by, the Prophet, teach us definitely that God "comprehendeth all things, and all things are before him, and all things are round about him, and he is above all things, and in all things, and is through all things, and is round about all things; and all things are by him, and of him, even God, for ever and ever." (D. & C. Sec. 88:41.) **Moreover** when I talk to these mourners, what have they lost? Their relatives and friends are only separated from their bodies for a short season: their spirits which existed with God have left the tabernacle of clay only for a little moment, as it were; and they now exist in a place where they converse together the same as we do on the earth,

I am dwelling on the immortality of the spirit of man. Is it logical to say that the intelligence of spirits is immortal, and yet that it has a beginning? The intelligence of spirits had no beginning, neither will it have an end. That is good logic. That which has a beginning may have an end. There never was a time when there were not spirits;** for they are co-equal [co-eternal] with our Father in heaven.

I want to reason more on the spirit of man; for I am dwelling on the body and spirit of man—on the subject of the dead. I take my ring from my finger and liken it unto the mind of man—the immortal part, because it had no beginning. Suppose you cut it in two; then it has a beginning and an end; but join it again, and it continues one eternal round. So with the spirit of man. As the Lord liveth, if it had a beginning, it will have an end. All the fools and learned and wise men from the beginning of creation, who say that the spirit of man had a beginning, prove that it must have an end; and if that doctrine is true, then the doctrine of annihilation would be true. But if I am right, I might with boldness proclaim from the house-tops that God never had the power to create the spirit of man at all. God himself could not create himself.

Intelligence is eternal and exists upon a self-existent principle. It is a spirit from age to age and there is no creation about it.* All the minds and spirits that God ever sent into the world are susceptible of enlargement.

in the Book of Abraham we read that the Lord said to Abraham: "These two facts do exist, that there are two spirits, one being more intelligent than the other; there shall be another more intelligent than they: I am the Lord thy God, I am more intelligent than they all." (Abraham 3:19.)

It appears to be very clear that the Prophet had in mind the **intelligence, when he said "the soul—the mind of man—the immortal spirit," was not created or made, and that there never was a time when there were not spirits for they are co-eternal with God. It is the doctrine of the scriptures, both in the Bible and in the Doctrine and Covenants, that we are the offspring of God. He is our Father; we are begotten sons and daughters unto Him. So Paul taught the Greeks on Mars' Hill. (Acts 17: 26-29.) It was taught by the resurrected Lord to Mary at the tomb, (John 20:17.) and by the Lord to the Prophet and Sidney Rigdon in the great vision (Sec. 76:22-24.) The reader is referred further to the official statement of the First Presidency and the Council of the Twelve Apostles, under the caption, **The Father and The Son,** in the **Improvement Era,** August, 1916.

"Man was also in the beginning with God. Intelligence, or the light of truth, was not created or made, neither indeed can be." (D. & C. Sec. 93.)

*It is clear in this statement that the terms "intelligence" and "spirit" are used synonymously and that the intelligent uncreated entity, spoken of as intelligence, is meant.

The first principles of man are self-existent with God. God himself, finding he was in the midst of spirits and glory, because he was more intelligent, saw proper to institute laws whereby the rest could have a privilege to advance like himself. The relationship we have with God places us in a situation to advance in knowledge. He has power to institute laws to instruct the weaker intelligences, that they may be exalted with Himself, so that they might have one glory upon another, and all that knowledge, power, glory, and intelligence, which is requisite in order to save them in the world of spirits.**

This is good doctrine. It tastes good. I can taste the principles of eternal life, and so can you. They are given to me by the revelations of Jesus Christ; and I know that when I tell you these words of eternal life as they are given to me, you taste them, and I know that you believe them. You say honey is sweet, and so do I. I can also taste the spirit of eternal life. I know that it is good; and when I tell you of these things which were given me by inspiration of the Holy Spirit, you are bound to receive them as sweet, and rejoice more and more.

The Relation of Man to God

I want to talk more of the relation of man to God. I will open your eyes in relation to the dead. All things whatsoever God in his infinite wisdom has seen fit and proper to reveal to us, while we are dwelling in mortality, in regard to our mortal bodies, are revealed to us in the abstract, and independent of affinity of this mortal tabernacle, but are revealed to our spirits precisely as though we had no bodies at all; and those revelations which will save our spirits will save our bodies. God reveals them to us in view of no eternal dissolution of the body, or tabernacle. Hence the responsibility, the awful responsibility, that rests upon us in relation to our dead; for all the spirits who have not obeyed the Gospel in the flesh must either

**"Behold this is my work and my glory—to bring to pass the immortality and eternal life of man."—(The Lord to Moses, Book of Moses, Chapt. 1:39: Pearl of Great Price)—that is "to bring to pass the immortality and eternal life of man," as man. This passage has reference doubtless to man as composed of spirit and body—a proper soul (see D. & C. Sec. 88:15-16)—"For the spirit and the body is the soul of man; and the resurrection of the dead is the redemption of the soul." In other words, the "work" and the "glory" of God are achieved in bringing to pass the "immortality and eternal life of man," as man, in the eternal union of the spirit and body of man through the resurrection—through the redemption of the soul. This brings into eternal union "spirit and element" declared by the word of God to be essential to a fulness of joy—"The elements are eternal, and spirit and element, inseparably connected, receive a fulness of joy; and when separated man cannot receive a fulness of joy." (D. & C. Sec. 93). Also "Adam fell that man might be: and men are that they might have joy." (2 Nephi 2:25). Indeed, the whole purpose of God in bringing to pass the earth-life of man is to inure to the welfare and enlargement of man as urged in the teaching of the Prophet in the paragraph above. God affects man only to his advantage. Note by Elder B. H. Roberts.

obey it in the spirit or be damned. Solemn thought!—dreadful thought! Is there nothing to be done?—no preparation—no salvation for our fathers and friends who have died without having had the opportunity to obey the decrees of the Son of Man? Would to God that I had forty days and nights in which to tell you all! I would let you know that I am not a "fallen prophet."

Our Greatest Responsibility

What promises are made in relation to the subject of the salvation of the dead? and what kind of characters are those who can be saved, although their bodies are mouldering and decaying in the grave? When His commandments teach us, it is in view of eternity; for we are looked upon by God as though we were in eternity; God dwells in eternity, and does not view things as we do.

The greatest responsibility in this world that God has laid upon us is to seek after our dead. The apostle says, "They without us cannot be made perfect"; for it is necessary that the sealing power should be in our hands to seal our children and our dead for the fulness of the dispensation of times—a dispensation to meet the promises made by Jesus Christ before the foundation of the world for the salvation of man.

Now, I will speak of them. I will meet Paul half way. I say to you, Paul, you cannot be perfect without us. It is necessary that those who are going before and those who come after us should have salvation in common with us; and thus hath God made it obligatory upon man. Hence, God said, "I will send you Elijah the prophet before the coming of the great and dreadful day of the Lord: he shall turn the heart of the fathers to the children, and the heart of the children to their fathers, lest I come and smite the earth with a curse."

The Unpardonable Sin

I have a declaration to make as to the provisions which God hath made to suit the conditions of man—made from before the foundation of the world. What has Jesus said? All sins, and all blasphemies, and every transgression, except one, that man can be guilty of, may be forgiven; and there is a salvation for all men, either in this world or the world to come, who have not committed the unpardonable sin, there being a provision either in this world or the world of spirits. Hence God hath made a provision that every spirit in the eternal world can be ferreted out and saved unless he has committed that unpardonable sin which cannot be remitted to him either in this world or the world of spirits. God has wrought out a salvation for all men, unless they have committed a certain sin; and every man who has a friend in the eternal world can save him, unless he has committed the unpardonable sin. And so you can see how far you can be a savior.

A man cannot commit the unpardonable sin after the dissolution of the body, and there is a way possible for escape. Knowledge saves a man; and in the world of spirits no man can be exalted but by knowledge. So long as a man will not give heed to the commandments, he must abide without salvation. If a man has knowledge, he can be saved; although, if he has been guilty of great sins, he will be punished for them. But when he consents to obey the gospel, whether here or in the world of spirits, he is saved.

A man is his own tormentor and his own condemner. Hence the saying, They shall go into the lake that burns with fire and brimstone. The torment of disappointment in the mind of man is as exquisite as a lake burning with fire and brimstone. I say, so is the torment of man.

I know the scriptures and understand them. I said, no man can commit the unpardonable sin after the dissolution of the body, nor in this life, until he receives the Holy Ghost; but they must do it in this world. Hence the salvation of Jesus Christ was wrought out for all men, in order to triumph over the devil; for if it did not catch him in one place, it would in another; for he stood up as a Savior. All will suffer until they obey Christ himself.

The contention in heaven was—Jesus said there would be certain souls that would not be saved; and the devil said he would save them all, and laid his plans before the grand council, who gave their vote in favor of Jesus Christ. So the devil rose up in rebellion against God, and was cast down, with all who put up their heads for him. (Book of Moses—Pearl of Great Price, Ch. 4:1-4; Book of Abraham, Ch. 3:23-28.)

The Forgiveness of Sins

All sins shall be forgiven, except the sin against the Holy Ghost; for Jesus will save all except the sons of perdition. What must a man do to commit the unpardonable sin? He must receive the Holy Ghost, have the heavens opened unto him, and know God, and then sin against him. After a man has sinned against the Holy Ghost, there is no repentance for him. He has got to say that the sun does not shine while he sees it; he has got to deny Jesus Christ when the heavens have been opened unto him, and to deny the plan of salvation with his eyes open to the truth of it; and from that time he begins to be an enemy. This is the case with many apostates of the Church of Jesus Christ of Latter-day Saints.

When a man begins to be an enemy to this work, he hunts me, he seeks to kill me, and never ceases to thirst for my blood. He gets the spirit of the devil—the same spirit that they had who crucified the Lord of Life—the same spirit that sins against the Holy Ghost.

You cannot save such persons; you cannot bring them to repentance; they make open war, like the devil, and awful is the consequence.

I advise all of you to be careful what you do, or you may by-and-by find out that you have been deceived. Stay yourselves; do not give way; don't make any hasty moves, you may be saved. If a spirit of bitterness is in you, don't be in haste. You may say, that man is a sinner. Well, if he repents, he shall be forgiven. Be cautious: await. When you find a spirit that wants bloodshed,—murder, the same is not of God, but is of the devil. Out of the abundance of the heart of man the mouth speaketh.

The best men bring forth the best works. The man who tells you words of life is the man who can save you. I warn you against all evil characters who sin against the Holy Ghost; for there is no redemption for them in this world nor in the world to come.

I could go back and trace every object of interest concerning the relationship of man to God, if I had time. I can enter into the mysteries; I can enter largely into the eternal worlds; for Jesus said, "In my Father's house are many mansions; if it were not so, I would have told you. I go to prepare a place for you." (John 14:2). Paul says, "There is one glory of the sun, and another glory of the moon, and another glory of the stars; for one star differeth from another star in glory. So also is the resurrection of the dead." (I Cor. 15:41). What have we to console us in relation to the dead? We have reason to have the greatest hope and consolation for our dead of any people on the earth; for we have seen them walk worthily in our midst, and seen them sink asleep in the arms of Jesus; and those who have died in the faith are now in the celestial kingdom of God. And hence is the glory of the sun.

You mourners have occasion to rejoice, speaking of the death of Elder King Follett; for your husband and father is gone to wait until the resurrection of the dead—until the perfection of the remainder; for at the resurrection your friend will rise in perfect felicity and go to celestial glory, while many must wait myriads of years before they can receive the like blessings; and your expectations and hopes are far above what man can conceive; for why has God revealed it to us?

I am authorized to say, by the authority of the Holy Ghost, that you have no occasion to fear; for he is gone to the home of the just. Don't mourn, don't weep. I know it by the testimony of the Holy Ghost that is within me; and you may wait for your friends to come forth to meet you in the morn of the celestial world.

Rejoice, O Israel! Your friends who have been murdered for the truth's sake in the persecutions shall triumph gloriously in the celestial world, while their murderers shall welter for ages in torment, even until they shall have paid the uttermost farthing. I say this for the benefit of strangers.

I have a father, brothers, children, and friends who have gone to a world of spirits. They are only absent for a moment. They are in the spirit, and we shall soon meet again. The time will soon arrive when the trumpet shall sound. When we depart, we shall hail our mothers, fathers, friends, and all whom we love, who have fallen asleep in Jesus. There will be no fear of mobs, persecutions, or malicious lawsuits and arrests; but it will be an eternity of felicity.

A question may be asked—"Will mothers have their children in eternity?" Yes! Yes! Mothers, you shall have your children; for they shall have eternal life, for their debt is paid. There is no damnation awaiting them for they are in the spirit. But as the child dies, so shall it rise from the dead, and be for ever living in the learning of God. It will never grow [in the grave]; it will still be the child, in the same precise form [when it rises] as it appeared before it died out of its mother's arms, but possessing all the intelligence of a God. Children dwell in the mansions of glory and exercise power, but appear in the same form as when on earth. Eternity is full of thrones, upon which dwell thousands of children, reigning on thrones of glory, with not one cubit added to their stature.*

I will leave this subject here, and make a few remarks on the subject of baptism. The baptism of water, without the baptism of fire and the Holy Ghost attending it, is of no use; they are necessarily and inseparably connected. An individual must be born of water and the spirit in order to get into the kingdom of God. In the German, the text bears me out the same as the revelations which I have given and taught for the past fourteen years on that subject. I have the testimony to put in their teeth. My testimony has been true all the time. You will find it in the declaration of John the Baptist. (Reads from the German.) John says, "I baptize you with water, but when Jesus comes, who has the power (or keys) He shall administer the baptism of fire and the Holy Ghost." Great God! Where is now all the sectarian world? And if this testimony is true, they are all damned as clearly as anathema can do it. I know the text is true. I call upon all you Germans who know that it is true to say, Eye. (Loud shouts of "Aye.")

Alexander Campbell, how are you going to save people with water alone? For John said his baptism was good for nothing without the baptism of Jesus Christ. "Therefore, *not* leaving the principles of

*It is clearly evident that in this passage concerning little children and their salvation and glorification after the resurrection, we do not have from the brethren, who made the notes, a perfect report on the status of little children after the resurrection. There was some lack of interpretation in the report of the Prophet's remarks, for he taught that little children would come forth from the dead in the same form and size in which their bodies were laid down but that they would grow after the resurrection to the full stature of the spirit. For an account of this teaching those who desire to investigate the matter more fully may consult the **Documentary History of the Church,** Vol. 4:556-7 and the footnote.

the doctrine of Christ, let us go on unto perfection; not laying again the foundation of repentance from dead works, and of faith towards God, of the doctrine of baptism, and of laying on of hands, and of resurrection of the dead, and of eternal judgment. And this will we do, if God permit." (Heb. 6:1-3).

There is one God, one Father, one Jesus, one hope of our calling, one baptism. All these three baptisms only make one. Many talk of baptism not being essential to salvation; but this kind of teaching would lay the foundation of their damnation. I have the truth, and am at the defiance of the world to contradict me, if they can.

I have now preached a little Latin, a little Hebrew, Greek, and German; and I have fulfilled all. I am not so big a fool as many have taken me to be. The Germans know that I read the German correctly.

The Second Death

Hear it, all ye ends of the earth—all ye priests, all ye sinners, and all men. Repent! Repent! Obey the gospel. Turn to God; for your religion won't save you, and you will be damned. I do not say how long. There have been remarks made concerning all men being redeemed from hell; but I say that those who sin against the Holy Ghost cannot be forgiven in this world or in the world to come; they shall die the second death. Those who commit the unpardonable sin are doomed to *Gnolom*—to dwell in hell, worlds without end. As they concocted scenes of bloodshed in this world, so they shall rise to that resurrection which is as the lake of fire and brimstone. Some shall rise to the everlasting burnings of God; for God dwells in everlasting burnings and some shall rise to the damnation of their own filthiness, which is as exquisite a torment as the lake of fire and brimstone.

I have intended my remarks for all, both rich and poor, bond and free, great and small. I have no enmity against any man. I love you all; but I hate some of your deeds. I am your best friend, and if persons miss their mark it is their own fault. If I reprove a man, and he hates me, he is a fool; for I love all men, especially these my brethren and sisters.

I rcjoice in hearing the testimony of my aged friends. You don't know me; you never knew my heart. No man knows my history. I cannot tell it: I shall never undertake it. I don't blame any one for not believing my history. If I had not experienced what I have, I would not have believed it myself. I never did harm any man since I was born in the world. My voice is always for peace.

I cannot lie down until all my work is finished. I never think any evil, nor do anything to the harm of my fellow-man. When I am called by the trump of the archangel and weighed in the balance, you will all know me then. I add no more. God bless you all. Amen.

CHAPTER XV.

GENERAL CONFERENCE FOR APRIL, 1844, CONCLUDED—THE ANNOUNCEMENT THAT THE WHOLE LAND OF AMERICA IS ZION—INSTRUCTIONS TO ELDERS SET APART FOR MISSIONS—A GENERAL CONFERENCE IN ENGLAND.

Monday, April 8, 1844.—[*Conference Report Continued.*]

At three-quarters past 9 a. m., President Joseph Smith took his seat on the stand and requested the choir to sing a hymn. He called upon Elder Brigham Young to read 1st Corinthians, 15th chapter, as his own lungs were injured.

Elder Brigham Young said—to continue the subject of President Smith's discourse yesterday, I shall commence by reading the 15th chapter of 1st Corinthians, from an old Bible; and requested W. W. Phelps to read it.

Prayer by Elder Brigham Young, after which the choir sang a hymn.

President Joseph Smith's Remarks—The Whole of America Zion.

President Joseph Smith said:—It is just as impossible, for me to continue the subject of yesterday as to raise the dead. My lungs are worn out. There is a time to all things, and I must wait. I will give it up, and leave the time to those who can make you hear, and I will continue the subject of my discourse some other time. I want to make a proclamation to the Elders. I wanted you to stay, in order that I might make this proclamation. You know very well that the Lord has led this Church by revelation. I have another revelation in relation to economy in the Church—a great, grand, and glorious revelation. I shall not be able to dwell as largely upon it now as at some other time; but I will give you the first principles. You know there has been great discussion in relation to Zion—where it is, and where the gathering of the dispensation is, and which I am now going to tell you. The prophets have spoken and written upon it; but I will make a proclamation that will cover a broader ground. *The whole of America is Zion itself*

from north to south, and is described by the Prophets, who declare that it is the Zion where the mountain of the Lord should be, and that it should be in the center of the land. When Elders shall take up and examine the old prophecies in the Bible, they will see it.

The declaration this morning is, that as soon as the Temple and baptismal font are prepared, we calculate to give the Elders of Israel their washings and anointings, and attend to those last and more impressive ordinances, without which we cannot obtain celestial thrones. But there must be a holy place prepared for that purpose. There was a proclamation made during the time that the foundation of the Temple was laid to that effect, and there are provisions made until the work is completed, so that men may receive their endowments and be made kings and priests unto the Most High God, having nothing to do with temporal things, but their whole time will be taken up with things pertaining to the house of God. There must, however, be a place built expressly for that purpose, and for men to be baptized for their dead. It must be built in this the central place; for every man who wishes to save his father, mother, brothers, sisters and friends, must go through all the ordinances for each one of them separately, the same as for himself, from baptism to ordination, washings and anointings, and receive all the keys and powers of the Priesthood, the same as for himself.

I have received instructions from the Lord that from henceforth wherever the Elders of Israel shall build up churches and branches unto the Lord throughout the States, there shall be a stake of Zion. In the great cities, as Boston, New York, &c., there shall be stakes. It is a glorious proclamation, and I reserved it to the last, and designed it to be understood that this work shall commence after the washings, anointings and endowments have been performed here.

The Lord has an established law in relation to the matter: there must be a particular spot for the salvation of our dead. I verily believe there will be a place, and hence men who want to save their dead can come and bring their families, do their work by being baptized and attending to the other ordinances for their dead, and then may go back again to live and wait till they go to receive their reward. I shall leave my brethren to enlarge on this subject: it is my duty to teach the doctrine. I would teach it more fully—the spirit is willing but the flesh is weak. God is not willing to let me gratify you; but I must teach the Elders, and they should teach you. God made Aaron to be the mouth piece for the children of Israel,* and He will make me be god to you in

* The scripture alluded to in the text is as follows:—Moses pleaded to be excused from the appointment to deliver Israel on the plea that he was not eloquent; whereupon the Lord said: "Is not Aaron the Levite thy brother? I know that he can speak well. And also, behold, he cometh forth to meet thee; and when he

His stead, and the Elders to be mouth for me; and if you don't like it, you must lump it. I have been giving Elder Adams instruction in some principles to speak to you, and if he makes a mistake, I will get up and correct him.

Elder G. J. Adams preached a discourse which occupied three hours, and which could be heard a great distance.

President Joseph Smith turned over the conference into the hands of the Twelve.

Choir sang a hymn. Prayer.

President Hyrum Smith called the conference to order at twenty-five minutes to four p. m., and spoke to the assembly one hour and a half.

He treated upon the subject of Elders preaching abroad. He said it was a matter of consequence that the Elders of Israel should know what they were about when they go to preach the Gospel. They should, like Paul, be ready to give a reason for the hope of their calling. When they are sent to preach the Gospel, they should preach the Gospel and nothing else, if they wish to stand approved themselves. The Elders are sent into the world to preach faith, repentance, baptism for the remission of sins, and the laying on of hands for the reception of the Holy Ghost and they should let the mysteries alone.

God has commanded you to preach repentance to this generation; and if this generation will not receive the first principles of the Gospel and the Book of Mormon, they will receive nothing greater. Just go and do as you are told and God will bless you.

It is the power of God that is going to convert the world, and nothing but the power of God. Every man who knows me knows that I have taught these principles from the beginning. It is the honest and pure in heart that will harken to the everlasting covenant. They are those who are noble and good; they will feed and clothe you and receive your testimony; and we want the Elders to gather out the good seed to Nauvoo. The day will come when you will see the wicked flee when no man pursueth. I want you to be wise as serpents and harmless as doves. Preach principles that will stand the test of ages; teach them good precepts and save souls, go forth as men of God, and you will find friends wherever you go. Drink deep of the Spirit of Truth and a great and mighty work shall be wrought in the world; hundreds

seeth thee, he will be glad in his heart. And thou shalt speak unto him, and put words in his mouth; * * * And he shall be thy spokesman unto the people: * * * * he shall be to thee instead of a mouth, and thou shalt be to him instead of God" (Exodus iv: 14-16.)

Somewhat later this passage occurs: "And the Lord said unto Moses, See, I have made thee a god to Pharaoh; and Aaron thy brother shall be thy prophet" (Exodus vii: 1.)

and tens of thousands shall flock to the standard and go up to Zion.

Many other remarks were made by the speaker.

After which Sidney Rigdon made a few remarks, and concurred in what Brother Hyrum had said.

Twelve minutes to six, adjourned to April 9th, at eight o'clock, a. m.

Special Meeting of Elders.

Tuesday, 9.—[*Conference Report Continued*]. At 8 a. m., the Elders assembled at the stand, (President Brigham Young presiding,) and were addressed by Elder Amasa Lyman; after which: President Brigham Young said—

Address of Brigham Young.

What has been given is correct; the speech and conduct of Elders one towards another is frequently wrong; one Elder will speak evil of another; and while you trample others you will sink yourself. A man has sinking principles; but if his feelings are elevated, he will build up others and build up himself. Just as sure as one Elder tries to build himself upon the destruction of another, he will surely sink himself.

I would like to sit and hear the brethren teach for a week; but as business is pressing, we must hurry through. Preach repentance to this generation. Faith must go before repentance, and of course all men must follow the course and obey the laws and ordinances for the remission of sins, so as to receive the gift of the Holy Ghost, and then your mission is done. Let a man who goes into the vineyard build up all he can. If a man preaches anything in error, pray to God that no man may remember it any more. No Elder will correct another in public before unbelievers unless he has the sinking principle. I call all the Elders together to witness that I always use charity, for it covers a multitude of sins.

North and South America Zion.

Let us obey the proclamation of Joseph Smith concerning the Elders going forth into the vineyard to build up the Temple, get their endowments, and be prepared to go forth and preach the Gospel. You may build up Zion, and learn to be men, and not children. It was a perfect sweepstakes when the Prophet called North and South America Zion. Let us go to and build the Temple with all our might, that we may build up the kingdom when established and her cords lengthened. It is a perfect knock-down to the devil's kingdom. There is not a faithful Elder who cannot, if he is humble and diligent, build up the Church. There are many men who will give you large sums to build a

Stake of Zion where they live. It proves the words of the Prophet of the last days.

The Priesthood is fitted to every capacity in the world. There are blessings and conditions in that Priesthood that suit every man. This will suit the condition of thousands, because it is as broad as the heavens, deep as hell, and wide as eternity.

I am asked all sorts of questions about making gods and devils, and organizing the eternal worlds; but we could not get it precisely into our understandings so as to make them. The God we serve is the God of Abraham, Isaac, and Jacob. There is no need of breaking the law of the land if you keep the law of the Lord. I want a wife that can take care of my children when I am away, who can pray, lay on hands, anoint with oil, and baffle the enemy; and this is a spiritual wife.

The sweepstakes is a perfect knock-down to the devil. We will build up churches and establish Zion and her stakes. This is a fire which, cannot be put out: it has spread far faster than ever it did before. If you kick us and cuff us, we will turn the world upside down, and make the cart draw the horse. We want to build the Temple and have the roof on this fall, in the name of Israel's God. There are hundreds of Elders who will sell their property to build up the Temple. Let us pay up our tithing. If there are any men who have not paid their tithing, they will not get in there. Let the branches send teams with provisions to work all the year.

We are aquainted with the views of Gen. Smith, the Democrats and Whigs and all factions. It is now time to have a President of the United States. Elders will be sent to preach the Gospel and electioneer. The government belongs to God. No man can draw the dividing line between the government of God and the government of the children of men. You can't touch the Gospel without infringing upon the common avocations of men. They may have helps and governments in the Church, but it is all one at last.

Address of Hyrum Smith the Patriarch.

Patriarch Hyrum Smith said: I never knew a proclamation to be understood at once. President Brigham Young wished to draw the attention of the brethren, first to build the Temple and get your washings, anointings, and endowments; after that to build up branches throughout the nations. We must do all we can to build up the Temple, and after that to build churches. The gathering will continue here until the Temple is so far finished that the Elders can get their endowments; and after that the gathering will be from the nations to North and South America, which is the land of Zion. North and South America, are the symbols of the wings. The gathering from the old countries will always be to headquarters, and I have no doubt this conference will do a great deal of good.

We have every power and principle to teach the people. Say what God says, and say no more. Never deviate one fraction from what God tells you. Elder Rigdon's remarks were very correct. Give out the simple principles. A man never fails who only says what he knows; and if any man says more,and can't give reasons, he falls short. Preach the first principles of the Gospel—preach them over again: you will find that day after day new ideas and additional light concerning them will be revealed to you. You can enlarge upon them so as to comprehend them clearly. You will then be able to make them more plainly understood by those who teach, so that you will meet with scarcely any honest man but will obey them, and none who can oppose. Adduce sufficient reason to prove all things, and you can convert every honest man in the world.The knowledge of the Gospel of Jesus Christ is not prevalent in the world, although it is written in the Holy Book. You can prove it by the Holy Book they profess to believe in, and your arguments will be so strong and convincing,that people will hear and obey it by thousands. The Savior says that to you it is given to know the mysteries of God, but to the world it is not given. You have power; you are authorized to put down every foolish thing you hear. A wise man will put it out of existence as he goes along; for light cleaveth unto light, knowledge to knowledge, and intelligence to intelligence.

We engage in the election the same as in any other principle: you are to vote for good men, and if you do not do this it is a sin: to vote for wicked men, it would be sin. Choose the good and refuse the evil. Men of false principles have preyed upon us like wolves upon helpless lambs. Damn the rod of tyranny; curse it. Let every man use his liberties according to the Constitution. Don't fear man or devil; electioneer with all people, male and female, and exhort them to do the thing that is right. We want a President of the U. S , not a party President, but a President of the whole people; for a party President disfranchises the opposite party. Have a President who will maintain every man in his rights.

I wish all of you to do all the good you can. We will try and convert the nations into one solid union. I despise the principle that divides the nation into party and faction. I want it to grow up like a green bay tree. Damn the system of splitting up the nation into opposite belligerent parties. Whatever are the rights of men guaranteed by the Constitution of these United States, let them have them. Then, if we were all in union, no one dare attempt to put a warlike foot on our soil. I don't like to see the rights of Americans trampled down. I am opposed to the policy of all such persons as would allow Great Britain or any other power to take from us Oregon or any portion of our national territory; and damn all who attempt it. Lift up your voices like thunder: there is power and influence enough among us to put in a President. I don't wonder at the old Carthagenian lawyer being afraid of Joseph Smith being elected.

[A unanimous vote was passed by the immense assembly for Joseph Smith to be the candidate for the next President.]

Address of Heber C. Kimball.

Elder Heber C. Kimball arose and said—What Brother Hyrum has told you is God's truth, and will eventually come to pass. As he was making his observations to the Elders, it made me think of the first time that I went out into the vineyard to preach. I dwelt on one subject till it branched like unto a tree that was cultivated, until the branches shot forth in all directions. Suppose you had only one seed to plant, and that seed was an acorn, and you spend your time in cultivating it till it comes forth a great and mighty tree, branching forth with many branches, and bearing fruit abundantly after its own kind. So it is with the first principles of the Gospel, they branch out in all directions, unfolding new light continually. They are eternal principles. I never preached anything else but the first principles. When first we went to England, we preached nothing else, and never even touched on the gathering, as there was no place of gathering, the Church having been driven from Jackson County and also from Kirtland, and the Prophets, Patriarchs, Apostles and Saints were wandering in the wilderness seeking for a home; but as soon as the people were baptized and received the Holy Ghost, the most of them had the spirit of prophecy, and prophesied of coming to this land, as being the land of Zion; and the time would come that they should come here. Yet we never taught the doctrine of the gathering or Book of Doctrine and Covenants.

If you tell the people to stay, they will gather here stronger than ever. If you want to cut anything off, you should know how to restore. You should never cut off the ears of the people until you are able to make them others.It is no matter what way you convert them so you do convert them to believe the doctrines of the very Bible they have always professed to believe. It is no use attempting to teach them other things until you can make them believe the principles contained in the Bible which they have been taught to reverence and believe from their infancy. It teaches the gathering and all the principles of the Gospel necessary to be taught to the unbelieving world. This is the thrashingfloor, where the wheat is gathered to be thrashed. There are a great many green heads, and they of course have to be pelted a little harder. After the wheat is thrashed, it has to go through the fanning-mill, and then the screen, and then the smut-mill; then it has to be ground and to be bolted: but many bolt away and leave. If you get a cudgeling, don't be mad, for your heads are green. We are going to arrange a plan for Conferences, and we design to send Elders to all the different States to get up meetings and protracted meetings, and electioneer for Joseph to be the next President.

A great many of the Elders will necessarily have to leave their families, and the mothers will have to assume the responsibility of governing and taking care of the children to a much greater extent than when their husbands were at home. I therefore exhort them to be humble, faithful, and diligent, seeking to the Lord for wisdom to rear up their children in righteousness and prepare them to roll on the work of the Lord when their fathers shall have been worn out in the ministry. The mothers, therefore, are the persons who will more or less have to train the children.

Twenty minutes to 11: A call was made for the volunteers to go preaching to pass out to the green. A great company moved out and returned to the right of the stand, and were numbered 244.

Twenty minutes to 1: Adjourned for one hour.

Met according to adjournment. The names of the volunteers were called, and places assigned to each.

Brigham Young's Instruction to the Elders.

President Brigham Young said: Take care of yourselves, be wise, be humble, and you will prosper. I curse all who degrade themselves with corruption and licentiousness, as many have done. Magnify your calling, keep yourselves pure and innocent, and your path shall be clear as the horizon. We have all manner of prejudices to contend with. We thank God for the Gospel, the Book of Mormon, and the Temple, and sing glory to God; and yet there are characters among us who from mere covetousness will squeeze a sixpence two inches long, and we have all their iniquity to bear.

We have the honor to be the first fruits of this dispensation, and have to contend with floods of oppression. Go humbly and prayerfully, trusting and believing in God, and what you desire to do you will accomplish. Cease not to ask the Father what you shall do, and He will give you the Spirit. You know not the day of your visitation. What is asked for in the name of Jesus Christ will be granted. J. C. Bennett's power fell like the lightning. God was asked not to let Joe Duncan be governor, and it was so. We asked the Lord to deliver us from Governor Reynolds, of Missouri; and he shot himself, and has gone to hell. As for Squire Warren, of Quincy, it takes two of him to make a shadow.

The Lord is cutting off the bitterest branches. Look at the explosion of the big gun on board of the *Princeton* war-steamer at Washington. God will deliver His faithful Saints. You will be innocent, and do a good work: you will come back, and bring your sheaves with you, rejoicing. Every man has the privilege of practicing godliness and virtue, and of manifesting himself as a servant of the Most High God. Doctor Foster lost his money by gambling, and joined blacklegs. Those men who say there is evil in the Church are evil themselves. This doctrine is the best for any man to practice, and will do him good. Ask of God that you may have wisdom to do all things. If you hear anything of an Elder preaching false doctrine, ask of God in full faith that it may be taken off the minds of the people.

A contribution was taken up for President Joseph Smith, $100 was raised, and another $100 loaned.

Comment of President Smith on the Conference.

Tuesday, *April 9th*, [*Continued*]:—The weather has been beautiful for the conference; and they have been the greatest, best, and most glorious five consecutive days ever enjoyed by this generation. Much good was done. Many spectators were present from Quincy, Alton, Warsaw, Fort Madison, and other towns. When we consider the immense number present, and the good order that was preserved, it speaks much in favor of the morality of the city.

In the afternoon I rode out with Emma, Dr. Goforth, and others to the mound. The peach trees look beautiful.

The Mayor and Marshal received a notification to produce docket and other papers in case of O. F. Bostwick, before the circuit court at Carthage; also a similar notification to produce papers in case of Amos Davis, appealed before Circuit Court.

A General Conference in England Beginning April 6th, and Continuing Until April 9th, 1844.

According to previous announcement, the general conference of the various branches of the Church of Jesus Christ of Latter-day Saints, commenced its sittings in the Music Hall, Liverpool, on the 6th of April,

1844, Elder Reuben Hedlock, president of the mission, presiding, and Elder J. S. Cantwell, acting as clerk.

Morning Session.

After opening meeting by singing and prayer, it was voted unanimously that Elder Reuben Hedlock preside over the conference and that Elder J. S. Cantwell, act as clerk.

The number of officers present at the opening are as follows:—High Priests, 10; Elders, 23; Priests, 5; Teachers, 3; Deacons, 2. The representation of the various conferences was then called for:—

Manchester Conference represented by Elder Charles Miller, including the branches of Manchester, Stockport, Ashton, Duckenfield, Newton Moor, Mottram, Bolton, Edgeworth Moor, Edgerton, Leith, Chewmoor, Breightmet Fold, Bradshaw, Tottington, Summerseat, Bury, Haslingden, Royton, Oldham, Rochdale, Eccles, Pendlebury, Heatons, Ratcliffe, Halfare. Crossmoor, Didsbury, Middleton, Crompton Fold, Marble Bridge, Ashworth Tops, Vale House. Comprises 1583 members, 2 High Priests, 41 Elders, 100 Priests, 56 Teachers, 19 Deacons. Baptized since last general conference, 194.

Liverpool Conference represented by Elder Mitchelson, including Liverpool, the Isle of Man, Chester, part of Wales, Warrington, St. Helens, and Graseby. Comprises 596 members, 3 High Priests, 29 Elders, 39 Priests, 19 Teachers, 11 Deacons. Baptized since last general conference, 107.

Preston Conference represented by Elder John Banks, including Preston, Lancaster, Kendal, Brigsteer Holme, Heskin, Hunter's Hill. Euxton, Leyland, Southport, and Longton. Comprises 594 members, 1 High Priest, 16 Elders, 23 Priests, 17 Teachers, 4 Deacons. Baptized since last general conference, 21.

London Conference represented by Elder John Cairns, including London, Newbury, Woolwich, Dover, and Luton. Comprises 324 members, 1 High Priest, 11 Elders, 21 Priests, 5 Teachers, 5 Deacons. Baptized since last general conference, 47.

Macclesfield Conference represented by Elder Galley, including Macclesfield, Bollington, Middlewich, Northwich, Plumbley, and Crewe. Comprises 219 members, 1 High Priest, 10 Elders, 22 Priests, 14 Teachers, 7 Deacons. Baptized since last general conference, 15.

Birmingham Conference represented by Elder Crook, including Birmingham, Gritsgreen, Oldbury, Wolverhampton, Dudley, Brittlelane, Bilston, Kidderminster, Leamington, Bloxwich, Stratford-upon-Avon, Catthorpe, Westbromwich, Penydarren, Abersychan, Beaufort, Rumny, Tredegar, Merthyr Tydvil, Aberdare. Comprises 707 members,

38 Elders, 49 Priests, 27 Teachers, 12 Deacons. Baptized since last general conference, 200.

Wooden Box represented by Elder Robert Crook, including Wooden Box, Dunstall, Branstone, Barton, and Colebille. Comprises 96 members, 9 Elders, 10 Priests, 6 Teachers, 5 Deacons. Baptized since last general conference, 60.

Staffordshire Conference represented by Elder George Simpson, including Burslem, Hanley, Stoke-upon-Trent, Newcastle, Baddely Edge, Bradley Green, Knutton Heath, Longton, Coxbank, Prees, Tunstall, Leek, Longport, Hassell Green, Allsager's Bank. Comprises 370 members, 1 High Priest, 29 Elders, 48 Priests, 20 Teachers, 11 Deacons.

Edinburgh Conference represented by Elder George P. Waugh, including Edinburgh, Wemyss, Sterling, and Pathead. Comprises 330 members, 11 Elders, 16 Priests, 7 Teachers, 3 Deacons. Baptized since November, 1843, 37.

Garaway Conference represented by Elder Blakey, including Garaway, Llanfoist, Buckle, Ewaisharold, Llanthony, and Llanvano. Comprises 172 members, 4 Elders, 9 Priests, 8 Teachers, 1 Deacon.

Glasgow Conferennce represented by Elder James Houston, including Glasgow, Paisley, Kilbirnie, Bridge of Weir, Thorny Bank and Shaws, Campsie, Renfrew, Greenock, Ayr, Bonhill, Balfrone, Johnstone, Airdrie, Irvine, and Calry. Comprises 833 members, 1 High Priest, 26 Elders, 39 Priests, 30 Teachers, 19 Deacons.

Sheffield Conference represented by letter, including Sheffield, Woodhouse, Dennington, and Brampton. Comprises 201 members, 5 Elders, 9 Priests, 5 Teachers, 3 Deacons.

Bradford Conference represented by Elder William Speakman, including Bradford, Idle, Leeds, Doncaster. Comprises 206 members, 9 Elders, 15 Priests, 8 Teachers, 6 Deacons. Baptized since last general conference, 44.

Ireland represented by Elder Sloan, including Hillsborough, Crawfordsburn, and Melusk, Comprises 52 members, 5 Elders, 1 Priest, 1 Teacher.

Lincolnshire Conference represented by letter. Comprises 27 members, 2 Elders, 2 Priests, 1 Teacher, 1 Deacon. Baptized since last general conference, 17.

Worcestershire Conference represented by Elder Thomas Smith, including Earls Common, Pinvin, Flyford Flavel, Worcester, Bromsgrove, Randan Woods, Barford, St. John's, and Milton. Comprises 140 members, 6 Elders, 10 Priests. 3 Teachers, 3 Deacons. Baptized since last general conference, 28.

Clitheroe Conference represented by Elder William Snalam, including

Clitheroe, Chatburn, Downham. Waddington, Ribchester, Chaigley, and Settle. Comprises 299 members, 16 Elders, 22 Priests, 18 Teachers, 4 Deacons. Baptized since last general conference, 14.

Leicester Conference represented by Elder Thomas Margetts, including Leicester and Nottingham. Comprises 127 members, 5 Elders, 10 Priests, 1 Teacher, 2 Deacons.

Cheltenham Conference represented by letter, consisting of 18 branches. Comprises 532 members, 17 Elders, 30 Priests, 13 Teachers, 5 Deacons. Baptized since last General Conference, 90.

Bath represented by letter, comprising 31 members, 1 Elder, 2 Priests.

Wolverton represented by letter. Comprises 8 members, 1 Elder, 2 Priests.

Carlisle represented by letter. Comprises 160 members, 8 Elders, 19 Priests, 8 Teachers, 3 Deacons; and contains four branches.

Littlemoor represented by letter. Comprises 6 members, 1 Priest.

Bedfordshire Conference represented by letter, including 12 branches Comprises 184 members, 14 Elders, 20 Priests, 9 Teachers, 2 Deacons.

The number of members and authorities of each conference being ascertained as nearly as possible, it was determined that the delegates should represent the condition of each conference, and what alterations or measures were necessary to be adopted for the wellbeing of each other.

Elder Charles Miller having remarked that he had been challenged to discussion, and had accepted it, it led to some remarks from Elder Ward as to the very little good effected in general by discussions; and that it was beneath the servants of God to turn aside from the path of duty to wrangle and dispute like the people of the world; and that while the professors of modern religion were in a manner devouring each other, the path of the Saints ought to be onward in the proclamation of the principles of truth.

Elder Hedlock agreed with the remarks of Elder Ward, and stated that they were in perfect accordance with the advice of the First Presidency, and that the evil ought to be guarded against as much as possible.

[The remaining sessions of the conference were devoted to hearing reports from the several conferences comprising the mission, giving instruction relative to ordaining men to the ministry, and the manner of conducting the ministry of the Church to make it effective. Among other items of interest was a communication from the Twelve in Nauvoo making the nomination of Elders Reuben Hedlock and Thomas Ward to preside over the British Mission, which nomination was accepted by the conference, and these brethren were unanimously sustained as the presidency of the mission. The publication of the *Millennial Star* had been ordered suspended by the Twelve, but the conference voted by unanimous acclamation that this conference request the quorum of the Twelve to permit the continued publication of that periodical. The minutes of the conference state that—

"Elder Hedlock addressed the assembly on the subject of the publications, and was desirous of taking the sense of that meeting on the same. It was true that the quorum of the Twelve had advised that the publication of the *Millennial Star* be stopped, and had given him authority to publish a circular as occasion might require; but he believed most sincerely that the stoppage of the *Star* would have a most injurious tendency.

"Several having spoken to the same effect, Elder Ward remarked that, if a publication was to be issued at all, it appeared trifling with the interest of the cause to change the name, inasmuch as the office had received the name of the *Millennial Star* Office, and many letters came to them with that address."

[Then followed the action of the conference upon the subject noted above. Permission must have been given soon afterwards to renew the publication of the *Star*, since it missed but one issue, that of May, 1844 —it was then published monthly. See vols. v and vi.]

CHAPTER XVI.

DIFFICULTIES WITH THE HIGBEES AND FOSTERS—CONFERENCES APPOINTED BY THE TWELVE THROUGHOUT THE UNITED STATES—INSTRUCTIONS TO REUBEN HEDLOCK, PRESIDENT OF THE BRITISH MISSION—PREPARATIONS FOR ENLARGEMENT OF THE WORK—FRANCIS M. HIGBEE'S SUIT AGAINST PRESIDENT SMITH—THE PROPHET RELEASED.

Wednesday, April 10, 1844.—The Twelve were in council arranging a plan for appointing conferences.

Thursday, 11.—In general council in Masonic Hall, morning and afternoon. Had a very interesting time. The Spirit of the Lord was with us, and we closed the council with loud shouts of Hosanna!

Friday, 12.—The Twelve met in council. Rode out with Brothers Parker and Clayton to look at some land.

A conference was held at Cypry, Tuscaloosa County, Alabama. Elder Benjamin L. Clapp, president, and John Brown, clerk. Seven branches were represented, consisting of 192 members, 12 Elders, 5 Priests, 4 Teachers, and 2 Deacons, all in good standing.

Saturday, 13.—At 10 a. m. met in City Council. George P. Styles was appointed City Attorney. I advise that the council take such a course as would protect the innocent: that in many cases the attorney would get his pay off the individual employing him; that the appointment would be a valuable consideration, and for one year a salary of $100 would be sufficient; perhaps $160 the next year, &c., increasing as the city increases; and if $100 would not satisfy, we had better have no attorney. "I would rather give my services as counselor, &c., than levy a tax the people are not able to pay; and that every man ought to be willing to help prop the city by bearing a share of the burden till the city is able to pay a higher salary. My opinion is that the officers of the city should be satisfied with a very small compensation for their services. I have never received twenty-five dollars for my services; [as counselor] but the peace I have enjoyed in the rights and liberties of the city has been ample compensation."

I suggested the propriety of inserting a clause in the ordinance to be made relating to the City Attorney, authorizing him to claim fees of parties in certain cases, and the small salary satisfy the attorney in cases where he can get no fees from his client. "I would rather be docked $100 in my salary than have the $200 given to the City Attorney by the city."

I also proposed that the Council take into consideration the payment of the police; also proposed that a public meeting be called in each ward to see if they will not, then the council will take the case into consideration.

At 1 p. m., the Municipal Court sat in the assembly room, where I asked Dr. R. D. Foster if he bore my expenses to Washington, or any part thereof.

Foster replied he did not.

I stated that Dr. Goforth had said that he was taken in a secret council when Foster told him he had paid my expenses.

Dr. Foster replied he never had a secret interview with Dr. Goforth, and gave his version of the meeting.

I then asked him—"Have I ever misused you any way?

Foster said—"I do not feel at liberty to answer this question, under existing circumstances?"

I again asked him—"Did I ever misuse you?"

He again replied—"I do not feel at liberty to answer under existing circumstances"

I then asked—"Did I ever wrong you in deal, or personally misuse you in any shape?"

Foster said, "I do not feel at liberty to answer. I have treated you Christianly and friendly too, so far as I have had the ability."

I then asked him to tell me where I had done wrong, and I will ask his forgiveness; for I want you to prove to this company by your testimony that I have treated you honorably.

Foster then said—"I shall testify no further at present."

I then asked Justice Aaron Johnson—"Did I ever make oath before you against Simpson?"

He replied—"Not before the prosecution."

I then told the whole story.

Andrew Colton then came up before the Municipal Court on *habeas corpus*, and was discharged on the insufficiency of the papers.

After which, I preferred the following charge before the High Council against Dr. Robert D. Foster "for unchristianlike conduct in general, for abusing my character privily, for throwing out slanderous insinuations against me, for conspiring against my peace and safety, for conspiring against my life, for conspiring against the peace of my family, and for lying."

A charge was preferred against Harrison Sagers for teaching spiritual wife doctrine and neglecting his family, which was handed over to the High Council to act upon.

At 2 p. m., Elder John Taylor delivered a political discourse.

About 5 p. m., the "*Maid of Iowa*" arrived at the Nauvoo House wharf, filled with passengers from England, led by William Kay. 210 souls started from Liverpool, and nearly all arrived in good health and spirits, one smaller company having previously arrived.

Sunday, 14.—Rainy day. No meeting at the stand. I preached on board the "*Maid of Iowa.*"

Committee of the Council met in the afternoon at my office.

Monday, 15.—At home settling with Dan Jones for steamboat "*Maid of Iowa.*" She has returned in debt about $1,700. After much conversation and deliberation, I agreed to buy out Jones, by giving him property in the city worth $1,231, and assuming the debts.

I rode out in the afternoon.

The Twelve Apostles arranged the appointments for the general conferences in the United States as follows:

Quincy, Ill.,	Sat. and Sun.	May	4 and	5
Princess Grove, Ill.,	" "	"	11	12
Ottowa, Ill.,	" "	"	18	19
Chicago, Ill.,	" "	"	25	26
Comstock, Kallamazoo county, Mich.,	" "	June	1	2
Pleasant Valley, Mich.,	" "	"	8	9
Frankland, Oakland county, Mich,	" "	"	15	16
Kirtland, Ohio,	" "	"	22	23
G. A. Neal's six miles west of Lockport, N.Y.	" "	"	29	30
Batavia, N. Y,	" "	July	6	7
Portage, Alleghany county, N. Y.,	" "	"	13	14
Hamilton, Madison county, N. Y.,	" "	"	20	21
Oswego, N. Y.,	" "	June	29	30
Adams, Jefferson county, N. Y.,	" "	July	6	7
London, Caledonia county, N. Y.	" "	June	15	16
Northfield, Washington county, ten miles of Montpelier, at Lyman Houghton's, N.Y.	" "	"	29	30
Fairfield, Essex Co., at Elder Tracy's, N. Y.	" "	July	13	14
Boston, Mass.,	" "	June	29	30
Salem, "	" "	July	6	7
New Bedford, Mass.,	" "	"	13	14
Peterboro, N. H.,	" "	"	13	14
Lowell, Mass.,	" "	"	27	28
Scarboro, Maine,	" "	"	6	7
Vinal Haven "	" "	"	13	14
Westfield, Mass.,	" "	"	27	28
Farmington, Mass.,	" "	Aug.	3	4
New Haven, Conn.,	" "	"	10	11
Canaan, Conn.,	" "	"	17	18
Norwalk, "	" "	"	24	25
New York City, N. Y.,	" "	"	17	18
Philadelphia, Pa.,	" "	Aug.	31	Sep. 1
Dresden, Weekly county, Tenn.,	" "	May	25	26

Eagle Creek, Benton county, Tenn.,	Sat and Sun	June 8	9
Dyer county, C. H.,	" "	" 22	23
Rutherford county, C. H., Tenn.,	" "	July 20	21
Lexington, Henderson county, Tenn.,	" "	Aug. 3	4
New Albany, Clinton county, Ky.,	" "	June 29	30
Alquina, Fayette county, Ia.,	" "	" 1	2
Pleasant Garden, Ia.,	" "	" 15	16
Fort Wayne, Ia.,	" "	" 29	30
Northfield, Boon county, Ia.,	" "	July 13	14
Cincinnati, Ohio,	" "	May 18	19
Pittsburgh, Pa.,	" "	June 1	2
Leechburg, "	" "	" 15	16
Running Water Branch, Noxuble Co., Miss.,	" "	" 1	2
Tuscaloosa, Ala.,	" "	" 22	23
Washington City, D. C.,	Sept. 7, 8, 9, 10, 11, 12, 13, 14, 15.		

We also publish the names of the Elders who are appointed to the several states, together with their appointments. Those who are numbered with the figures 1 and 2 will take the presidency of the several states to which they are appointed.

MAINE.

J. Butterfield, 1st
Elbridge Tufts, 2nd
S. B. Stoddard
Jonathan H. Hale
Henry Herriman,
John Moon

NEW HAMPSHIRE.

W. Snow, 1st
Howard Egan, 2nd
Alvin Cooley
John S. Twiss,
Charles A. Adams,
Bethuel Miller
A. D. Boynton.
Harley Morley
Israel Barlow
David Clough, Sen.
Calvin Reed
Chilion Mack
Isaac Burton

MASSACHUSETTS.

Daniel Spencer, 1st
Milton F. Bartlett
Daniel Loveland
Joseph J. Woodbury
W. H. Woodbury
John R. Blanchard
George Lloyd
Orlando D. Hovey
Nathaniel Ashby
Samuel P. Hoyt
Daniel W. Gardner

RHODE ISLAND.

William Seabury, 1st
Thomas McTaggart
Melvin Wilbur

CONNECTICUT.

E. H. Davis, 1st
Quartus S. Sparks

VERMONT.

Erastus Snow, 1st
William Hyde
Denman Cornish,
Jeremiah Hatch
Martin Titus
William Haight
John D. Chase
Josiah H. Perry
Amos Hodges.
Warren Snow
Dominicus Carter
Levi W. Hancock
Alfred Cordon
Charles Snow
James C. Snow
A. M. Harding
Isaac Houston

NEW YORK.

C. W. Wandell, 1st
Marcellus Bates, 2nd
Truman Gillett
A. A. Farnham
Edmund Ellsworth,
Gregory Bentley
Homer C. Hoyt
Isaac Chase,
Simeon A. Dunn
Daniel Shearer
James W. Phippin
J. H. Van Natta
Samuel P. Bacon
Bradford W, Elliott
J. R. G. Phelps
Joseph P. Noble
John Tanner
Thomas Fuller
O. M. Duel
Samuel White
W. R. R. Stowell
William D. Pratt
Marcellus McKeown
Horace S. Eldredge
William Newland
Allen Wait
William H. Parshall,
C. H. Wheelock
Timothy B. Foote
George W. Fowler
Henry L. Cook
William W. Dryer
Elijah Reed
Solon Foster
Hiram Bennett
Chandler Holbrook
Lyman Hall
William Felshaw
Daniel Fisher,
D. H. Redfield
Martin H. Tanner
G. D, Goldsmith
Charles Thompson
B. C. Elsworth
Archibald Bates
David Pettigrew
Ellis Eames

NEW JERSEY.

Ezra T. Benson, 1st
John Pack

PENNSYLVANIA.

D. D. Yearsley, 1st
Edson Whipple, 2nd
John Duncan
Stephen Post
G. W. Crouse
Jacob Shoemaker
Stephen Winchester
Hyrum Nyman
J. M. Cole
Charles Warner.
Wm. P. McIntyre
Jacob Zundall
Orrin D. Farlin
Henry Mouer
G. Chamberlain
Thomas Hess
A. J. Glæfke
Henry Dean
James Downing

DELAWARE.

John Jones
Warren Snow
Jonathan O. Duke
Justus Morse

MARYLAND.

Jacob Hamblin
Lyman Stoddard.
Patrick Norris

VIRGINIA.

B. Winchester, 1st
S. C. Shelton, 2nd
Geo. D. Watt, 3rd
Chapman Duncan
Joseph King
Peter Fife
Robert Hamilton
James Park
A. W. Whitney
Pleasant Ewell
W. E. Higginbottom
John F. Betts
Alfred B. Lambson
David Evans

NORTH CAROLINA.

A. McRae, 1st
Aaron Razer, 2nd
Thomas Guymon
George Watt.
John Holt
John Houston
James Sanderson

SOUTH CAROLINA.

Alonzo LeBaron, 1st
John M. Emell
William D. Lyman.
Ekells Truly
William Smith

GEORGIA.

Morgan L. Gardner
Isaac Beebe
Miles Anderson
S. E. Carpenter

KENTUCKY.

John D. Lee, 1st
D. H. Rogers
Samuel B. Frost
John O. Angus
Charles Spry
John H. Reid
William Watkins.
D. D. Hunt
M. B. Welton
Horace B. Owens
Joseph Holbrook
Hiram W. Mikesell
Garret W. Mikesell

TENNESSEE.

A. O. Smoot, 1st
Alphonzo Young, 2nd
W. W. Riley
Amos Davis
L. T. Coon
Jackson Smith
W. P. Vance
H. D. Buys
A. D. Young
Joseph Younger
G. W. Langley
G. Penn
J. J. Castell
J. A. Kelting
J. Hampton
Alfred Bell
Armstead Moffitt
D. P. Rainey
James Holt,
Warren Smith
J. J. Sasnett
H. B. Jacobs
John L. Fullmer
Joseph Mount

ALABAMA.

B. L. Clapp, 1st
G. W. Brandon
L. D. Butler
T. J. Brandon

MISSISSIPPI.

J. B. Walker
Ethan Barrus.
Daniel Tyler

LOUISIANA.

J. B. Bosworth, 1st
H. H. Wilson
Wm. Nelson
John Kelly
George Pew
Lorenzo Moore

ARKANSAS.

A. A. Simmons
Darwin Chase
J. A. McIntosh
Nathaniel Leavitt

OHIO.

Lorenzo Snow, 1st
L. Brooks, 2nd
Alfred Brown
J. J. Riser
William Batson
G. C. Riser
Clark Lewis
B. W. Wilson

J. Carroll
L. O. Littlefield
J. M. Powers
Milo Andrus
John Lovelace
W. H. Folsom
John Cooper
S. Carter
John Nichols
David Jones
Nathaniel Childs
Jesse Johnson
J. A. Casper
Joseph Rose
W. Brothers
Jared Porter
John W. Roberts
A. W. Condit
Loren Babbitt
Elijah Newman
Milton Stow
Edson Barney
Hiram Dayton
Jacob Morris
Ezra Strong
J. M. Emmett
Allen Tulley
P. H. Young
S. P. Hutchins
J. H. Foster
Nathan T. Porter
Ezra Vincent
Lysander Dayton

INDIANA.

Amasa Lyman, 1st
G. P. Dykes, 2nd
A. L. Lamoreaux
Charles Hopkins
F. M. Edwards
Salmon Warner
F. D. Richards
S. W. Richards
John Mackey
James Newberry
Abraham Palmer
John G. Smith
U. V. Stewart
Washington Lemon
Edward Carlin
L. D. Young
Wm. Snow
Nathan Tanner
Wm. Martindale
Henry Elliott
A. F. Farr
John Jones
Frederick Ott

MICHIGAN.

Charles C. Rich, 1st
Harvey Green, 2nd
Thomas Dunn
R. C. Sprague
Joseph Curtis
Zebedee Coltrin
Reuben W. Strong
L. N. Kendall
Wm. Savage
David Savage
Graham Coltrin
Samuel Parker
Jeremiah Curtis
C. W. Hubbard
S. D. Willard
Wm. Gribble

ILLINOIS.

E. H. Groves, 1st
Morris Phelps, 2nd

John Vance
H. Olmstead, Galena
H. W. Barnes, do.
Hiram Mott,
David Candland
W. A. Duncan
Wm. O. Clark
Almon Bathrick
P. H. Buzzard
Zachariah Hardy
John Hammond
G. W. Hickerson
Daniel Allen
David Judah
Thomas Dobson
James Nelson
David Lewis
S. Mulliner
John Gould
Zenus H. Gurley
Jefferson Hunt
Jacob L. Burnham
D. J. Kershner
N. Leavitt
John Laurence
Nathan A. West
Levi Jackman
Abel Lamb
Howard Coray
Stephen Markham
Levi Stewart
James Graham
Timothy S. Hoit
Duncan McArthur

MISSOURI.

A. H. Perkins, 1st
John Lowry 2nd
Wm. G. Rule
Wm. Coray
O. M. Allen
Wm. H. Jordan

WISCONSIN TERRITORY.

S. H. Briggs

FREE.

F. Nickerson, 1st
A. C. Nickerson
L. S. Nickerson

Those Elders who are numbered in the foregoing list to preside over the different states will appoint conferences in all places in their several states where opportunities present, and will attend all the conferences, or send experienced and able Elders, who will preach the truth in righteousness, and present before the people "General Smith's Views of the Powers and Policy of the General Government," and seek diligently to get up electors who will go for him for the Presidency. All the Elders will be faithful in preaching the Gospel in its simplicity and beauty, in all meekness, humility, long-suffering and prayerfulness; and the Twelve will devote the season to traveling, and will attend as many conferences as possible.

Elder B. Winchester is instructed to pass through Mississippi, Alabama, Georgia, North and South Carolina and Virginia, to visit the churches, hold conferences, and preside over them.

BRIGHAM YOUNG, President

W. RICHARDS, Clerk of the Quorum of the Twelve.

Tuesday, 16.—Rode out to Brother Greenwood's, but he had not returned. Five p. m. had a long talk with Chauncey L. Higbee and Esq. Marr, in front of my house, and read to them Dr. A. B. Williams' and M. G. Eaton's affidavit before Esq. Wells.

The Twelve Apostles met in council.

Wednesday 17.—Rode out with Brother Heber C. Kimball and William Clayton to the steamboat landing. Remainder of the day at home.

Thursday, 18.—Nine a. m. went into general council until noon and introduced J. W. Coolidge, D. S. Hollister, and added Lyman Wight's name.

While at dinner I made mention of the report that Foster, Higbee, *et al.* were paying someone's board at my table so as to catch something against me; so that, if the report is true, they may have something to carry back.

Two to five thirty p. m. in council.

At 6 p. m. Brigham Young, Willard Richards, John Taylor, George A. Smith, Heber C. Kimball, Wilford Woodruff, of the Twelve Apostles; Alpheus Cutler, Samuel Bent, George W. Harris, A. Johnson, William Marks, of the City Council; Charles C. Rich, Amasa M. Lyman, of the High Council; William W. Phelps, Newel K. Whitney, John Smith, John M. Bernhisel, Joseph Fielding, George J. Adams, Erastus Snow, Reynolds Cahoon, J. W. Coolidge, John Scott, John D. Lee, Levi W. Hancock, S. Williams, Jos. Young, John P. Greene, John D. Parker, Alexander McRae, George D. Watt, and William Clayton held a council and unanimously cut off Robert D. Foster, Wilson Law, William Law and Jane Law, of Nauvoo, and Howard Smith of Scott county, Illinois, from the Church of Jesus Christ of Latter-day Saints, for unchristianlike conduct; and their names were published in the *Times and Seasons*.

Excommunication of the Laws, Fosters, *et al.*

Friday, 19.—A company of about eighty Saints arrived. In the evening rode to the upper steamboat landing.

Saturday, 20.—Emma started for St. Louis to purchase goods.

I rode out with Dr. Bernhisel and my boys Frederick and Alexander to the prairie, which is now very green.

Elders Brigham Young and Wilford Woodruff rode to Lima and spent the night with Father Morley.

Sunday, 21.—At home; rainy day. A meeting at the Stand. Elder Erastus Snow preached on "The Law of Nature."

Elders Young and Woodruff attended a conference and preached to the Saints in Lima, where twenty-six Elders volunteered to go out preaching.

Elder Kimball attended a conference at Ramus.

Monday, 22.—All night lightning, thundering, raining, with strong east wind which continued through the day.

The river very high; all the mills in the city stopped on account of the high water.

This morning a man, who had put up at my house told me he wanted to see me alone. I went into my room with him, when he told me he was a prophet of God, that he came from Vermont, and he prophecied that this Government, was about to be overthrown, and the kingdom which Daniel speaks of was about to be established somewhere in the West, and he thought in Illinois.

My brother William arrived from New Jersey with some forty or fifty Saints. I spent some time with him in the evening.

Elders Young and Woodruff started for Nauvoo; but on account of a tremendous storm of hail and rain, they were glad to take shelter at Brother William Draper's, where they spent the night.

Tuesday, 9.—From 9 to 12 a general meeting of citizens friendly to my election, was held in the hall, to elect a delegate to go to the Baltimore Convention, to be held on the first Monday in May. D. S. Hollister was elected.

From 3 to 5 p. m. again assembled, and many speeches were made, &c.; and appointed the second Monday in May to hold a State Convention at Nauvoo.

In the evening, visited Agnes, my brother Carlos' widow, and Dr. Richards, with Hyrum.

Wednesday, *24*.—Rode up to the steamboat landing, where we found Elder J. M. Grant, who introduced me to Judge William Richards, of New Jersey, took him to Brother Winchester's.

In the evening Brother Ezra Thayer, Dr. Richards, and Dr. Williams were in my room, and a man who boarded at the Masonic Hall. At their request, I gave them a history of the Laws' proceedings, in part, in trying to make a difficulty in my family, &c.

Gave recommendations to Elders Amasa M. Lyman and D. S. Hollister.

Thursday, *25*.—Emma returned from St. Louis.

A brother who works in the *St. Louis Gazette* office came up at the same time, and wanted to know by what principle I got so much power, how many inhabitants and armed men we had, &c. I told him I obtained power on the principles of truth and virtue, which would last when I was dead and gone, &c.

In general council from 10 till 12, and from 2 to 5, when they adjourned *sine die*, after appointing a State Convention to meet in Nauvoo on 17th May. The council then dispersed to go abroad in the nations.

Instructed Dr. Richards to make out a writ of *habeas corpus* for Mr. Jeremiah Smith, of Iowa, who was expecting to be arrested by the U. S. Marshal for getting money which was due him, as he says, at Washington.

A play on rational amusement was to commence this evening, but a most tremendous shower of rain and large hail from the southwest commenced about six p. m. which prevented it. The small creeks rose over four feet high, overflowed their banks, sweeping away fences, and doing considerable damage.

The Mississippi river is higher at this place than ever known by the oldest inhabitant.

Friday 26.—At home. At 10 a. m. the Marshal went up on the hill to arrest Augustine Spencer for an assault on his brother, Orson Spencer, in his own house. Robert D. Foster, Charles Foster and Chauncey L. Higbee came down. Charles Foster drew a pistol pointed towards me, and threatened to shoot while standing on the steps of my office. I ordered him to be arrested and the pistol taken from him, when a struggle ensued, in which Charles Foster, Robert D. Foster and Chauncey L. Highbee resisted, and I ordered them to be arrested also, and I as the Mayor ordered the policemen to be called; then went on to try Augustine Spencer. He was fined $100, and required to give bonds in $100 to keep the peace for six months. He appealed the case at once to the Municipal Court.

Violence of the Fosters and Higbees.

Robert D. Foster, Chauncey L. Higbee, and Charles Foster were also tried for resisting the authorities of the city.

O. P. Rockwell sworn. Marshal John P. Greene sworn:—Said Dr. Foster swore by God that he would not assist the Marshal, and swore by God they would see the Mayor in hell before they would go; and that Charles Foster drew a pistol and presented at the Mayor, which was being wrested from him when Dr. Robert D. Foster interfered. Charles Foster and Chauncey L. Higbee said they would be G— d——d if they would not shoot the Mayor. They breathed out many hard threatenings and menacing sayings. They said they would consider themselves the favored of God for the privilege of shooting or ridding the world of such a tyrant (referring to the Mayor).

Joseph W. Coolidge sworn, and confirmed the Marshal's testimony.

Elbridge Tufts sworn, and confirmed the foregoing statements.

Robert D. Foster, Charles Foster and Chauncey L. Higbee were each fined $100. They immediately took an appeal to the Municipal Court.

I issued a warrant for Robert D. Foster, on complaint of Willard Richards, for a breach of ordinance, in that Foster said to Richards: "You," shaking his fist in the doctor's face, "are another d—ned black-hearted villain! You tried to seduce my wife on the boat, when she was going to New York and I can prove it; and the oath is out against you."

Saturday, 27.—A large company of gentlemen from St. Louis and other places on the river, called at the Mansion. After spending some time, they returned to the boat, but it was gone, when they again returned to the Mansion.

At 9 a. m. the case of Dr. Robert D. Foster came up for trial before the Municipal Court. I had a conversation with Foster in which he charged me with many crimes, and said that Daniteism was in Nauvoo; and he used a great variety of vile and false epithets and charges.

The court adjourned to Monday, the 29th at 9 a. m.

Foster agreed to meet me on the second Monday in May, at the Stand, and have a settlement, and he would publish the result of it in the Warsaw papers. I told him if he did not agree to be quiet, and not attempt to raise a mob, I would not meet him; if he would agree to be quiet, I would be willing to publish the settlement in the *Neighbor*. But Foster would not agree to be quiet. I then told him I had done my duty; the skirts of my garments were free from his (Foster's) blood; I had made the last overtures of peace to him; and then delivered him into the hands of God, and shook my garments against him as a testimony thereof.

I continued in the office some time afterwards in conversation, and then went into the big room and read in the *Warsaw Signal* a vile article against the Saints.

Elder Hiram Smith arrived from Liverpool accompanied by one hundred and fifty immigrating Saints.

There was a meeting at the Stand at one o'clock, to give instructions to the Elders going out electioneering. They were addressed by President Rigdon and William Smith.

Dr. Richards prosecuted Robert D. Foster for slander, &c.

Sunday, *28*.—At home. A beautiful clear day.

My brother Hyrum preached at the Stand in the morning, and among other things, said the time will shortly come that when one man makes another an offender for a word, he shall be cut off from the Church of Jesus Christ. There were prophets before, but Joseph has the spirit and power of all the prophets.

President Brigham Young also spoke very pointedly and very truly about Dr. Foster and others. Dr. Foster was cursed, and the people cried "Amen."

Several persons were baptized in the river at the foot of Main street.

There was a meeting of the Twelve Apostles, Seventies and others, in the Seventies' Hall, in the afternoon.

Prayer meeting in the evening: the brethren prayed for the sick, a deliverance from our enemies, a favorable termination to lawsuits, &c., &c. I had been suddenly taken sick, and was therefore unable to attend.

A conference of Elders assembled at Yelrome, or Morley Settlement, Lima, Isaac Morley presiding, when a quorum of High Priests was organized, consisting of thirty-one members. Horace Rawson president, Philip Gardner and Joseph S. Allen, his counselors, and James C. Snow, clerk.

There was a meeting at Wilson Law's, near the sawmill, of those who had been cut off from the Church, and their dupes. Several affidavits which they had taken against me and others were read. William Law, Wilson

Law, Austin A. Cowles, John Scott, Sen., Francis M. Higbee, Robert D. Foster, and Robert Pierce were appointed a committee to visit the different families in the city, and see who would join the new church; *i. e.*, as they had decided that I was a fallen prophet, &c.; and they appointed William Law in my place, who chose Austin Cowles and Wilson Law as his counselors. Robert D. Foster and Francis M. Higbee to be two of the Twelve Apostles, &c., &c., as report says.

Elder James Blackeslee preached in the forenoon, bearing a faithful testimony of the truth of the work and my being a true prophet, and in the afternoon joined the "Anties." They chose Charles Ivins Bishop.

A conference was held in Sheffield, England, representing 215 members, 7 Elders, 19 Priests, 5 Teachers, and 3 Deacons.

Monday, 29.—At home; received a visit from L. R. Foster of New York, who gave me a good pencil case, sent me by Brother Theodore Curtis, who is now in New York; and the first words I wrote with it were, "God bless the man!"

At 11 a. m., Robert D. Foster came up for trial. I transferred the case to Alderman William Marks. Foster objected to the jurisdiction of the court, also to an informality in the writ, &c.

The court decided he had not jurisdiction. Esquire Noble, from Rock river, assisted the City Attorney. Esquire Patrick was present.

I called a special session of the City Council at 3:30 p. m., when it was voted that W. W. Phelps take the place of John Taylor during his absence this season; also Aaron Johnson in place of Orson Hyde; Phineas Richards in place of Heber C. Kimball; Edward Hunter in place of Daniel Spencer; Levi Richards in place of Brigham Young as councilors in the City Council; and Elias Smith as alderman in place of George A. Smith.

Lieutenant Williams filed his affidavit *versus* Major-

General Wilson Law, and he was suspended from office to await his trial before a court-martial of the Nauvoo Legion for ungentlemanly conduct, &c.; and he was notified of his command in the Legion being suspended, and Charles C. Rich was notified to take command, and also notified seven officers to sit as a court-martial.

William Law was supended for trial about the same time.

Steamer *Mermaid* touched at Nauvoo House, landing at 5 p. m. for a short time when going down.

John P. Greene published the following in the *Neighbor:* (Impression of May 1st.)

The Foster-Higbee Embroilment.

All is peace at Nauvoo, among the Saints:

But, Mr. Taylor, I wish you to give the following outrage an insertion in the *Neighbor*, that the public mind may be disabused, and the disgrace and shame fall on those who have justly deserved it and merited the people's rebuke!

On Friday morning, the 26th inst., I was informed by Mr. Orrin P. Rockwell that one Mr. Augustine Spencer had committed an assault on the person of Alderman Orson Spencer, and the Mayor of the city had sent for Augustine Spencer, and found him in Mr. Marr's law office, made him a prisoner, and informed him he must go with me to the Mayor's office, when he said he would not go.

I then called upon Robert D. Foster, Chauncey L. Higbee, and Charles A. Foster to assist me in taking said Spencer to the Mayor's office; but they swore they would not, and used many threatening oaths and aspersions, saying they would see the Mayor and the city damned, and then they would not; but soon followed me and Mr. Augustine Spencer to the office door, when the Mayor ordered me to arrest these three men for refusing to assist me in the discharge of my duty; and when attempting to arrest them, they all resisted, and with horrid imprecations threatened to shoot.

I called for help, and there not being sufficient, the Mayor laid hold on the two Fosters at the same time. At that instant Charles A. Foster drew a double-barrel pistol on Mr. Smith, but it was instantly wrenched from his hand; and afterwards he declared he would have shot the Mayor, if we had let his pistol alone, and also he would thank God for the privilledge of ridding the world of a tyrant! Chauncey L. Higbee responded to Foster's threats, and swore that he would do it.

However, the three were arrested and brought before the Mayor, whereupon Orrin P. Rockwell, Joseph Coolidge, John P. Greene and E. Tufts testified to the amount of the above statements; upon which evidence the court assessed a fine of one hundred dollars to each of the above-named aggressors, who appealed to the Municipal Court.

I wish the public to know who it is that makes insurrections and disturbs the peace and quiet of the people of the city of Nauvoo; and in order to do this I need only to tell the world that this Robert D. Foster is a county magistrate, and the same Robert D. Foster that was fined for gambling a few weeks since; and that this Chauncey L. Higbee is a lawyer and notary public of Hancock county, and the same Chauncey L. Higbee that was fined for insulting the city officers (the marshal and constable) when in the discharge of their official duties, a few weeks since.

"When the wicked rule the people mourn, but righteousness exalteth any nation"—SOLOMON.

J. P. GREENE, City Marshal.

N. B.—We wish it to be distinctly understood that neither of the three above-named individuals are members of the Church of Latter-day Saints, but we believe Charles A. Foster is a Methodist.—J. P. G.

Tuesday, 30.—At home counseling the brethren about many things; received much company, &c.

In the afternoon in council with Hiram Clark and Brigham Young, at Brigham Young's house, on the affairs of the Church in England.

A complaint was commenced against William and Wilson Law in the Masonic Lodge, &c.

Sent notification to two more officers to sit in the court-martial on the trial of William and Wilson Law.

The *Osprey* steamer touched at the Nauvoo House landing in the evening.

Wednesday, May 1.—Heavy rain and wind last night.

At home counseling the brethren, and rode out a short time in the afternoon with a gentleman from Quincy.

Elder Lyman Wight and Bishop George Miller arrived from the Pine country.

Mr. Thomas A. Lyne, a tragedian from New York, assisted by George J. Adams and others, got up a theatrical exhibition in the lower room of the Masonic Hall, which was fitted up with very tasteful scenery. They performed "Pizarro," "The Orphan of Geneva," "Douglas," "The Idiot Witness," "Damon and Pythias," and other plays with marked success. The Hall was well attended each evening, and the audience expressed their entire satisfaction and approbation.

Thursday, 2.—Very windy all night, breaking down large trees; a thunder storm also.

At home and counseling the brethren.

Sent William Clayton to Wilson Law to find out why he refused paying his note, when he brought in some claims as a set-off which Clayton knew were paid, leaving me no remedy but the glorious uncertainty of the law.

At 10 a. m. the *Maid of Iowa* steamer started for Rock River for a load of wheat and corn to feed the laborers on the Temple.

William Clayton and Colonel Stephen Markham started to attend court at Dixon, on the case of "Joseph Smith vs. Harmon T. Wilson and Joseph H. Reynolds."

In the afternoon I rode to the prairie to sell some land, and during my absence Lucien Woodworth returned from Texas.

Lieut. Aaron Johnson made the following affidavit:

NAUVOO, May 2nd, 1844.

STATE OF ILLINOIS, HANCOCK CO., } ss
CITY OF NAUVOO. }

Personally appeared before me, John Taylor, Judge-Advocate of the Nauvoo Legion, Aaron Johnson; and being duly sworn deposes and says that on or about the 28th day of April, 1844, at the dwelling house of Wilson Law in Nauvoo aforesaid, Colonel R. D. Foster, Surgeon-in-Chief, and Brevet Brigadier-General of said Nauvoo Legion, while talking about General Joseph Smith, said that General Smith kept a gang of robbers and plunderers about his house for the purpose of robbing and plundering, and he (Smith) received half the spoils; also that said General Joseph Smith tried to get him (Foster) to go and kill Boggs, with many other ungentlemanly and unofficer-like observations concerning said General Smith and others.

AARON JOHNSON,
2nd Lieut., 1st Comp., 1st Regiment, 2nd Cohort, Nauvoo Legion.

Personally appeared, Aaron Johnson, the signer of the above complaint, and made oath the same was true according to the best of his knowledge and belief, the day and year above written before me.

JOHN TAYLOR,
Judge-Advocate of the Nauvoo Legion.

Friday, 3.—At home giving advice to brethren who were constantly calling to ask for counsel. Several thunder showers during the day.

In general council from 2 to 6, and from 8 to 10 p. m. Lucien Woodworth gave an account of his mission.

Wrote a letter to Uncle John Smith, and requested him to attend general council next Monday.

The following letter was written:

Letter: Brigham Young and Willard Richards to Reuben Hedlock—Instructions on Immigration Matters.

NAUVOO, May 3rd, 1844.

Elder Reuben Hedlock:

DEAR BROTHER—Your long communication by Elder Kay was received two weeks last Saturday, also the one by Elder Clark last Saturday, and we feel to thank you for the care you have taken to write us so particularly. We are glad to receive such communications, and wish you to continue the same course as opportunities present. The brethren have all had good passages (four ships). Elder Clark was only five weeks and three days to New Orleans. All things safe.

All things are going on gloriously at Nauvoo. We shall make a great wake in the nation. Joseph for President. Your family is well, and friends generally. We have already received several hundred volunteers to go out electioneering and preaching and more offering. We go for storming the nation. But we must proceed to realities.

The whisperings of the Spirit to us are that you do well to content yourself awhile longer in old England, and let your wife remain where she is. We hope the Temple may be completed, say one year from this spring, when in many respects changes will take place. Until then, who can do better in England than yourself! But we will not leave you comfortless; we will send Elders to your assistance. For three or four months we want all the help we can get in the United States; after which you may expect help.

In the meantime you are at liberty to print as many *Stars*, pamphlets hymn books, tracts, cards, &c., as you can sell; and make all the money you can in righteousness. Don't reprint everything you get from Nauvoo. Many things are printed here not best to circulate in England. Select and write doctrine, and matter, (new) such as will be useful to the Saints in England and new to us; so that when we exchange papers all will be edified. God shall give you wisdom, if you will seek to Him, and you shall prosper in your printing.

We also wish you to unfurl your flag on your shipping office, and send all the Saints you can to New York, or Boston, or Philadelphia or any other port of the United States, but not at our expense any longer. We have need of something to sustain us in our labors, and we want you to go ahead with printing and shipping, and make enough to support yourself and help us a bit. You will doubtless find it necessary to employ Brother Ward. Keep all your books straight, so that we in the end can know every particular.

Ship everybody to America you can get the money for—Saint and sinner—a general shipping-office. And we would like to have our shipping-agent in Liverpool sleep on as good a bed, eat at as respectable a house, keep as genteel an office, and have his boots shine as bright, and blacked as often as any other office-keeper. Yes sir; make you money enough to wear a good broadcloth, and show the world that you represent gentlemen of worth, character and respectability.

We will by-and-by have offices from the rivers to the ends of the earth, and we will begin at Liverpool from this time and increase and increase and *increase* the business of the office as fast as it can be done in safety, and circumstances will permit. Employ a runner, if necessary, and show the world you can do a better and more honorable business than anybody else, and more of it. Don't be afraid to blow your trumpet.

We need not say, deal with everybody so that they will want to deal with you again, and make all the money you honestly can. Send no more emigrants on emigration books or *Star* money. Temple orders for emigrants may be filled on Temple funds. Keep account of all moneys in their separate departments and favor us with a report occasionally.

Sell the Books of Mormon the first opportunity, if it be at a reduced price, and forward the money by the first safe conveyance to Brigham Young.

We will pay your wife as you requested in your letter, as soon as possible. We wish you to take care of yourself and family, and withal help us besides; and we have now put you in possession of means to do it.

Let nobody know your business but the underwriters. Our wives know not all our business, neither does any wise man's wife know all things, for the secret of the Lord is with those that fear Him and do His business. A hint to the wise is sufficient. But we will add, if you want us to do anything for your wife, write us, and we will do it; but keep our business from your wife and from everybody else

We are glad to hear a door is open in France, and sure we have no objections to your going over and preaching, &c.; but we think perhaps you will now find as much to do in England as you can find time to do it in; if not, go by all means. We are in hopes of sending a special messenger to France in a few days; if so, very likely he may call on you, and you pass over and give him an introduction: this would be pleasant for you all.

Brother Hedlock, a word with you privately. Joseph said, last con ference, that Zion included all North and South America; and after the Temple was done, and the Elders endowed, they would spread and build up cities all over the United States; but at present we are not to teach this doctrine. Nay, hold your tongue. But by this you can see why it is wsidom for the Saints to get into the United States—anywhere rather than stay in England to starve.

The prophet has a charter for a dam from the lower line of the city to the island opposite Montrose, and from thence to the sand-bar above in the Mississippi. Could five, six or seven thousand dollars be raised to commence the dam at the lower extremity, and erect a building, any machinery might be propelled by water. The value of a steam-engine would nearly build the dam sufficient for a cotton-factory, which we much need. Start some capitalists, if you can: 'tis the greatest speculation in the world: a world of cotton and woollen goods are wanted here.

We have proposed to Brother Clark to return to your assistance in the shipping business soon; also to enter into exchanges of goods and produce. Which he will do, he has not decided. What will hinder your doing a good business in shipping this season? Good? Yes, in competing with the first offices in the city, and by next season taking the lead, if not this! When the Saints get to New York, Boston, &c., let them go to work, spread abroad in the land, or come to Nauvoo, as they find convenient and have means, and when the season arrives, start again for New Orleans. Write soon after the receipt of this, and let us know the prospect.

Tell the Saints, when they arrive in America, to make themselves as comfortable as they can, and be diligent in business, and not be over-anxious if they cannot come to Nauvoo. They will find Elders in all the states who will be ready to give them instruction; and if they can gather something by the way by their industry to assist themselves with when they arrive here, it will be well for them.

We have dropped the Nauvoo House until the Temple can be completed, and the Temple is going on finely. We have had an open winter and a forward spring. The Twelve are holding general conferences all over the United States. They will go East soon, and Brother Young will write to you as soon as he gets the information to tell what house you can remit the book money to in New York.

We shall have a State Convention at Nauvoo on the 17th inst.,—an election. A great many are believing the doctrine. If any of the brethren wish to go to Texas, we have no particular objection. You may send a hundred thousand there if you can, in eighteen months, though we expect before that you will return to receive your endowments; and then we will consult your interest, with others who may be going abroad, about taking their families with them.

The kingdom is organized; and, although as yet no bigger than a grain of mustard seed, the little plant is in a flourishing condition, and our prospects brighter than ever. Cousin Lemuel is very friendly, and cultivating the spirit of peace and union in his family very extensively.

William and Wilson Law, Robert D. Foster, Chauncey L. and Francis Higbee, Father Cowles, &c., have organized a new church. (Laws and Fosters were first cut off). William Law is Prophet; James Blakesley and Cowles, Counselors; Higbee and Foster of the Twelve. Cannot learn all particulars. Charles Ivins, Bishop; old Dr. Green and old John Scott, his counselors. They are talking of sending a mission to England. but it will probably be after this when they come among you. 'Tis the same old story over again—"The doctrine is right, but Joseph is a fallen prophet."

Your brethren in the new covenant,

BRIGHAM YOUNG,
WILLARD RICHARDS.

Elder Parley P. Pratt wrote from Richmond, Mass., as follows:

Letter: Parley P. Pratt to Joseph Smith et al., Denouncing Augustine Spencer.

Dear Brother Joseph and Brother Orson Spencer, or whom it may concern:

This is to forewarn you that you have a snake in the grass—a base traitor and hypocrite in your midst, of whom perhaps you may not be fully aware. You may think these harsh terms, but I speak from good evidence and speak the truth.

Mr. Augustine Spencer, brother to Elder Orson Spencer, has written a letter from Nauvoo, which is now going the rounds in this neighborhood, and is fraught with the most infamous slander and lies concerning Joseph Smith and others, and which is calculated to embitter the minds of the people who read or hear it. It affirms that Joseph Smith is in the habit of drinking, swearing, carousing, dancing all night, &c.,

and that he keeps six or seven young females as wives, &c., and many other such like insinuations.

At the same time he cautions the people to whom he writes to keep the letter in such a way that a knowledge of its contents may not reach Nauvoo, as he says he is on intimate terms and confidential friendship with the "Prophet Joe" and the Mormons, and that he hopes to get into office by their means. This is his own acknowledgment of his own baseness, imposition and hypocrisy. I have not seen the letter myself, but have carefully examined the testimony of those who have, and I have also seen and witnessed its baneful effect upon the people here.

Now, I say to the Saints, Let such a man alone severely; shun him as they would the pestilence; be not deceived by a smooth tongue nor flattering words; neither accept of any excuse or apology until he boldly contradicts and counteracts his lying words abroad; but rather expose and unmask him in your midst, that he may be known and consequently become powerless, if he is not already so. I am well and expect to be in Boston tomorrow.

I remain, as ever, your friend and brother, in the love of truth,

P. P. PRATT.

RICHMOND, MASS., May 3rd, 1844.

Saturday, 4.—Rode out on the prairie to sell some land. The stone work for four circular windows finished cutting for the middle story of the Temple. Elder Wilford Woodruff moved into his new brick house.

A court-martial was detailed as follows:

HEADQUARTERS NAUVOO LEGION May 4, 1844.

To Alanson Ripley, Sergeant-Major, 2nd Cohort, Nauvoo Legion:

You are hereby forthwith commanded to notify the following named officers of the Nauvoo Legion to assemble at the office of Lieut.-General Joseph Smith, on Friday, the 10th inst., at 9 o'clock a. m., as members of a court-martial detailed for the trial of Robert D. Foster, Surgeon-in-Chief and Brevet Brigadier-General of the Nauvoo Legion, on the complaint of Lieut. Aaron Johnson for unofficer-like and unbecoming conduct, and hereof fail not, and make returns of your proceedings to the President of the Court on the first day of its sitting—*viz.*

Brig.,-Gen. George Miller as President; Brevet Brig.-Gen. Hugh McFall, Brevet Brig.-General Daniel H. Wells, Brevet Brig.-Gen. John S. Fullmer, Colonel Jonathan Dunham, Colonel Stephen Markham, Colonel Hosea Stout, Colonel John Scott, Lieut.-Colonel John D. Parker, Lieut.-Colonel Jonathan H. Hale, Lieut.-Colonel Theodore Turley, as members of said court, and Colonel John Taylor as Judge-Advocate

Also to summons Willard Richards and Aaron Johnson to appear at the same time and place as witnessses.

Given under my hand the day and year above written.

CHARLES C. RICH,

Major-General N. L., Commanding.

Dr. Richards wrote a letter, at President Brigham Young's request, to Reuben Hedlock.

Sunday, *5.*—At home. Rainy day. Elder Jedediah M. Grant preached at the Mansion at 2 p. m. A large company of friends at my house afternoon and evening, whom I addressed on the true policy of this people in our intercourse with the national government.

A conference was held at Marsh Hill, (formerly Froom's Hill) England, comprising 681 members, 22 Elders, 43 Priests, 15 Teachers, 7 Deacons.

Monday, *6.*—Attended general council all day. Elder J. M. Grant was added to the council. Voted to send Almon W. Babbitt on a mission to France and Lucien Woodworth to Texas. Sidney Rigdon was nominated as a candidate for the Vice-Presidency of the United States.

I had a warrant served on me by John D. Parker, issued by the clerk of the Circuit Court at Carthage, on the complaint of Francis M. Higbee, who had laid his damages at $5,000, but for what the writ does not state. I petitioned the Municipal Court for a writ of *habeas corpus*, which I obtained.

At 6 p. m. I was in conversation with Jeremiah Smith and a number of gentlemen, in my office on the subject of Emma's correspondence with Governor Carlin.

Beautiful day. West wind.

Tuesday 7.—Rode out on the prairie at nine a. m., with some gentlemen, to sell them some land. A tremendous thunder shower in the afternoon, with a strong wind and rain, which abated about sunset, and I stayed at my farm all night.

Esquire Daniel H. Wells issued a writ of ejectment against all persons who had bought land of Robert D.

Foster on the block east of the Temple, Foster having given them warranty deeds, but not having paid for the land himself.

An opposition printing press arrives at Dr. Foster's.

The following notice was issued by the Recorder:

STATE OF ILLINOIS, }
CITY OF NAUVOO. }

To the Marshal of the said City, greeting:

You are hereby required to notify Phineas Richards, Edward Hunter and Levi Richards, that they have been elected members of the City Council of said city; and Elias Smith, that he has been elected Alderman of said city by said City Council; and the said Councilors and Alderman and Gustavus Hills are required to appear, receive their oath of office, and take seats in said Council on Saturday, the 8th of June, 1844, at 10 o'clock a. m., at the Council Chamber. By order of the Council.

Witness my hand and corporation seal this 7th May, 1844.

[L. S.] W. RICHARDS. Recorder.

Thursday, 8.—Returned home. At 10 a. m. went before the Municipal Court on the case, "Francis M. Higbee *versus* Joseph Smith."

The Prophet's Petition for Writ of Habeas Corpus.

MUNICIPAL COURT, CITY OF NAUVOO, ILLINOIS.

Third day, regular term, May 8, 1844.

Before Alderman N. K. Whitney, acting Chief Justice, and Aldermen Daniel H. Wells, William Marks, Orson Spencer, George W. Harris, Gustavus Hills, George A. Smith and Samuel Bennett, Associate Justices presiding.

Ex-parte Joseph Smith, Sen., on *habeas corpus*. } Messrs. Styles and Rigdon, Counsel for Smith.

This case came before the court upon a return to a writ of *habeas corpus*, which was issued by this court on the 6th of May instant, upon the petition of Joseph Smith, Sen., as follows:

STATE OF ILLINOIS, }
CITY OF NAUVOO, } Sct.

To the Honorable Municipal Court and for the City of Nauvoo:

The undersigned, your petitioner, most respectfully represents that he is an inhabitant of said city. Your petitioner further represents that he is under arrest in said city, and is now in the custody of one John D. Parker, deputy sheriff of the county of Hancock, and state of

Illinois; and that the said Parker holds your petitioner by a writ of *Capias ad respondendum*, issued by the clerk of the Circuit Court of the county of Hancock and state of Illinois, at the instance of one Francis M. Higbee of said county, requiring your petitioner to answer the said Francis M. Higbee, "of a plea of the case;" damage, five thousand dollars. Your petitioner further represents that the proceedings against him are illegal; that the said warrant of arrest is informal, and not of that character which the law recognizes as valid; that the said writ is wanting and deficient in the plea therein contained; that the charge or complaint which your petitioner is therein required to answer is not known to the law.

Your petitioner further avers that the said writ does not disclose in any way or manner whatever any cause of action; which matter your petitioner most respectfully submits for your consideration, together with a copy of the said warrant of arrest which is hereunto attached.

Your petitioner further states that this proceeding has been instituted against him without any just or legal cause; and further that the said Francis M. Higbee is actuated by no other motive than a desire to persecute and harass your petitioner for the base purpose of gratifying feelings of revenge, which, without any cause, the said Francis M. Higbee has for a long time been fostering and cherishing.

Your petitioner further states that he is not guilty of the charge preferred against him, or of any act against him, by which the said Francis M. Higbee could have any charge, claim or demand whatever against your petitioner.

Your petitioner further states that he verily believes that another object the said F. M. Higbee had in instituting the proceeding was and is to throw your petitioner into the hands of his enemies, that he might the better carry out a conspiracy which has for some time been brewing against the life of your petitioner.

Your petitioner further states that the suit which has been instituted against him has been instituted through malice, private pique and corruption.

Your petitioner would therefore most respectfully ask your honorable body to grant him the benefit of the writ of *habeas corpus*, that the whole matter may be thoroughly investigated, and such order made as the law and justice demand in the premises: and your petitioner will ever pray.

JOSEPH SMITH, SEN.

Order of the Municipal Court.

STATE OF ILLINOIS,
CITY OF NAUVOO, } Sct.

NAUVOO, May 6th, 1844.

The people of the State of Illinois, to the Marshal of said city, greeting:

Whereas application has been made before the Municipal Court of said city, that the body of one Joseph Smith, Senior, of the said city of Nauvoo, is in the custody of John D. Parker, deputy sheriff of Hancock county and state aforesaid.

These are therefore to command the said John D. Parker, of the county aforesaid, to safely have the body of said Joseph Smith, Senior, of the city aforesaid, in his custody detained, as it is said, together with the day and cause of his caption and detention, by whatsoever name the said Joseph Smith, Senior, may be known or called, before the Municipal Court of said city forthwith, to abide such order as the said court shall make in this behalf; and further, if the said John D. Parker, or other person or persons, having said Joseph Smith, Senior, of said city of Nauvoo, in custody, shall refuse or neglect to comply with the provisions of this writ, you, the marshal of said city, or other person authorized to serve the same, are hereby required to arrest the person or persons so refusing or neglecting to comply as aforesaid, and bring him or them, together with the person or persons in his or their custody, forthwith before the Municipal Court aforesaid, to be dealt with according to law; and herein fail not and bring this writ with you.

Witness, Willard Richards, clerk of the Municipal Court at Nauvoo, this 6th day of May, in the year of our Lord one thousand eight hundred and forty-four.

WILLARD RICHARDS,
Clerk M. C. C. N.

I hold the within-named Joseph Smith, Senior, under arrest, by virtue of a *capias ad respondendum.*

HANCOCK COUNTY COURT.
To May Term, A. D. 1844.

Francis M. Higbee
vs.
Joseph Smith
} In case.

The day of his caption, May 6th, 1844.
To damage five thousand dollars.

WM. BACKENSTOS, S. H. C.
By J. D. PARKER, D. S.

STATE OF ILLINOIS,
HANCOCK COUNTY.
} ss

The people of the state of Illinois to the Sheriff of said county, greeting:

We command you that you take Joseph Smith, if to be found within your county, and him safely keep, so that you have his body before the Circuit Court of said county of Hancock on the first day of the next term thereof, to be holden at the Courthouse in Carthage on the third

Monday in the month of May instant, to answer Francis M. Higbee, of a plea of the case; damage, the sum of five thousand dollars, as he says; and you have then there this writ, and make due return thereon in what manner you execute the same.

[Seal] Witness, J. B. Backenstos, clerk of said Circuit Court at Carthage, this first day of May, in the year of our Lord, one thousand eight hundred and forty-four.

J. C. BACKENSTOS, Clerk.
By D. E. HEAD, Deputy.

This is a true copy of the original now in the possession of William B. Backenstos, Sheriff of Hancock county.

By J. D. PARKER, Deputy.

STATE OF ILLINOIS,
HANCOCK COUNTY, } Sct.
CITY OF NAUVOO.

To Mr. Francis M. Higbee:

SIR.—You will please to take notice that Joseph Smith, Senior, has petioned for a writ of *habeas corpus* from the Municipal Court of said city, praying that he may be liberated from the custody of John D. Parker, deputy sheriff of Hancock county, by whom he is held in custody on a *capias ad respondendum*, issued by the Circuit Court of Hancock county, on the first day of May instant, to answer Francis M. Higbee on a plea of the case, etc.; which writ is granted; and you will have the opportunity to appear before the Municipal Court at 10 o'clock a. m. on the 7th of May instant, at the Council Chamber in said city, and show cause why said Joseph Smith, Senior, should not be liberated on said *habeas corpus*.

[Seal] Witness my hand and seal of court this 5th day of May, 1844.

WILLARD RICHARDS, CLERK M. C. C. N.

The case was argued at length by Messrs. George P. Styles and Sidney Rigdon. After which the court allowed the petitioner and his counsel to proceed with the case. Whereupon President Joseph Smith, Brigham Young, Sidney Rigdon, Hyrum Smith, Orrin Porter Rockwell, Cyrus H. Wheelock, Joel S. Miles, Henry G. Sherwood, Heber C. Kimball, were permitted to testify proving (1) the very bad and immoral character of Francis M. Higbee; and (2) the maliciousness of his prosecution of Joseph Smith. In the course of his testimony the Prophet said: "The only sin I ever committed was in exercising sympathy and covering up their [the Higbees', Fosters', Laws' and Dr. Bennett's] iniquities, on their solemn promise to reform, and of this I am ashamed, and will never do so again." After hearing these witnesses the Judge said: "It is considered and ordained by the court—

"1st. That the said Joseph Smith, Senior, be discharged from the said arrest and imprisonment complained of in said petition, on the illegality of the writ upon which he was arrested, as well as upon the writ of the case, and that he go hence without day.

"2nd. Francis M. Higbee's character having been so fully shown as infamous, the court is convinced that this suit was instituted through malice, private pique, and corruption, and ought not to be countenanced; and it is ordained by the court that the said Francis M. Higbee pay the costs."

[Seal] In testimony whereof I hereunto set my hand and affix the seal of said court at the city of Nauvoo, this 8th day of May, 1844.

WILLARD RICHARDS, Clerk.

I copy the following from the *Neighbor* of this date:

Hurrah for the General! The following which we extract from the *St. Louis Organ*, shows how the public mind is turning, and what their feelings are in regard to the Prophet, his views and theirs also in regard to the Presidency.

Forebear awhile—we'll hear a little more. The matter is now settled with Messrs. Clay, Tyler and Van Buren. Let Mr. Clay return at once from his political perambulations in the South, Mr. Tyler abandon his hopes of re-election by aid of the "immediate annexation" of Texas, and let Mr. Van Buren be quiet at Kinderhook, that he may watch the operations of the "sober second thought" of the people!

General Joseph Smith, the acknowledged modern Prophet, has got them all in the rear; and from the common mode of testing the success of candidates for the Presidency, to wit., by steamboat elections, he (Smith) will beat all the other aspirants to that office two to one. We learn from the polls of the steamboat *Osprey*, on her last trip to this city, that the vote stood for General Joseph Smith, 20 gents and 5 ladies; Henry Clay, 16 gents and 4 ladies; Van Buren, 7 gents and 0 ladies.

Attended theatre in the evening.

CHAPTER XVII.

ADDRESS OF THE PROPHET—HIS PROPHETIC CALLING AND THE RESURRECTION—STATUS OF AFFAIRS AT NAUVOO—HYDE'S REPORTS FROM WASHINGTON ON THE WESTERN MOVEMENT—OREGON.

Thursday, May 9, 1844.—A court-martial was held in my office for the trial of Major-General Wilson Law, on a charge of ungentlemanly and unofficer-like conduct. Present—Generals Hyrum Smith, Charles C. Rich, Lyman Wight, George Miller and Albert P. Rockwood; Cols. John Scott and Hosea Stout; Judge-Advocate John Taylor; and Secretary Thomas Bullock. The charge was sustained and Wilson Law cashiered.

Theatricals in Nauvoo.

Evening, attended theatre, and saw "Damon and Pythias," and "The Idiot Witness" performed.

Elders Wilford Woodruff and George A. Smith called upon me this morning, and said they were ready to start on their mission to attend the conferences appointed throughout the north of Illinois, Indiana and Michigan. I blessed them in the name of the Lord, and told them to go, and they should prosper and always prosper. They left in company with Elders Jedediah M. Grant and Ezra Thayer.

Friday, 10—Rode out after breakfast to the prairie to sell some land to some brethren.

The court-martial was held in the Mayor's office on the charge against Robert D. Foster, Surgeon-General, for unbecoming and unofficer-like conduct, &c.; Brigadier-General George Miller presiding. The charges were sustained.

A prospectus of the *Nauuoo Expositor* was distributed among the people by the apostates.

The jury of Lee county, Illinois, awarded $40 damages and the costs against Joseph H. Reynolds and Harmon T. Wilson for illegal imprisonment and abuse, which I suffered from them last June in that county.

Saturday, 11.—At 10 a. m. I attended City Council, and stayed till half-past eleven; but there not being a quorum, adjourned until next regular session. At 1 p. m. at my office, and had a conversation with Mr. Lyne on the theatre; and at 6 p. m. attended prayer meeting: John P. Greene and Sidney Rigdon present. Several showers of rain during the day. The Nauvoo Legion had a company muster.

Sunday, 12.—At 10 a. m. I preached at the Stand. The following brief synopsis of my discourse was reported by my clerk, Thomas Bullock:

President Joseph Smith's Address—Defense of his Prophetic Calling—Resurrection of the Dead—Fullness of Ordinances Necessary Both for the Living and Dead.

The Savior has the words of eternal life. Nothing else can profit us. There is no salvation in believing an evil report against our neighbor. I advise all to go on to perfection, and search deeper and deeper into the mysteries of Godliness. A man can do nothing for himself unless God direct him in the right way; and the priesthood is for that purpose.

The last time I spoke on this stand it was on the resurrection of the dead, when I promised to continue my remarks upon that subject. I still feel a desire to say something on this subject. Let us this very day begin anew, and now say, with all our hearts, we will forsake our sins and be righteous. I shall read the 24th chapter of Matthew, and give it a literal rendering and reading; and when it is rightly understood, it will be edifying. [He then read and translated it from the German].

I thought the very oddity of its rendering would be edifying anyhow —"*And it will preached be, the Gospel of the kingdom, in the whole world, to a witness over all people: and then will the end come.*" I will now read it in German [which he did, and many Germans who were present said he translated it correctly].

The Savior said when these tribulations should take place, it should be committed to a man who should be a witness over the whole world:

the keys of knowledge, power and revelations should be revealed to a witness who should hold the testimony to the world. It has always been my province to dig up hidden mysteries—new things—for my hearers. Just at the time when some men think that I have no right to the keys of the Priesthood—just at that time I have the greatest right. The Germans are an exalted people. The old German translators are the most correct—most honest of any of the translators; and therefore I get testimony to bear me out in the revelations that I have preached for the last fourteen years. The old German, Latin, Greek and Hebrew translations all say it is true: they cannot be impeached, and therefore I am in good company.

All the testimony is that the Lord in the last days would commit the keys of the priesthood to a witness over all people. Has the Gospel of the kingdom commenced in the last days? And will God take it from the man until He takes him Himself? I have read it precisely as the words flowed from the lips of Jesus Christ. John the Revelator saw an angel flying through the midst of heaven, having the everlasting Gospel to preach unto them that dwell on the earth.

The scripture is ready to be fulfilled when great wars, famines, pestilence, great distress, judgments, &c., are ready to be poured out on the inhabitants of the earth. John saw the angel having the holy priesthood, who should preach the everlasting Gospel to all nations. God had an angel—a special messenger—ordained and prepared for that purpose in the last days. Woe, woe be to that man or set of men who lift up their hands against God and His witness in these last days: for they shall deceive almost the very chosen ones!

My enemies say that I *have* been a true prophet. Why, I had rather be a fallen true prophet than a false prophet. When a man goes about prophesying, and commands men to obey his teachings, he must either be a true or false prophet. False prophets always arise to oppose the true prophets and they will prophesy so very near the truth that they will deceive almost the very chosen ones.

The doctrine of eternal judgments belongs to the first principles of the Gospel, in the last days. In relation to the kingdom of God, the devil always sets up his kingdom at the very same time in opposition to God. Every man who has a calling to minister to the inhabitants of the world was ordained to that very purpose in the Grand Council of heaven before this world was. I suppose that I was ordained to this very office in that Grand Council. It is the testimony that I want that I am God's servant, and this people His people. The ancient prophets declared that in the last days the God of heaven should set up a kingdom which should never be destroyed, nor left to other people; and the very time that was calculated on, this people were struggling to bring it out. He that arms himself with gun, sword, or pistol, except in the defense of truth, will sometime be sorry for it. I never carry any weapon with me bigger than my penknife. When I was dragged before the cannon and muskets in Missouri, I was unarmed. God will always protect me until my mission is fulfilled.

I calculate to be one of the instruments of setting up the kingdom of Daniel by the word of the Lord, and I intend to lay a foundation that will revolutionize the whole world. I once offered my life to the Missouri mob as a sacrifice for my people, and here I am. It will not be by sword or gun that this kingdom will roll on: the power of truth is such that all nations will be under the necessity of obeying the Gospel. The prediction is that army will be against army: it may be that the Saints will have to beat their ploughs into swords, for it will not do for men to sit down patiently and see their children destroyed.

My text is on the resurrection of the dead, which you will find in the 14th chapter of John—"In my Father's house are many mansions." It should be—"In my Father's kingdom are many kingdoms," in order that ye may be heirs of God and joint-heirs with me. I do not believe the Methodist doctrine of sending honest men and noble-minded men to hell, along with the murderer and the adulterer. They may hurl all their hell and fiery billows upon me, for they will roll off me as fast as they come on. But I have an order of things to save the poor fellows at any rate, and get them saved; for I will send men to preach to them in prison and save them if I can.

There are mansions for those who obey a celestial law, and there are other mansions for those who come short of the law, every man in his own order. There is baptism, &c., for those to exercise who are alive, and baptism for the dead who die without the knowledge of the Gospel.

I am going on in my progress for eternal life. It is not only necessary that you should be baptized for your dead, but you will have to go through all the ordinances for them, the same as you have gone through to save yourselves. There will be 144,000 saviors on Mount Zion, and with them an innumerable host that no man can number. Oh! I beseech you to go forward, go forward and make your calling and your election sure; and if any man preach any other Gospel than that which I have preached, he shall be cursed; and some of you who now hear me shall see it, and know that I testify the truth concerning them.

In regard to the law of the priesthood, there should be a place where all nations shall come up from time to time to receive their endowments; and the Lord has said this shall be the place for the baptisms for the dead. Every man that has been baptized and belongs to the kingdom has a right to be baptized for those who have gone before; and as soon as the law of the Gospel is obeyed here by their friends who act as proxy for them, the Lord has administrators there to set them free.

A man may act as proxy for his own relatives; the ordinances of the Gospel which were laid out before the foundations of the world have thus been fulfilled by them, and we may be baptized for those whom we have much friendship for; but it must first be revealed to the man of God, lest we should run too far. "As in Adam all die, even so in Christ shall all be made alive;" all shall be raised from the dead. The Lamb of God hath brought to pass the resurrection, so that all shall rise from the dead.

God Almighty Himself dwells in eternal fire; flesh and blood cannot go there, for all corruption is devoured by the fire. "Our God is a consuming fire." When our flesh is quickened by the Spirit, there will be no blood in this tabernacle. Some dwell in higher glory than others.

Those who have done wrong always have that wrong gnawing them. Immortality dwells in everlasting burnings. I will from time to time reveal to you the subjects that are revealed by the Holy Ghost to me. All the lies that are now hatched up against me are of the devil, and the influence of the devil and his servants will be used against the kingdom of God. The servants of God teach nothing but principles of eternal life, by their works ye shall know them. A good man will speak good things and holy principles, and an evil man evil things. I feel, in the name of the Lord, to rebuke all such bad principles, liars, &c., and I warn all of you to look out whom you are going after. I exhort you to give heed to all the virtue and the teachings which I have given you. All men who are immortal dwell in everlasting burnings. You cannot go anywhere but where God can find you out. All men are born to die, and all men must rise; all must enter eternity.

In order for you to receive your children to yourselves you must have a promise—some ordinance; some blessing, in order to ascend above principalities, or else it may be an angel. They must rise just as they died; we can there hail our lovely infants with the same glory—the same loveliness in the celestial glory, where they all enjoy alike. They differ in stature, in size, the same glorious spirit gives them the likeness of glory and bloom; the old man with his silvery hairs will glory in bloom and beauty. No man can describe it to you—no man can write it.

When did I ever teach anything wrong from this stand? When was I ever confounded? I want to triumph in Israel before I depart hence and am no more seen. I never told you I was perfect; but there is no error in the revelations which I have taught. Must I, then, be thrown away as a thing of naught?

I enjoin for your consideration—add to your faith virtue, love, &c. I say, in the name of the Lord, if these things are in you, you shall be fruitful. I testify that no man has power to reveal it but myself—things in heaven, in earth and hell; and all shut your mouths for the future. I commend you all to God, that you may inherit all things; and may God add His blessing. Amen.

My brother Hyrum and Elder Lyman Wight also addressed the Saints.

My brother Hyrum received an anonymous letter, supposed to have been written by Joseph H. Jackson, threatening his life, and calling upon him to make his peace with God for he would soon have to die.

At 3 p. m. I attended prayer meeting in the council room. William Smith and Almon W. Babbitt were present. The room was full and we all prayed for deliverance from our enemies and exaltation to such offices as will enable the servants of God to execute righteousness in the earth.

I copy the following from the *Times and Seasons:*

FOR THE NEIGHBOR.

Nauvoo and President Smith.

Before taking my farewell of your beautiful and growing city, I avail myself of a few leisure moments in expressing some of my views and conclusions of the "Prophet Joe" and the Mormons. In the first place, allow me to say that the Mormons, as a people, have been most woe fully misrepresented and abused, and, in ninety-nine instances out of a hundred, by persons who know nothing of their principles and doctrines.

Before visiting the place, my mind was very much prejudiced against the Mormons, from reports which I had listened to in traveling through the different states; and I presume, if I had never taken occasion to inform myself of their religion and views, my mind would have remained in the same condition. There is not a city within my knowledge that can boast of a more enterprising and industrious people than Nauvoo. Her citizens are enlightened, and possess many advantages in the arts and sciences of the day, which other cities of longer standing cannot boast: in a word, Nauvoo bids fair to soon outrival any city in the West.

General Smith is a man who understands the political history of his country as well as the religious history of the world, as perfectly as any politician or religionist I have ever met with. He advances ideas which if carried into effect would greatly benefit the nation in point of commerce and finance; and while he maintains and philosophically shows that our country is approaching a fearful crisis, which, if not arrested, will end in disgrace to the country, and cause our national banner to hug its mast in disgust and shame, clearly points out the remedy.

Shall the liberty which our fathers purchased at so dear a price be wrenched from the hand of their children? Shall our national banner, which floated so proudly in the breeze at the Declaration of Independence, be disgraced and refuse to show its motto? Shall we, as American citizens, fold our arms and look quietly on, while the shackles of slavery are being fastened upon our hands, and while men only seek office for the purpose of exalting themselves into power? I say, shall we still rush blindly on and hasten on our own destruction by placing men in power who neither regard the interests of the people nor the prayers of the oppressed? Every American citizen will shout at the top of his voice—no!

Mr. Smith's "Views of the Powers and Policy of the Government" manifest a Republican spirit, and if carried out, would soon place the nation in a prosperous condition and brighten the prospects of those who now toil so incessantly to suppport the profligate expenditures and luxurious equipage of the present rulers and representatives of our nation.

Joseph Smith is a man who is in every way calculated to make a free people happy. He is liberal in his sentiments and allows every man the free expression of his feelings on all subjects; he is sociable and easy in his manners, is conversant and familiar on all exciting topics, expresses himself freely and plainly on the different methods of administering the Government, while he is not ashamed to let the world know his views and criticise upon his opinions.

I am, sir, in no way connected with the Mormon Church, but am disposed to listen to reason in all cases. I have heretofore been a warm advocate of the measures of the Whig party; but, considering General Smith's views and sentiments to be worthy the applause of every citizen of the United States, and especially the yeomanry of the country, I shall in every instance advocate his principles and use my utmost influence in his favor. I am, sir, yours in haste,

AN AMERICAN.

NAUVOO MANSION, May 12, 1844.

Monday 13.—Heavy thunder showers during the night. At 10 a. m. went to my office and conversed with several of the brethren. Sold Ellis M. Sanders one hundred acres of land, received $300 in cash, and his note for $1,000, and $20 for the Temple. Paid Sisson Chase $298 and took up a note of Young, Kimball & Taylor, given for money they had borrowed for me; and gave $10 to Heber C. Kimball.

At 2 p. m. attended meeting of the general council, at which the following letter from Orson Hyde was read:

Letter: Elder Orson Hyde's Report of Labors in Washington: President Smith's Memorial for Western Movement Before Congressmen.

WASHINGTON, April 25, 1844.

HONORED SIR:—I take the liberty to transmit through you to the council of our Church the result of my labors thus far. I arrived in this place on the 23rd instant, by way of Pittsburg. Philadelphia, and New Jersey.

I found Elder Orson Pratt here, Elder Page having been called home to Pittsburg on account of his wife's ill health. Elder Orson Pratt has been indefatigable in his exertions in prosecuting the business entrusted to his charge. His business has been before the Senate, and referred to the Committee on the Judiciary; and the report of said committee is not yet rendered, which is the cause of his delay in writing to you.

Yesterday we conversed with Messrs. Hoge, Hardin, Douglas and Wentworth; and last evening we spent several hours with the Hon. Mr. [James] Semple.* They all appear deeply interested in the Oregon question, and received us with every demonstration of respect that we could desire. Mr. Hoge thought the bill would not pass, from the fact that there already exists between England and America a treaty for the joint occupancy of Oregon, and that any act of our government authorizing an armed force to be raised, and destined for that country, would be regarded by England as an infraction of that treaty, and a cause of her commencing hostilities against us.

But my reply was, These volunteers are not to be considered any part or portion of the army of the United States, neither acting under the direction or authority of the United States; and, said I, for men to go there and settle in the character of emigrants cannot be regarded by our government as deviating in the least degree from her plighted faith, unless she intends to tamely submit to British monopoly in that country.

Mr. Hoge said he would present the memorial, if we desired it. I thanked him for his kind offer, but observed that I was not yet prepared for the bill to be submitted, but wished to elicit all the facts relative to the condition of Oregon, and also advise with many other members relative to the matter; and we could better determine then how the bill

* This was Illinois' senior Senator at the time.

should be introduced. We do not want it presented and referred to a standing committee, and stuck away with five or ten cords of petitions, and that be the last of it; but we want the memorial read, a move made to suspend the rules of the House, and the bill printed, &c.

Mr. Wentworth said, "I am for Oregon, any how. You may set me down on your list, and I will go for you if you will go for Oregon."

Judge Douglas has been quite ill, but is just recovered; he will help all he can; Mr. Hardin likewise. But Major Semple says that he does not believe anything will be done about Texas or Oregon this session, for it might have a very important effect upon the presidential election; and politicians are slow to move when such doubtful and important matters are likely to be effected by it. He says that there are already two bills before the House for establishing a territorial government in Oregon, and to protect the emigrants there; and now, he says, "Were your bill to be introduced, it might be looked upon that you claimed the sole right of emigrating to and settling the new country to the exclusion of others. He was in favor of the Oregon being settled, and he thought the bills already before the House would extend equal protection to us; and equal protection to every class of citizens was what the Government could rightly do, but particular privileges to any one class they could not rightly do."

I observed that the bill asks for no exclusive rights. It asks not for exclusive rights in Oregon, neither do we wish it. Other people might make a move to Oregon, and no prejudices bar their way, and their motives would not be misinterpreted.

But, said I, Missouri knows her guilt; and should we attempt to march to Oregon without the government throwing a protective shield over us, Missouri's crimes would lead her first to misinterpret our intentions, to fan the flame of popular excitement against us, and scatter the firebrands of a misguided zeal among the combustible materials of other places, creating a flame too hot for us to encounter—too desolating for us to indulge the hope of successfully prosecuting the grand and benevolent enterprise we have conceived.* We have been compelled to

*The reason for this reference to Missouri and of possible difficulty arising from the Saints going to Oregon without a guarantee of protection from the general government grew out of the fact that nearly all the early settlers of the Oregon territory were from Missouri. Even in this month of May, 1844, Cornelius Gilliam, the inveterate enemy of the Saints, and who took so prominent a part in the troubles about Far West, was collecting a large company at Independence, Missouri, numbering over three hundred persons, to start for Oregon that season; and all along the Oregon route on the south side of the Platte river, the road was thronged during the next several years by emigrants, very many of whom, and for some time the most of whom, were from Missouri. (*See Western Missouri Expositor*, May 18 1844. Also Bancroft's *Oregon* Vol. I, page 449, *Passim*).

relinquish our rights in Missouri. We have been forcibly driven from our homes, leaving our property and inheritances as spoil to the oppressor; and more or less in Illinois we have been subject to the whims and chimeras of illiberal men, and to threats, to vexatious prosecutions and lawsuits.

Our government professes to have no power to help us, or to redress the wrongs which we have suffered; and we now ask the government to protect us while raising our volunteers. And when we get into Oregon we will protect ourselves and all others who wish our protection. And after subduing a new country, encountering all its difficulties and hardships, and sustaining the just claims of our nation to its soil, we believe that the generosity of our government towards us will be equal to our enterprise and patriotism; and that they will allow us a grant or territory of land, which will be both honorable to them and satisfactory to us.

This, he says, is all very just and reasonable. But still he thinks that Congress will take no step in relation to Oregon, from the fact that his resolution requesting the President of the United States to give notice to the British Government for the abolition of the treaty of joint occupation was voted down; and while that treaty is in force, our government dare do nothing in relation to that country. This resolution was introduced by Mr. Semple to pave the way for the passage of those bills in relation to a territorial government in Oregon.

All our members [Illinois delegation] join in the acknowledgment that you now have an undoubted right to go to Oregon with all the emigrants you can raise. They say the existing laws protect you as much as law can protect you; and should Congress pass an additional law, it would not prevent wicked men from shooting you down as they did in Missouri. All the Oregon men in Congress would be glad we would go to that country and settle it.

I will now give you my opinion in relation to this matter. It is made up from the spirit of the times in a hasty manner, nevertheless I think time will prove it to be correct:—That Congress will pass no act in relation to Texas or Oregon at present. She is afraid of England, afraid of Mexico, afraid the Presidential election will be twisted by it. The members all appear like unskillful players at checkers—afraid to move, for they see not which way to move advantageously. All are figuring and play round the grand and important questions. In the days of our Lord the people neglected the weightier matters of the law, but tithed mint, rue, anise and cummin; but I think here in Washington they do little else than tithe the *mint*.

A member of Congress is in no enviable situation; if he will boldly advocate true principles, he loses his influence and becomes unpopular;

and whoever is committed and has lost his influence has no power to benefit his constituents, so that all go to figuring and playing around the great points.

Mr. Semple said that Mr. Smith could not constitutionally be constituted a member of the army by law; and this, if nothing else, would prevent its passage. I observed that I would in that case strike out that clause. Perhaps I took an unwarrantable responsibility upon myself; but where I get into a straight place I can do no better than act according to what appears most correct.

I do not intend the opinion that I have hastily given shall abate my zeal to drive the matter through, but I have given the opinion for your benefit that your indulgence of the hope that Congress will do something for us may not cause you to delay any important action.

There is already a government established in Oregon to some extent; magistrates have been chosen by the people, &c. This is on the south of the Columbia. North of that river the Hudson Bay Company occupy. There is some good country in Oregon, but a great deal of sandy, barren desert. I have seen a gentleman who has been there, and also in California.

The most of the settlers in Oregon and Texas are our old enemies, the mobocrats of Missouri. If, however, the settlement of Oregon and Texas be determined upon, the sooner the move is made the better; and I would not advise any delay for the action of our government, for there is such jealousy of our rising power already, that government will do nothing to favor us. If the Saints possess the kingdom I think they will have to take it; and the sooner it is done the more easily it is accomplished.

Your superior wisdom must determine whether to go to Oregon, to Texas, or to remain within these United States, and send forth the most efficient men to build up churches, and let them remain the time being; and in the meantime send some wise men among the Indians, and teach them civilization and religion, to cultivate the soil, to live in peace with one another and with all men. But whatever you do, don't be deluded with the hope that government will foster us and thus delay an action for which the present perhaps is the most proper time that ever will be.

Oregon is becoming a popular question: the fever of emigration begins to rage. If the Mormons become the early majority, others will not come; if the Mormons do not become the early majority, the others will not allow us to come.

Elder Pratt is faithful, useful and true; he has got the run of matters here very well, and is with me in all my deliberations, visitings, &c.

Major Semple goes with us this evening to introduce us to the President and to view the White House.

My heart and hand are with you. May heaven bless you and me. As ever, I am

ORSON HYDE.

To the Council of the Church of Jesus Christ of Latter-day Saints.

Also the following letter:

Letter: Orson Hyde's Second Letter from Washington Anent the Western Movement of the Church—the Probable Route.

WASHINGTON, April 26, 1844.

DEAR SIR:—Today I trouble you with another communication, which you will please have the goodness to lay before our council.

We were last evening introduced to the President at the White House by the politeness of Major Semple, where we spent an hour very agree ably. The President is a very plain, homespun, familiar, farmer-like man. He spoke of our troubles in Missouri, and regretted that we had met with such treatment. He asked us how we were getting along in Illinois. I told him that we were contending with the difficulties of a new country, and laboring under disadvantageous consequences of being driven from our property and homes in Missouri.

We have this day had a long conversation with Judge Douglas. He is ripe for Oregon and the California. He said he would resign his seat in Congress if he could command the force that Mr. Smith could, and would be on the march to the country in a month.

I learn that the eyes of many aspiring politicians in this place are upon that country, and that there is so much jealousy between them that they will probably pass no bill in relation to it. Now all these politicians rely upon the arm of the government to protect them there; and if government were to pass an act establishing a Territorial Government west of the Rocky Mountains there would be at once a tremendous rush of emigration; but if government pass no act in relation to it, these men have not stamina or sufficient confidence in themselves and their own resources to hazard the enterprise.

The Northern Whig members are almost to a man against Texas and Oregon; but should the present administration succeed in annexing Texas, then all the Whigs would turn around in favor of Oregon; for if Texas be admitted slavery is extended to the South; then free states must be added to the West to keep up a balance of power between the slave and the free states.

Should Texas be admitted, war with Mexico is looked upon as inevitable. The Senate have been in secret session on the ratification of the treaty of annexation; but what they did we cannot say. General Gaines who was boarding at the same house with Judge Douglas, was secretly ordered to repair to the Texan frontier four days ago, and left immediately. I asked Judge Douglas if that did not speak loud for annexation. He says no. Santa Anna, being a jealous, hot-headed pate, might be suspicious the treaty would be ratified by the Senate, and upon mere suspicion might attempt some hostilities, and Gaines has been ordered there to be on the alert and ready for action, if necessary. Probably our navy will in a few days be mostly in the Guif of Mexico.

There are many powerful checks upon our government, preventing her from moving in any of these important matters; and for aught I know these checks are permitted to prevent our government from extending her jurisdiction over the territory which God designs to give to His Saints. Judge Douglas says he would equally as soon go to that country without an act of Congress as with; "and that in five years a noble state might be formed; and then if they would not receive us into the Union, we would have a government of our own." He is decidedly of the opinion that Congress will pass no act in favor of any particular man going there; but he says if any man will go and desires that privilege, and has confidence in his own ability to perform it, he already has the right, and the sooner he is off the better for his scheme.

It is the opinion here among politicians that it will be extremely difficult to have any bill pass in relation to the encouragement of emigration to Oregon; but much more difficult to get a bill passed designating any particular man to go. But all concur in the opinion that we are authorized already.

In case of a removal to that country, Nauvoo is the place of general rendezvous. Our course from thence would be westward through Iowa bearing a little north until we came to the Missouri River, leaving the state of Missouri on the left, thence onward, until we came to the Platte, thence up the north fork of the Platte to the mouth of the Sweetwater river in longitude 107 degree, 45 W.; and thence up said Sweetwater river to the South Pass of the Rocky Mountains, about eleven hundred miles from Nauvoo; and from said South Pass, in latitude 42°28 north, to the Umpqua and Klamet valleys in Oregon, bordering on California, is about six hundred miles, making the distance from Nauvoo to the best portions of Oregon one thousand seven hundred miles.

There is no government established there; and it is so near California that when a government shall be estalished there, it may readily embrace that country likewise. There is much barren country, rocks and mountains in Oregon; but the valleys are very fertile. I am persuaded that Congress will pass no act in relation to that country, from the fact that the resolution requesting the President to give notice to the British Government for the discontinuance of the treaty of joint occupation of Oregon was voted down with a rush; and this notice must be given before any action can be had unless Congress violates the treaty; at least so say the politicians here.

Judge Douglas has given me a map of Oregon, and also a report on an exploration of the country lying between the Missouri river and the Rocky Mountains on the line of the Kansas and great Platte rivers, by Lieut. J. C. Fremont, of the corps of Topographical Engineers. On receiving it I expressed a wish that Mr. Smith could see it. Judge Douglas says "It is a public document, and I will frank it to him." I accepted his offer, and the book will be forthcoming to you. The people are so eager for it here that they have even stolen it out of the library. The author is Mr. Benton's son-in-law.* Judge Douglas borrowed it of Mr. Benton. I was not to tell any one in this city where I got it. The book is a most valuable document to any one contemplating a journey to Oregon. The directions which I have given may not be exactly correct, but the book will tell correctly. Judge Douglas says he can direct Mr. Smith to several gentlemen in California who will be able to give him any information on the state of affairs in that country: and when he returns to Illinois, he will visit Mr. Smith.

Brother Pratt and myself drafted a bill this morning, and handed it into the committee on the judiciary from the Senate, asking an appropriation of two million dollars for the relief of the sufferers among our people in Missouri in 1836-9, to be deposited in the hands of the City Council of Nauvoo, and by them dealt out to the sufferers in proportion to their loss. We intend to tease them until we either provoke them or get them to do something for us. I have learned this much—that if we want Congress to do anything for us in drawing up our memorial, we must not ask what is right in the matter, but we must ask what kind of a thing will Congress pass? Will it suit the politics of the majority? Will it be popular or unpopular? For you might as well drive a musket ball through a cotton bag, or the Gospel of Christ through the heart of a priest, case-hardened by sectarianism, bigotry and superstition, or a camel through the eye of a needle, as to drive anything through Congress that will operate against the popularity of politicians.

I shall probably leave here in a few days, and Brother Pratt will remain. I go to get money to sustain ourselves with.

I shall write again soon, and let you know what restrictions, if any, are laid upon our citizens in relation to passing through the Indian Territories. I shall communicate everything I think will benefit. In the meantime, if the council have any instructions to give us, we shall be happy to receive them here or at Philadelphia.

John Ross is here; we intend to see him. It is uncertain when Con-

* This was John C. Fremont.

gress rises. It will be a long pull, in my opinion. As ever, I am, yours sincerely,

ORSON HYDE.

P. S.—Elder Pratt's best respects to the brethren.

Willard Richards was instructed to answer the above letters, and Elders Lyman Wight and Heber C. Kimball were instructed to carry the answers.

Council adjourned at 6 p. m.

The steamer *Maid of Iowa* returned from Rock River with four hundred bushels of corn, and two hundred bushels of wheat, which had been purchased for the Temple. At 8 p. m. I went on board with Dr. Willard Richards, and visited Captain Dan Jones.

I insert a lettter which I received from Henry Clay:

Letter: Henry Clay to the Prophet.

ASHLAND, November 15, 1843.

DEAR SIR.—I have received your letter in behalf of the Church of Jesus Christ of Latter-day Saints, stating that you understand that I am a candidate for the presidency, and inquiring what will be my rule of action relative to you as a people should I be elected.

I am profoundly grateful for the numerous and strong expressions of the people in my behalf as a candidate for president of the United States; but I do not so consider myself. That must depend upon future events and upon my sense of duty.

Should I be a candidate, I can enter into no engagements, make no promises, give no pledge to any particular portion of the people of the United States. If I ever enter into that high office I must go into it free and unfettered, with no guarantees but such as are to be drawn from my whole life, character and conduct.

It is not inconsistent with this declaration to say that I have viewed with lively interest the progress of the Latter-day Saints; that I have sympathized in their sufferings under injustice, as it appeared to me, which have been inflicted upon them; and I think, in common with other religious communities, they ought to enjoy the security and protection of the Constitution and the laws.

I am, with great respect, your friend and obedient servant,

H. CLAY.

To Joseph Smith, Esq.

The Prophet's Answer to Clay's Letter.

[Under the date of the Journal's entry here being followed, May 13,

1844, President Smith sent a reply to the above eminent statesman's letter, taking him severely to task for his evident desire to be non-committal with reference to the problem presented by the wrongs which had been inflicted upon the Latter-day Saints by Missouri. Vexed by remembrance of the cruelty and injustice endured by the Saints in Missouri and the general indifference to their suffering among public men, the letter was written in a caustic and, at times, vehement vein.]

I instructed Thomas Bullock to take charge of the books of the *Maid of Iowa* and go on board as clerk.

Tuesday, 14.—Rode out about 7 a. m. The *Maid of Iowa* started for St. Louis at 8:30 a. m.

This afternoon, Mr. Reid, my old lawyer* gave a lecture on the stand, relating the history of some of my first persecutions. I spoke after he closed, and continued my history to the present time, relating some of the doings of the apostates in Nauvoo.

At 4 p. m. prayer meeting; few present. Prayed for Elder Woodworth's daughter, who was sick. Elder Lyman Wight was present.

Wednesday, 15.—At home; much rain through the day; river rising rapidly. Mr. Adams, son of John Quincy Adams, with Dr. Goforth, called to see me at the Mansion.

At 5 p. m. went to my office, and heard my letter to Mr. Clay read. At 7 p. m. rode to the upper landing with Mr. Adams.

I insert the following from the *Times and Seasons:*

STATUS OF AFFAIRS AT NAUVOO.

We take pleasure in announcing to the Saints abroad that Nauvoo continues to flourish, and the little one has become a thousand. Quite a number of splendid houses are being erected, and the Temple is rapidly progressing, insomuch that there is one universal expectation that before next winter closes in upon us the cap-stone will have been raised and the building enclosed.

The Saints continue to flock together from all parts of the wide-spread continent and from the islands of the sea. Three ship's com-

* For the part taken by Mr. Reid in defending the Prophet in those early experiences, see this HISTORY Vol. I, pp. 89-96 and *note* p. 94 *et seq.*

panies have arrived this spring from England, and are now rejoicing in the truths of the everlasting Gospel.

The Prophet is in good health and spirits, and unwearied in his anxiety and labors to instruct the Saints in the things of God and the mysteries of the Kingdom of Jesus Christ. Indeed we may truly say that those who come to scoff remain to pray.

Many have come here filled with prejudice and strange anticipations, but have been convinced that report with her thousand tongues is false, and have almost invariably left a testimony behind them. Instead of finding Mr. Smith the cunning, crafty, and illiterate character that he had been represented to be, they have found in him the gentleman and scholar—open, generous, and brave.

But it is his immediate connections and associates alone that can appreciate his virtues and his talents. While his face is set as a flint against iniquity from every quarter, the cries of the oppressed ever reach his heart, and his hand is ever ready to alleviate the sufferings of the needy.

A few heartless villains can always be found who are watching for his downfall or death; but the Lord has generally caused them to fall into their own pit, and no weapon formed against him has prospered. One or two disaffected individuals have made an attempt to spread dissension; but it is like a tale that is nearly told, and will soon be forgotten.

It was first represented as a monster calculated to spread desolation around; but we are credibly informed by a person who attended their first meeting, that there was much difficulty in raising a committee of seven, for there was some objection to Father——; but as none could be found to fill the vacuum, he constituted one of the seven *stars!*

It will be unneccessary for us to say much about those luminaries of the last days, as they shine forth in their true colors in our columns this week in the trial of President Smith. But to say anything by way of warning to the brethren abroad would resemble the "ocean into tempest tossed, to waft a feather or drown a fly." "By their fruits ye shall know them. Do men gather grapes of thorns or figs of thistles?"

The glad tidings of salvation and the fullness of the Gospel are fast spreading from city to city and from nation to nation. The little stone will still increase till the knowledge of God covers the earth and righteousness and truth extend from pole to pole.

I copy from the *Neighbor*:

WITHDRAWAL OF WILLIAM SMITH AS CANDIDATE FOR THE LEGISLATURE.

To the Friends and Voters of Hancock County: Elder William Smith (late representative) wishes to say to the friends and voters of Hancock county, that in consequence of the sickness of his family, now in the hands of a doctor in the city of Philadelphia, he relinquishes the idea of offering himself as a candidate for a seat in the next Legislature of Illinois; but, as a matter of the highest consideration, would recommend his brother Hyrum Smith as a suitable and capable person to fill that office and worthy of the people's confidence and votes.

We know of no person that would be more qualified to fill his station than General Hyrum Smith (his, William's, brother). We are not informed whether the General will accept of the office or not. If he will, we don't know of any gentleman in Hancock county who would be more competent. General Smith is a man of sterling integrity, deep penetration and brilliant talents. He is well versed in politics and as unchangeable as the everlasting hills. He is a man of probity and virtue, and an unwavering patriot.

If General Hyrum Smith will allow his name to be brought forth, we go it for him; and we know from the confidence and respect that are entertained for him as a gentleman and a patriot, he will be elected. What say you, General?

Thursday, 16.—Went to my office at 8 a. m., and heard a letter written by Elder Willard Richards, in behalf of the council to Elders Orson Hyde and Orson Pratt at Washington.

I ordered the Municipal Court to meet at one p. m. and spent the morning in reading.

Session of Municipal Court—Case of Jeremiah Smith.

At one p, m. I presided in Municipal Court. The case of Jeremiah Smith, Sen., who had been arrested by Jones on the charge of procuring money under false pretenses, came up on *habeas corpus*. The complainant, T. B. Johnson, by his counsel, Chauncey L. Higbee, asked for and obtained an adjournment for one week in order to procure witnesses. The petitioner by his counsel, George P. Stiles, objected to the plea, supposing the prosecuting party always ready for a trial. The court decided that it was an important case, and it was not best to be in haste; and if the prisoner is discharged on the merits of the case after a full investigation, he goes free forever. The majority of the court decided to adjourn until Thursday next.

I was about home the rest of the day and read in the

Neighbor the report of the trial in the Municipal Court on the 8th inst.

The following appears in the *Times and Seasons:*

LETTER: WILLIAM CLAYTON DESCRIBING THE FARCICAL PROCEEDINGS OF THE COURT AT DIXON IN THE CASE OF JOSEPH SMITH VS. JOSEPH H. REYNOLDS OF MISSOURI AND HARMON T. WILSON.

DEAR SIR.—I have just returned from the north part of this state, where I have been on business for our beloved President Joseph Smith; and it feels so good to breathe the pure air of liberty and friendship after spending some three or four days in a swamp, or rather a slough of religious prejudice and political hypocrisy, which are equally nauseous and offensive, that I cannot let this opportunity pass without giving vent to some of my feelings in regard to what passed while I remained at Dixon, on Rock River.

My principle business was to appear in the Lee county Circuit Court as a witness in the case of Joseph Smith, *vs.* Joseph H. Reynolds and Harmon T. Wilson, for false imprisonment and using unnecessary force and violence in arresting the plaintiff.

A plea had been entered in this suit by this counsel for the defendants, to which the counsel for the plaintiff demurred. The demurrer was argued on Wednesday morning, the 8th inst., and the parties finally joined issue on the charge of using unnecssary force and violence; and the court gave permission, by consent of the bar, to proceed with the trial, but the counsel not being fully prepared, it was laid over until the following morning, the 9th inst.

On Thursday morning, after the usual preliminaries of opening court, the above case was called up for trial, and the clerk ordered to impanel a jury; and here, sir, a scene took place which ought to make every honest American citizen blush and weep for the credit and honor of his country and laws. A number of men were called up, and when questioned as to whether they had previously expressed opinions in relation to the suit now pending, nearly the whole answered in the affirmative. The further question was then put as to whether they had any prejudice against either of the parties; to which a great majority replied they had against Smith. They were then questioned as to what their prejudice had reference—his religious sentiments, or general course of conduct. The greater part replied, to his religious sentiments; and the remainder said they were opposed to his general course of conduct.

About twenty men had to be called upon, one after another, out of the number the court finally selected twelve as competent jurors though the majority of these decidedly expressed their feelings of prejudice against the plaintiff. They were, however, accepted on the ground that they said they thought they could do justice to both parties, although some of them expressed a doubt whether they could do justice or not.

The jury being sworn, the court, or rather the counsel, proceeded to examine the witnesses on the part of the plaintiff, which occupied nearly the whole day. But little of the real matter of fact could be set before the court on account of their being confined to the charge of unnecesary force and violence; but this was proven in the clearest point of light.

I must refer to the testimony of old Mr. Dixon, whose silvery locks seem to tell an age of many years. His evidence related to the circumstance of the Missouri sheriff refusing for a length of time to give the plaintiff the privilege of *habeas corpus*, and threatening to drag him to Missouri in fifteen minutes from the time they arrived at Dixon. The old gentleman seemed to tremble with indignation while relating the simple facts as they transpired at the time; and, like a true lover of his country, appeared proud of the privilege of telling those men that the citizens of Dixon would not suffer themselves to be disgraced by permitting them to drag away a citizen of this state to a foreign state for trial, without the privilege of a trial by *habeas corpus*—a privilege which is guaranteed to every individual under like circumstances, and especially when it was understood that he was to be dragged to Missouri, amongst a people whose hands are yet dripping with the blood of murdered innocence, and who thirst for the blood of General Joseph Smith as the howling wolf thirsts for his prey. Surely such a picture would melt the heart of anything but an adamantine. There are those, and men too who profess to be the followers of the Lord Jesus Christ, who can hear such things and still wish the Missourians had got General Smith to Missouri to murder him without judge or jury, and surely they are no better than murderers themselves, and only lack the opportunity to make them shedders of innocent blood.

After the evidence was through on the part of the plaintiff, the witness for the defense was examined, which only occupied a few minutes. The arguments were then advanced on both sides, during which time I could not help noticing how apt the respectable gentleman of the opposite counsel was to sing the song of "old Joe Smith," &c., which might appear very gentlemanly in his mind, but to me it seemed as contemptible as the voice of a stupid ass, or the tongue of slander.

Finally the case was submitted to the jury, who were charged by the court, and then ordered to retire and bring in a sealed verdict the following morning at nine o'clock. Friday morning came and with it the verdict, and it proved to be in favor of the plaintiff and against the detendants for forty dollars and costs of suit. I confess I was astonished when I heard it, and could not help thinking that prejudice sometimes overrules justice even in the jury box. I could not help comparing the results of this trial with one which came off the day previous, wherein a certain person complained of another for destroying his cow by setting his dogs on the animal until they worried her. It appeared the cow of the plaintiff had seen fit to break into the defendant's lot without asking leave, and the defendant, or rather his men, not liking such treatment, set the dogs on her and destroyed her. Well, the result of this trial was a verdict of damages for the plaintiff of thirty dollars and costs!

Now, sir, compare the two cases. On the one hand here is a citizen of the United States near two hundred miles from his home and his friends; he is on a visit with his family, not dreaming of danger or difficulty. Two men—or rather wolves in sheep's clothing—for it is a fact that when Wilson and Reynolds made inquiry for General Smith at Dixon at the time of the arrest, they said they were "Mormon Elders," and wanted to see President Smith, &c.—two men, I say, while he is thus enjoying himself with his family, came upon him with each a loaded pistol in his hand, and threatened to shoot him dead if he offered the least resistance, although no resistance had been offered. They then began to haul him about; and when he asked them what they wanted with him, and what was their authority, they replied they were going to take him to Missouri; and jamming their pistols at his side, swore that was their authority. He requested them to let him go into the house to bid his family good-by; but this they positively refused, not even giving him the privilege to get his hat. They then forced him into the wagon and placing themselves one on each side, with a loaded pistol pressed close against his side, and repeatedly striking him with them, so as to make him lame and sore for two weeks afterwards, they drove him to Dixon, and ordered horses ready in fifteen minutes to drag him among his murderers, and otherwise abused, insulted, threatened, and treated him in the cruelest manner possible, filling his family with the most excruciating pangs, and rending the heart of his beloved companion with grief to witness their ferocious cruelty, not knowing but his life would be sacrificed before morning; and finally pursued their persecutions until it cost him from $3,500 to $5,000 expenses; and all this without a cause; and when he sues for justice against these men, he obtains damages to the amount of forty dollars!

On the other hand, a man loses a cow which had broke into his neighbor's lot, and he obtained damages to the amount of thirty dollars.

Now, sir, if this is not the effects of prejudice amounting to oppression, then I am no judge of right and wrong. I am very much inclined to think that if General Joseph Smith or any of his friends had treated any citizen of this state or any other state in the manner he was treated by these men, and they had sued for damages as he did, the case would have terminated very differently. However, so it is.

The idea of a man yielding to such a degree of prejudice as to render him incapable of executing justice between man and man, merely from rumor and report, is to me perfectly ridiculous and contemptible,as well as wicked and unjust. And when a man is all the day long boasting of the rights and privileges guaranteed to every citizen of the United States under the Constitution and laws, and at the same time is so prejudiced against one of the most peaceable citizens that he does not know whether he can render him justice in a court of equity,but would rather strengthen the hands of mobocrats and law-breakers, the inference that one must naturally draw is that such a man is a consummate scoundrel and hypocrite, or that he is guilty of the most flagrant violation of the most sacred constitutional principles embraced in the fundamental doctrines of this republic. I am happy, sir, to have evidence daily that no such corrupt prejudice exists in the heart of General Joseph Smith, nor in the community, so far as I have been able to discover.

Now, as to the exceptions these men have taken in regard to General Smith's religious views or general course of conduct, it matters not much. His religious views are his inalienable right, and are nobody's business; and the man who cannot render him justice on that account is a wilful violator of the laws he professes to admire; and, sir, I have for more than two years last past been a close observer of General Smith's general course of conduct, as well as his private life; and justice to him, to myself, and the community at large, compels me to say that, in all my intercourse with men, I never associated with a more honorable, upright, charitable, benevolent,and law-abiding man than is the much persecuted General Smith; and, sir, when I hear men speak reproachfully of him, I never ask for a second evidence of their corruptness and baseness. General Smith, sir, is a man of God, a man of truth, and a lover of his country; and never did I hear him breathe out curses or raillery at any man because he saw fit to differ in religious matters. Shame on the principle—shame on the man or set of men who show themselves so degraded and miserably corrupt.

The last night of our stay at Dixon, I had the privilege of speaking on the principles of my religion to a number of individuals in a kind of argument with two men; and, sir, although it is near some four years since I have made a practice of preaching, it felt as sweet as ever. Truth to an honest heart is sweet, but to a wicked man is like a piercing sword, as was manifest on that occasion; for although the principles of the Gospel were laid down so plain and clear that it was impossible to misunderstand, yet the opposing party repeatedly misconstrued my language, and even his own admission.

I cannot persuade myself that the prejudice referred to above is a general thing. There are many honorable exceptions, and I presume if the Mormons had signified their intentions of supporting the Democratic candidate for the presidency at the ensuing election, instead of nominating an independent candidate of their own choice, their prejudice would not have been so great at the trial of Reynolds and Wilson, and perhaps General Smith would have obtained a judgment somewhat equivalent to the injuries he sustained from that unholy prosecution. But the Mormon people are too noble-minded to be bought or biased by fear or favor, and have been too often deceived by the plausible pretensions of demagogues to put trust in any but tried friends. General Smith has ever been an undeviating friend, not only to this community, but to the oppressed of every name or society, and we consider him as competent and qualified for the highest office of the United States as any other man, and a little more so; and a great deal more worthy of it.

In conclusion, let me say that whatever others may say, I consider it an honor to be associated with such a man as General Joseph Smith, and all true followers of the Lord Jesus Christ; and the more wicked men despise and misrepresent the principles and conduct of President Smith, the more I love him and delight in his society; and this I can do without prejudice or animosity against any man or set of men. I believe in the broad principle of equal rights and privileges, so far as religion or politics are concerned; and while I seek to enjoy my religion according to the knowledge in me, I will interfere with the rights of no man, nor persecute because my neighbor does not think as I do.

A multitude of business compels me to close, and I must forbear. I have the honor to be your brother in the everlasting covenant.

WILLIAM CLAYTON.

NAUVOO, May 16, 1844.

From the *Neighbor*:—

STEAMBOAT ELECTION.

On the last upward voyage of the *Osprey* from St. Louis to this place as usual, the merits of the several candidates for the next Presidential election were discussed. A vote was taken, and the following was the state of the polls as handed to us by a gentleman who came as passenger:—

General Joseph Smith, 26 gentlemen, 3 ladies.

Henry Clay, 6 gentlemen, 2 ladies.

Van Buren, 2 gentlemen, 0 ladies.

The ladies are altogether forsaking Van Buren, and the gentlemen as a matter of course are following after. There is a wonderful shrinkage in Henry Clay, but the General is going it with a rush. *Hurrah for the General!*

CHAPTER XVIII.

THE STATE PRESIDENTIAL CONVENTION AT NAUVOO—THE STATES REPRESENTED—SPEECH OF JOHN S. REID, ESQ.—EARLY DAYS WITH THE PROPHET.

Friday, May 17, 1844.—The State Convention met in the assembly room. I copy the minutes.

State Convention at Nauvoo.

Convention met according to appointment, and was organized by appointing General Uriah Brown to the chair, and Dr. F. Merryweather secretary.

Dr. G. W. Goforth presented the following letter, and took his seat in the convention. Several letters of the same character were presented by other gentlemen, but we have not room to insert them.

MUSCOUTAH, ST. CLAIR COUNTY, ILL., May 4th, 1844.

Mr. G. W. Goforth:

Sir,—At various meetings held in this county, where I had the honor of attending, and the interesting topic of the selection of a suitable person for the high station of President of the United States being at this time the most important to Americans, and with the names that are now before the people, Joseph Smith of Nauvoo is recognized respectfully as a candidate, declarative in the principles of Jeffersonianism, or Jefferson democracy, free trade, and sailor's rights, and the protection of person and property.

A convention being about to be held in the City of Nauvoo on the 17th of this month (May), your name has been on every occasion given as a delegate to said convention, and through me the message to be imparted you, asking you to represent our expressions in the case.

Please say for us, as Americans, that we will support General Joseph Smith in preference to any other man that has given, or suffered his name to come before us as a candidate. And at the great Baltimore Convention, to be held on the 13th of July, our delegation to said convention be authorized to proclaim for us submission to the nominee as may be by them brought before the people, in case of a failure to nominate Joseph Smith (our choice), and unite approbatively for his support.

Respectfully, sir, this communication and authority usward is forwarded you as your voucher at said convention, with our hearty prayers for the success of him whose special name is given in the important affairs.

HENRY B. JACOBS,
Agent for the friends of General Joseph Smith.

Mr. Clay's letter to General Joseph Smith was then read by Mr. Phelps, and also General Joseph Smith's rejoinder, which was applauded by three cheers.

It was moved and seconded that the following gentlemen be appointed a committee to draft resolutions for the adoption of this convention:—

Dr. G. W. Goforth, John Taylor, Wm. W. Phelps, William Smith, and Lucian R. Foster.

It was moved and seconded that he correspondence of the Central Committee for Government Reform of New York be read by W. W. Phelps, also General Joseph Smith's answer to the same.

NEW YORK, April 20, 1844.

Joseph Smith, Esq.,

SIR,—The subscribers, the Central Committee of the National Reform Association, in accordance with a duty prescribed by their constitution, respectively solicit an expression of your views as a candidate for public office, on a subject that, as they think, vitally affects the rights and interests of their constituents.

We see this singular condition of affairs, and while wealth in our country is rapidly accumulating, while internal improvements of every description are fast increasing, and while machinery has multiplied the power of production to an immense extent, yet with all these national advantages, the compensation for useful labor is getting less and less.

We seek the cause of this anomaly, and we trace it to the monopoly of the land, which places labor at the mercy of capital. We therefore desire to abolish the monopoly, not by interfering with the conventional rights of persons now in possession of the land, but by arresting the further sale of all lands not yet appropriated as private property, and by allowing these lands hereafter to be freely occupied by those who may choose to settle on them.

We propose that the public lands hereafter shall not be owned, but occupied only, the occupant having the right to sell or otherwise dispose of improvements to any one not in possession of other land; so that, by preventing any individual from becoming possessed of more than a limited quantity, every one may enjoy the right.

This measure, we think, would gradually establish an equilibrium between the agricultural and other useful occupations, that would ensure to all full employment and fair compensation for their labor, on the lands now held as private property, and to each individual on the public lands the right to work for himself on his own premises, or for another, at his option.

An answer, as soon as convenient, will much oblige your fellow-citizens.

JOHN WINDT,
EGBERT S. MANNING,
JAMES MAXWELL,
LEWIS MASQUERIER,
DANIEL WITTER,
GEORE H. EVANS.
ELLIS SMALLEY.

NAUVOO, ILL., May 16th, 1844.

To John Windt, Egbert S. Manning, James Maxwell, Lewis Masquerier, Daniel Witter, George H. Evans, and Ellis Smalley, Esqrs.

GENTLEMEN:—

Your communication of April 20th, soliciting my views relative to the public lands, is before me; and I answer, that as soon as the greater national evils could be remedied by the consolidated efforts of a virtuous people and the judicious legislation of wise men, so that slavery could not occupy one-half of the United States for speculation, competition, prodigality, and fleshy capital, and so that enormous salaries, stipends, fees, perquisites, patronage, and the wages of spiritual wickedness in ermine and lace could not swallow up forty or fifty millions of public revenue, I would use all honorable means to bring the wages of mechanics and farmers up,and salaries of public servants down,increase labor and money by a judicious tariff, and advise the people—who are only the sovereigns of the soil—to petition Congress to pass a uniform land law! that the air, the water, and the land, of the asylum of the oppressed, might be free to free men!

With consideration of the highest regard for unadulterated freedom I have the honor to be your obedient servant.

JOSEPH SMITH.

After which, the meeting adjourned for one hour.

It was moved and seconded that the following gentlemen be constituted a committee to appoint electors for this State:—

Dr. G. W. Goforth, L. Robinson, L. N. Scoville, Peter Hawes, and John S. Reid.

It was moved and seconded that the following gentlemen be constituted a central committee of correspondence, having power to increase their number:—

Dr. Willard Richards, Dr. J. M. Bernhisel, W. W. Phelps, and Lucian R. Foster.

The following delegates from the different states of the Union were then received by vote:—

NAMES.	COUNTIES.	STATES.
Dr. G. W. Goforth	St. Clair	Illinois
Meyers, Esq.,	Adams	"
J. Sene,	Quincy	"
A. Badlock,	Joe Davis,	"
J. C. Wright,	Scott,	"
L. Wight,	Crawford,	"
S. Brown,	Brown,	"
W. B. Idle,	Sangamon,	"
J. Browning,	Adams,	"
W. W Phelps,	Hancock,	"
W. Green,	"	"
Ebenezer Robinson,	"	"
Johh Taylor,	"	"
Henry G. Sherwood,	"	"
F. Merryweather,	"	"
John S. Reid, Esq.,	Chemung	New York.
E. Reece, Esq.,	Buffalo,	"
L. R. Foster,	New York City,	"
Dr. J. M. Bernhisel,	"	"
Hugh Herinshaw,	West Chester,	"
E. Thompson,	"	"
S. A. Perry,	Essex,	"
Wm. Miller,	Livingston,	"
Mr. Dorlan,	Kings,	"
E. Swakhammer,	New York City,	"
P. Bowen,	Chester,	Pennsylvania.
W. Smith,	Philadelphia,	"
J. H. Newton,	"	"
Edward Hunter,	West Chester,	"
E. Woolley,	Columbiana.	Ohio
W. G. Ware,	Cincinnati,	"
Thos. Martin,	Hamilton,	"
C. Brooks,	Lake,	"
Dusten Arne,	"	"
W. W. Dryer,	Lorain,	"
M. J. Coltrin,	Cuyahoga,	"
W. Vanausdell,	Green Briar,	Virginia.
L. B. Lewis,		Massachusetts

Dr. Willard Richards,	Berkshire,	Massachusetts.
E. Dougherty,	Essex,	New Jersey.
W. Richardson,	Burlington,	"
J. Horner,	Monmouth,	"
Thomas Atkins,	Burlington,	"
Capt. R. Jones,	New Orleans,	Louisiana.
E. Ludington,	"	"
J. Harman	Monroe,	Mississippi.
Mr. Palman,	"	"
S. Gully,	Lawrence,	"
E. M. Sanders,	"	Delaware.
E. F. Sheets,	"	"
J. Hatch,	Alice,	Vermont.
J. Houston,	Madison,	"
J. A. Mikesell,	"	Missouri.
Col. Cowan,	Oxford,	Maine.
M. Anderson,	Rutherford,	Tennessee.
H. Stout,	Mercer,	Kentucky.
Gen. G. Miller,	Madison,	"
Mr. Hunt,	Switzerland,	Indiana.
A. Johnson,	Middletown,	Connecticut.
L. N. Scovil,		Maryland.
Dr. L. Richards,	Providence,	Rhode Island.
M. Wilber,		"
J. S. Swiss,		New Hampshire.
Dr. Shenask,		Michigan.
Abraham Williams,		Georgia.
J. Haws,		Alabama.
R. Alexander,	Union District,	South Carolina.
Y. Maccauslin,	Randolph,	North Carolina.
D. J. Putton,		Iowa.
Capt. Hathaway,*		Arkansas.

It was moved, seconded, and carried by acclamation. that General Joseph Smith, of Illinois, be the choice of this convention for President of the United States.

It was moved, seconded, and carried by acclamation, that Sidney Rigdon, Esq., of Pennsylvania, be the choice of the Convention for Vice-President of the United States.

The nine following resolutions were then adopted, the fifth of which was carried by acclamation.

Resolutions.

1. *Resolved*, that from all the facts and appearances that are now

* It is to be observed that these delegates named from the various States were now, and for some time past had been, residents of Nauvoo, Ill.

visible in the United States. we believe that much imbecility and fraud is practiced by the officers of Government; and that to remedy these evils it is highly necessary that a virtuous people should arise in the panoply of their might, and with one heart and one mind correct these abuses by electing wise and honorable men to fill the various offices of Government.

2. *Resolved*, that as union is power, the permanency and continuance of our political institutions depend upon the correction of the abuses.

3. *Resolved*, that as all political parties of the present day have degraded themselves by adhering more or less to corrupt principles and practices, by fomenting discord and division among the people, being swallowed in the vortex of party spirit and sectional prejudices, until they have become insensible to the welfare of the people and the general good of the country; and knowing that there are good men among all parties, in whose bosoms burn the fire of pure patriotism, we invite them, by the love of liberty, by the sacred honor of freemen, by the patriotism of the illustrious fathers of our freedom, by the glorious love of country, and by the holy principles of '76, to come over and help us to reform the Government.

4. *Resolved*, that to redress all wrongs, the government of the United States, with the President at its head, is as powerful in its sphere as Jehovah is in His.

5. *Resolved*, that the better to carry out the principles of liberty and equal rights, Jeffersonian democracy, free trade, and sailor's rights, and the protection of person and property, we will support General Joseph Smith, of Illinois, for the President of the United States at the ensuing election.

6, *Resolved*, that we will support Sidney Rigdon, Esq., of Pennsylvania, for the Vice-Presidency.

7. *Resolved*, that we will hold a National Convention at Baltimore on Saturday, the 13th day of July.

8. *Resolved*, that we call upon the honest men of all parties in each state to send their delegates to said convention.

9. *Resolved*, that all honest editors throughout the United States are requested to publish the above resolutions.

10. *Resolved*, that those gentlemen who stand at the head of the list, who have gone to the several states to take charge of our political interests, be requested to use every exertion to appoint electors in the several electoral districts of the States which they represent, and also to send delegates to the Baltimore Convention.

11. *Resolved*, that Dr. Goforth and John S. Reid, Esq., be requested to furnish a copy of their speeches for publication.

12. *Resolved*, that the electors be instructed to make stump speeches in their different districts.

13. *Resolved*, that the thanks of this meeting be given to Mr. Hancock for his patriotic song.

It was moved and seconded that Orson Hyde, Heber C. Kimball, David S. Hollister, Orson Pratt, and Lyman Wight represent this convention at the convention to be held in Baltimore on the 13th of July next.

Sidney Rigdon, Esq., then addressed the meeting, and was succeeded by the following gentlemen:—Gen. Joseph Smith, Dr. G. W. Goforth, Lyman Wight, W. W. Phelps, John Taylor, Hyrum Smith, and John S. Reid, Esq.

It was moved, seconded, and carried, that the thanks of this meeting be given to the chairman and secretary.

The Convention was addressed in an eloquent speech by Sidney Rigdon, Esq., showing the political dishonesty of both Henry Clay and Martin VanBuren, and stating his views, and the present condition of the country.

Dr. Goforth rose and addressed the convention. [Dr. Goforth dealt chiefly with the past glories of the republic, and the wrongs suffered by the Latter-day Saints in Missouri].

*Synopsis of the Remarks of Hon. John S. Reid.**

Mr. Chairman:

I cannot leave this subject and do justice to my own feelings and the character of Gen. Smith, without giving a short history of the first persecution that came upon him in the counties of Chenango and Broome, in the State of New York, commenced by that class of people calling themselves Christians.

The first acquaintance I had with Gen. Smith was about the year 1823. He came into my neighborhood, being then about eighteen years of age, and resided there two years; during which time I became intimately acquainted with him. I do know that his character was irreproachable; that he was well known for truth and uprightness; that he moved in the first circles of the community, and he was often spoken of as a young man of intelligence and good morals, and possessing a mind susceptible of the highest intellectual attainments.

I early discovered that his mind was constantly in search of truth, expressing an anxious desire to know the will of God concerning His children here below, often speaking of those things which professed Christians believe in. I have often observed to my best informed friends

* This was the "former lawyer" who defended the Prophet in his first prosecution in the State of New York, before local justices of the peace in Chenango and Broome counties, 1830; see this HISTORY, vol. I, ch. XX.

(those that were free from superstition and bigotry) that I thought Joseph was predestinated by his God from all eternity to be an instrument in the hands of the great Dispenser of all good to do a great work. What it was I knew not. After living in that neighborhood about three years, enjoying the good feelings of his acquaintance as a worthy youth, he told his particular friends that he had had a revelation from God to go to the west about eighty miles to his father's, in which neighborhood he should find hid in the earth an old history written on golden plates, which would give great light and knowledge concerning the will of God towards His people in this generation, unfolding the destiny of all nations, kindreds and tongues. He said that he distinctly heard the voice of him that spake. Joseph Knight, one of the fathers of your Church, a worthy man, and my intimate friend, went with him. When I reflect upon our former friendship, Mr. Chairman, and upon the scenes that he had passed through in consequence of mal-administration, mobocracy and cruelty, I feel to lift up my voice to high heaven, and pray God to bless the aged veteran, and that his silver locks may go down to the grave in peace, like a shock of corn fully ripe. In a few days his friends [Joseph Smith's] returned with the glad news that Joseph had found the plates and had gone down to his father-in-law's for the purpose of translating them. I believe he remained there until he finished the translation. After the book was published, he came to live in the neighborhood of Father Knight's, about four miles from me, and began to preach the Gospel; and many were pricked in their hearts, believed, and were baptized in the name of the Lord Jesus. He soon formed a Church at Colesville; his meetings were numerously attended, and the eyes of all people were upon him with astonishment. Oh, Mr. Chairman, the world was turned upside down at once, and the devil,—always ready to assist and help along in all difficulties that arise among men—personified in some of the religionists, began to prick up his ears and jump, and kick and run about, like Jim Crow, calling for rotten eggs to help in the wake. You would have thought, sir, that Gog and Magog were let loose on the young man. He called upon the world's people (as they are called) but got no help; he then flew about in the sectarian churches, like lightning, and they immediately came to his aid, and uniting their efforts, roared against him like the thunders of Mount Sinai. When those fiery bigots were let loose, they united in pouring the red hot vials of their wrath upon his head. Their cry of "False Prophet! False Prophet!" was sounded from village to village, and every foul epithet that malice and wicked ingenuity could invent were heaped upon him. Yes, sir; the same spirit that influenced the Presbyterians of Massachusetts about one hundred and fifty years ago, in their persecution of the Quakers, when they first began to preach their doctrines in that state, was fully manifested by those religious bigots, who were afraid if they let them alone, their own doctrines would come to naught. What was the result of the persecution in Massachusetts? Why, sir, warrants were made out by those churches having authority, and the Quakers were tried for heresy. But what was the result of those trials. The sentence of death was passed upon the Quakers for heresy by those religious fanatics, and three of them were hanged by the neck on Bloody Hill, in Boston, to make expiation for that unpardonable crime. "Tell it not in Gath," nor publish it not on the tops of the mountains in this boasted land of freedom, that the Puritans of New England, who had fled from the Old World in consequence of religious intolerance, that they might enjoy the sweets of liberty, so soon became persecutors themselves, and shed innocent blood, which still cries aloud from the dust for vengeance upon their heads. Let shame cover our faces when we mention the name of freedom in our grand republic.

O my God! when in one portion of our country blood is flowing from the crime of worshiping our Creator according to the dictates of conscience, or as the Spirit directs, and in the other are great rejoicings in consequence thereof, where, I ask, is the boasted freedom for which our fathers fought and bled?

O Thou who holdest the destinies of all things in Thine hands here below, return these blessings unto us, that we may keep them as precious jewels till time is no more. But, Mr. Chairman, I am wandering too far from the subject. I will return to the persecutions which followed General Smith, when his cheeks blossomed with the beauty of youth, and his eyes sparkled with innocence.

These bigots soon made up a false accusation against him, and had him arraigned before Joseph Chamberlain, a justice of the peace, a man who was always ready to deal out justice to all, and a man of great discernment of mind.

The case came up about 10 o'clock a. m. I was called upon to defend the prisoner, the prosecutors employed the best counsel they could get, and ransacked the town of Bainbridge and county of Chenango for witnesses that would swear hard enough to convict the prisoner; but they entirely failed. Yes, sir; let me say to you that not one blemish nor spot was found against his character. He came from that trial, notwithstanding the mighty efforts that were made to convict him of crime by his vigilant persecutors, with his character unstained by even the appearance of guilt.

The trial closed about twelve o'clock at night. After a few moments' deliberation, the court pronounced the words, "Not guilty," and the prisoner was discharged. But, alas! the devil, not satisfied with his defeat, stirred up a man not unlike himself, who was more fit to dwell among the fiends of hell than to belong to the human family, to go to Colesville and get another writ and take him to Broome county for another trial. They were sure they could send that boy to hell or to Texas, they did not care which; and in half an hour after he was discharged by the court, he was arrested again, and on the way to Colesville for another trial.

I was again called upon by his friends to defend him against his malignant persecutors, and clear him from the false charges they had preferred against him. I made every reasonable excuse I could, as I was nearly worn down through fatigue and want of sleep, as I had been engaged in lawsuits for two days and nearly the whole of two nights. But I saw the persecution was great against him; and here let me say, Mr. Chairman, singular as it may seem, while Mr. Knight was pleading with me to go, a peculiar impression or thought struck my mind that I must go and defend him, for he was the Lord's anointed. I did not know what it meant, but thought I must go and clear the Lord's anointed. I said I would go, and started with as much faith as the Apostles had when they could remove mountains, accompanied by Father Knight, who was like the old patriarch that followed the ark of God to the city of David.

We rode on till we came to the house of Hezekiah Peck, where a number of Mormon women were assembled, as I was informed, for the purpose of praying for the deliverance of the Prophet of the Lord. The women came out to our wagon, and Mrs. Smith among the rest.

O my God, sir, what were my feeling when I saw that woman who had but a few days before given herself, heart and hand, to be a consort for life, and that so soon her crimson cheeks must be wet with tears that came streaming from her eyes! Yes, sir; it seemed that her very heart strings would be broken with grief. My feelings, sir, were moved with pity and sorrow for the afflicted, and on the other hand they were wrough up to the highest pitch of indignation against those fiends of hell who had thus caused the innocent to suffer.

The next morning about ten o'clock, the court was organized. The prisoner was to be tried by three justices of the peace, that his departure out of the county might be made sure. Neither talents nor money were wanting to ensure them success. They employed the ablest lawyer in that county, and introduced twenty witnesses before dark, but proved nothing.

They sent out runners and ransaked the hills and vales, grog-shops and ditches, gathered together a company that looked as if they had come from hell, and had been whipped by the soot-boy thereof, which they brought forward to testify one after another, but with no better success. Although they wrung and twisted into every shape, in trying to tell something that would criminate the prisoner, nothing was proven against him whatever.

Having got through with the examination of their witnesses about two o'clock in the morning, the case was argued about two hours. There was not one particle of testimony against the prisoner. No, sir; he came out like the three children from the fiery furnace, without the smell of fire upon his garments.

The court deliberated upon the case for half an hour with closed doors, and then we were called in. The court arraigned the prisoner and said—"Mr. Smith, we have had your case under consideration, examined the testimony, and find nothing to condemn you; and therefore you are discharged."

They then proceeded to reprimand him severely—not because anything derogatory to his character in any shape had been proven against him by the host of witnesses that had testified during the trial, but merely to please those fiends in human shape who were engaged in the unhallowed persecution of an innocent man, sheerly on account of his religious opinions.

After they had got through, I arose and said—"This court puts me in mind of a certain trial held before Felix of old, when the enemies of Paul arraigned him before that venerable judge for some alleged crime, and nothing was found in him worthy of death or bonds. Yet, to please the Jews who were his accusers, he was left bound, contrary to law, and the court had served Mr. Smith in the same way, by their unlawful and uncalled for reprimand after his discharge to please his accusers."

We got him away that night from the midst of three hundred people without his receiving any injury; but I am well aware that we were assisted by some higher power than man; for to look back on the scene, I cannot tell how we succeeded in getting him away. I take no glory to myself: it was the Lord's work, and marvelous in our eyes.

This, Mr. Chairman, is a true history of the first persecution that came upon General Smith in his youth among professed Christians, and in a country heralded to the ends of the earth as a land of freedom, where all men have the constitutional right to worship as they please and believe what they please, without molestation, so long as they do not interfere with the rights and privileges of others—yes, sir; a persecution got up through the influence of religious bigotry by as vile a set of men as ever disgraced the family of man. But their devices against him were brought to naught by the Overruling Power that controls all things and brings to naught the counsels of the wicked.

Mr. Chairman, little did I think that I was defending a boy that would rise to eminence like this man—a man whom God delights to honor as a

Prophet and leader of His people—one to whom He has given the keys of heaven and earth, and the power of David, and said to him, Whatever you bind on earth shall be bound in heaven, and the gates of hell shall not prevail against you. And may he live to put his foot upon the neck of his enemies in love and meekness! I know, sir, that God has made him a leader of many thousands of people; and may he teach them in meekness and with that wisdom and judgment that God shall direct.

I add no more.

The Convention adjourned *sine die*

URIAH BROWN, President,
F. MERRRYWEATHER, Secretary.

I rode out in the afternoon.

About 6 p. m., a caucus was held; but, Emma being sick, I could not attend. At night a large assemblage burned a barrel of tar in the street. I went out to see what was the matter, and found they were giving toasts; and as soon as they became aware of my presence, they carried me on their shoulders twice round the fire, and escorted me to the Mansion by a band of music.

Elders Eranklin D. Richards and Joseph A. Stratton were ordained High Priests and set apart to go on a mission to England by Elders Brigham Young and Heber C. Kimball and Willard Richards.

CHAPTER XIX.

CHARGES AGAINST PRESIDENT SMITH BEFORE THE CIRCUIT COURT—HIS VOLUNTARY APPEARANCES AT COURT—TREATMENT—RETURN TO NAUVOO.

Saturday, May 18, 1844.—At 9 a. m., I went with Heber C. Kimball to visit President Brigham Young, and afterwards went out to the regimental training, and also in the afternoon riding on my horse, "Joe Duncan."

At 5 p. m., two cannons were fired opposite my old house, and the regiments were dismissed.

The high Council cut off from the Church James Blakesley, Francis M. Higbee, Charles Ivins, and Austin Cowles, for apostasy.

Sunday, 19.—Cloudy morning; rain about noon. I remained at home. Elder Lyman Wight preached at the stand in the morning. The usual prayer meeting at 2 p m. was dispensed with on account of the mud and rain.

In the evening I talked to the brethren at my house, Esquire Reid, my old lawyer, being present. W. W. Phelps read my last letter to Henry Clay to the company.

Monday, 20.—Emma continued very sick, and I was with her most of the time.

At 10 a. m., there was a meeting at the stand for the purpose of collecting means to enable Elder Lyman Wight to go to Washington.

Court Session at Carthage.

The Circuit Court commenced its sitting at Carthage, Judge Thomas presiding. Brother Phelps and many of the brethren went to Carthage. Phelps returned in the evening with the intelligence that a summons was supposed to be issued for me to appear on the same case on which I was set free by *habeas corpus* on the 8th inst.* The lawyers agreed to move an abatement. A good influence in favor of the Saints appears to have prevailed.

A general court-martial of the Legion was held, Brevet Major General Hyrum Smith presiding. It was adjourned to the 10th of June next.

Tuesday, 21.—A very pleasant morning. I rode out on horseback to the prairie, with Porter Rockwell and Mr. Reid. At 7 a. m., Elders Brigham Young, Heber C. Kimball, Lyman Wight, and about a hundred Elders, left this city on the steamer *Osprey* (Captain Anderson) for St. Louis.

The *Maid of Iowa* arrived at 8 a. m., with sixty-two Saints from the Eastern States on board, all in good health and spirits. The clerk, Thomas Bullock, reported the fields on each side of the river covered with water to the depth of upwards of sixteen feet, and all the farms on the flats of the Mississippi river were submerged, and the river was still rising eight inches per day. The *Maid of Iowa* started up the river for Wapello on the Iowa river at 3 p. m.

I was at home towards night with Emma, who is somewhat better. I shoveled dirt out of the ditch, while Wasson stood on the corner of the fence to watch. An officer arrived having a summons and an attachment to take me to Carthage, but he could not find me. I rode out in the evening to see David Yearsley's child, who was sick, and returned home at 9 p. m.

I copy from the *Times and Seasons*:—

LETTER: GEORGE A. SMITH TO "TIMES AND SEASONS"—CONFERENCE AT NEWARK, ILLINOIS.

"NEWARK, KENDALL COUNTY, ILL., May 21, 1844.

Editor of the Times and Seasons:—

DEAR SIR,—We arrived at Ottawa on the 17th inst., after driving

* Case of Chauncey L. Higbee vs. Joseph Smith, see Ch. XVI.

four days through the constant rains, and over roads almost impassable for man or beast. We were soon informed that the conference was removed twenty miles up Fox River, at the Newark Branch.

Notice had been given for a political address to be delivered in the Court House in the evening by one of the Twelve; several hundred citizens assembled, and were addressed by Elder G. A. Smith. The speaker considered General Smith the smartest man in the United States, and best calculated to fill the presidential chair, which was applauded by the assembly. His political views as presented on that occasion seemed to please most of the people. At the close of the speech the congregation quietly dispersed. Elder Woodruff continued his journey ten miles, and held a meeting with the LaSalle Branch of 46 members, mostly emigrants from Norway. On the 18th we arrived at Newark, and attended the Conference according to appointment.

The following is a copy of the minutes, which we forward for publication:—

NEWARK, KENDALL COUNTY, ILL., May 18, 1844.

Conference convened pursuant to notice.

There were present two of the quorum of the Twelve, one High Priest, two Seventies, nine Elders, one Priest, and one Teacher.

Conference called to order by Elder Woodruff.

Elder George A. Smith called to the chair.

Conference opened by singing, and prayer by the president.

Representation of the several branches was called for, when the following branches were represented as follows:

Newark Branch, 35 members, 1 Elder. 1 Teacher; La Salle Branch, 46 members, 2 Elders: Ottawa Branch, 16 members. 2 Elders; Bureau Branch, 15 members. 3 Elders; Pleasant Grove, McHenry County, 19 members, 2 Elders; Indian Creek Branch, 5 members; Big Vermillion Branch, 4 members; French Creek Grove Branch, 2 members. Total 133 members, 10 Elders, and 1 Teacher,

Canute Petersen, Severt Olson. Zimri H. Baxter, Levi Lightfoot, S. D. Huffaker, Mades Madison, Vance Jacobs, and Oder Jacobson, were ordained Priests; Ole Johnson and Peter Maclin ordained Teachers, under the hands of Elders Wilford Woodruff, Geo. A. Smith, and Ezra Thayer.

Appropriate remarks were then made by Elders Woodruff and Smith by way of counsel and instruction to those who had been ordained; followed by Elder David Savage.

Adjourned until Sunday morning, 10 o'clock.

Sunday, 19th.

Met according to adjournment.

Opened by singing and prayer by Elder A. M. Wilsey.

A discourse was then delivered by Elder Wilford Woodruff, in which he instructed the Elders to be careful to preach the first principles of the Gospel and doctrines of Christ, and not to spend their time in warring with the opinions of other men; showed the importance of revelation, and the necessity of a Prophet of God, as the head of the Church on earth, being as necessary in order to exist and advance in knowledge as for a natural body to possess a head in order to live. He considered we were enjoying the society of as good a Prophet in this day as any people ever enjoyed in any age of the world, and believed all good men would think so, if they were fully acquainted with him and his principles.

He was followed by Elder Geo. A. Smith, who bore testimony to the truth of the fullness of the Gospel, counseled the Elders to be humble, and not get head and shoulders above their brethren, lest they fall, like the tallest trees of the forest, that are first swept down by the raging storm.

Two o'clock, met according to adjournment, when the sacrament was administered, and many testimonies given from the Elders and members present concerning the truth of the work they had received.

Conference was dismissed amid the best of feelings, which were manifested not only by all the Saints, but by the whole congregation of citizens that attended. Good order prevailed through the whole conference. Attention, kindness, and civility, were manifested by all.

GEO. A. SMITH, President.

ASA MANCHESTER, Clerk.

At the close of the Conference, Elders C. C. Rich, David Fullmer, Norton Jacobs, and Moses Smith arrived direct from Nauvoo, on their way to Michigan.

20th—We have appointed a political meeting in Newark, this evening, and one at Joliet tomorrow evening, where we expect to present to the citizens General Smith's Views of the Powers and Policy of the Government, and discuss the subject of politics.

WILFORD WOODRUFF.
GEO. A. SMITH.

Wednesday, 22.—At home, watching, as the officers from Carthage were after me.

Visit of Sac and Fox Indians to Nauvoo.

At 10 a. m., about 40 Indians of the Sacs and Foxes came up in front of the Mansion, four or five of them being mounted, among whom was Black Hawk's brother, Kis-kish-kee, &c. I was obliged to send word I could not see them at present. They encamped in the Council Chamber afternoon and night. I was with the police on duty, and saw several individuals lurking around.

Very pleasant day.

President Brigham Young preached to the brethren in St. Louis this evening.

Thursday, 23.—Emma rather better. Read Hebrew with Neibaur, and counseled with various friends.

At 10 a. m., the Municipal Court met, Newel K. Whitney presiding; but there not being a quorum present, adjourned for one week.

At one p. m., had a talk with the Sac and Fox Indians in my back kitchen. They said—"When our fathers first came here, this land was inhabited by the Spanish; when the Spaniards were driven off, the French came, and then the English and Americans; and our fathers talked a great deal with the Big Spirit." They complained that they had been robbed of their lands by the whites, and cruelly treated.

Address of the Prophet to the Indians

I told them I knew they had been wronged, but that we had bought this land and paid our money for it. I advised them not to sell any more land, but to cultivate peace with the different tribes and with all men, as the Great Spirit wanted them to be united and to live in peace. "The Great Spirit has enabled me to find a book [showing them the Book of Mormon], which told me about your fathers, and Great Spirit told me, 'You must send to all the tribes that you can, and tell them to live in peace;' and when any of our people come to see you, I want you to treat them as we treat you."

At 3 p. m., the Indians commenced a war dance in front of my old house. Our people commenced with music and firing cannon. After the dance, which lasted about two hours, the firing of cannon closed the exercise, and with our music marched back to the office. Before they commenced dancing, the Saints took up a collection to get the Indians food.

A. A. Lathrop came to my clerk, Dr. Richards, and told him an officer was on his way with an attachment for him, and that the grand jury had found a bill against me for adultery, on the testimony of William Law; he had come from Carthage in two hours and thirty minutes to bring the news. Dr. Richards came to my house and stayed all night.

Aaron Johnson came from Carthage, and said that Foster had been swearing that I swore to the complaint on which Simpson was arrested. I instructed Johnson and Rockwell to go to Carthage in the morning, and have him indicted for perjury, as I never did swear to the complaint. The officer was after John D. Parker also, and report says Brigham Young, Heber C. Kimball and W. Clayton.

Past nine p. m., I walked a little way with Dr. Richards for exercise.

Hyrum's Caution to the Prophet on the Freedom of Speaking.

My brother Hyrum called in the evening, and cautioned me against speaking so freely about my enemies, &c., in such a manner as to make it actionable. I told him that six months would not roll over his head before they would swear twelve as palpable lies about him as they had about me.

President Brigham Young left St. Louis at noon in the steamboat *Louis Philippe*.

Friday, 24.—With my family all day.

Aaron Johnson and Orrin P. Rockwell went to Carthage to get Robert D. Foster indicted; but they returned again as the grand jury had risen. Joseph H. Jackson was at Carthage, and had sworn falsely against me.

At 6 p. m., went to Dr. Bernhise 's room, and had counsel with Brothers Richards and Phelps. I ordered a meeting of the City Council for tomorrow, and returned to my family after being absent about one hour.

The Central Committee wrote a letter to Hugh Clark Esq.:—

Letter: Central Campaign Committee to Hugh Clark, Esq.,—Presidential Election Matters.

NAUVOO, ILLINOIS, May 24, 1844.

SIR.—Having received your address through our mutual friend, Mr. Edward Doughty, we forward with this per next mail the Nauvoo *Neighbor* of the 22nd inst., through which you will learn the doings of a State Convention held in this place on the 17th; and this communication has been drawn forth, in a great degree, through our sympathies for a people who are now being mobbed in the city of brotherly love (Philadelphia) as we have been for many years in Missouri; and for what? For our religion, although called by another name.

The Mormons and the Catholics are the most obnoxious to the sectarian world of any people, and are the only two who have not persecuted each other and others in these the United States, and the only two who have suffered from the cruel hand of mobocracy for their religion under the name of foreigners; and to stay this growing evil, and establish Jeffersonian democracy, free trade and sailor's rights, and protection of person and property," we have nominated General Joseph Smith for the next president of the nation—a man with whom we are thoroughly acquainted, and have no fear in pledging our lives, our fortunes and our sacred honor, that, if elected, he will give and secure these inestimable blessings to every individual and society of men, no matter what their religious faith. Help us to elect this man, and we will help you to secure these privileges which belong to you, and break every yoke.

You will please to consider yourself a member of the corresponding committee with us, agreeable to the resolution of the State Convention, and lay this subject before your people, giving us your views on receipt hereof, and open such correspondence as wisdom shall dictate.

General Smith's prospects are brightening every day. With sentiments of the highest consideration, we are your obedient servants,

WILLARD RICHARDS,
JOHN M. BERNHISEL,
W. W. PHELPS,
LUCIAN R. FOSTER,

Central Committee of Correspondence for the Election of General Joseph Smith to the Presidency.

HUGH CLARK, ESQ. Alderman.
Corner of Fourth and Masters Street, Northern Liberties, Philadelphia.

Rainy evening.

A conference was held at Chicago, Alfred Cordon, president, and James Burgess, clerk. Eleven Elders were present, and a very favorable impression was made upon the minds of the people.

Saturday, 25.—At home, keeping out of the way of the expected writs from Carthage. Towards evening, Edward Hunter and William Marks, of the grand jury returned from Carthage; also Marshal John P. Greene and Almon W. Babbitt, who informed me there were two indictments found against me, one charging me with false swearing on the testimony of Joseph H. Jackson and Robert D. Foster, and one charging me with polygamy, or something else, on the testimony of William Law, that I had told him so! The particulars of which I shall learn hereafter. There was much false swearing before the grand jury. Francis M. Higbee swore so hard that I had received stolen property, &c., that his testimony was rejected. I heard that Joseph H. Jackson had come into the city. I therefore instructed the officers to arrest him for threatening to take life, &c.

Reported Indictments of the Prophet.

I had a long talk with Edward Hunter, my brother Hyrum, Dr. Richards, William Marks, Almon W. Babbitt, Shadrach Roundy, Edward Romney and others, and concluded not to keep out of the way of the officers any longer.

At 2 p. m. I was in council in my north room, and heard the letters from Elder O. Hyde read, and instructed Dr. Richards to write an answer, which he did as follows:

Letter: Willard Richards to Orson Hyde—Answering Hyde's Letter on Western Movement.

NAUVOO, May 26, 1844.

Orson Hyde, Esq.:

SIR.—Yours of April 30th is received. The council convened this afternoon, and, after investigation, directed an answer, which must be brief to correspond with the press of business.

All the items you refer to had previously received the deliberation of the council.

Messrs. Lyman Wight and Heber C. Kimball will doubtless be in Washington before you receive this, from whom you will learn all things relative to Texas, &c. Our great success at present depends upon our faith in the doctrine of election; and our faith must be made manifest by our works and every honorable exertion made to elect Gen. Smith.

Agricultural pursuits will take care of themselves, regulating their own operations and the rich also; but the poor we must gather and take care of, for they are to inherit the kingdom.

Nauvoo will be a "corner stake of Zion" forever, we most assuredly expect. Here are the house and the ordinance, extend where else we may.

Press the bills through the two houses, if possible. If Congress will not pass them, let them do as they have a mind with them. If they will not pass our bills, but will give us "something," they will give what they please, and it will be at our option to accept or reject.

Men who are afraid of "hazarding their influence" in the council or political arena are good for nothing. 'Tis the fearless, undaunted and persevering who will gain the conquest of the forum.

Sidney Rigdon, Esq., is about to resign the postoffice at Nauvoo, in favor of Gen. Joseph Smith, the founder of the city. He has the oldest petitions now on file in the general postoffice for that station, and has an undoubted claim over every other petitioner, by being the founder and supporter of the city, and by the voice of nineteen-twentieths of the people, and every sacred consideration; and it is the wish of the council that you engage the Illinois delegation to use their influence to secure the office to General Smith without fail, and have them ready to act on the arrival of Mr. Rigdon's resignation, and before too, if expedient.

We are also writing to Justin Butterfield, Esq., U. S. Attorney for the district of Illinois, who has kindly offered his services to secure the post office to the General, he having been here and seen for himself the situation; and probably his letter to the department will arrive nearly as soon as this.

The election on the principle of Jeffersonian democracy, free trade, and protection of person and property, is gaining ground in every quarter. All is well in Nauvoo, although some of the Anties are trying to do us injury; but their efforts are palsied, and they make very little headway. You remember the Preston motto, "Truth will prevail!* Therefore we go ahead.

* Referring to the motto that was displayed in the streets of Preston, England, on the arrival of Elders Kimball and Hyde as missionaries to that city in 1837. See this HISTORY, vol. II, pp. 498-9.

You have the best wishes of the council and friends here. I am, sir, most respectfully yours,

W. RICHARDS, Recorder.

By order of the council.

N. B. Your families and friends were well last information.

Sidney Rigdon resigned the office of postmaster of Nauvoo, and recommended me as his successor.

The *Maid of Iowa* arrived at five p. m.

The High Council have directed the following testimony to be published in the *Neighbor*, I copy it with the editor's remarks, to show the character of the men who are now seeking to destroy my life and usefulness, and overthrow the work of the Lord which He has commenced through my instrumentality:

[Here follow the affidavits of Margaret J. Nyman, Matilda J. Nyman, Sarah Miller, and an extract from the testimony of Catherine Warren before the High Council of the Church to the effect that Chauncey L. Higbee had brought about their ruin by deceit in representing that Joseph Smith taught that promiscuous sexual relations were not sinful when kept secret, and by this misrepresentation he, the said Chauncey L. Higbee, accomplished his wicked purposes].

Editorial Comment.

We have abundance of like testimony on hand which may be forthcoming if we are compelled; at present the foregoing may suffice.

"Why have you not published this before?" We answer—on account of the humility and entreaties of Higbee at the time; and on account of the feelings of his parents, who are highly respectable, we have forborne until now. The character of Chauncey L. Higbee is so infamous, and his exertions such as to destroy every principle of righteousness, that forbearance is no longer a virtue.

After all that this Chauncey L. Higbee has done in wickedly and maliciously using the name of Joseph Smith to persuade innocent females to submit to gratify his hellish lusts, and then blast the character of the most chaste, pure, virtuous and philanthropic man on earth, he, to screen himself from the law of the land and the just indignation of an insulted people, and save himself from the penitentiary, or whatever punishment his unparalleled crimes merit, has entered into a conspiracy with the Laws and others against the lives of those who are knowing to his abandoned conduct, thus hoping to save himself from the disgrace which must follow an exposure, and wreak his vengeance and gratify his revenge for his awful disappointment.

A two days' conference was held in Jefferson county, New York, at 10 a. m. Present 300 Saints, 150 of whom had embraced the Gospel since last autumn. Nine branches were represented, containing 289 members, 16 Elders, 8 Priests and 1 Teacher. An immense concourse of people assembled to hear the Elders preach. Elder Benjamin Brown was President, and J. W. Crosby, Clerk.

Conference in Jefferson Co., N. Y.

A three days' conference was held at Dresden, Weakly county, Tennessee. Elder A. O. Smoot was chosen president, and D. P. Raney, secretary. A large congregation assembled, but the proceedings were interrupted by a mob headed by some of the leading men of the county; yet a candidate for elector was appointed by my friends.

Conference, Dresden, Tenn.

Sunday, 26.—At 10 a. m. I preached at the Stand. The following synopsis was reported by Mr. Thos. Bullock, clerk of the steamer, *Maid of Iowa.*

Address of the Prophet—His Testimony Against the Dissenters at Nauvoo.

President Joseph Smith read the 11th Chap. II Corinthians. My object is to let you know that I am right here on the spot where I intend to stay. I, like Paul, have been in perils, and oftener than anyone in this generation. As Paul boasted, I have suffered more than Paul did. I should be like a fish out of water, if I were out of persecutions. Perhaps my brethren think it requires all this to keep me humble. The Lord has constituted me so curiously that I glory in persecution. I am not nearly so humble as if I were not persecuted. If oppression will make a wise man mad, much more a fool. If they want a beardless boy to whip all the world, I will get on the top of a mountain and crow like a rooster: I shall always beat them. When facts are proved, truth and innocence will prevail at last. My enemies are no philosophers: they think that when they have my spoke under, they will keep me down; but for the fools, I will hold on and fly over them.

God is in the still small voice. In all these affidavits, indictments, it is all of the devil—all corruption. Come on! ye prosecutors! ye false swearers! All hell, boil over! Ye burning mountains, roll down your lava! for I will come out on the top at last. I have more to boast of than ever any man had. I am the only man that has ever been able to keep a whole church together since the days of Adam. A large majority of the whole have stood by me. Neither Paul, John, Peter, nor Jesus ever did it. I boast that no man ever did such a work as I. The followers of Jesus ran away from Him; but the Latter-day Saints never ran away from me yet. You know my daily walk and conversation. I am in the bosom of a virtuous and good people. How I do love to hear the wolves howl! When they can get rid of me, the devil will also go. For the last three years I have a record of all my acts and proceedings, for I have kept several good, faithful, and efficient clerks in constant employ: they have accompanied me everywhere, and carefully kept my history, and they have written down what I have done, where I have been, and what I have said; therefore my enemies cannot charge me with any day, time, or place, but what I have written testimony to prove my actions; and my enemies cannot prove anything against me. They have got wonderful things in the land of Ham. I think the grand jury have strained at a gnat and swallowed the camel.

A man named Simpson says I made an affidavit against him, &c. Mr. Simpson says I arrested him. I never arrested Mr. Simpson in my life. He says I made an affidavit against him. I never made an affidavit against him in my life. I will prove it in court. I will tell you how it was: Last winter I got ready with my children to go to the farm to kill hogs. Orrin P. Rockwell was going to drive. An Englishman came in and wanted a private conversation with me. I told him I did not want any private conversations. "I demand one of you!" Such a one I am bound to obey anyhow. Said he—"I want a warrant against the man who stabbed Brother Badham. He said it was a man who boarded at Davis'. He said it was Mr. Simpson—it answered his description. I said I had no jurisdiction out of the city. He said—"The man must be arrested, or else he will go away." I told him—"You must go to Squire Wells, Johnson, or Foster." Mr. Lytle stepped up and said—"I am a policeman." I jumped into my carriage, and away I went.

When I came back I met Mr. Jackson. He said—"You did wrong in arresting Mr. Simpson." I told him I did not do it. I went over and sat down, and related the circumstances. He turned round and said—"Mr. Smith, I have nothing against you; I am satisfied." He went and supped with me. He declared in the presence of witnesses, that he had nothing against me. I then said—"I will go over to Esquire Johnson, and testify what the Englishman told me." I told him not to make out that I believe he is the man, but that I believe he is innocent. I don't want to swear that he is the man. Messrs. Coolidge, Rockwell, Hatfield, and Hawes were present.

Mr. Johnson made one [a complaint] out in due form: and as I sat down in a bustle the same as I do when one of the clerks brings a deed for me to sign. Johnson read it. I said—"I can't swear to that affidavit; I don't believe it: tear up that paper." Mr. Simpson agreed to come before Badham and make it up. I did not swear to it [*i. e.* to the complaint.]

After a while, Dr. Foster and others came in. They called me up to testify. I told it all the same as I do here. Mr. Simpson rose up, and asked—"Do you believe now that I am the man who stabbed Mr. Badham?" I replied—"No sir, I do not now, nor ever did: the magistrate says I did not swear to it." He considered, and made a public declaration that he was satisfied with me.

Aaron Johnson went before the grand jury and swore I did not swear to it, when Dr. Foster goes and swears that I swore to it, and that he was in the room when he was not in. Chauncey wanted me to stay and have a conversation. Dr. Foster asked Aaron Johnson for the writ and affidavit. He handed them to Dr. Foster, who read them, and then threw them into the fire. I said—"Doctor, you ought not to have burned it; it was my paper." Dr. Foster goes to the grand jury and swears he did not burn only one; but I say he burnt both. This is a fair sample of the swearing that is going on against me.

The last discharge was the 40th; now the 41st, 42nd, 43rd; all through falsehood. Matters of fact are as profitable as the Gospel, and which I can prove. You will then know who are liars, and who speak the truth I want to retain your friendship on holy grounds.

Another indictment has been got up against me. It appears a holy prophet has arisen up, and he has testified against me: the reason is, he is so holy. The Lord knows I do not care how many churches are in the world. As many as believe me, may. If the doctrine that I preach is true, the tree must be good. I have prophesied things that have come to pass, and can still.

Inasmuch as there is a new church, this must be old, and of course we ought to be set down as orthodox. From henceforth let all the churches now no longer persecute orthodoxy. I never built upon any other man's ground. I never told the old Catholic that he was a fallen true prophet God knows, then, that the charges against me are false.

I had not been married scarcely five minutes, and made one proclamation of the Gospel, before it was reported that I had seven wives. I mean to live and proclaim the truth as long as I can.

This new holy prophet [William Law] has gone to Carthage and swore that I had told him that I was guilty of adultery. This spiritual wifeism! Why, a man dares not speak or wink, for fear of being accused of this.

William Law testified before forty policemen, and the assembly room full of witnesses, that he testified under oath that he never had heard or seen or knew anything immoral or criminal against me. He testified under oath that he was my friend, and not the "Brutus." There was a cogitation who was the "Brutus." I had not prophesied against William Law. He swore under oath that he was satisfied that he was ready to lay down his life for me, and he swears that I have committed adultery.

I wish the grand jury would tell me who they are—whether it will be a curse or blessing to me. I am quite tired of the fools asking me.

A man asked me whether the commandment was given that a man may have seven wives; and now the new prophet has charged me with adultery. I never had any fuss with these men until that Female Relief Society brought out the paper against adulterers and adulteresses.

Dr. Goforth was invited into the Laws' clique, and Dr. Foster and the clique were dissatisfied with that document, and they rush away and leave the Church, and conspire to take away my life; and because I will not countenance such wickedness, they proclaim that I have been a true prophet, but that I am now a fallen prophet.

Jackson has committed murder, robbery, and perjury; and I can prove it by half-a-dozen witnesses. Jackson got up and said—"By God, he is innocent," and now swears that I am guilty. He threatened my life.

There is another Law, not the prophet, who was cashiered for dishonesty and robbing the government. Wilson Law also swears that I told him I was guilty of adultery. Brother Jonathan Dunham can swear to the contrary. I have been chained. I have rattled chains before in a dungeon for the truth's sake. I am innocent of all these charges, and you can bear witness of my innocence, for you know me yourselves.

When I love the poor, I ask no favors of the rich. I can go to the cross—I can lay down my life; but don't forsake me. I want the friendship of my brethren.—Let us teach the things of Jesus Christ. Pride goes before destruction, and a haughty spirit before a downfall.

Be meek and lowly, upright and pure; render good for evil, If you bring on yourselves your own destr uction, I will complain. It is not right for a man to bear down his neck to the oppressor always. Be humble and patient in all circumstances of life; we shall then triumph more gloriously. What a thing it is for a man to be accused of committing adultery, and having seven wives, when I can only find one.

I am the same man, and as innocent as I was fourteen years ago; and I can prove them all perjurers. I labored with these apostates myself until I was out of all manner of patience; and then I sent my brother Hyrum, whom they virtually kicked out of doors.

I then sent Mr. Backenstos, when they declared that they were my enemies. I told Mr. Backenstos that he might tell the Laws, if they had any cause against me I would go before the Church, and confess it to the world. He [Wm. Law] was summoned time and again, but refused to come. Dr. Bernhisel and Elder Rigdon know that I speak the truth. I cite you to Captain Dunham, Esquires Johnson and Wells, Brother Hatfield and others, for the truth of what I have said. I have said this to let my friends know that I am right.

As I grow older, my heart grows tenderer for you. I am at all times willing to give up everything that is wrong, for I wish this people to have a virtuous leader, I have set your minds at liberty by letting you know the things of Christ Jesus. When I shrink not from your defense will you throw me away for a new man who slanders you? I love you for your reception of me. Have I asked you for your money? No; you know better. I appeal to the poor. I say, Cursed be that man or woman who says that I have taken of your money unjustly. Brother Babbitt will address you. I have nothing in my heart but good feelings.

I rode out in the afternoon. On my return, my lawyers, Col. Richardson and Almon W. Babbitt, called upon me on the subject of the writs which were out against me.

Threat to Kidnap Jeremiah Smith.

A man called and informed me that John Eagle and several others intended to kidnap Jeremiah Smith during the night. I therefore stationed an extra police in order to protect him.

President Brigham Young arrived at Cincinnati at 5 p.m.

President Smith Voluntarily goes to Carthage to Meet Indictments.

Monday, *27.*—About 8 a. m., I started on horsback with a few friends, went by the Temple, and pursued my course towards Carthage, thinking it best for me to meet my enemies before the Circuit Court, and have the indictments against me investigated. After I had passed my farm on the prairie, most of the following brethren joined my company, and the remainder soon after my arrival in Carthage—viz: Aaron Johnson, Dr. Bernhisel, Joseph W. Coolidge, John Hatfield, Orrin P. Rockwell, Lorenzo Rockwell, William Walker, Harrison Sagers, Hyrum Smith, John P. Greene, Judge William Richards, Shadrach Roundy, Theodore Turley, Jedediah M. Grant, John Lytle, Joseph B. Noble, Edward Bonney, Lucien Woodworth, Cornelius P. Lott, Johathan Dunham, and other friends.

We arrived at Hamilton's hotel about noon. Charles A. Foster overtook us three or four miles from the city, and accompanied us to Carthage. I had considerable conversation with him, and he appeared to be more mild than previously, and as though he was almost persuaded that he had been influenced to some extent by false reports.

Joseph H. Jackson, Francis M. Higbee, and Chauncey L. Higbee were in Hamilton's hotel when we arrived. Soon after our arrival there, Charles A. Foster took me into a private room and told me in a friendly manner that there was a conspiracy against my life. Robert D. Foster told some of the brethren (with tears in his eyes) that there was evil determined against me; and that there were some persons who were determined I should not go out of Carthage alive. Jackson was seen to reload his pistols, and was heard to swear he would have satisfaction of me and Hyrum.

I had a short interview with Judge Thomas, who treated me with the utmost courtesy. He is a great man and a gentleman. After dinner (at the second or third table) we retired to our room, when Jackson, who had been to the Court House, came towards the hotel. Some person told him Hyrum had arrived, when he immediately turned towards the Court House again.

My lawyers, Messrs. Richardson, Babbitt, and Skinner, used all reasonable exertions to bring forward my trial on the charge of perjury; but the prosecuting party were not ready,—one Withers, a material witness (as they asserted in court), being absent.

My attorneys frequently called on me to report the state of things in court, and I was ready to go in at a moment's warning, being anxious for my trial; but the case was deferred till next term. I was left to give bail to the sheriff at his option. He told me I might go home, where he would call and take bail at his own convenience.

We immediately called for our horses; and while they

were being harnessed, Chauncey L. Higbee came to me and wanted me to stay as a witness in a certain case in which he was employed as attorney. He urged me considerably, but I told him I did not recollect the occurrence he referred to particularly enough to testify in the case, and got him to excuse me.

At half-past four p. m., we started on our return; but when we had got as far as Brother George D. Grant's, a heavy shower of rain commenced, and I went into the house, while most of the brethren went into the barn until the shower abated. After the storm had subsided, we went forward, and I, Hyrum, and some others arrived at home about 9 p. m., and found Emma sick. My carriage, with Joseph B. Noble, arrived a little after. It was upset on the Temple Hill, but no one was hurt. I rode on horseback all the way on "Joe Duncan."

The Return to Nauvoo.

As we left the tavern in Carthage, and passed the Court House, there were many people about in small groups. Jackson stood on the green with one or two men some distance off.

While at Hamilton's, Chauncey L. Higbee offered some insulting language concerning me to Orrin P. Rockwell, who resented it nobly as a friend ought to do. Hamilton, seeing it, turned Rockwell out of doors.

It was afterwards reported to me by James Flack that Robert D. Foster, Charles A. Foster, Wm. H. Rollinson, and the Higbees were on the hill when I passed in the morning. They immediately gathered their pistols, mounted their horses, and were in Carthage before me, excepting Charles A. Foster.

Also Mr. Powers was talking with Mr. Davies, a tailor, about my going to Carthage, and said they would attempt to kill Joseph Smith. Mr. Davies replied, "O no, I think not." Mr. Powers rejoined, "They will, by G—; and you know it, by G—."

Samuel Smith, of Montebello, heard at five this morning, that I had been taken prisoner to Carthage by a mob. He immediately gathered a company of twenty-five men for the purpose of assisting me, and arrived at Carthage about the time I did.

CHAPTER XX.

CASE OF JEREMIAH SMITH BEFORE MUNICIPAL COURT AT NAUVOO—AFFIDAVITS OF CRIMES OF CHAUNCEY L. HIGBEE —APPEARANCE OF THE "EXPOSITOR."

Tuesday, 28.—At home all day. Rain in the afternoon. The *Maid of Iowa* started for the Iowa river at 11 a. m.

I received a letter from Mr. J. Bronder, dated Philadelphia, May 20th, expressing his strong desires that I should allow my name to stand as candidate for the Presidency of the United States, urging many reasons for his request.

Wednesday, 29.—At home. Rain in the morning.

Arrest of Jeremiah Smith, by U. S. Authority.

Luther W. Hicock, of Burlington, Iowa, came in and arrested Jeremiah Smith on a warrant issued by Nathanial Pope, Judge of the U. S. Circuit Court. During our conversation in the afternoon we learned to our mutual joy that Jeremiah Smith and I were of one origin.

Received the following letter:

Letter: D. S. Hollister to Joseph Smith—Presidential Election Matters.

BALTIMORE, May 9th, 1844.

DEAR BROTHER JOSEPH.—From the time of my departue to that of my arrival here on Saturday last, I was blessed with prosperity. The feelings manifested by the passengers on the boat to St. Louis were quite favorable.

At St. Louis I embarked on board the steamer *Valley Forge*, with about 125 cabin passengers. I gradually introduced myself to those whose faces gave indications of honest hearts and intelligent minds.

On Sunday I was invited to give, in a public discourse, the points of difference between faith of the Latter-day Saints and other professors of the Christian religion. There was a Methodist preacher on board, with whom arrangements were made, to follow me and blow Mormonism to the four winds. Well, I led off in a discourse of an hour and a half. After dinner the Methodists tried to rally their preacher; but he could not be induced to undertake the fulfillment of his engagements.

I spent the time in conversing with groups of inquirers, and giving further information to those who sought it. After tea, the Methodist priest was, by much persuasion, induced to preach; but, to the astonishment of all, never once mentioned "Mormonism."

By-the-by, we had a beautiful specimen of Missouri treatment of the Saints on board. While I was speaking, I referred to the many false statements which found their way to the public through the papers. A case in point was that of Joseph Smith having just discarded his wife.

After I had finished speaking, and was standing on the guard of the boat, a Missourian stepped up to me, asking me if I wished to be understood that all who said Jo Smith had discarded his wife were liars. On my answering him in the affirmative, he drew his bowie knife on me; but some passengers, who had heard him threaten my life, were watching,and caught him as he was in the act of striking and I in the act of pitching him overboard; but they saved him, and I am glad of it. The whole affair turned much to my advantage. It was an occular demonstration to the crowd of Missourians' feeling toward the Church of Christ.

By this time the way was pretty well paved for introducing national matters; and from this on to our arrival at Wheeling, the time was principally occupied on that subject—reading your views on political economy, &c.

On arriving at Wheeling, a stranger might have imagined me to be a man of some consequence, for it was, "Will you take a seat in our coach?" "Go with us in this stage." "Hold on, and take a seat with us," says the third. In fact, the Mormon was quite a lion among the passengers.

But passing the minutiæ, I arrived in the city two days after the great Whig convention. All is joy and enthusiasm among the Whigs, while doubt and consternation are manifested among the Democrats. The convention has been got up at an immense expense; hundreds of thousands of dollars have been expended.

The Democratic convention comes off on the 27th inst. In the meantime I shall do what is in my power for the promotion of the good cause, and endeavor to be well accoutred for that oocasion. I expect to co-operate with Hyde, Pratt and Page, though as yet I have not heard from them.

I shall expect to receive from you the proceedings of the convention held at Nauvoo on Monday last, together with such instructions as you deem proper to give.

D. S. Hollister.

Thursday, *30*.—Municipal Court met at 10 a. m., over which I presided as mayor and chief justice. Present, William Marks, Orson Spencer, George W. Harris, Gustavus Hills and Samuel Bennett, alderman, associate justices. Jeremiah Smith, Sen., was brought up on *habeas corpus* from the custody of T. B. Johnson, the complainant.

Municipal Court—Case of Jeremiah Smith.

T. B. Johnson being called by the court answered that he did not acknowledge the jurisdiction of this court; that his writ was only to keep Smith until he could get another writ for him; that Mr. Hickock had a writ from Judge Pope, and he considered Mr. Smith his prisoner, and he attended this court as a matter of courtesy; and if any one offered resistance, he was instructed by Government to give their names, &c., and wrote the names of the court, &c.

Smith's counsel replied to such a subterfuge writ.

The court thought it due the court to hear the reasons why the jurisdiction of the court was not regarded.

T. B. Johnson said he did not come to make a speech; but was instructed to arrest the man. He intended to make no defense. He was an agent of the United States. "Your writ of *habeas corpus* had nothing more to do with this case than with a man in the moon. I have not been able to get authority, and did not come to make defense." Read from Charles B. Penrose's handwriting (so purporting) 33 sec. of Act Sept. 24th, 1789, Act of Congress. Had agreed to wait the decision of this court, but had not agreed to abide the decision.

James A. McCanse was called by the court and asked, "Do you subscribe to the decision of Mr. Johnson in the matter?"

McCanse would not decide. Would like counsel.

T. B. Johnson said he did not ask any favors of the court. He was a United States agent.

Councilor Hugins said—"If McCanse surrenders his claim we will not go into the merits of the case; but if McCanse claims the prisoner, we will go into the merits."

Councilor Hugins read a petition of Jeremiah Smith for another writ of *habeas corpus*. G. P. Stiles, counsel for prisoner, said that Johnson had given up the prisoner on the first claim.

T. B. Johnson said he did not surrender his claim; had nothing to say about it. "Take your own course, gentlemen."

Stiles said he has given him up on the first writ, and now says he says nothing about it; and upon this ground we claim a discharge.

T. B. Johnson said—"We would be defending the writ before Judge Pope. I come here as an agent of the United States. The prisoner has been taken out of my hand, I consider illegally. I do not come here to prosecute or to defend a writ of *habeas corpus*. There is no law for these proceedings. I know my rights. If this court thinks it right to discharge the prisoner, let them do it—let them do it. I do not ask any favors of the court—I ask justice. The laws of Illinois have no power over the United States laws. Let this court discharge him, and I shall take another course—I do not say against you as a court. I came here to arrest Jeremiah Smith."

Justice Harris asked if he meant to intimidate the court by threats.

The chief justice remarked that it was the duty of the United States and Federal Government to treat their subjects and constituents with all that complacency and good feeling which they wished in return, and to avoid every threatening aspect, every intimidating and harsh treatment. He respected the United States laws, but would not yield up any right ceded to the court. The United States have no right to trample our laws under their feet.

The court is bound by oath to support the Constitution of the United States, and State of Illinois and writ of *habeas corpus*. The Constitution of the United States and *habeas corpus* shall not be denied. If the court deny the writ of *habeas corpus*, they perjure themselves. The United States have no right to usurp power to intimidate, and the court would see them all destroyed before he would perjure himself. We have asked no power. Mr. Smith asked us to investigate. We were bound to do so. Let the Federal Government hurl on us their forces, dragoons, &c.; we are not to be intimidated. The court is clothed with *habeas corpus*, [power] and will execute it according to the law. "I understand some law and more justice, and know as much about the rights of American citizens as any man."

T. B. Johnson said—"If I did say anything indecorus to the court, I take it back."

Court responded—"All is right."

Court ordered that the prisoner be discharged, the complainant having refused to prosecute his claim; and that judgment be entered up *v*. T. B. Johnson, as agent, for costs of suit.

Afterwards another petition for another writ of *habeas corpus* was presented and the writ issued and tried. I copy the minutes from the municipal docket:

Municipal Court Minutes in the case of Jeremiah Smith.

State of Illinois, }
City of Nauvoo, } Municipal Court.

United States, vs. Jeremiah Smith, on Habeas Corpus.

May 30th, 1844, came Jeremiah Smith, and upon the reading and filing the petition for a writ of *habeas corpus* to be directed to one Luther W. Hickock to have forthwith before the Municipal Court the body of the said Jeremiah Smith upon said writ. Said writ was granted by the court in accordance with the prayer of the petitioner.

The writ of *habeas corpus* was served instanter by the Marshal in cour and petitioner present; which writ with Marshal's return thereon, is on file in the clerk's office.

The foregoing petition of said Jeremiah Smith, together with a certified copy of the warrant, by virtue of which the said Hickock held the said Jeremiah Smith in custody, are on file in the clerk's office.

Present, Joseph Smith, mayor and chief justice; and William Marks, Orson Spencer, George W. Harris, Gustavus Hills, and Samuel Bennett, aldermen, associate justices.

Luther W. Hickock was called by the court to answer in the case, who said he had a writ from Judge Pope, and should consider Smith his prisoner until he was compelled to give him up. Wanted an adjournment.

The court informed Hickock that Smith was their prisoner.

H. T. Hugins and George P. Stiles, counsel for Smith. objected to an adjournment, as there had been two weeks' adjournment for the Government to procure witnesses in another suit which had closed, arising out of the same case, and which had been abandoned by the prosecuting party.

T. B. Johnson appeared before the court and said—"I stand here as an agent for the Government to act in the case of Smith in any state where he may be found; and if we are to go into an investigation on the merits of the case, and go behind the writ, I must have time to send to Washington for witnesses; and I am instructed to consult with Justin Butterfield, Esq., Governor Chambers of Iowa, and Mr. McPherson of St. Louis.

The marshal, J. P. Greene, presented the prisoner for trial.

The court ordered the marshal to take charge of the prisoner, and have him forthcoming from time to time for trial.

Hickock asked for an adjournment until afternoon.

Hugins said—"If they want to go into the merits of the case, we will give them any time; but we propose to dispense with the merits, and move a discharge on the insufficiency of the papers. Dr. Hickock has no legal authority to arrest the prisoner," and read from page 51, Revised Statutes of Illinois, sec. 399.

T. B. Johnson said he could show the law different, and asked for one week's adjournment.

One o'clock p. m., court adjourned until after dinner to hear the pleas.

Three o'clock, p. m., court sat, the same as in the morning.

H. T. Hugins and George P. Stiles, counsel for Smith, read and filed their plea, moving the court that said Smith be discharged, and suffered to go at large.

1st. Because the person issuing the warrant on which he has been arrested is unauthorized to issue the same.

2nd. Because the process has been issued in a case and under circumstances where the law does not allow process.

3rd. Because the person having custody of said Smith is unauthorized to execute the warrant under which he is acting, and is not the person empowered by law to detain him.

4th. Because said Smith has been, by and before a competent court, legally examined and discharged in relation to the subject matter set forth in said warrant.

5th. Because said writ is defective in a substantial form required by law.

L. W. Hickock was called, and persisted in considering the authority under which he acted good and sufficient.

Counselor Hugins urged the first and second count in his plea, and read from the Constitution of the United States, Art. 4, 2nd sec, 2nd part. 3rd count, read Revised Statutes of Illinois, page 51, sec. 399, and page 324; 4th count, read the certificate of John S. Dunlap, clerk of the District Court for the county of DesMoines, Iowa Territory, dated May 21st, 1844, a copy of which is on file in the clerk's office.

L. W. Hickock said he had nothing to say; and the case was submitted.

DECISION—The court are of opinion, when they take into consideration their oath to support the Constitution of the United States, that the certificate of John S. Dunlap, clerk of the District Court for the county of DesMoines, Territory of Iowa, is sufficient to authorize the discharge or the prisoner, because the Constitution says no person shall twice be put in jeopardy of life for the same offense. The decision of the court is that the prisoner be discharged on all the points for which plea has been made in his behalf, and that judgment be entered against the prosecutor for cost.

Evening, T. B. Johnson was going to Burlington. Jeremiah Smith swore out an execution for $77.75. Mr. Johnson acknowledged the fee bill, and afterwards threatened to bring the dragoons in order to get Jeremiah Smith.

Mr. Hickock called for a copy of the proceedings of the Municipal Court.

I wrote the following letter to Judge Pope:—

Letter: Joseph Smith to Judge Pope Introducing Jeremiah Smith.

NAUVOO, May 30, 1844.

SIR,—Permit me to introduce to your particular notice and confidence as "brethren of the mystic tie," Mr. Jeremiah Smith of Iowa Territory, and Mr. H. T. Hugins, of Burlington, in said Territory Mr. Smith is a gentleman whose statements can be relied on, and Mr. Hugins a lawyer, of sound principles, as well as promising talents; and I always take pleasure in extending the reputations of honorable men among honorable men, especially when it appears to me that the benevolence and clemency extended by me is needed and merited by worthy men. Conscious, too, that your Honor is liberal and just in your sphere, and will appreciate "the golden rule," I have only to greet you with my best wishes for your welfare and happiness.

Respectfully, I have the honor to be,

Your humble servant,
JOSEPH SMITH.

JUDGE POPE.

A Presidential election was recently held on board the *Osprey* and the result was as follows:—

Joseph Smith, 65 gentlemen and 6 ladies.
Henry Clay, 27 " " 3 "
Van Buren, 12 " " 0 "

Friday, 31st.—

Affidavit H. T. Hugins, Anent Threat to Bring Dragoons Against Nauvoo.

STATE OF ILLINOIS, }
CITY OF NAUVOO, } SS.

May 31, 1844.

Then and there personally appeared before me, Joseph Smith, Mayor of the City of Nauvoo, the undersigned H. T. Hugins, of Burlington, Iowa Territory, and made solemn oath that Thomas B. Johnson did, on the 30th day of May, 1844, declare in his presence that he intended to bring dragoons and troops of the United States from Iowa Territory into this city, for the purpose of resisting the authority and power of the Municipal Court of said city, and that he should disregard entirely the authority of said court, and that he deemed the authority of said court of no effect. Deponent further states that said Johnson, in his said conversation, had reference to the case of Jeremiah Smith, which had been decided by said court.

H. T. HUGINS.

Subscribed and sworn to before me, this 31st day of May, 1844.

WM. W. PHELPS, Clerk M. C.

Upon the foregoing affidavit, I issued a *capias* to arrest Thomas B. Johnson for threatening the peace of the city with United States dragoons. At 10 a. m., called at my office. At 1 p. m., called to see Sister Richards, who was sick. I administered to her the laying on of hands, when she felt better. Afternoon I attended general council, when Brother Emmett made his report. Rode out in the evening to Van Orden's, and paid him $100. Two or three Indians staid in the hall at night.

Saturday, *June 1.*—At home. Some gentle showers.

At one, p. m., I rode out with Dr. Richards and Orrin P. Rockwell. Called on Davis at the boat. Paid Manhard $90. Met George J. Adams, and paid him $50. Then went to John P. Greene's, and paid him and another brother $200. Called at William Clayton's, while Dr. Richards and Orrin P. Rockwell called at the doctor's new house. Returned home at 4:30 p. m.

At 8 p. m., Peter Maughan, John Saunders, and Jacob Peart called at Dr. Richards' to consult about a coal-bed on Rock River. I suggested it would be profitable to employ the *Maid of Iowa* in the business of carrying the coal, &c; and all approved of this plan.

President Brigham Young and Elder John E. Page held a conference in Pittsburg.

I received the following letter:—

Joel H. Walker to Joseph Smith—Proposes to Join Prophet in Western Volunteer Movement.

BOSTON, May 9th, 1844.

MY DEAR SIR.—Being so closely confined in the postoffice in this city, where I have been but a short time, I have not, before this morning been aware that you had petitioned Congress in relation to raising a military force to protect our Southern Frontier.

My purpose in addressing you is to offer my services, either in military or civil duty, as I am so much confined that my health must suffer if I remain a great length of time.

If I can make myself known to you by reputation which I think possible, I have every confidence, if in your power, you will favor my wishes.

At any rate, I hope you will write me at your earliest convenience upon receipt of this.

I was born in Peacham, Vermont, October 14th, 1813. My father is Col. Joel Walker, now of Belvidere, Illinois. Hon. E. Peck, of Springfield, Illinois, is my brother-in-law. I was in the mercantile business in Chicago from 1836 to '39, (one of the firm of King, Walker & Co.,) since which time I have been here, with the exception of a year; have been in the military since the age of sixteen, and am considered somewhat proficient, having devoted much attention to the study of its principles, and an ardent love for the art. I have received a good academical and mercantile education; and if there is in your place anything which would be for our mutual advantage,

I am yours respectfully,

JOEL HAMILTON WALKER.

GENERAL JOSEPH SMITH, Nauvoo.

I replied as follows:

Letter: Joseph Smith to Joel H. Walker.

NAUVOO, ILLINOIS, June 1st, 1844.

SIR.—Yours of May 9th is before me, and according to my custom I answer off hand. I have not yet ascertained whether Congress will, by special act, authorize me to protect our beloved country. If it should, I have not a doubt but your services could be agreeably used.

As to what you could do in Nauvoo, I am unable to say. Gentlemen with a small capital, or a large one, can easily employ it to good advantage, our city is so rapidly improving.

Truth, virtue, and honor, combined with energy and industry, pave the way to exaltation, glory and bliss.

Respectfully, I have the honor to be your obedient servant,

JOSEPH SMITH.

JOEL HAMILTON WALKER, Boston, Mass.

Conference at Kalamazoo, Michigan.

A conference was held at Kalamazoo, Michigan. Present, Wilford Woodruff, George A. Smith, of the Twelve; S. Bent, C C Rich and B. Fullmer, of the High Council; also 5 High Priests, 8 Seventies, 14 Elders, 2 Priests, and 1 Deacon. Elder Wilford Woodruff presided. Seven branches were represented, containing 126 members, 15 Elders, 4 Priests, 1 Teacher and 2 Deacons. Two Elders were ordained; also 1 Priest and 1 Teacher.

A conference was held at Alquina, Fayette Co.,

Indiana. Elder Amasa Lyman presided. 5 High Priests, 2 Seventies and 4 Elders present.

Sunday, *2*.—At home. Pleasant day.

Conference at Glasgow, Scotland.

A conference was held in Glasgow, Scotland, representing 1,018 members, including 1 High Priest, 30 Elders, 46 Priests, 36 Teachers and 20 Deacons.

Monday, *3*.—At home. Received the following letter:

Letter: "Horace" to President Joseph Smith—Threatened Invasion of Nauvoo.

BURLINGTON, IOWA, June 2nd, 1844.

FRIEND SMITH.—I have just received intimation that there is a project on foot here to visit Nauvoo with a body of from five to six hundred armed men, for the purpose of liberating Dr. Hickock, who, it is stated, is confined in your prison. I, as a friend to your society, consider it my duty to make you aware of the danger you may be in, that you may be prepared to meet them. I think it best to keep my name from you, for were it known here that I had given notice of their proceedings, it would not be safe for me to remain. Do not think it a humbug, and treat it lightly; but prepare yourselves for the coming storm. From what I can learn, they intend going on the the next boat. I hope this may reach you in time.

I am, with respect, your friend,

HORACE.

Rode out on the hill about 9 a. m.

Municipal Court sat. I was not present. The appealed cases of Augustine Spencer, Chauncey L. Higbee, Charles A. Foster, and Robert D. Foster, came up; but as they failed to appear, the cases were referred back to the court below.

At 5 p. m. I read German with Alexander Neibaur.

President Brigham Young left Pittsburg, and preached in the evening to an attentive congregation in Old Britain.

Tuesday, *4*.—At home.

Arthur Morrison and Pulaski Cahoon proposed to give $100 per month for the use of the *Maid of Iowa*. Made out their own bonds with their own security; but I would not receive them.

In the afternoon I went out to my farm, and accidentally broke the whippletree of my buggy.

Wrote the following letter to Mr. Tewkesbury, Boston.

Letter: Joseph and Hyrum Smith to Mr. Tewkesbury—Seeking to Restore Latter to Fellowship.

NAUVOO, ILLINOIS, June 4th, 1844.

SIR.—We understand that you have been cut off from the Church of Jesus Christ of Latter-day Saints; and feeling an ardent desire for the salvation of the souls of men, we take pleasure in feeling after you; and therefore would, in the sincerity of men of God, advise you to be rebaptized by Elder Nickerson, one of the servants of God, that you may again receive the sweet influences of the Holy Ghost, and enjoy the fellowship of the Saints.

The law of God requires it, and you cannot be too good. Patience is heavenly, obedience is noble, forgiveness is merciful, and exaltation is godly; and he that holds out faithful to the end shall in no wise lose his reward. A good man will endure all things to honor Christ, and even dispose of the whole world, and all in it, to save his soul. Grace for grace is a heavenly decree, and union is power where wisdom guides.

Respectfully,

JOSEPH SMITH,
HYRUM SMITH.

The Municipal Court issued an execution against Francis M. Higbee for \$36.26½ for costs incurred on 8th May last.

At 6 p. m. I was in council with Elders John Taylor, Hyrum Smith, Willard Richards, Almon W. Babbitt, Lucien Woodworth, and William W. Phelps on the propriety of prosecuting the Laws and Fosters for perjury, slander, &c. Counseled Taylor to go on with the prosecution in behalf of Maria Lawrence. I concluded to go to Quincy with Taylor, and give up my bonds of guardianship as administrator of the Lawrence estate.

Prosecution of the Laws and Fosters Discussed.

Alpheus Cutler and Reynolds Cahoon are so anxious to get property, they will all flat out as soon as the Temple is completed and the faith of the Saints ceases from them, &c.

At 7 p. m. I walked out with Lucien Woodworth.

Wednesday, 5.—I went to the prairie to show some land, and returned home towards night.

At 8 p. m. I walked out with Dr. Richards. The lightning in the north was most beautiful. About 10 a shower of rain passed over, with continued distant thunder. There has not been any rain for some days back. Thermometer stood at 94½ degrees in the shade. Very warm.

I received a book entitled "*An Original History of the Religious Denominations at Present Existing in the United States,*"* and wrote the following acknowledgment:

Letter: Joseph Smith to L. Daniel Rupp—Book on Religious Sects.

NAUVOO, ILLINOIS, June 5th, 1844.

DEAR SIR.—He pasa Ek-klesia, &c., together with your note, has safely reached me, and I feel very thankful for so valuable a treasure. The design, the propriety, the wisdom of letting every sect tell its own story, and the elegant manner in which the work appears, have filled my breast with encomiums upon it, wishing you God speed.

Although all is not gold that shines, any more than every religious creed is sanctioned with the so eternally sure word of prophecy, satisfying all doubt with "Thus saith the Lord;" yet, "by proving contraries," truth is made manifest," and a wise man can search out "old paths, wherein righteous men held communion with Jehovah, and were exalted through obedience.

I shall be pleased to furnish further information at a proper time, and render you such further service as the work and vast extension of our Church may demand for the benefit of truth, virtue and holiness.

Your work will be suitably noticed in our papers for your benefit.

With great respect, I have the honor to be,

Your obedient servant,

JOSEPH SMITH.

L. D. RUPP, ESQ., Lancaster City, Pa.

Thursday, 6.—About 9 a. m. I ordered my carriage for a ride; but it stood at the door till nearly noon, while I read my lettter to Henry Clay to many strangers, in the

* An article prepared by President Smith, under the title "The Latter-day Saints," is published in this work.

bar-room,* among whom was one who advocated the claims of Henry Clay for the presidency. I argued with him for a long time to show the subject in its true light, and that no man could honestly vote for a man like Clay, who had violated his oath, and not acted on constitutional principles.

About half-past twelve Dimick B. Huntington came and said that Robert D. Foster felt very bad, and he thought there was a chance for his return, if he could be reinstated in his office in the Legion, &c., &c.; and that Foster had all the affidavits of the anti-Mormons under his control. I told Huntington that if Foster would return, withdraw all the suits he had commenced, and do right, he should be restored.

I rode out in the carriage with several persons for an hour or two. At 7 p. m. a heavy shower of rain, accompanied by thunder and lightning, and another shower at 9. p. m.

I issued the following caution to the public:

Having once notified the public against receiving a certain currency called "Kirtland Safety Society;" I again caution all persons against receiving or trading in said paper money, as all that was issued as genuine was redeemed. After the first officers who signed said bills retired, a new set of officers were appointed, and the vault of the institution was broken open and robbed of several hundred thousand dollars, the signatures forged upon the said stolen bills, and those bills are being slyly bartered or had in trade, for the purpose of wilful and malicious prosecution and collection.

In the first place the bills are not collectable by law in an unchartered institution. In the second place, they are spurious, the signature being a forgery, and every person passing or trading a bill is guilty of passing counterfeit money, besides the bare-faced act of swindling. And lastly, he that uses said bills in any way, as a medium of trade is guilty of fraud, and shows a wicked and corrupt determination to wilfully, maliciously and feloniously rob the Latter-day Saints; and if the executors of the laws are as ready to mete out even handed justice to such

*This was the public sitting room of the Mansion, which, it will be remembered was used at this time as a hotel.

men as the Mormons, more indictments will indicate more honesty. Time will show.

JOSEPH SMITH.

Nauvoo, June 6, 1844.

Prophet's Conversation with Dr. Foster.

Friday, 7.—Robert D. Foster called professedly to make some concessions in order to return to the Church. He wanted a private interview, which I declined. I had some conversation with him in the hall, in the presence of several gentlemen. I told him I would meet with him in the presence of friends. I would choose three or four, and he might choose an equal number, and that I was willing to settle everything on righteous principles. In the evening a report was circulated that Foster had said that I would receive him back on any terms, and give him a hatful of dollars into the bargain.

I went to the printing office about 2 p. m., and instructed Elder John Taylor to answer a certain bill or receipt of George W. Harris.

First number of the *Expositor*.

The first and only number of the *Nauvoo Expositor* was published, edited by Sylvester Emmons.

In the evening I received an extremely saucy and insulting letter from Robert D. Foster. Pleasant evening.

Saturday, 8.—From 10 a. m. to 1 p. m. in City Council; also from 3 to 6:30 p. m. The subject the *Nauvoo Expositor* was taken under consideration. An ordinance was passed concerning the City Attorney and his duties.

Elder Jedediah M. Grant preached in the Mansion this evening. Thunder and rain this evening and during the night.

A ferry-boat came down from Burlington with a pleasure party, and landed at the Nauvoo House at 2 p. m.

I sent William Clayton to Carthage to give in some lots for assessments; and while there Backenstos told him that Walter Bagby had been gone eight days to Missouri to try to get another writ for me. Brother Clayton also got news that the Democrats had dropped Van Buren, and substituted James K. Polk, of Tennessee for president, and Silas Wright of New York, for vice-president.

I walked out in the evening with Brother Clayton.

A conference was held at Pleasant Valley, Michigan. Present of the Twelve, Wilford Woodruff, and George A. Smith. Elder Wilford Woodruff presided. Six branches were represented, comprising 89 members, 5 Elders, 2 Priests, 4 Teachers, and 3 Deacons. Five Elders were ordained.

Conference at Pleasant Vallay, Michigan.

Sunday, 9.—At home. My health not very good, in consequence of my lungs being impaired by so much public speaking. My brother Hyrum preached at the Stand.

At 2 p. m. several passengers of the steamer *Osprey* from St. Louis and Quincy arrived, and put up at the Mansion. I helped to carry in their trunks, and chatted with them in the bar-room.

There was a meeting at the Mansion at 6 p. m.

CHAPTER XXI.

THE DESTRUCTION OF THE "NAUVOO EXPOSITOR"—PROCEEDINGS OF THE NAUVOO CITY COUNCIL AND MAYOR.

Monday, June 10, 1844.—I was in the City Council from 10 a. m., to 1:20 p. m., and from 2:20 p. m. to 6:30 p. m. investigating the merits of the *Nauvoo Expositor*, and also the conduct of the Laws, Higbees, Fosters, and others, who have formed a conspiracy for the purpose of destroying my life, and scattering the Saints or driving them from the state.

Nauvoo Expositor before Nauvoo City Council.

An ordinance was passed concerning libels. The Council passed an ordinance declaring the *Nauvoo Expositor* a nuisance, and also issued an order to me to abate the said nuisance. I immediately ordered the Marshal to destroy it without delay, and at the same time issued an order to Jonathan Dunham, acting Major-General of the Nauvoo Legion, to assist the Marshal with the Legion, if called upon so to do.

Ordinance on Libels.

About 8 p. m., the Marshal returned and reported that he had removed the press, type, printed paper, and fixtures into the street, and destroyed them. This was done because of the libelous and slanderous character of the paper, its avowed intention being to destroy the municipality and drive the Saints from the city. The *posse* accompanied by some hundreds of the citizens, returned with the Marshal to the front of the Mansion, when I gave them a short address, and told them they had done right and that not a hair of their heads should be hurt for it; that they had executed the orders which were given me by the City Council; that I would never submit to have another libelous publication established in the city; that I did not care how many papers were printed in the city, if they would print the truth: but would submit to no libels or slanders from them. I then blessed them in the name of the Lord. This speech was loudly greeted by the assembly with three-times-three cheers. The *posse* and assembly then dispersed all in good order. Francis M. Higbee and others made some threats.

East wind. Very cold and cloudy.

I here insert the

Ordinance Concerning Libels and for Other Purposes.

Whereas the Saints in all ages of the world have suffered persecution and death by wicked and corrupt men under the garb of a more holy appearance of religion; and whereas the Church of Jesus Christ of Latter day Saints, from the moment that its first truth sprang out of the earth till now, has been persecuted with death, destruction, and extermination; and, whereas men to fulfill the Scriptures that a man's enemies are they of his own household, have turned traitors in the Church, and combined and leagued with the most corrupt scoundrels and villains that disgrace the earth unhung, for the Heaven-daring and damnable purpose of revenge on account of disappointed lust, disappointed projects of speculation, fraud, and unlawful designs to rob and plunder mankind with impunity; and, whereas such wicked and corrupt men have greatly facilitated their unlawful designs, horrid intentions, and murderous plans by polluting, degrading and converting the blessings and utility of the press to the sin-smoking and blood-stained ruin of innocent communities—by publishing lies, false statements, coloring the truth, slandering men, women, children, societies, and countries—by polishing the characters of blacklegs, highwaymen, and murderers as virtuous; and whereas a horrid, bloody, secret plan, upheld, sanctioned and largely patronized by men in Nauvoo and out of it, who boast that all they want for the word *go*, to exterminate or ruin the Latter day Saints, is for them to do one unlawful act, and the work shall be done, is now fostered, cherished, and maturing in Nauvoo,—by men, too, who helped to obtain the very charter they would break, and some of them drew up and voted for the very ordinances they are striving to use as a scarecrow to frighten the surrounding country in rebellion, mobbing,and war; and whereas, while the blood of our brethren from wells, holes and naked prairies, and the ravishment of female virtue from Missouri, and the smoke from the altars of infamy, prostituted by John C. Bennett, and continued in the full tide of experiment and disgraceful damnation by the very self-called fragments of a body of degraded men that have got up a press in Nauvoo to destroy the charter of the city—to destroy Mormonism, men, women, and children as Missouri did; by force of arms—by fostering laws that emanate from corruption and betray with a kiss; wherefore to honor the State of Illinois, and those patriots who gave the charter, and for the benefit, convenience, health, and happiness of said city:—

Sec. 1. Be it ordained by the City Council of Nauvoo that if any person or persons shall write or publish in said city any false statement or libel any of the citizens, for the purpose of exciting the public mind against the chartered privileges, peace, and good order of said city, or shall slander (according to the definition of slander or libel by Blackstone or Kent, or the act in the statute of Illinois,) any portion of the inhabitants of said city, or bribe any portion of the citizens of said city for malicious purposes, or in any manner or form excite the prejudice of the community against any portion of the citizens of said city, for evil purposes, he, she, or they shall be deemed disturbers of the peace; and, upon conviction before the Mayor or Municipal Court, shall be fined in any sum not exceeding five hundred dollars, or imprisoned six months, or both, at the discretion of said Mayor or court.

Sec. 2. Be it further ordained that nothing in the foregoing section shall be so construed as to interfere with the right of any person to be tried by a jury of his vicinage, with the freedom of speech or the liberty of the press, according to the most liberal meaning of the Constitution, the dignity of freemen, the voice of truth, and the rules of virtue.

Sec. 3. And be it further ordained that this ordinance shall be in force from and after its passage.

Passed June 10th, 1844.

GEO. W. HARRIS, President, pro tem.

W. RICHARDS, Recorder.

I also insert a brief synopsis of the proceedings of the City Council of the city of Nauvoo, relative to the destruction of the press and fixtures of the *Nauvoo Expositor*.

Synopsis of Proceedings in the City Council against the Nauvoo Expositor.

CITY COUNCIL, REGULAR SESSION,
June 8th, 1844.

In connection with other business as stated in last week's paper, the

Mayor remarked that he believed it generally the case, that when a man goes to law, he has an unjust cause, and wants to go before some one who wants business, and that he had very few cases on his docket; and referring to Councilor Emmons, editor of the *Nauvoo Expositor*, suggested the propriety of first purging the City Council; and, referring to the character of the paper and proprietors, called up Theodore Turley, a mechanic, who being sworn, said that the Laws (William and Wilson,) had brought bogus dies to him to fix.

Councilor Hyrum Smith inquired what good Foster and his brother and the Higbees and Laws had ever done. While his brother Joseph was under arrest from the Missouri persecution, the Laws and Robert D. Foster would have been ridden on a rail, if he had not stepped forward to prevent it, on account of their oppressing the poor.

Mayor said, while he was under arrest by writ from Governor Carlin William Law sued him for $40 he was owing Law, and it took the last expense money he had to pay it.

Councilor Hyrum Smith referred to J. H. Jackson's coming to this city, &c. Mayor said that William Law had offered Jackson $500 to kill him.

Councilor Hyrum Smith continued—Jackson told him he (Jackson) meant to have his daughter, and threatened him if he made any resistance. Jackson related to him a dream, that Joseph and Hyrum were opposed to him, but that he would execute his purposes; that Jackson had laid a plan with four or five persons to kidnap his daughter, and threatened to shoot any one that should come near after he had got her in the skiff; that Jackson was engaged in trying to make bogus, which was his principal business. Referred to the revelation read to the High Council of the Church, which has caused so much talk, about multiplicity of wives; that said revelation was in answer to a question concerning things which transpired in former days. That when sick, William Law confessed to him that he had been guilty of adultery, and was not fit to live, and had sinned against his own soul, &c., and inquired who was Judge Emmons? When he came here he had scarce two shirts to his back; but he had been dandled by the authorities of the city, &c., and was now editor of the *Nauvoo Expositor*, and his right hand man, was Francis M. Higbee, who had confessed to him that he had had the———!

Washington Peck sworn, said—"Soon after Joseph H. Jackson came here, he came to witness to borrow money, which witness loaned him and took some jewelry as security.

Soon after a man from across the river came after the jewelry. Jackson had stolen the jewelry from him.

At another time wanted to get money of witness. Asked witness if he would do anything dishonorable to get a living. Witness said he would not. Jackson said witness was a damn fool, for he could get a living, a deal easier than he was then doing, by making bogus; and some men high in the Church, are engaged in the business.

Witness asked if it was Joseph. "No," said Jackson; "I dare not tell it to Joseph." Witness understood him the Laws are engaged in it. Jackson said he would be the death of witness, if he ever went to Joseph, or anyone else, to tell what he had said.

Afternoon.—Ordered by the Council that Sylvester Emmons be suspended until his case could be investigated, for slandering the City Council. That the Recorder notify him of his suspension, and that his case would come up for investigation at the next regular session of the Council. (The order is in the hands of the Marshal).

Councilor John Taylor said that Counci or Emmons helped to make the ordinances of the city, and had never lifted his voice against them in the Council, and was now trying to destroy the ordinances and the charter.

Lorenzo Wasson sworn, said Josoph H. Jackson had told witness that bogus-making was going on in the city; but it was too damned small business. Wanted witness to help him to procure money, for the General (Smith) was afraid to go into it; and with $500 he could get an engraving for bills on the Bank of Missouri, and one on the State of New York, and could make money. Said many times witness did not know him. Believed the General had been telling witness something. "G—d d—n him; if he has, I will kill him. Swore he would kill any man that should prove a traitor to him," Jackson said, if he could get a company of men to suit him, he would go into the frontiers and live by highway robbery; had got sick of the world.

Mayor suggested that the Council pass an ordinance to prevent misrepresentations and libelous publications and conspiracies against the peace of the city; and, referring to the reports that Dr. Foster had set afloat, said he had never made any proposals to Foster to come back to the Church. Foster proposed to come back; came to Mayor's house, and wanted a private interview. Had some conversation with Foster in the hall, in presence of several gentlemen, on the 7th inst. Offered to meet him and have an interview in presence of friends, three or four, to be selected by each party; which Foster agreed to, and went to bring his friends for the interview; and the next notice he had of him was the following letter:—

To General Joseph Smith:

June 7th, 1844.

Sir,—I have consulted my friends in relation to your proposals of settlement, and they as well as myself, are of opinion that your conduct, and that of your unworthy, unprincipled clan, is so base, that it would be morally wrong, and detract from the dignity of gentlemen, to hold any conference with you. The repeated insults and abuses I, as well as my friends, have suffered from your unlawful course towards us, demands honorable resentment. We are resolved to make this our motto.

Nothing on our part has been done to provoke your anger, but have done all things as become men. You have trampled upon everything we hold dear and sacred. You have set all law at defiance, and profaned the name of the Most High to carry out your damnable purposes; and I have nothing more to fear from you than you have already threatened; and I, as well as my friends, will stay here and maintain and magnify the law as long as we stay; and we are resolved never to leave until we sell or exchange our property that we have here.

The proposals made by your agent, Dimick Huntington, as well as the threats you sent to intimidate me, I disdain and despise as I do their unhallowed author. The right of my family and my friends demands at my hand a refusal of all your offers. We are united in virtue and truth, and we set hell at defiance, and all her agents. Adieu.

R. D. Foster.

Mayor continued—And when Foster left his house, he went to a shoe shop on the hill, and reported that Joseph said to him, if he would come back he would give him Law's place in the Church, and a hat-full of specie.

Lucien Woodworth sworn. Said that the conversation as stated by the Mayor was correct. Was at the Mansion June 7th, when Dr. Foster rode up and inquired if General Smith was at home. Dr. Foster went into the house; witness followed. Dr. Foster was there, the General, and others, looking at some specimens of penmanship. Something was said respecting a conversation at that time between the General and the Doctor, Gen. Smith observed to Foster, if he had a conversation, he would want others present. The Doctor said he would have a word with him by himself, and went into the hall. Witness went to the door that he might see and hear what was passing. They still continued to talk on the subject of a conversation that they might have afterwards with others present, whom Mr. Smith and Foster might choose. Foster left, and went for those that he said he wanted present, and would return soon with them. He heard all the conversation. Heard nothing about Gen. Smith's making any offers to Foster to settle.

Mayor said he wished it distinctly understood that he knew nothing about Dimick Huntington going to see Foster.

Woodworth said he sent Dimick Huntington to Foster, and Joseph knew nothing about it.

Councilor Hyrum Smith said Dimick Huntington came to him on the 7th inst. and said he had had an interview with Dr. Foster, and thought he was about ready to come back, and a word from him or Joseph would bring it about.

Mayor said—"The conduct of such men and such papers are calculated to destroy the peace of the city, and it is not safe that such things should exist, on account of the mob spirit which they tend to produce." He had made the statements he had, and called the witnesses to prepare the council to act in the case.

Emmons was blackguarded out of Philadelphia, and dubbed with the title of Judge (as he had understood from citizens of Philadelphia); was poor, and Mayor helped him to cloth for a coat before he went away last fall, and he (Emmons) labored all winter to get the postoffice from Mr. Rigdon (as informed).

Mayor referred to a writing from Dr. Goforth, showing that the Laws presented the communication from the Female Relief Society in the *Nauvoo Neighbor* to Dr. Goforth, as the bone of contention, and said if God ever spake by any man, it will not be five years before this city is in ashes and we in our graves, unless we go to Oregon, California or some other place, if the city does not put down everything which tends to mobocracy, and put down murderers, bogus-makers, and scoundrels. All the sorrow he ever had in his family in this city has arisen through the influence of William Law.

Councilor H. Smith spoke in relation to the Laws, Fosters, Higbees, editor of the *Signal*, &c., and of the importance of suppressing that spirit which has driven us from Missouri, &c.; that he would go in for an effective ordinance.

Mayor said, at the time Governor Carlin was pursuing him with his writs, William Law came to his house with a band of Missourians for the purpose of betraying him. Came to his gate, and was prevented by Daniel Carn, who was set to watch. Law came within his gate and called, "Mayor," and the Mayor reproved Law for coming at that time of night with a company of strangers.

Daniel Carn sworn. Said that about ten o'clock at night a boat came up the river with about a dozen men. William Law came to the gate with them. Witness on guard, stopped them. Law called Joseph to the door, and wanted an interview. Joseph said—"Brother Law, you know better than to come here at this hour of the night," and Law retired. Next morning Law wrote a letter to apologize, which witness heard read, which was written apparently to screen himself from the censure of a conspiracy; and the letter betrayed a conspiracy on the face of it.

Adjourned at half-past 6 p. m.. till Monday, 10th, 10 o'clock a. m.

Ajourned session, June 10th, 10 o'clock a, m. Alderman Harris presiding.

Mayor referred to Dr. Foster, and again read his letter of the 7th instant (as before quoted).

Cyrus Hills (a stranger) sworn. Said one day last week, believed it Wednesday, a gentleman whom witness did not know, came into the sitting room of the Nauvoo Mansion, and requested the Hon. Mayor to step aside; he wanted to speak with him. Mayor stepped through the door into the entry by the foot of the stairs, and the General (Mayor) asked him what he wished? Foster (as witness learned since was his name) said he wanted some conversation on some business witness did not understand at the time. The General refused to go any farther, and said he would have no conversation in private, and what should be said should be in public, and told Foster, if he would choose three or four men, he would meet him with the same number of men (among whom was his brother Hyrum), and they would have a cool and calm investigation of the subject; and by his making a proper satisfaction, things should be honorably adjusted. Witness judged, from the manner in which Foster expressed himself, that he agreed to the Mayor's proposals, and would meet him the same day in the presence of friends. Heard no proposals made by Mayor to Foster for settlement. Heard nothing about any offers of dollars, or money, or any other offer except those mentioned before. Nothing said about William Law. Was within hearing of the parties at the time conversation was going on.

Orrin P. Rockwell sworn. Some day last week saw Dr. Foster ride up to the Nauvoo Mansion and go in. Witness went in and found the Mayor and Dr. Foster in conversation. General Smith was naming the men he would have present, among whom were Hyrum Smith, William Marks, Lucien Woodworth, and Peter Haws; and Dr. Foster had leave to call an equal number of his friends, as witness understood, for the purpose of having an interview on some matters in contention.

The Doctor's brother was proposed. General said he had no objection; wanted him present. Dr. Foster started, saying he would be back shortly. Before Dr. Foster left, the men whom General Smith had named to be present at the conversation were sent for.

Cross-examined. Witness went into the house as Mayor and Dr. Foster were coming out of the bar-room into the hall Nothing said by the Mayor to Dr. Foster about his coming back. Made no offer to Foster about a settlement.

Mayor said the first thing that occurred to his mind, when he stepped into the hall with Foster, was that he wanted to assassinate him. He saw something shining below his vest. Mayor put his finger on it and said—"What is that?" Foster replied—"It's my pistol," and immediately took out the pistol, and showed it openly, and wanted the Mayor to go with him alone. Mayor said he would not go alone. Mayor never saw the pistol before. Had a hook on its side to hang on his waist-band.

Andrew L. Lamoreaux sworn. Said that in 1839 or '40, while President Joseph Smith, Elder Rigdon, Judge Higbee, Orrin P. Rockwell, and Dr. Robert D. Foster were on their way to Washington, called at witness' house in Dayton, Ohio; that the evening was spent very agreeably, except some dissatisfaction on the part of certain females with regard to the conduct of Dr. Foster. On their return from Washington, witness informed President Smith of Foster's conduct. President Smith said he had frequently reproved Foster for such conduct, and he had promised to do better, and told witness to reprove Foster, if he saw anything out of the way. That evening Foster refused to join the company, and walked through the town till about 8 o'clock, when he came in and interrupted President Smith, who was expounding some passages of the Scripture, and changed the conversation. Soon after the company were invited to Mr. Brown's at the next door, whither they all repaired. While at Mr. Brown's, conversation was going on, and the room much crowded. Dr. Foster and one of the ladies he had paid so much attention to before took their seats in one corner of the room. [Here follows statement of such lewdness in speech and conduct on the part of Foster that it would violate propriety to print it.] Next morning witness went in while Foster and others were at breakfast, and related what he had seen. Foster denied it. President Smith told him not to deny it, for he saw it himself, and was ashamed of it. Foster confessed it was true, and promised to reform.

Peter Haws sworn. Said that he came to Nauvoo before the Laws and brought considerable property. It was a short time after the Church had been driven out of Missouri, and had arrived in this place. The families having been robbed of all in Missouri, were in a starving condition. By the counsel of the Presidency, witness converted his funds to feeding the poor, bringing in meat and flour, &c.; and while thus engaged, drew upon the Laws, who were at that time engaged in merchandise, to the amount of some six hundred dollars, which, on account of expenditure for the poor, he was not able to pay within seventy or eighty dollars, which they pressed him for as soon as they wanted it, although he offered them good property at considerable less than the market value, as witness was obliged to leave the city on Church business for a little season. William Law threatened and intimidated witness' family during his absense for the pay.

Dr. Foster made a public dinner on the 4th of July. Witness was obliged to be absent, and deposited meat, flour, &c., with William Law to give to the poor at that dinner, and Law handed it out as his own private property. Witness carried a load of wheat to Law's mill to be ground. Law would not grind it only to give a certain quantity of flour in return by weight. Law used up the flour, promising from time to time he would refund it. As witness was about to start on a mission to the south with his valise in his hand saw Law before his door talking with Hyrum Smith. Called on Law, and told him he was going away, and his family wanted the flour. Law promised on the honor of a gentleman and a Saint, that his family should have the flour when they wanted.

Councilor Hyrum Smith said he recollected the time and circumstance.

Hawes said when he returned he found his family must have starved, if they had not borrowed money to get food somewhere else; could not get it of Law; and Law was preaching punctuality, *punctuality*, *punctuality*, as the whole drift of his discourses to the Saints, and abusing them himself and grinding the poor.

Mayor said, if he had a City Council who felt as he did, the establishment (referring to the *Nauvoo Expositor*) would be declared a nuisance before night; and then he read an editorial from the *Nauvoo Expositor*. He then asked who ever said a word against Judge Emmons until he attacked this Council? or even against Joseph H. Jackson or the Laws, until they came out against the city? Here is a paper (*Nauvoo Expositor*) that is exciting our enemies abroad. Joseph H. Jackson has been proved a murderer before the Council, and he declared the paper a nuisance—a greater nuisance than a dead carcass. They make it a criminality for a man to have a wife on the earth while he has one in heaven, according to the keys of the Holy Priesthood; and he then read a statement of William Law's from the *Expositor*, where the truth of God was transformed into a lie concerning this thing. He then read several statements of Austin Cowles in the *Expositor* concerning a private interview, and said he never had any private conversations with Austin Cowles on these subjects; that he preached on the stand from the Bible, showing the order in ancient days. What the opposition party want is to raise a mob on us and take the spoil from us, as they did in Missouri. He said it was as much as he could do to keep his clerk, Thompson, from publishing the proceeding of the Laws and causing the people to rise up against them. Said he would rather die tomorrow and have the thing smashed, than live and have it go on, for it was exciting the spirit of mobocracy among the people, and bringing death and destruction upon us.

Peter Hawes recalled a circumstance which he had forgotten to mention concerning a Mr. Smith who came from England and soon after died. The children had no one to protect them. There was one girl sixteen or seventeen years old, and a younger sister. Witness took these girls into his family out of pity. Wilson Law, then Major-General of the Nauvoo Legion, was familiar with the oldest daughter. Witness cautioned the girl. Wilson was soon there again, and went out in the evening with the girl, who, when charged by the witness' wife, confessed that Wilson Law had seduced her. Witness told her he could not keep her. The girl wept, made much ado, and many promises. Witness told her if she would do right she might stay; but she did not keep her promise. Wilson came again and she went out with him. Witness then required her to leave the house.

Mayor said certain women came to complain to his wife that they had caught Wilson Law with the girl [in compromising relations] at Mr. Hawes' in the night.

Councilor Hyrum Smith proceeded to show the falsehood of Austin Cowles in the *Expositor*, in relation to the revelation referred to.

Mayor said he had never preached the revelation in private; but he had public. Had not taught to the anointed in the Church in private, which statement many present confirmed; that on inquiring concerning the passage on the resurrection concerning "they neither marry nor are given in marriage," &c., he received for answer, "Man in this life must marry in view of eternity, otherwise they must remain as angels, or be single in heaven," which was the doctrine of the revelation referred to; and the Mayor spoke at considerable length in explanation of this principle, and was willing, for one, to subscribe his name to declare the *Expositor* and whole establishment a nuisance.

Two o'clock p. m. Willard Richards, the clerk of the Council, bore testimony of the good character and high standing of Mr. Smith and his family, whose daughter was seduced by Wilson Law, as stated by the last witness before the morning council; that Mrs. Smith died near the mouth of the Mississippi, and the father and eldest daughter died soon after their arrival in this place; and that the seduction of such a youthful, fatherless and innocent creature, by such a man in high standing as the Major-General of the Nauvoo Legion, was one of the darkest, damnedest, and foulest deeds on record.

Councilor Hyrum Smith concurred in the remarks made by the clerk concerning the excellent character of Mr. Smith and his family.

Mayor said the Constitution did not authorize the press to publish libels, and proposed that the Council make some provision for putting down the *Nauvoo Expositor*.

Councilor Hyrum Smith called for a prospectus of the *Expositor*.

Councilor Phelps read article 8, sec. 1, Constitution of Illinois.

Mayor called for the charter.

The clerk read the prospectus of the *Nauvoo Expositor* as follows:

PROSPECTUS OF THE "NAUVOO EXPOSITOR."

The *Nauvoo Expositor* will be issued on Friday of each week, on an imperial sheet, with a new press and materials of the best quality, and rendered worthy of the patronage of a discerning and enlightened public.

The *Expositor* will be devoted to a general diffusion of useful knowledge, and its columns open for the admission of all courteous communications of a religious, moral, social, literary, or political character without taking a decided stand in favor of either of the great political parties in the country. A part of its columns will be devoted to a few primary objects, which the publishers deem of vital importance to the public welfare. Their particular locality gives them a knowledge of the many *gross abuses exercised under the "pretended" authorities of the Charter of the City of Nauvoo*, by the legislative authorities of said city and the *insupportable oppression* of the *Ministerial powers in carrying out the unjust, illegal and unconstitutional ordinances of the same.* The publishers therefore deem it a sacred duty they owe to their country and their fellow-citizens to advocate through the columns of the *Expositor* THE UNCONDITIONAL REPEAL OF THE NAUVOO CITY CHARTER, to restrain and correct the abuses of the UNIT POWER, to ward off the iron rod which is held over the devoted heads of the citizens of Nauvoo and the surrounding country, to advocate unmitigated DISOBEDIENCE TO POLITICAL REVELATIONS, and to censure and decry gross moral imperfections wherever found, either in the plebeian, patrician or SELF-CONSTITUTED MONARCH—to advocate the pure principles of morality, the pure principles of truth, designed not to destroy, but to strengthen the mainspring of God's moral government—to advocate and exercise the freedom of speech in Nauvoo, independent of the ordinances abridging the same—*to give free toleration to every man's religious sentiment*, and sustain ALL in worshiping their God according to the monitions of their consciences, as guaranteed by the Constitution of our country, and to oppose with uncompromising hostility any UNION OF CHURCH AND STATE, or any preliminary step tending to the same—to sustain ALL *however humble*, in their equal and constitutional rights, and oppose the sacrifice of the liberty, the property and the happiness of the MANY, to the *pride* and *ambition* of the FEW; in a word, to give a full, candid and succinct statement of FACTS AS THEY REALLY EXIST IN THE CITY OF NAUVOO *fearless of whose particular case the facts may apply*—being governed by the laws of editorial courtesy, and the inherent dignity which is inseparable from honorable minds, at the same time exercising their own judgment in cases of flagrant abuses of moral delinquencies,—to use such terms and names as they deem proper, when the object is of such high importance that the end will justify the means. In this great and indispensable work, we confidently look to an enlightened public to aid us in our laudable effort.

The columns of the *Expositor* will be open to the discussion of all matters of public interest, the production of all correspondents, subject to the decision of the editor alone, who shall receive or reject at his option. National questions will be in place, but no preference given to either of the political parties. The editorial department will contain the political news of the day, proceedings of Congress, election returns &c. Room will be given for articles on agriculture, the mechanic arts, commercial transactions, &c.

The first number of the *Expositor* will be issued on Friday, the 7th day of June, 1844. The publishers bind themselves to issue the paper weekly for one year, and forward 52 copies to each subscriber during the year. Orders should be forwarded as soon as possible, that the publishers may know what number of copies to issue.

The publishers take pleasure in announcing to the public that they have engaged the service of Sylvester Emmons, Esq., who will have entire charge and supervision of the editorial department. From an acquaintance with the dignity of character and literary qualifications of this gentleman, they feel assured that the *Nauvoo Expositor* must and will sustain a high and honorable reputation.

All letters and communications must be addressed to Charles A. Foster, Nauvoo, Ill., postpaid, in order to insure attention.

WILLIAM LAW,
WILSON LAW,
CHARLES IVINS,
FRANCIS M. HIGBEE,
CHAUNCEY L. HIGBEE,
ROBERT D. FOSTER,
CHARLES A. FOSTER,
Publishers.

Nauvoo, Ill., May 10th, 1844.

Mayor read the statements of Francis M. Higbee from the *Expositor*, and asked—"Is it not treasonable against all chartered rights and privileges, and against the peace and happiness of the city?"

Councilor Hyrum Smith was in favor of declaring the *Expositor* a nuisance.

Councilor Taylor said no city on earth would bear such slander, and he would not bear it, and was decidedly in favor of active measures.

Mayor made a statement of what William Law said before the City Council under oath, that he was a friend to the Mayor, &c., and asked if there were any present who recollected his statement, when scores responded, Yes.

Councilor Taylor continued—Wilson Law was President of this Council during the passage of many ordinances, and referred to the records. "William Law and Emmons were members of the Council, and Emmons has never objected to any ordinance while in the Council, but has been more like a cipher, and is now become editor of a libelous paper, and is trying to destroy our charter and ordinances." He then read from the Constitution of the United States on the freedom of the press, and said—"We are willing they should publish the truth; but it is unlawful to publish libels. The *Expositor* is a nuisance, and stinks in the nose of every honest man."

Mayor read from Illinois Constitution, article 8, section 12, touching the responsibility of the press for its constitutional liberty.

Councilor Stiles said a nuisance was anything that disturbs the peace of a community, and read Blackstone on private wrongs, vol. 2, page 4; and the whole community has to rest under the stigma of these falsehoods (referring to the *Expositor*); and if we can prevent the issuing of any more slanderous communications, he would go in for it. It is right for this community to show a proper resentment; and he would go in for suppressing all further publications of the kind.

Councilor Hyrum Smith believed the best way was to smash the press and pi the type.

Councilor Johnson concurred with the Councilors who had spoken.

Alderman Bennett referred to the statement of the *Expositor* concerning the Municipal Court in the case of Jeremiah Smith as a libel, and considered the paper a public nuisance.

Councilor Warrington considered his a peculiar situation, as he did not belong to any church or any party. Thought it might be considered rather harsh for the Council to declare the paper a nuisance, and proposed giving a few days limitation, and assessing a fine of $3,000 for every libel; and if they would not cease publishing libels, to declare it a nuisance; and said the statutes made provisions for a fine of $500.

Mayor replied that they threatened to shoot him when at Carthage, and the women and others dare not go to Carthage to prosecute; and read a libel from the *Expositor* concerning the imprisonment of Jeremiah Smith.

Councilor Hyrum Smith spoke of the *Warsaw Signal*, and disapprobated its libelous course.

Mayor remarked he was sorry to have one dissenting voice in declaring the *Expositor* a nuisance.

Councilor Warrington did not mean to be understood to go against the proposition; but would not be in haste in declaring a nuisance.

Councilor Hyrum Smith referred to the mortgages and property of the proprietors of the *Expositor*, and thought there would be little chance of collecting damages for libels.

Alderman Elias Smith considered there was but one course to pursue that the proprietors were out of the reach of the law; that our course was to put an end to the things at once. Believed by what he had heard that if the City Council did not do it, others would.

Councilor Hunter believed it to be a nuisance. Referred to the opinion of Judge Pope on *habeas corpus*, and spoke in favor of the charter, &c. Asked Francis M. Higbee, before the jury, if he was not the man he saw at Joseph's house making professions of friendship. Higbee said he was not. (Hundreds know this statement to be false.) He also asked R. D. Foster if he did not state before hundreds of people that he believed Joseph to be a Prophet. "No," said Foster. They were under oath when they said it. (Many hundreds of people are witness to this perjury).

Alderman Orson Spencer accorded with the views expressed, that the *Nauvoo Expositor* is a nuisance. Did not consider it wise to give them time to trumpet a thousand lies. Their property could not pay for it. If we pass only a fine or imprisonment, have we any confidence that they will desist? None at all. We have found these men covenant-breakers with God, with their wives, &c. Have we any hope of their doing better? Their characters have gone before them. Shall they be suffered to go on, and bring a mob upon us, and murder our women and children, and burn our beautiful city! No! I had rather my blood would be spilled at once, and would like to have the press removed as soon as the ordinance would allow; and wish the matter might be put into the hands of the Mayor, and everybody stand by him in the execution of his duties, and hush every murmur.

Councilor Levi Richards said he had felt deeply on this subject, and concurred fully in the view General Smith had expressed of it this day; thought it unnecessary to repeat what the Council perfectly understood; considered private interest as nothing in comparison with the public good. Every time a line was formed in Far West, he was there—for what? To defend it against just such scoundrels and influence as the *Nauvoo Expositor* and its supporters were directly calculated to bring against us again. Considered the doings of the Council this day of immense moment, not to this city alone, but to the whole world; would go in to put a stop to the thing at once. Let it be thrown out of this city, and the responsibility of countenancing such a press be taken off our shoulders and fall on the State, if corrupt enough to sustain it.

Councilor Phineas Richards said that he had not forgotten the transaction at Haun's Mill, and that he recollected that his son George Spencer then lay in the well referred to on the day previous, without a winding-sheet, shroud or coffin. He said he could not sit still when he saw the same spirit raging in this place. He considered the publication of the *Expositor* as much murderous at heart as David was before the death of Uriah; was prepared to take stand; by the Mayor, and whatever he proposes; would stand by him to the last. The quicker it is stopped the better

Councilor Phelps had investigated the Constitution, Charter, and laws. The power to declare that office a nuisance is granted to us in the Springfield Charter, and a resolution declaring it a nuisance is all that is required.

John Birney sworn. Said Francis M. Higbee and Wm. Law declared they had commenced their operations, and would carry them out, law or no law.

Stephen Markham sworn. Said that Francis M. Higbee said the interest of this city is done the moment a hand is laid on their press.

Councilor Phelps continued, and referred to Wilson Law in destroying the character of a child—an orphan child, who had the charge of another child.

Warren Smith sworn. Said F. M. Higbee came to him, and proposed to have him go in as a partner in making bogus money. Higbee said he would not work for a living; that witness might go in with him if he would advance fifty dollars; and showed him (witness) a half-dollar which he said was made in his dies.

Councilor Phelps continued and he felt deeper this day than ever he felt before, and wanted to know, by "Yes," if there was any person who wanted to avenge the blood of that innocent female who had been seduced by the then Major-General of the Nauvoo Legion, Wilson Law; when "Yes!" resounded from every quarter of the house. He then referred to the tea plot at Boston, and asked if anybody's rights were taken away with that transaction; and are we offering, or have we offered to take away the rights of anyone these two days? ("No!" resounded from every quarter.) He then referred also to Law's grinding the poor during the scarcity of grain, while the poor had nothing but themselves to grind; and spoke at great length in support of active measures to put down iniquity, and suppress the spirit of mobocracy.

Alderman Harris spoke from the chair, and expressed his feelings that the press ought to be demolished.

The following resolution was then read and passed unanimously, with the exception of Councilor Warrington:—

"Resolved, by the City Council of the city of Nauvoo, that the printing-office from whence issues the *Nauvoo Expositor* is a public nuisance and also all of said *Nauvoo Expositors* which may be or exist in said establishment; and the Mayor is instructed to cause said printing establishment and papers to be removed without delay, in such manner as he shall direct.

GEORGE W. HARRIS,
President, *pro tem*.

W. RICHARDS, Recorder.

The following order was immediately issued by the Mayor:—

STATE OF ILLINOIS,
CITY OF NAUVOO, } SS.

To the Marshal of said City, greeting.

You are here commanded to destroy the printing press from whence issues the *Nauvoo Expositor*, and pi the type of said printing establishment in the street, and burn all the *Expositors* and libelous handbills found in said establishment; and if resistance be offered to your execution of this order by the owners or others, demolish the house; and if anyone threatens you or the Mayor or the officers of the city, arrest those who threaten you, and fail not to execute this order without delay, and make due return hereon.

By order of the City Council,
JOSEPH SMITH, Mayor.

Marshal's return—"The within-named press and type is destroyed and pied according to order, on this 10th day of June, 1844, at about 8 o'clock p. m.

J. P. GREENE, C. M.

HEADQUARTERS, NAUVOO LEGION,
June 10th, 1844.

To Jonathan Dunham, acting Major-General of the Nauvoo Legion.

You are hereby commanded to hold the Nauvoo Legion in readiness forthwith to execute the city ordinances, and especially to remove the printing establishment of the *Nauvoo Expositor;* and this is what you are required to do at sight, under the penalty of the laws, provided the Marshal shall require it and need your services.

JOSEPH SMITH,
Lieut-General, Nauvoo Legion.

Tuesday 11.—Spent the forenoon in council with the brethren at my house. Went to the office and conversed with my brother Hyrum, Dr. Richards, George G. Adams, and others.

I issued the following.

PROCLAMATION.

By virtue of my office as Mayor of the city of Nauvoo, I do hereby strictly enjoin it upon the municipal officers and citizens of said city to use all honorable and lawful means in their power to assist me in maintaining the public peace and common quiet of said city. As attempts have already been made to excite the jealousy and prejudice of the people of the surrounding country, by libels and slanderous articles upon the citizens and City Council, for the purpose of destroying the charter of said city, and for the purpose of raising suspicion, wrath, and indignation among a certain class of the less honorable portion of mankind, to commit acts of violence upon the innocent and unsuspecting, in a certain newspaper called the *Nauvoo Expositor*, recently established for such purposes in said city, and which has been destroyed as a nuisance, according to the provision of the charter. I further call upon every officer, authority, and citizen to be vigilant in preventing, by wisdom the promulgation of false statements, libels, slanders, or any other malicious or evil-designed concern that may be put in operation to excite and ferment the passions of men to rebel against the rights and privileges of the city, citizens, or laws of the land; to be ready to suppress the gathering of mobs; to repel, by gentle means and noble exertion, every foul scheme of unprincipled men to disgrace and dishonor the city, or state, or any of their legally-constituted authorities; and, finally to keep the peace by being cool, considerate, virtuous, unoffending, manly, and patriotic, as the true sons of liberty ever have been, and honorably maintain the precious boon our illustrious fathers won.

In witness whereof I have hereunto set my hand and affixed the seal of said corporation at the city of Nauvoo, this 11th day of June, 1844.

JOSEPH SMITH, Mayor.

I had an interview with Elder G. J. Adams out of doors and then returned home to dinner.

At 2 p. m. I went into court. Many people were present. I talked an hour or two on passing events, the mob party, &c., and told the people I was ready to fight, if the mob compelled me to, for I would not be in bondage. I asked the assembly if they would stand by me, and they cried "Yes" from all quarters. I returned home.

The Recorder issued a summons for Sylvester Emmons to attend the City Council on the second Saturday in July, at 10 a. m. to answer charges then and there to be preferred against him for slandering the City Council.

Dr. Richards came to me at my room as I was talking to my brother Hyrum, Eaton Bonney and others, and read the following letter:

Letter: L. W. Hickok to Joseph Smith—Probability of Indictment of the Prophet et al, at Springfield.

SPRINGFIELD, ILL., June 6th, 1844.

General Joseph Smith or Dr. Richards:

GENTLEMEN.—I arrived at this place on yesterday, safe and sound, in company with Major Smith, who is in good health, and wishes to be remembered to you and all his friends.

I have just learned that T. B. Johnson, the individual who figured so large at Nauvoo is about to present the case, or his case, before the grand jury at this place. This is to inform you of the fact, that you may take the necessary precaution, or do what you think advisable in the case. From what I can gather, you are all to be indicted who were present in the case according to the law of the city of Nauvoo.

I remain a friend to humanity, "equal rights," and justice to all mankind.

L. W. HICKOK.

P. S.—I have just learned that Elder Wight is in this place, and shall put this in his hands, thinking that he may act with more efficiency than the mail.

I am, &c.,
L. W. H.

Our communications by mail appear to be cut off, as no part of our extensive correspondence has come to hand by the U. S. mail for the last three weeks, and Dr. Hickok seems to be aware of it. Instructed Dr. Richards to answer Dr. Hickok's letter, and then rode out with O. P. Rockwell.

I received the following letter:

Letter: H. T. Hugins to Joseph Smith—Warning the Prophet of Probable Indictment.

SPRINGFIELD, ILL., June 6, 1844.

DEAR SIR.—I have just received information that T. B. Johnson is making an effort to procure from the grand jury for the United States, now in session at this place, an indictment against the members of your Municipal Court for exercising their legal and constitutional rights, and discharging their sworn duty in acting in the matter of Jeremiah Smith's petition for *habeas corpus*. I could hardly have supposed that he would succeed, had I not been informed that there is no doubt that he will accomplish his object. I give you this information that you may be able to act as circumstances may require. Mr. Smith has not had a hearing, and will not till tomorrow morning.

Yours truly,

H. T. HUGINS.

GENERAL JOSEPH SMITH, Nauvoo.

Elders Jedediah M. Grant and George J. Adams preached at my house in the evening. Cloudy and cool day.

The captain of the steamer *Osprey* called this forenoon at the printing office to see me. I rode with him to his boat, which was at the upper landing. When I came up, Charles A. Foster called the passengers to see the meanest man in the world. Mr. Eaton stopped him, and told the passengers that it was Foster who was the meanest man in the world. Rollison attempted to draw a pistol, but Eaton silenced him, and kept them all down.

David Harvey Redfield reported that last evening, while on the hill, just before the police arrived, Francis M. Higbee said while speaking of the printing press of the *Nauvoo Expositor*, if they lay their hands upon it or break it, they may date their downfall from that very hour, and in ten days there will not be a Mormon left in Nauvoo. What they do, they may expect the same in return. Addison Everett also heard him.

Jason R. Luse reported that Ianthus Rolf said, while the press was burning that before three weeks the Mansion House would be strung to the ground, and he would help to do it; and Tallman Rolf said the city would be strung to the ground within ten day. Moses Leonard also heard him, Joshua Miller being also present.

Bryant, (merchant of Nauvoo) said before he would see such things, he would wade to his knees in blood.

It is reported that runners have gone out in all directions to try to get up a mob; and the mobbers are selling their houses in Nauvoo and disposing of their property.

CHAPTER XXII.

PRESIDENT SMITH ARRESTED FOR RIOT IN RELATION TO "EXPOSITOR" AFFAIR—HABEAS CORPUS PROCEEDINGS BEFORE MUNICIPAL COURT—A CALL FROM ARKANSAS—THE PROPHETS'S DREAMS—MASS MEETING AT WARSAW—LETTERS TO GOVERNOR FORD ON "EXPOSITOR" AFFAIR.

Wednesay, June 12, 1844.—At 10 a. m. in my office.

At half-past one I was arrested by David Bettisworth on the following writ:

STATE OF ILLINOIS, }
HANCOCK COUNTY, } ss.

The People of the State of Illinois to all Constables, Sheriffs and Coroners of State, Greeting: ·

Whereas complaint hath been made before me, one of the justices of the peace within and for the county of Hancock aforesaid, upon the oath of Francis M. Higbee of said county, that Joseph Smith, Samuel Bennett, John Taylor and William W. Phelps, Hyrum Smith, John P. Greene, Stephen Perry, Dimick B. Huntington, Jonathan Dunham, Stephen Markham, William Edwards, Jonathan Holmes, Jesse P. Harmon, John Lytle, Joseph W. Coolidge, Harvey D. Redfield, Porter Rockwell and Levi Richards, of said county did on the 10th day of June instant commit a riot at and within the county aforesaid, wherein they, with force and violence broke into the office of the *Nauvoo Expositor*, and unlawfully and with force burned and destroyed the printing press, type and fixtures of the same, being the property of William Law, Wilson Law, Charles Ivins, Francis M. Higbee, Chauncey L. Higbee, Robert D. Foster, and Charles A. Foster.

These are therefore to command you forthwith to apprehend the said Joseph Smith, Samuel Bennett, John Taylor, William W. Phelps, Hyrum Smith, John P. Greene, Stephen Perry, Dimick B. Huntington, Jonathan Dunham, Stephen Markham, William Edwards, Jonathan Holmes, Jesse P. Harmon, John Lytle, Joseph W. Coolidge, Harvey D. Redfield, Porter Rockwell and Levi Richards, and bring them before me or some other justice of the peace, to answer the premises, and further to be dealt with according to Law.

Given under my hand and seal at Carthage, in the county aforesaid, this 11th day of June, A. D. 1844.

[Seal] THOMAS MORRISON, J. P.

The Prophet Asserts his Rights Under the Law.

After the officer got through reading the writ, I referred him to the clause in the writ—"Before me or some other justice of the peace of said county," saying, "We are ready to go to trial before Esquire Johnson or any justice in Nauvoo, according to the requirements of the writ;" but Bettisworth swore he would be damned but he would carry them to Carthage before Morrison, who issued the writ and seemed very wrathy. I asked him if he intended to break the law, for he knew the privilege of the prisoners, and they should have it. I called upon all present to witness that I then offered myself (Hyrum did the same) to go forthwith before the nearest justice of the peace, and also called upon them to witness whether the officer broke the law or not.

I felt so indignant at his abuse in depriving me of the privilege of the statute of Illinois in going before "some other justice," that I determined to take out a writ of *habeas corpus*, and signed the following petition:

The Prophet's Petition for Writ of Habeas Corpus.

STATE OF ILLINOIS, CITY OF NAUVOO.

To the Honorable Municipal Court in and for the said City of Nauvoo:

Your petitioner, Joseph Smith, respectfully represents that he is now under arrest in the said city of Nauvoo.

That he is in the custody of one David Bettisworth, a constable in and for said county of Hancock, who holds your petitioner, as he says by virtue of a warrant issued by one Thomas Morrison, an acting justice of the peace in and for the said county of Hancock, and State of Illinois, which warrant was issued upon the affidavits of one Francis M. Higbee, charging your petitioner with being guilty of a riot, or of having committed a riot within the county aforesaid.

Your petitioner further represents that the warrant of arrest, by virture of which the said David Bettisworth has made this arrest, does not disclose sufficiently clear and explicit the charge they have preferred.

Your petitioner further avers that this proceeding against him has been instituted through malice, private pique and corruption.

Your petitioner further avers that the design and intention of the said F. M. Higbee in commencing this prosecution is to commit and carry out more easily a conspiracy against the life of your petitioner; and that the said Higbee has publicly declared that it was his determination to do everything in his power to throw your petitioner into the hands of his enemies: and that there is a determination upon the part of said Higbee and his unhallowed coadjutors to commit an unlawful act, and to set the rights and privileges of your petitioner at defiance, and bring down upon his head this corrupt and unhallowed prosecution.

Your petitioner further avers that he is not guilty of the charge preferred against him; that he seeks an investigation before an impartial tribunal, and fears not the result.

Your petitioner would therefore ask your honorable body to grant him the benefit of the writ of *habeas corpus*, that this matter may be investigated upon legal principles, and that the legal and constitutional rights of your petitioner may be determined by your honorable body. And your petitioner, as in duty bound, will ever pray.

JOSEPH SMITH.

Subscribed and sworn to this 12th day of June, 1844, before me.

WILLARD RICHARDS, M. C. C. N.

Whereupon the clerk issued the following:

Petition of the Prophet Granted.

STATE OF ILLINOIS, CITY OF NAUVOO.

The People af the State of Illinois to the Marshal of Said City Greeting:

Whereas, application has been made before the Municipal Court of said city, that the body of one Joseph Smith, of the city aforesaid, is in the custody of one David Bettisworth, constable of the couuty of Hancock, and State aforesaid.

These are therefore to command the said David Bettisworth, constable as aforesaid, to safely have the body of said Joseph Smith, of the city aforesaid, in his custody detained, as it is said, together with the day and cause of his caption and detention, by whatsoever name the said Joseph Smith may be known or called, before the Municipal Court of the said city forthwith, to abide such order as the said court shall make in his behalf. And further, if the said David Bettisworth, or other person or persons having said Joseph Smith of said city of Nauvoo in custody shall refuse or neglect to comply with the provisions of this writ, you, the marshal of said city, or other person authorized to serve the same, are hereby required to arrest the person or persons so refusing or neglecting to comply, as aforesaid, and bring him or them together with the person or persons in his or their custody, forthwith before the Municipal Court aforesaid, to be dealt with according to law. And herein fail not, and bring this writ with you.

Witness, Willard Richards, clerk of the Municipal Court at Nauvoo, this 12th day of June, in the year of our Lord one thousand eight hundred and forty-four.

[Seal] WILLARD RICHARDS,
Clerk of the Municipal Court of the City of Nauvoo.

At 5 p. m. I appeared before the Municipal Court on the above *habeas corpus*. The following is a copy of their docket.

Hearing on the Expositor affairs Before the Municipal Court of Nauvoo—Habeas Corpus Proceedings.

Special session, June 12th, 1844, 5 o'clock p. m.

Present—Alderman N. K. Whitney, Orson Spencer, George W. Harris, Gustavus Hills, Elias Smith, and Samuel Bennett, associate justices. The Mayor being on trial, George W. Harris was elected president *pro tem*.

John P. Greene, Marshal, made his return on the writ of *habeas corpus;* "the body of Joseph Smith in court."

David Bettisworth made his return on the copy of the warrant which was attached to the petition as follows:—"I hold the body of Joseph Smith by virtue of a writ, of which the within is a copy. David Bettisworth, constable."

7th section of Addenda of City Ordinance read by Councilor George P. Styles. Resolution of City Council June 10th, 1844, declaring printing establishment of the *Nauvoo Expositor* a nuisance read. Mayor's order to the Marshal to execute the same was also read, and Lieut.-General's order of June 10th, 1844, to Major-General Dunham to assist the Marshal to destroy said printing establishment.

Theodore Turley sworn, said that the order of the Marshal was executed quietly and peaceably. There was no riot or disturbance, no noise, no exultation; the Marshal endeavored to keep peace and silence, and the officers did also. The two companies under command of Dunham and Markham retired in perfect order; no exultation or shouting. Marched in front of the Mansion, and were dismissed.

J.R. Wakefield confirmed the statements of Theodore Turley: said the Marshal stated his authority, and demanded the keys of the building, which Higbee denied; and Marshal ordered the door to be forced, and the press was broken, and type pied in the street.

James Jackson, sworn, confirmed the statements of previous witnesses; heard no noise on opening the door. Most of the confusion he heard was Higbee and his company throwing blackguard language to the posse, which they did not regard: saw the whole proceedings till they were dismissed; all was done in order. Higbee's blackguard language was not answered to at all by the ranks. Heard nothing said about shooting. Heard some one damn the city authorities. Understood it was Charles Foster. I am a stranger in this place.

John Kay, Robert Clift, Augustus A. Farnham, Joseph A. Kelting, Henry G. Sherwood, Augustus Stafford, Cyrus Canfield, John Gleason sworn.

Henry G. Sherwood confirmed the statements of previous witnesses. Pullin called for Dr. Foster and the officer commanded silence. Francis M. Higbee's threats have been lavish towards General Smith and Hyrum for a long time; has threatened injury upon them and the property of the Smiths. His conspiracies and threats have not been a little.

Orrin P. Rockwell sworn. Some three or four weeks ago said Francis M. Higbee said he would go his death against Joseph and Hyrum Smith. Francis said, "I know my course is wrong; but if I stop I shall get hell, and if I go on I shall only get hell;" and would do what he intended at the risk of his life, and would destroy the General if possible. Said the Council had ordered the press destroyed and "who lays his hands on the press it is death to them." Witness has frequently heard Higbee tell lies about the General to injure his character.

John Hughes, Joseph Dalton, William Clayton and James Goff sworn. John Hughes said, Higbee said, "By God, all I want to live for is to see this city sunk down to the lowest hell, and by God it shall!" This was just previous to the Marshal's arriving on the 10th. William Clayton said two years ago this June Francis M. Higbee confessed he was concerned with John C. Bennett in his iniquity, and had a bad disorder: said he knew his character was ruined. From time to time since that, witness knew Higbee had been threatening General Smith's character and property.

Leonard Soby heard Higbee threaten to shoot General Smith at Rollinson's store, and Higbee said the destinies of this people are this day sealed in the archives of heaven, and there shall not be left one stone upon another on that temple.

Jonn P. McEwan: Higbee said, in reference to Joseph Smith, "G— d-- him, I will shoot him and all that pertains to him; and before ten suns shall go over our heads, the Temple, Nauvoo House and Mansion shall all be destroyed, and it will be the total downfall of this community."

Cyrus Canfield: Higbee said he would never let things go till he had accomplished the downfall of General Smith; that he did not value his life to produce the downfall of General Smith.

Joseph Dalton: Higbee said, if they laid their hands on the press, from that hour they might date their downfall; that ten suns should not roll over their heads till the city was destroyed.

Court decided that Joseph Smith had acted under proper authority in destroying the establishment of the *Nauvoo Expositor* on the 10th inst.; that his orders were executed in an orderly and judicious manner, without noise or tumult; that this was a malicious prosecution on the part of Francis M. Higbee; and that said Higbee pay the costs of suit, and that Joseph Smith be honorably discharged from the accusations and of the writ, and go hence without delay.

I received the following letter:

Letter: Washington Tucker to President Smith—Asking that Elders be Sent to Arkansas.

ELDORADO, UNION COUNTY, ARKANSAS, May 4th, 1844.

To General Joseph Smith of Nauvoo, Illinois:

REVEREND SIR.—Last winter, while in the State of Mississippi, I became acquainted with one of your missionaries who was laboring at the time in that state. Also at the same time, I had an opportunity of perusing some of your sacred books; and from what I have been able to learn, as well from reading as from observation, I am constrained to be very favorably impressed towards the new doctrine. Although to me it certainly appears quite novel, yet I cannot do otherwise than believe there is great reality in it; so much so, indeed, that I am extremely anxious to become better informed on this all important and truly vital matter.

And, moreover, I am not the only one in this part who is an ardent seeker after truth. Indeed, the subject is beginning to produce a great deal of inquiry and some excitement in this country. Hundreds who never before heard of the new revelation are opening their eyes and staring and gaping to know more about it.

Some few days ago, several emigrants arrived here from Mississippi, who speak in the highest terms of the Latter-day Saints. Their report has greatly increased the inquiry and excitement previously going the rounds in this quarter. I hear a number speak of visiting Nauvoo, some of taking their families with them, and so remain there. But it is the general wish of a great many here in Union county for you to send a minister here immediately to instruct us and lead us more fully into the light of this wonderful and new revealed religion, and direct us into the true road to salvation.

This is the only subject on which my thoughts dwell both day and night; for, indeed, during my waking hours nothing diverts my meditation from this absorbing topic, and while asleep I dream of nothing else.

If you please, be so good as to send a laborer among us immediately; for indeed the harvest is great, and the laborers but few, or none at all, I have not the least doubt but that a Latter-day Saint would succeed here as well as the most sanguine could promise himself. His labors, I am sure, would be crowned with success, and the salvation of many a precious yet perishing soul might be rescued from death and prove the rich fruits of the missionary's toil.

The principal denominations here are the Methodists, the Baptists and Campbellites. A great many of the people, however, are none-professors, the greater majority of whom are quite moral, and many of them religiously inclined.

I shall look for a minister from you within two or three months. When he does come, I will see that he is hospitably received and entertained.

Your obedient and humble servant,

WASHINGTON TUCKER.

To which I wrote the following reply:

Letter: Joseph Smith to Washington Tucker, Promising that an Elder Should be Sent.

NAUVOO, ILLINOIS, June 12th, 1844.

SIR.—Your letter, dated May 4th, has reached me, and its contents duly considered. A multiplicity of business keeps me from writing as freely to correspondents as I could wish; still my heart is large enough for all men, and my sensibilities keen enough to have compassion for every case when justice, mercy, virtue, or humanity require it. Be pleased to accept my thanks for your very kind letter; study the Bible, and as many of our books as you can get; pray to the Father in the name of Jesus Christ, have faith in the promises made to the fathers, and your mind will be guided to the truth. An Elder shall be sent as soon as the Twelve can make the necessary arrangements.

In the Gospel of our Lord Jesus Christ,

I am your obedient servant,

JOSEPH SMITH.

WASHINGTON TUCKER, Eldorado, Arkansas.

The editor of the *Neighbor* writes:

RETRIBUTIVE JUSTICE.

A knot of base men, to further their wicked and malicious designs towards the Church of Jesus Christ of Latter-day Saints and to bolster up the intents of blacklegs and bogus-makers,and advocate the characters of murderers, established a press in this city last week, and issued a paper entitled the *Nauvoo Expositor.* The prospectus showed an intention to destroy the charter, and the paper was filled with libels and slanderous articles upon the citizens and City Council from one end to the other.

"A burnt child dreads the fire." The Church as a body and individually has suffered till "forebearance has ceased to be a virtue." The cries and pleadings of men, women and children, with the authorities were, "Will you suffer that servile, murderous paper to go on and vilify and slander the innocent inhabitants of this city, and raise another mob to drive and plunder us again as they did in Missouri?" Under these pressing cries and supplications of afflicted innocence, and in the character, dignity, and honor of the corporate powers of the charter, as granted to the city of Springfield, and made and provided as a part of our charter for legislative purposes—viz., "to declare what shall be a nuisance and to prevent and remove the same." The City Council of Nauvoo on Monday, the 10th instant, declared the establishment and *Expositor* a nuisance; and the city marshal, at the head of the police, in the evening, took the press, materials and paper into the street and burned them.

And in the name of freemen, and in the name of God, we beseech all men who have the spirit of honor in them to cease from persecuting us, collectively or individually. Let us enjoy our religion, rights and peace like the rest of mankind. Why start presses to destroy rights and privileges, and bring upon us mobs to plunder and murder? We ask no more than what belongs to us—the rights of Americans.

Further Action of Municipal Court on *Expositor* Case.

Thursday, *13.*—At nine a. m. presided in Municipal Court, which sat in the Seventies' Hall. Present, William Marks, Newel K. Whitney, George W. Harris, Gustavus Hills, and Elias Smith, associate justices. Hyrum Smith, John P. Greene, William W. Phelps, Stephen Markham, Harvey D. Redfield, John Lytle, Dimick B. Huntington, John Taylor, Levi Richards, Stephen Perry, Jonathan H. Holmes, Jonathan Dunham, Samuel Bennett and William W. Edwards were arrested on the complaint of Francis M. Higbee, before Thomas Morrison, J. P., of

Carthage, by David Bettisworth, constable of Hancock county. They petitioned for and obtained a writ of *habeas corpus*. I sat as chief-justice; William Marks, Newel K. Whitney, George W. Harris, Gustavus Hills, and Elias Smith as associate justices.

Addison Everett and James Jackson gave their testimony under oath, when they were all honorably discharged from the accusations and arrest, the court deciding that said Higbee pay the costs; whereupon execution was issued for the amount.

In the evening I attended meeting in the Seventies' Hall. George J. Adams preached and I made some observations afterwards, and related a dream which I had a short time since. I thought I was riding out in my carriage, and my guardian angel was along with me. We went past the Temple, and had not gone much further before we espied two large snakes so fast locked together that neither of them had any power. I inquired of my guide what I was to understand by that. He answered, "Those snakes represent Dr. Foster and Chauncey L. Higbee. They are your enemies and desire to destroy you; but you see they are so fast locked together that they have no power of themselves to hurt you. I then thought I was riding up Mulholland street, but my guardian angel was not along with me. On arriving at the prairie, I was overtaken and siezed by William and Wilson Law and others, saying, "Ah! ah! we have got you at last! We will secure you and put you in a safe place!" and, without any ceremony dragged me out of my carriage, tied my hands behind me, and threw me into a deep, dry pit, where I remained in a perfectly helpless condition, and they went away. While struggling to get out, I heard Wilson Law screaming for help hard by. I managed to unloose myself so as to make a spring, when I caught hold of some grass which grew at the edge of the pit.

The Prophet's Dreams on Condition of Apostates at Nauvoo.

I looked out of the pit and saw Wilson Law at a little distances attacked by ferocious wild beasts, and heard him cry out, "Oh! Brother Joseph, come and save me!" I replied, "I cannot, for you have put me into this deep pit." On looking out another way, I saw William Law with outstretched tongue, blue in the face, and the green poison forced out of his mouth, caused by the coiling of a large snake around his body. It had also grabbed him by the arm, a littte above the elbow, ready to devour him. He cried out in the intensity of his agony, "Oh, Brother Joseph, Brother Joseph, come and save me, or I die!" I also replied to him, "I cannot, William; I would willingly, but you have tied me and put me in this pit, and I am powerless to help you or liberate myself." In a short time after my guide came and said aloud, "Joseph, Joseph, what are you doing there?" I replied, "My enemies fell upon me, bound me and threw me in." He then took me by the hand, drew me out of the pit, set me free, and we went away rejoicing.

Threats of Carthage Mob against Nauvoo.

Two of the brethren arrived this evening from Carthage, and said that about three hundred mobbers were assembled there, with the avowed intention of coming against Nauvoo; also that Hamilton was paying a dollar per bushel for corn to feed their animals.

The following was published in the *Warsaw Signal* office. I insert it as a specimen of the unparalleled corruption and diabolical falsehood of which the human race has become capable in this generation:

MASS MEETING AT WARSAW.

At a mass meeting of the citizens of Hancock county, convened at Carthage on the 13th day of June, 1844 Mr. Knox was appointed president, John Doty and Lewis F. Evans, vice-presidents; and William Y. Head, secretary.

Henry Stephens, Esq., presented the following resolutions, passed at a meeting of the citizens of Warsaw, and urged the adoption of them as the sense of this meeting.

Preamble and Resolutions.

Whereas information has reached us, about which there can be no question, that the authorities of Nauvoo did recently pass an ordinance declaring a printing press and newspaper published by the opponents of the Prophet a nuisance, and in pursuance thereof did direct the Marshal of the city and his adherents to enter by force the building from whence the paper was issued, and violently (if necessary) to take possession of the press and printing materials, and thereafter to burn and destroy the same; and whereas, in pursuance of said ordinance, the Marshal and his adherents, together with a mob of Mormons, did, after sunset on the evening of the 10th instant, violently enter said building in a tumultuous manner, burn and destroy the press and other materials found on the premises.

And whereas Hyrum Smith did, in the presence of the City Council and the citizens of Nauvoo, offer a reward for the destruction of the printing press and materials of the *Warsaw Signal*, a newspaper also opposed to his interests;

And whereas the liberty of the press is one of the cardinal principles of our government, firmly guaranteed by the several constitutions of the states, as well as the United States;

And whereas, Hyrum Smith has within the last week publicly threatened the life of one of our valued citizens, Thomas C. Sharp, the editor of the *Signal;*

Therefore, be it solemnly

Resolved by the citizens of Warsaw in public meeting assembled, that we view the recent ordinance of the city of Nauvoo, and the proceedings thereunder as an outrage of an alarming character, revolutionary and tyrannical in tendency, and being under color of law as calculated to subvert and destroy in the minds of the community all reliance on the law.

Resolved, that as a community we feel anxious, when possible, to redress our grievances by legal remedies; but the time has now arrived when the law has ceased to be a protection to our lives and property. A mob at Nauvoo, under a city ordinance, has violated the highest privilege in government; and to seek redress in the ordinary mode would be utterly ineffectual.

Resolved, that the public threat made in the Council of the city, not only to destroy our printing-press, but to take the life of its editor, is sufficient, in connection with the recent outrage, to command the efforts and the services of every good citizen to put an immediate stop to the career of the mad prophet and his demoniac coadjutors. We must not only defend ourselves from danger, but we must resolutely carry the war into the enemy's camp. We do therefore declare that we will sustain our press and the editor at all hazards; that we will take full vengeance, terrible vengeance, should the lives of any of our citizens be lost in the effort; that we hold ourselves at all times in readiness to co-operate with our fellow-citizens in this state, Missouri and Iowa, to exterminate, utterly exterminate the wicked and abominable Mormon leaders, the authors of our troubles.

Resolved, that a committee of five be appointed forthwith to notify all persons in our township suspected of being the tools of the prophet to leave immediately on pain of instant vengeance. And we do recommend the inhabitants of the adjacent townships to do the same, hereby pledging ourselves to render all the assistance they may require.

Resolved, that the time, in our opinion, has arrived, when the adherents of Smith, as a body, should be driven from the surrounding settlements into Nauvoo. That the prophet and his miscreant adherents should then be demanded at their hands; and, if not surrendered, a war of extermination should be waged to the entire destruction, if necessary for our protection, of his adherents. And we hereby recommend this resolution to the consideration of the several townships, to the Mass Convention to be held at Carthage, hereby pledging ourselves to aid to the utmost the complete consummation of the object in view, that we may thereby be utterly relieved of the alarm, anxiety and trouble to which we are now subjected.

Resolved that every citizen arm himself to be prepared to sustain the resolutions herein contained.

Mr. Roosevelt rose and made a brief but eloquent speech, and called upon the citizens throughout the country to render efficient aid in carrying out the spirit of the resolutions. Mr. Roosevelt then moved a committee of seven be appointed by the chair to draft resolutions expressive of our action in future.

Mr. Catlin moved to amend the motion of Mr. Roosevelt, so that the committee should consist of one from each precinct; which motion, as amended, was adopted.

The chair then appointed the following: Col. Levi Williams, Rocky Run precinct; Joel Catlin, Augusta; Samuel Williams, Carthage; Elisha Worrell, Chili; Captain Maddison, St. Mary's; John M. Ferris, Fountain Green; James Rice, Pilot Grove; John Carns, Bear Creek; C. L. Higbee, Nauvoo; George Robinson, La Harpe; and George Rockwell, Warsaw, were appointed said committee.

On motion of Mr. Sympson, Walter Bagby, Esq., was requested to address the meeting during the absence of the committee. He spoke long and eloquently upon the couse of our grievances, and expressed his belief that the time was now at hand when we were individually and collectively called upon to repel the innovations upon our liberties, and suggested that points be designated as places of encampment at which to rendezvous our forces, that we may be ready when called upon for efficient action.

Dr Barnes, one of the persons who went with the officers to Nauvoo for the purpose of arresting the rioters, having just arrived, came into the meeting and reported the result of their proceedings, which was, that the persons charged in the writs were duly arrested, but taken from the officers' hands on a writ of *habeas corpus* from the Municipal Court, and discharged, and the following potent words entered upon the records—*honorably released.*

On motion of O. C. Skinner, Esq., a vote of thanks was tendered to Dr. Barnes for volunteering his services in executing said writs.

Francis M. Higbee was now loudly called for. He stated his personal knowledge of the Mormons from their earliest history—throughout their hellish career in Missouri and this state—which has been characterized by the darkest and most diabolical deeds which have ever disgraced humanity.

The committee appointed to draft resolutions brought in the following report, which, after some considerable discussion, was unanimously adopted:

Whereas, the officer charged with the execution of a writ against Joseph Smith and others, for riot in the county of Hancock, which said writ said officer has served upon said Smith and others; and whereas said Smith and others refuse to obey the mandate of said writ; and whereas in the opinion of this meeting, it is impossible for said officer so raise a posse of sufficient strength to execute said writ; and whereas it is the opinion of this meeting that the riot is still progressing and that violence is meditated and determined on, it is the opinion of this meeting that the circumstances of the case require the interposition of executive power. Therefore,

Resolved, that a deputation of two discreet men be sent to Springfield to solicit such interposition.

2nd, Resolved, that said deputation be furnished with a certified copy of the resolution, and be authorized to obtain evidence, by affidavits and otherwise, in regard to the violence which has already been committed, and is still further meditated.

Dr. Evans here arose and expressed his wish that the above resolutions would not retard our operations, but that we would each one arm and equip ourselves forthwith.

The resolutions passed at Warsaw were again read by Dr. Barnes, and passed by acclamation.

On motion of A. Sympson, Esq., the suggestion of Mr. Bagby,

appointing places of encampment, was adopted—to-wit., Warsaw, Carthage, Green Plains, Spilman's landing, Chili and La Harpe.

On motion, O. C. Skinner and Walter Bagby, Esqs., were appointed a committee to bear the resolutions adopted by this meeting to his Excellency the Governor, requiring his executive interposition.

On motion of J. H. Sherman, a central corresponding committee was appointed.

Order that J. H. Sherman, H. T. Wilson, Chauncey Robinson, William S. Freeman, Thomas Morrison, F. M. Higbee, Lyman Prentiss, and Stephen H. Tyler be said committee.

On motion of George Rockwell,

Resolved that constables in the different precincts hold themselves in readiness to obey the officer in possession of the writs, whenever called upon, in summoning the posse.

On motion, the meeting adjourned.

JOHN KNOX, President.
JOHN DOTY,
LEWIS F. EVANS, Vice-Presidents.
W. Y. HEAD, Secretary.

Friday, 14.—Wrote to Governor Ford as follows:

Letter: Joseph Smith to Governor Ford—Explaining Action of City Council in Proceedings in "Expositor" Affairs.

NAUVOO, June 14, 1844.

His Excellency Thomas Ford:

SIR.—I write you this morning, briefly, to inform you of the facts relative to the removal of the press and fixtures of the *Nauvoo Expositor* as a nuisance.

The 8th and 10th instant were spent by the City Council of Nauvoo in receiving testimony concerning the character of the *Expositor*, and the character and designs of the proprietors.

In the investigation it appeared evident to the council that the proprietors were a set of unprincipled, lawless debauchers, counterfeiters, bogus-makers, gamblers, peace-disturbers, and that the grand object of said proprietors was to destroy our constitutional rights and chartered privileges. To overthrow all good and wholesome regulations in society, to strengthen themselves against the municipality, to fortify themselves against the Church of which I am a member, and destroy all our religious rights and privileges by libels, slanders, falsehoods, perjury, &c., and sticking at no corruption to accomplish their hellish purposes; and that said paper of itself was libelous of the deepest dye, and very injurious as a vehicle of defamation, tending to corrupt the morals and disturb the peace, tranquility and happiness of the whole community, and especially that of Nauvoo.

After a long and patient investigation, of the *Expositor* and the character and design of its proprietors, the constitution, the charter, (see Addenda to Nauvoo Charter from the Springfield Charter, sec.7) and all the best authorities on the subject; (See Chitty's Blackstone Bk. iii: v, and n., &c., &c.) the City Council decided that it was necessary for the "peace, benefit, good order and regulations" of said city, "and for the protection of property," and for "the happiness and prosperity of the citizens of Nauvoo," that said *Expositor* should be removed, and declaring said *Expositor* a nuisance ordered the Mayor to cause them to be removed without delay; which order was committed to the Marshal by due process, and by him executed the same day, by removing the paper, press and fixtures into the streets and burning the same; all which was done without riot, noise, tumult or confusion, as has already been proved before the municipality of the city; and the particulars of the whole transaction may be expected in our next *Nauvoo Neighbor*.

I send you this hasty sketch that your Excellency may be aware of the lying reports that are now being circulated by our enemies that there has been a "mob at Nauvoo," and "blood and thunder," and "swearing that two men were killed," &c., &c., as we hear from abroad, are false—false as Satan himself could invent, and that nothing has been transacted here but what has been in perfect accordance with the strictest principles of law and good order on the part of the authorities of this city; and if your Excellency is not satisfied, and shall not be satisfied after reading the whole proceedings which will be forthcoming soon, and shall demand an investigation of our municipality before Judge Pope, or any legal tribunal at the Capitol, you have only to write your wishes, and we will be forthcoming. We will not trouble you to fill a writ or send an officer for us.

I remain, as ever, a friend of truth, good order, and your Excellency's humble servant,

JOSEPH SMITH.

The following letters were also written:

Letter: John M. Bernhisel to Governor Ford—Confirming Correctness of the Prophet's Report of "Expositor" Affair.

NAUVOO, June 14th, 1844.

To His Excellency Governor Ford:

SIR.—Though I have not the honor of a personal acquaintance with you, I take the liberty of stating to you that I arrived here from the city of New York about a year since, where I was engaged in the practice of medicine for many years; that General Smith's letter to you of this date has been read in my hearing; that the statement contained therein in relation to the proceedings of the municipal authorities for the removal of the press whence issued a scandalous sheet entitled the *Nauvoo Expositor* are correct, having been an eye- and ear-witness of them.

The whole affair was conducted by the City Marshal and his posse in the most quiet and orderly manner, without the least noise, riot or tumult; and when the nuisance was abated, they immediately retired and were dismissed.

Having been a boarder in General Smith's family for more than nine months, and having therefore had abundant opportunities of contemplating his character and observing his conduct, I have concluded to give you a few of my "impressions" of him.

General Joseph Smith is naturally a man of strong mental powers, and is possessed of much energy and decision of character, great penetration, and a profound knowlege of human nature. He is a man of calm judgment, enlarged views, and is eminently distinguished by his love of justice. He is kind and obliging, generous and benevolent, sociable and cheerful, and is possessed of a mind of a contemplative and reflective character. He is honest, frank, fearless and independent, and as free from dissimulation as any man to be found.

But it is in the gentle charities of domestic life, as the tender and affectionate husband and parent, the warm and sympathizing friend, that the prominent traits of his character are revealed, and his heart is felt to be keenly alive to the kindest and softest emotions of which human nature is susceptible; and I feel assured that his family and friends formed one of the greatest consolations to him while the vials of wrath were poured upon his head, while his footsteps were pursued by malice and envy, and reproach and slander were strewn in his path, as well as during numerous and cruel persecutions, and severe and protracted sufferings in chains and loathsome prisons, for worshiping God according to the dictates of his own conscience.

He is a true lover of his country, and a bright and shining example of integrity and moral excellence in all the relations of life. As a religious teacher, as well as a man, he is greatly beloved by this people. It is almost superfluous to add that the numerous ridiculous and scandalous reports in circulation respecting him have not the least foundation in truth.

In haste, I have the honor to be your Excellency's most obedient and humble servant,

JOHN M. BERNHISEL.

Letter: Wakefield to Governor Ford—Anent the "Expositor" Affair.

CITY OF NAUVOO, June 14th, 1844.

Hon. Governor Ford:

Being a stranger in the city of Nauvoo, but fully acquainted with the facts as stated in Gen. Smith's letter of June 14th, I assert that they are true in every particular, and that the press, in the minds of all unprejudiced people, was a nuisance of the worst character, and that the authorities acted perfectly proper in destroying it; and in accomplishing the act there was no noise, tumult or riot. Furthermore, having remained for a few weeks at General Smith's house, I think it my duty to state that I have seen nothing in his deportment but what is correct in all his domestic relations, being a kind husband and an affectionate father; and all his affairs, both domestic and official, have not only been free from censure, but praiseworthy, and ought to be imitated by every one desirous of order and peace.

Yours, sir, most obediently,

J. R. WAKEFIELD, M. D.

Letter: Sidney Rigdon to Governor Ford—"Expositor" Affair.

POST OFFICE, NAUVOO, ILL., June 14 1844.

His Ecellency, Thomas Ford:

DEAR SIR.—I address this letter to your Excellency by the hand of Mr. Samuel James, in consequence of the difficulties now existing in this county, difficulties in which I have had no concern; and fearing as I do, that in the midst of an excitement so great as I have understood now exists in this county, (I say understood, for it is by report only that I speak) there may be attempts made to prejudice your mind to take some measures of a violent character that may seriously affect the citizens of this place, and injure innocent and unoffending persons, which I am satisfied would grieve your Excellency, as well as every other thinking and humane man.

There have for a length of time difficulties existed between a number of the citizens of this place, which kept increasing. One of the parties had recourse to the *Warsaw Signal* as a medium through which they communicate their difficulties to the world. These productions were inflammatory to a high degree, and the party thus assailed charged the matter as libelous and highly abusive. To these exposures responses appeared in the papers of this place, charging the matter as being false and the authors as defamers and slanderers.

Things continued thus until a paper was established in this place called the *Nauvoo Expositor*. The first number of this paper made its appearance, and it was inflammatory and abusive to an extreme. This raised the excitement to a degree beyond control, and threatened serious consequence.

At this particular juncture all the authorities of the city feeling a common interest in the peace and quiet of the place, and fearing the worst consequences must follow if something were not done, the City Council met and took the matter into consideration, and, after deliberating on the subject and examining the charter, came to the conclusion to hazard all the consequences of declaring the press a nuisance, and accordingly ordered its removal. The city marshal, in obedience to this order, went and removed the press and destroyed it. This was done without tumult or disorder. When the press was destroyed, all returned home, and everything has been perfectly quiet ever since.

Within the last three days warrants have been issued from a justice of the peace in Carthage, calling for the bodies of the persons who destroyed the press. The officer having the matter in charge, refuses the persons a hearing before any other justices of the peace than the one issuing the warrants. With this demand they refused to comply, as there is a large assembly of persons assembled at Carthage making threats of violence; and they say, and I have no doubt they verily believe that by going there their lives will be in danger; and from the intelligence which I received last evening from a person in no way connected with the affair, and one of undoubted veracity, I must think so myself. This gentleman informs me that he has been in Carthage since Monday last at the land sales, and he heard threatenings by the persons assembled there that if they could get into Nauvoo they would murder indiscriminately, and those who wanted to escape must leave. This your Excellency would abhor as I do.

The citizens of this county who do not reside in Nauvoo, and those of other counties, have indeed no interest of a personal kind at stake in this matter. There are no persons disturbing them, nor going to do so; and this great excitement does savor of something else to me than a regard for the laws. Why not let the parties, as in all other cases of the kind settle their difficulties as the laws of the country in such cases have provided.

Have the citizens of Nauvoo ever interfered with cases of difficulty existing in other parts of the county, held public meetings to inflame the public mind in favor of one party, and prejudice it against the other party? Most assuredly they have not. Why, then, must the citizens of this place be scourged with such attempts?

If the citizens of Hancock want the supremacy of the laws maintained let these tumultuous assemblies disperse, and let the civil officers, if resisted, do as in other cases—call for aid instead of assembling in advance, and then call for persons to be brought into their midst as prisoners amidst threats and insults.

From the confidence I have in your Excellency's superior intelligence, and sound discretion, I doubt not that your Excellency will arrive at just conclusions when the matter is submitted to your consideration, as I understand it is about being.

I can see no need for executive interference in this case, but disperse all uncalled for assemblies, and let the laws have their regular course, which they can have if these assemblies will disperse. If not, I fear the consequences.

I send this to your Excellency as confidential, as I wish not to take any part in the affair, or be known in it.

With consideration of high regard, I am, dear sir, your Excellency's most obedient servant,

SIDNEY RIGDON.

I read the doings of the City Council to Dr. Wakefield, and gave him a volume of the *Times and Seasons*. About 4 p. m., I rode out with Dr. Bernhisel. Pleasant and warm day. Towards night some clouds.

A Mr. Norton was tried before Esq. Aaron Johnson, J. P., on a charge of firing Foster's printing office, and acquitted.

Saturday, *15*.—At home. Two brethren came from Lima, and said that Colonel Levi Williams had demanded the arms belonging to the Mormons in that neighborhood. They wished my advice on the subject. I told them that when they gave up their arms, to give up their lives with them as dearly as possible.

The Prophet's Advice on giving up Arms.

It is reported that a company of men were constantly training at Carthage. Mr. John M. Crane, from Warsaw, said that several boxes of arms had arrived at Warsaw from Quincy. There was some considerable excitement, but expected they were going to wait the meeting at Carthage, which was fixed for the middle of next week.

The *Maid of Iowa* arrived at half-past two p. m., while I was examining the painting, "Death on the Pale Horse," by Benjamin West, which has been exhibiting in my reading room for the last three days. The *Maid* had lost her lighter, which was loaded at the time with corn and lumber, it having broken in two on a snag in the Iowa river.

This morning Samuel James started for Springfield to carry letters and papers to Governor Ford concerning the destruction of the *Expositor* press.

About 7 p. m. I rode out with Orrin P. Rockwell.

I received the following letter:

Letter: A. Ladd to Joseph Smith—Wharfage Matter.

FORT MADISON, June 15th, 1844.

Gen. Joseph Smith:

DEAR SIR.—I have been informed that a writ was issued against the steam ferry, *New Purchase*, for wharfage, on Tuesday last, but no such writ has been served or shown to me, and I am anxious to learn the facts of the case. If it is required, I will pay wharfage with the greatest of pleasure; but I would dislike to have cost to pay in addition. I expect to visit this place with my boat at least once a week during the season. You will confer a favor on me by informing me in relation to the ordinance, &c.

It has been rumored that the *New Purchase* was employed to convey to Nauvoo an armed force to attack the citizens in connection with other companies, on account of the late difficulties at your place; but it is not true. I assure you that the boat will not be employed in any unlawful enterprise, and I further assure you that there is no unkind feeling existing in our place against the people of your place.

I remain yours with respect,

A. LADD.

Captain of the *New Purchase*.

GEN. JOSEPH SMITH, Nauvoo, Ill.

CHAPTER XXIII.

DISCOURSE OF THE PROPHET—THE GODHEAD—THE MOB UPRISING—ARREST OF PRESIDENT SMITH, ET AL. OVER THE "EXPOSITOR" AFFAIR—TRIAL BEFORE ESQUIRE WELLS.

A conference was held at Franklin, Michigan. Present of the Twelve, Wilford Woodruff and George A. Smith; Elder George A. Smith presided. Nine branches were represented, comprising 170 members, 8 Elders, 5 Priests, 5 Teachers and 3 Deacons. There were ordained 1 High Priest, 9 Elders, 2 Priests, and 1 Deacon, under the hands of Elders Wilford Woodruff, George A. Smith and Charles C. Rich.

Conference in Michigan.

Sunday, June 16, 1844.—I preached at the stand at 10 a. m. Before I closed my remarks it rained severely. The following synopsis was reported by Elder Thomas Bullock, whom I had transferred from the duties of clerk of the *Maid of Iowa* to my office.

SERMON BY THE PROPHET—THE CHRISTIAN GODHEAD—PLURALITY OF GODS.

Meeting in the Grove, east of the Temple, June 16, 1844.

Prayer by Bishop Newel K. Whitney.

Choir sang, "Mortals Awake."

President Joseph Smith read the 3rd chapter of Revelation, and took for his text 1st chapter, 6th verse—"And hath made us kings and priests unto God and His Father: to Him be glory and dominion forever and ever. Amen.

It is altogether correct in the translation. Now, you know that of late some malicious and corrupt men have sprung up and apostatized from the Church of Jesus Christ of Latter-day Saints, and they declare that the Prophet believes in a plurality of Gods, and, lo and behold! we have discovered a very great secret, they cry—"The Prophet says there are many Gods, and this proves that he has fallen."

It has been my intention for a long time to take up this subject and lay it clearly before the people, and show what my faith is in relation to this interesting matter. I have contemplated the saying of Jesus (Luke 17th chapter, 26th verse)—"And as it was in the days of Noah, so shall it be also in the days of the Son of Man." And if it does rain, I'll preach this doctrine, for the truth shall be preached.

I will preach on the plurality of Gods. I have selected this text for that express purpose. I wish to declare I have always and in all congregations when I have preached on the subject of the Deity, it has been the plurality of Gods. It has been preached by the Elders for fifteen years.

I have always declared God to be a distinct personage, Jesus Christ a separate and distinct personage from God the Father, and that the Holy Ghost was a distinct personage and a Spirit: and these three constitute three distinct personages and three Gods. If this is in accordance with the New Testament, lo and behold! we have three Gods anyhow, and they are plural: and who can contradict it?

Our text says "And hath made us kings and priests unto God and His Father." The Apostles have discovered that there were Gods above, for Paul says God was the Father of our Lord Jesus Christ. My object was to preach the scriptures, and preach the doctrine they contain, there being a God above, the Father of our Lord Jesus Christ. I am bold to declare I have taught all the strong doctrines publicly, and always teach stronger doctrines in public than in private.

John was one of the men, and apostles declare they were made kings and priests unto God, the Father of our Lord Jesus Christ. It reads just so in the Revelation. Hence, the doctrine of a plurity of Gods is as prominent in the Bible as any other doctrine. It is all over the face of the Bible. It stands beyond the power of controversy. A wayfaring man, though a fool, need not err therein.

Paul says there are Gods many and Lords many. I want to set it forth in a plain and simple manner; but to us there is but one God—that is *pertaining to us;* and he is in all and through all. But if Joseph Smith says there are Gods many and Lords many, they cry, "Away with him! Crucify him! crucify him!"

Mankind verily say that the scriptures are with them. Search the scriptures, for they testify of things that these apostates would gravely pronounce blasphemy. Paul, if Joseph Smith is a blasphemer, you are. I say there are Gods many and Lords many, but to us only one, and we are to be in subjection to that one, and no man can limit the bounds or the eternal existence of eternal time. Hath he beheld the eternal world, and is he authorized to say that there is only one God? He makes himself a fool if he thinks or says so, and there is an end of his career or progress in knowledge. He cannot obtain all knowledge, for he has sealed up the gate to it.

Some say I do not interpret the scripture the same as they do. They say it means the heathen's gods. Paul says there are Gods many and Lords many; and that makes a plurality of Gods, in spite of the whims of all men. Without a revelation, I am not going to give them the knowledge of the God of heaven. You know and I testify that Paul had no allusion to the heathen gods. I have it from God, and get over it if you can. I have a witness of the Holy Ghost, and a testimony that Paul had no allusion to the heathen gods in the text. I will show from the Hebrew Bible that I am correct, and the first word shows a plurality of Gods; and I want the apostates and learned men to come here and prove to the contrary, if they can. An unlearned boy must give you a little Hebrew. *Berosheit baurau Eloheim ait aushamayeen vehau auraits*, rendered by King James' translators, "In the beginning God created the heaven and the earth." I want to analyze the word *Berosheit*. *Rosh*, the head; *Sheit*, a grammatical termination, The *Baith* was not originally put there when the inspired man wrote it, but it has been since added by an old Jew. *Baurau* signifies to bring forth; *Eloheim* is from the word *Eloi*, God, in the singular number; and by adding the word *heim*, it renders it Gods. It read first, "In the beginning the head of the Gods brought forth the Gods," or, as others have translated it, "The head of the Gods called the Gods together." I want to show a little learning as well as other fools—

A little learning is a dangerous thing.
Drink deep, or taste not the Pierian spring,
There shallow draughts intoxicate the brain,
And drinking largely sobers us up again.

All this confusion among professed translators is for want of drinking another draught.

The head God organized the heavens and the earth. I defy all the world to refute me. In the beginning the heads of the Gods organized the heavens and the earth. Now the learned priests and the people rage, and the heathen imagine a vain thing. If we pursue the Hebrew text further, it reads, "*Berosheit baurau Eloheim ait aashamayeen vehau auraits*"—"The head one of the Gods said, Let us make a man in our own image." I once asked a learned Jew, "If the Hebrew language compels us to render all words ending in *heim* in the plural, why not render the first *Eloheim* plural?" He replied, "That is the rule with few exceptions; but in this case it would ruin the Bible." He acknowledged I was right. I came here to investigate these things precisely as I believe them. Hear and judge for yourselves; and if you go away satisfied, well and good.

In the very beginning the Bible shows there is a plurality of Gods beyond the power of refutation. It is a great subject I am dwelling on. The word *Eloheim* ought to be in the plural all the way through—Gods. The heads of the Gods appointed one God for us; and when you take [that] view of the subject, it sets one free to see all the beauty, holiness and perfection of the Gods. All I want is to get the simple, naked truth, and the whole truth.

Many men say there is one God; the Father, the Son and the Holy Ghost are only one God! I say that is a strange God anyhow—three in one, and one in three! It is a curious organization. "Father, I pray not for the world, but I pray for them which thou hast given me." "Holy Father, keep through Thine own name those whom thou hast given me, that they may be one as we are." All are to be crammed into one God, according to sectarianism. It would make the biggest God in all the world. He would be a wonderfully big God—he would be a giant or a monster. I want to read the text to you myself—"I am agreed with the Father and the Father is agreed with me, and we are agreed as one." The Greek shows that it should be agreed. "Father, I pray for them which Thou hast given me out of the world, and not for those alone, but for them also which shall believe on me through their word, that they all may be agreed, as Thou, Father, art with me, and I with Thee, that they also may be agreed with us," and all come to dwell in unity, and in all the glory and everlasting burnings of the Gods; and then we shall see as we are seen, and be as our God and He as His Father. I want to reason a little on this subject. I learned it by translating the papyrus which is now in my house. I learned a testimony concerning Abraham, and he reasoned concerning the God of heaven. "In order to do that," said he, "suppose we have two facts: that supposes another fact may exist—two men on the earth, one wiser than the other, would logically show that another who is wiser than the wisest may exist. Intelligences exist one above another, so that there is no end to them."

If Abraham reasoned thus—If Jesus Christ was the Son of God, and John discovered that God the Father of Jesus Christ had a Father, you may suppose that He had a Father also. Where was there ever a son without a father? And where was there ever a father without first being a son? Whenever did a tree or anything spring into existence without a progenitor? And everything comes in this way. Paul says that which is earthly is in the likeness of that which is heavenly, Hence if Jesus had a Father, can we not believe that *He* had a Father also? I despise the idea of being scared to death at such a doctrine, for the Bible is full of it.

I want you to pay particular attention to what I am saying. Jesus said that the Father wrought precisely in the same way as His Father had done before Him. As the Father had done before. He laid down His life, and took it up the same as His Father had done before. He did as He was sent, to lay down His life and take it up again; and then was committed unto Him the keys, &c. I know it is good reasoning.

I have reason to think that the Church is being purged. I saw Satan fall from heaven, and the way they ran was a caution. All these are wonders and marvels in our eyes in these last days. So long as men are under the law of God, they have no fears—they do not scare themselves.

I want to stick to my text, to show that when men open their lips against these truths they do not injure me, but injure themselves. To the law and to the testimony, for these principles are poured out all over the scriptures. When things that are of the greatest importance are passed over by weak-minded men without even a thought, I want to see truth in all its bearings and hug it to my bosom. I believe all that God ever revealed, and I never hear of a man being damned for believing too much; but they are damned for unbelief.

They found fault with Jesus Christ because He said He was the Son of God, and made Himself equal with God. They say of me, like they did of the apostles of old, that I must be put down. What did Jesus say? "Is it not written in your law, I said, Ye are Gods? If He called them Gods unto whom the word of God came, and the scriptures cannot be broken, say ye of Him whom the Father had sanctified and sent into the world, Thou blasphemest, because I said I am the Son of God?" It was through Him that they drank of the spiritual rock. Of course He would take the honor to Himself. Jesus, if they were called Gods unto whom the word of God came, why should it be thought blasphemy that I should say I am the son of God?

Oh, poor, blind apostates! did you never think of this before? These are the quotations that the apostates take from the scriptures. They swear that they believe the Bible, the Book of Mormon and the Doctrine and Covenants and then you will get from them filth, slander, and bogus-makers plenty. One of the apostate Church official members prophesied that Joseph would never preach any more, and yet I am now preaching.

Go and read the vision in the Book of Covenants. There is clearly illustrated glory upon glory—one glory of the sun, another glory of the moon, and a glory of the stars; and as one star differeth from another star in glory, even so do they of the telestial world differ in glory, and every man who reigns in celestial glory is a God to his dominions. By the apostates admitting the testimony of the Doctrine and Covenants, they damn themselves. Paul, what do you say? They impeached Paul and all went and left him. Paul had seven churches, and they drove him off from among them; and yet they cannot do it by me. I rejoice in that. My testimony is good.

Paul says, "There is one glory of the sun, and another glory of the moon, and another glory of the stars; for one star differeth from another star in glory. So is also the resurrection of the dead." They who obtain a glorious resurrection from the dead, are exalted far above principalities, powers, thrones, dominions and angels, and are expressly declared to be heirs of God and joint heirs with Jesus Christ,all having eternal power.

The scriptures are a mixture of very strange doctrines to the Christian world, who are blindly led by the blind. I will refer to another scripture. "Now," says God, when He visited Moses in the bush, (Moses was a stammering sort of a boy like me) God said, "Thou shalt be a God unto the children of Israel." God said, "Thou shalt be a God unto Aaron, and he shall be thy spokeman." I believe those Gods that God reveals as Gods to be sons of God, and all can cry, "Abba, Father!" Sons of God who exalt themselves to be Gods, even from before the foundation of the world, and are the only Gods I have a reverence for.

John said he was a king. "And from Jesus Christ, who is the faithful witness, and the first begotten of the dead, and the Prince of the kings of the earth. Unto Him that loved us, and washed us from our sins in His own blood, and hath made us kings and priests unto God, and His Father; to him be glory and dominion forever and ever Amen." Oh, Thou God who art King of kings and Lord of lords, the sectarian world, by their actions, declare, "We cannot believe Thee."

The old Catholic church traditions are worth more than all you have said. Here is a principle of logic that most men have no more sense than to adopt. I will illustrate it by an old apple tree. Here jumps off a branch and says, I am the true tree, and you are corrupt. If the whole tree is corrupt, are not its branches corrupt? If the Catholic religion is a false religion, how can any true religion come out of it? If the Catholic church is bad, how can any good thing come out of it? The character of the old churches have always been slandered by all apostates since the world began.

I testify again, as the Lord lives, God never will acknowledge any traitors or apostates. Any man who will betray the Catholics will betray you; and if he will betray me, he will betray you. All men are liars who say they are of the true Church without the revelations of Jesus Christ and the Priesthood of Melchisedek, which is after the order of the Son of God.

It is in the order of heavenly things that God should always send a new dispensation into the world when men have apostatized from the truth and lost the priesthood; but when men come out and build upon other men's foundations, they do it on their own responsibility, without authority from God; and when the floods come and the winds blow, their foundations will be found to be sand, and their whole fabric will crumble to dust.

Did I build on any other man's foundation? I have got all the truth which the Christian world possessed, and an independent revelation in the bargain, and God will bear me off triumphant. I will drop this subject. I wish I could speak for three or four hours; but it is not expedient on account of the rain: I would still go on, and show you proof upon proofs; all the Bible is equal in support of this doctrine, one part as another.

[On account of the rain it was impossible for Thomas Bullock to report any more].

Judge Jesse B. Thomas came to Nauvoo, and advised me to go before some justice of the peace of the county, and have an examination of the charges specified in the writ from Justice Morrison of Carthage; and if acquitted or bound over, it would allay all excitement, answer the law and cut off all legal pretext for a mob, and he would be bound to order them to keep the peace.

Advice of Judge Thomas on *Expositor* Affair.

Some forty gentlemen from Madison came down on a steamer to inquire into our difficulties. I met them at the Masonic Hall at 2 p. m., and gave them the desired information. Dr. Richards, the city recorder, read the minutes of the council declaring the *Nauvoo Expositor* a nuisance. They expressed themselves satisfied. I then went to the Temple stand and met some thousands of the brethren. I instructed them to keep cool, and prepare their arms for defense of the city, as it was reported that a mob was collecting in Carthage and other places. I exhorted them to be quiet and make no disturbance, and instructed the brethren to organize into the capacity of a public meeting and send delegates to all the surrounding towns and villages, to explain the cause of the disturbance, and show

Inquiry of Delegation from Madison.

them that all was peace at Nauvoo, and that there was no cause for any mobs.

A messenger arrived stating that the clerk of the county court expected to be driven out of Carthage tomorrow, and the only way to prevent the shedding of blood was to get the Governor in person to come down with his staff.

I wrote to Governor Ford stating the facts as follows:

Letter: Joseph Smith to Governor Ford—Inviting the Governor to Nauvoo.

NAUVOO, ILLINOIS, June 16th, 1844.

His Excellency Thomas Ford:

SIR.—I am informed from credible sources, as well as from the proceedings of a public meeting at Carthage, &c., as published in the *Warsaw Signal* extra, that an energetic attempt is being made by some of the citizens of this and the surrounding counties to drive and exterminate "the Saints" by force of arms; and I send this information to your Excellency by a special messenger, Hugh McFall, Adjutant-General, Nauvoo Legion, who will give all particulars; and I ask at your hands immediate counsel and protection.

Judge Thomas has been here and given his advice in the case, which I shall strictly follow until I hear from your Excellency, and in all cases shall adhere to the Constitution and laws.

The Nauvoo Legion is at your service to quell all insurrection and support the dignity of the common weal.

I wish, urgently wish your Excellency to come down in person with your staff and investigate the whole matter without delay, and cause peace to be restored to the country; and I know not but this will be the only means of stopping an effusion of blood.

The information referred to above is before me by affidavit.

I remain, sir, the friend of peace, and your Excellency's humble servant,

JOSEPH SMITH.

I enclosed a copy of the following affidavit:

Affidavit: Mob Movements.

STATE OF ILLINOIS, HANCOCK CO., }
CITY OF NAUVOO. } ss.

June 16th, 1844. Personally appeared before me Willard Richards, clerk of the Municipal Court of the City of Nauvoo, Thomas G. Wilson; and after being duly sworn according to law, deposeth and saith that during the last evening Robert Johnson, of the county aforesaid, told deponent that fifteen hundred Missourians would assemble at Warsaw, in said county, on the morning of the 17th instant; that the arms of the Quincy Greys had been sent up to Warsaw; that they had five cannon at Warsaw; that said Missourians, and others who would join them, would proceed to Carthage, and the Quincy Greys and other companies from Adams county were to meet the Missourians in Carthage at the time before stated; that from Carthage they were going round to the branches of the Church of Latter-day Saints in said county, and inform them that they must deny Joseph's being a Prophet, and if they did not deny Joseph, they must leave immediately: and on Thursday next the whole mob were to proceed to Nauvoo and demand Joseph and Hyrum Smith, and the City Council of said city, and if Joseph and Hyrum and the City Council were not given up they would blow up the city, and kill and exterminate all the inhabitants of said city.

THOMAS G. WILSON.

[Seal of Municipal Court.]

Subscribed and sworn to before me, Willard Richards, clerk. In testimony whereof I have hereunto set my hand and seal of the Municipal Court of said city, at the time and place above written.

WILLARD RICHARDS,
Clerk of the Municipal Court, City of Nauvoo.

I have compared the within affidavit with the original, and find it a true copy.

In witness whereof I have hereunto set my hand and seal of court at the city of Nauvoo, this 16th day of June, 1844.

WILLARD RICHARDS.
Clerk of the Municipal Court, City of Nauvoo.

Brother Butler, from Bear Creek, came in and made affidavit before the Recorder that fifteen hundred Missourians were to cross the Mississippi to Warsaw the next morning, on their way to Carthage.

I received a letter from Father Morley:

Letter: Isaac Morley to Joseph Smith—Mob Threats.

President Joseph Smith:

SIR.—Believing it to be my duty to inform you of the proceedings of a wicked clan against the Saints in this place, I improve this opportunity. On yesterday, George Baker, in company with Joseph Barber, a Mr. John Banks, Luther Perry and one more, (his name I have not got) came to my house. Mr. Baker came to my door and said he had some business, and wished to speak with me. I went out into my dooryard with him, and he came in company with a Mr. Banks and others. They informed me they were a committee appointed to inform me and our people that they had three propositions to make to us. In the first place, yourself and about seventeen others had broken the law and good order of society; that we, the Mormon people, must take up arms and proceed with them for your arrest, or take our effects and proceed immediately to Nauvoo, otherwise give up our arms, and remain quiet until the fuss is over. We have until Monday morning next to make up our minds. We have made up our minds that we shall not comply with any of these proposals, but stand in our own defense. We have no signature from the Governor, or any official officer, to accept of such wicked proposals.

We are informed that the company must be at Col. Williams' tomorrow morning at eight o'clock to proceed to Nauvoo.

I have thought it my duty to inform you of the proceedings here.

This from your humble servant,

ISAAC MORLEY.

June 16th, 1844,

We certify the above is true.

GARDNER SNOW,
EDMUND DURFEE,
IRA WILLSEY.

I sent the following answer by Joseph S. Allen:

Letter: Joseph Smith to Isaac Morley—Instructions on Resisting Mob.

HEADQUARTERS NAUVOO LEGION, NAUVOO.
LIEUT-GENERAL'S OFFICE,
June 16th, 1844.

Col. Isaac Morley:

SIR.—In reply to yours of this date, you will take special notice of the movements of the mob party that is stirring up strife and endeavoring to excite rebellion to the government and destroy the Saints, and cause all the troops of said Legion in your vicinity to be in readiness to act at a moment's warning; and if the mob shall fall upon the Saints by force of arms, defend them at every hazard unless prudence dictate the retreat of the troops to Nauvoo, in which case the mob will not disturb your women and children; and if the mob move towards Nauvoo, either come before them or in their rear and be ready to co-operate with the main body of the Legion. Instruct the companies to keep cool, and let all things be done decently and in order.

Give information by affidavit before a magistrate and special messengers to the Governor of what has occurred,and every illegal proceeding that shall be had on the subject, without delay. Also notify me of the same, and demand instruction and protection from the Governor.

JOSEPH SMITH.
Lieut.-Gen. Nauvoo Legion.

I insert the minutes of a public meeting:

Minutes of a Public Meeting at Nauvoo.

A public meeting was held in the city of Nauvoo on Sunday evening, the 16th inst.

Mr. John Taylor was unanimously called to the chair, and William Clayton appointed clerk.

The chairman stated briefly the object of the meeting, whereupon it was unanimously

Resolved, that inasmuch as many false reports are being circulated through this county by designing characters for the purpose of bringing persecution upon the peaceable citizens of this city we will use our endeavors to disabuse the public mind, and present a true statement of facts before them as speedily as possible.

Resolved that for the more speedy accomplishment of this object, this meeting appoint delegates to go to the different precincts throughout the county to lay a true statement of facts before the public.

The following delegates were then appointed;

To Warsaw precinct, Messrs. Joseph A. Kelting, Hugh McFall and John T. Barnett.

Rocky Run precinct, Messrs. Anson Call, E. Horner, Nicholas Boscow and David Evans.

Carthage precinct, Messrs. Lewis Robinson, Jeremiah Hatch, Jun., and Dr. Robinson.

Lima precinct, Messrs. William Allen, Elam Luddington,and Charles Warner.

La Harpe and Pilot Grove, Messrs. Benjamin Warrington and Hiram Kimball.

Spilman's Landing and Appanoose, Messrs. Elijah R. Swackhammer, and Truman Gillett, Jun.

St. Mary's and Chili, Messrs. Philander Colton and Averett.

Fountain Green and Macedonia, Messrs. Moses Claire and Andrew H. Perkins.

Augusta and Plymouth, Messrs. Peter Slater, Darwin Chase and John McIllwrick.

On motion, meeting adjourned *sine die.*

JOHN TAYLOR, President.
WILLIAM CLAYTON, Secretary.

And I issued the following:

PROCLAMATION.

MAYOR'S OFFICE, NAUVOO, June 16th, 1844.

As there are a number of statements in circulation which have for their object the injury of the Latter-day Saints, all of which are false and prompted by black-hearted villains, I therefore deem it my duty to disabuse the public mind in regard to them, and to give a plain statement of facts which have taken place in the city within a few days past, and which have brought upon us the displeasure of the unprincipled and the uninformed, and seems to afford an opportunity to our enemies to unite and arouse themselves to mob. And already they have commenced their hellish operations by driving a few defenseless "Mormons" from their houses and homes in the vicinity of Warsaw and Carthage.

A short time since a press was started in this city which had for its object the destruction of the institutions of the city, both civil and religious. Its proprietors are a set of unprincipled scoundrels, who attempted in every possible way to defame the character of the most virtuous of our community, and change our peaceful and prosperous city into a place as evil and polluted as their own black hearts. To rid the city of a paper so filthy and pestilential as this became the duty of every good citizen who loves good order and morality. A complaint was made before the City Council, and after a full and impartial investigation it was voted (without one dissenting voice) a public nuisance, and to be immediately destroyed. The peace and happiness of the place demanded it, the virtue ot our wives and daughters demanded it, and our consciences demanded it at our hands as conservators of the public peace.

That we acted right in this matter we have the assurance of one of the ablest expounders of the laws of England, namely, Blackstone, the Constitution of the state of Illinois, and our own chartered rights,

If, then, our charter gives us the power to decide what shall be a nuisance, and cause it to be removed, where is the offense? What law is violated? If, then, no law has been violated, why this ridiculous excitement and bandying with lawless ruffians to destroy the happiness of a people whose religious motto is "Peace and good will toward all men?"

Our city is infested with a set of blacklegs, counterfeiters and debauchers, and that the proprietors of this press were of that class the minutes of the Municipal Court fully testify, and in ridding our young and flourishing city of such characters we are abused by not only villainous demagogues, but by some who from their station and influence in society, ought rather to raise than repress the standard of human excellence.

We have no disturbance nor excitement among us, save what is made by the thousand-and-one idle rumors afloat in the country. Everyone is protected in his person and property, and but few cities of a population of twenty thousand people, in the United States, have less of dissipation or vice of any kind than the city of Nauvoo.

Of the correctness of our conduct in this affair, we appeal to every high court in the state, and to its ordeal we are willing to appear at any time that his Excellency, Governor Ford, shall please call us before it. I therefore, in behalf of the Municipal Court of Nauvoo, warn the lawless not to be precipitate in any interference in our affairs; for, as sure as there is a God in Israel, we shall ride triumphant over all oppression.

JOSEPH SMITH, Mayor.

I received a letter from my uncle, John Smith:

Letter: John Smith to Joseph Smith—Accompanying Delegation to the Prophet.

MACEDONIA, ILLINOIS, Sunday, June 16th, 1844.

President Smith:

DEAR SIR.—We send you Brothers Perkins, two faithful brethren, who will give you all the information which is within our knowledge of the proceedings of our enemies; and as we have not heard or received communication from Nauvoo as regards the course we should pursue, we now ask your counsel, and you will please forward per Brother Perkins. We should have sought your counsel sooner, only on account of high water. Please communicate in writing the course we in this part of the country should pursue. The brethren in these parts are in good faith, spirits, and health generally, and may be relied on.

Respectfully,

JOHN SMITH.

GENERAL JOSEPH SMITH.

Monday, 17.—I wrote the following to my uncle, John Smith:

Letter: Joseph Smith to John Smith—Instructions in Case of Mob Violence.

NAUVOO, June 17th, 1844.

Uncle John:

DEAR SIR.—The brethren from Ramus arrived here this morning. We were glad to see them, and to hear that you were all alive in the midst of the ragings of an infatuated and blood thirsty mob. I write these few lines to inform you that we feel determined in this place not to be dismayed if hell boils over all at once. We feel to hope for the best, and determined to prepare for the worst; and we want this to be your motto in common with us, "That we will never ground our arms until we give them up by death." Free trade and sailor's rights, protection of persons and property, wives and families.

If a mob annoy you, defend yourselves to the very last; and if they fall upon you with a superior force, and you think you are not able to compete with them, retreat to Nauvoo. But we hope for better things. But remember, if your enemies do fall upon you, be sure and take the best and most efficient measures the emergency of the case may require.

Remember the front and the rear of your enemies, because if they should come to Nanvoo to attack it unlawfully and by mob force, a little annoyance upon the rear with some bold fellows would be a very good thing to weaken the ranks of an enemy.

It is impossible to give you correct information what to do beforehand; but act according to the emergency of the case, but never give up your arms, but die first.

The brethren will give you information of the conversation between us. We have sent to the Governor, and are about to send again, and we want you to send affidavits and demand the attention of the Governor, and request protection at his hand, in common with the rest of us that by our continual wearying we may get him to come and investigate the whole matter.

I now conclude with my best wishes, and must refer you to the brethren for further information.

JOSEPH SMITH.
Mayor of the City of Nauvoo, and Lieut.-General of the Nauvoo Legion.

My brother Hyrum wrote the following letter to President Brigham Young.

Letter: Hyrum Smith to Brigham Young—Calling Home the Twelve.

CITY OF NAUVOO, June 17th, 1844.

Dear Brother Brigham Young:

There has been for several days a great excitement among the inhabitants in the adjoining counties. Mass meetings are held upon mass meetings drawing up resolutions to utterly exterminate the Saints. The excitement has been gotten up by the Laws, Fosters and the Higbees, and they themselves have left the city and are engaged in the mob. They have sent their runners into the State of Missouri to excite them to murder and bloodshed, and the report is that a great many hundreds of them will come over to take an active part in murdering the Saints. The excitement is very great indeed.

It is thought best by myself and others for you to return without delay, and the rest of the Twelve, and all the Elders that have gone out from this place, and as many more good, faithful men as feel disposed to come up with them. Let wisdom be exercised; and whatever they do, do it without a noise. You know we are not frightened, but think it best to be well prepared and be ready for the onset; and if it is extermination, extermination it is, of course.

Communicate to the others of the Twelve with as much speed as possible, with perfect stillness and calmness. A word to the wise is sufficient; and a little powder, lead and a good rifle can be packed in your luggage very easy without creating any suspicion.

There must be no excuses made, for wisdom says that a strict compliance with our request will be for our safety and welfare.

In haste, I remain yours in the firm bonds of the new and everlasting covenant,

HYRUM SMITH.

P. S.—Large bodies of armed men, cannon and munitions of war are coming on from Missouri in steamboats. These facts are communicated to the Governor and President of the United States, and you will readily see that we have to prepare for the onset.

In the bonds of the new and everlasting covenant, I remain yours,

JOSEPH SMITH.

Arrest of the Prophet *et al.* for Destroying the *Expositor*.

This morning [17th of June] I was arrested, together with Samuel Bennett, John Taylor, William W. Phelps, Hyrum Smith, John P. Greene, Dimick B. Huntington, Jonathan Dunham, Stephen Markham, Jonathan H. Holmes, Jesse P. Harmon, John Lytle, Joseph W. Coolidge, H. David Redfield, O. P. Rockwell, and Levi Richards, by Constable Joel S. Miles, on a writ issued by Daniel H. Wells, on complaint of W. G. Ware, for a riot on the 10th inst. in destroying the *Nauvoo Expositor* press. At 2 p. m. we went before Justice Wells at his house; and after a long and close examination we were discharged. The following is a copy of the minutes of this trial.

Minutes of the Trial of Joseph Smith et al. Before Esquire Wells—"Expositor" Affair.

FOR THE "NEIGHBOR."

STATE OF ILLINOIS }
COUNTY OF HANCOCK. } SS.

Justice's Court, June 17th. 1844, Daniel H. Wells, Justice of the Peace, presiding.

State of Illinois *v.* Joseph Smith, Samuel Bennett, John Taylor, William W. Phelps, Hyrum Smith, John P. Greene, Stephen Perry, Dimick B. Huntington, Jonathan Dunham, Stephen Markham, Jonathan H. Holmes, Jesse P. Harmon, John Lytle, Joseph W. Coolidge, H. David Redfield, Orrin Porter Rockwell and Levi Richards,

Defendants were brought before the court by Joel S. Miles, constable of the county aforesaid, by virtue of a warrant issued by the court on complaint of W. G. Ware, for a "riot committed in the city of Nauvoo, county aforesaid, on or before the 10th day of June, 1844, by forcibly entering a brick building in said city, occupied as a printing office and taking therefrom by force, and with force of arms, a printing-press, types and paper, together with other property, belonging to William Law, Wilson Law, Robert D. Foster, Charles A. Foster, Francis M. Higbee, Chauncey L. Higbee and Charles Ivins, and breaking in pieces and burning the same in the streets.

George P. Stiles, Esq., appeared as counsel for the defense, and Edward Bonny, Esq., for the prosecution.

W. G. Ware sworn. Said he was present when the City Council passed an order for the destruction of the press. Went up to the Temple and heard the Marshal read the order of the Mayor. Did not know how they got into the building. The press was taken out and destroyed.

Defendants' counsel objected to witness' stating who voted for the passage of the bill in the council and read Burns' definition of a riot, and said there could be no accessory.

Councilor Bonny read from the statute, page 173, and pleaded there might be an accessory to a riot. Court decided there might be an accessory to any crime either before or after the fact.

Witness knew some who voted for the order in the City Council. Heard Gen. Dunham give orders for the destruction of the press. Dunham, Redfield and Richards took an active part in the destruction of the press. Did not know all the persons.

Cross-examined: City Council considered the press a nuisance, and ordered it to be abated. Was present at the execution of the Mayor's orders. No unnecessary noise. All was done peaceably. Saw no disorder. Heard no language by the prisoners calculated to disturb the peace.

Henry O. Norton sworn. Was at the printing office. Heard Marshal Greene give orders to open the door. Markham carried out the press and type. Recollected Dunham. Could not identify any others. No contention between the marshal and Higbee. Marshal asked Charles A. Foster for the key, which he refused to give. Heard no threats concerning the destruction of the press any time.

O. F. Moesseur sworn. Saw many of the people gather around the printing office. Went over, back, and over again. Could not identify any person. Heard no loud talking or noise.

P. T. Rolfe sworn. Was at work in the printing office last Monday night. Chauncey Higbee came in and said the Council was about to destroy the press, and took some papers from the desk. Marshal Greene came with a company and demanded the key. Foster and Higbee forbade him. Door was opened by Lytle, as witness thought. The press and fixtures were destroyed, and some paper and a desk belonging to Dr. Foster, containing several thousand dollars of property, four thousand dollars auditor's warrants, and other valuable papers.

Cross-examined, Did not know the amount of warrants and papers. Presumed they were destroyed, Did not know whether they were destroyed. Was from the office long enough to have them taken out. Said Greene, Dunham, Markham, Holmes, Perry, Edwards and Harmon helped to move the press. Never knew anything against Joseph Smith personally.

B. Warrington sworn. Was present at the Council when the bill passed to destroy the press.

Joseph Smith objected to calling in question the doings of the City Council, and referred to the proceedings of Congress to show that all legislative bodies have a right to speak freely on any subject before them, and that Congress is not responsible for a riot which might arise on the execution of their order by the Marshal; that the execution of such order could not be a riot, but a legal transaction; that the doings of the City Council could only be called in question by the powers above them, and that a magistrate had not that power; that the City Council was not arraigned here for trial, but individuals were arraigned for a riot. If the City Council had transcended their powers, they were amenable to the Supreme Court; and that Judge Thomas had decided that an action could not lie if no riot had been committed.

Councilor Bonny said, if the act was committed under an ordinance of the city, they might show it in justification.

Court decided that the gentlemen arraigned were arraigned in their individual capacity, and could not be recognized by the court in their official capacity.

Witness said that all he heard the prisoners say was said as councilors.

Testimony on the prosecution closed.

Councilor Stiles moved that the prisoners be dismissed for want of a case being made out.

Councilor Bonny read the riot act, and pleaded a case had been made out.

Motion overruled by the Court.

Dr. Wakefield, Willard Richards and Edward Wingott sworn.

Dr. J. R. Wakefield, of New York, said he went on the hill after the order passed the Council. Saw some portion of the Legion collected, walking quietly along as though they were walking to the "Dead March in Saul." There was no noise or tumult. Higbee asked the Marshal his authority, Marshal stated his authority from the Mayor for abating the nuisance. Higbee set them all at defiance. Some twelve men were called out, who went up stairs and opened the door. Did not know how the door was opened. There was not more than one thump. Marshal Greene asked one of the officers if anything was destroyed except what belonged to the press? and the officer replied, "No." All was done in perfect order—as peaceably as people move on a Sunday. Was present all the time. All that was done was done in their official capacity as officers of the city.

Councilor Bonny objected to the testimony, as it was not before the Court that there was any city.

Court decided that any knowledge in possession of the Court was testimony in the Court.

E. Wingott, of Boston, concurred in Dr. Wakefield's statements. Was by the door when it was opened, and knew that nothing more than a knee was put against it. All was done quietly. Was present in the City Council when the order passed. Nothing said in Council except what was said in capacity of councilors and aldermen. Was by the door all the time when the press and type and things used in connection with the press were destroyed. There was no other property taken from the building.

Cross-examined: Did not know the name of the man who opened the door. Knew Orrin P. Rockwell.

Willard Richards read the resolutions of the City Council of the 10th instant, declaring the press a nuisance, &c., and the Mayor's order to the Marshal to destroy the press, and the Lieut.-General's order to Major-General Dunham to assist the Marshal with the Legion, if needed, to abate the nuisance, and the Marshal's return that the press and type were destroyed (as published in the *Neighbor*, June 19).

Court queried about the destruction of the desk.

Dr. Wakefield was again called up. Heard Marshal tell the officers and men to hurt no property, except the press, type and fixtures; and after the abatement, Marshal inquired if his order had been obeyed, and the officers said it had.

E. Wingott called again. Heard Mr. Foster ask Higbee for the key of the office, and afterward saw him deliver the key to Mr. Higbee. There was nothing destroyed but what pertained to the press.

Addison Everett of New York, sworn. Saw the press and type taken out and burned. Saw no other property burned. Desk might have been taken away before. Should not have seen it, if it had been. Saw no desk burned. Does not believe any desk was burned.

Joel S. Miles sworn. Foster said his docket was not burned. Witness was sure that Dr. Foster said he had taken other papers out of the desk.

W. G. Ware called again. Saw Charles Foster coming from the office and go into Foster's house with books under his arm. Looked like account books. Saw nothing but the press and fixtures brought out, except a chair, and the Marshal ordered it to be carried back.

E. Wingott recalled. Stood close by the door. Could see all that was done. Did not believe a desk could be brought out and he not see it.

Dr. Wakefield recalled. Joseph Smith and Hyrum were not on the hill at all that evening.

Joseph W. Coolidge was discharged by the Court and sworn. Charles Foster asked Francis Higbee for the key to the office. Higbee hesitated. Foster said he wanted to get a desk that had some valuable papers in it. Foster got the key and went in. Did not see him remove the desk. Might have removed it, and witness not see it. There was no desk burned.

The councilors submitted the case without plea, and the court discharged the prisoners.

CHAPTER XXIV.

RUMORS OF INVASION FROM MISSOURI—THE LEGION ORDERED TO ASSIST THE CITY MARSHAL—NAUVOO PLACED UNDER MARTIAL LAW—THE MAYOR'S ADDRESS TO THE LEGION.

Monday, June, 17, 1844, (continued).—Edward Hunter, Philip B. Lewis and Major John Bills started with the affidavit of Thomas G. Wilson and my letter, &c., to take to Governor Ford. I charged Edward Hunter, under oath, to tell Governor Ford all he knew concerning me, good or bad, as he has known me for several years; and I said to him, "Brother Hunter, you have always wished you had been with us from the commencement. If you will go to Springfield and do this business for me now in this time of danger, it shall be as though you had been in Missouri and had always been with us."

Stephen Markham made the following affidavit:

Affidavit of Stephen Markham—Nauvoo to be Attacked.

STATE OF ILLINOIS }
CITY OF NAUVOO. } ss.

On the 17th day of June, 1844, came Stephen Markham before me, Willard Richards, recorder of said city; and after being duly sworn, deposeth and saith that, from the public papers, especially the Warsaw papers, and from reports from the various precincts, a mob may be expected to make an immediate attack upon the citizens and city of Nauvoo, on account of the gatherings at the various precincts, and threats to exterminate the Latter-day Saints.

STEPHEN MARKHAM.

Sworn and subscribed to before me this 17th day of June, 1844.

WILLARD RICHARDS.
Recorder of the city of Nauvoo.

As soon as the affidavit came to my knowledge, I issued the following:

PROCLAMATION.

NAUVOO, June 17th, 1844.

To John P. Greene, Marshal of the City of Nauvoo, &c.:

SIR.—Complaint having been made to me on oath that a mob is collecting at sundry points to make an attack on this city, you will therefore take such measures as shall be necessary to preserve the peace of said city according to the provisions of the charter and the laws of the state; and with the police and the Legion, see that no violent act is committed. General Dunham is hereby instructed to act with the Marshal in keeping the peace, according to law.

JOSEPH SMITH, Mayor.

And also:

ORDER TO THE LEGION.

HEADQUARTERS NAUVOO LEGION,
NAUVOO, June 17th, 1844.

To Major General in Command, Jonathan Dunham:

Complaint having been made on oath that a mob is preparing to make an attack upon this city and citizens of Nauvoo, and having directed the Marshal to keep the peace, you are hereby commanded to order the Nauvoo Legion to be in readiness to assist said Marshal in keeping the peace, and doing whatever may be necessary to preserve the dignity of the state and city.

JOSEPH SMITH, Lieut.-General N. L.

Also:

LEGION PLACED AT COMMAND OF CITY MARSHAL.

HEADQUARTERS NAUVOO LEGION, June 17th, 1844.

To Major-General in Command, Jonathan Dunham:

You are hereby instructed to execute all orders of the Marshal, and perform all services with as little noise and confusion as possible, and take every precaution to prevent groups of citizens, &c., from gathering on the bank of the river, on the landing of boats or otherwise, and allay every cause and pretext of excitement as well as suspicion, and let your operations be efficient and decided.

JOSEPH SMITH, Lieut.-Gen. N. L.

I also issued an order to Col. A. P. Rockwood to call out

my guard and staff immediately to my headquarters; and I also ordered the Legion to parade tomorrow at 10 a. m.

HEADQUARTERS NAUVOO LEGION,
LIEUT.-GENERAL'S OFFICE
June 17th, 1844.

To Col. A. P. Rockwood:

You are hereby commanded to notify my guard and staff to appear at headquarters without delay, armed and equipped according to law for military duty and inspection, with powder and ball.

JOSEPH SMITH, Lieut.-Gen. N. L.

I advised my brother Hyrum not to mail his letter to President Young at present.

I directed my clerk, Thomas Bullock, to remain in the Masonic Hall and take affidavits of the men who are constantly coming in with news of the movements of the mob and preserve copies to forward to the Governor.

I received the following letter:

Letter: H. T. Hugins to Joseph Smith—Probable Indictment of the Prophet at Springfield.

BURLINGTON, IOWA TERRITORY,
June 17th, 1844.

DEAR SIR.—I write to inform you that Jeremiah Smith arrived here yesterday in safety and free from arrest. He desires, through me, to thank you for your kindness and attention to him while at Nauvoo.

I wrote from Springfield to apprise you that an effort was making to procure an indictment against the members of your Municipal Court for the part they acted in trying the *habeas corpus* petitions. Through the efforts of myself and Dr. Hickock, that result was prevented, and T. B. Johnson exposed. The boat is casting off, and I must close. Dr. Dunlop will write to apprise you of the William and Wilson Law's proceedings here. You will hear from me again soon.

Yours truly,
H. T. HUGINS.

GENERAL JOSEPH SMITH, Nauvoo, Ill.

The mob is still increasing in numbers at Carthage and other places.

It is reported that William and Wilson Law have laid a plan to burn the printing office of the *Nauvoo Neighbor* this night. I therefore stationed a strong police round the premises and throughout the city.

The captain of the steamer *Osprey* called upon me.

Charge of Threats Against Foster's Life.

About 11 p. m. a negro came into my office with an open letter, without any date or name, and said that Dr. Foster gave it to him at Madison to give Henry O. Norton. In that letter Foster said that Dunham and Richards swore in my presence that they would kill him (Foster) in two days, and that there was a man in Madison would swear he had heard them say so at my house.

I closed the issuing of orders about 12 at night, ready to retire to rest. Pleasant weather.

To refute the lying slanders of the *Warsaw Signal*, as published in the proceedings of a meeting held at Carthage an the 13th instant, I insert the following certificate.*

TO THE PUBLIC.

We, whose names are undersigned, having seen in the *Warsaw Signal*, containing the proceedings of a meeting held at Carthage on the 13th instant, many statements calculated to arouse the indignation and wrath of the people against the citizens of Nauvoo, do certify that Hyrum Smith did not make any threats, nor offer any reward against the *Signal* or its editor in the City Council.

JOHN TAYLOR,	GEORGE W. HARRIS,
AARON JOHNSON,	PHINEHAS RICHARDS,
WILLIAM BOLES,	THOMAS SMITH,
GEORGE P. STILES,	EDWARD HUNTER,
W. W. PHELPS,	MOSES F. CLARK,
ALANSON RIPLEY,	LEVI RICHARDS,
ORSON SPENCER,	ADDISON EVERETT,
JOHN P. GREENE,	PHILIP B. LEWIS.

NAUVOO, June 17, 1844.

* This was published in the *Nauvoo Neighbor* impressions of June 19 1844.

A *Nauvoo Neighbor* extra was issued with the following editorial:

TO THE PUBLIC.

As a soft breeze on a hot day mellows the air, so does the simple truth calm the feelings of the irritated; and so we proceed to give the proceedings of the City Council relating to the removal of the *Nauvoo Expositor* as a nuisance. We have been robbed, mobbed and plundered with impunity some two or three times; and as every heart is more apt to know its own sorrows, the people of Nauvoo had ample reason, when such characters as the proprietors and abettors of the *Nauvoo Expositor* proved to be before the City Council, to be alarmed for their safety.

The men who got up the press were constantly engaged in resisting the authority or threatening something. If they were fined, an appeal was taken, but the slander went on; and when the paper came, the course and the plan to destroy the city was marked out. The destruction of the city charter and the ruin of the Saints was the all-commanding topic.

Our lives, our city, our charter and our characters are just as sacred, just as dear, and just as good as other people's; and while no friendly arm has been extended from the demolition of our press in Jackson county, Missouri, without law, to this present day, the City Council with all the law of nuisance, from Blackstone down to the Springfield charter, knowing that if they exceeded the law of the land a higher court could regulate the proceedings, abated the *Nauvoo Expositor*.

The proceedings of the Council show, as sketched out, that there was cause for alarm. The people, when they reflect, will at once say that the feelings and rights of men ought to be respected. All persons otherwise, who, without recourse to justice, mercy or humanity, come out with inflammatory publications, destructive resolutions, or more especially extermination, show a want of feeling a want of respect and a want of religious toleration that honorable men will deprecate among Americans as they would the pestilence, famine, or horrors of war. It cannot be that the people are so lost to virtue as to coolly go to murdering men, women and children. No; candor and common sense forbid it!

Dr. Richards and Thomas Bullock sat up all last night writing the proceedings of the City Council for the press.

Tuesday, 18.—At 8 a. m. the Legion assembled according to orders, and organized at 9 a. m., under Acting Major-General Jonathan Dunham. The first cohort under the command of Colonel Stephen Markham, acting

Brigadier-General, and the second cohort under Colonel Hosea Stout, acting Brigadier-General.

Just before, I was informed that there were several boxes of arms landed at the upper stone house, which were secured by the Marshal. Soon after it was discovered that the arms (40 stand) had been sent by Henry G. Sherwood, and the Marshal bought them for the city.

About 1:45 p. m. I proclaimed the city under martial law, and caused the following orders to be issued from the Mayor's office:

DECLARATION OF MARTIAL LAW.

PROCLAMATION.

MAYOR'S OFFICE, CITY OF NAUVOO,
June 18th, 1844.

To the Marshal of the City of Nauvoo:

From the newspapers around us, and the current reports as brought in from the surrounding country, I have good reason to fear that a mob is organizing to come upon this city, and plunder and destroy said city, as well as murder the citizens; and by virtue of the authority vested in me as Mayor, and to preserve the city and the lives of the citizens, I do hereby declare the said city, within the limits of its incorporation, under martial law. The officers, therefore, of the Nauvoo Legion, the police as well as all others, will strictly see that no persons or property pass in or out of the city without due orders.

JOSEPH SMITH, Mayor.

About 2 p. m. the Legion was drawn up in the street close by the Mansion. I stood in full uniform on the top of the frame of a building.

Judge Phelps read the *Warsaw Signal* extra of the 17th, wherein all the "old citizens" were called upon to assist the mob in exterminating the leaders of the Saints and driving away the people.

I addressed the Legion for about an hour and a half.

[The following synopsis of this address was compiled by George A. Smith, from the verbal reports of Joseph G. Hovey, William G. Sterrett, Robert Campbell and many others who heard the Prophet on the occasion]:

The Last Speech of President Smith to the Legion.

It is thought by some that our enemies would be satisfied with my destruction; but I tell you that as soon as they have shed my blood they will thirst for the blood of every man in whose heart dwells a single spark of the spirit of the fullness of the Gospel. The opposition of these men is moved by the spirit of the adversary of all righteousness. It is not only to destroy me, but every man and woman who dares believe the doctrines that God hath inspired me to teach to this generation.

We have never violated the laws of our country. We have every right to live under their protection, and are entitled to all the privileges guaranteed by our state and national constitutions. We have turned the barren, bleak prairies and swamps of this state into beautiful towns, farms and cities by our industry; and the men who seek our destruction and cry thief, treason, riot, &c., are those who themselves violate the laws, steal and plunder from their neighbors, and seek to destroy the innocent, heralding forth lies to screen themselves from the just punishment of their crimes by bringing destruction upon this innocent people. I call God, angels and all men to witness that we are innocent of the charges which are heralded forth through the public prints against us by our enemies; and while they assemble together in unlawful mobs to take away our rights and destroy our lives, they think to shield themselves under the refuge of lies which they have thus wickedly fabricated.

We have forwarded a particular account of all our doings to the Governor. We are ready to obey his commands, and we expect that protection at his hands which we know to be our just due.

We have taken the counsel of Judge Thomas, and have been tried before a civil magistrate on the charge of riot—not that the law required it, but because the Judge advised it as a precautionary measure, to allay all possible pretext for excitement. We were legally acquitted by Esq. Wells, who is a good judge of law. Had we been before the Circuit, the Supreme, or any other court of law in the state or nation, we would have been acquitted, for we have broken no law.

Constable Bettisworth came here with a writ requiring us to go before Mr. Morrison, "or some other justice of the peace of the county," to answer to the charge of riot. We acknowledged ourselves his prisoners, and were ready to go before any magistrate in any precinct in this part of the county, or anywhere else where our lives could be protected from the mob who have published the resolutions for our extermination which you have just heard read. This is a privilege the law guarantees to us, and which the writ itself allows. He broke the law and refused us this privilege, declaring that we should go before Morrison in Carthage, and no one else, when he knew that a numerous mob was collected there who are publicly pledged to destroy our lives.

It was under these circumstances that we availed ourselves of the legal right of the ancient, high, and constitutional privilege of the writ of *habeas corpus*, and were brought before the Municipal Court of this city and discharged from the illegal detention under which we were held by Constable Bettisworth. All mob-men, priests, thieves. and bogus makers, apostates and adulterers, who combine to destroy this people, now raise the hue and cry throughout the state that we resist the law, in order to raise a pretext for calling together thousands more of infuriated mob-men to murder, destroy, plunder and ravish the innocent.

We are American citizens. We live upon a soil for the liberties of which our fathers periled their lives and spilt their blood upon the battlefield. Those rights so dearly purchased, shall not be disgracefully trodden under foot by lawless marauders without at least a noble effort on our part to sustain our liberties.

Will you all stand by me to the death, and sustain at the peril of your lives, the laws of our country, and the liberties and privileges which our fathers have transmitted unto us, sealed with their sacred blood? ("Aye!" shouted thousands.) He then said, "It is well. If you had not done it, I would have gone out there (pointing to the west) and would have raised up a mightier people."

I call upon all men, from Maine to the Rocky Mountains, and from Mexico to British America, whose hearts thrill with horror to behold the rights of freemen trampled under foot, to come to the deliverance of this people from the hand of oppression, cruelty, anarchy and misrule to which they have long been made subject. Come, all ye lovers of liberty, break the oppressor's rod, loose the iron grasp of mobocracy, and bring to condign punishment all those who trample under foot the glorious Constitution and the people's rights. [Drawing his sword, and presenting it to heaven, he said] I call God and angels to witness that I have unsheathed my sword with a firm and unalterable determination that this people shall have their legal rights, and be protected from mob violence, or my blood shall be spilt upon the ground like water, and my body consigned to the silent tomb. While I live, I will never tamely submit to the dominion of cursed mobocracy. I would welcome death rather than submit to this oppression; and it would be sweet, oh, sweet, to rest in the grave rather than submit to this oppression, agitation, annoyance, confusion, and alarm upon alarm, any longer.

I call upon all friends of truth and liberty to come to our assistance; and may the thunders of the Almighty and the forked lightnings of heaven and pestilence, and war and bloodshed come down on those ungodly men who seek to destroy my life and the lives of this innocent people.

I do not regard my own life. I am ready to be offered a sacrifice for this people; for what can our enemies do? Only kill the body, and their power is then at an end. Stand firm, my friends; never flinch. Do not seek to save your lives, for he that is afraid to die for the truth, will lose eternal life. Hold out to the end, and we shall be resurrected and become like Gods, and reign in celestial kingdoms, pricipalities, and eternal dominions, while this cursed mob will sink to hell, the portion of all those who shed innocent blood.

God has tried you. You are a good people; therefore I love you with all my heart. Greater love hath no man than that he should lay down his life for his friends. You have stood by me in the hour of trouble, and I am willing to sacrifice my life for your preservation.

May the Lord God of Israel bless you for ever and ever. I say it in the name of Jesus of Nazareth, and in the authority of the Holy Priesthood, which He hath conferred upon me.

(The people said "Amen.")

Hyrum said that the statement of Sharp in the *Warsaw Signal*, that he (Hyrum) had threatened to take his life, was false as hell—there was not a syllable of truth in it.

About 3:15 p. m., I took the command, and with my staff rode in front of the Legion, marched up Main Street, and returned to our former parade ground. The number on parade was very large, considering the number of Elders who had been sent on missions. After dismissing the Legion to their several commands, I returned home and gave orders to the several commanders only to receive official communications through my aides-de-camp, the proper official channel. I appointed Edward Bonney one of my aids-de-camp.

Truman Gillett, Jr., made the following affidavit:

Affidavit: Truman Gillett—the Treachery of William Law.

STATE OF ILLINOIS, }
CITY OF NAUVOO, } SS.

June 18th, 1844.—Personally appeared Truman Gillett, Jr., before me, Willard Richards, recorder of the city of Nauvoo; and after being duly sworn, deposeth and saith that on or about the first day of June, 1842, while passing up the Ohio river on the steamboat *Massachusetts*, deponent overheard two men, one a resident of Missouri and the other of Ohio, as reported, conversing together concerning incidents on the Upper Mississippi, when one said to the other. "If Law could have succeeded in getting an introduction for us to Joe Smith, damn him, we would have gagged him and nabbed him; and, damn him, all hell could not have rescued him from our hands."

The next morning deponent got in conversation with the man before mentioned from Missouri, who stated that he had been on the Upper Mississippi on business; that he stopped at Nauvoo on his way down with some twelve or fourteen other men, who laid a plan to kidnap Joe Smith; that some of the company queried about getting access to him, but one of them said he knew they could if he could find William Law. They called on William Law in the evening to get an introduction to their great Prophet, and Law went with them to the gate, where they were stopped by the police; "and it was well for him that we did not succeed in getting an introduction to him."

Deponent said, "Did William Law know your business?" And he said "Yes." Deponent asked, "What have you against Joseph Smith? Did he ever injure you?" The man replied, "No; but he has others." "Did you ever see him?" "Yes. I was one who helped to run the Mormons from Missouri," and related many circumstances concerning the Missouri mob.

Deponent said to the man, he was acquainted with William Law; considered he was an honorable man, and was led to doubt his being engaged with them in a conspiracy against Joseph Smith. He replied, "G—d d—n you, it is true, whether you believe it or not," and repeatedly affirmed it. Deponent did not believe the statements of the man from Missouri as mentioned above until after hearing the recent developments before the City Council. TRUMAN GILLETT, JR.

[Seal] Sworn and subscribed at the time and place above written, before me.

WILLARD RICHARDS, Recorder C. N.

At 8 p. m. I wrote the following:

Letter: Joseph Smith to H. T. Hugins—Congratulating Jeremiah Smith on his release.

NAUVOO, ILL., June 18th, 1844.

H. T. Hugins, Esq.

SIR.—I received your communication from Burlington per Captain Anderson; also Dr. Hickock's from Springfield; and I feel grateful for your favors, and congratulate you and Mr. Smith also.

The enemy, or mob, is prowling in the southern and eastern part of the county, and threatening us with extermination; and we ask the friends of peace and good government everywhere to use their influence in suppressing the spirit of mobocracy, and sustain us in our righteous course.

So far as you can conscientiously speak in our behalf, and lend your influence in our favor for the public good your favors will be highly appreciated.

Please show this to Dr. Hickock and such confidential friends as you think proper. Also request Mr. Dunlop to direct his letter to me.

The bearer, Dr. Wakefield, will give you all particulars.

In haste, I remain your friend, respectfully,

JOSEPH SMITH.

I sent the letter by Dr. Wakefield to Burlington.

Nine messengers arrived from Carthage, and report that the mob had received intelligence from the Governor, who would take no notice of them; and they damned the Governor as being as bad as Joe Smith. They did not care for him, and they were just as willing he would not help them as if he would.

Governor Ford's Treatment of the Mob.

There was a body of armed men in Carthage, and a mob meeting at Fountain Green, which attracted considerable attention.

Shadrach Roundy, a policeman, reported at 10 p. m., after I had retired, that a man by the name of Norton had threatened to shoot me. An examination was immediately had, but no proof was found.

Threat Against the Prophet's Life

This evening I appointed Theodore Turley Armorer-General of the Legion.

I insert the following affidavit:

Affidavit, Canfield and Belknap—Concerning Threats of Invasion from Missouri.

STATE OF ILLINOIS, }
CITY OF NAUVOO, } SS.

HANCOCK COUNTY, June 18, 1844.

Personally appeared before me, Aaron Johnson, a justice of the peace, Cyrus Canfield and Gilbert Belknap, of Hancock county; and being duly sworn depose and say that on yesterday, June 17th, 1844, certain persons—to-wit, Dr. Barnes and Joseph H. Jackson, having entered into conversation with your deponents, among other things declared that the Governor of Illinois was as big a scoundrel as Joseph Smith, and that he is the d—dest scoundrel that was ever suffered to live; that they did not care for the Governor, and had rather that the Governor would side with Smith; that they (the mob) were coming to Nauvoo with a sufficient force to take Smith; and if the people endeavored to prevent them, they should kill the people; and that if Smith had left Nauvoo, they had determined to destroy the Mansion and other buildings. And your deponents further say that one John Eller declared that he had lived in Missouri and was at the massacre of the Mormons at Haun's Mill, that he had killed one Mormon, and that he had left Missouri on purpose to fight the Mormons, and would hunt a Mormon as he would a deer. And your deponents further say that they heard that about one hundred persons had already arrived from Missouri, and were expecting as many more from that State. And your deponents further say, that they heard in Carthage that they had already received a number of guns and ammunition and provisions from St. Louis, in order to prosecute their attack upon Nauvoo. And, further your deponents say not.

CYRUS CANFIELD,
GILBERT BELKNAP.

Sworn and subscribed to before me, this eighteenth day of June, 1844.

AARON JOHNSON,
A Justice of the Peace.

CHAPTER XXV.

ATTEMPTS TO DRAFT SAINTS INTO MOB SERVICE AGAINST NAUVOO—THREATENED INVASION FROM MISSOURI—JAMES A. BENNETT URGED TO COME TO NAUVOO.

Wednesday, *June 19*, *1844*.—The Legion assembled on the parade-ground. A company of the Legion came in from Green Plains about 11 a. m. I met them at the front of the Mansion, and an escort came down from the parade-ground below the Temple and escorted them to the ground.

At 1 p. m. a company of volunteers arrived from Iowa and were also escorted to the parade-ground.

On Sunday, the 16th, a committee of the mob, headed by James Charles, a constable of Hancock county, went to the house of Captain Chester Loveland, who lives four miles southeast of Warsaw, and required him to call out his company to join the *posse* of David Bettisworth to go to Nauvoo and arrest me and the City Council. He peremptorily refused to comply with their request. The same *posse* returned on the 17th with an order, as they stated, from the Governor, which Loveland believed (and no doubt correctly) to be a forgery, and therefore still refused to go on any terms. The *posse* then reported his refusal to Colonel Williams, who appointed a committee of twelve to lynch, tar and feather Captain Loveland on the 18th; which committee went that evening and arrived about midnight.

Effort to Draft Chester Loveland into Mob Service.

Loveland, who had been informed of Williams' order, prepared himself for defense and kept watch. As soon as they came and he saw their number, and that they were provided with tar bucket, bag of feathers and a bundle of withes, in addition to their fire-arms, he blew out his light and placed himself in a suitable position to defend the door (which he had fastened) and the window. They went around his house several times, tried his door, rapped, called him by name, and consulted together. Some were for breaking the door; others thought it too dangerous. They knew he must be in there, for they were near his door when the light was blown out. Finally their courage failed; and notifying him to leave the country immediately, they took their departure. During this trying time Loveland did not speak.

Roads Leading into Nauvoo Picketed.

In the afternoon I gave orders to General Dunham to have a picket-guard under Col. Markham, posted on all the roads leading out of the city; also an inner guard, under Major Jesse P. Harmon, posted in all the streets and alleys in the city, and also on the river bank. I also gave orders to have all the powder and lead in the city secured, and to see that all the arms were in use, and that all unclaimed arms be put in the hands of those who could use them.

I insert the affidavit of Anson Call, David Evans and William E. Horner:

Affidavit: Call, Evans and Horner—Treatment of Nauvoo Committee by Levi Williams, et al.

STATE OF ILLINOIS, }
CITY OF NAUVOO, } ss.

HANCOCK COUNTY, June 19, 1844.

Personally appeared before me, Aaron Johnson, justice of the peace of said county, Anson Call, David Evans and William E. Horner, of Hancock county and state aforesaid; and being duly sworn, depose and say that on Monday, the 17th instant, we started for Rocky Run precinct, and arived yesterday. We then went to Col. Williams' of that place, and there soon assembled twenty or thirty men. We were informed that Col. Williams had gone to Lima to get the colonel there to bring on his regiment. We then informed them that we were delegated on behalf of the people of Nauvoo to transact business with them

They informed us they had a committee set apart to do their business, and that one was absent, and the other two would shortly be here. That while a person was seeking the two men, we observed to the people that General Smith was willing to be tried in any state, for any crime or supposed crime that he had ever committed, except in the state of Missouri.

One of the persons objected to General Smith being tried by the Municipal Court in Nauvoo, and declared that nothing else would do but for him to be taken upon the old writ, and by the same person who took him in custody before, and tried at the place where the writ was issued.

It was then observed that Judge Thomas had advised General Smith to enter into bonds to be tried before the Circuit Court, and this would allay all the excited feelings of the people.

It was then moved by one of their company, and sanctioned by the people, that a committee should wait on the Judge who gave General Smith this advice, and give him a coat of tar and feathers; when one John Elliott, of notoriety, agreed to find the tar and feathers for that purpose.

After some further conversation, a man whom they called Lawyer Stephens came in from Warsaw, and asked where Col. Williams was. He was told that he had gone to Lima. They then observed to the lawyer that we were delegates from Nauvoo, when he replied. "We are expecting delegates, too, at Warsaw;" and he said the people were talking of introducing them to the Mississippi river; and says he, "Gentlemen, you can do with your delegates what you think proper."

A Mr. Crawford, one of the committee, observed that he went against such proceedings, and advised them as a body to keep cool. They then told the lawyer the advice that the Judge of the Circuit Court had given to General Smith, when he said it was unlawful advice, and it was a second time moved and assented to that a committee should wait on Judge Thomas and give him a coat of tar and feathers. The remainder of the committee having come in, they stated to us that they had written to the Governor to obtain aid from other counties; and if the Governor did not send them aid, they were too weak to go themselves now, but were summoning all the people that would come into the county until they got force enough to come up and take Joseph Smith with the first warrant, and take him to the place where the writ was first issued; and nothing less than that would satisfy the people.

ANSON CALL,
DAVID EVANS,
WM. E. HORNER.

Sworn and subscribed to this 19th day of June, 1844.

AARON JOHNSON, J. P.

From the best information they could learn, there were two hundred armed men at Rocky Run precinct, two hundred at Warsaw, two hundred in Missouri, and the whole receiving constant additions.

At 9 p. m. I was at home. The city all quiet.

Thursday, *20*.—At daybreak I went with my staff and Major-General Dunham to the prairie, to view the situation of the ground, and to devise plans for the defense of the city, and select the proper locations to meet the mob, and made arrangements for provisions for the city, instructing my agent to pledge my farms for the purpose.

Preparations for an Attack.

At 10 a. m. Dr. Southwick from Louisiana arrived, and reported that there was not much excitement in St. Louis; that a cannon had arrived at Warsaw from Quincy, and that it had been reported to him that there was great excitement in Upper Missouri.

Report of Dr. Southwick.

At 11, I reviewed the Legion facing the Mansion, and went to parade on the banks of the river.

I insert the affidavit of Carlos W. Lyon.

Affidavit: Carlos W. Lyon.

STATE OF ILLINOIS, } ss
CITY OF NAUVOO. }

On the 20th day of June, 1844, came before me, Willard Richards, recorder of the city aforesaid, Carlos W. Lyon; and after being duly sworn, deposeth and saith that while at St. Louis, Mo., on Monday, the 17th instant, it was a common topic that they were furnishing arms and ammunition to be sent by steamboat to Warsaw, Illinois; and said if the people of Warsaw need five hundred men, to give notice by the steamer *Boreas*, and the men should be sent from St. Louis to Warsaw; and that your said affiant also saw a cannon landed from the steamer *Mermaid* at Warsaw; and further he saith not.

CARLOS W. LYON.

Subscribed and sworn to before me this 20th day of June, 1844.

WILLARD RICHARDS,
Recorder of the City of Nauvoo.

Wrote to John Tyler, President of the United States, as follows:

An Appeal to President Tyler.

CITY OF NAUVOO, ILLINOIS, June 20th, 1844.

SIR.— I have just enclosed to the Governor of the State of Illinois copies of the enclosed affidavits and extra. I am sorry to say that the State of Missouri, not contented with robbing, driving and murdering many of the Latter-day Saints, are now joining the mob of this state for the purpose of the "utter extermination" of the Mormons, as they have resolved. And now, sir, as President of the United States, will you render that protection which the Constitution guarantees in case of "insurrection and rebellion," and save the innocent and oppressed from such horrid persecution?

With great respect, I have the honor to be your obedient servant,

JOSEPH SMITH, Mayor.

JOHN TYLER, President of the U. S., Washington, D. C.

I here insert affidavits of Hiram B. Mount and John Cunningham:

Affidavit: Mount and Cunningham—Attempt to Draft them into the Mob Service.

STATE OF ILLINOIS, }
HANCOCK COUNTY, } ss.

CITY OF NAUVOO, June 20th, 1844.

Personally appeared before me, Aaron Johnson, an acting justice of the peace in and for the county of Hancock, Hiram B. Mount and John Cunningham, who being duly sworn, depose and say that George Baker, John Banks, Joseph Barber, and two others came to your deponents on Saturday the 15th inst., at Morley Settlement, in said county, and demanded our arms. We replied that we had none, when they required of us to go with them to Nauvoo to take Joseph Smith and other prisoners, and they promised to supply us with arms. Second, if we would not do so, that we were required to leave our homes and go to Nauvoo. We must either go against Smith, or take part with him.

They then told us they intended to go to Nauvoo to take Smith; and if they could not take him, they would take some of the head men of Smith's clan, and hold them under bonds of death until Smith was delivered up to them. And your deponents further say that John Banks told them if they could not get volunteers enough, they would get a force that would take him.

HIRAM B. MOUNT,
JOHN CUNNINGHAM, (x—his mark).

[Seal] Subscribed and sworn to this 20th day of June, 1844, before me,

AARON JOHNSON, J. P.

Affidavit: Allen T. Wait—Attempt to Draft him into Mob Service.

STATE OF ILLINOIS, }
HANCOCK COUNTY. } ss

CITY OF NAUVOO, June 20th, 1844.

Personally appeared before me, Aaron Johnson, an acting justice of the peace in and for said county, Allen T. Wait, of Morley Settlement in said county; and being first duly sworn, deposeth and saith that on Saturday morning he was at the house of Colonel Levi Williams, when he told me that I must take up arms and go and fight against Joseph Smith, or I must leave the place immediately, or else I must give up my arms and stay at home.

He also said they would take Smith by law if they could; or if the Governor would not grant a writ to take him they would take him anyhow. He also said, if the people would not give Smith up, they would lay the whole city of Nauvoo in ashes.

I inquired what they would do with those people of Nauvoo who would not fight? He said they must make some signal, or else they must share the same fate—they must all perish, men, women, and children.

I then left in order to go home, when Captain Harrison P. Crawford overtook me, and told me if the Governor would not help them they did not care for the Governor anyhow. He said Governor Ford was an unconstitutional man; he had issued two illegal writs, and they were done so on purpose: and any such man ought not to hold any office whatever; and they intended to proceed against the Mormons whether they got any authority from the Governor or not.

ALLAN T. WAIT.

[Seal] Subscribed and sworn to this 20th day of June, 1844, before me,

AARON JOHNSON, J. P.

Likewise the affidavit of Isaac Morley, Gardner Snow John Edmiston and Edmund Durfee.

Affidavit: Isaac Morley et al.—Attempt to Draft them into Mob Service,

STATE OF ILLINOIS, }
HANCOCK COUNTY, } ss

CITY OF NAUVOO, June 20th, 1844.

Personally appeared before me, Aaron Johnson, an acting justice of the peace in and for said county, Isaac Morley, Gardner Snow, John Edmiston and Edmund Durfee, all of Hancock county aforesaid; and being first duly sworn, depose and say that on Saturday, the 15th day of June, 1844, at Morley Settlement in said county, certain persons—to wit.,George Baker, farmer, John Banks, Esq., Luther Perry, constable, Joseph Barber, farmer; and another person whose name we do not know, called upon your deponent, Isaac Morley, when John Banks said they waited on him to make three propositions—namely: first, that we were to take up arms, join with, and go along with them to Nauvoo, to arrest one Joseph Smith and others, about seventeen in number, living in Nauvoo; second, to remove our effects to Nauvoo; or third, to give up our arms to them and remain neutral. And said Isaac Morley was required to notify all the brethren in the neighborhood, and report to the said committee, which of these propositions we accepted, by 8 o'clock on Monday morning following; and that one of the above resolutions was to be complied with within that time.

On the same day said Joseph Barber and Luther Perry went to where your deponent, Edmund Durfee, was at work in a field in the same neighborhood, and said they had come to notify him that said Durfee must comply with one of the above propositions; if not that said Durfee would smell thunder.

And all your deponents further depose and say that they have been compelled to leave their homes and flee to Nauvoo for protection. "For we were afraid to stay there on account of the mobs threatening to utterly exterminate us," according to a *Warsaw Signal* extra of June, 14th, 1844, if we stayed at home; and further your deponents say not.

ISAAC MORLEY,
GARDNER SNOW,
JOHN EDMISTON,
EDMUND DURFEE.

[Seal] Subscribed and sworn to this 20th day of June, 1844, before me,

AARON JOHNSON, J. P.

Also the affidavit of Solomon Hancock, William Garner, and John G. Lofton:

Affidavit: Hancock, Garner, Lofton—Attempt to Draft them into Mob Service.

STATE OF ILLINOIS, } ss
HANCOCK COUNTY. }

CITY OF NAUVOO, June 20th, 1844.

Personally appeared before me, Aaron Johnson, an acting justice of the peace, Solomon Hancock, William Garner and John G. Lofton, who being first duly sworn, depose and say that on Saturday, the 15th day of June, 1844, at Morley Settlement in said county, certain persons, —to wit., John Clark, John Crawford, Jeremiah Bently, and three others, all farmers, came to your deponents and made three several propositions to them, to wit: first, that we were to take up our arms and join with them in going to Nauvoo, to take Joseph Smith and others prisoners; second, to remove with our effects to Nauvoo immediately; or, third, to give up our arms to Col. Levi Williams and remain neutral.

We were ordered to give in our decision on Monday then next by 8 o'clock in the morning; and if we would not agree to their decision, we must abide the consequences. And in consequence of mobs gathering in the neighborhood, we have been obliged to leave our homes in order to save our lives, and are come to Nauvoo for protection.

Solomon Hancock further deposeth and saith that said John Clark did on Tuesday, 18th instant, inform your deponent that one of their party had gone to St. Louis and had obtained three cannon, and were expecting three companies of volunteers from St. Louis to join them in going to Nauvoo to exterminate the Mormons; and further your deponents say not.

SOLOMON HANCOCK,
WILLIAM GARNER,
JOHN G. LOFTON.

[Seal] Subscribed and sworn to this 20th day of June, 1844, before me,

AARON JOHNSON.

Also the affidavit of James Guyman:

Affidavit: James Guyman—Threats of Invasion from Missouri.

STATE OF ILLINOIS, } ss
HANCOCK COUNTY. }

CITY OF NAUVOO, June 20th, 1844.

Personally appeared before me, Aaron Johnson, an acting justice of the peace in and for said county, James Guyman, of Green Plains precinct in said county; and being first duly sworn deposeth and saith that on Saturday morning, the 15th instant, he was at Rocky Run precinct, when one Captain Wyers, captain of an "Independent Anti-Mormon Minute Men Company," came to a house where your deponent was staying. He inquired for a drum. He wanted either to borrow it or buy it until the affray with the Mormons was over.

I asked him how he was going to proceed to take Smith. He then said Missouri had offered to send over two thousand men, to come over to assist and take him.

I asked whether it was legal for them to come over here. He replied when they came over the constables were going to summons them, and also to summons every man who was in or would come into the county.

I asked if it was according to law to proceed that way, and he replied it was, and he went in for the law and democracy. He said they had sent two men to the Governor to order the militia out in their favor to help to take those criminals; and if he would not do just right, they would execute him by taking his head from his shoulders.

I replied, "You said you were a democracy man, and went for the law." I said, "Do you call that democracy or mobocracy?"

He said if they went that far, and if the Governor ordered the militia against them instead of in favor of them, he would turn mob, and the militia would join him, and they would take the Governor's head from his shoulders. He repeated it two or three times.

I enquired if it was law to go and drive those innocent Mormons who were living in the neighborhood, or tyrannically compel them to do things not agreeable to their will? He allowed that in this case it was.

I asked what he was going to do with these old settlers who would neither take up arms and fight against Smith nor in favor of him; when he replied they must fight either for one side or the other, or they must share the same fate as the Mormons.

Your deponent further saith that he is not a Mormon, and does not belong to the Church of Jesus Christ of Latter-day Saints; and further saith not.

JAMES GUYMAN.

[Seal] Subscribed and sworn to this 20th day of June, 1844, before me,

AARON JOHNSON, J. P.

Also the affidavit of Obadiah Bowen:

Affidavit: Obadiah Bowen—Attempt to Draft him into Service of Mob.

STATE OF ILLINOIS, } ss
HANCOCK COUNTY. }

CITY OF NAUVOO, June 20th, 1844.

Personally appeared before me, Aaron Johnson, an acting justice of the peace, in and for said county, Obadiah Bowen, of Morley Settlement, in said county; and being first duly sworn, deposeth and saith that on Saturday the 15th instant, John Clark rode up to where I was at work in Morley Settlement, and said he was afraid the Mormons would come and destroy their property; "and," said he, "if I have any destroyed by any person, I shall make my resort upon the nearest Mormons, and take their property in place of that which shall be taken away;" wherever he could find it, so long as it was a Mormon's; and that on Tuesday, the 18th instant, as I was coming from my house to the road leading to Lima, a mob was at the forks of the road standing still and consulting together; I came on the road about twenty rods ahead of them. In a few moments Colonel Levi Williams, John Clark and five others rode along the same road after me.

I heard them talking about shooting the Mormons, when Clark said, "It is no disgrace to shoot a Mormon, anyhow," when they all laughed. They overtook me, and Col. Williams asked me where I lived. I replied in Morley Settlement. He asked me if I was a Mormon, when Clark said it was no odds—he is on their part.

Col. Williams then threatened me, and said I must be sure and be at his house by nine o'clock in the morning; if not I must either get out of Morley Settlement, or be served the same sauce as the Mormons. He gave me to understand that they were going to make a total destruction of Morley Settlement tomorrow, and I had better get out of it.

He then talked about Joseph Smith, when I replied I understood Joseph Smith had a fair trial and was bound over to the Supreme Court. He said, "If he is not, we do not care, it is illegally done;" and he should go ahead. He should gather the troops, and there would be two thousand men landed tomorrow from Missouri. He said they were volunteers. They should meet next day at Carthage, and then go against Joseph Smith and demolish the city of Nauvoo, for have him at any rate they would. He was in a very great passion, and let out a great many oaths and [said] other things that I have not mentioned.

In consequence of their threats, and to save our lives, we were obliged to leave our homes in a very stormy night, and had to cross a dangerous stream that was swollen by the rain, and was unable to protect myself from great sufferings and hardships, and came to the city of Nauvoo for protection.

OBADIAH BOWEN.

[Seal] Subscribed and sworn to this 20th day of June, 1844, before me,

AARON JOHNSON, J. P.

Also the affidavit of Alvah Tippitts:

Affidavit: Alvah Tippetts—Violence of John Williams Upon.

STATE OF ILLINOIS,
HANCOCK COUNTY. } ss

CITY OF NAUVOO. June 20th, 1844.

Personally appeared before me, Aaron Johnson, a justice of the peace in and for the said county, Alvah Tippetts, of Warsaw, in Hancock county and state aforesaid; and being first duly sworn, deposeth and saith that on Wednesday, June 12th, at Green Plains, one Col. Levi Williams came to your deponent about sunrise, and ordered me out of the house that very day.

I replied he was very hasty. He again ordered me out of the house, and said, if I spoke a word, he would put me out of the house immediately.

I then took away part of my goods and left the house accordingly, because I was afraid to stay there another night.

The next day I went back after the remainder of my property, and called at the house of Col. Levi Williams for some things belonging to me.

When I arrived there John Williams, the son of said Levi Williams, aged about twenty-eight years, abused me for placing confidence in Joseph Smith and the people of Nauvoo. He then took me by the back of my neck and pushed me away, and said he would not have such stuff in his house. The second time he pushed me by the neck, and his foot to my back. He pushed me several times and kicked me. Again, when in the street, he kept kicking and pushing me, and abusing me with his tongue. I am sixty-one years old. I did not say anything to him to cause this abuse; but it was all on account of my believing that Joseph Smith and the people of Nauvoo would do nothing but what was according to law.

ALVAH TIPPETTS.

[Seal] Subscribed and sworn to this 20th day of June, 1844, before me,

AARON JOHNSON, J. P.

Reinforcement for Nauvoo from Ramus.

I had sent orders to Captain Almon W. Babbitt, commander of the company at Ramus, to come immediately with his company to Nauvoo, and help to defend the place; and this morning my brother-in-law, William McLeary, informs me that when the letter was read to the company, Babbitt refused to come, and said it was a foolish move, and objected to any of the company coming. The company was marshaled into line, when Babbitt said, "If any of you go, not one will ever get to Nauvoo alive," when immediately my Uncle John Smith stepped in front of the line and said, "Every man that goes at the call of the Prophet shall go and return safe, and not a hair of his head shall be lost; and I bless you in the name of the Lord."

The company immediately threw the command upon Uriah H. Yager, who accepted of it, and started for Nauvoo, although many of them were destitute of boots or shoes. The company had not traveled five miles before they suddenly came upon double their number of the mob, who had two red flags flying, and who had paraded their company and taken a position in a wood that commanded the road. The company from Macedonia opened file about ten feet apart and marched past them within rifle shot, while the mob fired several guns at them, the balls whizzing past their heads. They came here at daybreak this morning, and I directed the quartermaster to furnish those who needed with shoes.

I wrote the following letter:

Letter: Joseph Smith to Ballantyne and Slater—Advice on moving into Nauvoo.

NAUVOO, June 20th, 1844.

BROTHERS BALLANTYNE AND SLATER:—On information from you by J. McIlrick, I would advise that your families remain where they are and be quiet, as the mob will not be likely to disturb them; but any amount of wheat or provisions you may have you had better remove without delay to Nauvoo, as it will be better for you to bring it here and have your pay than to leave it for the mob to consume and destroy.

I remain your brother in Christ Jesus,

JOSEPH SMITH.

BALLANTYNE AND SLATER, Doyles Mills, near Plymouth, Ill.

I here insert the affidavit of John P. Greene and John M. Bernhisel:

Affidavit: Greene and Bernhisel—Threatened Invasion from Missouri.

STATE OF ILLINOIS,
COUNTY OF HANCOCK. } ss

CITY OF NAUVOO.

On the 20th day of June, 1844, personally appeared before me, Aaron Johnson, a justice of the peace within and for said county, John P. Greene, marshal of said city, and John M. Bernhisel; and after being duly sworn, depose and say that a body of citizens, in a mass meeting convened on the 13th instant at Carthage, resolved to exterminate the Latter-day Saints of the said city of Nauvoo, and for that purpose, according to the purport of the *Warsaw Signal* extra, dated June 14, 1844, bodies of armed men are coming from the State of Missouri, and also from the territory of Iowa, and the cannon and ammunition are being transported from the state of Missouri to Illinois for the purpose of utterly exterminating the Latter-day Saints. And your affiants would further state that these bodies of armed men, cannon, arms, and munitions of war are transported in steamboats navigating the waters of the United States, and that the name of one of these boats is the *Die Vernon.*

JOHN P. GREENE,
JOHN M. BERNHISEL.

[Seal] Subscribed and sworn to before me, this 20th day of June, 1844.

AARON JOHNSON, J. P.

Dr. Richards wrote the following:

Letter: Willard Richards to Jas Arlington Bennett—Affairs in Nauvoo—Western Movement.

MAYOR'S OFFICE, NAUVOO, June 20th, 1844.

DEAR GENERAL.—Yours of the 14th of April was received at a late date. A multiplicity of business on account of the peculiar state of affairs, has prevented a reply till now. Your views about the nomination of General Smith for the Presidency are correct. We will gain popularity and external influence. But this is not all: we mean to elect him, and nothing shall be wanting on our part to accomplish it; and why? Because we are satisfied, fully satisfied, that this is the best or only method of saving our free institutions from a total overthrow.

You will discover by this day's extra *Nauvoo Neighbor*, and previous papers which I shall forward with this, that we are already being surrounded by an armed mob; and, if we can believe a hundredth part of their statements we have no alternative but to fight or die. All the horrors of Missouri's murders are crowding thick upon us, and the citizens of this county declare in mass-meetings, "No peace till the Mormons are utterly exterminated from the earth." And for what?

A band of thieves, counterfeiters, bogus-makers, gamblers, debauchers, murderers, and all that is vile, established a printing-press in this city for the purpose of carrying on all their hellish plans and overthrowing every principle of righteousness; and after publishing one number, called the *Nauvoo Expositor*, filled on every column with lies and libel the most dark and damnable it were possible for men or demons on the earth or in the shades of Gehenna, calculated to destroy every chartered right to our peaceful city, and constitutional principles to our nation, being destitute of every vestige of truth, and without one redeeming quality, either in the paper or the characters of its publishers.

The City Council, on the 10th instant, ordered the press and fixtures to be abated as a nuisance which order was executed by the proper authorities without delay, without noise, tumult or confusion.

The proprietors immediately evacuated their houses and the city, and the night following fired one or more of their buildings, just as they did in Missouri, thinking to raise a hue-and-cry that the Mormons had done it, and by that means bring a mob on us without a moment's delay; but our vigilant police discovered the fire and abated that also.

Chagrined at their disappointment, and drunk with madness, they next went to Carthage, the county seat and headquarters of mobocracy, and swore that Joseph and about seventeen others had committed a riot, and sent a warrant for their apprehension. They offered to go before any magistrate in the vicinity and answer to the charge. The officer would not consent, but would take them to Carthage. They had threatened their lives at Carthage and did not consider it safe to go thither, and prayed out a writ of *habeas corpus* from the Municipal Court, and were set free.

This only enraged the mob the more, and another writ was issued by a county magistrate in the vicinity, not a Mormon, before whom they were brought, and every exertion made to convict them, but the magistrate discharged them.

This does not satisfy them. They are determined to have "Joe Smith," brought before themselves for trial at the headquarters of mobocracy swearing that all they want is to get him out of the city; and they will shoot the "damned rascal."

Cannon, ammunition and men are passing over the Mississippi from Missouri to Illinois, and the mob is collected by hundreds at different points in the county swearing everlasting vengeance; and when their oaths and writs will end, God knows.

We have sent messengers to the Governor, but had no returns, and shall dispatch messages to the President of the United States next boat.

If the virtuous part of the community, the state, the nation, will come to the rescue of innocence and the rights our fathers bled to purchase, that our peace and happiness may be secured to us in common with others, it is all we ask; but if they will not, and the mob goes on, we say a dishonorable life is worse than an honorable death, and we are ready for the onset; and we call upon all patriots, far and near, to lend a helping hand to put down the mob and restore peace.

If this is not done immediately, and the mob attempt to execute their threats, you may soon have the opportunity of beholding that glorious "vision in the west" you have sublimely contemplated in your letter.

I write you at this time at the request of the Prophet, and I invite you to come to our assistance with as many volunteers as you can bring. And if the mob cannot be dispersed, and the Government will not espouse our righteous cause, you may soon, very soon, behold the second birth of our nation's freedom; for live without the free exercise of thought, and the privilege of worshiping God according to the dictates of our consciences, we will not! We will die rather, and go where the wicked cease to trouble. But we firmly believe there are virtuous men and patriots enough yet left to sustain those principles which alone are worth living for. Will you come?

Here is Oregon. Here is California. Where is your ambition? Patriotism? Your "separate and independent empire," if you sit calmly still and see the most virtuous and noble people that ever trod upon the footstool of Jehovah ground to powder by a miscreant mob and not stretch forth your potent arm for their defense in all the majesty of a God? If you do not, your turn may come next; and where will it cease?

Let the first blow be struck upon us from this hour, and this field is open for every honest patriot from the east to the west sea, and from the river Mississippi to the ends of the earth.

General, will you stand neutral? Come, and you will know for yourself.

I close in haste, with good wishes to yourself and family.

W. Richards.

General J. A. Bennett,
Arlington House, N. Y.

CHAPTER XXVI.

THE TWELVE CALLED FROM EASTERN MISSION—GOVERNOR FORD AT CARTHAGE—NAUVOO DELEGATION TO GOVERNOR—THREATS AND CONSPIRACY AGAINST THE PROPHET'S LIFE—GOVERNOR FORD INVITED TO NAUVOO TO INVESTIGATE CONDITIONS.

Thursday, June 20, 1844 [*continued*].—I wrote to those of the Twelve Apostles who are absent on missions to come home immediately, namely, Brigham Young, Boston; Heber C. Kimball, Washington; Orson Hyde, Philadelphia; Parley P. Pratt, New York; Orson Pratt, Washington; Wilford Woodruff, Portage, New York; William Smith, Philadelphia; George A. Smith, Peterboro; John E. Page, Pittsburg; and Lyman Wight, Baltimore. Also to Amasa Lyman, Cincinnati, Ohio, and George Miller, Richmond, Madison county, Kentucky. I sent the letters by express by Aaron M. York to the Illinois river, on account of the stoppage of the mails.

The Apostles Called Home.

At 8 p. m. Thomas Bullock came and read to me the affidavits of Isaac Morley, Gardner Snow, John Edmiston, Edmund Durfee, Solomon Hancock, Allen T. Waite, James Guyman, Obadiah Bowen, Alvah Tippetts, Hiram B. Mount, and John Cunningham, with the affiants; and afterward the affidavits were all sworn to before Aaron Johnson, Esquire.

Ten p. m. John Pike and Henry Gates went to the quarters of the Major-General, and informed him they had seen a number of men driving about three hundred head of cattle in the direction of the mob camp. The drovers reported themselves as having come from Missouri, and were about nine miles from Nauvoo.

I gave directions to Theodore Turley to commence the manufacture of artillery. He asked me if he should not rent a building, and set some men to repairing the small arms which were out of order. I told him in confidence that there would not be a gun fired on our part during this fuss.

A Prophecy—No Gun Fired on Part of Saints.

I extract the following from a letter from Robert D. Foster dated "Carthage, June 20th, 1844, to John Proctor, Sen., Nauvoo."

Letter: Robert D. Foster to John Proctor—Fragment—Instruction as to Property.

We have a hundred barrels of flour here for the folks, and Nauvoo has no means to live, only from the country, and that is cut off sure There are thousands of armed men ready now and thousands more coming from Missouri and the country around. Tell John to sleep in the barn, and take care of fire and robbery, and all my things there, as I shall be home soon. Tell Amos Davis to keep his eyes open, as we learn that consecration law will soon commence on him. This we know, and he had better look out sharp. Let him read this sheet. Tell Norton Gibbs and all my boys that I should be glad to see them a minute, but I cannot come. They must be patient and faithful, and I will be there and reward every man according to his desert; and I won't forget the perjured villains there either.

I advised my brother Hyrum to take his family on the next steamboat and go to Cincinnati. Hyrum replied, "Joseph, I can't leave you." Whereupon I said to the company present, "I wish I could get Hyrum out of the way, so that he may live to avenge my blood, and I will stay with you and see it out."

Hyrum Smith's Fidelity to the Prophet.

Friday, 21.—About 10 a. m. I rode out with my guard up Main Street past the Major-General's quarters, and reviewed the Legion. I returned to headquarters about 2:30 p. m., having met Col. Elam L. Freeman and Mr. Bartlett, who came as express from the Governor who had arrived at Carthage this morning, and they delivered me the following letter:

Letter: Governor Ford to Mayor and Council of Nauvoo Asking Representatives to Meet him at Carthage.

HEADQUARTERS CARTHAGE, June 21st, 1844.

To the Honorable the Mayor and Common Council of the City of Nauvoo:

GENTLEMEN.—Having heard of the excitement in this part of the country, and judging that my presence here might be necessary to preserve the peace and enforce the laws, I arrived at this place this morning. Both before and since my arrival, complaints of a grave character have been made to me of certain proceedings of your honorable body. As chief magistrate, it is my duty to see that impartial justice shall be done, uninfluenced either by the excitement here or in your city.

I think before any decisive measure shall be adopted, that I ought to hear the allegations and defenses of all parties. By adopting this course I have some hope that the evils of war may be averted, and, at any rate, I will be enabled by it to understand the true merits of the present difficulties, and shape my course with reference to law and justice.

For these reasons I have to request that you will send out to me at this place, one or more well-informed and discreet persons, who will be capable of laying before me your version of the matter, and of receiving from me such explanations and resolutions as may be determined on.

Col. Elam L. Freeman will present you this note in the character of a herald from the Governor. You will respect his character as such and permit him to pass and repass free from molestation.

Your messengers are assured of protection in person and property, and will be returned to you in safety.

I am, gentlemen, with high consideration most respectfully,

Your obedient servant,

THOMAS FORD.

Governor and Commander in Chief.

Joseph H. Jackson at Nauvoo.

I immediately notified the City Council to meet in session at 4 p. m. About 11 a. m. a rumor was circulated at General Dunham's headquarters that Joseph H. Jackson was seen at Davidson Hibberd's. He [Dunham] ordered out a *posse* to arrest him, which went accordingly, but returned without success.

At 4 p. m. I met with the City Council, when the affidavits of the following persons were read—namely

Isaac Morley, Gardner Snow, John Edmiston, Edward Durfee, Solomon Hancock, William Gardner, John G. Lofton, Allen T. Waite, James Guyman, Obadiah Bowen, Alvah Tippetts, Hiram B. Mount, John Cunningham, Cyrus Canfield, Gilbert Belknap, Anson Call, David Evans, William E. Horner, Stephen Markham, Thomas G. Wilson, John P. Greene, John M. Bernhisel, Truman Gillett, Jr., Carlos W. Lyon, and H. T. Hugins; when Dr. J. M. Bernhisel, Councilor John Taylor, and Dr. Willard Richards were appointed by the council to return with the express to the Governor at Carthage, and carry said affidavits with the following letter:

Letter: Joseph Smith to Governor Ford—Submitting Documents.

NAUVOO, June 21, 1844.

SIR —The affidavits and handbills herewith connected, are submitted for your Excellency's consideration.

Respectfully, I have the honor to be your Excellency's obedient servant,

JOSEPH SMITH.

THOMAS FORD, Governor of Illinois, Carthage.

Messrs. Taylor and Bernhisel went accordingly, but Dr. Richards tarried to prepare additional documents.

The following affidavit was taken:

Affidavit: John P. Greene—Joseph H. Jackson,—Threatens Prophet's Life.

STATE OF ILLINOIS, HANCOCK CO., }
CITY OF NAUVOO. } ss.

June 21st, 1844.—Personally appeared John P. Greene before me, Willard Richards, recorder of said city; and after being duly sworn, deposeth and saith that on or about the 27th day of May, 1844, while at Hamilton's tavern, in Carthage, county aforesaid, in company with Joseph Smith and others, Robert D. Foster called deponent into a private room, and there and then said, "For God's sake, don't suffer that man, Joseph Smith, to go out of doors; for if he steps outside of the door his blood will be spilt;" to which statement deponent replied he had no such fears; when said Foster confirmed said statements with considerable emotion, and said he knew that Smith could not go out of doors, but his blood would be spilt.

Deponent asked Foster who would do it. Foster said he would not tell; but he knew the proud spirit of Jackson, that he would not be insulted, and that he would kill Joseph Smith if he had to die on the spot; and there were many others in Carthage who would assist to do the same thing. Joseph H. Jackson was in the house below at the time.

A day or two previous to the above conversation, while at Carthage aforesaid, deponent heard Joseph H. Jackson say that Joseph Smith was the damnedest rascal in the world, and he would be damned if he did not take vengeance on him, if he had to follow him to the Rocky Mountains; and said Jackson made many more such like threats against Joseph Smith and Hyrum Smith.

JOHN P. GREENE.

Sworn and subscribed this 21st day of June, 1844, before me,

[Seal] WILLARD RICHARDS,
Recorder of the city of Nauvoo.

And as this affidavit confirms what was told me in Carthage, I made the following affidavit:

Affidavit: Joseph Smith—Conspiracy Against Affiant's Life.

STATE OF ILLINOIS,
COUNTY OF HANCOCK. } ss

CITY OF NAUVOO, June 21st, 1844.

Personally appeared Joseph Smith before me, Willard Richards, recorder of the City of Nauvoo; and after being duly sworn deposeth and saith that while at Hamilton's tavern at Carthage, in the county aforesaid, on or about the 27th day of May, 1844, whither deponent had gone to transact business in the Circuit Court of the county aforesaid, Charles A. Foster took deponent into a private room, and told deponent there was a conspiracy against the life of deponent, and that deponent had not better go out of doors. If he did, his blood would be shed. Foster said he was deponent's friend, and did not want to see bloodshed.

JOSEPH SMITH.

[Seal] Sworn and subscribed this 21st day of June, 1844, before me,

WILLARD RICHARDS,
Recorder of the City of Nauvoo.

I instructed my clerks, Willard Richards, William Clayton, Thomas Bullock and John McEwan, to prepare all necessary papers and affidavits ready to be sent to the Governor tomorrow morning.

Joseph Jackson made the two following affidavits:

Affidavit: Joseph Jackson—Francis M. Higbee's Threat to Kill the Prophet.

STATE OF ILLINOIS, } ss
CITY OF NAUVOO. }

On the 21st day of June, 1844, came before me, W. W. Phelps, clerk of the Mayor's Court, Joseph Jackson; and after being duly sworn, deposeth and saith that on Tuesday, the 11th instant, he was in Nauvoo, when Francis M. Higbee, while speaking of the destruction of the printing press, said he was very sorry, for the proprietors had set up that press for the destruction of the city, and that he meant to kill Joseph Smith and Hyrum Smith; and he saith no further.

JOSEPH JACKSON.

Subscribed and sworn to before me, this 21st day of June, 1844.

WILLIAM W. PHELPS, Clerk M. C.

Affidavit: Joseph Jackson—Reporting Mob at Pilot Grove.

STATE OF ILLINOIS, } ss
CITY OF NAUVOO. }

On the 21st day of June, 1844, came before me, W. W. Phelps, clerk of the Mayor's Court for said city, Joseph Jackson; and after being duly sworn, deposeth and saith, that on the 19th day of June instant, at his residence near Pilot Grove, in the afternoon, about twenty-four persons fired about twenty-six guns at him, and that the balls whistled close by his head. Thus this mob, of which John McKay was one, fired about one hundred guns, but not all at your affiant; and that this mob was very noisy, cursing and swearing that they would kill every damned Mormon; and he says no further.

JOSEPH JACKSON.

Subscribed and sworn to before me, this 21st day of June, 1844.

WILLIAM W. PHELPS, Clerk M. C.

At 7 p. m. James Emmett went by order of the Sergeant of the Guard at the Stone House to the Major-General and reported the crew of the *Maid of Iowa* for firing five guns contrary to orders, which were, that any firing of guns was an alarm.

After the news had reached the city of the Governor's

arrival at Carthage, an express was sent to Keokuk to stop an express which I had sent to the Governor at Springfield before I had learned of his arrival at Carthage.

An officer of the United States army, having arrested a deserter, came to Nauvoo, and stayed at my house all night.

Col. Brewer and lady arrived at the Mansion about 9 p. m. Also James W. Woods, Esq., my attorney from Burlington.

At 10 p. m., Private ——— Minor gave information that as he was passing, an hour since, about two miles out of the city to his home, he was fired upon by some unknown person. General Stephen Markham ordered out a detachment to proceed to the designated place, scour that part of the country, and see that all was right.

[*Saturday, June 22.—*]

Letter: Joseph Smith to Governor Ford—Inviting the Governor to Come to Nauvoo and Investigate Conditions.

NAUVOO, Saturday Morning, June 22, 1844.

To His Excellency Thomas Ford, Governor:

DEAR SIR.—I this morning forward you the remainder of the affidavits which are ready to present to you, by the hands of a gentleman who is fully competent to give you information on the whole subject which has been the cause of the origin of our present difficulties. I would respectfully recommend the bearer, Col. Woodworth, as one of my aides, and a man whose testimony can be relied upon.

I presume you are already convinced that it would be altogether unsafe for me or any of the City Council to come to Carthage on account of the vast excitement which has been got up by false report and libelous publications. Nothing could afford me a greater pleasure than a privilege of investigating the whole subject before your Excellency in person; for I have ever held myself in readiness to comply with your orders and answer for my proceedings before any legal tribunal in the state.

I would hereby respectfully pray your Excellency to come to Nauvoo, if congenial with your feelings, and give us a privilege of laying the whole matter before you in its true colors, and where abundance of testimony can be forthcoming, to prove every point by disinterested persons—men of character and of worth and notoriety, strangers—who were here all the time. But I am satisfied your Excellency does not wish men to expose the lives of the citizens of this place by requiring them to put themselves into the power of an infuriated, blood-thirsty mob, a part of whom have already several times fired upon our people without the least shadow of cause or provocation.

I am informed this morning that some gentleman has made affidavit that he had a private conversation with me, in which I stated that I had secret correspondence with you, &c. If any person has been wicked enough to do this, he is a perjured villain; for in the first place, I do not suffer myself to hold private conversation with any stranger; and, in the second place, I have never even intimated anything of the kind as having secret correspondence with your Excellency.

Our troubles are invariably brought upon us by falsehoods and misrepresentations by designing men. We have ever held ourselves amenable to the law; and, for myself, sir, I am ever ready to conform to and support the laws and Constitution, even at the expense of my life. I have never in the least offered any resistence to law or lawful process, which is a well-known fact to the general public; all of which circumstances make us the more anxious to have you come to Nauvoo and investigate the whole matter.

Now, sir, is it not an easy matter to distinguish between those who have pledged themselves to exterminate innocent men, women and children, and those who have only stood in their own defense, and in defense of their innocent families, and that, too, in accordance with the Constitution and laws of the country, as required by the oaths, and as good and law-abiding citizens?

In regard to the destruction of the press, the truth only needs to be presented before your Excellency to satisfy you of the justice of the proceedings. The press was established by a set of men who had already set themselves at defiance of the law and authorities of the city, and had threatened the lives of some of its principal officers, and who also made it no private matter that the press was established for the express purpose of destroying the city, as will be shown by the affidavit of Joseph Jackson, and as they stated to me in their threats.

Mr. Babbitt informs me that reports are in circulation that we have taken property which belongs to the Messrs. Law and others. There has been no property meddled with, to my knowledge, belonging to any person, except property we have purchased of the rightful owners.

Mr. Law turned over some property to a Mr. Hicks, to pay a debt. This I purchased of Mr. Hicks, and I am responsible to him for the amount. We have been especially careful to preserve the property of those who are exciting the public against us, inasmuch as we know that every means would be used which could be invented to raise excitement; and we have appointed the police to watch this property and see that no harm was done to it by any person, as they had tried to fire their own building and were detected in the act. The fire was extinguished by the policemen, and no property damaged.

There have been no prisoners taken in this city, neither any person held as hostage, only some who are residents of this place, who had broken the laws. No stranger has been interfered with or detained in the city under any circumstances.

In haste, I have the honor to remain, dear sir, your most obedient servant,

JOSEPH SMITH.
Lieut.-Gen. N. L.

This letter was accompanied by other affidavits, and was sent by Lucien Woodworth, who was delegated to go in place of Dr. Richards. He started at noon in company with Squire Woods of Burlington.

CHAPTER XXVII.

PREPARATIONS TO DEFEND NAUVOO—MOB MOVEMENTS ON CARTHAGE ROAD—GOVERNOR FORD'S REVIEW OF HANCOCK COUNTY DIFFICULTIES—JOSEPH SMITH'S ACCOUNT OF THE SAME DIFFICULTIES, DEFENSE OF HIS OWN AND ASSOCIATES' COURSE.

Saturday, June 22 [*continued*].—Legion met as usual; and after receiving instructions, were dismissed until 6 p. m., when they met again.

Orders for Nauvoo's Entrenchment.

At 7 p. m. I instructed General Dunham to cause the regiment of the 2nd cohort to turn out tomorrow, and work by turns three or four hours each, with entrenching tools, and to take the best measures in case of attack. I also gave orders that a standard be prepared for the nations.

Almon W. Babbitt arrived from Carthage this morning, having come at the request of the Governor, who thought it not wisdom to have Richards and Phelps and others of the City Council go to Carthage.

Edward Robinson made the following affidavit:

Affidavit: Edward Robinson—Threats Against Nauvoo.

STATE OF ILLINOIS, }
CITY OF NAUVOO, } SS

On the 22nd day or June, 1844, came before me, W. W. Phelps, clerk of the Mayor's Court, in said city, Dr. Edward Robinson, who, after being duly sworn, deposeth and saith that while at Carthage, on the 18th and 19th instant, I heard several persons who had assembled together for warlike purposes, (having their arms and one cannon with them) say that they were gathering together for the purpose of destroying the property of General Joseph Smith, or, as they said, "Joe Smith," and his followers, and the City Council, with the exception of one; and finally said they would destroy the town and exterminate the Latter-day Saints.

EDWARD ROBINSON.

Subscribed and sworn to before me this 22nd day of June, 1844.

WILLIAM W. PHELPS, Clerk M. C.

James Olive made the following affidavit:

Affidavit: James Olive—Mob Movements on the Carthage Road.

STATE OF ILLINOIS, }
HANCOCK COUNTY. } ss

CITY OF NAUVOO, June 22nd, 1844.

Personally appeared before me, Aaron Johnson, a justice of the peace in and for said county, James Olive; who being first duly sworn, deposeth and saith that on Friday afternoon, the 21st instant, about 3 o'clock, he was at his own house, about two miles from Appanoose. In a southeasterly direction, he saw a four-horse wagon with some men before it, all traveling towards Appanoose. They went about a quarter of a mile beyond my house; there met a two horse wagon and a company of men, about fifteen in number. Both parties then took the road towards the Big Mound. A part of the men were mounted and a part were on foot. The mounted men were forward; and after passing my house, they wheeled and rode back to the footmen who were some little distance behind, and said to them, "There are some fellows on the Mound; you had better hurry on, and we will take those fellows and carry them to Carthage." They used profane language. I watched them until they got near the Mound, and saw the guard on the Mound turn and run towards Nauvoo. After that the company went on to the Mound, and halted near the spot where the guard had run from.

On the same evening, about sundown, there was a man by the name of Milton Hamilton came into my house and told me to arm and equip myself according to the law and stand in readiness; that the Governor had demanded Joseph Smith according to law, and that he would not come it (meaning that Joseph Smith would not surrender); that the General had issued orders for the militia to be in readiness to take said Smith. I asked him what general, and he observed that he believed it was Col. Williams. I asked him if it was done by orders of the Governor, and he said that was the understanding. He told me he acted under the orders of Captain McAuley; and further saith not.

JAMES OLIVE.

[Seal] Subscribed and sworn to this 22nd day of June, 1844, before me,

AARON JOHNSON, J. P.

Phebe Levett states that she saw Finch, Rollison, Foster, and Squire McAuley in the company who fired on the guard on the La Harpe road.

George G. Johnstone made the following affidavit:

Affidavit: George G. Johnstone—Militia Under Governor to Move on Nauvoo.

STATE OF ILLINOIS,
COUNTY OF HANCOCK. } ss

CITY OF NAUVOO, June 22nd, 1844.

Personally appeared before me, Aaron Johnson, a justice of the peace in and for the county of Hancock, George G. Johnstone, living on Spring Creek in McDonough county; who, being first duly sworn, deposeth and saith that yesterday, Napoleon Hardin came to your deponent and said that the Governor had sent orders for the militia to be called out for today at 4 o'clock p. m., and to start on the 22nd to Carthage, there to wait until all were ready from the different counties in the state, and then they should march out to the prairie. They should stop on the prairie and send a flag of truce to Nauvoo, and demand the body of General Joseph Smith. If the people of Nauvoo refused to give him up, then they should exterminate the whole of them.

GEORGE G. JOHNSTONE.

[Seal] Subscribed and sworn to this 22nd day of June, 1844, before me,

AARON JOHNSON, J. P.

Gideon Gibbs made the following affidavit:

Affidavit: Gideon Gibbs—Mob on La Harpe Road.

STATE OF ILLINOIS,
CITY OF NAUVOO. } ss

On the 22nd day of June, 1844, came before me, William W. Phelps, clerk of the Mayor's Court for said city, Gideon Gibbs, and after being duly sworn deposeth and saith that on the afternoon of the 21st instant, about a half-mile southeast of the Big Mound on the La Harpe road, a party of about eight or ten men, in a warlike attitude, in company with two teams, passed your said affiant, and one of them said he fired at two men near the Big Mound. Thought he killed them both; and your deponent saith no further.

GIDEON GIBBS.

Subscribed and sworn to before me, this 22nd day of June, 1844.

WILLIAM W. PHELPS, Clerk M. C.

Luman H. Calkins made the following affidavit:

Affidavit: Luman H. Calkins—Nauvoo Conspiracy Against the Prophet's Life.

STATE OF ILLINOIS, } ss
CITY OF NAUVOO, }

June 22nd, 1844.

Personally appeared before me, George W. Harris, an alderman acting in and for the city of Nauvoo, Luman H. Calkins; and being first duly sworn, deposeth and saith that about seven weeks ago I came on the steamboat *Ohio* from St. Louis to Nauvoo, when William Nesbit, who was on board, entered into conversation with your deponent.

I asked him if he knew anything about the conspiracy in Nauvoo to kill Joseph and Hyrum, and all that believed on them. He said he did. It was intended that they should be killed between then and the 1st of July.

I asked him who was at the head of the conspiracy. He replied he was sworn not to tell who the head one was. I asked him if there were any in Nauvoo concerned. He replied there was, and named the two Laws, two Fosters, two Higbees, Charles Ivins, and several others. I asked if it was to be made a public thing. He replied the first blow was to be struck in Nauvoo by those who were opposed to Joseph. I asked how many they could rely on in Nauvoo. He said they could rely on five hundred, if they could only get arms for them.

He said as soon as the first blow was struck in Nauvoo, there were about seven thousand men ready in Missouri to join them to exterminate all who believed on Joseph Smith. He also told me that the *Die Vernon*, when she came on her pleasure-trip to Nauvoo, that there were none but spies, and who came on purpose to see the places in order to know how to strike when the time comes to strike; and he also said "the Reformers" had got spies continually passing Nauvoo in order to spy out all that took place; that there was not a thing took place in Nauvoo but what was made known to them in St. Louis as soon as a steamboat landed.

I told him I should think he would be afraid to stop here. He said he should stay in Nauvoo and carry on his butchering as usual, as if there was nothing taking place; that he had as good a gun as any man ever put to his face, and that the first shot he should fire would be to kill Joseph and Hyrum. Said I, "The people will surely kill you then." He replied he would rush through a thousand people to wash his hands in Joseph's blood, and especially in Hyrum's, if he was to be immediately cut into a thousand pieces. He said he should be willing to die as soon as he had killed them.

About five weeks since I had another conversation with William Nesbit, when he confirmed the whole of the foregoing conversation; and he also said he had made arrangements with Mr. Bostwick of St. Louis to send him a brace of the best pistols, for the purpose of being ready when he wanted them. He also said that he would kill Hyrum any time he could get an opportunity without being detected. I then asked him if Hyrum could be put in his way so that no man would mistrust him, would you kill him? He said, "By God, I would." I asked if he would not be afraid to kill him in cold blood. He replied, "No, I would not; I would do it in a moment if I could get an opportunity."

The day following I left for Galena, and returned on Tuesday, the 18th instant, and on the 19th I saw William Nesbit in the ranks, and I cautioned Richard Brazier to keep an eye on Nesbit, for he had sworn to wash his hands in Joseph's and Hyrum's blood.

LUMAN H. CALKINS.

Subscribed and sworn to this 22nd day of June, 1844, before me,

GEORGE W. HARRIS,
Alderman of the City of Nauvoo.

At 12, noon, orders were sent to the different guards and pickets to let persons pass and repass without hailing until further orders.

I issued the following:

GENERAL ORDERS.

MAYOR'S OFFICE AND HEADQUARTERS, OF THE NAUVOO LEGION,
NAUVOO, June 22nd, 1844.

To Col. Jonathan Dunham, Acting Major-General Nauvoo Legion:

SIR.—You will proceed without delay, with the assistance of the Nauvoo Legion, to prepare the background [Eastern part] of said city for defense against an invasion by mobs, cause the Legion to be furnished with tents, and make your encampment in the vicinity of your labor.

JOSEPH SMITH,
Mayor of the City of Nauvoo, and Lieut.-Gen. Nauvoo Legion.

To COL. JONATHAN DUNHAM, Major-General in command Nauvoo Legion.

At 6 p. m. I prophesied that in the sickly seasons sickness would enter into the houses of the mob and vex them until they would fain repent in dust and ashes. They will be smitten with the scab, &c.

A Prophecy.

At 7 p. m. I received the following:

A Petition to Hear the Prophet Speak.

We, the undersigned citizens of Hancock county, respectfully request General Joseph Smith to preach on tomorrow, and that we have liberty of seats near enough to the stand to hear, inasmuch as we have an opportunity to hear him but seldom, and some of us have not heard him at all.

Yours respectfully,

JAMES HAMILTON AND CO., Capt. at the Liberty Branch.

NATHANIEL CASE, Capt. 7th Co., 4th Reg., 2nd Cohort, N. L. from La Harpe.

URIAH H. YAGER AND CO., Captain at the Branch of Macedonia, 2nd Cohort.

HIRAM CLARK 1st Lieut. at the Midland Branch Company.

Z. D. WILSON'S COMPANY.

ALNA L. TIPPETT'S COMPANY.

S. HANCOCK, Major of the First Battalion of the 3rd Regiment.

WARREN SNOW, Captain and Co., 4th Reg. 2nd Cohort of N. Legion.

At 10 p. m. I received the following letter by the hands of Captain Yates, who accompanied Elder John Taylor and Dr. John M. Bernhisel on their return from Carthage:

Letter: Governor Ford to Mayor and Council of the City of Nauvoo:

HEADQUARTERS CARTHAGE, June 22nd, 1844.

To the Mayor and Council of the City of Nauvoo:

GENTLEMEN.—After examining carefully all the allegations on the part of the citizens of the country in Hancock county, and the defensive matters submitted to me by the committee of your citizens concerning the existing disturbances, I find that there appears to be but little contradiction as to important facts, so that it may be safely assumed that the immediate cause of the existing excitement is the destruction of the press and *Nauvoo Expositor*, and the subsequent refusal of the individuals accused to be accountable therefor according to the general laws of this state, and the insisting on your parts to be accountable only before your own municipal court, and according to the ordinances of your city.

Many other facts have been asserted on both sides as tending to increase the excitement; but as they mostly relate merely to private persons, and committed by individuals, and tend simply to show the present state of affairs, I will not further notice them in this communication.

The material facts to be noticed are that a newspaper called the *Nauvoo Expositor* was established in Nauvoo; that this newspaper was deemed offensive to the people of that city; that the Common Council, without notice or process to the owners, entered into a trial and heard statements not under oath, and evidence which was under oath, in relation to the character, conduct and designs of the owners and editors of the press; that, upon hearing such statements and evidence, the Common Council passed an ordinance or resolution declaring said press and paper to be a public nuisance, and ordered the same to be abated as such; that a writ was issued by the Mayor to the Marshal of the city for that purpose; that a military order was issued at the same time by the Mayor, who is also Lieutenant-General of the Nauvoo Legion, to the Major-General in command of that Legion, for a force sufficient to ensure the execution of the writ aforesaid.

It appears also the press was destroyed in obedience to the foregoing ordinance and writ, according to a return on the same by the Marshal in the following words: "The within press and type is destroyed and pied according to order on this 10th day of June, 1844, at about six o'clock p. m.—J. P. GREENE, C. M."

It appears also that the owners of the press obtained from a justice of the peace at Carthage a warrant against the authors of this destruction for a riot; that the constable charged with the execution of this process, arrested some of the persons accused, who immediately obtained writs of *habeas corpus* from the Municipal Court of your city, by virtue of which they were tried in Nauvoo and discharged from arrest, and that they have ever since refused to be arrested or to submit to a trial at any other place or before any other court, except in the city and before the Municipal Court aforesaid.

It has also been reported to me that martial law has been declared in Nauvoo; that persons and property have been and are now forcibly imprisoned and detained there, and that the Legion has been ordered under arms to resist any attempt to arrest the persons accused. I have not particularly inquired into the truth of these latter reports; for although they may become matters of great importance in the sequel, they are not necessary to be ascertained and acted upon at present.

I now express to you my opinion that your conduct in the destruction of the press was a very gross outrage upon the laws and the liberties of the people. It may have been full of libels, but this did not authorize you to destroy it.

There are many newspapers in this state which have been wrongfully abusing me for more than a year, and yet such is my regard for the liberty of the press and the rights of a free people in a republican government that I would shed the last drop of my blood to protect those presses from any illegal violence. You have violated the Constitution in at least four particulars. You have violated that part of it which declares that the printing presses shall be free,being responsible for the abuse thereof, and that the truth may be given in evidence.

This article of the Constitution contemplates that the proprietors of a libelous press may be sued for private damages, or may be indicted criminally, and that upon trial they should have the right to give the truth in evidence. In this case the proprietors had no notice of the proceeding.

The Constitution also provides that the people shall be protected against unreasonable searches and seizures of their property and "That no man shall be deprived of life, liberty or property, except by the judgment of his peers (which means a jury trial) and the law of the land," which means due process of law and notice to the accused.

You have also violated the Constitution and your own charter in this: Your Council, which has no judicial powers, and can only pass ordinances of a general nature,have undertaken to pass judgment as a court and convict without a jury a press of being libelous and a nuisance to the city.

The Council at most could only define a nuisance by general ordinance, and leave it to the courts to determine whether individuals or particulars accused came within such definition.

The Constitution abhors and will not tolerate the union of legislative and judicial power in the same body of magistracy, because, as in this case, they will first make a tyrannical law, and then execute it in a tyrannical manner.

You have also assumed to yourselves more power than you are entitled to in relation to writs of *habeas* under your charter. I know that you have been told by lawyers, for the purpose of gaining your favor that you have this power to any extent. In this they have deceived you for their own base purposes. Your charter supposes that you may pass ordinances, a breach of which will result in the imprisonment of the offender.

For the purpose of insuring more speedy relief to such persons, authority was given to the Municipal Court to issue writs of *habeas corpus* in all cases arising under the ordinances of the city.

It was never supposed by the Legislature, nor can the language of your charter be tortured to mean that a jurisdiction was intended to be conferred which would apply to all cases of imprisonment under the general laws of the state or of the United States, as well as the city ordinances.

It has also been reserved to you to make the discovery that a newspaper charged to be scurrilous and libellous may be legally abated or removed as a nuisance. In no other state, county, city, town or territory in the United States has ever such a thing been thought of before. Such an act at this day would not be tolerated even in England. Just such another act in 1830 hurled the king of France from his throne, and caused the imprisonment of four of his principal ministers for life. No civilized country can tolerate such conduct, much less can it be tolerated in this free country of the United States.

The result of my deliberations on this subject is, that I will have to require you and all persons in Nauvoo accused or sued to submit in all cases implicitly to the process of the court, and to interpose no obstacles to an arrest, either by writ of *habeas corpus* or otherwise; and that all of the people of the city of Nauvoo shall make and continue the most complete submission to the laws of the state, and the process of the courts and justices of the peace.

In the particular case now under consideration, I require any and all of you who are or shall be accused to submit yourselves to be arrested by the same constable, by virtue of the same warrant and be tried before the same magistrate whose authority has heretofore been resisted. Nothing short of this can vindicate the dignity of violated law and allay the just excitement of the people.

I am anxious to preserve the peace. A small indiscretion may bring on a war. The whole country is now up in arms, and a vast number of people are ready to take the matter into their own hands. Such a state of things might force me to call out the militia to prevent a civil war. And such is the excitement of the country that I fear the militia, when assembled, would be beyond legal control.

You are wrong in the first instance, and I can call out no portion of the militia for your defense until you submit to the law. You have made it necessary that a *posse* should be assembled to execute legal process; and that *posse*, as fast as it assembles is in danger of being imbued with the mobocratic spirit. If you, by refusing to submit, shall make it necessary to call out the militia, I have great fears that your city will be destroyed, and your people many of them exterminated.

You know the excitement of the public mind. Do not tempt it too far. A very little matter may do a very great injury; and if you are disposed to continue the causes of excitement and render a force necessary to coerce submission, I would say that your city was built, as it were, upon a keg of powder which a very little spark may explode.

It is my intention to do all I can to preserve the peace, and even, if obliged, to call the militia to prosecute the war so as not to involve the innocent and comprehend all in the same punishment. But excitement is a mattter which grows very fast upon men when assembled. The affair, I much fear, may assume a revolutionary character, and the men may disregard the authority of their officers.

I tell you plainly that if no such submission is made as I have indicated, I will be obliged to call out the militia; and if a few thousand will not be sufficient, many thousands will be.

I sincerely hope that your people may do nothing which will make such a proceeding necessary. I hope also that they will be well-disposed to co-operate with me in allaying the excitement of the public mind. Immediately discharge such persons as you have under martial law. Let them go without molestation. Abstain from all injury to private property. Let people go where they please without swearing them first to take no part against you. All such proceedings tend only to inflame the public mind, and raise up ten men disposed to fight you for every one thus foolishly disabled.

Your committee assures me that you are sincerely desirous of preserving the peace; and if so, I hope you will co-operate with me in everything necessary to allay the excitement in the minds of the people.

The following-named persons are reported to me as being detained against their will by martial law: John A. Hicks, H. O. Norton, A. J. Higbee, John Eagle, P. J. Rolf, Peter Lemon, and T. J. Rolf. It will tend greatly to allay excitement if they shall be immediately discharged and suffered to go without molestation.

It is also reported here, and generally believed, (but whether true or not I have not yet learned) that there are many foraging parties abroad from Nauvoo committing depredations upon the cattle and property in the vicinity These acts, if correctly reported, must absolutely cease immediately, if you expect any person here to have the power to preserve the peace.

In case the persons accused should make no resistance to arrest, it will be against orders to be accompanied by others. If it should become necessary to have witnesses on the trials, I will see that such persons shall be duly summoned, *and I will also guarantee the safety of all such persons as may thus be brought to this place from Nauvoo either for trial or as witnesses for the accused.*

If the individuals accused cannot be found when required by the constable it will be considered by me as an equivalent to a refusal to be arrested, and the militia will be ordered accordingly.

I am, gentlemen, with great respect, your obedient servant,

THOMAS FORD,
Governor and Commander-in-Chief.

To which I wrote the following answer:

Letter: Joseph Smith to Governor Ford—Defending the action of the City Council in the "Expositor" Affair.

NAUVOO, June 22nd, 1844, 12 o'clock p. m.

To His Excellency, Thomas Ford:

SIR.—Yours of this date is received by Messrs. Taylor and Bernhisel. A part of the same delegation, Mr. Woodworth, who was detained yesterday, started for Carthage at 12 noon, this date, who, we perceive, had not arrived at your last date. Some documents conveyed by him would tend to counteract some of the views expressed in your Excellency's communication, and we feel confident, if all the facts could be before your Excellency, you would have come to different conclusions.

Our "insisting to be accountable only before our own Municipal Court," is totally incorrect. We plead a *habeas corpus* as a last resort to save us from being thrown into the power of the mobocrats, who were then threatening us with death, and it was with great reluctance we went before the Municipal Court, on account of the prejudice which might arise in the minds of the unbiased; and we did not petition for a *habeas corpus* until we had told the constable that on our lives we dare not go to Carthage for trial, and plead with him to go before any county magistrate he pleased in our vicinity, (which occurrence is common in legal proceedings) and not a member of our society, so that our lives might be saved from the threats thus already issued against us.

The press was declared a nuisance under the authority of the charter as written in 7th section of Addenda, the same as in the Springfield charter, so that if the act declaring the press a nuisance was unconstitutional, we cannot see how it is that the charter itself is not unconstitutional: and if we have erred in judgment, it is an official act, and belongs to the Supreme Court to correct it, and assess damages *versus* the city to restore property abated as a nuisance. If we have erred in this thing, we have done it in good company, for Blackstone on "Wrongs," asserts the doctrine that scurrilous prints may be abated as nuisances.

As to martial law, we truly say that we were obliged to call out the forces to protect our lives; and the Constitution guarantees to every man that privilege; and our measures were active and efficient, as the necessity of the case required; but the city is and has been continually under the special direction of the marshal all the time. No person, to our knowledge, has been arrested only for violation of the peace, and those some of our own citizens, all of whom we believe are now discharged. And if any property has been taken for public benefit without a compensation, or against the will of the owner, it has been done without our knowledge or consent, and when shown shall be corrected, if the people will permit us to resume our usual labors.

If we "have committed a gross outrage upon the laws and liberties of the people," as your Excellency represents, we are ready to correct that outrage when the testimony is forthcoming. All men are bound to act in their sphere on their own judgment, and it would be quite impossible for us to know what your Excellency's judgment would have been in the case referred to; consequently acted on our own and according to our best judgment, after having taken able counsel in the case. If we have erred, we again say we will make all right if we can have the privilege.

"The Constitution also provides that the people shall be protected against all unreasonable search and seizure." True. The doctrine we believe most fully, and have acted upon it; but we do not believe it unreasonable to search so far as it is necessary to protect life and property from destruction.

We do not believe in the "union of legislative and judicial power," and we have not so understood the action of the case in question.

Whatever power we have exercised in the *habeas corpus* has been done in accordance with the letter of the charter and Constitution as we confidently understood them, and that, too, with the ablest counsel; but if it be so that we have erred in this thing, let the Supreme Court correct the evil. We have never gone contrary to constitutional law, so far as we have been able to learn it. If lawyers have belied their profession to abuse us, the evil be on their heads.

You have intimated that no press has been abated as a nuisance in the United States. We refer your Excellency to Humphrey *versus* Press in Ohio, who abated the press by his own arm for libel, and the courts decided on prosecution no cause of action. And we do know that it is common for police in Boston, New York, &c., to destroy scurrilous prints: and we think the loss of character by libel and the loss of life by mobocratic prints to be a greater loss than a little property, all of which, life alone excepted, we have sustained, brought upon us by the most unprincipled outlaws, gamblers, counterfeiters, and such characters as have been standing by me, and probably are now standing around your Excellency—namely, those men who have brought these evils upon us.

We have no knowledge of men's being sworn to pass our city. And upon receipt of your last message the Legion was disbanded and the city left to your Excellency's disposal.

How it could be possible for us now to be tried constitutionally by the same magistrate who first issued the writ at Carthage we cannot see, for the Constitution expressly says no man shall twice be put in jeopardy of life and limb for the same offense; and all you refer to, have been, since the issuance of the *habeas corpus*, complied with for the same offense, and trial before Daniel H. Wells, justice of the peace for Hancock county, and, after a full investigation, were discharged. But, notwithstanding this, we would not hesitate to stand another trial according to your Excellency's wish, were it not that we are confident our lives would be in danger. We dare not come. Writs, we are assured, are issued against us in various parts of the country. For what? To drag us from place to place, from court to court, across the creeks and prairies, till some bloodthirsty villain could find his opportunity to shoot us. We dare not come, though your Excellency promises protection. Yet, at the same time, you have expressed fears that you could not control the mob, in which case we are left to the mercy of the merciless. Sir, we dare not come, for our lives would be in danger, and we are guilty of no crime.

You say, "It will be against orders to be accompanied by others, if we come to trial." This we have been obliged to act upon in Missouri; and when our witnesses were sent for by the court, (as your honor promises to do) they were thrust into prison, and we left without witnesses. Sir, you must not blame us, for "a burnt child dreads the fire." And although your Excellency might be well-disposed in the matter, the appearance of the mob forbids our coming. We dare not do it.

We have been advised by legal and high-minded gentlemen from abroad, who came on the boat this evening to lay our grievances before the Federal Government, as the appearance of things is not only treasonable against us, but against the state on the part of Missouri, unless the same has been requested of Governor Ford by the Federal Government. And we suppose your Excellency is well aware by this time that the mass-meetings of the county declared utter extermination of the Mormons, and that the Legion was not called out until complaints were made to the Mayor, and the citizens were afraid of their lives, and losing their confidence in the authorities of the city, and that nothing on the part of the city authorities had been wanting, legally and judiciously, to allay excitement and restore peace. We shall leave the city forthwith to lay the facts before the General Government, and, as before stated, the city is left open and unprotected; and by everything that is sacred, we implore your Excellency to cause our helpless women and children to be protected from mob violence, and let not the blood of innocence cry to heaven against you. We again say, if anything wrong has been done on our part, and we know of nothing, we will make all things right if the Government will give us the opportunity. Disperse the mob, and secure to us our constitutional privileges, that our lives may not be endangered when on trial.

I remain most respectfully, your Excellency's humble servant,

JOSEPH SMITH,
Mayor, and Lieut.-Gen. N. L.

CHAPTER XXVIII.

GOVERNOR FORD'S WRONG VIEWPOINT—ELDER TAYLOR'S ACCOUNT OF THE INTERVIEW WITH THE GOVERNOR AT CARTHAGE—CLOSE OF THE PROPHET'S JOURNAL NARRATIVE OF HIS LIFE.

Gov. Ford's Biased Judgment.

[S*aturday*, *June 22nd*, *1844*, *continued*].—It appears that the Governor, on arriving at Carthage, ordered the entire mob into service, adopted the lies and misrepresentations circulated against us by our enemies as truth, turned Supreme Court, and decided on the legality of our municipal ordinances and proceedings, which is the business of the judiciary alone. He charges us in his letter, based upon most cursed falsehoods, with violations of law and order, which have never been thought of by us. He treated our delegates very rudely. My communications that were read to him were read in the presence of a large number of our worst enemies, who interrupted the reader at almost every line with, "That's a damned lie!" and "That's a G— d——d lie!" He never accorded to them the privilege of saying one word to him only in the midst of such interruptions as, "You lie like hell!" from a crowd of persons present. These facts show conclusively that he is under the influence of the mob spirit, and is designedly intending to place us in the hands of murderous assassins, and is conniving at our destruction, or else that he is so ignorant and stupid that he does not understand the corrupt and diabolical spirits that are around him.

Elder John Taylor gave the following account of his interview with the Governor:

Elder John Taylor's Account of Interview With Governor Ford at Carthage.

After waiting the Governor's pleasure for some time, we had an audience—but such an audience! He was surrounded by some of the vilest and most unprincipled men in creation. Some of them had an appearance of respectability, but many of them lacked even that. Wilson, and, I believe, William Law were there, Foster, Frank and Chauncey Higbee, Mr. Marr, a lawyer from Nauvoo, a mobocratic merchant from Warsaw, Joseph H. Jackson, a number of his associates, and the Governor's secretary—in all fifteen or twenty persons, most of whom were recreant to virtue, honor, integrity and everything that is considered honorable among men. I can well remember the feelings of disgust that I had in seeing the Governor surrounded by such an infamous group, and on being introduced to men of so questionable a character; and had I been on private business, I should have turned to depart, and told the Governor that if he thought proper to associate with such questionable characters, I should beg leave to be excused; but coming, as we did, on public business, we could not of course consult our private feelings.

We then stated to the Governor that, in accordance with his request, General Joseph Smith had, in response to his call, sent us to him as a committee of conference; that we were acquainted with most of the circumstances that had transpired in and about Nauvoo lately, and were prepared to give him the information; that, moreover, we had in our possession testimony and affidavits confirmatory of what we should say, which had been forwarded to him by General Joseph Smith; that communications had been forwarded to his Excellency by Messrs. Hunter, James and others, some of which had not reached their destination, but of which we had duplicates with us. We then in brief related an outline of the difficulties, and the course we had pursued from the commencement of the troubles up to the present, and, handing him the documents, respectfully submitted the whole. During our conversation and explanations with the Governor, we were frequently rudely and impudently contradicted by the fellows he had around him, and of whom he seemed to take no notice.

He opened and read a number of the documents himself, and as he proceeded he was frequently interrupted by, "That's a lie!" "That's a G— d——d lie!" "That's an infernal falsehood!" "That's a blasted lie!" &c.

These men evidently winced on an exposure of their acts, and thus vulgarly, impudently and falsely repudiated them. One of their number, Mr. Marr, addressed himself several times to me while in conversation with the Governor. I did not notice him until after a frequent repetition of his insolence, when I informed him that my business at that time was with Governor Ford, whereupon I continued my conversation with his Excellency.

During the conversation the Governor expressed a desire that Joseph Smith and all parties concerned in passing or executing the city law in relation to the press had better come to Carthage; that however repugnant it might be to our feelings, he thought it would have a tendency to allay public excitement and prove to the people what we professed—that we wished to be governed by law.

We represented to him the course we had taken in relation to this matter, our willingness to go before another magistrate other than the Muncipal Court, the illegal refusal by the constable, of our request, our dismissal by the Municipal Court, a legally constituted tribunal, our subsequent trial before Esq. Wells at the instance of Judge Thomas (the circuit judge), and our dismissal by him; that we had fulfilled the law in every particular; that it was our enemies who were breaking the law, and, having murderous designs, were only making use of this as a pretext to get us into their power.

The Governor stated that the people viewed it differently, and that, notwithstanding our opinions, he would recommend that the people should be satisfied.

We then remarked to him that, should Joseph Smith comply with his request, it would be extremely unsafe, in the present excited state of the country, to come without an armed force; that we had a sufficiency of men, and were competent to defend ourselves, but that there might be danger of collision should our forces and those of our enemies be brought in such close proximity.

He strenuously advised us not to bring any arms, and pledged his faith as Governor, and the faith of the state, that we should be protected, and that he would guarantee our perfect safety.

At the termination of our interview, and previous to our withdrawal, after a long conversation and the perusal of the documents which we had brought, the Governor informed us that he would prepare a written communication for General Joseph Smith, which he desired us to wait for. We were kept waiting for this instrument some five or six hours.

About five o'clock in the afternoon we took our departure with not the most pleasant feelings. The associations of the Governor, the spirit that he manifested to compromise with these scoundrels, the length of time that he had kept us waiting, and his general deportment, together with the infernal spirit that we saw exhibited by those whom he admitted to his counsels, made the prospect anything but promising.

I had a consultation for a little while with my brother Hyrum, Dr. Richards, John Taylor and John M. Bernhisel, and determined to go to Washington and lay the matter before President Tyler.*

About 7 p. m. I requested Reynolds Cahoon and Alpheus Cutler to stand guard at the Mansion, and not to admit any stranger inside the house.

At sundown I asked O. P. Rockwell if he would go with me a short journey, and he replied he would.

[Abraham C. Hodge says that soon after dusk, Joseph called Hyrum, Willard Richards, John Taylor, William W. Phelps, A. C. Hodge, John L. Butler, Alpheus Cutler, William Marks and some others, into his upper room and said, "Brethren, here is a letter from the Governor which I wish to have read. After it was read through Joseph remarked, "There is no mercy—no mercy here." Hyrum said, "No; just as sure as we fall into their hands we are dead men." Joseph replied, "Yes; what shall we do, Brother Hyrum?" He replied, "I don't know." All at once Joseph's countenance brightened up and he said, "The way is open. It is clear to my mind what to do. All they want is Hyrum and myself; then tell everybody to go about their business, and not to collect in groups, but to scatter about. There is no doubt they will come here and search for us. Let them search; they will not harm you in person or property, and not even a hair of your head. We will cross the river tonight, and

* "At this juncture the council was interrupted by the withdrawal of President Smith to give an interview to two gentlemen—one of whom was a son of John C. Calhoun—who had arrived at the Mansion and were anxious to meet with the Prophet" (Life of John Taylor, page 125). Elder Taylor withdrew at a late hour from the council because of great weariness. "Shortly after he [Elder Taylor] retired, however, the Prophet returned, and the informal council meeting was resumed. The project of laying the case before President Tyler was abandoned. Joseph had received an inspiration to go west and all would be well" (Ibid).

go away to the West.'' He made a move to go out of the house to cross the river. When out of doors he told Butler and Hodge to take the *Maid of Iowa*, (in charge of Repsher) get it to the upper landing, and put his and Hyrum's families and effects upon her; then go down the Mississippi and up the Ohio river to Portsmouth, where they should hear from them. He then took Hodge by the hand and said, "Now, Brother Hodge, let what will come, don't deny the faith, and all will be well.'']

*I told Stephen Markham that if I and Hyrum were ever taken again we should be massacred, or I was not a prophet of God. I want Hyrum to live to avenge my blood, but he is determined not to leave me.**

* Here the direct narrative of the Prophet ends; what happened in the next few days of his life occurred under such circumstances as not to permit of his dictating an account of it to his secretary or clerks, as was his custom.

Concerning the statement in the text about the Prophet's desire to have Hyrum live, and the purpose of it, Mr. Edward Tullidge, in his *Life of Joseph the Prophet*, gives a different version of it. He states it: "*I want Hyrum to live to lead the Church, but he is determined not to leave me*'' (Tullidge, p. 491). On what authority Mr. Tullidge makes the change is not known; but there is evidence in addition to his statement that the Prophet did desire Hyrum Smith to succeed him in the presidency of the Church, and even "ordained'' him to take that place. At the October conference following the martyrdom of the two brothers, President Brigham Young said: "*Did Joseph ordain any man to take his place? He did. Who was it? It was Hyrum. But Hyrum fell a martyr before Joseph did*'' (*Times and Seasons* Vol. V, page 683.

CHAPTER XXIX.

THE PROPHET STARTS FOR THE ROCKY MOUNTAINS—THE COUNSEL OF FALSE BRETHREN—THE RETURN TO NAUVOO —THE SURRENDER AND ARRIVAL AT CARTHAGE.

An account of the arrest, imprisonment and martyrdom of President Joseph Smith and Patriarch Hyrum Smith in Carthage jail, Hancock county, Illinois, as collected from the journal kept at the time by Willard Richards and the statements published by John Taylor, Messrs. Reid and Woods and John S. Fullmer, and the writings and statements of Dan Jones, Cyrus H. Wheelock, Stephen Markham and many other persons, who were personally acquainted with the transactions.—By the Historian.†*

Saturday, June 22, 1844.—About 9 p. m. Hyrum came out of the Mansion and gave his hand to Reynolds Cahoon, at the same time saying, "A company of men are seeking to kill my brother Joseph, and the Lord has warned him to flee to the Rocky Mountains to save his life. Good-by, Brother Cahoon, we shall see you again." In a few minutes afterwards Joseph came from his family. His tears were flowing fast. He held a handkerchief to his face, and followed after Brother Hyrum without uttering a word.

The Warning to Flee to the Rocky Mountains.

Between 9 and 10 p. m. Joseph, Hyrum and Willard, while waiting on the banks of the river for the skiff, sent

* This is the title of the first *Compilation of Data* as it appears in the *Millennial Star*, Vol. XXIV, p. 332. A *Second Compilation* was made by the Church Historian, extending from the 22nd of June to the 8th of August, 1844, at which time the Twelve were accepted for the time as the Presiding Council of the Church; and the claims of Sidney Rigdon rejected.

† George A. Smith was the Historian from 1854 to 1875. Consequently this pilation was made under his supervision.

for William W. Phelps, and instructed him to take their families to Cincinnati by the second steamboat, arriving at Nauvoo; and when he arrived there to commence petitioning the President of the United States and Congress for redress of grievances, and see if they would grant the Church liberty and equal rights. Joseph then said: "Go to our wives, and tell them what we have concluded to do, and learn their feelings on the subject; and tell Emma you will be ready to start by the second steamboat, and she has sufficient money wherewith to pay the expenses. If you ascertain by tomorrow morning that there is anything wrong, come over the river to Montrose, to the house of Captain John Killien, and there you will learn where we are."

About midnight, Joseph, Hyrum and Dr. Richards called for Orrin P. Rockwell at his lodgings, and all went up the river bank until they found Aaron Johnson's boat, which they got into, and started about 2 a. m to cross the Mississippi river. Orrin P. Rockwell rowed the skiff, which was very leaky, so that it kept Joseph, Hyrum and the doctor busy baling out the water with their boots and shoes to prevent it from sinking.

Preparations for the Western Journey.

Sunday, *23*.—At daybreak arrived on the Iowa side of the river. Sent Orrin P. Rockwell back to Nauvoo with instructions to return the next night with horses for Joseph and Hyrum, pass them over the river in the night secretly, and be ready to start for the Great Basin in the Rocky Mountains.

Joseph, Hyrum and Dr. Richards walked up to Captain John Killien's house, where they arrived at sunrise; but he not being at home, they went from thence to Brother William Jordan's. About 9 a. m. Dr. Bernhisel came over the river to visit Joseph; also Reynolds Cahoon, who made some explanations respecting Governor Ford's letter.

Early in the morning a *posse* arrived in Nauvoo to

arrest Joseph, but as they did not find him, they started back to Carthage immediately, leaving one man of the name of Yates behind them, who said to one of the brethren that Governor Ford designed that if Joseph and Hyrum were not given up, he would send his troops and guard the city until they were found, if it took three years to do it.

Arrival of the Constable's *Posse.*

At 1 p. m. Emma sent over Orrin P. Rockwell, requesting him to entreat of Joseph to come back. Reynolds Cahoon accompanied him with a letter which Emma had written to the same effect, and she insisted that Cahoon should persuade Joseph to come back and give himself up. When they went over they found Joseph, Hyrum and Willard in a room by themselves, having flour and other provisions on the floor ready for packing.

Emma's Message to the Prophet.

Reynolds Cahoon informed Joseph what the troops intended to do, and urged upon him to give himself up, inasmuch as the Governor had pledged his faith and the faith of the state to protect him while he underwent a legal and fair trial. Reynolds Cahoon, Lorenzo D. Wasson and Hiram Kimball accused Joseph of cowardice for wishing to leave the people, adding that their property would be destroyed, and they left without house or home. Like the fable, when the wolves came the shepherd ran from the flock, and left the sheep to be devoured. To which Joseph replied, "If my life is of no value to my friends it is of none to myself."

Joseph said to Rockwell, "What shall I do?" Rockwell replied, "You are the oldest and ought to know best; and as you make your bed, I will lie with you." Joseph then turned to Hyrum, who was talking with Cahoon, and said, "Brother Hyrum, you are the oldest, what shall we do?" Hyrum said, "Let us go back and give ourselves up, and see the thing out." After studying a few moments, Joseph said, "If

Consultation with Rockwell.

you go back I will go with you, but we shall be butchered." Hyrum said, "No, no; let us go back and put our trust in God, and we shall not be harmed. The Lord is in it. If we live or have to die, we will be reconciled to our fate."

After a short pause, Joseph told Cahoon to request Captain Daniel C. Davis to have his boat ready at half-past five to cross them over the river.

Joseph and Hyrum then wrote the following letter:

Letter: Joseph and Hyrum Smith to Governor Ford—Consenting to go to Carthage.

BANK OF THE RIVER MISSISSIPPI,
Sunday, June 23rd, 1844, 2 p. m.

His Excellency Governor Ford:

SIR.—I wrote you a long communication at 12 last night, expressive of my views of your Excellency's communication of yesterday. I thought your letter rather severe, but one of my friends has just come to me with an explanation from the captain of your *posse* which softened the subject matter of your communication, and gives us greater assurance of protection, and that your Excellency has succeeded in bringing in subjection the spirits which surround your Excellency to some extent. And I declare again the only objection I ever had or ever made on trial by my country at any time, was what I have made in my last letter—on account of assassins, and the reason I have to fear deathly consequences from their hands.

But from the explanation, I now offer to come to you at Carthage on the morrow, as early as shall be convenient for your *posse* to escort us into headquarters, provided we can have a fair trial, not be abused nor have my witnesses abused, and have all things done in due form of law, without partiality, and you may depend on my honor without the show of a great armed force to produce excitement in the minds of the timid.

We will meet your *posse*, if this letter is satisfactory, (if not, inform me) at or near the Mound, at or about two o'clock tomorrow afternoon. which will be as soon as we can get our witnesses and prepare for trial. We shall expect to take our witnesses with us, and not have to wait a subpœna or part at least, so as not to detain the proceedings, although we may want time for counsel.

We remain most respectfully, your Excellency's humble servants,

JOSEPH SMITH.
HYRUM SMITH.

Also wrote to Horace T. Hugins, Esquire:

Letter: Joseph Smith to H. T. Hugins—Engaging Counsel.

NAUVOO, Sunday, June 23, 1844.

H. T. Hugins, Esq:

SIR.—I have agreed to meet Governor Ford at Carthage tomorrow to attend an examination before Justice Morrison, and request your attendance professionally with the best attorney you can bring.

I meet the Governor's *posse* on the Mound at 10 a. m.; in Carthage at 12 noon. Do not fail me, and oblige,

Yours respectfully,
JOSEPH SMITH.
per W. RICHARDS, Clerk.

P. S.—Dr. J. R. Wakefield I wish as witness, &c.

And also to Dr. J. Wakefield as follows:

Letter: Joseph Smith to J. R. Wakefield Soliciting Latter's Attendance as Witness.

NAUVOO, June 23, 1844.

Dr. J R. Wakefield:

SIR.—I would respectfully solicit your attendance at court in Carthage tomorrow at 12 noon, as witness in case "State of Illinois on complaint of Francis M. Higbee, *versus* Joseph Smith and others." Dear sir, do not fail me, and oblige your old friend,

JOSEPH SMITH,
per WILLARD RICHARDS, Clerk.

P. S.—Esq. Hugins and co-partner are expected. We meet the Governor's *posse* on the Mound at 10 a. m.: at Carthage at 12 noon. Bearer will give particulars.

The Prophet Returns to Nauvoo.

About 4 p. m. Joseph, Hyrum, the Doctor and others started back. While walking towards the river, Joseph fell behind with Orrin P. Rockwell. The others shouted to come on. Joseph replied, "It is of no use to hurry, for we are going back to be slaughtered," and continually expressed himself that he would like to get the people once more together, and talk to them tonight. Rockwell said if that was his wish he would get the people together, and he could talk to them by starlight.

It was the strong persuasions of Reynolds Cahoon, Lorenzo D. Wasson and Hiram Kimball, who were carrying out Emma's instructions, that induced Joseph and Hyrum to start back to Nauvoo. They re-crossed the river at half-past five. When they arrived at the Mansion in Nauvoo, Joseph's family surrounded him, and he tarried there all night, giving up the idea of preaching to the Saints by starlight.

He sent the letter of this date to Governor Ford by Col. Theodore Turley and Elder Jedediah M. Grant, who carried it to Carthage, where they arrived about 9 p.m. They gave the letter to Governor Ford, who first agreed to send a *posse* to escort General Smith in safety to Carthage. Immediately afterwards Mr. Skinner came in and made a very bitter speech to the Governor, in which Wilson Law and Joseph H. Jackson joined, telling him naught but lies, which caused Elder Grant to ask if messengers to him were to be insulted in that manner. The Governor treated them coldly, and rescinded his previous promise, and refused to send or allow an escort to go with Joseph, as he said it was an honor not given to any other citizen. He would not allow the messengers to stay in Carthage through the night, but ordered them to start at 10 o'clock, and return to Nauvoo with orders for General Smith to be in Carthage at 10 o'clock tomorrow morning without an escort; and he threatened that if General Smith did not give himself up at that time, that Nauvoo would be destroyed and all the men, women and children that were in it. Messrs. Grant and Turley immediately started; but on account of their horses being wearied, they did not arrive in Nauvoo until about four a. m. of the 24th, when they went to General Smith to report to him the state of excitement in Carthage. He would not hear one word of the warning, as he was determined to go to Carthage and give himself up to the Governor.

Vacillation of Governor Ford.

At night Joseph conversed with Captain Anderson, who reported that the mob at Warsaw had stopped his boat, and threatened to fire into her with his cannon. He gave the following certificate:

Certificate: Captain Anderson—on Retention of People in Nauvoo.

NAUVOO, June 23rd, 1844.

This is to certify that on Tuesday morning last, I stated to General Joseph Smith that the number of passengers leaving that day might produce the effect on the public mind that they were afraid of being attacked, and prove injurious; and I further observed, in order to preserve peace and good order, that it would be better to use his endeavors to retain those in the city until the excitement should abate.

GEORGE C. ANDERSON,
Captain steamer *Osprey*.

Joseph received the following letter:

Letter: Ed. Johnston to Joseph Smith—About Counsel.

Sunday Evening, June 23rd, 1844.

General Joseph Smith:

SIR.—I have this moment received your favor of this day per the hands of Mr. Adams. I regret to say, in reply, that I am now awaiting every moment a boat for St. Louis, whither my business requires me to go, and which, of course will deter me from acceding to your request. I have introduced Mr. Adams to a friend who is entirely competent to do full justice to your cause.

In great haste, yours respectfully,

ED. JOHNSTON.

PORT MADISON, IOWA.

Preparations are making for an early start tomorrow morning for Carthage. Joseph gave directions to gather some horses for the purpose of carrying him and his friends to Carthage tomorrow.

Preparations for Going to Carthage.

Although the Governor has threatened to send his troops into the city, none have appeared as yet.

Monday, 24.—Francis M. Higbee having sworn out a writ before Thomas Morrison, a justice of the peace at

Carthage on the 11th instant, against Joseph Smith, Hyrum Smith, Samuel Bennet, John Taylor, William W. Phelps, John P. Greene, Stephen C. Perry, Dimick B. Huntington, Jonathan Dunham, Stephen Markham, William W. Edwards, Jonathan Holmes, Jesse P. Harmon, John Lytle, Joseph W. Coolidge, David Harvey Redfield, Orrin P. Rockwell and Levi Richards for riot, in destroying the *Nauvoo Expositor* press, the property of William and Wilson Law and others, on the 10th instant, and Governor Ford having sent word by the *posse* that those eighteen persons should be protected by the militia of the state, they, upon the assurance of that pledge at half-past six a. m. started for Carthage, Willard Richards, Dan Jones, Henry G. Sherwood, Alfred Randall, James Davis, Cyrus H. Wheelock, A. C. Hodge and several other brethren, together with James W. Woods as counsel, accompanying them.

Defendants in the *Expositor* Case.

When they arrived at the top of the hill, Joseph sent Rockwell with a horse for Dr. Southwick, a Southern gentleman who had been staying some days at the Mansion, and who wished General Joseph Smith to buy considerable property in Texas; but Ed. Bonny took possession of the horse, so that Dr. Southwick could not then go.

Incidents *en route* for Carthage.

Joseph paused when they got to the Temple, and looked with admiration first on that, and then on the city, and remarked, "This is the loveliest place and the best people under the heavens; little do they know the trials that await them." As he passed out of the city, he called on Daniel H. Wells, Esq., who was unwell, and on parting he said, "Squire Wells, I wish you to cherish my memory, and not think me the worst man in the world either."

At ten minutes to 10 a. m. they arrived at Albert G. Fellows' farm, four miles west of Carthage, where they met Captain Dunn with a company of about sixty mounted militia, on seeing which Joseph said, "Do not be alarmed, brethren, for they

Meeting with Captain Dunn.

cannot do more to you than the enemies of truth did to the ancient Saints—they can only kill the body." The company made a halt, when Joseph, Hyrum and several others went into Fellows' house with Captain Dunn, who presented an order from Governor Ford for all the state arms in possession of the Nauvoo Legion, which Joseph immediately countersigned.

A Pathetic Prophecy.

Henry G. Sherwood went up to Joseph and said, "Brother Joseph, shall I return to Nauvoo and regulate about getting the arms and get the receipts for them?" Joseph inquired if he was under arrest, or expected to be arrested. Sherwood answered "No," when Joseph directed him to return ahead of the company, gather the arms and do as well as he could in all things. Joseph then said to the company who were with him, "*I am going like a lamb to the slaughter, but I am calm as a summer's morning. I have a conscience void of offense toward God and toward all men. If they take my life I shall die an innocent man, and my blood shall cry from the ground for vengeance, and it shall be said of me 'He was murdered in cold blood!'*" He then said to Father Sherwood, "Go, and God bless you." Sherwood then rode as swiftly as he could to Nauvoo.

Esquire Woods left the company there, and continued his journey to Carthage.

This order for the delivery of the state arms was evidently designed to drive the citizens of Nauvoo to desperation, so that in the heat of their indignation they might commit some overt act which the Governor could construe into treason, and thus have a shadow of excuse for his mob militia to destroy the Mormons.

Dunn's Request that the Prophet Return to Nauvoo:

Captain Dunn requested the company to return to Nauvoo to assist in collecting the arms, and pledged his word as a military man, that Joseph and his friends should be protected even if it were at the expense of his own life, and his men responded to the pledge by three cheers. Captain Dunn, no doubt feared that the order of the Governor would excite the inhabitants of Nauvoo beyond endurance, and therefore chose to depend on the well-known integrity of General Smith than to risk the chances of exciting the feelings of a much-abused people. At the same time Joseph sent a messenger to the Governor with the following letter:

Letter: Joseph Smith to Governor Ford—Explaining his Return to Nauvoo.

FOUR MILES WEST OF CARTHAGE MOUND,
HANCOCK COUNTY, ILLINOIS,
Monday, 10 o'clock.

His Excellency Governor Ford:

DEAR SIR.—On my way to Carthage to answer your request this morning, I here met Captain Dunn, who has here made known to me your orders to surrender the state arms in possession of the Nauvoo Legion, which command I shall comply with; and that the same may be done properly and without trouble to the state, I shall return with Captain Dunn to Nauvoo, see that the arms are put into his possession, and shall then return to headquarters in his company, when I shall most cheerfully submit to any requisition of the Governor of our state.

With all due respect to your Excellency, I remain your obedient servant.

JOSEPH SMITH.

He also issued the following order:

Order: Joseph Smith to General Dunham—Complying with Governor Ford's Demand for State Arms.

HEADQUARTERS NAUVOO LEGION,
Prairie Four Miles West of Carthage,
June 24th, 1844, 10 o'clock and 10 minutes.

To Major-General Jonathan Dunham and all commissioned and non-commissioned officers and privates of the Nauvoo Legion:

You are hereby ordered to comply strictly with the within order of the Commander-in-Chief, Governor Ford.

JOSEPH SMITH.
Lieut.-Gen. Nauvoo Legion.

And requested that the state arms should be taken to the Masonic Hall without delay.

Messenger Sent to Carthage.

Hyrum then said to Abram C. Hodge, "You go on into Carthage and see what is going on, and hear what is said on this matter."

Joseph and his company then returned with Captain Dunn, and arrived in Nauvoo at half-past two p. m.

When Hodge arrived at Carthage, he met with Rev. Mr. Dodge, who had some time previously been very kindly treated by Hyrum. He warned Hodge that as sure as Joseph and Hyrum came to Carthage, they would be killed. Hodge also saw Hamilton, the innkeeper, who, pointing to the Carthage Greys, said, "Hodge, there are the boys that will settle you Mormons." Hodge replied, "We can take as many men as there are there out of the Nauvoo Legion, and they would not be missed."

Surrender of State Arms.

When the fact of the order for the state arms was known in Nauvoo, many of the brethren looked upon it as another preparation for a Missouri massacre; nevertheless, as Joseph requested that it should be complied with, they very unwillingly gave up the arms.

About 6 p. m., when all the states' arms were collected, and the company were ready to start, Captain Dunn and Quartermaster-General Buckmaster made a short speech, expressing their gratitude at the peaceable conduct of the citizens of Nauvoo, and that while they thus conducted themselves they would protect them.

It appears that Governor Ford feared that the Nauvoo Legion, although disbanded, might avenge any outrage that might hereafter be committed on the persons of their leaders, and so thought he had better disarm them as he had previously disbanded them; yet the mob was suffered to retain their portion of the state's arms, even when within a half-day's march of Nauvoo, and they in a threatening and hostile attitude, while the Nauvoo Legion had not evinced the least disposition whatever, except to defend their city in case it should be attacked; and they had not set a foot outside the limits of the corporation.

Joseph rode down home twice to bid his family farewell. He appeared solemn and thoughtful, and expressed himself to several individuals that he expected to be murdered. There appeared no alternative but that he must either give himself up, or the inhabitants of the city would be massacred by a lawless mob under sanction of the Governor.

The Prophet's Farewell to his Family.

The company (about fifteen) then started again for Carthage, and when opposite to the Masonic Hall, Joseph said, "Boys, if I don't come back, take care of yourselves; I am going like a lamb to the slaughter." When they passed his farm he took a good look at it, and after they had passed it, he turned round several times to look again, at which some of the company made remarks, when Joseph said: "If some of you had got such a farm and knew you would not see it any more, you would want to take a good look at it for the last time." When they got to the edge of the woods near Nauvoo, they met A. C. Hodge returning from Carthage. He reported to Hyrum what he had heard in Carthage, told him what his feelings were and said, "Brother Hyrum, you are now clear, and if it was my duty to counsel you, I would say, do not go another foot, for they say they will kill you, if you go to Carthage," but as other persons gathered around, nothing further was said. About this time Joseph received the following letter:

Looking Back-Sadness.

Letter: Messrs. Reid and Woods to Joseph Smith—Documents for Defense.

CARTHAGE, 5 o'clock p. m.

General Joseph Smith:

DEAR SIR.—In accordance with previous arrangements with Elder Adams, I am here at your service; and it will be necessary for us to have, on the examination here before the justice, a certified copy of the city ordinance for the destruction of the *Expositor* press, or a copy which has been published by authority. We also wish the original order issued by you to the marshal for the destruction of said press, and such witnesses as may be necessary to show by whom the press was destroyed, and that the act was not done in a riotous or tumultuous manner.

Yours respectfully,

H. T. REID.

DEAR SIR.—I concur fully as to the above, and will add, from an interview with Governor Ford, you can, with the utmost safety, rely on his protection, and that you will have as impartial an investigation as could be expected from those opposed to you. The excitement is much allayed, and your opponents (those who wish to make capital out of you) do not want you to come to Carthage. Mr. Johnson has gone east, and that will account for Mr. Reed being here.

Respectfully, your obedient servant,

JAMES W. WOOD.

CARTHAGE, 24th June, 1844.

The Prophet's Arrival at Carthage.

The company arrived at Fellows' house, four miles west of Carthage, about 9 p. m., where they stopped about half an hour, and partook of such refreshments as they had brought with them. Captain Dunn and his company of mounted militia, returning with the state arms from Nauvoo, joined them here, and escorted them into Carthage, where they arrived at five minutes before 12 at night, and went to Hamilton's tavern. While passing the public square many of the troops, especially the Carthage Greys, made use of the following expressions, which were re-echoed in the ears of the Governor and hundreds of others, "Where is the damned prophet?" "Stand away, you McDonough boys, and let us shoot the damned Mormons." "G—d—— you, old Joe, we've got you now." "Clear the way and let us have a view of Joe Smith, the prophet of God. He has seen the last of Nauvoo. We'll use him up now, and kill all the damned Mormons." The rear platoon of the Carthage Greys repeatedly threw their guns over their heads in a curve, so that the bayonets struck the ground with the breech of their guns upward, when they would run back and pick them up, at the same time whooping, yelling, hooting and cursing like a pack of savages.

The Governor Pacifies the Mob.

On hearing the above expressions, the Governor put his head out of the window and very fawningly said, "I know your great anxiety to see Mr. Smith, which is natural enough, but it is quite too late tonight for you to have the opportunity; but I assure you, gentlemen, you shall have that privilege tomorrow morning, as I will cause him to pass before the troops upon the square, and I now wish you, with this assurance, quietly and peaceably to return to your quarters." When this declaration was made, there was a faint "Hurrah for Tom Ford," and they instantly obeyed his wish.

The Apostates at Carthage.

There was a company of apostates also quartered at Hamilton's hotel—namely William and Wilson Law, the Higbees and Fosters, Augustine Spencer, Henry O. Norton, John A. Hicks, (formerly president of the Elder's quorum) and others. Hicks stated to C. H. Wheelock that it was determined to shed the blood of Joseph Smith by not only himself, but by the Laws, Higbees, Fosters, Joseph H. Jackson, and many others, whether he was cleared by the law or not. Jackson talked freely and unreservedly on that subject, as though he were discoursing upon the most common occurrence of his life. Said he, you will find me a true prophet in this respect. Wheelock told Ford what Hicks had said, but he treated it with perfect indifference, and suffered Hicks and his associates to run at liberty and mature their murderous plans.

A writ was also issued by Robert F. Smith against Joseph W. Coolidge on complaint of Chauncey L. Higbee, charging him with the illegal detention of Charles A. Foster.

CHAPTER XXX.

ARREST OF JOSEPH AND HYRUM SMITH ON A CHARGE OF TREASON—FALSE IMPRISONMENT—ELDER TAYLOR'S PROTEST—FALSE IMPRISONMENT.

Tuesday, June 25, 1844.—This morning the prisoners voluntarily surrendered themselves to the constable, Mr. Bettisworth, who held the writ against them. The Governor was at headquarters in person, and had pledged his own faith and the faith of the state of Illinois, that the Smiths and other persons should be protected from personal violence, and should have a fair and impartial trial, if they would surrender themselves to be dealt with according to law. During the Governor's stay in Carthage, he repeatedly expressed to the legal counselors of the Smiths his determination to protect the prisoners, and to see that they should have a fair and impartial examination.

The Governor's Pledge of Protection.

At 8 a. m. President Smith had an interview with William G. Flood of Quincy, U. S. Receiver of Public Moneys. While in conversation with him, Constable David Bettisworth arrested Joseph for treason against the state of Illinois, with the following writ, which had been granted on the oath of Augustine Spencer:

The Arrest for Treason.

Writ of Arrest on the Charge of Treason—Joseph Smith.

STATE OF ILLINOIS, }
CITY OF NAUVOO. } SS

The people of the State of Illinois, to all sheriffs, coroners and constables of said state greeting:

Whereas complaint has been made before me, one of the justices of the peace in and for said county aforefaid, upon the oath of Augustine Spencer, that Joseph Smith, late of the county aforesaid, did, on or about the nineteenth day of June. A. D. 1844, at the county and state aforesaid, commit the crime of treason against the government and people of the State of Illinois aforesaid.

These are therefore to command you to take the said Joseph Smith if he be found in your county, or if he shall have fled, that you pursue after the said Smith into another county within this state, and take and safely keep the said Joseph Smith, so that you have his body forthwith before me to answer the said complaint,and be further dealt with according to law.

[Seal] Given under my hand and seal this 24th day of June, A. D. 1844.

R. F. SMITH, J. P.

Hyrum Smith was also arrested at the same time for treason on the same writ, granted on the affidavit of Henry O. Norton:

Writ of Arrest for Treason—Hyrum Smith.

STATE OF ILLINOIS,
HANCOCK COUNTY. } ss

The people of the State of Illinois, to all sheriffs, coroners and constables, greeting:

Whereas complaint has been made before me, one of the justices of the peace, in and for the county of Hancock, upon the oath of one Henry O. Norton, that one Hyrum Smith, late of the county of Hancock and state of Illinois, did, on the 19th day of June, 1844, commit the crime of treason against the government and people of the state of Illinois aforesaid.

These are therefore to command you to take the body of the said Hyrum Smith, if he be found in your county, or if he shall have fled that you pursue after the said Hyrum Smith into any county within this state, and take and safely keep the said Hyrum Smith, so that you have his body forthwith before me, to answer unto the said complaint, and be further dealt with according to law.

[Seal] Given under my hand and seal, this 24th day of June, 1844.

R. F. SMITH, J. P.

8:30 a. m.—Governor Ford called all the troops and ordered them to form a hollow square on the public ground near the Court House; and when formed, he mounted an old table, and addressed them in a most inflammatory manner, exciting the feelings of indignation against Generals Joseph and Hyrum Smith which were already burning in their breasts, occasioned by the falsehoods and misrepresentations that were in circulation, giving his assent and sanction to the rumors that had gathered them together, and stating that although they were dangerous men in the community, and guilty of all that they might have alleged against them, still they were in the hands of the law, which must have its course. He continued speaking twenty or thirty minutes.

Governor Ford's Speech to the Troops.

9:15 a. m.—The Governor came in and invited Joseph to walk with him through the troops. Joseph solicited a few moments' private conversation with him, which the Governor refused. While refusing, the Governor looked down at his shoes, as though he was ashamed. They then walked through the crowd with Brigadier-General Miner R. Deming and Dr. Richards, to General Deming's quarters. The people appeared quiet until a company of Carthage Greys flocked around the doors of General Deming in an uproarious manner, of which notice was sent to the Governor. In the meantime the Governor had ordered the McDonough troops to be drawn up in line for Joseph and Hyrum to pass in front of them, they having requested that they might have a clear view of the Generals Smith. Joseph had a conversation with the Governor for about ten minutes, when he again pledged the faith of the state that he and his friends should be protected from violence.

The Prophet's Request for an Interview with Gov. Ford.

Robinson, the postmaster, said, on report of martial law being proclaimed in Nauvoo, he had stopped the mail and notified the Postmaster-General of the state of things in Hancock county.

From the General's quarters Joseph and Hyrum went in front of the lines, in a hollow square of a company of

Carthage Greys. At seven minutes before ten they arrived in front of the lines, and passed before the whole, Joseph being on the right of General Deming, and Hyrum on his left, Elders Richards, Taylor and Phelps following. Joseph and Hyrum were introduced by the Governor about twenty times along the line, as General Joseph Smith and General Hyrum Smith, the Governor walking in front on the left. The Carthage Greys refused to receive them by that introduction, and some of the officers threw up their hats drew their swords and said they would introduce themselves to the damned Mormons in a different style. The Governor mildly entreated them not to act so rudely, but their excitement increased. The Governor, however, succeeded in pacifying them by making a speech, and promising them that they should have "full satisfaction." General Smith and party returned to their lodgings at five minutes past ten.

The Prophet Presented to the Troops.

10:30.—News reached Joseph at the hotel that the Carthage Greys had revolted, and were put under guard by General Deming. Joseph told all his friends to stay in the two rooms occupied by them in the hotel.

Revolt of the Carthage Greys.

10:50.—Quietness was apparently restored among the Carthage Greys.

11:15.—News arrived that the Warsaw troops were near Carthage, and had come of their own accord.

Mr. Prentice, U. S. Marshal for Illinois, called to see Joseph.

12 minutes before 1.—Intelligence was given to Joseph that the Laws, Higbees, Fosters and others, were going to Nauvoo to plunder. The Governor called at the door with some gentlemen, when Joseph informed him of what he had heard, and requested him to send a guard to protect the city of Nauvoo.

Threats of Apostates to Plunder Nauvoo.

Willard Richards wrote a letter to his wife.

1:30 p. m.—After dinner, Mark Aldrich of Warsaw called to see Joseph.

2:30.—The Governor communicated that he had ordered Captain Singleton with a company of men from McDonough county, to march to Nauvoo to co-operate with the police in keeping the peace; and he would call out the Legion, if necessary.

Joseph wrote to Emma as follows:

Letter: The Prophet to Emma Smith—Governor Ford Going to Nauvoo.

CARTHAGE, June 25th, 1844.
2:30 o'clock p. m.

DEAR EMMA.—I have had an interivew with Governor Ford, and he treats us honorably. Myself and Hyrum have been again arrested for treason because we called out the Nauvoo Legion; but when the truth comes out we have nothing to fear. We all feel calm and composed.

This morning Governor Ford introduced myself and Hyrum to the militia in a very appropriate manner, as General Joseph Smith and General Hyrum Smith. There was a little mutiny among the Carthage Greys, but I think the Governor has and will succeed in enforcing the laws. I do hope the people of Nauvoo will continue pacific and prayerful.

Governor Ford has just concluded to send some of his militia to Nauvoo to protect the citizens, and I wish that they may be kindly treated. They will co-operate with the police to keep the peace. The Governor's orders will be read in the hearing of the police and officers of the Legion, as I suppose.

3 o'clock.—The Governor has just agreed to march his army to Nauvoo, and I shall come along with him. The prisoners, all that can, will be admitted to bail. I am as ever,

JOSEPH SMITH.

EMMA SMITH.

The Prophet's Warning to Rockwell.

Joseph also sent a message to Orrin P. Rockwell not to come to Carthage, but to stay in Nauvoo, and not to suffer himself to be delivered into the hands of his enemies, or to be taken a prisoner by any one.

It was reported by Israel Barlow that he had heard resolutions of the Warsaw troops read, to the effect that they would return to Warsaw at 3 p. m., then go to Golden's Point on Thursday, and thence to Nauvoo.

Several of the officers of the troops in Carthage, and other gentlemen, curious to see the Prophet, visited Joseph in his room. General Smith asked them if there was anything in his appearance that indicated he was the desperate character his enemies represented him to be; and he asked them to give him their honest opinion on the subject. The reply was, "No, sir, your appearance would indicate the very contrary, General Smith; but we cannot see what is in your heart, neither can we tell what are your intentions." To which Joseph replied, "Very true, gentlemen, you cannot see what is in my heart, and you are therefore unable to judge me or my intentions; but I can see what is in your hearts, and will tell you what I see. I can see that you thirst for blood, and nothing but my blood will satisfy you. It is not for crime of any description that I and my brethren are thus continually persecuted and harassed by our enemies, but there are other motives, and some of them I have expressed, so far as relates to myself; and inasmuch as you and the people thirst for blood, I prophesy, in the name of the Lord, that you shall witness scenes of blood and sorrow to your entire satisfaction. Your souls shall be perfectly satiated with blood, and many of you who are now present shall have an opportunity to face the cannon's mouth from sources you think not of; and those people that desire this great evil upon me and my brethren, shall be filled with regret and sorrow because of the scenes of desolation and distress that await them. They shall seek for peace, and shall not be able to find it. Gentlemen, you will find what I have told you to be true."

The Prophet's Interview with Militia Officers.

12 minutes to 4.—Report came to Joseph that William and Wilson Law, Robert D. Foster, Chauncey L. Higbee and Francis M. Higbee had said *that there was nothing against these men; the law could not reach them but powder and ball would*, and they should not go out of Carthage alive.

Law Cannot Reach Them —Powder and Ball Must.

Arraigned on the *Expositor* Affair.

Joseph, Hyrum and thirteen others, were taken before Robert F. Smith, a justice of the peace residing in Carthage (he being also captain of the Carthage Greys) on the charge of riot destroying the printing press of the *Nauvoo Expositor*.

It is worthy of notice here, that when the defendants went before Esquire Wells, the prosecution objected, and insisted that they should be taken before the justice who issued the writ—viz., Thomas Morrison, and that Governor Ford had also stated in his letter to General Joseph Smith that he must go before the justice in Carthage who issued the writ. But when the prosecution had the defendants in their own power in Carthage, they could then ride over their own objections by taking them before another justice, who was known to be a greater enemy to the defendants than Justice Morrison, and moreover, before one who was not only a justice of the peace, but also the military commander of a company of Carthage Greys, who had already been arrested for mutiny.

Chauncey L. Higbee, one of the prosecutors, moved an adjournment.

H. T. Reid and James W. Woods on behalf of the defendants, objected to an adjournment, and said that the court was not authorized to take recognizance without their acknowledging their guilt, or having witnesses to prove it, and we admit the press was destroyed by order of the Mayor, it having been condemned by the City Council as a nuisance.

They read law to show that justices could not recognize without admission of guilt, and offered to give bail.

Mr. Reid stated that the law quoted by the prosecution belonged to civil, not criminal cases.

The prosecution insisted to have a commission of the crime acknowledged.

After a good deal of resistance on the part of the prosecution, court asked if the parties admitted that there was

Prophet *et al.* Bound over to Circuit Court.

sufficient cause to bind over, and the counsel for the defense admitted there was, and offered to enter into cognizance in the common form, in order to prevent, if possible, any increase of excitement.

5 p. m.—Court acknowledged the admission and ordered recognizances, whereupon Joseph Smith, Hyrum Smith, John Taylor, William W. Phelps, John P. Greene, Stephen C. Perry, Dimick B. Huntington, Jonathan Dunham, Stephen Markham, Jonathan H. Holmes, Jesse P. Harmon, John Lytle, Joseph W. Coolidge, David Harvey Redfield, and Levi Richards gave bonds, with John S. Fullmer, Edward Hunter, Dan Jones, John Benbow, and other unexceptionable sureties, in the sum of $500 for each of the defendants, total $7,500, for their appearance at the next term of the Circuit Court for Hancock county.

The Sureties for the Prophet.

It was evident that the magistrate intended to overreach the wealth of the defendants and their friends, so as to imprison them for want of bail; but it happened that there was strength to cover the demand, for some of the brethren went security to the full extent of their property; and Justice Smith adjourned his court over, and left the court house without calling on Joseph and Hyrum to answer to the charge of treason, or even intimating to those prisoners, or their counsel that they were expected to enter into an examination that night.

Captain Smith, the only magistrate who could grant subpoenas for witnesses, disappeared until a late hour, as if purposely to prevent the appearing of the defendant's witnesses, and in keeping with the conviction expressed by Joseph's enemies the previous day, that the law cannot touch them, but that powder and ball will.

About 6:30 p. m.—Dan Jones heard Wilson Law, whilst endeavoring to get another warrant against Joseph Smith for treason, declare that while he (Mr. Smith) was once preaching from Daniel 2nd chapter, 44th verse, said that the kingdom referred to was already set up, and that he was the king over it. He also heard Joseph H. Jackson, and other leaders of the mob, declare that they had eighteen accusations against Joseph, and as one failed, they would try another to detain him there, and that they had had so much trouble and hazard, and worked so hard in getting him to Carthage, that they would not let him get out of it alive. Jackson pointed to his pistols and said, "The balls are in there that will decide his case." Jones immediately went up stairs to Joseph and informed him what he had heard Jackson say.

Another Warrant Sought—Daniel's Kingdom and Treason.

About 7:30 p. m.—Dr. Levi Richards and most of the brethren, after they had signed the bonds, left for Nauvoo when Joseph and Hyrum went into the Governor's room and spoke with him, as Governor Ford had promised them an interview. After a few moments' conversation, the Governor left them to order the captain of the guard to give the brethren some passes. They then went to supper.

8 p. m.—Constable Bettisworth appeared at the lodgings of Joseph and Hyrum, and insisted that they should go to jail. Joseph demanded a copy of the mittimus, which was refused. Messrs. Woods and Reid, as counsel, insisted that the prisoners were entitled to be brought before a justice of the peace for examination before they could be sent to jail. The constable, to their surprise, then exhibited the following mittimus:

Illegal Imprisonment of the Smith Brothers.

The False Mittimus.

STATE OF ILLINOIS,
HANCOCK COUNTY, } ss.

The people of the State of Illinois to the keeper of the jail of said County, Greeting:

Whereas Joseph Smith and Hyrum Smith, of the county aforesaid, have been arrested upon oath of Augustine Spencer and Henry O. Norton, for the crime of treason, and have been brought before me as a justice of the peace in and for the said county, for trial at the seat of justice thereof, which trial has been necessarily postponed by reason of the absence of the material witnesses—to wit, Francis M. Higbee and others. Therefore, I command you, in the name of the people, to receive the said Joseph Smith and Hyrum Smith into your custody in the jail of the county aforesaid, there to remain until discharged by due course of law.

[Seal] Given under my hand and seal this 25th day of June, A. D. 1844.

(Signed) R. F. SMITH J. P.

Joseph remonstrated against such bare-faced, illegal, and tyrannical proceedings, but the constable still insisted that they should go to jail. Lawyer Woods requested the officer to wait until he could see Governor Ford, and was told by Bettisworth that he could only wait five minutes.

Joseph and Hyrum again remonstrated, and the constable waited until about nine o'clock, when they heard by Mr. Wood that the Governor did not think it within the sphere of his duty to interfere, as they were in the hands of the civil law, and therefore he had not the power to stay process, or the due course of law, and that he could not interrupt a civil officer in the discharge of his duty.

Governor Ford Refuses to Interfere with Illegal Proceedings.

Governor Ford knew this [proceeding] was illegal, (for he had formerly been an associate-justice of the Supreme Court of the state) and when he was appealed to by Captain Robert F. Smith to know what he must do, as he had found his mittimus as a magistrate was illegal, and therefore that it was a false committal, Governor Ford replied, "You have the Carthage Greys at your command." *Captain Smith* therefore commanded his "Greys" to execute and carry into effect his illegal mittimus as *a magistrate*, thus practically blending the civil and military in the same person at the same time; and the prisoners were violently and illegally dragged to jail without any examination whatever, while his Excellency was in the the adjoining room from that from which they were thus taken. So much for his professions that *the law must be executed.*

Thus a justice of the peace acting as a military officer also by virtue of his commission as such, orders his command to appear under arms and to incarcerate the prisoners whom he had just before ordered to commit to jail by *mittimus without having them brought before him for examination;* and the Governor, having been himself at one time a judge upon the bench, knew and well understood the illegality of the above proceedings.

He also well knew that military power and [civil] authority had been used by one and the same person, and yet he, acting at that time as Commander-in-Chief, which gave him the supervision over all his officers, and in fact made him responsible for all their acts and movements, refused to interfere when requested by the prisoners to interpose his authority in their behalf against an illegal civil process, and also refused to countermand the illegal, oppressive and unofficer-like order of one of his captains.

Moreover, having taken the oath of office, as Governor of ths state of Illinois, he was by virtue of that oath bound to see the laws faithfully executed, and not, as in this instance, see them violated and trodden under foot, and even prompt one of his officers in his lawless course. Thus he violated his solemn pledges and oath of office.

Elder Taylor's Remonstrance with Governor Ford.

Elder John Taylor says, "As I was informed of this illegal proceeding, I went immediately to the Governor and informed him of it; whether he was apprized of it before or not, I do not know, but my opinion is that he was. I represented to him the character of the parties who had made oath, the outrageous nature of the charge, the indignity offered to men in the position which they [the prisoners] occupied, and that he knew very well that it was a vexatious prosecution, and that they were not guilty of any such thing."

The Governor replied that he was very sorry that the

thing had occurred; that he did not believe the charges, but that he thought that the best thing to be done in the premises was to let the law take its course.

"I then reminded him that we had come out there at his instance, not to satisfy the law, which we had done before, but the prejudices of the people in relation to the affair of the press; that we had given bonds, which we could not by law be required to do, to satisfy the people at his instance, and that it was asking too much to require gentlemen in their position in life to suffer the degradation of being immured in a jail at the instance of such worthless scoundrels as those who had made this affidavit.

"The Governor replied that it was an unpleasant affair, and looked hard, but that it was a matter over which he had no control, as it belonged to the judiciary; that he, as the executive could not interfere with their proceedings, and that he had no doubt but that they would be immediately dismissed.

"I told him that we had looked to him for protection from such insults, and that I thought we had a right to do so from the solemn promises he had made to me and Dr. Bernhisel in relation to our coming without a guard or arms; that we had relied upon his faith and had a right to expect him to fulfill his engagements, after we had placed ourselves implicitely under his care, and complied with all his requests, although extra-judicial.

"He replied that he would detail a guard, if we required it, and see us protected, but that he could not interfere with the judiciary.

"I expressed my dissatisfaction at the course taken, and told him that if we were to be subject to mob rule, and to be dragged contrary to law into prison, at the instance of every infernal scoundrel whose oath could be bought for a dram of whiskey, his protection availed very little, and we had miscalculated his promises.

"Seeing there was no prospect of redress from the Governor, I returned to the room and found the Constable,

Bettisworth, very urgent to hurry Brothers Joseph and Hyrum to prison, whilst the brethren were remonstrating with him.

"At the same time a great rabble was gathered in the streets and around the door, and from the rowdyism manifested, I was afraid there was a design to murder the prisoners on the way to the jail.

"Without conferring with any person, my next feeling was to procure a guard, and seeing a man habited as a soldier in the room, I went to him and said, "I am afraid there is a design against the lives of the Messrs. Smith, will you go immediately and bring your captain, and if not convenient, any other captain of a company, and I will pay you well for your trouble."

Elder Taylor Takes Independent Action.

"He said he would, and departed forthwith, and soon returned with his captain, whose name I have forgotten* and introduced him to me.

"I told him of my fears, and requested him immediately to fetch his company. He departed forthwith, and arrived at the door with them, just as the time that the constable was hurrying the brethren downstairs.

"A number of brethren went along, and one or two strangers, and all of us safely lodged in prison, remained there during the night."

As Esquire Woods went to the door he met Captain Dunn, with some twenty men, they having come to guard the prisoners in jail. Mr. Woods accompanied Governor Ford to (Captain) Justice Robert F. Smith, who gave as a cause for issuing the warrant of committal, that the prisoners were not personally safe at the hotel. Mr. Woods then requested the Governor to have a company of troops from some other county detailed to guard the jail.

Captain Dunn, with his company, escorted Joseph and

*This was Captain Dunn, of Augusta township, who had been sent to Nauvoo a few days before to collect the state arms at Nauvoo, and who afterwards escorted the Prophet and his friends into Carthage.

Hyrum Smith from their lodgings, together with Willard Richards, John Taylor, John P. Greene, Stephen Markham, Dan Jones, John S. Fullmer, Dr. Southwick, and Lorenzo D. Wasson, to the jail. Markham had a very large hickory cane, which he called "the rascal-beater." Dan Jones had a smaller walking-stick, and they walked on either side of Joseph and Hyrum, keeping off the drunken rabble, who several times broke through the ranks.

In Carthage Jail.

They were received by the jailer, Mr. George W. Stigall, and put into the criminal's cell; but he afterwards gave them the debtors' apartment, where the prisoners and their friends had amusing conversations on various interesting subjects, which engaged them till late. Prayer was offered, which made Carthage prison into the gate of heaven for a while. They laid promiscuously on the floor, where they all slept from 11:30 until 6 a. m. of the 26th.

Counselor H. T. Reid, in his published statement, writes as follows: "The recitals of the mittimus, so far as they relate to the prisoners, having been brought before the justice for trial, and it there appearing that the necessary witnesses of the prosecution were absent, are wholly untrue, unless the prisoners could have appeared before the justice, without being present in person or by counsel; nor is there any law of Illinois which permits a justice to commit persons charged with crimes to jail, without examination as to the probability of their guilt."

CHAPTER XXXI.

INTERVIEW IN CARTHAGE PRISON BETWEEN GOVERNOR FORD AND THE PROPHET—TAYLOR'S REPORT OF THE INTERVIEW—TESTIMONY TO THE EXISTENCE OF A CARTHAGE CONSPIRACY AGAINST THE PROPHET'S LIFE.

Wednesday, June 26, 1844; 7 a. m.—Joseph Hyrum, and the rest of the brethren, took breakfast with Stigall, and were then removed to the room upstairs.

Dr. Southwick went to see the Governor

At 7:30 a. m., Markham, Wasson, and Jones were severally sent by Joseph with messages to the Governor, but at 8 a. m., got no return. He also sent word to his counsel that he wanted a change of venue to Quincy, Adams County.

Messages to the Governor

At 8 a. m., Joseph and Hyrum had a conversation with the jailor, Mr. Stigall, who said a week last Wednesday the mob were calculating to have made an attack on Nauvoo, and they expected about 9000 persons, but only about 200 came. They had sent runners to Missouri, and all around the counties in Illinois.

At ten minutes past 8 o'clock a. m. Joseph wrote to Governor Ford, as follows and sent it by Mr. Stigall:—

Letter—Joseph Smith to Governor Ford—Soliciting an Interview.

CARTHAGE JAIL, June 26, 1844.
Ten minutes past 8 a. m.

His Excellency Governor Ford:

SIR,—I would again solicit your excellency for an interview having been much disappointed the past evening. I hope you will not deny me this privilege any longer than your public duties shall absolutely require.

We have been committed under a false mittimus, and consequently the proceedings are illegal, and we desire the time may be hastened when all things shall be made right, and we relieved from this imprisonment.

Your servant,

JOSEPH SMITH.

P. S.—Please send an answer per bearer.

At 8:30 a. m., Markham and Jones returned, stating that the Governor said he was taken by surprise last evening, and was very sorry. Was afraid we would think he had forfeited his word about having an interview, that the wrath of the people was about to turn on the head of Jackson, the mob, &c. That the Governor was doing as fast as he could.

Word from Governor Ford.

Twelve minutes before 9. Received the following reply on the same sheet:—

"The interview will take place at my earliest leisure to-day.

"GOVERNOR FORD."

Ten minutes to 9. Mr. Reid and others arrived at the jail and investigated the merits of the case, and concluded to take a change of venue before Justice Greenleaf, of Augusta, Hancock county, and to send for Dr. James H. Lyon, Col. J. Brewer, Edward Bonney, M. G. Eaton, Dr. Abiathar Williams, Thomas A. Lyne, George J. Adams, Dr. J. M. Bernhisel, Daniel H. Wells, Daniel Spencer, Orson Spencer, Dr. J. R. Wakefield, George P. Stiles, Jonathan Dunham, Albert P. Rockwood, Captain G. C. Anderson, William Marks, Hiram Kimball, Lorenzo D. Wasson, and Samuel Searles, as witnesses.

Consultation With Counsel

9:27 a. m. The Governor, in company with Col. Thomas Geddes, arrived at the jail, when a lengthy conversation was entered into in relation to our difficulties; and after some preliminary remarks, at the Governor's request Brother Joseph gave him a general outline of the state of the coun-

Interview with Gov. Ford.

try, the tumultuous, mobocratic movements of our enemies, the precautionary measures used by himself, (Joseph Smith) the acts of the City Council, the destruction of the press, and the moves of the mob and ourselves up to that time.

The Following Account of this Interview is from the Manuscript History of the Church in the Historian's Office, and not Hitherto Published.

Joseph Smith stated to them [Governor Ford and Col. Geddes] the origin of the difficulty, the facts relating to the *Expositor* press, the course pursued by the City Council; the legality, as they thought, of their legislation; the pledges that he had made by letter and sent by expresses to his Exellency, that he was willing to satisfy all legal claims in case it should be shown that the City Council had transcended their legal bounds, etc., and that the Legion had been called out for the protection of the city, while it was threatened with immediate hostilities by an infuriated mob, until his Excellency could afford relief, and not for the purpose of invasion. (The Governor seemed to be satisfied that this was the truth, but still he did not interfere in their illegal imprisonment). Joseph adverted to all the leading causes which gave rise to the difficulties under consideration in a brief, but lucid, energetic and impressive manner. The Governor said he was satisfied it was the truth. General Smith then read copies of the orders and proceedings of the City Council of Nauvoo, concerning the destruction of the *Expositor* press, and of the correspondence forwarded to his Excellency, in relation thereto; and also informed him concerning the calling out of the Legion, and the position they occupied of absolute necessity, not to make war upon, or invade the rights of any portion of the citizens of the State; but it was the *last resort*, and *only* defense, *in the absence of executive protection*, against a large, organized military and mobocratic foe.

General Smith reminded his Excellency that the question in dispute [the *Expositor* case] was a *civil* matter, and to settle which needed no resort to arms, and that he was ready at any time, and had always been ready to answer any charge that might be preferred against him, either as the Lieutenant General of the Legion, the Mayor of the City, or as a private individual, in any court of justice, which was unintimidated by a mob or military array, *and make all the satisfaction that the law required, if any, etc.* The Governor said he had not called out this force; [i. e., the one then gathered at Carthage] but found it assembled in military array, without his orders, on his arrival at Carthage, and that the laws *must be enforced*, but that the prisoners must and should be protected, and he again pledged his word, and the faith and honor of the State, that they should be protected. He also stated that he intended to march his forces (that is, those who had assembled for mobocratic purposes; and whom he had mustered into his service) to Nauvoo to gratify *them*, and that the prisoners should accompany them, and then return again to attend the trial before the said magistrate, which he said had been postponed for the purpose of making this visit. (John S. Fullmer) Joseph alluded to the coming of Constable Bettisworth when he gave himself up, also to his offer to go before *any other justice of the peace*, and called upon some twenty bystanders to witness that he submitted to the writ, but for fear of his life if he went to Carthage he had preferred to go before Esq. Daniel H. Wells, a gentleman of high legal attainments, who is in no way connected with the Mormon Church.

Joseph also said that he had sent frequent expresses and letters to the Governor; that Dr. J. R. Wakefield, Dr. J. M. Bernhisel and Mr. Sidney Rigdon also had written letters to the Governor; that he had written another letter to the Governor which was sent on the 15th of June by Mr. James; that he had written again on the 16th of June, enclosing affidavits, and sent them by Messrs. Edward Hunter, Phillip B. Lewis and John Bills. He also read Captain Anderson's certificate of the proceedings of the mob at Warsaw; also his Proclamation, his orders as Lieutenant General to Major General Dunham, the proceed ings of the City Council of Nauvoo, and copies of communications forwarded to Springfield; also his letter of the 21st of June which was sent by Dr. Bernhisel, and Mr. John Taylor, and his letter of the 22nd, which was sent by Lucien Woodworth and Squire Woods.

Marshal John P. Greene explained about giving passes to persons going in and out of the city, and denied that any arrests had been made.

The Governor referred to the trial before Esq. Wells, which did not satisfy the feelings of the people in and about Carthage. The Governor admitted that sufficient time had not been allowed by the posse for the defendants to get ready, or to gather their witnesses, said it can be very safely admitted that your statements are true, and was satisfied now that the people of Nauvoo had acted according to the best of their judgment.

Mr. Reid said that it was very evident from the excitement created by Mr. Smith's enemies it would have been unsafe for him to come to Carthage, for under such circumstances he could not have had an impartial trial.

The Governor said he came here to enforce the laws on all the people whether Mormons or not; and then expressed his feelings about the destruction of the *Expositor* press.

Joseph spoke of his imprisonment in Missouri, and of the shameful kidnapping of his witnesses, and their being thrust into prison to prevent them from giving their testimony in his favor.

Governor Ford spoke of the Constitution.

Joseph said we were willing to pay for the press, as he did not want the owners to suffer any loss by it, [i. e. its suppression] neither did he wish such a libelous paper to be published in Nauvoo. As for calling out the Nauvoo Legion, if it was intended to resist the government of the State, it would be treason; but, as they believed, they were endeavoring to defend themselves, and had no such intention as to resist the government—it was all right.

The following report is by Elder John Taylor.*

Elder John Taylor's Account of Governor Ford's and President Smith's Interview.

Governor—General Smith, I believe you have given me a general outline of the difficulties that have existed in the country, in the documents forwarded to me by Dr. Bernhisel and Mr. Taylor; but, unfortunately, there seems to be a discrepancy between your statements and those of your enemies. It is true that you are substantiated by evidence and affidavit, but for such an extraordinary excitement as that which is now in the country, there must be some cause, and I attribute the last outbreak to the destruction of the *Expositor*, and to your refusal to comply with the writ issued by Esq. Morrison. The press in the United States is looked upon as the great bulwark of American freedom, and its destruction in Nauvoo was represented and looked upon as a high-handed measure, and manifests to the people a disposi-

*This report of the Prophet's interview with Governor Ford, it is only proper to say, was not written until a number of years after the interview took place. (See ms. Statement, Feb. 22, 1847, on Atlantic Ocean; also in *Taylor's Journal*, kept at Nauvoo, c. f. with "The Martyrdom of Joseph and Hyrum Smith, opening paragraphs, published in Tyler's "Mormon Battalion.") The extract above quoted is taken from "Taylor's Martyrdom of Joseph and Hyrum Smith." written at the request of George A. Smith and Wilford Woodruff "Church Historian," hence no earlier than 1854-1856, since Geo. A. Smith did not become Historian until the year first given, and Wilford Woodruff, assistant Historian in the second. The interview therefore, though given in dialogue form, can only be Elder Taylor's recollection of it, and could not be a *verbatum* report.

tion on your part to suppress the liberty of speech and of the press; this, with your refusal to comply with the requisition of a writ, I conceive to be the principal cause of this difficulty, and you are, moreover, represented to me as turbulent and defiant of the laws and institutions of your country.

Gen. Smith.—Governor Ford, you, sir, as Governor of this State, are aware of the prosecutions and persecutions that I have endured. You know well that our course has been peaceable and law-abiding, for I have furnished this State, ever since our settlement here, with sufficient evidence of my pacific intentions, and those of the people with whom I am associated, by the endurance of every conceivable indignity and lawless outrage perpetrated upon me and upon this people since our settlement here, and you yourself know that I have kept you well posted in relation to all matters associated with the late difficulties. If you have not got some of my communications, it has not been my fault.

Agreeably to your orders, I assembled the Nauvoo Legion for the protection of Nauvoo and the surrounding country against an armed band of marauders, and ever since they have been mustered I have almost daily communicated with you in regard to all the leading events that have transpired; and whether in the capacity of mayor of the city, or lieutenant-general of the Nauvoo Legion, I have striven to preserve the peace and administer even-handed justice to all; but my motives are impugned, my acts are misconstrued, and I am grossly and wickedly misrepresented. I suppose I am indebted for my incarceration here to the oath of a worthless man that was arraigned before me and fined for abusing and maltreating his lame, helpless brother.

That I should be charged by you, sir, who know better, of acting contrary to law, is to me a matter of surprise. Was it the Mormons or our enemies who first commenced these difficulties? You know well it was not us; and when this turbulent, outrageous people commenced their insurrectionary movements, I made you acquainted with them, officially, and asked your advice, and have followed strictly your counsel in every particular.

Who ordered out the Nauvoo Legion? I did, under your direction. For what purpose? To suppress these insurrectionary movements. It was at your instance, sir, that I issued a proclamation calling upon the Nauvoo Legion to be in readiness, at a moment's warning, to guard against the incursions of mobs, and gave an order to Jonathan Dunham acting major-general, to that effect. Am I then to be charged for the acts of others; and because lawlessness and mobocracy abound, am I when carrying out your instructions, to be charged with not abiding the law? Why is it that I must be held accountable for other men's acts? If there is trouble in the country, neither I nor my people made it, and all that we have ever done, after much endurance on our part, is to maintain and uphold the Constitution and institutions of our country, and to protect an injured, innocent, and persecuted people against misrule and mob violence.

Concerning the destruction of the press to which you refer, men may differ somewhat in their opinions about it; but can it be supposed that after all the indignities to which we have been subjected outside, that this people could suffer a set of worthless vagabonds to come into our city, and right under our own eyes and protection, vilify and calumniate not only ourselves, but the character of our wives and daughters, as was impudently and unblushingly done in that infamous and filthy sheet? There is not a city in the United States that would have suffered such an indignity for twenty-four hours.

Our whole people were indignant, and loudly called upon our city authorities for redress of their grievances, which, if not attended to they themselves would have taken the matter into their ow n hands, and have summarily punished the audacious wretches, as they deserved.

The principles of equal rights that have been instilled into our bosoms from our cradles, as American citizens, forbid us submitting to every foul indignity, and succumbing and pandering to wretches so infamous as these. But, independent of this, the course that we pursued we considered to be strictly legal; for, notwithstanding the insult we were anxious to be governed strictly by law, and therefore convened the City Council; and being desirous in our deliberations to abide law, summoned legal counsel to be present on the occasion.

Upon investigating the matter, we found that our City Charter gave us power to remove all nuisances; and, furthermore, upon consulting Blackstone upon what might be considered a nuisance, that distinguished lawyer, who is considered authority, I believe, in all our courts, states, among other things, that a libelous and filthy press may be considered a nuisance, and abated as such.

Here, then one of the most eminent English barristers, whose works are considered standard with us, declares that a libelous press may be considered a nuisance; and our own charter, given us by the legislature of this State, gives us the power to remove nuisances; and by ordering that press abated as a nuisance, we conceived that we were acting strictly in accordance with law. We made that order in our corporate capacity, and the City Marshal carried it out. It is possible there may have been some better way, but I must confess that I could not see it.

In relation to the writ served upon us, we were willing to abide the consequences of our own acts, but were unwilling, in answering a writ of that kind, to submit to illegal exactions sought to be imposed upon us under the pretense of law, when we knew they were in open violation of it.

When that document was presented to me by Mr. Bettisworth, I offered, in the presence of more than 20 persons, to go to any other magistrate, either in our city or Appanoose, or any other place where we should be safe, but we all refused to put ourselves into the power of a mob.

What right had that constable to refuse our request? He had none according to law; for you know, Governor Ford, that the statute law in Illinois is, that the parties served with the writ shall go before him who issued it, or some other justice of the peace. Why, then, should we be dragged to Carthage, where the law does not compel us to go? Does not this look like many others of our prosecutions with which you are acquainted? And had we not a right to expect foul play?

This very act was a breach of law on his part—an assumption of power that did not belong to him, and an attempt, at least, to deprive us of our legal and constitutional rights and privileges. What could we do under the circumstances different from what we did do? We sued for, and obtained a writ of *habeas coprus* from the Municipal Court, by which we were delivered from the hands of Constable Bettisworth, and brought before and acquitted by the Municipal Court.

After our acquittal, in a conversation with Judge Thomas, although he considered the acts of the party illegal, he advised, that to satisfy the people, we had better go before another magistrate who was not in our Church.

In accordance with his advice we went before Esq. Wells, with whom you are well acquainted; both parties were present, witnesses were called on both sides, the case was fully investigated, and we were again dismissed.

And what is this pretended desire to enforce law, and these lying, base rumors put into circulation for, but to seek, through mob influence, under pretense of law, to make us submit to requisitions that are contrary to law, and subversive of every principle of justice?

And when you, sir, reqired us to come out here, we came, not because it was legal, but because you required it of us, and we were desirous of showing to you and to all men that we shrunk not from the most rigid investigation of our acts.

We certainly did expect other treatment than to be immured in a jail at the instance of these men, and I think, from your plighted faith, we had a right to, after disbanding our own forces, and putting ourselves entirely in your hands; and now, after having fulfilled my part, sir, as a man and an American citizen, I call upon you, Governor Ford, and think I have a right to do so, to deliver us from this place, and rescue us from this outrage that is sought to be practiced upon us by a set of infamous scoundrels.

Gov. Ford—But you have placed men under arrest. detained men as prisoners, and given passes to others, some of which I have seen.

John P. Greene, City Marshal—Perhaps I can explain. Since these difficulties have commenced, you are aware that we have been placed under very peculiar circumstance,our city has been placed under a very rigid police guard; in addition to this, frequent guards have been placed outside the city to prevent any sudden surprise, and those guards have questioned suspected or suspicious persons as to their business.

To strangers, in some instances, passes have been given, to prevent difficulty in passing those guards. It is some of those passes that you have seen. No person, sir, has been imprisoned without a legal cause in our city.

Gov.—Why did you not give a more speedy answer to the *posse* that I sent out?

Gen. Smith.—We had matters of importance to consult upon. Your letter showed anything but an amicable spirit. We have suffered immensely in Missouri from mobs, in loss of property, imprisonment, and otherwise.

It took some time for us to weigh duly these matters. We could not decide upon the matters of such importance immediately,and your *posse* were too hasty in returning. We were consulting for a large people, and vast interests were at stake.

We had been outrageously imposed upon, and knew not how far we could trust anyone; besides, a question necessarily arose, how shall we come? Your request was that we should come unarmed. It became a matter of serious importance to decide how far promises could be trusted, and how far we were safe from mob violence.

Geddes—It certainly did look from all I have heard, from the general spirit of violence and mobocracy that here prevails, that it was not safe for you to come unprotected.

Gov.—I think that sufficient time was not allowed by the *posse* for you to consult and get ready. They were too hasty; but I suppose they found themselves bound by their orders. I think, too, there is a great deal of truth in what you say, and your reasoning is plausible; yet, I must beg leave to differ from you in relation to the acts of the City Council. That council in my opinion, had no right to act in a legislative capacity, and in that of the judiciary.

They should have passed a law in relation to the matter, and then the Municipal Court, upon complaint, could have removed it; but for the City Council to take upon themselves the law-making and the execution of the laws, in my opinion, was wrong; besides, these men ought to have had a hearing before their property was destroyed; to destroy it without was an infringement of their rights; besides, it is so contrary to the feelings of the American people to interfere with the press.

And furthermore, I cannot but think that it would have been more judicious for you to have gone with Mr. Bettisworth to Carthage, notwithstanding the law did not require it. Concerning your being in jail, I am sorry for that, I wish it had been otherwise. I hope you will soon be released, but I cannot interfere.

Joseph Smith—Governor Ford, allow me, sir, to bring one thing to your mind, that you seem to have overlooked. You state that you think it would have been better for us to have submitted to the requisition of Constable Bettisworth, and to have gone to Carthage.

Do you not know, sir, that that writ was served at the instance of an anti-Mormon mob, who had passed resolutions and published them to the effect that they would exterminate the Mormon leaders; and are you not informed that Captain Anderson was not only threatened when coming to Nauvoo, but had a gun fired at his boat by this said mob at Warsaw, when coming up to Nauvoo, and that this very thing was made use of as a means to get us into their hands, and we could not, without taking an armed force with us, go there without, according to their published declarations, going into the jaws of death?

To have taken a force would only have fanned the excitement, as they would have stated that we wanted to use intimidation, therefore we thought it the most judicious to avail ourselves of the protection of the law.

Gov.—I see, I see.

Joseph Smith—Furthermore, in relation to the press, you say that you differ with me in opinion; be it so, the thing after all is a legal difficulty, and the courts I should judge competent to decide on that matter.

If our act was illegal, we are willing to meet it; and although I cannot see the distinction that you draw about the acts of the City Council, and what difference it could have made in point of fact, law, or justice, between the City Council's acting together or separate, or how much more legal it would have been for the Municipal Court, who were a part of the City Council, to act separate, instead of with the councilors.

Yet, if it is deemed that we did a wrong in destroying that press, we refuse not to pay for it. We are desirous to fulfill the law in every particular, and are responsible for our acts.

You say that the parties ought to have had a hearing. Had it been a civil suit, this of course would have been proper; but there was a flagrant violation of every principle of right, a nuisance, and it was abated on the same principle that any nuisance, stench, or putrified carcase would have been removed.

Our first step, therefore, was to stop the foul, noisome, filthy sheet, and then the next, in our opinion, would have been to have prosecuted the men for a breech of public decency.

And furthermore, again, let me say, Governor Ford, I shall look to you for our protection. I believe you are talking of going to Nauvoo; if you go, sir, I wish to go along. I refuse not to answer any law, but I do not consider myself safe here.

Gov. I am in hopes that you will be acquitted; but if I go, I will certainly take you along. I do not, however, apprehend danger. I think you are perfectly safe, either here or anywhere else. I cannot, however, interfere with the law. I am placed in peculiar circumstances and seem to be blamed by all parties.

Joseph Smith—Governor Ford, I ask nothing but what is legal. I have a right to expect protection at least from you; for, independent of law, you have pledged your faith, and that of the State, for my protection, and I wish to go to Nauvoo.

Gov.—And you shall have protection, General Smith. I did not make this promise without consulting my officers, who all pledged their honor to its fullfillment. I do not know that I shall go tomorrow to Nauvoo, but if I do, I will take you along.*

*Thomas Gregg, author of the History of Hancock County, page 372, gives the following statement of Col. Thomas Geddes mentioned in the above interview as the companion of Governor Ford. If true, and it is quite in keeping with all the circumstances and with both the character and subsequent actions of the Governor, then it is a very important statement as showing the double dealing of which Governor Ford was always suspected in relation to his course with reference to the difficulties between the citizens of Nauvoo and their enemies. And now Col. Geddes as reported by Gregg:

"While the Smiths were in jail, I went to the jail in company with Governor Ford, and there we conversed with them for some time, the burden of Smith's

10:15 a. m.—The Governor left after saying that the prisoners were under his protection, and again pledging himself that they should be protected from violence, and telling them that if the troops marched the next morning to Nauvoo, as he then expected, they should probably be taken along, in order to insure their personal safety, with how much sincerity may be seen by the following affidavits:—

Affidavit—Alfred Randall—Threats Against the Prophet's Life in Carthage.

TERRITORY OF UTAH, }
GREAT SALT LAKE CITY. } SS

Personally appeared before me, Thomas Bullock, Recorder of Great Salt Lake County, Alfred Randall, who deposes and says, that about ten o'clock on the morning of the (26th) twenty sixth day of June, one thousand eight hundred and forty-four, he was in Carthage, Hancock county, Illinois, and as the troops, under Governor Thomas Ford, were in squads around the square, he went up to several of them, and heard one of the soldiers say: "When I left home I calculated to see old Joe dead before I returned," when several others said, "So did I," "So did I," and "I'll be damned if I don't," was the general reply.

One fellow then spoke up and said "I shouldn't wonder if there is some damned Mormon hearing all we have to say." Another who stood next to Randall, replied, "If I knew there was, I would run him through with my bayonet."

In a few minutes Randall went to another crowd of soldiers, and heard one say, "I guess this will be the last of old Joe." From there Randall went to Hamilton's Hotel, where Governor Thomas Ford was standing by the fence side, and heard another soldier tell Governor Thomas Ford, "The soldiers are determined to see Joe Smith dead before they leave here." Ford replied, "If you know of any such thing keep it to yourself."

In a short time Randall started for his own home, stayed all night, and arrived in Nauvoo on the twenty-seventh of June, when Governor

talk being that they were only acting in self-defense, and only wanted to be let alone. After leaving the jail, and while returning from it, the Governor and I had still further conversation about the subject matter. After some time the Governor exclaimed, "O, it's all nonsense; you will have to drive these Mormons out yet!" I then said: "If we undertake that, Governor, when the proper time comes, will you interfere?" "No, I will not," said he; then, after a pause, adding, "until you are through!"

Ford was making his notorious speech to the citizens. And further this deponent saith not.

ALFRED RANDALL.

Subscribed and sworn to before me this twelfth day of February, one thousand eight hundred and fifty-five.

THOMAS BULLOCK,
Recorder, Great Salt Lake County.

Affidavit—Jonathan C. Wright—Conspiracy against the Prophet's Life at Carthage.

On the 26th day of June, A. D. 1844, near the mansion in the city of Nauvoo, I fell in company with Col. Enoch C. March and Geo. T. M. Davis, Esq., from Alton, Illinois, editor of the *Telegraph*, who had just arrived from Carthage, where they said they had been for some days, in company with Governor Ford and others, in council upon the subject of the arrest and trial of Joseph and Hyrum Smith, who were then prisoners in the county jail in Carthage.

After considerable conversation between myself and them on the subject of the Mormon religion, and the reasons why I had embraced that faith, and renounced my former religious discipline—viz, that of the Methodists, Mr. March asked me what I thought of Joe Smith, and if I had any hopes of his return to Nauvoo in safety.

I answered that I knew Joseph Smith was a true Prophet of the living God, as good and virtuous a man as ever lived upon the earth; that the Book or Mormon was true as holy writ, and was brought forth precisely in the way and manner it purported to be, by the gift and power of the Lord Almighty, and from no other source; and that the revelations he had received and published were eternal truth, and heaven and earth would pass away before one jot or tittle of the same should fail, and all that he pretended and testified to concerning the ministration of holy angels from the heavens to him, the Urim and Thummim, the voice of God, his correspondence with the heavens, was the truth and nothing but the truth; and that in relation to his return I had no doubt but that he would be honorably discharged upon his trial by the court, and would be preserved in safety from the power of his enemies; that he was in the hands of his God, whom he loved and faithfully served; and He, who held the destinies of nations in His own hands, would deliver him from his enemies, as He had done hundreds of times before.

Col. March replied, "Mr. Wright, you are mistaken, and I know it; you do not know what I know; I tell you they will kill Joe Smith before he leaves Carthage, and I know it, and you never will see him alive again." Said I, "Enoch, I do not believe it, he is in the hands of God, and God will deliver him." Says he, "I know better; when you hear of him again, you will hear he is dead, and I know it. The people at Carthage wanted permission from the Governor to kill you all and burn up your city, and Ford (the Governor) asked me if I thought it was best to suffer it. I replied, "No, no, for God's sake, Ford, don't suffer it, that will never do, no never. Just see for a moment, Ford, what that would do; it would be the means of murdering thousands of innocent men, women and children, and destroying thousands of dollars' worth of property, and that would never do, it would not be sanctioned, it would disgrace the nation. You have now got the principle men here under your own control, they are all you want, what more do you want? When they are out of the way the thing is settled, and the people will be satisfied, and that is the easiest way you can dispose of it; and Governor Ford concluded upon the whole that was the best policy, and I know it will be done."

MAYOR'S OFFICE, GREAT SALT LAKE CITY, UTAH TERRITORY,
Jan. 13th, A. D. 1855.

Personally appeared before me, Jedediah M. Grant, Mayor of said City, Jonathan Calkins Wright, who being duly sworn, deposeth and saith that the foregoing statements contained in his report of the conversation between himself and Enoch C. March, in presence of Geo. T. M. Davis, Esq., on the 26th day of June, 1844, in the city of Nauvoo, is true to the best of his knowledge and belief; and further this deponent saith not.

JONATHAN CALKINS WRIGHT.

Sworn to and subscribed before me, this 13th day of January, 1855, in Great Salt Lake City, Utah Territory.

J. M. GRANT,
Mayor of Great Salt Lake City.

Affidavit:—Orrin P. Rockwell—Gov. Ford in Nauvoo.

Personally appeared before me, Thomas Bullock, County Recorder in and for Great Salt Lake County, in the Territory of Utah, Orrin P. Rockwell, who being first duly sworn, deposeth and saith that about the hour of 3 o'clock in the afternoon of the 27th day of June, one thousand eight hundred forty-four, a short time only before Governor Ford addressed the citizens of Nauvoo, he (Ford) and his suit occupied an upper room in the mansion of Joseph Smith, in the city of Nauvoo, when he, the said Rockwell, had of necessity to enter said upper room for his hat, and as he entered the door, all were sitting silent except one man, who was standing behind a chair making a speech, and while in the act of dropping his right hand from an uplifted position, said. "The deed is done before this time," which were the only words I heard while in the room, for on seeing me they all hushed in silence. At that time I conld not comprehend the meaning of the words, but in a few hours after I understood them as referring to the murder of Joseph and Hyrum Smith in Carthage jail.

ORRIN P. ROCKWELL,

Subscribed and sworn to before me, the fourteenth day of April, 1856.

THOMAS BULLOCK.
Recorder of Great Salt Lake County.

Affidavit:—Wm. G. Sterrett—Conduct of Gov. Ford and Posse While in Nauvoo.

STATE OF DESERET, GREAT SALT LAKE COUNTY.

Personally appeared before me, Thomas Bullock, Recorder in and for Great Salt Lake County, this third day of October, one thousand eight hundred and fifty, William G. Sterrett, who being first duly sworn, deposeth and saith that on the twenty-seventh day of June, one thousand eight hundred and forty-four, in the city of Nauvoo, county of Hancock, and State of Illinois, I heard Thomas Ford, Governor of Illinois, address an assembly of several thousand citizens, gathered around the frame of a building situated at the corner of Water and Main streets. He reproached the people in severe terms for the course they had taken in resising the *posse comitatus*, and among other things, "The retribution thereof will be terrible, and you must make up your minds for it. I hope you will not make any more trouble, but be a law-abiding people, for if I have to come again it will be worse for you."

And your deponent further saith, that about half-past five in the afternoon the said Governor Thomas Ford and his guard visited the Temple and the workshops on the Temple block,

Mr. Alpheus Cutler, one of the building committee of the Temple, sent me to watch them in and about the Temple. I was close to the Governor when one of his men called him to look at one of the oxen of the font in the basement of the Temple, that had part of one horn broken off. The Governor stepped up to it, and laying his hand on it remarked, "This is the cow with the crumply horn, that we read of." One of the staff continued, "That tossed the maiden all forlorn," and they all had a laugh about it.

Several of the horns were broken off the oxen by the Governor's attendants. A man who stood behind me said, "I'll be damned but I should like to take one of those horns home with me, to show as a curiosity, but it is a pity to break them off."

After they had passed round the font, one of them remarked, "This temple is a curious piece of workmanship, and it was a damned shame that they did not let Joe Smith finish it, so that we could have seen what sort of a finish he would have put on it, for it is altogether a different style of architecture from any building I have ever seen or read about." Another said, "But he is dead by this time, and he will never see this temple again."

I replied, "They cannot kill him until he has finished his work." The Governor thereupon gave a very significant grin, when one of his suit who stood next to me said, "Whether he has finished his work or not by God he will not see this place again, for he's finished before this time."

Another of his suit pulled out his watch and said, "Governor, it's time we were off, we have been here too long already. Whether you go or not, I'm going to leave, and that damned quick." The Governor said, "Yes, it's time for us to be going." They then all left the stone shop, mounted their horses, which were hitched near the temple, and went out of the city towards Carthage by way of Mulholland Street, taking with them one of the horns that the company had knocked off. Further this deponent saith not.

WM. G. STERRETT.

Sworn to and subscribed before me, this day and year first above written.

THOMAS BULLOCK,
Great Salt Lake County Recorder.

While Joseph was writing at the jailor's desk, William Wall stepped up, wanting to deliver a verbal message to him from his uncle John Smith. He turned round to speak to Wall, but the guard refused to allow them any communication.

At noon Joseph wrote to Judge Thomas as follows:

Letter: Joseph Smith to Judge Thomas—Engaging Thomas as Legal Counsel.

CARTHAGE JAIL, June 26, 1844.

His Hon. Judge Thomas.

DEAR SIR,—You will perceive by my date that I am in prison. Myself and brother Hyrum were arrested yesterday on charge of treason without bringing us before the magistrate; last evening we were committed on a mittimus from Justice Robert F. Smith, stating that we had been before the magistrate, which is *utterly false*; but from the appearance of the case at present, we can have no reasonable prospect of anything but partial decisions of law, and all the prospect we have of justice being done is to get our case on *habeas corpus* before an impartial judge; the excitement and prejudice is such in this place, testimony is of little avail.

Therefore, sir, I earnestly request your honor to repair to Nauvoo without delay, and make yourself at home at my house until the papers can be in readiness for you to bring us on *habeas corpus*. Our witnesses are all at Nauvoo, and there you can easily investigate the whole matter, and I will be responsible to you for all the trouble and expense.

CHAPTER XXXII.

THE PROPHET IN CARTHAGE PRISON—THE UNION OF JUDICIAL, EXECUTIVE, AND MILITARY AUTHORITY IN DEALING WITH THE PRISONERS—THE LAST NIGHT IN PRISON.

Wednesday, June 26, 1844.—(Noon)—Willard Richards made copies of the orders of Joseph Smith as Mayor to Marshal John P. Greene, and as Lieut.-General to Major-General Jonathan Dunham.

The Prophet's Anxiety for His own Safety.

Joseph remarked, "I have had a good deal of anxiety about my safety since I left Nauvoo, which I never had before when I was under arrest. I could not help those feelings, and they have depressed me." Most of the forenoon was spent by Dan Jones and Col. Stephen Markham in hewing with a pen-knife a warped door to get it on the latch, thus preparing to fortify the place against any attack.

The Prophet, Patriarch, and their friends took turns preaching to the guards, several of whom were relieved before their time was out, because they admitted they were convinced of the innocence of the prisoners. They frequently admitted they had been imposed upon, and more than once it was heard, "Let us go home, boys, for I will not fight any longer against these men."

Hyrum as Comforter.

During the day Hyrum encouraged Joseph to think that the Lord, for his Church's sake, would release him from prison. Joseph replied, "Could my brother, Hyrum but be liberated, it would not matter so much about me. Poor Rigdon, I am glad he is gone to Pittsburg out of the way; were he to preside he would lead the Church to destruction in less than five years."

Dr. Richards was busily engaged writing as dictated by the Prophet, and Elder Taylor amused him by singing. Joseph related his dream about William and Wilson Law, also his dream about trying to save a steamboat in a storm.

One of the counsel for the prosecution expressed a wish to Esq. Reid, that the prisoners should be brought out of jail for examination on the charge of treason.

Status of Prisoners Under the Law.

He was answered that the prisoners had already been committed "until discharged by due course of law," and therefore the justice and constable had no further control of the prisoners, and that if the prosecutors wished the prisoners brought out of jail, they might bring them out on a writ of *habeas corpus*, or some other "due course of law," when we would appear and defend.

12:30, noon—Dr. Bernhisel arrived at the jail.

Mr. Reid came with the following letter from General Deming.

Letter—Gen. Miner R. Deming to Joseph Smith—Protection and Admission to Presence of the Prophet.

Messrs. Smith,—I was requested by the governor to order you such protection as circumstances might require. The guard have been acting upon the supposition that your protection excluded all persons but those admitted by a pass. I have caused the officer of the guard to be correctly instructed of his duties, so that you need suffer no further inconvenience.

M. R. DEMING, Brig.-Gen'l.

Headquarters,
Carthage, June 26, 1844.

Effect of a False Commitment.

Counselor Reid said that he had got the magistrate on a pin hook, for the magistrate had committed them without examination, and had no further jurisdiction in the case, and he would not agree to a trial unless (Captain) Justice Smith would consent to go to Nauvoo for examination, where witnesses could be had.

Reid said that a week ago, Harmon T. Wilson and another, had concocted a scheme for a writ to take Joseph, and when he was apprehended, to take him to Missouri; and Harmon T. Wilson returned from Missouri the night before the burning of the press.

1 p. m.—Willard Richards wrote to his wife, and sent the letter by Cyrus C. Canfield.

Threats in the Governor's Presence.

It was common conversation on the camp ground and in the dining-room of the hotel, in the presence of Governor Ford, "The law is too short for these men, but they must not be suffered to go at large;" and, "if the law will not reach them, powder and ball must."

Loyalty of Mr. Stigall to His prisoners.

Half past 2—Constable Bettisworth came with Alexander Simpson, and wanted to come in, with an order to the jailor demanding the prisoners; but as Mr. Stigall, the jailor, could find no law authorizing a justice of the peace to demand prisoners committed to his charge, he refused to give them up until discharged from his custody by due course of the law.

Conference of Gov. Ford and Justice Smith.

Justice Robert F. Smith then inquired what he must do. Governor Ford replied, "We have plenty of troops; there are the Carthage Greys under your command, bring them out." Joseph sent Lorenzo D. Wasson to inform the Governor of what had just taken place, and also to inform his counsel, Messrs. Reid and Woods.

Twenty minutes to 3—Dr. Bernhisel returned from the Governor, and said apparently the Governor was doing all he could.

3 p. m.—Wrote to Messrs. Woods and Reid as follows which was carried by Elder John Taylor.

Letter: Joseph Smith to Messrs. Woods and Reid—Anent Excitement in Carthage.

CARTHAGE JAIL, June 26, 3 p. m.

Messrs. Woods and Reid.

SIRS,—Constable Bettisworth called a little while since, and wanted to come in, the guard would not [allow it]. We have since learned that he wanted to take us before the magistrate, and we have since learned that there is some excitement because we did not go, and we wish to see you without delay.

We are informed that Dr. Foster has said that they can do nothing with us, only by powder and ball, as we have done nothing against the law.

Yours,
JOSEPH SMITH,
Per W. RICHARDS.

Joseph and Hyrum Smith Forced from Prison.

Twenty minutes to 4—Upon the refusal of the jailor to give up the prisoners, the constable with the company of Carthage Greys, under the command of Frank Worrell, marched to the jail, and by intimidation and threats, compelled the jailor, against his will and conviction of duty, to deliver Joseph and Hyrum to the Constable, who forthwith, and contrary to their wishes, compulsorily took them.

Joseph, seeing the mob gathering and assuming a threatening aspect, concluded it best to go with them then, and putting on his hat, walked boldly into the midst of a hollow square of the Carthage Greys; yet evidently expecting to be massacred in the streets before arriving at the Court House, politely locked arms with the worst mobocrat he could see, and Hyrum locked arms with Joseph, followed by Dr. Richards, and escorted by a guard. Elders Taylor, Jones, Markham, and Fullmer followed, outside the hollow square, and accompanied them to the court room.

4 o'clock.—Case called by Robert F. Smith, Captain of

the Carthage Greys. The counsel for the prisoners then appeared, and called for subpoenas for witnesses on the part of the prisoners, and expressed their wish to go into the examination as soon as the witnesses could be brought from Nauvoo to Carthage. This was objected to most vehemently by the opposite counsel.

Prisoners Before the Court.

4:25.—Took copy of order to bring prisoners from jail for trial, as follows:—

Copy of Order to Bring Prisoners into Court.

STATE OF ILLINOIS, }
HANCOCK COUNTY. } SS

To David Bettisworth, Constable of said county.

You are hereby commanded to bring the bodies of Joseph Smith and Hyrum Smith from the jail of said county, forthwith before me at my office, for an examination on the charge of treason, they having been committed for safe keeping until trial could be had on such examination, and the state now being ready for such examination.

Given under my hand and seal this 26th day of June, 1844.

(Signed) R. F. SMITH, J. P. [L. S.]

4:30—Made a copy of the list of witnesses.

4:35—C. L. Higbee, O. C. Skinner, Thos. Sharp, Sylvester Emmons and Thos. Morrison, appeared as counsel for the State.

The writ was returned, endorsed,

"Served on June 25th," which was false.

Mr. Wood said, they were committed to jail without any examination whatever.

Mr. Reid urged a continuance of the case till the witnesses could be obtained from Nauvoo for the defense.

4:45 p. m.—Mr. Skinner suggested that the court adjourn until 12 o'clock tomorrow.

Mr. Wood proposed that the court adjourn until witnesses could be got together, or until tomorrow at any time, and again adjourn if they are not ready, without bringing the prisoners into court.

Mr. Reid hoped no compulsory measures would be made

use of by the prosecution in this enlightened country.

Mr. Skinner: "If witnesses cannot be had after due diligence by the defense, a continuance will be granted.

Court said this writ was served yesterday, (which was not the case, unless it could be served without the prisoners or their counsel knowing it).

On motion of counsel for the prisoners, examination was postponed till tomorrow at 12 o'clock noon, and subpoenas were granted to get witnesses from Nauvoo, twenty miles distance, whereupon the prisoners were remanded to prison with the following mittimus:—

Examination Postponed.

Second Mittimus Remanding Smith Brothers to Prison.

STATE OF ILLINOIS, }
HANCOCK COUNTY. } ss

To the keeper of the jail of Hancock County, Illinois, greeting:

Whereas Joseph Smith and Hyrum Smith have been arrested and brought before me, Robert F. Smith, a justice of the peace in and for said county, for examination on the charge of treason against the State of Illinois, and have applied for a continuance, which is granted until the 27th June, 1844, at 12 o'clock, m.

These are therefore to command you to receive the said Joseph Smith and Hyrum Smith into your custody in the jail of the county, there to remain until they are brought before me for said examination according to law.

Given under my hand and seal this 26th day of June, 1844.

R. F. SMITH, J. P. [L. S.]

5:30.—Returned to jail, and Joseph and Hyrum were thrust into close confinement.

Patriarch John Smith came from Macedonia to jail to see his nephews Joseph and Hyrum. The road was thronged with mobbers. Three of them snapped their guns at him, and he was threatened by many others who recognized him. The guard at the jail refused him admittance.

Brave Patriarch John Smith.

Joseph saw him through the prison window, and said to

the guard, "Let the old gentleman come in, he is my uncle." The guard replied they did not care who the hell he was uncle to, he should not go in.

Joseph replied, "You will not hinder so old and infirm a man as he is from coming in," and then said, "Come in uncle;" on which, after searching him closely the guard let him pass into the jail, where he remained about an hour. He asked Joseph if he thought he should again get out of the hands of his enemies, when he replied, "My brother Hyrum thinks I shall. I wish you would tell the brethren in Macedonia that they can see by this, that it has not been safe for me to visit them; and tell Almon W. Babbitt I want him to come and assist me as an attorney at my expected trial tomorrow before Captain R. F. Smith."

Pathetic Interview Between the Prophet and "Uncle John."

Father Smith then left the jail to convey this message to A. W. Babbitt, who was at Macedonia.

6 p. m.—Copied witnesses' names and mittimus.

Dr. Bernhisel brought the following:—

The Governor's Suggestions to the Jailor.

I would advise the jailor to keep the Messrs. Smith in the room in which I found them this morning, unless a closer confinement should be clearly necessary to prevent an escape.

THOMAS FORD,
Governor and Commander-in-Chief.

June 26th, 1844.

6:15 p. m.—Received the following letter from William Clayton:—

Letter:—William Clayton to Joseph Smith—Conditions in Nauvoo.

NAUVOO, June 26, 1844.

DEAR PRESIDENT,—

I write this line to inform you that Mr. Marsh, who lives down the river, and of whom you have had corn, pork, etc., has sent word if you want any bail he is ready for one to any amount; and further, that he has got some corn left which he wants you to have, lest the mob get it. (We will endeavor to obtain it.)

They have already taken two loads, but he has charged them a dollar a bushel for it.

The *Amaranth* has just landed at the foot of Main Street, and unloaded 200 bbls. flour,—95 for Mr. Kimball, and the balance for Bryant.

Captain Singleton, who came at the head of the police this morning, is sending a request to the Governor to call them home. He says he finds no difficulties to settle here, but there is plenty to settle at home. He furthermore says that while the police were at Carthage they were treated as soldiers, but since they came to Nauvoo they have been treated as gentlemen.

The company all got home safe and well last night.

A messenger is about to start forthwith to Judge Thomas.

All is peace in Nauvoo. Many threats keep coming that the mob are determined to attack the city in your absence, but we have no fears.

With fervency and true friendship, I remain yours eternally,

WILLIAM CLAYTON.

This letter was sent from Nauvoo by Joel S. Miles. Joseph instructed Cahoon to return to Nauvoo with all haste, and fetch a number of documents for the promised trial.

Twenty-five minutes to 7.—Sent a message to Counselor Woods to get subpoenas for Samuel James, Edward Hunter, and Philip B. Lewis, with instructions to bring with them the papers that they carried to the Governor at Springfield, and which the Governor had not seen, as he had started for Carthage before they arrived at Springfield.

Fifteen minutes to 8.—Supper.

Militia Council meeting at Carthage.

8 p. m.—Counselors Woods and Reid called with Elder John P. Greene, and said that the Governor and military officers had held a council which had been called by the Governor, and they decided that the Governor and all the troops should march to Nauvoo at eight o'clock to-morrow, except one company of about 50 men, in order to gratify the troops, and return next day, the company of fifty men to be selected by the Governor from those of the troops whose fidelity he could most rely on, to guard the prisoners, who should be left in Carthage jail; and that their trial be deferred until Saturday, the 29th.

After the consultation, the justice, (Robert F. Smith), who was one of the officers in command, altered the return of the subpoenas until the 29th. This was done without consulting either the prisoners or their counsel.

About 8:15, p. m.—Patriarch John Smith met Lawyer Babbitt, and delivered the message, when Babbitt replied "You are too late, I am already engaged on the other side."

9 p. m.—Messrs. Woods, Reid, and Greene returned to Hamilton's Hotel.

9:15.—Elder John Taylor prayed. Willard Richards, John Taylor, John S. Fullmer, Stephen Markham, and Dan Jones stayed with Joseph and Hyrum in the front room.

During the evening the Patriarch Hyrum Smith read and commented upon extracts from the Book of Mormon, on the imprisonments and deliverance of the servants of God for the Gospel's sake. Joseph bore a powerful testimony to the guards of the divine authenticity of the Book of Mormon, the restoration of the Gospel, the administration of angels, and that the kingdom of God was again established upon the earth, for the sake of which he was then incarcerated in that prison, and not because he had violated any law of God or man.

The Last Night in Carthage Prison.

They retired to rest late. Joseph and Hyrum occupied the only bedstead in the room, while their friends lay side by side on the matresses on the floor. Dr. Richards sat up writing until his last candle left him in the dark. The report of a gun fired close by caused Joseph to arise, leave the bed, and lay himself on the floor, having Dan Jones on his left, and John S. Fullmer on his right.

Joseph laid out his right arm, and said to John S. Fullmer, "Lay your head on my arm for a pillow, Brother John;" and when all were quiet they conversed in a low tone about the prospects of their deliverance. Joseph gave expression to several presentiments that he had to die, and said "I would like to see my family again." and "I would to God that I could preach to the Saints in Nauvoo once more." Fullmer tried to rally his spirits, saying he thought he would often have that privilege, when Joseph thanked him for the remarks and good feelings expressed to him.

Conversation with John S. Fullmer.

Soon after Dr. Richards retired to the bed which Joseph had left, and when all were apparently fast asleep, Joseph whispered to Dan Jones, "are you afraid to die?" Dan said, "Has that time come, think you? Engaged in such a cause I do not think that death would have many terrors." Joseph replied, "You will yet see Wales, and fulfill the mission appointed you before you die."

Prophecy on the Head of Dan Jones.

CHAPTER XXXIII.

THE DAY OF MARTYRDOM—THREATS—REPEATED WARNINGS OF THE PRISONERS' DANGER GIVEN TO GOVERNOR FORD—THE CARTHAGE GREYS AS GUARDS.

Tuesday, *27*, *5 a. m.*—John P. Greene and William W. Phelps called at the jail, on their way to Nauvoo.

Threats of Frank Worrell.

5:30 a. m.—Arose. Joseph requested Dan Jones to descend and inquire of the guard the cause of the disturbance in the night. Frank Worrel, the officer of the guard, who was one of the Carthage Greys, in a very bitter spirit said, "We have had too much trouble to bring Old Joe here to let him ever escape alive, and unless you want to die with him you had better leave before sundown; and you are not a damned bit better than him for taking his part, and you'll see that I can prophesy better than Old Joe, for neither he nor his brother, nor anyone who will remain with them will see the sun set today."

Governor Ford Warned of Worrell's Threat.

Joseph directed Jones to go to Governor Ford and inform him what he had been told by the officer of the guard. While Jones was going to Governor Ford's quarters, he saw an assemblage of men, and heard one of them, who was apparently a leader, making a speech, saying that, "Our troops will be discharged this morning in obedience to orders, and for a sham we will leave the town; but when the Governor and the McDonough troops have left for Nauvoo this afternoon, we will return and kill those men, if we have to tear the jail down." This sentiment was applauded by three cheers from the crowd.

Captain Jones went to the Governor, told him what had occurred in the night, what the officer of the guard had said, and what he had heard while coming to see him, and earnestly solicited him to avert the danger.

His Excellency replied, "You are unnecessarily alarmed for the safety of your friends, sir, the people are not that cruel."

Irritated by such a remark, Jones urged the necessity of placing better men to guard them than professed assassins, and said, "The Messrs. Smith are American citizens, and have surrendered themselves to your Excellency upon your pledging your honor for their safety; they are also Master Masons, and as such I demand of you protection of their lives."

Jones' Warning to Gov. Ford.

Governor Ford's face turned pale, and Jones remarked, "If you do not do this, I have but one more desire, and that is if you leave their lives in the hands of those men to be sacrificed——"

"What is that, sir?" he asked in a hurried tone.

"It is," said Jones, "that the Almighty will preserve my life to a proper time and place, that I may testify that you have been timely warned of their danger."

Jones then returned to the prison, but the guard would not let him enter. He again returned to the hotel, and found Governor Ford standing in front of the McDonough troops, who were in line ready to escort him to Nauvoo.

The disbanded mob retired to the rear, shouting loudly that they were only going a short distance out of town, when they would return and kill old Joe and Hyrum as soon as the Governor was far enough out of town.

Boasts of the Mob.

Jones called the attention of the Governor to the threats

then made, but the Governor took no notice of them, although it was impossible for him to avoid hearing them.

Jones then requested the Governor to give him passports for himself and friends to pass in and out of the prison, according to his promise made to the prisoners. He refused to give them, but he told General Deming to give one to Dr. Willard Richards, Joseph Smith's private secretary.

Chauncey L. Higbee's Declared Intention to Kill the Prophet

While obtaining this, Jones' life was threatened, and Chauncey L. Higbee said to him in the street, "We are determined to kill Joe and Hyrum, and you had better go away to save yourself."

At 7 a. m., Joseph, Hyrum, Dr. Richards, Stephen Markham and John S. Fullmer ate breakfast together. Mr. Crane ate with them, and wanted to know if the report was true that Joseph fainted three times on Tuesday, while being exhibited to the troops. He was told it was a false report.

8 a. m.—Cyrus H. Wheelock, at Joseph's request, applied to the Governor, and obtained the following passes:

Cyrus H. Wheelock's Passes.

Suffer Mr. C. H. Wheelock to pass in to visit General Joseph Smith and friends in Carthage jail unmolested.

THOMAS FORD.
Governor and Commander-in-Chief.

June, 27th, 1844.

Protect Mr. C. H. Wheelock in passing to and from Carthage and Nauvoo.

THOMAS FORD,
Governor and Commander-in-Chief.

June 27th, 1844.

While receiving these passes he related to the Governor the numerous threats he had heard.

John S. Fullmer went to the Governor to get a pass.

8:20 a. m.—Joseph wrote to Emma as follows:

Letter: Joseph Smith to Emma Smith—Prophet's Instruction as to Reception of the Governor.

CARTHAGE JAIL, June 27th, 1844.
20 minutes past eight a. m.

DEAR EMMA.—The Governor continues his courtesies, and permits us to see our friends. We hear this morning that the Governor will not go down with his troops today to Nauvoo, as we anticipated last evening; but if he does come down with his troops you will be protected; and I want you to tell Brother Dunham to instruct the people to stay at home and attend to their own business, and let there be no groups or gathering together, unless by permission of the Governor, they are called together to receive communications from the Governor, which would please our people, but let the Governor direct.

Brother Dunham of course will obey the orders of the government officers, and render them the assistance they require. There is no danger of any extermination order. Should there be a mutiny among the troops (which we do not anticipate, excitement is abating) a part will remain loyal and stand for the defense of the state and our rights.

There is one principle which is eternal; it is the duty of all men to protect their lives and the lives of the household, whenever necessity requires, and no power has a right to forbid it, should the last extreme arrive, but I anticipate no such extreme, but caution is the parent of safety.

JOSEPH SMITH.

P. S.—Dear Emma, I am very much resigned to my lot, knowing I am justified, and have done the best that could be done. Give my love to the children and all my friends, Mr. Brewer, and all who inquire after me; and as for treason, I know that I have not committed any, and they cannot prove anything of the kind, so you need not have any fears that anything can happen to us on that account. May God bless you all. Amen.

8:30.—John S. Fullmer returned to jail.

9:40 a. m.—Mr. Woods and Mr. Reid called. They said another consultation of the officers had taken place, and the former orders of the Governor for marching to Nauvoo with the whole army were countermanded.

Dr. Southwick was in the meeting, seeing what was going on. He afterward told Stephen Markham that the purport of the meeting was to take into consideration the best way to stop Joseph Smith's career, as his views on government were widely circulated and took like wildfire. They said if he did not get into the Presidential chair this election, he would be sure to the next time; and if Illinois and Missouri would join together and kill him, they would not be brought to justice for it. There were delegates in said meeting from every state in the Union except three. Governor Ford and Captain Smith were also in the meeting.

Dr. Southwick's Report of the Carthage Meeting.

Captain Dunn and his company were ordered to accompany the Governor to Nauvoo. The Carthage Greys, who had but two days before been under arrest for insulting the commanding general, and whose conduct had been more hostile to the prisoners than that of any other company, were selected by Governor Ford to guard the prisoners at the jail; and other troops composed of the mob whom the Governor had found at Carthage, and had mustered into the service of the State and who had been promised "full satisfaction" and that they should be marched to Nauvoo, were disbanded and discharged in Carthage; yet Governor Ford suffered two or three hundred armed men to remain encamped about eight miles off on the Warsaw road,* apparently under the control of Col. Levi Williams, a notoriously sworn enemy to Joseph, and who had on many occasions threatened the destruction of Nauvoo and the death of Joseph. Moreover it was the duty of

Appointment of the Carthage Greys to Guard the Prisoners.

* It is the record of the case, however, that Governor Ford did send an order disbanding the regiment from Warsaw which he had ordered to rendezvous at Golden's Point for the purpose of marching with the rest of the Governor's troops into Nauvoo. "The Governor," remarks the late John Hay, who is the authority for the incident of disbanding the Warsaw troops—"the Governor, fearing he could not control the inflammable material he had gathered together, had determined to scatter it again" (*Atlantic Monthly*, December, 1869). The courier of the Governor to the Warsaw troops was Mr. David Matthews, a well-known citizen of Warsaw. But after receiving the order for disbandment, while most of the troops returned to their homes, about one hundred and fifty volunteered to follow several of the militia captains—leaders on their own responsibilty—to Nauvoo; of whom about seventy-five reached that place and participated in the murder of the Brothers Smith.

the Governor to dismiss the troops into the hands of their several officers in order to be marched home and there disbanded, and not to have disbanded them at a distance from home, and at a time and place when they were predisposed to acts of lawless violence, rapine and murder.

Cyrus H. Wheelock, states that previous to leaving Carthage he said to the Governor, "Sir, you must be aware by this time that the prisoners have no fears in relation to any lawful demands made against them, but you have heard sufficient to justify you in the belief that their enemies would destroy them if they had them in their power; and now, sir, I am about to leave for Nauvoo, and I fear for those men; they are safe as regards the law, but they are not safe from the hands of traitors, and midnight assassins who thirst for their blood and have determined to spill it; and under these circumstances I leave with a heavy heart."

Wheelock's Remonstrance to Gov. Ford.

Ford replied: "I was never in such a dilemma in my life; but your friends shall be protected, and have a fair trial by the law; in this *pledge* I am not alone; I have obtained the *pledge* of the whole of the army to sustain me."

After receiving these assurances, Wheelock prepared to visit the prison. The morning being a little rainy, favored his wearing an overcoat, in the side pocket of which he was enabled to carry a six shooter, and he passed the guard unmolested. During his visit in the prison he slipped the revolver into Joseph's pocket. Joseph examined it, and asked Wheelock if he had not better retain it for his own protection.

Arms Given to the Prisoners.

This was a providential circumstance, as most other persons had been very rigidly searched. Joseph then handed the single barrel pistol which had been given him by John S. Fullmer, to his brother Hyrum, and said,

"You may have use for this." Brother Hyrum observed, "I hate to use such things or to see them used." "So do I," said Joseph, "but we may have to, to defend ourselves;" upon this Hyrum took the pistol.

Wheelock was intrusted with a verbal request to the commanders of the Legion to avoid all military display, or any other movement calculated to produce excitement during the Governor's visit. He was especially charged to use all the influence he possessed to have the brethren and friends of Joseph remain perfectly calm and quiet, inasmuch as they respected the feelings and well-being of the Prophet and Patriarch.

Reflections of the Prophet on Exposing Wickedness.

Said Joseph, "Our lives have already become jeopardized by revealing the wicked and bloodthirsty purposes of our enemies; and for the future we must cease to do so. All we have said about them is truth, but it is not always wise to relate all the truth. Even Jesus, the Son of God had to refrain from doing so, and had to restrain His feelings many times for the safety of Himself and His followers, and had to conceal the righteous purposes of His heart in relation to many things pertaining to His Father's kingdom. When still a boy He had all the intelligence necessary to enable Him to rule and govern the kingdom of the Jews, and could reason with the wisest and most profound doctors of law and divinity, and make their theories and practice to appear like folly compared with the wisdom He possessed; but He was a boy only, and lacked physical strength even to defend His own person, and was subject to cold, to hunger and to death. So it is with the Church of Jesus Christ of Latter-day Saints; we have the revelation of Jesus, and the knowledge within us is sufficient to organize a righteous government upon the earth, and to give universal peace to all mankind, if they would receive it, but we lack the physical strength, as did our Savior when a child, to defend our principles, and we have of necessity to be afflicted, persecuted and smitten, and to bear it patiently until Jacob is of age, then he will take care of himself.''

Wheelock took a list of witnesses' names that were wanted for the expected trial on Saturday. When the list was read over, a number of names were stricken out, among whom were Alpheus Cutler and Reynolds Cahoon, it being deemed by Brother Hyrum unnecessary for them to attend. Brother Joseph asked why they should not come. Hyrum answered, ''They may be very good men, but they don't know enough to answer a question properly.'' Brother Joseph remarked, ''That is sufficient reason.''

The Prisoners' Messages to Friends in Nauvoo.

The prisoners also sent many verbal messages to their families. They were so numerous that Dr. Richards proposed writing them all down, fearing Wheelock might forget, but Brother Hyrum fastened his eyes upon him, and with a look of penetration said, ''Brother Wheelock will remember all that we tell him, and he will never forget the occurrences of this day.''

Joseph related the following dream which he had last night:

The Prophet's Dream of his Kirtland Farm

''I was back in Kirtland, Ohio, and thought I would take a walk out by myself, and view my old farm, which I found grown up with weeds and brambles, and altogether bearing evidence of neglect and want of culture. I went into the barn, which I found without floor or doors, with the weather-boarding off, and was altogether in keeping with the farm.

''While I viewed the desolation around me, and was contemplating how it might be recovered from the curse upon it, there came rushing into the barn a company of furious men, who commenced to pick a quarrel with me.

''The leader of the party ordered me to leave the barn and farm, stating it was none of mine, and that I must give up all hope of ever possessing it.

''I told him the farm was given me by the Church, and

although I had not had any use of it for some time back, still I had not sold it, and according to righteous principles it belonged to me or the Church.

"He then grew furious and began to rail upon me, and threaten me, and said it never did belong to me nor to the Church.

"I then told him that I did not think it worth contending about, that I had no desire to live upon it in its present state, and if he thought he had a better right I would not quarrel with him about it but leave; but my assurance that I would not trouble him at present did not seem to satisfy him, as he seemed determined to quarrel with me, and threatened me with the destruction of my body.

"While he was thus engaged, pouring out his bitter words upon me, a rabble rushed in and nearly filled the barn, drew out their knives, and began to quarrel among themselves for the premises, and for a moment forgot me, at which time I took the opportunity to walk out of the barn about up to my ankles in mud.

"When I was a little distance from the barn, I heard them screeching and screaming in a very distressed manner, as it appeared they had engaged in a general fight with their knives. While they were thus engaged, the dream or vision ended."

Testimony of Joseph and Hyrum to the Book of Mormon.

Both Joseph and Hyrum bore a faithful testimony to the Latter-day work, and the coming forth of the Book of Mormon, and prophesied of the triump of the Gospel over all the earth, exhorting the brethren present to faithfulness and persevering diligence in proclaiming the Gospel, building up the Temple, and performing all the duties connected with our holy religion.

Joseph dictated the following postscript to Emma:

Letter: Postscript.

P. S.—20 minutes to 10.—I just learn that the Governor is about to disband his troops, all but a guard to protect us and the peace, and come himself to Nauvoo and deliver a speech to the people. This is right as I suppose.

He afterwards wrote a few lines with his own hand, which were not copied.

The letter was sent by Joel S. Mills and Cyrus H. Wheelock.

Gov. Ford Warned of the Conspiracy Against Prisoners' Lives.

John P. Greene, (Nauvoo city marshal) told Governor Ford that if he went to Nauvoo, leaving only the Carthage Greys to guard the jail, that there was a conspiracy on foot to take the lives of Joseph and Hyrum Smith during his absence, to which the Governor replied, "Marshal Greene, you are too enthusiastic."

CHAPTER XXXIV.

DEPARTURE OF GOVERNOR FORD FOR NAUVOO—THE AFTERNOON IN CARTHAGE PRISON—THE ASSAULT ON THE PRISON—THE MARTYRDOM OF JOSEPH AND HYRUM SMITH.

Thursday, *June 27*, [*continued*] *10:30.*,—Governor Ford went to Nauvoo some time this forenoon, escorted by a portion of his troops, most friendly to the prisoners, and leaving the known enemies of the Prophet, ostensibly to guard the jail, having previously disbanded the remainder.

Joseph sent a request to the Governor by Dan Jones for a pass for his private secretary, Dr. Willard Richards.

11 a. m.—John S. Fullmer left the jail for Nauvoo, with a verbal charge to assist Wheelock in gathering and forwarding witnesses for the promised trial.

James W. Woods, Esq., Joseph's principal lawyer, left Carthage for Nauvoo.

11:20 a. m.—Dan Jones returned with the following pass for Dr. Richards:—

Pass for Willard Richards.

Permit Dr. Richards, the private secretary of Joseph Smith, to be with him, if he desires it, and to pass and repasss the guard.

THOMAS FORD,
Commander-in-Chief.

June 27th, 1844.

Jones said he could not get one for himself.

Dan Jones met Almon W. Babbitt in the street, and informed him that Joseph wanted to see him.

11:30.—A. W. Babbitt arrived at the jail and read a letter from Oliver Cowdery.

Joseph, Hyrum, and Dr. Richards tried to get Jones past the guard, but they persisted in refusing to admit him.

12:20 noon.—Joseph wrote for Lawyer Browning of Quincy to come up on Saturday as his attorney, as follows:—

Letter: Joseph Smith to O. H. Browning—Engaging Browning as Legal Counsel.

CARTHAGE JAIL, June 27th, 1844.

Lawyer Browning:—

SIR,—Myself and brother Hyrum are in jail on charge of treason, to come up for examination on Saturday morning, 29th inst., and we request your professional services at that time, on our defense, without fail.

Most respectfully, your servant,
JOSEPH SMITH.

P. S.—There is no cause of action, for we have not been guilty of any crime, neither is there any just cause of suspicion against us; but certain circumstances make your attendance very necessary.

J. S.

The Guard's False Alarm Over the Nauvoo Legion.

Almon W. Babbitt took the letter and left the jail. He handed it to Jones, with directions to take it to Quincy forthwith. The guard being aware of the letter, told the mob that, "old Joe" had sent orders to raise the Nauvoo Legion to come and rescue him. The mob gathered around Jones, and demanded the letter; some of them wanted to take it from him by force, and said that Jones should not get out of Carthage alive, as a dozen men had started off with their rifles to waylay him in the woods. Having previously ordered his horse, Jones took advantage of their disagreement, and started off at full speed. He, by mistake, took the Warsaw road, and so avoided the men who were lying in wait for him. When he emerged on the prairie, he saw the Governor and his posse, whereupon he left the Warsaw road for the Nauvoo road.

Dr. Southwick called at the jail. Joseph gave him a note to Governor Ford or General Deming, requesting them to furnish him with a pass.

1:15. p. m.—Joseph, Hyrum, and Willard dined in their room. Taylor and Markham dined below.

Markham Forced out of Carthage.

1:30 p. m.—Dr. Richards was taken sick, when Joseph said, "Brother Markham, as you have a pass from the Governor to go in and out of the jail, go and get the doctor something that he needs to settle his stomach," and Markham went out for medicine. When he had got the remedies desired, and was returning to jail, a man by the name of Stewart called out, "Old man, you have got to leave town in five minutes." Markham replied, "I shall not do it." A company of Carthage Greys gathered round him, put him on his horse, and forced him out of the town at the point of the bayonet.

3:15. p. m.—The guard began to be more severe in their operations, threatening among themselves, and telling what they would do when the excitement was over.

Elder Taylor sang the following:—

The Poor Wayfaring Man of Grief.

A poor wayfaring man of grief
Had often crossed me on my way,
Who sued so humbly for relief
That I could never answer, Nay.

I had not power to ask his name;
Whither he went or whence he came;
Yet there was something in his eye
That won my love, I knew not why.

Once, when my scanty meal was spread,
He entered—not a word he spake!
Just perishing for want of bread;
I gave him all; he blessed it, brake,

And ate, but gave me part again;
Mine was an angel's portion then,
For while I fed with eager haste,
The crust was manna to my taste.

I spied him where a fountain burst,
Clear from the rock—his strength was gone,
The heedless water mock'd his thirst,
He heard it, saw it hurrying on.

I ran and raised the suff'rer up;
Thrice from the stream he drain'd my cup,
Dipp'd, and returned it running o'er;
I drank and never thirsted more.

'Twas night, the floods were out, it blew
A winter hurricane aloof;
I heard his voice, abroad, and flew
To bid him welcome to my roof.

I warmed, I clothed, I cheered my guest,
I laid him on my couch to rest;
Then made the earth my bed, and seem'd
In Eden's garden while I dream'd.

Stripp'd, wounded, beaten nigh to death,
I found him by the highway side;
I rous'd his pulse, brought back his breath,
Revived his spirit, and supplied

Wine, oil, refreshment—he was heal'd;
I had myself a wound conceal'd;
But from that hour forgot the smart,
And peace bound up my broken heart,

In pris'n I saw him next—condemned
To meet a traitor's doom at morn;
The tide of lying tongues I stemmed.
And honored him 'mid shame and scorn.

My friendship's utmost zeal to try,
He asked, if I for him would die;
The flesh was weak, my blood ran chill,
But the free spirit cried, "I will!"

Then in a moment to my view,
The stranger started from disguise:
The tokens in his hands I knew,
The Savior stood before mine eyes.

He spake—and my poor name he named—
"Of me thou hast not been asham'd;
These deeds shall thy memorial be;
Fear not thou didst them unto me."

When he got through, Joseph requested him to sing it again, which he did.

Hyrum read extracts from Josephus.

4 p. m.—The guard was again changed, only eight men being stationed at the jail, whilst the main body of the Carthage Greys were in camp about a quarter of a mile distant, on the public square.

4:15 p. m.—Joseph commenced conversing with the guard about Joseph H. Jackson, William and Wilson Law, and others of his persecutors.

Hyrum and Dr. Richards conversed together until quarter past five.

5 p. m.—Jailor Stigall returned to the jail, and said that Stephen Markham had been surrounded by a mob, who had driven him out of Carthage, and he had gone to Nauvoo.

Stigall suggested that they would be safer in the cell. Joseph said, "After supper we will go in." Mr. Stigall went out, and Joseph said to Dr. Richards, "If we go into the cell, will you go in with us?" The doctor answered, "Brother Joseph you did not ask me to cross the river with you—you did not ask me to come to Carthage—you did not ask me to come to jail with you—and do you think I would forsake you now? But I will tell you what I will do; if you are condemned to be hung for treason, I will be hung in your stead, and you shall go free." Joseph said, "You cannot." The doctor replied, "I will."

Anxiety of the Jailor.

Before the jailor came in, his boy brought in some water, and said the guard wanted some wine. Joseph gave Dr. Richards two dollars to give the guard; but the guard said one was enough, and would take no more.

Wine for the Guard.

The guard immediately sent for a bottle of wine, pipes, and two small papers of tobacco; and one of the guards brought them into the jail soon after the jailor went out. Dr. Richards uncorked the bottle, and presented a glass to Joseph, who tasted, as also Brother Taylor and the doctor, and the bottle was then given to the guard, who turned to go out. When at the top of the stairs some one below called him two or three times, and he went down.

Immediately there was a little rustling at the outer door of the jail, and a cry of surrender, and also a discharge of three or four firearms followed instantly. The doctor glanced an eye by the curtain of the window, and saw about a hundred armed men around the door.

The Assault on the Jail.

It is said that the guard elevated their firelocks, and boisterously threatening the mob discharged their firearms over their heads. The mob encircled the building, and some of them rushed by the guard up the flight of stairs, burst open the door, and began the work of death, while others fired in through the open windows.

In the meantime Joseph, Hyrum, and Elder Taylor had their coats off. Joseph sprang to his coat for his six-shooter, Hyrum for his single barrel, Taylor for Markham's large hickory cane, and Dr. Richards for Taylor's cane. All sprang against the door, the balls whistled up the stairway, and in an instant one came through the door.

The Prisoners' Defense.

Joseph Smith, John Taylor and Dr. Richards sprang to the left of the door, and tried to knock aside the guns of the ruffians.

Hyrum was retreating back in front of the door and snapped his pistol, when a ball struck him in the left side of his nose, and he fell on his back on the floor saying, "I am a dead man!" As he fell on the floor another ball from the outside entered his left side, and passed through his body with such force that it completely broke to pieces the watch he wore in his vest pocket, and at the same instant another ball from the door grazed his breast, and entered his head by the throat; subsequently a fourth ball entered his left leg.

Death of Hyrum Smith.

A shower of balls was pouring through all parts of the room, many of which lodged in the ceiling just above the head of Hyrum.

Joseph reached round the door casing, and discharged his six shooter into the passage, some barrels missing fire. Continual discharges of musketry came into the room. Elder Taylor continued parrying the guns until they had got them about half their length into the room, when he found that resistance was vain, and he attempted to jump out of the window, where a ball fired from within struck him on his left thigh, hitting the bone, and passing through to within half an inch of the other side. He fell on the window sill, when a ball fired from the outside struck his watch in his vest pocket, and threw him back into the room.

The "Handsome Fight" of Joseph Smith and John Taylor.

After he fell into the room he was hit by two more balls, one of them injuring his left wrist considerably, and the other entering at the side of the bone just below the left knee. He rolled under the bed, which was at the right of the window in the south-east corner of the room.

Taylor Wounded and Helpless.

While he lay under the bed he was fired at several times from the stairway; one ball struck him on the left hip, which tore the flesh in a shocking manner, and large quantities of blood were scattered upon the wall and floor.

When Hyrum fell, Joseph exclaimed, "Oh dear, brother Hyrum!" and opening the door a few inches he discharged his six shooter in the stairway (as stated before), two or three barrels of which missed fire.

Joseph, seeing there was no safety in the room, and no doubt thinking that it would save the lives of his brethren in the room if he could get out, turned calmly from the door, dropped his pistol on the floor, and sprang into the window when two balls pierced him from the door, and one entered his right breast from without, and he fell outward into the hands of his murderers, exclaiming. "O Lord, my God!"

The Death of the Prophet.

Dr. Richards' escape was miraculous; he being a very large man, and in the midst of a shower of balls, yet he stood unscathed, with the exception of a ball which grazed the tip end of the lower part of his left ear. His escape fulfilled literally a prophecy which Joseph made over a year previously, that the time would come that the balls would fly around him like hail, and he should see his friends fall on the right and on the left, but that there should not be a hole in his garment.

Willard Richards' Remarkable Escape.

The following is copied from the *Times and Seasons*:—

TWO MINUTES IN JAIL.

Possibly the following events occupied near three minutes, but I think only about two, and have penned them for the gratification of many friends.

CARTHAGE, June 27, 1844.

A shower of musket balls were thrown up the stairway against the door of the prison in the second story, followed by many rapid footsteps.

While Generals Joseph and Hyrum Smith, Mr. Taylor, and myself, who were in the front chamber, closed the door of our room against the entry at the head of the stairs, and placed ourselves against it, there being no lock on the door, and no catch that was usable.

The door is a common panel, and as soon as we heard the feet at the stairs head, a ball was sent through the door, which passed between us, and showed that our enemies were desperadoes, and we must change our position.

General Joseph Smith, Mr. Taylor and myself sprang back to the front part of the room, and General Hyrum Smith retreated two-thirds across the chamber directly in front of and facing the door.

A ball was sent through the door which hit Hyrum on the side of his nose, when he fell backwards, extended at length, without moving his feet.

From the holes in his vest (the day was warm, and no one had his coat on but myself), pantaloons, drawers, and shirt, it appears evident that a ball must have been thrown from without, through the window, which entered his back on the right side, and passing through, lodged against his watch, which was in his right vest pocket, completely pulverizing the crystal and face, tearing off the hands and mashing the whole body of the watch. At the same instant the ball from the door entered his nose.

As he struck the floor he exclaimed emphatically, "I am a dead man." Joseph looked towards him and responded, "Oh, dear brother Hyrum!" and opening the door two or three inches with his left hand, discharged one barrel of a six shooter (pistol) at random in the entry, from whence a ball grazed Hyrum's breast, and entering his throat passed into his head, while other muskets were aimed at him and some balls hit him.

Joseph continued snapping his revolver round the casing of the door into the space as before, three barrels of which missed fire, while Mr. Taylor with a walking stick stood by his side and knocked down the bayonets and muskets which were constantly discharging through the doorway, while I stood by him, ready to lend any assistance, with another stick, but could not come within striking distance without going directly before the muzzle of the guns.

When the revolver failed, we had no more firearms, and expected an immediate rush of the mob, and the doorway full of muskets, half way in the room, and no hope but instant death from within.

Mr. Taylor rushed into the window, which is some fifteen or twenty feet from the ground. When his body was nearly on a balance, a ball from the door within entered his leg, and a ball from without struck his watch, a patent lever, in his vest pocket near the left breast, and smashed it into "pie," leaving the hands standing at 5 o'clock, 16 minutes, and 26 seconds, the force of which ball threw him back on the floor, and he rolled under the bed which stood by his side, where he lay motionless, the mob from the door continuing to fire upon him, cutting away a piece of flesh from his left hip as large as a man's hand, and were hindered only by my knocking down their muzzles with a stick; while they continued to reach their guns into the room, probably left handed, and aimed their discharge so far round as almost to reach us in the corner of the room to where we retreated and dodged, and then I recommenced the attack with my stick.

Joseph attempted, as the last resort, to leap the same window from whence Mr. Taylor fell, when two balls pierced him from the door, and one entered his right breast from without, and he fell outward, exclaiming, "Oh Lord, my God!" As his feet went out of the window my head went in, the balls whistling all around. He fell on his left side a dead man.

At this instant the cry was raised, "He's leaped the window!" and the mob on the stairs and in the entry ran out.

I withdrew from the window, thinking it of no use to leap out on a hundred bayonets, then around General Joseph Smith's body.

Not satisfied with this I again reached my head out of the window, and watched some seconds to see if there were any signs of life, regardless of my own, determined to see the end of him I loved. Being fully satisfied that he was dead, with a hundred men near the body and more coming round the corner of the jail, and expecting a return to our room, I rushed towards the prison door, at the head of the stairs, and through the entry from whence the firing had proceeded, to learn if the doors into the prison were open.

When near the entry, Mr. Taylor called out, "Take me." I pressed my way until I found all doors unbarred, returning instantly, caught Mr. Taylor under my arm and rushed by the stairs into the dungeon, or inner prison, stretched him on the floor and covered him with a bed in such a manner as not likely to be perceived, expecting an immediate return of the mob.

I said to Mr. Taylor, "This is a hard case to lay you on the floor, but if your wounds are not fatal, I want you to live to tell the story." I expected to be shot the next moment, and stood before the door awaiting the onset. WILLARD RICHARDS.

While Willard Richards and John Taylor were in the cell, a company of the mob again rushed up stairs, but finding only the dead body of Hyrum, they were again descending the stairs, when a loud cry was heard, "The Mormons are coming!" which caused the whole band of murderers to flee precipitately to the woods.

The following communication was written and sent to Nauvoo:—

First Message to Nauvoo.

CARTHAGE JAIL, 8:05 o'clock, p. m., June 27th, 1844.

Joseph and Hyrum are dead. Taylor wounded, not very badly.* I am well. Our guard was forced, as we believe, by a band of Mis-

* This statement was made at Elder Taylor's request, that he might not alarm his family; he was, however, severely wounded, as the narrative in the text bears witness. When the note above was being prepared, Elder Taylor said, "Brother Richards, say I am *slightly* wounded;" and when it was brought to him he signed his name as quickly as he could, lest the tremor of his hand should be noticed, and the fears of his family aroused (*The Life of John Taylor*, pp. 144-5).

sourians from 100 to 200. The job was done in an instant, and the party fled towards Nauvoo instantly. This is as I believe it. The citizens here are afraid of the Mormons attacking them. I promise them no!

W. RICHARDS.
JOHN TAYLOR.

N. B.—The citizens promise us protection. Alarm guns have been fired.

The above note was addressed to Governor Ford, Gen. Dunham, Col. Markham, Emma Smith, Nauvoo.

This letter was given to William and John Barnes, two mobocrats, who were afraid to go to Nauvoo, fearing that the Mormons would kill them and lay everything waste about Carthage; they therefore carried it to Arza Adams, who was sick with the ague and fever, about two and a half miles north of Carthage. He was afraid to go on the main road; and after two hours persuasion Mr. Benjamin Leyland consented to pilot Adams by "a blind road," and about midnight they started, and arrived in Nauvoo a little after sunrise. They found the news had arrived before them, for about a dozen men were talking about it at the Mansion, but not knowing what to believe until Adams handed in the above official letter.

CHAPTER XXXV.

GOVERNOR FORD IN NAUVOO—NEWS OF THE MARTYRDOM—MESSAGES TO NAUVOO—ARRIVAL OF THE BODIES—SORROWFUL SCENES—THE BURIAL.

Thursday, June 27th (continued).—In the meantime the Governor was making to the Saints in Nauvoo one of the most infamous and insulting speeches that ever fell from the lips of an executive. Among other things he said, "A great crime has been done by destroying the *Expositor* press and placing the city under martial law, and a severe atonement must be made, so prepare your minds for the emergency. Another cause of excitement is the fact of your having so many firearms. The public are afraid that you are going to use them against government. I know there is a great prejudice against you on account of your peculiar religion, but you ought to be praying Saints, not military Saints. Depend upon it, a little more misbehavior from the citizens, and the torch, which is already lighted, will be applied, and the city may be reduced to ashes, and extermination would inevitably follow; and it gives me great pain to think that there is danger of so many innocent women and children being exterminated. If anything of a serious character should befall the lives or property of the persons who are prosecuting your leaders, you will be held responsible."

Governor Ford in Nauvoo.

The Governor was solicited to stay until morning, but he declined, and left Nauvoo at about 6:30 p. m.; and in passing up Main Street his escort performed the sword exercise, giving all the passes, guards, cuts and thrusts, taking up the entire width of

Military Display.

the street, and making as imposing a show as they could, until they passed Lyon's store, near the Masonic Hall. This was apparently done to intimidate the people, as the Governor had remarked in his speech that they need not expect to set themselves up against such "well disciplined troops."

Soon after Captain Singleton and his company left for home.

Gov. Ford's Interception of Grant and Bettisworth.

When the Governor and his party had proceeded about three miles from Nauvoo, they met two messengers (George D, Grant and David Bettisworth) hastening with the sad news to Nauvoo. The Governor took them back to Grant's house, one and one-half miles east of Carthage, with him in order to prevent their carrying the news until he and the authorities had removed the county records and public documents, and until most of the inhabitants had left Carthage. The Governor then proceeded towards Carthage, when Grant took another horse and rode into Nauvoo with the news that night.

Second Message to Nauvoo.

12 o'clock at night, 27th June.
CARTHAGE, HAMILTON'S TAVERN,

To Mrs. Emma Smith and Major-General Dunham, &c.:

The Governor has just arrived; says all things shall be inquired into. and all right measures taken.

I say to all the citizens of Nauvoo, my brethren, be still, and know that *God reigns. Don't rush out of the city*—don't rush to Carthage—stay at home, and be prepared for an attack from Missouri mobbers. The Governor will render every assistance possible—has sent out orders for troops. Joseph and Hyrum are dead. We will prepare to move the bodies as soon as possible.

The people of the county are greatly excited, and fear the Mormons will come out and take vengeance. I have pledged my word the Mormons will stay at home as soon as they can be informed, and no violence will be on their part, and say to my brethren in Nauvoo, in the name of the Lord, be still, be patient, only let such friends as choose come here to see the bodies. Mr. Taylor's wounds are dressed and not serious. I am sound.

WILLARD RICHARDS.
JOHN TAYLOR,
SAMUEL H. SMITH.

Defend yourselves until protection can be furnished necessary. June 27th, 1844.

THOMAS FORD,
Governor and Commander-in-Chief.

Mr. Orson Spencer:

DEAR SIR:—Please deliberate on this matter—prudence may obviate material destruction. I was at my residence when this horrible crime was committed. It will be condemned by three-fourths of the citizens of the county. Be quiet, or you will be attacked from Missouri.

M. R. DEMING.

It was near midnight before Dr. Richards could obtain any help or refreshment for John Taylor, who was badly wounded, nearly all the inhabitants of Carthage having fled in terror.

Departure of the Governor from the Danger Zone.

Friday, *28.—1 a. m.* The Governor said the matter should be investigated, and that there was a great responsibility resting upon him. He also said he would send a messenger with an express for Dr. Richards, and wrote an order for the citizens of Nauvoo to defend themselves.

He then went to the public square, and advised all who were present to disperse, as he expected the Mormons would be so exasperated that they would come and burn the town, whereupon the citizens of Carthage fled in all directions, and the Governor and his *posse* fled towards Quincy, and did not consider themselves safe until they had reached Augusta, eighteen miles distant from Carthage.

Captain Singleton, of Brown county arrived in Carthage from Nauvoo with his troops.

About 8 a. m. Dr. Richards started for Nauvoo with the bodies of Joseph and Hyrum on two wagons, accompanied by their brother Samuel H. Smith, Mr. Hamilton, and a guard of eight soldiers who had been detached for that purpose by General Deming. The bodies were covered with bushes to keep them from the hot sun. They were met by a great assemblage of citizens of Nauvoo, on Mulholland Street, about a mile east of the Temple, about three p. m. under direction of the city marshal.

The Start for Nauvoo with the Bodies of the Martyrs.

The City Council, the Lieut.-General's staff, Major. General Jonathan Dunham and staff, the acting Brigadier-General Hosea Stout and staff, commanders and officers of the Legion, and several thousands of the citizens were there amid the most solemn lamentations and wailings that ever ascended into the ears of the Lord of Hosts to be avenged of their enemies.

When the procession arrived, the bodies were both taken into the Nauvoo Mansion. The scene there cannot be described.

About eight or ten thousand persons were addressed by Dr. Willard Richards, William W. Phelps, Esquires Woods and Reid of Iowa, and Col. Stephen Markham. Dr. Richards admonished the people to keep the peace, stating that he had pledged his honor, and his life for their good conduct, when the people with one united voice resolved to trust to the law for a remedy of such a high-handed assassination, and when that failed, to call upon God to avenge them of their wrongs.

The Address of Dr. Richards *et al.*

O, Americans, weep, for the glory of freedom has departed!

When the bodies of Joseph and Hyrum arrived at the Mansion, the doors were closed immediately. The people were told to go quietly home, and the bodies would be viewed the next morning at eight o'clock.

Dimick B. Huntington, with the assistance of William Marks and William D. Huntington, washed the bodies from head to foot. Joseph was shot in the right breast, also under the heart, in the lower part of his bowels and the right side, and on the back part of the right hip. One ball had come out at the right shoulder-blade. Cotton soaked in camphor was put into each wound, and the bodies laid out with fine plain drawers and shirt, white neckerchiefs, white cotton stockings and white shrouds. (Gilbert Goldsmith was doorkeeper at the time).

Preparation of the Bodies for Burial.

After this was done, Emma (who at the time was pregnant) also Mary (Hyrum's wife) with the children of the martyred Prophet and Patriarch, were admitted to see the bodies. On first seeing the corpse of her husband, Emma screamed and fell back, but was caught and supported by Dimick B. Huntington. She then fell forward to the Prophet's face and kissed him, calling him by name, and begged him to speak to her once. Mary, (the Patriarch's wife) manifested calmness and composure throughout the trying scene, which was affecting in the extreme. Relatives and particular friends were also permitted to view the remains during the evening.

Saturday 29.—At 7 a. m. the bodies were put into the coffins which were covered with black velvet fastened with brass nails. Over the face of each corpse a lid was hung with brass hinges, under which was a square of glass to protect the face, and the coffin was lined with white cambric. The coffins were then each put into a rough pine box.

At 8 a. m. the room was thrown open for the Saints to view the bodies of their martyred Prophet and Patriarch, and it is estimated that over ten thousand persons visited the remains that day, as there was a perfect living stream of people entering in at the west door of the Man sion and out at the north door from 8 a. m. to 5 p. m., at which hour a request was made

Lying in State.

that the Mansion should be cleared, so that the family could take their farewell look at the remains.

The coffins were then taken out of the boxes into the little bedroom in the northeast corner of the Mansion, and there concealed and the doors locked. Bags of sand were then placed in each end of the boxes, which were nailed up, and a mock funeral took place, the boxes being put into a hearse and driven to the graveyard by William D. Huntington, and there deposited in a grave with the usual ceremonies.

This was done to prevent enemies of the martyred Prophet and Patriarch getting possession of the bodies, as they threatened they would do. As the hearse passed the meeting ground accompanied by a few men, William W. Phelps was preaching the funeral sermon.

The Real Burial.

About midnight the coffins containing the bodies were taken from the Mansion by Dimick B. Huntington, Edward Hunter, William D. Huntington, William Marks, Jonathan H. Holmes, Gilbert Goldsmith, Alpheus Cutler, Lorenzo D. Wasson, and Philip B. Lewis, preceded by James Emmett as guard with his musket.

They went through the garden, round by the pump, and were conveyed to the Nauvoo house, which was then built to the first joists of the basement, and buried in the basement story.

After the bodies were interred, and the ground smoothed off as it was before, and chips of wood and stone and other rubbish thrown over, so as to make it appear like the rest of the ground around the graves, a most terrific shower of rain, accompanied with thunder and lightning, occurred, and obliterated all traces of the fact that the earth had been newly dug.

The bodies remained in the cellar of the Nauvoo House where they were buried, until the fall, when they were removed by Dimick B. Huntington, William D. Huntington, Jonathan H. Holmes, and Gilbert Goldsmith, at Emma's request, to near the Mansion, and buried side by side, and the bee house then moved and placed over their graves.

The deceased children of Joseph were afterwards removed and interred in the same place. It was found at this time that two of Hyrum's teeth had fallen into the inside of his mouth, supposed to have been done by a ball at the time of the martyrdom, but which was not discovered at the time he was laid out, in consequence of his jaws being tied up.

* * * * * * *

[It is thought proper that this volume, which brings the HISTORY OF THE CHURCH to the close of its first Period—the administration of its First President, and, by way of pre-eminence *the* Prophet of the New Dispensation of the Gospel, should close with the official statement of the Martyrdom of the Prophet and the Patriarch. A statement so true, and conservative, and excellent that now for a long time it has been published in the "Doctrine and Covenants."]

MARTYRDOM OF JOSEPH SMITH, THE PROPHET, AND HIS BROTHER HYRUM.

(*From the Doctrine and Covenants*).

To seal the testimony of this book and the Book of Mormon, we announce the Martyrdom of Joseph Smith the Prophet, and Hyrum Smith the Patriarch. They were shot in Carthage jail, on the 27th of June, 1844, about 5 o'clock p. m., by an armed mob, painted black—of from 150 to 200 persons. Hyrum was shot first and fell calmly, exclaiming, "*I am a dead man!*" Joseph leaped from the window and was shot dead in the attempt, exclaiming, "*O Lord, my God!*" They were both shot after they were dead in a brutal manner, and both received four balls.

John Taylor and Willard Richards, two of the Twelve, were the only persons in the room at the time; the former was wounded in a savage manner with four balls, but has since recovered; the latter through the providence of God, escaped, "without even a hole in his robe."

Joseph Smith, the Prophet and Seer of the Lord, has done more (save Jesus only) for the salvation of men in this world, than any other man that ever lived in it. In the short space of twenty years he has brought forth the Book of Mormon, which he translated by the gift and power of God, and has been the means of publishing it on two continents; has sent the fullness of the everlasting Gospel which it contained to the four quarters of the earth; has brought forth the revelations and commandments which compose this Book of Doctrine and Covenants, and many other wise documents and instructions for the benefit of the children of men; gathered many thousands of the Latter-day Saints, founded a great city; and left a fame and name that cannot be slain. He lived great, and he died great in the eyes of God and his people, and like most of the Lord's anointed in ancient times, has sealed his mission and his works with his own blood—and so has his brother Hyrum. In life they were not divided, and in death they were not separated!

When Joseph went to Carthage to deliver himself up to the pretended requirements of the law, two or three days previous to his assassination, he said:

"I am going like a lamb to the slaughter; but I am calm as a summer's morning; I have a conscience void of offense towards God and towards all men. I shall die innocent, and it shall yet be said of me—he was murdered in cold blood."

The same morning after Hyrum had made ready to go—shall it be said to the slaughter? Yes, for so it was,—he read the following paragraph near the close of the fifth chapter of Ether, in the Book of Mormon, and turned down the leaf upon it:

"And it came to pass that I prayed unto the Lord that He would give unto the Gentiles grace that they might have charity. And it came to pass that the Lord said unto me, if they have not charity, it mattereth not unto you, thou hast been faithful; wherefore thy garments are clean. And because thou hast seen thy weakness thou shalt be made strong, even unto the sitting down in the place which I have prepared in the mansions of my Father. And now I . . . bid farewell unto the Gentiles; yea, and also unto my brethren whom I love, until we shall meet before the judgment-seat of Christ where all men shall know that my garments are not spotted with your blood."

The testators are now dead, and their testament is in force.

Hyrum Smith was forty-four years old, February, 1844, and Joseph Smith was thirty-eight in December, 1843: and henceforward their names will be classed among the martyrs of religion; and the reader in every nation will be reminded that the Book of Mormon and this Book of Doctrine and Covenants of the Church, cost the best blood of the nineteenth century to bring them forth for the salvation of a ruined world; and that if the fire can scathe a *green tree* for the glory of God, how easy it will burn up the "dry trees" to purify the vineyard of corruption. They lived for glory, they died for glory; and glory is their eternal reward. From age to age shall their names go down to posterity as gems for the sanctified.

They were innocent of any crime, as they had often been proved before, and were only confined in the jail by the conspiracy of traitors and wicked men; and their innocent blood on the floor of Carthage jail, is a broad seal affixed to "Mormonism" that cannot be rejected by any court on earth; and their *innocent blood* on the escutcheon of the State of Illinois with the broken faith of the State, as pledged by the Governor, is a witness to the truth of the everlasting gospel, that all the world cannot impeach; and their *innocent blood* on the banner of liberty, and on the *magna charta* of the United States is an ambassador for the religion of Jesus Christ that will touch the hearts of honest men among all nations; and their *innocent blood* with the *innocent blood* of all the martyrs under the altar that John saw, will cry unto the Lord of Hosts, till He avenges that blood on the earth. Amen.

(END OF PERIOD I.)

INDEX TO VOLUME VI.

A

B

I

J

K

L

M

T

HISTORY

OF THE

CHURCH OF JESUS CHRIST

OF

LATTER-DAY SAINTS

PERIOD II

FROM THE MANUSCRIPT HISTORY OF BRIGHAM YOUNG AND OTHER ORIGINAL DOCUMENTS

VOLUME VII

AN INTRODUCTION AND NOTES

BY

B. H. ROBERTS

PUBLISHED BY THE CHURCH

DESERET BOOK COMPANY
SALT LAKE CITY, UTAH

1980

Lithographed by

in the United States of America

MOUNT ENSIGN

(Cover Indent-gravure)

"All ye inhabitants of the world, and dwellers on the earth, see ye, when he lifteth up an Ensign on the mountains; and when he bloweth a trumpet, hear ye."—(*Isa. xviii*:3)

On the cover of each of the six preceding volumes of this series of the *History of the Church,* Period I, there has appeared in low relief an indent-gravure of some prominent place: the Hill Cumorah, the Kirtland Temple, the Liberty Prison, the Nauvoo Mansion, and the Carthage Jail; and for this Period II, volume VII, since it brings us in its action into Salt Lake valley, a Utah subject of first importance is selected, *viz.* "Mount Ensign". It is generally referred to as "Ensign Peak". Elder Woodruff, among those who first climbed the Mount, says in his Journal entry of that date—July 26, 1847:

"We went on the top of a high peak in the edge of the mountain, which we considered a good place to raise an Ensign. So we named it 'Ensign Peak', or 'Hill'."

Captain J. W. Gunnison, refers to it in his *The Mormons,* 1856, (pp. 33-4), as "Ensign Mound".

President Young refers to the Mount as "Ensign Hill", on the occasion of recording the incident of Addison Pratt receiving his endowments on its summit, in October, 1849. (See *Comprehensive History of the Church,* Century I, vol. iii, p. 386, footnote 10); so that while referred to generally in early days as "Ensign Peak", it was not exclusively known by that name; and as it was dedicated for such purpose and used as a "House of the Lord" for giving the sacred mysteries of the Temple ritual—a new sanctity attaches to it. It is a sacred "Mount", as much so as "Mount Lebanon", the "Mount of Transfiguration", "Mount Sinai", or "Mount Zion", where the Temple of Jerusalem stood. And since this western mountain in the edge of a group of mountains was used as a Temple of God, "Mount" is both more euphonious and implies sacredness rather than "Peak" does. Hence the name here used is suggested—"Mount Ensign".

The significance of "Ensign" in the literature of the Church of the New Dispensation—in connection with this "Mount"—is that it has reference to the intent of the church "in these last days", to raise an "Ensign" to the nations, known as the "Standard of Zion", which would be an "Ensign" made up of the flags of all nations, indicating that its message was to be to "every nation, kindred, tongue and people", symbolized in this flag, or "Ensign". The matter is referred to in some remarks of President Young made on the 29th of May, 1847, when he mentioned to his Camp of Pioneers the raising of such an "Ensign" in the place to which they were going. Elder Woodruff made note of it in his daily Journal of that date, and drew in the margin of his Journal the rough outline of such a flag. It was to this "Ensign" that the small group of Pioneers referred to when on the top of the "Mount" to which they had climbed, as being "a good place to raise an Ensign."

TABLE OF CONTENTS

VOLUME VII

PART I

CHURCH HISTORIANS' EXCERPT FROM FORD'S HISTORY OF ILLINOIS

CHAPTER I

CONDITIONS IN HANCOCK COUNTY REVIEWED BY GOVERNOR FORD—THE STATE ARMS OF THE LEGION SURRENDERED ON THE DEMAND OF THE GOVERNOR

CHAPTER II

SUBMISSION OF THE PROPHET TO THE REQUIREMENTS OF THE GOVERNOR—GATHERING OF THE ENEMY FORCES OF THE PROPHET—GOVERNOR FORD'S DEFENSIVE JUSTIFICATION FOR HIS PLACEMENT OF THE HOSTILE FORCES AT CARTHAGE AND THE DISMISSAL OF OTHERS

CHAPTER III

GOVERNOR FORD'S VISIT TO NAUVOO—FEARS ON THE WAY—INSULTING SPEECH TO THE CITIZENS—RESENTED—HEARS OF THE ASSASSINATION OF JOSEPH AND HYRUM SMITH

PART II

EXTENSION OF QUOTATIONS FROM FORD'S HISTORY OF ILLINOIS

CHAPTER IV

GOVERNOR FORD'S COMMENTS ON THE CHARACTER OF JOSEPH SMITH AND HIS FOLLOWERS—HIS CONJECTURES ON THE FUTURE OF MORMONISM

CHAPTER V

POLITICAL CONSIDERATIONS OF THE PERIOD FOLLOWING THE DEATH OF THE PROPHET—"TRIAL" OF THE MURDERERS—STATUS OF CIVIL GOVERNMENT IN HANCOCK COUNTY

PART III

MEMOIRS OF THE LATE PRESIDENT JOHN TAYLOR RESPECTING AFFAIRS AT NAUVOO LEADING UP TO THE MARTYRDOM OF THE PROPHET AND PATRIARCH: GOVERNOR FORD'S RESPONSIBILITY THEREIN

CHAPTER VI

THE MARTYRDOM OF JOSEPH SMITH: REVIEW OF CONDITIONS IN ILLINOIS PRECEDING THAT EVENT

CHAPTER VII

JOHN TAYLOR AND DOCTOR BERNHISEL'S INTERVIEW WITH GOVERNOR FORD PLEDGE OF GOVERNOR FORD FOR THE SECURITY OF JOSEPH SMITH IF HE WOULD COME TO CARTHAGE

CHAPTER VIII

INTERVIEW BETWEEN JOSEPH SMITH AND GOVERNOR THOMAS FORD

CHAPTER IX

THE ASSAULT UPON THE PRISON—THE MURDER OF JOSEPH AND HYRUM SMITH

CHAPTER X

WAS GOVERNOR FORD RESPONSIBLE FOR THE MURDER OF THE PROPHET AND PATRIARCH OF THE NEW DISPENSATION

PART IV

HISTORIANS' SECOND COMPILATION OF HISTORICAL ITEMS OF CHURCH HISTORY, FROM 22ND OF JUNE, 1844 TO 8TH OF AUGUST, 1844

CHAPTER XI

MISCELLANEOUS EVENTS APART FROM THE MAJOR FACTS OF THE MARTYRDOM OF THE PROPHET AND PATRIARCH FROM JUNE 22ND, 1844 TO JUNE 29TH, 1844

CHAPTER XII

MOVEMENTS IN HANCOCK COUNTY, CARTHAGE, NAUVOO, WARSAW AND QUINCY, FOR THE MAINTENANCE OF PEACE FOLLOWING THE MARTYRDOM: LIST OF THE NAMES OF THOSE WHO WERE IN THE MOB ASSEMBLED TO SLAY THE PROPHET

CHAPTER XIII

THE MARTYRDOM IN POETRY—EFFORTS FOR FOOD SUPPLIES AND PROTECTION FOR THE PEOPLE OF NAUVOO—THE DANIELS AFFIDAVIT ON THE MARTYRDOM

CHAPTER XIV

A CHAPTER OF SUNDRY EVENTS AT VARIOUS PLACES AND DOCUMENTS FOLLOWING THE MARTYRDOM: UNITED STATES PRESS COMMENTS ON THE MURDER

CHAPTER XV

CHAPTER OF MISCELLANEOUS DOCUMENTS, PRESS EXCERPTS AND MOVEMENTS OF LEADING ELDERS OF THE CHURCH AT NAUVOO AND ELSEWHERE

CHAPTER XVI

THE MOVEMENTS OF THE APOSTLES AND OTHER LEADING BRETHREN IN THE EAST AND AT NAUVOO—IMPORTANT COMMUNICATION FROM GOVERNOR FORD

CHAPTER XVII

GATHERING OF THE TWELVE AND OTHER LEADING ELDERS AT NAUVOO—DEATH OF ELDER SAMUEL H. SMITH, BROTHER OF THE PROPHET, EARLY MISSIONARY OF THE CHURCH AND ONE OF THE EIGHT WITNESSES OF THE BOOK OF MORMON

CHAPTER XVIII

THE GATHERING OF THE TWELVE APOSTLES FROM THE EAST TO NAUVOO: PRELIMINARY MEETINGS LOOKING TO THE SETTLEMENT OF THE QUESTION OF THE PRESIDENCY OF THE CHURCH

CHAPTER XIX

THE SETTLEMENT OF CHURCH LEADERSHIP—THE TWELVE APOSTLES ACCEPTED AS THE PRESIDENCY OF THE CHURCH, BRIGHAM YOUNG AT THEIR HEAD

PART V

EXCERPTS FROM THE MANUSCRIPT HISTORY OF BRIGHAM YOUNG FROM AUGUST 9, 1844, TO OCTOBER 8, 1848

CHAPTER XX

EVENTS IMMEDIATELY FOLLOWING THE SUSTAINING OF THE QUORUM OF THE TWELVE AS THE PRESIDENCY OF THE CHURCH—RESUMPTION OF THE CHURCH ACTIVITIES—PERPETUATION OF THE POLICY OF THE PROPHET

CHAPTER XXI

FORMAL TRIAL AND EXCOMMUNICATION OF PRESIDENT SIDNEY RIGDON—RESTLESS MOVEMENTS OF JAMES EMMETT—MISSION ACTIVITIES OF THE CHURCH—MOVEMENTS OF STATE OFFICIALS AND THE MOB OF HANCOCK COUNTY

CHAPTER XXII

EPISTLE OF THE TWELVE TO THE CHURCH—MORAL AND SPIRITUAL GUIDANCE

CHAPTER XXIII

MINUTES OF THE IMPORTANT CONFERENCE OF OCTOBER 6TH TO 8TH, 1844—THE CHURCH SET IN ORDER—DUTIES OF THE PRIESTHOOD EXPOUNDED—ECONOMICS CONSIDERED

CHAPTER XXIV

THE PRELIMINARY STEPS TO THE FORTHCOMING PROSECUTION OF THE MURDERERS OF JOSEPH AND HYRUM SMITH—THE WORK IN THE SOCIETY ISLANDS—TEMPLE AFFAIRS—FINANCIAL EMBARRASSMENT

CHAPTER XXV

PROGRESS OF WORK ON THE TEMPLE—MISCELLANEOUS MOVEMENTS IN CHURCH AND STATE

CHAPTER XXVI

THE GREAT CONFERENCE OF THE SEVENTIES AT NAUVOO—ORGANIZATION OF NEW QUORUMS—DEDICATION OF THE SEVENTIES' HALL—NOTABLE DISCOURSES—DOCTRINAL INSTRUCTIONS BY PRESIDENT BRIGHAM YOUNG ON PRIESTHOOD—THE TWELVE—THE SEVENTY—AND THE BISHOPRIC

CHAPTER XXVII

CAMPAIGN AGAINST WICKEDNESS BOTH BY THE CHURCH AUTHORITIES AND THE NAUVOO CITY COUNCIL—VILLAINY OF NAUVOO'S ENEMIES

CHAPTER XXVIII

THE STORY OF CONTINUED PROGRESS OF THE CHURCH IN NAUVOO, IN EUROPE AND IN THE UNITED STATES—PLEA FOR THE RETURN OF JAMES EMMETT'S COMPANY

CHAPTER XXIX

THE JAMES EMMETT COMPANY OFFICIALLY VISITED—APRIL CONFERENCE OF 1845—MUNICIPAL CORPORATIONS UNDER GENERAL STATE LAW—WESTERN MOVEMENT PROPOSED BY GOVERNOR FORD

CHAPTER XXX

AN APPEAL TO LYMAN WIGHT TO BE UNITED WITH THE TWELVE—LETTERS TO THE PRESIDENT OF THE UNITED STATES AND THE GOVERNORS OF THE RESPECTIVE STATES—LETTERS OF GOVERNOR FORD TO STATE MILITARY LEADERS—IMPORTANT DOCTRINAL LETTER OF THE TWELVE TO THE CHURCH

CHAPTER XXXI

SUNDRY EVENTS GROUPED TOGETHER LOOKING TO AN UNDERSTANDING WITH THE STATE GOVERNMENT AT NAUVOO—HARVEST FEAST AT NAUVOO

CHAPTER XXXII

PREPARATIONS FOR WESTWARD JOURNEY—THE FINAL WORD: THE CHURCH MUST LEAVE ILLINOIS—DETAIL OF THE PLANS—AMERICAN GOVERNMENT FAILS IN THE CASE OF THE LATTER-DAY SAINTS

CHAPTER XXXIII

LAST CONFERENCE AT NAUVOO—PLEA OF THE "MOTHER OF PROPHETS"—PATHETIC

CHAPTER XXXIV

OFFICIAL MESSAGE TO THE SAINTS IN THE UNITED STATES—REMOVAL OF THE CHURCH TO THE WEST—ORGANIZATION—OLIVER COWDERY'S TENDER OF SERVICES—THE BIGELOW CASE—WARREN-YOUNG-TAYLOR OUTRAGE—THE POWER OF PRAYER *vs.* MOBOCRACY—APPEAL TO GOVERNOR FORD

CHAPTER XXXV

IMPORTANT LETTERS, FRIENDLY AND OTHERWISE—SUMMARY OF RECENT PROCEDURE IN AND ABOUT NAUVOO WITH COMMENT OF AN EDITORIAL FROM THE TIMES AND SEASONS

CHAPTER XXXVI

MURDERS BY MOBS CONTINUED—CONFESSION OF DR. ROBERT D. FOSTER—FAREWELL OF ORSON PRATT TO EASTERN SAINTS—WESTWARD BY SHIPPING—THE DURFEE MURDER CASE

CHAPTER XXXVII

DEDICATION OF PARTS OF THE TEMPLE—ENDOWMENTS GIVEN—ROMAN CATHOLIC EFFORTS TO PURCHASE THE TEMPLE AND OTHER NAUVOO PROPERTY—THE CHURCH IN ENGLAND—UNITED STATES FEDERAL CHARGES OF COUNTERFEITING AGAINST CHURCH AUTHORITIES—CHURCH PUBLICATIONS FOR 1845

CHAPTER XXXVIII

LARGE NUMBER OF PERSONS ENDOWED IN THE TEMPLE—JANUARY AND FEBRUARY, 1846—CATHOLIC CHURCH EFFORTS TO PURCHASE L. D. S. PROPERTY—FRIENDLY ATTITUDE OF JUDGE JOSIAH LAMBORN—REPEATED HOSTILE EFFORTS OF STATE OFFICIALS—DEPARTURE OF THE TWELVE HASTENED BY FALSE REPORTS CIRCULATED BY GOVERNOR FORD

CHAPTER XXXIX

DEPARTURE OF BRIGHAM YOUNG FROM NAUVOO—PROPOSITION OF "A. G. BENSON & CO."—PROPOSED CONTRACT—PUBLIC MEETING IN THE TEMPLE—MISSISSIPPI BRIDGED BY ICE—LIMITED NUMBER WHO CROSSED ON THE ICE WITH TEAMS AND FAMILIES—PETITION TO THE GOVERNOR OF IOWA—REFLECTIONS ON COMMENCEMENT OF EXODUS FROM NAUVOO

CHAPTER XL

DISCONTINUANCE OF DAILY QUOTATIONS FROM THE MANUSCRIPT HISTORY OF BRIGHAM YOUNG—SUNDRY EVENTS IN THE MARCHING ENCAMPMENT FROM THE CLOSE OF FEBRUARY TO MID-JUNE

CHAPTER XLI

THE RETURN TO WINTER QUARTERS—THE ORGANIZATION OF AND UNIVERSAL ACCEPTANCE OF THE FIRST PRESIDENCY OF THE CHURCH, BRIGHAM YOUNG, HEBER C. KIMBALL AND WILLARD RICHARDS—1847-8 PRESIDENT YOUNG'S LAST JOURNEY OVER THE PLAINS

INTRODUCTION

Volume VII is divided into six parts:

I. *Church Historians' Excerpt from Ford's History of Illinois,* pp. 1 to 31.

II. *Later Church Historians' Extension of Quotations from Ford's History of Illinois,* pp. 33 to 51.

III. *Personal Account of the Martyrdom of Joseph and Hyrum Smith by the Late President John Taylor,* pp. 53 to 126.

IV. *Second Compilation of Historical Items of Period I of Church History, From 22nd of June,* 1844, *to 8th of August,* 1844 (Compiled by Church Historians George A. Smith and Wilford Woodruff, from the Journals of Elders Willard Richards, Wilford Woodruff and others), pp. 127 to 243.

V. *Excerpts from the Manuscript History of Brigham Young from August* 9, 1844, *to October* 8, 1848—Apostolic Interregnum—Inauguration of, and Sustaining of the Second First Presidency of Three, pp. 245 to 630.

The Church Documentary History, Period I, (The History of Joseph Smith the Prophet by Himself—his daily Journal in fact), necessarily closed with Joseph's martyrdom to which was added a brief account of his obsequies, and of his various services to humanity. The Historians of the Church who brought to a close that Period, George A. Smith, cousin of the Prophet and one of the Twelve Apostles, and Wilford Woodruff, also one of the Twelve Apostles, immediately followed that close by publishing a long and unbroken excerpt from Governor Thomas Ford's *History of Illinois,* which was published in 1854, about six months after the governor's death. This posthumous work gave large space to the activities and adventures of the Prophet and his people in Illinois, from 1839 to 1846. This, in fact, constitutes about the only part of Ford's *History* that is of permanent value or importance.

George A. Smith and Wilford Woodruff's excerpt from Ford's *History of Illinois* extends from page 328 to page 354; which is about two-thirds of what the governor wrote on the Mormons. Their quotation ends in the middle of a sentence, this because they were unwilling, doubtless, to include the vicious assault upon the character of the Prophet with which the sentence ends. The saints may now, however, be indifferent to such assaults upon the character and life's work of their Prophet, since time has placed the true value upon his character and the success of his work, vindicating both; rendering the "pelting of his memory with vile epithets" as supremely vain. Besides Ford's treatise of the Mormons in Illinois has some valuable material for their history not to be had elsewhere. And the student will have the satisfaction of knowing that he has practically all that the governor-enemy of the saints has said against them, and that the Prophet's followers have not blanched from all that is written of him by this opponent. The governor closes his chapter xi with the account of the trial of the murderers of the Prophet and Patriarch with the concession that government in Illinois had failed so far as protecting the Latter-day Saints in their rights, and adds that "there can be no government in a free country where the people do not voluntarily obey the laws;" which, of course, closes his connection with the events that occurred during the lifetime of the Prophet.

For the rest of Ford's connection with the History of the Church of the Latter-day Saints, excerpts are given including official letters, etc., as the events are developed; and are chosen and used in this present edition, and constitute Part II of this volume.

Governor Ford's contributions to the history of that period are followed by a review and commentary upon them by the late President John Taylor, who was a contemporary with Governor Ford and a leading participant in those events. This constitutes Part III of this volume. It is a review and commentary of the period of highest value, a statesman-like paper, a document of highest historical value of the times; and one marvels at the high tone with which the document is planned, being dispassionate, and one might say, written unexpectedly in an impartial spirit. The balancing of the *pros* and *cons* as to the responsibility of Governor Ford for the murder of the martyred being surprisingly fair to the governor. In my study of historical documents in which judgment is rendered upon such questions, without exception I can say that I have examined nothing that is equal in spirit and justice to this review by President Taylor of Governor Ford's responsibility for the murder. The Church of Jesus Christ of Latter-day Saints can well be proud of this performance of their great Apostle and later President of the Church. It deserves to live forever.

Part IV treats the Apostolic succession to the Presidency of the Church, from the death of the Prophet to August 8, 1844, a compilation made by the Church Historians George A. Smith and Wilford Woodruff from the Journals of Elders Willard Richards and Wilford Woodruff and others. It considers, and settles the claims of guardianship to the church made by Sidney Rigdon; finally disposes of his case; and installs the Presidency of the Twelve Apostles which continued until the First Presidency of Three could be re-established.

This touches what may be regarded as an important factor in the matter of arranging the transition from one administration in the Presidency of the Church to another. On the 6th of April, 1830, it was declared that a record should be kept in the church and that in it Joseph Smith should be called a "seer, a translator, a prophet, an apostle of Jesus Christ, an elder of the church through the will of God the Father, and the grace of your Lord Jesus Christ, being inspired of the Holy Ghost to lay the foundation thereof and to build it up unto the Most Holy Faith."*

It will be recognized that there were thus provided, even on the day the church was organized, very great powers of Presidency and administrative functions for Joseph Smith in the leadership of the church.

Later the Lord referred to the matter again and that by way of warning to the Prophet: "And I have sent forth the fulness of my gospel by the hand of my servant Joseph; and in weakness have I blessed him; and I have given unto him the keys of the mystery of those things which have been sealed, even things which were from the foundation of the world, and the things which shall come from this time until the time of my coming, *if he abide in me*, and *if not, another will I plant in his stead*."†

In another revelation the Lord enlarged upon this theme as follows: "Hearken ye elders of my church, and give ear to the words which I shall speak unto you. For behold, verily, verily, I say unto you, that ye have received a commandment for a law unto my church, through him whom I have appointed unto you to receive commandments and revelation from my hand. And this ye shall know assuredly—that there is none other appointed unto you to receive commandments and revelations until he be taken *if he abide in me*. But verily, verily, I say unto you, that none else shall be appointed unto this gift except it be through him, for if it be taken from him he shall not have power except to *appoint another in his stead*."‡

This makes known the fact that though the Prophet should not even abide in the Lord he would still have power left to appoint another in his stead; and how much more would he be competent to appoint another in his stead if he continued to abide in the Lord!

This right to appoint another in his stead the Prophet Joseph exercised, occasioned by his own approaching martyrdom. At the October Conference—the 6th, 1844—the conference following the martyrdom of the Prophet—in the presence of thousands making up the congregation, President Young asked the question: "Did Joseph ordain any man to take his place? He did. Who was it? It was Hyrum [his brother], but Hyrum fell a martyr before Joseph did".§ Holding in mind that the Lord has said that the Prophet Joseph Smith should not have taken from him the splendid powers of Presidency given to him for the guidance of the church—if he would "abide in the Lord".|| And in the event of his *not* abiding in the Lord, then he should not have power—"except to appoint another in his stead." It is clear that the Prophet was acting within his rights to appoint another to succeed himself in the Presidency of the Church when he appointed

**Doctrine and Covenants*, sec. xxi:1, 2

†*Doctrine and Covenants*, sec. xxxv:17-18.

‡*Doctrine and Covenants*, sec. xliii, 1-4.

§*Times and Seasons*, October 15, 1844, p. 683

||*Doctrine and Covenants*, sec. xxxv:18

Hyrum to succeed him. For surely, if when *not* abiding in the Lord he would still have power to appoint another in the prophetic office, and to succeed him in the Presidency of the Church, much more would he have the right to make the appointment when continuing to abide in the Lord. And this power he exercised; according to President Young he even "ordained" Hyrum to succeed him; but Hyrum, according to Joseph's own statement, would not leave him.*

In like manner the Christ designated St. Peter to succeed him in the leadership of the church, by saying: "I will give unto thee the keys of the kingdom of heaven, and whatsoever thou shalt bind on earth shall be bound in heaven: and whatsoever thou shalt loose on earth shall be loosed in heaven."† Thus did the Christ before his crucifixion appoint his successor in the Presidency of the Church in that dispensation.

Thus the Prophet Joseph Smith in appointing Hyrum Smith to be his successor in the leadership of the New Dispensation Church, did but follow the example of his divine Lord. But with Hyrum Smith falling a martyr before the Prophet Joseph Smith himself did, there was, of course, an end to that appointment: it had no chance to be presented to the people for approval, which, of course, would have been necessary as in the case of all officers in the church, or before the sub-division of it over which it is proposed they should exercise presiding jurisdiction.‡ Also it amounts to certainty that had Hyrum Smith survived his brother, and his name had been presented to the church as its President, he would have been overwhelmingly sustained by the saints for the office. But Hyrum dead before the Prophet was killed, it left no one else designated for the place of President, and hence choice and reconstruction of the Presidency devolved upon the next quorum in authority—the Twelve Apostles, which also is not only the "next" quorum in authority, but also "equal" in authority to the First Presidency,§ and therefore capable of doing whatever the First Presidency could do. It was under this quorum and its authority that President Brigham Young and his fellow Apostles proceeded to their construction of the First Presidency.

Part V of volume VII constitutes the larger section of the volume and consists of transcriptions from the *Manuscript History of Brigham Young*, to the close of the year 1848, and is the most important quotation of original documents to be had covering that period of time, setting forth the administration of the Twelve Apostles under the leadership of President Young. The value of this collection from original sources is beyond instant realization. As in the quotations from the Journal of Joseph Smith in the preceding six volumes of this

*See *Comprehensive History of the Church*, Century I, vol. ii, p. 424, footnote.
†*Matt.* xvi:19.
‡*Doctrine and Covenants*, sec. xx:65; and elsewhere.
§*Doctrine and Covenants*, sec. cvii:24.

series, so this section in volume VII gives the day by day and incident by incident transactions of the Apostles, disclosing the very spirit and administrative effects of the procedure and policies of their period. It is a most profitable contribution to the annals of the Church of Jesus Christ of Latter-day Saints. In it are revealed the truly and highly spiritual and unselfish efforts of the Twelve in directing the affairs of the church to the advantage of the organization and to the welfare of the saints. Their solicitude, watchfulness and prayerful interest in all the departments of the work of God are marvelous. The missionary service of the church in all the world was universal and untiring: throughout the United States, the Pacific groups of islands, the work in England. Also the local interests: the building up of Nauvoo, the completion of the Temple, the unstinted pouring of the contributed wealth of the people into its structural completion and interior embellishment, notwithstanding that they knew they could hold possession of it but a few months, and then it must be abandoned. It was the heroic and unselfish adherence to a completion of a commandment of God.

Nor did their zeal and sacrifices go unrewarded; for from December 10th, 1845, when the first endowments were given, to the 7th of February, 1846—when the Temple was closed for ordinance work—5,669 ordinances had been performed. These mostly for full endowment ceremonies, as the church in the main knows those ordinances today. However, some baptisms for the dead merely may have been recorded in the enumeration; also there may be slight variations above or below the figures here given; as the daily numbers, from which this total is made up, are occassionally given in round numbers. But think of the work accomplished, 5,669 endowments given! After full allowance is made for all slight variations that may have occurred, the official report makes it certain that over 5,500 endowments had been given in the Nauvoo Temple! So many of the saints entrusted with the sacred mysteries of the House of the Lord!

Meantime both the officers and church membership were making every exertion to prepare the church for removal to the west in fulfillment of the predictions of the Prophet Joseph Smith sometime previous to his death. In addition to this was their contention with authorities in high station in the state, more menacing to their security than the murderous assaults of mobs. In all things there was manifested a union of spirit and effort of the Apostles that proclaimed them true disciples of the Lord. They were a perfect example of a group united in one, a well-nigh perfect unanimity of purpose and action seemed to prevail. The spirit of the Christian religion was manifested in their forebearance and long continued patience with men of restless ambition who sought to divide the people and lead away groups of them. Such men as James Emmett who led a company of people into the western wilderness; Lyman Wight one of the Quorum of the

Twelve, who led a company of people into Texas; Bishop George Miller, always restive under restraint, who broke away from the main group of the people, impatient with what he thought was the too slow action of President Young and his brethren; their patience with Wm. Smith, one of the Twelve, then, and later Patriarch to the church, and brother of the Prophet. Their action in his trying case was a model of brotherly forbearance. Their uniform kindness and care for the Mother of the Prophet exhibited a truly Christian spirit and disproves the charges against the Twelve, that are sometimes made by dissentients, of tyranny, self-aggrandizement, and inordinate, and self-seeking ambition.

In all things the Twelve manifested their faith in prayer. God was their only refuge, as manifested in their constant appeal, to him in their days of trial. No one can read the annals of this volume and be in doubt of that; in sickness, in danger; in missionary undertakings; against the violence of mobs; in coping with the cunningly devised plans of political leaders, corrupted courts and scheming adventurers —against all these forces they employed the power of faith and prayer. But read the annals of the trying years covered by this volume of the History of the Church of Jesus Christ of Latter-day Saints, and you have in hand the world's finest example of faith and trust in God through prayer. Was one sick, the others prayed; was some group wayward, and rebellious, a circle met in prayer; did influential men in high places meet to conspire against them, the brethren sought to thwart their plans by an appeal to God through prayer; was one or more unjustly haled into the courts before unjust judges, prayer softened their hearts or confused their judgments; did mobs assail, did hell rage—prayer was both sword and shield. That all this may appear I take a cross section in Nauvoo experiences for an illustration which is but characteristic of the whole period.

I select items from the record of the months of August and September, 1844—in free quotation—and set down the direct experiences which illustrate the procedure of these presiding brethren that will indicate the spirit of the work they undertook and carried through. Under date of August 10, 1844, the day following the settlement of the Twelve Apostles as the Presiding Authority of the Church—this:

"The city council subscribed about $80.00 for the aid of the police. In addition to this really inadequate compensation Brigham Young, Heber C. Kimball, George A. Smith and Hyrum Kimball relinquished their dues as councilors that the taxes might be lessened and the police be paid.* * * Daniel Spencer was elected to fill the remainder of the term of the late Mayor Joseph Smith. An ordinance was passed allowing $100.00 per year to the mayor, and $1.00 a day to the councilors and aldermen while in session. * * * Also an ordinance prohibiting brothels and for suppressing disorderly characters was passed.

Wednesday, August 14.—[Brigham Young recording the incidents throughout] I attended meeting of the Twelve, Temple Committee and Nauvoo House Committee and the stone cutters for the Temple. * * * Agreed to raise the wages of the windlass men to $1.50 per day. The meeting terminated in a feeling of renewed determination to prosecute the work on the Temple.

Thursday, August 15.—The Quorum of the Twelve Apostles met at my house. * * * The council resolved to bear off the kingdom of God in all the world in truth, virtue and holiness, and to continue to set their faces as a flint against every species of wickedness, vice and dishonesty in all its forms: I met in a prayer circle with the Twelve and a few others in the afternoon and prayed for the sick."

RECOGNIZING THE PROPHET JOSEPH'S PLACE IN THE NEW DISPENSATION

"Let no man presume for a moment that his place will be filled by another, for, remember, he stands in his own place, and always will; and the Twelve Apostles of this dispensation stand in their own place and always will both in time and eternity to minister, preside and regulate the affairs of the whole church. * * * How vain are the imaginations of the children of men to presume for a moment that the slaughter of one, two, or a hundred of the leaders of this church could destroy an organization so perfect in itself and so harmoniously arranged that it will stand while one member of it is left upon the earth."

PROPHET'S COPY OF THE NEW TRANSLATION OF THE BIBLE

"*Monday, August* 19.—Elder Willard Richards called on Emma Smith, widow of the Prophet, for the new translation of the *Bible*. She said she did not feel disposed to give it up at present.

Wednesday, August 21.—Council of the Twelve Apostles at my house to meet Elder Lyman Wight. Elder John Taylor went after him with a carriage; found him sick and unable to attend. Sociable gathering of a number of the Twelve at Wilford Woodruff's. The brethren were accompanied with their wives. Elder Woodruff was blessed and set apart for his mission to England under the hands of the members of the quorum of the Twelve Apostles present."

BAPTISM FOR THE DEAD RESUMED

Several of the Twelve Apostles were baptized for their dead this same afternoon. This (August 24th) was the first renewal of baptisms for the dead since the death of the Prophet Joseph. The ordinance took place in the temporary baptismal font in the Temple.

"*Tuesday, August* 27.—Met with the officers of the Nauvoo Legion in council. Six of the Apostles were present. The council decided that they would carry out all the views of their martyred Prophet: The brethren felt very spirited on the subject.

Thursday, August 29.—This was fast day and I attended meeting at the stand and laid hands on several of the sick.

Wednesday, September 4.—Willard Richards sick. The Twelve

Apostles and a few others met at my house in the evening and prayed for the preservation of the church and ourselves and that the Lord might bind up the apostates and preserve the honest in heart.

Thursday, September 5.—Everyone attended public prayer meeting and exposed the false prophets.

Friday, September 6.—Elder Heber C. Kimball and I visited the sick until 2 p. m.

Saturday, September 7.—Accompanied by Elder Kimball I waited upon Elder John P. Greene and attended to ordinances for him: He was on his deathbed.

Monday, September 9.—I attended council with the Quorum of the Twelve at Elder Heber C. Kimball's. Thence I went in company with Elder Kimball through the city attending to business and visiting Elder John P. Greene and Parley P. Pratt who were sick.

Monday, September 9.—[The wayward labored with] Elder Heber C. Kimball and George A. Smith labored diligently with James Emmett that he might be persuaded to desist from his intended course of taking away a party of misguided saints into the wilderness.

Friday, September 13.—In company with Brother Heber C. Kimball and his wife, Vilate, I visited Mother Lucy Smith, Mother of the Prophet.

Same day.—Reports concerning the movement of the mob who are making preparations for what they call a 'wolf hunt' on the 26th and 27th of this month. * * * They design coming and attempting to drag some more authorities of the church out to Carthage to murder them.

Saturday, September 14.—In company with Elders Heber C. Kimball and George A. Smith I called on Sister Hyrum Smith.

Elder Amasa M. Lyman being very sick and reported to be dying, Brothers Kimball and George A. Smith and I retired to my upper room (prayer room) and prayed for him; he was healed from that very hour.

Evening, visited Brother Amasa M. Lyman (sick nigh unto death).

Monday, September 16.—Building of an arsenal in Nauvoo near the Temple for housing the arms of the people. I went to the ground secured for the Arsenal. We uncovered our heads and lifted our hands to heaven and I dedicated the ground by prayer to the God of the armies of Israel. I took the spade and broke the ground for the cellar.

Thursday, September 19.—At home, waiting upon my wife who is very sick. The saints called upon me for counsel and direction.

Friday, September 20.—Attending to ordinances in behalf of the saints and laying hands on the sick. The Lord is with me continually.

Sunday, September 22.—Governor's agent arrived in Nauvoo. Elder John Taylor made affidavits against T. C. Sharp and Levi Williams, two of the murderers of Joseph Smith.

Monday, September 23.—This evening Sheriff Deming came into Nauvoo for a Mormon *posse* to take Sharp and Williams. The Twelve decided that it was imprudent to take Mormons for that purpose and advised him accordingly.

Tuesday, September 24.—I attended council at Winsor P. Lyons. Six of the brethren of the Twelve were present, and Elder Joseph Young [senior President of the Seventy]. We selected seventy presidents to preside over the seventies—over the ten quorums of the seventies then in contemplation, and fifty high priests to preside over different sections of the country.

Thursday, September 26.—The Quincy militia [state troops] were escorted about town by the Nauvoo band—(act of courtesy on the part of the Nauvoo band).

Held a council at the Temple office and appointed four watchmen to watch the Temple tonight. Some of Wight's Company have come to town and they report that they have come to deface the capitals [placed upon the columns of the Temple] and burn the lumber around the Temple.

Friday, September 27.—This was the day set apart by the anti-Mormons for the great 'wolf hunt'.

Governor's troops came into Nauvoo to revert the purpose of it and the hunt failed. Several of the staff officers of the Nauvoo Legion appeared in uniform without arms, which the governor regarded as a hint to remind him of his disarming the Legion previous to the massacre of Joseph and Hyrum Smith.

Sunday, September 29.—I attended meeting. * * * Afternoon, I went to the Seventies' Hall *and ordained* the sixty-three members of the First Quorum of Seventy to be presidents over the quorums from the second to the tenth inclusive.

Monday, September 30.—I breakfasted at Elder Heber C. Kimball's. We laid hands on the sick and visited Mother Lucy Smith.

The Twelve used their influence to prevent the brethren and sisters from attending the ball given by William Marks. The same was to come off on Wednesday evening in the dining room of the Mansion, which was still stained with the blood which flowed from Joseph and Hyrum as their bodies lay in said room preparatory to burial.

Tuesday, October 1, 1844.—Evening, attended a meeting of the Quorum of the Twelve for prayer. A very interesting session."

So throughout. These men, Apostles of the Lord Jesus Christ, were devoted to prayer and the power thereof, nor could aught shake them from that anchorage. It was *par excellence* the period of prayer in the church; and of works, too, for nothing could exceed their activity; faith and works were evenly balanced; none could be more thoroughly convinced than they that "faith without works is dead, being alone." And so faith and works went hand in hand in this period, and held a great and disinherited and expatriated people together; and transported them across the plains and over the mountains to where they found refuge from their temporary ills, and sanctuary; and place and means to lengthen their cords and strengthen their stakes—a period for development.

In no other way can men of this and future generations so well learn "the faith of their fathers", or their character, than by a study of this sector of the Church History recorded in the annals of volume VII.

I
CHURCH HISTORIANS' EXCERPTS FROM FORD'S HISTORY OF ILLINOIS

HISTORY

OF THE

CHURCH OF JESUS CHRIST

OF

LATTER-DAY SAINTS

PERIOD II

FROM THE MANUSCRIPT HISTORY OF BRIGHAM YOUNG AND OTHER ORIGINAL DOCUMENTS

CHAPTER I.

CONDITIONS IN HANCOCK COUNTY REVIEWED BY GOVERNOR FORD—THE STATE ARMS OF THE LEGION SURRENDERED ON THE DEMAND OF THE GOVERNOR

Explanation

THE following lengthy excerpt from the *History of Illinois* by Thomas Ford, Governor of that State from 1842-6 was made by the Historians of the Church of Jesus Christ of Latter-day Saints, George A. Smith and Wilford Woodruff—1862—and published in the *Millennial Star* of that year (Vol. xxiv, pp. 519-584 *passim*). It is taken from Ford's *History* in unbroken quotation from page 329 to page 354. In a brief paragraph preceding this quotation (p. 328) the governor had said in commenting upon the character of the Mormon people: "Upon the whole, if one-half of these reports had been true [i. e. reports derogatory of their character] the Mormon community must have been the most intolerable collection of rogues ever assembled; or, if one-half them were false, they were the most maligned and abused." The beginning of the Historians' excerpt:

REVIEW OF GOVERNOR FORD'S PERFORMANCES

"Governor Ford is certainly a man who performed mighty wonders. He not only compelled two innocent men, by virtue of his office as Governor of Illinois, to go before two different magistrates on the same charge, contrary to the Constitution and laws of the state; to surrender themselves into the custody of a mob magistrate (not the one who issued the writ); go to prison under a military guard on an illegal mittimus, granted contrary to law, without any examination; put in a criminal cell without having been examined for crime; brought them out of prison contrary to law; thrust them back again under the most solemn and sacred pledges of his personal faith, and the faith of the state, for their protection; guarded them with men whom he knew to be treacherous, and to have resolved on the death of the prisoners, until they were murdered in cold blood, and then professed to be 'thunderstruck'!

It is our wish to do strict justice to the memory of this heroic governor, who, in addition to the abovenamed mighty achievements, on his deathbed bequeathed to the astounded world a volume of 447 pages, entitled, '*History of Illinois* from 1818 to 1847, containing a full account of the rise, progress, and fall of Mormonism', etc., from which we copy the following:—

GOVERNOR FORD'S STATEMENT

Cause of Popular Fury.

'But the great cause of popular fury was, that the Mormons at several preceding elections had cast their vote as a unit, thereby making the fact apparent that no one could aspire to the honors or offices of the country, within the sphere of their influence, without their approbation and votes. It appears to be one of the principles by which they insist upon being governed as a community, to act as a unit in all matters of government and religion. They express themselves to be fearful that if division should be encouraged in politics, it would soon extend to their religion, and rend their church with schism and into sects.

This seems to me to be an unfortunate view of the subject, and more unfortunate in practice, as I am well satisfied that it must be the fruitful source of excitement, violence, and mobocracy, whilst it is persisted in. It is indeed unfortunate for their peace that they do not divide in elections, according to their individual preferences or political principles, like other people.

This one principle and practice of theirs arrayed against them in deadly hostility all aspirants for office who were not sure of their support, all who have been unsuccessful in elections, and all who were too proud to court their influence, with all their friends and connections.

These also were the active men in blowing up the fury of the people, in hopes that a popular movement might be set on foot which would result in the expulsion or extermination of the Mormon voters. For this purpose, public meetings had been called, inflammatory speeches had been made, exaggerated reports had been extensively circulated, committees had been appointed, who rode night and day to spread the reports, and solicit the aid of neighboring counties. And at a public meeting at Warsaw, resolutions were passed to expel or exterminate the Mormon population.

Methods of Blowing up the Fury.

This was not, however, a movement which was unanimously concurred in. The county contained a goodly number of inhabitants in favor of peace, or who at least desired to be neutral in such a contest. These were stigmatized by the name of *Jack-Mormons,* and there were not a few of the more furious exciters of the people who openly expressed their intention to involve them in the common expulsion or extermination.

A system of excitement and agitation was artfully planned and executed with tact. It consisted in spreading reports and rumors of the most fearful character.

Illustrations of False Reports.

As examples: On the morning before my arrival at Carthage [June 21, 1844], I was awakened at an early hour by the frightful report, which was asserted with confidence and apparent consternation, that the Mormons had already commenced the work of burning, destruction, and murder, and that every man capable of bearing arms was instantly wanted at Carthage for the protection of the country. We lost no time in starting; but when we arrived at Carthage we could hear no more concerning this story.

Again: during the few days that the militia were encamped at Carthage, frequent applications were made to me to send a force here and a force there, and a force all about the country, to prevent murders, robberies, and larcenies, which it was said were threatened by the Mormons. No such forces were sent, nor were any such offenses committed at that time, except the stealing of some provisions, and there was never the least proof that this was done by a Mormon.

Again: on my late visit to Hancock county, I was informed by some of their violent enemies that the larcenies of the Mormons had become unusually numerous and insufferable. They indeed admitted that but little had been done in this way in their immediate vicinity; but they insisted that sixteen horses had been stolen by the Mormons in one night, near Lima, in the county of Adams.

At the close of the expedition, I called at this same town of Lima, and upon inquiry was told that no horses had been stolen in that neighborhood, but that sixteen horses had been stolen in one night in Hancock county. This last informant being told of the Hancock story, again changed the venue to another distant settlement in the northern edge of Adams.

As my object in visiting Hancock [county] was expressly to assist in the execution of the laws, and not to violate them, or to witness or permit their violation, as I was convinced that the Mormon leaders had committed a crime in the destruction of the press, and had resisted the execution of process, I determined to exert the whole force of the state, if necessary, to bring them to justice.

Governor Ford's Zeal for the Law!

But seeing the great excitement in the public mind, and the manifest tendency of this excitement to run into mobocracy, I was of opinion that before I acted I ought to obtain a pledge from the officers and men to support me in strictly legal measures, and to protect the prisoners in case they surrendered; for I was determined, if possible, that the forms of law should not be made the catspaw of a mob, to seduce these people to a quiet surrender, as the convenient victims of popular fury.

I therefore called together the whole force then assembled at Carthage, and made an address, explaining to them what I could, and what I could not legally do, and also adducing to them various reasons why they, as well as the Mormons, should submit to the laws, and why, if they had resolved upon revolutionary proceedings, their purpose should be abandoned.

Illinois Militia Promise to Sustain Legal Procedure Only.

The assembled troops seemed much pleased with the address, and upon its conclusion the officers and men unanimously voted, with acclamation, to sustain me in a strictly legal course, and that the prisoners should be protected from violence.

Upon the arrival of additional forces from Warsaw, McDonough, and Schuyler, similar addresses were made, with the same result.

It seemed to me that these votes fully authorized me to promise the accused Mormons the protection of the law in case they surrendered.

They were accordingly duly informed that if they surrendered they would be protected, and if they did not, the whole force of the state would be called out, if necessary, to compel their submission. A force of ten men was despatched with the constable to make the arrests and to guard the prisoners to headquarters.

In the meantime, Joe Smith, as Lieutenant-General of the Nauvoo Legion, had declared martial law in the city. The Legion was assembled, and ordered under arms. The members of it residing in the country were ordered into town. The Mormon settlements obeyed the summons of their leader, and marched to his assistance. Nauvoo was one great military camp, strictly guarded and watched, and no ingress or egress was allowed except upon the strictest examination.

Martial Law in Nauvoo.

In one instance, which came to my knowledge, a citizen of McDonough, who happened to be in the city, was denied the privilege of returning until he made oath that he did not belong to the party at Carthage, that he would return home without calling at Carthage, and that he would give no information of the movement of the Mormons.

However, upon the arrival of the constable and guard, the mayor, Joseph Smith, and common council at once signified their willingness to surrender, and stated their readiness to proceed to Carthage next morning at eight o'clock. Martial law had previously been abolished.

The hour of eight o'clock came, and the accused failed to make their appearance. The constable and his escort returned. The constable made no effort to arrest any of them, nor would he or the guard delay their departure one minute beyond the time, to see whether an arrest could be made.

Upon their return they reported that they had been informed that the accused had fled and could not be found.

I immediately proposed to a council of officers to march into Nauvoo with the small force then under my command, but the officers were of opinion that it was too small, and many of them insisted upon a further call of the militia.

Upon reflection I was of opinion that the officers were right in the estimate of our force, and the project for immediate action was abandoned.

I was soon informed, however, of the conduct of the constable and guard, and then I was perfectly satisfied that a most base fraud had been attempted; that, in fact, it was feared that the Mormons would submit, and thereby entitle themselves to the protection of the law.

A Base Fraud Attempted.

It was very apparent that many of the bustling, active spirits were afraid that there would be no occasion for calling out an overwhelming militia force, for marching it into Nauvoo, for probable mutiny when there, and for the extermination of the Mormon race. It appeared that the constable and the escort were fully in the secret, and acted well their part to promote the conspiracy.

Seeing this to be the state of the case, I delayed any further call of the militia, to give the accused another opportunity to surrender, for indeed I was most anxious to avoid a general call for the militia at that critical season of the year.

The whole spring season preceding had been unusually wet. No ploughing of corn had been done, and but very little planting. The season had just changed to be suitable for ploughing. The crops which had been planted were universally suffering, and the loss of two weeks, or even of one, at that time, was likely to produce a general famine all over the country.

The wheat harvest was also approaching; and if we got into a war, there was no foreseeing when it would end, or when the militia could safely be discharged.

In addition to these considerations, all the gristmills in all that section of the country had been swept away, or disabled, by the high waters, leaving the inhabitants almost without meal or flour, and making it impossible then to procure provisions by impressment or otherwise, for the sustenance of any considerable force.

This was the time of the high waters, of astonishing floods in all the rivers and creeks in the western country. The Mississippi river at St. Louis was several feet higher than it was ever known before; it was up into the second stories of the warehouses on Water Street. The steamboats ran up to these warehouses, and could scarcely receive their passengers from the second stories. The whole American [Missouri] bottom was overflowed from eight to twenty feet deep, and steamboats freely crossed the bottom along the road from St. Louis to the opposite bluffs in Illinois. Houses and fences and stock of all kinds were swept away, the fields near the river, after the water subsided, being covered with sand from a foot to three feet deep, which was generally thrown into ridges and washed into gullies, so as to spoil the land for cultivation.

Flood Conditions.

Families had great difficulty in making their escape. Through the active exertions of Mr. Pratt, the mayor of St. Louis, steamboats were sent in every direction to their relief. The boats found many of the families on the tops of their houses, just ready to be floated away.

The inhabitants of the bottom lost nearly all their personal property. A large number of them were taken to St. Louis in a state of entire destitution, and their necessities were supplied by the contributions of the charitable of that city. A larger number were forced out on to the Illinois bluffs, where they encamped, and were supplied with provisions by the neighboring inhabitants.

This freshet nearly ruined the ancient village of Kaskaskia. The inhabitants were driven away and scattered, many of them never to return.

For many years before this flood there had been a

flourishing institution at Kaskaskia, under the direction of an order of nuns of the Catholic Church. They had erected an extensive building, which was surrounded and filled by the waters to the second story; but they were all safely taken away, pupils and all, by a steamboat which was sent to their relief, and which ran directly up to the building and received its inmates from the second story. This school was now transferred to St. Louis, where it yet remains.

All the rivers and streams in Illinois were as high, and did as much damage in proportion to their length and the extent of their bottoms, as the Mississippi.

This great flood destroyed the last hope of getting provisions at home, and I was totally without funds belonging to the state, with which to purchase at more distant markets, and there was a certainty that such purchases could not have been made on credit abroad. For these reasons I was desirous of avoiding a war, if it could be avoided.

State Arms Demanded.

In the meantime, I made a requisition upon the officers of the Nauvoo Legion for the state arms in their possession. It appears that there was no evidence in the quartermaster-general's office of the number and description of arms with which the Legion had been furnished.

Dr. Bennett, after he had been appointed quartermaster-general, had joined the Mormons, and had disposed of the public arms as he pleased, without keeping or giving any account of them.

On this subject I applied to General Wilson Law for information. He had lately been the major-general of the Legion. He had seceded from the Mormon party; was one of the owners of the proscribed press, had left the city, as he said, in fear of his life; and was one of the party asking for justice against its constituted authorities. He was interested to exaggerate the number of arms rather than to place it at too low an estimate.

From his information I learned that the Legion had

received three pieces of cannon and about two hundred and fifty stand of small arms and their accoutrements. Of these, the three pieces of cannon and two hundred and twenty stand of small arms were surrendered. These arms were demanded because the Legion was illegally used in the destruction of the press and in enforcing martial law in the city, in open resistance to legal process and the *posse comitatus.*

I demanded the surrender also on account of the great prejudice and excitement which the possession of these arms by the Mormons had kindled in the minds of the people.

A large portion of the people, by pure misrepresentation, had been made to believe that the Legion had received of the state as many as thirty pieces of artillery and five or six thousand stand of small arms, which in all probability, would soon be wielded for the conquest of the country, and for their subjection to Mormon domination.

I was of opinion that the removal of these arms would tend much to allay this excitement and prejudice, and, in point of fact, although wearing a severe aspect, would be an act of real kindness to the Mormons themselves.' "

CHAPTER II.

SUBMISSION OF THE PROPHET TO THE REQUIREMENTS OF THE GOVERNOR — GATHERING OF THE ENEMY FORCES OF THE PROPHET — GOVERNOR FORD'S DEFENSIVE JUSTIFICATION FOR HIS PLACEMENT OF THE HOSTILE FORCES AT CARTHAGE AND THE DISMISSAL OF OTHERS

" 'ON the 23rd or 24th day of June, Joe Smith, the mayor of Nauvoo, together with his brother Hyrum, and all the members of the council, and all others demanded, came into Carthage and surrendered themselves prisoners to the constable on the charge of riot.

Surrender of Nauvoo's Mayor and City Council.

They all voluntarily entered into a recognizance before the justice of the peace for their appearance at court to answer the charge, and all of them were discharged from custody except Joe and Hyrum Smith, against whom the magistrate had issued a new writ on a complaint of treason. They were immediately arrested by the constable on this charge, and retained in his custody to answer it.

The overt act of treason charged against them consisted in the alleged levying of war against the state by declaring martial law in Nauvoo, and in ordering out the Legion to resist the *posse comitatus.* Their actual guiltiness of the charge would depend upon circumstances.

If their opponents had been seeking to put the law in force in good faith, and nothing more, then an array of military force in open resistance to the *posse comitatus* and the militia of the state most probably would have amounted to treason.

But if those opponents merely intended to use the process of the law, the militia of the state, and the *posse comitatus,* as catspaws to compass the possessions of their persons for the purpose of murdering them afterwards, as the sequel demonstrated the fact to be, it might well be doubted whether they were guilty of treason.

Soon after the surrender of the Smiths, at their request I dispatched Captain Singleton with his company from Brown county to Nauvoo, to guard the town, and I authorized him to take command of the Legion. He reported to me afterwards, that he called out the Legion for inspection, and that upon two hours' notice two thousand of them assembled, all of them armed, and this after the public arms had been taken away from them. So it appears that they had a sufficiency of private arms for any reasonable purpose.

The Nauvoo Legion.

After the Smiths had been arrested on the new charge of treason, the justice of the peace postponed the examination, because neither of the parties were prepared with their witnesses for trial. In the meantime, he committed them to the jail of the county for greater security.

In all this matter the justice of the peace and constable, though humble in office, were acting in a high and independent capacity, far beyond any legal power in me to control. I considered that the executive power could only be called in to assist, and not to dictate or control their action; that in the humble sphere of their duties they were as independent, and clothed with as high authority by the law, as the executive department, and that my province was simply to aid them with the force of the state.

Question of Jurisdiction.

It is true, that so far as I could prevail on them by advice, I endeavored to do so. The prisoners were not in military custody, or prisoners of war, and I could no more legally control these officers than I could the superior courts of justice.

Some persons have supposed that I ought to have had them sent to some distant and friendly part of the state for confinement and trial, and that I ought to have searched them for concealed arms; but these surmises and suppositions are readily disposed of by the fact, that they were not my prisoners, but were the prisoners of the constable and jailor, under the direction of the justice of the peace; and, also, by the fact that by law they could be tried in no other county than Hancock.

The jail in which they were confined is a considerable stone building, containing a residence for the jailor, cells for the close and secure confinement of the prisoners, and one larger room, not so strong, but more airy and comfortable than the cells. They were put into the cells by the jailor; but upon their remonstrance and request, and by my advice, they were transferred to the larger room, and there they remained until the final catastrophe. Neither they nor I seriously apprehended an attack on the jail through the guard stationed to protect it, nor did I apprehend the least danger on their part of an attempt to escape, for I was very sure that any such an attempt would have been the signal of their immediate death. Indeed, if they had escaped, it would have been fortunate for the purposes of those who were anxious for the expulsion of the Mormon population, for the great body of that people would most assuredly have followed their Prophet and principal leaders, as they did in their flight from Missouri.

I learned afterwards that the leaders of the anti-Mormons did much to stimulate their followers to the murder of the Smiths in jail, by alleging that the governor intended to favor their escape. If this had been true, and could have been well carried out, it would have been the best way of getting rid of the Mormons. These leaders of the Mormons would never have dared to return, and they would have been followed in their flight by all their church. *I had such plan in my mind,* but I had never breathed it to a living soul, and was thus thwarted in ridding the state of the Mormons two years before they actually left, by the insane frenzy of the anti-Mormons.

Joe Smith, when he escaped from Missouri, had no difficulty in again collecting his sect about him at Nauvoo; and so the Twelve Apostles, after they had been at the head of affairs long enough to establish their authority and influence as leaders, had no difficulty in getting nearly the whole body of Mormons to follow them into the wilderness two years after the death of their pretended Prophet.

Forces at Carthage and Warsaw.

The force assembled at Carthage amounted to about twelve or thirteen hundred men, and it was calculated that four or five hundred more were assembled at Warsaw. Nearly all that portion resident in Hancock were anxious to be marched into Nauvoo.

This measure was supposed to be necessary to search for counterfeit money and the apparatus to make it, and also to strike a salutary terror into the Mormon people by an exhibition of the force of the state, and thereby prevent future outrages, murders, robberies, burnings, and the like, apprehended as the effect of Mormon vengeance on those who had taken a part against them.

On my part, at one time, this arrangement was agreed to. The morning of the 27th day of June was appointed for the march, and Golden's Point, near the Mississippi river, and about equi-distant from Nauvoo and Warsaw, was selected as the place of rendezvous.

I had determined to prevail on the justice to bring out his prisoners, and take them along. A council of officers, however, determined that this would be highly inexpedient and dangerous, and offered such substantial reasons for their opinions as induced me to change my resolution.

Two or three days' preparation had been made for this expedition. I observed that some of the people became more and more excited and inflammatory the further the preparations were advanced. Occasional threats came to my ears of destroying the city and murdering or expelling the inhabitants.

I had no objection to ease the terrors of the people by such a display of force, and was most anxious also to search for the alleged apparatus for making counterfeit money; and, in fact, to inquire into all the charges against that people, if I could have been assured of my command against mutiny and insubordination. But I gradually learned, to my entire satisfaction, that there was a plan to get the troops into Nauvoo, and there to begin the war, probably by some of our own party, or some of the seceding Mormons taking advantage of the night to fire on our own force, and then laying it on the Mormons.

Threats of Violence Within the Governor's Forces.

I was satisfied that there were those amongst us fully capable of such an act, hoping that in the alarm, bustle and confusion of a militia camp, the truth could not be discovered, and that it might lead to the desired collision.

I had many objections to be made the dupe of any such or similar artifice. I was openly and boldly opposed to any attack on the city, unless it should become necessary, to arrest prisoners legally charged and demanded. Indeed, if anyone will reflect upon the number of women, inoffensive and young persons, and innocent children, which must be contained in such a city of twelve or fifteen thousand inhabitants, it would seem to me his heart would relent and rebel against such violent resolutions. Nothing but the most blinded and obdurate fury could incite a person, even if he had the power, to the willingness of driving such persons, bare and houseless, on to the prairies, to starve, suffer, and even steal, as they must have done, for subsistence. No one who has children of his own would think of it for a moment.

Besides this, if we had been ever so much disposed to commit such an act of wickedness, we evidently had not the power to do it. I was well assured that the Mormons, at a short notice, could muster as many as two or three thousand well-armed men. We had not more than seventeen hundred, with three pieces of cannon, and about twelve hundred stand of small arms. We had provisions for two days only, and would be compelled to disband at the end of that time. To think of beginning a war under such circumstances was a plain absurdity.

Pro et con of Militia-Mob Treachery.

If the Mormons had succeeded in repulsing our attack, as most likely would have been the case, the country must necessarily be given up to their ravages until a new force could be assembled, and provisions made for its subsistence. Or if we should have succeeded in driving them from their city, they would have scattered; and, being justly incensed at our barbarity, and suffering with privation and hunger, would have spread desolation all over the country, without any possibility on our part, with the force we then had, of preventing it. Again, they would have had the advantage of being able to subsist their force in the field by plundering their enemies.

All these considerations were duly urged by me upon the attention of a council of officers, convened on the morning of the 27th of June. I also urged upon the council that such wanton and unprovoked barbarity on their part would turn the sympathy of the people in the surrounding counties in favor of the Mormons, and therefore it would be impossible to raise a volunteer militia force to protect such a people against them. Many of the officers admitted that there might be danger of collision. But such was the blind fury prevailing at the time, though not showing itself by much visible excitement, that a small majority of the council adhered to the first resolution of marching into Nauvoo; most of the officers of the Schuyler and McDonough militia voting against it, and most of those of the county of Hancock voting in its favor.

A very responsible duty now devolved upon me, to determine whether I would, as commander-in-chief, be governed by the advice of this majority. I had no hesitation in deciding that I would not; but on the contrary, I ordered the troops to be disbanded, both at Carthage and Warsaw, with the exception of three companies, two of which were retained as a guard to the jail, and the other was retained to accompany me to Nauvoo.

The officers insisted much in council upon the necessity of marching to that place to search for apparatus to make counterfeit money, and more particularly to terrify the Mormons from attempting any open or secret measures of vengeance against the citizens of the county, who had taken a part against them or their leaders.

To ease their terrors on this head, I proposed to them that I would myself proceed to the city, accompanied by a small force, make the proposed search, and deliver an address to the Mormons, and tell them plainly what degree of excitement and hatred prevailed against them in the minds of the whole people, and that if any open or secret violence should be committed on the persons or property of those who had taken part against them, that no one would doubt but that it had been perpetrated by them, and that it would be sure and certain means of the destruction of their city and the extermination of their people.

Capt. R. F. Smith and the Carthage Greys left to Guard the Prisoners.

I ordered two companies, under the command of Captain R. F. Smith, of the Carthage Greys, to guard the jail. In selecting these companies, and particularly the company of the Carthage Greys for this service, I have been subjected to some censure. It has been said that this company had already been guilty of mutiny, and had been ordered to be arrested whilst in the encampment at Carthage, and that they and their officers were the deadly enemies of the prisoners. Indeed, it would have been difficult to find friends of the prisoners under my command, unless I had called in the Mormons as a guard, and this I was satisfied would have led to the immediate war and the sure death of the prisoners.

It is true that this company had behaved badly towards the brigadier-general* in command on the occasion when the prisoners were shown along the line of the McDonough militia. This company had been ordered as a guard. They were under the belief that the prisoners, who were arrested for a capital offense, were shown to the troops in a kind of triumph, and that they had been called on as a triumphal escort to grace the procession. They also entertained a very bad feeling towards the brigadier-general who commanded their service on the occasion.

The truth is, however, that this company was never ordered to be arrested; that the Smiths were not shown to the McDonough troops as a mark of honor and triumph, but were shown to them at the urgent request of the troops themselves, to gratify their curiosity in beholding persons who had made themselves so notorious in the country.

When the Carthage Greys ascertained what was the true motive in showing the prisoners to the troops, they were perfectly satisfied. All due atonement was made on their part for their conduct to the brigadier-general, and they cheerfully returned to their duty.

The Governor's Defensive Explanations.

Although I knew that this company were the enemies of the Smiths, yet I had confidence in their loyalty and integrity, because their captain was universally spoken of as a most respectable citizen and honorable man. The company itself was an old independent company, well armed,

*This was Brigadier-General M. R. Deming, see *Millennial Star* vol. xxiv, p. 423. B. H. R.

uniformed and drilled, and the members of it were the elite of the militia of the county.*

I relied upon this company especially because it was an independent company, for a long time instructed and practiced in military discipline and subordination. I also had their word and honor, officers and men, to do their duty according to law.

Besides all this, the officers and most of the men resided in Carthage, in the near vicinity of Nauvoo, and, as I thought, must know that they would make themselves and their property convenient and conspicuous marks of Mormon vengeance in case they were guilty of treachery.

I had at first intended to select a guard from the county of McDonough, but the militia of that county were very much dissatisfied to remain; their crops were suffering at home, they were in a perfect fever to be discharged, and I was destitute of provisions to supply them for more than a few days. They were far from

*The reader should be reminded that these statements of Governor Ford in justification of his placing the Carthage Greys on guard at the prison with Captain Robert F. Smith in command, is a labored defense written some years after the events, and for the purpose of justifying his course of procedure. A very lame and impotent defense it is. The governor should have remembered that in addition to the rebellious conduct of this company of Carthage Greys on the occasion of Joseph Smith and his brother Hyrum being introduced to the McDonough troops, there was the likewise boisterous reception of the Prophet and his company the night they arrived at Carthage, and under the very window of the hotel where the governor lodged, and within his hearing. On that occasion they exclaimed: "Where is the damned prophet?" "Stand away, you McDonough boys, and let us shoot the damned Mormons." "G—d— you, old Joe, we've got you now." "Clear the way and let us have a view of Joe Smith, the prophet of God. He has seen the last of Nauvoo. We'll use him up now, and kill all the damned Mormons." The rear platoon of the Carthage Greys repeatedly threw their guns over their heads in a curve so that the bayonets struck the ground with the breech of their guns upward, when they would run back and pick them up at the same time whooping, yelling, hooting and cursing like a pack of savages. Governor Ford was a witness of all this. For on hearing the above expressions, he put his head out of the window of the Hamilton Hotel at which he was stopping and very fawningly said, "I know your anxiety to see Mr. Smith, which is natural enough, but it is quite too late tonight for you to have the opportunity, but I assure you, gentlemen, you shall have that privilege tomorrow morning, as I will cause him to pass before the troops upon the square, and I now wish you, with this assurance quietly and peaceably to return to your quarters." When this declaration was made there was a faint "Hurrah for Tom Ford", and they instantly obeyed his wish. From all which it must appear that the governor could not fail but know the style of character of this company of militia, made up perhaps of the bitterest enemies of the Prophet and the Mormon people (See vol. vi, this *History*, Period I, pp. 559-60). B. H. R.

home, where they could not supply themselves, whilst the Carthage company could board at their own houses, and would be put to little inconvenience in comparison.

What gave me greater confidence in the selection of this company as a prudent measure was, that the selection was first suggested and urged by the brigadier-general in command, who was well known to be utterly hostile to all mobocracy and violence towards the prisoners, and who was openly charged by the violent party with being on the side of the Mormons.

At any rate, I knew that the jail would have to be guarded as long as the prisoners were confined; that an imprisonment for treason might last the whole summer and the greater part of the autumn before a trial could be had in the circuit court; that it would be utterly impossible, in the circumstances of the country, to keep a force there from a foreign county for so long a time; and that a time must surely come when the duty of guarding the jail would necessarily devolve on the citizens of the county.

It is true, also, that at this time I had not believed or suspected that any attack was to be made upon the prisoners in jail. It is true that I was aware that a great deal of hatred existed against them, and that there were those who would do them an injury if they could. I had heard of some threats being made, but none of an attack upon the prisoners whilst in jail. These threats seemed to be made by individuals not acting in concert. They were no more than the bluster which might have been expected, and furnished no indication of numbers combining for this or any other purpose.

I must here be permitted to say, also, that frequent appeals had been made to me to make a clean and thorough work of the matter by exterminating the Mormons or expelling them from the state. An opinion seemed generally to prevail that the sanction of executive authority would legalize the act; and all persons of any influence, authority, or note, who conversed with me on the subject, frequently and repeatedly stated their total unwillingness to act without my direction, or in any mode except according to law.

This was a circumstance well calculated to conceal from me the secret machinations on foot. I had constantly contended against violent measures, and so had the brigadier-general in command; and I am convinced that unusual pains were taken to conceal from both of us the secret measures resolved upon. It has been said, however, that some person named 'Williams',* in a public speech at Carthage, called for volunteers to murder the Smiths, and that I ought to have had him arrested. Whether such a speech was really made or not is yet unknown to me.' "

*Yet so prominent was this "some person named 'Williams' " that he was the "Colonel Levi Williams" in charge of the mob forces from Warsaw (See *History of Hancock County*, Gregg. p. 324). B. H. R.

CHAPTER III.

GOVERNOR FORD'S VISIT TO NAUVOO—FEARS ON THE WAY — INSULTING SPEECH TO THE CITIZENS — RESENTED — HEARS OF THE ASSASSINATION OF JOSEPH AND HYRUM SMITH

" 'HAVING ordered the guard, and left General Deming in command in Carthage, and discharged the residue of the militia, I immediately departed for Nauvoo, eighteen miles distant, accompanied by Colonel Buckmaster, quartermaster-general, and Captain Dunn's company of dragoons.

Uncertainty of the Reflections and Actions of Governor Ford.

After we had proceeded four miles, Colonel Buckmaster intimated to me a suspicion that an attack would be made upon the jail. He stated the matter as a mere suspicion, arising from having seen two persons converse together at Carthage with some air of mystery. I myself entertained no suspicion of such an attack; *at any rate, none before the next day in the afternoon,** because it was notorious that we had departed from Carthage with the declared intention of being absent at least two days.† I could not believe that any person would attack the jail whilst we were in Nauvoo, and thereby expose my life and the life of my companions to the sudden vengeance of the Mormons upon hearing of the death of their leaders. Nevertheless, acting upon

*Italics are the Church Historians', George A Smith and Wilford Woodruff. B. H. R.

†The governor is most unfortunate here in his admissions that he did not expect an attack "until the afternoon of the next day" following his departure for Nauvoo; for since he had made provision for being absent in Nauvoo "two days" then he did expect, from the language he here uses, that an attack would be made upon the jail and the prisoners on the second day after his departure, and while he would still be absent from Carthage. B. H. R.

the principle of providing against mere possibilities, I sent back one of the company with a special order to Captain Smith to guard the jail strictly, and at the peril of his life, until my return.

We proceeded on our journey four miles further. By this time I had convinced myself that no attack would be made on the jail that day or night. I supposed that a regard for my safety, and the safety of my companions, would prevent an attack until those to be engaged in it could be assured of our departure from Nauvoo. I still think that this ought to have appeared to me to be a reasonable supposition.

I therefore determined at this point to omit making the search for counterfeit money at Nauvoo, and defer an examination of all the other abominations charged on that people, in order to return to Carthage that same night, that I might be on the ground, in person, in time to prevent an attack upon the jail, if any had been meditated. To this end we called a halt; the baggage wagons were ordered to remain where they were until towards evening, and then return to Carthage.

Having made these arrangements, we proceeded on our march, and arrived at Nauvoo about four o'clock of the afternoon of the 27th day of June. As soon as notice could be given, a crowd of the citizens assembled to hear an address which I proposed to deliver to them. The number present has been variously estimated from one to five thousand.

Governor Ford in Nauvoo.

In this address I stated to them how and in what their functionaries had violated the laws; also the many scandalous reports in circulation against them, and that these reports, whether true or false, were generally believed by the people. I distinctly stated to them the amount of hatred and prejudice which prevailed everywhere against them, and the causes of it, at length.

I also told them, plainly and emphatically, that if any vengeance should be attempted openly or secretly against the persons or property of the citizens who had taken part against their leaders, that the public hatred and excitement was such, that thousands would assemble for the total destruction of their city and the extermination of their people, and that no power in the state would be able to prevent it.

People of Nauvoo Resent Charges.

During this address some impatience and resentment were manifested by the Mormons at the recital of the various reports enumerated concerning them, which they strenuously and indignantly denied to be true. They claimed to be a law-abiding people, and insisted that as they looked to the law alone for their protection, so were they careful themselves to observe its provisions.

Upon the conclusion of this address I proposed to take a vote on the question, whether they would strictly observe the laws even in opposition to their Prophet and leaders. The vote was unanimous in favor of this proposition.

The anti-Mormons contended that such a vote from the Mormons signified nothing; and truly the subsequent history of that people showed clearly that they were loudest in their professions of attachment to the law whenever they were guilty of the greatest extravagancies; and, in fact, that they were so ignorant and stupid about matters of law that they had no means of judging of the legality of their conduct only as they were instructed by their spiritual leaders.*

Word of the Assassination of the Prophet Received.

A short time before sundown we departed on our return to Carthage. When we had proceeded two miles, we met two individuals, one of them a Mormon, who informed us that the Smiths had been assassinated in jail, about five or six o'clock of that day. The intelligence seemed to strike every one with a kind of dumbness. As to

*Governor Ford is not justified in making these observations based on anything in the "subsequent history" of the people. Examination of their conduct in "subsequent history" will reveal the fact that they had as an intelligent understanding of law as a community, far exceeding the average of American community in respect to things of the law. B. H. R.

myself it was perfectly astounding, and I anticipated the very worst consequences from it.

The Mormons had been represented to me as a lawless, infatuated and fanatical people, not governed by the ordinary motives which influence the rest of mankind. If so, most likely an exterminating war would ensue, and the whole land would be covered with desolation.

Acting upon this supposition, it was my duty to provide as well as I could for the event. I therefore ordered the two messengers into custody, and to be returned with us to Carthage. This was done to get time to make such arrangements as could be made, and to prevent any sudden explosion of Mormon excitement before they could be written to by their friends at Carthage.

I also dispatched messengers to Warsaw, to advise the citizens of the event. But the people there knew all about the matter before my messengers arrived. They, like myself, anticipated a general attack all over the country. The women and children were removed across the river, and a committee was dispatched that night to Quincy for assistance.

The next morning, by daylight, the ringing of the bells in the city of Quincy announced a public meeting. The people assembled in great numbers at an early hour. The Warsaw committee stated to the meeting that a party of Mormons had attempted to rescue the Smiths out of jail; that a party of Missourians and others had killed the prisoners to prevent their escape; that the governor and his party were at Nauvoo at the time when intelligence of the fact was brought there; that they had been attacked by the Nauvoo Legion, and had retreated to a house where they were then closely besieged; that the governor had sent out word that he could maintain his position for two days, and would be certain to be massacred if assistance did not arrive by the end of that time.

False Rumors at Quincy and Warsaw.

It is unnecessary to say that this entire story was a fabrication. It was of a piece with the other reports put into circulation by the anti-Mormon party, to influence the public mind and call the people to their assistance. The effect of it, however, was that by ten o'clock on the 28th of June, between two and three hundred men from Quincy, under the command of Major Flood, embarked on board of a steamboat for Nauvoo, to assist in raising the siege, as they honestly believed.

As for myself, I was well convinced that those, whoever they were, who assassinated the Smiths, meditated in turn my assassination by the Mormons. The very circumstances of the case fully corroborated the information which I afterwards received, that upon consultation of the assassins it was agreed amongst them that the murder must be committed whilst the governor was at Nauvoo; that the Mormons would naturally suppose that he had planned it; and that in the first outpouring of their indignation they would assassinate him by way of retaliation; and that thus they would get clear [rid] of the Smiths and the governor all at once. They also supposed, that if they could so contrive the matter as to have the governor of the state assassinated by the Mormons, the public excitement would be greatly increased against that people, and would result in their expulsion from the state at least.

Upon hearing of the assassination of the Smiths, I was sensible that my command was at an end, that my destruction was meditated as well as that of the Mormons, and that I could not reasonably confide longer in the one party or in the other.

The Governor's Plight.

The question then arose, what would be proper to be done. A war was expected by everybody. I was desirous of preserving the peace. I could not put myself at the head of the Mormon force with any kind of propriety, and without exciting greater odium against them than already existed. I could not put myself at the head of the anti-Mormon party, because they had justly forfeited my confidence, and my command over them was put an end to by mutiny and treachery. I could not put myself at the head of either of these forces, because both of them in turn had violated the law, and, as I then believed, meditated further aggression. It appeared to me that if a war ensued, I ought to have a force in which I could confide, and that I ought to establish my headquarters at a place where I could learn the truth as to what was going on.

For these reasons I determined to proceed to Quincy, a place favorably situated for receiving the earliest intelligence, for issuing orders to raise an army if necessary, and for providing supplies for its subsistence. But first, I determined to return back to Carthage and make such arrangements as could be made for the pacification and defense of the country.

The Governor Establishes Headquarters at Quincy.

When I arrived there, about ten o'clock at night, I found that great consternation prevailed. Many of the citizens had departed with their families, and others were preparing to go. As the country was utterly defenseless, this seemed to me to be a proper precaution. One company of the guard stationed by me to guard the jail had disbanded and gone home before the jail was attacked, and many of the Carthage Greys departed soon afterwards.

General Deming, who was absent in the country during the murder, had returned. He volunteered to remain in command of a few men, with orders to guard the town, observe the progress of events, and to retreat if menaced by a superior force.

Here, also, I found Dr. Richards and John Taylor, two of the principal Mormon leaders, who had been in the jail at the time of the attack, and who voluntarily addressed a most pacific exhortation to their fellow citizens, which was the first intelligence of the murder which was received at Nauvoo. I think it very probable that the subsequent good conduct of the Mormons is attributable to the arrest of the messengers, and to the influence of this letter.

Having made these arrangements, I departed for Quincy. On my road thither, I heard of a body of militia marching from Schuyler, and another from Brown [counties]. It appears that orders had been sent out in my name, but without my knowledge, for the militia of Schuyler county. I immediately countermanded their march, and they returned to their homes.

When I arrived at Columbus, I found that Captain Jonas had raised a company of one hundred men, who were just ready to march. By my advice they postponed their march to await further orders.

I arrived at Quincy on the morning of the 29th of June, about eight o'clock, and immediately issued orders, provisionally, for raising an imposing force, when it should seem to be necessary.

I remained at Quincy for about one month, during which time a committee from Warsaw waited on me, with a written request that I would expel the Mormons from the state. It seemed that it never occurred to these gentlemen that I had no power to exile a citizen; but they insisted that if this were not done, their party would abandon the state. This requisition was refused, of course.

Demands Upon the Governor to Expel the Saints from Illinois.

During this time also, with the view of saving expense, keeping the peace, and having a force which would be removed from the prejudices in the country, I made application to the United States for five hundred men of the regular army, to be stationed for a time in Hancock county, which was subsequently refused.*

*The application here referred to by Governor Ford was unquestionably mere subterfuge. It is true he made application for a United States force of 500 men, but he made it in such form that it could not be otherwise than that he knew that the requisition would not be granted, for he made application for it at the wrong source; namely he wrote to Colonel S. W. Kearney (U. S. A.) Commander of the Third Military Department of the United States, at St. Louis, and made the appli-

During this time also, I had secret agents amongst all parties, observing their movements, and was accurately informed of everything that was meditated on both sides. It appeared that the anti-Mormon party had not relinquished their hostility to the Mormons, nor their determination to expel them, but had deferred further operations until the fall season, after they had finished their summer's work on their farms.

When I first went to Carthage, and during all this difficult business, no public officer ever acted from purer or more patriotic intentions than I did. I was perfectly conscious of the utmost integrity in all my actions, and felt lifted up far above all mere party considerations. But I had scarcely arrived at the scene of action before the whig press commenced the most violent abuse, and attributed to me the basest motives.

Perplexities of Governor Ford —Political Parties.

It was alleged in the *Sangamon Journal*, and repeated in the other whig newspapers, that the governor had merely gone over to cement an alliance with the Mormons; that the leaders would not be brought to punishment, but that a full privilege would be accorded to them to commit crimes of every hue and grade, in return for their support of the democratic party. I mention this not by way of complaint, for it is only the privilege of the minority to complain, but for its influence upon the people.

I observed that I was narrowly watched in all my proceedings by my whig fellow citizens, and was suspected of an intention to favor the Mormons.

I felt that I did not possess the confidence of the

cation for the above mentioned force to him instead of making application to the President of the United States; and this fact General Kearney mentioned in his letter replying to Governor Ford, a copy of which reply Governor Ford included in his letter to the General Authorities of the Church at Nauvoo. Kearney's letter bears date of July 11, 1844, and in it he said to Governor Ford: "I have not the power of complying with your request, but will forward by tomorrow's mail a copy of your communication to be read before the authorities in Washington City." The letter of Governor Ford, explaining this matter, including also Kearney's letter will be found in *The Comprehensive History of the Church of Jesus Christ of Latter-day Saints*, Century I, vol. ii, pp. 302-7. B. H. R.

men I commanded, and that they had been induced to withhold it by the promulgation of the most abominable falsehoods.

I felt the necessity of possessing their confidence, in order to give vigor to my action, and exerted myself in every way to obtain it, so that I could control the excited multitude who were under my command. I succeeded better for a time than could have been expected; but who can control the action of a mob without possessing their entire confidence?

It is true, also, that some unprincipled democrats all the time appeared to be very busy on the side of the Mormons, and this circumstance was well calculated to increase suspicion of every one who had the name of democrat.

Movements of the Mob from Warsaw.

It was many days after the assassination of the Smiths before the circumstances of the murder fully became known. It then appeared that, agreeably to previous orders, the *posse* at Warsaw had marched on the morning of the 27th of June in the direction of Golden's Point, with a view to join the force from Carthage, the whole body then to be marched into Nauvoo.

But by the time they had gone eight miles, they were met by the order to disband; and learning at the same time that the governor was absent at Nauvoo, about two hundred of these men, many of them being disguised by blacking their faces with powder and mud, hastened immediately to Carthage.

There they encamped, at some distance from the village, and soon learned that one of the companies left as a guard had disbanded and returned to their homes. The other company, the Carthage Greys, was stationed by the captain in the public square, a hundred and fifty yards from the jail, whilst eight men were detailed by him, under the command of Sergeant Franklin A. Worrell, to guard the prisoners.

A Communication was soon established between the conspirators and the company, and it was arranged that the guard should have their guns charged with blank cartridges, and fire at the assailants when they attempted to enter the jail.

The Attack Upon the Prison.

General Deming, who was left in command, being deserted by some of his troops, and perceiving the arrangement with the others, and having no force upon which he could rely, for fear of his life retired from the village.

The conspirators came up, jumped the slight fence around the jail, were fired upon by the guard, which, according to arrangement, was overpowered immediately, and the assailants entered the prison, to the door of the room where the two prisoners were confined, with two of their friends, who voluntarily bore them company.

An attempt was made to break open the door, but Joe Smith being armed with a six-barrelled pistol, furnished by his friends, fired several times as the door was bursted open, and wounded three of the assailants. At the same time several shots were fired into the room, by some of which John Taylor received four wounds, and Hyrum Smith was instantly killed.

Joe Smith now attempted to escape by jumping out of the second story window, but the fall so stunned him that he was unable to rise; and being placed in a sitting posture by the conspirators below, they dispatched him with four balls shot through his body.

Thus fell Joe Smith, the most successful impostor in modern times*.' " * * * * *

*Here ends the former Church Historians' (George A. Smith and Wilford Woodruff) quotation from Ford's *History of Illinois*. B. H. R.

II

EXTENSION OF QUOTATIONS FROM FORD'S *HISTORY OF ILLINOIS*

Explanation

THE former Historians of the Church, George A. Smith and Wilford Woodruff (see *Millennial Star*, Vol. xxiv, p. 584, 1862) end their quotation from Ford's *History of Illinois* at p. 354, and in the middle of an unfinished sentence. There are other matters however in the book that should be preserved to history, which deal with subsequent events of Mormon affairs in Hancock county, and as it is not likely that Ford's *History of Illinois* will ever be published again, and inasmuch also as his treatise upon Mormon affairs is the most important part of the book, we shall do a service both to the History of the Church and to the History of Illinois by publishing further excerpts. These quotations will make up chapters iv and v.

CHAPTER IV.

GOVERNOR FORD'S COMMENTS ON THE CHARACTER OF JOSEPH SMITH AND HIS FOLLOWERS—HIS CONJECTURES ON THE FUTURE OF MORMONISM

IT is necessary to repeat the part of the sentence with which the last chapter closed:

"Thus fell Joe Smith, the most successful impostor in modern times; a man who though ignorant and coarse, had some great natural parts, which fitted him for temporary success, but which were so obscured and counteracted by the inherent corruption and vices of his nature that he never could succeed in establishing a system of policy which looked to permanent success in the future.* His lusts, his love of money and power, always set him to studying present gratification and convenience, rather than the remote consequences of his plans. It seems that no power of intellect can save a corrupt man from this error. The strong cravings of the animal nature will never give fair play to a fine understanding, the judgment is never allowed

Governor Ford's Estimate of the Prophet's Character.

*In the light of the signal success which has attended upon the church which Joseph Smith under God founded, after one hundred years of existence, his followers may smile now at this pronouncement of his enemy, Governor Thomas Ford; as also they may quote without fear of creating disparagement for the Prophet the unfavorable estimate of his character. Joseph Smith belongs now to the ages; and nothing that Governor Ford said, or that any of his enemies have said could stay his triumphant march to an honorable place in the world's history, or prevent the church he founded from winning a permanent place in the world that is the astonishment of the thoughtful. "Traitors and tyrants now fight him in vain."

"The man who established a religion in this age of free debate, who was and is today accepted by hundreds of thousands [three quarters of a million now living, to say nothing of the hundreds of thousands of faithful disciples who have died in the faith within the first century of the existence of the church founded by him] as a direct emissary of the Most High—such a rare human being is not to be disposed of by pelting his memory with unsavory epithets" (*Figures of the Past*, "Joseph Smith at Nauvoo", Josiah Quincy, p. 376, Ed. 1901). B. H. R.

to choose that good which is far away, in preference to enticing evil near at hand. And this may be considered a wise ordinance of Providence, by which the counsels of talented but corrupt men, are defeated in the very act which promised success.

Characterization of Joseph Smith.

It must not be supposed that the pretended Prophet practiced the tricks of a common impostor; that he was a dark and gloomy person, with a long beard, a grave and severe aspect, and a reserved and saintly carriage of his person; on the contrary, he was full of levity, even to boyism romping; dressed like a dandy, and at times drank like a sailor and swore like a pirate. He could, as occasion required, be exceedingly meek in his deportment; and then again rough and boisterous as a highway robber; being always able to satisfy his followers of the propriety of his conduct. He always quailed before power, and was arrogant to weakness. At times he could put on the air of a penitent, as if feeling the deepest humiliation for his sins, and suffering unutterable anguish, and indulging in the most gloomy forebodings of eternal woe. At such times he would call for the prayers of the brethren in his behalf, with a wild and fearful energy and earnestness. He was full six feet high, strongly built, and uncommonly well muscled. No doubt he was as much indebted for his influence over an ignorant people, to the superiority of his physical vigor, as to his greater cunning and intellect.

Character of the Followers of Joseph Smith.

His followers were divided into the leaders and the led; the first division embraced a numerous class of broken-down, unprincipled men of talents, to be found in every country, who, bankrupt in character and fortune, had nothing to lose by deserting the known religions, and carving out a new one of their own. They were mostly infidels, who holding all religions in derision, believed that they had as good a right as Christ or Mahomet, or any of the founders of former systems, to create one for themselves; and if they could impose it upon mankind, to live upon the labor of their dupes. Those of the second division, were the credulous wondering part of men, whose easy belief and admiring natures, are always the victims of novelty, in whatever shape it may come, who have a capacity to believe any strange and wonderful matter, if it only be new, whilst the wonders of former ages command neither faith nor reverence; they were men of feeble purposes, readily subjected to the will of the strong, giving themselves up entirely to the direction of their leaders; and this accounts for the very great influence of those leaders in controlling them. In other respects some of the Mormons were abandoned rogues, who had taken shelter in Nauvoo, as a convenient place for the headquarters of their villainy; and others were good, honest, industrious people, who were the sincere victims of an artful delusion. Such as these were more the proper objects of pity than persecution. With them, their religious belief was a kind of insanity; and certainly no greater calamity can befall a human being, than to have a mind so constituted as to be made the sincere dupe of a religious impostor. * * *

* * * The world now indulged in various conjectures as to the further progress of the Mormon religion. By some persons it was believed that it would perish and die away with its founder. But upon the principle that 'the blood of the martyrs is the seed of the church', there was now really more cause than ever to predict its success. The murder of the Smiths, instead of putting an end to the delusion of the Mormons and dispersing them, as many believed it would, only bound them together closer than ever, gave them new confidence in their faith and an increased fanaticism.

World's Conjecture of the Mormon Religion.

The Mormon Church had been organized with a First Presidency, composed of Joe and Hyrum Smith and Sidney Rigdon, and Twelve Apostles of Jesus

Christ. The Twelve Apostles were now absent, and until they could be called together the minds of the 'saints' were unsettled, as to the future government of the church. Revelations were published that the Prophet, in imitation of the Savior, was to rise again from the dead. Many were looking in gaping wonderment for the fulfilment of this revelation, and some reported that they had already seen him, attended by a celestial army coursing the air on a great white horse.* Rigdon, as the only remaining member of the First Presidency, claimed the government of the church, as being successor to the Prophet. When the Twelve Apostles returned from foreign parts, a fierce struggle for power ensued between them and Rigdon. Rigdon fortified his pretensions by alleging the will of the Prophet in his favor, and pretending to have several new revelations from heaven, amongst which was one of a very impolitic nature. This was to the effect, that all the wealthy Mormons were to break up their residence at Nauvoo, and follow him to Pittsburg. This revelation put both the rich and the poor against him. The rich, because they did not want to leave their property; and the poor, because they would not be deserted by the wealthy. This was fatal to the ambition of Rigdon; and the Mormons, tired of the despotism of a one-man government, were now willing to decide in favor of the Apostles. Rigdon was expelled from the church as being a false prophet, and left the field with a few followers, to establish a little delusion of his own, near Pittsburg; leaving the government of the main church in the hands of the Apostles, with Brigham Young, a cunning but vulgar man, at their head, occupying the place of Peter in the Christian hierarchy.

Settlement of the Question of Church Leadership.

Missionaries were dispatched to all parts to preach

*No such revelation is extant; and I know of no other writing where it is to be found. B. H. R.

in the name of the 'martyred Joseph'; and the Mormon religion thrived more than ever. For a while it was doubtful whether the reign of the military saints in Nauvoo would not in course of time supplant the meek and lowly system of Christ. There were many things to favor their success. The different Christian sects had lost much of the fiery energy by which at first they were animated. They had attained to a more subdued, sober, learned, and intellectual religion. But there is at all times a large class of mankind who will never be satisfied with anything in devotion, short of a heated and wild fanaticism. The Mormons were the greatest zealots, the most confident in their faith, and filled with a wilder, fiercer, and more enterprising enthusiasm, than any sect on the continent of America; their religion gave promise of more temporal and spiritual advantages for less labor, and with less personal sacrifice of passion, lust, prejudice, malice, hatred, and ill will, than any other perhaps in the whole world. Their missionaries abroad, to the number of two or three thousand,* were most earnest and indefatigable in their efforts to make converts; compassing sea and land to make one proselyte. When abroad, they first preached doctrines somewhat like those of the Campbellites; Sidney Rigdon, the inventor of the system, having once been a Campbellite preacher; and when they had made a favorable impression, they began in far-off allusions to open up their mysteries, and to reveal to their disciples that a perfect 'fulness of the gospel' must be expected. This 'fulness of the gospel' was looked for by the dreamy and wondering disciple, as an indefinite something not yet to be comprehended, but which was essential to complete happiness and salvation. He was then told that God required him to remove to the place of gathering, where alone this sublime 'fulness of the gospel' could be fully revealed, and completely enjoyed. When he arrived at the place of gathering,

Launching of Missionary Activities.

*If this means at one time, it is a gross exaggeration. B. H. R.

he was fortified in the new faith by being withdrawn from all other influences; and by seeing and hearing nothing but Mormons and Mormonism; and by association with those only who never doubted any of the Mormon dogmas. Now the 'fulness of the gospel' could be safely made known. If it required him to submit to the most intolerable despotism; if it tolerated and encouraged the lusts of the flesh and a plurality of wives; if it claimed all the world for the saints; universal dominion for the Mormon leaders; if it sanctioned murder, robbery, perjury, and larceny, at the command of their priests, no one could now doubt but that this was the 'fulness of the gospel', the liberty of the saints, with which Christ had made them free.

Possible Future of Mormonism.

The Christian world, which has hitherto regarded Mormonism with silent contempt, unhappily may yet have cause to fear its rapid increase. Modern society is full of material for such a religion. At the death of the Prophet, fourteen years after the first Mormon Church was organized, the Mormons in all the world numbered about two hundred thousand souls (one-half million according to their statistics); a number equal, perhaps, to the number of Christians, when the Christian Church was of the same age.* It is to be feared that in course of a century, some gifted man like Paul, some splendid orator, who will be able by his eloquence to attract crowds of the thousands who are ever ready to hear, and be carried away by, the sounding brass and tinkling cymbal of sparkling oratory, may command a hearing, may succeed in breathing a new life into this modern Mahometanism, and make the name of the martyred Joseph ring as loud, and stir the souls of men as much, as the mighty name of Christ itself. Sharon, Palmyra, Manchester, Kirtland, Far West, Adamon Diahmon [Adam-ondi-Ahman], Ramus, Nauvoo, and the Carthage Jail, may become holy and

*Needless to say, these numbers are great exaggerations. B. H. R.

venerable names, places of classic interest, in another age; like Jerusalem, the Garden of Gethsemane, the Mount of Olives, and Mount Calvary to the Christian, and Mecca and Medina to the Turk. And in that event, the author of this *History* feels degraded by the reflection, that the humble governor of an obscure state, who would otherwise be forgotten in a few years, stands a fair chance, like Pilate and Herod, by their official connection with the true religion, of being dragged down to posterity with an immortal name, hitched on to the memory of a miserable impostor. There may be those whose ambition would lead them to desire an immortal name in history, even in those humbling terms. I am not one of that number.

About one year after the Apostles were installed into power, they abandoned for the present the project of converting the world to the new religion. All the missionaries and members abroad were ordered home; it was announced that the world had rejected the gospel by the murder of the Prophet and Patriarch, and was to be left to perish in its sins. In the meantime, both before and after this, the elders at Nauvoo quit preaching about religion. The Mormons came from every part, pouring into the city; the congregations were regularly called together for worship, but instead of expounding the new gospel, the zealous and infuriated preachers now indulged only in curses and strains of abuse of the Gentiles, and it seemed to be their design to fill their followers with the greatest amount of hatred to all mankind excepting the 'saints'. A sermon was no more than an inflammatory stump speech, relating to their quarrels with their enemies, and ornamented with an abundance of profanity. From my own personal knowledge of this people, I can say with truth, that I have never known much of any of their leaders who was not addicted to profane swearing. No other kind of discourses than these were heard in the city. Curses upon their enemies, upon the country, upon government, upon all public officers, were now the lessons taught by the elders, to inflame their people with the highest degree of spite and malice against all who were not of the Mormon Church, or its obsequious tools. The reader can readily imagine how a city of fifteen thousand inhabitants could be wrought up and kept in a continual rage by the inflammatory harangues of its leaders.*

In the meantime, the anti-Mormons were not idle; they were more than ever determined to expel the Mormons; and being passionately inflamed against them, they made many applications for executive assistance. On the other hand, the Mormons invoked the assistance of government to take vengeance upon the murderers of the Smiths. The anti-Mormons asked the governor to violate the Constitution, which he was sworn to support, by erecting himself into a military despot and exiling the Mormons. The Mormons, on their part, in their newspapers, invited the governor to assume absolute power, by taking a summary vengeance upon their enemies, by shooting fifty or a hundred of them, without judge or jury. Both parties were thoroughly disgusted with constitutional provisions restraining them from the summary attainment of their wishes for vengeance; each was ready to submit to arbitrary power, to the fiat of a dictator, to make me a king for the time being, or at least that I might exercise the power of a king, to abolish both the forms and spirit of free government, if the despotism to be erected upon its ruins could only be wielded for its benefit, and to take vengeance on its enemies. It seems that, notwithstanding all our strong professions of attachment to liberty, there is all the time an unconquerable leaning to the principles of monarchy and despotism, whenever the forms, the delays, and the restraints of republican government fail to correct

Demand and Counter-Demand.

Reflections of Governor Ford.

*Reference to Part V of this volume where much of the preaching of the Apostles is given both in synopses of discourses and verbatim reports will prove how utterly untrue the above statements of Governor Ford are. B. H. R.

great evils. When the forms of government in the United States were first invented, the public liberty was thought to be the great object of governmental protection. Our ancestors studied to prevent government from doing harm, by depriving it of power. They would not trust the power of exiling a citizen upon any terms; or of taking his life, without a fair and impartial trial in the courts, even to the people themselves, much less to their government. But so infatuated were these parties, so deep did they feel their grievances, that both of them were enraged in their turn, because the governor firmly adhered to his oath of office; refusing to be a party to their revolutionary proceedings; to set aside the government of the country, and execute summary vengeance upon one or the other of them."

CHAPTER V.

POLITICAL CONSIDERATIONS OF THE PERIOD FOLLOWING THE DEATH OF THE PROPHET—"TRIAL" OF THE MURDERERS — STATUS OF CIVIL GOVERNMENT IN HANCOCK COUNTY

"ANOTHER election was to come off in August, 1844, for members of congress, and for the legislature; and an election was pending throughout the nation for a president of the United States. The war of party was never more fierce and terrible than during the pendency of these elections. The parties in many places met separately almost every night; not to argue the questions in dispute, but to denounce, ridicule, abuse, and belittle each other, with sarcasm, clamor, noise, and songs, during which nothing could be heard but hallooing, hurrahing, and yelling, and then to disperse through town, with insulting taunts and yells of defiance on either side.

In all this they were but little less fanatical and frantic on the subject of politics, than were the Mormons about religion. Such a state of excitement could not fail to operate unfavorably upon the Mormon question, involved as it was in the questions of party politics, by the former votes of the Mormons. As a means of allaying excitement, and making the question more manageable, I was most anxious that the Mormons should not vote at this election, and strongly advised them against doing so. But Colonel E. D. Taylor went to their city a few days before the election, and the Mormons, being ever disposed to follow the worst advice they could get, were induced by him and others to vote for all the democratic candidates. Colonel Taylor found them very hostile to the

Political Fanaticism of the anti-Mormon Party.

Political Course of Col. E. D. Taylor—Democrat.

governor, and on that account much disposed not to vote at this election. The leading whig anti-Mormons, believing that I had an influence over the Mormons, for the purpose of destroying it had assured them that the governor had planned and been favorable to the murder of their Prophet and Patriarch. The Mormons pretended to suspect that the governor had given some countenance to the murder, or at least had neglected to take the proper precautions to prevent it. And yet it is strange that at this same election, they elected General Deming to be the sheriff of the county, when they knew that he had first called out the militia against them, had concurred with me in all the measures subsequently adopted, had been left in command at Carthage during my absence at Nauvoo, and had left his post when he saw that he had no power to prevent the murders. As to myself, I shared the fate of all men in high places, who favor moderation, who see that both parties in the frenzy of their excitement are wrong—espousing the cause of neither; which fate always is to be hated by both parties. But Colonel Taylor, like a skillful politician, denied nothing, but gave countenance to everything the Mormons said of the governor; and by admitting to them that the governor was a great rascal; by promising them the support of the democratic party, an assurance he was not authorized to make, but which they were foolish enough to believe, and by insisting that the governor was not the democratic party, he overcame their reluctance to vote. Nevertheless, for mere political effect, without a shadow of justice, the whig leaders and newspapers everywhere, and some enemies in the democratic ranks, immediately charged this vote of the Mormons to the governor's influence; and this charge being believed by many, made the anti-Mormon party more famous than ever in favor of the expulsion of the Mormons.

In the course of the fall of 1844, the anti-Mormon leaders sent printed invitations to all the militia captains in Hancock, and to the captains of militia in all the neighboring counties in Illinois, Iowa, and Missouri, to be present with their companies at a great wolf hunt in Hancock; and it was privately announced that the wolves to be hunted were the Mormons and Jack-Mormons. Preparations were made for assembling several thousand men, with provisions for six days; and the anti-Mormon newspapers, in aid of the movement, commenced anew the most awful accounts of thefts and robberies, and meditated outrages by the Mormons. The whig press in every part of the United States, came to their assistance. The democratic newspapers and leading democrats, who had received the benefit of the Mormon votes to their party, quailed under the tempest, leaving no organ for the correction of public opinion, either at home or abroad, except the discredited Mormon newspaper at Nauvoo. But very few of my prominent democratic friends would dare to come up to the assistance of their governor, and but few of them dared openly to vindicate his motives in endeavoring to keep the peace. They were willing and anxious for Mormon votes at elections, but they were unwilling to risk their popularity with the people, by taking a part in their favor, even when law and justice, and the Constitution, were all on their side. Such being the odious character of the Mormons, the hatred of the common people against them, and such being the pusillanimity of leading men, in fearing to encounter it.

A Proposed "Wolf Hunt".

In this state of the case I applied to Brigadier-General J. J. Hardin, of the state militia, and to Colonels Baker and Merriman, all whigs, but all of them men of military ambition, and they, together with Colonel William Weatherford, a democrat* with my own exertions, succeeded in raising about five hundred volunteers; and thus did these whigs, that which my own

*Of the officers who were out with me in this expedition, General Hardin, Colonels Baker and Weatherford, and Major Warren, afterwards greatly distinguished themselves in the Mexican War. Ford.

political friends, with two or three exceptions, were slow to do, from a sense of duty and gratitude.

With this little force under the command of General Hardin, I arrived in Hancock county on the 25th of September. The malcontents abandoned their design, and all the leaders of it fled to Missouri. The Carthage Greys fled almost in a body, carrying their arms along with them. During our stay in the county the anti-Mormons thronged into the camp, and conversed freely with the men, who were fast infected with their prejudices, and it was impossible to get any of the officers to aid in expelling them. Colonels Baker, Merriman and Weatherford, volunteered their services if I would go with them, to cross with a force into Missouri, to capture three of the anti-Mormon leaders, for whose arrest writs had been issued for the murder of the Smiths. To this I assented, and procured a boat, which was sent down in the night, and secretly landed a mile above Warsaw. Our little force arrived at that place about noon; that night we were to cross to Missouri at Churchville, and seize the accused there encamped with a number of their friends; but that afternoon Colonel Baker visited the hostile encampment, and on his return refused to participate in the expedition, and advised all his friends against joining it. There was no authority for compelling the men to invade a neighboring state, and for this cause, much to the vexation of myself and several others, the matter fell through.

Wolf Hunt Dispersed.

It seems that Colonel Baker had already partly arranged the terms for the accused to surrender. They were to be taken to Quincy for examination under a military guard; the attorney for the people was to be advised to admit them to bail, and they were to be entitled to a continuance of their trial at the next court at Carthage; upon this, two of the accused came over and surrendered themselves prisoners.

The Accused Murderers of the Prophet Dictate their Own Terms of Surrender.

But at that time I was held responsible for this

compromise with the murderers. The truth is, that I had but little of the moral power to command in this expedition. Officers, men, and all under me, were so infected with the anti-Mormon prejudices that I was made to feel severely the want of moral power to control them. It would be thought very strange in any other government that the administration should have the power to direct, but no power to control. By the Constitution the governor can neither appoint nor remove a militia officer. He may arrest and order a court martial. But a court martial composed of military officers, elected in times of peace, in many cases upon the same principles upon which Colonel Pluck was elected in New York City, is not likely to pay much attention to executive wishes in opposition to popular excitement. So, too, in Illinois, the governor has no power to appoint, remove, or in anywise control sheriffs, justices of the peace, nor even a constable; and yet the active cooperation of such officers with the executive, is indispensable to the success of any effort the governor may take to suppress civil war. If anyone supposes that the greatest amount of talents will enable anyone to govern under such circumstances, he is mistaken. It may be thought that the governor ought to create a public sentiment in favor of his measures, to sway the minds of those under him to his own course, but if anyone supposes that even the greatest abilities could succeed in such an effort against popular feeling, and against the inherent love of numerous demagogues for popularity, he is again mistaken.

GOVERNOR FORD'S PLEDGE OF SAFETY TO THE PROPHET ADMITTED

I had determined from the first that some of the ringleaders in the foul murder of the Smiths should be brought to trial. If these men had been the incarnation of satan himself, as was believed by many, their murder was a foul and treacherous action, alike disgraceful to those who perpetrated the crime, to the state, and to the governor, whose word had been pledged for the protection of the prisoners in jail, and which had been so shamefully violated; and required that the most vigorous means should be used to bring the assassins to punishment. As much as anything else the expedition under General Hardin had been ordered with a view to arrest the murderers.

Determination of the Governor to Have the Ringleaders of the Murderers of the Prophet and Patriarch Tried.

Accordingly, I employed able lawyers to hunt up the testimony, procure indictments, and prosecute the offenders. A trial was had before Judge Young in the summer of 1845. The sheriff and panel of jurors, selected by the Mormon court, were set aside for prejudice, and elisors were appointed to select a new jury. One friend of the Mormons and one anti-Mormon were appointed for this purpose; but as more than a thousand men had assembled under arms at the court, to keep away the Mormons and their friends, the jury was made up of these military followers of the court, who all swore that they had never formed or expressed any opinion as to the guilt or innocence of the accused. The Mormons had one principal witness, who was with the troops at Warsaw, had marched with them until they were disbanded, heard their consultations, went before them to Carthage, and saw them murder the Smiths. But before the trial came on, they had induced him to become a Mormon; and being much more anxious for the glorification of the Prophet than to avenge his death, the leading Mormons made him publish a pamphlet giving an account of the murder; in which he professed to have seen a bright and shining light descend upon the head of Joe Smith, to strike some of the conspirators with blindness, and that he heard supernatural voices in the air confirming his mission as a Prophet! Having published this in a book, he was compelled to swear to it in court, which of course destroyed the credit of his evidence. This witness was afterwards expelled from the Mormons, but no doubt they will cling to his evidence in favor of the divine mission of the Prophet.*

THE "TRIAL"! THE STATE OF THE COURT

Many other witnesses were examined, who knew the facts, but under the influence of the demoralization of faction, denied all knowledge of them. It has been said, that faction may find men honest, but it scarcely ever leaves them so. This was verified to the letter in the history of the Mormon quarrel. The accused were all acquitted.

During the progress of these trials, the judge was compelled to permit the courthouse to be filled and surrounded by armed bands, who attended court to browbeat and overawe the administration of justice. The judge himself was in a duress, and informed me that he did not consider his life secure any part of the time. The consequence was, that the crowd had everything their own way; the lawyers for the defense defended their clients by a long and elaborate attack on the governor; the armed mob stamped with their feet and yelled their approbation at every sarcastic and smart thing that was said; and the judge was not only forced to hear it, but to lend it a kind of approval. Josiah Lamborn was attorney for the prosecution; and O. H. Browning, O. C. Skinner, Calvin A. Warren, and William A. Richardson, were for the defense.

At the next term, the leading Mormons were tried and acquitted for the destruction of the heretical press. It appears that, not being interested in objecting to

*The witness here referred to was one Wm. M. Daniels, and he is doubtless worthy of all the scorn that Governor Ford here heaps upon him. But the "Mormons" do not "cling to his evidence in favor of the divine mission of the Prophet" since they concede the unreasonableness of his testimony as also the testimony of one Benjamin Brackenbury, as will be seen by the treatment of the testimony of these witnesses in *The Comprehensive History of the Church,* Century I, vol. ii, ch. lx, pp. 324-6, notes 14-15. B. H. R.

the sheriff or the jury selected by a court elected by themselves, they in their turn got a favorable jury determined upon acquittal, and yet the Mormon jurors all swore that they had formed no opinion as to the guilt or innocence of their accused friends. It appeared that the laws furnished the means of suiting each party with a jury. The Mormons could have a Mormon jury to be tried by, selected by themselves; and the anti-Mormons, by objecting to the sheriff and regular panel, could have one from the anti-Mormons. From henceforth no leading man on either side could be arrested without the aid of an army, as the men of one party could not safely surrender to the other for fear of being murdered; when arrested by a military force the Constitution prohibited a trial in any other county without the consent of the accused. No one would be convicted of any crime in Hancock; and this put an end to the administration of the criminal law in that distracted county. Government was at an end there, and the whole community were delivered up to the dominion of a frightful anarchy. If the whole state had been in the same condition, then indeed would have been verified to the letter what was said by a wit, when he expressed an opinion that the people were neither capable of governing themselves nor of being governed by others. And truly there can be no government in a free country where the people do not voluntarily obey the laws."*

Nauvoo Authorities Acquitted for Destruction of Expositor Press.

*Ford's *History of Illinois*, pp. 354-369.

III

MEMOIRS OF THE LATE PRESIDENT JOHN TAYLOR RESPECTING AFFAIRS AT NAUVOO LEADING UP TO THE MARTYRDOM OF THE PROPHET AND PATRIARCH: GOVERNOR FORD'S RESPONSIBILITY THEREIN

Explanation

FOLLOWING the preceding excerpts from Ford's *History of Illinois,* setting forth his views of Latter-day Saint affairs in the state of Illinois during his incumbency of the office of governor of that state, and also what really amounts to a defense of himself in relation to those events, I deem it important that a Latter-day Saint statement covering the same period of time and events, with comments thereon, should be made. Such a statement and comments I find in an historical document written by John Taylor, late President [the third] of the Church of Jesus Christ of Latter-day Saints, a close participant in these events; and second only in nearness to the Prophet Joseph Smith and his brother Hyrum in them; and who also was nearly made a complete martyr to the cause in which they suffered, being savagely wounded in Carthage Prison, and only narrowly escaping the death visited upon them. This statement and the comments upon this eventful period were made at a time far enough removed from the excitement of those days to enable the writer to speak temperately upon the events of that period, and at the same time in a judicial and statesmanlike spirit, that greatly enhances the value of the document.

As seen by the introductory paragraph, the paper was prepared at the request of George A. Smith and Wilford Woodruff, Church Historians, under the title of "The Martyrdom of Joseph Smith"; and was filed in the Historian's Office, Salt Lake City.

This document will make up chapters vi to x inclusive.

CHAPTER VI.

THE MARTYRDOM OF JOSEPH SMITH: REVIEW OF CONDITIONS IN ILLINOIS PRECEDING THAT EVENT

"BEING requested by Elders George A. Smith and Wilford Woodruff, Church Historians, to write an account of events that transpired before, and took place at, the time of the martyrdom of Joseph Smith, in Carthage Jail, in Hancock county, state of Illinois, I write the following, principally from memory, not having access at this time to any public documents relative thereto farther than a few desultory items contained in Ford's *History of Illinois*. I must also acknowledge myself considerably indebted to George A. Smith, who was with me when I wrote it, and who, although not there at the time of the bloody transaction, yet, from conversing with several persons who were in the capacity of Church Historians, and aided by an excellent memory, has rendered me considerable service.

Introduction.

These and the few items contained in the note at the end of this account are all the aid I have had. I would farther add that the items contained in the letter, in relation to dates especially, may be considered strictly correct.

After having written the whole, I read it over to the Hon. J. M. Bernhisel, who with one or two slight alterations, pronounced it strictly correct. Brother Bernhisel was present most of the time. I am afraid that, from the length of time that has transpired since the occurrence, and having to rely almost exclusively upon my memory, there may be some slight inaccuracies, but I believe that in general it is strictly correct. As I figured in those transactions from the commencement to the end, they left no slight impression on my mind.

In the year 1844, a very great excitement prevailed in some parts of Hancock, Brown and other neighboring counties of Illinois, in relation to the 'Mormons', and a spirit of vindictive hatred and persecution was exhibited among the people, which was manifested in the most bitter and acrimonious language, as well as by acts of hostility and violence, frequently threatening the destruction of the citizens of Nauvoo and vicinity, and utter annihilation of the 'Mormons' and 'Mormonism', and in some instances breaking out in the most violent acts of ruffianly barbarity. Persons were kidnapped, whipped, persecuted, and falsely accused of various crimes; their cattle and houses injured, destroyed, or stolen; vexatious prosecutions were instituted to harass, and annoy. In some remote neighborhoods they were expelled from their homes without redress, and in others violence was threatened to their persons and property, while in others every kind of insult and indignity were heaped upon them, to induce them to abandon their homes, the county, or the state.

Threatening Portents in Illinois, 1844.

These annoyances, prosecutions, and persecutions were instigated through different agencies and by various classes of men, actuated by different motives, but all uniting in the one object—prosecution, persecution, and extermination of the saints.

There were a number of wicked and corrupt men living in Nauvoo and its vicinity, who had belonged to the church, but whose conduct was incompatible with the gospel; they were accordingly dealt with by the church and severed from its communion. Some of these had been prominent members, and held official stations either in the city or church. Among these were John C. Bennett, formerly mayor; William Law, counselor to Joseph Smith; Wilson

Apostates at Nauvoo.

Law, his natural brother, and general in the Nauvoo Legion; Dr. R. D. Foster, a man of some property, but with a very bad reputation; Francis and Chauncey Higbee, the latter a young lawyer, and both sons of a respectable and honored man in the church, known as Judge Elias Higbee, who died about twelve months before.

Besides these, there were a great many apostates, both in the city and county, of less notoriety, who for their delinquencies, had been expelled from the church. John C. Bennett and Francis and Chauncey Higbee were cut off from the church; the former was also cashiered from his generalship for the most flagrant acts of seduction and adultery; and the developments in their cases were so scandalous that the high council, before whom they were tried, had to sit with closed doors.

William Law, although counselor to Joseph, was found to be his most bitter foe and maligner, and to hold intercourse [it was alleged], contrary to all law, in his own house, with a young lady resident with him; and it was afterwards proven that he had conspired with some Missourians to take Joseph Smith's life, and (the Prophet) was only saved by Josiah Arnold and Daniel Garn, who, being on guard at his house, prevented the assassins from seeing him. Yet, although having murder in his heart, his manners were generally courteous and mild, and he was well calculated to deceive.

General Wilson Law was cut off from the church for seduction, falsehood, and defamation; both the above were also court-martialed by the Nauvoo Legion, and expelled. Foster was also cut off I believe, for dishonesty, fraud, and falsehood. I know he was eminently guilty of the whole, but whether these were the specific charges or not, I don't know, but I do know that he was a notoriously wicked and corrupt man.

Besides the above characters and 'Mormonic' apostates, there were other three parties. The first of these may be called religionists, the second politicians, and the third counterfeiters, blacklegs, horse thieves, and cutthroats.

Other anti-Mormon Parties.

The religious party were chagrined and maddened because 'Mormonism' came in contact with their religion, and they could not oppose it from the scriptures. Thus like the ancient Jews, when enraged at the exhibition of their follies and hypocrisies by Jesus and his Apostles, so these were infuriated against the 'Mormons' because of their discomfiture by them; and instead of owning the truth and rejoicing in it, they were ready to gnash upon them with their teeth, and to persecute the believers in principles which they could not disprove.

The political party were those who were of opposite politics to us. There were always two parties, the whigs and democrats, and we could not vote for one without offending the other, and it not unfrequently happened that candidates for office would place the issue of their election upon opposition to the 'Mormons', in order to gain political influence from religious prejudice, in which case the 'Mormons' were compelled, in self-defense, to vote against them, which resulted almost invariably against our opponents. This made them angry; and although it was of their own making, and the 'Mormons' could not be expected to do otherwise, yet they raged on account of their discomfiture, and sought to wreak their fury on the 'Mormons'. As an instance of the above, when Joseph Duncan was candidate for the office of governor of Illinois, he pledged himself to his party that, if he could be elected, he would exterminate or drive the 'Mormons' from the state.* The consequence was that Governor Ford was elected. The whigs, seeing that they had been out-generaled by the democrats in securing the 'Mormon' vote, became seri-

Whigs and Democrats.

*See his remarks as contained in Ford's *History of Illinois*, p. 269.

ously alarmed, and sought to repair their disaster by raising a crusade against the people. The whig newspapers teemed with accounts of the wonders and enormities of Nauvoo, and of the awful wickedness of a party which could consent to receive the support of such miscreants. Governor Duncan, who was really a brave, honest man, and who had nothing to do with getting the 'Mormon' charters passed through the legislature, took the stump on this subject in good earnest, and expected to be elected governor almost on this question alone.

The third party, composed of counterfeiters, blacklegs, horse thieves, and cutthroats, were a pack of scoundrels that infested the whole of the western country at that time. In some districts their influence was so great as to control important state and county offices. On this subject Governor Ford has the following:

'Then, again, the northern part of the state was not destitute of its organized bands of rogues, engaged in murders, robberies, horse-stealing, and in making and passing counterfeit money. These rogues were scattered all over the north, but the most of them were located in the counties of Ogle, Winnebago, Lee and De Kalb.

Lawlessness in Northern Illinois.

'In the county of Ogle they were so numerous, strong, and well organized that they could not be convicted for their crimes. By getting some of their numbers on the juries, by producing a host of witnesses to sustain their defense, by perjured evidence, and by changing the venue of one county to another, by continuances from term to term, and by the inability of witnesses to attend from time to time at distant and foreign counties, they most generally managed to be acquitted.'*

There was a combination of horse thieves extending from Galena to Alton. There were counterfeiters engaged in merchandizing, trading, and storekeeping in most of the cities and villages, and in some districts, I have been credibly informed by men to whom they have disclosed their secrets; the judges, sheriffs, con-

*Ford's *History of Illinois*, p. 246.

stables, and jailors, as well as professional men, were more or less associated with them. These had in their employ the most reckless, abandoned wretches, who stood ready to carry into effect the most desperate enterprises, and were careless alike of human life and property. Their object in persecuting the 'Mormons' was in part to cover their own rascality, and in part to prevent them from exposing and prosecuting them; but the principal reason was plunder, believing that if they [the 'Mormons'] could be removed or driven, they would be made fat on 'Mormon' spoils, besides having in the deserted city a good asylum for the prosecution of their diabolical pursuits.

This conglomeration of apostate 'Mormons', religious bigots, political fanatics and blacklegs, all united their forces against the 'Mormons', and organized themselves into a party, denominated 'anti-Mormons'. Some of them, we have reason to believe, joined the church in order to cover their nefarious practices, and when they were expelled for their unrighteousness only raged with greater violence. They circulated every kind of falsehood that they could collect or manufacture against the 'Mormons'. They also had a paper to assist them in their infamous designs, called the *Warsaw Signal,* edited by a Mr. Thomas Sharp, a violent and unprincipled man, who shrunk not from any enormity. The anti-'Mormons' had public meetings, which were very numerously attended, where they passed resolutions of the most violent and inflammatory kind, threatening to drive, expel and exterminate the 'Mormons' from the state, at the same time accusing them of every evil in the vocabulary of crime.

They appointed their meetings in various parts of Hancock, McDonough, and other counties, which soon resulted in the organization of armed mobs, under the direction of officers who reported to their headquarters, and the reports of which were published in the anti-'Mormon' paper, and circulated through the adjoining counties. We also published in the *Times and Seasons* and the *Nauvoo Neighbor* (two papers published and edited by me at that time) an account, not only of their proceedings, but our own. But such was the hostile feeling, so well arranged their plans, and so desperate and lawless their measures, that it was with the greatest difficulty that we could get our papers circulated; they were destroyed by postmasters and others, and scarcely ever arrived at the place of their destination, so that a great many of the people, who would have been otherwise peaceable, were excited by their misrepresentations, and instigated to join their hostile or predatory bands.

Emboldened by the acts of those outside, the apostate 'Mormons', associated with others, commenced the publication of a libelous paper in Nauvoo, called the *Nauvoo Expositor*.

The Nauvoo Expositor.

This paper not only reprinted from the others, but put in circulation the most libelous, false, and infamous reports concerning the citizens of Nauvoo, and especially the ladies. It was, however, no sooner put in circulation than the indignation of the whole community was aroused; so much so, that they threatened its annihilation; and I do not believe that in any other city in the United States, if the same charges had been made against the citizens, it would have been permitted to remain one day. As it was among us, under these circumstances, it was thought best to convene the city council to take into consideration the adoption of some measures for its removal, as it was deemed better that this should be done legally than illegally. Joseph Smith, therefore, who was mayor, convened the city council for that purpose; the paper was introduced and read, and the subject examined. All, or nearly all present, expressed their indignation at the course taken by the *Expositor*, which was owned by some of the aforesaid apostates, associated with one or two others. Wilson Law, Dr. Foster, Charles Ivins and the Higbees before referred to, some lawyers, storekeepers, and others in Nauvoo who were not 'Mormons', together with the anti-'Mormons' outside of the city, sustained it. The calculation was, by false statements, to unsettle the minds of many in the city, and to form combinations there similar to the anti-'Mormon' associations outside of the city. Various attempts had heretofore been made by the party to annoy and irritate the citizens of Nauvoo; false accusations had been made, vexatious lawsuits instituted, threats made, and various devices resorted to, to influence the public mind, and, if possible, to provoke us to the commission of some overt act that might make us amenable to the law. With a perfect knowledge therefore, of the designs of these infernal scoundrels who were in our midst, as well as those who surrounded us, the city council entered upon an investigation of the matter. They felt that they were in a critical position, and that any move made for the abating of that press would be looked upon, or at least represented, as a direct attack upon the liberty of speech, and that, so far from displeasing our enemies, it would be looked upon by them as one of the best circumstances that could transpire to assist them in their nefarious and bloody designs. Being a member of the city council, I well remember the feeling of responsibility that seemed to rest upon all present; nor shall I soon forget the bold, manly, independent expressions of Joseph Smith on that occasion in relation to this matter. He exhibited in glowing colors the meanness, corruption and ultimate designs of the anti-'Mormons'; their despicable characters and ungodly influences, especially of those who were in our midst. He told of the responsibility that rested upon us, as guardians of the public interest, to stand up in the defense of the injured and oppressed, to stem the current of corruption, and as men and saints, to put a stop to this flagrant outrage upon this people's rights.

He stated that no man was a stronger advocate for

the liberty of speech and of the press than himself; yet, when this noble gift is utterly prostituted and abused, as in the present instance, it loses all claim to our respect, and becomes as great an agent for evil as it can possibly be for good; and notwithstanding the apparent advantage we should give our enemies by this act, yet it behooved us, as men, to act independent of all secondary influences, to perform the part of men of enlarged minds, and boldly and fearlessly to discharge the duties devolving upon us by declaring as a nuisance, and removing this filthy, libelous, and seditious sheet from our midst.

Mental Attitude of the Prophet.

The subject was discussed in various forms, and after the remarks made by the mayor, every one seemed to be waiting for some one else to speak.

After a considerable pause, I arose and expressed my feelings frankly, as Joseph had done, and numbers of others followed in the same strain; and I think, but am not certain, that I made a motion for the removal of that press as a nuisance. This motion was finally put, and carried by all but one; and he conceded that the measure was just, but abstained through fear.

Several members of the city council were not in the church. The following is the bill referred to:

*BILL FOR REMOVING OF THE PRESS OF THE NAUVOO EXPOSITOR**

'Resolved by the city council of the city of Nauvoo, that the printing office from whence issues the *Nauvoo Expositor* is a public nuisance; and also of said *Nauvoo Expositors* which may be or exist in said establishment; and the mayor is instructed to cause said establishment and papers to be removed without delay, in such manner as he shall direct.

'Passed June 10th, 1844. GEO. W. HARRIS, President *pro tem*.

'W. RICHARDS, Recorder.'

After the passage of the bill, the marshal, John P. Greene was ordered to abate or remove, which he forthwith proceeded to do by summoning a *posse* of men for

**Deseret News*, No. 29, September 23, 1857, p. 226.

that purpose. The press was removed or broken, I don't remember which, by the marshal, and the types scattered in the street.

This seemed to be one of those extreme cases that require extreme measures, as the press was still proceeding in its inflammatory course. It was feared that, as it was almost universally execrated, should it continue longer, an indignant people might commit some overt act which might lead to serious consequences, and that it was better to use legal than illegal means.

This, as was foreseen, was the very course our enemies wished us to pursue, as it afforded them an opportunity of circulating a very plausible story about the 'Mormons' being opposed to the liberty of the press and of free speech, which they were not slow to avail themselves of. Stories were fabricated, and facts perverted; false statements were made, and this act brought in as an example to sustain the whole of their fabrications; and, as if inspired by satan, they labored with an energy and zeal worthy of a better cause. They had runners to circulate their reports, not only through Hancock county, but in all the surrounding counties. These reports were communicated to their anti-'Mormon' societies, and these societies circulated them in their several districts. The anti-'Mormon' paper, the *Warsaw Signal,* was filled with inflammatory articles and misrepresentations in relation to us, and especially to this act of destroying the press. We were represented as a horde of lawless ruffians and brigands, anti-American and anti-republican, steeped in crime and iniquity, opposed to freedom of speech and of the press, and all the rights and immunities of a free and enlightened people; that neither person nor property was secure, that we had designs upon the citizens of Illinois and of the United States, and the people were called upon to rise *en masse,* and put us down, drive us away, or exterminate us as a pest to society, and alike dangerous to our neighbors, the state, and the commonwealth.

These statements were extensively copied and circulated throughout the United States. A true statement of the facts in question was published by us both in the *Times and Seasons* and the *Nauvoo Neighbor;* but it was found impossible to circulate them in the immediate counties, as they were destroyed at the post offices or otherwise by the agents of the anti-'Mormons', and, in order to get the mail to go abroad, I had to send the papers a distance of thirty or forty miles from Nauvoo, and sometimes to St. Louis (upward of two hundred miles), to insure their proceeding on their route, and then one-half or two-thirds of the papers never reached the place of destination, being intercepted or destroyed by our enemies.

Uncertainty of U. S. Mail.

These false reports stirred up the community around, of whom many, on account of religious prejudice, were easily instigated to join the anti-'Mormons' and embark in any crusade that might be undertaken against us; hence their ranks swelled in numbers, and new organizations were formed, meetings were held, resolutions passed, and men and means volunteered for the extirpation of the 'Mormons'.

On these points Governor Ford writes:

'These also were the active men in blowing up the fury of the people, in hopes that a popular movement might be set on foot, which would result in the expulsion or extermination of the 'Mormon voters. For this purpose public meetings had been called, inflammatory speeches had been made, exaggerated reports had been extensively circulated, committees had been appointed, who rode night and day to spread the reports and solicit the aid of neighboring counties, and at a public meeting at Warsaw resolutions were passed to expel or exterminate the 'Mormon' population. This was not, however, a movement which was unanimously concurred in. The county contained a goodly number of inhabitants in favor of peace, or who at least desired to be neutral in such a contest. These were stigmatized by the name of 'Jack-Mormons', and there were not a few of the more furious exciters of the people who openly expressed their intention to involve them in the common expulsion or extermination.

'A system of excitement and agitation was artfully planned and executed with tact. It consisted in spreading reports and rumors of the most fearful character. As examples: On the morning before my arrival at Carthage, I was awakened at an early hour by the frightful report, which was asserted with confidence and apparent consternation that the 'Mormons' had already commenced the work of burning, destruction, and murder, and that every man capable of bearing arms was instantly wanted at Carthage for the protection of the county.

Systematic anti-Mormon Agitation.

'We lost no time in starting; but when we arrived at Carthage we could hear no more concerning this story. Again, during the few days that the militia were encamped at Carthage, frequent applications were made to me to send a force here, and a force there, and a force all about the country, to prevent murders, robberies, and larcenies which, it was said, were threatened by the 'Mormons'. No such forces were sent, nor were any such offenses committed at that time, except the stealing of some provisions, and there was never the least proof that this was done by a 'Mormon'. Again, on my late visit to Hancock county, I was informed by some of their violent enemies that the larcenies of the 'Mormons' had become unusually numerous and insufferable.

'They admitted that but little had been done in this way in their immediate vicinity, but they insisted that sixteen horses had been stolen by the 'Mormons' in one night near Lima, and, upon inquiry, was told that no horses had been stolen in that neighborhood, but that sixteen horses had been stolen in one night in Hancock county. This last informant being told of the Hancock story, again changed the venue to another distant settlement in the northern edge of Adams.'*

In the meantime legal proceedings were instituted against the members of the city council of Nauvoo. A writ, here subjoined, was issued upon the affidavit of the Laws, Fosters, Higbees, and Ivins, by Mr. Morrison, a justice of the peace in Carthage, and the county seat of Hancock, and put into the hands of one David Bettisworth, a constable of the same place.

WRIT ISSUED UPON AFFIDAVIT BY THOMAS MORRISON, J. P., STATE OF ILLINOIS, HANCOCK COUNTY, ss

'The people of the state of Illinois, to all constables, sheriffs, and coroners of the said state, greeting:

'Whereas complaint hath been made before me, one of the justices of the peace in and for the county of Hancock aforesaid, upon the oath

*Ford's *History of Illinois*, pp. 330, 331.

of Francis M. Higbee, of the said county, that Joseph Smith, Samuel Bennett, John Taylor, William W. Phelps, Hyrum Smith, John P. Greene, Stephen Perry, Dimick B. Huntington, Jonathan Dunham, Stephen Markham, William Edwards, Jonathan Holmes, Jesse P. Harmon, John Lytle, Joseph W. Coolidge, Harvey D. Redfield, Porter Rockwell, and Levi Richards of said county, did on the 10th day of June instant, commit a riot at and within the county aforesaid, wherein they with force and violence broke into the printing office of the *Nauvoo Expositor*, and unlawfully and with force burned and destroyed the printing press, type and fixtures of the same, being the property of William Law, Wilson Law, Charles Ivins, Francis M. Higbee, Chauncey L. Higbee, Robert D. Foster, and Charles A. Foster.

'These are therefore to command you forthwith to apprehend the said Joseph Smith, Samuel Bennett, John Taylor, William W. Phelps, Hyrum Smith, John P. Greene, Stephen Perry, Dimick B. Huntington, Jonathan Dunham, Stephen Markham, William Edwards, Jonathan Holmes, Jesse P. Harmon, John Lytle, Joseph W. Coolidge, Harvey D. Redfield, Porter Rockwell, and Levi Richards, and bring them before me, or some other justice of the peace, to answer the premises, and farther to be dealt with according to law.

'Given under my hand and seal at Carthage, in the county aforesaid, this 11th day of June, A. D., 1844.

[Signed] THOMAS MORRISON, J. P.' (Seal) *

Action of the City Council.

The council did not refuse to attend to the legal proceedings in the case, but as the law of Illinois made it the privilege of the persons accused to go 'or appear before the issuer of the writ, *or any other justice of peace*', they requested to be taken before another magistrate, either in the city of Nauvoo or at any reasonable distance out of it.

This the constable, who was a mobocrat, refused to do, and as this was our legal privilege, we refused to be dragged, contrary to law, a distance of eighteen miles, when at the same time we had reason to believe that an organized band of mobocrats were assembled for the purpose of extermination or murder, and among whom it would not be safe to go without a superior force of armed men. A writ of *habeas corpus* was called for, issued by the municipal court of Nauvoo, taking us out of the hands of Bettisworth, and placing us in the charge of the city marshal. We went

**Deseret News*, No. 30, Sept. 30, 1857, p. 233.

before the municipal court and were dismissed. Our refusal to obey this illegal proceeding was by them construed into a refusal to submit to law, and circulated as such, and the people either did believe, or professed to believe, that we were in open rebellion against the laws and the authorities of the state. Hence mobs began to assemble, among which all through the country inflammatory speeches were made, exciting them to mobocracy and violence. Soon they commenced their depredations in our outside settlements, kidnaping some, and whipping and otherwise abusing others.

The persons thus abused fled to Nauvoo as soon as practicable, and related their injuries to Joseph Smith, then mayor of the city, and lieutenant-general of the Nauvoo Legion. They also went before magistrates, and made affidavits of what they had suffered, seen, and heard. These affidavits, in connection with a copy of all our proceedings were forwarded by Joseph Smith to Mr. Ford, then governor of Illinois, with an expression of our desire to abide law, and a request that the governor would instruct him how to proceed in the case of arrival of an armed mob against the city. The governor sent back instructions to Joseph Smith that, as he was lieutenant-general of the Nauvoo Legion, it was his duty to protect the city and surrounding country, and issued orders to that effect. Upon the reception of these orders Joseph Smith assembled the people of the city, and laid before them the governor's instructions; he also convened the officers of the Nauvoo Legion for the purpose of conferring in relation to the best mode of defense. He also issued orders to the men to hold themselves in readiness in case of being called upon. On the following day General Joseph Smith, with his staff, the leading officers of the Legion, and some prominent strangers who were in our midst, made a survey of the outside boundaries of the city, which was very extensive, being about five miles up and down the river, and about two and a half back in the center, for the purpose of ascertaining the position of the ground, and the feasibility of defense, and to make all necessary arrangements in case of an attack.

It may be well here to remark that numbers of gentlemen, strangers to us, either came on purpose or were passing through Nauvoo, and upon learning the position of things, expressed their indignation against our enemies, and avowed their readiness to assist us by their counsel or otherwise. It was some of these who assisted us in reconnoitering the city, and finding out its adaptability for defense, and how to protect it best against an armed force. The Legion was called together and drilled, and every means made use for defense. At the call of the officers, old and young men came forward, both from the city and the country, and mustered to the number of about five thousand.

Military Defensive Measures.

In the meantime our enemies were not idle in mustering their forces and committing depredations, nor had they been; it was, in fact, their gathering that called ours into existence; their forces continued to accumulate; they assumed a threatening attitude, and assembled in large bodies, armed and equipped for war, and threatened the destruction and extermination of the 'Mormons'.

An account of their outrages and assemblages was forwarded to Governor Ford almost daily; accompanied by affidavits furnished by eyewitnesses of their proceedings. Persons were also sent out to the counties around with pacific intentions, to give them an account of the true state of affairs, and to notify them of the feelings and dispositions of the people of Nauvoo, and thus, if possible, quell the excitement. In some of the more distant counties these men were very successful, and produced a salutary influence upon the minds of many intelligent and well-disposed men. In neighboring counties, however, where anti-'Mormon' influence prevailed, they produced little effect. At the same time guards were stationed around Nauvoo, and picket guards in the distance. At length opposing forces gathered so near that more active measures were taken; reconnoitering parties were sent out, and the city proclaimed under martial law. Things now assumed a belligerent attitude, and persons passing through the city were questioned as to what they knew of the enemy, while passes were in some instances given to avoid difficulty with the guards. Joseph Smith continued to send on messengers to the governor (Philip B. Lewis and other messengers were sent). Samuel James, then residing at La Harpe, carried a message and dispatches to him, and in a day or two after Bishop Edward Hunter and others went again with fresh dispatches, representations, affidavits, and instructions; but as the weather was excessively wet, the rivers swollen, and the bridges washed away in many places, it was with great difficulty that they proceeded on their journeys. As the mobocracy had at last attracted the governor's attention, he started in company with some others from Springfield to the scene of trouble, and missed, I believe, both Brothers James and Hunter on the road, and, of course, did not see their documents. He came to Carthage, and made that place, which was a regular mobocratic den, his headquarters; as it was the county seat, however, of Hancock county, that circumstance might, in a measure, justify his staying there.

To avoid the appearance of all hostility on our part, and to fulfill the law in every particular, at the suggestion of Judge Thomas, judge of that judicial district, who had come to Nauvoo at the time, and who stated that we had fulfilled the law, but, in order to satisfy all he would counsel us to go before Esquire Wells, who was not in our church, and have a hearing, we did so, and after a full hearing we were again dismissed.

The governor on the road collected forces, some

of whom were respectable, but on his arrival in the neighborhood of the difficulties he received as militia all the companies of the mob forces who united with him. After his arrival at Carthage he sent two gentlemen from there to Nauvoo as a committee to wait upon General Joseph Smith, informing him of the arrival of his excellency, with a request that General Smith would send out a committee to wait upon the governor and represent to him the state of affairs in relation to the difficulties that then existed in the county. We met this committee while we were reconnoitering the city to find out the best mode of defense as aforesaid. Dr. J. M. Bernhisel and myself were appointed as a committee by General Smith to wait upon the governor. Previous to going, however, we were furnished with affidavits and documents in relation both to our proceedings and those of the mob; in addition to the general history of the transaction, we took with us a duplicate of those documents which had been forwarded by Bishop Hunter, Brother James, and others. We started from Nauvoo in company with the aforesaid gentlemen at about 7 o'clock on the evening of the 21st of June, and arrived at Carthage about 11 p. m.

Governor Ford's Arrival at Carthage.

We put up at the same hotel with the governor, kept by a Mr. Hamilton. On our arrival we found the governor in bed, but not so with the other inhabitants. The town was filled with a perfect set of rabble and rowdies, who, under the influence of bacchus, seemed to be holding a grand saturnalia, whooping, yelling and vociferating as if bedlam had broken loose.

On our arrival at the hotel, and while supper was preparing, a man came to me, dressed as a soldier, and told me that a man named Daniel Garn had just been taken prisoner, and was about to be committed to jail, and wanted me to go bail for him. Believing this to be a ruse to get me out alone, and that some violence was intended, after consulting with Dr. Bernhisel, I told the man that I was well acquainted with Mr. Garn, that I knew him to be a gentleman, and did not believe that he had transgressed law, and, moreover, that I considered it a very singular time to be holding courts and calling for security, particularly as the town was full of rowdyism.

I informed him that Dr. Bernhisel and myself would, if necessary, go bail for him in the morning, but that we did not feel ourselves safe among such a set at that late hour of the night.

After supper, on retiring to our room, we had to pass through another, which was separated from ours only by a board partition, the beds in each room being placed side by side, with the exception of this fragile partition. On the bed that was in the room which we passed through I discovered a man by the name of Jackson, a desperate character, and a reputed, notorious cutthroat and murderer. I hinted to the doctor that things looked rather suspicious, and looked to see that my arms were in order. The doctor and I occupied one bed. We had scarcely laid down when a knock at the door, accompanied by a voice announced the approach of Chauncey Higbee, the young lawyer and apostate before referred to.

John Taylor and Dr. Bernhisel at Carthage.

He addressed himself to the doctor, and stated that the object of his visit was to obtain the release of Daniel Garn; that Garn he believed to be an honest man; that if he had done anything wrong, it was through improper counsel, and that it was a pity that he should be incarcerated, particularly when he could be so easily released; he urged the doctor, as a friend, not to leave so good a man in such an unpleasant situation; he finally prevailed upon the doctor to go and give bail, assuring him that on his giving bail Garn would be immediately dismissed.

During this conversation I did not say a word.

Higbee left the doctor to dress, with the intention of

returning and taking him to the court. As soon as Higbee had left, I told the doctor that he had better not go; that I believed this affair was all a ruse to get us separated; that they knew we had documents with us from General Smith to show to the governor; that I believed their object was to get possession of those papers, and, perhaps, when they had separated us, to murder one or both. The doctor, who was actuated by the best of motives in yielding to the assumed solicitude of Higbee, coincided with my views; he then went to Higbee and told him that he had concluded not to go that night, but that he and I would both wait upon the justice and Mr. Garn in the morning.

That night I lay awake with my pistols under my pillow, waiting for any emergency. Nothing more occurred during the night. In the morning we arose early, and after breakfast sought an interview with the governor, and were told that we could have an audience, I think, at 10 o'clock. In the meantime we called upon Mr. Smith, a justice of the peace, who had Mr. Garn in charge. We represented that we had been called upon the night before by two different parties to go bail for a Mr. Daniel Garn, whom we were informed he had in custody, and that, believing Mr. Garn to be an honest man, we had now come for that purpose, and were prepared to enter into recognizance for his appearance, whereupon Mr. Smith, the magistrate, remarked that, under the present excited state of affairs, he did not think he would be justified in receiving bail from Nauvoo, as it was a matter of doubt whether property would not be rendered valueless there in a few days.

Knowing the party we had to deal with, we were not much surprised at this singular proceeding; we then remarked that both of us possessed property in farms out of Nauvoo in the country, and referred him to the county records. He then stated that such was the nature of the charge against Mr. Garn that he believed he would not be justified in receiving any bail. We were thus confirmed in our opinion that the night's proceedings before, in relation to their desire to have us give bail, was a mere ruse to separate us. We were not permitted to speak with Garn, the real charge against whom was that he was traveling in Carthage or its neighborhood; what the fictitious one was, if I knew, I have since forgotten, as things of this kind were of daily occurrence."

CHAPTER VII.

JOHN TAYLOR AND DR. BERNHISEL'S INTERVIEW WITH GOVERNOR FORD—PLEDGE OF GOVERNOR FORD FOR THE SECURITY OF JOSEPH SMITH IF HE WOULD COME TO CARTHAGE

"AFTER waiting the governor's pleasure for some time we had an audience; but such an audience!

He was surrounded by some of the vilest and most unprincipled men in creation; some of them had an appearance of respectability, and many of them lacked even that. Wilson, and, I believe, William Law, were there; Foster, Frank and Chauncey Higbee, Mr. Mar, a lawyer from Nauvoo, a mobocratic merchant from Warsaw, the aforesaid Jackson, a number of his associates, among whom was the governor's secretary; in all, some fifteen or twenty persons, most of whom were recreant to virtue, honor, integrity, and everything that is considered honorable among men.

The Character of Men Surrounding the Governor.

I can well remember the feelings of disgust that I had in seeing the governor surrounded by such an infamous group, and on being introduced to men of so questionable a character; and had I been on private business, I should have turned to depart, and told the governor that if he thought proper to associate with such questionable characters, I should beg leave to be excused; but coming as we did on public business, we could not, of course, consult our private feelings.

We then stated to the governor that, in accordance with his request, General Smith had, in response to his call, sent us to him as a committee of conference; that we were acquainted with most of the circumstances that had transpired in and about Nauvoo lately, and were prepared to give him all information; that, moreover, we had in our possession testimony and affidavits confirmatory of what we should say, which had been forwarded to him by General Joseph Smith; that communications had been forwarded to his excellency by Messrs. Hunter, James, and others, some of which had not reached their destination, but of which we had duplicates with us. We then, in brief, related an outline of the difficulties, and the course we had pursued from the commencement of the troubles up to the present, and handing him the documents, respectfully submitted the whole.

During our conversation and explanations with the governor we were frequently rudely and impudently contradicted by the fellows he had around him, and of whom he seemed to take no notice.

He opened and read a number of the documents himself, and as he proceeded he was frequently interrupted by 'That's a lie!' 'That's a G—— d——ned lie!' 'That's an infernal falsehood!' 'That's a blasted lie!' etc.

These men evidently winced at an exposure of their acts, and thus vulgarly, impudently and falsely repudiated them. One of their number, Mr. Mar, addressed himself several times to me while in conversation with the governor. I did not notice him until after a frequent repetition of his insolence, when I informed him that 'my business at that time was with Governor Ford', whereupon I continued my conversation with his excellency. During the conversation, the governor expressed a desire that Joseph Smith, and all parties concerned in passing or executing the city law in relation to the press, had better come to Carthage; that, however repugnant it might be to our feelings, he thought it would have a tendency to allay public excitement, and prove to the people what we professed, that we wished to be governed by law. We represented to him the course we had taken in relation to this matter, and our willingness to go before another magistrate other than the municipal court; the illegal refusal of our request by the constable; our dismissal by the municipal court, a legally constituted tribunal; our subsequent trial before Squire Wells at the instance of Judge Thomas, the circuit judge, and our dismissal by him; that we had fulfilled the law in every particular; that it was our enemies who were breaking the law, and, having murderous designs, were only making use of this as a pretext to get us into their power. The governor stated that the people viewed it differently, and that, notwithstanding our opinions, he would recommend that the people should be satisfied. We then remarked to him that, should Joseph Smith comply with his request, it would be extremely unsafe, in the present excited state of the country, to come without an armed force; that we had a sufficiency of men, and were competent to defend ourselves, but there might be danger of collision should our forces and those of our enemies be brought into such close proximity. He strenuously advised us not to bring our arms, and *pledged his faith as governor, and the faith of the state, that we should be protected, and that he would guarantee our perfect safety.*

Governor and State's Pledge of Security.

We had at that time about five thousand men under arms, one thousand of whom would have been amply sufficient for our protection.

At the termination of our interview, and previous to our withdrawal, after a long conversation and the perusal of the documents which we had brought, the governor informed us that he would prepare a written communication for General Joseph Smith, which he desired us to wait for. We were kept waiting for this instrument some five or six hours.

About five o'clock in the afternoon we took our departure with not the most pleasant feelings. The associations of the governor, the spirit he manifested to compromise with these scoundrels, the length of time that he had kept us waiting, and his general deportment, together with the infernal spirit that we saw exhibited by those whom he had admitted to his counsels, made the prospect anything but promising.

We returned on horseback, and arrived at Nauvoo, I think, at about eight or nine o'clock at night accompanied by Captain Yates in command of a company of mounted men, who came for the purpose of escorting Joseph Smith and the accused in case of their complying with the governor's request, and going to Carthage. We went directly to Brother Joseph's when Captain Yates delivered to him the governor's communication. A council was called, consisting of Joseph's brother, Hyrum, Dr. Richards, Dr. Bernhisel, myself, and one or two others.

We then gave a detail of our interview with the governor. Brother Joseph was very much dissatisfied with the governor's letter* and with his general deportment, and so were the council, and it became a serious question as to the course we should pursue. Various projects were discussed, but nothing definitely decided upon for some time.

In the interim two gentlemen arrived; one of them, if not both, sons of John C. Calhoun. They had come to Nauvoo, and were very anxious for an interview with Brother Joseph.

These gentlemen detained him for some time; and as our council was held in Dr. Bernhisel's room in the Mansion House, the doctor lay down; and as it was now between 2 and 3 o'clock in the morning, and I had had no rest on the previous night, I was fatigued, and thinking that Brother Joseph might not return, I left for home and rest.

Being very much fatigued, I slept soundly, and was somewhat surprised in the morning by Mrs. Thompson entering my room about 7 o'clock, and exclaiming in surprise, 'What, you here! the brethren have crossed the river some time since.'

The Prophet's Start for the West.

*See Letter file in Church Historian's Office, "Ford", 1844. Contents of this letter sufficiently given in the conversation between Joseph Smith and Governor Ford in Carthage prison. (See chapter viii).

'What brethren?' I asked.

'Brother Joseph, and Hyrum, and Brother Richards', she answered.

I immediately arose upon learning that they had crossed the river, and did not intend to go to Carthage. I called together a number of persons in whom I had confidence, and had the type, stereotype plates, and most of the valuable things removed from the printing office, believing that should the governor and his force come to Nauvoo, the first thing they would do would be to burn the printing office, for I know that they would be exasperated if Brother Joseph went away. We had talked over these matters the night before, but nothing was decided upon. It was Brother Joseph's opinion that, should we leave for a time, public excitement, which was then so intense, would be allayed; that it would throw on the governor the responsibility of keeping the peace; that in the event of an outrage, the onus would rest upon the governor, who was amply prepared with troops, and could command all the forces of the state to preserve order; and that the act of his own men would be an overwhelming proof of their seditious designs, not only to the governor, but to the world. He moreover thought that, in the east, where he intended to go, public opinion would be set right in relation to these matters, and its expression would partially influence the west, and that, after the first ebullition, things would assume a shape that would justify his return.

I made arrangements for crossing the river, and Brother Elias Smith and Joseph Cain, who were both employed in the printing office with me, assisted all that lay in their power together with Brother Brower and several hands in the printing office. As we could not find out the exact whereabouts of Joseph and the brethren, I crossed the river in a boat furnished by Brother Cyrus H. Wheelock and Alfred Bell; and after the removal of the things out of the printing office, Joseph Cain brought the account books to me, that we might make arrangements for their adjustment; and Brother Elias Smith, cousin to Brother Joseph, went to obtain money for the journey, and also to find out and report to me the location of the brethren.

As Cyrus Wheelock was an active, enterprising man, and in the event of not finding Brother Joseph I calculated to go to Upper Canada for the time being, and should need a companion, I said to Brother Cyrus H. Wheelock, 'Can you go with me ten or fifteen hundred miles?'

He answered, 'Yes'.

'Can you start in half an hour?'

'Yes.'

However, I told him that he had better see his family, who lived over the river, and prepare a couple of horses and the necessary equippage for the journey, and that, if we did not find Brother Joseph before, we would start at nightfall.

Elder John Taylor in Disguise.

A laughable incident occurred on the eve of my departure. After making all the preparations I could, previous to leaving Nauvoo, and having bid adieu to my family, I went to a house adjoining the river, owned by Brother Eddy. There I disguised myself so as not to be known, and so effectually was the transformation that those who had come after me with a boat did not know me. I went down to the boat and sat in it. Brother Bell, thinking it was a stranger, watched my moves for some time very impatiently, and then said to Brother Wheelock, 'I wish that old gentleman would go away; he has been pottering around the boat for some time, and I am afraid Elder Taylor will be coming.' When he discovered his mistake, he was not a little amused.

The Prophet's Return to Nauvoo.

I was conducted by Brother Bell to a house that was surrounded by timber on the opposite side of the river. There I spent several hours in a chamber with Brother Joseph Cain, adjusting my accounts; and I made arrangements for the stereotype plates of the *Book of Mormon* and

Doctrine and Covenants to be forwarded east, thinking to supply the company with subsistence money through the sale of these books in the east.

My horses were reported ready by Brother Wheelock, and funds on hand by Brother Elias Smith. In about half an hour I should have started, when Brother Elias Smith came to me with word that he had found the brethren; that they had concluded to go to Carthage, and wished me to return to Nauvoo and accompany them. I must confess that I felt a good deal disappointed at this news, but I immediately made preparations to go. Escorted by Brother Elias Smith, I and my party went to the neighborhood of Montrose, where we met Brother Joseph, Hyrum, Brother Richards and others. Dr. Bernhisel thinks that W. W. Phelps was not with Joseph and Hyrum in the morning, but that he met him, myself, Joseph and Hyrum, Willard Richards and Brother Cahoon, in the afternoon, near Montrose returning to Nauvoo.

On meeting the brethren I learned that it was not Brother Joseph's desire to return, but that he came back by request of some of the brethren, and that it coincided more with Brother Hyrum's feelings than those of Brother Joseph. In fact, after his return, Brother Hyrum expressed himself as perfectly satisfied with the course taken, and said he felt much more at ease in his mind than he did before. On our return the calculation was to throw ourselves under the immediate protection of the governor, and to trust to his word and faith for our preservation.

A message was, I believe, sent to the governor that night, stating that we should come to Carthage in the morning, the party that came along with us to escort us back, in case we returned to Carthage, having returned.

It would seem from the following remarks of Governor Ford, that there was a design on foot, which was, that if we refused to go to Carthage at the governor's request, there should be an increased force called for by the governor, and that we should be destroyed by them. In accordance with this project, Captain Yates returned with his *posse*, accompanied by the constable who held the writ.

The following is the governor's remark in relation to this affair:

The Constable's Report to Governor Ford.

'The constable and his escort returned. The constable made no effort to arrest any of them, nor would he or the guard delay their departure one minute beyond the time, to see whether an arrest could be made. Upon their return they reported that they had been informed that the accused had fled, and could not be found. I immediately proposed to a council of officers to march into Nauvoo with the small force then under my command, but the officers were of the opinion that it was too small, and many of them insisted upon a further call of the militia. Upon reflection I was of the opinion that the officers were right in the estimate of our force, and the project for immediate action was abandoned.

'I was soon informed, however, of the conduct of the constable and guard, and then I was perfectly satisfied that a most base fraud had been attempted; that, in fact, it was feared that the 'Mormons' would submit, and thereby entitle themselves to the protection of the law. It was very apparent that many of the bustling, active spirits were afraid that there would be no occasion for calling out an overwhelming militia force, for marching it into Nauvoo, for probable mutiny when there, and for the extermination of the 'Mormon' race. It appeared that the constable and the escort were fully in the secret, and acted well their part to promote the conspiracy.'*

In the morning Brother Joseph had an interview with the officers of the Legion, with the leading members of the city council, and with the principal men of the city. The officers were instructed to dismiss their men, but to have them in a state of readiness to be called upon in any emergency that might occur.

About half past six o'clock the members of the city council, the marshal, Brothers Joseph and Hyrum, and a number of others, started for Carthage, on horseback. We were instructed by Brother Joseph Smith not to take any arms, and we consequently left

*Ford's *History of Illinois*, p. 333.

them behind. We called at the house of Brother Fellows on our way out. Brother Fellows lives about four miles from Carthage.

Demand for the State's Arms at Nauvoo

While at Brother Fellows' house, Captain Dunn, accompanied by Mr. Coolie, one of the governor's aid-de-camps, came up from Carthage en route for Nauvoo with a requisition from the governor for the state arms. We all returned to Nauvoo with them; the governor's request was complied with, and after taking some refreshments, we all returned to proceed to Carthage. We arrived there late in the night. A great deal of excitement prevailed on and after our arrival. The governor had received into his company all of the companies that had been in the mob; these fellows were riotous and disorderly, hallooing, yelling, and whooping about the streets like Indians, many of them intoxicated; the whole presented a scene of rowdyism and lowbred ruffianism only found among mobocrats and desperadoes, and entirely revolting to the best feelings of humanity. The governor made a speech to them to the effect that he would show Joseph and Hyrum Smith to them in the morning.

About here the companies with the governor were drawn up in line, and General Deming, I think, took Joseph by the arm and Hyrum (Arnold says that Joseph took the governor's arm), and as he passed through between the ranks, the governor leading in front, very politely introduced them as General Joseph Smith and General Hyrum Smith.*

**The Deseret News* gives the following account of Joseph and Hyrum Smith's passing through the troops in Carthage:

'Carthage, June 25th, 1844.

'Quarter past 9. The governor came and invited Joseph to walk with him through the troops. Joseph solicited a few moment's private conversation with him, which the governor refused.

'While refusing, the governor looked down at his shoes, as though he was ashamed. They then walked through the crowd, with Brigadier-General Miner, R. Deming, and Dr. Richards, to General Deming's quarters. The people appeared quiet until a company of Carthage Greys flocked round the doors of General Deming in an uproarious manner, of which notice was sent to the governor. In the meantime the governor had ordered the McDonough troops to be drawn up in line, for Joseph

All were orderly and courteous except one company of mobocrats—the Carthage Greys—who seemed to find fault on account of too much honor being paid to the 'Mormons'. There was afterward a row between the companies, and they came pretty near having a fight; the more orderly not feeling disposed to endorse or submit to the rowdyism of the mobocrats. The result was that General Deming, who was very much of a gentleman, ordered the Carthage Greys, a company under the command of Captain [R. F.] Smith, a magistrate in Carthage, and a most violent mobocrat, under arrest. This matter, however, was shortly afterward adjusted, and the difficulty settled between them.

The City Council of Nauvoo Arraigned Before Justice Smith.

The mayor, aldermen, councilors, as well as the marshal of the city of Nauvoo, together with some persons who had assisted the marshal in removing the press in Nauvoo, appeared before Justice Smith, the aforesaid captain and mobocrat, to again answer the charge of destroying the press; but as there was so much excitement, and as the man was an unprincipled villain before whom we were to have our hearing, we thought it most prudent to give bail, and consequently became security for each other in $500 bonds each, to appear

and Hyrum to pass in front of them, they having requested that they might have a clear view of the Generals Smith. *Joseph had a conversation with the governor for about ten minutes, when he again pledged the faith of the state that he and his friends should be protected from violence.*

'Robinson, the postmaster, said, on report of martial law being proclaimed in Nauvoo, he had stopped the mail, and notified the postmaster-general of the state of things in Hancock county.

'From the general's quarters Joseph and Hyrum went in front of the lines, in a hollow square of a company of Carthage Greys. At seven minutes before ten they arrived in front of the lines, and passed before the whole, Joseph being on the right of General Deming and Hyrum on his left, Elders Richards, Taylor and Phelps following. Joseph and Hyrum were introduced by Governor Ford about twenty times along the line as General Joseph Smith and General Hyrum Smith, the governor walking in front on the left. The Carthage Greys refused to receive them by that introduction, and some of the officers threw up their hats, drew their swords, and said they would introduce themselves to the damned 'Mormons' in a different style. The governor mildly entreated them not to act so rudely, but their excitement increased; the governor, however, succeeded in pacifying them by making a speech, and promising them that they should have 'full satisfaction'. General Smith and party returned to their lodgings at five minutes past ten' (*Deseret News*, No. 35, Nov. 4, 1857, p. 274).

before the county court at its next session. We had engaged as counsel a lawyer by the name of Wood, of Burlington, Iowa; and Reed, I think, of Madison, Iowa. After some little discussion the bonds were signed, and we were all dismissed.

Almost immediately after our dismissal, two men—Augustine Spencer and Norton—two worthless fellows, whose words would not have been taken for five cents, and the first of whom had a short time previously been before the mayor in Nauvoo for maltreating a lame brother, made affidavits that Joseph and Hyrum Smith were guilty of treason, and a writ was accordingly issued for their arrest, and the Constable Bettisworth, a rough, unprincipled man, wished immediately to hurry them away to prison without any hearing. His rude, uncouth manner in the administration of what he considered the duties of his office made him exceedingly repulsive to us all. But, independent of these acts, the proceedings in this case were altogether illegal. Providing the court was sincere, which it was not, and providing these men's oaths were true, and that Joseph and Hyrum were guilty of treason, still the whole course was illegal.

The Charge of Treason Against the Prophet.

The magistrate made out a mittimus, and committed them to prison without a hearing, which he had no right legally to do. The statute of Illinois expressly provides that 'all men shall have a hearing before a magistrate before they shall be committed to prison'; and Mr. Robert F. Smith, the magistrate, had made out a mittimus committing them to prison contrary to law without such hearing. As I was informed of this illegal proceeding, I went immediately to the governor and informed him of it. Whether he was apprised of it before or not, I do not know; but my opinion is that he was.

I represented to him the characters of the parties who had made oath, the outrageous nature of the charge, the indignity offered to men in the position which they occupied, and declared to him that he knew very well it was a vexatious proceeding, and that the accused were not guilty of any such crime. The governor replied, he was very sorry that the thing had occurred; that he did not believe the charges, but that he thought the best thing to be done was to let the law take its course. I then reminded him that we had come out there at his instance, not to satisfy the law, which we had done before, but the prejudices of the people, in relation to the affair of the press; that at his instance we had given bonds, which we could not by law be required to do to satisfy the people, and that it was asking too much to require gentlemen in their position in life to suffer the degradation of being immured in a jail at the instance of such worthless scoundrels as those who had made this affidavit. The governor replied that it was an unpleasant affair, and looked hard; but that it was a matter over which he had no control, as it belonged to the judiciary; that he, as the executive, could not interfere with their proceedings, and that he had no doubt but that they would immediately be dismissed. I told him that we had looked to him for protection from such insults, and that I thought we had a right to do so from the solemn promises which he had made to me and to Dr. Bernhisel in relation to our coming without guard or arms; that we had relied upon his faith, and had a right to expect him to fulfill his engagements after we had placed ourselves implicitly under his care, and complied with all his requests, although extra-judicial.

Governor Ford's Reaction to the Representation of John Taylor.

He replied that he would detail a guard, if we required it, and see us protected, but that he could not interfere with the judiciary. I expressed my dissatisfaction at the course taken, and told him that, if we were to be subject to mob rule, and to be dragged, contrary to law, into prison at the instance of every infernal scoundrel whose oaths could be bought for a dram of whiskey, his protection availed very little, and we had miscalculated his promises.

Seeing there was no prospect of redress from the governor, I returned to the room, and found the Constable Bettisworth very urgent to hurry Brothers Joseph and Hyrum to prison, while the brethren were remonstrating with him. At the same time a great rabble was gathered in the streets and around the door, and from the rowdyism manifested I was afraid there was a design to murder the prisoners on the way to jail.

Without conferring with any person, my next feelings were to procure a guard, and, seeing a man habited as a soldier in the room, I went to him and said, 'I am afraid there is a design against the lives of the Messrs. Smith; will you go immediately and bring your captain; and, if not convenient any other captain of a company, and I will pay you well for your trouble?' He said he would, and departed forthwith, and soon returned with his captain, whose name I have forgotten, and introduced him to me. I told him of my fears, and requested him immediately to fetch his company.

He departed forthwith, and arrived at the door with them just at the time when the constable was hurrying the brethren downstairs. A number of the brethren went along, together with one or two strangers; and all of us safely lodged in prison, remained there during the night."

CHAPTER VIII.

INTERVIEW BETWEEN JOSEPH SMITH AND GOVERNOR THOMAS FORD

"At the request of Joseph Smith for an interview with the governor, he came the next morning, Thursday, June 26th, at half past 9 o'clock, accompanied by Colonel Thomas Geddes, when a lengthy conversation was entered into in relation to the existing difficulties; and after some preliminary remarks, at the governor's request, Brother Joseph gave him a general outline of the state of affairs in relation to our difficulties, the excited state of the country, the tumultuous mobocratic movements of our enemies, the precautionary measures used by himself (Joseph Smith), the acts of the city council, the destruction of the press, and the moves of the mob and ourselves up to that time.

The following report is, I believe, substantially correct:

Governor—'General Smith, I believe you have given me a general outline of the difficulties that have existed in the country in the documents forwarded to me by Dr. Bernhisel and Mr. Taylor; but, unfortunately, there seems to be a great discrepancy between your statements and those of your enemies. It is true that you are substantiated by evidence and affidavit, but for such an extraordinary excitement as that which is now in the country there must be some cause, and I attribute the last outbreak to the destruction of the *Expositor*, and to your refusal to comply with the writ issued by Esquire Morrison. The press in the United States is looked upon as the great bulwark of American freedom, and its destruction in Nauvoo was represented and looked upon as a high-handed measure, and manifests to the people a disposition on your part to suppress the liberty of speech and of the press. This, with your refusal to comply with the requisition of a writ, I conceive to be the principal cause of this difficulty; and you are moreover represented to me as turbulent, and defiant of the laws and institutions of your country.'

General Smith—'Governor Ford, you, sir, as governor of this state, are aware of the persecutions that I have endured. You know well that our course has been peaceable and law-abiding for I have furnished this state ever since our settlement here with sufficient evidence of my pacific intentions, and those of the people with whom I am associated, by the endurance of every conceivable indignity and lawless outrage perpetrated upon me and upon this people since our settlement here; and you yourself know that I have kept you well posted in relation to all matters associated with the late difficulties. If you have not got some of my communications, it has not been my fault.

'Agreeably to your orders, I assembled the Nauvoo Legion for the protection of Nauvoo and the surrounding country against an armed band of marauders; and ever since they have been mustered I have almost daily communicated with you in regard to all the leading events that have transpired; and whether in the capacity of mayor of the city, or lieutenant-general of the Nauvoo Legion, I have striven, according to the best of my judgment to preserve the peace, and to administer even-handed justice; but my motives are impugned, my acts are misconstrued, and I am grossly and wickedly misrepresented. I suppose I am indebted for my incarceration to the oath of a worthless man, who was arraigned before me and fined for abusing and maltreating his lame, helpless brother. That I should be charged by you, sir, who know better, of acting contrary to law, is to me a matter of surprise. Was it the 'Mormons' or our enemies who first commenced these difficulties? You know well it was not us; and when this turbulent, outrageous people commenced their insurrectionary movements I made you acquainted with them officially, and asked your advice, and have followed strictly your counsel in every particular. Who ordered out the Nauvoo Legion? I did, under your direction. For what purpose? To suppress the insurrectionary movements. It was at your instance, sir, that I issued a Proclamation calling upon the Nauvoo Legion to be in readiness at a moment's warning to guard against the incursions of mobs, and gave an order to Jonathan Dunham, acting major-general, to that effect.

'Am I, then, to be charged with the acts of others? and because lawlessness and mobocracy abound, am I, when carrying out your instructions, to be charged with not abiding law? Why is it that I must be made accountable for other men's acts? If there is trouble in the country, neither I nor my people made it; and all that we have ever done, after much endurance on our part, is to maintain and uphold the Constitution and institutions of our country, and to protect an injured, innocent, and persecuted people against misrule and mob violence.

'Concerning the destruction of the press to which you refer, men may differ somewhat in their opinions about it; but can it be supposed that after all the indignities to which they have been subjected outside, that people would suffer a set of worthless vagabonds to come into their city, and, right under their own eyes and protection, vilify and calumniate not only themselves, but the character of their wives and daughters, as was impudently and unblushingly done in that infamous and filthy sheet?

'There is not a city in the United States that would have suffered such an indignity for twenty-four hours. Our whole people were indignant, and loudly called upon our city authorities for a redress of their grievances, which, if not attended to, they themselves would have taken into their own hands, and have summarily punished the audacious wretches as they deserved. The principle of equal rights that has been instilled into our bosoms from our cradles as American citizens forbids us submitting to every foul indignity, and succumbing and pandering to wretches so infamous as these. But, independent of this, the course that we pursued we consider to be strictly legal; for, notwithstanding the result, we were anxious to be governed strictly by law, and therefore we convened the city council; and being desirous in our deliberations to abide by law, we summoned legal counsel to be present on the occasion. Upon investigating the matter, we found that our city charter gave us power to remove all nuisances. Furthermore, after consulting Blackstone upon what might be considered a nuisance, it appeared that that distinguished lawyer, who is considered authority, I believe, in all courts, states among other things that 'a libelous and filthy *press* may be considered a nuisance, and abated as such.'* Here, then, one of the most eminent English barristers, whose works are considered standard with us, declares that a libelous and filthy press may be considered a nuisance; and our own charter, given us by the legislature of this state, gives us the power to remove nuisances; and by ordering that press to be abated as a nuisance, we conceived that we were acting strictly in accordance with law. We made that order in our corporate capacity, and the city marshal carried it out. It is possible there may have been some better way, but I must confess that I could not see it.

'In relation to the writ served upon us, we were willing to abide the consequences of our own acts, but

*The author referred to (Blackstone) says: "A fourth species of remedy by the mere act of the party injured, is the abatement, or removal of nuisances." On this the following commentary is made in note 6. "So it seems that a *libelous print, or paper* [not the printing *press* on which they may have been printed] affecting a private individual may be destroyed; or, which is the better course, taken and delivered to a magistrate" (See Chitty's *Blackstone*, bk. ii, chs. i, iv, note 6). The destruction of libelous *"prints and papers"* can scarcely be held to sustain the action of destroying a *"printing press."*

were unwilling, in answering a writ of that kind, to submit to illegal exactions, sought to be imposed upon us under the pretense of law, when we knew they were in open violation of it. When that document was presented to me by Mr. Bettisworth, I offered, in the presence of more than twenty persons, to go to any other magistrate, either in our city, in Appanoose, or any other place where we should be safe, but we all refused to put ourselves into the power of a mob. What right had that constable to refuse our request? He had none according to law; for you know, Governor Ford, that the statute law in Illinois is, that the parties served with the writ 'shall go before him who issued it, *or some other justice of the peace.*' Why, then, should we be dragged to Carthage, where the law does not compel us to go? Does not this look like many others of our persecutions with which you are acquainted? and have we not a right to expect foul play? This very act was a breach of law on his part, an assumption of power that did not belong to him, and an attempt, at least, to deprive us of our legal and constitutional rights and privileges. What could we do, under the circumstances, different from what we did do? We sued for, and obtained a writ of *habeas corpus* from the municipal court, by which we were delivered from the hands of Constable Bettisworth, and brought before and acquitted by the municipal court. After our acquittal, in a conversation with Judge Thomas, although he considered the acts of the party illegal, he advised that, to satisfy the people, we had better go before another magistrate who was not in our church. In accordance with his advice, we went before Esquire Wells, with whom you are well acquainted; both parties were present, witnesses were called on both sides, the case was fully investigated, and we were again dismissed. And what is this pretended desire to enforce law, and wherefore are these lying, base rumors put into circulation but to seek, through mob influence, under pretense of law, to make us submit to requisitions which are contrary to law and subversive of every principle of justice? And when you, sir, required us to come out here, we came, not because it was legal, but because you required it of us, and we were desirous of showing to you, and to all men, that we shrunk not from the most rigid investigation of our acts. We certainly did expect other treatment than to be immured in a jail at the instance of these men, and I think, from your plighted faith, we had a right so to expect, after disbanding our own forces, and putting ourselves entirely in your hands. And now, after having fulfilled my part, sir, as a man and an American citizen, I call upon you, Governor Ford, to deliver us from this place, and rescue us from this outrage that is sought to be practiced upon us by a set of infamous scoundrels.'

Governor Ford—'But you have placed men under arrest, detained men as prisoners, and given passes to others, some of which I have seen.'

John P. Greene, City Marshal—'Perhaps I can explain. Since these difficulties have commenced, you are aware that we have been placed under very peculiar circumstances; our city has been placed under a very rigid police guard; in addition to this, frequent guards have been placed outside the city to prevent any sudden surprise, and those guards have questioned suspected or suspicious persons as to their business. To strangers, in some instances, passes have been given to prevent difficulty in passing those guards; it is some of these passes that you have seen. No person, sir, has been imprisoned without a legal cause in our city.'

Governor—'Why did you not give a more speedy answer to the *posse* that I sent out?'

General Smith—'We had matters of importance to consult upon; your letter showed anything but an amiable spirit. We have suffered immensely in Missouri from mobs, in loss of property, imprisonment, and otherwise. It took some time for us to weigh duly these matters; we could not decide upon matters of such importance immediately, and your *posse* were too hasty in returning; we were consulting for a large people, and vast interests were at stake. We had been outrageously imposed upon, and knew not how far we could trust anyone, besides, a question necessarily arose, how shall we come? Your request was that we should come unarmed. It became a matter of serious importance to decide how far promises could be trusted, and how far we were safe from mob violence.'

Colonel Geddes—'It certainly did look from all I have heard, from the general spirit of violence and mobocracy that here prevails, that it was not safe for you to come unprotected.'*

Governor Ford—'I think that sufficient time was not allowed by the *posse* for you to consult and get ready. They were too hasty; but I suppose they found themselves bound by their orders. I think, too, there is a great deal of truth in what you say, and your reasoning is plausible, but I must beg leave to differ from you in relation to the acts of the city council. That council, in my opinion, had no right to act in a legislative capacity and in that of the judiciary. They should have passed a law in relation to the matter, and then the municipal court, upon complaint, could have removed it [i. e., the *Expositor* press]; but for the city council to take upon themselves the law-making and the execution of the law, is, in my opinion, wrong; besides, these men ought to have had a hearing before their property was destroyed; to destroy it without was an infringement on their rights; besides, it is so contrary to the feelings of American people to interfere with the press. And,

*Notwithstanding this sympathetic allusion by Colonel Geddes upon the situation, it is stated by Gregg that Geddes was really unfriendly to the Prophet and had no sympathy with him and the injustice which had been done him in his arrest and imprisonment, for after leaving the prison and carrying on a conversation with Governor Ford, he represents the governor as saying to him: "O, it's all nonsense; you will have to drive these Mormons out yet"! Then Geddes said to the governor: "If we undertake that governor, when the proper time comes, will you interfere?" "No, I will not", said the governor, after a pause adding, *"until you are through"* (Gregg's *History of Hancock County*, p. 372).

furthermore, I cannot but think that it would have been more judicious for you to have gone with Mr. Bettisworth to Carthage, notwithstanding the law did not require it. Concerning your being in jail, I am sorry for that; I wish it had been otherwise. I hope you will soon be released, but I can not interfere.'

Joseph Smith—'Governor Ford, allow me, sir, to bring one thing to your mind that you seem to have overlooked. You state that you think it would have been better for us to have submitted to the requisition of Constable Bettisworth, and to have gone to Carthage. Do you not know, sir, that that writ was served at the instance of an anti-'Mormon' mob, who had passed resolutions, and published them, to the effect that they would exterminate the 'Mormon' leaders? And are you not informed that Captain Anderson was not only threatened but had a gun fired at his boat by this said mob in Warsaw when coming up to Nauvoo, and that this very thing was made use of as a means to get us into their hands; and we could not, without taking an armed force with us, go there without, according to their published declarations, going into the jaws of death? To have taken a force with us would only have fanned the excitement, and they would have stated that we wanted to use intimidation; therefore, we thought it the most judicious to avail ourselves of the protection of law.'

Governor Ford—'I see, I see.'

Joseph Smith—'Furthermore, in relation to the press, you say that you differ from me in opinion. Be it so; the thing, after all, is only a legal difficulty, and the courts, I should judge, are competent to decide on that matter. If our act was illegal, we are willing to meet it and although I can not see the distinction that you draw about the acts of the city council, and what difference it could have made in point of fact, law, or justice between the city council's acting together or separate, or how much more legal it would have been for the municipal court, who were a part of the city council, to act separately instead of with the councilors, yet if it is deemed that we did a wrong in destroying that press, we refuse not to pay for it; we are desirous to fulfill the law in every particular, and are responsible for our acts. You say that the parties ought to have had a hearing. Had it been a civil suit, this, of course, would have been proper; but there was a flagrant violation of every principle of right—a nuisance; and it was abated on the same principle that any nuisance, stench, or putrefied carcass would have been removed. Our first step, therefore, was to stop the foul, noisome, filthy sheet, and then the next in our opinion would have been to have prosecuted the man for a breach of public decency. And, furthermore, again let me say, Governor Ford, I shall look to you for our protection. I believe you are talking of going to Nauvoo; if you go, sir, I wish to go along. I refuse not to answer any law, but I do not consider myself safe here.'

Governor—'I am in hopes that you will be acquitted, and if I go I will certainly take you along. I do not, however, apprehend danger. I think you are perfectly safe either here or anywhere else. I can not, however, interfere with the law. I am placed in peculiar circumstances, and seem to be blamed by all parties.'

Joseph Smith—'Governor Ford, I ask nothing but what is legal; I have a right to expect protection, at least from you; for, independent of law, you have pledged your faith and that of the state for my protection, and I wish to go to Nauvoo.'

Governor—'And you shall have protection, General Smith. I did not make this promise without consulting my officers, who all pledged their honor to its fulfillment. I do not know that I shall go tomorrow to Nauvoo, but if I do I will take you along.'

At a quarter past ten o'clock the governor left."

CHAPTER IX

THE ASSAULT UPON THE PRISON—THE MURDER OF JOSEPH AND HYRUM SMITH

"At about half past twelve o'clock, Mr. Reed, one of Joseph's counsel, came in, apparently much elated; he stated that, upon an examination of the law, he found that the magistrate had transcended his jurisdiction, and that, having committed them without an examination, his jurisdiction ended; that he had him upon a pinhook; that he ought to have examined them before he committed them, and that, having violated the law in this particular, he had no farther power over them; for, once committed, they were out of his jurisdiction, as the power of the magistrate extended no farther than their committal, and that now they could not be brought out except at the regular session of the circuit court, or by a writ of *habeas corpus;* but that if Justice Smith would consent to go to Nauvoo for trial, he would compromise matters with him, and overlook this matter.

The Magistrate Exceeds His Jurisdiction.

Mr. Reed farther stated that the anti-'Mormons', or mob had concocted a scheme to get a writ from Missouri, with a demand upon Governor Ford for the arrest of Joseph Smith, and his conveyance to Missouri, and that a man by the name of Wilson had returned from Missouri the night before the burning of the press for this purpose.

At half past two o'clock Constable Bettisworth came to the jail with a man named Simpson, professing to have some order, but he would not send up his name, and the guard would not let him pass. Dr.

Bernhisel and Brother Wasson went to inform the governor and council of this. At about twenty minutes to three Dr. Bernhisel returned, and stated that he thought the governor was doing all he could. At about ten minutes to three Hiram Kimball appeared with news from Nauvoo.

Soon after Constable Bettisworth came with an order from Esquire Smith to convey the prisoners to the courthouse for trial. He was informed that the process was illegal, that they had been placed there contrary to law, and that they refused to come unless by legal process. I was informed that Justice [Robert F.] Smith (who was also captain of the Carthage Greys) went to the governor and informed him of the matter, and that the governor replied, 'You have your forces, and of course can use them.' The constable certainly did return, accompanied by a guard of armed men, and by force, and under protest, hurried the prisoners to the court.

Prisoners Illegally Forced into Court.

About four o'clock the case was called by Captain Robert F. Smith, J. P. The counsel for the prisoners called for subpoenas to bring witnesses. At twenty-five minutes past four he took a copy of the order to bring the prisoners from jail to trial, and afterwards he took names of witnesses.

Counsel present for the state; Higbee, Skinner, Sharp, Emmons, and Morrison. Twenty-five minutes to five the writ was returned as served, June 25th.

Many remarks were made at the court that I paid but little attention to, as I considered the whole thing illegal and a complete burlesque. Wood objected to the proceedings *in toto,* in consequence of its illegality, showing that the prisoners were not only illegally committed, but that, being once committed, the magistrate had no farther power over them; but as it was the same magistrate before whom he was pleading who imprisoned them contrary to law, and the same who, as captain, forced them from jail, his arguments availed but little. He then urged that the prisoners be remanded until witnesses could be had, and applied for a continuance for that purpose. Skinner suggested until twelve o'clock next day. Wood again demanded until witnesses could be obtained; that the court meet at a specified time, and that, if witnesses were not present, again adjourn, without calling the prisoners. After various remarks from Reed, Skinner, and others, the court stated that the writ was served yesterday, and that it will give until tomorrow at twelve m. to get witnesses.

We then returned to jail. Immediately after our return Dr. Bernhisel went to the governor, and obtained from him an order for us to occupy a large open room containing a bedstead. I rather think that the same room had been appropriated to the use of debtors; at any rate, there was free access to the jailor's house, and no bars or locks except such as might be on the outside door of the jail. The jailor, Mr. George W. Steghall, and his wife, manifested a disposition to make us as comfortable as they could; we ate at their table, which was well provided, and, of course, paid for it.

Some Concessions of Comfort to the Prisoners.

I do not remember the names of all who were with us that night and the next morning in jail, for several went and came; among those that we considered stationary were Stephen Markham, John S. Fullmer, Captain Dan Jones, Dr. Willard Richards, and myself. Dr. Bernhisel says that he was there from Wednesday in the afternoon until eleven o'clock next day. We were, however, visited by numerous friends, among whom were Uncle John Smith, Hiram Kimball, Cyrus H. Wheelock, besides lawyers, as counsel. There was also a great variety of conversation, which was rather desultory than otherwise, and referred to circumstances that had transpired, our former and present grievances, the spirit of the troops around us, and the disposition of the governor; the devising for legal and other plans for deliverance, the nature of testimony required; the gathering of proper witnesses, and a variety of other topics, including our religious hopes, etc.

During one of these conversations Dr. Richards remarked: 'Brother Joseph, if it is necessary that you die in this matter, and if they will take me in your stead, I will suffer for you.' At another time, when conversing about deliverance, I said, 'Brother Joseph, if you will permit it, and say the word, I will have you out of this prison in five hours, if the jail has to come down to do it.' My idea was to go to Nauvoo, and collect a force sufficient, as I considered the whole affair a legal farce, and a flagrant outrage upon our liberty and rights. Brother Joseph refused.

Elder Cyrus H. Wheelock came in to see us, and when he was about leaving drew a small pistol, a six-shooter, from his pocket, remarking at the same time, 'Would any of you like to have this?' Brother Joseph immediately replied, 'Yes, give it to me,' whereupon he took the pistol, and put it in his pantaloons pocket. The pistol was a six-shooting revolver, of Allen's patent; it belonged to me, and was one that I furnished to Brother Wheelock when he talked of going with me to the east, previous to our coming to Carthage. I have it now in my possession. Brother Wheelock went out on some errand, and was not suffered to return. The report of the governor having gone to Nauvoo without taking the prisoners along with him caused very unpleasant feelings, as we were apprised that we were left to the tender mercies of the Carthage Greys, a company strictly mobocratic, and whom we knew to be our most deadly enemies; and their captain, Esquire [Robert F.] Smith, was a most unprincipled villain. Besides this, all the mob forces, comprising the governor's troops, were dismissed, with the exception of one or two companies, which the governor took with him to Nauvoo. The great part of the mob was liberated, the remainder was our guard.

Cyrus H. Wheelock's Visit to the Prison.

We looked upon it not only as a breach of faith on

the part of the governor, but also as an indication of a desire to insult us, if nothing more, by leaving us in the proximity of such men. The prevention of Wheelock's return was among the first of their hostile movements.

Colonel Markham went out, and he was also prevented from returning. He was very angry at this, but the mob paid no attention to him; they drove him out of town at the point of the bayonet, and threatened to shoot him if he returned. He went, I am informed, to Nauvoo for the purpose of raising a company of men for our protection. Brother Fullmer went to Nauvoo after witnesses: it is my opinion that Brother Wheelock did also.

Harsh Treatment of Col. Markham.

Sometime after dinner we sent for some wine. It has been reported by some that this was taken as a sacrament. It was no such thing; our spirits were generally dull and heavy, and it was sent for to revive us. I think it was Captain Jones who went after it, but they would not suffer him to return. I believe we all drank of the wine, and gave some to one or two of the prison guards. We all of us felt unusually dull and languid, with a remarkable depression of spirits. In consonance with those feelings I sang a song, that had lately been introduced into Nauvoo, entitled, 'A Poor Wayfaring Man of Grief', etc.*

Wine Obtained.

The song is pathetic, and the tune quite plaintive, and was very much in accordance with our feelings at the time for our spirits were all depressed, dull and gloomy and surcharged with indefinite ominous forebodings. After a lapse of some time, Brother Hyrum requested me again to sing that song. I replied, 'Brother Hyrum, I do not feel like singing;' when he remarked, 'Oh, never mind; commence singing, and you will get the spirit of it.'

'A Poor Wayfaring Man of Grief.'

*The song is published in full this *History*, vol. vi, pp. 614-15. It was the composition of Montgomery. B. H. R.

At his request I did so. Soon afterwards I was sitting at one of the front windows of the jail, when I saw a number of men, with painted faces, coming around the corner of the jail, and aiming towards the stairs.

The Assault.

The other brethren had seen the same, for, as I went to the door, I found Brother Hyrum Smith and Dr. Richards already leaning against it. They both pressed against the door with their shoulders to prevent its being opened, as the lock and latch were comparatively useless. While in this position, the mob, who had come upstairs, and tried to open the door, probably thought it was locked, and fired a ball through the keyhole; at this Dr. Richards and Brother Hyrum leaped back from the door, with their faces towards it; almost instantly another ball passed through the panel of the door, and struck Brother Hyrum on the left side of the nose, entering his face and head. At the same instant, another ball from the outside entered his back, passing through his body and striking his watch. The ball came from the back, through the jail window, opposite the door, and must, from its range, have been fired from the Carthage Greys, who were placed there ostensibly for our protection, as the balls from the firearms, shot close by the jail, would have entered the ceiling, we being in the second story, and there never was a time after that when Hyrum could have received the latter wound. Immediately, when the ball struck him, he fell flat on his back, crying as he fell, 'I am a dead man!' He never moved afterwards.

I shall never forget the deep feeling of sympathy and regard manifested in the countenance of Brother Joseph as he drew nigh to Hyrum, and, leaning over him, exclaimed, 'Oh! my poor, dear brother Hyrum!' He, however, instantly arose, and with a firm, quick step, and a determined expression of countenance, approached the door, and pulling the six-shooter left by Brother Wheelock from his pocket, opened the door slightly, and snapped the pistol six successive times;

only three of the barrels, however, were discharged. I afterwards understood that two or three were wounded by these discharges, two of whom, I am informed, died. I had in my hands a large, strong hickory stick, brought there by Brother Markham, and left by him, which I had seized as soon as I saw the mob approach; and while Brother Joseph was firing the pistol, I stood close behind him. As soon as he had discharged it he stepped back, and I immediately took his place next to the door, while he occupied the one I had done while he was shooting. Brother Richards, at this time, had a knotty walking-stick in his hands belonging to me, and stood next to Brother Joseph, a little farther from the door, in an oblique direction, apparently to avoid the rake of the fire from the door. The firing of Brother Joseph made our assailants pause for a moment; very soon after, however, they pushed the door some distance open, and protruded and discharged their guns into the room, when I parried them off with my stick, giving another direction to the balls.

It certainly was a terrible scene: streams of fire as thick as my arm passed by me as these men fired, and, unarmed as we were, it looked like certain death. I remember feeling as though my time had come, but I do not know when, in any critical position, I was more calm, unruffled, energetic, and acted with more promptness and decision. It certainly was far from pleasant to be so near the muzzles of those firearms as they belched forth their liquid flames and deadly balls. While I was engaged in parrying the guns, Brother Joseph said, 'That's right, Brother Taylor, parry them off as well as you can.' These were the last words I ever heard him speak on earth.

Every moment the crowd at the door became more dense, as they were unquestionably pressed on by those in the rear ascending the stairs, until the whole entrance at the door was literally crowded with muskets and rifles, which, with the swearing, shouting, and demoniacal expressions of those outside the door and on the stairs, and the firing of the guns, mingled with their horrid oaths and execrations, made it look like pandemonium let loose, and was, indeed, a fit representation of the horrid deed in which they were engaged.

Taylor's Effort to Escape by the Window.

After parrying the guns for some time, which now protruded thicker and farther into the room, and seeing no hope of escape or protection there, as we were now unarmed, it occurred to me that we might have some friends outside, and that there might be some chance of escape in that direction, but here there seemed to be none. As I expected them every moment to rush into the room—nothing but extreme cowardice having thus far kept them out—as the tumult and pressure increased, without any other hope, I made a spring for the window which was right in front of the jail door, where the mob was standing, and also exposed to the fire of the Carthage Greys, who were stationed some ten or twelve rods off. The weather was hot, we all of us had our coats off, and the window was raised to admit air. As I reached the window, and was on the point of leaping out, I was struck by a ball from the door about midway of my thigh, which struck the bone, and flattened out almost to the size of a quarter of a dollar, and then passed on through the fleshy part to within about half an inch of the outside. I think some prominent nerve must have been severed or injured for, as soon as the ball struck me, I fell like a bird when shot, or an ox when struck by a butcher, and lost entirely and instantaneously all power of action or locomotion. I fell upon the window-sill, and cried out, 'I am shot!' Not possessing any power to move, I felt myself falling outside of the window, but immediately I fell inside, from some, at that time, unknown cause. When I struck the floor my animation seemed restored, as I have seen it sometimes in squirrels and birds after being shot. As soon as I felt the power of motion I crawled under the bed, which was in a corner of the room, not far from the window where I received my wound. While on my way and under the bed I was wounded in three other places; one ball entered a little below the left knee, and never was extracted; another entered the forepart of my left arm, a little above the wrist, and, passing down by the joint, lodged in the fleshy part of my hand, about midway, a little above the upper joint of my little finger; another struck me on the fleshy part of my left hip, and tore away the flesh as large as my hand, dashing the mangled fragments of flesh and blood against the wall.

My wounds were painful, and the sensation produced was as though a ball had passed through and down the whole length of my leg. I very well remember my reflections at the time. I had a very painful idea of becoming lame and decrepid, and being an object of pity, and I felt as though I would rather die than be placed in such circumstances.

It would seem that immediately after my attempt to leap out of the window, Joseph also did the same thing, of which circumstance I have no knowledge only from information. The first thing that I noticed was a cry that he had leaped out of the window. A cessation of firing followed, the mob rushed downstairs, and Dr. Richards went to the window. Immediately afterward I saw the doctor going towards the jail door, and as there was an iron door at the head of the stairs adjoining our door which led into the cells for criminals, it struck me that the doctor was going in there, and I said to him, 'Stop, Doctor, and take me along.' He proceeded to the door and opened it, and then returned and dragged me along to a small cell prepared for criminals.

Summary of Movements.

Brother Richards was very much troubled, and exclaimed, 'Oh! Brother Taylor, is it possible that they have killed both Brother Hyrum and Joseph? it cannot surely be, and yet I saw them shoot them;' and, elevating his hands two or three times, he exclaimed, 'Oh Lord, my God, spare Thy servants!' He then said, 'Brother Taylor, this is a terrible event;' and he dragged me farther into the cell, saying, 'I am sorry I can not do better for you;' and, taking an old, filthy mattress, he covered me with it, and said, 'That may hide you, and you may yet live to tell the tale, but I expect they will kill me in a few moments!' While lying in this position I suffered the most excruciating pain.

Soon afterwards Dr. Richards came to me, informed me that the mob had precipitately fled, and at the same time confirmed my worst fears that Joseph was assuredly dead. I felt a dull, lonely, sickening sensation at the news. When I reflected that our noble chieftain, the Prophet of the living God, had fallen, and that I had seen his brother in the cold embrace of death, it seemed as though there was a void or vacuum in the great field of human existence to me, and a dark gloomy chasm in the kingdom, and that we were left alone. Oh, how lonely was that feeling! How cold, barren and desolate! In the midst of difficulties he was always the first in motion; in critical positions his counsel was always sought. As our Prophet he approached our God, and obtained for us his will; but now our Prophet, our counselor, our general, our leader, was gone, and amid the fiery ordeal that we then had to pass through, we were left alone without his aid, and as our future guide for things spiritual or temporal, and for all things pertaining to this world, or the next, he had spoken for the last time on earth.

The Murder Accomplished—Reflections.

These reflections and a thousand others flashed upon my mind. I thought, why must the good perish, and the virtuous be destroyed? Why must God's nobility, the salt of the earth, the most exalted of the human family, and the most perfect types of all excellence, fall victims to the cruel, fiendish hate of incarnate devils?

The poignancy of my grief, I presume, however, was somewhat allayed by the extreme suffering that I endured from my wounds.

Soon afterwards I was taken to the head of the stairs and laid there, where I had a full view of our beloved and now murdered brother, Hyrum. There he lay as I had left him; he had not moved a limb; he lay placid and calm, a monument of greatness even in death; but his noble spirit had left its tenement, and was gone to dwell in regions more congenial to its exalted nature. Poor Hyrum! He was a great and good man, and my soul was cemented to his. If ever there was an exemplary, honest, and virtuous man, an embodiment of all that is noble in the human form, Hyrum Smith was its representative.

While I lay there a number of persons came around, among whom was a physician. The doctor, on seeing a ball lodged in my left hand, took a penknife from his pocket and made an incision in it for the purpose of extracting the ball therefrom, and having obtained a pair of carpenter's compasses, made use of them to draw or pry out the ball, alternately using the penknife and compasses. After sawing for some time with a dull penknife, and prying and pulling with the compasses, he ultimately succeeded in extracting the ball, which weighed about half an ounce. Some time afterwards he remarked to a friend of mine that I had 'nerves like the devil', to stand what I did in its extraction. I really thought I had need of nerves to stand such surgical butchery, and that, whatever my nerves may be, his practice was devilish.

Rough Surgery.

This company wished to remove me to Mr. Hamilton's Hotel, the place where we had stayed previous to our incarceration in jail. I told them, however, that I did not wish to go: I did not consider it safe. They protested that it was, and that I was safe with them; that it was a perfect outrage for men to be used as we had been; that they were my friends; that it was for my good they were counseling me, and that I could be better taken care of there than here.

I replied, 'I don't know you. Whom am I among?

I am surrounded by assassins and murderers; witness your deeds. Don't talk to me of kindness or comfort; look at your murdered victims. Look at me! I want none of your counsel nor comfort. There may be some safety here; I can be assured of none anywhere,' etc.

They G— d— their souls to hell, made the most solemn asseverations, and swore by God and the devil, and everything else that they could think of, that they would stand by me to death and protect me. In half an hour every one of them fled from the town.

Soon after a coroner's jury were assembled in the room over the body of Hyrum. Among the jurors was Captain Smith of the 'Carthage Greys', who had assisted in the murder, and the same justice before whom we had been tried. I learned of Francis Higbee as being in the neighborhood. On hearing his name mentioned, I immediately arose and said, 'Captain Smith, you are a justice of the peace; I have heard his name mentioned; I want to swear my life against him.' I was informed that word was immediately sent to him to leave the place, which he did.

Activities of Willard Richards.

Brother Richards was busy during this time attending to the coroner's inquest, and to the removal of the bodies, and making arrangements for their removal from Carthage to Nauvoo.

Flight of the People from Carthage.

When he had a little leisure, he again came to me, and at his suggestion I was removed to Hamilton's Tavern. I felt that he was the only friend, the only person, that I could rely upon in that town. It was with difficulty that sufficient persons could be found to carry me to the tavern; for immediately after the murder a great fear fell upon all the people, and men, women, and children fled with great precipitation, leaving nothing nor anybody in the town but two or three women and children and one or two sick persons.

It was with great difficulty that Brother Richards

prevailed upon Mr. Hamilton, hotelkeeper, and his family, to stay; they would not until Brother Richards had given a solemn promise that he would see them protected, and hence I was looked upon as a hostage. Under these circumstances, notwithstanding, I believe they were hostile to the 'Mormons', and were glad that the murder had taken place, though they did not actually participate in it; and, feeling that I should be a protection to them they stayed.

The whole community knew that a dreadful outrage had been perpetrated by those villains, and fearing lest the citizens of Nauvoo, as they possessed the power, might have a disposition to visit them with a terrible vengeance, they fled in the wildest confusion. And, indeed, it was with very great difficulty that the citizens of Nauvoo could be restrained. A horrid, barbarous murder had been committed, the most solemn pledge violated, and that, too, while the victims were, contrary to the requirements of the law, putting themselves into the hands of the governor to pacify a popular excitement. This outrage was enhanced by the reflection that our people were able to protect themselves against not only all the mob, but against three times their number and that of the governor's troops put together. They were also exasperated by the speech of the governor in town.

The whole events were so faithless, so dastardly, so mean, cowardly, and contemptible, without one extenuating circumstance, that it would not have been surprising if the citizens of Nauvoo had arisen *en masse*. and blotted the wretches out of existence. The citizens of Carthage knew they would have done so under such circumstances, and, judging us by themselves, they were all panic-stricken, and fled. Colonel Markham, too, after his expulsion from Carthage, had gone home, related the circumstances of his ejectment, and was using his influence to get a company to go out. Fearing that when the people heard that their Prophet and Patriarch had been murdered under the above circumstances they might act rashly, and knowing that, if they once got roused, like a mighty avalanche they would lay the country waste before them and take a terrible vengeance—as none of the Twelve were in Nauvoo, and no one, perhaps, with sufficient influence to control the people, Dr. Richards, after consulting me, wrote the following note, fearing that my family might be seriously affected by the news. I told him to insert that I was slightly wounded.

*WILLARD RICHARDS' NOTE FROM CARTHAGE JAIL TO NAUVOO**

'Carthage Jail, 8 o'clock 5 min. p. m., June 27th, 1844.

'Joseph and Hyrum are dead. Taylor wounded, not very badly. I am well. Our guard was forced, as we believe, by a band of Missourians from 100 to 200. The job was done in an instant, and the party fled towards Nauvoo instantly. This is as I believe it. The citizens here are afraid of the 'Mormons' attacking them; I promise them no.

[Signed] W. RICHARDS.

'N. B.—The citizens promise us protection; alarm guns have been fired.

[Signed] JOHN TAYLOR.

I remember signing my name as quickly as possible, lest the tremor of my hand should be noticed, and the fears of my family excited.

A messenger was dispatched immediately with the note, but he was intercepted by the governor, who, on hearing a cannon fired at Carthage, which was to be the signal for the murder, immediately fled with his company, and fearing that the citizens of Nauvoo, when apprised of the horrible outrage, would immediately rise and pursue, he turned back the messenger, who was George D. Grant. A second one was sent, who was treated similarly; and not until a third attempt could news be got to Nauvoo.

News of the Assassination Intercepted by Governor Ford.

Samuel H. Smith, brother to Joseph and Hyrum, was the first brother I saw after the outrage; I am not

**Deseret News*, No. 38, Nov. 25, 1857, p. 297.

Attempt on the Life of Samuel H. Smith, Brother of the Prophet.

sure whether he took the news or not; he lived at the time in Plymouth, Hancock county, and was on his way to Carthage to see his brothers, when he was met by some of the troops, or rather mob, that had been dismissed by the governor, and who were on their way home. On learning that he was Joseph Smith's brother they sought to kill him, but he escaped, and fled into the woods, where he was chased for a length of time by them; but, after severe fatigue, and much danger and excitement, he succeeded in escaping, and came to Carthage. He was on horseback when he arrived, and was not only very much tired with the fatigue and excitement of the chase, but was also very much distressed in feelings on account of the death of his brothers. These things produced a fever, which laid the foundation for his death, which took place on the 30th of July. Thus another of the brothers fell a victim, although not directly, but indirectly to this infernal mob.

I lay from about five o'clock until two next morning without having my wounds dressed, as there was scarcely any help of any kind in Carthage, and Brother Richards was busy with the dead bodies, preparing them for removal. My wife Leonora started early the next day, having had some little trouble in getting a company or a physician to come with her; after considerable difficulty she succeeded in getting an escort, and Dr. Samuel Bennett came along with her. Soon after my father and mother arrived from Oquakie, near which place they had a farm at that time, and hearing of the trouble, hastened along.

General Deming, brigadier-general of the Hancock county militia, was very much of a gentleman, and showed me every courtesy, and Colonel Jones also was very solicitous about my welfare.

I was called upon by several gentlemen of Quincy and other places, among whom was Judge Ralston, as well as by our own people, and a medical man extracted a ball from my left thigh that was giving me much pain; it lay about half an inch deep, and my thigh was considerably swollen. The doctor asked me if I would be tied during the operation; I told him no; that I could endure the cutting associated with the operation as well without, and I did so; indeed, so great was the pain I endured that the cutting was rather a relief than otherwise.

A very laughable incident occurred at the time; my wife, Leonora, went into an adjoining room to pray for me, that I might be sustained during the operation. While on her knees at prayer, a Mrs. Bedell, an old lady of the Methodist association, entered, and, patting Mrs. Taylor on her back with her hand, said, 'There's a good lady, pray for God to forgive your sins; pray that you may be converted, and the Lord may have mercy on your soul.'

The scene was so ludicrous that Mrs. Taylor knew not whether to laugh or be angry. Mrs. Taylor informed me that Mr. Hamilton, the father of the Hamilton who kept the house, rejoiced at the murder, and said in company that 'it was done up in the best possible style, and showed good generalship,' and she farther believed that the other branches of the family sanctioned it. These were the associates of the old lady referred to, and yet she could talk of conversion and saving souls in the midst of blood and murder: such is man and such consistency!

The Hamiltons and the Murder.

The ball being extracted was the one that first struck me, which I before referred to; it entered on the outside of my left thigh, about five inches from my knee, and passing rather obliquely towards my body, had, it would seem, struck the bone, for it was flattened out nearly as thin and large as a quarter of a dollar.

The governor passed on, staying at Carthage only a few minutes, and he did not stop until he got fifty miles from Nauvoo."

CHAPTER X.

WAS GOVERNOR FORD RESPONSIBLE FOR THE MURDER OF THE PROPHET AND PATRIARCH OF THE NEW DISPENSATION

"THERE had been various opinions about the complicity of the governor in the murder, some supposing that he knew all about it, and assisted or winked at its execution. It is somewhat difficult to form a correct opinion; from the facts presented it is very certain that things looked more than suspicious against him.

In the first place, he positively knew that we had broken no law.

Secondly. He knew that the mob had not only passed inflammatory resolutions, threatening extermination to the 'Mormons', but that they had actually assembled armed mobs and commenced hostilities against us.

Thirdly. He took those very mobs that had been arrayed against us, and enrolled them as his troops, thus legalizing their acts.

Fourthly. He disbanded the Nauvoo Legion, which had never violated law, and disarmed them, and had about his person in the shape of militia known mobocrats and violators of the law.

Fifthly. He requested us to come to Carthage without arms, promising protection, and then refused to interfere in delivering us from prison, although Joseph and Hyrum were put there contrary to law.

Sixthly. Although he refused to interfere in our behalf, yet, when Captain Smith went to him and informed him that the persons refused to come out, he told him that he had a command and knew what to do, thus sanctioning the use of force in the violation of law when opposed to us, whereas he would not for us interpose his executive authority to free us from being incarcerated contrary to law, although he was fully informed of all the facts of the case, as we kept him posted in the affairs all the time.

Seventhly. He left the prisoners in Carthage jail contrary to his plighted faith.

Eighthly. Before he went he dismissed all the troops that could be relied upon, as well as many of the mob, and left us in charge of the 'Carthage Greys', a company that he knew were mobocratic, our most bitter enemies, and who had passed resolutions to exterminate us, and who had been placed under guard by General Deming only the day before.

Ninthly. He was informed of the intended murder, both before he left and while on the road, by several different parties.

Incriminating Circumstances Against Governor Ford.

Tenthly. When the cannon was fired in Carthage, signifying that the deed was done, he immediately took up his line of march and fled. How did he know that this signal portended their death if he was not in the secret? It may be said some of the party told him. How could he believe what the party said about the gun signal if he could not believe the testimony of several individuals who told him in positive terms about the contemplated murder?

He has, I believe, stated that he left the 'Carthage Greys' there because he considered that, as their town was contiguous to ours, and as the responsibility of our safety rested solely upon them, they would not dare suffer any indignity to befall us. This very admission shows that he did really expect danger; and then he knew that these people had published to the world that they would exterminate us, and his leaving us in their hands and taking of their responsibilities was like leaving a lamb in charge of a wolf, and trusting to its humanity and honor for its safe-keeping.

It is said, again, that he would not have gone to Nauvoo, and thus placed himself in the hands of the 'Mormons', if he had anticipated any such event, as he would be exposed to their wrath. To this it may be answered that the 'Mormons' did not know their signals, while he did; and they were also known in Warsaw, as well as in other places; and as soon as the gun was fired, a merchant of Warsaw jumped upon his horse and rode directly to Quincy, and reported, 'Joseph and Hyrum killed, and those who were with them in jail.' He reported farther that 'they were attempting to break jail, and were all killed by the guard.' This was their story; it was anticipated to kill all, and the gun was to be the signal that the deed was accomplished. This was known in Warsaw. The governor also knew it and fled; and he could really be in no danger in Nauvoo, for the 'Mormons' did not know it, and he had plenty of time to escape, which he did.

It is said that he made all his officers promise solemnly that they would help him to protect the Smiths; this may or may not be. At any rate, some of these same officers helped to murder them.

The strongest argument in the governor's favor, and one that would bear more weight with us than all the rest put together, would be that he could not believe them capable of such atrocity; and, thinking that their talk and threatenings were a mere ebullition of feeling, a kind of braggadocio, and that there was enough of good moral feeling to control the more violent passions, he trusted to their faith. There is, indeed, a degree of plausibility about this, but when we put it in juxtaposition to the amount of evidence that he was in possession of it weighs very little. He had nothing to inspire confidence in them, and everything to make him mistrust them. Besides, why his broken faith? Why his disregard of what was told him by several parties? Again, if he knew not the plan how did he understand the signal? Why so oblivious to everything pertaining

Argument in Favor of Governor Ford.

to the 'Mormon' interest, and so alive and interested about the mobocrats? At any rate, be this as it may, he stands responsible for their blood, and it is dripping on his garments. If it had not been for his promise of protection, they would have protected themselves; it was plighted faith that led them to the slaughter; and, to make the best of it, it was a breach of that faith and a nonfulfillment of that promise, after repeated warning, that led to their death.

Having said so much, I must leave the governor with my readers and with his God. Justice, I conceive, demanded this much, and truth could not be told with less; as I have said before, my opinion is that the governor would not have planned this murder, but he had not sufficient energy to resist popular opinion, even if that opinion led to blood and death.

Were National Characters Implicated in the Murder.

It was rumored that a strong political party, numbering in its ranks many of the prominent men of the nation, were engaged in a plot for the overthrow of Joseph Smith, and that the governor was of this party, and Sharp, Williams, Captain Smith, and others, were his accomplices, but whether this was the case or not I do not know. It is very certain that a strong political feeling existed against Joseph Smith, and I have reason to believe that his letters to Henry Clay were made use of by political parties opposed to Mr. Clay, and were the means of that statesman's defeat. Yet, if such a combination as the one referred to existed, I am not apprised of it.

While I lay at Carthage, previous to Mrs. Taylor's arrival, a pretty good sort of a man, who was lame of a leg, waited upon me, and sat up at night with me; afterwards Mrs. Taylor, mother, and others waited upon me.

Many friends called upon me, among whom were Richard Ballantyne, Elizabeth Taylor, several of the Perkins family, and a number of the brethren from Macedonia and La Harpe. Besides these, many strangers from Quincy, some of whom expressed indignant feelings against the mob and sympathy for myself. Brother Alexander Williams called upon me, who suspected that they had some designs in keeping me there, and stated that he had, at a given point in some woods, fifty men, and if I would say the word he would raise other fifty, and fetch me out of there. I thanked him, but told him I thought there was no need. However, it would seem that I was in some danger; for Colonel Jones, before referred to, when absent from me, left two loaded pistols on the table in case of an attack, and some time afterwards, when I had recovered and was publishing the affair, a lawyer, Mr. Backman, stated that he had prevented a man by the name of Jackson, before referred to, from ascending the stairs, who was coming with a design to murder me, and that now he was sorry he had not let him do the deed.

Visitors to John Taylor.

There were others also, of whom I heard, that said I ought to be killed, and they would do it, but that it was too damned cowardly to shoot a wounded man; and thus, by the chivalry of murderers, I was prevented from being a second time mutilated or killed. Many of the mob came around and treated me with apparent respect, and the officers and people generally looked upon me as a hostage, and feared that my removal would be the signal for the rising of the 'Mormons'.

I do not remember the time that I stayed at Carthage, but I think three or four days after the murder, when Brother Marks with a carriage, Brother James Allred with a wagon, Dr. Ells, and a number of others on horseback, came for the purpose of taking me to Nauvoo. I was very weak at the time, occasioned by the loss of blood and the great discharge of my wounds, so when my wife asked me if I could talk I could barely whisper no. Quite a discussion arose as to the propriety of my removal, the physicians and people of Carthage protesting that it would be my death, while my friends were anxious for my removal if possible.

I suppose the former were actuated by the above-named desire to keep me. Colonel Jones was, I believe, sincere; he had acted as a friend all the time, and he told Mrs. Taylor she ought to persuade me not to go, for he did not believe I had strength enough to reach Nauvoo. It was finally agreed, however, that I should go; but as it was thought that I could not stand riding in a wagon or carriage, they prepared a litter for me; I was carried downstairs and put upon it. A number of men assisted to carry me, some of whom had been engaged in the mob. As soon as I got downstairs, I felt much better and strengthened, so that I could talk; I suppose the effect of the fresh air.

Taylor's Painful Journey to Nauvoo.

When we had got near the outside of the town I remembered some woods that we had to go through, and telling a person near to call for Dr. Ells, who was riding a very good horse, I said, 'Doctor, I perceive that the people are getting fatigued with carrying me; a number of 'Mormons' live about two or three miles from here, near our route; will you ride to their settlement as quick as possible, and have them come and meet us?' He started off on a gallop immediately. My object in this was to obtain protection in case of an attack, rather than to obtain help to carry me.

Very soon after the men from Carthage made one excuse after another, until they had all left, and I felt glad to get rid of them. I found that the tramping of those carrying me produced violent pain, and a sleigh was produced and attached to the hind end of Brother James Allred's wagon, a bed placed upon it, and I propped up on the bed. Mrs. Taylor rode with me, applying ice water to my wounds. As the sleigh was dragged over the grass on the prairie, which was quite tall, it moved very easily and gave me very little pain.

When I got within five or six miles of Nauvoo the brethren commenced to meet me from the city, and they increased in number as we drew nearer, until there was a very large company of people of all ages and both sexes, principally, however, men.

For some time there had been almost incessant rain, so that in many low places on the prairie it was from one to three feet deep in water, and at such places the brethren whom we met took hold of the sleigh, lifted it, and carried it over the water; and when we arrived in the neighborhood of the city, where the roads were excessively muddy and bad, the brethren tore down the fences, and we passed through the fields.

Never shall I forget the differences of feeling that I experienced between the place that I had left and the one that I had now arrived at. I had left a lot of reckless, bloodthirsty murderers, and had come to the City of the Saints, the people of the living God; friends of truth and righteousness, thousands of whom stood there with warm, true hearts to offer their friendship and services, and to welcome my return. It is true it was a painful scene, and brought sorrowful remembrance to my mind, but to me it caused a thrill of joy to find myself once more in the bosom of my friends, and to meet with the cordial welcome of true, honest hearts. What was very remarkable, I found myself very much better after my arrival at Nauvoo than I was when I started on my journey, although I had traveled eighteen miles.

The next day, as some change was wanting, I told Mrs. Taylor that if she could send to Dr. Richards, he had my purse and watch, and they would find money in my purse.

Time Registrar of the Massacre.

Previous to the doctor leaving Carthage, I told him that he had better take my purse and watch, for I was afraid the people would steal them. The doctor had taken my pantaloon's pocket, and put the watch in it with the purse, cut off the pocket, and tied a string around the top; it was in this position when brought home. My family, however, were not a little startled to find that my watch had been struck with a ball. I sent for my vest, and, upon examination, it was found that there was a cut as if with a knife, in the vest pocket which had contained my watch. In the pocket the fragments of the glass were found literally ground to powder. It then occurred to me that a ball had struck me at the time I felt myself falling out of the window, and that it was this force that threw me inside. I had often remarked to Mrs. Taylor the singular fact of finding myself inside the room, when I felt a moment before after being shot, that I was falling out, and I never could account for it until then; but here the thing was fully elucidated, and was rendered plain to my mind. I was indeed falling out, when some villain aimed at my heart. The ball struck my watch, and forced me back; if I had fallen out I should assuredly have been killed, if not by the fall, by those around, and this ball, intended to dispatch me, was turned by an overruling Providence into a messenger of mercy, and saved my life. I shall never forget the feelings of gratitude that I then experienced towards my heavenly Father; the whole scene was vividly portrayed before me, and my heart melted before the Lord. I felt that the Lord had preserved me by a special act of mercy; that my time had not yet come, and that I had still a work to perform upon the earth.

[Signed] JOHN TAYLOR.

JOHN TAYLOR'S NOTES

"In addition to the above I give the following:

Dr. Bernhisel informed me that Joseph, looking him full in the face, and as solemn as eternity, said, 'I am going as a lamb to the slaughter, but I am as calm as a summer's morning. I have a conscience void of offense toward God and man.' I heard him state, in reply to an interrogatory, made either by myself or some one in my hearing, in relation to the best course to pursue: 'I am not now acting according to my judgment: others must counsel, and not me, for the present,' or in words to the same effect.

COMMENT ON THE EXPOSITOR AFFAIR

The governor's remarks about the press may be partially correct, so far as the legal technicality was concerned, and the order of administering law. The proper way would perhaps have been for the city council to have passed a law in regard to the removal of nuisances, and then for the municipal court to have ordered it to be abated on complaint. Be this as it may, it was only a variation in form, not in fact, for the municipal court formed part of the city council, and all voted; and, furthermore, some time after the murder, Governor Ford told me that the press ought to have been removed, but that it was bad policy to remove it as we did; that if we had only let a mob do it, instead of using the law, we could have done it without difficulty, and no one would have been implicated. Thus the governor, who would have winked at the proceedings of a mob, lent his aid to, or winked at, the proceedings of mob violence in the assassination of Joseph and Hyrum Smith for removing a nuisance according to law, because of an alleged informality in the legal proceedings or a legal technicality.

I must here state that I do not believe Governor Ford would have planned the murder of Joseph and Hyrum Smith; but being a man that courted popular opinion, he had not the firmness to withstand the mob, even when that mob were seeking to imbrue their hands in the blood of innocence; he lent himself to their designs and thus became a partaker of their evil deeds.

I will illustrate this vexed question with the following official paper, which appeared in the *Deseret News*, No. 30.

'Two of the brethren arrived this evening (June 13th, 1844), from Carthage, and said that about 300 mobbers were assembled there, with the avowed intention of coming against Nauvoo. Also that Hamilton [the hotel proprietor] was paying a dollar per bushel for corn to feed their animals.'

The following was published in the *Warsaw Signal* Office; I insert it as a specimen of the unparalleled corruption and diabolical falsehood of which the human race has become capable in this generation:

'At a mass meeting of the citizens of Hancock county, convened at Carthage on the 11th day of June, 1844, Mr. Knox was appointed president, John Doty and Lewis F. Evans, vice presidents, and William Y. Head, secretary.

'Henry Stephens, Esq. presented the following resolutions, passed at a meeting of the citizens of Warsaw, and urged the adoption of them as the sense of this meeting:

PREAMBLE AND RESOLUTIONS

'Whereas information has reached us, about which there can be no question, that the authorities of Nauvoo did recently pass an ordinance declaring a printing press and newspaper published by the opponents of the Prophet a nuisance, and in pursuance thereof did direct the marshal of the city and his adherents to enter by force the building from whence the paper was issued, and violently (if necessary) to take possession of the press and printing materials, and thereafter to burn and destroy the same; and whereas, in pursuance of said ordinance, the marshal and his adherents, together with a mob of Mormons, did, after sunset on the evening of the 10th inst., violently enter said building in a tumultuous manner, burn and destroy the press and other materials found on the premises;

And whereas Hyrum Smith did, in the presence of the city council and the citizens of Nauvoo, offer a reward for the destruction of the printing press and materials of the *Warsaw Signal*, a newspaper also opposed to his interest;

And whereas the liberty of the press is one of the cardinal principles of our government, firmly guaranteed by the several Constitutions of the states as well as the United States;

And whereas Hyrum Smith has within the last week publicly threatened the life of one of our valued citizens, Thos. C. Sharp, the editor of the *Signal*:

Therefore, be it solemnly *Resolved* by the citizens of Warsaw in public meeting assembled,

That we view the recent ordinance of the city of Nauvoo, and the proceedings thereunder, as an outrage of an alarming character, revolutionary and tyrannical in its tendency, and being under color of law, as calculated to subvert and destroy in the minds of the community all reliance on the law.

Resolved, That as a community we feel anxious, when possible, to redress our grievances by legal remedies; but the time has now arrived when the law has ceased to be a protection to our lives and property; a mob at Nauvoo, under a city ordinance, has violated the highest privilege in our government, and to seek redress in the ordinary mode would be utterly ineffectual.

Resolved, That the public threat made in the council of the city not only to destroy our printing press, but to take the life of its editor, is sufficient, in connection with the recent outrage, to command the efforts and the services of every good citizen to put an immediate stop to the career of the mad Prophet and his demoniac coadjutors. We must not only defend ourselves from danger, but we must resolutely carry the war into the enemy's camp. We do therefore declare that we will sustain our press and the editor at all hazards. That we will take full vengeance—terrible vengeance, should the lives of any of our citizens be lost in the effort. That we hold ourselves at all times in readiness to cooperate with our fellow citizens in this state, Missouri, and Iowa, to *exterminate*—UTTERLY EXTERMINATE, the wicked and abominable Mormon leaders, the authors of our troubles.

Resolved, That a committee of five be appointed forthwith to notify all persons in our township suspected of being the tools of the Prophet to leave immediately on pain of INSTANT VENGEANCE. And we do recommend the inhabitants of the adjacent townships to do the same, hereby pledging ourselves to render all the assistance they may require.

Resolved, That the time, in our opinion, has arrived when the adherents of Smith as a body, shall be driven from the surrounding settlements into Nauvoo; that the Prophet and his miscreant adherents should then be demanded at their hands, and if not surrendered, A WAR OF EXTERMINATION SHOULD BE WAGED, to the entire destruction, if necessary for our protection, of his adherents. And we do hereby recommend this resolution to the consideration of the several townships to the mass convention to be held at Carthage, hereby pledging ourselves to aid to the utmost the complete consummation of the object in view, that we may thereby be utterly relieved of the alarm, anxiety, and trouble to which we are now subjected.

Resolved, That every citizen arm himself, to be prepared to sustain the resolutions herein contained.

Mr. Roosevelt rose and made a brief but eloquent speech, and called upon the citizens throughout the country to render efficient aid in carrying out the spirit of the resolutions. Mr. Roosevelt then moved that a committee of seven be appointed by the chair to draft resolutions expressive of our action in future.

Mr. Catlin moved to amend the motion of Mr. Roosevelt so that the committee should consist of one from each precinct; which motion as amended, was adopted.

The chair then appointed the following as said committee: Colonel Levi Williams, Rocky Run precinct; Joel Catlin, Augusta; Samuel Williams, Carthage; Elisha Worrell, Chili; Captain Maddison, St.

Mary's; John M. Ferris, Fountain Green; James Rice, Pilot Grove; John Carns, Bear Creek; C. L. Higbee, Nauvoo; George Robinson, La Harpe, and George Rockwell, Warsaw.

On motion of Mr. Sympson, Walter Bagby, Esq. was requested to address the meeting during the absence of the committee. He spoke long and eloquently upon the cause of our grievances, and expressed his belief that the time was now at hand when we were individually and collectively called upon to repel the innovations upon our liberties, and suggested that points be designated as places of encampment at which to rendezvous our forces, that we may be ready, when called upon, for efficient action.

Dr. Barnes, one of the persons who went with the officers to Nauvoo for the purpose of arresting the rioters, having just arrived, came into the meeting, and reported the result of their proceedings, which was, that the persons charged in the writs were duly arrested, but taken from the officer's hands on a writ of *habeas corpus* from the municipal court and discharged, and the following potent words entered upon the records—HONORABLY DISCHARGED.

On motion of O. C. Skinner, Esq. a vote of thanks was tendered to Dr. Barnes for volunteering his services in executing said writs.

Francis M. Higbee was now loudly called for. He stated his personal knowledge of the Mormons from their earliest history, throughout their hellish career in Missouri and this state, which had been characterized by the darkest and most diabolical deeds which had ever disgraced humanity.

The committee appointed to draft resolutions brought in the following report, which after some considerable discussion, was unanimously adopted:

REPORT OF THE COMMITTEE

'Whereas the officer charged with the execution of a writ against Joseph Smith and others, for riot in the county of Hancock, which said writ said officer has served upon said Smith and others; and whereas said Smith and others refuse to obey the mandate of said writ; and whereas, in the opinion of this meeting, it is impossible for the said officer to raise a *posse* of sufficient strength to execute said writ; and whereas it is the opinion of this meeting that the riot is still progressing, and that violence is meditated and determined on, it is the opinion of this meeting that the circumstances of the case require the interposition of executive power: Therefore,

'*Resolved,* That a deputation of two discreet men be sent to Springfield to solicit such interposition.

'2d. *Resolved,* That a said deputation be furnished with a certified copy of the resolution, and be authorized to obtain evidence by affidavit and otherwise in regard to the violence which has already been committed and is still farther meditated.'

Dr. Evans here rose and expressed his wish that the above resolutions would not retard our operations, but that we would each one arm and equip ourselves forthwith.

The resolutions passed at Warsaw were again read by Dr. Barnes, and passed by acclamation.

On motion of A. Sympson, Esq., the suggestion of Mr. Bagby appointing places of encampment, was adopted to wit: Warsaw, Carthage, Green Plains, Spilman's Landing, Chili, and La Harpe.

On motion, O. C. Skinner and Walter Bagby, Esqrs. were appointed a committee to bear the resolutions adopted by this meeting to his excellency the governor, requiring his executive interposition.

On motion of J. H. Sherman, a Central Corresponding Committee was appointed.

Ordered, That J. H. Sherman, H. T. Wilson, Chauncey Robinson, Wm. S. Freeman, Thomas Morrison, F. M. Higbee, Lyman Prentiss, and Stephen H. Tyler be said committee.

On motion of George Rockwell,

Resolved, That constables in the different precincts hold themselves in readiness to obey the officer in possession of the writs, whenever called upon, in summoning the *posse.*

On motion, the meeting adjourned.

JOHN KNOX, President.
JOHN DOTY
LEWIS F. EVANS
Vice Presidents.

W. Y. Head, Secretary.'

The following will conclude the *'Expositor* Question':

JOSEPH SMITH'S ACCOUNT OF THE EXPOSITOR AFFAIR

'Nauvoo, June 14th, 1844.

'Sir,—I write you this morning briefly to inform you of the facts relative to the removal of the press and fixtures of the *Nauvoo Expositor* as a nuisance.

'The 8th and 10th instant were spent by the city council of Nauvoo in receiving testimony concerning the character of the *Expositor*, and the character and designs of the proprietors.

'In the investigation it appeared evident to the council that the proprietors were a set of unprincipled, lawless debauches, counterfeiters, bogus-makers, gamblers, peace-disturbers, and that the grand object of said proprietors was to destroy our constitutional rights and chartered privileges; to overthrow all good and wholesome regulations in society; to strengthen themselves against the municipality; to fortify themselves against the church of which I am a member, and destroy all our religious rights and privileges by libels, slanders, falsehoods, perjury, etc. and sticking at no corruption to accomplish their hellish purposes; and that said paper of itself was libelous of the deepest dye.

and very injurious as a vehicle of defamation, tending to corrupt the morals, and disturb the peace, tranquility, and happiness of the whole community, and especially that of Nauvoo.

'After a long and patient investigation of the character of the *Expositor*, and the characters and designs of its proprietors, the Constitution, the Charter (see Addenda to Nauvoo Charter from the *Springfield Charter*, sec. 7), and all the best authorities on the subject (see *Blackstone*, iii, 5, and n, etc., etc.), the city council decided that it was necessary for the 'peace, benefit, good order, and regulations' of said city, 'and for the protection of the property', and for 'the happiness and prosperity of the citizens of Nauvoo', that said *Expositor* should be removed; and declaring said *Expositor* a nuisance, ordered the mayor to cause them to be removed without delay, which order was committed to the marshal by due process, and by him executed the same day, by removing the paper, press, and fixtures into the streets, and burning the same; all which was done without riot, noise, tumult, or confusion, as has already been proved before the municipality of the city; and the particulars of the whole transaction may be expected in our next *Nauvoo Neighbor*.

'I send you this hasty sketch that your excellency may be aware of the lying reports that are now being circulated by our enemies, that there has been a 'mob at Nauvoo', and 'blood and thunder', and 'swearing that two men were killed', etc. etc., as we hear from abroad, are false—false as satan himself could invent, and that nothing has been transacted here but what has been in perfect accordance with the strictest principles of law and good order on the part of the authorities of this city; and if your excellency is not satisfied, and shall not be satisfied, after reading the whole proceedings, which will be forthcoming soon, and shall demand an investigation of our municipality before Judge Pope, or any legal tribunal at the Capitol, you have only to write your wishes, and we will be forthcoming; we will not trouble you to file a writ, or send an officer for us.

'I remain, as ever, a friend to truth, good order, and your excellency's humble servant,

[Signed] JOSEPH SMITH.

'His Excellency Thomas Ford.' "*

*See Tyler's *History of the Mormon Battalion*, Introduction, in which the Taylor document is published almost completely, also Captain Richard F. Burton's *City of the Saints*, 1862, Appendix III, pp. 517-547. The letter inserted by Burton at pp. 526-7. however, is not the letter to which Joseph Smith took exception (see p. 78 this volume) but is the letter received from Governor Ford written on his arrival at Carthage June 21, 1844, in which he asks for a committee to be sent to him giving the Latter-day Saint version of the proceedings which had taken place in Nauvoo up to that time. B. H. R.

IV

HISTORIANS' SECOND COMPILATION OF HISTORICAL ITEMS OF CHURCH HISTORY, FROM 22ND OF JUNE, 1844, TO 8TH OF AUGUST, 1844.

Explanation

PART IV is a second compilation following Period I of this *History*, made by the Church Historians George A. Smith and Wilford Woodruff from the Journals of Willard Richards, Wilford Woodruff and others and was published in the *Millennial Star*, 1862, Vol. xxiv, pp. 598-792; and 1863, Vol. xxv, pp. 6-280. See also *Deseret News*, Vol. vii, Dec. 9, 1857 to Jan. 20, 1858. This will comprise chapters xi to xix inclusive.

CHAPTER XI

MISCELLANEOUS EVENTS APART FROM THE MAJOR FACTS OF THE MARTYRDOM OF THE PROPHET AND PATRIARCH FROM JUNE 22, 1844, TO JUNE 29, 1844.

"*Saturday, June* 22, 1844.—In the evening Major-General Dunham issued orders to all the guards and sentries on the road to La Harpe, to let persons pass and repass, until further orders, except they discover companies of men, when they must report the same to headquarters immediately.

Varied Incidents of Activity in the Church.

A conference was held at Eagle, Benton county, Tennessee, Elder A. O. Smoot presiding, during which a branch was organized of seventeen members. One elder, one priest and one teacher were ordained.

Sunday, 23.—At 5 a. m., [at Nauvoo] A. P. Rockwood and John Scott asked advice what to do with the cannon, etc.

William Clayton got the public records together and buried them.

5 *p. m.*—Captain Anderson, of the steamer *Osprey,* conversed with Joseph, saying the mob at Warsaw threatened firing into his vessel.

President Brigham Young attended meeting at Lowell, Massachusetts.

Elder Heber C. Kimball preached at Wilmington, Delaware, in the forenoon, to an attentive congregation: he had a chill after he got through. Elder Lyman Wight spoke in the afternoon.

A conference was held at Kirtland, and was addressed by Elder Lorenzo Snow and others. Twelve persons were baptized and confirmed, and eight ordained elders.

Monday, 24.—

AFFIDAVIT OF J. R. WAKEFIELD

'Territory of Iowa, } sct.
Henry County. }

Dr. J. R. Wakefield being duly sworn, deposeth and sayeth, that on the 10th of June he, in company with two others, went on the hill in the city of Nauvoo, and in the neighborhood of the printing press of the *Nauvoo Expositor*, when a company of men approached, headed by the marshal of the city, Mr. Greene, some armed, but not many. After marching in front of the printing office, the marshal demanded the keys of the office, in behalf of the mayor and municipal court of Nauvoo, to destroy the press, type and appurtenances of said press, and burn them in the street.

Calm Procedure in Destroying the Nauvoo Expositor Press.

Mr. Higbee replied, in behalf of the whole of the editors of said newspaper, that he would not give up the key—that he set the court and city at defiance, and should hold them and the marshal responsible for their acts in this affair.

Accordingly orders were given to an officer of the company to forcibly take from the building the press, and destroy it according to order. It was done without any noise, or confusion, shouting, or riotous proceedings, and further deponent saith not.

[Signed] J. R. WAKEFIELD.

Sworn to and subscribed before me this 24th day of June, 1844.

A. McKINNEY, J. P.'

Tuesday, 25.—Elder Cahoon returned from Carthage for some papers, which were sent out by A. P. Rockwood.

Orrin P. Rockwell met F. M. Higbee about 4 p. m. and accused him of seeking Joseph's life. Higbee made use of some very insulting language in reply, when a scuffle ensued, during which a letter dropped out of Higbee's hat, which stated that there were seventy of the mob ready in Iowa to come upon Nauvoo tonight.

F. M. Higbee's Designs Against the Prophet's Life.

It is currently reported that the mob intend to make a rush on the jail tonight.

A strong guard placed in and round the city.

About 9 p. m. it began to rain very heavily.

Wednesday, 26.— 8 a. m., Captain Singleton arrived, with about sixty mounted militia, to protect the city in case a mob should come against it. He was authorized to take command of the police, and to use such measures as he might consider necessary.

Arrival of Capt. Singleton of the Illinois Militia in Nauvoo to Keep the Peace.

He read his orders from the governor, and wanted to know if our men would obey his orders, when the brethren responded 'yes', whereupon notification was sent to the police to meet at 6 p. m., in the Masonic Hall. He further reported that Dr. Foster had given him information at Carthage, where he would find three presses in Nauvoo, for making bogus money, and said that he wanted to get hold of them.

6 *p. m.*—The police assembled in the Seventies' Hall, and entered into a temporary organization to act under Captain Singleton. Many of the regular police being officers of the Legion, and on active service, their places were filled for the time.

At midnight Captain Singleton sent a notification to the major-general's quarters, that he wanted the Nauvoo Legion to be in readiness for parade at an hour's notice, when notifications were sent to the colonels of the several regiments accordingly.

Thursday, 27.—About 9 a. m., John P. Greene arrived in Nauvoo with subpœnas for witnesses for the expected trial on Saturday the 29th instant.

At 10 a. m., orders were received from Captain Singleton, to call out that portion of the Nauvoo Legion resident within the limits of the city, for review at noon. General Dunham immediately issued similar orders to the commandants.

At noon about two-thirds of the Legion turned out to parade, nearly all of whom were well armed, although all the state arms had been taken away, which caused Captain Singleton and his company to express their astonishment. The captain made a remark to the effect that it would not do to come against such a force as this. The Legion was soon dismissed, on account of a messenger from the governor reporting that all the troops were dismissed, except a small escort which was with him.

The Arrival of Governor Ford in Nauvoo.

5 *p. m.*—Governor Ford, with about fifty men arrived at the Mansion, and gave notice that he would shortly address the citizens. In about half an hour he ascended the frame of a building opposite the Mansion, and addressed the people.

WHEREABOUTS OF THE TWELVE—THEIR DEPRESSION OF SPIRIT

We here insert the location of the Twelve Apostles on this memorable day:—

President Brigham Young and Elder Wilford Woodruff spent a portion of the day together in the city of Boston, and were sitting together in the railway depot at the time of the massacre of the Prophets; they felt very sorrowful, and depressed in spirits, without knowing the cause.

Elders Heber C. Kimball and Lyman Wight traveled from Philadelphia to New York by railway and steamboat. Elder Kimball felt very mournful as though he had lost some friend, and knew not the cause.

Elder Orson Hyde was in the hall occupied by the saints in Boston, examining maps, and designating or pointing out each man's district or field of labor, in company with Elders Brigham Young, Wilford Woodruff and others, a part of the day. He felt very heavy and sorrowful in spirit, and knew not the cause, but felt no heart to look on the maps. He retired to the further end of the hall alone, and walked the floor; tears ran down his face * * * . He never felt so before, and knew no reason why he should feel so then.

Elder Parley P. Pratt was on the canal boat between Utica and Buffalo, N. Y., on his return to Nauvoo, and was much depressed in spirit; his brother William Pratt came on board of the same boat, and Parley asked him if he had any books or pamphlets containing the gospel of Christ, or the words of life; if so, to put them under lock and key, for the people are not worthy of them for, said Parley, 'I feel that the spirit of murder is in the hearts of the people through the land.'

Elders Willard Richards and John Taylor were the only two of the Quorum of the Twelve who were not on missions, and the only two men who were with the martyrs when they fell and sealed their testimony with their blood.

Elder George A. Smith rode with Elder Crandall Dunn, from Napoleon, to Elder Noah Willis Bartholemew's, near Jacksonburg, Jackson county, Michigan, and felt unusually cast down and depressed in spirits. About five o'clock he repaired to an oak grove, and called upon the Lord, endeavoring to break the spell of horror which had dominion over his mind. He remained there a long time without finding any relief, and then went back to Brother Bartholomew's, and went to bed with Elder Crandall Dunn; he could not sleep, but spent the night in a series of miserable thoughts and reflections. Once it seemed to him that some fiend whispered in his ear, 'Joseph and Hyrum are dead; ain't you glad of it?'

Elder Amasa Lyman was in the city of Cincinnati, and felt that depression of spirit mentioned by his brethren.

News of the Martyrdom of the Prophets Brought to Nauvoo.

Friday, 28.—News arrived in Nauvoo at daylight, that Joseph and Hyrum were murdered yesterday while in jail, committed upon an illegal mittimus by Robert F. Smith, justice of the peace and captain of the company stationed at the jail.

General Deming issued the following proclamation:

PROCLAMATION OF GENERAL DEMING TO THE PEOPLE OF HANCOCK COUNTY

'Headquarters, June 28, 1844.
4 o'clock, a. m.

To the Citizens of Carthage and Hancock County:

In pursuance of an order from Governor Ford, instructing me to the exercise of such discretionary powers as I may deem necessary for the preservation of the public safety, and the lives and property of our citizens; I hereby invite all citizens to remain at their several homes in Hancock county and cooperate with me in establishing tranquility and safety throughout the county.

The most efficient means have been put in requisition for concentrating the military force of the neighboring counties at Carthage, and in twelve hours there will be a sufficient force for the protection of every citizen in the county.

I confidently believe there is no just apprehension of an attack upon any place by the Mormon citizens of our county. And I hereby strictly command all citizens of Hancock county to abstain from violence towards the Mormon population, under penalty of the severest inflictions of military law, and act in no case only on the defensive.

The corpses of the murdered men will be forthwith removed to Nauvoo, under an escort from headquarters.

Given under my hand this 28th June, 1844, 4 o'clock, a. m.

[Signed] M. R. DEMING, Brigadier-General.
4th Brigade and 5th Division.

It is hoped and expected that the governor will be at headquarters in a few hours.'

The Nauvoo Legion Ordered Out—"Keep Quiet".

At 7½ a. m., General Dunham issued orders for the whole of the Legion to meet on the parade ground, east of the Temple, at 10 a. m. They met accordingly, when addresses were delivered, and exhortations given to the saints to keep quiet, and not to let their violently outraged feelings get the better of them.

About noon a council of officers of the Legion was held, and from thence they went to meet the sad procession that accompanied the bodies of the murdered Prophet and Patriarch.

Arrival of the Bodies of the Martyrs at Nauvoo.

At 2½ p. m., the corpses arrived at Mulholland Street, on two wagons, guarded by a few men from Carthage, and nearly all the citizens collected together and followed the bodies to the Mansion, where the multitude were addressed by Dr. Richards, W. W. Phelps, and Messrs. Woods and Reid, who exhorted the people to be peaceable and calm and use no threats.

NAMES OF THE PROPHET'S BODYGUARD

We here insert the names of Joseph's bodyguard:—

Alpheus Cutler, capt.	John Snyder,
Amos C. Hodge,	Christian Kreymer,
James Allred,	Lewis D. Wilson,
Thomas Grover,	William Marks,
Reynolds Cahoon,	James Emmet,
Shadrach Roundy,	John S. Butler,

Samuel H. Smith,
Edward Hunter, herald and armor bearer.

The following are the names of the martial band:—

NAMES OF THE NAUVOO LEGION BAND

E. P. Duzette, major,
L. W. Hancock, fife major,
Dimick B. Huntington, drum major,
Elisha Everett, leader,

William Carter,	——— Lyon,
Dominicus Carter,	Aroet Hale,
James W. Cummings,	Abram Day,
Joseph Richards,	L. W. Hardy,
Geo. W. Taggart,	Willard Smith,
Wm. D. Huntington,	Stephen Wilber,
Jesse Earl,	Lewis Hardy,
J. M. King,	James Leithead,
H. B. Jacobs,	J. M. Frink,
A. J. Clothier,	Eleazer King,
Sylvester Duzette,	——— Sprague.

In the afternoon Elders Heber C. Kimball, Lyman Wight, William Smith and wife, went by railway cars and steamboat to Boston.

Saturday, 29.—The Legion was out all last night, expecting a mob to come.

The following is from a letter addressed to President Joseph Smith, from Elders Lyman Wight and Heber C. Kimball:—

LETTER FROM ELDERS LYMAN WIGHT AND HEBER C. KIMBALL TO JOSEPH SMITH

'Philadelphia, Pa., June 19, 1844.

To my well beloved brother and fellow prisoner, President Joseph Smith*—

I take this opportunity of giving you an abridged history of my transactions, together with Brother Heber C. Kimball, my fellow traveler. We left Nauvoo the 21st day of May, amidst the acclamations of three cheers from the shore, 'Joseph Smith, the next President of the United States!'

We passed smoothly down the river; there were 165 passengers on board the boat *Osprey*. I was called upon to deliver a political address, and to show what right Joseph Smith had to the presidential chair, which I did to the entire satisfaction of nearly all the passengers on board, not forgetting at the same time to show that the other candidates had disqualified themselves to all the right and title, by acts of meanness.

Lyman Wight's Political Address.

Whilst speaking of their mean acts I was frequently interrupted with loud laughing and clapping of hands, by way of approbation. A vote being taken on the presidential question, Joseph Smith received a large majority over all the other candidates.

We reached St. Louis on the 22nd at 10 a. m. Here Brothers Young and Kimball called the church together and instructed them spiritually and politically. We learned that the church at St. Louis numbered nearly 700 souls.

On the 23rd we left St. Louis on board the boat *Louis Phillippe*, at half past 12 o'clock, with about 200 passengers on board; many of the same that were on the *Osprey*, together with many new passengers.

Brigham Young's Address on the Steamboat.

There were at first some little prejudices existing, but President Brigham Young, being called upon, delivered a discourse upon the principles of our doctrine, which entirely allayed the prejudices.

Next evening Brother William Smith was called upon to deliver an address, which he did in the power and demonstration of the spirit, and we were afterwards looked upon as their superiors.

On the 26th we reached Cincinnati, at 6 o'clock, p. m. Elders Young and Kimball went to visit the church in that city, whilst I changed our luggage on board the boat *Neptune* for Pittsburgh. All the passengers on board the *Louis Phillippe* being bound for Pittsburgh, came with us.

At 8 a. m. on the 27th, we held a conference with the elders in Cincinnati. I addressed them on the subject of politics, and perseverance in duty, and the great necessity of reform in government. I was followed by Brothers Kimball and Young on the same subjects.

Members of the Twelve in Conference at Cincinnati.

*This has reference to their imprisonment together in Liberty prison, Missouri, winter of 1838. B. H. R.

We then instructed them to have 2,000 copies of your views on the Powers and Policy of the Government printed, and for the elders to scatter them with the velocity of lightning and the voice of thunder.

I had nearly forgotten to mention an important occurrence on board of the *Louis Phillippe*, with a Mr. David Guard, of Lawrenceburgh, Indiana: he is worth from $200,000 to $300,000; he emigrated to Cincinnati when there were but three log cabins in that place. He gave me his views on politics, which completely corresponded with yours. I then gave him two copies of your 'Views'. He was highly pleased with them, and pledged his word he would have them published in both the Lawrenceburgh papers, as they were both published under his roof, and if they did not comply with so reasonable a request, they (the editors) would have to seek shelter elsewhere.

A Pioneer Cincinnatian for Joseph Smith for President of the United States.

He also stated that Joseph Smith was the first man since the days of Washington and Jefferson, who had been frank and honest enough to give his views to the people before being elected; and said, that he would go his whole length for such a man, and that if you were not elected this time, you would be the next: let this be an ensample of numerous other cases, as you know it would be too irksome to write them all, or read them.

To return to the subject, at ten o'clock this morning (the 27th), we left for Pittsburgh with an addition of passengers. On this boat I was called upon to deliver an address showing the utility of the *Book of Mormon*, and the present situation of the world, which I did, and by this time we had a complete victory over both priests and people. On this boat a large majority of votes were given for yourself for president.

The Apostles en route for Pittsburgh.

We arrived at Pittsburgh on the 30th at 6 p. m. Here we left President Brigham Young. Brothers William Smith, Heber C. Kimball and myself left Pittsburgh on the 31st of May, at 10 o'clock, from thence by steamer, stage and railway, we passed over hills and dales, arriving at Washington city [D. C.] on the 2nd of June, preaching to, and thorning everybody with politics that came in our way.

Thus after a journey of thirteen days we arrived in the great metropolis of the United States; which, by-the-by, with the exception of the Pennsylvania Avenue, more resembles the *Methodist slough of despond* than anything like a decent city.

Lyman Wight in Washington, D. C.—Impressions.

At this time, being near the close of the session, [congress] it was filled up with demagogues, jackleg lawyers and blackleg gamblers, and *everything else but intelligence.* The senators and representatives generally rise at 8 o'clock in the morning, prepare themselves for business about 11 o'clock, commonly return at 3 and 4 in the afternoon. From 6 till 9 is the only time we could do any business whatever, hence we prepared and watched our opportunity, and did all the business we could betwixt those hours, for ten days, pleading the cause of the poor and oppressed.

We have got a petition signed, with our names attached, in behalf of the church, asking for a remuneration for our losses, and not for our rights, or redress, for they would not receive such a petition from us. It was thought by Judge Semple, Judge Douglas, General [David R.] Atchison and Major Hughs, that our petition would carry if it was not too late in the season. Judge Semple handed it to the chairman of the Committee on Public Lands. He said he would do the best he could for us. General Atchison is of the opinion if we could sue the state of Missouri for redress of grievances, that there was virtue enough in the state to answer our demands, 'for', said he, *'they are ashamed of their conduct.'* Douglas and Semple are of the same opinion.

Petition to Congress for "Remuneration of Losses" of the Church in Missouri.

Brother Kimball and myself spared no pains during our stay at Washington: we found six members of the church, and many attentive hearers. We purpose sending a steady, faithful elder, who we think can build up a large church. We found our time too limited to meet the conferences and transact our business, to tarry longer at present, but shall return, if we find it necessary, after the Baltimore Convention; for we will never leave them, nor forsake them, nor return home, while we think there is a stone unturned, or a conscience that is not harrowed up by our continued preaching.

On the 11th instant we left Washington, and arrived at Brother Saunders', Wilmington, Delaware, at 5 o'clock the same evening, distance 114 miles. We can assure you we found everything right in this place, and adjacent to it. We found about 100 members, and held two meetings with them, appointing a conference on the 22nd and 23rd inst.

On the 13th at 2 p. m., we left this place for Philadelphia, and arrived at Brother William Smith's at 5 p. m. Brother Kimball being exposed, had a slight attack of the chills and fever. Since that time we have preached alternately.

Members of the Twelve at Philadelphia—Righteousness and Union of Joseph and the Twelve Affirmed.

The church here numbers nearly 200, out of which number many have commenced sickening, and were growing faint at the many false reports in circulation, fearing that the Prophet had fallen and the Twelve were in transgression, but they have since learned that the Prophet is right, and that the Twelve are with him, and they are beginning to revive; they have stood six tremendous shocks, and I think if they stand the seventh, which is to come tomorrow evening they will survive.

We shall call on them to know whether they intend to gather with the living and sustain the cause of God by the mouth of his Prophets and Apostles, or die in Philadelphia. If they should choose the latter, we shall attend to the funeral ceremonies, and leave them to rest with the dead, and we will go on our way among the living.

If they should choose the former, we shall expect a glorious work in this place.

We shall leave here on the 21st for Wilmington, to attend conference, we shall then return to this place, and from here to New York and Boston, to meet the conferences in those cities, and so continue from place to place until we shall have accomplished the mission appointed unto us."*

*This letter represents Elder Lyman Wight at his best, and shows him to be an Apostle of the Lord Jesus of no inferior order. B. H. R.

CHAPTER XII

MOVEMENTS IN HANCOCK COUNTY, CARTHAGE, NAUVOO, WARSAW AND QUINCY, FOR THE MAINTENANCE OF PEACE FOLLOWING THE MARTYRDOM: LIST OF THE NAMES OF THOSE WHO WERE IN THE MOB ASSEMBLED TO SLAY THE PROPHET

"*Saturday, June 29th,* 1844.—About noon, General H. Swazey, of Iowa, called at Nauvoo and offered assistance to the people.

The following article from Governor Ford, was published in the *Times and Seasons*:—

GOVERNOR FORD TO THE PEOPLE OF THE STATE OF ILLINOIS

'I desire to make a brief, but true statement of the recent disgraceful affair at Carthage, in regard to the Smiths, so far as circumstances have come to my knowledge.

The Smiths, Joseph and Hyrum, have been assassinated in jail, by whom it is not known, but will be ascertained. I pledged myself for their safety, and upon the assurance of that pledge they surrendered as prisoners. The Mormons surrendered the public arms in their possession, and the Nauvoo Legion submitted to the command of Captain Singleton, of Brown county, deputed for that purpose by me.

All these things were required to satisfy the old citizens of Hancock that the Mormons were peaceably disposed, and to allay jealousy and excitement in their minds.

It appears, however, that the compliance of the Mormons with every requisition made upon them, failed of that purpose. The pledge of security to the Smiths was not given upon my individual responsibility. Before I gave it, I obtained a pledge of honor by a unanimous vote from the officers and men under my command, to sustain me in performing it. If the assassination of the Smiths was committed by any portion of these, they have added treachery to murder, and have done all they could to disgrace the state, and sully the public honor.

On the morning of the day the deed was committed, we had proposed to march the army under my command into Nauvoo. I had, however, discovered on the evening before, that nothing but utter destruction of the city would satisfy a portion of the troops; and that if we marched into the city, pretexts would not be wanting for commencing hostilities. The Mormons had done everything required, or which ought to have been required of them. Offensive operations on our part would have been as unjust and disgraceful as they would have been impolitic in the present critical season of the year, the harvest and the crops. For these reasons I decided, in a council of officers to disband the army, except three companies, two of which were reserved as a guard for the jail.

With the other company I marched into Nauvoo, to address the inhabitants there, and tell them what they might expect in case they designedly or imprudently provoked a war. I performed this duty as I think plainly and emphatically, and then set out to return to Carthage.

When I had marched about three miles, a messenger informed me of the occurrences at Carthage. I hastened on to that place. The guard, it is said, did their duty, but were overpowered. Many of the inhabitants of Carthage had fled with their families. Others were preparing to go. I apprehended danger to the settlements from the sudden fury and passion of the Mormons, and sanctioned their movements in this respect.

General Deming volunteered to remain with a few troops to observe the progress of events, to defend property against small numbers, and with orders to retreat if menaced by a superior force. I decided to proceed immediately to Quincy, to prepare a force sufficient to suppress disorders, in case it should ensue from the foregoing transactions, or from any other cause. I have hopes that the Mormons will make no further difficulties. In this I may be mistaken. The other party may not be satisfied. They may recommence aggression.

I am determined to preserve the peace against all breakers of the same, at all hazards. I think present circumstances warrant the precaution of having a competent force at my disposal, in readiness to march at a moment's warning. My position at Quincy will enable me to get the earliest intelligence, and to communicate orders with great celerity.

I have decided to issue the following general orders:

GOVERNOR FORD'S GENERAL ORDERS TO THE MILITIA IN THE WESTERN COUNTIES OF ILLINOIS

'Headquarters, Quincy,
June 29, 1844.

It is ordered that the commandants of regiments in the counties of Adams, Marquette, Pike, Brown, Schuyler, Morgan, Scott, Cass, Fulton and McDonough, and the regiments composing General Stapp's brigade, will call their respective regiments and battalions together immediately upon the receipt of this order, and proceed by voluntary enlistment to enroll as many men as can be armed in their respective regiments. They will make arrangements for a campaign of twelve days, and will provide themselves with arms, ammunition and provisions accordingly, and hold themselves in readiness immediately to march upon the receipt of further orders.

The independent companies of riflemen, infantry, cavalry, and artillery in the above-named counties, and in the county of Sangamon will hold themselves in readiness in like manner.

[Signed] Thomas Ford,
Governor and Commander-in-Chief.'

Movement of Quincy Troops to Warsaw.

Saturday, 29, 1 p. m.—Mayor Wood and ex-Mayor Conyers, from Quincy, arrived from the governor's headquarters, and said 244 troops from Quincy had arrived in Warsaw to protect the innocent, and they had come to ascertain the feelings of the people, and adopt measures to allay excitement.

We copy the following letter from Sheriff J. B. Backenstos:—

ROLL OF CARTHAGE GREYS AND OFFICERS JUNE 27th, *A. D.* 1844.

Robert F. Smith, Captain.
F. A. Worrell,
S. O. Williams,
M. Barnes, Jun., } Lieutenants.

Guard at the Jail, June 27, 1844.

F. A. Worrell, officer of the guard.
Franklin Rhodes.
William Baldwin.
Levi Street, lives near Mendon, Adams county, Illinois.
Joseph Hawley, lives in Carthage, Illinois.
Anthony Barkman, lives in Carthage, Illinois.
Clabourn Wilson, lives in Carthage, Illinois.

Balance of [*Company of*] *Greys.*

Edwin Baldwin, lives near Carthage, Ill.
James D. Barnes, " "
Frederick Loring, in "
Leyrand Doolittle, " "

Marvin Hamilton, lives in Carthage, Ill.
Ebenezer Rand, " "
John W. Maith, " "
Thomas Griffith, " "
Lewis C. Stevenson, " "
Noah M. Reckard, " "
Eli H. Williams, " "
H. T. Wilson, " "
Albert Thompson, " "
Walter Bagby, left the country, gone to Louisiana, and died.
George C. Waggoner, lives 2½ miles north of Carthage.
Crocket Wilson, lives 8 miles east of Carthage.
Thomas J. Dale, 5 " " "
Richard Dale, 5 " " "

The Carthage Greys never numbered more than about thirty, rank and file; during the June mob war, several joined for the time only, who reside at other places, and whose names are unknown to me. The Carthage Greys were nearly to a man parties in the June massacre.

Green Plains.

Captain Weir's company of about sixty men.

Warsaw.

Captain J. C. Davis' company of about sixty men.

Captain Wm. N. Grover's company of about sixty men.

Captain Mark Aldrich's company of about sixty men, comprising the entire settlement in and about Warsaw and Green Plains, with the exception of the Walkers, Gillhams, Paytons, Bledsors, Gallahers, Byrrs, Kimballs, Worthens, Summervilles, and Bedells, and the Mormon families who resided in that part of the county at that time.

Those active in the massacre at Carthage—supplied by Sheriff J. B. Backenstos

The leaders of the Hancock mob, and those who took an active part in the massacre of Joseph and Hyrum Smith are—

Thomas C. Sharp, *Warsaw Signal*, Illinois, editor.
Colonel Levi Williams, Green Plains, Illinois, farmer.
William N. Grover, Warsaw, Illinois, lawyer.
Jacob C. Davis, Warsaw, Illinois, lawyer.
Mark Aldrich, Warsaw, Illinois, no business.
Henry Stephens, Warsaw, Illinois, lawyer.
George Rockwell, Warsaw, Illinois, druggist.

James H. Wood, Warsaw, Illinois, blacksmith.
Calvin Cole, Warsaw, Illinois, tavernkeeper.
William B. Chipley, Warsaw, Illinois, doctor.
——— Hays, Warsaw, Illinois, doctor.
J. D. Mellen, Warsaw, Illinois, merchant.
E. W. Gould, Warsaw, Illinois, merchant.
Samuel Fleming, Warsaw, Illinois, constable.
John Montague, Warsaw, Illinois, no business.
Jas. Gregg, Warsaw, Illinois, no business.
J. C. Elliot, Warsaw, Illinois, no business.
Lyman Prentiss, Warsaw, Illinois, no business.
D. W. Matthews, now St. Louis, Missouri, merchant.
J. B. Matthews, now St. Louis, Missouri, merchant.
Trueman Hosford, Warsaw, Illinois, farmer.
Four of the Chittendens, Warsaw, Illinois, different occupations.
J. W. Athey, Warsaw, Illinois, no business.
Onias C. Skinner, now of Quincy, Illinois, lawyer.
Calvin A. Warren, Quincy, Illinois, lawyer.
George W. Thatcher, Carthage, Illinois, county clerk.
James W. Brattle, Carthage, Illinois, land shark.
Alexander Sympson, Carthage, Illinois, land shark.
Jason H. Sherman, Carthage, Illinois, lawyer.
Michael Reckard, one-half mile west of Carthage, Illinois, farmer.
Thomas Morrison, Carthage, Illinois, lawyer.
E. S. Freeman, Carthage, Illinois, blacksmith.
Thomas L. Barnes, Carthage, Illinois, quack doctor.
John Wilson, Carthage, Illinois, tavernkeeper.
Edward Jones, 5 miles north of Carthage, farmer.
Captain James E. Dunn, Augusta, Illinois, tavernkeeper.
Joel Catlin, Augusta, Illinois, farmer, etc.
William D. Abernethy, Augusta, Illinois, farmer, etc.
Erastus Austin, constable, etc.
——— Austin, loafer.
Reuben Graves, St. Mary's, Illinois, farmer.
Henry Garnett, St. Mary's, Illinois, farmer.
F. J. Bartlett, St. Mary's, Illinois, miller.
Valentine Wilson, St. Mary's, Illinois, farmer.
Sylvester M. Bartlett, editor of the *Quincy Whig*.
Major W. B. Warren, a damned villain.
Colonel ——— Gettis, Fountain Green, Illinois, farmer.
Matthews McClaughny, Fountain Green, Illinois, farmer.
Nickerson Wright, Fountain Green, Illinois, farmer.
John McAuley, Camp Creek Precinct, Illinois, one of the worst men in Hancock.
William H. Rollason, Pontusuc, Illinois.
John M. Finch, Pontusuc, Illinois.
Francis M. Higbee, Pontusuc, Illinois.

———— Douglass, Pontusuc, Illinois, schoolmaster.

George Backman, one of the Durfee murderers.*

———— Moss or Morse, one of the Durfee murderers.

Jacob Beck, one of the Durfee murderers.

Backman lives in Carthage, Moss or Morse, and Jacob Beck have left the country, but expect to return.

The foregoing is a pretty large list: there are others of the smaller fry which I deem unworthy of notice, inasmuch as they were led on through the influence of the leaders, and whiskey. I most cheerfully give you any information in my power in reference to this matter; the only thing that I regret about is, that these things I am fearful will be put off so long that I will not live to see or hear of the awful vengeance which will in the end overtake the Hancock assassins. I have long been of the opinion that forebearance is no longer a virtue, let the guilty be made to answer for their crimes. Let justice be done, and all will be well.

The bloodhounds are still determined on taking my life; I can hear from them every once in a while. I will have to be exceedingly careful this summer, or they will have my scalp. They still act upon the principle that had it not been for me in September last, Worrell and McBradney would not have been killed, and the city of Nauvoo burned to the ground. They want to hold me responsible for everything that was done to put them down in their mob doings last year.

In reference to my correspondence with the governor, I will say that I received but two letters from him during the difficulty, neither of which were received until after the arrival of General Hardin and the [state] government troops.

In my communications to Governor Ford, in relation to the riots in Hancock county, I made but one request of him, and that was, that no troops ought to be brought into Hancock county; that I had sufficient power within the limits of the county to suppress any further riots, and prevent any more burning.

I am certain that the letters which I received from the governor were either left in your hands, or in the hands of some one in your office at Nauvoo; at least I have not got them now. I recollect that you desired to get them for future use, and am sorry that I cannot forward them to you. You will find in my Proclamations† the historical part of the last mob war in Hancock.'

The following list is from the pen of Dr. Willard Richards:—

*The Durfee murder occurred at Green Plains in Hancock county, Illinois, during the renewal of mob violence in the latter part of 1845 (See Jenson's *Chronology*, November, 1845, also *Comprehensive History of the Church*, Century I, vol. ii, ch. lxvii). B. H. R.

†These Proclamations are five in number, and will be found *in extenso* in the *Comprehensive History of the Church*, Century I, vol. ii, pp. 490-503. B. H. R.

LIST OF THE MOB AT CARTHAGE ACCORDING TO WILLARD RICHARDS

'William Law,
Wilson Law,
Robert D. Foster,
Charles A. Foster,
Francis M. Higbee,
Chauncey L. Higbee,
Joseph H. Jackson,
John M. Finch,
Wm. A. Rollason,
Wm. H. J. Marr,
S. M. Marr,
Sylvester Emmons,
Alexander Sympson,
John Eagle,
Henry O. Norton,
Augustine Spencer.

The foregoing have been aided and abetted by—Charles Ivins and family, P. T. Rolfe, N. J. Higbee.

William Cook, and Sarah, his wife, formerly Sarah Crooks, of Manchester.'

Sunday, 30.—The governor wrote to General Deming, as follows:—

COMMUNICATION OF GOVERNOR FORD TO GENERAL DEMING

'Headquarters, Quincy, June 30, 1844.

Sir.—It is my present opinion that the Mormons will not commit any outbreak, and that no further alarm need be apprehended. I regret to learn that the party in Hancock, who are in favor of violent measures have circulated a thousand false rumors of danger, for the purpose of getting men together without my authority, hoping that when assembled, they may be ready to join in their violent councils. This is a fraud upon the country, and must not be endured.

I am afraid that the people of Hancock are fast depriving themselves of the sympathy of their fellow citizens, and of the world. I strictly order and enjoin on you that you permit no attack on Nauvoo or any of the people there without my authority. I think it would be best to disband your forces, unless it should be necessary to retain them to suppress violence on either side: of this you must be the judge at present.

I direct that you immediately order all persons from Missouri and Iowa to leave the camp and return to their respective homes without delay.

I direct, also, that you cause all mutinous persons, and all persons who advise tumultuous proceedings to be arrested; and that you take energetic measures to stop the practice of spreading false reports put in circulation to inflame the public mind.

[Signed] THOMAS FORD, Commander-in-Chief.

To Brigadier-General Deming, Carthage, Ill.'

A few of the brethren met in council, and agreed to send Brother George J. Adams to bear the news of the massacre to the Twelve.

Elder Willard Richards wrote the following, and sent it by George J. Adams:—

WILLARD RICHARDS TO BRIGHAM YOUNG—NAUVOO AFFAIRS, INCLUDING THE MARTYRDOM

'Nauvoo, Sunday, June 30, 1844,
6 p. m.

Beloved Brother Brigham Young,—For the first moment we have had the opportunity, by request of such brethren of the council as we could call, we write to inform you of the situation of affairs in Nauvoo and elsewhere.

On the 24th inst., Joseph, Hyrum, and thirteen others went to Carthage, and gave themselves up to Robert F. Smith, a justice of the peace, on charge of riot, for destroying the *Nauvoo Expositor* press and apparatus.

25*th*. Were exhibited by Governor Ford to the troops assembled, like elephants,—gave bonds for appearance at court, were arrested on charge of treason, and committed to jail without examination.

26*th*. Brought out to the courthouse contrary to law, for examination,—returned to jail till witnesses could be procured.

27*th*. A little before 6 p. m. the jail was forced by an armed, disguised mob, of from 150 to 200; the guard was frustrated, Hyrum shot in the nose and throat and two other places, only saying, '*I am a dead man*'. Elder Taylor received four balls in left leg and left wrist and hand. Joseph received four bullets, one in right collar bone, one in right breast, and two others in his back, he leaped from the east window of the front room, and was dead in an instant. I remained unharmed. The bodies were removed to Nauvoo on the 28th, and buried on the 29th. Elder Taylor remains at Hamilton's Tavern yet; we heard today he is better.

Elder George J. Adams is deputed to convey this to you, together with today's *Extra Nauvoo Neighbor,* and other papers giving particulars which you may rely on.

The effect of this hellish butchery was like the bursting of a tornado on Carthage and Warsaw; those villages were without inhabitants, as in an instant they ran for their lives, lest the Mormons should burn and kill them suddenly—'the wicked flee when no man pursueth'.

The excitement has been great, but the indignation more terrible: a reaction is taking place, and men of influence are coming from abroad to learn the facts, and going away satisfied that the Mormons are not the aggressors.

You now know our situation, and the request of the council is, that the Twelve return to Nauvoo. The lives of twelve more are threatened with deadly threats. It has been suggested by the council, that if the Twelve approved, President Brigham Young, Heber C. Kimball, George A. Smith, Wilford Woodruff and Orson Pratt return immediately; and William Smith, whose life is threatened, with all the Smiths, John E. Page, Lyman Wight, Parley P. Pratt and Orson Hyde spend a little time in publishing the news in the eastern cities, and getting as many in the church as possible. This is for you to decide.

The saints have borne this trial with great fortitude and forbearance. They must keep cool at present. We have pledged our faith not to prosecute the murderers at present, but leave it to Governor Ford; if he fails, time enough for us by and by; vengeance is in the heavens. We have been in close quarters some time,—money and provisions are scarce. Will the eastern brethren contribute to our relief?

Governor Ford has taken away the state arms from the Legion. Your families are well, for aught I know. Sister Hyde has gone to Kirtland, I suppose. I have not been able to get any means for myself or anybody else.

The council consider it best for all the traveling elders to stop preaching politics—preach the gospel with double energy, and bring as many to the knowledge of the truth as possible.

The great event of 1844, so long anticipated, has arrived, without a parallel since the birth of Adam.

Jackson [W. H.] and his gang will try to waylay you coming up the river, if not before: look out for yourselves.

A little while since Parley wrote to Hyrum about Elder George J. Adams' proceedings and teachings in Boston. I heard Joseph tell Hyrum to let Adams alone, let Adams go back there and make all things right, that Parley had misapprehended some things, and acted in the matter rather injudiciously.

The saints have entered into covenants of peace with the governor and government officers, not to avenge the blood of the martyrs, but leave it with the executive, who had pledged the faith of the state for their safe-keeping. The elders cannot be too careful in all the world, to keep from saying anything to irritate and vex the governor, etc., for at present we must conciliate: it is *for our salvation*. The governor has *appeared* to act with honest intentions; we bring no charge against him—will wait patiently his proceedings in the matter. Let the elders keep cool, *vengeance rests in heaven*.—Yours as ever,

WILLARD RICHARDS'.

Peace Council at Nauvoo.

A council was held by the brethren, at which Messrs. Wood and Conyers from Quincy were present, also Colonel Richardson, lawyer, from Rushville. The council again expressed their determination to preserve the peace in the city, and requested those gentlemen to use their influence to allay the excitement abroad, which they promised to do.

Colonel Richardson agreed to use all his influence to stay all illegal writs, and all writs for the present.

General Dunham requested a guard might be sent to Golden's Point, to protect the people there from the mob.

Father John Smith was present, and spoke of the destruction of crops by the McDonough troops.

We extract from Elder Woodruff's Journal:—

EXCERPTS FROM WILFORD WOODRUFF'S JOURNAL—THE TWELVE IN BOSTON

'The Boston branch of the Church of Jesus Christ of Latter-day Saints, and many elders from various parts, met in conference in Franklin Hall, Boston, on the 29th day of June, 1844.

Present: a majority of the Quorum of the Twelve, *viz.*, President Brigham Young, presiding; Elders Heber C. Kimball, Orson Hyde, Orson Pratt, William Smith, Wilford Woodruff, and Lyman Wight.

Conference opened by prayer.

Elder Orson Hyde occupied the forenoon in an interesting manner.

Elders Young, Kimball, and Wight severally addressed the meeting in the afternoon, much to the edification of the people.

Resolved that James H. Glines and Wm. Henderson be ordained elders: they were ordained under the hands of Elders Brigham Young and Heber C. Kimball.

Conference adjourned till Sunday morning.

The Twelve met in council in the evening.

30*th*. 10 *a. m.* Conference met pursuant to adjournment.

Elder Orson Pratt addressed the meeting, and ably removed the objections generally urged against new revelation.

In the afternoon, Elder Lyman Wight preached on the immortality of the body and the spirit, and also the principle of charity, connecting it with baptism for the dead.

In the evening, Elder Wilford Woodruff preached from the words of Jesus: 'Ye are my friends, if ye do whatsoever I command you.'

The house was full through the day and evening, and much instruction was given during the conference by those who spoke.'

A. Jonas and Col. Fellows at Nauvoo—Their Instructions.

Monday, July 1.—A. Jonas and Colonel Fellows arrived in Nauvoo, with a message from the governor to the city council. We copy their instructions:—

THE GOVERNOR'S INSTRUCTIONS

'Colonel Fellows and Captain Jonas are requested to proceed by the first boat to Nauvoo, and ascertain what is the feeling, disposition, and determination of the people there, in reference to the late disturbances; ascertain whether any of them propose in any manner to avenge themselves, whether any threats have been used, and what is proposed generally to be done by them.

They are also requested to return to Warsaw and make similar inquiries there; ascertain how far false rumors have been put afloat for the purpose of raising forces; what is the purpose of the militia assembled, whether any attack is intended on Nauvoo.

Ascertain also, whether any person from Missouri or Iowa intends to take part in the matter, and in my name forbid any such interference, without my request, on pain of being demanded for punishment.

[Signed] THOMAS FORD.

June 30th, 1844.'

They wrote as follows:—

COMMISSIONERS' NOTE TO THE NAUVOO CITY COUNCIL

'Nauvoo, July 1, 1844.

To the City Council of Nauvoo:

Gentlemen,—With this you will receive a copy of instructions from Governor Ford to us. You will understand from them what we desire from you in action on your part, as the only authorities of your city now known to the country, of such a character as will pacify the public mind and satisfy the governor of your determination to sustain the supremacy of the laws, which will, we are sure, be gratifying to him, and as much so to

Yours respectfully,
[Signed] HART FELLOWS,
A. JONAS.'

We copy from the *Times and Seasons*:—

RESOLUTIONS OF THE CITY COUNCIL OF NAUVOO

'At a meeting of the city council, held in the council room, in the city of Nauvoo, on the first day of July, 1844, having received instructions from Governor Ford, through the agency of A. Jonas, Esq., and Colonel Fellows, it was unanimously

Resolved, For the purpose of insuring peace, and promoting the welfare of the county of Hancock and surrounding country, that we will rigidly sustain the laws and the governor of the state, so long as they and he, sustain us in all our constitutional rights.

Resolved, secondly, That to carry the foregoing resolutions into complete effect, that inasmuch as the governor has taken from us the public arms, that we solicit of him to do the same with all the rest of the public arms of the state.

Resolved, thirdly, To further secure the peace, friendship and happiness of the people, and allay the excitement that now exists, we will reprobate private revenge on the assassinators of General Joseph Smith and General Hyrum Smith by any of the Latter-day Saints. That instead of 'an appeal to arms', we appeal to the majesty of the law, and will be content with whatever judgment it shall award and should the law fail, we leave the matter with God.

Resolved, unanimously, That this city council pledge themselves for the city of Nauvoo, that no aggressions by the citizens of said city shall be made on the citizens of the surrounding country, but we invite them, as friends and neighbors, to use the Savior's golden rule, and 'do unto others as they would have others do unto them', and we will do likewise.

Resolved, lastly, That we highly approve of the present public pacific course of the governor to allay excitement and restore peace among the citizens of the country; and while he does so, and will use his influence to stop all vexatious proceedings in law, until confidence is restored, so that the citizens of Nauvoo can go to Carthage, or any other place, for trial, without exposing themselves to the violence of assassins, we will uphold him, and the law, by all honorable means.

[Signed] GEORGE W. HARRIS, President *pro tem.*
Willard Richards, Recorder.'

'A Jonas, Esq., and Colonel Fellows:—

Messrs.,—In reply to your communication to the city council of the city of Nauvoo, on behalf of His Excellency Governor Ford, I have been instructed by the council to communicate the foregoing resolutions which I respectfully solicit for your consideration, and at the same time would inform you that a public meeting of our citizens will take place at the stand, east of the Temple, at 4 p. m., and solicit your attendance.

Most respectfully, your obedient servant,
[Signed] W. RICHARDS.'

ACTION OF THE CITY COUNCIL—EXPRESSIONS OF APPRECIATION

'At a meeting of a large portion of the citizens of Nauvoo, convened at the stand, in the afternoon of July 1, 1844, after hearing the above instructions and resolutions of the city council read, and being addressed by A. Jonas, Esq., and others, the meeting responded to the same with a hearty AMEN!

The citizens then passed a vote of thanks to the governor's agents for their kindly interference in favor of peace among the citizens of Hancock county and elsewhere around us.

They also passed a vote of thanks to Messrs. Woods and Reid, the counsel for the Generals Smith, for their great exertions to have even-handed justice meted to the Latter-day Saints, and they also passed a vote of thanks to Messrs. Chambers and Field, the former one of the editors of the *Missouri Republican*, and the latter, one of the editors of the *Reveille*, of St. Louis, for their honorable course of coming to Nauvoo for facts, instead of spreading rumors concerning the Latter-day Saints.

Mr. Chambers made a very appropriate speech, containing inuendos for the benefit of our citizens, that appeared as the wise man said, *'like apples of gold in pictures of silver'*.

They also passed a vote of thanks to Messrs. Wood and Conyers, mayor and ex-mayor of Quincy, for their friendly disposition in establishing peace in this region, and we are happy to say that all appears to be *peace at Nauvoo*.'

ADDRESS TO THE CHURCH OF JESUS CHRIST OF LATTER-DAY SAINTS —A WORD OF CONSOLATION

'Deeply impressed for the welfare of all, while mourning the great loss of President Joseph Smith, our 'Prophet and Seer', and President Hyrum Smith, our 'Patriarch', we have considered the occasion demanded of us a word of consolation.

As has been the case in all ages, these saints have fallen martyrs for the truth's sake, and their escape from the persecution of a wicked world, in blood to bliss, only strengthens our faith, and confirms our religion as pure and holy.

We, therefore, as servants of the Most High God, having the *Bible*, *Book of Mormon*, and the *Book of Doctrine and Covenants*, together with thousands of witnesses, for Jesus Christ, would beseech the Latter-day Saints, in Nauvoo and elsewhere, to hold fast to the faith that has been delivered to them in the last days, abiding in the perfect law of the gospel.

Be peaceable, quiet citizens, doing the works of righteousness, and as soon as the Twelve and other authorities can assemble, or a majority of them, the onward course to the great gathering of Israel, and the final consummation of the dispensation of the fulness of times will be pointed out, so that the murder of Abel, the assassination of hundreds, the righteous blood of all the holy Prophets, from Abel to Joseph, sprinkled with the best blood of the Son of God, as the crimson sign of remission, only carries conviction to the bosoms of all intelligent beings, that the cause is just and will continue; and blessed are they that hold out faithful to the end, while apostates, consenting to the shedding of innocent blood, have no forgiveness in this world nor in the world to come.

Union is peace, brethren, and eternal life is the greatest gift of God. Rejoice, then, that you are found worthy to live and die for God. Men may kill the body, but they *cannot* hurt the soul, and wisdom shall be justified of her children. Amen.

[Signed] W. W. PHELPS,
WILLARD RICHARDS,
JOHN TAYLOR.

July 1, 1844'."

CHAPTER XIII

THE MARTYRDOM IN POETRY—EFFORTS FOR FOOD SUPPLIES AND PROTECTION FOR THE PEOPLE OF NAUVOO—THE DANIELS AFFIDAVIT ON THE MARTYRDOM

"THE following appropriate and expressive poetry we copy from the *Times and Seasons*:—

THE ASSASSINATION OF GENERALS JOSEPH AND HYRUM SMITH, FIRST PRESIDENT AND SECOND PATRIARCH OF THE CHURCH OF LATTER-DAY SAINTS, WHO WERE MASSACRED BY A MOB, IN CARTHAGE, HANCOCK COUNTY, ILLINOIS, ON THE 27TH OF JUNE, 1844

BY MISS ELIZA R. SNOW

'And when he had opened the fifth seal, I saw under the altar the souls of them that were slain for the word of God, and for the testimony which they held.

And they cried with a loud voice, saying, how long, O Lord, holy and true, dost thou not judge and avenge our blood on them that dwell on the earth?

And white robes were given unto every one of them; * * * that they should rest yet for a litle season, until their fellow servants also, and their brethren, that should be killed as they were, should be fulfilled' (*Rev.* vi:9, 10, 11).

'Ye heavens attend! Let all the earth give ear.
Let God and seraphs, men and angels hear—
The worlds on high—the universe shall know
What awful scenes are acted here below!
Had nature's self a heart, that heart would bleed
At the recital of that horrid deed;
For never, since the Son of Man was slain
Has blood so noble flowed from human vein
As that which now on God for vengeance calls
From freedom's ground—from Carthage prison walls.

Oh! Illinois! thy soil has drank the blood
Of Prophets martyr'd for the truth of God.
Once lov'd America, what can atone
For the pure blood of innocence thou'st sown?
Were all thy streams in teary torrents shed
How vain the tribute, for the noblest worth
That graced thy surface, O degraded earth!
Oh wretched murd'rers! fierce for human blood!
You've slain the Prophets of the living God,
Who've borne oppression from their early youth,
To plant on earth the principles of truth.

Shades of heroic fathers! Can it be
Beneath your blood-stained flag of liberty,
The firm supporters of our country's cause,
Are butchered while submissive to her laws?
Yes, blameless men, defam'd by hellish lies,
Have thus been offered as a sacrifice
T'appease the ragings of a brutish clan,
That has defied the laws of God and man!
'Twas not for crime or guilt of theirs they fell—
Against the laws they never did rebel;
True to their country, yet her plighted faith
Has proved an instrument of cruel death!
Where are thy far-famed laws—Columbia, where
Thy boasted freedom—thy protecting care?
Is this a land of rights? Stern facts shall say,
If legal justice here maintains its sway.
The official pow'rs of State are sheer pretense
When they're exerted in the Saints' defense.

Great men have fallen, and mighty men have died—
Nations have mourn'd their fav'rites and their pride;
But TWO so wise, so virtuous, great and good,
Before on earth, at once, have never stood
Since the creation—men whom God ordain'd
To publish truth where error long had reign'd,
Of whom the world itself unworthy prov'd,
It *knew them not;* but men with hatred mov'd,

And with infernal spirits have combin'd
Against the best, the noblest of mankind.
Oh persecution! shall thy purple hand
Spread utter desolation through the land?
Shall freedom's banner be no more unfurled?
Has peace indeed been taken from the world?

Thou God of Jacob, in this trying hour
Help us to trust in thy Almighty power;
Support thy Saints beneath this awful stroke,
Make bare thine arm to break oppression's yoke.
We mourn thy Prophet, from whose lips have flow'd
The words of life thy Spirit has bestow'd—
A depth of thought no human art could reach
From time to time, roll'd in sublimest speech
From the celestial fountain, through his mind,
To purify and elevate mankind;
The rich intelligence by him brought forth,
Is like the sunbeam spreading o'er the earth.

Now Zion mourns—she mourns an earthly head;
The Prophet and the Patriarch are dead!
The blackest deed that men or devils know,
Since Calv'ry's scene, has laid the brothers low!
One in their life, and one in death—they prov'd
How strong their friendship—how they truly lov'd;
True to their mission until death they stood,
Then seal'd their testimony with their blood.
All hearts with sorrow bleed, and every eye
Is bath'd in tears—each bosom heaves a sigh—
Heartbroken widows' agonizing groans
Are mingled with the helpless orphans' moans!
Ye Saints! be still, and know that God is just—
With steadfast purpose in his promise trust;
Girded with sackcloth, own his mighty hand,
And wait his judgment on this guilty land!
The noble martyrs now have gone to move
The cause of Zion in the courts above.

Nauvoo, July 1st, 1844.'

Tuesday, July 2, 1844.—We extract the following from Elders Kimball and Wight's letter:—

*SECOND LETTER FROM ELDERS WIGHT AND KIMBALL—MOVEMENTS OF THE TWELVE**

'June 21st, 1844.

We again resume the pen to give you a few further particulars. We met the church in the city of Philadelphia last evening, pursuant to adjournment, the members being all present. The vote was taken to know whether they would sustain the First Presidency and the Twelve in their calling, and follow their counsel spiritually and temporally, lay aside all their prejudice and fears, and follow them through evil as well as through good report. There was not a dissenting vote. We think the church is in a good condition. There will be some added next Sabbath by baptism, and we trust more ere long. For our manner of preaching and instructing the church, we refer you to brothers Forgeus and Price.

We leave here today, at 4 o'clock, for the Wilmington conference; many of the brethren and sisters from this place are going with us. We have so many calls in this place, from those in the church and out of it, that we cannot stop a night in a place. We are at this time at Sister McMinn's, whose family treat us with all the kindness and attention that the servants of God could ask. They wish to be remembered to the Prophet and family, and so do all the saints in this place; and they are now determined to uphold you by their prayers in all things. I must confess this was not the case when we came here, with all. We learned that it is too much the case that the Twelve often find their way hedged up by the presiding elders endeavoring to exalt themselves and debase us, but you will find it different with your case in Philadelphia.

June 24th, 1844.

Just returned from Wilmington conference, accompanied by several of the brethren and sisters who went from this place. We can truly say that this was one of the most pleasant trips in our life. We went down on the steamer *Balloon*, and returned by railway.

Our conference commenced on Saturday, the 22nd. The brethren came in from the adjacent country, and after much instruction from Brothers Kimball and Wight, we took a vote to know whether they would go withersoever the Presidency, Patriarch and Twelve went, should it be to Oregon, Texas, or California, or any other place directed by the wisdom of Almighty God. The saints, numbering about 100, rose to their feet and exclaimed, Whithersoever they go, we go, without a dissenting voice. This was truly an interesting meeting. We have not the least idea that anyone will back out;

*For first letter see chapter xi this volume.

they are nearly all men of wealth, and have commenced this morning to offer all surplus property for sale, that whenever you say go, they are ready. We ordained ten as promising young elders as we ever laid hands upon. They pledged themselves to start this week and go through the state of Delaware from house to house, and proclaim that the kingdom of heaven is at hand.

On Sabbath, the 23rd, we preached alternately to a large and respectable congregation, and left the warmest of friends in that place, both in and out of the church. We have hundreds of pleasant sceneries in our journals, which are too numerous to mention at present.

Yours as ever,
[Signed] HEBER C. KIMBALL,
LYMAN WIGHT.'

Tuesday, 2—Elder John Taylor was brought home from Carthage to the joy of his friends.

ACTION OF CITY COUNCIL ON SUPPLYING FOOD FOR NAUVOO

'A special session of the city council was called to devise ways and means for supplying the city with provisions. Dr. Richards, Colonel Dunham, Marshal Greene, and others, stated to the council that many were destitute, and that unless active measures were taken, many must suffer with hunger, as some had already; wherefore it was

Resolved, by the city council of the city of Nauvoo ,that special committees be appointed to visit the different sections of the surrounding country, and solicit the benevolent for donations, or provisions and means for supplying the wants of the destitute of this city; and so far as donations fail, supply the deficiency by loans.

Resolved, That Charles Patten, W. H. Jordan, and L. S. Dalrymple be this committee for Iowa; that D. M. Repsher, A. Morrison, and Captain Ross go to Madison, Burlington, and the north country; that Benjamin Clapp, Samuel James, and Hiram Clark visit Ramus, La Harpe, and the eastern country, and that Isaac Morley assist the south to carry out the foregoing resolutions.

Resolved, That L. N. Scovil, Edwin D. Woolley, and William M. Gheen, be a standing committee to negotiate for all necessary supplies to those who are on duty by order of government.

Resolved, That each of said committees keep an accurate account of all donations and loans, and make returns of the same to the marshal of the city.

Passed July 2nd, 1844, 6 p. m.

[Signed] ORSON SPENCER, President *pro tem.*

W. Richards, Recorder.'

GEORGE J. ADAMS—MESSENGER TO BRIGHAM YOUNG—FAILURE OF

'*To whom it may concern*—

Elder George J. Adams has been deputed by council of the church to bear despatches to Elder Young, president of the Quorum of the Twelve, relative to the death of the Prophet Joseph, and his brother Hyrum Smith, and the brethren are requested to see that no means are wanting to speed him on his important mission.

In behalf of the church,

[Signed] WILLARD RICHARDS,

Clerk of the Quorum of the Twelve.'

George J. Adams failed to perform this mission, although he had plenty of means, but Jedediah M. Grant went right through, and carried the word.

General Dunham wrote as follows:—

LETTER OF GENERAL DUNHAM TO GOVERNOR FORD—CALL FOR MORE MILITIA TROOPS TO CHECK MOB AT WARSAW AND GOLDEN'S POINT

'*His Excellency Governor Ford.*

I am sorry to inform you that the mob is still prowling between Warsaw and Golden's Point, waiting for an opportunity to come in and burn and destroy. The mob party are continually threatening us, and are driving our people away from their homes, and they are obliged to come here for protection.

I want you to send about one hundred or two hundred men whom you can depend upon as loyal, to quarter in the woods between here and Golden's Point, so that they can be between us and the mob, and protect us. Our troops are worn out, and I shall soon expect an order from you to discharge my men from the duty they are obliged to perform, to fulfil your order.

I am your Excellency's obedient servant,

[Signed] JONATHAN DUNHAM,

Major-General Commanding Nauvoo Legion.

July 2, 1844, 8 p. m.'

Council of the Twelve at Boston.

At a council of the Twelve and other elders, held in the Franklin Hall, Boston, there were ordained two elders, and arrangements made for dividing off into different parts of the vineyard. Each of the Twelve were appointed to attend several conferences.

Elders Wilford Woodruff and Milton Holmes took steamer for Portland, Maine.

Colonel Lyman Wight delivered a political address at Bunker Hill, at 4 p. m.

Wednesday, 3.—We copy from the *Neighbor*:—

THE ANSWER OF GOVERNOR FORD TO THE WARSAW COMMITTEE— REVIEW OF MURDER OF THE GENERALS SMITH

'Quincy, July 3, 1844.

To the Warsaw Committee:

Gentlemen,—I have received your communication on behalf of the citizens of Warsaw, stating their unalterable determination to compel the Mormons of your county to leave the state; or otherwise to abandon their own homes and evacuate the county, and asking my interference and influence to assist you in procuring the removal of the Mormons.

I have no reply whatever to make to that part of your letter which treats of the history, character, and offenses of the Mormons. I deem this, however, a fit occasion to remark somewhat upon the character of the events which have just transpired. These events present reasons for my determination which must be noticed.

When I came to your county I announced the policy by which I intended to be governed. The law was to be my guide; and this you well understand. I announced this determination in numerous public addresses, and uniformly in my private conversations. I successively obtained a vote to sustain me in this course from every troop stationed at Carthage, or who was visiting there.

From the detachment of your town and vicinity, who visited Carthage the day before the surrender of the Smiths, I obtained a similar pledge. I met them on the prairie, before they arrived in town, and as they must testify, stated to them at length, the reason which ought to influence them to keep the peace and abide the operation of the laws. They gave every demonstration of satisfaction, and signified, with unanimous acclamation, that they would stand by me in taking a strictly legal course.

All the other portion of the Hancock forces under my command were repeatedly and deeply pledged to sustain me in the same course. Under the firm and confident assurance of support thus obtained, I demanded the surrender of the Smiths, and promised them security.

In doing so, I now acknowledge that I erred, and erred grievously, in relying with too much confidence upon men with whom I was but little acquainted. The idea that men could be treacherous under such circumstances was abhorrent to my nature, and rejected with indignation.

Whatever your hatred of the Smiths might be, I was too confident you would respect your honor—the honor of your country and state, and the rights of defenseless prisoners. I could not believe that so much stupidity and baseness as was necessary for such an enterprise as the murder of defenseless prisoners in jail would be, could be mustered in Hancock county.

What aggravates the transaction, as a matter personal to myself, is that you betrayed my honor as well as your own, and that of the state; and you selected a time to commit the deed when you believed I was in Nauvoo, in the power of the Mormons, and would most probably be murdered by them by way of retaliation.

Upon the whole I cannot too strongly express my indignation and abhorrence of the base and profligate act which has disgraced the state and raised suspicions in the minds of many in regard to my conduct in the matter of the most painful character to my feelings.

I am happy, however, to learn that these denunciations apply only to a small portion of the people of Warsaw and Hancock county. All the most responsible inhabitants ought to be acquitted of any direct participation with the conspirators.

If they are culpable at all, it is for not using their influence against the act, and for not communicating to me information which would have enabled me to prevent it. The intention of the people must, to some extent, have been whispered about and understood, and ought to have been communicated to me as commander-in-chief.

Under these circumstances I am in but a poor situation to use influence with the Mormons, to procure their removal. Your own people have destroyed whatever influence I might otherwise have possessed in that quarter to serve you.

Your own conduct has placed me in a painfully suspicious attitude; and I have no hopes that I could now have a more persuasive influence with the Mormons than I had with the perpetrators of the horrid deed which I sought to prevent. Under the circumstances I cannot ask the Mormons to confide in me.

It must appear to them that they have been betrayed by somebody, and they do not know by whom.

If you mean to request me to exercise a forcible influence to expel them from the state, I answer you now, as I have uniformly done, that the law is my guide, and that I know of no law authorizing their expulsion. From this determination I have not swerved for an instant from the beginning until this time.

I see nothing now requiring any deviation, and besides, if I were ever so much determined to drive them out, I believe such is the abhorrence against the base deed which some of you have committed, that I could not obtain voluntary aid from the people.

I suppose that you are aware that a call for volunteers is the only mode in which a force can be raised, and the force when raised must be provisioned by voluntary contribution.

You had better not make too loud a call upon your fellow citizens; you may want their aid for defense; and may yet be glad to receive aid for defense rather than aggression.

I know the apprehensions which you entertain of Mormon violence; I will not now say whether your fears are well or ill founded; a little time will develop what may be expected.

Taking the law for my guide, I can assure you that, although some of you have treated me badly, in thwarting my policy and violating my honor, and have acted basely towards defenseless prisoners, yet you are entitled to, and are assured of all the force of the state to prevent or avenge illegal violence towards any of you. An inquiry must be made concerning the murderers; they must for the honor and credit of the state be dealt with according to law.

You ask a small force to be stationed in your county as a protection against small parties. You have not probably duly considered how large a force would be necessary for this purpose. A small force could protect but a few points of attack, and must necessarily leave the residue of the county exposed.

A large force cannot be stationed there permanently. Your best protection is the assurance that upon the first aggression or well defined threats, an overpowering force is ready to march directly for the scene of action.

I am informed that a design is still entertained at Warsaw of attacking Nauvoo. In this you will not be sustained by myself or the people; it is a part of my policy that you remain quiet, and if you please, watchful, but strictly on the defensive; and I now announce to you that I will not be thwarted in this policy with impunity.

I am, most respectfully,

Your obedient servant,
[Signed] THOMAS FORD.'

The Members of the Mob Wounded at Carthage.

Wednesday, 3.—Messrs. John B. Kimball, of Warsaw, and Elias Smith, of Nauvoo, reported that John Patrick Wells and W. Voorhees were wounded in the affray at Carthage.

Elders Brigham Young and Heber C. Kimball spent the day together in the city of Boston, and in the evening visited the museum.

Thursday, 4.—Elder Samuel H. Smith received a letter from Richard Ballantyne, introducing Mr. William M. Daniels.

Mr. Daniels made the following affidavit:—

AFFIDAVIT OF WILLIAM M. DANIELS

'State of Illinois,
Hancock county, } ss.

On the 4th day of July, 1844, came William M. Daniels before me, Aaron Johnson, a justice of the peace within and for said county, and after being duly sworn, deposeth and saith that on Saturday, the 22nd day of June, 1844, he came to the town of Warsaw, in said county of Hancock, and continued there until the Thursday following, the 27th day of June; that on that morning your affiant joined the rifle company commanded by Jacob Davis;

that the lieutenant and ——— Chittenden, Esq., said that as the governor would be absent from Carthage that day, that they would send ten men from each of the two companies to join the Carthage Greys, and kill the two Generals Smith, and if the governor opposed, to kill him too; that among those twenty men were Mr. Houck, a tailor, and Mr. Stephens, a cooper; the rest of the two companies marched towards Golden's Point to the railroad crossing, when they were met by the governor's order to disband all the troops, and Colonel Williams disbanded them.

That then the captains called them to order, saying they had no command over them, but wished them to form in line, which they did; that then Mr. Sharp, the editor of the *Warsaw Signal*, urged by a speech the necessity of *killing the two Smiths*, and a vote was then called who would go and do it.

Captain Davis and about twenty men went home, the residue, eighty-four men, went to Carthage, having six runners ahead to stop the twenty men who had before started for Carthage.

Soon after they started, one of the Carthage Greys met them with a letter, saying it was a most delightful time, the governor had gone, they could now kill Joseph and Hyrum Smith, and must do it quick before the governor returned; that they then turned to the left between the Warsaw and Nauvoo roads, and were not seen again by your affiant till they arrived at the jail in Carthage; that among the names of those who committed the murder at the jail in Carthage, Hancock county aforesaid, on the 27th day of June, 1844, at about 5 o'clock and 20 minutes, was Colonel Levi Williams, of Green Plains precinct, Captain Wires, ———— Chittenden, Esq., of Warsaw. ——— Houck, the tailor, Captain Grovenor, three brothers by the name of Stephens, coopers, ——— Allen, a cooper, all of Warsaw, and a man by the name of Mills, who was wounded in the right arm.

That your affiant would further state that this company before mentioned were painted black; that the guns of the guard at the jail were loaded with blank cartridges; that this was an arrangement entered into by the Carthage Greys, as said the messenger who came to meet said company in the morning.

That your said affiant saw Joseph Smith leap from the window of the jail, and that one of the company picked him up and placed him against the well curb, and several shot him, Colonel Williams exclaiming, 'Shoot him! Damn him! Shoot him!' and further your affiant saith not.* [Signed] WILLIAM M. DANIELS.'

*It is unfortunate that this affiant did not keep his subsequent statements at the trial within the limits of this affidavit as he would then have been a much more efficient witness at the subsequent trial of the murderers of the Prophet at which he was a witness and testified; but with the aid of a young typo in the *Times and Seasons* printing office at Nauvoo, he enlarged his affidavit to a sensational pamphlet detailing many miraculous occurrences in connection with the martyrdom which discredited him as a witness and did much towards making the murderers of the Prophet farcical.

The following anonymous letter was written:—

A PLEA FOR LIBERTY AND JUSTICE—ANONYMOUS

'For the *Lee County Democrat*,

Mr. Editor: Lee County, Iowa, July 4, 1844.

Sir,—On this birthday of our common country, I am admonished

This pamphlet detailing the alleged miraculous incidents in the murder was brought out in the trial and Daniels confronted with it, swore to the statements. The counsel for the defendants asked the court to eliminate all consideration of such testimony from the record. The court granted the request in the following terms:

"That in making up their (the jury's) verdict they will exclude from their consideration all that was said by Daniels, Brackenbury, and Miss Graham (witnesses)."

It was supposed that the testimony of Brackenbury and Miss Graham would support the testimony of Daniels, but this support failed to appear. We quote what is alleged to be a reproduction of much of it, in a book published in Utah under the title of *The Martyrs*. The excerpt begins with the appearance of the Prophet in the window of the prison under the fire of the mob:—

"He sprang into the window; but just as he was preparing to descend, he saw such an array of bayonets below, that he caught by the window casing, where he hung by his hands and feet, with his head to the north, feet to the south, and his body swinging downwards. He hung in that position three or four minutes, during which time he exclaimed, two or three times, 'O, Lord, My God!!!' and fell to the ground. While he was hanging in that position, Colonel Williams hallooed, 'Shoot him! G—d d—n him! shoot the dam'd rascal!' However, none fired at him.

He seemed to fall easy. He struck partly on his right shoulder and back, his neck and head reaching the ground a little before his feet. He rolled instantly on his face. From this position he was taken by a young man, who sprang to him from the other side of the fence, who held a pewter fife in his hand, was barefoot and bareheaded, having no coat, with his pants rolled above his knees, and shirtsleeves above his elbows. He set President Smith against the south side of the well curb, that was situated a few feet from the jail. While doing this, the savage muttered aloud, 'This is Old Jo; I know him. I know you, Old Jo. Damn you; you are the man that had my daddy shot.' The object he had in talking in this way, I supposed to be this: He wished to have President Smith and the people in general, believe he was the son of Governor Boggs, which would lead to the opinion that it was the Missourians who had come over and committed the murder. This was the report that they soon caused to be circulated; but this was too palpable an absurdity to be credited.

* * * The ruffian, of whom I have spoken, who set him against the well curb, now secured a bowie knife for the purpose of severing his head from his body. He raised the knife and was in the attitude of striking, when a light, so sudden and powerful burst from the heavens upon the bloody scene, (passing its vivid chain between Joseph and his murderers), that they were struck with terrified awe and filled with consternation. This light, in its appearance and potency, baffles all powers of description. The arm of the ruffian, that held the knife, fell powerless; the muskets of the four, who fired, fell to the ground, and they all stood like marble statues, not having power to move a single limb of their bodies.

By this time most of the men had fled in great disorder. I never saw so frightened a set of men before. Colonel Williams saw the light and was also badly frightened; but he did not entirely lose the use of his limbs or speech. Seeing the condition of these men, he hallooed to some who had just commenced to retreat, for God's sake to come and carry off these men. They came back and carried them by main strength towards the baggage wagons. They seemed as helpless as if they were dead" (*The Martyrs*, pp. 79-81. For treatment somewhat in full see *Comprehensive History of the Church*, Century I, vol. ii, ch.lx, pp. 321-34; also *History of Hancock County*, Gregg, pp. 323-31). B. H. R.

by surrounding circumstances that something must be done by the friends of liberty, and that speedily too, or the star spangled banner of the American Eagle must soon cease to wave its golden pinions o'er the heads of freemen.

I was aroused to these reflections by the statements of Messrs, Reid and Woods in the *Nauvoo Neighbor Extra,* of Sunday, June 30th, 1844, 3 p. m., also of the *Neighbor* of yesterday. Mr. H. T. Reid is a gentleman of high legal attainments, of Madison, in our county, possessed of a character for truth and veracity not to be impeached. Mr. J. W. Woods is an attorney, of Burlington, in this territory, of the same character and standing. His word may be relied on; and as these gentlemen were in the midst of the circumstances which led to the horrid butchery of Generals Joseph and Hyrum Smith at Carthage, on the 27th ult., and as they, like myself, are no Mormons, and live in a neighboring territory, I hope the citizens of these United States will give their statements of this horrid affair, that confidence and calm deliberation which the case solemnly demands.

If the freeborn sons of American liberty can be incarcerated in prison for some supposed or real crime without the privilege of an investigation, and be murdered by a ruthless mob in that defenseless state, in open daylight, and in the presence of the authorities of the land too, where, I ask in the name of freemen, where is our freedom? Where is our security for all the blessings for which our fathers fought and bled? Who will ere long dare lay his head upon his pillow in his own habitation and say, I am safe? If the strong walls of a prison are not sufficient to guarantee safety to citizens of this republic, what may we soon expect who live in unwalled houses? I ask in the name of humanity, are not American liberties on the verge of a mighty precipice, just ready to plunge into the whirlpool of utter dissolution?

Perhaps it may be said the Mormons are to blame; and supposing they are, does this warrant death and destruction to be hurled at them without judge or jury? The riots at Philadelphia and other places have been sufficiently alarming, but the recent tragedy at Carthage mocks all parallel—history has no equal.

The page of time till June 27th, 1844, has been unstained by such a blot. I mourn for my country. How has the soil of an independent state been crimsoned with innocent blood? I say innocent, for the law holds every man innocent till he is proved guilty. Were the Smiths proved guilty? No! they had no trial. Where is the plighted faith of the state?

How is the honor of all this western country tarnished! How will the jealousies of the eastern states be excited by this unheard of butchery!

I am a native of New England. I know the prejudices of the eastern people concerning the west and south. They feel that a man cannot travel in safety in our region, in Illinois, in Iowa, and the surrounding states and territories, without a pistol and a bowie knife, and that we almost belong to another race of beings; and when our eastern friends shall read the true and frightful tale of Messrs. Reid and Woods, well may their fears be increased, their jealousies aroused, and they led to believe that all they had anticipated was true concerning us. But, Mr. Editor, I would undeceive them; and although not one palliating circumstance, to my knowledge, offers itself to the public mind in relation to the occurrence at Carthage, yet I would say to my friends in New England, and to all men, the citizens of the west do not approbate such proceedings.

More than nineteen-twentieths of the citizens of Iowa, and, I am confident, of Illinois, reprobate with unqualified abhorrence the atrocious deed.

The wise, the virtuous, the patriotic of all sects and denominations and parties, political or religious, hurl their anathemas at the barbarous deed which was transacted by a lawless mob, a few scores of desperadoes, if we can believe the most authentic intelligence from the scene of trouble.

The great, great mass of the people deprecate the event as much as would the inhabitants of Vermont, Massachusetts, or any other state, and why not? We are their sons, their brothers, their sisters, their daughters, nursed by the same mothers, cradled by the same firesides.

I repeat what is well known, I am no Mormon, and that they may be guilty of some things as a society. If they are, I do not know it. So far as I have seen their leaders, their teachings have been moral and upright, and their publications state if they have erred in anything, they have erred unintentionally, and they are ready to be set right by the powers above them.

Why then should not the law have its course? Why should any man be condemned without a hearing? If this thing is suffered to go any further, God knows where it will end; I fear a general civil war, and I do hope that every good man in the union will arise and stamp with infamy any such unlawful proceedings.

If the city of Nauvoo erred in declaring the printing press of the *Expositor* a nuisance, what then? I am no lawyer, but I suppose it could be no more than a trespass—they liable for damage only; and if they erred in judgment, it is not the first time a legislative body has erred. Congress might have done as much, and not be killed for it; then why kill them?

Mr. Editor, is the action of the government to bring the murderers of the Generals Smith to justice? I ask for information. Have the perpetrators been discovered? Have arrests been made? Have rewards been made? Have rewards been offered by the governor of Illinois? or has he been dilatory in his duties, as the respectable part of the community think him to be?

If he does his duty, I trust justice will be done to the assassins;

but it is not enough to deprecate alone, action, decided action should be had in the case, that our country may be saved from mobocracy and violence, and order and law bear rule again in our land.*

I am, sir,

[Signed] A FRIEND TO EQUAL RIGHTS.' "

*It is appreciated that this is an anonymous communication, and anonymous letters are not often woven into serious historical statements; but it must be remembered that this anonymous letter was written for and published in the *Lee County Democrat* of Iowa, and is such a truthful statement of the main facts connected with the martyrdom of Joseph and Hyrum Smith and discusses the points at issue in such a temperate and striking manner that it represents a fixed and important view of the whole case; and for these valuable elements in it, notwithstanding its defects of composition, is here presented for preservation. B. H. R.

CHAPTER XIV

A CHAPTER OF SUNDRY EVENTS AT VARIOUS PLACES AND DOCUMENTS FOLLOWING THE MARTYRDOM: UNITED STATES PRESS COMMENTS ON THE MURDER

"*Thursday, July* 4, 1844.—Elders Brigham Young and Heber C. Kimball, with several other elders, visited the grand exhibition of fireworks on the Boston Common this evening. A great multitude were present.

Sundry Events and Activities.

Friday, 5.—Mr. Daniels started about 9 a. m. to go and see the governor, and tell him what he knew in relation to the massacre of the Generals Smith.

A raft of pine lumber arrived from the upper country.

Elders Young and Kimball took cars from Boston, and proceeded to Linn.

Saturday, 6.—General Deming and Mr. Robertson arrived in the city at 2 p. m. They expressed themselves abundantly satisfied with Dr. Richards' proceedings and agreement at Carthage, and said they believed the governor would do all in his power to quell further outrages, and preserve the peace.

William Clayton took charge of the raft of lumber which arrived yesterday, as agent for the trustee.

William Clayton saw the governor's reply to the letter from the Warsaw Committee of Safety, and recorded in his journal thus:—'The governor seems disposed to make the best of his situation, and try to restore the credit of the state by bringing the assassins to justice.'

A conference was held in Genessee, New York. Four branches were represented, containing 95 members, including 23 elders. Elder C. W. Wandell presided.

Sunday, 7.—Meeting at the stand.

Judge W. W. Phelps read Governor Ford's letter in reply to the Warsaw Committee.

President Marks addressed the meeting.

Dr. Willard Richards advised some of the people to go out and harvest, and others who stay to go on with the Temple, and make work in the city.

R. D. Foster arrived in the city. His presence produced some excitement in consequence of the saints believing he was accessory to the murder of the Prophets.

The following was sent to General Deming:—

LETTER TO GENERAL DEMING

'Nauvoo, Sunday, July 7, 1844.

General Deming, Acting-Commander of the Forces of Hancock County.

Sir,—We are informed that Dr. R. D. Foster is in this city, and that he has an order from Governor Ford to call out Captain Dunn's company of militia to guard him while here transacting business.

You must be aware, sir, at sight of such communication, the situation in which such an order of things must place this people, and of the difficulties which might grow out of such a course, and we earnestly desire your immediate action as agent of the governor for this county, to prevent any such occurrence.

We request General Deming to interfere in this matter. We request that no troops be quartered among us, for any such purpose, lest excitement arise between them and the citizens.

We desire that Dr. Foster's business be transacted by agency, or some way, so that there may be no cause of contention or excitement in our midst. Nothing shall be wanted on our part to keep the peace; but without the cooperation of government, it would seem impossible to accomplish it.

We are, sir, most respectfully, your servants and the friends of peace,

WILLARD RICHARDS,
W. W. PHELPS,
JOHN P. GREENE.

P. S.—General Deming knows the threats which have been made by Dr. Foster, and the cause we have to fear his presence, as well as troops in such a case.'

Apostles at Salem, Mass.

Elder Kimball's journal records a conference held this day at Salem. He preached in the forenoon, Elder Lyman Wight in the afternoon, and Elder Orson Pratt in the evening.

The conference went off well, the brethren realizing they had a good time.

A conference was held in the Presbyterian meeting-house in Scarborough, Maine, which continued through the 6th and 7th. Elder Wilford Woodruff presided.

The conference was addressed, and business attended to by Elders Wilford Woodruff, M. Holmes, E. Tufts, and Samuel Parker.

Religious Riot at Philadelphia.

A large mob assembled in Philadelphia on the 6th, and gathered in front of St. Philip's Church, with the intention of burning it, because of some difficulty existing between the Protestants and the Irish Catholics. The mob continued two days. The governor of the state called out 3,000 of the militia. There were 14 killed and 50 wounded during the riot.

Monday, 8.—About this time a letter was received from D. S. Hollister, reporting progress for the Baltimore convention to nominate candidates for the presidency.

Elders Brigham Young, Heber C. Kimball, Orson Pratt, Lyman Wight, Erastus Snow, Daniel Spencer and J. L. Heywood, held three meetings in the concert hall, Salem. The house was full and the brethren felt well.

The following is extracted from the *New York Tribune*:—

THE TROUBLES AT NAUVOO

'We begin almost to fear that the terrible scenes of cruelty, devastation of peaceful homes, and indiscriminate hunting down of men, women and children, which disgraced Missouri a few years since, during the expulsion of the Mormons from that state, are to be reenacted in Illinois.

The history of these deeds has never been, and probably never will be written; but enough of their atrocities has been heard from casual recitals of eye and ear witnesses to make the soul sicken with horror at their contemplation.

We are not the apologists of Joe Smith, or of the mummeries of Mormonism; we are ready to admit that the existence of that sect in the shape which it would seem Smith is bent on imparting to it, is fraught with danger, and should be looked to by the proper power; but in the name of common humanity, we stand up for the lives and security of helpless women and innocent children.

The executives of Illinois and Missouri have had loud and fair warning by the meetings in Carthage, Warsaw and St. Louis, of the dreadful scheme of arson and assassination that is going on to exterminate the Mormons; and if they permit the monstrous crime of the sacking of a city, the murder of men in cold blood, and the sacrifice of women and children to the demoniac fury of an inflamed mob, they will not, they cannot be held guiltless.

There are other means by which the course of the Mormons, if unlawful or destructive of the rights of others, can be restrained and punished; but, even if there be no immediate legal redress, are murder, rapine, desolation, the brand of civil war hurled among those who should be friends and neighbors—are these a suitable substitute for a little time and patience?

Let the citizens of Illinois *look to their votes* when next they approach the ballot box, and examine well for whom and for what principles they are cast, and they can restore the government of their state to hands that will remove their grievances and reassure them in their rights much more speedily than they can rebuild one log hut sacrificed to brutal war, or atone for the blood of a single human victim.'

Tuesday, 9.—Elders Willard Richards and John Taylor wrote as follows:—

LETTER OF INSTRUCTION AND INFORMATION TO THE PRESIDENT OF THE BRITISH MISSION

'Nauvoo, Illinois, U. S.,
July 9th, 1844.

Elder Reuben Hedlock, Presiding Elder of the Church of Jesus Christ in England, and the Saints in the British Empire.

Beloved Brethren,—As Elder James Parsons is about to leave for England, we embrace this, as the first opportunity, to communicate to you one of the most signal events which has ever transpired in the history of the church.

It has been declared by all the former Prophets and Apostles, that God had reserved unto himself a peculiar people for the last days, who would not only be zealous in good works, but who should be purified as gold in the furnace seven times, and who would have to endure through faith and patience in all long-suffering, in meekness, forbearance, love, and every God-like virtue unto the end as good soldiers, and meet all the scorn, scoff, and derision and chiding, buffeting and persecution a wicked world could heap upon them, and even death itself, not counting their lives dear unto themselves, that they might obtain their inheritance in that kingdom of their heavenly Father, which Jesus, their elder brother, had gone to prepare for them.

It is in this period of time that we are permitted to live. It is at the dawning of that day of days in which our heavenly Father is about to usher in that glorious period when times and seasons shall be changed and earth renewed, when after rumors and commotions, turmoils, strife, confusion, blood and slaughter, the sword shall be beaten into ploughshares, and peace and truth triumphantly prevail o'er all the footstool of Jehovah. The day of these events has dawned, although to human view a cloud has o'erspread the horizon.

You are acquainted with the general history of the church to which we belong. From our lips and pens you have learned its rise and progress; you have heard of the persecution of the saints in Missouri, and their expulsion from thence, together with their kind reception by the citizens of Illinois, where we have been located for the last four years.

For some months past we have been troubled with the wicked proceedings of certain apostates in our midst, who have striven to overthrow the church and produce trouble and anguish in the mind of every virtuous being, but their designs having been frustrated by the wise and judicious management on the part of the Prophet and the saints.

These apostates, reckless of all consequences, made a deadly thrust at our overthrow, leaving the city suddenly, and, afterwards, by themselves or agents, fired their own buildings, doubtless thinking they would charge it upon the saints, and by that means excite a mob in the surrounding country, who would fall upon and burn the city, but in this they were disappointed, our vigilant police discovered and extinguished the flames.

Their next course was to arrest the Prophet, the Patriarch, and others, by legal process and false pretense, and take them to Carthage, the county seat, for investigation; but they gave themselves up to the requisition of the law, on the pledge of Governor Ford that they should be protected from all personal violence, and went voluntarily to Carthage, without even the attendance of the officer.

Considerable excitement prevailed in the neighborhood, to allay which they voluntarily gave bonds for their appearance at the next session of the circuit court. Their voluntary and noble conduct should have satisfied every mind, but certain individuals of the basest sort swore out a writ for treason against the Prophet Joseph and the Patriarch Hyrum Smith, and they were thrust into jail *without trial, without examination, without any legal course or procedure,* on the 25th of June, where they remained till the next day, when they were brought before the magistrate, that a day might be set for their examination.

They were immediately remanded to prison, where they remained until the 27th, when but few of their friends were permitted to see them.

Between five and six o'clock p. m., of that day, a company of 150 or 200 armed, disguised and painted men rushed upon the guard who were set to watch the prison door, overpowered them, rushed upstairs into the entry adjoining the room where Joseph Smith and Hyrum Smith were, and John Taylor and Willard Richards sitting with them to keep them company.

As soon as the mob arrived at the head of the stairs, they fired through the door and shot Hyrum in the face. He fell instantly, exclaiming, 'I am a dead man'.

The mob instantly forced open the door with the points of the bayonets, and recommenced an indiscriminate discharge of firearms upon all in the room.

Mr. Taylor, in attempting to leap from the window, was shot and fell back in the chamber. Joseph, in attempting to leap from the same window, was shot, and fell on the outside, about 20 feet descent, when the mob gathered instantly round him and again shot him.

Joseph and Hyrum received each four balls, and were killed instantly. Elder Taylor received four balls in his left wrist and left leg—is doing well and is likely to recover.

Dr. Richards was marked on his left ear and cheek, otherwise remained unharmed. The whole scene occupied only two minutes, when the mob fled rapidly towards Warsaw.

The bodies of the murdered men were removed to Nauvoo on the 28th, and were buried on the 29th. This event has caused the deepest mourning among the saints, but they have not attempted to avenge the outrage.

The governor has promised that the whole treacherous proceedings shall be investigated according to law, and the saints have agreed to leave it with him, and with God to avenge their wrongs in this matter. There has been considerable excitement in the surrounding country, which is now in a great measure allayed. The action of the saints has been of the most pacific kind, remembering that God has said, 'Vengeance is mine, I will repay'.

For further particulars we refer you to the statements of Messrs. Reid and Woods, and other statements in the *Nauvoo Neighbor*, which we send you with this; and now, beloved brethren, we say to you all, as we say to the saints here, be still and know that God reigns. This is one of those fiery trials that is to try the saints in the last days.

These servants of God have gone to heaven by fire—the fire of an ungodly mob. Like the Prophets of ancient days they lived as long as the world would receive them; and this is one furnace in which the saints were to be tried, to have their leaders cut off from their midst, and not be permitted to avenge their blood.

God has said, 'Vengeance is mine; I have not called mine elders to fight their battles; I will fight their battles for them;' and we know, assuredly, that he will do it in his own due time, and we have only to wait in patience and pray for the fulfilment of the promise.

This event is one of the most foul and damnable that ever disgraced the earth, having no parallel in time. Innocent men imprisoned without law, without justice, and murdered in cold blood in the enlightened nineteenth century, in an enlightened country in open daylight.

It will call down the wrath and indignation of all nations upon the perpetrators of the horrid deed, and will prove the truth of the saying, 'The blood of the martyrs is the seed of the church.' They died for the word of God and the testimony of Jesus Christ.

God has not left his church without witnesses; as in former days, so shall it be in the latter days, when one falls another will arise to occupy a similar station. Our heavenly Father always has had a leader to his people, always will have, and the gates of hell can never prevail against the chosen of heaven.

The murder of Joseph will not stop the work; it will not stop the Temple; it will not stop the gathering; it will not stop the honest-in-heart from believing the truth and obeying it; but it is a proof of the revelations we have received from heaven through him. He has sealed his testimony with his blood. He was willing to die, and desired only to live for the sake of the brethren.

Two better men than Joseph and Hyrum Smith never lived. Two better men God never made. The memorial of their godly lives is embalmed, printed with indelible ink in the memory of every honest heart who knew their upright walk and conversation; but they are taken away by the hands of assassins, and of the foolish things of the earth God will raise up others to comfort and lead his people, and not one item of his word can fail.

Jerusalem must be rebuilt and Zion must be redeemed, the earth be cleansed from blood by fire, Jesus return to his own, and all who shall continue faithful unto the end shall rest in everlasting peace and blessedness.

We alone, of the Quorum of the Twelve Apostles, are here at this time to write to you, the remaining ten are in the eastern states preaching the gospel, and we expect them soon to return; and as soon as God will, we will write you again.

Proceed onward with all your labors as though nothing had happened, only, preach Joseph martyred for his religion, instead of living, and God will pour out his Spirit upon you, and hasten his work from this time.

Believe not every spirit, but try the spirits; believe not every report, for every false rumor that men and demons can invent is set afloat to gull the world. What we have told you by letter and papers is true, but time will not permit to tell you every particular now.

Be humble, prayerful, watchful, and let not the adversary get any advantage of one of you, and may the choicest blessings of Israel's God rest upon you and abide with you, that you may endure faithful in all tribulation and affliction, and be prepared to be gathered unto Mount Zion, and enter into celestial glory, is the earnest prayer of your brethren in the new and everlasting covenant. Amen.

[Signed] WILLARD RICHARDS,
JOHN TAYLOR.

P. S.—We would have said that while Joseph was on his way to Carthage, and on the prairie, he said to his friends around him, 'I am going like a lamb to the slaughter, but my mind is calm as the summer's morning, I have a conscience void of offense towards God and towards all men.' Joseph also said to his friends, 'I am going voluntarily to give myself up, and it shall be said of me that I *was murdered in cold blood*.'

Members of the Twelve in Boston.

Elders Brigham Young and Orson Pratt were at Boston when they first heard the rumors of the massacre of the Prophets, but did not believe the accounts were correct.

Elders Kimball and Wight were in Salem this morning, [July 9th] and heard of the death of the Prophets. Elder Kimball recorded he was unwilling to believe it, though it struck him to the heart. They took cars for Boston in the morning, where they stayed during the day. In the evening they proceeded to New York.

Elder Wilford Woodruff was in Portland, Maine, and ready to step on board of a steamer for Fox Islands, when he received the *Boston Times* newspaper, containing an account of the death of the Prophets. He immediately took cars and returned to Boston, stopping over night at Scarborough.

Wednesday, 10.—Elder Willard Richards, Patriarch John Smith, Elders Samuel H. Smith and W. W. Phelps, met in council in the council chamber.

Elder Willard Richards wrote as follows:—

LETTER TO A. JONAS—'ALL PEACE AT NAUVOO'

'Nauvoo, July 10, 1844.

A. Jonas, Esq.

Dear Sir,—Yours of the 6th, per Mr. Meetze, is received, and I have only time to thank you for the information it contained, and all your endeavors for the promotion of truth and justice, and can still give you the fullest assurance that all is perfect peace at Nauvoo, calmly waiting the fulfilment of Governor Ford's pledge to redeem the land from blood by legal process. You can do much to allay the excitement of the country in your travels, and the friends of peace will appreciate your labors.

Most respectfully,
WILLARD RICHARDS.'

Elder Parley P. Pratt arrived at Nauvoo.

Appeal of Nauvoo Ladies to Governor Ford.

A committee of nine ladies, among whom were Mrs. Hyrum Smith, Mrs. John Taylor, Mrs. Arthur Milliken and Mrs. W. W. Phelps, waited upon Mr. R. D. Foster, and told him they would not bear his taunts and insults any longer. They ordered him to leave the city forthwith, or he would be visited by a stronger force tomorrow. These ladies having good reason to believe that Foster was accessory to the murder of their relatives, the Prophets, took the liberty of pursuing this course towards him.

Mr. Hiram Kimball obligated himself that Foster should leave before morning, accordingly he got his team ready and took him out of the city that evening.

We copy from the *Neighbor*:—

ELDER JOHN TAYLOR AND ITEMS OF THE MARTYR-TRAGEDY

'Elder Taylor is recovering as fast as can be expected. His wounds are doing well.

The senior editor of this paper, Mr. Taylor, at the horrible assassination of Joseph and Hyrum Smith in Carthage jail, on the afternoon of the 27th day of June, received three wounds in his left thigh and knee, and one in his left wrist; besides which a *fifth ball* spent its force against his *watch* in his *left* vest pocket. This ball, but for the *timely* interference of this valuable watch, must have caused instant death, as it would have passed directly into his lungs. This watch, though dreadfully shattered, is a friend that points to the very moment when he stood between *life* and *death*, the hands pointing to 5 o'clock, 10 minutes and 26 seconds.

While upon this subject, Mr. Taylor and his friends wish, through this channel, to tender their thanks to Mr. Hamilton and family, and to all who assisted him in any manner during his stay at Carthage, while unable to be removed to his own home. Kindness, assistance, and the tender offices of humanity in such times of deep distress, give the noble mind a chance to appreciate *help when it is needed*, and to remember such friends in future. Nor should the assistance rendered to lay out the bodies of the Messrs. Smith, preparatory to their removal to Nauvoo, be forgotten. Though the people of Carthage, under the excitement of the moment, generally fled, yet those who did stay did all they could to forward the bodies, as well as to make Mr. Taylor as comfortable as the circumstances of the case would permit.

One thing further: In this awful tragedy, Dr. Willard Richards, equally exposed to the shower of bullets which were fired into the room at the door and windows, *escaped unhurt*, and while he would render thanksgiving and praise to his God for this signal preservation of his life, he would also return his grateful acknowledgments to the Messrs. Hamilton and others, who rendered all the assistance in their power in this awful hour of murder and woe at Carthage.'

Elders Brigham Young and Orson Pratt went from Boston to Lowell.

Movments of Some of the Twelve—Boston, Philadelphia.

Elders Kimball, Wight and William Smith, proceeded by railway from New York to Philadelphia.

The *Neighbor* has the following notice:—

'THE PROPHET'—A NEW L. D. S. PUBLICATION

'A well disposed newspaper called *The Prophet*, was started in New York, in the month of May last. The *ruptures* of our neighbors, and the murder of our best friends, have prevented us from giving our readers *timely* notice. It is published by a society for the promotion of truth, and we must say that in a city so large as New York, if the people have virtue, holiness, and the kindred spirits which have ever won the affections of humanity, they will sustain the *Prophet* liberally. Nor should the country be less magnanimous: by comparing opinions, and proving contrarieties, *truth* manifests itself.'

PUBLIC OPINION ON THE MURDER OF JOSEPH AND HYRUM SMITH FROM VARIOUS NEWSPAPERS

We copy from the *St. Louis Evening Gazette*:—

'Public opinion of the press on the assassination of Joseph and Hyrum Smith by a mob in the jail at Carthage, while under the sacred pledge of the state for the protection of their lives.

'With reference to the recent bloody affair at Carthage, the *O. S. Democrat* says:—

'From all the facts now before us, we regard these homicides as nothing else than murder in cold blood—murder against the plighted faith of the chief magistrate of Illinois—murder of a character so atrocious and so unjustifiable as to leave the blackest stain on all its perpetrators, their aiders, abettors, and defenders.'

The *Republican* pronounces the deed 'unprovoked murder'.

The *Reporter* says:—'The conduct of the mob at Carthage cannot be justified'.

The *Reveille* says:—'Joe Smith has been *'Lynched'* while under the protection of the *'Laws'*.'

The *New Era* says:—'It was cruel and cowardly to murder the unarmed prisoners when they had surrendered themselves, and were in custody of the laws.'

In fact, the press of St. Louis denounces this bloody deed without a dissenting voice*.'

From the *Lee County* (*Iowa*) *Democrat*:

'We also endorse the whole of the sentiments of the St. Louis press, and say it was a *premeditated murder,* and that the offenders ought to be ferreted out and dealt with according to the strict sense of the law.'

From the *Illinois State Register*:—

JOSEPH SMITH, THE MORMON PROPHET, AND HIS BROTHER, HYRUM, MURDERED IN PRISON

'The following particulars of the most disgraceful and cold-blooded murder ever committed in a Christian land, is copied from an extra from the office of the *Quincy Herald*. Rumors of the bloody deed reached this city several days ago, but were not believed until Tuesday evening, when there was no further room left for doubt. Next week we will have all the particulars. Every effort will be made to bring the assassins to punishment.'

FROM THE QUINCY HERALD EXTRA OF SATURDAY

'Governor Ford arrived in this city this morning, much worn down by travel and fatigue, having left Carthage yesterday. It is now certain that only Joe and Hyrum Smith are killed, and they were murdered in cold blood.

*This denunciation by the St. Louis press "without a dissenting voice" is all the more worthy of note because it was in western Missouri—in which state St. Louis is situated—that the same kind of lawless assault upon the Church of the Latter-day Saints was made and the murder of many of its membership occurred but a few years before; and the like proceedings in Illinois might have been held up as a justification of the action of mobs in western Missouri against the saints. B. H. R.

It seems that while Governor Ford was absent from Carthage to Nauvoo, for the purpose of ascertaining satisfactorily the strength of the Mormon force, an excited mob assembled near Carthage, disfigured themselves by painting their faces, and made a rush upon the jail where Joe and his fellow prisoners were confined.

The guard placed by the governor to protect the jail were overpowered by superior numbers, the doors of the jail forced, and Joe and Hyrum both shot.

Hyrum was instantly killed by a ball, which passed through his head. Joe was in the act of raising the window, when he was shot both from without and within, and fell out of the window to the ground.

Richards, whom we supposed yesterday was dead, escaped unhurt. Mr. Taylor, the editor of the *Nauvoo Neighbor*, was in the room with the Smiths, and received three balls in his leg, and one in his arm. He is not considered dangerous. Three of the assailants were slightly wounded.

It will probably never be known who shot Joseph and Hyrum Smith, but their murder was a *cold-blooded, cowardly act,* which will consign the perpetrators, if discovered, to *merited infamy and disgrace.* They have broken their pledges to the governor, disgraced themselves and the state to which they belong. *They have crimsoned their perfidy with blood.*

The dead bodies of the Smiths were conveyed to Nauvoo, by order of the governor yesterday. It was supposed by many, that the Mormons on seeing them would break away from all restraints and commence a war of extermination.

But nothing of the kind occurred. They received their murdered friends in sorrow—laid down their arms and remained quiet. Colonel Singleton and his company of 60 men are still in Nauvoo, and the Mormons submitted to their authority.

The 300 that left our city yesterday on the *Boreas* are at present in Warsaw. A man was knocked down with a musket in Warsaw yesterday, for *presuming* to express disapprobation at the murder of the Smiths.'

From the *Sangamon Journal*:—

THE MORMON DIFFICULTIES

'Notwithstanding all the rumors which are afloat, we are unable to state anything very definite in relation to affairs at Nauvoo, or in the region round about that city.

It is certain that the governor has called out some of the neighboring militia; that bodies of armed men had collected without waiting a call from the governor; that the governor had accepted the services of militia at St. Louis under certain contingencies; that he had demanded of Smith the state arms at Nauvoo; that it had been reported that they were given up; that Smith and his council had given themselves up to be tried by our laws for alleged offenses.

Thus far our news seems to be certain. Rumor says further, that on Thursday of last week Joe Smith, Hyrum Smith and Dr. Richards were shot by a mob at Carthage.

We are incredulous in regard to the truth of this rumor. We cannot think, under the circumstances of the case, the excitement against these men among the anti-Mormons, Governor Ford would have received them as prisoners, to be tried under our laws, had pledged himself for their protection, and then placed them in a situation where they would be murdered. The rumor is too preposterous for belief. We wait with much anxiety to hear the truth on this subject; and this feeling is general in this community.'

From the *Missouri Republican*:—

'*The Murders at Carthage.*—A letter from the editor, one from G. T. M. Davis, Esq., and a proclamation from Governor Ford, give all the information which we have been able to collect from the seat of civil commotion and murder in Illinois.

They were issued in an extra form yesterday morning, and are transferred to our columns today for the benefit of our numerous readers abroad.

All our information tends to fix upon the people concerned in the death of the *Smiths*, the odium of perfidious, blackhearted, cowardly *murder*—so wanton as to be without any justification—so inhuman and treacherous as to find no parallel in savage life under any circumstances.

Governor Ford declares his intention to seek out the murderers; and he owes it to his own honor and to that of the state, whose faith was most grossly violated, never to cease his exertions for this purpose.

The Mormons, it will be seen, were quiet, and not disposed to commit any acts of aggression; their enemies, on the other hand, were evidently disposed to push them to extremities, and to force them from the state.

This feeling may be checked by the alacrity with which Governor Ford's orders were being executed, but it will be some time before peace and order can be restored—the disgrace of past acts cannot be wiped out.'

The following extract of a letter from a highly respectable gentleman to his friend in Nauvoo, we copy from the *Nauvoo Neighbor*:—

'Fair Haven, Ct. July 10, 1844.

I have, by the papers, within a day or two, been informed of the murder of Joseph and Hyrum Smith. This is an event which will be deeply lamented by all Mormons, and will appear, probably, to those who are not Mormons, as the final overthrow of their religious tenets.

I will, however, make the prediction that this diabolical butchery makes more Mormons than the *friendship* of half the inhabitants in Illinois could have done by their most devoted exertions.

The blood of saints is the seed of the church. It will be considered by an extensive portion of the world that the Smiths have suffered martyrdom for their religion, and their profoundest sympathies will be aroused in favor of those believing the same creed.

The inflammatory appeals to the bloodthirsty passions of the anti-Mormon populace will be universally condemned by the reflecting and moral part of every community, and thousands will now examine your tenets, who never thought of such a thing before.

Carthage and Warsaw will be denounced by the honorable, and the indelible disgrace with which they now stand covered, will cause them to be avoided by every person who has any regard to his personal safety.

It is now known here that the lazy speculators of Warsaw, and the still lazier office drones at Carthage, cared nothing for Joe Smith personally, or for his tenets either; but the prosperity of Nauvoo increasing as it did, beyond any former parallel, even in the western world, excited in their bosoms envy, hatred and all ungodliness.

This is the true secret of all their barbarous movements against Mormonism; and they supposed by destroying the Smiths they should extinguish their religion, disperse the Mormons, depopulating and desolating Nauvoo. Their folly and wickedness will produce a result exactly the reverse; Mormons will increase an hundredfold; they will, if possible, be more devoutly attached to their religion; will concentrate more closely together, for self-preservation, and their united industry will produce such a city at Nauvoo as does not exist west of the mountains.

From all accounts which have been published here, it does not appear that the slightest resistance was made to the execution of the law, and the inquiry is now made, what was all this clamor, excitement and military parade for?

The editor of the *Warsaw Signal* can answer the question; and if he had his deserts, it is probable no more unprincipled and inflammatory addresses to an infuriated mob would ever emanate from his pen. Not that I would wish any violence to him, but he should be tried by the laws of the state, and see how far his course renders him accountable for the murders which have been committed.

Nothing has ever given me greater gratification than the calm, dignified submission to the laws shown at Nauvoo since the death of the Smiths. This forbearance on your part is beyond all praise; let it continue. Give not the shadow of a pretext for another appeal to popular fury. The demons are foiled, and let them gnash their teeth in silence over their disappointment.

The increase of population at Nauvoo can no more be prevented than the Mississippi can be stopped in its course. Its triumph is inevitable, because the engine by which it is to be accomplished is irresistible.

What earthly power has ever yet stood before the overpowering energies of a religious creed? But when religion is protected by law, as your religion ought to be, and will soon be, in Illinois, then such advances will be made by the Mormons as have never been dreamed of by the greatest enthusiast.'

The editor of the *Neighbor* adds:—

'Upon this letter, let it be remembered that the writer is not a Mormon or a western man, but a citizen of Connecticut, loving law, liberty and life.'

From the *Tompkins* (N. Y.) *Democrat,* we extract the following:—

'The report that a battle had been fought between the Mormons and anti-Mormons, in which some five hundred were slain, is all a hoax. Such vile statements only serve to give strength to the Prophet's views. Indeed, we do not know which has the worst effect on the community, the doctrines of Smith or the ten thousand false rumors constantly put in circulation against him. One thing is certain, his name will survive when those who grossly misrepresent him have become blanks on the page of the future.' "

CHAPTER XV

CHAPTER OF MISCELLANEOUS DOCUMENTS, PRESS EXCERPTS, AND MOVEMENTS OF LEADING ELDERS OF THE CHURCH AT NAUVOO AND ELSEWHERE

'*Tuesday, July* 11, 1844.—Elder Willard Richards called upon Elder Parley P. Pratt, likewise Brothers Samuel Russell, Hiram Kimball and Stephen Markham; also upon Brother Elijah Fordham, to inquire about the lumber for the Temple.

Movements of the Twelve *et al.*

Elders Brigham Young and Orson Pratt traveled to Peterboro, for the purpose of attending conference.

Elders Kimball, Wight and others went to Wilmington, and preached in the evening: several saints from Chester county were present.

Elder Wilford Woodruff preached in Boston this evening, and endeavored to console the saints who were mourning the loss of the martyred Prophet and Patriarch.

Friday, 12.—President Marks consulted with William Clayton about calling a meeting of the presidents of various quorums to appoint a trustee-in-trust in behalf of the Church of Jesus Christ of Latter-day Saints.

At Nauvoo Question of Trustee-in-Trust.

A council was held at 3 p. m.; but as Dr. Willard Richards and Bishop Whitney considered it premature, the council was adjourned till Sunday evening, the 14th.

Messrs. Bedell and Backenstos arrived in Nauvoo, and reported that the governor had demanded the public arms at Warsaw, and was refused.

Governor's Order Disregarded at Warsaw.

President Brigham Young spent the day with the brethren in Peterboro .

We learn from Elder Kimball's journal, that in company with Elder Lyman Wight and delegates to the convention from Pennsylvania, Delaware and Maryland, he proceeded to Baltimore. He and Brother Wight, hearing so many contradictory reports concerning the death of the Prophets, felt very anxious to obtain some correct information. They went into their closets and prayed to the Lord to open the way whereby they might know the truth concerning it. Immediately Elder Kimball went to the post office, and got letters up to the 24th of June from his wife, informing him that Presidents Joseph and Hyrum Smith had delivered themselves up into the hands of their enemies to be tried, upon reading which they were immediately satisfied that the Prophets were massacred.

Premonitory Anxieties.

Elder Wilford Woodruff wrote a letter of exhortation to the saints, which was published in *The Prophet*.

Elder John E. Page wrote a long letter on Mormonism, which appeared in the *People's Organ,* of Pittsburgh.

Saturday, 13.—Dr. Willard Richards proposed the organization of a fishing company to help to supply the city of Nauvoo with food.

Elders Kimball and Wight returned to Wilmington, and from thence to Philadelphia, where they read letters giving a particular account of the martyrdom of their brethren.

Sunday, 14.—Meeting at the stand: Elder Parley P. Pratt preached.

Dr. Willard Richards proposed that the church postpone electing a trustee until the Twelve returned, and called a special conference.

6 *p. m.* Several councilors came to the council chamber to investigate the subject of choosing trustees, but decided to wait until the Twelve arrived.

We extract the following from President Brigham Young's Journal:—

EXCERPTS FROM PRESIDENT YOUNG'S JOURNAL

'*Friday,* 12.—We held a meeting in Peterboro in the evening, preparatory to the conference tomorrow.

Saturday, 13.—Had a good time at conference all day. The brethren were very glad to see us, and the Lord gave us many good things to say to them. I preached to the saints and showed the organization and establishment of the kingdom of God upon the earth: that the death of one or a dozen could not destroy the priesthood, nor hinder the work of the Lord from spreading throughout all nations.

Sunday, 14.—Held three meetings, ordained 28 elders. We enjoyed ourselves well, and had an excellent conference.'

Elders Kimball and Wight went to meeting in Philadelphia, and read the account of the massacre to the saints, who all felt very sorrowful, and agreed to dress in mourning in token of their love and respect for the martyred Prophets.

Elder Kimball recorded, 'O Lord, how can we part with our dear brethren—O Lord, save thy servants the Twelve.'

Elder Woodruff Preaches in Boston.

The saints in Boston met in the Franklin Hall; the house was crowded to overflowing, and many could not get into the room. Numbers who had not been in the habit of attending the meetings, came to see what course the saints would pursue now their leaders were slain. Elder Wilford Woodruff, being the only one of the Twelve in the city, addressed the saints during the day, and also in the evening. He preached in the forenoon from *Rev.,* ch. vi, 9, 10 and 11th verses; in the afternoon from *Rev.,* ch. xiv, 6, 7 and 8th verses, and in the evening on the parable of the fig tree, as recorded by *St. Luke* in ch. xxi; and, in connection, read some of the revelations given through the martyred Prophet of our day. The Spirit of the Lord rested powerfully upon the speaker and the saints, and their hearts were comforted.

Movements at Nauvoo.

Monday, 15.—Elders Parley P. Pratt, Willard Richards, W. W. Phelps and the bishops, with many brethren, assembled to organize a company of fishermen to supply the city with fish; twenty-eight volunteered, with eight boats and skiffs.

Isaac Higbee was appointed president, John S. Higbee and Peter Shirts counselors.

The *Times and Season* has the following editorial:—

REVIEW OF THE MURDER AT CARTHAGE

'*General Joseph Smith,* who was murdered in cool blood, in Carthage jail, on Thursday, the 27th day of June, was one of the best men that ever lived on the earth.

The work he has thus far performed, towards establishing pure religion and preparing the way for the great gathering of Israel, in the short space of twenty years, since the time when the angel of the Lord made known his mission and gave him power to move the cause of Zion, exceeds anything of the kind on record.

Without learning, without means, and without experience, he has met a learned world, a rich century, a hard-hearted, wicked and adulterous generation, with truth that could not be resisted, facts that could not be disproved, revelations whose spirit had so much God in them that the servants of the Lord could not be gainsaid or resisted, but, like the rays of light from the sun, they have tinged everything they lit upon with a lustre and livery which has animated, quickened and adorned.

The pages of General Smith's history, though his enemies never ceased to persecute him and hunt for offenses against him, are as unsullied as virgin snow; on about fifty prosecutions for supposed criminal offenses, he came out of the *legal fire,* heated like Nebuchadnezzar's furnace, seven times hotter than it was wont to be, *without the smell of fire,* or a thread of his garments scorched.

His foes of the world and enemies of his own household, who have sought occasions against him, in order secretly to deprive him of his life, because his goodness, greatness and glory exceeded theirs, have a poor excuse to offer the world for shedding his innocent blood, and no apology to make to the Judge of all the earth at the day of judgment. They have murdered him because they feared his righteousness.

His easy, goodnatured way, allowing everyone was honest, drew around him hypocrites, wicked and mean men, with the virtuous, and in the hour of trouble or trial, when the wheat was cleansed by water, the light kernels and smut rose upon the top of the water and had to be poured off, that the residue might be clean; or, to be still plainer, when they went through the machine for cleansing the grain, the chaff, light grain and smut, were blown off among the rubbish.

False brethren, or to call them by their right name, 'apostates', have retarded the work more, and combined more influence to rob him of life, than all Christendom; for they, having mingled in his greatness, knew where and when to take advantage of his weakness.

Their triumph, however, is one that disgraces their state and nation, ruins them in time and in eternity.

They cannot outgrow it, they cannot outlive it, and they cannot outdie it, from him that winked at it to him that shot the fatal ball, wherever there is moral honesty, humanity, love of life, liberty and the pursuit of happiness, there the breath of indignation, the whisper of 'those murders', the story of mobocracy and the vengeance of God will haunt the whole gang and their offspring and abettors with a fury like Milton's gates of hell,

'* * * grating harsh thunder.'

In thus descanting upon the glory of General Joseph Smith and the cowardly disgrace of his assassins, let his noble-minded brother Hyrum have no less honor shown him. He lived so far beyond the ordinary walk of man, that even the tongue of the vilest slanderer could not touch his reputation.

He lived godly and he died godly, and his murderers will yet have to confess that it would have been better for them to have a millstone tied to them, and they cast into the depths of the sea, and remain there while eternity goes and eternity comes, than to have robbed that noble man of heaven of his life.

If there be such a thing as the greatest and least crimes among the archives of the better world, the wilful murder of Joseph and Hyrum Smith will be first and worst, without forgiveness in this world or the world to come, 'for no murderer hath eternal life abiding in him.'

The Savior said, woe unto the world because of offenses, but offenses must needs come; but woe unto him by whom they come!

Prophets have been sent, according to the sacred history, which all enlightened nations use as a guide of morality here, or for a rule to obtain heaven hereafter, to instruct and lead the people according to the pure purposes of God, and yet from Cain down to two or three hundred Americans, Illinoians, Missourians, Christians, even freemen, the lives of mostly all these good men, the servants of God, not omitting his own Son, have been taken from them by those who professed to be the most wise, enlightened, intelligent and religious, (that is nationally) that were on the earth when the hellish deeds were done.

But what has the next generation said? Ah! time thou art older and abler to tell the story than they that did the solemn act. No wonder the heathen nations will be God's in the day of his power; they have not killed the Prophets.

When General Smith went to Carthage, just as the cavalry met him for the purpose of obtaining the state arms, he said to a friend, '*I am going like a lamb to the slaughter; but I am calm as a summer's morning: I have a conscience void of offense toward God, and toward all men: I shall die innocent.'*

Now ye great men who boast of great wisdom, what think ye of the Prophet's last prediction? How glorious! How mild! How God-like! No wonder the sympathies of all honest men are kindled in his behalf; the goodness of his deeds merit them.

The want of a perfect knowledge of the servants of God, of the Son of God, in all ages, down to this last, horrid, heart-sickening butchery of those two unoffending American freemen, must have been the great first cause of taking life contrary to the law of God or man.

Leaving religion out of the case, where is the lover of his country, and his posterity, that does not condemn such an outrageous murder, and will not lend all his powers, energies and influence to bring the offenders to justice and judgment?

Every good man will do it when he remembers that these two innocent men were confined in jail for a supposed crime, deprived of any weapons to defend themselves, had the pledged faith of the state of Illinois, by Governor Ford, for their protection, and were then shot to death, while with uplifted hands they gave such signs of distress as would have commanded the interposition and benevolence of savages or pagans.

They were both Masons in good standing.

Ye brethren of 'the mystic tie', what think ye! Where are our good Masters Joseph and Hyrum? Is there a pagan, heathen or savage nation on the globe that would not be moved on this great occasion, as the trees of the forest are moved by a mighty wind? Joseph's last exclamation was, *'O Lord, my God'*.

If one of these murderers, their abettors or accessories before or after the fact, are suffered to cumber the earth without being dealt with according to law, what is life worth, and what is the benefit of laws? and more than all, what is the use of institutions which savages would honor, where civilized beings murder without cause or provocation?

Will the Americans look over the vast concerns that must, sooner or later, touch their welfare at home and abroad, and exalt or disgrace them among the kingdoms of the great family of man, and learn whether anarchy, mobbery and butchery are not swiftly hurrying the constituted authorities of our country into irretrievable ruin, while the inhabitants of the land must sink into wretchedness, bloodshed, revenge and woe?

Elder John Taylor and Dr. Willard Richards, who were in the jail at the time, innocently, as friends of these men, have only to thank God that their lives were spared.

Elder Taylor was wounded with four bullets, and a fifth ball, which, had it not been for his watch in his left vest pocket, would have passed into his vitals and destroyed his life instantly.

This memorable and very valuable watch saved his life, and will remain with its hands permanently pointing to '5 o'clock, 16 minutes and 26 seconds', as the moment when so small a machine interposed between time and eternity.

Dr. Richards was not wounded by a single ball, though one passed so near his ear as to leave a mark.

If such scenes do not awaken the best feelings of freemen for personal safety, what will? We pause! solemnly pause for the opinion of millions, because all are interested; life is the last boon, all is blank without it, death blots the rest, and where is man?

To conclude, if the good people of our common country, and our common world, do not arise with a union of feeling and energy to help to wash off the blood of these two innocent men from Hancock county, from the plighted faith of Illinois, from the boasted and widespreading fame of the United States, and from the dignity of our globe, then let all but the righteous be smitten with a curse; but, methinks I see a 'union of all honest men', aside from religion, stand forth to magnify the law, who will never rest till justice and judgment have made the offenders, abettors and accessories, whether apostates, officers or mere *men, atone for the innocent blood of Joseph and Hyrum Smith.'*

The following was written by the undersigned members of the council [i. e. of the Twelve]:—

LETTER TO THE SAINTS ABROAD

'Dear Brethren,—On hearing of the martyrdom of our beloved Prophet and Patriarch, you will doubtless need a word of advice and comfort, and look for it from our hands.

We would say, therefore, first of all, be still and know that the Lord is God, and that he will fulfil all things in his own due time, and not one jot or tittle of all his purposes and promises shall fail.

Remember, REMEMBER that the priesthood and the keys of power are held in eternity as well as in time, and, therefore, the servants of God who pass the veil of death are prepared to enter upon a greater and more effectual work, in the speedy accomplishment of the restoration of all things spoken of by his holy prophets.

Remember that all the prophets and saints who have existed since the world began, are engaged in this holy work, and are yet in the vineyard, as well as the laborers of the eleventh hour, and are all pledged to establish the kingdom of God on the earth, and to give judgment unto the saints: therefore, none can hinder the rolling on of the eternal purposes of the great Jehovah.

And we have now every reason to believe that the fulfilment of his great purposes are much nearer than we had supposed, and that not many years hence we shall see the kingdom of God coming with power and great glory to our deliverance.

As to our country and nation, we have more reason to weep for them than for those they have murdered, for they are destroying themselves and their institutions, and there is no remedy; and as to feelings of revenge, let them not have place for one moment in our bosoms, for God's vengeance will speedily consume to that degree that we would fain be hid away and not endure the sight.

Let us then humble ourselves under the mighty hand of God, and endeavor to put away all our sins and imperfections as a people and as individuals, and to call upon the Lord with the spirit of grace and supplication, and wait patiently on him until he shall direct our way.

Let no vain and foolish plans or imaginations scatter us abroad and divide us asunder as a people, to seek to save our lives at the expense of truth and principle, but rather let us live or die together and in the enjoyment of society and union.

Therefore, we say, let us haste to fulfil the commandments which God has already given us. Yea, let us haste to build the Temple of our God, and to gather together thereunto, our silver and our gold with us, unto the name of the Lord, and then we may expect that he will teach us of his ways, and we will walk in his paths.

We would further say, that in consequence of the great rains which have deluged the western country, and, also, in consequence of persecution and excitement, there has been but little done here, either in farming or building, this season; therefore, there is but little employment and but little means of subsistence at the command of the saints in this region; therefore, let the saints abroad and others who feel for our calamities and wish to sustain us, come on with their money and means without delay, and purchase lots and farms, and build buildings and employ hands, as well as to pay their tithings into the Temple and their donations to the poor.

We wish it distinctly understood abroad that we greatly need the assistance of every lover of humanity, whether members of the church or otherwise, both in influence and in contributions for our aid, succor and support.

Therefore, if they feel for us, now is the time to show their liberality and patriotism towards a poor and persecuted, but honest and industrious people.

Let the elders who remain abroad continue to preach the gospel in its purity and fulness, and to bear testimony of the truth of these things which have been revealed for the salvation of this generation.

[Signed] PARLEY P. PRATT,
WILLARD RICHARDS,
JOHN TAYLOR,
W. W. PHELPS.

Nauvoo, July 15, 1844.'

Elder Jedediah M. Grant returned to Philadelphia. Two weeks since he left Nauvoo, and reported that all was quiet and peace in the city since the burial of the martyrs.

LAMENTATION

Of a Jew Among the Afflicted and Mourning Sons and Daughters of Zion, at the Assassination of the Two Chieftains in Israel, Joseph and Hyrum Smith.

'Blessed the people knowing the shout of Jehovah,
In the light of his countenance they will walk.
How can we, a people in sackcloth,
Open our lips before thee?
They have rejected and slain our leaders,
Thine anointed ones.
Our eyes are dim, our hearts heavy;
No place of refuge being left.
Redeem the people that in thee only trusts:
There is none to stand between and inquire;
Thou art our helper,
The refuge of Israel in time of trouble.
O look in righteousness upon thy faithful servants,
Who have laid bare their lives unto death,
Not withholding their bodies;
Being betrayed by false brethren, and their lives cut off,
Forbidding their will before thine:
Having sanctified thy great name,
Never polluting it;
Ready for a sacrifice;—standing in the breach,
Tried, proved and found perfect.
To save the blood of the fathers;
Their children, brothers, and sisters;
Adding theirs unto those who are gone before them;
Sanctifying thy holy and great name upon the earth;
Cover and conceal not their blood.
Give ear unto their cries until thou lookest
And shewest down from heaven-taking vengeance
And avenging their blood—avenging thy people and
thy law,

According to thy promises made
Unto our forefathers, Abraham, Isaac and Jacob.
Hasten the acceptable and redeeming year;
Shadday: remember unto us thy covenants:
All this heaviness has reached us;
Can any one be formed to declare
What has befallen us?
All this we bear, and the name of our God
We will not forget, nor deny,
The 'Hebrews' God' he is called,
Thou art clothed with righteousness,
But we are vile.
Come not in judgment with us.
Before thee nothing living is justified by their works.
But be with us as thou wast with our fathers.
Help thou, O Father; unto thee
We will lift our souls,
Our hearts in our hands;
We look to heaven,
Lifting our eyes unto the mountains,
From whence cometh our help.
Turn away thine anger,
That we be not spoiled.
O return and leave a blessing behind thee.'*

Tuesday, 16.—William Clayton finished measuring the last raft of lumber for the Temple, from the pineries, amounting to 87,732 feet.

The following was received by Dr. Willard Richards:—

LETTER REPORTING THREATENING PORTENTS AGAINST NAUVOO

'De Kalb, Hancock Co., Ill.,
July 1, 1844.
[In confidence]

Dr. Richards.

Dear Sir,—I hope the subject upon which this communication

*_Times and Seasons_, vol. v, p. 591. The author of this poem is Alexander Neibaur who is also the author of the hymn "Come Thou Glorious Day of Promise", see _L. D. S. Hymn Books_, current. The strong Hebraic character of the above poem will appear to the reader.

is written will be a sufficient apology for the privilege I have taken in addressing you, with whom I have not had the pleasure of an acquaintance.

I wish to apprise you that reports are in circulation, which no doubt are true, that the Warsaw and Green Plains mobocrats are making strong exertions to raise forces sufficient to mob and drive the people of your city from their present residences.

I think you should keep a steady lookout, for it seems that the cold-hearted murder of Generals Joseph and Hyrum Smith in Carthage jail has not satisfied the bloodthirsty dispositions of those demons, but they desire to prosecute their wretched purposes still further.

I, as one of General Deming's staff, have used my influence against calling out a large force to be stationed at Carthage, fearing that some might be influenced by those mobocrats to join them in their wretched purpose, for I have no idea they can get forces enough to leave their homes, neither in Illinois nor Missouri, for that purpose, to overcome you.

If we could have four or five hundred troops stationed at Carthage, of the right sort, that could be depended on, to suppress mobs, I should like it, but, fearing the influence of those desperadoes might cause them to disobey all orders and join the mob against you, I think it best not to risk it.

The murder of Generals Joseph and Hyrum Smith is deprecated by the community, almost at large, that is, those who are not lost to the principles of humanity; and there seems to be a general feeling of sympathy resting on the public mind.

I was pleased to hear of the prudent course that your people resolved to pursue, in acting only on the defensive and abiding the law, which is on your side.

In haste, yours, etc.,

THOS. H. OWEN.'

To which Dr. Willard Richards replied as follows:—

DECLARED INTENTION OF THE CHURCH TO TAKE NO PART IN THE TRIAL OF THE MURDERERS OF THE PROPHETS

'Nauvoo, July 16, 1844.

Sir,—I am sorry that there has been delay which caused your letter to arrive so late to hand, and I feel thankful for the very kind and sympathetic manner in which you express yourself towards us as a people, and shall be very thankful if you will continue your favors to me whenever anything may occur, and you may depend upon my doing the same to yourself.

In regard to the assassination of the Generals Smith, we do not intend to take any action in the case whatever, but leave ourselves entirely in the hands of the governor and the majesty of the law, to mete out just and retributive justice in the matter.

You may rest perfectly assured that we never did act on the offensive, or against the law, but shall continue the same course, which appears to have given you so much satisfaction, and act entirely on the defensive, and abide the law.

In haste, sir, I remain yours, etc.,
WILLARD RICHARDS.

Thos. H. Owen, Esq.'

Elder Wilford Woodruff wrote the following:—

WOODRUFF'S LETTER TO BRIGHAM YOUNG—REPORTING THE PROPHETS' DEATH

'Boston, July 16, 1844.

Elders Brigham Young and Orson Pratt.

Dear Brethren.—I hasten to inform you that I returned to this city on hearing the report of the death of Joseph and Hyrum, expecting to see you. I have waited a number of days in deep suspense, to obtain word I could rely on.

This morning two letters were put into my hands by Sister Phelps, one from Erastus Snow and one from John E. Page of Pittsburgh, both confirming the report of the death of Joseph and Hyrum—they were murdered in Carthage jail.

It is not for me to counsel you, but I would ask if it would not be well for you to come direct to Boston, and hold a council with the Twelve and decide what course to pursue. Things are still very critical in the west; we don't know where it will end.

I spent the Sabbath here, spoke three times, comforted the saints all I could and had a good time. The saints bear the shock well. I am well and in good spirits. I do not know where I can address my letters to reach you. I shall write to Lowell, Peterboro and Bradford, hoping they may reach you in one of those places.

I shall go immediately to Farmington, New Haven, Ct., and New York; if you wish to write to me, direct to Farmington, Ct.

Yours in the kingdom of God,
WILFORD WOODRUFF.'

President Young having received Elder Woodruff's letter at Peterboro, started for Boston, but on arriving at Lowell remained all night.

Movement Respecting the Prophet's Estate.

Wednesday, 17.—Mrs. Emma Smith, in company with Messrs. Woods and Wasson, went to Carthage for letters of administration on the estate of her deceased husband, Joseph Smith.

The following is from Elder Woodruff's Journal:—

EXCERPT

'Elder Brigham Young arrived in Boston this morning. I walked with him to 57 Temple Street, and called upon Sister Vose. Brother Young took the bed and gave vent to his feelings in tears. I took the big chair, and veiled my face, and for the first time gave vent to my grief and mourning for the Prophet and Patriarch of the church, Joseph and Hyrum Smith, who were murdered by a Gentile mob. After being bathed in a flood of tears I felt composed. Elder Young left the city. I spent the night at Brother Phelps.'

The following is extracted from the *St. Louis Transcript,* taken from the report of the editor of the *Republican*:—

REPORTS OF MOVEMENTS IN ILLINOIS OBSERVED FROM WARSAW

'On our return we stopped at Warsaw, where the state commissioners were joined by Colonel Wood, the mayor of Quincy, and Mr. Conyers. These gentlemen had returned from Nauvoo through Carthage, and had been laboring to establish peace between the parties.

The people of Hancock county, however, appear to be averse to any compromise short of the removal of the Mormons from the county. They assert that it is now absolutely necessary to peace and quietness that either the Mormons or citizens quit the county, and that sooner or later one must go, even if force be necessary to accomplish it.

Mr. Jonas, one of the commissioners, addressed the citizens of Warsaw, and called upon them to say whether they would support the governor in enforcing the law and upholding the Constitution, and they unanimously refused to give the pledge.

The same evening a Mr. Skinner of Carthage, who professed to speak in the name of the citizens of Hancock, uttered the same sentiment. He deprecated, as impossible, the idea of settlement if the Mormons were to remain.

A committee of the citizens waited upon Governor Ford, informing him of their fixed conviction that it was necessary one of the parties should leave the county, and desiring him to decide.

The governor replied that it was not for him to decide such a question, or to order any body of citizens, whether Mormons or anti-Mormons, out of the county or state.

From the feeling evinced by the most active in the anti-Mormon ranks, we came to the conclusion that nothing but a dread of consequences would prevent further outbreaks. The flame has been smothered for a time, but the fire has not been quenched, and slight causes may make it burst forth more fiercely than before.

Governor Ford has a most arduous duty to perform. Of his ability to discharge it we will not now speak. At our latest dates he was still at Quincy, and avowed the intention of maintaining the ascendancy of the law at all hazards. He has dismissed all the troops, and they have returned to their homes.' "

CHAPTER XVI

THE MOVEMENTS OF THE APOSTLES AND OTHER LEADING BRETHREN IN THE EAST AND AT NAUVOO—IMPORTANT COMMUNICATION FROM GOVERNOR FORD

"*Thursday, July 18th* 1844.—No rain since the night of the 29th ult., of any moment: excessively warm. Thermometer 92½ ° F. After sunset the clouds gathered dense and black, accompanied by lightning, which became so constant, and the flashes so near each other, as to be almost one continued flash, lighter than noonday; the rain descended in torrents, the wind tremendous, prostrating many trees and some houses.

Storm—Status of Weather.

The following is from Elder Woodruff's Journal:—

EXCERPTS

'President Brigham Young arrived in the city of Boston, also Elders Orson Hyde, Heber C. Kimball and Orson Pratt. We met together in council, and agreed to counsel the elders and brethren having families at Nauvoo, to return immediately to them. Elder Hyde advertised that he would preach on the subject of the massacre of Joseph and Hyrum Smith, the Prophet and Patriarch of the church.

Movements of the Twelve in the East.

According to appointment the saints and friends met in a hall in Washington Street. Elder Hyde preached from words in chapter xxiv of *St. Matthew*, 9th to 14th verse, and concluded with the following remarks:—

DISCOURSE OF ELDER ORSON HYDE AT WASHINGTON, D. C.

'In consequence of the death of the Prophets, the editors seem to get the spirit of prophecy, and say the work is done, and will stop and die; but, as I am in the midst of the prophetic editors, like Saul

I catch some of the spirit of prophecy, and so I will prophesy that instead of the work dying, it will be like the mustard stock that was ripe, that a man undertook to throw out of his garden, and scattered seed all over it, and next year it was nothing but mustard. It will be so by shedding the blood of the Prophets—it will make ten saints where there is one now.

Some said that he would be president [i. e. of the U. S.], but is now dead; now, what will he do? The Revelator says, 'He that overcometh will I give power over the nations, and he shall rule them with a rod of iron'; I don't know but he may hold the keys of the plagues that are to be poured out in the last days upon this and other nations.

Angels appeared anciently to John, who were his fellow servants, the Prophets. Joseph may appear in this day to his brethren.

This gospel of the kingdom must be preached in all the world for a testimony, then shall the end come; though they should be persecuted, if they endured to the end, they should be saved.

This generation speak much about the clouds and weather; they discern the face of the sky, but why can they not discern the signs of the times? The fig trees are leafing, and all things indicate the second advent of Christ.'

REMARKS OF BRIGHAM YOUNG

Elder Brigham Young arose, and said he felt disposed to add his testimony; be of good cheer. The testimony is not in force while the testator liveth; when he died it was in force; so it is with Joseph.

On the Day of Pentecost there were but 120 of the saints, but at that time there were added 3,000 souls. When God sends a man to do a work, all the devils in hell cannot kill him until he gets through his work; so with Joseph, he prepared all things, gave the keys to men on the earth, and said, 'I may soon be taken from you'.'

The following Epistle of the Twelve was published in the *Prophet*:—

AN EPISTLE OF THE APOSTLES TO THE SAINTS

'Boston, July 18, 1844.

To the Elders and Saints Scattered Abroad, Greeting.

Dear Brethren,—We take this method to notify you that the advice and counsel of the Twelve is, that all the brethren who have families in the west should return to them as soon as convenient, and that all the churches should remain humble and watch unto prayer, and follow the teachings that have been given them by the servants of God, and leave all things in the hands of God: all will be right; the name of the Lord will be glorified and his work will prosper. And we would warn the saints in all the world against receiving the teachings of any man or set of men who come professing to be elders of the Church of Jesus Christ of Latter-day Saints, who preach any doctrine contrary to the plain and holy principles of the gospel of Jesus Christ which have been delivered unto them.

We wish to see all the authorities of the church residing at Nauvoo, who at this time may be absent, such as the presidents of the different quorums, high priests, high council, seventies and bishops, that we may meet them in council as soon as convenient, as we expect to return immediately to Nauvoo.

Dear brethren, we are sensible that the account of the death of the Prophet and Patriarch of the church will be painful to your hearts: it is to ours. We feel and mourn their loss, but they have sealed their testimony with their blood; they have not counted their lives as dear unto themselves as the lives of the church; they have died in the Lord and their works will follow them.

The eyes of the Lord are upon those who have shed the blood of the Lord's anointed, and he will judge them with a righteous judgment. Let the saints cultivate a meek and quiet spirit, and all things shall in the end work together for your good.

By order of the Quorum of the Twelve,

[Signed] BRIGHAM YOUNG, *President,*
WILFORD WOODRUFF, *Clerk.*'

We copy from the *Prophet*:—

WARNING AGAINST FALSE DOCTRINES

'*Mr. Editor,*—I am requested to say to the saints, through the *Prophet,* by the counsel of the Twelve, that whereas certain strange doctrines have been taught and practiced in Boston and elsewhere, by men claiming higher authority than the Twelve,—

This is, therefore, to warn you, in the name of our Lord Jesus Christ, that you give no heed to men making these high pretensions, when they teach you things that are not in accordance with principles which you know to be correct.

And we would seriously caution all men to beware how they offer strange fire upon the altars of pure and innocent hearts, lest that flame consume them, root and branch, in an unexpected hour; for the authorities of God's house are not to be rode over by any man, and he escape without the rod.

A ship that carries more sail than her ballast will admit of, will surely capsize when the storm strikes her. This is a figure, and let it be remembered.

Yours truly,
ORSON HYDE.'

Friday, 19.—Elders Parley P. Pratt, Willard Richards, John Taylor and W. W. Phelps spent the afternoon in council.

Elders at Nauvoo.

Elder Kimball went to Salem, and preached to the saints in the evening.

Saturday, 20.—Elders Brigham Young and Heber C. Kimball spent the day together in the city of Boston. Elders Orson Hyde and Orson Pratt left for New York, and Elder Wilford Woodruff for Connecticut.

Movements of Elders in the East.

Sunday, 21.—Meeting at the stand. Elder Parley P. Pratt preached from the *Book of Mormon,* quoting from Moroni, 'Widows mourning for their husbands'.

Meetings at Nauvoo.

Afternoon.—The sacrament was administered. Elders Pratt, Cahoon and Richards spoke.

Elders Young and Kimball preached to the saints in Boston during the day and evening; congregations very attentive.

Monday, 22.—The following is from Governor Thomas Ford:—

LETTER OF GOVERNOR FORD TO WILLARD RICHARDS AND W. W. PHELPS

'Quincy, July 17, 1844.
[Confidential]

Gentlemen,—I have just returned from St. Louis. I should have gone on directly to Nauvoo, but I was aware that a visit to your place at this time would certainly be misrepresented by the public. I want very much to see some of you solely on the business of the late outrages at Carthage.

The mode of proceeding to be adopted is a matter for careful consideration. I wish to see some of you to consult on that one subject alone. Can one of you come down? If so, come immediately, or let me know.

I am, most respectfully,

Your obedient servant,
[Signed] THOMAS FORD.

Dr. Willard Richards,
W. W. Phelps, Esq.'

To which the annexed was sent in reply:—

REPLY OF RICHARDS AND PHELPS

'Nauvoo, July 22, 1844.

[Confidential]

His Excellency Governor Ford.

Sir,—We have, at this late hour, received your letter of the 17th inst., and would be gratified with an interview, agreeably to your Excellency's request; but the murder of our best men makes our time precious, and compels us to forego the interview.

We have delegated our friend, Mr. Orson Spencer, one of the aldermen of our city, to meet your Excellency on the arrival of the morning boat, answer any queries, and attend to all necessary business, having the fullest confidence in his ability and integrity to discharge the mission to your Excellency's satisfaction and the best interest of our bleeding and long-loved country.

We are, sir, most respectfully,

Your obedient servants,

[Signed] WILLARD RICHARDS,

W. W. PHELPS.'

Sister Leonora Taylor wrote as follows:—

LEONORA TAYLOR'S WOMANLY LETTER TO GOVERNOR FORD

'Nauvoo, July 22, 1844.

To His Excellency Thomas Ford.

Sir,—The peculiarity of my situation will, I hope, plead my excuse for troubling your Excellency on the present occasion.

Mr. Taylor, who was severely wounded in the jail at Carthage, is still ill, and obliged to be lifted in and out of bed; his wounds are slowly healing, and we hope he will finally get well, if suffered to do so. But, sir, I am sorry to say the murderers and mobbers are still at large in our neighborhood; as there has been no steps taken to bring them to justice, they have taken fresh courage and held meetings to carry out their work of destruction. I have been told they have sent messengers to Missouri to collect all the force they can, to come and exterminate the Mormons after harvest.

I have enclosed your Excellency a communication sent Mr. Taylor yesterday, which is a sample of many that are daily coming in. He does not know of my writing this letter. Nothing but the urgency of the case could have induced me to remind your Excellency of your promise to bring the *murderers* to *justice*. If a step of that kind is not taken soon, I much fear that it cannot benefit us as a people.

We are without arms, in a great measure, having delivered them up at your Excellency's request, and we are forbid to stand even in our own defense. In this peculiar position, without resources, we can only look to your Excellency for defense, to you, sir, for protection; and if it is not granted, we must be murdered in cold blood.

My feelings as a wife, and mother of helpless children, together with the afflictions of an injured people, all constrain me to beseech of you to exert the power and authority which the people and God has given you, in the cause of the oppressed. You shall have our prayers, that wisdom may be given you from on high to act in this case to the glory of God, your own honor and that of the state we live in.

Your Excellency was warned of our brethren's danger, who were murdered, but could not believe that men were so base and degraded. The same men are now plotting our destruction.

As an individual who feels herself injured, and also in behalf of an oppressed, injured and persecuted people, I again beg your official interference. Your Excellency cannot now be mistaken in the men nor their design; I beseech you then, for the honor of our bleeding country, for the sake of suffering innocence and the cause of humanity, by the wounds of my husband and the blood of those murdered victims, to use prompt measures for our protection and the bringing to justice of those murderers.

Sincerely praying that you, sir, may become a terror to evildoers and the praise of those that do well, with great respect

I have the honor to be

Your Excellency's humble servant,

LEONORA TAYLOR.'

Movements of Prominent Elders.

Elder Wilford Woodruff went to Farmington, Ct., and spent the night at his father's house. He ordained his father a high priest.

Tuesday, 23.—10 a. m. Elder Orson Spencer went down on the *Osprey* to Quincy, to wait upon the governor.

Elders Brigham Young and Heber C. Kimball spent the day in Boston. They attended meeting in the evening and ordained thirty-two elders.

Elder Woodruff parted with his father and mother at Farmington, and proceeded to New York.

Wednesday, 24.—Elders Parley P. Pratt, Willard Richards, W. W. Phelps, George Miller and L. Woodworth met in council. They anointed and administered to Elder Samuel H. Smith, who was very sick.

Elder Phelps received the following communication from the governor:—

IMPORTANT AND CONFIDENTIAL LETTER OF GOVERNOR FORD TO ELDER W. W. PHELPS

'Quincy, July 22, 1844.

Sir,—On Thursday last I wrote to Dr. Richards and yourself, requesting you to come or send some person to me at this place, to confer with me in relation to the time and mode of proceeding against the murderers of the Messrs. Smith; and I therein stated that I would have come to Nauvoo for that purpose were it not for the certainty that my motives and objects for so doing would be misinterpreted. As none of you have come, and have probably not received my letter, I have concluded to write you again and send this letter by special messenger.

In this letter I will say to you what I intended to say in a personal conference. In the beginning, then, you must allow me to say that my position forbids that I should be a partisan on either side of your unhappy controversy.

I may, for aught I know, have stern duties to perform in relation to both parties. This, however, will depend on which side may be the aggressor. Thus far, since the death of the Smiths, your people have behaved well; much better than could have been expected under the circumstances, and much better than the opposite party. I anxiously hope that they may have the grace to continue in the same line of conduct.

An unresisting, passive, peaceable, but defensive course on your parts, will do much to disarm prejudices in the surrounding country. That such prejudices do exist in the minds of the people you know as well as I, though you may not be fully aware of their extent, or the ferocity which they engender.

If I speak of those prejudices and the causes of them, I do not wish you to misunderstand me, as some of you did on a former occasion, and suppose that I am speaking my own opinions and feelings.

I say now, once for all, that I have nothing to do with those prejudices further than as a practical man; they obtrude themselves on my consideration, as presenting obstacles to me in the discharge of my official duty. The more prejudice and bad feeling which is gotten up against your people, whether by their own imprudence or the malice of their enemies, the more difficult it is for me to do anything effectually to protect either party according to law.

There are, I am informed, some few inflammatory and hot-blooded individuals amongst you, who, by their imprudence and rashness, continue to give cause for those prejudices, and, of course, by so doing, continue to involve you all in a common danger; I speak of the danger of a mob.

I am also informed that most of you entertain the opinion that there has been a great and universal reaction in the public mind since the death of the Smiths.

On this subject I desire to tell you the naked truth. I am aware that you scarcely ever hear the truth, as to public sentiment abroad, from those who visit you in your city. The complaisance of such persons, and their desire to please, will induce them to omit the statement of disagreeable truths, and to say such things only as are pleasing and complimentary. You are bound, as men of sense, to receive all such statements with a great deal of allowance.

On my part, without desiring to please any of you, or to conciliate your favor, but certainly without any design to insult your misfortunes, and in a pure spirit of friendly concern for the peace and safety of all who repose under the shade of our political fig tree, I desire to state to you frankly, candidly and thoroughly, what I do know on this subject.

The naked truth then is, that most well-informed persons condemn in the most unqualified manner the mode in which the Smiths were put to death, but nine out of every ten of such accompany the expression of their disapprobation by a manifestation of their pleasure that they are dead.

The disapproval is most unusually cold and without feeling. It is a disapproval which appears to be called for, on their part, by decency, by a respect for the laws and a horror of mobs, but does not flow warm from the heart.

The unfortunate victims of this assassination were generally and thoroughly hated throughout the country, and it is not reasonable to suppose that their death has produced any reaction in the public mind resulting in active sympathy; if you think so, you are mistaken.

Most that is said on the subject is merely from the teeth out; and your people may depend on the fact, that public feeling is now, at this time, as thoroughly against them as it has ever been.

I mention this, not for the purpose of insulting your feelings, but to show you clearly how careful your people ought to be in future to avoid all causes of quarrel and excitement, and what little reliance could be placed on any militia force which I could send in your favor.

I ought, perhaps, to qualify what I have said, by remarking that but few persons from the surrounding counties could now be procured to join a mob force against you, without further cause of excitement to be ministered by some misguided imprudence of your people. But what I mean to say, and to say truly, is, that in the present temper of the public mind I am positively certain that I cannot raise a militia force in the state who would be willing to fight on your side, or to hazard their lives to protect you from an attack of your enemies.

The same state of things exists in relation to any force which might be ordered to arrest the murderers. If troops should be ordered for that purpose, I would expect that they would behave as the militia did in the late Philadelphia riots. The militia in that case sympathized with the native party and against their opponents. It was an unpopular service, and rather than fight they suffered themselves to be defeated and driven from the field.

It is true that I might call upon the Mormons themselves, and then I would have a reliable force. This, however, would be a dangerous experiment, and would, in my mind, inevitably lead to civil war, the result of which no man can foresee.

I think I may safely say, that if the Nauvoo Legion should be called out against the old citizens, the crimes which are sought to be punished would be instantly forgotten in the general and burning indignation which would be kindled.

Men would rally to their assistance who would otherwise be neutral. Your Legion has ever been regarded with a jealous eye; the arming and drilling of your people, with such exceeding industry, in a season of peace, (not wrong in itself,) has been looked upon by the great body of the people with suspicion, and as intended in due time for the subversion of the public liberty: in the beginning you would have been much better without it. If your people had never made any military pretensions, no military feeling would ever have been aroused against you.

This much I hope you will consider has been said from a friendly motive, and for the further purpose of showing you what a dangerous experiment it would be, and how well calculated to excite a civil war, in which your city might be utterly destroyed, if I should attempt to call out the hated Legion against the old citizens.

You may be disposed to ask, What use is there for law and government if these things be so? I answer you, that cases like the present do not seem to be fully provided for by our Constitutions; they were not anticipated to occur.

Upon the first institution of our governments, it was a season of internal peace and union among our people. The population was homogeneous, and all agreed together as brothers. It was supposed that the great body of the people would be always willingly submissive to the laws which they themselves had made. It was not foreseen that great and hostile parties would soon spring up and combine in large numbers to set the law at defiance.

A voluntary submission and obedience was supposed as the basis of government, for this reason no adequate provision was made in our state constitutions for coercing this submission, when the laws were to be trampled upon by the concerted action of large numbers.

The states are prohibited from maintaining standing armies; the only military force at their command, without aid from the general government, is the militia; and, as I have already shown you, this force can only be relied on to do effectual service where that service is popular and jumps with their inclinations.

For this same reason, I must beg leave to say that a party, as in your case, which is the object of popular odium, cannot be too circumspect in their behavior, so as to give no color to the hatred of your enemies. 'Truth is great and will prevail'.

From this you may be assured that if the conduct of your people shall be uniformly peaceably honest and submissive to the laws, even if they have to bear persecution for a season, such conduct must result in dissipating the unhappy prejudices which exist against you.

Truth and candor, however, compel me to say that the Mormons have not always acted in such a manner as if they intended to avoid the creation of prejudices.

The pretensions of your municipal court, the unheard of description of ordinances passed by your city council, the assault on Mr. Bagby, the attempt to kidnap persons from Missouri, the formal destruction of a printing office and the general tone of arrogance and defiance of some of your leaders, were well calculated to inflame the public mind against you.

I think that I have considered this difficult subject in every possible point of view. I am afraid to rely on the militia in the present temper of the public mind. To call on the Nauvoo Legion would be suicidal to any effort as pacification of existing troubles, and for that reason would fail to bring about an enforcement of the laws.

If the laws are to be enforced at all in your county, out of the ordinary way by courts alone, it must be done by a force which is indifferent as to both parties.

To call in one party to put down and subdue the other, would lead to the most disastrous consequences; all the pride of conquest and victory; all the shame of defeat by, and submission to an adversary; all the fury of unconquerable hate and exasperated feeling would necessarily be mingled with the contest, and render it bloody and bitter beyond anything we know of in this country.

For these reasons I have called upon the officers now in command, in the absence of General Gains, of the 3rd Military Department of the United States, for five hundred men of the regular army to be stationed in Hancock county, with whose aid I hope to be able to preserve order and proceed against all criminals whomsoever they may be. The following is a copy of the answer to the application:—

'Headquarters, 3rd Mil. Dept.,
St. Louis, Mo., July 11, 1844.

'Sir,—I have the honor to acknowledge the receipt of your Excellency's communication of this date, relating to the difficulties which have occurred between the Mormons and the people of Hancock county, Illinois, and the further difficulties apprehended by you, and requesting of me a force of some five hundred men from the regular army of the United States to be stationed for a time in Hancock county, and to act in conjunction with such forces as may be ordered on the part of the state of Illinois.

'I have not the power of complying with your request, but will forward by tomorrow's mail a copy of your communication to be laid before the authorities in Washington city, and will advise your Excellency of the result as soon as ascertained.

With great respect,
Your most obedient servant,
[Signed] S. W. KEARNEY,
Col. 1st Drags.

His Excellency Thomas Ford,
Governor of Illinois, St. Louis, Mo.'

By the above letter you will perceive that I cannot yet be enabled to say with certainty whether the application will be successful: we will know in two weeks, I think, at most.

The anti-Mormon party intend to renew the war this fall, and if it were known with certainty that the troops of the regular army would be obtained to prevent their operations, they would, most likely, hasten their plans and do all the mischief in their power before the force arrives. They are not afraid of the state militia, and would give themselves but little concern in fear of such opposition.

I therefore caution you not to let it be known beyond your most trusted men that a regular force is expected. I have myself not informed anyone who would make the matter public, and yet, most unaccountably, the fact has got into the newspapers.

Another caution I would give you, your people cannot pay too much attention to it. It is very natural and probable to suppose that with the prospect of such a force, and the increased security it may give, some of your people may be prompted to such audacity and imprudence as will tend to prolong angry feelings. They may thus be induced to do and say foolish and wicked things, uselessly vexatious and mortifying to the opposing party.

There are no doubt wicked people in Nauvoo, ready for the commission of crime, as well as in every other city of the same number of inhabitants. The well-disposed amongst you must restrain those persons, and, if need be, bring them to punishment. The public at large will not distinguish among you, but will involve you all in a common obloquy.

I have dwelt more, perhaps, than may be agreeable to you on this point; but I have done so in my anxiety that the Mormons may demonstrate to the world that they are no more deserving than their enemies.

Three or four of your people are reported to me as having already been threatening life, and publicly following men about the city with clubs, and that no effort was made to restrain them. An effectual stop must be put to all such vaporings, if you expect it to stop on the other side. You are interested in bringing all such men to immediate justice, if you can. If pacification is what you ask, you must restrain your own hostility.

It may be thought that there has already been too much delay in proceeding against the murderers, that a further delay will give an opportunity for many of the guilty to escape, and that the apparent impunity for the present will greatly encourage further outrages against you.

This last consideration is one of considerable force, and on that account I could wish to proceed without delay, if it could be done without exciting further troubles, or if I had a force at my command on which I could rely to suppress them.

I do not fear that any of the leaders will escape or flee from justice: they are determined to remain and brave it out to the end.

In my humble opinion there is no utility in proceeding against any but the leaders.

As to the misguided multitude who were the mere followers of others and the instruments of mischief, it has never been the practice of civilized states to proceed against them with rigor.

The punishment of some of the principal offenders has always been looked upon as sufficient to vindicate the majesty of the law and to deter others from the commission of like offenses, and this is the whole object of human punishment.

I do not apprehend that anything requiring my further stay here will happen immediately, and will return home tomorrow.

I am, most respectfully,

Your obedient servant,

[Signed] THOMAS FORD.

William W. Phelps, Esq., Nauvoo, Illinois.' "*

*This lengthy communication of Governor Ford to W. W. Phelps is quite characteristic of Thomas Ford in nearly all his relationships with the Latter-day Saints, both before and after the martyrdom of the Prophets; and bears witness of his weakness, and inclination to double-dealing with them. In nothing is this more apparent than in the letter enclosed in the above communication to Colonel S. W. Kearney of the First Dragoons, headquarters of the Third Military Department at St. Louis. Ford's appeal to this local commander of the First Dragoons can be no other than mere pretense at applying for U. S. military assistance to quell the riotous uprising of mobs and the rebellion of state military units inclined to mobocracy in western Illinois. The Constitution of the United States makes it possible by application of the legislature or of the executive of a state when the legislature can not be convened to appeal to the federal government for protection against invasion or against "domestic violence". But this application must be made to the federal government for the fulfillment of the guarantee against domestic violence and with his knowledge of the law governing the case, the inconsistency of the appeal of Governor Ford to Colonel Kearney could not be other than a mere pretense at securing aid against the domestic violence in western Illinois at that period. It was a mere "seeming" to invoke federal aid, well knowing that it could not be granted from that source, and in that manner; and evidently the governor sought to satisfy the leading elders at Nauvoo that he had vainly attempted to exercise this power lodged in him by the Constitution. His ignorance could not be pleaded in excuse of such artful dodging in the case. B. H. R.

CHAPTER XVII

GATHERING OF THE TWELVE AND OTHER LEADING ELDERS AT NAUVOO—DEATH OF ELDER SAMUEL H. SMITH, BROTHER OF THE PROPHET, EARLY MISSIONARY OF THE CHURCH AND ONE OF THE EIGHT WITNESSES OF THE BOOK OF MORMON

"*Wednesday, July* 24, 1844.—The brethren of the Twelve were delayed in Boston several days, waiting upon Elder Lyman Wight to accompany them to Nauvoo.

Preparations of the Twelve to Start for Nauvoo.

Elders Young, Kimball and Wight left Boston by railway in the morning for Nauvoo. On their arrival at Albany, in the evening, they were joined by Elders Orson Hyde, Orson Pratt, Wilford Woodruff and Sister Ruth Sayers, who had arrived from New York. They continued their journey by railway during the night.

Thursday, 25.—Elder Orson Spencer returned from Quincy.

Dr. Richards received the following from President Brigham Young:—

LETTER OF ELDER BRIGHAM YOUNG TO WILLARD RICHARDS

'Salem, July 8, 1844.

Beloved Brother Willard Richards:

I sit down a few minutes to write you, as Brother Erastus Snow is going to start for Nauvoo tomorrow. He has been laboring in Vermont.

We cannot get one word from our families by letter of late. Sister Ruth Sayers has received a letter from her husband, that, I understand, gives some information which seems to be satisfactory.

According to what we hear in this country about the 'Mormons' in the west, I should suppose that there is an election about to take place, or the Prophet had offered himself for some office in the United States; for of all the howlings of devils and devil's whelps, this season cannot be beat.

Sometimes the 'Mormons' are all killed; sometimes they are half killed; sometimes the blood is shoe-deep in Nauvoo; sometimes 'Old Joe', as they call him, is taken by the mob and carried to Missouri; sometimes he is gone to Washington; sometimes he has run away; then again he is given up to the authorities, etc., etc. One might suppose him to be a sectarian God, without body, parts or passions, his center everywhere and his circumference nowhere.

Since I left Nauvoo I have heard a great many expressions about the Prophet, but the prevailing opinion is, that he is the smartest man in the Union, and the people are afraid of his smartness. Some will vote for him for the novelty of the thing, and some to see what a Prophet will do at the head of government. We had a fine passage on the rivers; preached and lectured all the way round.

I lectured at Pittsburgh and in Kirtland. We held political meetings at Shalorsville and Hiram. I preached in the first house west of old Father Johnson's, where Brothers Joseph and Sidney were mobbed. I looked at the house a great many times.

I left Brothers Snow and Brooks in Ohio, doing well. The Twelve have been faithful in all things. Brother William Smith is a great man in his calling in this country. Brother Lyman Wight has never been with us before; he is a great, good, noble-hearted man. I love my brethren more and more.

I want to see you and the rest of the brethren in Nauvoo. Give my best love to Brothers Joseph and Hyrum. I cannot be there to see them, but I pray for them continually, and for you and all the brethren in our beloved city, and I pray my heavenly Father to preserve my brethren, my family and the whole city. I pray that we may finish the Temple and get our endowments.

We had a large congregation in Boston at our convention, though in the evening there were some who came in that made some disturbance. This proves that the voice of the people rules; that is, the voice of the rabble. One of the watch got some hurt, but all this did us good in Boston. Brother Heywood, from Quincy, is here with us and is doing much good. He is a faithful witness for Brother Joseph and the principles of righteousness.

We have baptized a good many since we left. The gospel is going ahead. All the stories that are going the rounds make no difference, the people will believe the gospel.

You might ask what we think about Brother Joseph's getting the election this year? You know all about it. We shall do all we can and leave the event with God—the God of heaven will do just as he pleases about it.

Brother Daniel Spencer and many others are here; they are awake to the subject. We are now in the concert hall in Salem. Brother Erastus Snow is now speaking.

We shall attend the conferences in this country, and then leave for the western states to attend the conferences, and get home as quickly as possible. If you are to have a little trouble there, we wish to have a hand in it with you.

I wish you would see my family and speak comfortably to them. Brother Tur, I hope all will go on well with him. If you get a chance to dispose of our property at a good rate, do so. If my wife can get anything to help her I should be pleased. Give my love to Sister Jennetta and all the household, and to all the saints.

Brothers Kimball and Wight will start for Baltimore tomorrow. The brethren in this country inquire after you and all the elders that they have seen; they are warm-hearted. I suppose you have received a letter from the Boston church, with Parley P. Pratt's name to it.

May the Lord bless you all,

BRIGHAM YOUNG.'

Elder Samuel H. Smith remains very sick.

Elder Erastus Snow, and many other elders, returned home today; all seemed weighed down with gloom.

Elders Young, Kimball, Hyde, Pratt, Woodruff and Wight arrived in Buffalo, and remained all night.

Friday, 26.—President Young and company took steamboat at Buffalo for Detroit.

Elder Orson Hyde took leave of his brethren at Fairport, to visit his family at Kirtland.

Saturday, 27.—We copy from the *Times and Seasons* the following from the pen of Miss E. R. Snow:—

TO ELDER JOHN TAYLOR

'Thou Chieftain of Zion! henceforward thy name
Will be classed with the martyrs and share in their fame;
Through ages eternal, of thee will be said,
'With the greatest of Prophets he suffered and bled'.
When the shafts of injustice were pointed at him—
When the cup of his suff'ring was filled to the brim—
When his innocent blood was inhumanly shed,
You shared his afflictions and with him you bled.
When around you, like hailstones, the rifle balls flew—
When the passage of death opened wide to your view—
When the Prophet's freed spirit, through martyrdom fled,
In your gore you lay welt'ring—with martyrs you bled.
All the scars from your wounds, like the trophies of yore,
Shall be ensigns of honor till you are no more;
And by all generations, of thee shall be said,
'With the best of the Prophets in prison he bled'.'

The brethren of the Twelve arrived at Detroit in the evening, and remained over night at the railroad hotel.

Sunday, 28.—Elders Parley P. Pratt, W. W. Phelps and others addressed the saints in Nauvoo.

Elders Returning to Nauvoo.

On hearing of the death of the Prophet and Patriarch, Elders Charles C. Rich, David Fullmer, Graham Coltrin, Samuel Bent, Ira Miles and George A. Smith were together in Michigan. Elder George A. Smith counselled the elders to return home. They accordingly started for Nauvoo. The roads were muddy, the waters high, and many of the bridges were gone. As they approached Nauvoo they found the people very hostile, however they preached at several places by the way.

Elder George A. Smith, and the brethren with him, arrived at Nauvoo near midnight.

The following is from Elder Wilford Woodruff's Journal:—

EXCERPT

'The brethren of the Twelve took the propeller *Hercules* for Chicago at 10 a. m. Fare in the cabin $7. We had comfortable staterooms. We spent the day in writing and in social conversation with each other concerning the death of Joseph and Hyrum and the welfare of the church and our families. A variety of subjects were called up, each one expressing his feelings freely. President Brigham Young said he wished me to keep an account of things as they were passing, as he should look to me for his journal at a future day. Elder Wight said that Joseph told him, while in Liberty jail, Missouri, in 1839, he would not live to see forty years, but he was not to reveal it till he was dead.'

Monday, 29.—Elder George A. Smith visited the Prophet's family.

Elders Willard Richards and George A. Smith visited Elder Samuel H. Smith and laid hands upon him. He expressed a strong desire to live: he was very low, being in the last stages of bilious fever.

Elders Richards and Smith met at Elder Richards',

and ordained two elders who were about leaving the the city. Brother Richards signed their licenses:—

'TWELVE APOSTLES,
President.

Willard Richards, Clerk.'

George Miller called on them and requested the privilege of passing some resolutions against the murderers of Joseph and Hyrum. The brethren told him to be quiet and wait and see what the governor and the state authorities would do, that Dr. Richards had pledged himself that the brethren would be quiet, and the Lord had said, 'Vengeance is mine, I will repay'. Miller left the council, saying, 'Fat men for patience'.

Bishop George Miller's Restiveness.

In the evening Elders Richards and Smith visited Elder Taylor.

Tuesday, 30.—Elder Samuel H. Smith, brother of the martyred Prophet and Patriarch, died.

DEATH OF SAMUEL H. SMITH

Elders W. Richards and George A. Smith met in council with Elder Taylor at his house. Bishop George Miller and Alexander Badlam wanted them to call together the Council of Fifty and organize the church. They were told that the Council of Fifty was not a church organization, but was composed of members irrespective of their religious faith, and organized for the purpose of consulting on the best manner of obtaining redress of grievances from our enemies, and to devise means to find and locate in some place where we could live in peace; and that the organization of the church belonged to the priesthood alone.

The Council of Fifty.

The brethren of the Twelve arrived at Mackinaw. The steamer stopped a short time, took in some fish, and took some boats with Indians in tow. There was a feeling of prejudice manifested by the passengers of the boat against the

Returning Elders not of the World.

brethren, because they did not mingle with them in their nonsense and folly, and this spirit is more or less manifest throughout the world.

Wednesday, 31.—Elder Amasa Lyman arrived in Nauvoo.

The following from the governor appeared in the *Neighbor*:—

GOVERNOR FORD TO THE PEOPLE OF WARSAW IN HANCOCK COUNTY

'I am continually informed of your preparations and threats to renew the war and exterminate the 'Mormons'. One would suppose that you ought to rest satisfied with what you have already done.

The 'Mormon' leaders, if they ever resisted the law, have submitted to its authority. They have surrendered the public arms, and appeared to be ready to do anything required to make atonement for whatever wrong may have been done.

Since the assassination of their two principal leaders, under circumstances well calculated to inflame their passions and drive them to excesses for the purposes of revenge, they have been entirely peaceful and submissive, and have patiently awaited the slow operation of the laws to redress the wrongs of which they complained. There has been no retaliation, no revenge, and, for anything I can ascertain, there will be none.

Those of your people who are charged with being the most hostile to them have lived, if they knew it, in perfect security from illegal violence.

I am anxious for a pacification of your difficulties. You cannot drive out or exterminate the 'Mormons'. Such an effort would be madness, and would not be permitted by the people of the state. You cannot be sustained in it either by force or law. You are binding yourselves to your weakness, and keeping up an agitation which must fail of the purpose intended and recoil with terrible energy upon your own heads.

I exhort you to reconsider your infatuated resolutions. Try your 'Mormon' neighbors again, and if you cannot dwell together in amity, you may at least refrain from injuring each other.

From the moderation of the 'Mormons', under what they conceive to be the deepest injury, you might well hope that if they ever entertained designs inconsistent with your liberty and happiness, that those designs have been abandoned. They are also interested in preserving the peace.

It is not natural to suppose that they, any more than yourselves, wish to live in continual alarm. They hope for quietness, and will be peaceful and submissive in order to enjoy it. But you are continually driving them to desperation by an insane course of threatening and hostility, and depriving yourselves of peace by the same means used to disquiet them.

If I have said anything severe in this address, I pray you attribute it to my deep conviction that your course is improper and unwarrantable. Such is the opinion of the people at large in the state and all over the country.

From being right in the first instance you have put yourselves in the wrong, and there are none who sustain you. As men of sense you are bound to see, if you will open your eyes, that you cannot effect your purposes. Nevertheless, you are still training and drilling, and keeping together, and threatening a renewal of the war.

I have said to you often that you cannot succeed; by this time you ought to see it yourselves. What can your small force do against two thousand armed men, entrenched in a city, and defending themselves, their wives and their children?

Besides, if you are the aggressors, I am determined that all the power of the state shall be used to prevent your success. I can never agree that a set of infatuated and infuriated men shall barbarously attack a peaceful people who have submitted to all the demands of the law, and when they had full power to do so, refrained from inflicting vengeance upon their enemies. You may count on my most determined opposition—upon the opposition of the law, and upon that of every peaceful, law-abiding citizen of the country.

This is not spoken in anger. God knows I would do no injury unless compelled to do so to sustain the laws. But mob violence must be put down. It is threatening the whole country with anarchy and ruin. It is menacing our fair form of government, and destroying the confidence of the patriot in the institutions of his country.

I have been informed that the 'Mormons' about Lima and Macedonia have been warned to leave the settlements. They have a right to remain and enjoy their property. As long as they are good citizens they shall not be molested, and the sooner those misguided persons withdraw their warning and retrace their steps, the better it will be for them.

[Signed] THOMAS FORD.

July 25, 1844.

Thursday, August 1.—The remains of the deceased Elder Samuel H. Smith were interred this morning at 10 a. m.

We extract the following from his obituary:—

BIOGRAPHICAL NOTE OF SAMUEL H. SMITH, BROTHER OF THE PROPHET—IMPORTANT TESTIMONY TO THE BOOK OF MORMON

'Samuel Harrison Smith, the fourth son of Joseph and Lucy, was born in the town of Tunbridge, Orange county, Vermont, on the 13th day of March, 1808.

In his early life he assisted his father in farming. He possessed a religious turn of mind, and at an early age joined the Presbyterian Church, to which sect he belonged until he visited his brother Joseph in May, 1829, when Joseph informed him that the Lord was about to commence his latter-day work.

He also showed him that part of the *Book of Mormon* which he had translated, and labored to persuade him concerning the gospel of Jesus Christ which was about to be revealed in its fulness.

Samuel was not, however, very easily persuaded of these things; but after much inquiry and explanation he retired and prayed that he might obtain from the Lord wisdom to enable him to judge for himself; the result was that he obtained revelation for himself sufficient to convince him of the truth of the testimony of his brother Joseph.

On the 15th day of May, 1829, having been commanded of the Lord, Joseph Smith and Oliver Cowdery were baptized, and as they were returning from the water to the house, they overheard Samuel engaged in secret prayer. Joseph said that he considered that a sufficient testimony of his being a fit subject for baptism; and as they had now received authority to baptize, they spoke to Samuel upon the subject, and he went straightway to the water with them, and was baptized by Oliver Cowdery, he being the third person baptized into the Church of Jesus Christ in the last dispensation.

He was one of the eight witnesses of the *Book of Mormon*.

He was present at the organization of the church, April 6, 1830, and was one of the six who at that time constituted the members of the church. He was ordained to the priesthood on the 6th of April, 1830.

On the 30th of June following the organization of the church, he took some *Books of Mormon* and started out on his mission, to which he had been set apart by his brother Joseph, and on traveling twenty-five miles, which was his first day's journey, he stopped at a number of places in order to sell his books, but was turned out of doors as soon as he declared his principles.

When evening came on he was faint and almost discouraged; but coming to an inn, which was surrounded with every appearance of plenty, he called to see if the landlord would buy one of his books. On going in, Samuel inquired of him if he did not wish to purchase a history of the origin of the Indians.

'I do not know', replied the host, 'how did you get hold of it?'

'It was translated', rejoined Samuel, 'by my brother, from some gold plates that he found buried in the earth.'

'You damned liar', cried the landlord, 'get out of my house—you shan't stay one minute with your books.'

Samuel was sick at heart, for this was the fifth time he had been turned out of doors that day. He left the house and traveled a short distance, and washed his feet in a small brook as a testimony against the man.

He then proceeded five miles further on his journey, and seeing an apple tree a short distance from the road, he concluded to pass the night under it; and here he lay all night upon the cold, damp ground.

In the morning he arose from his comfortless bed, and observing a small cottage at no great distance, he drew near, hoping to get a little refreshment. The only inmate was a widow, who seemed very poor. He asked her for food, relating the story of his former treatment. She prepared him some victuals, and, after eating, he explained to her the history of the *Book of Mormon*. She listened attentively, and believed all that he told her; but, in consequence of her poverty, she was unable to purchase one of the books. He presented her with one, and proceeded to Bloomington, which was eight miles further.

Here he stopped at the house of one John P. Greene, who was a Methodist preacher and was at that time about starting on a preaching mission. He, like the others, did not wish to make a purchase of what he considered at that time to be a nonsensical fable; however, he said that he would take a subscription paper, and if he found any one on his route who was disposed to purchase, he would take his name, and in two weeks Samuel might call again, and he would let him know what the prospect was of selling. After making this arrangement, Samuel left one of his books with him and returned home.

At the time appointed, Samuel started again for the Rev. John P. Greene's, in order to learn the success which this gentleman had met with in finding sale for the *Book of Mormon*. This time his father and mother accompanied him, and it was their intention to have passed near the tavern where Samuel was so abusively treated a fortnight previous, but just before they came to the house a sign of smallpox intercepted them.

They turned aside, and meeting a citizen of the place they inquired of him to what extent this disease prevailed. He answered that the tavernkeeper and two of his family had died with it not long since, but he did not know that anyone else had caught the distemper, and that it was brought into the neighborhood by a traveler who stopped at the tavern over night.

Samuel performed several short missions with the books, and gave the following account of his third mission to Livonia:—

'When I arrived at Mr. Greene's, Mrs. Greene informed me that her husband was absent from home, that there was no prospect of selling my books, and even the one which I had left with them she expected I would have to take away, as Mr. Greene had no disposition to purchase it, although she had read it herself and was much pleased with it.

'I then talked with her a short time, and, binding my knapsack upon my shoulders, rose to depart; but, as I bade her farewell, it was impressed upon my mind to leave the book with her. I made her a present of it, and told her that the Spirit forbade my taking it away. She burst into tears, and requested me to pray with her. I did so, and afterwards explained to her the most profitable manner of reading the book* which I had left with her, which was, to ask God, when she read it, for a testimony of the truth of what she had read, and she would receive the Spirit of God which would enable her to discern the things of God. I then left her and returned home.'

In December, 1830, Samuel was sent to preach in Kirtland, Ohio, and the surrounding country. About that time Joseph, the Prophet, went to Kirtland to preside, accompanied by Hyrum and many of the saints, and soon after Joseph Smith, Sen's. family, and the saints who were located in Waterloo, in Fayette township, also moved to Kirtland.

In June, 1831, he was called by revelation to go to Missouri on a mission, in company with Reynolds Cahoon. They immediately started, and while on their way called upon William E. McLellin, and preached the gospel to him and a large assembly in a room which he procured. William, being troubled about the things he heard, closed up his business and proceeded after the brethren to Missouri, where he was baptized before they arrived.

On their route to Missouri they [Elders Smith and Cahoon] preached the gospel, traveling without purse or scrip, and enduring much for the want of food and rest.

When they started for Missouri, about fifty brethren set out for the same place, and when they all arrived, they met on the spot for the Temple, in Jackson county, and dedicated the ground unto God.

Brothers Smith and Cahoon spent several days in Jackson county, attended several conferences and were with Joseph when he received several revelations. While in Missouri they were required to remain together on their return mission until they reached home, which was in September following.

Soon after their arrival in Kirtland they took a mission into the southern townships and counties of Ohio. Brother Cahoon returned after laboring about six weeks, but Samuel continued preaching through the winter, strengthening the churches and comforting the saints.

*This *Book of Mormon* left at the home of the Greene's who were relatives of the Young's finally fell into the hands of Brigham Young, and Heber C. Kimball and was the means not only of bringing them directly to the knowledge of the New Dispensation gospel, but was the means also of their conversion. This copy of the *Book of Mormon* came into the hands of Phineas Young, the brother of Brigham Young, and was by him given into the possession of Joseph F. Smith, nephew of the Prophet Joseph and subsequently President of the Church. He in turn presented it to his son Joseph Fielding Smith, who still (1932) has it in his possession.

In a revelation given January, 1832, Orson Hyde and Samuel H. Smith were called to go on a mission to the eastern country; accordingly they started in March, and traveled and preached the gospel through the states of Ohio, New York, Pennsylvania, Connecticut, Rhode Island, Massachusetts and Maine. They baptized several in Spafford, N. Y., in Boston and Linn, Mass., in Providence, R. I., and in Saco, Maine, preaching much from house to house, as well as in public congregations, and returning to Kirtland in November or December.

During the year 1833, Samuel preached among the churches as he had opportunity, and spent a good portion of his time laboring with his hands.

On the 17th of February, 1834, he was ordained and set apart as one of the high council in Kirtland, in which office he officiated until he went to Missouri in 1838.

August 13th, 1834, he married Mary Bailey, who was born in Bedford, Hillsborough county, New Hampshire, Dec. 20th, 1808.

September 16th, 1835, he was appointed, in company with David Whitmer, as a committee and general agent to act in the name of, and for the Literary firm. In the winter of 1835-6 he chopped cordwood for Lorenzo D. Young.

In 1838 he traveled, in company with his brother Joseph, from Kirtland to Missouri. He passed through the mobbing of that year in Far West and Adam-ondi-Ahman in Missouri, and his family suffered nigh unto death from exposure, as they were driven about by the mob.

He was in the Crooked River battle; and immediately after, by the counsel of President Brigham Young, with Brothers C. C. Rich, B. L. Clapp, L. D. Young and about twenty others, they fled for Illinois by the wilderness, through the north part of Missouri and the southern part of Iowa.

Messengers overtook them and informed them that General Clark had sent a company of fifty well armed men to follow them, with strict orders not to return until they had brought back the company either dead or alive.

When this word came a halt was called, and Samuel asked what they should do in case the enemy overtook them. After a few moments' consultation, the whole company covenanted with uplifted hands to Heaven, that if they were overtaken they would fight till they died, and not a man would fall into the hands of the enemy alive.

They then traveled on ten miles and camped on the edge of some timber on the north side of a four-mile prairie, and they afterwards learned that their enemies camped on the south edge of the same prairie, and would have overtaken them next day had not the Lord sent a heavy snowstorm during the night; and when the brethren arose in the morning, Phineas H. Young remarked that that snowstorm was their salvation. The air was so full of snow that they could hardly find their horses to saddle them, but they soon mounted their horses and continued their journey as fast as they could. The storm was from the north and in their faces; it filled their tracks in a few moments, so that Clark's men could not follow.

It was reported that this company of men, on their return, informed the general that they could not overtake the 'damned Mormons' for they were stopped by a 'damned snowstorm'.

After they had got some distance on their journey, the company divided into three parts, the three brethren named fell in company with Samuel; their provisions gave out, and, after spending several days without food, except eating linden buds and slippery elm bark, they camped upon a small stream, and the company, numbering eight, held a council and appointed Samuel president, that they might receive the word of the Lord in relation to the situation of Joseph the Prophet and those who were with him, also in relation to their families, and what they were to do to obtain food. They all knelt down in a circle, and each one prayed, then the Spirit of the Lord came upon Samuel, and, being filled with the Holy Ghost, he arose and said:—

'Thus saith the Lord—My servant Joseph is not injured, nor any of his brethren that are with him, but they will all be delivered out of the hands of their enemies. Your families are all well, but anxious about you. Let your hearts be comforted, for I, the Lord, will provide food for you on the morrow.'

They went to bed with glad hearts, and arose in the morning and prayed again, and went out two by two to hunt for food. Brother Clapp saw several squirrels and shot at them, but could not hit them. They were only to stay one hour. At the end of the time they all returned except C. C. Rich and Samuel.

Feeling very faint, one of the brethren proposed killing a horse. Brother Clapp said that when Brothers Rich and Samuel returned they would have food, as he never knew the Lord to give a false revelation to his servants; and, while conversing upon the matter, the brethren made their appearance with two silk handkerchiefs tied up full of bread and dried meat.

Samuel's mind was led in a certain direction, and following it they came to an Indian camp. They made known to the Indians by signs that they were hungry; upon this the squaw, with all possible speed, baked them some cakes, and gave each of them two, sending two to each of the six brethren in camp, giving them to understand that she would be glad to send more, but she had but little flour, and her papooses (children) would be hungry.

When they arrived in camp, all felt to rejoice. They formed a circle around the food and asked a blessing upon it. The bread was very good, being shortened with raccoon's oil. After eating they started upon their journey, and obtained food sufficient, so that none perished.

Samuel arrived in Quincy, and was there to assist his father and mother over the river on their arrival, and hired a house for them, into which he also assisted four other families of the saints; and, according to the word of the Lord unto him, his brothers, Joseph and Hyrum, were deliverød, and they arrived in Quincy in April, 1839.

He moved, in company with Don Carlos, on to a farm which he rented near Macombe, McDonough county, where he spent the season farming.

Elders Wilford Woodruff and John Taylor called upon them as they went on their missions to England, and held a meeting with the saints in that place (Oct. 11th, 1839). Don Carlos preached, and was followed by Samuel, who enjoyed much of the Holy Spirit, and bore a strong testimony to the truth of the work of God. He assisted the brethren upon their journey.

In September, 1840, Samuel received the following blessing from under the hands of his father, Joseph Smith, Sen., upon his dying bed:—

'Samuel, you have been a faithful and obedient son. By your faithfulness you have brought many into the church. The Lord has seen your diligence, and you are blessed in that he has never chastised you, but has called you home to rest; and there is a crown laid up for you which shall grow brighter and brighter unto the perfect day.

'When the Lord called you he said, 'Samuel, I have seen thy sufferings, have heard thy cries and beheld thy faithfulnes; thy skirts are clear from the blood of this generation'. Because of these things, I seal upon your head all the blessings which I have heretofore pronounced upon you; and this, my dying blessing, I now seal upon you. Even so. Amen.'

His wife bore to him four children—*viz.*, Susannah B., Mary B., Samuel Harrison Bailey and Lucy B. His wife Mary died January 25th, 1841.

In April, 1841, he was sent on a mission to preach the gospel in Scott and adjoining counties, Illinois. May 3rd, he married Levira Clark, daughter of Gardner and Delecta, born in Livonia, Livingston county, New York, July 30th, 1815. He preached during the summer and fall, his wife remaining with his father-in-law.

In the month of November he returned to Nauvoo, taking his family with him, where he remained during the winter, and also the summer of 1842, during which time he worked mostly for Joseph and harvested in the country.

In the fall of 1842 he removed to his brother William's tavern at Plymouth. In the summer of 1843 he was often at Nauvoo. In the fall he chopped wood, and prepared his farm by making fences and clearing off the timber, preaching the gospel in the vicinity as he had opportunity.

In the spring of 1844 he cultivated his farm, and upon hearing of the imprisonment of his brothers in Carthage jail, he repaired thither on horseback to see them. While on the way he was pursued by the mobocrats; but in consequence of the fleetness of his horse, he was enabled to reach Carthage in safety, from whence he went to Nauvoo in company with the bodies of his martyred brothers, Joseph and Hyrum.

His wife, Levira, bore to him three daughters—*viz.*, Levira A. C., Louisa C. and Lucy J. C.

He was soon after taken sick of bilious fever, and died on the 30th of July, aged 36 years.'

The following extract is from his obituary notice, published in the *Times and Seasons*:—

'The exit of this worthy man, so soon after the *horrible butchery* of his brothers, Joseph and Hyrum, in Carthage jail, is a matter of deep solemnity to the family, as well as a remediless loss to all. If ever there lived a good man upon the earth, Samuel H. Smith was that person. His labors in the church from first to last, carrying glad tidings to the eastern cities, and finally his steadfastness as one of the [eight special] *witnesses* to the *Book of Mormon*, and many saintly traits of virtue, knowledge, temperance, patience, godliness, brotherly kindness and charity, shall be given of him hereafter as a man of God.' "

CHAPTER XVIII

THE GATHERING OF THE TWELVE APOSTLES FROM THE EAST TO NAUVOO: PRELIMINARY MEETINGS LOOKING TO THE SETTLEMENT OF THE QUESTION OF THE PRESIDENCY OF THE CHURCH

"*Thursday, August* 1, 1844.—The brethren of the Twelve arrived in Chicago in the evening, and tarried over night at the Lake Street house.

Political Election in Hancock Co., Illinois.

Friday, 2.—A meeting of the citizens of Hancock county was held at the grove, west of the Temple. Great excitement prevailed through the county. The mob party were determined to elect officers who would screen the murderers of Joseph and Hyrum Smith and exterminate the Mormons.

The meeting resolved to support candidates who were in favor of preserving order and enforcing the laws. The following candidates were agreed upon:—Miner* R. Deming, sheriff; Daniel H. Wells, coroner; George Coulson, commissioner; J. B. Backenstos and A. W. Babbitt, representatives.

Movements of Brigham Young.

President Young and company took stage at seven a. m., for Galena; passed over delightful country, but very bad roads; had to walk over mudholes and bad places, and had to carry poles or rails on their backs to pry out the stage coach.

Movements of Sidney Rigdon.

Saturday, 3.—Elder Sidney Rigdon arrived at Nauvoo from Pittsburgh.

Elders Parley P. Pratt, Willard Richards and George A. Smith invited President Rigdon to meet in council at eight o'clock tomorrow morning, which he agreed to.

*Sometimes spelled "Minor".

The Twelve continued their journey through the day and night by stage. While upon their journey they overtook a company of Norwegians who were traveling with oxteams, and heavily loaded wagons, one of which was stuck fast in the mud, blocking up the road, while several of them were whipping the oxen and bawling to them in the Norwegian language, which seemed to frighten the oxen, but they were unable to move the wagons on.

Brigham Young as Oxteamster—Anecdote.

After sitting and looking at them a moment, President Young got out of the coach and stepped up, and took the whip out of the hands of one of the Norwegians, telling them all to stand out of the way.

He then talked to the oxen in a tongue which was not understood by Norwegians or English, and touching them lightly with the whip, they instantly pulled the wagon out of the mud and continued the journey, much to the astonishment of the Norwegians and the surprise and amusement of the passengers on the stage.

Sunday, 4.—Elders Parley P. Pratt, Willard Richards and George A. Smith met in council, and waited an hour for Elder Rigdon, who excused himself afterwards by saying he was engaged with a lawyer.

Sunday Service at Nauvoo—Sermon of Sidney Rigdon.

10 *a. m.* Meeting at the stand. Elder Rigdon preached from the words, 'For my thoughts are not as your thoughts, neither are your ways my ways, saith the Lord.' He related a vision which he said the Lord had shown him concerning the situation of the church, and said there must be a guardian appointed to build the church up to Joseph, as he had begun it.

He said he was the identical man that the ancient prophets had sung about, wrote and rejoiced over, and that he was sent to do the identical work that had been the theme of all the prophets in every preceding generation. He said that the Lord's ways were not as our ways, for the Lord said he would 'hiss for the fly from the uttermost part of the rivers of Egypt, and for the bee that is in the land of Assyria,' and thereby destroy his enemies; that the time was near at hand when he would see one hundred tons of metal per second thrown at the enemies of God, and that the blood would be to the horses' bridles; and that he expected to walk into the palace of Queen Victoria and lead her out by the nose, when none would have power to say, 'why do ye so?' and if it were not for two or three things which he knew, this people would be utterly destroyed, and not a soul left to tell the tale.

Parley P. Pratt's Comment on Rigdon's Sermon.

Elder Parley P. Pratt, in referring to the remarks of Brother Rigdon, on a subsequent occasion, said, 'I am the identical man the prophets *never* sang nor wrote a word about.'

Public service meeting continued; afternoon: Elders Murdock and Rich preached. Elder William Marks, president of the stake, gave public notice (at the request of Elder Rigdon), that there would be a special meeting of the church at the stand, on Thursday, the 8th inst., for the purpose of choosing a guardian, (President and Trustee).

Appointment Attempted to Choose a "Guardian" for the Church.

Elder Thomas Grover proposed waiting to examine the revelation.

Elder Marks said President Rigdon wanted the meeting on Tuesday, but he put it off till Thursday; that Elder Rigdon was some distance from his family, and wanted to know if this people had anything for him to do; if not, he wanted to go on his way, for there was a people numbering thousands and tens of thousands who would receive him; that he wanted to visit other branches around, but he had come here first.

Elder Rich called upon William Clayton, and said he was dissatisfied with the hurried movement of Elder Rigdon. He considered, inasmuch as the Twelve had been sent for and were soon expected home, the notice for meeting was premature, and it seemed to him a plot laid to take advantage of the situation of the saints.

President Young and his associates arrived at Galena at eight o'clock this morning (August 4th), nearly exhausted with fatigue, having traveled 48 hours without stopping, except to take meals and change horses, distance about 160 miles.

From the *Millennial Star*:—

MARK OF RESPECT SHOWN BY THE LATTER-DAY SAINTS IN LIVERPOOL FOR THE MARTYRS

'On Sunday, August 4th, very numerous congregations attended at the Music Hall, the majority of the saints in deep mourning, whilst the platform or raised gallery, where the priesthood sat, was handsomely decorated with black drapery. We would suggest to the saints generally, as far as their means will allow them, to pay respect to the memory of our lamented brethren.'

Monday, 5.—Elders Parley P. Pratt, Willard Richards, John Taylor, George A. Smith, Amasa Lyman and Bishop Whitney, waited upon Elder Rigdon in the morning. He said he would meet them in council at Elder Taylor's after dinner.

The Agitation of Sidney Rigdon.

They accordingly met in council, and when Elder Rigdon came in, he paced the room and said, 'Gentlemen, you're used up; gentlemen, you are all divided; the anti-Mormons have got you; the brethren are voting every way, some for James, some for Deming, some for Coulson, and some for Bedell; the anti-Mormons have got you, you cannot stay in the county, everything is in confusion, you can do nothing, you lack a great leader, you want a head, and unless you unite upon that head you are blown to the four winds, the anti-Mormons will carry the election—a guardian must be appointed.'

Elder George A. Smith said, 'Brethren, Elder Rigdon is entirely mistaken, there is no division; the brethren are united; the election will be unanimous, and the friends of law and order will be elected by a thousand majority. There is no occasion to be alarmed. President Rigdon is inspiring fears there are no grounds for.

The result was that it was one of the most unanimous elections held in Nauvoo, as there were only five opposition votes polled in the city, and in the county the majority for the law and order candidates was over one thousand, notwithstanding the anti-Mormons smuggled a great many votes from other counties.

Result of the Election.

Elder Rigdon said he did not expect the people to choose a guardian on Thursday, but to have a prayer meeting and interchange of thought and feeling, and warm up each other's hearts.

Jesse Price made the following affidavit:—

AFFIDAVIT OF JESSE PRICE BEFORE AARON JOHNSON—MURDEROUS INTENTIONS OF WILLIAM LAW

'State of Illinois, County of Hancock, ss.

On the 5th day of August, 1844, personally appeared before me, Aaron Johnson, justice of the peace in and for said county, Jesse Price; and after being duly sworn according to law, deposeth and saith, that on or about the 18th of April, 1844, in the city of Nauvoo, county aforesaid, William Law said, 'I put pistols in my pockets one night, and went to Joseph Smith's house, determined to blow his infernal brains out, but I could not get the opportunity to shoot him then, but I am determined I will shoot him the first opportunity, and you will see blood and thunder and devastation in this place, but I shall not be here;' and deponent saith not further.'

The following letter was sent to Dr. Richards:—

LETTER OF JOSEPH M. COLE—ELECTION RETURNS THREATENED

'La Harpe, August 5, 1844.

Brother Richards,—I hasten to inform you that intelligence has arrived in this place today, by several persons, that the mobocrats at Carthage have concocted a plan to intercept the returns of the election at Nauvoo, and destroy them before they arrive at Carthage. The information is of such a nature that I deemed it necessary that you should be informed of the same, that you may act accordingly.

Respectfully,

JOSEPH M. COLE.'

President Young and the Apostles with him went on board the steamer *St. Croix* at Galena, for Nauvoo. They started in the afternoon.

Elder Kimball recorded the following dream:—

Elder Heber C. Kimball's Dream.

'I dreamed of speaking before a large congregation on the policy of the nation and the policy of our religion. I said that Joseph the Prophet had laid the foundation, and we would have to carry out his measures. Joseph was present, and heard all I said and sanctioned it. All seemed perfectly natural.'

Tuesday, 6.—Elders Parley P. Pratt, Willard Richards, John Taylor, George A. Smith and Bishop Whitney met in council at Elder Taylor's.

Activities of Elder Willard Richards.

From the death of Joseph until the arrival of President Brigham Young and the Twelve, Elder Willard Richards was the principal counselor of the saints in Nauvoo, and had scarcely a moment's rest. He answered the calls and inquiries of hundreds of the brethren, and was engaged every day until a late hour, or until exhaustion compelled him to lie down.

The following is extracted from Elder Woodruff's Journal:—

EXCERPT

'We (the brethren of the Twelve returning to Nauvoo) stopped at various places while going down the Mississippi, among others, the town of Burlington, after which we prepared our minds to once more behold the city of Nauvoo and embrace our families and friends.

We were landed at the upper stone house at eight in the evening, and were welcomed with joy by all the citizens we met. We hired a coach, and I accompanied my brethren to their families, after which I was conveyed to my own, and truly felt to rejoice to once more meet with my wife, children and friends. Thus it is with me, I have spent but one summer either at home or with the body of the church for the last ten years, as my lot has been cast abroad in the vineyard most of the time.

When we landed in the city a deep gloom seemed to rest over the city of Nauvoo, which we never experienced before.'

Majority of the Twelve in Council—Nauvoo.

Wednesday, 7.—Elders Brigham Young, Heber C. Kimball, Parley P. Pratt, Orson Pratt, Willard Richards, Wilford Woodruff, George A. Smith and Lyman Wight met in council with Elder Taylor at his house. They found him recovering from his wounds received at the massacre of the Prophets.

The Twelve felt to rejoice at having the privilege of again meeting in council together, after having passed through such trying scenes, and to be welcomed by the saints who considered it very providential for the Twelve to arrive at this particular juncture, when their minds were agitated, their hearts sorrowful, and darkness seemed to cloud their path, feeling like sheep without a shepherd, their beloved Prophet having been taken away.

4 p. m.—Meeting of the Twelve Apostles, high council and high priests at the Seventies' Hall.

Meeting of Church Authorities at Nauvoo.

President William Marks prayed.

President Brigham Young called upon President Rigdon to make a statement to the church concerning his message to the saints, and the vision and revelation he had received.

President Rigdon said:—

'The object of my mission is to visit the saints and offer myself to them as a guardian. I had a vision at Pittsburgh, June 27th. This was presented to my mind not as an open vision, but rather a continuation of the vision mentioned in the *Book of Doctrine and Covenants.**

The Proposition of Elder Rigdon to Become "Guardian" to the Church.

It was shown to me that this church must be built up to Joseph, and that all the blessings we receive must come through him. I have been ordained a spokesman to Joseph, and I must come to Nauvoo and see that the church is governed in a proper manner. Joseph sustains the same relationship to this church as he has always done. No man can be the successor of Joseph.

The kingdom is to be built up to Jesus Christ through Joseph; there must be revelation still. The martyred Prophet is still the head of this church; every quorum should stand as you stood in your washings and consecrations. I have been consecrated a spokesman to Joseph, and I was commanded to speak for him. The church is not disorganized though our head is gone.

We may have a diversity of feelings on this matter. I have been called to be a spokesman unto Joseph, and I want to build up the church unto him; and if the people want me to sustain this place, I

*Undoubtedly Elder Rigdon referred to the continuation of the "Vision" of The Three Glories, now published in section lxxvi of the current edition of the *Doctrine and Covenants*, though what the connection could be is difficult to see.

want it upon the principle that every individual shall acknowledge it for himself.

I propose to be a guardian to the people; in this I have discharged my duty and done what God has commanded me, and the people can please themselves whether they accept me or not.'

President Brigham Young said:—

'I do not care who leads the church, even though it were Ann Lee; but one thing I must know, and that is what God says about it. I have the keys and the means of obtaining the mind of God on the subject.

Attitude of Brigham Young—The Twelve Hold the "Keys".

I know there are those in our midst who will seek the lives of the Twelve as they did the lives of Joseph and Hyrum. We shall ordain others and give the fulness of the priesthood, so that if we are killed the fulness of the priesthood may remain.

Joseph conferred upon our heads all the keys and powers belonging to the Apostleship which he himself held before he was taken away, and no man or set of men can get between Joseph and the Twelve in this world or in the world to come.

How often has Joseph said to the Twelve, 'I have laid the foundation and you must build thereon, for upon your shoulders the kingdom rests.'

The Twelve, as a quorum, will not be permitted to tarry here long; they will go abroad and bear off the kingdom to the nations of the earth, and baptize the people faster than mobs can kill them off. I would like, were it my privilege, to take my valise and travel and preach till we had a people gathered who would be true.

My private feelings would be to let the affairs of men and women alone, only go and preach and baptize them into the kingdom of God; yet, whatever duty God places upon me, in his strength I intend to fulfill it.

I want to see this people, with the various quorums of the priesthood, assembled together in special conference on Thursday* next at 10 a. m.'

Which was carried unanimously by vote."

*In the previous publication of this historical item (*Millennial Star*, vol. xxv, p. 216) the language is "I want to see this people with their various quorums of the priesthood assembled together in special conference on *Tuesday* next." This would have brought the meeting on Tuesday the 13th of August. Evidently the word "Tuesday" was a misprint and should have been, as changed above in the text, "Thursday", which was the day following the council meeting and as a matter of fact it was the next day following, August 8th, that the general public meeting of the church with the quorums assembled in their order to settle this matter of the presiding council in the church that the meeting was held. B. H. R.

CHAPTER XIX

THE SETTLEMENT OF CHURCH LEADERSHIP—THE TWELVE APOSTLES ACCEPTED AS THE PRESIDENCY OF THE CHURCH, BRIGHAM YOUNG AT THEIR HEAD

"*Thursday, August 8th,* 1844.—At a special meeting of the Church of Jesus Christ of Latter-day Saints held in Nauvoo, at 10 a. m. on Thursday, August 8, 1844, by the request of President William Marks, (who was then presiding over that stake of Zion) to choose a guardian, or President and Trustee, Sidney Rigdon took his position in a wagon, about two rods in front of the stand, and harangued the saints for about one and a half hours, upon choosing a guardian for the church. The meeting was then dismissed, when President Brigham Young gave out an appointment for the brethren to assemble at 2 p. m.

Special Public Meeting of the Church.

At the appointed time the brethren came together. Present, of the Twelve, Brigham Young, Heber C. Kimball, Parley P. Pratt, Orson Pratt, Willard Richards, Wilford Woodruff, George A. Smith.* The several quorums were organized on and around the stand according to order.

THE REMARKS OF PRESIDENT YOUNG IN BEHALF OF THE CLAIM OF THE TWELVE TO LEAD THE CHURCH IN THE ABSENCE OF THE FIRST PRESIDENCY

The meeting being opened, President Brigham Young arose and said:—

*It will be observed that there were seven of the Apostles present, a majority of the quorum. Of the absent ones, John Taylor was confined to his home, not yet recovered from his wounds, Orson Hyde, John E. Page, and Wm. Smith had not yet arrived in Nauvoo; and Lyman Wight was still in the east.

'Attention all! This congregation makes me think of the days of King Benjamin, the multitude being so great that all could not hear. I request the brethren not to have any feelings for being convened this afternoon, for it is necessary; we want you all to be still and give attention, that all may hear. Let none complain because of the situation of the congregation, we will do the best we can.

For the first time in my life, for the first time in your lives, for the first time in the kingdom of God in the 19th century, without a Prophet at our head, do I step forth to act in my calling in connection with the Quorum of the Twelve, as Apostles of Jesus Christ unto this generation—Apostles whom God has called by revelation through the Prophet Joseph, who are ordained and anointed to bear off the keys of the kingdom of God in all the world.

This people have hitherto walked by sight and not by faith. You have had the Prophet in your midst. Do you all understand? You have walked by sight and without much pleading to the Lord to know whether things were right or not.

Heretofore you have had a Prophet as the mouth of the Lord to speak to you, but he has sealed his testimony with his blood, and now, for the first time, are you called to walk by faith, not by sight.

The first position I take in behalf of the Twelve and the people is, to ask a few questions. I ask the Latter-day Saints: do you, as individuals, at this time, want to choose a Prophet or a guardian? Inasmuch as our Prophet and Patriarch are taken from our midst, do you want some one to guard, to guide and lead you through this world into the kingdom of God, or not? All that want some person to be a guardian or a Prophet, a spokesman or something else, signify it by raising the right hand. (No votes).

When I came to this stand I had peculiar feelings and impressions. The faces of this people seem to say, we want a shepherd to guide and lead us through this world. *All that want to draw away a party from the church after them, let them do it if they can, but they will not prosper.*

If any man thinks he has influence among this people to lead away a party, let him try it, and he will find out that there is power with the Apostles which will carry them off victorious through all the world, and build up and defend the church and kingdom of God.

What do the people want? I feel as though I wanted the privilege to weep and mourn for thirty days at least, then rise up, shake myself, and tell the people what the Lord wants of them; although my heart is too full of mourning to launch forth into business transactions and the organization of the church, I feel compelled this day to step forth in the discharge of those duties God has placed upon me.

I now wish to speak of the organization of the Church of Jesus Christ of Latter-day Saints. If the church is organized, and you want to know how it is organized, I will tell you. I know your feelings—do you want me to tell your feelings?

Here is President Rigdon, who was counselor to Joseph. I ask, where are Joseph and Hyrum? They are gone beyond the veil; and if Elder Rigdon wants to act as his counselor, he must go beyond the veil where he is.

There has been much said about President Rigdon being President of the Church, and leading the people, being the head, etc. Brother Rigdon has come 1,600 miles to tell you what he wants to do for you. If the people want President Rigdon to lead them they may have him; but I say unto you that the Quorum of the Twelve have the keys of the kingdom of God in all the world.

The Twelve are appointed by the finger of God. Here is Brigham, have his knees ever faltered? Have his lips ever quivered? Here is Heber and the rest of the Twelve, an independent body who have the keys of the priesthood—the keys of the kingdom of God to deliver to all the world: this is true, so help me God. They stand next to Joseph, and are as the First Presidency of the Church.

I do not know whether my enemies will take my life or not, and I do not care, for I want to be with the man I love.

You cannot fill the office of a prophet, seer and revelator: God must do this. You are like children without a father and sheep without a shepherd. You must not appoint any man at our head; if you should, the Twelve must ordain him. You cannot appoint a man at our head; but if you do want any other man or men to lead you, take them and we will go our way to build up the kingdom in all the world.

I know who are Joseph's friends, and who are his enemies. I know where the keys of the kingdom are, and where they will eternally be. You cannot call a man to be a prophet; you cannot take Elder Rigdon and place him above the Twelve; if so, he must be ordained by them.

I tell you there is an overanxiety to hurry matters here. You cannot take any man and put him at the head; you would scatter the saints to the four winds, you would sever the priesthood. So long as we remain as we are, the heavenly Head is in constant cooperation with us; and if you go out of that course, God will have nothing to do with you.

Again, perhaps some think that our beloved Brother Rigdon would not be honored, would not be looked to as a friend; but if he does right and remains faithful he will not act against our counsel nor we against his, but act together, and we shall be as one.

I again repeat, no man can stand at our head, except God reveals it from the heavens.

I have spared no pains to learn my lesson of the kingdom in this world and in the eternal worlds; and if it were not so, I could go and live in peace; but for the gospel and your sakes I shall stand in my place. We are liable to be killed all the day long. You have never lived by faith.

Brother Joseph, the Prophet, has laid the foundation for a great work, and we will build upon it; you have never seen the quorums built one upon another. There is an almighty foundation laid, and we can build a kingdom such as there never was in the world: we can build a kingdom faster than satan can kill the saints off.

What do you want? Do you want a patriarch for the whole church? To this we are perfectly willing. If Brother Samuel H. Smith had been living, it would have been his right and privilege; but he is dead, he is gone to Joseph and Hyrum, he is out of the reach of bullets and spears, and he can waft himself with his brothers, his friends and the saints.

Do you want a patriarch? Here is brother William [Smith] left; here is Uncle John Smith, uncle to the Prophet Joseph left; it is their right. The right of patriarchal blessings belongs to Joseph's family.

Do you want a Trustee-in-Trust? Has there been a bishop who has stood in his lot yet? What is his business? To take charge of the temporal affairs, so that the Twelve and the elders may go on their business. Joseph condescended to do their business for them. Joseph condescended to offer himself for president of the United States, and it was a great condescension.

Do you want a spokesman? Here are Elder Rigdon, Brother Amasa Lyman [whom Joseph expected to take as a counselor] and myself. Do you want the church properly organized, or do you want a spokesman to be chief cook and bottle-washer? Elder Rigdon claims to be spokesman to the Prophet. Very well, he was; but can he now act in that office? If he wants now to be a spokesman to the Prophet, he must go to the other side of the veil, for the Prophet is there, but Elder Rigdon is here. Why will Elder Rigdon be a fool? Who knows anything of the priesthood, or of the organization of the kingdom of God.* I am plain.

*It is rather singular that in the remarks of President Young and by none of the leading elders who spoke on that eventful 8th of August, 1844, that no adequate unfolding of the relationship of the respective presiding councils of the church was given. In the above I follow the punctuation as it stands in the records of the church, that is, as will be seen, the sentence, "Who knows anything of the priesthood, or of the organization of the kingdom of God", ends with a period. I wonder if the speaker's intent was not to make of it a question (?) For so far as the speeches are concerned there really was no adequate relationship of presiding councils of the priesthood given. It is quite possible that they had not been studied by the elders from the viewpoint of the relationship of these respective councils. In section cvii of the *Doctrine and Covenants*, which is *par excellence* the revelation on priesthood of the church, it is pointed out that "of necessity there are presidents, or presiding officers growing out of, or appointed from among those who are ordained to the several offices in these two priesthoods [Melchizedek and Aaronic. I refer only to the Melchizedek].

(1). "Of the Melchizedek priesthood three Presiding High Priests chosen by

Does this church want it as God organized it? Or do you want to clip the power of the priesthood, and let those who have the keys of the priesthood go and build up the kingdom in all the world, wherever the people will hear them?

If there is a spokesman, if he is a king and priest, let him go and build up a kingdom unto himself; that is his right and it is the right of many here, but the Twelve are at the head of it.

I want to live on the earth and spread truth through all the world. You saints of latter-days want things right. If 10,000 men rise up and say they have the Prophet Joseph Smith's shoes, I know they are imposters. In the priesthood you have a right to build up a kingdom, if you know how the church is organized.

Now, if you want Sidney Rigdon or William Law to lead you, or anybody else, you are welcome to them; but I tell you, in the name of the Lord that no man can put another between the Twelve and the Prophet Joseph. Why? Because Joseph was their file leader, and he has committed into their hands the keys of the kingdom in this last dispensation, for all the world; don't put a thread between the priesthood and God.

I will ask, who has stood next to Joseph and Hyrum? I have, and I will stand next to him. We have a head, and that head is the Apostleship, the spirit and power of Joseph, and we can now begin to see the necessity of that Apostleship.

Brother Rigdon was at his side—not above. No man has a right to counsel the Twelve but Joseph Smith. Think of these things. You cannot appoint a prophet; but if you let the Twelve remain and act in their place, the keys of the kingdom are with them and they can manage the affairs of the church and direct all things aright.

Now, all this does not lessen the character of President Rigdon; let him magnify his calling, and Joseph will want him beyond the veil—

the body, appointed and ordained to that office and upheld by the confidence, faith, and prayer of the church, form a quorum of the Presidency of the Church.

(2) "The Twelve traveling councilors are called to be the Twelve Apostles, or special witnesses of the name of Christ in all the world. * * * They form a quorum equal in authority and power to the Three Presidents previously mentioned.

(3) "The Seventy are also called to preach the gospel and to be especial witnesses unto the Gentiles and in all the world. * * * And they form a quorum equal in authority to that of the Twelve special witnesses or Apostles just named" (*Doctrine and Covenants*, sec. cvii).

It is not necessary to quote further, but it stands to reason that if for any cause the First Presidency goes out of existence, the council which is next to the first and equal in authority and power to it—the second council upon which presiding responsibility rests—is the Council of the Twelve. Hence the Council of the Twelve Apostles logically and according to the constitutional organization of the church, becomes the *de facto* presiding authority of the church. But this was not at the time definitely pointed out.

let him be careful what he does, lest that thread which binds us together is cut asunder. May God bless you all.'*

(Much more was said by President Young, but not written).

SPEECH OF AMASA M. LYMAN†

Amasa Lyman said:—

'I do not rise to electioneer. I am gratified with the open, frank and plain exposition of President Young. He has seen the relation I bear to my deceased brother [i. e. Joseph Smith]. I never did conceive it gave me a precedence to go before the Twelve.

I do not make exceptions to anything he has said. I believe there is no power, or officer, or means wanted to carry on the work, but

*It was while delivering this speech that a transformation of President Brigham Young is said to have occurred, that is to say in voice, person and manner. He seemed to be the personification of Joseph Smith, on the testimony of many who were present. The late President George Q. Cannon of this event said:

"If Joseph had arisen from the dead and again spoken in their hearing, the effect could not have been more startling than it was to many present at that meeting; it was the voice of Joseph himself; and not only was it the voice of Joseph which was heard, but it seemed in the eyes of the people as if it were the very person of Joseph which stood before them. A more wonderful and miraculous event than was wrought that day in the presence of that congregation we never heard of. The Lord gave his people a testimony that left no room for doubt as to who was the man chosen to lead them" (*Life of Brigham Young*, Tullidge, 1877, p. 115).

In the Journal of Elder Wm. C. Staines of the date of August 8, 1844, the following statement is recorded: "Brigham Young said: 'I will tell you who your leaders or guardians will be—the Twelve—I at their head.' This was with the voice like the voice of the Prophet Joseph. I thought it was he, and so did thousands who heard it. This was very satisfactory to the people, and a vote was taken to sustain the Twelve in their office, which with a few dissenting voices, was passed."

Wilford Woodruff described the event as follows: "If I had not seen him with my own eyes, there is no one that could have convinced me that it was not Joseph Smith, and anyone can testify to this who was acquainted with these two men" (*Deseret Evening News*, March 12, 1892).

†Amasa M. Lyman here making this speech had been ordained an Apostle (August 20, 1842) during a brief suspension of Elder Orson Pratt from the Quorum of the Twelve owing to a misunderstanding between Elder Pratt and President Joseph Smith; but on the reconciliation of Elders Pratt and Smith and the former's reinstatement into the Quorum of the Twelve, Elder Lyman had been taken by President Smith into the First Presidency (*History of the Church*, Period I, vol. v, pp. 255-6). However he was never formally presented to the people in that capacity, but meantime he had continued to act with the leaders of the church—the Apostles—and a few days following this 8th of August meeting, namely on the 12th of August at a council of the Twelve Apostles, he was received by vote as a member of the Quorum of the Twelve (See *History of Brigham Young, Ms.*, August 12, 1844, p. 3).

what is in the Twelve. I am satisfied that no man can carry on the work, but the power that is in the Twelve, as has been stated.

There is one thing to secure the salvation of this people, and that is not in union alone, it is for you to know the right and be united—it has been presented to you by President Young, and I will back him up. All I design to do is to redeem my pledge.

President Young has stood next to the Prophet Joseph, with the Twelve, and I have stood next to them, and I will stand next to them. I have been at the back of Joseph Smith, and will be at the back of the Twelve forever, and then we will be saved.

There is no need of a President, we have a head here. What is that head? The Quorum of the Twelve Apostles are the head. We now see the necessity of the Apostleship.

I might rise up as well as any other man to ask for the Presidency, but I could not do it without endangering my salvation. This is the power that turns the key to bestow salvation through all the land, in the way that Joseph commenced it, the first one called to do the same in all the world. If Joseph Smith had any power to bear off the kingdom of God, the Twelve have the same.

I could not advocate a choosing of a President, and myself a candidate; so then you know the place I occupy is, to stand to the Twelve the same as the Twelve did to Joseph, either on one side or the other. I do not want to go before them or to fall asleep. I want to see the kingdom roll forth by our united faith and efforts.'

President Rigdon called upon W. W. Phelps to speak in his behalf, as he could not speak.

SPEECH OF ELDER W. W. PHELPS—NO SUPPORT TO SIDNEY RIGDON

W. W. Phelps arose and said: —

'With the knowledge that I have I cannot suppose but that this congregation will act aright this day. I believe enough has been said to prepare the minds of the people to act.

I have known many of them for 14 years, and I have always known them to submit with deference to the authorities of the church. I have seen the elders of Israel and the people—take their lives in their hands and go without purse or scrip in winter and in summer. I have seen them prepare for war, and ready to pour out their hearts' blood, and that is an evidence that they will walk by counsel.

I am happy to see this little lake of faces, and to see the same spirit and disposition manifested here today, as it was the day after the bloody tragedy, when Joseph and Hyrum Smith were brought home dead to this city. Then you submitted to the law's slow delay, and handed the matter over to God; and I see the same thing today—

you are now determined as one man to sustain the authorities of the church, and I am happy that the men who were on Joseph's right and left hand submit themselves to the authority of the priesthood.

I have feelings about this, especially for President Rigdon, and I want to say that there is a quorum that the Twelve belong to, and that the people will receive an endowment. I brought President Rigdon into that quorum, and he received in part the blessings. I could not bear the thought of President Rigdon going into the world without his endowment. He did obtain part, and I hope he will submit.

I want Brother Amasa to stand on the side of the Twelve, and they are wanted there still—let them go on and sustain them in that high office. You cannot put in a guardian of the church.

We have hitherto walked by sight, and if a man wanted to know anything he had only to go to Brother Joseph. Joseph has gone, but he has not left us comfortless.

I want to say that Brother Joseph came and enlightened me two days after he was buried. He came the same as when he was alive, and in a moment appeared to me in his own house. He said, 'Tell the drivers to drive on.' I asked if the building was on wheels? He said, 'certainly'. I spoke, and away it went. We drove all round the hills and valleys. He then told the drivers to drive on over the river into Iowa. I told him Devil Creek was before us. He said, 'Drive over Devil Creek; I don't care for Devil Creek or any other creek;' and we did so. Then I awoke.

There is a combination of persons in this city who are in continual intercourse with William and Wilson Law, who are at the bottom of the matter to destroy all that stand for Joseph, and there are persons now in this city who are only wanting power to murder all the persons that still hold on to Joseph; but let us go ahead and build up the Temple, and then you will be endowed. When the Temple is completed all the honorable mothers in Israel will be endowed, as well as the elders.

If you want to do right, uphold the Twelve. If they die, I am willing to die with them; but do your duty and you will be endowed. I will sustain the Twelve as long as I have breath.

When Joseph was going away he said he was going to die, and I said I was willing to die with him; but as I am now alive, as a lawyer in Israel, I am determined to live.

I want you all to recollect that Joseph and Hyrum have only been removed from the earth, and they now counsel and converse with the Gods beyond the reach of powder and ball.'

REMARKS OF ELDER PARLEY P. PRATT

Parley P. Pratt said:—

'What has been said has been well said. If there are men here who are our enemies, I'll tell you when they will cease to be here: they will be here while you will deal with them. If I exchange property or deal with men, I do it with those whom I know to be faithful.

If there are wicked men here, it is because we support them. Stop dealing with them, and they will go away. Will I support them? No, I would deal with all honest men whom I know to be such.

I am willing to do good to all men, especially to the household of faith. Our enemies will cease to dwell here when you cease to deal with them. Mobs and wicked men will cease when you cease to support them.

I know we can all live and be happy too, when we deal with honest men. If a man wants a doctor or a lawyer, he will send directly for the worst man he can find.

I would die a natural death sooner than I would have a wicked doctor to help me off. I would go without sueing all the days of my life before I would go to a lawyer to sue. I will not say anything about the merchants, because you all know them.

PRESIDENT BRIGHAM YOUNG'S SECOND SPEECH

President Brigham Young again arose and said:—

'There is more business than can be done this afternoon, but we can accomplish all we want to have done without calling this convention of the whole church. I am going to present to you the leading items.

I do not ask you to take my counsel or advice alone, but every one of you act for yourselves; but if Brother Rigdon is the person you want to lead you, vote for him, but not unless you intend to follow him and support him as you did Joseph. Do not say so without you mean to take his counsel hereafter.

And I would say the same for the Twelve, don't make a covenant to support them unless you intend to abide by their counsel; and if they do not counsel you as you please, don't turn round and oppose them.

I want every man, before he enters into a covenant, to know what he is going to do; but we want to know if this people will support the priesthood in the name of Israel's God. If you say you will, do so.

We want men appointed to take charge of the business that did lay on the shoulders of Joseph. Let me say to you that this kingdom will spread more than ever.

The Twelve have the power now—the seventies, the elders and all of you can have power to go and build up the kingdom in the name of Israel's God. Nauvoo will not hold all the people that will come into the kingdom.

We want to build the Temple, so as to get our endowment; and if we do our best, and satan will not let us build it, we will go into the wilderness and we will receive the endowment, for we will receive an endowment anyhow.

Will you abide our counsel? I again say, my soul for any man's, if they will abide our counsel, that they will go right into heaven. We have all the signs and tokens to give to the porter at the door, and he will let us in.

I will ask you as quorums, Do you want Brother Rigdon to stand forward as your leader, your guide, your spokesman. President Rigdon wants me to bring up the other question first, and that is, Does the church want, and is it their only desire to sustain the Twelve as the First Presidency of this people?

Here are the Apostles, the *Bible*, the *Book of Mormon*, the *Doctrine and Covenants*—they are written on the tablet of my heart. If the church want the Twelve to stand as the head, the First Presidency of the Church, and at the head of this kingdom in all the world, stand next to Joseph, walk up into their calling, and hold the keys of this kingdom, every man, every woman, every quorum is now put in order, and you are now the sole controllers of it.

All that are in favor of this, in all the congregation of the saints, manifest it by holding up the right hand. (There was a universal vote). If there are any of the contrary mind, every man and every woman who does not want the Twelve to preside, lift up your hands in like manner. (No hands up). This supersedes the other question, and trying it by quorums.

We feel as though we could take Brother Rigdon in our bosom along with us; we want such men as Brother Rigdon. He has been sent away by Brother Joseph to build up a kingdom; let him keep the instructions and calling; let him raise up a mighty kingdom in Pittsburgh, and we will lift up his hands to Almighty God. I think we may have a printing office and a gathering there. If the devil still tries to kill us he will have enough to do.

The next is President Marks. Our feelings are to let him stand as president of the stake, as heretofore. We can build the Temple, etc.

You did not know who you had amongst you. Joseph so loved this people that he gave his life for them; Hyrum loved his brother and this people unto death. Joseph and Hyrum have given their lives for the church. But very few knew Joseph's character; he loved you unto death—you did not know it until after his death: he has now sealed his testimony with his blood.

If the Twelve had been here we would not have seen him given up—he should not have been given up. He was in your midst, but you did not know him; he has been taken away, for the people are not worthy of him.

The world is wide. I can preach in England, Ireland, Scotland, France, Germany, etc. I can preach in all the world, and the devils cannot find us. I'll swear to you I will not be given up.

There is much to be done. You have men among you who sleep with one eye open. The foundation is laid by our Prophet, and we will build thereon; no other foundation can be laid but that which is laid, and we will have our endowment, if the Lord will.

As the authorities do not want us to do military duty, don't do it. If it is necessary, my neck is ready for the knife; as for myself, I am determined to build up the kingdom of God: and by and by there will be a gleaning of grapes, and it may be said, 'To your tents, O Israel'.

We can build on the foundation that was laid by the Prophet. Joseph has finished his work, and all the devils in hell and all the mobbers on earth could not take his life until he had accomplished his work. God said, I will put a veil over his eyes and lead him up to the slaughter like a sheep to be killed, for the people are not worthy of him, though God loves this people.

Let no man suppose that the kingdom is rent from you; that it is not organized. If all the quorums of the church were slain, except the high priests, they would rise up with the keys of the kingdom, and have the powers of the priesthood upon them, and build up the kingdom, and the devil cannot help himself.

You can go to a healthy country, buy the land, and don't let a cursed scoundrel get in your midst. Let there be good men, good women, and whenever a man comes with a wheelbarrow-full of goods don't sell him land, don't let him a house, nor buy of him.

Suppose we had ten thousand such places, and increasing in greatness, perfectly free from these poor devils, we should feel better than we do now. Let us all be humble and get our endowments—all be humble, industrious and prudent, what sort of a kingdom would it be? The foundation is laid for more than we can think or talk about today.

Is it the will of this congregation that they will be tithed until the Temple is finished, as they have hitherto been? If so, signify it by the uplifted hand. (The vote was unanimous).

The men will act that have never acted before, and they will have the power and authority to do it. Is it the mind of this congregation to loose the hands of the Twelve, and enable us to go and preach to all the world? We want to know the feelings of the people. Is it your will to support the Twelve in all the world in their missions? (The congregation sustained this question by a unanimous vote). Will you leave it to the Twelve to dictate about the finances of the church? and will it be the mind of this people that the Twelve teach what will be the duties of the bishops in handling the affairs of the church? I want this, because twelve men can do it just as well as calling this immense congregation together at any other time. (A unanimous vote).

We shall have a patriarch, and the right is in the family of Joseph Smith, his brothers, his sons, or some one of his relations. Here is Uncle John, he has been ordained a patriarch. Brother Samuel would have taken the office if he had been alive; it would have been his right;

the right is in Uncle John, or one of his brothers (read sec. iii, par. 17, *Doctrine and Covenants**). I know that it would have belonged to Samuel. But as it is, if you leave it to the Twelve, they will wait until they know who is the man. Will you leave it to the Twelve, and they dictate the matter. (A unanimous vote). I know it will be let alone for the present.

I feel to bring up Brother Rigdon; we are of one mind with him and he with us. Will this congregation uphold him in the place he occupies by the prayer of faith and let him be one with us and we with him. (Unanimous). The Twelve will dictate and see to other matters. There will be a committee for the Temple; and now let men stand to their posts and be faithful.'

Adjourned to Oct. 6, Conference.
Benediction by Elder Parley P. Pratt.

COMMENT OF THE CHURCH HISTORIANS WHO COMPILED THIS DATA OF THE CHURCH HISTORY

Thus closes the History of Joseph Smith, the great Prophet, Seer and Revelator, whom God has chosen to lay the foundation for the establishment of his church and kingdom upon the earth in the last dispensation and fulness of times.

He performed as great and mighty a work as any man that ever tabernacled in the flesh, save Jesus only. His mission lasted nearly seventeen years; from the time he received the plates from the angel Moroni on the 22nd day of Sept., 1827, to the 27th of June, 1844, when he was martyred in Carthage Jail, under the pledged protection of the governor of Illinois, Thomas Ford.

The History of Joseph Smith is now before the world, and we are satisfied that a history more correct in its details than this was never published. To have it strictly correct, the greatest possible pains have been taken by the historians and clerks engaged in the work. They were eye and ear witnesses of nearly all the transactions recorded in this history, most of which were reported as they transpired, and, where they were

*This would be the Nauvoo edition of the *Doctrine and Covenants*. In the current edition the passage is found in sec. cvii:39.

not personally present, they have had access to those who were.

Moreover, since the death of the Prophet Joseph, the history has been carefully revised under the strict inspection of President Brigham Young, and approved of by him.

TESTIMONY OF THE CHURCH HISTORIANS

We, therefore, hereby bear our testimony to all the world, unto whom these words shall come, that the History of Joseph Smith is true, and is one of the most authentic histories ever written.

We were, much of the time, associated with him in his travels and ministry since he organized the Church of Christ upon the earth. He labored diligently for the salvation and benefit of the human family. He ever taught and practiced, in public and in private, virtue, holiness and truth.

His brother Hyrum was martyred at the same time with him. He, also, was a great and good man, a wise counselor to his brother Joseph and a Prophet and Patriarch in the church, and the spirit of his office was with him up to the time of his death.

They were slain for the word of God and the testimony of Jesus Christ, and the people and nation who have persecuted them unto death and shed their blood will assuredly find their words fulfilled upon their heads, even in speedy and certain destruction, as were the words of the Savior fulfilled upon the Jewish nation for stoning and killing the Prophets and shedding the blood of the Lord's Anointed.

GEORGE A. SMITH,
WILFORD WOODRUFF, } Historians."

V

EXCERPTS FROM THE MANUSCRIPT HISTORY OF BRIGHAM YOUNG FROM AUGUST 9, 1844 TO OCTOBER 8, 1848

Explanation

PART V deals with the actual beginning of the authorized administration by the Twelve Apostles in their Presidency of the Church; and gives the detail of their administration from August 9, 1844 to December 5, 1847, when Brigham Young was nominated by the Council of the Twelve Apostles near Winter Quarters; and by October 8, 1848, the nomination had been presented and unanimously sustained by all the major divisions of the church. The subject matter of the period is taken almost exclusively from *The History of Brigham Young, (Ms.)*

This period officially shows the administration of the Quorum of the Twelve acting as the Presidency of the Church, and vindicates that Presidency for harmony and effectiveness. It has never before been published and will be found a rich mine of original information that will be of high value to the church for all time, in that it will constitute an appeal to ultimate authority for events of this period, and a vindication of the men who functioned in the Presidency of the Church during that time.

The main features covered in the period are the church life in Nauvoo; the completion of the Temple with the administration of the sacred ordinances therein; the establishment of the quorums of the priesthood, especially the high priests and the seventies. It may be said that it is especially a period of instruction for the ministry of the church and important in developing the seventies' organization therein. The period also deals with the exodus of the church from Nauvoo, the journey to the Missouri frontiers, thence westward over the plains and the mountains to the Salt Lake Valley; the beginning of settlements there and the installation of the second First Presidency of the Church—Brigham Young, Heber C. Kimball and Willard Richards.

CHAPTER XX

EVENTS IMMEDIATELY FOLLOWING THE SUSTAINING OF THE QUORUM OF THE TWELVE—AS THE PRESIDENCY OF THE CHURCH—RESUMPTION OF CHURCH ACTIVITIES—PERPETUATION OF THE POLICY OF THE PROPHET

"*Friday, August* 9, 1844.—I met in council with Elders Heber C. Kimball, Parley P. Pratt, Orson Pratt, Wilford Woodruff, Willard Richards, George A. Smith, Amasa M. Lyman and eleven others at my house.

Administrative Acts Following the Appointment of the Apostles to the Presidency.

On motion of Elder Heber C. Kimball, Bishop Newel K. Whitney and George Miller were appointed to settle the affairs of the late Trustee-in-Trust, Joseph Smith, and be prepared to enter upon their duties as Trustees of the Church of Jesus Christ of Latter-day Saints.

The Nauvoo House Committee were instructed to wind up their business and report.

Patriarch John Smith [local] had the privilege of appointing another president at Macedonia in his stead and locating in Nauvoo at his option.*

Conversation ensued relative to the affairs and liabilities of the church and the building of the Nauvoo House.

Saturday, 10.—The following is an extract from the Minutes of the Nauvoo City Council:

'City council met at 9 a. m. and subscribed about $80.00 for the

*This was Patriarch "Uncle" John Smith, from now on prominent in the history of the church, and who was made Presiding Patriarch to the whole church Dec 24, 1847. He was paternal uncle of the Prophet Joseph.

Heretofore in this volume the footnotes are from various writers. Those supplied by the present editor up to now have been signed with his initials. Hereafter, as he supplies all the footnotes, they will not be so signed.

aid of the police. Councilors (city) Brigham Young, Heber C. Kimball, George A. Smith and Hyrum Kimball in addition relinquished their dues as councilors that the taxes might be lessened and the police be paid. * * * Captain Hosea Stout said the police were willing to watch the city while it was necessary and all they wanted was to live [i. e. have their living provided for] while they did it.

Action of the City Council for the Suppression of Vice.

Daniel Spencer was elected to fill the remainder of the term of the late martyred Mayor Joseph Smith.

An ordinance was passed allowing $100.00 per year to the mayor, and $1.00 a day to the councilors and aldermen while in session.

Also an ordinance prohibiting brothels and disorderly characters.'*

Sunday, 11.—Forenoon meeting. At the stand Elder Lyman Wight preached about leading a company away into the wilderness. Afternoon, Elder Wm. Hyde preached. At 3 p. m. a few of the authorities met at my house to pray for deliverance from the mob.

At a conference held in Southfield Center, Oakland county, Michigan on the 9th, 10th and 11th inst. there were represented 14 branches, containing upwards of 200 members and 37 officers. Elders W. Burton and Mephiboseth Sirrine, presidents.

Monday, 12.—The Twelve Apostles met in council and made the following appointments:

That Elder Amasa Lyman, who was ordained an Apostle by the direction of President Joseph Smith August 20, 1842, stand as a member of the Quorum of the Twelve;

Definite Assignments to Labors.

That Elder John Taylor hire the printing office and establishment of the *Nauvoo Neighbor* and the *Times and Seasons* from the church;

*The ordinance was signed by George W. Harris, president *protem* and Willard Richards, recorder. The ordinance was quite drastic. It declared such places (brothels) public nuisances and that the owners or keepers of such houses be fined in the sum of not less than $50.00, nor more than $2,500.00 and imprisonment for six months for each offense of one day's continuance of such establishments, and that any person frequenting such establishments (except on lawful business) is to be fined in any sum of not less than $50.00 or more than $500.00 and six months imprisonment for each offense and further for every act of adultery or fornication which can be proved. The party is to be imprisoned six months and fined in the sum of not less than $50.00 and not more than $2,500.00, and that the individual's own acknowledgment shall be considered evidence in the case.

That Elder Wilford Woodruff go on a mission to England and preside over the churches there and on the adjacent isles and continent, taking charge of the printing and take his family with him;

That the general superintendencies' direction and control of the emigration from England be in the name of Brigham Young, President of the Quorum of the Twelve;

That the continent of America be organized into districts and high priests appointed to preside over each district;

That Brigham Young, Heber C. Kimball, and Willard Richards direct the continent and appoint presidents to manage the general affairs of the church;

That Lyman Wight go to Texas as he chooses, with his company, also George Miller and Lucine Woodworth, if they desire to go;

That Willard Richards continue the history of the church and be supported;

Elder Hyde arrived at Nauvoo from his eastern mission.

Wednesday, 14.—I attended meeting of the Twelve, Temple and Nauvoo House Committees and the stonecutters for the Temple at the Seventies' Hall. Agreed to raise the wages of the windlass men to $1.50 per day. The meeting terminated in a feeling of renewed determination to prosecute the work upon the Temple.

Thursday, 15.—The Quorum of the Twelve Apostles met at my house. Many matters were talked over.

Righteous Resolutions of the Twelve.

The council resolved to bear off the kingdom of God in all the world, in truth, honesty, virtue and holiness, and to continue to set their faces as a flint against every species of wickedness, vice and dishonesty in all its forms.

I met in a prayer circle with the Twelve and a few others in the afternoon and prayed for the sick.

The following is from the *Times and Seasons*:

AN EPISTLE OF THE TWELVE TO THE CHURCH OF JESUS CHRIST OF LATTER-DAY SAINTS, IN NAUVOO AND ALL THE WORLD—GREETING:

'*Beloved Brethren*:—Forasmuch as the saints have been called to suffer deep affliction and persecution, and also to mourn the loss of our beloved Prophet and also our Patriarch who have suffered a cruel martyrdom for the testimony of Jesus, having voluntarily yielded themselves to cruel murderers who had sworn to take their lives, and thus like good shepherds have laid down their lives for the sheep, therefore it becomes necessary for us to address you at this time on several important subjects.

The Saints Bereft of Their Prophet.

You are now without a prophet present with you in the flesh to guide you; but you are not without Apostles, who hold the keys of power to seal on earth that which shall be sealed in heaven, and to preside over all the affairs of the church in all the world; being still under the direction of the same God, and being dictated by the same spirit, having the same manifestations of the Holy Ghost to dictate all the affairs of the church in all the world, to build up the kingdom upon the foundation that the Prophet Joseph has laid, who still holds the keys of this last dispensation, and will hold them to all eternity, as a king and priest unto the Most High God, ministering in heaven, on earth, or among the spirits of the departed dead, as seemeth good to him who sent him.

The Prophet Still at the Head of His Dispensation.

Let no man presume for a moment that his place will be filled by another; for, *remember he stands in his own place*, and always will; and the Twelve Apostles of this dispensation stand in their own place and always will, both in time and in eternity, to minister, preside and regulate the affairs of the whole church.

How vain are the imaginations of the children of men, to presume for a moment that the slaughter of one, two or a hundred of the leaders of this church could destroy an organization, so perfect in itself and so harmoniously arranged that it will stand while one member of it is left alive upon the earth. Brethren be not alarmed, for if the Twelve should be taken away still there are powers and offices in existence which will bear the kingdom of God triumphantly victorious in all the world. This church may have prophets many, and apostles many, but they are all to stand in due time in their proper organization, under the direction of those who hold the keys.

Nauvoo the Place for the Gathering for the Present.

On the subject of the gathering, let it be distinctly understood that the city of Nauvoo and the Temple of our Lord are to continue to be built up according to the pattern which has been commenced, and which has progressed with such rapidity thus far.

The city must be built up and supported by the gathering of those who have capital, and are willing to lay it out for the erection of every branch of industry and manufacture, which is necessary for the employment and support of the poor, or of those who depend wholly on their labor; while farmers who have capital must come on and purchase farms in the adjoining country, and improve and cultivate the same.—In this way all may enjoy plenty, and our infant city may grow and flourish, and be strengthened an hundred fold; and unless this is done, it is impossible for the gathering to progress, because those who have no other dependence cannot live together without industry and employment.

Therefore, let capitalists hasten here; and they may be assured we have nerves, sinews, fingers, skill and ingenuity sufficient in our midst to carry on all the necessary branches of industry.

The Temple must be completed by a regular system of tithing, according to the commandments of the Lord, which he has given as a law unto this church, by the mouth of his servant Joseph.

The Law of Tithing to be Enforced.

Therefore, as soon as the Twelve have proceeded to a full and complete organization of the branches abroad, let every member proceed immediately to tithe himself or herself, a tenth of all their property and money, and pay it into the hands of the Twelve; or into the hands of such bishops as have been, or shall be appointed by them to receive the same, for the building of the Temple for the support of the priesthood according to the scriptures, and the revelations of God; and then let them continue to pay in a tenth of their income from that time forth, for this is a law unto this church as much binding on their conscience as any other law or ordinance. And let this law or ordinance be henceforth taught to all who present themselves for admission into this church, that they may know the sacrifice and tithing which the Lord requires, and perform it; or else not curse the church with a mock membership as many have done heretofore. This will furnish a steady public fund for all sacred purposes, and save the leaders from constant debt and embarrassment, and the members can then employ the remainder of their capital in every branch of enterprize, industry, and charity, as seemeth them good; only holding themselves in readiness to be advised in such manner as shall be for the good of themselves and the whole society; and thus all things can move in harmony, and for the general benefit and satisfaction of all concerned.

The U. S. to be Organized into Church Districts Administered by High Priests.

The United States and adjoining provinces will be immediately organized by the Twelve into proper districts, in a similar manner as they have already done in England and Scotland, and high priests will be appointed over each district, to preside over the same, and to call quarterly conferences for the regulation and representation of the branches included in the same, and for the furtherance of the gospel; and also to take measures for a yearly representation in a general conference. This will save the trouble and confusion of the running to and fro of elders; detect false doctrine and false teachers, and make every elder abroad accountable to the conference in which he may happen to labor. Bishops will also be appointed in the larger branches, to attend to the management of the temporal funds, such as tithings and funds for the poor, according to the revelations of God and to be judges in Israel.

The gospel in its fulness and purity, must now roll forth through every neighborhood of this widespread country, and to all the world; and millions will awake to its truths and obey its precepts; and the kingdoms of this world will become the kingdoms of our Lord and of his Christ.

Suggestion as to Policies.

As rulers and people have taken counsel together against the Lord, and against his anointed, and have murdered him who would have reformed and saved the nation, it is not wisdom for the saints to have anything to do with politics, voting, or president-making, at present. None of the candidates who are now before the public for that high office, have manifested any disposition or intention to redress wrong or restore right, liberty or law; and therefore woe unto him who gives countenance to corruption, or partakes of murder, robbery, or other cruel deeds. Let us then stand aloof from all their corrupt men and measures, and wait, at least, till a man is found, who, if elected, will carry out the enlarged principles, universal freedom, and equal rights and protection, expressed in the views of our beloved Prophet and martyr, General Joseph Smith.

We do not, however, offer this political advice as binding on the consciences of others; we are perfectly willing that every member of this church should use his own freedom in all political matters; but we give it as our own rule of action, and for the benefit of those who may choose to profit by it.

Closing Admonition.

Now, dear brethren, to conclude our present communication, we would exhort you in the name of the Lord Jesus Christ, to be humble and faithful before God, and before all the people, and give no occasion for any man to speak evil of you, but preach the gospel in its simplicity and purity, and practice righteousness, and seek to establish the influence of truth, peace and love among mankind, and in so doing the Lord will bless you, and make you a blessing to all people.

You may expect to hear from us again.

[Signed] BRIGHAM YOUNG
President of the Twelve.

Nauvoo, August 15th, 1844.

August 15, (*continued*).—Elders Noah Rogers and Benjamin F. Grouard wrote from Tahiti of this date that they and Elder Addison Pratt had arrived at the Society Islands. Their vessel had stopped at Toboui to refit and obtain supplies, where, being favorably received by the natives Elder Pratt remained. Elders Rogers and Grouard proceeded to Tahiti and found the people in great confusion in consequence of an invasion by the French. The English missionaries opposed the elders bitterly, but having become alarmed in consequence of the war between the French and the Islanders they had mostly left the island. The elders found great difficulty in engaging the attention of the people in consequence of the excitement of the war. Queen Pomare's force having been defeated, the natives retired to the interior. Elder Pratt had baptized several Americans who were residing at Toboui which is a small island about 300 miles from Tahiti.

Report of Mission Movements in the Pacific Islands.

Saturday, 17.—In company with Elders Kimball, Woodruff and others I went on to the Temple walls, viewed the country, encouraged the workmen and counseled Brother Woodruff in relation to his mission to England.

Afternoon, spent considerable time in the Tithing Office.

Mission Movements in the Southern States.

Elder John Brown wrote from Monroe county, Mississippi, of his preaching in Kentucky, and in Hickman, Williamson, and Sumner counties, Tennessee; also in Tuscaloosa county, Alabama; thence he proceeded to Perry county, Alabama, where he found a branch of fifteen raised up by Elder James Brown, and where he and Brother Haden W. Church, baptized forty-five. They continued their labors during last winter in Alabama and Mississippi. A conference was held in Alabama, in April, at which several elders were ordained. From this conference, Brother Church went to Tennessee and Brother B. L. Clapp and John Brown to Mississippi. Brother Clapp soon returned to Nauvoo and Brother Brown held a conference in July when thirty-nine were reported as having been baptized since last conference.

Sunday, 18.—I preached to the saints in the morning. The following synopsis of my discourse and minutes of the meeting were reported by Elder Woodruff:

PRESIDENT BRIGHAM YOUNG'S DISCOURSE

'I have many things to speak of. It was my mind in the first place that we should have a suitable time to meditate upon all matters, and weigh them, even every subject wherein we felt interested. When the question was asked me if the elders should continue to baptize for the dead, I replied that I had no counsel to give upon that subject at present, but thought it best to attend to other matters in the meantime.

Restless Elements at Nauvoo.

I have learned some things I did not know when I came home. I discover a disposition in the sheep to scatter, now the shepherd is taken away. I do not say that it will never be right for this people to go from here or scatter abroad; but I do say wait until the time comes, or until you are counseled to do so. The report has gone forth through the city that the Twelve have a secret understanding with those men who are going away and taking companies with them, that they shall take away all they can; and although the Twelve will blow it up in public, yet privately they wish it to go on, but if they were the last words I had to say before going into the eternal worlds I would swear by the Holy Trinity that such a report is utterly false, and there is not a word of truth in it. There is no man who has any right to lead away one soul out of this city by the consent of the Twelve, except Lyman Wight and George Miller, they have had the privilege of taking the 'Pine Company'* where they pleased, but not another soul has the consent of the Twelve to go with them. There is no man who has any liberty to lead away people into the wilderness

*This has reference to a company of men under the leadership of Lyman Wight to go into the pine country in the north to get out timber for the Temple.

from this church, or to lead them anywhere else, by the consent of the Twelve or the church, except in the case above named—and I tell you in the name of Jesus Christ that if Lyman Wight and George Miller take a course contrary to our counsel and will not act in concert with us, they will be damned and go to destruction—and if men will not stop striving to be great and exalted, and lead away parties from us, thereby weakening our hands, they will fall and not rise again—and I will destroy their influence in this church with the help of God and my brethren. I wish you to distinctly understand that the counsel of the Twelve is for every family that does not belong to the Pine Company to *stay here in Nauvoo,* and build up the Temple and get your endowments; do not scatter; 'united we stand, divided we fall'. It has been whispered about that all who go into the wilderness with Wight and Miller will get their endowments, but they cannot give an endowment in the wilderness. If we do not carry out the plan Joseph has laid down and the pattern he has given for us to work by, we cannot get any further endowment—I want this to sink deep into your hearts that you may remember it. If you stir up the flame of dissension, will you get an endowment? No! You get a party to run here and another there, to divide our strength, and weaken our hands, and our enemies will flock around us and destroy us—in that case you will not get your endowments, but will sink and not rise;—go to hell and not to the bosom of Abraham. Do the people leave here because they are afraid? Are you cowards? Do you fear those who have power to kill the body only? If you leave this place for fear of the mob, before God tells you to go, you will have no place of rest, but you will flee from place to place and go like the Jews, until God raises up some other people to redeem you, for if the devil scares you from this place he will scare you from all other places. Let no man go from this place but the pine country brethren, but stay here and sow, plant, build, and put your plowshares into the prairies: one plowshare will do more to drive off the mob than two guns. Let us stay here where the bones of Joseph, Hyrum, Samuel, Don Carlos, and Father Smith are. While Joseph was alive he said 'If I am slain in battle or fall by the hands of my enemies I want my body brought to Nauvoo and laid in the tomb I have prepared.' I would rather have the dead body of the Prophet than some men who are alive and I would rather have the clothes of the Prophet stuffed with straw for president of the United States than any man whose name is now before the nation as a candidate, for the straw would not do any harm.

We want to build the Temple in this place, if we have to build it as the Jews built the walls of the Temple in Jerusalem, with a sword in one hand and the trowel in the other. How easily some men are scared! I have not been frightened yet, and I know of other men who have not.

The Church not to be Deprived of Revelations.

Do you suppose the mouth of God is closed, to be opened no more unto us? If this were the case I would not give the ashes of a rye straw for the salvation of the church. If God has ceased to speak by the Holy Ghost, or to give revelation, there is no salvation; but this is not the case.

There seems to be a disposition by many to leave Nauvoo and go into the wilderness or somewhere else. Suppose we should all go into the wilderness and then ask God to give us an endowment, and he should ask if we were driven from Nauvoo, and who drove us? The devil drove us would be the answer; he might say, well, did you not know that I had power over the devil? Yes, but one said I would not give a jackknife for all Nauvoo, and another said, I would not give a pair of mules for the best farm in Hancock county and I was afraid; would the Lord give an endowment to a people who would be frightened away from their duty?

Concerning those who are wishing to lead away parties contrary to counsel, I would not wish them damned worse, than to have a company after their own liking go with them, for they will soon quarrel among themselves; and if we should go to the wilderness and ask the Lord to give us an endowment, he might ask us, saying, Did I not give you rock in Nauvoo to build the Temple with? Yes. Did I not through my providence furnish men to quarry and cut the stone and prepare it for the building? Yes. Did I not give you means to build the Temple there? Yes. Very well, had you died in Nauvoo, on the walls of the Temple, or in your fields, I would have taken you to myself and raised up men to officiate for you, and you would have enjoyed the highest glory. Did you make a sacrifice by tithing? No. Well I do not wonder you did not believe I had power over the devil.

Such may go away but I want to have the faithful stay here to build the Temple and settle the city. We shall require the tenth of all your property as a tithing for the building of the Temple and for the poor and for the priesthood. I want my support and living by the church hereafter, so that I can give my whole time to the business of the church. I have always supported myself heretofore in all my travels and labors, with the aid of my brethren.

The Law of Tithing to be Enforced.

Joseph has always been preserved from his enemies, until now, but he has sealed his testimony with his blood, and his testament is now in force. While the testator lived it was all in his hands, but now he is dead.

There is no remission of sins without the shedding of blood.* You will soon wake up and know things as they are—there has been a great debt paid; there will be no need of more blood of the saints being shed at present, by and by you will understand and see that all is right.

Woe! woe! woe! unto all who have shed the blood of the saints and the Lord's anointed. It must needs be that offenses come, but woe unto that man through whom they come.

Woe! to Those by Whom Offenses Come.

*Heb. ix:22.

To those who want to go away from this place, I would say wait until the time comes. I will give you the key. North and South America is Zion and as soon as the Temple is done and you get your endowments you can go and build up stakes, but do not be in haste, wait until the Lord says go. If you have the Spirit of God you can discover right from wrong—when all is right with the priesthood and a man rises up and speaks by the Spirit of God and just right, all will say, Amen, but when a man rises up and talks as smooth as oil, if he is not right, there will be many queries about it, it will not edify the body [i. e. the people]. I give this as a key. You may go all over North and South America and build up stakes when the time comes. The whole continent of America must be organized into districts and presiding elders appointed over each district: the time has come when all things must be set in order.

The Whole of America Zion.

I wish the saints to let their bickerings cease, and a strict order of things be introduced: we shall not harbor blacklegs, counterfeiters and bogus-makers; we know all about them, they have been in our midst long enough. I advise all the saints to have no dealings with such men; let them alone. The time has come that they should be wiped out of our midst, let the ungodly dealers alone; and as to the doctors who are in our midst, who are our enemies, I say let them alone, for I have no doubt but that three to one who have died in this place had a doctor. I say woe unto you lawyers, for your whole study is to put down truth and put a lie in its stead. I want the lawyers to know that we have common sense. They want to make you believe that when you spell 'baker' it means cider or whiskey. Now let the lawyers and doctors alone and leave off bitterness and evil speaking, and you will build the Temple and get an endowment. All ye lawyers go away and let us alone and when we get full of the devil and want you, we will send for you, we may then have a more convenient season.

I want to say to all who profess to be saints, do not harbor blacklegs, counterfeiters and bogus-makers, wipe them away; it is time to carry out the design of our Prophet; do cease to employ doctors, lawyers, and merchants who will empty your purses and then mob you. Store your grain in Nauvoo for you will want it here to eat while you are building the Temple. I say to the hands on the Temple, be united; and to the Temple Committee, do not turn away any person because he is an Englishman, Scotchman, Irishman or of any other nation; but employ every man you can and build the Temple and your homes. I would rather pay out every cent I have to build up this place and get an endowment, if I were driven the next minute without anything to take with me. As to the doctors, let them go. I can prove that a doctor in this place doctored a woman that was in the family way, and did not know it until she was delivered, and both woman and child died, and if you will employ them, you will all die.

The Ungodly Not to be Tolerated.

There is a distinction between the law of the land and the law of the church. You have the privilege of keeping all shops that do not come in contact with the law of the state, county, or city; so I will evade the law of the land, says the dealer, and give away whiskey and sell a little tobacco or something else and charge enough for both; but the law of the church will reach such men and if they are members they should be cut off. I dreamed that I saw a fruit tree in which I went in search of fruit. I soon discovered that some of the main branches on the top were dead. It seemed to me necessary to cut off the dead branches in order to save the tree so I told some person to help me cut them off. The person stepped on to a large green limb and was afraid it would break so I put my shoulder under it and held it up till the dead branch was cut off, the green limb cracked but did not break. After all the

Evasions not to be Practiced in Administering the Law of the Church.

The Removal of Dead Branches.

dry limbs were cut off the wounds healed up and the tree grew finely.

Let us cut off the dead branches of the church that good fruit may grow and a voice will soon be heard, go and build up Zion and the Temple of the Lord.

The seventies will be organized and a presidency of seven men will be chosen out of the first quorum to preside over the first ten quorums.'*

The Work of the Church in the South.

August 18, (*continued*).—At a conference in Tazewell county, Virginia, Richard H. Kinnamon presiding, Elders Hamilton and Park were appointed to labor in Tazewell, Smith and Washington counties. Elders King and Lambson were appointed to labor in Greenbrier and Monroe counties, Elders Carter and Biles in Giles and Roanoke counties, Elder Hyatt in Patrick county, Elder Pitts in Giles county, Elders R. H. Kinnamon and Stephen Litz in South Carolina and Elder J. T. Crow was sent on a mission south.

Several were called to the priesthood; during conference the sacrament was administered and one person baptized. Elder Robert Hamilton preached.

The Prophet's "Translation" of the Bible Sought.†

Monday, 19.—Elder Willard Richards called on Emma Smith, widow of the Prophet, for the new translation of the *Bible*: She said she did not feel disposed to give it up at present.

I met in council with Elders Heber C. Kimball, Parley P. Pratt, Orson Pratt, Willard Richards, Wilford Woodruff, George A. Smith, Amasa M. Lyman, Erastus Snow, William W. Phelps and Jonathan Dunham at my house, when it was voted that Dan Jones

*These groups constituting the councils for the first ten quorums however did not cease to be members of the first quorum, on the contrary they continued to be the First Quorum of the Seventy one of the three great councils (the third) of the priesthood. The First Presidency and the Twelve being the other two. (*Doctrine and Covenants,* sec. cvii).

†It will be observed that I place "translation" in the sideheading in quotation marks. I do this because the work of the Prophet was not really a translation of the *Bible* from ancient languages, but was a revision of the *English Bible* (King James' version), under inspiration. (See this *History,* vol. i, p. 324, especially footnote; and p. 341; vol. iv, p. 137).

receive an order on Elder Woodruff, Liverpool, for five hundred dollars to assist him on his mission to Wales, having confidence that the Lord would bless him in preaching the gospel to that nation; Brother Jones having relinquished a certain sum due him to be applied to the benefit of the Temple.

Elder Willard Richards read a letter he received from James Arlington Bennett, in which he relates his dreams relative to the murder of Joseph and Hyrum. Elder Richards was instructed to write Bennett in reply, which was done. Afternoon, with Elder Kimball and Richards I visited Mr. Davidson Hibbard on business.

James Arlington Bennett.

Wednesday, 21.—Council of the Twelve Apostles at my house to meet Elder Lyman Wight. Elder John Taylor went after him with a carriage; found him sick and unable to attend.

I spent the evening and partook of supper at Elder Woodruff's with Elders Heber C. Kimball, Willard Richards, John Taylor and their wives.

Friday, 23.—The brethren of the Twelve got ready to go and dine at Father Mikesell's; but were called to go and see Lyman Wight near the upper stone house: he and thirty others were sick in the same house.

Saturday, 24.—Council of the Twelve Apostles, the Temple and Nauvoo House Committees and other elders at my house, when it was voted that I should take such measures as should seem best to gather men and means to this place to complete the Temple. Elder Lyman Wight was counselled to go north instead of going south.

Council Meeting to Give Impetus to Build the Temple.

After transacting the business presented, Elder Woodruff was blessed and set apart to his mission to England under the hands of the members of the Quorum of the Twelve Apostles present: Several of the Twelve Apostles were baptized for their dead this afternoon.*

*Also see p. 264, where President Young extended the privilege for the saints generally to be baptized for the dead. It is to be presumed that this was the

DISCOURSE OF ELDER WILFORD WOODRUFF

Sunday, 25.—Meeting at the stand. Elder Wilford Woodruff preached, he said:

'There is a spirit in man and the inspiration of the Almighty giveth it understanding. It is through this principle that this congregation is assembled together at this place; you had understanding of the things of God

announcement of the resumption of attending to baptisms for the dead under the administration of Brigham Young and the Twelve Apostles which baptisms may well have been interrupted during the exciting period just previous to and following the martyrdom of the Prophet. While Elijah revealed the keys of the priesthood pertaining to this ordinance in the Kirtland Temple in 1836—April 3—the Prophet Joseph did not begin teaching baptism for the dead until in October, 1840 (See letter of President Smith to the "Traveling High Council"—the Twelve Apostles, then in England—this *History*, vol. iv, p. 231).

On the introduction of this doctrine to the church it made a very strong appeal to the members thereof and there was generally an earnest desire to attend to this ordinance for the dead. Some irregularities ensued, such as improper representatives being baptized for the departed dead, and in some few instances women being baptized for men and *vice versa*. These ordinances for some time were performed in the Mississippi river. This procedure however was finally cancelled and at the October conference, 1841, the Prophet Joseph made the announcement that there should be no more baptisms for the dead until the ordinance could be attended to in the Temple then building. "For thus saith the Lord", declared the Prophet (this *History*, vol. iv, p. 426).

Also there had been some irregularities in the matter of neglecting to make proper records of baptisms for the dead. These irregularities were corrected by careful instructions from the Prophet. (See two epistles of his in *Doctrine and Covenants*, sec. cxxvii and cxxviii, bearing date of Sept. 1, 1842 and Sept. 6, 1842.) Meantime a rather fine temporary baptismal font was erected in the basement of the Temple and enclosed by a temporary frame building. built of split oak clapboards (See this *History*, vol. vi, p. 46). Baptisms in this font were very numerous, even in the days of the Prophet. And now such baptisms were resumed under the direction of President Brigham Young and his brethren.

The mission of Elijah in the New Dispensation was foreshadowed even on the occasion of Moroni's first visit to the Prophet Joseph Smith on September 21, 1823, when Moroni, in quoting prophecies of the scriptures which were soon to be fulfilled, made reference to this mission of Elijah, saying: that the Lord would reveal unto the Prophet Joseph the priesthood by the hand of Elijah before the coming of the great and dreadful day of the Lord; and that he would plant in the hearts of the children the promises made to the fathers, etc. (See Writings of Joseph Smith. *Pearl of Great Price*, p. 21, current edition). In section xx of the *Doctrine and Covenants*, vv. 25-27. it is said "that as many as would believe and be baptized in his holy name [in the New Dispensation then coming forth] and endure in faith to the end, should be saved. Not only those who believed *after* he came in the Meridian of time in the flesh, but all those *from the beginning*, even as many as were *before* he came who believed in the words of the holy prophets, who spake as they were inspired by the gift of the Holy Ghost, who truly testified of him in all things—should have eternal life as well as those who should come *after*, who should believe in the gifts and callings of God, by the Holy Ghost, which beareth record of the Father and of the Son." So that almost from the commencement of the New Dispensation the work for the dead may be said to be in contemplation.

by the Spirit of God, and I have now one important declaration to make unto you, and that is, that inasmuch as you will be united in heart, mind and action in supporting your counsellors, the authorities of the church, the priesthood of God, and follow the counsel given you, as you have endeavored to follow the counsel of the Prophet while he was living, you will be safe and blessed and will prosper; but if you are divided and reject the counsel of God you will fall: union and faithfulness is your salvation. You have been led by one of the best men that ever graced humanity or tabernacled in flesh; but he has gone; he has sealed his testimony with his blood; he loved this people unto death.

Exhortation to Unity.

I call upon this people to be united in building upon the foundation which the Prophet Joseph has laid. You have been called to suffer much in the cause in which you are engaged, but if judgment begins at the House of God, Babylon will not escape; and if there is fire in a green tree, a dry tree will not escape, and there are none more prepared for the shock that is coming upon the earth than the Latter-day Saints. The object we have in view is to secure blessings beyond the veil in the first resurrection; this is what we are preparing for. Again, I would say let not the saints be troubled because they have lost their Prophet. I would ask, because the Prophet has sealed his testimony with his blood, if that destroys the gospel—takes away the power of God—annihilates truth—or buries the priesthood? I tell you, nay! it does not. His testament is now in force; therefore my counsel is to follow the example of those who have gone before and be faithful unto death. If you will be united and go too with your mights in building the Temple you will have power to accomplish it and get an endowment. I exhorted the saints to faithfulness—and requested their prayers, and asked their forgiveness for anything that I might have done wrong and bade them farewell.'

The Prophet Joseph Sealed his Testimony with his Blood.

Baptism for the Dead Resumed.

I [Brigham Young] spoke a few words to the saints; told them they were at liberty to be baptized for their dead relatives.

Elders Orson Hyde and Parley P. Pratt bore testimony that Joseph the Prophet had ordained, anointed and appointed the Twelve to lead the church, and had given them the keys of the kingdom for that purpose.

Testimonies on Various Things.

Elder John Taylor bore testimony against those that murdered Joseph and Hyrum Smith; he said they should be cursed and the congregation said, Amen.

Elder William W. Phelps and Reynolds Cahoon bore testimony that Joseph said unto the Twelve 'upon you must rest the responsibility of bearing off the kingdom of God in all the world, therefore round up your shoulders and bear it.'*

Monday, 26.—Attended council held at my house. Afternoon attended a court martial.

Tuesday, 27.—I met with the officers of the Nauvoo Legion in council; six of the Apostles were present. The council decided that they would carry out all the views of our martyred Prophet: the brethren felt very spirited on the subject.

Departure of Elders Woodruff and Jones for England.

Wednesday, 28.—Elders Wilford Woodruff, Dan Jones, and Hiram Clark with their families started this afternoon for England.

Thursday, 29.—The Quorum of the Twelve Apostles met at my house, having notified Elders Rigdon and Marks to attend. This was fast day and I attended meeting at the stand and laid hands on several of the sick.

Elders Rigdon and Marks Cited Before the Twelve.

Friday, 30.—In company with my brethren of the

*This is important as corroborating a statement made many years subsequently by William Smith, brother of the Prophet at a court in Independence. He testified in that court in what is known as the "Temple Lot Suit" to obtain title to the Kirtland Temple by the organization known as the Josephite Church, *vs.* the Hedrickite Church, when he said President Joseph Smith ordained "him [Wm. Smith, who was one of the original members of the Quorum of the Twelve Apostles at Kirtland] a prophet, seer, revelator, and translator, and then informed him that he had all the necessary ordinations to lead the church in his time" (See *Succession in the Presidency of the Church*, B. H. Roberts, second edition, p. 104).

Twelve, Father John Smith and many others I visited at Father Mikesell's, partook of dinner and an abundance of peaches from his orchard: the family were glad to see us and we spent a pleasant day. Many of the brethren in the city being apprehensive that we might fall into the hands of the mob, took their guns and went a 'hunting' around and below Mikesell's along the timbered bluffs on the Mississippi River.

A Social Function Under Armed Guards.

Saturday, 31.—Visiting the sick. Afternoon attended general meeting of the officers of the Nauvoo Legion. I was unanimously elected lieutenant-general and Charles C. Rich, major-general of the Nauvoo Legion. Evening, attended a school meeting."

CHAPTER XXI.

FORMAL TRIAL AND EXCOMMUNICATION OF PRESIDENT SIDNEY RIGDON—RESTLESS MOVEMENTS OF JAMES EMMETT—MISSION ACTIVITIES OF THE CHURCH—MOVEMENTS OF STATE OFFICIALS AND THE MOB OF HANCOCK COUNTY

Rigdon's Vagaries—Gog and Magog.

"*Sunday, September* 1, 1844.—I [Brigham Young] went to the stand* in the forenoon. Elder Sidney Rigdon preached. His discourse was complicated and somewhat confused; he said he had all things shown to him from this time to the winding-up scene, or the great battle of Gog and Magog; there were great things to take place, but he did not tell what the saints should do to save themselves.

I met with the high priests' quorum in the afternoon and spoke at some length to the brethren. Elder Heber C. Kimball addressed the meeting; afterwards, we proceeded to the Seventies' Hall and instructed the seventies pertaining to the organization of their quorums.

Conference in Philadelphia.

A conference was held at Philadelphia, August 31st, and September 1st, at which Elder William Smith [Apostle and brother of the Prophet] presided. Elder Jedediah M. Grant represented three hundred and thirty-four members, including officers and gave much good instruction pertaining to the duties of the saints, in building a Temple and strengthening the hands of the saints at Nauvoo. Elders Wm. Smith and William I. Appleby preached.

Monday, 2.—Visited Elders Willard Richards and John P. Greene who were very sick.

*"I went to the stand." This had reference to an outdoor place of meeting on the Temple site and was the only place of meeting sufficient to accommodate the large congregations that were wont to assemble in Nauvoo during the summer time.

I wrote the following which was published in the *Times and Seasons*:

CONCENTRATION AT NAUVOO

'The Twelve would invite the brethren abroad, in obedience to the commandments of the Lord, to gather to Nauvoo with their means to help build up the city, and complete the Temple, which is now going forward faster than it has at any time since it commenced. Beware of the speculations about the Prophet! Believe no tales on the subject: Time will tell who are the friends of Joseph Smith, who laid down his life for his brethren. We have no new commandments, but beseech the brethren to honor and obey the old ones, for, wheresoever the carcass is, there will the eagles be gathered together.'

Tuesday, 3.—I had an interview with Brother Sidney Rigdon. He said he had power and authority above the Twelve Apostles and did not consider himself amenable to their counsel. In the evening, the Twelve had an interview with Brother Rigdon, who was far from feeling an interest with the Twelve. His license was demanded, which he refused to give up, and said the church had not been lead by the Lord for a long time, and he should come out and expose the secrets of the church.

Rigdon's License Demanded.

Wednesday, 4.—Elder Willard Richards sick. The Twelve Apostles and a few others met at my house in the evening and prayed for the preservation of the church and ourselves; and that the Lord might bind up the apostates and preserve the honest in heart.

Thursday, 5.—Brother Wm. Marks came to see me in relation to President Rigdon and his revelations. Afternoon, attended public prayer meeting and exposed the false prophets. Evening, Elder Hyde preached in the Masonic Hall on Elder Rigdon's conduct since his return to Nauvoo.

Friday, 6.—Elder Heber C. Kimball and I visited the sick till two p. m.

Brother Alonzo W. Whitney informed us of the proceedings of Elder Rigdon and others.

Elder Orson Pratt preached in the Seventies' Hall.

Saturday, 7.—Accompanied by Elder Kimball I waited upon Elder John P. Greene, and attended to ordinances for him: he was on his deathbed.*

Leonard Soby was disfellowshipped by the high council for following Elder Rigdon.

Sunday, 8.—I insert the following synopsis of minutes of Elder Sidney Rigdon's trial:

THE FORMAL TRIAL OF ELDER SIDNEY RIGDON

'Minutes of a meeting of the Church of Jesus Christ of Latter-day Saints held on the meeting ground in the city of Nauvoo. Present, of the Quorum of the Twelve, President Brigham Young, Heber C. Kimball, Parley P. Pratt, Orson Pratt, Orson Hyde, George A. Smith, John Taylor and Amasa M. Lyman.

The high council was organized with Bishop Newel K. Whitney at their head.†

Testimony of Elder Brigham Young.

President Young briefly addressed the congregation and introduced the business of the day, which he said would be this: All those who are for Joseph and Hyrum, the *Book of Mormon, Book of Doctrine and Covenants,* the Temple and Joseph's measures, they being one party, will be called upon to manifest their principles openly and boldly, the opposite party to enjoy the same liberty and be as decided and manifest their principles as boldly as they do in their secret meetings and private councils. If they are for Sidney Rigdon, and believe he is the man to be the first President and leader of this people, they are requested to manifest it as freely as they do in other places, because this will form another party: President Young alluded to the course of Elder Rigdon.

Other Witnesses.

Elders Orson Hyde, Parley P. Pratt, Amasa M. Lyman, John Taylor, William W. Phelps, Heber C. Kimball and William Marks bore testimony in relation to the course of Elder Rigdon, which is published in full in the fifth volume of the *Times and Seasons.*

Elder W. W. Phelphs [after the above hearing] moved that Elder Sidney Rigdon be cut off from the church, and delivered over to the buffetings of satan until he repent.

The Judgment.

Bishop Newel K. Whitney then presented the motion to the high council [who was trying the case] and the vote was unanimous in the affirmative.

*These were doubtless the usual ordinances for the sick and dedicating him to the Lord.

†This was the special high council provided for in the church for the trial of a president in the Presidency of the High Priesthood of the Church, which is presided over by the bishop of the church, assisted by twelve high priests chosen for the occasion. (See *Doctrine and Covenants,* sec. cvii:82-84). In this case Bishop Newel K. Whitney was the presiding bishop of the special court and the Apostles—the Twelve—were the accusers.

Elder Phelps then offered the same motion to the church, upon which President Young arose and requested the congregation to place themselves so that all could be seen who voted. He then called upon the church to signify whether they were in favor of the motion: the vote was nearly unanimous.

Those who were for Sidney Rigdon were requested to make it manifest: there were ten who voted for him.

Elder Phelps then moved that all who have voted to follow Elder Rigdon be suspended until they can have a trial before the high council. An amendment was offered as follows: 'or shall hereafter be found advocating his principles.'

The vote was unanimous in the affirmative.

President Young arose and delivered Sidney Rigdon over to the buffetings of satan in the name of the Lord, and all the people said, Amen.'*

Monday, 9.—I attended council with the Quorum of the Twelve at Elder Heber C. Kimball's; thence I went in company with Elder Kimball through the city, attending to business and visiting Elders John P. Greene and Parley P. Pratt who were sick.

Labors with James Emmett.

Elder Heber C. Kimball and George A. Smith labored diligently with James Emmett that he might be persuaded to desist from his in-

*This is a very brief statement of the trial and final dismissal of Elder Sidney Rigdon from the church. The minutes of the trial with objections and remarks and complaints were published in the *Times and Seasons* of Sept. 15, Oct. 2, and Oct. 15, 1844, running through three numbers, and in all making fifteen pages of closely printed matter. Very serious charges are made against Elder Rigdon for insubordination, for claiming to hold keys and authority above any man or set of men in the church, even superior authority and keys thereof than those held by the Twelve; and likewise he had ordained men to positions—places and offices not recognized as properly belonging to the church. Among other things he somewhere about this time predicted that the building of the Temple would cease and prophesied that there would not be another stone raised upon the walls of the Temple. At one of the meetings where this was said, a Brother Wm. W. Player determined that Elder Rigdon should not prove a true prophet, in this instance at least, and took with him Archibald and John Held, and set a stone upon the Temple wall, making this prediction a failure; and of course the Temple was subsequently completed and dedicated, and ordinance work performed therein. The statement of Wm. W. Player is signed and recorded in the *History of Brigham Young, Ms.*, for December, 1844, p. 67.

After this trial at Nauvoo Sidney Rigdon returned to Pittsburg in Pennsylvania where he had something of a following; and he undertook to organize a church, choosing twelve apostles, etc.; his efforts however amounted to but little. He sent missionaries to many branches of the church to represent his claims, but his organization was never strong either in membership of leading men, and it soon crumbled into decay. Sidney Rigdon himself sank out of sight and in 1876 he died in obscurity in Allegheny county, state of New York. (See *Succession in the Presidency of the Church*, by the present writer, second edition).

tended course of taking away a party of misguided saints into the wilderness.*

Tuesday, 10.—Elder John P. Greene died.

Elder Orson Hyde started for Kirtland.

I attended council with the Twelve and others when orders to the mob given by Colonel Levi Williams were read. General Deming [sheriff of Hancock county] said he did not consider that a mob large enough to do any mischief could be raised.

Afternoon, with Elder Kimball visiting the saints.

Evening, attended a meeting of officers of the Legion, when a resolution was passed to build an arsenal and gunsmith's shop: one hundred and thirty dollars was subscribed towards the erection of the building.

Wednesday, 11.—Elder John P. Greene buried. * *

I attended council at Elder Erastus Snow's; afterwards in company with several officers of the Legion looking out a location for the arsenal.

Friday, 13.—I went to the parade ground where the officers were drilling. Jonathan Dunham was elected brigadier-general of the second cohort of the Nauvoo Legion: I addressed the officers.

In company with Brother Heber C. Kimball and his wife, Vilate, I visited Mother [Lucy] Smith.

The "Wolf Hunt" Preparation.

There are many reports concerning the movements of the mob; who are making preparations for what they call a 'wolf hunt' on the 26th and 27th of this month; but the general apprehension is that they design coming and attempting to drag some more authorities of the church out to Carthage to murder them.

Saturday, 14.—In company with Elders Heber C. Kimball and George A. Smith I called on Sister Hyrum Smith.

*James Emmett, born on February 22, 1803, in Boone county, Kentucky. He was quite active in the affairs of the church in Missouri; but just a bit uncertain in his conduct. In May of 1837, fellowship was withdrawn from him by a meeting of the presidency and high council of the church at Far West "for unwise conduct, until he should make satisfaction". This he did, and was returned to fellowship; but he was always a restless, impatient man and ambitious of leadership which led him into great trouble and final separation from the church as we shall see.

Elder Amasa M. Lyman being very sick and reported to be dying, Brothers Kimball, George A. [Smith] and I retired to my upper room and prayed for him: he was healed from that very hour.

Attended city council, Jonathan C. Wright was elected marshal and W. W. Phelps recorder of deeds. George A. Smith was elected councilor.

At two p. m., the second cohort of the Nauvoo Legion inspected: Brother John Taylor and I attended.

Evening, visited Brother Amasa M. Lyman.

Sunday, 15.—Elder Parley P. Pratt preached in the forenoon and Elder Orson Pratt in the afternoon.

Monday, 16.—At six a. m., accompanied by Elder Heber C. Kimball, Generals C. C. Rich, Jonathan Dunham and other officers of the Legion, I went to the ground secured for the arsenal, near the Temple. We uncovered our heads and lifted our hands to heaven and I dedicated the ground, by prayer, to the God of the armies of Israel. I took the spade and broke the ground for the cellar.

The Dedication of the Nauvoo Arsenal.

Evening, I attended council; Jared Carter was present and made confession and promised to return to the church.

Tuesday, 17.—The Legion trained. Afterwards the officers met when George A. Smith was elected quartermaster-general of the Nauvoo Legion, with the rank of colonel.

The following is from Elder Addison Pratt, Tubuai [sometimes written Tooboui or Toboui], Society Islands, of date of July 26, 1844.

LETTER OF ELDER ADDISON PRATT FROM THE SOCIETY ISLANDS

'July 26th, I baptized nine persons, four Americans, one Scotchman and four natives, having previously baptized one. On the 29th, I organized the Tubuai branch of the Church of Jesus Christ of Latter-day Saints, numbering eleven members, all in good standing.

On the 5th of August, I administered the sacrament. For wine I substituted cocoanut milk,* that was a pure beverage, which never

**Doctrine and Covenants,* sec. xxvii.

had come to the open air till we broke the nut for that purpose. On the 8th I baptized another person.

The inhabitants here have resolved to build me a house. This climate is fine, never so cold as to freeze, though in July and August it is as cold as it can be and not freeze. January and February are the warmest months, though the heat is never so scorching as some days we have at home. In summer, however, the mosquitoes are innumerable and in winter the fleas are equally plentiful, though we have means to guard against them.

Before I came here King Tommatooah buried his wife; on the 14th July I married him to Toupah his queen; he has been very friendly with me ever since I came here.

Sometimes when I get to thinking about home I feel that I could leave all and return as quickly as possible. A few evenings since I fell into a train of thoughts and told my brethren. I went to bed, fell asleep and dreamed I had deserted my post and got to Nauvoo; the people all knew I had left without counsel and treated me with coolness and neglect. This mortified my feelings so much that I never thought of my family; I saw Brother Young, he was busily employed in sending a company of elders to Europe; I felt an anxiety to go with them, but I had deserted one station, and they never intended to send me to another. I then thought I would go back to the one I had left, but I had no means to get back, or to help myself with: I thought my shame was greater than I could bear, and with these reflections I awoke.*

I have lived at Mattaoora since I came here till the 23rd of August. I then removed to this place called Mahoo, which is the place where I first landed.

The second sabbath after I came here, the church [i. e. the saints] came over to visit me, and I baptized seven more, all natives and heads of families. I administered the sacrament and we felt that we were greatly blessed.

It is now a year since I have heard a syllable from home, and three months since I have heard from the brethren at Tahiti, though I have sent word by eight vessels bound thither.

On learning that missionaries [i. e. of sectarian churches] had arrived from Tahiti I called to see them. I had heard so much of their iniquity and I wanted to see how they looked; to me they looked guilty indeed. One of them named Howe very sanctimoniously remarked, 'I understand you have come among the Islands in the capacity of a preacher.' I answered, 'yes.' 'And what do you preach?' 'The sacred truths of the *Bible,*' I replied. 'I suppose you are aware,' said he, 'that many years ago the London Missionary Society established a mission here at a very great expense;' the whole stress was on the great expense, the cost of translating the *Bible,* etc.

*This is a very common experience with missionaries of the Church of the Latter-day Saints, as thousands will testify who read these words.

'Well,' said I, 'and now you are opposed to having the *Bible* preached after you have accomplished the translation?' He said, no: he had no objections to my preaching the *Bible,* but he understood I had another book I preached from. I told him that was a mistake, and went on to tell him what it was; a long dialogue ensued in which they all questioned me on the fundamental principles of the gospel, but they had to drop several points they introduced for fear of trapping themselves; at length they told me they found no fault with me as far as the *Bible* was concerned, but the *Book of Mormon* they had read and it was a bad book. I told them to show me some specimens of bad doctrine in it: they turned to the place where it says, 'Adam fell that man might be,' at which they flounced considerably, but I soon succeeded in proving that it was not contrary to *Bible* doctrine; they said they could find a worse place than that and turned to the passage:

'Adam had to know misery before he knew happiness.' This they spouted upon me in a great rage. I referred them to the temptations of the Savior and his sufferings that he might be perfected.

I questioned them about their belief in the *Bible,* and the coming of the Son of God the second time; contrasted this with the dispensation of Noah, told them the world was now being warned, and the consequences that would ensue if men did not give heed. I then raised my right hand towards heaven and called on all the heavenly hosts to witness the testimony I bore; that I knew Brother Joseph Smith to be a good man and a Prophet of the Lord. * * * The Spirit of the Lord rested upon me; it threw them into confusion, they knew not what to say. They finally told me as long as I preached the truth they would pray that I might be upheld, but if I preached error they should pray that it might fall to the ground. Then, I said, our prayers will be united.'

Wednesday, 18.—I attended council with the Twelve Apostles and Bishops Whitney and Miller, at Elder Taylor's. Several communications from the elders abroad were read.

Disposition of the Profits Arising from the Sale of the Church Works.

It was voted that the profits arising from the publication of the *Book of Mormon* and *Book of Doctrine and Covenants* be devoted to the priesthood for the building up of the kingdom of God.

Thursday, 19.—At home waiting upon my wife who was very sick. The saints called upon me for counsel and direction.

Friday, 20.—Attending to ordinances in behalf of

the saints, and laying hands on the sick. The Lord is with me continually.

Saturday, 21.—I visited the saints accompanied by Elders Kimball and Lyman. Received a letter from Elder Jedediah M. Grant relating the slanderous course pursued by Elder B. Winchester against the Twelve, and informing us that at the Philadelphia conference he refused to vote to sustain the Twelve asserting that they gagged him while on his trial at Nauvoo.

Opposition of Benjamin Winchester Reported.

Sunday, 22.—I preached to the congregation of the saints on the priesthood: had a good time.

High priests' quorum met at the Masonic Hall. Elder George A. Smith preached.

Evening, attended council.

Murray McConnel, Esq., governor's agent from Morgan county arrived in Nauvoo, and Elder John Taylor made affidavit against Thomas C. Sharp and Levi Williams, two of the murderers of Joseph and Hyrum Smith.

Affidavit Against the Murderers of the Prophet.

Monday, 23.—The first capital weighing about two tons was raised on to the walls of the Temple.

This evening, Sheriff Deming came into Nauvoo for a Mormon *posse* to take Sharp and Williams. The Twelve decided that it was imprudent to take [use] Mormons for that purpose and advised him accordingly.

Received some arms and ammunition from the brethren in St. Louis, by the hands of Thomas McKenzie.

Tuesday, 24.—I attended a council at Winsor P. Lyons; six of the brethren of the Twelve were present, and Elder Joseph Young; we selected seventy presidents to preside over the seventies* and fifty high priests to preside over different sections of the country.

Selection of Presiding Seventies and High Priests.

The Quincy Greys under Captain Morgan and a company of Germans under Captain Swinder arrived

*See ch. xxii.

from Quincy and encamped in the east part of the city. These captains expected a general officer to direct their movements and expressed their astonishment at his non-arrival.

Received a letter from David Clayton containing an account of the sayings and doings of Lyman Wight, his opposition to the Twelve and Clayton's reasons for leaving Wight's company.

Attempt to Arrest Murderers of the Prophet.

Wednesday, 25.—Sheriff Deming asked for wagons to take the Quincy militia to Warsaw to arrest Sharp. The marshal furnished teams and wagons, when the militia said they had no orders from the governor to go.

An attempt was made under the directions of the governor's agent to arrest Thomas C. Sharp, but failed; it was reported that Colonel Levi Williams ran away.

Received a letter from Elder William A. Moore pertaining to the malicious and wicked course of Ben Winchester.

Thursday, 26.—I attended a council held at my house. Benjamin Winchester and wife were cut off from the church.

The Quincy militia escorted about town by the Nauvoo Band.

Night Watchman Appointed for the Temple.

Held a council at the Temple Office and appointed four watchmen to watch the Temple tonight, some of Wight's company have come to town and they report that they have come to deface the capitals, and burn the lumber round the Temple.

General Charles C. Rich wrote the following:

'*To His Excellency, Thomas Ford, Governor of the State of Illinois and Commander-in-chief of the Militia.*

Sir: I received your letter by the hand of Major Bills last evening after dark and hastened to lay before you such information as is in my possession in regard to the movements at Warsaw and Carthage. The deputy sheriff arrived here last evening and informed us that he was at Warsaw and apprehended Thomas C. Sharp who was rescued from his hands by the citizens of Warsaw who stated that they would not let him be taken, law or no law, governor or no governor.

Judge Lot who also arrived here last evening from Quincy, passed through the neighborhood of Warsaw, and informed us that the country was in commotion, and that they had dispatched runners in all directions to raise a force and have it in readiness to act in defiance of all law; from all we have learned there is not much force assembled as yet in Carthage or Warsaw.

Everything is perfectly quiet here; we were, however, a little surprised on the arrival of two companies of militia from Quincy, such things being altogether unsuspected by us, having received no information from you in regard to such movements.

I had a conference with General Miller since the receipt of your letter, who informs me that he has as yet received no letter from you, though he has been expecting an answer for several days, consequently we are left in the dark in regard to your instructions for our intended movements.

Permit me sir, to introduce to your acquaintance Major John Pack and Mr. Snow, gentlemen, in whom we repose the utmost confidence and to whom you can communicate anything you wish concerning us.'

I received the following:

'*SPECIAL ORDER NO.* 10

Camp Pulasky, Sept. 26, 1844.

To the Commander of the Nauvoo Legion:

General Hardin having been commanded by the governor and commander-in-chief to take command of the Nauvoo Legion in the event of their being called into service will review the Legion tomorrow the 27th at 1 o'clock, p. m. It is not intended as a muster of the Legion into service but as a parade for inspection and review.

By order of Brigadier-General,

[Signed] J. J. HARDIN,

W. B. Warren, Brigade-Major. Commanding Illinois Volunteers.

Friday, 27.—This was the day set apart by the anti-Mormons for the great 'wolf hunt'.

A little before noon the governor and two of his aids arrived in Nauvoo. After viewing the Temple they went down towards the Mansion. About two p. m. his troops marched into the city, about five hundred in number. They had three six-pounders with them, two of which were brass. The whole company halted on the first vacant block on the flat and tarried there some time. Many of the men visited the font and the Temple; they appeared astonished, but were civil.

I received my commission as lieutenant-general, and Charles C. Rich his as major-general.

Governor Ford said he had come to execute the law and was ready to proceed against the murderers of Joseph and Hyrum Smith as fast as the people get out writs. He issued a Proclamation offering a reward of two hundred dollars each for the arrest of Sharp, Jackson and Williams, and announced his intention of taking all the arms from this part of the state. His troops numbered four hundred and seventy, all that would volunteer in nine counties to help maintain the supremacy of the laws in Hancock and bring murderers to justice.

Saturday, 28.—I sent the following:

PRESIDENT YOUNG'S LETTER TO GOVERNOR FORD

'Headquarters, Nauvoo Legion,
Sept. 28, 1844.

His Excellency, Thomas Ford, Governor and Commander-in-Chief:

Sir: The review of the Nauvoo Legion will take place this day at twelve m., at which time the commander-in-chief, with his staff, is respectfully solicited to accept an escort from the Legion and be present at the review.

[Signed] BRIGHAM YOUNG,
Lieutenant-General, Nauvoo Legion.

By E. H. Derby, Secretary.'

I reviewed the Legion. The governor, General J. J. Hardin and staff were present. Appropriate salutes were fired on the occasion.

The Legion made a creditable and soldier-like appearance. Several of the staff officers of the Legion appeared in uniform without arms, which the governor regarded as a hint to remind him of his disarming the Legion previous to the massacre of Joseph and Hyrum Smith.

Four p. m., the governor marched his militia force about three miles down the river and camped in the woods.

Preparatoin of Boats for Governor Ford.

The governor called upon General George Miller to furnish boats to convey his command in the night to Warsaw, who after making the necessary arrangements, accompanied by Cyrus H. Wheelock, two other brethren and one of the governor's officers, started to inform his Excellency that the boats were ready. On reaching the neighborhood of the camp the officer requested the brethren to wait until he would go in and speak to the governor; after waiting a few minutes the brethren attempted to go in and see the governor for themselves but were prevented by a sentinel who cocked his gun. Soon after three rounds of musketry were discharged by a detachment of the governor's troops, the bullets whistled all around Brother Miller and party, one ball taking effect upon the sentinel who cried out very loudly, 'I am a dead man': the officers subsequently remarked that they had forgotten to call in their sentinel. Brother Miller and party rendered the wounded sentinel all the assistance they could until his comrades from the camp came to his relief, when Brother Miller learned the boats were not wanted; whereupon, accompanied by his party he started back for Nauvoo, when they got a few rods off twenty or thirty guns were fired after them; some of the balls skimmed the road near their feet; but they were preserved by the hand of God."

CHAPTER XXII.

EPISTLE OF THE TWELVE TO THE CHURCH—MORAL AND SPIRITUAL GUIDANCE

"*Sunday, September* 29, 1844.—I [Brigham Young] attended meeting. Elder Parley P. Pratt preached on the duties of saints and advised all the drunkards and thieves to either quit their wickedness or leave the city, and not claim the name of Mormons, he exhorted the saints in the spirit of meekness to cherish the fruits of the Spirit and walk uprightly before God, and deal justly with all men and to shew by their walk and conduct that they had not taken upon them the name of Christ in vain, giving their enemies no occasion to say or print anything against them that was evil.

I made a few remarks endorsing the sisters' penny subscription* for the purpose of procuring glass and nails for the Temple and requested the saints to prepare themselves to entertain the elders who may be in attendance at conference.

All the First Quorum of the Seventy Ordained Presidents.

Afternoon, I went to the Seventies' Hall and ordained the sixty-three members of the First Quorum of the Seventy to be presidents over the quorums from the second to the tenth inclusive.

The high priests' quorum met.

Considerable sickness reported throughout the city and many deaths.

Monday, 30.—I breakfasted at Elder Heber C. Kimball's. We laid hands on the sick and visited Mother Smith.

Evening, went to the military school held at the Masonic Hall. Afterwards attended council with the

*This sisters' "penny fund" system was instituted by Patriarch Hyrum Smith.

Twelve and concluded to use our influence to prevent the brethren and sisters from attending the ball which William Marks, landlord of the Nauvoo Mansion was making arrangements for; the same to come off on Wednesday evening in the dining room of the Mansion, which was still stained with the blood which flowed from Joseph and Hyrum, as their bodies lay in said room preparatory to burial.

Elder Marks' Ball Boycotted.

Tuesday, October 1.—Evening, attended a meeting of the quorum for prayer: a very interesting session.

AN EPISTLE OF THE TWELVE,

'*To the Church of Jesus Christ of Latter-day Saints—Greeting*:

Dear Brethren: Having promised in our former epistles to address you from time to time, we now proceed to give you further information relative to the welfare of the church both temporally and spiritually; the building up of Nauvoo; the gathering of the saints; the building of the Temple; the establishment of manufacturing and various branches of industry; the support of the poor, and the preserving of peace, good order, union, love, and truth: to the suppression of vice, and every kind of disorder, evil, and immorality.

Subjects of the Epistle.

The Temple, as a great and glorious public work, immediately connected with the completion of our preparation, and ordinances, touching our salvation and exaltation, and that of our dead, necessarily claims our first, and most strict attention. And we rejoice to say for the encouragement of all, that its walls are now ready to receive the capitals, and the arches of the upper story windows; and in fact, seven of the capitals are already reared. The timbers are also being framed, and reared on the inside. In short it is progressing with a rapidity which is truly astonishing.

The Temple.

The gathering, next claims our attention as a work of salvation, to be accomplished in wisdom and prudence. Your Prophets and Apostles, have often told you, that the saints cannot gather together in large numbers, and be able to enjoy the comforts and necessaries of life, without the necessary calculations and preparations for their employment and support. Not only must farms be cultivated, houses built, and mills to grind the corn, but there must be something produced bv industry, to send off to market in exchange for cash, and for such other articles as we need. This must be produced, not by singing, or praying, or going to meeting, or visiting, or friendly greetings, or conversation, *But, by the united industry, skill, and economy of the whole people.* Men, women,

The Gathering.

and children must be well, and constantly employed. In order the more effectually to do this, we must turn our attention to the erection of workshops for the manufacture of every useful article; and wares thus manufactured must find a market, not in Nauvoo alone but in all the wide country, and in cities and towns abroad.

If the saints will commence and follow out this plan, and lay out their cash for the raw material, and employ their friends and themselves at home, instead of sending away all our cash for manufactured goods, we can soon produce millions of wealth, and the poor will have no cause of complaint; for among a temperate people thus employed there would soon be no poor except the widow, the orphan, or the infirm, and these could be abundantly provided for.

Economic Advantages at Nauvoo.

The fact is, we have a country abundantly supplied with natural resources, and calculated for the production of wool, flax, hemp, cotton, and many other articles; and we have water power to any amount; and after all our troubles, a prospect of peace and protection; in short everything for the encouragement of capitalists and workmen. Come on then, all ye ends of the earth, take hold together, and with a long, strong, steady and united exertion, let us build up a stronghold of industry and wealth, which will stand firm and unshaken amid the wreck of empires and the crash of thrones.

The Consciousness of Sound Doctrine.

In regard to principle and doctrine, we know that we are founded upon the plain and manifest truth as revealed from on high; and which is sufficiently manifest and plain to convince all honest men who look into it, and to confound all who oppose. The main object then which remains to be carried out is to practice accordingly, and to live according to our knowledge.

Let the saints now send in their young men who are strong to labor, together with money, provisions, clothing, tools, teams, and every necessary means, such as they know they will want when they arrive, for the purpose of forwarding this work.

Brethren, bring all your tithings into the storehouse and prove the Lord, and see if he will not pour out a blessing, that there will not be room enough to receive.

Awaiting Spiritual Blessings.

Yes, brethren, we verily know and bear testimony, that a cloud of blessing and of endowment, and of the keys of the fulness of the priesthood, and of things pertaining to eternal life, is hanging over us, and ready to burst upon us; or upon as many as live worthy of it, so soon as there is a place found on earth to receive it. Therefore, let no cunningly devised fable, no false delusive spirit, or vision, no man or set of men who go out from us, but are not of us, have any influence on your minds for a moment, to draw your minds away from this all important work. But enter steadily and regularly upon a strict observance of the law of tithing, and of freewill offerings, till Jehovah shall say it is enough; your offerings are accepted: then come up to the House of the Lord, and be taught in his ways, and walk in his paths; yea, enter his sanctuary; and receive the oil of joy for mourning, and the garment of praise for the spirit of heaviness.

In order to do this we must not only be industrious and honest, in providing abundantly for our temporal wants, and for those for whom duty and charity bind us to act, but we must abstain from all intemperance, immorality and vice of whatever name or nature; we must set an example of virtue, modesty, temperance, continency, cleanliness, and charity. And be careful not to mingle in the vain amusements and sins of the world.

Against Vice in All its Forms.

In nearly all cities or towns of an extensive population there are certain vices, or crimes, not exactly tolerated by law, but yet, borne with by the people as a kind of unavoidable or necessary evil; such, for instance, as gambling, drunkenness, vain and wicked amusements and allurements, directly calculated to corrupt the morals of the people and lead them from the paths of virtue and truth. Among the most conspicuous and fashionable of these we might mention, balls, dances, corrupt and immodest theatrical exhibitions, magical performances, etc., all of which are apt not only to have an evil tendency in themselves, but to mingle the virtuous and the vicious in each others society; not for the improvement of the vicious but rather to corrupt the virtuous.

Nauvoo is now becoming one of the largest towns of the west, and as it was founded, and is still in a great measure managed by the saints, we greatly desire the united influence of all wellwishers to our society, and to good order and morality, to cooperate with us in preserving the general peace and quiet, and in suppressing these and all other vices and evils.

Or, to be plain on the subject, we wish to suppress all grogshops, gambling houses, and all other disorderly houses or proceedings in our city, and to tolerate no intemperance or vice in our midst. And so far at least as the members of the church are concerned, we would advise that balls, dances, and other vain and useless amusements be neither countenanced nor patronized; they have been borne with, in some instances heretofore for the sake of peace and good will. But it is not now a time for dancing or frolics but a time of mourning, and of humiliation and prayer.

If the people were all righteous, it would do to dance, and to have music, feasting and merriment. But what fellowship has Christ with Belial? Or what fellowship has light with darkness? or what union have the sons and daughters of God with the children of this world, who fear not God nor regard man. All amusements in which saints and sinners are mingled tends to corruption, and has a baneful influence in religious society.

There are amusements which are at once both innocent, instructive, and entertaining; and which the saints can enjoy, in honor to themselves, and without mingling with the world. Such for instance, as musical concerts, philosophical and astronomical exhibitions, etc. These, together with our religious devotions, and the increase of light, knowledge and intelligence which flows like a flood of glory from the upper world, are quite sufficient to exercise all our powers of enjoyment.

As the business of the conference is now fast crowding upon our time, we must cut short this communication by informing you that an organization and arrangement is now in progress, by which high priests and presiding officers will be appointed over each district of country, throughout the union, who will have entire charge, under the direction of the Twelve of all spiritual matters, superintending the labors of the elders and the calling of conferences. Arrangements will also be made, for the proper payment and reception of tithing, so that it may be duly received by responsible agents and recorded. Of these particulars you will receive further communication from us soon.

Organization for Effective Administration.

Done in council at Nauvoo, this first day of October, A. D. 1844.

[Signed] BRIGHAM YOUNG, President.'

Wednesday, 2.—At ten a. m., a council of the Twelve met at Elder Kimball's.

Elder A. W. Babbitt read a letter from Oliver Cowdery.

Governor Ford disbanded his troops. Sharp and Williams have given themselves up and gone to Quincy under a contract with the governor.

Sharp and Williams, Alleged Murderers of the Prophet Surrender.

Friday, 4.—I went up to the Temple in the forenoon. Attended council with the Twelve, the bishops and the Temple Committee at Sister Emma Smith's and expressed our feelings and intentions to her.

Elder Woodruff preached through the eastern states while traveling on his mission to England. He had an interesting time among his relatives at his father's house in Farmington, Connecticut, and this evening ordained his Uncle, Ozem Woodruff, a high priest."

Labors of Elder Woodruff Among Relatives.

CHAPTER XXIII.

MINUTES OF THE IMPORTANT CONFERENCE OF OCTOBER 6TH TO 8TH, 1844—THE CHURCH SET IN ORDER—DUTIES OF THE PRIESTHOOD EXPOUNDED—ECONOMICS CONSIDERED

"*Sunday, October* 6, 1844.—From the *Times and Seasons* (p. 682).

OCTOBER CONFERENCE MINUTES

'City of Nauvoo, Oct. 6, 1844.

Thousands having arrived on the ground by ten o'clock a. m. Elder Parley P. Pratt called the people to order. Singing by the choir—prayer by Elder Phelps. Some instructions were given by Elder Pratt, when President Brigham Young having arrived, arose to lay before the brethren the matters to be attended to during the conference.

THE DISCOURSE OF PRESIDENT BRIGHAM YOUNG

'This day' [he said], 'will be devoted to preaching and instruction, and we will attend to business tomorrow. If the Twelve could have had their desires when they returned home, they would have set their houses in order, and devoted themselves to fasting and prayer.

The Reasons Given for Haste in Settling the Question of Leadership Before Convening the Conference.

It has not been the Twelve who desired to have business which pertains to this conference transacted previous, it was others who urged it on. Some elders who have known the organization of the church from the beginning, have faltered and become darkened. We feel to give the necessary instruction pertaining to the church, and how it has been led, etc. It is necessary that the saints should also be instructed relative to building the Temple, and spreading the principles of truth from sea to sea, and from land to land until it shall have been preached to all nations, and then according to the testimony of the ancients, the end will come. When the Lord commences to work upon the earth he always does it by revealing his will to some man on the earth, and he to others. The church is built up by revelation, given from day to day according to the requirements of the people. The Lord will not cease to give revelations to the people, unless, the people trample on his laws and forsake and reject him. I request that the Latter-day Saints may pray that we may have the outpouring of the Spirit that we may hear, and I wish them to pray for me that I may have strength, and that I may make every principle I speak upon so perfectly plain, that we may all understand as quick as when we talk together upon our daily matters.

The Church Led by Revelation.

'This church has been led by revelation, and unless we forsake the Lord entirely, so that the priesthood is taken from us, it will be led by revelation all the time. The question arises with some who has the right to revelation? I will not ascend any higher than a priest, and ask the priest what is your right? You have the right to receive the administration of angels. If an angel was to come to you and tell you what the Lord was going to do in this day, you would say you had a revelation. The president of the priests has a right to the Urim and Thummim, which gives revelation. He has the right of receiving visits from angels. Every priest then in the church has the right of receiving revelations. Every member has the right of receiving revelations for themselves, both male and female. It is the very life of the church of the living God, in all ages of the world. The Spirit of Truth is sent forth into all the world to reprove the world of sin and unrighteousness, and of a judgment to come. If we were here today and had never heard this gospel, and a man was to come bounding into our midst, saying, he had come to preach the gospel, to tell us that God was about to restore the priesthood, and save the people, etc., it would be your privilege, and my privilege to ask God in the name of Jesus Christ, as individuals, concerning this thing, whether it was of God, and get a testimony from God that it was true, and this would be revelation. Let us take some of these old fathers for an example, they have heard the gospel, they have been baptized, etc., had hands laid on them for the gift of the Holy Ghost—he has got a family of children, he has been led all his days by his own spirit, but now begins to come to understand he has the right to bow before the Lord and receive instruction from God, from day to day, how to manage his family, his farm, his merchandise, and to govern all the affairs of his house. I will take some of my younger brethren who have received the gospel, they have been ordained an elder to hold the keys, etc. What is your privilege? It is your privilege to go and preach the gospel to the world, and to go by the power of the Holy Ghost, and you have no right to go without it. You have been ordained to go forth and build up the kingdom to a certain extent. No man ever preached a gospel discourse, nor ever will, unless he does it by revelation. You will do it by the Holy Ghost, or when you tell the history of the gospel, the gospel will not be there. It has got to be done by revelation or the gospel you have not got, and when you preach, the people will still be left without the gospel. There never was a prophet on the earth that dictated to the people, but he dictated their temporal affairs as well as spiritual. It is the right of an individual to get revelations to guide himself. It is the right of the head of a family to get revelations to guide and govern his family. It is the right of an elder when he has built up a church to get revelations to guide and lead that people until he leads them and delivers them up to his superiors. An elder will always be a little in advance of those whom he has raised up if he is faithful.'

Self-Guidance by Revelation.

He [President Young] next showed how the saints are delivered up in their progress from those who give them up to the high council, and from the high council to the prophet, and from the prophet to the son, the elder brother, and from the son to his father. (Then continued)—

'Are the keys of the kingdom taken from Joseph? Oh no; well then he still lives. He that believes in Jesus as Joseph did, they will never die. They may lay down their lives, but they still hold the keys. You are not going to be led without revelation. The Prophet has stepped behind the veil and you have the right to obtain revelations for your own salvation. Who stood next to the Prophet when he was here. You have all acknowledged that the Twelve were the Presidents of the whole church when Joseph was not; and now he has stepped behind the veil, he is not here, and the Twelve are the Presidents of the whole church. When did Joseph become a Prophet? I can tell you, when he became an Apostle.* Years and years before he had the right of holding the keys of the Aaronic priesthood, he was a Prophet, even before he was baptized. There has been a perfect flood of revelation poured from this stand all the time and you did not know it. Every spirit that confesses that Joseph Smith is a Prophet, that he lived and died a Prophet and that the *Book of Mormon* is true, is of God, and every spirit that does not is of anti-Christ.

The Keys of Leadership not Taken from Joseph.

'It is the test of our fellowship to believe and confess that Joseph lived and died a Prophet of God in good standing; and I don't want

The Test of Fellowship.

*This remark is a bit confusing because as a matter of fact Joseph Smith did not receive the Apostleship before he was baptized, for he was baptized on the visit of John the Baptist who restored the keys of the Aaronic priesthood May 15, 1829; and the restoration of the Apostleship came to him and Oliver Cowdery somewhat later, most likely sometime in June, 1829. But President Young had in mind the fact of Joseph Smith becoming a Prophet from the time when he received his First Vision of God the Father and of the Son, early in the spring of 1820 and this constituted him a witness for God and likewise a Prophet; but he did not become authoritatively a Prophet to the church until he had been made an Apostle; for as stated by St. Paul, the order of these officers in the church is—"God hath set some in the church first apostles, secondarily prophets," etc. (I Cor. xii:28.)

anyone to fellowship the Twelve who says that Joseph is fallen. If you don't know whose right it is to give revelations, I will tell you, It is I. There never has a man stood between Joseph and the Twelve, and unless we apostatize there never will. If Hyrum had lived he would not have stood between Joseph and the Twelve, but he would have stood for Joseph.—Did Joseph ordain any man to take his place? He did. Who was it? It was Hyrum, but, Hyrum fell a martyr before Joseph did. If Hyrum had lived he would have acted for Joseph, and then when we had gone up, the Twelve would have sat down at Joseph's right hand, and Hyrum on the left hand. The *Bible* says God hath set in the church, first Apostles, then comes Prophets, afterwards, because the keys and power of the Apostleship are greater than that of the Prophets. Sidney Rigdon cannot hold the keys without Joseph, if he had held the keys with Joseph and been faithful he would have been with us. If the Twelve do not apostatize they carry the keys of this kingdom wherever they go.'

Hyrum Smith Ordained to Take the Prophet's Office.

He [President Young] concluded by requesting all the brethren to tarry with us until all the business is through.

The meeting adjourned by blessing from Elder Heber C. Kimball, until 2 o'clock.

ELDER JOHN TAYLOR'S DISCOURSE

Two o'clock p. m.—The meeting was opened as usual by singing; and prayer by Elder W. W. Phelps. After which Elder John Taylor arose and addressed the people. He said it was with peculiar feelings that he arose to address the congregation.

'This is the first general conference' [he said], 'that has been held, where your beloved Prophet and Patriarch are not present. When I look at the many difficulties and severe trials we have passed through it fills me with peculiar feelings. I feel happy to see that the people still

Adherence to Principles Given by Revelation.

seem determined to hold on to those principles which have been given to us through revelation. Nothing shall separate us from those principles which we have imbibed, neither life nor death. By the voice of Jehovah we have been sustained and will be sustained so long as we put our trust in him. We have not followed 'cunningly devised fables', but those principles which have come from God. So long as we are sustained and upheld by the arm of Jehovah, we shall stand: mobs may rage, and the rulers may imagine vain things; but God has said, touch not mine anointed and do my people no harm; and if harm does befall them, woe to that man by whom it comes. If our Prophets have been taken, they are gone to plead our cause before the Father. And if we are deprived of their persons, presence and counsel, that is no reason why we should be deprived of the counsel of God to direct us in all our movements whilst pressing on our journey here below. We are in possession of the same principles, the same priesthood, the same medium of communication and intelligence, and of those things which will not only secure our happiness here, but hereafter. When we speak of these matters, we speak of things which we know assuredly, and although our Prophet and Patriarch are taken, all things pertaining to our salvation will roll on and progress with as great rapidity, and can be as effectually secured and accomplished as if they [Joseph and Hyrum] were here themselves. God has secured to us those things in relation to our salvation which have been in his bosom since the world began. He has in his providence seen fit to call our brethren to himself; but he has left others to take their places, who can teach us principles and lead us to those things whereby we may ultimately be clothed with glory, honor, immortality, and eternal life. If we had built upon a false foundation we might have made a mistake in relation to our gathering together to be instructed; but we had not; our present revelations agree with the past. The prophets said

Perpetuation of the Plan of Salvation.

that the people would gather together, 'those who had made a covenant with God by sacrifice', and the word and purpose of God must stand unchanged, they do not rest upon any mere casualty. Did the Prophet ever tell us that if a certain man should happen to die we should scatter abroad? No! no such thing ever emanated from the lips of God. We assembled together to fulfill the revelations of the Great Jehovah, to bring about the dispensation of the fulness of times, to build up a Zion to the Most High; that he might be glorified. We assembled here to bring about great events, to fulfill the things spoken of by the prophets and secure to ourselves an inheritance in the everlasting kingdom of God. Shall we then be led about by the foolish notions of any man? No! we will not, but we will accomplish those things which are commanded us. We will not be diverted from our course, though earth and hell oppose. Shall we fear the puny arm of man, or the prating of a wretched mobocrat? No! What have we to fear? We have nothing but God to fear.

Hopes of the Saints Beyond the Grave.

'It is true we have not much to live for, and if we have no hope beyond the grave we should be of all men most miserable. We are oppressed, and slandered and persecuted all the day long; all that I care for is to do the will of God, and secure to myself all those blessings which the gospel will warrant me. I have been brought to the gates of death, but I don't fear it; I care nothing about it. You feel as I do in relation to these matters, for your conduct has proven it during the late difficulties. I know that the majority of the people are endeavoring to serve God with all their hearts, and are they not prepared to die? There is nothing in death we have to fear; it is not half as much to die as it is to be persecuted all the day long. Our great object then is to accomplish the thing that we set out for. When we gathered together we expected to meet tribulation; the elders that preached to you told you this or else they did not do their duty. We have been told there would be earthquakes in divers places, and pestilence, and war, and persecution, and distress, and famine. Do these things move us? If the bud is so bitter I wonder what the fruit will be. Don't you expect to be worse off than you are now. John saw an innumerable company and wanted to know where they came from; it was told to him that they are they which came out of great tribulation. That is the path we have to tread. The scripture says: 'woe unto you when all men shall speak well of you'; but that curse has never come upon us, for there are some few here and there who will not speak well of us. But 'blessed are ye when men shall revile you, and persecute you, and say all manner of evil against you falsely for Christ's sake.' Do you think there is any more evil that they have not said? If there is, let it come. What is it that makes you to be evil spoken of? you used to have a good name and reputation where you resided; what is the reason you are now so much spoken against? You have dared to believe the gospel; you have dared to obey it; and that is the reason why the world hates you. I know there is not a better set of men than these by which I am surrounded; I know there is not a more virtuous set of people on the earth, and yet all manner of evil is spoken of you. Shall we cry and go mourning all day long? No, we will rejoice and be exceeding glad, for great is our reward in heaven. I feel to rejoice; we have cause to rejoice for all manner of evil is spoken against us falsely, and I will say hallelujah, for the Lord God Omnipotent reigneth. What did we know of God, of religion, of heaven or hell, until it was made known to us through this gospel? We knew nothing. Why are we taking so much pains to build that Temple? That we may fulfill certain ordinances, and receive certain endowments and secure to ourselves an inheritance in the eternal world. Every man, woman and child within the sound of my voice, are interested in the

Expectation of Tribulation.

High Standing of the Saints of the New Dispensation.

building of that Temple. We know very little as a people yet, we don't know so much as the former day saints. The Savior said to his disciples, 'whither I go ye know, and the way ye know'; but how many of you know the locality of the Savior and the way to go to him? I know there are some here who know how to save themselves and their families, and it is this which occupies their attention all the day long, and it was this which occupied the attention of our beloved Prophet. Abraham obtained promises through the gospel, from God, for himself and his posterity. There were some upon this continent who also obtained promises, in consequence of which the *Book of Mormon* came forth. The first thing we have got to do is to build the Temple, where we can receive those blessings which we so much desire. Never mind mobocrats, but let us do what God has commanded us. You that are living at a distance, don't fear these cursed scoundrels; we are all in the hands of God; we are all the servants of God; and we are going forth to do the things of God.'

To Build the Temple the First Duty.

He [Elder Taylor] exhorted the saints to be virtuous, humble and faithful, and concluded by blessing the saints.

He said further, in relation to the baptisms for the dead, that it would be better for the saints to go on and build the Temple before we urge our baptisms too much. There are cases which require being attended to, and there are provisions made for them; but as a general thing he would advise them not to be in too great a hurry. He said one of the clerks had asked whether any should be baptized who had not paid their tithing; it is our duty to pay our tithing, one-tenth of all we possess, and then one-tenth of our increase, and a man who has not paid his tithing is unfit to be baptized for his dead. It is as easy for a man who has ten thousand dollars to pay one thousand, as it is for a man who has but

Baptism for the Dead and Tithing.

a little to pay one-tenth. It is our duty to pay our tithing. If a man has not faith enough to attend to these little things, he has not faith enough to save himself and his friends. It is a man's duty to attend to these things. The poor are not going to be deprived of these blessings because they are poor; no, God never reaps where he has not sown. This command is harder for the rich than the poor; a man who has one million dollars, if he should give one hundred thousand, he would think he was beggared forever. The Savior said, how hardly do they that have riches enter the kingdom of heaven.

BISHOP MILLER'S REMARKS

Bishop Miller arose to say that on yesterday the bishops had to go in debt to get some wood to save some poor from suffering; and they wanted to take up a collection to pay the amount; he was opposed to taking up a collection in the congregation, but necessity required it on this occasion.

After the collection was taken up the conference adjourned until tomorrow morning at 10 o'clock.

Monday, October 7th, 1844, 10 o'clock, a. m.—Conference met pursuant to adjournment, and opened by singing, and prayer by Elder Parley P. Pratt, after which President Young arose to exhort the saints to keep their minds on the business before them, and not to be in a hurry to get away.

SUSTAINING OF THE SEVERAL AUTHORITIES OF THE CHURCH

The first business that we shall attend to will be to present the several quorums before the conference, for the purpose of taking an expression of the brethren and sisters, whether they will sustain the officers according to their several appointments.

I shall therefore give way, and I am to hear motions and present them to the conference for their action: wherefore,

It was moved by Elder Heber C. Kimball, that we

as a church endeavor to carry out the principles and measures heretofore adopted and laid down by Joseph Smith as far as in us lies, praying Almighty God to help us to do it. This motion was put to the conference by President Young and carried unanimously.

Policies of Joseph and Hyrum Smith Sustained by Vote.

President Young said by way of explanation. that this is as much as to say that we receive and acknowledge Joseph Smith as a Prophet of God; being called of God and maintaining his integrity and acceptance until death.

Elder Heber C. Kimball then moved that we carry out all the measures of Hyrum Smith, a Prophet and Patriarch in the church, so far as in us lies [the power], by the help of God.

This motion was also carried unanimously.

President Young said, this is an acknowledgment that he lived approved of God and died a martyr for the truth.

Elder W. W. Phelps moved that we uphold Brigham Young the president of the Quorum of the Twelve, as one of the Twelve and the First Presidency of the Church.

This motion was duly seconded, and put to the church by Elder John Smith (Uncle of the Prophet) and carried unanimously.

Moved by President John Smith and seconded, that we receive Elder Heber C. Kimball as one of the Twelve, and that he be sustained as such by the church. Carried unanimously.

Moved and seconded, that we receive Elder Orson Hyde as one of the Twelve, and that he be sustained as such by the church. Carried unanimously.

Moved and seconded, that we receive Elder Parley P. Pratt as one of the Twelve, and that he be sustained as such by the church. Carried unanimously.

Moved and seconded, that we receive Elder William Smith as one of the Twelve, and that he be sustained as such by the church. Carried unanimously.

Moved and seconded, that we receive Elder Orson Pratt as one of the Twelve, and that he be sustained as such by the church. Carried unanimously.

Moved and seconded, that we receive Elder John E. Page as one of the Twelve, and that he be sustained as such by the church. Carried unanimously.

Moved and seconded, that we receive Elder Willard Richards as one of the Twelve, and that he be sustained as such by the church. Carried unanimously.

Moved and seconded, that we receive Elder Wilford Woodruff as one of the Twelve, and that he be sustained as such by the church. Carried unanimously.

Moved and seconded, that we receive Elder John Taylor as one of the Twelve, and that he be sustained as such by the church. Carried unanimously.

Moved and seconded that we receive Elder George A. Smith as one of the Twelve, and that he be sustained as such by the church. Carried unanimously.

Moved by Elder H. C. Kimball, that Elder Amasa Lyman *stand in his lot.** The motion was seconded.

An Explanation by President Young.

President Young said by way of explanation that Elder Amasa Lyman is one of the Twelve, just in the same relationship as he sustained to the First Presidency. He is one in our midst and a counselor with us.

The motion was then presented and carried unanimously.

Moved and seconded, and after some discussion, carried unanimously that Elder Lyman Wight be sustained in his office to fill the place of Elder David W. Patten [martyred at Crooked River Battle, Missouri], but not

*Lyman "to stand in his lot". It will be observed here that if Amasa M. Lyman had been accounted as one of the Quorum of the Twelve Apostles, the quorum would have had thirteen in it instead of twelve. Elder Lyman had been ordained as an Apostle, and filled a vacancy that had been made by dropping Orson Pratt from the quorum before the death of the Prophet, but when Orson Pratt had been reinstated in his quorum, and the Prophet had decided that the action of the Twelve was illegal because it was not a majority that acted in the case, President Smith took Elder Lyman into the Council of the First Presidency and he was the Prophet's counselor. and now he was made counselor to the Twelve. as he had been to the Prophet—hence "Lyman to stand in his lot". (c. f. This *History*, vol. v, ch. xiii).

to take his crown, for that, as the Lord has said, no man can take.*

Elder Snow moved that George Miller be received as president of the high priests' quorum. Carried unanimously.

President John Smith moved that William Marks be sustained in his calling as president of this [Nauvoo] stake.

Elder W. W. Phelps objected inasmuch as the high council had dropped him from their quorum.

Elder S. Bent explained and said the reason why the high council dropped Elder Marks, was because he did not acknowledge the authority of the Twelve, but the authority of Elder Rigdon.

Difference of Effect in Dropping Officers from Positions.

President Young said that a president of a stake could be dropped without taking his standing from him in the church. But not so with the First Presidency or the Twelve. A president of a stake is only called for the time being, if you drop him he will fall back into the high priests' quorum.

The motion was then put, but there were only two votes. The contrary vote was put and carried by an overwhelming majority.

Elder H. C. Kimball moved that Elder John Smith stand as the president of this stake. Carried unanimously.

President Young then said, the Macedonia church must select their own man for a president, as Elder John Smith is coming here.

President John Smith moved that Elder Charles C. Rich be one of his council. Carried unanimously.

The High Council.

Moved and seconded, that S. Bent, James Allred, Dunbar Wilson, George W. Harris, Wm. Huntington, Sen., Newel Knight, Alpheus Cutler, Aaron Johnson, Henry G. Sherwood, Thomas Grover, Ezra T. Benson, and David Fullmer, be sustained as the high council. Carried unanimously.

*_Doctrine and Covenants_, sec. cxxiv:130.

Elder H. C. Kimball moved that Elder Joseph Young stand as First President over all the quorums of the seventies. Carried unanimously.

The First Council of the Seventy.

Moved and seconded, that Levi W. Hancock be sustained as one of the Presidents of Seventies. Carried unanimously.

Moved and seconded, that Daniel S. Miles be sustained as one of the Presidents of Seventies. Carried unanimously.

Moved and seconded, that Zerah Pulsipher, be sustained as one of the Presidents of Seventies. Carried unanimously.

Moved and seconded, that Josiah Butterfield be cut off from the church. Carried unanimously.

President Young showed that it was because he had got a little money, and was lifted up.

Moved and seconded, that Henry Harriman be sustained as one of the Presidents of Seventies. Carried unanimously.

President Young said, that the Seventies [First Council] had dropped James Foster, and cut him off, and we need not take an action upon his case.

Moved and seconded, that Jedediah M. Grant take the place of J. Butterfield in the Quorum of Seventies. Carried unanimously.

Elder H. C. Kimball moved that N. K. Whitney stand as our first bishop in the Church of Jesus Christ of Later-day Saints. Carried unanimously.

The Bishopric.

Moved and seconded, that George Miller stand as second bishop. Carried unanimously.

Moved and seconded, that Samuel Williams retain his office as president of [in] the elders' quorum. Carried unanimously.

The Elders.

Moved and seconded, that Jesse Baker and Joshua Smith be sustained as his counselors. Carried unanimously.

The Lesser Priesthood.

Moved and seconded, that Stephen M. Farnsworth retain his office as president of the priests. Carried unanimously.

Moved and seconded, that E. Averett retain his standing as president of the teachers. Carried unanimously.

Moved and seconded, that Jonathan H. Hale, Isaac Higbee, John Murdock, David Evans, Hezekiah Peck, Daniel Garns, Jacob Foutz, Tarlton Lewis, and Israel Calkins, be sustained as bishops in their several wards. Carried unanimously.

ELDER PARLEY P. PRATT'S DISCOURSE

President Young being fatigued gave place for Elder Parley P. Pratt, who got up to preach his 'old sermon', [not said in derision] *viz.*: that we continue our united and ceaseless exertions to build this Temple. He referred to the discoveries of Elders Rigdon and Samuel James. They said nothing about building the Temple, the city, feeding the poor, etc. We heard a great deal about the Mount of Olives—Brook Kedron—Queen Victoria—great battles, etc. This brought to my mind a good text in Webster's spelling book, 'The Country Maid and the Milk Pail'. He then went on to show the importance of building the Temple. He bore testimony that the people had hearkened to the voice of the Lord and to his commandments, and that they were still hearkening, and consequently we should be sustained here until we shall complete the Temple and receive our endowments. He showed the consequences if we did not build it, 'that we should be rejected as a people with our dead.' When the elders go abroad to teach the people, let them teach what we have to do, and what is depending on us and not spend their time in quoting multitudes of scripture to prove one point. We want to build up Nauvoo, never mind Gog and Magog, the Brook Kedron, etc., never mind the old countries; God has something to do there by and by, but not just now. He recommended the brethren to make improvements and enlarge themselves without fear, for we shall not be moved till God suffers it. We are the only people who do not fear death, we have no need to fear it. He next said he would give the people a little religious advice. He advised those who had means to go to getting sheep to consume the vegetation and raise wool, by which means our women would be well employed in manufacturing the wool. He said in a proper time we will have gold and silver, and food and clothing, and palaces in abundance, we will create it by our labor.

President Young advised the saints to come after intermission prepared to tarry till evening if necessary. They [the authorities] have much instruction to give and want an opportunity to give it. He advised the saints to call and get Orson Pratt's *Mormon Almanac* which is something new. After some few exhortations he closed the meeting till 2 o'clock by blessing.

Two o'clock p. m.—Meeting opened by singing, and prayer by Elder John Taylor, after which Elder Taylor presented a communication from Mr. Small declaring his full faith in Elder Rigdon's doctrine. Moved and seconded, that he be cut off from the church. Carried unanimously.

A Rigdonite Excommunicated.

ELDER HEBER C. KIMBALL'S DISCOURSE

Elder Heber C. Kimball addressed the congregation on the principles of salvation by the celestial law. He went on to show the order of the resurrection and that there are different orders or degrees, wherever death finds us the resurrection will take hold of us. 'We desire to obtain a fulness of celestial glory, but many will be disappointed. It is for this that we pray every day that the Lord will spare our lives that we may obtain it. President Joseph Smith never rested till he had endowed the Twelve with all the power of the priesthood, because he was about to pass within the veil. He designed that we should give it to you and

The Resurrection.

you cannot be saved without it. You cannot obtain these things until that house [The Temple] is built. I and my brethren are willing to do all that lays in our power to finish that house for your benefit, that you may go where Joseph is gone. We have got to carry out Joseph's measures and you have got to assist us. When Jesus was upon the earth his time was spent in endowing the Twelve Apostles that they might do the things he had left undone and carry out his measures, and upon the same principle we carry out Joseph's measures. We have no rest—don't sleep half as much as you do. We need your prayers.

All Evil to be put Away.

'It is necessary to put away all wickedness from our midst, all grogshops and bad houses. Drunkenness and such things will be our overthrow if we are ever overthrown. The best way to put these things away is to never frequent such places. It is necessary for us to put away all this frolicking and dancing over the blood of the Prophet, where it was drenched by the blood from the coffin.* When the Prophet had a dance at his house he said everything against it he could, and now men go and practice the same things. Shall we put these things away? I say yes. We have got an ungodly race here among us who are leading our young people away. They will open their doors and let men go in and say everything against the Twelve and the church they are capable of. I never frequent such places; I cast them far from me. Are you not under the same obligations and responsibility, ye elders, high priests, teachers, deacons and members?'

He then went on to show that the saints could not obtain the blessings they want until the Temple is finished. We want all to pay their tithing that they may receive the blessings.

PRESIDENT YOUNG PRESENTS A PATRIARCH

President Young arose and said that it had been

*See page 280 this volume.

moved and seconded that Asael Smith* should be ordained to the office of patriarch. He went on to show that the right to the office of Patriarch to the whole church belonged to William Smith† as a legal right by descent. Uncle Asael [however] ought to receive the office of [a] patriarch in the church.

The motion was put and carried unanimously.

President Young wanted to say a few words on the principle of tithing. 'There has been so much inquiry it becomes irksome: the law is for a man to pay one-tenth of all he possesses for the erecting of the House of God, the spread of the gospel, and the support of the priesthood. When a man comes into the church he wants to know if he must reckon his clothing, bad debts, lands, etc. It is the law to give one-tenth of what he has got, and then one-tenth of his increase or one-tenth of his time. A man comes and says he was sick six months and what is required of me? Why go and pay your tithing for the time you are able to work. Some say they have been preaching and want to know if that doesn't pay their tithing? Well, it will if you want to have it so.' He then went on to recommend the brethren not to sell their grain but to bring it into the city and store it, and not take it to Warsaw.

The Principle of Tithing Expounded.

He next referred to Lyman Wight's going away be-

*This was the son of Asael Smith, brother of the Prophet Joseph's father, who was the first Presiding Patriarch to the church. Asael Smith, here proposed as a patriarch in the church, was not made the Presiding Patriarch to the church, as that position was filled at this time by William Smith, the brother of Hyrum Smith, the martyr, who had succeeded his father Joseph Smith, known in our annals as Joseph Smith, Sen.

†William Smith was subsequently ordained to be the Presiding Patriarch to the whole church. On this subject President Young says in his *Ms. History* under date of May 24, 1845: "The brethren present expressed their feelings towards Elder William Smith to which he responded. The Twelve then laid their hands upon him and ordained him to be Patriarch to the whole church. There was a warm interchange of good feelings between William Smith and the Quorum" (*History of Brigham Young, Ms.* 1845, p. 84) But before he was sustained in that position by the church, which in the due order of events would have taken place at the October conference, 1845, his iniquitous life came fully to light and he was rejected by the conference both as a member of the Quorum of the Twelve, and as Presiding Patriarch to the church. (See Minutes of the Conference for October 1845, *Times and Seasons,* vol. vi, p. 1009). On the 12th of October, 1845 he was excommunicated from the church (*Ibid*).

cause he was a coward, but he will come back and his company, and James Emmett and his company will come back. How easy would it be for the Lord if an army of mobs was to come within one mile of this place, to turn the northwest winds upon them and with snow, hail and rain, make them so that they would be glad to take care of themselves and leave us alone. He then referred to the Missourians when Joseph and others went to jail, snapping their guns at the brethren but they would not go off, etc. The Lord never let a prophet fall on the earth until he had accomplished his work: and the Lord did not take Joseph until he had finished his work, and it is the greatest blessing to Joseph and Hyrum God could bestow to take them away, for they had suffered enough. They are not the only martyrs that will have to die for the truth. There are men before me today who will be martyrs, and who will have to seal their testimony with their blood. I believe this people is the best people of their age that ever lived on the earth, the church of Enoch not excepted. We want you to come on with your tithes and offerings to build this Temple, and when it is finished we want you to spend a year in it and we will tell you things you never thought of.

Reference to Lyman Wight's and James Emmett's Going Away.

The Twelve then proceeded to ordain Asael Smith as follows:

THE ORDINATION OF A PATRIARCH—ASAEL SMITH

'Brother Asael Smith in the name of the Lord Jesus Christ of Nazareth, we lay our hands upon your head to ordain you to the office of Patriarch in this last Church of Jesus Christ, and we bestow upon you the keys and power, and the right and authority of blessing as *a patriarch in the Church of Jesus Christ*—and we say unto thee, thou shalt be a father to many. Thou shalt feel the Spirit of the Lord more than thou hast ever done before. Thy heart shall be enlarged, and it shall be thy delight to bless thy family, and thy posterity, and the fatherless and widow; and the Spirit of the Lord will rest upon you to predict upon the heads of those on whom you lay your hands, things that shall be hereafter even in the eternal world. We ask thee O Lord in the name of Jesus Christ that thou wouldst send thy Spirit upon this thy servant, that his heart may circumscribe the wisdom and knowledge of this world, and be enlarged so as to comprehend the things of eternity. We say unto thee, thou art blessed: thou art of the royal blood, and of thy lineage shall arise great and powerful men in the earth. We seal upon you the powers we have mentioned with the keys thereof upon your head in the name of Jesus Christ. Thou art the anointed of the Lord, one who shall stand in the latter days and be a pillar in the church of the living God, and one in whom the saints of God may trust to ask counsel. These blessings we seal upon you in the name of Jesus Christ: Amen.'

THE BUSINESS OF THE CONFERENCE FOR OCTOBER 8TH OUTLINED

President Young then said, we want the conference to continue tomorrow for business. We want the high priests' quorum together. President Miller will organize them on the right of the stand.

The Presidents of Seventies will organize all the seventies. We want to select a number of high priests to go through the states to preside over congressional districts. Then we want to have the elders' quorum organized that we can take out of the elders' quorum and fill up the seventies. We want all the seventies to be here and their presidents. We want them organized and begin to fill up the second quorum and then the third and the fourth to the tenth. The business of the day will be to ordain the Presidents of the Seventies and then fill the quorums of seventies from the elders' quorums, and select men from the quorum of high priests to go abroad and preside.

The conference then adjourned until tomorrow at nine o'clock, by blessing from President John Smith.

REMARKS OF ELDER JOHN TAYLOR ON ECONOMIC POLICY TO BE INAUGURATED AT NAUVOO

Tuesday Morning, October 8th, 1844.—Previous to opening the services of the day, Elder John Taylor made some remarks on our temporal economy. He proceeded to say that we have the means of wealth within ourselves.

'We have mechanics of every description from every country; men who are capable of carrying through any branch of manufacture. We want capital to commence with; but it is not necessary to wait for a very large amount, for it is safer to go to work with small means, than with an immense sum; for a rich man is very apt to overlook himself, and for want of proper calculation often scatters his means without accomplishing any benefit to the community. We can be made rich by our own enterprise and labor. Look at Great Britain; how have they obtained it? They have obtained it by encouraging their own manufacturers. It is true the poor are oppressed there; but it is not the manufacturers that oppress the people. We are not going to start anything on a large scale; our calculation is to have the saints manufacture everything we need in Nauvoo, and all kinds of useful articles to send abroad through the states and bring money here. Franklin says, 'time is money', and we want to spend our time in something that is useful and beneficial. Since we came here we have labored under every disadvantage. We have purchased Nauvoo, and much of the surrounding country, which has taken all our money. We have no need now to purchase more land; we now want to hit upon a plan to enable you to take your hands out of your pockets and build work shops and other places of industry. We have silk weavers, and cotton weavers, and every kind of mechanics that can be thought of. We want these to come together, and we want those who have money to lay it out and find them work. We have men here who can take the raw silk and from that carry it through every process and manufacture the shawls and dresses our women wear. We want to purchase raw cotton and manufacture it into wearing apparel, etc. If we can manufacture cotton, silk and woolen goods, we can keep our money at home; we will encourage home manufacture, as the Quakers do. We want all the cutlers to get together and manufacture our knives and forks, etc., etc. I know that we, as a community, can manufacture every thing we need. But I must now desist as the time to commence meeting has arrived.'

ORGANIZATION OF THE HIGH PRIESTS AND THE SEVENTY

Elder Heber C. Kimball now appeared and took charge of the meeting, which was opened by singing and prayer by Elder W. W. Phelps.

Elder George A. Smith moved that all in the elders' quorum under the age of thirty-five should be ordained into the seventies', if they are in good standing, and worthy, and will accept it. The motion was seconded and carried unanimously.

Elder Heber C. Kimball stated that President Joseph Young's wife was very sick and he wished to have her blessed, that brother Young might tarry and perform the duties of his office, and if the congregation would bless her let them say amen, and all the congregation said, amen.

He then recommended all those elders who are under the age of thirty-five, and also all the priests, teachers, deacons and members, who are recommended to be ordained, to withdraw and receive an ordination into the seventies, which was done.

SPECIAL MISSION APPOINTED TO THE HIGH PRIESTS

President Brigham Young then appeared and proceeded to select men from the high priests' quorum, to go abroad in all the congressional districts of the United States, to preside over the branches of the church, as follows:

David Evans
A. O. Smoot
Edson Whipple
Harvey Green
J. S. Fullmer
J. G. Divine
J. H. Johnson
Lester Brooks
J. B. Noble
Rufus Fisher
D. B. Huntington
Joseph Holbrook
John Lawson
Abel Lamb
J. H. Hale
G. D. Watt
J. W. Johnson
L. T. Coons
J. L. Robinson
Howard Coray
M. Sirrine
Pelatiah Brown

Jefferson Hunt
Lorenzo Snow
William Snow
Noah Packard
A. L. Tippets
J. C. Kingsbury
Jacob Foutz
Peter Haws
Thomas Gates
Simeon Carter
Albert Brown
Levi Gifford
Elijah Fordham
Edward Fisher
Franklin D. Richards
Isaac Clark
J. S. Holman
Wandell Mace
Charles Thompson
John Murdock
John Chase
A. L. Lamoreaux
E. T. Benson
Thomas Grover
C. L. Whitney
Addison Everett
Moses Clawson
William Parks
George Colson
H. W. Miller
Isaac Higbee
Daniel Garn
E. H. Groves
G. P. Dykes
Willard Snow
Wm. Felshaw
Winslow Farr
Shadrach Roundy
S. B. Stoddard
E. D. Woolley
Solomon Hancock
Abraham Palmer
James Brown
R. McBride
W. D. Pratt
Martin H. Peck
Morris Phelps
D. McArthur
Archibald Patten
L. H. Ferry
Charles Crismon
Lyman Stoddard
Arnold Stevens
David Fullmer
Joseph Allen
Andrew Perkins
Daniel Carter
Wm. G. Perkins
Graham Coltrin
D. H. Redfield
Titus Billings
Harvey Olumstead
Daniel Stanton

EXPLANATION OF THE MISSION

President Young explained the object for which these high priests were being sent out, and informed them that it was not the design to go and tarry six months and then return, but to go and settle down, where they can take their families and tarry until the

Temple is built, and then come and get their endowments, and return to their families and build up a stake as large as this.

President Young then selected from the elders' quorums some to be ordained high priests, whose names for the want of room are omitted for the present.

He also selected a number more to go into the seventies after which the remainder of the morning was spent in calling out the several quorums of seventies, and giving charges to the several presidents.

Brother Joseph L. Heywood was ordained under the hands of Elder Brigham Young, Heber C. Kimball and Parley P. Pratt, to be a bishop to the church in Quincy, Illinois.

Previous to adjournment the Presidents of the Seventies ordained upwards of 400 into the quorums of the seventies, and the presidents of the high priests' quorum ordained 40 into their quorum.

The meeting then adjourned until 2 o'clock p. m.

INSTRUCTIONS TO SEVENTIES AND ELDERS

Two o'clock p. m.—Conference resumed business. Those presidents of the seventies who were present and had not received an ordination to the presidency over the seventies, were called out and ordained, under the hands of President Joseph Young and others.

The remainder of the afternoon was spent in filling up the quorums of seventies, and at the close, eleven quorums were filled and properly organized, and about 40 elders organized as a part of the twelfth quorum.

President Brigham Young then said that the elders young men who are capable of preaching, will be ordained; 'but do not be anxious. You must now magnify your calling. Elders who go to borrowing horses or money, and running away with it, will be cut off from the church without any ceremony. They will not have as much lenity as heretofore. The seventies will have to be subject to their presidents and council. We do not want any man to go to preaching until he is sent. If an elder wants to go to preaching let him go into the seventies. *You are all apostles to the nations to carry the gospel;* and when we send you to build up the kingdom, we will give you the keys, and power and authority. If the people will let us alone we will convert the world, and if they persecute us we will do it the quicker. I would exhort all who go from this place to do right and be an honor to the cause. Inasmuch as you will go forth and do right you shall have more of the spirit than you have heretofore. We have had a good conference; we have had beautiful weather and no accidents; and if you will go and do honor to the Lord for this, say amen;' and all the people said amen.

On motion the conference adjourned until the 6th of April next, at 10 o'clock a. m.

Meeting dismissed by prayer from Elder Heber C. Kimball.

[Signed] BRIGHAM YOUNG, President.
Wm. Clayton, Clerk.'

At this conference there were about sixty brethren ordained high priests and four hundred and thirty ordained seventies.

Wednesday, 9.—A council of the Twelve was held at my house.

At a meeting of the trades called for the purpose of discussing the propriety of manufacturing instead of importing articles of common use in the city of Nauvoo, —John Taylor was appointed chairman and W. W. Phelps, secretary.

An Industrial Committee Appointed.

Elders John Taylor, Orson Spencer and Phineas Richards were appointed a general committee to devise plans, and confer with the special committees of the several trades."

CHAPTER XXIV

PRELIMINARY STEPS TO THE FORTHCOMING PROSECUTION OF THE MURDERERS OF JOSEPH AND HYRUM SMITH—THE WORK IN THE SOCIETY ISLANDS—TEMPLE AFFAIRS—FINANCIAL EMBARRASSMENT

"*Wednesday, October* 9, 1844 (*continued*):—Governor Ford wrote the following:

LETTER OF GOVERNOR FORD AUTHORIZING THE USE OF THE NAUVOO LEGION FOR PROTECTION OF THE COURTS

'State of Illinois, Executive Department,
Springfield, October 9th, 1844.

To Lieutenant-General Brigham Young of the Nauvoo Legion:

Sir: It may be probable that there may be further disturbances in Hancock county by those opposed to the prosecutions against the murderers of Joseph and Hyrum Smith. They may combine together in arms to subvert justice and prevent those prosecutions from going on. They may also attack or resist the civil authorities of the state in that county and they may attack some of the settlements or people there with violence.

The sheriff of the county may want a military force to guard the court and protect it or its officers or the jurors thereof or the witnesses attending court from the violence of a mob.

In all these cases you are hereby ordered and directed to hold in readiness a sufficient force under your command of the Nauvoo Legion to act under the direction of the said sheriff for the purposes aforesaid; and also to suppress mobs which may be collected in said county to injure the persons or property of any of the citizens. In testimony whereof I have hereunto set my hand and affixed the seal of state the day and year first herein above written.

[Signed] THOMAS FORD,
Governor and Commander-in-Chief.'

NOTE ACCOMPANYING THE GOVERNOR'S LETTER

'The enclosed order is one of great delicacy to execute. I have conversed with Mr. Backenstos and others and my opinion is the same as theirs that employing the Legion even legally may call down the vengeance of the people against your city. It if should be the means of getting up a civil war in Hancock I do not know how much force

I could bring to the aid of government. A force to be efficient would have to be called out as volunteers; a draft would bring friends and enemies alike. I called for twenty-five hundred before and by ordering out independent companies got four hundred and seventy-five. Three of those companies, the most efficient, have since been broken up and would refuse to go again. I should anticipate but a small force to be raised by volunteers. I would not undertake to march a drafted militia there. Two-thirds of them would join the enemy. The enclosed order is more intended as a permission to use the Legion in the manner indicated, if upon the whole matter it is thought advisable, than a compulsory command.

Your most wise and discreet councilors and county officers will have to act according to their best judgment.

[Signed] THOMAS FORD.'

Thursday, 10.—Elder Heber C. Kimball and myself spent most of the day at Father Ezra Chase's.

Friday, 11.—Evening, I attended prayer meeting at Elder Kimball's.

Saturday, 12.—I met with the city council.

Sunday, 13.—Meeting at the stand; Elder Parley P. Pratt preached.

The seventies met at their hall; Elder Orson Pratt preached and instructed the seventies in relation to their duties.

President Young's Visit to the East.

Tuesday, 15.—Accompanied by Elder Heber C. Kimball and my brother Lorenzo D. Young I started for Ottoway. We traveled to Ramus and stayed with Brother Erastus Bingham, where Parley P. Pratt joined us.

A meeting of delegates from Trades Committees was held in the Masonic Hall, Nauvoo, John Taylor chairman; at which it was reported that enough had been made manifest to ensure the practicability of making Nauvoo a great manufacturing depot.

Wednesday, 16.—Accompanied by the brethren before named I traveled to Brother Justus Ames's near Galesburg, forty miles. Next day, we traveled to LaFayette and stayed with Brother Austin Grant, and on the following day traveled to Providence encountering a wet snowstorm from which I took cold and suffered from diarrhea: we stayed at a tavern.

Saturday, 19.—We drove forty-four miles and arrived at Ottoway.

Sunday, 20.—We held two meetings at Brother Busard's.

Elders Heber C. Kimball and Parley P. Pratt and I preached: we had a profitable time.

The seventies met in their hall at Nauvoo.

After ordaining presidents who had been selected to preside over the quorums, a call was made by request of the major-general for thirty wagons and teams to be in readiness at the hall by daylight tomorrow, with three days' provisions and horse feed sufficient for the journey. This call was made to convey witnesses to Carthage in safety, and for protection during the trials at court: as two of our best men were murdered in Carthage in June and that too under the faith and pledge of the state and since caution is the parent of safety, it was deemed inadvisable to venture upon the pledges and promises of others.

Large Party of Witnesses From Nauvoo go to Carthage.

Monday, 21.—About one hundred and fifty brethren went from Nauvoo to Carthage early this morning and encamped near Crooked Creek; although they exhibited no arms their appearance created much excitement. The company consisted of the city council, police and those concerned in abating the *Nauvoo Expositor* nuisance with the witnesses and others who had business in Carthage: by encamping they avoided the necessity of paying hotel bills to enemies and the risk of being murdered in their beds.

With the brethren accompanying me I dined at Brother Reuben Miller's, crossed Fox river and proceeded to Brother Dunavan's and remained all night.

Tuesday, 22.—We visited the Norwegian branch in La Salle county, and met with the saints in the evening.

Misconduct of William Smith *et al* Reported.

I received a lengthy communication from Elder Wilford Woodruff relative to the injudicious course pursued by Elders William Smith, George J. Adams and Samuel Brannan.

A correspondent wrote from Carthage to the *Nauvoo Neighbor* as follows:

Mob Movements at Carthage

'Court is in session. The mob is here but not in great numbers. They are fierce and vindictive and disposed to do harm if they dare. They had a violent warlike meeting in the courthouse last night, in which they tried to get up a story that there were two hundred Mormons and three hundred Indians encamped near this place in hostile array for the purpose of an attack on the town. They passed panic resolutions, advising the court to adjourn and threatened if that was not done that they would raise an armed force as they say to protect themselves, but as all know, for the purpose of awing the court and juries and driving off witnesses. Rosevelt, Sharp, Williams and company were the leaders in getting up the excitement. They hope to get it believed abroad that they are about to be attacked by the Mormons as an excuse for some outrage which they wish, but have not the courage to perpetrate.'

A Norwegian Branch Organized

Wednesday, 23.—In company with Elder Heber C. Kimball, Parley P. Pratt and Lorenzo D. Young, I called the brethren together as a conference of the Norwegian branch. We taught the principles of the gospel to them and appointed George P. Dykes, high priest, to preside over the Norwegian branch and the saints in that vicinity of country, and ordained Reuben Miller a bishop.

We bought one hundred acres of land from Brothers Goodman and Anderson, and thereupon laid out a city. We selected the ground for a meetinghouse and drove the southeast corner stake. We called the city Norway and dedicated it to the Lord. Evening, we ordained Brother Phillip Hammond Busard a high priest and set him apart as a counselor to Brother Dykes.

Thursday, 24.—We left Ottoway and drove forty-three miles to Brother Parley P. Pratt's farm. We found his brother, Anson Pratt, and family well: they were glad to see us.

The brethren who went to Carthage returned home to Nauvoo. The members of the city council who were not indicted by the grand jury, were released from their bonds; eleven brethren were indicted for riot: the judge and attorney advised the brethren to return to Nauvoo to allay the excitement. The trials are continued until next spring term of court: the Nauvoo Legion is a terror.

Return of the Nauvoo Witnesses.

Brother Hyrum Smith prophesied that the governor would call upon the Nauvoo Legion to maintain the supremacy of the law, which has been fulfilled according to [by] the governor's late order.

Willard Richards was subpoenaed to appear before the grand jury, but being unable and unwilling to go to Carthage application was made to the court to get an attachment for his person, the attorney averring that it was necessary to have someone to prove that Joseph and Hyrum were dead, and he presumed that Richards was in possession of that knowledge; the court however refused the attachment as they considered that fact could be proved without bringing a sick man out of his bed. The Twelve all left Nauvoo during the court except Elder Willard Richards who was confined to his bed, and Elder George A. Smith who gave such counsel as the excitement of the times required.

Willard Richards Subpoenaed a Witness at the Carthage Trial.

WORK IN SOCIETY ISLANDS REPORTED

Elder Noah Rogers wrote from Huahine, Society Islands, of date as follows:

'I have left Tahiti and am now on the Island of Huahine, which is about ninety or one hundred miles distant. The work on Tahiti has got a good start. We baptized several whites, and several more said that they believed and would be baptized soon, and several natives told me when I left Tahiti that they meant to be baptized soon.

I left Brother Grouard there, who has got the language very well, and I have no doubt of his faithfulness, because he is a firm and faithful brother, and seeks the good of the kingdom of God.

I have been but one week on Huahine. I expect soon to obtain a house and preach as there is one or two that show some disposition to assist me in getting one. Almost every white man on this island keeps a grogshop and a gambling house, which is a very bad example for the natives. If you say anything to them about it, they will say that the whites learned [taught] us. They are full of licentiousness, which the sailors are very willing to encourage. When I see so much iniquity and abomination, it makes me sick to the very heart, and I wonder that the Lord has spared the world so long as he has. There is but one missionary [i. e. sectarian] here, who rules the island, as it were. All the people say that he is a very nice man, but I cannot say so much of him as he refuses to talk with me.'

President Young's Return to Nauvoo.

Monday, 28.—I returned to Nauvoo with my brethren, we found our families well. During our absence it was unknown to the people whither we had gone.

The Neighbor announced that true bills of indictment had been found against several persons of Hancock county, for the murder of Joseph and Hyrum Smith on the 27th of June last. Among the most conspicuous are, Colonel Levi Williams, Thomas C. Sharp, Mark Aldrich and Jacob C. Davis. The latter a senator in the legislature of Illinois.

Indictment of the Prophet's Murderers.

I attended a council with my brethren of the Twelve, the Trustees, the Temple Committee and Brother William Weeks the architect at the Temple Office, settling the differences existing between the Temple Committee and Brother Weeks.

Thursday, 31.—Elder Heber C. Kimball and I visited the Temple. I called at Sister Snively's with Brother Parley P. Pratt.

Friday, November 1, 1844.—The seventies met at 10 a. m.; President Joseph Young took the lead of business. Brother Eleazur Miller was ordained a president and twenty brethren were ordained seventies. I addressed the meeting on the subject of Elections, and voting for party candidates. I told them I wish I could communicate my feelings to them without speaking; and gave some of my views in relation to political men, and their principles.

Seventies' Meeting.

Sunday, 3.—I went to the Seventies' Hall in the forenoon, attended the high priests' quorum in the afternoon, and met again with the seventies in the evening.

At a conference held in Livonia, Wayne county, Michigan, on the 1st, 2nd and 3d inst., fourteen branches were represented, five elders volunteered to go and preach the gospel, and a resolution was passed to sustain the Twelve and all the authorities in carrying out the commandments of God that have been given through Joseph Smith, our martyred Prophet. The sacrament was administered, and much instruction given on the first principles of the gospel.*

Thursday, 7.—With Elders John Taylor and George A. Smith, I visited the Trustees, afterwards visited at Brother Joseph Bates Noble's with Elder Amasa M. Lyman, Sister Olive Frost and others.

A conference was held in New Trenton, Franklin county, Indiana, on the 6th and 7th inst. A good feeling prevailed, the Spirit of God was made manifest. President David Pettegrew baptized nine persons, and many were believing.

Friday, 8.—I went out to Fisher's Brick Yard and laid hands on the sick.

Saturday, 9.—I met with the city council. They passed an ordinance to prohibit the vending of spirituous liquors in the city under a penalty of not less than $25.00.

Sunday, 10.—I preached about two hours to the saints at the meeting ground; many present; had a good time.

Evening, seventies met: after the ordinations and business were attended to, Elder George A. Smith addressed the meeting on the progress of the kingdom.

At a quarterly conference held at St. Louis, present of the Twelve—1, high priests—4, seventies—15,

*The minutes of the conference were signed by Lyman Stoddard, President, William Burton, Clerk.

Conference at St. Louis.

elders—21, priests—13, teachers—2, deacons—5, members—172. The congregation was large, and notwithstanding the crowd strict attention was given to the interesting discourse of Elder Orson Hyde.

During conference seventeen persons joined the branch by letter, and one by baptism.

Monday, 11.—Attended council with the Twelve, bishops, high council, mayor and policemen, and transacted business for the welfare of the church.

Tuesday, 12.—I went to the Temple; called on Elders Kimball and Richards and found them recovering. I attended and addressed a meeting of the various trades of the city; a committee of three were appointed to see to the erection of a cotton factory, inasmuch as the machinery could be obtained. Elders John Taylor and Orson Spencer addressed the meeting.

William Clayton recorded the following:

'As I was walking along Front Street, St. Louis, I saw a man engaged cutting a stone monument. I was amazed to see these words already cut on the monument, *viz.* 'Highwater June 27th, 1844', that was the day when this generation rejected the Prophet of God, when he and his brother Hyrum, the Patriarch, were murdered at Carthage jail by a wicked mob, and this was the day when the waters overflowed the Missouri at the highest, when the Front Street of St. Louis was covered eight feet deep with the flood.'

Thursday, 14.—Elder B. L. Clapp wrote the following brief account of his mission:

Mission of Elder B. L. Clapp.

'I left Nauvoo August 12th, 1843, on a special mission to the south, and returned June 7th, 1844, during which time I traveled 4,444 miles, held 176 meetings and baptized 118 souls in the states of Alabama and Mississippi.'

Friday, 15.—I met with the authorities and held a council in relation to building the arsenal and carrying on the public works.

Sunday, 17.—Ten a. m. seventies met, Joseph Young presiding; twelve brethren were ordained to be seventies; several were recommended to the high priests' quorum. I attended in the evening and addressed the meeting.

Tuesday, 19.—Elder Orson Hyde and I visited the sick. A trades meeting was held in the Masonic Hall addressed by Elders Taylor, Scovil, Hunter and others. Elder J. W. Crosby wrote the following:

MISSION IN CANADIAN PROVINCES

'In August, 1843, Elder B. Brown and myself (having been appointed to visit the British provinces) proceeded to western New York, where we spent the winter. We organized several branches of the church, baptized upward of 150 souls, and held two conferences. After tarrying eight months, we went to Montreal and Quebec, making a short stay in each of these Catholic cities, preached some and circulated some books, pamphlets, etc. We proceeded to New Brunswick, and amid much opposition, persecution and personal violence, baptized 47; organized them into two branches, both in the county of York, above Frederickston. We returned to Boston in October and have spent a few weeks in the regions round about.'

Saturday, 23.—Bishop N. K. Whitney met with the lesser priesthood at the house of Samuel Gulley, and filled up the different quorums. I attended and in company with Elder Kimball and Bishop Whitney, ordained Brother Edward Hunter bishop, and set him apart to the care of the fifth ward [Nauvoo].

Edward Hunter Ordained a Bishop.

Sunday, 24.—Ten a. m. meeting of seventies in their hall. The seven presidents of the thirteenth quorum were ordained. Twenty brethren were ordained seventies, President Joseph Young preached.

Monday, 25.—A remonstrance against the division of Hancock county, numerously signed was placed in the hands of A. W. Babbitt, Esq., for presentation to the legislature of Illinois.

Saturday, 30.—Received a letter from Elder Wilford Woodruff, giving a particular account of the eastern branches of the church, which he had visited on his way to New York.

Sunday, December 1, 1844.—Elder Parley P. Pratt was appointed to go to the city of New York, and take charge of the press, regulate and counsel the immigration that may come that way from Europe and take the presidency of all the eastern branches of the church.

Eleven a. m., seventies met in their hall, Joseph Young presiding; sixteen brethren were ordained seventies; Elder George A. Smith preached at length on the subject of Apostasy.

Monday, 2.—I extract from the *Times and Seasons* (p. 728) the following:—

A VOICE FROM THE TEMPLE

By the Temple Committee

'We would say to all those who wish to bring tithes for the building of the Temple in the city of Nauvoo, that we have deemed it wisdom to remove our office, for the better accommodation of business, and of all who visit us on business, to the new and commodious brick store of Elder Parley P. Pratt, situated one block north from the west end of the Temple; at which place we will attend every day in the week (Sunday excepted) from morning till evening, to receive donations for the Temple and also attend to all other matters of business pertaining to the Trustees. We publish this notice that the brethren may not need to inquire where they shall deposit their donations. We have only one place of deposit in the city of Nauvoo and that is the above mentioned brick store.

Change of Office Location.

We would also once more offer a word of caution to all the saints for their benefit, inasmuch as there are those who are going round amongst the branches of the church to collect funds for the Temple without authority, and who are all the while practicing impositions upon the brethren. They generally use the property for their own individual benefit, and make no returns of it to us, and consequently when the donors come to see the records their names are not there. Many have felt to censure us on this account, but censure in such a case is unjust, for we have published notices repeatedly, warning the saints not to credit any man's testimony as to his being an agent unless he can show written authority from us or the Quorum of the Twelve, and all those who entrust their means in the hands of unauthorized agents, do it at their own risk, and not ours.

A Word of Caution Against Frauds.

The presiding elders in the branches have a right to call for, and to see the authority of any and every man professing to be an agent for the church, and if he is an honest servant and a man of authority he will always be ready to produce his testimonials to proper authority, but if he is an impostor he will either make excuses, or he will probably scorn at the idea of your questioning a man of God as to his authority. In some

The Right to Demand Identification of Agents.

instances men have considered themselves insulted when asked by the presiding elders for their authority, but this is only an evidence either of their own wickedness, or that they come on an errand on which they were never legally sent. Beware of wolves in sheep's clothing!

We are more particular on this subject because there have been instances, not a few, wherein men who are not Latter-day Saints, but on the contrary our most bitter enemies, have gone round gulling the churches and professing to be 'Mormons' and agents to collect funds for the building of the 'Temple and Nauvoo House', etc.; and they have taken advantage of the liberality of the brethren by all kinds of fine speeches and persuasive inducements to get away with their money, until they have accomplished their objects, and then they become 'missing'. It is not our wish to see the brethren cheated so barefacedly after all the persecutions we have suffered, and we once more repeat the caution, be wise and careful.

There are instances where the saints rarely see an authorized agent, in consequence of the distance from Nauvoo, or, in consequence of their residing some distance from a regularly organized branch. In such cases, when they want to send up their donations, let them do it by some man with whom they are well acquainted, and who they are well satisfied will do right, and carry their donation safe to its destination. And it would be well in all cases, where the brethren abroad send donations by authorized agents, to send a letter by mail (post paid), to the Trustees-in-Trust, informing them of the facts, and by whom their donations were sent, etc., and a good man will not blame you for being thus careful, for the same law that guards your rights will guard his rights, and the rights of every man.

List of Church Agents to be Published.

It is our intention for the future to publish the names of our agents in the *Nauvoo Neighbor* and the *Times and Seasons,* which we consider to be safer and better than written authority, inasmuch as the latter can be 'forged', but the former can not, and the agents can carry a copy of the paper, having their authority with them wherever they go.

Promised Change of Labor for Money.

There is also another subject which we would touch upon in this notice. There have been instances wherein men have gone amongst the branches of the church, collecting money and agreeing to pay the same amount in labor on the Temple, which they represent will answer as good a purpose as the money. We have to say on this subject that all such transactions are regarded as fraud, and is only a more crafty way of cheating the brethren. It would be folly for us to tell a man that ten days labor on the Temple would answer the law of tithing as well as ten dollars in money, when he was possessed of one hundred dollars in money. We know better, and every faithful brother and sister in the church will know better when they understand the principles of salvation as well as old Abraham, Isaac and Jacob did. For Jacob said of all thou givest me, one-tenth I will give unto thee, and whoever will read the history of the ancients with care will find that the law was, that they must pay one-tenth of all in its kind, whether cattle, horses, sheep, or fruits of the field. 'Tis true there were laws of redemption, whereby a man might redeem 'ought of his tithing' but it was so strict, that it is far easier to pay the tithing in kind rather than redeem it.

Jesus said, all who do the works of Abraham are the children of Abraham, and he (Abraham) paid tithes of all. The Savior also said to the Pharisees, 'ye pay tithes of mint and annis and cummin, but neglect the weightier matters of the law, judgment, mercy and faith, these ought ye to have done, and not have left the others undone.'

We make reference to these subjects that the brethren may take the hint, and think for themselves for just so sure as there are laws established from before the foundation of the world for the government of the Church of Christ just so sure will we fail of obtaining a fulness of salvation if we do not abide by those laws. No man can obtain a celestial glory if he will not abide a celestial law, and the law of tithing is a celestial law, and always was in force where the Melchizedek priesthood was inherited.

Operation of the Law of Tithing.

Why did the Savior say, 'how hardly shall they that have riches enter the kingdom of heaven?' Just converse with a rich man upon the subject of tithing, and you will soon see a reason why the rich can hardly enter the kingdom of heaven. When you converse with a man who has got ten thousand dollars in money in his hands, and tell him that his tithing will be one thousand dollars in money, you generally will see the force of the words of Jesus. That man would consider himself almost ruined if he should donate his one thousand dollars, whereas a man who has only ten dollars in money in the world, will come forward with cheerfulness and donate his tenth with joy. Remember the widow with her two mites.

The Saints Will Desire to Know.

No man or woman who really desires to secure a fulness of salvation will wish to be kept ignorant of those principles, and laws and ordinances on which his salvation depends, and consequently we are free to give a hint on the subject of tithing, not because we take it upon us to instruct the people, but because we realize in some measure the importance of it ourselves to set the saints to 'thinking for themselves' on the subject.

The Twelve Willing to Impart Instructions

When the saints ask for instructions, the Twelve are the proper authorities to refer to, and they will deal it out as fast as the saints are willing to obey.

Progress on the Temple.

We are happy to have to say that the Temple has progressed more rapidly than our most sanguine expectations could have imagined. All the capitals are on the walls, except one, which if the weather permit, will be up in a few days. The weather has been remarkably favorable and continues so to the present. The feelings of the saints are good and their hearts are cheered while they look upon the House of God and reflect on the prospects of its speedy completion. Their toils and poverty and persecutions are all swallowed up in the cheering prospects of their reward, only a little ways ahead.

Peace smiles upon our beloved city. And the great God looks down upon this people with sympathy and compassion from day to day, dispensing his heavenly blessings upon all the families of his saints according to his infinite wisdom and their willingness to receive them. The hearts of the saints are united firmer than ever, notwithstanding the vigorous efforts made by satan and dissenters to sow amongst us discord, strife, and confusion, and every evil work, scattering not excepted. Many houses are in progress of erection, which on account of the lateness of the season will have to stand unfinished until next spring. Every effort is being made to establish and put in operation various branches of manufacture for the employment of the saints, and the prospects are good, but not unattended with difficulty, toil and anxiety. But diligence, economy, and steady perseverance in a good cause, never fails to bring its reward, and very often the sweetest roses are surrounded by the sharpest thorns, and the greatest treasures deposited in places the most difficult of access, where we have to dig, and dig long and deep in order to obtain them.

Status of the Saints and the Work at Nauvoo.

We might prolong these remarks, but perhaps we have said enough for once. We will leave the subject, praying the blessings of our heavenly Father to rest upon all good men, and especially upon the saints, that they may have peace and joy in the Holy Ghost, and attain to that knowledge which will obtain for them an inheritance in the eternal kingdom of our God.

Benediction.

We have the honor to be
Your most obedient servants, and brethren in the faith of Christ,

N. K. WHITNEY,
GEORGE MILLER,
Trustees-in-Trust.

By Wm. Clayton, Recorder.
Nauvoo, Dec. 2, 1844.'

Monday, December 2, (*continued*).—I attended a council at Elder Willard Richards: present—the brethren of the Twelve, the Trustees; the Temple Committee and architect. The duties of the Temple Committee and architect were explained.

Evening; the Presidents of Seventies met.

Tuesday, 3.—City police met. Captain Hosea Stout instructed them pertaining to their duties.

Thursday, 5.—I insert the following minutes:

COUNCIL MINUTES OF FINANCIAL AFFAIRS

'Afternoon, a council was held in the recorder's office, President Brigham Young and Heber C. Kimball of the Quorum of the Twelve were present, also N. K. Whitney and George Miller, Trustees and Alpheus Cutler and Reynolds Cahoon, the Temple Committee. The council was called for the purpose of devising means to raise the sum of $3,100, which is due from the Trustees to several individuals for church lands, and which will have to be paid within three months or the lands be forfeited, worth from ten to fifteen thousand dollars. About one thousand dollars of the aforesaid sum must be paid in a few days. After conversing some time on the prospects of raising funds, President Young said that his feelings were to draw the money lying in the possession of Sisters Mary Smith and Mercy R. Thompson and A. Cutler, which money has been donated by the sisters of the church, by paying one cent a week, for the purpose of purchasing the nails and glass for the Temple and which amounted to five or six hundred dollars already collected. It is considered wisdom to do this to save the church property from the hands of our enemies; and the straitened circumstances under which the Trustees labor in consequence of persecution and oppression—we consider sufficient to justify the course. It is also considered certain that the money will be ready by the time the nails and glass are needed for the Temple, and that the money will be saving so much interest, whereas at the present it is lying useless. The suggestion by President Young seemed to meet the feelings of all the brethren, and it was concluded to draw an order for the money on Mrs. Mary Smith, and Mercy R. Thompson, which was immediately done.'

Action on Finance.

LETTER OF PRESIDENT YOUNG TO RELIEF SOCIETY PRESIDENCY

'*To Mrs. Mary Smith and Mercy R. Thompson,*

Dear Sisters:

We are under the necessity of raising a considerable sum of money for the use of the church within a few days. We have counseled together on the subject, and have considered it wisdom to call upon you for the money in your hands, donated by the sisters as penny subscription. You will therefore please deliver the same to Bishop Whitney when he presents this order.

Done by order of the Quorum of the Twelve, for and in behalf of the Church of Jesus Christ of Latter-day Saints.

[Signed] BRIGHAM YOUNG,
President of the Quorum of the Twelve.

William Clayton, Clerk.
Dec. 5, 1844.

N. B. Elder W. Richards, the clerk of the Quorum of the Twelve is very sick and unable to attend to business, which is the reason of the above signature as clerk.' "

CHAPTER XXV

PROGRESS OF WORK ON THE TEMPLE—MISCELLANEOUS MOVEMENTS IN CHURCH AND STATE

"*Friday, December* 6, 1844.—I [Brigham Young] insert the following minutes:—

THE PLACING OF THE LAST CAPITAL ON THE TEMPLE

'The last of the capitals was placed on the walls of the Temple. The workmen commenced raising the stone at half after 10 o'clock, but when about half way up one of the block shives broke in two. This placed the matter in a dangerous position, it was impossible to raise the stone higher without a new shive, and to attempt to let it down would have cut off the rope instantly. After much labor the workmen secured the tackle so that it could not move and having this done, they fixed a new shive in the block and after about an hour and a half's delay, at half after one p. m. the stone was safely fixed in its place in the wall. This stone is the largest one among the capitals and is supposed to weigh over two tons. There are thirty capitals around the Temple, each one composed of five stones, *viz.* one base stone, one large stone representing the sun rising just above the clouds, the lower part obscured; the third stone represents two hands each holding a trumpet, and the last two stones form a cap over the trumpet stone, and these all form the capital, the average cost of which is about four hundred and fifty dollars each. These stones are very beautifully cut, especially the face and trumpet stones, and are an evidence of great skill in the architect and ingenuity on the part of the stonecutters. They present a very pleasing and noble appearance, and seem very appropriate in their places. The first capital was set on the 23d of September last, making but a little over ten weeks between the first and the last, and out of that time the workmen lost about three weeks through bad weather, and having to wait for stone.

There has not been the slightest accident attending the raising of these large stones, except the second one which was set, the workmen, undertook to move the stone a little nearer the building without having first fixed the guy ropes to the crane, and while in the attempt the crane fell over with a tremendous crash and fell within about a foot of Brother Thomas Jaap, one of the workmen, who ran as soon as he saw the crane falling but happened to run in the same direction in which it fell. Providentially no further damage was done than to the crane which was partially broken.

The weather has been very favorable most of the time, but on account of its being so late in the season, it was generally feared we would not succeed in getting them [the capitals] up before winter set in, but it seems as though the Lord held up the storms and the cold for our advantage, until this important piece of labor has been accomplished to our utmost satisfaction and delight.

There are yet twelve of the capitals without trumpet stones, and will have to remain so until spring; three of them however are finished and several others nearly so.

The weather changed this morning. It rained nearly all the time the men were at work; and about two hours after the last capital was set, it commenced snowing and continued until the ground was covered about four inches deep. Nine o'clock p. m., it now freezes very sharp and to all appearance stern winter has taken possession of the atmosphere in earnest.'

Departure of Elder Woodruff for England.

Elder Wilford Woodruff and family, in company with Elder H. Clark and Dan Jones and their families, and Elders Milton Holmes and Leonard W. Hardy sailed from New York in the packet ship, *John B. Skiddy,* for Liverpool.

Sunday, 8.—The seventies met in their hall. Eight brethren were ordained seventies. A letter was read from Elder B. F. Grouard from the Society Isles. Elder Henry Harriman, George A. Smith and Joseph Young instructed the elders.

Elder Willard Richards, city recorder, opened office in his new house, and appointed Thomas Bullock his deputy. Thomas [Bullock] commenced putting the city records in order, which had been neglected some four months in consequence of Brother Willard's inability through sickness.

Conference in Michigan.

Monday, 9.—A conference was held in Comstock, Kalamazoo county, Michigan on the 8th and 9th inst. Crandall Dunn presiding; five branches were represented numbering 107 members, 1 high priest, 16 elders, 1 teacher, and one deacon. Resolutions were passed to sustain the Twelve and agreeing to tithe themselves to aid in building the Temple. During the conference much good instruction was given by Elder Crandall Dunn, C. M. Webb, and D. Savage; one priest was ordained, 3 children blessed, and one person baptized.

Wednesday, 11.—Elder Willard Richards recommenced to gather materials for the Church History, assisted by W. W. Phelps.

Thursday, 12.—The high priests of the 5th ward met in the Concert Hall.

Friday, 13.—The Aaronic priesthood met. Bishop N. K. Whitney presided. He spoke on the subject of furnishing employment for the poor, the manufacturing of straw and palm leaf hats, and willow baskets. Two were ordained.

Saturday, 14.—Received a lengthy communication from A. W. Babbitt, Esq., house of representatives, Springfield. Advising in relation to his communications with the governor, the anticipated movements of the legislature, and his intended course pertaining to the chartered rights of the city of Nauvoo; to which a reply was written by Orson Spencer showing the injustice and unconstitutionality of a repeal of the Nauvoo Charter.

Repeal of Nauvoo Charters Proposed.

In company with Elder Heber C. Kimball, Orson Hyde, Orson Pratt, John Taylor, and George A. Smith, I attended city council. An ordinance was passed organizing the Seventies' Library and Institute Association. The council expressed their views in relation to the illegality of the legislature interfering with the chartered right of the city of Nauvoo; when those rights had never been exercised to the hurt or the prejudice of the innocent.

City Council Meeting.

Sunday, 15.—Ten a. m. meeting of seventies. President Joseph Young, presiding. Twenty-nine persons were unanimously received by vote and ordained to be seventies.

The ordinance of the city council in relation to the Seventies' Library and Institute Association was read.

Elder George A. Smith advised the elders to get up

schools, that all the seventies who would, might be taught in the branches of education, and prepare themselves that the least might be fully competent, to correspond with the wise men of the world.

School for Seventies.

Good and useful instruction relative to manners, order and good behavior were given by the president and some of his council.

Monday, 16.—I extract from the *Tithing Record No.* 2:—

'A few days ago the Twelve and the Trustees counseled together on the propriety of employing a suitable number of carpenters this winter to prepare the timbers for the Temple, so as to have them all ready when the stone work was finished.

They concluded to employ fifteen persons steadily as carpenters, and that the architect be authorized to select such men as he has confidence in—men who are well qualified to do the work that is wanted. It was also concluded to fix up a shop in the Temple for the carpenters to work in. Accordingly the south side of the lower story was weatherboarded around and a convenient shop made of it on Saturday, and today, the men have gone to work.

Carpenters Selected to Work on the Temple.

The names of the carpenters selected as steady hands are as follows: *viz*: Truman O. Angel, William Felshaw, William F. Cahoon, Joseph S. Schofield, Samuel Rolfe, Zimri H. Baxter, Addison Everett, John Stiles, Hugh Riding, Miles Romney, Jabez Durfee, Stephen Longstroth, Benjamin Rolfe, Nicholas T. Silcock, William Carmichael, Hiram Mace, Daniel Avery, Gideon Gibbs, and Wandel Mace.

N. B.—Daniel Avery is employed to take care of the shop and the fires, etc.

The three last named are engaged in the sawmill shop.'

Tuesday, 17.—I copy the following minutes on file:—

PRESIDENCY APPOINTED FOR KIRTLAND

'The Quorum of the Twelve and others in council assembled at the office of President Brigham Young, at the corner of Kimball and Granger Streets.

Moved and seconded that Brother Reuben McBride take the presidency over all the affairs pertaining to the Church of Jesus Christ of Latter-day Saints in Kirtland—both spiritually and temporally—which was carried by a unanimous voice of said council.

A letter was then read before the council which President Young received from Brothers Joseph Parsons and James McDowell, residing in Pittsburgh, containing an acknowledgment that they had been deceived by Elder Rigdon's false pretensions to the Presidency, and after a calm and careful investigation of the *Book of Doctrine and Covenants* and *Book of Mormon*, they had renounced the pretensions of Sidney Rigdon as being false and felt satisfied that the Quorum of the Twelve held the keys of the kingdom.

Elder Rigdon Rejected by Elders in Pittsburgh.

Voted unanimously that their acknowledgment be received and they be received into full fellowship with the saints.'

I received a letter from Horace R. Hotchkiss proposing to dispose of lots in Nauvoo, to be compensated by improvements on adjoining lots; also on the subject of home manufactures and building up the city of Nauvoo; to which I replied informing him that property was not so high as it had been, and referred him to Elder Taylor for information on the trades operations.

Hotchkiss Interests in Nauvoo.

The brethren of the Twelve visited Elder Willard Richards who was sick.

Wednesday, 18.—Evening with Elder Heber C. Kimball and Bishop N. K. Whitney. I attended the practice of music at the Concert Hall.

Friday, 20.—In company with Elder Heber C. Kimball and George A. Smith I spent a portion of the day at the Tithing Office regulating matters pertaining to tithings; called on Brother Willard Richards, found him some better.

William Clayton records he 'had some conversation with Brother Cahoon respecting making a feast for the poor and proposed to do it on New Year's day. Daniel H. Wells, Esq., agreed to give ten dollars to aid the feast for the poor.'

Sunday, 22.—I met as usual with the Twelve Apostles and others for prayer.

Ten a. m., seventies met at their hall, Joseph Young presiding: five presidents and forty seventies were ordained; fourteenth quorum organized; two brethren were recommended to the high priests' quorum.

Monday, 23.—The Aaronic priesthood met; Bishop

N. K. Whitney presiding; four persons were ordained to the office of priest.

Tuesday, 24.—The stockholders of the Seventies' Library and Institute Association elected Elder George A. Smith, Amasa M. Lyman, Joseph Young, Levi W. Hancock, Albert Carrington, John D. Lee and James M. Monroe trustees.

Wednesday, 25.—I spent an agreeable time at Brother Coolidge's, in company with Elders Heber C. Kimball, George A. Smith, A. M. Lyman, John Taylor and their ladies. The band was in attendance. We partook of a substantial dinner; after which I made a few remarks expressive of my good feelings and love to my brethren. I remarked that the Lord would never suffer us to overcome our enemies while we cherished feelings of revenge, when we prevailed over our enemies it must be from a sense of duty and not of revenge.

Banquet and Party.

Friday, 27.—I went to the Trustee's Office.

Evening, there was a meeting in the Seventies' Hall of the city council, the high council and leading authorities of the church.

Governor Ford's special message to the legislature was read. It was a very meager attempt to excuse himself from participation in the assassination of Joseph and Hyrum Smith, being full of misrepresentations, exaggerations and contemptible falsehoods.

Governor Ford's Message to the Illinois Legislature.

Brother A. W. Babbitt made a report of his proceedings in Springfield.

Sunday, 29.—I published the following:

'*Brother Taylor on Church Periodicals.*—The question is asked in *The New York Prophet*: Why is it that there is no more interest manifested among the elders in enlisting support or subscriptions for our periodicals? For one I will answer the question. While I have been preaching abroad from place to place, the question being asked of me so many times by the saints, 'Why do not my papers come? I subscribed and sent the money long ago and have received but two or three numbers.' My reply has been, 'it seems the post office department is very uncertain.'

Realizing the very few that have been received by our brethren abroad, in proportion to the many that have been mailed at our establishment, my heart has fainted, and I have not asked men to pay their money fearing they would never receive their papers.' "

CHAPTER XXVI

THE GREAT CONFERENCE OF THE SEVENTIES AT NAUVOO—ORGANIZATION OF NEW QUORUMS—DEDICATION OF THE SEVENTIES' HALL—NOTABLE DISCOURSES—DOCTRINAL INSTRUCTIONS BY PRESIDENT BRIGHAM YOUNG ON PRIESTHOOD—THE TWELVE—THE SEVENTY—AND THE BISHOPRIC

"*Monday, December* 30, 1844.—The following is extracted from the *Times and Seasons,* Vol. vi, p. 794:—

DEDICATION OF THE SEVENTIES' HALL

(*Five Days, Dec.* 26-30, 1844. *A Memorable Conference*)

'*Thursday, December* 26, *A. D.* 1844.—The services commenced under the direction of President Joseph Young [the Senior President of the First Quorum of the Seventy], who organized the meeting in the following order:

Arrangement of the Meeting.

The stand was occupied by the Seven Presiding Presidents of the Seventy, and the Twelve or as many of them as were present. The senior president of each quorum was seated on the right, the choir of singers on the left, and the brass band in front. The second and third quorums in order, with their families, occupied the other seats for the day. Each day afforded a new congregation, that all the seventies, with their families, might in turn, participate in the privilege of the dedication, according to their respective quorums, there being fifteen quorums whose claims were equal, two of which convened in the hall each day, beginning with the second and third [quorums].

The excellent melody of the choir and band, mingling with the devout aspirations of a congregation of all saints, gave the commencement of their services an air of interest, felicity and glory, at once feeling, touching, pathetic, grand, sublime!

A hymn, composed by Elder W. W. Phelps, for the dedication, entitled 'A Voice from the Prophet: Come to Me', was sung:

A VOICE FROM THE PROPHET

'COME TO ME'

(By W. W. Phelps, to the Tune—'Indian Hunter')

'Come to me, will ye come to the saints that have died—
To the next better world, where the righteous reside;
Where the angels and spirits in harmony be.
In the joys of a vast Paradise? Come to me.

Come to me where the truth and the virtues prevail;
Where the union is one, and the years never fail;
Where the heart can't conceive, nor the nat'ral eye see,
What the Lord has prepar'd for the just: Come to me.

Come to me where there is no destruction or war;
Neither tyrants, nor mobbers, or nations ajar;
Where the system is perfect, and happiness free,
And the life is eternal with God: Come to me.

Come to me, will ye come to the mansions above
Where the bliss and the knowledge, the light, and the love,
And the glory of God, do eternally be?
Death, the wages of sin, is not here: Come to me.

Come to me, here are Adam and Eve at the head
Of a multitude quicken'd and rais'd from the dead:
Here's the knowledge that was, or that is, or will be—
In the gen'ral assembly of worlds: Come to me.

Come to me; here's the myst'ry that man hath not seen;
Here's our Father in heaven, and Mother, the Queen,
Here are worlds that have been, and the worlds yet to be,
Here's eternity,—endless; amen: Come to me.

Come to me all ye faithful and blest of Nauvoo:
Come ye Twelve, and ye High Priests, and Seventies, too;
Come ye Elders, and all of the great company;—
When you've finish'd your work on the earth: Come to me,

Come to me; here's the future, the present and past:
Here is Alpha, Omega, the first and the last;
Here's the fountain, the 'river of life', and the Tree;
Here's your Prophet and Seer, Joseph Smith: Come to me.'

The dedication prayer by President Brigham Young, was in substance as follows:

PRAYER: A SUPPLICATION TO THE THRONE OF GRACE

'Thou God who dwellest in the midst of thine own kingdoms, and doeth thy pleasure in the midst of the same. We realize that we are thy children, although we have long wandered from thee. Yet we feel that it is thy good pleasure to bless us, when we come unto thee with hearts of humility. Therefore we desire to present ourselves before thee as dutiful children to an earthly parent, knowing that we are thine and ask thee for those things we need. We feel, our Father, that we are in a world of darkness, and trouble, and death, where we cannot behold thy glory; yet we come unto thee in the name of Jesus Christ, thy Son, and ask thee to forgive our sins and past offenses. Fill us with thy Spirit, and accept our praise, while we dedicate ourselves unto thee, and as we have approximated to behold this beautiful morning, the day in which begins a new year. do thou, our heavenly Father, look down in compassion upon us, the creatures of thy care and protection, who dwell upon thy footstool. Increase our knowledge, wisdom, and understanding, that we, thy servants, may be enabled to administer salvation to thy people, even as thou hast committed a dispensation of the same unto us; and while we call on thy name we desire union in thy presence, our Father, to dedicate unto thee this hall, the ground upon which it stands, and all things that appertain unto it. We ask thee to let thy blessing rest upon thy servant Edward Hunter, our beloved brother, who has donated to us the ground upon which this sacred edifice has been erected. We pray thee to enrich him and his family, not only with the good things of this world, but with the riches of eternity also. We ask thee, our Father, to accept the dedication of our hearts this morning, and may we feel the prelude of that power and authority with which thy servants shall be clothed, when they shall go forth and open the door of salvation to the nations and kingdoms of the earth; even thy servants, the seventies, upon whom the burden of thy kingdom does rest, and to whom the keys of the same shall be committed from time to time. We now dedicate this hall unto thee, our Father, and ask thee in the name of thy Son Jesus Christ, to sanctify it and make it holy, and may no foul spirit be suffered to enter it, but may it be filled with thy Spirit that it may be called the gate of heaven, and may all who enter within its doors be made to feel thy love and power. We ask thee to pour out thy Spirit upon the Presidency of the Seventies; wilt thou endow them with knowledge and understanding that they may be enabled to instruct thy servants over whom they are called to preside; and do thou let the same blessings flow freely upon each quorum, that all thy servants may be filled with thy Spirit, and become mighty men before thee that they may go forth and gather the pure in heart, Zion redeemed and Jerusalem rebuilt. Help us O Lord to separate ourselves from all iniquity, that evildoers may not exist in our midst, but may this people become a holy people, peculiar to thyself, to show forth thy praise in all the world. Our Father in heaven, we humbly beseech thee to shield and protect us in this city; provide for and sustain us by thy power, that we may be enabled to accomplish the work which thou hast commanded us to do. Assist us to build the Temple and Nauvoo House; that the truth and light of the everlasting gospel may shine forth from this place, to the honor, praise and glory of thy name. Regard in mercy the Quorum of the Twelve, at whom the arrows of the destroyer are directed. Preserve them O Lord, by thine own omnipotent power, that they may stand in holy places and be enabled to disseminate the knowledge of thy kingdom to the inhabitants of the earth; wilt thou sustain us, our Father, that we may perform and accomplish the mighty work whereunto we are called.

'We feel to lament and mourn the loss of our beloved brothers, Joseph and Hyrum, the Prophet and Patriarch, whom thou hast suffered to be martyred for the testimony of the truth; but we thank thee our Father, that although they have been taken from us for the present, yet that same spirit which animated their bosoms, the fruits of which is peace and charity, still remains amongst thy people. We now commit ourselves into thy care, and ask thee to guide and control us by the council of heaven, through all the shifting and various scenes of mortality, that the numbers of our days may be filled up in usefulness, and we be prepared for that exalted station and rest that remains for the people of God, and the honor, praise, and glory of our salvation, we will ascribe unto thee; for thine is the kingdom, power and glory, worlds without end: Amen.'*

A hymn composed by Elder John Taylor for the dedication of the Seventies' Hall and dedicated to President Brigham Young, was sung by Elder John Kay, assisted by the band, entitled 'The Seer'.

THE SEER

'The Seer;—the Seer;—Joseph the Seer—
I'll sing of the Prophet ever dear,
His equal now cannot be found,—
By searching the wide world around.

*It is doubtful if Brigham Young ever did anything better in oral expression than this beautiful and timely prayer.

With Gods he soared in the realms of day;
And men he taught the heavenly way.
'Mid the foaming billows of angry strife—
He stood at the helm of the ship of life.
The earthly Seer; the heavenly Seer,
I love to dwell on his mem'ry dear;—
The chosen of God, and the friend of men,
He brought the priesthood back again,
He gazed on the past, on the present too;—
And ope'd the heavenly world to view.

Of noble seed—of heavenly birth,
He came to bless the sons of earth;
With keys by the Almighty given,
He opened the full rich stores of heaven,
O'er the world that was wrapt in sable night
Like the sun he spread his golden light.
He strove,—O, how he strove to stay,
The stream of crime in its reckless way—
He urged the wayward to reclaim;
With a mighty mind, and a noble aim.

The saints;—the saints; his only pride,
For them he lived, for them he died!
Their joys were his;—their sorrows too;—
He lov'd the saints;—he lov'd Nauvoo.
Unchanged in death, with a Savior's love
He pleads their cause, in the courts above.
The Seer;—the Seer—Joseph the Seer!
O, how I love his memory dear,
The just and wise, the pure and free,
A father he was, and is to me.
Let fiends now rage in their dark hour;
No matter, he is beyond their power.

He's free;—he's free;—the Prophet's free!
He is where he will ever be.
Beyond the reach of mobs and strife,
He rests unharm'd in endless life.
His home's in the sky;—he dwells with the Gods
Far from the furious rage of mobs.
He died; he died—for those he lov'd
He reigns;—he reigns in the realms above,

He waits with the just who have gone before,
To welcome the saints to Zion's shore;
Shout, shout ye saints—this boon is given,
We'll meet our martyr'd Seer in heaven.'*

REMARKS OF ELDER HEBER C. KIMBALL

Elder Heber C. Kimball addressed the congregation in plain though impressive language, and in his usual philanthropic manner, used a chain as a figure to illustrate the principle of gradation, while in pursuit of celestial enjoyment in worlds to come.

ELDER GEORGE A. SMITH'S DISCOURSE AND ADMONITION ON UNION

Elder George A. Smith offered some very appropriate remarks relative to union. He referred to the Zion Camp, and their expedition to Missouri, and after giving an interesting account on that subject, concluded with an exhortation to union, firmness, and perseverance. He said that if we were of one heart and mind, we might be as the angels are. Perfect union and harmony exist among them. Hence their concert of action, and consequently their influence and power with God; and upon the same principle [continued he] we could make a heaven wherever in the dispensation of Providence, we might be placed, possessing this principle, consonant with the honors, glory and immortality of angels.

At 12 o'clock, a recess of one hour was given each day. At 1 o'clock the house was called to order by President Joseph Young.

DISCOURSE OF ELDER ORSON HYDE ON UNION—AN ILLUSTRATION

Elder Orson Hyde took the stand, and continued the

*This hymn under the circumstances of its rendition would be very impressive in the congregation of the seventies and their families. John Kay had a rich, deep baritone voice and sang with excellent taste and the martyrdom of the Prophet being so recent, within six months, the saints would be greatly affected by the noble sentiments of Elder Taylor's hymn, accompanied with the musical rendition of it.

same subject, [unity of spirit and action], and introduced for a comparison the circumstance of the Assyrian king, who gave his son a bundle of arrows bound in a quiver, and commanded him to break them, which he in vain attempted to do while they were firmly bound together; but when they were unbound and separated, the object was easily effected. This circumstance he likened to this people, and said that if we were united we would be able to stand against all the fiery darts that could be hurled upon us by the adversary of our salvation. Some having a knowledge of this fact, have used every effort to divide this people, in order to accomplish their wicked designs. Some few have been led to the north, others to the west, and some to the east. Those who have separated may be broken; but those who remain together firmly united can never be broken.

Illustration of the Force in Unity.

After speaking of authorities in the church or kingdom of God, he observed that 'Apostles in the primitive age of Christianity were first made witnesses to all the nations of the earth. They were afterwards made judges of that same people. Hence the saying of the Apostles, 'know ye not that the saints shall judge the world?' that is, that generation or people to whom they were sent as witnesses. (See *I Cor.* vi:2,3). Indeed they were competent to sit in judgment upon them, having had an experimental knowledge of their course of conduct and barbarous treatment towards the servants of God that were sent to establish peace among them. Many of whom they did not only reject, but tortured and slew them in a cruel manner. This was the fate of the Prophets and Apostles who vainly attempted to restore them from their wickedness, assuring them, to use the language of the scripture: 'As you mete out to others, so shall it be measured to you again.'

Apostles Witnesses for God.

'The declaration of John while on the Isle of Patmos, through the Spirit of God, declaring things which would come to pass, says: Give her double for all her sins. The reason is obvious. The debt was of a long standing; she had exercised unceasing tyranny over the servants of God, and refused them justice and mercy. Therefore as they meted out, double measure shall be given them in return. I have no doubt,' said he, 'but the old scribes, and pharisees, after scourging the saints in the most horrid manner, and causing many to seal their testimony with their blood, would go into the Temple with all the sanctity imaginable and ask God to forgive their sins; when in reality he would have nothing to do with the matter, until they had first obtained forgiveness from those whom they had injured, by making ample satisfaction to them. For proof of this fact just examine the declaration of Jesus to the Apostles: Whose soever sins ye remit on earth, shall be remitted in heaven. And if they were retained on earth they were to be retained in heaven also.

Measure to Babylon Double.

'Neither can this generation get forgiveness from God, for the great injuries that they have done us as a people, without first rendering perfect satisfaction to us whom they have injured. The elders of this church have been swift witnesses to Missouri, and all the world. Hence in vain may they plead to have their sins remitted until the proper steps are taken.

'Our Prophet has been slain, and the burden of the kingdom has fallen upon us (the Twelve) and our lives are sought after; but while the angel that administers to man is still in attendance, his life is protected, for the guardian angel is stronger than death; but when he is withdrawn humanity is easily overcome. Hence it was with the Son of God while upon the cross, that even he, the Savior of the world, could but exclaim: My God, my God, why hast thou forsaken me! Referring to the protecting angel whom the Lord had called away, leaving Jesus in the arms of death; that he might be taken away from this world of misery and pain to the

Burden of the Kingdom Has Fallen Upon the Twelve.

mansions of God, where he should turn and rule the nations with a rod of iron [i. e. the law, or word of God]. For proof of my assertion I have only to call upon the same individual who exclaimed on the cross: My God why hast thou taken away my protecting angel.

'At the time of his arrest he commanded Peter to put up his sword and gave him to understand that if it were the will of God that he should not drink of the bitter cup (death) that he could call on his Father for ten legions of angels who would eagerly fly to his deliverance. But had he been delivered from the cross, how could the scriptures have been fulfilled? * * *

'Another word respecting the arrows, which by the Spirit of God was made manifest to me last summer.

Efforts to Break up the Unity of the Saints.

There were certain persons who endeavored to divide and draw away the saints from this place, by telling them in secret councils: I have the wink from the Twelve; their minds are to sanction our going to build up, etc. I have got my work laid out by revelation; but you must not say a word to them (the Twelve) about this matter, for if you do you will not get any satisfaction, they will disclaim in public any knowledge of such a move; but I understand them; all is right; and thus hold them in ignorance; also, bind them by solemn oath, not to disclose the matter to any human being, not even to their wives, under the penalty of death. Through hypocrisy and false statements, a few, and but a few, have been deceived and torn from the bundle of arrows by those who have led off from this place. This is an aspiring spirit and is from the devil, and every spirit that refuses to make manifest, is from Lucifer, the prince of darkness. Now let the saints, from this time forth be guarded against all such secrets, councils or confirmations.'

ELDER AMASA M. LYMAN'S DISCOURSE

Elder Amasa M. Lyman expressed his gratitude to

God for the favorable circumstances under which we were placed at present. Said he, when we contemplate the exalted station and high calling of this august body of elders, we can but associate it with their future destiny. They, as a people are only forming a character for heaven and immortal happiness. This certainly should stimulate each man of you to action, and remove every drowsy, careless, idle feeling from their minds, while in each heart the most lively sensations of joy should spring up. He advised them to embrace every opportunity afforded them to improve their minds and obtain useful knowledge. Just take the saints out of the world, said he, and soon destruction would sweep the land, as was the fact with Sodom and Gomorrah.

Effects of This Notable Meeting of Elders.

In speaking of the Seventies' Library and Institute Association, he remarked that the seventies were designed to be messengers to every land and kingdom under heaven, and consequently they will have ample opportunities to gather many antiquities, with various books, charts, etc., to deposit in the library for the advancement of art and science, which, with just principles, will go heart and hand unto perfection, being built upon truth, the foundation of the Apostles and Prophets, Jesus Christ the Chief Corner Stone, which shall sound out from this voluminous institute, and with its benign influence organize and harmonize the vast extent of the world.

The Seventies' Library and Institute.

Friday, December 27.—Fourth and fifth quorums met. Prayer by Elder George A. Smith.

The order of the meeting was explained by President Joseph Young.

HEBER C. KIMBALL'S ADDRESS

Elder Heber C. Kimball then delivered a short address upon the authorities of the kingdom of God, and in passing on, he set forth the order as to endowment, and informed the saints that every man and woman must stand in his proper place and station, being subject to the powers that be, in order to be exalted to glory, honor, and immortality in the eternal world. 'It is even so in the resurrection from the dead, as St. Paul informs us that Christ is the first fruits of the resurrection from the dead in the primitive age, and so will Joseph Smith be in this dispensation. Joseph will be the first man who will rise from the dead, and then all men according to their proper order.

Joseph Smith's Place in the Resurrection.

'I will tell the seventies and everybody else, if you cannot and will not submit to the authorities that God has placed in his church over you, you had better back out now, and not attempt to proceed further; if you are ever saved it will be by obedience to the order of God's kingdom here on the earth, and this order is in subordination to that order which is in the heavens. According to the important station the seventies are called to fill in this last dispensation, they should be careful to walk uprightly and act justly, shunning every appearance of evil and never condescend to do anything mean.'

Submit to the Powers That Be.

Adjourned one hour.

Met pursuant to adjournment.

ELDER JOHN TAYLOR'S DISCOURSE—RELATIONSHIP OF THE CHURCH TO GOD

Elder John Taylor took the stand and proceeded to lay before us the pure principles of life and salvation, reminding us that we were the people that the Lord had chosen and set apart to accomplish the great and mighty work of the last days, which was spoken of by the prophets of old. 'No other people,' said he, 'can possibly do this work, for unto us the keys of this last dispensation with the power of the priesthood is given; consequently there is no people under the whole heaven that sustain the same relationship with God, as we do. What knowledge have the world of God's laws or his ways? They don't know enough in reality to save a mosquito.

'I do not mean to say that there is no learning in the world, for I am aware of the fact that there is far more of what the world calls wisdom in the midst of the inhabitants of the earth than can be found here; but a learned fool is no better than an illiterate one, if the Apostle Paul's judgment can be admitted as proof. He told the people of his day that the wisdom of this world was foolishness with God. When I ask what knowledge the world has of God or his government, I mean to be understood as speaking of that knowledge that comes from God, communicated to us through the channel of revelation, for without it we know nothing correctly, no more than the brute beasts who are led by the instinct of nature. Consequently, brethren, when you go to declare the plain truth of the kingdom of God, the gospel of Jesus Christ, you should never shrink from your calling, nor succumb to the learned because of the advantage they have over you by reason of literary attainments, for God is with you, and will give you a mouth and wisdom by which you shall be delivered from the strong arm of violence.

The Elders of the Church and the Learning of the World.

'Remember the race is not to the swift nor the battle to the strong; but to those who trust in the Lord. When the Twelve were called to bear the gospel of this kingdom to the inhabitants of Europe, there were not many wise among them, speaking after the manner of men; yet we believed him faithful who had chosen us, and as little children we trusted in him for wisdom and understanding to do his will; for his will was our pleasure, and in the short space of two years, about two thousand souls were given to us in the ministry. I speak of these things that you may know in whom to put your trust and confidence; for should you desire self-esteem, and take the honor to yourselves, you soon would sink to shame and disgrace. You are the heralds of salvation, and through your faithfulness, obedience and persever-

The Race Not to the Swift Nor the Battle to the Strong.

ance, you may be exalted to kings and priests unto God in the eternal worlds.

Admonitions to the Seventies.

'Some of you may be called to go to foreign lands to administer salvation to nations that are to you unknown. The redemption of your deceased relatives are also required at your hands. Hence you discover your relationship with God and the responsibility under which you are acting. Be faithful in him who has called you, and he will deliver you from every snare, pit, and temptation that awaits you. I would rather trust in God for bread, than to trust in the princes of this world. I speak of these things for your interest; then let your hearts be comforted. When we (the Twelve) left this place, on our mission to England, a journey of near five thousand miles to be accomplished without a penny in our pockets, our only resource was to trust in the Disposer of all events to supply our returning wants. And our prayers were heard and answered according to the desires of our hearts.

Lift Up Your Heads Like Kings.

'When you go forth, lift up your heads like kings and trust in the name of Israel's God; for the very hairs of your head are numbered and will not fall to the ground without notice. Remembering at all times to uphold each other by the prayer and power of faith, and God will bless you and your labors.'

The following prayer was made by President Joseph Young on the fourth day of the dedication.

PRAYER OF PRESIDENT JOSEPH YOUNG—SECOND PRAYER OF DEDICATION

'O God, our heavenly Father, we humbly pray thee in the name of Jesus Christ, thy Son, to bless us with the remission of all our sins and vanities; for we are subject to follies and vanities. But we thank thee, our Father, that thou hast prepared a way and provided means whereby we may be enabled to overcome, and elude the grasp of the destroyer. We ask thee, our Father, to guide us by the Spirit, that we may feel thy love shed abroad in our hearts, and fully appreciate every blessing that flows from thy liberal hands. As thou hast seen fit to break the silence of heaven, and again communicated thy will to the sons of men that dwell upon the earth, we ask thee to indict our petitions as we present ourselves in thy presence to dedicate this hall, for we now dedicate it and ourselves unto thee, and ask thee to let a special blessing rest upon him who has bequeathed to us the ground upon which this hall now stands. We remember before thee, our Father, the Building Committee, who were appointed to build the Temple. Let their hands be strengthened to carry on the work, and grant that the house may be finished according to thy commandments unto thy people, that thy servants may receive their endowments and be clothed upon with power and authority, to carry thy word to the scattered remnants of thy people. Let the Council of the Twelve come in remembrance before thee. Bless them, O Lord, with all that pertains to them. Also the quorums of the seventies, who have built this hall, not particularly by thy commandment, but in honor of thy name. Bless them and their families when they shall go to the islands of the sea, to preach the acceptable year of the Lord, and declare the truth of heaven, the gospel of the Son of God. Let them become mighty men in pulling down the strongholds of satan, and bursting the prison doors of darkness, and spread the light of the everlasting gospel to earth's remotest bounds. Bless the poor who are destitute; open the hearts of the rich, so that the principle of sympathy and charity may predominate and reign in their bosoms, that they may impart of their substance to feed the poor. Finally our Father, we ask thee to guide the destinies of this meeting to thy praise, for thine is the kingdom, power and glory, worlds without end: Amen.'

REMARKS OF ELDER JOHN E. PAGE, ONE OF THE TWELVE

Elder John E. Page having arrived here a short time previous with his family from Pittsburgh, being present, was requested to render an account of his stewardship, which he cheerfully assented to.

The Seventies a Lever in the Hands of God.

He arose and proceeded in a concise manner and gave a very interesting narrative of the events connected with his mission during his absence from this city. He also made many pertinent remarks upon the principles of the kingdom of God, and the organization of the same. He then added that the seventies were in the hands of God as a lever, by which he would turn the world upside down and establish his covenant with the inhabitants of every land; that light and truth should prevail where the powers of darkness, superstition and error had long swayed universal dominion; and finally concluded by assuring the saints that he was one with them, and gave his testimony to the present organization of the church in the most solemn manner, and gave place.

THE GREAT DISCOURSE OF ELDER ORSON PRATT

Monday, December 30.—Elder Orson Pratt took the stand and after many appropriate remarks upon the principle of union, he made a quotation from the *Book of Mormon*: 'Adam fell that man might be—men are that they might have joy', and reasoned upon the correctness of the saying. He said that 'if Adam had not partaken of the fruit of the tree of life, he never could have obeyed the commandment enjoined upon him and the woman, which was to multiply and replenish the earth; (as will appear in the sequel) neither could he have appreciated the blessings of paradise without an experience of the opposite.

Adam Fell That Man Might Be

'The Apostle Paul plainly declared that the man was not in the transgression, but the woman; hence we infer that Adam was acquainted of the penalty annexed to the law of God, and with his future destiny, before he partook of the fruit. It might be said that out of two evils the man upon reflection chose the least. The first was the seduction of the woman, by the tempter, which evil would terminate in the banishment of the woman from the garden of paradise, it being one of the penalties annexed to the law for the offense already committed. Adam knowing this fact chose to suffer the penalty of the law with the woman, rather than to be deprived of her society; consequently he followed her into the transgression, as St. Paul remarks. The creature (Adam) was made subject to sin, not willingly; but by reason of him who has subjected the same in hope. The hope

Man and Woman in the Fall.

spoken of here, by Paul, must allude to the redemption of the woman and her posterity from the fall to immortality and eternal life.

'From this last quotation of the Apostle, we have reason to believe that Adam was encouraged to follow the woman into the transgression, and to people the earth. Whether Adam understood the law of redemption prior to the fall or not, I shall not decide; but shall be contented to submit the circumstance to your consideration. A word to the wise is sufficient.'

Comment on the Conference.

It was designed at the commencement to have continued each discourse throughout the week; but as that would occupy entirely too much space, we will conclude with these brief sketches, already given. Truly this was a time and season of rejoicing with the saints. Peace and harmony, brotherly love, kindness, and charity prevails throughout.

The remembrance of this glorious jubilee will never be erased from the minds of those who were participants. Each family was provided with fruits, nuts and every desert that heart could wish. Well might it be said that the saints enjoyed a feast of fat things.

JOHN D. LEE, Clerk.'

CHURCH PUBLICATIONS

The following works were published during the year 1844:

Times and Seasons, semi-monthly, twenty-three numbers, octavo, containing three hundred and sixty-seven pages.

Nauvoo Neighbor, folio, weekly.

Both of these papers were published at Nauvoo, John Taylor, editor. *The Times and Seasons* devoted principally to the publication of the faith and history of the church. The *Nauvoo Neighbor* included the principal items of news, general intelligence and advertisements.

Latter-day Saints Millennial Star, octavo 16 pp. monthly, Liverpool, England; Thomas Ward editor."

CHAPTER XXVII

CAMPAIGN AGAINST WICKEDNESS BOTH BY THE CHURCH AUTHORITIES AND THE NAUVOO CITY COUNCIL—VILLAINY OF NAUVOO'S ENEMIES

"*Wednesday, January* 1, 1845.—Accompanied by Elder Heber C. Kimball I went to Bishop David Evans' ward south of Nauvoo City, and solemnized a marriage.

The following was written in council:

A WORD TO THE CHURCHES ABROAD FROM THE TWELVE

(*First Greeting of* 1845)

'The Twelve, feeling a great anxiety for the unity and prosperity of the whole church, and, more especially, for the benefit of the branches of the church abroad in the world, would, after mature deliberation, and as a matter of counsel, (approving of the course, management, and matter of the *Times and Seasons* and *Nauvoo Neighbor*), recommend that suitable pains and exertions be taken by both elders and members, to obtain these papers from Nauvoo. A unity of effort, to circulate these papers, not only among the saints, but among the people at large, will greatly facilitate the labors of the traveling elders, while it disseminates correct principles, sanctioned by the highest authorities in the church, and at the same time, opens a channel of communication, best calculated to win the good feelings of the community, while the affections, and zeal of the brethren, are harmonized, by the same doctrines, the same rules; and the same laudable purposes.

The kingdoms of the world continue and extend by division, but the saints can only expect to prevail by wisdom and counsel; we therefore, in connection with the union which prevails among the saints here, and for the prosperity of the branches abroad, and as a reward of merit to the honorable standing of the *Times and Seasons* and *Nauvoo Neighbor*, and for their unyielding energies in the cause of truth 'through good and through evil report', bespeak for them a liberal subscription and ready remittance. May light and liberality be equal.

We have just entered upon the threshold of a new year, and may our Father in heaven, have so much respect to his saints and people, as to bless the pure in heart, pure in purpose, and coworkers for the redemption of man, until the light from Zion extends round the globe and 'all Israel shall be saved'; and then we can rejoice and say: it was good for us that we followed the counsel of the Lord.

Brethren, we greet you with peace, and may the Lord bless you with righteousness.

Done in council, this first day of January, 1845.

[Signed] BRIGHAM YOUNG, President.'

Elder Orson Hyde wrote an article which was published in the *Times and Seasons* advising the saints in the east to beware of land speculators professing to be Latter-day Saints, who were trying to sell lands in Illinois for lands and other property in the east.

ELDER ORSON HYDE'S LETTER OF CAUTION: BEWARE OF DECEPTION!

'Tidings have just reached us here [in Nauvoo] that certain men in the eastern countries, Ohio and other places, professing to be Latter-day Saints, are very busy in selling Illinois lands, and exchanging them for real estate and other property in the east. I would inform all the saints everywhere, that this operation is a field for greater and more extensive fraud than any other with which I am acquainted.

You may give some irresponsible, worthless creature a clear title to your homes in the east, with the expectation of finding good land here in exchange with a good title, etc., etc. But when you come, you may find your land in a swamp, in the middle of an extensive prairie, ten or fifteen miles from any timber. I will venture to give it as my opinion that those miserable speculators are knaves and villains; professing to be saints, and trying to help the church and build up the cause, when they have no license from the authorities of the church here.

I say again, beware of those 'wolves in sheep's clothing'. Whenever any such operation is deemed beneficial to the saints by those who know and understand these things, some competent responsible person will be sent, duly authorized with documents from under the hands of the Twelve that reside in this city. Otherwise you may find to your sorrow that you will have to pay for your lands twice over before you get good titles. I therefore warn you, as a watchman of your interests, to hold on upon your homes until you know certainly what you are doing.

[Signed] ORSON HYDE.'

In company with Elders Heber C. Kimball, Orson Pratt, George A. Smith, Willard Richards and Amasa

M. Lyman, I spent the afternoon and evening, with our wives, at Hiram Kimball's; had a pleasant time: the propriety of settling a new country was discussed.

Settling in a New Country Discussed.

Mr. Jacob B. Backenstos delivered a speech in the house of representatives, Springfield, against the senate bill for the unconditional repeal of the Nauvoo Charter, wherein he ably set forth the injuries and persecutions suffered by the citizens of Nauvoo.

Repeal of Nauvoo Charter Before Illinois Legislature.

Elder Parley P. Pratt, having been appointed to the presidency of the eastern churches, published a proclamation to the saints in his presidency explaining the duties of his calling and the several duties of the officers and members under his special charge.

Elder Parley P. Pratt's Proclamation.

Thursday, 2.—Elders Heber C. Kimball, Orson Pratt and myself held a council at the Tithing Office with Bishops Newel K. Whitney and George Miller, Trustees and Alpheus Cutler and Reynolds Cahoon, Temple Committee: the object of the council was to inspire the Temple Committee with confidence and satisfaction.

Evening, in company with Elders Heber C. Kimball, John Taylor, and others I took supper with Dr. Willard Richards: sixteen of the brethren and sisters who first embraced the work in Preston, England, were present.

First Preston Reunion of Elders and Saints.

Friday, 3.—Elder Wilford Woodruff and accompanying missionaries landed in Liverpool having been twenty-five days at sea.

Saturday, 4.—A conference was held in Hartford, Connecticut, at which thirty-six members were represented including six officers. Elder M. Sirrine presided.

Work in Connecticut Extended.

Evening, I met with the city police at the Seventies' Hall and gave them suitable instructions.

DISCOURSES OF ELDERS YOUNG AND KIMBALL AGAINST WICKEDNESS

Sunday, 5.—I went to the stand and addressed the saints on the necessity of having more order and putting down iniquity, and exhorted the brethren to rise up *en masse*, and put down the thieving, swearing, gambling, bogus-making, retailing spirituous liquors, bad houses, and all abominations practiced in our midst by our enemies, who, after they could not live among us any longer would go out to the world and publish that these things were practiced by us. I severely rebuked the civil authorities of the city for their want of energy in the discharge of their duty, and censured parents and guardians for not keeping their children from prowling round the streets at night; and remarked that if we did not as a people uproot such things, they would uproot us, and we would have to leave before we had done the things the Lord had commanded us to do. Elder Kimball followed me, treating on the same subject: a large congregation—pleasant day.

Movement of the Saints to California Considered.

Tuesday, 7.—I met in council with my brethren of the Twelve. The subject of sending a company to California was further discussed; also the propriety of sending to the branches of the church abroad for teams to help the expedition.

Wednesday, 8.—I attended a meeting which was got up by my brother, Joseph Young, of all our relatives and connections. Elder Phineas Richards presided. Elder Phineas Richards, John Haven, myself, Joseph Young, Heber C. Kimball, John Taylor, John Smith and Lucy Smith, mother of the Prophet, severally addressed the meeting.

The Young Family Social Reunion.

Evening, I met with the Twelve, bishops, high council, and city officials in relation to the election of city officers: the members of the Quorum of the Twelve present declined accepting any nomination.

The police held a meeting this afternoon; the Twelve

and Father John Smith attended and partook of dinner with them: it was an agreeable and interesting time.

Friday, 10.—The Twelve, the Temple Committee, the surveyors (Sherwood and Ripley) and Bishop Whitney, Trustee, met with the Committee of the Nauvoo Manufacturing Association respecting erecting the contemplated dam in the Mississippi.

The lesser priesthood met at the Music Hall. Bishop N. K. Whitney presided. He stated the object of the meeting was to fill up the quorums in order that the saints might be visited by the lesser priesthood; he recommended that the bishops establish in their respective wards the manufacturing of palm leaf and straw hats, willow baskets and other business that children are capable of learning, that they may be raised to industrious habits; he further stated his determination to have a feast prepared for the poor that their hearts might be made to rejoice. Bishops Edward Hunter, Isaac Higbee and others made some very interesting remarks. Bishop Whitney gave the lesser priesthood a faithful charge in relation to ferreting out iniquity. Four priests and ten teachers were ordained.

Lesser Priesthood Quorums Set in Order.

Saturday, 11.—City council met and transacted much business. Passed an ordinance authorizing and licensing Brigham Young to run a ferry across the Mississippi at Nauvoo in place of Joseph Smith, martyred.

With Elders Taylor, Richards and Phelps, I spent the evening writing an epistle to the churches on the gathering.

Sunday, 12.—A general meeting of the seventies convened at their hall; I attended and informed them that the Twelve designed to select a number of experienced elders from among the quorums to take short missions through this state and Iowa, for the purpose of frustrating the designs of wicked and ungodly men, who are endeavoring to poison the minds of the people by misrepresenting us and circulating base and false reports about us

Mission Projected for the Seventies.

as a people. There were a great many people who knew nothing about the true character of this church. From false reports many are led to suppose that we are all a set of thieves, blacklegs and bogus-makers, but we will undeceive them, that is, the honest in heart, who will listen to the elders sent among them. One hundred brethren were ordained into the seventies. The fifteenth and sixteenth quorums were organized.

IMPORTANT DISCOURSES BY ELDERS HEBER C. KIMBALL AND ORSON PRATT

Elder Heber C. Kimball preached to the saints in the Concert Hall on the subject of increase and expansion. Elder Orson Pratt advanced an idea pertaining to the magnitude of the planetary system, illustrative of the enlargement of the saints.

Elder Kimball and I attended the high priests' quorum and selected fifty of the members to go on missions till April 1st in the surrounding counties.

Evening, attended prayer meeting.

Monday, 13.—The city council met in Brother W. Richards' office, and adopted the following Preamble and Resolutions:

THE VOICE OF NAUVOO

(*Proceedings of the City Council*)

PREAMBLE

'It is with feelings of deep and inexpressible regret that we learn that the inhabitants of various parts of this state are seeking to accumulate all the real and supposed crimes of the whole community [of Nauvoo] for the secret or ostensible purpose of raising a tide of influence against the Mormon community that shall sweep them into irrecoverable ruin. This course of conduct, originating with our mortal enemies and gathering in its wake, other men that would revolt at the idea of lending a hand to oppress a long abused people that are struggling against foes within and foes without; [which] is at the present almost insupportable to our feelings. We have scarcely laid by our mourning weeds for murdered men, whom we promptly surrendered up to the state of Illinois for an equitable trial—And now we see in embryo another campaign to spill yet more blood and effect an utter extermination and massacre. We sought to rid our city of counterfeiters and blacklegs; these together with our foes without and within, had established a printing press of unparalleled rancor and malignity. But our efforts to obtain freedom from such vicious monsters cost us much tribulation and precious blood.

The impunity thus far granted the murderers by the senate and other authorities of the state of Illinois, has emboldened them and their apologists to set on foot a series of other exciting causes that they hope will either destroy this community, or prevent their criminals from being brought to punishment. We have not so much fear that our enemies will succeed in their fiendish designs against us, as we have that the peace and good order of the people of this state will be disturbed, and fearful anarchy and bloody misrule will ensue among those who listen to and countenance the fell designs of those who are stealing from quiet citizens of the state and palming upon them a spurious and false currency, and charging to the Mormons their own crimes. If they shall succeed, the citizens will be involved in continual larcenies, and neighborhood broils, and crimes, the end of which cannot now be foreseen. We deprecate such evils and calamities because we desire the good of all mankind; as the gratuitous labors of the greater portion of our citizens in spreading truth throughout the world under much poverty and suffering, abundantly prove.

As for us, our course is fixed, and while we are peaceable and loyal to the Constitution and laws of our country, and are ever willing to join hands with the honest, virtuous, and patriotic in suppressing crime and punishing criminals, we will leave our enemies to judge, whether it would not be better to make Nauvoo one universal burying ground, before we suffer ourselves to be driven from our hard-earned and lawful homes, by such high-handed oppression, and it may yet become a question to be decided by the community, whether the Mormons will, after having witnessed their best men murdered without redress, quietly and patiently, suffer their enemies to wrench from them the last shreds of their Constitutional rights; and whether they will not make their city one great sepulchre, rather than be the humble devotees at the shrine of mobocracy. But for the satisfaction of all concerned, we reiterate in the following resolutions, sentiments that we have always expressed in all places as occasion demanded:

Resolved; That the greater part of the thefts which have been complained of, are not, in our opinion, true in fact, but have been trumped up by inimical persons, in order to cover their aggressive doings, with plausibility, and entice honest and unwary citizens to unite with them in the same uncompromising hostility against this people.

Resolved; That we defy the world to substantiate a single instance, where we have concealed criminals, or screened them from justice; but, on the contrary, always have been, and now are, extremely anxious that they should be ferreted out and brought to justice; and to this end would esteem it a favor, that if any person should lose property, or have good and sufficient reason to suspect any place of containing apparatus for making bogus or counterfeit money, that such person would follow up, trace out, and make diligent search, for all such property and apparatus, and if they can trace it into this city, we pledge ourselves to assist them legally, to the extent of our abilities in so laudable an undertaking.

Resolved; That it is our opinion that very many scoundrels, such as thieves, robbers, bogus-makers, counterfeiters asd murderers, have been induced from reports published in the *Warsaw Signal,* to flock into this county in order to carry on their evil practices, knowing that it would be immediately charged upon the Mormons, and thereby they escape—and although we think that the reports of thefts have been very much exaggerated, yet we know from dear bought experience that such things do exist, and further we doubt not there may be some such characters prowling in and about our city.

Resolved; That we are extremely anxious to ferret out and bring to justice, all such persons, if any, that are within the limits of our city, and for this purpose we have authorized our mayor to enlarge the police, to any number, not exceeding five hundred, and we also pledge ourselves to double our diligence, and call upon our citizens to assist in ridding our city and country of all such infamous characters.

Done, in council, this 13th day of January, 1845.

[Signed] DANIEL SPENCER, Mayor.

W. Richards, Recorder.'

Tuesday, 14.—

MEETING OF THE CITIZENS

'At a large meeting of the citizens of Nauvoo, convened at the stand, on the 14th day of January, 1845, Daniel Spencer, mayor of the city, was called to the chair, and James Sloan appointed secretary; and Samuel Bent, Alpheus Cutler, Charles C. Rich, Phineas Richards, and David Fullmer, were appointed a committee, to draft a Preamble and Resolutions, expressive of the sense of this meeting on the proceedings of the city council, and for the action of this meeting. The committee retired and in a short time, returned the following, which were adopted unanimously:

PREAMBLE

'*Whereas,* the city council of the city of Nauvoo, have presented to this meeting, a Preamble and sundry Resolutions setting forth the fact, that enemies to the people of this city, and as we believe, enemies to the common welfare of the people of this state, are attempting to get up an extensive popular excitement, prejudicial to this people and the country at large; and *whereas,* said Resolutions set forth an unqualified reprobation of all unlawful and villainous conduct whether under the false color of Mormonism, or the real guise of mobbers, blacklegs, bogus-makers, thieves, 'wolf hunters', or murderers; *therefore*, we hereby express our perfect concurrence in the said Preamble and Resolutions.

And *whereas*, the *Warsaw Signal*, the *Alton Telegraph*, and the *Quincy Whig*, have been, as we believe, industriously engaged in circulating falsehood; disseminating discord, and the principles of mobocracy; and *whereas*, Mormon extermination, pillage, robbery, and murder, have received both countenance and apology in these scurrilous prints, as we believe; and *whereas*, the pen of murderers, as we believe, has occupied the columns of these papers in order to defend the cries of innocent blood that ascends to heaven for vengeance; and *whereas*, a large share of the thefts spoken of and blazed through the land, are wholly without existence when traced out, as appears not only from the instance recorded in the Governor's Message concerning horse stealing, but from other similar instances, too numerous to mention; and *whereas*, it has been zealously reported, that much stolen goods could be traced to Nauvoo, and that no citizen could enter our city to search for thieves, and stolen goods, because the thief and goods would be screened from detection by the Mormon fraternity, and the person in search, would be in jeopardy of his life; and *whereas*, thieves and counterfeiters have in some instances fled to our city, either under the mistaken apprehension that we would screen them, or from a malignant design to palm upon us their own crimes, and thereby draw us under the lash of persecution; and *whereas*, it can be proved that individuals, in order to swell the list of Mormon depredations, have reported property to be stolen, which at another time they have acknowledged, they sold the same property and received pay; and *whereas*, bee yards have been robbed, the hives left at Mormon doors, to palm the theft upon us, when the honey has been found in the houses of our enemies; and *whereas*, an innumerable number of such infamous tricks have been played upon us, by our enemies, as we believe, for the purpose of blackening our character in the eyes of honest men; and *whereas*, our city is nightly infested with a set of outlandish men, who we believe, visit us for no good purpose, who do not appear to have any lawful business, but rather, as we believe, are endeavoring to scatter amongst us, their bogus and counterfeits, prostitute the virtue of the place, deposit stolen goods, or steal from us, and by every means in their power, sow the seeds of discord, strife, confusion, mobocracy, and murder, that in the end, they may uproot our beautiful city; and *whereas*, that in some instances, when the ministers of justice have visited our city, at the dark hour of midnight, for the purpose of making legal arrests, as they say; we believe what is reported to us, that they have employed runners to steal the saddles and bridles from their own horses, while in our city, for the purpose of damning us in the eyes of the community.

And *whereas*, the chief magistrate of this state, after a second and protracted visit to this city, and much pains taken to investigate the charge of promiscuous stealing, reports to the legislature as follows:

'Justice, however, required me here to say, that I have investigated the charge of promiscuous stealing, and find it to be greatly exaggerated. I could not ascertain that there were a greater proportion of thieves in that community, than in any other of the same number of inhabitants; and perhaps if the city of Nauvoo, were compared with St. Louis, or any other western city, the proportion would not be so great.'

And *whereas,* the printing office of our open and avowed enemy Dr. Foster, was set on fire, in this city by himself, or by his instruction, as we believe, to fan the flame of mobocracy, which fire was only prevented by our vigilant police.

And *whereas,* we firmly believe, that our enemies in this city, have several times attempted to fire their own buildings and have only been prevented by the diligence of our officers—

Therefore, be it resolved, unanimously, that we will use all lawful means in our power to assist the public to prevent stealing and bogus-making, and bring the offenders to justice.

Resolved, that to prevent further depredations in our city, by lawless desperadoes from abroad, we approve the raising of 500 police by this city.

Resolved, unanimously, That we invite all honest men to watch closely their property, and arrest all thieves; and if they shall catch a thief in the act of stealing, challenge him to stand, and if he refuses so to do, and flees, so far as the Mormons are concerned, we will be satisfied if the owners of the property shall speedily send after him a writ of *habeas corpus* sealed with lead to arrest his progress, but after all, should the thief prove to be a mobocrat, alas! alas!! O what a pity!

Resolved, unanimously, That 50 delegates be sent to the surrounding country to inform the people of the designs of our enemies now concocting in their secret and public meetings, so that the honest part of the community, may unite with us, to prevent stealing and secure peace.

Resolved, That these proceedings be published in the papers at Nauvoo, with a request that other papers copy them.

[Signed] DANIEL SPENCER, Chairman.

James Sloan, Secretary.'*

AN EPISTLE OF THE TWELVE TO THE CHURCH OF JESUS CHRIST OF LATTER-DAY SAINTS IN ALL THE WORLD, GREETING

'*Beloved Brethren*:—

As the purposes of God roll forth and the work of the Lord hastens to its accomplishment, it is necessary that we, as watchmen upon the towers of Zion, communicate with you from time to time,

**Times and Seasons*, vol. vi, pp. 773-5.

and put you in possession of such information as may be deemed necessary for your welfare, for the furtherance of the cause of God, and for the fulfilling of these great purposes which our heavenly Father has designed in the rolling forth of the dispensation of the fulness of times, 'spoken of by all the prophets since the world was.'

The Temple has progressed very rapidly since the death of our beloved Prophet and Patriarch. The diligence of those employed, and the willingness of the saints to contribute, have brought it to a state of forwardness, which has far exceeded our most sanguine expectations. You have already been informed that the capitals of the columns were all on; we have now to announce to you that by the time the spring opens we expect that every stone will be cut to complete the Temple, and it will not take long to lay them, when they are all prepared.

Progress on the Temple Since the Prophet's Death.

Great numbers of carpenters, masons, and other workmen are daily engaged in this arduous undertaking, so that not only is stone being prepared, but the sash, flooring, seats, and other things are progressing rapidly; and it is our design, if possible, so to rush the work forward that the building will be enclosed, and certain portions of it in that state of forwardness, so that we shall be prepared to commence giving the saints their endowments next fall; that the elders of Israel may be prepared by the power and spirit of the great Jehovah, to fulfill with dignity and honor, the great work devolving upon them to perform.

We wish to inform you brethren that the work in which we are engaged is great and mighty, it is the work of God and we have to rush it forth against the combined powers of earth and hell, we feel it to be an arduous undertaking whilst you, many of you have been enjoying ease, prosperity, and peace at home. We have had to combat mobs and to wade through blood to fulfill the work devolving upon us, and you: we have been exerting our energies, expended our money; and employing our time, our labor, our influence, and means for the accomplishment of this purpose; and feeling confident dear brethren, that you would like to share with us the labor, as well as the glory, we make the following requests:

Difficulties Under Which the Work Had to be Carried on

We wish all the young, middle aged, and able bodied men who have it in their hearts to stretch forth this work with power, to come to Nauvoo, prepared to stay during the summer; and to bring with them means to sustain themselves with, and to enable us to forward this work; to bring with them teams, cattle, sheep, gold, silver, brass, iron, oil, paints and tools; and let those who are within market distance of Nauvoo bring with them provisions to sustain themselves and others during their stay. And let all the churches send all the money, cloth, and clothing, together with the raw material for manufacturing purposes; such as cotton,

A Call For Help.

cotton yarn, wool, steel, iron, brass, etc., etc., as we are preparing to go into extensive manufacturing operations, and all these things can be applied to the furtherance of the Temple.

Temporary Font in the Temple.

There was a font erected in the basement story of the Temple, for the baptism of the dead, the healing of the sick and other purposes; this font was made of wood, and was only intended for the present use; but it is now removed, and as soon as the stone cutters get through with the cutting of the stone for the walls of the Temple, they will immediately proceed to cut the stone for and erect a font of hewn stone. This font will be of an oval form and twelve feet in length and eight wide, with stone steps and an iron railing; this font will stand upon twelve oxen, which will be cast of iron or brass, or perhaps hewn stone. If of brass, polished; if of iron, bronzed;—upon each side of the font there will be a suite of rooms fitted up for the washings. In the recesses, on each side of the arch, on the first story, there will be a suite of rooms or ante-chambers, lighted with the first row of circular windows. As soon as a suitable number of those rooms are completed we shall commence the endowment.

Brethren, inasmuch as you have long desired blessings, come up to the help of the Lord, and help to forward the work that we are engaged in; for we trust that these rooms will be finished by the first of December next, so that you may enter therein and receive wisdom, knowledge, understanding, and the power of the priesthood, which you have so long desired; that you may be prepared to go forth to the nations of the earth and build up the kingdom in all parts of the world; gather up Israel, redeem Zion; rebuild Jerusalem; and fill the whole earth with the knowledge of God.

The Law of Tithing.

While upon this subject we would remind the brethren of their duty in tithing according to the laws, and commandments given through Joseph the Prophet, it is the duty of all saints to tithe themselves one-tenth of all they possess when they enter into the new and everlasting covenant; and then one-tenth of their interest, or income, yearly afterwards. If the brethren will attend to this strictly, and send up the sum by agents appointed by us, whose names you will see in this paper, then we shall hold ourselves responsible for all monies and properties delivered to those agents that the names of the several individuals who send their tithing by the legal agents may be entered upon the book of the *Law of the Lord;* if this is not attended to strictly by the branches of the church abroad, they may be disappointed when they find that they have sent their means by unauthorized agents, who have not made returns to the Trustees, and their names are not recorded as they would have been if they had hearkened to counsel. On the subject of regular appointed agencies we would refer you to an article written by the Trustees, Bishops Whitney and Miller, and published in the *Times and Seasons* of December, 1844.

We would further say to the brethren that if there should be any of the churches to whom these agents do not come, let them send their means by honest men whom they may select from among themselves, and in whom they can place confidence; but we cannot be responsible for the conduct of any agents that we do not send, and can only give credit for that we receive. And as the churches abroad have been much imposed upon by designing men, without authority, we would warn them against such persons, and advise them not to pay their funds to traveling elders and others without a written authority from us to which shall be attached the private seal of the Twelve and their names published as above stated. Those men that we shall select for agents will be men of honor, men of integrity and respectability, in whom we can confide, and who are responsible, and able, and willing to enter into bonds for the faithful performance of their duty. This course will prevent those many impositions which have heretofore been practiced by villains wearing the garb of saints, and place the churches in a situation that they can forward their tithings with safety.

There is now in the city eight of the Twelve all in good health and spirits; our city is progressing, and the work of the Lord is rolling forth with unprecedented rapidity.

Thus, dear brethren, we have given you, in part, some of the measures and calculations, which we mean to carry into effect for your salvation, and for the furtherance of the salvation of the world. We have commenced a new year, and, as the Lord says; 'All victory and glory is brought to pass unto you through diligence, faithfulness and prayers of faith,' so we cannot but hope, that you will renew your exertions, your prayers, and your tithings, for the benefit of Zion, that she may arise and shine for the good of all people.

We cannot say everything in one short epistle, therefore, from time to time, as the Lord puts into our hearts instructions, we shall give them unto you: solemnly praying that you will increase your faith, double your diligence, walk by light and obedience, and be instant in season, to do the will of our Father in heaven:—Beware of ungodly men, who creep among you unawares; they are clouds without water, driven about by winds, and will finally be blown into outer darkness.

Our counsel to the traveling elders abroad is for them to return to Nauvoo by the 6th of April, to conference or as soon as possible afterwards, and before they leave, it will be necessary for them to ordain good and wise men to preside over the branches during their absence.

May the grace of our Lord Jesus Christ, a veneration for the names of the first Martyrs, first Elders, and first Prophets of the nineteenth century, inspire your hearts, to hear counsel, to keep counsel, to practice holiness, live the life of saints, and 'die the death of the righteous, that your last end may be like his'.

Done in council, at Nauvoo, this 14th day of January, 1845.
[Signed] BRIGHAM YOUNG, President.
Willard Richards, Clerk.'*

Wednesday, 15.—I went to the Temple, afterwards to the stone quarry; Brother Albert P. Rockwood reported sixty-two hands and six teams engaged today in the quarry.

Evening, went to the Seventies' Hall. The brethren of the Twelve, the high council, Trustees-in-Trust, many high priests and seventies were present. The elders appointed on missions were assigned to their respective districts. Elder Kimball instructed the elders to be fathers and not masters, and to be wise in their requirements of tithing from the saints abroad. I gave some general instructions, and counseled the elders to gather all to Nauvoo who could leave their families and especially the young men to help complete the Temple. Heavy thunder, lightning and rain.

Assignment of Missionaries.

Thursday, 16.—I spent most of the day with Elder Kimball correcting his history.

Friday, 17.—Mr. Joseph A. Kelting, deputy sheriff of Hancock county published the following in the *Times and Seasons* (p. 775):

TO THE PUBLIC

'Nauvoo, Jan. 17, 1845.

As much has been said concerning stealing and secreting property in this city, for the purpose of giving an impression abroad that Nauvoo was a grand *depot* for concealing stolen property, and that the Mormon community was concerned in it,—I will state, that so far as my knowledge extends, concerning the matter, I have ascertained that stolen property has been brought by way of Nauvoo, from the country, and then crossed over the Mississippi river to Iowa, and back into the territory some ten or twelve miles; where the thieves have some friends to conceal stolen property.

There seems to be a connection of these friends thirty or forty miles back into the country on this side of the river, who, with five or six in this city, seem to have a line for running stolen property through Nauvoo to the territory of Iowa; and I have good reason to believe

**Times and Seasons,* vol. vi, p. 779-780.

that those in the country on this side of the river, those in the city, and those in the territory, are one clan, but they are not Mormons; nor have the Mormons any fellowship with them.

I have taken pains to go with a person from the country, with a writ, and have searched every house suspected, till the person was satisfied, and till I was satisfied myself that no such property, as claimed, was in the city.

I have good reason to believe that scoundrels stay in Nauvoo, and when stolen property comes into the city, they are ready to pass it on to the territory, and screen themselves under the cloak of Mormonism, in order that the Mormons may bear the blame. If people will satisfy themselves as I have done, they may find a *depot* in the regions of Iowa, containing the greater part of the property charged to the Mormons.

I would state further, that the Mormons had no agency in the searches I made, but that I made them, at the instance of men from the country, and that I spent three days in the territory of Iowa, searching into the facts and matters, and my statements are made up from personal observation.

[Signed] JOSEPH A. KELTING,
Deputy Sheriff of Hancock County.'

Evening of Friday, 17.—Elder H. C. Kimball, John Taylor and George A. Smith met with me in my upper room: we counseled and prayed."

CHAPTER XXVIII

THE STORY OF CONTINUED PROGRESS OF THE CHURCH IN NAUVOO, IN EUROPE AND IN THE UNITED STATES—PLEA FOR THE RETURN OF JAMES EMMETT'S COMPANY

"*Saturday, January* 18, 1845.—I called at Elder Willard Richards' and left some correspondence: proceeded to the Temple.

Sunday, 19.—The seventies met at their hall. Presidents for the sixteenth and seventeenth quorums were set apart; fifty persons were ordained. Afternoon the high priests' quorum met; President George Miller preached on the subject of Intemperance. In the evening I met the police and instructed them in their duties.

Monday, 20.—I called on Elder Willard Richards and found him engaged on the History.

Tuesday, 21.—Forenoon, with Elders Kimball and Richards at the Historian's Office. Wrote a letter to my brother, Phineas H., with counsel for the saints in Kirtland to come to Nauvoo, that all who have faith in the latter-day work may be united with us in building the Temple.

Evening, I met in council with Elders Heber C. Kimball, Willard Richards, George A. Smith and Amasa M. Lyman; we wrote to Elder Jedediah M. Grant, Philadelphia, counseling him to forward all the young men and other available help he could to build the Temple.

Wednesday, 22.—Forenoon, Elder Orson Pratt wrote a letter, in behalf of the council, to Elder Parley P. Pratt. Afternoon, I went to the Historian's Office accompanied by Elders Kimball and Taylor. The letters to Elders Grant and Pratt were read and approved. A copy of Elder Pratt's letter was sent to Wm. Smith.

Evening, accompanied by my wife I attended a party at Brother Woodruff's, Heber C. Kimball, John Taylor, George A. Smith, W. W. Phelps and their wives were present.

Elder Elias Smith received a letter from A. W. Babbitt, Springfield, Ill., with the information that he was before the Legislative House Committee on Banks and Corporations pertaining to the bill for the unconditional repeal of the Nauvoo Charter. Jacob A. Davis made a strong anti-Mormon speech before said committee and presented them with a full file of the *Nauvoo Neighbor* containing the ordinances passed by the city council. Mr. Backenstos was also before the committee and pleaded like an apostle for the rights of his constituents. The committee inquired of Mr. Babbitt as to 'bogus-making'—spiritual wife doctrine—and whether he believed in [Joseph] Smith's revelations. He had made two speeches before the committee, but believed they would recommend the passage of the bill.*

Thursday, 23.—I wrote to Elder Ezra T. Benson: called at the Trustees' Office; went to the Temple; called at Elder Richards', Kimball's, Taylor's and Hyde's. Found Brother John Scott at my house who said Brother Aaron Smith had just returned from Appanoose and said Wilson Law was there lecturing to the mob; counseling them to drive the 'Mormons' from Nauvoo before the Temple was done or they never could.

Friday, 24.—Elders Heber C. Kimball and N. K. Whitney were at my house. Elder Orson Hyde returned from St. Louis, Mo.

The plasterers finished plastering the Concert Hall. This building is thirty feet by fifty and eleven feet high. The ceiling is arched and has sounding jars. It has

*The speeches in the Illinois legislature will be found *in extenso* in the *Comprehensive History of the Church,* Century I, vol. ii, ch. lxvii.

been built amidst difficulty and discouragement in consequence of poverty, and has cost nearly one thousand dollars: much of the burden has laid on the Trustees, Stephen H. Goddard, Wm. F. Cahoon, and Wm. Clayton.

Saturday, 25.—I went to the Temple this morning, thence with Elder Kimball, my brother Joseph, and Marshal Jon. C. Wright, to Brother Richards' office.

Sunday, 26.—I attended the regular meeting of the high priests' quorum at the Masonic Hall. George Miller presiding, who introduced the subject of building a hall for the use of the quorums of high priests one hundred and twenty feet long by eighty wide, and about thirty-three feet high. I asked all that were in favor of having such a hall built, and were willing to do something towards building it, and not merely look on and see their brethren build it, to raise their hands; all hands were raised. I told them such a building as had been proposed would not cost less than fifteen thousand dollars. Two years ago or even one year ago we had not a public hall in this city. The room in Brother Joseph's store was the only one where a congregation could convene. A year ago last fall I said to the seventies that if I were as strong and numerous a body as they were, I would go to work and put up a building that I might have a place to worship in. They put up their building, but the plan being altered, at the suggestion of Brother Hyrum, they had to wait for timber and could not finish it that season. Should the high priests commence the erection of the building proposed, next fall will come and even winter and the quorum will still be without a place to meet in, and probably the next season would pass away before it could be finished. I proposed to the quorum to finish off the upper story of the Temple in which they could receive their washings and anointings and endowments instead of undertaking a building from the commencement: this proposition was received by unanimous vote.

High Priests' Hall Contemplated.

Elder Heber C. Kimball preached in the Concert Hall.

The seventies met in their hall. President Joseph Young presiding, James M. Munroe expressed his willingness to teach the seventies English grammar. Elder George A. Smith spoke on the benefits arising from education; he said, the saints should improve and be diligent in acquiring knowledge, this people and their gathering together has been made a political question, and we are a bone for all the world to pick at; Lawyer Babbitt had written that the legislature had repealed the city charter of Nauvoo, and there was a great rejoicing among the priests at their victory.

News of Nauvoo's Charter Being Repealed.

President Joseph Young spoke of the importance of being able to speak correctly. He lectured the youth who joined the quorums as to obedience; said, if he knew of a man belonging to these quorums stealing he would be cut off the church and published in the *Neighbor*. The saints had always taught honesty, virtue and uprightness—the lives of thousands were jeopardized by rascals and hypocrites, who would call you brother and pilfer your property; such were neither fit to be called saints nor decent human beings, they would go to hell. The names of several suspected of stealing were mentioned. James Dunn was cut off, two members were called in question for drunkenness.

Admonition by President Joseph Young.

Evening, I attended prayer meeting.

Monday, 27.—Attended to sending off fifty missionaries and forwarding letters to Elders Parley P. Pratt, Wm. Smith and J. M. Grant. Elder Kimball preached the funeral sermon of Sister Perrygrine Sessions.

Evening, at Dr. Richards' office; I dictated a letter to Joshua Grant and heard several articles read.

I insert minutes of meeting of the Presidents of Seventies:

MINUTES OF SEVENTIES COUNCIL

'Meeting opened by singing and prayer. President Joseph Young spoke upon the lack of wisdom and economy of the members of this church. As an example he quoted the teaching of a certain elder, a president of one of the quorums, who told the people he considered the Twelve Apostles to be God to us. This sentiment expressed to many was not only dangerous to the community, but was calculated to jeopardize the lives of the Twelve. The same allusion was made to Joseph, and the reply of the mob was, well if Jo Smith is their God we will kill their God, and so they did, and it may be so with the Twelve. The brethren should speak and act in wisdom for their own sake as well as for the truth's sake. There are brethren in these quorums and even presidents who are connected with a body of those consecrating thieves, who pretend to say that they have a right to consecrate from the Gentiles, but such will steal from their brethren as well as others.

Several elders spoke on the subject, expressing their sense of the propriety of expelling said members from the church and publishing their names.

The clerk, Elder John D. Lee, said that some of the brethren were probably too hasty in their decision according to his view of the matter. He considered that if the elders acted with discretion they must not be excited nor influenced by passion and remarked that did the elders possess the power of Jehovah in their present weak condition in less than twenty-four hours the earth would be depopulated, especially should the elders be vested with that power in turns, for what would be spared by one would likely be destroyed by another.

Forbearance With Sinners as Some May Repent.

President Brigham Young arose and said, 'When men have come into our midst who were as corrupt as the devil himself, many have supposed it would have been better to have cut their throats with a feather and exposed their sink of corruption, and let them go to hell where they belonged, than to have borne with them as Brother Joseph Smith did; but this course would meet with a conflicting argument. To stop a man in his career would be taking away his agency. Cain was permitted to live, peradventure, he might repent of his wickedness, and redeem a portion of his time, and thereby obtain a glory and salvation, though not a full salvation; and this is the reason that Brother Joseph bore so long with Jackson* and others, that peradventure they might, notwithstanding they had been guilty of murder and robbery, come to the waters of baptism through repentance, and redeem a part of their allotted time. If they were cut off from the earth they might with propriety come up in the day of judgment and say we took away their agency, which if we had let alone, they would

*This was a desperate character who appeared in Hancock county about the time the "Mormon" troubles approached a climax in the life of the Prophet. Jackson was supposed to be implicated in the murder of the Prophet. (See this *History*, vol. vi, pp. 149, 521, 560).

have repented of their sins and redeemed a part of their time. The presidents of seventies should be men of wisdom and know how to save men instead of destroying them; for example let a hot-headed president stand at the head of a quorum and let some of the members of his quorum be overtaken in a fault, it would make no difference how small or great the offense might be, the first steps that would be taken (instead of going in a private manner, as a prudent reflecting president should and teach the guilty the law of redemption, bind up the breach and thereby save a soul from ruin) would be to have the offense made public—have the accused arraigned before the quorum in order to ferret out the crime, thus increasing the wound, especially if it should be an interruption between a man and his wife; the offense having become public, confidence is lost, not only in the accused, but the parties concerned lose confidence in each other, their reputation sinks, consequently despair rushes into the troubled soul, who is thus rashly treated and he or they suppose they have not a friend on earth, consequently imagine it is useless for them to try to redeem their former standing, and in fact instances have been known of individuals under like circumstances giving up to intoxication and finally become the most miserable dissipated and abandoned wretches on earth; whereas, had wisdom been used, the soul might have been reclaimed and saved by casting the mantle of charity around them and thereby covering up a multitude of sins. This is what is meant by the mantle of charity that Paul speaks of [covering a multitude of sins].

We should be charitable, liberal, patient and forbearing with each other and above all never blast each others' characters, rather hide each others faults with the mantle of charity; for when but few know your faults they seem but few, but expose them and they become multitudes.'

U. S. Land Grant Sought in Michigan.

Tuesday, 28.—I met in council with Elders Heber C. Kimball, John Taylor, John E. Page, Bishops Whitney and Miller, Reynolds Cahoon and Elias Smith, when was read a letter from Wm. P. Richards, Esq., Macomb, McDonough county, Illinois, to Bishop George Miller suggesting the propriety of petitioning congress for a grant of land twenty-four miles square in the pineries or other uninhabited portions of public domain to be set apart as a reserve for the saints, with power to make our own local arrangements, and enact laws not repugnant to the Constitution of the United States. This he considers necessary in consequence of the irreconcilable feelings of the public in relation to us as a religious body: his communication with the correspondence thereon was published in the *Neighbor*.

Wednesday, 29.—I called at Elder Richards' office with Elder Kimball and Thomas Kingston and read a letter* from J. B. Backenstos informing us of the strong prejudice entertained by the members of the legislative assembly and the determined spirit evinced to repeal the Nauvoo City Charter; also informing us that John Dougherty, senator from Union county, openly justified the murder of Joseph and Hyrum Smith, and that the senate had discharged from arrest Jacob C. Davis, one of their number, who was indicted for murder. Mr. Backenstos had appealed to the sense of justice, equal rights, patriotism and humanity possessed by the members of the house of representatives in vain. His colleague Mr. Babbitt and himself had done their duty.

Backenstos Reports Prejudice in Illinois Legislature.

Afternoon, attended council.

Evening, I assisted Brother Kimball to prepare his Journal for the press, and blessed his child, Brigham Willard.

Thursday, 30.—Attended council with the authorities of the city, pertaining to the action of the legislature in repealing the City Charter. The council agreed to have the city election go on tomorrow, not knowing whether the governor would pass or veto the bill. A committee was appointed to confer with legal gentlemen in relation to the legitimacy of the legislature repealing a charter granted for the term of perpetual succession.

Legality of Repeal of Nauvoo Charters Questioned.

* * *

Friday, 31.—Elders Heber C. Kimball, John Taylor, Willard Richards and W. W. Phelps engaged in writing letters to eminent jurists, inquiring as to the constitutionality of the action of the Illinois legislature in repealing the City Charter of Nauvoo.

Received a letter from Elder Parley P. Pratt in rela-

*See letter file in Historian's Office, box 7.

tion to the prosperity of the church under his care, [i. e. N. Y.] and the great demand for *Books* of *Doctrine and Covenants* and *Hymn Books.*

A meeting was held in the Seventies' Hall, for the purpose of forming a Mercantile and Mechanical Association, Elder John Taylor, chairman. Twelve trustees were elected to control the association, *viz.* Daniel Garn, Samuel Bent, Shadrach Roundy, Charles C. Rich, John D. Lee, L. N. Scovil, Joseph Worthen, Joseph Horn, Hosea Stout, Edward Hunter, Gustavus Williams and Charles A. Davis.

Bishops Whitney and Miller, Trustees-in-Trust for the church published the following:

AGENTS APPOINTED FOR RECEIVING DONATIONS AND TITHING FOR BUILDING THE TEMPLE

'*To Whom It May Concern*: This certifies that the following named elders have been appointed by the proper authorities of the Church of Jesus Christ of Latter-day Saints, agents to collect donations and tithings for the Temple in Nauvoo and for other purposes; and have complied with all necessary requirements by entering into bonds to our entire satisfaction. We hope they will be received as such by all people wherever they may travel. [Then follow the names of 46 elders so appointed].

We hope also that the brethren will have confidence in them, inasmuch as we hold ourselves responsible to credit on the *Book of Law of the Lord,* for all donations put into their hands, to the names of the donors on their tithing.

Inasmuch as this is a very good opportunity, and inasmuch as we feel very anxious that all should double their exertions in order to finish the building of the Temple the next season, that the saints may receive their endowments; we hope the saints universally will embrace the opportunity, and donate liberally, that they may the more speedily receive their reward, for great things depend on our finishing the building of the Temple with speed.'

Saturday, February 1, 1845.—At ten a. m. I met with Elders John Taylor, Willard Richards, Orson Spencer, George Miller, W. W. Phelps and L. R. Foster in committee to complete the letters to eminent jurists [i. e. on legality of the repeal of the Nauvoo Charter].

Sunday, 2.—I preached in the Concert Hall, to a crowded assembly. Elder Orson Hyde preached in the

Masonic Hall. Elder Heber C. Kimball preached at Brother Gully's at candle light; Father John Smith and Bishop Miller made a few remarks.

The seventies met at their hall in the evening, Elders George A. Smith, Joseph Young and others preached; several were ordained into the quorums, and several presidents were set apart for the eighteenth quorum. I spent the evening at home with my family.

City Election at Nauvoo.

Monday, 3.—The following officers were elected without a dissenting vote (about 900 votes polled):

Mayor: Orson Spencer.

Aldermen: Daniel Spencer, N. K. Whitney, George W. Harris and Charles C. Rich.

Councilors: David Fullmer, John Pack, George Miller, W. W. Phelps, Jonathan C. Wright, Samuel Bent, Phineas Richards, James Sloan and Edward Hunter.

I received the following communication from the attorney-general of the state of Illinois:

A FRIENDLY LETTER FROM JOSIAH LAMBORN, STATE OFFICIAL

'Springfield, 28th Jan., 1845.

Dear Sir:

You and I were slightly acquainted heretofore, though I presume you have forgotten me. During my sojourn here this winter, I have carefully watched the progress of events and particularly so in reference to your friends and fellow citizens of Nauvoo. Throughout all the persecutions and abuses which have been heaped upon you, though I have been far removed from any political or pecuniary influence which might bias my mind; yet I have always considered that your enemies have been prompted by religious and political prejudices and by a desire for plunder and blood, more than for the common good. By the repeal of your charter and by refusing all amendments and modifications our legislature has given a kind of sanction to the barbarous manner in which you have been treated.

Your two representatives exerted themselves to the extent of their abilities in your behalf, but the tide of popular passion and frenzy was too strong to be resisted. It is truly a melancholy spectacle to witness the lawmakers of a sovereign state condescending to pander to the vices, ignorance and malevolence of a class of people who are at all times ready for riot, murder and rebellion. You had many true friends here. Most of the intelligent gentlemen out of the legislature felt that you were an injured and an outraged people. The members living nearest to your city and having better means of information than those living remotely, sustained and defended you to the last. The opposition was made up of the body of the whig party, together with such demagogues of the other party as could be cajoled and bamboozled by the whigs.

There is now presented to the house a new charter for your city. It is referred to a select committee. What its fate may be no man can tell. Your senator, Jacob C. Davis, has done much to poison the minds of members against anything in your favor. He walks at large in defiance of law, an indicted murderer. If a Mormon was in his position the senate would afford no protection, but he would be dragged forth to the jail or to the gallows or to be shot down by a cowardly and brutal mob.

All you have to do is to be quiet, submissive to the laws and circumspect in your conduct. Heap coals of fire on their heads by humility and kindness, and my word for it, there will be a mighty reaction in the public sentiment, which will ultimately overthrow all your enemies. The sober second thought of the people will always be right, and heaven will protect you against all the assaults of a corrupt and bloodthirsty rabble.

Excuse me for attempting to give you advice. I do not wish to interfere with your affairs or to dictate in any way to your minds. My motives are those of friendship springing warm from my heart and the same which would control in relation to all mankind.

Yours, etc.

[Signed] JOSIAH LAMBORN.'

Tuesday, 4.—I met in council with the authorities of the church. Afternoon, Elder Kimball visited Mother Smith.

Thursday, 6.—I preached in the Concert Hall to a large congregation on the occasion of the death of Alonzo W. N. Whitney.

Friday, 7.—A meeting was held of the Council of the Trades Association. Elders John Taylor, George A. Smith and Amasa M. Lyman attended.

Sunday, 9.—Elder Kimball and I preached at Brother Horner's Mill; had a good meeting with the brethren: many came to hear us.

Meeting at the stand: Elders John Taylor and George A. Smith preached on the necessity of the

Seventy's Quorums to be Purged of Wickedness.

people sustaining themselves by home productions and their industry; manufacturing their own clothing and being united and keeping such good order that the repeal of the city charters would be no injury to the community.

Afternoon, high priests' quorum met.

Seventies met in their hall. President Joseph Young said he meant by the assistance of the great God to cut off all liars, swearers, bogus-makers and bogus-circulators and endeavor to purify the bodies of the seventies from filth and wickedness. Seven presidents were set apart, and thirty members ordained for the nineteenth quorum. Elder Amasa M. Lyman addressed the meeting on the subject of order.

The branch at Quincy, Illinois, held a conference. There were represented one hundred members, including nine high priests, one seventy, twelve elders and two priests, one teacher and one deacon.

Monday, 10.—Meeting of the Presidents of Seventies at early candle light. After the business before the meeting was attended to, I instructed the elders on the subject of revelation; showing how the Lord dealt with his children in revealing to them here a little and there a little, as they were capacitated to receive, comprehend and improve upon, named baptism for the dead in which the Lord first revealed the principle, then the order. Elders John E. Page and George A. Smith bore testimony.

Revelation Doctrine.

Tuesday, 11.—Elders Kimball, Page, Taylor, Smith, Lyman and myself met with the Trades Committee.

Afternoon, attended meeting at Elder Taylor's with a Committee of the Agricultural and Manufacturing Society. It was proposed that the citizens be invited to subscribe twelve thousand days work, which it was estimated would put a sufficient dam in the Mississippi to propel machinery.

Mr. John C. Elliott, one of the murderers of Joseph and Hyrum Smith was arrested by John Kay.

With other items, I wrote Elder Woodruff the following:

PRESIDENT YOUNG'S LETTER TO ELDER WOODRUFF IN ENGLAND

'It will rejoice your heart to hear that we have a remarkable mild winter, clear and pleasant, no snow, and peace in the city, as it does ours to live here and enjoy it. Though the papers report a total repeal of the Nauvoo Charter by a large majority in both houses, we remain undisturbed, and city affairs go on as usual. We expect to appeal to the U. S. court.

The stone is nearly hewn for the Temple; a stone font is about to be erected, the woodwork is progressing rapidly under a temporary roof in the basement story, and we hope to commence the endowments next fall or early in the winter. We will not send many elders to England until after the endowment.

You will please call at Stationer's Hall, London, the first opportunity, and get or by some means procure a copy of the 'copyright of the *Book of Mormon*' and safely keep it until further notice. The saints are more engaged than ever to finish the Temple, and it is desirable that tithings be forwarded from all branches at the earliest safe conveyance.

Copyrights.

The different quorums are becoming perfected in their several organizations, by which means the elders are learning their duty. Union, love and peace were never more universal among the saints at Nauvoo, than at the present time. Brother Willard is convalescent, collecting materials for history and much regrets the absence of Elder Woodruff's Journals.'

Wednesday, 12.—Mr. Elliott was examined before Justices Aaron Johnson, Daniel H. Wells, Isaac Higbee and committed to Carthage jail to await his trial at the next term of the circuit court.

Thursday, 13.—I met in council with the Twelve and others. With Elders Willard Richards, George A. Smith, and others, I spent the evening at Elder Kimball's: had a good time.

Friday, 14.—Father Morley arrived from Yelrome near Lima, Adams county, bringing word that five of the brethren there had been arrested charged with larceny; he says that property had been concealed on their premises and recovered by a search warrant, on the principle 'those that hide can find'. These proceedings were had to produce

Brethren Arrested at Yelrome on False Pretenses.

excitement, and a warrant is said to be out for Father Morley. I met with the Twelve and others and prayed for the deliverance of these brethren. Father Morley was counseled to remove his family to Nauvoo and Solomon Hancock was appointed to preside over that branch. Dr. John M. Bernhisel was appointed a Traveling Bishop to visit the churches. Some conversation ensued on the subject of sending six brethren with Brother Lewis Dana to the west and especially to Texas.

Saturday, 15.—A conference was held in Lipsey, Tuscaloosa county, Alabama. Five branches were represented containing one hundred and forty-one members, including twenty-four officers, A. O. Smoot, presided.

Died—in Nauvoo, Asa Works, Sen., aged eighty-three years, after a sickness of six months.

A Soldier of the American Revolution Dies.

He served his country as a soldier in the American Revolution; was in the battles of Bennington and Monmouth, in the latter of which he received a wound in his left arm between the shoulder and elbow,—underwent a great deal of hardship, privation and hunger in helping to gain American independence.

In the year 1838, he emigrated to Far West, Missouri, at which place he was called to witness the violation of that liberty he fought to obtain. He endured with the Latter-day Saints all the persecution and suffering inflicted upon them in 1838 and 9 in Missouri; and since that time has lived in exile in the state of Illinois. Brother Asa Works was the father of my first wife, Miriam.

Sunday, 16.—Elder Amasa M. Lyman preached in the Masonic Hall. The seventies from the first to the eighth quorums met in their hall. Elder Zerah Pulsipher preached. Elder George A. Smith preached to the high priests: three persons were ordained high priests. Evening, I attended prayer meeting at the Trustees' Office.

Monday, 17.—Meeting of the Presidents of Seventies. Measures were adopted to facilitate the building of President Joseph Young's house.

Tuesday, 18.—The Board of the Mercantile and Mechanical Association met at the Masonic Hall and proceeded to organize.

I attended a council at President John Smith's, and ordained Wm. Perkins bishop of Macedonia and Andrew H. Perkins his counselor.

Thursday, 20.—I called at Elder W. Richards' office with Elders Joseph Young, George A. Smith and Amasa M. Lyman. I heard a recital of the Haun's Mill Massacre by my brother Joseph: afterwards went to the Temple.

Friday, 21.—I preached at Brother Robert Pierce's on the occasion of the funeral of Brother Morris Whitesides.

Saturday, 22.—I attended meeting of the high council in the Seventies' Hall: a full quorum present.

Sunday, 23.—I preached at Hiram Kimball's, Elders Heber C. Kimball and George A. Smith administered the sacrament: had a good meeting.

Meeting of seventies in their hall. Elders P. B. Lewis made a few remarks. President Joseph Young spoke of the principle of receiving revelation from God.

Meeting at Bishop Hale's. Elder Dunham preached, followed by Mother Smith, who gave a recital of the persecutions endured by her family, in establishing the church, and exhorted the brethren and sisters to bring up their children in the way they should go; there were meetings held in the Concert and Masonic Halls.

Afternoon, high priests quorum met, Elder Kimball preached.

Evening, the Twelve Apostles and others met in council and for prayer.

Monday, 24.—In company with Elders Heber C. Kimball, Orson Pratt, Amasa M. Lyman, George Miller, William Clayton, George D. Grant, E. D. Woolley, John Kay and John L. Smith I went to Macedonia:

we were armed with forty-six rounds, loaded pistols.

After the company partook of refreshments, we met at Brother Benjamin F. Johnson's and enjoyed a pleasant evening; Brother Kay sang a number of songs.

Evening, the Presidents of Seventies met in their hall. The charges against James Carrol and Hiram Gates, were investigated and they were expelled from the church. The brethren agreed to trade with those merchants who sustained good order and honored the laws of the city.

Tuesday, 25.—I spent the day in Macedonia, settling the church business with Elder B. F. Johnson. The company from Nauvoo dined at Elder Wm. G. Perkins'.

Afternoon, visited the saints. Evening. Elders Orson Pratt, Amasa M. Lyman, George Miller and I preached. Chatted at Brother Johnson's till after midnight. I told the brethren that all was not right and that we would have some of the brethren from Nauvoo before daybreak; George D. Grant and John Kay agreed to watch during the night. A rumor having reached Nauvoo that Elder Kimball and I were in Carthage jail, Elders John E. Page, John Taylor, Willard Richards, George A. Smith, and Charles C. Rich, met in Nauvoo at Elder Taylor's and investigated the report, and though they did not believe it, they deemed it prudent to dispatch Brother Hosea Stout and seven of the old police to Macedonia, as a protection for us.

Premonitions of President Young.

President John Smith very sick, several of the Twelve administered to him.

Wednesday, 26.—Brother Hosea Stout and company arrived in front of Brother Johnson's house; we at first thought it was the mob, but when Wm. H. Kimball cried out 'Father don't you know me', we immediately recognized the brethren and had a joyful meeting; they brought us word of the rumor which had arisen in Nauvoo from two suspi-

Friends Arrive—Not the Mob.

cious persons who had been at Brother Turley's inquiring for Elder Kimball and me.

At ten a. m. we started for Nauvoo, twenty-three of the brethren from Macedonia accompanying us through the timber about seven miles when we halted and Howard Egan recited a negro sermon; I made a few remarks by way of counsel to the Macedonia brethren and blessed them in the name of the Lord; they returned home; we proceeded and arrived in Nauvoo about three p. m.

Thursday, 27.—This morning in company with Elders George A. Smith, John E. Page, Willard Richards and John Taylor I proceeded to the bank of the river, in the lower part of the city, the site of the contemplated dam and in presence of about one hundred individuals consecrated the ground by prayer; Elder John E. Page being mouth. I made a few remarks.

Delegation Appointed to Visit James Emmett's Company in the Wilderness

The Twelve Apostles, Trustees, mayor, aldermen and councilors met in council. Moses Smith represented the condition of the company led into the wilderness by James Emmett. After mature deliberation on the situation and condition of James Emmett's company, it was unanimously voted that Elder Amasa M. Lyman visit them, and that he choose a companion to accompany him. Voted that Elder Orson Pratt write a fatherly epistle in behalf of this council and Elder Orson Spencer assist him: Elder Lyman chose Elder Daniel Spencer to accompany him.

The following is a copy of the letter written:

THE COUNCIL'S LETTER WRITTEN TO JAMES EMMETT AND COMPANY

'Nauvoo, February 27, 1845.

To James Emmett & Company,

Dear Brethren: We, the Twelve and some other of the authorities of the church, being in council assembled, send unto you this epistle by the hand of our beloved, trustworthy and faithful brother Amasa M. Lyman, whom we have counseled to visit you, and give you instruction for your good and salvation.

Though our counsel has been lightly esteemed and disregarded by Brother Emmett, yet we verily believe there are those among you who have been honestly and sincerely deceived by his vain pretenses and misrepresentations. We labored long and faithfully to persuade Brother Emmett to hearken to the counsel of his friends to whom were committed the power, authority and keys for the salvation of Zion and the redemption of her children together with the keys of endowment for the lifting up and exaltation of the heirs of promise—the remnant of Joseph—but our counsels, our persuasions, our entreaties, and all our labors with him were in vain. He still persisted in his course and has led you forth from our midst and separated you from the body and like a branch severed from a tree you must and will perish together with your posterity and your progenitors unless you are engrafted again thereon before you wither and die; and because we know your unfortunate condition, and because we feel for your safety as a kind father feels for his tender offspring we therefore stretch out our arms to you and would feign welcome you to the bosom of our counsels and rescue you from the vortex of ruin and destruction into which you will inevitably and irrecoverably plunge yourselves by continuing to hearken to the counsels of one who will not regard the advice and counsel of the proper authorities of the kingdom of God.

Do you wish, dear brethren, to see the house of our God built up, adorned, and prepared according to the commandment and pattern given? Do you wish to enter into its sacred courts and receive your washings and anointings, and the keys of knowledge and power? Do you desire the eternal seal of the priesthood placed upon your head by which your progenitors for ages past and your posterity for endless generations to come shall be secured to you in a covenant that is everlasting? Do you desire to take part with the servants of God in teaching, civilizing, saving and exalting the Lamanites? And, in fine, do you desire to stand forth with the servants of God and in the majesty and strength and greatness of the everlasting priesthood rescue the earth from violence, oppression and wickedness and seal all things unto the end of all things that the saints alone may have dominion.

All of you are ready to answer yes, and respond with a hearty affirmative. But remember that there is but one way by which you can realize or partake of these things; it is by hearkening to our counsel in all things; and for this reason we send unto you Brother Amasa [M. Lyman], who will counsel you in all things according to the mind and will of God, according to the circumstances in which you are placed.

If Brother Emmett will receive our advice and continue so to do, it shall yet be well with him, but if not we say in the name of the Lord that it shall be ill with him and all that follow him.'

Evening, called on Father John Smith, who was still sick; united with the brethren and prayed for him: he felt blessed.

Friday, 28.—I went to the Temple and visited the Trustees, and counseled with them pertaining to business: all things going on well.

Saturday, March 1, 1845.—I met with the 'General Council'* at the Seventies Hall. We decided to send nine brethren westward, to search out a location for the saints; many eloquent speeches were made on the present position of affairs: had a good meeting, which continued all day.

The high council met: no business.

The overflowing of rivers in the north of China submerged whole provinces with populations respectively larger than some of the second class kingdoms of Europe. When the waters receded thousands of corpses were left on the ground. Upwards of seventeen millions of human beings who have escaped from the inundations have spread over the adjacent provinces, beggared of all things and crying for bread.

Sunday, 2.—At home—unwell. Elders Heber C. Kimball and John E. Page preached in the Music Hall. The seventies and their families met in their hall. Elders Luman A. Shurtliff, Hiram Dayton, and Joseph Young preached.

Evening, visited Father John Smith and the mother of the Prophet.

Monday, 3.—I accompanied Elder Heber C. Kimball at his request on to the hill to transact some business: returned home quite sick and went to bed.

Evening, the Presidents of Seventies met, and investigated the characters of several of their members. The choir had a concert at the Music Hall; Elders Taylor and Kimball addressed the assembly spiritedly.

Tuesday, 4.—Continued sickly. General Council met at Seventies Hall; Elder Kimball presided; the subject of the western mission was discussed.

*"General Council is the Council of Fifty." This is the footnote in *President Young's Ms. History*. This Council of Fifty is the legislature of the kingdom of God which includes the church. (For treatise see Note at end of chapter.)

Thursday, 6.—Elders Kimball and Richards called on me this evening. I sat up a little and felt better.

Friday, 7.—I walked over to my brother Joseph's: felt considerably better. I had no doctor in my sickness, but the Lord, my wife, and the laying on of hands of the elders.

Saturday, 8.—I rode up to the Temple. High council met—no business—adjourned.

Sunday, 9.—I attended council with Elders Heber C. Kimball, John Taylor, George A. Smith, N. K. Whitney and George Miller, most of the day; afterwards met with the high priests' quorum and preached. Evening, attended seventies meeting and addressed the brethren.

Elder Wilford Woodruff attended conference at Preston, England. Five hundred and five members were represented.

Monday, 10.—Forenoon, with Elders Kimball and Richards. Afternoon, Elders George A. Smith assisted Elder Richards to get out historical items.

Tuesday, 11.—I attended the General Council. The subject of writing to Governor Ford; also the present movements of the mob were discussed. It was considered best for those who are hunted with writs to go on missions; as the policy of commencing a mob persecution has always been to get out vexatious writs in order to provoke resistance to the form of legal authority and thereby produce a collision between us and the state; so that we may, if possible, evade the blow until we can finish the Temple and the Nauvoo House. It was also decided that the workmen on the walls of the Temple commence work tomorrow.

Wednesday, 12.—The sheriff is here with writs for several of the brethren. He says that the mob have sent messengers to the governor to inform him that the Mormons have resisted the officers and requesting him to order a *posse comitatus* to come and take Brackenbury: Mr. Brackenbury was a witness against the murderers of Joseph and Hyrum Smith.

Wm. Marks left town suddenly.

A dreadful earthquake occurred in the city of Mexico at fifty-two minutes past three p. m., which caused a great amount of suffering and great destruction of property.

Thursday, 13.—Several brethren accompanied Mr. Brackenbury to Augusta.

Friday, 14.—I attended meeting in the Masonic Hall and proposed that deacons be appointed to take care of the poor, in every neighborhood, with bishops at their head: agreed to meet the bishops and their counselors at the Masonic Hall on Monday morning to organize.

Brother A. P. Rockwood recorded the following:

'For the three and a half years that I have been in charge of the Temple quarry, with from twenty to one hundred and fifty hands, Brother Moses Horn has been the first person that has met with an accident by blasting. During this time there has been burned, according to my judgment, about one hundred casks of powder. Brother Horn had retired to the usual distance while blasting; he was struck on the head by a stone weighing one and a half pounds which fractured his skull; we immediately conveyed him home, sent for Dr. Bernhisel and other physicians, who pronounced the wound mortal: he died in three hours.' "

NOTE

President Young in writing a letter (May 3, 1844) to Reuben Hedlock, president of the European Mission at the time, said to him: "The kingdom is organized; and although as yet no bigger than a grain of mustard seed, the little plant is in a flourishing condition and our prospects brighter than ever. Cousin Lemuel is very friendly [referring to the Indians] and cultivating the spirit of peace and union in his family very extensively."*

Again in a discourse under date of July 8, 1855,† President Young said: "As was observed by Brother Pratt [this morning] that kingdom [i. e. of God] is actually organized and the inhabitants of the earth do not know it. If this people know anything about it, all right; it is organized preparatory to taking effect in the due time of the Lord, and in the manner that shall please him. As observed by

**Millennial Star,* vol. xxiii, p. 422.

†*Deseret News,* August 1, 1855, vol. v, p. 162; see also *Journal of Discourses,* vol. ix, pp. 309-17.

one of the speakers this morning that kingdom grows out of the Church of Jesus Christ of Latter-day Saints, but it is not the church; for a man may be a legislator in that body which will issue laws to sustain the inhabitants of the earth in their individual rights and still not belong to the Church of Jesus Christ at all. And further though a man may not even believe in any religion it would be perfectly right, when necessary, to give him the privilege of holding a seat among that body which will make laws to govern all the nations of the earth and control those who make no profession of religion at all; for that body would be governed, controlled and dictated to acknowledge others in those rights which they wish to enjoy themselves. Then the Latter-day Saints would be protected, if a kingdom of this kind was on the earth, the same as all other people."

The late President George Q. Cannon while editor of the *Juvenile Instructor** said:

"We are asked, Is the Church of God, and the Kingdom of God the same organization? and we are informed that some of the brethren hold that they are separate.

This is the correct view to take. The Kingdom of God is a separate organization from the Church of God. There may be men acting as officers in the Kingdom of God who will not be members of the Church of Jesus Christ of Latter-day Saints. On this point the Prophet Joseph gave particular instructions before his death, and gave an example, which he asked the younger elders who were present to always remember. It was to the effect that men might be chosen to officiate as members of the Kingdom of God who had no standing in the Church of Jesus Christ of Latter-day Saints. The Kingdom of God when established will not be for the protection of the Church of Jesus Christ of Latter-day Saints alone, but for the protection of all men, whatever their religious views or opinions may be. Under its rule, no one will be permitted to overstep the proper bounds or to interfere with the rights of others."

Undoubtedly all this has reference to the time spoken of by St. John in *Revelation* when he said: "And the seventh angel sounded; and there were great voices in heaven, saying, The kingdoms of this world are become the kingdoms of our Lord, and of his Christ; and he shall reign forever and ever."†

However it is proper to note that sometimes these terms "the Church of Christ", "the Kingdom of God" and "the Kingdom of Heaven" are used interchangeably in the scriptures and hence the confusion in these terms sometimes obtains.

*Vol. xxxi, p 140.
†*Rev.* xi:15.

CHAPTER XXIX

THE JAMES EMMETT COMPANY OFFICIALLY VISITED—APRIL CONFERENCE OF 1845—MUNICIPAL CORPORATIONS UNDER GENERAL STATE LAW—WESTERN MOVEMENT PROPOSED BY GOVERNOR FORD

"*Saturday, March* 15, 1845.—Attended council at the Trustees' Office: present—a quorum of the Twelve Apostles, Presidency of the Seventies, Temple Committee, Trustees and Architect. We decided to put all our help on the Temple—build a drain for the font—a wall on the south side of the Temple block—keep three cranes going, and stop building the dam in the Mississippi till next winter.

Afternoon, I attended the high council in company with Elders Heber C. Kimball, Orson Pratt, John Taylor, George A. Smith, and John E. Page.

Elders Amasa M. Lyman and Daniel Spencer returned from their visit to Emmett's company.

At five p. m., the Twelve and Trustees repaired to the Mansion and heard Elder Lyman give an account of his late mission to Emmett's company. He found them on the Iowa river one hundred and fifty miles west of the settlements in a deplorable condition, caused chiefly by the rigid enforcement of Emmett's measures; he having limited their food to three gills of corn each per day. The company were much distressed and in all probability many would soon return to Nauvoo.

Lyman and Spencer's Report of Emmett's Company.

The Twelve and Trustees partook of supper provided by Brother John Pack at the Mansion; after which the band discoursed sweet music.

Mr. Brackenbury and company returned from

Augusta; he had not been brought to trial, the party prosecuting alleging they were not ready; Brackenbury offered to admit the charge, and give bonds for his appearance at next court, which was all the justice of the peace could require, if the trial had proceeded and the charge had been sustained; but the justice would not do it, so determined were the mob to annoy Brackenbury and get an opportunity to do him personal violence. Mr. Brackenbury was arrested for perjury; but the real intention of the mob was to get him into their hands to murder him, to prevent his being a witness against the murderers of Joseph and Hyrum Smith.

Brackenbury—Plot Against.

Sunday, 16.—Elder Amasa M. Lyman preached at the stand. He spoke as follows:

'I have been in the woods and have seen those people who have gone into the wilderness to get their endowment. They have suffered much—have been reduced in their rations to three gills of corn per day, and latterly to two gills, hence you will not be surprised when I tell you that they have grown very poor. This is the way they live in the wilderness, still they profess to abide the counsel of the Twelve. Emmett is trustee-in-trust and Butler is second in command. Their countenances brightened up when they saw Brother Spencer and me, and found they were not all entirely cut off. The majority of them were under the impression that their movement was directed by the orders of the Twelve.

Amasa M. Lyman's Further Report on the Emmett Company's Conditions.

Brother Emmett did not manifest any disposition to follow the counsel of the Twelve, he said if the Twelve would live among the Gentiles longer he had no objections, but that he had endured the driving from Missouri with patience, and that he was clear from the blood of the Gentiles. He seemed determined to go ahead against the advice of God, man or the devil. He got his company to consecrate wife, children, clothing and everything they had, and place all their property under the control of the bishop; there is not one who can control a second suit of clothes. Brother Hilmer wanted to come away. Emmett said to him, 'Did not you covenant to stand by us? If you want to be a covenant-breaker you can go.' They have more arms than men. More than one-half of the party were for stopping. Orders were given for the arms to be brought in and piled. Those who declared their determination to go ahead took the arms and the others were commanded to stand and have their tents searched. The suffering they have endured is too bad to talk about. Once in a while their cattle die; they have not the trouble of killing them; they then go to work and eat them. I stayed one night, my heart was sick; I left and wrote to them.'

REMARKS OF BRIGHAM YOUNG ON EMMETT'S COMPANY AND SUNDRY TOPICS

I [Brigham Young] also addressed the meeting and said: 'I will give a few of my own ideas in short. Living poor, being in the wilderness, etc., is nothing to me when I am called to endure it, but people who run headlong into misery and bring upon themselves suffering, do not arrive at anything but darkness and despair. There is not one of Emmett's company that can claim the protection of heaven or any blessing of the everlasting gospel; their sufferings add nothing to their exaltation, but if the Lord had called them to pass through trials, they would have visions, revelations and faith (if necessity required) to cause him to feed them like the children of Israel. We told James Emmett, if he went, he would get into trouble: this congregation can be led by a thread. Religion is one thing and fanaticism is another.

Spring is here; we covenanted to labor on the Temple until it was finished and do all we could towards its completion; but we have not done it; if the brethren had continued, they might have worked on those walls four days a week. The stonecutters and joiners have been at work; the joiners have far exceeded our expectations this winter. The timber holds out, we keep using and there is enough left; there will be no lack of timber. If the brethren will go to work now, there will be no lack of provisions. We want the brethren to pay up their tithing. If you will haul wood, timber, etc., and help on the Temple you will find that it will be made up to you in your crops.

Since N. K. Whitney and George Miller have taken charge of the business, no man has needed anything but what has been supplied. I can call scores of men around me, who would sooner sacrifice every dollar they have, than the work on the Temple should stop. We can set four hundred men to work on the Temple. I do not want any man to go to preach till he is sent. If the world want to hear preaching let them come here, and if they really want the gospel, let them clean [up] Carthage jail.

I have proposed to the leading men of the Water Power Company, to put their work on the Temple. I will call the stockholders together, and give my reasons to them. We want to press forward the work on the Temple. I now proclaim to all saints who control means, to go to the Trustees and see if they want means to procure provisions, etc., for the hands; and I ask you to use all your influence to strengthen the hands of the Trustees.

I swear by the God of heaven that we will not spend money in feeing lawyers. All the lawsuits that have been got up against the saints, have been hatched up to fee lawyers, tavernkeepers, etc. I would rather have a six-shooter than all the lawyers in Illinois. I am sworn not to pay lawyers, but to pay our debts, and it will relieve us from an immense tax. Do not let there be a lot laying vacant in this town, join fences, for there is land enough in this city without going on to the prairie. I am going to drop the name Nauvoo and call this the 'City of Joseph'. Tomorrow evening we want the bishops at the Masonic Hall, and we will organize them according to our notion of things. We have no police; the legislature has repealed our charter, and we mean to have the 'City of Joseph' organized. The streets shall be kept clear; and the poor cared for.

Brother Wm. Marks has gone without being 'whit-;led' out. He would hire a man for twenty-five cents a day and would make a man work two days in the harvest field for one bushel of wheat, which is one of the most low, dishonest, mean things a person can do.'

Departure of Wm. Marks from Nauvoo.

Elder Heber C. Kimball preached at Brother Luce's on the occasion of the death of Brother Moses Horn.

Monday, 17.—One hundred and five extra laborers and about thirty teams commenced work at the Temple this morning in obedience to the call of yesterday to hasten its completion.

Tuesday, 18.—I met with General Council all day.

Wednesday, 19.—Colonel Hosea Stout, who was on duty this evening at my house [i. e. as watchman] called upon me and I had some conversation with him in regard to the saints settling the country near the headwaters of the Colorado of the west.

Thursday, 20.—Elder Heber C. Kimball and I called on Elder Richards and found him and his clerks engaged on the history: we proceeded to the Temple.

Evening, attended prayer meeting at Brother Joseph B. Noble's.

Friday, 21.—In company with Elders Heber C. Kimball, Willard Richards, John E. Page and A. W. Babbitt, I went to the Trustees' Office and consulted in relation to the best course for Mr. Brackenbury to pursue. We agreed that he should sue out a writ of *habeas corpus* returnable before Judge Young at Quincy, and that Brother Babbitt should accompany him thither.

Movement as to Brackenbury.

Evening, attended prayer meeting at Brother Joseph B. Noble's.

Saturday, 22.—I attended the General Council. The

subject of the western mission was considered and occupied the most of the day: the Nauvoo House, Printing Office, Church History and organization of the city were also matters of consideration.

Sunday, 23.—Elder Heber C. Kimball preached in the Music Hall on the building of the Temple.

Elder Wilford Woodruff attended a conference in Edinburgh, Scotland; four hundred and nine members were represented.

Monday, 24.—In company with the Twelve Apostles I attended a meeting at the Concert Hall in the evening. We ordained bishops who were directed to set apart deacons in their wards to attend to all things needful and especially to watch; being without any city organization, we deemed it prudent to organize the priesthood more strictly that the peace and good order hitherto sustained by the city might still be preserved.

Tuesday, 25.—I attended council with the Twelve and prayer meeting in the evening.

Wednesday, 26.—Elder Amos Fielding with about fifty saints arrived this evening, being a portion of the company who left Liverpool, England, on the ship *Palmyra;* many of the company were unable to get further than St. Louis. At nine p. m., I rode to the upper landing and welcomed the saints, and directed the schoolhouse to be opened for the use of the company during the night.

Arrival of English Saints.

Brother Perkins from Macedonia, brought word that the mob were making active preparations to make a break upon us about court time, which is the third Monday in May: they were collecting artillery and organizing themselves for a general raid.

Mob Movements.

Thursday, 27.—I attended council with the Twelve, the Trustees, the Temple Committee and Brother Amos Fielding at Father Cutler's. Church matters and the plans of the mob were canvassed.

At three p. m., Brother Wm. W. Player finished setting the last trumpet stone on the capitals of the pilasters of the Temple. All the capitals and trumpet stones are now safe on the walls, which is a matter of rejoicing to all who love to witness the prosperity of the work. The weather has been sometimes very cold and at other times very windy, so that it has been impossible for the hands to continue on the walls, much of the time of late.

Friday, 28.—I attended a party at the Mansion; most of the Twelve and their families and about one hundred and forty others were present: the brass band performed some good pieces.

Saturday, 29.—Elder Kimball and I called on Elder Richards at the Historian's Office; thence we proceeded to the Temple.

Elder Orson Hyde preached at the stand on the occasion of a Masonic funeral.

Sunday, 30.—I preached to the saints. It was very windy. It rained in the afternoon.

Monday, 31.—Elder Wilford Woodruff attended a conference at Liverpool, England: twelve branches were represented containing six hundred and seventy-six members.

Advice Sought From Governor Ford.

I wrote to Governor Ford asking his counsel in relation to the reorganization of the militia of the city of Nauvoo, as the Legion was dissolved by a repeal of the charter, and soliciting his views on the great western measure: and also whether it would be the best policy to organize Nauvoo under the act for organizing towns.

Tuesday, April 1, 1845.—I commenced revising the History of Joseph Smith at Brother Richards' office: Elder Heber C. Kimball and George A. Smith were with me. President Joseph Smith had corrected forty-two pages before his massacre. It afforded us great satisfaction to hear Brother Richards read the history of the infancy of the church. Adjourned at eleven p. m. having read one hundred and forty pages in Book 'A'.

Wednesday, 2.—Engaged at Elder Richards' office

with Elders Kimball and Smith revising Church History.

Brother Jesse D. Hunter returned from his mission having visited the branches in the state of Tennessee since January last, and received two hundred and thirty dollars on tithing and offerings for the Temple mostly in property.

Thursday, 3.—Accompanied by Elders Heber C. Kimball, Willard Richards and George A. Smith, I went to the Temple.

Evening, the brethren of the Twelve and others met at Elder Richards' office and prayed; we remembered our enemies and prayed that their designs against Zion might fail; we felt the power of God.

Friday, 4.—I visited Brother Moore, who had been accidentally shot. Dr. Bernhisel decided that the wound was mortal; but by the blessing of God he recovered.

Elder Benjamin L. Clapp reported that he left Nauvoo on the twenty-third day of October, 1844, on a special mission to collect tithing throughout the southern states. He returned about this date, having held many meetings, baptized fifteen persons and collected one thousand and forty-seven dollars which he delivered to the Trustee-in-Trust.

Backenstos Threatened.

The mob left notice with Sheriff Backenstos of Carthage to leave by three p. m. today. The Jack-Mormons (the name attached to those friendly to Mormonism), say they will defend him and are gathering a company for that purpose. Backenstos says he will not be driven, but will stand his ground: report says the mob are divided among themselves.

Brother William W. Major exhibited a painting of the assassination of Joseph and Hyrum Smith by the mob at Carthage.

Sunday, 6.—The following Conference Minutes are extracted from the *Times and Seasons*;

CONFERENCE MINUTES

'Special conference of the Church of Jesus Christ of Latter-day Saints at Nauvoo, April 6, 1845; it being the first day of the sixteenth year (i. e. of the organization of the church).

The choir sang 'Hark the Jubilee' at quarter past ten o'clock, while the assembly was collecting.

Present—President Brigham Young, Heber C. Kimball, Orson Hyde, Orson Pratt, George A. Smith, John Taylor, John E. Page, Willard Richards, and Amasa M. Lyman of the Quorum of the Twelve—Father John Smith, president of the stake—Bishops Whitney and Miller—the high council—and about twenty-two thousand persons (in attendance).

Elder Kimball called the meeting to order at half past ten a. m.; and the choir sang the thirty-first hymn; followed by prayer by Elder Kimball; the choir then sang 'Come All Ye Sons of Zion'.

The morning was spent in teaching, on the baptism for the dead, by President Young.

Conference adjourned until two o'clock.

Two o'clock p. m.—Conference met pursuant to adjournment; the forepart of which was taken up by the blessing of children, but owing to the immense number it was found impossible to complete the whole, when it was accordingly dispensed with, and the remainder of the afternoon was occupied in exhortation from the stand, by Elder Page and President Young and the conference adjourned until tomorrow at ten o'clock a. m.

Monday, April 7, 1845, *ten o'clock a. m.*—Conference met pursuant to adjournment; after the conference was seated, in consequence of the high wind, it was thought best to remove into the valley, a little south; and the whole of this immense congregation was removed, and comfortably seated in the short space of about forty minutes. The choir sang 'The Heavenly Vision', and was followd by prayer, by Elder John Taylor, after which the choir sang another hymn. Elder Kimball then arose and stated to the congregation some of the items of business which would be necessary to attend to during the day, *viz.*: the building of the Temple, and the Nauvoo House; also, to take into consideration all old obligations against the church, which are pouring in like a torrent, also to ascertain the feelings of the people, in regard to sustaining the authorities of the church under the present organization.

President Brigham Young then arose, and said he would now present the first item of business, which would be to present the authorities of the church for the approval or disapproval of the conference. He also said he wanted to know if the saints are satisfied that Joseph Smith lived and died as a Prophet, Seer, and Revelator to this church.

The Saints Satisfied with Joseph Smith as a Prophet.

Whereupon Elder Phelps moved that we accept the labors of Joseph

Smith as a Prophet, Seer, and Revelator to the nineteenth century; and that we are satisfied that he lived according to his profession, and died a martyr to the truth. Carried unanimously.

Elder Phelps moved that we accept the labors of Hyrum Smith, believing that he lived according to his profession, and died a martyr to the truth. Carried unanimously.

Elder Phelps moved that this conference accept the Twelve as the First Presidency and leaders of this church. Carried unanimously. [After which each of the Twelve was sustained separately by unanimous vote].

* * *

The chairman then observed, concerning the course of Lyman Wight, his feelings are, that we should let him remain for the present, probably hereafter there may be a time that he will hearken to counsel, and do much good which he is capable of—for he is a noble-minded man.

Lyman Wight.

The chairman then stated that the next item of business would be, to present to the conference, the presidency of the stake; moved and seconded that Patriarch John Smith continue in his office, as president of this stake, and that he be sustained in his office. Carried unanimously.

Moved and seconded that Charles C. Rich be continued and sustained in his office of counselor to Father Smith. Carried unanimously.

Moved and seconded that George Miller be continued and sustained in his office, as president of the high priests' quorum. Carried unanimously.

Moved and seconded that William Snow and Noah Packard be continued and sustained in their office as counselors to President Miller. Carried unanimously.

Moved and seconded that Samuel Bent, be continued and sustained in his office as president of the high council. Carried unanimously.

Moved and seconded that George W. Harris, Alpheus Cutler, William Huntington Sen., James Allred, Henry G. Sherwood, Thomas Grover, Newel Knight, Lewis D. Wilson, David Fullmer, Ezra T. Benson, and Aaron Johnson be continued and sustained in their office as members of the high council. Carried unanimously.

Moved and seconded that Joseph Young be continued and sustained as President of the First Presidency of the Seventy. Carried unanimously.

Moved and seconded that Levi W. Hancock, Henry Harriman, Zerah Pulsipher, Jedediah M. Grant, and Daniel S. Miles be continued and sustained in their office, as Associate Presidents to President Joseph Young. Carried unanimously.

Moved and seconded that if Roger Orton will reform and become a good man, he be received and ordained as a member of this presidency. Carried unanimously.

Moved and seconded that Samuel Williams be continued and

sustained in his office as the president of the elders' quorum. Carried unanimously.

Moved and seconded that Jesse Baker, and Joshua Smith be continued, and sustained as counselors to President Williams. Carried unanimously.

Moved and seconded that Newel K. Whitney and George Miller be continued and sustained in their offices as Bishops and Trustees-in-Trust, to the Church of Jesus Christ of Latter-day Saints. Carried unanimously.

Moved and seconded that Alpheus Cutler and Reynolds Cahoon be continued and sustained as Temple Committee. Carried unanimously.

On the subject of the old church debts coming, it was moved and seconded that the debts of Kirtland, and Missouri, and the debts that are said to be accrued in consequence of purchasing the Galland tract in Iowa territory, be dropt, and come up no more, and the Trustees shall be dunned for them no more forever;—neither shall they be sold into the hands of the Gentiles. Carried unanimously.

Conference then adjourned until 2 o'clock.

Two o'clock p. m.—Conference met pursuant to adjournment.

The choir sang a hymn, which was followed by prayer from Elder Orson Pratt; after which the choir sang another hymn. By request of President Young, Elder Orson Pratt read the revelation, given January 19th, 1841, concerning the building of the Temple, Nauvoo House, etc. After which he read an extract from the *Law of the Lord,* page 240.

The chairman then stated that he wanted to lay before the conference, the subject of completing the Nauvoo House, whereupon—

Elder Phelps moved 'that we fulfill the revelation, by completing the Nauvoo House, as soon as possible.' Carried unanimously.

The chairman called for a show of hands from all those who could, and would, take one share of stock in the Nauvoo House, there were so many hands uplifted that they could not possibly be counted.

He next called for a show of hands from those who could and would, take two shares; quite a large number of hands were shown.

He then called for a show of hands from all, both male and female, who, after they had done all they could to finish the Temple are willing to sacrifice their all, to finish the Nauvoo House, rather than not have it done. Every hand was raised in the congregation.

The President then proclaimed to the conference, that on next Monday, the books for the Nauvoo House Association would be opened in the upper part of the brick store on Water Street.

The conference then adjourned until tomorrow at 10 o'clock a. m.

Tuesday, April 8, 1845.—Conference met pursuant to adjournment at 10 a. m. and was addressed by Elders Kimball and Young, upon the propriety of the saints staying in Hancock county, and in the afternoon Elders Young, Page, and Hyde addressed the assembly.

Perfect union and harmony prevailed throughout the conference and there was but one dissenting vote in the entire congregation.

Nauvoo becomes City of Joseph.

It was moved by the President, [Brigham Young] that henceforth and forever, this city shall be called 'The City of Joseph'. [Carried unanimously.]

Great praise is due to ex-Marshal A. P. Rockwood, and his associates for their unwearied exertion, to arrange and seat the numberless assembly, for the most perfect order was maintained by them throughout the whole city and the conference—and to the saints universally for seconding their movements.

On motion conference adjourned until the 6th of October next.

[Signed] BRIGHAM YOUNG, President.

William Clayton }
Thomas Bullock } Clerks of Conference.'

COMMENTS ON THE CONFERENCE

'Elder George D. Watt, whose valuable services to this church as Professor of Phonography, are highly appreciated; has taken down the speeches delivered on this occasion, and they will appear from time to time as circumstances will allow.

Never have we seen the time before when the people were more willing to receive and listen to counsel than now. The high council have only had one case in about seven weeks. Our magistrates have nothing to do. We have little or no use for charter or law. Every man is doing his best to cultivate the ground, and all are anxious to provide things honestly in the sight of all men—to honor our God, our country and its laws. Whenever a dispute or difficulty arises, a word from the proper source puts all to right, and no resort to law. May God ever save us from this snare of men, this drainer of the purse, and this fruitful source of contention and strife.'*

Monday, April 7, 1845.—The stockholders of the Nauvoo House Association met. Elders George A. Smith and Amasa M. Lyman were appointed trustees in the place of Lyman Wight and John Snider; L. R. Foster was appointed clerk.

Tuesday, 8.—I had a conversation with Dr. W. G. Goforth on the principles of the gospel and baptized him, and in company with Brothers Heber C. Kimball and George A. Smith confirmed him a member of the church and ordained him a high priest.

Brother Elijah Fordham returned from New York

**Times and Seasons,* vol. vi, pp. 869-871

and brought twelve hundred and sixty-three dollars for the Temple.

Wednesday, 9.—I met in council with the Twelve and bishops at the Trustees' Office. We agreed to advise Peter Maughan and Jacob Peart to return from Rock river whither they had been to work a coal mine; Reuben McBride to put the Kirtland property in the best state possible, without paying out money and to come to Nauvoo bye and bye. The bishops were instructed to sell the steamboat *Maid of Iowa* for what they could get for it.

Elder Lorenzo Snow returned to Nauvoo and brought some money and property and a six-pounder cannon on tithing.

Nauvoo to Become the Public Center for the Church.

Thursday, 10.—I met in council with Elders Heber C. Kimball, Orson Hyde, John Taylor, George A. Smith, Willard Richards and Amasa M. Lyman. We decided to print our own works at Nauvoo; remove the printing office into the Masonic Hall, and print the *Book of Doctrine and Covenants, Hymn Book* and *History* as soon as possible.

A resolution was passed to disfellowship George J. Adams and Sam Brannan, and a letter was written to Elder Parley P. Pratt on the subject.

The trustees of the Nauvoo House Association met and examined their books.

Evening, the Twelve and bishops met at the Historian's Office and prayed for rain; an abundant harvest; deliverance from our enemies and blessings on the saints.

Friday, 11.—I met with the General Council at the Masonic Hall.

Saturday, 12.—The trustees of the Nauvoo House Association met.

The old police invited the Twelve and their families to a party at the Masonic Hall, when a comfortable repast was partaken of. The police performed a new piece entitled, 'Father Marks' Return to Mormonism'.

Evening, the U. S. deputy marshal for the district of Illinois arrived in town with writs for myself and others.

Sunday, 13.—Meeting at the stand. Elders Heber C. Kimball and John Taylor preached. Several officers attended meeting. Elder Taylor gave them to understand that if they made an attempt to serve writs on him it would cost them their lives, and said, if they wished to magnify the law and make it honorable they should bring to justice the murderers of Joseph and Hyrum, two of our best men, who were treacherously butchered while in the custody of officers pledged for their safety; and that he would not submit any more to such outrages on our lives and liberties, for under present circumstances the law is only powerful to hold men still while the lawless massacre them.

I attended the high priests' quorum meeting and gave much counsel.

The following letter from the governor was read:

LETTER OF GOVERNOR FORD ON THE ORGANIZATION OF TOWN GOVERNMENT WITHIN NAUVOO

'Springfield, April 8, 1845.

General Brigham Young:

I have received your letter of March the 31st and have attentively considered its contents until this time. It is a matter of much delicacy and importance to answer in the best manner the inquiries contained in it. A town corporation under the general law, will evidently be insufficient for such a place as Nauvoo. The general law does not extend your limits over a mile square. This however may be remedied in some degree by making a number of corporations to include the whole territory of the city. In this case however you will be liable to a want of united action; and so many governments though less efficient must be more expensive than a city government.

I make no doubt also that you stand in need of a local court which however you cannot have higher than that of a justice of the peace under the present law. I would advise that you incorporate as many towns, one mile square as will cover the city; and I make no doubt but that your peaceable and orderly conduct, if continued, will be duly appreciated by the next session of the legislature. By that time the storm of passion produced by recent events will have subsided and I make no doubt a new charter will be granted.

The powers under your town charters will be but limited it is true.

They are to make and execute ordinances not inconsistent with law and the Constitution; to prevent and remove nuisances; to restrain and prohibit gaming and disorderly conduct; to prevent the indecent exhibition of horses; to license public shows; to sink and repair public wells; to open and repair the streets and alleys and make pavements and sidewalks, and to provide means to protect the town from injuries by fires, and to levy a tax on real estate for town purposes. These powers are somewhat better than none; and will give you some protection and provide somewhat for the advancement and comfort of your city. And I would advise the people to avail themselves of them until they can do better at another session. As to a want of legal united action, on the part of so many corporations in any common design for the good of the city; that must be supplied at present by their voluntary concurrence, which can be brought about by the influence of your leading citizens. There is no other way to do it that I can think of. Whether you have that spirit of unity amongst you which will enable them to do so, you know better than I can know.

As to your military affairs I have already written to the Hon. A. W. Babbitt concerning that subject and I refer you to that letter for my opinions at length as to your military organization. Since I wrote that letter I have been advised of the movement at Carthage in relation to the Hon. J. B. Backenstos, and also of the proceedings of the Carthagenians in removing the cannon from McComb. As yet I am ignorant of their design in this latter movement. Whether they intend it as a mere bravado, to keep up agitation and excitement, until after the trials; or whether there is to be a general move and renewal of the designs of last summer and fall I am not aware. I have seen the *Warsaw Signal* which again preached expulsion but beyond this I have seen nothing and know nothing of their designs. I have on Saturday last dispatched a bold and trusty man to demand the arms and cannon at Carthage and Warsaw. These events may for aught I know point to a new war against you. If they do you cannot be organized as a part of the state militia too soon.

I am aware that under such an organization there must be many persons exempt from military duty; but in case of danger no doubt they will voluntarily enroll themselves; there is no law to forbid their service; their exemption is not a disqualification to serve, but a privilege not to serve if they choose.

In case a mob should be raised against you it will be your privilege and one of your highest duties to society and yourselves to resist it. But you know your condition as a people. You know the prejudices which exist; and the disposition of the public mind to believe evil of you. You will therefore have to be cautious. Do nothing which will allow your opponents to say that you have begun a war. Place them clearly in the wrong and keep them so.

As to the great western measure if congress would grant you the land, I think it would be good policy for your people to move to some far distant country. Your religion is new and it surprises the people as any great novelty in religion generally does. They cannot rise above the prejudices excited by such novelty. However truly and sincerely your own people may believe in it; the impression on the public mind everywhere is that your leading men are impostors and rogues and that the others are dupes and fools. This impression in the minds of the great mass is sufficient to warrant them in considering and treating you as enemies and outcasts; as men to be cherished and trusted in nothing, because in their estimation some of you are deluded, and others designing in matters of religion. If you can get off by yourselves you may enjoy peace; but surrounded by such neighbors I confess that I do not foresee the time when you will be permitted to enjoy quiet. I was informed by General Joseph Smith last summer that he contemplated a removal west; and from what I learned from him and others at that time I think if he had lived he would have begun to move in the matter before this time. I would be willing to exert all my feeble abilities and influence to further your views in this respect if it was the wish of your people.

WESTERN MOVEMENT OF THE SAINTS SUGGESTED

I would suggest a matter in confidence, California now offers a field for the prettiest enterprise that has been undertaken in modern time. It is but sparsely inhabited and by none but the Indian or imbecile Mexican Spaniard. I have not inquired enough to know how strong it is in men and means. But this we know that if conquered from Mexico that country is so physically weak and morally distracted that she could never send a force there to conquer it. Why would it not be a pretty operation for your people to go out there, take possession of and conquer a portion of the vacant country, and establish an independent government of your own subject only to the laws of nations. [?] You would remain there a long time before you would be disturbed by the proximity of other settlements. If you conclude to do this your design ought not to be known or otherwise it would become the duty of the United States to prevent your emigration. But if you once cross the line of the United States territories you would be in no danger of being interfered with.

I am very respectfully
Your obedient Servant,
[Signed] THOMAS FORD.'*

Sunday 13, (*continued*).—At four p. m., I met with the Quorum of the Twelve.

Evening, in company with several brethren I visited the U. S. deputy marshal at the Mansion; he was very polite."

*A facsimile of this paragraph of Governor Ford's letter will be found in the *Comprehensive History of the Church*, Century I, vol. iii, p. 420.

CHAPTER XXX

AN APPEAL TO LYMAN WIGHT TO BE UNITED WITH THE TWELVE—LETTERS TO THE PRESIDENT OF THE UNITED STATES AND THE GOVERNORS OF THE RESPECTIVE STATES—LETTERS OF GOVERNOR FORD TO STATE MILITARY LEADERS—IMPORTANT DOCTRINAL LETTER OF THE TWELVE TO THE CHURCH

"*Monday, April* 14, 1845.—The public hands commenced the foundation of the wall around the Temple block.

Elder Richards and I attended the deacons' meeting. The deacons have become very efficient looking after the welfare of the saints; every part of the city is watched with the strictest care, and whatever time of night the streets are traveled at the corner of every block a deacon is found attending to his duty.

Tuesday, 15.—Brother Heber C. Kimball, George A. Smith and myself went to visit Philo Dibble, who was sick. We then went to Isaac Higbee's office and attended a council in relation to the organization of a town under the general incorporation act. Afterwards visited the arsenal and Uncle John Smith who let Dr. Cannon have his house and lot in Macedonia to cancel an obligation for four hundred dollars held by Dr. Cannon's wife and her sister against myself and Brother Kimball. Proceeded to Bishop Whitney's and administered to his wife who was sick; thence to the Seventies' Hall and attended General Council, where the letter from Governor Ford was read. If the advice of Governor Ford relative to organizing city government under the state law, were complied with to the letter, it would require

Towns Under General State Corporation Act Considered.

twelve incorporations, as limited by the state statutes to supply the place of the Nauvoo Charter and cover the limits of the city with this species of complicated, restricted town protection.

Wednesday, 16.—At sunset, Brother Heber C. Kimball and I laid hands on Brother W. Richards who was sick. A small portion of the city was incorporated as the town of Nauvoo and Alpheus Cutler, Orson Spencer, Charles C. Rich, Theodore Turley and David Fullmer were appointed trustees; they selected policemen, and appointed Hosea Stout captain, they also appointed assessors, collectors and other officers.

Thursday, 17.—I met in council with Elders Orson Pratt, George A. Smith, Amasa M. Lyman, C. C. Rich, and Samuel Bent, at Elder Richards'. We wrote as follows:

LETTER TO LYMAN WIGHT ET AL: A PLEA FOR UNION

'*To Brother Lyman Wight and All the Brethren With Him*—
Greeting:

We the Council of the Twelve being assembled and having learned your present circumstances and situation and also your future calculations with regard to your journey west, cannot feel justified without giving you a word of counsel and advice together with some information relative to our present prospects. We are prospering in this city both temporally and spiritually. Immigration continues to this city. Several hundred have arrived this spring. Great peace and union prevail among all the saints. There were many thousands present at our conference this month. All of our business was performed with the utmost peace and union and not a dissenting voice. We are rushing the Temple ahead with a strong hand. Tithings come in for the Temple more liberally than they have ever done before, and with but few exceptions the saints are willing to give their all for the Temple if required. There is every prospect of getting on the roof and finishing some rooms by next autumn when we shall commence administering the ordinances of endowment according to the commandment. We intend commencing again on the Nauvoo House within a few days. All the saints feel spirited and determined to carry out the measures of our martyred Prophet. There is no prospect of any mob at present, and all things bid fair for peace and prosperity.

And now, dear brethren, if you will hearken to our counsel you will give up all idea of journeying west at present. If you go westward before you have received your endowments in the Temple you will not prosper. And when you meet with trouble and difficulty let no one say that the counsel of the Twelve brought them into it, for we now in the name of the Lord counsel and advise you not to go west at present. We desire, dear brethren, that you should take hold with us and help us to accomplish the building of the Lord's houses. Come brethren, be one with us, and let us be agreed in all of our exertions to roll on the great wheel of the kingdom. We forward this letter by Brother Bent. He will give you further instructions relative to our proceedings and future calculations and we hope you will receive his counsel and do accordingly and all shall be well.'

Elder Samuel Bent was instructed to read the foregoing letter aloud to all the company.

Brother Lyman Wight has one hundred and thirty souls numbering forty able bodied men with him.

Evening, the Twelve and presiding bishops met and prayed.

Friday, 18.—As the workmen on the Temple had raised a large stone about fifteen hundred pounds weight, the chain broke and it fell fifty feet, but without injury to the building or any person.

Sunday, 20.—Elders Orson Pratt, Phineas H. Young and I preached. Afternoon, in council with the Twelve at the Seventies' Hall when four elders were set apart for missions.

Monday, 21.—Elder Wm. W. Player put up the first star on the southeast corner of the Temple. Elders Heber C. Kimball and William Clayton were watching the progress of the stone towards its destination: the 'stars' will add much to the beauty of the Temple.

Tuesday, 22.—Attended General Council.

Wednesday, 23.—Brother George A. Smith spent the evening with me.

Thursday, 24.—Elders Phineas H. Young, Jonathan Dunham, Charles Shumway, Lewis Dana and S. Tindale, started west on a mission to the Lamanites. Evening, attended prayer meeting with the Twelve at Elder Richards.

Realizing fully the insecurity of our position surrounded as we are by mob violence, and the constitution and laws of Illinois being powerless for our protection we deemed it wisdom, in General Council, to write as follows to the President of the United States and to the governor of every state in the Union except Missouri [and Illinois]:

LETTER TO THE PRESIDENT OF THE UNITED STATES AND THE GOVERNORS OF THE RESPECTIVE STATES

'Nauvoo, Illinois, April 24, 1845.

His Excellency James K. Polk,
President of the United States.
Hon. Sir:

Suffer us, Sir, in behalf of a disfranchised and long afflicted people to prefer a few suggestions for your serious consideration in hope of a friendly and unequivocal response, at as early a period as may suit your convenience, and the extreme urgency of the case seem to demand.

It is not our present design to detail the multiplied and aggravated wrongs that we have received in the midst of a nation that gave us birth. Most of us have long been loyal citizens of some one of these United States over which you have the honor to preside, while a few only claim the privileges of peaceable and lawful emigrants designing to make the Union our permanent residence.

We say we are a disfranchised people. We are privately told by the highest authorities of this state that it is neither prudent nor safe for us to vote at the polls; still we have continued to maintain our right to vote, until the blood of our best men has been shed, both in Missouri and Illinois, with impunity.

You are doubtless somewhat familiar with the history of our extermination from the state of Missouri, wherein scores of our brethren were massacred; hundreds died through want and sickness occasioned by their unparalleled sufferings; some millions of our property were confiscated or destroyed, and some fifteen thousand souls fled for their lives to the then hospitable and peaceful shores of Illinois; and that the state of Illinois granted to us a liberal charter (for the term of perpetual succession) under whose provision private rights have become invested, and the largest city in the state has grown up, numbering about twenty thousand inhabitants.

But Sir, the startling attitude recently assumed by the state of Illinois forbids us to think that her designs are any less vindictive than those of Missouri. She has already used the military of the state with the executive at their head to coerce and surrender up our best men to unparalleled murder, and that too under the most sacred pledges of protection and safety. As a salvo for such unearthly perfidy and guilt she told us through her highest executive officer, that the laws should be magnified and the murderers brought to justice; but the blood of her innocent victims had not been wholly wiped from the floor of the awful arena, where the citizens of a sovereign state pounced upon two defenseless servants of God our Prophet and our Patriarch, before the senate of that state rescued one of the indicted actors in that mournful tragedy from the sheriff of Hancock county and gave him an honorable seat in her hall of legislation, and all who were indicted by the grand jury of Hancock county for the murder of Generals Joseph and Hyrum Smith are suffered to roam at large watching for further prey.

To crown the climax of those bloody deeds the state has repealed all those chartered rights, by which we might have lawfully defended ourselves against aggressors. If we defend ourselves hereafter against violence whether it comes under the shadow of law or otherwise (for we have reason to expect it both ways) we shall then be charged with treason and suffer the penalty; and if we continue passive and non-resistant we must certainly expect to perish, for our enemies have sworn it.

And here, Sir, permit us to state that General Joseph Smith, during his short life, was arraigned at the bar of his country about fifty times charged with criminal offenses, but was acquitted every time by his country, his enemies, or rather his religious opponents, almost invariably being his judges. And we further testify that as a people, we are law abiding, peaceable, and without crime and we challenge the world to prove the contrary; and while other less cities in Illinois have had special courts instituted to try their criminals, we have been stripped of every source of arraigning marauders and murderers who are prowling around to destroy us except the common magistracy.

With these facts before you, Sir, will you write to us without delay as a father and friend and advise us what to do. We are members of the same great confederacy. Our fathers, nay some of us, have fought and bled for our country, and we love her Constitution dearly.

In the name of Israel's God and by virtue of multiplied ties of country and kindred, we ask your friendly interposition in our favor. Will it be too much for us to ask you to convene a special session of congress and furnish us an asylum, where we can enjoy our rights of conscience and religion unmolested? Or, will you in a special message to that body, when convened recommend a remonstrance against such unhallowed acts of oppression and expatriation as this people have continued to receive from the states of Missouri and Illinois? Or, will you favor us by your personal influence and by your official rank? Or will you express our views concerning what is called the 'Great Western Measure' of colonizing the Latter-day Saints in Oregon, the northwestern territory, or some location remote from the states, where the hand of oppression shall not crush every noble principle and extinguish every patriotic feeling?

And now, Honored Sir, having reached out our imploring hands to you, with deep solemnity, we would importune with you as a father, a friend, a patriot and the head of a mighty nation, by the Constitution of American Liberty, by the blood of our fathers who have fought for the independence of this Republic, by the blood of the martyrs which has been shed in our midst, by the wailings of the widows and orphans, by their murdered fathers and mothers, brothers and sisters, wives and children, by the dread of immediate destruction from secret combinations now forming for our overthrow, and by every endearing tie that binds man to man and renders life bearable, and that too, for aught we know for the last time, that you will lend your immediate aid to quell the violence of mobocracy, and exert your influence to establish us as a people in our civil and religious rights where we now are, or in some part of the United States, or at some place remote therefrom, where we may colonize in peace and safety as soon as circumstances will permit.

We sincerely hope that your future prompt measure towards us will be dictated by the best feelings that dwell in the bosom of humanity, and the blessings of a grateful people and of many ready to perish shall come upon you.

We are Sir,
with great respect,
Your Obt. Servts.
[Signed] BRIGHAM YOUNG,
WILLARD RICHARDS,
ORSON SPENCER,
ORSON PRATT,
W. W. PHELPS,
A. W. BABBITT,
J. M. BERNHISEL,

Committee in behalf of the Church of Jesus Christ of Latter-day Saints at Nauvoo, Illinois.'

'P.S. As many of our communications, postmarked at Nauvoo have failed of their destination and the mails around us have been intercepted by our enemies, we shall send this to some distant office by the hand of a special messenger.'

The letters to the governors were the same as the above with slight requisite alterations.

Saturday, 26.—In company with Brothers Heber C. Kimball, George A. Smith, Amasa M. Lyman, and others I attended Brother George D. Watt's phonographic class from nine a. m. till noon.

Sunday, 27.—Elders A. W. Babbitt and John Taylor preached at the stand. I met with the brethren of the Twelve at Elder W. Richards': we revised the conference minutes.

Evening, the Twelve Apostles, Presidents John Smith and Joseph Young met for prayer.

Monday, 28.—In council with Brothers H. C. Kimball, John Taylor and N. K. Whitney; we read letters from Parley P. Pratt in relation to his movements in the east; he thinks that he has influence with President Polk and other leading men of the nation, who are determined secretly to control the officers of Illinois so as to induce them to do away with mobs and mobocracy.

Tuesday, 29.—Evening, I attended General Council: Elder Samuel Bent reported the result of his visit to Lyman Wight's camp.

Thursday, May 1, 1845.—Accompanied by Brothers Heber C. Kimball, Newel K. Whitney, Alpheus Cutler and Wm. Clayton I rode to the river and bought lumber to the amount of sixteen hundred dollars. Brother Kimball and I gathered teams to draw it to the Temple. Evening, attended prayer meeting.

Saturday, 3.—Brother Ellis M. Sanders let the Trustees of the Temple have one thousand dollars in cash.

At a conference held in Batavia, N. Y., four branches containing seventeen elders, one priest and forty-two members were represented: Elder Winslow Farr presided.

Sunday, 4.—I attended meeting. Elder Orson Spencer and I preached. I dined at Brother Willard Richards' in company with Elders Kimball, Smith, Taylor and our wives. I met with the Twelve and wrote letters to Elders Parley P. Pratt and E. T. Benson, notifying the latter of his release and of Willard Snow's appointment as his successor in Massachusetts.

William Smith and family arrived from the east.

Elder Wilford Woodruff attended a conference in Blackburn, near Preston, England, and dedicated a new hall to worship; full house and interesting time.

Monday, 5.—Attended council of the Twelve at my house, on the case of Samuel Brannan and matters in the east. William Smith was present and expressed his satisfaction with the organization of the church.

Tuesday, 6.—The following was published in the *Nauvoo Neighbor*:

A VOICE FROM NAUVOO

'*Whereas* it is currently reported in various parts of this county, and in the adjoining counties, as we are creditably informed, that it is our intention to throng Carthage during the ensuing session of the circuit court of this county, for the purpose of awing or overruling the court so as to procure a conviction of certain men of the crime of murdering Joseph and Hyrum Smith; and *whereas* such reports are calculated to awaken an unjust prejudice against an innocent people; and *whereas* our enemies have jumped upon this stratagem as a hobby to raise an excitement against us; and *whereas* many honest and law abiding men are liable to be misled and imposed upon by these false, malicious, and envious reports; and *whereas* the governor of our state has solemnly pledged himself to us that the laws should be executed in justice in the premises; and *whereas* we did at that time pledge ourselves as a people to patiently wait their execution, and the action of the government; and *whereas* it is reported that certain individuals are trying to raise an excitement on the editorials of the *Nauvoo Neighbor*.

We *therefore*, in behalf of the church we represent do hereby publish to all men, that as a people and a council, we have no knowledge of the *Neighbor* until we read it as do others, and therefore cannot be responsible for it, and all we ask is the same consideration in the public mind, as is exercised towards the editorials of other papers in our land. And we further declare to all men, that as a people we are still determined to abide our pledge, and await the action of the executive and judiciary, and tarry at home and attend to our own business as usual during the sitting of the court except such as have lawful business with the court and are required to be in attendance, and hope that all men will do the same, and we wish, decidedly wish, that those whose business it is to keep the peace during court, should do it, and let us as a people alone, for we do not wish to be brought in collision with our neighbors and we are determined to abide the law.

In behalf of a General Council of the authorities of the Church of Jesus Christ of Latter-day Saints at Nauvoo.

[Signed] WILLARD RICHARDS, Committe.'

Evening, I attended General Council, when it was agreed that letters should be written to Governor Ford and J. B. Hoge, M. C., in relation to the threats of the mob; and to take measures for the brethren to hold themselves in readiness for defense in case of an attack, and to pursue a medium course avoiding extremes that might raise an excitement in the country.

The Twelve met with the old police at the Masonic Hall to make preparations to prevent our surprise by the mob.

Wednesday, 7.—Brother Orson Hyde reported that a mob of about two hundred men were collected at Appanoose who had prevented some of the brethren from going to work on the Island. The mob captain told the brethren that they had arranged matters so as to cut off all communication with the governor.

The officers of the Legion met at the Masonic Hall.

Evening, attended prayer meeting with the Twelve, N. K. Whitney, and Levi Richards.

Thursday, 8.—I called at Elder Richards' office at ten a. m., and remained till five p. m., when Elder Richards accompanied me to Elder Kimball's.

Evening, met and prayed with the Twelve.

The council wrote to Elder Woodruff as follows:

COUNCIL'S LETTER TO ELDER WILFORD WOODRUFF—ENGLAND

'It is a part of our religion to support any government, wherever we may be, that will protect us in common with other citizens; for, to this end governments are instituted; and as England has ever been true and faithful to us, as a people in common with others, the elders cannot be too particular to enjoin on all the saints to yield obedience to the laws, and respect every man in his office, letting politics wholly, entirely and absolutely alone, and preach the principles of the gospel of salvation; for to this end were they ordained and sent forth. We are for peace, we want no contention with any person or government, and should war commence between England and America, it will probably be wisdom for you and all the American elders to return immediately home, and leave all parties to fight their own battles. * *

The stones are in rapid progress for the new font [i. e. of the Temple]. The wall for the foundation of the pickets or railing around the Temple block, and the block west of the Temple (to be in one) is also commenced. The bricks are making for the Nauvoo House; one hundred and forty thousand feet of pine timber was received last Saturday for our public buildings; another raft is expected soon and we anticipate they will be enclosed early in the fall. Immigration has been greater than usual this season; perfect peace and union prevail. It is also a time of health.

We have thought it would be very agreeable to the feelings of the English saints to furnish a bell for the Temple, if this is their pleasure you can forward it the first conveyance, and we will have it hung as the building is going up. We are but little acquainted with the weight of bells; we have thought of two thousand pounds weight, but we leave this to your judgment; we want one that can be heard night or day.

We forward you with this in a package a letter of attorney constituting you an agent to transact all necessary business for the church in the United Kingdom of Great Britain, and on the continent of Europe.'

Friday, 9.—I met with the Twelve in council, also Elders N. K. Whitney and W. W. Phelps and J. B. Backenstos.

Saturday, 10.—Brother George A. Smith called upon me this morning and I accompanied him to the Historian's Office where we read and revised Church History.

Afternoon, met in General Council.

Sunday, 11.—Elders William and George A. Smith and I preached at the stand. Evening, attended prayer meeting.

Elder Woodruff attended a quarterly conference at Clitheroe, England, and ordained one elder and several to the lesser priesthood. He had an interesting and affectionate time with those churches built up by Elder Heber C. Kimball on his first mission to England.

Conference at Clitheroe England.

Monday, 12.—Evening, with Brothers Heber C. Kimball, W. Richards and George A. Smith at Brother Edward Hunter's revising history.

Tuesday, 13.—With Elders Heber C. Kimball, W. Richards and George A. Smith reading and revising Church History at Brother Edward Hunter's where we had retired to keep out of the way of writs reported to have been issued against us.

Governor Ford wrote the following letters:

LETTERS FROM GOVERNOR FORD TO GENERAL DEMING

'Executive Department,
Springfield, Ill, May 13, 1845.

M. R. Deming, Brigadier-General, Illinois Militia.

Sir: I have received information which I do not know whether to credit or not, that certain persons in Hancock county are preparing a force, with a view to prevent the witnesses on the part of the state in the murder cases, now pending, from attending court at the term to be held this month. If such should be the case, and if it should become necessary to protect the court, the jurors or the witnesses whose duty it may be to attend; or to secure the custody of prisoners, you are hereby fully authorized and empowered to call out and employ a sufficient force of militia from your brigade for that purpose. This order to include the militia of Nauvoo.

[Signed] THOMAS FORD, Governor and Commander-in-Chief.'

'Springfield, Ill., May 13, 1845.

Brigadier-General M. R. Deming:

Sir: I herewith send you authority to call out the militia of your brigade if necessary. The defendants in the murder cases have written here for Logan to defend them; and it is understood here that they do not intend to create any disturbance. The signs are not yet sufficiently certain to authorize me now to send militia there. I have employed Lamborn to assist in the prosecution. You will advise with him. If the defendants should organize a force to prevent a fair trial and keep off the witnesses I think it would be best to get the cases continued and at another term it will be so manifest that a force will be necessary to protect the court that I will be justified in sending one. But if at present I send one I will be laughed at and it will be universally believed that no necessity existed for it and that I have put the state to expense for nothing. If however you see that force is to be used and should think it most advisable to meet the crisis at this time, I give you power to employ your whole brigade including the Mormons of course. Upon the whole I think that they are the most fit material to be called on as their fidelity in doing their duty during the pending trials may be more thoroughly relied on than any troops I could send there.

I am most respectfully your obedient servant,
[Signed] THOMAS FORD.'

GOVERNOR FORD'S LETTER TO. A. W. BABBITT—VACILLATION

'Springfield, May 13, 1845.

Hon. A. W. Babbitt:

Dear Sir: I received your favor from Galena last evening. If I thought that I could have the least influence in preventing a disturbance in Hancock county I would cheerfully go over there. My opinion however is that my presence there, and that of Mr. Hoge would only aggravate matters. I have employed Mr. Lamborn to assist the prosecution and have sent a military order to General Deming giving him authority to call out his whole brigade, including the Mormons of course if necessary to protect the court, the witnesses, the jurors; or to secure the custody of prisoners. He will use this order with discretion. You can certainly raise a force in Hancock amply sufficient to overpower any mob forces which can be got together. The defendants have written here for counsel, and it is universally understood here, that they do not intend to resist. At any rate the signs are not so definite as to authorize me now to call the militia. If I were to do so, the people would be made to believe all over the state that there was no necessity for it, and that the public had been corruptly put to this expense to serve the Mormon vote. Besides I very much question whether I could raise a force now, when there is so little apparent necessity for it; and I also question whether any force which I could send could be relied on to act efficiently. You suggest in your letter that if there shall be a disturbance the distance to this place where I reside, would prevent a messenger from arriving until after the event had occurred. Nearly the same thing would happen if I were at Carthage. If I were to call on the militia (other than the Mormons) I would have to send back an order to this side of the Illinois river before I could begin to find any that I could rely on. It is evident to my mind that it would not do to call on any of the militia of the military tract. They would either stand idle or join the enemy. If a force shall really become necessary I can think of none which can be embodied so soon, or who would be likely to act with the requisite zeal and fidelity as the Mormons themselves. General Deming has my orders for this purpose; and as I do not pretend to be a military man I do not see why he cannot act as efficiently with this force in my absence as if I were present.

I would make another suggestion: Possibly, if a mob should be organized to keep away the witnesses it may be the best for the prosecution to move for a continuance of the indictments grounded on the absence of testimony setting forth all the circumstances calculated to prevent a fair trial. And if the case shall have to be continued on account of a mob, the necessity will then be apparent to all the world for a force at the next term. But until such a necessity is manifest it is the very worst policy to be making frequent calls of the militia. The very idea that the necessity for protecting the Mormons and putting the state to expense for that purpose continually exists, creates a prejudice against them and a strong desire everywhere of getting them out of the state. Besides the mob party have this advantage that if I send a force there capable of overpowering them they can and will swear that they never had the least intention of creating the least possible disturbance. And what is more they will make the whole people of the state believe it. They will believe in such a case that I have been humbugged; and humbugged by the Mormons. You may well conceive what a prejudice this impression will create. Upon the whole I am decidedly of opinion that the local militia under the command of General Deming ought to be relied on; that even this force ought not to be called out until it is manifestly apparent that it is needed for the protection of the law against actual violence and that in fact it might be better to suffer a continuance of the prosecutions if it will be the means of shewing to the world what the defendants and their friends will do if not prevented. I have made these same suggestions to Mr. Lamborn and General Deming.

I am most respectfully,

Your Obedient Servant,

[Signed] THOMAS FORD.'

Wednesday, 14.—Continued at Brother Edward Hunter's as yesterday; my health, and that of Brother Richards poor; but we read and revised history all day.

Thursday, 15.—I was quite unwell, Brother George A. Smith called in the forenoon and read the *Neighbor* to me: Brothers W. Richards and Amasa M. Lyman sick.

Fast day: all works were stopped. Meetings were held in the several wards and donations made to the bishops for the poor; enough was contributed to supply the wants of the poor until harvest. Evening, met at Brother Richards' for prayer.

Friday, 16.—I spent the day at Brother Hunter's in company with Brothers Heber C. Kimball, Willard Richards, George A. Smith and N. K. Whitney revising history: Thomas Bullock read for us. I wrote a letter to the architect directing him to place a stone in the west end (front) of the Temple with the inscription 'Holiness to the Lord' thereon. Isaac Chase agreed to let the church have one thousand dollars. Elder Orson Pratt called and reported that four hundred men had gone up the opposite side of the river.

Saturday, 17.—Revising history as yesterday, with the addition of Brother John Taylor: Brother Hunter and family were very kind to us. We wrote an epistle to the saints in Nauvoo dated at Point Clear and directed the same to Brother Orson Pratt.

Sunday, 18.—Elder Orson Pratt preached to the saints; also read the following epistle:

GENERAL LETTER OF THE TWELVE TO THE CHURCH FROM THEIR RETIREMENT

'Point Clear, Steamboat under way,
one o'clock Saturday morning,
May 17, 1845.

To the Church of Jesus Christ of Latter-day Saints in the City of Joseph—Greeting:

Beloved Brethren: Our whole souls bless you; and we are happy in the privilege of communicating to you a few thoughts. Much more would we rejoice were it our privilege to be in your midst the coming Sabbath and tell you all that is in our hearts; but we are pilgrims in a world of sorrow and woe. In our journeyings to proclaim the gospel and bring about salvation to the honest in heart, God is with us and we prosper; though weary, we are not cast down nor discouraged, for we know that victory is with the upright.

We are happy to hear of the great union and love manifested at your recent fast, which also the Spirit bore witness of to us, and of your liberality towards the poor, and may the abundance which you have so liberally contributed in your penury in dealing your bread to the hungry be the omen of an abundant harvest of the fruits of the earth into your granaries the present and all future seasons.

Since we commenced our journey we have discovered some letters from Brother Joseph Smith to Bishop Partridge from which we extract the following for your edification and instruction:

MESSAGE OF NEWLY DISCOVERED LETTERS OF THE PROPHET ON CONSECRATION

'I proceed to answer your questions concerning the consecration of property. First, it is not right to condescend to very great particulars in taking inventories. The fact is this, a man is bound by the law of the church, to consecrate to the bishop, before he can be considered a legal heir to the kingdom of Zion; and this too without constraint; and unless he does this, he cannot be acknowledged before the Lord, on the church book: therefore to condescend to particulars, I will tell you that every man must be his own judge how much he should receive, and how much he should suffer to remain in the hands of the bishop. I speak of those who consecrate more than they need for the support of themselves and their families.

'The matter of consecration must be done by the mutual consent of both parties; for to give the bishop power to say how much every man shall have, and he be obliged to comply with the bishop's judgment is giving to the bishop more power than a king has; and upon the other hand, to let every man say how much he needs and the bishop be obliged to comply with his judgment is to throw Zion into confusion and make a slave of the bishops. The fact is, there must be a balance or equilibrium of power, between the bishop and the people; and thus harmony and good-will will be preserved among you.'

THE PRINCIPLE OF FASTS DEFINED

Let this be an ensample to all saints, and there will never be any lack for bread: When the poor are starving, let those who have, fast one day and give what they otherwise would have eaten to the bishops for the poor, and every one will abound for a long time; and this is one great and important principle of fasts approved of the Lord. And so long as the saints will all live to this principle with glad hearts and cheerful countenances they will always have an abundance.

We will give you another extract from the same author in a letter to Elder Phelps when in Zion:

FATE OF THE SONS OF PERDITION NOT REVEALED

'Say to the brethren Hulets and to all others that the Lord never authorized them to say that the devil, or his angels, or the son of perdition should ever be restored; for their state of destiny was not revealed to man, is not revealed, nor ever shall be revealed save to those who are made partakers thereof; consequently those who teach this doctrine have not received it of the Spirit of the Lord. Truly Brother Oliver declared it to be the doctrine of devils. We, therefore, command that this doctrine be taught no more in Zion. We sanction the decision of the bishop and his council in relation to this doctrine being a bar of communion.'

Let this extract remind the elders and all saints that a wise head keeps a still tongue. And that it is far better many times for men, yes and women too to forget all they know, than to tell all they know. And better still to forget than to tell some great things which they do not know. Probably the elders in Zion know about as much about the devil's being redeemed, as the elders know about the great God of the Gods, of the God of this world, which some have spoken of, concerning which they know nothing. There are Lords many and Gods many. But who are they, and what their relation to us, or this earth? Who can answer? This is a subject not revealed, therefore let the elders be silent concerning it. And who knows anything about our suffering in this world for sins committed in a former state of existence? Let him who had the answer by revelation speak: and if no such revelation exists, let this subject also live where it belongs in eternal forgetfulness to the ignorant until they shall be instructed from the right source.

Wisdom is justified of her children, therefore beloved brethren be wise and live up to the holy religion which you profess—to mind your own business and let your neighbors alone. Plant your gardens and till your farms; acknowledge your heavenly Father in all things; continue to raise up his house; walk humbly before him; watch and pray without ceasing; for ye know not what hour the thief will come. But be ye sure of this the thief will never come while he sees the good man of the house watching for him.

If ye are one, says Jesus, then are ye mine, and whatsoever ye shall ask the Father in my name he will give it unto you. Then brethren continue to be one and ask unceasingly and God will deliver you from all your enemies, break the oppressor's power and continue peace in the beloved city. Brethren pray for us that we may be prospered on our journey, and be returned to the saints in peace and safety when we shall have completed our mission. We bless you and praying the God of our fathers, Abraham, Isaac and Jacob to bless you with every blessing even unto everlasting life and salvation in his presence in the name of Jesus Christ, Amen.'

Sunday, 18, (*continued*).—At five p. m., the Presidents of Seventies met. President Joseph Young spoke emphatically as to putting down wickedness and evil known to exist among members of the quorums.

Evening, attended council and prayer meeting with the Twelve at Brother Richards': adjourned at 2 a. m.

Elder Woodruff attended a conference at Carlisle, England, one hundred and sixty-five members were represented including thirty-seven officers.

A conference was held in Ilion, Herkimer county, New York, fifty-two members, nine elders and two priests were represented.

Monday, 19.—Associated with Brothers Heber C. Kimball, John Taylor, and George A. Smith, I spent the day at Brother Robert Pierce's; Brother Pierce had gone to Carthage as a juror, his family made us very comfortable. Brothers W. Richards and George A. Smith went to Brother Elijah Fordham's.

Many brethren went to Carthage to attend the trial of the murderers of Joseph and Hyrum Smith: George D. Watt attended court and reported the proceedings.

Tuesday, 20.—With the brethren named I remained at Brother Pierce's; Willard Richards and George A. Smith joined us. We read and revised fifty-seven pages of History of Joseph Smith from Book 'B': Brothers Amasa M. Lyman and others called to see us.

Wednesday, 21.—Brother Richards went to Brother Fordham's. Brother George A. [Smith] visited the families of the Twelve who were from home and spent the afternoon with Brother Richards. At nine p. m., Brothers H. C. Kimball, J. Taylor, G. A. Smith, W. H. Kimball, Bishop Garn and I called at Brother Richards' and remained till midnight.

The following letter was sent to Josiah Lamborn, attorney-general of Illinois [by George A. and John Smith]:

REVIEW OF DIFFICULTIES ATTENDANT UPON COLLECTION OF EVIDENCE FOR THE PROSPECTIVE TRIAL OF THOSE CHARGED WITH THE MURDER OF THE PROPHET AND PATRIARCH JOSEPH AND HYRUM SMITH

'*Sir*: We are this evening informed by Mr. Scott that it is your wish as prosecuting attorney *vs.* the murderers of the Generals Smith that the Mormons should hunt up the witnesses in the case, and that Mr. Murray McConnell had conveyed the idea that there was a committee in the county whose business it was to collect and arrange the testimony against the day of trial and that said committee are supposed to be Mormons, etc. etc.

Now, Sir, in behalf of the Church of Jesus Christ of Latter-day Saints; or, if you choose, the Mormon fraternity, we beg leave to state to you, what has been often reiterated by us, and which is a well known fact, both to our people and the state, *viz*: that the difficulty causing the pending trials is not between the Mormons and anti-Mormons; nor between the Mormons and the murderers; but it is between the state and the prisoners or offenders.

The facts are, the Messrs. Smiths were murdered while in the charge of the state, relying on the plighted faith of the state for protection, and not in the presence of Mormon witnesses, for the Mormons were not there, but doubtless in the presence of many who were not Mormons.

To show our loyalty to the institutions of our country and preserve peace in the county, as a people, we pledged ourselves to abide the operations of the law as directed by the proper authorities of the commonwealth; and that we would abide the decisions of the court, not taking vengeance into our own hands, (as was then feared by some) or commencing prosecutions, to which we have strictly adhered, and intend still to adhere, that our pledge may be honorably redeemed in the sight of all men, although we have been strongly solicited to enter the field of prosecution, and that, too, by the state or her agents: for instance when Mr. McConnell was engaged in preparation for the prosecution he came to Nauvoo and strongly solicited the Mormons to come out as complainants and assist in procuring witnesses, etc.; but we replied that we had had nothing to do with the affair, and wanted nothing to do with it; and for us to enlist in attempting to bring the murderers to justice, no matter how legal in our movements it would be construed into a persecution, or a desire to pick a quarrel on our part, which we were and still are determined to avoid, even every appearance of evil, and cut off every occasion of our enemies, or of those who are ready to seize upon any pretext to make us trouble.

We are decidedly for peace, and we ever have been and as the murders were committed while the murdered were in immediate charge of the state, all we ask is, that the state will prosecute the case to final judgment, and redeem her pledge, as we have ours; or if she choose to abandon the prosecution we shall submit peaceably; although, for public good, we would prefer that justice should take place.

We are unacquainted with the statute which suffers indicted murderers to roam at large month after month without arrest; or, after delivery, or surrender, to run at pleasure before trial, and we know not what other similar laws we might come in contact with, and be liable to break to our own endangering or disadvantage, should we attempt to have anything to do with the case in question.

It is reported to us, true or false we know not, that the sheriff of Hancock county and his deputies have been forbidden by the court to act in pending trials, and that the jurors have been discharged without impaneling. If this be true we are unacquainted with the statutes in the case and have nothing to say.

When Mr. McConnell was here last fall, at his earnest solicitation, we collected all the information in our possession and presented the same to him, supposing he would prosecute the case to final judgment. He took minutes at the time and probably has them now, if he has not handed them over, of which you must be acquainted, better than we, and of which we did not preserve minutes: we know of no new information since that period.

We were happy to hear that the trials had been committed to your able charge, and anticipated that you would have made us a visit before the sitting of the court; and we still anticipate that after court you will make us a visit, that we may have the pleasure of a more general acquaintance among our citizens; and we feel confident that such a visit would be higly appreciated by our friend, General Young, with whom we understand you are acquainted.

We shall be ever ready to assist in favoring the ends of right so far as we can do it and not give any occasion of excitement which would be detrimental to public peace.

We are Sir,

Most Respectfully
Your Servts.
[Signed] GEORGE A. SMITH,
JOHN SMITH.'

Thursday, 22.—Elder Kimball and I spent the day at Brother Parley P. Pratt's.

Caroline Grant, wife of Elder Wm. Smith, died, aged thirty years and four months.

Evening, I attended council and prayer meeting.

Friday, 23.—Forenoon, Elder Heber C. Kimball, Willard Richards, John Taylor, George A. Smith, John E. Page and myself at Brother Taylor's. Afternoon, Samuel Brannan arrived from New York and in company with Wm. Smith visited us.

Brother John Kay was engaged in drilling out a six-pounder cannon and preparing it for service.

Evening, in council with the Twelve and Bishop Whitney: the improper course of Wm. Smith was the subject of conversation.

Saturday, 24.—A large number of the saints assembled to witness the laying of the capstone on the southeast corner of the Temple. Of the Twelve there were present, besides myself, Heber C. Kimball, John Taylor, Willard Richards, Amasa M. Lyman, George A. Smith, John E. Page, Orson Hyde and Orson Pratt, also Newel K. Whitney and George Miller the Presiding Bishops and Trustees-in-Trust, Alpheus Cutler and Reynolds Cahoon, Temple Committee, William Clayton, Temple recorder, John Smith, patriarch and president of the stake and several members of the high council. The brass band arranged themselves and played the 'Nightingale'.

Laying the Capstone of the Temple.

At six o'clock and eight minutes a. m., Brother Wm. Player commenced spreading the mortar, perfect silence prevailing; the stone being lifted to its place. I stepped on the same and fitted it precisely to its position with the large beetle, at twenty-two minutes past six a. m., the capstone was pronounced set; the band played the 'Capstone March' composed for the occasion by Wm. Pitt. I said:

'The last stone is now laid upon the Temple and I pray the Almighty in the name of Jesus to defend us in this place and sustain us until the Temple is finished and we have all got our endowments.'

The whole congregation then shouted, 'Hosanna, Hosanna, Hosanna, to God and the Lamb, Amen, Amen, and Amen,' which was repeated a second and third time. I concluded by saying, 'So let it be, O Lord Almighty. This is the seventh day of the week or the Jewish Sabbath. It is the day on which the Almighty finished his work and rested from his labors; we have finished the walls of the Temple and we may rest today from our labors.'

I dismissed the workmen for the day and requested them to spend the day in giving thanks to God; and dismissed the congregation, and with the brethren of the Twelve retired to our places of retreat, out of the way of constables and officers who are prowling around the city from Carthage.

The morning was wet and cold, but those present were highly interested with the morning's services, and felt well in consideration that the walls of the Temple were completed, notwithstanding the prophecies of our enemies and apostates.

Elder Orson Pratt preached the funeral discourse of Caroline, the daughter of Joshua and Thalia Grant and wife of Elder Wm. Smith, to a large assembly at the stand; her remains were deposited in the tomb of Joseph: she has left two children to mourn her loss.

At three p. m., a council of the Twelve met at Elder Taylor's and took into consideration the case of Elder Samuel Brannan who had been disfellowshiped; an investigation was entered into and Elder Brannan introduced testimony to prove his innocence of the charges made against him: he was restored to fellowship.

Wm. Smith Made Patriarch to the Whole Church.

The brethren present expressed their feelings towards Elder Wm. Smith to which he responded. The Twelve then laid their hands upon him and ordained him to be a Patriarch to the whole church: there was a warm interchange of good feeling between William Smith and the quorum.

Sunday, 25.—Elder John E. Page preached at the stand. The Presidents of Seventies met and preached to each other. Evening, the Twelve and others met for prayer.

Monday, 26.—I met with several of the Twelve and others in the Phonographic School at Brother Richards'. The Twelve and Trustees met in council at Bishop Miller's and wrote a long communication to Elder Parley P. Pratt.

Tuesday, 27.—I received a respectful letter from Governor Drew in reply to our Memorial to him as governor of Arkansas; stating his inability to protect us in the state of Arkansas, and suggesting the propriety of our settling in Oregon, California, Nebraska or some other country where we will be out of the reach of our persecutors."*

*The letter of Governor Drew will be found *in extenso* in *The Comprehensive History of the Church*, Century I, vol. ii. p. 525-6.

CHAPTER XXXI

SUNDRY EVENTS GROUPED TOGETHER LOOKING TO AN UNDERSTANDING WITH THE STATE GOVERNMENT AT NAUVOO—HARVEST FEAST AT NAUVOO

"*Wednesday, May* 28, 1845.—This morning the workmen commenced to raise the attic story of the Temple.

Thursday, 29.—Evening, met at Brother Richards' for prayer in company with Brothers Heber C. Kimball, Orson Hyde, Orson Pratt, Willard Richards, John Taylor, Amasa M. Lyman, N. K. Whitney, George Miller, Joseph Young and Levi Richards. Prayed that the Lord would overrule the movements of Wm. Smith who is endeavoring to ride the Twelve down; also that the Lord would overrule the proceedings of the mob so that we may dwell in peace until the Temple is finished.

Prayer and its Objective.

The court at Carthage heard the lawyer's pleas on the defense in the case the state of Illinois *vs.* the murderers of Joseph and Hyrum Smith; the counsel for the defense exhibited a cruel and mendacious spirit. Calvin A. Warren of Quincy made the most inflammatory speech.

Friday, 30.—I attended council with the Twelve at Elder Taylor's.

The jury at Carthage brought in a verdict of acquittal in favor of Levi Williams, Thomas C. Sharp, Mark Aldrich, Jacob C. Davis and William N. Grover —as we had anticipated: the court, attorneys, jury and bystanders being all fully satisfied of their guilt.*

*John Hay, secretary of state in two presidential administrations—McKinley's and Roosevelt's, 1898-1905—who as a boy was reared in Hancock county, in the *Atlantic Monthly* for December, 1869, contributed an article on the "Mormon Prophet's Tragedy", in which he reviews this mass trial of the above named characters, where at one point he writes: "The case was closed, there was not a man on the jury, in the court, in the county, that did not know the defendants had done murder. But it was not proven, and the verdict of 'not guilty' was right in law." Rather a sad comment on justice in Illinois at that time (See *Comprehensive History of the Church,* Century I, vol. ii, p. 327).

Brother George D. Watt attended the trial and took lengthy minutes from which the following is extracted:

GEORGE D. WATT'S REPORT OF THE CARTHAGE TRIAL

'District Court of Illinois,
Carthage, Hancock County, State of Illinois,
May 19, 1845.

The Hon. Richard M. Young of Quincy on the bench. The forenoon was spent in organizing. Adjourned at twelve m.

Court met at two p. m.

Colonel Levi Williams, Thomas C. Sharp, editor of the *Warsaw Signal,* Jacob C. Davis, state senator, Mark Aldrich and William N. Grover were held to bail with each other for sureties, in the sum of one thousand dollars each, to make their appearance in court each day of the term; they were indicted for the murder of Joseph Smith at Carthage jail on the twenty-seventh day of June, 1844.

The court decided that their case would be tried on Wednesday morning, May 21st.

Accordingly the sheriff notified the witnesses for both parties to make their appearance on said morning at seven o'clock; the court then proceeded to other business.

Wednesday Morning, May 21st.

Court opened.

The names of the counsel for the defense are as follows: William A. Richardson, O. H. Browning, Calvin A. Warren.

Josiah Lamborn, Esq. for the people.

Colonel Wm. A. Richardson presented before the court two affidavits drawn out by the defendants to quash the array. The charge of prejudice, consanguinity and partiality was preferred by these affidavits against the county commissioners, the sheriff and his deputies in the arrangement of the present panel of jurors; that their design was to hurt and prejudice the present trial, and thus endanger the lives of the defendants. On these grounds the defendants pleaded for the quashing of the array. After referring to the statute to show the provision made for such a proceeding he submitted to the court.

The attorney for the people then arose and made the following observations, *viz.*: That the doctrine advanced by Colonel Richardson was a novelty to him, as the affidavits of the defendants predicated no charge against the present panel of jurors, either individually or collectively; he showed from the statute that the array could not be quashed upon the above principle, neither did he believe the officers of the county could be discharged upon a mere *exparte* affidavit, but the charges ought to be made and affidavits filed and a trial had before the court. He said it was the first time he had heard of such a proceeding to quash the array, at the same time nothing alleged against it individually or collectively.

He showed that the statute referred to by Colonel Richardson applied to civil and not criminal cases. He could not suffer the idea of having the panel quashed by the discharge of all the officers of the county upon a mere *exparte* affidavit, and that too made by five men indicted for murder. He asked for a precedent in all the experience of this state or any other in criminal cases; he defied them to produce a single case.

Mr. Browning, for the defense, said, that although there had not been a precedent in the United States for such a proceeding, the reason is there has never been a case like this in the United States. He contended that such a proceeding is fully warranted by the English statutes and the statutes of the United States, that in a case like this the county commissioners, the sheriff and his deputies can be discharged, and in their place can be appointed elisors for the purpose of choosing another jury.

The court ruled that the jury be discharged and elisors appointed.

The court then adjourned.

Thursday, May 22nd.

The court appointed Thomas H. Owen and William D. Abernethy elisors and they selected a full panel of jurors.

Four panels of jurors were successively called and out of the ninety-six men twelve were selected as a jury satisfactory to the defense.

Mr. Lamborn prosecuted before this jury in a manner which showed clearly to every bystander the certainty of the guilt of the prisoners who were honorably acquitted. Mr. Frank Worrell, who had command of the guard at the jail at the time of the massacre, being summoned as a witness, and being asked by the prosecuting attorney if the guard had their guns loaded with blank cartridges at the time of the attack on the jail refused to answer, assigning as a reason that he could not without incriminating himself.'

The *Nauvoo Neighbor* has the following:

THE CARTHAGE ASSASSINS

'On Friday last the trial terminated, and the prisoners were acquitted in the case of Joseph Smith. This accords with the vote of the city council last July, that when the law failed to atone for the blood of our Prophet and Patriarch shed at Carthage on the 27th of June last by a mob, we would refer the case to God for a righteous judgment, and we have never varied from that intention. If those men had been found guilty it would have been a novel case and a violation of all the rules of the world in all martyr cases before.

The murderers of Joseph and Hyrum Smith can rest assured that their case, independent of all earthly tribunals, will be tried by the Supreme Judge of the Universe, who has said, vengeance is mine and I will repay.'

Saturday, 31.—Brother George D. Watt returned from Carthage. Threats were made that his minutes should never go to Nauvoo, but he succeeded in passing them out of the court room about every hour.

Calvin A. Warren [counsel for the defense] said that if the prisoners were guilty of murder he himself was guilty alleging that it was the public opinion that the Smiths ought to be killed, and public opinion made the laws consequently it was not murder to kill the Smiths. [!]

Elder Orson Spencer made the following report:

REPORTED INTERVIEW WITH GOVERNOR FORD AND EX-GOVERNOR REYNOLDS

'By the appointment of the Twelve I went to Springfield, Illinois about the middle of June [a note in the manuscript changes this to 'the last of May'] in company with Brother Samuel Brannan in order to see Governor Ford. Immediately on our arrival we found his Excellency who received us politely and introduced us to the secretary of state, Mr. Campbell, and to ex-Governor Reynolds. After dinner we all repaired to the governor's office in the state house except Mr. Campbell. There we held a familiar interview for several hours; during which both governors spoke freely of the unreasonable prejudice of the people through the state especially in the southern part of it. They were requested to use their influence officially and personally to allay prejudice and rebut slanders that might ultimately endanger the safety of this people unless counteracted. Governor Reynolds said that he had attempted to speak in extenuation of the supposed faults of the saints at public meetings, but the people rudely resisted his efforts and accused him of being a 'Smithite' and a 'Mormon'; and he was seriously afraid they would mob us by making an attack by the cooperation of steamboats upon our city. Both governors strenuously urged the necessity that the saints should cease to gather in one place and also opposed my suggestion to buy out the anti-Mormons in the county. They alleged that we might spread through other counties as we had done in Hancock, which would increase the alarm in other counties and in the state generally. They said that our political influence was that which exasperated the people.

Governor Ford said he durst not trust the best militia in the state to defend the Mormons. They would go over to the side of the mob in the event of a collision. He said that even General Hardin could not be trusted in our defense against the mob. He further said that the conduct of Governor Boggs of Missouri was unlawful and barbarous and pledged himself never to act like him in driving the saints and confirmed a former pledge that he would never demand the leaders of this church on criminal writs to expose them to assassination as the Smiths had been, and to use his utmost endeavors to suppress all mobs. He said however that his official influence was only nominal, there was really no force in the government.

Large masses of people that might assemble for violent and tumultuous purposes could not be restrained by any law or government.

He was then assured that it was our intention as soon as we could finish the Temple to send off many of our people to distant parts of the earth and in the course of eighteen months very many of our people would colonize distant parts; and we were ready from that time forth to sell our property as soon as practicable and commence removals, if the people round about would buy us out.'

Sunday, June 1, 1845.—I attended meeting at the stand. Elder Heber C. Kimball preached.

[In the remarks of Elder Kimball the following occurs].

DISCOURSE OF ELDER KIMBALL

'I will mention one thing that we united in prayer for and called upon the Father in the name of Jesus: that our enemies should not have power to come in here with vexatious writs, for his servants during this court, and they have not done it. Is not this a miracle? Yes; and we have asked for rain, and it has rained; and we have asked for God to heal the sick, and he has healed them, or they are mending in answer to our prayers. Are not these great blessings? Does not this prove that God is with this people? Yes, verily, his name is to be praised, if this people will feel the same interest for the building up of this kingdom, and for the erecting of those houses, his will will be done, and there is no power that can stay them, and when that is done, I am satisfied; I do not care if I go into the wilderness the next day.'*

Elder John Taylor followed [Elder Kimball] on the subject of our persecutions. I made a few remarks.

At four p. m. the Presidents of Seventies met and preached to each other, and ordained four presidents for the twenty-seventh quorum.

Evening, I met for council and prayer with Elders H. C. Kimball, Orson Pratt, Willard Richards, John E. Page, John Taylor, George A. Smith, Amasa M.

***Times and Seasons*, p. 987, vol. vi.

Lyman, John Smith, N. K. Whitney, George Miller, Levi Richards, Joseph Young and Wm. Clayton. Voted that Brother Peter O. Hanson translate the *Doctrine and Covenants* and *Book of Mormon* into the Danish Norwegian language and that Elder Orson Pratt assist him. Voted that the Trustees give George D. Watt a quarter of a lot and build him a house and employ him as reporter for the church and let his labors go towards paying for his house and lot. We prayed that justice might overtake the murderers of Joseph and Hyrum and that George J. Adams be stopped in his mad career.

A conference was held in Merthyr-Tydvil, Wales, Elder William Henshaw presided; forty had been baptized since the April conference, and the brethren felt determined to spread the gospel.

At a special conference held in Cincinnati, thirty-two members were represented.

Monday, 2.—I met with the Twelve in council.

Thursday, 5.—I met for prayer with the Twelve and other brethren.

Elder Parley P. Pratt wrote to the Twelve of date, as follows:

ELDER PARLEY P. PRATT'S LETTER TO THE TWELVE IN NAUVOO—CONDITIONS IN NEW YORK CITY

'As it regards publishing in this city [New York], if all the political and religious influence and support we have combined will support a periodical, even allowing the editor to work for nothing and live on sawdust pudding, it will be more than we have yet done, or are likely to do at present. There is little prospect of a periodical being supported by church or state, even if we give our time *gratis*, and use the utmost economy; therefore to divide it and either of us succeed seems at present impracticable; and I doubt very much whether we can continue to publish. The churches are few in number, we decrease while you increase. The law of tithing, emigration, the strengthening and defense of the City of Joseph has occupied the attention and employed the energies of the saints so entirely, since we came from the west and laid before them their duty and the necessity of immediate action, that it seems almost vain to mention subscriptions for papers in this country. If they have a dollar to spare, it is handed in for tithing, or used for the purchase of arms, clothing and ammunition, or to help themselves to emigrate and settle in the west.

Our teachings and influence, aided by yours and by the Spirit of God, have tended to produce this state of things, and it pleases us so well that we do not like to counteract it in the least; but it rather embarrasses us as to immediate means to clothe or to furnish us money for necessary expenses and involves us in debt, besides devoting our entire time.

I have become convinced that I can do no good here. The public are entirely indifferent, and will neither come to meeting, hear, nor read the truth. The saints are few, about fifty of them attended a Sunday meeting in a large hall, and perhaps half a dozen strangers come in and out to gaze and gape and wonder and perish.

I have labored hard for six months without an idle moment, and have used economy in living, traveling and clothing. I feel as if I was now done with this city, and nearly so with the nation. My garments are clear, if they all perish. If I tarry a little longer in the east it will necessarily be in Boston and vicinity, where there is more interest manifested for the truth.'

Saturday, 7.—Elder W. Woodruff visited the saints in London and secured the copyright of the *Book of Doctrine and Covenants* at Stationer's Hall, having published three thousand copies at Liverpool: he presented a copy to the Library of the British Museum. The copyright was secured in forty-eight hours after the last sheets were obtained from the printers; which defeated a secret plan of some of our enemies who were taking measures to print the book and secure the copyright.

Sunday, 8.—At four p. m., I met with the Twelve and others for counsel and prayer: we decided that Elder Orson Hyde go to the east and buy canvas for a Tabernacle [tent], and type to print the History of Joseph Smith. General Conference of Seventies met and proceeded with the organization of the quorums.

A conference was held in Florence, St. Joseph county, Michigan, when one hundred and twenty-eight members, one high priest, sixteen elders and four of the lesser priesthood were represented; Elder Crandall Dunn, president and Elder E. M. Webb, clerk.

Tuesday, 10.—I met in council with the brethren of the Twelve, and discussed the title of the Church History.

Thursday, 12.—I spent the afternoon with several of the Twelve.

Sunday, 15.—Elder Orson Hyde preached at the stand; Elder George A. Smith advocated the building of the Nauvoo House, and was followed by Elders Amasa M. Lyman and George Miller on the same subject. The high priests' quorum met. Evening, I met with the Twelve. The seventies met; Elder Joseph Young and others preached.

Monday, 16.—Council met on the Temple walls.

Tuesday, 17.—The Council of the Twelve wrote the following:

LETTER OF THE TWELVE TO THE SAINTS ABROAD

'*To the Saints Abroad, Greeting*:

The walls of our Temple are completed and the roof is nearly on. Through the liberality of the brethren that building is in a rapid state of advancement; but it will only accommodate a small portion of our congregation when completed.

Pursuant to the counsel of Joseph Smith given previous to his martyrdom, we now intend to erect a Tabernacle for the congregation made of canvas. It will take about four thousand yards, which, with other fixtures, will cost between one and two thousand dollars.

Elder Hyde's Mission to Secure a Tent Tabernacle.

We have appointed Elder Orson Hyde one of our own quorum, a faithful, trusty and competent man of God, to go forth and raise all the necessary funds for the above purpose, to procure the materials and return with them to this place as soon as possible. Elder Hyde is authorized to raise the necessary funds by loan, by contribution, or tithing or donation; if by loan, the church here will refund the same in lands at a low rate, or in cash as soon as we can command it; and any contract that he may make in relation to the above, the church will be responsible for.

It is hoped that no brother or sister who has funds that he or she can spare for a season will withhold them from Brother Hyde, for it is the aid that he seeks for us. Also we hope that the saints will be liberal in their donations, and every other person that wishes well to the Temple of God and to the Tabernacle of the congregation in Zion. May God bless all that feel interested in the matter.'

Bishop Whitney started for St. Louis with $1,549 to purchase materials for the Temple.

Wednesday, 18.—I met with Elders Heber C. Kimball, John Taylor and George A. Smith at Brother Taylor's; we revised a portion of the History of Joseph Smith.

Elders Phineas H. Young and Charles Shumway returned from their missions and reported favorably.

Thursday, 19.—I spent the day with Brothers H. C. Kimball and George A. Smith revising history. Evening, the Twelve met for council and prayer.

I received a lengthy letter from Mr. H. R. Hotchkiss in relation to the necessity of establishing manufactories in Nauvoo for the employment of our rapidly increasing population of mechanics.

Friday, 20.—Elders H. C. Kimball, Orson Pratt, George A. Smith, and myself engaged revising Church History.

Sunday, 22.—Meeting at the stand; Elder Orson Pratt preached, but as it rained heavily, the meeting was dismissed. Evening, I met with the Twelve and others for prayer; Sister Jennetta Richards being very sick was administered to.

Arrest of Orrin Porter Rockwell. Other Attempted Arrests.

Monday, 23.—The sheriff came in with writs for a number of brethren and succeeded in arresting O. P. Rockwell and J. P. Harmon, but Rockwell got away from him. A constable from Le Harpe came in with writs for Brother Taylor, myself and others, but we kept out of the way.

Jonathan Dunham who was on a mission to the Lamanites received a notification from Ranes, the Indian Agent of the Neosha sub-agency to leave the country immediately.

Tuesday, 24.—I examined Church History with the brethren. Evening, Hiram Kimball and D. H. Wells returned from Carthage and brought word that Sheriff Deming had shot Sam Marshall.

William Smith *vs.* Nauvoo Police.

Wednesday, 25.—At three p. m., I met with the Quorum of the Twelve for prayer; and in council in relation to a difficulty between William Smith and Brother Elbridge Tufts.

After council the Twelve met with the police at the

Masonic Hall when Wm. Smith delivered a very pathetic speech, delineating in a sectarian tone, the wrongs that his brothers and himself had sustained; asserting that we were all dependent upon his family for the priesthood, and pronouncing the most fearful anathemas upon all those who should not sustain him in his course, justifying his assault upon Brother Tufts, and demanding of the Twelve to inform the police that it was their duty to take his counsel in relation to the manner they discharge their duty. I told him that as an officer Brother Tuft was subject to the magistrates, and had no right to discharge a prisoner only by the order of the proper officer; that he (Brother William Smith) had no more right to interfere with the police than I had; that when he beat Brother Tufts for refusing to discharge his prisoner, he was doing wrong, and meddling with that which was not his business and should make satisfaction; that we received the priesthood from God through Joseph Smith and not through William, and that he had no authority or power to curse the Twelve Apostles who received the priesthood from Joseph; that we were not influenced by his curses, and that his prayers and imprecations upon the heads of those who were seeking to fulfill the instructions of Joseph to the letter would rise no higher than the smoke from a dung hill.

Brother William appeared humbled and agreed to make ample satisfaction to Brother Tufts.

James Arlington Bennett.

Received a letter from James Arlington Bennett of New York, in which he applies to be consecrated a general of the Nauvoo Legion, that he may 'fight Napoleon's battles over again, either in Nauvoo or elsewhere.' This wild spirit of ambition has repeatedly manifested itself to us by many communications received from various sources, suggesting schemes of blood and empire, as if the work of the Lord was intended for personal aggrandisement.

Thursday, 26.—The Twelve met for council and

prayer: several children were blessed. The first stone for the new font was laid in the Temple.

Friday, 27.—Elders Heber C. Kimball, Orson Pratt, Amasa M. Lyman, George A. Smith, Willard Richards, John E. Page, George Miller, Joseph Young and John Taylor met for fasting, prayer and counsel.

I wrote the following letter to Elder Woodruff:

BRIGHAM YOUNG'S LETTER TO WILFORD WOODRUFF IN ENGLAND—PROGRESS AND UNITY IN NAUVOO

'Nauvoo, June 27th, 1845.

Dear Brother Woodruff.—We sit down to acknowledge the receipt of your letters, and it being one year this day since the massacre of our beloved brethren Joseph and Hyrum, we have concluded to spend the day in conversation, counsel and prayer, and also to write answers to your letters, well knowing that a little information from this place must be acceptable to you at all times, for we feel it as a source of comfort to us to hear of your prosperity. We have met from time to time to offer up our prayers and thanksgivings before the Lord for the salvation and peace of the saints, and that the Lord would enable us to finish the Temple and the Nauvoo House that the brethren might obtain their endowments, for this we have supplicated by night and by day, and hitherto we have been prospered in a manner beyond our most sanguine expectations. Another subject for which we have constantly supplicated is the welfare and success of our dear brethren in England, Brother Parley P. Pratt in New York, and the brethren on the Islands of the Pacific, these with our petitions for the sick in our midst, and that God will preserve us from internal broils, has been the theme of our prayers from time to time, and we are happy to say that God has heard and answered our prayers, and has done all things well. The most perfect union, peace and good feeling has invariably prevailed in our midst and still continues. It seems like a foretaste of celestial enjoyment and Millennial glory.

* * *

The capstone of the Temple was laid by the Twelve on Saturday morning the 24th of May, at six o'clock, in the presence of many saints. It would have pleased you to have heard the hosannas on that occasion, and to have witnessed the short but interesting ceremony. The frame work of the roof is on the building, and the next week the brethren expect to put on the shingles; the frame work around the foundation of the tower is all up, and the first timbers for the tower itself were raised this day. The new stone front is mostly cut, and the first stone was laid today at about four o'clock. We expect in about five or six weeks the attic story of the Temple and the font will be all finished and ready for dedication, and just as soon as they are ready we shall dedicate them. We have all the timbers for the Temple on the ground, and above one hundred thousand shingles for the roof. The lead for the eaves and the tin for the dome of the tower are also bought. We have paid near 4000 dollars this spring for lumber (pine, boards, etc.) and near 1000 dollars for lead and tin, and have as yet lacked nothing. There is the most perfect union prevailing among the saints, and every man seems determined to do all he can to roll on the work of the Temple as fast as possible. Elder Hyde started east, about ten days ago, to purchase the cloth for the Tabernacle; and Elder Egan is gone to St. Louis to buy about 125 dollars worth of hemp to make cords for it.

The brethren are clearing the ground round the Temple, and we expect to have the Tabernacle reared, so as to be ready to meet in this fall.

We are building a stone wall around the Temple block, eight feet high and about five feet thick at the base, the wall on the north side is nearly built, the most of the woodwork for the Temple is finished, all the windowframes and sashes are made, and the glaziers are ready to set the glass, which we expect here in a few days, the frame and ornamental work of the tower is all ready to be put up, and the whole is far on the way of completion. The Nauvoo House Committee have reorganized, and the saints have appointed Elders A. Lyman and George A. Smith on that committee, in the place of Lyman Wight and J. Snider. A large quantity of brick is already made for the Nauvoo House, and considerable means are on hand to prosecute the work. We calculate to have it covered in before winter. The arsenal is ready for the roof timbers and the timbers on the ground. There are many good buildings erecting in different parts of the city, there is not much sickness in the place, and there never was a more prosperous time, in general, amongst the saints, since the work commenced. Nauvoo, or, more properly, the 'City of Joseph', looks like a paradise. All the lots and land, which have heretofore been vacant and unoccupied, were enclosed in the spring, and planted with grain and vegetables, which makes it look more like a garden of gardens than a city; and the season has been so favorable, the prospect is, there will be enough raised within the limits of the corporation to supply the inhabitants with corn, potatoes, and other vegetables. Hundreds of acres of prairie land have also been enclosed, and are now under good cultivation, blooming with corn, wheat, potatoes, and other necessaries of life. Many strangers are pouring in to view the Temple and the city. They express their astonishment and surprise to see the rapid progress of the Temple, and the beauty and grandeur of Mormon looks. Many brethren are coming from abroad, who seem highly delighted with the place and all its appendages.

We now conclude with our best wishes and prayers for your health and prosperity with that of your family, and those associated with you. Please remember us to Brothers Clark, Hedlock and families, and those of all the brethren with you, and believe us to be as ever—yours in the bonds of truth and righteousness.

[Signed] BRIGHAM YOUNG.

P.S. *Sunday, June* 29.—This day the twenty-eighth quorum of the seventies has been organized, and is nearly full. There are twenty-seven quorums duly organized and all appear united in the same interest, and firm in the faith. Brother Milton Holmes is remembered by us in his station, he has been appointed one of the presidents of a quorum of seventies.'*

The saints in England observed this, the anniversary of the martyrdom of Joseph and Hyrum, by fasting and prayer: Elder Woodruff addressed a large assembly of saints at Birmingham.

Saturday, 28.—A number of brethren met and removed the stand and benches to the ground west of the Temple.

I rode out to the prairie with several of the Twelve: we felt thankful to God to see the crops looking so well.

Bonds for General Deming—a Contrast.

Some of our wealthy brethren went to Carthage and became sureties on the bond upon which General Deming was set at liberty: the sum required was ten thousand dollars. Each signer was required to swear to the lowest cash value of his property and that it did not lie in the City of Nauvoo and he was then taken for one-half the sworn amount, so that twenty thousand dollars in property at its lowest cash value was held in security for General Deming's appearance at court. This contrasts strangely with the clemency extended by the court to Sharp, Williams, Aldrich, Grover, and Davis who were admitted to bail at the last court for one thousand dollars each on their own security; Deming having killed Marshall in self-defense, while the others violated the solemn faith of the state, pledged by its executive, and murdered innocent, unoffending men while confined in helpless condition in a prison awaiting examination!

Thirteen hundred dwellings were burned in Quebec, Canada, and at least six thousand persons were rendered homeless.

*Millennial Star, vol. vi, pp. 91-2.

Father John Smith and Brother George A. Smith called upon William Smith in relation to his mother's visions. William evinced a very bitter spirit and declared himself President of the Church, and said that he would have his rights: his uncle reasoned with him and endeavored to show him the falsity of his position.

Attempted Reconciliation with William Smith and the Twelve.

Sunday, 29.—Elder Ezra T. Benson and I preached in the forenoon and Elders John Taylor and Amasa M. Lyman in the afternoon, at the grove west of the Temple. Evening, I met with the Twelve and others for prayer.

Monday, 30.—Visited Mother Smith in company with the Twelve and Bishops Whitney and Miller. William Smith was invited but did not attend. Mother Smith expressed herself satisfied with the Twelve and the course they were pursuing.

* * *

Tuesday, July 8, 1845.—Brother Joseph Toronto handed to me $2,500 in gold and said he wanted to give himself and all he had to the upbuilding of the church and kingdom of God; he said he should henceforth look to me for protection and counsel. I laid the money at the feet of the bishops.

Wednesday, 9.—Sister Jennetta Richards, wife of Dr. Willard Richards, died at 10:15 a. m.

At 2 p. m. the Smith family attended a public dinner at the Mansion which was given by Bishops Whitney and Miller in behalf of the church; seven widows and about fifty of the family were present. Brothers H. C. Kimball, John Taylor, Bishops Whitney, Miller and myself, assisted in waiting on the table; the band and a few friends attended: Mother Smith addressed her kindred and the audience in a feeling and pathetic manner.

* * *

Saturday, August 2, 1845.—In council with several of the Twelve and bishops. Brother Emmett desired in behalf of his company to be retained in the fellowship of the church. I informed him that if he and his company would follow the counsel of the Twelve we would fellowship them, but not otherwise.

James Emmett's Desire to be in Fellowship.

Afternoon, I rode out in the new church carriage with Brother Kimball and the bishops to look at two [city] blocks of Emma Smith's which she has agreed to sell the Trustees for $550.00. We selected blocks 96 and 97 and then went to Mother Smith's and brought her in the carriage to choose which of the two blocks she would have deeded to herself and her daughters. She selected block 96, and desired to have the church build her a house like Brother Kimball's. She asked for the carriage we rode in, a horse and a double carriage harness. We gave her the use of the carriage during her lifetime.

Kindness to Mother Lucy Smith.

Monday, 4.—Elders Daniel Spencer and Charles Shumway were appointed to go on a mission west in company with Brothers Herring and Otis.

Afternoon, in council with the Twelve, James Emmett and others. Emmett wished to be restored to the priesthood. He confessed his fault in leading away his company contrary to counsel and promised to make all the restoration in his power, he said he would abide counsel. Council decided he should be restored.

Wednesday, 6.—In council with Brothers H. C. Kimball, W. Richards, G. A. Smith and Amasa M. Lyman.

From the *New York Sun.*

TEMPLE AT NAUVOO

'The building of the Mormon Temple under all the troubles by which those people have been surrounded, seems to be carried on with a religious enthusiasm which reminds us of olden times, by the energy which controls all the movements towards its completion. It occupies the highest and most imposing position in Nauvoo and is built of fine limestone. Has thirty pilasters—six at each end and nine at each side—each surmounted by a capital on which is carved a human face with rays around it and two hands holding trumpets. The Temple is 88 feet by 128 feet; from floor to ceiling is 65 feet; and from the ground to the top of the spire is 165 feet. The baptismal font is in the basement, to be supported by stone oxen. Three hundred and fifty men are zealously at work upon the building, which it is supposed will be finished in a year and a half, probably at a cost of half a million of dollars. The spiritual concerns of the Mormons are governed by a Council of Twelve, composed of the following persons

Brigham Young—*The Lion of the Lord.*
H. C. Kimball—*The Herald of Grace.*
Parley P. Pratt—*The Archer of Paradise.*
Orson Hyde—*The Olive Branch of Israel.*
Willard Richards—*The Keeper of the Rolls.*
John Taylor—*The Champion of Right.*
Wm. Smith—*The Patriarchal, Jacob's Staff.*
Wilford Woodruff—*The Banner of the Gospel.*
George A. Smith—*The Entablature of Truth.*
Orson Pratt—*The Gauge of Philosophy.*
John E. Page—*The Sundial.*
Lyman Wight—*The Wild Ram of the Mountains.*

It is supposed that the Mormon inhabitants of this city are fully 12,000 souls, and of the surrounding country, 5,000 more. The only property owned in common is the Temple. The Mormons are industrious, good farmers, raise wheat plentifully, and are about to engage in manufactures. The whole community may be considered in their peculiar traits singular and remarkable and in after ages their Temple, like the ruins of Palenque may strike the beholder with wonder and history may be unable to explain what race worshiped there.'*

Tuesday, 12.—9 a. m., the Twelve, presiding bishops and others met in council, and wrote letters for H. G. Sherwood and John S. Fullmer, with authority to lead, direct and instruct Emmett's company who are now encamped among the Sioux on the Missouri river about thirty miles above the mouth of Big Sioux river. We laid our hands upon the heads of Brothers Sherwood, Fullmer and Emmett and blessed them for the mission. Brother Emmett declared he would be subject to counsel.

Sunday, 17.—I dreamed this morning I saw Brother Joseph Smith, and as I was going about my business, he said, 'Brother Brigham, don't be in a hurry', which was repeated the second and third times with a degree of sharpness.

*The author of the *Sun* article is supposed to be William W. Phelps, writing from Nauvoo.

Monday, 18.—I met with the brethren of the Council, and Trustees of the Nauvoo House on the walls of the building. Elder Kimball dedicated it to the Lord, asking his blessing to attend the work and those engaged upon it. The workmen then commenced: Brother Alonzo H. Raleigh laid the first brick.

Wednesday, 20.—A severe thunderstorm this morning, Brother Ralph was killed by lightning on Parley Street. Others were knocked down.

Governor Ford ordered the state arms in the possession of the Carthage Greys to be delivered to Sheriff Backenstos.

Friday, 22.—Elders W. Richards and George A. Smith commenced writing the History of Zion's Camp. Brother George A. Smith supplying many incidents from memory.

Sunday, 24.—Meeting at the stand: My brother Joseph Young, preached a funeral sermon. I made a few remarks.

Evening, the quorums all met at the stand and I instructed them about building the houses the Lord had commanded, called upon the bricklayers to come forward and put up the Nauvoo House, fifty came forward.

An L. D. S. American Revolution Soldier Dies.

Elder David Foote was buried. He was born, August 7, 1769, Harrington, Litchfield county, Connecticut. His father enlisted in the army of the Revolution and died in the service. David was reared by his uncle, Jonathan Barker.

In 1791 he married Irene, the eldest daughter of Matham and Dorcas Lane. He joined the Methodists and served as a class leader several years, he subsequently became a believer in universal restoration.

In the winter of 1830 he obtained a copy of the *Book of Mormon* which was read by himself and family, he considered it a true record. He was baptized by Elder John Murdock in Genesee, in the fall of 1833, and ordained an elder in 1834, commenced preaching and raised up a branch in Greenwood, New York, where he resided, and was called to preside over the same in 1835. Several elders visited him during the summer, and members were added to the branch.

In 1837, he moved with his family to Chester, near Kirtland, and in May, 1838, started for Missouri and arrived in Caldwell county in August in time to share in the persecutions that followed, and was driven to Adams county, Illinois. He was ordained a high priest in November, 1844.

August 14, 1845 he was taken sick with the chills and fever, his sickness continued till the night of the 22nd, when he fell asleep and all attempts to awake him proved ineffectual, he slept till 11 p. m., when he passed behind the veil without a struggle or a groan. Dying as he lived, a faithful saint.

Wednesday, 27.—Elder Parley P. Pratt gave an account of his mission in the east where he had been about 9 months (and returned on August 26th), preaching to and counseling the saints, and collecting tithing. Council voted they were satisfied with the course of Elder Pratt.

Monday, September 1, 1845. — Elders Daniel Spencer and Charles Shumway, who left Nauvoo on a mission to the west, on the fourth of last month returned with news confirmatory of the death of Brother Jonathan Dunham, which took place on the 28th of July last, a little before daylight.

Thursday, 4.—2 p. m., met for counsel and prayer with the Twelve and others.

A Harvest Feast Near Nauvoo.

Messrs. Elam Meacham, Phineas Richards, Levi R. Chase, Francisco Durphy, Isaac Houston, John Wait, Gardner Clark and Thomas Corbitt the trustees and officers of the Big Field Association having invited us to attend a public dinner, Elders H. C. Kimball, W. Richards, John Taylor, George A. Smith, Amasa Lyman, Father John Smith, Bishops George Miller and N. K. Whitney went to the field about six miles southeast from the city and partook with them of an excellent dinner. 616 adults sat down to the table: They had an ample bowery prepared for the occasion. I preached encouragingly to the brethren and advised them to store their grain in the city. They have 30,000 bushels of corn in the field."

CHAPTER XXXII

PREPARATIONS FOR WESTWARD JOURNEY—THE FINAL WORD: THE CHURCH MUST LEAVE ILLINOIS—DETAIL OF THE PLANS—AMERICAN GOVERNMENT FAILS IN THE CASE OF THE LATTER-DAY SAINTS

"*Tuesday, September* 9, 1845.—Forenoon, unwell.

Two p. m. General Council [Council of Fifty] met. Resolved that a company of 1500 men be selected to go to Great Salt Lake valley and that a committee of five be appointed to gather information relative to emigration, and report the same to the council.

Salt Lake Valley Considered as place of Settlement.

Wednesday, 10.—I dreamed last night that I was chased by a mob to a place like a barn full of corn or grain, one chased me so close that he got into the same room with me and it was Thomas Ford, who appeared only two and one-half feet high, I took his wrist between my fingers and stepped to the door and knocked down one after another of the mob with him till I discovered he was dead.

News arrived that the mob are burning the houses of the brethren at Yelrome.

Thursday, 11.—I received a letter from Sheriff J. B. Backenstos announcing the death of General Miner R. Deming, who died at half past ten o'clock yesterday of congestive fever; during his illness his life was repeatedly threatened by the mob, he was prevented from sleeping at night by their yells and hideous screams, as they kept up a continual row in the streets of Carthage near the general's residence which greatly aggravated his fever, and doubtless caused his death.

Death of Miner R. Deming.

I answered Sheriff Backenstos' letter assuring him of our regret at the loss the cause of liberty, law, and order had sustained in the unexpected death of General Deming, and informed him of the burning of the houses of the citizens of Morley Settlement by the mob yesterday, and requested him to take immediate steps to suppress the mob, advised him to inform the governor that he may take the necessary measures to protect the lives and property of the people in this country.

A messenger from Lima reports eight houses burned.

The Twelve met in council; it was agreed to dispatch a messenger to the Lima branch and counsel the brethren to propose to sell their property to the mob and bring their families and grain here, and to send a messenger to Michigan to advise the brethren to sell their farms for stock, sheep, etc., also to Ottawa and recommend the brethren there to gather all the hay they can.

Prayers were offered up that the Lord would give us wisdom to manage affairs with the mob so as to keep them off till we can accomplish what he requires at our hands in completing the Temple and Nauvoo House, also for wisdom to manage the affairs in regard to the western emigration.

A selection was made of members of the council to start westward next spring.

Friday, 12.—Nine a. m., council met at Historian's Office, wrote and dispatched the following letter by James H. Woodland:—

BRIGHAM YOUNG'S LETTER TO SOLOMON HANCOCK

'Nauvoo, Sept. 12, 1845.

President Solomon Hancock,

Dear Brother: We have received your communication of last eve and taken it into consideration in council, and decided that it is wisdom for you to remove the women and children from Yelrome as fast as you can with what teams you have got, and we will send you more as fast as we can, and not only remove the women and children but your grain and let all the brethren stay there and keep 'bachelor's hall' and watch movements of the mob.

The object of our enemies is to get opposition enough to raise popular excitement but we think it best to let them burn up our houses while we take care of our families and grain.

Let the sheriff of Hancock county attend to the mob, and let us see whether he and the Jack-Mormons, so-called, the friends of law and order, will calmly sit down and watch the funeral processions of Illinois liberty; if so, they will all fall under the same condemnation. At a future day our course will be plain.

Be calm and patient till all things are ready. What is a little property or a few lives, compared with the properties and lives of a great people, and the house and ordinances on which the salvation of that people depend?

You will employ the best scribe you have, or half a dozen of them, if necessary, to pen minutely all the movements of the enemy and friends, what houses are burned, by whom, at what hour, who were present, and who saw them do it, etc.: even every particular and forward us a daily copy, if opportunity permits.

[Signed] BRIGHAM YOUNG, President.

W. Richards, Clerk.'

SOLOMON HANCOCK'S ANSWER TO BRIGHAM YOUNG

By letter from Solomon Hancock, Yelrome, we learn that the mob have burned all the houses on the south side of the branch [brook], and left last evening for Lima, said they would return this morning as soon as light, and swear they will sweep through and burn everything to Nauvoo. Colonel Levi Williams is at the head of the mob.

The following notice was issued by the council:

'Nauvoo, Sept. 12, 1845.

To the Brethren in and About Nauvoo, Greeting:

Aid Sent to Morley Settlement.

The Council of the Church requests every man who has a team to go immediately to the Morley Settlement, and act in concert with President Solomon Hancock in removing the sick, the women, children, goods and grain to Nauvoo.

[Signed] BRIGHAM YOUNG, President.

W. Richards, Clerk.'

The brethren at Yelrome made the following proposition to the mob:—

'Yelrome, Sept. 12, 1845.

Conciliation Offered to the Mob.

We the undersigned, a committee appointed by the Morley and Hancock Settlement (a branch of the Mormon Church); *Whereas* there seemingly exists some difficulty between said body and anti-Mormons, we, as representatives of said body, wish to make some propositions so as to make peace;

we wish to sell our deeded lands as well as our improvements as low as it could be reasonably expected, reserving to ourselves the crops now on the premises; and will take in exchange, working cattle, beef cattle, cows, sheep, horses, wagons, harness, store goods, and any available property and give possession as soon as our crops can be taken care of and we receive pay for the same; the whole of which may be purchased from the undersigned acting as committee or from owners.

[Signed] DANIEL TYLER,
HORACE RAWSON,
MARCELLUS MCCOWN,
SAMUEL ALGER.'

An extra *Nauvoo Neighbor* was issued giving an account of the burning; and appealing to the citizens to come forward and magnify the laws.

Saturday, 13.—Brother H. C. Kimball and Andrew Perkins visited me. Brother Perkins wanted to know something about our going west; I told him that those who went must expect to go on the Apostles' doctrines and no man say aught that he has is his own, but all things are the Lord's: and we his stewards, and every man receive his stewardship.

Journey West to be made on the Apostles' Plan—"All things in common."

George W. Lang reported that he had been among the mob at Green Plains and Lima. Esquire Hill of Lima told him they did not design gathering in large bodies, but go on as they had done and finish burning Yelrome, then attack some other place and drive the Mormons all into Nauvoo, then they had further plans to move them from there by help from abroad.

Afternoon, I visited the sick and met the Committee on Emigration and others at Brother Daniel Spencer's. Father Bent was instructed to organize a company of 100 families.

George Miller said he went to Carthage with his wife and was transacting business at the county clerk's office, when he was arrested by Michael Barnes, constable, and taken before Captain Robert F. Smith, justice of the peace; was charged with treason and as the state was not ready for trial,

Arrest of George Miller —Resistance.

and the offense not bailable, Captain Smith ordered him to be committed to jail, upon which Miller told him there was not enough men in the little town to put him in jail. Said he had served the United States government in two wars—had made the roads into this country and had killed snakes, and it was an imposition for these slinks that followed his tracks to charge him with treason, but if they wished to have an examination, he would come and attend court, but would not go into that jail alive. Upon which Esquire Smith took his verbal recognizance for his appearance at Carthage the next Saturday.

Sunday, 14.—* * * I prophesied we would have a winter of peace in Nauvoo.

I said, in relation to the mob burning houses, I was willing they should do so, until the surrounding counties should be convinced that we were not the aggressors, peradventure they may conclude to maintain the supremacy of the law by putting down mob violence and bringing offenders to justice.

Resolution to Help the Saints from Yelrome to Nauvoo.

I counseled the brethren to bring their families and grain here, and called for volunteers with wagons and teams to aid in removing the saints to this place; one hundred and thirty-four teams were procured and started forthwith. The brethren agreed to continue until they had brought in all their families, effects and grain of the saints in the settlements attacked by the mob.

I received a letter from John Loveless and Westley Knight informing me that the Highland branch was embodied [organized] by order of the sheriff to protect their property.

SUBSTITUTION OF MILITARY MEASURES FOR CIVIC MUNICIPAL ORGANIZATION

As the repeal of our City Charter had deprived us of our military organization, the following was issued by the council:—

'*To Charles C. Rich*:
President of all the Organized Quorums of the Church of Jesus Christ of Latter-day Saints in Hancock County.

Greeting: You are hereby instructed to hold the same [i. e. quorums of the priesthood] in readiness for all duties that shall be necessary in all emergencies.

Done at the 'City of Joseph' this 14th day of September, A. D. 1845.

[Signed] BRIGHAM YOUNG, President.'

Monday, 15.—Seven a. m., the police met at my house and put me up a stable.

Sheriff Backenstos went to Warsaw and tried his best to summon a *posse* to stop the burning but could not raise one.

Forty-four buildings have been burned by the mob. Several houses have been burned in the Prairie branch, Green Plain precinct.

Arrest of Prominent Citizens of Nauvoo Attempted.

Michael Barnes a constable from Carthage, and his brother came into Nauvoo with writs for H. C. Kimball, Willard Richards, John E. Page, Daniel Garn, Wm. and George A. Smith, and myself, issued by Captain Smith of the Carthage Greys, on the complaint of ———— Backman. The charges were for aiding and abetting Joseph Smith in treasonable designs against the state, for being officers in the Nauvoo Legion, for building an arsenal, for keeping cannon in times of peace, for holding a private council in Nauvoo, and for holding correspondence with the Indians.

He called on General Miller and made known his business. Miller told him he would get the men together and they would meet him at the Masonic Hall at 4 o'clock p. m. The constable said he did not wish to see Wm. Smith, but was anxious for all the others; before the time appointed he concluded to leave the names of the parties with General Miller and requested them to meet the justice at A. G. Fellow's house on the Prairie four miles this side of Carthage.

I wrote Elder Samuel Brannan in regard to the continuation of the *New York Messenger* as follows:

'Do as you and Brother Pratt think best, only do not think to sustain it [the *Messenger*] from the tithing. You know your circumstances and whether the subscription list will warrant its continuation or not.

Publication of Eastern Papers Referred to the Brethren in the East.

I wish you together with your press, paper, and ten thousand of the brethren, were now in California at the Bay of San Francisco, and if you can clear yourself and go there, do so.'

I received a letter from J. B. Backenstos, dated, Carthage, September 15th, in which he stated his inability to raise law and order citizens to quell the mob and requested us to hold two thousand well armed men in readiness for immediate service at any hour that he may call for them and added: that if we will not defend our own lives and property that we cannot reasonably expect any considerable support from those citizens commonly called 'Jack-Mormons'. 'Colonel Levi Williams has ordered out his brigade of militia, I am certain the turnout will be slim, we must whip them.'

Steps Attempted at the Maintainance of "Law and Order".

In reply I advised him to wait a few days and see if there are any law and order citizens in the county that are not Mormons, and if it proved there were none else to stand up for the Constitution and laws of the state, it would then be time enough for us, as the old citizens had heretofore advised us to 'hold still'! 'Keep cool'! 'Be quiet'! etc., etc., we were determined to do so.

The first regiment, second cohort of the Nauvoo Legion met and organized, choosing the old officers, to place themselves in readiness to act at the sheriff's call.

'There is grain enough growing within ten miles of this city, raised by the saints, to feed the whole population for two years if they were to sit down and do nothing but gather it in and feast upon it, and worship God. We expect to bring it all into the city or near it and the people too. The mob seem determined to drive us to our duty in gathering, and then drive us to carry the fulness of the gospel from among them and carry it to Israel. We are all well.

[Signed] [BRIGHAM YOUNG].'

* * *

Tuesday, 16.—Sheriff Backenstos arrived in great haste and somewhat excited, said that the mob had driven him from his house in Carthage yesterday, and he went to Warsaw and stayed over night. He soon ascertained that the people were so enraged at him for trying to stop the house-burning that there was little probability of getting away alive, but finally prevailed on an influential mobocrat to escort him out of Warsaw this morning, who came with him about three and a half miles and on leaving cautioned him that if he saw two men together to avoid them for there were deep plans laid to kill him. Soon after he was pursued by a party of the mob on horseback, three of whom took the lead, one of the three had a swifter horse and gained a hundred yards in advance of his party in a short time when his horse stumbled and threw his rider. Backenstos maintained his speed, driving as fast as his horse could go.

Sheriff Backenstos Expelled from Carthage.

The mob took the nearest road to cross his track and on his arrival at the old railroad crossing, the mob were within about 200 yards, they being on horseback and he in a buggy, they had gained on him considerably.

Orrin P. Rockwell and John Redding were refreshing themselves near the crossing as they had been out to bring in some of the burnt-out families who were sick, and on looking up saw Backenstos coming down the hill at full speed, and asked what was the matter. Backenstos replied the mob were after and determined to kill him and commanded them in the name of the people of the state to protect him. Rockwell replied, fear not, we have 50 rounds (two fifteen-shooter rifles besides revolvers).

Sheriff Backenstos then turned to the mob and commanded them to stop, and as they continued to advance raising their guns, he ordered Rockwell to fire; he did so aiming at the clasp of the belt on one of the mob, which proved to be Frank Worrell,

Killing of Frank Worrell.

who fell from his horse and the rest turned back and soon brought up a wagon and put his body into it.

* * *

Tuesday, 30.—Met in General Council at the Seventies' Hall. * * *

Parley P. Pratt said he had made a calculation for an outfit that every family of five persons would require: one good wagon, three yoke of cattle, two cows, two beef cattle, three sheep, one thousand pounds of flour, twenty pounds of sugar, one rifle and ammunition, a tent and tent poles; and that the cost would be about $250.00 provided the family had nothing to begin with, only bedding and cooking utensils; and the weight would be about twenty-seven hundred including the family, and calculating them to walk considerably would reduce it to about nineteen hundred weight.

Outfit Required for the Westward Journey for a Family of Five Persons.

It was decided that all the council [i. e. of the Twelve] were to go west with their families, friends and neighbors.

General C. C. Rich reported that General J. J. Hardin with his troops had arrived in the city and were on the square northeast of the temple, waiting an interview with the Twelve and authorities of the place. Also that Sheriff Jacob B. Backenstos and Judge Stephen A. Douglas were at Elder Taylor's and wished to see me as soon as possible. Council adjourned.

Interview of Church Authorities with Commanding General Hardin *et al.*

I went with the Twelve to Elder Taylor's and saw Judge Douglas and Sheriff Backenstos.

They said it was hard to make the people, the other side of the Illinois river, believe that it was not the Mormons that were burning houses in Hancock county.

They wished us to go and see General Hardin. In company with H. C. Kimball, W. Richards, John Taylor, George A. Smith and Amasa M. Lyman, I went on to the hill and met General Hardin and staff surrounded by his troops, four hundred in number. He read us his orders from the governor to come here and keep the peace if he had to keep the county under martial law: said he wished to search for the bodies of two dead men who were last seen in Nauvoo and it was supposed they had been murdered.

I told him he was welcome to search for dead bodies or anything else he pleased. He inquired if I knew anything about them or of crimes having been committed in Nauvoo. I replied I knew nothing of the kind, but that I had reliable information that some hundred houses had been burned in the south part of the county and probably if he would go there, he would find the persons who had done it.

I tendered him the hospitality of the city and a home at my house, to which he replied drily, 'I always stay in camp.'

General Hardin marched his troops to, and searched the Temple, Masonic Hall, Nauvoo House, and the stables of the Mansion.

There were deposited some forty barrels of wild grape wine in the Masonic Hall which attracted the attention of some of the searchers and caused some delay.

While searching the Mansion stables, they found where a horse had been bled and sent for the landlord and demanded an explanation; after being shown the horse, the General and Judge Douglas ran their swords into the manure, as though they expected to prick some dead bodies and make them squeal. Almon W. Babbitt told them they must think we were fools to bury dead men in a stable when it was so easy to throw them into the Mississippi river, which was only a few rods off. They then marched off and camped on the south side of the city.

Caleb Baldwin was arrested and taken into camp, and examined as a witness. Most of the questions asked were designed to find out where the bodies of Joseph and Hyrum Smith were buried.

* * *

Wednesday, October 1, 1845.—Met in council at Elder Taylor's. General John J. Hardin, Hon. Stephen A. Douglas and J. A. McDougal were present.

Plans of the Saints' Proposition to Remove from Illinois.

E. A. Bedell, Esqr., asked General Hardin for three or four men to go to Warsaw and make arrests, which request was granted.

I asked the gentlemen present as to their feelings as friends and neighbors, and in relation to our propositions for removal.

General Hardin said he would do all in his power by counsel, etc., to help us, and approved of our proposed location at Vancouver's Island. He thought it desirable for our sakes that we should remove, also for the peace of the county.

Judge Douglas said Vancouver's Island was claimed by the United States, and he felt sure there would be no objection to its settlement, or to the settlement of Oregon.

General Hardin proposed that we should appoint trustees-in-trust to sell our property.

I proposed a committee of the whole on both sides, and informed them that we were not sowing any winter wheat, and a greater testimony of our intentions to remove should not be asked.

Propositions of the Saints Admitted to be "just and fair".

Judge Douglas said, all competent men must admit that the propositions of the committee of citizens of Nauvoo were just and fair.

General Hardin said he was satisfied we intended to remove but had not the assurance we could go if our property could not be sold.

We received the following:

LETTER FROM THE QUINCY COMMITTEE

'Nauvoo, October 1, 1845.

To the First President and Council of the Church at Nauvoo:

Having had a free and full conversation with you this day in reference to your proposed removal from this county, together with members

Church Leaders Requested to Place Terms of Departure in Writing.

of your church, we have to request you to submit the facts and intentions stated to us in the said conversation to writing, in order that we may lay them before the governor and the people of the state. We hope that by so doing it will have a tendency to allay the excitement at present existing in the public mind.

We have the honor to subscribe ourselves.

Respectfully yours etc.

[Signed] JOHN J. HARDIN,
W. B. WARREN,
S. A. DOUGLAS,
J. A. MCDOUGAL.'

Thursday, 2.—The council received the following from Camp Mississippi:

'*To the First President and High Council of the Church of the Latter-day Saints*:

Since our conference with you yesterday, we have arrived at this place and have held free conversation with the anti-Mormons of this and the surrounding counties. We have read to them your statement made to us on the 1st instant.

Acquiescence of the Citizens of Illinois to the Agreed Removal of the Saints.

We have informed them that you individually made similar statements to us, with the most solemn protestations of truth, and with every appearance of earnest determination to carry out your expressed intentions in good faith.

In the Resolutions which were adopted yesterday, in this place, by the delegates from nine counties, (the citizens of Hancock being excluded from the meeting), it was resolved (as we are informed, not having seen a copy of the Resolutions), to accept your proposition to remove in the spring.

Since we have made public the statement by you made to us, there seems to be a general acquiescence in it by citizens of other counties, and of this, so far as to agree to restrain and withhold all further violence, and that you be permitted to depart in peace next spring.

We are convinced that affairs have reached such a crisis, that it has become impossible for your church to remain in this country.

After what has been said and written by yourselves, it will be confidently expected by us and the whole community, that you will remove from the state with your whole church, in the manner you have agreed in your statement to us.

Should you not do so, we are satisfied, however much we may deprecate violence and bloodshed, that violent measures will be resorted to, to compel your removal, which will result in most disastrous consequences to yourselves and your opponents, and that the end will be your expulsion from the state.

We think that steps should be taken by you to make it apparent that you are actually preparing to remove in the spring.

By carrying out, in good faith, your proposition to remove as submitted to us, we think you should be, and will be permitted to depart peaceably next spring for your destination, west of the Rocky Mountains.

For the purpose of maintaining law and order in this county, the commanding general purposes to leave an armed force in this county which will be sufficient for that purpose and which will remain as long as the governor deems it necessary. And for the purpose of preventing the use of such force for vexatious or improper objects, we will recommend the governor of the state to send some competent legal officer to remain here, and have the power of deciding what process shall be executed by said military force.

We recommend to you to place every possible restraint in your power over the members of your church, to prevent them from committing acts of aggression or retaliation on any citizens of the state, as a contrary course may, and most probably will bring about a collision which will subvert all efforts to maintain the peace in this county; and we propose making a similar request of your opponents in this and the surrounding counties.

With many wishes that you may find peace and prosperity in the land of your destination, which you desire, we have the honor to subscribe ourselves,

[Signed] JOHN J. HARDIN,
W. B. WARREN,
S. A. DOUGLAS,
J. A. MCDOUGAL.'

Friday, 3.—The following Resolutions by the citizens of Quincy were published in the *Quincy Whig*, October 1st:—

RESOLUTIONS IN THE QUINCY WHIG

'First, *Resolved*, That we accept and recommend to the people of the surrounding counties to accept the proposition made by the Mormons to remove from the state next spring: but we accept it as an unconditional proposition to remove. We do not intend to bring ourselves under any obligations to purchase their property or to furnish purchasers for the same, but will expect them to dispose of their property and remove at the time appointed.

Secondly, That we do not endorse the enumeration of grievances made by the Mormons in their printed proposition to remove, or in any degree yield our assent thereto: that we do not believe them to be a persecuted people, but believe whatever grievances they may suffer to be the legitimate consequences of their own conduct.

Thirdly, *Resolved,* That it is now too late to attempt the settlement of the difficulties in Hancock county upon any other basis than that of the removal of the Mormons from the state.

Fourthly, *Resolved,* That whilst we shall endeavor by all means in our power to prevent the occurrence of anything which might operate against their removal, and afford the people of Nauvoo any ground of complaint, we shall equally expect good faith upon their part; and if they shall not comply with their own propositions, the consequences must rest upon those who violate faith. And we now solemnly pledge ourselves to be ready at the appointed time to act as the occasion may require, and that we will immediately adopt a preliminary military organization, for prompt future action if occasion should demand it.

Fifthly, *Resolved,* That we respectfully recommend to the people of the surrounding counties, to wait with patience the time appointed for removal, and that if in their opinion the Resolutions passed by this meeting are such as the occasion requires they adopt them and send copies to the church authorities at Nauvoo.

Sixthly, *Resolved,* That in our opinion the peace of Hancock county cannot be so far restored as to allow the desired progress to be made in preparing the way for the removal of the Mormons while J. B. Backenstos remains sheriff of said county and that he ought to resign said office.

Seventhly, *Resolved,* That we recommend to all parties in Hancock county that they suspend all legal prosecutions for alleged offenses during the present state of excitement; and that all should be permitted to return to their homes in peace.

Eighthly, *Resolved,* That in our opinion it will only be necessary for the people of Nauvoo to appoint commissioners on their part to whom applications for the purchase of real estate may be made, and that there is no necessity to appoint commissioners on the other side.

Ninthly, *Resolved,* That in order to manifest our sympathies with the unoffending poor, the widow and orphans of Nauvoo, a committee of twenty with a treasurer, be appointed by the chairman, whose duty it shall be to receive subscriptions from all those desirous of contributing pecuniary aid for such persons and that the amount collected be paid over to such persons as they shall appoint to receive it upon their being ready to start upon their journey of removal.

Tenthly, *Resolved,* That we expect as an indispensable condition to the pacification of the county that the old citizens of Hancock county be permitted to return to their homes unmolested by the present sheriff, and the Mormons for the offenses alleged against them, and that any attempt on their part to arrest or prosecute such citizens will inevitably lead to a renewal of the late disorders.

Eleventh, *Resolved,* That the judge of this judicial circuit be requested not to hold any court in Hancock county this fall, with a view to prevent unnecessary excitement and collision in said county, which might inflame the passions of its citizens and so endanger its peace, it being well known that the unpleasant difficulties already existing there have entirely prevented the due impartial administration of justice.

Twelfth, *Resolved,* That this meeting deem it proper to recommend that a small military force be stationed in Hancock county until next spring to prevent depredations upon private property and preserve the peace of said county and that it be respectfully yet earnestly recommended to the executive of this state to furnish the same for the purpose above named.'

ADDITIONAL RESOLUTIONS ADOPTED AT THE SAME MEETING

'*Resolved,* That a committee of five be appointed for the purpose of adopting and carrying into operation a volunteer military organization for Adams county, and said committee are hereby authorized to do all things lawful, necessary and proper for the purpose of preparing such a force, without delay, to be used to preserve the peace of this and the adjoining counties.

Resolved, That the committee appointed to visit Nauvoo deserve and receive our warmest thanks, for the prompt, able and efficient manner in which they discharged the duties confided to them.

Resolved, That the chairman of this meeting be and he is hereby vested with full power and authority to call an adjourned meeting at any time he may deem the public exigencies require it.

Resolved, That the proceedings of this meeting be published in the city papers and copies thereof transmitted to the governor of the state, and to the church authorities of Nauvoo by the chairman and secretary of this meeting.'

Saturday, 4.—Attended General Council at Seventies' Hall. While riding to the hall with Elders H. C. Kimball and W. Richards, Elder Richards prophesied that we should have means to move all the poor and want for nothing. Elder Kimball said, amen.

A Prophecy of Good.

The correspondence from General Hardin and suite, the governor, and the Resolutions by the citizens of Quincy were read to the council.

I proposed that we cease publishing the *Nauvoo Neighbor* and save our paper inasmuch as our papers rarely get beyond the hands of our enemies. Any information we want to send abroad we will publish in circulars and extras.

Resolution to Cease Publishing the *Nauvoo Neighbor* and the *Times and Seasons.*

Elder Richards moved that the next number of the *Times and Seasons* close that paper and that the minutes of the conference be published in the *Nauvoo Neighbor*.

I proposed that we appoint a committee of three to select and preserve the statements of the press of the United States concerning us, and proposed that Elders Parley P. Pratt, Orson Spencer and Wm. W. Phelps be a committee to write a pointed document relating to the treatment we have received from the United States.*

The committee who were appointed by the President to acquire and lay before the council all the necessary information in regard to the outfitting of families for emigration west of the mountains submit the following report obtained from calculation and from the best works on the subject:

REQUIREMENTS OF EACH FAMILY OF FIVE FOR THE JOURNEY ACROSS THE PLAINS

'Each family consisting of five adults, will require 1 good strong wagon, well covered. 3 good yokes of oxen between the ages of four and ten. Two or more cows. One or more good beeves, some sheep if they have them.

One thousand pounds of flour or other bread stuff and good sacks to put it in.

One bushel of beans.

One hundred pounds of sugar.

One good musket or rifle to each man.

One pound of powder and three lbs. lead (or perhaps more).

Two lbs. tea, 5 lbs. coffee.

Twenty-five pounds of salt.

A few pounds of dried beef, or bacon, as they choose.

A good tent and furniture to each two families.

From ten to fifty pounds of seed to a family.

And from twenty-five to one hundred pounds of farming or other tools.

Clothing and bedding to each family of five persons not to exceed five hundred pounds.

One or more sets of saw and gristmill irons to each company of one hundred families.

*This was in harmony with the revelation which was given some five years earlier to the Prophet Joseph Smith in which a commandment was given for the gathering up of all the libelous and damaging falsehoods that had been stated against the church by their enemies (See *Doctrine and Covenants*, sec. cxxiii, March, 1839).

Cooking utensils to consist of a bake-kettle, frying-pan, coffee pot, tin cups, plates, and forks, spoons, pans, etc., etc., as few as will do.

A few goods to trade with the Indians.

A little iron and steel, a few pounds of nails.

Each wagon supposed to be loaded on the start with one ton without the persons or twenty-eight hundred including them.

If going to the coast it is not necessary to carry seed wheat, oats or grass. Nor are cattle and sheep absolutely necessary except to live on while upon the journey, as the country abounds in both cattle and sheep. A few horses will be necessary for each company. Also a few cannon and ammunition for the same. The journey to the coast will require some four or five months, being upwards of two thousand miles.

There was also added two sets of pulley blocks and rope for crossing rivers to each company.

Two ferry boats to each company.

One keg of alcohol of five gallons for each two families.

Ten pounds of dried apples for each family.

Five pounds of dried peaches.

Twenty pounds of dried pumpkin.

Two pounds of black pepper.

One pound of cayenne.

One-half pound mustard.

Twelve nutmegs. One fish seine for each company. Hooks and lines for each family.' "

CHAPTER XXXIII

LAST CONFERENCE AT NAUVOO—PLEA OF THE "MOTHER OF PROPHETS"—PATHETIC

"*Sunday, October* 5, 1845.—

FIRST MEETING IN THE TEMPLE

Through the indefatigable exertions, unceasing industry, and heaven-blessed labors, in the midst of trials, tribulations, poverty, and worldly obstacles, solemnized in some instances, by death, about five thousand saints had the inexpressible joy and great gratification to meet for the first time in the House of the Lord in the City of Joseph. From mites and tithing millions had risen up to the glory of God, as a Temple, where the children of the last kingdom could come together and praise the Lord.

It certainly afforded a holy satisfaction to think that since the sixth of April, 1841, when the first stone was laid, amidst the most straitened circumstances, the Church of Jesus Christ of Latter-day Saints had witnessed their bread cast upon waters, or more properly, their obedience to the commandments of the Lord, appear in the tangible form of a Temple, entirely enclosed, windows in; with temporary floors, pulpits and seats to accommodate so many persons preparatory to a General Conference; no General Conference having been held for three years past, according to the declaration of our martyred Prophet:—

'There shall be no more baptisms for the dead, until the ordinance can be attended to in the font of the Lord's House; and the church shall not hold another General Conference, until they can meet in said house. *For thus saith the Lord.*'

I [Brigham Young] opened the services of the day by a dedicatory prayer, presenting the Temple, thus far completed, as a monument of the saints' liberality, fidelity, and faith, concluding: 'Lord, we dedicate this house and ourselves, to thee.' The day was occupied most agreeably in hearing instructions and teachings, and offering up the gratitude of honest hearts, for so great a privilege, as worshiping God within instead of without an edifice, whose beauty and workmanship will compare with any house of worship in America, and whose motto is:

'HOLINESS TO THE LORD'.

Monday, 6.—

CONFERENCE MINUTES

'Minutes of the first General Conference, which was ever held by the Church of Jesus Christ of Latter-day Saints, in the House of the Lord in the City of Joseph, commencing on Monday, October 6th, 1845, ten o'clock forenoon.

Present—Elder Brigham Young, President of the Quorum of the Twelve Apostles; also Elders Heber C. Kimball, Parley P. Pratt, Willard Richards, John Taylor, George A. Smith and Amasa M. Lyman; Patriarchs John Smith and Isaac Morley; Presiding Bishops Newel K. Whitney and George Miller; also the authorities of the church generally.

The conference was opened with singing by the choir, and prayer by Elder Parley P. Pratt. Elder Willard Richards then arose and read over some notices concerning lost property, concerts, etc. He then stated, that the President had waited from half past nine to near eleven o'clock, for the people to get together; he exhorted the brethren to be more punctual, as so much time lost could not be recalled, and we have a great amount of business, which must necessarily be attended to during conference. He next stated that General Hardin had requested us to make out a list of all the buildings belonging to our brethren which have been burned by our enemies, and also had requested that all those who have had their buildings or other property destroyed should make affidavit of the same before a justice of the peace, and have their affidavits ready to be forwarded to him at as early a season as possible.

FIRST BUSINESS—PRESENTATION OF AUTHORITIES FOR APPROVAL

President Brigham Young then rose and said: the first business that will come before this conference, will be to present the authorities of the church to ascertain whether they are in good standing.

Father John Smith, the president of the stake, then arose and presented the Twelve as the Presidents of the whole church; which was seconded and carried unanimously.

It was then moved that Brigham Young be continued and sustained as the President of the Quorum of the Twelve Apostles; seconded and carried unanimously.

It was next moved that Heber C. Kimball be continued and sustained as one of the Twelve Apostles: seconded and carried unanimously.

It was next moved that Orson Hyde be continued and sustained as one of the Twelve Apostles; seconded and carried unanimously.

It was next moved that Parley P. Pratt be continued and sustained as one of the Twelve Apostles; seconded and carried unanimously.

It was next moved that Orson Pratt be continued and sustained as one of the Twelve Apostles; seconded and carried unanimously.

Orson Pratt's Objection to Sustaining William Smith.

It was next moved, that William Smith be continued and sustained as one of the Twelve Apostles; seconded. Whereupon Elder Orson Pratt arose and said:

'I have an objection to Brother William continuing in that office. I feel, as an individual, that I cannot, conscientiously, uphold and sustain Brother William as one of the Twelve Apostles, until he thinks different from what he does now. I have many reasons for this, but I will merely mention one or two, which must suffice for the present. In the first place, I have proof positive that he is an aspiring man; that he aspires to uproot and undermine the legal Presidency of the Church, that he may occupy the place himself. This he has avowed openly in the east, which I can prove by good and substantial witnesses. In the second place, while Brother William was in the east, to my certain knowledge, his doctrine and conduct have not had a savory influence; but have produced death and destruction wherever he went. This also I am well prepared to prove. I have been waiting in all long suffering, for an alteration in Brother William's course, but up to the present time, I have been disappointed. For these two reasons, I would plead for one, that we no longer sustain him in his office, till a proper investigation can be had, and he make satisfaction. I do this individually; I leave others to do as they please.'

The motion being seconded, a vote was then taken to sustain him, but was *lost* unanimously.

It was next moved that John E. Page be continued and sustained as one of the Twelve Apostles; seconded and carried unanimously.

It was next moved that Willard Richards be continued and sustained as one of the Twelve Apostles; seconded and carried unanimously.

It was next moved, that Wilford Woodruff be continued and sustained as one of the Twelve Apostles; seconded and carried unanimously.

It was next moved that John Taylor be continued and sustained as one of the Twelve Apostles; seconded and carried unanimously.

It was next moved that George A. Smith be continued and sustained as one of the Twelve Apostles; seconded and carried unanimously.

It was next moved that Lyman Wight be continued and sustained as one of the Twelve Apostles; whereupon Elder A. W. Babbitt said:

A. W. Babbitt's Objection to Lyman Wight.

'As Elder Orson Pratt remarked, concerning William Smith, that he could not conscientiously vote to sustain him, so I say in regard to Lyman Wight, I cannot conscientiously give my vote in his favor. My reason is this: If there is a council in this church that ought to be united, and act in unison as one man, it is the Council of the Twelve. If the head is sick, the whole body is afflicted. If I am rightly informed concerning Brother Wight's conduct, for the past year, he has not acted in unison with the Twelve, nor according to their counsel. The last year has been one of affliction, persecution and sorrow, when the adversary has continually sought to destroy and mutilate the church; and it has required all the faith, prayers and perseverance of the leaders, to save this people from the grasp of the destroyer. If the counsel of Brother Wight had been followed, this Temple would not have been built, nor the baptismal font erected. He has sought to draw away a part of the force, which we ought to have had to build this Temple. His teachings have been contrary to the counsel of the church, and his conduct calculated to destroy it. Under circumstances of this kind, I cannot conscientiously vote to continue him in his standing, until he retracts, and makes satisfaction. Brother Wight's course has been calculated to divide the church, and prevent those things being accomplished, which were commanded of God by the Prophet Joseph.'

Elder Kimball arose and said:—

'It is well known, that Brother Wight's case was had before the conference last spring, and that he was dropt, and then again retained; that is, that we would let him be, and see what he would do, and what course he would take. He has been away ever since; and is with a small company somewhere; we cannot tell what he is doing; he may in his own mind, be acting in concert with the rest, and he may be acting for the good of this people. It would be my mind, to let his case lay over for the present, until we can learn something from him.'

Whereupon it was moved, that we let the case of Brother Lyman Wight lay over for the present until we hear from him. Seconded and carried unanimously.

It was next moved that Amasa M. Lyman be continued and sustained as one of the Twelve Apostles; seconded and carried unanimously.

Wm. Smith Rejected as Patriarch.

Elder Isaac Morley arose and said; he would next present William Smith as the Patriarch of the Church; and moved that he be continued and sustained in that office; seconded and *lost* unanimously.

President Brigham Young stated, that about three years ago, Elder Willard Richards was appointed by President Joseph Smith, as Historian for the Church, and general Church Recorder. We have previously acted on his appointment to office, as Recorder, but not as Historian. He would therefore move, that we receive the appointment of Brother Joseph, and that we continue and sustain Elder Richards as Historian for the Church,

Willard Richards Sustained as Church Historian.

and General Church Recorder; seconded and carried unanimously.

It was next moved that Father John Smith be continued and sustained as president of this stake of Zion; and that Isaac Morley and Charles C. Rich be continued and sustained as his counselors; seconded and carried unanimously.

It was next moved that Samuel Bent be continued and sustained in his office as president of the high council; seconded and carried unanimously.

It was next moved, that George W. Harris, Alpheus Cutler, James Allred, Thomas Grover, Henry G. Sherwood, William Huntington, Sen., Lewis D. Wilson, Newel Knight, David Fullmer, Aaron Johnson, and Ezra T. Benson each be continued and sustained as members of the high council; seconded and carried unanimously.

It was next moved that George Miller be continued and sustained as president of the high priests' quorum, and that William Snow and Noah Packard be continued as his counselors; seconded and carried unanimously.

It was next moved that Joseph Young be continued and sustained in his office as the Senior President of the First Quorum of the Seventy; seconded and carried unanimously.

It was next moved that Levi W. Hancock, Henry Harriman, Zera Pulsipher, Daniel S. Miles, Jedediah M. Grant, each be continued and sustained as one of the Seven Presidents over all the Seventies; seconded and carried unanimously.

Elder George A. Smith remarked that Roger Orton was one of the 'Old Camp'* and was selected a year ago to be one of the seven Presidents of the Seventy; but he had never received his ordination, nor done anything to magnify his calling. It is not to be expected that we

Elder Roger Orton dropped from First Council of Seventy.

*"Old Camp" (i. e. Zion's Camp) which went to Missouri to redeem Zion in 1834, and from which the Twelve Apostles and the first two quorums of Seventy were chosen.

shall wait year after year for men to come forward and fill their offices. Brother Orton was one of the Old Camp, and we love him on that account; we always called him the 'Big Major', and a first rate man; but he has not come forward since his appointment to magnify his calling.

Elder Joseph Young said:

'Last spring I visited Roger Orton and apprised him of his appointment. He agreed to come as early as convenient, and receive his ordination; and I gave him to understand, if he did not come and act in his office, he would be dropt. Brother Orton has always sustained Brother Joseph and the church, but he has very little of the spirit; he has been in the church about twelve years, but never has been active since his discharge from the camp that went up to Missouri in 1834. It was by the counsel of the Twelve that he was appointed one of the Presidents of the Seventy. I have no particular desire to plead for him, but if his case can be laid over, I think he can be saved in that office, but I will be subject to counsel. I have considerable feeling for him; he lost all his property in Missouri, and has since addicted himself to drinking whiskey; that seems to have ruined him, but he may be reclaimed.'

President Brigham Young arose and said, he would preach one of Dow's short sermons:—

'If you won't when you can, when you will you shan't'. 'I say if men will not act and magnify their calling, let more honorable men be appointed. Roger Orton is keeping a public house at Augusta and has had sufficient time to come and prove himself a worthy man in his office, but has not done it; and I say let a more honorable man take the crown. If he won't work now, when will he?'

It was then moved that we drop him; seconded and carried unanimously.

Moved that Samuel Williams be continued and sustained as president of the elders' quorum, and Jesse Baker and Joshua Smith be continued and sustained as his counselors; seconded and carried unanimously.

Moved that Newel K. Whitney be continued and sustained as the first Bishop of the Church; and that George Miller be continued and sustained as his associate; seconded and carried unanimously.

Moved that Stephen M. Farnsworth be continued

and sustained as president of the priests' quorum; and that William Carmichael and ---------- Betts be continued and sustained as his counselors; seconded and carried unanimously.

Moved that Elisha Averett be continued and sustained as president of the teachers' quorum; as also his former counselors; seconded and carried unanimously.

Council of Deacons in the Church Provided.

President Brigham Young moved, that there be a quorum of deacons selected, and a president over them, and that the Presiding Bishops see to it, as soon as possible, and make report to this conference before its close; seconded and carried unanimously.

Conference then adjourned till two o'clock p. m. Benediction by Elder G. A. Smith.

Two p. m.—The house was called to order by Elder Taylor; the choir sang 'The Prodigal Son'. Elder Taylor read a list of the sick, and offered up prayer; after which the choir sang another hymn.

Elder Parley P. Pratt on the Situation and Prospects of the Saints.

Whereupon Elder Parley P. Pratt addressed the conference on the subject of our present situation and prospects. He referred to the great amount of expense and labor we have been at to purchase lands, build houses, the Temple, etc.; we might ask, why is it that we have been at all this outlay and expense, and then are called to leave it? He would answer that the people of God always were required to make sacrifices, and if we have a sacrifice to make, he is in favor of its being something worthy of the people of God.

'We do not want to leave a desolate place, to be a reproach to us, but something that will be a monument to those who may visit the place of our industry, diligence and virtue. There is no sacrifice required at the hands of the people of God but shall be rewarded to them an hundred fold, in time or eternity.

'The Lord has another purpose to bring about and to fulfill. We know that the great work of God must all the while be on the increase and grow greater. The people must enlarge in numbers and extend their borders; they cannot always live in one city, nor in one county;

they cannot always wear the yoke; Israel must be the head and not the tail. The Lord designs to lead us to a wider field of action, where there will be more room for the saints to grow and increase, and where there will be no one to say we crowd them, and where we can enjoy the pure principles of liberty and equal rights.

'When we settle a country where the air, the water, soil and timber is equally free to every settler without money or without price, the climate healthy, and the people free from unjust and vexatious lawsuits, mobocracy, and oppression of every kind, we can become vastly more wealthy, have better possessions and improvements, and build a larger and better Temple in five years from this time than we now possess.

'It has cost us more for sickness, defense against mobs, vexatious prosecutions, and to purchase lands in this place, than as much improvement will cost in another.

'One small nursery may produce many thousands of fruit trees, while they are small. But as they expand towards maturity, they must needs be transplanted, in order to have room to grow and produce the natural fruits. It is so with us. We want a country where we have room to expand, and to put in requisition all our energies and the enterprise and talents of a numerous, intelligent and increasing people. In our natural state, ask yourselves if you could be brought to endure and enjoy a celestial law, without an experience of the kind we have passed through for the last fifteen years?

'In short, this people are fast approaching that point which ancient prophets have long since pointed out as the destiny of the saints of the last days.'

After many other spirited remarks touching similar points, he was succeeded by Elder George A. Smith, on the same subject. Elder Smith observed that a revelation was given in Missouri in regard to the saints consecrating their property which was not understood at the time; but they were soon brought to their understanding, for the Lord in his providence caused it all to be consecrated, for they were compelled to leave it.

George A. Smith.

He is glad of the prospect of leaving this county and seeking a place where we can enjoy the fruits of our labors and God himself be the sole proprietor of the elements.

Here is one principle in which he wants this whole people to unite. When we were to leave Missouri the saints entered into a covenant not to cease their exertions until every saint who wished to go was removed, which was done.

We are better off now than we were then, and he wants to see the same principle carried out now, that every man will give all to help to take the poor; and every honest industrious member who wants to go. He wants to see this influence extend from the west to the east sea.

After which President Brigham Young moved that we take all the saints with us, to the extent of our ability, that is, our influence and property; seconded by Elder Kimball, and carried unanimously. Elder Brigham Young continued:

'If you will be faithful to your covenant, I will now prophesy that the great God will shower down means upon this people, to accomplish it [the resolution] to the very letter. I thank God that the time has come so much sooner than I expected, that that scripture is being fulfilled, 'My people shall be willing in the day of my power'; and I almost feel to thank our friends abroad for hastening it on now.'

President Young's Prophecy of the Deliverance of the Saints.

Elder Parley P. Pratt made some remarks relative to the brethren being all on a level when they left Missouri. He referred to the Whitmer family monopolizing timber; advised liberality with wood.

Elder H. C. Kimball moved that every man who owned a woodlot should on application, let the poor, the sick, and the needy who wanted wood, have it; and those who have teams should assist in hauling it to them; seconded and carried unanimously.

It was requested by President Young that no man go into another's woods without the consent of the owner; and then take it clean and be careful of the timber.

Benediction by W. W. Phelps and adjourned until tomorrow at ten a. m.

Tuesday, October 7, 1845.—Conference met pursuant to adjournment at ten a. m. Meeting called to order by president of the stake. Choir sang a hymn. Prayer by Elder Phelps. Choir then sang another hymn.

Elder Heber C. Kimball then addressed the conference.

'This is a hard place for anyone to speak in, and there are many things still necessary to lay before this conference. For my part I am done preaching to this nation; at least for the present. I have been forth through the United States and Europe, in fact, I have spent my whole time at it, since I came into the church. It is now all counsel for me—We have a great many things to say today; and I suppose we shall always have plenty to do. I presume many have got out of business; but we will now have work enough, to get ready to go to some other country; to get there, and to plough our fields when we get there. I have seen people crying and weeping, and mourning, because they had nothing to do; but when we leave this place, you will never have cause to weep for not having anything to do, from this time forth, and forever more, if you are faithful to your calling. I am glad the time of our exodus is come; I have looked for it for years. It is necessary for us to be faithful and humble, and if we listen to counsel we shall prosper. And although we leave all our fine houses and farms here, how long do you think it will be before we shall be better off than we are now? I have no farm to leave; I never had that privilege. Many of the brethren have farms; but there are many who have spent their whole time in the service of the church, for fourteen or fifteen years, who never had a farm. When we get to a new country, some of these old veterans will be looked after first; and I rejoice in it. We are now about coming to the Apostolic religion; i. e., you will sell all, and come and lay it down at the Apostles' feet. But it has taken a good scourging for fifteen years to bring us to this. There may be individuals who will look at their pretty houses and gardens and say, 'it is hard to leave them'; but I tell you, when we start, you will put on your knapsacks, and follow after us. Before I was baptized, I believed we should come into an Apostolic religion. As for a Common Stock Business Religion, such as many preach, I do not believe in it. Every man will be a steward over his house and property; and if he is an unfaithful steward, his stewardship will be given to another. I will prophesy in the name of Heber C. Kimball, that in five years, we will be as well again off as we are now. Those brethren who have gone off and labored among the Gentiles, are not as well off as we are; some have eighty dollars, some an hundred, and some fifty dollars due them; and their 'friends' have driven them away penniless; and they have had to flee for safety to Nauvoo. Those who remained here, are better off. Since we have had an invitation from our 'friends' to leave

Elder Kimball

the county, many have asked, shall we go and labor for them? They may go, if they have a mind to; but I won't do it; I'll see them go the other way first.

'I positively know men, that have gone to labor for those, who with uplifted hands, swore they would take President Brigham Young's life and my own. If it is your feeling to tarry here, and labor for each other to get away, manifest it (clear vote). At the last conference, a vote was passed that the Gentiles were cut off; and now, why do you want to labor for them. Inasmuch as the Gentiles reject us, lo! we turn to the Jews.

'Again; there is a constant running to the Twelve, and saying 'Can't we go in your company?' We calculate you are all going in the first company, both old and young, rich and poor; for there will be but one company. Probably we will sometimes be the first, and then again the last, sometimes in one place, sometimes in another. Some say, 'ah! you are going ahead, and taking the band;' but we will be with all of you.

'We first made a selection of one hundred, and when we had done, we found we could not be satisfied without taking the whole; and so we finally concluded we would take you all with us, and have but one company. There is no use in making selections, for you are all good; but there is still a chance for us all to be a great deal better. We have no partiality; we have a common interest, for the welfare of this whole people, and we feel to advocate your cause like a father would advocate the cause of his children.

'When men come in here to divide you, and when the mob came, did we flee? No! No! the hireling fleeth, but we felt like a father, and if you had to die, we would die with you. We want to feed the sheep, to nourish them; they have a tremendous journey to take; and when we see one that is weak and feeble, we will take it up, put it into a wagon, and take you all with us. We have had sorrow and could not sleep on your accounts: if we had no anxiety for you, we should have fled into the wilderness and left you.

'We want to take you to a land, where a white man's foot never trod, nor a lion's whelps, nor the devil's; and there we can enjoy it, with no one to molest and make us afraid; and we will bid all the nations welcome, whether Pagans, Catholics, or Protestants. We are not accounted as white people, and we don't want to live among them. I had rather live with the buffalo in the wilderness; and I mean to go if the Lord will let me, and spare my life. Let us become passive as clay in the hands of the potter: if we don't we will be cut from the wheel and thrown back in the mill again, like the Fosters, Higbees, and others. They want to come into Nauvoo again; but we won't let them, until we have all the good clay out, and have made it into vessels of honor to our heavenly Father: then they may come and be ground.'

Elder Lyman next arose and remarked:

'President Young says, we did not calculate to be in a hurry. It would be a matter of gratification, if I could express my feelings; but I have so many of them that I can't do it.

Elder Lyman's Remarks.

'There has been in the progress of this church an ample manifestation of the various windings and dispositions of man. A person cannot fail to perceive it, when he will observe and reflect, and doubtless those who have reflected may be satisfied, that the course of this people is unalterably fixed. I am glad it is not controlled by any human being. We have contended with opposition when it appeared impossible for us to overcome, and yet we have triumphed; and this people are becoming great and numerous.

'Perhaps in the congregation before me there is every variety of feeling, which can be found on the face of the earth: yet we find their feelings undergoing a change, and that this people are approximating to a *Oneness;* the people are becoming one, and their interests one. When they first heard the gospel, they hailed and cherished it with joy; and they have come up here to receive additional instruction: yet perhaps, they have made but a limited calculation of how far they would have to go, in obedience and sacrifices, and to how much persecution and suffering they would be subject that they might come up out of the fire as gold seven times tried.

'It has been said, that after a time, the Lord will accomplish a certain something: That after men had endeavored to build up kingdoms, and seen them crumble to the dust and disappear; he had said, he would build up a kingdom which would stand forever, and become a universal kingdom: and moreover the Prophet said, 'it should break in pieces every other kingdom'. If any man had preached this, he would have been considered guilty of treason. But those whom the Christian world consider as better men than we are, have said it; men, whom they say were better, and had knowledge, power, and virtue, more than they will now admit is lawful for us in this enlightened age to enjoy.

'It has been said, that we should leave this country next spring; if the Lord is willing and the people have no objections. (And we don't care much whether they have or not; we calculate to go about next spring). And we calculate to go the same people we are now; preserving the same principles which have caused us to grow and expand as we have done. This people have grown until there is not room for them to grow, and now they need transplanting, where they can have more room: and however much the people may seem disposed to not go, the sails are set, the wind is fair, and we are bound to weather the point, whether we will or no; for we are not at the helm; and whine and complain as much as you please, you have got to weather the point. Brother Kimball says, the whiners will have to go behind! So if you want to go in the company of the Twelve, you must not whine. Some persons suppose that when they had once lost their all, they had suffered enough: to hear them talk you would suppose that John the Revelator, when they tried to boil him in oil, or the three Hebrew children in the fiery furnace, seven times heated—never suffered half as much, nor felt half so uncomfortable as they. They have to get rich, and be made poor, about twenty times over, before they will come straight. I expect the rich will have to be made poor until the poor are made rich; and then there will be nobody poor. When the rich are rich; and the poor are rich; then there will be nobody rich and nobody poor; for all will be on a level.

'God did not say, that this man or that man should build up the kingdom, that was to break in pieces all other kingdoms; but he said he would do it himself; and whenever this people were unwilling to do as the Lord would have them he has taken his rod and scourged them, until they were forced to do it. The Lord once said he would make Kirtland a stronghold for a time; and he has done it. He said in Missouri he would sustain the saints for a time; and he did it. And when we came here, the Lord said, that if the people of the state of Illinois would maintain us in our rights they would be blessed; if not we might find it to our advantage to leave them.'

The names of Company No. 5 were then called over, with orders to meet after meeting at the old stand.

Appeal in Behalf of the Poor.

Elder Taylor made some remarks in behalf of the suffering poor in the north part of town; and called upon all to come forward to aid the bishops in supplying these poor families.

Elder George A. Smith said there were many coming to get leaders of the companies appointed; and remarked you need not be in a hurry for the Twelve will take care to have proper captains appointed in due time; and all will move on like clockwork. But we must not hurry business.

The Patriarch, John Smith, appointed four bishops to stand at the door, to take a collection for the benefit of the poor.

The choir sang and the meeting was dismissed until 2 o'clock p. m.

Benediction by George A. Smith.

All the single men who want to come into the 1st

company or company of the Twelve, were notified to give in their names.

At 2 o'clock.—President Brigham Young came to the stand and dismissed the meeting until tomorrow at 10 o'clock a. m. This was done on account of a body of armed men having suddenly entered the city. Not knowing but this was a move by the mob, the President requested all the brethren to go home and prepare themselves for any emergency. He, however, soon ascertained that W. B. Warren, Esq. was at the head of the troops and that they had come in on business.

Early Adjournment of Conference—Report of Troops in the City.

The President then informed the people of this fact; and requested them to retire to their homes in peace; concluding his remarks with these words, 'Be ye also ready'.

Wednesday, October 8, 1845.—Conference opened at the usual hour with singing and prayer.

Mother Lucy Smith, the aged and honored parent of Joseph Smith, having expressed a wish to say a few words to the congregation, she was invited upon the stand. She spoke at considerable length and in an audible manner, so as to be heard by a large portion of the vast assembly.

Appearance of Mother Lucy Smith Before the Conference.

She commenced by saying that she was truly glad that the Lord had let her see so large a congregation. She had a great deal of advice to give, but Brother Brigham Young had done the errand, he had fixed it completely. There were comparatively few in the assembly who were acquainted with her family. She was the mother of eleven children, seven of whom were boys. She raised them in the fear and love of God, and never was there a more obedient family. She warned parents that they were accountable for their children's conduct; advised them to give them books and work to keep them from idleness; warned all to be full of love, goodness and kindness, and never to do in secret, what they would not do in the presence of millions. She wished to know of the congregation whether they considered her a mother in Israel (upon which President Brigham Young said: all who consider Mother Smith as a mother in Israel, signify it by saying yes!—One universal 'yes' rang throughout). She remarked that it was just eighteen years since Joseph Smith the Prophet had become acquainted with the contents of the plates; and then in a concise manner related over the most prominent points in the early history of her family; their hardships, trials, privations, persecutions, sufferings, etc.; some parts of which melted those who heard her to tears, more especially the part relating to a scene in Missouri, when her beloved son Joseph was condemned to be shot in fifteen minutes, and she by prodigious efforts was enabled to press through the crowd to where he was, and to give him her hand; but could not see his face; he took her hand and kissed it she said, let me hear your voice once more my son; he said, 'God bless you my dear mother!' She gave notice that she had written her history, and wished it printed before we leave this place. She then mentioned a discourse once delivered by Joseph after his return from Washington, in which he said that he had done all that could be done on earth to obtain justice for their wrongs; but they were all, from the president to the judge, determined not to grant justice. But, said he, keep good courage, these cases are recorded in heaven, and I am going to lay them before the highest court in heaven. 'Little', said she, 'did I then think he was so soon to leave us, to take the case up himself. And don't you think this case is now being tried? I feel as though God was vexing this nation a little, here and there, and I feel that the Lord will let Brother Brigham take the people away. Here, in this city, lay my dead; my husband and children; and if so be the rest of my children go with you, (and would to God they may all go), they will not go without me; and if I go, I want my bones brought back in case I die away, and deposited with my husband and children.' (Mother

Smith said many more good things, but the rest being inaudible to the reporters, they are lost).

President Brigham Young then arose and said he wanted to relate to the congregation the last closing remarks of Mother Smith; inasmuch as she could not be heard by all.

'Mother Smith proposes a thing which rejoices my heart: she will go with us. I can answer for the authorities of the church; we want her and her children to go with us; and I pledge myself in behalf of the authorities of the church, that while we have anything, they shall share with us. We have extended the helping hand to Mother Smith. She has the best carriage in the city and while she lives, shall ride in it when and where she pleases.

Considerate Pledges Made to the Smith Family.

'When William came here we furnished him a span of horses and a carriage and a house and Brother Kimball became responsible for the rent of it. He has run away in a time of trouble; but I suppose will come back when it is peace, and we mean to have him with us yet.'

(Mother Smith here interrupted President Young, but inaudible to the reporters). President Young continued:

'Mother Smith has been relating over the circumstances of her pecuniary life of late; she is perfectly satisfied, and all is right. I could have wished that the bishops would visit her more frequently; but they have done pretty well—and I say in the name of the Latter-day Saints, we will supply her wants; and I want the people to take anything they have for her to her, and let her do with it as she pleases. I have never asked her to go for she had told me she would not; but now she has offered it. Mother Smith proposes that she will go with us, if we will promise to bring back her remains in case of her death and deposit them with her husband's. Also Joseph once said, with outstretched arms, 'If I fall in battle in Missouri, I want you to bring my bones back, and deposit them in that sepulchre—I command you to do it in the name of the Lord.' And I pledge myself if Mother Smith goes with us and I outlive her, I will do my best to bring her bones back again, and deposit them with her children, and I want to know if this people are willing to enter into a covenant to do the same.' (Unanimous vote).

Pledge of President Young to Return the Remains of Mother Smith to Her Family at Nauvoo.

President Brigham Young continued:

'We are determined also to use every means in our power to do all that Joseph told us. And we will petition Sister Emma in the name of Israel's God, to let us deposit the remains of Joseph according as he commanded us. And if she will not consent to it, our garments are clear. Then when he awakes in the morning of the resurrection, he shall talk with them, not with me; the sin shall be upon her head, not ours.'

Meeting was adjourned to two p. m.

Benediction by President Brigham Young.

2 p. m.—Conference met pursuant to adjournment.

Meeting called to order by Elder Joseph Young. Choir sang 'The Spirit of God Like a Fire is Burning'. Prayer by Elder Taylor. Choir sang again.

Elder Taylor then arose and said:

Proposal to Withdraw Publication of the Printed Word.

'There is one piece of business which devolves upon me to bring before this conference; and that is the printing. As we have done preaching, so we have done printing to the people; and now let them alone and mind our own business, and let them print what they have a mind to. It has been thought best to publish the conference minutes, and let that finish the subject; but I have thought it would perhaps be better to continue the *Times and Seasons* until the volume be completed. And if we do not circulate them abroad, we can at home, in the neighborhood. There are reasons for it. First, many are anxious about items of doctrine which the saints want; and many want to have the volume completed. As to the *Nauvoo Neighbor*, it is more connected with temporal matters, news, etc., and we don't care so much about that. The world doesn't wish any news from us, and we don't wish to urge it upon them. I have read papers until I have become tired; for they are all villainy, corruption, deceit and abomination; and I shall be glad when we get to a place where we can be at peace. In regard to discontinuing the papers, I will do as I am counseled. Some may consider that they will be injured by stopping the paper; but I will give four or five dollars worth of obligations for everyone they can present against me. No man can say that I have asked pay for a paper, though hundreds here are owing me for it. I will abide counsel, but am willing to publish the *Times and Seasons* until the end of the volume.'

Elder Kimball moved that we discontinue the *Nauvoo Neighbor* after one number; and that the *Times and Seasons* continue from time to time, till the volume is closed; seconded and carried.

The next item of business is to appoint committees to sell houses, farms, lots, etc., that they can be referred to for sales,

Appointment of Utility Committees.

Nauvoo. — Winslow Farr, Edward Hunter, Rufus Beach, A. W. Babbit, Joseph L. Heywood, John Benbow, and Daniel Russell.

La Harpe.—Lyman Corey, John Clark and John L. Bartolph.

Macedonia.—Wm. G. Perkins, Isaac Clark and Andrew H. Perkins.

Camp Creek.—L. A. Bingham.

Bear Creek.—Nelson Higgins, Samuel Shepherd and Daniel Allen.

Knowlton's Settlement. — Sidney A. Knowlton, Eleazer Brown and James Rawlins.

Highland Branch.—James Duncan, Wm. A. Duncan, and John Loveless.

Montebello—Eleazer Miller and Jesse Spurgin.

Yelrome.—Solomon Hancock and Horace Rawson.

In Iowa, every man is appointed to act as a committee of the whole for the sale of lands.

Elder Kimball said; there is yet another piece of business of great importance to all who have families; that is, to have some school books printed for the education of our children, which will not be according to the Gentile order.

Elder W. W. Phelps said:

Provision made for the Publication of School Books for Children.

'As a people we are fast approaching a desired end, which may literally be called a beginning. Thus far, we cannot be reproached with being backward in instruction. By revelation, in 1831, I was appointed to 'do the work of printing, and of selecting and writing books for schools in this church, that little children might receive instruction;' and since then I have received a further sanction. We are preparing to go out from among the people, where we can serve God in righteousness; and the first thing is, to teach our children; for they are as the Israel of old. It is our children who will take the kingdom and bear it off to all the world. The first commandment with promise to Israel was, 'Honor thy father and thy mother, that thy days may be long in the land, which the Lord thy God giveth thee.' We will instruct our children in the paths of righteousness; and we want that instruction compiled in a book.'

Moved that W. W. Phelps write some school books for the use of children; seconded and carried.

Elder Kimball said; the next item of business is whether or not there shall be a general settlement with the Trustees-in-Trust, the Twelve, the Temple Committee, and all others, so that we may not go away indebted to the Lord, and I want to know if it is wisdom to take such a course or not. But if we go away in debt, let it be to each other.

President Brigham Young said:

'One object of this settlement with us is, some of the Latter-day Saints believe that the Twelve are supported out of the funds belonging to this house; and I am not disposed to go away under the idea that I am in debt to the Trustees, when I have put more into their hands than I have taken out. Perhaps it will be a matter of curiosity to some how I get my living. It is not by stealing!—but by good luck, and the providence of God and good men. Those men who have done the most, are the nearest square. I want the Twelve, and the committee, and all the people to settle with the Trustees, and not go away in debt to the Lord; and then we will have abundance to take away the poor.'

Proposals for the Settlement of All Accounts.

Elder Kimball moved, that the Twelve, the Temple Commitee, and all others settle with the Trustees-in-Trust; and that the Trustees-in-Trust settle with the Presidency of the Church; seconded and carried. Elder Kimball remarked, we shall now expect a settlement from all those who have the wherewith, or you need not expect an endowment in this house. President Joseph Smith said he would stand at the door with the books; you will not see him, but you will see his successors, who will carry out his designs.

Elder George A. Smith said the next item was of very great importance:

'There has been more powder and ball wasted within the last two weeks, than would supply all the people with meat for three months if they were in a game country. What is the use of this waste? You cannot wake up in the night, but you hear them cracking away. You can hardly walk the streets, but sometimes a bullet will whistle over your head. Men say they are afraid their guns won't go off, it is wet; then I am in favor of getting something to draw (the charge from) them; I hope there will be no more firing. If there was a mob in sight, you have time enough to load your guns and fire on them. I want the powder and lead saved, so that when you get to your journey's end, you can sustain yourselves with food. Save your powder, caps and lead. I move that this conference discountenance all firing in the city, by any man, by night or by day, in every possible manner.'

Seconded and carried.

Elder H. C. Kimball said:

'There are a good many complaints of late, and I am sorry to hear it, of some of the neighbors having had their cattle shot. Brother John Benbow has had fifteen wounded. I am ashamed of a man who will do such things. The man that will destroy his neighbor's property in that way, I will prophesy that the hand of God will be upon him until he makes restitution, and he will not prosper.'

Sundry Practical Considerations Adopted.

Moved, that all persons who have been guilty, or may be hereafter, of shooting cattle, shall be cut off from the church, unless they make restitution; seconded and carried.

Moved that all persons who will not take care of their unruly cattle, shall be cut off from the church; seconded and carried.

President Young said:

'I have a little corn, if it is destroyed it may all go before I will have revenge. I am for keeping orderly and obeying counsel. When we first (again) preached in the grove, I charged the brethren not to let their cattle get into the gardens of the widows and the sick; and if the widows shot them, I would stand between them and harm, and someone, on the Friday following shot my only cow. I would have given five half eagles to bring her back again. She was reared by my wife, while I was on my mission to England, and was so gentle that my children could sit under her and milk her and play between her horns without fear of being hurt. Take care of your cattle, and feed them with your corn stalks, cabbage, slops, etc.'

And he again charged the brethren not to touch any property which did not belong to them; even if it be only a rail. He said:

'In Quincy they have decided that we shall not have any more law suits. Judge Purple has agreed not to hold any more courts in this county: (though we hear that he will). They are going to collect funds, as they say, to assist the poor to move out of Nauvoo. If they have a mind to bestow anything, let them give it to the Trustees, to be dealt out by them. We don't know but they will yet do as they did in Missouri—take our own property, and sell or bestow it upon us again at an extortionate price, and call it a deed of charity. I will tell you what it will be—a stink offering.'

Brother William Clayton then read a letter from Major Warren, respecting the arrest of one Smith, for felony, yesterday.

Moved that this conference adjourn until the 6th of April next; seconded and carried.

WILLIAM CLAYTON,
THOMAS BULLOCK,
Clerks of Conference.' "*

**Times and Seasons*, vol. vi, pp. 1008-1016.

CHAPTER XXXIV

OFFICIAL MESSAGE TO THE SAINTS IN THE UNITED STATES—REMOVAL OF THE CHURCH TO THE WEST—ORGANIZATION — OLIVER COWDERY'S TENDER OF SERVICES — THE BIGELOW CASE — WARREN-YOUNG-TAYLOR OUTBREAK — THE POWER OF PRAYER *vs.* MOBOCRACY — APPEAL TO GOVERNOR FORD

"*Wednesday, October 8, 1845.*—

EPISTLE TO THE BRETHREN OF THE CHURCH OF JESUS CHRIST OF LATTER-DAY SAINTS, SCATTERED ABROAD THROUGH THE UNITED STATES OF AMERICA

'*The Following Circular is Hereby Sent, Greeting:*
Beloved Brethren:

You will perceive from the foregoing interesting Minutes of the General Conference, just held in the Temple in this place [see Chapter XXXIII] not only the unparalleled union of the great body of the saints convened, but also that a crisis of extraordinary and thrilling interests has arrived. The exodus of the nation of the only true Israel from these United States to a far distant region of the west, where bigotry, intolerance and insatiable oppression lose their power over them—forms a new epoch, not only in the history of the church, but of this nation. And we hereby timely advise you to consider well, as the spirit may give you understanding, the various and momentous bearings of this great movement, and hear what the spirit saith unto you by this our epistle.

Exodus Announced.

Jesus Christ was delivered up into the hands of the Jewish nation to save or condemn them, to be well or maltreated by them according to the determinate counsel and foreknowledge of God. And regard not that even in the light of a catastrophe wholly unlooked for. The spirit of prophecy has long since portrayed in the *Book of Mormon* what might be the conduct of this nation towards the Israel of the last days. The same spirit of prophecy that dwelt richly in the bosom of Joseph has time and again notified the counselors of this church of emergencies that might arise, of which this removal is one; and one too in which all the Latter-day Saints throughout the length and breadth of all the United States should have a thrilling and deliberate interest. The same evil that premeditated against Mordecai awaited equally all the families of his nation. If the authorities of this church cannot abide in peace within the pale of this nation, neither can those

The Interest of Removal of the Church to the West to be Universal.

who implicitly hearken to their wholesome counsel. A word to the wise is sufficient. You all know and have doubtless felt for years the necessity of a removal provided the government [U. S.] should not be sufficiently protective to allow us to worship God according to the dictates of our own consciences, and of the omnipotent voice of eternal truth. Two cannot walk together except they be agreed. Jacob must be expatriated while Esau held dominion. It was wisdom for the child of promise to go far away from him that thirsted for blood. Even the heir of universal kingdoms fled precipitately into a distant country until they that sought to murder (him) were dead. The ranklings of violence and intolerance and religious and political strife that have long been waking up in the bosom of this nation, together with the occasional scintilations of settled vengeance, and blood guiltiness cannot long be suppressed. And deplorable is the condition of any people that is constrained to be the butt of such discordant and revolutionary materials. The direful eruption must take place. It requires not the spirit of prophecy to foresee it. Every sensible man in the nation has felt and perhaps expressed his melancholy fears of the dreadful vortex into which partizan ambition, contempt of the poor, and trampling down the just as things of nought were fast leading the nation. We therefore write unto you beloved brethren, as wise men that will foresee the evil and hide yourselves until the indignation be overpast.

Threatening National Portents.

Concerning those who have more immediately instigated our removal by shedding the blood of our Prophet and Patriarch and burning the habitations of scores of families in the midst of the most desolating sickness ever known in the western valley; and who oblige us to watch for our lives night and day—we have nothing to say. We have told such tales to our father the president, and to all the high-minded governors, until we are weary of it. We look far beyond those by whom offenses come, and discover a merciful design in our heavenly Father towards all such as patiently endure these afflictions until he advises them that the day of their deliverance has come. It is our design to remove all the saints as early next spring as the first appearance of thrifty vegetation. In the meantime the utmost diligence of all the brethren at this place and abroad will be requisite for our removal, and to complete the unfinished part of the Lord's House, preparatory to dedication by the next General Conference. The font and other parts of the Temple will be in readiness in a few days to commence the administration of holy ordinances of endowments, for which the faithful have long diligently labored and fervently prayed, desiring above all things to see the beauty of the Lord and inquire in his holy Temple. We therefore invite the saints abroad generally so to arrange their affairs as to come with their families in sufficient time to receive their endowments, and aid in giving the last

The Church has Come to Silence.

Intent to Complete the Temple.

finish to the House of the Lord previous to the great emigration of the church in the spring. A little additional help in the heat of the day from those abroad, to those here, who have been often driven and robbed will sweeten the interchange of fellowship, and so far fulfill the law of Christ as to bear one another's burdens. The sacrifice of property that will probably accrue from a virtually coerced sale in a given short time together with the exhaustion of available means, that has arisen from an extensive improvement of farms, and the erection of costly public and private edifices together with persecutions and abundant labors of elders in preaching the gospel to the nations, and also in self-defense from traitors and foes, hypocrites and knaves, are things that will suggest themselves to all the thoughtful humane and philanthropic. And we are confident in our Lord Jesus Christ that the balm and cordial adequate to the present crisis of affairs, will come from the saints abroad to the utmost of their ability. And you cannot furnish it better, than to come up unitedly to the counsel of our epistle promptly, diligently and to the letter. Therefore dispose of your properties and inheritance, and interests for available means, such as money, wagons, oxen, cows, mules, and a few good horses adapted to journeying and scanty feed. Also for durable fabrics suitable for apparel and tents; and some other necessary articles of merchandise. Wake up, wake up, dear brethren, we exhort you, from the Mississippi to the Atlantic, and from Canada to Florida, to the present glorious emergency in which the God of heaven has placed you to prove your faith by your works, preparatory to a rich endowment in the Temple of the Lord, and the obtaining of promises and deliverances, and glories for yourselves and your children and your dead. And we are well persuaded you will do these things, though we thus stir up your pure minds to remembrance. In so doing, the blessings of many, ready to perish like silent dew upon the grass, and the approbation of generations to come, and the hallowed joys of eternal life will rest upon you. And we can not but assure you in conclusion of our most joyful confidence, touching your union and implicit obedience to the counsel of the Great God through the Presidency of the saints. With these assurances and hopes concerning you, we bless you and supplicate the wisdom and furtherance of the Great Head of the Church upon your designs and efforts.

Admonition to Preparation for Western Move.

[Signed] BRIGHAM YOUNG, President.

Willard Richards, Clerk.

N. B. Let all wagons that are hereafter built be constructed to the track of five feet width from center to center. Families may properly travel to this place during winter in their wagons.

There are said to be many good locations for settlements on the Pacific, especially at Vancouver's Island near the mouth of the Columbia.'

A general meeting of the seventies at 8 a. m.; twenty-two members were ordained for the thirty-first quorum.

Seventies' Affairs.

Thursday, 9.—The seventies met in general conference. President Joseph Young counseled the seventies to pay strict attention to the call of their presidents and strongly exhorted them to pray unto the Lord day and night, and trust in him for deliverance, for the fervent prayers and faith of the saints would accomplish more than the strength of their arms, for the Lord holds the destinies of all men in his hands and he will control them according to his will and he has power to deliver us.

General Hardin has pledged himself to the mob that he will come to Nauvoo with his troops and either arrest Orrin P. Rockwell and some others of the brethren or he 'will unroof every house in Nauvoo'. Three hundred of our enemies have volunteered to come with him from Quincy and they expect to be joined by others on the way.

General Hardin's Threat Against Nauvoo.

There seems to be no disposition abroad but to massacre the whole body of this people, and nothing but the power of God can save us from the cruel ravages of the bloodthirsty mob.

We concluded to plead with our heavenly Father to preserve his people, and the lives of his servants that the saints may finish the Temple and receive their endowments.

Reliance Upon Prayer.

Saturday, 11.—The council met at Elder Taylor's. We joined in prayer, and wrote a circular for the agents to take abroad with them.

Afternoon, I remained at home being worn down with fatigue.

7 p. m., met for counsel and prayer. After prayer we finished an extract from the conference minutes for the circular. Also appointed additional captains of hundreds, making twenty-five companies, as follows: 1st, The Twelve; 2nd, Samuel Bent; 3rd, Alpheus Cutler; 4th, Isaac Morley; 5th,

Organized Companies.

Shadrach Roundy; 6th, Reynolds Cahoon; 7th, Daniel Spencer; 8th, Peter Haws; 9th, Joseph Fielding; 10th, John D. Parker; 11th, David Fullmer; 12th, Charles Shumway; 13th, Charles C. Rich; 14th, Jedediah M. Grant; 15th, Erastus Snow; 16th, Benjamin F. Johnson; 17th, Andrew H. Perkins; 18th, George Coulson; 19th, David Evans; 20th, Daniel C. Davis; 21st, Jonathan H. Hale; 22nd, George P. Dykes, (Ottoway); 23rd, Mephiboseth Sirrine, (Michigan); 24th, Hosea Stout; 25th, Wm. Huntington.

Bishop Miller, Sheriff Backenstos, and those who went with them to Quincy, have all returned safely.

Various Movements of Friends and Foes.

Backenstos is bound over to court in three thousand dollar bonds.

General Hardin has gone to Springfield.

Tuesday, 14.—Major Warren came into the city with a detachment of the troops.

We prayed that they might not be permitted to do any injury to any of the saints; nor to interrupt our peace; they stayed but a short time.

Friday, 17.—Elder Orson Hyde returned from the east, having purchased between four and five thousand yards of canvas for the Tabernacle.

Wrote to General James Arlington Bennett in answer to several letters from him, and some he had written which we have not received, as he sent them by mail. We invited him to come out and see us, and make arrangements and go to the mountains with us.

Tender of Services from Oliver Cowdery.

I received a letter from Oliver Cowdery dated, Tiffin, Ohio, October 7th, advising us to seek aid from the United States government and offered his services as agent to see President Polk on the subject of removal westward if the council desired it.

2 p. m., attended council at Elder Heber C. Kimball's.

Last Meeting of High Council in Nauvoo.

The high council met for the last time in Nauvoo, at least, it is the last minutes in their book.

Sunday, 19.—The congregation met in the Temple. Elder Orson Hyde preached.

Excommunication of William Smith.

William Smith who has published a pamphlet against the Twelve was excommunicated from the church by unanimous vote.

4 p. m., I met with the first Emigrating Company and proceeded with the organization by appointing captains of fifties and tens.

The Tabernacle for the Wilderness.

Monday, 20.—Elder Orson Hyde made returns of money collected for the Tabernacle \$1415.38½c; he paid for canvas \$1050.56c and other expenses \$105.80c.

Views of James Arlington Bennett.

Evening, the Twelve met in council at Elder Taylor's, General James Arlington Bennett met with us, he expressed himself opposed to our selling out to gratify the mob, and would rather see us fight and maintain our ground.

Tuesday, 21.—We visited the Temple. General Bennett was highly pleased with it.

Judge Purple is holding a court in Carthage.

I received the following:

LETTER FROM J. B. BACKENSTOS

'Carthage, Illinois,
October 21, 1845.

My Dear Friend:

As yet nothing has been done to do us any good, the array of grand and petit jurors has been set aside upon an affidavit of one of the mobbers, William D. Abernethy, a notorious man has been appointed as an elisor. Thomas C. Owen is also appointed for the other elisor so things are taking a strong and decided stand against us and justice. Our judge has so far decidedly shown himself in favor of the mob faction, and has so far disgusted very many of the respectable persons at court, I confess I am perfectly displeased with such judicial 'humbugs'.

Our coroner, Henry W. Miller, has also been set aside as well as myself, so you may understand where we are, and what we may expect

Yours, etc.,
[Signed] J. B. BACKENSTOS.'

Wednesday, 22.—General J. A. Bennett and Mr.

Booth, editor of the *Quincy Herald,* called at Dr. Richards' and tarried till noon. The conversation turned upon the saints going west. General Bennett asked Mr. Booth 'why don't you go with them'? Mr. Booth replied, 'To tell you the truth, that is my business here and I am not alone, for a number of others in Quincy are thinking of the same thing.'

Mr. Booth offered to publish in his paper anything to help the saints in the sale of their property, and any other communication from us which would not conflict with public opinion so far as to drive away his subscribers.

Evening, I met with the Twelve at Elder Taylor's. A letter was read from Reuben McBride, Kirtland, stating that the apostates were doing everything they could to injure the saints. S. B. Stoddard, Jacob Bump, Hiram Kellogg, Leonard Rich, and Jewel Raney are the leaders of the rioters; they have broken into the House of the Lord, and taken possession of it, and are trying to take possession of the church farm.

Hostility in Kirtland.

Jesse P. Harmon and John Lytle who were charged with destroying the *Expositor* press were tried before Judge Purple.

The court decided in his charge to the jury, that the defendants acting under the municipal authorities of Nauvoo, were acting without authority, and if it could be proven that they had taken any part in the destruction of the press they were to be found guilty.

Prosecutions for the Expositor Affair.

Rollison was the principal witness for the prosecution and gave a minute detail of the manner in which the nuisance was abated and stated that Mr. Harmon took the lead of the police on the occasion. On being asked if it was Appleton M. Harmon or Jesse P. Harmon, he replied it was the policeman and on being informed they were both policemen, he became confused and said he could not tell which it was.

The witness was asked whether it was John Lytle or Andrew Lytle, he replied, it was the Policeman

Lytle, on being informed that they were both policemen, he answered it was the Blacksmith Lytle and on being told they were both blacksmiths, he declared that he could not identify the persons. The jury brought in a verdict of 'not guilty' and the defendants were acquitted accordingly.

A Muddled Witness.

Thus were the words of the Prophet Joseph fulfilled, who told the police (when they reported to him that they had abated the nuisance) that not one of them should ever be harmed for what they had done, and that if there were any expenses consequent he would foot the bill.

Thursday, 23.—A detachment of the governor's troops came in from Carthage to search for a bogus press. They searched Lucien Woodworth's house in vain.

In Search for a Bogus Press.

By letters from Jonathan H. Hale and Jacob B. Backenstos we learn that Alpheus Cutler, John Lytle, Jesse B. Harmon and ———— Holmes were acquitted, as the prosecution failed to prove they were the men who destroyed the *Expositor* press.

All the affidavits of the sufferers in the house-burning in Hancock county were called for to be presented before the grand jury.

Friday, 24.—Evening, council met at Elder Taylor's. Some of the mob went to Nathan Bigelow's near Camp Creek and ordered him to leave before Thursday for they were coming to burn his house, he sent his son to Nauvoo for counsel, and he was advised to go to Carthage and make the facts known to Major Warren.

He accordingly went and told Warren who replied, that the troops were gone elsewhere and he had nobody to send. But told the young man to tell his father to defend his house, and call on his neighbors to assist him. It appears that on Thursday the young man did not get back to tell his father that night. Soon after this, Warren sent five of his men to Father Bigelow's to defend his house.

Tragedy of the Bigelow Home Attack.

They missed their way and did not get there till 11 o'clock at night. On arriving they tied their horses; and their commander, Lieutenant Edwards from Quincy, went straight to the door and undertook to go in without knocking. Father Bigelow expected it was the mob coming and asked who was there, but the man did not answer but still attempted to open the door. Father Bigelow again asked who was there, and what he wanted, but could get no answer. He then told the man if he opened the door he should shoot him. The man finally opened the door and Father Bigelow discharged a pistol at him loaded with buckshot; he then snatched up a musket and shot that. The shot took effect on Edwards' hip and three balls entered his breast. He fell and called to the others to come and help him. They then told Father Bigelow they were the governor's troops and had come to protect him. Father Bigelow said if that was the case he was sorry, and went to work and made a fire and got the man in and took care of him. This morning they brought Father Bigelow to Carthage a prisoner, but his case was not disposed of when the brethren left. Warren justified the act.

Saturday, 25.—4 p. m., A. W. Babbitt arrived from Carthage and stated that when the brethren went in yesterday as witnesses of the house-burning the grand jury refused to hear their testimony, or to admit any of them into the jury room, which effectually shields the house-burners from justice and blockades the way for the sufferers to obtain redress.

Refused Hearing Before the Carthage Grand Jury.

The steamer *Sarah Ann* passed up the river, Doctor Foster and Lyman E. Johnson were on board. When the boat landed Jackson Redden was standing by and L. E. Johnson stepped up to him to counsel concerning his father and brother's case. Dr. R. D. Foster got a number of men from the boat and undertook to haul Redden on board and take him off with them. Redden knocked the first man down that undertook to lay hands on him; a few of the brethren who were not far off ran to Redden's assistance and with sticks and stones soon drove the whole crew on board; the captain started immediately, without unloading; the clerk left the bills of lading with a man who handed them to Albert P. Rockwood, but appeared not to know what he did. After the boat started Doctor Foster shot his pistol at the brethren but hurt no one. One of the brethren was cut on the back of the neck with a stone.

The Redden Affair.

This morning Hosea Stout and John Scott stationed themselves at the mound, seven miles east of Nauvoo, and extended a few men for miles north and south to ascertain and express any hostile movements which might be made towards Nauvoo.

Nauvoo Eastern Outpost.

Major Warren, Judge Purple, J. B. Backenstos, Judge Ralston and Mr. Brannan with a detachment of troops came into town and Warren demanded an explanation in relation to seeing some fifteen or twenty of our express men on the prairie.

I went to the Mansion and in plain but mild language stated the reason why our men were there. Warren in a great rage declared he would issue his manifesto on Monday morning and put the county under martial law. After this Elder John Taylor made some very just and spirited remarks in relation to the foul treachery or criminal imbecility of the governor's protection, telling Mr. Warren that we had placed our express men in a position to communicate the earliest intelligence should any mob violence be attempted upon our brethren while at Carthage and further said: 'We lack confidence in the governor's troops under your command while hundreds of murderers, robbers and house-burners roam at large unwhipped of justice. We shall take measures to protect ourselves. I, Sir, have been shot all to pieces under the 'protection' of the governor's troops. Our leading men have been murdered in Carthage and

Warren-Young-Taylor Outburst of Feeling.

we shall not trust ourselves unprotected again until the state gives some evidence more than it has done of its justice and humane intentions to enforce its laws.'

Judge Purple said: 'Mr. Taylor do not talk on such an exciting topic.'

Elder Taylor ordered wine for the company, Judge Purple and all except Warren drank.

Elder Hyde commenced to make an apology for Elder Taylor. Elder Taylor interrupted him, saying, 'Do not offer any apology for me'. Judge Purple said, 'We accept the wine for Mr. Taylor's apology.'

Evening, I met with the council at Elder Taylor's. We prayed that the Lord would overrule the matter and remove from Warren's heart the disposition to declare martial law or otherwise let his hand be heavy upon him with judgment that he may not be able to bring trouble upon the saints.

Resort to Prayer.

Brother Hedlock called upon Dr. Richards with a message from General Bennett, saying that he had left Carthage and gone to Quincy that he would write Dr. Richards soon, and that he would cross the Rocky Mountains with us in the spring.

James Arlington Bennett's Message.

Enos Curtis made the following affidavit:

MORE HOUSE-BURNING

'State of Illinois }
Hancock County } ss.

On the 25th day of October, A. D. 1845, personally appeared before me E. A. Bedell one of the justices of the peace in and for said county, Enos Curtis, who after being duly sworn according to law deposeth and saith:—that on or about the eighteenth day of October A. D. 1845, in the Morley Settlement in said county he saw two houses and three stables burning and also saw two mobbers armed with guns going away from the same. And the deponent further saith that on Monday the twenty-first inst. he saw another house burning, said to belong to the widow Boss containing her potatoes and other vegetables. And further the deponent saith not.

[Signed] ENOS CURTIS.

Subscribed and sworn to before me this 25th day of October, A. D. 1845.

[Signed] E. A. BEDELL, J. P.'

Sunday, 26.—This morning Bishop Miller waited upon Judges Purple and Ralston and showed them the Temple.

Eight a. m., the seventies met in the Temple and proceeded with the organization of the thirty-first quorum.

P. M., council met at Elder Taylor's. Elder Orson Spencer in behalf of the council wrote the following:

AN APPEAL TO GOVERNOR FORD

'City of Nauvoo, Oct. 26, 1845.

To his Excellency Thomas Ford.

Sir: Fresh occasion from an occurrence of last evening appears to have arisen for this council to address you by the bearers E. A. Bedell, Esq. and Mr. George Miller. Having learned two or three days since that a number of houses and outbuildings were burned in the south part of the county and the utter impotency or negligence of the state forces to stop the work of burning, and having also learned that the mob intended next to burn houses in the north part of the county, at Camp Creek, and application having been made to Major Warren without obtaining sufficient aid to protect the citizens a number of our men in small companies not exceeding four in a company were ranging on the prairies in order to make a prompt report of any fresh depredations that might be made upon our property or persons.

At this time last evening Judge Purple, Major Warren and a portion of the bar, after adjourning the court were crossing the prairie to this place, when Major Warren discovered a portion of our men, say fifteen or twenty in their detached order. An inquiry into their business was made, and the answers not being sufficiently definite and satisfactory owing to weariness of watching and sense of their wrongs, the major took considerable umbrage and immediately upon his arrival demanded a satisfactory explanation. It was promptly given by President Young in a conciliatory spirit.

The major peremptorily avowed that he would issue his manifesto tomorrow and put the whole county under martial law, after which Elder Taylor made some spirited but not unjust remarks on his own responsibility.

If the major should impose martial law upon the county it would be a matter greatly to be deplored.

It would tend to obstruct the ends of peace and prevent that arrangement of affairs so necessary to our peaceful departure with our poor and helpless in the spring. It has been our continued effort and prayer to God that we might be unmolested until we can depart in the spring. For this purpose we still desire of you as our honored chief magistrate and the friend of the oppressed that the state troops may be speedily withdrawn. From this no danger will arise, even to our worst enemies, as our past forbearance and long suffering will abundantly prove. We would respectfully apprise you that the work of burning still goes on in the southern part of the county, as affidavits forwarded showing a number of buildings burned in the last two weeks will prove.

Our people are continually harrassed with threats of burning, and assassination up to last evening: and as astonishing as it may seem to you some of the house-burners are actually in the *posse* of state troops and are prowling round in Nauvoo every few days. Judge then of our feelings and situation and show us that favor that will merit the blessings of thousands upon your honored head.

Concerning what has been written and other matters of importance to us, we refer your honor to the bearers, who will give you the necessary information.

With sentiments of high consideration I have the honor to remain in behalf of the council your obedient servant,

W. RICHARDS, Clerk.'

E. A. Bedell and George Miller started at 8 p. m. to convey the above communication to Governor Ford. The night was so dark they lost their way twice and it was with much difficulty they reached Crooked Creek where they remained till break of day.

I conversed with Judge Ralston in relation to selling our property to the Catholics. He advised us to sell to them and said he would use his influence with them in Quincy to come and settle here.

Major Warren said this morning that no man would be permitted to go into Carthage [to attend trial of the Prophet's murderers] with any kind of arms. He swore he should search every man. It was thought best that about one hundred of the brethren should go and about twenty advance into town without arms, and the balance remain behind until they could ascertain Warren's movements; and if he declared martial law, all return, as in that case there can be no court held.

Plans for Attending Trial at Carthage.

Monday, 27.—Bedell and Miller reached Macedonia early, breakfasted with Wm. G. Perkins, changed horses and pursued their journey.

Elder A. W. Babbitt returned from Carthage and

reported that Backenstos had obtained a change of venue to Peoria to have his trial in five weeks. He is in the hands of the coroner who has permission either to take bail or select his own guard, at the expense of the state. The court adjourned until next May. The grand jury found bills of indictment against several of our brethren, none of the witnesses who had been burned out by the mob were admitted into the jury room, or allowed any opportunity to testify of their sufferings and so the farce ended with adding insult to injury. All Governor Ford, General John J. Hardin, Major Warren and Mr. Brayman's promise of administering justice and punishing the house-burners simply ends in compelling the sufferers to leave their destitute and helpless families and bear the loss of time and expense of spending several days at court to be told: 'You d—— Mormons shall not be admitted into the jury room to testify against the old citizens who have burned your houses, barns and grain, and turned your sick and helpless families out of doors to perish without food or shelter on the eve of winter.'*

Brigham Young's Reflections on the Procedure of State Officials.

Babbitt states that Dr. Abiather Williams has been before one of the judges of Iowa and sworn that the Twelve made bogus at his house in Iowa.

Charge that the Twelve Made Bogus.

They have taken out a United States writ and made a demand on the governor of this state for them, and the deputy marshal of Iowa (Silas Haight) is at Carthage with writs for all the Twelve. Warren is coming with the troops tomorrow, to aid the marshal in making the arrests. They had these writs with them on Saturday evening and this deputy was also with them, but when Elder Taylor made his speech it bluffed them off and they were afraid to serve them; since then Warren has sent to some of the eastern counties for volunteers to join his ranks.

*This cannot be supposed to be an actual speech from the grand jury, but it is implied as what their action inferred. Otherwise it would be a bald confession of what the old settlers had done.

The brethren in council expressed their feelings and all felt satisfied that the Lord would overrule this matter also for our good. The brethren of the Twelve all concluded to leave their homes tonight, so that if the *posse* come in during the night there will be no danger.

Defense by Prayer.

Tuesday, 28.—Ten a. m., President John Smith, Elders Newell K. Whitney, Joseph Young, Wm. W. Phelps, Orson Spencer, Joseph C. Kingsbury, and Lucien Woodworth met at Elder Taylor's and prayed.

The Twelve being apprehensive of treachery hid themselves until towards evening, when I received word from Major Warren that he wished to have an interview with us.

In the afternoon the Twelve held a consultation with Major Warren: I copy from Elder Clayton's Journal:

INTERVIEW WITH MAJOR WARREN

'Warren stated that when he came in with his troops on Saturday he had writs against the Twelve for 'treason' but he considered it unjust to serve them, he considered that if the Twelve were to be harassed with writs this people could not get away in the spring, that from Elder Taylor's remarks he understood we meant that no writs of any kind should be served in Nauvoo but intended to resist. This was explained by President Young who told Warren that we did not intend to resist. He also drew out of Warren that he was going to Springfield tomorrow and one part of his errand was to get his friends and relatives to come here and purchase some of our farms, for he was delighted with them. It appears that the Lord has softened his heart in answer to our prayers, for which we felt thankful.'

The following is extracted from George Miller's Journal:

REPORT OF BISHOP MILLER'S INTERVIEW WITH GOVERNOR FORD

'We (Miller and Bedell) traveled during last night, it was very dark, but by the light of the burning prairie we were enabled to proceed, we stopped fourteen miles from Springfield the latter part of the night and had a short nap while our breakfast was preparing, at the house of Mr. Bell all that we had conversed with during the past day disapproved of the course of the anti-Mormons in Hancock county.

We arrived at Springfield soon after breakfast and delivered the letter and affidavits to Governor Ford, whereupon he read several letters from individuals in Hancock county and others from different parts of the state insisting on the necessity of quartering a force in the county all winter sufficient to maintain law and order.

Mr. Bedell and I urged with the most earnest solicitude the disbanding of the forces stationed in our county, as we believed them to be a greater curse upon us than the real mob, as they have the effect to embolden rather than deter them [the mob] from committing acts of violence. Governor Ford seemed to be friendly, he deplored deeply the situation of the country and said, if he were to exert the executive influence in our behalf as ought to be done in justice to us, it would result in his overthrow and ours also. He also said, his private opinion was that the whole state were a mob and that he could not trust them to act in any emergency where we as a community were a party: Our interview lasted about three hours.

His final conclusion was to go to Hancock, and take a conciliatory course so as to prevent a collision until we should get away next spring: and when we should be gone bring them to justice and hang every devil of them [house-burners and murderers].

We conversed with several citizens who approved of the course of Backenstos in allaying the disturbances in Hancock, and reprobated with much severity the conduct of the house-burners, and expressed sorrow that Sheriff Backenstos did not kill five hundred of them.'

I copy from the *Nauvoo Neighbor*:

ADDENDUM

'*Hancock Circuit Court*:

This court commenced its session on Monday the 20th inst. at Carthage. Present:—the Hon. Norman H. Purple, Judge; M. Brayman, states attorney *protem;* J. B. Backenstos, sheriff; Henry W. Miller, coroner; and E. D. Head, clerk.

After the grand jury were called an affidavit was presented to the court sworn to by a man named Michael Barnes, Jr., one of the known murderers of Joseph and Hyrum Smith, and also one of the grain and house-burners, which affidavit set forth that the county commissioners were prejudiced against him, and selected the grand jury with a view of having him indicted, whereupon the court set aside the array of grand jurors. When Sheriff Backenstos addressed the court among other things he stated that he had been recognized by his Honor to appear and answer whatever indictment the grand jury might find against him, and hoped that the court would excuse him or any and all of his deputies in the selection of grand jurors. The sheriff and his deputies were then excused from performing that duty, whereupon the court appointed Thomas H. Owen and William D. Abernethy, elisors: objections being made to Wm. D. Abernethy the court set him aside and appointed Captain Morgan of Adams county in his place.

The grand jury, as selected by the elisors, were called and sworn on Thursday, and retired to investigate the crimes which have been committed in Hancock county unanswered and true presentments made. Little if anything was done on Thursday.

On Friday a rush was made by the mob party. Witnesses were brought in and examined before the grand jury and on Saturday about 11 o'clock the grand jury came into court and presented a bill against Sheriff Backenstos for the murder of Worrell, also several bills were found against the Latter-day Saints. In the meantime on Friday afternoon about forty witnesses appeared in Carthage to enter their complaints against the house-burners for arson, larceny and other crimes, knocking at the door of the grand jury room to be heard, and applying individually to some of the grand jurors with their complaints; but nothing could be done. There being a determination on the part of the grand jury that no evidence should be heard nor bills found against any of the anti-Mormons, whether for murder, burning houses or other outrages perpetrated against the saints; when the grand jury presented the bills the sheriff was placed in the hands of the coroner. The prosecuting attorney entered a *nolle prosequi* as to the bills found against the saints.

The court adjourned until Monday the 27th instant when Sheriff Backenstos was to be tried: the sheriff appeared ready with his counsel and desired an immediate trial, but by some judicial legerdemain the cause was sent to Peoria county to be tried at a special term of a circuit court, which is to come off in about five weeks. On motion of council, it was ordered that Sheriff Backenstos be admitted to bail in the sum of $3000, for his appearance at Peoria circuit court, which bail price has been executed and the sheriff is going about his business. The sheriff is in good health and spirits, and bears persecution with all commendable forbearance. His Honor Judge Purple visited Nauvoo on Saturday afternoon in company with M. Brayman, states attorney, Major Warren, and several gentlemen of the bar, and heard the Latter-day Saints tell their own story.'

Brigham Young Incognito.

Wednesday, 29.—I remained incognito at Brother A. P. Rockwood's, Brothers George A. Smith and Amasa M. Lyman came to see me; also Brothers Henry G. Sherwood and John S. Fullmer who had just returned from their mission westward; Bishop Whitney and Brother Wm. Clayton also came to see me. Elder Sherwood made a report of their late mission, which was very satisfactory and gave us some very interesting information concerning our best route to the west.

I extract the following from John S. Fullmer's account of his mission to Vermilion:

FULLMER'S MISSION TO JAMES EMMETT'S ENCAMPMENT

'*August* 13, 1845: In company with Elder Henry G. Sherwood and James Emmett, I started from Nauvoo on a mission to James Emmett's company, encamped on the Vermillion, a tributary of the upper Missouri river.

We had one horse each, which carried us and all our provisions and bedding for the journey. Our course lay about west-north-west as far as Raccoon Barracks on the Desmoines river, seventy-five miles from Nauvoo.

Finding that we were suspected of being Indian traders we took a northwest course for four days and then turned towards Council Bluffs. While here Emmett's conduct became almost insupportable, and he appeared unwilling to pilot us to his camp, but finding Elder Sherwood and myself determined to push on at all hazards, he concluded to accompany us. Much of the country over which we traveled was very dry and water scarce so that we suffered considerably.

Finding there was some disturbance between the Pottawattomie and Sioux Indians we took our course up the river several miles from it keeping a sharp lookout for war parties and Indian campfires.

September 13.—We arrived at Emmett's camp (625 miles from Raccoon Barracks) and met our brethren. On our way we encountered many deep streams, with miry bottoms, and steep banks, also some severe storms which caused some of the streams to overflow their banks.

Emmett's camp contained about one hundred souls and were in a better condition than we expected to find them, they were tolerably well provided with provisions but somewhat destitute of clothing.

They feasted us on samp and milk and urged us to eat heartily of dried buffalo meat saying it would hurt no one, but we found to the contrary to our inconvenience and sorrow, its tendency is to swell to its natural dimensions as soon as eaten and this caused us to feel something like a beer barrel in a state of fermentation which no hoops can control.

Notwithstanding our caution and prudence, Elder Sherwood and myself were taken with violent ague and fever and for a week or more were unable to attend to business during which time Emmett sought to get the advantage of us, by intimating to the company that something was wrong with us, that the Lord was displeased with us, etc. John S. Butler and a few others had spirit enough to understand the spirit of these charges. Upon Elder Sherwood's recovery he rebaptized John S. Butler and reordained him. I was then carried to the river and rebaptized for my health by Elder J. S. Butler and walked back and was so far recovered in a few days as to be able to attend council.

We explained our mission to the people, and gave what instruction we could, as to their temporal welfare. We learned that many of them had been led away by Emmett's misrepresentations and such were glad to receive our counsel. Emmett opposed us and finally claimed equal authority with us. This drew forth our papers which gave us the presidency, while Emmett was only our conductor to the camp. The saints went forth and were all rebaptized by Elder John S. Butler.

To obviate any trouble with Emmett after we should be gone, we appointed him the president of the camp, with instructions. They were to remain where they were, build cabins for the winter, procure what buffalo meat they could, by sending out organized parties; to conciliate the friendship of the Indians, and prepare themselves for any instructions they might receive from Nauvoo in the spring, anticipating a removal to some place then unknown. After we had finished our business we appointed John S. Butler to attend us on our return, as we were yet too feeble to risk such a trip alone, and also to be the bearer of such instructions to the camp as might be given at headquarters. Emmett desired this appointment; but his recent behavior as a guide disqualified him.

A few days before we left a circumstance happened which came near proving fatal to the whole camp. Owing to our feeble health, we decided that it was impracticable to return on horseback: Accordingly we solicited Emmett to buy our horses for the use of the camp; but he gave us no satisfaction. We next applied to Brewyer, a French trader who gave us forty-five dollars for our horses: Emmett refused to deliver up the horses from his corral, although they had been paid for, stating that he wanted them for buffalo horses. This so enraged Brewyer that he immediately declared hostilities against the whole camp. There had been above a thousand Indians camped close by during our stay, but they had just started to the north. Brewyer who had married two of Eagle's (the chief's) daughters sent for him to return with all his warriors, which summons they promptly obeyed. He now stimulated them by giving them whiskey and sold them guns and ammunition on credit, in case they would wipe out the entire camp. Eagle promised to do so.

Fortunately there lived there a halfbreed named Ongee, an educated and influential man to whom Eagle communicated his intentions. Ongee opposed them with all the art he was master of. One device was this: Ongee said they would select the least baby they could find and kill it and he would give each of them a petticoat and make squaws of all them: to Eagle he said he should walk over his dead body first: but if they would desist Brewyer should have the horses he had bought, which we also determined he should have if that should settle up the affair.

Just before the difficulty was settled, an Indian brave appeared followed by a number of others on horseback, before Butler's tent, where Emmett was sitting and leveled his rifle at him: but was instantly prevented from firing by Ongee who was consulting with him on the subject at the time.

Ongee's wife also used what influence, tears and entreaties she had with the several chiefs, and with Eagle also, who was the head chief.

In ordinary circumstances these efforts would have proven unavailing but the Lord had compassion on his people and turned the wrath of the Indians aside.

Ongee had contracted a friendship towards our people which he so manfully displayed in the deliverance of the camp. And wishing to show his respect to the two strangers who visited the camp with authority, he made a feast, the best his table could furnish; and there was no mean variety of vegetables, fowls and meat served up in tolerably good style, and in great profusion. Among the latter variety was to them the choicest of all dishes, especially when they wish to do honor to their guests: that was a fine fat dog of small size. Being a dish of honor it became indispensable that we should partake of it, which of course we did, but I will not say, 'with a will', but with apparent good grace. It was also a rule with them that each guest must clear his plate or dish, however much it might contain, or of whatever kind or variety, or pay a horse in default; but from some cause or other, perhaps through respect for our feeble health, this rule was waived, in our behalf, to our no small gratification, for we had been served enough to do us half a week.

As we had concluded to return by the river we made a canoe of a large cottonwood tree and fell in company with a couple of traders who were going down the river with some furs.

We left camp on the third of October, taking provisions as we supposed to last us to Council Bluffs, but being unacquainted with the channel, and the river being low, we found ourselves out of provisions before we had got half the distance. About this time as we were camping (for we had to lay to by nights) we saw a large flock of turkeys going to roost near by. One of the trappers, Elders Butler and Sherwood started out for a hunt by moonlight, one shot nine, one eleven, and the other thirteen times without so much as ruffling a feather. The Frenchman cursed his luck and swore his gun had a spell on it.

In the morning Butler went out and at the first shot brought down his turkey, this served us one day, and now we had eaten our last bite and no prospects of anything but salt and Missouri river water. We continued our route watching for game, hours passed and we saw none. After camping for the night, the Frenchman who had cursed his luck, shot a fine buck deer, which lasted us to Council Bluffs, eight days.

Twenty miles above St. Joseph, Missouri, John S. Butler left us and struck across the country for Nauvoo, not wishing to go through Missouri.

At St. Joseph we took a steamer for St. Louis. The rest of our journey to Nauvoo was pleasant as we performed it by steamboat. It is reported that the apostates are trying to get up an influence with the president of the United States to prevent the saints emigrating westward, and that they have written to the president informing him of the resolutions of the General Council [Council of Fifty] to move westward, and representing that Council guilty of treason, etc.' "

CHAPTER XXXV

IMPORTANT LETTERS, FRIENDLY AND OTHERWISE—SUMMARY OF RECENT PROCEDURE IN AND ABOUT NAUVOO WITH COMMENT OF AN EDITORIAL FROM THE TIMES AND SEASONS

"*Wednesday, October* 29, 1845. — Evening, the Twelve met at Elder Taylor's. The following letter was read:

WILD SCHEMES PROPOSED BY 'BACKWOODSMAN' OF PALMYRA, MISSOURI, FOR THE CONJOINT OCCUPANCY OF 'CALIFORNIA' BY THE LATTER-DAY SAINTS AND MIGRATING CITIZENS FROM THE UNITED STATES, BUT TO LIVE IN SEPARATE COMMUNITIES—FOUNDING OF INDEPENDENT GOVERNMENT—'THE UNITED STATES OF THE WEST'

'Palmyra, Mo., Oct. 22, 1845.

Sir: Owing to particular circumstances, I make free to address you, though a stranger, and I do it with plainness and candor because I think candor is always best, and may prevent difficulty hereafter. I see from the papers that you Mormons as a body intend to remove next spring to California, I myself am one of a very large number who have for some time been making arrangements for a settlement there with a view to the ultimate and not very remote establishment of an independent government not with a view to annexation to this government at all, but for that and Oregon to form the 'United States of the West'.

General Leslie Combs of Kentucky and several sons of Mr. Clay, are of the number, and the design will be carried out, and it is folly in you to think of settling there, unless it be on terms of compromise, that will insure the peaceable enjoyment of your peculiar organization. Experience ought to have taught you by this time, that it is impossible for you to exist as a community collected together in a city in the midst of another community, governed by other laws, than those you esteem paramount to all laws. You cannot be tolerated long, in that manner of living, anywhere; it is contrary to human nature and to the nature of things. The very principles you inculcate, that as the Lord's chosen people you have a right to everything you need, are incompatible with civil government, and the rights of others, and will not be tolerated, I again say, in any place long. If therefore you locate in California when it has already commenced settling, you interfere with the settlers already there, and you will create a prejudice against you, and so soon as enough others join them, which will soon be the case, you will again be expelled, this is inevitable.

I freely acknowledge, that although I have never taken any part against you, yet, I have felt a strong prejudice against your community because I believe that the natural tendency of your institutions is to make a part of your community bad citizens. No people have a right to interfere with your religious views, but if your religious views tend to disturb or resist the laws, or trespass on the rights or property of others, then the community have the right to interfere, and such is the case, too well established to be doubted by any person of intelligence, after making all proper allowance for false reports against you, of which I doubt not there are many. I think I understand you about as well as you do yourselves. There are three classes among you, the leaders, the fanatics and the dishonest part. The whole design of the leaders is to obtain power and wealth, the fanatics are conscientious and honest in their belief that they are doing God's service, but a large proportion have joined you, just to get the license and impunity which your numbers and strength give them, to pilfer and steal. This is the real state of the case, and it is useless to deny it. I do not charge all your denomination with the faults of a part, but I charge that the nature of your organization inclines the body to protect those committing depredations. I know there are good and bad in all communities, but the fear of the law with us, checks the vicious, with you they are emboldened, because they think your numbers will shield them from punishment, hence they indulge to a greater degree in bad practices, not because they are worse than others, but because of the nature of your social system. Whenever men have the strength, they tyrannize and even well disposed persons may be induced to connive at such practices by such arguments as these: 'The earth is the Lord's and the fulness thereof, and he giveth it to his chosen people, we are his chosen people, therefore we have a right to everything we need'.

The country around and on the Bay of San Francisco and in the valley of the Sacramento has already commenced settling, and in that part our party will settle and if you settle there you cannot stay there for the two communities cannot and will not live together, but if you are wise and will consent to the arrangement we propose, you will neither infringe upon, nor be infringed upon.

Mr. Hastings describes California as being naturally divided into two sections which he denominates the western and eastern sections. (I suppose you have read his book). In the eastern section there are no settlements, that section is watered by the great river, the Colorado of the west, which puts into the Gulf of California, or rather into the Bay of Colorado which is connected with the gulf; Hastings says that the harbor at the estuary of the river is very capacious and good, this affords a very elegible situation for an extensive settlement, and large city of commercial business; here, as there are no settlements, you can safely locate without infringing upon anybody and by a prudent arrangement being made beforehand the settlement may be permanent. I hope you may see the necessity of such arrangements, and avoid all occasion for such continual agitation and commotion as have been heretofore in connection with your community. I was often deeply pained on seeing your women and children, moving from Missouri through the snow and inclement weather, but notwithstanding these were my feelings, my acquaintances with the world and with human nature is such, that I know you cannot live in your organized embodied state in the midst of another community. We are willing to come to an understanding with you and reduce it to something like the form of a treaty that you shall settle at the mouth of the Colorado of the west and have assigned you a certain district of country, sufficiently large on that river, and in the eastern section exclusively and that we will not intrude on you within those bounds, provided you do not intrude on us, or on others without those bounds, and on the further condition that you join us and the original settlers to revolutionize the country from the dominion of Mexico and erect it into an independent government in connection with Oregon under the denomination of the United States of the West. Oregon and California including lower California will form sufficient territory to form twenty states.

Lower California would be forced into the confederation because it would be cut off from communication with any part of Mexico. It would evidently be your interest to join in the revolution because the Catholic religion being the established religion of the Mexican government, you could not be tolerated in the enjoyment of your views, but establish an independent government with full toleration of all religions, and then by a division of territorial limits as I propose, all difference will be prevented, for as we would have nothing to do with each other's religious views, and if each party were confined within its own limits we would know each other only as citizens. equally bound to protect each other and the country against all foreign invasion, and consequently to protect each other in the enjoyment of our respective peculiar views, then there need be no interruption of friendship and we could forget the past, as prejudice would die away. We could have an arrangement by which a due proportion of governmental patronage would be bestowed upon and enjoyed by each party, according to their relative strength as citizens, and to be wielded for the good of the whole republic and not for the exclusive benefit of either party so that as citizens of the republic we would all be precisely on the same footing and know no distinction any more, than if you had no separate social organization at all.

I submit this for your serious consideration and I request an early understanding and a positive statement in writing whether you abide by the proposed agreement or not, to be stated so definitely that it will admit of no misunderstanding.

You can write to this place addressed to 'Backwoodsman', distinctly defining your position in relation to this matter. We must know soon as measures have already been taken to send a messenger round by sea to put the settlers and the authorities on their guard so as to prevent your settling there, if you do not close with and come into this arrangement.

If you accede to this offer, I wish you to keep this letter and take it with you as evidence for it is written in good faith.

[Signed] BACKWOODSMAN.'

BRIGHAM YOUNG'S COMMENT ON THE ABOVE PROPOSITION

The above letter contains the lucubrations of some of Senator Benton's mobocratic associations who, no doubt, desire to make us a barrier between them and the Mexican government. His falsehoods in relation to our social system, and interference with the rights and property of others, are too absurd to be noticed, but I copy the letter as a specimen of numerous others which I am constantly receiving and which show the vanity, folly and corruption to which the human heart has been prostituted.

We had prayers as usual.

I received a letter from Elder Willard Snow, dated at Boston, October 12th.

Thursday, 30.—Bishop George Miller and E. A. Bedell returned from Springfield at 10 a. m. and reported their interview with Governor Ford and informed us that the governor would be at Carthage today, and intends to see to matters himself and try to preserve peace until we can get away.

ORSON SPENCER'S LETTER TO GOVERNOR FORD (BUT WITH SANCTION OF PRESIDENT YOUNG AND HIS COUNCIL); OVERZEALOUS AND UNNECESSARILY HARSH TOWARD GOVERNOR FORD

'Nauvoo, City of Joseph,
October 23d, 1845.

To His Excellency Thomas Ford.

Sir: The familiar interview I have had the honor to share with you, and the portentious state of affairs in Hancock county induce me to write you. Not however without the impulse of President Young and his council. After our interview in June last, in presence of ex-Governor Reynolds and Samuel Brannan, Esq., I ventured unequivocally to assure the authorities in this place that you, Sir, would never, no never, lend your official influence to oppress or exterminate this people.

This was the prominent and emphatic object of my mission to Springfield, and made uppermost in our whole discourse, as you well recollect. The result of that interview was perfectly satisfactory to me and in the strength of your generous, noble avowal never to walk in the steps of Governor Boggs of Missouri, and never to jeopardize the lives of our leaders under writs and arrests as the Smiths had been, I made the most sanguine assurances to the council of your high-minded and patriotic bearing towards this people. You also will recollect that I labored to apprise you that by misrepresentation, and falsehood they might endeavor to array the state executive against us, before a full disclosure of facts could come to your knowledge. And, Sir, contrary to all these assurances and pleasing ground of joyful hope, that the high authority of the state would never be wielded against law and order, and consequently against a long persecuted and unoffending people, we find your troops, yes, *your troops,* clothed with the power of your own signature, and all the potency your official name can impart, right in our midst! And for what purpose have they been here the last six weeks? Let the facts speak, and what have they done?

Have they stayed the progress of crime? and spliced up the fragments of law and order? Have they looked with paternal charity after the fugitives that have been compelled to run for their lives, before the lurid flames of the incendiary? Have they administered to the sick, or afforded them shelter, when precipitated on the cold ground of autumn to die, under the excitement of threats, conflagration, and disease? Have they ever shielded those that humanely volunteered to go twenty miles and under to gather up scattered fragments of property and crops and dispersed cattle, hogs, and fowls that the wretched survivors might be protected? Have they come valiantly forward to help the high sheriff of the county in his perilous and arduous struggle, to stop the marauders in their hellish deeds of robbery, midnight arson, and murder? To all these inquiries I answer before all men, and before the Judge of quick and dead solemnly—no! But, Sir, the doings of *your* troops have been not only the negative, but the very ingenious and hypocritical counterpart of all this. In proof of this, if proof were necessary (when scores of journals and visiting spectators to these awful scenes have testified through the land), I ask you Sir, where now is the head and right arm of the law in Hancock county. Sheriff Backenstos severed; yes, completely amputated and severed. And for what and by whom, has this noble-hearted patriot, dared to break the midnight arson and the infuriated cupidity of fiends, and roll back the crimson current of onward desolation, and pick up the routed sick, and quench the rolling conflagration? In God's name and with retributive solemnity I ask where is this noble right arm of the law? Severed indeed but not by the mob: no— would to God it had been for the honor of our state and nation, and for the blushing glory of humanity. But it was not so, this 'valiant arm of the law', with the firmness and patriotism of Jackson, Samuel Adams and Patrick Henry had won a victory that will ever laurel his brow, or the circle of such worthies as Washington, Marion, and Howard for all time to come, he had rescued the sick from the tusks of the wild boar, and boldly struck down the midnight arson, with the torch in his hand, and routed the whole host of inhuman fiends when your troops arrived. Horrible to say, *your* troops Sir, forthwith arrested the benefactor and released 'Barrabas'. The sick and robbed hung aside their harps and mournfully exclaimed: Has Governor Ford become another Boggs? *Your* troops Sir, were immediately a safe-guard and shield to robbers and murderers, who speedily returned to their houses in quiet, while the veteran of law and order, with the whole *posse* of government were exposed to warrants and recognized for manslaughter. In no instance has an anti-Mormon malefactor been arrested. *Posses* of state troops continually throng our city and the vicinity with attempts at all hours of the night and day to make arrests. The consequence is, that peaceable, unoffending citizens, and those who have yielded prompt obedience to the order of the sheriff in authority, are filled with fearful apprehension of being ferreted out to undergo the like fate of the assassinated Smiths, and of being tried under the impanelment of the most notorious mobocrat as elisor. *Your* troops Sir, in the estimation of the public (soon after they were disbanded) murdered the defenseless Smiths in prison and the state force is now a perfectly legalized mob-sweetened arsenic—honeyed poison. The mob arsenic and poison when unadulterated we are not afraid of. But when they are administered to us by your potent arm, with all the authority of government our condition is appalling, and desperatives must be used. The only difference between *your* troops and the mob is like the difference between a keg of arsenic and a keg of choice flour fatally flavored with arsenic. The mob we dare to resist where they are purely mob: but the state force, though equally fatal we are obliged to submit to because of legal authority.

And now will you in the eyes of a nation and world that is canvassing your acts by their domestic firesides and in the reading room, continue to legalize the doings of an armed soldiery, that are more obnoxious to law than the mob. Then, Sir, for humanity's sake, speedily withdraw these troops, and allow us peace long enough to attend to our sick and prepare for a general departure in the spring.

Do not force us to blood shedding or a fatal dispersion in the inclement winter, when multitudes of the poor must inevitably perish, and your own exalted name, sink beneath that of Nero, Boggs and Williams. Withdraw then these troops and lend not a listening ear to aspiring politicians, or the cupidity of the cruel, but, let the oppressed bless your name, for permission to breathe the air of liberty long enough to escape in a warm season to the caves of the mountains, or to some distant island of the Pacific.

With high hopes of your bold philanthropic determination, in behalf of the council,

Your friend and obedient servant,
[Signed] ORSON SPENCER.'

GOVERNOR FORD'S REPUDIATION OF SPENCER'S LETTER

'Springfield, Ill.,
October 30, 1845.

Sir: I return your letter of the 23d instant as not being respectful: as containing undeserved censure and as being in many particulars false and libellous: When were the Mormon people exterminated by my order?

It is acknowledged on all hands that there are some thieves in your city as in all other cities. These your people say, you have no power to restrain and punish for want of a city government and court. If you cannot restrain them I can and will. This is not extermination, or following in the footsteps of Governor Boggs.

I am very respectfully
Your obedient servant,
[Signed] THOMAS FORD.

Orson Spencer, Esq.
Nauvoo, Illinois.'

GOVERNOR FORD'S LETTER TO GENERAL (BISHOP) GEORGE MILLER: FURTHER REPUDIATION OF SPENCER'S LETTER

'Springfield, October 30th, 1845.

General George Miller,

Sir: The two letters mentioned by you as having been mailed at Quincy by yourself and Mr. Spencer, were received the next morning after you left. Mr. Spencer is a man for whom I have felt a warm personal esteem but really his letter is a most uncalled for philippic containing the most extraordinary charge, that I have exterminated your people. It is true that I have sent troops to Hancock to quell disturbance. They were few in number and not sufficient for the work of extermination if they had been ever so willing. They were successful in everything except in arresting the rioters. This the sheriff's *posse* could not do, because they had run away. It is true also that the sheriff had apparently restored order before the arrival of General Hardin, but that order was not likely to continue. The anti-Mormons had fled from the county and were successfully enlisting forces in the neighboring counties. You may not believe it, but I assure you they would have raised four or five thousand men. Nothing has saved an attack on your city, by that number, but the march of General Hardin by my order. You may have beaten the assailants and a great number of good honest citizens, the dupes of anti-Mormon falsehoods, would have lost their lives, this was not to be permitted, it would have disgraced any government which would have permitted it.

Although neither your people nor the anti-Mormons were in a temper to appreciate the favor, it was no less my duty and that of General Hardin to stop you on both sides, both parties were so enraged that they were, as they said, anxious to be permitted to fight, though they were much like the two men whose disposition to fight increased as they were forced asunder by their neighbors; and their ardor sensibly abated when the obstacle to a fight should be removed.

It is supposed by your people that if the sheriff had not been interfered with by the state militia he could have kept the peace and preserved order. There are many reasons why this is not so. First, the anti-Mormons would have removed out of the county. The people of the surrounding counties were afraid in that event, that your people would get the whole of Hancock, and would be as troublesome to them as you had been to the anties of Hancock. For which reason they were determined to drive you off before you got stronger. They reasoned thus: these people, the Mormons, have for some cause or other been in difficulty with all the people they ever lived amongst. They were obliged to leave Ohio and Missouri and they have not agreed better with their neighbors of Hancock. If these neighbors move away their places will be occupied by Mormons, and we, the surrounding counties, will be their nearest neighbors and may expect with certainty to have the like difficulties with them. They said therefore we will take time by the forelock and drive them away before they get stronger and more capable of resistance.

Secondly, although the sheriff had put down the house-burners, he had not suppressed stealing and murder on the other side. One man had certainly been murdered between Carthage and Appanoose, another was missing in Nauvoo under circumstances which leave no doubt but that he was murdered in your city and most probably by order of some of your principal men. At least such is and was the popular belief. Stolen property has been traced to your city during the ascendency of the sheriff, and the owners who came to search were ordered away and fled for fear of their lives. None of the stolen property could be found and in fact the owners did not dare to go to look for it without the aid and protection of the state troops. You may say this is the work of only a few and that your people are not responsible for the few in your city any more than in any other city; this may be true, but its truth does not do away with the necessity for a military force. I have long believed that there are those in Nauvoo who carry on a pretty large business in stealing. Some have alleged that this gang are patronized by the church authorities. This charge, however, I never believed and would not believe it unless proved by the most satisfactory evidence. Be this as it may, the thieves are there and they do steal as is the case in all other cities of ten or twelve thousand inhabitants.

I think it likely that some of your people who were burnt out by the mob, have persuaded themselves that they have a right to indemnify themselves for their losses by taking the property of their enemies. It is also probable that many persons unconnected with the Mormons go to Hancock to steal on their credit. Be this as it may, stealing as well as burning has been done and the stolen property has been traced to your city. Other thieves have been captured whilst taking it there: all these things took place during the ascendency of the sheriff and was kept secret from him, or if he knew of it he had no power to prevent it. Under these circumstances it was considered advisable by General Hardin, Judge Douglas, Major Warren and Mr. McDougall the attorney-general to leave one hundred men as a permanent guard. General Hardin informs me by letter that your high council expressed a wish that this force might be left. It was also requested, as he says, by all the well disposed persons in the county and particularly by the Reverend Mr. Owen who has never been a mobocrat. I cannot hear that this force has annoyed your people in any other way than once in a while to be marched into your city in quest of stolen property. This must be what Mr. Spencer calls extermination, for I have never heard that the troops have annoyed you in any other way. Mr. Spencer complains that the presence of these troops prevents the Mormons from going on peaceably and quietly in making their arrangements to remove in the spring. I am at a loss to perceive how, unless it be really true that a part of those arrangements are intended to consist in making reprisals upon the property of your enemies to pay you for your losses. This must not be attempted and will not be permitted. A demonstration of your intention to this effect will cause an attempt by the anti-Mormon party to drive you out before spring. If there are more of you in Nauvoo than can live this winter, good sense would say scatter until spring and be making something by labor to live upon. At all events until I am better informed I will hold it to be my duty to continue a military force in Hancock, both to protect you from the attacks of your enemies, as well as to prevent stealing whether by the anti-Mormons on your credit; by the Mormons themselves; by interlopers who come to your city as a place of refuge or by those who have been burnt out and who may be tempted to take this method of indemnifying themselves for their losses; and if the civil law is not strong enough martial law must be resorted to. Because if these things are not put an end to, the surrounding counties will take up the guard and you may be driven in despite of the state, in the dead of winter.

In the course of my official duties I have had a great deal of trouble with both parties in Hancock. I have been called to do both of you some good and some harm. The harm is always remembered: the good is either not understood or is forgotten. I do not expect any gratitude or applause from either party; and you may be sure that the last things that I will think possible to be accomplished will be to please either you or the anti-Mormons, by any moderate conduct which, by taking the law for guide, repudiates the wildness and infatuation of both parties.

My health is bad or I should have started for Hancock on Wednesday morning last to see for myself what the state of things really are.

I am most respectfully your
obedient servant,
[Signed] THOMAS FORD.'

Friday, 31.—At the Tithing Office, writing a letter to Brother V. Shurtliff to receive tithing in the east, and donations to help away the poor.

P. M., council met at Elder Taylor's. We wrote the following to Bishop John B. Purcell of Cincinnati:—

LETTER TO REV. BISHOP PURCELL, ET AL, CINCINNATI

'City of Nauvoo, October 31, 1845.

To Reverend Bishop Purcell, and all Other Authorities of the Catholic Church—Greeting:

The Church of Jesus Christ of Latter-day Saints hereby take opportunity to inform you by letter and by our confidential messenger, Almon W. Babbit, Esq., that it is our fixed purpose to remove hence early next spring.

The hand of oppression and the lacerations of the tongue of calumny have compelled us to the determination to dispose of numerous lots, tenements, etc., in this city together with our public buildings, for instance our Temple, the Nauvoo House, the Academy, Seventies' Hall, Concert Hall, and other buildings, also our farms and other possessions in Hancock county, even all our effects and temporal interests. The individual members of our community have also determined *en masse* to do the same with their effects and have empowered agents to sell. The bearer, Mr. Babbitt, is empowered to represent as our authorized agent all our said property and interest in this city and county. Through the suggestion of Judge Ralston of Quincy and other friends to your faith we are disposed to invite the authorities of your church, either personally or by authorized agents, to visit our city that we may negotiate with them, at as early a period as possible, the sale of our property. We shall forbear any extensive sales to other communities until we learn your answer to this our epistle. The bearer may be relied upon as our confidential and highly esteemed brother who will furnish you any information preparatory to the proposed negotiation and sale.

With sentiments of high consideration, I have the honor to subscribe myself in behalf of the Council of the Church, your friend and obedient servant,

[Signed] W. RICHARDS, Clerk.'

I received a long epistle from Elder Woodruff dated Liverpool, October 1st, relative to the course pursued by Elder Reuben Hedlock and Thomas Ward.

I also received the following:

LETTER OF ORSON PRATT TO BRIGHAM YOUNG ON THE MATTER OF PURCHASING ARMS AND SELLING NAUVOO PROPERTY

'New York, October 31, 1845.

President Brigham Young and Council.

Dear Brethren:

I received a communication relative to obtaining six-barreled pistols for self-defense, (while journeying in western wilds). I immediately took active measures to obtain them and the present prospect is good. I think I shall obtain several hundred dollars for that purpose. The six-inch pistols can be obtained at retail for twelve dollars. The wholesale price is ten dollars but by agreeing to take some thirty or forty they can be obtained at nine and one-half dollars. As soon as I have raised the most of the funds that can be raised I shall make the purchase. I now have between one and two hundred dollars tithing subject to your order: tithing comes in very slowly since the exertions that were made for the canvass. The recent troubles in the west have put new life and zeal into the saints in the east, they are very anxious to assist all they can, and to gather westward.

The celebrated Robert Owen* has been to visit me several times. I have been endeavoring to persuade him to rent our houses and lands in Illinois, and he has quite a notion of so doing. He will let me know more about it in a few days: he thinks of locating the Owenites at Nauvoo.

Brother Brannan thinks it will be difficult to take his printing establishment and go to California unless he goes away dishonorably without paying debts. If we could sell he could pay his debts.

He is very anxious to go, and is willing to do anything he is counseled. He says that the church perhaps would consider it wisdom to buy his establishment and still keep up the paper.

I have not had an opportunity of visiting Philadelphia as yet, perhaps you may consider it wisdom to send two faithful elders to preside: one in Philadelphia, another in Boston.

Brother Willard Snow's pleadings to go home are almost irresistible, I believe that I will give him permission. I hope that it will meet with your approbation for I wish to do right. Since I heard of your

*This was the celebrated English communist seeking to establish his system in the United States.

persecutions and resolutions to leave Nauvoo in the spring I can hardly contain myself. I want to fly upon the wings of the wind and be with you, where you go, I want to go, where you stop, I want to stop. Brethren, give me counsel on this matter. Can I go with you in the spring? If so is it my privilege to return this fall? Count me worthy to receive counsel on these important items. Should my feelings get the upper hand of me and I start forthwith for Nauvoo I hope you will forgive me. I am willing to abide your counsel in all things.

I remain, dear brethren, your everlasting friend and fellow laborer,

[Signed] ORSON PRATT.'

Sundry Letters.

I received a letter from Charles A. Lovell, Mass., October 20th recommending us as a community to remove to California. Another from Thomas J. Farnhaus, New York, October 20th, on the same subject. Also one from Edward Warren, Boston, October 22nd portraying the Bay of San Francisco and country round as one well adapted for our location in the west.

Saturday, November 1, 1845.—I paid William Clayton one hundred and fifty dollars to purchase instruments for the brass band.

I met in council with the Twelve and Presiding Bishop, at 10 a. m.

The following editorial appeared in the *Times and Seasons*:

GREAT PERSECUTION OF THE CHURCH OF JESUS CHRIST OF LATTER-DAY SAINTS IN ILLINOIS

Summary of Persecutions up to Date.

'After we had begun to realize the abundance of one of the most fruitful seasons known for a long time, and while many hundreds of saints were laboring with excessive, and unwearied diligence to finish the Temple and rear the Nauvoo House, suddenly in the forepart of September, the mob commenced burning the houses and grain of the saints in the south part of Hancock county. Though efforts were made by the sheriff to stay the torch of the incendiary and parry off the deluge of arson, still a 'fire and sword' party continued the work of destruction for about a week, laying in ashes nearly two hundred buildings and much grain.

Nor is this all: as it was in the sickly season, many feeble persons, thrown out into the scorching rays of the sun, or wet with the dampening dews of the evening, died, being persecuted to death in a Christian land of law and order; and while they are fleeing and dying, the mob, embracing doctors, lawyers, statesmen, Christians of various denominations, with the military from colonels down, were busily engaged in filching or plundering, taking furniture, cattle and grain. In the midst of this horrid revelry, having failed to procure aid among the 'old citizens', the sheriff summoned a sufficient *posse* to stay the 'fire shower of ruin', but not until some of the offenders had paid for the aggression with their lives.

This, however, was not the end of the matter. Satan sits in the hearts of the people to rule for evil, and the surrounding counties began to fear that law, religion, and equal rights, in the hands of the Latter-day Saints, would feel after iniquity or terrify their neighbors to larger acts of 'reserved rights', and so they began to open a larger field of woe. To cut this matter short they urged the necessity (to stop the effusion of blood), to expel the church, or as they call them, the Mormons, from the United States, 'peaceably if they could, and forcibly if they must', unless they would transport themselves by next spring. Taking into consideration the great value of life, and the blessings of peace, a proposition upon certain specified conditions was made to a committee of Quincy, and which it was supposed from the actions of conventions was accepted. But we are sorry to say, that the continued depredations of the mob and the acts of a few individuals, have greatly lessened the confidence of every friend of law, honor and humanity, in everything promised by the committees and conventions, though we have already made great advances towards outfitting for a move next spring.

A few troops stationed in the county, have not entirely kept the mob at bay: several buildings have been burned in the month of October.

We shall, however, make every exertion on our part, as we have always done, to preserve the law and our engagements sacred, and leave the event with God, for he is sure.

It may not be amiss to say, that the continued abuses, persecutions, murders, and robberies practiced upon us by a horde of land pirates with impunity in a Christian republic, and land of liberty, (while the institutions of justice, have either been too weak to afford us protection or redress, or else they too have been a little remiss) have brought us to the solemn conclusion that our exit from the United States is the only alternative by which we can enjoy our share of the elements which our heavenly Father created free for all.

We can then shake the dust from our garments, suffering wrong rather than do wrong, leaving this nation alone in her glory, while the residue of the world, points the finger of scorn, till the indignation and consumption decreed, make a full end.

In our patience we wil possess our souls and work out a more exceeding and eternal weight of glory, preparing, by withdrawing the power and priesthood from the Gentiles, for the great consolation of Israel, when the wilderness shall blossom as the rose, and Babylon fall like a millstone cast into the sea. The just shall live by faith; but the folly of fools will perish with their bodies of corruption: then shall the righteous shine: Amen.' "

CHAPTER XXXVI

MURDERS BY MOBS CONTINUED—CONFESSION OF DR. ROBERT D. FOSTER—FAREWELL OF ORSON PRATT TO EASTERN SAINTS — WESTWARD BY SHIPPING — THE DURFEE MURDER CASE

"*Sunday, November* 2, 1845.—The first Emigration Company [for the west] organized by appointing captains of tens.

The second quorum of seventies held a festival at the Seventies Hall.

Monday, 3.—Brother Heber C. Kimball and I visited Dr. Willard Richards who was sick.

Evening, council met at Elder John Taylor's, Brothers Sherwood, Fullmer and Butler made a further report of the country west.

Abraham C. Hodge stated that he had some conversation with Robert D. Foster, who told him his feelings on the subject of Mormonism. He said, 'Hodge, you are going to the west—I wish I was going among you, but it can't be so, I am the most miserable wretch that the sun shines upon. If I could recall eighteen months of my life I would be willing to sacrifice everything I have upon earth, my wife and child not excepted. I did love Joseph Smith more than any man that ever lived, if I had been present I would have stood between him and death.' Hodge inquired, 'Why did you do as you have done? You were accessory to his murder.' He replied: 'I know that, and I have not seen one moment's peace since that time. I know that Mormonism is true, and the thought of meeting (Joseph and Hyrum) at the bar of God is more awful to me than anything else.'

Self-report of Dr. Robert D. Foster.

Organization of Westbound Company No. 1.

Tuesday, 4.—Emigrating Company No. 1 met in the Temple, eighteen companies of ten families each were filled up and Parley P. Pratt and Amasa Lyman appointed captains over the first and second hundreds.

At 5 p. m., council met for prayers at the Historian's Office, (Dr. Richards').

Joshua Smith died. He was born in Nobleborough, Kennebeck (now Lincoln) county, Maine, February 13th, 1788. He was the son of Stephen and Miriam, and the eldest of four pair of twins, who lived to be men except one. Joshua was baptized at Kirtland, by John Smith in June, 1836. He was poisoned by the militia while at Carthage where he was summoned to attend court; the militia searched for him and found a knife under his arm and arrested him, and while under arrest they gave him dinner, where no doubt he received the poison, he soon became very thirsty, and vomiting followed until death. He said, he had been poisoned by the militia and at a post mortem examination by Drs. John M. Bernhisel, Lucius P. Sanger and Jesse Brailey the suspicion was confirmed; he was a good man and his name will be registered among those who wear a martyr's crown.

Joshua Smith Died—Poisoned by Carthage Militia.

He was second counselor to Samuel Williams, president of the elders' quorum, at the time of his death.

Miscellaneous Items.

Wednesday, 5.—Attended council with the Twelve to direct the arrangement of the seats in the Temple.

Afternoon, in council at the Historian's Office.

Thursday, 6.—4 p. m., attended council and prayer meeting with the Twelve.

Friday, 7. — 4 p. m., attended council with the Twelve.

Saturday, 8.—Revising history in company with Brothers Heber C. Kimball, Willard Richards and George A. Smith till 4 p. m. Afterwards the Twelve and others met for council and prayer.

FAREWELL MESSAGE OF ORSON PRATT

'*To the Saints of the Eastern and Middle States, Greeting*:

Dear Brethren: The time is at hand for me to take a long and lasting farewell to these eastern countries, being included with my family, among the tens of thousands of American citizens who have the choice of death or banishment beyond the Rocky Mountains. I have preferred the latter. It is with the greatest of joy that I forsake this republic; and all the saints have abundant reasons to rejoice that they are counted worthy to be cast out as exiles from this wicked nation; for we have received nothing but one continual scene of the most horrid and unrelenting persecutions at their hands for the last sixteen years. If our heavenly Father will preserve us, and deliver us out of the hands of the bloodthirsty Christians of these United States and not suffer any more of us to be martyred to gratify their holy piety, I for one shall be very thankful. Perhaps we may have to suffer much in the land of our exile, but our sufferings will be from another cause—there will be no Christian bandit to afflict us all the day long—no holy pious priests to murder us by scores—no editors to urge on house-burning, devastation and death. If we die in the dens and caves of the Rocky Mountains, we shall die where freedom reigns triumphantly. Liberty in a solitary place, and in a desert, is far more preferable than martyrdom in these pious states.

Perhaps the rich may ask, how they are to dispose of their farms and houses so as to get to Nauvoo this winter and be ready to start early in the spring with the great company?—In reply to this inquiry, we observe that they can do it if they only have a disposition. Many of them might have disposed of their property years ago, but have been holding on to the same, for the purpose of getting a greater price, or for fear of losing their property by the ravages of mobs, if they gathered with the saints; thus they have not been willing to readily comply with the great commandment of God, concerning the gathering, and thus they are deprived of the privilege of sacrificing their property by being driven from the same: but still they can reprieve themselves in some measure, by selling immediately at all hazards, although they should not get one third of its real value.

The Lord requires a sacrifice, and he that is not willing, will fail of the blessing. Brethren now is the time for you to be up and doing, for unless you can get to Nauvoo this winter, it will be entirely needless for you to go in the spring, for you could not arrive in time to leave with the saints.

We would say to the poor in the east, that it will be of no use for them to go to Nauvoo, unless they have means sufficient to purchase horses, wagons, tents, etc., for it will be in vain for them to think of starting for the Rocky Mountains without these things; and the church at Nauvoo will have as much as they can possibly do to provide these things for the poor of that place. If they should have any

Mutual Helpfulness of Rich and Poor.

means left after having provided for their own poor, they would of course be willing to help the poor abroad; the rich in the branches abroad should help the poor to horses, wagons, etc.; and those who cannot possibly obtain these things, must raise means to pay their passage by sea around Cape Horn to the western coast of North America. Indeed our expenses by sea from here to the place of our destination would be but a trifle more, than our expenses from here to Nauvoo. Hence all the poor that can raise funds sufficient to go to Nauvoo, can with a little exertion, obtain sufficient to go by Cape Horn.

Company *via* Sea Provided.

Those who go by sea, can carry with them many articles which it would be impossible to carry over the mountains. Elder Samuel Brannan has been counseled to go by sea. He will sail about the middle of January. Those who wish to accompany him are requested to give him their names as early as possible. If one hundred and fifty or two hundred passengers can be obtained, he can venture to charter a vessel for them, and thus their fare will be scarcely nothing. The voyage can be performed in four or five months.

Brethren awake!—be determined to get out from this evil nation next spring. We do not want the saints to be left in the United States after that time. Let every branch in the east, west, north, and south, be determined to flee out of Babylon, either by land or by sea, as soon as then. Judgment is at the door; and it will be easier to go now, than to wait until it comes.

Those who go by sea, should go as soon as possible, as it will be almost impossible to double Cape Horn in our summer months; as the seasons there are directly the opposite of ours. Their coldest months are in July, and August, their warmest months in January and February. There is too much ice in our summer months to admit a safe passage round the Cape.

Elder Samuel Brannan Appointed to Head Sea-bound Company.

Elder Samuel Brannan is hereby appointed to preside over, and take charge of the company that go by sea; and all who go with him will be required to give strict heed to his instruction and counsel. He will point out to you the necessary articles to be taken, whether for food or for raiment, together with farming utensils, mechanical instruments, and all kinds of garden seeds, seeds of various kinds of fruits, etc., etc. Several have already given their names to go with him, and I think he will soon raise a company as large as can conveniently go in one vessel.

Brethren, if you all want to go, charter half a dozen or a dozen vessels, and fill each with passengers, and the fare among so many will be but a trifle. The most of those, however, who can get teams this winter, had better go by land.

Do not be fainthearted nor slothful, but be courageous and diligent, prayerful and faithful, and you can accomplish almost anything that you undertake. What great and good work cannot the saints do, if they take hold of it with energy and ambition?

Admonition.

We can do almost anything, for our Father in heaven will strengthen us, if we strengthen ourselves. He will work according to our faith. If we say we cannot go, God will not help us; but if we say, in the name of the Lord we will go! and set ourselves about it, he will help us. The saints must do greater things than these, before many years pass away, and now is the time to try your faith and ambition, and thus by experience be prepared for greater achievements.

Warning Against Apostate Prowling Wolves.

Brother Snow and myself are called upon to leave you, to visit our families and friends in the west. After our departure apostates will prowl around the branches here in the east, seeking to devour. They will present themselves before you as very pious and holy beings, mourning over the corruptions of the church while the Twelve Apostles of the Lamb will be represented as devils incarnate. But dear brethren, our works you have seen, and our diligence and anxiety for your salvation, you are not ignorant of. We have labored with all patience and diligence with you. We have prayed with you, and taught and instructed, and counseled you according as the Lord has given us wisdom—And I hereby testify unto you in the name of the Lord God of Joseph, that, if after all the instruction you have received, you suffer yourselves to be influenced and led away by apostates, such as [Sidney] Rigdon, [George J.] Adams, William Smith, and others who have been legally cut off from the church—your sins shall be upon your own heads—our garments are clean. Remember these words, and let nothing move you. Let no apostates be in the least welcome under your roof. Be ashamed and blush at the very idea of attending one of their wicked meetings. Despise their principles, and all their apostate doings, as you would the very gates of hell. Touch not—taste not, and handle not any of their accursed doctrines; for they shall utterly perish, and all that follow them. The day shall come when they shall weep and howl for vexation of spirit, for their miseries shall come upon them; and all shall know and discern between the righteous and the wicked—between saints and apostates.

When the saints get this message, I shall probably be on my way to the west. Should they wish to forward me letters or assistance, they can direct the same to Nauvoo. I hereby tender my thanks to the saints for such assistance as they have rendered me. I have received in the neighborhood of twenty dollars in fulfillment of my dream. Those who have responded to the same, have the warmest gratitude of my heart. I have just returned from a tour of about eight hundred miles, all at my own expense. And I assure you dear brethren, that it is a difficult matter for the servants of God to spend all their time in the ministry unless the saints uphold their hands. I should have probably visited more branches of the church in the east if I had been in the possession of sufficient funds to have paid my traveling expenses. I have no fault to find. The saints in the east have done well in the main; for they have responded to the call of our brethren in the west, in relation to tithing, tabernacle, etc.; and they shall in no wise lose their reward. We love the saints, both in the east and in the west, and it grieves our hearts that circumstances should force any of you to tarry in the states after next spring. If it were in our power, our hearts would leap for joy at the prospect of taking you all with us: and thus would the fulness of the gospel be fully brought from among the Gentiles.

Brethren and sisters, remember the *Book of Mormon,* the *Book of Covenants,* and the instructions, teachings, and counsels, which the faithful servants have given you from time to time. Be strictly virtuous, pure, upright, and honest in all things; and comply faithfully with the instructions upon these points, as pointed out in my message. You can now see the consequences attending those who have violated those virtuous principles. They have apostatized, and become the bitterest enemies of the servants of God: thus fulfilling the words of Jesus—'He that looketh on a woman to lust after her, or if anyone commit adultery in their hearts, they shall not have the spirit, but shall deny the faith.'*

It is a fearful thing to violate the commandments of God, and depart from the strict laws which he has given concerning these matters. There is a right way, and there are many wrong ways; and blessed is that person who findeth the right way, and walketh therein even unto the end, for they shall be crowned with great glory, and of the increase of their kingdom, there shall be no end. Such shall be honored among the sons and daughters of God, while the corrupt, the whoremongers, and the vile seducer, shall be abased, where there is wailing, and wretchedness indescribable.

Who then, for a moment's gratification, will sacrifice an eternal kingdom, where pure virtue, and love, and affection shall beam forth like the rays of the morning from every joyful countenance?

Apostrophy to Virtue.

O Virtue! How amiable thou art! Strength and beauty, and excellency, and dignity, and honor, and immortality, are thine offspring—Gentle peace, pure affection, unbounded love, and omnipotent power, shall reign triumphantly in thy habitations forevermore!

Commends the Saints to the Lord.

And now I must say to the saints in the eastern countries farewell. Farewell till we meet on distant lands. May our kind Father hasten that time. Yea, O Lord God, remember these my brethren and sisters, and save them. Behold O Lord, they have received thy servants, and the message thou

**Book of Covenants*, p. 204, 5th paragraph, stereotyped [Nauvoo] edition; current—1921—edition, sec. xlii:23

gavest them to declare. They have fed us and clothed us; they have given their tithes for the building of thy Temple, and now, O Father, reject not their offerings, neither cast away thy people who are called by thy name. Forgive their sins, and pity them even as a Father pitieth his own children. Behold O Lord, the desire of this thy people to go forth from among the Gentiles, who have sorely persecuted them all the day long. But thy people are poor. Wilt thou not help them? Wilt thou not deliver them out of the hands of all their enemies who hate them? And when thou shalt visit this nation in sore judgment, according to that which thou hast spoken, destroy not thy people who are poor, with the wicked; but hide them with thine own hand, and shield them from judgment.

Hear the prayer of thy servant kind Father, in behalf of his brethren, over whom he has presided, and whom he is now about to leave. For I ask thee for all these things, in the name of thy Son. Amen.

And again, with my heart full of blessings I say farewell.

[Signed] ORSON PRATT.

City of New York, Nov. 8, 1845.'

Sunday, 9.—No public meeting; the floor of the first story in the Temple having been taken up to put in new timbers, the sleepers which were put in at the commencement of the Temple having become rotten.

The brethren belonging to the different Emigrating Companies assembled in and around the Temple, and received instruction concerning emigration.

Eleven a. m., I addressed the saints.

Noon, I met with the captains of companies.

Two p. m., I met with Emigrating Company No. 1.

Suggested Purchase of Copyright of "Mother Smith's History."

Monday, 10.—I spent the day with Elders Heber C. Kimball, Willard Richards and George A. Smith revising Church History; several of the Twelve and others called in the afternoon; we consulted on the subject of purchasing the copyright of Mother Smith's *History;* and concluded to settle with Brother Howard Coray* for his labor in compiling the same.

*The work of compilation for Mother Lucy Smith was really done by his wife, Sister M. J. Coray, who was also her amanuensis throughout. The work was finally published under the direction of President Joseph F. Smith in Salt Lake City, Utah, October, 1901. It was revised by Elders George A. Smith and Elias Smith, close relatives of the author. See title page, etc.

Tuesday, 11.—Forenoon, Elders Willard Richards and George A. Smith revising history.

Afternoon, Elder Kimball and I joined them, and assisted in revising history.

Four p. m., the Twelve met, Elder Parley P. Pratt read an epistle to the churches which he had been instructed to write.

After council, accompanied by Brothers Heber C. Kimball and Levi Richards, I visited and administered to the sick.

Wednesday, 12.—Council met in the afternoon for prayer. A conference was held at New York City:

New York Conference

'The Church of Jesus Christ of Latter-day Saints met pursuant to appointment on the evening of the 12th of November at the American Hall. Many of the brethren were present from Long Island, Connecticut, and New Jersey.

On motion, Elder Orson Pratt was called to the chair, and G. T. Newell, secretary.

After prayer and a dedication of the assembly to God by the president, and a song of Zion by the whole assembly, the president arose and laid before the conference the present condition of the saints, and the necessity of all removing to the west. He exhorted them to a union of action for the benefit of the poor, that they might not be left behind. That as long as the church remained among the Gentiles, the fulness of the gospel could not be [said to have been] taken from them, and the *Book of Mormon* be fulfilled.

Elder Brannan then arose and presented the following Preamble and Resolutions, which were unanimously adopted by the whole assembly without a dissenting voice.

ELDER BRANNAN'S RESOLUTIONS

'*Whereas,* we as a people have sought to obey the great commandment of the dispensation of the fulness of times, by gathering ourselves together; and as often as we have done so, we have been sorely persecuted by the Protestant Christian Churches, our houses burned, and we disinherited of our possessions, and driven forth upon the charity of a cold-hearted world, to seek protection and sustenance for ourselves and families.

And *Whereas:*—Inasmuch as the people and authorities of the United States have sanctioned such proceedings, without manifesting any disposition to sustain us in our constitutional rights, but have rejected our many petitions to judges, governors, and presidents for the last twelve years, having hardened their hearts like Pharaoh of old, against the cries of the fatherless and the widow—That we now cease our cries, wipe away our tears, and prepare ourselves to 'enter into our chambers and shut our doors about us for a little season until the indignation be overpast.' Therefore,

'*Resolved,* That we hail with joy the Proclamation of our brethren from the City of Joseph [i. e. Nauvoo] to make preparations for our immediate departure, and give thanks and praise to our heavenly Father that the day of our deliverance is so near at hand.

'*Resolved,* That we look upon the Proclamation sent forth and published in the *Warsaw Signal* by our former brother, William Smith, as being actuated by purely selfish motives alone, for his own personal emolument and aggrandizement, at the sacrifice of the lives of his best friends, and the defamation of the character of the whole church; unchristianlike, even if true, because it brings persecution and affliction upon the innocent.

'*Resolved,* That we most heartily sanction the proceedings of the council and church at Nauvoo, in his excommunication; and that suffering innocence in this city by his hands, has demanded it long since. And in it we believe that prayers of the fatherless and widow have been answered. And further

'*Resolved,* That we caution all the honest in heart among the saints, where he has not visited in the east and elsewhere, that have not had an opportunity of proving his Apostleship as we have, to beware how they receive him into their houses, or bid him Godspeed, lest they bring condemnation upon themselves ignorantly.

'*Resolved,* That during the mission and ministry of our brethren, the Twelve, among us, since the absence of William Smith, their conduct has been of the most exemplary character, both in practice and precept; which we are sorry we are not able to say of our former Brother William Smith. And

'*Resolved,* That we advise him if he wishes to keep himself from trouble, shame, and disgrace—that if he has any feeling for the character of his family, and his martyred brethren, that he stay where he is, or go where he is not known. For we, the church in New York, have no desire to see him, unless he repent speedily, and go about making restitution for lifting his hand against the church and kingdom of God to destroy it.

'*Resolved,* That the church in this city move, one and all, west of the Rocky Mountains between this and next season, either by land or water; and that we most earnestly pray all our brethren in the eastern country to join with us in this determination, and carry it out effectually, to the delivery of the people of God from the daughters of Babylon, and not one left behind.

'*Resolved,* That there are no apologies required of those who do not go, but old age, sickness, infirmities, and poverty; 'For he that will not forsake father and mother, houses and lands, wives and children for me, and my name's sake, is not worthy of me'.'

Elder Brannan laid before the congregation his instructions from the authorities of the church directing him to go by water, and called upon all who wanted to accompany him, to come forward at the close of the meeting and put down their names. The conference was then dismissed by a benediction from the president.

[Signed] ORSON PRATT, President.

G. T. Newell, Secretary.'

Wednesday 12 (*continued*).—Brother Rice's farm-house on Camp Creek was burned by about thirty men of the mob who swore they were Governor Ford's troops, which was probably false, John M. Finch and Rollison were with them.

Action in Illinois.

Thursday, 13.—Forenoon, I rode out to the prairie with Dr. Richards, my brothers John and Joseph, E. T. Benson and G. D. Grant, and dined at Brother Chamberlain's.

4 p. m., attended council with the Twelve. It was decided that Mother Lucy Smith should be furnished with food, clothing, and wood for the winter.

We prayed as usual.

Dr. Richards and I visited Stephen Markham who was cutting and sawing wagon spokes, at his place in the woods. We helped him to cut and saw a while, and then took his rifle and shot at a mark, with my second shot I cut the pin that fastened the two-inch paper mark to a tree.

Brigham Young's Marksmanship.

I wrote a lengthy communication to Noah Rogers giving him the general items of church news since he left on his mission to the Pacific Islands.

Friday, 14.—Evening, the Twelve met at Dr. Richards'. James H. Flanigan reports:

A MISSIONARY'S REPORT

'Nauvoo, Illinois, Nov. 14, 1845.

Having just returned from a mission eastward, appointed by the spring conference of 1843; according to order established by the Church of Christ, that elders should report their stewardship; I thought, although I was among the least, yet I would not be among the last in confessing my ignorance, and stating unequivocally, that I am but an unprofitable servant.

During my mission, which was in the fall and spring of '43 and '44, in the states of New Jersey and Maryland, in company with my fellow laborer, S. H. Rogers, we endeavored, according to our ability, and the trust reposed in us, to help rear up the standard of Latter-day glory, and to facilitate the great and momentous work of God in these last days.

I will also say, that although we were weak, yet we were made strong by the hand of the mighty God of Jacob! And although we were little, yet we confounded the great; and although our wisdom consisted in the simplicity of Christ's gospel, yet the wisdom of man was confounded before our eyes.

Many honorable men were enamoured of the truth, and many honorable men instructed in the plan of salvation. We baptized thirty-five or forty for the remission of their sins, and organized one branch of twenty-five or thirty members in Maryland; and thus the words of God were fulfilled, that 'the weak should confound the wisdom of the mighty, and the poor among men rejoice, the meek increase their joy in the Lord, those who erred learn doctrine,' etc., etc. Thus was the mission, and thus it ended.

May God bless his people, redeem and save Israel, and hasten his work in its time.

JAMES H. FLANIGAN.'

Saturday, 15.—Elders Heber C. Kimball, Willard Richards, and I visited through the city.

Evening, the Twelve met for prayer.

DEATH OF EDMUND DURFEE—SHOT BY A MOB OF HOUSE-BURNERS

A considerable party of the mob set fire to a stack of straw near Solomon Hancock's barn and concealed themselves. Hancock and others went out to put out the fire which was the only way to save the building, when they were fired upon by the burners, and Elder Edmund Durfee killed on the spot, many balls flew around the rest of the brethren, but none of the rest were hurt.*

Elder Edmund Durfee was born in Rhode Island, October 3, 1788. He was baptized by Elder Simeon Carter in Ruggles township, Ashland county, Ohio, May, 1831. (He had been a Methodist). He was ordained an elder by Simeon Carter and Solomon Han-

*See footnote p. 145 this volume.

cock; and accompanied Elder Brackenbury on a mission to Chautauqua county, New York, in December, 1831.

Elder Joseph B. Brackenbury died at Pomfret from the effects of poison secretly administered to him by opposers, who afterwards boasted that Mormon elders had not faith enough to stand poison. The night after his burial there was a heavy snowstorm, about half past eleven o'clock Joel H. Johnson dreamed that some persons were digging up Brother Brackenbury's body, and was so exercised about it that he called up some of the brethren and went to the spot, about one mile distant, and found a party of doctors at work, who had nearly cleared the grave of earth; the men fled with utmost precipitation. David Johnson took after the largest one who was caught and bound over in one thousand dollar bonds for his appearance at court, but was never tried.

Case of Poison by Mob.

Body-Snatching.

DURFEE'S BIOGRAPHICAL NOTE

In the spring of 1832, Elder Durfee with nine others went up to Jackson county to put in grain, and build houses, and returned the same season.

He took another mission to the state of New York in the fall. In May, 1833, he moved to Kirtland. He was one of the twenty-four elders who laid the corner stones of the Temple in Kirtland, and moved to Caldwell county, Missouri, in 1837, and settled on Log Creek. In 1838 he was expelled from the state of Missouri with the saints, and settled in Yelrome, Hancock county, Illinois. After his death the mob boasted that they fired at Durfee on a bet of a gallon of whiskey that they could kill him the first shot, and they won.

Sunday, 16.—Meeting in the grove at 10 a. m.

Elders Orson Hyde, Heber C. Kimball and I preached.

I received the following:

BACKENSTOS' NOTE TO THE TWELVE

'*To the Twelve*:

On last night Elder Edmund Durfee was basely murdered by the mob in the Green Plains precinct, what shall be done to avenge his blood? the troops afford us no protection.

Yours, etc.,

November 16th, 1845. J. B. BACKENSTOS.'

Edmund Durfee's body was brought into the city to be buried.

I learned that Elder Theodore Turley has been arrested at Alton on a charge of bogus-making.

Afternoon, council of the Twelve assembled.

Orson Hyde in behalf of the council wrote the following letter:—

HYDE'S LETTER TO MAJOR WARREN REPORTING DURFEE'S MURDER

'Nauvoo, Nov. 17, 1845.

Major Warren,

Sir: Intelligence reached us last evening of the murder of Mr. Edmund Durfee in the south part of the county by the mob who fired a quantity of straw to decoy him out, and while he was engaged in raking the straw so that the fire might not communicate with the buildings, six shots were made at him, one of which took effect in his breast and he died immediately.

His remains are brought to this city for interment.

Mr. Durfee was one of the most quiet and inoffensive citizens in these United States and from our acquaintance with him, and from the nature of his business in securing his crops we are persuaded that his murder was wholly unprovoked.

The burning of the house of Mr. Rice has created little excitement in the city, but on this occasion, we look to you to take such steps and adopt such measures as you, in your wisdom, shall deem expedient, and that you will make your views public as early as consistent.

Shall we send a sufficient number of men into the south part of the county to protect themselves while gathering their crops? or will you send your men for that purpose, or at least, a sufficient number of them? Be so good as to inform us so soon as convenient.

Affidavits will probably soon reach you of the above transactions.

Very Respectfully, in behalf of the Council,

[Signed] ORSON HYDE'.

AN EPISTLE TO THE SAINTS

'All those who have letters, or documents of any kind in their possession, which in any way relate to the History of the Church of Jesus Christ of Latter-day Saints, are requested to leave them with the historian before tomorrow evening.

On Collection of Historical Items.

All elders who have been out on special missions within two years, and have not reported themselves in writing, are requested to do so before tomorrow evening.

Every individual who may be in possession of any fact, circumstance, incident, event, or transaction which they wish recorded in the *General History of the Church* will report it in writing before tomorrow evening.

The historian wants all books, maps, charts, papers, documents of every kind, name, and nature, and all information that may relate to, or have a bearing in any wise upon the History of the Church, before him, in his office within twenty-four hours.

Important items of history have frequently been presented at too late an hour to gain an insertion. Therefore I would say, that the history is written up to the year 1843, and the documents now wanting, are for the years 43-4 and 5. But if any of the brethren have any items of valuable history of any date, they may hand them in, and they will be filed away for future use.

The injunction of the Apostle 'owe no man anything' is excellent, and ought to be remembered by every one, and practiced, so far as circumstances will admit; this is a part of the religion of the celestial kingdom; I have endeavored to live up to it, and I am determined to live to it more perfectly if possible, therefore, I request every individual who has any account for or against me, to call and settle the same before next Sabbath; if they owe me I will not kill them, and if I owe them I will try and pay them, for I hope soon to start on a mission towards some Island in the Pacific ocean, and if I should go away in debt to God or man I should expect to be shipwrecked before I got there. And now, brethren, if you want to save me from such a dreadful calamity, don't fail to call and settle with me, for I expect that I owe some little accounts which have escaped my recollection and my mind cannot rest so as to prosecute my business in peace until these things are settled. Remember the time before next Sabbath and set me free for after that I have much business that will require my attention.

Payment of Debts.

May the God of Israel bless all the saints, help them to do right, prosper them in their business, and save them in his kingdom is the prayer of your brother,

[Signed] WILLARD RICHARDS.

City of Joseph [Nauvoo], Sunday Morning, November 16th, 1845.'

Monday, 17.—I met in council at 4 p. m. with Elders Heber C. Kimball, Orson Hyde, Parley P. Pratt, John Taylor, George A. Smith, Joseph Young and Bishop George Miller.

In obedience to the call of the historian many elders furnished reports of their missions: I insert the following:

JAMES C. SNOW'S MISSION TO THE EAST

'May 17th, 1844, I left Yelrome, Hancock county, Illinois, for Rush county, Indiana, on a special mission.

On the 27th I commenced to lay before the people the views and policy of President Joseph Smith relative to the government and laws of the United States, presenting him as a candidate for the ensuing presidential election; at first, I met with opposition until the people became better acquainted with his principles; prejudice then gave way, and hundreds in Rush and other counties were turned in favor of President Smith and the saints.

Twenty were baptized into the church. When the news arrived of his death the people were disappointed and the shock was universally felt. Some of the most influential men immediately predicted the downfall of the nation because they looked lamely on and sang lulla-by-baby.

JAMES C. SNOW.

City of Joseph [Nauvoo], November 17th, 1845.'

Tuesday, 18.—The Twelve met in council at Dr. Richards'.

Another Judicial Farce—Durfee's—to be Enacted.

Mr. Brayman, attorney for the state, wrote a letter to the council desiring witnesses against the murderers of Durfee to be sent to Carthage, also affidavits forwarded in relation to the burning of Rice's house, and advising us of the arrest of George Backman, Moss and Snyder, who were charged with the murder of Elder Edmund Durfee, Sen.

The council replied immediately and requested the witnesses to start in the morning for Carthage to perform their part in another judicial farce.

I received the following:

SOLOMON HANCOCK'S LETTER ON DURFEE'S MURDER

'Carthage, November 18th, 1845.

President Brigham Young:

I am convinced that Major Warren and Mr. Brayman are doing all they can to ferret out and convict the guilty who have recently been engaged in lawless transactions. They have stationed troops at my house to protect it from the incendiary and things generally appear to be working out right.

As there appears to be a disposition to act in support of law I think we ought to aid in getting witnesses so that the truth may be proven.

I have learned that Calvin Beebe, Lester Herrick and Nelson Herrick were in Lima on Saturday night, and know something of the intentions of the mob upon my property. I believe their evidence is necessary. They should come to Carthage in time for the examination.

Please send all who know anything about the recent lawless outrages.

Yours Respectfully, etc.

SOLOMON HANCOCK.'

JAMES ARLINGTON BENNETT'S REQUEST

Tuesday, 18 (*continued*).—I received a letter from James Arlington Bennett urging me to appoint him military commander-in-chief in the church, the spirit of the letter shows a thirst for personal aggrandizement unbecoming a servant of God.

NAUVOO NEIGHBOR — EXTRA

Nauvoo, November 19th, 1845

MURDER AND ARSON
EDMUND DURFEE SHOT—TWO HOUSES BURNED

'As may be seen by the affidavits below, it falls to our painful lot to chronicle two more outrages upon the lives and rights of the Latter-day Saints, since they have been using all diligence to secure their crops, build wagons, and leave next spring.

Mr. Durfee was one of the most industrious, inoffensive and good men that could be found, and having his house burnt in September last, moved to Nauvoo and went on Saturday last for a load of grain, was shot dead in cold blood, at midnight while striving with others to save property from the flames by an armed mob!

As to the destruction of the houses and property, and the treatment on that occasion—let the affidavit speak for itself.

We have nearly two thousand five hundred wagons commenced for our Pacific journey next spring, but such outrages certainly are not calculated to aid us in getting ready. We have borne the Missouri persecution; we have mourned the loss of the Prophet and Patriarch, Joseph and Hyrum Smith; we feel the destruction of one or two hundred houses the present season, and our hearts are pained at the murder of Edmund Durfee, because he was a good man; but, we, as in all cases of the saints, leave the disposition of these matters in the care of a wise God, and the perpetrators, to the mercy of (as they say), a country of laws, and be those laws honored or disgraced we cannot be charged with revenge; and we do beseech the people and the authorities not to impute crime to us, to raise excitement, when we see our accusers wiping the blood of innocent men, women, and children, from their garments, as though this was the realm of Nero.

If thieves and robbers escape to Nauvoo, our rule is to deliver them up to the law of the land, and that is all that we can do.

We believe there is virtue and humanity among high-minded men, that know what honor is, and we appeal to them to lend a helping hand, while we are outfitting for our intended removal in the spring. Give us peace, for you that hold the balances of power can! And when we have settled on the other side of America you will know of a truth that we were friends and not enemies to life, law, and liberty! That we were good men, engaged in a good cause, and will receive the meed of praise we deserve for universal benevolence, and everlasting friendship to goodness.

The jealousy of the present generation is so great against the saints, that we have deemed it our duty to give this and the accompanying affidavits, that the world may know the continued ravages, and bloody outrages of a midnight mob; and for another important reason, that as Major Warren has pledged himself to use every exertion in his power to allay excitement, prevent the destruction of property, and stop the shedding of blood, we cannot feel anything better than that he will exhibit his honor and clemency in our behalf, that we may prepare for our exodus in peace henceforth.'

AFFIDAVITS IN THE DURFEE MURDER CASE

'State of Illinois }
Hancock County } ss.

Personally appeared before me, Aaron Johnson a justice of the peace within and foresaid county, James H. Woodland, and after being duly sworn, deposeth and saith, that on the night of the 15th of November, 1845, in the south part of said county, near Solomon Hancock's house, about midnight, a stack of straw was discovered on fire and that several persons turned out to suppress the flames; they raked away the straw to prevent it from catching and firing the barn; while thus engaged, a whistle was heard east and one west; and presently a gun was fired at them, and they continued to fire till six guns were discharged at them; the ball of the fourth one entered the body of Edmund Durfee, just above his heart and he died instantly, and further deponent saith not.

[Signed] JAMES H. WOODLAND.

Sworn to and subscribed this 17th day of November, 1845.

[Signed] AARON JOHNSON, J. P. (LS).'

'State of Illinois }
Hancock County } ss.

Personally appeared before me, Isaac Higbee, a justice of the peace within said county, Joseph Swymler, who being duly sworn according to law, deposeth and saith, that on the night of the 13th day of November, 1845, at about half past twelve o'clock, a company of men about thirty in number, made their appearance at the residence of Samuel Hicks in said county, near the head of Camp Creek, and called for Samuel Hicks, who got up out of bed and went to the door and asked what was wanted, they said they were the governor's troops right from Carthage, and had a writ for William Rice, who they said was there, and was told that he was not there. They laid hold of Hicks and forced him away without anything on but his shirt, Hicks and his wife and child all being sick with the ague, part of the company remained; they then called deponent and his brother up who were there, and ordered them to carry out the goods of the said Hicks and while his brother was in the chamber, they set fire to the stairs, which prevented him from getting all their goods, and when the fire had got to burning through the roof, they came back with Hicks who had suffered much with cold and ague, and after giving many insults and threats they went away. Deponent recognized in the company Jospeh Agnew, John M. Finch, and a young man by the name of Moss, and further deponent saith not.

[Signed] JOSEPH SWYMLER.

Sworn and subscribed to before me, this 17th day of November, 1845.

[Signed] ISAAC HIGBEE, J. P.'

Thursday, 20.—Council of the Twelve met in the afternoon.

I wrote a letter to Elder Wilford Woodruff, Liverpool, England, in reply to his communications.

Friday, 21.—The Twelve met and prayed.

COURSE OF MAJOR WARREN REPORTED—BACKENSTOS

Sheriff Backenstos came into council about 7 p. m., and said that he had watched Major Warren very closely for the last four days, thought he had turned Jack-Mormon, that he had been very busy and energetic in arresting the murderers of Durfee and the burners of Rice's house, that he had several of them under guard at Carthage and was in pursuit of more and had chased one of them into Missouri and forced him back at the point of the pistol without any requisition from the governor. He admitted to Backenstos that Durfee would not have been murdered had the troops not been in the county; notwithstanding Governor Ford's late letter to the contrary.

Major Warren has made several very sharp speeches to the anti-Mormons and told them if they did not help to bring those murderers to justice he would withdraw his troops from the county, and leave them in the hands of Backenstos; he had also intimated that if he could not bring them to justice without, he would establish martial law for a little season, try them by court martial, and have them shot. Stephens of Green Plains issued his warrant for the apprehension of the murderers, and came to Carthage on the day of examination and claimed his privilege of trying his own writs. Warren knowing him to be a mobocrat, caused Mr. Bartlett to issue new writs and took the prisoners out of Stephens' hands.

The sheriff also stated, that the clerk of the commissioners' court had had an injunction served on him, and had refused to issue the orders granted by the last commissioners' court for the payment of the sheriff's *posse* in quieting the rioters and house-burners.

Dr. Richards sick.

Saturday, 22.—The Twelve met with thirty-eight of the brethren who were expelled from Jackson county, Missouri, in 1833. Several of them spoke, some of them saying they thought they were neglected and cast off poor.

Echo from Jackson Co. Expulsion.

I made a few remarks, and showed that many had been slothful and had not preached nor magnified their callings in the church.

The plasterers finished the attic story of the Temple.

Sunday, 23.—Eleven a. m., seventies met in the Concert Hall.

Progress of Organizing Companies for the West.

I met with the captains of Emigrating Companies and gave them appropriate counsel.

Families organized, 3285.

Wagons on hand, 1508.

Wagons commenced, 1892.

Afternoon, the Council of the Twelve met. Several letters were read. Many threats by our enemies were afloat.

Monday, 24.—Ten a. m., Brother Heber C. Kimball and I called at the Historian's Office and read history with Dr. Richards and George A. Smith.

The council wrote Elder Theodore Turley who is now in jail awaiting his examination.

We have learned that the persons who murdered Edmund Durfee as also those who burned Rice's and Hick's houses were discharged by the magistrate without examination. Our brethren went according to Major Warren and Mr. Brayman's request as witnesses thereby fulfilling their part towards magnifying and making the laws honorable, but returned unheard, and the farce closed sooner than he had anticipated, without even a grand jury on the case.

Afternoon, council met for prayers.

Wednesday, 26.—At the Historian's Office with Elder George A. Smith and revised fifty pages history.

Elder Heber C. Kimball accompanied me to the Temple and examined the rooms. We were also engaged borrowing means to aid the Trustees, that they may go on with the work.

The presidents of the different quorums of seventies met and made some arrangements to furnish two rooms in the Temple. Elder Jedediah M. Grant gave a brief narration of his faith and standing.

The painters finished painting the attic of the Temple.

Thursday, 27.—At the Trustees' Office, arranging business.

Afternoon, Erastus H. Derby called upon Dr. Richards and informed him that Silas Haight, a deputy United States marshal of Iowa and another suspicious fellow were loitering about the streets, and endeavoring to see some of the Twelve to serve writs on them.

Friday, 28.—I went to the Trustees' Office, attending to church business. Elders Willard Richards and George A. Smith read and revised history to the end of 1843.

Saturday, 29.—I met with the Twelve, Bishops Whitney and Miller and a few others in the Temple and laid the carpet on the main floor of the attic story, and also on several of the small rooms ready for the First Quorum [of the Seventy] to meet in."

CHAPTER XXXVII

DEDICATION OF PARTS OF THE TEMPLE — ENDOWMENTS GIVEN — ROMAN CATHOLIC EFFORTS TO PURCHASE THE TEMPLE AND OTHER NAUVOO PROPERTY—THE CHURCH IN ENGLAND—UNITED STATES FEDERAL CHARGES OF COUNTERFEITING AGAINST CHURCH AUTHORITIES—CHURCH PUBLICATIONS FOR 1845

"*Sunday, November* 30, 1845.—At ten a. m. I went to the attic story of the Temple with Elders Heber C. Kimball, Willard Richards, Parley P. Pratt, John Taylor, Orson Hyde, George A. Smith, and Amasa Lyman, of the Quorum of the Twelve; also Newel K. Whitney and George Miller, Presiding Bishops; John Smith, Patriarch and President of the Stake, Joseph Young, President of the Seventies, Alpheus Cutler and R. Cahoon, Temple Committee, Cornelius P. Lott, Levi Richards. Joseph C. Kingsbury, Orson Spencer, Wm. W. Phelps, Isaac Morley, Lucien Woodworth. At about 12 o'clock, sang 'Come All Ye Sons of Zion'.

Dedication of the Attic Story of the Temple—Brigham Young.

I requested Wm. Clayton to keep minutes. I then offered up prayer and dedicated the attic story of the Temple and ourselves to God, and prayed that God would sustain and deliver us his servants from the hands of our enemies, until we have accomplished his will in this house. Elder Taylor then sang 'A Poor Wayfaring Man of Grief', after which Elder Heber C. Kimball prayed, that the Lord would hear and answer the prayers of his servant Brigham, and break off the yoke of our enemies and inasmuch as they lay traps for the feet of his servants that they may fall into them themselves and be destroyed—that God would bless his servant Joseph Young, heal his wife, and bless his family—that God would bless and heal his own [Elder Kimball's] family and asked for the same blessings on all our families which he had asked for Joseph Young and himself.

Hans C. Hanson, the doorkeeper reported that there were two officers waiting at the foot of the stairs for me. I told the brethren that I could bear to tarry here where it was warm as long as they could stay in the cold waiting for me. Elder Amasa Lyman requested hands to be laid on him that he might be healed; five of the brethren laid hands on him.

Officers at the Door of the Temple Waiting for Brigham Young.

Joseph Young prayed that our enemies might have no power over our leaders, he prayed for our brethren in England and on the Islands of the Sea; Brothers Babbitt, Turley and the Reddens—also that the Trustees might have means to liquidate all the debts.

The side rooms were occupied as follows:

Assignment of Rooms in the Temple Attic.

The first, in the southeast corner as a private office.

The second by Heber C. Kimball, W. Richards and myself. The third and fourth by others of the Twelve; Fifth, by Joseph Young and Presidency of the Seventies; Sixth, for washing and anointing the elders.

On the north side: first, bishops and lesser priesthood. Second, president of the stake and high council; third and fourth, high priests' quorum; fifth elders quorum; sixth, washing and anointing room occupied by the sisters.

Hans C. and Peter O. Hanson were appointed to see to the fires, keep watch and guard the doors.

Every hundred have established one or more wagon shops; wheelrights, carpenters and cabinetmakers are nearly all foremen wagon makers, and many not mechanics are at work in every part of the town preparing timber for making wagons. The timber is cut and brought into the city green; hub, spoke, and felloe timber boiled in salt and water, and

Wagon Makers.

other parts kiln dried; shops are established at the Nauvoo House, Masonic Hall, and Arsenal, nearly every shop in town is employed in making wagons.

Teams are sent to all parts of the county to purchase iron; blacksmiths are at work night and day and all hands are busily engaged getting ready for our departure westward as soon as possible.

Very few sales of property are being made, the citizens of the country around instead of aiding us to sell our property, are using their influence to discourage sales and the authorities constantly haunt us with vexatious writs, efforts are making to bring us into collision with the authorities of the United States by means of vexatious writs from the federal courts. The brethren are doing their utmost to prepare amidst all the discouragements that surround us for a general exodus in the spring; but from the manner that our neighbors have kept their faith, it is very apparent that as soon as the strength of Israel is gone, that the remainder will be in danger of violence, from our cruel persecutors, the promises of governors, generals, judges, conventions of citizens, and mob leaders, and their hounds to the contrary notwithstanding; but we trust in God, we praise him that we have been thus far able to prepare his Temple for the ordinances of the priesthood, and we feel full of confidence that he will hear our prayers and deliver his unoffending people from the power of their enemies, and lead us to a land where we can enjoy peace for a season.

Conditions in Nauvoo.

FOREIGN AFFAIRS

Elder Wilford Woodruff attended the Glasgow conference (Scotland). The branches comprising the conference were represented and contained 1181 members, including one high priest, 44 elders, 31 priests, 40 teachers and 30 deacons; sixty-eight were baptized since last conference.

Elder James Houston left Nauvoo, November 1,

1842, on a mission to preach the gospel in company with Elder Samuel Mulliner. They labored in Niagara county, New York, until the following summer, when Elder Houston, according to counsel, proceeded to Scotland, where he labored for about two years, mostly in the Glasgow conference; raising up a branch in Lanark. While on his mission he baptized 95 persons. He left Liverpool in charge of the company of saints that sailed on the *Oregon* in September, 1845, and returned to Nauvoo, November 15th.

Monday, December 1, 1845.—I met with several of the Twelve, the Temple Committee, and Trustees in the council chamber over the store.

Roman Catholic Effort to Purchase the Public Buildings at Nauvoo.

Letters were read from J. B. Purcell,* Catholic bishop of Cincinnati, the Catholic bishop at Detroit, and other gentlemen, inquiring after the property and lands for sale in Nauvoo and vicinity.

Elder Almon W. Babbitt made a report of his mission to St. Louis, Cincinnati and Chicago, relative to the disposition of property in Hancock county; and said the Catholics were making considerable exertions to have the members of their church purchase our property. They were very anxious to lease the Temple, but were not able to buy it. Mr. Quarters, the bishop at Chicago, has sent an agent who may probably enter into some arrangements for our property, he is expected tomorrow.

Brother Albert P. Rockwood was instructed to rent the upper stream mill for four months.

Bishop Miller answered a letter from Thomas H. Owen,† giving him an estimate of lands for sale in the several settlements in Hancock county under cultivation.

Tuesday, 2.—I received a letter from Messrs. Dun-

*This was Arch-Bishop Purcell who held a notable public debate with Alexander Campbell at Cincinnati in 1837, it was known as "The Battle of the Giants"! "Authority of the Catholic Church" was the subject of the debate.

†This was Thomas H. Owen the English Communist, temporarily in the United States to establish his system.

can and Co. of Bloomington, stating that a heavy firm in Philadelphia wished to know the condition and situation of our property, terms, etc., as they wished to buy, and for their ability to do so, referred us to Sheriff Backenstos and others; they proposed to pay specie for the whole, if a bargain were concluded.

Offer to Sell Nauvoo Property at Fifty Per Cent Valuation.

The council returned answer by letter that if their agent or agents would come here and examine the property, that we would sell the whole or any part of the city of Nauvoo, owned by our people, or the farms in the county, for fifty per cent under the valuation of like property, similarly situated in this country.

I spent the day in the Temple making preparations for the endowments.

Evening, Elders Heber C. Kimball, Orson Hyde, Parley P. Pratt, George A. Smith and I ordained Albert P. Rockwood, Benjamin L. Clapp and Jedediah M. Grant Presidents over the First Quorum of Seventies, filling vacancies which had been occasioned by the death of Daniel S. Miles, the apostacy of Josiah Butterfield, and the neglect of Roger Orton.

Vacancies in the First Council of the Seventy Filled.

Spent an hour in prayer.

Thursday, 4.—I was engaged with several of the Twelve fitting up the Temple preparatory to administering the ordinances of endowment.

Evening, the council met for prayer in the Temple.

Friday, 5.—Eight a. m., Brother Heber C. Kimball and I called on Dr. Richards who was sick, we proceeded to the Temple and were engaged in fitting up the upper rooms.

The Lord's Sacrament in the Temple.

Sunday, 7.—I met with the Twelve and others in the Temple. We partook of the sacrament, exhorted each other and prayed.

Monday, 8.—I have been actively engaged in the Temple since the painters finished, fitting up the apartments and preparing the rooms for administering endowments.

Tuesday, 9.—Forenoon, in the Temple.

Four p. m., Elders Heber C. Kimball, Orson Hyde, Parley P. Pratt, Willard Richards, John Taylor, George A. Smith, Amasa Lyman, Joseph L. Haywood, and I met at the Historian's Office with Father Tucker from Quincy and Father Hamilton from Springfield.

Further Roman Catholic Inquiry into Purchase of Nauvoo Property.

Father Tucker stated that Father Hamilton and himself had come here by direction of the bishop of Chicago, to see and inquire into the situation of the land and property for sale in and around Nauvoo.

I informed them that we would so reduce the value of the property as to make it an object for a society or speculators; and we wish to hand it over to the Catholics and so keep out those who want to have our property for nothing.

Evening, we wrote out propositions for the sale of our lands for the benefit of the Catholic deputation.

Wednesday, 10.—Nine a. m., I went to the Temple, weather fine, but cold.

I fitted up the curtains on the east windows, Brother Heber C. Kimball and wife, Sisters Parley P. Pratt and N. K. Whitney assisted me.

Catholic Inspection of the Temple.

Eleven a. m., Messrs. Tucker and Hamilton, Catholics, were admitted into the Temple to an audience with the Quorum of the Twelve and a few other brethren.

The propositions for sale of our lands were handed, by Brother Orson Hyde, to Father Tucker, who perused them, and handed them to Father Hamilton, his colleague. I gave him an explanation of the design of the rooms in the Temple, with which they seemed well satisfied.

Father Tucker said he thought it would be wisdom to publish our propositions in all the Catholic papers and lay the matter plainly before their people.

Hopeful Prospect of Catholic Purchase.

He should also think it advisable for the Catholic bishop to send a competent committee to ascertain the value of our property, etc., etc. At the same time they will use all their influence to effect a sale as speedily as possible.

Father Tucker thought they had men in St. Louis, New York and other cities, who could soon raise the amount we want, but the time is so very short he does not know whether it can be done so soon.

He asked if we would be willing to have our propositions published in their papers.

I answered that we would have no objections, providing it was understood that we reserved the right to sell when we had an opportunity.

Father Hamilton wished to ascertain upon what conditions they could obtain two of our public buildings, one for a school and one for a church. They intended to write to the bishop, and wished to be able to supply him with some information on this subject.

I said I was well aware that there were many men in the Catholic Church who could furnish all the money we wanted immediately, but I supposed it was with them as it was with a Mr. Butler, a wealty banker, who, when asked, why he did not sign off more bills, replied it was a good deal of trouble to sign off bills!

Brigham Young's Comment on Proposed Catholic Purchase.

Perhaps it is too much trouble to dig their money out of their vaults, but I wished it distinctly understood that while we make liberal propositions to dispose of our property, we must have the means to help ourselves away.

I said I would like to add a note to our proposals before they are presented for publication, to this effect, that if a party agree to them, we will lease them the Temple for a period of from five to thirty-five years, at a reasonable price, the rent to be paid in finishing the unfinished parts of the Temple, the wall around the Temple block and the block west of the Temple, and keeping the Temple in repair.

The council agreed to the amendment, which was accordingly added to the proposals, and handed to Father Tucker.

Father Tucker gave much encouragement that an arrangement would speedily be entered into to accomplish the sale of our property; both of the gentlemen seemed highly pleased with the Temple and city.

Three p. m., Sisters Mary Ann Young, Vilate Kimball and Elizabeth Ann Whitney commenced administering the ordinances in the Temple [Dec. 10, 1845].

We consecrated oil.

ACQUITTAL OF SHERIFF BACKENSTOS FOR THE KILLING OF FRANK A. WORRELL

News has arrived that Sheriff Backenstos, who went to Peoria in charge of Henry W. Miller, coroner of Hancock county, and was tried before Judge Purple on the charge of the 'murder' of Frank A. Worrell, was acquitted. The moral atmosphere around the judge was so different, than when at Carthage, that in all his charges and rulings, he appeared like another judge, and as though he had never been afflicted with mobocratic mania.

The jury said if there had been no witnesses only on the part of the state, it would not have required more than two minutes to have made up their verdict. There are two of the mob witnesses in jail for perjury and Backenstos is gone to Springfield to request the governor to withdraw his troops.

Completion of the Temple East Room for Giving Endowments.

At 3:45 p. m., we completed the arrangements of the east room, preparatory to giving endowments.

The following persons were present on this occasion, *viz.*:—

Myself and wife, Mary Ann;
Heber C. Kimball and wife, Vilate;
Orson Hyde and Nancy Marinda;
Parley P. Pratt and Mary Ann;
John Taylor and Leonora;
George A. Smith and Bathsheba W.;
Willard Richards;
Amasa Lyman and Mariah Louisa;
John E. Page and Mary;

John Smith and Clarissa;
Mother Lucy Smith;
Newel K. Whitney and Elizabeth Ann;
George Miller and Mary Catharine;
William W. Phelps and Sally;
John M. Bernhisel;
Alpheus Cutler and Lois;
Levi Richards;
Reynolds Cahoon and Thirza;
William Clayton;
Lucien Woodworth and Phebe;
Orson Spencer and Catharine C.;
Agnes M. Smith;
Mercy R. Thompson;
Mary Smith.

Attic Rooms of the Temple.

The main room of the attic story is eighty-eight feet two inches long and twenty-eight feet eight inches wide. It is arched over, and the arch is divided into six spaces by cross beams to support the roof. There are six small rooms on each side about fourteen feet square. The last one on the east end on each side is a little smaller.

The first room on the south side beginning on the east is occupied by myself, the second by Elder Kimball, the third by Elders Orson Hyde, Parley P. Pratt and Orson Pratt; the fourth by John Taylor, George A. Smith, Amasa Lyman and John E. Page; the fifth by Joseph Young and Presidents of Seventies; the sixth, a preparation room.

On the north side, the first east room is for Bishop Whitney and the lesser priesthood, the second is for the high council, the third and fourth for President George Miller and the high priests' quorum, the fifth the elders' room, and the sixth the female preparation room.

Commencement of General Administering Temple Ordinances.

Four-twenty-five p. m., Elder Heber C. Kimball and I commenced administering the ordinances of endowment [Dec. 10, 1845].

Five o'clock, Isaac Morley and his wife

Lucy, Joseph Fielding, Joseph C. Kingsbury and Cornelius P. Lott came in.

Nine-thirty p. m., we assembled for prayers, Amasa Lyman was mouth.

We continued officiating in the Temple during the night until three-thirty a. m. of the 11th.

The following were administered to:

Willard Richards;
Heber C. Kimball and his wife, Vilate;
George A. Smith and Bathsheba W.;
Orson Hyde and Nancy Marinda;
John Smith and Clarissa;
Newel K. Whitney and Elizabeth Ann;
Brigham Young and Mary Ann;
William W. Phelps and Sally;
Parley P. Pratt and Mary Ann;
Amasa Lyman and Mariah Louisa;
George Miller and Mary Catharine;
John Taylor and Leonora;
Lucien Woodworth and Phebe;
John E. Page and Mary;
Joseph C. Kingsbury;
Mary Smith, widow of Hyrum;
Agnes Smith, widow of Don Carlos.

Thursday, 11.—Elder Heber C. Kimball and I went to Joseph Kingsbury's and ate breakfast and returned to the Temple.

Elder Orson Pratt returned from his eastern mission, bringing four hundred dollars worth of Allen's revolving six-shooting pistols (alias pepperboxes).

I officiated in the Temple with the brethren of the Twelve. We administered the ordinances of endowment to:

Isaac Morley and his wife, Lucy;
Orson Spencer and Catharine C.;
Joseph Young;
Alpheus Cutler and Lois;
Reynolds Cahoon and Thirza;

William Clayton and Ruth;
Cornelius P. Lott and Permelia;
Mother Lucy Smith and Mercy R. Thompson.

At eight a. m., we assembled for prayer, Elder John E. Page was mouth. After which I called the Twelve and bishops together and informed them that I had received a letter from Brother Samuel Brannan, stating that he had been at Washington and had learned that the secretary of war and other members of the cabinet were laying plans and were determined to prevent our moving west: alleging that it is against the law for an armed body of men to go from the United States to any other government.

Extermination Proposed.

They say it will not do to let the Mormons go to California nor Oregon, neither will it do to let them tarry in the states, and they must be obliterated from the face of the earth.

We prayed that the Lord would defeat and frustrate all the plans of our enemies, and inasmuch as they lay plans to exterminate this people and destroy the priesthood from off the earth, that the curse of God may come upon them, and all the evil which they design to bring upon us, may befall themselves; and that the Lord would preserve the lives of his servants and lead us out of this ungodly nation in peace.

I said we should go out from this place in spite of them all, and the brethren all felt that God would deliver us from the grasp of this ungodly and mobocratic nation.

Brother Amasa Lyman and I tarried in the Temple all night.

Friday, 12.—In company with my brethren of the Twelve I officiated in the Temple until midnight.

Orson Pratt and his wife, Sarah Marinda, the First Presidency of the Seventy and their wives and others numbering in all twenty-eight males and twenty-seven females received the ordinances of endowment.

Several tarried in the Temple all night.

Saturday, 13.—We continued officiating in the Temple; twenty-five males and twenty females were administered unto.

I drafted rules for the preservation of order in the House of the Lord.

Rules Drafted for Order in the Temple.

News arrived from Springfield that Lucien B. Adams, son of the late Judge Adams, has effected a complete revolution in the minds of the inhabitants of Springfield, so much so, that Judge Pope is convinced that Elder Turley is imprisoned through persecution and says he shall discharge him when he arrives at Springfield.

Courts of Springfield Modified Toward the Saints.

Sunday, 14.—The Twelve and others with our wives met in the attic story of the Temple.

After prayer and singing, Elders Isaac Morley and Charles C. Rich administered, and we partook of the sacrament.

I introduced the subject of establishing rules for the preservation of order in the House of the Lord which were agreed to and ordered to be printed.

Rules for the Establishment of Order for the House of the Lord.

* * * * * * * * *

There is too much covetousness in the church, and too much disposition amongst the brethren to seek after power and has been from the beginning, but this feeling is diminishing and the brethren begin to know better. In consequence of such feelings Joseph [Smith] left the people in the dark on many subjects of importance and they still remain in the dark. We have got to rid such principles from our hearts.

The Prophet Left the People Uninformed on Some Matters.

I referred to the manner in which the corner stones of this Temple were laid as published in the *Times and Seasons,* and said that the perfect order would have been for the presidency of the stake to lay the first or southeast corner; the high council the second or southwest corner; the bishops the northeast corner; but the high priests laid the southwest corner, though they had no right to do it.

Proper Order of Laying Temple Corner Stones.

I spoke of the brethren making objections to persons being permitted to receive the ordinances, and added, that when objections were made I should feel bound to determine whether the person making the objections was a responsible person, and if he is not, I should do as I pleased about listening to the objections; but if he was a responsible person I should listen to them.

To constitute a man responsible he must have the power and ability not only to save himself but to save others; but there are those who are not capable of saving themselves and will have to be saved by others.

When a man objects to another receiving the ordinances he becomes responsible to answer to God for that man's salvation; and who can tell but if he received the ordinances he would be saved, but if we refuse to give him the means he cannot be saved and we are responsible for it.

There is no law to prevent any man from obtaining all the blessings of the priesthood if he will walk according to the commandments, pay his tithes and seek after salvation, but he may deprive himself of them.

After much profitable instruction we united in prayer, Orson Hyde being mouth.

Meeting adjourned for one week.

Two p. m., many of those who had received their ordinances the past week met and received instructions from Elders Parley P. Pratt and William W. Phelps.

The Twelve met and read some letters, also an account of Sheriff Backenstos' travel from the *Peoria Register*.

We went down to the lower room and counseled on the arrangement of the pulpits.

I remained in the Temple all night.

Meeting in England.

Elder Wilford Woodruff attended a special conference of the churches in the British Isles in the Hall of Science, Manchester.

10,956 members were represented; including 8 high priests, 392 elders, 590 priests, 311 teachers, and 188 deacons; 1570 were baptized since April last.

Monday, 15.—The ordinances of endowment were administered to sixty-four brethren and sisters.

Administrations in the Temple.

The Twelve and others officiated.

Tuesday, 16.—I have been busy in the Temple dictating the order of business, appointing brethren to officiate in the various departments, and giving much instruction at different intervals; Elder Kimball assisted me. Sixty-nine brethren and sisters received their ordinances.

Wednesday, 17.—We continued our labors in the Temple, administered the ordinances of endowment to sixty-nine brethren and sisters.

Ten twenty-five p. m., eighteen persons assembled in my room and joined with me in prayer.

My son, Joseph A., remained with me in the Temple all night.

Letters to Government Officials Anent Movement of the Saints to the West.

Letters were written to Stephen A. Douglas, M. C., J. P. Hoge, M. C., Wm. S. Marcy, Secretary of War, John Wentworth, M. C., and John Chapman in relation to our movement to the west, in consequence of learning that attempts were made to induce government to prevent our removal.

Thursday, 18.—Sixty-six persons were administered to in the Temple. I retired to bed about midnight.

Anxiety for Continuance of Temple Ordinances.

In consequence of the great pressure of business during the past week, it had been decided to devote Saturday to the purpose of washing robes and garments used, but there being a general desire in the minds of all those officiating in the ordinances that the work should not cease, it was determined that the clothes should be washed during the night.

Temple Workers Appointed.

Friday, 19.—I appointed the following elders to officiate and labor in the Temple today:

Heber C. Kimball,	George Miller,
George A. Smith,	Phineas H. Young,
Joseph Young,	Lucius N. Scovil,

Aaron Johnson,
Wm. W. Phelps,
Hosea Stout,
Wm. Crosby,
A. O. Smoot,
Erastus Snow,
Jesse D. Harmon,
Orson Hyde,
Amasa Lyman,
Orson Pratt,
John Smith,
Jedediah M. Grant,
John Scott,
Charles C. Rich,
Daniel Garn,
John L. Butler,
John Brown,
Alexander McRae,
Benj. L. Clapp,
Franklin D. Richards.

7 p. m., I met with the Twelve in Elder Kimball's room for prayer; after which we counseled on the propriety of sending certain brethren to England.

Ninety-eight persons received ordinances.

I remained in the Temple.

Reading of Col. John Fremont's Works.

Saturday, 20.—Beautiful morning. I dictated the arrangements for the day. Afterwards, with a few of the Twelve and others heard F. D. Richards read *Fremont's Journal,* giving an account of his travels to California.

We considered it prudent to devote today to cleaning and washing, and suspend operations in the Temple; but on account of the anxiety of the saints to receive their ordinances, the brethren and sisters volunteered to wash clothes every night. Ninety-five persons received their ordinances.

Sunday, 21.—According to appointment on Sunday last, a meeting was held in the Temple today of some of those who had received their ordinances.

Seventy-five persons were present.

Elder Heber C. Kimball presiding.

Sacrament Administered in the Temple.

The sacrament was administered by Father John Smith and Bishop George Miller. Elders George A. Smith and Heber C. Kimball preached, others made a few remarks confirming what had been said.

Elder John Taylor was mouth in prayer.

Meeting dismissed at 2:10 p. m.

Three p. m., many others who had been invited met according to appointment.

Elders Amasa Lyman and Heber C. Kimball preached.

Provision Made for the Seventy in the Temple.

At ten a. m., the seventies met in the Music Hall. The thirty-second quorum of seventies was organized; and arrangements made to finish an upper room in the Temple for the benefit of the seventies.

Monday, 22.—I stayed in the Temple last night and early this morning gave direction for the arrangements of the day, assisted by George Miller,* as the day was set apart more especially for the high priests.

One hundred and six persons received ordinances.

Tuesday, 23.—Early this morning the drying house of Captain Charles C. Rich's Emigrating Co. No. 13 was burned to the ground, consuming $300.00 worth of wagon timber.

The high council met in the Temple for prayer.

United States Authorities to Arrest Brigham Young.

One-five p. m., Almon W. Babbitt came into the Temple and informed me that there were some federal officers from Springfield accompanied by several of the state troops in the city for the purpose of arresting some of the Twelve, especially Amasa Lyman and myself.

It was soon reported that they were at the door of the Temple and were intending to search it. George D. Grant, my coachman, went below and drove my carriage up to the door as if he was waiting for me to come down.

The Bogus Brigham Incident.

William Miller put on my cap and Brother Kimball's cloak and went downstairs meeting the marshal and his assistants at the door, as he was about getting into my carriage the marshal arrested him, on a writ from the United States court, charging him with counterfeiting the coin of the United States. Miller told him there must be some mistake about it, as he was not guilty of anything of the kind, but the marshal insisted it was right.

*Brother Miller was president of the high priests.

Miller desired the marshal to go down to the Mansion where he could get counsel and ascertain if the proceedings were legal. On reaching the Mansion they went into a private room where Esq. Edmonds examined the writ and pronounced it legal. Miller gave Edmonds the name of four witnesses for subpoena for him, and asked the marshal to remain until morning; he consented, but soon got uneasy and said he must go to Carthage. Miller then inquired if he would wait three quarters of an hour until he could get his witnesses, but in fifteen minutes he said he must go, and would wait no longer. Miller got into his carriage, Esq. Edmonds rode with the marshal's guard and they started for Carthage, Miller protesting there was some mistake about it, for he certainly was not guilty of any such things as were charged in the writ: on the way to Carthage the marshal was very social, and remarked that the people had got quite a joke upon him for letting Turley give him the dodge. As they approached Carthage the troops began to whoop and holloa and went into town in high glee, performing the journey which was eighteen miles in two hours.

The marshal put up at Hamilton's Tavern, and the rumor soon spread through the town that Brigham Young was in the custody of the marshal at Hamilton's. Among others, George W. Thatcher, county commissioner's clerk, who was well acquainted with Miller came into the tavern to see me. The marshal at his request took Miller into a private room. After a little conversation one of the guards came in and the marshal went out. The marshal soon returned and said to Mr. Miller, 'I am informed you are not Mr. Young;' 'Ah!' exclaimed Miller, 'then if I should prove not to be Mr. Young, it would be a worse joke on you than the Turley affair,' he replied, 'I'll be damned if it won't.'

The marshal asked Miller if his name was Young, he answered, 'I never told you my name was Young, did I?' 'No,' replied the marshal, 'but one of my men professed to be acquainted with Mr. Young, and pointed you out to me to be him.' William Backenstos was called in and he told them William Miller was not Brigham Young. Another man came, and said he could swear Miller was not Brigham Young. The marshal said he was sorry, and asked Miller his name, he replied, 'it is William Miller'.

The marshal left the room and soon returned accompanied by Edmonds who was laughing heartily at him. Edmonds inquired if he had anything more to do with 'Mr. Young'. The marshal replied that he did not know that he had anything further to do with Mr. Miller.

Eighty-seven persons received the ordinances.

Seven-thirty p. m., I met with the Twelve in prayer, and thanked the Lord for deliverance from the snares of our enemies.

Prayer and Retirement from Enemies.

Eight-twenty, I left the Temple disguised and shortly after Brothers Heber C. Kimball, Parley P. Pratt, George A. Smith and Amasa Lyman left, to elude the vexatious writs of our persecutors.

Wednesday, 24.—All the Twelve have been absent from the Temple the greater part of this day except Orson Pratt. One hundred twenty-two persons received the ordinances.

At 11:20, Elder Heber C. Kimball and I returned to the Temple and remained all night.

Aftermath of the "Bogus Brigham" Incident.

William Miller remained last night at Carthage at Jacob B. Backenstos'. Miller said he could not sleep being interrupted by Edmonds' continued roars of laughter at the marshal's discomfiture.

Miller saw two of the marshal's guards, one of whom threatened his life. Miller came in with the stage, the driver told him that the officers said it would be like searching for a needle in a hay mow now, to undertake to find Brigham Young in Nauvoo.

Thursday, 25.—12:15 p. m., George D. Grant brought word that the United States marshal is in the city again. Elder Kimball sent a message to him by Elder Grant, and at 1:15 Elder Kimball and I left the Temple.

Six p. m., the high council met for prayer in room No. 4; the high priests met in room No. 8.

At twenty minutes before six, Amasa Lyman, George A. Smith, Orson Hyde, and John Taylor went into the Temple, at 6:10 Parley P. Pratt and Orson Pratt, and at 6:18 Brother Heber C. Kimball and I went in.

The Twelve met in my room for counsel and prayer. After considerable conversation about the western country we united in prayer: George A. Smith was mouth.

One hundred seven persons received their ordinances. The business of the day closed at twenty minutes past ten o'clock, and notice was given that no more washings and anointings would be attended to at present. Brother Kimball and I, with some few others, remained in the Temple all night.

Friday, 26.—Elders Heber C. Kimball, Orson Pratt and I were present in the Temple this morning and a few of those who had been officiating: I called them together in the east room about 11:30 a. m., and told them there would be no business done today and that they were all dismissed except the two Brothers Hanson, and three brethren for officers.

Instructions of Brigham Young on Temple Procedure.

I said we shall have no more anointing at present, and if the brethren do not get anything more than they have already received, they have got all they have worked for in building this house; and if there is any more to be received it is because the Lord is merciful and gracious.

The high council and high priests will meet together once a day as usual for prayer.

Two hundred sixty-eight high priests were reported to have received their endowments.

I further remarked, that when we began again we should pay no respect to quorums. Every man that comes in, is washed and anointed by good men and it makes no difference. Every man that gets his endowments, whether he is a high priest or seventy may go into any part of the world and build up the kingdom if he has the keys. We have been ordained to the Melchizedek priesthood which is the highest order of the priesthood, and it has many branches or appendages.

I said, my feelings were to rest a few days and let the Temple rest, and when we commenced work again I would make a selection of hands who will remain and officiate daily. No persons will be allowed to come in unless they are invited, and I shall feel insulted if they remain here. I felt it impressed upon me to rest a few days and make these regulations, and as our oil is done we cannot do much anyway.

Six p. m., the Twelve, the high council, the high priests and the Presidents of Seventies met for prayer, each quorum in their own apartment.

Sheriff Backenstos informed me that the United States deputy marshal was in town with writs for the Twelve and Brother George Miller.

Eight p. m., Elder Kimball and I left the Temple.

Saturday, 27.—This morning was a very pleasant one, moderately cold, the sun shining clear and bright in the heavens.

Orson Pratt was the only one of the Twelve present in the Temple.

A U. S. Deputy Marshal *et al* Visit the Temple.

Ten-fifteen a. m., the United States Deputy Marshal Roberts, went to the Temple in company with Almon W. Babbitt and searched for the Twelve and others. He was freely admitted to every part of the Temple, to which he desired access; he went into the tower, on to the roof, into the attic story and while viewing the city from the tower he expressed his astonishment at its magnificence and extent and said considering the unfavorable circumstances with which the people had been surrounded it seemed almost impossible that so much should have been accomplished. He passed through the various departments into the east room where he very intently examined the portraits, and made inquiries as to whose they were.

On entering the attic hall he was requested to take off his boots and uncover his head, to which he complied; after remaining about half an hour he departed.

About two p. m., the marshal returned accompanied by a gentleman whom he introduced as from New Orleans, and Sheriff Backenstos. They visited the middle room and the tower and departed after about half an hour.

Letter of Emma Smith to *New York Sun.*

Dr. Bernhisel went to the Temple about one p. m. and borrowed the *New York Sun* of December 9, 1845, which contains a letter said to have been written by Emma Smith, to the editor.

Lewis Robbins is cleaning and putting in order the washing rooms and furniture, Peter Hanson is translating the *Book of Mormon* into the Danish language, Elisha Averett is doorkeeper, John L. Butler, fireman, David Candland and L. R. Foster, clerks. Orson Pratt has been engaged in making astronomical calculations. From several observations he makes the latitude of Nauvoo 40°35′48″ north.

Orson Pratt makes Astronomical Observations from the Temple.

In the evening I went to the Temple and met with Brothers Heber C. Kimball, Parley P. Pratt, Orson Pratt, Amasa Lyman and George A. Smith.

We retired to my room for prayer at six-forty-five. Elder John Taylor came in and joined us. Elder Heber C. Kimball was mouth. Elder Hyde arrived after prayers, and informed us he could not come at the hour as the officers were watching his house.

The high council met and prayed for me and all the Twelve, that we might be preserved from our enemies that the faithful saints may be permitted to receive all the ordinances of the Lord's House—that the Lord would bless the quorums, and for several sick persons.

Nauvoo High Council in Prayer.

The high priests met in rooms Nos. 6 and 8 and prayed that those persons who are seeking our hurt may find themselves hedged up—for deliverance from bondage—means to remove, that I and all the quorums in the church may be sustained—for the sick—Elders Woodruff, Grouard [in the Pacific Islands] and all the missionaries on the globe, etc.

High Priests in Prayer.

The First Presidency of the Seventies met for prayer.

The Presidency of the Seventy in Prayer.

After prayers a general conversation ensued, in which the Twelve and bishops, J. M. Grant, and several others took part. The visit of the marshal and the emigration to California were the prominent topics. Elder Parley P. Pratt read from Hastings' account of California.

Nine-thirty-five the Twelve met in council and selected the names of persons who would be called upon to labor in the Temple the ensuing week.

The names of Other Temple Workers Given.

The list is as follows, *viz.*:

Joseph Young,	Lorenzo Snow,
Abraham O. Smoot,	Lewis Robbins,
Wm. Crosby,	Benj. L. Clapp,
Henry Harriman,	Charles C. Rich,
J. M. Grant,	William Snow,
Erastus Snow,	Ezra T. Benson,
Orson Spencer,	Franklin D. Richards,
Willard Snow,	Elisha Averett,

John L. Butler.

The above in addition to those of the Twelve who will be present are considered sufficient to perform the work.

Elders Heber C. Kimball, Amasa Lyman, George A. Smith, Newel K. Whitney, and a few others remained in the Temple all night.

Sunday, 28.—About two hundred of the brethren and sisters met at ten-thirty a. m. in the attic story of the Temple, some of the

A Sacramental Meeting Held in the Temple.

side rooms were filled, and the curtains withdrawn.

After singing and prayer, I addressed the meeting.

The sacrament was administered. Elder Kimball made a few remarks. After prayer the meeting was dismissed by benediction from Elder Orson Hyde.

High Council and High Priests in Prayer.

Six p. m., the high council and the high priests met for prayer.

Elder Kimball and I remained in the Temple.

Monday, 29.—Elder Kimball and I assisted by our wives, and the laborers in the Temple, cleaned up and arranged the furniture in the rooms.

Dragoons from Carthage at Nauvoo.

Four dragoons came in from Carthage and searched Nauvoo for hogs, said to have been stolen from Mr. Hibbard.

Elders George A. Smith and Amasa Lyman revised history.

Elder Parley P. Pratt read *Fremont's Journal* to Brother Kimball and me.

Report of Mission in Society Islands.

Three-fifteen p. m., Elder Noah Rogers just arrived from his mission to the Society Islands, in the South Pacific Ocean; he was accompanied by Mr. Tower, a fellow passenger on board ship, whom he baptized. He brings a favorable report of the progress of the gospel on those Islands. He came on foot from Paducah on the Ohio river.

1000 Received Ordinances to this Date.

Three-forty, a company numbering twelve commenced receiving their ordinances; this makes 1000 who have received the ordinances.

Six p. m., the high council, the high priests and the seventies met for prayer.

The Twelve in Prayer.

The Twelve met for prayer. We prayed for deliverance from our enemies, and that we might be spared to give the faithful saints their endowments, Orson Hyde being mouth.

I spent an hour reading, and with Brothers Kimball and Lyman remained in the Temple all night.

Tuesday, 30.—At eight-ten a. m., commenced to

administer the ordinances. Elders Heber C. Kimball, Parley P. Pratt, George A. Smith, Amasa Lyman, Joseph Young and myself consecrated oil.

Departure of the Marshal from Nauvoo.

Eleven-thirty, Almon W. Babbitt reported that the marshal had left for Springfield, and there would probably be no more danger of writs for the present.

Eighty-eight persons received ordinances.

Pioneer Company of 1000 for the West.

Elder Parley P. Pratt has been engaged part of the time in forming a schedule for a Pioneer Company of 1000 men to precede the body of emigrants, to find a proper location and put in seed early in the summer.

Recreation in the Temple.

The labors of the day having been brought to a close at so early an hour, *viz.*: eight-thirty, it was thought proper to have a little season of recreation, accordingly Brother Hanson was invited to produce his violin, which he did, and played several lively airs accompanied by Elisha Averett on his flute, among others some very good lively dancing tunes. This was too much for the gravity of Brother Joseph Young who indulged in dancing a hornpipe, and was soon joined by several others, and before the dance was over several French fours were indulged in. The first was opened by myself with Sister Whitney and Elder Heber C. Kimball and partner. The spirit of dancing increased until the whole floor was covered with dancers, and while we danced before the Lord, we shook the dust from off our feet as a testimony against this nation.

Other forms of Entertainment—Singing in Tongues.

After the dancing had continued about an hour, several excellent songs were sung, in which several of the brethren and sisters joined. The 'Upper California' was sung by Erastus Snow, after which I called upon Sister Whitney who stood up and invoking the gift of tongues, sang a beautiful song of Zion in tongues. The interpretation was given by her husband, Bishop Whitney, and me, it related to our efforts to build this house to the privilege we now have of meeting in it, our departure shortly to the country of the Lamanites, their rejoicing when they hear the gospel and of the ingathering of Israel.

I spoke in a foreign tongue; likewise, Brother Kimball.

After a little conversation of a general nature I closed the exercises of the evening by prayer.

Six p. m., the high council, and two companies of high priests met for prayer.

Wednesday, December 31, 1845.—Elder Heber C. Kimball and I superintended the operations in the Temple, examined maps with reference to selecting a location for the saints west of the Rocky Mountains, and reading various works written by travelers in those regions; also made selections of names of persons to be invited to receive their endowments.

Readings of the "West" and Selection of Locations for the Saints.

Eighty-four persons were received into the Temple.

Six p. m., the high council, high priests, and seventies met in their respective rooms and prayed.

CHURCH PUBLICATIONS FOR THE PERIOD

During the year 1845 there was published the *Times and Seasons,* fortnightly, octavo, edited by John Taylor, Nauvoo, Illinois.

The *Nauvoo Neighbor,* weekly, folio, edited by John Taylor, Nauvoo, Illinois.

The *Millennial Star,* fortnightly, octavo, edited by Wilford Woodruff and Thomas Ward, Liverpool.

The *Prophet,* weekly, folio, edited by Samuel Brannan, New York, which ended May 24th and was succeeded by

The *New York Messenger,* July 25th, quarto, edited by Parley P. and Orson Pratt.

Proclamation of the Twelve to the Kings of the World, pamphlet, 8 vo. 16 pages, written by Parley P. Pratt, and published by Wilford Woodruff, Liverpool.

Speech of Elder Orson Hyde, delivered at Nauvoo upon the course and conduct of Sidney Rigdon.

The *Voice of Truth,* containing some of the public writings, and a synopsis of a sermon of President Joseph Smith, as reported by Thomas Bullock, Nauvoo.

Account of the Murder of Generals Joseph and Hyrum Smith, by William M. Daniels, Nauvoo.

A Dialogue Between Joseph Smith and the Devil, which first appeared in the *New York Herald,* by Elder Parley P. Pratt.

Prophetic Almanac, by Orson Pratt, New York."

CHAPTER XXXVIII

LARGE NUMBER OF PERSONS ENDOWED IN THE TEMPLE—JANUARY AND FEBRUARY, 1846—CATHOLIC CHURCH EFFORTS TO PURCHASE L. D. S. NAUVOO PROPERTY—FRIENDLY ATTITUDE OF JUDGE JOSIAH LAMBORN—REPEATED HOSTILE EFFORTS OF STATE OFFICIALS—DEPARTURE OF THE TWELVE HASTENED BY FALSE REPORTS CIRCULATED BY GOVERNOR FORD

"*Thursday, January* 1, 1846.—At an early hour, Elder Heber C. Kimball and I went to the Temple. The plasterers have commenced to plaster the arched ceiling of the lower hall, the floor is laid, the framework of the pulpits and seats for the choir and band are put up; and the work of finishing the room for dedication progresses rapidly.

6:30 p. m., the high priests met and prayed, eighty-nine persons received ordinances.

10:20 p. m., after finishing the labors of the day, the company assembled in the large room in the attic story and united in prayer with Elder Heber C. Kimball, thanking God for his great mercy and goodness to us in granting this opportunity of meeting together in the House of the Lord, asking him that he would continue to bless us, that he would bless President Brigham Young with health and wisdom, that he might be able to lead and direct this people; and that the same blessings might be extended to all his brethren of the Twelve and all the saints; and that God would bless our wives and give unto them strength of body that they might live and administer to the servants of God, that they might see three score years and ten, and behold the kingdom of God established in the earth; and that we might be enabled to continue in Nauvoo in peace, until all the faithful saints

Ordinance Work in the Temple—Prayer.

had received their endowments; and that when the time to leave here should arrive that we might be able to sell our possessions and obtain those things that we need to enable us to go away in comfort. Also, that God would bless our children, and all that pertains to us.

Friday, 2.—Sixty-four persons received ordinances.

At 6 p. m., the high council, high priests, and seventies met in their several apartments for prayer.

Heber C. Kimball's Dream.

This morning Elder Heber C. Kimball related the following dream: Last evening, before retiring to bed he asked God to enlighten his mind with regard to the work of endowment; while sleeping he beheld a large field of corn that was fully ripe, he and a number of others were commanded to take baskets and pick off the corn with all possible speed, for there would soon be a storm that would hinder the gathering of the harvest. The hands engaged in gathering the harvest, were heedless and unconcerned and did not haste, as they were commanded; but he and the man he assisted had a much larger basket than the rest, and picked with all their might of the largest ears of the field, they once in a while would pick an ear that had a long tail on each end and but a few grains scattering over the center of the cob, which were very light.

Interpretation.

The interpretation of the dream is, that the field represented the church, the good corn represented good saints, the light corn represented the light and indifferent saints, the laborers are those appointed to officiate in the Temple, the storm is trouble that is near upon us, and requires an immediate united exertion of all engaged in giving the endowments to the saints, or else we will not get through before we will be obliged to flee for our lives.

Elder Kimball having invited Brothers William Pitt, William Clayton, J. F. Hutchinson and James Smithies [musicians], they performed several very beautiful pieces of music.

After a short time spent in dancing, Elder Orson

Hyde delivered a short address and requested the company present to unite with him in prayer.

I addressed the brethren at length, alluding to the privileges we enjoy—of the order of administering endowments; that the way to grow and thrive was to serve the Lord in all we did, exhorted the brethren to remember their covenants and not to speak evil of each other, and related some of the efforts made to arrest me and persecute the saints. If Joseph Smith had been living, we should have already been in some other country, and we would go where we would be 'the old settlers', and build larger Temples than this.

The High Privileges of the Saints.

Saturday, 3.—One hundred and fourteen persons received their ordinances.

At 5 p. m., several companies of high priests met for prayer.

At 7, the seventies met for prayer.

I had a chill today, accompanied by fever, and felt unable to attend to business. I remained in the Temple all night.

Sunday, 4.—No public meeting was held in the Temple this day, on account of the floor being insufficient to support a large congregation.

I attended a council of the Twelve in the Temple. David Candland was appointed a mission to England.

A letter was received from Samuel Brannan, New York, also one from Pittsburg, signed Wm. W. Salt; both of which were answered.

The different quorums met in their respective rooms for prayer, at the usual hour.

Sheriff Backenstos received the following:

LETTER OF GOVERNOR FORD TO SHERIFF BACKENSTOS

'Springfield, December 29, 1845.

Dear Sir: In the matter of the late attempt to make arrests by the deputy marshal in Nauvoo, you will understand that that was entirely an affair of the U. S. government, in which this state took no official part. A demand was made on me by the marshal for troops which was promptly refused. I am not yet advised that the troops under the command of Major Warren took any part. If they did they had no orders from me, and I cannot think that they did take any part in assisting the deputy marshal for that would have been contrary to the settled and solemn understanding between Major Warren and myself. I had heard some rumor of the matter before I received your letter, from which I inferred that some of the men may have gone with the deputy marshal as a mere personal guard.

You know that the impression has become pretty general that no officer can go with safety unattended to Nauvoo to arrest any of their principal men. The idea is, that an officer thus exposed would be liable to be murdered. This may be all idle supposition, yet it is sufficient to account for the men going with the marshal without supposing they went to assist him.

This indictment in the U. S. court against the leading Mormons puts a new face on the matter. It will bring them and the United States for the first time into collision. It is impossible for me to guess, with any certainty, as to the course of Mr. Polk in the matter, but I would think it likely that he will order up a regiment or two of the regular army, and perhaps call on me for the militia, in which event I will be compelled to order them as you know.

I hope that the administration will not act in the matter this winter. If the Mormons remain in the state a strong force will be ordered to Nauvoo by the secretary of war, to remain there until arrests can be made. This you know is all guess work, as I have no such official relations with the government at Washington as would enable me to know it certainly. I also think that it is very likely that the government at Washington will interfere to prevent the Mormons from going west of the Rocky Mountains. Many intelligent persons sincerely believe that they will join the British if they go there, and be more trouble than ever, and I think that this consideration is likely to influence the government.

If it should be the case that government will order and station a large force at Nauvoo, and they can keep their soldiers there with as little expense as anywherelse, and shall interfere to prevent their emigration, it will put the Mormon leaders who are indicted in a worse box than they have yet been.*

They will have to separate from their people and become fugitives in the earth, or submit to a trial on their indictments. These are all

*The statement in this letter about the probability of the United States government being likely to intercept the departure of the church leaders from Nauvoo is a most diabolical and self-conceived trick on the part of Governor Ford. For in his *History of Illinois*, (p. 413), after confessing that he purposely tried to mislead the church authorities to a belief of this kind he says:

"With a view to hasten their removal they were made to believe that the president would order the regular army to Nauvoo as soon as the navigation opened in the spring. This had its intended effect; the Twelve with about two thousand of their followers, immediately crossed the Mississippi before the breaking up of the ice."

mere speculations of mine, but it will be for you and them to calculate whether the results guessed at, are not probable.

I am most respectfully
Your Obedient Servant,
[Signed] THOMAS FORD.'

Should Governor Ford's speculations and suppositions in relation to U. S. troops prove correct, and the government send a regular force to arrest us, we will run no risk of being murdered by them as our leaders have been; and as to fearing a trial before the courts it is all gammon for our danger consists only in being held still by the authorities while mobs massacre us as Governor Ford held Joseph and Hyrum Smith while they were butchered.

Monday, 5.—My health being better I was ready for duty at an early hour. Spent the morning in hearing letters and newspapers [read], and giving directions as to the business of the day.

8:45 a. m., commenced washing and anointing [i. e. in the Temple].

Seventeen bottles of oil were consecrated.

One hundred four persons received their endowments.

The high council, two companies of high priests, and the seventies met in their respective rooms for prayer.

9 p. m., the labors of the day being over, Brothers Hanson and E. Averett played on the violin and flute and enlivened the spirits of the saints present: some embraced the opportunity and danced to the lively strains of music.

Dancing in the Temple.

Elder Heber C. Kimball and I returned home about midnight.

The county commissioners' court met at Carthage. Messrs. Coulson and Perkins, being in attendance, and while allowing some bills for provisions and provender furnished to Backenstos' *posse*—during the late difficulties—Mr. Thatcher, the clerk, stated that an injunction had been served on him, which had been issued by the clerk of the circuit court,

Bills Protested.

forbidding all proceedings in relation to bills presented for the support of said *posse*, and this injunction he was determined to obey, and would not, therefore, place the order just made on record. The commissioners refused to recognize the legality of the injunction, on the ground that there was no provision in the statutes of the state to authorize such an interference with the county commissioners' court.

Tuesday, 6.—Seventeen bottles of oil were consecrated.

Ninety persons received ordinances.

6 p. m., Elder H. C. Kimball and I with our wives attended a party at Elder John Taylor's.

Three companies of high priests, the high council, and the seventies met for prayer in their respective rooms in the Temple.

Several musicians were present in the evening, some of the brethren danced.

I returned to the Temple about 10 p. m. and took part in the exercises. Brothers Erastus Snow and Levi W. Hancock sang hymns.

Wednesday, 7.—This morning there was an immense crowd at the reception room waiting for admission. The brethren brought all kinds of provisions for the use of those who are attending on the ordinances of the Lord's House.

Catholic Proposal to Rent Public Buildings in Nauvoo.

A letter was received this morning from Father Tucker, informing us that the Catholic bishop could not raise money enough to purchase our property, but would either purchase or rent one of our public buildings, but would not insure it against fire or mobs.

One hundred twenty-one persons received ordinances.

The supply of provisions brought in today has been very abundant, and much has been sent away to those families that are destitute.

The high council and three companies of high priests met for prayer.

The Presidents of Seventies met in council, in relation to keeping order in the Temple. The Twelve delegated to them the government of the Temple, while the ordinances were being administered to their quorums.

Service of Seventies in the Temple.

This afternoon, the new altar was used for the first time, and four individuals and their wives were sealed. The altar is about two and one-half feet high and two and one-half feet long and about one foot wide, rising from a platform about 8 or 9 inches high and extending out on all sides about a foot, forming a convenient place to kneel upon. The top of the altar and the platform for kneeling upon are covered with cushions of scarlet damask cloth; the sides of the upright part or body of the altar are covered with white linen.

A Temple Sealing Altar Erected.

The Twelve and presiding bishops with their wives were present at the dedication of the altar this afternoon.

* * *

Thursday, 8.—* * * Eighty-one persons received ordinances.

* * *.

Friday, 9.—One hundred and five persons received ordinances in the Temple. I attended to ordinances at the altar. The several quorums met for prayer.

I observed to the brethren that it was my wish that all dancing and merriment should cease, lest the brethren and sisters be carried away by vanity; and that the name of the Deity should be held in reverence, with all the due deference that belongeth to an infinite being of his character.

Dancing in the Temple Discontinued.

I received a letter from Samuel J. Hastings, of Boston, proposing to ship passengers, merchandise and freight to the Pacific coast for the saints.

Saturday, 10.—* * * One hundred and eighteen

received ordinances. I received a letter from Elder Wilford Woodruff, Liverpool, informing me that he had made arrangements to send his family home by New Orleans and return himself by Boston, calling in Maine and Connecticut, to bring his kindred to Nauvoo to start with the church westward in their exodus from the United States.

Announcement of Elder Woodruff's Return from England.

Sunday, 11.—The General Council met and arranged to make an early start west.

Monday, 12.—One hundred and forty-three persons received their endowments in the Temple. I officiated at the altar. Such has been the anxiety manifested by the saints to receive the ordinances [of the Temple], and such the anxiety on our part to administer to them, that I have given myself up entirely to the work of the Lord in the Temple night and day, not taking more than four hours sleep, upon an average, per day, and going home but once a week.

Anxious to Receive Temple Ordinances.

Elder Heber C. Kimball and the others of the Twelve Apostles were in constant attendance but in consequence of close application some of them had to leave the Temple to rest and recruit their health.

Tuesday, 13.—A council was held in the Temple.

The captains of fifties and tens made reports of the number in their respective companies, who were prepared to start west immediately, should the persecutions of our enemies compel us to do so: one hundred and forty horses and seventy wagons were reported ready for immediate service.

* * *

Thursday, 15.—I received a letter from George B. Wallace containing information that Samuel Brannan had chartered a ship to take a company of saints to San Francisco at twelve hundred dollars per month.

Elder Wallace had proposed to the brethren to purchase a ship, by shares of fifty dollars each to emigrate the saints to the Pacific coast; he gave an account of the progress of the work in the east.

Friday, 16.—A company of about forty saints including a portion of Elder Woodruff's family, consisting of his wife, Phebe, and two children, left Liverpool, on board of the ship *Liverpool,* for New Orleans. Flder Woodruff forwarded his family, he having to go by way of New York to Maine and Connecticut for his parents and daughter.

* * *

Saturday, 17.—Thirty-six persons received ordinances in the Temple.

I received the following [from Attorney-General Josiah Lamborn]:

JOSIAH LAMBORN PROPOSES TO WRITE HISTORY OF THE "MORMONS"

'Springfield, Illinois.
(Confidential) 17th Jan., 1846.

Dear Sir: I have been thinking of preparing for publication of a brief History of the Mormons and their difficulties in the different states where they have resided. My object would be to present to the public, the political, religious, and sectional motives, which have led to the persecutions of the Mormons. A well arranged statement of all these matters in a popular style of literature would have a tendency to correct public opinion and do much good.

I have lived in this state for many years, and have been intimately acquainted with the policy of office holders and office seekers, and without any particular intimacy with the Mormons themselves, I have become familiar with their peculiar condition.

A history of this kind would come with a good grace from one who has never had any personal, political or religious connection with your people. I presume that you are aware of the fact, that my feelings are as liberal and friendly as the feelings of any public man in the state. At no time have I failed to correct misrepresentations against you; and in some instances I have done so at the peril of losing favor and influence with men in high official stations.

I could prepare a work of the kind proposed and sell the copyright in New York, for five thousand dollars.

My object in addressing myself to you is to ascertain whether the Mormons would afford me any facilities in getting correct information, etc. If I should engage in anything of the kind I would wish to visit Nauvoo and have personal intercourse with some of the intelligent and respectable citizens for four or five weeks. Nothing could be done without some aid from your citizens, and if they will lend me their aid I will endeavor to make manifest my gratitude in a becoming manner. You can consult in confidence, with your friends upon this proposition, and let me know at an early day your views, etc.

Respectfully yours,
[Signed] J. LAMBORN.'

I attended a concert in the Music Hall; while my coachman, Brother George D. Grant, was taking his last passenger home, my horses fell through a bridge on Parley Street; I was in bed when I heard of it, but immediately arose, put on my clothes and hastened to the rescue of my team; on arriving I found they had lain nearly an hour between the timbers of the bridge, totally unable to extricate themselves from their distressing situation, and notwithstanding they were dumb animals they were sensible of their condition. We soon tore the timbers away and let down the horses one at a time, and rolling them over placed them where they could help themselves. (The depth of the gully was about six feet.) I returned home and washed the horses all over with spirits, using about half a gallon of whiskey in bathing them, which prevented stiffness and colds, so that in a few days they were able for service again.

President Young's Interest in His Team.

Sunday, 18.—A meeting of the captains of Emigrating Companies was held in the attic story of the Temple, to ascertain the number ready and willing to start should necessity compel our instant removal, being aware that evil is intended towards us, and that our safety alone will depend upon our departure from this place, before our enemies shall intercept and prevent our going.

Preparation for Instant Flight from Nauvoo.

A general interest in the movement was manifested by the whole council, every man felt willing to yield to the circumstances that surround us, and let their property be used for the purpose of accomplishing the removal and salvation of this people.

We selected Almon W. Babbitt, Joseph L. Heywood, John S. Fullmer, Henry W. Miller and John M. Bernhisel, a committee to dispose of our property and effects and aid such in emigrating as may have to go, it was agreed that they should have letters of attorney to authorize them to act for us legally.

They were instructed to enclose the Nauvoo House and complete the first story of the Temple.

Meetings for prayer in the several rooms.

Monday, 19.—I administered at the altar all day with the exception of thirty minutes in which I took some refreshments.

Evening, I attended a concert in the Music Hall.

Tuesday, 20.—One hundred and ninety-five persons received ordinances in the Temple.

Public prejudice being so strong against us, and the excitement becoming alarming we determined to continue the administration of the ordinances of endowment night and day.

The high council published the following:

A CIRCULAR OF THE HIGH COUNCIL TO THE CHURCH

'*To the Members of the Church of Jesus Christ of Latter-day Saints, and to all Whom it May Concern—Greeting*:

Beloved Brethren and Friends: We the members of the high council of the church by the voice of all her authorities, have unitedly and unanimously agreed, and embrace this opportunity to inform you; that we intend to send out into the western country from this place, sometime in March, a Company of Pioneers, consisting mostly of young, hardy men, with some families. These are destined to be furnished with an ample outfit; taking with them a printing press, farming utensils of all kinds, with mill irons and bolting cloths, seeds of all kinds, grain, etc.

The object of this early move is to put in a spring crop, to build houses, and to prepare for the reception of families who will start so soon as grass shall be sufficiently grown to sustain teams and stock.

Our Pioneers are instructed to proceed west until they find a good place to make a crop, in some good valley in the neighborhood of the Rocky Mountains, where they will infringe upon no one, and not be likely to be infringed upon. Here we will make a resting place, until we can determine a place for a permanent location. In the event of the president's [U. S.] recommendation to build block houses and stockade forts on the route to Oregon, becoming a law, we have encouragements of having that work to do; and under our peculiar circumstances, we can do it with less expense to the government than any other people.

We also further declare for the satisfaction of some who have concluded that our grievances have alienated us from our country, that our patriotism has not been overcome by fire—by sword—by daylight, nor by midnight assassinations, which we have endured; neither have they alienated us from the institutions of our country.

Should hostilities arise between the government of the United States and any other power, in relation to the right of possessing the territory of Oregon, we are on hand to sustain the claims of the United

States' government to that country. It is geographically ours; and of right, no foreign power should hold dominion there; and if our services are required to prevent it, those services will be cheerfully rendered according to our ability. We feel the injuries that we have sustained, and are not insensible of the wrongs we have suffered; still we are Americans, and should our country be invaded we hope to do, at least, as much as did the 'conscientious' Quaker who took his passage on board a merchant ship and was attacked by pirates. The pirates boarded the merchantman and one of the enemies' men fell into the water between the two vessels, but seized a rope that hung over and was pulling himself up on board the merchantman. The conscientious Quaker saw this, and though he did not like to fight, he took his jack-knife and quickly moved to the scene, saying to the pirate, 'If thee wants that piece of rope I will help thee to it.' He cut the rope asunder—the pirate fell—and a watery grave was his resting place.

Much of our property will be left in the hands of competent agents for sale at a low rate, for teams, for goods and for cash. The funds arising from the sale of property will be applied to the removal of families from time to time as fast as consistent, and it now remains to be proven whether those of our families and friends who are necessarily left behind for a season to obtain an outfit, through the sale of property shall be mobbed, burnt, and driven away by force. Does any American want the honor of doing it? or will Amercians suffer such acts to be done, and the disgrace of them to rest on their character under existing circumstances? If they will, let the world know it. But we do not believe they will.

We agreed to leave the country for the sake of peace, upon the condition that no more vexatious prosecutions be instituted against us. In good faith we have labored to fulfill this engagement. Governor Ford has also done his duty to further our wishes in this respect. But there are some who are unwilling that we should have an existence anywhere. But our destinies are in the hands of God, and so also is their's.

We venture to say that our brethren have made no counterfeit money: and if any miller has received fifteen hundred dollars base coin in a week, from us, let him testify. If any land agent of the general government has received wagonloads of base coin from us in payment for lands, let him say so. Or if he has received any at all from us, let him tell it. Those witnesses against us have spun a long yarn: but if our brethren had never used an influence against them to break them up, and to cause them to leave our city, after having satisfied themselves that they were engaged in the very business of which they accuse us, their revenge might never have been roused to father upon us their own illegitimate and bogus productions.

We have never tied a black strap around any person's neck, neither have we cut their bowels out, nor fed any to the 'catfish'. The systematic order of stealing of which these grave witnesses speak, must certainly be original with them. Such a plan could never originate with any person, except someone who wished to fan the flames of death and destruction around us. The very dregs of malice and revenge are mingled in the statements of those witnesses alluded to by the *Sangamon Journal*. We should think that every man of sense might see this. In fact, many editors do see it, and they have our thanks for speaking of it.

We have now stated our feelings, our wishes, and our intentions: and by them we are willing to abide; and such editors as are willing that we should live and not die; and have a being on the earth while heaven is pleased to lengthen out our days, are respectfully requested to publish this article. And men who wish to buy property very cheap, to benefit themselves and are willing to benefit us, are invited to call and look: and our prayer shall ever be that justice and judgment—mercy and truth may be exalted, not only in our own land, but throughout the world, and the will of God be done on earth as it is done in heaven.

Done in council [stake high council] at the city of Nauvoo, on the 20th day of January, 1846.

[Signed]	SAMUEL BENT	JAMES ALLRED
	GEORGE W. HARRIS	WM. HUNTINGTON
	HENRY G. SHERWOOD	ALPHEUS CUTLER
	NEWEL KNIGHT	LEWIS D. WILSON
	EZRA T. BENSON	DAVID FULLMER
	THOMAS GROVER	AARON JOHNSON.'

Wednesday, 21.—Two hundred and eight persons received ordinances. I received a letter from Hon. J. H. Ralston, Quincy, concerning our removal, etc., he says:

Admonition to "Suffer and Forgive!"

'I have long known many of the Mormons, who I have always thought good citizens, let them now show that they can suffer and forgive, and that amidst oppression their patriotism grows the brighter.'

Thursday, 22.—One hundred and ninety-eight persons received ordinances in the Temple. Elder Heber C. Kimball received a letter from Dr. Alphonzo Young of the 21st inst. in which he says:

Warning of Hostilities in Iowa.

'I have learned that the mob have been making preparations in Iowa to harass the brethren. Yesterday they got up a war dance in Keokuk and those participating in it were dressed in Indian garb, and as the report is widely circulated that the Twelve will soon leave for the west, I have no doubt but that the meeting was got up to concoct schemes to take the Twelve, when they cross the Mississippi or soon after.'

Friday, 23.—One hundred and twenty-eight persons received ordinances in the Temple. Elder Woodruff and Joseph A. Stratton sailed from Liverpool on board the packet ship *Ashburton* for New York.

Saturday, 24.—One hundred and fifty-one persons received ordinances in the Temple. I attended a general meeting of the official members of the church held in the second story of the Temple, for the purpose of arranging the business affairs of the church prior to our exit from this place.

The meeting being organized previous to my arrival Elder Orson Pratt was appointed chairman.

Trustees Appointed to Take Charge of Property at Nauvoo.

I explained to the brethren the object of appointing trustees, and informed them that the trustees would act in concert with Bishops Whitney and Miller while they remained here; and that when the Twelve left the bishops would accompany them, and that the trustees now appointed would carry on the finishing of the Temple and the Nauvoo House, also dispose of our property, fit out the saints and send them westward. It is wisdom to take this course that we may have efficient men to act for and in behalf of the church and people. I want Bishops Whitney and Miller here while we are here, and when we go, they will go with us.

We intend to start a company of young men and some few families perhaps within a few weeks. This company will travel until they can find a good location beyond the settlements, and there stop and put in a summer crop, that we may have something to subsist upon, and a portion of us remain there until we can make further discoveries.

We are forced to this policy by those who are in authority [i. e. in the state]. I find no fault with the Constitution or laws of our country, they are good enough. It is the abuse of those laws which I despise, and which God, good men and angels abhor.

I hope we will find a place, where no self-righteous neighbors can say that we are obnoxious to them; I exhort you brethren not to be self-important. We have covenanted to remove the poor that are worthy, and this we intend to do, God being our helper.

Let us walk humbly before the Lord, be upright and sustain yourselves and realize that we are engaged in a great and important movement. If any want to go with us that are not members of the church bid them welcome; for I look upon every man that is a true republican as bone of my bone and flesh of my flesh; and if any wish to follow Sidney Rigdon or J. J. Strang I say let them go; we will cut them off from the church, and let them take their own course for salvation.

President Favors Liberty.

I know where the power of the priesthood lies and I know that the enemy of all righteousness seeks our downfall, but God is our preserver.

A set of bogus-makers who recently commenced operations in this city, who are determined to counterfeit coin here by wagonloads and make it pass upon the community as land office money; [they] are determined to be revenged upon us, because we would not permit them to pursue their wicked business in Nauvoo, they have scattered through the country circulating their bogus money and spreading lies and every species of falsehood, saying that we are engaged in bogus-making in order thereby to conceal their crimes, and screen themselves from observation and punishment, and at the same time be avenged upon us for not consenting to the establishment of their bogus mints at Nauvoo.

Of Bogus Makers.

Nevertheless, we may have to suffer repeated wrongs in consequence of those falsehoods that are and which will be circulated about us; but my faith is that God will rule the elements, and the Prince and power of the air will be stayed, and the Lord will fight our battles, as in the days of Moses; and we will see the deliverance brought to pass. Although, there may be bloodshed frequently, still this must needs be that the scriptures may be fulfilled.

It is but a small matter for us to lay down our lives if we are prepared for the change; when we take our exit from this world we go into the society of disembodied spirits, and there become one of those who await the resurrection of the body; if humility and faithfulness has characterized our lives, our condition will be much better than the present. This nation is fearful that we will turn the world upside down and accomplish wonderful things in the land; our elders have confounded the wise men if they have not converted them. The nation are afraid that we will convert the savages of the forest; we will teach them and all with whom we may have intercourse, and further we will yet bring salvation to this nation if they will cease their hostilities against us, and repent of their sins. The Lord has said he would fight our battles, and if this nation still continues to be actuated towards us with a persecuting spirit, vengeance shall come from the Lord upon them, until they shall be utterly wasted; but I intend to preach and do all the good that I can.

Unimportance of Death to the Saints.

When the time comes to start westward we will continue to gather, until Israel is gathered; let there be no feelings about who shall go first; those who go first will lay a foundation for those who shall come after, and none will be neglected in their time.

I have one request to make of all the saints that expect to emigrate with us, that they be subject to their leaders, with their property and means, and if this is done I can say there never will be a lack in the church. If any man can say that he has been wronged out of his money by the bishops, let him speak and it shall be restored to him again; but I am aware it is not so. Keep your money in circulation and it will enable you to do good and you will be blessed in so doing; retain your money when the poor around you are crying for bread and it will prove a curse to you. Be honorable in all your

Justice in Financial Affairs Assured.

dealings, prompt and punctual to pay all your debts and restore confidence, let promptness and punctuality be the standard with you and the God of peace will pour out blessings upon you that there shall not be room enough to receive them.

We intend to finish the Temple and the Nauvoo House, as far as putting on the roof and putting in the windows are concerned, and we shall drop all political operations and church government, and by so doing we may preserve our public buildings from the torch. I propose that all the saints lay down their property to be used in building the Temple, the Nauvoo House and helping the poor away, such as must go in the first company.

The Committee of Trustees.

I nominated Almon W. Babbitt, Joseph L. Heywood, and John S. Fullmer, trustees for the building of the Temple and Henry W. Miller and John M. Bernhisel, trustees or committee for the building of the Nauvoo House, which nominations were seconded and carried without a dissenting voice.

Two p. m., on motion, the meeting adjourned, after which I ascended the stairs—called at the dining room and partook of some refreshment, then repaired to room No. 1 where I continued administering at the altar until midnight.

Sunday, 25.—I attended to ordinances in the Temple.

Monday, 26.—Nine a. m., I went to the Temple and commenced the ordinances in the different departments which were set apart for the purpose; the washing and anointing was suspended until tomorrow.

Tuesday, 27.—One hundred and twenty-six persons received ordinances.

The "Higher Ordinances" of the Temple.

Elders Heber C. Kimball, Orson Hyde, Parley P. Pratt, Orson Pratt, Amasa Lyman, and I officiated in the higher ordinances. Elders George A. Smith and Willard Richards were absent, being sick.

Sheriff Backenstos has returned from Springfield, and says, that Governor Ford has turned against us, and that Major Warren is making calculations to prevent our going away.

Increasing Unfriendliness of Governor Ford.

I received a letter from Josiah Lamborn, Esq., Springfield, stating that Governor Ford was decidedly in favor of General J. J. Hardin's policy, which is, that of suspending all civil offices, the collection of taxes, and placing the county under martial law.

I officiated at the altar until 10 p. m. and remained in the Temple all night.

Wednesday, 28.—One hundred and seventy-two persons received ordinances in the Temple.

Nine-thirty p. m., the labors of the day closed. I remained in the Temple.

Thursday, 29.—I continued giving endowments in the Temple in connection with my brethren of the Twelve and others. One hundred and thirty-three persons received ordinances.

Quite a number of the governor's troops are prowling around our city; I am informed that they are seeking to arrest some of the leading men of the church.

This evening I read a letter from S. Brannan in which he said he had ascertained from Amos Kendall, the late postmaster-general, that government intended to intercept our movements by stationing strong forces in our way to take from us all firearms on the pretense that we were going to join another nation.

More Rumors of "Interception".

Brannan said this jealousy originated from Arlington Bennett's letters in relation to our movements. We ask God our heavenly Father to exert his power in our deliverance that we may be preserved to establish truth upon all the face of the earth.

Friday, 30.—One hundred and seventy-two persons received the ordinances of endowment.

Nine a. m., the [wind] vane was put upon the tower of the Temple.

The weather is stormy, yet not cold. At ten a. m., I entered the Temple where I labored until evening.

Saturday, 31.—Two hundred and thirty-three persons received ordinances.

About noon, Brother Amasa Lyman came into the Temple being quite feeble; Elder H. C. Kimball administered to him.

The labors in the Temple came to a close at 10:39 p. m. I called the house to order and Elder Charles C. Rich prayed and we retired to rest.

Sunday, February 1, 1846.—Public meeting in the second story of the Temple. Elder Orson Pratt and myself addressed the meeting.

Sunday Service in the Temple.

After meeting, I returned to the attic and partook of some refreshments.

Elder Heber C. Kimball, Amasa Lyman, and I administered at the altar.

Monday, 2.—Two hundred and thirty-four persons received ordinances.

Ten a. m., the Twelve, Trustees and a few others met in council, to ascertain the feelings of the brethren that were expecting to start westward. We agreed that it was imperatively necessary to start as soon as possible. I counseled the brethren to procure boats and hold them in readiness to convey our wagons and teams over the river, and let everything for the journey be in readiness, that when a family is called to go, everything necessary may be put into the wagon within four hours, at least, for if we are here many days, our way will be hedged up. Our enemies have resolved to intercept us whenever we start. I should like to push on as far as possible before they are aware of our movements. In order to have this counsel circulated, I sent messengers to notify the captains of hundreds and fifties to meet at 4 p. m. at Father Cutlers'.

Early Departure of the Twelve from Nauvoo Imperative.

At four o'clock, I met with the captains of hundreds and fifties, and laid my counsel before them, to which they all consented, and dispersed to carry it into execution.

I received letters from England and the eastern states.

At sundown, I returned to the Temple and continued there until 9 p. m. Before leaving I gave instructions to my clerks not to stop recording until the records of the endowments were finished.

Elder H. C. Kimball and I went to Willard Richards' office, where we remained in council with him. In the course of our council we walked out into the garden, and examined his grove of chestnut trees, and his wife, Jennetta's grave, and after returning to the office made inquiries of the Lord as to our circumstances and the circumstances of the saints and received satisfactory answers. Retired about 1 a. m.

At the Home of Willard Richards.

Tuesday, 3.—Notwithstanding that I had announced that we would not attend to the administration of the ordinances, the House of the Lord was thronged all day, the anxiety being so great to receive, as if the brethren would have us stay here and continue the endowments until our way would be hedged up, and our enemies would intercept us. But I informed the brethren that this was not wise, and that we should build more Temples, and have further opportunities to receive the blessings of the Lord, as soon as the saints were prepared to receive them. In this Temple we have been abundantly rewarded, if we receive no more. I also informed the brethren that I was going to get my wagons started and be off. I walked some distance from the Temple supposing the crowd would disperse, but on returning I found the house filled to overflowing.

Great Anxiety of the Saints to Receive Endowments.

Looking upon the multitude and knowing their anxiety, as they were thirsting and hungering for the word, we continued at work diligently in the House of the Lord.

Two hundred and ninety-five persons received ordinances.

Brother Player and two others altering Jennetta Richards' grave. I stayed at home until 6 p. m. I went to the Temple and returned again in an hour, busy preparing for my journey to the west.

Grave of Jennetta Richards Opened.

Jennetta's coffin was opened, and the whole family looked at the corpse, which was but little decayed.

Wednesday, 4.—I continued loading up my wagons, preparatory to starting west.

Elder G. D. Watt received his letter of recommendation to preach the gospel in England.

Brother Player and others completed Jennetta's grave placing the inscription stone across her breast, one stone below, and another above, for a covering of the whole. It was first covered with a plank. A line passing ten feet south of the house, in a range with the west side of the building, thence west at a right angle twenty feet, thence descend at a right angle about three feet, and it will reach about the center of the vault containing the coffin.

Friday, 6.—Five hundred and twelve persons received the first ordinances of endowment in the Temple.

Bishop George Miller and family crossed the Mississippi river. They had six wagons.

Saturday, 7.—According to G. A. Smith's Journal upwards of six hundred received the ordinances [i. e. of the Temple]: One hundred and twenty-six of which were reported in the Seventies Record.

Sunday, 8.—I met with the Council of the Twelve in the southeast corner room of the attic of the Temple. We knelt around the altar, and dedicated the building to the Most High. We asked his blessing upon our intended move to the west; also asked him to enable us some day to finish the Temple, and dedicate it to him, and we would leave it in his hands to do as he pleased; and to preserve the building as a monument to Joseph Smith. We asked the Lord to accept the labors of his servants in this land. We then left the Temple.

Prayer for the Nauvoo. Temple.

I addressed the saints in the grove and informed them that the company going to the west would start this week across the river.

John Smith, president of the stake, and family crossed the river, accompanied by his clerk, Albert Carrington, and family.

Monday, 9.—A detachment of the governor's troops came into the city and apprehended a man named Samuel Smith, who soon escaped.

Elder George A. Smith sent his family across the river.

Three-thirty p. m., the roof of the Temple was discovered to be on fire. An alarm was immediately given, when the brethren marched steadily to its rescue. I saw the flames from a distance, but it was out of my power to get there in time to do any good towards putting out the fire, and I said if it is the will of the Lord that the Temple be burned, instead of being defiled by the Gentiles, Amen to it.

Roof of the Temple on Fire.

I went to the Temple as soon as I could, after the fire had been extinguished, the brethren gave a loud shout of Hosannah, while standing on the deck roof.

Willard Richards called on the brethren to bring out all their buckets, to fill them with water, and pass them on. Lines inside were formed, and the buckets passed in quick succession. The fire raged near half an hour. It was caused by the stovepipe being overheated, drying the clothing in the upper room. It burned from the west stovepipe from the ridge to the railing, about sixteen feet north and south, and about ten feet east and west on the north side. The shingles on the north were broken in several places.

By the advice of President H. C. Kimball the brethren dispersed.

Several of the troops went to the Temple and attempted to enter, but were prevented by the brethren at the door.

At the same time that the Temple was on fire a

number of brethren were crossing the river in a flatboat, when in their rear a man and two boys were in a skiff in a sinking condition, on account of being overloaded and the unskilfulness of the helmsman. They hailed to the flatboat, which soon turned, and rendered them assistance. As soon as they got the three on board the flatboat, a filthy wicked man squirted some tobacco juice into the eyes of one of the oxen attached to Thomas Grover's wagon, which immediately plunged into the river, dragging another ox with him, and as he was going overboard he tore off one of the sideboards which caused the water to flow into the flatboat, and as they approached the shore the boat sank to the bottom, before all the men could leap off. Several of the brethren were picked up in an exhausted condition. Two oxen were drowned and a few things floated away and were lost. The wagon was drawn out of the river with its contents damaged.

A River Disaster Incident.

The crossing of the river was superintended by the police, under the direction of Hosea Stout. They gathered several flatboats, some old lighters, and a number of skiffs, forming altogether quite a fleet, and were at work night and day, crossing the saints.

The undersigned wrote as follows:

JOHN E. PAGE OF THE COUNCIL OF THE TWELVE DISFELLOWSHIPED

'Nauvoo, Feb. 9, 1846.

To the Saints of God.

Dear Brethren and Sisters: We take this opportunity to say to you that we have no fellowship with Elder John E. Page, in consequence of his murmuring disposition, and choosing to absent himself from our councils, and then saying that he is made a servant and slave of by his quorum, and has had no privileges in the Temple, when the plain truth is, he has chosen to stand aside from us, and because we would let him do so, he has murmured about it. He has been on the background and in the shade ever since he failed to fulfill his mission to Jerusalem in company with Elder Hyde.

Now, beloved brethren, you are not bound to look to him as one of the Twelve Apostles, for he has yielded himself up to temptation, and he cannot resist the spirit of apostasy which inspired him to find fault with the organization of the church.

We, therefore, your brethren in solemn council, being grieved at his murmurings and dissension, and also at his yielding himself up to temptation willingly and without cause, have withdrawn the hand of fellowship from him until he comes to us and gives satisfaction for his dissension; and the saints are released from all covenants and obligations to abide his counsel.

Done in council the day and date above written.

[Signed] BRIGHAM YOUNG, President,
HEBER C. KIMBALL,
PARLEY P. PRATT,
GEORGE A. SMITH,
ORSON PRATT,
JOHN TAYLOR,
WILLARD RICHARDS.

Orson Hyde, Clerk.' "

CHAPTER XXXIX

DEPARTURE OF BRIGHAM YOUNG FROM NAUVOO—PROPOSITION OF "A. G. BENSON & CO."—PROPOSED CONTRACT—PUBLIC MEETING IN THE TEMPLE—MISSISSIPPI BRIDGED BY ICE—LIMITED NUMBER WHO CROSSED ON THE ICE WITH TEAMS AND FAMILIES—PETITION TO THE GOVERNOR OF IOWA—REFLECTIONS ON COMMENCEMENT OF EXODUS FROM NAUVOO

"*Tuesday, February* 10, 1846.—Dr. Richards had a very comfortable chat with Elder Noah Rogers who had just returned from the Society Islands. Elder Rogers related an account of Wm. Law and others attempting to take the life of the Prophet Joseph.

THE SENIOR PRESIDENT OF THE FIRST COUNCIL OF THE SEVENTY APPOINTED PRESIDENT OF THE CHURCH AT NAUVOO

Joseph Young was appointed to preside over the church during the stay of the saints in Nauvoo and received his letter of appointment from the Quorum of the Twelve.

Wednesday, 11.—President Joseph Young met in the Temple with a company of saints for prayer, and organized companies for prayer to meet every night.

Thursday, 12.—The Twelve Apostles making preparations to start on their journey westward.

Twelve brethren met in the Temple and prayed in two companies. Elders Ransom Shepherd and Joseph Young were mouth in prayer.

Friday, 13.—Two companies met for prayer in the House of the Lord this evening, and prayed for the preservation of the Twelve, and that they might have wisdom to guide the saints in the paths of peace and safety; for the healing of the sick, etc.

Saturday, 14.—Eleven of the brethren met for prayer in two companies.

Sunday, 15.—I crossed the river with my family accompanied by W. Richards and family and George A. Smith. We traveled on four miles, when we came to the bluff. I would not go on until I saw all the teams up. I helped them up the hill with my own hands. At dusk started on, and reached Sugar Creek about 8 p. m., having traveled nine miles. The roads were very bad. * * *

President Young Departs from Nauvoo.

Monday, 16.—I was very busy in organizing the camp on Sugar Creek, Ambrosia township, Lee county, Iowa territory, where there was plenty of timber and water.

Ten a. m., I walked up the valley with Amasa Lyman and Willard Richards where we united in prayer, and I read to them a communication received two days previously, then returned to camp and continued the organization, acting the part of a father to everybody.

The night was clear and cold. Two companies met this evening in the Temple and prayed.

Tuesday, 17.—Nine-fifty a. m., all the brethren of the camp assembled near the bridge, when I arose in a wagon and cried with a loud voice—'Attention! the whole Camp of Israel'. I proceeded to explain the cause of delay of the camp, which was, in short, that Bishop Whitney and Elders H. C. Kimball and Wm. Clayton were not ready, or were waiting to secure and bring with them church property needed in the camp. Some of the brethren have been here nearly two weeks, and if all had come on according to counsel, I should have been here sooner, if I had come without a shirt to my back.

Explanation of Delay of Movements.

I wish the brethren to stop running to Nauvoo, hunting, fishing, roasting their shins, idling away their time, and fix nosebaskets for their horses, and save their corn, and fix comfortable places for their wives and children to ride, and never borrow without asking leave, and be sure

Instructions on Camp Deportment.

and return what was borrowed, lest your brother be vexed with you and in his anger curse you, and then you would be cursed according to the power of the priesthood that brother possesses, and evil will come upon you. That all dogs in the camp should be killed, if the owners would not tie them up; and any man who would keep a horse in camp, that had the horse distemper, ought to forfeit all his horses. [This because horse distemper was rife in the camp and contagious.]

We will have no laws we cannot keep, but we will have order in the camp. If any want to live in peace when we have left this, they must toe the mark.

I then called upon all who wanted to go with the camp, to raise their right hands, and all hands were up.

Camp Commissary Appointed.

I said we must wait here until we get the artillery, canvas, and public property; that the brethren must build a pen for corn and hay. George W. Harris was appointed commissary. That all spare men were for pioneers, guards, watchmen, and that all men of families must be organized into companies of tens, fifties, and hundreds. Wm. Clayton would be general clerk of the camp.

I requested the brethren to report all matters of history which might arise, to Willard Richards, historian.

At eleven o'clock, I returned to my tent and commenced organizing my division of the camp, consisting of four companies of tens, including the historian, his family, and teams.

Elder Heber C. Kimball arrived in camp at the same hour, and at half past one he and I dined on bean porridge in George D. Grant's tent.

Villainous Proposition of Amos Kendall "A. G. Benson and Co."

Two-thirty, accompanied by Elders Heber C. Kimball, Orson Hyde, Orson Pratt, John Taylor, George A. Smith, and Willard Richards. I went up the valley east of the camp about half a mile and counseled. A letter from

Samuel Brannan and a copy of an agreement between Brannan and Benson were read.

Amos Kendall, of Kentucky, who was postmaster-general from May, 1835, till May, 1840, A. G. Benson and others represented to Samuel Brannan that unless the leaders of the church would sign an agreement with them, to which the president of the United States was a silent party, the government would not permit the Latter-day Saints to proceed on their journey westward. This agreement requires the Latter-day Saints to transfer to 'A. G. Benson and Company' the odd number of all the land and town lots they may acquire in the country where they may settle, and in case they refuse to sign said agreement, the president would issue a proclamation that it was the intention of the Latter-day Saints to take sides with other nations against the United States, and order them to be disarmed and dispersed. Brannan becoming fully satisfied that this was the secret intention of the government, and that the president was a principal party, signed it.

LETTER OF SAMUEL BRANNAN ON "A. G. BENSON AND CO."

'New York, Jan. 12, 1846.

Brother Young: I have written you three letters of late from Boston, Washington and New York, and I fear they have been intercepted on the way and I have thought it prudent to direct this to some obscure individual that it may reach [you] in safety; I have received positive information that it is the intention of the government to disarm you after you have taken up your line of march in the spring, on the ground of the law of nations, or the treaty existing between the United States and Mexico, 'That an armed *posse* of men shall not be allowed to invade the territory of a foreign nation.'

Amos Kendall was in the city last week, and positively declared that that was the intention of the government, and I thought it my duty to let you know that you might be on your guard. I declare to all that you are not going to California but Oregon, and that my information is official. Kendall has also learned that we have chartered the ship *Brooklyn* and that Mormons are going out in her, and it is thought that she will be searched for arms, and if found taken from us, and if not, an order will be sent to Commodore Stockton on the Pacific to search our vessel before we land.

Kendall will be in the city next Thursday again, and then an effort will be made to bring about a reconciliation. I will make you acquainted with the result before I leave. My company now numbers about one hundred and seventy-five. I chartered the whole ship, put her in the market and have already obtained one thousand dollars worth of freight for the Sandwich Islands, and a good prospect for more. I now have it in my power to learn every movement of the government in relation to us, which I shall make you acquainted with from time to time. God is at work in the east and so is the devil, but Moses' rod will be too hard for him. I feel my weakness and inability and desire your blessing and prayers that I may be successful. My cares and labors weigh me down day and night, but I trust in God that I shall soon have a happy deliverance.

All the saints in the east are praying and crying for deliverance; but I must now close by subscribing myself, your brother in the everlasting covenant.

[Signed] SAMUEL BRANNAN.'

FURTHER REPORT OF SAMUEL BRANNAN

'New York, Jan. 26, 1846.

Dear Brother Young: I haste to lay before your honorable body the result of my movements since I wrote you last, which was from this city, stating some of my discoveries in relation to the contemplated movements of the general government, in opposition to our removal.

I had an interview with Amos Kendall in company with Mr. Benson, which resulted in a compromise, the conditions of which you will learn by reading the contract, between them and us, which I shall forward by this mail. I shall also leave a copy of the same with Elder Appleby, who was present when it was signed. Kendall is now our friend and will use his influence in our behalf in connection with twenty-five of the most prominent demagogues of the country. You will be permitted to pass out of the states unmolested. Their counsel is to go well armed, but keep them well secreted from the rabble.

I shall select the most suitable spot on the Bay of San Francisco for the location of a commercial city.

When I sail, which will be next Saturday at 1 o'clock, I shall hoist a flag with Oregon on it. Immediately on the reception of this letter you must write to Messrs. A. G. Benson [and Co.] and let them know whether you are willing to coincide with the contract I have made for our deliverance. I am aware that it is a covenant with death, but we know that God is able to break it, and will do it, the children of Israel from Egypt had to make covenants for their safety and leave it for God to break them, and the Prophet has said 'as it was then so shall it be in the last days.' And I have been led by a remarkable train of circumstances to say, amen—and I feel and hope you will do the same. Mr. Benson thinks the Twelve should leave and get out of the country first and avoid being arrested if it is a possible thing, but if you are arrested you will find a staunch friend in him, and you will find friends, and that a host, to deliver you from their hands—if any of you are arrested, don't be tried west of the Allegheny Mountains. In the east you will find friends that you little think of. It is the prayer of the saints in the east night and day for your safety and it is mine first in the morning and the last in the evening. I must now bring my letter to a close. Mr. Benson's address is No. 39 South Street —and the sooner you can give him an answer the better it will be for us. He will spend one month in Washington to sustain you—and he will do it, no mistake. But everything must be kept as silent as death on our part—names of the parties in particular. I now commit this sheet to the post praying that Israel's God may prevent it from falling into the hands of wicked men. You will hear from me again on the day of sailing if it is the Lord's will. Amen.

Yours truly,
A friend and brother in God's Kingdom,
[Signed] SAMUEL BRANNAN.'

'New York, Jan. 27th.

Brother Young: Your letter confirming the contract I have made, which I directed you to address to A. G. Benson, must be written to me, and on the outside addressed to A. G. Benson and all will go well.

Yours very respectfully in haste,
[Signed] S. BRANNAN.'

The following is a copy of a contract entered into between A. G. Benson of New York for Amos Kendall and others of one part, and Samuel Brannan of the other, done at the city of New York, previous to the ship *Brooklyn* sailing for California.

"CONTRACT" BETWEEN "A. G. BENSON AND CO." AND SAMUEL BRANNAN

'*Whereas*, the Latter-day Saints generally known under the name of Mormons, though devotedly attached to the principles on which the government of the United States and of the several states are founded, have become satisfied that owing to the prejudices against them which designing men have created in the minds of the great mass of the community, who do not appreciate their character, nor understand their designs, they cannot, under the jurisdiction of any of the present states, enjoy the privileges and security which their constitutions and laws promise to all sects and creeds.

And whereas, they have resolved to seek for liberty and security beyond the jurisdiction of the states, and under the fostering care of the United States, within their territories, not doubting that in becoming a nucleus on the shores of the Pacific, around which a new state shall grow up, constituted of a people, who, from their more intimate knowledge of them will be free from those prejudices, which now drive them into exile, thereby affording them peace and security, the only boons they ask at the hands of man, and

Whereas, it is their earnest desire to depart in peace, and reach their future homes, without that molestation on their pilgrimage which the government of the United States might, under a misapprehension as to their designs, feel themselves called upon to offer; and *whereas,* A. G. Benson states that he has it in his power to correct any misrepresentations which may be made to the president of United States, and prevent any authorized interference with them on their journey, and also to extend to them facilities for emigration, especially by sea, and afford them great commercial facilities and advantages at their new homes; *wherefore,*

It is covenanted and agreed between A. G. Benson aforesaid, on behalf of himself and such as he may hereafter associate with him on the one part, and Samuel Brannan, for and in behalf of the Latter-day Saints, by their principal men, duly authorized on the other part, that the said ______________ shall take the necessary steps to guard the said Latter-day Saints against the effects of misapprehension, and prevent interference with them, by the officers or agents of the United States, on their journey westward, and shall, as far as in his power, facilitate trade with them in their new settlement, and promote emigration, to strengthen them there; and on the part of the said ______________ for and on behalf of the Latter-day Saints aforesaid, it is covenanted and agreed that, in case the said saints shall be enabled to reach their new homes without molestation from the government of the United States, and they or any of them shall acquire lands from the said United States or from any other source, then one-half of the said lands shall belong and be conveyed to the said Benson, and those whom by written contract, he may have associated with him, his and their heirs and assigns, said lands if not surveyed to be held in common until a survey shall be made when they shall be *ipso facto* divided by alternate sections, the odd numbers belonging to the said Latter-day Saints, and the even numbers belonging to the said Benson and his associates; but if surveyed they shall be divided by sections, half sections, quarter sections, or otherwise, so as to carry into effect this agreement in its true nature and intent; and if the said saints or any of them, or the said Brannan or any of his associates, assigns or heirs shall within ten years, lay off and establish any city or cities, town or towns on the lands acquired by them or any of them, each alternate lot in said cities and towns, shall belong and be conveyed to the said ______________ and his associates and assigns as hereinbefore stipulated by the said Brannan, that the said saints shall exert all their lawful authority and influence to prevent the imposition of any tax on the vacant lands held by said ______________, his associates and assigns, so long as they use due diligence to settle the same, or any higher tax upon vacant city and town lots held by him and them, than shall be imposed on vacant lots held by resident citizens.

And it is further stipulated and agreed by the said Brannan in behalf of said Latter-day Saints, that they shall not in any manner on their journey, or after their arrival in the west, violate the laws or Constitution of the United States, it being hereby solemnly declared by him, that their dearest object, and most earnest desire is to enjoy for themselves, their wives, children and neighbors, of whatever religion or political faith, the protection which that Constitution and those laws promise to all men of whatever creed.

Witness our hands and seals at the city of New York on the --------- day of January, 1846.

[Signed] SAMUEL BRANNAN, A. G. BENSON.

Witness: W. I. APPLEBY.'

'This is only a copy of the original which I have filled out. It is no gammon but will be carried through if you say, amen—it was drawn up by Kendall's own hand—but no person must be known but Mr. Benson.'

Samuel Brannan urged upon the council the necessity of signing the document.

The council considered the subject, and concluded that as our trust was in God and that we looked to him for protection, we would not sign any such unjust and oppressive agreement.

This was a plan of political demagogues to rob the Latter-day Saints of millions and compel them to submit to it, by threats of federal bayonets.

This evening was severely cold.

Thirty elders met in the Temple for prayer in two companies.

Wednesday, 18.—I called the brethren together and instructed the captains of hundreds to raise money in their respective companies and send for cloth for tent ends and wagon covers; and informed the Pioneer Company that it would be their duty to prepare roads, look out camp grounds, dig wells, when necessary, and ascertain where hay and corn could be purchased for the camp; that if the brethren could not bring their minds to perfect order, they had better leave the camp and I would have no feelings against them; that after dark no man must leave the camp without the countersign, nor approach the guard abruptly; that every family must call on the Lord night and morning at every tent or wagon, and

Instructions to the "Pioneer Company."

we shall have no confidence in the man who does not; that the police would be night and day guard; that every captain of ten would keep one man on watch every night; that Benjamin F. Johnson be authorized to receive and preserve for the owners all the lost property found; and that when I wanted to see the brethren together, a white flag should be hoisted, and that when the captains are wanted together a blue or colored flag should be raised; the captains of hundreds were instructed to form their companies in circles, without the circle surrounding the stand; Captain Hosea Stout formed the police; Captain Stephen Markham the Pioneers.

Elder Parley P. Pratt called out the companies of the Twelve. Captain Wm. Pitt called out the musicians. Captains George Miller, Shadrach Roundy, Charles C. Rich, Charles Shumway, Peter Haws, Samuel Bent, and Daniel Spencer called out their respective companies.

Those not organized were instructed to join the Pioneers, and all to organize into companies of tens.

I told the brethren they were the best set of fellows in the world, still there was a great chance for improvement: I blessed them in the name of the Lord.

Twelve-twenty p. m., Lyman O. Littlefield called on me in company with Dr. Clayton Tiffin of St. Louis, who was baptized last evening at Nauvoo, and wanted counsel.

I counseled Dr. Tiffin to meet the camp on the Missouri in April, bringing groceries principally.

The artillery was brought into camp in charge of Colonel John Scott, two six-pounders, one three-pounder and one short twelve-pounder carronade [cannon].

Elder Kimball, myself and a few others returned to Nauvoo: the night was moderate.

Twenty-four elders met for prayer in the Temple.

Thursday, 19.—From Dr. Richards' *Camp Journal*:

'The wind blew steadily from the northwest accompanied by snow which fell to the depth of seven or eight inches, but much thawed as it fell, the storm was unceasing, and the evening was very cold, which caused much suffering in the camp, for there were many who had no tents or any comfortable place to lodge: many tents were blown down, some of them were unfinished and had no ends.'

A Fierce Storm.

Twenty-five elders met for prayer in the Temple. Elders Phineas Richards and Curtis E. Bolton were mouth.

Friday, 20.—From the historian's *Camp Journal*:

'Extremely cold, considerable ice floating on the Mississippi river.

About fifteen hundred bushels of tithing corn which had previously been gathered up in Lee county, together with a large amount of potatoes, turnips, and other vegetables and grain had been mostly consumed by the camp.

Dr. Richards was sick in bed with a severe cough, and at one p. m. invited Elders Parley P. Pratt, Orson Pratt, George A. Smith, Amasa Lyman, and Bishop George Miller to his tent; the council voted to purchase three hundred bushels of corn of Wm. Leffingwell and one yoke of oxen of Wm. Hawkes. The cold increased through the day, the night was very severe, at many points ice fastened on the banks of the Mississippi river.'

Twenty-five elders met in the Temple and prayed. Elders Franklin D. and Samuel W. Richards were mouth.

Saturday, 21.—From the *Camp Journal*:

'Cold continues. Two-thirty p. m., Elders Orson Pratt, Amasa Lyman, George A. Smith, George Miller and Albert P. Rockwood in council in the historian's tent.

Elder Willard Richards proposed that Bishop Miller assisted by Elder Charles C. Rich purchase five hundred or more bushels of corn and procure hay and straw to any amount—that Captain Stephen Markham of the Pioneers cause all the tithing wheat and rye at Ambrosia tithing office, and one hundred bushels of corn, to be ground immediately, and report to the council; that one load of wheat in care of David Dixon be ground and reported, and that John Scott cause the wheat in care of Captain Davis to be carried to the Buonaparte mills, floured and stored until further orders; also that the brethren meet at ten a. m. and at 4 p. m. on each day until President Young returns, to all of these propositions the council agreed unanimously.

Camp Provisions Secured.

The day was pleasant but the cold severe; the saints in camp were patient, and endured all their privations without murmuring.'

Twelve elders met in the Temple for prayer, Wm. Felshaw was mouth.

Sunday, 22.—I attended meeting at the Temple, the room was crowded and a great weight caused the new truss floor to settle nearly to its proper position. While settling, an inch-board or some light timber underneath was caught and cracked, the sound of which created great alarm in the congregation and some jumped out of the windows, smashing the glass and all before them. Philo Farnsworth smashed the northeast window while others ran out of the doors and many of those who remained jumped up and down with all their might crying Oh! Oh!! Oh!!! as though they could not settle the floor fast enough, but at the same time so agitated that they knew not what they did.

The Settling Temple Floor —Confusion— Hysteria.

I attempted to call the assembly to order to explain the cause of the settling of the floor, but failing to get their attention I adjourned the meeting to the grove. I went below, examined the floor and found it had hardly settled to its designed position, passed on to the assembly in the grove where the snow was about a foot deep, and told the people they might jump up and down as much as they pleased.

One man who jumped out of the window broke his arm and mashed his face, another broke his leg; both were apostates.

Afternoon, Elders Heber C. Kimball, John Taylor and I started for the camp; the ice was running in the river so there was no possibility of crossing only with a skiff which we accomplished with difficulty and danger, the skiff being very heavily laden, and arrived at camp at 7 o'clock.

From the [*Camp*] *Journal*:

'Ten a. m., Elders Orson Pratt, George A. Smith, Amasa Lyman and Willard Richards, in council.

Bishop Miller reported that he had purchased two hundred and fifteen baskets of corn.

Voted that Elder George A. Smith have a milk cow, which he had obtained on tithing, that Brother Thomas Grover have ropes to tie his oxen, and that Brothers Rockwood and Lee examine a load of tin belonging to Pulaski Cahoon and purchase such, as quality and prices would warrant, and raise forty or fifty dollars to send for such articles of tinware as were needed by the camp.

General Charles C. Rich reported that he had procured three hundred and fifty bushels of corn mostly on tithing.

Lucien Woodworth stated to the council that he could probably obtain five hundred bushels of corn, besides potatoes and other provisions, among the brethren in the vicinity, by donation: the council delegated to him that mission.

Voted that the brethren be lectured on domestic economy that the guard be instructed to lay aside their heavy arms during the day, that the Pioneer Company burn charcoal and that the blacksmiths and wagon makers organize and prepare for their several duties in the camp.

Camp Lecture.

One p. m., the brethren came together at the raising of the flag. Elders Orson Pratt and Amasa Lyman lectured on the health, comfort, success, peace, prosperity and salvation of the camp.

Four p. m., the council convened as in the morning with the addition of Elder Parley P. Pratt.

Resolved that the second hundred bushels of corn be prepared for mill on the return of the meal of the first—that Bishop George Miller authorize Captain John Scott, of the artillery to gather provisions on tithing; that Parley P. Pratt and Amasa Lyman have leave to go tomorrow to the Clark Settlement for oxen, corn and provisions, etc.'

Twenty-five elders met for prayer in the Temple.

Monday, 23.—I met in council with the Twelve and captains of hundreds as to moving the camp.

We agreed to pass up the divide between the waters of the Des Moines and Missouri rivers.

Henry G. Sherwood was appointed Pioneer Commissary to obtain grain and provisions for the camp.

Captain Stephen Markham was instructed to send a company of Pioneers to find a camping ground between Sugar Creek Encampment and Bonaparte Mills.

Captain Samuel Bent was instructed to move his company, consisting of twenty-five wagons, in the morning.

Several guns were discharged in and about the camp.

During the council Benjamin Stewart came up to the tent fire of the guards, caught up a large pistol and discharged it across the fire; it contained three small rifle balls which entered the left thigh of Abner Blackburn, son of Anthony Blackburn, two balls passed out the opposite side and one hit the bone and passed down remaining in the leg.

Evening, the Pioneers returned and reported a good camping ground ten miles from this, and corn plenty at 18¾ cents; 12¾ cents being the market price at Sugar Creek and Montrose.

PROSPECTUS OF THE HANCOCK EAGLE—"THE NEW ORDER OF THINGS"

W. E. Matlock issued the prospectus of the *Hancock Eagle* [Nauvoo], from which I extract the following·

'Our object in commencing the publication at this juncture, is to anticipate *the new order of things* which will inevitably result from the changes now taking place in the civil, ecclesiastical, and domestic polity of this large city and the country adjacent.

Nauvoo and its immediate suburbs, until recently, contained over 15,000 inhabitants—the greater part of whom were known as 'Mormons'—of these, some two or three thousand have already left together with an equal number from the country. A majority of those remaining, will, in due season depart upon their pilgrimage towards the setting sun. The high council is dissolved, and the church organization has been entirely broken up to be reestablished, we opine, in some distant region whose waters flow into the Pacific Ocean. The Twelve with their thousands of followers have abandoned their Temple and their city; with them, goes all that the enemies of Mormonism regard as inimical to the genius of our institutions and the well being of the community at large.'

Twenty-eight elders met for prayer in the Temple.

Tuesday, 24.—A son was born to John Redding in camp.

The cold has been severe the past night, a snowstorm this morning which continued during the forenoon, blowing from the northwest, which prevented Captain Bent's Company from moving; the cold was severe through the day and increased as night approached.

I was busy in unloading, weighing and loading my wagons preparatory to a removal.

I handed out to many of the brethren cloth for tent ends and wagon covers.

Evening, I met with Elders Heber C. Kimball and Willard Richards at his [the latter's] tent, to investigate some disaffection which existed between Bishop Miller and the guards which proved to be a misunderstanding.

Seven p. m., thermometer 12 degrees below zero, Fah. Mississippi river frozen over above Montrose.

Twenty-five elders met for prayer in the Temple in two companies.

Wednesday, 25.—The morning was colder than any one since the encampment, but the sun rose clear, the whole camp appeared cheerful and happy.

Nine a. m., the blast of the bugle and the raising of the flag called the brethren together.

President Young stated to the assembly that he had been informed by Bishop Miller, that jobs of chopping cord wood and splitting rails could be obtained to advantage by the brethren on the Desmoines river, at, and above Farmington; Bishop Miller said, that he had received his information from Mr. Crook, a merchant of Farmington. President Young asked, shall we go where we can get work? when the brethren responded in the affirmative, then, said the President, we will browse our cattle till Bishop Whitney comes up.

Prospects of Camp Employment.

President Young then spoke against thieving, cutting strings from wagon covers, and said the brethren had gone contrary to counsel in cutting rail timber, etc., on the camp ground and they must stop all such practices; that they had not made him their leader of the camp as yet, but if they should do it, when they get out of the settlements where his orders could be executed, they would have justice done them, and, said he, I should be perfectly willing to see thieves have their throats cut; some of you may say, if that is your feelings Brigham, we'll lay you aside sometime, well, do it if you can; I would rather die by the hands of the meanest of all men, false brethren, than to live among thieves. He then called upon the captains of companies to report those who were most destitute and he would divide among them the corn and oats he had brought for horse feed; there is no need of stealing, if one suffers we will all suffer, this great 'I' and little 'you', I cannot bear, if the guard consider the Twelve as privileged characters they must consider the high council also, and if the high council, the high priests, etc., and we

Irregularities in Camp Life.

should all be privileged characters; and what is the use of any guard? None at all. When I want to pass the guard I will go to the sergeant and get the password, and I want all the brethren to do the same. Let no man crowd upon the guard and let the guard know no man as a privileged character.

President Young retired from the meeting and went to distributing his grain among the needy.'

About eleven a. m., Captain Charles C. Rich arrived from Nauvoo and reported that he had walked over the Mississippi river on the ice at Montrose.

Seven a. m., thermometer at 6° Fah.; one p. m., thermometer 18° Fah. Latitude of the Camp of Israel by a meridian observation of the sun taken by Professor Orson Pratt this day was 40° 31′ 50″, longitude 91° 16′ 0″.

Bishop George Miller with about sixteen wagons and thirty or forty Pioneers started for the Des Moines.

At seven p. m., thermometer stood 10° Fah.

This afternoon, Captain Samuel J. Hastings arrived from Boston and in the evening was in council with the Twelve at the recorder's office, Dr. Richards' tent; when Mr. Hastings answered our queries in a previous letter by stating that he would take emigrants from New York, Boston and the Atlantic cities to California and the western coast generally for $150.00 including provisions; that from New Orleans there would be an additional expense of about $4000 for every two hundred passengers and to enter the Columbia river there would be an additional expense of about five per cent. Mr. Hastings received a letter of introduction from the council to the Trustees at Nauvoo. He retired in my tent about 11 o'clock.

Captain Samuel J. Hastings—Pathfinder of the West.

Two companies of elders met and prayed in the Temple, thirty present.

Cold Intensity.

Thursday, 26.—Six-thirty a. m., thermometer stood at 2° below zero, Fah.

The weather being so cold it was not considered

prudent to remove the tents of families as had been contemplated.

John Gool let Thomas Grover, whose oxen were drowned on the 9th, have a span of horses and wagon to help him forward to be returned from the journey's end. This morning John Gool's wife came into camp and demanded the team; I tried to persuade her that it would be loss to her to take away the team under existing circumstances; but she persisted in her demand and took the team and drove off: I told Brother Grover to trust in the Lord.

Dr. Levi and Samuel W. Richards arrived in camp about eleven a. m. on a visit.

The trustees, Babbitt, Heywood and Fullmer arrived about noon.

The historian has been mostly confined to his bed since his arrival in camp, with a severe cough, and unable to write, but has dictated the *Camp Journal* from his pillow for the pen of Wm. Coray, scribe, since the 17th inst.

About noon, someone presented Brother Grover with a team.

Mr. Prentice, U. S. marshal, and several of the governor's troops from Carthage, came into camp and inquired for a grey horse which they said was stolen from McDonough county two weeks previously; that they had traced the horse to within six miles of Nauvoo and had caught the thief in Nauvoo but he was not a Mormon.

An Appeal to be Made to the Governor of Iowa.

In the evening I met in council with Elders Orson Pratt, John Taylor and Willard Richards in my tent and decided to write to the governor of Iowa and ascertain his views about the saints stopping on the public land in Iowa to raise a crop this season; read the prospectus of the *Hancock Eagle;* also the *New York Messenger Extra,* which gave an account of the sailing of the *Brooklyn* with Elder Samuel Brannan and company of two hundred and thirty souls, or one hundred and seventy-five passengers.

The sky was clear in the forenoon, in the afternoon cloudy, and the wind veering to the southeast. Six p. m., thermometer 10° above zero, Fah.

George A. Smith went to Nauvoo.

Twenty-three elders met for prayer in the Temple.

Friday, 27.—Six a. m., thermometer 5° above zero, Fah.

This morning Captain Albert P. Rockwood slaughtered a fine ox which had been sprained, and distributed it amongst the most needy of the camp.

James Wallace came into camp and thought he ought to have pay for the timber which the brethren had cut; he was willing to leave it to them what the timber was worth.

Over the Mississippi on the Ice.

William Clayton arrived at three thirty p. m.; having crossed the Mississippi with his teams on the ice.

The sky was clouded through the day, the wind in the southeast and very chilly, and towards night a little fine hail fell; the camp generally healthy and happy.

Six p. m., 21° above zero, Fah.

Brother McKee protested my order for corn to the amount of $15.00, which he promised to the camp yesterday; when the teams called for the corn this morning, McKee told them he had concluded to keep the corn to help off the poor with, which caused the teams in camp to be fed on five ears of corn each.

Eleven elders met for prayer in the Temple.

Saturday, 28.—Six a. m., thermometer 20° above zero, Fah. Wind variable, changing toward the north.

Some of the Pioneers, Daniel Spencer, Charles Shumway, and part of Captain Bent's Company moved on four miles.

I met in council with the Twelve in my tent. We read and approved the following to the governor of Iowa:—

COMMUNICATION TO THE GOVERNOR OF IOWA

'*To His Excellency,*
Governor of the Territory of Iowa,

Honored Sir: The time is at hand, in which several thousand free citizens of this great Republic, are to be driven from their peaceful homes and firesides, their property and farms, and their dearest constitutional rights—to wander in the barren plains, and sterile mountains of western wilds, and linger out their lives in wretched exile far beyond the pale of professed civilization; or else be exterminated upon their own lands by the people, and authorities of the state of Illinois. As life is sweet we have chosen *banishment* rather than death. But Sir, the terms of our banishment are so rigid that we have not sufficient time allotted us to make the necessary preparations to encounter the hardships and difficulties of those dreary and uninhabited regions. We have not time allowed us to dispose of our property, dwellings, and farms, consequently, many of us will have to leave them unsold, without the means of procuring the necessary provisions, clothing, teams, etc. to sustain us but a short distance beyond the settlements: hence our persecutors have placed us in very unpleasant circumstances.

To stay, is death by 'fire and sword', to go into banishment unprepared, is death by starvation. But yet under these heart-rending circumstances, several hundreds of us have started upon our dreary journey, and are now encamped in Lee county, Iowa, suffering much from the intensity of the cold. Some of us are already without food, and others barely sufficient to last a few weeks: hundreds of others must shortly follow us in the same unhappy condition.

Therefore, we, the Presiding Authorities of the Church of Jesus Christ of Latter-day Saints, as a committee in behalf of several thousand suffering exiles, humbly ask your Excellency to shield and protect us in our constitutional rights, while we are passing through the territory over which you have jurisdiction. And should any of the exiles be under the necessity of stopping in this territory for a time, either in the settled or unsettled parts, for the purpose of raising crops, by renting farms or upon the public lands, or to make the necessary preparations for their exile in any lawful way, we humbly petition your Excellency to use an influence and power in our behalf: and thus preserve thousands of American citizens, together with their wives and children from intense sufferings, starvation and death.

And your petitioners will ever pray.'

Three-thirty p. m., I rode out two or three miles in company with several of the council and the band, and met Bishop Whitney, saluted him and returned.

I was so afflicted with the rheumatism it was with difficulty I could walk.

Bishop Whitney arrived in camp about 4:30.

Some of the brethren were engaged this day in building a log house to pay James Wallace for his wood which the camp had burned on his claim.

Noon, thermometer 41° above zero Fah., six p. m., thermometer 21° above zero Fah.

The camp consisted of nearly four hundred wagons all very heavily loaded with not over one-half of the teams necessary to make a rapid journey. Most of the families were provided with provisions for several months. A considerable number, regardless of counsel, had started in a destitute condition, and some others, with only provisions for a few days.

Shortage of Teams.

Colonel Stephen Markham had about one hundred Pioneers to prepare the road in advance of the main body.

Colonel Hosea Stout with about one hundred men acted as police for the encampment; they were generally armed with rifles.

Colonel John Scott with about one hundred men accompanied the artillery.

A considerable number of the teams were to be returned as soon as an encampment could be selected for putting in spring crops; others expected to return as soon as the loads of provisions and forage which they hauled were exhausted.

Our encampment on Sugar Creek has had a tendency to check the movements of the mob, as they were generally of opinion, that our fit out was so insufficient that in a short time we would break to pieces and scatter.

The great severity of the weather and not being able to sell any of our property, the difficulty of crossing the river during many days of running ice all combined to delay our departure, though for several days the bridge of ice across the Mississippi greatly facilitated the crossing and compensated, in part, for the delay caused by the running ice.

President Young's Reflections.

The fact is worthy of remembrance that several thousand persons left their homes in midwinter and exposed themselves without shelter, except that afforded by a scanty supply of tents and wagon covers, to a cold which effectually made an ice bridge over the Mississippi river which at Nauvoo is more than a mile broad. We could have remained sheltered in our homes had it not been for the threats and hostile demonstrations of our enemies, who, notwithstanding their solemn agreements had thrown every obstacle in our way, not respecting either life, liberty or property, so much so, that our only means of avoiding a rupture was by starting in midwinter.

Our homes, gardens, orchards, farms, streets, bridges, mills, public halls, magnificent Temple, and other public improvements we leave as a monument of our patriotism, industry, economy, uprightness of purpose and integrity of heart; and as a living testimony of the falsehood and wickedness of those who charge us with disloyalty to the Constitution of our country, idleness and dishonesty."

CHAPTER XL

DISCONTINUANCE OF DAILY QUOTATIONS FROM THE MANUSCRIPT HISTORY OF BRIGHAM YOUNG—SUNDRY EVENTS IN THE MARCHING ENCAMPMENT FROM THE CLOSE OF FEBRUARY TO MID-JUNE.

With the close of February, 1846, I shall discontinue following the daily Journal known as the *History of Brigham Young, Ms.,* because of the inadequacy of the space in this volume to continue daily entries from that Journal, to the close of the period designed—October 8, 1848. The last hundred pages or so from the daily entries of that Journal up to now have been added to this volume at the suggestion of a committee of the Twelve Apostles to whom the manuscript was submitted, because they felt the desire to have the narrative of President Young continued throughout the crucial period of the exodus from Nauvoo; the importance of the official documents connected with the last days of Nauvoo being considered by them of such historical value that they ought not to be omitted from this volume. But these daily entries may not now be further continued if volume vii of the *History* is to be kept somewhat uniform in size with the previous six volumes, and hence I cover the period from the close of February, 1846, to the arrival at Council Bluffs in elliptical narrative with occasional verbatim brief quotations from the Journal at crucial points.

Breaking up of the Camp on Sugar Creek.

The first of March witnessed the breaking up of the encampment at Sugar Creek where some of the saints had been stationed for several weeks. Thence this encampment and others which followed on from Nauvoo continued marching intermittently westward amid renewing storms of the early spring months which with the breaking up of the frost in the mellow soil of the territory of Iowa made the roads well-nigh impassable and the discomfort of the westward moving wagons of the really one encampment extremely slow and wearisome.

Incompleteness of Preparations for the Westward Trek.

The hastened departure from Nauvoo of these early companies had enforced upon them an incompleted preparation, all which was unnecessarily enforced upon them by the constantly outbreaking hostility of their enemies, and Governor Ford repeatedly harassing the leaders of the church with manufactured statements about the likely intentions of the general government to hinder the departure of the people westward, and the arrest of the leading authorities of the church. This also prevented the perfect organization of the camps that had been projected for the departure from Nauvoo, resulting in some confusion in the organization projected, which in reality was not perfected until about half the journey between Nauvoo and Council Bluffs was accomplished. After that the organization as designed in the first place was carried into effect. Of course with the weather improvements which came in the latter part of March, and of April and May, many of the discomforts and distresses of the month of February and early part of March disappeared; and the great encampment, swelled into thousands both of people and wagons with large herds of oxteams, loose cattle and horses and mules, as it approached the Missouri frontiers.

Development of Methods of Travel *en Marche.*

With the first sections of the moving camps a company of Pioneers was organized to forge ahead of the oncoming companies selecting the route, bridging some sloughs and streams, including the Chariton river. As springtime advanced selections of lands were made at different places, the prairie broken up and sown to early crops, which were left to be harvested by later companies as they arrived at these sections.

Meantime in the march individuals and small companies were sent to the north and south of the route to exchange household goods, excess bedding, crockery ware, etc., for corn, oats and other provisions for men and animals. Occasionally contracts for plowing, rail-splitting, building houses, etc., were secured from the settlers in this new country, for which compensation was had in provisions, corn and hay for the struggling teams, more especially in the time when spring had not brought forth the prairie grass for grazing the stock.

Thus the line of encampments resembled in many respects an industrial column, that had to be largely self-sustaining *en marche*.

A brass band led by Captain William Pitt to enliven the march of the camp segments was sometimes invited to give concerts at villages near to the line of march, which did much to change the feelings of hostility which occasionally was manifested in such places. Thus this band proved a very great benefit to the marching column, besides cheering the spirits of the pilgrims.

"Camp of Israel."

"Camp of Israel" was the name given to sections of the moving caravans, but more especially to the part of the encampment graced by the presence of President Brigham Young and his associate Apostles; from which headquarters instructions and orders were issued to the encampments along the whole line of march.

Prominent Encampments.

Principal and somewhat permanent encampments were formed at Richardson's Point, about 55miles west of Nauvoo. Here President Young remained from the 7th of March to the 19th of that month, as heavy rains made the roads and swollen streams impassable. A similar encampment was formed on the Chariton river where the leader established his headquarters on the 27th of March and remained until the first of April. Thence he moved to an encampment on Locust river, reached on the 6th of April. Garden Grove, named by the marching saints, was headquarters of the camp on the 25th of April—150 miles from Nauvoo. Here extensive crops were planted; and again at Mount Pisgah some distance westward. This somewhat permanent encampment was located and named by Elder Parley P. Pratt. His description of arriving at the place and naming it is given in his *Autobiography* as follows:

> "Riding about three or four miles through beautiful prairies I came suddenly to some round and sloping hills, grassy, and crowned with beautiful groves of timber; while alternate open groves and forests seemed blended in all the beauty and harmony of an English park. While beneath and beyond, on the west, rolled a main branch of Grand river, with its rich bottoms of alternate forest and prairie. As I approached this lovely scenery, several deer and wolves, being startled at the sight of me, abandoned the place and bounded away till lost from my sight amid the groves. Being pleased and excited at the varied beauty before me, I cried out, 'this is Mount Pisgah.'"

Mount Pisgah

When he reported the place that evening in camp, the name was adopted by the council, and Mount Pisgah thereafter became a permanent encampment to the marching hosts of Israel. Also extensive crops were planted there that spring.

Arrival at Council Bluffs.

The march under constantly improving weather conditions was continued until Council Bluffs on the Missouri river was reached in mid-June from which point it was proposed to send out into the western wilderness, beyond the Rocky Mountains, a company of one hundred Pioneers to search out a place where crops could be planted and a resting place, as an objective, be established for the saints until perhaps more permanent locations could be determined upon.

Irregularities *en Marche.*

It could not be otherwise in such a mixed company of people drawn together by the proclamation of the New Dispensation from so many sections of the United States, Great Britain and Canada, then that there would crop out in the great encampments some irregularities that bespoke uncertain training in righteousness and the outcropping of defective human nature. However, for the most part, the great leader of the expedition from Nauvoo could justly speak in high praise of the general character of the people whom he was leading into a distant wilderness.

On Sunday, April 12, he (President Young) met with the saints attended by his usual associates of the Council of the Twelve together with Bishops Whitney and Miller, Elder Charles C. Rich and about thirty of the brethren at the encampment of Elder Heber C. Kimball. Following is the report of Brigham Young of the services held that day:

President Young's High Praise of the Camps.

"I told them that I was satisfied that we were taking a course that would prove to be salvation, not only to this camp, but to the saints that were still behind. I did not think there had ever been a body of people since the days of Enoch placed under the same unpleasant circumstances that this people have been, where there was so little grumbling; and I was satisfied that the Lord was pleased with the majority of the 'Camp of Israel'. But there had been some things done which were wrong. There were among us those who were passing counterfeit money and had done it all the time since we left Nauvoo. There were men among us who would steal; some pleaded our suffering from persecution, and said they were justified in stealing from our enemies because they had robbed us; *but such a course tends to destroy the kingdom of God.*

I propose that we proceed to the purchase [of lands] on Grand river, Iowa, and fence in a field of two miles square, build about twenty log cabins, plow some land and put in spring crops and thus spend our time until the weather settles; select men and families to take care of our improvements and the rest proceed westward. We will also send men back from Grand river to look out a new and better road to pilot the next company so that they may avoid the creeks, bad roads and settlements through which we have passed. Then those who follow can tarry on Grand river or go on to the Missouri bottoms and other places, where there will be plenty of feed for their cattle and tarry through the winter, and come on another season as soon as they can make their way through. I also propose that we select a number of men out of each company and send them tomorrow to Judge [i. e. Bishop] Miller's in the neighborhood of Grand river to work and get corn and other provisions for the camp. Also that we select a company to start about Tuesday and go on the northern route to Grand river, find the best road and good location and let the camp follow at short stages. One hundred wagons will be sufficient to cross the mountains this season.

Heber C. Kimball moved and it was voted that my views be carried out. I moved and the council voted to proceed direct to Council Bluffs. Heber C. Kimball, Parley P. Pratt, John Taylor, Orson Pratt, George A. Smith, Joshua H. Holman, Henry G. Sherwood, William L. Cutler and myself were selected to proceed to Grand river."

In this brief account of that meeting on Sunday, April 12, 1846, is given a picture of the spirit and nature of the many events that make up the history of that strange march.*

Bogus Again.

The matter of counterfeit money spoken of in the above remarks, is again referred to in the *Manuscript History of Brigham Young.*† It appears that the man who had the counterfeit money in his possession had let another brother have some of it on shares, which he was to exchange among the settlers north and south of the line of march in exchange for goods, etc. This man had not shared the profits with the man who gave him the bogus and hence a quarrel between them. President Young being brought to the scene of the quarrel reproved them for dealing in base coin and told the originator of the trouble that he could not govern himself, his family or a company; and unless he repented and forsook such dishonesty the hand of the Lord would be against him and all those who partook of such corruption.‡

Challenge to a Duel.

In another case two brethren had a disagreement over some wrongs sustained, fancied or real, and a challenge was issued by James M. Hemmic to Wilbur J. Earl to fight a duel. The matter coming to the ears of President Young, a council was called and an immediate judgment pronounced in this language—"That James M. Hemmic be discharged from the service of this camp forthwith by order of the

*History of Brigham Young, Ms., 1846, pp. 141-3.

†P. 171, for 1846.

‡The words of President Young were fulfilled: "The chief actor in the business," wrote George Q. Cannon, years afterwards, "and his whole family became apostates and very disreputable people, and the hand of the Lord was visibly against him. The man also to whom he gave bogus money to pass eventually lost his standing in the church and went down" (History of the Church, Cannon, *Juvenile Instructor,* vol. xvii, p. 293).

council." This was signed by Willard Richards, clerk.

After entering the Pottawattomie Indian country a piece of bogus money was passed upon an Indian; making the discovery, the red man and his friends took an ox from the next passing company and killed it. When the matter was reported to President Young he declared "the Indian had done just right".

Desire to Return to Nauvoo for Families.

Many of the brethren in the first companies leaving Nauvoo had left their families behind until the advanced companies could be well under way, and President Young and the council were quite severely tried by a number of these brethren constantly bringing up the request that they be allowed to return to Nauvoo to bring back their families. A number indeed did so return without the consent of the leaders. However, by the time the companies had reached Richardson's Point, quite a list of these men in the Pioneer Companies and those in charge of the artillery with other special detachments were formally released by official action to go back for their families, and gradually the number who were desiring to return to Nauvoo fell off until the annoyance ceased to exist.

Improvised Mail Service.

Those returning to Nauvoo, however, were able to be of service by carrying letters from the camp segments back to their friends, and letters also were forwarded from Nauvoo to the headquarters of the Camp of Israel, and thus was maintained a sort of postal service, the tent of Willard Richards being known as the General Post Office, both for outgoing and incoming mail. Sometimes this service was kept up by the appointment of men to go back and forth along the line of movement.

Prayers Well-nigh Constant.

Letters from Nauvoo brought the acceptable news that companies of brethren—high priests, seventies, and elders—met in groups, almost daily, in the Temple to engage in prayer in behalf of the Camp of Israel and also for the benefit of the saints everywhere in the church. Especial prayer service was also frequently celebrated in the camps by appointment. Indeed, if one notices the frequency of prayer both in the camps and in the Temple, he is led to exclaim—If prayer can really serve its high purpose, then there was never a time like this in the church where the service of prayer was so constantly used, or more fervent appeals made to God for the deliverance of the saints!

Meantime, during this march of the saints from Nauvoo to Council Bluffs, two important things happened which had an effect upon the intended movements of the exiles. The first was the activity of Jesse C. Little at Washington, D. C., who had been appointed to preside over the Eastern States Mission with instructions to visit Washington and if possible secure the assignment for the saints in assisting the general government to settle California in anticipation of a conquest of that country by the United States then entering upon a war with Mexico. Elder Little contacted the federal administration and upon his representing the condition of the Latter-day Saint community at Nauvoo, and their westward traveling encampments, obtained the promise of President James K. Polk that an opportunity would be given for a company of at least 500 men to march with the "Army of the West" to California. They would be employed for one year, receive the usual compensation allowed to soldiers of the army of the United States, and be allowed to keep their arms and all their army equipment at the end of that time. Elder Little had proposed to raise 1000 settlers for California in the eastern branches of the church and 1000 men from their encampments on the Missouri, but the administration decided to take into service only 500 men.

J. C. Little at Washington.

The second thing was the order sent to General Stephen W. Kearny at Ft. Leavenworth to take the necessary steps to raise this Battalion of 500 men. The carrier of the dispatches to General Kearny was Thomas L. Kane who had

Raising the Mormon Battalion.

cooperated with Elder Little in presenting the cause of the Church of the Latter-day Saints to the administration and other friends in Washington.

The first knowledge of this opportunity of service with the "Army of the West" reached the Camp of Israel at Mount Pisgah, where on the 26th of June Captain James Allen of the United States army arrived, accompanied by three dragoons. The camp at Mount Pisgah was momentarily thrown into great confusion and excitement by this event, since the rumors, first set on foot at Nauvoo, that the United States would intercept the removal of the saints from the United States, was remembered, and the cry was echoed from tent to tent —"The United States troops are upon us!" "The United States troops are upon us!!" But as Captain Allen soon presented the intention of his visit, the excitement subsided, and Elder Wilford Woodruff of the Twelve Apostles, who at the time was at the encampment, referred Captain Allen's request for the enlistment of volunteers to President Young, then at Council Bluffs, and Captain Allen proceeded on his journey westward to make known his mission to the leader. Upon the proposition being submitted to President Young to raise a company of 500 volunteers the subject was referred to the council and a favorable decision rendered. Whereupon for several weeks the different sections of the encampment were visited as far east as Mount Pisgah—and word was sent on by letter to Garden Grove—150 miles west of Nauvoo, it will be remembered. These sectors of the camp were canvassed and men gathered together at Council Bluffs to enlist in the service of the United States.

Misapprehensions of the Motives of the U. S.

Unfortunately there were many misapprehensions concerning the enlistment of this company of volunteers. For a long time it was represented as current traditional history that the opportunity given for enlistment was a "demand" or "requisition" or "draft"–sometimes one, sometimes another–

of the United States government, unjust and out of all proportion to the membership of the church, and made from sinister motives of encompassing the destruction of the moving caravans either by scattering or annihilating them. First, in that if they refused to enlist, an excuse for halting their departure from the United States and their utter destruction would be justified; and on the other hand, if they complied and furnished the 500 young men, necessarily it would deplete their fighting force that they would fall victims to the large tribes of war-like Indians upon the plains and through the mountains. Nothing of this kind, of course, could be implied in the action of the administration at Washington, still it was so reported and believed.* In the first place, a much larger offer than 500 men was tendered to the administration, and the service was almost piteously pleaded for by a representative of the church —the president of the Eastern States Mission. In addition to that it was utterly impossible for the administration at Washington to make a "demand" or a "draft" for this service from the Mormon people, for at the utmost the president could only call for "volunteers"; since the law authorizing the president to organize an army to make war upon Mexico empowered him only to call for volunteers, 50,000 of them apportioned among the states. The quota in most of the states was over-subscribed by three times the number asked for, and the United States did not really need the service of the Mormon Battalion of 500 men in the sense that there was a lack of volunteers. The war was a very popular one.

Misapprehension also arose as to the time in which the Battalion was enlisted. It was popularly supposed that three days only were occupied in raising the Battalion. It is true the Battalion was mustered upon the rolls and commanders of companies were chosen from among the volunteers, and the Battalion put in march-

*See Sergeant Daniel Tyler's *History of the Mormon Battalion,* pp. 348-55.

Time Element in Raising the Battalion.

ing order under Captain James Allen to be marched to Ft. Leavenworth in three days. But before these three days of mustering in the Battalion at Council Bluffs, more than three weeks had been used by the principal brethren of the Camp of Israel in going through the various segments of the marching column selecting and deciding upon those who should form the membership of this Battalion. The remarks accredited to Brigham Young that he said to Captain Allen:—"You shall have your Battalion, Sir; and if there are not young men enough we will take old men, and if they are not enough, we will take women!"—was undoubtedly intended for humor; for after several weeks of recruiting throughout the camps from Council Bluffs to Mount Pisgah, President Young must have been well advised that the 500 volunteers were on hand to be registered in the service of the United States.

For further and full details concerning the calling of the Mormon Battalion, its departure from Council Bluffs and Ft. Leavenworth, its record march of two thousand miles through what is now the states of Kansas, New Mexico, Arizona, and California, to San Diego on the Pacific coast, and its record in California, see *Comprehensive History of the Church of Jesus Christ of Latter-day Saints,* Century I, vol. iii, chapters lxxiii, lxxiv, lxxv, lxxxvii. Also the final and cruel expulsion* of the remnant of the church members left in Nauvoo, in the latter part of September, 1846, and all their sufferings on the west bank of the Mississippi, their journey through Iowa, and their final union with their fellow exiles at Council Bluffs will be found and given in detail in the *Comprehensive History of the Church,* Century I, vol. iii, chapters lxx, lxxii and lxxvi.

Reference to the *Comprehensive History of the Church.*

The founding of Winter Quarters and the trek during the summer of 1847 of the Pioneer Companies to

*It was in this final expulsion of the remnants of the saints from Nauvoo in which Daniel H. Wells figured so prominently, and so bravely, which won for him the title of "Defender of Nauvoo", (See references above to *Comprehensive History*).

the valley of the Great Salt Lake, their arrival and settlement there—all this is also treated in sufficient detail in the *Comprehensive History of the Church of Jesus Christ of Latter-day Saints,* Century I, and it will not be necessary to repeat these things in greater detail by following further the *Manuscript History of Brigham Young.* But the return of the Pioneers to Winter Quarters, late in 1847, and the steps taken to organize again the First Presidency of Three in December of that year, together with acceptance of the action by the various great divisions of the church, as then existing, is of sufficient importance to have the official account of it given from *President Young's Manuscript History* and with that account as given, chiefly by himself, we will close this seventh volume.

CHAPTER XLI

THE RETURN TO WINTER QUARTERS—THE ORGANIZATION OF AND UNIVERSAL ACCEPTANCE OF THE FIRST PRESIDENCY OF THE CHURCH, BRIGHAM YOUNG, HEBER C. KIMBALL, AND WILLARD RICHARDS—1847-8—PRESIDENT YOUNG'S LAST JOURNEY OVER THE PLAINS

After having settled the Pioneer Company and the contingent Mormon Battalion, invalided sections, which had wintered at Pueblo, and who arrived in Salt Lake City five days after the Pioneer Company, President Young, a number of the Twelve Apostles, (a majority), and some of the Pioneer Company returned to Winter Quarters late in 1847 to further the migration of the saints still encamped on the Missouri frontiers.

Under date of October 30, 1847, President Young records in his *Manuscript History* the following:

"*Saturday, October* 30, 1847.—At sunset about 20 wagons arrived from Winter Quarters with Bishop N. K. Whitney, John S. Fullmer, Wm. Kay and many friends, bringing food and grain.

Sunday, 31.—When we were about one mile from Winter Quarters the wagons of the Twelve came to the front, when I remarked:

The Thanks of the Leader —His Report of the Pioneer Journey.

'Brethren, I will say to the Pioneers, I wish you to receive my thanks for your kindness and willingness to obey orders; I am satisfied with you: you have done well. We have accomplished more than we expected. Out of one hundred forty-three men who started, some of them sick, all of them are well; not a man has died; we have not lost a horse, mule, or ox, but through carelessness; the blessings of the Lord have been with us. If the brethren are satisfied with me and the Twelve, please signify it, (which was unanimously done). I feel to bless you all in the name of the Lord God of Israel. You are dismissed to go to your own homes.'

We drove into the town in order, about an hour before sunset. The streets were crowded with people to shake hands as we passed through the lines; we were truly rejoiced to once more behold our wives, children and friends after an absence of over six months, having traveled over 2000 miles, sought out a location for the saints to dwell in [in] peace, and accomplished the most interesting mission in this last dispensation. Not a soul of our camp died, and no serious accident happened to any, for which we praise the Lord.

* * *.

Wednesday, November 3, 1847.—The Twelve met in council at my house. John S. Fullmer reported the proceedings of the trustees in Nauvoo; when it was voted that the trustees gather all the papers and books pertaining to church affairs in Nauvoo, and as many of the poor saints together with as much church property as they can, and remove hither [i. e. Winter Quarters]. It was also voted that the saints in Garden Grove be advised to remove to Winter Quarters next spring.

Friday, 5.—I met in council with the Twelve. I signed a letter addressed to Colonel J. C. Little instructing him to resume his presidency over the eastern churches, and one to Elder John Brown and the saints in the southern states; also one to the trustees at Nauvoo recommending them to leave the keys of the Temple in care of Judge Owens and the building itself in the hands of the Lord*. The minutes of the con-

*DESTRUCTION OF THE MORMON [NAUVOO] TEMPLE

"*November* 19, 1848: 'On Monday the 19th of November, our citizens were awakened by the alarm of fire, which, when first discovered, was bursting out through the spire of the Temple, near the small door that opened from the east side to the roof, on the main building. The fire was seen first about three o'clock in the morning, and not until it had taken such hold of the timbers and roof as to make useless any effort to extinguish it. The materials of the inside were so dry, and the fire spread so rapidly, that a few minutes were sufficient to wrap this famed edifice in a sheet of flame. It was a sight too full of mournful sublimity. The mass of material which had been gathered there by the labor of many years afforded a rare opportunity for this element to play off some of its wildest sports. Although

ference of September 24, 1846, of the Chain Island group in the Pacific ocean were read, comprising thirteen branches on nine islands, containing 804 members, four elders, seven priests, thirteen teachers and twenty deacons.

Saturday, 6.—Evening, I met with the council and School of the Seventy.

Sunday, 7.—Elder Orson Pratt preached in the Council House. He gave an account of the Pioneer journey and described some of the lakes and valleys of the mountains.

Monday, 8.—I met with the Twelve, when it was voted that the saints vacate Winter Quarters in the spring and go westward. Elder Hyde informed the council that fellowship was withdrawn from George Miller, also James Emmett and his company; which was approved.

Tuesday, 9.—The Apostles, high council, Bishop

the morning was tolerably dark, still, when the flames shot upwards, the spire, the streets, and the houses for nearly a mile distant were lighted up, so as to render even the smallest objects discernible. The glare of the vast torch, pointing skyward, indescribably contrasted with the universal gloom and darkness around it; and men looked on with faces sad as if the crumbling ruins below were consuming all their hopes.

It was evidently the work of an incendiary. There had been, on the evening previous, a meeting in the lower room; but no person was in the upper part where the fire was first discovered. Who it was, and what could have been his motives, we have now no idea. Some feeling infinitely more unenviable than that of the individual who put the torch to the beautiful Ephesian structure of old, must have possessed him. To destroy a work of art, at once the most elegant and the most renowned in its celebrity of any in the whole west, would, we should think, require a mind of more than ordinary depravity; and we feel assured that no one in this community could have been so lost to every sense of justice, and every consideration of interest as to become the author of the deed' (*Nauvoo Patriot*).

November 1, 1856: Lewis A. Bidamon, (who married Emma Smith, widow of the Prophet Joseph, on December 23, 1847), [L. D. S. Biographical Encyclopedia, Jenson, vol. i, p. 692], landlord of the Nauvoo Mansion, Illinois, stated to Elders George A. Smith and Erastus Snow, that the inhabitants of Warsaw, Carthage, Pontusuc and surrounding settlements in consequence of jealousy that Nauvoo would still retain its superior importance as a town and might induce the Mormons to return contributed a purse of five hundred dollars which they gave to Joseph Agnew in consideration of his burning the Temple; and that said Agnew was the person who set the building on fire.

Bidamon further stated, that the burning of the Temple had the effect of diminishing the importance of Nauvoo; for his 'Mansion' or 'Hotel' had not since the conflagration one-fourth the custom it previously had" (*History of Brigham Young, Ms.*, 1848, pp. 79-81).

Whitney, Presidents of Seventy and others, met in the Council House on business.

Wednesday, 10.—I met with the Twelve, high council and Seventies on business.

Thursday, 11.—I met with Elders Orson Pratt, Willard Richards, George A. Smith and Joseph Young to see to the distribution of the Nauvoo library which had been forwarded by the trustees.

Sunday, 14.—I met with the saints in public meeting; referred to our healthy locality in the mountains; suggested that those who could not go west next spring should vacate Winter Quarters and return to the east side of the river. The saints voted to leave Winter Quarters next spring.

Monday, 15.—I met with the high priests. Evening, I met with the seventies and high priests who were addressed by Elder Kimball and myself on the necessity of a reformation. I remarked that the government officials were looking on us more eagerly than when we were in Jackson, Caldwell and Clay counties, Missouri.

Tuesday, 16.—The council convened at noon in the Council House. Bishop Whitney was directed to preside over the high priests for the time being.

Thursday, 18.—I visited the sick and attended a high priests' meeting. The official members of the First Emigrating Division met at 7 p. m., and decided to fill up the old organization by new members.

Friday, 19.—The council wrote to Major Miller requesting his views and opinions on the saints vacating their winter quarters on the Omaha lands.

Saturday, 20.—The Council of the Twelve met in the Council House and selected twenty-seven persons to go on missions to preach.

Sunday, 21.—I was sickly. Elders Orson Pratt and Wilford Woodruff preached at the stand.

Oliver Cowdery Exhorted to be Rebaptized.

Monday, 22.—The Council of the Twelve met in Dr. Richards' office and wrote a letter to Oliver Cowdery, exhorting him to be rebaptized.

Tuesday, 23.—The Twelve and Presidents of Seventy met and selected seventeen elders to go on missions.

Thursday, 25.—I met with the Twelve and officers of the Emigrating Companies and instructed them pertaining to their further organization. We wrote to Elder N. H. Felt, St. Louis, to forward the emigrating saints to Winter Quarters.

Friday, 26.—I wrote a letter to Elder Orson Spencer giving particulars of Pioneer journey, their labors in Salt Lake valley and other interesting items.

Sunday, 28.—I met with the Twelve and high council in the forenoon, Theodore Turley and Joseph Fielding were voted members of the high council. In the evening I preached to the seventies and high priests concerning gathering to the Bluffs, and from there to the mountains, and aiding each other until all are located in a healthy country.

* * *

Friday, December 3, 1847.—The Twelve traveled to the Block House branch and met the high council and others, when I preached, followed by Elders George A. Smith, Amasa Lyman and Wilford Woodruff. Afternoon, I introduced the subject of organizing a Carrying Company hence to the Salt Lake country, for the purpose of taking as many thither as possible. I recommended the brethren to build a house 50 by 100 feet in time to accommodate the conference next spring, and called for help to assist the bishops on the west side of the river, who have to support three hundred poor persons daily. Elder Kimball preached.

Council met at Brother Daley's. Elder Wm. I. Appleby presented the gold pens and pencils sent by Colonel T. L. Kane to the Twelve Apostles. He reported the condition of the churches east.

Saturday, 4.—I attended conference and proposed building a big log house in the hollow, for temporary use, telling the congregation not to be surprised if a city should be built there. The conference voted that

Henry W. Miller be a committee of one to superintend the building, under the dictation of the Twelve. I told the conference that we must recommend ourselves as a people by our good works, to the Lord God Almighty. The conference was adjourned till December 24th to meet in the new house to be built.

The Twelve selected the site to build the house on and proceeded to Father Ezra Chase's Settlement.

Sunday, 5.—We traveled to Elder Hyde's house where all of the Council [i. e. of the Twelve] assembled in the evening. After remarks by myself, Heber C. Kimball, Orson Hyde, Willard Richards, Wilford Woodruff, George A. Smith, Amasa Lyman, and Ezra T. Benson [8 of the Quorum of the Twelve], I was unanimously elected President of the Church of Jesus Christ of Latter-day Saints, with authority to nominate my two counselors, which I did by appointing Heber C. Kimball my first counselor and Willard Richards my second counselor, and the appointments were unanimously sustained.*

*En route from Salt Lake valley, President Young conversed with his brethren of the Apostles on the subject of reorganizing the First Presidency of the Church. His conversation with Elder Woodruff on the subject is thus related by the latter in his Journal:

"*October* 12, 1847.—I had a question put to me by President Young: What my opinion was concerning one of the Twelve Apostles being appointed as the President of the Church with his two counselors. I answered that a quorum like the Twelve who had been appointed by revelation, confirmed by revelation from time to time—I thought it would require a revelation to change the order of that quorum. [But] whatever the Lord inspires you to do in this matter. I am with you" (*Woodruff's Journal,* entry for October 12, 1847).

In some remarks made by President Young while in St. George in 1862, he said to Isaac Morley and Levi Jackman, who were present with him: "You are both Jackson county members and I want you to live to go back to Jackson county with me." He also said: "Here is Brother Woodruff [who was present], he was the first man that I felt by the spirit to speak to about the organization of the church [i. e. First Presidency of the Church] (*Wilford Woodruff's Journal,* August 23, 1862; also copied into *Brigham Young's History, Ms.,* same date, pp. 779-80).

Wilford Woodruff also records concerning this meeting at Orson Hyde's house, that before the choice of Brigham Young for President of the Church "many interesting remarks were made by the various individuals who spoke, [this included all the members of the Twelve present], and we were followed by President Young. After which Orson Hyde moved that Brigham Young be the President of the Church of Jesus Christ of Latter-day Saints and that he nominate his two counselors, and they three form the First Presidency. Seconded by Wilford Woodruff and carried unanimously. President Young nominated Heber C. Kimball as his first counselor; seconded, and carried unanimously. President Young nominated Willard Richards as his second counselor; seconded, and carried unanimously" (*Woodruff's Journal,* entry for December 5, 1847).

Monday, 6.—The council met in the afternoon in Brother Orson Hyde's house and attended to several items of business; conversed about building a Temple in Salt Lake City and voted that Uncle John Smith be the Patriarch to the whole church; that Orson Hyde go to the east to procure means to help us and that E. T. Benson go with him; that Luke Johnson be ordained an elder, [formerly one of the original Quorum of the Twelve]; that Orson Pratt go to England and take charge of the affairs of the church there; that Amasa Lyman go to the southern states to get help.

Tuesday, 7.—Returned to Winter Quarters having accomplished much important business during this visit.

Thursday, 9—During my absence the past summer the Omahas [Indians] have killed more than twenty of my cows and calves.

Colonel Thomas L. Kane wrote me and enclosed a printed circular of a 'Meeting for the Relief of the Mormons in Philadelphia', copies of which had been sent to the president and vice-president of the United States, and to the members of congress; showing the colonel's great anxiety in behalf of a persecuted and suffering people.

Friday, 10.—Accompanied by Dr. Richards I visited Elder Kimball. I met Dr. J. M. Bernhisel and heard his report concerning the Nauvoo House affairs; also visited General Johnson, and attended meeting of First Division of Emigration.

Saturday, 11.—Philemon C. Merrill with fifteen others of the Mormon Battalion arrived in Winter Quarters; they left Great Salt Lake City, October 8th. * * *.

Thursday, 23.—I started for Council Point and attended a meeting there at the schoolhouse when Elders Wilford Woodruff and Joseph Young preached.

Friday, 24.—Proceeded to Miller's Hollow, [later called Kanesville], where the brethren had built a log house forty by sixty feet, capable of seating about one thousand persons. The house was dedicated by Elder Orson Pratt as a house of prayer and thanksgiving. The congregation was addressed by Elders Wilford Woodruff and Orson Pratt and in the afternoon by Elders Amasa Lyman, George A. Smith and myself. Elder Wm. I. Appleby preached during the evening service.

Saturday, 25.—The council went to the Log Tabernacle and attended meeting. The congregation voted that the high council on the east side of the river have all municipal power given to them by this people, and that the bishops' courts have authority as civil magistrates among the people, until the laws of Iowa are extended over us.

* * *.

Monday, 27.—Conference convened again when Elder Kimball spoke, followed by Elder Joseph Young, myself, Elders George A. Smith, Orson Pratt and Amasa Lyman, when I was unanimously elected [sustained] President of the Church of Jesus Christ of Latter-day Saints.* Heber C. Kimball and Willard Richards were in like manner elected [sustained] respectively my first and second counselors. Uncle John

*This was a General Conference of the whole church from Winter Quarters, Kanesville and Council Bluffs. "The spirit of the Lord at this time," said Brigham Young a month later, "rested upon the people in a powerful manner, insomuch that the saints' hearts were filled with joy unspeakable; every power of their mind and nerve of their bodies was awakened." A dead silence reigned in the congregation while the President spoke following the vote which had been taken (See Letter of President Young to Orson Spencer, then in England, *Millennial Star*, vol. x, p. 115).

Subsequently this action of the saints in the settlements on the Missouri river in conference assembled—being the largest number of church members in one body, with several high councils presiding in various divisions of the church in those settlements—was ratified by unanimous vote by the saints of Salt Lake valley and in the General Conference of the church held in that place on the 8th of October, 1848; there being about 5000 people in the valley by that time.

Elder Parley P. Pratt nominated Brigham Young at that conference as the First President of the Church and the motion was carried *without a dissenting vote*. (See *Comprehensive History of the Church*, Century I, vol. iii, p. 318, note).

The action was also ratified by the saints of the British Isles in General Conference assembled at Manchester, England, August 14, 1848, at which there were present delegates from 28 different conferences with a membership of 17,902. (See *Millennial Star*, vol. x. p. 252. where the names of the officers are given; also the

Smith was unanimously elected [sustained] Patriarch to the whole church.

I spoke again referring to what had been accomplished by the saints and other topics; bore testimony that the communion of the Holy Spirit was enjoyed by those present, when the conference was adjourned till the 6th of April at the Log Tabernacle.

After benediction by Elder George A. Smith the congregation shouted three times 'Hosannah, Hosannah, Hosannah to God and the Lamb, Amen, Amen and Amen!'*

Tuesday, 28.—Wrote a letter to Elder Orson Spencer, Liverpool, England, with instructions to send the British saints *via* New Orleans and St. Louis to Council Bluffs.

Wednesday, 29.—The First Presidency, the Twelve, high council, and several others met in the Council House in Winter Quarters and attended to business. * * *.

GENERAL ANNUAL CONFERENCE OF THE CHURCH, 1848

"*Thursday, April* 6, 1848.—I attended a conference at the Log Tabernacle, Miller's Hollow (named at this conference Kanesville), held on the 6th, 7th and 8th. I nominated, and Elder Orson Hyde was chosen, president [i. e. of the conference meetings]. The constituted authorities of the church were sustained, also the high council and other authorities in Pottawattomie. Elders Orson Hyde, George A. Smith, Orson Pratt, Wilford Woodruff, Joseph Young, Heber C. Kimball, myself and others preached. William Draper, Sen., was called to the office of patriarch. The appointments

names of the conferences and the statistics in detail; see also *Manuscript History of Brigham Young* under date of August 14, 1848, pp. 48-49, where the statistics are also given in detail.)

*This shout of "Hosanna" is given only on very great occasions. It is usually given three times in immediate succession; and when voiced by thousands and sometimes tens of thousands in unison, and at their utmost strength, it is most impressive and inspiring. It is impossible to stand unmoved on such an occasion. It seems to fill the prairie or woodland, mountain wilderness or tabernacle, with mighty waves of sound; and the shout of men going into battle cannot be more stirring. It gives wonderful vent to religious emotions, and is followed by a feeling of reverential awe—a sense of oneness with God.

of Elders Orson Hyde and George A. Smith to labor in Pottawattomie, Elder Orson Pratt in Great Britain and Elder Wilford Woodruff to the eastern states, Nova Scotia and Canada were sustained. A vote of gratitude was accorded to the saints at St. Louis for their liberality to the presidency and the saints at Winter Quarters during the past year. Committees were appointed to select locations and settle the poor of Winter Quarters on the Pottawattomie lands: Luke Johnson was recommended as a physician.

Appointments to Missions.

* * *

Sunday, May 21.—During this month I attended meetings each Sunday which were held at the stand. On the 14th, I preached at length and blessed the land at Winter Quarters and on the Pottawattomie purchase, for the benefit of the saints who should occupy it.

Friday, 26.—On the 26th I started from Winter Quarters on my journey to the mountains, leaving my houses, mills and the temporary furniture I had acquired during our sojourn there. This was the fifth time I had left my home and property since I embraced the gospel of Jesus Christ. All of my company had left Winter Quarters and were mostly, on the last day of this month, on the west side of the Elkhorn river, the place of rendezvous for organization.

President Young's Departure for the West.

Wednesday, 31.—On the 31st the organization was commenced by appointing Zera Pulsipher captain of a hundred with John Benbow and Daniel Wood captains of fifties; also, Lorenzo Snow captain of a hundred, with Heman Hyde and John Stoker captains of fifties. I gave some general instructions as to the necessity of observing order in camp—taking care of the cattle and not allowing them to be abused; not to have yelling nor bawling in camp; but to attend prayers—put out the fires and go to bed by 9 p. m.

Organization of President Young's Company.

Elder James H. Flanigan received a license to preach the gospel in Great Britain, under the direction of the presidency there. I gave my brother, Phineas H. Young a recommend to travel and preach in the states, and gather means to help himself and the saints westward. I also signed a letter of recommendation in behalf of Brother Willard Richards authorizing him to travel and preach in the United States and Europe and gather means to fit him out for his journey to the mountains. At the same time, I counseled him to gather up what teams and wagons he could and come on after us, as soon as he was able, even if he had to leave a portion of his family another year.

Heber C. Kimball's Company.

Thursday, June 1.—On the 1st Brother Heber C. Kimball with a company of fifty-five wagons arrived on the east bank of the Elkhorn river.

I proceeded to a further organization of my company. William G. Perkins was chosen captain of a hundred with John D. Lee and Eleazer Miller captains of fifties; also Allen Taylor captain of a hundred with John Harvey and Daniel Garn captains of fifties. The company voted that I should act as General Superintendent of the Emigrating Companies and Daniel H. Wells was sustained as my aid-de-camp. Isaac Morley was sustained as president of the company, with Reynolds Cahoon and William W. Major as his counselors. Horace S. Eldredge was chosen marshal, and Hosea Stout captain of the night guard. Captain Lorenzo Snow's Company moved out to the Platte river, and Captain Pulsipher's Company started out a few miles.

Elders Orson Hyde, Wilford Woodruff and Ezra T. Benson visited the organized camps at the Horn [Elkhorn] and returned to Winter Quarters on the third. The remainder of my company started from the Horn on the fifth.

Brother H. C. Kimball's Company started from the Horn on the 7th, and on the 9th they elected the following officers, *viz.* Henry Harriman, captain of the first hundred, Titus Billings and John Pack, captains of fifties; subsequently, Isaac Higbee was appointed a captain of fifty.

Wednesday, 14.—On the 14th my company reached the Loupe Fork whence I sent Brothers Daniel H. Wells and Daniel Wood back to Brother Heber C. Kimball's Camp, by whom Brother Kimball sent me a letter detailing the particulars of an unfortunate occurrence between William H. Kimball, Howard Egan, Thomas E. Ricks and Noah W. Bartholomew and the Indians; in which Brother Ricks was shot with three buckshot and Brother Egan was shot in the wrist. Dr. Bernhisel had dressed their wounds and both were doing well.

Indian Difficulties—Wounding of Thomas E. Ricks.

Thursday, 15.—I crossed the Loupe Fork on the 15th. Brother Kimball's Company came up on the 16th, and next day with the assistance of some of the best teams in my company, his company crossed.

Thomas Bullock, clerk, reported the statistics of my company to be 1,229 souls, 397 wagons, 74 horses, 19 mules, 1,275 oxen, 699 cows, 184 loose cattle, 411 sheep, 141 pigs, 605 chickens [and a variety of smaller domestic animals].

Statistics of President Young's and Kimball's Companies.

Subsequently the statistics of Brother Kimball's Company were obtained and showed 662 souls, 226 wagons, 57 horses, 25 mules, 737 oxen, 284 cows, 150 loose cattle, 243 sheep, 96 pigs, 299 chickens [and a number of smaller domestic animals].

Sunday, 18.—Brother Kimball and I gathered the companies together on the 18th, and preached to them.

In consequence of depredations committed by the Indians the saints on the Pottawattomie side of the Missouri prepared to organize themselves as militia by electing Charles M. Johnson, colonel, Abraham C. Hodge, lieutenant-colonel, and Philemon C. Merrill, major.

Pottawattomie Indian Depredations.

Winter Quarters, after its vacation by Elder Kimball's Company and mine, presented a desolate aspect.

Desolation of Winter Quarters.

A terrific thunder storm passed over, accompanied by a hurricane which tore wagon covers to shreds and whistled fearfully through the empty dwellings. A few straggling Indians camped in the vacated premises and subsisted upon the cattle which had died by poverty and what [else] they [could] pick up.

Some Indians stole three oxen from John Scott, who, assisted by others, pursued them and recovered the beeves.

Wednesday, September 20.—My company arrived in Great Salt Lake valley on and after the 20th and Elder Kimball's a few days after.

* * *

Friday, October 6.—The Semi-Annual Conference [in Salt Lake valley] was opened on the 6th, but postponed till Sunday the 8th, in consequence of the Battalion brethren having set apart the 5th to celebrate their return home, which day was so unfavorable that the celebration was deferred and came off on the 6th, by partaking of a dinner, firing of cannon at intervals, and meeting, which dismissed at sundown.

THE FIRST PRESIDENCY SUSTAINED

Sunday, 8.—On the 8th, the [regular church] conference met, when I was sustained by unanimous vote as President of the Church, with Heber C. Kimball and Willard Richards as my counselors.

The following officers were also sustained by unanimous vote:

THE TWELVE APOSTLES

Orson Hyde, Parley P. Pratt, Orson Pratt, Lyman Wight, Wilford Woodruff, John Taylor, George A. Smith, Amasa Lyman, and Ezra T. Benson, members of the Quorum of the Twelve Apostles.

THE PATRIARCH TO THE CHURCH

John Smith, Patriarch to the church. [This was

"Uncle John" Smith, brother of the Prophet's father, who was the first Patriarch to the church].

FIRST SEVEN PRESIDENTS OF THE SEVENTY

Joseph Young, Levi W. Hancock, Zera Pulsipher, Albert P. Rockwood, Henry Harriman, Jedediah M. Grant, and Benjamin L. Clapp, First Presidents of the Seventies.

PRESIDING BISHOP

Newel K. Whitney, presiding bishop [i. e. of the whole church].

PRESIDENCY OF THE SALT LAKE STAKE

Charles C. Rich, president of the stake, with John Young and Erastus Snow, counselors.

HIGH COUNCIL OF SALT LAKE STAKE

Henry G. Sherwood, Levi Jackman, Daniel Spencer, Ira Eldredge, Shadrach Roundy, Willard Snow, John Murdock, Lewis Abbott, Edson Whipple, John Vance and Abraham O. Smoot, members of the high council.

Arrangements were entered into for the building of a Council House.

I preached on the holy priesthood, showing the necessity of a First Presidency over the Church; for God had told me we would fall, if we did not organize a First Presidency."*

This acceptance by sustaining the action of a majority of the Quorum of the Twelve at Winter Quarters on the 5th of December, 1847, sustained also by the Annual Conference of the Church at Miller's Hollow (Council Point, at that particular conference named Kanesville, and subsequently Council Bluffs); and by all the branches in that region; by the church in Salt Lake valley, with more than 5000 members; and by the saints in conference assembled in Great Britain

**History of Brigham Young, Ms.*, 1845-6-7-8.

(then numbering, as stated in the text, 17,902 members); and by the churches in the Pacific Islands; completed the installation of Brigham Young and his counselors as the second First Presidency of the Church, of three Presiding High Priests, and bridges over the period of time and historic ground between the passing of the First Presidency in the administration of Joseph Smith, the Prophet, and the establishment again of the First Presidency by the selection and inauguration of Brigham Young, official Prophet in the Church of Jesus Christ of Latter-day Saints. And with this, Period II of the *Documentary History of the Church* may be considered closed.

END OF VOLUME VII.

INDEX TO VOLUME VII

I

J

K

L

M

N

P

Q

R

S

HISTORY

of

THE CHURCH OF JESUS CHRIST

of

LATTER-DAY SAINTS

INDEX

Compiled and edited by
E. Keith Howick

Deseret Book Company,
Salt Lake City, Utah

Printed in the U.S.A.

Reprint May 1983

PREFACE

In preparing this index to the History of The Church of Jesus Christ of Latter-day Saints, it is felt that a source of knowledge and heritage of unequaled importance is given to the members of the Church and to the world. The History consists of seven volumes which were compiled by the Church historians, with introduction and notes written by B. H. Roberts. It offers to the student of religious history, and particularly to the Church member, an exciting reference into the foundations of the Church of Jesus Christ in the last days.

Each of these volumes contains a small index. However, in the great and voluminous work of compiling the main body of the manuscript, the index placed in each volume becomes merely a touchstone to some important people and events in Church history. Each index is chronological in nature, which adds to the difficulty in use, making the researcher view all of each index in order to discover any particular point of interest or research. Further, it has been necessary to go to each of the seven volumes individually if the researcher was to discover information concerning the entire Joseph Smith period of the Church.

Because of the importance of the Documentary History and the valuable materials found therein, including not only doctrinal items discoursed by Joseph Smith and other leading members of the Church, but also the details of the persecutions which befell the people of early Church history and the miracles and stories which have been unparalleled since the time of Christ, the author decided some years ago to do a complete and comprehensive index of the Joseph Smith period of Church history. Therefore, the index which follows was developed and offers to the individual some unique and valuable materials for the study of Church history.

The following is a simple explanation of the index and its use: first, the index is totally alphabetical. The index includes the introductions, main body, and all footnotes within each volume, and each item includes all references within all seven volumes. No attempt has been made to reference every time a name or occurrence takes place, but all important events are indexed.

Since all but two of the sections of the Doctrine and Covenants are found in the Documentary History of the Church, it should be noted that the body of the Doctrine and Covenants is not here indexed. For references therein, refer to the complete index in the Doctrine and Covenants itself. Sections and revelations in the Doctrine and Covenants are, however, included in this index.

Second, the index is complete as to proper names. It offers a genealogy of activities in Church history and, although some names are listed as a last name only, or are indexed as merely "mentioned" in the pages of the manuscript, they were indexed to give a complete and full account of all persons who played a part in the pages of history.

Third, there are cross-references within titles; and, in some important events, the title may be listed several places and under several different titles. However, the user is directed to go to the other obvious cross-references or individual listings in order to fully discover the materials available.

Fourth, there are several unique sources available in the index. As an example, the title "STORIES." Under this heading the attempt was made to compile in one place the most important and most interesting sagas of Church history. Other such titles exist, and the user need only use his imagination to be directed to them.

Fifth, in different titles, the author has annotated suggested cross-references. No attempt has been made to be exhaustive, and the user should again proceed with his imagination and common sense to fully research any given topic.

It is hoped that the compilation and publication of this index will be of value to the student of Church history and allow more people to acquaint themselves with episodes and circumstances of a heritage second to none.

The author gratefully acknowledges the valuable assistance which was rendered to him by his wife, who aided in the proofreading of the manuscript and who gave encouragement to proceed in the work; and his secretary, Joan Moon, whose tireless efforts in typing and correcting the manuscript are appreciated.

E. Keith Howick

INDEX TO THE HISTORY OF THE CHURCH OF JESUS CHRIST OF LATTER-DAY SAINTS

—A—

—B—

—C—

—F—

—G—

—H—

—I—

—K—

—L—

LATTER-DAY SAINTS, CHURCH OF JESUS CHRIST OF (continued)

LETTERS (continued)

LETTERS (continued)

LETTERS (continued)

—M—

—N—

NAUVOO (continued)

—O—

—P—

PERSECUTIONS, ILLINOIS (continued)

PERSECUTIONS, MISSOURI (continued)

—Q—

—R—

—S—

SMITH, JOSEPH (continued)

SMITH, JOSEPH (continued)

SMITH JOSEPH (continued)

—T—

—U—

—V—

—W—

—Y—